The International Student Bible for Catholics

New American Bible

THOMAS NELSON PUBLISHERS
Nashville

The International Student Bible for Catholics

Old Testament Real-Life Application Notes,
10 Old Testament "Believe It or Nots,"
Things You'll Discover in the Old Testament

The New American Bible
NIHIL OBSTAT: Stephen J. Hartdegen, O.F.M., S.S.L.
Christian P. Ceroke, O. Carm., S.T.D.
IMPRIMATUR: †Patrick Cardinal O'Boyle, D.D.
Archbishop of Washington
July 27, 1970

The Revised New Testament
NIHIL OBSTAT: Stephen J. Hartdegen, O.F.M., S.S.L.
Censor Deputatus
IMPRIMATUR: †James Cardinal Hickey, S.T.D., J.C.D.
Archbishop of Washington
August 27, 1986

Revised Psalms of the New American Bible
IMPRIMATUR: Most Reverend Daniel E. Pilarczyk
President, National Conference of Catholic Bishops
October 10, 1991

What's Inside and **Real-Life Application Notes**
derived from The International Student Bible for Catholics
New Testament Edition
NIHIL OBSTAT: Reverend Monsignor Joseph Pollard, S.T.D.
Censor Deputatus
IMPRIMATUR: †Roger Cardinal Mahony
Archbishop of Los Angeles
May 20, 1993

Topical Index
derived from the Biblical Cyclopedic Index of
The New Catholic Study Bible
St. Jerome Edition
IMPRIMATUR: †John Cardinal Krol
Archbishop of Philadelphia
CENSORES DEPUTATI: The Reverend Daniel A. Murray
The Reverend John P. Murray, C.M.
March 25, 1985

Printed in the United States of America
19 20 21 22 23 24 25 -- 06 05 04 03 02

CONTENTS

Note of Thanks

The Publisher wishes to thank Paul Lauer of *YOU!* Magazine and Tom Ehart for their creative talents and care in preparing the featured articles, *What's Inside,* and the real-life application notes included in the topical index of this Bible.

Warning: Use of this book has been known to cause radical positive life alterations.

What's Inside:

What the Church Says About the Bible

"Since everything asserted by the inspired authors or sacred writers must be held to be asserted by the Holy Spirit, it follows that the books of Scripture must be acknowledged as teaching solidly, faithfully and without error that truth which God wanted put into the sacred writings for the sake of our salvation."

(Dogmatic Constitution on Divine Revelation: Second Vatican Council)

HAVE YOU HEARD THE NEWS?

Have you heard the latest news? "13-year-old shoots his family to death and then kills himself. Westside teen gets raped. 2-year-old child starves to death in Africa. 10-year-old boy arrested selling drugs to stay alive in New York City. Stay tuned for the weather forecast. . . ."

It sounds like a movie or something. But it's real life. And maybe you've even seen some of it firsthand. Well, God has seen all of it. Every act of violence, every word of hatred, every murder, rape, and suicide takes place right before God's very eyes. God knows the news better than CNN will ever know it.

"Why doesn't God do something about all these problems?" you ask. Well, as you venture through this book, you're going to find the answer to that question. You're going to discover that God is doing all that is necessary. And you're going to realize that the tool God wants to use to change the world for the better is none other than . . . YOU.

Jesus has no arms to touch people with but our arms, and no heart to love people with but our hearts. And in order for our arms and hearts to work for Christ, we must become like him. We must grow into the complete person that he wants us to be. Following him we will obtain the self-confidence, strength, goodness, and "power" to stand for what we believe in and to become the leaders of a new generation of youth who will change the world for the better.

THE BIBLE: AN INCREDIBLE ADVENTURE!

Question: What's the best-selling, most widely read book of all time?
Answer: The Bible.

That's right, folks. More people have read the "Good Book" than any other book in history. Millions of Bibles are printed each year throughout the world in many, many languages. And the Bible so far outsells every other book that the people who make up the best-seller lists don't even include it anymore!

What's the deal with this book? What's made it so popular for so long? Does it have romance? Adventure? Intrigue? Life-and-death situations? Excitement? Tear-jerking tragedies? Life-altering messages?

Yes to all the above. The Bible is absolutely the most moving, exciting, life-altering book you will ever read. But that's because the Bible is more than just a book. The Bible contains the words of Jesus Christ, who presented the mind and heart of God his Father. So when you read it, you literally come into contact with God, the Holy Spirit, who reaches out to your heart and soul as the words enter your mind!

Reading any other book is just a normal, natural event. But reading the Bible is a *supernatural* event! And that's more than any *New York Times'* best-seller can offer.

About 250 years ago, a famous skeptic named Voltaire held a Bible in his hand and said, "In one hundred years, this book will be forgotten, eliminated!"

Guess what? Almost one hundred years later, Voltaire's house was bought and made into offices for the Geneva Bible Society! The group began shipping Bibles out of Voltaire's former home. Before long, they had grown into an international Bible distribution network!

Where Did the Bible Come From?

Where did the Bible come from?

The Bible was written over a time span of nearly two thousand years. Yeah, that's 20 centuries! Remember Moses, the great leader of the Jewish people? Well, he and many other Jewish leaders, like the prophets, wrote the Old Testament first, and then the New Testament was written by the followers of Jesus Christ after his death and resurrection.

Some of the people who wrote the Bible were highly educated. Others were simple farmers. Several were political leaders. Only a few were what we'd call professors. Peter was a fisherman. Luke may have been a physician, and Matthew was a tax collector. Most of these authors never even met each other.

Leave it up to God. Only God could put together such a diverse group of people and get them to write something that blends together as well as the Bible does.

Think about it. If you were able to pick out a bunch of your friends and ask them to write about religion, morals, the creation of the world, the meaning of life, and the end of the world, the book would end up being like lunch in the school cafeteria! But the Bible isn't that way. Its writers and subjects fit together and make sense!

But weren't these people like sinners and ordinary human beings who make major mistakes?

Sure they were! That's what's so amazing. Despite all the obstacles and human error (you know, like ink spilling on the paper or the dog chewing up chapter three right before it's supposed to be copied), the Bible ended up being the most important book of all time. It's almost as though someone was putting it all together. Someone *was*—the EDITOR IN CHIEF . . . the Holy Spirit. The Holy Spirit inspired (*inspired* means "breathed into") the writers to put in Scripture the teachings God wanted communicated to the world. That's why we call the Bible God's word and Matthew's word or John's word at the same time.

If the parts of the Bible were written by different people, how were they compiled into one book we now call the Bible?

Great question! Most of the Old Testament part of the Bible was already written and compiled by the Jewish people by the time Jesus was born. The New Testament was compiled from letters and records which were written by the followers of Jesus between the years A.D. 50 and 125 (shortly after Jesus' death and resurrection). But because there were so many writings and letters circulating in the early days of Christianity, the Church had to determine which documents were truly inspired by God. This process took many years, but by A.D. 397, at the Council of Carthage, the same books which we have today in the Catholic Bible were listed as inspired. The Council of Trent in the sixteenth century called this the "canon"—or official books—of the Bible, and set down once and for all that these books were inspired and inerrant.

Why are Protestant and Catholic Bibles different?

In the New Testament, Catholic and Protestant Bibles have the same amount of books: 27. But in the Old Testament, the Catholic Bible has a total of 46 books, while the Protestant Bible only has 39. That's because during the Protestant Reformation of the sixteenth century, the Protestant reformers removed some of the books that they considered "questionable." We call these the Deuterocanonical books. The Catholic

Church still holds that they are fully inspired by God; but the Protestants, while respecting the books, don't hold them on par with the rest of the books of the Bible. Some Protestant Bibles include them while others do not. In Protestant Bibles, they are called the Apocrypha.

What will God say to me in the Bible?

Wouldn't it be great if God would sit right in front of you and talk to you about your life—your hopes, your dreams, your fears? Well, guess what? God is present in a special way when you open the Bible. Reading the Bible is a way to listen to God, and you'll be amazed at how many times your reading will relate perfectly to something going on in your life.

The Bible wasn't written to conceal (hide) God's plan. It was written to reveal (to make open) God's plan. And it's clear enough for any of us to understand and to live by.

Things you'll discover in the Old Testament:

- The roots and history of God's relationship with humanity—forming the basis for three major world religions: Judaism, Christianity, and Islam
- The epic stories of Creation, Adam and Eve, Cain and Abel, Noah and the Great Flood, the Tower of Babel, Abraham's covenant with God, Joseph and his amazing "dream coat," Moses and the prophets, the Promised Land, Samson and Delilah, David and Goliath, Daniel in the lions' den, Jonah in the belly of the fish, and so many more!
- The rise and fall of kings and nations
- Real-life stories of love and hate, peace and war, and God's justice and mercy.

Things you'll discover in the New Testament:

- Who Jesus is
- What Jesus said and did
- How much he loves you
- What God is like
- What pleases or displeases God
- How to get to know God better
- How to love ourselves and love our neighbors, and much more!

Throughout the Bible, you'll see how you can be forgiven and how you can forgive others. And you'll learn how to live happily and have courage even in the face of death. You'll also get the lowdown on how to get ready for heaven.

The Bible answers important questions, too, such as:

- "Where did I come from?"
- "Why am I here on earth, anyhow?"

(continued on p. 11)

Are There Errors in the Bible?

"I think the Bible has errors in it."

Can you give an example?

"Well, not really. I've just heard that from other people."

Yeah, that's the way most rumors start. Sometimes people don't really know what the issues are; they're just going along with what others are saying.

"So you're saying there are no errors in the Bible?"

It depends on what you mean by errors. If you take everything in the Bible to be absolutely literal, then it looks like there are errors. For instance, in John's gospel, Jesus chased the merchants out of the temple in the early part of the story (Jn 2:13–16). In Matthew's account, Jesus did this near the end of his ministry (Mt 21:12). One of the writers must be wrong.

"Right!"

Not necessarily. The Church teaches in *Sancta Mater Ecclesia,* a document from the Pontifical Biblical Commission of 1964, as follows:

> for the truth of the narrative is not affected in the slightest by the fact that the evangelists report the sayings or doings of Our Lord in a different order and that they use different words to express what he said, not keeping to the very letter, but nevertheless, preserving the sense.

There is more than one way of telling the truth.

"But with all the copying of the manuscripts, how do we know that the writers didn't change or miss anything?"

Well, it's true that in Bible times, they didn' t have printing presses as we do today, so every copy of the Bible had to be copied by hand. And yes, copyists did make some errors. But most of those errors were minor. Usually, they had to do with the spelling or repetition of a word, and these were easy enough to spot.

"But that can add up to a lot over two thousand years."

Well, of the thousands of manuscripts and parts of manuscripts that modern archaeologists have discovered, none of them contain any doctrinal differences. In other words, the Bible that you have is the same message between Genesis and Revelation that the Christians had in the first century. You can trust your Bible. It's true.

- "Where am I going?"
- "How can I find and know the truth?"

And the answers to these questions aren't coming from some new religion or cult of the twentieth century. These are time-tested answers that have been leading millions of people to happiness for thousands of years!

Some skeptics say that we can't trust the Bible, but they're overlooking some very important—the most important—evidence regarding the Bible: the good that it has done in the world. Literally billions of people have benefited by the Bible's messages of peace, love, justice, mercy, forgiveness, redemption, and the meaning of life. Very few people in all of history have ever said the words of the Bible have not helped humanity. Nearly everyone recognizes its importance.

Besides, Jesus himself said that we could trust the words of Scripture (Jn 10:35) and that God's words would never pass away (Mt 5:18). And if it's good enough for Jesus, it's good enough for us.

Also see *Catechism of the Catholic Church,* 80, 81, 95, 101–141.

HOW TO GET THE MOST OUT OF MY BIBLE

Read some of the Bible every day. Try to set a reachable goal of reading through the Bible in one year. God won't be offended if you miss a day, but you'll feel the difference in your spiritual life. Have you ever gone without eating for a day? You feel hungry. The same thing happens spiritually if you go without nourishing yourself with spiritual reading and prayer.

Not only that. Your daily Bible reading will become a solid foundation you can build your life on. It will comfort you, advise you, and bring you closer to God. In fact, it's like getting a letter every day from someone you love. Because it's God's love letter to you. You want to open your letters every day.

Tips for a Good Read

Seek to answer these main questions as you read the Bible:

- What does this part of the Scripture actually say?
  - —Who is speaking?
  - —Where are they?
  - —What are they trying to say?
  - —Why are they saying it?
  - —Why did God want them to say it?
- What is God specifically saying to me in this Scripture?
  - —What aspects of my life relate to this Scripture?
  - —Can I relate to one of its characters?
  - —How can I put God's guidance to work in my life?

More Tips:

- Pray before you begin, and ask God to speak to you through the Bible.
- Read your Bible slowly. You want to get the whole story, but take your time. After each paragraph, ask yourself, "What does this mean and what does it have to do with me?"
- Keep a notebook with you while you read the Bible. If you have questions, jot them down, so you can ask others about it later.
- Read regularly with a friend.
- Check out Bible references and commentaries to help you understand more.
- If you have questions, check with your youth minister, teacher, parish priest, or someone else with a strong Bible background.

"How Can I Put What I'm Learning to Work in My Life?"

Reading the Bible merely to gain knowledge is very noble, but it won't change your life. You have to make it part of your life and put it into action. You have to apply its teachings to your daily living.

To apply the truth you have learned, ask yourself some tough questions. You may want to record the answers to these in a notebook:

- What does this passage teach me about Jesus? about God? about the Holy Spirit? about God's love?
- Does the passage show me any area of my life I need to change—maybe a sin that I need to confess or turn away from? Or my attitude? Or a need for restitution (making a wrong right, if possible—for example, paying back money that you have stolen, or apologizing to somebody whom you have hurt)?
- Is there a promise in the passage that I can believe and live by?
- Is there something here I should pray about?
- What can I thank the Lord for as a result of this truth?

Strange things I'll find in the New Testament:

- A young pregnant woman who was a virgin (Matthew 1; Luke 1)
- A guy who was so hungry he almost ate pig food (Luke 15:16)
- A guy who fell asleep at church and fell out a window (Acts 20:7–9)
- A lake of fire (Revelation 20:14–15)
- A book-burning party (Acts 19:19)
- Huge hailstones that weigh a hundred pounds (Revelation 16:21)

- The blasting and the blessing (Acts 5:1–16)
- An angel who argued with the devil (Jude 9)

Also see *Catechism of the Catholic Church*, 109–119.

DOES GOD EXIST?

A lot of people today say that God doesn't really exist. They say science has proven that we evolved from amoebas instead of being made by God. (They haven't figured out who made the amoebas yet, though.) They say that God was just invented to explain the things we couldn't understand. (Is that why Isaac Newton was such a religious man?) And they say that religion has done nothing but cause wars. (It's funny that Attila the Hun, William the Conqueror, Napoleon, Stalin, and Hitler were not religious people.)

But the real reason people deny God's existence is because they haven't seen God *for themselves.* Most of us have to see to believe. And if we have doubts about God, it's because we haven't recognized the power and love of God in our life.

Seeing Is Believing

God knew that many people have to see to believe, so Jesus, the Son of God, came to show God *in the flesh.* Jesus is God in human flesh. Through his miracles, he showed us the power God has over all creation. Through his teachings, he laid out the path we must travel to attain happiness and fulfillment. Through his death on the cross and resurrection from the dead, he conquered sin and death and opened the door to everlasting life.

But what about those of us who were born too late to meet this incredible God-man? Does God expect us to believe *without* seeing? Not really. And that's why Jesus is still here—even two thousand years after he returned to heaven. How? you ask. In three ways. First, he lives and moves in the people who follow him, are baptized, and make up the Church. (These people are called Christians; altogether they make up the "body of Christ.") Second, he lives in the Eucharist, which we celebrate and share in when we receive Holy Communion at Mass. Third, he lives in the words of the Bible—words to which you give new life when you read them or listen to them.

God on Board

That's why this book is so incredible! The mind and heart and "secrets" of God—the words of Jesus Christ—are right here in your hands. And in some ways you' re even luckier than those who saw Jesus in person, because they only got to hear part of his teaching before he moved on to another town. Through the Bible, you get the "best" or "greatest hits" of his teachings, thanks to the early Christians who recorded it and compiled it.

God is far from dead. God's Word is right in your hands, waiting to find a home in your life, to nourish you with spiritual food that leads to everlasting life.

Also see *Catechism of the Catholic Church*, 27–49.

IS JESUS CHRIST GOD?

Jesus Christ is both true man and true God. During his life on earth, we can see that as a person, Jesus was like us in everything except sin (Heb 4:15). He cried; he was tempted; he experienced hunger, thirst, and tremendous physical pain; he even felt the loneliness and frustration of being abandoned by his best friends. Jesus became a complete person so that he could become fully one with us in our human existence (Phil 2:6–7).

But at the same time, Jesus is the Son of God. He allowed himself to be worshiped as God, something no other Jewish person would dream of doing. When Thomas said to Jesus, "My Lord and my God!" (Jn 20:28), Jesus did not say, "No, Thomas, don't call me that." Jesus accepted Thomas's worship.

Some people want to think of Jesus as merely a great moral teacher. But Jesus did not stop there. He said he was the Son of God many times (for an example, see Matthew 26:63–64), and he even made himself equal to God the Father (Jn 10:30). And he could not have been a "great moral teacher" if he was lying or even crazy.

Jesus said, "I am the way and the truth and the life. No one comes to

Do You Love Me?

You love me. And you want to show it. So you say it—with a word. The love you have exists inside of you, but if you want to express it to me, you have to transfer it from your mind and heart into words or actions. That way your love enters the physical world.

God loves you. And God wants to show it—with a word. The love that God has for us is expressed in the Son of God, Jesus Christ. He's God's love made into human form.

In Jesus, the mind and heart of God are placed right before our very eyes. We need only open our eyes to see how beautiful they really are.

the Father except through me" (Jn 14:6). That's because he and God the Father and God the Holy Spirit are actually three Persons united in one God. That is why we call God the "Holy Trinity" *(trinity* means "three").

3 People Jesus Raised From the Dead

- Jairus's daughter (Mark 5:22–43)
- A widow's son in the town of Nain (Luke 7:11–15)
- Jesus' friend Lazarus (John 11:1–44)

8 Miracles That Show Jesus Has Power Over Nature

- Jesus turned water into wine (John 2:1–10).
- He calmed a bad storm (Matthew 8:23–27; Mark 4:35–41; Luke 8:22–25).
- He fed more than 5,000 people with only five loaves of bread and two small fish (Matthew 14:13–21; Mark 6:34–44; Luke 9:12–17; John 6:5–15).
- He walked on the water in the middle of a lake (Matthew 14:22–33; Mark 6:45–52; John 6:16–21).
- He fed more than 4,000 people (Matthew 15:32–39; Mark 8:1–9).
- He told Peter where to catch a fish with a coin in its mouth (Matthew 17:24–27).
- He caused the disciples to haul in a huge catch of fish (Luke 5:1–11).
- And then there was another big catch of fish (John 21:1–11).

Also see *Catechism of the Catholic Church,* 430–455, 464–469.

WHAT DOES THE OLD TESTAMENT HAVE TO DO WITH JESUS?

If we want to read the story of Jesus, we turn to the New Testament. But if we want to truly understand why Jesus did the things he did, we also need to know about the Old Testament. It's part of God's word to us, too.

A testament, or covenant, is a promise between two parties. The Old Testament is the story of God's dealings with humanity under the old covenant, and everything Jesus did in the New Testament was based upon it. Jesus said, "Do not think that I have come to abolish the law or the prophets. I have come not to abolish but to fulfill" (Mt 5:17).

Jesus Used the Old Testament

The Old Testament was the Bible of Jesus' day. He accepted it as Scripture and quoted it regularly. Jesus also taught his disciples from the Old Testament, and many of the stories he told had their roots in it, including his descriptions of his second coming (see Matthew 24:29–31). He prayed the same psalms that we do. And some of his final words, as he died on the cross, were verses from the Old Testament. (Jesus quoted Psalms 22:2 and 31:6. You can read these in Mark 15:34 and Luke 23:46.)

Jesus believed the Old Testament. His life, ministry, death, and resurrection were all based on it. The New Testament is built firmly on the foundation of the Old Testament. Over two hundred prophecies in the Old Testament predicted Jesus' coming. For instance, the Bible predicted that he would:

- be born into the family of Judah
- be born to a virgin
- be born in Bethlehem
- go down to Egypt
- heal the sick
- be rejected by his own people
- be betrayed by a friend
- be sold for thirty pieces of silver
- be crucified with sinners
- be pierced in his side
- be raised from the dead
- ascend into heaven

We believe all of these prophecies were fulfilled in Jesus.

10 Old Testament "Believe It or Nots"

1. The opening of the Red Sea (Exodus 14)
2. Water from a rock and bread from Heaven (Exodus 15—16)
3. Walls of Jericho fall down (Joshua 6)
4. Gideon gets his signs from God (Judges 6)
5. Samson pulls down a temple with his bare hands (Judges 16)
6. David defeats the giant Goliath (1 Samuel 17)
7. Elijah roasts a soaked bull (1 Kings 18)
8. Elisha raises the dead (2 Kings 4)

9. 3 young men survive a fiery furnace (Daniel 3)
10. Daniel survives the lions' den (Daniel 6)

5 REASONS YOU CAN BE SURE JESUS IS RISEN FROM THE DEAD

The resurrection of Jesus Christ is the central issue of Christianity. Unlike other religions such as Islam or Buddhism, Christianity rises or

3 Faith-Builders When You Have Doubts

Almost all Catholics have questions and doubts about their faith at one point or another. Jesus never became angry with his friends because of their doubts. When you have questions or doubts, here are three reminders that will help boost your faith:

1. Look at the physical world around you. This earth could not have "just happened" by some cosmic accident. Imagine that thousands of auto parts were floating around out in space, and one day they all fell to earth in the form of a brand new sports car. Pretty silly, huh?

Now multiply that by the billions of objects on earth that have complex designs, and you begin to realize how silly it would be to believe that the world "just happened." No, it didn't "just happen." God created the heavens and the earth. And God created you. (Read Psalm 148 and Isaiah 44:23; 55:12; 64:1–4 for more on God's glory in creation.)

2. The resurrection of Jesus Christ. When you have doubts, just remember: Jesus arose from the dead. Nobody has ever been able to explain that one away (although many have tried). Over five hundred people saw Jesus alive within a short time after he had been crucified, pronounced dead, and buried. (Read John 20—21 and Acts 1:3.)

3. Jesus has changed your life. A changed life is still the best proof of Christianity. When you find yourself in doubt, remember what Jesus has already done for you. Some people may not understand. Others may not believe you. But nobody can argue with you when you can honestly say, "Jesus changed my life!" (See Galatians 2:20.)

falls with the resurrection. Even the apostle Paul said, "And if Christ has not been raised, then empty [too] is our preaching; empty, too, your faith. . . . But now Christ has been raised from the dead" (1 Cor 15:14, 20).

Evidence of the Resurrection

The resurrection of Jesus Christ really happened. Here are five reasons why you can be sure of it:

1. The Bible, which is God's Word, tells you it happened, over and over again and in many different ways.

2. The tomb was empty. The testimonies of Matthew, Mark, Luke, John, Peter, and Mary all agree: On the Sunday after Jesus was crucified, his tomb was empty. Jesus was gone.

What happened?

Some say the women and the disciples went to the wrong tomb. But if that were true, why couldn't anyone take them to the "right" tomb and produce the body of Jesus?

Some say that Jesus didn't really die on the cross, but that he just "appeared" to die. That's an insult to the Roman soldiers, who knew how to kill a man and who knew a dead man when they saw one. Not only that, it doesn't explain how Jesus rolled the stone away. Nor does it explain how a severely beaten, battered, and bloody Jesus could have the energy or the ability to convince everyone that he had risen miraculously from the grave, much less look the part.

Others say that the appearances of Jesus must have been hallucinations. The disciples and others who "saw" Jesus after he had been crucified, they say, were just "seeing things." But that doesn't make sense either. Besides the impossibility of mass hallucinations, it still doesn't explain where the real body of Jesus was or is. Some say that somebody stole Jesus' body. But who would have wanted it? His friends? They were afraid to even come near the cross when Jesus was dying. It is unlikely that they would have been brave enough to tangle with the Roman guards posted at the grave (Mt 27:62–66).

The enemies of Jesus would have had no reason to steal his dead body either. Even if they had, when the disciples began preaching that Jesus was alive, his enemies could have ended Christianity with one deadening thud. All they had to do was produce the body. But they couldn't. He was alive!

3. The change in the lives of Paul and James. Some skeptics say that Jesus appeared only to his loyal followers after the resurrection. But that is not true. He appeared to two very strict Jews, Paul and James.

Paul, known as Saul before he met the risen Jesus, hated everything about Jesus. He hated those who said that Jesus was alive, and he had legal permission from the Jewish leaders to persecute any Jews who were followers of Jesus. But then Jesus himself appeared to Saul as he was on his way to Damascus (Acts 9).

Saul was converted. He later became known as "Paul," and spent the rest of his life telling people about the resurrection of our Lord Jesus Christ.

James was Jesus' cousin, but he had not believed in Jesus. Yet James became a leader in the early Christian church. What happened? The apostle Paul explains:

> For I handed on to you as of first importance what I also received: that Christ died for our sins in accordance with the scriptures; that he was buried; that he was raised on the third day in accordance with the scriptures; that he appeared to Kephas, then to the Twelve. After that, he appeared to more than five hundred brothers at once, most of whom are still living, though some have fallen asleep. After that he appeared to James, then to all the apostles. Last of all, as to one born abnormally, he appeared to me (1 Cor 15:3–8).

4. The eyewitness accounts. Within a few days of his execution, all sorts of people were claiming to have seen Jesus, alive from the dead! Think of the list:

- Mary Magdalene
- Peter
- John
- the other disciples
- Thomas (the skeptic)
- the two travelers on the road to Emmaus (Lk 24:13–15)
- five hundred others
- Saul of Tarsus (some time later than the others)

All of these people said the same thing: "Jesus is alive! Christ is risen!"

5. The effect on the people who saw Jesus. Have you ever wondered what happened to the disciples? Christian tradition tells us that all of them, except for John, died violent deaths rather than deny that Jesus was alive. John lived the longest after Jesus' death. He died of natural causes. The others gave their testimonies with their lives.

Skeptics object, "Yes, but men and women often give their lives for a cause they believe in. That's no proof that Jesus arose." True, many people will die for something they *believe* to be true, but people will not lay down their lives for something they *know* to be false. Yet, one by one, each of the disciples gave up their lives. If Jesus had not risen, wouldn't at least one of them have said, "Wait a minute! Why should I die for a lie about a dead man?"

But they didn't. They were convinced that Jesus is alive.

> "Christianity begins where religion ends . . . with the resurrection."—Anonymous

Also see *Catechism of the Catholic Church*, 638–658.

"WHEN ARE YOU COMING BACK, JESUS?"

The world has not seen the last of Jesus Christ! He came once in human history; he lives now in the Church, in the Eucharist, and in the Bible's word; and the Bible says he will come again. The Bible has over three hundred prophecies about the *second* coming of Jesus Christ.

When Is Jesus Coming?

Jesus' disciples were wondering that same thing. One day they asked Jesus directly: "Tell us, when will this happen, and what sign will there be of your coming, and of the end of the age?" (Mt 24:3).

Jesus didn't tell his disciples that he would return on a specific date. Any time you read or hear of people saying they know the date when Jesus is coming, beware. Jesus never set a date. He said that no one knows the day or the hour (Mt 24:36).

He did give us certain signs to look for, though.

What Are Some of the Signs?

1. False messiahs and false prophets (Mt 24:5, 11, 24). Jesus said that many will come claiming to be him, saying that they are the Christ, the Messiah. These false prophets will fool a lot of people. They will even try to fool God's chosen ones (Mt 24:24).

2. Wars and threats of wars (Mt 24:6). Some people say, "We've always had wars." And they're right. But Jesus is talking about cosmic wars. At the end of World War II, General Douglas

MacArthur warned, "We have had our last chance. If we do not now devise some greater and more equitable system, Armageddon will be at our door." (The Armageddon MacArthur was referring to is the final battle between good and evil in which Jesus will be victorious.)

In August, 1945, the United States dropped the first atomic bomb to be used in war on the Japanese city of Hiroshima. In the city of 500,000 people, 70,000 were killed instantly. Another 70,000 were injured, and many of that number died in the hours that followed.

An area of 4.7 square miles (over 3,000 acres) in the downtown part of the city was completely leveled. Shock waves blasted from the center of the explosion at speeds of over 600 miles per hour. The waves crumbled walls that were more than a mile from town. Heat waves *millions* of degrees in intensity melted flesh, stone, and anything else in their path.

The really scary part is that the bomb dropped on Hiroshima was a small one compared to what we have today. It was equal to about 20,000 tons of dynamite, not exactly a firecracker, but only one-fiftieth of a megaton. Now, however, the world is armed with *one-hundred megaton* nuclear warheads!

3. Famines (Mt 24:7). Jesus said that before his coming, the world would once again know severe famine. "People will starve to death," he said. Today, despite lots of hunger relief projects, millions of people still starve to death. Before another day passes, 10,000 human beings will die of starvation. Ten thousand more will die tomorrow, and the next day, and the next.

Jesus said it would be that way. That doesn't mean we should do nothing and let people die. Jesus said those things would happen to make us wake up to our own Christian responsibilities. Christians should be leading the way to help feed and clothe a needy world.

Other Signs of the Times

4. Earthquakes in various places (Mt 24:7).

5. Evil will spread and love will grow cold (Mt 24:12).

6. The good news will be preached in all the world (Mt 24:14). Jesus didn't say that everyone would believe the good news. Read the verse carefully for yourself: "And this gospel of the kingdom will be preached throughout the world as a witness to all nations, and then the end will come" (Mt 24:14).

Most of the people living in the world have not yet heard the good news. We may have the technical potential to bring the good news of Jesus to the whole world, but the same technical power can be used to block it. The mission is just as urgent today as when it was first given to the apostles.

What Should We Do?

When Jesus concluded his long discussion about his return, he added a great word of hope. He said, "But when these signs begin to happen, stand erect and raise your heads because your redemption is at hand" (Lk 21:28).

But Jesus also told us that no one knows the date or the hour. Too many preachers are running around today trying to convert people by planting seeds of fear in them regarding the end of the world. It doesn't matter when the end of the world will come—whether it's this century or centuries from now. That's up to God.

The important thing is that we commit our lives to the service of God today—and not put it off until tomorrow. Because even if the world is still around tomorrow, we may not be.

For each one of us, it's important to think about when the end comes for you and for me.

Also see *Catechism of the Catholic Church*, 668–682.

WHO IS THE HOLY SPIRIT?

The Holy Spirit is the third Person of the Holy Trinity, which includes the Father and the Son (Jesus). The Spirit is the love between the Father and the Son. That's why when we say "God is love," we are referring especially to the Holy Spirit, who makes us keenly aware of the love shared in the Trinity. This is the same Holy Spirit that we receive in a special way at our Confirmation.*

What Else Does the Holy Spirit Do?

The Holy Spirit is the One who "sanctifies" us (makes us holy) by making us into the image of Jesus. Some of the ways the Holy Spirit does this are:

- Showing us what is true (Jn 16:13)
- Teaching us what Jesus wants us to know (Jn 14:26; 16:7–15)
- Helping us know Jesus better (1 Cor 2:1–13)
- Enabling us to think as Jesus does (1 Cor 2:16)
- Helping us avoid sin and do what is right (1 Cor 6:11)

The Multiplication of Jesus

When Jesus walked the earth in person, he could only be at one place, at one time. Now he can be with all of us, at all times, by his Spirit, in the Sacraments, and wherever Christians gather in his name.

The Holy Spirit produces *spiritual fruit* in our lives. St. Paul tells us what this "fruit" is like: "The fruit of the Spirit is love, joy, peace, patience, kindness, generosity, faithfulness, gentleness, self-control" (Gal 5:22–23). The Holy Spirit also gives each believer a spiritual gift or gifts (see Romans 12; 1 Corinthians 12:4–11; Ephesians 4). These gifts are to be used to build up the entire body of Christ. The Holy Spirit wants you to use your gifts to grow in holiness, to help others, and to lead them to Jesus.

Christ in You

The Holy Spirit is the Spirit of God, alive in you. God wants to fill your life with the Spirit's presence (Eph 5:18). This will make the "real you" come alive, because we only become fully ourselves through our connection with God and with other people alive with God's Spirit.

---

*For more on how we receive the Holy Spirit in a special way at our Confirmation, see page 40.

Also see *Catechism of the Catholic Church*, 687–747.

SIN: A CRIME OF THE HEART

Nobody's perfect, that's for sure. But Jesus told us to strive to be the best we could be: "Be perfect, just as your heavenly Father is perfect" (Mt 5:48). The truth is, God wants us to avoid sin for *our* sake, because sin harms us—physically, mentally, and spiritually—and it harms everybody else around us. It's true that God loves us just the way we are. But God also loves us too much to let us remain less than we have the potential to be.

What Is Sin?

Scholars have all sorts of definitions for sin. Some define sin as "a willful disobedience to God." When you know what is right and you willfully decide to do wrong, that is sin. James puts it this way: "For one who knows the right thing to do and does not do it, it is a sin" (Jas 4:17).

The real essence of sin, though, is that it's a failure to love the way God wants us to love. Jesus summed up the Ten Commandments into just two: Love the Lord your God, and love your neighbor as yourself (see Mark 12:29–31). So if we've sinned, it means we've failed to truly love.

But love is a big word, and we often distort it to mean things it really doesn't. For instance, a parent might say, "I whipped my son because I love him." But in reality, the whipping might have been out of anger, not out of love. Another person might say, "I love that woman, so we're going to have sex." But all this guy might mean is, "I want to satisfy myself." That's not love. If the two commit adultery, that's anything but love.

The Ten Commandments: A Recipe for Love

That's the reason God had to *define* what real love is by giving us the Ten Commandments, and sending Jesus to be a walking example of love on earth. Jesus showed us that each commandment is not only a way of saying "no" to sin, but more importantly, it's saying "yes" to love.

For example, looking at the Sixth Commandment ("You shall not commit adultery," Ex 20:14), we can see that all forms of sexuality that say "yes" to extramarital sex and lust violate the commandment, while forms of sexuality that say "yes" to *true* love—faithful marriage, sexual self-control, unselfish expression of love—uphold the commandment.

The Ten Commandments

1. You shall not have other gods besides me.
2. You shall not take the name of the LORD, your God, in vain.
3. Remember to keep holy the sabbath day.
4. Honor your father and your mother.
5. You shall not kill.
6. You shall not commit adultery.
7. You shall not steal.
8. You shall not bear false witness against your neighbor.
9. You shall not covet your neighbor's house.
10. You shall not covet your neighbor's wife.

Also see *Catechism of the Catholic Church*, 2052–2557.

The Beatitudes: Love Further Defined

In his famous "Sermon on the Mount" (Mt 5—7), Jesus spelled out what it really means to say "yes" to love—to love the way he loved. The sermon contains teachings on forgiveness, helping the needy, and living a virtuous life, as well as the "Lord's Prayer" or "Our Father." It also contains the " Beatitudes," eight teachings of Christ which show ways that we can be blessed by God. The Beatitudes are:

1. Blessed are the poor in spirit, for theirs is the kingdom of heaven.
2. Blessed are they who mourn, for they will be comforted.
3. Blessed are the meek, for they will inherit the land.
4. Blessed are they who hunger and thirst for righteousness, for they will be satisfied.
5. Blessed are the merciful, for they will be shown mercy.
6. Blessed are the clean of heart, for they will see God.
7. Blessed are the peacemakers, for they will be called children of God.
8. Blessed are they who are persecuted for the sake of righteousness, for theirs is the kingdom of heaven.

(See Matthew 5:3–10.)

How Can My Sins Be Forgiven?

St. Paul says, "All have sinned and are deprived of the glory of God" (Rom 3:23). Okay. So we've all sinned. What can we do about it? How can we get free from sin and its effects? The Bible says, "If we say, 'We are without sin,' we deceive ourselves, and the truth is not in us. If we acknowledge our sins, he is faithful and just and will forgive our sins and cleanse us from every wrongdoing" (1 Jn 1:8–9).

So the real key to forgiveness is simply acknowledging our sin before God and asking forgiveness. As Catholics, we have a special way to do this in the Sacrament of Reconciliation (see page 42 for more information).

To Repent Means "To Turn Around"

Repentance is more than just saying, "I'm sorry." To repent means "to turn away" from your sin and "to turn around" in your living, recentering your life in God. Lots of people are sorry for their sins, but they won't turn away from them. In the New Testament, even Judas, the disciple who betrayed Jesus, was sorry for what he had done. But he didn't ask Jesus for forgiveness. Nor did he turn away from his sin. Instead, he went out and hanged himself (Mt 27:5).

St. Peter betrayed Jesus as well, but unlike Judas, Peter turned from his sin and renewed his love for Jesus. Peter had denied Jesus three times, so Jesus asked Peter three times, "Do you love me?" to which Peter replied three times, "Yes, Lord, you know that I love you!" (Jn 21:15–17). In the Old Testament, we see how the entire city of Nineveh truly turned away from sin, and God therefore did not destroy it (see the Book of Jonah).

God Is Always Ready to Forgive

God will never deny us forgiveness (see Ps 32:1–2). No matter what we've done, our loving Father will always welcome us back with open arms as the father welcomed back his "lost son" (Lk 15:11–32). All we need to do is admit our failings and sincerely try, with God's help, to avoid them in the future.

Also see *Catechism of the Catholic Church*, 386–389, 1472, 1846–1876.

WOULD GOD REALLY SEND ME TO HELL FOR BEING BAD?

God doesn't send people to hell for being bad. If he did, heaven would be one lonely place, because we're all bad to one degree or another. People go to hell only because they reject God and the offer of salvation that Jesus Christ earned for us. At their death, God simply honors their decision not to be part of his family. Without God, we are already beginning to live in hell. Because the greatest tragedy of hell is that it's a place completely separated from God. There is no love, no compassion, and no peace. Why? Because all of those blessings come from God alone. So when we've lost God, we've lost all the rest.

Does Hell Really Exist?

Count on it. The Bible has four different words for hell. The word used most often for "hell" in the Old Testament is *sheol*. Sheol is a dark, gloomy underworld. It is the place of the dead. Nothing is said about fire and brimstone, but sheol is not exactly the kind of place where you would enjoy living forever.

In the New Testament, the word *hades* means much the same as sheol. Another word, *Tartarus,* is used once by the apostle Peter. It describes the place where disobedient angels were sent when they sinned (2 Pt 2:4).

The most common word for hell in the New Testament is *Gehenna*. Ten of the eleven times it is used, it comes from the mouth of Jesus himself. *Gehenna* was a valley near Jerusalem where people burned refuse. Jesus used it to mean "a final place of punishment for the ungodly." These four words might not all refer to precisely the same existence. But the idea is definitely that *heaven* is where you want to be.

The Garbage Dump of Human History

Most of what we know about hell comes from the mouth of Jesus himself. He said, "Whoever says, 'You fool,' will be liable to fiery

Gehenna" (Mt 5:22). It was Jesus who rebuked his friends for fearing what mere humans could do to them: "Do not be afraid of those who kill the body but cannot kill the soul; rather, be afraid of the one who can destroy both soul and body in Gehenna" (Mt 10:28). He compared hell to Gehenna, a place just outside of Jerusalem. It had once been the site where human sacrifices were offered to the heathen god Molech. But by the time of Christ it had become a garbage dump full of worms and rats. To help reduce the health hazard, the garbage was set on fire all the time. Fire, smoke, and awful smells were always part of Gehenna. When Jesus wanted to describe the horrors of hell in human terms, he used the word *Gehenna*. He called it a place of everlasting punishment; a place of outer, absolute darkness. It's the garbage dump of human history.

Hell Wasn't Made for People

God never intended for anyone to go to hell. Hell is a place for the devil and his fallen angels (Mt 25:41) once they revolted against God. If you go to hell, it will be your own fault, not God's.

God loves you with an infinite love. Jesus, the Son of God, even gave his own life to reconcile you to God so that you could freely enter heaven. "The wages of sin is death, but the gift of God is eternal life in Christ Jesus our Lord" (Rom 6:23).

Also see *Catechism of the Catholic Church*, 1033–1037.

KNOCKIN' ON HEAVEN'S DOOR?

Most people believe there's a heaven. But where is heaven? What does it look like? How can we get there? Why don't the astronauts bump into it in outer space? Good questions.

The Bible says quite a bit about heaven. The subject is mentioned fifty-two times in the Book of Revelation alone! Hundreds of other references to heaven are sprinkled throughout the Scripture. Jesus sometimes used the phrase "kingdom of heaven." By this, he meant his spiritual kingdom, not necessarily an actual place (see Matthew 5:3; 10:7; 16:19). But the Bible also pictures a *place* called heaven. This is the "home" of God, the "place" completely filled with God's presence.

Your Future Home?

Not only is heaven Jesus' home, it is the future home of those who do the will of God. The night before he was killed, Jesus told his disciples, "Do not let your hearts be troubled. You have faith in God; have faith also in me. In my Father's house there are many dwelling places. If there were not, would I have told you that I am going to prepare a place for you? And if I go and prepare a place for you, I will come back again and take you to myself, so that where I am you also may be" (Jn 14:1–3).

Can your mind imagine the place that the all-powerful God is preparing for you? It will be beyond our wildest dreams!

What Is Heaven Like?

In heaven we will see God face-to-face! This is called the "beatific vision" and is not granted to us until we finally reach heaven. When Jesus returns to earth, every person who ever lived will see him—even those who crucified him. The author of the Book of Revelation wrote: "Behold, he is coming amid the clouds, and every eye will see him, even those who pierced him" (Rv 1:7). But this is not the "beatific vision" which introduces us among the blessed of God.

In Revelation, John describes heaven in physical terms, though we know heaven is really a spiritual state of being. This "New Jerusalem" or "holy city" is symbolically described as a huge, golden city fifteen hundred miles in each direction, including fifteen hundred miles high! (See Revelation 21:16.) Its walls are made of jasper (Rv 21:18), and it has twelve gates (Rv 21:21). A river flows through it with crystal clear, life-giving waters. "On either side of the river grew the tree of life that produces fruit twelve times a year, once each month; the leaves of the trees serve as medicine for the nations" (Rv 22:2).

Obviously, since heaven is a spiritual state of being, we can't expect to find a *physical* metropolis when we get there. But at the end of time, when our bodies are reunited with our souls in the resurrection (this is what we refer to when we say, "I believe in the resurrection of the body," in the Apostle's Creed), the physical universe as we know it will be renewed in God's love as well (see Revelation 21). It is then that our experience of heaven may take on a "physical" nature, like the "physical" nature of the resurrected Jesus, who was solid enough for Thomas to touch (Jn 20:27), yet was still able to pass through walls like a spirit (Jn 20:26). There is more than one kind of "physical" nature.

What Will We Do in Heaven?

Nobody knows for sure what we'll do in heaven. Some people say part of our time in heaven will be spent working. Work is a joyous activity when it's done in the right spirit. Others say that we may also be ruling over some parts of God's universe. Maybe so, but the Bible doesn't say these things specifically.

What the Bible does say is that there will be no more suffering, sickness, or sadness in heaven, so we will have complete freedom to love and be loved there.

Think of the best relationships you've had in this life—those great moments of joy shared with family or friends. The feeling of being congratulated or honored for something you've done well . . . the feeling of receiving a special gift from a loved one . . . the feeling of laughing and celebration. These types of experiences will be yours forever in heaven as you and all the other saints and angels share a perfect love for each other—without the fighting, jealousy, misunderstanding, and the other hassles that sometimes mess up our relationships on earth.

You'll even be able to meet all the spiritual "giants" you've read about and heard about all these years—people like Moses, King David, St. Paul, St. Peter, St. Francis, St. Mary Magdalene, and the Blessed Virgin Mary.

You'll also meet all your relatives and friends who have reached heaven before you. In heaven you'll fully realize that *every* human being there is your relative as a fellow child of God.

Oneness With God

But by far the greatest part of heaven will be God, because God is the source of all the life, happiness, and love that you'll experience in heaven. The Bible says that there is no need for a sun or a moon in heaven, for God's glory gives it light (Rv 21:23). God's light will permeate our entire being, and we will bask in it with far greater pleasure than we now bask in the sun at the ocean on a summer day.

This "beatific vision" of God will bring us deep into the infinite mysteries of God and creation. We will enter into the mind of God that created the universe. We will enter the heart of God and love more fully than we have loved on earth. For all eternity, we will be opening the treasure chest of God's glory and finding new gifts with our name on them. We will finally understand everything in ways unimaginable. And we will never want anything more.

What Won't Be in Heaven?

It is interesting to note what will not be in heaven:

- No tears, death, mourning, crying, or pain (Rv 21:4)
- No church or temple (Rv 21:22; the whole place will be the temple of God!)
- No sun or moon (Rv 21:23; God's love will be the source of light there)
- No night; no closing of the city gates (Rv 21:25)
- Nothing unclean (Rv 21:27)
- No more hassles with the devil (Rv 20:10; he can't get in there)
- No sea (Rv 21:1; some Bible scholars believe this means we will no longer be separated from our loved ones)
- No one who does abominable things (Rv 21:27)
- No one who tells lies (Rv 21:27)
- No curse of sin; it will be broken (Rv 22:3)

Will Everyone Reach Heaven?

None of us knows for sure who will or will not reach heaven. God alone knows the heart of every person and how much he or she loved God and neighbor.

What we do know, though, is that:

Heaven Is a Holy Place

Everything about heaven is holy. The Lord of heaven is holy. The angels and the other creatures who are worshiping the Lord Jesus are holy. The redeemed saints of God are holy. That's why it's necessary for *us* to be holy to get in!

We have to be redeemed by Jesus and be sincerely *trying* to become holy like him. Alone we could never become holy, so we rely totally on the grace of God. But God relies totally on our willingness to cooperate with that grace.

No Excuses This Time!

You may be a pro at putting things off until some other time, but your passage out of this life and into the next one will be one meeting you will not miss. You may try to avoid God all of your life on earth. You may attempt to shut God out of your life. You may even reject God, but you can count on meeting him someday, whether you want to or not.

Jesus made it clear that each of us will stand before him at death and give an account of what we have done (or not done) in our lives. If we have sincerely tried to know God and follow his commandments, then we will have become true sons and daughters of God (brothers and sisters of Jesus) in this life, and will share the inheritance that God has prepared for us in heaven.

By seeking God in this life, we begin to live in the "kingdom of heaven" even before we die. Passing into heaven then becomes a natural progression of what we're already doing.

If we deny God in this life, however, then we'll be completely unprepared for heaven. Going into heaven like that would be like putting a fish on dry land. It just doesn't work.

Also see *Catechism of the Catholic Church*, 1023–1029.

WHY DO I NEED TO GO TO CHURCH? CAN'T I WORSHIP GOD AT HOME?

Sometimes you wonder why you should go to church at all. I mean, it's Sunday and there are a hundred other fun things you want to do. Besides, this is your one chance to sleep in, and church is going to be boring anyway. Can't you just stay home and worship God in your way for once?

Sure, you *could* worship God at home—and you *should* every day of the week. But on Sundays God wants you to worship with other Catholics—as a community. It's the one day of the week when God wants all the "family" of sons and daughters together for a "family gathering" of worship and thanksgiving. That is what the Catholic Church teaches.

No Person Is an Island

Missing Mass is like missing a family gathering, such as Thanksgiving dinner. Maybe people won't notice you're not there as they would at Thanksgiving, but God notices. And besides, the main person who will notice is *you*. Why? Because "no man is an island" (John Donne). Besides, Sunday Mass is a time to witness to your faith.

We all need things from other people, and we all have things to give other people. That's why God wants us to celebrate Eucharist together on Sundays. Your church might not have the greatest Mass, but part of that might be because you're not doing anything to make it better.

The Bible says: "We should not stay away from our assembly, as is the custom of some, but encourage one another" (Heb 10:25).

Why Is Mass So Special Anyway?

Besides, what goes on at Mass is not something you could just do by yourself in your own home. It's doing what Jesus asked us to do in memory of him. It's the Lord's Supper, in which Jesus offers himself to us as the "bread of life," changing bread and wine into his own body and blood so that his followers would achieve complete union with him. The Mass is also a memorial—a reenactment that makes present Jesus' death on the cross, in which he offered himself to the Father as a sacrifice for our sins.

We call the Mass the "Eucharist," which means "thanksgiving," because it's joining Jesus in thanking God for the gift of life, love, and salvation given us in Jesus Christ. In the Mass, we join the priest, who stands in the place of Christ, offering himself to the Father for us. With the whole Church, we make up the body of Christ and offer ourselves in love to the Father.

That's why it's so important for us to be there!

A Catholic Church: Set Aside for Worship

And besides, a Catholic Church is consecrated especially for this worship of God. A bishop actually comes and blesses the site, making it a place where God will dwell in us his people, in the Eucharist, and in our sharing of God's Word. That 's why Catholic churches are such special places. Every Catholic Church is a house for God's people, the Church.

It's Not the Building That Makes the Church

Still, the church building is not nearly as important as the people in it. (In some parts of the world, Catholics can't afford to build a church, or are forced to worship outside of one.) The real Church is the body of believers gathered in Jesus' name.

Also see *Catechism of the Catholic Church*, 1066–1075.

IS THE CHURCH FULL OF HYPOCRITES?

Question: I've heard all about priests and other leaders in the Church who commit terrible sins. How can I follow a Church that has these people in it?

Answer: With that reasoning, how could you follow anything on earth? How could you follow any government, any school, any institution whatsoever? *Every* human institution has *some* corrupt people! As Jesus said, no one is fully righteous. We are all sinners.

Question: But I thought the Church was founded by Jesus, and therefore it couldn't have any evil in it.

Answer: Okay, let me explain. The Church *was* founded by Jesus Christ, and he said that "the gates of the netherworld shall not prevail against it" (Mt 16:18), which means it will never die. That's because the Holy Spirit is the real leader and sustainer of the Church. And therefore, the Church and its basic teachings on faith and morals will be safeguarded from error by the power of the Holy Spirit.

However, Jesus appointed *human beings* to operate and spread the Church throughout the world, and human beings are not perfect. Christ's gospel and his Church are not corrupt, but each of us—everyone in the Church—is a sinner, and some can be downright corrupt.

Question: I still don't see how that justifies the Church, if they're supposed to be representing Christ.

Answer: Let me put it to you another way. Suppose the constitution of your country's government was the best constitution you could imagine—perfect rights for everyone, perfect laws, and so on. So the basis of your government would be perfect. But now you have governors, mayors, and other politicians who have to put that constitution into effect. Chances are, even though the constitution is a great document, it's still going to have its problems in practice because of the weaknesses of those politicians. It's the same with the Church. Its basic doctrines, as laid down by Jesus Christ and inspired by the Holy Spirit, are perfect.

But the people in charge of spreading that faith, like everyone else (including each one of us), don't always practice what they preach, or they may preach a message that is in keeping with their own lifestyle rather than with God's plan.

Jesus encountered the same problem in his time. Even though the Jewish religion came from God, some of those who were leading it (the "scribes" and "Pharisees") were very corrupt. But since the religion was basically good, Jesus told the people to continue to follow it, but without imitating those who were corrupting it: "Do and observe all things whatsoever they tell you, but do not follow their example. For they preach but they do not practice" (Mt 23:3).

Despite the sinfulness of its members, including those leading it, the Church has successfully brought people to know Jesus Christ and his truth for nearly two thousand years. During Mass, the priest prays to God, "Look not on the sins of your people, but on the faith of your Church. . . ." We should say the same, always praying that the faith Christ has given us will transform all members of the Church (including us) into good and holy people.

Also see *Catechism of the Catholic Church*, 823–825.

WHAT DOES "CATHOLIC" MEAN?

Okay, you're at Mass on Sunday. You just listened to the priest's homily and you're either A) very inspired or B) falling asleep. You hear the thunder of the congregation as they launch into their best rendition of the Creed. "We believe in One God the Father, the Almighty. . . ." You zone out.

A minute later you zone back in, "We believe in one, holy, catholic, and apostolic Church"—cut—back up—rewind . . . "hcruhC cilotsopa dna, cilohtac"—right there—stop. That's the word. Say it forward: *Catholic*. Yes! What does that mean? Any clue? Check it out: It's Greek, and guess what it means? *Universal! Catholic* means "universal." And why did we name the Church "universal"? Here it is in a nutshell:

• **The Church is universal in time:** From the moment Jesus commissioned the apostles to right now, the Church has continued to exist, working to spread the message and truth of salvation in Christ. In other words, the Church has been (and will be) there from its foundation to last week, to now, to tomorrow, to the end of time! Therefore, it's *universal* in time.

• **The Church is universal in place:** The Church is for all land and all peoples—all races, nationalities, shapes, sizes, and colors. The Catholic Church can be found in more countries than any other religion.

You name the country, and the gospel of Jesus is there. You name the language, and the Bible's probably in it.

And every single day, throughout the world, one common prayer echoes in literally thousands of languages: the Catholic Mass. When we go to Mass, we're uniting spiritually in the same prayer that is being said *all over the world.* When we lift up our hearts in repentance at the beginning of Mass, there are Chinese, Japanese, Germans, Indians, Africans, Australians, and people from every other country in the world lifting their hearts with us in spirit. When we give the sign of peace, they're reaching out in peace as well. When we recite the Creed, they're professing the same faith. When we say, "Our Father, who art in heaven," they're praying the same words in many other languages. This is the meaning of *universal* in place. *Universal* means for all peoples.

• **The Church is universal in doctrine:** No matter where the Catholic faith is practiced, it maintains the same Christian doctrine. And how, you might ask, after 2,000 years of it spreading through so many different cultures and times, can its doctrine still be unchanged? Because through all the centuries, the Holy Spirit has guided it! Sure, people (even popes) within the Church have made mistakes, but ultimately, despite human error, the Church's doctrine has remained intact. Saying the doctrine does not change doesn't mean it doesn't develop. For example, you can't find the word *trinity* in the New Testament. It's like the acorn and the oak. The giant oak doesn't look like the acorn, but it still came from it.

It is this doctrine that holds the Catholic faith together all over the world. All united under the Pope, we Catholics profess the same faith and remain committed to the same Church. Sure, there's plenty of variety within our ranks, but there is unity in that diversity. And that unity is what makes us Catholic. That unity is *universal*!

Also see *Catechism of the Catholic Church,* 813–822, 830–835.

WHY DO WE HAVE A POPE?

"Why do we need a Pope? And, for that matter, why do we need bishops and priests and. . ." Okay, don't get carried away. The easiest way to answer that question is to use the constitution analogy. Imagine if you made photocopies of your country's constitution and gave one to each citizen, saying, "Read it. Interpret it. And live it the way you think you should." What would you get? Mayhem. Anarchy. Nearly everyone would interpret and live the constitution a little differently, and there would be no unity. That's why every country needs a *government* to put its constitution into effect and maintain unity.

Jesus didn't make photocopies of the Bible and pass it out to all his followers and say, "Read it. Interpret it. And live it the way you think you should." Instead, he laid the foundation for a Church whose leaders would safeguard and help the Church to understand his teachings and maintain unity.

Jesus selected twelve apostles whom he trained for this leadership task. But even *they* needed a leader, so Jesus told Simon Peter, the son of Jonah, "You are Peter, and upon this rock I will build my church, and the gates of the netherworld shall not prevail against it. I will give you the keys to the kingdom of heaven" (Mt 16:18–19). We consider St. Peter the first Pope, or leader of the Church, even though he wasn't called "Pope." And since Peter was the bishop of Rome, almost all of his successors have been situated there; and all have been the bishop of Rome even when situated elsewhere, which is the main reason our faith is called the *Roman* Catholic faith. Pope John Paul II is the 266th successor of St. Peter in a nearly 2,000-year line of unbroken succession.

How About All These Priests and Bishops?

The Pope, bishops, priests, and deacons have a special leadership role in the mission of today's Church, just as the first apostles and disciples whom Jesus chose had a special role in the early Church.

Jesus told those first disciples, "Whoever listens to you listens to me" (Lk 10:16), and he commanded them to teach the world everything he had taught them, promising that he would be with them, "always, until the end of the age" (Mt 28:20). And just as Jesus appointed twelve apostles, they appointed others to help them carry on the mission of the Church in their own time and through all time. We should respect and obey our leaders in the Church, because they act with the authority that Jesus himself gave to them. (For more information, see "The Sacrament of Holy Orders" on page 44.)

We're All Called!

Did you realize that we're *all* part of the "holy priesthood" of Christ because of our baptism? And as part of the broader priesthood, we're all called to be ministers of Christ to the world. These days, the Church is using the talents of lay (nonordained) leaders in its mission more than ever before. Some are teachers or social workers; others are theologians or writers; still others are Eucharistic ministers or lectors. There are many vocations in both the ordained and lay areas of life. What part of this holy ministry are *you* called to?

Also see *Catechism of the Catholic Church,* 880–887.

WHO ARE MARY AND ALL THE SAINTS?

Some people think that when Catholics pray to Mary and the saints it's idol worship and a negative in God's eyes. Let's look at what this stuff is all about . . .

"Hey, Man, Will You Pray for Me?"

John: Paul, you gotta pray for my dad, 'cause he's really sick right now and he's going into the hospital for tests.

Paul: Really? Okay, yeah, I'll definitely say some prayers for him, and I'll also ask St. Francis of Assisi to pray for him as well.

John: St. Francis? You mean the guy who lived seven hundred years ago in Italy? How can he pray for me? He's been dead for centuries! Besides, Jesus told us that he was the only mediator between us and God.

Paul: Then why are you asking *me* to pray for your dad?

John: Well, because we should all pray for each other. Jesus said, "I say to you, if two of you agree on earth about anything for which they are to pray, it shall be granted to them by my heavenly Father" (Mt 18:19).

Paul: I totally agree. So if I can pray for you or your dad now, don't you think I can keep praying for you after I die? If I died tomorrow knowing that your dad needs prayers, don't you think I'd still pray for him once I got to heaven?

John: Yeah, I guess.

Paul: And guess what? If I pray for him today—which I will—my prayers are still somewhat limited by my sins and my lack of faith. But once I reach heaven, I won't sin anymore. Therefore, my love and my prayers will be even more powerful before God.

"But They Don't Even Know My Name!"

John: Well, maybe it's true that you could pray for me once you're in heaven, but the rest of the saints in heaven don't even know who I am.

Paul: How do you know? The saints can see everything God allows them to see because God sees everything.

John: So you're saying that these saints are just like our friends and relatives on earth, except that they're in heaven?

Paul: Exactly. It's what we call "The Communion of Saints." It's the big family of the children of God, composed of those living on earth, those being purified in purgatory, and those who have already made it to heaven. We're one big family of Christians supporting each other on our trek to reach heaven.

John: So we don't really pray to the saints as if they were God, we just ask them to help us by praying *with* us?

Paul: Right! And then we get a lot more prayer power. That's why prayers with the saints have worked so well since the beginning of the Church.

John: You mean they did this in the early church as well?

Paul: You bet. If you go into the catacombs (you know, the caves under the ground where poor Romans, including many early Christians, were buried), you'll see the names of Christian martyrs together with messages asking them to pray for those who were still alive. They were an inspiration for the early Christians.

John: But why do we need any inspiration other than Christ?

Paul: Because God wants us to inspire each other. That's why St. Paul wrote, "Be imitators of me, as I am of Christ" (1 Cor 11:1). In the lives of the saints, the power of Jesus is acted out in every age and every situation. And that helps us relate to Jesus even better.

John: Doesn't that take away from Christ?

Paul: Not at all. It's like the *Mona Lisa*. The more you admire the painting, the more you praise the painter. The saints always said their holiness came from God, not themselves. So in honoring the saints, you automatically praise God.

"What's So Special About Mary?"

John: So why is the Virgin Mary so special of all the saints?

Paul: Because her "yes" to God was the beginning of our salvation, the moment the Holy Spirit conceived Jesus in Mary's womb. Jesus took his humanity from Mary. Mary was his mother. He obeyed her. He loved her. And she loved him more than anyone else ever loved him. (Generally, who loves a child more than his own mother?)

John: Are you saying that Mary was closer to Jesus than anyone else?

Paul: Absolutely. As the mother of Jesus (Mary conceived Jesus by the power of the Holy Spirit), Mary was more united to God than anyone who has ever lived. Not even Moses had this kind of relationship with God. He carried God's Commandments on stone tablets. Mary carried the author of those Commandments in her womb! Moses obeyed God. But in the little home in Nazareth, the Son of God obeyed his mother Mary!

And then, don't forget that Jesus entrusted John and all of us to Mary as he was dying on the cross.

John: But God is God, and Mary is just a creature.

Paul: That's right, she is only a creature, and anyone who says Mary is anything more than a creature is committing idolatry. But nonetheless, some of God's creatures become more united to God than others, and Mary united herself *completely* to God. That unity with God makes her prayers especially powerful. Remember the wedding at Cana (see John 2:1–11)? They ran out of wine, and Mary asked Jesus for a miracle. Even though he resisted at first, he changed the water into wine because his mother had asked him to help.

In heaven, Mary still asks Jesus to help us in many ways, and Jesus says "yes" to his mother like any good son would.

John: Well, does all this mean that I should always pray to the saints, and never to God?

Paul: Of course not! You should *always* pray directly to God. And then you should also ask others on earth and the saints in heaven to pray for you as well. All of those prayers are ultimately directed to God, who alone holds the power to answer them.

Also see *Catechism of the Catholic Church*, 487–511, 946–959, 1717, 2030, 2156, 2683–2684.

THE SEVEN SACRAMENTS: AWESOME SPIRITUAL TREASURES!

Before Jesus left us, he wanted to leave a visible sign of his love and care for us . . . something to help us continue to believe in him. He could have left a huge monument of himself in stone, but he knew that would crumble away or be tumbled sooner or later. He could have left that star in Bethlehem shining brightly, but he knew that would burn out someday. And if he had left us with only the Bible, he knew that some people who couldn't read or get to a Bible might miss out on his offer of new life and salvation.

So Jesus figured out a way to leave us a treasure that could not deteriorate, or burn out, or be missed because of language or culture. It's a treasure that only becomes valuable when it's placed into a person's soul—where no one else can ever touch it or take it away. This treasure was the greatest gift Jesus ever gave us. And this treasure is the Sacraments, seven of them, seven sacramental acts for a Church that is the sacramental presence of Christ in the world.

The Sacraments (Baptism, Reconciliation, Eucharist, Confirmation, Matrimony, Holy Orders, and Anointing of the Sick) are the outward signs of the inward treasures—graces—that Jesus is planting in our souls. Each sacrament is a spiritual event in concrete terms—water or oil combined with the grace of God—which produces a brilliant diamond of holiness in a person's soul and gives a responsibility in the Church.

As Catholics, we believe Jesus instituted each of the Seven Sacraments, although it took the Church many years to develop the various and sometimes changing ways in which we practice them. For instance, going to daily Mass and receiving Holy Communion daily is a relatively new practice. In the early Church, Christians celebrated Eucharist once a week. And in the early Church, the Sacrament of Confirmation was not given mainly to teenagers as it is today. It was connected with Baptism. Indeed, the way we practice the Sacraments may change from age to age, but the basics of the Sacraments remain the same. Here's a rundown of the basics of the Seven Sacraments in about seven minutes.

BAPTISM: Big Baby Gets a Bath

It's no news that when a baby is born, one of the first things it gets is a bath. That's because it has gook and slime all over it, and in order to keep it healthy, it needs to be washed clean. The same can be said about our souls. Before we're baptized, we're like "spiritual babies" and our souls need to be washed to remove the gook and slime caused by "original sin." Original sin—which was the result of our first parents' disobedience to God (see Genesis 3)—caused a division in our relationship with God, and cut us off from God's gift of eternal life: "The moment you eat from it (the tree of knowledge of good and bad) you are surely doomed to die" (Gn 2:17).

Through our baptism into Christ, our relationship with God is reconciled, and the door to eternal life is once again opened to us. Whether we're 6 seconds old or 60 years old, Baptism is our spiritual birthday into the family of God. Through this sacrament, our original sin is washed away, and we begin a new life united to Christ and the whole Christian community. Baptism is the beginning of an awesome journey. We're now part of the death and resurrection of Christ, and that means we're called to become "other Christs" to the world by living out the teachings of Jesus in our own lives. Actually, we are purified in Baptism because we join Christ in his dying—giving our lives for others—and rising with him.

Baptism is a sacrament we only receive once in life. Any sins we commit throughout our life (called "personal sins") *after* our Baptism are forgiven through the grace we continue to receive when we pray, follow God's will, and receive the other sacraments (especially the Sacrament of Reconciliation in the case of any serious sins).

CONFIRMATION: Bigger Baby Takes the Plunge

Remember when you were a little kid? Water was a big event. In the winter you had a blast in the bathtub, and in the summer you splashed around in a plastic pool. But one day someone showed you a lake, or better yet, the ocean. There was a twinge of fear. But you knew you just had to take the plunge. There's something great about being able to let go and *go for it*.

The same thing happens when you get confirmed. You got your feet wet when you were baptized and now it's time to take a major life-altering, soul-transforming, radical step into committed, responsible, full-force Christian living. No one's making the decisions for you now. It's just you and God and a huge ocean of life ahead, challenging you to sail through it on the wind of the Spirit. In Confirmation you take the full ownership of the commitment made in Baptism.

When the Bishop anoints your head and tells you to "receive the Holy Spirit," you'd better believe that the Holy Spirit is going to move some mountains inside of you.

Remember Pentecost (see Acts 2)? The Holy Spirit came to the apostles then. In a way, that was their Confirmation. It confirmed once and for all that they were believers who could witness to Christ. And they were "baptized in fire." They received the gifts of the Holy Spirit, like wisdom and understanding, and also other gifts, like the ability to make bold statements about God or to speak in everybody's languages.

You get various gifts, too, at your Confirmation; each person receives the special gifts God wants to give that person. You might not notice them right away, but they're there nonetheless. It's like starting off in a new school. You have to learn the ropes and listen to the directions of your new teacher . . . yeah, you guessed it, the Holy Spirit.

But the Holy Spirit is more than a teacher. The Spirit is a comforter, a helper, a friend when everyone else is gone. It's God's Holy Spirit that fills our hearts, minds, and souls with a burning desire to enflame the world with the love of God. It's a fire of peace and forgiveness. It's a fire that some choose to extinguish. But by our act of being confirmed, we are choosing to let the fire grow!

EUCHARIST: A Great Mystery

In the early days of the Church, some people were scared of Christians because they heard that they were eating the flesh and blood of a man. Well, they were right about Christians eating the Body of Christ, but it certainly wasn't what they thought it was.

The Eucharist, also called the Mass, is the prayer of Christ. In the Mass, Christ offers his whole life to God, the Father. In the Mass, we join Christ in that prayer. In the Mass, Jesus gives us his Body and Blood in the Holy Eucharist, but he gives it to us in the form of ordinary bread and wine. Jesus told us, "Whoever eats my flesh and drinks my blood has eternal life, and I will raise him on the last day. For my flesh is true food, and my blood is true drink" (Jn 6:54–55; see also 1 Corinthians 11).

Some people wonder how this can be. St. Ignatius of Antioch, who knew St. John the Apostle, even wrote, "The Docetae (a group of Christians who had separated themselves from the Church) abstain from the Eucharist . . . because they refuse to admit that the Eucharist is the flesh of our Lord Jesus Christ."

Sometimes people argue, "How could God enter a piece of bread?" "How could a piece of bread become the body of Christ?" For that matter, how could an infinite God enter the microscopic human body that Jesus became at the moment of conception in Mary's womb? How could the Word of God become flesh? That, too, seems impossible. But with God all things are possible.

The fact is, we believe Jesus speaks for himself regarding the Eucharist. When he told people that they would have to eat his body, many people were offended because they thought he meant it literally. He could have said, "Hey, I don't mean that literally. I'm just using a symbol." That way a lot of people would have accepted his statement. But instead Jesus just reasserted what he had said. Even after many of the people began to leave him because of this statement, he *still* didn't change his words!

And then, at the Last Supper, Jesus took the bread, broke it and said, "This is my body." Notice, he didn't say, "This is *like* my body," or "This *represents* (or is a symbol of) my body." No, he said it was his body! And Christ's followers believed it. St. Justin Martyr, who died in 165, wrote, "As God's Word Jesus Christ became flesh and blood for our salvation, so also have we been taught that the food made Eucharist by the word of prayer is both flesh and blood of that Jesus who was made flesh."

At Mass, the priest stands in the place of Christ, and through the power of the Holy Spirit, the bread and wine become Christ's body and blood. We don't know *how* this happens because it's a mystery, which the Church calls "transubstantiation." But we do understand *why* it happens.

It happens so that God can fully communicate and become one with us. In the Old Testament, the Jewish priest would offer a sacrificial lamb or goat to God to ask pardon for the people's sins. This offering would then be eaten by both the priest and the people. It was a "meal" of reconciliation, forgiveness, and thanksgiving.

In the New Testament, Jesus offered *himself* as the sacrificial lamb to obtain pardon for all people's sins ("the Lamb of God who takes away the sin of the world"). And by making himself truly present to us in the Eucharist, we can share a communion with God—a "meal" of reconciliation and thanksgiving. St. Paul called this meal "the Lord's Supper" (1 Cor 11:20).

This "breaking of the bread" has gone on since the very the beginning of the Church (see Acts 2:46) because Jesus told his apostles to continue doing it in memory of him. This spiritual food has nourished the greatest saints in the Church and brought them to a deeper love for God. It will do the same for us if we let it!

RECONCILIATION: Somebody Get Me a Doctor!

Is there anything better than a doctor when you're feeling really sick? Okay, maybe a mom, dad, or good friend. Well, that's just what God is for us in the Sacrament of Reconciliation. When our souls are aching or "ill" from sin, it's then that we can turn to the Divine Doctor, who will comfort and instruct us like a parent or good friend and who will restore us to spiritual health.

Jesus gave his Church and especially the apostles the power to administer this divine healing. He breathed his Holy Spirit on them and said, "Receive the Holy Spirit. Whose sins you forgive are forgiven them, and whose sins you retain are retained" (Jn 20:22–23).

But a doctor can only heal you if you tell him what's wrong. That's why we Catholics go to confession. The priest acts as God's "physical" representative, listens to our problems and counsels us, and then speaks God's words of healing by saying the words, "I absolve (release) you from your sins. . . ."

Jesus knew that confessing our sins to another person would help us get those sins off our chest (St. James wrote, "Confess your sins to one another," 5:16). Besides, when we sin, we sin not only against ourselves but against the whole Church of believers, the body of Christ. So we should also seek forgiveness from the Church, which the priest represents.

Reconciliation is one of the greatest sacraments to keep us growing in our Catholic faith. And unlike visiting therapists, psychiatrists, and other "soul and mind doctors," reconciliation is absolutely free. We should take advantage of it, because in every Catholic Church in the world, you'll find the "doctor" will be in.

ANOINTING OF THE SICK: Somebody Get Me the Doctor Again!

The same is true when we are *physically* sick or near death. God's minister anoints us with oil, prays with us and helps us offer our sufferings to God with patience and endurance. This is called the "Anointing of the Sick." Check out James 5:14–15, where he writes, "Is anyone among you sick? He should summon the presbyters of the church, and they should pray over him and anoint [him] with oil in the name of the Lord, and the prayer of faith will save the sick person, and the Lord will raise him up. If he has committed any sins, he will be forgiven."

Jesus made it a point to express his love and mercy through his physical touch and healing. And he left the Church this sacrament to carry on that healing. But more important than the physical healing that may or may not come (according to God 's plan for the person's life), we can always count on spiritual healing from this sacrament.

MATRIMONY: Baby I Love U

Marci and Marvin had it made. They were in love. This was better than the movies. Then Marci brought up the big "M," and Marvin miraculously disappeared. It was fun being in love, he thought, but being "in love" and "loving" are two different things. Sharing your life with another person, for the rest of your life, means more than kissing under the mistletoe.

Someone once said that friendship is "a single soul dwelling in two bodies." But marriage is "two souls dwelling in one body." When two people marry each other in the Catholic Church, they bind themselves together as one for life. That's because marriage is a *sacrament*. It's not just a contract between two people though; God also becomes part of their covenant to help them toward a deeper and transformed life through marriage.

Just as Jesus witnessed and approved the marriage in Cana, God is still part of the marriage sacrament. The apostle Paul even compared Christ's love for the Church to the love that spouses have for each other (see Ephesians 5:25). That's because married love is meant to be unconditional, like God's love is for us. Two people make a commitment in marriage to love each other exclusively and unconditionally, without any time limits.

Sounds like a pretty tough recipe to follow, huh? It is. That's why God's a part of it—a *necessary* ingredient. Without God, a marriage lacks the "glue" it needs to stay together. But with God, we can make it through the "sickness and health, richer and poorer, good times and bad times."

And in marriage, a couple has the opportunity to become *creators* of life, like God! And since God created out of love, it's only right that humans should create out of love as well. That's why new life (a baby) happens as a result of "making love." And that's why sex is so holy when it happens within marriage. It not only unites the couple in love, it unites the couple to God's creative, life-giving powers!

HOLY ORDERS: A Bad Boy Gets a Heavenly Call

In high school, Kenny was wild. Although from time to time he was aware of God's presence, Kenny loved girls, sports, parties, and lived life in the fast lane. After high school, he still tried to leave God out of his life. He became a first-class steward on a prestigious airline, an interpreter on the ocean liner *Queen Elizabeth,* a soldier in the British Army Intelligence Corps, got engaged, and traveled the world. But God wouldn't leave him alone. God kept calling him, kept asking him, kept whetting his appetite with glimpses of a better life beyond all his luxuries. And then one day God called, and Kenny answered.

No one knows how or why God chooses some guys to be priests. It just happens. Jesus chose his apostles, and he chose Kenny (now well-known priest/lecturer Fr. Ken Roberts). He handpicked them and told them to go out and bring his salvation to all the world.

Jesus could have just yelled out to a random crowd and told them, "Hey, you can all go out and forgive sins now, okay." But he didn't. He "called" people out of that crowd to represent him in a special way and carry on some of the very special, sacramental aspects of his ministry. They were meant to lead the others after Jesus was gone, because we all need leaders.

As Catholics we believe that Jesus chose the first apostles and made them "bishops," or leaders, of the Church. This process is called "ordination." This was the origin of the Sacrament of Holy Orders. The apostles in turn chose other bishops and other priests, through the power of the Holy Spirit working in this sacrament. And to this day that "passing on of the torch" is accomplished as bishops lay hands on new priests throughout the world, ordaining them for the work of God.

Also see *Catechism of the Catholic Church,* 1113–1134.

HOW DO I BECOME A BETTER CATHOLIC? THE TEN STEPS

A jailer at Philippi asked Paul and Silas the most important question in life: "What must I do to be saved?" They answered him, "Believe in the Lord Jesus and you and your household will be saved" (Acts 16:30–31). The jailer believed this message about Jesus and the good news. The jailer gave his life to Christ and so did his family members. But that doesn't mean the rest of his life was a fairy tale.

To be a Christian means to be a follower of Jesus Christ. But that doesn't just mean lip service. It means a radical commitment. We are saying, "Jesus, I believe in you. I trust you with my life. I want to live for you. I believe that you died on the cross to take my place, so I could be forgiven. Because of that, I am willing to turn away from my sinful way of living to follow you." If you're ready to be radical for God, here are 10 steps to help you become a faith-filled, on-fire Catholic.

1. Read your Bible! Read the Word of God every day. Start with one chapter a day, beginning with Genesis. It won't take long to read the whole Bible. As you read, ask the Lord to speak to your heart, your mind, and your conscience. There may be verses you don't understand, or words you can't pronounce. Your Bible has some notes to help you with these. Just hang in there. God will "fill you in" on exactly what you need to know right now, at this point in your life. And keep an open mind. The Bible was meant to accompany you your whole life long.

2. Pray every day. Prayer is God's toll-free number. Just dial, 1-800-GOD-TIME and God'll pick up before it even rings. Then start talking. You don't need to use big words or "religious-sounding" phrases. Just talk to God as you'd talk to a good friend. Be respectful. But be yourself, too.

Talk about the good things in your life. And talk about the bad. God's interested in all of it. But remember, prayer is communication, and communication is a two-way street. Sometimes just sitting in silence is the best prayer we can offer God. Our silence gives God a chance to "talk."

If you have problems figuring out what to say, there are plenty of prayers that others have written, including the "Our Father," which Jesus himself gave us (Mt 6:9–13). The Rosary is also a powerful prayer, which has helped countless Catholics get closer to God over the centuries.

3. Tell someone you respect about your new commitment to Christ. Find someone who can support you in your decision to become a better Catholic. It could be a teacher, a parish priest, your parents, a youth minister or even a friend who's a committed Catholic. Sharing your faith with this person will give you a sense of responsibility and commitment.

4. Go to church. Start this weekend, if not before! Remember, we go to church to worship God with a community of believers, so try to go with an open mind and heart. Be attentive to the people around you. As the New Testament puts it, they are your "brothers and sisters." Don't be a snoozehead—get involved! Participate! Sing! (Remember, singing is praying twice—even if it's off key!) Say the responses and the prayers like you *mean* them. We don't have problems talking loud at parties or concerts, so why should we respond like dead robots at Mass? And if you have a talent for reading or singing, or if you feel called to be an altar server or a eucharistic minister, get to it. Your church life will only be as vibrant as *you* make it.

5. Go for the sacraments. Especially for the Eucharist and Reconciliation. Take advantage of these great gifts Jesus gave us. The body and blood of Christ are given to you as the Bread of Life and the cup of salvation. If you're having trouble believing in the presence of Jesus in the Eucharist, ask Jesus to increase your faith. After all, Jesus said, "Ask and you will receive" (Lk 11:9–13). Jesus wants to give us the gift of faith. Remember, Jesus is present in the community, in the Word of God, and in you, as well as in the signs of bread and wine.

Jesus also wants us to live our lives free from sin and guilt. When we hurt ourselves and others by doing things that are against God's will, there is a need in our hearts and souls for forgiveness. When we go to the Sacrament of Reconciliation (confession), we show God we're sorry for our failures and we want to be forgiven. And when the priest says, "I absolve you from your sins," we know without a doubt that our souls are once again "right with God."

6. Keep a daily journal. You can write notes to yourself about your spiritual journey. And you can write notes to God (love notes, of course). And write down questions you have about your faith, so that you can later ask someone for help with them. Most of all, a spiritual journal is a way to keep yourself in touch with who you are and who God is in your life. It's actually a prayer written down.

7. Find out more about what the Catholic Church teaches and why. You don't understand something about our faith? Find out! Get answers! You can ask your pastor, a youth minister, other Catholics, or attend meetings or conventions or retreats. You can get a good spiritual book, maybe on the life of a saint. You can even rent a Catholic video or movie (there *are* a few in existence!), or even visit a Catholic Web site. There's a lot of stuff out there to help us understand our faith; we just have to look for it.

8. Share your faith with others—especially other young people. It may be hard at first to share your faith—especially with those closest to you, who may not understand the changes in your life—but eventually they'll get used to it, and more often than not they'll like the changes they see.

Try not to scare people away by getting too enthusiastic. Sometimes just sharing how God has changed your life is the easiest way to start and it gives your friends something they can easily relate to. Your good example is the best testimony of your faith.

Another way to help others find Jesus is by inviting them to go to church with you. After Mass, you can talk about what you heard. You can also invite your friends to fun activities, such as youth group meetings, retreats, and other church events.

9. Put your faith into practice. God is definitely calling you to put your faith into actions. Can you sing or play an instrument? Can you teach? Can you visit the shut-ins (people who are sick, old, or for some other reason can't get to church)? Can you help other people who are less fortunate than you are? And, hey, have you ever considered becoming a priest or religious sister or brother? Don't be afraid to answer God's call, no matter what it is!

The greatest joy you'll experience in life will come from allowing Jesus to do things in and through your life! When you become his hands and his heart to the world, his Holy Spirit will pass through you like wind rushing through a flute. And the music that will come from it will bring peace and fulfillment to you and those you've touched. That's what the Christian life is all about—Jesus Christ alive in you!

You don't have to be especially talented in order for Jesus to use you. It's not your *ability* that he is looking for. It's your *availability*. Make (or continue) your commitment to him right now. "Jesus, I'm available to you. Here's my life. You are welcome to work through me any way you wish. I just want to bring honor and glory to you and change my world for the better!" Amen!

10. Thank God every day that you've received this gift of faith. Nothing you ever find in life will compare!

Also see *Catechism of the Catholic Church*, 2012–2016.

HOW TO GET ALONG WITH MY CHRISTIAN FRIENDS IN OTHER DENOMINATIONS

Marci: Hi, you guys. What's up?

Sharleen: Hi, Marci. We were just talking about going to youth group tonight.

Marci: Really? Where do you guys go?

Karin: Oh, we go to Christ Hope Fellowship in the valley.

Marci: What's that?

Sharleen: Are you for real? It's a church!

Marci: What I meant was, what kind of church?

Brent: Oh, it's a nondenominational Christian. Where do you go?

Marci: I go to St. Patrick's on 86th Street.

Brent: Isn't that Catholic?

Marci: Yeah.

Sharleen: Like, I didn't know you were *Catholic!*

Marci: Yeah, I am. Why?

Sharleen: I'm just surprised, that's all. I thought you were Christian.

Marci: Whaddya mean? I *am* Christian.

Brent: Not if you're Catholic, you're not. Christians aren't supposed to worship idols. That's the very first commandment. You Catholics do. You worship statues and Mary and other dead people.

Marci: Oh, right! We do not.

Sharleen: Yeah, and how come you call priests "Father" when Jesus says right in the Bible to call no man father because our Father in heaven is our only father?

Marci: Well, first of all, St. Paul calls himself a "father" of the other Christians.

Sharleen: And, like, why do you tell your sins to a priest? It doesn't say to do that in the Bible. And what about purgatory, and . . .

Marci: You guys, that's about a hundred different things, and if you'd give me a chance to answer, maybe I can explain.

Brent: Well, we kinda have to run or we're gonna be late. Maybe you can come to our church sometime to see what Christians are really like.

Marci: Yeah . . . maybe. See ya later.

Three days later

Marci: . . . I don't know what to do. I really like them and I know they're really good people, but I'm afraid they won't hang out with me because they think I'm not Christian.

Fr. Aldon: Well, I think it's really important for you to stress the things you *do* have in common with them. It's so easy to pick out certain differences and harp on those. People hear all kinds of distorted truths about us, and unless someone takes the time to explain the truth to them, they'll never know we *are* Christians.

Marci: Like what?

Fr. Aldon: Well, start with the things all Christians believe in. The easiest way is to start with the Creed. Tell them you believe in one God. You believe in the Trinity and the resurrection; you believe in heaven and hell. Tell them that you believe that Christ died to save all of us. These are things most Christians believe.

And ask them what else they believe. Then ask them *why* they believe it. You might find that they might know a lot of "stuff," but they may be kind of unsure about why.

Marci: But what about when they get to the other things?

Fr. Aldon: Then you need to explain in a nice way what we believe, and if there's something you don't know, be honest. Tell them you're not sure, or that you don't know, but that you'll ask me or your parents, or read up on it. You might find that they've taken a lot at face value, too, and they may need to do a little bit of homework of their own.

Marci: Do you really think we'll be able to be good friends?

Fr. Aldon: There's no reason why Catholics and Christians of other denominations can't be the closest of friends. After all, we share the fundamental belief and love of Jesus, and as Christians we're all called to love God and one another. If any of you have a problem loving each other, then you need to reevaluate your beliefs! I've found that one of the best ways to reinforce such a friendship is to pray with your Christian friends and pray for things you do together, like school and extracurricular activities. That would please God a lot more than all the arguing!

Also see *Catechism of the Catholic Church*, 818–819, 836–856, 2106.

WHO DO YOU THINK YOU ARE?

How you see yourself is one of the key factors in your life. Some people refer to this as self-image, or self-esteem. Self-esteem is that deep-down feeling you have about your own personal worth. It's your opinion of yourself. It's that feeling that says, "I like myself" or "I dislike myself."

Why Does It Matter?

The reason your self-concept is so important is because you talk, act, and react like the person you think you are. Sure, even with a poor self-image you may break out of the pattern and belt one out of the park, or ace the big test, or get a date with Mr. or Miss Perfect.

On the other hand, even guys and girls with good self-images blow it from time to time. Usually, though, your mind will complete the picture you tell it to paint of yourself.

If you see yourself as ugly, fat, stupid, or slow, you'll probably act that way. If your self-worth is low, you may think of yourself as a born loser. You may think that you're even unworthy of God's love or anybody else's.

You may slip into the habit of putting yourself down. Here are a few of the phrases that a person with poor self-esteem often uses:

- I can never do anything right.
- Why me?
- I'll never amount to anything.
- I guess God loves me, but I sure can't stand myself.
- I'm good for nothing.
- God could never use somebody like me.

Sound Familiar?

A lot of young people these days suffer from this lack of self-respect. That's because society today defines us not by *who* we are but by *what* we are. In other words, we have to *be something* in order to be worthwhile. We have to look a certain way, act a certain way, wear certain clothes, drive a certain car, and so on and so on.

The media pumps this into our heads for one reason: to make money from us. By trying to make us into something we're not, they can make a lot of money from us. They'll sell us everything we need to get there!

But the fact is we never make it—even if we're born beautiful. As long as we try to attain the image of false perfection that the media convinces us to be, we'll never be happy with ourselves and our shortcomings.

Who We Are, Not What We Are

God looks at us in a way completely different from the way modern society does. Only in understanding who you are in God's eyes can you realize that who you are will always be far more important than what you are. And who are you? You are a child of God, created in the image of God.

You are more important and powerful than any animal or plant, or even the entire earth, sun, and solar system. Because all of those things will someday disappear. The earth and everything on it will someday be gone, and even the sun will eventually burn out. But you, in God, will live *forever!* You will still be alive long after the sun itself has burned out!

The Most Important Thing in the Universe?

Of all the creatures that God placed on the earth, God gave this gift of eternal life to human beings. And because God loves you and wants so badly to spend eternity with you, Jesus died to make that gift available to you.

This is so much more important than any fashion, fad, or fancy car!

God will love you unconditionally, no matter what you wear, what you say, or what you drive. Because of that, you can honestly say, "Thanks, Lord, for creating me. I know you have a purpose for making me the way you did. I'm glad to be me. I'd rather be me than any other person on earth. Thanks, Lord, for what you are going to do in and through my life."

Common Errors Concerning Self-Image

1. Thinking too lowly of ourselves. This causes us to wallow in low self-esteem. We know that we're "fallen sinners," so we think we're worthless. Like Adam and Eve, we feel naked and ashamed, and we fear being exposed (see Genesis 3:10).

Here's the key: When you've sinned, *admit* that you've hurt someone else, or yourself, or God, rather than shaking it off like it's no big deal. Once you've asked God's forgiveness (and received the Sacrament of Reconciliation in the case of a very serious sin) and made amends to those you've hurt, it's over and in the past. Don't keep giving yourself a hard time about it.

Sometimes a person you hurt won't want to "forgive and forget." You can only ask. Even if the person would rather stay mad, you want to know you've done all you could. God knows, too.

Next time you feel down on yourself, read 1 Corinthians 12 to see how each of us is valuable in God's plan.

2. Eating humble pie. True humility is one of the best qualities a person can have. But some people confuse godly humility with putting themselves down.

You know this sort of person. They go around dragging themselves through the dirt. "I can't do anything right. I think I'll eat some worms!" They think they're being humble, but this is not the type of humility that God desires, because rejecting yourself is also rejecting the Spirit of God that is within you.

Others have difficulty accepting a compliment. They say, "Oh, be serious, it was no big deal." So when someone says something nice about you, thank them and say to yourself (and maybe even to them), "Thank you, God, for the gifts you've given me."

3. Whining for compliments. Whiners spend most of their time advertising their mistakes. "Did I mess up?" "Was that all right? I think I blew that last part."

In a weird way, whiners are trying to get somebody else to support their own self-esteem. They really crave compliments and flattery, but their self-images are so low they are afraid to ask for an honest opinion. They hang negative comments out on the line, hoping that someone will come along and take them down.

4. Thinking too highly of ourselves. This is a negative form of pride that leads people to think or act like they're better than everyone else. They keep telling you how great they are. They're always right, at least in their own minds. They're show-offs, and often they're loud, crude, and rude. They might even think they call the shots in their life, rather than God.

But in reality, this pride is usually fake, and inside they're really struggling with a low self-image. That's why they're trying to call attention to themselves. What they are really saying is: "Help! I need attention. Please look at me!"

People with good self-images have healthy respect for God and healthy regard for themselves.

They don't need to crawl, and they don't need to boast. They can do without expensive toys or trinkets. They know who they are in Christ, so they can afford to be modest. Their self-esteem doesn't depend upon whether or not they "win" in the eyes of the world. Their view of themselves is based upon the source of all truly lasting success—Jesus Christ.

Tips to Improve Your Self-Image

Improving your self-image may take some time and some work, but with God's help, you can do it. Here are some suggestions that will help, too.

1. Remember, God loves you and accepts you, no strings attached. YOU MATTER TO GOD!

2. Accept God's forgiveness. It's tough to feel good about yourself when you know you are dirty on the inside. Forgiveness is needed.

First, seek and receive God's forgiveness in the Sacrament of Reconciliation. Admit what you've done, and ask God to forgive you. Ask God for the power to do better in the future. Then make sure you've sincerely forgiven yourself. If God can forgive you, you can forgive yourself!

Next, seek forgiveness from those you may have hurt. You might be surprised at how fast most people are to forgive. (Most people.)

Finally, forgive those who have hurt you. Even if they never find out about it, forgive them from your heart. Jesus said, "If you forgive others their transgressions, your heavenly Father will forgive you. But if you do not forgive others, neither will your Father forgive your transgressions" (Mt 6:14–15). Try it! You'll feel a burden lifted from your shoulders, and your self-esteem will rise.

3. Find a friend in whom you can confide. You don't need many friends to help improve your self-image. But if you can find even one with whom you can share your inner feelings, it may be a large step forward for your self-esteem. This friend should be somebody you trust—someone who will tell you the truth about yourself.

Don't think you're a weirdo for seeking help. Just the opposite is true. We all need encouragement. Even Jesus had friends.

4. Read about good heroes you want to imitate. Read the stories of some of the people who have truly had an impact on their world—people such as Abraham Lincoln, Thomas Edison, Mother Theresa, or any of the many saints in our faith. Read about St. Francis, who embraced poverty and charity as a way to perfection. Or St. Maria Goretti, who was stabbed to death defending her sexual purity. Or St. Maximillian Kolbe, who died in another man's place in the Nazi death camps. There are hundreds of testimonies of people who have reached holiness in every age. You can read about how, despite their human failings and weaknesses, they still accomplished great things in the world. Learn from them. And if they're still living, listen to them speak, in person or on tape.

The apostle Paul tells us:

"Be renewed in the spirit of your minds, and put on the new self" (Eph 4:23–24). Cheer up and feel good about yourself! God is on your side.

5. Smile, and show it in how you look. Not only does smiling improve your self-image, it will make you more interesting to others. Your outward appearance does make a statement—to others and to yourself. This doesn't mean you have to have a perfect body and the perfect clothes. It just means that you should look and act in a way that will make you feel good about yourself.

Also see *Catechism of the Catholic Church*, 355–368, 1701–1715.

I'M ALL STRESSED OUT

Stress. A lot of us feel it. Parents, teachers, business professionals, even priests. Teenagers are especially sensitive to stress. Stress at home, at work, at school with your friends, pressure from your peers, difficult decisions about dating, drugs, sex, or alcohol, grappling with your grades . . . whew! The stress can really get to you.

What Causes Stress?

Most stress in your life can be traced to one of three sources:

- Other people
- Events or circumstances
- Inner confusion or frustration

Other people can put pressure on you in many different ways. Parents can pressure you to do better at school, to get a part-time job, or to be home on time. Brothers and sisters can be a source of stress, too. Not

Stress Finder

Stress can sneak up on you. Many times you don't even notice it until it's too late. But being aware of a few signs of stress can help you avoid being caught by surprise.

Read over the list below and think back over the past few days or weeks. Then check off those signs you have noticed in your life recently. More than three checkmarks, and you may be headed for burnout. Review the suggestions, and if necessary, seek help:

- ❏ Extreme tension between you and your parents
- ❏ Temper tantrums
- ❏ Headaches
- ❏ Avoiding being with other people
- ❏ Frequent stomach knots or pains
- ❏ Problems with your peers
- ❏ Nightmares
- ❏ Too much sleep
- ❏ Too little sleep
- ❏ Declining interest in enjoyable activities
- ❏ Attempting to escape your problems through music, movies, TV and the Internet, or drugs, sex, alcohol, or the occult

all of this pressure is bad, but it may feel that way when you're experiencing it.

Sometimes other people simply bother you. Stress strikes when your friends have ignored you, criticized you, or attempted to get you to do something you'd rather avoid.

Events and circumstances, especially those over which you have no control, pour on the pressure. For example, you pass your driver's test, but don't have a car of your own to drive. Your parents need theirs, and not many friends will allow you to borrow an automobile. So you're stuck. All dressed up and no way to go.

Or, you studied like mad for that big test, and you really did pretty well, but "Billy the Brain" blew the curve by blitzing the test and scoring a perfect paper. Another "C" for you. Or, you've been hoping and praying for a date to homecoming, but nobody wants to go with you. What's the result? Frustration, anger, and, you guessed it, more pressure.

Sometimes the stress comes from **turmoil inside** that you can't explain. It's just there. Fear of failure, or rejection, or not being popular, or that you aren't smart enough or good-looking, or that you won't be able to succeed in the career you want to pursue. All of these things bring about stress.

How Can You Handle Stress?

1. Notice the warning signs. Your heart always seems to be racing. Your stomach feels as though it's tied in knots. These are often the first warnings of too much stress.

2. Recognize that everyone gets stressed out once in a while. Even strong Christians have to deal with the pressures of life. The pressures don't go away with age. They simply take a different form.

3. Try various methods of coping. When the pressure is on, some people will close their eyes and relax for a few minutes. Others suggest that you blink hard. This breaks the train of thought that has been racing through your mind. Sometimes it helps to take a deep breath and let it out very slowly. Do this several times and you will begin to feel your body relaxing.

Take a walk. Take a break. Jump in a lake. Change your routine or usual pattern of doing things. Often, physical exercise is a great stress reducer. Go swimming or jogging. Play some basketball.

Check your diet. Are you eating healthy, or are you stuffing your body with junk food? It does make a difference.

4. Realize that there are some things you can't control. For example, you can't control whether or not your parents will get a divorce, but you can control whether or not you will get to school or work on time. Concentrate on those things you can change, and leave the rest up to God.

5. Seek support. Everyone needs to talk with someone who cares. Don't be bashful about seeking help from someone who has been where you are right now. Possibly your parents, or a priest, nun, teacher, or youth leader can relate to what you are going through. Be willing to go to them and ask for their advice. They may never know you are hurting unless you talk to them. Your friends may be able to help, too, but keep in mind, their views are probably close to your own, so it might be best to get other opinions as well.

6. Talk to God. This is your first line of defense against stress, so pray every day! When you pray, talk honestly with the Lord. Say what you're feeling, and ask for help. God has the answers and help you're looking for.

Sometimes the best part of praying takes place when you simply keep quiet and listen for God to speak to your heart and mind. In other words, relax and listen.

Also see *Catechism of the Catholic Church*, 1718–1719.

WHY AM I SO DEPRESSED?

Sid Imsosad is bummed today. He's not really sure why, but it's those same old feelings of distress, failure, hopelessness, gloom, doom, and despair that are flooding his mind once again. Why is it he feels this way, and how in the world can he overcome it?

What Causes Depression?

- Sometimes people who are prone toward depression have a poor self-image. They feel badly about themselves, so it's hard to feel good about much else.
- Sometimes depression is caused by feelings of guilt or shame, self-criticism, or embarrassment. If these feelings are the result of sin, the sin should be confessed. Often depression will go away when a person knows that he or she is forgiven.
- Sometimes, though, none of the above reasons are the cause of the depression. You simply feel "down" and you don't really have a good reason. Well, you're not alone. Some of the greatest

saints fought periodic bouts with depression! Your depression may just be an opportunity to grow closer to God.

Is Depression a Sin?

It's not a sin to get depressed. But God doesn't want you to *stay* depressed—especially if the depression is caused by self-centeredness.

But keep in mind, people don't simply "snap out of" depression. It may take time. Be patient with yourself. Perhaps a physical, chemical imbalance in your body is the cause. If you seem always depressed, an exam by a doctor may be the place to start. Check your diet carefully. Are you eating right? Getting enough sleep? Exercising?

Other Possibilities

Are you a perfectionist? You say nothing ever seems quite good enough for you? If so, you will probably be depressed much of your life.

Do you have some wrong concepts about God or others whom you look up to for recognition? Maybe you think that you can never please God or your parents; that you must always work harder and harder; that you are doomed to be a failure. If so, no wonder you get depressed! God is not like that, and, hopefully, neither are your parents. God loves you, period. You don't have to earn that love. Nothing you ever do will keep God from loving you. Hopefully, the same is true for your parents. But if it isn't, you have to realize that your real value is that you're a child of God, infinitely loved and infinitely valuable regardless of what you achieve in life.

Whatever the reason for your depression, don't ignore it. If you find yourself often feeling down for long periods of time, seek counsel. Your parish priest, teacher, or youth leader can probably help you, but the first step will be up to you.

Talk to God and read your Bible (try Matthew 11:28–30 and 1 Peter 5:7 for starters) to get a life energizer. God wants to deliver you from depression. You should want that healing as well!

> "You can make more friends in two months by becoming interested in other people than you can in two years by trying to get other people interested in you."
> —Dale Carnegie

WHY AM I SO LONELY?

Liz Allalone is having another typical Saturday night. She's home alone with the TV. She has three rented videos, a bag of instant popcorn, and some ice cream. But not even a gallon of ice cream will fill the void she feels inside. She feels unwanted, uninvited, and unnecessary. No matter how hard she tries, she just doesn't feel like she belongs.

Liz's biggest problem is that she has a hard time talking to other people, and she lacks the confidence to try. "Who would even give me the time of day?" she wonders. So, of course, no one talks to her either. And no one invites her to the parties. That's why Liz is home alone again on a Saturday night.

Help! I Want to Get Out!

How can you break the loneliness mode?

1. **Begin by praying, and reading some of the Bible every day.** John 14:1–3, 15–21, 23 are great passages that show us God never leaves us lonely; and in the Old Testament, Psalms 68, 84, and 107 are great loneliness busters! When you pray and open up to God by reading the Bible, you begin to feel the presence of God. Then, even when it looks like you're alone, you are no longer lonely. Your Best Friend is right there with you.

2. **Get involved with your local church or youth group.** Think about what you can give to the group, rather than what you can get. Just being around other Catholic youth is a help. Laugh. Have fun. Try new things. Tell somebody else about the joy you have found in Jesus.

3. **If possible, mend any "broken fences" with your own family.** Maybe the reason you feel so alone is because you broke off your relationship with your parents or brothers and sisters. Do whatever you can to patch things up.

4. **Call or visit someone else you think might be lonely.** Offer to buy the soft drinks, coffee, or pizza, and go spend some time together. You'll both feel better. Or you might choose to visit an older relative, or even volunteer to visit in a retirement home or hospital. You'll find plenty of people there who would love to share your company!

Also see *Catechism of the Catholic Church*, 1878–1885.

HOW CAN I FIND FRIENDS WHO LIKE ME FOR WHO I AM?

One thing is for sure: You won't make true friends by letting down your values or by going along with the crowd. Sure, you'll get some attention for a while that way. But not for long, and the attention you get won't make you feel great about yourself. Nowadays, people respect someone who dares to "go against the flow."

Where Can I Meet Friends?

New friends might be just about anywhere! You usually make your closest friends where you spend most of your time. Here are some tips:

1. School, work, sports teams or events, and church activities are some possibilities. *Go where the kind of friends you want hang out:* Christian concerts, working with the church youth group, missions trips, or just hanging out together.

Remember: New friends aren't just going to arrive at your door. You have to go out and meet them. So if you're just locking yourself into a place in front of the TV, you might as well go out and buy an inflatable friend, prop it up in the corner, and pretend "he" or "she" is your best friend. The real people aren't on TV; they're outside waiting for you.

2. *Be a bit bold.* Don't be shy about saying hello to new people at school or church. If the person turns down your attention, just move on to someone else.

3. *Let your friendships grow and multiply.* Don't take advantage of your friends, but allow them to introduce you to their friends. Do the same for them.

4. The old saying is true: *"To have a friend you must be a friend."* Take an interest in your friends. Let them know that they're important to you. Send a card or a note of encouragement once in a while. Most everybody loves to get mail, especially when it's telling them that they matter to someone else. Tell your friends why you admire or appreciate them. Don't flatter, just be yourself. Be a friend.

5. Most important, *make sure Jesus is in charge of your friendships.* Keep first things first. Look at Matthew 6:25–34 and check out your priorities as you read.

Also see *Catechism of the Catholic Church,* 1929–1933.

GOD, ME . . . AND SEX

God created sex. And God never makes a mistake. Let's find out more about sex in the following conversation between Brendon (a teenage guy) and God.

Brendon: It seems like you're so strict about my sexuality, God. Don't you want me to enjoy myself?

God: It may seem like I'm strict, but actually my teachings on sexuality are based in love, and they're designed to be the best for you. After all, I made you in the first place. And I also made sex. I gave it as a gift to you and the rest of humanity as a powerful expression of love and life that you could share with each other. But because I made sex so powerful, it's important that you follow my directions in using it. Otherwise it can cause a lot of problems.

Brendon: Like what kind of problems?

God: Look at what you have today from misusing your sexuality: unwanted pregnancies, divorce, diseases, AIDS, abortion. None of those were part of my plan for the gift of sexuality I gave to humanity. These are the result of humanity's misusing the gift.

Brendon: Well, you know how difficult it is today. I mean, everywhere you look someone's telling you to have sex.

God: I know. Many people use it to sell things. Their greed leads them to abuse sexuality for these purposes. They use your sexual impulses to sell you cars, alcohol, perfume, and more. But the plan I gave you for sexuality is *free*. It can't be sold. And that's why greedy people aren't interested in promoting it.

Brendon: But what if I really love the girl I want to have sex with?

God: I know how strong your emotions can be for another person. But you have to use your intellect as well to balance your emotions and physical desires. If you really love a person, then you'll want what's best for her, instead of what's most physically or emotionally satisfying for you. Besides, you may think you love your girlfriend, but sometimes you can be blinded by mere infatuation. My plan for discovering true love is that you explore the other parts of your relationship—your personalities, likes, and dislikes. This part of the relationship is the most important part, because this is what lasts for a lifetime. The physical part of love is important as well, but when it's developed too early, it overpowers the other parts of a relationship. You end up using a person for his or her body instead of really getting to know the person's heart and mind.

Brendon: But some of my friends tell me that sex brought them closer to their girlfriends.

God: That's only because I put a special bonding mechanism in sex. But this was meant to keep *married* people together, not people who are just dating. Sex, as I planned it, creates an automatic bonding that says,

"I give all of myself to you, unconditionally, *forever.*" I made it that way to strengthen the bond in marriage. But when you're not married, you really can't make that "forever" commitment, which means your bodies are lying to each other when you have sex. And unfortunately, that leads to big problems later on.

Brendon: Like what?

God: Well, once you've bonded to a number of different people through sex, and that bond has been broken because your relationships with those people ended, you often find that you can no longer bond as well. Your ability to stay loyal has been weakened. That's one reason there is so much divorce nowadays. People come into marriage unable to stay committed because they've been with so many other people already. When things get tough, their life pattern tells them to just move on to the next person.

Brendon: That makes sense, Lord. It's just so hard when your friends are pressuring you to prove yourself by sleeping with someone.

God: Maybe you need to find some new friends. *Real* friends. Sex has nothing to do with proving yourself—unless you're an animal. But you're not. I set up human sexuality very differently from animal sexuality. Animals can't control their sexuality; they follow their natural instincts. But I gave humans free will, and that means *you* control your sexuality. If you don't control your sexuality, it controls you—and you end up *worse* than animals.

Brendon: Lord, I'm confused about why we have all these sexual urges in the first place. Why would you give me these sexual attractions if you didn't want me to act on them?

God: I gave you many urges and drives. The drive to eat. The need to sleep. Each of your urges serves a purpose in my love for you, but each must be controlled. If you eat too much, you can become overweight. If you sleep too much, you can get lazy. Your sexual energy must be controlled as well. That's why I give you all these sexual urges at such a young age.

Brendon: To teach me control?

God: Exactly. Through puberty, I give your mind and intellect a wonderful crash course in learning how to control your body. If you follow my plan to the best of your ability, puberty leads you to the virtues of responsibility, maturity, and self-control. And do you know why I want you to learn those virtues at this stage in your life?

Brendon: Why, Lord?

God: Because you're almost an adult! And in order to really succeed in life, you need maturity and self-control. During puberty your body is maturing so quickly that it *forces* your mind to mature as well, and that's how I make a *real* adult out of you. That's why it's so important not to let your sexual desires overrule your mind, because that can stunt your maturity. That's one reason why some adults still act like children who can't control themselves.

Brendon: Well, Lord, you do make a lot of sense. And I know you know what's best for me. But it's going to be difficult.

God: Brendon, it's very difficult. And that's why you need me. Don't forget that I'm there to help, and I'm there to pick you back up if you fall.

Brendon: Thanks, Lord.

God: And Brendon, remember that you and most other guys out there would much rather marry a virgin than a girl who's slept with a bunch of other guys. Because you know that girl has kept herself pure for you. So if you really love a girl, defend her purity. She'll thank you for it some day. And so will I. Sexuality is a great gift, and I want you and your future spouse to get the most out of it. So open the gift when all other wedding presents are meant to be opened—*after* the wedding.

What the Bible Says About Sex

God always speaks favorably about sex when it's within marriage. But God labels all sexual conduct outside of marriage as sin. The apostle Paul wrote:

> Do you not know that the unjust will not inherit the kingdom of God? Do not be deceived; neither fornicators nor idolaters nor adulterers nor boy prostitutes nor practicing homosexuals . . . will inherit the kingdom of God (1 Cor 6:9–10).
>
> Avoid immorality. Every other sin a person commits is outside the body, but the immoral person sins against his own body. Do you not know that your body is a temple of the Holy Spirit within you, whom you have from God, and that you are not your own? For you have been purchased at a price. Therefore, glorify God in your body (1 Cor 6:18–20).

That sounds pretty harsh by today's standards. But the message is clear: God doesn't want us messing around with sex outside of marriage.

5 Reasons to Practice Chastity

What is chastity? Chastity is sexual self-control. It's saving sex for marriage and being faithful to your spouse in marriage. It's God's plan for real love, health, happiness, and success!

1. True Love Chastity helps us express our love, affection, and sexuality in ways that lead us to give and receive true love. Limiting our *physical* sexual expressions in a dating relationship allows us time to develop other important aspects of the relationship through talking, listening, and sharing. Many couples have explored each other's bodies, but have never gotten to *know* each other. It's almost a rule: The more physical your relationship before marriage, the less *real* communication and the less you *really* know each other.

2. Self-Control=Success Learning self-control is an important lesson in life. Self-control helps us overcome selfishness, and helps us focus more on the concerns of others. This not only makes us more likable people; it also enables us to be more like Christ and reach out to others in need. Self-control leads to responsibility and commitment, which are important for our success as adults. And self-control also gives us a healthy sense of self-esteem, because we recognize our ability to "overcome" personal challenges.

3. Chastity out of Marriage=Success in Marriage Studies statistically show that people who practice chastity before marriage are more successful in marriage. In other words, there are fewer cases of divorce, sexual abuse, and adultery in marriages of persons who remained chaste before marriage. Why? Because chastity is sexual self-control. And if one learns sexual self-control out of marriage, one will be able to practice it within marriage as well! Then sex within marriage becomes a beautiful part of living out the sacrament of love between two spouses.

4. Health and Happiness Chastity is effective in preventing dangerous, sometimes deadly, sexually transmitted diseases and unwanted pregnancies. Chastity has no negative side effects, is 100 percent pure, and costs nothing. Chastity is God's plan for health and happiness.

5. A Clear Conscience Even though our society may say it's okay to have premarital sex, we still feel guilty when we do it because we know deep inside that God says sex outside of marriage is wrong. This guilt is our conscience speaking to us, and it can often affect us in negative ways when we don't deal with it by seeking forgiveness for our sins. And though God is always ready to forgive us, practicing chastity is a great way to avoid having to bear those feelings of guilt for sexual sin. Chastity helps us go home after a date and feel good about what we've done (or not done). It keeps our hearts and minds pure so God can use us to do great things in this world!

But I Already Did It

If you've already made some mistakes regarding premarital sex, remember that God loves you and wants to forgive you and cleanse you. This is just the sort of thing Jesus died for. Remember the woman caught in adultery in the Bible? She had committed a great sexual sin. But Jesus saw her tears, her sorrow, and her great desire for real love, so he forgave her. You, too, can come back to God whenever you want to. All you have to do is ask. God is waiting to forgive, heal, and continue loving you.

Also see *Catechism of the Catholic Church*, 2337–2356.

HOW TO UNPLUG THE SEXUAL PRESSURE COOKER

Here are eight great tips to help keep your sexuality in check:

1. Hang around with the right crowd. St. Paul does not pull any punches when he warns us, "Do not be led astray: 'Bad company corrupts good morals' " (1 Cor 15:33). The people we're hanging out with are going to have an impact on us—for better or worse. That's why it's great to hang around other serious Christians. They'll help lift us up, rather than pull us down. Also, if we're part of a Christian group, we can get *positive* peer pressure working for us.

2. See beauty, not lust. It's not necessarily wrong to think, "Wow, what a cute guy (or girl)!" when you see an attractive person. After all, *God* made the person beautiful. But when we begin undressing that person in our minds, then our admiration has turned to lust. Jesus himself warned us that these thoughts—if uncontrolled—are almost as bad as physically committing the sexual acts we're imagining (see Matthew 5:28). So keep your thoughts clean by acknowledging beauty where you see it, and then respecting it by seeing it in the pure way that God sees it.

3. Keep your mouth clean. One of the better results of the "sexual revolution" is that we now talk more openly about sex. But hey, don't cheapen God's beautiful gift of sexuality by talking about sex in an obscene or profane way—you know, dirty jokes and suggestive remarks.

It's not wrong to talk about sex. Just be sure that your words are honoring to God who created the whole idea.

4. Dress for success . . . not distress. Your personal appearance makes a statement. You can represent the Lord well by dressing attractively and modestly. Or, you can transmit sexual signals that attract members of the opposite sex to your body. Take a good look in a mirror and ask yourself, "What message am I transmitting by my appearance?" If the message is not one that would please God, it's time to change your "look."

5. Just do it (stay busy). What we do with our time can either make or break us. Remember King David? He had a sexual affair with Bathsheba when most of his best buddies were on the battlefield (see 2 Samuel 11). He let down his guard, and he lost his own battle against lust. The same thing could happen to us if we're not wise. Don't get lazy or bored. Keep busy doing things for God and others, and you won't have time to fall into selfish desires that lead to sin.

6. Fill your engine with good gas so it will run clean. Choosing carefully what movies, videos, TV programs, Internet sites, magazines, and music we expose ourselves to is important. Watching sexy movies and reading sexy magazines aren't the greatest ways to resist sexual temptation, because what goes into us will eventually come out of us!

We should instead fill our minds with images of real beauty and purity. St. Paul said, "Whatever is true, whatever is honorable, whatever is just, whatever is pure, whatever is lovely, whatever is gracious, if there is any excellence and if there is anything worthy of praise, think about these things" (Phil 4:8).

7. Pet your dog, not your date! We hardly talk about petting nowadays. Today, it's more like advanced mauling! Petting could be defined as "any intimate sex play short of sexual union." This includes any physical activity that is meant to excite sexual passion in another person. The Bible says, "Can a man take fire to his bosom, and his garments not be burned? Or can a man walk on live coals, and his feet not be scorched?" (Prv 6:27–28). The same goes for petting. Once you get the fires hot, you're almost sure to get burned!

So girls, if he puts his hands on your body where you know he shouldn't, gently but firmly move them away. You don't need to bite him, slam his hand in the car door, or stick his finger in an electric socket. Just move his hands. He'll get the hint. If he doesn't, punch him! (Just kidding. Just don't go out with him again.) The same goes for guys. If a girl makes sexual advances toward you, be man enough to put a stop to it.

Cool off, and refocus your energy into learning more about your date's mind than his or her body.

8. Pick the right locations for your dates. Lovers' Point is not the best place to retain your virginity. But too often we don't plan ahead, and we end up in compromising situations, doing things we hadn't planned on doing. No plan is a bad plan.

So decide before your date where you're going, and choose places where you won't be tempted to go too far. For example, don't lie down on the floor together to watch TV when no one else is around.

Plan your dates with other couples, and pick activities that involve action and dialogue—like dancing or games or sports. These kind of activities leave a good taste in your mouth, because you've had fun without compromising your values or turning your back on God.

Also see *Catechism of the Catholic Church*, 2337–2356.

ABORTION: THE NEW HOLOCAUST

More and more pregnant young women are choosing to abort their babies. Why? First, because it's legal. On January 22, 1973, the United States Supreme Court said it was okay to kill an unborn baby. Since then, an average of one and a half million babies have been destroyed every year in the United States alone (55 million a year worldwide!). That's over four thousand U.S. babies a day.

Less than one percent of those abortions are performed to protect the health of the mother, or because of rape or incest. Most are done to free young couples from the responsibilities of premarital pregnancies and parenthood. Other abortions are done because of sex selection (they wanted a boy instead of a girl). Others are done because the unborn baby is discovered to be less than perfect.

But most are done as a "last-ditch" method of birth control. The attitude is: "If I get pregnant, I can always get an abortion."

And for young people, that appears to be the easiest way out, rather than facing parents, friends, and the knowing looks of others in school or in town. Saving face, no matter what the cost, is the crucial issue.

It's a Child . . . Not a Choice

Have you ever noticed that most people who are in favor of abortion never talk about the baby? They talk about the *fetus,* which is Latin for "unborn child." Why? Because "terminating a fetus" sounds like getting rid of some sort of toxic waste product. Destroying a *baby* sounds much different, doesn't it?

Did you know that from the moment of conception, the instant your life began, your tiny one-celled "fetus" had all the ingredients for *you*? In that one cell were the characteristics that make up your height, the color of your hair and eyes, and your many other traits. All of you was already there. Only time and food were necessary for you to grow into the "larger" person you are today.

Did you know that your heart was beating at three weeks, your brain was starting to function at six weeks, your skeleton, head, face, arms, legs, fingers (with fingerprints!), toes, and major muscle systems were in place by eight weeks, and you were making facial expressions by the twelfth week of your life in the womb?

When somebody talks about aborting a fetus, don't let them kid you. They're talking about killing a human being. What else could it be? A plant? An animal?

When a woman plans to abort her child, she calls it a "fetus." But when she wants to bring it to term, she calls it a "baby."

Abortion: The Reality

Aborted babies suffer a brutally painful death. In one type of abortion, the baby is burned to death by a saltwater solution injected into the mother. In another method of abortion, the baby is pulled from its mother's womb by cutting the baby's little body apart. Another method uses a powerful suction (like a vacuum cleaner) to suck the baby's body out of the womb. And perhaps the worst of all is the partial-birth abortion. In this unbelievably cruel method, the baby is pulled out of the womb feet first until only the head remains in the womb. Then, while the baby is still alive, scissors are inserted into the child's skull, and its brains are extracted! That's the reality, folks.

And doctors are trying to devise new, less painful methods of abortion. Some methods involve pregnant women taking pills or receiving injections. But the fact remains, no matter what methods are created to perform abortions, the result is the killing of an innocent human life.

What Does God Say About Abortion?

Murder is a sin. As part of the Ten Commandments, God says, "You shall not kill" (Ex 20:13). Abortion is the murder of an innocent human child, whether the government says so or not.

Beyond that, God is the one who's forming the child in the mother's womb, not the doctors or the government. King David described it this way:

> You formed my inmost being;
> you knit me in my mother's womb.
> I praise you, so wonderfully you made me;
> wonderful are your works!
> My very self you knew;
> my bones were not hidden from you,
> When I was being made in secret,
> fashioned as in the depths of the earth.
>
> —Psalm 139:13–15

God told the prophet Jeremiah something similar: "Before I formed you in the womb I knew you; before you were born I dedicated you, a prophet to the nations I appointed you" (Jer 1:5).

The Bible always talks about the unborn child as a baby, not as a fetus, a problem, or "an accident." From the moment Mary conceived Jesus in her womb, she was considered to be carrying the Son of God, not a "fetus" or a "potential" human being. (For a beautiful example of this, see Luke 1:39–45.)

After an Abortion

Maybe you or a person close to you has already had an abortion. Perhaps you didn't know any better. Or maybe you knew it was wrong. Your conscience screamed at you like a siren, but you were afraid to do anything else. Whatever the case, here are a few things a person who has had an abortion should know:

- **Don't give up on yourself.** God hasn't given up on you and still loves you. God wants you to be free of guilt and feeling whole again.

  Abortion is not the unpardonable sin. You can be forgiven. Read the story about the woman who was caught in bed with a man who was not her husband (see John 8:3–11). Notice how tenderly, yet how firmly, Jesus dealt with her. He forgave her when everyone else wanted to kill her. He'll do the same for you.

(continued)

(continued)

- **Ask God to come into your life and heal you.** And get to the Sacrament of Reconciliation right away. It will help you to get it off your chest, and you'll be reconciled in your faith. Sometimes it can also help to have a special Mass offered for the aborted child. Talk this over with your priest.
- **There are also support groups** for women who have suffered the trauma of abortion and its side effects. Contact WEBA (Women Exploited by Abortion) in your area, your diocesan Pro-Life office, or Project Rachel (for contact with a priest who has been trained to deal with post-abortion women). *Remember:* You are not alone. There is help. There is hope. And there is a new life waiting for you after abortion.

Also see *Catechism of the Catholic Church*, 2270–2275.

"MY BUDDY'S GAY"

Brad: Why do I have to give you a reason why? It's none of your business, okay?

Brendon: Well, maybe I don't like seeing my two best friends going from being best buds to enemies.

Brad: Look, Brendon, we don't hate each other. I'm just a little confused about him right now. Remember the party over at Christy's house about a month ago? When I drove Pat home, he started bawling his eyes out. He said he was tired of living a lie and trying to fool everyone. He said he had to tell someone 'cause he couldn't stand it anymore. I told him he could tell me anything. And he did. He told me he was gay.

Brendon: Wow. That's intense.

Brad: I know. And I'm trying to figure out how I'm supposed to deal with it.

Brendon: Well listen, I'm taking Sister Carol's human sexuality class, and there's a whole section on homosexuality. So maybe I can help.

Brad: Really?

Brendon: Yeah. Let me grab my notes. Okay, let's see here, we just got this handout from the *Catechism of the Catholic Church*. It's not always the easiest stuff to understand, but let's give it a try . . . sections 2357 and 2358. It says, "Homosexuality refers to relations between men or between women who experience an exclusive or predominant sexual attraction toward persons of the same sex. . . . Its psychological genesis"—I guess that means where it comes from—"remains largely unexplained."

Brad: So they're saying it's still not fully understood what causes homosexuality?

Brendon: Yeah. Let's read on. "Basing itself on the Bible, which presents homosexual acts as acts of great depravity (see Genesis 19:1–29; Romans 1:24–27; 1 Corinthians 6:10; 1 Timothy 1:10), tradition has always declared that 'homosexual acts are intrinsically disordered' (Personna Humana 8). They are contrary to the natural law. They close the sexual act to the gift of life. They do not proceed from a genuine affective and sexual complementarily. Under no circumstances can they be approved."

Brad: Hum. So it says homosexual acts can't be accepted. But then how are we supposed to act toward homosexuals—especially our friends?

Brendon: That's a good question. I remember Sister Carol saying it was really important not to reject them, because Christ never rejects anyone. Here's what the Catechism says: "The number of men and women who have deep-seated homosexual tendencies is not negligible. They do not choose their homosexual condition; for most of them it is a trial. They must be accepted with respect, compassion, and sensitivity. Every sign of unjust discrimination in their regard should be avoided. These persons are called to fulfill God's will in their lives and, if they are Christians, to unite to the sacrifice of the Lord's Cross the difficulties they may encounter from their condition."

Brad: So we've gotta support Pat, even though we can't approve of gay sex.

Brendon: Yeah. A lot of times people get so angry when they find out, they condemn the person and wipe them off their list. But Christ taught us to love everyone—no matter what.

Brad: So how can Pat deal with his homosexual attractions?

Brendon: Listen, just because we feel a certain way, it doesn't mean we have to act upon that inclination or that the situation is hopeless. I mean, *all* unmarried Christians are called to abstain from sex, so even you and I aren't supposed to act on the heterosexual feelings we might have toward a girl until we're married.

Brad: Yeah, I guess we're in the same boat in that sense.

Brendon: It used to be that there was nowhere for homosexuals to turn for help. But now there's a lot of support available. We should encourage Pat to try to find a homosexual support group he could be part of at church. Some of them even have information about what's sometimes called "reorientation," which helps some homosexuals reorient themselves to a heterosexual lifestyle, although that's really hard to do. The bottom line is, there's a lot of hope for those who are struggling with their sexuality. We just need to support them, love them, and have faith. *(Catechism quotes taken verbatim from Catechism of the Catholic Church, Catholic Book Publishing Co., New York—English translation of the Catechism of the Catholic Church for the United States of America copyright 1994, United States Catholic Conference.)*

Homosexual Support Groups

- Courage, *A support group for Catholic homosexuals*—St. Michael's Rectory, 424 W. 34th St., New York, NY 10001
- Exodus International, *A nondenominational Christian support group*—P.O. Box 2121, San Rafael, CA 94912
- Desert Stream Ministries, *A nondenominational Christian support and healing ministry*—12488 Venice Blvd., Los Angeles, CA 90066-3804

If You Are Tempted Toward Homosexual Acts

If you are attracted to members of the same sex, it is important to realize a few things:

- First: Understand that God still loves you.
- Second: No matter how you feel, you *can* be in control of your behavior. If you feel homosexual temptations pulling at you to engage in sexual activity, you can resist those desires just as heterosexual persons must resist sexual activity outside of marriage. Resisting is difficult but *not* impossible, if it's done with the help of the Holy Spirit.
- Third: A solid prayer life, frequent reception of the sacraments, especially the Eucharist and Reconciliation, and a church-based homosexual support group can give you the power to live a holy life. If you fall, never forget that Jesus will always welcome you back.

Also see *Catechism of the Catholic Church,* 2357–2359.

AIDS 101

Lots of people are talking about AIDS these days. Every day we hear another news report about it, or hear some expert warning people about it on a talk show. What's the truth about AIDS?

What Is It?

AIDS is a short term for a disease with a long name: Acquired Immune Deficiency Syndrome. When a person gets AIDS, his or her body's immune system is broken down by the disease. As a result, the body cannot protect itself against infections and other diseases. It's caused by a virus with another long name: human immunodeficiency virus (HIV).

How's It Spread?

AIDS is spread mainly in two ways: (1) through semen-to-blood contact; (2) through blood-to-blood contact. Most people get AIDS as a result of sexual activity with an infected person, or through dirty needles and syringes used by intravenous drug abusers. (Intravenous drug users inject drugs directly into their veins.)

Some doctors suggest you can get AIDS by deep "French kissing" if infected blood should mix in saliva, due to bleeding gums or cuts in the mouth. However, there are no *documented* cases of this.

It's possible to get AIDS from a blood transfusion in which infected blood is used, although many thorough precautions are now taken which greatly reduce the chances of this. It is also possible for a pregnant mother with AIDS to pass on the infection to her baby. These cases, however, are rare compared to the total number of people who get AIDS. Most people still get AIDS through sexual contact.

How's It Not Spread?

You don't get AIDS by hugging a person with AIDS. You don't get it by shaking hands, being sneezed on, using the same toilet or water fountain, or even eating from the same dishes that an AIDS-infected person has used.

But remember, anyone who is sexually active is a target for AIDS. AIDS symptoms may not show up in a person's body for five to eight years (or longer) after they are infected. That means, if you have sex with anybody, you are open to the disease if your partner has had sex with anyone other than you within the past eight years! In other words, you may not know for as long as eight years whether you have been infected after having sexual relations with someone. Any person who is infected with the HIV virus, whether or not they have symptoms of AIDS, can still infect another person.

Safe? Safer? Safest!

"So I'll use a condom." The media and condom manufacturers and many others want us to believe condoms are the answer. They're not. No condom is 100 percent safe. Condoms can come off during sex. They can also break. They must also be used correctly in order to be effective. To put it simply, if we know condoms fail in preventing pregnancy, why would we fool ourselves into believing they'll prevent AIDS?

The Cure

There is no complete cure for AIDS, though thankfully researchers are discovering new ways to limit the impact it has on people and prolong their lives. Research is going forward, but so far nearly everyone who has contracted AIDS has eventually died, often within a few years.

BUT you *can* greatly reduce the likelihood of ever getting AIDS! How? Don't do drugs, and keep yourself sexually pure before marriage and completely faithful to your partner within marriage (and make sure your husband or wife was pure before marriage too—or that their HIV test is negative). If you do that, your chances of getting AIDS are almost zero.

Wake Up Call

In Jesus' day, leprosy was an awful skin disease. It was so bad that nobody wanted to be near a person who had it. That person was known as a leper.

Most people ran away from the lepers in Jesus' day. Healthy people feared that they would "catch" leprosy if they got close to a leper. By law, when a leper walked down the street, he or she had to warn people to stay away. They rang handbells and cried out, "Unclean! Unclean!"

But Jesus loved lepers. He reached out to them in love and healed them. (For an example, see Mark 1:40–42.)

In our day, AIDS victims are thought of as "unclean." Few people want to be near someone who has AIDS. Many are afraid that if they touch a person with AIDS, they, too, will catch the disease. That's not true. So what can we do?

Jesus Needs Your Hands to Reach Out

The AIDS problem may be our best chance to put our Christian talk into actions. Many persons with AIDS think Christians hate them. We can show them that we care, by reaching out to them with the love of Jesus.

How can we do this? Maybe somebody you know has AIDS. You could visit that person at home or in the hospital. Talk to that person.

Spending time with someone who is dying from AIDS is a ministry that almost anyone can perform. You don't have to have all the answers. Just being there shows you care.

Most AIDS patients who are in the advanced stages are dying. And some are dying without Jesus. Maybe you can tell the person you visit about the Lord who loved lepers . . . and how Jesus still loves those who are suffering today!

And remember, not every person with AIDS is "dying." Some are doing their best to carry on with their lives and accomplish the work God has put them here to do. We must support and respect these people as we would any other person. Perhaps they can teach us all about the true meaning of life—a life they no longer take for granted.

Also see *Catechism of the Catholic Church*, 1499–1532, 1929–1933, 2196.

"LOVE THE ONE YOU'RE WITH"

We show our love for God by showing our love for people. That starts with a healthy and humble love for ourselves, based on our belief that Jesus lives in us. Knowing that we are "temples of the Holy Spirit" we are called to cherish, respect, and nourish our bodies, souls, and minds. In doing so, we'll be able to do the same with our families . . . our first "little societies."

From there we are called to express our love to the rest of society—to those in our schools, hospitals, governments . . . and even to those in our streets. As long as there are people being unjustly treated or lacking the necessities of life, we, as followers of Jesus, are called to speak up, give of ourselves, and love unceasingly so that everyone may share in the gifts God has given us.

Giving for Life

Sometimes that means sacrificing part of ourselves and our things for the benefit of those who don't have. But that's exactly what Jesus did: He sacrificed himself for the sake of all of us who were spiritually starving and dying. And his sacrifice brought us life. He calls us to do the same for others.

5 Boredom Busters (Things You Can Do to Help Others)

1. **Adopt-a-grandparent:** Every community has elderly people. Some of them are in retirement homes or nursing homes,

some live alone, some are shut-ins, and some are even homeless. All it takes is one of us to adopt one of them.

It's amazing what a smile can do to make another person feel better. Just spending the time to talk with them, to hold their hands, to take a walk together, or to write a letter for them is a small, but very worthwhile, investment. You may be surprised, too, at how much you and they have in common and at the things you can learn from each other!

2. Volunteer: There are so many places to volunteer—hospitals, schools, libraries, churches, St. Vincent de Paul Societies, YMCAs, Salvation Army or Goodwill stores, your local congress representative's office, an AIDS hospice, soup kitchens, or homeless shelters. You name it. Check with your local church and youth group. Tons of places need reliable volunteers to do hundreds of different things.

3. Do a drive: Everyone has clothes and canned goods that they never use. But someone needs to get them all together. Organize a neighborhood, church or school clothing or canned goods drive to help those in your area who can't afford to buy them. Get your friends to help, too. Set a definite date, publicize it, make sure the proper authorities know (so people don't call the police), and then rake in the goods. This is a once or twice a year thing that can really be a benefit bash.

4. Help babies and their parents: Many couples need help with their children. They need tutors, baby-sitters (even while they're home cooking or working) and mother's helpers, chore helpers, errand runners, help walking the kids home from school or taking them to the library. Parents need all the help they can get, and the help you give can also prepare you for when you become a parent.

5. Raise funds: Great charities always need money to continue their work. You can help even if you don't have any money. Here's how. Do a penny drive at school or church. Get everyone to bring their pennies for a month or a couple of months and then give the money to a charity. Your parish or school can even adopt a child or teen in a foreign country for a year with just pennies a day. Or how about trying a bowl-a-thon or jog-a-thon to raise money?

Remember: You can make the difference . . . it just takes some time and effort!

What Is Abuse?

The term *abuse* covers a wide group of subjects these days. Some of the most common forms of abuse are verbal, physical, and sexual abuse.

Verbal Abuse

This is where one person is always saying terrible things to or about another. The abuser may curse or swear, yell or scream. The verbal abuser does not just get mad once in a while. He or she often gets furious, sometimes violently angry.

Verbal abusers like to call people terrible names. By putting down someone else, they think they are building themselves up. They also blame other people for their troubles. Most verbal abusers refuse to take responsibility for their own actions.

Physical Abuse

This includes hitting, punching, kicking, pulling hair, slapping, or any cruel or undeserved punishment. Physical abuse is not the light spanking that parents may choose to do to discipline their children. The abuser spanks too hard and too often, many times for no real reason except to vent his or her anger.

Other kinds of physical abuse may include being locked in a room, purposely not given enough food, or being badly beaten with a belt, board, or some other object.

Sexual Abuse

Sexual abuse does not always have to include sexual intercourse. Sexual abuse can include someone touching or exposing the private parts of another person's body. Sometimes sexual abuse can be committed by somebody in the victim's own family (a father or mother, a brother or sister, a stepparent, or a relative). Girls are not the only ones being abused. Many boys have also been abused.

All three of the above abuses are *sin.*

I KNOW SOMEONE BEING ABUSED

What should you do if you know a victim of abuse?

Don't ignore it!

This is very important. Don't pretend that it isn't happening. Don't try to find an excuse or reason for the abuse. It is not right, no matter how you look at it.

Get help.

Go and tell a "neutral" person, someone you trust, what you think is going on. This person could be a pastor, youth leader, guidance counselor, or teacher.

The abused person has little hope of getting free unless the offender is stopped. That's why you must tell somebody. Once the problem is reported to the proper authorities, the abused person and the abuser can get help. (By the way, never tell a lie about abuse. Say only what you *know*. Accusing someone falsely is called slander. It is a serious crime and violates God's Eighth Commandment.)

What Spiritual Advice Should I Give an Abused Person?

1. *Tell* the victim of abuse that even though he or she may feel dirty, a victim is not a bad person. Someone may have been forced or tricked into doing bad things, but that doesn't make that person evil.

What happened was wrong, but the victim was not responsible. An abused person doesn't need to feel guilty, worthless, helpless, or afraid. It was right to tell about the problem.

2. *Remind* the abused person of God's love. "God loves you" are powerful words. Tell the victim of abuse that he or she is special. Jesus cares about that person and so do you.

3. *Pray* with and for the abused person. Commit the problem to the Lord. Encourage the victim to forgive the abuser. It will do no good to hold on to hatred or bitterness. Forgiveness, though, does not mean that you should do nothing about the abuse. Continue the steps listed above, and seek help for all the parties involved.

4. *Encourage* the abused person to talk with a priest, sister, or youth leader. If he or she doesn't know one, recommend someone you know and arrange an introduction.

Caution: Fragile

Abused girls and guys can be fragile. They sometimes break easily because they have already been severely damaged. They can also have a low self-image, and may think they're bad. They may suffer from depression and even think of suicide.

These symptoms can affect their concentration in school and lead to poor grades. Others may run away from home. Some get involved with drugs or alcohol. Sometimes abused people slip into other forms of sexual immorality because they feel that they are already "used."

You can help in this situation only with lots of care and prayer. Without our Lord Jesus Christ and his forgiveness, it is very hard for the abused to recover. Give them all the help and love that you can.

And if the abused person is *you*, take these words to heart:

- Don't ignore it!
- Get help.
- Remember that you are not a bad person.
- Jesus loves you, and he will help you.
- Pray and commit the problem to him.
- Forgive the person who abused you.
- Talk to someone who can help you soon!

Also see *Catechism of the Catholic Church*, 1929–1933.

WHAT'S WRONG WITH A FEW DRINKS?

In the Bible we read that Jesus turned water into wine. (To read about this event, see John 2:1–10.) So it must be okay to drink, right?

Not exactly. First of all, the wine they drank back then was a lot less alcoholic than much of what we have available now. It was probably similar to what we call grape juice today. An ounce of grape juice was mixed with about two ounces of water. Some wines had as much as ten ounces of water for every two ounces of grape syrup.

Today's wines, beers, wine coolers, and hard liquors have a higher alcohol content, sometimes referred to as the "proof" of the beverage. Some whiskeys, for example, are ninety "proof," which is 45 percent pure alcohol! Wines today are about 11 to 15 percent alcohol, whereas the stronger wines in the Bible were only about 7 to 10 percent alcohol.

Still, with even that low amount of alcohol, some wines of Bible times were strong enough to be used as medicines. Wine was also used as an antiseptic, to kill germs, by pouring it on a cut or wound (see the story of the Good Samaritan in Luke 10:25–37).

Paul also told Timothy to "have a little wine for the sake of your stomach" (1 Tm 5:23). They didn't have antacids back then, you know.

Wine was also used as a painkiller in Jesus' day. It was especially strong when it was mixed with "gall," a bitter substance squeezed from a plant. This drink was offered to Jesus while he was on the cross, but he turned it down (see Matthew 27:34).

Drink This In

The Old Testament, too, warns about the dangers of strong drink. Movies and TV make drinking look glamorous, but that's not the picture the Bible paints!

Drink this in:

Who scream? Who shriek?
Who have strife? Who have anxiety?
Who have wounds for nothing?
Who have black eyes?
Those who linger long over wine,
those who engage in trials of blended wine.
Look not on the wine when it is red,
when it sparkles in the glass.
It goes down smoothly;
but in the end it bites like a serpent,
or like a poisonous adder.
Your eyes behold strange sights,
and your heart utters disordered thoughts;
You are like one now lying in the depths of the sea,
now sprawled at the top of the mast.
"They struck me, but it pained me not;
They beat me, but I felt it not;
When shall I awake
to seek wine once again?"

—Proverbs 23:29–35

Is Drinking a Sin?

The Bible doesn't say that drinking a glass of wine, beer, or a mixed drink is a sin. It does say that it's wrong for a Christian to get *drunk*. Being drunk is listed right along with other major sins in the New Testament (see Romans 13:13; 1 Corinthians 6:9–10; Galatians 5:19–21; and 1 Peter 4:3). Paul also taught that Christian leaders should never be drunk (see 1 Timothy 3:2–3; Titus 1:7).

Who Needs It Anyway?

A good question to ask yourself is: "Why do I want to drink anyway?" Most people don't like beer or whiskey the first few times they try it. They have to force themselves to enjoy the taste. But they still drink it. Why?

The truth is, many of us feel we need to drink to fit in with the crowd. What else could move us to down a shot of hard liquor that nearly makes us heave? Peer pressure. And if that is what's causing us to drink, what does that say about our self-image and our individuality? Do we really need to have a drink in our hand to look cool, or is that just a crutch?

What Are We Escaping From?

Other people drink to escape themselves or their problems. Alcohol numbs their feelings of anger, sadness, or even their inability to relate to others. But booze is just a temporary escape, and the problems are back in a few hours, or until the next drink.

This is a dangerous trap to fall into. It often leads people into alcoholism. The more they depend on alcohol to take their troubles away, the

Four Things to Think About

1. Remember, your body is a temple of the Holy Spirit. Alcohol abuse destroys blood vessels and brain cells and can also damage your liver. Is God pleased by that?

2. Abusive drinking kills. Every year nearly ten thousand young Americans under the age of twenty-five die in drinking-related traffic accidents. Besides that, overconsumption of alcohol is a leading contributor to divorce, rape, child and wife abuse, and violent crime in America.

3. With this in mind, what message are you giving to your friends when you get drunk? Some people say, "Well, drinking doesn't bother me. I don't get drunk." Maybe so. Unfortunately, a lot of your friends can't stop with only one drink. Because of your bad example, they may end up getting in trouble, or worse.

4. The apostle Paul gave us a good example to follow. He decided to not eat or drink anything that would cause a weaker Christian to sin. He called this "the Law of Love." You can find his advice on this subject in Romans 14—15, and 1 Corinthians 8—10. Beyond that, St. Paul said, "Do not get drunk on wine, in which lies debauchery, but be filled with the Spirit" (Eph 5:18).

more the alcohol traps them into emotionally and *physically* needing it.

God doesn't want us to become slaves to anything. If we're drinking for recognition, liberation, or to escape, we're blowing it big time. We can only face our problems and become appealing to others when we face *ourselves* and let others see us as we really are.

Freedom, liberation, and self-confidence come through our connection with God. As Jesus said, "You will know the truth, and the truth will set you free" (Jn 8:32). "I am the way and the truth and the life" (Jn 14:6). Jesus wants us to receive his life and enjoy it to the fullest, naturally.

Also see *Catechism of the Catholic Church*, 2290.

DEADLY RUSH

What do these people have in common: rock stars Elvis Presley, Janis Joplin, Jimi Hendrix, Keith Moon, and Sid Vicious; All-American basketball star Len Bias; pro-football player Don Rogers; and actor John Belushi? You guessed it. They're all dead because of drugs.

Unfortunately, it's not hard to get drugs these days. People are making billions of dollars from drugs, and when there's money like that involved it's almost impossible to make the dealers stop dealing.

They've set up shop everywhere—not just in the sleazy part of town. And they're after people from all walks of life: rich kids, poor kids, bright kids, slower kids. If you've got the dough, they've got the dope.

Why Do People Take Drugs, Anyway?

1. Curiosity Some people take drugs out of curiosity. "I just wanted to see what it was like." We forget that "curiosity killed the cat." And drugs are killing thousands every year.

2. Peer Pressure A lot of people take drugs because they want to be accepted by friends—the ones who come and say, "Hey, check this out. Don't be a wimp. Try it." There's also that feeling of nervous excitement—wanting to be "one of the few," bold enough to do what is wrong.

The fact is, people who do drugs are not among the few anymore. Lots of people are doing them. It's really not bold at all. It's far bolder to say no. That takes a lot more courage when you know your reputation with your friends is on the line.

But are your friends going to say, "Let's not hang out with Paul, 'cause he won't do drugs"? You call those *friends?* People who won't accept you for who you are? Those aren't real friends.

Besides, in taking drugs, they're really trying to escape something. Maybe they're trying to run away from troubles at home or at school. Sometimes they are running from their own anger or loneliness.

3. As an Escape Many people take drugs to fill a void in their own lives. They may put up a pretty good front. They may look or act tough. Or maybe they try to act super-cool. Inside, though, they're hurting.

One Teenage Drug User's Testimony

"I was 13 when my older sister gave me my first joint. I didn't want to do it, but I knew she and her friends would make fun of me if I didn't. I knew it was wrong for a lot of reasons, but I did it anyway.

"A couple weeks later I found out my brother was smoking dope, too. We partied with his friends and I got really high. His friends thought I was cool, so I began to get high every weekend. But pot didn't seem to get me high enough, so I started doing speed and other pills, and then coke and acid and all kinds of weird stuff.

"For some reason I couldn't seem to stop. The more drugs I did, the more I had to have. I would steal drugs from the medicine cabinets in every home I went into, and I'd steal money from everyone, especially my parents, just to buy more. By the time I was 17, I was a dealer and was getting high every day.

"Without even knowing it, I became a different person. I looked the same on the outside. But lying became a way of life, and I became vicious and verbally abusive, especially with my parents. We fought all the time, mainly because I was flunking some of my classes.

"Even my friends changed. I was hanging out with people I wouldn't have been caught dead with a year before. It got to the point where I didn't even know who my friends were, but that didn't matter, because I didn't even know who I was anymore.

"Then one day I overdosed and almost died. I remember coming out of it in the hospital and something finally clicked in me, like a voice that was saying, 'Jason, there's more; just keep looking.' I didn't believe in God, but I knew that there was something I had to find. I tried to stop doing drugs, and it took me about four more years of trashing myself and crashing before I finally got free of drugs. That was when God came into my life once and for all and taught me a new way of living . . . without drugs."

Have you ever felt that way? Have your weaknesses caused you, too, to start taking drugs?

During the early teenage years, especially, you may feel awkward or ugly. Your body is changing. You're not a child anymore, but you're not an adult yet, either. You feel like you don't fit in anywhere. Your self-image goes down the tubes and drugs look like a way to temporarily escape the hassles.

But Jesus came that you might have life in its fullest (see John 10:10)—real life, not a fake, momentary, drug-induced "rush." Jesus wants to give you lasting peace. And it won't cost you a dime.

Also see *Catechism of the Catholic Church*, 2291.

GENERATION X

They call us the X Generation because they're not really sure what we stand for—X is the unknown. But if an alien came and immersed himself in our music, TV, movies, and the Internet, he might get an image of us that's more like Generation X-treme. Extremely troubled, that is.

Modern media has become the "voice" for every bizarre, kinky, obscene, and violent expression we can dream up. Sex is presented as the ultimate meaning of life—women are useful only as sex objects. And, of course, guys desire nothing but sex—as well as crude violence, satanic symbols, rebellion, self-centeredness and materialism.

Is that really the voice of all of our generation? Is that *your* voice?

- Crude, demeaning language is commonplace on TV now.
- The networks compete to come up with the most extramarital sex, divorce, abuse, rape, incest, violence, and murder—both with actors and in REAL LIFE! They say this is what sells. If that's true, what does that say about us?
- And how about the "voice" of our music? When our most creative songwriters, singers, and musicians are obsessed with negativity, hopelessness, and thoughts of suicide, rape, and murder, are they really representing us?
- Even the Internet is now the new frontier where people go for imitation love and countless hours of wasted time.

What About the Good Stuff?

We have to give a good listen to the voice of our generation. What do we really want to say about our generation that people will someday read in their history books? Does everything have to be negative, selfish, and sinful? Can't we still make good, positive videos, TV shows, movies, and music? Can't we use art and expression to be positive about life . . . in other words, to give the world hope?

Can't we point out social concerns and inequalities from a constructive instead of destructive approach? This is what God wants us to use our musical talents for! Art should serve society, not only as a form of entertainment, but also as a positive influence in our lives. How much of the stuff out there right now is accomplishing that?

Freedom of Expression

Our right to express ourselves should never be allowed to become harmful or fatal to other human beings. Adolf Hitler had a right to express himself and his dissatisfaction with the world. But when his "expression" was corrupting others and convincing them to kill millions of people, his "right" had gone too far.

And if the media really want to present reality, why don't they give us *both sides* of the coin? Isn't it funny we don't hear the truth about abortion coming across those airwaves, or see the characters on TV getting sexually transmitted diseases or AIDS even though they're sleeping with everything that moves? And why don't we hear much about God, faith, and morals? The truth is, if we want to talk about censorship, God and God's teachings are the things being censored!

Back to the Future

It's up to us to make the media responsible now and in the future. We can write to them and tell them to bag the trash, recycle the garbage, and dump the waste. We can become the writers, actors, singers, directors, and producers of tomorrow and clean up the media by bringing good and positive shows, videos, films, and music back to our homes and theaters. If we keep buying the filth they try to sell us, they'll keep selling it to us. But if we boycott their businesses, we can help the next generation be a GOD generation.

Also see *Catechism of the Catholic Church,* 1157, 2493–2513.

WHAT IS THE OCCULT?

Judd: Hey Jim, I heard Christy talking about how her brother is getting into the occult. She says she's really worried about him. Do you know what that occult stuff is all about?

Jim: Yeah. Actually, we're studying that right now in our religion class because a lot of us were asking the same question. Miss Thomas told us that the occult is a catchall term that's used to describe a bunch of different spiritual practices. Occult actually means "secret," or "concealed."

Judd: So what kind of stuff do they do?

Astrology

Jim: Well, the most typical form of the occult is astrology.

Judd: You mean, like the science class?

Jim: No, that's *astronomy,* which is a real form of science. I'm talking about astrology—you know, reading horoscopes and stuff.

Judd: Oh, yeah. Like they have in the Sunday paper.

Jim: Right. It's the belief that your future can be told by studying the position of the sun, moon, and planets with relation to the stars. These people offer advice based on a chart with the signs of the zodiac, an imaginary path that the planets supposedly travel.

Judd: Yeah, I've read my horoscope a couple of times. Sometimes they almost get it right!

Jim: But that's because the advice is so general it could apply to almost anyone. It's like, "Today you'll have an important decision to make. Make it wisely." Besides, even if they could tell the future, by some weird demonic powers, they're totally going against God's Word. It's saying the stars and planets control our destiny.

Fortune-Telling and Games

Judd: How about stuff like fortune-telling?

Jim: Same thing. Only instead of looking at the planets, they tell the future by reading your palms, looking into a glass ball, or reading tea leaves or cards. And they're usually making a lot of money from you in the process. But can you imagine that your palms would actually tell your future? I mean, what if you were born without hands? Does that mean you have no future?

Judd: Or how about those tarot cards? I guess it's a bit crazy to think that your life could be determined by the shuffle of a deck of cards!

Jim: It's games, man. And God doesn't play games. Speaking of which, you should watch out for games like Ouija boards and "Dungeons and Dragons," too.

Judd: Why? I thought that stuff was pretty innocent fun.

Jim: Yeah, most of the time it is. But they can also be doorways to trouble. They have you invoking all kinds of unseen spiritual powers that are anything but Jesus and the saints. And kids have actually been known to commit serious crimes that they say were connected with those games.

Clairvoyance, Mental Telepathy, E.S.P. and Psychic Powers

Judd: I watched a show once on E.S.P. Where does that fit in?

Jim: That's when certain people have "extrasensory" abilities. They may be able to read somebody's mind, or "sense" when something is going to happen. Some people really do have these abilities, but beware of anyone who uses this power independently of God and Jesus Christ.

Judd: Why?

Jim: Because they can use it to make money, do evil, or manipulate other people. Besides, you don't know where their power is coming from. Some people, like cult leader and mass murderer Jim Jones, have shown miraculous powers to lure in followers, only to lead them ultimately into evil.

Judd: Whoa. Never thought of that.

Witchcraft

Judd: How about witchcraft?

Jim: Miss Thomas had us read up on that, too. Witchcraft is an old form of pagan spirituality—meaning they don't worship God but rather things on earth, and in the unseen world that they think have powers. They do rituals and chants that invoke these powers. But St. Paul said that people who practice witchcraft are offending God: "Those who do such things will not inherit the kingdom of God" (Gal 5:21).

Satanism

Judd: Are witches into Satanism though?

Jim: Most of them are not. Satanism is a more direct worshiping of Satan. Just as Christians consider Jesus their Lord and Savior, so Satanists consider Satan their lord. They offer their lives and souls to him in elaborate rituals. They also offer other sacrifices, including human beings, to the devil, because these sacrifices are thought to give them more power. Of all of the occult, Satanism is the most extreme and the most disgusting.

Judd: I know; I've read about some of what they've found out about satanic human sacrifices.

Jim: And the amazing thing is, people actually do it. They believe that Satanism gives the right to do anything, because they believe they

> **What the Bible Says About the Occult**
>
> "Let the astrologers stand forth to save you, the stargazers who forecast at each new moon what would happen to you. Lo, they are like stubble, fire consumes them; They cannot save themselves from the spreading flames. . . . Each wanders his own way, with none to save you" (Is 47:13–15).

are a superior, "chosen" race of people who will reign forever with Satan. It's a complete reversal of Christianity.

Judd: And it's a big lie.

Jim: That's right. The devil promises power, but the people that have come out of heavy involvement in Satanism say you really live a life of fear and guilt. Whereas those who follow God receive a true sense of peace and the *real* power of Jesus Christ, who defeated the devil a long time ago, once and for all.

Also see *Catechism of the Catholic Church*, 210–217.

DOES THE DEVIL REALLY EXIST?

Is the devil for real, or is he just something someone made up to make certain types of music seem even more radical and rebellious? Are people who call themselves Satanists ignorantly worshiping someone who never really existed?

What Does the Bible Say About the Devil?

The Bible says a lot about the devil, or Satan, and other evil spirits. We first see the devil popping up in the form of a serpent to tempt Adam and Eve (Gn 3), and he makes other cameo appearances throughout the Old Testament (see 1 Chronicles 21:1; Job 1:6; 2:1; Zechariah 3:1).

In the New Testament, we learn that evil spirits were continually at war with Jesus during his public life, but they never seemed to be a match for the power of God. Whoever or whatever they were, they didn't stand a chance against Jesus. (See examples of Jesus dealing with these spirits in Matthew 8:28–32; 17:14–18; Mark 1:34; 5:1–13; Luke 8:26–33.)

Where Did the Devil Come From?

The Bible speaks of a battle which took place in heaven between the angel Lucifer, who rebelled against God, and Michael (the Archangel), who was loyal to God (Rv 12). Lucifer lost the fight and was cast out of heaven, together with all the angels who had rebelled with him (one-third of all the angels according to a common interpretation of Revelation 12:4).

Lucifer is now called Satan or the devil, and the rest of the fallen angels are known as demons.

There are a number of new cults that worship Lucifer as an "angel of light," and those who follow Satanism worship him as an angel of darkness, power, and pleasure.

What Should We Do?

The fact is, the devil—or any other form of evil—cannot overcome the person who is right with God. (That's why it's important to reconcile yourself with God if you haven't already!) But if you are severely troubled, see a priest and discuss the matter. You may be suffering from something spiritual, but then again it may be something emotional or even physiological.

Regardless of the source of the problem, God has the power to heal you.

So rather than worry about demons, we need to keep focused on Jesus Christ. In Christ we stay joyful, not preoccupied with negatives. Then we can confidently say, "My power is in the name and authority of Jesus" (see Acts 16:18). And when Jesus is with us, we have nothing to fear.

Also see *Catechism of the Catholic Church*, 391–395.

WHAT IS A CULT?

Cults are popping up all over the place these days. They're usually composed of a bunch of people who follow a new religious creed founded by one central leader. Their leader is almost always a dynamic, convincing person who claims to have discovered new "truths" that must be shared with the rest of the world—usually for its salvation.

Few of these leaders ever show any miraculous powers or notable holiness to back up their claims to be "appointed by God." They just have some quality that spiritually hungry or insecure people are attracted to, and pretty soon their following reaches cult status.

Most Deny Jesus Is God

Most of these new cults will talk about Jesus or other traditional religious images. But they do this only to make their cult look harmless. In reality, however, most of them will deny that Jesus is God (see Colossians 1:15–16) or that we have any need for the salvation that he won for us on the cross.

Cults mix in half-truths that sound Christian, but are actually departures from the historical Christian faith. Cults thrive on ignorance and uncertainty. Christians who do not know what they believe—or why they believe—are prime targets for cults. Also, Christians who are discouraged or dissatisfied with their own churches often are attracted to cults. They are lured by the love and the life they see displayed by cult members.

"Gimme Something to Believe In"

Actually, cults do not attract the "down-and-out" as much as the "up-and-out." Many cult members are upper-middle class, white, young men and women, ages eighteen to twenty-four. They often have grown up with "absent" parents and have a strong need for approval.

Many cultists are very sincere. They desire to see a better world and are frustrated at society's inability or unwillingness to change. Many cult members have had troubles in their families. Some lean toward a cult because of a recent failure in a relationship or job. Some have tried church and gotten "turned off." All cult members are looking for something spiritual to believe in.

Unfortunately, though, they've found an imitation faith instead of the real thing.

Cults Add to the Bible

A mind-boggling variety of cults operates in the United States and around the world. All teach their followers to worship false gods, or one god in a false form. Some look to their leader as their savior. And to justify their beliefs, some cults even add to what the Bible says. The apostle Paul rebuked this type of falsehood. He wrote:

> I am amazed that you are so quickly forsaking the one who called you . . . for a different gospel (not that there is another). . . . But even if we or an angel from heaven should preach [to you] a gospel other than the one that we preached to you, let that one be accursed! (Gal 1:6–8).

The main thing to remember about cult members is that they have been deceived. It will do little good to argue with them. If you know someone in a cult, the best thing you can do is to read up on that cult, and try to show the person how its teachings contradict the teachings of Jesus. Then pray hard that God gives them the grace to see the truth.

WHAT'S THE NEW AGE RAGE?

Does anybody really know what the New Age is? It sounds good. It seems pretty peaceful. But what exactly does a "New Age" person believe? There are no New Age lists of rules or commandments. There is no official New Age sacred book. Basically, it's just a bunch of people tossing around a bunch of different spiritual ideas that collectively claim to be able to lead the world into its "new age" of enlightenment.

Sounds pretty harmless, huh?

Then What's the Big Deal?

The big deal is that even though it sounds harmless, the New Age movement is really dangerous. It takes pure beliefs from different religions, especially from Christianity and Buddhism, and it mixes them all up to suit the beliefs and lifestyles of the individual. It's a perfect form of spirituality for those who want a custom-made religion to go along with their custom car, custom house, and custom meals. It's perfect for the "me generation" people who say, "I want to do it my way."

But "my way" may not be God's way, as we'll see by looking at some of the basic New Age philosophies . . .

What's It All About?

From ancient times, people have worshiped things and people rather than God. It goes back to the story of Adam, Eve, and the Serpent. The Serpent tempted Adam and Eve by promising that if they ate of the forbidden fruit they would "be like gods" (Gn 3:5). Boy, did that plan backfire!

It's the most basic problem of humanity: Pride. It's wanting to make our own decisions and control our destiny. In essence, it's saying, "I'm God. And you're God. We're all God. So, hey, we're in control." And the sad thing is, it's *almost* true. Almost.

As baptized Christians the Holy Spirit dwells in us, and therefore God is in us. And all human beings are created "in the image of God." But that doesn't mean we *are* God. God is God, and we are *creatures,* totally dependent on God for every breath we take.

Sure, we have to take control of our destiny to build a world of love, peace, and justice. But we will never achieve that without being humble before God and putting our trust in Jesus Christ our Redeemer.

Beware of False Prophets

Jesus said that many "false prophets" would come to the world claiming to be the "Christ" returning to earth, but Jesus warned us not to follow them (Mt 24:23–27). In reality, they would be leading us to a god other than the Father, Son, and Holy Spirit.

If a person doesn't know the truth of God's Word, he or she can easily be misled. In the days ahead, don't be surprised if more and more books, movies, and music have "spiritual" themes. But the "spirit" may not be the Holy Spirit. It may be a spirit that leads us to worship ourselves, not Jesus Christ.

What Are Some New Age Practices?

- **Channeling.** Channelers are people who claim to have or to be "spirit guides." They say that the spirit of someone who died (usually thousands of years ago) can pass (channel) information through them back to you. This information usually claims to unlock the "secrets" of life and the supernatural world. And it doesn't come cheap. Channelers charge a lot of money for tickets to enter their "channeling" sessions.

The Bible says stay away from this stuff:

Let there not be found among you anyone who immolates his son or daughter in the fire, nor a fortune-teller, soothsayer, charmer, diviner, or caster of spells, nor one who consults ghosts and spirits or seeks oracles from the dead (Dt 18:10–11).

Channelers often speak about "opening up to higher beings." Watch out! The only higher beings you want to open up to are Jesus and the saints!

- **Crystals.** Many believers in the New Age have a collection of crystals. They believe the crystals have power to heal them or bring them peace, love, good luck, or success. But only God has the power to give those things—not a rock.

Also see *Catechism of the Catholic Church*, 210–217.

REINCARNATION: HAVE WE REALLY BEEN HERE BEFORE?

Many people, particularly those who practice Eastern religions like Hinduism and Buddhism, believe they have been on earth in various forms for thousands of years. They believe the soul progresses or digresses from one life to the next, depending on the degree of virtue or perfection it attains in each life.

A soul can take the form of anything on earth, from a plant, to an animal, to a human being. The goal is to eventually reach spiritual perfection and enlightenment ("heaven" or "nirvana"), at which point the soul becomes free of the material world, and no longer returns to earth in any physical form. Although some of this philosophy is in agreement with our Christian beliefs—for instance, the importance of attaining virtue in order to enter into heaven—the basic idea of reincarnation contradicts the teaching of the Bible and our Christian faith. Jesus never said we had an unlimited number of chances to "get it right" and reach heaven. He stressed the importance of getting it right *now* in this life, and he indicated many times that the life following this one would be in the spiritual world—in heaven or hell. That's why the Bible says, "It is appointed that human beings die once, and after this the judgment" (Heb 9:27).

There are many good people who believe in reincarnation, but this is one belief that Christians can't accept. We know that through our faith in Jesus we will be with *God* in the next life!

EVOLUTION: WAS MY GRANDMA AN ORANGUTAN?

There I was in the checkout line of the local supermarket. Yes, I, Craig Argyle, the skateboarder who gets kicked out of everyone's parking lots and abandoned swimming pools, ventured into the essence of suburbia . . . Ralph's. So like any bored customer, I glanced at all the candy bars, gum, and okay, I'll admit it—I feasted my eyes on the cover of one of those sensationalistic newspapers. Why? Because it read, "PREHISTORIC FAMILY FOUND ALIVE!" I lost it. All I could think of was a Neanderthal Man riding an eohippus (the two-foot high ancestor of Mr. Ed the Talking Horse).

Are We Not Apes?

I thought about that poster up on the wall in the bio lab at school. What is the deal with this evolution stuff anyway? Some people say the world and everything in it gradually evolved over a long, long, long period of time. I guess I can agree with that. But only if that "evolution" happened by the hand of God.

Science may someday prove its *theory* that our great, great, great (etc.) grandma was something like an orangutan, but it will never be able to explain where all of this energy and life—from the Big Bang to Big Foot—came from.

There has to be some power behind all of this, a power that wasn't caused by some other power before it—a power that is independent of time. As Christians, we call this power *God*.

Shouldn't We Take the Genesis Creation Story Literally?

Some Christians take the Bible's account of Creation literally. Creationists believe that all living species were created separately just as they appear today—and they were created during the six-day period described in the Bible (see Genesis 1), which is said to have taken place only six thousand years ago.

But the Bible says, "With the Lord one day is like a thousand years" (2 Pt 3:8), meaning God measures time differently than we do, and "six days" or six thousand years could mean any amount of time—even billions of years.

The Catholic Church takes a less literal approach to the Creation story in Genesis, seeing it as a literary device the author used to describe something almost indescribable. The Church attributes all of the work of Creation to God, while respecting science's discoveries concerning the complex way in which God accomplished that creation.

We believe that evolution could have occurred in God's creation—God allowing nature to develop according to the natural laws he created. In fact, while some people have said that the scientific evidence of evolution proves that God *doesn't* exist, we say it actually supports the existence of God.

God and Science Actually Agree!

Our faith tells us that as long as science doesn't contradict what God has said, then it's okay. If it does seem to contradict, somebody may be wrong—and it's not God.

But here's something really great: The order in which God is said to have created the world (stars and planets, then water and land, then ocean creatures, then land creatures, then people, etc.) corresponds perfectly with the order in which science believes creation occurred.

In fact, they're saying now that the universe's entire trillions and quadrillions of planets, stars, lights, masses, and energies all exploded into being from an original hyper-compacted speck of incredible energy that was smaller than a single molecule. It's like the whole universe came out of nothing! One researcher even said, "If you're a believer, what we're looking at here is the face of God."

God's Breath of Life

One question remains, however: How can evolution of the *physical* universe account for the *spiritual* or *rational* nature of humankind? How could an irrational ape climbing a tree have become a rational human being driving a car? What is the "missing link" between the animal world and the human world that science still hasn't been able to discover?

The Church teaches that what makes us different from the animals is that we have a soul and we were created in the image of God. Our "rational soul" is what gives us the power of reasoning and free will—the power that enables us to write symphonies and take spaceships to the moon.

But where did we get this special power? The Bible says that when God created the first human beings, he breathed his life into them (Gn 2:7), a specific action that our Creator had not done for any other creature. This breath of life from God is what set us apart and gave us dominion over the rest of the world. And it's this breath that is the "missing link" scientists have been looking for.

Also see *Catechism of the Catholic Church*, 279–324.

HOW CAN I KNOW THE WILL OF GOD?

Ever thought you were meant to do something that you're not doing yet? Welcome to the club. Club Clueless, that is. Membership over five billion worldwide (every human being). No dues. I mean, no *dos*. Because if you knew what to do, you wouldn't be in the club.

What to do. Get a job? Which job? Go to college? Which college? Get married? To whom? When? Why? Where? How? Huh? Face it, you're a card-carrying member of Club Clueless.

Wouldn't you just love it if God would sit down at breakfast with you and say, "Here's what I want you to do." But it never happens like that. So you flip a coin instead. It comes up tails. "That's not what I wanted to hear. Let's try two out of three. . . ."

And so you meander deeper into Club Clueless's dark rooms, never realizing that right smack in the middle of the Club there's an emergency exit leading to the land of . . . God's will!

Let's call it Club Clued-In. It's that wonderful existence we enter into when we're in sync with God's plan for our life. Perhaps you've never been a member of Club Clued-In? It's a lot harder to get into than Club Clueless. Let's look at how you join . . .

From Club Clueless to Club Clued-In

How can you find the will of God—you know, get in sync with God's plan for your life? Well, in the Old Testament, God spoke personally to people like Abraham and Moses to reveal the "big plan." Jesus appeared to St. Paul, throwing him from his horse, to give him his new mission as a leading apostle. Some of us might get lucky and receive very clear signals from God.

But most of us have to find God's will in other ways. St. Paul gives us a clue on how to begin. He says, "This is the will of God, your holiness" (1 Thes 4:3). In other words, more than anything else, Jesus wants you to become sanctified, or close to him. So the answer to the question, "What does God want me to do?" is "What can bring me closer to God?"

With each little decision you make, you ask yourself, "Which of these choices will lead me closer to God?" And then take the step toward God. That's the emergency exit in Club Clueless that leads to the land of Club Clued-In.

Sometimes It's Not That Easy

That's easy for the small decisions, like choosing whether or not to break the law or one of God's commandments. But sometimes it's still hard to figure out the bigger decisions in life. For instance, you might think that becoming a priest or a nun would certainly lead you closer to God, but then again so would being single or married. Every vocation in life can be a road to God—it just depends on how we live that vocation.

Here are some other ways to see what God's will would be:

A Checklist for Discovering the Big Plan

1. **What do the Bible and the Church say about the matter?** God's will never contradicts the teachings of Christ. That's why it's so important to know what Christ taught, both through reading

the Bible and through learning your Catholic faith. This helps form your conscience so that you can think clearly and see things the way God sees them.

For example, should you steal food from the cafeteria, or rip off the place where you work? Of course not. How do you know? Because God's Word says so: "The thief must no longer steal, but rather labor, doing honest work with his [own] hands, so that he may have something to share with one in need" (Eph 4:28). God says it even more bluntly in the Old Testament: "You shall not steal" (Ex 20:15). That's number eight on God's Top Ten List.

Not only does Scripture tell you what *not* to do, it also tells you what to do. Jesus summed it up by saying, "Love God, and love your neighbor as yourself" (see Luke 10:27).

2. What do wise counselors say? All through Scripture, God tells you to seek the advice of the spiritual leaders: "The way of a fool seems right in his own eyes, but he who listens to advice is wise" (Prv 12:15). Your spiritual counselors may include your parents (if they are close to God), a priest, religious brother or sister, a church youth leader, an older, more experienced person (a teacher or coach), or a professional Christian counselor. Talk to one or more of these leaders when you are trying to make an important decision.

Should you also consult your friends? Of course. But remember, they might not have the experience that other people have. And sometimes friends are too close to you to really give you an unbiased opinion.

No matter who gives you advice, be careful. Even good people can give you bad advice. If someone gives you advice that doesn't line up with what God or the Church teaches, then look for advice somewhere else.

3. What do you think about it? God gives each of us an incredible brain. And we're expected to use it. Don't depend entirely upon your own ideas and longings, but don't ignore them either. God may be trying to tell you something. Just because *we want* to do something, it doesn't mean *God doesn't want* us to do it. Sometimes we think we're supposed to give up all our dreams to serve God, but we forget that those dreams may have come from God!

Jesus told us to use our talents to the fullest. Our talents, abilities, goals, and aspirations may be the very things God wants us to use to change the world for the better. The real key is to make sure that God is first, and all the rest is second. And sometimes God asks us to give up certain things to make sure that's the case.

God asked Abraham to sacrifice his only son, Isaac (see Genesis 22). Abraham loved Isaac more than anything, but to show that he was willing to do God's will no matter what, he prepared to sacrifice his son. God was testing Abraham's obedience, and Abraham passed the test. God sent an angel to tell Abraham he could spare his son after all. God even made Isaac the leader of his nation!

The point is, God wants us to use the things we love in life, but we have to make sure we've put God first. Some people say, for example, "I'm going to become rich so that I can use my money to serve God and help the poor." Wrong. What we should say is, "I'm going to serve God and help the poor. I trust that God will provide for me—whether I'm rich, poor, or otherwise."

4. Take time for prayer. Before we make serious decisions, we should always pray. Sometimes God is trying to tell us the way to go—through the advice of others or the guidance of the Bible or the Church—but because we haven't prayed enough, we're not able to recognize these spiritual signals. In other words, God is speaking, but we're not listening! That's why we have to pray. Prayer gives us ability to recognize God. And remember, hearing what God has to say requires *listening,* not just talking.

Different Strokes for Different Folks

God has given each of us different gifts. Be honest with yourself and try to cultivate the things you do well. God will use some of them, while others may fall by the wayside. Be open to anything. Be willing to change. You may give up one talent because you feel God calling you somewhere else. Don't be afraid. You'll discover new talents and longings you never even knew you had.

God is always loving and patient. If you put the Lord first in your life, you'll gradually move down your path to fulfillment in this life. It may not always be easy, but in the long run you'll see how wise God was in letting you experience what you did.

Remember that there are no "accidents" in life—God knows everything, and nothing happens unless God causes or allows it to happen. And as St. Paul says, "We know that all things work for good for those who love God" (Rom 8:28).

Pray that you will always have the strength to say "yes" to God as Mary did (see Luke 1:38). When the angel came to Mary and told her she would be the mother of the Savior, she was amazed. But she trusted in God's will. She accepted the incredible and difficult mission. She said "yes." (See also Psalm 32:8.)

God has a specific mission for you as well. And it's something only you can do. Don't be afraid to answer the call. Because that's where your true joy awaits you.

Also see *Catechism of the Catholic Church,* 1704, 2822–2827.

THE NEW AMERICAN BIBLE

Translated from the Original Languages
with Critical Use of All the Ancient Sources
and
THE REVISED NEW TESTAMENT
AUTHORIZED BY THE BOARD OF TRUSTEES
of the
CONFRATERNITY OF CHRISTIAN DOCTRINE
and
APPROVED BY THE ADMINISTRATIVE
COMMITTEE/BOARD
of the
NATIONAL CONFERENCE OF CATHOLIC BISHOPS
and the
UNITED STATES CATHOLIC CONFERENCE

NAB

CATHOLIC BIBLE PRESS
a division of
THOMAS NELSON PUBLISHERS
Nashville • Atlanta • London • Vancouver

299

THE NEW AMERICAN BIBLE

NIHIL OBSTAT: Stephen J. Hartdegen, O.F.M., S.S.L.
Christian P. Ceroke, O. Carm., S.T.D.

IMPRIMATUR: †Patrick Cardinal O'Boyle, D.D.
Archbishop of Washington

July 27, 1970

THE REVISED NEW TESTAMENT

NIHIL OBSTAT: Stephen J. Hartdegen, O.F.M., S.S.L.
Censor Deputatus

IMPRIMATUR: †James Cardinal Hickey, S.T.D., J.C.D.
Archbishop of Washington

August 27, 1986

REVISED PSALMS OF THE NEW AMERICAN BIBLE

IMPRIMATUR: Most Reverend Daniel E. Pilarczyk
President, National Conference of
Catholic Bishops

October 10, 1991

For "English Versions of the Bible"

NIHIL OBSTAT: Nicholas Tranter, S.T.L.
Lionel Swain, S.T.L., L.S.S.
Censors

IMPRIMATUR: †John Cardinal Heenan
Archbishop of Westminster

April 25, 1969

Printed in the United States of America
19 20 21 22 23 24 25 -- 06 05 04 03 02

For the faithful in all English-speaking countries the publication of *The New American Bible* represents a notable achievement. Its pages contain a new Catholic version of the Bible in English, along with illustrations and explanations that facilitate the understanding of the text.

For more than a quarter of a century, members of the Catholic Biblical Association of America, sponsored by the Bishops' Committee of the Confraternity of Christian Doctrine, have labored to create this new translation of the Scriptures from the original languages or from the oldest extant form in which the texts exist.

In so doing, the translators have carried out the directive of our predecessor, Pius XII, in his famous Encyclical *Divino Afflante Spiritu,* and the decree of the Second Vatican Council *(Dei Verbum),* which prescribed that 'up-to-date and appropriate translations be made in the various languages, by preference from the original texts of the sacred books,' and that 'with the approval of Church authority, these translations may be produced in cooperation with our separated brethren' so that 'all Christians may be able to use them.'

The holy task of spreading God's word to the widest possible readership has a special urgency today. Despite all his material achievements, man still struggles with the age-old problems of how to order his life for the glory of God, for the welfare of his fellows and the salvation of his soul. Therefore we are gratified to find in this new translation of the Scriptures a new opportunity for men to give themselves to frequent reading of, and meditation on, the living Word of God. In its pages we recognize His voice, we hear a message of deep significance for every one of us. Through the spiritual dynamism and prophetic force of the Bible, the Holy Spirit spreads his light and his warmth over all men, in whatever historical or sociological situation they find themselves.

On all who have contributed to this translation, and all who seek in its pages the sacred teaching and the promise of salvation of Jesus Christ our Lord, we gladly bestow our paternal Apostolic Blessing.

From the Vatican, September 18, 1970

Paulus PP. VI

COLLABORATORS ON THE OLD TESTAMENT OF THE NEW AMERICAN BIBLE

Bishops' Committee of the Confraternity of Christian Doctrine

Most Rev. Charles P. Greco, D.D., Chairman
Most Rev. Joseph T. McGucken, S.T.D.
Most Rev. Vincent S. Waters, D.D.
Most Rev. Romeo Blanchette, D.D.
Most Rev. Christopher J. Weldon, D.D.

EDITORS IN CHIEF

Rev. Louis F. Hartman, C.SS.R., S.S.L., Ling. Or. L., Chairman
Rev. Msgr. Patrick W. Skehan, S.T.D., LL.D., Vice-Chairman
Rev. Stephen J. Hartdegen, O.F.M., S.S.L., Secretary

ASSOCIATE EDITORS AND TRANSLATORS

Rev. Edward P. Arbez, S.S., S.T.D.
Rev. Msgr. Edward J. Byrne, Ph.D., S.T.D.
Rev. Edward A. Cerny, S.S., S.T.D.
Rev. James E. Coleran, S.J., S.T.L., S.S.L.
Rev. John J. Collins, S.J., M.A., S.S.L.
Sr. M. Emmanuel Collins, O.S.F., Ph.D.
Prof. Frank M. Cross, Jr., Ph.D.
Rev. Patrick Cummins, O.S.B., S.T.D.
Rev. Antonine A. De Guglielmo, O.F.M., S.T.D., S.S.L., S.S. Lect. Gen.
Rev. Alexander A. Di Lella, O.F.M., S.T.L., S.S.L., Ph.D.
Most Rev. John J. Dougherty, S.T.L., S.S.D.
Rev. William A. Dowd, S.J., S.T.D., S.S.L.
Prof. David Noel Freedman, Ph.D.
Rev. Michael J. Gruenthaner, S.J., S.T.D., S.S.D.
Rev. Msgr. Maurice A. Hofer, S.S.L.
Rev. Justin Krellner, O.S.B., S.T.D.
Rev. Joseph L. Lilly, C.M., S.T.D., S.S.L.
Rev. Roderick F. MacKenzie, S.J., M.A., S.S.D.
Rev. Edward A. Mangan, C.SS.R., S.S.L.
Rev. Daniel W. Martin, C.M., S.T.L., S.S.L.
Rev. William H. McClellan, S.J.
Rev. James McGlinchey, C.M., S.T.D.
Rev. Frederick Moriarty, S.J., S.S.L., S.T.D.
Rev. Richard T. Murphy, O.P., S.T.D., S.S.D.
Rev. Roland E. Murphy, O. Carm., M.A., S.T.D., S.S.L.
Rev. Msgr. William R. Newton, M.S., S.S.D.
Rev. Eberhard Olinger, O.S.B.
Rev. Charles H. Pickar, O.S.A., S.T.L., S.S.L.
Rev. Christopher Rehwinkel, O.F.M., S.T.D., S.S. Lect. Gen.
Rev. Msgr. John R. Rowan, S.T.D., S.S.L.
Prof. J. A. Sanders, Ph.D.
Rev. Edward F. Siegman, C.PP.S., S.T.D., S.S.L.
Rev. Msgr. Matthew P. Stapleton, S.T.D., S.S.L.
Rev. Msgr. John E. Steinmueller, S.T.D., S.S.L.
Rev. John Ujlaki, O.S.B., Litt.D.
Rev. Bruce Vawter, C.M., S.T.L., S.S.D.
Rev. John B. Weisengoff, S.T.D., S.S.L.

COLLABORATORS ON THE REVISED EDITION OF THE NEW TESTAMENT OF THE NEW AMERICAN BIBLE

BISHOPS' AD HOC COMMITTEE

Most Rev. Theodore E. McCarrick, D.D.
Most Rev. Richard J. Sklba, D.D.
Most Rev. J. Francis Stafford, D.D.
Most Rev. John F. Whealon, D.D., Chairman

BOARD OF EDITORS

Rev. Msgr. Myles M. Bourke
Rev. Francis T. Gignac, S.J., Chairman
Rev. Stephen J. Hartdegen, O.F.M., Secretary
Rev. Claude J. Peifer, O.S.B.
Rev. John H. Reumann

REVISERS

Rev. Msgr. Myles M. Bourke
Rev. Frederick W. Danker
Rev. Alexander A. Di Lella, O.F.M.
Rev. Charles H. Giblin, S.J.
Rev. Francis T. Gignac, S.J.
Rev. Stephen J. Hartdegen, O.F.M.
Dr. Maurya P. Horgan
Rev. John R. Keating, S.J.
Rev. John Knox
Dr. Paul J. Kobelski
Dr. J. Rebecca Lyman
Bro. Elliott C. Maloney, O.S.B.
Dr. Janet A. Timbie

CONSULTANTS

The Rev. Joseph Jensen, O.S.B.
The Rev. Aidan Kavanagh, O.S.B.
Dr. Marianne Sawicki

BUSINESS MANAGER

Charles A. Buggé

WORD PROCESSOR

Suzanna Jordan

COLLABORATORS ON THE REVISED PSALMS of the NEW AMERICAN BIBLE

BISHOPS' AD HOC COMMITTEE

Most Rev. Enrique San Pedro, S.J.
Most Rev. Richard Sklba, D.D.
Most Rev. Donald W. Troutman, S.T.D., S.S.L.
Most Rev. Emil A. Wcela
Most Rev. John F. Whealon, S.S.L., Chairman

BOARD OF EDITORS

Rev. Richard Clifford, S.J.
Br. Aloysius Fitzgerald, F.S.C.
Rev. Joseph Jensen, O.S.B.
Rev. Roland Murphy, O. Carm.
Sr. Irene Nowell, O.S.B.
Dr. Judith Sanderson

REVISERS

Prof. Gary Anderson
Rev. Michael L. Barré
Rev. Christopher T. Begg
Dr. Joseph Blenkinsopp
Rev. Anthony R. Ceresko, O.S.F.S.
Rev. Richard J. Clifford, S.J.
Rev. Aelred Cody, O.S.B.
Prof. Michael D. Coogan
Rev. Alexander A. Di Lella, O.F.M.
Dr. Robert A. Di Vito
Br. Aloysius Fitzgerald, F.S.C.
Rev. Michael D. Guinan, O.F.M.
Rev. William L. Holladay
Rev. William Irwin, C.S.B.
Rev. Joseph Jensen, O.S.B.
Rev. John S. Kselman
Dr. Conrad E. L'Heureux
Rev. Leo Laberge, O.M.I.
Dr. Paul G. Mosca
Rev. Dr. Roland E. Murphy, O. Carm.
Dr. Michael Patrick O'Connor
Rev. Brian J. Peckham, S.J.
Prof. Jimmy J. Roberts
Sr. Eileen M. Schuller, O.S.U.
Dr. Byron E. Shafer
Prof. Mark S. Smith
Prof. Matitiahu Tsevat
Dr. Eugene C. Ulrich
Prof. James C. VanderKam
Rev. Jerome T. Walsh

BUSINESS MANAGER

Charles A. Buggé

CONTENTS

THE OLD TESTAMENT

THE NEW TESTAMENT

PREFACE TO THE NEW AMERICAN BIBLE OLD TESTAMENT

On September 30, 1943, His Holiness Pope Pius XII issued his now famous encyclical on scripture studies, *Divino afflante Spiritu*. He wrote: "We ought to explain the original text which was written by the inspired author himself and has more authority and greater weight than any, even the very best, translation whether ancient or modern. This can be done all the more easily and fruitfully if to the knowledge of languages be joined a real skill in literary criticism of the same text."

Early in 1944, in conformity with the spirit of the encyclical, and with the encouragement of Archbishop Cicognani, Apostolic Delegate to the United States, the Bishops' Committee of the Confraternity of Christian Doctrine requested members of The Catholic Biblical Association of America to translate the sacred scriptures from the original languages or from the oldest extant form of the text, and to present the sense of the biblical text in as correct a form as possible.

The first English Catholic version of the Bible, the Douay-Rheims (1582–1609/10), and its revision by Bishop Challoner (1750) were based on the Latin Vulgate. In view of the relative certainties more recently attained by textual and higher criticism, it has become increasingly desirable that contemporary translations of the sacred books into English be prepared in which due reverence for the text and strict observance of the rules of criticism would be combined.

The New American Bible has accomplished this in response to the need of the church in America today. It is the achievement of some fifty biblical scholars, the greater number of whom, though not all, are Catholics. In particular, the editors-in-chief have devoted twenty-five years to this work. The collaboration of scholars who are not Catholic fulfills the directive of the Second Vatican Council, not only that "correct translations be made into different languages especially from the original texts of the sacred books," but that, "with the approval of the church authority, these translations be produced in cooperation with separated brothers" so that "all Christians may be able to use them."

The text of the books contained in *The New American Bible* is a completely new translation throughout. From the original and the oldest available texts of the sacred books, it aims to convey as directly as possible the thought and individual style of the inspired writers. The better understanding of Hebrew and Greek, and the steady development of the science of textual criticism, the fruit of patient study since the time of St. Jerome, have allowed the translators and editors in their use of all available materials to approach more closely than ever before the sense of what the sacred authors actually wrote.

Where the translation supposes the received text—Hebrew, Aramaic, or Greek, as the case may be—ordinarily contained in the best-known editions, as the original or the oldest extant form, no additional remarks are necessary. But for those who are happily able to study the original text of the scriptures at firsthand, a supplementary series of textual notes pertaining to the Old Testament was added originally in an appendix to the typical edition. (It is now obtainable in a separate booklet from The Catholic Biblical Association of America, The Catholic University of America, Washington, DC 20064.) These notes furnish a guide in those cases in which the editorial board judges that the manuscripts in the original languages, or the evidence of the ancient versions, or some similar source, furnish the correct reading of a passage, or at least a reading more true to the original than that customarily printed in the available editions.

The Massoretic text of 1 and 2 Samuel has in numerous instances been corrected by the more ancient manuscripts Samuel a, b, and c from Cave 4 of Qumran, with the aid of important evidence from the Septuagint in both its oldest form and its Lucianic recension. Fragments of the lost Book of Tobit in Aramaic and in Hebrew, recovered from Cave 4 of Qumran, are in substantial agreement with the Sinaiticus Greek recension used for the translation of this book. The lost original Hebrew text of 1 Maccabees is replaced by its oldest extant form in Greek. Judith, 2 Maccabees, and parts of Esther are also translated from the Greek.

The basic text for the Psalms is not the Massoretic but one which the editors considered closer to the original inspired form, namely the Hebrew text underlying the new Latin Psalter of the Church, the *Liber Psalmorum* (1944[1], 1945[2]). Nevertheless they retained full liberty to establish the reading of the original text on sound critical principles.

The translation of Sirach, based on the original Hebrew as far as it is preserved and corrected from the ancient versions, is often interpreted in the light of the traditional Greek text. In the Book of Baruch the basic text is the Greek of the Septuagint, with some readings derived from an underlying Hebrew form no longer extant. In the deuterocanonical sections of Daniel (3, 24–90; 13, 1–14, 42), the basic text is the Greek text of Theodotion, occasionally revised according to the Greek text of the Septuagint.

In some instances in the Book of Job, in Proverbs, Sirach, Isaiah, Jeremiah, Ezekiel, Hosea, Amos, Micah, Nahum, Habakkuk, and Zechariah there is good reason to believe that the original order of lines was accidentally disturbed in the transmission of the text. The verse numbers given in such cases are always those of the current Hebrew text, though the arrangement differs. In these instances the textual notes advise the reader of the difficulty. Cases of exceptional dislocation are called to the reader's attention by footnotes.

The Books of *Genesis to Ruth* were first published in 1952; the Wisdom Books, *Job to Sirach,* in 1955; the Prophetic Books, *Isaiah to Malachi,* in 1961; and the Books, *Samuel to Maccabees,* in 1969. In the present edition of *Genesis to Ruth* there are certain new features: a general introduction to the Pentateuch, a retranslation of the text of Genesis with an introduction, cross-references, and revised textual notes, besides new and expanded exegetical notes which take into consideration the various sources or literary traditions.

The revision of *Job to Sirach* includes changes in strophe division in Job and Proverbs and in titles of principal parts and sections of Wisdom and Ecclesiastes. Corrections in the text of Sirach are made in 39, 27—44, 17 on the basis of the Masada text, and in 51, 13–30 on the basis of the occurrence of this canticle in the Psalms scroll from Qumran Cave 11. In this typical edition, new corrections are reflected in the textual notes of Job, Proverbs, Wisdom, and Sirach. In the Psalms, the enumeration found in the Hebrew text is followed instead of the double enumeration, according to both the Hebrew and the Latin Vulgate texts, contained in the previous edition of this book.

In the Prophetic Books *Isaiah to Malachi,* only minor revisions have been made in the structure and wording of the texts, and in the textual notes.

The spelling of proper names in *The New American Bible* follows the customary forms found in most English Bibles since the Authorized Version.

The work of translating the Bible has been characterized as "the sacred and apostolic work of interpreting the word of God and of presenting it to the laity in translations as clear as the difficulty of the matter and the limitations of human knowledge permit" (A. G. Cicognani, Apostolic Delegate, in *The Catholic Biblical Quarterly,* 6, [1944], 389–90). In the appraisal of the present work, it is hoped that the words of the encyclical *Divino afflante Spiritu* will serve as a guide: "Let all the sons of the church bear in mind that the efforts of these resolute laborers in the vineyard of the Lord should be judged not only with equity and justice but also with the greatest charity; all moreover should abhor that intemperate zeal which imagines that whatever is new should for that very reason be opposed or suspected."

Conscious of their personal limitations for the task thus defined, those who have prepared this text cannot expect that it will be considered perfect; but they can hope that it may deepen in its readers "the right understanding of the divinely given Scriptures," and awaken in them "that piety by which it behooves us to be grateful to the God of all providence, who from the throne of his majesty has sent these books as so many personal letters to his own children" *(Divino afflante Spiritu).*

THE BOOKS OF

THE OLD TESTAMENT
AND
THEIR ABBREVIATIONS

[ ] indicates a gloss

THE PENTATEUCH

The Pentateuch, which consists of the first five books of the Bible (Genesis, Exodus, Leviticus, Numbers, Deuteronomy), enjoys particular prestige among the Jews as the "Law," or "Torah," the concrete expression of God's will in their regard. It is more than a body of legal doctrine, even though such material occupies many chapters, for it contains the story of the formation of the People of God: Abraham and the patriarchs, Moses and the oppressed Hebrews in Egypt, the birth of Israel in the Sinai covenant, the journey to the threshold of the Promised Land, and the "discourses" of Moses.

The grandeur of this historic sweep is the result of a careful and complex joining of several historical traditions, or sources. These are primarily four: the so-called Yahwist, Elohist, Priestly and Deuteronomic strands that run through the Pentateuch. (They are conveniently abbreviated as J, E, P and D.) Each brings to the Torah its own characteristics, its own theological viewpoint—a rich variety of interpretation that the sensitive reader will take pains to appreciate. A superficial difference between two of these sources is responsible for their names: the Yahwist prefers the name Yahweh *(represented in translation as* LORD*) by which God revealed himself to Israel; the Elohist prefers the generic name for God,* Elohim. *The Yahwist is concrete, imaginative, using many anthropomorphisms in its theological approach, as seen, e.g., in the narrative of creation in Gn 2, compared with the Priestly version in Gn 1. The Elohist is more sober, moralistic. The Priestly strand, which emphasizes genealogies, is more severely theological in tone. The Deuteronomic approach is characterized by the intense hortatory style of Dt 5–11, and by certain principles from which it works, such as the centralization of worship in the Jerusalem temple.*

However, even this analysis of the Pentateuch is an over-simplification, for it is not always possible to distinguish with certainty among the various sources. The fact is that each of these individual traditions incorporates much older material. The Yahwist was himself a collector and adapter. His narrative is made up of many disparate stories that have been reoriented, and given a meaning within the context in which they now stand; e.g., the story of Abraham and Isaac in Gn 22. Within the J and P traditions one has to reckon with many individual units; these had their own history and life-setting before they were brought together into the present more or less connected narrative.

This is not to deny the role of Moses in the development of the Pentateuch. It is true we do not conceive of him as the author of the books in the modern sense. But there is no reason to doubt that, in the events described in these traditions, he had a uniquely important role, especially as lawgiver. Even the later laws which have been added in P and D are presented as a Mosaic heritage. Moses is the lawgiver par excellence, *and all later legislation is conceived in his spirit, and therefore attributed to him. Hence, the reader is not held to undeviating literalness in interpreting the words, "the* LORD *said to Moses." One must keep in mind that the Pentateuch is the crystallization of Israel's age-old relationship with God.*

In presenting the story of the birth of the People of God, the Pentateuch looks back to the promises made to the patriarchs, and forward to the continuing fulfillment of these promises in later books of the Bible. The promises find their classic expression in Gn 12, 1ff. The "God of the Fathers" challenges Abraham to believe: the patriarch is to receive a people, a land, and through him the nations will somehow be blessed.

The mysterious and tortuous way in which this people is brought into being is described: Despite Sarah's sterility, Isaac is finally born—to be offered in sacrifice! The promises are renewed to him eventually, and also to the devious Jacob, as if to show that the divine design will be effected, with or without human cunning. The magnificent story of Joseph is highlighted by the theme of Providence; the promise of a people is taking shape.

Israel is not formed in a vacuum, but amid the age-old civilization of Mesopotamia and the Nile. Oppression in Egypt provokes a striking intervention of God.

Yahweh reveals himself to Moses as a savior, and the epic story of deliverance is told in Exodus. This book also tells of the Sinai covenant, which is rightfully regarded as the key to the Old Testament. Through the covenant Israel becomes Yahweh's people, and Yahweh becomes Israel's God. This act of grace marks the fulfillment of the first promise; that Abraham will be the father of a great nation, God's special possession. The laws in Exodus and Leviticus (P tradition) are both early and late. They spell out the proper relationship of the federation of the Twelve tribes with the LORD. *He is a jealous God, demanding exclusive allegiance; he cannot be imaged; he takes vengeance upon the wicked, and shows mercy to the good. Slowly the* LORD *reveals himself to his people; with remarkable honesty, Israel records the unsteady response—the murmurings and rebellions and infidelities through the desert wanderings up to the plain of Moab.*

This sacred history was formed within the bosom of early Israel, guided by the spirit of God. It was sung beside the desert campfires; it was commemorated in the liturgical feasts, such as Passover; it was transmitted by word of mouth from generation to generation—until all was brought together in writing, about the sixth century B.C., when the literary formation of the Pentateuch came to an end.

The Book of Deuteronomy has a history quite peculiar to itself. Its old traditions and law code (12—26) are put forth in the form of "discourses" of Moses before his death. The extraordinarily intense and hortatory tone fits the mood of a discourse. The book contains possibly the preaching of the Levites in the northern kingdom of Israel before its fall in 721 B.C. If this book is situated in its proper historical perspective, its true impact is more vividly appreciated. It is the blueprint of the great "Deuteronomic" reform under King Josiah (640-609 B.C.). This was an attempt to galvanize the people into a whole-hearted commitment to the covenant ideals, into an obedience motivated by the great commandment of love (Dt 6, 4ff). Israel has yet another chance, if it obeys. The people are poised between life and death; and they are exhorted to choose life—today (26, 16-19; 30, 15-20).

The Book of

GENESIS

Genesis, the first book of the Bible, opens with the Hebrew word bereshit, *which means "in the beginning." The title "Genesis" was given to the Septuagint (Greek) translation of the book because of its concern with the origin of the world (Gn 1, 1; 2, 4), of the human race, and, in particular, of the Hebrew people.*

Eleven structural units (toledoth), *of unequal length and importance, present the unity and purpose of the book in terms of God's universal sovereignty, his dealings with men, and his choice and formation of a special people to be the instrument of his plan of salvation.*

The tracing of the direct descendance from Adam to Jacob constitutes the major part of the book, while the genealogical tables of lateral branches are not so developed nor of such interest as those that pertain to the story of the Israelite people. In fact, these lateral branches gradually disappear from the narrative. And with the introduction of Abraham and his covenant with God, the history of humanity as such becomes contracted to the story of the descendants of Abraham through Isaac and Jacob—the chosen people.

Despite its unity of plan and purpose, the book is a complex work, not to be attributed to a single original author. Several sources, or literary traditions, that the final redactor used in his composition are discernable. These are the Yahwist (J), Elohist (E) and Priestly (P) sources, which in turn reflect older oral traditions (see Introduction to the Pentateuch).

In Genesis, the Yahwist source is the most important by reason of its teaching, its antiquity, and the continuity it gives the book. It constitutes a sacred history, continually drawing attention to the working out of God's design through his interventions in the affairs of men. The Elohist source, less well preserved, is found in fragmentary form only, depicting God's manifestations through visions and dreams rather than theophanies. Angels are God's intermediaries with men. Moreover, there is a solicitude for the divine transcendence and greater sensitivity toward the moral order. The Priestly source contains those elements—chronological data, lists, genealogies—that construct the framework of Genesis and bind its contents together. To the J and E sources it adds such legal institutions as the sabbath rest, circumcision, and the alliances between God and Noah and God and Abraham.

The interpreter of Genesis will recognize at once the distinct object that sets chapters 1—11 apart: the recounting of the origin of the world and of man (primeval history). To make the truths contained in these chapters intelligible to the Israelite people destined to preserve them, they needed to be expressed through elements prevailing among that people at that time. For this reason, the truths themselves must therefore be clearly distinguished from their literary garb.

With the story of the patriarchs Abraham, Isaac and Jacob (11, 27—50, 26), the character of the narrative changes. While we do not view the account of the patriarchs as history in the strict sense, nevertheless certain of the matters recounted from the time of Abraham onward can be placed in the actual historical and social framework of the Near East in the early part of the second millennium B.C. (2000-1500), and documented by non-biblical sources.

Genesis contains many religious teachings of basic importance: the preexistence and transcendence of God, his wisdom and goodness, his power through which all things are made and on which they all depend; the special creation of man in God's image and likeness, and of woman from the substance of man; the institution of marriage as the union of one man with one woman; man's original state of innocence; man's sin of pride and disobedience; its consequences for the protoparents and their posterity. Despite the severity of their punishment, hope of reconciliation is offered by God through the first as well as the subsequent promises of salvation and blessing. Abraham is blessed for his faith and obedience, and he is to be a blessing for all nations through his offspring, Isaac, Jacob, and Jacob's sons (Gn 12, 3; 18, 18; 22, 18), of whom the Messiah, mankind's greatest blessing, will eventually be born (Gal 3, 8).

Frequent references to Genesis are found in the New Testament. Christ becomes the antithesis of Adam: sin and death come to mankind through Adam, justification and life through Jesus Christ (Rom 5, 12.17ff). Noah's ark becomes the symbol of the Church, by which men are saved from destruction through the waters of baptism (1 Pt 3, 20ff); Abraham's faith is the model for all believers; the sacrifice of his son Isaac typifies the sacrifice of Christ, Son of the Father. The Liturgy, too, relates the persons of Abel, Abraham and Melchizedek to Christ in his act of sacrifice.

The Book of Genesis is divided as follows:

I: The Primeval History (1, 1—11, 26)
II: The Patriarch Abraham (11, 27—25, 18)
III: The Patriarchs Isaac and Jacob (25, 19—36, 43)
IV: Joseph and His Brothers (37, 1—50, 26)

I: THE PRIMEVAL HISTORY

CHAPTER 1

First Story of Creation. 1*† In the be-
ginning, when God created the heavens
and the earth, 2*† the earth was a form-
less wasteland, and darkness covered
the abyss, while a mighty wind swept
over the waters.
3* Then God said, "Let there be light,"
and there was light. 4 God saw how good
the light was. God then separated the
light from the darkness. 5† God called
the light "day," and the darkness he
called "night." Thus evening came, and
morning followed—the first day.
6 Then God said, "Let there be a dome
in the middle of the waters, to separate
one body of water from the other." And
so it happened: 7* God made the dome,
and it separated the water above the
dome from the water below it. 8 God
called the dome "the sky." Evening
came, and morning followed—the sec-
ond day.
9* Then God said, "Let the water un-
der the sky be gathered into a single ba-
sin, so that the dry land may appear."
And so it happened: the water under the
sky was gathered into its basin, and the
dry land appeared. 10 God called the dry
land "the earth," and the basin of the
water he called "the sea." God saw how
good it was. 11* Then God said, "Let the
earth bring forth vegetation: every kind
of plant that bears seed and every kind
of fruit tree on earth that bears fruit with
its seed in it." And so it happened: 12 the
earth brought forth every kind of plant
that bears seed and every kind of fruit
tree on earth that bears fruit with its
seed in it. God saw how good it was.
13 Evening came, and morning fol-
lowed—the third day.
14* Then God said: "Let there be lights
in the dome of the sky, to separate day
from night. Let them mark the fixed
times, the days and the years, 15 and
serve as luminaries in the dome of the
sky, to shed light upon the earth." And
so it happened: 16* God made the two
great lights, the greater one to govern
the day, and the lesser one to govern the
night; and he made the stars. 17 God set
them in the dome of the sky, to shed light
upon the earth, 18 to govern the day and
the night, and to separate the light from
the darkness. God saw how good it was.
19 Evening came, and morning fol-
lowed—the fourth day.
20* Then God said, "Let the water teem
with an abundance of living creatures,
and on the earth let birds fly beneath
the dome of the sky." And so it hap-
pened: 21 God created the great sea mon-
sters and all kinds of swimming
creatures with which the water teems,
and all kinds of winged birds. God saw
how good it was, 22* and God blessed
them, saying, "Be fertile, multiply, and
fill the water of the seas; and let the birds
multiply on the earth." 23 Evening came,
and morning followed—the fifth day.
24* Then God said, "Let the earth bring

---

*

1, 1: 2, 1.4; Pss 8, 4; 38—39; 90, 2; Wis 11, 17; Sir 16, 24, Jer 10, 12; 2 Mc 7, 28; Acts 14, 15; Col 1, 16f; Heb 1, 2f; 3, 4; 11, 3; Rv 4, 11.
2: Jer 4, 23.
3: 2 Cor 4, 6.
7: Prv 8, 27f; 2 Pt 3, 5.
9: Jb 38, 8; Ps 33, 7; Jer 5, 22.
11: Ps 104, 14.
14: Jb 26, 10; Ps 19, 1f; Bar 3, 33.
16: Dt 4, 19; Ps 136, 7ff; Wis 13, 2ff; Jer 31, 35.
20: Jb 12, 7-10.
22: 8, 17.
24: Sir 16, 27f; Bar 3, 32.

---

†

1, 1—2, 4a: This section introduces the whole Pentateuch. It shows how God brought an orderly universe out of primordial chaos.

1, 2: *The abyss:* the primordial ocean according to the ancient Semitic cosmogony. After God's creative activity, part of this vast body forms the salt-water seas (vv 9f); part of it is the fresh water under the earth (Ps 33, 7; Ez 31, 4), which wells forth on the earth as springs and fountains (Gn 7, 11; 8, 2; Prv 3, 20). Part of it, "the upper water" (Ps 148, 4; Dn 3, 60), is held up by the dome of the sky (Gn 1, 6f), from which rain descends on the earth (Gn 7, 11; 2 Kgs 7, 2.19; Ps 104, 13). *A mighty wind:* literally, "a wind of God," or "a spirit of God"; cf Gn 8, 1.

1, 5: In ancient Israel a day was considered to begin at sunset. According to the highly artificial literary structure of Gn 1, 1—2, 4a, God's creative activity is divided into six days to teach the sacredness of the sabbath rest on the seventh day in the Israelite religion (2, 2f).

forth all kinds of living creatures: cattle,
creeping things, and wild animals of all
kinds." And so it happened: 25 God made
all kinds of wild animals, all kinds of cat-
tle, and all kinds of creeping things of
the earth. God saw how good it was.
26*† Then God said: "Let us make man
in our image, after our likeness. Let
them have dominion over the fish of the
sea, the birds of the air, and the cattle,
and over all the wild animals and all the
creatures that crawl on the ground."

27 God created man in his image;
in the divine image he created him;
male and female he created them.

28* God blessed them, saying: "Be fertile
and multiply; fill the earth and subdue
it. Have dominion over the fish of the
sea, the birds of the air, and all the living
things that move on the earth." 29* God
also said: "See, I give you every seed-
bearing plant all over the earth and ev-
ery tree that has seed-bearing fruit on
it to be your food; 30 and to all the ani-
mals of the land, all the birds of the air,
and all the living creatures that crawl
on the ground, I give all the green plants
for food." And so it happened. 31* God
looked at everything he had made,
and he found it very good. Evening
came, and morning followed—the sixth
day.

CHAPTER 2

1* Thus the heavens and the earth and
all their array were completed. 2* Since
on the seventh day God was finished
with the work he had been doing, he
rested on the seventh day from all the
work he had undertaken. 3* So God
blessed the seventh day and made it
holy, because on it he rested from all
the work he had done in creation.
4† Such is the story of the heavens and
the earth at their creation.
Second Story of Creation. At the time
when the LORD God made the earth and
the heavens—5 while as yet there was no
field shrub on earth and no grass of the
field had sprouted, for the LORD God had
sent no rain upon the earth and there
was no man to till the soil, 6 but a stream
was welling up out of the earth and was
watering all the surface of the ground—
7*† the LORD God formed man out of the
clay of the ground and blew into his nos-
trils the breath of life, and so man be-
came a living being.
8*† Then the LORD God planted a gar-
den in Eden, in the east, and he placed
there the man whom he had formed.
9* Out of the ground the LORD God made
various trees grow that were delightful
to look at and good for food, with the
tree of life in the middle of the garden
and the tree of the knowledge of good
and bad.
10† A river rises in Eden to water the
garden; beyond there it divides and be-
comes four branches. 11 The name of the
first is the Pishon; it is the one that winds
through the whole land of Havilah,
where there is gold. 12 The gold of that
land is excellent; bdellium and lapis la-
zuli are also there. 13* The name of the
second river is the Gihon; it is the one
that winds all through the land of Cush.
14 The name of the third river is the Ti-
gris; it is the one that flows east of As-
shur. The fourth river is the Euphrates.
15* The LORD God then took the man
and settled him in the garden of Eden,
to cultivate and care for it. 16* The LORD
God gave man this order: "You are free
to eat from any of the trees of the garden
17* except the tree of knowledge of good
and bad. From that tree you shall not
eat; the moment you eat from it you are
surely doomed to die."
18* The LORD God said: "It is not good
for the man to be alone. I will make a
suitable partner for him." 19 So the LORD
God formed out of the ground various
wild animals and various birds of the air,

*

26f: 5, 1.3; 9, 6; Ps 8, 5f; Wis 2, 23; 10, 2; Sir 17, 1.3f; Jas 3, 7; 1 Cor 11, 7; Eph 4, 24; Col 3, 10; Mt 19, 4; Mk 10, 6.
28: 8, 17; 9, 1; Pss 8, 6-9; 115, 16; Wis 9, 2.
29f: 9, 3; Ps 104, 14f.
31: 1 Tm 4, 4.
2, 1: Is 45, 12; Jn 1, 3.
2: Ex 20, 9ff; 31, 17; Heb 4, 4.10.
3: Ex 20, 11; Dt 5, 14; Neh 9, 14.
7: 3, 19; 18, 27; Tb 8, 6; Jb 34, 15; Pss 103, 14; 104, 29; Eccl 3, 20; 12, 7; Wis 7, 1; Sir 33, 10; 1 Cor 15, 45.
8: Is 51, 3; Ez 31, 9.
9: 3, 22; Prv 3, 18; Rv 2, 7; 22, 2.14.
13: Sir 24, 25.
15: Sir 7, 15.
16: Ps 104, 14.
17: 3, 2f; Rom 6, 23.
18: Tb 8, 6; Sir 36, 24; 1 Cor 11, 9; 1 Tm 2, 13.

†

1, 26: Man is here presented as the climax of God's creative activity; he resembles God primarily because of the dominion God gives him over the rest of creation.

2, 4b-25: This section is chiefly concerned with the creation of man. It is much older than the narrative of 1, 1—2, 4a. Here God is depicted as creating man before the rest of his creatures, which are made for man's sake.

2, 7: God is portrayed as a potter molding man's body out of clay. There is a play on words in Hebrew between *adam* ("man") and *adama* ("ground"). *Being:* literally, "soul."

2, 8: *Eden:* used here as the name of a region in southern Mesopotamia; the term is derived from the Sumerian word *eden,* "fertile plain." A similar-sounding Hebrew word means "delight"; the *garden in Eden* could therefore be understood as the "garden of delight," so that, through the Greek version, it is now known also as "paradise," literally, a "pleasure park."

2, 10-14: *Rises:* in flood to overflow its banks. *Beyond there:* as one travels upstream. *Branches:* literally, "heads," i.e., upper courses. Eden is near the head of the Persian Gulf, where the Tigris and the Euphrates join with two other streams to form a single river. *The land of Cush* here and in 10, 8, is not Ethiopia (Nubia) as elsewhere, but the region of the Kassites, east of Mesopotamia.

and he brought them to the man to see
what he would call them; whatever the
man called each of them would be its
name. 20 The man gave names to all the
cattle, all the birds of the air, and all the
wild animals; but none proved to be the
suitable partner for the man.
21* So the LORD God cast a deep sleep
on the man, and while he was asleep,
he took out one of his ribs and closed
up its place with flesh. 22 The LORD God
then built up into a woman the rib that
he had taken from the man. When he
brought her to the man, 23† the man said:

"This one, at last, is bone of my
bones
and flesh of my flesh;
This one shall be called 'woman,'
for out of 'her man' this one has
been taken."

24*† That is why a man leaves his father
and mother and clings to his wife, and
the two of them become one body.
25 The man and his wife were both
naked, yet they felt no shame.

CHAPTER 3

The Fall of Man. 1 Now the serpent
was the most cunning of all the animals
that the LORD God had made. The ser-
pent asked the woman, "Did God really
tell you not to eat from any of the trees
in the garden?" 2 The woman answered
the serpent: "We may eat of the fruit of
the trees in the garden; 3* it is only about
the fruit of the tree in the middle of the
garden that God said, 'You shall not eat
it or even touch it, lest you die.'" 4* But
the serpent said to the woman: "You cer-
tainly will not die! 5† No, God knows well
that the moment you eat of it your eyes
will be opened and you will be like gods
who know what is good and what is bad."
6* The woman saw that the tree was
good for food, pleasing to the eyes, and
desirable for gaining wisdom. So she
took some of its fruit and ate it; and she
also gave some to her husband, who was
with her, and he ate it. 7 Then the eyes
of both of them were opened, and they
realized that they were naked; so they
sewed fig leaves together and made loin-
cloths for themselves.
8*† When they heard the sound of the
LORD God moving about in the garden
at the breezy time of the day, the man
and his wife hid themselves from the
LORD God among the trees of the gar-
den. 9 The LORD God then called to the
man and asked him, "Where are you?"
10 He answered, "I heard you in the gar-
den; but I was afraid, because I was
naked, so I hid myself." 11 Then he
asked, "Who told you that you were
naked? You have eaten, then, from the
tree of which I had forbidden you to
eat!" 12 The man replied, "The woman
whom you put here with me—she gave
me fruit from the tree, and so I ate it."
13* The LORD God then asked the
woman, "Why did you do such a thing?"
The woman answered, "The serpent
tricked me into it, so I ate it."
14* Then the LORD God said to the ser-
pent:

"Because you have done this, you
shall be banned
from all the animals
and from all the wild creatures;
On your belly shall you crawl,
and dirt shall you eat
all the days of your life.

15*† I will put enmity between you and
the woman,
and between your offspring and
hers;
He will strike at your head,
while you strike at his heel."

16* To the woman he said:

"I will intensify the pangs of your
childbearing;
in pain shall you bring forth chil-
dren.
Yet your urge shall be for your hus-
band,
and he shall be your master."

17* To the man he said: "Because you
listened to your wife and ate from the
tree of which I had forbidden you to eat,

---

*

21: Sir 17, 1; 1 Cor 11, 8f; 1 Tm 2, 13.
24: Mt 19, 5; Mk 10, 7; 1 Cor 7, 10f; Eph 5, 31.
3, 3: 2, 17; Rom 6, 23.
4f: Wis 2, 24; Sir 25, 14; Is 14, 14; Jn 8, 44; 2 Cor 11, 3.
6: 3, 22; 1 Tm 2, 14.
8: Jer 23, 24.
13: 2 Cor 11, 3.
14: Is 65, 25; Mi 7, 17; Rv 12, 9.
15: Is 7, 14; 9, 5; Rom 16, 20; 1 Jn 3, 8; Rv 12, 17.
16: 1 Cor 11, 3; Eph 5, 22f; 1 Tm 2, 12.
17: 5, 29; Rom 5, 12; 8, 20; Heb 6, 8.

---

†

2, 23: There is a play on the similar-sounding Hebrew words *ishsha* ("woman") and *ishah* ("her man, her husband").

2, 24: *One body:* literally "one flesh"; classical Hebrew has no specific word for "body." The sacred writer stresses the fact that conjugal union is willed by God.

3, 5: *Like gods who know:* or "like God who knows."

3, 8: *The breezy time of the day:* literally "the wind of the day." On most days in Palestine a cooling breeze blows from the sea shortly before sunset.

3, 15: *He will strike . . . at his heel:* since the antecedent for *he* and *his* is the collective noun *offspring,* i.e., all the descendants of the woman, a more exact rendering of the sacred writer's words would be, "They will strike . . . at their heels." However, later theology saw in this passage more than unending hostility between snakes and men. The serpent was regarded as the devil (Wis 2, 24; Jn 8, 44; Rv 12, 9; 20, 2), whose eventual defeat seems implied in the contrast between *head* and *heel.* Because "the Son of God was revealed to destroy the works of the devil" (1 Jn 3, 8), the passage can be understood as the first promise of a Redeemer for fallen mankind. The woman's offspring then is primarily Jesus Christ.

"Cursed be the ground because of
you!
In toil shall you eat its yield
all the days of your life.
18 Thorns and thistles shall it bring
forth to you,
as you eat of the plants of the field.
19* By the sweat of your face
shall you get bread to eat,
Until you return to the ground,
from which you were taken;
For you are dirt,
and to dirt you shall return."

20† The man called his wife Eve, because she became the mother of all the living.
21 For the man and his wife the LORD
God made leather garments, with which
he clothed them. 22* Then the LORD God
said: "See! The man has become like one of us, knowing what is good and what is bad! Therefore, he must not be allowed to put out his hand to take fruit from the tree of life also, and thus eat
of it and live forever." 23 The LORD God
therefore banished him from the garden of Eden, to till the ground from which
he had been taken. 24† When he expelled
the man, he settled him east of the garden of Eden; and he stationed the cherubim and the fiery revolving sword, to guard the way to the tree of life.

CHAPTER 4

Cain and Abel. 1† The man had relations with his wife Eve, and she conceived and bore Cain, saying, "I have produced a man with the help of the
LORD." 2 Next she bore his brother Abel.
Abel became a keeper of flocks, and Cain
a tiller of the soil. 3 In the course of time
Cain brought an offering to the LORD
from the fruit of the soil, 4* while Abel,
for his part, brought one of the best firstlings of his flock. The LORD looked with
favor on Abel and his offering, 5 but on
Cain and his offering he did not. Cain greatly resented this and was crest-
fallen. 6 So the LORD said to Cain: "Why
are you so resentful and crestfallen?
7*† If you do well, you can hold up your head; but if not, sin is a demon lurking at the door: his urge is toward you, yet you can be his master."
8* Cain said to his brother Abel, "Let us go out in the field." When they were in the field, Cain attacked his brother
Abel and killed him. 9 Then the LORD
asked Cain, "Where is your brother Abel?" He answered, "I do not know.
Am I my brother's keeper?" 10 The LORD
then said: "What have you done! Listen: your brother's blood cries out to me from
the soil! 11* Therefore you shall be banned from the soil that opened its mouth to receive your brother's blood
from your hand. 12 If you till the soil, it
shall no longer give you its produce. You shall become a restless wanderer on the
earth." 13 Cain said to the LORD: "My
punishment is too great to bear. 14 Since
you have now banished me from the soil, and I must avoid your presence and become a restless wanderer on the earth,
anyone may kill me at sight." 15† "Not
so!" the LORD said to him. "If anyone kills Cain, Cain shall be avenged sevenfold." So the LORD put a mark on Cain, lest anyone should kill him at sight.
16† Cain then left the LORD's presence and settled in the land of Nod, east of Eden.

Descendants of Cain and Seth.
17† Cain had relations with his wife, and
she conceived and bore Enoch. Cain also became the founder of a city, which he
named after his son Enoch. 18 To Enoch
was born Irad, and Irad became the father of Mehujael; Mehujael became the father of Methusael, and Methusael be-
came the father of Lamech. 19 Lamech
took two wives; the name of the first was
Adah, and the name of the second Zillah.
20 Adah gave birth to Jabal, the ancestor
of all who dwell in tents and keep cattle.
21 His brother's name was Jubal; he was
the ancestor of all who play the lyre
and the pipe. 22 Zillah, on her part, gave
birth to Tubalcain, the ancestor of all who forge instruments of bronze and iron. The sister of Tubalcain was Naamah.
23 Lamech said to his wives:

"Adah and Zillah, hear my voice;
wives of Lamech, listen to my utterance:

*

19: 2, 7; Jb 10, 9; 34, 15; Pss 90, 3; 103, 14; Eccl 3, 20; 12, 7; Wis 15, 8; Sir 10, 9; 17, 2; Rom 5, 12; 1 Cor 15, 21; Heb 9, 27.	4, 4: Ex 34, 19; Heb 11, 4.
22: 2, 9; Rv 22, 2.14.	7: Sir 7, 1; Jude 11.
	8: Wis 10, 3; Mt 23, 35; Lk 11, 51; 1 Jn 3, 12; Jude 11.
	11: Dt 27, 24.

†

3, 20: This verse seems to be out of place; it would fit better after v 24. The Hebrew name *hawwa* ("Eve") is related to the Hebrew word *hay* ("living").

3, 24: The above rendering is based on the ancient Greek version; that of the current Hebrew is, When he expelled the man, he settled, east of the garden of Eden, the cherubim.

4, 1: The Hebrew name *qayin* ("Cain") and the term *qaniti* ("I have produced") present another play on words.

4, 7: *Demon lurking:* in Hebrew, *robes,* literally "croucher," is used here, like the similar Akkadian term *rabisu,* to designate a certain kind of evil spirit.

4, 15: *A mark:* probably a tattoo. The use of tattooing for tribal marks has always been common among the nomads of the Near Eastern deserts.

4, 16: *The land of Nod:* not a definite geographic region. The term merely means "the land of nomads."

4, 17-22: In vv 12-16 Cain was presented as the archetype of nomadic peoples. The sacred author in this section follows another ancient tradition that makes Cain the prototype of sedentary peoples with higher material culture.

I have killed a man for wounding
me,
a boy for bruising me.
[24] If Cain is avenged sevenfold,
then Lamech seventy-sevenfold."

[25]† Adam again had relations with his
wife, and she gave birth to a son whom
she called Seth. "God has granted me
more offspring in place of Abel," she
said, "because Cain slew him." [26]* To
Seth, in turn, a son was born, and he
named him Enosh.
At that time men began to invoke the
LORD by name.

CHAPTER 5

Generations: Adam to Noah. [1]*† This
is the record of the descendants of
Adam. When God created man, he made
him in the likeness of God; [2] he created
them male and female. When they were
created, he blessed them and named
them "man."
[3]* Adam was one hundred and thirty
years old when he begot a son in his like-
ness, after his image; and he named him
Seth. [4] Adam lived eight hundred years
after the birth of Seth, and he had other
sons and daughters. [5] The whole lifetime
of Adam was nine hundred and thirty
years; then he died.
[6] When Seth was one hundred and five
years old, he became the father of
Enosh. [7] Seth lived eight hundred and
seven years after the birth of Enosh, and
he had other sons and daughters. [8] The
whole lifetime of Seth was nine hundred
and twelve years; then he died.
[9] When Enosh was ninety years old,
he became the father of Kenan. [10] Enosh
lived eight hundred and fifteen years
after the birth of Kenan, and he had
other sons and daughters. [11] The whole
lifetime of Enosh was nine hundred and
five years; then he died.
[12] When Kenan was seventy years old,
he became the father of Mahalalel.
[13] Kenan lived eight hundred and forty
years after the birth of Mahalalel, and
he had other sons and daughters. [14] The
whole lifetime of Kenan was nine hun-
dred and ten years; then he died.
[15] When Mahalalel was sixty-five
years old, he became the father of Jared.
[16] Mahalalel lived eight hundred and
thirty years after the birth of Jared, and
he had other sons and daughters. [17] The
whole lifetime of Mahalalel was eight
hundred and ninety-five years; then he
died.
[18] When Jared was one hundred and
sixty-two years old, he became the fa-
ther of Enoch. [19] Jared lived eight hun-
dred years after the birth of Enoch, and
he had other sons and daughters. [20] The
whole lifetime of Jared was nine hun-
dred and sixty-two years; then he died.
[21] When Enoch was sixty-five years
old, he became the father of Methuselah.
[22] Enoch lived three hundred years after
the birth of Methuselah, and he had
other sons and daughters. [23] The whole
lifetime of Enoch was three hundred
and sixty-five years. [24]*† Then Enoch
walked with God, and he was no longer
here, for God took him.
[25] When Methuselah was one hundred
and eighty-seven years old, he became
the father of Lamech. [26] Methuselah
lived seven hundred and eighty-two
years after the birth of Lamech, and he
had other sons and daughters. [27] The
whole lifetime of Methuselah was nine
hundred and sixty-nine years; then he
died.
[28] When Lamech was one hundred and
eighty-two years old, he begot a son
[29]*† and named him Noah, saying, "Out
of the very ground that the LORD has
put under a curse, this one shall bring
us relief from our work and the toil of
our hands." [30] Lamech lived five hun-
dred and ninety-five years after the
birth of Noah, and he had other sons and
daughters. [31] The whole lifetime of La-
mech was seven hundred and seventy-
seven years; then he died.
[32]* When Noah was five hundred years
old, he became the father of Shem, Ham,
and Japheth.

*

26: 1 Chr 1, 1; Lk 3, 38.
5, 1: 1, 27; Wis 2, 23; Sir 17, 1; 1 Cor 11, 7; Jas 3, 9.
3: 4, 25.
3-32: 1 Chr 1, 1-4; Lk 3, 36ff.
24: Wis 4, 10f; Sir 44, 16; 49, 14; Heb 11, 5.
29: 3, 17ff.
32: 6, 10; 10, 1.

†

4, 25f: *Has granted:* Hebrew *shat,* a wordplay on the name *shet* ("Seth"). *Enosh:* in Hebrew, a synonym of *adam* ("man"). *At that time . . . name:* men began to call God by his personal name, Yahweh, rendered as "the LORD" in this version of the Bible. The ancient, so-called Yahwist, source used here employs the name Yahweh long before the time of Moses. Another ancient source, the Elohist (from its use of the term *Elohim,* "God," instead of *Yahweh,* "Lord," for the pre-Mosaic period), makes Moses the first to use Yahweh as the proper name of Israel's God, previously known by other names as well; cf Ex 3, 13ff.

5, 1-32: Although this chapter, with its highly schematic form, belongs to the relatively late "Priestly document," it is based on very ancient traditions. Together with 11, 10-26, its primary purpose is to bridge the genealogical gap between Adam and Abraham. Adam's line is traced through Seth, but several names in the series are the same as, or similar to, certain names in Cain's line (4, 17ff). The long lifespans attributed to these ten antediluvian patriarchs have a symbolic rather than a historical value. Babylonian tradition also recorded ten kings with fantastically high ages who reigned successively before the flood.

5, 24: In place of the usual formula, *Then he died,* the change to *Enoch walked with God* clearly implies that he did not die, but like Elijah (2 Kgs 2, 11f) was taken alive to God's abode.

5, 29: There is a similarity in sound between the Hebrew word *noah,* "Noah," and the verbal phrase *yenahamenu,* "he will bring us relief"; this latter refers both to the curse put on the soil because of the fall of man (3, 17ff) and to Noah's success in agriculture, especially in raising grapes for wine (9, 20f).

CHAPTER 6

Origin of the Nephilim. 1† When men
began to multiply on earth and daugh-
ters were born to them, 2*† the sons of
heaven saw how beautiful the daughters
of man were, and so they took for their
wives as many of them as they chose.
3† Then the LORD said: "My spirit shall
not remain in man forever, since he is
but flesh. His days shall comprise one
hundred and twenty years."
4*† At that time the Nephilim ap-
peared on earth (as well as later), after
the sons of heaven had intercourse with
the daughters of man, who bore them
sons. They were the heroes of old, the
men of renown.
Warning of the Flood. 5*† When the
LORD saw how great was man's wicked-
ness on earth, and how no desire that
his heart conceived was ever anything
but evil, 6 he regretted that he had made
man on the earth, and his heart was
grieved.
7 So the LORD said: "I will wipe out
from the earth the men whom I have
created, and not only the men, but also
the beasts and the creeping things and
the birds of the air, for I am sorry that
I made them." 8 But Noah found favor
with the LORD.
9* These are the descendants of Noah.
Noah, a good man and blameless in that
age, 10 for he walked with God, begot
three sons: Shem, Ham, and Japheth.
11* In the eyes of God the earth was
corrupt and full of lawlessness. 12* When
God saw how corrupt the earth had be-
come, since all mortals led depraved
lives on earth, 13* he said to Noah: "I
have decided to put an end to all mortals
on earth; the earth is full of lawlessness
because of them. So I will destroy them
and all life on earth.
Preparation for the Flood. 14† "Make
yourself an ark of gopherwood, put vari-
ous compartments in it, and cover it in-
side and out with pitch. 15† This is how
you shall build it: the length of the ark
shall be three hundred cubits, its width
fifty cubits, and its height thirty cubits.
16† Make an opening for daylight in the
ark, and finish the ark a cubit above it.
Put an entrance in the side of the ark,
which you shall make with bottom, sec-
ond and third decks. 17* I, on my part,
am about to bring the flood [waters] on
the earth, to destroy everywhere all
creatures in which there is the breath
of life; everything on earth shall perish.
18* But with you I will establish my cove-
nant; you and your sons, your wife and
your sons' wives, shall go into the ark.
19 Of all other living creatures you shall
bring two into the ark, one male and one
female, that you may keep them alive
with you. 20 Of all kinds of birds, of
all kinds of beasts, and of all kinds of
creeping things, two of each shall come
into the ark with you, to stay alive.
21 Moreover, you are to provide yourself
with all the food that is to be eaten, and
store it away, that it may serve as provi-
sions for you and for them." 22 This Noah
did; he carried out all the commands
that God gave him.

CHAPTER 7

1* Then the LORD said to Noah: "Go
into the ark, you and all your household,
for you alone in this age have I found
to be truly just. 2 Of every clean animal,
take with you seven pairs, a male and

GENESIS

*

6, 2: Mt 24, 38; Lk 17, 26f.
4: Wis 14, 6; Bar 3, 26.
5: Ps 14, 2f.
9: Wis 10, 4; Sir 44, 17.
11: Jb 22, 15ff.
12: Ps 14, 2.
13: Sir 40, 9f; 44, 17; Mt 24, 37ff.
17: 7, 4.21; 2 Pt 2, 5.
18: 9, 9; Wis 14, 6; Heb 11, 7; 1 Pt 3, 20.
7, 1: Wis 10, 4; Sir 44, 17; 2 Pt 2, 5.

†

6, 1-4: This is apparently a fragment of an old legend that had borrowed much from ancient mythology. The sacred author incorporates it here, not only in order to account for the prehistoric giants of Palestine, whom the Israelites called *the Nephilim,* but also to introduce the story of the flood with a moral orientation—the constantly increasing wickedness of mankind.

6, 2: *The sons of heaven:* literally "the sons of the gods" or "the sons of God," i.e., the celestial beings of mythology.

6, 3: *My spirit:* the breath of life referred to in 2, 7. *His days . . . years:* probably the time God would still let men live on earth before destroying them with the flood, rather than the maximum span of life God would allot to individual men in the future.

6, 4: *As well as later:* According to Nm 13, 33, when the Israelites invaded Palestine and found there the tall aboriginal Anakim, they likened them to *the Nephilim;* cf Dt 2, 10f. Perhaps the huge megalithic structures in Palestine were thought to have been built by a race of giants, whose superhuman strength was attributed to semi-divine origin. *The heroes of old:* the legendary worthies of ancient mythology.

6, 5—8, 22: The story of the great flood here recorded is a composite narrative based on two separate sources interwoven into an intricate patchwork. To the Yahwist source, with some later editorial additions, are usually assigned 6, 5-8; 7, 1-5.7-10.12.16b.17b.22-23; 8,2b-3a.6-12.13b.20-22. The other sections come from the "Priestly document." The combination of the two sources produced certain duplications (e.g., 6, 13-22 of the Yahwist source, beside 7, 1-5 of the Priestly source); also certain inconsistencies, such as the number of the various animals taken into the ark (6, 19f; 7, 14f of the Priestly source, beside 7, 2f of the Yahwist source), and the timetable of the flood (8, 3-5.13f of the Priestly source, beside 7, 4.10.12.17b; 8, 6.10.12 of the Yahwist source). Both biblical sources go back ultimately to an ancient Mesopotamian story of a great flood, preserved in the eleventh tablet of the Gilgamesh Epic. The latter account, in some respects remarkably similar to the biblical account, is in others very different from it.

6, 14: *Gopherwood:* an unidentified wood not mentioned elsewhere; *gopher* is merely the Hebrew word for it.

6, 15: The dimensions of Noah's ark were approximately 440 × 73 × 44 feet, a foot and a half to the cubit. The ark of the Babylonian flood story was an exact cube, 120 cubits in length, width and height.

6, 16: *Opening for daylight:* a conjectural rendering of the Hebrew word *sohar,* occurring only here. The reference is probably to an open space on all sides near the top of the ark to admit light and air. The ark also had a window or hatch, which could be opened and closed (8, 6).

GENESIS

its mate; and of the unclean animals, one
pair, a male and its mate; 3 likewise, of
every clean bird of the air, seven pairs,
a male and a female, and of all the un-
clean birds, one pair, a male and a fe-
male. Thus you will keep their issue alive
over all the earth. 4* Seven days from
now I will bring rain down on the earth
for forty days and forty nights, and so
I will wipe out from the surface of the
earth every moving creature that I have
made." 5 Noah did just as the LORD had
commanded him.

The Great Flood. 6 Noah was six hun-
dred years old when the flood waters
came upon the earth. 7* Together with
his sons, his wife, and his sons' wives,
Noah went into the ark because of the
waters of the flood. 8 Of the clean ani-
mals and the unclean, of the birds, and
of everything that creeps on the ground,
9* [two by two] male and female entered
the ark with Noah, just as the LORD had
commanded him. 10 As soon as the seven
days were over, the waters of the flood
came upon the earth.

11† In the six hundredth year of Noah's
life, in the second month, on the seven-
teenth day of the month: it was on that
day that

All the fountains of the great abyss
burst forth,
and the floodgates of the sky were
opened.

12 For forty days and forty nights heavy
rain poured down on the earth.

13 On the precise day named, Noah
and his sons Shem, Ham, and Japheth,
and Noah's wife, and the three wives of
Noah's sons had entered the ark,
14 together with every kind of wild beast,
every kind of domestic animal, every
kind of creeping thing of the earth, and
every kind of bird. 15 Pairs of all crea-
tures in which there was the breath of
life entered the ark with Noah. 16 Those
that entered were male and female, and
of all species they came, as God had
commanded Noah. Then the LORD shut
him in.

17 The flood continued upon the earth
for forty days. As the waters increased,
they lifted the ark, so that it rose above
the earth. 18 The swelling waters in-
creased greatly, but the ark floated on
the surface of the waters. 19 Higher and
higher above the earth rose the waters,
until all the highest mountains every-
where were submerged, 20 the crest ris-
ing fifteen cubits higher than the
submerged mountains. 21* All creatures
that stirred on earth perished: birds,
cattle, wild animals, and all that
swarmed on the earth, as well as all
mankind. 22 Everything on dry land with
the faintest breath of life in its nostrils
died out. 23 The LORD wiped out every
living thing on earth: man and cattle,
the creeping things and the birds of the
air; all were wiped out from the earth.
Only Noah and those with him in the ark
were left.

CHAPTER 8

7:24 The waters maintained their crest
over the earth for one hundred and fifty
days, 8:1 and then God remembered
Noah and all the animals, wild and
tame, that were with him in the ark. So
God made a wind sweep over the earth,
and the waters began to subside. 2 The
fountains of the abyss and the floodgates
of the sky were closed, and the down-
pour from the sky was held back.
3 Gradually the waters receded from the
earth. At the end of one hundred and
fifty days, the waters had so diminished
4† that, in the seventh month, on the sev-
enteenth day of the month, the ark came
to rest on the mountains of Ararat. 5 The
waters continued to diminish until the
tenth month, and on the first day of the
tenth month the tops of the mountains
appeared.

6† At the end of forty days Noah
opened the hatch he had made in the
ark, 7 and he sent out a raven, to see if
the waters had lessened on the earth.
It flew back and forth until the waters
dried off from the earth. 8 Then he sent
out a dove, to see if the waters had less-
ened on the earth. 9 But the dove could
find no place to alight and perch, and
it returned to him in the ark, for there
was water all over the earth. Putting out
his hand, he caught the dove and drew
it back to him inside the ark. 10 He waited
seven days more and again sent the
dove out from the ark. 11 In the evening
the dove came back to him, and there
in its bill was a plucked-off olive leaf!
So Noah knew that the waters had less-
ened on the earth. 12 He waited still an-
other seven days and then released the
dove once more; and this time it did not
come back.

13 In the six hundred and first year of
Noah's life, in the first month, on the first
day of the month, the water began to
dry up on the earth. Noah then removed
the covering of the ark and saw that the
surface of the ground was drying up.

---

*

4: 6, 17; 2 Pt 2, 5.
7: Wis 14, 6; 1 Pt 3, 20; 2 Pt 2, 5.
9: 6, 19.
21ff: Jb 22, 16; Mt 24, 39; Lk 17, 27; 2 Pt 3, 6.

†

7, 11: *Abyss:* the subterranean ocean; see note on 1, 2.

8, 4: *Ararat:* ancient Urartu, north of the Mesopotamian plain, part of modern Armenia.

8, 6: In the original Yahwist source, from which this verse is taken, the forty days refer to the full period of the flood itself (cf 7, 4.17); in the present context, however, they seem to refer to a period following the date just given in v 5 from the Priestly source.

14 In the second month, on the twenty-
seventh day of the month, the earth was
dry.
15 Then God said to Noah: 16 "Go out
of the ark, together with your wife and
your sons and your sons' wives. 17* Bring
out with you every living thing that is
with you—all bodily creatures, be they
birds or animals or creeping things of
the earth—and let them abound on the
earth, breeding and multiplying on it."
18 So Noah came out, together with his
wife and his sons and his sons' wives;
19 and all the animals, wild and tame,
all the birds, and all the creeping crea-
tures of the earth left the ark, one kind
after another.
20 Then Noah built an altar to the
LORD, and choosing from every clean
animal and every clean bird, he offered
holocausts on the altar. 21*† When the
LORD smelled the sweet odor, he said to
himself: "Never again will I doom the
earth because of man, since the desires
of man's heart are evil from the start;
nor will I ever again strike down all liv-
ing beings, as I have done.

22* As long as the earth lasts,
seedtime and harvest,
cold and heat,
Summer and winter,
and day and night
shall not cease."

CHAPTER 9

Covenant with Noah. 1* God blessed
Noah and his sons and said to them: "Be
fertile and multiply and fill the earth.
2 Dread fear of you shall come upon all
the animals of the earth and all the birds
of the air, upon all the creatures that
move about on the ground and all the
fishes of the sea; into your power they
are delivered. 3*† Every creature that is
alive shall be yours to eat; I give them
all to you as I did the green plants.
4*† Only flesh with its lifeblood still in
it you shall not eat. 5* For your own life-
blood, too, I will demand an accounting:
from every animal I will demand it, and
from man in regard to his fellow man
I will demand an accounting for human
life.

6* If anyone sheds the blood of man,
by man shall his blood be shed;
For in the image of God
has man been made.

7* Be fertile, then, and multiply; abound
on earth and subdue it."
8 God said to Noah and to his sons with
him: 9* "See, I am now establishing my
covenant with you and your descen-
dants after you 10 and with every living
creature that was with you: all the birds,
and the various tame and wild animals
that were with you and came out of the
ark. 11* I will establish my covenant with
you, that never again shall all bodily
creatures be destroyed by the waters of
a flood; there shall not be another flood
to devastate the earth." 12 God added:
"This is the sign that I am giving for all
ages to come, of the covenant between
me and you and every living creature
with you: 13* I set my bow in the clouds
to serve as a sign of the covenant be-
tween me and the earth. 14 When I bring
clouds over the earth, and the bow ap-
pears in the clouds, 15* I will recall the
covenant I have made between me and
you and all living beings, so that the
waters shall never again become a flood
to destroy all mortal beings. 16 As the
bow appears in the clouds, I will see it
and recall the everlasting covenant that
I have established between God and all
living beings—all mortal creatures that
are on earth." 17 God told Noah: "This
is the sign of the covenant I have estab-
lished between me and all mortal crea-
tures that are on earth."
Noah and His Sons. 18*† The sons of
Noah who came out of the ark were
Shem, Ham and Japheth. (Ham was the
father of Canaan.) 19 These three were
the sons of Noah, and from them the
whole earth was peopled.
20 Now Noah, a man of the soil, was
the first to plant a vineyard. 21* When
he drank some of the wine, he became
drunk and lay naked inside his tent.

GENESIS

*

8, 17: 1, 22.28.
21: Sir 44, 18; Is 54, 9; Rom 7, 18.
22: Jer 33, 20.25.
9, 1: 1, 22.28; 8, 17; Jas 3, 7.
3: 1, 29f; Dt 12, 15.
4: Lv 7, 26f; 17, 4; Dt 12, 16.23; 1 Sm 14, 33; Acts 15, 20.
5: 4, 10f; Ex 21, 12.
6: 1, 26f; Lv 24, 17; Nm 35, 33; Jas 3, 9.
7: 1, 28; 8, 17; 9, 2.
9: 6, 18.
11: Sir 44, 18; Is 54, 9.
13: Sir 43, 12.
15: Is 54, 9.
18: 5, 32; 10, 1.
21: Lam 4, 21; Heb 2, 15.

†

8, 21: *From the start:* literally "from his youth." It is uncertain whether this means from the beginning of the human race or from the early years of the individual.

9, 3: Antediluvian creatures, including man, are depicted as vegetarians (1, 29f), becoming carnivorous only after the flood.

9, 4: Because a living being dies when it loses most of its blood, the ancients regarded blood as the seat of life, and therefore as sacred. Although in itself the prohibition against eating meat with blood in it is comparable to the ritual laws of the Mosaic code, the Jews considered it binding on all men, because it was given by God to Noah, the new ancestor of all mankind; therefore the early Christian Church retained it for a time (Acts 15, 20.29).

9, 18-27: This story seems to be a composite of two earlier accounts; in the one, Ham was guilty, whereas, in the other, it was Canaan. One purpose of the story is to justify the Israelites' enslavement of the Canaanites because of certain indecent sexual practices in the Canaanite religion. Obviously the story offers no justification for enslaving African Negroes, even though Canaan is presented as a "son" of Ham because the land of Canaan belonged to Hamitic Egypt at the time of the Israelite invasion.

22 Ham, the father of Canaan, saw his
father's nakedness, and he told his two
brothers outside about it. 23 Shem and
Japheth, however, took a robe, and hold-
ing it on their backs, they walked back-
ward and covered their father's na-
kedness; since their faces were turned
the other way, they did not see their fa-
ther's nakedness. 24 When Noah woke up
from his drunkenness and learned what
his youngest son had done to him, 25* he
said:

"Cursed be Caanan!
The lowest of slaves
shall he be to his brothers."

26† He also said:

"Blessed be the LORD, the God of
Shem!
Let Canaan be his slave.
27† May God expand Japheth,
so that he dwells among the tents
of Shem;
and let Canaan be his slave."

28 Noah lived three hundred and fifty
years after the flood. 29 The whole life-
time of Noah was nine hundred and fifty
years; then he died.

CHAPTER 10

Table of the Nations. 1† These are the
descendants of Noah's sons, Shem,
Ham, and Japheth, to whom sons were
born after the flood.

2*† The descendants of Japheth:
Gomer, Magog, Madai, Javan,
Tubal, Meshech, and Tiras.
3† The descendants of Gomer:
Ashkenaz, Riphath, and To-
garmah.
4† The descendants of Javan:
Elishah, Tarshish, the Kittim, and
the Rodanim.

5 These are the descendants of Ja-
pheth, and from them sprang the mari-
time nations, in their respective lands—
each with its own language—by their
clans within their nations.

6† The descendants of Ham:
Cush, Mizraim, Put, and Canaan.
7 The descendants of Cush:
Seba, Havilah, Sabtah, Raamah,
and Sabteca.
The descendants of Raamah: Sheba
and Dedan.

8† Cush became the father of Nimrod,
who was the first potentate on earth. 9 He
was a mighty hunter by the grace of the
LORD; hence the saying, "Like Nimrod,
a mighty hunter by the grace of the
LORD." 10† The chief cities of his king-
dom were Babylon, Erech, and Accad,
all of them in the land of Shinar.
11† From that land he went forth to As-
shur, where he built Nineveh, Rehoboth-
Ir, and Calah, 12† as well as Resen, be-
tween Nineveh and Calah, the latter
being the principal city.

13* Mizraim became the father of the
Ludim, the Anamim, the Lehabim, the
Naphtuhim, 14† the Pathrusim, the Cas-
luhim, and the Caphtorim from whom
the Philistines sprang.

15† Canaan became the father of Si-
don, his first-born, and of Heth; 16 also
of the Jebusites, the Amorites, the Gir-
gashites, 17 the Hivites, the Arkites, the
Sinites, 18 the Arvadites, the Zemarites,
and the Hamathites. Afterward, the
clans of the Canaanites spread out, 19† so
that the Canaanite borders extended
from Sidon all the way to Gerar, near
Gaza, and all the way to Sodom, Gomor-
rah, Admah and Zeboiim, near Lasha.

*

25: Dt 27, 16; Wis 12, 11.
10, 2-8: 1 Chr 1, 5-10.
2: Ez 38, 2.
13-18: 1 Chr 1, 11-16.

†

9, 26: *Blessed . . . Shem:* Perhaps the text read originally, "Blessed of the LORD be Shem," which would be expected in the context.

9, 27: In the Hebrew text there is a play on the words *yapt* ("expand") and *yepet* ("Japheth").

10, 1-32: This chapter presents a remarkably good classification of the various peoples known to the ancient Israelites; it is theologically important at stressing the basic family unity of all men on earth. The relationship between the various peoples is based partly on linguistic, partly on geographic, and partly on political grounds *according to their . . . languages, . . . lands and nations* (v 31). In general, *the descendants of Japheth* (vv 2-5) are the peoples of the Indo-European languages to the north and west of Mesopotamia and Syria; *the descendants of Ham* (vv 6-20) are the Hamitic-speaking peoples of northern Africa; and *the descendants of Shem* (vv 21-31) are the Semitic-speaking peoples of Mesopotamia, Syria and Arabia. But there are many exceptions to this rule; the Semitic-speaking peoples of Canaan, for instance, are considered descendants of Ham, because at the time they were subject to Hamitic Egypt (vv 6.15-19). This chapter is a composite from the Yahwist source (vv 8-19.21.24-30) of about the ninth century B.C., and the Priestly source (vv 1-7.20.22f.31f) of a few centuries later. That is why certain tribes of Arabia are listed under both Ham (v 7) and Shem (vv 26ff).

10, 2: *Gomer:* the Cimmerians; *Madai:* the Medes; *Javan:* the Greeks.

10, 3: *Ashkenaz:* the Scythians.

10, 4: *Elishah:* Cyprus; *the Kittim:* certain inhabitants of Cyprus; *the Rodanim:* the inhabitants of Rhodes.

10, 6: *Cush:* Biblical Ethiopia, modern Nubia; *Mizraim:* Egypt; *Put:* either Punt in East Africa or Libya.

10, 8: *Cush:* here, the Kassites; see note on 2, 10-14. *Nimrod:* probably Tukulti-Ninurta I (thirteenth century B.C.), the first Assyrian conqueror of Babylonia and a famous city-builder at home.

10, 10: *Shinar:* ancient Sumer in southern Mesopotamia, mentioned also in 11, 2; 14, 1.

10, 11: *Asshur:* Assyria. *Rehoboth-Ir:* literally "wide-streets city," was probably not the name of another city, but an epithet of Nineveh; cf Jon 3, 3.

10, 12: *Calah:* Assyrian Kalhu, the capital of Assyria in the ninth century B.C.

10, 14: *The Pathrusim:* the people of upper (southern) Egypt; cf Is 11, 11; Jer 44, 1; Ez 29, 14; 30, 14. *Caphtorim:* Crete; for Caphtor as the place of origin of the Philistines, cf Dt 2, 23; Am 9, 7; Jer 47, 4.

10, 15: *Heth:* the biblical Hittites; see note on Gn 23, 3.

10, 19: *Lasha:* the reading of this name is uncertain; perhaps it should be "Bela"; cf 14, 2.

20 These are the descendants of Ham,
according to their clans and languages,
by their lands and nations.
21 To Shem also, Japheth's oldest
brother and the ancestor of all the chil-
dren of Eber, sons were born.

22* The descendants of Shem:
Elam, Asshur, Arpachshad, Lud,
and Aram.
23 The descendants of Aram:
Uz, Hul, Gether, and Mash.

24 Arpachshad became the father of
Shelah, and Shelah became the father
of Eber. 25† To Eber two sons were born:
the name of the first was Peleg, for in
his time the world was divided; and the
name of his brother was Joktan.
26 Joktan became the father of Almo-
dad, Sheleph, Hazarmaveth, Jerah,
27 Hadoram, Uzal, Diklah, 28 Obal,
Abimael, Sheba, 29 Ophir, Havilah, and
Jobab. All these were descendants of
Joktan. 30 Their settlements extended all
the way to Sephar, the eastern hill coun-
try.
31 These are the descendants of Shem,
according to their clans and languages
by their lands and nations.
32 These are the groupings of Noah's
sons, according to their origins and by
their nations. From these the other na-
tions of the earth branched out after the
flood.

CHAPTER 11

The Tower of Babel. 1† The whole
world spoke the same language, using
the same words. 2† While men were mi-
grating in the east, they came upon a
valley in the land of Shinar and settled
there. 3 They said to one another,
"Come, let us mold bricks and harden
them with fire." They used bricks for
stone, and bitumen for mortar. 4† Then
they said, "Come, let us build ourselves
a city and a tower with its top in the sky,
and so make a name for ourselves; oth-
erwise we shall be scattered all over the
earth."
5 The LORD came down to see the city
and the tower that the men had built.
6 Then the LORD said: "If now, while they
are one people, all speaking the same
language, they have started to do this,
nothing will later stop them from doing
whatever they presume to do. 7 Let us
then go down and there confuse their
language, so that one will not under-
stand what another says." 8 Thus the
LORD scattered them from there all over
the earth, and they stopped building the
city. 9† That is why it was called Babel,
because there the LORD confused the
speech of all the world. It was from that
place that he scattered them all over the
earth.

The Line from Shem to Abraham.
10*† This is the record of the descen-
dants of Shem. When Shem was one
hundred years old, he became the father
of Arpachshad, two years after the flood.
11 Shem lived five hundred years after
the birth of Arpachshad, and he had
other sons and daughters.
12† When Arpachshad was thirty-five
years old, he became the father of She-
lah. 13 Arpachshad lived four hundred
and three years after the birth of Shelah,
and he had other sons and daughters.
14 When Shelah was thirty years old,
he became the father of Eber. 15 Shelah
lived four hundred and three years after
the birth of Eber, and he had other sons
and daughters.
16† When Eber was thirty-four years
old, he became the father of Peleg.
17 Eber lived four hundred and thirty
years after the birth of Peleg, and he
had other sons and daughters.
18 When Peleg was thirty years old, he
became the father of Reu. 19 Peleg lived
two hundred and nine years after the
birth of Reu, and he had other sons and
daughters.
20 When Reu was thirty-two years old,
he became the father of Serug. 21 Reu
lived two hundred and seven years after
the birth of Serug, and he had other sons
and daughters.
22 When Serug was thirty years old, he
became the father of Nahor. 23 Serug
lived two hundred years after the birth
of Nahor, and he had other sons and
daughters.

*

22-29: 1 Chr 1, 17-23. 11, 10-26: 1 Chr 1, 24-27; Lk 3, 34ff.

†

10, 25: In the Hebrew text there is a play on the name *Peleg* and the word *niplega,* "was divided."

11, 1-9: This story, based on traditions about the temple towers or ziggurats of Babylonia, is used by the sacred writer primarily to illustrate man's increasing wickedness, shown here in his presumptuous effort to create an urban culture apart from God. The secondary motive in the story is to present an imaginative origin of the diversity of languages among the various peoples inhabiting the earth, as well as an artificial explanation of the name "Babylon."

11, 2: *Shinar:* see note on 10, 10.

11, 4: *Tower with its top in the sky:* a direct reference to the chief ziggurat of Babylon, the *E-sag-ila,* signifying "the house that raises high its head." Babylonian ziggurats were the earliest skyscrapers.

11, 9: *Babel:* the Hebrew form of the name "Babylon"; the native name, *Bab-ili,* means "gate of the gods." The Hebrew word *balil,* "he confused," has a similar sound. Apparently the name referred originally only to a certain part of the city, the district near the gate that led to the temple area.

11, 10-26: This section is a continuation of the genealogical record given in 5, 1–32; see note there. Although the ages of the patriarchs in this list are much lower than those of the antediluvian patriarchs, they are still artificial and devoid of historical value. The ages given here are from the current Hebrew text; the Samaritan and Greek texts have divergent sets of numbers in most cases.

11, 12: The Greek text has a certain Kenan (cf 5, 9f) between Arpachshad and Shelah. This text is followed in Lk 3, 36.

11, 16: *Eber:* the eponymous ancestor of the Hebrews, "descendants of Eber" (10, 21.24-30); see note on 14, 13.

24 When Nahor was twenty-nine years
old, he became the father of Terah.
25 Nahor lived one hundred and nineteen
years after the birth of Terah, and he
had other sons and daughters.
26* When Terah was seventy years old,
he became the father of Abram, Nahor
and Haran.

II: THE PATRIARCH ABRAHAM

Terah. 27 This is the record of the de-
scendants of Terah. Terah became the
father of Abram, Nahor, and Haran, and
Haran became the father of Lot.
28† Haran died before his father Terah,
in his native land, in Ur of the Chalde-
ans. 29* Abram and Nahor took wives;
the name of Abram's wife was Sarai,
and the name of Nahor's wife was Mil-
cah, daughter of Haran, the father of
Milcah and Iscah. 30 Sarai was barren;
she had no child.
31*† Terah took his son Abram, his
grandson Lot, son of Haran, and his
daughter-in-law Sarai, the wife of his
son Abram, and brought them out of Ur
of the Chaldeans, to go to the land of
Canaan. But when they reached Haran,
they settled there. 32† The lifetime of
Terah was two hundred and five years;
then Terah died in Haran.

CHAPTER 12

Abram's Call and Migration. 1* The
LORD said to Abram: "Go forth from the
land of your kinsfolk and from your fa-
ther's house to a land that I will show
you.

2* "I will make of you a great nation,
and I will bless you;
I will make your name great,
so that you will be a blessing.
3*† I will bless those who bless you
and curse those who curse you.
All the communities of the earth
shall find blessing in you."

4* Abram went as the LORD directed
him, and Lot went with him. Abram was
seventy-five years old when he left
Haran. 5† Abram took his wife Sarai, his
brother's son Lot, all the possessions
that they had accumulated, and the per-
sons they had acquired in Haran, and
they set out for the land of Canaan.
When they came to the land of Canaan,
6 Abram passed through the land as far
as the sacred place at Shechem, by the
terebinth of Moreh. (The Canaanites
were then in the land.)
7* The LORD appeared to Abram and
said, "To your descendants I will give
this land." So Abram built an altar there
to the LORD who had appeared to him.
8 From there he moved on to the hill
country east of Bethel, pitching his tent
with Bethel to the west and Ai to the east.
He built an altar there to the LORD and
invoked the LORD by name. 9† Then
Abram journeyed on by stages to the
Negeb.
Abram and Sarai in Egypt. 10* There
was famine in the land; so Abram went
down to Egypt to sojourn there, since
the famine in the land was severe.
11 When he was about to enter Egypt, he
said to his wife Sarai: "I know well how
beautiful a woman you are. 12 When the
Egyptians see you, they will say, 'She
is his wife'; then they will kill me, but
let you live. 13*† Please say, therefore,
that you are my sister, so that it may
go well with me on your account and my
life may be spared for your sake."
14 When Abram came to Egypt, the
Egyptians saw how beautiful the woman
was; and when Pharaoh's courtiers saw
her, 15 they praised her to Pharaoh. So
she was taken into Pharaoh's palace.

---

*

26: Jos 24, 2; 1 Chr 1, 27.
29: 17, 15; 20, 12.
31: Jos 24, 3; Neh 9, 7; Jdt 5, 6-9; Acts 7, 4.
12, 1: Acts 7, 3; Heb 11, 8.
2: 17, 6; Sir 44, 20; Rom 4, 17-22.
3: 18, 18; 22, 18; Acts 3, 25; Gal 3, 8.
4f: 11, 31; Jos 24, 3; Acts 7, 4.
7: Ex 33, 1; Dt 34, 4; Acts 7, 5.
10: 26, 1.
13: 20, 12f; 26, 7.

---

†

11, 28: *Ur of the Chaldeans:* Ur was an extremely ancient city of the Sumerians (later, of the Babylonians) in southern Mesopotamia. The Greek text has "the land of the Chaldeans." In either case, the term *Chaldeans* is an anachronism, because the Chaldeans were not known to history until approximately a thousand years after Abraham's time.

11, 31: The Samaritan and Greek texts include Nahor and his wife in Terah's migration to Haran. Although this is probably due to scribal harmonization, Nahor's family actually did migrate to Haran; cf 24, 10; 27, 43.

11, 32: Since Terah was seventy years old when his son Abraham was born (v 26), and Abraham was seventy-five when he left Haran (12, 4), Terah lived in Haran for sixty years after Abraham's departure. According to the tradition in the Samaritan text, Terah died when he was one hundred and forty-five years old, therefore, in the same year in which Abraham left Haran. This is the tradition followed in St. Stephen's speech: Abraham left Haran "after his father died" (Acts 7, 4).

12, 3: *Shall find blessing in you:* the sense of the Hebrew expression is probably reflexive, "shall bless themselves through you" (i.e., in giving a blessing they shall say, "May you be as blessed as Abraham"), rather than passive, "shall be blessed in you." Since the term is understood in a passive sense in the New Testament (Acts 3, 25; Gal 3, 8), it is rendered here by a neutral expression that admits of both meanings. So also in the blessings given by God to Isaac (26, 4) and Jacob (28, 14).

12, 5: *Persons:* slaves and retainers that formed the social aggregate under the leadership of Abraham; cf 14, 14.

12, 9: *The Negeb:* the semidesert land of southern Palestine.

12, 13: *You are my sister:* although Abraham's deceit may not be fully defensible, his statement was at least a half-truth; Sarah was indeed his relative, called "a sister" in Hebrew; cf 20, 12. Moreover, the ancient traditions on which this story and the parallel ones in 20, 1-18 and 26, 6-11 are based, probably come from the Hurrian custom of wife-sister marriage. Among the Hurrians, with whom Abraham's clan lived in close contact at Haran, a man could adopt his wife as his sister and thus give her higher status.

16† On her account it went very well with
Abram, and he received flocks and
herds, male and female slaves, male and
female asses, and camels.
17* But the LORD struck Pharaoh and
his household with severe plagues be-
cause of Abram's wife Sarai. 18 Then
Pharaoh summoned Abram and said to
him: "How could you do this to me! Why
didn't you tell me she was your wife?
19 Why did you say, 'She is my sister,'
so that I took her for my wife? Here,
then, is your wife. Take her and be
gone!"
20 Then Pharaoh gave men orders con-
cerning him, and they sent him on his
way, with his wife and all that belonged
to him.

CHAPTER 13

Abram and Lot Part. 1* From Egypt
Abram went up to the Negeb with his
wife and all that belonged to him, and
Lot accompanied him. 2* Now Abram
was very rich in livestock, silver, and
gold. 3 From the Negeb he traveled by
stages toward Bethel, to the place be-
tween Bethel and Ai where his tent had
formerly stood, 4* the site where he had
first built the altar; and there he invoked
the LORD by name.
5 Lot, who went with Abram, also had
flocks and herds and tents, 6 so that the
land could not support them if they
stayed together; their possessions were
so great that they could not dwell to-
gether. 7 There were quarrels between
the herdsmen of Abram's livestock and
those of Lot's. (At this time the Canaan-
ites and the Perizzites were occupying
the land.)
8 So Abram said to Lot: "Let there be
no strife between you and me, or be-
tween your herdsmen and mine, for we
are kinsmen. 9 Is not the whole land at
your disposal? Please separate from me.
If you prefer the left, I will go to the right;
if you prefer the right, I will go to the
left." 10 Lot looked about and saw how
well watered the whole Jordan Plain was
as far as Zoar, like the LORD's own gar-
den, or like Egypt. (This was before the
LORD had destroyed Sodom and Gomor-
rah.) 11 Lot, therefore, chose for himself
the whole Jordan Plain and set out east-
ward. Thus they separated from each
other; 12 Abram stayed in the land of Ca-
naan, while Lot settled among the cities
of the Plain, pitching his tents near
Sodom. 13* Now the inhabitants of
Sodom were very wicked in the sins they
committed against the LORD.
14* After Lot had left, the LORD said
to Abram: "Look about you, and from
where you are, gaze to the north and
south, east and west; 15* all the land that
you see I will give to you and your de-
scendants forever. 16* I will make your
descendants like the dust of the earth;
if anyone could count the dust of the
earth, your descendants too might be
counted. 17 Set forth and walk about in
the land, through its length and breadth,
for to you I will give it." 18* Abram
moved his tents and went on to settle
near the terebinth of Mamre, which is
at Hebron. There he built an altar to the
LORD.

CHAPTER 14

The Four Kings. 1† In the days of
. . . , Amraphel king of Shinar, Arioch
king of Ellasar, Chedorlaomer king of
Elam, and Tidal king of Goiim 2 made
war on Bera king of Sodom, Birsha king
of Gomorrah, Shinab king of Admah,
Shemeber king of Zeboiim, and the king
of Bela (that is, Zoar). 3† All the latter
kings joined forces in the Valley of Sid-
dim (that is, the Salt Sea). 4 For twelve
years they had been subject to Chedor-
laomer, but in the thirteenth year they
rebelled. 5† In the fourteenth year Che-
dorlaomer and the kings allied with him
came and defeated the Rephaim in Ash-
teroth-karnaim, the Zuzim in Ham, the
Emim in Shaveh-kiriathaim, 6* and the
Horites in the hill country of Seir, as far
as El-paran, close by the wilderness.
7 They turned back and came to En-
mishpat (that is, Kadesh), and they sub-
dued the whole country both of the
Amalekites and of the Amorites who
dwelt in Hazazon-tamar. 8 Thereupon
the king of Sodom, the king of Gomor-
rah, the king of Admah, the king of Ze-
boiim, and the king of Bela (that is,
Zoar) marched out, and in the Valley
of Siddim they went into battle against
them: 9 against Chedorlaomer king of
Elam, Tidal king of Goiim, Amraphel
king of Shinar, and Arioch king of Ella-
sar—four kings against five. 10 Now the
Valley of Siddim was full of bitumen pits;
and as the kings of Sodom and Gomor-
rah fled, they fell into these, while the

*

17: Ps 105, 14.
13, 1: 12, 9.
2: Ps 112, 1ff; Prv 10, 22.
4: 12, 8.
13: 18, 20; Ez 16, 49; 2 Pt 2, 6 ff; Jude 1, 7.
14: 28, 14.
15: 12, 7; Mt 5, 4; Lk 1, 55; Acts 7, 5; Gal 3, 16.
16: 22, 17; Nm 23, 10.
18: 14, 13.
14, 6: Dt 2, 12.

†

12, 16: *Camels:* domesticated camels probably did not come into common use in the ancient Near East until the end of the second millennium B.C. Thus the mention of camels at the time of the patriarchs (24, 11-64; 30, 43; 31, 17.34; 32, 8.16; 37, 25) is seemingly an anachronism.

14, 1: *In the days of . . . :* the personal name by which the event is dated has not been preserved.

14, 3: *The Salt Sea:* now known as the Dead Sea.

14, 5f: The five kings came from north to south through the land east of the Jordan.

rest fled to the mountains. 11 The victors
seized all the possessions and food sup-
plies of Sodom and Gomorrah and then
went their way, 12* taking with them
Abram's nephew Lot, who had been liv-
ing in Sodom, as well as his possessions.
13† A fugitive came and brought the
news to Abram the Hebrew, who was
camping at the terebinth of Mamre the
Amorite, a kinsman of Eshcol and Aner;
these were in league with Abram.
14 When Abram heard that his nephew
had been captured, he mustered three
hundred and eighteen of his retainers,
born in his house, and went in pursuit
as far as Dan. 15 He and his party de-
ployed against them at night, defeated
them, and pursued them as far as Ho-
bah, which is north of Damascus. 16 He
recovered all the possessions, besides
bringing back his kinsman Lot and his
possessions, along with the women and
the other captives.
17 When Abram returned from his vic-
tory over Chedorlaomer and the kings
who were allied with him, the king of
Sodom went out to greet him in the Val-
ley of Shaveh (that is, the King's Valley).
18*† Melchizedek, king of Salem,
brought out bread and wine, and being
a priest of God Most High, he blessed
Abram with these words:

19† "Blessed be Abram by God Most High,
the creator of heaven and earth;
20† And blessed be God Most High,
who delivered your foes into your hand."

Then Abram gave him a tenth of every-
thing.
21 The king of Sodom said to Abram,
"Give me the people; the goods you may
keep." 22† But Abram replied to the king
of Sodom: "I have sworn to the LORD,
God Most High, the creator of heaven
and earth, 23 that I would not take so
much as a thread or a sandal strap from
anything that is yours, lest you should
say, 'I made Abram rich.' 24 Nothing for
me except what my servants have used
up and the share that is due to the men
who joined me—Aner, Eshcol and
Mamre; let them take their share."

CHAPTER 15

The Covenant with Abram. 1 Some
time after these events, this word of the
LORD came to Abram in a vision:

"Fear not, Abram!
I am your shield;
I will make your reward very great."

2 But Abram said, "O Lord GOD, what
good will your gifts be, if I keep on being
childless and have as my heir the stew-
ard of my house, Eliezer?" 3 Abram
continued, "See, you have given me no
offspring, and so one of my servants will
be my heir." 4* Then the word of the
LORD came to him: "No, that one shall
not be your heir; your own issue shall
be your heir." 5* He took him outside
and said: "Look up at the sky and count
the stars, if you can. Just so," he added,
"shall your descendants be." 6*† Abram
put his faith in the LORD, who credited
it to him as an act of righteousness.
7* He then said to him, "I am the LORD
who brought you from Ur of the Chalde-
ans to give you this land as a posses-
sion." 8 "O Lord GOD," he asked, "How
am I to know that I shall possess it?"
9*† He answered him, "Bring me a
three-year-old heifer, a three-year-old
she-goat, a three-year-old ram, a turtle-
dove, and a young pigeon." 10 He
brought him all these, split them in two,
and placed each half opposite the other;
but the birds he did not cut up. 11 Birds
of prey swooped down on the carcasses,
but Abram stayed with them. 12 As the
sun was about to set, a trance fell upon
Abram, and a deep, terrifying darkness
enveloped him.
13* Then the LORD said to Abram:

*

12: 13, 10ff.
18: Ps 110, 4; Heb 5, 6.10; 7, 1.
15, 4: 17, 16.
5: 22, 17; 28, 14; Ex 32, 13; Dt 1, 10; Sir 44, 21; Rom 4, 18; Heb 11, 12.
6: 1 Mc 2, 52; Rom 4, 3.9.22; Gal 3, 6f; Jas 2, 23.
7: 11, 31; 12, 1; Ex 32, 13; Neh 9, 7f; Acts 7, 2f.
9: Lv 1, 14.
13: Ex 12, 40; Nm 20, 15; Jdt 5, 9f; Is 52, 4; Acts 13, 20; Gal 3, 17.

†

14, 13: *Abram the Hebrew:* elsewhere in the Old Testament, until the last pre-Christian centuries, the term "Hebrew" is used only by non-Israelites, or by Israelites in speaking to foreigners, since it evidently had a disparaging connotation—something like "immigrant." The account in this chapter may, therefore, have been taken originally from a non-Israelite source, in which Abraham, a warlike sheik of Palestine, appears as a truly historical figure of profane history.

14, 18: *Salem:* traditionally identified with Jerusalem (Ps 76, 3), but the Hebrew text is not certain; instead of the present *melek shalem* ("king of Salem"), the original may have been *melek shelomo* ("a king allied to him"). In Heb 7, 2, "king of Salem" is interpreted as "king of peace" *(shalom).*

14, 19: *God Most High:* in Hebrew, *el-elyon.* In Canaanite texts, each element may occur separately as the name of a specific deity, or they may be applied together to a single deity, as is done here by the Canaanite priest Melchizedek. For the Israelites, *el* became a poetic synonym for *elohim* ("God"); *elyon* ("Most High") became one of the titles of their God Yahweh.

14, 20: *Abram gave him:* literally "he gave him"; but *Abram* is to be understood as the subject of the sentence, for the tithes were the tenth part assigned to priests; cf Heb 7, 4-10.

14, 22: Abraham uses the name of the Canaanite god *el-elyon* ("God the Most High") in apposition to the name of his God, *yahweh* ("the LORD").

15, 6: Abraham's *faith* in God's promises was regarded as *an act of righteousness,* i.e., as expressing the "right" attitude of man toward God. In turn, God credited this to Abraham, i.e., gave him title to the fulfillment of God's promises. St. Paul (Rom 4, 1-25; Gal 3, 6-9) makes Abraham's faith a model for that of Christians.

15, 9: *Three-year-old:* ritually mature.

"Know for certain that your descen-
dants shall be aliens in a land not their
own, where they shall be enslaved and
oppressed for four hundred years.
14* But I will bring judgment on the na-
tion they must serve, and in the end they
will depart with great wealth. 15 You,
however, shall join your forefathers in
peace; you shall be buried at a contented
old age. 16*† In the fourth time-span the
others shall come back here; the wicked-
ness of the Amorites will not have
reached its full measure until then."
17† When the sun had set and it was
dark, there appeared a smoking brazier
and a flaming torch, which passed be-
tween those pieces. 18*† It was on that
occasion that the LORD made a covenant
with Abram, saying: "To your descen-
dants I give this land, from the Wadi of
Egypt to the Great River [the Euphra-
tes], 19* the land of the Kenites, the
Kenizzites, the Kadmonites, 20 the Hit-
tites, the Perizzites, the Rephaim, 21 the
Amorites, the Canaanites, the Girgash-
ites, and the Jebusites."

CHAPTER 16

Birth of Ishmael. 1*† Abram's wife
Sarai had borne him no children. She
had, however, an Egyptian maidservant
named Hagar. 2* Sarai said to Abram:
"The LORD has kept me from bearing
children. Have intercourse, then, with
my maid; perhaps I shall have sons
through her." Abram heeded Sarai's re-
quest. 3 Thus, after Abram had lived ten
years in the land of Canaan, his wife Sa-
rai took her maid, Hagar the Egyptian,
and gave her to her husband Abram to
be his concubine. 4* He had intercourse
with her, and she became pregnant.
When she became aware of her preg-
nancy, she looked on her mistress with
disdain. 5* So Sarai said to Abram: "You
are responsible for this outrage against
me. I myself gave my maid to your em-
brace; but ever since she became aware
of her pregnancy, she has been looking
on me with disdain. May the LORD de-
cide between you and me!" 6 Abram told
Sarai: "Your maid is in your power. Do
to her whatever you please." Sarai then
abused her so much that Hagar ran
away from her.
7*† The LORD's messenger found her
by a spring in the wilderness, the spring
on the road to Shur, 8 and he asked, "Ha-
gar maid of Sarai, where have you come
from and where are you going?" She an-
swered, "I am running away from my
mistress, Sarai." 9 But the LORD's mes-
senger told her: "Go back to your mis-
tress and submit to her abusive
treatment. 10* I will make your descen-
dants so numerous," added the LORD's
messenger, "that they will be too many
to count. 11† Besides," the LORD's mes-
senger said to her:

"You are now pregnant and shall
bear a son;
you shall name him Ishmael,
For the LORD has heard you,
God has answered you.
12* He shall be a wild ass of a man,
his hand against everyone,
and everyone's hand against him;
In opposition to all his kin
shall he encamp."

13*† To the LORD who spoke to her she
gave a name, saying, "You are the God
of Vision"; she meant, "Have I really
seen God and remained alive after my
vision?" 14† That is why the well is called
Beer-lahai-roi. It is between Kadesh and
Bered.
15* Hagar bore Abram a son, and
Abram named the son whom Hagar
bore him Ishmael. 16 Abram was eighty-
six years old when Hagar bore him Ish-
mael.

CHAPTER 17

Covenant of Circumcision. 1* † When
Abram was ninety-nine years old, the
LORD appeared to him and said: "I am
God the Almighty. Walk in my presence
and be blameless. 2* Between you and

*

14: Ex 3, 8.21f.
16: 1 Kgs 21, 26.
18: Ex 32, 13; Neh 9, 8; Ps 105, 11; Sir 44, 21.
19f: Dt 7, 1.
16, 1: 11, 30.
2: 21, 8f; Gal 4, 22.
4: Sm 1, 6; Prv 30, 23.
5-16: 21, 10-19.
7: Ex 15, 22.
10: 17, 20; 21, 13.18; 25, 12-18.
12: 21, 20; 25, 18.
13: 24, 62.
15: 16, 2; Gal 4, 22.
17, 1: 35, 11; Ex 6, 3.
2: 12, 2; 13, 16; Ex 32, 13.

†

15, 16: *Time-span:* the Hebrew term *dor* is commonly rendered as "generation," but it may signify a period of varying length. Neither this passage nor the statement about the four hundred years has any value for determining how long the Israelites were in Egypt.

15, 17: *Brazier:* literally "oven"; a portable one is meant here. The smoke and fire represent God's presence. Although the text does not mention it, Abraham no doubt also walked between the split carcasses. For the meaning of this strange ceremony, see note on Jer 34, 18f.

15, 18: *Made a covenant:* literally "cut a covenant"; the expression derives from the ceremony of cutting the animals in two.

16, 1-6: Sarah's actions are all in keeping with the laws of the time, as known from ancient extra-biblical sources.

16, 7: *The LORD's messenger:* a manifestation of God in human form; therefore in v 13 the messenger is identified with the Lord himself.

16, 11: *Ishmael:* in Hebrew the name means "God has heard."

16, 13: *The God of Vision:* In Hebrew, *el-roi;* hence the name of the spring. *Remained alive:* for the ancient notion that a person died on seeing God, cf 32, 31; Ex 20, 19; Dt 4, 33; Jgs 13, 22.

16, 14: *Beer-lahai-roi:* probably "the well of living sight," i.e., the well where one can see (God) and yet live.

17, 1: *The Almighty:* traditional but incorrect rendering of the divine title *shaddai,* of uncertain meaning.

me I will establish my covenant, and I
will multiply you exceedingly."
3 When Abram prostrated himself,
God continued to speak to him: 4* "My
covenant with you is this: you are to be-
come the father of a host of nations.
5*† No longer shall you be called Abram;
your name shall be Abraham, for I am
making you the father of a host of na-
tions. 6 I will render you exceedingly fer-
tile; I will make nations of you; kings
shall stem from you. 7* I will maintain
my covenant with you and your descen-
dants after you throughout the ages as
an everlasting pact, to be your God and
the God of your descendants after you.
8* I will give to you and to your descen-
dants after you the land in which you
are now staying, the whole land of Ca-
naan, as a permanent possession; and
I will be their God."
9 God also said to Abraham: "On your
part, you and your descendants after
you must keep my covenant throughout
the ages. 10* This is my covenant with
you and your descendants after you that
you must keep: every male among you
shall be circumcised. 11* Circumcise the
flesh of your foreskin, and that shall be
the mark of the covenant between you
and me. 12* Throughout the ages, every
male among you, when he is eight days
old, shall be circumcised, including
houseborn slaves and those acquired
with money from any foreigner who is
not of your blood. 13 Yes, both the house-
born slaves and those acquired with
money must be circumcised. Thus my
covenant shall be in your flesh as an ev-
erlasting pact. 14 If a male is uncircum-
cised, that is, if the flesh of his foreskin
has not been cut away, such a one shall
be cut off from his people; he has broken
my covenant."
15† God further said to Abraham: "As
for your wife Sarai, do not call her Sarai;
her name shall be Sarah. 16* I will bless
her, and I will give you a son by her.
Him also will I bless; he shall give rise
to nations, and rulers of peoples shall
issue from him." 17*† Abraham pros-
trated himself and laughed as he said
to himself, "Can a child be born to a man
who is a hundred years old? Or can
Sarah give birth at ninety?" 18 Then Ab-
raham said to God, "Let but Ishmael live
on by your favor!" 19* God replied:
"Nevertheless, your wife Sarah is to
bear you a son, and you shall call him
Isaac. I will maintain my covenant with
him as an everlasting pact, to be his God
and the God of his descendants after
him. 20* As for Ishmael, I am heeding
you: I hereby bless him. I will make him
fertile and will multiply him exceed-
ingly. He shall become the father of
twelve chieftains, and I will make of him
a great nation. 21* But my covenant I will
maintain with Isaac, whom Sarah shall
bear to you by this time next year."
22 When he had finished speaking with
him, God departed from Abraham.
23 Then Abraham took his son Ishmael
and all his slaves, whether born in his
house or acquired with his money—ev-
ery male among the members of Abra-
ham's household—and he circumcised
the flesh of their foreskins on that same
day, as God had told him to do.
24* Abraham was ninety-nine years old
when the flesh of his foreskin was cir-
cumcised, 25 and his son Ishmael was
thirteen years old when the flesh of his
foreskin was circumcised. 26 Thus, on
that same day Abraham and his son Ish-
mael were circumcised; 27 and all the
male members of his household, includ-
ing the slaves born in his house or ac-
quired with his money from foreigners,
were circumcised with him.

CHAPTER 18

Abraham's Visitors. 1 The LORD ap-
peared to Abraham by the terebinth of
Mamre, as he sat in the entrance of his
tent, while the day was growing hot.
2* Looking up, he saw three men stand-
ing nearby. When he saw them, he ran
from the entrance of the tent to greet
them; and bowing to the ground, 3† he
said: "Sir, if I may ask you this favor,
please do not go on past your servant.
4 Let some water be brought, that you
may bathe your feet, and then rest your-
selves under the tree. 5 Now that you
have come this close to your servant,
let me bring you a little food, that you
may refresh yourselves; and afterward
you may go on your way." "Very well,"

*

4: Sir 44, 21; Rom 4, 17.
5: Neh 9, 7.
7: Ps 105, 42; Lk 1, 72f; Gal 3, 16.
8: Ex 32, 13; Dt 1, 8; 14, 2; Lk 1, 55; Acts 7, 5.
10: Jn 7, 22; Acts 7, 8; Rom 4, 11.
11: Sir 44, 21.
12: Lv 12, 3; Lk 1, 59; 2, 21.
16: 18, 10; Gal 4, 23.
17: Rom 4, 19; Heb 11, 11f.
19: 11, 30; 21, 2; Ex 32, 13; Sir 44, 22.
20: 16, 10; 21, 13.18; 25, 12-16.
21: 18, 14; 21, 2; 26, 2-5; Rom 9, 7.
24: 17, 10; Rom 4, 11.
18, 2: Heb 13, 1f; 2 Kgs 4, 16; Rom 9, 9.

†

17, 5: *Abram* and *Abraham* are merely two forms of the same name, both meaning, "the father is exalted"; another variant form is Abiram (Nm 16, 1; 1 Kgs 16, 34). The additional *-ha-* in the form Abraham is explained by folk etymology as coming from *ab-hamon goyim,* "father of a host of nations."

17, 15: *Sarai* and *Sarah* are variant forms of the same name, both meaning "princess."

17, 17: *Laughed: yishaq,* which is the Hebrew form of the name "Isaac"; other similar explanations of the name are given in 18, 12 and 21, 6.

18, 3: Abraham addresses the leader of the group, whom he does not yet recognize as Yahweh; in the next two verses he speaks to all *three men.* The other two are later (19, 1) identified as messengers.

they replied, "do as you have said."
6† Abraham hastened into the tent and
told Sarah, "Quick, three seahs of fine
flour! Knead it and make rolls." 7 He ran
to the herd, picked out a tender, choice
steer, and gave it to a servant, who
quickly prepared it. 8† Then he got some
curds and milk, as well as the steer that
had been prepared, and set these before
them; and he waited on them under the
tree while they ate.
9 "Where is your wife Sarah?" they
asked him. "There in the tent," he re-
plied. 10*† One of them said, "I will
surely return to you about this time next
year, and Sarah will then have a son."
Sarah was listening at the entrance of
the tent, just behind him. 11* Now Abra-
ham and Sarah were old, advanced in
years, and Sarah had stopped having
her womanly periods. 12† So Sarah
laughed to herself and said, "Now that
I am so withered and my husband is so
old, am I still to have sexual pleasure?"
13 But the LORD said to Abraham: "Why
did Sarah laugh and say, 'Shall I really
bear a child, old as I am?' 14* Is anything
too marvelous for the LORD to do? At
the appointed time, about this time next
year, I will return to you, and Sarah will
have a son." 15 Because she was afraid,
Sarah dissembled, saying, "I didn't
laugh." But he said, "Yes you did."

Abraham Intercedes for Sodom.
16 The men set out from there and looked
down toward Sodom; Abraham was
walking with them, to see them on their
way. 17 The LORD reflected: "Shall I hide
from Abraham what I am about to do,
18* now that he is to become a great and
populous nation, and all the nations of
the earth are to find blessing in him?
19 Indeed, I have singled him out that he
may direct his sons and his posterity to
keep the way of the LORD by doing what
is right and just, so that the LORD may
carry into effect for Abraham the prom-
ises he made about him." 20*† Then the
LORD said: "The outcry against Sodom
and Gomorrah is so great, and their sin
so grave, 21 that I must go down and see
whether or not their actions fully corre-
spond to the cry against them that
comes to me. I mean to find out."
22 While the two men walked on far-
ther toward Sodom, the LORD remained
standing before Abraham. 23 Then
Abraham drew nearer to him and said:
"Will you sweep away the innocent with
the guilty? 24 Suppose there were fifty in-
nocent people in the city; would you wipe
out the place, rather than spare it for
the sake of the fifty innocent people
within it? 25* Far be it from you to do
such a thing, to make the innocent die
with the guilty, so that the innocent and
the guilty would be treated alike! Should
not the judge of all the world act with
justice?" 26 The LORD replied, "If I find
fifty innocent people in the city of
Sodom, I will spare the whole place for
their sake." 27* Abraham spoke up
again: "See how I am presuming to
speak to my Lord, though I am but dust
and ashes! 28 What if there are five less
than fifty innocent people? Will you de-
stroy the whole city because of those
five?" "I will not destroy it," he an-
swered, "if I find forty-five there." 29 But
Abraham persisted, saying, "What if
only forty are found there?" He replied,
"I will forebear doing it for the sake of
the forty." 30 Then he said, "Let not my
Lord grow impatient if I go on. What if
only thirty are found there?" He replied,
"I will forebear doing it if I can find but
thirty there." 31 Still he went on, "Since
I have thus dared to speak to my Lord,
what if there are no more than twenty?"
"I will not destroy it," he answered, "for
the sake of the twenty." 32* But he still
persisted: "Please, let not my Lord grow
angry if I speak up this last time. What
if there are at least ten there?" "For the
sake of those ten," he replied, "I will not
destroy it."
33 The LORD departed as soon as he
had finished speaking with Abraham,
and Abraham returned home.

GENESIS

CHAPTER 19

Destruction of Sodom and Gomorrah.
1 The two angels reached Sodom in the
evening, as Lot was sitting at the gate
of Sodom. When Lot saw them, he got
up to greet them; and bowing down with
his face to the ground, 2*† he said,
"Please, gentlemen, come aside into

*

10: 17, 19; 21, 1.
11: 17, 17; Rom 4, 19; Heb 11, 11f.
14: Mt 19, 26; Mk 10, 27; Lk 1, 37; 18, 27; Rom 4, 21.
18: Lk 1, 55.
20: 19, 13; Is 3, 9; Lk 17, 28; Jude 1, 7.
25: Dt 32, 4; Jb 8, 3.20; Wis 12, 15.
27: Sir 10, 9; 17, 27.
32: Jer 5, 1; Ez 22, 30.
19, 2: Wis 10, 6; Sir 16, 8; Ez 16, 50; Heb 13, 1f.

†

18, 6: *Three seahs:* one ephah, about half a bushel.

18, 8: *Curds:* a type of soft cheese or yoghurt.

18, 10: *One of them:* i.e., the Lord. Abraham now realizes this for the first time when he hears the prediction of a miraculous birth. *About this time next year:* literally "when the time becomes alive," i.e., at the time when birth is due after the period of gestation; the conception is understood as taking place soon after the prediction.

18, 12: *Sarah laughed:* see note on 17, 17.

18, 20: Israelite tradition was unanimous in ascribing the destruction of Sodom and Gomorrah to the wickedness of these cities, but tradition varied in regard to the nature of this wickedness. According to the present account of the Yahwist, the sin of Sodom was homosexuality (19, 4f), which is therefore also known as sodomy; but according to Isaiah (1, 9f; 3, 9), it was a lack of social justice; Ezekiel (16, 46-51) described it as a disregard for the poor, whereas Jeremiah (23, 14) saw it as general immorality.

19, 2: *Gentlemen:* Lot does not yet know that the distinguished-looking men are God's messengers; cf 18, 3.

your servant's house for the night, and
bathe your feet; you can get up early to
continue your journey." But they re-
plied, "No, we shall pass the night in the
town square." 3 He urged them so
strongly, however, that they turned
aside to his place and entered his house.
He prepared a meal for them, baking
cakes without leaven, and they dined.
4* Before they went to bed, all the
townsmen of Sodom, both young and
old—all the people to the last man—
closed in on the house. 5 They called to
Lot and said to him, "Where are the men
who came to your house tonight? Bring
them out to us that we may have intima-
cies with them." 6 Lot went out to meet
them at the entrance. When he had shut
the door behind him, 7 he said, "I beg
you, my brothers, not to do this wicked
thing. 8 I have two daughters who have
never had intercourse with men. Let me
bring them out to you, and you may do
to them as you please. But don't do any-
thing to these men, for you know they
have come under the shelter of my
roof." 9* They replied, "Stand back! This
fellow," they sneered, "came here as an
immigrant, and now he dares to give or-
ders! We'll treat you worse than them!"
With that, they pressed hard against
Lot, moving in closer to break down the
door. But his guests put out their hands,
10 pulled Lot inside with them, and
closed the door; 11† at the same time they
struck the men at the entrance of the
house, one and all, with such a blinding
light that they were utterly unable to
reach the doorway.
12*† Then the angels said to Lot: "Who
else belongs to you here? Your sons
[sons-in-law] and your daughters and
all who belong to you in the city—take
them away from it! 13* We are about to
destroy this place, for the outcry reach-
ing the LORD against those in the city
is so great that he has sent us to destroy
it." 14† So Lot went out and spoke to his
sons-in-law, who had contracted mar-
riage with his daughters. "Get up and
leave this place," he told them; "the
LORD is about to destroy the city." But
his sons-in-law thought he was joking.
15 As dawn was breaking, the angels
urged Lot on, saying, "On your way!
Take with you your wife and your two
daughters who are here, or you will be
swept away in the punishment of the
city." 16 When he hesitated, the men, by
the LORD's mercy, seized his hand and
the hands of his wife and his two daugh-
ters and led them to safety outside the
city. 17* As soon as they had been
brought outside, he was told: "Flee for
your life! Don't look back or stop any-
where on the Plain. Get off to the hills
at once, or you will be swept away."
18 "Oh, no, my lord!" replied Lot. 19 "You
have already thought enough of your
servant to do me the great kindness of
intervening to save my life. But I cannot
flee to the hills to keep the disaster from
overtaking me, and so I shall die.
20† Look, this town ahead is near enough
to escape to. It's only a small place. Let
me flee there—it's a small place, isn't
it?—that my life may be saved." 21 "Well,
then," he replied, "I will also grant you
the favor you now ask. I will not over-
throw the town you speak of. 22* Hurry,
escape there! I cannot do anything until
you arrive there." That is why the town
is called Zoar.
23* The sun was just rising over the
earth as Lot arrived in Zoar; 24* at the
same time the LORD rained down
sulphurous fire upon Sodom and Go-
morrah [from the LORD out of heaven].
25*† He overthrew those cities and the
whole Plain, together with the inhabit-
ants of the cities and the produce of the
soil. 26* But Lot's wife looked back, and
she was turned into a pillar of salt.
27 Early the next morning Abraham
went to the place where he had stood
in the LORD's presence. 28*† As he
looked down toward Sodom and Gomor-
rah and the whole region of the Plain,
he saw dense smoke over the land rising
like fumes from a furnace.
29 Thus it came to pass: when God de-
stroyed the Cities of the Plain, he was
mindful of Abraham by sending Lot
away from the upheaval by which God
overthrew the cities where Lot had been
living.

*

4-9: Jgs 19, 22-25; Jude 1, 7.
9: 13, 12; 2 Pt 2, 7f.
12: 2 Pt 7, 9.
13: Is 1, 7.9; Zep 2, 9; Lk 17, 29.
17: Wis 10, 6.
22: Wis 10, 6.
23: Pss 9, 6; 11, 6; 107, 34.
24: Wis 10, 7; Is 1, 9; 13, 19; Lam 4, 6; 17, 29; 2 Pt 2, 6.
25: Dt 29, 22; Jer 50, 40; Am 4, 11.
26: Wis 10, 7; Lk 17, 32.
28: Rv 9, 2; 14, 10f.

†

19, 11: *Blinding light:* a preternatural flash that temporarily dazed the wicked men and revealed to Lot the true nature of his guests.

19, 12: Since Lot apparently had no *sons,* a glossator interpreted the term to mean *sons-in-law.*

19, 14: It is uncertain whether Lot's *sons-in-law* were fully married to his daughters or only "engaged" to them (Israelite "engagement" was the first part of the marriage ceremony), or even whether the daughters involved were the same as, or different from, the two daughters who were still in their father's house.

19, 20: *A small place:* the Hebrew word *misar,* literally "a little thing," has the same root consonants as the name of the town *Zoar* in v 22.

19, 25: *Overthrew:* The consistent use of this term, literally "turned upside down," to describe the destruction of the Cities of the Plain seems to imply that their upheaval (v 29) was caused primarily by an earthquake; this would naturally be accompanied by a disastrous fire, especially in a region containing bitumen (14, 10) and its accompanying gases.

19, 28f: From the height east of Hebron, Abraham could easily see the region at the southern end of the Dead Sea, where the *Cities of the Plain* were probably located.

Moabites and Ammonites. [30]† Since
Lot was afraid to stay in Zoar, he and
his two daughters went up from Zoar
and settled in the hill country, where he
lived with his two daughters in a cave.
[31] The older one said to the younger:
"Our father is getting old, and there is
not a man on earth to unite with us as
was the custom everywhere. [32] Come, let
us ply our father with wine and then lie
with him, that we may have offspring
by our father." [33] So that night they plied
their father with wine, and the older one
went in and lay with her father; but he
was not aware of her lying down or her
getting up. [34] Next day the older one said
to the younger: "Last night it was I who
lay with my father. Let us ply him with
wine again tonight, and then you go in
and lie with him, that we may both have
offspring by our father." [35] So that night,
too, they plied their father with wine,
and then the younger one went in and
lay with him; but again he was not aware
of her lying down or her getting up.
[36] Thus both of Lot's daughters be-
came pregnant by their father. [37]*† The
older one gave birth to a son whom she
named Moab, saying, "From my fa-
ther." He is the ancestor of the Moabites
of today. [38]*† The younger one, too, gave
birth to a son, and she named him Am-
mon, saying, "The son of my kin." He
is the ancestor of the Ammonites of to-
day.

CHAPTER 20

Abraham at Gerar. [1]† Abraham jour-
neyed on to the region of the Negeb,
where he settled between Kadesh and
Shur. While he stayed in Gerar, [2] he said
of his wife Sarah, "She is my sister." So
Abimelech, king of Gerar, sent and took
Sarah. [3] But God came to Abimelech in
a dream one night and said to him, "You
are about to die because of the woman
you have taken, for she has a husband."
[4] Abimelech, who had not approached
her, said: "O Lord, would you slay a man
even though he is innocent? [5] He himself
told me, 'She is my sister,' and she her-
self also stated, 'He is my brother.' I did
it in good faith and with clean hands."
[6] God answered him in the dream: "Yes,
I know you did it in good faith. In fact,
it was I who kept you from sinning
against me; that is why I did not let you
touch her. [7]† Therefore, return the
man's wife—as a spokesman he will in-
tercede for you—that your life may be
saved. If you do not return her, you can
be sure that you and all who are yours
will certainly die."
[8] Early the next morning Abimelech
called all his court officials and informed
them of everything that had happened,
and the men were horrified. [9] Then
Abimelech summoned Abraham and
said to him: "How could you do this to
us! What wrong did I do to you that you
should have brought such monstrous
guilt on me and my kingdom? You have
treated me in an intolerable way.
[10] What were you afraid of," he asked
him, "that you should have done such
a thing?" [11] "I was afraid," answered
Abraham, "because I thought there
would surely be no fear of God in this
place, and so they would kill me on ac-
count of my wife. [12]* Besides, she is in
truth my sister, but only my father's
daughter, not my mother's; and so she
became my wife. [13] When God sent me
wandering from my father's house, I
asked her: 'Would you do me this favor?
In whatever place we come to, say that
I am your brother.' "
[14] Then Abimelech took flocks and
herds and male and female slaves and
gave them to Abraham; and after he re-
stored his wife Sarah to him, [15] he said,
"Here, my land lies at your disposal; set-
tle wherever you please." [16]† To Sarah
he said: "See, I have given your brother
a thousand shekels of silver. Let that
serve you as a vindication before all who
are with you; your honor has been pre-
served with everyone." [17] Abraham then
interceded with God, and God restored
health to Abimelech, that is, to his wife
and his maidservants, so that they could
bear children; [18] for God had tightly
closed every womb in Abimelech's
household on account of Abraham's wife
Sarah.

CHAPTER 21

Birth of Isaac. [1]* The LORD took note
of Sarah as he had said he would; he
did for her as he had promised. [2]* Sarah
became pregnant and bore Abraham a
son in his old age, at the set time that
God had stated. [3]* Abraham gave the

---

*

37: Dt 2, 9.
38: Dt 2, 19.
20, 12: 12, 13.
21, 1: 17, 19; 18, 10.
2: Gal 4, 23; Heb 11, 11.
3: Mt 1, 2; Lk 3, 34.

---

†

19, 30-38: This Israelite tale about the origin of Israel's neighbors east of the Jordan and the Dead Sea was told partly to ridicule these racially related but rival nations and partly to give folk etymologies for their names.

19, 37: *From my father:* in Hebrew, *meabi,* similar in sound to the name "Moab."

19, 38: *The son of my kin:* in Hebrew, *ben-ammi,* similar in sound to the name "Ammonites."

20, 1-18: This story from the Elohist source (see note on 4, 25) combines elements found in the two very similar but distinct stories of the Yahwist source, in 12, 10-20 and 26, 6-11.

20, 7: *Spokesman:* the Hebrew term *nabi* used here is regularly translated as "prophet," but it simply means "one who speaks on behalf of another," whether the latter is God, as in almost all cases, or another man, as in Ex 4, 16.

20, 16: *A thousand shekels of silver:* not a gift distinct from that of the animals and the slaves (v 14), but the monetary value of these.

name Isaac to this son of his whom Sarah bore him. 4* When his son Isaac was eight days old, Abraham circumcised him, as God had commanded. 5 Abraham was a hundred years old when his son Isaac was born to him. 6* Sarah then said, "God has given me cause to laugh, and all who hear of it will laugh with me. 7 Who would have told Abraham," she added, "that Sarah would nurse children! Yet I have borne him a son in his old age." 8 Isaac grew, and on the day of the child's weaning, Abraham held a great feast.

9† Sarah noticed the son whom Hagar the Egyptian had borne to Abraham playing with her son Isaac; 10* so she demanded of Abraham: "Drive out that slave and her son! No son of that slave is going to share the inheritance with my son Isaac!" 11 Abraham was greatly distressed, especially on account of his son Ishmael. 12* But God said to Abraham: "Do not be distressed about the boy or about your slave woman. Heed the demands of Sarah, no matter what she is asking of you; for it is through Isaac that descendants shall bear your name. 13 As for the son of the slave woman, I will make a great nation of him also, since he too is your offspring."

14† Early the next morning Abraham got some bread and a skin of water and gave them to Hagar. Then, placing the child on her back, he sent her away. As she roamed aimlessly in the wilderness of Beer-sheba, 15 the water in the skin was used up. So she put the child down under a shrub, 16 and then went and sat down opposite him, about a bowshot away; for she said to herself, "Let me not watch the child die." As she sat opposite him, he began to cry. 17* God heard the boy's cry, and God's messenger called to Hagar from heaven: "What is the matter, Hagar? Don't be afraid; God has heard the boy's cry in this plight of his. 18 Arise, lift up the boy and hold him by the hand; for I will make of him a great nation." 19 Then God opened her eyes, and she saw a well of water. She went and filled the skin with water, and then let the boy drink.

20 God was with the boy as he grew up. He lived in the wilderness and became an expert bowman, 21 with his home in the wilderness of Paran. His mother got a wife for him from the land of Egypt.

The Pact at Beer-sheba. 22† About that time Abimelech, accompanied by Phicol, the commander of his army, said to Abraham: "God is with you in everything you do. 23† Therefore, swear to me by God at this place that you will not deal falsely with me or with my progeny and posterity, but will act as loyally toward me and the land in which you stay as I have acted toward you." 24 To this Abraham replied, "I so swear."

25 Abraham, however, reproached Abimelech about a well that Abimelech's men had seized by force. 26 "I have no idea who did that," Abimelech replied. "In fact, you never told me about it, nor did I ever hear of it until now."

27 Then Abraham took sheep and cattle and gave them to Abimelech and the two made a pact. 28 Abraham also set apart seven ewe lambs of the flock, 29 and Abimelech asked him, "What is the purpose of these seven ewe lambs that you have set apart?" 30 Abraham answered, "The seven ewe lambs you shall accept from me that thus I may have your acknowledgment that the well was dug by me." 31† This is why the place is called Beer-sheba; the two took an oath there. 32 When they had thus made the pact in Beer-sheba, Abimelech, along with Phicol, the commander of his army, left and returned to the land of the Philistines.

33† Abraham planted a tamarisk at Beer-sheba, and there he invoked by name the LORD, God the Eternal. 34 Abraham resided in the land of the Philistines for many years.

CHAPTER 22

The Testing of Abraham. 1*† Some time after these events, God put Abra-

---

*

4: 17, 10ff; Acts 7, 8.
6: 17, 17.
10: Jgs 11, 2; Gal 4, 30.
12: Rom 9, 7; Heb 11, 18.
17: 16, 7.
22, 1: Sir 44, 20.

†

21, 9-19: This story of Hagar's expulsion, in the Elohist source, is in general a duplicate of the one from the Yahwist source in 16, 5-14; but the two stories differ greatly in detail.

21, 14: *Placing the child on her back:* the phrase is translated from an emended form of the Hebrew text. In the current faulty Hebrew text, Abraham put the bread and the waterskin on Hagar's back, while her son apparently walked beside her. This reading seems to be a scribal attempt at harmonizing the present passage with the data of the Priestly source, in which Ishmael would have been at least fourteen years old when Isaac was born; compare 16, 16 with 21, 5; cf 17, 25. But in the present Elohist story Ishmael is obviously a little boy, not much older than Isaac; cf vv 15, 18.

21, 22: Here and in v 32 the Greek text has ". . . Abimelech, accompanied by Ahuzzath, his councilor, and Phicol . . ."; but this is probably a secondary harmonization with 26, 26. Abimelech took Phicol with him in order to intimidate Abraham by a show of strength.

21, 23: *This place:* Beer-sheba (v 31). Abimelech had come from Gerar (20, 2), about thirty miles west of Beer-sheba.

21, 31: *Beer-sheba:* the Hebrew name really means, "the well of the seven," i.e., the place where there are seven wells, alluded to in the episode of the *seven ewe lambs,* vv 28ff; but it can also be interpreted to mean "the well of the oath."

21, 33: *God the Eternal:* in Hebrew, *el olam,* perhaps the name of the deity of the pre-Israelite sanctuary at Beer-sheba, but used by Abraham merely as a title of Yahweh; cf Is 40, 28.

22, 1: *God put Abraham to the test:* to prove the firmness of Abraham's faith in God's promise that through Isaac all the nations of the earth would find blessing; cf 18, 10.18; 21, 12.

ham to the test. He called to him, "Abra-
ham!" "Ready!" he replied. 2*† Then
God said: "Take your son Isaac, your
only one, whom you love, and go to the
land of Moriah. There you shall offer
him up as a holocaust on a height that
I will point out to you." 3 Early the next
morning Abraham saddled his donkey,
took with him his son Isaac, and two of
his servants as well, and with the wood
that he had cut for the holocaust, set out
for the place of which God had told him.
4 On the third day Abraham got sight
of the place from afar. 5 Then he said
to his servants: "Both of you stay here
with the donkey, while the boy and I go
on over yonder. We will worship and
then come back to you." 6 Thereupon
Abraham took the wood for the holo-
caust and laid it on his son Isaac's shoul-
ders, while he himself carried the fire
and the knife. 7 As the two walked on
together, Isaac spoke to his father Abra-
ham. "Father!" he said. "Yes, son," he
replied. Isaac continued, "Here are the
fire and the wood, but where is the sheep
for the holocaust?" 8 "Son," Abraham
answered, "God himself will provide the
sheep for the holocaust." Then the two
continued going forward.
9* When they came to the place of
which God had told him, Abraham built
an altar there and arranged the wood
on it. Next he tied up his son Isaac, and
put him on top of the wood on the altar.
10* Then he reached out and took the
knife to slaughter his son. 11 But the
LORD's messenger called to him from
heaven, "Abraham, Abraham!" "Yes,
Lord," he answered. 12* "Do not lay your
hand on the boy," said the messenger.
"Do not do the least thing to him. I know
now how devoted you are to God, since
you did not withhold from me your own
beloved son." 13 As Abraham looked
about, he spied a ram caught by its horns
in the thicket. So he went and took the
ram and offered it up as a holocaust in
place of his son. 14† Abraham named the
site Yahweh-yireh; hence people now
say, "On the mountain the LORD will
see."
15 Again the LORD's messenger called
to Abraham from heaven 16* and said:
"I swear by myself, declares the LORD,
that because you acted as you did in not
withholding from me your beloved son,
17* I will bless you abundantly and make
your descendants as countless as the
stars of the sky and the sands of the sea-
shore; your descendants shall take pos-
session of the gates of their enemies,
18* and in your descendants all the na-
tions of the earth shall find blessing—all
this because you obeyed my command."
19 Abraham then returned to his ser-
vants, and they set out together for
Beer-sheba, where Abraham made his
home.

Nahor's Descendants. 20† Some time
afterward, the news came to Abraham:
"Milcah too has borne sons, to your
brother Nahor: 21 Uz, his first-born, his
brother Buz, Kemuel (the father of
Aram), 22 Chesed, Hazo, Pildash, Jid-
laph, and Bethuel." 23 Bethuel became
the father of Rebekah. These eight Mil-
cah bore to Abraham's brother Nahor.
24 His concubine, whose name was Reu-
mah, also bore children: Tebah, Gaham,
Tahash, and Maacah.

CHAPTER 23

Purchase of a Burial Place. 1 The span
of Sarah's life was one hundred and
twenty-seven years. 2 She died in Kir-
iath-arba (that is, Hebron) in the land
of Canaan, and Abraham performed the
customary mourning rites for her.
3† Then he left the side of his dead
one and addressed the Hittites:
4*† "Although I am a resident alien
among you, sell me from your holdings
a piece of property for a burial ground,
that I may bury my dead wife." 5 The
Hittites answered Abraham: "Please,
sir, 6 listen to us! You are an elect of God
among us. Bury your dead in the choic-
est of our burial sites. None of us would
deny you his burial ground for the burial
of your dead." 7 Abraham, however, be-
gan to bow low before the local citizens,
the Hittites, 8 while he appealed to them:
"If you will allow me room for burial of
my dead, listen to me! Intercede for me
with Ephron, son of Zohar, asking him
9 to sell me the cave of Machpelah that
he owns; it is at the edge of his field. Let

*

2: 2 Chr 3, 1; 1 Mc 2, 52; Heb 11, 17.
9: Jas 2, 21.
10: Wis 10, 5.
12: Rom 8, 32; 1 Jn 4, 9.
16f: 15, 5; Ex 32, 13; Lk 1, 73; Rom 4, 13; Heb 6, 13f; 11, 12.
17: 24, 60.
18: 12, 3; 18, 18; 26, 4; Sir 44, 21; Acts 3, 25; Gal 3, 16.
23, 4: 33, 19; Acts 7, 16; Heb 11, 9.

†

22, 2: *Only one:* uniquely precious, especially loved; therefore the same term is rendered in vv 12.17 as "beloved."

22, 14: *Yahweh-yireh:* a Hebrew expression meaning "the Lord will see"; the reference is to the words in v 8, "God himself will see to it."

22, 20-24: A list of Aramean tribes who lived to the east and northeast of Israel, twelve in number, like the twelve tribes of Israel (35, 23) and the twelve tribes of Ishmael (25, 12-16).

23, 3: *The Hittites:* a non-Semitic people in Canaan; their relationship to the well-known Hittites of Asia Minor is uncertain.

23, 4: *A resident alien:* literally "a sojourner and a settler," i.e., a long-term resident alien. Such a one would normally not have the right to own property. The importance of Abraham's purchase of the field in Machpelah, which is worded in technical legal terms, lies in the fact that it gave his descendants their first, though small, land rights in the country that God had promised the patriarch they would one day inherit as their own. Abraham therefore insists on purchasing the field and not receiving it as a gift.

him sell it to me in your presence, at
its full price, for a burial place."
10† Now Ephron was present with the
Hittites. So Ephron the Hittite replied to
Abraham in the hearing of the Hittites
who sat on his town council: 11 "Please,
sir, listen to me! I give you both the field
and the cave in it; in the presence of my
kinsmen I make this gift. Bury your
dead!" 12 But Abraham, after bowing low
before the local citizens, addressed
Ephron in the hearing of these men:
13 "Ah, if only you would please listen
to me! I will pay you the price of the
field. Accept it from me, that I may bury
my dead there." 14 Ephron replied to
Abraham, "Please, 15† sir, listen to me!
A piece of land worth four hundred
shekels of silver—what is that between
you and me, as long as you can bury
your dead?" 16*† Abraham accepted
Ephron's terms; he weighed out to him
the silver that Ephron had stipulated in
the hearing of the Hittites, four hundred
shekels of silver at the current market
value.
17* Thus Ephron's field in Machpelah,
facing Mamre, together with its cave
and all the trees anywhere within its
limits, was conveyed 18 to Abraham by
purchase in the presence of all the Hit-
tites who sat on Ephron's town council.
19 After this transaction, Abraham bur-
ied his wife Sarah in the cave of the field
of Machpelah, facing Mamre (that is,
Hebron) in the land of Canaan. 20 Thus
the field with its cave was transferred
from the Hittites to Abraham as a burial
place.

CHAPTER 24

Isaac and Rebekah. 1 Abraham had
now reached a ripe old age, and the
LORD had blessed him in every way.
2*† Abraham said to the senior servant
of his household, who had charge of all
his possessions: "Put your hand under
my thigh, 3* and I will make you swear
by the LORD, the God of heaven and the
God of earth, that you will not procure
a wife for my son from the daughters
of the Canaanites among whom I live,
4 but that you will go to my own land
and to my kindred to get a wife for my
son Isaac." 5 The servant asked him:
"What if the woman is unwilling to fol-
low me to this land? Should I then take
your son back to the land from which
you migrated?" 6 "Never take my son
back there for any reason," Abraham
told him. 7* "The LORD, the God of
heaven, who took me from my father's
house and the land of my kin, and who
confirmed by oath the promise he then
made to me, 'I will give this land to your
descendants'—he will send his messen-
ger before you, and you will obtain a wife
for my son there. 8 If the woman is un-
willing to follow you, you will be released
from this oath. But never take my son
back there!" 9 So the servant put his
hand under the thigh of his master
Abraham and swore to him in this un-
dertaking.
10† The servant then took ten of his
master's camels, and bearing all kinds
of gifts from his master, he made his
way to the city of Nahor in Aram Naha-
raim. 11 Near evening, at the time when
women go out to draw water, he made
the camels kneel by the well outside the
city. 12† Then he prayed: "LORD, God of
my master Abraham, let it turn out fa-
vorably for me today and thus deal gra-
ciously with my master Abraham.
13 While I stand here at the spring and
the daughters of the townsmen are com-
ing out to draw water, 14 if I say to a girl,
'Please lower your jug, that I may drink,'
and she answers, 'Take a drink, and let
me give water to your camels, too,' let
her be the one whom you have decided
upon for your servant Isaac. In this way
I shall know that you have dealt gra-
ciously with my master."
15* He had scarcely finished these
words when Rebekah (who was born to
Bethuel, son of Milcah, the wife of Abra-
ham's brother Nahor) came out with a
jug on her shoulder. 16 The girl was very
beautiful, a virgin, untouched by man.
She went down to the spring and filled
her jug. As she came up, 17 the servant
ran toward her and said, "Please give
me a sip of water from your jug."
18 "Take a drink, sir," she replied, and
quickly lowering the jug onto her hand,
she gave him a drink. 19 When she had

*

16: Acts 7, 16.
17f: 49, 29f.
24, 2f: 47, 29.
3: 24, 37; 28, 1f; Jgs 14, 3; Tb 4, 12.
7: 12, 7; Ex 6, 8; Tb 5, 17; Gal 3, 16.
15: 22, 23.

†

23, 10: *Who sat on his town council:* probable meaning of the literal translation, "who came in at the gate of his city"; so also in v 18.

23, 15: *Four hundred shekels:* probably an exorbitant sum; Jeremiah (32, 9) paid only seventeen shekels for his field in Anathoth, though the Babylonian invasion no doubt helped to reduce the price.

23, 16: *The current market value:* the standard weight called a shekel varied according to time and place.

24, 2: *Put your hand under my thigh:* the symbolism of this act was apparently connected with the Hebrew concept of children issuing from their father's "thigh" (46, 26; Ex 1, 5). Perhaps the man who took such an oath was thought to bring the curse of sterility on himself if he did not fulfill his sworn promise. Jacob made Joseph swear in the same way (Gn 47, 29). In both these instances, the oath was taken to carry out the last request of a man upon his death.

24, 10: *Nahor:* it is uncertain whether this is to be understood as the name of Abraham's brother (11, 27), Rebekah's grandfather (24, 15), or the city of the same name (as known from the Mari documents): *Aram Naharaim,* situated near Haran (11, 31) in northern Mesopotamia.

24, 12: *Let it turn out favorably for me:* let me have a favorable omen; cf end of v 14.

let him drink his fill, she said, "I will draw water for your camels, too, until they have drunk their fill." 20 With that, she quickly emptied her jug into the drinking trough and ran back to the well to draw more water, until she had drawn enough for all the camels. 21 The man watched her the whole time, silently waiting to learn whether or not the LORD had made his errand successful. 22 When the camels had finished drinking, the man took out a gold ring weighing half a shekel, which he fastened on her nose, and two gold bracelets weighing ten shekels, which he put on her wrists. 23 Then he asked her: "Whose daughter are you? Tell me, please. And is there room in your father's house for us to spend the night?" 24 She answered: "I am the daughter of Bethuel the son of Milcah, whom she bore to Nahor. 25 There is plenty of straw and fodder at our place," she added, "and room to spend the night." 26 The man then bowed down in worship to the LORD, 27 saying: "Blessed be the LORD, the God of my master Abraham, who has not let his constant kindness toward my master fail. As for myself also, the LORD has led me straight to the house of my master's brother."

28 Then the girl ran off and told her mother's household about it. 29* Now Rebekah had a brother named Laban. 30 As soon as he saw the ring and the bracelets on his sister Rebekah and heard her words about what the man had said to her, Laban rushed outside to the man at the spring. When he reached him, he was still standing by the camels at the spring. 31 So he said to him: "Come, blessed of the LORD! Why are you staying outside when I have made the house ready for you, as well as a place for the camels?" 32 The man then went inside; and while the camels were being unloaded and provided with straw and fodder, water was brought to bathe his feet and the feet of the men who were with him. 33 But when the table was set for him, he said, "I will not eat until I have told my tale." "Do so," they replied.

34 "I am Abraham's servant," he began. 35 "The LORD has blessed my master so abundantly that he has become a wealthy man; he has given him flocks and herds, silver and gold, male and female slaves, and camels and asses. 36 My master's wife Sarah bore a son to my master in her old age, and he has given him everything he owns. 37 My master put me under oath, saying: 'You shall not procure a wife for my son among the daughters of the Canaanites in whose land I live; 38 instead, you shall go to my father's house, to my own relatives, to get a wife for my son.' 39 When I asked my master, 'What if the woman will not follow me?,' 40* he replied: 'The LORD, in whose presence I have always walked, will send his messenger with you and make your errand successful, and so you will get a wife for my son from my own kindred of my father's house. 41 Then you shall be released from my ban. If you visit my kindred and they refuse you, then, too, you shall be released from my ban.'

42 "When I came to the spring today, I prayed: 'LORD, God of my master Abraham, may it be your will to make successful the errand I am engaged on! 43 While I stand here at the spring, if I say to a young woman who comes out to draw water, Please give me a little water from your jug, 44 and she answers, Not only may you have a drink, but I will give water to your camels, too—let her be the woman whom the LORD has decided upon for my master's son.'

45 "I had scarcely finished saying this prayer to myself when Rebekah came out with a jug on her shoulder. After she went down to the spring and drew water, I said to her, 'Please let me have a drink.' 46 She quickly lowered the jug she was carrying and said, 'Take a drink, and let me bring water for your camels, too.' So I drank, and she watered the camels also. 47 When I asked her, 'Whose daughter are you?' she answered, 'The daughter of Bethuel, son of Nahor, borne to Nahor by Milcah.' So I put the ring on her nose and the bracelets on her wrists. 48 Then I bowed down in worship to the LORD, blessing the LORD, the God of my master Abraham, who had led me on the right road to obtain the daughter of my master's kinsman for his son. 49 If, therefore, you have in mind to show true loyalty to my master, let me know; but if not, let me know that, too. I can then proceed accordingly."

50* Laban and his household said in reply: "This thing comes from the LORD; we can say nothing to you either for or against it. 51 Here is Rebekah, ready for you; take her with you, that she may become the wife of your master's son, as the LORD has said." 52 When Abraham's servant heard their answer, he bowed to the ground before the LORD. 53 Then he brought out objects of silver and gold and articles of clothing and presented them to Rebekah; he also gave costly presents to her brother and mother. 54* After he and the men with him had eaten and drunk, they spent the night there.

When they were up the next morning, he said, "Give me leave to return to my master." 55 Her brother and mother replied, "Let the girl stay with us a short while, say ten days; after that she may

---

29: 27, 43.
40: Tb 5, 17; 10, 13.
50f: Tb 7, 12.
54: Tb 7, 14; 8, 20.

go." 56 But he said to them, "Do not de-
tain me, now that the LORD has made
my errand successful; let me go back
to my master." 57 They answered, "Let
us call the girl and see what she herself
has to say about it." 58 So they called Re-
bekah and asked her, "Do you wish to
go with this man?" She answered, "I
do." 59 At this they allowed their sister
Rebekah and her nurse to take leave,
along with Abraham's servant and his
men. 60* Invoking a blessing on Re-
bekah, they said:

"Sister, may you grow
into thousands of myriads;
And may your descendants gain
possession
of the gates of their enemies!"

61 Then Rebekah and her maids started
out; they mounted their camels and fol-
lowed the man. So the servant took Re-
bekah and went on his way.
62* Meanwhile Isaac had gone from
Beer-lahai-roi and was living in the re-
gion of the Negeb. 63† One day toward
evening he went out . . . in the field, and
as he looked around, he noticed that
camels were approaching. 64 Rebekah,
too, was looking about, and when she
saw him, she alighted from her camel
65 and asked the servant, "Who is the
man out there, walking through the
fields toward us?" "That is my master,"
replied the servant. Then she covered
herself with her veil.
66 The servant recounted to Isaac all
the things he had done. 67 Then Isaac
took Rebekah into his tent; he married
her, and thus she became his wife. In
his love for her Isaac found solace after
the death of his mother Sarah.

CHAPTER 25

Abraham's Sons by Keturah.
1*† Abraham married another wife,
whose name was Keturah. 2 She bore
him Zimran, Jokshan, Medan, Midian,
Ishbak, and Shuah. 3* Jokshan became
the father of Sheba and Dedan. The de-
scendants of Dedan were the Asshurim,
the Letushim, and the Leummim. 4 The
descendants of Midian were Ephah,
Epher, Hanoch, Abida, and Eldaah. All
of these were descendants of Keturah.
5 Abraham deeded everything that he
owned to his son Isaac. 6† To his sons
by concubinage, however, he made
grants while he was still living, as he sent
them away eastward, to the land of
Kedem, away from his son Isaac.
Death of Abraham. 7 The whole span
of Abraham's life was one hundred and
seventy-five years. 8 Then he breathed
his last, dying at a ripe old age, grown
old after a full life; and he was taken
to his kinsmen. 9* His sons Isaac and
Ishmael buried him in the cave of Mach-
pelah, in the field of Ephron, son of Zo-
har the Hittite, which faces Mamre,
10 the field that Abraham had bought
from the Hittites; there he was buried
next to his wife Sarah. 11 After the death
of Abraham, God blessed his son Isaac,
who made his home near Beer-lahai-roi.
Descendants of Ishmael. 12 These are
the descendants of Abraham's son Ish-
mael, whom Hagar the Egyptian, Sar-
ah's slave, bore to Abraham. 13* These
are the names of Ishmael's sons, listed
in the order of their birth: Nebaioth (Ish-
mael's first-born), Kedar, Adbeel, Mib-
sam, 14 Mishma, Dumah, Massa,
15 Hadad, Tema, Jetur, Naphish, and
Kedemah. 16* These are the sons of Ish-
mael, their names by their villages and
encampments; twelve chieftains of as
many tribal groups.
17 The span of Ishmael's life was one
hundred and thirty-seven years. After
he had breathed his last and died, he
was taken to his kinsmen. 18*† The Ish-
maelites ranged from Havilah-by-Shur,
which is on the border of Egypt, all the
way to Asshur; and each of them pitched
camp in opposition to his various kins-
men.

III: THE PATRIARCHS ISAAC AND JACOB

Birth of Esau and Jacob. 19 This is the
family history of Isaac, son of Abraham;
Abraham had begotten Isaac. 20* Isaac
was forty years old when he married Re-
bekah, the daughter of Bethuel the Ara-
mean of Paddan-aram and the sister of
Laban the Aramean. 21 Isaac entreated
the LORD on behalf of his wife, since she
was sterile. The LORD heard his en-
treaty, and Rebekah became pregnant.
22 But the children in her womb jostled
each other so much that she exclaimed,
"If this is to be so, what good will it do

*

60: 22, 17.
62: 16, 13f; 25, 11.
25, 1-4: 1 Chr 1, 32f.
3: Is 21, 13.
9f: 23, 3-20.
13-16: 1 Chr 1, 29ff.
13: Is 60, 7.
16: 17, 20.
18: 16, 12.
20: 24, 66.

†

24, 63: *He went out:* the meaning of the Hebrew term that follows this is obscure.

25, 1-11: Though mentioned here, Abraham's marriage to a concubine, or wife of secondary rank, and his death are not to be understood as happening chronologically after the events narrated in the preceding chapter.

25, 6: *The land of Kedem:* or "the country of the East," the region inhabited by the Kedemites or Easterners (29, 1; Jgs 6, 3.33; Jb 1, 3; Is 11, 14). The names mentioned in vv 2ff, as far as they can be identified, are those of tribes in the Arabian desert.

25, 18: *Pitched camp:* literally "fell"; the same Hebrew verb is used in Jgs 7, 12 in regard to the hostile encampment of Bedouin tribes. The present passage shows the fulfillment of the prediction contained in Gn 16, 12.

me!" She went to consult the LORD,
23* and he answered her:

"Two nations are in your womb,
two peoples are quarreling while
still within you;
But one shall surpass the other,
and the older shall serve the
younger."

24* When the time of her delivery came,
there were twins in her womb. 25† The
first to emerge was reddish, and his
whole body was like a hairy mantle; so
they named him Esau. 26*† His brother
came out next, gripping Esau's heel; so
they named him Jacob. Isaac was sixty
years old when they were born.
27* As the boys grew up, Esau became
a skillful hunter, a man who lived in the
open; whereas Jacob was a simple man,
who kept to his tents. 28 Isaac preferred
Esau, because he was fond of game; but
Rebekah preferred Jacob. 29 Once, when
Jacob was cooking a stew, Esau came
in from the open, famished. 30† He said
to Jacob, "Let me gulp down some of
that red stuff; I'm starving." (That is why
he was called Edom.) 31*† But Jacob
replied, "First give me your birthright
in exchange for it." 32 "Look," said Esau,
"I'm on the point of dying. What good
will any birthright do me?" 33* But Jacob
insisted, "Swear to me first!" So he sold
Jacob his birthright under oath. 34 Jacob
then gave him some bread and the lentil
stew; and Esau ate, drank, got up, and
went his way. Esau cared little for his
birthright.

CHAPTER 26

Isaac and Abimelech. 1* There was a
famine in the land (distinct from the
earlier one that had occurred in the days
of Abraham), and Isaac went down to
Abimelech, king of the Philistines in Ge-
rar. 2 The LORD appeared to him and
said: "Do not go down to Egypt, but con-
tinue to camp wherever in this land I
tell you. 3* Stay in this land, and I will
be with you and bless you; for to you
and your descendants I will give all
these lands, in fulfillment of the oath that
I swore to your father Abraham. 4* I will
make your descendants as numerous as
the stars in the sky and give them all
these lands, and in your descendants all
the nations of the earth shall find bless-
ing—5 this because Abraham obeyed
me, keeping my mandate (my com-
mandments, my ordinances, and my in-
structions)."
6† So Isaac settled in Gerar. 7 When the
men of the place asked questions about
his wife, he answered, "She is my sis-
ter." He was afraid, if he called her his
wife, the men of the place would kill him
on account of Rebekah, since she was
very beautiful. 8 But when he had been
there for a long time, Abimelech, king
of the Philistines, happened to look out
of a window and was surprised to see
Isaac fondling his wife Rebekah. 9 He
called for Isaac and said: "She must cer-
tainly be your wife! How could you have
said, 'She is my sister'?" Isaac replied,
"I thought I might lose my life on her
account." 10 "How could you do this to
us!" exclaimed Abimelech. "It would
have taken very little for one of the men
to lie with your wife, and you would
have thus brought guilt upon us!"
11 Abimelech therefore gave this warn-
ing to all his men: "Anyone who molests
this man or his wife shall forthwith be
put to death."
12† Isaac sowed a crop in that region
and reaped a hundredfold the same
year. Since the LORD blessed him, 13* he
became richer and richer all the time,
until he was very wealthy indeed. 14 He
acquired such flocks and herds, and so
many work animals, that the Philistines
became envious of him. 15* (The Philis-
tines had stopped up and filled with dirt
all the wells that his father's servants
had dug back in the days of his father
Abraham.) 16 So Abimelech said to
Isaac, "Go away from us; you have be-
come far too numerous for us." 17 Isaac
left there and made the Wadi Gerar his
regular campsite. 18 (Isaac reopened the
wells which his father's servants had
dug back in the days of his father Abra-
ham and which the Philistines had
stopped up after Abraham's death; he

*

23: 27, 29; Nm 24, 18; Mal 1, 2-5; Rom 9, 11f.
24: Hos 12, 3.
26: Mt 1, 2.
27: 27, 6f.
31: Dt 21, 17.
33: Heb 12, 16.
26, 1-14: 12, 10-20.
1: 12, 1.
3: 12, 7; 15, 18; Ex 32, 13; Ps 105, 9; Sir 44, 22; Heb 11, 9.
4: 12, 3; 22, 17f; 28, 14; Ex 32, 13.
13f: Jb 1, 3.
15-24: 21, 25-31.

†

25, 25: *Reddish:* in Hebrew, *admoni,* a reference to Edom, another name for Esau (v 30; 36, 1). Edom, however, was really the name of the country south of Moab where the descendants of Esau lived. It was called the "red" country because of its reddish sandstone. *Hairy:* in Hebrew, *sear,* a reference to Seir, another name for Edom (36, 8). One might expect the text to say, "So they named him Seir"; but Esau (*esaw*) also means "hairy."

25, 26: *Esau's heel:* the Hebrew is *baaqeb esaw,* a reference to the name Jacob; cf 27, 36. Probably, however, the name Jacob has no true etymological connection with the Hebrew word for "heel" (*aqeb*) but is instead a shortened form of some such name as *yaaqob-el* ("may God protect").

25, 30: *Red stuff:* in Hebrew, *adom;* another play on the word "Edom," the "red" land.

25, 31: *Birthright:* the privilege that entitled the first-born son to a position of honor in the family and to a double share in the possessions inherited from the father.

26, 6-11: The Yahwist's version of the wife-sister episode at Gerar; the Elohist's version (20, 1-18) is connected with Abraham and Sarah.

26, 12-33: The Yahwist's version of the story about the wells at Beer-sheba; again, the Elohist's version (21, 22f) is connected with Abraham. A redactor joined the two accounts by means of the parenthetical verses 15 and 18.

gave them the same names that his fa-
ther had given them.) 19 But when
Isaac's servants dug in the wadi and
reached spring water in their well,
20† the shepherds of Gerar quarreled
with Isaac's servants, saying, "The
water belongs to us!" So the well was
called Esek, because they had chal-
lenged him there. 21† Then they dug an-
other well, and they quarreled over that
one too; so it was called Sitnah. 22 When
he had moved on from there, he dug still
another well; but over this one they did
not quarrel. It was called Rehoboth, be-
cause he said, "The LORD has now given
us ample room, and we shall flourish in
the land."

23 From there Isaac went up to Beer-
sheba. 24* The same night the LORD ap-
peared to him and said: "I am the God
of your father Abraham. You have no
need to fear, since I am with you. I will
bless you and multiply your descen-
dants for the sake of my servant Abra-
ham." 25 So he built an altar there and
invoked the LORD by name. After he had
pitched his tent there, his servants be-
gan to dig a well nearby.

26* Abimelech had meanwhile come to
him from Gerar, accompanied by Ahuz-
zath, his councilor, and Phicol, the gen-
eral of his army. 27 Isaac asked them,
"Why have you come to me, seeing that
you hate me and have driven me away
from you?" 28 They answered: "We are
convinced that the LORD is with you, so
we propose that there be a sworn agree-
ment between our two sides—between
you and us. Let us make a pact with you:
29 you shall not act unkindly toward us,
just as we have not molested you, but
have always acted kindly toward you
and have let you depart in peace. Hence-
forth, 'The LORD's blessing be upon
you!' " 30 Isaac then made a feast for
them, and they ate and drank. 31 Early
the next morning they exchanged oaths.
Then Isaac bade them farewell, and they
departed from him in peace.

32 That same day Isaac's servants
came and brought him news about the
well they had been digging; they told
him, "We have reached water!" 33† He
called it Shibah; hence the name of the
city, Beer-sheba, to this day.

34*† When Esau was forty years old,
he married Judith, daughter of Beeri the
Hittite, and Basemath, daughter of Elon
the Hivite. 35 But they became a source
of embitterment to Isaac and Rebekah.

CHAPTER 27

Jacob's Deception. 1† When Isaac was
so old that his eyesight had failed him,
he called his older son Esau and said
to him, "Son!" "Yes, father!" he replied.
2 Isaac then said, "As you can see, I am
so old that I may now die at any time.
3 Take your gear, therefore—your
quiver and bow—and go out into the
country to hunt some game for me.
4† With your catch prepare an appetiz-
ing dish for me, such as I like, and bring
it to me to eat, so that I may give you
my special blessing before I die."

5* Rebekah had been listening while
Isaac was speaking to his son Esau. So
when Esau went out into the country to
hunt some game for his father,
6 Rebekah said to her son Jacob, "Listen!
I overheard your father tell your brother
Esau, 7 'Bring me some game and with
it prepare an appetizing dish for me to
eat, that I may give you my blessing with
the LORD's approval before I die.' 8 Now,
son, listen carefully to what I tell you.
9 Go to the flock and get me two choice
kids. With these I will prepare an appe-
tizing dish for your father, such as he
likes. 10 Then bring it to your father to
eat, that he may bless you before he
dies." 11* "But my brother Esau is a
hairy man," said Jacob to his mother
Rebekah, "and I am smooth-skinned!
12 Suppose my father feels me? He will
think I am making sport of him, and I
shall bring on myself a curse instead of
a blessing." 13 His mother, however, re-
plied: "Let any curse against you, son,
fall on me! Just do as I say. Go and get
me the kids."

14 So Jacob went and got them and
brought them to his mother; and with
them she prepared an appetizing dish,
such as his father liked. 15 Rebekah then

---

*

24: 46, 3.
26-33: 21, 22-31; Prv 16, 7.
34f: 27, 46.
27, 5: 25, 28.
11: 25, 25.

†

26, 20: *Esek:* "challenge."

26, 21: *Sitnah:* "opposition"; one might expect the text to be continued by some such words as "because they were in opposition there."

26, 33: *Shibah:* "seven," for the sake of a closer assonance with Beer-sheba; but the present version of the story says nothing about there being seven wells there as implied in 21, 28-31. The Greek version understood the Hebrew text more logically as *shebua,* "oath," in keeping with the present story.

26, 34f: These verses from the Priestly source, which have no logical connection with the preceding stories, serve as an introduction to the following section on Esau's loss of his birthright by suggesting a motivation for this in Isaac's and Rebekah's dislike for Esau's Canaanite wives.

27, 1-45: What Jacob did in deceiving his father and thereby cheating Esau out of Isaac's deathbed blessing is condemned as blameworthy, not only by Hosea (12, 4) and Jeremiah (9, 3), but also, indirectly, by the Yahwist narrator of the present story, who makes the reader sympathize with Esau as the innocent victim of a cruel plot, and shows that Jacob and his mother, the instigator of the plot, paid for it by a lifelong separation from each other. The story was told because it was part of the mystery of God's ways in salvation history—his use of weak, sinful men to achieve his own ultimate purpose.

27, 4: *My special blessing:* "the blessing of my soul." The same expression is used also in vv 19, 25, 31. In the context it must mean something like a solemn deathbed blessing, believed to be especially efficacious.

took the best clothes of her older son
Esau that she had in the house, and gave
them to her younger son Jacob to wear;
16 and with the skins of the kids she cov-
ered up his hands and the hairless parts
of his neck. 17 Then she handed her son
Jacob the appetizing dish and the bread
she had prepared.
18 Bringing them to his father, Jacob
said, "Father!" "Yes?" replied Isaac.
"Which of my sons are you?" 19 Jacob
answered his father: "I am Esau, your
first-born. I did as you told me. Please
sit up and eat some of my game, so that
you may give me your special blessing."
20 But Isaac asked, "How did you suc-
ceed so quickly, son?" He answered,
"The LORD, your God, let things turn out
well with me." 21 Isaac then said to Ja-
cob, "Come closer, son, that I may feel
you, to learn whether you really are my
son Esau or not." 22 So Jacob moved up
closer to his father. When Isaac felt him,
he said, "Although the voice is Jacob's,
the hands are Esau's." 23 (He failed to
identify him because his hands were
hairy, like those of his brother Esau; so
in the end he gave him his blessing.)
24 Again he asked him, "Are you really
my son Esau?" "Certainly," he replied.
25 Then Isaac said, "Serve me your
game, son, that I may eat of it and then
give you my blessing." Jacob served it
to him, and Isaac ate; he brought him
wine, and he drank. 26 Finally his father
Isaac said to him, "Come closer, son,
and kiss me." 27* As Jacob went up and
kissed him, Isaac smelled the fragrance
of his clothes. With that, he blessed him,
saying,

"Ah, the fragrance of my son
is like the fragrance of a field
that the LORD has blessed!

28 "May God give to you
of the dew of the heavens
And of the fertility of the earth
abundance of grain and wine.

29* "Let peoples serve you,
and nations pay you homage;
Be master of your brothers,
and may your mother's sons bow
down to you.
Cursed be those who curse you,
and blessed be those who bless
you."

30 Jacob had scarcely left his father,
just after Isaac had finished blessing
him, when his brother Esau came back
from his hunt. 31 Then he too prepared
an appetizing dish with his game, and
bringing it to his father, he said, "Please,
father, eat some of your son's game, that
you may then give me your special
blessing." 32 "Who are you?" his father
Isaac asked him. "I am Esau," he re-
plied, "your first-born son." 33 With that,
Isaac was seized with a fit of uncontrol-
lable trembling. "Who was it, then," he
asked, "that hunted game and brought
it to me? I finished eating it just before
you came, and I blessed him. Now he
must remain blessed!" 34 On hearing his
father's words, Esau burst into loud, bit-
ter sobbing. "Father, bless me too!" he
begged. 35 When Isaac explained, "Your
brother came here by a ruse and carried
off your blessing," 36*† Esau exclaimed,
"He has been well named Jacob! He has
now supplanted me twice! First he took
away my birthright, and now he has
taken away my blessing." Then he
pleaded, "Haven't you saved a blessing
for me?" 37 Isaac replied: "I have al-
ready appointed him your master, and
I have assigned to him all his kinsmen
as his slaves; besides, I have enriched
him with grain and wine. What then can
I do for you, son?" 38* But Esau urged
his father, "Have you only that one
blessing, father? Bless me too!" Isaac,
however, made no reply; and Esau wept
aloud. 39* Finally Isaac spoke again and
said to him:

"Ah, far from the fertile earth
shall be your dwelling;
far from the dew of the heavens
above!

40* "By your sword you shall live,
and your brother you shall serve;
But when you become restive,
you shall throw off his yoke from
your neck."

41* Esau bore Jacob a grudge because
of the blessing his father had given him.
He said to himself, "When the time of
mourning for my father comes, I will kill
my brother Jacob." 42 When Rebekah
got news of what her older son Esau had
in mind, she called her younger son Ja-
cob and said to him: "Listen! Your
brother Esau intends to settle accounts
with you by killing you. 43 Therefore,
son, do what I tell you: flee at once to
my brother Laban in Haran, 44 and stay
with him a while until your brother's
fury subsides 45 [until your brother's an-
ger against you subsides] and he forgets
what you did to him. Then I will send
for you and bring you back. Must I lose
both of you in a single day?"

*

27: 22, 17f; Heb 11, 20.
29: 25, 23; 49, 8; Nm 24, 9.
36: 25, 26. 29-34; Hos 12, 4.
38: Heb 12, 17.
39: Heb 11, 20.
40: 2 Kgs 8, 20.22; 2 Chr 21, 8.
41: Wis 10, 10; Ob 1, 10.

†

27, 36: *He has now supplanted me:* in Hebrew, *wayyaqebeni,* a wordplay on the name Jacob, *yaaqob;* see Jer 9, 3 and note, as well as Gn 25, 26. There is also a play between the Hebrew words *bekora* ("birthright") and *beraka* ("blessing").

Jacob Sent to Laban. 46*† Rebekah said to Isaac: "I am disgusted with life because of the Hittite women. If Jacob also should marry a Hittite woman, a native of the land, like these women, what good would life be to me?"

CHAPTER 28

1* Isaac therefore called Jacob, greeted him with a blessing, and charged him: "You shall not marry a Canaanite woman! 2* Go now to Paddan-aram, to the home of your mother's father Bethuel, and there choose a wife for yourself from among the daughters of your uncle Laban. 3 May God Almighty bless you and make you fertile, multiply you that you may become an assembly of peoples. 4* May he extend to you and your descendants the blessing he gave to Abraham, so that you may gain possession of the land where you are staying, which he assigned to Abraham." 5* Then Isaac sent Jacob on his way; he went to Paddan-aram, to Laban, son of Bethuel the Aramean, and brother of Rebekah, the mother of Jacob and Esau.

6 Esau noted that Isaac had blessed Jacob when he sent him to Paddan-aram to get himself a wife there, charging him, as he gave him his blessing, not to marry a Canaanite woman, 7 and that Jacob had obeyed his father and mother and gone to Paddan-aram. 8 Esau realized how displeasing the Canaanite women were to his father Isaac, 9* so he went to Ishmael, and in addition to the wives he had, married Mahalath, the daughter of Abraham's son Ishmael and sister of Nebaioth.

Jacob's Dream at Bethel. 10 Jacob departed from Beer-sheba and proceeded toward Haran. 11† When he came upon a certain shrine, as the sun had already set, he stopped there for the night. Taking one of the stones at the shrine, he put it under his head and lay down to sleep at that spot. 12*† Then he had a dream: a stairway rested on the ground, with its top reaching to the heavens; and God's messengers were going up and down on it. 13* And there was the LORD standing beside him and saying: "I, the LORD, am the God of your forefather Abraham and the God of Isaac; the land on which you are lying I will give to you and your descendants. 14* These shall be as plentiful as the dust of the earth, and through them you shall spread out east and west, north and south. In you and your descendants all the nations of the earth shall find blessing. 15* Know that I am with you; I will protect you wherever you go, and bring you back to this land. I will never leave you until I have done what I promised you."

16 When Jacob awoke from his sleep, he exclaimed, "Truly, the LORD is in this spot, although I did not know it!" 17† In solemn wonder he cried out: "How awesome is this shrine! This is nothing else but an abode of God, and that is the gateway to heaven!" 18*† Early the next morning Jacob took the stone that he had put under his head, set it up as a memorial stone, and poured oil on top of it. 19*† He called that site Bethel, whereas the former name of the town had been Luz.

20 Jacob then made this vow: "If God remains with me, to protect me on this journey I am making and to give me enough bread to eat and clothing to wear, 21 and I come back safe to my father's house, the LORD shall be my God. 22 This stone that I have set up as a memorial stone shall be God's abode. Of everything you give me, I will faithfully return a tenth part to you."

CHAPTER 29

Arrival in Haran. 1*† After Jacob resumed his journey, he came to the land of the Easterners. 2* Looking about, he

*

46: 26, 34f.
28, 1: 24, 3f; 26, 35.
2: 22, 22; 17, 1f.4f.
4: Ex 32, 13.
5: Jdt 8, 26.
9: 36, 2f.
12: Jn 1, 51.
13: Dt 1, 8; Mi 7, 28.
14: 12, 3; 13, 14f; 15, 5f; 18, 18; 22, 17f; 26, 4; Dt 19, 8; Sir 44, 21.
15: 31, 3.
18: 31, 13; 35, 14f.
19: 35, 6; 48, 3; Jos 18, 13; Jgs 1, 23; Hos 12, 4.
29, 1: Wis 10, 10.
2: 24, 11f.

†

27, 46—28, 9: This section, which is from the Priestly source and a direct sequel of 26, 34f, presents a different, though not contradictory, reason for Jacob's going to Paddan-aram: namely, to preserve racial purity among the chosen people. The account of Esau's marriages is given for the purpose of explaining the racial mixture of the Edomites, who were descended in part from tribes related to Israel, in part from older peoples in Edom called Hittites, Horites or Hivites, and in part from the Ishmaelite (Arabian) tribes who later invaded the region.

28, 11: *Shrine:* literally "place," often used specifically of a sacred site. Here the place was Bethel (v 19), a sacred site as early as the time of Abraham (12, 8).

28, 12: *Stairway:* in Hebrew, *sullam,* traditionally but inaccurately translated as "ladder." The corresponding verb, *salal,* means "to heap up" something, such as dirt for a highway or ramp. The imagery in Jacob's dream is derived from the Babylonian ziggurat or temple tower, "with its top in the sky" (11, 4), and with brick steps leading up to a small temple at the top.

28, 17: *This:* the stone Jacob used as a headrest; cf v 22. *That:* the stairway Jacob saw in his dream.

28, 18: *Memorial stone:* in Hebrew, *Masseba,* a stone which might vary in shape and size, set upright and usually intended for some religious purpose. Since the custom of erecting such "sacred pillars" in Palestine went back to its pre-Israelite period, their pagan associations were often retained; therefore, later Israelite religion forbade their erection (Lv 26, 1; Dt 16, 22) and ordered the destruction of those that were associated with paganism (Ex 34, 31; Dt 12, 3).

28, 19: *Bethel:* i.e., "house of God"; the reference is to the abode of God in v 17.

29, 1: *Easterners:* see note on 25, 6.

saw a well in the open country, with
three droves of sheep huddled near it,
for droves were watered from that well.
A large stone covered the mouth of the
well. 3 Only when all the shepherds were
assembled there could they roll the stone
away from the mouth of the well and
water the flocks. Then they would put
the stone back again over the mouth of
the well.

4 Jacob said to them, "Friends, where
are you from?" "We are from Haran,"
they replied. 5* Then he asked them,
"Do you know Laban, son of Nahor?"
"We do," they answered. 6 He inquired
further, "Is he well?" "He is," they an-
swered; "and here comes his daughter
Rachel with his flock." 7 Then he said:
"There is still much daylight left; it is
hardly the time to bring the animals
home. Why don't you water the flocks
now, and then continue pasturing
them?" 8 "We cannot," they replied,
"until all the shepherds are here to roll
the stone away from the mouth of the
well; only then can we water the flocks."

9 While he was still talking with them,
Rachel arrived with her father's sheep;
she was the one who tended them. 10 As
soon as Jacob saw Rachel, the daughter
of his uncle Laban, with the sheep of his
uncle Laban, he went up, rolled the stone
away from the mouth of the well, and
watered his uncle's sheep. 11† Then Ja-
cob kissed Rachel and burst into tears.
12 He told her that he was her father's
relative, Rebekah's son, and she ran to
tell her father. 13 When Laban heard the
news about his sister's son Jacob, he
hurried out to meet him. After embrac-
ing and kissing him, he brought him to
his house. Jacob then recounted to La-
ban all that had happened, 14† and La-
ban said to him, "You are indeed my
flesh and blood."

Marriage to Leah and Rachel. After
Jacob had stayed with him a full month,
15 Laban said to him: "Should you serve
me for nothing just because you are a
relative of mine? Tell me what your
wages should be." 16 Now Laban had two
daughters; the older was called Leah,
the younger Rachel. 17† Leah had lovely
eyes, but Rachel was well formed and
beautiful. 18† Since Jacob had fallen in
love with Rachel, he answered Laban,
"I will serve you seven years for your
younger daughter Rachel." 19 Laban
replied, "I prefer to give her to you
rather than to an outsider. Stay with
me." 20* So Jacob served seven years for
Rachel, yet they seemed to him but a
few days because of his love for her.

21 Then Jacob said to Laban, "Give me
my wife, that I may consummate my
marriage with her, for my term is now
completed." 22 So Laban invited all the
local inhabitants and gave a feast. 23 At
nightfall he took his daughter Leah and
brought her to Jacob, and Jacob con-
summated the marriage with her.
24 (Laban assigned his slave girl Zilpah
to his daughter Leah as her maidser-
vant.) 25† In the morning Jacob was
amazed: it was Leah! So he cried out to
Laban: "How could you do this to me!
Was it not for Rachel that I served you?
Why did you dupe me?" 26 "It is not the
custom in our country," Laban replied,
"to marry off a younger daughter before
an older one. 27*† Finish the bridal week
for this one, and then I will give you the
other too, in return for another seven
years of service with me."

28 Jacob agreed. He finished the bridal
week for Leah, and then Laban gave him
his daughter Rachel in marriage.
29 (Laban assigned his slave girl Bilhah
to his daughter Rachel as her maidser-
vant.) 30* Jacob then consummated his
marriage with Rachel also, and he loved
her more than Leah. Thus he remained
in Laban's service another seven years.

Jacob's Children. 31 When the LORD
saw that Leah was unloved, he made her
fruitful, while Rachel remained barren.
32*† Leah conceived and bore a son, and
she named him Reuben; for she said, "It
means, 'The LORD saw my misery; now
my husband will love me.' " 33† She con-
ceived again and bore a son, and said,
"It means, 'The LORD heard that I was
unloved,' and therefore he has given me
this one also"; so she named him Sim-
eon. 34† Again she conceived and bore
a son, and she said, "Now at last my hus-
band will become attached to me, since
I have now borne him three sons"; that
is why she named him Levi. 35*† Once

*

5: Tb 7, 4.	30: Dt 21, 15ff.
20: Hos 12, 13.	32: 49, 3.
27: Hos 12, 13.	35: Mt 1, 2; Lk 3, 33.

†

29, 11: *Burst into tears:* literally "raised his voice and wept," i.e., for joy.

29, 14: *Flesh and blood:* literally "bone and flesh," i.e., a close relative; on the Hebrew idiom, see 2, 23.

29, 17: *Lovely eyes:* the adjective modifying *eyes* is often translated as "weak," but "lovely" is the more probable word.

29, 18: Jacob offers to render service (Jos 15, 16f; 1 Sm 17, 25; 18, 17) in lieu of the customary bridal price (Ex 22, 16f; Dt 22, 29).

29, 25: *Jacob was amazed:* he had not recognized Leah because a bride was veiled when she was brought to her bridegroom; cf 24, 65.

29, 27: *The bridal week:* an ancient wedding lasted for seven days of festivities; cf Jgs 14, 12.

29, 32: *Reuben:* the literal meaning of the Hebrew name is "look, a son!" But in this case, as also with the names of all the other sons of Jacob, a symbolic rather than an etymological interpretation of the name is given, because the name and the persons were regarded as closely interrelated. The symbolic interpretation of Reuben's name, according to the Yahwist source, is based on the similar-sounding *raa beonyi,* "he saw my misery." In the Elohist source, the name is explained by the similar-sounding *yeehabani,* "he will love me."

29, 33: *Simeon:* in popular etymology, related to *shama,* "he heard."

29, 34: *Levi:* related to *yillaweh,* "he will become attached."

29, 35: *Judah:* related to *odeh,* "I will give grateful praise."

more she conceived and bore a son, and she said, "This time I will give grateful praise to the LORD"; therefore she named him Judah. Then she stopped bearing children.

CHAPTER 30

1* When Rachel saw that she failed to bear children to Jacob, she became envious of her sister. She said to Jacob, "Give me children or I shall die!" 2* In anger Jacob retorted, "Can I take the place of God, who has denied you the fruit of the womb?" 3*† She replied, "Here is my maidservant Bilhah. Have intercourse with her, and let her give birth on my knees, so that I too may have offspring, at least through her." 4† So she gave him her maidservant Bilhah as a consort, and Jacob had intercourse with her. 5 When Bilhah conceived and bore a son, 6† Rachel said, "God has vindicated me; indeed he has heeded my plea and given me a son." Therefore she named him Dan. 7 Rachel's maidservant Bilhah conceived again and bore a second son, 8† and Rachel said, "I engaged in a fateful struggle with my sister, and I prevailed." So she named him Naphtali.

9 When Leah saw that she had ceased to bear children, she gave her maidservant Zilpah to Jacob as a consort. 10 So Jacob had intercourse with Zilpah, and she conceived and bore a son. 11† Leah then said, "What good luck!" So she named him Gad. 12 Then Leah's maidservant Zilpah bore a second son to Jacob; 13† and Leah said, "What good fortune!"—meaning, "Women call me fortunate." So she named him Asher.

14† One day, during the wheat harvest, when Reuben was out in the field, he came upon some mandrakes which he brought home to his mother Leah. Rachel asked Leah, "Please let me have some of your son's mandrakes." 15 Leah replied, "Was it not enough for you to take away my husband, that you must now take my son's mandrakes too?" "Very well, then!" Rachel answered. "In exchange for your son's mandrakes, Jacob may lie with you tonight." 16 That evening, when Jacob came home from the fields, Leah went out to meet him. "You are now to come in with me," she told him, "because I have paid for you with my son's mandrakes." So that night he slept with her, 17 and God heard her prayer; she conceived and bore a fifth son to Jacob. 18† Leah then said, "God has given me my reward for having let my husband have my maidservant"; so she named him Issachar. 19 Leah conceived again and bore a sixth son to Jacob; 20† and she said, "God has brought me a precious gift. This time my husband will offer me presents, now that I have borne him six sons"; so she named him Zebulun. 21 Finally, she gave birth to a daughter, and she named her Dinah.

22 Then God remembered Rachel; he heard her prayer and made her fruitful. 23* She conceived and bore a son, and she said, "God has removed my disgrace." 24† So she named him Joseph, meaning, "May the LORD add another son to this one for me!"

Jacob Outwits Laban. 25 After Rachel gave birth to Joseph, Jacob said to Laban: "Give me leave to go to my homeland. 26 Let me have my wives, for whom I served you, and my children, too, that I may depart. You know very well the service that I have rendered you." 27 Laban answered him: "If you will please. . . .

"I have learned through divination that it is because of you that God has blessed me. 28 So," he continued, "state what wages you want from me, and I will pay them." 29 Jacob replied: "You know what work I did for you and how well your livestock fared under my care; 30 the little you had before I came has grown into very much, since the LORD's blessings came upon you in my company. Therefore I should now do something for my own household as well." 31 "What should I pay you?" Laban asked. Jacob answered: "You do not have to pay me anything outright. I will again pasture and tend your flock, if you

*

30, 1: Prv 30, 16. 2: 2 Kgs 5, 7. 3: 16, 2ff. 23: Lk 1, 25.

†

30, 3: *On my knees:* in the ancient Near East, a father would take a newborn child in his lap to signify that he acknowledged it as his own; Rachel uses this ceremony in order to adopt the child and establish her legal rights to it.

30, 4: *Consort:* The Hebrew word normally means "wife," but here it refers to a wife of secondary rank, who did not have the full legal rights of an ordinary wife.

30, 6: *Dan:* explained by the term *dannanni,* "he has vindicated me."

30, 8: *Naphtali:* explained by the phrase *"Naptule elohim niptalti,"* literally, "in a divine wrestling match I have wrestled," perhaps implying the concept of an ordeal; hence the above rendering, *I engaged in a fateful struggle.*

30, 11: *Gad:* explained by the Hebrew term *begad,* literally "in luck," i.e., *what good luck!*

30, 13: *Asher:* explained by the term *beoshri,* literally "in my good fortune," i.e., *what good fortune,* and by the term *ishsheruni* "they call me fortunate."

30, 14: *Mandrakes:* an herb whose root was anciently thought to promote conception. The Hebrew word for mandrakes, *dudaim,* has erotic connotations, since it sounds like the words *daddayim* ("breasts") and *dodim* ("sexual pleasure").

30, 18: *Issachar:* explained by the terms *sekari,* "my reward," and in v 16, *sakor sekartika,* literally "I have hired you," i.e., *I have paid for you.*

30, 20: *Zebulun:* related to the Akkadian word *zubullum,* "bridegroom's gift," is explained by the terms *zebadani . . . zebed tob,* "he has brought me a precious gift," and *yizbeleni,* "he will offer me presents."

30, 24: *Joseph:* explained by the words *yosep,* "may he add," and in v 23, *asap,* "he has removed."

do this one thing for me: 32† go through
your whole flock today and remove from
it every dark animal among the sheep
and every spotted or speckled one
among the goats. Only such animals
shall be my wages. 33 In the future,
whenever you check on these wages of
mine, let my honesty testify against me:
any animal in my possession that is not
a speckled or spotted goat, or a dark
sheep, got there by theft!" 34 "Very
well," agreed Laban. "Let it be as you
say."
35† That same day Laban removed the
streaked and spotted he-goats and all
the speckled and spotted she-goats, all
those with some white on them, as well
as the fully dark-colored sheep; these he
left . . . in charge of his sons. 36 Then
he put a three days' journey between
himself and Jacob, while Jacob contin-
ued to pasture the rest of Laban's flock.
37 Jacob, however, got some fresh
shoots of poplar, almond and plane
trees, and he made white stripes in them
by peeling off the bark down to the white
core of the shoots. 38 The rods that he
had thus peeled he then set upright in
the watering troughs, so that they would
be in front of the animals that drank
from the troughs. When the animals
were in heat as they came to drink,
39† the goats mated by the rods, and so
they brought forth streaked, speckled
and spotted kids. 40 The sheep, on the
other hand, Jacob kept apart, and he set
these animals to face the streaked or
fully dark-colored animals of Laban.
Thus he produced special flocks of his
own, which he did not put with Laban's
flock. 41 Moreover, whenever the hardier
animals were in heat, Jacob would set
the rods in the troughs in full view of
these animals, so that they mated by the
rods; 42 but with the weaker animals he
would not put the rods there. So the fee-
ble animals would go to Laban, but the
sturdy ones to Jacob. 43 Thus the man
grew increasingly prosperous, and he
came to own, not only large flocks, but
also male and female servants and cam-
els and asses.

CHAPTER 31

Flight from Laban. 1 Jacob learned
that Laban's sons were saying, "Jacob
has taken everything that belonged to
our father, and he has accumulated all
this wealth of his by using our father's
property." 2 Jacob perceived, too, that
Laban's attitude toward him was not
what it had previously been. 3* Then the
LORD said to Jacob, "Return to the land
of your fathers, where you were born,
and I will be with you."
4 So Jacob sent for Rachel and Leah
to meet him where he was in the field
with his flock. 5 There he said to them:
"I have noticed that your father's atti-
tude toward me is not as it was in the
past; but the God of my father has been
with me. 6 You well know what effort I
put into serving your father; 7* yet your
father cheated me and changed my
wages time after time. God, however,
did not let him do me any harm.
8† Whenever your father said, 'The
speckled animals shall be your wages,'
the entire flock would bear speckled
young; whenever he said, 'The streaked
animals shall be your wages,' the entire
flock would bear streaked young. 9 Thus
God reclaimed your father's livestock
and gave it to me. 10 Once, in the breed-
ing season, I had a dream in which I
saw mating he-goats that were streaked,
speckled and mottled. 11 In the dream
God's messenger called to me, 'Jacob!'
'Here!' I replied. 12 Then he said: 'Note
well. All the he-goats in the flock, as they
mate, are streaked, speckled and mot-
tled, for I have seen all the things that
Laban has been doing to you. 13* I am
the God who appeared to you in Bethel,
where you anointed a memorial stone
and made a vow to me. Up, then! Leave
this land and return to the land of your
birth.' "
14 Rachel and Leah answered him:
"Have we still an heir's portion in our
father's house? 15† Are we not regarded
by him as outsiders? He not only sold
us; he has even used up the money that
he got for us! 16* All the wealth that God
reclaimed from our father really be-
longs to us and our children. Therefore,
do just as God has told you." 17 Jacob
proceeded to put his children and wives

*

31, 3: 26, 3; 28, 15; 32, 10.
7: Jdt 8, 26.
13: 28, 18.
16: Wis 10, 10f.

†

30, 32: *Dark . . . sheep . . . spotted or speckled goats:* In the Near East the normal color of sheep is light gray, whereas that of goats is uniform dark brown or black. Ordinarily, therefore, Jacob would have received but few animals.

30, 35: By giving the abnormally colored animals to his sons, Laban not only deprived Jacob of his first small wages, but he also designed to prevent in this way the future breeding of such animals in the part of his flock entrusted to Jacob.

30, 39-42: Jacob's stratagem was based on the widespread notion among simple people that visual stimuli can have prenatal effects on the offspring of breeding animals. Thus, the rods on which Jacob had whittled stripes or bands or chevron marks were thought to cause the female goats that looked at them to bear kids with lighter-colored marks on their dark hair, while the gray ewes were thought to bear lambs with dark marks on them simply by visual crossbreeding with the dark goats.

31, 8-12: This Elohist account of the miraculous increase in Jacob's flock differs somewhat from the Yahwist account given in 30, 32-42.

31, 15: *Outsiders:* literally "foreign women"; they lacked the favored legal status of native women. *Used up:* literally "eaten, consumed"; the bridal price that a man received for giving his daughter in marriage was legally reserved as her inalienable dowry.

on camels, 18 and he drove off with all
his livestock and all the property he had
acquired in Paddan-aram, to go to his
father Isaac in the land of Canaan.
19*† Now Laban had gone away to
shear his sheep, and Rachel had mean-
while appropriated her father's house-
hold idols. 20† Jacob had hoodwinked
Laban the Aramean by not telling him
of his intended flight. 21 Thus he made
his escape with all that he had. Once he
was across the Euphrates, he headed for
the highlands of Gilead.
22 On the third day, word came to La-
ban that Jacob had fled. 23† Taking his
kinsmen with him, he pursued him for
seven days until he caught up with him
in the hill country of Gilead. 24* But that
night God appeared to Laban the Ara-
mean in a dream and warned him,
"Take care not to threaten Jacob with
any harm!"

Jacob and Laban in Gilead. 25 When
Laban overtook Jacob, Jacob's tents
were pitched in the highlands; Laban
also pitched his tents there, on Mount
Gilead. 26† "What do you mean," Laban
demanded of Jacob, "by hoodwinking
me and carrying off my daughters like
war captives? 27 Why did you dupe me
by stealing away secretly? You should
have told me, and I would have sent you
off with merry singing to the sound of
tambourines and harps. 28 You did not
even allow me a parting kiss to my
daughters and grandchildren! What you
have now done is a senseless thing. 29 I
have it in my power to harm all of you;
but last night the God of your father said
to me, 'Take care not to threaten Jacob
with any harm!' 30 Granted that you had
to leave because you were desperately
homesick for your father's house, why
did you steal my gods?" 31 "I was fright-
ened," Jacob replied to Laban, "at the
thought that you might take your
daughters away from me by force. 32 But
as for your gods, the one you find them
with shall not remain alive! If, with my
kinsmen looking on, you identify any-
thing here as belonging to you, take it."
Jacob, of course, had no idea that Rachel
had stolen the idols.
33 Laban then went in and searched
Jacob's tent and Leah's tent, as well as
the tents of the two maidservants; but
he did not find the idols. Leaving Leah's
tent, he went into Rachel's. 34* Now Ra-
chel had taken the idols, put them inside
a camel cushion, and seated herself
upon them. When Laban had rummaged
through the rest of her tent without find-
ing them, 35 Rachel said to her father,
"Let not my lord feel offended that I
cannot rise in your presence; a woman's
period is upon me." So, despite his
search, he did not find his idols.
36 Jacob, now enraged, upbraided La-
ban. "What crime or offense have I com-
mitted," he demanded, "that you should
hound me so fiercely? 37 Now that you
have ransacked all my things, have you
found a single object taken from your
belongings? If so, produce it here before
your kinsmen and mine, and let them
decide between us two.
38 "In the twenty years that I was un-
der you, no ewe or she-goat of yours ever
miscarried, and I have never feasted on
a ram of your flock. 39*† I never brought
you an animal torn by wild beasts; I
made good the loss myself. You held me
responsible for anything stolen by day
or night. 40 How often the scorching heat
ravaged me by day, and the frost by
night, while sleep fled from my eyes!
41 Of the twenty years that I have now
spent in your household, I slaved four-
teen years for your two daughters and
six years for your flock, while you
changed my wages time after time. 42* If
my ancestral God, the God of Abraham
and the Awesome One of Isaac, had not
been on my side, you would now have
sent me away empty-handed. But God
saw my plight and the fruits of my toil,
and last night he gave judgment."
43† Laban replied to Jacob: "The
women are mine, their children are
mine, and the flocks are mine; every-
thing you see belongs to me. But since
these women are my daughters, I will
now do something for them and for the
children they have borne. 44 Come, then,
we will make a pact, you and I; the LORD
shall be a witness between us."
45* Then Jacob took a stone and set it
up as a memorial stone. 46 Jacob said to
his kinsmen, "Gather some stones." So
they got some stones and made a
mound; and they had a meal there at

*

19: 19, 34; 1 Sm 19, 13.
24: Wis 10, 12.
34: 31, 19.
39: Ex 22, 12.
42: 19, 24.29.
45: 28, 18; 35, 14.

†

31, 19: *Household idols:* in Hebrew, *teraphim,* figurines used in divination (Ez 21, 26; Zec 10, 2). Laban calls them his "gods" (v 30).

31, 20: *Hoodwinked:* literally "stolen the heart of," i.e., lulled the mind of. *Aramean:* The earliest extra-biblical references to the Arameans date from several centuries after the time of Jacob; to call Laban an *Aramean* and to have him speak Aramaic (v 47) would seem to be an anachronism.

31, 23: *For seven days:* literally "a way of seven days," a general term to designate a long distance; it would have taken a camel caravan many more days to travel from Haran to Gilead, the region east of the northern half of the Jordan.

31, 26: *War captives:* literally "women captured by the sword"; the women of a conquered people were treated as part of the victor's booty; cf 1 Sm 30, 2; 2 Kgs 5, 2.

31, 39: Laban's actions were contrary to the customs of the ancient Near East, as recorded in the Code of Hammurabi: "If in a sheepfold an act of god has occurred, or a lion has made a kill, the shepherd shall clear himself before the deity, and the owner of the fold must accept the loss" (par. 266); cf Ex 22, 12.

31, 43-54: In this account of the treaty between Laban and Jacob, the Yahwist and Elohist sources are closely interwoven. The *mound* or cairn of stones comes from the Yahwist source, the *memorial stone* or stele from the Elohist.

the mound. 47† Laban called it Jegar-sa-
hadutha, but Jacob named it Galeed.
48 "This mound," said Laban, "shall be
a witness from now on between you and
me." That is why it was named Galeed—
49† and also Mizpah, for he said: "May
the LORD keep watch between you and
me when we are out of each other's sight.
50 If you mistreat my daughters, or take
other wives besides my daughters, re-
member that even though no one else
is about, God will be witness between you
and me."
51 Laban said further to Jacob: "Here
is this mound, and here is the memorial
stone that I have set up between you and
me. 52 This mound shall be witness, and
this memorial stone shall be witness,
that, with hostile intent, neither may I
pass beyond this mound into your terri-
tory, nor may you pass beyond it into
mine. 53 May the God of Abraham and
the god of Nahor [their ancestral dei-
ties] maintain justice between us!" Ja-
cob took the oath by the Awesome One
of Isaac. 54 He then offered a sacrifice
on the mountain and invited his kinsmen
to share in the meal. When they had
eaten, they passed the night on the
mountain.

CHAPTER 32

1 Early the next morning, Laban
kissed his grandchildren and his daugh-
ters goodbye; then he set out on his jour-
ney back home, 2 while Jacob continued
on his own way. Then God's messengers
encountered Jacob. 3† When he saw
them he said, "This is God's encamp-
ment." So he named that place Maha-
naim.

Embassy to Esau. 4* Jacob sent mes-
sengers ahead to his brother Esau in the
land of Seir, the country of Edom, 5 with
this message: "Thus shall you say to my
lord Esau: 'Your servant Jacob speaks
as follows: I have been staying with La-
ban and have been detained there until
now. 6 I own cattle, asses and sheep, as
well as male and female servants. I am
sending my lord this information in the
hope of gaining your favor.' " 7 When the
messengers returned to Jacob, they
said, "We reached your brother Esau.
He is now coming to meet you, accompa-
nied by four hundred men."
8 Jacob was very much frightened. In
his anxiety, he divided the people who
were with him, as well as his flocks,
herds and camels, into two camps. 9 "If
Esau should attack and overwhelm one
camp," he reasoned, "the remaining
camp may still survive." 10* Then he
prayed: "O God of my father Abraham
and God of my father Isaac! You told
me, O LORD, 'Go back to the land of your
birth, and I will be good to you.' 11 I am
unworthy of all the acts of kindness that
you have loyally performed for your
servant: although I crossed the Jordan
here with nothing but my staff, I have
now grown into two companies. 12* Save
me, I pray, from the hand of my brother
Esau! Otherwise I fear that when he
comes he will strike me down and slay
the mothers and children. 13 You your-
self said, 'I will be very good to you, and
I will make your descendants like the
sands of the sea, which are too numer-
ous to count.' "
14 After passing the night there, Jacob
selected from what he had with him the
following presents for his brother Esau:
15 two hundred she-goats and twenty he-
goats; two hundred ewes and twenty
rams; 16 thirty milch camels and their
young; forty cows and ten bulls; twenty
she-asses and ten he-asses. 17 He put
these animals in charge of his servants,
in separate droves, and he told the ser-
vants, "Go on ahead of me, but keep a
space between one drove and the next."
18 To the servant in the lead he gave this
instruction: "When my brother Esau
meets you, he may ask you, 'Whose man
are you? Where are you going? To whom
do these animals ahead of you belong?'
19 Then you shall answer, 'They belong
to your brother Jacob, but they have
been sent as a gift to my lord Esau; and
Jacob himself is right behind us.' " 20 He
gave similar instructions to the second
servant and the third and to all the oth-
ers who followed behind the droves,
namely: "Thus and thus shall you say
to Esau, when you reach him; 21 and be
sure to add, 'Your servant Jacob is right
behind us.' " For Jacob reasoned, "If I
first appease him with gifts that precede
me, then later, when I face him, perhaps
he will forgive me." 22 So the gifts went
on ahead of him, while he stayed that
night in the camp.

Struggle with the Angel. 23 In the
course of that night, however, Jacob
arose, took his two wives, with the two
maidservants and his eleven children,
and crossed the ford of the Jabbok.
24 After he had taken them across the
stream and had brought over all his pos-
sessions, 25† Jacob was left there alone.

*

32, 4: 36, 6.
10: 31, 3.
12: 28, 14; 48, 16; Ex 32, 13; Heb 11, 12.

†

31, 47: *Jegar-sahadutha:* an Aramaic term meaning "mound of witness." *Galeed:* in Hebrew, *galed,* with the same meaning; also offers an explanation of the regional name Gilead.

31, 49: *Mizpah:* a town in Gilead; cf Jgs 10, 17; 11, 11.34; Hos 5, 1. The Hebrew name *mispa* ("lookout") is allied to *yisep yhwh* ("may the Lord keep watch"), and also echoes the word *masseba* ("memorial pillar").

32, 3: *Mahanaim:* a town in Gilead (Jos 13, 26.30; 21, 38; 2 Sm 2, 8; etc.). The Hebrew name means "two camps." There are other allusions to the name in vv 8.11.

32, 25: *Some man:* a messenger of the Lord in human form, as is clear from vv 29ff.

Then some man wrestled with him until
the break of dawn. 26* When the man
saw that he could not prevail over him,
he struck Jacob's hip at its socket, so
that the hip socket was wrenched as they
wrestled. 27 The man then said, "Let me
go, for it is daybreak." But Jacob said,
"I will not let you go until you bless me."
28* "What is your name?" the man
asked. He answered, "Jacob." 29† Then
the man said, "You shall no longer be
spoken of as Jacob, but as Israel, be-
cause you have contended with divine
and human beings and have prevailed."
30 Jacob then asked him, "Do tell me
your name, please." He answered, "Why
should you want to know my name?"
With that, he bade him farewell.
31*† Jacob named the place Peniel, "Be-
cause I have seen God face to face," he
said, "yet my life has been spared."
32 At sunrise, as he left Penuel, Jacob
limped along because of his hip. 33 That
is why, to this day, the Israelites do not
eat the sciatic muscle that is on the hip
socket, inasmuch as Jacob's hip socket
was struck at the sciatic muscle.

CHAPTER 33

Jacob and Esau Meet. 1 Jacob looked
up and saw Esau coming, accompanied
by four hundred men. So he divided his
children among Leah, Rachel and the
two maidservants, 2 putting the maids
and their children first, Leah and her
children next, and Rachel and Joseph
last. 3 He himself went on ahead of them,
bowing to the ground seven times, until
he reached his brother. 4 Esau ran to
meet him, embraced him, and flinging
himself on his neck, kissed him as he
wept.
5 When Esau looked about, he saw the
women and children. "Who are these
with you?" he asked. Jacob answered,
"They are the children whom God has
graciously bestowed on your servant."
6 Then the maidservants and their chil-
dren came forward and bowed low;
7 next, Leah and her children came for-
ward and bowed low; lastly, Rachel and
her children came forward and bowed
low. 8 Then Esau asked, "What did you
intend with all those droves that I en-
countered?" Jacob answered, "It was to
gain my lord's favor." 9 "I have plenty,"
replied Esau; "you should keep what is
yours, brother." 10 "No, I beg you!" said
Jacob. "If you will do me the favor,
please accept this gift from me, since to
come into your presence is for me like
coming into the presence of God, now
that you have received me so kindly.
11 Do accept the present I have brought
you; God has been generous toward me,
and I have an abundance." Since he so
urged him, Esau accepted.
12 Then Esau said, "Let us break camp
and be on our way; I will travel alongside
you." 13 But Jacob replied: "As my lord
can see, the children are frail. Besides,
I am encumbered with the flocks and
herds, which now have sucklings; if
overdriven for a single day, the whole
flock will die. 14 Let my lord, then, go on
ahead of me, while I proceed more
slowly at the pace of the livestock before
me and at the pace of my children, until
I join my lord in Seir." 15 Esau replied,
"Let me at least put at your disposal
some of the men who are with me." But
Jacob said, "For what reason? Please
indulge me in this, my lord." 16 So on the
same day that Esau began his journey
back to Seir, 17† Jacob journeyed to Suc-
coth. There he built a home for himself
and made booths for his livestock. That
is why the place was called Succoth.
18* Having thus come from Paddan-
aram, Jacob arrived safely at the city
of Shechem, which is in the land of Ca-
naan, and he encamped in sight of the
city. 19*† The plot of ground on which
he had pitched his tent he bought for a
hundred pieces of bullion from the de-
scendants of Hamor, the founder of She-
chem. 20* He set up a memorial stone
there and invoked "El, the God of Is-
rael."

CHAPTER 34

The Rape of Dinah. 1† Dinah, the
daughter whom Leah had borne to Ja-
cob, went out to visit some of the women
of the land. 2† When Shechem, son of
Hamor the Hivite, who was chief of the

*

26: Hos 12, 4.
28: 35, 10; 1 Kgs 18, 31; 2 Kgs 17, 34.
31: Jgs 13, 22.
33, 18: 12, 6; Jn 4, 6.
19: Jos 24, 32; Jn 4, 5; Acts 7, 16.
20: Jgs 6, 24.

†

32, 29: *Israel:* the first part of the Hebrew name *Yisrael* is given a popular explanation in the word *sarita,* "you contended"; the second part is the first syllable of *elohim,* "divine beings." The present incident, with a similar allusion to the name Israel, is referred to in Hos 12, 5, where the mysterious wrestler is explicitly called an angel.

32, 31: *Peniel:* a variant of the word Penuel (v 32), the name of a town on the north bank of the Jabbok in Gilead (Jgs 8, 8f.17; 1 Kgs 12, 25). The name is explained as meaning "the face of God," *peni-el. Yet my life has been spared:* see note on 16, 13.

33, 17: *Succoth:* an important town near the confluence of the Jabbok and the Jordan (Jos 13, 27; Jgs 8, 5-16; 1 Kgs 7, 46). *Booths:* in Hebrew, *sukkot,* of the same sound as the name of the town.

33, 19: *Pieces of bullion:* in Hebrew, *kesita,* a monetary unit of which the value is now unknown. *Descendants of Hamor:* Hamorites, "the men of Hamor"; cf Jgs 9, 28. Hamor was regarded as the eponymous ancestor of the pre-Israelite inhabitants of Shechem.

34, 1-31: Behind the story of the rape of Dinah and the revenge of Jacob's sons on the men of the city of Shechem there probably lies a dimly recollected historical event connected with an armed conflict between the earliest Israelite tribes invading central Canaan and the Hurrian inhabitants of the Shechem region.

34, 2: *Hivite:* The Greek text has "Horite"; the terms were apparently used indiscriminately to designate the Hurrian or other non-Semitic elements in Palestine.

region, saw her, he seized her and lay
with her by force. [3] Since he was strongly
attracted to Dinah, daughter of Jacob,
indeed was really in love with the girl,
he endeavored to win her affection.
[4] Shechem also asked his father Hamor,
"Get me this girl for a wife."
[5] Meanwhile, Jacob heard that She-
chem had defiled his daughter Dinah;
but since his sons were out in the fields
with his livestock, he held his peace until
they came home. [6] Now Hamor, the fa-
ther of Shechem, went out to discuss the
matter with Jacob, [7]* just as Jacob's
sons were coming in from the fields.
When they heard the news, the men
were shocked and seethed with indigna-
tion. What Shechem had done was an
outrage in Israel; such a thing could not
be tolerated.
[8] Hamor appealed to them, saying:
"My son Shechem has his heart set on
your daughter. Please give her to him
in marriage. [9] Intermarry with us; give
your daughters to us, and take our
daughters for yourselves. [10] Thus you
can live among us. The land is open be-
fore you; you can settle and move about
freely in it, and acquire landed property
here." [11] Then Shechem, too, appealed
to Dinah's father and brothers: "Do me
this favor, and I will pay whatever you
demand of me. [12] No matter how high
you set the bridal price, I will pay you
whatever you ask; only give me the
maiden in marriage."
Revenge of Jacob's Sons. [13] Jacob's
sons replied to Shechem and his father
Hamor with guile, speaking as they did
because their sister Dinah had been de-
filed. [14] "We could not do such a thing,"
they said, "as to give our sister to an
uncircumcised man; that would be a dis-
grace for us. [15] We will agree with you
only on this condition, that you become
like us by having every male among you
circumcised. [16] Then we will give you our
daughters and take yours in marriage;
we will settle among you and become
one kindred people with you. [17] But if you
do not comply with our terms regarding
circumcision, we will take our daughter
and go away."
[18] Their proposal seemed fair to Ha-
mor and his son Shechem. [19] The young
man lost no time in acting in the matter,
since he was deeply in love with Jacob's
daughter. Moreover he was more highly
respected than anyone else in his clan.
[20] So Hamor and his son Shechem went
to their town council and thus presented
the matter to their fellow townsmen:
[21] "These men are friendly toward us.
Let them settle in the land and move
about in it freely; there is ample room
in the country for them. We can marry
their daughters and give our daughters
to them in marriage. [22] But the men will
agree to live with us and form one kin-
dred people with us only on this condi-
tion, that every male among us be cir-
cumcised as they themselves are.
[23] Would not the livestock they have ac-
quired—all their animals—then be ours?
Let us, therefore, give in to them, so that
they may settle among us."
[24]† All the able-bodied men of the town
agreed with Hamor and his son She-
chem, and all the males, including every
able-bodied man in the community,
were circumcised. [25]* On the third day,
while they were still in pain, Dinah's full
brothers Simeon and Levi, two of Ja-
cob's sons, took their swords, advanced
against the city without any trouble, and
massacred all the males. [26]* After they
had put Hamor and his son Shechem to
the sword, they took Dinah from She-
chem's house and left. [27] Then the other
sons of Jacob followed up the slaughter
and sacked the city in reprisal for their
sister Dinah's defilement. [28] They seized
their flocks, herds and asses, whatever
was in the city and in the country
around. [29]* They carried off all their
wealth, their women, and their children,
and took for loot whatever was in the
houses.
[30] Jacob said to Simeon and Levi: "You
have brought trouble upon me by mak-
ing me loathsome to the inhabitants of
the land, the Canaanites and the Periz-
zites. I have so few men that, if these
people unite against me and attack me,
I and my family will be wiped out." [31] But
they retorted, "Should our sister have
been treated like a harlot?"

CHAPTER 35

Bethel Revisited. [1]* God said to Ja-
cob: "Go up now to Bethel. Settle there
and build an altar there to the God who
appeared to you while you were fleeing
from your brother Esau." [2]† So Jacob
told his family and all the others who
were with him: "Get rid of the foreign
gods that you have among you; then pu-
rify yourselves and put on fresh clothes.
[3] We are now to go up to Bethel, and I
will build an altar there to the God who
answered me in my hour of distress and
who has been with me wherever I have
gone." [4]† They therefore handed over to

---

*

34, 7: 2 Sm 13, 12.
25: 49, 6.
26: Jdt 9, 2.
29: Jdt 9, 3f.
35, 1: 28, 12f.

---

†

34, 24: *Every able-bodied man in the community:* literally "all those who go out at the gate of the city," apparently meaning the men who go out to war. By temporarily crippling them through circumcision, Jacob's sons deprived the city of its defenders.

35, 2: *Foreign gods:* pagan images, including household idols (see note on 31, 19), that Jacob's people brought with them from Paddan-aram.

35, 4: *Rings:* Earrings were often worn as amulets connected with pagan magic.

Jacob all the foreign gods in their pos-
session and also the rings they had in
their ears. 5 Then, as they set out, a ter-
ror from God fell upon the towns round
about, so that no one pursued the sons
of Jacob.
6* Thus Jacob and all the people who
were with him arrived in Luz [that is,
Bethel] in the land of Canaan. 7* There
he built an altar and named the place
Bethel, for it was there that God had re-
vealed himself to him when he was flee-
ing from his brother.
8† Death came to Rebekah's nurse
Deborah; she was buried under the oak
below Bethel, and so it was called Allon-
bacuth.
9 On Jacob's arrival from Paddan-
aram, God appeared to him again and
blessed him. 10* God said to him:

"You whose name is Jacob
shall no longer be called Jacob,
but Israel shall be your name."

Thus he was named Israel. 11 God also
said to him:

"I am God Almighty;
be fruitful and multiply.
A nation, indeed an assembly of na-
tions,
shall stem from you,
and kings shall issue from your
loins.
12* The land I once gave
to Abraham and Isaac
I now give to you;
And to your descendants after you
will I give this land."

13 Then God departed from him. 14* On
the site where God had spoken with him,
Jacob set up a memorial stone, and upon
it he made a libation and poured out oil.
15 Jacob named the site Bethel, because
God had spoken with him there.
Jacob's Family. 16 Then they de-
parted from Bethel; but while they still
had some distance to go on the way to
Ephrath, Rachel began to be in labor
and to suffer great distress. 17 When her
pangs were most severe, her midwife
said to her, "Have no fear! This time,
too, you have a son." 18† With her last
breath—for she was at the point of
death—she called him Ben-oni; his fa-
ther, however, named him Benjamin.
19*† Thus Rachel died; and she was bur-
ied on the road to Ephrath [that is, Beth-
lehem]. 20 Jacob set up a memorial stone
on her grave, and the same monument
marks Rachel's grave to this day.
21 Israel moved on and pitched his tent
beyond Migdal-eder. 22* While Israel
was encamped in that region, Reuben
went and lay with Bilhah, his father's
concubine. When Israel heard of it, he
was greatly offended.
The sons of Jacob were now twelve.
23 The sons of Leah: Reuben, Jacob's
first-born, Simeon, Levi, Judah, Issa-
char, and Zebulun; 24† the sons of Rachel:
Joseph and Benjamin; 25 the sons of Ra-
chel's maid Bilhah: Dan and Naphtali;
26 the sons of Leah's maid Zilpah: Gad
and Asher. These are the sons of Jacob
who were born to him in Paddan-aram.
27 Jacob went home to his father Isaac
at Mamre, in Kiriath-arba [that is, He-
bron], where Abraham and Isaac had
stayed. 28 The lifetime of Isaac was one
hundred and eighty years; then he
breathed his last. 29 After a full life, he
died as an old man and was taken to
his kinsmen. His sons Esau and Jacob
buried him.

CHAPTER 36

Edomite Lists. 1 These are the de-
scendants of Esau [that is, Edom].
2*† Esau took his wives from among the
Canaanite women: Adah, daughter of
Elon the Hittite; Oholibamah, grand-
daughter through Anah of Zibeon the
Hivite; 3 and Basemath, daughter of Ish-
mael and sister of Nebaioth. 4* Adah
bore Eliphaz to Esau; Basemath bore
Reuel; 5* and Oholibamah bore Jeush,
Jalam and Korah. These are the sons
of Esau who were born to him in the land
of Canaan.
6* Esau took his wives, his sons, his
daughters, and all the members of his
household, as well as his livestock com-
prising various animals and all the prop-
erty he had acquired in the land of

*

6: 28, 19; Jos 18, 13; Jgs 1, 22f.
7: 28, 12f.
10: 1 Kgs 18, 31; 2 Kgs 17, 34.
12: Ex 32, 13; Heb 11, 9.
14: 28, 18; 31, 45.
19: 48, 7; 1 Sm 10, 2; Mi 5, 2.
22: 49, 4; 1 Chr 5, 1.
36, 2: 26, 34.
4: 1 Chr 1, 35.
5: 1 Chr 1, 35.
6: 32, 4.

†

35, 8: This verse may have stood originally in some other context. Rebekah's nurse is spoken of without a name in 24, 59. *Allon-bacuth:* the Hebrew name means "oak of weeping."

35, 18: *Ben-oni:* either "son of my vigor" or, more likely in the context, "son of affliction." *Benjamin:* "son of the right hand." This may be interpreted to signify a son who is his father's help and support, but more likely its original meaning was "southerner." In the Hebrew idiom, the south lies to one's right hand, and Benjamin was the southernmost of the Rachel tribes.

35, 19: *Bethlehem:* the gloss comes from a later tradition that identified the site with Bethlehem, also called Ephrath or Ephratha (Jos 15, 59; Ru 4, 11; Mi 5, 1). But Rachel's grave was actually near Ramah (Jer 31, 15), a few miles north of Jerusalem, in the territory of Benjamin (1 Sm 10, 2).

35, 24ff: Benjamin is here said to have been born in *Paddan-aram,* either because all twelve sons of Jacob are considered as a unit, or because the Priestly source, from which vv 23-29 are taken, follows a tradition different from that of the Elohistic source found in vv 16-20.

36, 2-14: The names of Esau's wives and of their fathers given here differ considerably from their names cited from other old sources in 26, 34 and 28, 9. *Zibeon the Hivite:* in v 20 he is called a *Horite;* see note on 34, 2.

Canaan, and went to the land of Seir,
out of the way of his brother Jacob.
7 Their possessions had become too
great for them to dwell together, and the
land in which they were staying could
not support them because of their live-
stock. 8* So Esau settled in the highlands
of Seir. [Esau is Edom.] 9 These are the
descendants of Esau, ancestor of the
Edomites, in the highlands of Seir.

10 These are the names of Esau's sons:
Eliphaz, son of Esau's wife Adah; and
Reuel, son of Esau's wife Basemath.
11* The sons of Eliphaz were Teman,
Omar, Zepho, Gatam, and Kenaz.
12 (Esau's son Eliphaz had a concubine
Timna, and she bore Amalek to Eli-
phaz.) These are the descendants of
Esau's wife Adah. 13* The sons of Reuel
were Nahath, Zerah, Shammah, and
Mizzah. These are the descendants of
Esau's wife Basemath. 14* The descen-
dants of Esau's wife Oholibamah—
granddaughter through Anah of Zib-
eon—whom she bore to Esau were
Jeush, Jalam, and Korah.

15 The following are the clans of Esau's
descendants. The descendants of Eli-
phaz, Esau's first-born: the clans of Te-
man, Omar, Zepho, Kenaz, 16 Korah,
Gatam, and Amalek. These are the clans
of Eliphaz in the land of Edom; they are
descended from Adah. 17 The descen-
dants of Esau's son Reuel: the clans of
Nahath, Zerah, Shammah, and Mizzah.
These are the clans of Reuel in the land
of Edom; they are descended from
Esau's wife Basemath. 18 The descen-
dants of Esau's wife Oholibamah: the
clans of Jeush, Jalam, and Korah. These
are the clans of Esau's wife Oholibamah,
daughter of Anah. 19 Such are the de-
scendants of Esau [that is, Edom] ac-
cording to their clans.

20*† The following are the descendants
of Seir the Horite, the original settlers
in the land: Lotan, Shobal, Zibeon, Anah,
21 Dishon, Ezer, and Dishan; they are the
Horite clans descended from Seir, in the
land of Edom. 22* Lotan's descendants
were Hori and Hemam, and Lotan's sis-
ter was Timna. 23 Shobal's descendants
were Alvan, Mahanath, Ebal, Shepho,
and Onam. 24 Zibeon's descendants were
Aiah and Anah. (He is the Anah who
found water in the desert while he was
pasturing the asses of his father Zibeon.)
25 The descendants of Anah were Dishon
and Oholibamah, daughter of Anah.
26 The descendants of Dishon were Hem-
dan, Eshban, Ithran, and Cheran. 27 The
descendants of Ezer were Bilhan, Zaa-
van, and Akan. 28 The descendants of
Dishan were Uz and Aran. 29 These are
the Horite clans: the clans of Lotan, Sho-
bal, Zibeon, Anah, 30 Dishon, Ezer, and
Dishan; they were the clans of the Hor-
ites, clan by clan, in the land of Seir.

31*† The following are the kings who
reigned in the land of Edom before any
king reigned over the Israelites. 32 Bela,
son of Beor, became king in Edom; the
name of his city was Dinhabah. 33 When
Bela died, Jobab, son of Zerah, from
Bozrah, succeeded him as king. 34 When
Jobab died, Husham, from the land of
the Temanites, succeeded him as king.
He defeated the Midianites in the coun-
try of Moab; the name of his city was
Avith. 35 When Husham died, Hadad,
son of Bedad, succeeded him as king.
36 When Hadad died, Samlah, from Mas-
rekah, succeeded him as king. 37 When
Samlah died, Shaul, from Rehoboth-on-
the-River, succeeded him as king.
38 When Shaul died, Baal-hanan, son of
Achbor, succeeded him as king. 39 When
Baal-hanan died, Hadar succeeded him
as king; the name of his city was Pau.
(His wife's name was Mehetabel; she
was the daughter of Matred, son of Me-
zahab.)

40 The following are the names of
the clans of Esau individually accord-
ing to their subdivisions and localities:
the clans of Timna, Alvah, Jetheth,
41 Oholibamah, Elah, Pinon, 42 Kenaz,
Teman, Mibzar, 43 Magdiel, and Iram.
These are the clans of the Edomites, ac-
cording to their settlements in their ter-
ritorial holdings. [Esau was the father
of the Edomites.]

IV: JOSEPH AND HIS BROTHERS

CHAPTER 37

Joseph Sold into Egypt. 1 Jacob set-
tled in the land where his father had
stayed, the land of Canaan. 2 This is his
family history. When Joseph was seven-
teen years old, he was tending the flocks
with his brothers; he was an assistant
to the sons of his father's wives Bilhah
and Zilpah, and he brought his father
bad reports about them.

3 Israel loved Joseph best of all his
sons, for he was the child of his old age;
and he had made him a long tunic.
4 When his brothers saw that their father
loved him best of all his sons, they hated
him so much that they would not even
greet him.

5* Once Joseph had a dream, which he
told to his brothers: 6 "Listen to this
dream I had. 7 There we were, binding

---

*

8: Dt 2, 4f; Jos 24, 4.
11f: 1 Chr 1, 36.
13: 1 Chr 1, 37.
14: 1 Chr 1, 35.
20f: 1 Chr 1, 38.
22-28: 1 Chr 1, 39-42.
31-43: 1 Chr 1, 43-54.
37, 5: 42, 9.

†

36, 20: *Seir the Horite:* according to Dt 2, 12, the highlands of Seir were inhabited by Horites before they were occupied by the Edomites.

36, 31: *Before any king reigned over the Israelites:* obviously this statement was written after the time of Saul, Israel's first king.

sheaves in the field, when suddenly my
sheaf rose to an upright position, and
your sheaves formed a ring around my
sheaf and bowed down to it." [8]* "Are you
really going to make yourself king over
us?" his brothers asked him. "Or impose
your rule on us?" So they hated him all
the more because of his talk about his
dreams.

[9] Then he had another dream, and this
one, too, he told to his brothers. "I had
another dream," he said; "this time, the
sun and the moon and eleven stars were
bowing down to me." [10] When he also
told it to his father, his father reproved
him. "What is the meaning of this dream
of yours?" he asked. "Can it be that I
and your mother and your brothers are
to come and bow to the ground before
you?" [11] So his brothers were wrought
up against him but his father pondered
the matter.

[12] One day, when his brothers had
gone to pasture their father's flocks at
Shechem, [13] Israel said to Joseph, "Your
brothers, you know, are tending our
flocks at Shechem. Get ready; I will send
you to them." "I am ready," Joseph an-
swered. [14] "Go then," he replied; "see if
all is well with your brothers and the
flocks, and bring back word." So he sent
him off from the valley of Hebron. When
Joseph reached Shechem, [15] a man met
him as he was wandering about in the
fields. "What are you looking for?" the
man asked him. [16] "I am looking for my
brothers," he answered. "Could you
please tell me where they are tending
the flocks?" [17] The man told him, "They
have moved on from here; in fact, I
heard them say, 'Let us go on to Do-
than.' " So Joseph went after his broth-
ers and caught up with them in Dothan.
[18] They noticed him from a distance, and
before he came up to them, they plotted
to kill him. [19] They said to one another:
"Here comes that master dreamer!
[20]* Come on, let us kill him and throw
him into one of the cisterns here; we
could say that a wild beast devoured
him. We shall then see what comes of
his dreams."

[21]† When Reuben heard this, he tried
to save him from their hands, saying:
"We must not take his life. [22]* Instead
of shedding blood," he continued, "just
throw him into that cistern there in the
desert; but don't kill him outright." His
purpose was to rescue him from their
hands and restore him to his father. [23] So
when Joseph came up to them, they
stripped him of the long tunic he had
on; [24] then they took him and threw him
into the cistern, which was empty and
dry.

[25]* They then sat down to their meal.
Looking up, they saw a caravan of Ish-
maelites coming from Gilead, their
camels laden with gum, balm and resin
to be taken down to Egypt. [26]* Judah
said to his brothers: "What is to be
gained by killing our brother and con-
cealing his blood? [27] Rather, let us sell
him to these Ishmaelites, instead of do-
ing away with him ourselves. After all,
he is our brother, our own flesh." His
brothers agreed. [28]*† They sold Joseph
to the Ishmaelites for twenty pieces of
silver.

Some Midianite traders passed by,
and they pulled Joseph up out of the cis-
tern and took him to Egypt. [29] When
Reuben went back to the cistern and saw
that Joseph was not in it, he tore his
clothes, [30] and returning to his brothers,
he exclaimed: "The boy is gone! And I—
where can I turn?" [31] They took Joseph's
tunic, and after slaughtering a goat, dip-
ped the tunic in its blood. [32] Then they
sent someone to bring the long tunic to
their father, with the message: "We
found this. See whether it is your son's
tunic or not." [33]* He recognized it and
exclaimed: "My son's tunic! A wild beast
has devoured him! Joseph has been torn
to pieces!" [34] Then Jacob rent his
clothes, put sackcloth on his loins, and
mourned his son many days. [35]* Though
his sons and daughters tried to console
him, he refused all consolation, saying,
"No, I will go down mourning to my son
in the nether world." Thus did his father
lament him.

[36]* The Midianites, meanwhile, sold
Joseph in Egypt to Potiphar, a courtier
of Pharaoh and his chief steward.

CHAPTER 38

Judah and Tamar. [1]† About that time
Judah parted from his brothers and
pitched his tent near a certain Adullam-

*

8: 50, 17.
20: 44, 28.
22: 42, 22.
25: 43, 11.
26: Jb 16, 18.
28: Ps 105, 17; Wis 10, 13; Acts 7, 9.
33: 44, 28.
35: 42, 38.
36: Ps 105, 17.

†

37, 21-36: The chapter thus far is from the Yahwist source, as are also vv 25-28a. But vv 21-24 and 28b-36 are from the Elohist source. In the latter, Reuben tries to rescue Joseph, who is taken in Reuben's absence by certain Midianites; in the Yahwist source, it is Judah who saves Joseph's life by having him sold to certain Ishmaelites. Although the two variant forms in which the story was handed down in early oral tradition differ in these minor points, they agree on the essential fact that Joseph was brought as a slave into Egypt because of the jealousy of his brothers.

37, 28: *They sold Joseph . . . silver:* in the Hebrew text, these words occur between *out of the cistern* and *and* (*they*) *took him to Egypt* at the end of the verse.

38, 1-30: This chapter, from the Yahwist source, has nothing to do with the Joseph story in which Judah is still living with his father and brothers. The sacred author inserted this independent account from the life of Judah at this place to mark the long lapse of time during which Joseph's family knew nothing of his life in Egypt. This is apparently a personalized history of the early days of the tribe of Judah, which interbred with several Canaanite clans, though some of these soon became extinct.

ite named Hirah. 2* There he met the
daughter of a Canaanite named Shua,
married her, and had relations with her.
3 She conceived and bore a son, whom
she named Er. 4 Again she conceived
and bore a son, whom she named Onan.
5*† Then she bore still another son,
whom she named Shelah. They were in
Chezib when he was born.

6 Judah got a wife named Tamar for
his first-born, Er. 7* But Er, Judah's
first-born, greatly offended the LORD; so
the LORD took his life. 8*† Then Judah
said to Onan, "Unite with your brother's
widow, in fulfillment of your duty as
brother-in-law, and thus preserve your
brother's line." 9 Onan, however, knew
that the descendants would not be
counted as his; so whenever he had rela-
tions with his brother's widow, he wasted
his seed on the ground, to avoid contrib-
uting offspring for his brother. 10 What
he did greatly offended the LORD, and
the LORD took his life too. 11 Thereupon
Judah said to his daughter-in-law Ta-
mar, "Stay as a widow in your father's
house until my son Shelah grows up"—
for he feared that Shelah also might die
like his brothers. So Tamar went to live
in her father's house.

12 Years passed, and Judah's wife, the
daughter of Shua, died. After Judah
completed the period of mourning, he
went up to Timnah for the shearing of
his sheep, in company with his friend
Hirah the Adullamite. 13 When Tamar
was told that her father-in-law was on
his way up to Timnah to shear his sheep,
14* she took off her widow's garb, veiled
her face by covering herself with a
shawl, and sat down at the entrance to
Enaim, which is on the way to Timnah;
for she was aware that, although Shelah
was now grown up, she had not been
given to him in marriage. 15 When Judah
saw her, he mistook her for a harlot,
since she had covered her face. 16 So he
went over to her at the roadside, and
not realizing that she was his daughter-
in-law, he said, "Come, let me have in-
tercourse with you." She replied, "What
will you pay me for letting you have in-
tercourse with me?" 17 He answered, "I
will send you a kid from the flock."
"Very well," she said, "provided you
leave a pledge until you send it."
18† Judah asked, "What pledge am I to
give to you?" She answered, "Your seal
and cord, and the staff you carry." So
he gave them to her and had intercourse
with her, and she conceived by him.
19 When she went away, she took off her
shawl and put on her widow's garb
again.

20 Judah sent the kid by his friend the
Adullamite to recover the pledge from
the woman; but he could not find her.
21† So he asked the men of the place,
"Where is the temple prostitute, the one
by the roadside in Enaim?" But they an-
swered, "There has never been a temple
prostitute here." 22 He went back to Ju-
dah and told him, "I could not find her;
and besides, the men of the place said
there was no temple prostitute there."
23 "Let her keep the things," Judah re-
plied; "otherwise we shall become a
laughingstock. After all, I did send her
the kid, even though you were unable
to find her."

24 About three months later, Judah
was told that his daughter-in-law Ta-
mar had played the harlot and was then
with child from her harlotry. "Bring her
out," cried Judah; "she shall be burned."
25 But as they were bringing her out, she
sent word to her father-in-law, "It is by
the man to whom these things belong
that I am with child. Please verify," she
added, "whose seal and cord and whose
staff these are." 26 Judah recognized
them and said, "She is more in the right
than I am, since I did not give her to
my son Shelah." But he had no further
relations with her.

27* When the time of her delivery
came, she was found to have twins in
her womb. 28 While she was giving birth,
one infant put out his hand; and the mid-
wife, taking a crimson thread, tied it on
his hand, to note that this one came out
first. 29*† But as he withdrew his hand,
his brother came out; and she said,
"What a breach you have made for
yourself!" So he was called Perez.
30*† Afterward his brother came out; he
was called Zerah.

*

38, 2: 1 Chr 2, 3.
5: 1 Chr 4, 21.
7: 1 Chr 2, 3.
8: Dt 25, 5; Mt 22, 24; Mk 12, 19; Lk 20, 28.
14: Prv 7, 10.
27: 1 Chr 2, 4.
29: Rv 4, 12; Mt 1, 3; Lk 3, 33.
30: Nm 26, 20; 1 Chr 2, 4; Mt 1, 3.

†

38, 5: *Chezib:* a variant form of Achzib (Jos 15, 44; Mi 1, 14), a town in the Judean Shephelah.

38, 8: *Preserve your brother's line:* literally "raise up seed for your brother." The ancient Israelites regarded as very important their law of levirate, or "brother-in-law" marriage; see notes on Dt 25, 5; Ru 2, 20. In the present story, it is primarily Onan's violation of this law, rather than the means he used to circumvent it, that brought on him God's displeasure (vv 9f).

38, 18: *Seal and cord:* the cylinder seal, through which a hole was bored lengthwise so that it could be worn from the neck by a cord, was a distinctive means of identification. Apparently a man's staff was also marked with his name (Nm 17, 16f) or other sign of identification.

38, 21: *Temple prostitute:* the Hebrew term *qedesha,* literally "consecrated woman," designates a woman who had ritual intercourse with men in pagan fertility rites; cf Dt 23, 18; Hos 4, 14, where the same Hebrew word is used. Hirah the Adullamite uses a word that refers to a higher social class than that designated by the term *zona,* common "harlot," used in vv 15.24.

38, 29: *He was called Perez:* the Hebrew word means "breach."

38, 30: *He was called Zerah:* a name connected here by popular etymology with a Hebrew verb for the red light of dawn, alluding apparently to the crimson thread.

CHAPTER 39

Joseph's Temptation. 1† When Joseph
was taken down to Egypt, a certain
Egyptian (Potiphar, a courtier of Pha-
raoh and his chief steward) bought him
from the Ishmaelites who had brought
him there. 2* But since the LORD was
with him, Joseph got on very well and
was assigned to the household of his
Egyptian master. 3 When his master saw
that the LORD was with him and brought
him success in whatever he did, 4* he
took a liking to Joseph and made him
his personal attendant; he put him in
charge of his household and entrusted
to him all his possessions. 5 From the
moment that he put him in charge of
his household and all his possessions,
the LORD blessed the Egyptian's house
for Joseph's sake; in fact, the LORD's
blessing was on everything he owned,
both inside the house and out. 6 Having
left everything he owned in Joseph's
charge, he gave no thought, with Joseph
there, to anything but the food he ate.
Now Joseph was strikingly handsome
in countenance and body. 7 After a time,
his master's wife began to look fondly
at him and said, "Lie with me." 8 But
he refused. "As long as I am here," he
told her, "my master does not concern
himself with anything in the house, but
has entrusted to me all he owns. 9 He
wields no more authority in this house
than I do, and he has withheld from me
nothing but yourself, since you are his
wife. How, then, could I commit so great
a wrong and thus stand condemned be-
fore God?" 10* Although she tried to en-
tice him day after day, he would not
agree to lie beside her, or even stay near
her.
11 One such day, when Joseph came
into the house to do his work, and none
of the household servants were then in
the house, 12 she laid hold of him by his
cloak, saying, "Lie with me!" But leav-
ing the cloak in her hand, he got away
from her and ran outside. 13 When she
saw that he had left his cloak in her hand
as he fled outside, 14 she screamed for
her household servants and told them,
"Look! my husband has brought in a He-
brew slave to make sport of us! He came
in here to lie with me, but I cried out
as loud as I could. 15 When he heard me
scream for help, he left his cloak beside
me and ran away outside."
16 She kept the cloak with her until his
master came home. 17 Then she told him
the same story: "The Hebrew slave
whom you brought here broke in on me,
to make sport of me. 18 But when I
screamed for help, he left his cloak be-
side me and fled outside." 19 As soon as
the master heard his wife's story about
how his slave had treated her, he be-
came enraged. 20* He seized Joseph and
threw him into the jail where the royal
prisoners were confined.
But even while he was in prison, 21* the
LORD remained with Joseph; he showed
him kindness by making the chief jailer
well-disposed toward him. 22 The chief
jailer put Joseph in charge of all the pris-
oners in the jail, and everything that had
to be done there was done under his
management. 23 The chief jailer did not
concern himself with anything at all that
was in Joseph's charge, since the LORD
was with him and brought success to all
he did.

CHAPTER 40

The Dreams Interpreted. 1 Some time
afterward, the royal cupbearer and
baker gave offense to their lord, the king
of Egypt. 2 Pharaoh was angry with his
two courtiers, the chief cupbearer and
the chief baker, 3 and he put them in cus-
tody in the house of the chief steward
(the same jail where Joseph was con-
fined). 4 The chief steward assigned Jo-
seph to them, and he became their
attendant.
After they had been in custody for
some time, 5 the cupbearer and the
baker of the king of Egypt who were
confined in the jail both had dreams on
the same night, each dream with its own
meaning. 6 When Joseph came to them
in the morning, he noticed that they
looked disturbed. 7 So he asked Pha-
raoh's courtiers who were with him in
custody in his master's house, "Why do
you look so sad today?" 8* They an-
swered him, "We have had dreams, but
there is no one to interpret them for us."
Joseph said to them, "Surely, interpre-
tations come from God. Please tell the
dreams to me."
9 Then the chief cupbearer told Joseph
his dream. "In my dream," he said, "I
saw a vine in front of me, 10 and on the
vine were three branches. It had barely
budded when its blossoms came out,
and its clusters ripened into grapes.
11 Pharaoh's cup was in my hand; so I
took the grapes, pressed them out into
his cup, and put it in Pharaoh's hand."
12 Joseph said to him: "This is what it

*

39, 2: 1 Sm 3, 19; 10, 7; 18, 14; 2 Sm 5, 10; 2 Kgs 18, 7; Acts 7, 9.
4: Dn 1, 9.
10: 1 Mc 2, 53.
20: Ps 105, 18.
21: Acts 7, 9f.
40, 8: 41, 16.

†

39, 1: (*Potiphar . . . chief steward*): These words in the text serve to harmonize ch 39 from the Yahwist source with 37, 36 and 40, 1-23 from the Elohist. In the former, the Ishmaelites who bought Joseph from his brothers (37, 28) sold him to the unnamed "Egyptian master" of ch 39. In the latter, the Midianites who kidnaped Joseph (37, 28; 40, 15) sold him to Potiphar, Pharaoh's chief steward (37, 36), whose house was used as a royal prison (40, 2f).

means. The three branches are three
days; 13† within three days Pharaoh will
lift up your head and restore you to your
post. You will be handing Pharaoh his
cup as you formerly used to do when
you were his cupbearer. 14 So if you will
still remember, when all is well with you,
that I was here with you, please do me
the favor of mentioning me to Pharaoh,
to get me out of this place. 15 The truth
is that I was kidnaped from the land of
the Hebrews, and here I have not done
anything for which I should have been
put into a dungeon."
16 When the chief baker saw that Jo-
seph had given this favorable interpre-
tation, he said to him: "I too had a
dream. In it I had three wicker baskets
on my head; 17 in the top one were all
kinds of bakery products for Pharaoh,
but the birds were pecking at them out
of the basket on my head." 18 Joseph said
to him in reply: "This is what it means.
The three baskets are three days;
19 within three days Pharaoh will lift up
your head and have you impaled on a
stake, and the birds will be pecking the
flesh from your body."
20 And in fact, on the third day, which
was Pharaoh's birthday, when he gave
a banquet to all his staff, with his court-
iers around him, he lifted up the heads
of the chief cupbearer and chief baker.
21 He restored the chief cupbearer to his
office, so that he again handed the cup
to Pharaoh; 22 but the chief baker he im-
paled—just as Joseph had told them in
his interpretation. 23 Yet the chief cup-
bearer gave no thought to Joseph; he
had forgotten him.

CHAPTER 41

Pharaoh's Dream. 1 After a lapse of
two years, Pharaoh had a dream. He
saw himself standing by the Nile, 2 when
up out of the Nile came seven cows,
handsome and fat; they grazed in the
reed grass. 3 Behind them seven other
cows, ugly and gaunt, came up out of
the Nile; and standing on the bank of
the Nile beside the others, 4 the ugly,
gaunt cows ate up the seven handsome,
fat cows. Then Pharaoh woke up.
5 He fell asleep again and had another
dream. He saw seven ears of grain, fat
and healthy, growing on a single stalk.
6 Behind them sprouted seven ears of
grain, thin and blasted by the east wind;
7 and the seven thin ears swallowed up
the seven fat, healthy ears. Then Pha-
raoh woke up, to find it was only a dream.
8 Next morning his spirit was agitated.
So he summoned all the magicians and
sages of Egypt and recounted his
dreams to them; but no one could inter-
pret his dreams for him. 9 Then the chief
cupbearer spoke up and said to Pha-
raoh: "On this occasion I am reminded
of my negligence. 10 Once, when Pha-
raoh was angry, he put me and the chief
baker in custody in the house of the chief
steward. 11 Later, we both had dreams
on the same night, and each of our
dreams had its own meaning. 12* There
with us was a Hebrew youth, a slave of
the chief steward; and when we told him
our dreams, he interpreted them for us
and explained for each of us the mean-
ing of his dream. 13 And it turned out just
as he had told us: I was restored to my
post, but the other man was impaled."
14* Pharaoh therefore had Joseph
summoned, and they hurriedly brought
him from the dungeon. After he shaved
and changed his clothes, he came into
Pharaoh's presence. 15 Pharaoh then
said to him: "I had certain dreams that
no one can interpret. But I hear it said
of you that the moment you are told a
dream you can interpret it." 16* "It is not
I," Joseph replied to Pharaoh, "but God
who will give Pharaoh the right an-
swer."
17 Then Pharaoh said to Joseph: "In
my dream, I was standing on the bank
of the Nile, 18 when up from the Nile
came seven cows, fat and well-formed;
they grazed in the reed grass. 19 Behind
them came seven other cows, scrawny,
most ill-formed and gaunt. Never have
I seen such ugly specimens as these in
all the land of Egypt! 20 The gaunt, ugly
cows ate up the first seven fat cows.
21 But when they had consumed them,
no one could tell that they had done so,
because they looked as ugly as before.
Then I woke up. 22 In another dream I
saw seven ears of grain, fat and healthy,
growing on a single stalk. 23 Behind them
sprouted seven ears of grain, shriveled
and thin and blasted by the east wind;
24 and the seven thin ears swallowed up
the seven healthy ears. I have spoken
to the magicians, but none of them can
give me an explanation."
25 Joseph said to Pharaoh: "Both of
Pharaoh's dreams have the same mean-
ing. God has thus foretold to Pharaoh
what he is about to do. 26 The seven
healthy cows are seven years, and the
seven healthy ears are seven years—the
same in each dream. 27 So also, the seven
thin, ugly cows that came up after them
are seven years, as are the seven thin,
wind-blasted ears; they are seven years
of famine. 28 It is just as I told Pharaoh:

GENESIS

*

41, 12: Dn 1, 17. 16: 40, 8.
14: Ps 105, 20.

†

40, 13: *Lift up your head:* signifying "pardon you." In v 19 "to lift up the head" means "to behead"; and finally, in v 20, the same expression means "to review the case (of someone)." Joseph couches his interpretation of the dreams in equivocal terms.

God has revealed to Pharaoh what he
is about to do. 29 Seven years of great
abundance are now coming throughout
the land of Egypt; 30 but these will be fol-
lowed by seven years of famine, when
all the abundance in the land of Egypt
will be forgotten. When the famine has
ravaged the land, 31 no trace of the abun-
dance will be found in the land because
of the famine that follows it—so utterly
severe will that famine be. 32 That Pha-
raoh had the same dream twice means
that the matter has been reaffirmed by
God and that God will soon bring it
about.

33 "Therefore, let Pharaoh seek out
a wise and discerning man and put
him in charge of the land of Egypt.
34 Pharaoh should also take action to ap-
point overseers, so as to regiment the
land during the seven years of abun-
dance. 35 They should husband all the
food of the coming good years, collecting
the grain under Pharaoh's authority, to
be stored in the towns for food. 36 This
food will serve as a reserve for the coun-
try against the seven years of famine
that are to follow in the land of Egypt,
so that the land may not perish in the
famine."

37* This advice pleased Pharaoh and
all his officials. 38 "Could we find another
like him," Pharaoh asked his officials,
"a man so endowed with the spirit of
God?" 39 So Pharaoh said to Joseph:
"Since God has made all this known to
you, no one can be as wise and discern-
ing as you are. 40* You shall be in charge
of my palace, and all my people shall
dart at your command. Only in respect
to the throne shall I outrank you.
41 Herewith," Pharaoh told Joseph, "I
place you in charge of the whole land
of Egypt." 42† With that, Pharaoh took
off his signet ring and put it on Joseph's
finger. He had him dressed in robes of
fine linen and put a gold chain about his
neck. 43† He then had him ride in the
chariot of his vizier, and they shouted
"Abrek!" before him.

Thus was Joseph installed over the
whole land of Egypt. 44 "I, Pharaoh, pro-
claim," he told Joseph, "that without
your approval no one shall move hand
or foot in all the land of Egypt."
45† Pharaoh also bestowed the name of
Zaphenath-paneah on Joseph, and he
gave him in marriage Asenath, the
daughter of Potiphera, priest of Heliopo-
lis. 46 Joseph was thirty years old when
he entered the service of Pharaoh, king
of Egypt.

After Joseph left Pharaoh's presence,
he traveled throughout the land of
Egypt. 47 During the seven years of
plenty, when the land produced abun-
dant crops, 48 he husbanded all the food
of these years of plenty that the land of
Egypt was enjoying and stored it in the
towns, placing in each town the crops
of the fields around it. 49 Joseph gar-
nered grain in quantities like the sands
of the sea, so vast that at last he stopped
measuring it, for it was beyond measure.

50* Before the famine years set in, Jo-
seph became the father of two sons,
borne to him by Asenath, daughter of
Potiphera, priest of Heliopolis. 51† He
named his first-born Manasseh, mean-
ing, "God has made me forget entirely
the sufferings I endured at the hands of
my family"; 52† and the second he
named Ephraim, meaning, "God has
made me fruitful in the land of my afflic-
tion."

53 When the seven years of abundance
enjoyed by the land of Egypt came to
an end, 54* the seven years of famine set
in, just as Joseph had predicted. Al-
though there was famine in all the other
countries, food was available throughout
the land of Egypt. 55 When hunger came
to be felt throughout the land of Egypt
and the people cried to Pharaoh for
bread, Pharaoh directed all the Egyp-
tians to go to Joseph and do whatever
he told them. 56 When the famine had
spread throughout the land, Joseph
opened all the cities that had grain and
rationed it to the Egyptians, since the
famine had gripped the land of Egypt.
57 In fact, all the world came to Joseph
to obtain rations of grain, for famine had
gripped the whole world.

CHAPTER 42

***The Brothers' First Journey to
Egypt.*** 1 When Jacob learned that grain
rations were available in Egypt, he said
to his sons: "Why do you keep gaping
at one another? 2* I hear," he went on,

*

37: Acts 7, 10.
40: Ps 105, 21; Wis 10, 14; 1 Mc 2, 53; Acts 7, 10.
50: 46, 20; 48, 5.
54: Ps 105, 16; Acts 7, 11.
42, 2: Acts 7, 12.

†

41, 42: *Signet ring:* a finger ring in which was set a stamp seal, different from the cylinder seal such as Judah wore; see note on 38, 18. This is an authentic detail. By receiving Pharaoh's signet ring, Joseph was made vizier of Egypt (v 43); the vizier was known as "seal-bearer of the king of Lower Egypt." Another authentic detail is the *gold chain,* a symbol of high office in ancient Egypt.

41, 43: *Abrek:* apparently a cry of homage, though the word's derivation and actual meaning are uncertain.

41, 45: *Zaphenath-paneah:* a Hebrew transcription of an Egyptian name meaning "the god speaks and he (the new-born child) lives." *Asenath:* means "belonging to (the Egyptian goddess) Neith." *Potiphera:* means "he whom Ra (the Egyptian god) gave"; a shorter form of the same name was borne by Joseph's master (37, 36). *Heliopolis:* in Hebrew, *On,* a city seven miles northeast of modern Cairo, site of the chief temple of the sun god; it is mentioned also in v 50; 46, 20; Ez 30, 17.

41, 51: *Manasseh:* allusion to this name is in the Hebrew expression, *nishshani,* "he made me forget."

41, 52: *Ephraim:* related to the Hebrew expression *hiphrani,* "(God) has made me fruitful."

"that rations of grain are available in
Egypt. Go down there and buy some for
us, that we may stay alive rather than
die of hunger." 3 So ten of Joseph's
brothers went down to buy an emer-
gency supply of grain from Egypt. 4 It
was only Joseph's full brother Benjamin
that Jacob did not send with the rest,
for he thought some disaster might be-
fall him. 5* Thus, since there was famine
in the land of Canaan also, the sons of
Israel were among those who came to
procure rations.
6* It was Joseph, as governor of the
country, who dispensed the rations to all
the people. When Joseph's brothers
came and knelt down before him with
their faces to the ground, 7 he recognized
them as soon as he saw them. But he
concealed his own identity from them
and spoke sternly to them. "Where do
you come from?" he asked them. They
answered, "From the land of Canaan,
to procure food."
8 When Joseph recognized his broth-
ers, although they did not recognize him,
9*† he was reminded of the dreams he
had about them. He said to them: "You
are spies. You have come to see the
nakedness of the land." 10 "No, my
lord," they replied. "On the contrary,
your servants have come to procure
food. 11 All of us are sons of the same
man. We are honest men; your servants
have never been spies." 12 But he an-
swered them: "Not so! You have come
to see the nakedness of the land."
13* "We your servants," they said, "were
twelve brothers, sons of a certain man
in Canaan; but the youngest one is at
present with our father, and the other
one is gone." 14 "It is just as I said," Jo-
seph persisted; "you are spies. 15 This is
how you shall be tested: unless your
youngest brother comes here, I swear
by the life of Pharaoh that you shall not
leave here. 16 So send one of your num-
ber to get your brother, while the rest
of you stay here under arrest. Thus shall
your words be tested for their truth; if
they are untrue, as Pharaoh lives, you
are spies!" 17 With that, he locked them
up in the guardhouse for three days.
18 On the third day Joseph said to
them: "Do this, and you shall live; for
I am a God-fearing man. 19 If you have
been honest, only one of your brothers
need be confined in this prison, while the
rest of you may go and take home provi-
sions for your starving families. 20* But
you must come back to me with your
youngest brother. Your words will thus
be verified, and you will not die." To this
they agreed. 21* To one another, how-
ever, they said: "Alas, we are being pun-
ished because of our brother. We saw
the anguish of his heart when he pleaded
with us, yet we paid no heed; that is why
this anguish has now come upon us."
22* "Didn't I tell you," broke in Reuben,
"not to do wrong to the boy? But you
wouldn't listen! Now comes the reckon-
ing for his blood." 23 They did not know,
of course, that Joseph understood what
they said, since he spoke with them
through an interpreter. 24 But turning
away from them, he wept. When he was
able to speak to them again, he had
Simeon taken from them and bound be-
fore their eyes. 25 Then Joseph gave or-
ders to have their containers filled with
grain, their money replaced in each
one's sack, and provisions given them
for their journey. After this had been
done for them, 26 they loaded their don-
keys with the rations and departed.
27† At the night encampment, when
one of them opened his bag to give his
donkey some fodder, he was surprised
to see his money in the mouth of his bag.
28 "My money has been returned!" he
cried out to his brothers. "Here it is in
my bag!" At that their hearts sank.
Trembling, they asked one another,
"What is this that God has done to us?"
29 When they got back to their father
Jacob in the land of Canaan, they told
him all that had happened to them.
30 "The man who is lord of the country,"
they said, "spoke to us sternly and put
us in custody as if we were spying on
the land. 31 But we said to him: 'We are
honest men: we have never been spies.
32 There were twelve of us brothers, sons
of the same father; but one is gone, and
the youngest one is at present with our
father in the land of Canaan.' 33 Then the
man who is lord of the country said to
us: 'This is how I shall know if you are
honest men: leave one of your brothers
with me, while the rest of you go home
with rations for your starving families.
34 When you come back to me with your
youngest brother, and I know that you
are honest men and not spies, I will re-
store your brother to you, and you may
move about freely in the land.'"
35 When they were emptying their
sacks, there in each one's sack was his
moneybag! At the sight of their money-
bags, they and their father were dis-
mayed. 36 Their father Jacob said to
them: "Must you make me childless? Jo-
seph is gone, and Simeon is gone, and

*

5: Jdt 5, 10; Acts 7, 11.
6: Ps 105, 21.
9: 37, 5.
13: 44, 20.
20: 43, 5.
21: 37, 18-27.
22: 37, 22.

†

42, 9.12: *The nakedness of the land:* the military weakness of the land, like human nakedness, should not be seen by strangers.

42, 27-28: These two verses are from the Yahwist source, whereas the rest of the chapter is from the Elohist source, in which the men find the money in their sacks (not "bags"—a different Hebrew word) only when they arrive home (v 35); cf 43, 21.

now you would take away Benjamin!
Why must such things always happen
to me?" 37 Then Reuben told his father:
"Put him in my care, and I will bring
him back to you. You may kill my own
two sons if I do not return him to you."
38* But Jacob replied: "My son shall not
go down with you. Now that his full
brother is dead, he is the only one left.
If some disaster should befall him on the
journey you must make, you would send
my white head down to the nether world
in grief."

CHAPTER 43

The Second Journey to Egypt. 1† Now
the famine in the land grew more severe.
2 So when they had used up all the ra-
tions they had brought from Egypt, their
father said to them, "Go back and pro-
cure us a little more food." 3* But Judah
replied: "The man strictly warned us,
'You shall not appear in my presence
unless your brother is with you.' 4 If you
are willing to let our brother go with us,
we will go down to procure food for you.
5* But if you are not willing, we will not
go down, because the man told us, 'You
shall not appear in my presence unless
your brother is with you.' " 6 Israel de-
manded, "Why did you bring this trou-
ble on me by telling the man that you
had another brother?" 7 They answered:
"The man kept asking about ourselves
and our family: 'Is your father still liv-
ing? Do you have another brother?' We
had to answer his questions. How could
we know that he would say, 'Bring your
brother down here'?"

8* Then Judah urged his father Israel:
"Let the boy go with me, that we may
be off and on our way if you and we and
our children are to keep from starving
to death. 9* I myself will stand surety for
him. You can hold me responsible for
him. If I fail to bring him back, to set
him in your presence, you can hold it
against me forever. 10 Had we not dilly-
dallied, we could have been there and
back twice by now!"

11* Their father Israel then told them:
"If it must be so, then do this: Put some
of the land's best products in your bag-
gage and take them down to the man
as gifts: some balm and honey, gum and
resin, and pistachios and almonds.
12 Also take extra money along, for you
must return the amount that was put
back in the mouths of your bags; it may
have been a mistake. 13 Take your
brother, too, and be off on your way back
to the man. 14 May God Almighty dis-
pose the man to be merciful toward you,
so that he may let your other brother
go, as well as Benjamin. As for me, if I
am to suffer bereavement, I shall suffer
it."

15 So the men got the gifts, took double
the amount of money with them, and,
accompanied by Benjamin, were off on
their way down to Egypt to present
themselves to Joseph. 16 When Joseph
saw Benjamin with them, he told his
head steward, "Take these men into the
house, and have an animal slaughtered
and prepared, for they are to dine with
me at noon." 17 Doing as Joseph had or-
dered, the steward conducted the men
to Joseph's house. 18 But on being led to
his house, they became apprehensive.
"It must be," they thought, "on account
of the money put back in our bags the
first time, that we are taken inside; they
want to use it as a pretext to attack us
and take our donkeys and seize us as
slaves." 19 So they went up to Joseph's
head steward and talked to him at the
entrance of the house. 20* "If you please,
sir," they said, "we came down here
once before to procure food. 21* But
when we arrived at a night's encamp-
ment and opened our bags, there was
each man's money in the mouth of his
bag—our money in the full amount! We
have now brought it back. 22 We have
brought other money to procure food
with. We do not know who put the first
money in our bags." 23 "Be at ease," he
replied; "you have no need to fear. Your
God and the God of your father must
have put treasures in your bags for you.
As for your money, I received it." With
that, he led Simeon out to them.

24 The steward then brought the men
inside Joseph's house. He gave them
water to bathe their feet, and got fodder
for their donkeys. 25 Then they set out
their gifts to await Joseph's arrival at
noon, for they had heard that they were
to dine there. 26 When Joseph came
home, they presented him with the gifts
they had brought inside, while they
bowed down before him to the ground.
27* After inquiring how they were, he
asked them, "And how is your aged fa-
ther, of whom you spoke? Is he still in
good health?" 28 "Your servant our fa-
ther is thriving and still in good health,"
they said, as they bowed respectfully.
29* When Joseph's eye fell on his full
brother Benjamin, he asked, "Is this
your youngest brother, of whom you told
me?" Then he said to him, "May God
be gracious to you, my boy!" 30 With that,
Joseph had to hurry out, for he was so
overcome with affection for his brother

*

38: 37, 35.
43, 3: 44, 23.
5: 42, 20.
8: 42, 37.
9: 44, 32.
11: 45, 23.
20: 42, 3.
21: 42, 27f.
27: Tb 7, 4.
29: 42, 13.

†

43, 1-34: This chapter and the following one are from the Yahwist source, in which Judah, not Reuben as in the Elohist source, volunteers to go surety for Benjamin.

that he was on the verge of tears. He
went into a private room and wept there.
31 After washing his face, he reap-
peared and, now in control of himself,
gave the order, "Serve the meal." 32† It
was served separately to him, to the
brothers, and to the Egyptians who par-
took of his board. (Egyptians may not
eat with Hebrews; that is abhorrent to
them.) 33 When they were seated by his
directions according to their age, from
the oldest to the youngest, they looked
at one another in amazement; 34† and as
portions were brought to them from
Joseph's table, Benjamin's portion was
five times as large as anyone else's. So
they drank freely and made merry with
him.

CHAPTER 44

Final Test. 1† Then Joseph gave his
head steward these instructions: "Fill
the men's bags with as much food as
they can carry, and put each man's
money in the mouth of his bag. 2 In the
mouth of the youngest one's bag put also
my silver goblet, together with the
money for his rations." The steward car-
ried out Joseph's instructions. 3 At day-
break the men and their donkeys were
sent off. 4 They had not gone far out of
the city when Joseph said to his head
steward: "Go at once after the men!
When you overtake them, say to them,
'Why did you repay good with evil? Why
did you steal the silver goblet from me?
5† It is the very one from which my mas-
ter drinks and which he uses for divina-
tion. What you have done is wrong.'"
6 When the steward overtook them and
repeated these words to them, 7 they re-
monstrated with him: "How can my lord
say such things? Far be it from your
servants to do such a thing! 8 We even
brought back to you from the land of Ca-
naan the money that we found in the
mouths of our bags. Why, then, would
we steal silver or gold from your mas-
ter's house? 9 If any of your servants is
found to have the goblet, he shall die,
and as for the rest of us, we shall become
my lord's slaves." 10 But he replied,
"Even though it ought to be as you pro-
pose, only the one who is found to have
it shall become my slave, and the rest
of you shall be exonerated." 11 Then
each of them eagerly lowered his bag
to the ground and opened it; 12 and when
a search was made, starting with the
oldest and ending with the youngest, the
goblet turned up in Benjamin's bag. 13 At
this, they tore their clothes. Then, when
each man had reloaded his donkey, they
returned to the city.
14 As Judah and his brothers reentered
Joseph's house, he was still there; so
they flung themselves on the ground be-
fore him. 15 "How could you do such a
thing?" Joseph asked them. "You should
have known that such a man as I could
discover by divination what happened."
16† Judah replied: "What can we say to
my lord? How can we plead or how try
to prove our innocence? God has uncov-
ered your servants' guilt. Here we are,
then, the slaves of my lord—the rest of
us no less than the one in whose posses-
sion the goblet was found." 17 "Far be
it from me to act thus!" said Joseph.
"Only the one in whose possession the
goblet was found shall become my slave;
the rest of you may go back safe and
sound to your father."
18 Judah then stepped up to him and
said: "I beg you, my lord, let your ser-
vant speak earnestly to my lord, and do
not become angry with your servant, for
you are the equal of Pharaoh. 19† My
lord asked your servants, 'Have you a
father, or another brother?' 20* So we
said to my lord, 'We have an aged father,
and a young brother, the child of his old
age. This one's full brother is dead, and
since he is the only one by that mother
who is left, his father dotes on him.'
21 Then you told your servants, 'Bring
him down to me that my eyes may look
on him.' 22 We replied to my lord, 'The
boy cannot leave his father; his father
would die if he were to leave him.' 23* But
you told your servants, 'Unless your
youngest brother comes back with you,
you shall not come into my presence
again.' 24 When we returned to your
servant our father, we reported to him
the words of my lord.
25 "Later, our father told us to come
back and buy some food for the family.
26 So we reminded him, 'We cannot go
down there; only if our youngest brother
is with us can we go, for we may not
see the man if our youngest brother is
not with us.' 27 Then your servant our fa-
ther said to us, 'As you know, my wife
bore me two sons. 28* One of them, how-

*

44, 20: 42, 13.
23: 43, 3.
28: 37, 20.33.

†

43, 32: *Separately to him:* that Joseph did not eat with the other Egyptians was apparently a matter of rank.

43, 34: *Five times as large as:* probably an idiomatic expression for "much larger than."

44, 1f: Replacement of the money in the men's bags is probably a redactional addition here, taken from the Yahwist account of the first visit. It is only the goblet in Benjamin's bag, not any replaced money, that plays a part in the rest of the chapter.

44, 5: *Divination:* seeking omens through liquids poured into a cup or bowl was a common practice in the ancient Near East; cf v 15. Even though divination was frowned on in later Israel (Lv 19, 31), it is in this place an authentic touch which the sacred author does not hesitate to ascribe to Joseph, the wisest man in Egypt.

44, 16: *Guilt:* in trying to do away with Joseph when he was young.

44, 19: *My lord. . . your servants:* such frequently repeated expressions in Judah's speech show the formal court style used by a subject in speaking to a high official.

ever, disappeared, and I had to conclude
that he must have been torn to pieces
by wild beasts; I have not seen him since.
29 If you now take this one away from
me too, and some disaster befalls him,
you will send my white head down to
the nether world in grief.'
30 "If then the boy is not with us when
I go back to your servant my father,
whose very life is bound up with his, he
will die as soon as he sees that the boy
is missing; 31 and your servants will thus
send the white head of our father down
to the nether world in grief. 32* Besides,
I, your servant, got the boy from his fa-
ther by going surety for him, saying, 'If
I fail to bring him back to you, father,
you can hold it against me forever.'
33 Let me, your servant, therefore, re-
main in place of the boy as the slave of
my lord, and let the boy go back with
his brothers. 34 How could I go back to
my father if the boy were not with me?
I could not bear to see the anguish that
would overcome my father."

CHAPTER 45

The Truth Revealed. 1 Joseph could
no longer control himself in the presence
of all his attendants, so he cried out,
"Have everyone withdraw from me!"
Thus no one else was about when he
made himself known to his brothers.
2 But his sobs were so loud that the
Egyptians heard him, and so the news
reached Pharaoh's palace. 3* "I am Jo-
seph," he said to his brothers. "Is my
father still in good health?" But his
brothers could give him no answer, so
dumbfounded were they at him.
4 "Come closer to me," he told his
brothers. When they had done so, he
said: "I am your brother Joseph, whom
you once sold into Egypt. 5* But now do
not be distressed, and do not reproach
yourselves for having sold me here. It
was really for the sake of saving lives
that God sent me here ahead of you.
6 For two years now the famine has been
in the land, and for five more years till-
age will yield no harvest. 7 God, there-
fore, sent me on ahead of you to ensure
for you a remnant on earth and to save
your lives in an extraordinary deliver-
ance. 8† So it was not really you but God
who had me come here; and he has
made of me a father to Pharaoh, lord
of all his household, and ruler over the
whole land of Egypt.
9*† "Hurry back, then, to my father
and tell him: 'Thus says your son Joseph:
God has made me lord of all Egypt;
come to me without delay. 10† You will
settle in the region of Goshen, where you
will be near me—you and your children
and grandchildren, your flocks and
herds, and everything that you own.
11 Since five years of famine still lie
ahead, I will provide for you there, so
that you and your family and all that
are yours may not suffer want.'
12 Surely, you can see for yourselves,
and Benjamin can see for himself, that
it is I, Joseph, who am speaking to you.
13 Tell my father all about my high posi-
tion in Egypt and what you have seen.
But hurry and bring my father down
here." 14 Thereupon he flung himself on
the neck of his brother Benjamin and
wept, and Benjamin wept in his arms.
15 Joseph then kissed all his brothers,
crying over each of them; and only then
were his brothers able to talk with
him.
16 When the news reached Pharaoh's
palace that Joseph's brothers had come,
Pharaoh and his courtiers were pleased.
17 So Pharaoh told Joseph: "Say to your
brothers: 'This is what you shall do: Load
up your animals and go without delay
to the land of Canaan. 18* There get your
father and your families, and then come
back here to me; I will assign you the
best land in Egypt, where you will live
off the fat of the land.' 19 Instruct them
further: 'Do this. Take wagons from the
land of Egypt for your children and your
wives and to transport your father on
your way back here. 20 Do not be con-
cerned about your belongings, for the
best in the whole land of Egypt shall be
yours.' "
21 The sons of Israel acted accordingly.
Joseph gave them the wagons, as Pha-
raoh had ordered, and he supplied them
with provisions for the journey. 22 He
also gave to each of them fresh clothing,
but to Benjamin he gave three hundred
shekels of silver and five sets of gar-
ments. 23 Moreover, what he sent to his
father was ten jackasses loaded with the
finest products of Egypt and ten jennies
loaded with grain and bread and other
provisions for his journey. 24 As he sent
his brothers on their way, he told them,
"Let there be no recriminations on the
way."
25 So they left Egypt and made their
way to their father Jacob in the land of
Canaan. 26 When they told him, "Joseph
is still alive—in fact, it is he who is ruler

*

32: 43, 9. 15.
45, 3f: Acts 7, 13. 9: Acts 7, 14.
5: 50, 20; Sir 49, 18: Acts 7, 14.

†

45, 8: *Father to Pharaoh:* a term applied to a vizier in ancient Egypt.

45, 9-15: In these verses, as in 46, 31—47, 5a, all from the Yahwist source, Joseph in his own name invites his father and brothers to come to Egypt. Only after their arrival is Pharaoh informed of the fact. On the other hand, in 45, 16-20, from the Elohist source, it is Pharaoh himself who invites Joseph's kinsmen to migrate to his domain.

45, 10: *The region of Goshen:* modern Wadi Tumilat in the eastern part of the Nile Delta.

of all the land of Egypt," he was dumb-
founded; he could not believe them.
27 But when they recounted to him all
that Joseph had told them, and when he
saw the wagons that Joseph had sent for
his transport, the spirit of their father
Jacob revived. 28 "It is enough," said Is-
rael. "My son Joseph is still alive! I must
go and see him before I die."

CHAPTER 46

Migration to Egypt. 1 Israel set out
with all that was his. When he arrived
at Beer-sheba, he offered sacrifices to
the God of his father Isaac. 2 There God,
speaking to Israel in a vision by night,
called, "Jacob! Jacob!" "Here I am," he
answered. 3† Then he said: "I am God,
the God of your father. Do not be afraid
to go down to Egypt, for there I will
make you a great nation. 4 Not only will
I go down to Egypt with you; I will also
bring you back here, after Joseph has
closed your eyes."
5 So Jacob departed from Beer-sheba,
and the sons of Israel put their father
and their wives and children on the wag-
ons that Pharaoh had sent for his trans-
port. 6* They took with them their
livestock and the possessions they had
acquired in the land of Canaan. Thus Ja-
cob and all his descendants migrated to
Egypt. 7 His sons and his grandsons, his
daughters and his granddaughters—all
his descendants—he took with him to
Egypt.
8* These are the names of the Israel-
ites, Jacob and his descendants, who mi-
grated to Egypt.
Reuben, Jacob's first-born, 9*† and
the sons of Reuben: Hanoch, Pallu,
Hezron, and Carmi. 10* The sons of
Simeon: Nemuel, Jamin, Ohad, Jachin,
Zohar, and Shaul, son of a Canaanite
woman. 11* The sons of Levi: Gershon,
Kohath, and Merari. 12* The sons of Ju-
dah: Er, Onan, Shelah, Perez, and
Zerah—but Er and Onan had died in the
land of Canaan; and the sons of Perez
were Hezron and Hamul. 13* The sons
of Issachar: Tola, Puah, Jashub, and
Shimron. 14* The sons of Zebulun: Sered,
Elon, and Jahleel. 15 These were the sons
whom Leah bore to Jacob in Paddan-
aram, along with his daughter Dinah—
thirty-three persons in all, male and fe-
male.
16* The sons of Gad: Zephon, Haggi,
Shuni, Ezbon, Eri, Arod, and Areli.
17* The sons of Asher: Imnah, Ishvah,
Ishvi, and Beriah, with their sister
Serah; and the sons of Beriah: Heber and
Malchiel. 18 These were the descendants
of Zilpah, whom Laban had given to his
daughter Leah; these she bore to Ja-
cob—sixteen persons in all.
19 The sons of Jacob's wife Rachel: Jo-
seph and Benjamin. 20* In the land of
Egypt Joseph became the father of Ma-
nasseh and Ephraim, whom Asenath,
daughter of Potiphera, priest of Heliopo-
lis, bore to him. 21* The sons of Benja-
min: Bela, Becher, Ashbel, Gera,
Naaman, Ahiram, Shupham, Hupham,
and Ard. 22 These were the sons whom
Rachel bore to Jacob—fourteen persons
in all.
23* The sons of Dan: Hushim. 24* The
sons of Naphtali: Jahzeel, Guni, Jezer,
and Shillem. 25 These were the sons of
Bilhah, whom Laban had given to his
daughter Rachel; these she bore to Ja-
cob—seven persons in all.
26* Jacob's people who migrated to
Egypt—his direct descendants, not
counting the wives of Jacob's sons—
numbered sixty-six persons in all.
27*† Together with Joseph's sons who
were born to him in Egypt—two per-
sons—all the people comprising Jacob's
family who had come to Egypt
amounted to seventy persons in all.
28 Israel had sent Judah ahead to Jo-
seph, so that he might meet him in
Goshen. On his arrival in the region of
Goshen, 29 Joseph hitched the horses to
his chariot and rode to meet his father
Israel in Goshen. As soon as he saw him,
he flung himself on his neck and wept
a long time in his arms. 30 And Israel
said to Joseph, "At last I can die, now
that I have seen for myself that Joseph
is still alive."
31 Joseph then said to his brothers and
his father's household: "I will go and in-
form Pharaoh, telling him: 'My brothers
and my father's household, whose home
is in the land of Canaan, have come to

*

46, 6: Ex 1, 1; Jos 24, 4; Jdt 5, 10; Acts 7, 15.
8: Ex 1, 2.
9: Ex 6, 14; Nm 26, 5; 1 Chr 5, 3.
10: Ex 6, 15; Nm 26, 12; 1 Chr 4, 24.
11: Ex 6, 16; Nm 3, 17; 26, 57; 1 Chr 6, 1.
12: 38, 3-10, 29f; Nm 26, 19; Rv 4, 18-22; 1 Chr 2, 5.
13: Nm 26, 23f; 1 Chr 7, 1.
14: Nm 26, 26.
16: Nm 26, 15f.
17: Nm 26, 44; 1 Chr 7, 30f.
20: 41, 50; Nm 26, 28.35.
21: Nm 26, 38; 1 Chr 7, 6; 8, 1-4.
23: Nm 26, 42.
24: Nm 26, 48f; 1 Chr 7, 13.
26: Ex 1, 5.
27: Ex 1, 5; Dt 10, 22; Acts 7, 14.

†

46, 3: *I am God:* more precisely according to the Hebrew text, "I am El." "El" is here a divine name, not the common noun "god."

46, 9-27: This genealogical list has here been inserted by a redactor who bases it on the clan lists (Nm 26, 5-50) at the time of Moses. Therefore it includes some of Jacob's grandchildren, who would hardly have been born when Joseph was still a relatively young man. The number *fourteen* (v 22) is based on a garbled version of the genealogical list.

46, 27: *Seventy persons:* either to be understood as a round number, or arrived at by including Jacob and Joseph with the preceding persons, who add up to sixty-eight.

me. 32 The men are shepherds, having
long been keepers of livestock; and they
have brought with them their flocks and
herds, as well as everything else they
own.' 33 So when Pharaoh summons you
and asks what your occupation is, 34 you
must answer, 'We your servants, like our
ancestors, have been keepers of live-
stock from the beginning until now,' in
order that you may stay in the region
of Goshen, since all shepherds are
abhorrent to the Egyptians."

CHAPTER 47

Settlement in Goshen. 1 Joseph went
and told Pharaoh, "My father and my
brothers have come from the land of Ca-
naan, with their flocks and herds and
everything else they own; and they are
now in the region of Goshen." 2 He then
presented to Pharaoh five of his brothers
whom he had selected from their full
number. 3 When Pharaoh asked them
what their occupation was, they an-
swered, "We your servants, like our an-
cestors, are shepherds. 4* We have
come," they continued, "in order to stay
in this country, for there is no pasture
for your servants' flocks in the land of
Canaan, so severe has the famine been
there. Please, therefore, let your ser-
vants settle in the region of Goshen."
5 Pharaoh said to Joseph, "They may
settle in the region of Goshen; and if you
know any of them to be qualified, you
may put them in charge of my own live-
stock."

Thus, when Jacob and his sons came
to Joseph in Egypt, and Pharaoh, king
of Egypt, heard about it, Pharaoh said
to Joseph, "Now that your father and
brothers have come to you, 6 the land of
Egypt is at your disposal; settle your fa-
ther and brothers in the pick of the
land." 7 Then Joseph brought his father
Jacob and presented him to Pharaoh.
After Jacob had paid his respects to
Pharaoh, 8 Pharaoh asked him, "How
many years have you lived?" 9† Jacob
replied: "The years I have lived as a
wayfarer amount to a hundred and
thirty. Few and hard have been these
years of my life, and they do not com-
pare with the years that my ancestors
lived as wayfarers." 10 Then Jacob bade
Pharaoh farewell and withdrew from his
presence.

11† As Pharaoh had ordered, Joseph
settled his father and brothers and gave
them holdings in Egypt on the pick of
the land, in the region of Rameses.
12 And Joseph sustained his father and
brothers and his father's whole house-
hold, down to the youngest, with food.

Joseph's Land Policy. 13 Since there
was no food in any country because of
the extreme severity of the famine, and
the lands of Egypt and Canaan were lan-
guishing from hunger, 14 Joseph gath-
ered in, as payment for the rations that
were being dispensed, all the money that
was to be found in Egypt and Canaan,
and he put it in Pharaoh's palace.
15 When all the money in Egypt and Ca-
naan was spent, all the Egyptians came
to Joseph, pleading, "Give us food or we
shall perish under your eyes; for our
money is gone." 16 "Since your money
is gone," replied Joseph, "give me your
livestock, and I will sell you bread in re-
turn for your livestock." 17 So they
brought their livestock to Joseph, and
he sold them food in return for their
horses, their flocks of sheep and herds
of cattle, and their donkeys. Thus he got
them through that year with bread in
exchange for all their livestock. 18 When
that year ended, they came to him in
the following one and said: "We cannot
hide from my lord that, with our money
spent and our livestock made over to my
lord, there is nothing left to put at my
lord's disposal except our bodies and our
farm land. 19 Why should we and our
land perish before your very eyes? Take
us and our land in exchange for food,
and we will become Pharaoh's slaves
and our land his property; only give us
seed, that we may survive and not per-
ish, and that our land may not turn into
a waste."

20 Thus Joseph acquired all the farm
land of Egypt for Pharaoh, since with
the famine too much for them to bear,
every Egyptian sold his field; so the land
passed over to Pharaoh, 21 and the peo-
ple were reduced to slavery, from one
end of Egypt's territory to the other.
22 Only the priests' lands Joseph did not
take over. Since the priests had a fixed
allowance from Pharaoh and lived off
the allowance Pharaoh had granted
them, they did not have to sell their land.

23 Joseph told the people: "Now that I
have acquired you and your land for
Pharaoh, here is your seed for sowing
the land. 24 But when the harvest is in,
you must give a fifth of it to Pharaoh,
while you keep four-fifths as seed for
your fields and as food for yourselves
and your families [and as food for your
children]." 25 "You have saved our
lives!" they answered. "We are grateful

*

47, 4: Ex 23, 9; Dt 23, 8.

†

47, 9: *Wayfarer . . . wayfarers:* man is merely a sojourner on earth; cf Ps 39, 13.

47, 11: *The region of Rameses:* same as the region of Goshen; see note on 45, 10. The name Rameses, however, is an anachronism, since this royal name did not come into use before the end of the fourteenth century B.C., long after the time of Joseph.

to my lord that we can be Pharaoh's
slaves." 26 Thus Joseph made it a law for
the land in Egypt, which is still in force,
that a fifth of its produce should go to
Pharaoh. Only the land of the priests did
not pass over to Pharaoh.

***Jacob Blesses Ephraim and
Manasseh.*** 27* Thus Israel settled in the
land of Egypt, in the region of Goshen.
There they acquired property, were fer-
tile, and increased greatly. 28 Jacob lived
in the land of Egypt for seventeen years;
the span of his life came to a hundred
and forty-seven years. 29 When the time
approached for Israel to die, he called
his son Joseph and said to him: "If you
really wish to please me, put your hand
under my thigh as a sign of your con-
stant loyalty to me; do not let me be bur-
ied in Egypt. 30* When I lie down with
my ancestors, have me taken out of
Egypt and buried in their burial place."
31† "I will do as you say," he replied. But
his father demanded, "Swear it to me!"
So Joseph swore to him. Then Israel
bowed at the head of the bed.

CHAPTER 48

1 Some time afterward, Joseph was in-
formed, "Your father is failing." So he
took along with him his two sons, Ma-
nasseh and Ephraim. 2 When Jacob was
told, "Your son Joseph has come to
you," he rallied his strength and sat up
in bed.

3*† Jacob then said to Joseph: "God
Almighty appeared to me at Luz in the
land of Canaan, and blessing me, 4 he
said, 'I will make you fertile and numer-
ous and raise you into an assembly of
tribes, and I will give this land to your
descendants after you as a permanent
possession.' 5 Your two sons, therefore,
who were born to you in the land of
Egypt before I joined you here, shall be
mine; Ephraim and Manasseh shall be
mine as much as Reuben and Simeon
are mine. 6 Progeny born to you after
them shall remain yours; but their heri-
tage shall be recorded in the names of
their two brothers. 7*† I do this because,
when I was returning from Paddan,
your mother Rachel died, to my sorrow,
during the journey in Canaan, while we
were still a short distance from Ephrath;
and I buried her there on the way to
Ephrath [that is, Bethlehem]."

8 When Israel saw Joseph's sons, he
asked, "Who are these?" 9 "They are my
sons," Joseph answered his father,
"whom God has given me here." "Bring
them to me," said his father, "that I may
bless them." 10 (Now Israel's eyes were
dim from age, and he could not see well.)
When Joseph brought his sons close to
him, he kissed and embraced them.
11 Then Israel said to Joseph, "I never
expected to see your face again, and now
God has allowed me to see your descen-
dants as well!"

12 Joseph removed them from his fa-
ther's knees and bowed down before him
with his face to the ground. 13 Then Jo-
seph took the two, Ephraim with his
right hand, to Israel's left, and Manas-
seh with his left hand, to Israel's right,
and led them to him. 14 But Israel, cross-
ing his hands, put out his right hand and
laid it on the head of Ephraim, although
he was the younger, and his left hand
on the head of Manasseh, although he
was the first-born. 15* Then he blessed
them with these words:

"May the God in whose ways
my fathers Abraham and Isaac
walked,
The God who has been my shepherd
from my birth to this day,
16 The Angel who has delivered me
from all harm,
bless these boys
That in them my name be recalled,
and the names of my fathers
Abraham and Isaac,
And they may become teeming mul-
titudes
upon the earth!"

17 When Joseph saw that his father had
laid his right hand on Ephraim's head,
this seemed wrong to him; so he took
hold of his father's hand, to remove it
from Ephraim's head to Manasseh's,
18 saying, "That is not right, father; the
other one is the first-born; lay your right
hand on his head!" 19 But his father re-
sisted. "I know it, son," he said, "I know.
That one too shall become a tribe, and
he too shall be great. Nevertheless, his
younger brother shall surpass him, and
his descendants shall become a multi-
tude of nations." 20* So when he blessed
them that day and said, "By you shall
the people of Israel pronounce blessings;
may they say, 'God make you like
Ephraim and Manasseh,'" he placed
Ephraim before Manasseh.

21 Then Israel said to Joseph: "I am

*

27: Ex 1, 7.
30: 50, 5.
48, 3f: 28, 12-15; 35, 6.
7: 35, 19.
15: Heb 11, 21.
20: Heb 11, 21.

†

47, 31: *Israel bowed at the head of the bed:* meaning perhaps that he gave a nod of assent and appreciation as he lay on his bed. By reading with different vowels the Hebrew word for "bed," the Greek version translated it as "staff," and understood the phrase to mean that he bowed in worship, leaning on the top of his staff; it is thus quoted in Heb 11, 21.

48, 3: *Luz:* an older name of Bethel (28, 19).

48, 7: Since her early death prevented Rachel from bearing more than two sons, Jacob feels justified in treating her two grandsons as if they were her own offspring.

about to die. But God will be with you
and will restore you to the land of your
fathers. 22*† As for me, I give to you, as
to the one above his brothers, Shechem,
which I captured from the Amorites with
my sword and bow."

CHAPTER 49

Jacob's Testament. 1 Jacob called his
sons and said: "Gather around, that I
may tell you what is to happen to you
in days to come.

2 "Assemble and listen, sons of Jacob,
listen to Israel, your father.

3 "You, Reuben, my first-born,
my strength and the first fruit of my manhood,
excelling in rank and excelling in power!
4* Unruly as water, you shall no longer excel,
for you climbed into your father's bed
and defiled my couch to my sorrow.

5† "Simeon and Levi, brothers indeed,
weapons of violence are their knives.
6* Let not my soul enter their council,
or my spirit be joined with their company;
For in their fury they slew men,
in their willfulness they maimed oxen.
7 Cursed be their fury so fierce,
and their rage so cruel!
I will scatter them in Jacob,
disperse them throughout Israel.

8 "You, Judah, shall your brothers praise
—your hand on the neck of your enemies;
the sons of your father shall bow down to you.
9* Judah, like a lion's whelp,
you have grown up on prey, my son.
He crouches like a lion recumbent,
the king of beasts—who would dare rouse him?
10† The scepter shall never depart from Judah,
or the mace from between his legs,
While tribute is brought to him,
and he receives the peoples' homage.
11† He tethers his donkey to the vine,
his purebred ass to the choicest stem.
In wine he washes his garments,
his robe in the blood of grapes.
12 His eyes are darker than wine,
and his teeth are whiter than milk.

13 "Zebulun shall dwell by the seashore
[This means a shore for ships],
and his flank shall be based on Sidon.

14 "Issachar is a rawboned ass,
crouching between the saddlebags.
15 When he saw how good a settled life was,
and how pleasant the country,
He bent his shoulder to the burden
and became a toiling serf.

16† "Dan shall achieve justice for his kindred
like any other tribe of Israel.
17 Let Dan be a serpent by the roadside,
a horned viper by the path,
That bites the horse's heel,
so that the rider tumbles backward.

18 "[I long for your deliverance, O LORD!]

19† "Gad shall be raided by raiders,
but he shall raid at their heels.

20 "Asher's produce is rich,
and he shall furnish dainties for kings.

21 "Naphtali is a hind let loose
which brings forth lovely fawns.

22 "Joseph is a wild colt,
a wild colt by a spring,
a wild ass on a hillside.
23 Harrying and attacking,
the archers opposed him;
24 But each one's bow remained stiff,
as their arms were unsteady,
By the power of the Mighty One of Jacob,

* 22: Jos 17, 14.17f; Jn 4, 5. 49, 4: 35, 22; 1 Chr 5, 1f. 6: 34, 25. 9: 1 Chr 5, 2.

†

48, 22: Both the meaning of the Hebrew and the historical reference in this verse are obscure. By taking the Hebrew word for Shechem as a common noun meaning shoulder or mountain slope, some translators render the verse, "I give you one portion more than your brothers, which I captured. . . ." The reference may be to the capture of Shechem by the sons of Jacob (34, 24-29). Shechem lay near the border separating the tribal territory of Manasseh from that of Ephraim (Jos 16, 4-9; 17, 1f.7).

49, 5: *Knives:* if this is the meaning of the obscure Hebrew word here, the reference may be to the knives used in circumcising the men of Shechem (34, 24; cf Jos 5, 2).

49, 10: *While tribute is brought to him:* this translation is based on a slight change in the Hebrew text, which, as it stands, would seem to mean, "until he comes to Shiloh." A somewhat different reading of the Hebrew text would be, "until he comes to whom it belongs." This last has been traditionally understood in a Messianic sense. In any case, the passage foretells the supremacy of the tribe of Judah, which found its fulfillment in the Davidic dynasty and ultimately in the Messianic Son of David, Jesus Christ.

49, 11: *In wine . . . the blood of grapes:* Judah's clothes are poetically pictured as soaked with grape juice from trampling in the wine press, the rich vintage of his land; cf Is 63, 2.

49, 16: In Hebrew the verb for *achieve justice* is from the same root as the name *Dan.*

49, 19: In Hebrew there is a certain assonance between the name *Gad* and the words for "raided," "raiders" and "raid."

because of the Shepherd, the Rock
of Israel,
25† The God of your father, who helps
you,
God Almighty, who blesses you,
With the blessings of the heavens
above,
the blessings of the abyss that
crouches below,
The blessings of breasts and womb,
26 the blessings of fresh grain and
blossoms,
The blessings of the everlasting
mountains,
the delights of the eternal hills.
May they rest on the head of Joseph,
on the brow of the prince among
his brothers.

27 "Benjamin is a ravenous wolf;
mornings he devours the prey,
and evenings he distributes the
spoils."

Farewell and Death. 28 All these are
the twelve tribes of Israel, and this is
what their father said about them, as he
bade them farewell and gave to each of
them an appropriate message. 29 Then
he gave them this charge: "Since I am
about to be taken to my kindred, bury
me with my fathers in the cave that lies
in the field of Ephron the Hittite, 30* the
cave in the field of Machpelah, facing
on Mamre, in the land of Canaan, the
field that Abraham bought from Ephron
the Hittite for a burial ground. 31 There
Abraham and his wife Sarah are buried,
and so are Isaac and his wife Rebekah,
and there, too, I buried Leah—32 the field
and the cave in it that had been purchased from the Hittites."
33 When Jacob had finished giving
these instructions to his sons, he drew
his feet into the bed, breathed his last,
and was taken to his kindred.

CHAPTER 50

Jacob's Funeral. 1 Joseph threw him-
self on his father's face and wept over
him as he kissed him. 2 Then he ordered
the physicians in his service to embalm
his father. When they embalmed Israel,
3 they spent forty days at it, for that is
the full period of embalming; and the
Egyptians mourned him for seventy
days. 4 When that period of mourning
was over, Joseph spoke to Pharaoh's
courtiers. "Please do me this favor," he
said, "and convey to Pharaoh this re-
quest of mine. 5* Since my father, at the
point of death, made me promise on oath
to bury him in the tomb that he had prepared for himself in the land of Canaan,
may I go up there to bury my father and
then come back?" 6 Pharaoh replied,
"Go and bury your father, as he made
you promise on oath."
7 So Joseph left to bury his father; and
with him went all of Pharaoh's officials
who were senior members of his court
and all the other dignitaries of Egypt,
8 as well as Joseph's whole household,
his brothers, and his father's household;
only their children and their flocks and
herds were left in the region of Goshen.
9 Chariots, too, and charioteers went up
with him; it was a very large retinue.
10† When they arrived at Goren-
ha-atad, which is beyond the Jordan,
they held there a very great and solemn
memorial service; and Joseph observed
seven days of mourning for his father.
11 When the Canaanites who inhabited
the land saw the mourning at Goren-
ha-atad, they said, "This is a solemn fu-
neral the Egyptians are having." That
is why the place was named Abel-
mizraim. It is beyond the Jordan.
12 Thus Jacob's sons did for him as he
had instructed them. 13* They carried
him to the land of Canaan and buried
him in the cave in the field of Machpelah,
facing on Mamre, the field that Abra-
ham had bought for a burial ground
from Ephron the Hittite.
14 After Joseph had buried his father
he returned to Egypt, together with his
brothers and all who had gone up with
him for the burial of his father.

Plea for Forgiveness. 15 Now that
their father was dead, Joseph's brothers
became fearful and thought, "Suppose
Joseph has been nursing a grudge
against us and now plans to pay us back
in full for all the wrong we did him!"
16 So they approached Joseph and said:
"Before your father died, he gave us
these instructions: 17 'You shall say to
Joseph, Jacob begs you to forgive the
criminal wrongdoing of your brothers,
who treated you so cruelly.' Please,
therefore, forgive the crime that we, the
servants of your father's God, commit-
ted." When they spoke these words to
him, Joseph broke into tears. 18 Then his
brothers proceeded to fling themselves
down before him and said, "Let us be
your slaves!" 19 But Joseph replied to
them: "Have no fear. Can I take the

---

* 30: 23, 17. 50, 5: 47, 30. 13: 23, 16; Acts 7, 16.

---

† 49, 25f: A very similar description of the agricultural riches of the tribal land of Joseph is given in Dt 33, 13-16.

50, 10f: *Goren-ha-atad:* "Threshing Floor of the Brambles." *Abel-mizraim:* although the name really means "watercourse of the Egyptians," it is understood here, by a play on the first part of the term, to mean "mourning of the Egyptians." The site has not been identified through either reading of the name. But it is difficult to see why the mourning rites should have been held in the land *beyond the Jordan* when the burial was at Hebron. Perhaps an earlier form of the story placed the mourning rites beyond the wadi of Egypt, the traditional boundary between Canaan and Egypt (Nm 34, 5; Jos 15, 4.47).

place of God? [20]* Even though you
meant harm to me, God meant it for
good, to achieve his present end, the sur-
vival of many people. [21]* Therefore have
no fear. I will provide for you and for
your children." By thus speaking kindly
to them, he reassured them.
[22] Joseph remained in Egypt, together
with his father's family. He lived a hun-
dred and ten years. [23]* He saw
Ephraim's children to the third genera-
tion, and the children of Manasseh's son
Machir were also born on Joseph's
knees.

Death of Joseph. [24]* Joseph said to his
brothers: "I am about to die. God will
surely take care of you and lead you out
of this land to the land that he promised
on oath to Abraham, Isaac and Jacob."
[25]* Then, putting the sons of Israel under
oath, he continued, "When God thus
takes care of you, you must bring my
bones up with you from this place."
[26]* Joseph died at the age of a hundred
and ten. He was embalmed and laid to
rest in a coffin in Egypt.

20: 45, 5; Sir 49, 15.
21: 47, 12.
23: Nm 32, 39; Jos 17, 1.
24: Ex 3, 8; Jos 24, 32; Heb 11, 22.
25: Ex 13, 19; Heb 11, 22.
26: Sir 49, 15.

The Book of

EXODUS

The second book of the Pentateuch is called Exodus from the Greek word for "departure," because the central event narrated in it is the departure of the Israelites from Egypt. It continues the history of the chosen people from the point where the Book of Genesis leaves off. It recounts the oppression by the Egyptians of the ever-increasing descendants of Jacob and their miraculous deliverance by God through Moses, who led them across the Red Sea to Mount Sinai where they entered into a special covenant with the Lord.

These events were of prime importance to the chosen people, for they became thereby an independent nation and enjoyed a unique relationship with God. Through Moses God gave to the Israelites at Mount Sinai the "law": the moral, civil and ritual legislation by which they were to become a holy people, in whom the promise of a Savior for all mankind would be fulfilled.

The principal divisions of Exodus are:

I: The Israelites in Egypt (1, 1—12, 36)
II: The Exodus from Egypt and the Journey to Sinai (12, 37—18, 27)
III: The Covenant at Mount Sinai (19, 1—24, 18)
IV: The Dwelling and Its Furnishings (25, 1—40, 38)

I: THE ISRAELITES IN EGYPT

CHAPTER 1

Jacob's Descendants in Egypt.
1† These are the names of the sons of
Israel who, accompanied by their house-
holds, migrated with Jacob into Egypt:
2† Reuben, Simeon, Levi and Judah;
3 Issachar, Zebulun and Benjamin; 4 Dan
and Naphtali; Gad and Asher. 5*† The
total number of the direct descendants
of Jacob was seventy. Joseph was al-
ready in Egypt.
6* Now Joseph and all his brothers and
that whole generation died. 7 But the Is-
raelites were fruitful and prolific. They
became so numerous and strong that the
land was filled with them.
The Oppression. 8*† Then a new king,
who knew nothing of Joseph, came to
power in Egypt. 9 He said to his subjects,
"Look how numerous and powerful the
Israelite people are growing, more so
than we ourselves! 10 Come, let us deal
shrewdly with them to stop their in-
crease; otherwise, in time of war they
too may join our enemies to fight against
us, and so leave our country."
11*† Accordingly, taskmasters were
set over the Israelites to oppress them
with forced labor. Thus they had to build
for Pharaoh the supply cities of Pithom
and Raamses. 12 Yet the more they were
oppressed, the more they multiplied and
spread. The Egyptians, then, dreaded
the Israelites 13 and reduced them to
cruel slavery, 14† making life bitter for
them with hard work in mortar and
brick and all kinds of field work—the
whole cruel fate of slaves.
Command to the Midwives. 15 The
king of Egypt told the Hebrew midwives,
one of whom was called Shiphrah and
the other Puah, 16† "When you act as
midwives for the Hebrew women and
see them giving birth, if it is a boy, kill
him; but if it is a girl, she may live."
17 The midwives, however, feared God;
they did not do as the king of Egypt had
ordered them, but let the boys live. 18 So
the king summoned the midwives and
asked them, "Why have you acted thus,
allowing the boys to live?" 19 The mid-
wives answered Pharaoh, "The Hebrew
women are not like the Egyptian

---

*

1, 5: Gn 46, 27; Dt 10, 22; Acts 7, 14.	6: Gn 50, 26. 8ff: Acts 7, 18. 11: Dt 26, 6.

†

1, 1: *Sons of Israel:* here literally the first-generation sons of Jacob. Cf v 5. However, beginning with 1, 7 the same Hebrew phrase refers to the more remote descendants of Jacob; hence, from there on, it is ordinarily rendered as "the Israelites." *Households:* the family in its fullest sense, including wives, children and servants.

1, 2: The sons of Jacob are listed here according to the respective mothers. Cf Gn 29, 31; 30, 20; 35, 16-26.

1, 5: *Direct descendants:* literally, persons coming from the loins of Jacob; hence, wives and servants are here excluded. Cf Gn 46, 26.

1, 8: *Who knew nothing of Joseph:* this king ignored the services that Joseph had rendered to Egypt.

1, 11: *Pharaoh:* not a personal name, but a title common to all the kings of Egypt.

1, 14: *Mortar:* either the wet clay with which the bricks were made, as in Na 3, 14, or the cement used between the bricks in building, as in Gn 11, 3.

1, 16: *And see them giving birth:* the Hebrew text is uncertain.

women. They are robust and give birth before the midwife arrives." 20 Therefore God dealt well with the midwives. The people, too, increased and grew strong. 21 And because the midwives feared God, he built up families for them. 22*† Pharaoh then commanded all his subjects, "Throw into the river every boy that is born to the Hebrews, but you may let all the girls live."

CHAPTER 2

Birth and Adoption of Moses. 1* Now a certain man of the house of Levi married a Levite woman, 2* who conceived and bore a son. Seeing that he was a goodly child, she hid him for three months. 3† When she could hide him no longer, she took a papyrus basket, daubed it with bitumen and pitch, and putting the child in it, placed it among the reeds on the river bank. 4 His sister stationed herself at a distance to find out what would happen to him.

5 Pharaoh's daughter came down to the river to bathe, while her maids walked along the river bank. Noticing the basket among the reeds, she sent her handmaid to fetch it. 6 On opening it, she looked, and lo, there was a baby boy, crying! She was moved with pity for him and said, "It is one of the Hebrews' children." 7 Then his sister asked Pharaoh's daughter, "Shall I go and call one of the Hebrew women to nurse the child for you?" 8 "Yes, do so," she answered. So the maiden went and called the child's own mother. 9 Pharaoh's daughter said to her, "Take this child and nurse it for me, and I will repay you." The woman therefore took the child and nursed it. 10*† When the child grew, she brought him to Pharaoh's daughter, who adopted him as her son and called him Moses; for she said, "I drew him out of the water."

Moses' Flight to Midian. 11*† On one occasion, after Moses had grown up, when he visited his kinsmen and witnessed their forced labor, he saw an Egyptian striking a Hebrew, one of his own kinsmen. 12 Looking about and seeing no one, he slew the Egyptian and hid him in the sand. 13 The next day he went out again, and now two Hebrews were fighting! So he asked the culprit, "Why are you striking your fellow Hebrew?" 14 But he replied, "Who has appointed you ruler and judge over us? Are you thinking of killing me as you killed the Egyptian?" Then Moses became afraid and thought, "The affair must certainly be known."

15* Pharaoh, too, heard of the affair and sought to put him to death. But Moses fled from him and stayed in the land of Midian. As he was seated there by a well, 16 seven daughters of a priest of Midian came to draw water and fill the troughs to water their father's flock. 17 But some shepherds came and drove them away. Then Moses got up and defended them and watered their flock. 18† When they returned to their father Reuel, he said to them, "How is it you have returned so soon today?" 19† They answered, "An Egyptian saved us from the interference of the shepherds. He even drew water for us and watered the flock!" 20 "Where is the man?" he asked his daughters. "Why did you leave him there? Invite him to have something to eat." 21 Moses agreed to live with him, and the man gave him his daughter Zipporah in marriage. 22*† She bore him a son, whom he named Gershom; for he said, "I am a stranger in a foreign land."

The Burning Bush. 23* A long time passed, during which the king of Egypt died. Still the Israelites groaned and cried out because of their slavery. As their cry for release went up to God, 24* he heard their groaning and was mindful of his covenant with Abraham, Isaac and Jacob. 25 He saw the Israelites and knew. . . .

CHAPTER 3

1† Meanwhile Moses was tending the flock of his father-in-law Jethro, the priest of Midian. Leading the flock across the desert, he came to Horeb, the

*

22: Acts 7, 19.
2, 1: 6, 20; Nm 26, 59.
2: Acts 7, 20; Heb 11, 23.
10: Acts 7, 21; Heb 11, 24.
11-14: Acts 7, 23-28.
15: Acts 7, 29; Heb 11, 27.
22: 18, 3.
23: 3, 7.9; Dt 26, 7.
24: 6, 5; Pss 105, 8f; 106, 44f.

†

1, 22: *The river:* the Nile, which was "the" river for the Egyptians.

2, 3: *Basket:* literally, "chest" or "ark"; the same Hebrew word is used in Gn 6, 14 for Noah's ark. Here, however, the chest was made of papyrus stalks.

2, 10: *When the child grew:* probably when he was weaned or a little later. *Moses:* in Hebrew, *Mosheh;* the Hebrew word for "draw out" is *mashah.* This explanation of the name is not intended as a scientific etymology but as a play on words. The name is probably derived from an Egyptian word for "has been born," referring the birth to a god thought to be its sponsor.

2, 11: *After Moses had grown up:* Acts 7, 23 indicates that this was after an interval of nearly forty years. Cf Ex 7, 7. *Striking:* probably in the sense of "flogging"; according to some, "slaying."

2, 18: *Reuel:* he was also called Jethro. Cf 3, 1; 4, 18; 18, 1.

2, 19: *An Egyptian:* Moses was probably wearing Egyptian dress, or spoke Egyptian to Reuel's daughters.

2, 22: *Gershom:* the name is explained as if it came from the Hebrew word *ger,* "stranger," joined to the Hebrew word *sham,* "there." Some Greek and Latin manuscripts add here a passage taken from 18, 4.

3, 1: *The mountain of God:* probably given this designation because of the divine apparitions which took place there, such as on this occasion and when the Israelites were there after the departure from Egypt.

mountain of God. 2*† There an angel of
the LORD appeared to him in fire flaming
out of a bush. As he looked on, he was
surprised to see that the bush, though
on fire, was not consumed. 3 So Moses
decided, "I must go over to look at this
remarkable sight, and see why the bush
is not burned."

The Call of Moses. 4 When the LORD
saw him coming over to look at it more
closely, God called out to him from the
bush, "Moses! Moses!" He answered,
"Here I am." 5* God said, "Come no
nearer! Remove the sandals from your
feet, for the place where you stand is
holy ground. 6*† I am the God of your
father," he continued, "the God of Abra-
ham, the God of Isaac, the God of Ja-
cob." Moses hid his face, for he was
afraid to look at God. 7 But the LORD
said, "I have witnessed the affliction of
my people in Egypt and have heard
their cry of complaint against their slave
drivers, so I know well what they are
suffering. 8*† Therefore I have come
down to rescue them from the hands of
the Egyptians and lead them out of that
land into a good and spacious land, a
land flowing with milk and honey, the
country of the Canaanites, Hittites, Am-
orites, Perizzites, Hivites and Jebusites.
9 So indeed the cry of the Israelites has
reached me, and I have truly noted that
the Egyptians are oppressing them.
10 Come, now! I will send you to Pharaoh
to lead my people, the Israelites, out of
Egypt."

11† But Moses said to God, "Who am
I that I should go to Pharaoh and lead
the Israelites out of Egypt?" 12 He an-
swered, "I will be with you; and this shall
be your proof that it is I who have sent
you: when you bring my people out of
Egypt, you will worship God on this very
mountain." 13 "But," said Moses to God,
"when I go to the Israelites and say to
them, 'The God of your fathers has sent
me to you,' if they ask me, 'What is his
name?' what am I to tell them?" 14† God
replied, "I am who am." Then he added,
"This is what you shall tell the Israelites:
I AM sent me to you."

15* God spoke further to Moses, "Thus
shall you say to the Israelites: The LORD,
the God of your fathers, the God of
Abraham, the God of Isaac, the God of
Jacob, has sent me to you.

"This is my name forever;
this is my title for all generations.

16† "Go and assemble the elders of the
Israelites, and tell them: The LORD, the
God of your fathers, the God of Abra-
ham, Isaac and Jacob, has appeared to
me and said: I am concerned about you
and about the way you are being treated
in Egypt; 17 so I have decided to lead you
up out of the misery of Egypt into the
land of the Canaanites, Hittites, Amo-
rites, Perizzites, Hivites and Jebusites,
a land flowing with milk and honey.

18* "Thus they will heed your message.
Then you and the elders of Israel shall
go to the king of Egypt and say to him:
The LORD, the God of the Hebrews, has
sent us word. Permit us, then, to go a
three days' journey in the desert, that
we may offer sacrifice to the LORD, our
God.

19 "Yet I know that the king of Egypt
will not allow you to go unless he is
forced. 20 I will stretch out my hand,
therefore, and smite Egypt by doing all
kinds of wondrous deeds there. After
that he will send you away. 21* I will even
make the Egyptians so well-disposed to-
ward this people that, when you leave,
you will not go empty-handed. 22† Every
woman shall ask her neighbor and her
house guest for silver and gold articles
and for clothing to put on your sons and
daughters. Thus you will despoil the
Egyptians."

CHAPTER 4

Confirmation of Moses' Mission.
1 "But," objected Moses, "suppose they
will not believe me, nor listen to my plea?

*

3, 2-10: Acts 7, 30-35.
5: Jos 5, 15.
6: 4, 5; Mt 22, 32; Mk 12, 36; Lk 20, 37.
8f: Gn 15, 19ff.
15: Ps 135, 13.
18: 5, 3.
21f: 11, 2f; 12, 35f.

†

3, 2: *An angel of the LORD:* the visual form under which God appeared and spoke to men is referred to indifferently in some Old Testament texts either as God's angel or as God himself. Cf Gn 16, 7.13; Ex 14, 19.24f; Nm 22, 22-35; Jgs 6, 11-18.

3, 6: The appearance of God caused fear of death, since it was believed that no one could see God and live; cf Gn 32, 30. *The God of Abraham . . . Jacob:* cited by Christ in proof of the resurrection since the patriarchs, long dead, live on in God who is the God of the living. Cf Mt 22, 32; Mk 12, 26; Lk 20, 37.

3, 8: *I have come down:* a figure of speech signifying an extraordinary divine intervention in human affairs. Cf Gn 11, 5.7. *Flowing with milk and honey:* an expression denoting agricultural prosperity, which seems to have been proverbial in its application to Palestine. Cf 13, 5; Nm 13, 27; Jos 5, 6; Jer 11, 5; 32, 22; Ez 20, 6.15.

3, 11: *Who am I:* besides naturally shrinking from such a tremendous undertaking, Moses realized that, as a fugitive from Pharaoh, he could hardly hope to carry out a mission to him. Perhaps he also recalled that on one occasion even his own kinsmen questioned his authority. Cf 2, 14.

3, 14: *I am who am:* apparently this utterance is the source of the word *Yahweh,* the proper personal name of the God of Israel. It is commonly explained in reference to God as the absolute and necessary Being. It may be understood of God as the Source of all created beings. Out of reverence for this name, the term *Adonai,* "my Lord," was later used as a substitute. The word LORD in the present version represents this traditional usage. The word "Jehovah" arose from a false reading of this name as it is written in the current Hebrew text.

3, 16: *Elders:* the Israelite leaders, who were usually older men. They were representatives of the people.

3, 22: *Articles:* probably jewelry. *Despoil:* this was permissible, that the Israelites might compensate themselves for their many years of servitude; besides, the Egyptians would give these things willingly. Cf 12, 33-36.

For they may say, 'The LORD did not
appear to you.' " 2 The LORD therefore
asked him, "What is that in your hand?"
"A staff," he answered. 3* The LORD
then said, "Throw it on the ground."
When he threw it on the ground it was
changed into a serpent, and Moses shied
away from it. 4 "Now, put out your
hand," the LORD said to him, "and take
hold of its tail." So he put out his hand
and laid hold of it, and it became a staff
in his hand. 5 "This will take place so that
they may believe," he continued, "that
the LORD, the God of their fathers, the
God of Abraham, the God of Isaac, the
God of Jacob, did appear to you."

6 Again the LORD said to him, "Put
your hand in your bosom." He put it in
his bosom, and when he withdrew it, to
his surprise his hand was leprous, like
snow. 7 The LORD then said, "Now, put
your hand back in your bosom." Moses
put his hand back in his bosom, and
when he withdrew it, to his surprise it
was again like the rest of his body. 8 "If
they will not believe you, nor heed the
message of the first sign, they should be-
lieve the message of the second. 9* And
if they will not believe even these two
signs, nor heed your plea, take some
water from the river and pour it on the
dry land. The water you take from the
river will become blood on the dry land."

Aaron's Office as Assistant. 10* Moses,
however, said to the LORD, "If you
please, LORD, I have never been elo-
quent, neither in the past, nor recently,
nor now that you have spoken to your
servant; but I am slow of speech and
tongue." 11 The LORD said to him, "Who
gives one man speech and makes an-
other deaf and dumb? Or who gives sight
to one and makes another blind? Is it
not I, the LORD? 12 Go, then! It is I who
will assist you in speaking and will teach
you what you are to say." 13† Yet he in-
sisted, "If you please, Lord, send some-
one else!" 14 Then the LORD became
angry with Moses and said, "Have you
not your brother, Aaron the Levite? I
know that he is an eloquent speaker. Be-
sides, he is now on his way to meet you.
15* When he sees you, his heart will be
glad. You are to speak to him, then, and
put the words in his mouth. I will assist
both you and him in speaking and will
teach the two of you what you are to do.
16† He shall speak to the people for you:
he shall be your spokesman, and you
shall be as God to him. 17† Take this staff
in your hand; with it you are to perform
the signs."

Moses' Return to Egypt. 18† After this
Moses returned to his father-in-law
Jethro and said to him, "Let me go back,
please, to my kinsmen in Egypt, to see
whether they are still living." Jethro
replied, "Go in peace." 19* In Midian the
LORD said to Moses, "Go back to Egypt,
for all the men who sought your life are
dead." 20 So Moses took his wife and his
sons, and started back to the land of
Egypt, with them riding the ass. The
staff of God he carried with him. 21† The
LORD said to him, "On your return to
Egypt, see that you perform before
Pharaoh all the wonders I have put in
your power. I will make him obstinate,
however, so that he will not let the people
go. 22* So you shall say to Pharaoh: Thus
says the LORD: Israel is my son, my first-
born. 23* Hence I tell you: Let my son
go, that he may serve me. If you refuse
to let him go, I warn you, I will kill your
son, your first-born."

24† On the journey, at a place where
they spent the night, the Lord came
upon Moses and would have killed him.
25* But Zipporah took a piece of flint and
cut off her son's foreskin and, touching
his person, she said, "You are a spouse
of blood to me." 26 Then God let Moses
go. At that time she said, "A spouse of
blood," in regard to the circumcision.

27 The LORD said to Aaron, "Go into
the desert to meet Moses." So he went,
and when they met at the mountain of
God, Aaron kissed him. 28 Moses in-
formed him of all the LORD had said in
sending him, and of the various signs
he had enjoined upon him. 29 Then Mo-
ses and Aaron went and assembled all
the elders of the Israelites. 30 Aaron told
them everything the LORD had said to
Moses, and he performed the signs be-
fore the people. 31 The people believed,
and when they heard that the LORD was
concerned about them and had seen
their affliction, they bowed down in wor-
ship.

CHAPTER 5

Pharaoh's Obduracy. 1 After that,
Moses and Aaron went to Pharaoh and

*

4, 3: 7, 10.	19: 2, 15.23.
9: 7, 17.19f.	22: Sir 36, 11.
10: 6, 12.	23: 11, 5; 12, 29.
15f: 7, 1.	25: Is 6, 2; 7, 20.

†

4, 13: *Send someone else:* literally, "Send by means of him whom you will send," that is, "Send whom you will."

4, 16: *Spokesman:* literally, "mouth"; Aaron was to serve as a mouthpiece for Moses, as a prophet does for God; hence the relation between Moses and Aaron is compared to that between God and his prophet. Cf 7, 1.

4, 17: *This staff:* probably the same as that of vv 2ff; but some understand it here of a new staff now given by God to Moses.

4, 18: Moses did not tell his father-in-law his main reason for returning to Egypt, but this secondary motive which he offered was also true.

4, 21: *Make him obstinate:* literally, "harden his heart." God permitted Pharaoh to be stubborn in his opposition to the departure of the Israelites. Cf Rom 9, 17f.

4, 24ff. Apparently God was angry with Moses for having failed to keep the divine command given to Abraham in Gn 17, 10ff. Moses' life is spared when his wife circumcises their son.

said, "Thus says the LORD, the God of
Israel: Let my people go, that they may
celebrate a feast to me in the desert."
2 Pharaoh answered, "Who is the LORD,
that I should heed his plea to let Israel
go? I do not know the LORD; even if I
did, I would not let Israel go." 3* They
replied, "The God of the Hebrews has
sent us word. Let us go a three days'
journey in the desert, that we may offer
sacrifice to the LORD, our God; otherwise
he will punish us with pestilence or the
sword."

4 The king of Egypt answered them,
"What do you mean, Moses and Aaron,
by taking the people away from their
work? Off to your labor! 5 Look how nu-
merous the people of the land are al-
ready," continued Pharaoh, "and yet
you would give them rest from their la-
bor!"

6† That very day Pharaoh gave the
taskmasters and foremen of the people
this order: 7† "You shall no longer sup-
ply the people with straw for their brick-
making as you have previously done.
Let them go and gather straw them-
selves! 8 Yet you shall levy upon them
the same quota of bricks as they have
previously made. Do not reduce it. They
are lazy; that is why they are crying, 'Let
us go to offer sacrifice to our God.'
9 Increase the work for the men, so that
they keep their mind on it and pay no
attention to lying words."

10 So the taskmasters and foremen of
the people went out and told them,
"Thus says Pharaoh: I will not provide
you with straw. 11 Go and gather the
straw yourselves, wherever you can find
it. Yet there must not be the slightest re-
duction in your work." 12 The people,
then, scattered throughout the land of
Egypt to gather stubble for straw,
13 while the taskmasters kept driving
them on, saying, "Finish your work, the
same daily amount as when your straw
was supplied."

Complaint of the Foremen. 14 The
foremen of the Israelites, whom the
taskmasters of Pharaoh had placed over
them, were beaten, and were asked,
"Why have you not completed your pre-
scribed amount of bricks yesterday and
today, as before?"

15 Then the Israelite foremen came
and made this appeal to Pharaoh: "Why
do you treat your servants in this man-
ner? 16 No straw is supplied to your ser-
vants, and still we are told to make
bricks. Look how your servants are
beaten! It is you who are at fault."
17 Pharaoh answered, "It is just because
you are lazy that you keep saying, 'Let
us go and offer sacrifice to the LORD.'
18 Off to work, then! Straw shall not be
provided for you, but you must still de-
liver your quota of bricks."

19 The Israelite foremen knew they
were in a sorry plight, having been told
not to reduce the daily amount of bricks.
20 When, therefore, they left Pharaoh
and came upon Moses and Aaron, who
were waiting to meet them, 21 they said
to them, "The LORD look upon you and
judge! You have brought us into bad
odor with Pharaoh and his servants and
have put a sword in their hands to slay
us."

Renewal of God's Promise. 22 Moses
again had recourse to the LORD and said,
"Lord, why do you treat this people so
badly? And why did you send me on
such a mission? 23 Ever since I went to
Pharaoh to speak in your name, he has
maltreated this people of yours, and you
have done nothing to rescue them."

CHAPTER 6

1 Then the LORD answered Moses,
"Now you shall see what I will do to
Pharaoh. Forced by my mighty hand,
he will send them away; compelled by
my outstretched arm, he will drive them
from his land."

2 God also said to Moses, "I am the
LORD. 3* As God the Almighty I ap-
peared to Abraham, Isaac and Jacob,
but my name, LORD, I did not make
known to them. 4* I also established my
covenant with them, to give them the
land of Canaan, the land in which they
were living as aliens. 5* And now that I
have heard the groaning of the Israel-
ites, whom the Egyptians are treating
as slaves, I am mindful of my covenant.
6 Therefore, say to the Israelites: I am
the LORD. I will free you from the forced
labor of the Egyptians and will deliver
you from their slavery. I will rescue you
by my outstretched arm and with
mighty acts of judgment. 7* I will take
you as my own people, and you shall
have me as your God. You will know that
I, the LORD, am your God when I free
you from the labor of the Egyptians
8 and bring you into the land which I
swore to give to Abraham, Isaac and Ja-
cob. I will give it to you as your own pos-
session—I, the LORD!" 9 But when Moses
told this to the Israelites, they would not
listen to him because of their dejection
and hard slavery.

10 Then the LORD said to Moses, 11 "Go
and tell Pharaoh, king of Egypt, to let

*

5, 3: 3, 18.
6, 3: Gn 17, 1; 35, 11.
4: Gn 15, 18; 17, 4-8.
5: 2, 24.
7: Lv 26, 12.

†

5, 6: *The taskmasters and foremen:* the former were higher officials and probably Egyptians; the latter were lower officials, chosen from the Israelites themselves. Cf v 14.

5, 7: Straw was mixed with the clay to give the sun-dried bricks greater consistency.

the Israelites leave his land." 12* But
Moses protested to the LORD, "If the Is-
raelites would not listen to me, how can
it be that Pharaoh will listen to me, poor
speaker that I am!" 13 Still, the LORD, to
bring the Israelites out of Egypt, spoke
to Moses and Aaron and gave them his
orders regarding both the Israelites and
Pharaoh, king of Egypt.

Genealogy of Moses and Aaron.
14*† These are the heads of the ancestral
houses. The sons of Reuben, the first-
born of Israel, were Hanoch, Pallu,
Hezron and Carmi; these are the clans
of Reuben. 15* The sons of Simeon were
Jemuel, Jamin, Ohad, Jachin, Zohar and
Shaul, who was the son of a Canaanite
woman; these are the clans of Simeon.
16* The names of the sons of Levi, in
their genealogical order, are Gershon,
Kohath and Merari. Levi lived one hun-
dred and thirty-seven years.

17* The sons of Gershon, as heads of
clans, were Libni and Shimei. 18* The
sons of Kohath were Amram, Izhar, He-
bron and Uzziel. Kohath lived one hun-
dred and thirty-three years. 19* The sons
of Merari were Mahli and Mushi. These
are the clans of Levi in their genealogi-
cal order.

20*† Amram married his aunt Joch-
ebed, who bore him Aaron, Moses and
Miriam. Amram lived one hundred and
thirty-seven years. 21 The sons of Izhar
were Korah, Nepheg and Zichri. 22 The
sons of Uzziel were Mishael, Elzaphan
and Sithri. 23* Aaron married Ammina-
dab's daughter, Elisheba, the sister of
Nahshon; she bore him Nadab, Abihu,
Eleazar and Ithamar. 24 The sons of Ko-
rah were Assir, Elkanah and Abiasaph.
These are the clans of the Korahites.
25 Aaron's son, Eleazar, married one of
Putiel's daughters, who bore him Phin-
ehas. These are the heads of the ances-
tral clans of the Levites. 26 This is the
Aaron and this the Moses to whom the
LORD said, "Lead the Israelites from the
land of Egypt, company by company."
27 These are the ones who spoke to Pha-
raoh, king of Egypt, to bring the Israel-
ites out of Egypt—the same Moses and
Aaron.

Moses and Aaron before Pharaoh.
28 On the day the LORD spoke to Moses
in Egypt 29 he said, "I am the LORD. Re-
peat to Pharaoh, king of Egypt, all that
I tell you." 30* But Moses protested to the
LORD, "Since I am a poor speaker, how
can it be that Pharaoh will listen to me?"

CHAPTER 7

1*† The LORD answered him, "See! I
have made you as God to Pharaoh, and
Aaron your brother shall act as your
prophet. 2 You shall tell him all that I
command you. In turn, your brother
Aaron shall tell Pharaoh to let the Israel-
ites leave his land. 3 Yet I will make
Pharaoh so obstinate that, despite the
many signs and wonders that I will work
in the land of Egypt, 4 he will not listen
to you. Therefore I will lay my hand on
Egypt and by great acts of judgment I
will bring the hosts of my people, the Is-
raelites, out of the land of Egypt, 5 so that
the Egyptians may learn that I am the
LORD, as I stretch out my hand against
Egypt and lead the Israelites out of their
midst."

6 Moses and Aaron did as the LORD
had commanded them. 7 Moses was
eighty years old and Aaron eighty-three
when they spoke to Pharaoh.

The Staff Turned into a Snake. 8 The
LORD told Moses and Aaron, 9* "If Pha-
raoh demands that you work a sign or
wonder, you shall say to Aaron: Take
your staff and throw it down before
Pharaoh, and it will be changed into a
snake." 10 Then Moses and Aaron went
to Pharaoh and did as the LORD had
commanded. Aaron threw his staff
down before Pharaoh and his servants,
and it was changed into a snake.
11* Pharaoh, in turn, summoned wise
men and sorcerers, and they also, the
magicians of Egypt, did likewise by their
magic arts. 12 Each one threw down his
staff, and it was changed into a snake.
But Aaron's staff swallowed their staffs.
13 Pharaoh, however, was obstinate and
would not listen to them, just as the LORD
had foretold.

***First Plague: Water Turned into
Blood.*** 14† Then the LORD said to Moses,
"Pharaoh is obdurate in refusing to let
the people go. 15 Tomorrow morning,
when he sets out for the water, go and
present yourself by the river bank, hold-
ing in your hand the staff that turned
into a serpent. 16 Say to him: The LORD,

*

12: 6, 30.
14: Nm 26, 5f; 1 Chr 5, 3.
15: Nm 26, 12; 1 Chr 4, 24.
16: Nm 3, 17; 1 Chr 6, 1.16; 23, 6.
17: Nm 3, 21; 1 Chr 6, 17; 23, 7.
18: Nm 3, 27; 1 Chr 6, 2.18.
19: Nm 3, 20; 1 Chr 6, 19; 23, 21.
20: Nm 26, 59.
23: Ru 4, 19f; 1 Chr 2, 10.
30: 6, 12.
7, 1: 4, 15f.
9: 4, 3.
11: 2 Tm 3, 8.

†

6, 14: The purpose of the genealogy here is to give the line from which Moses and Aaron sprang. Reuben and Simeon are first mentioned because, as older brothers of Levi, their names occur before his in the genealogy.

6, 20: *His aunt:* more exactly, "his father's sister." Later on such a marriage was forbidden. Cf Lv 18, 12. Hence, the Greek and Latin versions render here, "his cousin."

7, 1: Just as God had his prophets to speak to men in his name, so Moses had Aaron as his "prophet" to speak to Pharaoh. Cf 4, 16.

7, 14: Most of the ten plagues of Egypt seem to be similar to certain natural phenomena of that country; but they are represented as supernatural at least in their greater intensity and in their occurring exactly according to Moses' commands.

the God of the Hebrews, sent me to you
with the message: Let my people go to
worship me in the desert. But as yet you
have not listened. 17* The LORD now
says: This is how you shall know that I
am the LORD. I will strike the water of
the river with the staff I hold, and it shall
be changed into blood. 18 The fish in the
river shall die, and the river itself shall
become so polluted that the Egyptians
will be unable to drink its water."
19 The LORD then said to Moses, "Say
to Aaron: Take your staff and stretch out
your hand over the waters of Egypt—
their streams and canals and pools, all
their supplies of water—that they may
become blood. Throughout the land of
Egypt there shall be blood, even in the
wooden pails and stone jars."
20 Moses and Aaron did as the LORD
had commanded. Aaron raised his staff
and struck the waters of the river in full
view of Pharaoh and his servants, and
all the water of the river was changed
into blood. 21 The fish in the river died,
and the river itself became so polluted
that the Egyptians could not drink its
water. There was blood throughout the
land of Egypt. 22 But the Egyptian magi-
cians did the same by their magic arts.
So Pharaoh remained obstinate and
would not listen to Moses and Aaron, just
as the LORD had foretold. 23 He turned
away and went into his house, with no
concern even for this. 24 All the Egyp-
tians had to dig in the neighborhood of
the river for drinking water, since they
could not drink the river water.
Second Plague: the Frogs. 25 Seven
days passed after the LORD had struck
the river. 26*† Then the LORD said to Mo-
ses, "Go to Pharaoh and tell him: Thus
says the LORD: Let my people go to wor-
ship me. 27 If you refuse to let them go,
I warn you, I will send a plague of frogs
over all your territory. 28 The river will
teem with frogs. They will come up into
your palace and into your bedroom and
onto your bed, into the houses of your
servants, too, and your subjects, even
into your ovens and your kneading
bowls. 29 The frogs will swarm all over
you and your subjects and your ser-
vants."

CHAPTER 8

1 The LORD then told Moses, "Say to
Aaron: Stretch out your hand and your
staff over the streams and canals and
pools, to make frogs overrun the land
of Egypt." 2 Aaron stretched out his
hand over the waters of Egypt, and the
frogs came up and covered the land of
Egypt. 3 But the magicians did the same
by their magic arts. They, too, made
frogs overrun the land of Egypt.
4 Then Pharaoh summoned Moses and
Aaron and said, "Pray the LORD to re-
move the frogs from me and my sub-
jects, and I will let the people go to offer
sacrifice to the LORD." 5 Moses answered
Pharaoh, "Do me the favor of appoint-
ing the time when I am to pray for you
and your servants and your subjects,
that the frogs may be taken away from
you and your houses and be left only in
the river." 6 "Tomorrow," said Pharaoh.
Then Moses replied, "It shall be as you
have said, so that you may learn that
there is none like the LORD, our God.
7 The frogs shall leave you and your
houses, your servants and your subjects;
only in the river shall they be left."
8 After Moses and Aaron left Pha-
raoh's presence, Moses implored the
LORD to fulfill the promise he had made
to Pharaoh about the frogs; 9† and the
LORD did as Moses had asked. The frogs
in the houses and courtyards and fields
died off. 10 Heaps and heaps of them
were gathered up, and there was a
stench in the land. 11 But when Pharaoh
saw that there was a respite, he became
obdurate and would not listen to them,
just as the LORD had foretold.
Third Plague: the Gnats.
12*† Thereupon the LORD said to Moses,
"Tell Aaron to stretch out his staff and
strike the dust of the earth, that it may
be turned into gnats throughout the land
of Egypt." 13 They did so. Aaron
stretched out his hand, and with his staff
he struck the dust of the earth, and gnats
came upon man and beast. The dust of
the earth was turned into gnats through-
out the land of Egypt. 14* Though the
magicians tried to bring forth gnats by
their magic arts, they could not do so.
As the gnats infested man and beast,
15† the magicians said to Pharaoh, "This
is the finger of God." Yet Pharaoh re-
mained obstinate and would not listen
to them, just as the LORD had foretold.
Fourth Plague: the Flies. 16 Again the
LORD told Moses, "Early tomorrow
morning present yourself to Pharaoh
when he goes forth to the water, and say
to him: Thus says the LORD: Let my peo-
ple go to worship me. 17 If you will not
let my people go, I warn you, I will loose
swarms of flies upon you and your ser-
vants and your subjects and your
houses. The houses of the Egyptians and

*

17-21: 4, 9; Pss 78, 44; 105, 29; Wis 11, 5-7.
26-29: Pss 78, 45; 105, 30.
8, 12f: Ps 105, 31.
14: Wis 17, 7.

†

7, 26—8, 28: This is 8, 1-32 in the verse enumeration of the Vulgate.
8, 9: *Courtyards:* some render "farmhouses."
8, 12.17: *Gnats, flies:* it is uncertain what species of troublesome insects are here meant.
8, 15: *The finger of God:* understood by the magicians as the *staff* mentioned in 8, 13. Cf Lk 11, 20.

the very ground on which they stand
shall be filled with swarms of flies. 18 But
on that day I will make an exception of
the land of Goshen: there shall be no flies
where my people dwell, that you may
know that I am the LORD in the midst
of the earth. 19 I will make this distinc-
tion between my people and your people.
This sign shall take place tomorrow."
20* This the LORD did. Thick swarms of
flies entered the house of Pharaoh and
the houses of his servants; throughout
Egypt the land was infested with flies.
21 Then Pharaoh summoned Moses
and Aaron and said to them, "Go and
offer sacrifice to your God in this land."
22† But Moses replied, "It is not right to
do so, for the sacrifices we offer to the
LORD, our God, are an abomination to
the Egyptians. If before their very eyes
we offer sacrifices which are an abomi-
nation to them, will not the Egyptians
stone us? 23 We must go a three days'
journey in the desert to offer sacrifice
to the LORD, our God, as he commands
us." 24 "Well, then," said Pharaoh, "I will
let you go to offer sacrifice to the LORD,
your God, in the desert, provided that
you do not go too far away and that you
pray for me." 25 Moses answered, "As
soon as I leave your presence I will pray
to the LORD that the flies may depart to-
morrow from Pharaoh and his servants
and his subjects. Pharaoh, however,
must not play false again by refusing to
let the people go to offer sacrifice to the
LORD." 26 When Moses left Pharaoh's
presence, he prayed to the LORD; 27 and
the LORD did as Moses had asked. He
removed the flies from Pharaoh and his
servants and subjects. Not one re-
mained. 28 But once more Pharaoh be-
came obdurate and would not let the
people go.

CHAPTER 9

Fifth Plague: the Pestilence. 1 Then
the LORD said to Moses, "Go to Pharaoh
and tell him: Thus says the LORD, the
God of the Hebrews: Let my people go
to worship me. 2 If you refuse to let them
go and persist in holding them, 3 I warn
you, the LORD will afflict all your live-
stock in the field—your horses, asses,
camels, herds and flocks—with a very
severe pestilence. 4 But the LORD will
distinguish between the livestock of Is-
rael and that of Egypt, so that none be-
longing to the Israelites will die." 5 And
setting a definite time, the LORD added,
"Tomorrow the LORD shall do this in the
land." 6* And on the next day the LORD
did so. All the livestock of the Egyptians
died, but not one beast belonging to the
Israelites. 7 But though Pharaoh's mes-
sengers informed him that not even one
beast belonging to the Israelites had
died, he still remained obdurate and
would not let the people go.
Sixth Plague: the Boils. 8 Then the
LORD said to Moses and Aaron, "Take
a double handful of soot from a furnace,
and in the presence of Pharaoh let Mo-
ses scatter it toward the sky. 9 It will then
turn into fine dust over the whole land
of Egypt and cause festering boils on
man and beast throughout the land."
10 So they took soot from a furnace and
stood in the presence of Pharaoh. Moses
scattered it toward the sky, and it
caused festering boils on man and beast.
11 The magicians could not stand in Mo-
ses' presence, for there were boils on the
magicians no less than on the rest of the
Egyptians. 12 But the LORD made Pha-
raoh obstinate, and he would not listen
to them, just as the LORD had foretold
to Moses.
Seventh Plague: the Hail. 13 Then the
LORD told Moses, "Early tomorrow
morning present yourself to Pharaoh
and say to him: Thus says the LORD, the
God of the Hebrews: Let my people go
to worship me, 14 or this time I will hurl
all my blows upon you and your servants
and your subjects, that you may know
that there is none like me anywhere on
earth. 15 For by now I would have
stretched out my hand and struck you
and your subjects with such pestilence
as would wipe you from the earth.
16*† But this is why I have spared you:
to show you my power and to make my
name resound throughout the earth!
17 Will you still block the way for my peo-
ple by refusing to let them go? 18 I warn
you, then, tomorrow at this hour I will
rain down such fierce hail as there has
never been in Egypt from the day the
nation was founded up to the present.
19 Therefore, order all your livestock and
whatever else you have in the open fields
to be brought to a place of safety. What-
ever man or beast remains in the fields
and is not brought to shelter shall die
when the hail comes upon them."
20 Some of Pharaoh's servants feared the
warning of the LORD and hurried their
servants and livestock off to shelter.
21 Others, however, did not take the
warning of the LORD to heart and left
their servants and livestock in the fields.
22 The LORD then said to Moses,
"Stretch out your hand toward the sky,
that hail may fall upon the entire land
of Egypt, on man and beast and every

*

20: Pss 78, 45; 105, 31; Wis 16, 9.
9, 6: Ps 78, 48.
16: Rom 9, 17.

†

8, 22: The Egyptians would fiercely resent the sacrifice of any animal they considered sacred. Certain animals were worshiped in Egypt, at least as the symbols of various deities.

9, 16: *To show you:* some ancient versions read, "to show through you." Cf Rom 9, 17.

growing thing in the land of Egypt."
23* When Moses stretched out his staff
toward the sky, the LORD sent forth hail
and peals of thunder. Lightning flashed
toward the earth, and the LORD rained
down hail upon the land of Egypt; 24 and
lightning constantly flashed through the
hail, such fierce hail as had never been
seen in the land since Egypt became a
nation. 25 It struck down every man and
beast that was in the open throughout
the land of Egypt; it beat down every
growing thing and splintered every tree
in the fields. 26 Only in the land of
Goshen, where the Israelites dwelt, was
there no hail.
27 Then Pharaoh summoned Moses
and Aaron and said to them, "I have
sinned again! The LORD is just; it is I
and my subjects who are at fault. 28 Pray
to the LORD, for we have had enough of
God's thunder and hail. Then I will let
you go; you need stay no longer."
29 Moses replied, "As soon as I leave the
city I will extend my hands to the LORD;
the thunder will cease, and there will be
no more hail. Thus you shall learn that
the earth is the LORD's. 30 But you and
your servants, I know, do not yet fear
the LORD God."
31 Now the flax and the barley were
ruined, because the barley was in ear
and the flax in bud. 32 But the wheat and
the spelt were not ruined, for they grow
later.
33 When Moses had left Pharaoh's
presence and had gone out of the city,
he extended his hands to the LORD. Then
the thunder and the hail ceased, and the
rain no longer poured down upon the
earth. 34 But Pharaoh, seeing that the
rain and hail and thunder had ceased,
sinned again: he with his servants be-
came obdurate, 35 and in his obstinacy
he would not let the Israelites go, as the
LORD had foretold through Moses.

CHAPTER 10

Eighth Plague: the Locusts. 1 Then the
LORD said to Moses, "Go to Pharaoh, for
I have made him and his servants obdu-
rate in order that I may perform these
signs of mine among them 2* and that
you may recount to your son and grand-
son how ruthlessly I dealt with the Egyp-
tians and what signs I wrought among
them, so that you may know that I am
the LORD."
3 So Moses and Aaron went to Pharaoh
and told him, "Thus says the LORD, the
God of the Hebrews: How long will you
refuse to submit to me? Let my people
go to worship me. 4 If you refuse to let
my people go, I warn you, tomorrow I
will bring locusts into your country.
5 They shall cover the ground, so that
the ground itself will not be visible. They
shall eat up the remnant you saved un-
hurt from the hail, as well as all the fo-
liage that has since sprouted in your
fields. 6 They shall fill your houses and
the houses of your servants and of all
the Egyptians; such a sight your fathers
or grandfathers have not seen from the
day they first settled on this soil up to
the present day." With that he turned
and left Pharaoh.
7 But Pharaoh's servants said to him,
"How long must he be a menace to us?
Let the men go to worship the LORD,
their God. Do you not yet realize that
Egypt is being destroyed?" 8 So Moses
and Aaron were brought back to Pha-
raoh, who said to them, "You may go
and worship the LORD, your God. But
how many of you will go?" 9 "Young and
old must go with us," Moses answered,
"our sons and daughters as well as our
flocks and herds must accompany us.
That is what a feast of the LORD means
to us." 10† "The LORD help you," Pha-
raoh replied, "if I ever let your little ones
go with you! Clearly, you have some evil
in mind. 11† No, no! Just you men can
go and worship the LORD. After all, that
is what you want." With that they were
driven from Pharaoh's presence.
12* The LORD then said to Moses,
"Stretch out your hand over the land of
Egypt, that locusts may swarm over it
and eat up all the vegetation and what-
ever the hail has left." 13† So Moses
stretched out his staff over the land of
Egypt, and the LORD sent an east wind
blowing over the land all that day and
all that night. At dawn the east wind
brought the locusts. 14 They swarmed
over the whole land of Egypt and settled
down on every part of it. Never before
had there been such a fierce swarm of
locusts, nor will there ever be. 15 They
covered the surface of the whole land,
till it was black with them. They ate up
all the vegetation in the land and the
fruit of whatever trees the hail had
spared. Nothing green was left on any
tree or plant throughout the land of
Egypt.
16 Hastily Pharaoh summoned Moses
and Aaron and said, "I have sinned
against the LORD, your God, and against
you. 17 But now, do forgive me my sin

*

23f: Pss 78, 47; 105, 32f.
10, 2: Dt 6, 20ff.
12ff: Pss 78, 46; 105, 34f.

†

10, 10: *The LORD help you . . . :* literally, "May the LORD be with you in the same way as I let you . . . "; a sarcastic blessing intended as a curse.

10, 11: Pharaoh realized that if the men alone went they would have to return to their families. He suspected that the Hebrews had no intention of returning.

10, 13: *East wind:* coming across the desert from Arabia, the strong east wind brings Egypt the burning sirocco and, at times, locusts. Cf 14, 21.

once more, and pray the LORD, your God, to take at least this deadly pest from me." 18 When Moses left the presence of Pharaoh, he prayed to the LORD, 19† and the LORD changed the wind to a very strong west wind, which took up the locusts and hurled them into the Red Sea. But though not a single locust remained within the confines of Egypt, 20 the LORD made Pharaoh obstinate, and he would not let the Israelites go.

Ninth Plague: the Darkness. 21† Then the LORD said to Moses, "Stretch out your hand toward the sky, that over the land of Egypt there may be such intense darkness that one can feel it." 22* So Moses stretched out his hand toward the sky, and there was dense darkness throughout the land of Egypt for three days. 23 Men could not see one another, nor could they move from where they were, for three days. But all the Israelites had light where they dwelt.

24 Pharaoh then summoned Moses and Aaron and said, "Go and worship the LORD. Your little ones, too, may go with you. But your flocks and herds must remain." 25 Moses replied, "You must also grant us sacrifices and holocausts to offer up to the LORD, our God. 26 Hence, our livestock also must go with us. Not an animal must be left behind. Some of them we must sacrifice to the LORD, our God, but we ourselves shall not know which ones we must sacrifice to him until we arrive at the place itself." 27 But the LORD made Pharaoh obstinate, and he would not let them go. 28 "Leave my presence," Pharaoh said to him, "and see to it that you do not appear before me again! The day you appear before me you shall die!" 29 Moses replied, "Well said! I will never appear before you again."

CHAPTER 11

Tenth Plague: the Death of the First-born. 1 Then the LORD told Moses, "One more plague will I bring upon Pharaoh and upon Egypt. After that he will let you depart. In fact, he will not merely let you go; he will drive you away. 2* Instruct your people that every man is to ask his neighbor, and every woman her neighbor, for silver and gold articles and for clothing." 3 The LORD indeed made the Egyptians well-disposed toward the people; Moses himself was very highly regarded by Pharaoh's servants and the people in the land of Egypt.

4* Moses then said, "Thus says the LORD: At midnight I will go forth through Egypt. 5* Every first-born in this land shall die, from the first-born of Pharaoh on the throne to the first-born of the slave-girl at the handmill, as well as all the first-born of the animals. 6 Then there shall be loud wailing throughout the land of Egypt, such as has never been, nor will ever be again. 7 But among the Israelites and their animals not even a dog shall growl, so that you may know how the LORD distinguishes between the Egyptians and the Israelites. 8* All these servants of yours shall then come down to me, and prostrate before me, they shall beg me, 'Leave us, you and all your followers!' Only then will I depart." With that he left Pharaoh's presence in hot anger.

9 The LORD said to Moses, "Pharaoh refuses to listen to you that my wonders may be multiplied in the land of Egypt." 10 Thus, although Moses and Aaron performed these various wonders in Pharaoh's presence, the LORD made Pharaoh obstinate, and he would not let the Israelites leave his land.

CHAPTER 12

The Passover Ritual Prescribed. 1 The LORD said to Moses and Aaron in the land of Egypt, 2*† "This month shall stand at the head of your calendar; you shall reckon it the first month of the year. 3 Tell the whole community of Israel: On the tenth of this month every one of your families must procure for itself a lamb, one apiece for each household. 4† If a family is too small for a whole lamb, it shall join the nearest household in procuring one and shall share in the lamb in proportion to the number of persons who partake of it. 5 The lamb must be a year-old male and without blemish. You may take it from either the sheep or the goats. 6 You shall keep it until the fourteenth day of this month, and then, with the whole assembly of Israel present, it shall be slaughtered during the evening twilight. 7 They shall take some of its blood and apply it to the two doorposts and the lintel of every house in which they partake of the lamb. 8 That same night they shall eat

---

*

22: Ps 105, 28.
11, 2f: 3, 21f; 12, 35f.
4: 12, 12.
5f: 12, 29f.
8: 12, 31ff.
12, 2-20: Lv 23, 5-8; Nm 9, 2-5; 28, 16ff; Dt 16, 1-8.

†

10, 19: *The Red Sea:* according to the traditional translation, but the Hebrew is literally, "the Reed Sea"; hence the Red Sea of Exodus was probably a body of shallow water somewhat to the north of the present deep Red Sea.

10, 21: *Darkness:* at times a storm from the south, called the *khamsin,* blackens the sky of Egypt with sand from the Sahara; the dust in the air is then so thick that the darkness can, in a sense, "be felt."

12, 2: *This month:* Abib, the month of "ripe grain." Cf 13, 4; 23, 15; 34, 18; Dt 16, 1. It occurred near the vernal equinox, March-April. Later it was known by the Babylonian name of Nisan. Cf Neh 2, 1; Est 3, 7.

12, 4: *Share in the lamb:* probably, in the expenses of its purchase. Some explain, "reckon for the lamb the number of persons required to eat it." Cf 12, 10.

its roasted flesh with unleavened bread
and bitter herbs. 9 It shall not be eaten
raw or boiled, but roasted whole, with
its head and shanks and inner organs.
10 None of it must be kept beyond the
next morning; whatever is left over in
the morning shall be burned up.
11† "This is how you are to eat it: with
your loins girt, sandals on your feet and
your staff in hand, you shall eat like
those who are in flight. It is the Passover
of the LORD. 12 For on this same night I
will go through Egypt, striking down ev-
ery first-born of the land, both man and
beast, and executing judgment on all the
gods of Egypt—I, the LORD! 13* But the
blood will mark the houses where you
are. Seeing the blood, I will pass over
you; thus, when I strike the land of
Egypt, no destructive blow will come
upon you.
14 "This day shall be a memorial feast
for you, which all your generations shall
celebrate with pilgrimage to the LORD,
as a perpetual institution. 15 For seven
days you must eat unleavened bread.
From the very first day you shall have
your houses clear of all leaven. Whoever
eats leavened bread from the first day
to the seventh shall be cut off from Is-
rael. 16 On the first day you shall hold
a sacred assembly, and likewise on the
seventh. On these days you shall not do
any sort of work, except to prepare the
food that everyone needs.
17* "Keep, then, this custom of the un-
leavened bread. Since it was on this very
day that I brought your ranks out of the
land of Egypt, you must celebrate this
day throughout your generations as a
perpetual institution. 18 From the eve-
ning of the fourteenth day of the first
month until the evening of the twenty-
first day of this month you shall eat un-
leavened bread. 19 For seven days no
leaven may be found in your houses.
Anyone, be he a resident alien or a na-
tive, who eats leavened food shall be cut
off from the community of Israel.
20 Nothing leavened may you eat; wher-
ever you dwell you may eat only unleav-
ened bread."
Promulgation of the Passover. 21 Mo-
ses called all the elders of Israel and said
to them, "Go and procure lambs for your
families, and slaughter them as Pass-
over victims. 22*† Then take a bunch of
hyssop, and dipping it in the blood that
is in the basin, sprinkle the lintel and
the two doorposts with this blood. But
none of you shall go outdoors until
morning. 23 For the LORD will go by,
striking down the Egyptians. Seeing the
blood on the lintel and the two doorposts,
the LORD will pass over that door and
not let the destroyer come into your
houses to strike you down.
24 "You shall observe this as a perpet-
ual ordinance for yourselves and your
descendants. 25 Thus, you must also ob-
serve this rite when you have entered
the land which the LORD will give you
as he promised. 26* When your children
ask you, 'What does this rite of yours
mean?' 27 you shall reply, 'This is the
Passover sacrifice of the LORD, who
passed over the houses of the Israelites
in Egypt; when he struck down the
Egyptians, he spared our houses.' "
Then the people bowed down in wor-
ship, 28 and the Israelites went and did
as the LORD had commanded Moses and
Aaron.
Death of the First-born. 29* At mid-
night the LORD slew every first-born in
the land of Egypt, from the first-born
of Pharaoh on the throne to the first-
born of the prisoner in the dungeon, as
well as all the first-born of the animals.
30 Pharaoh arose in the night, he and all
his servants and all the Egyptians; and
there was loud wailing throughout
Egypt, for there was not a house without
its dead.
Permission to Depart. 31 During the
night Pharaoh summoned Moses and
Aaron and said, "Leave my people at
once, you and the Israelites with you!
Go and worship the LORD as you said.
32 Take your flocks, too, and your herds,
as you demanded, and be gone; and you
will be doing me a favor."
33 The Egyptians likewise urged the
people on, to hasten their departure
from the land; they thought that other-
wise they would all die. 34 The people,
therefore, took their dough before it
was leavened, in their kneading bowls
wrapped in their cloaks on their shoul-
ders. 35* The Israelites did as Moses had
commanded: they asked the Egyptians
for articles of silver and gold and for
clothing. 36 The LORD indeed had made
the Egyptians so well-disposed toward
the people that they let them have what-
ever they asked for. Thus did they de-
spoil the Egyptians.

II: THE EXODUS FROM EGYPT AND THE JOURNEY TO SINAI

Departure from Egypt. 37* The Israel-
ites set out from Rameses for Succoth,

*

13: Heb 11, 28.
17: 13, 3.
22f: 12, 7.13.
26f: 13, 8.14; Dt 6, 20f.
29f: 11, 4ff; Pss 78, 51; 105, 36; 136, 10; Wis 18, 10-16.
35f: 3, 21f; 11, 2f; Ps 105, 37f.
37: Nm 33, 3ff.

†

12, 11: *Passover:* in Hebrew, *pesach,* in Aramaic, *pascha.* In the following verses the same root is used in the verb "to pass over." The word may be originally Egyptian, *pesach,* "the blow," i.e., the final plague which destroyed the Egyptian first-born.

12, 22: *Hyssop:* a plant with many woody branchlets that made a convenient sprinkler.

about six hundred thousand men on
foot, not counting the children. 38† A
crowd of mixed ancestry also went up
with them, besides their livestock, very
numerous flocks and herds. 39 Since the
dough they had brought out of Egypt
was not leavened, they baked it into un-
leavened loaves. They had been rushed
out of Egypt and had no opportunity
even to prepare food for the journey.
40†* The time the Israelites had stayed
in Egypt was four hundred and thirty
years. 41 At the end of four hundred and
thirty years, all the hosts of the LORD
left the land of Egypt on this very date.
42 This was a night of vigil for the LORD,
as he led them out of the land of Egypt;
so on this same night all the Israelites
must keep a vigil for the LORD through-
out their generations.
Passover Regulations. 43 The LORD
said to Moses and Aaron, "These are the
regulations for the Passover. No for-
eigner may partake of it. 44 However,
any slave who has been bought for
money may partake of it, provided you
have first circumcised him. 45 But no
transient alien or hired servant may
partake of it. 46*† It must be eaten in one
and the same house; you may not take
any of its flesh outside the house. You
shall not break any of its bones. 47* The
whole community of Israel must keep
this feast. 48 If any aliens living among
you wish to celebrate the Passover of the
LORD, all the males among them must
first be circumcised, and then they may
join in its observance just like the na-
tives. But no man who is uncircumcised
may partake of it. 49 The law shall be the
same for the resident alien as for the na-
tive."
50 All the Israelites did just as the LORD
had commanded Moses and Aaron.
51 On that same day the LORD brought
the Israelites out of Egypt company by
company.

CHAPTER 13

Consecration of First-born. 1 The
LORD spoke to Moses and said,
2* "Consecrate to me every first-born
that opens the womb among the Israel-
ites, both of man and beast, for it belongs
to me."
3* Moses said to the people, "Remem-
ber this day on which you came out of
Egypt, that place of slavery. It was with
a strong hand that the LORD brought you
away. Nothing made with leaven must
be eaten. 4 This day of your departure
is in the month of Abib. 5 Therefore, it
is in this month that you must celebrate
this rite, after the LORD, your God, has
brought you into the land of the Canaan-
ites, Hittites, Amorites, Hivites and
Jebusites, which he swore to your fa-
thers he would give you, a land flowing
with milk and honey. 6 For seven days
you shall eat unleavened bread, and the
seventh day shall also be a festival to
the LORD. 7 Only unleavened bread may
be eaten during the seven days; no
leaven and nothing leavened may be
found in all your territory. 8 On this day
you shall explain to your son, 'This is
because of what the LORD did for me
when I came out of Egypt.' 9* It shall
be as a sign on your hand and as a re-
minder on your forehead; thus the law
of the LORD will ever be on your lips,
because with a strong hand the LORD
brought you out of Egypt. 10 Therefore,
you shall keep this prescribed rite at its
appointed time from year to year.
11 "When the LORD, your God, has
brought you into the land of the Canaan-
ites, which he swore to you and your fa-
thers he would give you, 12* you shall
dedicate to the LORD every son that
opens the womb; and all the male first-
lings of your animals shall belong to the
LORD. 13 Every first-born of an ass you
shall redeem with a sheep. If you do not
redeem it, you shall break its neck. Ev-
ery first-born son you must redeem. 14 If
your son should ask you later on, 'What
does this mean?' you shall tell him, 'With
a strong hand the LORD brought us out
of Egypt, that place of slavery. 15 When
Pharaoh stubbornly refused to let us go,
the LORD killed every first-born in the
land of Egypt, every first-born of man
and of beast. That is why I sacrifice to
the LORD everything of the male sex that
opens the womb, and why I redeem ev-
ery first-born of my sons.' 16* Let this,
then, be as a sign on your hand and as
a pendant on your forehead: with a
strong hand the LORD brought us out of
Egypt."
Toward the Red Sea. 17† Now, when
Pharaoh let the people go, God did not
lead them by way of the Philistines'
land, though this was the nearest; for he

---

*

40: Gn 15, 13; Acts 7, 6; Gal 3, 17.
46: Nm 9, 12; Jn 19, 36.
47f: Nm 9, 14.
13, 2: 13, 12-15.
3-10: 12, 2-20.
9: 13, 16; Dt 6, 8; 11, 18.
12-15: 13, 2; 22, 29f; 34, 19f; Nm 3, 12f; 8, 16; 18, 15; Dt 15, 19.
16: 13, 9.

†

12, 38: *Mixed ancestry:* half-Hebrew and half-Egyptian. Cf Nm 11, 4; Lv 24, 10f.

12, 40: *In Egypt:* according to some ancient sources, "in Canaan and Egypt," thus reckoning from the time of Abraham. Cf Gal 3, 17.

12, 46: *You shall not break any of its bones:* the application of these words to our Lord on the cross shows that the Paschal lamb was a prophetic type of Christ, immolated to free men from the bondage of sin. Cf also 1 Cor 5, 7; 1 Pt 1, 19.

13, 17: *By way of the Philistines' land:* the most direct route from Egypt to Palestine, along the shore of the Mediterranean.

thought, should the people see that they
would have to fight, they might change
their minds and return to Egypt.
18 Instead, he rerouted them toward the
Red Sea by way of the desert road. In
battle array the Israelites marched out
of Egypt. 19* Moses also took Joseph's
bones along, for Joseph had made the
Israelites swear solemnly that, when
God should come to them, they would
carry his bones away with them.
20* Setting out from Succoth, they
camped at Etham near the edge of the
desert.
21*† The LORD preceded them, in the
daytime by means of a column of cloud
to show them the way, and at night by
means of a column of fire to give them
light. Thus they could travel both day
and night. 22 Neither the column of cloud
by day nor the column of fire by night
ever left its place in front of the people.

CHAPTER 14

1 Then the LORD said to Moses,
2*† "Tell the Israelites to turn about and
camp before Pi-hahiroth, between Mig-
dol and the sea. You shall camp in front
of Baal-zephon, just opposite, by the sea.
3 Pharaoh will then say, 'The Israelites
are wandering about aimlessly in the
land. The desert has closed in on them.'
4 Thus will I make Pharaoh so obstinate
that he will pursue them. Then I will re-
ceive glory through Pharaoh and all his
army, and the Egyptians will know that
I am the LORD."
This the Israelites did. 5* When it was
reported to the king of Egypt that the
people had fled, Pharaoh and his ser-
vants changed their minds about them.
"What have we done!" they exclaimed.
"Why, we have released Israel from our
service!" 6 So Pharaoh made his chari-
ots ready and mustered his soldiers—
7 six hundred first-class chariots and all
the other chariots of Egypt, with war-
riors on them all. 8 So obstinate had the
LORD made Pharaoh that he pursued the
Israelites even while they were march-
ing away in triumph. 9 The Egyptians,
then, pursued them; Pharaoh's whole
army, his horses, chariots and chario-
teers, caught up with them as they lay
encamped by the sea, at Pi-hahiroth, in
front of Baal-zephon.
Crossing of the Red Sea. 10 Pharaoh
was already near when the Israelites
looked up and saw that the Egyptians
were on the march in pursuit of them.
In great fright they cried out to the
LORD. 11 And they complained to Moses,
"Were there no burial places in Egypt
that you had to bring us out here to die
in the desert? Why did you do this to
us? Why did you bring us out of Egypt?
12 Did we not tell you this in Egypt, when
we said, 'Leave us alone. Let us serve
the Egyptians'? Far better for us to be
the slaves of the Egyptians than to die
in the desert." 13 But Moses answered
the people, "Fear not! Stand your
ground, and you will see the victory the
LORD will win for you today. These
Egyptians whom you see today you will
never see again. 14 The LORD himself will
fight for you; you have only to keep still."
15 Then the LORD said to Moses, "Why
are you crying out to me? Tell the Israel-
ites to go forward. 16 And you, lift up
your staff and, with hand outstretched
over the sea, split the sea in two, that
the Israelites may pass through it on dry
land. 17 But I will make the Egyptians
so obstinate that they will go in after
them. Then I will receive glory through
Pharaoh and all his army, his chariots
and charioteers. 18 The Egyptians shall
know that I am the LORD, when I receive
glory through Pharaoh and his chariots
and charioteers."
19 The angel of God, who had been
leading Israel's camp, now moved and
went around behind them. The column
of cloud also, leaving the front, took up
its place behind them, 20† so that it came
between the camp of the Egyptians and
that of Israel. But the cloud now became
dark, and thus the night passed without
the rival camps coming any closer to-
gether all night long. 21* Then Moses
stretched out his hand over the sea, and
the LORD swept the sea with a strong east
wind throughout the night and so turned
it into dry land. When the water was thus
divided, 22 the Israelites marched into
the midst of the sea on dry land, with
the water like a wall to their right and
to their left.
Destruction of the Egyptians. 23 The
Egyptians followed in pursuit; all Pha-
raoh's horses and chariots and chario-
teers went after them right into the
midst of the sea. 24 In the night watch

*

19: Gn 50, 25; Jos 24, 32.
20: Nm 33, 6.
21f: 40, 38; Nm 9, 15-22; Dt 1, 33; Neh 9, 19; Pss 78, 14; 105, 39; Wis 10, 17.
14, 2: Nm 33, 7f.
5-8: Wis 19, 3; 1 Mc 4, 9.
21f: 15, 19; Pss 66, 6; 78, 13; 136, 13f; Wis 10, 18; 19, 7f; Is 63, 12f; Heb 11, 29.

†

13, 21: *A column of cloud . . . a column of fire:* probably one and the same preternatural phenomenon, a central nucleus of fire surrounded by smoke; only at night was its luminous nature visible. Cf 40, 38.

14, 2: These places have not been definitively identified. Even the relative position of *Pi-hahiroth* and *Baal-zephon* is not clear; perhaps the former was on the west shore of the sea, where the Israelites were, and the latter on the opposite shore.

14, 20: *The cloud now became dark:* the light which it ordinarily cast at night would now have been a help to the Egyptians; its present obscurity serves as a shield for the Israelites. However, the reading of the original text here is not quite certain.

just before dawn the LORD cast through
the column of the fiery cloud upon the
Egyptian force a glance that threw it
into a panic; 25 and he so clogged their
chariot wheels that they could hardly
drive. With that the Egyptians sounded
the retreat before Israel, because the
LORD was fighting for them against the
Egyptians.
26 Then the LORD told Moses, "Stretch
out your hand over the sea, that the
water may flow back upon the Egyp-
tians, upon their chariots and their char-
ioteers." 27 So Moses stretched out his
hand over the sea, and at dawn the sea
flowed back to its normal depth. The
Egyptians were fleeing head on toward
the sea, when the LORD hurled them into
its midst. 28* As the water flowed back,
it covered the chariots and the chario-
teers of Pharaoh's whole army which
had followed the Israelites into the sea.
Not a single one of them escaped. 29 But
the Israelites had marched on dry land
through the midst of the sea, with the
water like a wall to their right and to
their left. 30 Thus the LORD saved Israel
on that day from the power of the Egyp-
tians. When Israel saw the Egyptians ly-
ing dead on the seashore 31* and beheld
the great power that the LORD had
shown against the Egyptians, they
feared the LORD and believed in him and
in his servant Moses.

CHAPTER 15

1*† Then Moses and the Israelites sang
this song to the LORD:

I will sing to the LORD, for he is glori-
ously triumphant;
horse and chariot he has cast into
the sea.

2* My strength and my courage is the
LORD,
and he has been my savior.
He is my God, I praise him;
the God of my father, I extol him.

3 The LORD is a warrior,
LORD is his name!
4 Pharaoh's chariots and army he
hurled into the sea;
the elite of his officers were sub-
merged in the Red Sea.
5* The flood waters covered them,
they sank into the depths like a
stone.

6 Your right hand, O LORD, magnifi-
cent in power,
your right hand, O LORD, has
shattered the enemy.
7 In your great majesty you over-
threw your adversaries;
you loosed your wrath to consume
them like stubble.
8 At a breath of your anger the waters
piled up,
the flowing waters stood like a
mound,
the flood waters congealed in the
midst of the sea.

9 The enemy boasted, "I will pursue
and overtake them;
I will divide the spoils and have
my fill of them;
I will draw my sword; my hand
shall despoil them!"
10 When your wind blew, the sea cov-
ered them;
like lead they sank in the mighty
waters.

11 Who is like to you among the gods,
O LORD?
Who is like to you, magnificent in
holiness?
O terrible in renown, worker of won-
ders,
12 when you stretched out your right
hand, the earth swallowed
them!

13 In your mercy you led the people
you redeemed;
in your strength you guided them
to your holy dwelling.

14 The nations heard and quaked;
anguish gripped the dwellers in
Philistia.
15 Then were the princes of Edom dis-
mayed;
trembling seized the chieftains of
Moab;
All the dwellers in Canaan melted
away;
16* terror and dread fell upon them.
By the might of your arm they were
frozen like stone,
while your people, O LORD, passed
over,
while the people you had made
your own passed over.

17 And you brought them in and
planted them on the mountain
of your inheritance—
the place where you made your
seat, O LORD,
the sanctuary, O LORD, which
your hands established.
18 The LORD shall reign forever and
ever.

19* They sang thus because Pharaoh's
horses and chariots and charioteers
had gone into the sea, and the LORD

---

*

28f: Dt 11, 4; Ps 106, 11.
31f: Ps 106, 12; Wis 10, 20.
15, 1: 15, 21.
2: Ps 118, 14; Is 12, 2.
5: Neh 9, 11.
16f: Ps 78, 53ff.
19: 14, 21-29.

†

15, 1-21: This canticle (used in Christian liturgy) celebrates God's saving power, miraculously delivering his people from their enemies, and leading them to the victorious conquest of the Promised Land.

made the waters of the sea flow back
upon them, though the Israelites had
marched on dry land through the midst
of the sea. 20 The prophetess Miriam,
Aaron's sister, took a tambourine in her
hand, while all the women went out after
her with tambourines, dancing; 21*† and
she led them in the refrain:

> Sing to the LORD, for he is gloriously
> triumphant;
> horse and chariot he has cast into
> the sea.

At Marah and Elim. 22* Then Moses
led Israel forward from the Red Sea, and
they marched out to the desert of Shur.
After traveling for three days through
the desert without finding water, 23 they
arrived at Marah, where they could not
drink the water, because it was too bit-
ter. Hence this place was called Marah.
24 As the people grumbled against Mo-
ses, saying, "What are we to drink?"
25* he appealed to the LORD, who pointed
out to him a certain piece of wood. When
he threw this into the water, the water
became fresh.

It was here that the LORD, in making
rules and regulations for them, put them
to the test. 26* "If you really listen to the
voice of the LORD, your God," he told
them, "and do what is right in his eyes:
if you heed his commandments and
keep all his precepts, I will not afflict you
with any of the diseases with which I af-
flicted the Egyptians; for I, the LORD, am
your healer."

27* Then they came to Elim, where
there were twelve springs of water and
seventy palm trees, and they camped
there near the water.

CHAPTER 16

The Desert of Sin. 1† Having set out
from Elim, the whole Israelite commu-
nity came into the desert of Sin, which
is between Elim and Sinai, on the fif-
teenth day of the second month after
their departure from the land of Egypt.
2 Here in the desert the whole Israelite
community grumbled against Moses
and Aaron. 3 The Israelites said to them,
"Would that we had died at the LORD's
hand in the land of Egypt, as we sat by
our fleshpots and ate our fill of bread!
But you had to lead us into this desert
to make the whole community die of
famine!"

The Quail and Manna. 4*† Then the
LORD said to Moses, "I will now rain
down bread from heaven for you. Each
day the people are to go out and gather
their daily portion; thus will I test them,
to see whether they follow my instruc-
tions or not. 5 On the sixth day, however,
when they prepare what they bring in,
let it be twice as much as they gather
on the other days." 6* So Moses and
Aaron told all the Israelites, "At evening
you will know that it was the LORD who
brought you out of the land of Egypt;
7 and in the morning you will see the
glory of the LORD, as he heeds your
grumbling against him. But what are we
that you should grumble against us?
8 When the LORD gives you flesh to eat
in the evening," continued Moses, "and
in the morning your fill of bread, as he
heeds the grumbling you utter against
him, what then are we? Your grumbling
is not against us, but against the LORD."

9 Then Moses said to Aaron, "Tell the
whole Israelite community: Present
yourselves before the LORD, for he has
heard your grumbling." 10 When Aaron
announced this to the whole Israelite
community, they turned toward the
desert, and lo, the glory of the LORD ap-
peared in the cloud! 11 The LORD spoke
to Moses and said, 12 "I have heard the
grumbling of the Israelites. Tell them:
In the evening twilight you shall eat
flesh, and in the morning you shall have
your fill of bread, so that you may know
that I, the LORD, am your God."

13* In the evening quail came up and
covered the camp. In the morning a dew
lay all about the camp, 14 and when the
dew evaporated, there on the surface of
the desert were fine flakes like hoarfrost
on the ground. 15*† On seeing it, the Isra-
elites asked one another, "What is this?"
for they did not know what it was. But
Moses told them, "This is the bread
which the LORD has given you to eat.

Regulations Regarding the Manna.
16 "Now, this is what the LORD has com-
manded. So gather it that everyone has
enough to eat, an omer for each person,

*

21: 15, 1.
22f: Nm 33, 8.
25: Sir 38, 5.
26: Dt 7, 15.
27: Nm 33, 9.
16, 4: Pss 78, 24f; 105, 40; Jn 6, 31f; 1 Cor 10, 3.
6f: 16, 12.
13: Nm 11, 31; Ps 78, 27f.
15: Dt 8, 3.

†

15, 21: *She led them:* Miriam's refrain re-echoes the first verse of this song and was probably sung as an antiphon after each verse.

16, 1: *On the fifteenth day of the second month:* just one full month after their departure from Egypt. Cf 12, 2.51; Nm 33, 3f. They encamped in the desert of Sin on a Friday; the murmuring (vv 2f) occurred on the sabbath, the arrival of the quail (v 13) the evening before Sunday, followed by six mornings (vv 14-27) of collecting manna before the next sabbath.

16, 4: *Bread from heaven:* as a gift from God, the manna is said to come down from the sky. Cf Ps 78, 25; Wis 16, 20. Perhaps it was similar to a natural substance that is still found in small quantities on the Sinai peninsula, but here it is, at least in part, clearly miraculous. Our Lord referred to the manna as a type of the Blessed Eucharist. Cf Jn 6, 32.49-52.

16, 15: *What is this:* the original *man hu* is thus rendered by the ancient versions, which understood the phrase as a popular etymology of the Hebrew word *man,* "manna"; some render, "This is manna."

as many of you as there are, each man
providing for those of his own tent."
17 The Israelites did so. Some gathered
a large and some a small amount.
18*† But when they measured it out by
the omer, he who had gathered a large
amount did not have too much, and he
who had gathered a small amount did
not have too little. They so gathered that
everyone had enough to eat. 19 Moses
also told them, "Let no one keep any of
it over until tomorrow morning." 20 But
they would not listen to him. When some
kept a part of it over until the following
morning, it became wormy and rotten.
Therefore Moses was displeased with
them.

21 Morning after morning they gath-
ered it, till each had enough to eat; but
when the sun grew hot, the manna
melted away. 22 On the sixth day they
gathered twice as much food, two omers
for each person. When all the leaders
of the community came and reported
this to Moses, 23 he told them, "That is
what the LORD prescribed. Tomorrow is
a day of complete rest, the sabbath, sa-
cred to the LORD. You may either bake
or boil the manna, as you please; but
whatever is left put away and keep for
the morrow." 24 When they put it away
for the morrow, as Moses commanded,
it did not become rotten or wormy.
25 Moses then said, "Eat it today, for to-
day is the sabbath of the LORD. On this
day you will not find any of it on the
ground. 26 On the other six days you can
gather it, but on the seventh day, the
sabbath, none of it will be there." 27 Still,
on the seventh day some of the people
went out to gather it, although they did
not find any. 28 Then the LORD said to
Moses, "How long will you refuse to keep
my commandments and laws? 29 Take
note! The LORD has given you the sab-
bath. That is why on the sixth day he
gives you food for two days. On the sev-
enth day everyone is to stay home and
no one is to go out." 30 After that the peo-
ple rested on the seventh day.

31*† The Israelites called this food
manna. It was like coriander seed, but
white, and it tasted like wafers made
with honey.

32 Moses said, "This is what the LORD
has commanded. Keep an omerful of
manna for your descendants, that they
may see what food I gave you to eat in
the desert when I brought you out of the
land of Egypt." 33*† Moses then told
Aaron, "Take an urn and put an omer
of manna in it. Then place it before the
LORD in safekeeping for your descen-
dants." 34† So Aaron placed it in front
of the commandments for safekeeping,
as the LORD had commanded Moses.

35* The Israelites ate this manna for
forty years, until they came to settled
land; they ate manna until they reached
the borders of Canaan. 36 [An omer is
one tenth of an ephah.]

CHAPTER 17

Water from the Rock. 1* From the
desert of Sin the whole Israelite commu-
nity journeyed by stages, as the LORD
directed, and encamped at Rephidim.

Here there was no water for the people
to drink. 2* They quarreled, therefore,
with Moses and said, "Give us water to
drink." Moses replied, "Why do you
quarrel with me? Why do you put the
LORD to a test?" 3 Here, then, in their
thirst for water, the people grumbled
against Moses, saying, "Why did you
ever make us leave Egypt? Was it just
to have us die here of thirst with our
children and our livestock?" 4 So Moses
cried out to the LORD, "What shall I do
with this people? A little more and they
will stone me!" 5* The LORD answered
Moses, "Go over there in front of the
people, along with some of the elders of
Israel, holding in your hand, as you go,
the staff with which you struck the river.
6 I will be standing there in front of you
on the rock in Horeb. Strike the rock,
and the water will flow from it for the
people to drink." This Moses did, in the
presence of the elders of Israel. 7*† The
place was called Massah and Meribah,
because the Israelites quarreled there
and tested the LORD, saying, "Is the
LORD in our midst or not?"

Battle with Amalek. 8*† At Rephidim,
Amalek came and waged war against
Israel. 9 Moses, therefore, said to
Joshua, "Pick out certain men, and to-
morrow go out and engage Amalek in
battle. I will be standing on top of the
hill with the staff of God in my hand."
10 So Joshua did as Moses told him: he
engaged Amalek in battle after Moses

---

*
18: 2 Cor 8, 15.
31: Nm 11, 7.
33: Heb 9, 4.
35: Jos 5, 12.
17, 1: Nm 33, 12ff.
2-7: Nm 20, 2-13.
5f: Dt 8, 15; Pss 78, 15f; 105, 41; Wis 11, 4; Is 43, 20; 48, 21.
7: Ps 95, 8f.
8: Dt 25, 17; 1 Sm 15, 2.

---

†
16, 18: St. Paul cites this passage as an example of equitable sharing. Cf 2 Cor 8, 15.

16, 31: *Coriander seed:* small, round, aromatic seeds of bright brown color; the comparison, therefore, refers merely to the size and shape, not to the taste or color of the manna.

16, 33: *Urn:* according to the Greek translation, which is followed in Heb 9, 4, this was a golden vessel.

16, 34: *The commandments:* the two tablets of the ten commandments, which were kept in the ark. Cf 25, 16.21f.

17, 7: *Massah . . . Meribah:* Hebrew words meaning respectively, "the (place of the) test," and, "the (place of the) quarreling."

17, 8: *Amalek:* the Amalekites were an aboriginal people of southern Palestine and the Sinai peninsula. Cf Nm 24, 20.

had climbed to the top of the hill with
Aaron and Hur. 11 As long as Moses kept
his hands raised up, Israel had the better
of the fight, but when he let his hands
rest, Amalek had the better of the fight.
12 Moses' hands, however, grew tired; so
they put a rock in place for him to sit
on. Meanwhile Aaron and Hur sup-
ported his hands, one on one side and
one on the other, so that his hands re-
mained steady till sunset. 13 And Joshua
mowed down Amalek and his people
with the edge of the sword.
14* Then the LORD said to Moses,
"Write this down in a document as
something to be remembered, and recite
it in the ears of Joshua: I will completely
blot out the memory of Amalek from un-
der the heavens." 15† Moses also built an
altar there, which he called Yahweh-
nissi; 16 for he said, "The LORD takes in
hand his banner; the LORD will war
against Amalek through the centuries."

CHAPTER 18

Meeting with Jethro. 1 Now Moses' fa-
ther-in-law Jethro, the priest of Midian,
heard of all that God had done for Moses
and for his people Israel: how the LORD
had brought Israel out of Egypt. 2 So his
father-in-law Jethro took along Zippo-
rah, Moses' wife, whom Moses had sent
back to him, 3* and her two sons. One
of these was called Gershom; for he said,
"I am a stranger in a foreign land." 4 The
other was called Eliezer; for he said,
"My father's God is my helper; he has
rescued me from Pharaoh's sword."
5 Together with Moses' wife and sons,
then, his father-in-law Jethro came to
him in the desert where he was en-
camped near the mountain of God, 6 and
he sent word to Moses, "I, Jethro, your
father-in-law, am coming to you, along
with your wife and her two sons."
7 Moses went out to meet his father-
in-law, bowed down before him, and
kissed him. Having greeted each other,
they went into the tent. 8 Moses then told
his father-in-law of all that the LORD
had done to Pharaoh and the Egyptians
for the sake of Israel, and of all the hard-
ships they had had to endure on their
journey, and how the LORD had come
to their rescue. 9 Jethro rejoiced over all
the goodness that the LORD had shown
Israel in rescuing them from the hands
of the Egyptians. 10 "Blessed be the
LORD," he said, "who has rescued his
people from the hands of Pharaoh and
the Egyptians. 11 Now I know that the
LORD is a deity great beyond any other;
for he took occasion of their being dealt
with insolently to deliver the people from
the power of the Egyptians." 12 Then
Jethro, the father-in-law of Moses,
brought a holocaust and other sacrifices
to God, and Aaron came with all the el-
ders of Israel to participate with Moses'
father-in-law in the meal before God.
Appointment of Minor Judges. 13 The
next day Moses sat in judgment for the
people, who waited about him from
morning until evening. 14 When his fa-
ther-in-law saw all that he was doing for
the people, he inquired, "What sort of
thing is this that you are doing for the
people? Why do you sit alone while all
the people have to stand about you from
morning till evening?" 15 Moses an-
swered his father-in-law, "The people
come to me to consult God. 16 Whenever
they have a disagreement, they come to
me to have me settle the matter between
them and make known to them God's
decisions and regulations."
17 "You are not acting wisely," his fa-
ther-in-law replied. 18* "You will surely
wear yourself out, and not only yourself
but also these people with you. The task
is too heavy for you; you cannot do it
alone. 19 Now, listen to me, and I will give
you some advice, that God may be with
you. Act as the people's representative
before God, bringing to him whatever
they have to say. 20 Enlighten them in
regard to the decisions and regulations,
showing them how they are to live and
what they are to do. 21* But you should
also look among all the people for able
and God-fearing men, trustworthy men
who hate dishonest gain, and set them
as officers over groups of thousands, of
hundreds, of fifties, and of tens. 22 Let
these men render decisions for the peo-
ple in all ordinary cases. More important
cases they should refer to you, but all
the lesser cases they can settle them-
selves. Thus, your burden will be light-
ened, since they will bear it with you.
23 If you do this, when God gives you or-
ders you will be able to stand the strain,
and all these people will go home satis-
fied."
24 Moses followed the advice of his fa-
ther-in-law and did all that he had sug-
gested. 25 He picked out able men from
all Israel and put them in charge of the
people as officers over groups of thou-
sands, of hundreds, of fifties, and of tens.
26 They rendered decisions for the peo-
ple in all ordinary cases. The more diffi-
cult cases they referred to Moses, but
all the lesser cases they settled them-
selves. 27 Then Moses bade farewell to
his father-in-law, who went off to his
own country.

*

14: Nm 24, 20; 1 Sm 15, 3.20.
18, 3: 2, 22.
18: Nm 11, 14.
21.25: Dt 1, 15; 16, 18.

†

17, 15: *Yahweh-nissi:* meaning, "the LORD is my banner."

III: THE COVENANT AT MOUNT SINAI

CHAPTER 19

Arrival at Sinai. 1* In the third month
after their departure from the land of
Egypt, on its first day, the Israelites
came to the desert of Sinai. 2 After the
journey from Rephidim to the desert of
Sinai, they pitched camp.
While Israel was encamped here in
front of the mountain, 3 Moses went up
the mountain to God. Then the LORD
called to him and said, "Thus shall you
say to the house of Jacob; 4* tell the Isra-
elites: You have seen for yourselves how
I treated the Egyptians and how I bore
you up on eagle wings and brought you
here to myself. 5* Therefore, if you
hearken to my voice and keep my cov-
enant, you shall be my special posses-
sion, dearer to me than all other people,
though all the earth is mine. 6*† You
shall be to me a kingdom of priests, a
holy nation. That is what you must tell
the Israelites." 7 So Moses went and
summoned the elders of the people.
When he set before them all that the
LORD had ordered him to tell them, 8 the
people all answered together, "Every-
thing the LORD has said, we will do."
Then Moses brought back to the LORD
the response of the people.
9* The LORD also told him, "I am com-
ing to you in a dense cloud, so that when
the people hear me speaking with you,
they may always have faith in you also."
When Moses, then, had reported to the
LORD the response of the people, 10 the
LORD added, "Go to the people and have
them sanctify themselves today and to-
morrow. Make them wash their gar-
ments 11 and be ready for the third day;
for on the third day the LORD will come
down on Mount Sinai before the eyes of
all the people. 12* Set limits for the peo-
ple all around the mountain, and tell
them: Take care not to go up the moun-
tain, or even to touch its base. If anyone
touches the mountain, he must be put
to death. 13 No hand shall touch him; he
must be stoned to death or killed with
arrows. Such a one, man or beast, must
not be allowed to live. Only when the
ram's horn resounds may they go up to
the mountain." 14 Then Moses came
down from the mountain to the people
and had them sanctify themselves and
wash their garments. 15 He warned
them, "Be ready for the third day. Have
no intercourse with any woman."
The Great Theophany. 16* On the
morning of the third day there were
peals of thunder and lightning, and a
heavy cloud over the mountain, and a
very loud trumpet blast, so that all the
people in the camp trembled. 17 But Mo-
ses led the people out of the camp to
meet God, and they stationed them-
selves at the foot of the mountain.
18 Mount Sinai was all wrapped in
smoke, for the LORD came down upon
it in fire. The smoke rose from it as
though from a furnace, and the whole
mountain trembled violently. 19 The
trumpet blast grew louder and louder,
while Moses was speaking and God an-
swering him with thunder.
20 When the LORD came down to the
top of Mount Sinai, he summoned Moses
to the top of the mountain, and Moses
went up to him. 21 Then the LORD told
Moses, "Go down and warn the people
not to break through toward the LORD
in order to see him; otherwise many of
them will be struck down. 22 The priests,
too, who approach the LORD must sanc-
tify themselves; else he will vent his an-
ger upon them." 23 Moses said to the
LORD, "The people cannot go up to
Mount Sinai, for you yourself warned us
to set limits around the mountain to
make it sacred." 24 The LORD repeated,
"Go down now! Then come up again
along with Aaron. But the priests and
the people must not break through to
come up to the LORD; else he will vent
his anger upon them." 25 So Moses went
down to the people and told them this.

CHAPTER 20

The Ten Commandments. 1† Then
God delivered all these commandments:
2* "I, the LORD, am your God, who
brought you out of the land of Egypt,
that place of slavery. 3 You shall not
have other gods besides me. 4* You shall
not carve idols for yourselves in the
shape of anything in the sky above or
on the earth below or in the waters be-
neath the earth; 5*† you shall not bow
down before them or worship them. For
I, the LORD, your God, am a jealous God,

*

19, 1f: Nm 33, 15.
4: Dt 32, 11.
5: Dt 7, 6; 14, 2; 26, 18f; 32, 8f.
6: 1 Pet 2, 9.
9: 20, 21; 24, 15-18.
12f: 34, 3; Heb 12, 18f.
16ff: Dt 4, 10ff.
20, 2-17: Dt 5, 6-21.
2: Lv 26, 13; Ps 81, 10; Hos 13, 4.
4: 34, 17; Lv 26, 1; Dt 4, 15-19; 27, 15.
5: 34, 7.14; Nm 14, 18; Dt 4, 24; 6, 15.

†

19, 6: *Kingdom of priests:* inasmuch as the whole Israelite nation was consecrated to God in a special way, it formed a race of royal priests who participated in the liturgical sacrifices, even though the actual offering of the sacrifices was the exclusive prerogative of the Aaronic priesthood. The same condition exists in the New Dispensation as regards the whole Christian people and the Christian priesthood in the strict sense. Cf Is 61, 6; 1 Pt 2, 5.9.

20, 1-17: The precise division of these precepts into "ten commandments" is somewhat uncertain. Traditionally among Catholics vv 1-6 are considered as only one commandment, and v 17 as two. Cf Dt 5, 6-21.

20, 5: *Jealous:* demanding exclusive allegiance, such as a wife must have for her husband.

inflicting punishment for their fathers'
wickedness on the children of those who
hate me, down to the third and fourth
generation; 6 but bestowing mercy down
to the thousandth generation, on the
children of those who love me and keep
my commandments.
7* "You shall not take the name of the
LORD, your God, in vain. For the LORD
will not leave unpunished him who takes
his name in vain.
8* "Remember to keep holy the sab-
bath day. 9 Six days you may labor and
do all your work, 10 but the seventh day
is the sabbath of the LORD, your God.
No work may be done then either by you,
or your son or daughter, or your male
or female slave, or your beast, or by the
alien who lives with you. 11* In six days
the LORD made the heavens and the
earth, the sea and all that is in them;
but on the seventh day he rested. That
is why the LORD has blessed the sabbath
day and made it holy.
12* "Honor your father and your
mother, that you may have a long life
in the land which the LORD, your God,
is giving you.
13* "You shall not kill.
14* "You shall not commit adultery.
15* "You shall not steal.
16* "You shall not bear false witness
against your neighbor.
17* "You shall not covet your neigh-
bor's house. You shall not covet your
neighbor's wife, nor his male or female
slave, nor his ox or ass, nor anything
else that belongs to him."
The Fear of God. 18* When the people
witnessed the thunder and lightning, the
trumpet blast and the mountain smok-
ing, they all feared and trembled. So
they took up a position much farther
away 19 and said to Moses, "You speak
to us, and we will listen; but let not God
speak to us, or we shall die." 20 Moses
answered the people, "Do not be afraid,
for God has come to you only to test you
and put his fear upon you, lest you
should sin." 21 Still the people remained
at a distance, while Moses approached
the cloud where God was.
22 The LORD told Moses, "Thus shall
you speak to the Israelites: You have
seen for yourselves that I have spoken
to you from heaven. 23* Do not make
anything to rank with me; neither gods
of silver nor gods of gold shall you make
for yourselves.
24*† "An altar of earth you shall make
for me, and upon it you shall sacrifice
your holocausts and peace offerings,
your sheep and your oxen. In whatever
place I choose for the remembrance of
my name I will come to you and bless
you. 25* If you make an altar of stone
for me, do not build it of cut stone, for
by putting a tool to it you desecrate it.
26 You shall not go up by steps to my al-
tar, on which you must not be indecently
uncovered.

CHAPTER 21

Laws Regarding Slaves. 1† "These
are the rules you shall lay before them.
2* When you purchase a Hebrew slave,
he is to serve you for six years, but in
the seventh year he shall be given his
freedom without cost. 3 If he comes into
service alone, he shall leave alone; if he
comes with a wife, his wife shall leave
with him. 4 But if his master gives him
a wife and she bears him sons or daugh-
ters, the woman and her children shall
remain the master's property and the
man shall leave alone. 5 If, however, the
slave declares, 'I am devoted to my mas-
ter and my wife and children; I will not
go free,' 6† his master shall bring him
to God and there, at the door or door-
post, he shall pierce his ear with an awl,
thus keeping him as his slave forever.
7 "When a man sells his daughter as
a slave, she shall not go free as male
slaves do. 8† But if her master, who had
destined her for himself, dislikes her, he
shall let her be redeemed. He has no
right to sell her to a foreigner, since he
has broken faith with her. 9 If he destines
her for his son, he shall treat her like a
daughter. 10 If he takes another wife, he
shall not withhold her food, her clothing,
or her conjugal rights. 11 If he does not
grant her these three things, she shall
be given her freedom absolutely, without
cost to her.
Personal Injury. 12* "Whoever strikes
a man a mortal blow must be put to

*

7: Lv 19, 12; 24, 16.
8ff: 23, 12; 31, 13-16; 34, 21; 35, 2; Lv 23, 3.
11: 31, 17; Gn 2, 2f.
12-16: Mt 19, 18f; Mk 10, 19; Lk 18, 20; Rom 13, 9.
12: Mt 15, 4; Mk 7, 10; Eph 6, 2f.
13: Mt 5, 21.
14: Lv 18, 20; 20, 10; Dt 22, 22; Mt 5, 27.
15: Lv 19, 11.
16: 23, 1; Dt 19, 16ff; Prv 19, 5.9; 24, 28.
17: Rom 7, 7.
18-21: Dt 4, 11; 5, 22-27; 18, 16; Heb 12, 18f.
23: 20, 3f.
24: Dt 12, 5.11; 14, 23; 16, 6.
25: Dt 27, 5; Jos 8, 31.
21, 2-6: Lv 25, 39ff; Dt 15, 12-18; Jer 34, 14.
12ff: Lv 24, 17; Nm 35, 15-29; Dt 4, 41f; 19, 2-5.

†

20, 24: *I choose for the remembrance of my name:* literally, "where I make my name to be remembered": at the sacred site where God wishes to be worshiped and his name revered.

21, 1: *Rules:* judicial precedents to be used in settling questions of law and custom. This introductory phrase serves as the title of the following collection of civil and religious laws (chapters 21-23) which is called in 24, 7, *the book of the covenant.*

21, 6: *To God:* to the sanctuary; or perhaps the phrase is to be rendered, "to the gods," in the sense of "to the judges." Cf Ps 82, 1. Since the expression "to have an open ear" meant "to obey," a pierced ear lobe was an ancient symbol of obedience. Cf Ps 40, 7.

21, 8: *Destined her:* intended her as a wife of second rank.

death. 13 He, however, who did not hunt
a man down, but caused his death by
an act of God, may flee to a place which
I will set apart for this purpose. 14 But
when a man kills another after mali-
ciously scheming to do so, you must take
him even from my altar and put him to
death. 15 Whoever strikes his father or
mother shall be put to death.
16* "A kidnaper, whether he sells his
victim or still has him when caught, shall
be put to death.
17* "Whoever curses his father or
mother shall be put to death.
18 "When men quarrel and one strikes
the other with a stone or with his fist,
not mortally, but enough to put him in
bed, 19 the one who struck the blow shall
be acquitted, provided the other can get
up and walk around with the help of his
staff. Still, he must compensate him for
his enforced idleness and provide for his
complete cure.
20 "When a man strikes his male or fe-
male slave with a rod so hard that the
slave dies under his hand, he shall be
punished. 21 If, however, the slave sur-
vives for a day or two, he is not to be
punished, since the slave is his own
property.
22* "When men have a fight and hurt
a pregnant woman, so that she suffers
a miscarriage, but no further injury, the
guilty one shall be fined as much as the
woman's husband demands of him, and
he shall pay in the presence of the
judges. 23† But if injury ensues, you shall
give life for life, 24 eye for eye, tooth for
tooth, hand for hand, foot for foot,
25 burn for burn, wound for wound,
stripe for stripe.
26 "When a man strikes his male or fe-
male slave in the eye and destroys the
use of the eye, he shall let the slave go
free in compensation for the eye. 27 If he
knocks out a tooth of his male or female
slave, he shall let the slave go free in
compensation for the tooth.
28 "When an ox gores a man or a
woman to death, the ox must be stoned;
its flesh may not be eaten. The owner
of the ox, however, shall go unpunished.
29 But if an ox was previously in the habit
of goring people and its owner, though
warned, would not keep it in; should it
then kill a man or a woman, not only
must the ox be stoned, but its owner also
must be put to death. 30 If, however, a
fine is imposed on him, he must pay in
ransom for his life whatever amount is
imposed on him. 31 This law applies if
it is a boy or a girl that the ox gores.
32 But if it is a male or a female slave
that it gores, he must pay the owner of
the slave thirty shekels of silver, and the
ox must be stoned.
Property Damage. 33 "When a man
uncovers or digs a cistern and does not
cover it over again, should an ox or an
ass fall into it, 34 the owner of the cistern
must make good by restoring the value
of the animal to its owner; the dead ani-
mal, however, he may keep.
35 "When one man's ox hurts another's
ox so badly that it dies, they shall sell
the live ox and divide this money as well
as the dead animal equally between
them. 36 But if it was known that the ox
was previously in the habit of goring and
its owner would not keep it in, he must
make full restitution, an ox for an ox;
but the dead animal he may keep.
37*† "When a man steals an ox or a
sheep and slaughters or sells it, he shall
restore five oxen for the one ox, and four
sheep for the one sheep.

CHAPTER 22

1† "[If a thief is caught in the act of
housebreaking and beaten to death,
there is no bloodguilt involved. 2 But if
after sunrise he is thus beaten, there is
bloodguilt.] He must make full restitu-
tion. If he has nothing, he shall be sold
to pay for his theft. 3 If what he stole is
found alive in his possession, be it an
ox, an ass or a sheep, he shall restore
two animals for each one stolen.
4† "When a man is burning over a field
or a vineyard, if he lets the fire spread
so that it burns in another's field, he
must make restitution with the best
produce of his own field or vineyard. 5 If
the fire spreads further, and catches on
to thorn bushes, so that shocked grain
or standing grain or the field itself is
burned up, the one who started the fire
must make full restitution.
Trusts and Loans. 6 "When a man
gives money or an article to another for
safekeeping and it is stolen from the lat-
ter's house, the thief, if caught, must
make twofold restitution. 7† If the thief
is not caught, the owner of the house
shall be brought to God, to swear that

*

16: Dt 24, 7.
17: Lv 20, 9; Prv 20, 20; Mt 15, 4; Mk 7, 10.
22-25: Lv 24, 18-21; Dt 19, 21; Mt 5, 38.
37: 2 Sm 12, 6.

†

21, 23ff: This section is known as the *lex talionis,* the law of tit for tat. The purpose of this law was not merely the enforcement of rigorous justice, but also the prevention of greater penalties than would be just. Christ refers to this passage when he exhorts Christians to cede their lawful rights for the sake of charity. Cf Mt 5, 38ff.

21, 37—22, 30: In the Vulgate, 22, 1-31.

22, 1f: *If a thief is caught:* this seems to be a fragment of what was once a longer law on housebreaking, which has been inserted here into the middle of a law on stealing animals. At night the householder would be justified in killing a burglar outright, but not so in the daytime, when the burglar could more easily be caught alive. *He must make full restitution:* this stood originally immediately after 21, 37.

22, 4: The Greek and Latin versions understood this verse as a prohibition against allowing one's cattle to graze in the field of another.

22, 7: *Brought to God:* see note on 21, 6. Cf also 22, 10.

he himself did not lay hands on his
neighbor's property. 8 In every question
of dishonest appropriation, whether it be
about an ox, or an ass, or a sheep, or a
garment, or anything else that has dis-
appeared, where another claims that the
thing is his, both parties shall present
their case before God; the one whom
God convicts must make twofold restitu-
tion to the other.
9 "When a man gives an ass, or an ox,
or a sheep, or any other animal to an-
other for safekeeping, if it dies, or is
maimed or snatched away, without any-
one witnessing the fact, 10 the custodian
shall swear by the LORD that he did not
lay hands on his neighbor's property;
the owner must accept the oath, and no
restitution is to be made. 11 But if the cus-
todian is really guilty of theft, he must
make restitution to the owner. 12* If it
has been killed by a wild beast, let him
bring it as evidence, and he need not
make restitution for the mangled ani-
mal.
13 "When a man borrows an animal
from his neighbor, if it is maimed or dies
while the owner is not present, the man
must make restitution. 14 But if the
owner is present, he need not make res-
titution. If it was hired, this was covered
by the price of its hire.
Social Laws. 15* "When a man se-
duces a virgin who is not betrothed, and
lies with her, he shall pay her marriage
price and marry her. 16† If her father
refuses to give her to him, he must still
pay him the customary marriage price
for virgins.
17* "You shall not let a sorceress live.
18* "Anyone who lies with an animal
shall be put to death.
19* "Whoever sacrifices to any god, ex-
cept to the LORD alone, shall be doomed.
20* "You shall not molest or oppress
an alien, for you were once aliens your-
selves in the land of Egypt. 21 You shall
not wrong any widow or orphan. 22 If
ever you wrong them and they cry out
to me, I will surely hear their cry. 23 My
wrath will flare up, and I will kill you
with the sword; then your own wives will
be widows, and your children orphans.
24* "If you lend money to one of your
poor neighbors among my people, you
shall not act like an extortioner toward
him by demanding interest from him.
25 If you take your neighbor's cloak as
a pledge, you shall return it to him be-
fore sunset; 26 for this cloak of his is the
only covering he has for his body. What
else has he to sleep in? If he cries out
to me, I will hear him; for I am compas-
sionate.
27*† "You shall not revile God, nor
curse a prince of your people.
28 "You shall not delay the offering of
your harvest and your press. You shall
give me the first-born of your sons.
29* You must do the same with your oxen
and your sheep; for seven days the first-
ling may stay with its mother, but on
the eighth day you must give it to me.
30* "You shall be men sacred to me.
Flesh torn to pieces in the field you shall
not eat; throw it to the dogs.

CHAPTER 23

1* "You shall not repeat a false report.
Do not join the wicked in putting your
hand, as an unjust witness, upon any-
one. 2 Neither shall you allege the exam-
ple of the many as an excuse for doing
wrong, nor shall you, when testifying in
a lawsuit, side with the many in pervert-
ing justice. 3* You shall not favor a poor
man in his lawsuit.
4* "When you come upon your ene-
my's ox or ass going astray, see to it that
it is returned to him. 5 When you notice
the ass of one who hates you lying pros-
trate under its burden, by no means de-
sert him; help him, rather, to raise it up.
6 "You shall not deny one of your
needy fellow men his rights in his law-
suit. 7 You shall keep away from any-
thing dishonest. The innocent and the
just you shall not put to death, nor shall
you acquit the guilty. 8* Never take a
bribe, for a bribe blinds even the most
clear-sighted and twists the words even
of the just. 9* You shall not oppress an
alien; you well know how it feels to be
an alien, since you were once aliens
yourselves in the land of Egypt.
Religious Laws. 10* "For six years you
may sow your land and gather in its
produce. 11 But the seventh year you
shall let the land lie untilled and unhar-
vested, that the poor among you may
eat of it and the beasts of the field may
eat what the poor leave. So also shall you
do in regard to your vineyard and your
olive grove.
12* "For six days you may do your
work, but on the seventh day you must
rest, that your ox and your ass may also

EXODUS

*

22, 12: Gn 31, 39.
15f: Dt 22, 28f.
17: Lv 19, 26.31; 20, 6.27; Dt 18, 10f. 7f.17f.
18: Lv 18, 23; Dt 27, 21.
19: Dt 13; 17, 2-7.
20-23: 23, 9; Lv 19, 33f; Dt 10, 18f; 24, 17f; 27, 19; Zec 7, 10.
24-26: Lv 25, 35-38; Dt 23, 19f; 24, 10-13; Ez 18,
27: Acts 23, 5.
29: 13, 2; 34, 19; Lv 22, 27; Dt 15, 19.
30: Lv 7, 24; 17, 15; 22, 8.
23, 1f: Dt 19, 16ff.
3: Lv 19, 15.
4: Dt 22, 1ff.
8: Dt 16, 19; 27, 25; Sir 20, 28.
9: 22, 21.
10f: Lv 25, 3-7.
12: 20, 8.

†

22, 16: *The customary marriage price for virgins:* fifty shekels according to Dt 22, 29.

22, 27: *God:* or perhaps "the gods," in the sense of "the judges," as the parallel with *a prince of your people* suggests.

have rest, and that the son of your maid-
servant and the alien may be refreshed.
13 Give heed to all that I have told you.
"Never mention the name of any other
god; it shall not be heard from your lips.
14*† "Three times a year you shall cel-
ebrate a pilgrim feast to me. 15† You
shall keep the feast of Unleavened
Bread. As I have commanded you, you
must eat unleavened bread for seven
days at the prescribed time in the month
of Abib, for it was then that you came
out of Egypt. No one shall appear before
me empty-handed. 16 You shall also
keep the feast of the grain harvest with
the first of the crop that you have sown
in the field; and finally, the feast at the
fruit harvest at the end of the year, when
you gather in the produce from the
fields. 17 Thrice a year shall all your men
appear before the Lord GOD.
18* "You shall not offer the blood of my
sacrifice with leavened bread; nor shall
the fat of my feast be kept overnight till
the next day. 19† The choicest first fruits
of your soil you shall bring to the house
of the LORD, your God.
"You shall not boil a kid in its mother's
milk.

Reward of Fidelity. 20* "See, I am
sending an angel before you, to guard
you on the way and bring you to the
place I have prepared. 21† Be attentive
to him and heed his voice. Do not rebel
against him, for he will not forgive your
sin. My authority resides in him. 22 If you
heed his voice and carry out all I tell
you, I will be an enemy to your enemies
and a foe to your foes.
23* "My angel will go before you and
bring you to the Amorites, Hittites, Per-
izzites, Canaanites, Hivites and Jebu-
sites; and I will wipe them out.
24† Therefore, you shall not bow down
in worship before their gods, nor shall
you make anything like them; rather,
you must demolish them and smash
their sacred pillars. 25 The LORD, your
God, you shall worship; then I will bless
your food and drink, and I will remove
all sickness from your midst; 26 no
woman in your land will be barren or
miscarry; and I will give you a full span
of life.
27* "I will have the fear of me precede
you, so that I will throw into panic every
nation you reach. I will make all your
enemies turn from you in flight, 28† and
ahead of you I will send hornets to drive
the Hivites, Canaanites and Hittites out
of your way. 29 But not in one year will
I drive them all out before you; else the
land will become so desolate that the
wild beasts will multiply against you.
30 Instead, I will drive them out little by
little before you, until you have grown
numerous enough to take possession of
the land. 31*† I will set your boundaries
from the Red Sea to the sea of the Philis-
tines, and from the desert to the River;
all who dwell in this land I will hand over
to you to be driven out of your way.
32* You shall not make a covenant with
them or their gods. 33 They must not
abide in your land, lest they make you
sin against me by ensnaring you into
worshiping their gods."

CHAPTER 24

Ratification of the Covenant. 1 Moses
himself was told, "Come up to the LORD,
you and Aaron, with Nadab, Abihu, and
seventy of the elders of Israel. You shall
all worship at some distance, 2 but Moses
alone is to come close to the LORD; the
others shall not come too near, and the
people shall not come up at all with Mo-
ses."
3* When Moses came to the people and
related all the words and ordinances of
the LORD, they all answered with one
voice, "We will do everything that the
LORD has told us." 4† Moses then wrote
down all the words of the LORD and, ris-
ing early the next day, he erected at the
foot of the mountain an altar and twelve
pillars for the twelve tribes of Israel.
5* Then, having sent certain young men
of the Israelites to offer holocausts and
sacrifice young bulls as peace offerings
to the LORD, 6 Moses took half of the
blood and put it in large bowls; the other
half he splashed on the altar. 7 Taking
the book of the covenant, he read it aloud
to the people, who answered, "All that
the LORD has said, we will heed and do."

*

14-17: 34, 18.22ff; Lv 23; Dt 16, 1-17.
18f: 34, 25f.
20: 14, 19; 32, 34; 33, 2.
23f: 34, 10-16; Nm 33, 51f; Dt 7, 24ff.
27ff: Dt 2, 25; 7, 20ff.
31: Gn 15, 18; Dt 11, 24; Jos 1, 4.
32f: 34, 12-16; Dt 7, 2ff.
24, 3: 19, 8.
5-8: Heb 9, 18ff.

†

23, 14: These three feasts are elsewhere called the Passover, Pentecost and Booths. Cf 34, 18-26; Lv 23; Dt 16.

23, 15: *Appear before me:* the original expression was "see my face"; so also in several other places, as 23, 17; 34, 23f; Dt 16, 16; 31, 11.

23, 19: *Boil a kid in its mother's milk:* this was part of a Canaanite ritual; hence it is forbidden here as a pagan ceremony.

23, 21: *My authority resides in him:* literally, "My name is within him."

23, 24: *Make anything like them:* some render, "act according to their conduct." *Sacred pillars:* objects of religious veneration at Canaanite sanctuaries.

23, 28: *Hornets:* some understand this figuratively of various troublesome afflictions; others translate the Hebrew word as "leprosy." Cf Dt 7, 20; Jos 24, 12; Wis 12, 8.

23, 31: *The sea of the Philistines:* the Mediterranean. *The River:* the Euphrates. Only in the time of David and Solomon did the territory of Israel come near to reaching such distant borders.

24, 4: *Pillars:* stone shafts or slabs, erected as symbols of the fact that each of the twelve tribes had entered into this covenant with God; not idolatrous as in 23, 24, although the same Hebrew word is used in both passages. See note on Gn 28, 18.

8 Then he took the blood and sprinkled
it on the people, saying, "This is the
blood of the covenant which the LORD
has made with you in accordance with
all these words of his."
9 Moses then went up with Aaron, Na-
dab, Abihu, and seventy elders of Israel,
10 and they beheld the God of Israel. Un-
der his feet there appeared to be sap-
phire tilework, as clear as the sky itself.
11† Yet he did not smite these chosen Is-
raelites. After gazing on God, they could
still eat and drink.
Moses on the Mountain. 12* The LORD
said to Moses, "Come up to me on the
mountain and, while you are there, I will
give you the stone tablets on which I
have written the commandments in-
tended for their instruction." 13 So Moses
set out with Joshua, his aide, and went
up to the mountain of God. 14 The elders,
however, had been told by him, "Wait
here for us until we return to you. Aaron
and Hur are staying with you. If anyone
has a complaint, let him refer the matter
to them." 15 After Moses had gone up,
a cloud covered the mountain. 16* The
glory of the LORD settled upon Mount
Sinai. The cloud covered it for six days,
and on the seventh day he called to Mo-
ses from the midst of the cloud. 17* To
the Israelites the glory of the LORD was
seen as a consuming fire on the moun-
taintop. 18* But Moses passed into the
midst of the cloud as he went up on the
mountain; and there he stayed for forty
days and forty nights.

IV: THE DWELLING AND ITS FURNISHINGS

CHAPTER 25

Collection of Materials. 1* This is what
the LORD then said to Moses: 2 "Tell the
Israelites to take up a collection for me.
From every man you shall accept the
contribution that his heart prompts him
to give me. 3* These are the contri-
butions you shall accept from them:
gold, silver and bronze; 4 violet, purple
and scarlet yarn; fine linen and goat
hair; 5† rams' skins dyed red, and ta-
hash skins; acacia wood; 6 oil for the
light; spices for the anointing oil and for
the fragrant incense; 7 onyx stones and
other gems for mounting on the ephod
and the breastpiece.
8* "They shall make a sanctuary for
me, that I may dwell in their midst.
9* This Dwelling and all its furnishings
you shall make exactly according to the
pattern that I will now show you.
Plan of the Ark. 10* "You shall make
an ark of acacia wood, two and a half
cubits long, one and a half cubits wide,
and one and a half cubits high. 11 Plate
it inside and outside with pure gold, and
put a molding of gold around the top of
it. 12 Cast four gold rings and fasten them
on the four supports of the ark, two rings
on one side and two on the opposite side.
13 Then make poles of acacia wood and
plate them with gold. 14 These poles you
are to put through the rings on the sides
of the ark, for carrying it; 15 they must
remain in the rings of the ark and never
be withdrawn. 16 In the ark you are to
put the commandments which I will give
you.
17† "You shall then make a propitia-
tory of pure gold, two cubits and a half
long, and one and a half cubits wide.
18† Make two cherubim of beaten gold
for the two ends of the propitiatory,
19 fastening them so that one cherub
springs direct from each end. 20 The
cherubim shall have their wings spread
out above, covering the propitiatory with
them; they shall be turned toward each
other, but with their faces looking to-
ward the propitiatory. 21 This propitia-
tory you shall then place on top of the
ark. In the ark itself you are to put the
commandments which I will give you.
22 There I will meet you and there, from
above the propitiatory, between the two
cherubim on the ark of the command-
ments, I will tell you all the commands
that I wish you to give the Israelites.
The Table. 23* "You shall also make a
table of acacia wood, two cubits long, a
cubit wide, and a cubit and a half high.
24 Plate it with pure gold and make a
molding of gold around it. 25† Surround
it with a frame, a handbreadth high,
with a molding of gold around the frame.
26 You shall also make four rings of gold
for it and fasten them at the four cor-
ners, one at each leg, 27 on two opposite
sides of the frame as holders for the

*

12: 31, 18; 32, 15f; Dt 5, 22.
16: Sir 45, 4.
17: 19, 18; Heb 12, 18.
18: 34, 28; Dt 9, 9.
25, 1-7: 35, 4-9. 20-29.
3: 35, 4-9.
8f: 26, 1-30; 36, 8-38.
9: Acts 7, 44.
10-22: 37, 1-9; Heb 9, 1-5.
23-30: 37, 10-16.

†

24, 11: *After gazing on God:* the ancients thought that the sight of God would bring instantaneous death. Cf 33, 20; Gn 16, 13; 32, 31; Jgs 6, 22f; 13, 22. *Eat and drink:* partake of the sacrificial meal.

25, 5: *Tahash:* perhaps the name of a marine animal, such as the dugong or the porpoise. The Greek and Latin versions took it for the color hyacinth.

25, 17: *Propitiatory:* this traditional rendering of the Hebrew term, which may mean merely "cover," is derived from its connection with the ceremony of the Day of Atonement whereby God was rendered "propitious." Cf Lv 16, 14ff.

25, 18ff: *Cherubim:* probably in the form of human-headed winged lions. The cherubim over the ark formed the throne for the invisible Lord. Cf Ps 80, 2. For a more detailed description of the somewhat different cherubim in the temple of Solomon, see 1 Kgs 6, 23-28; 2 Chr 3, 10-13.

25, 25: *A frame:* probably placed near the bottom of the legs to keep them steady. The golden table of Herod's temple is pictured thus on the Arch of Titus.

poles to carry the table. 28 These poles for carrying the table you shall make of acacia wood and plate with gold. 29† Of pure gold you shall make its plates and cups, as well as its pitchers and bowls for pouring libations. 30* On the table you shall always keep showbread set before me.

The Lampstand. 31* "You shall make a lampstand of pure beaten gold—its shaft and branches—with its cups and knobs and petals springing directly from it. 32 Six branches are to extend from the sides of the lampstand, three branches on one side, and three on the other. 33† On one branch there are to be three cups, shaped like almond blossoms, each with its knob and petals; on the opposite branch there are to be three cups, shaped like almond blossoms, each with its knob and petals; and so for the six branches that extend from the lampstand. 34† On the shaft there are to be four cups, shaped like almond blossoms, with their knobs and petals, 35 including a knob below each of the three pairs of branches that extend from the lampstand. 36 Their knobs and branches shall so spring from it that the whole will form but a single piece of pure beaten gold. 37*† You shall then make seven lamps for it and so set up the lamps that they shed their light on the space in front of the lampstand. 38† These, as well as the trimming shears and trays, must be of pure gold. 39 Use a talent of pure gold for the lampstand and all its appurtenances. 40* See that you make them according to the pattern shown you on the mountain.

CHAPTER 26

The Tent Cloth. 1*† "The Dwelling itself you shall make out of sheets woven of fine linen twined and of violet, purple and scarlet yarn, with cherubim embroidered on them. 2 The length of each shall be twenty-eight cubits, and the width four cubits; all the sheets shall be of the same size. 3 Five of the sheets are to be sewed together, edge to edge; and the same for the other five. 4 Make loops of violet yarn along the edge of the end sheet in one set, and the same along the edge of the end sheet in the other set. 5 There are to be fifty loops along the edge of the end sheet in the first set, and fifty loops along the edge of the corresponding sheet in the second set, and so placed that the loops are directly opposite each other. 6 Then make fifty clasps of gold, with which to join the two sets of sheets, so that the Dwelling forms one whole.

7† "Also make sheets woven of goat hair, to be used as a tent covering over the Dwelling. 8 Eleven such sheets are to be made; the length of each shall be thirty cubits, and the width four cubits: all eleven sheets shall be of the same size. 9† Sew five of the sheets, edge to edge, into one set, and the other six sheets into another set. Use the sixth sheet double at the front of the tent. 10 Make fifty loops along the edge of the end sheet in one set, and fifty loops along the edge of the end sheet in the second set. 11 Also make fifty bronze clasps and put them into the loops, to join the tent into one whole. 12 There will be an extra half sheet of tent covering, which shall be allowed to hang down over the rear of the Dwelling. 13 Likewise, the sheets of the tent will have an extra cubit's length to be left hanging down on either side of the Dwelling to protect it. 14 Over the tent itself you shall make a covering of rams' skins dyed red, and above that, a covering of tahash skins.

The Wooden Walls. 15* "You shall make boards of acacia wood as walls for the Dwelling. 16 The length of each board is to be ten cubits, and its width one and a half cubits. 17† Each board shall have two arms that shall serve to fasten the boards in line. In this way all the boards of the Dwelling are to be made. 18 Set up the boards of the Dwelling as follows: twenty boards on the south side, 19 with forty silver pedestals under the twenty boards, so that there are two pedestals under each board, at

*

30: Lv 24, 5ff.
31-40: 37, 17-24.
37: Lv 24, 2ff; Nm 8, 2.
40: Heb 8, 5.
26, 1-14: 36, 8-19.
15-30: 36, 20-34.

†

25, 29f: The *plates* held the showbread, that is, the holy bread which was placed upon the table every sabbath as an offering to God, and was later eaten by the priests. The *cups* held the incense which was strewn upon the bread. Cf Lv 24, 5-9. The libation wine was poured from the *pitchers* into the *bowls*. All these vessels were kept on the golden table.

25, 33: In keeping with the arrangement of the ornaments on the shaft, the three sets of ornaments on each branch were probably so placed that one was at the top and the other two equally spaced along the length of the branch. *Knob:* the cup-shaped seed capsule at the base of a flower.

25, 34f: Of the four ornaments on the shaft, one was at the top and one was below each of the three sets of side branches.

25, 37: The lamps were probably shaped like small boats, with the wick at one end; the end with the wick was turned toward the front of the lampstand.

25, 38: *Trays:* small receptacles for the burnt-out wicks.

26, 1: *Sheets:* strips of tapestry, woven of white linen, the colored threads being used for the cherubim which were embroidered on them. These sheets were stretched across the top of the Dwelling to form a roof, their free ends hanging down inside the boards which formed walls.

26, 7: *Tent covering:* the cloth made of sheets of goat hair to cover the Dwelling.

26, 9: Half the width of the end strip was folded back at the front of the Dwelling, thus leaving another half-strip to hang down at the rear. Cf v 12.

26, 17: *Arms:* literally, "hands." According to some, they served as "tongue and groove" to mortise the boards together; according to others, they were pegs at the bottom of the boards and fitted into sockets in the pedestals.

its two arms; 20 twenty boards on the other side of the Dwelling, the north side, 21 with their forty silver pedestals, two under each board; 22 six boards for the rear of the Dwelling, to the west; 23 and two boards for the corners at the rear of the Dwelling. 24 These two shall be double at the bottom, and likewise double at the top, to the first ring. That is how both boards in the corners are to be made. 25 Thus, there shall be in the rear eight boards, with their sixteen silver pedestals, two pedestals under each board. 26 Also make bars of acacia wood: five for the boards on one side of the Dwelling, 27 five for those on the other side, and five for those at the rear, toward the west. 28 The center bar, at the middle of the boards, shall reach across from end to end. 29 Plate the boards with gold, and make gold rings on them as holders for the bars, which are also to be plated with gold. 30 You shall erect the Dwelling according to the pattern shown you on the mountain.

The Veils. 31* "You shall have a veil woven of violet, purple and scarlet yarn, and of fine linen twined, with cherubim embroidered on it. 32† It is to be hung on four gold-plated columns of acacia wood, which shall have hooks of gold and shall rest on four silver pedestals. 33 Hang the veil from clasps. The ark of the commandments you shall bring inside, behind this veil which divides the holy place from the holy of holies. 34 Set the propitiatory on the ark of the commandments in the holy of holies.

35 "Outside the veil you shall place the table and the lampstand, the latter on the south side of the Dwelling, opposite the table, which is to be put on the north side. 36† For the entrance of the tent make a variegated curtain of violet, purple and scarlet yarn and of fine linen twined. 37 Make five columns of acacia wood for this curtain; have them plated with gold, with their hooks of gold; and cast five bronze pedestals for them.

CHAPTER 27

The Altar of Holocausts. 1* "You shall make an altar of acacia wood, on a square, five cubits long and five cubits wide; it shall be three cubits high. 2 At the four corners there are to be horns, so made that they spring directly from the altar. You shall then plate it with bronze. 3 Make pots for removing the ashes, as well as shovels, basins, forks and fire pans, all of which shall be of bronze. 4† Make a grating of bronze network for it; this to have four bronze rings, one at each of its four corners. 5 Put it down around the altar, on the ground. This network is to be half as high as the altar. 6 You shall also make poles of acacia wood for the altar, and plate them with bronze. 7 These poles are to be put through the rings, so that they are on either side of the altar when it is carried. 8† Make the altar itself in the form of a hollow box, just as it was shown you on the mountain.

Court of the Dwelling. 9* "You shall also make a court for the Dwelling. On the south side the court shall have hangings a hundred cubits long, woven of fine linen twined, 10 with twenty columns and twenty pedestals of bronze; the hooks and bands on the columns shall be of silver. 11 On the north side there shall be similar hangings, a hundred cubits long, with twenty columns and twenty pedestals of bronze; the hooks and bands on the columns shall be of silver. 12 On the west side, across the width of the court, there shall be hangings, fifty cubits long, with ten columns and ten pedestals. 13 The width of the court on the east side shall be fifty cubits. 14 On one side there shall be hangings to the extent of fifteen cubits, with three columns and three pedestals; 15 on the other side there shall be hangings to the extent of fifteen cubits, with three columns and three pedestals.

16 "At the entrance of the court there shall be a variegated curtain, twenty cubits long, woven of violet, purple and scarlet yarn and of fine linen twined. It shall have four columns and four pedestals.

17 "All the columns around the court shall have bands and hooks of silver, and pedestals of bronze. 18 The enclosure of the court is to be one hundred cubits long, fifty cubits wide, and five cubits high. Fine linen twined must be used, and the pedestals must be of bronze. 19 All the fittings of the Dwelling, whatever be their use, as well as all its tent pegs and all the tent pegs of the court, must be of bronze.

Oil for the Lamps. 20* "You shall order the Israelites to bring you clear oil of crushed olives, to be used for the light, so that you may keep lamps burning regularly. 21 From evening to morning

*

31: 2 Chr. 3, 14.
31-37: 36, 35-38.
27, 1-8: 38, 1-7.
9-19: 38, 9-20.
20f: Lv 24, 1-4.

†

26, 32: *Hooks:* probably placed near the tops of the columns, to hold the rope from which the veils and curtains hung.

26, 36: *Variegated:* without definite designs such as the cherubim on the inner veil.

27, 4: *Grating:* it is not clear whether this was flush with the altar or at some small distance from it; in the latter case the space between the altar and the grating would be filled with stones and serve as a platform around the altar, which would otherwise be too high for the priest to reach conveniently.

27, 8: *Hollow:* probably filled with earth or stones when in use. Cf 20, 24f.

Aaron and his sons shall maintain them
before the LORD in the meeting tent, out-
side the veil which hangs in front of the
commandments. This shall be a perpet-
ual ordinance for the Israelites through-
out their generations.

CHAPTER 28

The Priestly Vestments. 1* "From
among the Israelites have your brother
Aaron, together with his sons Nadab,
Abihu, Eleazar and Ithamar, brought to
you, that they may be my priests. 2 For
the glorious adornment of your brother
Aaron you shall have sacred vestments
made. 3 Therefore, to the various expert
workmen whom I have endowed with
skill, you shall give instructions to make
such vestments for Aaron as will set him
apart for his sacred service as my priest.
4 These are the vestments they shall
make: a breastpiece, an ephod, a robe,
a brocaded tunic, a miter and a sash.
In making these sacred vestments
which your brother Aaron and his sons
are to wear in serving as my priests,
5 they shall use gold, violet, purple and
scarlet yarn and fine linen.

The Ephod and Breastpiece. 6*† "The
ephod they shall make of gold thread
and of violet, purple and scarlet yarn,
embroidered on cloth of fine linen
twined. 7 It shall have a pair of shoulder
straps joined to its two upper ends. 8 The
embroidered belt of the ephod shall ex-
tend out from it and, like it, be made
of gold thread, of violet, purple and scar-
let yarn, and of fine linen twined.

9 "Get two onyx stones and engrave on
them the names of the sons of Israel:
10 six of their names on one stone, and
the other six on the other stone, in the
order of their birth. 11 As a gem-cutter
engraves a seal, so shall you have the
two stones engraved with the names of
the sons of Israel and then mounted in
gold filigree work. 12 Set these two stones
on the shoulder straps of the ephod as
memorial stones of the sons of Israel.
Thus Aaron shall bear their names on
his shoulders as a reminder before the
LORD. 13* Make filigree rosettes of gold,
14 as well as two chains of pure gold,
twisted like cords, and fasten the cord-
like chains to the filigree rosettes.

15*† "The breastpiece of decision you
shall also have made, embroidered like
the ephod with gold thread and violet,
purple and scarlet yarn on cloth of fine
linen twined. 16 It is to be square when
folded double, a span high and a span
wide. 17† On it you shall mount four rows
of precious stones: in the first row, a car-
nelian, a topaz and an emerald; 18 in the
second row, a garnet, a sapphire and a
beryl; 19 in the third row, a jacinth, an
agate and an amethyst; 20 in the fourth
row, a chrysolite, an onyx and a jasper.
These stones are to be mounted in gold
filigree work, 21 twelve of them to match
the names of the sons of Israel, each
stone engraved like a seal with the name
of one of the twelve tribes.

22 "When the chains of pure gold,
twisted like cords, have been made for
the breastpiece, 23 you shall then make
two rings of gold for it and fasten them
to the two upper ends of the breastpiece.
24 The gold cords are then to be fastened
to the two rings at the upper ends of the
breastpiece, 25 the other two ends of the
cords being fastened in front to the two
filigree rosettes which are attached to
the shoulder straps of the ephod. 26 Make
two other rings of gold and put them on
the two lower ends of the breastpiece,
on its edge that faces the ephod. 27 Then
make two more rings of gold and fasten
them to the bottom of the shoulder
straps next to where they join the ephod
in front, just above its embroidered belt.
28 Violet ribbons shall bind the rings of
the breastpiece to the rings of the ephod,
so that the breastpiece will stay right
above the embroidered belt of the ephod
and not swing loose from it.

29 "Whenever Aaron enters the sanc-
tuary, he will thus bear the names of the
sons of Israel on the breastpiece of deci-
sion over his heart as a constant re-
minder before the LORD. 30*† In this
breastpiece of decision you shall put the
Urim and Thummim, that they may be
over Aaron's heart whenever he enters
the presence of the LORD. Thus he shall
always bear the decisions for the Israel-
ites over his heart in the LORD's pres-
ence.

Other Vestments. 31* "The robe of the
ephod you shall make entirely of violet

---

*

28, 1-5: 39, 1; Sir 45, 7.
6-12: 39, 2-7; Sir 45, 8-14.
13f: 28, 22.25; 39, 15.18.
15-21: 39, 15-21.
30: Lv 8, 8; Sir 45, 11.
31-35: 39, 20ff; Lv 8, 9; Sir 45, 10.

†

28, 6: *Ephod:* this Hebrew word is retained in the translation because it is the technical term for a peculiar piece of the priestly vestments, the exact nature of which is uncertain. It seems to have been a sort of apron that hung from the shoulders of the priest by *shoulder straps* (v 7) and was tied around his waist by the loose ends of the attached belt (v 8).

28, 15-30: *Breastpiece:* in shape like a modern altar burse, it was a pocketlike receptacle for holding the *Urim* and *Thummim* (v 30), and formed an integral part of the ephod, to which it was attached by an elaborate system of rings and chains. Both the ephod and its breastpiece were made of brocaded linen.

28, 17-20: The translation of the Hebrew names of some of these gems is quite conjectural.

28, 30: *Urim and Thummim:* both the meaning of these Hebrew words and the exact nature of the objects so designated are uncertain. They were apparently lots of some kind which were drawn or cast by the priest to ascertain God's decision in doubtful matters. Hence, the burse in which they were kept was called "the breastpiece of decision."

material. 32 It shall have an opening for
the head in the center, and around this
opening there shall be a selvage, woven
as at the opening of a shirt, to keep it
from being torn. 33 All around the hem
at the bottom you shall make pome-
granates, woven of violet, purple and
scarlet yarn and fine linen twined, with
gold bells between them; 34 first a gold
bell, then a pomegranate, and thus alter-
nating all around the hem of the robe.
35 Aaron shall wear it when ministering,
that its tinkling may be heard as he en-
ters and leaves the LORD's presence in
the sanctuary; else he will die.

36 "You shall also make a plate of pure
gold and engrave on it, as on a seal en-
graving, 'Sacred to the LORD.' 37* This
plate is to be tied over the miter with a
violet ribbon in such a way that it rests
on the front of the miter, 38 over Aaron's
forehead. Since Aaron bears whatever
guilt the Israelites may incur in conse-
crating any of their sacred gifts, this
plate must always be over his forehead,
so that they may find favor with the
LORD.

39* "The tunic of fine linen shall be bro-
caded. The miter shall be made of fine
linen. The sash shall be of variegated
work.

40 "Likewise, for the glorious adorn-
ment of Aaron's sons you shall have tu-
nics and sashes and turbans made.
41† With these you shall clothe your
brother Aaron and his sons. Anoint and
ordain them, consecrating them as my
priests. 42* You must also make linen
drawers for them, to cover their naked
flesh from their loins to their thighs.
43 Aaron and his sons shall wear them
whenever they go into the meeting tent
or approach the altar to minister in the
sanctuary, lest they incur guilt and die.
This shall be a perpetual ordinance for
him and for his descendants.

CHAPTER 29

Consecration of the Priests. 1* "This is
the rite you shall perform in consecrat-
ing them as my priests. Procure a young
bull and two unblemished rams. 2 With
fine wheat flour make unleavened cakes
mixed with oil, and unleavened wafers
spread with oil, 3 and put them in a bas-
ket. Take the basket of them along with
the bullock and the two rams. 4 Aaron
and his sons you shall also bring to the
entrance of the meeting tent, and there
wash them with water. 5 Take the vest-
ments and clothe Aaron with the tunic,
the robe of the ephod, the ephod itself,
and the breastpiece, fastening the em-
broidered belt of the ephod around him.
6 Put the miter on his head, the sacred
diadem on the miter. 7 Then take the
anointing oil and anoint him with it,
pouring it on his head. 8 Bring forward
his sons also and clothe them with the
tunics, 9* gird them with the sashes, and
tie the turbans on them. Thus shall the
priesthood be theirs by perpetual law,
and thus shall you ordain Aaron and his
sons.

Ordination Sacrifices. 10* "Now bring
forward the bullock in front of the meet-
ing tent. There Aaron and his sons shall
lay their hands on its head. 11 Then
slaughter the bullock before the LORD,
at the entrance of the meeting tent.
12 Take some of its blood and with your
finger put it on the horns of the altar.
All the rest of the blood you shall pour
out at the base of the altar. 13 All the fat
that covers its inner organs, as well as
the lobe of its liver and its two kidneys,
together with the fat that is on them, you
shall take and burn on the altar. 14* But
the flesh and hide and offal of the bullock
you must burn up outside the camp,
since this is a sin offering.

15 "Then take one of the rams, and
after Aaron and his sons have laid their
hands on its head, 16 slaughter it. The
blood you shall take and splash on all
the sides of the altar. 17 Cut the ram into
pieces; its inner organs and shanks you
shall first wash, and then put them with
the pieces and with the head. 18 The en-
tire ram shall then be burned on the al-
tar, since it is a holocaust, a sweet-
smelling oblation to the LORD.

19 "After this take the other ram, and
when Aaron and his sons have laid their
hands on its head, 20 slaughter it. Some
of its blood you shall take and put on
the tip of Aaron's right ear and on the
tips of his sons' right ears and on the
thumbs of their right hands and the
great toes of their right feet. Splash
the rest of the blood on all the sides of
the altar. 21 Then take some of the blood
that is on the altar, together with some
of the anointing oil, and sprinkle this on
Aaron and his vestments, as well as on
his sons and their vestments, that his
sons and their vestments may be sacred.

22† "Now, from this ram you shall take
its fat: its fatty tail, the fat that covers
its inner organs, the lobe of its liver, its
two kidneys with the fat that is on them,
and its right thigh, since this is the ordi-

*

37: 39, 31; Lv 8, 9.
39-43: 39, 27ff.
42: Ez 44, 18.
29, 1-8: Lv 8, 1-9.
9: Lv 8, 13.
10-26: Lv 8, 14-30.
14: Heb 13, 11.

†

28, 41: *Ordain them:* literally, "fill their hands," a technical expression used solely for the installation of priests. The phrase probably originated in the custom of placing in the priests' hands the instruments or other symbols of the sacerdotal office.

29, 22: *Fatty tail:* the thick layer of fat surrounding the tails of sheep and rams bred in Palestine even today. It is regarded as a choice food. Cf Lv 3, 9.

nation ram; 23 then, out of the basket of
unleavened food that you have set be-
fore the LORD, you shall take one of the
loaves of bread, one of the cakes made
with oil, and one of the wafers. 24† All
these things you shall put into the hands
of Aaron and his sons, so that they may
wave them as a wave offering before the
LORD. 25 After you have received them
back from their hands, you shall burn
them on top of the holocaust on the altar
as a sweet-smelling oblation to the LORD.
26 Finally, take the breast of Aaron's or-
dination ram and wave it as a wave of-
fering before the LORD; this is to be your
own portion.

27*† "Thus shall you set aside the
breast of whatever wave offering is
waved, as well as the thigh of whatever
raised offering is raised up, whether this
be the ordination ram or anything else
belonging to Aaron or to his sons. 28 Such
things are due to Aaron and his sons
from the Israelites by a perpetual ordi-
nance as a contribution. From their
peace offerings, too, the Israelites shall
make a contribution, their contribution
to the LORD.

29* "The sacred vestments of Aaron
shall be passed down to his descendants,
that in them they may be anointed and
ordained. 30 The descendant who suc-
ceeds him as priest and who is to enter
the meeting tent to minister in the sanc-
tuary shall be clothed with them for
seven days.

31* "You shall take the flesh of the or-
dination ram and boil it in a holy place.
32 At the entrance of the meeting tent
Aaron and his sons shall eat the flesh
of the ram and the bread that is in the
basket. 33 They themselves are to eat of
these things by which atonement was
made at their ordination and consecra-
tion; but no layman may eat of them,
since they are sacred. 34 If some of the
flesh of the ordination sacrifice or some
of the bread remains over on the next
day, this remnant must be burned up;
it is not to be eaten, since it is sacred.
35* Carry out all these orders in regard
to Aaron and his sons just as I have
given them to you.

"Seven days you shall spend in or-
daining them, 36*† sacrificing a bullock
each day as a sin offering, to make
atonement. Thus also shall you purge
the altar in making atonement for it; you
shall anoint it in order to consecrate it.
37 Seven days you shall spend in making
atonement for the altar and in conse-
crating it. Then the altar will be most
sacred, and whatever touches it will be-
come sacred.

38*† "Now, this is what you shall offer
on the altar: two yearling lambs as the
sacrifice established for each day; 39 one
lamb in the morning and the other lamb
at the evening twilight. 40 With the first
lamb there shall be a tenth of an ephah
of fine flour mixed with a fourth of a hin
of oil of crushed olives and, as its liba-
tion, a fourth of a hin of wine. 41 The
other lamb you shall offer at the evening
twilight, with the same cereal offering
and libation as in the morning. You shall
offer this as a sweet-smelling oblation
to the LORD. 42 Throughout your genera-
tions this established holocaust shall be
offered before the LORD at the entrance
of the meeting tent, where I will meet
you and speak to you.

43* "There, at the altar, I will meet the
Israelites; hence, it will be made sacred
by my glory. 44 Thus I will consecrate
the meeting tent and the altar, just as
I also consecrate Aaron and his sons to
be my priests. 45 I will dwell in the midst
of the Israelites and will be their God.
46 They shall know that I, the LORD, am
their God who brought them out of the
land of Egypt, so that I, the LORD, their
God, might dwell among them.

CHAPTER 30

Altar of Incense. 1* "For burning in-
cense you shall make an altar of acacia
wood, 2 with a square surface, a cubit
long, a cubit wide, and two cubits high,
with horns that spring directly from it.
3 Its grate on top, its walls on all four
sides, and its horns you shall plate with
pure gold. Put a gold molding around
it. 4 Underneath the molding you shall
put gold rings, two on one side and two
on the opposite side, as holders for the
poles used in carrying it. 5 Make the
poles, too, of acacia wood and plate them
with gold. 6* This altar you are to place
in front of the veil that hangs before the
ark of the commandments where I will
meet you.

7 "On it Aaron shall burn fragrant in-
cense. Morning after morning, when he
prepares the lamps, 8 and again in the
evening twilight, when he lights the
lamps, he shall burn incense. Through-
out your generations this shall be the es-

*

27f: Lv 7, 31-34; 10, 14f; Nm 18, 18f; Dt 18, 3.
29: Nm 20, 26.28.
31-34: Lv 8, 31f.
35: Lv 8, 36.
36f: Lv 8, 33ff.
38-42: Nm 28, 3-8.
43: 25, 22.
30, 1-5: 37, 25-28.
6: 40, 26.

†

29, 24-26: *Wave offering:* the portions of a peace offering, breast and right thigh, which the officiating priest moved to and fro (waved) in the presence of the Lord. They were reserved for Aaron and his sons.

29, 27-30: These verses are a parenthetical interruption of the ordination ritual; v 31 belongs logically immediately after v 26.

29, 36f: *Purge the altar:* the construction of an altar by profane hands rendered it impure. The anointing and consecration of the altar purified it and made it sacred.

29, 38-42: A parenthesis inserted into the rubrics for consecrating the altar; v 43 belongs directly after v 37.

tablished incense offering before the LORD. 9 On this altar you shall not offer up any profane incense, or any holocaust or cereal offering; nor shall you pour out a libation upon it. 10* Once a year Aaron shall perform the atonement rite on its horns. Throughout your generations this atonement is to be made once a year with the blood of the atoning sin offering. This altar is most sacred to the LORD."

Census Tax. 11 The LORD also said to Moses, 12* "When you take a census of the Israelites who are to be registered, each one, as he is enrolled, shall give the LORD a forfeit for his life, so that no plague may come upon them for being registered. 13* Everyone who enters the registered group must pay a half-shekel, according to the standard of the sanctuary shekel, twenty gerahs to the shekel. This payment of a half-shekel is a contribution to the LORD. 14 Everyone of twenty years or more who enters the registered group must give this contribution to the LORD. 15 The rich need not give more, nor shall the poor give less, than a half-shekel in this contribution to the LORD to pay the forfeit for their lives. 16* When you receive this forfeit money from the Israelites, you shall donate it to the service of the meeting tent, that there it may be the Israelites' reminder before the LORD, of the forfeit paid for their lives."

The Laver. 17 The LORD said to Moses, 18* "For ablutions you shall make a bronze laver with a bronze base. Place it between the meeting tent and the altar, and put water in it. 19* Aaron and his sons shall use it in washing their hands and feet. 20 When they are about to enter the meeting tent, they must wash with water, lest they die. Likewise when they approach the altar in their ministry, to offer an oblation to the LORD, 21 they must wash their hands and feet, lest they die. This shall be a perpetual ordinance for him and his descendants throughout their generations."

The Anointing Oil. 22 The LORD said to Moses, 23 "Take the finest spices: five hundred shekels of free-flowing myrrh; half that amount, that is, two hundred and fifty shekels, of fragrant cinnamon; two hundred and fifty shekels of fragrant cane; 24 five hundred shekels of cassia—all according to the standard of the sanctuary shekel; together with a hin of olive oil; 25* and blend them into sacred anointing oil, perfumed ointment expertly prepared. 26* With this sacred anointing oil you shall anoint the meeting tent and the ark of the commandments, 27 the table and all its appurtenances, the lampstand and its appurtenances, the altar of incense 28 and the altar of holocausts with all its appurtenances, and the laver with its base. 29 When you have consecrated them, they shall be most sacred; whatever touches them shall be sacred. 30* Aaron and his sons you shall also anoint and consecrate as my priests. 31 To the Israelites you shall say: As sacred anointing oil this shall belong to me throughout your generations. 32 It may not be used in any ordinary anointing of the body, nor may you make any other oil of a like mixture. It is sacred, and shall be treated as sacred by you. 33 Whoever prepares a perfume like this, or whoever puts any of this on a layman, shall be cut off from his kinsmen."

The Incense. 34* The LORD told Moses, "Take these aromatic substances: storax and onycha and galbanum, these and pure frankincense in equal parts; 35 and blend them into incense. This fragrant powder, expertly prepared, is to be salted and so kept pure and sacred. 36 Grind some of it into fine dust and put this before the commandments in the meeting tent where I will meet you. This incense shall be treated as most sacred by you. 37 You may not make incense of a like mixture for yourselves; you must treat it as sacred to the LORD. 38 Whoever makes an incense like this for his own enjoyment of its fragrance, shall be cut off from his kinsmen."

CHAPTER 31

Choice of Artisans. 1* The LORD said to Moses, 2 "See, I have chosen Bezalel, son of Uri, son of Hur, of the tribe of Judah, 3 and I have filled him with a divine spirit of skill and understanding and knowledge in every craft: 4 in the production of embroidery, in making things of gold, silver or bronze, 5 in cutting and mounting precious stones, in carving wood, and in every craft. 6 As his assistant I have appointed Oholiab, son of Ahisamach, of the tribe of Dan. I have also endowed all the experts with the necessary skill to make all the things I have ordered you to make: 7* the meeting tent, the ark of the commandments with the propitiatory on top of it, all the furnishings of the tent, 8 the table with its appurtenances, the pure gold lampstand with all its appurtenances, the altar of incense, 9 the altar of holocausts with all its appurtenances, the laver with its base, 10† the service cloths, the sacred

*

10: Lv 16, 18.
12: Nm 1, 2f; 26, 2.
13: Mt 17, 24-27.
16: 38, 25.
18: 38, 8; 40, 7.30.
19ff: 40, 31f.
25: 37, 29.
26-29: 40, 9ff; Lv 8, 10; Nm 7, 1.
30: 29, 7; Lv 8, 12.
34ff: 25, 6; 37, 29.
31, 1-6: 35, 30-35.
7-11: 35, 10-19.

†

31, 10: *The service cloths:* so the Greek. They were perhaps the colored cloths mentioned in Nm 4, 4-15.

vestments for Aaron the priest, the vest-
ments for his sons in their ministry,
11 the anointing oil, and the fragrant in-
cense for the sanctuary. All these things
they shall make just as I have com-
manded you."

Sabbath Laws. 12* The LORD said to
Moses, 13 "You must also tell the Israel-
ites: Take care to keep my sabbaths, for
that is to be the token between you and
me throughout the generations, to show
that it is I, the LORD, who make you holy.
14 Therefore, you must keep the sabbath
as something sacred. Whoever dese-
crates it shall be put to death. If anyone
does work on that day, he must be rooted
out of his people. 15 Six days there are
for doing work, but the seventh day is
the sabbath of complete rest, sacred to
the LORD. Anyone who does work on the
sabbath day shall be put to death. 16 So
shall the Israelites observe the sabbath,
keeping it throughout their generations
as a perpetual covenant. 17 Between me
and the Israelites it is to be an everlast-
ing token; for in six days the LORD made
the heavens and the earth, but on the
seventh day he rested at his ease."

18* When the LORD had finished speak-
ing to Moses on Mount Sinai, he gave
him the two tablets of the command-
ments, the stone tablets inscribed by
God's own finger.

CHAPTER 32

The Golden Calf. 1* When the people
became aware of Moses' delay in com-
ing down from the mountain, they gath-
ered around Aaron and said to him,
"Come, make us a god who will be our
leader; as for the man Moses who
brought us out of the land of Egypt, we
do not know what has happened to him."
2 Aaron replied, "Have your wives and
sons and daughters take off the golden
earrings they are wearing, and bring
them to me." 3 So all the people took off
their earrings and brought them to
Aaron, 4* who accepted their offering,
and fashioning this gold with a graving
tool, made a molten calf. Then they cried
out, "This is your God, O Israel, who
brought you out of the land of Egypt."
5† On seeing this, Aaron built an altar
before the calf and proclaimed, "Tomor-
row is a feast of the LORD." 6* Early the
next day the people offered holocausts
and brought peace offerings. Then they
sat down to eat and drink, and rose up
to revel.

7* With that, the LORD said to Moses,
"Go down at once to your people, whom
you brought out of the land of Egypt,
for they have become depraved. 8 They
have soon turned aside from the way I
pointed out to them, making for them-
selves a molten calf and worshiping it,
sacrificing to it and crying out, 'This is
your God, O Israel, who brought you out
of the land of Egypt!' 9* I see how stiff-
necked this people is," continued the
LORD to Moses. 10 "Let me alone, then,
that my wrath may blaze up against
them to consume them. Then I will make
of you a great nation."

11* But Moses implored the LORD, his
God, saying, "Why, O LORD, should your
wrath blaze up against your own people,
whom you brought out of the land of
Egypt with such great power and with
so strong a hand? 12 Why should the
Egyptians say, 'With evil intent he
brought them out, that he might kill
them in the mountains and exterminate
them from the face of the earth'? Let
your blazing wrath die down; relent in
punishing your people. 13* Remember
your servants Abraham, Isaac and Is-
rael, and how you swore to them by your
own self, saying, 'I will make your de-
scendants as numerous as the stars in
the sky; and all this land that I promised,
I will give your descendants as their
perpetual heritage.' " 14 So the LORD re-
lented in the punishment he had threat-
ened to inflict on his people.

15* Moses then turned and came down
the mountain with the two tablets of the
commandments in his hands, tablets
that were written on both sides, front
and back; 16* tablets that were made by
God, having inscriptions on them that
were engraved by God himself. 17 Now,
when Joshua heard the noise of the peo-
ple shouting, he said to Moses, "That
sounds like a battle in the camp." 18 But
Moses answered, "It does not sound like
cries of victory, nor does it sound like
cries of defeat; the sounds that I hear
are cries of revelry." 19* As he drew near
the camp, he saw the calf and the danc-
ing. With that, Moses' wrath flared up,
so that he threw the tablets down and
broke them on the base of the mountain.
20*† Taking the calf they had made, he
fused it in the fire and then ground it
down to powder, which he scattered on

*

12-17: 20, 8-11; 35, 1-3.
18: 24, 12; 32, 15f; Dt 5, 22.
32, 1: 32, 23; Acts 7, 40.
4: 32, 8; 1 Kgs 12, 28.
6: 1 Cor 10, 7.
7f: Dt 9, 12.16.
9f: Dt 9, 13; Ps 106, 23.
11f: Nm 14, 13ff; Dt 9, 28.
13: Gn 22, 16f.
15: Dt 9, 15.
16: 31, 18.
19: Dt 9, 16f.
20: Dt 9, 21.

†

32, 5: *The calf . . . a feast of the* LORD: from this it is clear that the golden calf was intended as an image, not of a false god, but of the LORD himself, his strength being symbolized by the strength of a young bull. The Israelites, however, had been forbidden to represent the Lord under any visible form. Cf 20, 4.

32, 20: *The water:* the stream that flowed down Mount Sinai. Cf Dt 9, 21.

the water and made the Israelites drink.
21 Moses asked Aaron, "What did this
people ever do to you that you should
lead them into so grave a sin?" 22 Aaron
replied, "Let not my lord be angry. You
know well enough how prone the people
are to evil. 23 They said to me, 'Make us
a god to be our leader; as for the man
Moses who brought us out of the land
of Egypt, we do not know what has hap-
pened to him.' 24 So I told them, 'Let any-
one who has gold jewelry take it off.'
They gave it to me, and I threw it into
the fire, and this calf came out."
25 When Moses realized that, to the
scornful joy of their foes, Aaron had let
the people run wild, 26* he stood at the
gate of the camp and cried, "Whoever
is for the LORD, let him come to me!"
All the Levites then rallied to him,
27† and he told them, "Thus says the
LORD, the God of Israel: Put your sword
on your hip, every one of you! Now go
up and down the camp, from gate to
gate, and slay your own kinsmen, your
friends and neighbors!" 28 The Levites
carried out the command of Moses, and
that day there fell about three thousand
of the people. 29† Then Moses said, "To-
day you have been dedicated to the
LORD, for you were against your own
sons and kinsmen, to bring a blessing
upon yourselves this day."
The Atonement. 30* On the next day
Moses said to the people, "You have
committed a grave sin. I will go up to
the LORD, then; perhaps I may be able
to make atonement for your sin." 31 So
Moses went back to the LORD and said,
"Ah, this people has indeed committed
a grave sin in making a god of gold for
themselves! 32† If you would only forgive
their sin! If you will not, then strike me
out of the book that you have written."
33 The LORD answered, "Him only who
has sinned against me will I strike out
of my book. 34 Now, go and lead the peo-
ple whither I have told you. My angel
will go before you. When it is time for
me to punish, I will punish them for their
sin."
35 Thus the LORD smote the people for
having had Aaron make the calf for
them.

CHAPTER 33

1* The LORD told Moses, "You and the
people whom you have brought up from
the land of Egypt, are to go up from here
to the land which I swore to Abraham,
Isaac and Jacob I would give to their
descendants. 2* Driving out the Canaan-
ites, Amorites, Hittites, Perizzites, Hi-
vites and Jebusites, I will send an angel
before you 3 to the land flowing with milk
and honey. But I myself will not go up
in your company, because you are a
stiff-necked people; otherwise I might
exterminate you on the way." 4 When
the people heard this bad news, they
went into mourning, and no one wore
his ornaments.
5 The LORD said to Moses, "Tell the Is-
raelites: You are a stiff-necked people.
Were I to go up in your company even
for a moment, I would exterminate you.
Take off your ornaments, therefore; I
will then see what I am to do with you."
6 So, from Mount Horeb onward, the Is-
raelites laid aside their ornaments.
Moses' Intimacy with God. 7*† The
tent, which was called the meeting tent,
Moses used to pitch at some distance
away, outside the camp. Anyone who
wished to consult the LORD would go to
this meeting tent outside the camp.
8 Whenever Moses went out to the tent,
the people would all rise and stand at
the entrance of their own tents, watching
Moses until he entered the tent. 9 As Mo-
ses entered the tent, the column of cloud
would come down and stand at its en-
trance while the LORD spoke with Moses.
10 On seeing the column of cloud stand
at the entrance of the tent, all the people
would rise and worship at the entrance
of their own tents. 11* The LORD used to
speak to Moses face to face, as one man
speaks to another. Moses would then re-
turn to the camp, but his young assis-
tant, Joshua, son of Nun, would not
move out of the tent.
12* Moses said to the LORD, "You, in-
deed, are telling me to lead this people
on; but you have not let me know whom
you will send with me. Yet you have said,
'You are my intimate friend,' and also,
'You have found favor with me.' 13 Now,
if I have found favor with you, do let
me know your ways so that, in knowing
you, I may continue to find favor with
you. Then, too, this nation is, after all,
your own people." 14† "I myself," the
LORD answered, "will go along, to give

*

26-29: Dt 33, 8f.
30-34: Dt 9, 18ff.
33, 1: Gn 12, 7.
2: 23, 23.
7: 29, 42f.
11: Nm 12, 8; Dt 34, 10; Sir 45, 4-6.
12: 32, 34.

†

32, 27: *Slay your own kinsmen . . . :* those who were especially guilty of the idolatry.

32, 29: *Dedicated to the LORD:* because of their zeal for the true worship of the Lord, the Levites were chosen to be special ministers of the ritual service. However, the meaning of the Hebrew here is somewhat disputed.

32, 32: *The book that you have written:* the list of God's intimate friends. In a similar sense St. Paul wished to be anathema from Christ for the sake of his brethren. Cf Rom 9, 3.

33, 7-11: *The meeting tent* is mentioned here by anticipation; its actual construction is described in the following chapters.

33, 14: *I myself:* literally, "my face," that is, "my presence." *To give you rest:* in the Promised Land; some understand, "to put your mind at rest"; others, by a slight emendation in the text, render, "to lead you."

you rest." 15 Moses replied, "If you are not going yourself, do not make us go up from here. 16 For how can it be known that we, your people and I, have found favor with you, except by your going with us? Then we, your people and I, will be singled out from every other people on the earth." 17 The LORD said to Moses, "This request, too, which you have just made, I will carry out, because you have found favor with me and you are my intimate friend."

18 Then Moses said, "Do let me see your glory!" 19* He answered, "I will make all my beauty pass before you, and in your presence I will pronounce my name, 'LORD'; I who show favors to whom I will, I who grant mercy to whom I will. 20* But my face you cannot see, for no man sees me and still lives. 21 Here," continued the LORD, "is a place near me where you shall station yourself on the rock. 22 When my glory passes I will set you in the hollow of the rock and will cover you with my hand until I have passed by. 23† Then I will remove my hand, so that you may see my back; but my face is not to be seen."

CHAPTER 34

Renewal of the Tablets. 1* The LORD said to Moses, "Cut two stone tablets like the former, that I may write on them the commandments which were on the former tablets that you broke. 2 Get ready for tomorrow morning, when you are to go up Mount Sinai and there present yourself to me on the top of the mountain. 3* No one shall come up with you, and no one is even to be seen on any part of the mountain; even the flocks and the herds are not to go grazing toward this mountain." 4 Moses then cut two stone tablets like the former, and early the next morning he went up Mount Sinai as the LORD had commanded him, taking along the two stone tablets.

5 Having come down in a cloud, the LORD stood with him there and proclaimed his name, "LORD." 6* Thus the LORD passed before him and cried out, "The LORD, the LORD, a merciful and gracious God, slow to anger and rich in kindness and fidelity, 7 continuing his kindness for a thousand generations, and forgiving wickedness and crime and sin; yet not declaring the guilty guiltless, but punishing children and grandchildren to the third and fourth generation for their fathers' wickedness!" 8 Moses at once bowed down to the ground in worship. 9 Then he said, "If I find favor with you, O Lord, do come along in our company. This is indeed a stiff-necked people; yet pardon our wickedness and sins, and receive us as your own."

Religious Laws. 10 "Here, then," said the LORD, "is the covenant I will make. Before the eyes of all your people I will work such marvels as have never been wrought in any nation anywhere on earth, so that this people among whom you live may see how awe-inspiring are the deeds which I, the LORD, will do at your side. 11* But you, on your part, must keep the commandments I am giving you today.

"I will drive out before you the Amorites, Canaanites, Hittites, Perizzites, Hivites and Jebusites. 12* Take care, therefore, not to make a covenant with these inhabitants of the land that you are to enter; else they will become a snare among you. 13† Tear down their altars; smash their sacred pillars, and cut down their sacred poles. 14† You shall not worship any other god, for the LORD is 'the Jealous One'; a jealous God is he. 15 Do not make a covenant with the inhabitants of that land; else, when they render their wanton worship to their gods and sacrifice to them, one of them may invite you and you may partake of his sacrifice. 16 Neither shall you take their daughters as wives for your sons; otherwise, when their daughters render their wanton worship to their gods, they will make your sons do the same.

17* "You shall not make for yourselves molten gods.

18* "You shall keep the feast of Unleavened Bread. For seven days at the prescribed time in the month of Abib you are to eat unleavened bread, as I commanded you; for in the month of Abib you came out of Egypt.

19* "To me belongs every first-born male that opens the womb among all your livestock, whether in the herd or in the flock. 20 The firstling of an ass you shall redeem with one of the flock; if you do not redeem it, you must break its neck. The first-born among your sons you shall redeem.

---

*

19: Rom 9, 15.
20: Jn 1, 18; 1 Tm 6, 16.
34, 1: Dt 10, 1f.
3: 19, 12f.21.
6f: 20, 5f; Nm 14, 18; Dt 5, 9f; Jer 32, 18.
11: 13, 5; 33, 2.
12-16: 23, 32f; Dt 7, 1-5; 12, 2f.
17: Lv 19, 4; 5, 8f.
18: 12, 15ff; 13, 3f.
19f: 13, 2.12f; 23, 15.

†

33, 23: *You may see my back:* man can see God's glory as reflected in creation, but his "face," that is, God as he is in himself, mortal man cannot behold. Cf 1 Cor 13, 12.

34, 13: *Sacred poles:* "Ashera" was the name of a Canaanite goddess. In her honor wooden poles (*asherot*) were erected, just as stone pillars (*massebot*) were erected in honor of the god Baal. Both were placed near the altar in a Canaanite shrine.

34, 14: *The LORD is "the Jealous One":* see note on 20, 5. Some, by a slight emendation, render, "The LORD is jealous for his name." Cf Ez 39, 25.

"No one shall appear before me
empty-handed.
21* "For six days you may work, but
on the seventh day you shall rest; on that
day you must rest even during the sea-
sons of plowing and harvesting.
22*† "You shall keep the feast of Weeks
with the first of the wheat harvest; like-
wise, the feast at the fruit harvest at the
close of the year. 23 Three times a year
all your men shall appear before the
Lord, the LORD God of Israel. 24 Since I
will drive out the nations before you to
give you a large territory, there will be
no one to covet your land when you go
up three times a year to appear before
the LORD, your God.
25* "You shall not offer me the blood
of sacrifice with leavened bread, nor
shall the sacrifice of the Passover feast
be kept overnight for the next day.
26 "The choicest first fruits of your soil
you shall bring to the house of the LORD,
your God.
"You shall not boil a kid in its mother's
milk."
Radiance of Moses' Face. 27 Then the
LORD said to Moses, "Write down these
words, for in accordance with them I
have made a covenant with you and with
Israel." 28* So Moses stayed there with
the LORD for forty days and forty nights,
without eating any food or drinking any
water, and he wrote on the tablets the
words of the covenant, the ten com-
mandments.
29 As Moses came down from Mount
Sinai with the two tablets of the com-
mandments in his hands, he did not
know that the skin of his face had be-
come radiant while he conversed with
the LORD. 30 When Aaron, then, and the
other Israelites saw Moses and noticed
how radiant the skin of his face had be-
come, they were afraid to come near
him. 31 Only after Moses called to them
did Aaron and all the rulers of the com-
munity come back to him. Moses then
spoke to them. 32 Later on, all the Israel-
ites came up to him, and he enjoined on
them all that the LORD had told him on
Mount Sinai. 33*† When he finished
speaking with them, he put a veil over
his face. 34 Whenever Moses entered the
presence of the LORD to converse with
him, he removed the veil until he came
out again. On coming out, he would tell
the Israelites all that had been com-
manded. 35 Then the Israelites would see
that the skin of Moses' face was radiant;
so he would again put the veil over his
face until he went in to converse with
the LORD.

CHAPTER 35

Sabbath Regulations. 1* Moses as-
sembled the whole Israelite community
and said to them, "This is what the LORD
has commanded to be done. 2 On six
days work may be done, but the seventh
day shall be sacred to you as the sabbath
of complete rest to the LORD. Anyone
who does work on that day shall be put
to death. 3 You shall not even light a fire
in any of your dwellings on the sabbath
day."
Collection of Materials. 4 Moses told
the whole Israelite community, "This is
what the LORD has commanded: 5* Take
up among you a collection for the LORD.
Everyone, as his heart prompts him,
shall bring, as a contribution to the
LORD, gold, silver and bronze; 6 violet,
purple and scarlet yarn; fine linen and
goat hair; 7 rams' skins dyed red, and
tahash skins; acacia wood; 8 oil for the
light; spices for the anointing oil and for
the fragrant incense; 9 onyx stones and
other gems for mounting on the ephod
and on the breastpiece.
Call for Artisans. 10* "Let every ex-
pert among you come and make all that
the LORD has commanded: the Dwelling,
11 with its tent, its covering, its clasps,
its boards, its bars, its columns and its
pedestals; 12 the ark, with its poles, the
propitiatory, and the curtain veil; 13 the
table, with its poles and all its appurte-
nances, and the showbread; 14 the lamp-
stand, with its appurtenances, the
lamps, and the oil for the light; 15 the al-
tar of incense, with its poles; the anoint-
ing oil, and the fragrant incense; the
entrance curtain for the entrance of the
Dwelling; 16 the altar of holocausts, with
its bronze grating, its poles, and all its
appurtenances; the laver, with its base;
17 the hangings of the court, with their
columns and pedestals; the curtain for
the entrance of the court; 18 the tent pegs
for the Dwelling and for the court, with
their ropes; 19 the service cloths for use
in the sanctuary; the sacred vestments
for Aaron, the priest, and the vestments
worn by his sons in their ministry."
The Contribution. 20 When the whole
Israelite community left Moses' pres-
ence, 21 everyone, as his heart suggested
and his spirit prompted, brought a con-

---

*

21: 20, 9f.
22f: 23, 16f; Dt 16, 10.13.16.
25f: 23, 18f.
28: 24, 18; Dt 9, 9.18; 10, 2.4.
33f: 2 Cor 3, 13.16.
35, 1-3: 31, 13-17.
5-9: 25, 2-7.
10-19: 31, 6-11.

---

†

34, 22: *Feast of Weeks:* the festival of thanksgiving for the harvest, celebrated seven weeks or fifty days after the beginning of the harvest. It was also called Pentecost (fiftieth) and coincided with the giving of the law on Mount Sinai, fifty days after the offering of the first fruits (Lv 23, 10f; Dt 16, 9).

34, 33: *He put a veil over his face:* St. Paul sees in this a symbol of the failure of the Jews to recognize Jesus as the promised Messiah: the true spiritual meaning of the writings of Moses and the prophets is still veiled from the unbelieving Jews. Cf 2 Cor 3, 7-18.

tribution to the LORD for the construc-
tion of the meeting tent, for all its ser-
vices, and for the sacred vestments.
22* Both the men and the women, all as
their heart prompted them, brought
brooches, earrings, rings, necklaces and
various other gold articles. Everyone
who could presented an offering of gold
to the LORD. 23 Everyone who happened
to have violet, purple or scarlet yarn,
fine linen or goat hair, rams' skins dyed
red or tahash skins, brought them.
24 Whoever could make a contribution of
silver or bronze offered it to the LORD;
and everyone who happened to have
acacia wood for any part of the work,
brought it. 25 All the women who were
expert spinners brought hand-spun vio-
let, purple and scarlet yarn and fine
linen thread. 26 All the women who pos-
sessed the skill, spun goat hair. 27 The
princes brought onyx stones and other
gems for mounting on the ephod and on
the breastpiece; 28 as well as spices, and
oil for the light, anointing oil, and fra-
grant incense. 29 Every Israelite man
and woman brought to the LORD such
voluntary offerings as they thought best,
for the various kinds of work which the
LORD had commanded Moses to have
done.

The Artisans. 30* Moses said to the Is-
raelites, "See, the LORD has chosen Bez-
alel, son of Uri, son of Hur, of the tribe
of Judah, 31 and has filled him with a di-
vine spirit of skill and understanding
and knowledge in every craft: 32 in the
production of embroidery, in making
things of gold, silver or bronze, 33 in cut-
ting and mounting precious stones, in
carving wood, and in every other craft.
34 He has also given both him and Oho-
liab, son of Ahisamach, of the tribe of
Dan, the ability to teach others. 35 He has
endowed them with skill to execute all
types of work: engraving, embroidering,
the making of variegated cloth of violet,
purple and scarlet yarn and fine linen
thread, weaving, and all other arts and
crafts.

CHAPTER 36

1* "Bezalel, therefore, will set to work
with Oholiab and with all the experts
whom the LORD has endowed with skill
and understanding in knowing how to
execute all the work for the service of
the sanctuary, just as the LORD has com-
manded."

2 Moses then called Bezalel and Oho-
liab and all the other experts whom the
LORD had endowed with skill, men
whose hearts moved them to come and
take part in the work. 3 They received
from Moses all the contributions which
the Israelites had brought for establish-
ing the service of the sanctuary. Still,
morning after morning the people con-
tinued to bring their voluntary offerings
to Moses. 4 Thereupon the experts who
were executing the various kinds of
work for the sanctuary, all left the work
they were doing, 5 and told Moses, "The
people are bringing much more than
is needed to carry out the work which
the LORD has commanded us to do."
6 Moses, therefore, ordered a proclama-
tion to be made throughout the camp:
"Let neither man nor woman make any
more contributions for the sanctuary."
So the people stopped bringing their of-
ferings; 7 there was already enough at
hand, in fact, more than enough, to com-
plete the work to be done.

The Tent Cloth and Coverings. 8* The
various experts who were executing the
work, made the Dwelling with its ten
sheets woven of fine linen twined, having
cherubim embroidered on them with
violet, purple and scarlet yarn. 9 The
length of each sheet was twenty-eight
cubits, and the width four cubits; all the
sheets were of the same size. 10 Five of
the sheets were sewed together, edge to
edge; and the same for the other five.
11 Loops of violet yarn were made along
the edge of the end sheet in the first set,
and the same along the edge of the end
sheet in the second set. 12 Fifty loops
were thus put on one inner sheet, and
fifty loops on the inner sheet in the other
set, with the loops directly opposite each
other. 13 Then fifty clasps of gold were
made, with which the sheets were joined
so that the Dwelling formed one whole.

14 Sheets of goat hair were also woven
as a tent over the Dwelling. Eleven such
sheets were made. 15 The length of each
sheet was thirty cubits and the width
four cubits; all eleven sheets were the
same size. 16 Five of these sheets were
sewed edge to edge into one set; and the
other six sheets into another set. 17 Fifty
loops were made along the edge of the
end sheet in one set, and fifty loops along
the edge of the corresponding sheet in
the other set. 18 Fifty bronze clasps were
made with which the tent was joined so
that it formed one whole. 19 A covering
for the tent was made of rams' skins
dyed red, and above that, a covering of
tahash skins.

The Boards. 20* Boards of acacia
wood were made as walls for the Dwell-
ing. 21 The length of each board was ten
cubits, and the width one and a half cu-
bits. 22 Each board had two arms, fas-
tening them in line. In this way all the
boards of the Dwelling were made.
23 They were set up as follows: twenty
boards on the south side, 24 with forty
silver pedestals under the twenty

---

* 22-28: 25, 3-7.
30-35: 31, 1-6.
36, 1f: 31, 1.6.
8-19: 26, 1-14.
20-34: 26, 15-29.

boards, so that there were two pedestals under each board, at its two arms; 25 twenty boards on the other side of the Dwelling, the north side, 26 with their forty silver pedestals, two under each board; 27 six boards at the rear of the Dwelling, to the west; 28 and two boards at the corners in the rear of the Dwelling. 29 These were double at the bottom, and likewise double at the top, to the first ring. That is how both boards in the corners were made. 30 Thus, there were in the rear eight boards, with their sixteen silver pedestals, two pedestals under each board. 31 Bars of acacia wood were also made, five for the boards on one side of the Dwelling, 32 five for those on the other side, and five for those at the rear, to the west. 33 The center bar, at the middle of the boards, was made to reach across from end to end. 34 The boards were plated with gold, and gold rings were made on them as holders for the bars, which were also plated with gold.

The Veil. 35* The veil was woven of violet, purple and scarlet yarn, and of fine linen twined, with cherubim embroidered on it. 36 Four gold-plated columns of acacia wood, with gold hooks, were made for it, and four silver pedestals were cast for them.

37 The curtain for the entrance of the tent was made of violet, purple and scarlet yarn, and of fine linen twined, woven in a variegated manner. 38 Its five columns, with their hooks as well as their capitals and bands, were plated with gold; their five pedestals were of bronze.

CHAPTER 37

The Ark. 1* Bezalel made the ark of acacia wood, two and a half cubits long, one and a half cubits wide, and one and a half cubits high. 2 The inside and outside were plated with gold, and a molding of gold was put around it. 3 Four gold rings were cast and put on its four supports, two rings for one side and two for the opposite side. 4 Poles of acacia wood were made and plated with gold; 5 these were put through the rings on the sides of the ark, for carrying it.

6 The propitiatory was made of pure gold, two and a half cubits long and one and a half cubits wide. 7 Two cherubim of beaten gold were made for the two ends of the propitiatory, 8 one cherub fastened at one end, the other at the other end, springing directly from the propitiatory at its two ends. 9 The cherubim had their wings spread out above, covering the propitiatory with them. They were turned toward each other, but with their faces looking toward the propitiatory.

The Table. 10* The table was made of acacia wood, two cubits long, one cubit wide, and one and a half cubits high. 11 It was plated with pure gold, and a molding of gold was put around it. 12 A frame a handbreadth high was also put around it, with a molding of gold around the frame. 13 Four rings of gold were cast for it and fastened, one at each of the four corners. 14 The rings were alongside the frame as holders for the poles to carry the table. 15 These poles were made of acacia wood and plated with gold. 16 The vessels that were set on the table, its plates and cups, as well as its pitchers and bowls for pouring libations, were of pure gold.

The Lampstand. 17* The lampstand was made of pure beaten gold—its shaft and branches as well as its cups and knobs and petals springing directly from it. 18 Six branches extended from its sides, three branches on one side and three on the other. 19 On one branch there were three cups, shaped like almond blossoms, each with its knob and petals; on the opposite branch there were three cups, shaped like almond blossoms, each with its knob and petals; and so for the six branches that extended from the lampstand. 20 On the shaft there were four cups, shaped like almond blossoms, with their knobs and petals, 21 including a knob below each of the three pairs of branches that extended from the lampstand. 22 The knobs and branches sprang so directly from it that the whole formed but a single piece of pure beaten gold. 23 Its seven lamps, as well as its trimming shears and trays, were made of pure gold. 24 A talent of pure gold was used for the lampstand and its various appurtenances.

The Altar of Incense. 25* The altar of incense was made of acacia wood, on a square, a cubit long, a cubit wide, and two cubits high, having horns that sprang directly from it. 26 Its grate on top, its walls on all four sides, and its horns were plated with pure gold; and a molding of gold was put around it. 27 Underneath the molding gold rings were placed, two on one side and two on the opposite side, as holders for the poles to carry it. 28 The poles, too, were made of acacia wood and plated with gold.

29* The sacred anointing oil and the fragrant incense were prepared in their pure form by a perfumer.

CHAPTER 38

The Altar of Holocausts. 1* The altar of holocausts was made of acacia wood,

*

35-8: 26, 31-37.
37, 1-9: 25, 10-22.
10-16: 25, 23-30.
17-24: 25, 31-39.
25-28: 30, 1-5.
29: 30, 23ff.34ff.
38, 1-7: 27, 1-8; 2 Chr 1, 5.

on a square, five cubits long and five cubits wide; its height was three cubits. 2 At the four corners horns were made that sprang directly from the altar. The whole was plated with bronze. 3 All the utensils of the altar, the pots, shovels, basins, forks and fire pans, were likewise made of bronze. 4 A grating of bronze network was made for the altar and placed round it, on the ground, half as high as the altar itself. 5 Four rings were cast for the four corners of the bronze grating, as holders for the poles, 6 which were made of acacia wood and plated with bronze. 7 The poles were put through the rings on the sides of the altar for carrying it. The altar was made in the form of a hollow box.

8*† The bronze laver, with its bronze base, was made from the mirrors of the women who served at the entrance of the meeting tent.

The Court. 9* The court was made as follows. On the south side of the court there were hangings, woven of fine linen twined, a hundred cubits long, 10 with twenty columns and twenty pedestals of bronze, the hooks and bands of the columns being of silver. 11 On the north side there were similar hangings, one hundred cubits long, with twenty columns and twenty pedestals of bronze, the hooks and bands of the columns being of silver. 12 On the west side there were hangings, fifty cubits long, with ten columns and ten pedestals, the hooks and bands of the columns being of silver. 13 On the east side the court was fifty cubits long. 14 Toward one side there were hangings to the extent of fifteen cubits, with three columns and three pedestals; toward the other side, 15 beyond the entrance of the court, there were likewise hangings to the extent of fifteen cubits, with three columns and three pedestals. 16 The hangings on all sides of the court were woven of fine linen twined. 17 The pedestals of the columns were of bronze, while the hooks and bands of the columns were of silver; the capitals were silver-plated, and all the columns of the court were banded with silver.

18 At the entrance of the court there was a variegated curtain, woven of violet, purple and scarlet yarn and of fine linen twined, twenty cubits long and five cubits wide, in keeping with the hangings of the court. 19 There were four columns and four pedestals of bronze for it, while their hooks were of silver. 20 All the tent pegs for the Dwelling and for the court around it were of bronze.

Amount of Metal Used. 21 The following is an account of the various amounts used on the Dwelling, the Dwelling of the commandments, drawn up at the command of Moses by the Levites under the direction of Ithamar, son of Aaron the priest. 22* However, it was Bezalel, son of Uri, son of Hur, of the tribe of Judah, who made all that the Lord commanded Moses, 23 and he was assisted by Oholiab, son of Ahisamach, of the tribe of Dan, who was an engraver, an embroiderer, and a weaver of variegated cloth of violet, purple and scarlet yarn and of fine linen.

24 All the gold used in the entire construction of the sanctuary, having previously been given as an offering, amounted to twenty-nine talents and seven hundred and thirty shekels, according to the standard of the sanctuary shekel. 25 The amount of the silver received from the community was one hundred talents and one thousand seven hundred and seventy-five shekels, according to the standard of the sanctuary shekel; 26* one bekah apiece, that is, a half-shekel apiece, according to the standard of the sanctuary shekel, was received from every man of twenty years or more who entered the registered group; the number of these was six hundred and three thousand five hundred and fifty men. 27 One hundred talents of silver were used for casting the pedestals of the sanctuary and the pedestals of the veil, one talent for each pedestal, or one hundred talents for the one hundred pedestals. 28 The remaining one thousand seven hundred and seventy-five shekels were used for making the hooks on the columns, for plating the capitals, and for banding them with silver. 29 The bronze, given as an offering, amounted to seventy talents and two thousand four hundred shekels. 30 With this were made the pedestals at the entrance of the meeting tent, the bronze altar with its bronze gratings and all the appurtenances of the altar, 31 the pedestals around the court, the pedestals at the entrance of the court, and all the tent pegs for the Dwelling and for the court around it.

CHAPTER 39

The Vestments. 1* With violet, purple and scarlet yarn were woven the service cloths for use in the sanctuary, as well as the sacred vestments for Aaron, as the LORD had commanded Moses.

2* The ephod was woven of gold thread and of violet, purple and scarlet yarn and of fine linen twined. 3 Gold was first hammered into gold leaf and then cut up into threads, which were woven with

*

8: 30, 18-21.
9-20: 27, 9-19.
22f: 31, 2.6; 35, 30.34; 36, 1.
26: Nm 1, 46.
39, 1: 31, 10.
2-10: 28, 6-12.

†

38, 8: The reflecting surface of ancient mirrors was usually of polished bronze. *The women who served:* cf 1 Sm 2, 22.

the violet, purple and scarlet yarn into
an embroidered pattern on the fine
linen. 4 Shoulder straps were made for
it and joined to its two upper ends. 5 The
embroidered belt on the ephod extended
out from it, and like it, was made of
gold thread, of violet, purple and scar-
let yarn, and of fine linen twined, as
the LORD had commanded Moses.
6 The onyx stones were prepared and
mounted in gold filigree work; they were
engraved like seal engravings with the
names of the sons of Israel. 7 These
stones were set on the shoulder straps
of the ephod as memorial stones of the
sons of Israel, just as the LORD had com-
manded Moses.

8* The breastpiece was embroidered
like the ephod, with gold thread and vio-
let, purple and scarlet yarn on cloth of
fine linen twined. 9 It was square and
folded double, a span high and a span
wide in its folded form. 10 Four rows of
precious stones were mounted on it: in
the first row a carnelian, a topaz and an
emerald; 11 in the second row, a garnet,
a sapphire and a beryl; 12 in the third
row a jacinth, an agate and an amethyst;
13 in the fourth row a chrysolite, an onyx
and a jasper. They were mounted in gold
filigree work. 14 These stones were
twelve, to match the names of the sons
of Israel, and each stone was engraved
like a seal with the name of one of the
twelve tribes.

15* Chains of pure gold, twisted like
cords, were made for the breastpiece,
16 together with two gold filigree rosettes
and two gold rings. The two rings were
fastened to the two upper ends of the
breastpiece. 17 The two gold chains were
then fastened to the two rings at the ends
of the breastpiece. 18 The other two ends
of the two chains were fastened in front
to the two filigree rosettes, which were
attached to the shoulder straps of the
ephod. 19 Two other gold rings were
made and put on the two lower ends of
the breastpiece, on the edge facing the
ephod. 20 Two more gold rings were
made and fastened to the bottom of the
two shoulder straps next to where they
joined the ephod in front, just above
its embroidered belt. 21 Violet ribbons
bound the rings of the breastpiece to the
rings of the ephod, so that the breast-
piece stayed right above the embroi-
dered belt of the ephod and did not swing
loose from it. All this was just as the
LORD had commanded Moses.

The Other Vestments. 22 The robe of
the ephod was woven entirely of violet
yarn, 23 with an opening in its center like
the opening of a shirt, with selvage
around the opening to keep it from being
torn. 24 At the hem of the robe pome-
granates were made of violet, purple
and scarlet yarn and of fine linen twined;
25 bells of pure gold were also made
and put between the pomegranates all
around the hem of the robe: 26 first a bell,
then a pomegranate, and thus alternat-
ing all around the hem of the robe which
was to be worn in performing the minis-
try—all this, just as the LORD had com-
manded Moses.

27* For Aaron and his sons there were
also woven tunics of fine linen; 28 the mi-
ter of fine linen; the ornate turbans of
fine linen; drawers of linen [of fine linen
twined]; 29 and sashes of variegated
work made of fine linen twined and of
violet, purple and scarlet yarn, as the
LORD had commanded Moses. 30* The
plate of the sacred diadem was made
of pure gold and inscribed, as on a seal
engraving: "Sacred to the LORD." 31 It
was tied over the miter with a violet rib-
bon, as the LORD had commanded Mo-
ses.

Presentation of the Work to Moses.
32 Thus the entire work of the Dwelling
of the meeting tent was completed. The
Israelites did the work just as the LORD
had commanded Moses. 33 They then
brought to Moses the Dwelling, the tent
with all its appurtenances, the clasps,
the boards, the bars, the columns, the
pedestals, 34 the covering of rams' skins
dyed red, the covering of tahash skins,
the curtain veil; 35 the ark of the
commandments with its poles, the pro-
pitiatory, 36 the table with all its
appurtenances and the showbread,
37 the pure gold lampstand with its lamps
set up on it and with all its appurte-
nances, the oil for the light, 38 the golden
altar, the anointing oil, the fragrant in-
cense; the curtain for the entrance of the
tent, 39 the altar of bronze with its bronze
grating, its poles and all its appurte-
nances, the laver with its base, 40 the
hangings of the court with their columns
and pedestals, the curtain for the en-
trance of the court with its ropes and
tent pegs, all the equipment for the ser-
vice of the Dwelling of the meeting tent;
41 the service cloths for use in the sanctu-
ary, the sacred vestments for Aaron the
priest, and the vestments to be worn by
his sons in their ministry. 42 The Israel-
ites had carried out all the work just as
the LORD had commanded Moses. 43 So
when Moses saw that all the work was
done just as the LORD had commanded,
he blessed them.

CHAPTER 40

Erection of the Dwelling. 1 Then the
LORD said to Moses, 2*† "On the first day

---

*

8-14: 28, 15-21.
15-21: 28, 31-35.
27ff: 28, 39-42.
30f: 28, 36f.
40, 2-8: 40, 16-33.
2: 26, 30.

†

40, 2: *On the first day of the first month:* almost a year after the departure of the Israelites from Egypt. Cf v 17.

of the first month you shall erect the
Dwelling of the meeting tent. [3]* Put the
ark of the commandments in it, and
screen off the ark with the veil. [4] Bring
in the table and set it. Then bring in the
lampstand and set up the lamps on it.
[5] Put the golden altar of incense in front
of the ark of the commandments, and
hang the curtain at the entrance of the
Dwelling. [6] Put the altar of holocausts in
front of the entrance of the Dwelling of
the meeting tent. [7] Place the laver be-
tween the meeting tent and the altar,
and put water in it. [8] Set up the court
round about, and put the curtain at the
entrance of the court.

[9]* "Take the anointing oil and anoint
the Dwelling and everything in it, con-
secrating it and all its furnishings, so
that it will be sacred. [10] Anoint the altar
of holocausts and all its appurtenances,
consecrating it, so that it will be most
sacred. [11] Likewise, anoint the laver with
its base, and thus consecrate it.

[12]* "Then bring Aaron and his sons to
the entrance of the meeting tent, and
there wash them with water. [13] Clothe
Aaron with the sacred vestments and
anoint him, thus consecrating him as my
priest. [14] Bring forward his sons also,
and clothe them with the tunics. [15] As
you have anointed their father, anoint
them also as my priests. Thus, by being
anointed, shall they receive a perpetual
priesthood throughout all future genera-
tions."

[16] Moses did exactly as the LORD had
commanded him. [17] On the first day of
the first month of the second year the
Dwelling was erected. [18] It was Moses
who erected the Dwelling. He placed its
pedestals, set up its boards, put in its
bars, and set up its columns. [19] He
spread the tent over the Dwelling and
put the covering on top of the tent, as
the LORD had commanded him. [20]* He
took the commandments and put them
in the ark; he placed poles alongside the
ark and set the propitiatory upon it. [21] He
brought the ark into the Dwelling and
hung the curtain veil, thus screening off
the ark of the commandments, as the
LORD had commanded him. [22] He put the
table in the meeting tent, on the north
side of the Dwelling, outside the veil,
[23]* and arranged the bread on it before
the LORD, as the LORD had commanded
him. [24] He placed the lampstand in the
meeting tent, opposite the table, on the
south side of the Dwelling, [25] and he set
up the lamps before the LORD, as the
LORD had commanded him. [26] He placed
the golden altar in the meeting tent, in
front of the veil, [27] and on it he burned
fragrant incense, as the LORD had com-
manded him. [28] He hung the curtain at
the entrance of the Dwelling. [29] He put
the altar of holocausts in front of the en-
trance of the Dwelling of the meeting
tent, and offered holocausts and cereal
offerings on it, as the LORD had com-
manded him. [30]* He placed the laver be-
tween the meeting tent and the altar,
and put water in it for washing. [31] Moses
and Aaron and his sons used to wash
their hands and feet there, [32] for they
washed themselves whenever they went
into the meeting tent or approached the
altar, as the LORD had commanded Mo-
ses. [33] Finally, he set up the court around
the Dwelling and the altar and hung the
curtain at the entrance of the court. Thus
Moses finished all the work.

God's Presence in the Dwelling.
[34]* Then the cloud covered the meeting
tent, and the glory of the LORD filled the
Dwelling. [35] Moses could not enter the
meeting tent, because the cloud settled
down upon it and the glory of the LORD
filled the Dwelling. [36] Whenever the
cloud rose from the Dwelling, the Israel-
ites would set out on their journey. [37] But
if the cloud did not lift, they would not
go forward; only when it lifted did they
go forward. [38] In the daytime the cloud
of the LORD was seen over the Dwelling;
whereas at night, fire was seen in the
cloud by the whole house of Israel in all
the stages of their journey.

3ff: 26, 33ff.
9ff: 30, 26-29.
12-15: 28, 41; 29, 4-9; Lv 8, 1-13.
20ff: 25, 16.21; 26, 33ff.
23: 25, 30.
30ff: 30, 18ff.
34-38: Nm 9, 15-22.

The Book of
LEVITICUS

The name "Leviticus" was bestowed on the third book of the Pentateuch by the ancient Greek translators because a good part of this book consists of sacrificial and other ritual laws prescribed for the priests of the tribe of Levi.

Continuing the legislation given by God to Moses at Mount Sinai, Leviticus is almost entirely legislative in character; the rare narrative portions are subordinate to the main legislative theme. Generally speaking, the laws contained in this book serve to teach the Israelites that they should always keep themselves in a state of legal purity, or external sanctity, as a sign of their intimate union with the Lord. Accordingly, the central idea of Leviticus is contained in its oft-repeated injunction: "You shall be holy, because I, the LORD, am holy."

The main divisions of Leviticus are:

I: RITUAL OF SACRIFICES

CHAPTER 1

Holocausts. 1 The LORD called Moses,
and from the meeting tent gave him this
message: 2*† "Speak to the Israelites
and tell them: When any one of you
wishes to bring an animal offering to the
LORD, such an offering must be from the
herd or from the flock.
3*† "If his holocaust offering is from
the herd, it must be a male without blem-
ish. To find favor with the LORD, he shall
bring it to the entrance of the meeting
tent 4* and there lay his hand on the
head of the holocaust, so that it may be
acceptable to make atonement for him.
5* He shall then slaughter the bull before
the LORD, but Aaron's sons, the priests,
shall offer up its blood by splashing it
on the sides of the altar which is at the
entrance of the meeting tent. 6 Then he
shall skin the holocaust and cut it up into
pieces. 7 After Aaron's sons, the priests,
have put some burning embers on the
altar and laid some wood on them, 8 they
shall lay the pieces of meat, together
with the head and the suet, on top of the
wood and embers on the altar. 9* The in-
ner organs and the shanks, however, the
offerer shall first wash with water. The
priest shall then burn the whole offering
on the altar as a holocaust, a sweet-
smelling oblation to the LORD.
10 "If his holocaust offering is from the
flock, that is, a sheep or a goat, he must
bring a male without blemish. 11 This he
shall slaughter before the LORD at the
north side of the altar. Then Aaron's
sons, the priests, shall splash its blood
on the sides of the altar. 12 When the of-
ferer has cut it up into pieces, the priest
shall lay these, together with the head
and suet, on top of the wood and the fire
on the altar. 13 The inner organs and the
shanks, however, the offerer shall first
wash with water. The priest shall offer
them up and then burn the whole offer-
ing on the altar as a holocaust, a sweet-
smelling oblation to the LORD.
14* "If he offers a bird as a holocaust
to the LORD, he shall choose a turtledove
or a pigeon as his offering. 15* Having
brought it to the altar where it is to be
burned, the priest shall snap its head
loose and squeeze out its blood against
the side of the altar. 16 Its crop and feath-
ers shall be removed and thrown on the
ash heap at the east side of the altar.
17 Then, having split the bird down the
middle without separating the halves,
the priest shall burn it on the altar, over

---

*

1, 2: 22, 18. 19.
3: Ex 12, 5.
4: 3, 2.8. 13; 4, 15; 8, 14.22; 16, 21; Ex 29, 10.15.
5: 3, 8.
9: 3, 5.16; Ex 29, 18.
14: 5, 7; 12, 8; Lk 2, 24.
15: 5, 8.

†

1, 2: *From the herd or from the flock:* the only animals which could be used as sacrificial victims were either of the bovine class (bulls, cows and calves) or the ovine class (sheep and lambs, goats and kids). Excluded, therefore, were not only all wild animals, but also such "unclean" domestic animals as the camel and the ass. See note on 11, 1ff.

1, 3: *Holocaust:* from the Greek word meaning "wholly burned," this is the technical term for the special type of sacrifice in which an entire animal except its hide was consumed in the fire on the altar. The primary purpose of this complete gift was to render glory and praise to God.

the wood on the fire, as a holocaust, a
sweet-smelling oblation to the LORD.

CHAPTER 2

Cereal Offerings. 1* "When anyone
wishes to bring a cereal offering to the
LORD, his offering must consist of fine
flour. He shall pour oil on it and put
frankincense over it. 2*† When he has
brought it to Aaron's sons, the priests,
one of them shall take a handful of this
fine flour and oil, together with all the
frankincense, and this he shall burn on
the altar as a token offering, a sweet-
smelling oblation to the LORD. 3* The
rest of the cereal offering belongs to
Aaron and his sons. It is a most sacred
oblation to the LORD.
4 "When the cereal offering you pre-
sent is baked in an oven, it must be in
the form of unleavened cakes made of
fine flour mixed with oil, or of unleav-
ened wafers spread with oil. 5* If you
present a cereal offering that is fried on
a griddle, it must be of fine flour mixed
with oil and unleavened. 6 Such a cereal
offering must be broken into pieces, and
oil must be poured over it. 7 If you pre-
sent a cereal offering that is prepared
in a pot, it must be of fine flour, deep-
fried in oil. 8 A cereal offering that is
made in any of these ways you shall
bring to the LORD, offering it to the
priest, who shall take it to the altar. 9 Its
token offering the priest shall then lift
from the cereal offering and burn on the
altar as a sweet-smelling oblation to the
LORD. 10 The rest of the cereal offering
belongs to Aaron and his sons. It is a
most sacred oblation to the LORD.
11* "Every cereal offering that you
present to the LORD shall be unleavened,
for you shall not burn any leaven or
honey as an oblation to the LORD. 12 Such
you may indeed present to the LORD in
the offering of first fruits, but they are
not to be placed on the altar for a pleas-
ing odor. 13*† However, every cereal of-
fering that you present to the LORD shall
be seasoned with salt. Do not let the salt
of the covenant of your God be lacking
from your cereal offering. On every of-
fering you shall offer salt.
14 "If you present a cereal offering of
first fruits to the LORD, you shall offer
it in the form of fresh grits of new ears
of grain, roasted by fire. 15 On this cereal
offering you shall put oil and frankin-
cense. 16 For its token offering the priest
shall then burn some of the grits and oil,
together with all the frankincense, as an
oblation to the LORD.

CHAPTER 3

Peace Offerings. 1*† "If someone in
presenting a peace offering makes his
offering from the herd, he may offer be-
fore the LORD either a male or a female
animal, but it must be without blemish.
2* He shall lay his hand on the head of
his offering, and then slaughter it at the
entrance of the meeting tent; but Aar-
on's sons, the priests, shall splash its
blood on the sides of the altar. 3* From
the peace offering he shall offer as an
oblation to the LORD the fatty membrane
over the inner organs, and all the fat that
adheres to them, 4† as well as the two
kidneys, with the fat on them near the
loins, and the lobe of the liver, which he
shall sever above the kidneys. 5* All this
Aaron's sons shall then burn on the altar
with the holocaust, on the wood over the
fire, as a sweet-smelling oblation to the
LORD.
6 "If the peace offering he presents to
the LORD is from the flock, he may offer
either a male or a female animal, but
it must be without blemish. 7 If he pre-
sents a lamb as his offering, he shall
bring it before the LORD, 8 and after lay-
ing his hand on the head of his offering,
he shall slaughter it before the meeting
tent; but Aaron's sons shall splash its
blood on the sides of the altar. 9*† As
an oblation to the LORD he shall present
the fat of the peace offering: the whole
fatty tail, which he must sever close to
the spine, the fatty membrane over the
inner organs, and all the fat that adheres
to them, 10 as well as the two kidneys,
with the fat on them near the loins, and
the lobe of the liver, which he must sever
above the kidneys. 11 All this the priest
shall burn on the altar as the food of the
LORD's oblation.
12 "If he presents a goat, he shall bring
it before the LORD, 13 and after laying
his hand on its head, he shall slaughter
it before the meeting tent; but Aaron's
sons shall splash its blood on the sides

*

2, 1: Nm 15, 4.
2: 6, 15.
3: 7, 9f; Sir 7, 31; 1 Cor 9, 13.
5: 1 Chr 23, 29.
11: 6, 16f; Mt 16, 12; Mk 8, 15; Lk 12, 1; 1 Cor 5, 7; Gal 5, 9.
13: Ez 43, 24.
3, 1: 22, 21.
2: 1, 4.
3: Ex 29, 13.22.
5: 6, 12.
9: 9, 19.

†

2, 2: *Token offering:* literally, "reminder." Instead of burning the whole cereal offering, they burned only this part of it on the altar; it thus corresponded to the fat of the peace offering. See note on 3, 1.

2, 13: *The salt of the covenant of your God:* the partaking in common of salt by those seated together at table was an ancient symbol of friendship and alliance. Cf Mk 9, 49 and Col 4, 6; and see note on Nm 18, 19.

3, 1: *Peace offering:* thus the ancient versions have rendered the Hebrew word, which perhaps means more exactly, "fulfillment sacrifice," offered up in fulfillment of a vow. Cf Prv 7, 14. Its characteristic feature was the sacred banquet at which the offerer and his guests partook of the meat of the sacrificed animal. Cf 7, 11-21.

3, 4: *The lobe of the liver:* some render, "the fatty covering of the liver."

3, 9: *The whole fatty tail:* see note on Ex 29, 22.

of the altar. [14] From it he shall offer as an oblation to the LORD the fatty membrane over the inner organs, and all the fat that adheres to them, [15] as well as the two kidneys, with the fat on them near the loins, and the lobe of the liver, which he must sever above the kidneys. [16] All this the priest shall burn on the altar as the food of the sweet-smelling oblation. All the fat belongs to the LORD. [17]*† This shall be a perpetual ordinance for your descendants wherever they may dwell. You shall not partake of any fat or any blood."

CHAPTER 4

Sin Offerings: For Priests. [1] The LORD said to Moses, [2]*† "Tell the Israelites: When a person inadvertently commits a sin against some command of the LORD by doing one of the forbidden things, [3]*† if it is the anointed priest who thus sins and thereby makes the people also become guilty, he shall present to the LORD a young, unblemished bull as a sin offering for the sin he committed. [4]* Bringing the bullock to the entrance of the meeting tent, before the LORD, he shall lay his hand on its head and slaughter it before the LORD. [5] The anointed priest shall then take some of the bullock's blood and bring it into the meeting tent, [6]* where, dipping his finger in the blood, he shall sprinkle it seven times before the LORD, toward the veil of the sanctuary. [7]* The priest shall also put some of the blood on the horns of the altar of fragrant incense which is before the LORD in the meeting tent. The rest of the bullock's blood he shall pour out at the base of the altar of holocausts which is at the entrance of the meeting tent. [8] From the sin-offering bullock he shall remove all the fat: the fatty membrane over the inner organs, and all the fat that adheres to them, [9] as well as the two kidneys, with the fat on them near the loins, and the lobe of the liver, which he must sever above the kidneys. [10] This is the same as is removed from the ox of the peace offering; and the priest shall burn it on the altar of holocausts. [11]* The hide of the bullock and all its flesh, with its head, legs, inner organs and offal, [12] in short, the whole bullock, shall be brought outside the camp to a clean place where the ashes are deposited and there be burned up in a wood fire. At the place of the ash heap, there it must be burned.

For the Community. [13]* "If the whole community of Israel inadvertently and without even being aware of it does something that the LORD has forbidden and thus makes itself guilty, [14] should it later on become known that the sin was committed, the community shall present a young bull as a sin offering. They shall bring it before the meeting tent, [15]* and here, before the LORD, the elders of the community shall lay their hands on the bullock's head. When the bullock has been slaughtered before the LORD, [16] the anointed priest shall bring some of its blood into the meeting tent, [17] and dipping his finger in the blood, he shall sprinkle it seven times before the LORD, toward the veil. [18] He shall also put some of the blood on the horns of the altar of fragrant incense which is before the LORD in the meeting tent. The rest of the blood he shall pour out at the base of the altar of holocausts which is at the entrance of the meeting tent. [19] All of its fat he shall take from it and burn on the altar, [20] doing with this bullock just as he did with the other sin-offering bullock. Thus the priest shall make atonement for them, and they will be forgiven. [21] This bullock must also be brought outside the camp and burned, just as has been prescribed for the other one. This is the sin offering for the community.

For the Princes. [22] "Should a prince commit a sin inadvertently by doing one of the things which are forbidden by some commandment of the LORD, his God, and thus become guilty, [23] if later on he learns of the sin he committed, he shall bring as his offering an unblemished male goat. [24] Having laid his hands on its head, he shall slaughter the goat as a sin offering before the LORD, in the place where the holocausts are slaughtered. [25] The priest shall then take some of the blood of the sin offering on his finger and put it on the horns of the altar of holocausts. The rest of the blood he shall pour out at the base of this altar. [26]* All of the fat he shall burn on the altar like the fat of the peace offering. Thus the priest shall make atonement for the prince's sin, and it will be forgiven.

For Private Persons. [27]* "If a private person commits a sin inadvertently by doing one of the things which are forbid-

*

17: 17, 10-14; Gn 9, 4; Dt 12, 16.23; 15, 23.
4, 2: 5, 15.17; Nm 15, 22-29.
3: Heb 7, 27.
4: 1, 3f.
6: 8, 11.
7: 8, 15; 9, 9; 16, 18; Ex 29, 12.
11: 8, 17; 9, 11; Ex 29, 14; Nm 19, 5.
13: 5, 2-4; Nm 15, 24-26.
15: 1, 4.
26: 3, 3-5.
27: Nm 15, 27.

†

3, 17: *Any fat:* only the fat mentioned in vv 9f.14f is meant; other fat could be eaten by the Israelites.

4, 2: *A sin:* not necessarily a moral fault; included are all the cases of ritual uncleanness which people necessarily incurred in certain unavoidable circumstances.

4, 3: *The anointed priest:* his violation of the ceremonial law brought a sort of collective guilt on all the people whom he represented before God. *Sin offering:* more exactly, "sacrifice for remitting sin"; sin is here understood as explained above.

den by the commandments of the LORD, and thus becomes guilty, 28 should he later on learn of the sin he committed, he shall bring an unblemished she-goat as the offering for his sin. 29* Having laid his hand on the head of the sin offering, he shall slaughter it at the place of the holocausts. 30 The priest shall then take some of its blood on his finger and put it on the horns of the altar of holocausts. The rest of the blood he shall pour out at the base of the altar. 31* All the fat shall be removed, just as the fat is removed from the peace offering, and the priest shall burn it on the altar for an odor pleasing to the LORD. Thus the priest shall make atonement for him, and he will be forgiven.

32 "If, however, for his sin offering he presents a lamb, he shall bring an unblemished female. 33 Having laid his hand on its head, he shall slaughter this sin offering in the place where the holocausts are slaughtered. 34 The priest shall then take some of the blood of the sin offering on his finger and put it on the horns of the altar of holocausts. The rest of the blood he shall pour out at the base of the altar. 35* All the fat shall be removed, just as the fat is removed from the peace-offering lamb, and the priest shall burn it on the altar with the other oblations of the LORD. Thus the priest shall make atonement for the man's sin, and it will be forgiven.

CHAPTER 5

For Special Cases. 1* "If any person refuses to give the information which, as a witness of something he has seen or learned, he has been adjured to give, and thus commits a sin and has guilt to bear; 2* or if someone, without being aware of it, touches any unclean thing, as the carcass of an unclean wild animal, or that of an unclean domestic animal, or that of an unclean swarming creature, and thus becomes unclean and guilty; 3 or if someone, without being aware of it, touches some human uncleanness, whatever kind of uncleanness this may be, and then recognizes his guilt; 4* or if someone, without being aware of it, rashly utters an oath to do good or evil, such as men are accustomed to utter rashly, and then recognizes that he is guilty of such an oath; 5* then whoever is guilty in any of these cases shall confess the sin he has incurred, 6 and as his sin offering for the sin he has committed he shall bring to the LORD a female animal from the flock, a ewe lamb or a she-goat. The priest shall then make atonement for his sin.

7* "If, however, he cannot afford an animal of the flock, he shall bring to the LORD as the sin offering for his sin two turtledoves or two pigeons, one for a sin offering and the other for a holocaust. 8* He shall bring them to the priest, who shall offer the one for the sin offering first. Snapping its head loose at the neck, yet without breaking it off completely, 9* he shall sprinkle some of the blood of the sin offering against the side of the altar. The rest of the blood shall be squeezed out against the base of the altar. Such is the offering for sin. 10 The other bird shall be offered as a holocaust in the usual way. Thus the priest shall make atonement for the sin the man committed, and it will be forgiven.

11 "If he is unable to afford even two turtledoves or two pigeons, he shall present as a sin offering for his sin one tenth of an ephah of fine flour. He shall not put oil or frankincense on it, because it is a sin offering. 12 When he has brought it to the priest, the latter shall take a handful of this flour as a token offering, and this he shall burn as a sin offering on the altar with the other oblations of the LORD. 13* Thus the priest shall make atonement for the sin that the man committed in any of the above cases, and it will be forgiven. The rest of the flour, like the cereal offerings, shall belong to the priest."

Guilt Offerings. 14 The LORD said to Moses, 15† "If someone commits a sin by inadvertently cheating in the LORD's sacred dues, he shall bring to the LORD as his guilt offering an unblemished ram from the flock, valued at two silver shekels according to the standard of the sanctuary shekel. 16* He shall also restore what he has sinfully withheld from the sanctuary, adding to it a fifth of its value. This is to be given to the priest, who shall then make atonement for him with the guilt-offering ram, and he will be forgiven.

17*† "If someone, without being aware of it, commits such a sin by doing one of the things which are forbidden by some commandment of the LORD, that he incurs guilt for which he must an-

---

*

29: 1, 4.
31: 1, 9; 3, 3-5.
35: 3, 3.9.
5, 1: Prv 29, 24.
2: 11, 24.31.39; 12; 13; 15.
4: Jgs 11, 30f; 1 Sm 14, 24; Mk 6, 23; Acts 23, 12.
5: 26, 40; Nm 5, 7.
7: 12, 8; Lk 2, 24.
8: 1, 15.17.
9: 1, 15.
13: 4, 26.35.
16: 22, 14.
17: 4, 2.

†

5, 15: *Cheating:* not offering the full amount in tithes, first fruits, etc. *Guilt offering:* its characteristic was a certain additional penalty imposed as reparation for the injustice involved in the fault which was atoned for by this sacrifice. However, in certain passages, e.g., 14, 12f; Nm 6, 12; Ezr 10, 19, the term "guilt offering" is used for more important cases of "sin offerings" where no apparent injustice is involved.

5, 17: *Without being aware of it:* the case naturally presupposes that later on the offender learns of his mistake. Cf 4, 13f.

swer, [18] he shall bring as a guilt offering to the priest an unblemished ram of the flock of the established value. The priest shall then make atonement for the fault which was unwittingly committed, and it will be forgiven. [19] Such is the offering for guilt; the penalty of the guilt must be paid to the LORD."

[20] The LORD said to Moses, [21] "If someone commits a sin of dishonesty against the LORD by denying his neighbor a deposit or a pledge or a stolen article, or by otherwise retaining his neighbor's goods unjustly, [22] or if, having found a lost article, he denies the fact and swears falsely about it with any of the sinful oaths that men make in such cases, [23] he shall therefore, since he has incurred guilt by his sin, restore the thing that was stolen or unjustly retained by him or the deposit left with him or the lost article he found [24] or whatever else he swore falsely about; on the day of his guilt offering he shall make full restitution of the thing itself, and in addition, give the owner one fifth of its value. [25] As his guilt offering he shall bring to the LORD an unblemished ram of the flock of the established value. When he has presented this as his guilt offering to the priest, [26] the latter shall make atonement for him before the LORD, and he will be forgiven whatever guilt he may have incurred."

CHAPTER 6

The Daily Holocaust. [1] The LORD said to Moses, [2]† "Give Aaron and his sons the following command: This is the ritual for holocausts. The holocaust is to remain on the hearth of the altar all night until the next morning, and the fire is to be kept burning on the altar. [3] The priest, clothed in his linen robe and wearing linen drawers on his body, shall take away the ashes to which the fire has reduced the holocaust on the altar, and lay them at the side of the altar. [4] Then, having taken off these garments and put on other garments, he shall carry the ashes to a clean place outside the camp. [5] The fire on the altar is to be kept burning; it must not go out. Every morning the priest shall put firewood on it. On this he shall lay out the holocaust and burn the fat of the peace offerings. [6] The fire is to be kept burning continuously on the altar; it must not go out.

Daily Cereal Offering. [7] "This is the ritual of the cereal offering. One of Aaron's sons shall first present it before the LORD, in front of the altar. [8] Then he shall take from it a handful of its fine flour and oil, together with all the frankincense that is on it, and this he shall burn on the altar as its token offering, a sweet-smelling oblation to the LORD. [9] The rest of it Aaron and his sons may eat; but it must be eaten in the form of unleavened cakes and in a sacred place: in the court of the meeting tent they shall eat it. [10] It shall not be baked with leaven. I have given it to them as their portion from the oblations of the LORD; it is most sacred, like the sin offering and the guilt offering. [11] All the male descendants of Aaron may partake of it as their rightful share in the oblations of the LORD perpetually throughout your generations. Whatever touches the oblations becomes sacred."

[12]† The LORD said to Moses, [13] "This is the offering that Aaron and his sons shall present to the LORD [on the day he is anointed]: one tenth of an ephah of fine flour for the established cereal offering, half in the morning and half in the evening. [14] It shall be well kneaded and fried in oil on a griddle when you bring it in. Having broken the offering into pieces, you shall present it as a sweet-smelling oblation to the LORD. [15] Aaron's descendant who succeeds him as the anointed priest shall do likewise. This is a perpetual ordinance: for the Lord the whole offering shall be burned. [16] Every cereal offering of a priest shall be a whole burnt offering; it may not be eaten."

Sin Offerings. [17] The LORD said to Moses, [18]* "Tell Aaron and his sons: This is the ritual for sin offerings. At the place where holocausts are slaughtered, there also, before the LORD, shall the sin offering be slaughtered. It is most sacred. [19]* The priest who presents the sin offering may partake of it; but it must be eaten in a sacred place, in the court of the meeting tent. [20] Whatever touches its flesh shall become sacred. If any of its blood is spilled on a garment, the stained part must be washed in a sacred place. [21]* A clay vessel in which it has been cooked shall thereafter be broken; if it is cooked in a bronze vessel, this shall be scoured afterward and rinsed with water. [22]* All the males of the priestly line may partake of the sin offering, since it is most sacred. [23]* But no one may partake of any sin offering of which some blood has been brought into the

*

6, 18: 7, 2.
19: 10, 17.
21: 11, 33; 15, 12.
22: 7, 6; Nm 18, 10.
23: 4, 5; Heb 13, 11.

†

6, 2: *Ritual:* literally, "law, instruction." Here, and in the following paragraphs, are given additional prescriptions for various kinds of sacrifices which were, in part, treated of in the preceding chapters.

6, 12-16: This is another law about the daily or "established" cereal offering. It differs in some respects from the preceding law (vv 7-11) and also from the law in Ex 29, 38-42. Hence, the words *on the day he is anointed* were probably added by some later scribe in order to avoid the difficulty of harmonizing this law with the other two laws on the same matter.

meeting tent to make atonement in the sanctuary; such an offering must be burned up in the fire.

CHAPTER 7

Guilt Offerings. 1 "This is the ritual for guilt offerings, which are most sacred. 2* At the place where the holocausts are slaughtered, there also shall the guilt offering be slaughtered. Its blood shall be splashed on the sides of the altar. 3* All of its fat shall be taken from it and offered up: the fatty tail, the fatty membrane over the inner organs, 4 as well as the two kidneys with the fat on them near the loins, and the lobe of the liver, which must be severed above the kidneys. 5 All this the priest shall burn on the altar as an oblation to the LORD. This is the guilt offering. 6* All the males of the priestly line may partake of it; but it must be eaten in a sacred place, since it is most sacred.

7 "Because the sin offering and the guilt offering are alike, both having the same ritual, the guilt offering likewise belongs to the priest who makes atonement with it. 8 Similarly, the priest who offers a holocaust for someone may keep for himself the hide of the holocaust that he has offered. 9* Also, every cereal offering that is baked in an oven or deep-fried in a pot or fried on a griddle shall belong to the priest who offers it, 10* whereas all cereal offerings that are offered up dry or mixed with oil shall belong to all of Aaron's sons without distinction.

Peace Offerings. 11 "This is the ritual for the peace offerings that are presented to the LORD. 12 When anyone makes a peace offering in thanksgiving, together with his thanksgiving sacrifice he shall offer unleavened cakes mixed with oil, unleavened wafers spread with oil, and cakes made of fine flour mixed with oil and well kneaded. 13† His offering shall also include loaves of leavened bread along with the victim of his peace offering for thanksgiving. 14 From each of his offerings he shall present one portion as a contribution to the LORD; this shall belong to the priest who splashes the blood of the peace offering.

15* "The flesh of the thanksgiving sacrifice shall be eaten on the day it is offered; none of it may be kept till the next day. 16 However, if the sacrifice is a votive or a free-will offering, it should indeed be eaten on the day the sacrifice is offered, but what is left over may be eaten on the next day. 17 Should any flesh from the sacrifice be left over on the third day, it must be burned up in the fire. 18 If, therefore, any of the flesh of the peace offering is eaten on the third day, it shall not win favor for him nor shall it be reckoned to his credit; rather, it shall be considered as refuse, and anyone who eats of it shall have his guilt to bear. 19 Should the flesh touch anything unclean, it may not be eaten, but shall be burned up in the fire.

"All who are clean may partake of this flesh. 20 If, however, someone while in a state of uncleanness eats any of the flesh of a peace offering belonging to the LORD, that person shall be cut off from his people. 21 Likewise, if someone touches anything unclean, whether the uncleanness be of human or of animal origin or from some loathsome crawling creature, and then eats of a peace offering belonging to the LORD, that person, too, shall be cut off from his people."

Prohibition against Blood and Fat. 22 The LORD said to Moses, 23*† "Tell the Israelites: You shall not eat the fat of any ox or sheep or goat. 24* Although the fat of an animal that has died a natural death or has been killed by wild beasts may be put to any other use, you may not eat it. 25 If anyone eats the fat of an animal from which an oblation is made to the LORD, such a one shall be cut off from his people. 26 Wherever you dwell, you shall not partake of any blood, be it of bird or of animal. 27* Every person who partakes of any blood shall be cut off from his people."

The Portions for Priests. 28 The LORD said to Moses, 29 "Tell the Israelites: He who presents a peace offering to the LORD shall bring a part of it as his special offering to him, 30† carrying in with his own hands the oblations to the LORD. The fat is to be brought in, together with the breast, which is to be waved as a wave offering before the LORD. 31* The priest shall burn the fat on the altar, but the breast belongs to Aaron and his sons. 32 Moreover, from your peace offering you shall give to the priest the right leg as a raised offering. 33 The descendant of Aaron who offers up the blood and fat of the peace offering shall have the right leg as his portion, 34* for from the peace offerings of the Israelites I have

*

7, 2: 6, 18.
3-5: 3, 4.9f.14-16; 4, 8f.
6: 6, 22.
9: 2, 3-10; Nm 18, 9; Ez 44, 29.
10: 2, 14f.
15-18: 19, 6f.
23: 3, 17.
24: 22, 8.
27: 17, 10.
31: 3, 11.16.
34: Ex 29, 27f.

†

7, 13: *Leavened bread:* these loaves were not burned on the altar (cf 2, 11), but were eaten at the "communion" meal which followed the sacrifice. See note on 3, 1.

7, 23: *The fat:* only the particular portions specified in 3, 9f.14f are meant. *Ox or sheep or goat:* such animals as could be sacrificed; the fat of other clean animals could be eaten.

7, 30-34: *A wave offering . . . a raised offering:* these ceremonies are described in Ex 29, 24-28. The Hebrew word for "raised offering" is also rendered, in certain contexts, as "contribution."

taken the breast that is waved and the
leg that is raised up, and I have given
them to Aaron, the priest, and to his sons
by a perpetual ordinance as a contri-
bution from the Israelites."
35† This is the priestly share from the
oblations of the LORD, allotted to Aaron
and his sons on the day he called them
to be the priests of the LORD; 36 on the
day he anointed them the LORD ordered
the Israelites to give them this share by
a perpetual ordinance throughout their
generations.
37 This is the ritual for holocausts, ce-
real offerings, sin offerings, guilt offer-
ings, [ordination offerings] and peace
offerings, 38 which the LORD enjoined on
Moses at Mount Sinai at the time when
he commanded the Israelites in the wil-
derness of Sinai to bring their offerings
to the LORD.

II: CEREMONY OF ORDINATION

CHAPTER 8

Ordination of Aaron and His Sons.
1*† The LORD said to Moses, 2† "Take
Aaron and his sons, together with the
vestments, the anointing oil, the bullock
for a sin offering, the two rams, and the
basket of unleavened food. 3 Then as-
semble the whole community at the en-
trance of the meeting tent." 4 And Moses
did as the LORD had commanded. When
the community had assembled at the en-
trance of the meeting tent, 5 Moses told
them what the LORD had ordered to be
done. 6* Bringing forward Aaron and his
sons, he first washed them with water.
7* Then he put the tunic on Aaron,
girded him with the sash, clothed him
with the robe, placed the ephod on him,
and girded him with the embroidered
belt of the ephod, fastening it around
him. 8*† He then set the breastpiece on
him, with the Urim and Thummim in
it, 9* and put the miter on his head, at-
taching the gold plate, the sacred dia-
dem, over the front of the miter, at his
forehead, as the LORD had commanded
him to do.
10* Taking the anointing oil, Moses
anointed and consecrated the Dwelling,
with all that was in it. 11 Then he sprin-
kled some of this oil seven times on the
altar, and anointed the altar, with all its
appurtenances, and the laver, with its
base, thus consecrating them. 12* He
also poured some of the anointing oil on
Aaron's head, thus consecrating him.
13 Moses likewise brought forward Aar-
on's sons, clothed them with tunics,
girded them with sashes, and put tur-
bans on them, as the LORD had com-
manded him to do.
Ordination Sacrifices. 14 When he had
brought forward the bullock for a sin of-
fering, Aaron and his sons laid their
hands on its head. 15* Then Moses
slaughtered it, and taking some of its
blood, with his finger he put it on the
horns around the altar, thus purifying
the altar. He also made atonement for
the altar by pouring out the blood at its
base when he consecrated it. 16* Taking
all the fat that was over the inner organs,
as well as the lobe of the liver and the
two kidneys with their fat, Moses burned
them on the altar. 17 The bullock, how-
ever, with its hide and flesh and offal
he burned in the fire outside the camp,
as the LORD had commanded him to do.
18 He next brought forward the holo-
caust ram, and Aaron and his sons laid
their hands on its head. 19 When he had
slaughtered it, Moses splashed its blood
on all sides of the altar. 20 After cutting
up the ram into pieces, he burned the
head, the cut-up pieces and the suet;
21 then having washed the inner organs
and the shanks with water, he also
burned these remaining parts of the ram
on the altar as a holocaust, a sweet-
smelling oblation to the LORD, as the
LORD had commanded him to do.
22 Then he brought forward the second
ram, the ordination ram, and Aaron and
his sons laid their hands on its head.
23* When he had slaughtered it, Moses
took some of its blood and put it on the
tip of Aaron's right ear, on the thumb
of his right hand, and on the big toe of
his right foot. 24 Moses had the sons of
Aaron also come forward, and he put
some of the blood on the tips of their
right ears, on the thumbs of their right
hands, and on the big toes of their right
feet. The rest of the blood he splashed
on the sides of the altar. 25 He then took
the fat: the fatty tail and all the fat over
the inner organs, the lobe of the liver
and the two kidneys with their fat, and
likewise the right leg; 26 from the basket
of unleavened food that was set before
the LORD he took one unleavened cake,
one loaf of bread made with oil, and one
wafer; these he placed on top of the por-
tions of fat and the right leg. 27 He then
put all these things into the hands of
Aaron and his sons, whom he had wave
them as a wave offering before the LORD.
28 When he had received them back, Mo-
ses burned them with the holocaust on

*

8, 1-36: cf Ex 29.
6f: Ex 40, 12f.
7ff: Sir 45, 8-13.
8: Ex 28, 30.
9: Ex 28, 36.
10: Ex 30, 26.
12: Sir 45, 15.
15: 4, 7; Heb 9, 22.
16f: 3, 4; 4, 8-11.
23: 14, 14.

†

7, 35: *The priestly share:* literally, "the anointed part."
8, 1—9, 21: Though presented in the form of a narrative, this description of Aaron's ordination was intended to serve as a guide for all future ordinations.
8, 2: *The vestments, etc.:* already described in Ex 28—29.
8, 8: *The Urim and Thummim:* see note on Ex 28, 30.

the altar as the ordination offering, a sweet-smelling oblation to the LORD. 29 He then took the breast and waved it as a wave offering before the LORD; this was Moses' own portion of the ordination ram. All this was in keeping with the LORD's command to Moses. 30 Taking some of the anointing oil and some of the blood that was on the altar, Moses sprinkled with it Aaron and his vestments, as well as his sons and their vestments, thus consecrating both Aaron and his vestments and his sons and their vestments.

31 Finally, Moses said to Aaron and his sons, "Boil the flesh at the entrance of the meeting tent, and there eat it with the bread that is in the basket of the ordination offering, in keeping with the command I have received: 'Aaron and his sons shall eat of it.' 32 What is left over of the flesh and the bread you shall burn up in the fire. 33 Moreover, you are not to depart from the entrance of the meeting tent for seven days, until the days of your ordination are completed; for your ordination is to last for seven days. 34† The LORD has commanded that what has been done today be done to make atonement for you. 35 Hence you must remain at the entrance of the meeting tent day and night for seven days, carrying out the prescriptions of the LORD; otherwise, you shall die; for this is the command I have received." 36 So Aaron and his sons did all that the LORD had commanded through Moses.

CHAPTER 9

Octave of the Ordination. 1 On the eighth day Moses summoned Aaron and his sons, together with the elders of Israel, 2 and said to Aaron, "Take a calf for a sin offering and a ram for a holocaust, both without blemish, and offer them before the LORD. 3 Tell the elders of Israel, too: Take a he-goat for a sin offering, a calf and a lamb, both unblemished yearlings, for a holocaust, 4 and an ox and a ram for a peace offering, to sacrifice them before the LORD, along with a cereal offering mixed with oil; for today the LORD will reveal himself to you." 5 So they brought what Moses had ordered. When the whole community had come forward and stood before the LORD, 6 Moses said, "This is what the LORD orders you to do, that the glory of the LORD may be revealed to you. 7 Come up to the altar," Moses then told Aaron, "and offer your sin offering and your holocaust in atonement for yourself and for your family; then present the offering of the people in atonement for them, as the LORD has commanded."

8 Going up to the altar, Aaron first slaughtered the calf that was his own sin offering. 9 When his sons presented the blood to him, he dipped his finger in the blood and put it on the horns of the altar. The rest of the blood he poured out at the base of the altar. 10 He then burned on the altar the fat, the kidneys and the lobe of the liver that were taken from the sin offering, as the LORD had commanded Moses; 11 but the flesh and the hide he burned up in the fire outside the camp. 12 Then Aaron slaughtered his holocaust. When his sons brought him the blood, he splashed it on all sides of the altar. 13 They then brought him the pieces and the head of the holocaust, and he burned them on the altar. 14 Having washed the inner organs and the shanks, he burned these also with the holocaust on the altar.

15 Thereupon he had the people's offering brought up. Taking the goat that was for the people's sin offering, he slaughtered it and offered it up for sin as before. 16 Then he brought forward the holocaust, other than the morning holocaust, and offered it in the usual manner. 17 He then presented the cereal offering; taking a handful of it, he burned it on the altar. 18 Finally he slaughtered the ox and the ram, the peace offering of the people. When his sons brought him the blood, Aaron splashed it on all sides of the altar. 19* The portions of fat from the ox and from the ram, the fatty tail, the fatty membrane over the inner organs, the two kidneys, with the fat that is on them, and the lobe of the liver, 20 he placed on top of the breasts and burned them on the altar, 21* having first waved the breasts and the right legs as a wave offering before the LORD, in keeping with the LORD's command to Moses.

Revelation of the Lord's Glory. 22 Aaron then raised his hands over the people and blessed them. When he came down from offering the sin offering and holocaust and peace offering, 23* Moses and Aaron went into the meeting tent. On coming out they again blessed the people. Then the glory of the LORD was revealed to all the people. 24* Fire came forth from the LORD's presence and consumed the holocaust and the remnants of the fat on the altar. Seeing this, all the people cried out and fell prostrate.

---

* 9, 19f: 3, 3ff.
21: 7, 31f.
23: Nm 6, 23-26.
24: 1 Kgs 18, 38; 2 Chr 7, 1.

---

† 8, 34: The sense is not quite clear. Either the verse gives merely the reason why God ordered this ceremony, or it contains God's command that the same ceremony be used in all future ordinations, or it decrees a repetition of the entire ceremony on each of the seven days. At least a sin offering for atonement was made on each of these days. Cf Ex 29, 29-36.

CHAPTER 10

Nadab and Abihu. 1*† During this time Aaron's sons Nadab and Abihu took their censers and, strewing incense on the fire they had put in them, they offered up before the LORD profane fire, such as he had not authorized. 2*† Fire therefore came forth from the LORD's presence and consumed them, so that they died in his presence. 3*† Moses then said to Aaron, "This is as the LORD said:

> Through those who approach me I
> will manifest my sacredness;
> In the sight of all the people I will
> reveal my glory."

But Aaron said nothing. 4 Then Moses summoned Mishael and Elzaphan, the sons of Aaron's uncle Uzziel, with the order, "Come, remove your kinsmen from the sanctuary and carry them to a place outside the camp." 5† So they went in and took them, in their tunics, outside the camp, as Moses had commanded.

Conduct of the Priests. 6*† Moses said to Aaron and his sons Eleazar and Ithamar, "Do not bare your heads or tear your garments, lest you bring not only death on yourselves but God's wrath also on the whole community. Your kinsmen, the rest of the house of Israel, shall mourn for those whom the LORD's fire has smitten; 7 but do not you go beyond the entry of the meeting tent, else you shall die; for the anointing oil of the LORD is upon you." So they did as Moses told them.

8 The LORD said to Aaron, 9* "When you are to go to the meeting tent, you and your sons are forbidden under pain of death, by a perpetual ordinance throughout your generations, to drink any wine or strong drink. 10* You must be able to distinguish between what is sacred and what is profane, between what is clean and what is unclean; 11* you must teach the Israelites all the laws that the LORD has given them through Moses."

The Eating of the Priestly Portions. 12* Moses said to Aaron and his surviving sons, Eleazar and Ithamar, "Take the cereal offering left over from the oblations of the LORD, and eat it beside the altar in the form of unleavened cakes. Since it is most sacred, 13 you must eat it in a sacred place. This is your due from the oblations of the LORD, and that of your sons; such is the command I have received. 14* With your sons and daughters you shall also eat the breast of the wave offering and the leg of the raised offering, in a clean place; for these have been assigned to you and your children as your due from the peace offerings of the Israelites. 15 The leg of the raised offering and the breast of the wave offering shall first be brought in with the oblations, the fatty portions, that are to be waved as a wave offering before the LORD. Then they shall belong to you and your children by a perpetual ordinance, as the LORD has commanded."

16† When Moses inquired about the goat of the sin offering, he discovered that it had all been burned. So he was angry with the surviving sons of Aaron, Eleazar and Ithamar, and said, 17* "Why did you not eat the sin offering in the sacred place, since it is most sacred? It has been given to you that you might bear the guilt of the community and make atonement for them before the LORD. 18 If its blood was not brought into the inmost part of the sanctuary, you should certainly have eaten the offering in the sanctuary, in keeping with the command I had received." 19 Aaron answered Moses, "Even though they presented their sin offering and holocaust before the LORD today, yet this misfortune has befallen me. Had I then eaten of the sin offering today, would it have been pleasing to the LORD?" 20 On hearing this, Moses was satisfied.

III: LAWS REGARDING LEGAL PURITY

CHAPTER 11

Clean and Unclean Food. 1† The LORD said to Moses and Aaron, 2 "Speak to the

LEVITICUS

---

*

10, 1: 16, 1; Nm 3, 4; 26, 61; 1 Chr 24, 2.
2: Nm 16, 35.
3: 21, 17.21.
6: 21, 10.
9: Ez 44, 21.
10: 11, 47; 20, 25; Ez 22, 26; 44, 23.
11: Sir 45, 16.
12: 6, 16.
14f: 7, 34.
17: 6, 18f.

---

†

10, 1: *Nadab and Abihu:* the older sons of Aaron. Cf Ex 6, 23f.

10, 2: *Fire:* perhaps after the manner of lightning.

10, 3: *I will manifest my sacredness:* the presence of God is so sacred that it strikes dead those who approach him without the proper holiness. Cf Nm 20, 13; Ez 28, 22.

10, 5: *In their tunics:* they were buried just as they were, with no shroud or funeral solemnities.

10, 6: *Bare your heads:* go without the customary head covering, as a sign of mourning. Some interpreters, however, understand it as the cutting off of one's hair, which ordinarily all the Israelites, men as well as women, let grow long. Cf Is 15, 2; Jer 7, 29. Still others understand the verb to mean "to let one's hair hang loose and wild." Cf 13, 45; 21, 10, where the same phrase is used.

10, 16-19: *Eleazar and Ithamar* burned the entire goat of the sin offering (9, 15) instead of eating it in a sacred place (6, 19) to bear the guilt of the community. Aaron defends this action of his sons against Moses' displeasure by implying that they did not have sufficient sanctity to eat the flesh of the victim and thus perform the expiation of the people. They themselves still labored under the blow of the divine anger which struck their brothers Nadab and Abihu.

11, 1ff: These distinctions between edible and inedible meats were probably based on traditional ideas of hygiene, but they are here given a moral, religious basis: the inedible varieties are classified as "unclean" to remind the Israelites that they are to be a pure and holy people, dedicated to the Lord.

Israelites and tell them: Of all land ani-
mals these are the ones you may eat:
3 any animal that has hoofs you may eat,
provided it is cloven-footed and chews
the cud. 4 But you shall not eat any of
the following that only chew the cud or
only have hoofs: the camel, which in-
deed chews the cud, but does not have
hoofs and is therefore unclean for you;
5† the rock badger, which indeed chews
the cud, but does not have hoofs and is
therefore unclean for you; 6 the hare,
which indeed chews the cud, but does
not have hoofs and is therefore unclean
for you; and the pig, 7 which does indeed
have hoofs and is cloven-footed, but
does not chew the cud and is therefore
unclean for you. 8 Their flesh you shall
not eat, and their dead bodies you shall
not touch; they are unclean for you.

9 "Of the various creatures that live in
the water, you may eat the following:
whatever in the seas or in river waters
has both fins and scales you may eat.
10 But of the various creatures that crawl
or swim in the water, whether in the sea
or in the rivers, all those that lack either
fins or scales are loathsome for you,
11 and you shall treat them as loathsome.
Their flesh you shall not eat, and their
dead bodies you shall loathe. 12 Every
water creature that lacks fins or scales
is loathsome for you.

13† "Of the birds, these you shall loathe
and, as loathsome, they shall not be
eaten: the eagle, the vulture, the osprey,
14 the kite, the various species of falcons,
15 the various species of crows, 16 the os-
trich, the nightjar, the gull, the various
species of hawks, 17 the owl, the cormo-
rant, the screech owl, 18 the barn owl, the
desert owl, the buzzard, 19† the stork, the
various species of herons, the hoopoe,
and the bat.

20 "The various winged insects that
walk on all fours are loathsome for you.
21 But of the various winged insects that
walk on all fours you may eat those that
have jointed legs for leaping on the
ground; 22† hence of these you may eat
the following: the various kinds of lo-
custs, the various kinds of grasshoppers,
the various kinds of katydids, and the
various kinds of crickets. 23 All other
winged insects that have four legs are
loathsome for you.

24† "Such is the uncleanness that you
contract, that everyone who touches
their dead bodies shall be unclean until
evening, 25 and everyone who picks up
any part of their dead bodies shall wash
his garments and be unclean until eve-
ning. 26† All hoofed animals that are not
cloven-footed or do not chew the cud are
unclean for you; everyone who touches
them becomes unclean. 27† Of the vari-
ous quadrupeds, all those that walk on
paws are unclean for you; everyone who
touches their dead bodies shall be un-
clean until evening, 28 and everyone who
picks up their dead bodies shall wash
his garments and be unclean until
evening. Such is their uncleanness for
you.

29 "Of the creatures that swarm on the
ground, the following are unclean for
you: the rat, the mouse, the various
kinds of lizards, 30 the gecko, the chame-
leon, the agama, the skink, and the mole.
31 Among the various swarming crea-
tures, these are unclean for you. Every-
one who touches them when they are
dead shall be unclean until evening.
32 Everything on which one of them falls
when dead becomes unclean. Any such
article that men use, whether it be an
article of wood, cloth, leather or goat
hair, must be put in water and remain
unclean until evening, when it again be-
comes clean. 33 Should any of these crea-
tures fall into a clay vessel, everything
in it becomes unclean, and the vessel it-
self you must break. 34 Any solid food
that was in contact with water, and any
liquid that men drink, in any such vessel
become unclean. 35 Any object on which
one of their dead bodies falls, becomes
unclean; if it is an oven or a jar-stand,
this must be broken to pieces; they are
unclean and shall be treated as unclean
by you. 36† However, a spring or a cis-
tern for collecting water remains clean;
but whoever touches the dead body be-
comes unclean. 37 Any sort of cultivated
grain remains clean even though one of
their dead bodies falls on it; 38 but if the
grain has become moistened, it becomes
unclean when one of these falls on it.

39 "When one of the animals that you
could otherwise eat, dies of itself, anyone
who touches its dead body shall be un-
clean until evening; 40* and anyone who
eats of its dead body shall wash his gar-
ments and be unclean until evening; so
also, anyone who removes its dead body

*

11, 40: 17, 15; 22, 8.

†

11, 5f: According to modern zoology, *the rock badger* (hyrax Syriacus) is classified as an ungulate, and *the hare* as a rodent; neither is a ruminant. They appear to chew their food as the true ruminants do, and it is upon this appearance that the classification in the text is based.

11, 13-19.30: The identification of the various Hebrew names for these birds and reptiles is in many cases uncertain.

11, 19: *The bat:* actually a mammal, but listed here with the birds because of its wings.

11, 22: The Hebrew distinguishes four classes of edible locust-like insects, but the difference between them is quite uncertain. Cf Mt 3, 4.

11, 24-28: This paragraph sharpens the prohibition against unclean animals: not only is their meat unfit for food, but contact with their dead bodies makes a person ritually unclean.

11, 26: *All hoofed animals that are not cloven-footed:* such as the horse and the ass.

11, 27: *All those that walk on paws:* such as dogs and cats.

11, 36: *Whoever touches the dead body:* to remove the dead insect from the water supply.

shall wash his garments and be unclean
until evening.
41 “All the creatures that swarm on the
ground are loathsome and shall not be
eaten. 42 Whether it crawls on its belly,
goes on all fours, or has many legs, you
shall eat no swarming creature: they are
loathsome. 43* Do not make yourselves
loathsome or unclean with any swarm-
ing creature through being contami-
nated by them. 44* For I, the LORD, am
your God; and you shall make and keep
yourselves holy, because I am holy. You
shall not make yourselves unclean, then,
by any swarming creature that crawls
on the ground. 45 Since I, the LORD,
brought you up from the land of Egypt
that I might be your God, you shall be
holy, because I am holy.
46 “This is the law for animals and
birds and for all the creatures that move
about in the water or swarm on the
ground, 47* that you may distinguish be-
tween the clean and the unclean, be-
tween creatures that may be eaten and
those that may not be eaten.”

CHAPTER 12

Uncleanness of Childbirth. 1 The
LORD said to Moses, 2*† “Tell the Israel-
ites: When a woman has conceived and
gives birth to a boy, she shall be unclean
for seven days, with the same unclean-
ness as at her menstrual period. 3* On
the eighth day, the flesh of the boy's
foreskin shall be circumcised, 4 and then
she shall spend thirty-three days more
in becoming purified of her blood; she
shall not touch anything sacred nor en-
ter the sanctuary till the days of her pu-
rification are fulfilled. 5 If she gives birth
to a girl, for fourteen days she shall be
as unclean as at her menstruation, after
which she shall spend sixty-six days in
becoming purified of her blood.
6* “When the days of her purification
for a son or for a daughter are fulfilled,
she shall bring to the priest at the en-
trance of the meeting tent a yearling
lamb for a holocaust and a pigeon or a
turtledove for a sin offering. 7 The priest
shall offer them up before the LORD to
make atonement for her, and thus she
will be clean again after her flow of
blood. Such is the law for the woman who
gives birth to a boy or a girl child. 8*† If,
however, she cannot afford a lamb, she
may take two turtledoves or two pigeons,
the one for a holocaust and the other for
a sin offering. The priest shall make
atonement for her, and thus she will
again be clean.”

CHAPTER 13

Leprosy. 1 The LORD said to Moses
and Aaron, 2*† “If someone has on his
skin a scab or pustule or blotch which
appears to be the sore of leprosy, he shall
be brought to Aaron, the priest, or to one
of the priests among his descendants,
3 who shall examine the sore on his skin.
If the hair on the sore has turned white
and the sore itself shows that it has pen-
etrated below the skin, it is indeed the
sore of leprosy; the priest, on seeing this,
shall declare the man unclean. 4 If, how-
ever, the blotch on the skin is white, but
does not seem to have penetrated below
the skin, nor has the hair turned white,
the priest shall quarantine the stricken
man for seven days. 5 On the seventh
day the priest shall again examine him.
If he judges that the sore has remained
unchanged and has not spread on the
skin, the priest shall quarantine him for
another seven days, 6 and once more ex-
amine him on the seventh day. If the
sore is now dying out and has not spread
on the skin, the priest shall declare the
man clean; it was merely eczema. The
man shall wash his garments and so be-
come clean. 7 But if, after he has shown
himself to the priest to be declared clean,
the eczema spreads at all on his skin,
he shall once more show himself to the
priest. 8 Should the priest, on examining
it, find that the eczema has indeed
spread on the skin, he shall declare the
man unclean; it is leprosy.
9 “When someone is stricken with lep-
rosy, he shall be brought to the priest.
10 Should the priest, on examining him,
find that there is a white scab on the skin
which has turned the hair white and that
there is raw flesh in it, 11 it is skin leprosy
that has long developed. The priest shall
declare the man unclean without first
quarantining him, since he is certainly
unclean. 12† If leprosy breaks out on the
skin and, as far as the priest can see,
covers all the skin of the stricken man

*

43f: 20, 25f.
44: 19, 2; 20, 7.26; Mt 5, 48; 1 Pt 1, 16.
47: 10, 10.
12, 2: 15, 19.
3: Gn 17, 12; Jn 7, 22.
6: Lk 2, 22.
8: 1, 14; Lk 2, 24.
13, 2: Dt 24, 8.

†

12, 2f: The uncleanness of the woman was more serious during the first period, the seven days after the birth of a boy or the fourteen days after the birth of a girl; only during this period would the rules given in 15, 19-24 apply.

12, 8: Forty days after the birth of Jesus, his Virgin Mother made this offering of the poor (Lk 2, 22.24); since the holocaust was offered in thanksgiving for the birth of the child, this was most fittingly offered by Mary. However, because of her miraculous delivery, she was not really obliged to make the sin offering of purification.

13, 2ff: Various kinds of skin blemishes are treated here which were not contagious but simply disqualified their subjects from association with others, especially in public worship, until they were declared ritually clean. The Hebrew term used does not refer to Hansen's disease, currently called leprosy.

13, 12ff: *If leprosy breaks out on the skin:* the symptoms described here point to a form of skin disease which is merely on the surface and therefore easily cured.

from head to foot, 13 should the priest
then, on examining him, find that the
leprosy does cover his whole body, he
shall declare the stricken man clean;
since it has all turned white, the man
is clean. 14 But as soon as raw flesh ap-
pears on him, he is unclean; 15 on observ-
ing the raw flesh, the priest shall declare
him unclean, because raw flesh is un-
clean; it is leprosy. 16 If, however, the
raw flesh again turns white, he shall re-
turn to the priest; 17 should the latter, on
examining him, find that the sore has
indeed turned white, he shall declare the
stricken man clean, and thus he will be
clean.

18 "If a man who had a boil on his skin
which later healed, 19 should now in the
place of the boil have a white scab or a
pink blotch, he shall show himself to the
priest. 20 If the latter, on examination,
sees that it is deeper than the skin and
that the hair has turned white, he shall
declare the man unclean; it is the sore
of leprosy that has broken out in the boil.
21 But if the priest, on examining him,
finds that there is no white hair in it and
that it is not deeper than the skin and
is already dying out, the priest shall
quarantine him for seven days. 22 If it
has then spread on the skin, the priest
shall declare him unclean; the man is
stricken. 23 But if the blotch remains in
its place without spreading, it is merely
the scar of the boil; the priest shall there-
fore declare him clean.

24 "If a man had a burn on his skin,
and the proud flesh of the burn now be-
comes a pink or a white blotch, 25 the
priest shall examine it. If the hair has
turned white on the blotch and this
seems to have penetrated below the skin,
it is leprosy that has broken out in the
burn; the priest shall therefore declare
him unclean and stricken with leprosy.
26 But if the priest, on examining it, finds
that there is no white hair on the blotch
and that this is not deeper than the skin
and is already dying out, the priest shall
quarantine him for seven days. 27 Should
the priest, when examining it on the sev-
enth day, find that it has spread at all
on the skin, he shall declare the man un-
clean and stricken with leprosy. 28 But
if the blotch remains in its place without
spreading on the skin and is already dy-
ing out, it is merely the scab of the burn;
the priest shall therefore declare the
man clean, since it is only the scar of
the burn.

29 "When a man or a woman has a sore
on the head or cheek, 30† should the
priest, on examining it, find that the sore
has penetrated below the skin and that
there is fine yellow hair on it, the priest
shall declare the person unclean, for this
is scall, a leprous disease of the head or
cheek. 31 But if the priest, on examining
the scall sore, finds that it has not pene-
trated below the skin, though the hair
on it may not be black, the priest shall
quarantine the person with scall sore for
seven days, 32 and on the seventh day
again examine the sore. If the scall has
not spread and has no yellow hair on it
and does not seem to have penetrated
below the skin, 33 the man shall shave
himself, but not on the diseased spot.
Then the priest shall quarantine him for
another seven days. 34 If the priest, when
examining the scall on the seventh day,
finds that it has not spread on the skin
and that it has not penetrated below the
skin, he shall declare the man clean; the
latter shall wash his garments, and thus
he will be clean. 35 But if the scall spreads
at all on his skin after he has been de-
clared clean, 36 the priest shall again ex-
amine it. If the scall has indeed spread
on the skin, he need not look for yellow
hair; the man is surely unclean. 37 If,
however, he judges that the scall has re-
mained in its place and that black hair
has grown on it, the disease has been
healed; the man is clean, and the priest
shall declare him clean.

38 "When the skin of a man or a woman
is spotted with white blotches, 39† the
priest shall make an examination. If the
blotches on the skin are white and al-
ready dying out, it is only tetter that has
broken out on the skin, and the person
therefore is clean.

40 "When a man loses the hair of his
head, he is not unclean merely because
of his bald crown. 41 So too, if he loses
the hair on the front of his head, he is
not unclean merely because of his bald
forehead. 42 But when there is a pink sore
on his bald crown or bald forehead, it
is leprosy that is breaking out there.
43 The priest shall examine him; and if
the scab on the sore of the bald spot has
the same pink appearance as that of skin
leprosy of the fleshy part of the body,
44 the man is leprous and unclean, and
the priest shall declare him unclean by
reason of the sore on his head.

45 "The one who bears the sore of lep-
rosy shall keep his garments rent and
his head bare, and shall muffle his
beard; he shall cry out, 'Unclean, un-
clean!' 46* As long as the sore is on him
he shall declare himself unclean, since
he is in fact unclean. He shall dwell
apart, making his abode outside the
camp.

Leprosy of Clothes. 47† "When a lep-
rous infection is on a garment of wool

*

46: Nm 5, 2; 12, 14f; 2 Kgs 15, 5; Lk 17, 12.

†

13, 30: *Scall:* a scabby or scaly eruption of the scalp. According to some, "ringworm."

13, 39: *Tetter:* vitiligo, a harmless form of skin disease.

13, 47: *A leprous infection:* some mold or fungus growth resembling human leprosy.

or of linen, 48 or on woven or knitted material of linen or wool, or on a hide or anything made of leather, 49 if the infection on the garment or hide, or on the woven or knitted material, or on any leather article is greenish or reddish, the thing is indeed infected with leprosy and must be shown to the priest. 50 Having examined the infection, the priest shall quarantine the infected article for seven days.

51 "On the seventh day the priest shall again examine the infection. If it has spread on the garment, or on the woven or knitted material, or on the leather, whatever be its use, the infection is malignant leprosy, and the article is unclean. 52 He shall therefore burn up the garment, or the woven or knitted material of wool or linen, or the leather article, whatever it may be, which is infected; since it has malignant leprosy, it must be destroyed by fire. 53 But if the priest, on examining the infection, finds that it has not spread on the garment, or on the woven or knitted material, or on the leather article, 54 he shall give orders to have the infected article washed and then quarantined for another seven days.

55 "Then the priest shall again examine the infected article after it has been washed. If the infection has not changed its appearance, even though it may not have spread, the article is unclean and shall be destroyed by fire. 56 But if the priest, on examining the infection, finds that it is dying out after the washing, he shall tear the infected part out of the garment, or the leather, or the woven or knitted material. 57 If, however, the infection again appears on the garment, or on the woven or knitted material, or on the leather article, it is still virulent and the thing infected shall be destroyed by fire. 58 But if, after the washing, the infection has left the garment, or the woven or knitted material, or the leather article, the thing shall be washed a second time, and thus it will be clean. 59* This is the law for leprous infection on a garment of wool or linen, or on woven or knitted material, or on any leather article, to determine whether it is clean or unclean."

CHAPTER 14

Purification after Leprosy. 1 The LORD said to Moses, 2* "This is the law for the victim of leprosy at the time of his purification. He shall be brought to the priest, 3 who is to go outside the camp to examine him. If the priest finds that the sore of leprosy has healed in the leper, 4† he shall order the man who is to be purified, to get two live, clean birds, as well as some cedar wood, scarlet yarn, and hyssop. 5† The priest shall then order him to slay one of the birds over an earthen vessel with spring water in it. 6 Taking the living bird with the cedar wood, the scarlet yarn and the hyssop, the priest shall dip them all in the blood of the bird that was slain over the spring water, 7 and then sprinkle seven times the man to be purified from his leprosy. When he has thus purified him, he shall let the living bird fly away over the countryside. 8 The man being purified shall then wash his garments and shave off all his hair and bathe in water; only when he is thus made clean may he come inside the camp; but he shall still remain outside his tent for seven days. 9 On the seventh day he shall again shave off all the hair of his head, his beard, his eyebrows, and any other hair he may have, and also wash his garments and bathe his body in water; and so he will be clean.

Purification Sacrifices. 10 "On the eighth day he shall take two unblemished male lambs, one unblemished yearling ewe lamb, three tenths of an ephah of fine flour mixed with oil for a cereal offering, and one log of oil. 11 The priest who performs the purification ceremony shall place the man who is being purified, as well as all these offerings, before the LORD at the entrance of the meeting tent. 12 Taking one of the male lambs, the priest shall present it as a guilt offering, along with the log of oil, waving them as a wave offering before the LORD. 13 (This lamb he shall slaughter in the sacred place where the sin offering and the holocaust are slaughtered; because, like the sin offering, the guilt offering belongs to the priest and is most sacred.) 14* Then the priest shall take some of the blood of the guilt offering and put it on the tip of the man's right ear, the thumb of his right hand, and the big toe of his right foot. 15 The priest shall also take the log of oil and pour some of it into the palm of his own left hand; 16 then, dipping his right forefinger in it, he shall sprinkle it seven times before the LORD. 17 Of the oil left in his hand the priest shall put some on the tip of the man's right ear, the thumb of his right hand, and the big toe of his right foot, over the blood of the guilt offering. 18 The rest of the oil in his hand the priest shall put on the head of the man being purified. Thus shall the priest make atonement for him before the LORD. 19 Only after he has offered the sin

*

59: 14, 54.
14, 2: Mt 8, 4; Mk 1, 44; Lk 5, 14.
14: 8, 23f.

†

14, 4: *Scarlet yarn:* probably used for tying the hyssop sprig to the cedar branchlet.

14, 5: *Spring water:* literally, "living water," taken from some source of running water, not from a cistern.

offering in atonement for the man's un-
cleanness shall the priest slaughter the
holocaust 20 and offer it, together with
the cereal offering, on the altar before
the LORD. When the priest has thus
made atonement for him, the man will
be clean.

Poor Leper's Sacrifice. 21 "If a man is
poor and cannot afford so much, he shall
take one male lamb for a guilt offering,
to be used as a wave offering in atone-
ment for himself, one tenth of an ephah
of fine flour mixed with oil for a cereal
offering, a log of oil, 22† and two turtle-
doves or pigeons, which he can more
easily afford, the one as a sin offering
and the other as a holocaust. 23 On the
eighth day of his purification he shall
bring them to the priest, at the entrance
of the meeting tent before the LORD.
24 Taking the guilt-offering lamb, along
with the log of oil, the priest shall wave
them as a wave offering before the LORD.
25 When he has slaughtered the guilt-of-
fering lamb, he shall take some of its
blood, and put it on the tip of the right
ear of the man being purified, on the
thumb of his right hand, and on the big
toe of his right foot. 26 The priest shall
then pour some of the oil into the palm
of his own left hand 27 and with his right
forefinger sprinkle it seven times before
the LORD. 28 Some of the oil in his hand
the priest shall also put on the tip of the
man's right ear, the thumb of his right
hand, and the big toe of his right foot,
over the blood of the guilt offering. 29 The
rest of the oil in his hand the priest shall
put on the man's head. Thus shall he
make atonement for him before the
LORD. 30 Then, of the turtledoves or pi-
geons, such as the man can afford, 31 the
priest shall offer up one as a sin offering
and the other as a holocaust, along with
the cereal offering. Thus shall the priest
make atonement before the LORD for the
man who is to be purified. 32 This is the
law for one afflicted with leprosy who
has insufficient means for his purifica-
tion."

Leprosy of Houses. 33 The LORD said
to Moses and Aaron, 34 "When you come
into the land of Canaan, which I am giv-
ing you to possess, if I put a leprous in-
fection on any house of the land you
occupy, 35 the owner of the house shall
come and report to the priest, 'It looks
to me as if my house were infected.'
36 The priest shall then order the house
to be cleared out before he goes in to
examine the infection, lest everything in
the house become unclean. Only after
this is he to go in to examine the house.
37 If the priest, on examining it, finds that
the infection on the walls of the house
consists of greenish or reddish depres-
sions which seem to go deeper than the
surface of the wall, 38 he shall close the
door of the house behind him and quar-
antine the house for seven days. 39 On
the seventh day the priest shall return
to examine the house again. If he finds
that the infection has spread on the
walls, 40 he shall order the infected
stones to be pulled out and cast in an
unclean place outside the city. 41 The
whole inside of the house shall then be
scraped, and the mortar that has been
scraped off shall be dumped in an un-
clean place outside the city. 42 Then new
stones shall be brought and put in the
place of the old stones, and new mortar
shall be made and plastered on the
house.

43 "If the infection breaks out once
more after the stones have been pulled
out and the house has been scraped and
replastered, 44 the priest shall come
again; and if he finds that the infection
has spread in the house, it is corrosive
leprosy, and the house is unclean. 45 It
shall be pulled down, and all its stones,
beams and mortar shall be hauled away
to an unclean place outside the city.
46 Whoever enters a house while it is
quarantined shall be unclean until eve-
ning. 47 Whoever sleeps or eats in such
a house shall also wash his garments.
48 If the priest finds, when he comes to
examine the house, that the infection
has in fact not spread after the plaster-
ing, he shall declare the house clean,
since the infection has been healed. 49 To
purify the house, he shall take two birds,
as well as cedar wood, scarlet yarn, and
hyssop. 50 One of the birds he shall slay
over an earthen vessel with spring water
in it. 51 Then, taking the cedarwood, the
hyssop and the scarlet yarn, together
with the living bird, he shall dip them
all in the blood of the slain bird and the
spring water, and sprinkle the house
seven times. 52 Thus shall he purify the
house with the bird's blood and the
spring water, along with the living bird,
the cedar wood, the hyssop, and the
scarlet yarn. 53 He shall then let the liv-
ing bird fly away over the countryside
outside the city. When he has thus made
atonement for it, the house will be clean.

54 "This is the law for every kind of
human leprosy and scall, 55* for leprosy
of garments and houses, 56 as well as for
scabs, pustules and blotches, 57 so that
it may be manifest when there is a state
of uncleanness and when a state of
cleanness. This is the law for leprosy."

CHAPTER 15

Personal Uncleanness. 1 The LORD
said to Moses and Aaron, 2* "Speak to

*

55: 13, 47-58. 15, 2: Nm 5, 2.

†

14, 22: *Two turtledoves:* substitutes for the two additional lambs, similar to the offering of a poor woman after childbirth. Cf 12, 8.

the Israelites and tell them: Every man
who is afflicted with a chronic flow from
his private parts is thereby unclean.
3 Such is his uncleanness from this flow
that it makes no difference whether the
flow drains off or is blocked up; his un-
cleanness remains. 4 Any bed on which
the man afflicted with the flow lies, is
unclean, and any piece of furniture on
which he sits, is unclean. 5 Anyone who
touches his bed shall wash his garments,
bathe in water, and be unclean until eve-
ning. 6 Whoever sits on a piece of furni-
ture on which the afflicted man was
sitting, shall wash his garments, bathe
in water, and be unclean until evening.
7 Whoever touches the body of the af-
flicted man shall wash his garments,
bathe in water, and be unclean until eve-
ning. 8 If the afflicted man spits on a
clean man, the latter shall wash his gar-
ments, bathe in water, and be unclean
until evening. 9 Any saddle on which
the afflicted man rides, is unclean.
10 Whoever touches anything that was
under him shall be unclean until eve-
ning; whoever lifts up any such thing
shall wash his garments, bathe in water,
and be unclean until evening. 11 Anyone
whom the afflicted man touches with un-
rinsed hands shall wash his garments,
bathe in water, and be unclean until eve-
ning. 12 Earthenware touched by the af-
flicted man shall be broken; and every
wooden article shall be rinsed with
water.

13 "When a man who has been afflicted
with a flow becomes free of his affliction,
he shall wait seven days for his purifica-
tion. Then he shall wash his garments
and bathe his body in fresh water, and
so he will be clean. 14 On the eighth day
he shall take two turtledoves or two pi-
geons, and going before the LORD, to the
entrance of the meeting tent, he shall
give them to the priest, 15 who shall offer
them up, the one as a sin offering and
the other as a holocaust. Thus shall the
priest make atonement before the LORD
for the man's flow.

16 "When a man has an emission of
seed, he shall bathe his whole body in
water and be unclean until evening.
17 Any piece of cloth or leather with seed
on it shall be washed with water and be
unclean until evening.

18 "If a man lies carnally with a
woman, they shall both bathe in water
and be unclean until evening.

19* "When a woman has her menstrual
flow, she shall be in a state of impurity
for seven days. Anyone who touches her
shall be unclean until evening. 20 Any-
thing on which she lies or sits during her
impurity shall be unclean. 21 Anyone
who touches her bed shall wash his gar-
ments, bathe in water, and be unclean
until evening. 22 Whoever touches any
article of furniture on which she was sit-
ting, shall wash his garments, bathe in
water, and be unclean until evening.
23† But if she is on the bed or on the seat
when he touches it, he shall be unclean
until evening. 24* If a man dares to lie
with her, he contracts her impurity and
shall be unclean for seven days; every
bed on which he then lies also becomes
unclean.

25* "When a woman is afflicted with a
flow of blood for several days outside her
menstrual period, or when her flow con-
tinues beyond the ordinary period, as
long as she suffers this unclean flow she
shall be unclean, just as during her men-
strual period. 26 Any bed on which she
lies during such a flow becomes unclean,
as it would during her menstruation, and
any article of furniture on which she sits
becomes unclean just as during her
menstruation. 27 Anyone who touches
them becomes unclean; he shall wash
his garments, bathe in water, and be un-
clean until evening.

28 "If she becomes freed from her af-
fliction, she shall wait seven days, and
only then is she to be purified. 29 On the
eighth day she shall take two turtledoves
or two pigeons and bring them to the
priest at the entrance of the meeting
tent. 30 The priest shall offer up one of
them as a sin offering and the other as
a holocaust. Thus shall the priest make
atonement before the LORD for her un-
clean flow.

31 "You shall warn the Israelites of
their uncleanness, lest by defiling my
Dwelling, which is in their midst, their
uncleanness be the cause of their death.

32 "This is the law for the man who is
afflicted with a chronic flow, or who has
an emission of seed, and thereby be-
comes unclean; 33 as well as for the
woman who has her menstrual period,
or who is afflicted with a chronic flow;
the law for male and female; and also
for the man who lies with an unclean
woman."

CHAPTER 16

The Day of Atonement. 1 After the
death of Aaron's two sons, who died
when they approached the LORD's pres-
ence, the LORD spoke to Moses 2*† and

*

19: 12, 2.5.
24: 18, 19.
25: Mt 9, 20; Mk 5, 25; Lk 8, 43.
16, 2: Heb 9, 6-12.

†

15, 23: What is added to the legislation by this verse is uncertain in both the Hebrew and the Greek.

16, 2: *The sanctuary, inside the veil:* the innermost part of the sanctuary, known also as "the holy of holies." Cf Ex 26, 33f. Here the high priest was allowed to enter only once a year, on *Yom Kippur,* the Day of Atonement. In Heb 9, 3-12 this ceremony is applied to Christ's single act of Redemption, whereby he won for us an everlasting atonement. *Propitiatory:* see note on Ex 25, 17.

said to him, "Tell your brother Aaron
that he is not to come whenever he
pleases into the sanctuary, inside the
veil, in front of the propitiatory on the
ark; otherwise, when I reveal myself in
a cloud above the propitiatory, he will
die. 3 Only in this way may Aaron enter
the sanctuary. He shall bring a young
bullock for a sin offering and a ram for
a holocaust. 4 He shall wear the sacred
linen tunic, with the linen drawers next
his flesh, gird himself with the linen sash
and put on the linen miter. But since
these vestments are sacred, he shall not
put them on until he has first bathed his
body in water. 5* From the Israelite
community he shall receive two male
goats for a sin offering and one ram for
a holocaust.

6 "Aaron shall bring in the bullock, his
sin offering to atone for himself and for
his household. 7 Taking the two male
goats and setting them before the LORD
at the entrance of the meeting tent, 8† he
shall cast lots to determine which one
is for the LORD and which for Azazel.
9 The goat that is determined by lot for
the LORD, Aaron shall bring in and offer
up as a sin offering. 10 But the goat deter-
mined by lot for Azazel he shall set alive
before the LORD, so that with it he may
make atonement by sending it off to
Azazel in the desert.

11 "Thus shall Aaron offer up the bull-
ock, his sin offering, to atone for himself
and for his family. When he has slaugh-
tered it, 12 he shall take a censer full of
glowing embers from the altar before
the LORD, as well as a double handful
of finely ground fragrant incense, and
bringing them inside the veil, 13† there
before the LORD he shall put incense on
the fire, so that a cloud of incense may
cover the propitiatory over the com-
mandments; else he will die. 14* Taking
some of the bullock's blood, he shall
sprinkle it with his finger on the fore part
of the propitiatory and likewise sprinkle
some of the blood with his finger seven
times in front of the propitiatory.

15* "Then he shall slaughter the peo-
ple's sin-offering goat, and bringing its
blood inside the veil, he shall do with it
as he did with the bullock's blood, sprin-
kling it on the propitiatory and before
it. 16 Thus he shall make atonement for
the sanctuary because of all the sinful
defilements and faults of the Israelites.
He shall do the same for the meeting
tent, which is set up among them in the
midst of their uncleanness. 17 No one else
may be in the meeting tent from the time
he enters the sanctuary to make atone-
ment until he departs. When he has
made atonement for himself and his
household, as well as for the whole Isra-
elite community, 18* he shall come out
to the altar before the LORD and make
atonement for it also. Taking some of
the bullock's and the goat's blood, he
shall put it on the horns around the altar,
19 and with his finger sprinkle some of
the blood on it seven times. Thus he shall
render it clean and holy, purged of the
defilements of the Israelites.

The Scapegoat. 20 "When he has com-
pleted the atonement rite for the sanctu-
ary, the meeting tent and the altar,
Aaron shall bring forward the live goat.
21* Laying both hands on its head, he
shall confess over it all the sinful faults
and transgressions of the Israelites,
and so put them on the goat's head. He
shall then have it led into the desert
by an attendant. 22* Since the goat is to
carry off their iniquities to an isolated
region, it must be sent away into the des-
ert.

23† "After Aaron has again gone into
the meeting tent, he shall strip off and
leave in the sanctuary the linen vest-
ments he had put on when he entered
there. 24 After bathing his body with
water in a sacred place, he shall put on
his vestments, and then come out and
offer his own and the people's holocaust,
in atonement for himself and for the
people, 25 and also burn the fat of the sin
offering on the altar.

26 "The man who has led away the goat
for Azazel shall wash his garments and
bathe his body in water; only then may
he enter the camp. 27* The sin-offering
bullock and goat whose blood was
brought into the sanctuary to make
atonement, shall be taken outside the
camp, where their hides and flesh and
offal shall be burned up in the fire. 28 The
one who burns them shall wash his gar-
ments and bathe his body in water; only
then may he enter the camp.

The Fast. 29*† "This shall be an ever-
lasting ordinance for you: on the tenth
day of the seventh month every one of
you, whether a native or a resident alien,
shall mortify himself and shall do no
work. 30 Since on this day atonement is
made for you to make you clean, so that

*

5: Nm 29, 11.
14: Heb 9, 13.25.
15: Heb 5, 1; 6, 19.
18: Ex 30, 12.
21: Is 53, 6; 2 Cor 5, 21.
22: Is 53, 11. 12; Jn 1, 29; 1 Pt 2, 24.
27: Heb 13, 11.
29: 23, 27. 32; Nm 29, 7.

†

16, 8: *Azazel:* perhaps a name for Satan, used only in this chapter. The ancient versions translated this word as "the escaping goat," whence the English word "scapegoat."

16, 13: *Else he will die:* the smoke is to conceal the resplendent majesty of God, the sight of which would strike any man dead.

16, 23: This verse is best read after v 25. According to later Jewish practice the high priest again went into the holy of holies to remove the censer.

16, 29: *Mortify himself:* literally, "afflict his soul"; traditionally understood by the Jews as signifying abstinence from all food. This is the only fast day prescribed in the Mosaic law.

you may be cleansed of all your sins be-
fore the LORD, [31] by everlasting ordi-
nance it shall be a most solemn sabbath
for you, on which you must mortify
yourselves.
[32] "This atonement is to be made by
the priest who has been anointed and
ordained to the priesthood in succession
to his father. He shall wear the linen gar-
ments, the sacred vestments, [33] and
make atonement for the sacred sanctu-
ary, the meeting tent and the altar, as
well as for the priests and all the people
of the community. [34]* This, then, shall
be an everlasting ordinance for you:
once a year atonement shall be made
for all the sins of the Israelites."
Thus was it done, as the LORD had
commanded Moses.

IV: CODE OF LEGAL HOLINESS

CHAPTER 17

Sacredness of Blood. [1] The LORD said
to Moses, [2] "Speak to Aaron and his
sons, as well as to all the Israelites, and
tell them: This is what the LORD has
commanded. [3]† Any Israelite who
slaughters an ox or a sheep or a goat,
whether in the camp or outside of it,
[4] without first bringing it to the entrance
of the meeting tent to present it as an
offering to the LORD in front of his Dwell-
ing, shall be judged guilty of bloodshed;
and for this, such a man shall be cut off
from among his people. [5] Therefore,
such sacrifices as they used to offer up
in the open field the Israelites shall
henceforth offer to the LORD, bringing
them to the priest at the entrance of the
meeting tent and sacrificing them there
as peace offerings to the LORD. [6] The
priest shall splash the blood on the altar
of the LORD at the entrance of the meet-
ing tent and there burn the fat for an
odor pleasing to the LORD. [7]* No longer
shall they offer their sacrifices to the sa-
tyrs to whom they used to render their
wanton worship. This shall be an ever-
lasting ordinance for them and their
descendants.
[8] "Tell them, therefore: Anyone,
whether of the house of Israel or of the
aliens residing among them, who offers
a holocaust or sacrifice [9] without bring-
ing it to the entrance of the meeting tent
to offer it to the LORD, shall be cut off
from his kinsmen. [10]* And if anyone,
whether of the house of Israel or of the
aliens residing among them, partakes
of any blood, I will set myself against
that one who partakes of blood and will
cut him off from among his people.
[11]*† Since the life of a living body is in
its blood, I have made you put it on the
altar, so that atonement may thereby be
made for your own lives, because it is
the blood, as the seat of life, that makes
atonement. [12] That is why I have told
the Israelites: No one among you, not
even a resident alien, may partake of
blood.
[13] "Anyone hunting, whether of the Is-
raelites or of the aliens residing among
them, who catches an animal or a bird
that may be eaten, shall pour out its
blood and cover it with earth. [14]* Since
the life of every living body is its blood,
I have told the Israelites: You shall not
partake of the blood of any meat. Since
the life of every living body is its blood,
anyone who partakes of it shall be cut
off.
[15]* "Everyone, whether a native or an
alien, who eats of an animal that died
of itself or was killed by a wild beast,
shall wash his garments, bathe in water,
and be unclean until evening, and then
he will be clean. [16] If he does not wash
or does not bathe his body, he shall have
the guilt to bear."

CHAPTER 18

The Sanctity of Sex. [1] The LORD said
to Moses, [2] "Speak to the Israelites and
tell them: I, the LORD, am your God.
[3] You shall not do as they do in the land
of Egypt, where you once lived, nor shall
you do as they do in the land of Canaan,
where I am bringing you; do not conform
to their customs. [4] My decrees you shall
carry out, and my statutes you shall take
care to follow. I, the LORD, am your God.
[5]* Keep, then, my statutes and decrees,
for the man who carries them out will
find life through them. I am the LORD.
[6]† "None of you shall approach a close
relative to have sexual intercourse with
her. I am the LORD. [7]* You shall not dis-
grace your father by having intercourse
with your mother. Besides, since she is

*

34: Heb 9, 7. 25.
17, 7: Ex 34, 15; Dt 32, 17; 2 Chr 11, 15; 1 Cor 10, 20.
10: 3, 17.
11: Gn 9, 4.
14: 7, 26f.
15: 11, 39f; 22, 8.
18, 5: Gal 3, 12.
7-16: 20, 11-21.

†

17, 3ff: The ancients considered blood the seat and sign of life, and therefore something sacred, even in animals. Cf Gn 9, 4f. Hence, even the ordinary butchering of an animal for meat was looked upon as having a sacrificial character, so that it should be performed at the sanctuary. This law, however, could not be carried out without great difficulty when the Israelites were scattered throughout Palestine, and so was modified in Dt 12, 20ff.

17, 11: *That atonement may thereby be made for your own lives:* hence, the sacrifice of an animal was a symbolic act which substituted the victim's life for the life of the offerer, who thus acknowledged that he deserved God's punishments for his sins. This idea of sacrifice is applied in Heb 9-10 to the death of Christ, inasmuch as "without the shedding of blood there is no forgiveness" (Heb 9, 22).

18, 6-18: These laws are formulated as directed to the male Israelites only, but naturally the same norms of consanguinity and affinity would apply to the women as well. Marriage, as well as casual intercourse, is here forbidden between men and women of the specified degrees of relationship.

your own mother, you shall not have in-
tercourse with her. 8* You shall not have
intercourse with your father's wife, for
that would be a disgrace to your father.
9 You shall not have intercourse with
your sister, your father's daughter or
your mother's daughter, whether she
was born in your own household or born
elsewhere. 10 You shall not have inter-
course with your son's daughter or with
your daughter's daughter, for that
would be a disgrace to your own family.
11 You shall not have intercourse with
the daughter whom your father's wife
bore to him, since she, too, is your sister.
12* You shall not have intercourse with
your father's sister, since she is your fa-
ther's relative. 13 You shall not have in-
tercourse with your mother's sister,
since she is your mother's relative.
14* You shall not disgrace your father's
brother by being intimate with his wife,
since she, too, is your aunt. 15 You shall
not have intercourse with your daugh-
ter-in-law; she is your son's wife, and
therefore you shall not disgrace her.
16*† You shall not have intercourse with
your brother's wife, for that would be
a disgrace to your brother. 17 You shall
not have intercourse with a woman and
also with her daughter, nor shall you
marry and have intercourse with her
son's daughter or her daughter's daugh-
ter; this would be shameful, because
they are related to her. 18 While your
wife is still living you shall not marry
her sister as her rival; for thus you would
disgrace your first wife.
19 "You shall not approach a woman
to have intercourse with her while she
is unclean from menstruation. 20 You
shall not have carnal relations with your
neighbor's wife, defiling yourself with
her. 21*† You shall not offer any of your
offspring to be immolated to Molech,
thus profaning the name of your God.
I am the LORD. 22* You shall not lie with
a male as with a woman; such a thing
is an abomination. 23* You shall not have
carnal relations with an animal, defiling
yourself with it; nor shall a woman set
herself in front of an animal to mate with
it; such things are abhorrent.
24 "Do not defile yourselves by any of
these things by which the nations whom
I am driving out of your way have de-
filed themselves. 25 Because their land
has become defiled, I am punishing it
for its wickedness, by making it vomit
out its inhabitants. 26 You, however,
whether natives or resident aliens, must
keep my statutes and decrees forbidding
all such abominations 27 by which the
previous inhabitants defiled the land;
28 otherwise the land will vomit you
out also for having defiled it, just as it
vomited out the nations before you.
29 Everyone who does any of these
abominations shall be cut off from
among his people. 30* Heed my charge,
then, not to defile yourselves by observ-
ing the abominable customs that have
been observed before you. I, the LORD,
am your God."

CHAPTER 19

Various Rules of Conduct. 1 The LORD
said to Moses, 2* "Speak to the whole Is-
raelite community and tell them: Be
holy, for I, the LORD your God, am holy.
3* Revere your mother and father, and
keep my sabbaths. I, the LORD, am your
God.
4* "Do not turn aside to idols, nor
make molten gods for yourselves. I, the
LORD, am your God.
5 "When you sacrifice your peace of-
fering to the LORD, if you wish it to be
acceptable, 6 it must be eaten on the very
day of your sacrifice or on the following
day. Whatever is left over until the third
day shall be burned up in the fire. 7* If
any of it is eaten on the third day, the
sacrifice will be unacceptable as refuse;
8 whoever eats of it then shall pay the
penalty for having profaned what is sa-
cred to the LORD. Such a one shall be
cut off from his people.
9* "When you reap the harvest of your
land, you shall not be so thorough that
you reap the field to its very edge, nor
shall you glean the stray ears of grain.
10 Likewise, you shall not pick your vine-
yard bare, nor gather up the grapes that
have fallen. These things you shall leave
for the poor and the alien. I, the LORD,
am your God.
11* "You shall not steal. You shall not
lie or speak falsely to one another.
12* You shall not swear falsely by my
name, thus profaning the name of your
God. I am the LORD.
13* "You shall not defraud or rob your
neighbor. You shall not withhold over-
night the wages of your day laborer.

*

8: Dt 23, 1; 27, 20; 1 Cor 5, 1.
12f: 20, 19.
14: 20, 20.
16: 20, 21; Mt 14, 3f; Mk 6, 18.
21: 20, 2-5; Dt 18, 10; 2 Kgs 16, 3; 21, 6.
22: 20, 13; Rom 1, 27; 1 Cor 6, 9f.
23: 20, 15f; Ex 22, 18.
30: 20, 23; Dt 18, 9.
19, 2: 11, 44; Mt 5, 48; 1 Pt 1, 16.
3: Ex 20, 12.
4: 26, 1; Ex 20, 3-5; 34, 17; Dt 27, 15.
7: 7, 18.
9: 23, 22; Dt 24, 19ff.
11: Ex 20, 15f.
12: Ex 20, 7; Mt 5, 33.
13: Dt 24, 14f.

†

18, 16: *With your brother's wife:* it was the violation of this law which aroused the wrath of John the Baptist against Herod Antipas. Cf Mk 6, 18. An exception to this law is made in Dt 25, 5.

18, 21: *Immolated to Molech:* the reference is to the Canaanite custom of sacrificing children to the god Molech. The little victims were first slain and then cremated. Cf Ez 16, 20ff; 20, 26.31; 23, 37.

14 You shall not curse the deaf, or put
a stumbling block in front of the blind,
but you shall fear your God. I am the
LORD.
15* "You shall not act dishonestly in
rendering judgment. Show neither par-
tiality to the weak nor deference to the
mighty, but judge your fellow men
justly. 16 You shall not go about spread-
ing slander among your kinsmen; nor
shall you stand by idly when your neigh-
bor's life is at stake. I am the LORD.
17* "You shall not bear hatred for your
brother in your heart. Though you may
have to reprove your fellow man, do not
incur sin because of him. 18*† Take no
revenge and cherish no grudge against
your fellow countrymen. You shall love
your neighbor as yourself. I am the
LORD.
19 "Keep my statutes: do not breed any
of your domestic animals with others of
a different species; do not sow a field of
yours with two different kinds of seed;
and do not put on a garment woven with
two different kinds of thread.
20† "If a man has carnal relations with
a female slave who has already been liv-
ing with another man but has not yet
been redeemed or given her freedom,
they shall be punished but not put to
death, because she is not free. 21 The
man, moreover, shall bring to the en-
trance of the meeting tent a ram as his
guilt offering to the LORD. 22 With this
ram the priest shall make atonement be-
fore the LORD for the sin he has commit-
ted, and it will be forgiven him.
23† "When you come into the land and
plant any fruit tree there, first look upon
its fruit as if it were uncircumcised. For
three years, while its fruit remains un-
circumcised, it may not be eaten. 24 In
the fourth year, however, all of its fruit
shall be sacred to the LORD as a thanks-
giving feast to him. 25 Not until the fifth
year may you eat its fruit. Thus it will
continue its yield for you. I, the LORD,
am your God.
26* "Do not eat meat with the blood still
in it. Do not practice divination or sooth-
saying. 27*† Do not clip your hair at the
temples, nor trim the edges of your
beard. 28 Do not lacerate your bodies for
the dead, and do not tattoo yourselves.
I am the LORD.
29 "You shall not degrade your daugh-
ter by making a prostitute of her; else
the land will become corrupt and full of
lewdness. 30* Keep my sabbaths, and
reverence my sanctuary. I am the LORD.
31* "Do not go to mediums or consult
fortune-tellers, for you will be defiled by
them. I, the LORD, am your God.
32 "Stand up in the presence of the
aged, and show respect for the old; thus
shall you fear your God. I am the LORD.
33* "When an alien resides with you in
your land, do not molest him. 34* You
shall treat the alien who resides with you
no differently than the natives born
among you; have the same love for him
as for yourself; for you too were once
aliens in the land of Egypt. I, the LORD,
am your God.
35 "Do not act dishonestly in using
measures of length or weight or capac-
ity. 36* You shall have a true scale and
true weights, an honest ephah and an
honest hin. I, the LORD, am your God,
who brought you out of the land of
Egypt. 37 Be careful, then, to observe all
my statutes and decrees. I am the
LORD."

CHAPTER 20

Penalties for Various Sins. 1 The LORD
said to Moses, 2* "Tell the Israelites:
Anyone, whether an Israelite or an alien
residing in Israel, who gives any of his
offspring to Molech shall be put to death.
Let his fellow citizens stone him. 3* I my-
self will turn against such a man and
cut him off from the body of his people;
for in giving his offspring to Molech, he
has defiled my sanctuary and profaned
my holy name. 4 Even if his fellow citi-
zens connive at such a man's crime of
giving his offspring to Molech, and fail
to put him to death, 5 I myself will set
my face against that man and his family
and will cut off from their people both
him and all who join him in his wanton
worship of Molech. 6* Should anyone
turn to mediums and fortune-tellers and
follow their wanton ways, I will turn
against such a one and cut him off from

*

15: Ex 23, 2f; Dt 1, 17; 16, 19; Ps 82, 2; Prv 24, 23.
17: Mt 18, 15; Lk 17, 3; Gal 6, 1; 1 Jn 3, 14.
18: Mt 5, 43; 19, 19; 22, 39; Mk 12, 31; Rom 13, 9; Gal 5, 14; Jas 2, 8.
26: 3, 17; Dt 18, 10; 2 Kgs 17, 17; 21, 6; 2 Chr 33, 6.
27: 21, 5.
30: 26, 2; Ex 20, 8.
31: 20, 6.27; Dt 18, 11; Is 8, 19.
33: Ex 22, 20; 23, 9; Jer 22, 3; Mal 3, 5.
34: Dt 10, 19.
36: Dt 25, 13.15; Prv 11, 1; 16, 11; 20, 10; Ez 45, 10.
20, 2: 18, 21.
3: Ez 23, 39.
6: 19, 31.

†

19, 18: *You shall love your neighbor as yourself:* cited by our Lord as the second of the two most important commandments of God. Cf Mt 22, 39; Mk 12, 31. Although in the present context the word "neighbor" is restricted to "fellow countrymen," in Lk 10, 29-37 Christ extends its meaning to embrace all men, even enemies. Cf also Mt 5, 43ff.

19, 20ff: This law seems out of its proper context here; perhaps it stood originally after 20, 12. *Female slave . . . given her freedom:* reference is to the case treated of in Ex 21, 7-11.

19, 23ff: *Uncircumcised:* by analogy with a newborn boy, the newly planted tree was considered impure until "circumcised" by offering to the Lord all the fruit it bore in the fourth year.

19, 27: See note on 21, 5.

his people. 7* Sanctify yourselves, then,
and be holy; for I, the LORD, your God,
am holy. 8 Be careful, therefore, to ob-
serve what I, the LORD, who make you
holy, have prescribed.
9* "Anyone who curses his father or
mother shall be put to death; since he
has cursed his father or mother, he has
forfeited his life. 10* If a man commits
adultery with his neighbor's wife, both
the adulterer and the adulteress shall be
put to death. 11* If a man disgraces his
father by lying with his father's wife,
both the man and his stepmother shall
be put to death; they have forfeited their
lives. 12* If a man lies with his daughter-
in-law, both of them shall be put to
death; since they have committed an
abhorrent deed, they have forfeited
their lives. 13* If a man lies with a male
as with a woman, both of them shall be
put to death for their abominable deed;
they have forfeited their lives. 14* If a
man marries a woman and her mother
also, the man and the two women as well
shall be burned to death for their shame-
ful conduct, so that such shamefulness
may not be found among you. 15* If a
man has carnal relations with an ani-
mal, the man shall be put to death, and
the animal shall be slain. 16* If a woman
goes up to any animal to mate with it,
the woman and the animal shall be slain;
let them both be put to death; their lives
are forfeit. 17* If a man consummates
marriage with his sister or his half-sis-
ter, they shall be publicly cut off from
their people for this shameful deed; the
man shall pay the penalty of having had
intercourse with his own sister. 18* If a
man lies in sexual intercourse with a
woman during her menstrual period,
both of them shall be cut off from their
people, because they have laid bare the
flowing fountain of her blood. 19* You
shall not have intercourse with your
mother's sister or your father's sister;
whoever does so shall pay the penalty
of incest. 20 If a man disgraces his uncle
by having intercourse with his uncle's
wife, the man and his aunt shall pay the
penalty by dying childless. 21 If a man
marries his brother's wife and thus dis-
graces his brother, they shall be child-
less because of this incest.
22 "Be careful to observe all my stat-
utes and all my decrees; otherwise the
land where I am bringing you to dwell
will vomit you out. 23* Do not conform,
therefore, to the customs of the nations
whom I am driving out of your way, be-
cause all these things that they have
done have filled me with disgust for
them. 24* But to you I have said: Their
land shall be your possession, a land
flowing with milk and honey. I am giving
it to you as your own, I, the LORD, your
God, who have set you apart from the
other nations. 25* You, too, must set
apart, then, the clean animals from the
unclean, and the clean birds from the
unclean, so that you may not be contam-
inated with the uncleanness of any beast
or bird or of any swarming creature in
the land that I have set apart for you.
26* To me, therefore, you shall be sacred;
for I, the LORD, am sacred, I, who have
set you apart from the other nations to
be my own.
27*† "A man or a woman who acts as
a medium or fortune-teller shall be put
to death by stoning; they have no one
but themselves to blame for their
death."

CHAPTER 21

Sanctity of the Priesthood. 1*† The
LORD said to Moses, "Speak to Aaron's
sons, the priests, and tell them: None of
you shall make himself unclean for any
dead person among his people, 2 except
for his nearest relatives, his mother or
father, his son or daughter, his brother
3 or his maiden sister, who is of his own
family while she remains unmarried; for
these he may make himself unclean.
4 But for a sister who has married out
of his family he shall not make himself
unclean; this would be a profanation.
5*† "The priests shall not make bare
the crown of the head, nor shave the
edges of the beard, nor lacerate the
body. 6† To their God they shall be sa-
cred, and not profane his name; since
they offer up the oblations of the LORD,
the food of their God, they must be holy.
7* "A priest shall not marry a woman
who has been a prostitute or has lost her
honor, nor a woman who has been di-
vorced by her husband; for the priest is
sacred to his God. 8 Honor him as sacred

*

7: 11, 44; 19, 2; 1 Pt 1, 16.
9: Ex 21, 17; Prv 20, 20; Mt 15, 4; Mk 7, 10.
10: 18, 20; Dt 22, 22; Jn 8, 5.
11: 18, 7f.
12: 18, 15.
13: 18, 22.
14: 18, 17; Dt 27, 23.
15: Ex 22, 18; Dt 27, 21.
16: 18, 23.
17: 18, 9; Dt 27, 22.
18: 18, 19.
19: 18, 12f.
23: 18, 30.
24: Ex 3, 8.17; 6, 8.
25: 11, 2-47; Dt 14, 4-20.
26: 11, 44; Ex 19, 6; 1 Pt 1, 16.
27: 19, 31; Ex 22, 17; Dt 18, 11.
21, 1: Ez 44, 25.
5: Ez 44, 20.
7: Ez 44, 22.

†

20, 27: This verse is best read immediately after v 6.

21, 1: *Unclean for any dead person:* by preparing the corpse for burial. Cf Nm 6, 6; 19, 11-19.

21, 5: Such mourning customs of the Canaanites were forbidden to all the Israelites, but especially to the priests. Cf 19, 27f.

21, 6: *Sacred:* the same Hebrew word has both the active meaning of "holy," that is, keeping oneself free from profane impurities, and the passive meaning of "sacred," that is, set apart from what is profane and therefore treated with religious reverence.

who offers up the food of your God; treat him as sacred, because I, the LORD, who have consecrated him, am sacred.

[9] "A priest's daughter who loses her honor by committing fornication and thereby dishonors her father also, shall be burned to death.

[10]† "The most exalted of the priests, upon whose head the anointing oil has been poured and who has been ordained to wear the special vestments, shall not bare his head or rend his garments, [11] nor shall he go near any dead person. Not even for his father or mother may he thus become unclean [12]* or leave the sanctuary; otherwise he will profane the sanctuary of his God, for with the anointing oil upon him, he is dedicated to his God, to me, the LORD.

[13] "The priest shall marry a virgin. [14]* Not a widow or a woman who has been divorced or a woman who has lost her honor as a prostitute, but a virgin, taken from his own people, shall he marry; [15] otherwise he will have base offspring among his people. I, the LORD, have made him sacred."

Irregularities. [16] The LORD said to Moses, [17] "Speak to Aaron and tell him: None of your descendants, of whatever generation, who has any defect shall come forward to offer up the food of his God. [18] Therefore, he who has any of the following defects may not come forward: he who is blind, or lame, or who has any disfigurement or malformation, [19] or a crippled foot or hand, [20] or who is humpbacked or weakly or walleyed, or who is afflicted with eczema, ringworm or hernia. [21] No descendant of Aaron the priest who has any such defect may draw near to offer up the oblations of the LORD; on account of his defect he may not draw near to offer up the food of his God. [22] He may, however, partake of the food of his God: of what is most sacred as well as of what is sacred. [23] Only, he may not approach the veil nor go up to the altar on account of his defect; he shall not profane these things that are sacred to me, for it is I, the LORD, who make them sacred."

[24] Moses, therefore, told this to Aaron and his sons and to all the Israelites.

CHAPTER 22

Sacrificial Banquets. [1] The LORD said to Moses, [2] "Tell Aaron and his sons to respect the sacred offerings which the Israelites consecrate to me; else they will profane my holy name. I am the LORD.

[3] "Tell them: If any one of you, or of your descendants in any future generation, dares, while he is in a state of uncleanness, to draw near the sacred offerings which the Israelites consecrate to the LORD, such a one shall be cut off from my presence. I am the LORD.

[4]* "No descendant of Aaron who is stricken with leprosy, or who suffers from a flow, may eat of these sacred offerings, unless he again becomes clean. Moreover, if anyone touches a person who has become unclean by contact with a corpse, or if anyone has had an emission of seed, [5]* or if anyone touches any swarming creature or any man whose uncleanness, of whatever kind it may be, is contagious, [6]* the one who touches such as these shall be unclean until evening and may not eat of the sacred portions until he has first bathed his body in water, [7] then when the sun sets, he again becomes clean. Only then may he eat of the sacred offerings which are his food. [8]* He shall not make himself unclean by eating of any animal that has died of itself or has been killed by wild beasts. I am the LORD.

[9] "They shall keep my charge and not do wrong in this matter; else they will die for their profanation. I am the LORD who have consecrated them.

[10]* "Neither a lay person nor a priest's tenant or hired servant may eat of any sacred offering. [11] But a slave whom a priest acquires by purchase or who is born in his house may eat of his food. [12] A priest's daughter who is married to a layman may not eat of the sacred contributions. [13] But if a priest's daughter is widowed or divorced and, having no children, returns to her father's house, she may then eat of her father's food as in her youth. No layman, however, may eat of it. [14]* If such a one eats of a sacred offering through inadvertence, he shall make restitution to the priest for the sacred offering, with an increment of one fifth of the amount. [15]* The sacred offerings which the Israelites contribute to the LORD the priests shall not allow to be profaned [16] nor in the eating of the sacred offering shall they bring down guilt that must be punished; it is I, the LORD, who make them sacred."

Unacceptable Victims. [17] The LORD said to Moses, [18] "Speak to Aaron and his sons and to all the Israelites, and tell them: When anyone of the house of Israel, or any alien residing in Israel, who wishes to offer a sacrifice, brings a holocaust as a votive offering or as a free-

---

*

12: 10, 7.
14: Ez 44, 22.
22, 4: 7, 20; 15, 16.
5: 11, 24.43.
6: Heb 10, 22.
8: 17, 15; Dt 14, 21; Ez 44, 31.
10: 1 Sm 21, 6; Mt 12, 4.
14: 5, 16; 27, 13.15.19.
15: 19, 8; Nm 18, 32.

---

†

21, 10: *Bare his head:* see note on 10, 6.

will offering to the LORD, 19* if it is to
be acceptable, the ox or sheep or goat
that he offers must be an unblemished
male. 20* You shall not offer one that has
any defect, for such a one would not be
acceptable for you. 21* When anyone
presents a peace offering to the LORD
from the herd or the flock in fulfillment
of a vow, or as a free-will offering, if it
is to find acceptance, it must be unblem-
ished; it shall not have any defect. 22 One
that is blind or crippled or maimed, or
one that has a running sore or mange
or ringworm, you shall not offer to the
LORD; do not put such an animal on the
altar as an oblation to the LORD. 23 An
ox or a sheep that is in any way ill-pro-
portioned or stunted you may indeed
present as a free-will offering, but it will
not be acceptable as a votive offering.
24 One that has its testicles bruised or
crushed or torn out or cut off you shall
not offer to the LORD. You shall neither
do this in your own land 25* nor receive
from a foreigner any such animals to
offer up as the food of your God; since
they are deformed or defective, they will
not be acceptable for you."

26 The LORD said to Moses, 27* "When
an ox or a lamb or a goat is born, it shall
remain with its mother for seven days;
only from the eighth day onward will it
be acceptable, to be offered as an obla-
tion to the LORD. 28 You shall not slaugh-
ter an ox or a sheep on one and the same
day with its young. 29 Whenever you of-
fer a thanksgiving sacrifice to the LORD,
so offer it that it may be acceptable for
you; 30* it must, therefore, be eaten on
the same day; none of it shall be left over
until the next day. I am the LORD.

31 "Be careful to observe the com-
mandments which I, the LORD, give you,
32 and do not profane my holy name; in
the midst of the Israelites I, the LORD,
must be held as sacred. It is I who made
you sacred 33 and led you out of the land
of Egypt, that I, the LORD, might be your
God."

CHAPTER 23

Holy Days. 1 The LORD said to Moses,
2 "Speak to the Israelites and tell them:
The following are the festivals of the
LORD, my feast days, which you shall
celebrate with a sacred assembly.

3* "For six days work may be done;
but the seventh day is the sabbath rest,
a day for sacred assembly, on which you
shall do no work. The sabbath shall be-
long to the LORD wherever you dwell.

Passover. 4* "These, then, are the fes-
tivals of the LORD which you shall cele-
brate at their proper time with a sacred
assembly. 5* The Passover of the LORD
falls on the fourteenth day of the first
month, at the evening twilight. 6* The
fifteenth day of this month is the LORD's
feast of Unleavened Bread. For seven
days you shall eat unleavened bread.
7* On the first of these days you shall
hold a sacred assembly and do no sort
of work. 8 On each of the seven days you
shall offer an oblation to the LORD. Then
on the seventh day you shall again hold
a sacred assembly and do no sort of
work."

9 The LORD said to Moses, 10 "Speak to
the Israelites and tell them: When you
come into the land which I am giving
you, and reap your harvest, you shall
bring a sheaf of the first fruits of your
harvest to the priest, 11† who shall wave
the sheaf before the LORD that it may
be acceptable for you. On the day after
the sabbath the priest shall do this. 12 On
this day, when your sheaf is waved, you
shall offer to the LORD for a holocaust
an unblemished yearling lamb. 13 Its ce-
real offering shall be two tenths of an
ephah of fine flour mixed with oil, as a
sweet-smelling oblation to the LORD; and
its libation shall be a fourth of a hin of
wine. 14† Until this day, when you bring
your God this offering, you shall not eat
any bread or roasted grain or fresh ker-
nels. This shall be a perpetual statute for
you and your descendants wherever you
dwell.

Pentecost. 15* "Beginning with the
day after the sabbath, the day on which
you bring the wave-offering sheaf, you
shall count seven full weeks, 16*† and
then on the day after the seventh week,
the fiftieth day, you shall present the
new cereal offering to the LORD. 17 For
the wave offering of your first fruits to
the LORD, you shall bring with you from
wherever you live two loaves of bread
made of two tenths of an ephah of fine

*

19: 1, 3.10.
20: Dt 15, 21; 17, 1; Mal 1, 8.14.
21: 3, 1.6.
25: Mal 1, 14.
27: Ex 22, 29.
30: 7, 15.
23, 3: Ex 20, 8-11; 23, 12; 31, 14f; 34, 21; Dt 5, 12-15; Lk 13, 14.
4: Ex 23, 14-19.
5: Nm 9, 2f; 28, 16.
6: Ex 12, 18; 13.3.10; 23, 15; 34, 18.
7: Ex 12, 15; Nm 28, 18.25.
15: Ex 34, 22; Nm 28, 26; Dt 16, 9.
16: Acts 2, 1.

†

23, 11: *The sabbath:* according to the Jewish tradition this was the feast day itself, the fifteenth of Nisan, which was a special day of rest. Cf v 7. However, some understand here the Saturday of the Passover week, cf Jn 19, 31, or even the Saturday following it.

23, 14: *Any bread:* made from the new grain. The harvest had first to be sanctified for man's use by this offering to God.

23, 16: *The fiftieth:* from the Greek word for this we have the name "Pentecost." Cf 2 Mc 12, 31; Acts 2, 1. It was also called "the feast of the Seven Weeks," or simply "the feast of Weeks" (Nm 28, 26; Dt 16, 10; Tb 2, 1). *The new cereal offering:* of flour made from the new grain. Pentecost was the thanksgiving feast at the end of the grain harvest, which began after Passover. Later tradition made it a commemoration of the giving of the law at Sinai.

flour and baked with leaven. 18 Besides the bread, you shall offer to the LORD a holocaust of seven unblemished yearling lambs, one young bull, and two rams, along with their cereal offering and libations, as a sweet-smelling oblation to the LORD. 19* One male goat shall be sacrificed as a sin offering, and two yearling lambs as a peace offering. 20 The priest shall wave the bread of the first fruits and the two lambs as a wave offering before the LORD; these shall be sacred to the LORD and belong to the priest. 21 On this same day you shall by proclamation have a sacred assembly, and no sort of work may be done. This shall be a perpetual statute for you and your descendants wherever you dwell.

22 "When you reap the harvest of your land, you shall not be so thorough that you reap the field to its very edge, nor shall you glean the stray ears of your grain. These things you shall leave for the poor and the alien. I, the LORD, am your God."

New Year's Day. 23 The LORD said to Moses, 24 "Tell the Israelites: On the first day of the seventh month you shall keep a sabbath rest, with a sacred assembly and with the trumpet blasts as a reminder; 25 you shall then do no sort of work, and you shall offer an oblation to the LORD."

The Day of Atonement. 26* The LORD said to Moses, 27* "The tenth of this seventh month is the Day of Atonement, when you shall hold a sacred assembly and mortify yourselves and offer an oblation to the LORD. 28 On this day you shall not do any work, because it is the Day of Atonement, when atonement is made for you before the LORD, your God. 29 Anyone who does not mortify himself on this day shall be cut off from his people, 30 and if anyone does any work on this day, I will remove him from the midst of his people. 31 This is a perpetual statute for you and your descendants wherever you dwell: you shall do no work, 32 but shall keep a sabbath of complete rest and mortify yourselves. Beginning on the evening of the ninth of the month, you shall keep this sabbath of yours from evening to evening."

The Feast of Booths. 33 The LORD said to Moses, 34*† "Tell the Israelites: The fifteenth day of this seventh month is the LORD's feast of Booths, which shall continue for seven days. 35 On the first day there shall be a sacred assembly, and you shall do no sort of work. 36 For seven days you shall offer an oblation to the LORD, and on the eighth day you shall again hold a sacred assembly and offer an oblation to the LORD. On that solemn closing you shall do no sort of work.

37 "These, therefore, are the festivals of the LORD on which you shall proclaim a sacred assembly, and offer as an oblation to the LORD holocausts and cereal offerings, sacrifices and libations, as prescribed for each day, 38 in addition to those of the LORD's sabbaths, your donations, your various votive offerings and the free-will offerings that you present to the LORD.

39* "On the fifteenth day, then, of the seventh month, when you have gathered in the produce of the land, you shall celebrate a pilgrim feast of the LORD for a whole week. The first and the eighth day shall be days of complete rest. 40† On the first day you shall gather foliage from majestic trees, branches of palms and boughs of myrtles and of valley poplars, and then for a week you shall make merry before the LORD, your God. 41* By perpetual statute for you and your descendants you shall keep this pilgrim feast of the LORD for one whole week in the seventh month of the year. 42 During this week every native Israelite among you shall dwell in booths, 43* that your descendants may realize that, when I led the Israelites out of the land of Egypt, I made them dwell in booths. I, the LORD, am your God."

44 Thus did Moses announce to the Israelites the festivals of the LORD.

CHAPTER 24

The Sanctuary Light. 1 The LORD said to Moses, 2* "Order the Israelites to bring you clear oil of crushed olives for the light, so that you may keep lamps burning regularly. 3 In the meeting tent, outside the veil that hangs in front of the commandments, Aaron shall set up the lamps to burn before the LORD regularly, from evening till morning. Thus, by a perpetual statute for you and your descendants, 4* the lamps shall be set up on the pure gold lampstand, to burn regularly before the LORD.

The Showbread. 5* "You shall take

*

19: Nm 28, 30.
26: 25, 9.
27: 16, 29f; Nm 29, 7.
34: Nm 29, 12; Dt 16, 13; 2 Mc 1, 9.18; Jn 7, 2.
39: Ex 23, 16; Dt 16, 13.
41: Nm 29, 12-38.
43: Dt 31, 10-13.
24, 2: Ex 27, 20f.
4: Ex 25, 31.
5: Ex 25, 30; 1 Kgs 7, 48; 2 Chr 4, 19; 13, 11; Heb 9.2.

†

23, 34: *Feasts of Booths:* the joyful observance of the vintage and fruit harvest. Cf Dt 16, 13. During the seven days of the feast the Israelites camped in booths of branches erected on the roofs of their houses or in the streets in commemoration of their wanderings in the desert, where they dwelt in booths.

23, 40: *Foliage:* literally, "fruit," but here probably used in the general sense of "produce, growth." These branches were used for constructing the "booths" or huts in which the people lived during the feast. Cf Neh 8, 15. However, from about the time of Christ on, the Jews have understood this of "fruit" in the strict sense; hence, branches of lemons and oranges were carried with the other branches in joyous procession.

fine flour and bake it into twelve cakes, using two tenths of an ephah of flour for each cake. 6 These you shall place in two piles, six in each pile, on the pure gold table before the LORD. 7 On each pile put some pure frankincense, which shall serve as an oblation to the LORD, a token offering for the bread. 8* Regularly on each sabbath day this bread shall be set out afresh before the LORD, offered on the part of the Israelites by an everlasting agreement. 9 It shall belong to Aaron and his sons, who must eat it in a sacred place, since, as something most sacred among the various oblations to the LORD, it is his by perpetual right."

Punishment of Blasphemy. 10 Among the Israelites there was a man born of an Israelite mother (Shelomith, daughter of Dibri, of the tribe of Dan) and an Egyptian father. 11 This man quarreled publicly with another Israelite and cursed and blasphemed the LORD's name. So the people brought him to Moses, 12 who kept him in custody till a decision from the LORD should settle the case for them. 13 The LORD then said to Moses, 14 "Take the blasphemer outside the camp, and when all who heard him have laid their hands on his head, let the whole community stone him. 15 Tell the Israelites: Anyone who curses his God shall bear the penalty of his sin; 16* whoever blasphemes the name of the LORD shall be put to death. The whole community shall stone him; alien and native alike must be put to death for blaspheming the LORD's name.

17* "Whoever takes the life of any human being shall be put to death; 18* whoever takes the life of an animal shall make restitution of another animal. A life for a life! 19 Anyone who inflicts an injury on his neighbor shall receive the same in return. 20* Limb for limb, eye for eye, tooth for tooth! The same injury that a man gives another shall be inflicted on him in return. 21 Whoever slays an animal shall make restitution, but whoever slays a man shall be put to death. 22* You shall have but one rule, for alien and native alike. I, the LORD, am your God."

23* When Moses told this to the Israelites, they took the blasphemer outside the camp and stoned him; they carried out the command that the LORD had given Moses.

CHAPTER 25

The Sabbatical Year. 1 The LORD said to Moses on Mount Sinai, 2 "Speak to the Israelites and tell them: When you enter the land that I am giving you, let the land, too, keep a sabbath for the LORD. 3* For six years you may sow your field, and for six years prune your vineyard, gathering in their produce. 4* But during the seventh year the land shall have a complete rest, a sabbath for the LORD, when you may neither sow your field nor prune your vineyard. 5† The aftergrowth of your harvest you shall not reap, nor shall you pick the grapes of your untrimmed vines in this year of sabbath rest for the land. 6 While the land has its sabbath, all its produce will be food equally for you yourself and for your male and female slaves, for your hired help and the tenants who live with you, 7 and likewise for your livestock and for the wild animals on your land.

The Jubilee Year. 8 "Seven weeks of years shall you count—seven times seven years—so that the seven cycles amount to forty-nine years. 9 Then, on the tenth day of the seventh month let the trumpet resound; on this, the Day of Atonement, the trumpet blast shall reecho throughout your land. 10*† This fiftieth year you shall make sacred by proclaiming liberty in the land for all its inhabitants. It shall be a jubilee for you, when every one of you shall return to his own property, every one to his own family estate. 11 In this fiftieth year, your year of jubilee, you shall not sow, nor shall you reap the aftergrowth or pick the grapes from the untrimmed vines. 12 Since this is the jubilee, which shall be sacred for you, you may not eat of its produce, except as taken directly from the field.

13 "In this year of jubilee, then, every one of you shall return to his own property. 14 Therefore, when you sell any land to your neighbor or buy any from him, do not deal unfairly. 15* On the basis of the number of years since the last jubilee shall you purchase the land from him; and so also, on the basis of the number of years for crops, shall he sell it to you. 16 When the years are many, the

*

8: 1 Chr 9, 32.
16: 1 Kgs 21, 10.13; Mt 26, 65f; Jn 10, 33.
17: Gn 9, 5f; Ex 21, 12; Nm 35, 31; Dt 19, 11f.
18: Ex 21, 33f.
20: Dt 19, 21; Mt 5, 38.
22: 19, 34; Ex 12, 49; Nm 15, 16.
23: Acts 7, 57f.
25, 3: Ex 23, 10f.
4: 1 Mc 6, 49.53.
10: Nm 36, 4; Is 61, 2; Ez 46, 17; Lk 4, 19.
15: 27, 18.23.

†

25, 5ff: As long as the produce of the sabbatical year remains on the field, it remains available to everyone; cf v 12. In Ex 23, 10f the poor and the wild beasts that have no other source of nourishment are alone mentioned.

25, 10: *Fiftieth year:* to arrive at this number, the preceding year of jubilee is included in the count, and therefore this is more exactly the forty-ninth year, the seventh sabbatical year. *Liberty:* Israelite slaves were set free (v 50) and landed property was returned to its original owner (v 13): two important laws for preserving the social and economic equilibrium. *Jubilee:* derived from the Hebrew word *yobel,* "ram's horn," which was blown on this occasion.

price shall be so much the more; when the years are few, the price shall be so much the less. For it is really the number of crops that he sells you. 17 Do not deal unfairly, then; but stand in fear of your God. I, the LORD, am your God.

18 "Observe my precepts and be careful to keep my regulations, for then you will dwell securely in the land. 19* The land will yield its fruit and you will have food in abundance, so that you may live there without worry. 20* Therefore, do not say, 'What shall we eat in the seventh year, if we do not then sow or reap our crop?' 21 I will bestow such blessings on you in the sixth year that there will then be crop enough for three years. 22* When you sow in the eighth year, you will continue to eat from the old crop; and even into the ninth year, when the crop comes in, you will still have the old to eat from.

Redemption of Property. 23* "The land shall not be sold in perpetuity; for the land is mine, and you are but aliens who have become my tenants. 24 Therefore, in every part of the country that you occupy, you must permit the land to be redeemed. 25* When one of your countrymen is reduced to poverty and has to sell some of his property, his closest relative, who has the right to redeem it, may go and buy back what his kinsman has sold. 26 If, however, the man has no relative to redeem his land, but later on acquires sufficient means to buy it back in his own name, 27 he shall make a deduction from the price in proportion to the number of years since the sale, and then pay back the balance to the one to whom he sold it, so that he may thus regain his own property. 28* But if he does not acquire sufficient means to buy back his land, what he has sold shall remain in the possession of the purchaser until the jubilee, when it must be released and returned to its original owner.

29 "When someone sells a dwelling in a walled town, he has the right to buy it back during the time of one full year from its sale. 30 But if such a house in a walled town has not been redeemed at the end of a full year, it shall belong in perpetuity to the purchaser and his descendants; nor shall it be released in the jubilee. 31 However, houses in villages that are not encircled by walls shall be considered as belonging to the surrounding farm land; they may be redeemed at any time, and in the jubilee they must be released.

32 "In levitical cities the Levites shall always have the right to redeem the town houses that are their property. 33 Any town house of the Levites in their cities that had been sold and not redeemed, shall be released in the jubilee; for the town houses of the Levites are their hereditary property in the midst of the Israelites. 34* Moreover, the pasture land belonging to their cities shall not be sold at all; it must always remain their hereditary property.

35* "When one of your fellow countrymen is reduced to poverty and is unable to hold out beside you, extend to him the privileges of an alien or a tenant, so that he may continue to live with you. 36 Do not exact interest from your countryman either in money or in kind, but out of fear of God let him live with you. 37* You are to lend him neither money at interest nor food at a profit. 38 I, the LORD, am your God, who brought you out of the land of Egypt to give you the land of Canaan and to be your God.

39* "When, then, your countryman becomes so impoverished beside you that he sells you his services, do not make him work as a slave. 40 Rather, let him be like a hired servant or like your tenant, working with you until the jubilee year, 41 when he, together with his children, shall be released from your service and return to his kindred and to the property of his ancestors. 42 Since those whom I brought out of the land of Egypt are servants of mine, they shall not be sold as slaves to any man. 43 Do not lord it over them harshly, but stand in fear of your God.

44 "Slaves, male and female, you may indeed possess, provided you buy them from among the neighboring nations. 45 You may also buy them from among the aliens who reside with you and from their children who are born and reared in your land. Such slaves you may own as chattels, 46* and leave to your sons as their hereditary property, making them perpetual slaves. But you shall not lord it harshly over any of the Israelites, your kinsmen.

47 "When one of your countrymen is reduced to such poverty that he sells himself to a wealthy alien who has a permanent or a temporary residence among you, or to one of the descendants of an immigrant family, 48 even after he has thus sold his services he still has the right of redemption; he may be redeemed by one of his own brothers, 49 or by his uncle or cousin, or by some other relative or fellow clansman; or, if he acquires the means, he may redeem himself. 50 With his purchaser he shall compute the years from the sale to the jubilee, distributing the sale price over these years as though he had been hired as a day laborer. 51 The more such years

*

19: 26, 5.
20: Mt 6, 25.31; Lk 12, 22.29.
22: 26, 10.
23: 1 Pt 2, 11.
25: Ru 2, 20; 4, 4.6; Jer 32, 7f.
28: 27, 24.
34: Nm 35, 3.
35: Dt 15, 7.8.
37: Dt 23, 19.
39: 1 Kgs 9, 22.
46: Is 14, 1f.

there are, the more of the sale price he
shall pay back as ransom; 52 the fewer
years there are left before the jubilee
year, the more he has to his credit; in
proportion to his years of service shall
he pay his ransom. 53 The alien shall
treat him as a servant hired on an an-
nual basis, and he shall not lord it over
him harshly under your very eyes. 54* If
he is not thus redeemed, he shall never-
theless be released, together with his
children, in the jubilee year. 55 For to me
the Israelites belong as servants; they
are servants of mine, because I brought
them out of the land of Egypt, I, the
LORD, your God.

CHAPTER 26

The Reward of Obedience. 1* "Do not
make false gods for yourselves. You
shall not erect an idol or a sacred pillar
for yourselves, nor shall you set up a
stone figure for worship in your land; for
I, the LORD, am your God. 2* Keep my
sabbaths, and reverence my sanctuary.
I am the LORD.

3† "If you live in accordance with my
precepts and are careful to observe my
commandments, 4* I will give you rain
in due season, so that the land will bear
its crops, and the trees their fruit; 5 your
threshing will last till vintage time, and
your vintage till the time for sowing, and
you will have food to eat in abundance,
so that you may dwell securely in your
land. 6 I will establish peace in the land,
that you may lie down to rest without
anxiety. I will rid the country of rav-
enous beasts, and keep the sword of war
from sweeping across your land. 7 You
will rout your enemies and lay them low
with your sword. 8 Five of you will put
a hundred of your foes to flight, and a
hundred of you will chase ten thousand
of them, till they are cut down by your
sword. 9 I will look with favor upon you,
and make you fruitful and numerous, as
I carry out my covenant with you. 10* So
much of the old crops will you have
stored up for food that you will have to
discard them to make room for the new.
11* I will set my Dwelling among you,
and will not disdain you. 12 Ever present
in your midst, I will be your God, and
you will be my people; 13 for it is I, the
LORD, your God, who brought you out
of the land of the Egyptians and freed
you from their slavery, breaking the
yoke they had laid upon you and letting
you walk erect.

Punishment of Disobedience. 14 "But
if you do not heed me and do not keep
all these commandments, 15 if you reject
my precepts and spurn my decrees, re-
fusing to obey all my commandments
and breaking my covenant, 16 then I, in
turn, will give you your deserts. I will
punish you with terrible woes—with
wasting and fever to dim the eyes and
sap the life. You will sow your seed in
vain, for your enemies will consume the
crop. 17* I will turn against you, till you
are beaten down before your enemies
and lorded over by your foes. You will
take to flight though no one pursues you.

18 "If even after this you do not obey
me, I will increase the chastisement for
your sins sevenfold, 19 to break your
haughty confidence. I will make the sky
above you as hard as iron, and your soil
as hard as bronze, 20 so that your
strength will be spent in vain; your land
will bear no crops, and its trees no fruit.

21 "If then you become defiant in your
unwillingness to obey me, I will multiply
my blows another sevenfold, as your
sins deserve. 22 I will unleash the wild
beasts against you, to rob you of your
children and wipe out your livestock, till
your population dwindles away and
your roads become deserted.

23 "If, with all this, you still refuse to
be chastened by me and continue to defy
me, 24* I, too, will defy you and will smite
you for your sins seven times harder
than before. 25 I will make the sword, the
avenger of my covenant, sweep over
you. Though you then huddle together
in your walled cities, I will send in pesti-
lence among you, till you are forced to
surrender to the enemy. 26* And as I cut
off your supply of bread, ten women will
need but one oven for baking all the
bread they dole out to you in rations—
not enough food to still your hunger.

27 "If, despite all this, you still persist
in disobeying and defying me, 28 I, also,
will meet you with fiery defiance and will
chastise you with sevenfold fiercer pun-
ishment for your sins, 29*† till you begin
to eat the flesh of your own sons and
daughters. 30* I will demolish your high
places, overthrow your incense stands,
and cast your corpses on those of your
idols. In my abhorrence of you, 31 I will
lay waste your cities and devastate your
sanctuaries, refusing to accept your

*

54: Ex 21, 2f.
26, 1: 19, 4; Ex 20, 4; Nm 33, 52; Dt 5, 8.
2: Ex 20, 8.
4: Ps 85, 13.
10: 25, 22.
11f: Ex 29, 45; Ez 37, 26ff; 2 Cor 6, 16.
17: Dt 28, 25.
24f: Jer 2, 30; Ez 5, 17; 14, 17.
26: Is 9, 19; Ez 4, 16; 5, 16; 14, 13; Mi 6, 14.
29: Is 9, 18.
30: 2 Chr 14, 5; 34, 3.4.7; Ez 6, 3-6.

†

26, 3-45: Since God's covenant was with the Israelite nation as a whole, these promises and threats are made primarily to the entire community. The rewards and punishments are of a temporal nature because the community as such exists only here on earth, not in the hereafter.

26, 29: *Eat the flesh of your own sons and daughters:* extreme famine in cities under siege often forced their inhabitants to such dire means of subsistence. Cf Dt 28, 53; Jer 19, 9; Ez 5, 10; 2 Kgs 6, 28f.

sweet-smelling offerings. 32* So devas-
tated will I leave the land that your very
enemies who come to live there will
stand aghast at the sight of it. 33* You
yourselves I will scatter among the na-
tions at the point of my drawn sword,
leaving your countryside desolate and
your cities deserted. 34* Then shall the
land retrieve its lost sabbaths during all
the time it lies waste, while you are in
the land of your enemies; then shall the
land have rest and make up for its sab-
baths 35 during all the time that it lies
desolate, enjoying the rest that you
would not let it have on the sabbaths
when you lived there.

36 "Those of you who survive in the
lands of their enemies I will make so
fainthearted that, if leaves rustle behind
them, they will flee headlong, as if from
the sword, though no one pursues them;
37 stumbling over one another as if to es-
cape a weapon, while no one is after
them—so helpless will you be to take a
stand against your foes! 38 You will be
lost among the Gentiles, swallowed up
in your enemies' country. 39* Those of
you who survive in the lands of their en-
emies will waste away for their own and
their fathers' guilt.

40 "Thus they will have to confess that
they and their fathers were guilty of
having rebelled against me and of hav-
ing defied me, 41 so that I, too, had to
defy them and bring them into their ene-
mies' land. Then, when their uncircum-
cised hearts are humbled and they make
amends for their guilt, 42* I will remem-
ber my covenant with Jacob, my cove-
nant with Isaac, and my covenant with
Abraham; and of the land, too, I will be
mindful. 43 But the land must first be rid
of them, that in its desolation it may
make up its lost sabbaths, and that they,
too, may make good the debt of their
guilt for having spurned my precepts
and abhorred my statutes. 44 Yet even
so, even while they are in their enemies'
land, I will not reject or spurn them, lest,
by wiping them out, I make void my
covenant with them; for I, the LORD, am
their God. 45* I will remember them be-
cause of the covenant I made with their
forefathers, whom I brought out of the
land of Egypt under the very eyes of the
Gentiles, that I, the LORD, might be their
God."

46† These are the precepts, decrees
and laws which the LORD had Moses
promulgate on Mount Sinai in the pact
between himself and the Israelites.

V: REDEMPTION OF OFFERINGS

CHAPTER 27

Redemption of Votive Offerings. 1 The
LORD said to Moses, 2 "Speak to the Isra-
elites and tell them: When anyone fulfills
a vow of offering one or more persons
to the LORD, who are to be ransomed at
a fixed sum of money, 3 for persons be-
tween the ages of twenty and sixty, the
fixed sum, in sanctuary shekels, shall be
fifty silver shekels for a man, 4 and thirty
shekels for a woman; 5 for persons be-
tween the ages of five and twenty, the
fixed sum shall be twenty shekels for a
youth, and ten for a maiden; 6 for per-
sons between the ages of one month and
five years, the fixed sum shall be five
silver shekels for a boy, and three for
a girl; 7 for persons of sixty or more, the
fixed sum shall be fifteen shekels for a
man, and ten for a woman. 8 However,
if the one who took the vow is too poor
to meet the fixed sum, the person must
be set before the priest, who shall deter-
mine the sum for his ransom in keeping
with the means of the one who made the
vow.

9 "If the offering vowed to the LORD
is an animal that may be sacrificed, ev-
ery such animal, when vowed to the
LORD, becomes sacred. 10 The offerer
shall not present a substitute for it by
exchanging either a better for a worse
one or a worse for a better one. If he
attempts to offer one animal in place of
another, both the original and its substi-
tute shall be treated as sacred. 11 If the
animal vowed to the LORD is unclean
and therefore unfit for sacrifice, it must
be set before the priest, 12† who shall de-
termine its value in keeping with its good
or bad qualities, and the value set by the
priest shall stand. 13* If the offerer
wishes to redeem the animal, he shall
pay one fifth more than this valuation.

14 "When someone dedicates his house
as sacred to the LORD, the priest shall
determine its value in keeping with its
good or bad points, and the value set by
the priest shall stand. 15 If the one who
dedicated his house wishes to redeem it,
he shall pay one fifth more than the price
thus established, and then it will again
be his.

16 "If the object which someone dedi-
cates to the LORD is a piece of his heredi-

*

32: 1 Kgs 9, 8; Jer 9, 11; 18, 16; 19, 8; 25, 18; Ez 5, 15.
33: Jer 9, 16; Zec 7, 14.
34: 25, 2; 2 Chr 36, 21.
39: Ez 4, 17; 24, 23; 33, 10.
42: Ex 6, 5; 2 Kgs 13, 23; Ps 106, 45; Ez 16, 20.
45: Ex 12, 51.
27, 13: 22, 14.

†

26, 46: The Book of Leviticus seems originally to have ended here; the following chapter is an appendix.

27, 12: *Determine its value:* fix the price at which the animal may be sold to someone else. Only the original owner must pay the twenty percent tax, as a penalty for buying back what he had vowed to God. So also for houses and fields that are vowed to the Lord, as treated of in the following verses. The money from the sale or from the redemption of such vowed property naturally goes to the sanctuary.

tary land, its valuation shall be made according to the amount of seed required to sow it, the acreage sown with a homer of barley seed being valued at fifty silver shekels. 17 If the dedication of a field is made at the beginning of a jubilee period, the full valuation shall hold; 18* but if it is some time after this, the priest shall estimate its money value according to the number of years left until the next jubilee year, with a corresponding rebate on the valuation. 19 If the one who dedicated his field wishes to redeem it, he shall pay one fifth more than the price thus established, and so reclaim it. 20 If, instead of redeeming such a field, he sells it to someone else, it may no longer be redeemed; 21 but at the jubilee it shall be released as sacred to the LORD; like a field that is doomed, it shall become priestly property.

22 "If the field that some man dedicates to the LORD is one he had purchased and not a part of his hereditary property, 23 the priest shall compute its value in proportion to the number of years until the next jubilee, and on the same day the price thus established shall be given as sacred to the LORD; 24* at the jubilee, however, the field shall revert to the hereditary owner of this land from whom it had been purchased.

25 "Every valuation shall be made according to the standard of the sanctuary shekel. There are twenty gerahs to the shekel.

Offerings Not To Be Redeemed.
26* "Note that a first-born animal, which as such already belongs to the LORD, may not be dedicated by vow to him. If it is an ox or a sheep, it shall be ceded to the LORD; 27† but if it is an unclean animal, it may be redeemed by paying one fifth more than its fixed value. If it is not redeemed, it shall be sold at its fixed value.

28* "Note, also, that any one of his possessions which a man vows as doomed to the LORD, whether it is a human being or an animal or a hereditary field, shall be neither sold nor ransomed; everything that is thus doomed becomes most sacred to the LORD. 29† All human beings that are doomed lose the right to be redeemed; they must be put to death.

30* "All tithes of the land, whether in grain from the fields or in fruit from the trees, belong to the LORD, as sacred to him. 31 If someone wishes to buy back any of his tithes, he shall pay one fifth more than their value. 32 The tithes of the herd and the flock shall be determined by ceding to the LORD as sacred every tenth animal as they are counted by the herdsman's rod. 33 It shall not matter whether good ones or bad ones are thus chosen, and no exchange may be made. If any exchange is attempted, both the original animal and its substitute shall be treated as sacred, without the right of being bought back."

34 These are the commandments which the LORD gave Moses on Mount Sinai for the Israelites.

---

*

18: 25, 15f.
24: 25, 10.28.41.
26: Ex 13, 2.
28: 1 Sm 15, 21.
30: Nm 18, 21.24; 2 Chr 31, 5f.12; Mal 3, 8.10.

†

27, 27: *An unclean animal:* such as the first-born of an ass, which was unfit for sacrifice. According to Ex 13, 13; 34, 20, a first-born ass was to be redeemed by offering a sheep in its stead, or was to have its neck broken. The present law is probably a later modification of the earlier one.

27, 29: *All human beings that are doomed:* according to some interpreters, this signifies the idolatrous Canaanites, who were doomed to destruction by divine authority; according to others, this drastic law was enacted for the purpose of discouraging private persons from rashly vowing their slaves or other dependents as offerings to God. Cf Ex 22, 19; Dt 13, 13-19.

The Book of

NUMBERS

The Book of Numbers derives its name from the account of the two censuses of the Hebrew people taken, one near the beginning and the other toward the end of the journey in the desert (chapters 1 and 26). It continues the story of that journey, begun in Exodus, and describes briefly the experiences of the Israelites for a period of thirty-eight years, from the end of their encampment at Sinai to their arrival at the border of the Promised Land. Numerous legal ordinances are interspersed in the account, making the book a combination of law and history.

The various events described clearly indicate the action of God, who punishes the murmuring of the people by prolonging their stay in the desert, at the same time preparing them by this discipline to be his witnesses among the nations.

In the New Testament Christ and the Apostles derive useful lessons from such events in the Book of Numbers as the brazen serpent (Jn 3, 14f), the sedition of Korah and its consequences (1 Cor 10, 10), the prophecies of Balaam (2 Pt 2, 15f), and the water gushing from the rock (1 Cor 10, 4).

The chief divisions of the Book of Numbers are as follows:

I: Preparation for the Departure from Sinai (1, 1—10, 10)
II: From Sinai to the Plains of Moab (10, 11—22, 1)
III: On the Plains of Moab (22, 2—36, 13)

I: PREPARATION FOR THE DEPARTURE FROM SINAI

CHAPTER 1

The Census. 1 In the year following
that of the Israelites' departure from the
land of Egypt, on the first day of the sec-
ond month, the LORD said to Moses in
the meeting tent in the desert of Sinai:
2*† "Take a census of the whole commu-
nity of the Israelites, by clans and an-
cestral houses, registering each male in-
dividually. 3 You and Aaron shall enroll
in companies all the men in Israel of
twenty years or more who are fit for mil-
itary service.
Moses' Assistants. 4 "To assist you
there shall be a man from each tribe,
the head of his ancestral house. 5* These
are the names of those who are to assist
you:
from Reuben: Elizur, son of Shedeur;
6 from Simeon: Shelumiel, son of Zurishaddai;
7 from Judah: Nahshon, son of Amminadab;
8 from Issachar: Nethanel, son of Zuar;
9 from Zebulun: Eliab, son of Helon;
10 from Ephraim: Elishama, son of Ammihud,
and from Manasseh: Gamaliel, son of Pedahzur, for the descendants of Joseph;
11 from Benjamin: Abidan, son of Gideoni;
12 from Dan: Ahiezer, son of Ammishaddai;
13 from Asher: Pagiel, son of Ochran;
14 from Gad: Eliasaph, son of Reuel;
15 from Naphtali: Ahira, son of Enan."
16*† These were councilors of the com-
munity, princes of their ancestral tribes,
chiefs of the troops of Israel. 17 So Moses
and Aaron took these men who had been
designated, 18 and assembled the whole
community on the first day of the second
month. Every man of twenty years or
more then declared his name and lin-
eage according to clan and ancestral
house, 19 as the LORD had commanded
Moses.
Count of the Twelve Tribes. This is
their census as taken in the desert of Si-
nai. 20 Of the descendants of Reuben, the
first-born of Israel, registered by lineage
in clans and ancestral houses: when all
the males of twenty years or more who
were fit for military service were polled,
21 forty-six thousand five hundred were
enrolled in the tribe of Reuben.
22 Of the descendants of Simeon, regis-
tered by lineage in clans and ancestral
houses: when all the males of twenty

---

* 1, 2f: 14, 29; 26, 2-51. 5-15: 10, 14-27. 16: Ex 18, 21.25.

---

† 1, 2: All Israel was divided into tribes, each tribe into clans, and each clan into ancestral houses.

1, 16: *Troops:* literally "thousands"; this division of the Israelites, with its subdivisions of "hundreds, fifties and tens," was primarily for military and judicial purposes. Cf Ex 18, 21; 2 Sm 18, 1.

years or more who were fit for military
service were polled, 23 fifty-nine thou-
sand three hundred were enrolled in the
tribe of Simeon.
24 Of the descendants of Gad, regis-
tered by lineage in clans and ancestral
houses: when all the males of twenty
years or more who were fit for military
service were polled, 25 forty-five thou-
sand six hundred and fifty were enrolled
in the tribe of Gad.
26 Of the descendants of Judah, regis-
tered by lineage in clans and ancestral
houses: when all the males of twenty
years or more who were fit for military
service were polled, 27 seventy-four
thousand six hundred were enrolled in
the tribe of Judah.
28 Of the descendants of Issachar, reg-
istered by lineage in clans and ancestral
houses: when all the males of twenty
years or more who were fit for military
service were polled, 29 fifty-four thou-
sand four hundred were enrolled in the
tribe of Issachar.
30 Of the descendants of Zebulun, reg-
istered by lineage in clans and ancestral
houses: when all the males of twenty
years or more who were fit for military
service were polled, 31 fifty-seven thou-
sand four hundred were enrolled in the
tribe of Zebulun.
32 Of the descendants of Joseph—
Of the descendants of Ephraim, regis-
tered by lineage in clans and ancestral
houses: when all the males of twenty
years or more who were fit for military
service were polled, 33 forty thousand
five hundred were enrolled in the tribe
of Ephraim.
34 Of the descendants of Manasseh,
registered by lineage in clans and ances-
tral houses: when all the males of twenty
years or more who were fit for military
service were polled, 35 thirty-two thou-
sand two hundred were enrolled in the
tribe of Manasseh.
36 Of the descendants of Benjamin,
registered by lineage in clans and ances-
tral houses: when all the males of twenty
years or more who were fit for military
service were polled, 37 thirty-five thou-
sand four hundred were enrolled in the
tribe of Benjamin.
38 Of the descendants of Dan, regis-
tered by lineage in clans and ancestral
houses: when all the males of twenty
years or more who were fit for military
service were polled, 39 sixty-two thou-
sand seven hundred were enrolled in the
tribe of Dan.
40 Of the descendants of Asher, regis-
tered by lineage in clans and ancestral
houses: when all the males of twenty
years or more who were fit for military
service were polled, 41 forty-one thou-
sand five hundred were enrolled in the
tribe of Asher.
42 Of the descendants of Naphtali, reg-
istered by lineage in clans and ancestral
houses: when all the males of twenty
years or more who were fit for military
service were polled, 43 fifty-three thou-
sand four hundred were enrolled in the
tribe of Naphtali.
44 It was these who were registered,
each according to his ancestral house,
in the census taken by Moses and Aaron
and the twelve princes of Israel. 45 The
total number of the Israelites of twenty
years or more who were fit for military
service, registered by ancestral houses,
46 was six hundred and three thousand,
five hundred and fifty.

Levites Omitted in the Census.
47*† The Levites, however, were not reg-
istered by ancestral tribe with the oth-
ers. 48 For the LORD had told Moses,
49 "The tribe of Levi alone you shall not
enroll nor include in the census along
with the other Israelites. 50* You are to
give the Levites charge of the Dwelling
of the commandments with all its equip-
ment and all that belongs to it. It is they
who shall carry the Dwelling with all its
equipment and who shall be its minis-
ters. They shall therefore camp around
the Dwelling. 51* When the Dwelling is
to move on, the Levites shall take it
down; when the Dwelling is to be
pitched, it is the Levites who shall set
it up. Any layman who comes near it
shall be put to death. 52* While the other
Israelites shall camp by companies,
each in his own division of the camp,
53* the Levites shall camp around the
Dwelling of the commandments. Other-
wise God's wrath will strike the Israelite
community. The Levites, then, shall
have charge of the Dwelling of the com-
mandments." 54 All this the Israelites
fulfilled as the LORD had commanded
Moses.

CHAPTER 2

Arrangement of the Tribes. 1 The
LORD said to Moses and Aaron: 2* "The
Israelites shall camp, each in his own
division, under the ensigns of their an-
cestral houses. They shall camp around
the meeting tent, but at some distance
from it.
3† "Encamped on the east side, toward

*

47: 2, 33; 3, 14-39; 26, 57-62.
50: 3, 7f; 4, 2-49; 1 Chr 6, 48.
51: 3, 10.38; 18, 7; 2 Sm 6, 6f; 1 Chr 13, 10.
52: 2, 2.34.
53: 3, 7f.38; 8, 19; 18, 4f.
2, 2: 1, 52.

†

1, 47: The Levites were not enrolled in this census, which was principally for military purposes, but a separate census was made of them. Cf 3, 15f.39.

2, 3-31: A similar arrangement of the tribes around the central sanctuary in the ideal Israelite state is given in Ez 48.

the sunrise, shall be the divisional camp
of Judah, arranged in companies. [The
prince of the Judahites was Nahshon,
son of Amminadab, 4 and his soldiers
amounted in the census to seventy-four
thousand six hundred.] 5 With Judah
shall camp the tribe of Issachar [Their
prince was Nethanel, son of Zuar, 6 and
his soldiers amounted in the census to
fifty-four thousand four hundred.] 7 and
the tribe of Zebulun. [Their prince was
Eliab, son of Helon, 8 and his soldiers
amounted in the census to fifty-seven
thousand four hundred. 9 The total num-
ber of those registered by companies in
the camp of Judah was one hundred and
eighty-six thousand four hundred.]
These shall be first on the march.
10 "On the south side shall be the divi-
sional camp of Reuben, arranged in
companies. [Their prince was Elizur,
son of Shedeur, 11 and his soldiers
amounted in the census to forty-six
thousand five hundred.] 12 Beside them
shall camp the tribe of Simeon [Their
prince was Shelumiel, son of Zurishad-
dai, 13 and his soldiers amounted in the
census to fifty-nine thousand three hun-
dred.] 14 and next the tribe of Gad.
[Their prince was Eliasaph, son of
Reuel, 15 and his soldiers amounted in
the census to forty-five thousand six
hundred and fifty. 16 The total number
of those registered by companies in the
camp of Reuben was one hundred and
fifty-one thousand four hundred and
fifty.] These shall be second on the
march.
17 "Then the meeting tent and the
camp of the Levites shall set out in the
middle of the line. As in camp, so also
on the march, every man shall be in his
proper place, with his own division.
18 "On the west side shall be the divi-
sional camp of Ephraim, arranged in
companies. [Their prince was Elishama,
son of Ammihud, 19 and his soldiers
amounted in the census to forty thou-
sand five hundred.] 20 Beside them shall
camp the tribe of Manasseh [Their
prince was Gamaliel, son of Pedahzur,
21 and his soldiers amounted in the cen-
sus to thirty-two thousand two hun-
dred.] 22 and the tribe of Benjamin.
[Their prince was Abidan, son of Gid-
eoni, 23 and his soldiers amounted in the
census to thirty-five thousand four hun-
dred. 24 The total number of those regis-
tered by companies in the camp of
Ephraim was one hundred and eight
thousand one hundred.] These shall be
third on the march.
25 "On the north side shall be the divi-
sional camp of Dan, arranged in compa-
nies. [Their prince was Ahiezer, son of
Ammishaddai, 26 and his soldiers
amounted in the census to sixty-two
thousand seven hundred.] 27 Beside
them shall camp the tribe of Asher
[Their prince was Pagiel, son of Ochran,
28 and his soldiers amounted in the cen-
sus to forty-one thousand five hundred.]
29 and next the tribe of Naphtali. [Their
prince was Ahira, son of Enan, 30 and
his soldiers amounted in the census to
fifty-three thousand four hundred.
31 The total number of those registered
by companies in the camp of Dan was
one hundred and fifty-seven thousand
six hundred.] These shall be the last of
the divisions on the march."
32* This was the census of the Israel-
ites taken by ancestral houses. The total
number of those registered by compa-
nies in the camps was six hundred and
three thousand five hundred and fifty.
33 The Levites, however, were not regis-
tered with the other Israelites, for so the
LORD had commanded Moses. 34 The Is-
raelites did just as the LORD had com-
manded Moses; both in camp and on the
march they were in their own divisions,
every man according to his clan and his
ancestral house.

CHAPTER 3

The Sons of Aaron. 1 The following
were the descendants of Aaron and Mo-
ses at the time that the LORD spoke to
Moses on Mount Sinai. 2* The sons of
Aaron were Nadab his first-born, Abihu,
Eleazar, and Ithamar. 3 These are the
names of the sons of Aaron, the anointed
priests who were ordained to exercise
the priesthood. 4* But when Nadab and
Abihu offered profane fire before the
LORD in the desert of Sinai, they met
death in the presence of the LORD, and
left no sons. Thereafter only Eleazar and
Ithamar performed the priestly func-
tions under the direction of their father
Aaron.
Levites in Place of the First-born.
5 Now the LORD said to Moses: 6* "Sum-
mon the tribe of Levi and present them
to Aaron the priest, as his assistants.
7* They shall discharge his obligations
and those of the whole community be-
fore the meeting tent by serving at the
Dwelling. 8 They shall have custody of
all the furnishings of the meeting tent
and discharge the duties of the Israelites
in the service of the Dwelling. 9* You
shall give the Levites to Aaron and his
sons; they have been set aside from
among the Israelites as dedicated to me.
10* But only Aaron and his descendants
shall you appoint to have charge of the
priestly functions. Any layman who
comes near shall be put to death."
11 The LORD said to Moses, 12* "It is I

---

*

32-33: 1, 46-49.
3, 2: Ex 6, 23.
4: 26, 61; Lv 10, 1f; 1 Chr 24, 2.
6: 18, 2.
7: 8, 24.
9: 8, 19.
10: 1, 51; 18, 7.
12f: 3, 41; 8, 16f; Ex 13, 2. 12.15.

who have chosen the Levites from the Israelites in place of every first-born that opens the womb among the Israelites. The Levites, therefore, are mine, [13] because every first-born is mine. When I slew all the first-born in the land of Egypt, I made all the first-born in Israel sacred to me, both of man and of beast. They belong to me; I am the LORD."

Census of the Levites. [14] The LORD said to Moses in the desert of Sinai, [15]* "Take a census of the Levites by ancestral houses and clans, registering every male of a month or more." [16] Moses, therefore, took their census in accordance with the command the LORD had given him.

[17]* The sons of Levi were named Gershon, Kohath and Merari. [18] The descendants of Gershon, by clans, were named Libni and Shimei. [19] The descendants of Kohath, by clans, were Amram, Izhar, Hebron and Uzziel. [20] The descendants of Merari, by clans, were Mahli and Mushi. These were the clans of the Levites by ancestral houses.

Duties of the Levitical Clans. [21] To Gershon belonged the clan of the Libnites and the clan of the Shimeites; these were the clans of the Gershonites. [22] When all their males of a month or more were registered, they numbered seven thousand five hundred. [23] The clans of the Gershonites camped behind the Dwelling, to the west. [24] The prince of their ancestral house was Eliasaph, son of Lael. [25]*† At the meeting tent they had charge of whatever pertained to the Dwelling, the tent and its covering, the curtain at the entrance of the meeting tent, [26] the hangings of the court, the curtain at the entrance of the court enclosing both the Dwelling and the altar, and the ropes.

[27] To Kohath belonged the clans of the Amramites, the Izharites, the Hebronites, and the Uzzielites; these were the clans of the Kohathites. [28] When all their males of a month or more were registered, they numbered eight thousand three hundred. They had charge of the sanctuary. [29] The clans of the Kohathites camped at the south side of the Dwelling. [30] The prince of their ancestral house was Elizaphan, son of Uzziel. [31]† They had charge of whatever pertained to the ark, the table, the lampstand, the altars, the utensils with which the ministry of the sanctuary was exercised, and the veil. [32] The chief prince of the Levites, however, was Eleazar, son of Aaron the priest; he was supervisor over those who had charge of the sanctuary.

[33] To Merari belonged the clans of the Mahlites and the Mushites; these were the clans of Merari. [34] When all their males of a month or more were registered, they numbered six thousand two hundred. [35] The prince of the ancestral house of the clans of Merari was Zuriel, son of Abihail. They camped at the north side of the Dwelling. [36]† The Merarites were charged with the care of whatever pertained to the boards of the Dwelling, its bars, columns, pedestals, and all its fittings, [37] as well as the columns of the surrounding court with their pedestals, pegs and ropes.

[38] East of the Dwelling, that is, in front of the meeting tent, toward the sunrise, were camped Moses and Aaron and the latter's sons. They discharged the obligations of the sanctuary for the Israelites. Any layman who came near was to be put to death.

[39] The total number of male Levites a month old or more whom Moses had registered by clans in keeping with the LORD's command, was twenty-two thousand.

Census and Ransom of First-born. [40] The LORD then said to Moses, "Take a census of all the first-born males of the Israelites a month old or more, and compute their total number. [41] Then assign the Levites to me, the LORD, in place of all the first-born of the Israelites, as well as their cattle in place of all the first-born among the cattle of the Israelites." [42] So Moses took a census of all the first-born of the Israelites, as the LORD had commanded him. [43] When all the first-born males of a month or more were registered, they numbered twenty-two thousand two hundred and seventy-three.

[44] The LORD said to Moses: [45] "Take the Levites in place of all the first-born of the Israelites, and the Levites' cattle in place of their cattle, that the Levites may belong to me. I am the LORD. [46] As ransom for the two hundred and seventy-three first-born of the Israelites who outnumber the Levites, [47]* you shall take five shekels for each individual, according to the standard of the sanctuary shekel, twenty gerahs to the shekel.

*

15: 3, 39; 26, 62.
17-20: 26, 57; Gn 46, 11; Ex 6, 16-19; 1 Chr 6, 1f.16-19.
25-26: Ex 26, 7.14. 36; 36, 14.
47: 18, 16; Ex 30, 13; Lv 27, 25; Ez 45, 12.

†

3, 25f: The Gershonites had two wagons for transporting these things; cf 7, 7. For a description of *the Dwelling,* see Ex 26, 1-6; *the tent,* Ex 26, 7-13; *its covering,* Ex 26, 14; *the curtain at the entrance,* Ex 26, 36; *the hangings of the court,* Ex 27, 9-15; *the curtain at the entrance of the court,* Ex 27, 16; *the ropes* of the Dwelling, Ex 35, 18.

3, 31: The Kohathites had to carry these sacred objects on their shoulders; cf 7, 9. For a description of *the ark,* see Ex 25, 10-22; *the table,* Ex 25, 23-30; *the lampstand,* Ex 25, 31-40; *the altars,* Ex 27, 1-8; 30, 1-10.

3, 36f: The Merarites had four wagons for transporting this heavy material; cf 7, 8. For a description of *the boards, bars, etc., of the Dwelling,* see Ex 26, 15-30; *the columns, pedestals etc., of the court,* Ex 27, 9-19.

[48] Give this silver to Aaron and his sons as ransom for the extra number." [49] So Moses took the silver as ransom from those who were left when the rest had been redeemed by the Levites. [50] From the first-born of the Israelites he received in silver one thousand three hundred and sixty-five shekels according to the sanctuary standard. [51] He then gave this ransom silver to Aaron and his sons, as the LORD had commanded him.

CHAPTER 4

Duties Further Defined. [1] The LORD said to Moses and Aaron: [2] "Among the Levites take a total of the Kohathites, by clans and ancestral houses, all the men of the Kohathites [3]*† between thirty and fifty years of age; these are to undertake obligatory tasks in the meeting tent.

[4] "The service of the Kohathites in the meeting tent concerns the most sacred objects. [5]† In breaking camp, Aaron and his sons shall go in and take down the screening curtain and cover the ark of the commandments with it. [6] Over these they shall put a cover of tahash skin, and on top of this spread an all-violet cloth. They shall then put the poles in place. [7] On the table of the Presence they shall spread a violet cloth and put on it the plates and cups, as well as the bowls and pitchers for libations; the established bread offering shall remain on the table. [8] Over these they shall spread a scarlet cloth and cover all this with tahash skin. They shall then put the poles in place. [9] They shall use a violet cloth to cover the lampstand with its lamps, trimming shears, and trays, as well as the various containers of oil from which it is supplied. [10] The lampstand with all its utensils they shall then enclose in a covering of tahash skin, and place on a litter. [11]† Over the golden altar they shall spread a violet cloth, and cover this also with a covering of tahash skin. They shall then put the poles in place. [12] Taking the utensils of the sanctuary service, they shall wrap them all in violet cloth and cover them with tahash skin. They shall then place them on a litter. [13]† After cleansing the altar of its ashes, they shall spread a purple cloth over it. [14]† On this they shall put all the utensils with which it is served: the fire pans, forks, shovels, basins, and all the utensils of the altar. They shall then spread a covering of tahash skin over this, and put the poles in place.

[15]* "Only after Aaron and his sons have finished covering the sacred objects and all their utensils on breaking camp, shall the Kohathites enter to carry them. But they shall not touch the sacred objects; if they do they will die. These, then, are the objects in the meeting tent that the Kohathites shall carry.

[16] "Eleazar, son of Aaron the priest, shall be in charge of the oil for the light, the fragrant incense, the established cereal offering, and the anointing oil. He shall be in charge of the whole Dwelling with all the sacred objects and utensils that are in it."

[17] The LORD said to Moses and Aaron: [18] "Do not let the group of Kohathite clans perish from the body of the Levites. [19] That they may live and not die when they approach the most sacred objects, this is what you shall do for them: Aaron and his sons shall go in and assign to each of them his task and what he must carry; [20]* but the Kohathites shall not go in to look upon the sacred objects, even for an instant; if they do, they will die."

[21] The LORD said to Moses, [22] "Take a total among the Gershonites also, by ancestral houses and clans, [23] of all the men between thirty and fifty years of age; these are to undertake obligatory tasks in the meeting tent. [24] This is the task of the clans of the Gershonites, what they must do and what they must carry: [25] they shall carry the sheets of the Dwelling, the meeting tent with its covering and the outer wrapping of tahash skin, the curtain at the entrance of the meeting tent, [26] the hangings of the court, the curtain at the entrance of the court that encloses both the Dwelling and the altar, together with their ropes and all other objects necessary in their use. Whatever is to be done with these things shall be their task. [27] The service of the Gershonites shall be entirely under the direction of Aaron and his sons, with regard to what they must do and what they must carry; you shall make each man of them responsible for what he is to carry. [28] This, then, is the task of the Gershonites in the meeting tent; and they shall be under the supervision of Ithamar, son of Aaron the priest.

[29] "Among the Merarites, too, you shall enroll by clans and ancestral houses [30] all their men between thirty

*

4, 3: 8, 24; 1 Chr 23, 24-27.
15: 2 Sm 6, 6f; 1 Chr 13, 9f.
20: 1 Sm 6, 19.

†

4, 3: *Thirty:* at a later period the Levites began to serve when they were twenty-five (8, 24) or even only twenty years old (1 Chr 23, 24.27; 2 Chr 31, 17; Ezr 3, 8; but cf 1 Chr 23, 3).

4, 5: *The screening curtain:* the veil between the inner and the outer rooms of the sanctuary. Cf Ex 26, 31-33.

4, 11: *The golden altar:* the altar of incense. Cf Ex 30, 1-6.

4, 13: *The altar:* the bronze altar of holocausts. Cf Ex 27, 1-8.

4, 14: *Forks:* used in turning over the sacrificed animal on the fire of the altar. *Basins:* to receive the sacrificial blood; cf Zec 9, 15.

and fifty years of age; these are to un-
dertake obligatory tasks in the meeting
tent. 31* This is what they shall be re-
sponsible for carrying, all the years of
their service in the meeting tent: the
boards of the Dwelling with its bars, col-
umns and pedestals, 32 and the columns
of the surrounding court with their ped-
estals, pegs and ropes. You shall desig-
nate for each man of them all the objects
connected with his service, which he
shall be responsible for carrying. 33 This,
then, is the task of the clans of the Me-
rarites during all their service in the
meeting tent under the supervision of
Ithamar, son of Aaron the priest."

Number of Adult Levites. 34 So Moses
and Aaron and the princes of the com-
munity made a registration among the
Kohathites, by clans and ancestral
houses, 35 of all the men between thirty
and fifty years of age. These were to un-
dertake obligatory tasks in the meeting
tent; 36 as registered by clans, they num-
bered two thousand seven hundred and
fifty. 37 Such was the census of all the
men of the Kohathite clans who were to
serve in the meeting tent, which Moses
took, together with Aaron, as the LORD
bade him.

38 The registration was then made
among the Gershonites, by clans and
ancestral houses, 39 of all the men be-
tween thirty and fifty years of age. These
were to undertake obligatory tasks in the
meeting tent; 40 as registered by clans
and ancestral houses, they numbered
two thousand six hundred and thirty.
41 Such was the census of all the men of
the Gershonite clans who were to serve
in the meeting tent, which Moses took,
together with Aaron, at the LORD's bid-
ding.

42 Then the registration was made
among the Merarites, by clans and an-
cestral houses, 43 of all the men from
thirty up to fifty years of age. These were
to undertake obligatory tasks in the
meeting tent; 44 as registered by clans,
they numbered three thousand two hun-
dred. 45 Such was the census of the men
of the Merarite clans which Moses took,
together with Aaron, as the LORD bade
him.

46 Therefore, when Moses and Aaron
and the Israelites princes had completed
the registration among the Levites, by
clans and ancestral houses, 47 of all the
men between thirty and fifty years of
age who were to undertake tasks of ser-
vice or transport of the meeting tent,
48 the total number registered was eight
thousand five hundred and eighty.
49 According to the LORD's bidding to
Moses, they gave them their individual
assignments for service and for trans-
port; so the LORD had commanded Mo-
ses.

CHAPTER 5

The Unclean Expelled. 1 The LORD
said to Moses: 2*† "Order the Israelites
to expel from camp every leper, and ev-
eryone suffering from a discharge, and
everyone who has become unclean by
contact with a corpse. 3* Male and fe-
male alike, you shall compel them to go
out of the camp; they are not to defile
the camp in which I dwell." 4 The Isra-
elites obeyed the command that the
LORD had given Moses; they expelled
them from the camp.

Unjust Possession. 5† The LORD said
to Moses, 6* "Tell the Israelites: If a man
(or a woman) commits a fault against
his fellow man and wrongs him, thus
breaking faith with the LORD, 7 he shall
confess the wrong he has done, restore
his ill-gotten goods in full, and in addi-
tion give one fifth of their value to the
one he has wronged. 8† However, if the
latter has no next of kin to whom resto-
ration of the ill-gotten goods can be
made, the goods to be restored shall be
the LORD's and shall fall to the priest;
this is apart from the atonement ram
with which the priest makes amends for
the guilty man. 9* Likewise, every sa-
cred contribution that the Israelites are
bound to make shall fall to the priest.
10* Each Israelite man may dispose of
his own sacred contributions; they be-
come the property of the priest to whom
he gives them."

Ordeal for a Suspected Adultress.
11 The LORD said to Moses, 12 "Speak to
the Israelites and tell them: If a man's
wife goes astray and becomes unfaithful
to him 13* by having intercourse with an-
other man, though her husband has not
sufficient evidence of the fact, so that her
impurity remains unproved for lack of
a witness who might have caught her
in the act; 14 or if a man is overcome by
a feeling of jealousy that makes him sus-
pect his wife, whether she was actually
impure or not: 15 he shall bring his wife
to the priest and shall take along as an
offering for her a tenth of an ephah of

*

31: 3, 36f.
5, 2: 19, 11.13; Lv 13, 46; 21, 1; 22, 4.
3: 35, 34.
6ff: Lv 5, 21-25.
9: Dt 18, 3f; Ez 44, 29f.
10: Lv 10, 12-15.
13: Lv 18, 20; Jn 8, 4.

†

5, 2: For the laws regarding victims of leprosy, see Lv 13-14; those *suffering from a discharge,* Lv 15; the *unclean by contact with a corpse,* 19, 11-22; Lv 21, 1-4.

5, 5-10: The basic law on unjust possession is given in Lv 5, 14-26. The new item here concerns the case where the injured party has died and left no heirs, in which case the restitution must be made to the priest.

5, 8: *Next of kin:* literally "redeemer," a technical term denoting the nearest relative, upon whom devolved the obligation of "redeeming" the family property, in order to keep it within the family. Cf Lv 25, 25; Ru 4, 1-6.

barley meal. However, he shall not pour
oil on it nor put frankincense over it,
since it is a cereal offering of jealousy,
a cereal offering for an appeal in a ques-
tion of guilt.
16 "The priest shall first have the
woman come forward and stand before
the LORD. 17*† In an earthen vessel he
shall meanwhile put some holy water,
as well as some dust that he has taken
from the floor of the Dwelling. 18† Then,
as the woman stands before the LORD,
the priest shall uncover her head and
place in her hands the cereal offering
of her appeal, that is, the cereal offering
of jealousy, while he himself shall hold
the bitter water that brings a curse.
19 Then he shall adjure the woman, say-
ing to her, 'If no other man has had in-
tercourse with you, and you have not
gone astray by impurity while under the
authority of your husband, be immune
to the curse brought by this bitter water.
20 But if you have gone astray while un-
der the authority of your husband and
have acted impurely by letting a man
other than your husband have inter-
course with you'— 21† so shall the priest
adjure the woman with this oath of
imprecation—'may the LORD make you
an example of malediction and impre-
cation among your people by causing
your thighs to waste away and your belly
to swell! 22*† May this water, then, that
brings a curse, enter your body to make
your belly swell and your thighs waste
away!' And the woman shall say, 'Amen,
amen!' 23 The priest shall put these
imprecations in writing and shall then
wash them off into the bitter water,
24 which he is to have the woman drink,
so that it may go into her with all its
bitter curse. 25 But first he shall take the
cereal offering of jealousy from the
woman's hand, and having waved this
offering before the LORD, shall put it
near the altar, 26* where he shall take
a handful of the cereal offering as its to-
ken offering and burn it on the altar.
Only then shall he have the woman
drink the water. 27 Once she has done
so, if she has been impure and unfaithful
to her husband, this bitter water that
brings a curse will go into her, and her
belly will swell and her thighs will waste
away, so that she will become an exam-
ple of imprecation among her people.
28 If, however, the woman has not defiled
herself, but is still pure, she will be im-
mune and will still be able to bear chil-
dren.
29 "This, then, is the law for jealousy:
When a woman goes astray while under
the authority of her husband and acts
impurely, 30 or when such a feeling of
jealousy comes over a man that he be-
comes suspicious of his wife, he shall
have her stand before the LORD, and the
priest shall apply this law in full to her.
31† The man shall be free from guilt, but
the woman shall bear such guilt as she
may have."

CHAPTER 6

Laws Concerning Nazirites. 1† The
LORD said to Moses: 2 "Speak to the Isra-
elites and tell them: When a man (or a
woman) solemnly takes the nazirite vow
to dedicate himself to the LORD, 3* he
shall abstain from wine and strong
drink; he may neither drink wine vine-
gar, other vinegar, of any kind of grape
juice, nor eat either fresh or dried
grapes. 4 As long as he is a nazirite he
shall not eat anything of the produce of
the vine; not even unripe grapes or
grapeskins. 5* While he is under the
nazirite vow, no razor shall touch his
hair. Until the period of his dedication
to the LORD is over, he shall be sacred,
and shall let the hair of his head grow
freely. 6* As long as he is dedicated to
the LORD, he shall not enter where a
dead person is. 7 Not even for his father
or mother, his sister or brother, should
they die, may he become unclean, since
his head bears his dedication to God.
8 As long as he is a nazirite he is sacred
to the LORD.
9 "If someone dies very suddenly in his
presence, so that his dedicated head be-
comes unclean, he shall shave his head
on the day of his purification, that is, on
the seventh day. 10 On the eighth day he
shall bring two turtledoves or two pi-
geons to the priest at the entrance of the
meeting tent. 11 The priest shall offer up
the one as a sin offering and the other

*

17: 19, 17.
22: Ps 109, 18.
26: Lv 5, 12.
6, 3f: Jgs 13, 7.14.
5: Jgs 13, 5; 16, 17; 1 Sm 1, 11.
6: 19, 11.16; Lv 21, 11.

†

5, 17: *Holy water:* water from the laver that stood in the court of the Dwelling.

5, 18: *Appeal:* by which she invokes the Lord and refers her case to his decision.

5, 21: *An example of malediction and imprecation:* the woman's name would be used in curses and oaths to invoke a similar misfortune on another person or on oneself. Cf Is 65, 15; Jer 29, 22.

5, 22: *Amen:* a Hebrew word meaning, "certainly, truly," used to give assent to a statement, a curse, a blessing, a prayer, or the like; in this sense of "so be it," the Christian liturgy also uses it after prayers and blessings.

5, 31: *Free from guilt:* by fulfilling his obligation of obtaining a decision in the matter.

6, 1ff: *Nazirite:* from the Hebrew word *nazir,* meaning "set apart as sacred, dedicated, vowed." The nazirite vow could be either for a limited period or for life. Those bound by this vow had to abstain from all the products of the grapevine, from cutting or shaving their hair, and from contact with a corpse. They were regarded as men of God like the prophets; cf Am 2, 11f. Examples of lifelong nazirites were Samson (Jgs 13, 4f.7; 16, 17), Samuel (1 Sm 1, 11), and John the Baptizer (Lk 1, 15). At the time of Christ the practice of taking the nazirite vow for a limited period seems to have been quite common, even among the early Christians; cf Acts 18, 18; 21, 23f.26.

as a holocaust, thus making atonement for him for the sin he has committed by reason of the dead person. On the same day he shall reconsecrate his head [12] and begin anew the period of his dedication to the LORD as a nazirite, bringing a yearling lamb as a guilt offering. The previous period is not valid, because his dedicated head became unclean.

[13]* "This is the ritual for the nazirite: On the day he completes the period of his dedication he shall go to the entrance of the meeting tent, [14] bringing as his offering to the LORD one unblemished yearling lamb for a holocaust, one unblemished yearling ewe lamb for a sin offering, one unblemished ram as a peace offering, along with their cereal offerings and libations, [15] and a basket of unleavened cakes of fine flour mixed with oil and of unleavened wafers spread with oil. [16] The priest shall present them before the LORD, and shall offer up the sin offering and the holocaust for him. [17] He shall then offer up the ram as a peace offering to the LORD, with its cereal offering and libation, and the basket of unleavened cakes. [18]* Then at the entrance of the meeting tent the nazirite shall shave his dedicated head, collect the hair, and put it in the fire that is under the peace offering. [19] After the nazirite has shaved off his dedicated hair, the priest shall take a boiled shoulder of the ram, as well as one unleavened cake and one unleavened wafer from the basket, and shall place them in the hands of the nazirite. [20] The priest shall then wave them as a wave offering before the LORD. They become sacred and shall belong to the priest, along with the breast of the wave offering and the leg of the raised offering. Only after this may the nazirite drink wine.

[21] "This, then, is the law for the nazirite; this is the offering to the LORD which is included in his vow of dedication apart from anything else which his means may allow. Thus shall he carry out the law of his dedication in keeping with the vow he has taken."

The Priestly Blessing. [22] The LORD said to Moses: [23] "Speak to Aaron and his sons and tell them: This is how you shall bless the Israelites. Say to them:

[24] The LORD bless you and keep you!
[25]† The LORD let his face shine upon you, and be gracious to you!
[26]† The LORD look upon you kindly and give you peace!

[27] So shall they invoke my name upon the Israelites, and I will bless them."

CHAPTER 7

Offerings of Princes. [1]* Now, when Moses had completed the erection of the Dwelling and had anointed and consecrated it with all its equipment (as well as the altar with all its equipment), [2] an offering was made by the princes of Israel, who were heads of ancestral houses; the same princes of the tribes who supervised the census. [3] The offering they brought before the LORD consisted of six baggage wagons and twelve oxen, that is, a wagon for every two princes, and an ox for every prince. These they presented as their offering before the Dwelling.

[4] The LORD then said to Moses, [5] "Accept their offering, that these things may be put to use in the service of the meeting tent. Assign them to the Levites, to each group in proportion to its duties." [6] So Moses accepted the wagons and oxen, and assigned them to the Levites. [7]* He gave two wagons and four oxen to the Gershonites in proportion to their duties, [8] and four wagons and eight oxen to the Merarites in proportion to their duties, under the supervision of Ithamar, son of Aaron the priest. [9]* He gave none to the Kohathites, because they had to carry on their shoulders the sacred objects which were their charge.

[10]* For the dedication of the altar also, the princes brought offerings before the altar on the day it was anointed. [11] But the LORD said to Moses, "Let one prince a day present his offering for the dedication of the altar."

[12]† The one who presented his offering on the first day was Nahshon, son of Amminadab, prince of the tribe of Judah. [13] His offering consisted of one silver plate weighing a hundred and thirty shekels according to the sanctuary standard and one silver basin weighing seventy shekels, both filled with fine flour mixed with oil for a cereal offering; [14] one gold cup of ten shekels' weight filled with incense; [15] one young bull, one ram, and one yearling lamb for a holocaust; [16] one goat for a sin offering; [17] and two oxen, five rams, five goats, and five yearling lambs for a peace offering. This was the offering of Nahshon, son of Amminadab.

[18] On the second day Nethanel, son of Zuar, prince of Issachar, made his offering. [19] He presented as his offering one silver plate weighing a hundred and thirty shekels according to the sanctuary standard and one silver basin

*

13: Acts 21, 24.26.
18: Acts 18, 18; 21, 24.
7, 1: Ex 40, 17.
7f: 4, 24-33.
9: 3, 31; 4, 4-15.
10: 7, 84.

†

6, 25: *Let his face shine:* a Hebrew idiom for "smile."
6, 26: *Peace:* the Hebrew word includes the idea of "prosperity, happiness."
7, 12-88: The repetitious account of the same offerings brought by each of the twelve tribal princes and the summary of them are characteristic of an official registration.

weighing seventy shekels, both filled
with fine flour mixed with oil for a cereal
offering; 20 one gold cup of ten shekels'
weight filled with incense; 21 one young
bull, one ram, and one yearling lamb for
a holocaust; 22 one goat for a sin offering;
23 and two oxen, five rams, five goats,
and five yearling lambs for a peace of-
fering. This was the offering of Nethanel,
son of Zuar.

24 On the third day it was the turn of
Eliab, son of Helon, prince of the Zebu-
lunites. 25 His offering consisted of one
silver plate weighing a hundred and
thirty shekels according to the sanctu-
ary standard and one silver basin
weighing seventy shekels, both filled
with fine flour mixed with oil for a cereal
offering; 26 one gold cup of ten shekels'
weight filled with incense; 27 one young
bull, one ram, and one yearling lamb for
a holocaust; 28 one goat for a sin offering;
29 and two oxen, five rams, five goats,
and five yearling lambs for a peace of-
fering. This was the offering of Eliab, son
of Helon.

30 On the fourth day it was the turn of
Elizur, son of Shedeur, prince of the
Reubenites. 31 His offering consisted of
one silver plate weighing a hundred and
thirty shekels according to the sanctu-
ary standard and one silver basin
weighing seventy shekels, both filled
with fine flour mixed with oil for a cereal
offering; 32 one gold cup of ten shekels'
weight filled with incense; 33 one young
bull, one ram, and one yearling lamb for
a holocaust; 34 one goat for a sin offering;
35 and two oxen, five rams, five goats,
and five yearling lambs for a peace of-
fering. This was the offering of Elizur,
son of Shedeur.

36 On the fifth day it was the turn of
Shelumiel, son of Zurishaddai, prince of
the Simeonites. 37 His offering consisted
of one silver plate weighing a hundred
and thirty shekels according to the sanc-
tuary standard and one silver basin
weighing seventy shekels, both filled
with fine flour mixed with oil for a cereal
offering; 38 one gold cup of ten shekels'
weight filled with incense; 39 one young
bull, one ram, and one yearling lamb for
a holocaust; 40 one goat for a sin offering;
41 and two oxen, five rams, five goats,
and five yearling lambs for a peace of-
fering. This was the offering of Shelu-
miel, son of Zurishaddai.

42 On the sixth day it was the turn of
Eliasaph, son of Reuel, prince of the
Gadites. 43 His offering consisted of one
silver plate weighing a hundred and
thirty shekels according to the sanctu-
ary standard and one silver basin
weighing seventy shekels, both filled
with fine flour mixed with oil for a cereal
offering; 44 one gold cup of ten shekels'
weight filled with incense; 45 one young
bull, one ram, and one yearling lamb for
a holocaust; 46 one goat for a sin offering;
47 and two oxen, five rams, five goats,
and five yearling lambs for a peace of-
fering. This was the offering of Eliasaph,
son of Reuel.

48 On the seventh day it was the turn
of Elishama, son of Ammihud, prince of
the Ephraimites. 49 His offering con-
sisted of one silver plate weighing a hun-
dred and thirty shekels according to the
sanctuary standard and one silver basin
weighing seventy shekels, both filled
with fine flour mixed with oil for a cereal
offering; 50 one gold cup of ten shekels'
weight filled with incense; 51 one young
bull, one ram, and one yearling lamb for
a holocaust; 52 one goat for a sin offering;
53 and two oxen, five rams, five goats,
and five yearling lambs for a peace of-
fering. This was the offering of Elish-
ama, son of Ammihud.

54 On the eighth day it was the turn
of Gamaliel, son of Pedahzur, prince of
the Manassehites. 55 His offering con-
sisted of one silver plate weighing a hun-
dred and thirty shekels according to the
sanctuary standard and one silver basin
weighing seventy shekels, both filled
with fine flour mixed with oil for a cereal
offering; 56 one gold cup of ten shekels'
weight filled with incense; 57 one young
bull, one ram, and one yearling lamb for
a holocaust; 58 one goat for a sin offering;
59 and two oxen, five rams, five goats,
and five yearling lambs for a peace of-
fering. This was the offering of Gamaliel,
son of Pedahzur.

60 On the ninth day it was the turn of
Abidan, son of Gideoni, prince of the
Benjaminites. 61 His offering consisted of
one silver plate weighing a hundred and
thirty shekels according to the sanctu-
ary standard and one silver basin
weighing seventy shekels, both filled
with fine flour mixed with oil for a cereal
offering; 62 one gold cup of ten shekels'
weight filled with incense; 63 one young
bull, one ram, and one yearling lamb for
a holocaust; 64 one goat for a sin offering;
65 and two oxen, five rams, five goats,
and five yearling lambs for a peace of-
fering. This was the offering of Abidan,
son of Gideoni.

66 On the tenth day it was the turn of
Ahiezer, son of Ammishaddai, prince of
the Danites. 67 His offering consisted of
one silver plate weighing a hundred and
thirty shekels according to the sanctu-
ary standard and one silver basin
weighing seventy shekels, both filled
with fine flour mixed with oil for a cereal
offering; 68 one gold cup of ten shekels'
weight filled with incense; 69 one young
bull, one ram, and one yearling lamb for
a holocaust; 70 one goat for a sin offering;
71 and two oxen, five rams, five goats,
and five yearling lambs for a peace of-
fering. This was the offering of Ahiezer,
son of Ammishaddai.

72 On the eleventh day it was the turn
of Pagiel, son of Ochran, prince of the
Asherites. 73 His offering consisted of
one silver plate weighing one hundred
and thirty shekels according to the sanc-
tuary standard and one silver basin
weighing seventy shekels, both filled
with fine flour mixed with oil for a cereal
offering; 74 one gold cup of ten shekels'
weight filled with incense; 75 one young
bull, one ram, and one yearling lamb for
a holocaust; 76 one goat for a sin offering;
77 and two oxen, five rams, five goats,
and five yearling lambs for a peace of-
fering. This was the offering of Pagiel,
son of Ochran.

78 On the twelfth day it was the turn
of Ahira, son of Enan, prince of the
Naphtalites. 79 His offering consisted of
one silver plate weighing a hundred and
thirty shekels according to the sanctu-
ary standard and one silver basin
weighing seventy shekels, both filled
with fine flour mixed with oil for a cereal
offering; 80 one gold cup of ten shekels'
weight filled with incense; 81 one young
bull, one ram, and one yearling lamb for
a holocaust; 82 one goat for a sin offering;
83 and two oxen, five rams, five goats,
and five yearling lambs for a peace of-
fering. This was the offering of Ahira,
son of Enan.

84 These were the offerings for the ded-
ication of the altar, given by the princes
of Israel on the occasion of its anointing:
twelve silver plates, twelve silver basins,
and twelve gold cups. 85 Each silver
plate weighed a hundred and thirty
shekels, and each silver basin seventy,
so that all the silver of these vessels
amounted to two thousand four hundred
shekels, according to the sanctuary
standard. 86 The twelve gold cups that
were filled with incense weighed ten
shekels apiece, according to the sanctu-
ary standard, so that all the gold of the
cups amounted to one hundred and
twenty shekels. 87 The animals for the
holocausts were, in all, twelve young
bulls, twelve rams, and twelve yearling
lambs, with their cereal offerings; those
for the sin offerings were twelve goats.
88 The animals for the peace offerings
were, in all, twenty-four oxen, sixty
rams, sixty goats, and sixty yearling
lambs. These, then, were the offerings
for the dedication of the altar after it was
anointed.

The Voice. 89* When Moses entered
the meeting tent to speak with him, he
heard the voice addressing him from
above the propitiatory on the ark of the
commandments, from between the two
cherubim; and it spoke to him. . . .

CHAPTER 8

The Lamps Set Up. 1 The LORD spoke
to Moses, and said, 2* "Give Aaron this
command: When you set up the seven
lamps, have them throw their light to-
ward the front of the lampstand."
3 Aaron did so, setting up the lamps to
face toward the front of the lampstand,
just as the LORD had commanded Moses.
4* The lampstand was made of beaten
gold in both its shaft and its branches,
according to the pattern which the LORD
had shown Moses.

Purification of the Levites. 5 The LORD
said to Moses: 6† "Take the Levites from
among the Israelites and purify them.
7† This is what you shall do to them to
purify them. Sprinkle them with the
water of remission; then have them
shave their whole bodies and wash their
clothes, and so purify themselves. 8 They
shall take a young bull, along with its
cereal offering of fine flour mixed with
oil; you shall take another young bull for
a sin offering. 9 Then have the Levites
come forward in front of the meeting
tent, where you shall assemble also the
whole community of the Israelites.
10 While the Levites are present before
the LORD, the Israelites shall lay their
hands upon them. 11 Let Aaron then offer
the Levites before the LORD as a wave
offering from the Israelites, thus devot-
ing them to the service of the LORD.
12 The Levites in turn shall lay their
hands on the heads of the bullocks,
which shall then be immolated, the one
as a sin offering and the other as a holo-
caust to the LORD, in atonement for the
Levites. 13 Thus, then, shall you have the
Levites stand before Aaron and his sons,
to be offered as a wave offering to the
LORD; 14* and thus shall you set aside
the Levites from the rest of the Israel-
ites, that they may be mine.

15 "Only then shall the Levites enter
upon their service in the meeting tent.
You shall purify them and offer them
as a wave offering; 16* because they,
among the Israelites, are strictly dedi-
cated to me; I have taken them for my-
self in place of every first-born that
opens the womb among the Israelites.
17* Indeed, all the first-born among the
Israelites, both of man and of beast, be-
long to me; I consecrated them to myself
on the day I slew all the first-born in
the land of Egypt. 18 But in place of all
the first-born Israelites I have taken the

*

89: Ex 25, 22.
8, 2: Ex 25, 37.
4: Ex 25, 31.40.
14: 3, 45.
16: 3, 12.45.
17: 3, 13; 13, 2; Lk 2, 23.

†

8, 6: *Purify them:* in the language of the Pentateuch only the priests were "consecrated," that is, made sacred or set aside for the Lord, in an elaborate ceremony described in Ex 29; Lv 8. The Levites were merely "purified," that is, made ritually clean for their special work.

8, 7: *Water of remission:* literally, "water of sin," that is, for the remission of sin.

Levites; 19* and I have given these dedi-
cated Israelites to Aaron and his sons
to discharge the duties of the Israelites
in the meeting tent and to make atone-
ment for them, so that no plague may
strike among the Israelites should they
come near the sanctuary."
20 Thus, then, did Moses and Aaron
and the whole community of the Israel-
ites deal with the Levites, carrying out
exactly the command which the LORD
had given Moses concerning them.
21† When the Levites had cleansed
themselves of sin and washed their
clothes, Aaron offered them as a wave
offering before the LORD, and made
atonement for them to purify them.
22 Only then did they enter upon their
service in the meeting tent under the su-
pervision of Aaron and his sons. The
command which the LORD had given
Moses concerning the Levites was car-
ried out.
Age Limits for Levitical Service. 23 The
LORD said to Moses: 24* "This is the rule
for the Levites. Each from his twenty-
fifth year onward shall perform the re-
quired service in the meeting tent.
25 When he is fifty years old, he shall re-
tire from the required service and work
no longer. 26 His service with his fellow
Levites shall consist in sharing their re-
sponsibilities in the meeting tent, but he
shall not do the work. This, then, is how
you are to regulate the duties of the Le-
vites."

CHAPTER 9

Second Passover. 1 In the first month
of the year following their departure
from the land of Egypt, the Lord said
to Moses in the desert of Sinai, 2 "Tell
the Israelites to celebrate the Passover
at the prescribed time. 3* The evening
twilight of the fourteenth day of this
month is the prescribed time when you
shall celebrate it, observing all its rules
and regulations." 4 Moses, therefore,
told the Israelites to celebrate the Pass-
over. 5 And they did so, celebrating the
Passover in the desert of Sinai during
the evening twilight of the fourteenth
day of the first month, just as the LORD
had commanded Moses.
6 There were some, however, who were
unclean because of a human corpse and
so could not keep the Passover that day.
These men came up to Moses and Aaron
that same day 7 and said, "Although we
are unclean because of a corpse, why
should we be deprived of presenting the
LORD's offering at its proper time along
with the other Israelites?" 8 Moses an-
swered them, "Wait until I learn what
the LORD will command in your regard."
9 The LORD then said to Moses:
10 "Speak to the Israelites and say: If any
one of you or of your descendants is un-
clean because of a corpse, or if he is ab-
sent on a journey, he may still keep the
LORD's Passover. 11* But he shall keep
it in the second month, during the eve-
ning twilight of the fourteenth day of
that month, eating it with unleavened
bread and bitter herbs, 12* and not leav-
ing any of it over till morning, nor break-
ing any of its bones, but observing all
the rules of the Passover. 13 However,
anyone who is clean and not away on
a journey, who yet fails to keep the Pass-
over, shall be cut off from his people,
because he did not present the LORD's
offering at the prescribed time. That
man shall bear the consequences of his
sin.
14*† "If an alien who lives among you
wishes to keep the LORD's Passover, he
too shall observe the rules and regula-
tions for the Passover. You shall have
the same law for the resident alien as
for the native of the land."
The Fiery Cloud. 15*† On the day
when the Dwelling was erected, the
cloud covered the Dwelling, the tent of
the commandments; but from evening
until morning it took on the appearance
of fire over the Dwelling. 16 It was always
so: during the day the Dwelling was cov-
ered by the cloud, which at night had
the appearance of fire. 17* Whenever the
cloud rose from the tent, the Israelites
would break camp; wherever the cloud
came to rest, they would pitch camp.
18* At the bidding of the LORD the Israel-
ites moved on, and at his bidding they
encamped. As long as the cloud stayed
over the Dwelling, they remained in
camp.
19 Even when the cloud tarried many
days over the Dwelling, the Israelites
obeyed the LORD and would not move
on; 20 yet sometimes the cloud was over
the Dwelling only for a few days. It was
at the bidding of the LORD that they
stayed in camp, and it was at his bidding
that they departed. 21 Sometimes the
cloud remained there only from evening
until morning; and when it rose in the
morning, they would depart. Or if the
cloud lifted during the day, or even at
night, they would then set out.
22 Whether the cloud tarried over the

*

19: 3, 9f.
24: 4, 3.23.
9, 3: Ex 12, 6; Lv 23, 5.
11: 2 Chr 30, 2-15.
12: Ex 12, 46; Jn 19, 36.
14: Ex 12, 48f.
15: Ex 13, 21.
17: Wis 18, 3.
18: 1 Cor 10, 1.

†

8, 21: *Cleansed themselves of sin:* by having the "water of remission" sprinkled on them as prescribed in v 7.

9, 14: *An alien:* this passage presupposes that he is already circumcised as prescribed in Ex 12, 48.

9, 15: *The cloud:* already mentioned at the departure from Egypt; cf Ex 13, 21f.

Dwelling for two days or for a month or longer, the Israelites remained in camp and did not depart; but when it lifted, they moved on. 23 Thus, it was always at the bidding of the LORD that they encamped, and at his bidding that they set out; ever heeding the charge of the LORD, as he had bidden them through Moses.

CHAPTER 10

The Silver Trumpets. 1 The LORD said to Moses: 2 "Make two trumpets of beaten silver, which you shall use in assembling the community and in breaking camp. 3 When both are blown, the whole community shall gather round you at the entrance of the meeting tent; 4 but when one of them is blown, only the princes, the chiefs of the troops of Israel, shall gather round you. 5 When you sound the first alarm, 6 those encamped on the east side shall set out; when you sound the second alarm, those encamped on the south side shall set out; when you sound the third alarm, those encamped on the west side shall set out; when you sound the fourth alarm, those encamped on the north side shall set out. Thus shall the alarm be sounded for them to depart. 7 But in calling forth an assembly you are to blow an ordinary blast, without sounding the alarm.

8 "It is the sons of Aaron, the priests, who shall blow the trumpets; and the use of them is prescribed by perpetual statute for you and your descendants. 9* When in your own land you go to war against an enemy that is attacking you, you shall sound the alarm on the trumpets, and the LORD, your God, will remember you and save you from your foes. 10*† On your days of celebration, your festivals, and your new-moon feasts, you shall blow the trumpets over your holocausts and your peace offerings; this will serve as a reminder of you before your God. I, the LORD, am your God."

II: FROM SINAI TO THE PLAINS OF MOAB

Departure from Sinai. 11 In the second year, on the twentieth day of the second month, the cloud rose from the Dwelling of the commandments. 12 The Israelites moved on from the desert of Sinai by stages, until the cloud came to rest in the desert of Paran.

13 The first time that they broke camp at the bidding of the LORD through Moses, 14* the camp of the Judahites, under its own standard and arranged in companies, was the first to set out. Nahshon, son of Amminadab, was over their host, 15 and Nethanel, son of Zuar, over the host of the tribe of Issachar, 16 and Eliab, son of Helon, over the host of the tribe of Zebulun. 17 Then, after the Dwelling was dismantled, the clans of Gershon and Merari set out, carrying the Dwelling. 18 The camp of the Reubenites, under its own standard and arranged in companies, was the next to set out, with Elizur, son of Shedeur, over their host, 19 and Shelumiel, son of Zurishaddai, over the host of the tribe of Simeon, 20 and Eliasaph, son of Reuel, over the host of the tribe of Gad. 21 The clan of Kohath then set out, carrying the sacred objects for the Dwelling, which was to be erected before their arrival. 22 The camp of the Ephraimites next set out, under its own standard and arranged in companies, with Elishama, son of Ammihud, over their host, 23 and Gamaliel, son of Pedahzur, over the host of the tribe of Manasseh, 24 and Abidan, son of Gideoni, over the host of the tribe of Benjamin. 25 Finally, as rear guard for all the camps, the camp of the Danites set out, under its own standard and arranged in companies, with Ahiezer, son of Ammishaddai, over their host, 26 and Pagiel, son of Ochran, over the host of the tribe of Asher, 27 and Ahira, son of Enan, over the host of the tribe of Naphtali. 28 This was the order of departure for the Israelites, company by company.

Hobab as Guide. As they were setting out, 29 Moses said to his brother-in-law Hobab, son of Reuel the Midianite, "We are setting out for the place which the LORD has promised to give us. Come with us, and we will be generous toward you, for the LORD has promised prosperity to Israel." 30† But he answered, "No, I will not come. I am going instead to my own country and to my own kindred." 31 Moses said, "Please, do not leave us; you know where we can camp in the desert, and you will serve as eyes for us. 32 If you come with us, we will share with you the prosperity the LORD will bestow on us."

Into the Desert. 33*† They moved on from the mountain of the LORD, a three days' journey, and the ark of the covenant of the LORD which was to seek out their resting place went the three days' journey with them. 34 And when they set

*

10, 9: 2 Chr 13, 14.
10: 29, 1; 2 Chr 29, 26ff.
14ff: 2, 3.5.7.
33: Dt 1, 33.

†

10, 10: *Days of celebration:* special holidays, such as the occasion of a victory. *Festivals:* the great annual feasts of the Passover, Pentecost and Booths described in Lv 23; Nm 28-29.

10, 30ff: Hobab wished to be coaxed before granting the favor. From Jgs 1, 16 it seems probable that he did accede to Moses' request.

10, 33: *The mountain of the LORD:* Sinai (Horeb), elsewhere always called "the mountain of God."

out from camp, the cloud of the LORD
was over them by day.
35* Whenever the ark set out, Moses
would say,

"Arise, O LORD, that your enemies
may be scattered,
and those who hate you may flee
before you."

36 And when it came to rest, he would
say,

"Return, O LORD, you who ride upon
the clouds,
to the troops of Israel."

CHAPTER 11

Discontent of the People. 1* Now the
people complained in the hearing of the
LORD; and when he heard it his wrath
flared up so that the fire of the LORD
burned among them and consumed the
outskirts of the camp. 2 But when the
people cried out to Moses, he prayed to
the LORD and the fire died out. 3† Hence
that place was called Taberah, because
there the fire of the LORD burned among
them.
4* The foreign elements among them
were so greedy for meat that even the
Israelites lamented again, "Would that
we had meat for food! 5* We remember
the fish we used to eat without cost in
Egypt, and the cucumbers, the melons,
the leeks, the onions, and the garlic.
6 But now we are famished; we see noth-
ing before us but this manna."
7*† Manna was like coriander seed
and had the appearance of bdellium.
8 When they had gone about and gath-
ered it up, the people would grind it be-
tween millstones or pound it in a mortar,
then cook it in a pot and make it into
loaves, which tasted like cakes made
with oil. 9* At night, when the dew fell
upon the camp, the manna also fell.
10 When Moses heard the people, fam-
ily after family, crying at the entrance
of their tents, so that the LORD became
very angry, he was grieved. 11 "Why do
you treat your servant so badly?" Moses
asked the LORD. "Why are you so dis-
pleased with me that you burden me
with all this people? 12 Was it I who con-
ceived all this people? or was it I who
gave them birth, that you tell me to
carry them at my bosom, like a foster
father carrying an infant, to the land you
have promised under oath to their fa-
thers? 13 Where can I get meat to give
to all this people? For they are crying
to me, 'Give us meat for our food.' 14 I
cannot carry all this people by myself,
for they are too heavy for me. 15 If this
is the way you will deal with me, then
please do me the favor of killing me at
once, so that I need no longer face this
distress."

The Seventy Elders. 16 Then the LORD
said to Moses, "Assemble for me seventy
of the elders of Israel, men you know
for true elders and authorities among
the people, and bring them to the meet-
ing tent. When they are in place beside
you, 17 I will come down and speak with
you there. I will also take some of the
spirit that is on you and will bestow it
on them, that they may share the burden
of the people with you. You will then not
have to bear it by yourself.
18 "To the people, however, you shall
say: Sanctify yourselves for tomorrow,
when you shall have meat to eat. For
in the hearing of the LORD you have
cried, 'Would that we had meat for food!
Oh, how well off we were in Egypt!'
Therefore the LORD will give you meat
for food, 19 and you will eat it, not for
one day, or two days, or five, or ten, or
twenty days, 20 but for a whole month—
until it comes out of your very nostrils
and becomes loathsome to you. For you
have spurned the LORD who is in your
midst, and in his presence you have
wailed, 'Why did we ever leave Egypt?' "
21 But Moses said, "The people around
me include six hundred thousand sol-
diers; yet you say, 'I will give them meat
to eat for a whole month.' 22 Can enough
sheep and cattle be slaughtered for
them? If all the fish of the sea were
caught for them, would they have
enough?" 23 The LORD answered Moses,
"Is this beyond the LORD's reach? You
shall see now whether or not what I have
promised you takes place."
The Spirit on the Elders. 24 So Moses
went out and told the people what the
LORD had said. Gathering seventy el-
ders of the people, he had them stand
around the tent. 25† The LORD then came
down in the cloud and spoke to him.
Taking some of the spirit that was on
Moses, he bestowed it on the seventy
elders; and as the spirit came to rest on
them, they prophesied.
26 Now two men, one named Eldad and
the other Medad, were not in the gather-
ing but had been left in the camp. They
too had been on the list, but had not gone
out to the tent; yet the spirit came to rest

*

35: Ps 68, 2.
11, 1: Dt 9, 22.
4: Ps 78, 18.
5f: 21,5; Ex 16, 3; Acts 7, 39.
7f: Ex 16, 14f.31; Ps 78, 24; Wis 16, 20; Jn 6, 31.
9: Ex 16, 14f.

†

11, 3: *Taberah* means "the burning."

11, 7: *Coriander seed:* see note on Ex 16, 31. *Bdellium:* a transparent, amber-colored gum resin, which is also mentioned in Gn 2, 12.

11, 25: *They prophesied:* in the sense, not of foretelling the future, but of speaking in enraptured enthusiasm. Such manifestations of mystic exaltation occurred in the early days of Hebrew prophecy (1 Sm 10, 10ff; 19, 20ff) and in the first years of the Church (Acts 2, 6-11.17; 19, 6; 1 Cor 12-14).

on them also, and they prophesied in the
camp. 27 So, when a young man quickly
told Moses, "Eldad and Medad are
prophesying in the camp," 28 Joshua,
son of Nun, who from his youth had been
Moses' aide, said, "Moses, my lord, stop
them." 29 But Moses answered him, "Are
you jealous for my sake? Would that all
the people of the LORD were prophets!
Would that the LORD might bestow his
spirit on them all!" 30 Then Moses retired
to the camp, along with the elders of Is-
rael.

The Quail. 31*† There arose a wind
sent by the LORD, that drove in quail
from the sea and brought them down
over the camp site at a height of two cu-
bits from the ground for the distance of
a day's journey all around the camp.
32*† All that day, all night, and all the
next day the people gathered in the
quail. Even the one who got the least
gathered ten homers of them. Then they
spread them out all around the camp.
33 But while the meat was still between
their teeth, before it could be consumed,
the LORD's wrath flared up against the
people, and he struck them with a very
great plague. 34† So that place was
named Kibroth-hattaavah, because it
was there that the greedy people were
buried.
35 From Kibroth-hattaavah the people
set out for Hazeroth.

CHAPTER 12

Jealousy of Aaron and Miriam.
1† While they were in Hazeroth, Miriam
and Aaron spoke against Moses on the
pretext of the marriage he had con-
tracted with a Cushite woman. 2† They
complained, "Is it through Moses alone
that the LORD speaks? Does he not speak
through us also?" And the LORD heard
this. 3* Now, Moses himself was by far
the meekest man on the face of the
earth. 4 So at once the LORD said to Mo-
ses and Aaron and Miriam, "Come out,
you three, to the meeting tent." And the
three of them went. 5 Then the LORD
came down in the column of cloud, and
standing at the entrance of the tent,
called Aaron and Miriam. When both
came forward, 6 he said, "Now listen to
the words of the LORD:

Should there be a prophet among
you,
in visions will I reveal myself to
him,
in dreams will I speak to him;
7* Not so with my servant Moses!
Throughout my house he bears my
trust:
8* face to face I speak to him,
plainly and not in riddles.
The presence of the LORD he be-
holds.
Why, then, did you not fear to speak
against my servant Moses?"

Miriam's Leprosy. 9 So angry was the
LORD against them that when he de-
parted, 10*† and the cloud withdrew
from the tent, there was Miriam, a snow-
white leper! When Aaron turned and
saw her a leper, 11 "Ah, my lord!" he said
to Moses, "please do not charge us with
the sin that we have foolishly commit-
ted! 12 Let her not thus be like the still-
born babe that comes forth from its
mother's womb with its flesh half con-
sumed." 13 Then Moses cried to the
LORD, "Please, not this! Pray, heal her!"
14 But the LORD answered Moses, "Sup-
pose her father had spit in her face,
would she not hide in shame for seven
days? Let her be confined outside the
camp for seven days; only then may she
be brought back." 15 So Miriam was con-
fined outside the camp for seven days,
and the people did not start out again
until she was brought back.
16 After that the people set out from
Hazeroth and encamped in the desert
of Paran.

CHAPTER 13

The Twelve Scouts. 1 The LORD said to
Moses, 2 "Send men to reconnoiter the
land of Canaan, which I am giving to
the Israelites. You shall send one man
from each ancestral tribe, all of them
princes." 3* So Moses dispatched them
from the desert of Paran, as the LORD
had ordered. All of them were leaders
among the Israelites; 4 by name they
were:

Shammua, son of Zaccur, of the
tribe of Reuben;

---

*

31: Ps 78, 26ff.
32f: Ps 78, 26-31; 1 Cor 10, 6-7.
12, 3: Sir 45, 1f.
7: Sir 45, 3; Heb 3, 2.5.
8: Ex 33, 11; Dt 34, 10.
10: Dt 24, 9.
13, 3-33: Dt 1, 22-28.

†

11, 31: *At a height of two cubits from the ground:* exhausted by the storm, the quail could take but short, low flights, so that they were easily captured. To give food to the hungry people, God may have used the natural phenomenon of the annual migration of quail across the Sinai Peninsula. In the spring large flocks of these birds cross the Gulf of Aqabah flying toward the west; in the fall they fly back eastward from the Mediterranean. *The sea* mentioned here probably refers to the former body of water.

11, 32: *They spread them out:* to cure by drying.

11, 34: *Kibroth-hattaavah* means "graves of greed."

12, 1: *Cushite woman:* apparently Zipporah, the Midianitess, is meant; cf Ex 2, 21. Perhaps the term is used here merely in the sense of "despised foreigner."

12, 2: The real reason for Miriam's quarrel with her brother Moses was her jealousy of his superior position; his *Cushite* wife served only as an occasion for the dispute. Aaron merely followed his sister in her rebellion; hence she alone was punished.

12, 10: *A snow-white leper:* afflicted with "white leprosy," a skin disease that generally is not serious or of long duration. Cf Lv 13, 3-6.

5 Shaphat, son of Hori, of the tribe of Simeon;
6 Caleb, son of Jephunneh, of the tribe of Judah;
7 Igal [son of Joseph], of the tribe of Issachar;
10 Gaddiel, son of Sodi, of the tribe of Zebulun;
11 Gaddi, son of Susi, of the tribe of Manasseh, for the Josephites, with
8 Hoshea, son of Nun, of the tribe of Ephraim;
9 Palti, son of Raphu, of the tribe of Benjamin;
12 Ammiel, son of Gemalli, of the tribe of Dan;
13 Sethur, son of Michael, of the tribe of Asher;
14 Nahbi, son of Vophsi, of the tribe of Naphtali;
15 Geuel, son of Machi, of the tribe of Gad.

16† These are the names of the men
whom Moses sent out to reconnoiter the
land. But Hoshea, son of Nun, Moses
called Joshua.
17 In sending them to reconnoiter the
land of Canaan, Moses said to them, "Go
up here in the Negeb, up into the high-
lands, 18 and see what kind of land it is.
Are the people living there strong or
weak, few or many? 19 Is the country in
which they live good or bad? Are the
towns in which they dwell open or forti-
fied? 20 Is the soil fertile or barren,
wooded or clear? And do your best to
get some of the fruit of the land." It was
then the season for early grapes.
21† So they went up and reconnoitered
the land from the desert of Zin as far
as where Rehob adjoins Labo of Ha-
math. 22*† Going up by way of the
Negeb, they reached Hebron, where
Ahiman, Sheshai and Talmai, descen-
dants of the Anakim, were living. [He-
bron had been built seven years before
Zoan in Egypt.] 23† They also reached
the Wadi Eshcol, where they cut down
a branch with a single cluster of grapes
on it, which two of them carried on a
pole, as well as some pomegranates and
figs. 24* It was because of the cluster the
Israelites cut there that they called the
place Wadi Eshcol.
Their Return. 25 After reconnoitering
the land for forty days they returned,
26* met Moses and Aaron and the whole
community of the Israelites in the desert
of Paran at Kadesh, made a report to
them all, and showed them the fruit of
the country. 27 They told Moses: "We
went into the land to which you sent us.
It does indeed flow with milk and honey,
and here is its fruit. 28* However, the
people who are living in the land are
fierce, and the towns are fortified and
very strong. Besides, we saw descen-
dants of the Anakim there. 29 Amalekites
live in the region of the Negeb; Hittites,
Jebusites and Amorites dwell in the
highlands, and Canaanites along the
seacoast and the banks of the Jordan."
30 Caleb, however, to quiet the people
toward Moses, said, "We ought to go up
and seize the land, for we can certainly
do so." 31 But the men who had gone
up with him said, "We cannot attack
these people; they are too strong for us."
32* So they spread discouraging reports
among the Israelites about the land they
had scouted, saying, "The land that we
explored is a country that consumes its
inhabitants. And all the people we saw
there are huge men, 33*† veritable giants
[the Anakim were a race of giants]; we
felt like mere grasshoppers, and so we
must have seemed to them."

CHAPTER 14

Threats of Revolt. 1 At this, the whole
community broke out with loud cries,
and even in the night the people wailed.
2* All the Israelites grumbled against
Moses and Aaron, the whole community
saying to them, "Would that we had died
in the land of Egypt, or that here in the
desert we were dead! 3 Why is the LORD
bringing us into this land only to have
us fall by the sword? Our wives and little
ones will be taken as booty. Would it not
be better for us to return to Egypt?" 4 So
they said to one another, "Let us appoint
a leader and go back to Egypt."
5 But Moses and Aaron fell prostrate
before the whole assembled community
of the Israelites; 6 while Joshua, son of
Nun, and Caleb, son of Jephunneh, who
had been in the party that scouted the
land, tore their garments 7* and said to
the whole community of the Israelites,
"The country which we went through

*

22: Jos 11, 21f.
24: 32, 9; Dt 1, 24f.
26f: Ex 3, 8.17.
28f: Dt 9, 1f.
32: 32, 9; Jos 14, 8.
33: Dt 2, 10.
14, 2: Ex 16, 3; Ps 106, 25.
7f: Dt 1, 25.

†

13, 16: *Joshua:* in Hebrew, "Jehoshua," which was later modified to "Jeshua," the Hebrew pronunciation of the name "Jesus." Hoshea and Joshua are variants of one original name meaning "the LORD saves." Cf Mt 1, 21.

13, 21: *The desert of Zin:* north of Paran and southwest of the Dead Sea. It is quite distinct from "the desert of Sin" near the border of Egypt (Ex 16, 1; 17, 1; Nm 33, 11). *Labo of Hamath:* a town near Riblah (Jer 39, 5f) at the southern border of *Hamath,* an independent kingdom in southern Syria. David's conquests extended as far as Hamath (2 Sm 8, 9ff), and Labo thus formed the northern border of the ideal extent of Israel's possessions (34, 7ff; Ez 47, 15; 48, 1). Some commentators think that this verse is a later addition to the text; cf Dt 1, 24.

13, 22.28: *Anakim:* an aboriginal race in southern Palestine, largely absorbed by the Canaanites before the Israelite invasion. Either because of their tall stature or because of the massive stone structures left by them the Israelites regarded them as giants.

13, 23: *Eshcol* means "cluster."

13, 33: *Giants:* in Hebrew, "nephilim." Cf Gn 6, 4.

and explored is a fine, rich land. 8 If the
LORD is pleased with us, he will bring
us in and give us that land, a land flow-
ing with milk and honey. 9*† But do not
rebel against the LORD! You need not be
afraid of the people of that land; they
are but food for us! Their defense has
left them, but the LORD is with us. There-
fore, do not be afraid of them." 10 In an-
swer, the whole community threatened
to stone them.

The Lord's Sentence. But then the
glory of the LORD appeared at the meet-
ing tent to all the Israelites. 11* And the
LORD said to Moses, "How long will this
people spurn me? How long will they re-
fuse to believe in me, despite all the signs
I have performed among them? 12* I will
strike them with pestilence and wipe
them out. Then I will make of you a na-
tion greater and mightier than they."
13* But Moses said to the LORD: "Are
the Egyptians to hear of this? For by
your power you brought out this people
from among them. 14* And are they to
tell of it to the inhabitants of this land?
It has been heard that you, O LORD, are
in the midst of this people; you, LORD,
who plainly reveal yourself! Your cloud
stands over them, and you go before
them by day in a column of cloud and
by night in a column of fire. 15 If now
you slay this whole people, the nations
who have heard such reports of you will
say, 16* 'The LORD was not able to bring
this people into the land he swore to give
them; that is why he slaughtered them
in the desert.' 17 Now then, let the power
of my Lord be displayed in its greatness,
18* even as you have said, 'The LORD is
slow to anger and rich in kindness, for-
giving wickedness and crime; yet not
declaring the guilty guiltless, but pun-
ishing children to the third and fourth
generation for their fathers' wicked-
ness.' 19* Pardon, then, the wickedness
of this people in keeping with your great
kindness, even as you have forgiven
them from Egypt until now."
20 The LORD answered: "I pardon them
as you have asked. 21 Yet, by my life and
the LORD's glory that fills the whole
earth, 22* of all the men who have seen
my glory and the signs I worked in
Egypt and in the desert, and who never-
theless have put me to the test ten times
already and have failed to heed my
voice, 23 not one shall see the land which
I promised on oath to their fathers. None
of these who have spurned me shall see
it. 24* But because my servant Caleb has
a different spirit and follows me unre-
servedly, I will bring him into the land
where he has just been, and his descen-
dants shall possess it. 25† But now, since
the Amalekites and Canaanites are liv-
ing in the valleys, turn away tomorrow
and set out in the desert on the Red Sea
road."
26 The LORD also said to Moses and
Aaron: 27* "How long will this wicked
community grumble against me? I have
heard the grumblings of the Israelites
against me. 28† Tell them: By my life,
says the LORD, I will do to you just what
I have heard you say. 29* Here in the
desert shall your dead bodies fall. Of all
your men of twenty years or more, reg-
istered in the census, who grumbled
against me, 30 not one shall enter the
land where I solemnly swore to settle
you, except Caleb, son of Jephunneh,
and Joshua, son of Nun. 31* Your little
ones, however, who you said would be
taken as booty, I will bring in, and they
shall appreciate the land you spurned.
32 But as for you, your bodies shall fall
here in the desert, 33* here where your
children must wander for forty years,
suffering for your faithlessness, till the
last of you lies dead in the desert.
34 Forty days you spent in scouting the
land; forty years shall you suffer for
your crimes: one year for each day.
Thus you will realize what it means to
oppose me. 35 I, the LORD, have sworn
to do this to all this wicked community
that conspired against me: here in the
desert they shall die to the last man."
36* And so it happened to the men
whom Moses had sent to reconnoiter the
land and who on returning had set the
whole community grumbling against
him by spreading discouraging reports
about the land; 37 these men who had
given out the bad report about the land
were struck down by the LORD and died.
38* Of all the men who had gone to recon-
noiter the land, only Joshua, son of
Nun, and Caleb, son of Jephunneh, sur-
vived.

Unsuccessful Invasion. 39 When Mo-
ses repeated these words to all the Isra-
elites, the people felt great remorse.

---

*

9: Dt 7, 18.
11: Ps 78, 22.32.
12: Ex 32, 10.
13-16: Ex 32, 12; Dt 9, 26ff; Ps 106, 23.
14: Ex 13, 21; Jos 2, 9f.
16: Ex 32, 12; Dt 9, 28.
18: Ex 20, 5; 34, 6f: Pss 103, 8; 145, 8.
19: Ps 78, 38.
22f: Dt 1, 35.
24: Jos 14, 8f.
27: Ex 16, 7.12.
29: Dt 1, 35; Heb 3, 17.
31: Dt 1, 39.
33f: 13, 26; 32, 13; Ps 95, 10; Ez 4, 6.
36f: 13, 17.32f; 1 Cor 10, 10.
38: 26, 65.

†

14, 9: *They are but food for us:* that is, "we can easily consume and destroy them." This is the answer to the pessimistic report that this land "consumes its inhabitants" (13, 32).

14, 25: *The valleys:* the low-lying plains in the Negeb and along the seacoast and in the Jordan depression, as well as the higher valleys in the mountains farther north: cf 14, 45.

14, 28f: God punished the malcontents by giving them their wish; cf v 2. Their lack of faith and of confidence in God is cited in 1 Cor 10, 10, and Heb 3, 12-18, as a warning for Christians.

40* Early the next morning they started
up into the foothills, saying, "Here we
are, ready to go up to the place that the
LORD spoke of: for we were indeed doing
wrong." 41 But Moses said, "Why are you
again disobeying the LORD's orders?
This cannot succeed. 42* Do not go up,
because the LORD is not in your midst;
if you go, you will be beaten down before
your enemies. 43 For there the Amalek-
ites and Canaanites face you, and you
will fall by the sword. You have turned
back from following the LORD; therefore
the LORD will not be with you."
44* Yet they dared to go up into the
foothills, even though neither the ark of
the covenant of the LORD nor Moses left
the camp. 45† And the Amalekites and
Canaanites who dwelt in that hill coun-
try came down and defeated them, beat-
ing them back as far as Hormah.

CHAPTER 15

Secondary Offerings. 1 The LORD said
to Moses, 2† "Give the Israelites these in-
structions: When you have entered the
land that I will give you for your home-
steads, 3 if you make to the LORD a
sweet-smelling oblation from the herd
or from the flock, in holocaust, in fulfill-
ment of a vow, or as a freewill offering,
or for one of your festivals, 4 whoever
does so shall also present to the LORD
a cereal offering consisting of a tenth of
an ephah of fine flour mixed with a
fourth of a hin of oil, 5 as well as a libation
of a fourth of a hin of wine, with each
lamb sacrificed in holocaust or other-
wise. 6 With each sacrifice of a ram you
shall present a cereal offering of two
tenths of an ephah of fine flour mixed
with a third of a hin of oil, 7 and a libation
of a third of a hin of wine, thus making
a sweet-smelling offering to the LORD.
8 When you sacrifice an ox as a holo-
caust, or in fulfillment of a vow, or as
a peace offering to the LORD, 9 with it
you shall present a cereal offering of
three tenths of an ephah of fine flour
mixed with half a hin of oil, 10 and a liba-
tion of half a hin of wine, as a sweet-
smelling oblation to the LORD. 11 The
same is to be done for each ox, ram,
lamb or goat. 12 Whatever the number
you offer, do the same for each of them.
13 "All the native-born shall make
these offerings in the same way, when-
ever they present a sweet-smelling obla-
tion to the LORD. 14 Likewise, in any
future generation, any alien residing
with you permanently or for a time, who
presents a sweet-smelling oblation to the
LORD, shall do as you do. 15 There is but
one rule for you and for the resident
alien, a perpetual rule for all your de-
scendants. Before the LORD you and the
alien are alike, 16 with the same law
and the same application of it for the
alien residing among you as for your-
selves."
17 The LORD said to Moses, 18 "Speak
to the Israelites and tell them: When you
enter the land into which I will bring you
19* and begin to eat of the food of that
land, you shall offer the LORD a contri-
bution 20† consisting of a cake of your
first batch of dough. You shall offer it
just as you offer a contribution from the
threshing floor. 21 Throughout your gen-
erations you shall give a contribution
to the LORD from your first batch of
dough.
Sin Offerings. 22*† "When through in-
advertence you fail to carry out any of
these commandments which the LORD
gives to Moses, 23 and through Moses to
you, from the time the LORD first issues
the commandment down through your
generations: 24 if the community itself
unwittingly becomes guilty of the fault
of inadvertence, the whole community
shall offer the holocaust of one young
bull as a sweet-smelling oblation pleas-
ing to the LORD, along with its prescribed
cereal offering and libation, as well as
one he-goat as a sin offering. 25* Then
the priest shall make atonement for the
whole Israelite community; thus they
will be forgiven the inadvertence for
which they have brought their holocaust
as an oblation to the LORD. 26 Not only
the whole Israelite community, but also
the aliens residing among you, shall be
forgiven, since the fault of inadvertence
affects all the people.
27* "However, if it is an individual who
sins inadvertently, he shall bring a year-
ling she-goat as a sin offering, 28 and the
priest shall make atonement before the
LORD for him who sinned inadvertently;
when atonement has been made for him,
he will be forgiven. 29 You shall have but
one law for him who sins inadvertently,
whether he be a native Israelite or an
alien residing with you.
30* "But anyone who sins defiantly,
whether he be a native or an alien, in-

*

40: 13, 18; Dt 1, 41.
42: Dt 1, 42.
44: Dt 1, 43.
15, 19-20: Ez 44, 30.
22f: Lv 4, 13f.
25: Lv 4, 20.
27f: Lv 4, 27f.
30: Dt 17, 12.

†

14, 45: *Hormah:* one of the Canaanite royal cities in southern Judea (Jos 12, 14), known at this time as "Zephath"; the origin of the later name is told in 21, 3; Jgs 1, 17.

15, 2-16: These laws on sacrifice are complementary to those of Lv 1-3. Since the food of the Israelites consisted not only of meat but also of bread, oil and wine, so, besides the animal oblations, they offered flour, wine and oil in sacrifice to the Lord.

15, 20: *Dough:* some render, "barley grits." This word is used elsewhere only in Ez 44, 30 and Neh 10, 33; a related Hebrew word is used in Lv 2, 14.

15, 22ff: Although no moral guilt is incurred by an inadvertent violation of God's commandments, the sanctity of the law can require some reparation even for such violations.

sults the LORD, and shall be cut off from among his people. 31* Since he has despised the word of the LORD and has broken his commandment, he must be cut off. He has only himself to blame."

The Sabbath-breaker. 32 While the Israelites were in the desert, a man was discovered gathering wood on the sabbath day. 33 Those who caught him at it brought him to Moses and Aaron and the whole assembly. 34*† But they kept him in custody, for there was no clear decision as to what should be done with him. 35 Then the LORD said to Moses, "This man shall be put to death; let the whole community stone him outside the camp." 36 So the whole community led him outside the camp and stoned him to death, as the LORD had commanded Moses.

Tassels on the Cloak. 37 The LORD said to Moses, 38*† "Speak to the Israelites and tell them that they and their descendants must put tassels on the corners of their garments, fastening each corner tassel with a violet cord. 39 When you use these tassels, let the sight of them remind you to keep all the commandments of the LORD, without going wantonly astray after the desires of your hearts and eyes. 40 Thus you will remember to keep all my commandments and be holy to your God. 41* I, the LORD, am your God who, as God, brought you out of Egypt that I, the LORD, may be your God."

CHAPTER 16

Rebellion of Korah. 1† Korah, son of Izhar, son of Kohath, son of Levi, [and Dathan and Abiram, sons of Eliab, son of Pallu, son of Reuben] took 2 two hundred and fifty Israelites who were leaders in the community, members of the council and men of note. They stood before Moses, 3* and held an assembly against Moses and Aaron, to whom they said, "Enough from you! The whole community, all of them, are holy; the LORD is in their midst. Why then should you set yourselves over the LORD's congregation?"

4 When Moses heard this, he fell prostrate. 5 Then he said to Korah and to all his band, "May the LORD make known tomorrow morning who belongs to him and who is the holy one and whom he will have draw near to him! Whom he chooses, he will have draw near him. 6 Do this: take your censers [Korah and all his band] 7 and put fire in them and place incense in them before the LORD tomorrow. He whom the LORD then chooses is the holy one. Enough from you Levites!"

8 Moses also said to Korah, "Listen to me, you Levites! 9* Is it too little for you that the God of Israel has singled you out from the community of Israel, to have you draw near him for the service of the LORD's Dwelling and to stand before the community to minister for them? 10 He has allowed you and your kinsmen, the descendants of Levi, to approach him, and yet you now seek the priesthood too. 11 It is therefore against the LORD that you and all your band are conspiring. For what has Aaron done that you should grumble against him?"

Rebellion of Dathan and Abiram. 12† Moses summoned Dathan and Abiram, sons of Eliab, but they answered, "We will not go. 13 Are you not satisfied with having led us here away from a land flowing with milk and honey, to make us perish in the desert, that you must now lord it over us? 14† Far from bringing us to a land flowing with milk and honey, or giving us fields and vineyards for our inheritance, will you also gouge out our eyes? No, we will not go."

15* Then Moses became very angry and said to the LORD, "Pay no heed to their offering. I have never taken a single ass from them, nor have I wronged any one of them."

Korah. 16 Moses said to Korah, "You and all your band shall appear before the LORD tomorrow—you and they and Aaron too. 17 Then each of your two hundred and fifty followers shall take his own censer, put incense in it, and offer it to the LORD; and you and Aaron, each with his own censer, shall do the same." 18 So they all took their censers, and laying incense on the fire they had put in them, they took their stand by the en-

---

*

31: Prv 13, 13.
34: Lv 24, 12.
38: Dt 22, 12.
41: Lv 22, 32f.
16, 3: Ps 106, 16ff; Sir 45, 19; 1 Cor 10, 10.
9: Dt 10, 8.
15: 1 Sm 12, 3.

---

†

15, 34: *No clear decision:* they already knew that a willful violation of the sabbath was a capital offense, but they did not yet know how the death penalty was to be inflicted.

15, 38: *Tassels:* at the time of Christ these tassels were worn by all pious Jews, including our Lord (Mt 9, 20f; Mk 6, 56); the Pharisees wore very large ones in ostentation of their zeal for the law (Mt 23, 5).

16, 1ff: The evidence seems to show that there were two distinct rebellions: one of Korah and his band (27, 3) and the other of Dathan and Abiram (Dt 11, 6); cf Ps 106. The present account combines both events into one narrative; but even here it is rather easy to separate the two, once certain proper names (vv 1.6.24.32.35) have been identified as glosses. The rebellion of the Reubenites, Dathan and Abiram, was of a political nature, against Moses alone as the civil leader; these rebels were punished by being swallowed alive in an earthquake. The rebellion of Korah was of a religious nature, against the religious leadership of both Moses and Aaron; about two hundred and fifty malcontents joined Korah's *band;* they were punished by fire. The parts of the present section which refer to the rebellion of Dathan and Abiram are vv 12-15 and vv 25-34 of chapter 16; the rest of chapter 16 and all of chapter 17 concern the rebellion of Korah.

16, 12: *We will not go:* to appear before Moses' tribunal.

16, 14: *Gouge out our eyes:* blind us to the real state of affairs.

trance of the meeting tent along with
Moses and Aaron. 19 Then, when Korah
had assembled all his band against them
at the entrance of the meeting tent, the
glory of the LORD appeared to the entire
community, 20 and the LORD said to Mo-
ses and Aaron, 21 "Stand apart from this
band, that I may consume them at
once." 22 But they fell prostrate and
cried out, "O God, God of the spirits of
all mankind, will one man's sin make
you angry with the whole community?"
23 The LORD answered Moses, 24 "Speak
to the community and tell them: With-
draw from the space around the Dwell-
ing" [of Korah, Dathan and Abiram].

Punishment of Dathan and Abiram.
25† Moses, followed by the elders of Is-
rael, arose and went to Dathan and Abi-
ram. 26 Then he warned the community,
"Keep away from the tents of these
wicked men and do not touch anything
that is theirs: otherwise you too will be
swept away because of all their sins."
27 When Dathan and Abiram had come
out and were standing at the entrances
of their tents with their wives and sons
and little ones, 28 Moses said, "This is
how you shall know that it was the LORD
who sent me to do all I have done, and
that it was not I who planned it: 29 if these
men die an ordinary death, merely suf-
fering the fate common to all mankind,
then it was not the LORD who sent me.
30 But if the LORD does something en-
tirely new, and the ground opens its
mouth and swallows them alive down
into the nether world, with all belonging
to them, then you will know that these
men have defied the LORD." 31* No
sooner had he finished saying all this
than the ground beneath them split
open, 32 and the earth opened its mouth
and swallowed them and their families
[and all of Korah's men] and all their
possessions. 33 They went down alive to
the nether world with all belonging to
them; the earth closed over them, and
they perished from the community.
34 But all the Israelites near them fled
at their shrieks, saying, "The earth
might swallow us too!"

Punishment of Korah. 35† So they
withdrew from the space around the
Dwelling [of Korah, Dathan and Abi-
ram]. And fire from the LORD came
forth which consumed the two hundred
and fifty men who were offering the in-
cense.

CHAPTER 17

1 The LORD said to Moses, 2 "Tell Elea-
zar, son of Aaron the priest, to remove
the censers from the embers; and scatter
the fire some distance away, 3† for these
sinners have consecrated the censers at
the cost of their lives. Have them ham-
mered into plates to cover the altar, be-
cause in being presented before the
LORD they have become sacred. In this
way they shall serve as a sign to the Isra-
elites." 4 So Eleazar the priest had the
bronze censers of those burned during
the offering hammered into a covering
for the altar, 5 in keeping with the orders
which the LORD had given him through
Moses. This cover was to be a reminder
to the Israelites that no layman, no one
who was not a descendant of Aaron,
should approach the altar to offer in-
cense before the LORD, lest he meet the
fate of Korah and his band.

6 The next day the whole Israelite
community grumbled against Moses
and Aaron, saying, "It is you who have
slain the LORD's people." 7 But while the
community was deliberating against
them, Moses and Aaron turned toward
the meeting tent, and the cloud now cov-
ered it and the glory of the LORD ap-
peared. 8 Then Moses and Aaron came
to the front of the meeting tent, 9 and
the LORD said to Moses and Aaron,
10 "Depart from this community, that I
may consume them at once." But they
fell prostrate.

11* Then Moses said to Aaron, "Take
your censer, put fire from the altar in
it, lay incense on it, and bring it quickly
to the community to make atonement
for them; for wrath has come forth from
the LORD and the blow is falling."
12 Obeying the orders of Moses, Aaron
took his censer and ran in among the
community, where the blow was already
falling on the people. Then, as he offered
the incense and made atonement for the
people, 13 standing there between the liv-
ing and the dead, the scourge was
checked. 14 Yet fourteen thousand seven
hundred died from the scourge, in addi-
tion to those who died because of Korah.
15 When the scourge had been checked,
Aaron returned to Moses at the entrance
of the meeting tent.

Aaron's Staff. 16 The LORD now said to
Moses, 17† "Speak to the Israelites and
get one staff from them for each ances-
tral house, twelve staffs in all, one from

NUMBERS

*

31ff: 26, 10; Lv 10, 2; Dt 11, 6; Ps 106, 17f.

17, 11: Wis 18, 20f.

†

16, 25: Since Dathan and Abiram had refused to go to Moses (vv 12ff), he, with the elders as witnesses, was obliged to go to their tent.

16, 35: This verse continues v 24; the first sentence is transposed from v 27.

17, 3: Whatever was brought into intimate contact with something sacred shared in its sacredness. See note on 19, 20.

17, 17: The staff was not merely an article of practical use, but also a symbol of authority; cf Gn 49, 10; Nm 24, 17; Jer 48, 17. Hence, the staff of a leader of a tribe was considered the emblem of his tribe; in fact, certain Hebrew words for "staff" also mean "tribe." Perhaps for this reason, to avoid confusion, the author here uses the term "ancestral house" instead of the ordinary word for "tribe."

each of their tribal princes. Mark each man's name on his staff; 18† and mark Aaron's name on Levi's staff, for the head of Levi's ancestral house shall also have a staff. 19 Then lay them down in the meeting tent, in front of the commandments, where I meet you. 20 There the staff of the man of my choice shall sprout. Thus will I suppress from my presence the Israelites' grumbling against you."

21 So Moses spoke to the Israelites, and their princes gave him staffs, twelve in all, one from each tribal prince; and Aaron's staff was with them. 22 Then Moses laid the staffs down before the LORD in the tent of the commandments. 23 The next day, when Moses entered the tent, Aaron's staff, representing the house of Levi, had sprouted and put forth not only shoots, but blossoms as well, and even bore ripe almonds! 24 Moses thereupon brought out all the staffs from the LORD's presence to the Israelites. After each prince identified his own staff and took it, 25 the LORD said to Moses, "Put back Aaron's staff in front of the commandments, to be kept there as a warning to the rebellious, so that their grumbling may cease before me; if it does not, they will die." 26 And Moses did as the LORD had commanded him.

Charge of the Sacred Things. 27† Then the Israelites cried out to Moses, "We are perishing; we are lost, we are all lost! 28 Every time anyone approaches the Dwelling of the LORD, he dies! Are we to perish to the last man?"

CHAPTER 18

1† The LORD said to Aaron, "You and your sons as well as the other members of your ancestral house shall be responsible for the sanctuary; but the responsibility of the priesthood shall rest on you and your sons alone. 2† Bring with you also your other kinsmen of the tribe of Levi, your ancestral tribe, as your associates and assistants, while you and your sons are in front of the tent of the commandments. 3 They shall look after your persons and the whole tent; however, they shall not come near the sacred vessels or the altar, lest both they and you die. 4† As your associates they shall have charge of all the work connected with the meeting tent. But no layman shall come near you. 5 You shall have charge of the sanctuary and of the altar, that wrath may not fall again upon the Israelites.

6* "Remember, it is I who have taken your kinsmen, the Levites, from the body of the Israelites; they are a gift to you, dedicated to the LORD for the service of the meeting tent. 7*† But only you and your sons are to have charge of performing the priestly functions in whatever concerns the altar and the room within the veil. I give you the priesthood as a gift. Any layman who draws near shall be put to death."

The Priests' Share of the Sacrifices. 8*† The LORD said to Aaron, "I myself have given you charge of the contributions made to me in the various sacred offerings of the Israelites; by perpetual ordinance I have assigned them to you and to your sons as your priestly share. 9 You shall have the right to share in the oblations that are most sacred, in whatever they offer me as cereal offerings or sin offerings or guilt offerings; these shares shall accrue to you and to your sons. 10 In eating them you shall treat them as most sacred; every male among you may partake of them. As sacred, they belong to you.

11*† "You shall also have what is removed from the gift in every wave offering of the Israelites; by perpetual ordinance I have assigned it to you and to your sons and daughters. All in your family who are clean may partake of it. 12* I have also assigned to you all the best of the new oil and of the new wine and grain that they give to the LORD as their first fruits; 13 and likewise, of whatever grows on their land, the first products that they bring in to the LORD shall be yours; all of your family who are clean may partake of them. 14† Whatever is doomed in Israel shall be yours. 15* Every living thing that

---

*

18, 6: 3, 9; 8, 19.
7: 3, 10.
8: 5, 9.
11: Ex 29, 27f; Lv 7, 34, 10, 14.
12f: Dt 18, 4; 26, 2.
15: Ex 13, 2.

---

†

17, 18: *Levi's staff:* it is not clear whether this is considered as one of the twelve mentioned in the preceding verse, or as a thirteenth staff. Sometimes Levi is reckoned as one of the twelve tribes (e.g., Dt 27, 12f), but more often the number twelve is arrived at by counting the two sub-tribes of Joseph, i.e., Ephraim and Manasseh, as distinct tribes. In this passage also it seems probable that the tribe of Levi is considered apart from the other twelve.

17, 27f: Logically these two verses belong immediately after 16, 35.

18, 1ff: This law, which kept unqualified persons from contact with sacred things, is the answer to the Israelites' cry in 17, 28. It is followed by other laws concerning priests and Levites.

18, 2: *Associates:* in Hebrew this word alludes to the popular etymology of the name "Levi." Cf Gn 29, 34.

18, 4: *Layman:* here, "one who is not a Levite"; in v 7, "one who is not a priest."

18, 7: *Veil:* the outer veil, or "curtain," is probably meant.

18, 8ff: Two classes of offerings are here distinguished: the *most sacred* offering, which only the male members of the priestly families could eat (vv 8ff), and the other offerings, which even the women of the priestly families could eat (vv 11-19).

18, 11: *Wave offering:* this included the breast and right leg (v 18), the shoulder of the peace offering (Lv 7, 30-34), and portions of the nazirite sacrifice (Nm 6, 19f).

18, 14: *Doomed:* in Hebrew, *herem,* which means here "set aside from profane use and made sacred to the Lord." Cf Lv 27, 21.28.

opens the womb, whether of man or of
beast, such as are to be offered to the
LORD, shall be yours; but you must let
the first-born of man, as well as of un-
clean animals, be redeemed. 16 The ran-
som for a boy is to be paid when he is
a month old; it is fixed at five silver shek-
els according to the sanctuary standard,
twenty gerahs to the shekel. 17 But the
first-born of cattle, sheep or goats shall
not be redeemed; they are sacred. Their
blood you must splash on the altar and
their fat you must burn as a sweet-
smelling oblation to the LORD. 18* Their
meat, however, shall be yours, just as
the breast and the right leg of the wave
offering belong to you. 19† By perpetual
ordinance I have assigned to you and
to your sons and daughters all the con-
tributions from the sacred gifts which
the Israelites make to the LORD; this is
an inviolable covenant to last forever be-
fore the LORD, for you and for your de-
scendants." 20*† Then the LORD said to
Aaron, "You shall not have any heritage
in the land of the Israelites nor hold any
portion among them; I will be your por-
tion and your heritage among them.

Tithes Due the Levites. 21* "To the
Levites, however, I hereby assign all
tithes in Israel as their heritage in rec-
ompense for the service they perform
in the meeting tent. 22 The Israelites may
no longer approach the meeting tent;
else they will incur guilt deserving
death. 23 Only the Levites are to perform
the service of the meeting tent, and they
alone shall be held responsible; this is
a perpetual ordinance for all your gen-
erations. The Levites, therefore, shall
not have any heritage among the Israel-
ites, 24 for I have assigned to them as
their heritage the tithes which the Isra-
elites give as a contribution to the LORD.
That is why I have ordered that they are
not to have any heritage among the Isra-
elites."

Tithes Paid by the Levites. 25 The
LORD said to Moses, 26 "Give the Levites
these instructions: When you receive
from the Israelites the tithes I have as-
signed you from them as your heritage,
you are to make a contribution from
them to the LORD, a tithe of the tithes;
27 and your contribution will be credited
to you as if it were grain from the thresh-
ing floor or new wine from the press.
28 Thus you too shall make a contribution
from all the tithes you receive from the
Israelites, handing over to Aaron the
priest the part to be contributed to the
LORD. 29 From all the gifts that you re-
ceive, and from the best parts, you are
to consecrate to the LORD your own full
contribution.

30 "Tell them also: Once you have
made your contribution from the best
part, the rest of the tithes will be credited
to you Levites as if it were produce of
the threshing floor or of the winepress.
31 Your families, as well as you, may eat
them anywhere, since they are your rec-
ompense for service at the meeting tent.
32 You will incur no guilt so long as you
make a contribution of the best part. Do
not profane the sacred gifts of the Israel-
ites and so bring death on yourselves."

CHAPTER 19

Ashes of the Red Heifer. 1 The LORD
said to Moses and Aaron: 2 "This is the
regulation which the law of the LORD
prescribes. Tell the Israelites to procure
for you a red heifer that is free from ev-
ery blemish and defect and on which no
yoke has ever been laid. 3† This is to be
given to Eleazar the priest, to be led out-
side the camp and slaughtered in his
presence. 4† Eleazar the priest shall take
some of its blood on his finger and sprin-
kle it seven times toward the front of the
meeting tent. 5 Then the heifer shall be
burned in his sight, with its hide and
flesh, its blood and offal; 6 and the priest
shall take some cedar wood, hyssop and
scarlet yarn and throw them into the fire
in which the heifer is being burned. 7 The
priest shall then wash his garments and
bathe his body in water. He remains un-
clean until the evening, and only after-
ward may he return to the camp.
8 Likewise, he who burned the heifer
shall wash his garments, bathe his body
in water, and be unclean until evening.
9 Finally, a man who is clean shall
gather up the ashes of the heifer and de-
posit them in a clean place outside the
camp. There they are to be kept for pre-
paring lustral water for the Israelite
community. The heifer is a sin offering.
10 He who has gathered up the ashes of
the heifer shall also wash his garments
and be unclean until evening. This is a
perpetual ordinance, both for the Israel-

*

18: Lv 7, 31-34.
20: Dt 10, 9; 18, 1f; Jos 13, 33; Ez 44, 28.
21: Heb 7, 5.

†

18, 19: *An inviolable covenant:* literally, "a convenant of salt." Cf 2 Chr 13, 5. The reference may perhaps be to the preservative power of salt (cf Mt 5, 13); but more likely the phrase refers to the custom of partaking of the same salt in common to render a contract unbreakable. See note on Lv 2, 13.

18, 20: The priests and Levites were forbidden to own hereditary land such as the other Israelites possessed; therefore in the allotment of the land they were not to receive any portion of it. Certain cities, however, were assigned to them for their residence; cf 35, 1-8.

19, 3: *Outside the camp:* several Fathers of the Church saw in this a prefiguring of the sacrificial death of Christ outside the walls of Jerusalem; cf Jn 19, 20; Heb 13, 12; in the purifying water, into which the ashes of the red heifer were put, they saw a type of the water of Baptism.

19, 4: *Toward the front of the meeting tent:* since the tabernacle faced the east (Ex 26, 15-30), the killing of the heifer took place east of the camp; in later times it was done on the Mount of Olives, east of the Temple.

ites and for the aliens residing among
them.
Use of the Ashes. 11 “Whoever touches
the dead body of any human being shall
be unclean for seven days; 12 he shall pu-
rify himself with the water on the third
and on the seventh day, and then he
will be clean again. But if he fails to pu-
rify himself on the third and on the sev-
enth day, he will not become clean.
13* Everyone who fails to purify himself
after touching the body of any deceased
person, defiles the Dwelling of the LORD
and shall be cut off from Israel. Since
the lustral water has not been splashed
over him, he remains unclean: his un-
cleanness still clings to him.
14 “This is the law: When a man dies
in a tent, everyone who enters the tent,
as well as everyone already in it, shall
be unclean for seven days; 15 likewise,
every vessel that is open, or with its
lid unfastened, shall be unclean.
16 Moreover, everyone who in the open
country touches a dead person, whether
he was slain by the sword or died natu-
rally, or who touches a human bone or
a grave, shall be unclean for seven days.
17† For anyone who is thus unclean,
ashes from the sin offering shall be put
in a vessel, and spring water shall be
poured on them. 18 Then a man who is
clean shall take some hyssop, dip it in
this water, and sprinkle it on the tent
and on all the vessels and persons that
were in it, or on him who touched a bone,
a slain person or other dead body, or a
grave. 19 The clean man shall sprinkle
the unclean on the third and on the sev-
enth day; thus purified on the seventh
day, he shall wash his garments and
bathe his body in water, and in the eve-
ning he will be clean again. 20† Any un-
clean man who fails to have himself
purified shall be cut off from the commu-
nity, because he defiles the sanctuary of
the LORD. As long as the lustral water
has not been splashed over him, he re-
mains unclean. 21 This shall be a perpet-
ual ordinance for you.
“One who sprinkles the lustral water
shall wash his garments, and anyone
who comes in contact with this wa-
ter shall be unclean until evening.
22 Moreover, whatever the unclean per-
son touches becomes unclean itself, and
anyone who touches it becomes unclean
until evening.”

CHAPTER 20

Death of Miriam. 1† The whole Israel-
ite community arrived in the desert of
Zin in the first month, and the people
settled at Kadesh. It was here that Mir-
iam died, and here that she was buried.
Water Famine at Kadesh. 2 As the
community had no water, they held a
council against Moses and Aaron. 3 The
people contended with Moses, exclaim-
ing, “Would that we too had perished
with our kinsmen in the LORD’s pres-
ence! 4 Why have you brought the
LORD’s community into this desert
where we and our livestock are dying?
5 Why did you lead us out of Egypt, only
to bring us to this wretched place which
has neither grain nor figs nor vines nor
pomegranates? Here there is not even
water to drink!” 6 But Moses and Aaron
went away from the assembly to the en-
trance of the meeting tent, where they
fell prostrate.
Sin of Moses and Aaron. Then the
glory of the LORD appeared to them,
7 and the LORD said to Moses, 8 “Take
the staff and assemble the community,
you and your brother Aaron, and in their
presence order the rock to yield its
waters. From the rock you shall bring
forth water for the community and their
livestock to drink.” 9 So Moses took the
staff from its place before the LORD, as
he was ordered. 10* He and Aaron as-
sembled the community in front of the
rock, where he said to them, “Listen to
me, you rebels! Are we to bring water
for you out of this rock?” 11*† Then, rais-
ing his hand, Moses struck the rock
twice with his staff, and water gushed
out in abundance for the community and
their livestock to drink. 12† But the LORD
said to Moses and Aaron, “Because you
were not faithful to me in showing forth
my sanctity before the Israelites, you
shall not lead this community into the
land I will give them.”
13* These are the waters of Meribah,
where the Israelites contended against
the LORD, and where he revealed his
sanctity among them.
Edom’s Refusal. 14† From Kadesh

---

*

19, 13: Lv 15, 31.
20, 10: Ex 17, 5f.
11: Ps 78, 15f; Wis 11, 4; 1 Cor 10, 4.
13: 27, 14; Ex 17, 7.

---

†

19, 17ff: “If . . . the sprinkling of a heifer’s ashes can sanctify those who are defiled so that their flesh is cleansed, how much more will the blood of Christ . . . cleanse our consciences from dead works to worship the living God” (Heb 9, 13f).

19, 20: Ritual uncleanness is, as it were, contagious, so also sacredness; see note on 17, 3.

20, 1: *The first month:* we would expect the mention also of the day and of the year (after the exodus) when this took place; cf similar dates in 1, 1; 10, 11; 33, 38; Dt 1, 3. Here the full date seems to have been lost. Probably the Israelites arrived in Kadesh in the third year after the exodus. Cf Dt 1, 46. *The desert of Zin:* a barren region with a few good oases, southwest of the Dead Sea. See note on 13, 21.

20, 11: *Twice:* perhaps because he had not sufficient faith to work the miracle with the first blow. Cf v 12.

20, 12f: The sin of Moses and Aaron consisted in doubting God’s mercy toward the ever-rebellious people. *In showing forth my sanctity:* God’s sacred power and glory: an allusion to the name of the place, *Kadesh,* which means “sanctified, sacred.” *Meribah* means “contention.” Cf Ex 17, 7.

20, 14: *Your brother Israel:* the Edomites were descended from Esau, the brother of Jacob. Their country, to the southeast of the Dead Sea, was also known as Seir; cf Gn 25, 24ff; 36, 1.8f.

Moses sent men to the king of Edom with
the message: "Your brother Israel has
this to say: You know of all the hardships
that have befallen us, [15] how our fathers
went down to Egypt, where we stayed
a long time, how the Egyptians mal-
treated us and our fathers, [16]* and how,
when we cried to the LORD, he heard our
cry and sent an angel who led us out
of Egypt. Now here we are at the town
of Kadesh at the edge of your territory.
[17]† Kindly let us pass through your coun-
try. We will not cross any fields or vine-
yards, nor drink any well water, but we
will go straight along the royal road
without turning to the right or to the left,
until we have passed through your terri-
tory."
[18] But Edom answered him, "You shall
not pass through here; if you do, I will
advance against you with the sword."
[19] The Israelites insisted, "We want only
to go up along the highway. If we or our
livestock drink any of your water, we
will pay for it. Surely there is no harm
in merely letting us march through."
[20]* But Edom still said, "No, you shall
not pass through," and advanced
against them with a large and heavily
armed force. [21]* Therefore, since Edom
refused to let them pass through their
territory, Israel detoured around them.
Death of Aaron. [22]† Setting out from
Kadesh, the whole Israelite community
came to Mount Hor. [23] There at Mount
Hor, on the border of the land of Edom,
the LORD said to Moses and Aaron,
[24] "Aaron is about to be taken to his peo-
ple; he shall not enter the land I am giv-
ing to the Israelites, because you both
rebelled against my commandment at
the waters of Meribah. [25]* Take Aaron
and his son Eleazar and bring them up
on Mount Hor. [26] Then strip Aaron of his
garments and put them on his son Elea-
zar; for there Aaron shall be taken in
death."
[27] Moses did as the LORD commanded.
When they had climbed Mount Hor in
view of the whole community, [28]* Moses
stripped Aaron of his garments and put
them on his son Eleazar. Then Aaron
died there on top of the mountain. When
Moses and Eleazar came down from the
mountain, [29] all the community under-
stood that Aaron had passed away; and
for thirty days the whole house of Israel
mourned him.

CHAPTER 21

Victory over Arad. [1]*† When the Ca-
naanite king of Arad, who lived in the
Negeb, heard that the Israelites were
coming along the way of Atharim, he en-
gaged them in battle and took some of
them captive. [2]* Israel then made this
vow to the LORD: "If you deliver this peo-
ple into my hand, I will doom their cit-
ies." [3]*† Later, when the LORD heeded
Israel's prayer and delivered up the Ca-
naanites, they doomed them and their
cities. Hence that place was named Hor-
mah.
The Bronze Serpent. [4] From Mount
Hor they set out on the Red Sea road,
to by-pass the land of Edom. But with
their patience worn out by the journey,
[5]*† the people complained against God
and Moses, "Why have you brought us
up from Egypt to die in this desert,
where there is no food or water? We are
disgusted with this wretched food!"
[6]*† In punishment the LORD sent
among the people saraph serpents,
which bit the people so that many of
them died. [7] Then the people came to
Moses and said, "We have sinned in
complaining against the LORD and you.
Pray the LORD to take the serpents from
us." So Moses prayed for the people,
[8]† and the LORD said to Moses, "Make
a saraph and mount it on a pole, and if
anyone who has been bitten looks at it,
he will recover." [9]*† Moses accordingly
made a bronze serpent and mounted it
on a pole, and whenever anyone who
had been bitten by a serpent looked at
the bronze serpent, he recovered.
Journey around Moab. [10]* The Israel-
ites moved on and encamped in Oboth.

*

16: Ex 2, 23.
20: Jgs 11, 17.
21f: 33, 37.
25f: Dt 32, 50.
28: 33, 38.
21, 1: 33, 40.
2: Jos 6, 17; Jgs 1, 17.
3: 14, 45.
5: 11, 6; Ex 16, 3.
6: Dt 8, 15; Wis 16, 5; 1 Cor 10, 9.
9: Wis 16, 6f.10; Jn 3, 14f.
10: 33, 43f.

†

20, 17: *The royal road:* an important highway, running north and south along the plateau east of the Dead Sea. In ancient times it was much used by caravans and armies; later it was improved by the Romans, and large stretches of it are still clearly recognizable.

20, 22: *Mount Hor:* not definitively identified, but probably to be sought in the vicinity of Kadesh. According to Dt 10, 6, Aaron died at Moserah (cf "Moseroth" in Nm 33, 30f), which is apparently the name of the region in which Mount Hor is situated.

21, 1-3: The account of this episode seems to be a later insertion here, for 21, 4, belongs logically immediately after 20, 29. Perhaps this is the same event as that mentioned in Jgs 1, 16f.

21, 3: *Hormah:* related to the Hebrew word *herem,* meaning "doomed." See notes on 14, 45; 18, 14.

21, 5: *This wretched food:* apparently the manna is meant.

21, 6: *Saraph:* the Hebrew name for a certain species of venomous snakes; the word probably signifies "the fiery one," these snakes being so called from the burning effect of their poisonous bite.

21, 8: *If anyone who has been bitten looks at it, he will recover:* "and as Moses lifted up the serpent in the desert, even so must the Son of Man be lifted up, that those who believe in him may not perish, but may have life everlasting" (Jn 3, 14f).

21, 9: King Hezekiah, in his efforts to abolish idolatry, "smashed the bronze serpent which Moses had made" (2 Kgs 18, 4).

21, 11: *Iye-abarim* probably means "the ruins in the Abarim (Mountains)." See note on 27, 12.

11† Setting out from Oboth, they en-
camped in Iye-abarim in the desert
fronting Moab on the east. 12 Setting out
from there, they encamped in the Wadi
Zered. 13 Setting out from there, they en-
camped on the other side of the Arnon,
in the desert that extends from the terri-
tory of the Amorites; for the Arnon
forms Moab's boundary with the Amo-
rites. 14† Hence it is said in the "Book
of the Wars of the LORD":

"Waheb in Suphah and the wadies,
15 Arnon and the wadi gorges
That reach back toward the site of
Ar
and slant to the border of Moab."

16† From there they went to Beer,
where there was the well of which the
LORD said to Moses, "Bring the people
together, and I will give them water."
17 Then it was that Israel sang this song:

"Spring up, O well!—so sing to it—
18 The well that the princes sank,
that the nobles of the people dug,
with their scepters and their
staffs."

From Beer they went to Mattanah,
19 from Mattanah to Nahaliel, from Na-
haliel to Bamoth, 20† from Bamoth to the
cleft in the plateau of Moab at the head-
land of Pisgah that overlooks Jeshi-
mon.

Victory over Sihon. 21 Now Israel sent
men to Sihon, king of the Amorites, with
the message, 22 "Let us pass through
your country. We will not turn aside into
any field or vineyard, nor will we drink
any well water, but we will go straight
along the royal road until we have
passed through your territory." 23* Si-
hon, however, would not let Israel pass
through his territory, but mustered all
his forces and advanced into the desert
against Israel. When he reached Jahaz,
he engaged Israel in battle. 24 But Israel
defeated him at the point of the sword,
and took possession of his land from the
Arnon to the Jabbok and as far as the
country of the Ammonites, whose
boundary was at Jazer. 25* Israel seized
all the towns here and settled in these
towns of the Amorites, in Heshbon and
all its dependencies. 26 Now Heshbon
was the capital of Sihon, king of the Am-
orites, who had fought against the for-
mer king of Moab and had seized all his
land from Jazer to the Arnon. 27 That is
why the poets say:

"Come to Heshbon, let it be rebuilt,
let Sihon's capital be firmly con-
structed.
28 For fire went forth from Heshbon
and a blaze from the city of Sihon;
It consumed the cities of Moab
and swallowed up the high places
of the Arnon.
29† Woe to you, O Moab!
You are ruined, O people of Che-
mosh!
He let his sons become fugitives
and his daughters be taken cap-
tive
by the Amorite king Sihon.
30 Their plowland is ruined from Hesh-
bon to Dibon;
Ar is laid waste; fires blaze as far
as Medeba."

31 When Israel had settled in the land
of the Amorites, 32 Moses sent spies to
Jazer; Israel then captured it with its de-
pendencies and dispossessed the Amo-
rites who were there.

Victory over Og. 33* Then they turned
and went up along the road to Bashan.
But Og, king of Bashan, advanced
against them with all his people to give
battle at Edrei. 34* The LORD, however,
said to Moses, "Do not be afraid of him;
for into your hand I will deliver him with
all his people and his land. Do to him
as you did to Sihon, king of the Amorites,
who lived in Heshbon." 35 So they struck
him down with his sons and all his peo-
ple, until not a survivor was left to him,
and they took possession of his land.

CHAPTER 22

1† Then the Israelites moved on and
encamped in the plains of Moab on the
other side of the Jericho stretch of the
Jordan.

III: ON THE PLAINS OF MOAB

Balaam Summoned. 2 Now Balak, son
of Zippor, saw all that Israel did to the
Amorites. 3 Indeed, Moab feared the Is-
raelites greatly because of their num-
bers, and detested them. 4 So Moab said

*

23: Dt 2, 32; Jgs 11, 20.
25f: Jos 21, 39; Jgs 11, 26.
33: Dt 3, 1ff.
34: Ps 136, 17ff.

†

21, 14: *The "Book of the Wars of the LORD":* an ancient collection of Israelite songs, now lost. *Waheb in Suphah:* since neither place is mentioned elsewhere, it is quite uncertain whether these dubious Hebrew words are even to be considered as place names; some Hebrew words apparently lost must have preceded this phrase.

21, 16: *Beer* means a well.

21, 20: *Jeshimon:* "the wasteland"; in 1 Sm 23, 19.24, and 26, 1.3, this is the desert of Judah, on the western side of the Dead Sea, but here and in Nm 23, 28, it seems to refer to the southern end of the Jordan valley where Beth-jeshimoth was situated.

21, 29: *Chemosh:* the chief god of the Moabites, and mentioned as such in the famous inscription of Mesha, king of Moab, who was the contemporary of the dynasty of Omri in Israel. Cf 1 Kgs 11, 7.33; 2 Kgs 23, 13; Jer 48, 7.13.

22,1: *The plains of Moab:* the lowlands to the northeast of the Dead Sea, between the Jordan and the foothills below Mount Nebo. Here the Israelites remained until they crossed the Jordan, as told in Jos 1-4. Jericho lay to the west of the Jordan.

to the elders of Midian, "Soon this horde
will devour all the country around us as
an ox devours the grass of the field."
And Balak, Zippor's son, who was king
of Moab at that time, 5 sent messengers
to Balaam, son of Beor, at Pethor on the
Euphrates, in the land of the Amawites,
summoning him with these words, "A
people has come here from Egypt who
now cover the face of the earth and are
settling down opposite us! 6† Please
come and curse this people for us; they
are stronger than we are. We may then
be able to defeat them and drive them
out of the country. For I know that who-
ever you bless is blessed and whoever
you curse is cursed." 7 Then the elders
of Moab and of Midian left with the divi-
nation fee in hand and went to Balaam.
When they had given him Balak's mes-
sage, 8 he said to them in reply, "Stay
here overnight, and I will give you what-
ever answer the LORD gives me." So the
princes of Moab lodged with Balaam.
9 Then God came to Balaam and said,
"Who are these men visiting you?"
10 Balaam answered God, "Balak, son of
Zippor, king of Moab, sent me the mes-
sage: 11 'This people that came here from
Egypt now cover the face of the earth.
Please come and lay a curse on them
for us; we may then be able to give them
battle and drive them out.' " 12 But God
said to Balaam, "Do not go with them
and do not curse this people, for they
are blessed." 13 The next morning Ba-
laam arose and told the princes of Balak,
"Go back to your own country, for the
LORD has refused to let me go with you."
14 So the princes of Moab went back to
Balak with the report, "Balaam refused
to come with us."

Second Appeal to Balaam. 15 Balak
again sent princes, who were more nu-
merous and more distinguished than the
others. 16 On coming to Balaam they told
him, "This is what Balak, son of Zippor,
has to say: Please do not refuse to come
to me. 17 I will reward you very hand-
somely and will do anything you ask of
me. Please come and lay a curse on this
people for me." 18* But Balaam replied
to Balak's officials, "Even if Balak gave
me his house full of silver and gold, I
could not do anything, small or great,
contrary to the command of the LORD,
my God. 19 But, you too shall stay here
overnight, till I learn what else the LORD
may tell me."
20 That night God came to Balaam and
said to him, "If these men have come
to summon you, you may go with them;
yet only on the condition that you do ex-
actly as I tell you." 21 So the next morn-
ing when Balaam arose, he saddled his
ass, and went off with the princes of
Moab.

The Talking Ass. 22† But now the an-
ger of God flared up at him for going,
and the angel of the LORD stationed him-
self on the road to hinder him as he was
riding along on his ass, accompanied by
two of his servants. 23 When the ass saw
the angel of the LORD standing on the
road with sword drawn, she turned off
the road and went into the field, and Ba-
laam had to beat her to bring her back
on the road. 24 Then the angel of the
LORD took his stand in a narrow lane
between vineyards with a stone wall on
each side. 25 When the ass saw the angel
of the LORD there, she shrank against
the wall; and since she squeezed Ba-
laam's leg against it, he beat her again.
26 The angel of the LORD then went
ahead, and stopped next in a passage
so narrow that there was no room to
move either to the right or to the left.
27 When the ass saw the angel of the
LORD there, she cowered under Balaam.
So, in anger, he again beat the ass with
his stick.
28* But now the LORD opened the
mouth of the ass, and she asked Balaam,
"What have I done to you that you
should beat me these three times?"
29 "You have acted so willfully against
me," said Balaam to the ass, "that if I
but had a sword at hand, I would kill
you here and now." 30 But the ass said
to Balaam, "Am I not your own beast,
and have you not always ridden upon
me until now? Have I been in the habit
of treating you this way before?" "No,"
replied Balaam.
31 Then the LORD removed the veil
from Balaam's eyes, so that he too saw
the angel of the LORD standing on the
road with sword drawn; and he fell on
his knees and bowed to the ground.
32 But the angel of the LORD said to him,
"Why have you beaten your ass these
three times? It is I who have come
armed to hinder you because this rash
journey of yours is directly opposed to
me. 33 When the ass saw me, she turned
away from me these three times. If she
had not turned away from me, I would
have killed you; her I would have
spared." 34 Then Balaam said to the an-
gel of the LORD, "I have sinned. Yet I
did not know that you stood against me
to oppose my journey. Since it has dis-

*

22, 18: 24, 13. 28: 2 Pt 2, 16.

†

22, 6: *Curse this people for us:* Balak believed that if Balaam forecast an evil omen for Israel, this evil would come to pass, as if by magic. Balaam was a soothsayer or foreteller; cf Jos 13, 22.

22, 22: *The anger of God flared up:* not merely because Balaam was going to Balak, for he had God's permission for the journey (v 20), but perhaps because he was tempted by avarice to curse Israel against God's command. "Abandoning the straight road, they have gone astray, following the road of Balaam, the son of Bosor, who loved payment for wrongdoing" (2 Pt 2, 15); and "abandoned themselves to Balaam's error for the sake of gain" (Jude 11). Cf v 32 and compare Ex 4, 18-26.

pleased you, I will go back home." 35 But
the angel of the LORD said to Balaam,
"Go with the men; but you may say only
what I tell you." So Balaam went on with
the princes of Balak.
36 When Balak heard that Balaam was
coming, he went out to meet him at the
boundary city Ir-Moab on the Arnon at
the end of the Moabite territory. 37 And
he said to Balaam, "I sent an urgent
summons to you! Why did you not come
to me? Did you think I could not reward
you?" 38 Balaam answered him, "Well,
I have come to you after all. But what
power have I to say anything? I can
speak only what God puts in my mouth."
39 Then Balaam went with Balak, and
they came to Kiriath-huzoth. 40 Here Ba-
lak slaughtered oxen and sheep, and
sent portions to Balaam and to the
princes who were with him.
The First Oracle. 41 The next morning
Balak took Balaam up on Bamoth-baal,
and from there he saw some of the
clans.

CHAPTER 23

1 Then Balaam said to Balak, "Build
me seven altars, and prepare seven bull-
ocks and seven rams for me here." 2 So
he did as Balaam had ordered, offering
a bullock and a ram on each altar. And
Balak said to him, "I have erected the
seven altars, and have offered a bullock
and a ram on each." 3 Balaam then said
to him, "Stand here by your holocaust
while I go over there. Perhaps the LORD
will meet me, and then I will tell you
whatever he lets me see." He went out
on the barren height, 4 and God met him.
5 When he had put an utterance in Ba-
laam's mouth, the LORD said to him, "Go
back to Balak, and speak accordingly."
6 So he went back to Balak, who was still
standing by his holocaust together with
all the princes of Moab. 7*† Then Ba-
laam gave voice to his oracle:

From Aram has Balak brought me here,
Moab's king, from the Eastern Mountains:
"Come and lay a curse for me on Jacob,
come and denounce Israel."

8 How can I curse whom God has not cursed?
How denounce whom the LORD has not denounced?

9† For from the top of the crags I see him,
from the heights I behold him.
Here is a people that lives apart
and does not reckon itself among the nations.

10† Who has ever counted the dust of Jacob,
or numbered Israel's wind-borne particles?
May I die the death of the just,
may my descendants be as many as theirs!

11 "What have you done to me?" cried
Balak to Balaam. "It was to curse my
foes that I brought you here; instead, you
have even blessed them." 12 Balaam re-
plied, "Is it not what the LORD puts in
my mouth that I must repeat with care?"
The Second Oracle. 13† Then Balak
said to him, "Please come with me to
another place from which you can see
only some and not all of them, and from
there curse them for me." 14 So he
brought him to the lookout field on the
top of Pisgah, where he built seven altars
and offered a bullock and a ram on each
of them. 15 Balaam then said to Balak,
"Stand here by your holocaust, while I
seek a meeting over there." 16 Then the
LORD met Balaam, and having put an
utterance in his mouth, he said to him,
"Go back to Balak, and speak accord-
ingly." 17 So he went back to Balak, who
was still standing by his holocaust to-
gether with the princes of Moab. When
Balak asked him, "What did the LORD
say?" 18 Balaam gave voice to his oracle:

Be aroused, O Balak, and hearken;
give ear to my testimony, O son of Zippor!

19 God is not man that he should speak falsely,
nor human, that he should change his mind.
Is he one to speak and not act,
to decree and not fulfill?

20 It is a blessing I have been given to pronounce;
a blessing which I cannot restrain.

21† Misfortune is not observed in Jacob,
nor misery seen in Israel.
The LORD, his God, is with him;
with him is the triumph of his King.

22*† It is God who brought him out of Egypt,
a wild bull of towering might.

---

* 23, 7: 22, 6. 22: 24, 8.

---

†

23, 7: *Aram:* the ancient name of the region later known as Syria. *The Eastern Mountains:* the low ranges in the Syrian desert near the Euphrates and Balaam's town of Pethor; cf 22, 5.

23, 9: *A people that lives apart:* Israel, as the chosen people of God, occupied a unique place among the nations, from which they kept themselves aloof.

23, 10: *The dust of Jacob . . . Israel's wind-borne particles:* the Israelites will be as numerous as dust in a desert sandstorm. *May I . . . as many as theirs:* a formula by which Balaam swears he is speaking the truth; he sees the reward of virtue in having numerous descendants.

23, 13: *To another place:* Balak thought that if Balaam would view Israel from a different site, he could forecast a different kind of omen.

23, 21: *Misfortune . . . misery:* Balaam admits that he is unable to predict any evils for Israel.

23, 22: *A wild bull of towering might:* the reference is to Israel, rather than to God.

23 No, there is no sorcery against Jacob,
nor omen against Israel.
It shall yet be said of Jacob,
and of Israel, "Behold what God has wrought!"
24* Here is a people that springs up like a lioness,
and stalks forth like a lion;
It rests not till it has devoured its prey
and has drunk the blood of the slain.

25 "Even though you cannot curse
them," said Balak to Balaam, "at least
do not bless them." 26 But Balaam an-
swered Balak, "Did I not warn you that
I must do all that the LORD tells me?"
The Third Oracle. 27 Then Balak said
to Balaam, "Come, let me bring you to
another place; perhaps God will approve
of your cursing them for me from
there." 28 So he took Balaam to the top
of Peor, that overlooks Jeshimon.
29 Balaam then said to him, "Here build
me seven altars; and here prepare for
me seven bullocks and seven rams."
30 And Balak did as Balaam had or-
dered, offering a bullock and a ram on
each altar.

CHAPTER 24

1 Balaam, however, perceiving that
the LORD was pleased to bless Israel, did
not go aside as before to seek omens,
but turned his gaze toward the desert.
2 When he raised his eyes and saw Israel
encamped, tribe by tribe, the spirit of
God came upon him, 3 and he gave voice
to his oracle:

The utterance of Balaam, son of Beor,
the utterance of the man whose eye is true,
4 The utterance of one who hears what God says,
and knows what the Most High knows,
Of one who sees what the Almighty sees,
enraptured, and with eyes unveiled:
5 How goodly are your tents, O Jacob;
your encampments, O Israel!
6 They are like gardens beside a stream,
like the cedars planted by the LORD.
7 His wells shall yield free-flowing waters,
he shall have the sea within reach;
His king shall rise higher than. . . .
and his royalty shall be exalted.
8* It is God who brought him out of Egypt,
a wild bull of towering might.
He shall devour the nations like grass,
their bones he shall strip bare.
9* He lies crouching like a lion,
or like a lioness; who shall arouse him?
Blessed is he who blesses you,
and cursed is he who curses you!

10*† Balak beat his palms together in
a blaze of anger at Balaam and said to
him, "It was to curse my foes that I sum-
moned you here; yet three times now
you have even blessed them instead!
11 Be off at once, then, to your home. I
promised to reward you richly, but the
LORD has withheld the reward from
you!" 12 Balaam replied to Balak, "Did
I not warn the very messengers whom
you sent to me, 13* 'Even if Balak gave
me his house full of silver and gold, I
could not of my own accord to anything,
good or evil, contrary to the command
of the LORD'? Whatever the LORD says
I must repeat.
The Fourth Oracle. 14 "But now that
I am about to go to my own people, let
me first warn you what this people will
do to your people in the days to come."
15 Then Balaam gave voice to his oracle:

The utterance of Balaam, son of Beor,
the utterance of the man whose eye is true,
16 The utterance of one who hears what God says,
and knows what the Most High knows,
Of one who sees what the Almighty sees,
enraptured and with eyes unveiled.
17*† I see him, though not now;
I behold him, though not near:
A star shall advance from Jacob,
and a staff shall rise from Israel,
That shall smite the brows of Moab,
and the skulls of all the Shuthites,
18 Till Edom is dispossessed,
and no fugitive is left in Seir.
Israel shall do valiantly,
19 and Jacob shall overcome his foes.

NUMBERS

*

24: 24, 9; Gn 49.9.
24, 8: 23, 22.
9: 23, 24; Gn 12, 3; 27, 29; 49, 9.
10: 23, 11.
13: 22, 18.
17: 2 Sm 8, 2.

†

24, 10: *Balak beat his palms:* a sign of disclaiming any responsibility for paying the promised reward.

24, 17: *A star. . . a staff:* many of the Fathers have understood this as a Messianic prophecy, although it is not referred to anywhere in the New Testament; in this sense the *star* is Christ himself, just as he is the *staff from Israel;* cf Is 11, 1. But it is doubtful whether this passage is to be connected with the "star of the Magi" in Mt 2, 1-12. *The Shuthites:* mentioned in other documents of this period as nomads on the borders of Palestine.

20*† Upon seeing Amalek, Balaam gave
voice to his oracle:

First of the peoples was Amalek,
but his end is to perish forever.

21† Upon seeing the Kenites, he gave
voice to his oracle:

Your abode is enduring, O smith,
and your nest is set on a cliff;
22 Yet destined for burning—
even as I watch—are your inhabitants.

23† Upon seeing. . . . he gave voice to his
oracle:

Alas, who shall survive of Ishmael,
24 to deliver his people from the
hands of the Kittim?
When they have conquered Asshur
and conquered Eber,
He too shall perish forever.

25 Then Balaam set out on his journey
home; and Balak also went his way.

CHAPTER 25

Worship of Baal of Peor. 1*† While Is-
rael was living at Shittim, the people de-
graded themselves by having illicit
relations with the Moabite women.
2* These then invited the people to the
sacrifices of their god, and the people
ate of the sacrifices and worshiped their
god. 3* When Israel thus submitted to
the rites of Baal of Peor, the LORD's an-
ger flared up against Israel, 4*† and he
said to Moses, "Gather all the leaders
of the people, and hold a public execu-
tion of the guilty ones before the LORD,
that his blazing wrath may be turned
away from Israel." 5 So Moses told the
Israelite judges, "Each of you shall kill
those of his men who have submitted to
the rites of Baal of Peor."

Zeal of Phinehas. 6† Yet a certain Is-
raelite came and brought in a Midianite
woman to his clansmen in the view of
Moses and of the whole Israelite com-
munity, while they were weeping at the
entrance of the meeting tent. 7* When
Phinehas, son of Eleazar, son of Aaron
the priest, saw this, he left the assembly,
and taking a lance in hand, 8 followed
the Israelite into his retreat where he
pierced the pair of them, the Israelite
and the woman. Thus the slaughter of
Israelites was checked; 9 but only after
twenty-four thousand had died.

10 Then the LORD said to Moses,
11† "Phinehas, son of Eleazar, son of
Aaron the priest, has turned my anger
from the Israelites by his zeal for my
honor among them; that is why I did not
put an end to the Israelites for the of-
fense to my honor. 12* Announce, there-
fore, that I hereby give him my pledge
of friendship, 13 which shall be for him
and for his descendants after him the
pledge of an everlasting priesthood, be-
cause he was zealous on behalf of his
God and thus made amends for the Isra-
elites."

14† The Israelite slain with the Midian-
ite woman was Zimri, son of Salu, prince
of an ancestral house of the Simeonites.
15 The slain Midianite woman was Cozbi,
daughter of Zur, who was head of a clan,
an ancestral house, in Midian.

Vengeance on the Midianites. 16† The
LORD then said to Moses, 17* "Treat the
Midianites as enemies and crush them,
18 for they have been your enemies by
their wily dealings with you as regards
Peor and as regards their kinswoman
Cozbi, the daughter of a Midianite
prince, who was killed at the time of the
slaughter because of Peor."

CHAPTER 26

The Second Census. 19† After the
slaughter 1 the LORD said to Moses and
Eleazar, son of Aaron the priest,
2* "Take a census, by ancestral houses,
throughout the community of the Israel-

*

20: Ex 17, 14; 1 Sm 15, 3.
25, 1: 31, 16.
2: Ex 34, 15f.
3: Ps 106, 28; Hos 9, 10.
4: Dt 4, 3.
7: Ps 106, 30.
12f: Sir 45, 23f; Ps 106, 31; 1 Mc 2, 26.54.
17f: 31, 2-12.
26, 2: 1, 2f.

†

24, 20: *First:* literally "the beginning." Amalek was an aboriginal people in Palestine and therefore considered as of great antiquity. There is a deliberate contrast here between the words *first* and *end.*

24, 21: *The Kenites* lived in high strongholds in the mountains of southern Palestine and the Sinai Peninsula, and were skilled in working the various metals found in their territory. Their name is connected, at least by popular etymology, with the Hebrew word for "smith"; of similar sound is the Hebrew word for "nest"—hence the play on words in the present passage.

24, 23f: The translation of this short oracle is based on a reconstructed text and is rather uncertain. *Ishmael:* the survival of Ishmael is indicated in Gn 17, 20; 21, 13.18.

25, 1: *Shittim:* the full name was Abel-shittim, a locality at the foot of the mountains in the northeastern corner of *the plains of Moab* (33, 49). *Illicit relations:* perhaps as part of the licentious worship of Baal of Peor.

25, 4: Hold a public execution: the same phrase occurs in 2 Sm 21, 6-14, where the context shows that at least a part of the penalty consisted in being denied honorable burial. In both passages, dismemberment as a punishment for the breaking of covenant pledges is a current understanding of the phrase.

25, 6: *Midianite woman:* at this time the Midianites were leagued with the Moabites in opposing Israel; cf 22, 4.7. Balaam had induced both the Midianites (31, 16) and the Moabites (Ap 2, 14) to lure the Israelites to the obscene rites of Baal of Peor. *They were weeping:* on account of the plague that had struck them; cf v 8.

25, 11: *For my honor:* by taking vengeance on those who had made Baal of Peor a rival of the Lord.

25, 14f: The nobility of the slain couple is mentioned in order to stress the courage of Phinehas in punishing them. The zeal of Phinehas became proverbial; cf Ps 106, 30; Sir 45, 23; 1 Mc 2, 26.54.

25, 16ff: The account of the execution of this command is given in Nm 31, 1-18.

ites of all those of twenty years or more
who are fit for military service in Israel."
3 So on the plains of Moab along the Jeri-
cho stretch of the Jordan, Moses and the
priest Eleazar registered 4 those of
twenty years or more, as the LORD had
commanded Moses.

The Israelites who came out of the
land of Egypt were as follows:

5* Of Reuben, the first-born of Israel,
the Reubenites by clans were: through
Hanoch the clan of the Hanochites,
through Pallu the clan of the Palluites,
6 through Hezron the clan of the Hezron-
ites, through Carmi the clan of the Car-
mites. 7 These were the clans of the
Reubenites, of whom forty-three thou-
sand seven hundred and thirty men
were registered.

8 From Pallu descended Eliab, 9* and
the descendants of Eliab were Dathan
and Abiram—the same Dathan and Abi-
ram, councilors of the community, who
revolted against Moses and Aaron [like
Korah's band when it rebelled against
the LORD]. 10 The earth opened its mouth
and swallowed them as a warning [Ko-
rah too and the band that died when the
fire consumed two hundred and fifty
men. 11 The descendents of Korah, how-
ever, did not die out].

12† The Simeonites by clans were:
through Nemuel the clan of the Nemuel-
ites, through Jamin the clan of the Ja-
minites, through Jachin the clan of the
Jachinites, 13 through Sohar the clan of
the Soharites, through Shaul the clan of
the Shaulites. 14 These were the clans of
the Simeonites, of whom twenty-two
thousand two hundred men were regis-
tered.

15 The Gadites by clans were: through
Zephon the clan of the Zephonites,
through Haggi the clan of the Haggites,
through Shuni the clan of the Shunites,
16 through Ozni the clan of the Oznites,
through Eri the clan of the Erites,
17 through Arod the clan of the Arodites,
through Areli the clan of the Arelites.
18 These were the clans of the Gadites,
of whom forty thousand five hundred
men were registered.

19*† The sons of Judah who died in the
land of Canaan were Er and Onan.
20 The Judahites by clans were: through
Shelah the clan of the Shelahites,
through Perez the clan of the Perezites,
through Zerah the clan of the Zerahites.
21 The Perezites were: through Hezron
the clan of the Hezronites, through
Hamul the clan of the Hamulites.
22 These were the clans of Judah, of
whom seventy-six thousand five hun-
dred men were registered.

23 The Issacharites by clans were:
through Tola the clan of the Tolaites,
through Puvah the clan of the Puvahites,
24 through Jashub the clan of the Ja-
shubites, through Shimron the clan of
the Shimronites. 25 These were the clans
of Issachar, of whom sixty-four thou-
sand three hundred men were regis-
tered.

26 The Zebulunites by clans were:
through Sered the clan of the Seredites,
through Elon the clan of the Elonites,
through Jahleel the clan of the Jahleel-
ites. 27 These were the clans of the Zebu-
lunites, of whom sixty thousand five
hundred men were registered.

28 The sons of Joseph were Manasseh
and Ephraim. 29 The Manassehites by
clans were: through Machir the clan of
the Machirites, through Gilead, a de-
scendant of Machir, the clan of the
Gileadites. 30 The Gileadites were:
through Abiezer the clan of the Abi-
ezrites, through Helek the clan of the
Helekites, 31 through Asriel the clan of
the Asrielites, through Shechem the clan
of the Shechemites, 32 through Shemida
the clan of the Shemidaites, through
Hepher the clan of the Hepherites.
33* Zelophehad, son of Hepher, had no
sons, but only daughters, whose names
were Mahlah, Noah, Hoglah, Milcah and
Tirzah. 34 These were the clans of Ma-
nasseh, of whom fifty-two thousand
seven hundred men were registered.

35 The Ephraimites by clans were:
through Shuthelah the clan of the Shu-
thelahites, through Becher the clan of
the Bechrites, through Tahan the clan
of the Tahanites. 36 The Shuthelahites
were: through Eran the clan of the
Eranites. 37 These were the clans of the
Ephraimites, of whom thirty-two thou-
sand five hundred men were registered.

These were the descendants of Joseph
by clans.

38 The Benjaminites by clans were:
through Bela the clan of the Belaites,
through Ashbel the clan of the Ashbel-
ites, through Ahiram the clan of the Ahi-
ramites, 39 through Shupham the clan of
the Shuphamites, through Hupham the
clan of the Huphamites. 40 The descen-
dants of Bela were Arad and Naaman:
through Arad the clan of the Aradites,
through Naaman the clan of the Naa-
manites. 41 These were the Benjaminites
by clans, of whom forty-five thousand
six hundred men were registered.

42 The Danites by clans were: through
Shuham the clan of the Shuhamites.
These were the clans of Dan, 43 of whom
sixty-four thousand four hundred men
were registered.

*

5f: 1 Chr 5, 3. 12; 1 Chr 2, 3.
9f: 16, 1.32. 33: 27, 1; 36, 11;
19: Gn 38, 7.10; 46, Jos 17, 3.

†

26, 12: *Nemuel:* so also in Gn 46, 10; 1 Chr 4, 24. In Ex 6, 15, the same man is called "Jemuel"; it is uncertain which form is correct.

26, 19: This is the last verse of ch. 25.

[44] The Asherites by clans were:
through Imnah the clan of the Imnites,
through Ishvi the clan of the Ishvites,
through Beriah the clan of the Beriites,
[45] through Heber the clan of the Heber-
ites, through Malchiel the clan of the
Malchielites. [46] The name of Asher's
daughter was Serah. [47] These were the
clans of Asher, of whom fifty-three thou-
sand four hundred men were registered.
[48] The Naphtalites by clans were:
through Jahzeel the clan of the Jahzeel-
ites, through Guni the clan of the Gu-
nites, [49] through Jezer the clan of the
Jezerites, through Shillem the clan of the
Shillemites. [50] These were the clans of
Naphtali, of whom forty-five thousand
four hundred men were registered.
[51] These six hundred and one thousand
seven hundred and thirty were the Isra-
elites who were registered.
Allotment of the Land. [52]† The LORD
said to Moses, [53]* "Among these groups
the land shall be divided as their heri-
tage in keeping with the number of indi-
viduals in each group. [54]* To a large
group you shall assign a large heritage,
to a small group a small heritage, each
group receiving its heritage in propor-
tion to the number of men registered in
it. [55] But the land shall be divided by lot,
as the heritage of the various ancestral
tribes. [56] As the lot falls shall each group,
large or small, be assigned its heritage."
Census of the Levites. [57] The Levites
registered by clans were: through Ger-
shon the clan of the Gershonites,
through Kohath the clan of the Kohath-
ites, through Merari the clan of the Me-
rarites. [58] These also were clans of Levi:
the clan of the Libnites, the clan of the
Hebronites, the clan of the Mahlites, the
clan of the Mushites, the clan of the Ko-
rahites.
Among the descendants of Kohath
was Amram, [59] whose wife was named
Jochebed. She also was of the tribe of
Levi, born to the tribe in Egypt. To Am-
ram she bore Aaron and Moses and their
sister Miriam. [60] To Aaron were born
Nadab and Abihu, Eleazar and Ithamar.
[61] But Nadab and Abihu died when they
offered profane fire before the LORD.
[62]* The total number of male Levites
one month or more of age, who were reg-
istered, was twenty-three thousand.
They were not registered with the other
Israelites, however, for no heritage was
given them among the Israelites.
[63] These, then, were the men regis-
tered by Moses and the priest Eleazar
in the census of the Israelites taken on
the plains of Moab along the Jericho
stretch of the Jordan. [64] Among them
there was not a man of those who had
been registered by Moses and the priest
Aaron in the census of the Israelites
taken in the desert of Sinai. [65]* For the
LORD had told them that they would
surely die in the desert, and not one of
them was left except Caleb, son of Je-
phunneh, and Joshua, son of Nun.

CHAPTER 27

Zelophehad's Daughters. [1]* Zelophe-
had, son of Hepher, son of Gilead, son
of Machir, son of Manasseh, son of Jo-
seph, had daughters named Mahlah,
Noah, Hoglah, Milcah and Tirzah. They
came forward, [2] and standing in the
presence of Moses, the priest Eleazar,
the princes, and the whole community
at the entrance of the meeting tent, said:
[3]† "Our father died in the desert. Al-
though he did not join those who banded
together against the LORD [in Korah's
band], he died for his own sin without
leaving any sons. [4] But why should our
father's name be withdrawn from his
clan merely because he had no son? Let
us, therefore, have property among our
father's kinsmen."
Laws Concerning Heiresses. [5]† When
Moses laid their case before the LORD,
[6] the LORD said to him, [7] "The plea of
Zelophehad's daughters is just; you shall
give them hereditary property among
their father's kinsmen, letting their
father's heritage pass on to them.
[8] Therefore, tell the Israelites: If a man
dies without leaving a son, you shall let
his heritage pass on to his daughter; [9] if
he has no daughter, you shall give his
heritage to his brothers; [10] if he has no
brothers, you shall give his heritage to
his father's brothers; [11]* if his father had
no brothers, you shall give his heritage
to his nearest relative in his clan, who
shall then take possession of it." This is
the legal norm for the Israelites, as the
LORD commanded Moses.
Joshua To Succeed Moses. [12]* † The
LORD said to Moses, "Go up here into

---

*

53: Jos 11, 23.
54: 33, 54; 35, 8.
62: 3, 39.
65: 14, 22ff. 29.
27, 1: 26, 33; Jos 17, 3.
11: Jer 32, 6-9.
12: Dt 3, 27; 32, 49; 34, 1.

---

†

26, 52-56: The division of Canaan among the various tribes and clans and families was determined partly by the size of each group and partly by lot. Perhaps the lots determined the respective locality of each tribal land and the section reserved for each clan, while the relative size of the allotted locality and section depended on the numerical strength of each group. The Hebrews considered the outcome of the drawing of lots as an expression of God's will; cf Acts 1, 23-26.

27, 3: *He did not join . . . against the LORD:* had he done so, he and his heirs could have rightly been deprived of the privilege of receiving a portion in the Promised Land.

27, 5-11: The purpose of this law, as also that of the related laws in Nm 36, 2-10 (heiresses to marry within the same tribe), Dt 25, 5-10 (levirate marraige), and Lv 25, 10 (return of property in the jubilee year), was to keep the landed property within the proper domain of each tribe.

27, 12: *The Abarim Mountains:* the range on the eastern side of the Dead Sea.

the Abarim Mountains and view the land
that I am giving to the Israelites.
13* When you have viewed it, you too
shall be taken to your people, as was
your brother Aaron, 14* because in the
rebellion of the community in the desert
of Zin you both rebelled against my or-
der to manifest my sanctity to them by
means of the water." [This is the water
of Meribah of Kadesh in the desert of
Zin.]
15 Then Moses said to the LORD,
16† "May the LORD, the God of the spirits
of all mankind, set over the community
a man 17 who shall act as their leader
in all things, to guide them in all their
actions; that the LORD's community may
not be like sheep without a shepherd."
18*† And the LORD replied to Moses,
"Take Joshua, son of Nun, a man of
spirit, and lay your hand upon him.
19 Have him stand in the presence of the
priest Eleazar and of the whole commu-
nity, and commission him before their
eyes. 20 Invest him with some of your
own dignity, that the whole Israelite
community may obey him. 21† He shall
present himself to the priest Eleazar, to
have him seek out for him the decisions
of the Urim in the LORD's presence; and
as he directs, Joshua, all the Israelites
with him, and the community as a whole
shall perform all their actions."
22 Moses did as the LORD had com-
manded him. Taking Joshua and having
him stand in the presence of the priest
Eleazar and of the whole community,
23 he laid his hands on him and gave him
his commission, as the LORD had di-
rected through Moses.

CHAPTER 28

General Sacrifices. 1 The LORD said to
Moses, 2 "Give the Israelites this com-
mandment: At the times I have ap-
pointed, you shall be careful to present
to me the food offerings that are offered
to me as sweet-smelling oblations.
Each Morning and Evening.
3* † "You shall tell them therefore: This
is the oblation which you shall offer to
the LORD: two unblemished yearling
lambs each day as the established holo-
caust, 4 offering one lamb in the morning
and the other during the evening twi-
light, 5† each with a cereal offering of
one tenth of an ephah of fine flour mixed
with a fourth of a hin of oil of crushed
olives. 6 This is the established holocaust
that was offered at Mount Sinai as a
sweet-smelling oblation to the LORD.
7† And as the libation for the first lamb,
you shall pour out to the LORD in the
sanctuary a fourth of a hin of wine. 8 The
other lamb, to be offered during the eve-
ning twilight, you shall offer with the
same cereal offering and the same liba-
tion as in the morning, as a sweet-smell-
ing oblation to the LORD.
On the Sabbath. 9 "On the sabbath day
you shall offer two unblemished yearling
lambs, with their cereal offering, two
tenths of an ephah of fine flour mixed
with oil, and with their libations. 10 Each
sabbath there shall be the sabbath holo-
caust in addition to the established holo-
caust and its libation.
At the New-Moon Feast. 11† "On the
first of each month you shall offer as a
holocaust to the LORD two bullocks, one
ram, and seven unblemished yearling
lambs, 12 with three tenths of an ephah
of fine flour mixed with oil as the cereal
offering for each bullock, two tenths of
an ephah of fine flour mixed with oil as
the cereal offering for the ram, 13 and
one tenth of an ephah of fine flour mixed
with oil as the cereal offering for each
lamb, that the holocaust may be a sweet-
smelling oblation to the LORD. 14 Their
libations shall be half a hin of wine for
each bullock, a third of a hin for the ram,
and a fourth of a hin for each lamb. This
is the new moon holocaust for every new
moon of the year. 15 Moreover, one goat
shall be sacrificed as a sin offering to
the LORD. These are to be offered in ad-
dition to the established holocaust and
its libation.
At the Passover. 16*† "On the four-
teenth day of the first month falls the
Passover of the LORD, 17 and the fifteenth
day of this month is the pilgrimage feast.
For seven days unleavened bread is to
be eaten. 18* On the first of these days
you shall hold a sacred assembly, and

*

13f: 20, 12, 24.
14: Dt 32, 51.
18: Dt 34, 9.
28, 3-8: Ex 29, 38-42.
16: Ex 12, 18; Lv 23, 5; Dt 16, 1.
18: Ex 12, 16; Lv 23, 7.

†

27, 16: *The God of the spirits of all mankind:* the sense is either that God knows the character and abilities of all men and therefore knows best whom to appoint (cf Acts 1, 24), or, more probably, that God is Master of life and death and therefore can call Moses from this world whenever he wishes; cf the same phrase in Nm 16, 22, where "spirit" evidently means "the life principle."

27, 18: *A man of spirit:* literally, "a man in whom there is spirit": one who has the qualities of a good leader—courage, prudence, and strength of will. Cf Gn 41, 38; Dt 34, 9.

27, 21: *The Urim:* certain sacred objects which the Hebrew priests employed to ascertain the divine will, probably by obtaining a positive or negative answer to a given question. The full expression was "the Urim and Thummim"; cf Ex 28, 30; Lv 8, 8; Dt 33, 8; Ezr 2, 63; Neh 7, 65. Joshua was ordinarily not to receive direct revelations from God as Moses had received them.

28, 3: *The established holocaust:* "the *tamid* holocaust," the technical term for the daily sacrifice.

28, 5: *Oil of crushed olives:* this oil, made in a mortar, was purer and more expensive than oil extracted in the olive press.

28, 7: *In the sanctuary:* according to Sir 50, 15, it was at the base of the altar.

28, 11: *On the first of each month:* literally, "at the new moons"; beginning on the evening when the crescent of the new moon first appeared.

28, 16: *On the fourteenth day:* toward evening at the end of this day; cf Ex 12, 6.18.

do no sort of work. 19 As an oblation you
shall offer a holocaust to the LORD,
which shall consist of two bullocks, one
ram, and seven yearling lambs that you
are sure are unblemished, 20 with their
cereal offerings of fine flour mixed with
oil; offering three tenths of an ephah for
each bullock, two tenths for the ram,
21 and one tenth for each of the seven
lambs; 22 and offer one goat as a sin of-
fering in atonement for yourselves.
23 These offerings you shall make in ad-
dition to the established morning holo-
caust: 24 you shall make exactly the
same offerings each day for seven days
as food offerings, in addition to the es-
tablished holocaust with its libation, for
a sweet-smelling oblation to the LORD.
25* On the seventh day you shall hold
a sacred assembly, and do no sort of
work.

At Pentecost. 26*† "On the day of first
fruits, on your feast of Weeks, when you
present to the LORD the new cereal offer-
ing, you shall hold a sacred assembly,
and do no sort of work. 27 You shall offer
as a sweet-smelling holocaust to the
LORD two bullocks, one ram, and seven
yearling lambs that you are sure are un-
blemished, 28 with their cereal offerings
of fine flour mixed with oil; offering three
tenths of an ephah for each bullock, two
tenths for the ram, 29 and one tenth for
each of the seven lambs. 30 Moreover,
one goat shall be offered as a sin offering
in atonement for yourselves. 31 You shall
make these offerings, together with their
libations, in addition to the established
holocaust with its cereal offering.

CHAPTER 29

On New Year's Day. 1*† "On the first
day of the seventh month you shall hold
a sacred assembly, and do no sort of
work; it shall be a day on which you
sound the trumpet. 2 You shall offer as
a sweet-smelling holocaust to the LORD
one bullock, one ram, and seven un-
blemished yearling lambs, 3 with their
cereal offerings of fine flour mixed with
oil; offering three tenths of an ephah for
the bullock, two tenths for the ram, 4 and
one tenth for each of the seven lambs.
5 Moreover, one goat shall be offered as
a sin offering in atonement for your-
selves. 6 These are to be offered in addi-
tion to the ordinary new-moon holocaust
with its cereal offering, and in addition
to the established holocaust with its ce-
real offering, together with the libations
prescribed for them, as a sweet-smelling
oblation to the LORD.

On the Day of Atonement. 7*† "On the
tenth day of this seventh month you
shall hold a sacred assembly, and mor-
tify yourselves, and do no sort of work.
8 You shall offer as a sweet-smelling ho-
locaust to the LORD one bullock, one
ram, and seven yearling lambs that you
are sure are unblemished, 9 with their
cereal offerings of fine flour mixed with
oil; offering three tenths of an ephah for
the bullock, two tenths for the ram,
10 and one tenth for each of the seven
lambs. 11† Moreover, one goat shall be
sacrificed as a sin offering. These are to
be offered in addition to the atonement
sin offering, the established holocaust
with its cereal offering, and their liba-
tions.

On the Feast of Booths. 12*† "On the
fifteenth day of the seventh month you
shall hold a sacred assembly, and do no
sort of work; then, for seven days follow-
ing, you shall celebrate a pilgrimage
feast to the LORD. 13† You shall offer as
a sweet-smelling holocaust to the LORD
thirteen bullocks, two rams, and four-
teen yearling lambs that are unblem-
ished, 14 with their cereal offerings of fine
flour mixed with oil; offering three tenths
of an ephah for each of the thirteen bull-
ocks, two tenths for each of the two
rams, 15 and one tenth for each of the
fourteen lambs. 16 Moreover, one goat
shall be sacrificed as a sin offering.
These are to be offered in addition to the
established holocaust with its cereal of-
fering and libation.

17 "On the second day you shall offer
twelve bullocks, two rams, and fourteen
unblemished yearling lambs, 18 with
their cereal offerings and libations as
prescribed for the bullocks, rams and
lambs in proportion to their number,
19 as well as one goat for a sin offering,
besides the established holocaust with
its cereal offering and libation.

20 "On the third day you shall offer
eleven bullocks, two rams, and fourteen

*

25: Ex 12, 16; 13, 6; Lv 23, 8.
26: Ex 34, 22.
29,1: 10, 10; Lv 23, 24.
7: Lv 16, 29; 23, 27f.32.
12: Lv 23, 34f.

†

28, 26: *The day of first fruits:* a unique term for this feast, which is usually called "the feast of Weeks"; it was celebrated as a thanksgiving for the wheat harvest seven weeks after the barley harvest (Passover). In the time of Christ it was commonly known by the Greek word "Pentecost," that is, "fiftieth" (day after the Passover); see note on Lv 23, 16.

29, 1: *The first day of the seventh month* (about September-October) is now the Jewish New Year's Day. In the older calendar the year began with the first of Nisan (March-April); cf Ex 12, 2.

29, 7: *The tenth day of this seventh month:* the Day of Atonement. *Mortify yourselves:* literally, "afflict your souls," that is, with fasting.

29, 11: *The atonement sin offering:* the bullock prescribed in Lv 16, 11f.

29, 12: This feast of Booths celebrating the vintage harvest was the most popular of all and therefore had the most elaborate ritual. See note on Lv 23, 34.

29, 13: *Thirteen bullocks:* the number of bullocks sacrificed before the octave day was seventy, arranged on a descending scale so that the number on the seventh day was the sacred number seven.

unblemished yearling lambs, [21] with
their cereal offerings and libations as
prescribed for the bullocks, rams and
lambs in proportion to their number,
[22] as well as one goat for a sin offering,
besides the established holocaust with
its cereal offering and libation.
[23] "On the fourth day you shall offer
ten bullocks, two rams, and fourteen un-
blemished yearling lambs, [24] with their
cereal offerings and libations as pre-
scribed for the bullocks, rams and lambs
in proportion to their number, [25] as well
as one goat for a sin offering, besides
the established holocaust with its cereal
offering and libation.
[26] "On the fifth day you shall offer nine
bullocks, two rams, and fourteen un-
blemished yearling lambs, [27]* with their
cereal offerings and libations as pre-
scribed for the bullocks, rams and lambs
in proportion to their number, [28] as well
as one goat for a sin offering, besides
the established holocaust with its cereal
offering and libation.
[29] "On the sixth day you shall offer
eight bullocks, two rams, and fourteen
unblemished yearling lambs, [30] with
their cereal offerings and libations as
prescribed for the bullocks, rams and
lambs in proportion to their number,
[31] as well as one goat for a sin offering,
besides the established holocaust with
its cereal offering and libation.
[32] "On the seventh day you shall offer
seven bullocks, two rams, and fourteen
unblemished yearling lambs, [33] with
their cereal offerings and libations as
prescribed for the bullocks, rams and
lambs in proportion to their number,
[34] as well as one goat for a sin offering,
besides the established holocaust with
its cereal offering and libation.
[35]*† "On the eighth day you shall hold
a solemn meeting, and do no sort of
work. [36] You shall offer up in holocaust
as a sweet-smelling oblation to the LORD
one bullock, one ram, and seven un-
blemished yearling lambs, [37] with their
cereal offerings and libations as pre-
scribed for the bullocks, rams and lambs
in proportion to their number, [38] as well
as one goat for a sin offering, besides
the established holocaust with its cereal
offering and libation.
[39] "These are the offerings you shall
make to the LORD on your festivals, be-
sides whatever holocausts, cereal offer-
ings, libations, and peace offerings you
present as your votive or freewill offer-
ings."

CHAPTER 30

[1] Moses then gave the Israelites these
instructions, just as the LORD had or-
dered him.

Validity and Annulment of Vows.

[2] Moses said to the heads of the Israelite
tribes, "This is what the LORD has com-
manded: [3]*† When a man makes a vow
to the LORD or binds himself under oath
to a pledge of abstinence, he shall not
violate his word, but must fulfill exactly
the promise he has uttered.
[4] "When a woman, while still a maiden
in her father's house, makes a vow to
the LORD, or binds herself to a pledge,
[5] if her father learns of her vow or the
pledge to which she bound herself and
says nothing to her about it, then any
vow or any pledge she has made re-
mains valid. [6] But if on the day he learns
of it her father expresses to her his dis-
approval, then any vow or any pledge
she has made becomes null and void;
and the LORD releases her from it, since
her father has expressed to her his dis-
approval.
[7] "If she marries while under a vow
or under a rash pledge to which she
bound herself, [8] and her husband learns
of it, yet says nothing to her that day
about it, then the vow or pledge she had
made remains valid. [9] But if on the day
he learns of it her husband expresses to
her his disapproval, he thereby annuls
the vow she had made or the rash pledge
to which she had bound herself, and the
LORD releases her from it. [10] The vow of
a widow or of a divorced woman, or any
pledge to which such a woman binds
herself, is valid.
[11]† "If it is in her husband's house that
she makes a vow or binds herself under
oath to a pledge, [12] and her husband
learns of it yet says nothing to express
to her his disapproval, then any vow or
any pledge she has made remains valid.
[13] But if on the day he learns of them
her husband annuls them, then what-
ever she has expressly promised in her
vow or in her pledge becomes null and
void; since her husband has annulled
them, the LORD releases her from them.
[14] "Any vow or any pledge that she
makes under oath to mortify herself, her
husband can either allow to remain valid
or render null and void. [15] But if her hus-
band, day after day, says nothing at all
to her about them, he thereby allows as
valid any vow or any pledge she has

NUMBERS

*

27: 29, 30.37.
35: Lv 23, 36; Jn 7, 37.
30, 3: Dt 23, 22; Eccl 5, 3f.

†

29, 35: *A solemn meeting:* the Hebrew word is the technical term for the closing celebration of the three major feasts of the Passover, Pentecost and Booths, or of other special feasts that lasted for a week. Cf Lv 23, 36; Dt 16, 8; 2 Chr 7, 9; Neh 8, 18.

30, 3: *A vow . . . a pledge:* here the former signifies the doing of some positive good deed, in particular the offering of some sacrifice; the latter signifies the abstaining from some otherwise licit action or pleasure; cf v 14.

30, 11: *In her husband's house:* after her marriage. This contrasts with the case given in vv 7ff.

made; he has allowed them to remain
valid, because on the day he learned of
them he said nothing to her about them.
16† If, however, he countermands them
some time after he first learned of them,
he is responsible for her guilt."
17 These are the statutes which the
LORD prescribed through Moses con-
cerning the relationship between a hus-
band and his wife, as well as between
a father and his daughter while she is
still a maiden in her father's house.

CHAPTER 31

Extermination of the Midianites.
1† The LORD said to Moses, 2 "Avenge
the Israelites on the Midianites, and then
you shall be taken to your people." 3 So
Moses told the people, "Select men from
your midst and arm them for war, to
attack the Midianites and execute the
LORD's vengeance on them. 4 From each
of the tribes of Israel you shall send a
band of one thousand men to war."
5 From the clans of Israel, therefore, a
thousand men of each tribe were levied,
so that there were twelve thousand men
armed for war. 6 Moses sent them out
on the campaign, a thousand from each
tribe, with Phinehas, son of Eleazar, the
priest for the campaign, who had with
him the sacred vessels and the trumpets
for sounding the alarm. 7 They waged
war against the Midianites, as the LORD
had commanded Moses, and killed ev-
ery male among them. 8† Besides those
slain in battle, they killed the five Midi-
anite kings: Evi, Rekem, Zur, Hur and
Reba; and they also executed Balaam,
son of Beor, with the sword. 9 But the Is-
raelites kept the women of the Midian-
ites with their little ones as captives, and
all their herds and flocks and wealth as
spoil, 10 while they set on fire all the
towns where they had settled and all
their encampments. 11 Then they took all
the booty, with the people and beasts
they had captured, and brought the cap-
tives, together with the spoils and booty,
12 to Moses and the priest Eleazar and
to the Israelite community at their camp
on the plains of Moab, along the Jericho
stretch of the Jordan.
Treatment of the Captives. 13 When
Moses and the priest Eleazar, with all
the princes of the community, went out-
side the camp to meet them, 14 Moses be-
came angry with the officers of the
army, the clan and company command-
ers, who were returning from combat.
15 "So you have spared all the women!"
he exclaimed. 16* "Why, they are the
very ones who on Balaam's advice
prompted the unfaithfulness of the Isra-
elites toward the LORD in the Peor affair,
which began the slaughter of the LORD's
community. 17† Slay, therefore, every
male child and every woman who has
had intercourse with a man. 18 But you
may spare and keep for yourselves all
girls who had no intercourse with a man.
Purification after Combat. 19 "More-
over, you shall stay outside the camp for
seven days, and those of you who have
slain anyone or touched anyone slain in
battle shall purify yourselves on the
third and on the seventh day. This ap-
plies both to you and to your captives.
20 You shall also purify every article of
cloth, leather, goats' hair, or wood."
21 Eleazar the priest told the soldiers
who had returned from combat: "This
is what the law, as prescribed by the
LORD to Moses, ordains: 22 Whatever can
stand fire, such as gold, silver, bronze,
iron, tin and lead, 23† you shall put into
the fire, that it may become clean; how-
ever, it must also be purified with lustral
water. But whatever cannot stand fire
you shall put into the water. 24 On the
seventh day you shall wash your clothes,
and then you will again be clean. After
that you may enter the camp."
Division of the Booty. 25 The LORD
said to Moses: 26 "With the help of the
priest Eleazar and of the heads of the
ancestral houses, count up all the human
captives and the beasts that have been
taken; 27† then divide them evenly, giv-
ing half to those who took active part
in the war by going out to combat, and
half to the rest of the community. 28 You
shall levy a tax for the LORD on the war-
riors who went out to combat: one out
of every five hundred persons, oxen,
asses and sheep 29 in their half of the
spoil you shall turn over to the priest
Eleazar as a contribution to the LORD.
30 From the Israelites' half you shall take
one out of every fifty persons, and the
same from the different beasts, oxen,
asses and sheep, and give them to the
Levites, who have charge of the LORD's
Dwelling." 31 So Moses and the priest
Eleazar did this, as the LORD had com-
manded Moses.

*

31, 16: 2 Pt 2, 15; Rv 2, 14.

†

30, 16: *He countermands them:* he prevents their fulfillment. Since he has first allowed the vows to remain valid, he can no longer annul them.

31, 1ff: The narrative of Israel's relations with Midian, which was interrupted after 25, 18, is now resumed.

31, 8: *The five Midianite kings:* they are called "Midianite princes, Sihon's vassals" in Jos 13, 21.

31, 17: There are later references to Midian in Jgs 6-8; 1 Kgs 11, 18; Is 60, 6. The present raid was only against those Midianites who were dwelling at this time near the encampment of the Israelites.

31, 23: *Lustral water:* water mixed with the ashes of the red heifer as prescribed in Nm 19, 9.

31, 27: *Divide them evenly:* for a similar division of the booty into two equal parts, between those who engaged in the fray and those who stayed with the baggage, cf 1 Sm 30, 24. But note that here the tax on the booty of the noncombatants is ten times as much as that on the soldier's booty.

Amount of Booty. 32 This booty, what
was left of the loot which the soldiers
had taken, amounted to six hundred and
seventy-five thousand sheep, 33 seventy-
two thousand oxen, 34 sixty-one thou-
sand asses, 35 and thirty-two thousand
girls who were still virgins.
36 The half that fell to those who had
gone out to combat was: three hundred
and thirty-seven thousand five hundred
sheep, 37 of which six hundred and sev-
enty-five fell as tax to the LORD; 38 thirty-
six thousand oxen, of which seventy-two
fell as tax to the LORD; 39 thirty thousand
five hundred asses, of which sixty-one
fell as tax to the LORD; 40 and sixteen
thousand persons, of whom thirty-two
fell as tax to the LORD. 41 The taxes con-
tributed to the LORD, Moses gave to the
priest Eleazar, as the LORD had com-
manded him.
42 The half for the other Israelites,
which fell to the community when Moses
had taken it from the soldiers, was:
43 three hundred and thirty-seven thou-
sand five hundred sheep, 44 thirty-six
thousand oxen, 45 thirty thousand five
hundred asses, 46 and sixteen thousand
persons. 47 From this, the Israelites'
share, Moses, as the LORD had ordered,
took one out of every fifty, both of per-
sons and of beasts, and gave them to the
Levites, who had charge of the LORD's
Dwelling.
Gifts of the Officers. 48 Then the offi-
cers who had been clan and company
commanders of the army came up to
Moses 49 and said to him, "Your servants
have counted up the soldiers under our
command, and not one is missing. 50† So,
to make atonement for ourselves before
the LORD, each of us will bring as an of-
fering to the LORD some gold article he
has picked up, such as an anklet, a
bracelet, a ring, an earring, or a neck-
lace." 51 Moses and the priest Eleazar
accepted this gold from them, all of it
in well-wrought articles. 52 The gold that
they gave as a contribution to the LORD
amounted in all to sixteen thousand
seven hundred and fifty shekels. This
was from the clan and company com-
manders; 53 what the common soldiers
had looted each one kept for himself.
54 Moses, then, and the priest Eleazar
accepted the gold from the clan and
company commanders, and put it in the
meeting tent as a memorial for the Isra-
elites before the LORD.

CHAPTER 32

Request of Gad and Reuben. 1† Now
the Reubenites and Gadites had a very
large number of livestock. Noticing that
the land of Jazer and of Gilead was graz-
ing country, 2 they came to Moses and
the priest Eleazar and to the princes of
the community and said, 3† "The region
of Ataroth, Dibon, Jazer, Nimrah, Hesh-
bon, Elealeh, Sebam, Nebo and Baal-
meon, 4 which the LORD has laid low be-
fore the community of Israel, is grazing
country. Now, since your servants have
livestock," 5 they continued, "if we find
favor with you, let this land be given to
your servants as their property. Do not
make us cross the Jordan."
Moses' Rebuke. 6 But Moses answered
the Gadites and Reubenites: "Are your
kinsmen, then, to engage in war, while
you remain here? 7 Why do you wish to
discourage the Israelites from crossing
to the land the LORD has given them?
8* That is just what your fathers did
when I sent them from Kadesh-barnea
to reconnoiter the land. 9 They went up
to the Wadi Eshcol and reconnoitered
the land, then so discouraged the Israel-
ites that they would not enter the land
the LORD had given them. 10* At that
time the wrath of the LORD flared up,
and he swore, 11 'Because they have not
followed me unreservedly, none of these
men of twenty years or more who have
come up from Egypt shall ever see this
country I promised under oath to Abra-
ham and Isaac and Jacob, 12*† except
the Kenizzite Caleb, son of Jephunneh,
and Joshua, son of Nun, who have fol-
lowed the LORD unreservedly.' 13 So in
his anger with the Israelites the LORD
made them wander in the desert forty
years, until the whole generation that
had done evil in the sight of the LORD
had died out. 14 And now here you are,
a brood of sinners, rising up in your fa-
thers' place to add still more to the
LORD's blazing wrath against the Israel-
ites. 15 If you turn away from following
him, he will make them stay still longer
in the desert, and so you will bring about
the ruin of this whole nation."
Counter Proposal. 16 But they were in-
sistent with him: "We wish only to build
sheepfolds here for our flocks, and towns
for our families; 17* but we ourselves will
march as troops in the van of the Israel-

*

32, 8f: 13, 31ff; Dt 1, 22.
10f: Dt 1, 34f.
12: 14, 24; Dt 1, 36.
17: Jos 4, 12f.

†

31, 50: The precise nature and use of some of these articles of gold is not certain.

32, 1: *Gilead:* the name of the western part of the plateau east of the Jordan, sometimes signifying the whole region from the Yarmuk to the Jordan, sometimes only the northern part of this region, and sometimes, as here, only its southern part. *Jazer* lay to the east of southern Gilead.

32, 3: The places named in this verse, as well as the additional ones given in vv 34-38, were all in the former kingdom of Sihon, that is, in the region between the Jabbok and the Arnon. Cf 21, 23f; Jos 13, 19-21. 24-27.

32, 12: *Kenizzite:* a member of the clan of Kenaz, which, according to Gn 36, 11. 15. 42, was Edomitic; hence, although Caleb belonged to the tribe of Judah (Nm 13, 6; 34, 19), he must have had Edomite blood in his veins; cf also Jos 14, 6. 14.

ites, until we have led them to their des-
tination. Meanwhile our families can re-
main here in the fortified towns, safe
from attack by the natives. 18 We will not
return to our homes until every one of
the Israelites has taken possession of his
heritage, 19* and will not claim any her-
itage with them once we cross the Jor-
dan, so long as we receive a heritage for
ourselves on this eastern side of the Jor-
dan."

Agreement Reached. 20† Moses said
to them in reply: "If you keep your word
to march as troops in the LORD's van-
guard 21 and to cross the Jordan in full
force before the LORD until he has driven
his enemies out of his way 22* and the
land is subdued before him, then you
may return here, quit of every obligation
to the LORD and to Israel, and this region
shall be your possession before the
LORD. 23 But if you do not do this, you
will sin against the LORD, and you can
be sure that you will not escape the con-
sequences of your sin. 24 Build the towns,
then, for your families, and the folds for
your flocks, but also fulfill your express
promise."

25 The Gadites and Reubenites an-
swered Moses, "Your servants will do as
you command, my lord. 26* While our
wives and children, our herds and other
livestock remain in the towns of Gilead,
27 all your servants will go across as
armed troops to battle before the LORD,
just as your lordship says."

28 Moses, therefore, gave this order in
their regard to the priest Eleazar, to
Joshua, son of Nun, and to the heads of
the ancestral tribes of the Israelites:
29 "If all the Gadites and Reubenites
cross the Jordan with you as combat
troops before the LORD, you shall give
them Gilead as their property when the
land has been subdued before you. 30 But
if they will not go across with you as
combat troops before the LORD, you
shall bring their wives and children and
livestock across before you into Canaan,
and they shall have their property with
you in the land of Canaan."

31 To this the Gadites and Reubenites
replied, "We will do what the LORD has
commanded us, your servants. 32 We
ourselves will go across into the land of
Canaan as troops before the LORD, but
we will retain our hereditary property
on this side of the Jordan." 33*† So Moses
gave them [the Gadites and Reubenites,
as well as half the tribe of Manasseh,
son of Joseph, the kingdom of Sihon,
king of the Amorites, and the kingdom
of Og, king of Bashan,] the land with its
towns and the districts that surrounded
them.

34 The Gadites rebuilt the fortified
towns of Dibon, Ataroth, Aroer,
35 Atroth-shophan, Jazer, Jogbehah,
36 Beth-nimrah and Beth-haran, and
they built sheepfolds. 37 The Reubenites
rebuilt Heshbon, Elealeh, Kiriathaim,
38† Nebo, Baal-meon [names to be
changed!], and Sibmah. These towns,
which they rebuilt, they called by their
old names.

Other Conquests. 39 The descendants
of Machir, son of Manasseh, invaded
Gilead and captured it, driving out the
Amorites who were there. 40* [Moses
gave Gilead to Machir, son of Manasseh,
and he settled there.] 41* Jair, a Manas-
sehite clan, campaigned against the tent
villages, captured them and called them
Havvoth-jair. 42 Nobah also campaigned
against Kenath, captured it with its de-
pendencies and called it Nobah after his
own name.

CHAPTER 33

Stages on the Journey. 1† The follow-
ing are the stages by which the Israelites
journeyed up by companies from the
land of Egypt under the guidance of Mo-
ses and Aaron. 2 By the LORD's com-
mand Moses recorded the starting
places of the various stages. The starting
places of the successive stages were:

3† They set out from Rameses in the first month,
on the fifteenth day of the first month.
On the Passover morrow the Israelites went forth
in triumph, in view of all Egypt,

*

19: Jos 13, 8.
22: Jos 1, 15.
26: Jos 1, 14.
33: Dt 3, 12; 29, 7; Jos 12, 6; 13, 8.
40: Dt 3, 15.
41: Dt 3, 14.

†

32, 20ff: Since the ark of the Lord was borne into battle with the Israelite army, the vanguard was said to march *before the Lord.*

32, 33: The preceding is concerned solely with the two tribes of Gad and Reuben and with the land of the former kingdom of Sihon; hence it seems probable that the sudden reference here to the half-tribe of Manasseh and to their territory in Bashan, the former kingdom of Og, is a later addition to the text.

32, 38: The phrase in brackets is a gloss, warning the reader either to change the order of the preceding names, or, more probably, to read some other word, such as *bosheth,* "shame," for *Baal. They called by their old names:* literally, "they called by their names" (see Textual Notes); however, some understand the current Hebrew text to mean, "they called by new names."

33, 1ff: This list of camping sites was drawn up by Moses, as v 2 expressly states. However, in its present form it probably includes some glosses. Moreover, a comparison with the more detailed accounts of the journey as given elsewhere shows that this list is not complete. It records just forty camping sites, not counting the starting place, Rameses, and the terminus, the plains of Moab. This number, which corresponds exactly to the forty years of wandering in the desert, is probably a schematic device. Besides, it seems that in its present form the order of some of these names has been disturbed. Several names listed here are not recorded elsewhere.

33, 3f: These two verses were probably borrowed from some ancient song celebrating the exodus from Egypt.

4* While the Egyptians buried their
first-born
all of whom the LORD had struck
down;
on their gods, too, the LORD exe-
cuted judgments.

From Egypt to Sinai. 5 Setting out
from Rameses, the Israelites camped at
Succoth. 6 Setting out from Succoth, they
camped at Etham near the edge of the
desert. 7* Setting out from Etham, they
turned back to Pi-hahiroth, which is op-
posite Baal-zephon, and they camped
opposite Migdol. 8* Setting out from Pi-
hahiroth, they crossed over through the
sea into the desert, and after a three
days' journey in the desert of Etham,
they camped at Marah. 9* Setting out
from Marah, they came to Elim, where
there were twelve springs of water and
seventy palm trees, and they camped
there. 10 Setting out from Elim, they
camped beside the Red Sea. 11 Setting
out from the Red Sea, they camped in
the desert of Sin. 12 Setting out from the
desert of Sin, they camped at Dophkah.
13 Setting out from Dophkah, they
camped at Alush. 14* Setting out from
Alush, they camped at Rephidim, where
there was no water for the people to
drink. 15* Setting out from Rephidim,
they camped in the desert of Sinai.

From Sinai to Kadesh. 16 Setting out
from the desert of Sinai, they camped
at Kibroth-hattaavah. 17* Setting out
from Kibroth-hattaavah, they camped
at Hazeroth. 18 Setting out from Haze-
roth, they camped at Rithmah. 19 Setting
out from Rithmah, they camped at Rim-
mon-perez. 20 Setting out from Rimmon-
perez, they camped at Libnah. 21 Setting
out from Libnah, they camped at Ris-
sah. 22 Setting out from Rissah, they
camped at Kehelathah. 23 Setting out
from Kehelathah, they camped at
Mount Shepher. 24 Setting out from
Mount Shepher, they camped at Hara-
dah. 25 Setting out from Haradah, they
camped at Makheloth. 26 Setting out
from Makheloth, they camped at Ta-
hath. 27 Setting out from Tahath, they
camped at Terah. 28 Setting out from
Terah, they camped at Mithkah.
29 Setting out from Mithkah, they
camped at Hashmonah. 30† Setting out
from Hashmonah,—

From Mount Hor to Ezion-geber. They
camped at Moseroth. 31 Setting out from
Moseroth, they camped at Bene-jaakan.
32 Setting out from Bene-jaakan, they
camped at Mount Gidgad. 33 Setting out
from Mount Gidgad, they camped at
Jotbathah. 34 Setting out from Jotba-
thah, they camped at Abronah. 35 Set-
ting out from Abronah, they camped at
Ezion-geber. 36* Setting out from Ezion-
geber,—

From Kadesh to Mount Hor. They
camped in the desert of Zin, at Kadesh.
37 Setting out from Kadesh, they camped
at Mount Hor on the border of the land
of Edom. 38* [Aaron the priest ascended
Mount Hor at the LORD's command, and
there he died in the fortieth year from
the departure of the Israelites from the
land of Egypt, on the first day of the fifth
month. 39 Aaron was a hundred and
twenty-three years old when he died on
Mount Hor. 40† Now, when the Canaanite
king of Arad, who lived in the Negeb in
the land of Canaan, heard that the Isra-
elites were coming. . . .] 41† Setting out
from Mount Hor,—

***From Ezion-geber to the Plains of
Moab.*** They camped at Zalmonah.
42 Setting out from Zalmonah, they
camped at Punon. 43 Setting out from
Punon, they camped at Oboth. 44 Setting
out from Oboth, they camped at Iye-
abarim on the border of Moab. 45 Setting
out from Iye-abarim, they camped at
Dibon-gad. 46 Setting out from Dibon-
gad, they camped at Almon-diblathaim.
47 Setting out from Almon-diblathaim,
they camped in the Abarim Mountains
opposite Nebo. 48 Setting out from the
Abarim Mountains, they camped on the
plains of Moab along the Jericho stretch
of the Jordan. 49 Their camp along the
Jordan on the plains of Moab extended
from Beth-jeshimoth to Abelshittim.

Conquest and Division of Canaan.
50 The LORD spoke to Moses on the plains
of Moab beside the Jericho stretch of the
Jordan and said to him: 51 "Tell the Isra-
elites: When you go across the Jordan
into the land of Canaan, 52* drive out all
the inhabitants of the land before you;
destroy all their stone figures and mol-
ten images, and demolish all their high
places.

53 "You shall take possession of the
land and settle in it, for I have given you
the land as your property. 54* You shall
apportion the land among yourselves by
lot, clan by clan, assigning a large heri-
tage to a large group and a small heri-
tage to a small group. Wherever any-

*

33, 4f: Ex 12, 12. 29. 37.
7: Ex 14, 2.
8: Ex 15, 22.
9: Ex 15, 27.
14: Ex 17, 1.
15: Ex 19, 2.
17f: Nm 11, 34f.
36f: 20, 1.22.
38: 20, 25; Dt 32, 50.
52: Ex 23, 31; 34, 13; Dt 7, 5; 12, 3.
54: 26, 53ff.

†

33, 30-36: Moseroth is mentioned in Dt 10, 6 (in the form of "Moserah"), as the place where Aaron died. It must therefore have been close to Mount Hor; cf Nm 20, 22ff. It seems very probable that the section vv 36b-41a stood orginally immediately after v 30a.

33, 40: The verse begins the same account of the victory over Arad as is given in 21, 1ff, where it also follows the account of Aaron's death.

33, 41b-49: It seems that this section stood originally immediately after v 36a.

one's lot falls, there shall his property
be within the heritage of his ancestral
tribe.
55* "But if you do not drive out the in-
habitants of the land before you, those
whom you allow to remain will become
as barbs in your eyes and thorns in your
sides, and they will harass you in the
country where you live, 56 and I will treat
you as I had intended to treat them."

CHAPTER 34

The Boundaries. 1 The LORD said to
Moses, 2 "Give the Israelites this order:
When you enter the land of Canaan, this
is the territory that shall fall to you as
your heritage—the land of Canaan with
its boundaries:
3* "Your southern boundary shall be
at the desert of Zin along the border of
Edom; on the east it shall begin at the
end of the Salt Sea, 4* and turning south
of the Akrabbim Pass, it shall cross Zin,
and extend south of Kadesh-barnea to
Hazar-addar; thence it shall cross to Az-
mon, 5* and turning from Azmon to the
Wadi of Egypt, shall terminate at the
Sea.
6† "For your western boundary you
shall have the Great Sea with its coast;
this shall be your western boundary.
7† "The following shall be your bound-
ary on the north: from the Great Sea you
shall draw a line to Mount Hor, 8 and
shall continue it from Mount Hor to Labo
in the land of Hamath, with the bound-
ary extending through Zedad. 9 Thence
the boundary shall reach to Ziphron and
terminate at Hazar-enan. This shall be
your northern boundary.
10 "For your eastern boundary you
shall draw a line from Hazar-enan to
Shepham. 11 From Shepham the bound-
ary shall go down to Ar-Baal, east of
Ain, and descending further, shall strike
the ridge on the east side of the Sea of
Chinnereth; 12 thence the boundary shall
continue along the Jordan and termi-
nate with the Salt Sea.
"This is the land that shall be yours,
with the boundaries that surround it."
13 Moses also gave this order to the Is-
raelites: "This is the land, to be appor-
tioned among you by lot, which the LORD
has commanded to be given to the nine
and one half tribes. 14 For all the ances-
tral houses of the tribe of Reuben, and
the ancestral houses of the tribe of Gad,
as well as half of the tribe of Manasseh,
have already received their heritage;
15 these two and one half tribes have re-
ceived their heritage on the eastern side
of the Jericho stretch of the Jordan, to-
ward the sunrise."
Supervisors of the Allotment. 16 The
LORD said to Moses, 17 "These are the
names of the men who shall apportion
the land among you: Eleazar the priest,
and Joshua, son of Nun, 18* and one
prince from each of the tribes whom you
shall designate for this task. 19 These
shall be as follows:

from the tribe of Judah: Caleb, son of Jephunneh,
20 from the tribe of Simeon: Samuel, son of Ammihud;
21 from the tribe of Benjamin: Elidad, son of Chislon;
22 from the tribe of Dan: Bukki, son of Jogli;
23 from the tribe of Manasseh: Hanniel, son of Ephod; and
24 from the tribe of Ephraim: Kemuel, son of Shiphtan, for the descendants of Joseph;
25 from the tribe of Zebulun: Elizaphan, son of Parnach;
26 from the tribe of Issachar: Paltiel, son of Azzan;
27 from the tribe of Asher: Ahihud, son of Shelomi;
28 from the tribe of Naphtali: Pedahel, son of Ammihud."

29 These are they whom the LORD com-
manded to assign the Israelites their
heritage in the land of Canaan.

CHAPTER 35

Cities for the Levites. 1 The LORD gave
these instructions to Moses on the plains
of Moab beside the Jericho stretch of the
Jordan: 2* "Tell the Israelites that out of
their hereditary property they shall give
the Levites cities for homes, as well as
pasture lands around the cities. 3 The
cities shall serve them to dwell in, and
the pasture lands shall serve their herds
and flocks and other animals. 4 The pas-
ture lands of the cities to be assigned
the Levites shall extend a thousand cu-
bits from the city walls in each direction.
5 Thus you shall measure out two thou-
sand cubits outside the city along each
side—east, south, west and north—with
the city lying in the center. This shall
serve them as the pasture lands of their
cities.
6* "Now these are the cities you shall
give to the Levites: the six cities of asy-
lum which you must establish as places
where a homicide can take refuge, and
in addition forty-two other cities—7 a to-
tal of forty-eight cities with their pasture

*

55: Jos 23, 13; Jgs 2, 3.
34, 3: Jos 15, 1f.
4: Jos 15, 3.
5: Jos 15, 4.
18: 1, 4.
35, 2: Jos 14, 3f; 21, 2.
6: Dt 4, 41f; Jos 20, 2.

†

34, 6: *The Great Sea:* the Mediterranean.
34, 7f: *Mount Hor:* different from the one where Aaron died; cf Nm 20, 22; 33, 37f.

lands to be assigned the Levites. 8† In
assigning the cities from the property of
the Israelites, take more from a larger
group and fewer from a smaller one, so
that each group will cede cities to the
Levites in proportion to its own heri-
tage."

Cities of Asylum. 9 The LORD said to
Moses, 10* "Tell the Israelites: When you
go across the Jordan into the land of Ca-
naan, 11 select for yourselves cities to
serve as cities of asylum, where a homi-
cide who has killed someone uninten-
tionally may take refuge. 12† These cities
shall serve you as places of asylum from
the avenger of blood, so that a homicide
shall not be put to death unless he is first
tried before the community. 13 Six cities
of asylum shall you assign: 14 three be-
yond the Jordan, and three in the land
of Canaan. 15 These six cities of asylum
shall serve not only the Israelites but all
the resident or transient aliens among
them, so that anyone who has killed an-
other unintentionally may take refuge
there.

Murder and Manslaughter. 16*† "If a
man strikes another with an iron instru-
ment and causes his death, he is a mur-
derer and shall be put to death. 17 If a
man strikes another with a death-deal-
ing stone in his hand and causes his
death, he is a murderer and shall be put
to death. 18 If a man strikes another with
a death-dealing club in his hand and
causes his death, he is a murderer and
shall be put to death. 19 The avenger of
blood may execute the murderer, put-
ting him to death on sight.

20* "If a man pushes another out of ha-
tred, or after lying in wait for him throws
something at him, and causes his death,
21 or if he strikes another out of enmity
and causes his death, he shall be put to
death as a murderer. The avenger of
blood may execute the murderer on
sight.

22* "However, if a man pushes another
accidentally and not out of enmity, or
if without lying in wait for him he throws
some object at him, 23 or without seeing
him throws a death-dealing stone which
strikes him and causes his death, al-
though he was not his enemy nor seek-
ing to harm him: 24 then the community,
deciding the case between the slayer
and the avenger of blood in accordance
with these norms, 25* shall free the ho-
micide from the avenger of blood and
shall remand him to the city of asylum
where he took refuge; and he shall stay
there until the death of the high priest
who has been anointed with sacred oil.
26 If the homicide of his own accord
leaves the bounds of the city of asylum
where he has taken refuge, 27 and the
avenger of blood finds him beyond these
bounds and kills him, the avenger incurs
no bloodguilt; 28 the homicide was bound
to stay in his city of asylum until the
death of the high priest. Only after the
death of the high priest may the homi-
cide return to his own district.

29 "These shall be norms for you and
all your descendants, wherever you live,
for rendering judgment.

Witnesses. 30* "Whenever someone
kills another, the evidence of witnesses
is required for the execution of the mur-
derer. The evidence of a single witness
is not sufficient for putting a person to
death.

No Indemnity. 31 "You shall not ac-
cept indemnity in place of the life of a
murderer who deserves the death pen-
alty; he must be put to death. 32 Nor shall
you accept indemnity to allow a refugee
to leave his city of asylum and again
dwell elsewhere in the land before the
death of the high priest. 33 You shall not
desecrate the land where you live. Since
bloodshed desecrates the land, the land
can have no atonement for the blood
shed on it except through the blood of
him who shed it. 34* Do not defile the
land in which you live and in the midst
of which I dwell; for I am the LORD who
dwells in the midst of the Israelites."

CHAPTER 36

Property of Heiresses. 1 The heads of
the ancestral houses in the clan of de-
scendants of Gilead, son of Machir, son
of Manasseh—one of the Josephite
clans—came up and laid this plea before
Moses and the priest Eleazar and before
the princes who were the heads of the
ancestral houses of the other Israelites.
2* They said: "The LORD commanded
you, my lord, to apportion the land by
lot among the Israelites; and you, my
lord, were also commanded by the LORD
to give the heritage of our kinsman Zelo-
phehad to his daughters. 3 But if they
marry into one of the other Israelite
tribes, their heritage will be withdrawn
from our ancestral heritage and will be
added to that of the tribe into which they
marry; thus the heritage that fell to us

---

*

10ff: Dt 19, 2; Jos 20, 2ff.
16: Ex 21, 12; Lv 24, 17.
20: Ex 21, 14; Dt 19, 11.
22: Jos 20, 3.
25: Jos 20, 6.
30: Dt 17, 6; 19, 15; Jn 8, 17; 2 Cor 13, 1; 1 Tm 5, 19.
34: Ex 29, 45.
36, 2: 26, 55; 27, 6; Jos 17, 3f.

†

35, 8: This provision was hardly observed in the actual assignment of the levitical cities as narrated in Jos 21.

35, 12: *The avenger of blood:* one of the close relatives of the slain (2 Sm 14, 7) who, as executor of public justice, had the right and duty to take the life of the murderer; cf Dt 19, 6. 12; Jos 20, 3.5.9.

35, 16-25: Here, as also in Dt 19, 1-13, there is a casuistic development of the original law as stated in Ex 21, 12ff.

by lot will be diminished. 4† When the
Israelites celebrate the jubilee year, the
heritage of these women will be perma-
nently added to that of the tribe into
which they marry and will be withdrawn
from that of our ancestral tribe."

5† So Moses gave this regulation to the
Israelites according to the instructions
of the LORD: "The tribe of the Josephites
are right in what they say. 6 This is what
the LORD commands with regard to the
daughters of Zelophehad: They may
marry anyone they please, provided
they marry into a clan of their ancestral
tribe, 7 so that no heritage of the Israel-
ites will pass from one tribe to another,
but all the Israelites will retain their own
ancestral heritage. 8 Therefore, every
daughter who inherits property in any
of the Israelite tribes shall marry some-
one belonging to a clan of her own an-
cestral tribe, in order that all the
Israelites may remain in possession of
their own ancestral heritage. 9 Thus, no
heritage can pass from one tribe to an-
other, but all the Israelite tribes will re-
tain their own ancestral heritage."

10 The daughters of Zelophehad
obeyed the command which the LORD
had given to Moses. 11 Mahlah, Tirzah,
Hoglah, Milcah and Noah, Zelophehad's
daughters, married relatives on their fa-
ther's side 12 within the clans of the de-
scendants of Manasseh, son of Joseph;
hence their heritage remained in the
tribe of their father's clan.

Conclusion. 13 These are the com-
mandments and decisions which the
LORD prescribed for the Israelites
through Moses, on the plains of Moab
beside the Jericho stretch of the Jordan.

†

36, 4: Before the jubilee year various circumstances, such as divorce, could make such property revert to its original tribal owners; but in the jubilee year it became irrevocably attached to its new owners.

36, 5-9: This is a supplement to the law given in 27, 5-11.

The Book of

DEUTERONOMY

The fifth and last book of the Pentateuch is called Deuteronomy, meaning "second law." In reality, what it contains is not a new law but a partial repetition, completion and explanation of the law proclaimed on Mount Sinai. The historical portions of the book are also a résumé of what is related elsewhere in the Pentateuch.

The chief characteristic of this book is its vigorous oratorical style. In a series of eloquent discourses Moses presents the theme of covenant renewal in a vital liturgical framework. He exhorts, corrects and threatens his people, appealing to their past glory, their historic mission, and the promise of future triumph. His aim is to enforce among the Israelites the Lord's claim to their obedience, loyalty and love.

The events contained in the Book of Deuteronomy took place in the plains of Moab (1, 5) between the end of the wanderings in the desert (1, 3) and the crossing of the Jordan River (Jos 4, 19), a period of no more than forty days.

The Book of Deuteronomy, written after the Israelites had for centuries been resident in the Land of Promise, takes the form of a testament of Moses, the great leader and legislator, to his people on the eve of his death. At the time of our Lord's coming, it shared with the Psalms a preeminent religious influence among the Old Testament books.

The Savior quoted passages of Deuteronomy in overcoming the threefold temptation of Satan in the desert (Mt 4; Dt 6, 13.16; 8, 3; 10, 20), and in explaining to the lawyer the first and greatest commandment (Mt 22, 35-39; Dt 6, 4).

The book is divided as follows:

I: Historical Review and Exhortation (1, 1—4, 43)
II: God and His Covenant (4, 44—11, 32)
III: Exposition of the Law (12, 1—26, 19)
IV: Final Words of Moses (27, 1—34, 12)

I: HISTORICAL REVIEW AND EXHORTATION

CHAPTER 1

Introduction. 1† These are the words
which Moses spoke to all Israel beyond
the Jordan [in the desert, in the Arabah,
opposite Suph, between Paran and To-
phel, Laban, Hazeroth and Dizahab; 2 it
is a journey of eleven days from Horeb
to Kadesh-barnea by way of the high-
lands of Seir].
3 In the fortieth year, on the first day
of the eleventh month, Moses spoke to
the Israelites all the commands that the
LORD had given him in their regard.
4* After he had defeated Sihon, king of
the Amorites, who lived in Heshbon, and
Og, king of Bashan, who lived in Ashta-
roth and in Edrei, 5 Moses began to ex-
plain the law in the land of Moab beyond
the Jordan, as follows:
Departure from Horeb. 6 "The LORD,
our God, said to us at Horeb, 'You have
stayed long enough at this mountain.
7*† Leave here and go to the hill country
of the Amorites and to all the surround-
ing regions, the land of the Canaanites
in the Arabah, the mountains, the foot-
hills, the Negeb and the seacoast; to
Lebanon, and as far as the Great River
[the Euphrates]. 8* I have given that
land over to you. Go now and occupy
the land I swore to your fathers, Abra-
ham, Isaac and Jacob, I would give to
them and to their descendants.'
Appointment of Elders. 9† "At that
time I said to you, 'Alone, I am unable
to carry you. 10* The LORD, your God,
has so multiplied you that you are now
as numerous as the stars in the sky.
11 May the LORD, the God of your fa-
thers, increase you a thousand times

---

* 1, 4: 3, 2; Nm 21, 21-35.
7: Nm 13, 29.
8: Gn 12, 7; 15, 18; 17, 7f; 28, 13f.
10: 10, 22; Gn 15, 5.

---

† 1, 1: The local setting of all these discourses is *in the land of Moab beyond the Jordan* (cf v 5), also known as *the plains of Moab* (Nm 36, 13).

1, 7: The Amorites and the Canaanites formed the principal part of the pre-Israelite population of Palestine. *The foothills:* the hills on the western slope of the Judean mountain range. *The Arabah:* the valley of the Jordan and the depression south of the Dead Sea. *The Negeb:* the arid land in southern Palestine.

1, 9: *Carry you:* cf v 31.

over, and bless you as he promised!
[12] But how can I alone bear the crushing
burden that you are, along with your
bickering? [13*] Choose wise, intelligent
and experienced men from each of your
tribes, that I may appoint them as your
leaders.' [14] You answered me, 'We agree
to do as you have proposed.' [15] So I took
outstanding men of your tribes, wise and
experienced, and made them your lead-
ers as officials over thousands, over hun-
dreds, over fifties and over tens, and
other tribal officers. [16*] I charged your
judges at that time, 'Listen to complaints
among your kinsmen, and administer
true justice to both parties even if one
of them is an alien. [17] In rendering judg-
ment, do not consider who a person is;
give ear to the lowly and to the great
alike, fearing no man, for judgment is
God's. Refer to me any case that is too
hard for you and I will hear it.' [18] There-
upon I gave you all the commands you
were to fulfill.

The Twelve Scouts. [19*] "Then, in obe-
dience to the command of the LORD, our
God, we set out from Horeb and jour-
neyed through the whole desert, vast
and fearful as you have seen, in the di-
rection of the hill country of the Amo-
rites. We had reached Kadesh-barnea
[20] when I said to you, 'You have come
to the hill country of the Amorites, which
the LORD, our God, is giving us. [21] The
LORD, your God, has given this land over
to you. Go up and occupy it, as the LORD,
the God of your fathers, commands you.
Do not fear or lose heart.' [22*] Then all
of you came up to me and said, 'Let us
send men ahead to reconnoiter the land
for us and report to us on the road we
must follow and the cities we must take.'
[23] Agreeing with the proposal, I chose
twelve men from your number, one from
each tribe. [24] They set out into the hill
country as far as the Wadi Eshcol, and
explored it. [25] Then, taking along some
of the fruit of the land, they brought it
down to us and reported, 'The land
which the LORD, our God, gives us is
good.'

Threats of Revolt. [26*] "But you re-
fused to go up, and after defying the
command of the LORD, your God,
[27*†] you set to murmuring in your tents,
'Out of hatred for us the LORD has
brought us up out of the land of Egypt,
to deliver us into the hands of the Amo-
rites and destroy us. [28*] What shall we
meet with up there? Our kinsmen have
made us fainthearted by reporting that
the people are stronger and taller than
we, and their cities are large and forti-
fied to the sky; besides, they saw the
Anakim there.'

[29] "But I said to you, 'Have no dread
or fear of them. [30] The LORD, your God,
who goes before you, will himself fight
for you, just as he took your part before
your very eyes in Egypt, [31] as well as
in the desert, where you saw how the
LORD, your God, carried you, as a man
carries his child, all along your journey
until you arrived at this place.' [32] Despite
this, you would not trust the LORD, your
God, [33*] who journeys before you to find
you a resting place—by day in the cloud,
and by night in the fire, to show the way
you must go. [34*] When the LORD heard
your words, he was angry; [35] and he
swore, 'Not one man of this evil genera-
tion shall look upon the good land I
swore to give to your fathers, [36†] except
Caleb, son of Jephunneh; he shall see it.
For to him and to his sons I will give
the land he trod upon, because he has
followed the LORD unreservedly.'

[37*] "The LORD was angered against
me also on your account, and said, 'Not
even you shall enter there, [38*] but your
aide Joshua, son of Nun, shall enter. En-
courage him, for he is to give Israel its
heritage. [39*] Your little ones, who you
said would become booty, and your
children, who as yet do not know good
from bad—they shall enter; to them I will
give it, and they shall occupy it. [40] But
as for yourselves: turn about and pro-
ceed into the desert on the Red Sea
road.'

Unsuccessful Invasion. [41*] "In reply
you said to me, 'We have sinned against
the LORD. We will go up ourselves and
fight, just as the LORD, our God, com-
manded us.' And each of you girded on
his weapons, making light of going up
into the hill country. [42] But the LORD said
to me, 'Warn them: Do not go up and
fight, lest you be beaten down before
your enemies, for I will not be in your
midst.' [43] I gave you this warning but you
would not listen. In defiance of the
LORD's command you arrogantly
marched off into the hill country. [44] Then
the Amorites living there came out
against you and, like bees, chased you,
cutting you down in Seir as far as Hor-
mah. [45] On your return you wept before
the LORD, but he did not listen to your
cry or give ear to you. [46] That is why you
had to stay as long as you did at Kadesh.

*

13ff: Ex 18, 21-25.
16f: Ex 18, 26; 2 Chr 19, 6f; Prv 24, 23; Jn 7, 24; Jas 2, 9.
19: 8, 15; 32, 10.
22-28: Nm 13, 2-34.
26: 9, 23.
27: 9, 28; Nm 14, 1-4; Ps 106, 25.
28: 9, 1f.
33: Ex 13, 21; Nm 10, 33f; 14, 14.
34ff: Nm 14, 22f.28-38; Jos 14, 9.
37: 4, 21; 34, 4; Nm 20, 12.
38: 31, 3.7; Nm 27, 18ff; 34, 17.
39f: Nm 14, 31.
41-45: Nm 14, 40. 42-45.

†

1, 27: *In your tents:* among yourselves.

1, 36: *Except Caleb:* Joshua also was allowed to enter, but he is not referred to here because special mention is made of him in v 38 as the successor of Moses.

CHAPTER 2

Northward along Edom. 1* "When we
did turn and proceed into the desert on
the Red Sea road, as the LORD had com-
manded me, we circled around the high-
lands of Seir for a long time. 2 Finally
the LORD said to me, 3 'You have wan-
dered round these highlands long
enough; turn and go north. 4 Give this
order to the people: You are now about
to pass through the territory of your
kinsmen, the descendants of Esau, who
live in Seir. Though they are afraid of
you, be very careful 5 not to come in con-
flict with them, for I will not give you
so much as a foot of their land, since I
have already given Esau possession of
the highlands of Seir. 6 You shall pur-
chase from them with silver the food you
eat and the well water you drink. 7* The
LORD, your God, has blessed you in all
your undertakings; he has been con-
cerned about your journey through this
vast desert. It is now forty years that
he has been with you, and you have
never been in want.'

Along Moab. 8* "Then we left behind
us the Arabah route, Elath, Ezion-geber,
and Seir, where our kinsmen, the de-
scendants of Esau, live; and we went on
toward the desert of Moab. 9* And the
LORD said to me, 'Do not show hostility
to the Moabites or engage them in battle,
for I will not give you possession of any
of their land, since I have given Ar to
the descendants of Lot as their own.
10* [Formerly the Emim lived there, a
people strong and numerous and tall like
the Anakim; 11 like them they were con-
sidered Rephaim. It was the Moabites
who called them Emim. 12* In Seir, how-
ever, the former inhabitants were the
Horites; the descendants of Esau dispos-
sessed them, clearing them out of the
way and taking their place, just as the
Israelites have done in the land of their
heritage which the LORD has given
them.] 13* Get ready, then, to cross the
Wadi Zered.' So we crossed it. 14* Thirty-
eight years had elapsed between our de-
parture from Kadesh-barnea and that
crossing; in the meantime the whole
generation of soldiers had perished from
the camp, as the LORD had sworn they
should. 15 For it was the LORD's hand
that was against them, till he wiped them
out of the camp completely.

Along Ammon. 16 "When at length
death had put an end to all the soldiers
among the people, 17 the LORD said to
me, 18 'You are now about to leave Ar
and the territory of Moab behind. 19* As
you come opposite the Ammonites, do
not show hostility or come in conflict
with them, for I will not give you posses-
sion of any land of the Ammonites, since
I have given it to the descendants of Lot
as their own. 20 [This also was consid-
ered a country of the Rephaim from its
former inhabitants, whom the Ammon-
ites called Zamzummim, 21 a people
strong and numerous and tall like the
Anakim. But these, too, the LORD
cleared out of the way for the Ammon-
ites, who ousted them and took their
place. 22 He had done the same for the
descendants of Esau, who dwell in Seir,
by clearing the Horites out of their way,
so that the descendants of Esau have
taken their place down to the present.
23† So also the Caphtorim, migrating
from Caphtor, cleared away the Avvim,
who once dwelt in villages as far as
Gaza, and took their place.]

Defeat of Sihon. 24* " 'Advance now
across the Wadi Arnon. I now deliver
into your hands Sihon, the Amorite king
of Heshbon, and his land. Begin the oc-
cupation; engage him in battle. 25 This
day I will begin to put a fear and dread
of you into every nation under the heav-
ens, so that at the mention of your name
they will quake and tremble before you.'

26 "So I sent messengers from the
desert of Kedemoth to Sihon, king of
Heshbon, with this offer of peace: 27 'Let
me pass through your country by the
highway; I will go along it without turn-
ing aside to the right or to the left. 28 For
the food I eat which you will supply, and
for the water you give me to drink, you
shall be paid in silver. Only let me march
through, 29* as the descendants of Esau
who dwell in Seir and the Moabites who
dwell in Ar have done, until I cross the
Jordan into the land which the LORD, our
God, is about to give us.' 30 But Sihon,
king of Heshbon, refused to let us pass
through his land, because the LORD,
your God, made him stubborn in mind
and obstinate in heart that he might de-
liver him up to you, as indeed he has
now done.

31 "Then the LORD said to me, 'Now
that I have already begun to hand over
to you Sihon and his land, begin the ac-
tual occupation.' 32 So Sihon and all his
people advanced against us to join battle
at Jahaz; 33* but since the LORD, our
God, had delivered him to us, we de-
feated him and his sons and all his peo-
ple. 34*† At that time we seized all his

*

2, 1: 1, 40; Nm 14, 25; 21, 4.
7: 8, 2ff.
8: Jgs 11, 18.
9: Gn 19, 36f.
10: 1, 28.
12: Gn 36, 20f.
13: Nm 21, 12.
14: Nm 14, 29.33.35.
19: Gn 19, 38.
24: Nm 21, 13; Jgs 11, 19-22.
29: 2, 5.8f; Jgs 11, 17.
33: 29, 7; Nm 21, 23-32.
34: 3, 6; 29, 7f.

†

2, 23: *The Caphtorim:* members of one of the groups of sea peoples who invaded the coast of Egypt and the southern part of Palestine about 1200 B.C. *Caphtor:* the ancient name of the island of Crete. Cf Am 9, 7.

2, 34: *Doomed:* see notes on Nm 18, 14; 21, 3.

cities and doomed them all, with their
men, women and children; we left no
survivor. 35 Our only booty was the live-
stock and the loot of the captured cities.
36* From Aroer on the edge of the Wadi
Arnon and from the city in the wadi it-
self, as far as Gilead, no city was too
well fortified for us to whom the LORD
had delivered them up. 37* However, in
obedience to the command of the LORD,
our God, you did not encroach upon any
of the Ammonite land, neither the region
bordering on the Wadi Jabbok, nor the
cities of the highlands.

CHAPTER 3

Defeat of Og. 1* "Then we turned and
proceeded toward Bashan. But Og, king
of Bashan, advanced against us with all
his people to give battle at Edrei. 2* The
LORD, however, said to me, 'Do not be
afraid of him, for I have delivered him
into your hand with all his people and
his land. Do to him as you did to Sihon,
king of the Amorites, who lived in Hesh-
bon.' 3 And thus the LORD, our God, de-
livered into our hands Og, king of
Bashan, with all his people. We defeated
him so completely that we left him no
survivor. 4 At that time we captured all
his cities, none of them eluding our
grasp, the whole region of Argob, the
kingdom of Og in Bashan: sixty cities
in all, 5 to say nothing of the great num-
ber of unwalled towns. All the cities were
fortified with high walls and gates and
bars. 6* As we had done to Sihon, king
of Heshbon, so also here we doomed all
the cities, with their men, women and
children; 7 but all the livestock and the
loot of each city we took as booty for
ourselves.

8 "And so at that time we took from
the two kings of the Amorites beyond
the Jordan the territory from the Wadi
Arnon to Mount Hermon 9 [which is
called Sirion by the Sidonians and Senir
by the Amorites], 10 comprising all the
cities of the plateau and all Gilead and
all the cities of the kingdom of Og in
Bashan including Salecah and Edrei.
11† [Og, king of Bashan, was the last re-
maining survivor of the Rephaim. He
had a bed of iron, nine regular cubits
long and four wide, which is still pre-
served in Rabbah of the Ammonites.]

Allotment of the Conquered Lands.
12* "When we occupied the land at that
time, I gave Reuben and Gad the terri-
tory from Aroer, on the edge of the Wadi
Arnon, halfway up into the highlands of
Gilead, with the cities therein. 13 The rest
of Gilead and all of Bashan, the kingdom
of Og, the whole Argob region, I gave
to the half-tribe of Manasseh. [All this
region of Bashan was once called a land
of the Rephaim. 14* Jair, a Manassehite
clan, took all the region of Argob as far
as the border of the Geshurites and
Maacathites, and called it after his own
name Bashan Havvoth-jair, the name it
bears today.] 15 To Machir I gave Gilead,
16 and to Reuben and Gad the territory
from Gilead to the Wadi Arnon—includ-
ing the wadi bed and its banks—and to
the Wadi Jabbok, which is the border
of the Ammonites, 17* as well as the Ara-
bah with the Jordan and its eastern
banks from Chinnereth to the Salt Sea
of the Arabah, under the slopes of Pis-
gah.

18*† "At that time I charged them as
follows: 'The LORD, your God, has given
you this land as your own. But all you
troops equipped for battle must cross
over in the vanguard of your brother Is-
raelites. 19* Only your wives and chil-
dren, as well as your livestock, of which
I know you have a large number, shall
remain behind in the towns I have given
you, 20* until the LORD has settled your
kinsmen as well, and they too possess
the land which the LORD, your God, will
give them on the other side of the Jor-
dan. Then you may all return to the pos-
sessions I have given you.'

21 "It was then that I instructed
Joshua, 'Your eyes have seen all that the
LORD, your God, has done to both these
kings; so, too, will the LORD do to all the
kingdoms which you will encounter over
there. 22 Fear them not, for the LORD,
your God, will fight for you.'

Refusal to Moses. 23 "And it was then
that I besought the LORD, 24 'O Lord GOD,
you have begun to show to your servant
your greatness and might. For what god
in heaven or on earth can perform deeds
as mighty as yours? 25 Ah, let me cross
over and see this good land beyond the
Jordan, this fine hill country, and the
Lebanon!' 26* But the LORD was angry
with me on your account and would not
hear me. 'Enough!' the LORD said to me.
'Speak to me no more of this. 27* Go up
to the top of Pisgah and look out to the
west, and to the north, and to the south,
and to the east. Look well, for you shall
not cross this Jordan. 28* Commission

*

36: 3, 12; Jos 13, 9.16; Jgs 11, 26.
37: Nm 21, 24; Jos 12, 2.
3, 1: 29, 6; Nm 21, 33.
2f: Nm 21, 34f.
6: Ps 135, 10ff.
12f: Nm 32, 29.32f; Jos 13, 8.29.
14: Nm 32, 41; Jos 13, 11.13.
17: 4, 49; Jos 12, 3.
18: Jos 1, 14; 4, 12.
19: Nm 32, 1.4; Jos 1, 14.
20: Jos 22, 4.
26: 4, 21.
27: 34, 4; Nm 27, 12f.
28: 1, 38; 31, 7; Nm 27, 22f.

†

3, 11: *Bed of iron:* some translate, "a sarcophagus of basalt."

3, 18: *I charged them:* the words which follow were spoken to the men of Reuben and Gad (cf Nm 32).

Joshua, and encourage and strengthen
him, for he shall cross at the head of
this people and shall put them in posses-
sion of the land you are to see.' 29 This
was while we were in the ravine opposite
Beth-peor.

CHAPTER 4

Advantages of Fidelity. 1 "Now, Is-
rael, hear the statutes and decrees
which I am teaching you to observe, that
you may live, and may enter in and take
possession of the land which the LORD,
the God of your fathers, is giving you.
2* In your observance of the command-
ments of the LORD, your God, which I
enjoin upon you, you shall not add to
what I command you nor subtract from
it. 3* You have seen with your own eyes
what the LORD did at Baal-peor: the
LORD, your God, destroyed from your
midst everyone that followed the Baal
of Peor; 4 but you, who clung to the LORD,
your God, are all alive today. 5 There-
fore, I teach you the statutes and decrees
as the LORD, my God, has commanded
me, that you may observe them in the
land you are entering to occupy.
6 Observe them carefully, for thus will
you give evidence of your wisdom and
intelligence to the nations, who will hear
of all these statutes and say, 'This great
nation is truly a wise and intelligent peo-
ple.' 7* For what great nation is there
that has gods so close to it as the LORD,
our God, is to us whenever we call upon
him? 8 Or what great nation has statutes
and decrees that are as just as this whole
law which I am setting before you today?

Revelation at Horeb. 9* "However,
take care and be earnestly on your
guard not to forget the things which your
own eyes have seen, nor let them slip
from your memory as long as you live,
but teach them to your children and to
your children's children. 10*† There was
the day on which you stood before the
LORD, your God, at Horeb, and he said
to me, 'Assemble the people for me; I
will have them hear my words, that they
may learn to fear me as long as they
live in the land and may so teach their
children.' 11* You came near and stood
at the foot of the mountain, which blazed
to the very sky with fire and was en-
veloped in a dense black cloud. 12* Then
the LORD spoke to you from the midst
of the fire. You heard the sound of the
words, but saw no form; there was only
a voice. 13* He proclaimed to you his
covenant, which he commanded you to
keep: the ten commandments, which he
wrote on two tablets of stone. 14 The
LORD charged me at that time to teach
you the statutes and decrees which you
are to observe over in the land you will
occupy.

Danger of Idolatry. 15 "You saw no
form at all on the day the LORD spoke
to you at Horeb from the midst of the
fire. Be strictly on your guard, therefore,
16* not to degrade yourselves by fash-
ioning an idol to represent any figure,
whether it be the form of a man or a
woman, 17 of any animal on the earth or
of any bird that flies in the sky, 18 of any-
thing that crawls on the ground or of any
fish in the waters under the earth.
19* And when you look up to the heavens
and behold the sun or the moon or any
star among the heavenly hosts, do not
be led astray into adoring them and
serving them. These the LORD, your
God, has let fall to the lot of all other
nations under the heavens; 20*† but you
he has taken and led out of that iron
foundry, Egypt, that you might be his
very own people, as you are today.
21* Since the LORD was angered against
me on your account and swore that I
should not cross the Jordan nor enter
the good land which he is giving you as
a heritage, 22* I myself shall die in this
country without crossing the Jordan; but
you will cross over and take possession
of that good land. 23* Take heed, there-
fore, lest, forgetting the covenant which
the LORD, your God, has made with you,
you fashion for yourselves against his
command an idol in any form whatso-
ever. 24 For the LORD, your God, is a con-
suming fire, a jealous God.

God's Fidelity. 25† "When you have
children and grandchildren, and have
grown old in the land, should you then
degrade yourselves by fashioning an
idol in any form and by this evil done
in his sight provoke the LORD, your God,
26 I call heaven and earth this day to wit-
ness against you, that you shall all
quickly perish from the land which you
will occupy when you cross the Jordan.
You shall not live in it for any length
of time but shall be promptly wiped out.

*

4, 2: 13, 1.
3: Nm 25, 3-9.
7: 2 Sm 7, 23.
9: 11, 19; Ps 78, 3-6.
10: Heb 12, 18f.
11: Ex 19, 17f.
12: 4, 33.36; 5, 4.
13: Ex 24, 12; 31, 18; 34, 28.
16: 5, 8; Ex 20, 4.
19: 17, 3; Jb 31, 26ff.
20: 1 Kgs 8, 51; Jer 11, 4.
21: 1, 37; 3, 26.
22: 3, 27.
23: 4, 16.

†

4, 10: Beginning here and continuing on for several verses (at least to the end of v 14) is the "reminiscence," the account of the things that the Israelites should recall and teach their children.

4, 20: Egypt is called an *iron foundry,* or furnace for smelting iron, because God allowed the Israelites to be afflicted there for the sake of their spiritual purification; the same expression for Egypt occurs also in 1 Kgs 8, 51; Jer 11, 4; compare the expression, "the furnace of affliction," in Is 48, 10.

4, 25: *Grown old:* Israel will lose the freshness of its youthful fervor.

27* The LORD will scatter you among the nations, and there shall remain but a handful of you among the nations to which the LORD will lead you. 28* There you shall serve gods fashioned by the hands of man out of wood and stone, gods which can neither see nor hear, neither eat nor smell. 29* Yet there too you shall seek the LORD, your God; and you shall indeed find him when you search after him with your whole heart and your whole soul. 30 In your distress, when all these things shall have come upon you, you shall finally return to the LORD, your God, and heed his voice. 31* Since the LORD, your God, is a merciful God, he will not abandon and destroy you, nor forget the covenant which under oath he made with your fathers.

Proofs of God's Love. 32 "Ask now of the days of old, before your time, ever since God created man upon the earth; ask from one end of the sky to the other: Did anything so great ever happen before? Was it ever heard of? 33* Did a people ever hear the voice of God speaking from the midst of fire, as you did, and live? 34*† Or did any god venture to go and take a nation for himself from the midst of another nation, by testings, by signs and wonders, by war, with his strong hand and outstretched arm, and by great terrors, all of which the LORD, your God, did for you in Egypt before your very eyes? 35 All this you were allowed to see that you might know the LORD is God and there is no other. 36 Out of the heavens he let you hear his voice to discipline you; on earth he let you see his great fire, and you heard him speaking out of the fire. 37 For love of your fathers he chose their descendants and personally led you out of Egypt by his great power, 38 driving out of your way nations greater and mightier than you, so as to bring you in and to make their land your heritage, as it is today. 39* This is why you must now know, and fix in your heart, that the LORD is God in the heavens above and on earth below, and that there is no other. 40* You must keep his statutes and commandments which I enjoin on you today, that you and your children after you may prosper, and that you may have long life on the land which the LORD, your God, is giving you forever."

Cities of Refuge. 41* Then Moses set apart three cities in the region east of the Jordan, 42 that a homicide might take refuge there if he unwittingly killed his neighbor to whom he had previously borne no malice, and that he might save his life by fleeing to one of these cities: 43 Bezer in the desert, in the region of the plateau, for the Reubenites; Ramoth in Gilead for the Gadites; and Golan in Bashan for the Manassehites.

II: GOD AND HIS COVENANT

Introduction. 44 This is the law which Moses set before the Israelites. 45 These are the ordinances, statutes and decrees which he proclaimed to them when they had come out of Egypt 46 and were beyond the Jordan in the ravine opposite Beth-peor, in the land of Sihon, king of the Amorites, who dwelt in Heshbon and whom Moses and the Israelites defeated after coming out of Egypt. 47 They occupied his land and the land of Og, king of Bashan, as well—the land of these two kings of the Amorites in the region east of the Jordan: 48† from Aroer on the edge of the Wadi Arnon to Mount Sion (that is Hermon) 49* and all the Arabah east of the Jordan, as far as the Arabah Sea under the slopes of Pisgah.

CHAPTER 5

The Covenant at Horeb. 1 Moses summoned all Israel and said to them, "Hear, O Israel, the statutes and decrees which I proclaim in your hearing this day, that you may learn them and take care to observe them. 2* The LORD, our God, made a covenant with us at Horeb; 3 not with our fathers did he make this covenant, but with us, all of us who are alive here this day. 4 The LORD spoke with you face to face on the mountain from the midst of the fire. 5* Since you were afraid of the fire and would not go up the mountain, I stood between the LORD and you at that time, to announce to you these words of the LORD:

The Decalogue. 6* 'I, the LORD, am your God, who brought you out of the land of Egypt, that place of slavery. 7* You shall not have other gods besides me. 8* You shall not carve idols for yourselves in the shape of anything in the sky above or on the earth below or in the waters beneath the earth; 9*† you

*

27f: 28, 36.62. 64.
28: Ps 135, 15ff; Is 44, 9.
29: Jer 29, 13.
31: 31, 8.
33: 4, 36; 5, 24.26; Ex 20, 19.
34: 7, 19; 26, 8; 29, 2; Ex 7, 3; 15, 3-10; Jer 32, 21.
39: 4, 35.
40: 6, 2f; 12, 28.
41ff: 19, 2-13; Nm 35, 6-29; Jos 20, 8; 21, 27.36f; 1 Chr 6, 71.80.
49: 3, 17.
5, 2: 28, 69.
5: Ex 24, 2.
6-21: Ex 20, 2-17.
6: Ps 81, 11.
7: Ps 81, 10.
8: 27, 15; Lv 26, 1; Ps 97, 7.
9: Ex 34, 14.

†

4, 34: *Testings:* the demonstrations of God's power as in the ten great plagues of Egypt; cf 7, 19; 29, 2.

4, 48: *Sion:* another name for Mount Hermon, besides those mentioned in 3, 9.

5, 9f: God does not punish us for another's sins, but because of the solidarity of human society, the good or evil deeds of one generation may make their effects felt even in later generations. Yet note how God's mercy allows the good effects of virtue to last much longer than the bad effects of vice: a thousand generations compared to three or four.

shall not bow down before them or wor-
ship them. For I, the LORD, your God,
am a jealous God, inflicting punishments
for their fathers' wickedness on the
children of those who hate me, down to
the third and fourth generation 10* but
bestowing mercy, down to the thou-
sandth generation, on the children of
those who love me and keep my com-
mandments.
11* 'You shall not take the name of the
LORD, your God, in vain. For the LORD
will not leave unpunished him who takes
his name in vain.
12 'Take care to keep holy the sabbath
day as the LORD, your God, commanded
you. 13 Six days you may labor and do
all your work; 14* but the seventh day
is the sabbath of the LORD, your God.
No work may be done then, whether by
you, or your son or daughter, or your
male or female slave, or your ox or ass
or any of your beasts, or the alien who
lives with you. Your male and female
slave should rest as you do. 15* For re-
member that you too were once slaves
in Egypt, and the LORD, your God,
brought you from there with his strong
hand and outstretched arm. That is why
the LORD, your God, has commanded
you to observe the sabbath day.
16* 'Honor your father and your
mother, as the LORD, your God, has
commanded you, that you may have a
long life and prosperity in the land
which the LORD, your God, is giving you.
17* 'You shall not kill.
18 'You shall not commit adultery.
19 'You shall not steal.
20 'You shall not bear dishonest witness
against your neighbor.
21 'You shall not covet your neighbor's
wife.
'You shall not desire your neighbor's
house or field, nor his male or female
slave, nor his ox or ass, nor anything
that belongs to him.'
Moses as Mediator. 22 "These words,
and nothing more, the LORD spoke with
a loud voice to your entire assembly on
the mountain from the midst of the fire
and the dense cloud. He wrote them
upon two tablets of stone and gave them
to me. 23 But when you heard the voice
from the midst of the darkness, while
the mountain was ablaze with fire, you
came to me in the person of all your
tribal heads and elders, 24* and said,
'The LORD, our God, has indeed let us
see his glory and his majesty! We have
heard his voice from the midst of the
fire and have found out today that a man
can still live after God has spoken with
him. 25* But why should we die now?
Surely this great fire will consume us.
If we hear the voice of the LORD, our
God, any more, we shall die. 26 For what
mortal has heard, as we have, the voice
of the living God speaking from the
midst of fire, and survived? 27* Go
closer, you, and hear all that the LORD,
our God, will say, and then tell us what
the LORD, our God, tells you; we will lis-
ten and obey.'
28* "The LORD heard your words as
you were speaking to me and said to me,
'I have heard the words these people
have spoken to you, which are all well
said. 29 Would that they might always be
of such a mind, to fear me and to keep
all my commandments! Then they and
their descendants would prosper for-
ever. 30 Go, tell them to return to their
tents. 31 Then you wait here near me and
I will give you all the commandments,
the statutes and decrees you must teach
them, that they may observe them in the
land which I am giving them to possess.'
32 "Be careful, therefore, to do as the
LORD, your God, has commanded you,
not turning aside to the right or to the
left, 33* but following exactly the way
prescribed for you by the LORD, your
God, that you may live and prosper, and
may have long life in the land which you
are to occupy.

CHAPTER 6

1* "These then are the command-
ments, the statutes and decrees which
the LORD, your God, has ordered that
you be taught to observe in the land into
which you are crossing for conquest,
2* so that you and your son and your
grandson may fear the LORD, your God,
and keep, throughout the days of your
lives, all his statutes and command-
ments which I enjoin on you, and thus
have long life. 3 Hear then, Israel, and
be careful to observe them, that you may
grow and prosper the more, in keeping
with the promise of the LORD, the God
of your fathers, to give you a land flow-
ing with milk and honey.
The Great Commandment. 4*† "Hear,
O Israel! The LORD is our God, the LORD
alone! 5* Therefore, you shall love the

*

10: 7, 9; Ex 20, 6.
11: Mt 5, 33.
14: Gn 2, 2; Ex 20, 8; 23, 12; Heb 4, 4.
15: 15, 15; 16, 12; 24, 18.22.
16: Sir 3, 2-16; Mt 15, 4; Mk 7, 10; Lk 18, 20; Eph 6, 2.
17-20: Mt 5, 21.27; Lk 18, 20; Jas 2, 11.
24: 4, 33.
25: 18, 16.
27: Ex 20, 19.
28: 18, 17.
33: 4, 40.
6, 1: 4, 1; 5, 31; 12, 1.
2: 4, 40; 5, 29; 10, 12f.
4: Mk 12, 29.
5: 10, 12; 11, 13; Mt 22, 37; Mk 12, 30; Lk 10, 27.

†

6, 4f: This passage contains the basic principle of the whole Mosaic law, the keynote of the Book of Deuteronomy: since the Lord alone is God, we must love him with an undivided heart. Christ cited these words as "the greatest and the first commandment," embracing in itself the whole law of God (Mt 22, 37f and parallels).

LORD, your God, with all your heart, and
with all your soul, and with all your
strength. 6* Take to heart these words
which I enjoin on you today. 7 Drill them
into your children. Speak of them at
home and abroad, whether you are busy
or at rest. 8*† Bind them at your wrist
as a sign and let them be as a pendant
on your forehead. 9* Write them on the
doorposts of your houses and on your
gates.

Fidelity in Prosperity. 10* "When the
LORD, your God, brings you into the land
which he swore to your fathers, Abra-
ham, Isaac and Jacob, that he would
give you, a land with fine, large cities
that you did not build, 11 with houses full
of goods of all sorts that you did not gar-
ner, with cisterns that you did not dig,
with vineyards and olive groves that you
did not plant; and when, therefore, you
eat your fill, 12* take care not to forget
the LORD, who brought you out of the
land of Egypt, that place of slavery.
13*† The LORD, your God, shall you
fear; him shall you serve, and by his
name shall you swear. 14* You shall not
follow other gods, such as those of the
surrounding nations, 15 lest the wrath of
the LORD, your God, flare up against you
and he destroy you from the face of the
land; for the LORD, your God, who is in
your midst, is a jealous God.

16* "You shall not put the LORD, your
God, to the test, as you did at Massah.
17 But keep the commandments of the
LORD, your God, and the ordinances and
statutes he has enjoined on you. 18 Do
what is right and good in the sight of
the LORD, that you may, according to
his word, prosper, and may enter in and
possess the good land which the LORD
promised on oath to your fathers,
19* thrusting all your enemies out of
your way.

Instruction to Children. 20* "Later on,
when your son asks you what these ordi-
nances, statutes and decrees mean
which the LORD, our God, has enjoined
on you, 21* you shall say to your son, 'We
were once slaves of Pharaoh in Egypt,
but the LORD brought us out of Egypt
with his strong hand 22 and wrought be-
fore our eyes signs and wonders, great
and dire, against Egypt and against
Pharaoh and his whole house. 23 He
brought us from there to lead us into the
land he promised on oath to our fathers,
and to give it to us. 24 Therefore, the
LORD commanded us to observe all these
statutes in fear of the LORD, our God,
that we may always have as prosperous
and happy a life as we have today; 25 and
our justice before the LORD, our God, is
to consist in carefully observing all these
commandments he has enjoined on
us.'

CHAPTER 7

Destruction of Pagans. 1* "When the
LORD, your God, brings you into the land
which you are to enter and occupy, and
dislodges great nations before you—the
Hittites, Girgashites, Amorites, Canaan-
ites, Perizzites, Hivites and Jebusites:
seven nations more numerous and pow-
erful than you—2* and when the LORD,
your God, delivers them up to you and
you defeat them, you shall doom them.
Make no covenant with them and show
them no mercy. 3* You shall not inter-
marry with them, neither giving your
daughters to their sons nor taking their
daughters for your sons. 4 For they
would turn your sons from following me
to serving other gods, and then the
wrath of the LORD would flare up against
you and quickly destroy you.

5*† "But this is how you must deal with
them: Tear down their altars, smash
their sacred pillars, chop down their sa-
cred poles, and destroy their idols by
fire. 6* For you are a people sacred to
the LORD, your God; he has chosen you
from all the nations on the face of the
earth to be a people peculiarly his own.
7 It was not because you are the largest
of all nations that the LORD set his heart
on you and chose you, for you are really
the smallest of all nations. 8 It was be-
cause the LORD loved you and because
of his fidelity to the oath he had sworn
to your fathers, that he brought you out
with his strong hand from the place of
slavery, and ransomed you from the
hand of Pharaoh, king of Egypt.
9* Understand, then, that the LORD,
your God, is God indeed, the faithful God
who keeps his merciful covenant down
to the thousandth generation toward
those who love him and keep his com-
mandments, 10 but who repays with de-

*

6f: 4, 9; 11, 18; 32, 46.
8: 11, 18; Ex 13, 9.16; Mt 23, 5.
9: 11, 20.
10f: Jos 24, 13.
12: 5, 6.
13: 10, 20; Mt 4, 10; Lk 4, 8.
14f: 8, 19; 11, 16.28.
16: Nm 20, 1-13.
19: Ex 23, 27; 34, 11.
20: Ex 12, 26; 13, 14.
21: Ex 20, 2.
7, 1: Ex 23, 23; 33, 2.
2: Ex 34, 12.
3f: Ex 34, 16; 1 Kgs 11, 1f.
5: 12, 3; Ex 34, 13.
6: 14, 2; 26, 18; Ex 19, 6.
9f: 5, 9f.

†

6, 8: *Bind them . . . as a sign:* these injunctions were probably meant merely in a figurative sense; cf Ex 13, 9.16. However, the later Jews understood them literally, and tied on their wrists and foreheads "phylacteries," boxes containing strips of parchment on which these words were inscribed; cf Mt 23, 5.

6, 13: *Him shall you serve:* here, to "serve" God means especially to "worship" him; in this sense it is quoted by our Lord (Mt 4, 10) as an argument against worshiping the devil.

7, 5: *Sacred pillars . . . poles:* see note on Ex 34, 13.

struction the person who hates him; he does not dally with such a one, but makes him personally pay for it. 11 You shall therefore carefully observe the commandments, the statutes and the decrees which I enjoin on you today.

Blessings of Obedience. 12* "As your reward for heeding these decrees and observing them carefully, the LORD, your God, will keep with you the merciful covenant which he promised on oath to your fathers. 13* He will love and bless and multiply you; he will bless the fruit of your womb and the produce of your soil, your grain and wine and oil, the issue of your herds and the young of your flocks, in the land which he swore to your fathers he would give you. 14 You will be blessed above all peoples; no man or woman among you shall be childless nor shall your livestock be barren. 15 The LORD will remove all sickness from you; he will not afflict you with any of the malignant diseases that you know from Egypt, but will leave them with all your enemies.

16 "You shall consume all the nations which the LORD, your God, will deliver up to you. You are not to look on them with pity, lest you be ensnared into serving their gods. 17 * Perhaps you will say to yourselves, 'These nations are greater than we. How can we dispossess them?' 18 But do not be afraid of them. Rather, call to mind what the LORD, your God, did to Pharaoh and to all Egypt: 19* the great testings which your own eyes have seen, the signs and wonders, his strong hand and outstretched arm with which the LORD, your God, brought you out. The same also will he do to all the nations of whom you are now afraid. 20* Moreover, the LORD, your God, will send hornets among them, until the survivors who have hidden from you are destroyed. 21 Therefore, do not be terrified by them, for the LORD, your God, who is in your midst, is a great and awesome God. 22* He will dislodge these nations before you little by little. You cannot exterminate them all at once, lest the wild beasts become too numerous for you. 23* The LORD, your God, will deliver them up to you and will rout them utterly until they are annihilated. 24* He will deliver their kings into your hand, that you may make their names perish from under the heavens. No man will be able to stand up against you, till you have put an end to them. 25 The images of their gods you shall destroy by fire. Do not covet the silver or gold on them, nor take it for yourselves, lest you be ensnared by it; for it is an abomination to the LORD, your God. 26 You shall not bring any abominable thing into your house, lest you be doomed with it; loathe and abhor it utterly as a thing that is doomed.

CHAPTER 8

God's Care. 1* "Be careful to observe all the commandments I enjoin on you today, that you may live and increase, and may enter in and possess the land which the LORD promised on oath to your fathers. 2* Remember how for forty years now the LORD, your God, has directed all your journeying in the desert, so as to test you by affliction and find out whether or not it was your intention to keep his commandments. 3*† He therefore let you be afflicted with hunger, and then fed you with manna, a food unknown to you and your fathers, in order to show you that not by bread alone does man live, but by every word that comes forth from the mouth of the LORD. 4* The clothing did not fall from you in tatters, nor did your feet swell these forty years. 5 So you must realize that the LORD, your God, disciplines you even as a man disciplines his son.

Danger of Prosperity. 6 "Therefore, keep the commandments of the LORD, your God, by walking in his ways and fearing him. 7* For the LORD, your God, is bringing you into a good country, a land with streams of water, with springs and fountains welling up in the hills and valleys, 8 a land of wheat and barley, of vines and fig trees and pomegranates, of olive trees and of honey, 9 a land where you can eat bread without stint and where you will lack nothing, a land whose stones contain iron and in whose hills you can mine copper. 10 But when you have eaten your fill, you must bless the LORD, your God, for the good country he has given you. 11 Be careful not to forget the LORD, your God, by neglecting his commandments and decrees and statutes which I enjoin on you today: 12 lest, when you have eaten your fill, and have built fine houses and lived in them, 13 and have increased your herds and flocks, your silver and gold, and all your property, 14 you then become haughty of heart and unmindful of the LORD, your God, who brought you out of the land of Egypt, that place of slavery; 15* who guided you through the vast and terrible desert with its saraph serpents and scor-

*

12-16: 28, 1-14; Ex 23, 22-26; Lv 26, 3-13.
13: 30, 9.
17f: 1, 28ff.
19: 4, 34.
20: Ex 23, 28ff.
22: Ex 23, 29f.
23: 7, 2.
24: 11, 25.
8, 1: 4, 1; 6, 1.
2: 2, 7; 29, 4; Am 2, 10.
3: Ex 16, 12-15.35; Nm 11, 6-9; Mt 4, 4; Lk 4, 4.
4: 29, 4; Neh 9, 21.
7: 11, 10ff.
15: Wis 11, 4.

†

8, 3: *Not by bread alone,* etc: quoted by our Lord in Mt 4, 4. The sense is: God takes care of those who love him even when natural means seem to fail them.

pions, its parched and waterless ground;
who brought forth water for you from
the flinty rock 16 and fed you in the
desert with manna, a food unknown to
your fathers, that he might afflict you
and test you, but also make you prosper-
ous in the end. 17* Otherwise, you might
say to yourselves, 'It is my own power
and the strength of my own hand that
has obtained for me this wealth.'
18 Remember then, it is the LORD, your
God, who gives you the power to acquire
wealth, by fulfilling, as he has now done,
the covenant which he swore to your fa-
thers. 19* But if you forget the LORD,
your God, and follow other gods, serving
and worshiping them, I forewarn you
this day that you will perish utterly.
20 Like the nations which the LORD de-
stroys before you, so shall you too perish
for not heeding the voice of the LORD,
your God.

CHAPTER 9

Unmerited Success. 1* "Hear, O Is-
rael! You are now about to cross the Jor-
dan to enter in and dispossess nations
greater and stronger than yourselves,
having large cities fortified to the sky,
2* the Anakim, a people great and tall.
You know of them and have heard it said
of them, 'Who can stand up against the
Anakim?' 3* Understand, then, today
that it is the LORD, your God, who will
cross over before you as a consuming
fire; he it is who will reduce them to noth-
ing and subdue them before you, so that
you can drive them out and destroy
them quickly, as the LORD promised
you. 4* After the LORD, your God, has
thrust them out of your way, do not say
to yourselves, 'It is because of my merits
that the LORD has brought me in to pos-
sess this land'; for it is really because
of the wickedness of these nations that
the LORD is driving them out before you.
5 No, it is not because of your merits or
the integrity of your heart that you are
going in to take possession of their land;
but the LORD, your God, is driving these
nations out before you on account of
their wickedness and in order to keep
the promise which he made on oath to
your fathers, Abraham, Isaac and Ja-
cob. 6 Understand this, therefore: it is
not because of your merits that the
LORD, your God, is giving you this good
land to possess, for you are a stiff-
necked people.

The Golden Calf. 7* "Bear in mind
and do not forget how you angered the
LORD, your God, in the desert. From the
day you left the land of Egypt until you
arrived in this place, you have been re-
bellious toward the LORD. 8* At Horeb
you so provoked the LORD that he was
angry enough to destroy you, 9* when I
had gone up the mountain to receive the
stone tablets of the covenant which the
LORD made with you. Meanwhile I
stayed on the mountain forty days and
forty nights without eating or drinking,
10* till the LORD gave me the two tablets
of stone inscribed, by God's own finger,
with a copy of all the words that the
LORD spoke to you on the mountain from
the midst of the fire on the day of the
assembly. 11 Then, at the end of the forty
days and forty nights, when the LORD
had given me the two stone tablets of
the covenant, 12* he said to me, 'Go down
from here now, quickly, for your people
whom you have brought out of Egypt
have become depraved; they have al-
ready turned aside from the way I
pointed out to them and have made for
themselves a molten idol. 13 I have seen
now how stiff-necked this people is,' the
LORD said to me. 14 'Let me be, that I
may destroy them and blot out their
name from under the heavens. I will
then make of you a nation mightier and
greater than they.'

15* "When I had come down again
from the blazing, fiery mountain, with
the two tablets of the covenant in both
my hands, 16* I saw how you had sinned
against the LORD, your God: you had al-
ready turned aside from the way which
the LORD had pointed out to you by
making for yourselves a molten calf!
17 Raising the two tablets with both
hands I threw them from me and broke
them before your eyes. 18* Then, as be-
fore, I lay prostrate before the LORD for
forty days and forty nights without eat-
ing or drinking, because of all the sin
you had committed in the sight of the
LORD and the evil you had done to pro-
voke him. 19* For I dreaded the fierce
anger of the LORD against you: his wrath
would destroy you. Yet once again the
LORD listened to me. 20 With Aaron, too,
the LORD was deeply angry, and would
have killed him had I not prayed for him
also at that time. 21* Then, taking the
calf, the sinful object you had made, and
fusing it with fire, I ground it down to
powder as fine as dust, which I threw
into the wadi that went down the moun-
tainside.

22* "At Taberah, at Massah, and at
Kibroth-hattaavah likewise, you pro-
voked the LORD to anger. 23* And when

17: 9, 4.
19: 4, 25f; 30, 18.
9, 1: 1, 28; 4, 38.
2: Nm 13, 33.
3: 31, 3; Ex 23, 27.
4: 8, 17.
7: 31, 27; Ex 14, 11; Nm 14, 11.
8: Ex 32, 4; Ps 106, 19.
9: Ex 24, 12.18; 34, 28.
10: Ex 31, 18.
12ff: Ex 32, 7-10.
15: Ex 32, 15.
16f: Ex 32, 19.
18: Ex 32, 31; 34, 28.
19: 10, 10; Ex 32, 10.
21: Ex 32, 20.
22: Ex 17, 7; Nm 11, 1ff.34.
23: Nm 14, 1-4; Ps 106, 24f.

he sent you up from Kadesh-barnea to take possession of the land he was giving you, you rebelled against this command of the LORD, your God, and would not trust or obey him. 24 Ever since I have known you, you have been rebels against the LORD.

25 "Those forty days, then, and forty nights, I lay prostrate before the LORD, because he had threatened to destroy you. 26 This was my prayer to him: O Lord GOD, destroy not your people, the heritage which your majesty has ransomed and brought out of Egypt with your strong hand. 27 Remember your servants, Abraham, Isaac and Jacob. Look not upon the stubbornness of this people nor upon their wickedness and sin, 28* lest the people from whose land you have brought us say, 'The LORD was not able to bring them into the land he promised them'; or 'Out of hatred for them, he brought them out to slay them in the desert.' 29* They are, after all, your people and your heritage, whom you have brought out by your great power and with your outstretched arm.

CHAPTER 10

1* "At that time the LORD said to me, 'Cut two tablets of stone like the former; then come up the mountain to me. Also make an ark of wood. 2 I will write upon the tablets the commandments that were on the former tablets that you broke, and you shall place them in the ark.' 3* So I made an ark of acacia wood, and cut two tablets of stone like the former, and went up the mountain carrying the two tablets. 4* The LORD then wrote on them, as he had written before, the ten commandments which he spoke to you on the mountain from the midst of the fire on the day of the assembly. After the LORD had given them to me, 5* I turned and came down the mountain, and placed the tablets in the ark I had made. There they have remained, in keeping with the command the LORD gave me.

6* [The Israelites set out from Beeroth Bene-jaakan for Moserah, where Aaron died and was buried, his son Eleazar succeeding him in the priestly office. 7* From there they set out for Gudgodah, and from Gudgodah for Jotbathah, a region where there is water in the wadies.]

8* "At that time the LORD set apart the tribe of Levi to carry the ark of the covenant of the LORD, to be in attendance before the LORD and minister to him, and to give blessings in his name, as they have done to this day. 9* For this reason, Levi has no share in the heritage with his brothers; the LORD himself is his heritage, as the LORD, your God, has told him.

10 "After I had spent these other forty days and forty nights on the mountain, and the LORD had once again heard me and decided not to destroy you, 11* he said to me, 'Go now and set out at the head of your people, that they may enter in and occupy the land which I swore to their fathers I would give them.'

The Lord's Majesty. 12* "And now, Israel, what does the LORD, your God, ask of you but to fear the LORD, your God, and follow his ways exactly, to love and serve the LORD, your God, with all your heart and all your soul, 13 to keep the commandments and statutes of the LORD which I enjoin on you today for your own good? 14*† Think! The heavens, even the highest heavens, belong to the LORD, your God, as well as the earth and everything on it. 15* Yet in his love for your fathers the LORD was so attached to them as to choose you, their descendants, in preference to all other peoples, as indeed he has now done. 16† Circumcise your hearts, therefore, and be no longer stiff-necked. 17* For the LORD, your God, is the God of gods, the LORD of lords, the great God, mighty and awesome, who has no favorites, accepts no bribes; 18 who executes justice for the orphan and the widow, and befriends the alien, feeding and clothing him. 19* So you too must befriend the alien, for you were once aliens yourselves in the land of Egypt. 20* The LORD, your God, shall you fear, and him shall you serve; hold fast to him and swear by his name. 21 He is your glory, he, your God, who has done for you those great and terrible things which your own eyes have seen. 22* Your ancestors went down to Egypt seventy strong, and now the LORD, your God, has made you as numerous as the stars of the sky.

*

28: Nm 14, 14ff.
29: 4, 20; Ex 6, 6f.
10, 1: Ex 34, 1.
3: Ex 34, 4.
4: Ex 20, 1-17; 34, 28.
5: Ex 40, 20; 1 Kgs 8, 9.
6: Nm 33, 31.
7: Nm 33, 32f.
8: Nm 3, 6; 6, 23-27; 16, 9.
9: Nm 18, 20.
11: Ex 32, 34; 33, 1.
12: 6, 2.5.
14: Neh 9, 6.
15: 7, 6ff.
17: 2 Chr 19, 7; Jb 34, 19; Wis 6, 7; Acts 10, 34; Rom 2, 11; Gal 2, 6.
19: Ex 22, 21; 23, 9; Lv 19, 33f.
20: 6, 13; Mt 4, 10; Lk 4, 8.
22: Gn 46, 27; Ex 1, 5; Acts 7, 14.

†

10, 14: *Even the highest heavens:* literally, "and the heavens of the heavens"; compare the phrase, "the third heaven," in 2 Cor 12, 2.

10, 16: *Circumcise your hearts:* cf 30, 6; Jer 4, 4; Rom 2, 29. The "uncircumcised heart" (Lv 26, 41; Jer 9, 25; Ez 44, 7.9) is closed and unreceptive to divine grace and guidance, just as "uncircumcised ears" (Jer 6, 10) are closed to sound, and "uncircumcised lips" (Ex 6, 12.30) do not open well in speech.

CHAPTER 11

The Wonders of the Lord. 1 "Love the LORD, your God, therefore, and always heed his charge: his statutes, decrees and commandments. 2 It is not your children, who have not known it from experience, but you yourselves who must now understand the discipline of the LORD, your God; his majesty, his strong hand and outstretched arm; 3* the signs and deeds he wrought among the Egyptians, on Pharaoh, king of Egypt, and on all his land; 4* what he did to the Egyptian army and to their horses and chariots, engulfing them in the water of the Red Sea as they pursued you, and bringing ruin upon them even to this day; 5 what he did for you in the desert until you arrived in this place; 6* and what he did to the Reubenites Dathan and Abiram, sons of Eliab, when the ground opened its mouth and swallowed them up out of the midst of Israel, with their families and tents and every living thing that belonged to them. 7 With your own eyes you have seen all these great deeds that the LORD has done. 8 Keep all the commandments, then, which I enjoin on you today, that you may be strong enough to enter in and take possession of the land into which you are crossing, 9 and that you may have long life on the land which the LORD swore to your fathers he would give to them and their descendants, a land flowing with milk and honey.

The Gift of Rain. 10 "For the land which you are to enter and occupy is not like the land of Egypt from which you have come, where you would sow your seed and then water it by hand, as in a vegetable garden. 11* No, the land into which you are crossing for conquest is a land of hills and valleys that drinks in rain from the heavens, 12 a land which the LORD, your God, looks after; his eyes are upon it continually from the beginning of the year to the end. 13*† If, then, you truly heed my commandments which I enjoin on you today, loving and serving the LORD, your God, with all your heart and all your soul, 14† I will give the seasonal rain to your land, the early rain and the late rain, that you may have your grain, wine and oil to gather in; 15* and I will bring forth grass in your fields for your animals. Thus you may eat your fill. 16* But be careful lest your heart be so lured away that you serve other gods and worship them. 17 For then the wrath of the LORD will flare up against you and he will close up the heavens, so that no rain will fall, and the soil will not yield its crops, and you will soon perish from the good land he is giving you.

Reward of Fidelity. 18* "Therefore, take these words of mine into your heart and soul. Bind them at your wrist as a sign, and let them be a pendant on your forehead. 19 Teach them to your children, speaking of them at home and abroad, whether you are busy or at rest. 20 And write them on the doorposts of your houses and on your gates, 21 so that, as long as the heavens are above the earth, you and your children may live on in the land which the LORD swore to your fathers he would give them.

22 "For if you are careful to observe all these commandments I enjoin on you, loving the LORD, your God, and following his ways exactly, and holding fast to him, 23* the LORD will drive all these nations out of your way, and you will dispossess nations greater and mightier than yourselves. 24*† Every place where you set foot shall be yours: from the desert and from Lebanon, from the Euphrates River to the Western Sea, shall be your territory. 25* None shall stand up against you; the LORD, your God, will spread the fear and dread of you through any land where you set foot, as he promised you.

A Blessing and a Curse. 26* "I set before you here, this day, a blessing and a curse: 27 a blessing for obeying the commandments of the LORD, your God, which I enjoin on you today; 28 a curse if you do not obey the commandments of the LORD, your God, but turn aside from the way I ordain for you today, to follow other gods, whom you have not known. 29*† When the LORD, your God, brings you into the land which you are to enter and occupy, then you shall pronounce the blessing on Mount Gerizim, the curse on Mount Ebal. 30 [Are they not beyond the Jordan, on the other side of the western road in the country of the Canaanites who live in the Arabah, opposite the Gilgal beside the terebinth of Moreh?] 31 For you are about to cross

---

*

11, 3: 6, 22; Ps 78, 42-51.
4: Ex 14, 26ff; 15, 9; Pss 78, 53; 106, 11.
6: Nm 16, 31ff.
11f: 8 7.
13f: 10, 12; Lv 26, 4.
15: Ps 104, 14.
16f: 4, 25f; 6, 14.
18-21: 6, 6-9.
23: 7, 1; 9, 1.
24: Ex 23, 31.
25: 2, 25; 7, 24; Ex 23, 27.
26ff: 28, 2-45; 30, 1.15. 19.
29: 27, 12f.

---

†

11, 13ff: As often in the Prophets, the discourse passes into the words of God himself. Cf 7, 4; 17, 3; 28, 20; 29, 4f.

11, 14: *The early rain:* the rains which begin in October or November and continue intermittently throughout the winter. *The late rain:* the heavy showers of March and April. In Palestine the crops are sown in the autumn and reaped in the spring.

11, 24: *The Western Sea:* the Mediterranean.

11, 29: *You shall pronounce the blessing . . . the curse:* for the full ceremony, see chapters 27 and 28. *Gerizim . . . Ebal:* adjacent mountains in Samaria with a deep ravine between them. Their summits command an excellent view of the entire country.

the Jordan to enter and occupy the land which the LORD, your God, is giving you. When, therefore, you take possession of it and settle there, 32 be careful to observe all the statutes and decrees that I set before you today.

III: EXPOSITION OF THE LAW

CHAPTER 12

One Sanctuary. 1 "These are the statutes and decrees which you must be careful to observe in the land which the LORD, the God of your fathers, has given you to occupy, as long as you live on its soil. 2* Destroy without fail every place on the high mountains, on the hills, and under every leafy tree where the nations you are to dispossess worship their gods. 3 Tear down their altars, smash their sacred pillars, destroy by fire their sacred poles, and shatter the idols of their gods, that you may stamp out the remembrance of them in any such place.

4 "That is not how you are to worship the LORD, your God. 5* Instead, you shall resort to the place which the LORD, your God, chooses out of all your tribes and designates as his dwelling 6 and there you shall bring your holocausts and sacrifices, your tithes and personal contributions, your votive and freewill offerings, and the firstlings of your herds and flocks. 7 There, too, before the LORD, your God, you and your families shall eat and make merry over all your undertakings, because the LORD, your God, has blessed you. 8 You shall not do as we are now doing; here, everyone does what seems right to himself, 9 since you have not yet reached your resting place, the heritage which the LORD, your God, will give you. 10 But after you have crossed the Jordan and dwell in the land which the LORD, your God, is giving you as a heritage, when he has given you rest from all your enemies round about and you live there in security, 11 then to the place which the LORD, your God, chooses as the dwelling place for his name you shall bring all the offerings I command you: your holocausts and sacrifices, your tithes and personal contributions, and every special offering you have vowed to the LORD. 12 You shall make merry before the LORD, your God, with your sons and daughters, your male and female slaves, as well as with the Levite who belongs to your community but has no share of his own in your heritage. 13 Take care not to offer up your holocausts in any place you fancy, 14 but offer them up in the place which the LORD chooses from among your tribes; there you shall make whatever offerings I enjoin upon you.

Profane and Sacred Meals. 15 "However, in any of your communities you may slaughter and eat to your heart's desire as much meat as the LORD, your God, has blessed you with; and the unclean as well as the clean may eat it, as they do the gazelle or the deer. 16* Only, you shall not partake of the blood, but must pour it out on the ground like water. 17 Moreover, you shall not, in your own communities, partake of your tithe of grain or wine or oil, of the firstborn of your herd or flock, of any offering you have vowed, of your freewill offerings, or of your personal contributions. 18 These you must eat before the LORD, your God, in the place he chooses, along with your son and daughter, your male and female slave, and the Levite who belongs to your community; and there, before the LORD, you shall make merry over all your undertakings. 19* Take care, also, that you do not neglect the Levite as long as you live in the land.

20*† "After the LORD, your God, has enlarged your territory, as he promised you, when you wish meat for food, you may eat it at will, to your heart's desire; 21 and if the place which the LORD, your God, chooses for the abode of his name is too far, you may slaughter in the manner I have told you any of your herd or flock that the LORD has given you, and eat it to your heart's desire in your own community. 22 You may eat it as you would the gazelle or the deer: the unclean and the clean eating it alike. 23 But make sure that you do not partake of the blood; for blood is life, and you shall not consume this seat of life with the flesh. 24 Do not partake of the blood, therefore, but pour it out on the ground like water. 25 Abstain from it, that you and your children after you may prosper for doing what is right in the sight of the LORD. 26 However, any sacred gifts or votive offerings that you may have, you shall bring with you to the place which the LORD chooses, 27* and there you must offer both the flesh and the blood of your holocausts on the altar of the LORD, your God; of your other sacrifices the blood indeed must be poured out against the altar of the LORD, your God, but their flesh may be eaten. 28 Be careful to heed all these commandments I enjoin on you, that you and your descendants may always prosper for doing what is good and right in the sight of the LORD, your God.

Pagan Rites. 29 "When the LORD, your

*

12, 2f: 7, 5; Ex 23, 24; 34, 13.
5-7.11f: 14, 22-26; 15, 19f; 16, 2.10f. 14f; 26, 2.
16: 15, 23; Gn 9, 4; Lv 3, 17.
19: 14, 27.
20: 19, 8; Gn 28, 14; Ex 34, 24.
27: Lv 17, 11.

†

12, 20: *Meat for food:* as on special feasts. Meat was not eaten every day in Israel, even by the wealthy.

God, removes the nations from your way
as you advance to dispossess them, be
on your guard! Otherwise, once they
have been wiped out before you and you
have replaced them and are settled in
their land, 30 you will be lured into fol-
lowing them. Do not inquire regarding
their gods, 'How did these nations wor-
ship their gods? I, too, would do the
same.' 31* You shall not thus worship the
LORD, your God, because they offered
to their gods every abomination that the
LORD detests, even burning their sons
and daughters to their gods.

CHAPTER 13

Penalties for Idolatry. 1 "Every com-
mand that I enjoin on you, you shall be
careful to observe, neither adding to it
nor subtracting from it.
2† "If there arises among you a
prophet or a dreamer who promises you
a sign or wonder, 3 urging you to follow
other gods, whom you have not known,
and to serve them: even though the sign
or wonder he has foretold you comes to
pass, 4 pay no attention to the words of
that prophet or that dreamer; for the
LORD, your God, is testing you to learn
whether you really love him with all
your heart and with all your soul. 5 The
LORD, your God, shall you follow, and
him shall you fear; his commandment
shall you observe, and his voice shall
you heed, serving him and holding fast
to him alone. 6* But that prophet or that
dreamer shall be put to death, because,
in order to lead you astray from the way
which the LORD, your God, has directed
you to take, he has preached apostasy
from the LORD, your God, who brought
you out of the land of Egypt and ran-
somed you from that place of slavery.
Thus shall you purge the evil from your
midst.
7 "If your own full brother, or your son
or daughter, or your beloved wife, or
your intimate friend, entices you se-
cretly to serve other gods, whom you
and your fathers have not known, 8 gods
of any other nations, near at hand or
far away, from one end of the earth to
the other: 9 do not yield to him or listen
to him, nor look with pity upon him, to
spare or shield him, 10 but kill him. Your
hand shall be the first raised to slay him;
the rest of the people shall join in with
you. 11 You shall stone him to death, be-
cause he sought to lead you astray from
the LORD, your God, who brought you
out of the land of Egypt, that place of
slavery. 12 And all Israel, hearing of it,
shall fear and never again do such evil
as this in your midst.
13 "If, in any of the cities which the
LORD, your God, gives you to dwell in,
you hear it said 14 that certain scoun-
drels have sprung up among you and
have led astray the inhabitants of their
city to serve other gods whom you have
not known, 15 you must inquire carefully
into the matter and investigate it thor-
oughly. If you find that it is true and an
established fact that this abomination
has been committed in your midst,
16* you shall put the inhabitants of that
city to the sword, dooming the city and
all life that is in it, even its cattle, to the
sword. 17 Having heaped up all its spoils
in the middle of its square, you shall
burn the city with all its spoils as a whole
burnt offering to the LORD, your God. Let
it be a heap of ruins forever, never to
be rebuilt. 18 You shall not retain any-
thing that is doomed, that the blazing
wrath of the LORD may die down and
he may show you mercy and in his
mercy for you may multiply you as he
promised your fathers on oath; 19 be-
cause you have heeded the voice of the
LORD, your God, keeping all his com-
mandments which I enjoin on you today,
doing what is right in his sight.

CHAPTER 14

Pagan Mourning Rites. 1* "You are
children of the LORD, your God. You
shall not gash yourselves nor shave
the hair above your foreheads for the
dead. 2* For you are a people sacred
to the LORD, your God, who has chosen
you from all the nations on the face of
the earth to be a people peculiarly his
own.
Clean and Unclean Animals. 3* "You
shall not eat any abominable thing.
4* These are the animals you may eat:
the ox, the sheep, the goat, 5† the red
deer, the gazelle, the roe deer, the ibex,
the addax, the oryx, and the mountain
sheep. 6 Any animal that has hoofs you
may eat, provided it is cloven-footed
and chews the cud. 7 But you shall not
eat any of the following that only chew
the cud or only have cloven hoofs: the
camel, the hare and the rock badger,
which indeed chew the cud, but do not
have hoofs and are therefore unclean for
you; 8* and the pig, which indeed has
hoofs and is cloven-footed, but does not

*

31: Lv 18, 21; Jer 7, 31.
13, 6-10.14: 6, 14; 17, 2-7.
16f: Jos 6, 18.24; 7, 26; 8, 28.
14, 1: Lv 19, 28.
2: 7, 6.
3: Ez 4, 14; Acts 10, 14.
4-20: Lv 11, 2-23.
8: Lv 11, 26.

†

13, 2.4.6: *Dreamer:* a false prophet who pretended to have received revelations from God in his dreams; cf Jer 23, 25-32; Zec 10, 2. But dreams could also be a channel of true prophecy (Nm 12, 6; Jl 3, 1) and of genuine revelations (Gn 20, 3.6; 31, 10.24; 37, 5.9; Mt 1, 20; 2.12f.19; etc.).

14, 5: *The gazelle, the addax, the oryx:* species of antelopes. *The ibex:* a species of wild goat.

chew the cud and is therefore unclean
for you. Their flesh you shall not eat,
and their dead bodies you shall not
touch.
9 “Of the various creatures that live in
the water, whatever has both fins and
scales you may eat, 10 but all those that
lack either fins or scales you shall not
eat; they are unclean for you.
11 “You may eat all clean birds. 12 But
you shall not eat any of the following:
the eagle, the vulture, the osprey, 13 the
various kites and falcons, 14 all the vari-
ous species of crows, 15 the ostrich, the
nightjar, the gull, the various species of
hawks, 16 the owl, the screech owl, the
ibis, 17 the desert owl, the buzzard, the
cormorant, 18 the stork, the various
species of herons, the hoopoe, and the
bat. 19† All winged insects, too, are un-
clean for you and shall not be eaten.
20 But you may eat any clean winged
creatures.
21*† “You must not eat any animal
that has died of itself, for you are a peo-
ple sacred to the LORD, your God. But
you may give it to an alien who belongs
to your community, and he may eat it,
or you may sell it to a foreigner.

“You shall not boil a kid in its mother’s
milk.

Tithes. 22* “Each year you shall tithe
all the produce that grows in the field
you have sown; 23* then in the place
which the LORD, your God, chooses as
the dwelling place of his name you shall
eat in his presence your tithe of the
grain, wine and oil, as well as the first-
lings of your herd and flock, that you
may learn always to fear the LORD, your
God. 24† If, however, the journey is too
much for you and you are not able to
bring your tithe, because the place
which the LORD, your God, chooses for
the abode of his name is too far for you,
considering how the LORD has blessed
you, 25 you may exchange the tithe for
money and, with the purse of money in
hand, go to the place which the LORD,
your God, chooses. 26 You may then ex-
change the money for whatever you de-
sire, oxen or sheep, wine or strong drink,
or anything else you would enjoy, and
there before the LORD, your God, you
shall partake of it and make merry with
your family. 27* But do not neglect the
Levite who belongs to your community,
for he has no share in the heritage with
you.
28* “At the end of every third year you
shall bring out all the tithes of your pro-
duce for that year and deposit them in
community stores, 29 that the Levite who
has no share in the heritage with you,
and also the alien, the orphan and the
widow who belong to your community,
may come and eat their fill; so that the
LORD, your God, may bless you in all
that you undertake.

CHAPTER 15

Debts and the Poor. 1*† “At the end
of every seven-year period you shall
have a relaxation of debts, 2 which shall
be observed as follows. Every creditor
shall relax his claim on what he has
loaned his neighbor; he must not press
his neighbor, his kinsman, because a re-
laxation in honor of the LORD has been
proclaimed. 3* You may press a for-
eigner, but you shall relax the claim on
your kinsman for what is yours. 4 Nay,
more! since the LORD, your God, will
bless you abundantly in the land he will
give you to occupy as your heritage,
there should be no one of you in need.
5 If you but heed the voice of the LORD,
your God, and carefully observe all
these commandments which I enjoin on
you today, 6* you will lend to many na-
tions, and borrow from none; you will
rule over many nations, and none will
rule over you, since the LORD, your God,
will bless you as he promised. 7 If one
of your kinsmen in any community is
in need in the land which the LORD, your
God, is giving you, you shall not harden
your heart nor close your hand to him
in his need. 8* Instead, you shall open
your hand to him and freely lend him
enough to meet his need. 9 Be on your
guard lest, entertaining the mean
thought that the seventh year, the year
of relaxation, is near, you grudge help
to your needy kinsman and give him
nothing; else he will cry to the LORD
against you and you will be held guilty.
10 When you give to him, give freely and
not with ill will; for the LORD, your God,
will bless you for this in all your works
and undertakings. 11*† The needy will
never be lacking in the land; that is why
I command you to open your hand to

*

21: Ex 22, 30; 23, 19; 34, 26.	15, 1: Neh 10, 31.
22: Lv 27, 30.	3: 23, 20.
23f: 12, 5ff.	6: 28, 12f.
27: 12, 12.19.	8: Lv 25, 35; Sir 29, 1f; Mt 5, 42.
28f: 26, 12.	11: 15, 8; Sir 29, 12.

†

14, 19f: The apparent contradiction is to be resolved in the light of Lv 11, 20-23: the *unclean winged insects* are those that walk on the ground; the *clean winged creatures* are those that leap on the ground, such as certain species of locusts.

14, 21: *Boil a kid in its mother’s milk:* see note on Ex 23, 19.

14, 24: *Considering how the LORD has blessed you:* should the Israelite farmer be blessed with an abundant harvest, a tenth of this would be too much to transport for a great distance.

15, 1: *At the end of every seven-year period:* in every seventh, or sabbatical, year. Cf v 9; 31, 10; and compare Jer 34, 14 with Dt 15, 12. *A relaxation of debts:* it is uncertain whether a full cancellation of debts is meant, or merely a suspension of payment on them or on their interest among the Israelites. Cf Ex 23, 11 where the same Hebrew root is used of a field that is “let lie fallow” in the sabbatical year.

15, 11: *The needy will never be lacking:* compare the words of Christ, “The poor you will always have with you” (Mt 26, 11).

your poor and needy kinsman in your
country.
Hebrew Slaves. 12* “If your kinsman,
a Hebrew man or woman, sells himself
to you, he is to serve you for six years,
but in the seventh year you shall dismiss
him from your service, a free man.
13 When you do so, you shall not send
him away empty-handed, 14 but shall
weight him down with gifts from your
flock and threshing floor and wine press,
in proportion to the blessing the LORD,
your God, has bestowed on you. 15* For
remember that you too were once slaves
in the land of Egypt, and the LORD, your
God, ransomed you. That is why I am
giving you this command today. 16* If,
however, he tells you that he does not
wish to leave you, because he is devoted
to you and your household, since he
fares well with you, 17† you shall take an
awl and thrust it through his ear into
the door, and he shall then be your slave
forever. Your female slave, also, you
shall treat in the same way. 18 You must
not be reluctant to let your slave go free,
since the service he has given you for
six years was worth twice a hired man’s
salary; then also the LORD, your God,
will bless you in everything you do.
Firstlings. 19* “You shall consecrate
to the LORD, your God, all the male first-
lings of your herd and of your flock. You
shall not work the firstlings of your cat-
tle, nor shear the firstlings of your flock.
20* Year after year you and your family
shall eat them before the LORD, your
God, in the place he chooses. 21* If, how-
ever, a firstling is lame or blind or has
any other serious defect, you shall not
sacrifice it to the LORD, your God, 22 but
in your own communities you may eat
it, the unclean and the clean eating it
alike, as you would a gazelle or a deer.
23 Only, you shall not partake of its blood,
which must be poured out on the ground
like water.

CHAPTER 16

Feast of the Passover. 1*† “Observe
the month of Abib by keeping the Pass-
over of the LORD, your God, since it was
in the month of Abib that he brought you
by night out of Egypt. 2 You shall offer
the Passover sacrifice from your flock
or your herd to the LORD, your God, in
the place which he chooses as the dwell-
ing place of his name. 3* You shall not
eat leavened bread with it. For seven
days you shall eat with it only unleav-
ened bread, the bread of affliction, that
you may remember as long as you live
the day of your departure from the land
of Egypt; for in frightened haste you left
the land of Egypt. 4 Nothing leavened
may be found in all your territory for
seven days, and none of the meat which
you sacrificed on the evening of the first
day shall be kept overnight for the next
day.
5 “You may not sacrifice the Passover
in any of the communities which the
LORD, your God, gives you; 6 only at the
place which he chooses as the dwelling
place of his name, and in the evening
at sunset, on the anniversary of your de-
parture from Egypt, shall you sacrifice
the Passover. 7 You shall cook and eat
it at the place the LORD, your God,
chooses; then in the morning you may
return to your tents. 8 For six days you
shall eat unleavened bread, and on the
seventh there shall be a solemn meeting
in honor of the LORD, your God; on that
day you shall not do any sort of work.
Feast of Weeks. 9* “You shall count
off seven weeks, computing them from
the day when the sickle is first put to
the standing grain. 10† You shall then
keep the feast of Weeks in honor of the
LORD, your God, and the measure of
your own freewill offering shall be in
proportion to the blessing the LORD, your
God, has bestowed on you. 11* In the
place which the LORD, your God,
chooses as the dwelling place of his
name, you shall make merry in his pres-
ence together with your son and daugh-
ter, your male and female slave, and the
Levite who belongs to your community,
as well as the alien, the orphan and the
widow among you. 12 Remember that
you too were once slaves in Egypt, and
carry out these statutes carefully.
Feast of Booths. 13*† “You shall cele-
brate the feast of Booths for seven days,
when you have gathered in the produce
from your threshing floor and wine
press. 14* You shall make merry at your
feast, together with your son and daugh-
ter, your male and female slave, and
also the Levite, the alien, the orphan and
the widow who belong to your commu-
nity. 15 For seven days you shall cele-
brate this pilgrim feast in honor of the
LORD, your God, in the place which he
chooses; since the LORD, your God, has

*

12: Ex 21, 2; Jer 34, 14.
15: 5, 15.
16f: Ex 21, 5f.
19: Ex 13, 11.
20: 14, 23.
21ff: 12, 15f; Lv 22, 20.
16, 1-8: Ex 12, 2-20; 23, 15; Nm 28, 16ff.24f.
3f: Ex 13, 6f; 34, 18.
9-12: Lv 23, 15-21.
11: 12, 5.7.12.18.
13-15: Ex 23, 16; Lv 23, 34-43; Nm 29, 12-38.
14: 16, 11.

†

15, 17: *His ear:* cf Ex 21, 6 and the note there.
16, 1: *Abib:* “ear of grain, ripe grain,” the name of the month in which the barley harvest fell, corresponding to our March and April; at a later period this month received the Babylonian name of “Nisan.”
16, 10: *Feast of Weeks:* later known more commonly as “Pentecost.”
16, 13: See note on Lv 23, 34.

blessed you in all your crops and in all your undertakings, you shall do nought but make merry.

16* "Three times a year, then, every male among you shall appear before the LORD, your God, in the place which he chooses: at the feast of Unleavened Bread, at the feast of Weeks, and at the feast of Booths. No one shall appear before the LORD empty-handed, 17 but each of you with as much as he can give, in proportion to the blessings which the LORD, your God, has bestowed on you.

Judges. 18 "You shall appoint judges and officials throughout your tribes to administer true justice for the people in all the communities which the LORD, your God, is giving you. 19* You shall not distort justice; you must be impartial. You shall not take a bribe; for a bribe blinds the eyes even of the wise and twists the words even of the just. 20 Justice and justice alone shall be your aim, that you may have life and may possess the land which the LORD, your God, is giving you.

Pagan Worship. 21*† "You shall not plant a sacred pole of any kind of wood beside the altar of the LORD, your God, which you will build; 22 nor shall you erect a sacred pillar, such as the LORD, your God, detests.

CHAPTER 17

1* "You shall not sacrifice to the LORD, your God, from the herd or from the flock an animal with any serious defect; that would be an abomination to the LORD, your God.

2* "If there is found among you, in any one of the communities which the LORD, your God, gives you, a man or a woman who does evil in the sight of the LORD, your God, and transgresses his covenant, 3* by serving other gods, or by worshiping the sun or the moon or any of the host of the sky, against my command; 4 and if, on being informed of it, you find by careful investigation that it is true and an established fact that this abomination has been committed in Israel: 5† you shall bring the man (or woman) who has done the evil deed out to your city gates and stone him to death. 6* The testimony of two or three witnesses is required for putting a person to death; no one shall be put to death on the testimony of only one witness. 7* At the execution, the witnesses are to be the first to raise their hands against him; afterward all the people are to join in. Thus shall you purge the evil from your midst.

Judges. 8 "If in your own community there is a case at issue which proves too complicated for you to decide, in a matter of bloodshed or of civil rights or of personal injury, you shall then go up to the place which the LORD, your God, chooses, 9* to the levitical priests or to the judge who is in office at that time. They shall study the case and then hand down to you their decision. 10 According to this decision that they give you in the place which the LORD chooses, you shall act, being careful to do exactly as they direct. 11 You shall carry out the directions they give you and the verdict they pronounce for you, without turning aside to the right or to the left from the decision they hand down to you. 12† Any man who has the insolence to refuse to listen to the priest who officiates there in the ministry of the LORD, your God, or to the judge, shall die. Thus shall you purge the evil from your midst. 13 And all the people, on hearing of it, shall fear, and never again be so insolent.

The King. 14* "When you have come into the land which the LORD, your God, is giving you, and have occupied it and settled in it, should you then decide to have a king over you like all the surrounding nations, 15* you shall set that man over you as your king whom the LORD, your God, chooses. He whom you set over you as king must be your kinsman; a foreigner, who is no kin of yours, you may not set over you. 16*† But he shall not have a great number of horses; nor shall he make his people go back again to Egypt to acquire them, against the LORD's warning that you must never go back that way again. 17* Neither shall he have a great number of wives, lest his heart be estranged, nor shall he accumulate a vast amount of silver and

*

16: Ex 23, 14f.17; 34, 23; 2 Chr 8, 13.
19: 1, 17; Ex 23, 8.
21: 1 Kgs 14, 15; 2 Chr 33, 3.
17, 1: Lv 22, 20.
2-7: 13, 6-15.
3: 4, 19.
6: 19, 15; Nm 35, 30; Mt 18, 16; Jn 8, 17; 2 Cor 13, 1.
7: 13, 10.
9: 21, 5; 2 Chr 19, 8.
14: 1 Sm 8, 5.19f.
15: 1 Sm 9, 16; 10, 24; 16, 12.
16: 28, 68; 1 Kgs 4, 26; 10, 26.
17: 1 Kgs 11, 3f; Neh 13, 26.

†

16, 21—17, 7: This section seems to be out of its proper place, since it interrupts the natural sequence of the laws for the judges (16, 18-20 and 17, 8-13). It probably belongs to the similar section, 12, 29—14, 2.

16, 21f: *Sacred pole . . . sacred pillar:* see note on Ex 34, 13.

17, 5: *Out to your city gates:* outside the gates in an unclean place; cf Lv 24, 14; Nm 15, 36; Acts 7, 58; Heb 13, 12.

17, 12: *The priest:* the high priest; *the judge:* a layman. The former presided over the court in cases which directly concerned religion, the latter in cases of a more secular nature; cf 2 Chr 19, 8-11.

17, 16: *Horses:* chariotry for war. *The LORD's warning:* the same warning is also referred to in 28, 68, although it is not mentioned explicitly elsewhere in the Pentateuch. We know from other sources that Egypt used to export war horses to Palestine. The danger envisioned here is that some king might make Israel a vassal of Egypt for the sake of such military aid.

gold. [18]* When he is enthroned in his
kingdom, he shall have a copy of this
law made from the scroll that is in the
custody of the levitical priests. [19] He
shall keep it with him and read it all the
days of his life that he may learn to fear
the LORD, his God, and to heed and fulfill
all the words of this law and these stat-
utes. [20] Let him not become estranged
from his countrymen through pride, nor
turn aside to the right or to the left from
these commandments. Then he and his
descendants will enjoy a long reign in
Israel.

CHAPTER 18

Priests. [1]* "The whole priestly tribe of
Levi shall have no share in the heritage
with Israel; they shall live on the obla-
tions of the LORD and the portions due
to him. [2] Levi shall have no heritage
among his brothers; the LORD himself
is his heritage, as he has told him. [3] The
priests shall have a right to the following
things from the people: from those who
are offering a sacrifice, whether the vic-
tim is from the herd or from the flock,
the priest shall receive the shoulder, the
jowls and the stomach. [4]* You shall also
give him the first fruits of your grain and
wine and oil, as well as the first fruits
of the shearing of your flock; [5] for the
LORD, your God, has chosen him and his
sons out of all your tribes to be always
in attendance to minister in the name
of the LORD.

[6] "When a Levite goes from one of
your communities anywhere in Israel in
which he ordinarily resides, to visit, as
his heart may desire, the place which
the LORD chooses, [7] he may minister
there in the name of the LORD, his God,
like all his fellow Levites who are in at-
tendance there before the LORD. [8] He
shall then receive the same portions to
eat as the rest, along with his monetary
offerings and heirlooms.

Prophets. [9]* "When you come into the
land which the LORD, your God, is giving
you, you shall not learn to imitate the
abominations of the peoples there.
[10]*† Let there not be found among you
anyone who immolates his son or
daughter in the fire, nor a fortune-teller,
soothsayer, charmer, diviner, [11] or
caster of spells, nor one who consults
ghosts and spirits or seeks oracles from
the dead. [12]* Anyone who does such
things is an abomination to the LORD,
and because of such abominations the
LORD, your God, is driving these nations
out of your way. [13] You, however, must
be altogether sincere toward the LORD,
your God. [14] Though these nations whom
you are to dispossess listen to their
soothsayers and fortune-tellers, the
LORD, your God, will not permit you to
do so.

[15]*† "A prophet like me will the LORD,
your God, raise up for you from among
your own kinsmen; to him you shall lis-
ten. [16]* This is exactly what you re-
quested of the LORD, your God, at Horeb
on the day of the assembly, when you
said, 'Let us not again hear the voice of
the LORD, our God, nor see this great
fire any more, lest we die.' [17] And the
LORD said to me, 'This was well said. [18] I
will raise up for them a prophet like you
from among their kinsmen, and will put
my words into his mouth; he shall tell
them all that I command him. [19]* If any
man will not listen to my words which
he speaks in my name, I myself will
make him answer for it. [20]* But if a
prophet presumes to speak in my name
an oracle that I have not commanded
him to speak, or speaks in the name of
other gods, he shall die.'

[21] "If you say to yourselves, 'How can
we recognize an oracle which the LORD
has spoken?', [22] know that, even though
a prophet speaks in the name of the
LORD, if his oracle is not fulfilled or veri-
fied, it is an oracle which the LORD did
not speak. The prophet has spoken it
presumptuously, and you shall have no
fear of him.

CHAPTER 19

Cities of Refuge. [1] "When the LORD,
your God, removes the nations whose
land he is giving you, and you have
taken their place and are settled in their
cities and houses, [2]†* you shall set apart

---

*

18: 31, 9.26.
18, 1: Nm 18, 8f.20-24; 1 Cor 9, 13.
4: Nm 18, 12; 2 Chr 31, 5.
9: 12, 29ff; Lv 18, 26-30.
10f: Lv 18, 21; 19, 31; 20, 27; 1 Sm 28, 7; 2 Kgs 17, 17; 21, 6.
12: 9, 4.
15: Jn 1, 45; 6, 14; Acts 3, 22; 7, 37.
16: Ex 20, 19.
19: Acts 3, 23.
20.22: 13, 2ff.
19, 2: 4, 41ff; Ex 21, 13; Nm 35, 10-15; Jos 20, 2.8.

†

18, 10f: *Immolates his son or daughter in the fire:* to Molech. See note on Lv 18, 21. Such human sacrifices are classed here with other pagan superstitions because they were believed to possess magical powers for averting a calamity; cf 2 Kgs 3, 27. Three other forms of superstition are listed here: augury (by a *fortune-teller,* a *soothsayer* or a *diviner*): black magic (by a *charmer . . . or caster of spells*); and necromancy (by *one who consults ghosts and spirits or seeks oracles from the dead*).

18, 15: *A prophet like me:* from the context (opposition to the pagan soothsayers) it seems that Moses is referring in general to all the true prophets who were to succeed him. But since Christ is the Great Prophet in whom the prophetic office finds its fulfillment and completion, this passage was understood in a special Messianic sense both by the Jews (Jn 6, 14; 7, 40) and by the Apostles (Acts 3, 22; 7, 37).

19, 2: *Set apart three cities:* the Israelites were to have at least six cities of refuge, three in the land east of the Jordan and three in the land of Canaan west of the Jordan (Nm 35, 9-34); but since the three cities east of the Jordan had now been appointed (Dt 4, 41-43), reference is made here only to the three west of the Jordan. The execution of this command is narrated in Jos 20.

three cities in the land which the LORD, your God, is giving you to occupy. 3 You shall thereby divide into three regions the land which the LORD, your God, will give you as a heritage, and so arrange the routes that every homicide will be able to find a refuge.

4* "It is in the following case that a homicide may take refuge in such a place to save his life: when someone unwittingly kills his neighbor to whom he had previously borne no malice. 5 For example, if he goes with his neighbor to a forest to cut wood, and as he swings his ax to fell a tree, its head flies off the handle and hits his neighbor a mortal blow, he may take refuge in one of these cities to save his life. 6† Should the distance be too great, the avenger of blood may in the heat of his anger pursue the homicide and overtake him and strike him dead, even though he does not merit death since he had previously borne the slain man no malice. 7 That is why I order you to set apart three cities.

8* "But if the LORD, your God, enlarges your territory, as he swore to your fathers, and gives you all the land he promised your fathers he would give 9 in the event that you carefully observe all these commandments which I enjoin on you today, loving the LORD, your God, and ever walking in his ways: then add three cities to these three. 10 Thus, in the land which the LORD, your God, is giving you as a heritage, innocent blood will not be shed and you will not become guilty of bloodshed.

11* "However, if someone lies in wait for his neighbor out of hatred for him, and rising up against him, strikes him mortally, and then takes refuge in one of these cities, 12 the elders of his own city shall send for him and have him taken from there, and shall hand him over to be slain by the avenger of blood. 13 Do not look on him with pity, but purge from Israel the stain of shedding innocent blood, that you may prosper.

Removal of Landmarks. 14* "You shall not move your neighbor's landmarks erected by your forefathers in the heritage you receive in the land which the LORD, your God, is giving you to occupy.

False Witnesses. 15* "One witness alone shall not take the stand against a man in regard to any crime or any offense of which he may be guilty; a judicial fact shall be established only on the testimony of two or three witnesses.

16 "If an unjust witness takes the stand against a man to accuse him of a defection from the law, 17* the two parties in the dispute shall appear before the LORD in the presence of the priests or judges in office at that time; 18* and if after a thorough investigation the judges find that the witness is a false witness and has accused his kinsman falsely, 19 you shall do to him as he planned to do to his kinsman. Thus shall you purge the evil from your midst. 20 The rest, on hearing of it, shall fear, and never again do a thing so evil among you. 21* Do not look on such a man with pity. Life for life, eye for eye, tooth for tooth, hand for hand, and foot for foot!

CHAPTER 20

Courage in War. 1 "When you go out to war against your enemies and you see horses and chariots and an army greater than your own, do not be afraid of them, for the LORD, your God, who brought you up from the land of Egypt, will be with you.

2 "When you are about to go into battle, the priest shall come forward and say to the soldiers: 3 'Hear, O Israel! Today you are going into battle against your enemies. Be not weakhearted or afraid; be neither alarmed nor frightened by them. 4* For it is the LORD, your God, who goes with you to fight for you against your enemies and give you victory.'

5* "Then the officials shall say to the soldiers, 'Is there anyone who has built a new house and not yet had the housewarming? Let him return home, lest he die in battle and another dedicate it. 6 Is there anyone who has planted a vineyard and never yet enjoyed its fruits? Let him return home, lest he die in battle and another enjoy its fruits in his stead. 7* Is there anyone who has betrothed a woman and not yet taken her as his wife? Let him return home, lest he die in battle and another take her to wife.' 8* In fine, the officials shall say to the soldiers, 'Is there anyone who is afraid and weakhearted? Let him return home, lest he make his fellows as fainthearted as himself.'

9 "When the officials have finished speaking to the soldiers, military officers shall be appointed over the army.

Cities of the Enemy. 10 "When you march up to attack a city, first offer it terms of peace. 11 If it agrees to your terms of peace and opens its gates to

*

4: 4, 42; Nm 35, 15; Jos 20, 3.5.
8: Gn 15, 18-21; 28, 14; Ex 23, 31; 34, 24.
11ff: Ex 21, 12.14; Nm 35, 20f.
14: 27, 17; Prv 23, 10; Hos 5, 10.
15: 17, 6; Nm 35, 30; Mt 18, 16; Jn 8, 17; 2 Cor 13, 1.
17: 17, 8f.
18f: Dn 13, 61f.
21: Ex 21, 23f; Lv 24, 20; Mt 5.38.
20, 4: 1, 30; 3, 22; Jos 23, 10.
5ff: 1 Mc 3, 56.
7: 24, 5.
8: Jgs 7, 3.

†

19, 6: *The avenger of blood:* see note on Nm 35, 12.

you, all the people to be found in it shall
serve you in forced labor. 12 But if it re-
fuses to make peace with you and in-
stead offers you battle, lay siege to it,
13* and when the LORD, your God, deliv-
ers it into your hand, put every male in
it to the sword; 14 but the women and
children and livestock and all else in it
that is worth plundering you may take
as your booty, and you may use this
plunder of your enemies which the
LORD, your God, has given you.
15 "That is how you shall deal with any
city at a considerable distance from you,
which does not belong to the peoples of
this land. 16* But in the cities of those
nations which the LORD, your God, is
giving you as your heritage, you shall
not leave a single soul alive. 17 You must
doom them all—the Hittites, Amorites,
Canaanites, Perizzites, Hivites and Jeb-
usites—as the LORD, your God, has com-
manded you, 18 lest they teach you to
make any such abominable offerings as
they make to their gods, and you thus
sin against the LORD, your God.
Trees of a Besieged City. 19 "When you
are at war with a city and have to lay
siege to it for a long time before you cap-
ture it, you shall not destroy its trees by
putting an ax to them. You may eat their
fruit, but you must not cut down the
trees. After all, are the trees of the field
men, that they should be included in
your siege? 20 However, those trees
which you know are not fruit trees you
may destroy, cutting them down to build
siegeworks with which to reduce the city
that is resisting you.

CHAPTER 21

Expiation of Untraced Murder. 1† "If
the corpse of a slain man is found lying
in the open on the land which the LORD,
your God, is giving you to occupy, and
it is not known who killed him, 2 your
elders and judges shall go out and mea-
sure the distances to the cities that are
in the neighborhood of the corpse.
3 When it is established which city is
nearest the corpse, the elders of that city
shall take a heifer that has never been
put to work as a draft animal under a
yoke, 4† and bringing it down to a wadi
with an everflowing stream at a place
that has not been plowed or sown, they
shall cut the heifer's throat there in the
wadi. 5* The priests, the descendants of
Levi, shall also be present, for the LORD,
your God, has chosen them to minister
to him and to give blessings in his name,
and every case of dispute or violence
must be settled by their decision. 6† Then
all the elders of that city nearest the
corpse shall wash their hands over the
heifer whose throat was cut in the wadi,
7† and shall declare, 'Our hands did not
shed this blood, and our eyes did not see
the deed. 8 Absolve, O LORD, your people
Israel, whom you have ransomed, and
let not the guilt of shedding innocent
blood remain in the midst of your people
Israel.' Thus they shall be absolved from
the guilt of bloodshed, 9 and you shall
purge from your midst the guilt of inno-
cent blood, that you may prosper for do-
ing what is right in the sight of the LORD.
Marriage with a Female Captive.
10 "When you go out to war against your
enemies and the LORD, your God, deliv-
ers them into your hand, so that you take
captives, 11 if you see a comely woman
among the captives and become so en-
amored of her that you wish to have her
as wife, 12† you may take her home to
your house. But before she may live
there, she must shave her head and pare
her nails 13 and lay aside her captive's
garb. After she has mourned her father
and mother for a full month, you may
have relations with her, and you shall
be her husband and she shall be your
wife. 14 However, if later on you lose your
liking for her, you shall give her her
freedom, if she wishes it; but you shall
not sell her or enslave her, since she was
married to you under compulsion.
Rights of the First-born. 15 "If a man
with two wives loves one and dislikes the
other; and if both bear him sons, but the
first-born is of her whom he dislikes:
16 when he comes to bequeath his prop-
erty to his sons he may not consider as
his first-born the son of the wife he loves,
in preference to his true first-born, the
son of the wife whom he dislikes. 17 On
the contrary, he shall recognize as his
first-born the son of her whom he dis-
likes, giving him a double share of what-
ever he happens to own, since he is the
first fruits of his manhood, and to him
belong the rights of the first-born.

*

13f: Nm 31, 7.9.11; Jos 22, 8.
16f: 7, 1f; Jos 10, 40; 11, 14.
21, 5: 19, 17.

†

21, 1-9: This paragraph is best read immediately after 19, 21. The *slain man* may not necessarily have been murdered; he may have been killed by a wild beast. But the blood of the slain cries out to God from the soil where it was shed; cf Gn 4, 10. Therefore a religious ceremony of propitiation is here prescribed in order to avert God's anger on the community.

21, 4: *They shall cut the heifer's throat there in the wadi:* its blood is to be carried away by the stream, signifying thereby the removal of the human blood from the soil. This is not a sacrifice but a symbolic action; the priests are present merely as official witnesses.

21, 6: *Wash their hands:* a symbolic gesture in protestation of one's own innocence when human blood is unjustly shed; cf Mt 27, 24.

21, 7: *This blood:* the blood of the slain man as symbolized by the heifer's blood.

21, 12f: *Shave her head . . . :* these symbolic actions are meant to signify the purification of the woman from her pagan defilement or perhaps the end of her period of mourning for her previous husband.

The Incorrigible Son. 18 "If a man has
a stubborn and unruly son who will not
listen to his father or mother, and will
not obey them even though they chastise
him, 19† his father and mother shall have
him apprehended and brought out to the
elders at the gate of his home city,
20 where they shall say to those city el-
ders, 'This son of ours is a stubborn and
unruly fellow who will not listen to us;
he is a glutton and a drunkard.' 21 Then
all his fellow citizens shall stone him to
death. Thus shall you purge the evil
from your midst, and all Israel, on hear-
ing of it, shall fear.

Corpse of a Criminal. 22† "If a man
guilty of a capital offense is put to death
and his corpse hung on a tree, 23*† it
shall not remain on the tree overnight.
You shall bury it the same day; other-
wise, since God's curse rests on him who
hangs on a tree, you will defile the land
which the LORD, your God, is giving you
as an inheritance.

CHAPTER 22

Care for Lost Animals. 1* "You shall
not see your kinsman's ox or sheep
driven astray without showing concern
about it; see to it that it is returned to
your kinsman. 2 If this kinsman does not
live near you, or you do not know who
he may be, take it to your own place and
keep it with you until he claims it; then
give it back to him. 3 You shall do the
same with his ass, or his garment, or
anything else which your kinsman loses
and you happen to find; you may not be
unconcerned about them. 4 You shall not
see your kinsman's ass or ox foundering
on the road without showing concern
about it; see to it that you help him lift
it up.

Various Precepts. 5 "A woman shall
not wear an article proper to a man, nor
shall a man put on a woman's dress; for
anyone who does such things is an
abomination to the LORD, your God.

6 "If, while walking along, you chance
upon a bird's nest with young birds or
eggs in it, in any tree or on the ground,
and the mother bird is sitting on them,
you shall not take away the mother bird
along with her brood; 7 you shall let her
go, although you may take her brood
away. It is thus that you shall have pros-
perity and a long life.

8 "When you build a new house, put
a parapet around the roof; otherwise, if
someone falls off, you will bring blood-
guilt upon your house.

9*† "You shall not sow your vineyard
with two different kinds of seed; if you
do, its produce shall become forfeit, both
the crop you have sown and the yield
of the vineyard. 10 You shall not plow
with an ox and an ass harnessed to-
gether. 11* You shall not wear cloth of
two different kinds of thread, wool and
linen, woven together.

12*† "You shall put twisted cords on
the four corners of the cloak that you
wrap around you.

Crimes against Marriage. 13 "If a
man, after marrying a woman and hav-
ing relations with her, comes to dislike
her, 14 and makes monstrous charges
against her and defames her by saying,
'I married this woman, but when I first
had relations with her I did not find her
a virgin,' 15† the father and mother of
the girl shall take the evidence of her
virginity and bring it to the elders at the
city gate. 16 There the father of the girl
shall say to the elders, 'I gave my daugh-
ter to this man in marriage, but he has
come to dislike her, 17 and now brings
monstrous charges against her, saying:
I did not find your daughter a virgin.
But here is the evidence of my daugh-
ter's virginity!' And they shall spread
out the cloth before the elders of the city.
18† Then these city elders shall take the
man and chastise him, 19 besides fining
him one hundred silver shekels, which
they shall give to the girl's father, be-
cause the man defamed a virgin in Is-
rael. Moreover, she shall remain his
wife, and he may not divorce her as long
as he lives.

20 "But if this charge is true, and evi-
dence of the girl's virginity is not found,
21 they shall bring the girl to the entrance
of her father's house and there her
townsmen shall stone her to death, be-
cause she committed a crime against Is-
rael by her unchasteness in her father's
house. Thus shall you purge the evil
from your midst.

22* "If a man is discovered having re-
lations with a woman who is married to
another, both the man and the woman

*

23: Gal 3, 13.
22, 1-4: Ex 23, 4f.
9.11: Lv 19, 19.
12: Nm 15, 38; Mt 23, 5.
22: Lv 20, 10; Jn 8, 4f.

†

21, 19: *The gate:* in the city walls. This open space served as the forum for the administration of justice. Cf 22, 15; 25, 7; Ru 4, 1f.11; Is 29, 21; Am 5, 10.12.15.

21, 22: *Hung on a tree:* some understand, "impaled on a stake." In any case the hanging or impaling was not the means used to execute the criminal; he was first put to death by the ordinary means, stoning, and his corpse was then exposed on high as a salutary warning for others. Cf Jos 8, 29; 10, 26; 1 Sm 31, 10; 2 Sm 21, 9.

21, 23: *God's curse rests on him who hangs on a tree:* St. Paul quotes these words in Gal 3, 13, where he applies them to the crucified Savior, who "ransomed us from the curse of the law by becoming a curse for us."

22, 9: *Become forfeit:* to the sanctuary; cf Lv 19, 19; Jos 6, 19.

22, 12: *Twisted cords:* referred to as "tassels" on "violet cords" in Nm 15, 38. See note there.

22, 15: *The evidence of her virginity:* the bridal garment or sheet stained with a little blood from the first nuptial relations.

22, 18: *Chastise him:* flog him, as prescribed in 25, 1-3.

with whom he has had relations shall die. Thus shall you purge the evil from your midst.

23† "If within the city a man comes upon a maiden who is betrothed, and has relations with her, 24 you shall bring them both out to the gate of the city and there stone them to death: the girl because she did not cry out for help though she was in the city, and the man because he violated his neighbor's wife. Thus shall you purge the evil from your midst.

25 "If, however, it is in the open fields that a man comes upon such a betrothed maiden, seizes her and has relations with her, the man alone shall die. 26 You shall do nothing to the maiden, since she is not guilty of a capital offense. This case is like that of a man who rises up against his neighbor and murders him: 27 it was in the open fields that he came upon her, and though the betrothed maiden may have cried out for help, there was no one to come to her aid.

28* "If a man comes upon a maiden that is not betrothed, takes her and has relations with her, and their deed is discovered, 29 the man who had relations with her shall pay the girl's father fifty silver shekels and take her as his wife, because he has deflowered her. Moreover, he may not divorce her as long as he lives.

CHAPTER 23

1† "A man shall not marry his father's wife, nor shall he dishonor his father's bed.

Membership in the Community. 2 "No one whose testicles have been crushed or whose penis has been cut off may be admitted into the community of the LORD. 3 No child of an incestuous union may be admitted into the community of the LORD, nor any descendant of his even to the tenth generation. 4* No Ammonite or Moabite may ever be admitted into the community of the LORD, nor any descendants of theirs even to the tenth generation, 5* because they would not succor you with food and water on your journey after you left Egypt, and because Moab hired Balaam, son of Beor, from Pethor in Aram Naharaim, to curse you; 6 though the LORD, your God, would not listen to Balaam and turned his curse into a blessing for you, because he loves you. 7 Never promote their peace and prosperity as long as you live. 8* But do not abhor the Edomite, since he is your brother, nor the Egyptian, since you were an alien in his country. 9 Children born to them may in the third generation be admitted into the community of the LORD.

Cleanliness in Camp. 10 "When you are in camp during an expedition against your enemies, you shall keep yourselves from everything offensive. 11 If one of you becomes unclean because of a nocturnal emission, he shall go outside the camp, and not return until, 12 toward evening, he has bathed in water; then, when the sun has set, he may come back into the camp. 13 Outside the camp you shall have a place set aside to be used as a latrine. 14 You shall also keep a trowel in your equipment and with it, when you go outside to ease nature, you shall first dig a hole and afterward cover up your excrement. 15 Since the LORD, your God, journeys along within your camp to defend you and to put your enemies at your mercy, your camp must be holy; otherwise, if he sees anything indecent in your midst, he will leave your company.

Various Precepts. 16 "You shall not hand over to his master a slave who has taken refuge from him with you. 17† Let him live with you wherever he chooses, in any one of your communities that pleases him. Do not molest him.

18*† "There shall be no temple harlot among the Israelite women, nor a temple prostitute among the Israelite men. 19 You shall not offer a harlot's fee or a dog's price as any kind of votive offering in the house of the LORD, your God; both these things are an abomination to the LORD, your God.

20* "You shall not demand interest from your countrymen on a loan of money or of food or of anything else on which interest is usually demanded. 21 You may demand interest from a foreigner, but not from your countryman, so that the LORD, your God, may bless you in all your undertakings on the land you are to enter and occupy.

22 "When you make a vow to the LORD, your God, you shall not delay in fulfilling it; otherwise you will be held guilty, for the LORD, your God, is strict in requiring it of you. 23 Should you refrain from making a vow, you will not be held

*

28f: Ex 22, 16.
23, 4: Neh 13, 1f.
5: Nm 24, 10.
8: Gn 25, 24ff.
18: 1 Kgs 14, 24; 22, 46; 2 Kgs 23, 7.
20: Ex 22, 25; Lv 25, 37; Lk 6, 34f.

†

22, 23: *A maiden who is betrothed:* a girl who is married but not yet brought to her husband's home and whose marriage is therefore still unconsummated.

23,1: *Father's wife:* stepmother. *Dishonor:* cf 27, 20.

23, 17: *In any one of your communities:* from this it would seem that the slave in question is a fugitive from a foreign country.

23, 18f: The pagans believed that they could enter into special relationship with their gods and goddesses by having sexual relations with the pagan priests and priestesses who prostituted themselves for this purpose. The money paid for this was considered a sort of votive offering made to the pagan sanctuary. Such abominations were naturally forbidden in Israel. *A dog's price:* the money paid to the pagan priest for his indecent service.

guilty. 24 But you must keep your solemn
word and fulfill the votive offering you
have freely promised to the LORD.
25 "When you go through your neigh-
bor's vineyard, you may eat as many
of his grapes as you wish, but do not put
them in your basket. 26 When you go
through your neighbor's grainfield, you
may pluck some of the ears with your
hand, but do not put a sickle to your
neighbor's grain.

CHAPTER 24

Marriage Laws. 1† "When a man,
after marrying a woman and having re-
lations with her, is later displeased with
her because he finds in her something
indecent, and therefore he writes out a
bill of divorce and hands it to her, thus
dismissing her from his house: 2 if on
leaving his house she goes and becomes
the wife of another man, 3 and the sec-
ond husband, too, comes to dislike her
and dismisses her from his house by
handing her a written bill of divorce; or
if this second man who has married her,
dies; 4 then her former husband, who
dismissed her, may not again take her
as his wife after she has become defiled.
That would be an abomination before
the LORD, and you shall not bring such
guilt upon the land which the LORD, your
God, is giving you as a heritage.
5* "When a man is newly wed, he need
not go out on a military expedition, nor
shall any public duty be imposed on him.
He shall be exempt for one year for the
sake of his family, to bring joy to the
wife he has married.
Justice, Equity and Charity. 6† "No
one shall take a hand mill or even its
upper stone as a pledge for debt, for he
would be taking the debtor's sustenance
as a pledge.
7* "If any man is caught kidnaping a
fellow Israelite in order to enslave him
and sell him, the kidnaper shall be put
to death. Thus shall you purge the evil
from your midst.
8* "In an attack of leprosy you shall
be careful to observe exactly and to
carry out all the directions of the leviti-
cal priests. Take care to act in accor-
dance with the instructions I have given
them. 9* Remember what the LORD,
your God, did to Miriam on the journey
after you left Egypt.
10† "When you make a loan of any kind
to your neighbor, you shall not enter his
house to receive a pledge from him,
11 but shall wait outside until the man to
whom you are making the loan brings
his pledge outside to you. 12 If he is a poor
man, you shall not sleep in the mantle
he gives as a pledge, 13* but shall return
it to him at sunset that he himself may
sleep in it. Then he will bless you, and
it will be a good deed of yours before
the LORD, your God.
14* "You shall not defraud a poor and
needy hired servant, whether he be one
of your own countrymen or one of the
aliens who live in your communities.
15 You shall pay him each day's wages
before sundown on the day itself, since
he is poor and looks forward to them.
Otherwise he will cry to the LORD against
you, and you will be held guilty.
16* "Fathers shall not be put to death
for their children, nor children for their
fathers; only for his own guilt shall a
man be put to death.
17* "You shall not violate the rights of
the alien or of the orphan, nor take the
clothing of a widow as a pledge. 18 For,
remember, you were once slaves in
Egypt, and the LORD, your God, ran-
somed you from there; that is why I
command you to observe this rule.
19* "When you reap the harvest in
your field and overlook a sheaf there,
you shall not go back to get it; let it be
for the alien, the orphan or the widow,
that the LORD, your God, may bless you
in all your undertakings. 20 When you
knock down the fruit of your olive trees,
you shall not go over the branches a sec-
ond time; let what remains be for the
alien, the orphan and the widow.
21 When you pick your grapes, you shall
not go over the vineyard a second time;
let what remains be for the alien, the or-
phan, and the widow. 22 For remember
that you were once slaves in Egypt; that
is why I command you to observe this
rule.

CHAPTER 25

1 "When men have a dispute and bring
it to court, and a decision is handed

*

24, 5: 20, 7
7: Ex 21, 16.
8: Lv 13, 1-14.
9: Nm 12, 10-15.
13: Ex 22, 26.
14f: Lv 19, 13; Tb 4, 15; Sir 34, 25f; Jer 22, 13.
16: 2 Kgs 14, 6; 2 Chr 25, 4; Ez 18, 20.
17: Ex 22, 22; 23, 9.
19ff: Lv 19, 9f; 23, 22.

†

24, 1-4: This law is directly concerned only with forbidding divorced couples to remarry each other, and indirectly with checking hasty divorces, by demanding sufficient cause and certain legal formalities. Divorce itself is taken for granted and tolerated as an existing custom whose evils this law seeks to lessen. Cf 22, 19.29; Mal 2, 14ff. Christ gave the authentic interpretation of this law: "Because of the hardness of your hearts Moses allowed you to divorce your wives, but from the beginning it was not so" (Mt 19, 8f).

24, 1: *Something indecent:* a rather indefinite phrase, meaning perhaps "immodest conduct." At the time of Christ the rabbis differed in opinion concerning the sufficient grounds for divorce; cf Mt 19, 3.

24, 6: Since the Israelites ground their grain into flour only in sufficient quantity for their current need, to deprive a debtor of his hand mill was virtually equivalent to condemning him to starve to death.

24, 10f: The debtor had the right to select the pledge that the creditor demanded as a guarantee for his loan.

down to them acquitting the innocent
party and condemning the guilty party,
2 if the latter deserves stripes, the judge
shall have him lie down and in his pres-
ence receive the number of stripes his
guilt deserves. 3*† Forty stripes may be
given him, but no more; lest, if he were
beaten with more stripes than these,
your kinsman should be looked upon as
disgraced because of the severity of the
beating.
4*† "You shall not muzzle an ox when
it is treading out grain.
Levirate Marriage. 5*† "When broth-
ers live together and one of them dies
without a son, the widow of the deceased
shall not marry anyone outside the fam-
ily; but her husband's brother shall go
to her and perform the duty of a brother-
in-law by marrying her. 6* The first-
born son she bears shall continue the
line of the deceased brother, that his
name may not be blotted out from Israel.
7 If, however, a man does not care to
marry his brother's wife, she shall go
up to the elders at the gate and declare,
'My brother-in-law does not intend to
perform his duty toward me and refuses
to perpetuate his brother's name in Is-
rael.' 8 Thereupon the elders of his city
shall summon him and admonish him.
If he persists in saying, 'I am not willing
to marry her,' 9† his sister-in-law, in the
presence of the elders, shall go up to him
and strip his sandal from his foot and
spit in his face, saying publicly, 'This is
how one should be treated who will not
build up his brother's family!' 10 And his
lineage shall be spoken of in Israel as
'the family of the man stripped of his
sandal.'
Various Precepts. 11 "When two men
are fighting and the wife of one inter-
venes to save her husband from the
blows of his opponent, if she stretches
out her hand and seizes the latter by his
private parts, 12 you shall chop off her
hand without pity.
13* "You shall not keep two differing
weights in your bag, one large and the
other small; 14 nor shall you keep two dif-
ferent measures in your house, one large
and the other small. 15 But use a true and
just weight, and a true and just measure,
that you may have a long life on the land
which the LORD, your God, is giving you.
16 Everyone who is dishonest in any of
these matters is an abomination to the
LORD, your God.
17*† "Bear in mind what Amalek did
to you on the journey after you left
Egypt, 18 how without fear of any god
he harassed you along the way, weak
and weary as you were, and cut off at
the rear all those who lagged behind.
19* Therefore, when the LORD, your God,
gives you rest from all your enemies
round about in the land which he is giv-
ing you to occupy as your heritage, you
shall blot out the memory of Amalek
from under the heavens. Do not forget!

CHAPTER 26

Thanksgiving for the Harvest.
1 "When you have come into the land
which the LORD, your God, is giving you
as a heritage, and have occupied it and
settled in it, 2* you shall take some first
fruits of the various products of the soil
which you harvest from the land which
the LORD, your God, gives you, and put-
ting them in a basket, you shall go to
the place which the LORD, your God,
chooses for the dwelling place of his
name. 3 There you shall go to the priest
in office at that time and say to him, 'To-
day I acknowledge to the LORD, my God,
that I have indeed come into the land
which he swore to our fathers he would
give us.' 4 The priest shall then receive
the basket from you and shall set it in
front of the altar of the LORD, your God.
5*† Then you shall declare before the
LORD, your God, 'My father was a wan-
dering Aramean who went down to
Egypt with a small household and lived
there as an alien. But there he became
a nation great, strong and numerous.
6* When the Egyptians maltreated and
oppressed us, imposing hard labor upon
us, 7 we cried to the LORD, the God of

*

25, 3: 2 Cor 11, 24.
4: 1 Cor 9, 9; 1 Tm 5, 18.
5: Mt 22, 24; Mk 12, 19; Lk 20, 28.
6-9: Ru 4, 5-10.
13ff: Lv 19, 35f; Prv 16, 11; Ex 45, 10; Mi 6, 11.
17: Ex 17, 8
19: Ex 17, 14; 1 Sm 15, 2f.
26, 2: Ex 23, 19; 34, 26.
5: Gn 46, 6f; Acts 7, 14f.
6f: Ex 1, 8-22; 2, 23ff; 3, 9; Nm 20, 15f.

†

25, 3: *Forty stripes:* a relatively mild punishment in ancient times. Later Jewish practice limited the number to thirty-nine; cf 2 Cor 11, 24.

25, 4: St. Paul argues from this verse that a laborer has the right to live on the fruits of his labor; cf 1 Cor 9, 9; 1 Tm 5, 18.

25, 5: *When brothers live together:* when relatives of the same clan, though married, hold their property in common. It was only in this case that the present law was to be observed, since one of its purposes was to keep the property of the deceased within the same clan. Such a marriage of a widow with her brother-in-law is known as a "levirate" marriage from the Latin word *levir,* meaning "a husband's brother."

25, 9f: The penalty decreed for a man who refuses to comply with this law of family loyalty is public disgrace (the widow is to *spit in his face*) and the curse of poverty; sandals were proverbially a man's cheapest possession (cf Am 2, 6; 8, 6), and therefore "a man without sandals" was the poorest of the poor. Some commentators, however, connect this symbolic act with the ceremony mentioned in Ru 4, 7f.

25, 17-19: This attack on Israel by Amalek is not mentioned elsewhere in the Old Testament, although it probably was connected with the battle mentioned in Ex 17, 8. A campaign against Amalek was carried out by Saul; cf 1 Sm 15.

26, 5: *Aramean:* either in reference to the origin of the patriarchs from Aram Naharaim (cf Gn 24, 10; 25, 20; 28, 5; 31, 20.24), or merely in the sense of "nomad," in the same way as "Arab" was later used; cf Jer 3, 2.

our fathers, and he heard our cry and saw our affliction, our toil and our oppression. 8* He brought us out of Egypt with his strong hand and outstretched arm, with terrifying power, with signs and wonders; 9* and bringing us into this country, he gave us this land flowing with milk and honey. 10 Therefore, I have now brought you the first fruits of the products of the soil which you, O LORD, have given me.' And having set them before the LORD, your God, you shall bow down in his presence. 11* Then you and your family, together with the Levite and the aliens who live among you, shall make merry over all these good things which the LORD, your God, has given you.

Prayer with the Tithes. 12*† "When you have finished setting aside all the tithes of your produce in the third year, the year of the tithes, and you have given them to the Levite, the alien, the orphan and the widow, that they may eat their fill in your own community, 13 you shall declare before the LORD, your God, 'I have purged my house of the sacred portion and I have given it to the Levite, the alien, the orphan and the widow, just as you have commanded me. In this I have not broken or forgotten any of your commandments: 14† I have not eaten any of the tithe as a mourner; I have not brought any of it out as one unclean; I have not offered any of it to the dead. I have thus hearkened to the voice of the LORD, my God, doing just as you have commanded me. 15 Look down, then, from heaven, your holy abode, and bless your people Israel and the soil you have given us in the land flowing with milk and honey which you promised on oath to our fathers.'

The Covenant. 16 "This day the LORD, your God, commands you to observe these statutes and decrees. Be careful, then, to observe them with all your heart and with all your soul. 17* Today you are making this agreement with the LORD: he is to be your God and you are to walk in his ways and observe his statutes, commandments and decrees, and to hearken to his voice. 18* And today the LORD is making this agreement with you: you are to be a people peculiarly his own, as he promised you; and provided you keep all his commandments, 19 he will then raise you high in praise and renown and glory above all other nations he has made, and you will be a people sacred to the LORD, your God, as he promised."

IV: FINAL WORDS OF MOSES

CHAPTER 27

Ceremonies. 1 Then Moses, with the elders of Israel, gave the people this order: "Keep all these commandments which I enjoin on you today. 2 On the day you cross the Jordan into the land which the LORD, your God, is giving you, set up some large stones and coat them with plaster. 3* Also write on them, at the time you cross, all the words of this law, that you may thus enter into the land flowing with milk and honey, which the LORD, your God, and the God of your fathers, is giving you as he promised you. 4 When, moreover, you have crossed the Jordan, besides setting up on Mount Ebal these stones concerning which I command you today, and coating them with plaster, 5* you shall also build to the LORD, your God, an altar made of stones that no iron tool has touched. 6 You shall make this altar of the LORD, your God, with undressed stones, and shall offer on it holocausts to the LORD, your God. 7 You shall also sacrifice peace offerings and eat them there, making merry before the LORD, your God. 8† On the stones you shall inscribe all the words of this law very clearly."

9* Moses, with the levitical priests, then said to all Israel: "Be silent, O Israel, and listen! This day you have become the people of the LORD, your God. 10 You shall therefore hearken to the voice of the LORD, your God, and keep his commandments and statutes which I enjoin on you today."

11 That same day Moses gave the people this order: 12* "When you cross the Jordan, Simeon, Levi, Judah, Issachar, Joseph and Benjamin shall stand on Mount Gerizim to pronounce blessings over the people, 13 while Reuben, Gad, Asher, Zebulun, Dan and Naphtali shall stand on Mount Ebal to pronounce curses.

The Twelve Curses. 14 "The Levites shall proclaim aloud to all the men of Israel: 15*† 'Cursed be the man who makes a carved or molten idol—an abomination to the LORD, the product of a craftsman's hands—and sets it up in secret!' And all the people shall answer, 'Amen!'

16* 'Cursed be he who dishonors his father or his mother!' And all the people shall answer, 'Amen!'

*

8: Ex 12, 51.
9: Ex 3, 8.
11: 12, 7.12.
12: 14, 28f.
17: Ex 24, 7.
18f: 7, 6; 14, 2; 28, 1; Ex 19, 5.
27, 3: Jos 8, 32.
5: Ex 20, 25; Jos 8, 31.
9: 26, 17ff.
12f: 11, 29; Jos 8, 33f.
15: Ex 20, 4.23; Lv 19, 4; Wis 14, 8.
16: 21, 18-21; Ex 21, 17; Lv 20, 9.

†

26, 12: *And you have given them to the Levite, . . .* : as prescribed in 14, 28f.

26, 14: These are allusions to pagan religious practices.

27, 8: *On the stones:* cf vv 3f; not the stones of the altar.

27, 15-26: *Amen:* see note on Nm 5, 22.

17* 'Cursed be he who moves his neigh-
bor's landmarks!' And all the people
shall answer, 'Amen!'
18* 'Cursed be he who misleads a blind
man on his way!' And all the people shall
answer, 'Amen!'
19* 'Cursed be he who violates the
rights of the alien, the orphan or the
widow!' And all the people shall answer,
'Amen!'
20* 'Cursed be he who has relations
with his father's wife, for he dishonors
his father's bed!' And all the people shall
answer, 'Amen!'
21* 'Cursed be he who has relations
with any animal!' And all the people
shall answer, 'Amen!'
22* 'Cursed be he who has relations
with his sister or his half-sister!' And all
the people shall answer, 'Amen!'
23* 'Cursed be he who has relations
with his mother-in-law!' And all the peo-
ple shall answer, 'Amen!'
24* 'Cursed be he who slays his neigh-
bor in secret!' And all the people shall
answer, 'Amen!'
25 'Cursed be he who accepts payment
for slaying an innocent man!' And all
the people shall answer, 'Amen!'
26* 'Cursed be he who fails to fulfill any
of the provisions of this law!' And all the
people shall answer, 'Amen!'

CHAPTER 28

Blessings for Obedience. 1*† "Thus,
then, shall it be: if you continue to heed
the voice of the LORD, your God, and are
careful to observe all his command-
ments which I enjoin on you today, the
LORD, your God, will raise you high
above all the nations of the earth. 2 When
you hearken to the voice of the LORD,
your God, all these blessings will come
upon you and overwhelm you:

3 "May you be blessed in the city,
and blessed in the country!

4* "Blessed be the fruit of your womb,
the produce of your soil and the
offspring of your livestock,
the issue of your herds and the
young of your flocks!
5 "Blessed be your grain bin and your
kneading bowl!

6† "May you be blessed in your coming
in,
and blessed in your going out!

Victory and Prosperity. 7† "The LORD
will beat down before you the enemies
that rise up against you; though they
come out against you from but one di-
rection, they will flee before you in
seven. 8 The LORD will affirm his blessing
upon you, on your barns and on all your
undertakings, blessing you in the land
that the LORD, your God, gives you.
9* Provided that you keep the com-
mandments of the LORD, your God, and
walk in his ways, he will establish you
as a people sacred to himself, as he
swore to you; 10*† so that, when all the
nations of the earth see you bearing the
name of the LORD, they will stand in awe
of you. 11 The LORD will increase in more
than goodly measure the fruit of your
womb, the offspring of your livestock,
and the produce of your soil, in the land
which he swore to your fathers he would
give you. 12* The LORD will open up for
you his rich treasure house of the heav-
ens, to give your land rain in due season,
blessing all your undertakings, so that
you will lend to many nations and bor-
row from none. 13† The LORD will make
you the head, not the tail, and you will
always mount higher and not decline,
as long as you obey the commandments
of the LORD, your God, which I order
you today to observe carefully; 14 not
turning aside to the right or to the left
from any of the commandments which
I now give you, in order to follow other
gods and serve them.

Curses for Disobedience. 15* "But if
you do not hearken to the voice of the
LORD, your God, and are not careful to
observe all his commandments which I
enjoin on you today, all these curses
shall come upon you and overwhelm
you:

16 "May you be cursed in the city,
and cursed in the country!

17 "Cursed be your grain bin and your
kneading bowl!
18 "Cursed be the fruit of your womb,
the produce of your soil and the
offspring of your livestock,
the issue of your herds and the
young of your flocks!

19 "May you be cursed in your coming
in,
and cursed in your going out!

*

17: 19, 14.
18: Lv 19, 14.
19: 24, 17; Ex 22, 21f.
20: 22; 23, 1. Lv 18, 8; 20, 11.
21: Ex 22, 18; Lv 18, 23; 20, 15.
22: Lv 18, 9; 20, 17.
23: Lv 18, 17; 20, 14.
24: Ex 20, 13; 21, 12; Nm 35, 20f.
26: Gal 3, 10.
28, 1-68: Lv 26, 1-45.
1-14: 7, 12-16.
1: 26, 19.
4: 7, 13; 30, 9.
9: 26, 18; Ex 19, 5f.
10: 2, 25; 11, 25.
12: 15, 6.
15: Bar 1, 20; Dn 9, 11; Mal 2, 2.

†

28, 1-69: This chapter would read better immediately after chapter 26.

28, 6: *In your coming in . . . in your going out:* at the beginning and end of every action, or in all actions in general.

28, 7.25: *From but one direction . . . in seven:* in one compact mass, contrasted with many scattered groups.

28, 10: *You bearing the name of the LORD:* literally, "The LORD's name is called over you," an expression signifying ownership and protection. Cf 2 Sm 12, 28; 1 Kgs 8, 43; Is 4, 1; 63, 19; Jer 7, 10f; 14, 9; 15, 16; 25, 29; Am 9, 12.

28, 13: *The head, not the tail:* in the honorable position as leader. Cf Is 9, 14; 19, 15.

Sickness and Defeat. 20 “The LORD will put a curse on you, defeat and frustration in every enterprise you undertake, until you are speedily destroyed and perish for the evil you have done in forsaking me. 21 The LORD will bring a pestilence upon you that will persist until he has exterminated you from the land you are entering to occupy. 22* The LORD will strike you with wasting and fever, with scorching, fiery drought, with blight and searing wind, that will plague you until you perish. 23 The sky over your heads will be like bronze and the earth under your feet like iron. 24 For rain the LORD will give your land powdery dust, which will come down upon you from the sky until you are destroyed. 25* The LORD will let you be beaten down before your enemies; though you advance against them from one direction, you will flee before them in seven, so that you will become a terrifying example to all the kingdoms of the earth. 26 Your carcasses will become food for all the birds of the air and for the beasts of the field, with no one to frighten them off. 27* The LORD will strike you with Egyptian boils and with tumors, eczema and the itch, until you cannot be cured. 28 And the LORD will strike you with madness, blindness and panic, 29 so that even at midday you will grope like a blind man in the dark, unable to find your way.

Despoilment. “You will be oppressed and robbed continually, with no one to come to your aid. 30 Though you betroth a wife, another man will have her. Though you build a house, you will not live in it. Though you plant a vineyard, you will not enjoy its fruits. 31 Your ox will be slaughtered before your eyes, and you will not eat of its flesh. Your ass will be stolen in your presence, but you will not recover it. Your flocks will be given to your enemies, with no one to come to your aid. 32 Your sons and daughters will be given to a foreign nation while you look on and grieve for them in constant helplessness. 33 A people whom you do not know will consume the fruit of your soil and of all your labor, and you will be oppressed and crushed at all times without surcease, 34 until you are driven mad by what your eyes must look upon. 35† The LORD will strike you with malignant boils of which you cannot be cured, on your knees and legs, and from the soles of your feet to the crown of your head.

Exile. 36* “The LORD will bring you, and your king whom you have set over you, to a nation which you and your fathers have not known, and there you will serve strange gods of wood and stone, 37 and will call forth amazement, reproach and barbed scorn from all the nations to which the LORD will lead you.

Fruitless Labors. 38* “Though you spend much seed on your field, you will harvest but little, for the locusts will devour the crop. 39* Though you plant and cultivate vineyards, you will not drink or store up the wine, for the grubs will eat the vines clean. 40* Though you have olive trees throughout your country, you will have no oil for ointment, for your olives will drop off unripe. 41* Though you beget sons and daughters, they will not remain with you, but will go into captivity. 42 Buzzing insects will infest all your trees and the crops of your soil. 43 The alien residing among you will rise higher and higher above you, while you sink lower and lower. 44 He will lend to you, not you to him. He will become the head, you the tail.

45 “All these curses will come upon you, pursuing you and overwhelming you, until you are destroyed, because you would not hearken to the voice of the LORD, your God, nor keep the commandments and statutes he gave you. 46† They will light on you and your descendants as a sign and a wonder for all time. 47 Since you would not serve the LORD, your God, with joy and gratitude for abundance of every kind, 48 therefore in hunger and thirst, in nakedness and utter poverty, you will serve the enemies whom the LORD will send against you. He will put an iron yoke on your neck, until he destroys you.

Invasion and Siege. 49* “The LORD will raise up against you a nation from afar, from the end of the earth, that swoops down like an eagle, a nation whose tongue you do not understand, 50 a nation of stern visage, that shows neither respect for the aged nor pity for the young. 51 They will consume the offspring of your livestock and the produce of your soil, until you are destroyed; they will leave you no grain or wine or oil, no issue of your herds or young of your flocks, until they have brought about your ruin. 52 They will besiege you in each of your communities, until the great, unscalable walls you trust in come tumbling down all over your land. They will so besiege you in every community throughout the land which the LORD, your God, has given you, 53* that in the

*

22f: Lv 26, 19.
25: Lv 26, 17.37.
27: Ex 9, 9ff.
36f: 1 Kgs 9, 7ff; 2 Chr 7, 20ff; 33, 11; 36, 6.20.
38: Mi 6, 15; Hg 1, 6.
39: Zep 1, 13.
40: Mi 6, 15.
41: Lam 1, 5.
49-52: Jer 5, 15ff; Bar 4, 15f.
53: Lv 26, 29; 2 Kgs 6, 28f; Jer 19, 9; Lam 4, 10; Bar 2, 3.

†

28, 35: This verse is best read with v 27.
28, 46: *A sign and a wonder:* an ominous example, attracting attention; cf 29, 21-28.

distress of the siege to which your enemy subjects you, you will eat the fruit of your womb, the flesh of your own sons and daughters whom the LORD, your God, has given you. 54 The most refined and fastidious man among you will begrudge his brother and his beloved wife and his surviving children, 55 any share in the flesh of his children that he himself is using for food when nothing else is left him in the straits of the siege to which your enemy will subject you in all your communities. 56 The most refined and delicate woman among you, so delicate and refined that she would not venture to set the sole of her foot on the ground, will begrudge her beloved husband and her son and daughter 57 the afterbirth that issues from her womb and the infant she brings forth when she secretly uses them for food for want of anything else, in the straits of the siege to which your enemy will subject you in your communities.

Plagues. 58 "If you are not careful to observe every word of the law which is written in this book, and to revere the glorious and awesome name of the LORD, your God, 59 he will smite you and your descendants with severe and constant blows, malignant and lasting maladies. 60*† He will again afflict you with all the diseases of Egypt which you dread, and they will persist among you. 61 Should there be any kind of sickness or calamity not mentioned in this book of the law, that too the LORD will bring upon you until you are destroyed. 62* Of you who were numerous as the stars in the sky, only a few will be left, because you would not hearken to the voice of the LORD, your God.

Exile. 63* "Just as the LORD once took delight in making you grow and prosper, so will he now take delight in ruining and destroying you, and you will be plucked out of the land you are now entering to occupy. 64* The LORD will scatter you among all the nations from one end of the earth to the other, and there you will serve strange gods of wood and stone, such as you and your fathers have not known. 65† Among these nations you will find no repose, not a foot of ground to stand upon, for there the LORD will give you an anguished heart and wasted eyes and a dismayed spirit. 66 You will live in constant suspense and stand in dread both day and night, never sure of your existence. 67 In the morning you will say, 'Would that it were evening!' and in the evening you will say, 'Would that it were morning!' for the dread that your heart must feel and the sight that your eyes must see. 68*† The LORD will send you back in galleys to Egypt, to the region I told you that you were never to see again; and there you will offer yourselves for sale to your enemies as male and female slaves, but there will be no buyer."

69 These are the words of the covenant which the LORD ordered Moses to make with the Israelites in the land of Moab, in addition to the covenant which he made with them at Horeb.

CHAPTER 29

Past Favors Recalled. 1 Moses summoned all Israel and said to them, "You have seen all that the LORD did in the land of Egypt before your very eyes to Pharaoh and all his servants and to all his land; 2* the great testings your own eyes have seen, and those great signs and wonders. 3† But not even at the present day has the LORD yet given you a mind to understand, or eyes to see, or ears to hear. 4* 'I led you for forty years in the desert. Your clothes did not fall from you in tatters nor your sandals from your feet; 5 bread was not your food, nor wine or beer your drink. Thus you should know that I, the LORD, am your God.' 6* When we came to this place, Sihon, king of Heshbon, and Og, king of Bashan, came out to engage us in battle, but we defeated them 7* and took over their land, which we then gave as a heritage to the Reubenites, Gadites, and half the tribe of Manasseh. 8 Keep the terms of this covenant, therefore, and fulfill them, that you may succeed in whatever you do.

All Israel Bound to the Covenant. 9 "You are all now standing before the LORD, your God—your chiefs and judges, your elders and officials, and all of the men of Israel, 10 together with your wives and children and the aliens who live in your camp, down to those who hew wood and draw water for you— 11† that you may enter into the covenant of the LORD, your God, which he concluded with you today under this sanction of a curse; 12 so that he may now

*

60: 28, 27.
62: 1, 10; Jer 42, 2.
63: 30, 9.
64: Lv 26, 33.
68: Hos 8, 13; 9, 3.
29, 2: 4, 34; Ex 19, 4.
4: 8, 2.4.
6: 2, 24.32; 3, 1; Nm 21, 33ff.
7: 3, 16; Nm 32, 33.

†

28, 60: *He will again afflict you with all the diseases of Egypt:* such as the Lord had promised to remove from his people; cf 7, 15.

28, 65: *Wasted eyes:* worn out and disappointed in their longing gaze.

28, 68: *In galleys:* in the ships of the Phoenician slave traders (Ez 27, 13; Jl 4, 6; Am 1, 9), who also dealt with Egypt (Is 23, 3).

29, 3: *Eyes to see . . . ears to hear:* with inner, spiritual discernment. Cf Mt 13, 43.

29, 11: *Sanction of a curse:* the present pact binds under penalty of the curses mentioned in this book. Cf v 20.

establish you as his people and he may
be your God, as he promised you and
as he swore to your fathers Abraham,
Isaac and Jacob. [13] But it is not with you
alone that I am making this covenant,
under this sanction of a curse; [14]† it is
just as much with those who are not here
among us today as it is with those of us
who are now here present before the
LORD, our God.
Warning against Idolatry. [15] "You
know in what surroundings we lived in
the land of Egypt and what we passed
by in the nations we traversed, [16] and
you saw the loathsome idols of wood and
stone, of gold and silver, that they pos-
sess. [17] Let there be, then, no man or
woman, no clan or tribe among you, who
would now turn away their hearts from
the LORD, our God, to go and serve these
pagan gods! Let there be no root that
would bear such poison and wormwood
among you. [18]† If any such person, upon
hearing the words of this curse, should
beguile himself into thinking that he can
safely persist in his stubbornness of
heart, as though to sweep away both the
watered soil and the parched ground,
[19] the LORD will never consent to pardon
him. Instead, the LORD's wrath and jeal-
ousy will flare up against that man, and
every curse mentioned in this book will
alight on him. The LORD will blot out his
name from under the heavens [20] and will
single him out from all the tribes of Is-
rael for doom, in keeping with all the
curses of the covenant inscribed in this
book of the law.
Punishment for Infidelity. [21] "Future
generations, your own descendants who
will rise up after you, as well as the for-
eigners who will come here from far-off
lands, when they see the calamities of
this land and the ills with which the
LORD has smitten it— [22]* all its soil being
nothing but sulphur and salt, a burnt-
out waste, unsown and unfruitful, with-
out a blade of grass, destroyed like
Sodom and Gomorrah, Admah and Ze-
boiim, which the LORD overthrew in his
furious wrath— [23]* they and all the na-
tions will ask, 'Why has the LORD dealt
thus with this land? Why this fierce out-
burst of wrath?' [24] And the answer will
be, 'Because they forsook the covenant
which the LORD, the God of their fathers,
had made with them when he brought
them out of the land of Egypt, [25] and they
went and served other gods and adored
them, gods whom they did not know and
whom he had not let fall to their lot:
[26] that is why the LORD was angry with
this land and brought on it all the impre-
cations listed in this book; [27]* in his furi-
ous wrath and tremendous anger the
LORD uprooted them from their soil and
cast them out into a strange land, where
they are today.' [28]† [Both what is still
hidden and what has already been re-
vealed concern us and our descendants
forever, that we may carry out all the
words of this law.]

CHAPTER 30

Mercy for the Repentant. [1]* "When
all these things which I have set before
you, the blessings and the curses, are
fulfilled in you, and from among what-
ever nations the LORD, your God, may
have dispersed you, you ponder them in
your heart: [2]* then, provided that you
and your children return to the LORD,
your God, and heed his voice with all
your heart and all your soul, just as I
now command you, [3] the LORD, your
God, will change your lot; and taking
pity on you, he will again gather you
from all the nations wherein he has scat-
tered you. [4] Though you may have been
driven to the farthest corner of the
world, even from there will the LORD,
your God, gather you; even from there
will he bring you back. [5] The LORD, your
God, will then bring you into the land
which your fathers once occupied, that
you too may occupy it, and he will make
you more prosperous and numerous
than your fathers. [6]*† The LORD, your
God, will circumcise your hearts and the
hearts of your descendants, that you
may love the LORD, your God, with all
your heart and all your soul, and so may
live. [7] But all those curses the LORD, your
God, will assign to your enemies and the
foes who persecuted you. [8] You, how-
ever, must again heed the LORD's voice
and carry out all his commandments
which I now enjoin on you. [9]* Then the
LORD, your God, will increase in more
than goodly measure the returns from
all your labors, the fruit of your womb,
the offspring of your livestock, and the
produce of your soil; for the LORD, your
God, will again take delight in your pros-
perity, even as he took delight in your
fathers', [10] if only you heed the voice of
the LORD, your God, and keep his com-

*

22: Gn 14, 10f; 19, 24f.
23f: 1 Kgs 9, 8f; Jer 22, 8f.
27: Dn 9, 11-14.
30, 1: 11, 26ff.
2f: Neh 1, 9.
6: 6, 5.
9: 28, 11.

†

29, 14: *Not here among us:* this includes their descendants.
29, 18: *To sweep away both the watered soil and the parched ground:* apparently a proverb signifying that such an unfaithful Israelite will cause God to punish the good with the wicked, to root out the good plants growing in irrigated soil, together with the worthless plants growing in the dry ground.
29, 28: *What is still hidden:* the events of the future. *What has already been revealed:* God's law and the punishments in store for those who break it. Leave the future to God; our business is to keep his law.
30, 6: *Circumcise your hearts:* see note on 10, 16.

mandments and statutes that are written in this book of the law, when you return to the LORD, your God, with all your heart and all your soul.

God's Command Clear. 11† "For this command which I enjoin on you today is not too mysterious and remote for you. 12 It is not up in the sky, that you should say, 'Who will go up in the sky to get it for us and tell us of it, that we may carry it out?' 13 Nor is it across the sea, that you should say, 'Who will cross the sea to get it for us and tell us of it, that we may carry it out?' 14† No, it is something very near to you, already in your mouths and in your hearts; you have only to carry it out.

The Choice before Israel. 15 "Here, then, I have today set before you life and prosperity, death and doom. 16 If you obey the commandments of the LORD, your God, which I enjoin on you today, loving him, and walking in his ways, and keeping his commandments, statutes and decrees, you will live and grow numerous, and the LORD, your God, will bless you in the land you are entering to occupy. 17 If, however, you turn away your hearts and will not listen, but are led astray and adore and serve other gods, 18 I tell you now that you will certainly perish; you will not have a long life on the land which you are crossing the Jordan to enter and occupy. 19* I call heaven and earth today to witness against you: I have set before you life and death, the blessing and the curse. Choose life, then, that you and your descendants may live, 20 by loving the LORD, your God, heeding his voice, and holding fast to him. For that will mean life for you, a long life for you to live on the land which the LORD swore he would give to your fathers Abraham, Isaac and Jacob."

CHAPTER 31

The Lord's Leadership. 1 When Moses had finished speaking these words to all Israel, 2* he said to them, "I am now one hundred and twenty years old and am no longer able to move about freely; besides, the LORD has told me that I shall not cross this Jordan. 3* It is the LORD, your God, who will cross before you; he will destroy these nations before you, that you may supplant them. [It is Joshua who will cross before you, as the LORD promised.] 4* The LORD will deal with them just as he dealt with Sihon and Og, the kings of the Amorites whom he destroyed, and with their country. 5* When, therefore, the LORD delivers them up to you, you must deal with them exactly as I have ordered you. 6* Be brave and steadfast; have no fear or dread of them, for it is the LORD, your God, who marches with you; he will never fail you or forsake you."

Call of Joshua. 7* Then Moses summoned Joshua and in the presence of all Israel said to him, "Be brave and steadfast, for you must being this people into the land which the LORD swore to their fathers he would give them; you must put them in possession of their heritage. 8 It is the LORD who marches before you; he will be with you and will never fail you or forsake you. So do not fear or be dismayed."

The Reading of the Law. 9 When Moses had written down this law, he entrusted it to the levitical priests who carry the ark of the covenant of the LORD, and to all the elders of Israel, 10*† giving them this order: "On the feast of Booths, at the prescribed time in the year of relaxation which comes at the end of every seven-year period, 11† when all Israel goes to appear before the LORD, your God, in the place which he chooses, you shall read this law aloud in the presence of all Israel. 12 Assemble the people—men, women and children, as well as the aliens who live in your communities—that they may hear it and learn it, and so fear the LORD, your God, and carefully observe all the words of this law. 13 Their children also, who do not know it yet, must hear it and learn it, that they too may fear the LORD, your God, as long as you live on the land which you will cross the Jordan to occupy."

Commission of Joshua. 14† The LORD said to Moses, "The time is now approaching for you to die. Summon Joshua, and present yourselves at the meeting tent that I may give him his commission." So Moses and Joshua went and presented themselves at the meeting tent. 15 And the LORD appeared at the tent in a column of cloud, which stood still at the entrance of the tent.

A Command to Moses. 16* The LORD said to Moses, "Soon you will be at rest

---

*

19: 4, 26.
19: 11, 26ff; 28, 2.15.
31, 2: 34, 7; Nm 20, 12.
3: 9, 3.
4: Nm 21, 21-35.
5: 7, 2.
6: 20, 3f.
7f: Jos 1, 6f.9.
10f: 16, 13ff.
16: Jgs 2, 12.17.

---

†

30, 11-14: God has revealed his will so clearly that ignorance of his law can be no excuse. St. Paul in Rom 10, 6-10, applies these words to the ease with which we can come to faith and salvation in Christ.

30, 14: *In your mouths:* that you may readily talk about it; cf 6, 7; 11, 19. *And in your hearts:* that you may easily remember it; cf 6, 6; 11, 18.

31, 10: *The year of relaxation:* cf 15, 1ff and the note there.

31, 11ff: Reading the law not only instructed the people but also consoled them by the assurance of the divine goodness.

31, 14f.23: V 23 is best read immediately after v 15; perhaps the original order was vv 7-8.14-15.23.

with your fathers, and then this people
will take to rendering wanton worship
to the strange gods among whom they
will live in the land they are about to
enter. They will forsake me and break
the covenant which I have made with
them. 17 At that time my anger will flare
up against them; I will forsake them and
hide my face from them, so that they
will become a prey to be devoured, and
many evils and troubles will befall them.
At that time they will indeed say, 'Is it
not because our God is not among us that
these evils have befallen us?' 18 Yet I will
be hiding my face from them at that
time only because of all the evil they
have done in turning to other gods.
19* Write out this song, then, for your-
selves. Teach it to the Israelites and have
them recite it, so that this song may be
a witness for me against the Israelites.
20 For when I have brought them into the
land flowing with milk and honey which
I promised on oath to their fathers, and
they have eaten their fill and grown fat,
if they turn to other gods and serve
them, despising me and breaking my
covenant; 21 then, when many evils and
troubles befall them, this song, which
their descendants will not have forgot-
ten to recite, will bear witness against
them. For I know what they are inclined
to do even at the present time, before I
have brought them into the land which
I promised on oath to their fathers." 22 So
Moses wrote this song that same day,
and he taught it to the Israelites.

Commission of Joshua. 23* Then the
LORD commissioned Joshua, son of Nun,
and said to him, "Be brave and stead-
fast, for it is you who must bring the Is-
raelites into the land which I prom-
ised them on oath. I myself will be with
you."

The Law Placed in the Ark. 24* When
Moses had finished writing out on a
scroll the words of the law in their en-
tirety, 25 he gave the Levites who carry
the ark of the covenant of the LORD this
order: 26 "Take this scroll of the law and
put it beside the ark of the covenant of
the LORD, your God, that there it may
be a witness against you. 27 For I already
know how rebellious and stiff-necked
you will be. Why, even now, while I am
alive among you, you have been rebels
against the LORD! How much more,
then, after I am dead! 28* Therefore, as-
semble all your tribal elders and your
officials before me, that I may speak
these words for them to hear, and so
may call heaven and earth to witness
against them. 29* For I know that after
my death you are sure to become cor-
rupt and to turn aside from the way
along which I directed you, so that evil
will befall you in some future age be-
cause you have done evil in the LORD's
sight, and provoked him by your deeds."

The Song of Moses. 30 Then Moses re-
cited the words of this song from begin-
ning to end, for the whole assembly of
Israel to hear:

CHAPTER 32

A

1† Give ear, O heavens, while I speak;
let the earth hearken to the words of my mouth!

2 May my instruction soak in like the rain,
and my discourse permeate like the dew,
Like a downpour upon the grass,
like a shower upon the crops.

3 For I will sing the LORD's renown.
Oh, proclaim the greatness of our God!

4* The Rock—how faultless are his deeds,
how right all his ways!
A faithful God, without deceit,
how just and upright he is!

5* Yet basely has he been treated by his degenerate children,
a perverse and crooked race!

6* Is the LORD to be thus repaid by you,
O stupid and foolish people?
Is he not your father who created you?
Has he not made you and established you?

7* Think back on the days of old,
reflect on the years of age upon age.
Ask your father and he will inform you,
ask your elders and they will tell you:

8*† When the Most High assigned the nations their heritage,
when he parceled out the descendants of Adam,

*

19: 31, 21; 32, 1-43.
23: 31, 7f; Jos 1, 5ff.
24f: 31, 9.
28: 32, 1-43.
29: Jgs 2, 19.
32, 4: Ps 92, 15; Rv 15, 3.
5: 31, 29; Ps 78, 8; Lk 9, 41.
6: Ex 4, 22; Is 63, 16; 64, 8; Jer 31, 9.
7: 4, 32; Ps 44, 2.
8: Gn 10, 1-32; Acts 17, 26.

†

32, 1-43: In the style of the great prophets, the speaker is often God himself. The whole song is a poetic sermon, having for its theme God's benefits to Israel (vv 1-14) and Israel's ingratitude and idolatry in turning to the gods of the pagans, which sins will be punished by the pagans themselves (vv 15-29); in turn, the foolish pride of the pagans will be punished, and the Lord's honor will be vindicated (vv 30-43).

32, 8: *The sons of God:* the angels; cf Jb 1, 6; 2, 1; 38, 7; Ps 89, 7f. Here the various nations are portrayed as having their respective guardian angels. Cf Dn 10, 20f; 12, 1.

He set up the boundaries of the peoples
after the number of the sons of God;
9* While the LORD's own portion was Jacob,
His hereditary share was Israel.

10* He found them in a wilderness,
a wasteland of howling desert.
He shielded them and cared for them,
guarding them as the apple of his eye.

11* As an eagle incites its nestlings forth
by hovering over its brood,
So he spread his wings to receive them
and bore them up on his pinions.

12 The LORD alone was their leader,
no strange god was with him.
13† He had them ride triumphant over the summits of the land
and live off the products of its fields,
Giving them honey to suck from its rocks
and olive oil from its hard, stony ground;

14† Butter from its cows and milk from its sheep,
with the fat of its lambs and rams;
Its Bashan bulls and its goats,
with the cream of its finest wheat;
and the foaming blood of its grapes you drank.

B

15*†[So Jacob ate his fill,]
the darling grew fat and frisky;
you became fat and gross and gorged.
They spurned the God who made them
and scorned their saving Rock.
16* They provoked him with strange gods
and angered him with abominable idols.

17 They offered sacrifice to demons, to "no-gods,"
to gods whom they had not known before,
To newcomers just arrived,
of whom their fathers had never stood in awe.
18* You were unmindful of the Rock that begot you,
You forgot the God who gave you birth.

19 When the LORD saw this, he was filled with loathing
and anger toward his sons and daughters.

20* "I will hide my face from them," he said,
"and see what will then become of them.
What a fickle race they are,
sons with no loyalty in them!
21* "Since they have provoked me with their 'no-god'
and angered me with their vain idols,
I will provoke them with a 'no-people';
with a foolish nation I will anger them.

22* "For by my wrath a fire is enkindled
that shall rage to the depths of the nether world,
Consuming the earth with its yield,
and licking with flames the roots of the mountains.
23 I will spend on them woe upon woe
and exhaust all my arrows against them:

24 "Emaciating hunger and consuming fever
and bitter pestilence,
And the teeth of wild beasts I will send among them,
with the venom of reptiles gliding in the dust.
25* "Snatched away by the sword in the street
and by sheer terror at home
Shall be the youth and the maiden alike,
the nursing babe as well as the hoary old man.

26 "I would have said, 'I will make an end of them
and blot out their name from men's memories,'
27 Had I not feared the insolence of their enemies,
feared that these foes would mistakenly boast,
'Our own hand won the victory;
the LORD had nothing to do with it.' "

28† For they are a people devoid of reason,

---

*

9: Ex 19, 5; Ps 33, 12.
10: 8, 15; Jer 2, 6; Zec 2, 8.
11: Ex 19, 4.
15: 31, 20.
16: Nm 25, 2f; Ps 78, 58.
18: Jer 2, 32.
20: 31, 17.
21: Rom 10, 19.
22: Lam 4, 11.
25: Lv 26, 25.

†

32, 13: *The land:* Canaan.

32, 14: *Bashan:* a fertile grazing land east of the Jordan, famous for its strong cattle. Cf Ps 22, 13; Ez 39, 18; Am 4, 1.

32, 15: *The darling:* a probable meaning of the Hebrew word *yeshurun,* a term of endearment for "Israel." Cf 33, 5.26; Is 44, 2.

32, 28-35: The reference is to the pagan nations, not to Israel.

having no understanding.
29 If they had insight they would realize what happened,
they would understand their future and say,

C

30 "How could one man rout a thousand,
or two men put ten thousand to flight,
Unless it was because their Rock sold them
and the LORD delivered them up?"
31 Indeed, their "rock" is not like our Rock,
and our foes are under condemnation.

32 They are a branch of Sodom's vinestock,
from the vineyards of Gomorrah.
Poisonous are their grapes
and bitter their clusters.
33 Their wine is the venom of dragons
and the cruel poison of cobras.

34 "Is not this preserved in my treasury,
sealed up in my storehouse,
35 Against the day of vengeance and requital,
against the time they lose their footing?"
Close at hand is the day of their disaster
and their doom is rushing upon them!

36*† Surely, the LORD shall do justice for his people;
on his servants he shall have pity.
When he sees their strength failing,
and their protected and unprotected alike disappearing,

37* He will say, "Where are their gods whom they relied on as their 'rock'?
38 Let those who ate the fat of your sacrifices
and drank the wine of your libations
Rise up now and help you!
Let them be your protection!

39* "Learn then that I, I alone, am God,
and there is no god besides me.
It is I who bring both death and life,
I who inflict wounds and heal them,
and from my hand there is no rescue.

40 "To the heavens I raise my hand and swear:
As surely as I live forever,
41 I will sharpen my flashing sword,
and my hand shall lay hold of my quiver.
"With vengeance I will repay my foes
and requite those who hate me.
42 I will make my arrows drunk with blood,
and my sword shall gorge itself with flesh—
With the blood of the slain and the captured,
Flesh from the heads of the enemy leaders."

43 Exult with him, you heavens,
glorify him, all you angels of God;
For he avenges the blood of his servants
and purges his people's land.

44 So Moses, together with Joshua, son
of Nun, went and recited all the words
of this song for the people to hear.
Final Appeal. 45 When Moses had fin-
ished speaking all these words to all Is-
rael, 46* he said, "Take to heart all the
warning which I have now given you and
which you must impress on your chil-
dren, that you may carry out carefully
every word of this law. 47 For this is no
trivial matter for you; rather, it means
your very life, since it is by this means
that you are to enjoy a long life on the
land which you will cross the Jordan to
occupy."
Moses to View Canaan. 48 On that very
day the LORD said to Moses, 49* "Go up
on Mount Nebo, here in the Abarim
Mountains [it is in the land of Moab fac-
ing Jericho], and view the land of Ca-
naan, which I am giving to the Israelites
as their possession. 50* Then you shall
die on the mountain you have climbed,
and shall be taken to your people, just
as your brother Aaron died on Mount
Hor and there was taken to his people;
51* because both of you broke faith with
me among the Israelites at the waters
of Meribath-kadesh in the desert of Zin
by failing to manifest my sanctity
among the Israelites. 52* You may in-
deed view the land at a distance, but you
shall not enter that land which I am giv-
ing to the Israelites."

CHAPTER 33

Blessing upon the Tribes. 1 This is the blessing which Moses, the man of God,

*

36: 2 Mc 7, 6.
37f: Jgs 10, 14; Jer 2, 28.
39: 4, 35; Tb 13, 2; Wis 16, 13.
46: 4, 9.
49: Nm 27, 12; 33, 47f.
50: Nm 20, 24ff. 28; 27, 13; 33, 38.
51: Nm 20, 12; 27, 14.
52: 3, 27; 34, 4.

†

32, 36: *Their protected and unprotected:* the meaning of the Hebrew is uncertain; according to some, the idea is "slaves and freemen."

pronounced upon the Israelites before he died. 2*† He said:

"The LORD came from Sinai
and dawned on his people from Seir;
He shone forth from Mount Paran
and advanced from Meribath-kadesh,
While at his right hand a fire blazed forth
and his wrath devastated the nations.
3† But all his holy ones were in his hand;
they followed at his feet
and he bore them up on his pinions.
4* A law he gave to us;
he made the community of Jacob his domain,
5† and he became king of his darling.
When the chiefs of the people assembled
and the tribes of Israel came together.

6*† "May Reuben live and not die out,
but let his men be few."

7*† The following is for Judah. He said:

"The LORD hears the cry of Judah;
you will bring him to his people.
His own hands defend his cause
and you will be his help against his foes."

8*† Of Levi he said:

"To Levi belong your Thummim,
to the man of your favor your Urim;
For you put him to the test at Massah
and you contended with him at the waters of Meribah.
9† He said of his father, 'I regard him not';
his brothers he would not acknowledge,
and his own children he refused to recognize.
Thus the Levites keep your words,
and your covenant they uphold.
10* They promulgate your decisions to Jacob
and your law to Israel.
They bring the smoke of sacrifice to your nostrils,
and burnt offerings to your altar.
11 Bless, O LORD, his possessions
and accept the ministry of his hands.
Break the backs of his adversaries
and of his foes, that they may not rise."

12* Of Benjamin he said:

"Benjamin is the beloved of the LORD,
who shelters him all the day,
while he abides securely at his breast."

13* Of Joseph he said:

"Blessed by the LORD is his land
with the best of the skies above
and of the abyss crouching beneath;
14 With the best of the produce of the year,
and the choicest sheaves of the months;
15 With the finest gifts of the age-old mountains
and the best from the timeless hills;
16† With the best of the earth and its fullness,
and the favor of him who dwells in the bush.
These shall come upon the head of Joseph
and upon the brow of the prince among his brothers,
17 The majestic bull, his father's first-born,
whose horns are those of the wild ox
With which to gore the nations,
even those at the ends of the earth."
[These are the myriads of Ephraim,
and these the thousands of Manasseh.]

18* Of Zebulun he said:

"Rejoice, O Zebulun, in your pursuits,
and you, Issachar, in your tents!

*

33, 2: Ex 19, 18.20; Jgs 5, 4f.
4: Jn 1, 17; 7, 19.
6: Gn 49, 3f.
7: Gn 49, 8-12.
8: Gn 49, 5; Ex 17, 7; 28, 30; Nm 20, 13.
10: Ex 30, 7f.
12: Gn 49, 27.
13-17: Gn 49, 22-26.
18f: Gn 49, 13ff.

†

33, 2-5.26-29: These verses seem to form an independent hymn describing, in the form of a theophany, the conquest of Canaan. The first section of this hymn (vv 2-5) serves here as an introduction to the various "blessings"; the second section (vv 26-29), as their conclusion.

33, 3: *His holy ones were in his hand:* the Israelites were protected by the Lord.

33, 5.26: *The darling:* see note on 32, 15.

33, 6: In keeping with the other blessings, probably this verse was once introduced by the phrase, "Of Reuben he said." It is to be noted that there is no blessing here for Simeon.

33, 7: *Bring him to his people:* this probably refers to the isolated position of the tribe of Judah during the conquest of the Promised Land (cf Jgs 1, 17-19); according to some commentators the reference is to the divided kingdom.

33, 8: *Thummim . . . Urim:* see note on Ex 28, 30.

33, 9: The reference is probably to the Levites' slaughter of their brethren after the affair of the golden calf in the desert; cf Ex 32, 27-29.

33, 16: *Him who dwells in the bush:* a title given to the Lord because of his appearance to Moses in the burning bush; cf Ex 3.

19† You who invite the tribes to the mountains
where feasts are duly held,
Because you suck up the abundance of the seas
and the hidden treasures of the sand."

20* Of Gad he said:
"Blessed be he who has made Gad so vast!
He lies there like a lion
that has seized the arm and head of the prey.
21*†He saw that the best should be his
when the princely portion was assigned,
while the heads of the people were gathered.
He carried out the justice of the LORD
and his decrees respecting Israel."

22*† Of Dan he said:
"Dan is a lion's whelp,
that springs forth from Bashan!"

23*† Of Naphtali he said:
"Naphtali is enriched with favors
and filled with the blessings of the LORD;
The lake and south of it are his possession!"

24*† Of Asher he said:
"More blessed than the other sons be Asher!
May he be the favorite among his brothers,
as the oil of his olive trees runs over his feet!
25 May your bolts be of iron and bronze;
may your strength endure
through all your days!"
26 "There is no god like the God of the darling,
who rides the heavens in his power,
and rides the skies in his majesty;
27 He spread out the primeval tent;
he extended the ancient canopy.
He drove the enemy out of your way
and the Amorite he destroyed.
28* Israel has dwelt securely,
and the fountain of Jacob has been undisturbed
In a land of grain and wine,
where the heavens drip with dew.
29* How fortunate you are, O Israel!
Where else is a nation victorious in the LORD?
The LORD is your saving shield,
and his sword is your glory.
Your enemies fawn upon you,
as you stride upon their heights."

CHAPTER 34

Death and Burial of Moses. 1* Then
Moses went up from the plains of Moab
to Mount Nebo, the headland of Pisgah
which faces Jericho, and the LORD
showed him all the land—Gilead, and as
far as Dan, 2 all Naphtali, the land of
Ephraim and Manasseh, all the land of
Judah as far as the Western Sea, 3 the
Negeb, the circuit of the Jordan with the
lowlands at Jericho, city of palms, and
as far as Zoar. 4* The LORD then said
to him, "This is the land which I swore
to Abraham, Isaac and Jacob that I
would give to their descendants. I have
let you feast your eyes upon it, but you
shall not cross over." 5* So there, in the
land of Moab, Moses, the servant of the
LORD, died as the LORD had said; 6 and
he was buried in the ravine opposite
Beth-peor in the land of Moab, but to
this day no one knows the place of his
burial. 7* Moses was one hundred and
twenty years old when he died, yet his
eyes were undimmed and his vigor un-
abated. 8 For thirty days the Israelites
wept for Moses in the plains of Moab,
till they had completed the period of
grief and mourning for Moses.

9* Now Joshua, son of Nun, was filled
with the spirit of wisdom, since Moses
had laid his hands upon him; and so the
Israelites gave him their obedience, thus
carrying out the LORD's command to
Moses.

10* Since then no prophet has arisen
in Israel like Moses, whom the LORD
knew face to face. 11* He had no equal
in all the signs and wonders the LORD
sent him to perform in the land of Egypt
against Pharaoh and all his servants
and against all his land, 12 and for the
might and the terrifying power that Mo-
ses exhibited in the sight of all Israel.

*

20f: Gn 49, 19.
21: Nm 32, 1.5.16-19.31f; Jos 1, 12-15; 1 Chr 5, 18-22.
22: Gn 49, 16f.
23: Gn 49, 21; Jos 19, 32-39.
24f: Gn 49, 20.
28: Gn 27, 28.
29: 4, 7f.
34, 1: 3, 27.
4: 3, 27; 32, 52; Gn 12, 7; 15, 18.
5: 32, 50.
7: 31, 2.
9: Nm 27, 18.23; Jos 1, 17.
10: Ex 33, 11.
11: 4, 34.

†

33, 19: *The abundance of the seas:* perhaps the wealth that comes from sea-borne trade or from fishing. *The hidden treasures of the sand:* possibly an allusion to the valuable purple dye extracted from certain marine shells found on the coast of northern Palestine.

33, 21: *The princely portion:* Moses gave the tribe of Gad their land on the east of the Jordan only on condition that they would help the other tribes conquer the land west of the river; cf Nm 32; Jos 22.

33, 22: The sense is, "May he leap up like a lion of Bashan"; the heavily wooded hills of Bashan were notorious for their lions, but the tribe of Dan was not settled in this region.

33, 23: *The lake:* the Lake of Gennesaret on which the land of this tribe bordered.

33, 24: The land of the tribe of Asher was covered with olive groves.

The Book of

JOSHUA

The Book of Joshua derives its name from the successor of Moses, with whose deeds it is principally concerned. The purpose of the book is to demonstrate God's fidelity in giving to the Israelites the land he had promised them for an inheritance (Gn 15, 18ff; Jos 1, 2ff; 21, 41ff; 23, 14ff).

Their occupation of the country is begun with the crossing of the Jordan and the conquest of Jericho (ch 1—6), in both of which the Lord intervenes on their behalf. This is followed by a first foothold on the Palestinian mountain range, at Ai, Bethel, and Gibeon (ch 7—9), and two sweeping campaigns against the city states in the south of the country (ch 10) and in the north (ch 11), with a summary in ch 12. The broad claim to total sovereignty thus established is spelled out by a combined list of tribal boundaries and of the towns contained within each area or administrative district (ch 13—19), including cities of asylum and cities for the Levites (ch 20, 21). The book closes with a narrative about the tribes east of the Jordan (ch 22), a warning speech by Joshua (ch 23), and a renewal at Shechem (ch 24) of the covenant with the Lord, already affirmed there near the beginning of the conquest (8, 30–35).

Like the books which precede it, the Book of Joshua was built up by a long and complex process of editing traditional materials. Both Jewish and Christian believers have always regarded it as inspired.

The entire history of the conquest of the Promised Land is a prophecy of the spiritual conquest of the world through the Church under the leadership of Jesus the Messiah.

The Book of Joshua may be divided as follows:

I: Conquest of Canaan (1, 1—12, 24)
II: Division of the Land (13, 1—21, 45)
III: Return of the Transjordan Tribes and Joshua's Farewell (22, 1—24, 33)

I: CONQUEST OF CANAAN

CHAPTER 1

Divine Promise of Assistance. 1 After Moses, the servant of the LORD, had died, the LORD said to Moses' aide Joshua, son of Nun: 2 "My servant Moses is dead. So prepare to cross the Jordan here, with all the people into the land I will give the Israelites. 3* As I promised Moses, I will deliver to you every place where you set foot. 4† Your domain is to be all the land of the Hittites, from the desert and from Lebanon east to the great river Euphrates and west to the Great Sea. 5* No one can withstand you while you live. I will be with you as I was with Moses: I will not leave you nor forsake you. 6 Be firm and steadfast, so that you may give this people possession of the land which I swore to their fathers I would give them. 7* Above all, be firm and steadfast, taking care to observe the entire law which my servant Moses enjoined on you. Do not swerve from it either to the right or to the left, that you may succeed wherever you go. 8 Keep this book of the law on your lips. Recite it by day and by night, that you may observe carefully all that is written in it; then you will successfully attain your goal. 9 I command you: be firm and steadfast! Do not fear nor be dismayed, for the LORD, your God, is with you wherever you go."

10 So Joshua commanded the officers of the people: 11* "Go through the camp and instruct the people, 'Prepare your provisions, for three days from now you shall cross the Jordan here, to march in and take possession of the land which the LORD, your God, is giving you.' "

The Transjordan Tribes. 12 Joshua reminded the Reubenites, the Gadites, and the half-tribe of Manasseh: 13 "Remember what Moses, the servant of the LORD, commanded you when he said, 'The LORD, your God, will permit you to

---

*

1, 3f: 14, 9; Gn 15, 18; Dt 11, 24.
5: Dt 31, 8; Heb 13, 5.
7. 9: Dt 31, 7f.
11: Dt 11, 31.

†

1, 4: The ideal frontiers are given: in the south *the desert* of Sinai, in the north the *Lebanon* range, in the east the *Euphrates,* and in the west *the Great Sea,* the Mediterranean.

settle in this land.' [14]* Your wives, your
children, and your livestock shall re-
main in the land Moses gave you here
beyond the Jordan. But all the warriors
among you must cross over armed
ahead of your kinsmen and you must
help them [15]* until the LORD has settled
your kinsmen, and they like you possess
the land which the LORD, your God, is
giving them. Afterward you may return
and occupy your own land, which Mo-
ses, the servant of the LORD, has given
you east of the Jordan." [16] "We will do
all you have commanded us," they an-
swered Joshua, "and we will go wher-
ever you send us. We will obey you as
completely as we obeyed Moses. [17] But
may the LORD, your God, be with you
as he was with Moses. [18] If anyone rebels
against your orders and does not obey
every command you give him, he shall
be put to death. But be firm and stead-
fast."

CHAPTER 2

Spies Saved by Rahab. [1]*† Then
Joshua, son of Nun, secretly sent out two
spies from Shittim, saying, "Go, recon-
noiter the land and Jericho." When the
two reached Jericho, they went into the
house of a harlot named Rahab, where
they lodged. [2] But a report was brought
to the king of Jericho that some Israel-
ites had come there that night to spy out
the land. [3] So the king of Jericho sent
Rahab the order, "Put out the visitors
who have entered your house, for they
have come to spy out the entire land."
[4]* The woman had taken the two men
and hidden them, so she said, "True, the
men you speak of came to me, but I did
not know where they came from. [5] At
dark, when it was time for the gate to
be shut, they left, and I do not know
where they went. You will have to pursue
them immediately to overtake them."
[6]† Now, she had led them to the roof,
and hidden them among her stalks of
flax spread out there. [7] But the pursuers
set out along the way to the fords of the
Jordan, and once they had left, the gate
was shut.

[8]† Before the spies fell asleep, Rahab
came to them on the roof [9]* and said:
"I know that the LORD has given you the
land, that a dread of you has come upon
us, and that all the inhabitants of the
land are overcome with fear of you.
[10]* For we have heard how the LORD
dried up the waters of the Red Sea be-
fore you when you came out of Egypt,
and how you dealt with Sihon and Og,
the two kings of the Amorites beyond
the Jordan, whom you doomed to de-
struction. [11]* At these reports, we are
disheartened; everyone is discouraged
because of you, since the LORD, your
God, is God in heaven above and on
earth below. [12]* Now then, swear to me
by the LORD that, since I am showing
kindness to you, you in turn will show
kindness to my family; and give me an
unmistakable token [13] that you are to
spare my father and mother, brothers
and sisters, and all their kin, and save
us from death." [14] "We pledge our lives
for yours," the men answered her. "If
you do not betray this errand of ours,
we will be faithful in showing kindness
to you when the LORD gives us the land."

[15]† Then she let them down through
the window with a rope; for she lived in
a house built into the city wall. [16] "Go
up into the hill country," she suggested
to them, "that your pursuers may not
find you. Hide there for three days, until
they return; then you may proceed on
your way." [17] The men answered her,
"This is how we will fulfill the oath you
made us take: [18] When we come into the
land, tie this scarlet cord in the window
through which you are letting us down;
and gather your father and mother,
your brothers and all your family into
your house. [19] Should any of them pass
outside the doors of your house, he will
be responsible for his own death, and we
shall be guiltless. But we shall be respon-
sible if anyone in the house with you is
harmed. [20] If, however, you betray this
errand of ours, we shall be quit of the
oath you have made us take." [21] "Let it
be as you say," she replied, and bade
them farewell. When they were gone,
she tied the scarlet cord in the window.

[22] They went up into the hills, where
they stayed three days until their pur-
suers, who had sought them all along the
road without finding them, returned.
[23] Then the two came back down from
the hills, crossed the Jordan to Joshua,
son of Nun, and reported all that had
befallen them. [24] They assured Joshua,

*

14: Nm 32, 26.
15: 22, 4; Dt 3, 20.
2, 1: Mt 1, 5; Jas 2, 25.
4: 6, 17.
9: Ex 15, 15f; 23, 27.
10: 4, 23; Ex 14, 21; Nm 21, 23-26. 33ff.
11: Dt 4, 39.
12: 2, 18; 6, 23. 25.

†

2, 1: *Harlot:* this is the regular equivalent of the Hebrew word, but perhaps it is used here of Rahab in the broader sense of a woman who kept a public house. Joshua's spies hoped to remain undetected at such an inn.

2, 6: *Stalks of flax spread out:* to dry in the sun, after they had been soaked in water, according to the ancient process of preparing flax for linen-making. In the Near East the flax harvest occurs near the time of the feast of the Passover (4, 19; 5, 10); cf Ex 9, 31.

2, 8-11: Rahab's faith and good works are praised in the New Testament; cf Heb 11, 31; Jas 2, 25.

2, 15: *A house built into the city wall:* such houses, which used the city wall for their own inner walls, have been found at ancient sites. The upper story of Rahab's house was evidently higher than the city wall. It was through the window of such a house that St. Paul escaped from Damascus; cf Acts 9, 25; 2 Cor 11, 33.

"The LORD has delivered all this land
into our power; indeed, all the inhabit-
ants of the land are overcome with fear
of us."

CHAPTER 3

***Preparations for Crossing the Jor-
dan.*** 1* Early the next morning, Joshua
moved with all the Israelites from Shit-
tim to the Jordan, where they lodged be-
fore crossing over. 2 Three days later the
officers went through the camp 3 and is-
sued these instructions to the people:
"When you see the ark of the covenant
of the LORD, your God, which the leviti-
cal priests will carry, you must also
break camp and follow it, 4 that you may
know the way to take, for you have not
gone over this road before. But let there
be a space of two thousand cubits be-
tween you and the ark. Do not come
nearer to it." 5 Joshua also said to the
people, "Sanctify yourselves, for tomor-
row the LORD will perform wonders
among you." 6 And he directed the
priests to take up the ark of the covenant
and go on ahead of the people; and they
did so.

7* Then the LORD said to Joshua, "To-
day I will begin to exalt you in the sight
of all Israel, that they may know I am
with you, as I was with Moses. 8 Now
command the priests carrying the ark
of the covenant to come to a halt in the
Jordan when they reach the edge of the
waters."

9 So Joshua said to the Israelites,
"Come here and listen to the words of
the LORD, your God." 10* He continued:
"This is how you will know that there
is a living God in your midst, who at your
approach will dispossess the Canaanites,
Hittites, Hivites, Perizzites, Girgashites,
Amorites and Jebusites. 11 The ark of the
covenant of the LORD of the whole earth
will precede you into the Jordan.
12* [Now choose twelve men, one from
each of the tribes of Israel.] 13 When the
soles of the feet of the priests carrying
the ark of the LORD, the Lord of the
whole earth, touch the water of the Jor-
dan, it will cease to flow; for the water
flowing down from upstream will halt in
a solid bank."

The Crossing Begun. 14 The people
struck their tents to cross the Jordan,
with the priests carrying the ark of the
covenant ahead of them. 15† No sooner
had these priestly bearers of the ark
waded into the waters at the edge of the
Jordan, which overflows all its banks
during the entire season of the harvest,
16*† than the waters flowing from up-
stream halted, backing up in a solid
mass for a very great distance indeed,
from Adam, a city in the direction of
Zarethan; while those flowing down-
stream toward the Salt Sea of the
Arabah disappeared entirely. Thus the
people crossed over opposite Jericho.
17* While all Israel crossed over on dry
ground, the priests carrying the ark of
the covenant of the LORD remained mo-
tionless on dry ground in the bed of the
Jordan until the whole nation had com-
pleted the passage.

CHAPTER 4

Memorial Stones. 1 After the entire
nation had crossed the Jordan, 2* the
LORD said to Joshua, "Choose twelve
men from the people, one from each
tribe, 3* and instruct them to take up
twelve stones from this spot in the bed
of the Jordan where the priests have
been standing motionless. Carry them
over with you, and place them where
you are to stay tonight."

4 Summoning the twelve men whom he
had selected from among the Israelites,
one from each tribe, 5 Joshua said to
them: "Go to the bed of the Jordan in
front of the ark of the LORD, your God;
lift to your shoulders one stone apiece,
so that they will equal in number the
tribes of the Israelites. 6 In the future,
these are to be a sign among you. When
your children ask you what these stones
mean to you, 7* you shall answer them,
'The waters of the Jordan ceased to flow
before the ark of the covenant of the
LORD when it crossed the Jordan.' Thus
these stones are to serve as a perpetual
memorial to the Israelites." 8 The twelve
Israelites did as Joshua had com-
manded: they took up as many stones
from the bed of the Jordan as there were
tribes of the Israelites, and carried them
along to the camp site, where they
placed them, according to the LORD's di-
rection. 9 Joshua also had twelve stones
set up in the bed of the Jordan on the
spot where the priests stood who were
carrying the ark of the covenant. They
are there to this day.

*

3, 1: 2, 1.
7: 1, 5; 4, 14.
10: Ex 33, 2; Dt 7, 1.
12: 4, 2. 4.
16: Ps 114, 3.
17: 4, 7. 22.
4, 2: 3, 12.
3: 3, 13; 4, 8f; Dt 27, 2.
7: 3, 13. 16.

†

3, 15: *Season of the harvest:* toward the end of March and the beginning of April, when the grain and other crops that grew during the rainy season of winter were reaped. The crossing took place "on the tenth day of the first month" of the Hebrew year, which began with the first new moon after the spring equinox; cf 4, 19. At this time of the year the Jordan would be swollen as a result of the winter rains and the melting snow of Mount Hermon.

3, 16: The sudden damming of the river could have been caused by a landslide, as has happened on other occasions. The miraculous character of this event would not thereby be removed because God, who foretold it (3, 13), also caused it to take place at precisely the right moment (3, 15), whether or not he used natural forces to accomplish his will.

10† The priests carrying the ark re-
mained in the bed of the Jordan until
everything had been done that the LORD
had commanded Joshua to tell the peo-
ple. The people crossed over quickly,
11 and when all had reached the other
side, the ark of the LORD, borne by the
priests, also crossed to its place in front
of them. 12* The Reubenites, Gadites,
and half-tribe of Manasseh, armed,
marched in the vanguard of the Israel-
ites, as Moses had ordered. 13 About
forty thousand troops equipped for bat-
tle passed over before the LORD to the
plains of Jericho.
14* That day the LORD exalted Joshua
in the sight of all Israel, and thenceforth
during his whole life they respected him
as they had respected Moses.
15 Then the LORD said to Joshua,
16* "Command the priests carrying the
ark of the commandments to come up
from the Jordan." 17 Joshua did so,
18 and when the priests carrying the ark
of the covenant of the LORD had come
up from the bed of the Jordan, as the
soles of their feet regained the dry
ground, the waters of the Jordan re-
sumed their course and as before over-
flowed all its banks.
19 The people came up from the Jordan
on the tenth day of the first month, and
camped in Gilgal on the eastern limits
of Jericho. 20 At Gilgal Joshua set up the
twelve stones which had been taken
from the Jordan, 21 saying to the Israel-
ites, "In the future, when the children
among you ask their fathers what these
stones mean, 22 you shall inform them,
'Israel crossed the Jordan here on dry
ground.' 23* For the LORD, your God,
dried up the waters of the Jordan in
front of you until you crossed over, just
as the LORD, your God, had done at the
Red Sea, which he dried up in front of
us until we crossed over; 24 in order that
all the peoples of the earth may learn
that the hand of the LORD is mighty, and
that you may fear the LORD, your God,
forever."

CHAPTER 5

Rites at Gilgal. 1 When all the kings
of the Amorites to the west of the Jordan
and all the kings of the Canaanites by
the sea heard that the LORD had dried
up the waters of the Jordan before the
Israelites until they crossed over, they
were disheartened and lost courage at
their approach.
2 On this occasion the LORD said to
Joshua, "Make flint knives and circum-
cise the Israelite nation for the second
time." 3† So Joshua made flint knives
and circumcised the Israelites at Gib-
eath-haaraloth, 4* under these circum-
stances: Of all the people who came out
of Egypt, every man of military age had
died in the desert during the journey
after they left Egypt. 5 Though all the
men who came out were circumcised,
none of those born in the desert during
the journey after the departure from
Egypt were circumcised. 6* Now the Is-
raelites had wandered forty years in the
desert, until all the warriors among the
people that came forth from Egypt died
off because they had not obeyed the
command of the LORD. For the LORD
swore that he would not let them see the
land flowing with milk and honey which
he had promised their fathers he would
give us. 7* It was the children whom he
raised up in their stead whom Joshua
circumcised, for these were yet with
foreskins, not having been circumcised
on the journey. 8 When the rite had been
performed, the whole nation remained
in camp where they were, until they re-
covered. 9* † Then the LORD said to
Joshua, "Today I have removed the re-
proach of Egypt from you." Therefore
the place is called Gilgal to the present
day.
10*† While the Israelites were en-
camped at Gilgal on the plains of Jeri-
cho, they celebrated the Passover on the
evening of the fourteenth of the month.
11 On the day after the Passover they ate
of the produce of the land in the form
of unleavened cakes and parched grain.
On that same day 12* after the Passover
on which they ate of the produce of the
land, the manna ceased. No longer was
there manna for the Israelites, who that
year ate of the yield of the land of Ca-
naan.
Siege at Jericho. 13*† While Joshua
was near Jericho, he raised his eyes and

*

12: Dt 3, 18.
14: 3, 7.
16: 3, 6.
23: Ex 14, 21.
5, 4: Nm 14, 29; 26, 64f; Dt 2, 16; Ps 106, 26; 1 Cor 10, 5.
6: Nm 14, 29; Heb 3, 11. 17.
7: Dt 1, 39.
9: 4, 19.
10: Ex 12, 6; Lv 23, 5; Nm 9, 3-5.
12: Ex 16, 35.
13: Ex 23, 20.

†

4, 10–18: After the digression about the two sets of memorial stones, the author resumes the narrative by briefly repeating the story of the crossing, which he had already told in 3, 14-17.

5, 3: *Gibeath-haaraloth:* "Hill of the Foreskins."

5, 9: *The place is called Gilgal:* by popular etymology, because of the similarity of sound with the Hebrew word *gallōthi,* "I have removed." Gilgal probably means "(the place of) the circle of standing stones." Cf 4, 4-8.

5, 10: *The month:* the first month of the year, later called Nisan; see note on 3, 15. The crossing of the Jordan occurred, therefore, about the same time of the year as did the equally miraculous crossing of the Red Sea; cf Ex 12-14.

5, 13—6, 26: The account of the siege of Jericho embraces: (1) The command of the Lord, through his angel, to Joshua (5, 13—6, 5); (2) Joshua's instructions to the Israelites, with a brief summary of how these orders were carried out (6, 6-11); (3) a description of the action on each of the first six days (6, 12-14); (4) the events on the seventh day (6, 15-26).

saw one who stood facing him, drawn
sword in hand. Joshua went up to him
and asked, "Are you one of us or of our
enemies?" [14] He replied, "Neither. I am
the captain of the host of the LORD and
I have just arrived." Then Joshua fell
prostrate to the ground in worship, and
said to him, "What has my lord to say
to his servant?" [15*] The captain of the
host of the LORD replied to Joshua, "Re-
move your sandals from your feet, for
the place on which you are standing is
holy." And Joshua obeyed.

CHAPTER 6

[1] Now Jericho was in a state of siege
because of the presence of the Israelites,
so that no one left or entered. [2] And to
Joshua the LORD said, "I have delivered
Jericho and its king into your power.
[3] Have all the soldiers circle the city,
marching once around it. Do this for six
days, [4*] with seven priests carrying
ram's horns ahead of the ark. On the
seventh day march around the city
seven times, and have the priests blow
the horns. [5] When they give a long blast
on the ram's horns and you hear that
signal, all the people shall shout aloud.
The wall of the city will collapse, and
they will be able to make a frontal at-
tack."
[6] Summoning the priests, Joshua, son
of Nun, then ordered them to take up
the ark of the covenant with seven of
the priests carrying ram's horns in front
of the ark of the LORD. [7] And he ordered
the people to proceed in a circle around
the city, with the picked troops march-
ing ahead of the ark of the LORD. [8] At
this order they proceeded, with the
seven priests who carried the ram's
horns before the LORD blowing their
horns, and the ark of the covenant of
the LORD following them. [9] In front of the
priests with the horns marched the
picked troops; the rear guard followed
the ark, and the blowing of horns was
kept up continually as they marched.
[10] But the people had been commanded
by Joshua not to shout or make any
noise or outcry until he gave the word:
only then were they to shout. [11] So he
had the ark of the LORD circle the city,
going once around it, after which they
returned to camp for the night.
[12] Early the next morning, Joshua had
the priests take up the ark of the LORD.
[13] The seven priests bearing the ram's
horns marched in front of the ark of the
LORD, blowing their horns. Ahead of
these marched the picked troops, while
the rear guard followed the ark of the
LORD, and the blowing of horns was kept
up continually. [14] On this second day
they again marched around the city
once before returning to camp; and for
six days in all they did the same.
[15] On the seventh day, beginning at
daybreak, they marched around the city
seven times in the same manner; on that
day only did they march around the city
seven times. [16] The seventh time around,
the priests blew the horns and Joshua
said to the people, "Now shout, for the
LORD has given you the city [17*] and ev-
erything in it. It is under the LORD's ban.
Only the harlot Rahab and all who are
in the house with her are to be spared,
because she hid the messengers we sent.
[18*†] But be careful not to take, in your
greed, anything that is under the ban;
else you will bring upon the camp of Is-
rael this ban and the misery of it. [19] All
silver and gold, and the articles of
bronze or iron, are sacred to the LORD.
They shall be put in the treasury of the
LORD."

The Fall of Jericho. [20*†] As the horns
blew, the people began to shout. When
they heard the signal horn, they raised
a tremendous shout. The wall collapsed,
and the people stormed the city in a
frontal attack and took it. [21*] They ob-
served the ban by putting to the sword
all living creatures in the city: men and
women, young and old, as well as oxen,
sheep and asses.
[22*] Joshua directed the two men who
had spied out the land, "Go into the har-
lot's house and bring out the woman with
all her kin, as you swore to her you would
do." [23*] The spies entered and brought
out Rahab, with her father, mother,
brothers, and all her kin. Her entire
family they led forth and placed them
outside the camp of Israel. [24*] The city
itself they burned with all that was in
it, except the silver, gold, and articles
of bronze and iron, which were placed
in the treasury of the house of the LORD.
[25†] Because Rahab the harlot had hid-
den the messengers whom Joshua had
sent to reconnoiter Jericho, Joshua
spared her with her family and all her
kin, who continue in the midst of Israel
to this day.

*

15: Ex 3, 5; Acts 7, 33.
6, 4: Nm 10, 8f.
17: 2, 4; Dt 20, 17; Heb 11, 31.
18: 7, 12. 25; Dt 13, 18.
20: 2 Mc 12, 15; Heb 11, 30.
21: Dt 7, 2.
22: 2, 14.
23: 2, 13; Heb 11, 31.
24: 8, 2.

†

6, 18: *That is under the ban:* that is doomed to destruction; see notes on Lv 27, 29; Nm 18, 14; 21, 3.

6, 20: *The wall collapsed:* by the miraculous intervention of God. The blowing of the horns and the shouting of the people were a customary feature of ancient warfare, here intended by God as a test of the people's obedience and of their faith in his promise; cf Heb 11, 30.

6, 25: From Mt 1, 5, we learn that Rahab married Salmon of the tribe of Judah and thus became the great-great-grandmother of David, Christ's ancestor; cf Ru 4, 18-22.

26*† On that occasion Joshua imposed
the oath: Cursed before the LORD be the
man who attempts to rebuild this city,
Jericho. He shall lose his first-born when
he lays its foundation, and he shall lose
his youngest son when he sets up its
gates. 27* Thus the LORD was with
Joshua so that his fame spread through-
out the land.

CHAPTER 7

Defeat at Ai. 1* But the Israelites vio-
lated the ban; Achan, son of Carmi, son
of Zerah, son of Zara of the tribe of Ju-
dah, took goods that were under the ban,
and the anger of the LORD flared up
against the Israelites.
2 Joshua next sent men from Jericho
to Ai, which is near Bethel on its eastern
side, with instructions to go up and re-
connoiter the land. When they had ex-
plored Ai, 3 they returned to Joshua and
advised, "Do not send all the people up;
if only about two or three thousand go
up, they can overcome Ai. The enemy
there are few; you need not call for an
effort from all the people." 4 About three
thousand of the people made the attack,
but they were defeated by those at Ai,
5 who killed some thirty-six of them.
They pressed them back across the
clearing in front of the city gate till they
broke ranks, and defeated them finally
on the descent, so that the confidence
of the people melted away like wa-
ter.
6 Joshua, together with the elders of
Israel, rent his garments and lay pros-
trate before the ark of the LORD until
evening; and they threw dust on their
heads. 7 "Alas, O Lord GOD," Joshua
prayed, "why did you ever allow this
people to pass over the Jordan, deliver-
ing us into the power of the Amorites,
that they might destroy us? Would that
we had been content to dwell on the
other side of the Jordan. 8 Pray, Lord,
what can I say, now that Israel has
turned its back to its enemies? 9 When
the Canaanites and the other inhabitants
of the land hear of it, they will close in
around us and efface our name from the
earth. What will you do for your great
name?"
10 The LORD replied to Joshua: "Stand
up. Why are you lying prostrate?
11* Israel has sinned: they have violated
the covenant which I enjoined on them.
They have stealthily taken goods subject
to the ban, and have deceitfully put them
in their baggage. 12* If the Israelites can-
not stand up to their enemies, but must
turn their back to them, it is because
they are under the ban. I will not remain
with you unless you remove from among
you whoever has incurred the ban.
13* Rise, sanctify the people. Tell them
to sanctify themselves before tomorrow,
for the LORD, the God of Israel, says: You
are under the ban, O Israel. You cannot
stand up to your enemies until you re-
move from among you whoever has in-
curred the ban. 14 In the morning you
must present yourselves by tribes. The
tribe which the LORD designates shall
come forward by clans; the clan which
the LORD designates shall come forward
by families; the family which the LORD
designates shall come forward one by
one. 15 He who is designated as having
incurred the ban shall be destroyed by
fire, with all that is his, because he has
violated the covenant of the LORD and
has committed a shameful crime in Is-
rael."

Achan's Guilt and Punishment.
16† Early the next morning Joshua had
Israel come forward by tribes, and the
tribe of Judah was designated. 17* Then
he had the clans of Judah come forward,
and the clan of Zerah was designated.
He had the clan of Zerah come forward
by families, and Zabdi was designated.
18 Finally he had that family come for-
ward one by one, and Achan, son of
Carmi, son of Zabdi, son of Zerah of the
tribe of Judah, was designated. 19 Joshua
said to Achan, "My son, give to the
LORD, the God of Israel, glory and honor
by telling me what you have done; do
not hide it from me." 20 Achan answered
Joshua, "I have indeed sinned against
the LORD, the God of Israel. This is what
I have done: 21 Among the spoils, I saw
a beautiful Babylonian mantle, two hun-
dred shekels of silver, and a bar of gold
fifty shekels in weight; in my greed I took
them. They are now hidden in the
ground inside my tent, with the silver
underneath." 22 The messengers whom
Joshua sent hastened to the tent and
found them hidden there, with the silver
underneath. 23 They took them from the
tent, brought them to Joshua and all the
Israelites, and spread them out before
the LORD.
24 Then Joshua and all Israel took
Achan, son of Zerah, with the silver, the
mantle, and the bar of gold, and with
his sons and daughters, his ox, his ass
and his sheep, his tent, and all his pos-
sessions, and led them off to the Valley

*

26: 1 Kgs 16, 34.
27: 1, 5.
7, 1: 6, 18; 22, 20; 1 Chr 2, 7.
11: 6, 17-19.
12: 6, 18.
13: 3, 5; Lv 20, 7; 1 Sm 16, 5.
17: Nm 26, 20.

†

6, 26: *He shall lose his first-born . . . its gates:* this curse was fulfilled when Hiel rebuilt Jericho as a fortified city during the reign of Ahab, king of Israel; cf 1 Kgs 16, 34. Till then Jericho was merely an unwalled village; cf Jos 18, 12. 21; Jgs 3, 13; 2 Sm 10, 5.

7, 16ff: *Was designated:* probably by means of the Urim and Thummim; cf 1 Sm 14, 38-42. See note on Ex 28, 30.

of Achor. 25* Joshua said, "The LORD
bring upon you today the misery with
which you have afflicted us!" And all Is-
rael stoned him to death 26*† and piled
a great heap of stones over him, which
remains to the present day. Then the an-
ger of the LORD relented. That is why
the place is called the Valley of Achor
to this day.

CHAPTER 8

Capture of Ai. 1* The LORD then said
to Joshua, "Do not be afraid or dis-
mayed. Take all the army with you and
prepare to attack Ai. I have delivered
the king of Ai into your power, with his
people, city, and land. 2* Do to Ai and
its king what you did to Jericho and its
king; except that you may take its spoil
and livestock as booty. Set an ambush
behind the city." 3† So Joshua and all
the soldiers prepared to attack Ai. Pick-
ing out thirty thousand warriors, Joshua
sent them off by night 4 with these or-
ders: "See that you ambush the city from
the rear, at no great distance; then all
of you be on the watch. 5 The rest of the
people and I will come up to the city,
and when they make a sortie against us
as they did the last time, we will flee
from them. 6 They will keep coming out
after us until we have drawn them away
from the city, for they will think we are
fleeing from them as we did the last time.
When this occurs, 7 rise from ambush
and take possession of the city, which
the LORD, your God, will deliver into
your power. 8 When you have taken the
city, set it afire in obedience to the
LORD's command. These are my orders
to you." 9 Then Joshua sent them away.
They went to the place of ambush, tak-
ing up their position to the west of Ai,
toward Bethel. Joshua, however, spent
that night in the plain.

10 Early the next morning Joshua
mustered the army and went up to Ai
at its head, with the elders of Israel.
11 When all the troops he led were drawn
up in position before the city, they
pitched camp north of Ai, on the other
side of the ravine. 12 [He took about five
thousand men and set them in ambush
between Bethel and Ai, west of the city.]
13 Thus the people took up their stations,
with the main body north of the city and
the ambush west of it, and Joshua waited
overnight among his troops. 14 The king
of Ai saw this, and he and all his army
came out very early in the morning to
engage Israel in battle at the descent to-
ward the Arabah, not knowing that there
was an ambush behind the city.
15 Joshua and the main body of the Isra-
elites fled in seeming defeat toward the
desert, 16 till the last of the soldiers in
the city had been called out to pursue
them. 17 Since they were drawn away
from the city, with every man engaged
in this pursuit of Joshua and the Israel-
ites, not a soldier remained in Ai [or
Bethel], and the city was open and un-
protected.

18 Then the LORD directed Joshua,
"Stretch out the javelin in your hand to-
ward Ai, for I will deliver it into your
power." Joshua stretched out the javelin
in his hand toward the city, 19 and as
soon as he did so, the men in ambush
rose from their post, rushed in, captured
the city, and immediately set it on fire.
20 By the time the men of Ai looked back,
the smoke from the city was already
sky-high. Escape in any direction was
impossible, because the Israelites re-
treating toward the desert now turned
on their pursuers; 21 for when Joshua
and the main body of Israelites saw that
the city had been taken from ambush
and was going up in smoke, they struck
back at the men of Ai. 22* Since those
in the city came out to intercept them,
the men of Ai were hemmed in by Israel-
ites on either side, who cut them down
without any fugitives or survivors
23 except the king, whom they took alive
and brought to Joshua.

24 All the inhabitants of Ai who had
pursued the Israelites into the desert
were slain by the sword there in the
open, down to the last man. Then all Is-
rael returned and put to the sword those
inside the city. 25 There fell that day a
total of twelve thousand men and
women, the entire population of Ai.
26* Joshua kept the javelin in his hand
stretched out until he had fulfilled the
doom on all the inhabitants of Ai.
27 However, the Israelites took for them-
selves as booty the livestock and the
spoil of that city, according to the com-
mand of the LORD issued to Joshua.
28* Then Joshua destroyed the place by
fire, reducing it to an everlasting mound
of ruins, as it remains today. 29* He had
the king of Ai hanged on a tree until eve-
ning; then at sunset Joshua ordered the
body removed from the tree and cast at
the entrance of the city gate, where a
great heap of stones was piled up over

*

25: 6, 18; 22, 20; 1 Chr 2, 7.
26: 8, 29.
8, 1: 2, 24.
2: 6, 21. 24; Dt 20, 14.
22: Dt 7, 2.
26: Ex 17, 11ff.
28: Dt 13, 16.
29: 10, 26f; Dt 21, 22f; Jn 19, 31.

†

7, 26: *Achor:* "misery, affliction." The reference is to the saying of Joshua in v 25, with an allusion also to the similar-sounding name of Achan.

8, 3: *Thirty thousand warriors:* this figure of the Hebrew text, which seems extremely high, may be due to a copyist's error; some manuscripts of the Septuagint have "three thousand," which is the number of the whole army in the first, unsuccessful attack (7, 4); the variant reading in v 12 mentions "five thousand."

it, which remains to the present day.
Altar on Mount Ebal. 30† Later Joshua
built an altar to the LORD, the God of
Israel, on Mount Ebal, 31* of unhewn
stones on which no iron tool had been
used, in keeping with the command to
the Israelites of Moses, the servant of
the LORD, as recorded in the book of the
law. On this altar they offered holocausts
and peace offerings to the LORD.
32* There, in the presence of the Israel-
ites, Joshua inscribed upon the stones
a copy of the law written by Moses.
33* And all Israel, stranger and native
alike, with their elders, officers and
judges, stood on either side of the ark
facing the levitical priests who were car-
rying the ark of the covenant of the
LORD. Half of them were facing Mount
Gerizim and half Mount Ebal, thus car-
rying out the instructions of Moses, the
servant of the LORD, for the blessing of
the people of Israel on this first occasion.
34* Then were read aloud all the words
of the law, the blessings and the curses,
exactly as written in the book of the law.
35* Every single word that Moses had
commanded, Joshua read aloud to the
entire community, including the women
and children, and the strangers who had
accompanied Israel.

CHAPTER 9

Confederacy against Israel. 1* When
the news reached the kings west of the
Jordan, in the mountain regions and in
the foothills, and all along the coast of
the Great Sea as far as Lebanon: Hit-
tites, Amorites, Canaanites, Perizzites,
Hivites and Jebusites, 2 they all formed
an alliance to launch a common attack
against Joshua and Israel.
The Gibeonite Deception. 3* On learn-
ing what Joshua had done to Jericho and
Ai, the inhabitants of Gibeon 4 put into
effect a device of their own. They chose
provisions for a journey, making use of
old sacks for their asses, and old wine-
skins, torn and mended. 5 They wore old,
patched sandals and shabby garments;
and all the bread they took was dry and
crumbly. 6* Thus they journeyed to
Joshua in the camp at Gilgal, where they
said to him and to the men of Israel, "We
have come from a distant land to pro-
pose that you make an alliance with us."
7† But the men of Israel replied to the
Hivites, "You may be living in land that
is ours. How, then, can we make an alli-
ance with you?" 8 But they answered
Joshua, "We are your servants." Then
Joshua asked them, "Who are you?
Where do you come from?" 9* They an-
swered him, "Your servants have come
from a far-off land, because of the fame
of the LORD, your God. For we have
heard reports of all that he did in Egypt
10* and all that he did to the two kings
of the Amorites beyond the Jordan, Si-
hon, king of Heshbon, and Og, king of
Bashan, who lived in Ashtaroth. 11 So our
elders and all the inhabitants of our
country said to us, 'Take along provi-
sions for the journey and go to meet
them. Say to them: We are your ser-
vants; we propose that you make an alli-
ance with us.' 12 This bread of ours was
still warm when we brought it from
home as provisions the day we left to
come to you, but now it is dry and crum-
bled. 13 Here are our wineskins, which
were new when we filled them, but now
they are torn. Look at our garments and
sandals, which are worn out from the
very long journey." 14* Then the Israel-
ite princes partook of their provisions,
without seeking the advice of the LORD.
15* So Joshua made an alliance with
them and entered into an agreement to
spare them, which the princes of the
community sealed with an oath.
Gibeonites Made Vassals. 16 Three
days after the agreement was entered
into, the Israelites learned that these
people were from nearby, and would be
living in Israel. 17 The third day on the
road, the Israelites came to their cities
of Gibeon, Chephirah, Beeroth and Kir-
iath-jearim, 18 but did not attack them,
because the princes of the community
had sworn to them by the LORD, the God
of Israel. When the entire community
grumbled against the princes, 19 these all
remonstrated with the people, "We have
sworn to them by the LORD, the God of
Israel, and so we cannot harm them.
20 Let us therefore spare their lives and
so deal with them that we shall not be
punished for the oath we have sworn to
them." 21† Thus the princes recom-
mended that they be let live, as hewers
of wood and drawers of water for the
entire community; and the community
did as the princes advised them.

*

31: Ex 20, 24f; Dt 27, 5f.
32: Dt 27, 2. 8.
33: 3, 3; Dt 11, 27; 27, 12; 31, 9. 12.
34: Dt 28, 2-68; 30, 19; 31, 11; Neh 8, 2f.
35: Dt 31, 12.
9, 1: 3, 10; Ex 3, 8. 17; 23, 23; Dt 1, 7.
3: 6, 21. 24; 11, 19.
6: Ex 23, 32; Dt 7, 2.
9: 2, 10.
10: Nm 21, 25. 33.
14: Nm 27, 21.
15: 11, 19; 2 Sm 21, 2.

†

8, 30-35: These ceremonies were prescribed in Dt 11, 29 and 27, 2-26. See notes on those passages.

9, 7: *The Hivites:* apparently the Gibeonites belonged to this larger ethnic group (cf also 11, 19), although in 2 Sm 21, 2 they are classed as Amorites; both groups are listed among the *seven nations* in Canaan whom the Israelites were to exterminate; cf Dt 7, 1f.

9, 21: *Hewers of wood and drawers of water:* proverbial terms for the lowest social class in the Israelite community; cf Dt 29, 10f.

22 Joshua summoned the Gibeonites
and said to them, "Why did you lie to
us and say that you lived at a great dis-
tance from us, when you will be living
in our very midst? 23 For this are you
accursed: every one of you shall always
be a slave [hewers of wood and drawers
of water] for the house of my God."
24* They answered Joshua, "Your ser-
vants were fully informed of how the
LORD, your God, commanded his ser-
vant Moses that you be given the entire
land and that all its inhabitants be de-
stroyed before you. Since, therefore, at
your advance, we were in great fear for
our lives, we acted as we did. 25 And now
that we are in your power, do with us
what you think fit and right." 26† Joshua
did what he had decided: while he saved
them from being killed by the Israelites,
27* at the same time he made them, as
they still are, hewers of wood and draw-
ers of water for the community and for
the altar of the LORD, in the place of the
LORD's choice.

CHAPTER 10

The Siege of Gibeon. 1* Now Adonize-
dek, king of Jerusalem, heard that, in
the capture and destruction of Ai,
Joshua had done to that city and its king
as he had done to Jericho and its king.
He heard also that the inhabitants of
Gibeon had made their peace with Is-
rael, remaining among them, 2 and that
there was great fear abroad, because
Gibeon was large enough for a royal
city, larger even than the city of Ai, and
all its men were brave. 3 So Adonizedek,
king of Jerusalem, sent for Hoham, king
of Hebron, Piram, king of Jarmuth, Ja-
phia, king of Lachish, and Debir, king
of Eglon, 4* to come to his aid for an at-
tack on Gibeon, since it had concluded
peace with Joshua and the Israelites.
5† The five Amorite kings, of Jerusalem,
Hebron, Jarmuth, Lachish and Eglon,
united all their forces and marched
against Gibeon, where they took up siege
positions. 6* Thereupon, the men of
Gibeon sent an appeal to Joshua in his
camp at Gilgal: "Do not abandon your
servants. Come up here quickly and
save us. Help us, because all the Amorite
kings of the mountain country have
joined forces against us."

Joshua's Victory. 7 So Joshua
marched up from Gilgal with his picked
troops and the rest of his soldiers.
8 Meanwhile the LORD said to Joshua,
"Do not fear them, for I have delivered
them into your power. Not one of them
will be able to withstand you." 9 And
when Joshua made his surprise attack
upon them after an all-night march
from Gilgal, 10 the LORD threw them into
disorder before him. The Israelites in-
flicted a great slaughter on them at
Gibeon and pursued them down the
Beth-horon slope, harrassing them as
far as Azekah and Makkedah.
11*† While they fled before Israel along
the descent from Beth-horon, the LORD
hurled great stones from the sky above
them all the way to Azekah, killing
many. More died from these hailstones
than the Israelites slew with the sword.
12 On this day, when the LORD delivered
up the Amorites to the Israelites,

Joshua prayed to the LORD,
and said in the presence of Israel:
Stand still, O sun, at Gibeon,
O moon, in the valley of Aijalon!
13*† And the sun stood still,
and the moon stayed,
while the nation took vengeance
on its foes.

Is this not recorded in the Book of
Jashar? The sun halted in the middle of
the sky; not for a whole day did it resume
its swift course. 14 Never before or since
was there a day like this, when the LORD
obeyed the voice of a man; for the LORD
fought for Israel. 15 [Then Joshua and
all Israel returned to the camp at Gil-
gal.]

Execution of Amorite Kings. 16 Mean-
while the five kings who had fled, hid
in a cave at Makkedah. 17 When Joshua
was told that the five kings had been dis-
covered hiding in a cave at Makkedah,
18 he said, "Roll large stones to the
mouth of the cave and post men over
it to guard them. 19 But do not remain
there yourselves. Pursue your enemies,
and harry them in the rear. Do not allow
them to escape to their cities, for the
LORD, your God, has delivered them into
your power."
20 Once Joshua and the Israelites had
finally inflicted the last blows in this very

*

24: Ex 23, 27f; Dt 7. 1f.
27: Dt 12, 5.
10, 1: 9, 15; 6, 21. 24; 8, 26-29.
4: 9, 15.
6: 9, 6.
11: Job 38, 22.
13: Sir 46, 4; Is 28, 21; Heb 3, 11.

†

9, 26f: Later on, Saul violated the immunity of the Gibeonites, but David vindicated it; cf 2 Sm 21, 1-9.

10, 5: *Hebron . . . Eglon:* these four cities were to the south and southwest of Jerusalem.

10, 11: *Great stones from the sky:* the hailstones mentioned in the next sentence.

10, 13: *Is this not recorded:* the reference is to the preceding, poetic passage. Evidently the *Book of Jashar,* like the *Book of the Wars of the LORD* (Nm 21, 14), recounted in epic style the exploits of Israel's early heroes. *The sun halted:* though it is widely supposed that this passage describes in popular language and according to external appearances a miraculous lengthening of the day, it is equally probable that Joshua's prayer was rather for an abrupt obscuration of the sun, which would impede his enemies in their flight homeward and also prevent them from rallying their forces; this request would have been answered by the hailstorm (cf Sir 46, 5) and by a darkness relieved only twenty-four hours later, well into the next day.

great slaughter, and the survivors had escaped from them into the fortified cities, 21 all the army returned safely to Joshua and the camp at Makkedah, no man uttering a sound against the Israelites. 22 Then Joshua said, "Open the mouth of the cave and bring out those five kings to me." 23 Obediently, they brought out to him from the cave the five kings, of Jerusalem, Hebron, Jarmuth, Lachish and Eglon. 24 When they had done so, Joshua summoned all the men of Israel and said to the commanders of the soldiers who had marched with him, "Come forward and put your feet on the necks of these kings." They came forward and put their feet upon their necks. 25 Then Joshua said to them, "Do not be afraid or dismayed, be firm and steadfast. This is what the LORD will do to all the enemies against whom you fight." 26* Thereupon Joshua struck and killed them, and hanged them on five trees, where they remained hanging until evening. 27 At sunset they were removed from the trees at the command of Joshua and cast into the cave where they had hidden; over the mouth of the cave large stones were placed, which remain until this very day.

Conquest of Southern Canaan. 28* Makkedah, too, Joshua captured and put to the sword at that time. He fulfilled the doom on the city, on its king, and on every person in it, leaving no survivors. Thus he did to the king of Makkedah what he had done to the king of Jericho. 29 Joshua then passed on with all Israel from Makkedah to Libnah, which he attacked. 30 Libnah also, with its king, the LORD delivered into the power of Israel. He put it to the sword with every person there, leaving no survivors. Thus he did to its king what he had done to the king of Jericho. 31 Joshua next passed on with all Israel from Libnah to Lachish, where they set up a camp during the attack. 32 The LORD delivered Lachish into the power of Israel, so that on the second day Joshua captured it and put it to the sword with every person in it, just as he had done to Libnah. 33 At that time Horam, king of Gezer, came up to help Lachish, but Joshua defeated him and his people, leaving him no survivors. 34 From Lachish, Joshua passed on with all Israel to Eglon; encamping near it, they attacked it 35 and captured it the same day, putting it to the sword. He fulfilled the doom that day on every person in it, just as he had done at Lachish. 36 From Eglon, Joshua went up with all Israel to Hebron, which they attacked 37 and captured. They put it to the sword with its king, all its towns, and every person there, leaving no survivors, just as Joshua had done to Eglon. He fulfilled the doom on it and on every person there. 38 Then Joshua and all Israel turned back to Debir and attacked it, 39 capturing it with its king and all its towns. They put them to the sword and fulfilled the doom on every person there, leaving no survivors. Thus was done to Debir and its king what had been done to Hebron, as well as to Libnah and its king.

40* Joshua conquered the entire country; the mountain regions, the Negeb, the foothills, and the mountain slopes, with all their kings. He left no survivors, but fulfilled the doom on all who lived there, just as the LORD, the God of Israel, had commanded. 41† Joshua conquered from Kadesh-barnea to Gaza, and all the land of Goshen to Gibeon. 42 All these kings and their lands Joshua captured in a single campaign, for the LORD, the God of Israel, fought for Israel. 43 Thereupon Joshua with all Israel returned to the camp at Gilgal.

CHAPTER 11

Northern Confederacy. 1† When Jabin, king of Hazor, learned of this, he sent a message to Jobab, king of Madon, to the king of Shimron, to the king of Achshaph, 2* and to the northern kings in the mountain regions and in the Arabah near Chinneroth, in the foothills, and in Naphath-dor to the west. 3 These were Canaanites to the east and west, Amorites, Hittites, Perizzites and Jebusites in the mountain regions, and Hivites at the foot of Hermon in the land of Mizpah. 4 They came out with all their troops, an army numerous as the sands on the seashore, and with a multitude of horses and chariots. 5† All these kings joined forces and marched to the waters of Merom, where they encamped together to fight against Israel.

6 The LORD said to Joshua, "Do not fear them, for by this time tomorrow I will stretch them slain before Israel. You must hamstring their horses and burn their chariots." 7 Joshua with his whole army came upon them at the waters of Merom in a surprise attack. 8* The LORD

---

*

26f: 8, 29; Dt 21, 22f.
28: 6, 21.
40: Dt 20, 16f.
11, 2: 12, 3; Jgs 1, 27.
8: 13, 6.

---

†

10, 41: *Goshen:* a town and its surrounding district at the southern end of the Judean mountains (cf 11, 16; 15, 51); not to be confused with the *land of Goshen* in northeastern Egypt (Gn 45, 10), although in the current Hebrew Bible both names are spelled the same.

11, 1ff: *Hazor, Madon, Shimron,* and *Chinneroth:* cities and their surrounding districts in eastern Galilee. *Achshaph* and *Naphath-dor:* southwest of Galilee. *The mountain regions:* in central and northern Galilee.

11, 5: *The waters of Merom:* a stream in central Galilee that flows southeast to water the fertile Arabah, or plain of Chinneroth on the western shore of the Lake of Gennesaret.

delivered them into the power of the Is-
raelites, who defeated them and pursued
them to Greater Sidon, to Misrephoth-
maim, and eastward to the valley of
Mizpeh. They struck them all down,
leaving no survivors. [9] Joshua did to
them as the LORD had commanded: he
hamstrung their horses and burned
their chariots.

Conquest of Northern Canaan. [10] At
that time Joshua, turning back, cap-
tured Hazor and slew its king with the
sword; for Hazor formerly was the chief
of all those kingdoms. [11] He also fulfilled
the doom by putting every person there
to the sword, till none was left alive. Ha-
zor itself he burned. [12]* Joshua thus cap-
tured all those kings with their cities and
put them to the sword, fulfilling the
doom on them, as Moses, the servant of
the LORD, had commanded. [13] However,
Israel did not destroy by fire any of the
cities built on raised sites, except Hazor,
which Joshua burned. [14] The Israelites
took all the spoil and livestock of these
cities as their booty; but the people they
put to the sword, until they had extermi-
nated the last of them, leaving none
alive. [15]* As the LORD had commanded
his servant Moses, so Moses com-
manded Joshua, and Joshua acted ac-
cordingly. He left nothing undone that
the LORD had commanded Moses should
be done.

Survey of the Conquest. [16]* So Joshua
captured all this land: the mountain re-
gions, the entire Negeb, all the land of
Goshen, the foothills, the Arabah, as well
as the mountain regions and foothills of
Israel, [17]* from Mount Halak that rises
toward Seir as far as Baal-gad in the
Lebanon valley at the foot of Mount Her-
mon. All their kings he captured and put
to death. [18] Joshua waged war against
all these kings for a long time. [19]* With
the exception of the Hivites who lived
in Gibeon, no city made peace with the
Israelites; all were taken in battle.
[20]* For it was the design of the LORD to
encourage them to wage war against Is-
rael, that they might be doomed to de-
struction and thus receive no mercy, but
be exterminated, as the LORD had com-
manded Moses.

[21]*† At that time Joshua penetrated
the mountain regions and exterminated
the Anakim in Hebron, Debir, Anab, the
entire mountain region of Judah, and
the entire mountain region of Israel.
Joshua fulfilled the doom on them and
on their cities, [22] so that no Anakim were
left in the land of the Israelites. How-
ever, some survived in Gaza, in Gath,
and in Ashdod. [23]*† Thus Joshua cap-
tured the whole country, just as the
LORD had foretold to Moses. Joshua
gave it to Israel as their heritage, appor-
tioning it among the tribes. And the land
enjoyed peace.

CHAPTER 12

Lists of Conquered Kings. [1]† The
kings of the land east of the Jordan, from
the River Arnon to Mount Hermon, in-
cluding all the eastern section of the Ar-
abah, whom the Israelites conquered
and whose lands they occupied, were:
[2]* First, Sihon, king of the Amorites,
who lived in Heshbon. His domain ex-
tended from Aroer, which is on the bank
of the Wadi Arnon, to include the wadi
itself, and the land northward through
half of Gilead to the Wadi Jabbok, [3]* as
well as the Arabah from the eastern side
of the Sea of Chinnereth, as far south
as the eastern side of the Salt Sea of the
Arabah in the direction of Beth-jeshi-
moth, to a point under the slopes of Pis-
gah. [4]* Secondly, Og, king of Bashan, a
survivor of the Rephaim, who lived at
Ashtaroth and Edrei. [5] He ruled over
Mount Hermon, Salecah, and all Bashan
as far as the boundary of the Geshurites
and Maacathites, and over half of Gilead
as far as the territory of Sihon, king of
Heshbon. [6]* After Moses, the servant of
the LORD, and the Israelites conquered
them, he assigned their land to the
Reubenites, the Gadites, and the half-
tribe of Manasseh, as their property.

[7] This is a list of the kings whom
Joshua and the Israelites conquered
west of the Jordan and whose land, from
Baal-gad in the Lebanon valley to Mount
Halak which rises toward Seir, Joshua
apportioned to the tribes of Israel. [8] It
included the mountain regions and foot-
hills, the Arabah, the slopes, the desert,
and the Negeb, belonging to the Hittites,
Amorites, Canaanites, Perizzites, Hi-
vites and Jebusites. [9]* They were the
kings of Jericho, Ai (which is near
Bethel), [10]* Jerusalem, Hebron, [11] Jar-
muth, Lachish, [12]* Eglon, Gezer,
[13]* Debir, Geder, [14] Hormah, Arad,

*

12: Dt 7, 2; 20, 16f.
15: Dt 7, 2.
16: 10, 41; 12, 8.
17: 12, 7; Dt 7, 24.
19: 9, 3.7.15.
20: Dt 2, 30; 20, 16f.
21: Jos 15, 13f; Nm 13, 22; Dt 1, 28.
23: 14, 1—19, 51; Nm 34, 2-12.
12, 2-5: Nm 21, 21-26.33ff.
3: 13, 20.
4: 13, 11f.
6: Nm 32, 33; Dt 3, 12f.
9: 6, 2; 8, 23.
10f: 10, 23.
12: 10, 23.33.
13: 10, 38f; 15, 36.

†

11, 21ff: Most of the land assigned to the tribe of Judah was not conquered by it till the early period of the Judges. See note on Jgs 1, 1-36.

11, 23: *The land enjoyed peace:* of a limited and temporary nature. Many of the individual tribes had still to fight against the remaining Canaanites; cf 15, 13-17; 17, 12f. This verse forms the conclusion to the first part of the book. Cf note on 12, 1-24.

12, 1-24: This chapter, inserted between the two principal parts of the book (chapters 1-11 and 13-21), resembles the lists of conquered cities which are inscribed on monuments of the Egyptian and Assyrian monarchs. Perhaps it was copied here from some such public Israelite record.

15* Libnah, Adullam, 16* Makkedah,
Bethel, 17* Tappuah, Hepher, 18* Aphek,
Lasharon, 19* Madon, Hazor, 20* Shim-
ron, Achshaph, 21* Taanach, Megiddo,
22* Kedesh, Jokneam (at Carmel),
23* and Dor (in Naphath-dor), the for-
eign king at Gilgal, 24 and the king of Tir-
zah: thirty-one kings in all.

II: DIVISION OF THE LAND

CHAPTER 13

Division of Land Commanded.
1* When Joshua was old and advanced
in years, the LORD said to him: "Though
now you are old and advanced in years,
a very large part of the land still remains
to be conquered. 2† This additional land
includes all Geshur and all the districts
of the Philistines 3* (from the stream ad-
joining Egypt to the boundary of Ekron
in the north is reckoned Canaanite terri-
tory, though held by the five lords of the
Philistines in Gaza, Ashdod, Ashkelon,
Gath and Ekron); also where the Avvim
are in the south; 4 all the land of the Ca-
naanites from Mearah of the Sidonians
to Aphek, and the boundaries of the Am-
orites; 5 and the Gebalite territory; and
all the Lebanon on the east, from Baal-
gad at the foot of Mount Hermon to Labo
in the land of Hamath. 6* At the advance
of the Israelites I will drive out all the
Sidonian inhabitants of the mountain re-
gions between Lebanon and Misre-
photh-maim; at least include these areas
in the division of the Israelite heritage,
just as I have commanded you. 7 Now,
therefore, apportion among the nine
tribes and the half-tribe of Manasseh the
land which is to be their heritage."
The Eastern Tribes. 8* Now the other
half of the tribe of Manasseh as well as
the Reubenites and Gadites, had re-
ceived their heritage which Moses, the
servant of the LORD, had given them east
of the Jordan: 9 from Aroer on the bank
of the Wadi Arnon and the city in the
wadi itself, through the tableland of
Medeba and Dibon, 10 with the rest of the
cities of Sihon, king of the Amorites, who
reigned in Heshbon, to the boundary of
the Ammonites; 11 also Gilead and the
territory of the Geshurites and Ma-
acathites, all Mount Hermon, and all
Bashan as far as Salecah, 12 the entire
kingdom in Bashan of Og, a survivor of
the Rephaim, who reigned at Ashtaroth
and Edrei. Though Moses conquered
and occupied these territories, 13 the Is-
raelites did not dislodge the Geshurites
and Maacathites, so that Geshur and
Maacath survive in the midst of Israel
to this day. 14* However, to the tribe of
Levi Moses assigned no heritage since,
as the LORD had promised them, the
LORD, the God of Israel, is their heritage.
Reuben. 15* What Moses gave to the
Reubenite clans: 16 Their territory
reached from Aroer, on the bank of
the Wadi Arnon, and the city in the
wadi itself, through the tableland about
Medeba, 17 to include Heshbon and
all its towns which are on the tableland,
Dibon, Bamoth-baal, Beth-baal-meon,
18 Jahaz, Kedemoth, Mephaath, 19 Kiria-
thaim, Sibmah, Zereth-shahar on the
knoll within the valley, 20 Beth-peor, the
slopes of Pisgah, Beth-jeshimoth,
21* and the other cities of the tableland
and, generally, of the kingdom of Sihon.
This Amorite king, who reigned in Hesh-
bon, Moses had killed, with his vassals,
the princes of Midian, who were settled
in the land: Evi, Rekem, Zur, Hur and
Reba; 22* and among their slain follow-
ers the Israelites put to the sword also
the soothsayer Balaam, son of Beor.
23 The boundary of the Reubenites was
the bank of the Jordan. These cities and
their villages were the heritage of the
clans of the Reubenites.
Gad. 24* What Moses gave to the Gad-
ite clans: 25 Their territory included
Jazer, all the cities of Gilead, and half
the land of the Ammonites as far as
Aroer, toward Rabbah (that is, 26 from
Heshbon to Ramath-mizpeh and Bet-
onim, and from Mahanaim to the
boundary of Lodebar); 27 and in the Jor-
dan valley: Beth-haram, Beth-nimrah,
Succoth, Zaphon, the other part of the
kingdom of Sihon, king of Heshbon, with
the bank of the Jordan to the southeast-
ern tip of the Sea of Chinnereth. 28 These
cities and their villages were the heri-
tage of the clans of the Gadites.
Manasseh. 29* What Moses gave to the
clans of the half-tribe of Manasseh:
30* Their territory included Mahanaim,
all of Bashan, the entire kingdom of Og,
king of Bashan, and all the villages of
Jair, which are sixty cities in Bashan.
31 Half of Gilead, with Ashtaroth and
Edrei, once the royal cities of Og in
Bashan, fell to the descendants of Ma-
chir, son of Manasseh, for half the clans
descended from Machir.

*

15: 10, 29f; 15, 35.
16: 8, 17; 10, 28.
17: 15, 34.
18: 15, 53.
19: 11, 1.10.
20: 11, 1.
21: 17, 11.
22: 19, 37.
23: 11, 2.
13, 1: 23, 1.
3: Jgs 3, 3.
6: 11, 8.
8: 12, 6; Nm 32, 33.
14: 14, 3f; Nm 18, 20-24.
15-31: Dt 3, 12-17.
15-23: Nm 21, 25-31; 32, 37f.
21: Nm 21, 24; 31, 8; Dt 3, 10.
22: Nm 31, 8.
24-28: Nm 32, 34ff.
29-31: Nm 32, 39ff.
30: Nm 32, 41.

†

13, 2: *Geshur:* not to be confused with the large Aramaean district of the same name in Bashan (vv 11-13; Dt 3, 14); here it is a region to the south of the Philistine country, since vv 2-5 list the unconquered lands along the coast from south to north; cf also 1 Sm 27, 8.

32 These are the portions which Moses
gave when he was in the plains of Moab,
beyond the Jordan east of Jericho.
33* However, Moses gave no heritage to
the tribe of Levi, since the LORD himself,
the God of Israel, is their heritage, as
he promised.

CHAPTER 14

The Western Tribes. 1* Here follow
the portions which the Israelites re-
ceived in the land of Canaan. Eleazar
the priest, Joshua, son of Nun, and the
heads of families in the tribes of the Isra-
elites determined 2* their heritage by lot,
in accordance with the instructions the
LORD had given through Moses concern-
ing the remaining nine and a half tribes.
3* For to two and a half tribes Moses had
already given a heritage beyond the Jor-
dan; and though the Levites were given
no heritage among the tribes, 4* the de-
scendants of Joseph formed two tribes,
Manasseh and Ephraim. The Levites
themselves received no share of the land
except cities to live in, with their pasture
lands for the cattle and flocks.
5 Thus, in apportioning the land, did
the Israelites carry out the instructions
of the LORD to Moses.
Caleb's Portion. 6* When the Judah-
ites came up to Joshua in Gilgal, the
Kenizzite Caleb, son of Jephunneh, said
to him: "You know what the LORD said
to the man of God, Moses, about you and
me in Kadesh-barnea. 7* I was forty
years old when the servant of the LORD,
Moses, sent me from Kadesh-barnea to
reconnoiter the land; and I brought back
to him a conscientious report. 8* My fel-
low scouts who went up with me discour-
aged the people, but I was completely
loyal to the LORD, my God. 9 On that oc-
casion Moses swore this oath, 'The land
where you have set foot shall become
your heritage and that of your descen-
dants forever, because you have been
completely loyal to the LORD, my God.'
10* Now, as he promised, the LORD has
preserved me while Israel was journey-
ing through the desert, for the forty-five
years since the LORD spoke thus to Mo-
ses; and although I am now eighty-five
years old, 11* I am still as strong today
as I was the day Moses sent me forth,
with no less vigor whether for war or
for ordinary tasks. 12* Give me, there-
fore, this mountain region which the
LORD promised me that day, as you
yourself heard. True, the Anakim are
there, with large fortified cities, but if
the LORD is with me I shall be able to
drive them out, as the LORD promised."
13* Joshua blessed Caleb, son of Jephun-
neh, and gave him Hebron as his heri-
tage. 14 Therefore Hebron remains the
heritage of the Kenizzite Caleb, son of
Jephunneh, to the present day, because
he was completely loyal to the LORD, the
God of Israel. 15* Hebron was formerly
called Kiriath-arba, for Arba, the great-
est among the Anakim. And the land en-
joyed peace.

CHAPTER 15

Boundaries of Judah. 1* The lot for
the clans of the Judahite tribe fell in the
extreme south toward the boundary of
Edom, the desert of Zin in the Negeb.
2* The boundary there ran from the bay
that forms the southern end of the Salt
Sea, 3 southward below the pass of Ak-
rabbim, across through Zin, up to a point
south of Kadesh-barnea, across to
Hezron, and up to Addar; from there,
looping around Karka, 4 it crossed to Az-
mon and then joined the Wadi of Egypt
before coming out at the sea. [This is
your southern boundary.] 5 The eastern
boundary was the Salt Sea as far as the
mouth of the Jordan.
6* The northern boundary climbed
from the bay where the Jordan meets
the sea, up to Beth-hoglah, and ran
north of Beth-arabah, up to Eben-Bo-
han-ben-Reuben. 7* Thence it climbed
to Debir, north of the vale of Achor, in
the direction of the Gilgal that faces the
pass of Adummim, on the south side of
the wadi; from there it crossed to the
waters of En-shemesh and emerged at
En-rogel. 8*† Climbing again to the Val-
ley of Ben-hinnom on the southern flank
of the Jebusites [that is, Jerusalem], the
boundary rose to the top of the mountain
at the northern end of the Valley of
Rephaim, which bounds the Valley of
Hinnom on the west. 9* From the top of
the mountain it ran to the fountain
of waters of Nephtoah, extended to the
cities of Mount Ephron, and continued
to Baalah, or Kiriath-jearim. 10 From
Baalah the boundary curved westward
to Mount Seir and passed north of the
ridge of Mount Jearim (that is, Ches-

*

33: 18, 7; Nm 18, 20.
14, 1: 17, 4; 21, 1; Nm 34, 17f.
2: Nm 26, 55; 33, 54; 34, 13.
3: 13, 8.14.33.
4: 21, 3-40; Gn 48, 5.
6: Nm 14, 24.30; 32, 12; Dt 1, 36.38.
7: Nm 14, 6-9.
8: Nm 13, 31ff; 14, 24; 32, 12; Dt 1, 36.
10: Nm 14, 30.
11: Sir 46, 1ff.
12: 11, 21.
13: 10, 36f; 15, 13-19; 21, 11f.
15: Jgs 1, 10.
15, 1: Nm 34, 3.
2-4: Nm 34, 3ff.
6: 18, 18f.22.
7: 7, 26; 18, 16ff; 2 Sm 17, 17.
8: 18, 16.
9: 18, 15.

†

15, 8: *The Valley of Ben-hinnom:* the southern limit of Jerusalem. *Ben-hinnom* means "son of Hinnom." The place was also called *Valley of Hinnom,* in Hebrew *gē-hinnom,* whence the word "Gehenna" is derived.

alon); thence it descended to Beth-
shemesh, and ran across to Timnah. 11 It
then extended along the northern flank
of Ekron, continued through Shikkeron,
and across to Mount Baalah, thence to
include Jabneel, before it came out at
the sea. 12 The western boundary was the
Great Sea and its coast. This was the
complete boundary of the clans of the
Judahites.

Conquest by Caleb. 13* As the LORD
had commanded, Joshua gave Caleb,
son of Jephunneh, a portion among the
Judahites, namely, Kiriath-arba (Arba
was the father of Anak), that is, Hebron.
14* And Caleb drove out from there the
three Anakim, the descendants of Anak:
Sheshai, Ahiman and Talmai. 15* From
there he marched up against the inhab-
itants of Debir, which was formerly
called Kiriath-sepher. 16 Caleb said, "I
will give my daughter Achsah in mar-
riage to the one who attacks Kiriath-se-
pher and captures it." 17† Othniel, son
of Caleb's brother Kenaz, captured it,
and so Caleb gave him his daughter
Achsah in marriage. 18 On the day of her
marriage to Othniel, she induced him to
ask her father for some land. Then, as
she alighted from the ass, Caleb asked
her, "What is troubling you?" 19 She an-
swered, "Give me an additional gift!
Since you have assigned to me land in
the Negeb, give me also pools of water."
So he gave her the upper and the lower
pools.

Cities of Judah. 20† This is the heritage
of the clans of the tribe of Judahites:
21 The cities of the tribe of the Judahites
in the extreme southern district toward
Edom were: Kabzeel, Eder, Jagur,
22 Kinah, Dimonah, Adadah, 23 Kedesh,
Hazor and Ithnan; 24 Ziph, Telem, Bea-
loth, 25 Hazor-hadattah, and Kerioth-
hezron (that is, Hazor); 26 Amam,
Shema, Moladah, 27 Hazar-gaddah,
Heshmon, Beth-pelet, 28 Hazar-shual,
Beer-sheba and Biziothiah; 29 Baalah,
Iim, Ezem, 30 Eltolad, Chesil, Hormah,
31* Ziklag, Madmannah, Sansannah,
32 Lebaoth, Shilhim and En-rimmon; a
total of twenty-nine cities with their vil-
lages.

33† In the foothills: Eshtaol, Zorah,
Ashnah, 34 Zanoah, Engannim, Tap-
puah, Enam, 35 Jarmuth, Adullam, So-
coh, Azekah, 36 Shaaraim, Adithaim,
Gederah, and Gederothaim; fourteen
cities and their villages. 37 Zenan, Ha-
dashah, Migdal-gad, 38 Dilean, Mizpeh,
Joktheel, 39 Lachish, Bozkath, Eglon,
40 Cabbon, Lahmam, Chitlish, 41 Gede-
roth, Beth-dagon, Naamah and Makke-
dah; sixteen cities and their villages.
42 Libnah, Ether, Ashan, 43 Iphtah, Ash-
nah, Nezib, 44 Keilah, Achzib and Ma-
reshah; nine cities and their villages.
45 Ekron and its towns and villages;
46 from Ekron to the sea, all the towns
that lie alongside Ashdod, and their vil-
lages; 47 Ashdod and its towns and vil-
lages; Gaza and its towns and villages,
as far as the Wadi of Egypt and the coast
of the Great Sea.

48 In the mountain regions: Shamir,
Jattir, Socoh, 49 Dannah, Kiriath-san-
nah (that is, Debir), 50 Anab, Eshtemoh,
Anim, 51 Goshen, Holon and Giloh;
eleven cities and their villages. 52 Arab,
Dumah, Eshan, 53 Janim, Beth-tappuah,
Aphekah, 54 Humtah, Kiriath-arba (that
is, Hebron), and Zior; nine cities and
their villages. 55 Maon, Carmel, Ziph,
Juttah, 56 Jezreel, Jokdeam, Zanoah,
57 Kain, Gibbeah and Timnah; ten cities
and their villages. 58 Halhul, Beth-zur,
Gedor, 59 Maarath, Beth-anoth and El-
tekon; six cities and their villages.
Tekoa, Ephrathah (that is, Bethlehem),
Peor, Etam, Kulom, Tatam, Zores,
Karim, Gallim, Bether and Manoko;
eleven cities and their villages.
60* Kiriath-baal (that is, Kiriath-jearim)
and Rabbah; two cities and their vil-
lages.

61† In the desert: Beth-arabah, Mid-
din, Secacah, 62 Nibshan, Ir-hamelah
and En-gedi; six cities and their villages.
63* [But the Jebusites who lived in Jeru-
salem the Judahites could not drive out;
so the Jebusites dwell in Jerusalem be-
side the Judahites to the present day.]

CHAPTER 16

The Joseph Tribes. 1† The lot that fell
to the Josephites extended from the Jor-
dan at Jericho to the waters of Jericho
east of the desert; then the boundary
went up from Jericho to the heights at
Bethel. 2 Leaving Bethel for Luz, it
crossed the ridge to the border of the

*

13-19: Jgs 1, 10-15.
13: 14, 13ff.
14: Nm 13, 22; Jgs 1, 20.
15: 10, 38.
31: 1 Sm 27, 6.
60: 18, 14.
63: Jgs 1, 21; 2 Sm 5, 6.

†

15, 17-19: The story of Othniel is told again in Jgs 1, 13-15; cf also Jgs 3, 9-11.

15, 20-62: This elaborate list of the cities of Judah was probably taken from a document made originally for administrative purposes; the cities are divided into four provincial districts, some of which have further subdivisions. For similar lists of the cities of Judah, cf 19, 2-7; 1 Chr 4, 28-32; Neh 11, 25-30. This list has suffered in transmission, so that the totals given in vv 32 and 36 are not exact, and some of the names are probably misspelled; many of the cities cannot be identified.

15, 33: *In the foothills:* see note on Dt 1, 7.

15, 61: *In the desert:* in the Jordan rift near the Dead Sea.

16, 1—17, 18: The boundaries and cities of Judah, the most important tribe, having been given, the land of the next most important group, the two Josephite tribes of Ephraim and Manasseh, is now described, though it was separated from Judah by the territories of Benjamin (18, 11-20) and Dan (19, 40-48).

16, 1-3: This line formed the southern boundary of Ephraim and the northern boundaries of Benjamin and of Dan.

Archites at Ataroth, [3]* and descended
westward to the border of the Japhle-
tites, to that of the Lower Beth-horon,
and to Gezer, ending thence at the sea.
Ephraim. [4] Within the heritage of Ma-
nasseh and Ephraim, sons of Joseph,
[5]*† the dividing line for the heritage of
the clans of the Ephraimites ran from
east of Ataroth-addar to Upper Beth-
horon [6]* and thence to the sea. From
Michmethath on the north, their bound-
ary curved eastward around Taanath-
shiloh, and continued east of it to Ja-
noah; [7] from there it descended to Ata-
roth and Naarah, and skirting Jericho,
it ended at the Jordan. [8]* From Tappuah
the boundary ran westward to the Wadi
Kanah and ended at the sea. This was
the heritage of the clans of the Ephraim-
ites, [9]* including the villages that be-
longed to each city set aside for the
Ephraimites within the territory of the
Manassehites. [10]* But they did not drive
out the Canaanites living in Gezer, who
live on within Ephraim to the present
day, though they have been impressed
as laborers.

CHAPTER 17

Manasseh. [1]* Now as for the lot that
fell to the tribe of Manasseh as the first-
born of Joseph: since his eldest son, Ma-
chir, the father of Gilead, was a warrior,
who had already obtained Gilead and
Bashan, [2]* the allotment was now made
to the other descendants of Manasseh,
the clans of Abiezer, Helek, Asriel, She-
chem, Hepher and Shemida, the other
male children of Manasseh, son of Jo-
seph.
[3]* Furthermore, Zelophehad, son of
Hepher, son of Gilead, son of Machir,
son of Manasseh, had had no sons, but
only daughters, whose names were
Mahlah, Noah, Hoglah, Milcah, and Tir-
zah. [4]* These presented themselves to
Eleazar the priest, to Joshua, son of Nun,
and to the princes, saying, "The LORD
commanded Moses to give us a heritage
among our kinsmen." So in obedience
to the command of the LORD a heritage
was given to each of them among their
father's kinsmen. [5]* Thus ten shares fell
to Manasseh apart from the land of
Gilead and Bashan beyond the Jordan,
[6] since these female descendants of Ma-
nasseh received each a portion among
his sons. The land of Gilead fell to the
rest of the Manassehites.
[7]† Manasseh bordered on Asher.
From Michmethath near Shechem, an-
other boundary ran southward to in-
clude the natives of En-Tappuah,
[8] because the district of Tappuah be-
longed to Manasseh, although Tappuah
itself was an Ephraimite city on the bor-
der of Manasseh. [9]* This same boundary
continued down to the Wadi Kanah. The
cities that belonged to Ephraim from
among the cities in Manasseh were those
to the south of that wadi; thus the terri-
tory of Manasseh ran north of the wadi
and ended at the sea. [10] The land on the
south belonged to Ephraim and that on
the north to Manasseh; with the sea as
their common boundary, they reached
Asher on the north and Issachar on the
east.
[11]* Moreover, in Issachar and in Asher
Manasseh was awarded Beth-shean and
its towns, Ibleam and its towns, Dor and
its towns and the natives there, Endor
and its towns and natives, Taanach and
its towns and natives, and Megiddo and
its towns and natives [the third is
Naphath-dor]. [12] Since the Manasseh-
ites could not conquer these cities, the
Canaanites persisted in this region.
[13] When the Israelites grew stronger
they impressed the Canaanites as labor-
ers, but they did not drive them out.
Protest of Joseph Tribes. [14]* The de-
scendants of Joseph said to Joshua,
"Why have you given us only one lot and
one share as our heritage? Our people
are too many, because of the extent to
which the LORD has blessed us."
[15] Joshua answered them, "If you are too
many, go up to the forest and clear out
a place for yourselves there in the land
of the Perizzites and Rephaim, since the
mountain regions of Ephraim are so
narrow." [16]* For the Josephites said,
"Our mountain regions are not enough
for us; on the other hand, the Canaanites
living in the valley region all have iron
chariots, in particular those in Beth-
shean and its towns, and those in the val-
ley of Jezreel." [17] Joshua therefore said
to Ephraim and Manasseh, the house of
Joseph, "You are a numerous people
and very strong. You shall have not
merely one share, [18] for the mountain re-
gion which is now forest shall be yours
when you clear it. Its adjacent land shall
also be yours if, despite their strength

*

16, 3: 10, 10.33.
5: 18, 13.
6: 17, 7.
8: 17, 7.
9: 17, 9.
10: Jgs 1, 29.
17, 1: Gn 41, 51; 46, 20; 48, 18; 50, 23; Nm 26, 29; Dt 3, 13.15.
2: Nm 26, 29-32.
3: Nm 26, 33; 27, 1; 36, 2.
4: Nm 27, 6f; 36, 2.
5: 13, 30f.
9: 16, 8f.
11: 1 Chr 7, 29.
11ff: Jgs 1, 27f.
14: 16, 4; Gn 48, 19f.22.
16: Jgs 6, 33.

†

16, 5: *The dividing line:* separating Ephraim from Manasseh. Ephraim's northern border (v 5) is given in an east-to-west direction; its eastern border (v 6f) in a north-to-south direction.

17, 7: *Manasseh bordered on Asher:* only at the extreme northwestern section of Manasseh's territory. The boundary given in the following sentences (vv 7-10) is a more detailed description of the one already mentioned in 16, 5ff, as separating Manasseh from Ephraim.

and iron chariots, you drive out the Ca-
naanites."

CHAPTER 18

1* After they had subdued the land,
the whole community of the Israelites
assembled at Shiloh, where they set up
the meeting tent.
The Seven Remaining Portions.
2 Seven tribes among the Israelites had
not yet received their heritage. 3 Joshua
therefore said to the Israelites, "How
much longer will you put off taking steps
to possess the land which the LORD, the
God of your fathers, has given you?
4 Choose three men from each of your
tribes; I will commission them to begin
a survey of the land, which they shall
describe for purposes of inheritance.
When they return to me 5* you shall di-
vide it into seven parts. Judah is to retain
its territory in the south, and the house
of Joseph its territory in the north. 6 You
shall bring here to me the description
of the land in seven sections. I will then
cast lots for you here before the LORD,
our God. 7* For the Levites have no
share among you, because the priest-
hood of the LORD is their heritage; while
Gad, Reuben, and the half-tribe of Ma-
nasseh have already received the heri-
tage east of the Jordan which Moses, the
servant of the LORD, gave them."
8 When those who were to map out the
land were ready for the journey, Joshua
instructed them to survey the land, pre-
pare a description of it, and return to
him; then he would cast lots for them
there before the LORD in Shiloh. 9 So they
went through the land, listed its cities
in writing in seven sections, and re-
turned to Joshua in the camp at Shiloh.
10 Joshua then divided up the land for
the Israelites into their separate shares,
casting lots for them before the LORD in
Shiloh.
Benjamin. 11 One lot fell to the clans
of the tribe of Benjaminites. The terri-
tory allotted them lay between the de-
scendants of Judah and those of Joseph.
12*† Their northern boundary began at
the Jordan and went over the northern
flank of Jericho, up westward into the
mountains, till it reached the desert of
Beth-aven. 13* From there it crossed
over to the southern flank of Luz (that
is, Bethel). Then it ran down to Ataroth-
addar, on the mountaintop south of
Lower Beth-horon. 14 For the western
border, the boundary line swung south
from the mountaintop opposite Beth-
horon till it reached Kiriath-baal (that
is, Kiriath-jearim), which city belonged
to the Judahites. This was the western
boundary. 15 The southern boundary be-
gan at the limits of Kiriath-jearim and
projected to the spring at Nephtoah.
16* It went down to the edge of the moun-
tain on the north of the Valley of
Rephaim, where it faces the Valley of
Ben-hinnom; and continuing down the
Valley of Hinnom along the southern
flank of the Jebusites, reached En-rogel.
17 Inclining to the north, it extended to
En-shemesh, and thence to Geliloth, op-
posite the pass of Adummim. Then it
dropped to Eben-Bohan-ben-Reuben,
18* across the northern flank of the Ara-
bah overlook, down into the Aarabah.
19 From there the boundary continued
across the northern flank of Beth-hoglah
and extended to the northern tip of the
Salt Sea, at the southern end of the Jor-
dan. This was the southern boundary.
20 The Jordan bounded it on the east.
This was how the heritage of the clans
of the Benjaminites was bounded on all
sides.
21 Now the cities belonging to the
clans of the tribe of the Benjaminites
were: Jericho, Beth-hoglah, Emek-
keziz, 22 Beth-arabah, Zemaraim,
Bethel, 23 Avvim, Parah, Ophrah,
24 Chephar-ammoni, Ophni and Geba;
twelve cities and their villages. 25 Also
Gibeon, Ramah, Beeroth, 26 Mizpeh,
Chephirah, Mozah, 27 Rekem, Irpeel,
Taralah, 28 Zela, Haeleph, the Jebusite
city (that is, Jerusalem), Gibeah and
Kiriath; fourteen cities and their vil-
lages. This was the heritage of the clans
of Benjaminites.

JOSHUA

CHAPTER 19

Simeon. 1 The second lot fell to Sim-
eon. The heritage of the clans of the tribe
of Simeonites lay within that of the Ju-
dahites. 2* For their heritage they re-
ceived Beer-sheba, Shema, Moladah,
3 Hazar-shual, Balah, Ezem, 4 Eltolad,
Bethul, Hormah, 5 Ziklag, Bethmar-ca-
both, Hazar-susah, 6 Beth-lebaoth and
Sharuhen; thirteen cities and their vil-
lages. 7 Also En-rimmon, Ether and
Ashan; four cities and their villages,
8 besides all the villages around these
cities as far as Baalath-beer (that is, Ra-
moth-negeb). This was the heritage of
the clans of the tribe of the Simeonites.
9 This heritage of the Simeonites was
within the confines of the Judahites; for

*

18, 1: 19, 51.
5: 15, 1—17, 18.
7: 13, 8.33.
12: 16, 1.
13: 16, 2f.5; Gn 28, 19.
16: 15, 7f.
18: 15, 6.
19, 2-8: 1 Chr 4, 28-33.

†

18, 12-20: Benjamin's *northern boundary* (vv 12f) corresponded to part of the southern boundary of Ephraim (16, 1f). Their *western border* (v 14) was the eastern border of Dan (cf 19, 40-47). Their *southern boundary* (vv 15-19) corresponded to part of the northern boundary of Judah (15, 6-9).

since the portion of the latter was too
large for them, the Simeonites obtained
their heritage within it.
Zebulun. 10† The third lot fell to the
clans of the Zebulunites. The limit of
their heritage was at Sarid. 11 Their
boundary went up west . . . and through
Mareal, reaching Dabbesheth and the
wadi that is near Jokneam. 12 From
Sarid eastward it ran to the district of
Chisloth-tabor, on to Daberath, and up
to Japhia. 13 From there it continued
eastward to Gath-hepher and to Eth-ka-
zin, extended to Rimmon, and turned to
Neah. 14 Skirting north of Hannathon,
the boundary ended at the valley of Iph-
tahel. 15 Thus, with Kattath, Nahalal,
Shimron, Idalah and Bethlehem, there
were twelve cities and their villages 16 to
comprise the heritage of the clans of the
Zebulunites.
Issachar. 17† The fourth lot fell to Is-
sachar. The territory of the clans of the
Issacharites 18 included Jezreel, Chesul-
loth, Shunem, 19 Hapharaim, Shion,
Anaharath, 20 Rabbith, Kishion, Ebez,
21 Remeth, En-gannim, En-haddah and
Beth-pazzez. 22 The boundary reached
Tabor, Shahazumah and Beth-shemesh,
ending at the Jordan. These sixteen cit-
ies and their villages 23 were the heritage
of the clans of the Issacharites.
Asher. 24† The fifth lot fell to the clans
of the tribe of the Asherites. 25 Their ter-
ritory included Helkath, Hali, Beten,
Achshaph, 26 Allammelech, Amad and
Mishal, and reached Carmel on the west,
and Shihor-libnath. 27 In the other direc-
tion, it ran eastward of Beth-dagon,
reached Zebulun and the valley of Iph-
tahel; then north of Beth-emek and
Neiel, it extended to Cabul, 28* Mishal,
Abdon, Rehob, Hammon and Kanah,
near Greater Sidon. 29 Then the bound-
ary turned back to Ramah and to the
fortress city of Tyre; thence it cut back
to Hosah and ended at the sea. Thus,
with Mahalab, Achzib, 30 Ummah, Acco,
Aphek and Rehob, there were twenty-
two cities and their villages 31 to com-
prise the heritage of the clans of the tribe
of the Asherites.
Naphtali. 32† The sixth lot fell to the
Naphtalites. The boundary of the clans
of the Naphtalites 33 extended from He-
leph, from the oak at Zaanannim to Lak-
kum, including Adami-nekeb and
Jabneel, and ended at the Jordan. 34 In
the opposite direction, westerly, it ran
through Aznoth-tabor and from there
extended to Hukkok; it touched Zebulun
on the south, Asher on the west, and the
Jordan on the east. 35 The fortified cities
were Ziddim, Zer, Hammath, Rakkath,
Chinnereth, 36 Adamah, Ramah, Hazor,
37 Kedesh, Edrei, En-hazor, 38* Yiron,
Migdal-el, Horem, Beth-anath and
Beth-shemesh; nineteen cities and their
villages, 39 to comprise the heritage of
the clans of the tribe of the Naphta-
lites.
Dan. 40† The seventh lot fell to the
clans of the tribe of Danites. 41 Their her-
itage was the territory of Zorah, Eshtaol,
Ir-shemesh, 42* Shaalabbin, Aijalon,
Ithlah, 43 Elon, Timnah, Ekron,
44 Eltekoh, Gibbethon, Baalath, 45 Jehud,
Bene-berak, Gath-rimmon, 46 Me-jar-
kon and Rakkon, with the coast at
Joppa. 47*† But the territory of the Dan-
ites was too small for them; so the Dan-
ites marched up and attacked Leshem,
which they captured and put to the
sword. Once they had taken possession
of Leshem, they renamed the settlement
after their ancestor Dan. 48 These cities
and their villages were the heritage of
the clans of the tribe of the Danites.
Joshua's City. 49 When the last of them
had received the portions of the land
they were to inherit, the Israelites as-
signed a heritage in their midst to
Joshua, son of Nun. 50* In obedience to
the command of the LORD, they gave
him the city which he requested, Tim-
nah-serah in the mountain region of
Ephraim. He rebuilt the city and made
it his home.
51 These are the final portions into
which Eleazar the priest, Joshua, son of
Nun, and the heads of families in the
tribes of the Israelites divided the land
by lot in the presence of the LORD,
at the door of the meeting tent in Shi-
loh.

*

28f: Jgs 1, 31.
38: Jgs 1, 33.
42: Jgs 1, 35.
47: Jgs 18, 27-29.
50: 24, 30; Jgs 2, 9.

†

19, 10-16: Zebulun's territory was in the central section of the Plain of Esdraelon and of southern Galilee; it was bounded on the south by Manasseh, on the southeast by Issachar, on the northeast and north by Naphtali, and on the west by Asher. The site of the later city of Nazareth was within its borders. *Bethlehem* of Zebulun was, of course, distinct from the city of the same name in Judah. *Twelve cities:* apparently seven of the names are missing from v 15, unless some of the places mentioned in vv 12-14 are to be included in the number.

19, 17-23: Issachar's land was on the eastern watershed of the Plain of Esdraelon, but also included the southeastern end of the Galilean mountains. It was surrounded by Manasseh on the south and east, by Naphtali on the north, and by Zebulun on the west. *Jezreel* (v 18) dominated the plain to which it gave its name, the later form of which was Esdraelon.

19, 24-31: Asher inherited the western slope of the Galilean hills as far as the sea, with Manasseh to the south, Zebulun and Naphtali to the east, and Phoenicia to the north.

19, 32-39: Naphtali received eastern Galilee; Asher was to the west and Zebulun and Issachar were to the south, while the upper Jordan and Mount Hermon formed the eastern border. Part of the tribe of Dan later on occupied the northern extremity of Naphtali's lands, at the sources of the Jordan (v 47).

19, 40-46: The original territory of Dan was a small enclave between Judah, Benjamin, Ephraim and the Philistines.

19, 47: *Leshem:* called *Laish* in Jgs 18, where the story of the migration of the Danites is told at greater length.

CHAPTER 20

Cities of Asylum. 1† The LORD said to
Joshua: 2* "Tell the Israelites to desig-
nate the cities of which I spoke to them
through Moses, 3 to which one guilty of
accidental and unintended homicide
may flee for asylum from the avenger
of blood. 4 To one of these cities the killer
shall flee, and standing at the entrance
of the city gate, he shall plead his case
before the elders, who must receive him
and assign him a place in which to live
among them. 5 Though the avenger of
blood pursues him, they are not to de-
liver up the homicide who slew his fellow
man unintentionally and not out of pre-
vious hatred. 6* Once he has stood judg-
ment before the community, he shall live
on in that city till the death of the high
priest who is in office at the time. Then
the killer may go back home to his own
city from which he fled."

List of Cities. 7* So they set apart Ke-
desh in Galilee in the mountain region
of Naphtali, Shechem in the mountain
region of Ephraim, and Kiriath-arba
(that is, Hebron) in the mountain region
of Judah. 8* And beyond the Jordan east
of Jericho they designated Bezer on the
open tableland in the tribe of Reuben,
Ramoth in Gilead in the tribe of Gad,
and Golan in Bashan in the tribe of Ma-
nasseh. 9* These were the designated
cities to which any Israelite or stranger
living among them who had killed a per-
son accidentally might flee to escape
death at the hand of the avenger of
blood, until he could appear before the
community.

CHAPTER 21

Levitical Cities. 1*† The heads of the
Levite families came up to Eleazar the
priest, to Joshua, son of Nun, and to the
heads of families of the other tribes of
the Israelites 2* at Shiloh in the land of
Canaan, and said to them, "The LORD
commanded, through Moses, that cities
be given us to dwell in, with pasture
lands for our livestock." 3 Out of their
own heritage, in obedience to this com-
mand of the LORD, the Israelites gave
the Levites the following cities with their
pasture lands.

4 When the first lot among the Levites
fell to the clans of the Kohathites, the
descendants of Aaron the priest ob-
tained thirteen cities by lot from the
tribes of Judah, Simeon and Benjamin.
5 The rest of the Kohathites obtained ten
cities by lot from the clans of the tribe
of Ephraim, from the tribe of Dan, and
from the half-tribe of Manasseh. 6 The
Gershonites obtained thirteen cities by
lot from the clans of the tribe of Issa-
char, from the tribe of Asher, from the
tribe of Naphtali, and from the half-tribe
of Manasseh. 7 The clans of the Mera-
rites obtained twelve cities from the
tribes of Reuben, Gad and Zebulun.
8* These cities with their pasture lands
the Israelites allotted to the Levites in
obedience to the LORD's command
through Moses.

Cities of the Priests. 9* From the
tribes of the Judahites and Simeonites
they designated the following cities,
10 and assigned them to the descendants
of Aaron in the Kohathite clan of the
Levites, since the first lot fell to them:
11 first, Kiriath-arba (Arba was the fa-
ther of Anak), that is, Hebron, in the
mountain region of Judah, with the ad-
jacent pasture lands, 12* although the
open country and villages belonging to
the city had been given to Caleb, son of
Jephunneh, as his property. 13 Thus to
the descendants of Aaron the priest
were given the city of asylum for homi-
cides at Hebron, with its pasture lands;
also, Libnah with its pasture lands,
14 Jattir with its pasture lands, Esh-
temoa with its pasture lands, 15 Holon
with its pasture lands, Debir with its pas-
ture lands, 16 Ashan with its pasture
lands, Juttah with its pasture lands, and
Beth-shemesh with its pasture lands:
nine cities from the two tribes men-
tioned. 17 From the tribe of Benjamin
they obtained the four cities of Gibeon
with its pasture lands, Geba with its pas-
ture lands, 18* Anathoth with its pasture
lands, and Almon with its pasture lands.
19 These cities which with their pasture
lands belonged to the priestly descen-
dants of Aaron, were thirteen in all.

Cities of the Other Kohathites. 20* The
rest of the Kohathite clans among the
Levites obtained by lot, from the tribe
of Ephraim, four cities. 21 They were as-
signed, with its pasture lands, the city
of asylum for homicides at Shechem in
the mountain region of Ephraim; also

JOSHUA

*

20, 2: Ex 21, 13; Nm 35, 10-14; Dt 4, 41-43; 19, 2-9.
6: Nm 35, 12.24f.
7: 15, 13; 19, 37; 21, 21.
8: 21, 27.36f.
9: Nm 35, 15.
21, 1: Ex 6, 16-19; Nm 3, 17-20.
2: Nm 35, 2.
8: Nm 35, 2.
9-19: 1 Chr 6, 54-60.
12: 14, 14; 15, 13.
18: Jer 1, 1.
20-26: 1 Chr 6, 66-70.

†

20, 1-9: The laws concerning the cities of refuge are given in Nm 35, 9-28; Dt 19, 1-13; see notes on Nm 35, 16-25; Dt 19, 2.

21, 1: The order to establish special cities for the Levites is given in Nm 35, 1-8. The forty-eight cities listed here were hardly the exclusive possession of the Levites; at least the more important of them, such as Hebron, Shechem and Ramoth in Gilead, were certainly peopled for the most part by the tribe in whose territory they were situated. But in all these cities the Levites had special property rights which they did not possess in other cities; cf Lv 25, 32ff.

Gezer with its pasture lands, 22 Kibzaim
with its pasture lands, and Beth-horon
with its pasture lands. 23 From the tribe
of Dan they obtained the four cities of
Elteke with its pasture lands, Gibbethon
with its pasture lands, 24 Aijalon with its
pasture lands, and Gath-rimmon with
its pasture lands; 25 and from the half-
tribe of Manasseh the two cities of Taa-
nach with its pasture lands and Ibleam
with its pasture lands. 26 These cities
which with their pasture lands belonged
to the rest of the Kohathite clans were
ten in all.

Cities of the Gershonites. 27* The Ger-
shonite clan of the Levites received from
the half-tribe of Manasseh two cities: the
city of asylum for homicides at Golan,
with its pasture lands; and also Beth-
ashtaroth with its pasture lands. 28 From
the tribe of Issachar they obtained the
four cities of Kishion with its pasture
lands, Daberath with its pasture lands,
29 Jarmuth with its pasture lands, and
En-gannim with its pasture lands; from
the tribe of Asher, 30 the four cities of
Mishal with its pasture lands, Abdon
with its pasture lands, 31 Helkath with its
pasture lands, and Rehob with its pas-
ture lands; 32 and from the tribe of Naph-
tali, three cities: the city of asylum for
homicides at Kedesh in Galilee, with its
pasture lands; also Hammath with its
pasture lands, and Rakkath with its pas-
ture lands. 33 These cities which with
their pasture lands belonged to the Ger-
shonite clans were thirteen in all.

Cities of the Merarites. 34* The Mera-
rite clans, the last of the Levites, re-
ceived from the tribe of Zebulun the four
cities of Jokneam with its pasture lands,
Kartah with its pasture lands,
35 Rimmon with its pasture lands, and
Nahalal with its pasture lands; 36 also,
across the Jordan, from the tribe of Reu-
ben, four cities: the city of asylum for
homicides at Bezer with its pasture
lands, Jahaz with its pasture lands,
37 Kedemoth with its pasture lands, and
Mephaath with its pasture lands; 38 and
from the tribe of Gad a total of four cit-
ies: the city of asylum for homicides at
Ramoth in Gilead with its pasture lands,
also Mahanaim with its pasture lands,
39 Heshbon with its pasture lands, and
Jazer with its pasture lands. 40 The cities
which were allotted to the Merarite
clans, the last of the Levites, were there-
fore twelve in all.

41* Thus the total number of cities
within the territory of the Israelites
which, with their pasture lands, be-
longed to the Levites, was forty-eight.
42 With each and every one of these cities
went the pasture lands round about it.

43* And so the LORD gave Israel all the
land he had sworn to their fathers he
would give them. Once they had con-
quered and occupied it, 44 the LORD gave
them peace on every side, just as he had
promised their fathers. Not one of their
enemies could withstand them; the LORD
brought all their enemies under their
power. 45* Not a single promise that the
LORD made to the house of Israel was
broken; every one was fulfilled.

III: RETURN OF THE TRANSJORDAN TRIBES AND JOSHUA'S FAREWELL

CHAPTER 22

The Eastern Tribes Dismissed. 1 At
that time Joshua summoned the Reu-
benites, the Gadites, and the half-tribe
of Manasseh 2* and said to them: "You
have done all that Moses, the servant
of the LORD, commanded you, and have
obeyed every command I gave you.
3 For many years now you have not once
abandoned your kinsmen, but have
faithfully carried out the commands of
the LORD, your God. 4* Since, therefore,
the LORD, your God, has settled your
kinsmen as he promised them, you may
now return to your tents beyond the Jor-
dan; to your own land, which Moses, the
servant of the LORD, gave you. 5* But be
very careful to observe the precept and
law which Moses, the servant of the
LORD, enjoined upon you: love the LORD,
your God; follow him faithfully; keep his
commandments; remain loyal to him;
and serve him with your whole heart
and soul." 6 Joshua then blessed them
and sent them away to their own tents.

7* (For, to half the tribe of Manasseh
Moses had assigned land in Bashan; and
to the other half Joshua had given a por-
tion along with their kinsmen west of the
Jordan.) What Joshua said to them
when he sent them off to their tents with
his blessing was, 8* "Now that you are
returning to your own tents with great
wealth, with very numerous livestock,
with silver, gold, bronze and iron, and
with a very large supply of clothing, di-
vide these spoils of your enemies with
your kinsmen there." 9* So the Reuben-
ites, the Gadites, and the half-tribe of
Manasseh left the other Israelites at Shi-
loh in the land of Canaan and returned
to the land of Gilead, their own property,
which they had received according to
the LORD's command through Moses.

The Altar beside the Jordan. 10 When
the Reubenites, the Gadites, and the
half-tribe of Manasseh came to the re-
gion of the Jordan in the land of Canaan,

27-33: 1 Chr 6, 71-76.
34-38: 1 Chr 6, 77-81.
41: Nm 35, 7.
43: Gn 12, 7; 13, 15; 15, 18; 26, 3; 28, 4.13.
45: 23, 14f.
22, 2: 1, 16f; Nm 32, 20ff; Dt 3, 18ff.
4: 1, 13; 13, 8; Nm 32, 33.
5: Dt 6, 5f.17; 10, 12; 11, 1.13.22.
7: 17, 5.
8: Nm 31, 27.
9: 18, 1; Nm 32, 1.26.29.

they built there at the Jordan a conspic-
uously large altar. 11*† The other Israel-
ites heard the report that the
Reubenites, the Gadites, and the half-
tribe of Manasseh had built an altar in
the region of the Jordan facing the land
of Canaan, across from them, 12† and
therefore they assembled their whole
community at Shiloh to declare war on
them.

Accusation of the Western Tribes.
13* First, however, they sent to the Reu-
benites, the Gadites, and the half-tribe
of Manasseh in the land of Gilead an em-
bassy consisting of Phinehas, son of
Eleazar the priest, 14 and ten princes,
one from every tribe of Israel, each one
being both prince and military leader of
his ancestral house. 15 When these came
to the Reubenites, the Gadites, and the
half-tribe of Manasseh in the land of Gil-
ead, they said to them: 16* "The whole
community of the LORD sends this mes-
sage: What act of treachery is this you
have committed against the God of Is-
rael? You have seceded from the LORD
this day, and rebelled against him by
building an altar of your own! 17* For the
sin of Peor, a plague came upon the
community of the LORD. 18 We are still
not free of that; must you now add to
it? You are rebelling against the LORD
today and by tomorrow he will be angry
with the whole community of Israel!
19*† If you consider the land you now
possess unclean, cross over to the land
the LORD possesses, where the Dwelling
of the LORD stands, and share that with
us. But do not rebel against the LORD,
nor involve us in rebellion, by building
an altar of your own in addition to the
altar of the LORD, our God. 20*† When
Achan, son of Zerah, violated the ban,
did not wrath fall upon the entire com-
munity of Israel? Though he was but a
single man, he did not perish alone for
his guilt!"

Reply of the Eastern Tribes. 21 The
Reubenites, the Gadites, and the half-
tribe of Manasseh replied to the military
leaders of the Israelites: "The LORD is
the God of gods. 22† The LORD, the God
of gods, knows and Israel shall know.
If now we have acted out of rebellion or
treachery against the LORD, our God,
23 and if we have built an altar of our
own to secede from the LORD, or to offer
holocausts, grain offerings or peace of-
ferings upon it, the LORD himself will ex-
act the penalty. 24 We did it rather out
of our anxious concern lest in the future
your children should say to our children:
'What have you to do with the LORD, the
God of Israel? 25 For the LORD has
placed the Jordan as a boundary be-
tween you and us. You descendants of
Reuben and Gad have no share in the
LORD.' Thus your children would pre-
vent ours from revering the LORD. 26 So
we decided to guard our interests by
building this altar of our own: not for
holocausts or for sacrifices, 27* but as ev-
idence for you on behalf of ourselves and
our descendants, that we have the right
to worship the LORD in his presence with
our holocausts, sacrifices, and peace of-
ferings. Now in the future your children
cannot say to our children, 'You have
no share in the LORD.' 28† Our thought
was, that if in the future they should
speak thus to us or to our descendants,
we could answer: 'Look at the model of
the altar of the LORD which our fathers
made, not for holocausts or for sacri-
fices, but to witness between you and us.'
29 Far be it from us to rebel against the
LORD or to secede now from the LORD
by building an altar for holocaust, grain
offering, or sacrifice in addition to the
altar of the LORD, our God, which stands
before his Dwelling."

30 When Phinehas the priest and the
princes of the community, the military
leaders of the Israelites, heard what the
Reubenites, the Gadites and the Manas-
sehites had to say, they were satisfied.
31 Phinehas, son of Eleazar the priest,
said to the Reubenites, the Gadites and
the Manassehites, "Now we know that
the LORD is with us. Since you have not
committed this act of treachery against
the LORD, you have kept the Israelites
free from punishment by the LORD."

32 Phinehas, son of Eleazar the priest,
and the princes returned from the Reu-
benites and the Gadites in the land of
Gilead to the Israelites in the land of Ca-
naan, and reported the matter to them.

*

11: Dt 13, 13ff.
13: Ex 6, 25; Sir 45, 28.
16: Lv 17, 8f.
17: Nm 25, 3f; Dt 4, 3.
19: 18, 1.
20: 7, 1.5.
27: Dt 12, 5f.17f.

†

22, 11: *In the region of the Jordan facing the land of Canaan:* on the eastern side of the Jordan valley. The river itself formed the boundary between these eastern tribes and the rest of the tribes who lived in what was formerly Canaan—though the term *Canaan* could also be used of both sides of the Jordan valley (cf v 10). The Transjordan tribes naturally built their altar in their own territory.

22, 12: *To declare war on them:* the western Israelites considered this altar, which seemed to violate the customary unity of the sanctuary (cf Lv 17, 1-9; Dt 12, 4-14), as a sign of secession and dangerous to national unity. The motives for the war were political as well as religious.

22, 19: *Unclean:* not sanctified by the Dwelling of the Lord.

22, 20: *Achan . . . did not perish alone:* his guilt caused the failure of the first attack on Ai (7, 4-23); this fact is adduced as an argument for the solidarity and mutual responsibility of all the Israelites.

22, 22: *The LORD, the God of gods:* the Hebrew, which cannot be adequately rendered in English here, adds to the divine name Yahweh ("the LORD") two synonymous words for "God," *el* and *elohim.* The repetition of these three sacred words adds force to the protestations of fidelity and innocence.

22, 28: *To witness:* far from being destined to form a rival sanctuary, the *model of the altar* was intended by the eastern tribes solely as a means of teaching their children to be faithful to the one true sanctuary beyond the Jordan.

33 The report satisfied the Israelites, who
blessed God and decided against declar-
ing war on the Reubenites and Gadites
or ravaging the land they occupied.
34† The Reubenites and the Gadites
gave the altar its name as a witness
among them that the LORD is God.

CHAPTER 23

Joshua's Final Plea. 1* Many years
later, after the LORD had given the Isra-
elites rest from all their enemies round
about them, and when Joshua was old
and advanced in years, 2 he summoned
all Israel (including their elders, lead-
ers, judges and officers) and said to
them: "I am old and advanced in years.
3 You have seen all that the LORD, your
God, has done for you against all these
nations; for it has been the LORD, your
God, himself who fought for you. 4* Bear
in mind that I have apportioned among
your tribes as their heritage the nations
that survive [as well as those I de-
stroyed] between the Jordan and the
Great Sea in the west. 5 The LORD, your
God, will drive them out and dislodge
them at your approach, so that you
will take possession of their land as
the LORD, your God, promised you.
6* Therefore strive hard to observe and
carry out all that is written in the book
of the law of Moses, not straying from
it in any way, 7* or mingling with these
nations while they survive among you.
You must not invoke their gods, or swear
by them, or serve them, or worship
them, 8 but you must remain loyal to the
LORD, your God, as you have been to this
day. 9 At your approach the LORD has
driven out large and strong nations, and
to this day no one has withstood you.
10* One of you puts to flight a thousand,
because it is the LORD, your God, himself
who fights for you, as he promised you.
11 Take great care, however, to love the
LORD, your God. 12* For if you ever
abandon him and ally yourselves with
the remnant of these nations while they
survive among you, by intermarrying
and intermingling with them, 13 know for
certain that the LORD, your God, will no
longer drive these nations out of your
way. Instead they will be a snare and
a trap for you, a scourge for your sides
and thorns for your eyes, until you per-
ish from this good land which the LORD,
your God, has given you.
14† "Today, as you see, I am going the
way of all men. So now acknowledge
with your whole heart and soul that not
one of all the promises the LORD, your
God, made to you has remained unful-
filled. Every promise has been fulfilled
for you, with not one single exception.
15*† But just as every promise the LORD,
your God, made to you has been fulfilled
for you, so will he fulfill every threat,
even so far as to exterminate you from
this good land which the LORD, your
God, has given you. 16 If you transgress
the covenant of the LORD, your God,
which he enjoined on you, serve other
gods and worship them, the anger of the
LORD will flare up against you and you
will quickly perish from the good land
which he has given you."

CHAPTER 24

Reminder of the Divine Goodness.
1 Joshua gathered together all the tribes
of Israel at Shechem, summoning their
elders, their leaders, their judges and
their officers. When they stood in ranks
before God, 2*† Joshua addressed all the
people: "Thus says the LORD, the God
of Israel: In times past your fathers,
down to Terah, father of Abraham and
Nahor, dwelt beyond the River and
served other gods. 3* But I brought your
father Abraham from the region beyond
the River and led him through the entire
land of Canaan. I made his descendants
numerous, and gave him Isaac. 4* To
Isaac I gave Jacob and Esau. To Esau
I assigned the mountain region of Seir
in which to settle, while Jacob and his
children went down to Egypt.
5* "Then I sent Moses and Aaron, and
smote Egypt with the prodigies which
I wrought in her midst. 6* Afterward I
led you out of Egypt, and when you
reached the sea, the Egyptians pursued
your fathers to the Red Sea with chariots
and horsemen. 7* Because they cried out
to the LORD, he put darkness between
your people and the Egyptians, upon
whom he brought the sea so that it en-
gulfed them. After you witnessed what
I did to Egypt, and dwelt a long time
in the desert, 8* I brought you into the
land of the Amorites who lived east of
the Jordan. They fought against you, but

*

23, 1: 13, 1.
4: 13, 2-7; 14, 2; 18, 10; Ps 78, 55.
6: 1, 7.
7: Dt 7, 2ff.
10: Ex 14, 14; Lv 26, 8; Dt 3, 22.
12: Ex 34, 16; Dt 7, 3.
15: Lv 26, 14-39; Dt 28, 15-68.
24, 2: Gn 11, 26.31; 31, 53.
3: Gn 12, 1; Acts 7, 2-4.
4: Gn 25, 24ff; 36, 8; 46, 1.6; Acts 7, 15.
5: Ex 3, 10; 7, 14—12, 30.
6: Ex 12, 37.51; 14, 9.
7: Ex 14, 10.20.27f.
8: Nm 21, 21-35.

†

22, 34: The name of this altar was the Hebrew word for "witness," *'ed.*

23, 14: *Going the way of all men:* drawing near to death, the inevitable goal of all; cf 1 Kgs 2, 1f.

23, 15: *Every threat:* mentioned especially in Dt 28, 15-68.

24, 2: *Beyond the River:* east of the Euphrates; cf Gn 11, 28-31.

I delivered them into your power. You
took possession of their land, and I de-
stroyed them [the two kings of the Amo-
rites] before you. 9* Then Balak, son of
Zippor, king of Moab, prepared to war
against Israel. He summoned Balaam,
son of Beor, to curse you; 10* but I would
not listen to Balaam. On the contrary,
he had to bless you, and I saved you
from him. 11* Once you crossed the Jor-
dan and came to Jericho, the men of Jer-
icho fought against you, but I delivered
them also into your power. 12*† And I
sent the hornets ahead of you which
drove them [the Amorites, Perizzites,
Canaanites, Hittites, Girgashites, Hi-
vites and Jebusites] out of your way; it
was not your sword or your bow.

13* "I gave you a land which you had
not tilled and cities which you had not
built, to dwell in; you have eaten of vine-
yards and olive groves which you did
not plant.

14* "Now, therefore, fear the LORD and
serve him completely and sincerely.
Cast out the gods your fathers served
beyond the River and in Egypt, and
serve the LORD. 15*† If it does not please
you to serve the LORD, decide today
whom you will serve, the gods your fa-
thers served beyond the River or the
gods of the Amorites in whose country
you are dwelling. As for me and my
household, we will serve the LORD."

Renewal of the Covenant. 16 But the
people answered, "Far be it from us to
forsake the LORD for the service of other
gods. 17 For it was the LORD, our God,
who brought us and our fathers up out
of the land of Egypt, out of a state of
slavery. He performed those great mira-
cles before our very eyes and protected
us along our entire journey and among
all the peoples through whom we passed.
18 At our approach the LORD drove out
[all the peoples, including] the Amorites
who dwelt in the land. Therefore we
also will serve the LORD, for he is our
God."

19*† Joshua in turn said to the people,
"You may not be able to serve the LORD,
for he is a holy God; he is a jealous God
who will not forgive your transgressions
or your sins. 20 If, after the good he has
done for you, you forsake the LORD and
serve strange gods, he will do evil to you
and destroy you."

21 But the people answered Joshua,
"We will still serve the LORD." 22 Joshua
therefore said to the people, "You are
your own witnesses that you have cho-
sen to serve the LORD." They replied,
"We are, indeed!" 23 "Now, therefore,
put away the strange gods that are
among you and turn your hearts to
the LORD, the God of Israel." 24 Then
the people promised Joshua, "We will
serve the LORD, our God, and obey his
voice."

25 So Joshua made a covenant with the
people that day and made statutes and
ordinances for them at Shechem,
26* which he recorded in the book of the
law of God. Then he took a large stone
and set it up there under the oak that
was in the sanctuary of the LORD.
27* And Joshua said to all the people,
"This stone shall be our witness, for it
has heard all the words which the LORD
spoke to us. It shall be a witness against
you, should you wish to deny your God."
28* Then Joshua dismissed the people,
each to his own heritage.

Death of Joshua. 29* After these
events, Joshua, son of Nun, servant of
the LORD, died at the age of a hundred
and ten. 30* He was buried within the
limits of his heritage at Timnath-serah
in the mountain region of Ephraim
north of Mount Gaash. 31 Israel served
the LORD during the entire lifetime of
Joshua and that of the elders who out-
lived Joshua and knew all that the LORD
had done for Israel. 32*† The bones of
Joseph, which the Israelites had brought
up from Egypt, were buried in Shechem
in the plot of ground Jacob had bought
from the sons of Hamor, father of She-
chem, for a hundred pieces of money.
This was a heritage of the descendants
of Joseph. 33* When Eleazar, son of
Aaron, also died, he was buried on the
hill which had been given to his son
Phinehas in the mountain region of
Ephraim.

*

9: Nm 22, 2-5.
10: Nm 23, 1—24, 25.
11: 3, 14; 6, 1.
12: 11, 20: Ex 23, 28; Dt 7, 20.
13: Dt 6, 10f.
14: Dt 10, 12; 1 Sm 7, 3; 12, 24; Tb 14, 9.
15: Dt 30, 15-19.
19: Ex 20, 5; 23, 21; 34, 14; Lv 19, 2.
26: Gn 28, 18; 31, 45; Jgs 9, 6.
27: Gn 31, 48.52; Dt 31, 19.21.26.
28: Jgs 2, 6.
29ff: Jgs 2, 7ff.
30: 19, 50; Jgs 2, 9.
32: Gn 33, 19; 50, 24; Ex 13, 19.
33: 22, 13.

†

24, 12: *The hornets:* see note on Ex 23, 28.

24, 15: *The gods your fathers served:* Abraham's ancestors were polytheists.

24, 19: *You may not be able:* fidelity to God's service is not easy, and therefore those who take such solemn obligations on themselves must be ever vigilant against human weakness.

24, 32: *The bones of Joseph:* the mummified body of Joseph (Gn 50, 25f), which the Israelites took with them as they left Egypt (Ex 13, 19), was fittingly buried at the ancient city of Shechem, near the border between the two Josephite tribes of Ephraim and Manasseh.

The Book of

JUDGES

The Book of Judges derives its title from the twelve heroes of Israel whose deeds it records. They were not magistrates, but military leaders sent by God to aid and to relieve his people in time of external danger. They exercised their activities in the interval of time between the death of Joshua and the institution of the monarchy in Israel. Six of them—Othniel, Ehud, Barak, Gideon, Jephthah and Samson—are treated in some detail and have accordingly been styled the Major Judges. The other six, of whose activities this book preserves but a summary record, are called the Minor Judges. There were two other judges, whose judgeships are described in 1 Samuel—Eli and Samuel, who seem to have ruled the entire nation of Israel just before the institution of the monarchy. The twelve judges of the present book, however, very probably exercised their authority, sometimes simultaneously, over one or another tribe of Israel, never over the entire nation.

The purpose of the book is to show that the fortunes of Israel depended upon the obedience or disobedience of the people to God's law. Whenever they rebelled against him, they were oppressed by pagan nations; when they repented, he raised up judges to deliver them (cf 2, 10-23).

The accounts of various events, whether written shortly after their occurrence or orally transmitted, were later skillfully unified according to the moral purpose of the redactor some time during the Israelite monarchy.

The book is divided as follows:

- *I: Palestine after the Death of Joshua (1, 1—3, 6)*
- *II: Stories of the Judges (3, 7—16, 31)*
- *III: The Tribes of Dan and Benjamin in the Days of the Judges (17, 1—21, 25)*

I: PALESTINE AFTER THE DEATH OF JOSHUA

CHAPTER 1

Pagan Survivors in Palestine.
1*† After the death of Joshua the Israel-
ites consulted the LORD, asking, "Who
shall be first among us to attack the Ca-
naanites and to do battle with them?"
2 The LORD answered, "Judah shall at-
tack: I have delivered the land into his
power." 3 Judah then said to his brother
Simeon, "Come up with me into the ter-
ritory allotted to me, and let us engage
the Canaanites in battle. I will likewise
accompany you into the territory allot-
ted to you." So Simeon went with him.
4 When the forces of Judah attacked,
the LORD delivered the Canaanites and
Perizzites into their power, and they
slew ten thousand of them in Bezek. 5 It
was in Bezek that they came upon Ado-
nibezek and fought against him. When
they defeated the Canaanites and Periz-
zites, 6 Adonibezek fled. They set out in
pursuit, and when they caught him, cut
off his thumbs and his big toes. 7 At this
Adonibezek said, "Seventy kings, with
their thumbs and big toes cut off, used
to pick up scraps under my table. As I
have done, so has God repaid me." He
was brought to Jerusalem, and there he
died. 8 [The Judahites fought against Je-
rusalem and captured it, putting it to the
sword; then they destroyed the city by
fire.]
9* Afterward the Judahites went down
to fight against the Canaanites who lived
in the mountain region, in the Negeb,
and in the foothills. 10* Judah also
marched against the Canaanites who
dwelt in Hebron, which was formerly
called Kiriath-arba, and defeated
Sheshai, Ahiman and Talmai. 11 From
there they marched against the inhab-
itants of Debir, which was formerly
called Kiriath-sepher. 12 And Caleb said,
"I will give my daughter Achsah in mar-
riage to the one who attacks Kiriath-se-
pher and captures it." 13* Othniel, son

*

1, 1: 20, 18; Nm 27, 21.
9: Jos 10, 40; 11, 16; 12, 8.
10-15: Jos 15, 13-19.
10: Nm 13, 22; Jos 14, 15.
13: 3, 9.

†

1, 1-36: This chapter summarizes events most of which occurred shortly after the death of Joshua. Perhaps because they were planned and inaugurated by him, they are also attributed to him in the last half of the preceding book (Jos 14—22).

of Caleb's younger brother Kenaz, cap-
tured it; so Caleb gave him his daughter
Achsah in marriage. 14 On the day of her
marriage to Othniel she induced him to
ask her father for some land. Then, as
she alighted from the ass, Caleb asked
her, "What is troubling you?" 15 Give me
an additional gift," she answered.
"Since you have assigned land in the
Negeb to me, give me also pools of
water." So Caleb gave her the upper and
the lower pool. 16*† The descendants of
the Kenite, Moses' father-in-law, came
up with the Judahites from the city of
palms to the desert at Arad [which is
in the Negeb]. But they later left and set-
tled among the Amalekites.
17* Judah then went with his brother
Simeon, and they defeated the Canaan-
ites who dwelt in Zephath. After having
doomed the city to destruction, they re-
named it Hormah. 18* Judah, however,
did not occupy Gaza with its territory,
Ashkelon with its territory, or Ekron
with its territory. 19* Since the LORD was
with Judah, he gained possession of the
mountain region. Yet he could not dis-
lodge those who lived on the plain, be-
cause they had iron chariots. 20* As
Moses had commanded, Hebron was
given to Caleb, who then drove from it
the three sons of Anak.
21*† The Benjaminites did not dislodge
the Jebusites who dwelt in Jerusalem,
with the result that the Jebusites live in
Jerusalem beside the Benjaminites to
the present day.
22 The house of Joseph, too, marched
up against Bethel, and the LORD was
with them. 23* The house of Joseph had
a reconnaissance made of Bethel, which
formerly was called Luz. 24 The scouts
saw a man coming out of the city and
said to him, "Show us a way into the city,
and we will spare you." 25 He showed
them a way into the city, which they then
put to the sword; but they let the man
and his whole clan go free. 26 He then
went to the land of the Hittites, where
he built a city and called it Luz, as it is
still called.
27* Manasseh did not take possession
of Beth-shean with its towns or of Taa-
nach with its towns. Neither did he dis-
lodge the inhabitants of Dor and its
towns, those of Ibleam and its towns, or
those of Megiddo and its towns. The Ca-
naanites kept their hold in this district.
28 When the Israelites grew stronger,
they impressed the Canaanites as labor-
ers, but did not drive them out.
29* Similarly, the Ephraimites did not
drive out the Canaanites living in Gezer,
and so the Canaanites live in Gezer in
their midst.
30 Zebulun did not dislodge the inhab-
itants of Kitron or those of Nahalol; the
Canaanites live among them, but have
become forced laborers.
31* Nor did Asher drive out the inhab-
itants of Acco or those of Sidon, or take
possession of Mahaleb, Achzib, Helbah,
Aphik or Rehob. 32 The Asherites live
among the Canaanite natives of the
land, whom they have not dislodged.
33* Naphtali did not drive out the in-
habitants of Beth-shemesh or those of
Beth-anath, and so they live among the
Canaanite natives of the land. However,
the inhabitants of Beth-shemesh and
Beth-anath have become forced labor-
ers for them.
34* The Amorites hemmed in the Dan-
ites in the mountain region, not permit-
ting them to go down into the plain.
35 The Amorites had a firm hold in Har-
heres, Aijalon and Shaalbim, but as the
house of Joseph gained the upper hand,
they were impressed as laborers.
36 The territory of the Amorites ex-
tended from the Akrabbim pass to Sela
and beyond.

CHAPTER 2

Infidelities of the Israelites. 1* An an-
gel of the LORD went up from Gilgal to
Bochim and said, "It was I who brought
you up from Egypt and led you into the
land which I promised on oath to your
fathers. I said that I would never break
my covenant with you, 2* but that you
were not to make a pact with the inhabit-
ants of this land, and you were to pull
down their altars. Yet you have not
obeyed me. What did you mean by this?
3* For now I tell you, I will not clear them
out of your way; they shall oppose you
and their gods shall become a snare for
you."
4 When the angel of the LORD had
made these threats to all the Israelites,
the people wept aloud; 5† and so that
place came to be called Bochim. They
offered sacrifice there to the LORD.
6* When Joshua dismissed the people,
each Israelite went to take possession of
his own hereditary land. 7 The people

*

16: 4, 11; Nm 10, 29-32.
17: Nm 21, 3.
18: Jos 11, 22.
19: Jos 17, 16ff.
20: Jos 14, 9.13; 15, 14.
21: Jos 15, 63.
23: Gn 28, 19; 35, 6; 48, 3; Jos 18, 13.
27f: Jos 17, 11ff.
29: Jos 16, 10.
31f: Jos 19, 24-31.
33: Jos 19, 32-39.
34: Jos 19, 47f.
2, 1ff: 6, 8ff.
2: Ex 34, 12f. 15; Dt 7, 2.5; 12, 2f.
3: Nm 33, 55; Jos 23, 13.
6-9: Jos 24, 28-31.

†

1, 16: *Moses' father-in-law:* Reuel; cf Nm 10, 29-32 and note. *City of Palms:* Jericho (cf Dt 34, 3) or a town in the Negeb.

1, 21: According to Jos 18, 16, Jerusalem was assigned to the tribe of Benjamin. But it was not actually taken from the Jebusites until David captured it (2 Sm 5, 6-9) and made it his capital, outside the tribal organization.

2, 5: *Bochim:* the Hebrew word for "weepers."

served the LORD during the entire life-
time of Joshua, and of those elders who
outlived Joshua and who had seen all
the great work which the LORD had done
for Israel. 8 Joshua, son of Nun, the ser-
vant of the LORD, was a hundred and
ten years old when he died; 9* and they
buried him within the borders of his
heritage at Timnath-heres in the moun-
tain region of Ephraim north of Mount
Gaash.

10 But once the rest of that generation
were gathered to their fathers, and a
later generation arose that did not know
the LORD, or what he had done for Israel,
11*† the Israelites offended the LORD by
serving the Baals. 12 Abandoning the
LORD, the God of their fathers, who had
led them out of the land of Egypt, they
followed the other gods of the various
nations around them, and by their
worship of these gods provoked the
LORD.

13† Because they had thus abandoned
him and served Baal and the Ashtaroth,
14 the anger of the LORD flared up against
Israel, and he delivered them over to
plunderers who despoiled them. He al-
lowed them to fall into the power of their
enemies round about whom they were
no longer able to withstand. 15* What-
ever they undertook, the LORD turned
into disaster for them, as in his warning
he had sworn he would do, till they were
in great distress. 16 Even when the LORD
raised up judges to deliver them from
the power of their despoilers, 17 they did
not listen to their judges, but abandoned
themselves to the worship of other gods.
They were quick to stray from the
way their fathers had taken, and did
not follow their example of obedience
to the commandments of the LORD.
18 Whenever the LORD raised up judges
for them, he would be with the judge and
save them from the power of their ene-
mies as long as the judge lived; it was
thus the LORD took pity on their distress-
ful cries of affliction under their oppres-
sors. 19* But when the judge died, they
would relapse and do worse than their
fathers, following other gods in service
and worship, relinquishing none of their
evil practices or stubborn conduct.

20* In his anger toward Israel the LORD
said, "Inasmuch as this nation has vio-
lated my covenant which I enjoined on
their fathers, and has disobeyed me, 21 I
for my part will not clear away for them
any more of the nations which Joshua
left when he died." 22 Through these na-
tions the Israelites were to be made to
prove whether or not they would keep
to the way of the LORD and continue in
it as their fathers had done; 23 therefore
the LORD allowed them to remain in-
stead of expelling them immediately, or
delivering them into the power of Israel.

CHAPTER 3

1 The following are the nations which
the LORD allowed to remain, so that
through them he might try all those Is-
raelites who had no experience of the
battles with Canaan [just to instruct, by
training them in battle, 2 those genera-
tions only of the Israelites who would not
have had that previous experience]:
3*† the five lords of the Philistines; and
all the Canaanites, the Sidonians, and
the Hivites who dwell in the mountain
region of Lebanon between Baal-her-
mon and the entrance to Hamath.
4 These served to put Israel to the test,
to determine whether they would obey
the commandments the LORD had en-
joined on their fathers through Moses.
5 Besides, the Israelites were living
among the Canaanites, Hittites, Amo-
rites, Perizzites, Hivites and Jebusites.
6 In fact, they took their daughters in
marriage, and gave their own daughters
to their sons in marriage, and served
their gods.

II: STORIES OF THE JUDGES

Othniel. 7*† Because the Israelites
had offended the LORD by forgetting the
LORD, their God, and serving the Baals
and the Asherahs, 8 the anger of the
LORD flared up against them, and he al-
lowed them to fall into the power of
Cushan-rishathaim, king of Aram Na-
haraim, whom they served for eight
years. 9 But when the Israelites cried out
to the LORD, he raised up for them a sav-
ior, Othniel, son of Caleb's younger
brother Kenaz, who rescued them.
10* The spirit of the LORD came upon
him, and he judged Israel. When he went
out to war, the LORD delivered Cushan-
rishathaim, king of Aram, into his
power, so that he made him subject.

*

9: Jos 19, 50.
11.14: 3, 7f; 4, 1f; 6, 1; 10, 6f; 13, 1.
15: Dt 28, 15-68.
19: 3, 12; 4, 1; 6, 1; 8, 33.
20f: Jos 25, 16.
3,3: Jos 13, 2-6.
7: 2, 11ff.
10: 6, 34; 11, 29; 13, 25; 14, 6. 19; 15, 14.

†

2, 11: *Baals:* the chief god of the Canaanites and the Phoenicians was called "Baal," a word meaning "lord." He was honored by various titles, hence the plural form here, equivalent to "the pagan gods."

2, 13: *Ashtaroth:* the Canaanite Phoenician goddess of love and fertility was Astarte. The plural form used here refers to her various titles and images and is equivalent to "goddesses."

3, 3: *The Philistines:* non-Semitic invaders who gave their name to all Palestine, although they occupied only its southwestern plains. Their confederation embraced the five leading cities of Gaza, Ashkelon, Ashdod, Gath and Ekron.

3, 7: *Asherahs:* elsewhere rendered "sacred poles." See note on Ex 34, 13; and on Dt 7, 5. Here the word seems to mean "goddesses."

11* The land then was at rest for forty
years, until Othniel, son of Kenaz, died.
Ehud. 12 Again the Israelites offended
the LORD, who because of this offense
strengthened Eglon, king of Moab,
against Israel. 13 In alliance with the
Ammonites and Amalekites, he at-
tacked and defeated Israel, taking pos-
session of the city of palms. 14 The
Israelites then served Eglon, king of
Moab, for eighteen years.
15 But when the Israelites cried out to
the LORD, he raised up for them a savior,
the Benjaminite Ehud, son of Gera, who
was left-handed. It was by him that the
Israelites sent their tribute to Eglon,
king of Moab. 16 Ehud made himself a
two-edged dagger a foot long, and wore
it under his clothes over his right thigh.
17 He presented the tribute to Eglon, king
of Moab, who was very fat, 18 and after
the presentation went off with the tribute
bearers. 19 He returned, however, from
where the idols are, near Gilgal, and
said, "I have a private message for you,
O king." And the king said, "Silence!"
Then when all his attendants had left his
presence, 20 and Ehud went in to him
where he sat alone in his cool upper
room, Ehud said, "I have a message
from God for you." So the king rose from
his chair, 21 and then Ehud with his left
hand drew the dagger from his right
thigh, and thrust it into Eglon's belly.
22 The hilt also went in after the blade,
and the fat closed over the blade because
he did not withdraw the dagger from his
body.
23 Then Ehud went out into the hall,
shutting the doors of the upper room on
him and locking them. 24 When Ehud
had left and the servants came, they saw
that the doors of the upper room were
locked, and thought, "He must be easing
himself in the cool chamber." 25 They
waited until they finally grew suspicious.
Since he did not open the doors of the
upper room, they took the key and
opened them. There on the floor, dead,
lay their lord!
26 During their delay Ehud made good
his escape and, passing the idols, took
refuge in Seirah. 27 On his arrival he
sounded the horn in the mountain region
of Ephraim, and the Israelites went
down from the mountains with him as
their leader. 28* "Follow me," he said to
them, "for the LORD has delivered your
enemies the Moabites into your power."
So they followed him down and seized
the fords of the Jordan leading to Moab,
permitting no one to cross. 29 On that oc-
casion they slew about ten thousand Mo-
abites, all of them strong and valiant
men. Not a man escaped. 30 Thus was
Moab brought under the power of Israel
at that time; and the land had rest for
eighty years.
Shamgar. 31 After him there was
Shamgar, son of Anath, who slew six
hundred Philistines with an oxgoad. He,
too, rescued Israel.

CHAPTER 4

Deborah and Barak. 1 After Ehud's
death, however, the Israelites again of-
fended the LORD. 2* So the LORD allowed
them to fall into the power of the Ca-
naanite king, Jabin, who reigned in Ha-
zor. The general of his army was Sisera,
who dwelt in Harosheth-ha-goiim. 3 But
the Israelites cried out to the LORD; for
with his nine hundred iron chariots he
sorely oppressed the Israelites for
twenty years.
4 At this time the prophetess Deborah,
wife of Lappidoth, was judging Israel.
5 She used to sit under Deborah's palm
tree, situated between Ramah and
Bethel in the mountain region of Ephra-
im, and there the Israelites came up to her
for judgment. 6* She sent and sum-
moned Barak, son of Abinoam, from
Kedesh of Naphtali. "This is what the
LORD, the God of Israel, commands,"
she said to him; "go, march on Mount
Tabor, and take with you ten thousand
Naphtalites and Zebulunites. 7* I will
lead Sisera, the general of Jabin's army,
out to you at the Wadi Kishon, together
with his chariots and troops, and will de-
liver them into your power." 8 But Barak
answered her, "If you come with me, I
will go; if you do not come with me, I
will not go." 9 "I will certainly go with
you," she replied, "but you shall not gain
the glory in the expedition on which you
are setting out, for the LORD will have
Sisera fall into the power of a woman."
So Deborah joined Barak and journeyed
with him to Kedesh.
10* Barak summoned Zebulun and
Naphtali to Kedesh, and ten thousand
men followed him. Deborah also went
up with him. 11*† Now the Kenite Heber
had detached himself from his own peo-
ple, the descendants of Hobab, Moses'
brother-in-law, and had pitched his tent
by the terebinth of Zaanannim, which
was near Kedesh.
12 It was reported to Sisera that Barak,
son of Abinoam, had gone up to Mount
Tabor. 13 So Sisera assembled from Ha-
rosheth-ha-goiim at the Wadi Kishon all
nine hundred of his iron chariots and
all his forces. 14 Deborah then said to

*

11: 5, 31; 8, 28.
28: 4, 7.14; 7, 9. 15.
4, 2: Jos 11, 1. 10; Ps 83, 10; 1 Sm 12, 9.
6: Heb 11, 32.
7: 5, 21; Ps 83, 10.
10: 5, 18.
11: Nm 10, 29.

†

4, 11: Most of the Kenites occupied a district in the southern part of Judah (1, 16). A group of them, however, had detached themselves and settled in lower Galilee.

Barak, "Be off, for this is the day on
which the LORD has delivered Sisera into
your power. The LORD marches before
you." So Barak went down Mount Tabor,
followed by his ten thousand men.
15* And the LORD put Sisera and all his
chariots and all his forces to rout before
Barak. Sisera himself dismounted from
his chariot and fled on foot. 16 Barak,
however, pursued the chariots and the
army as far as Harosheth-ha-goiim. The
entire army of Sisera fell beneath the
sword, not even one man surviving.

17† Sisera, in the meantime, had fled
on foot to the tent of Jael, wife of the
Kenite Heber, since Jabin, king of Ha-
zor, and the family of the Kenite Heber
were at peace with one another. 18 Jael
went out to meet Sisera and said to him,
"Come in, my lord, come in with me; do
not be afraid." So he went into her tent,
and she covered him with a rug. 19* He
said to her, "Please give me a little water
to drink. I am thirsty." But she opened
a jug of milk for him to drink, and then
covered him over. 20 "Stand at the en-
trance of the tent," he said to her. "If
anyone comes and asks, 'Is there some-
one here?' say, 'No!' " 21* Instead Jael,
wife of Heber, got a tent peg and took
a mallet in her hand. While Sisera was
sound asleep, she stealthily approached
him and drove the peg through his tem-
ple down into the ground, so that he per-
ished in death. 22 Then when Barak
came in pursuit of Sisera, Jael went out
to meet him and said to him, "Come, I
will show you the man you seek." So he
went in with her, and there lay Sisera
dead, with the tent peg through his tem-
ple.

23 Thus on that day God humbled the
Canaanite king, Jabin, before the Israel-
ites; 24 their power weighed ever heavier
upon him, till at length they destroyed
the Canaanite king, Jabin.

CHAPTER 5

Canticle of Deborah. 1 On that day
Deborah [and Barak, son of Abinoam,]
sang this song:

2† Of chiefs who took the lead in Israel,
of noble deeds by the people who
bless the LORD,
3 Hear, O kings! Give ear, O princes!
I to the LORD will sing my song,
my hymn to the LORD, the God of
Israel.

4 O LORD, when you went out from
Seir,
when you marched from the land
of Edom,
The earth quaked and the heavens
were shaken,
while the clouds sent down show-
ers.
5* Mountains trembled
in the presence of the LORD, the
One of Sinai,
in the presence of the LORD, the
God of Israel.

6* In the days of Shamgar, son of
Anath,
in the days of slavery caravans
ceased:
Those who traveled the roads
went by roundabout paths.
7 Gone was freedom beyond the walls,
gone indeed from Israel.
When I, Deborah, rose,
when I rose, a mother in Israel,
8† New gods were their choice;
then the war was at their gates.
Not a shield could be seen, nor a
lance,
among forty thousand in Israel!

9 My heart is with the leaders of Is-
rael,
nobles of the people who bless the
LORD;
10 They who ride on white asses,
seated on saddlecloths as they go
their way;
11 Sing of them to the strains of the
harpers at the wells,
where men recount the just deeds
of the LORD,
his just deeds that brought free-
dom to Israel.

12 Awake, awake, Deborah!
awake, awake, strike up a song.
Strength! arise, Barak,
make despoilers your spoil, son of
Abinoam.
13 Then down came the fugitives with
the mighty,
the people of the LORD came down
for me as warriors.

14† From Ephraim, princes were in the
valley;

*

15: Ps 83, 10.
19: 5, 25.
21: 5, 26.
5, 5: Dt 33, 2; 2 Sm 22, 8; Pss 18, 8; 68, 9.
5: Ex 19, 16; Dt 4, 11; Ps 97, 5.
6: 3, 31.

†

4, 17-22: It is to be noted that the sacred author merely records the fact of the murder of Sisera. We must not construe this as approval of Jael's action.

5, 2-31: This canticle is an excellent example of early Hebrew poetry, even though some of its verses are now obscure.

5, 8: *New gods:* pagan deities; cf Dt 32, 16-18. God punished the idolatry of the Israelites by leaving them relatively unarmed before the attacks of their enemies, who had better weapons, made of iron; cf 1 Sm 13, 19-22.

5, 14-22: Praise for the tribes which formed the Israelite league against Sisera: Ephraim, Benjamin, Manasseh (represented by Machir), Zebulun, Issachar, and Naphtali (led by Barak). The tribes of Reuben, Gad (Gilead), Dan, and Asher are chided for their lack of co-operation. The more distant tribes of Judah and Simeon are not mentioned.

behind you was Benjamin, among
your troops.
From Machir came down commanders,
from Zebulun wielders of the marshal's staff.
15* With Deborah were the princes of Issachar;
Barak, too, was in the valley, his
course unchecked.

Among the clans of Reuben
great were the searchings of
heart.
16 Why do you stay beside your
hearths
listening to the lowing of the
herds?
Among the clans of Reuben
great were the searchings of
heart!

17 Gilead, beyond the Jordan, rests;
why does Dan spend his time in
ships?
Asher, who dwells along the shore,
is resting in his coves.
18* Zebulun is the people defying death;
Naphtali, too, on the open heights!

19* The kings came and fought;
then they fought, those kings of
Canaan,
At Taanach by the waters of Megiddo;
no silver booty did they take.
20*† From the heavens the stars, too,
fought;
from their courses they fought
against Sisera.
21* The Wadi Kishon swept them away;
a wadi . . . , the Kishon.
22 Then the hoofs of the horses
pounded,
with the dashing, dashing of his
steeds.

23† "Curse Meroz," says the LORD,
"hurl a curse at its inhabitants!
For they came not to my help,
as warriors to the help of the
LORD."

24* Blessed among women be Jael,
blessed among tent-dwelling
women.
25* He asked for water, she gave him
milk;
in a princely bowl she offered
curds.
26 With her left hand she reached for
the peg,
with her right, for the workman's
mallet.

She hammered Sisera, crushed his
head;
she smashed, stove in his temple.
27 At her feet he sank down, fell, lay
still;
down at her feet he sank and fell;
where he sank down, there he fell,
slain.

28 From the window peered down and
wailed
the mother of Sisera, from the lattice:
"Why is his chariot so long in coming?
why are the hoofbeats of his chariots delayed?"
29 The wisest of her princesses answers
her,
and she, too, keeps answering
herself:

30 "They must be dividing the spoil
they took:
there must be a damsel or two for
each man,
Spoils of dyed cloth as Sisera's spoil,
an ornate shawl or two for me in
the spoil."

31* May all your enemies perish thus,
O LORD!
but your friends be as the sun rising in its might!

And the land was at rest for forty
years.

CHAPTER 6

The Call of Gideon. 1 The Israelites of-
fended the LORD, who therefore deliv-
ered them into the power of Midian for
seven years, 2 so that Midian held Israel
subject. For fear of Midian the Israelites
established the fire signals on the moun-
tains, the caves for refuge, and the
strongholds. 3* And it used to be that
when the Israelites had completed their
sowing, Midian, Amalek and the Ked-
emites would come up, 4 encamp oppo-
site them, and destroy the produce of
the land as far as the outskirts of Gaza,
leaving no sustenance in Israel, nor
sheep, oxen or asses. 5 For they would
come up with their livestock, and their
tents would become as numerous as lo-
custs; and neither they nor their camels
could be numbered, when they came
into the land to lay it waste. 6 Thus was

*

15: 4, 14.
18: 4, 10.
19: 1, 27; Jos 17, 11.
20: 4, 15; Jos 10, 14.
21: 4, 7.13.
24: 4, 17; Jdt 13, 17; Lk 1, 28.42.
25f: 4, 19.21.
31: Ps 83, 10-19.
6, 3f: 7, 12; Dt 28, 30ff.

†

5, 20f: It would seem that nature aided the Hebrews in some way. Perhaps the torrential rains swelled the waters of Kishon, which then overwhelmed the Canaanites.

5, 23: *Meroz:* an unknown locality in which Hebrews probably resided, since its inhabitants are cursed for their failure to proffer aid.

Israel reduced to misery by Midian, and
so the Israelites cried out to the LORD.
7 When Israel cried out to the LORD be-
cause of Midian, 8* he sent a prophet to
the Israelites who said to them, "The
LORD, the God of Israel, says: I led you
up from Egypt; I brought you out of the
place of slavery. 9 I rescued you from
the power of Egypt and of all your other
oppressors. I drove them out before you
and gave you their land. 10 And I said
to you: I, the LORD, am your God; you
shall not venerate the gods of the Amo-
rites in whose land you are dwelling. But
you did not obey me."
11 Then the angel of the LORD came
and sat under the terebinth in Ophrah
that belonged to Joash the Abiezrite.
While his son Gideon was beating out
wheat in the winepress to save it from
the Midianites, 12 the angel of the LORD
appeared to him and said, "The LORD
is with you, O champion!" 13 "My lord,"
Gideon said to him, "if the LORD is with
us, why has all this happened to us?
Where are his wondrous deeds of which
our fathers told us when they said, 'Did
not the LORD bring us up from Egypt?'
For now the LORD has abandoned us and
has delivered us into the power of
Midian." 14 The LORD turned to him and
said, "Go with the strength you have and
save Israel from the power of Midian.
It is I who send you." 15 But he answered
him, "Please, my lord, how can I save
Israel? My family is the meanest in Ma-
nasseh, and I am the most insignificant
in my father's house." 16 "I shall be with
you," the LORD said to him, "and you
will cut down Midian to the last man."
17 He answered him, "If I find favor with
you, give me a sign that you are speak-
ing with me. 18 Do not depart from here,
I pray you, until I come back to you and
bring out my offering and set it before
you." He answered, "I will await your
return."
19 So Gideon went off and prepared a
kid and an ephah of flour in the form
of unleavened cakes. Putting the meat
in a basket and the broth in a pot, he
brought them out to him under the tere-
binth and presented them. 20* The angel
of God said to him, "Take the meat and
unleavened cakes and lay them on this
rock; then pour out the broth." When he
had done so, 21 the angel of the LORD
stretched out the tip of the staff he held,
and touched the meat and unleavened
cakes. Thereupon a fire came up from
the rock which consumed the meat and
unleavened cakes, and the angel of the
LORD disappeared from sight. 22* Gid-
eon, now aware that it had been the an-
gel of the LORD, said, "Alas, Lord GOD,
that I have seen the angel of the LORD
face to face!" 23 The LORD answered him,
"Be calm, do not fear. You shall not die."
24† So Gideon built there an altar to the
LORD and called it Yahweh-shalom. To
this day it is still in Ophrah of the Abi-
ezrites.
25† That same night the LORD said to
him, "Take the seven-year-old spare
bullock and destroy your father's altar
to Baal and cut down the sacred pole
that is by it. 26 You shall build, instead,
the proper kind of altar to the LORD,
your God, on top of this stronghold. Then
take the spare bullock and offer it as a
holocaust on the wood from the sacred
pole you have cut down." 27 So Gideon
took ten of his servants and did as the
LORD had commanded him. But through
fear of his family and of the townspeo-
ple, he would not do it by day, but did
it at night. 28 Early the next morning the
townspeople found that the altar of Baal
had been destroyed, the sacred pole
near it cut down, and the spare bullock
offered on the altar that was built.
29 They asked one another, "Who did
this?" Their inquiry led them to the con-
clusion that Gideon, son of Joash, had
done it. 30 So the townspeople said to
Joash, "Bring out your son that he may
die, for he has destroyed the altar of
Baal and has cut down the sacred pole
that was near it." 31 But Joash replied
to all who were standing around him,
"Do you intend to act in Baal's stead,
or be his champion? If anyone acts for
him, he shall be put to death by morning.
If he whose altar has been destroyed is
a god, let him act for himself!" 32*† So
on that day Gideon was called Jerub-
baal, because of the words, "Let Baal
take action against him, since he de-
stroyed his altar."
33 Then all Midian and Amalek and the
Kedemites mustered and crossed over
into the valley of Jezreel, where they en-
camped. 34 The spirit of the LORD enve-
loped Gideon; he blew the horn that
summoned Abiezer to follow him. 35 He
sent messengers, too, throughout Ma-
nasseh, which also obeyed his summons;
through Asher, Zebulun and Naphtali,
likewise, he sent messengers and these
tribes advanced to meet the others.
36 Gideon said to God, "If indeed you are
going to save Israel through me, as you
promised, 37 I am putting this woolen
fleece on the threshing floor. If dew
comes on the fleece alone, while all the
ground is dry, I shall know that you will
save Israel through me, as you prom-

*

8ff: 2, 1f; 10, 11-14.
20: 13, 19.
22f: Gn 32, 31; Dt 5,
24ff.
32: 1 Sm 12, 11.

†

6, 24: *Yahweh-shalom:* Hebrew for "the LORD is peace," a reference to the LORD's words, "Be calm," literally, "Peace be to you!"

6, 25: *The sacred pole:* see note on Ex 34, 13.

6, 32: *Jerubbaal:* similar in sound to the Hebrew words meaning, "Let Baal take action."

ised." 38 That is what took place. Early
the next morning he wrung the dew from
the fleece, squeezing out of it a bowlful
of water. 39 Gideon then said to God, "Do
not be angry with me if I speak once
more. Let me make just one more test
with the fleece. Let the fleece alone be
dry, but let there be dew on all the
ground." 40 That night God did so; the
fleece alone was dry, but there was dew
on all the ground.

CHAPTER 7

Defeat of Midian. 1* Early the next
morning Jerubbaal (that is, Gideon) en-
camped by En-harod with all his sol-
diers. The camp of Midian was in the
valley north of Gibeath-hammoreh.
2 The LORD said to Gideon, "You have
too many soldiers with you for me to de-
liver Midian into their power, lest Israel
vaunt itself against me and say, 'My own
power brought me the victory.' 3* Now
proclaim to all the soldiers, 'If anyone
is afraid or fearful, let him leave.' "
When Gideon put them to this test on
the mountain, twenty-two thousand of
the soldiers left, but ten thousand re-
mained. 4 The LORD said to Gideon,
"There are still too many soldiers. Lead
them down to the water and I will test
them for you there. If I tell you that a
certain man is to go with you, he must
go with you. But no one is to go if I tell
you he must not." 5† When Gideon led
the soldiers down to the water, the LORD
said to him, "You shall set to one side
everyone who laps up the water as a dog
does with its tongue; to the other, every-
one who kneels down to drink." 6 Those
who lapped up the water raised to their
mouths by hand numbered three hun-
dred, but all the rest of the soldiers knelt
down to drink the water. 7 The LORD said
to Gideon, "By means of the three hun-
dred who lapped up the water I will save
you and will deliver Midian into your
power. So let all the other soldiers go
home." 8 Their horns, and such supplies
as the soldiers had with them, were
taken up, and Gideon ordered the rest
of the Israelites to their tents, but kept
the three hundred men. Now the camp
of Midian was beneath him in the valley.
9 That night the LORD said to Gideon,
"Go, descend on the camp, for I have
delivered it up to you. 10 If you are afraid
to attack, go down to the camp with your
aide Purah. 11 When you hear what they
are saying, you will have the courage
to descend on the camp." So he went
down with his aide Purah to the outposts
of the camp. 12 The Midianites, Amalek-
ites, and all the Kedemites lay in the val-
ley, as numerous as locusts. Nor could
their camels be counted, for these were
as many as the sands on the seashore.
13† When Gideon arrived, one man was
telling another about a dream. "I had
a dream," he said, "that a round loaf
of barley bread was rolling into the
camp of Midian. It came to our tent and
struck it, and as it fell it turned the tent
upside down." 14 "This can only be the
sword of the Israelite Gideon, son of
Joash," the other replied. "God has de-
livered Midian and all the camp into his
power." 15 When Gideon heard the de-
scription and explanation of the dream,
he prostrated himself. Then returning to
the camp of Israel, he said, "Arise, for
the LORD has delivered the camp of
Midian into your power."
16 He divided the three hundred men
into three companies, and provided
them all with horns and with empty jars
and torches inside the jars. 17 "Watch me
and follow my lead," he told them. "I
shall go to the edge of the camp, and
as I do, you must do also. 18 When I and
those with me blow horns, you too must
blow horns all around the camp and cry
out, 'For the LORD and for Gideon!' "
19† So Gideon and the hundred men who
were with him came to the edge of the
camp at the beginning of the middle
watch, just after the posting of the
guards. They blew the horns and broke
the jars they were holding. 20 All three
companies blew horns and broke their
jars. They held the torches in their left
hands, and in their right the horns they
were blowing, and cried out, "A sword
for the LORD and Gideon!" 21 They all
remained standing in place around the
camp, while the whole camp fell to run-
ning and shouting and fleeing. 22* But
the three hundred men kept blowing the
horns, and throughout the camp the
LORD set the sword of one against an-
other. The army fled as far as Beth-shit-
tah in the direction of Zarethan, near the
border of Abel-meholah at Tabbath.
23 The Israelites were called to arms
from Naphtali, from Asher, and from all
Manasseh, and they pursued Midian.
24 Gideon also sent messengers through-
out the mountain region of Ephraim to
say, "Go down to confront Midian, and

*

7, 1: 6, 32.
3: Dt 20, 8.
22f: Ps 83, 10; Is 9, 4.

†

7, 5: The Lord desired not numerous but reliable soldiers. Those who drank from their hands were alert, standing ready to resist attack, whereas the others were careless and undependable. The cowardly soldiers had already been dismissed (v 3); cf Dt 20, 8.

7, 13: The barley loaf represents the agricultural Hebrews while the tent refers to the nomadic Midianites. The overthrow of the tent indicates the victory of the Hebrews over their Midianite oppressors.

7, 19: *At the beginning of the middle watch:* about two hours before midnight. The ancient Hebrews divided the night into three watches of about four hours each. At the beginning of a watch the sentinels were changed.

seize the water courses against them as
far as Beth-barah, as well as the Jor-
dan." So all the Ephraimites were called
to arms, and they seized the water
courses as far as Beth-barah, and the
Jordan as well. 25* They captured the
two princes of Midian, Oreb and Zeeb,
killing Oreb at the rock of Oreb and Zeeb
at the winepress of Zeeb. Then they pur-
sued Midian and carried the heads of
Oreb and Zeeb to Gideon beyond the
Jordan.

CHAPTER 8

1 But the Ephraimites said to him,
"What have you done to us, not calling
us when you went to fight against Mid-
ian?" And they quarreled bitterly with
him. 2* "What have I accomplished now
in comparison with you?" he answered
them. "Is not the gleaning of Ephraim
better than the vintage of Abiezer? 3 Into
your power God delivered the princes
of Midian, Oreb and Zeeb. What have I
been able to do in comparison with
you?" When he said this, their anger
against him subsided.

4 When Gideon reached the Jordan
and crossed it with his three hundred
men, they were exhausted and fam-
ished. 5 So he said to the men of Succoth,
"Will you give my followers some loaves
of bread? They are exhausted, and I am
pursuing Zebah and Zalmunna, kings of
Midian." 6† But the princes of Succoth
replied, "Are the hands of Zebah and
Zalmunna already in your possession,
that we should give food to your army?"
7 Gideon said, "Very well; when the
LORD has delivered Zebah and Zal-
munna into my power, I will grind your
flesh in with the thorns and briers of the
desert." 8 He went up from there to Pen-
uel and made the same request of them,
but the men of Penuel answered him as
had the men of Succoth. 9 So to the men
of Penuel, too, he said, "When I return
in triumph, I will demolish this tower."

10 Now Zebah and Zalmunna were in
Karkor with their force of about fifteen
thousand men; these were all who were
left of the whole Kedemite army, a hun-
dred and twenty thousand swordsmen
having fallen. 11 Gideon went up by the
route of the nomads east of Nobah and
Jogbehah, and attacked the camp when
it felt secure. 12 Zebah and Zalmunna
fled. He pursued them and took the two
kings of Midian, Zebah and Zalmunna,
captive, throwing the entire army into
panic.

13 Then Gideon, son of Joash, returned
from battle by the pass of Heres. 14 He
captured a young man of Succoth, who
upon being questioned listed for him the
seventy-seven princes and elders of
Succoth. 15 So he went to the men of Suc-
coth and said, "Here are Zebah and Zal-
munna, with whom you taunted me, 'Are
the hands of Zebah and Zalmunna al-
ready in your possession, that we should
give food to your weary followers?' "
16 He took the elders of the city, and
thorns and briers of the desert, and
ground these men of Succoth into them.
17 He also demolished the tower of Pen-
uel and slew the men of the city.

18 Then he said to Zebah and Zal-
munna, "Where now are the men you
killed at Tabor?" "They all resembled
you," they replied. "They appeared to
be princes." 19 "They were my brothers,
my mother's sons," he said. "As the
LORD lives, if you had spared their lives,
I should not kill you." 20 Then he said
to his first-born, Jether, "Go, kill them."
Since Jether was still a boy, he was
afraid and did not draw his sword.
21 Zebah and Zalmunna said, "Come, kill
us yourself, for a man's strength is like
the man." So Gideon stepped forward
and killed Zebah and Zalmunna. He also
took the crescents that were on the necks
of their camels.

22 The Israelites then said to Gideon,
"Rule over us—you, your son, and your
son's son—for you rescued us from the
power of Midian." 23 But Gideon an-
swered them, "I will not rule over you,
nor shall my son rule over you. The
LORD must rule over you."

24† Gideon went on to say, "I should
like to make a request of you. Will each
of you give me a ring from his booty?"
(For being Ishmaelites, the enemy had
gold rings.) 25 "We will gladly give
them," they replied, and spread out a
cloak into which everyone threw a ring
from his booty. 26 The gold rings that he
requested weighed seventeen hundred
gold shekels, in addition to the crescents
and pendants, the purple garments
worn by the kings of Midian, and the
trappings that were on the necks of their
camels. 27 Gideon made an ephod out of
the gold and placed it in his city Ophrah.
However, all Israel paid idolatrous hom-
age to it there, and caused the ruin of
Gideon and his family.

28 Thus was Midian brought into sub-
jection by the Israelites; no longer did
they hold their heads high. And the land
had rest for forty years, during the life-
time of Gideon.

Gideon's Son Abimelech. 29 Then Jer-

*

25: 8, 3; Ps 83, 12; Is 10, 26. 8, 2: 6, 34.

†

8, 6: *Are the hands . . . in your possession . . .?:* i.e., can you already boast of victory? The hands as well as the heads of slain enemies were cut off and counted as trophies; cf 2 Sm 4, 8; 2 Kgs 10, 7f; and the Ugaritic Anath Epic, V AB, II 10ff.

8, 24: *Ishmaelites:* here as in Gn 37, 25-28, the designation is not ethnic; it refers rather to their status as nomads.

ubbaal, son of Joash, went back home to stay. 30* Now Gideon had seventy sons, his direct descendants, for he had many wives. 31† His concubine who lived in Shechem also bore him a son, whom he named Abimelech. 32 At a good old age Gideon, son of Joash, died and was buried in the tomb of his father Joash in Ophrah of the Abiezrites. 33† But after Gideon was dead, the Israelites again abandoned themselves to the Baals, making Baal of Berith their god 34 and forgetting the LORD, their God, who had delivered them from the power of their enemies all around them. 35 Nor were they grateful to the family of Jerubbaal [Gideon] for all the good he had done for Israel.

CHAPTER 9

1* Abimelech, son of Jerubbaal, went to his mother's kinsmen in Shechem, and said to them and to the whole clan to which his mother's family belonged, 2 "Put this question to all the citizens of Shechem: 'Which is better for you: that seventy men, or all Jerubbaal's sons, rule over you, or that one man rule over you?' You must remember that I am your own flesh and bone." 3 When his mother's kin repeated these words to them on his behalf, all the citizens of Shechem sympathized with Abimelech, thinking, "He is our kinsman." 4 They also gave him seventy silver shekels from the temple of Baal of Berith, with which Abimelech hired shiftless men and ruffians as his followers. 5 He then went to his ancestral house in Ophrah, and slew his brothers, the seventy sons of Jerubbaal, on one stone. Only the youngest son of Jerubbaal, Jotham, escaped, for he was hidden. 6 Then all the citizens of Shechem and all Beth-millo came together and proceeded to make Abimelech king by the terebinth at the memorial pillar in Shechem.

7 When this was reported to him, Jotham went to the top of Mount Gerizim, and standing there, cried out to them in a loud voice: "Hear me, citizens of Shechem, that God may then hear you! 8* Once the trees went to anoint a king over themselves. So they said to the olive tree, 'Reign over us.' 9† But the olive tree answered them, 'Must I give up my rich oil, whereby men and gods are honored, and go to wave over the trees?' 10 Then the trees said to the fig tree, 'Come; you reign over us!' 11 But the fig tree answered them, 'Must I give up my sweetness and my good fruit, and go to wave over the trees?' 12 Then the trees said to the vine, 'Come you, and reign over us.' 13† But the vine answered them, 'Must I give up my wine that cheers gods and men, and go to wave over the trees?' 14 Then all the trees said to the buckthorn, 'Come; you reign over us!' 15 But the buckthorn replied to the trees, 'If you wish to anoint me king over you in good faith, come and take refuge in my shadow. Otherwise, let fire come from the buckthorn and devour the cedars of Lebanon.'

16† "Now then, if you have acted in good faith and honorably in appointing Abimelech your king, if you have dealt well with Jerubbaal and with his family, and if you have treated him as he deserved— 17 for my father fought for you at the risk of his life when he saved you from the power of Midian; 18* but you have risen against his family this day and have killed his seventy sons upon one stone, and have made Abimelech, the son of his handmaid, king over the citizens of Shechem, because he is your kinsman— 19 if, then, you have acted in good faith and with honor toward Jerubbaal and his family this day, rejoice in Abimelech and may he in turn rejoice in you. 20 But if not, let fire come forth from Abimelech to devour the citizens of Shechem and Beth-millo, and let fire come forth from the citizens and from Beth-millo to devour Abimelech." 21 Then Jotham went in flight to Beer, where he remained for fear of his brother Abimelech.

22 When Abimelech had ruled Israel for three years, 23 God put bad feelings between Abimelech and the citizens of Shechem, who rebelled against Abimelech. 24 This was to repay the violence done to the seventy sons of Jerubbaal and to avenge their blood upon their brother Abimelech, who killed them, and upon the citizens of Shechem, who encouraged him to kill his brothers. 25 The citizens of Shechem then set men in ambush for him on the mountaintops, and these robbed all who passed them on the road. But it was reported to Abimelech.

26 Now Gaal, son of Ebed, came over to Shechem with his kinsmen. The citizens of Shechem put their trust in him,

*

30: 9, 2.5. 8: 8, 22f.
9, 1: 8, 31. 18: 8, 31.

†

8, 31: *Concubine:* a wife of secondary rank.

8, 33: *Baal of Berith:* one of the titles of Baal as worshiped by the Canaanites of Shechem, meaning "the lord of the covenant."

9, 9: *Whereby men and gods are honored:* oil was used in the worship both of the true God and of false gods; it was prescribed in the worship of Yahweh (Lv 2, 1.6.15; 24, 2). It was also used to consecrate prophets, priests and kings (Ex 30, 25.30; 1 Sm 10, 1; 16, 13).

9, 13: *Cheers gods:* wine was used in the libations both of the Temple of Jerusalem and of pagan temples.

9, 16: Just as the noble trees refused the honor of royalty and were made subject to a mean plant, so did Abimelech of less noble birth than the seventy sons of Gideon now tyrannize over the people.

27 and went out into the fields, harvested their grapes and trod them out. Then they held a festival and went to the temple of their god, where they ate and drank and cursed Abimelech. 28* Gaal, son of Ebed, said, "Who is Abimelech? And why should we of Shechem serve him? Were not the son of Jerubbaal and his lieutenant Zebul once subject to the men of Hamor, father of Shechem? Why should we serve him? 29 Would that this people were entrusted to my command! I would depose Abimelech. I would say to Abimelech, 'Get a larger army and come out!' "

30 At the news of what Gaal, son of Ebed, had said, Zebul, the ruler of the city, was angry 31 and sent messengers to Abimelech in Arumah with the information: "Gaal, son of Ebed, and his kinsmen have come to Shechem and are stirring up the city against you. 32 Now rouse yourself; set an ambush tonight in the fields, you and the men who are with you. 33 Promptly at sunrise tomorrow morning, make a raid on the city. When he and his followers come out against you, deal with him as best you can."

34 During the night Abimelech advanced with all his soldiers and set up an ambush for Shechem in four companies. 35 Gaal, son of Ebed, went out and stood at the entrance of the city gate. When Abimelech and his soldiers rose from their place of ambush, 36 Gaal saw them and said to Zebul, "There are men coming down from the hilltops!" But Zebul answered him, "You see the shadow of the hills as men." 37 But Gaal went on to say, "Men are coming down from the region of Tabbur-Haares, and one company is coming by way of Elon-Meonenim." 38 Zebul said to him, "Where now is the boast you uttered, 'Who is Abimelech that we should serve him?' Are these not the men for whom you expressed contempt? Go out now and fight with them." 39 So Gaal went out at the head of the citizens of Shechem and fought against Abimelech. 40 But Abimelech routed him, and he fled before him; and many fell slain right up to the entrance of the gate. 41 Abimelech returned to Arumah, but Zebul drove Gaal and his kinsmen from Shechem, which they had occupied.

42 The next day, when the people were taking the field, it was reported to Abimelech, 43 who divided the men he had into three companies, and set up an ambush in the fields. He watched till he saw the people leave the city, and then rose against them for the attack. 44 Abimelech and the company with him dashed in and stood by the entrance of the city gate, while the other two companies rushed upon all who were in the field and attacked them. 45† That entire day Abimelech fought against the city, and captured it. He then killed its inhabitants and demolished the city, sowing the site with salt.

46 When they heard of this, all the citizens of Migdal-shechem went into the crypt of the temple of El-berith. 47 It was reported to Abimelech that all the citizens of Migdal-shechem were gathered together. 48 So he went up Mount Zalmon with all his soldiers, took his axe in his hand, and cut down some brushwood. This he lifted to his shoulder, then said to the men with him, "Hurry! Do just as you have seen me do." 49 So all the men likewise cut down brushwood, and following Abimelech, placed it against the crypt. Then they set the crypt on fire over their heads, so that every one of the citizens of Migdal-shechem, about a thousand men and women, perished.

50 Abimelech proceeded to Thebez, which he invested and captured. 51 Now there was a strong tower in the middle of the city, and all the men and women, in a word all the citizens of the city, fled there, shutting themselves in and going up to the roof of the tower. 52 Abimelech came up to the tower and fought against it, advancing to the very entrance of the tower to set it on fire. 53* But a certain woman cast the upper part of a millstone down on Abimelech's head, and it fractured his skull. 54* He immediately called his armor-bearer and said to him, "Draw your sword and dispatch me, lest they say of me that a woman killed me." So his attendant ran him through and he died. 55 When the Israelites saw that Abimelech was dead, they all left for their homes.

56 Thus did God requite the evil Abimelech had done to his father in killing his seventy brothers. 57 God also brought all their wickedness home to the Shechemites, for the curse of Jotham, son of Jerubbaal, overtook them.

CHAPTER 10

Tola. 1 After Abimelech there rose to save Israel the Issacharite Tola, son of Puah, son of Dodo, a resident of Shamir in the mountain region of Ephraim. 2 When he had judged Israel twenty-three years, he died and was buried in Shamir.

Jair. 3 Jair the Gileadite came after him and judged Israel twenty-two years. 4*† He had thirty sons who rode on thirty

---

*

28: Gn 34, 2.6.
53: 2 Sm 11, 21.
54: 1 Sm 31, 4; 1 Chr 10, 4.
10, 4: Dt 3, 14.

---

†

9, 45: *Sowing the site with salt:* a severe measure, which was a symbol of desolation, and even more, since it actually rendered the ground barren and useless.

10, 4: *Saddle-asses:* a sign of rank and wealth; cf 5, 10; 12, 14.

saddle-asses and possessed thirty cities
in the land of Gilead; these are called
Havvoth-jair to the present day. 5 Jair
died and was buried in Kamon.

Oppression by the Ammonites. 6 The
Israelites again offended the LORD, serv-
ing the Baals and Ashtaroth, the gods
of Aram, the gods of Sidon, the gods of
Moab, the gods of the Ammonites, and
the gods of the Philistines. Since they
had abandoned the LORD and would not
serve him, 7 the LORD became angry
with Israel and allowed them to fall into
the power of [the Philistines and] the
Ammonites. 8 For eighteen years they
afflicted and oppressed the Israelites in
Bashan, and all the Israelites in the Am-
orite land beyond the Jordan in Gilead.
9 The Ammonites also crossed the Jor-
dan to fight against Judah, Benjamin,
and the house of Ephraim, so that Israel
was in great distress.

10 Then the Israelites cried out to the
LORD, "We have sinned against you; we
have forsaken our God and have served
the Baals." 11* The LORD answered the
Israelites: "Did not the Egyptians, the
Amorites, the Ammonites, the Philis-
tines, 12* the Sidonians, the Amalekites,
and the Midianites oppress you? Yet
when you cried out to me, and I saved
you from their grasp, 13 you still forsook
me and worshiped other gods. Therefore
I will save you no more. 14 Go and cry
out to the gods you have chosen; let them
save you now that you are in distress."
15 But the Israelites said to the LORD,
"We have sinned. Do to us whatever you
please. Only save us this day." 16 And
they cast out the foreign gods from their
midst and served the LORD, so that he
grieved over the misery of Israel.

17* The Ammonites had gathered for
war and encamped in Gilead, while the
Israelites assembled and encamped in
Mizpah. 18* And among the people the
princes of Gilead said to one another,
"The one who begins the war against the
Ammonites shall be leader of all the in-
habitants of Gilead."

CHAPTER 11

Jephthah. 1 There was a chieftain, the
Gileadite Jephthah, born to Gilead of a
harlot. 2 Gilead's wife had also borne
him sons, and on growing up the sons
of the wife had driven Jephthah away,
saying to him, "You shall inherit nothing
in our family, for you are the son of an-
other woman." 3 So Jephthah had fled
from his brothers and had taken up resi-
dence in the land of Tob. A rabble had
joined company with him, and went out
with him on raids.

4 Some time later, the Ammonites
warred on Israel. 5 When this occurred
the elders of Gilead went to bring
Jephthah from the land of Tob.
6 "Come," they said to Jephthah, "be our
commander that we may be able to fight
the Ammonites." 7 "Are you not the ones
who hated me and drove me from my
father's house?" Jephthah replied to the
elders of Gilead. "Why do you come to
me now, when you are in distress?" 8 The
elders of Gilead said to Jephthah, "In
any case, we have now come back to
you; if you go with us to fight against
the Ammonites, you shall be the leader
of all of us who dwell in Gilead."
9 Jephthah answered the elders of Gil-
ead, "If you bring me back to fight
against the Ammonites and the LORD
delivers them up to me, I shall be your
leader." 10 The elders of Gilead said to
Jephthah, "The LORD is witness between
us that we will do as you say."

11* So Jephthah went with the elders
of Gilead, and the people made him their
leader and commander. In Mizpah,
Jephthah settled all his affairs before the
LORD. 12 Then he sent messengers to the
king of the Ammonites to say, "What
have you against me that you come to
fight with me in my land?" 13* He an-
swered the messengers of Jephthah,
"Israel took away my land from the Ar-
non to the Jabbok and the Jordan when
they came up from Egypt. Now restore
the same peaceably."

14 Again Jephthah sent messengers to
the king of the Ammonites, 15* saying to
him, "This is what Jephthah says: Israel
did not take the land of Moab or the land
of the Ammonites. 16 For when they
came up from Egypt, Israel went
through the desert to the Red Sea and
came to Kadesh. 17* Israel then sent
messengers to the king of Edom saying,
'Let me pass through your land.' But the
king of Edom did not give consent. They
also sent to the king of Moab, but he too
was unwilling. So Israel remained in Ka-
desh. 18* Then they went through the
desert, and by-passing the land of Edom
and the land of Moab, went east of the
land of Moab and encamped across the
Arnon. Thus they did not go through
the territory of Moab, for the Arnon is
the boundary of Moab. 19* Then Israel
sent messengers to Sihon, king of the
Amorites, king of Heshbon. Israel said
to him, 'Let me pass through your land
to my own place.' 20 But Sihon refused
to let Israel pass through his territory.
On the contrary, he gathered all his sol-
diers, who encamped at Jahaz and
fought Israel. 21 But the LORD, the God

JUDGES

*

11-14: 2, 1ff; 6, 8ff.
11: Nm 21, 21-32.
12: 6, 3.
17: 11, 29.
18: 11, 5-11.
11, 11: 10, 18.
13: Nm 21, 13.24ff.
15: Dt 2, 9.19.
17: Nm 20, 1.14.18-21; Dt 1, 46.
18: Nm 36, Dt 2, 8.
19-22: Nm 21, 21-26; Dt 2, 26-36.

of Israel, delivered Sihon and all his men
into the power of Israel, who defeated
them and occupied all the land of the
Amorites dwelling in that region, 22 the
whole territory from the Arnon to the
Jabbok, from the desert to the Jordan.
23 If now the LORD, the God of Israel, has
cleared the Amorites out of the way of
his people, are you to dislodge Israel?
24*† Should you not possess that which
your god Chemosh gave you to possess,
and should we not possess all that the
LORD, our God, has cleared out for us?
25* Again, are you any better than Ba-
lak, son of Zippor, king of Moab? Did
he ever quarrel with Israel, or did he
war against them 26* when Israel occu-
pied Heshbon and its villages, Aroer and
its villages, and all the cities on the
banks of the Arnon? Three hundred
years have passed; why did you not re-
cover them during that time? 27 I have
not sinned against you, but you wrong
me by warring against me. Let the LORD,
who is judge, decide this day between
the Israelites and the Ammonites!"
28 But the king of the Ammonites paid
no heed to the message Jephthah sent
him.

Jephthah's Vow. 29 The spirit of the
LORD came upon Jephthah. He passed
through Gilead and Manasseh, and
through Mizpah-Gilead as well, and
from there he went on to the Ammonites.
30† Jephthah made a vow to the LORD.
"If you deliver the Ammonites into my
power," he said, 31 "whoever comes out
of the doors of my house to meet me
when I return in triumph from the Am-
monites shall belong to the LORD. I shall
offer him up as a holocaust."

32 Jephthah then went on to the Am-
monites to fight against them, and the
LORD delivered them into his power, 33 so
that he inflicted a severe defeat on them,
from Aroer to the approach of Minnith
(twenty cities in all) and as far as Abel-
keramin. Thus were the Ammonites
brought into subjection by the Israelites.
34 When Jephthah returned to his house
in Mizpah, it was his daughter who came
forth, playing the tambourines and
dancing. She was an only child: he had
neither son nor daughter besides her.
35* When he saw her, he rent his gar-
ments and said, "Alas, daughter, you
have struck me down and brought ca-
lamity upon me. For I have made a vow
to the LORD and I cannot retract."
36 "Father," she replied, "you have
made a vow to the LORD. Do with me
as you have vowed, because the LORD
has wrought vengeance for you on your
enemies the Ammonites." 37† Then she
said to her father, "Let me have this fa-
vor. Spare me for two months, that I
may go off down the mountains to
mourn my virginity with my compan-
ions." 38 "Go," he replied, and sent her
away for two months. So she departed
with her companions and mourned her
virginity on the mountains. 39 At the end
of the two months she returned to her
father, who did to her as he had vowed.
She had not been intimate with man. It
then became a custom in Israel 40 for Is-
raelite women to go yearly to mourn the
daughter of Jephthah the Gileadite for
four days of the year.

CHAPTER 12

The Shibboleth Incident. 1* The men
of Ephraim gathered together and
crossed over to Zaphon. They said to
Jephthah, "Why do you go on to fight
with the Ammonites without calling us
to go with you? We will burn your house
over you." 2 Jephthah answered them,
"My soldiers and I were engaged in a
critical contest with the Ammonites. I
summoned you, but you did not rescue
me from their power. 3 When I saw that
you would not effect a rescue, I took my
life in my own hand and went on to the
Ammonites, and the LORD delivered
them into my power. Why, then, do you
come up against me this day to fight with
me?"

4 Then Jephthah called together all the
men of Gilead and fought against
Ephraim, whom they defeated; for the
Ephraimites had said, "You of Gilead
are Ephraimite fugitives in territory be-
longing to Ephraim and Manasseh."
5 The Gileadites took the fords of the Jor-
dan toward Ephraim. When any of the
fleeing Ephraimites said, "Let me pass,"
the men of Gilead would say to him,
"Are you an Ephraimite?" If he an-
swered, "No!" 6† they would ask him to

*

24: Nm 21, 29; 1 Kgs 11, 7.
25: Nm 22, 2; Jos 24, 9; Mi 6, 5.
26: Nm 21, 25; Dt 2, 36.
35: Nm 30,3.
12, 1: 8, 1.

†

11, 24: *Chemosh:* the chief god of the Moabites—not of the Ammonites, whose leading deity was called Molech or Milcom; cf Nm 21, 29; 1 Kgs 11, 7; 2 Kgs 23, 13. The error is probably due to an ancient copyist. Jephthah argues from the viewpoint of his adversaries, the Ammonites, that they were entitled to all the land they had conquered with the aid of their god. It does not necessarily follow that Jephthah himself believed in the actual existence of this pagan god.

11, 30-40: The text clearly implies that Jephthah vowed a human sacrifice, according to the custom of his pagan neighbors; cf 2 Kgs 3, 27. The inspired author merely records the fact; he does not approve of the action.

11, 37: *Mourn my virginity:* to bear children was woman's greatest pride; to be childless was regarded as a great misfortune. Hence Jephthah's daughter asks permission to mourn the fact that she will be put to death before she can bear children.

12, 6: *Shibboleth:* "an ear of grain." But this Hebrew word can also mean "flood water" as in Ps 69, 3.16. Apparently the Gileadites engaged the Ephraimites in conversation about the "flood water" of the Jordan. Differences in enunciating the initial sibilant of the Hebrew word betrayed different tribal affinities.

say "Shibboleth." If he said "Sibboleth,"
not being able to give the proper pronun-
ciation, they would seize him and kill
him at the fords of the Jordan. Thus
forty-two thousand Ephraimites fell at
that time.
7 After having judged Israel for six
years, Jephthah the Gileadite died and
was buried in his city in Gilead.
Ibzan. 8 After him Ibzan of Bethlehem
judged Israel. 9 He had thirty sons. He
also had thirty daughters married out-
side the family, and he brought in as
wives for his sons thirty young women
from outside the family. After having
judged Israel for seven years, 10 Ibzan
died and was buried in Bethlehem.
Elon. 11 After him the Zebulunite Elon
judged Israel. When he had judged Is-
rael for ten years, 12 the Zebulunite Elon
died and was buried in Elon in the land
of Zebulun.
Abdon. 13 After him the Pirathonite
Abdon, son of Hillel, judged Israel. 14 He
had forty sons and thirty grandsons who
rode on seventy saddle-asses. After
having judged Israel for eight years,
15 the Pirathonite Abdon, son of Hillel,
died and was buried in Pirathon in the
land of Ephraim on the mountain of the
Amalekites.

CHAPTER 13

The Birth of Samson. 1* The Israelites
again offended the LORD, who therefore
delivered them into the power of the
Philistines for forty years.
2 There was a certain man from Zorah,
of the clan of the Danites, whose name
was Manoah. His wife was barren and
had borne no children. 3* An angel of
the LORD appeared to the woman and
said to her, "Though you are barren and
have had no children, yet you will con-
ceive and bear a son. 4 Now, then, be
careful to take no wine or strong drink
and to eat nothing unclean. 5*† As for
the son you will conceive and bear, no
razor shall touch his head, for this boy
is to be consecrated to God from the
womb. It is he who will begin the deliver-
ance of Israel from the power of the
Philistines."
6 The woman went and told her hus-
band, "A man of God came to me; he
had the appearance of an angel of God,
terrible indeed. I did not ask him where
he came from, nor did he tell me his
name. 7 But he said to me, 'You will be
with child and will bear a son. So take
neither wine nor strong drink, and eat
nothing unclean. For the boy shall be
consecrated to God from the womb, until
the day of his death.' " 8 Manoah then
prayed to the LORD. "O LORD, I beseech
you," he said, "may the man of God
whom you sent, return to us to teach us
what to do for the boy who will be born."
9 God heard the prayer of Manoah,
and the angel of God came again to the
woman as she was sitting in the field.
Since her husband Manoah was not with
her, 10 the woman ran in haste and told
her husband. "The man who came to me
the other day has appeared to me," she
said to him; 11 so Manoah got up and fol-
lowed his wife. When he reached the
man, he said to him, "Are you the one
who spoke to my wife?" "Yes," he an-
swered. 12 Then Manoah asked, "Now,
when that which you say comes true,
what are we expected to do for the boy?"
13 The angel of the LORD answered Ma-
noah, "Your wife is to abstain from all
the things of which I spoke to her. 14 She
must not eat anything that comes from
the vine, nor take wine or strong drink,
nor eat anything unclean. Let her ob-
serve all that I have commanded her."
15 Then Manoah said to the angel of the
LORD, "Can we persuade you to stay,
while we prepare a kid for you?" 16 But
the angel of the LORD answered Manoah,
"Although you press me, I will not par-
take of your food. But if you will, you
may offer a holocaust to the LORD."Not
knowing that it was the angel of the
LORD, 17 Manoah said to him, "What is
your name, that we may honor you when
your words come true?" 18*† The angel
of the LORD answered him, "Why do you
ask my name, which is mysterious?"
19* Then Manoah took the kid with a ce-
real offering and offered it on the rock
to the LORD, whose works are mysteries.
While Manoah and his wife were looking
on, 20 as the flame rose to the sky from
the altar, the angel of the LORD ascended
in the flame of the altar. When Manoah
and his wife saw this, they fell prostrate
to the ground; 21* but the angel of the
LORD was seen no more by Manoah and
his wife. Then Manoah, realizing that it
was the angel of the LORD, 22 said to his
wife, "We will certainly die, for we have
seen God." 23 But his wife pointed out to
him, "If the LORD had meant to kill us,
he would not have accepted a holocaust
and cereal offering from our hands! Nor
would he have let us see all this just now,
or hear what we have heard."
24* The woman bore a son and named
him Samson. The boy grew up and the

*

13, 1: 10, 6.
3f: 1 Sm 1, 20; Lk 1, 31.
5: Nm 6, 5.
18: Gn 32, 29.
19f: 6, 19ff.
21f: 6, 22f.
24: Heb 11, 32.

†

13, 5: *Consecrated:* in Hebrew, *nazir.* Samson therefore was for life to be under the nazirite vow, which obliged him to abstain from drinking wine or having his hair cut; cf Nm 6, 2-8.

13, 18: *Mysterious:* incomprehensible, above human understanding. Hence, the angel speaks in the name of the Lord himself, to whom Manoah at once offers a sacrifice.

LORD blessed him; 25 the spirit of the
LORD first stirred him in Mahaneh-dan,
which is between Zorah and Eshtaol.

CHAPTER 14

Marriage of Samson. 1† Samson went
down to Timnah and saw there one of
the Philistine women. 2 On his return he
told his father and mother, "There is a
Philistine woman I saw in Timnah whom
I wish you to get as a wife for me." 3 His
father and mother said to him, "Can you
find no wife among your kinsfolk or
among all our people, that you must go
and take a wife from the uncircumcised
Philistines?" But Samson answered his
father, "Get her for me, for she pleases
me." 4* Now his father and mother did
not know that this had been brought
about by the LORD, who was providing
an opportunity against the Philistines;
for at that time they had dominion over
Israel.

5† So Samson went down to Timnah
with his father and mother. When they
had come to the vineyards of Timnah,
a young lion came roaring to meet him.
6 But the spirit of the LORD came upon
Samson, and although he had no weap-
ons, he tore the lion in pieces as one tears
a kid. 7 However, on the journey to speak
for the woman, he did not mention to
his father or mother what he had done.
8 Later, when he returned to marry the
woman who pleased him, he stepped
aside to look at the remains of the lion
and found a swarm of bees and honey
in the lion's carcass. 9 So he scooped the
honey out into his palms and ate it as
he went along. When he came to his fa-
ther and mother, he gave them some to
eat, without telling them that he had
scooped the honey from the lion's car-
cass.

10 His father also went down to the
woman, and Samson gave a banquet
there, since it was customary for the
young men to do this. 11† When they met
him, they brought thirty men to be his
companions. 12 Samson said to them,
"Let me propose a riddle to you. If within
the seven days of the feast you solve it
for me successfully, I will give you thirty
linen tunics and thirty sets of garments.
13 But if you cannot answer it for me, you
must give me thirty tunics and thirty
sets of garments." "Propose your rid-
dle," they responded; "we will listen to
it." 14 So he said to them,

> "Out of the eater came forth food,
> and out of the strong came forth
> sweetness."

15 After three days' failure to answer the
riddle, they said on the fourth day to
Samson's wife, "Coax your husband to
answer the riddle for us, or we will burn
you and your family. Did you invite us
here to reduce us to poverty?" 16 At Sam-
son's side, his wife wept and said, "You
must hate me; you do not love me, for
you have proposed a riddle to my coun-
trymen, but have not told me the an-
swer." He said to her, "If I have not told
it even to my father or my mother, must
I tell it to you?" 17 But she wept beside
him during the seven days the feast
lasted. On the seventh day, since she im-
portuned him, he told her the answer,
and she explained the riddle to her
countrymen.

18 On the seventh day, before the sun
set, the men of the city said to him,

> "What is sweeter than honey,
> and what is stronger than a lion?"

He replied to them,

> "If you had not plowed with my
> heifer,
> you would not have solved my rid-
> dle."

19 The spirit of the LORD came upon
him, and he went down to Ashkelon,
where he killed thirty of their men and
despoiled them; he gave their garments
to those who had answered the riddle.
Then he went off to his own family in
anger, 20* and Samson's wife was mar-
ried to the one who had been best man
at his wedding.

CHAPTER 15

Samson Defeats the Philistines.
1 After some time, in the season of the
wheat harvest, Samson visited his wife,
bringing a kid. But when he said, "Let
me be with my wife in private," her fa-
ther would not let him enter, 2 saying,
"I thought it certain you wished to repu-
diate her; so I gave her to your best man.
Her younger sister is more beautiful
than she; you may have her instead."
3 Samson said to them, "This time the
Philistines cannot blame me if I harm
them." 4 So Samson left and caught
three hundred foxes. Turning them tail

---

*

14, 4: 15, 11. 20: 15, 2.6.

---

†

14, 1-3: Marriages were arranged by the parents of the bridegroom as well as of the bride; cf Gn 24, 2-8; 34, 3-6. The Mosaic law specified only seven pagan nations, not including the Philistines, in the prohibition against mixed marriages; cf Dt 7, 1-4. But national and religious sentiment was against any marriage with a non-Israelite; cf Gn 28, 1f; 1 Kgs 11, 1-10.

14, 5ff: Although Samson was accompanied by his parents on the journey to Timnah, v 7 implies that he was not near them when *he tore the lion in pieces.*

14, 11: *Companions:* known at a later period as "the friends of the bridegroom" (1 Mc 9, 39; Mk 2, 19), the best man and his fellows. Here they are Philistines (v 16), appointed by the family of the bride, who would also have several bridesmaids; cf Mt 25, 1-13.

to tail, he tied between each pair of tails
one of the torches he had at hand. 5 He
then kindled the torches and set the
foxes loose in the standing grain of the
Philistines, thus burning both the shocks
and the standing grain, and the vine-
yards and olive orchards as well.
6* When the Philistines asked who had
done this, they were told, "Samson, the
son-in-law of the Timnite, because his
wife was taken and given to his best
man." So the Philistines went up and de-
stroyed her and her family by fire.
7 Samson said to them, "If this is how
you act, I will not stop until I have taken
revenge on you." 8 And with repeated
blows, he inflicted a great slaughter on
them. Then he went down and remained
in a cavern of the cliff of Etam.
9 The Philistines went up and, from a
camp in Judah, deployed against Lehi.
10 When the men of Judah asked, "Why
have you come up against us?" they an-
swered, "To take Samson prisoner; to do
to him as he has done to us." 11 Three
thousand men of Judah went down to
the cavern in the cliff of Etam and said
to Samson, "Do you not know that the
Philistines are our rulers? Why, then,
have you done this to us?" He answered
them, "As they have done to me, so have
I done to them." 12 They said to him, "We
have come to take you prisoner, to de-
liver you over to the Philistines." Sam-
son said to them, "Swear to me that you
will not kill me yourselves." 13* "No,"
they replied, "we will certainly not kill
you but will only bind you and deliver
you over to them." So they bound him
with two new ropes and brought him up
from the cliff. 14 When he reached Lehi,
and the Philistines came shouting to
meet him, the spirit of the LORD came
upon him: the ropes around his arms be-
came as flax that is consumed by fire
and his bonds melted away from his
hands. 15 Near him was the fresh jaw-
bone of an ass; he reached out, grasped
it, and with it killed a thousand men.
16 Then Samson said,

"With the jawbone of an ass
I have piled them in a heap;
With the jawbone of an ass
I have slain a thousand men."

17† As he finished speaking he threw
the jawbone from him; and so that place
was named Ramath-lehi. 18 Being very
thirsty, he cried to the LORD and said,
"You have granted this great victory by
the hand of your servant. Must I now
die of thirst or fall into the hands of the
uncircumcised?" 19† Then God split the
cavity in Lehi, and water issued from
it, which Samson drank till his spirit re-
turned and he revived. Hence that
spring in Lehi is called En-hakkore to
this day.

20* Samson judged Israel for twenty
years in the days of the Philistines.

CHAPTER 16

1 Once Samson went to Gaza, where
he saw a harlot and visited her.
2 Informed that Samson had come there,
the men of Gaza surrounded him with
an ambush at the city gate all night long.
And all the night they waited, saying,
"Tomorrow morning we will kill him."
3 Samson rested there until midnight.
Then he rose, seized the doors of the city
gate and the two gateposts, and tore
them loose, bar and all. He hoisted them
on his shoulders and carried them to the
top of the ridge opposite Hebron.

Samson and Delilah. 4 After that he
fell in love with a woman in the Wadi
Sorek whose name was Delilah. 5 The
lords of the Philistines came to her and
said, "Beguile him and find out the se-
cret of his great strength, and how we
may overcome and bind him so as to
keep him helpless. We will each give you
eleven hundred shekels of silver."
6 So Delilah said to Samson, "Tell me
the secret of your great strength and
how you may be bound so as to be kept
helpless." 7 "If they bind me with seven
fresh bowstrings which have not dried,"
Samson answered her, "I shall be as
weak as any other man." 8 So the lords
of the Philistines brought her seven
fresh bowstrings which had not dried,
and she bound him with them. 9* She
had men lying in wait in the chamber
and so she said to him, "The Philistines
are upon you, Samson!" But he snapped
the strings as a thread of tow is severed
by a whiff of flame; and the secret of
his strength remained unknown.
10 Delilah said to Samson, "You have
mocked me and told me lies. Now tell
me how you may be bound." 11* "If they
bind me tight with new ropes, with which
no work has been done," he answered
her, "I shall be as weak as any other
man." 12 So Delilah took new ropes and
bound him with them. Then she said to
him, "The Philistines are upon you,
Samson!" For there were men lying in
wait in the chamber. But he snapped
them off his arms like thread.
13 Delilah said to Samson again, "Up
to now you have mocked me and told
me lies. Tell me how you may be bound."
He said to her, "If you weave my seven
locks of hair into the web and fasten

*

6: 14, 20.
13: 16, 11f.
20: 16, 31.
16, 9: 15, 14.
11: 15, 13.

†

15, 17: *Ramath-lehi:* "heights of the jawbone."
15, 19: *En-hakkore:* "the spring of him who cries out," an allusion to Samson's cry in v 18.

them with the pin, I shall be as weak
as any other man." 14 So while he slept,
Delilah wove his seven locks of hair into
the web, and fastened them in with the
pin. Then she said, "The Philistines are
upon you, Samson!" Awakening from
his sleep, he pulled out both the weaver's
pin and the web.
15 Then she said to him, "How can you
say that you love me when you do not
confide in me? Three times already you
have mocked me, and not told me the
secret of your great strength!" 16 She im-
portuned him continually and vexed
him with her complaints till he was
deathly weary of them. 17* So he took
her completely into his confidence and
told her, "No razor has touched my
head, for I have been consecrated to God
from my mother's womb. If I am
shaved, my strength will leave me, and
I shall be as weak as any other man."
18 When Delilah saw that he had taken
her completely into his confidence, she
summoned the lords of the Philistines,
saying, "Come up this time, for he has
opened his heart to me." So the lords
of the Philistines came and brought up
the money with them. 19 She had him
sleep on her lap, and called for a man
who shaved off his seven locks of hair.
Then she began to mistreat him, for his
strength had left him. 20 When she said,
"The Philistines are upon you, Sam-
son!", and he woke from his sleep, he
thought he could make good his escape
as he had done time and again, for he
did not realize that the LORD had left
him. 21 But the Philistines seized him and
gouged out his eyes. Then they brought
him down to Gaza and bound him with
bronze fetters, and he was put to grind-
ing in the prison. 22 But the hair of his
head began to grow as soon as it was
shaved off.

The Death of Samson. 23*† The lords
of the Philistines assembled to offer a
great sacrifice to their god Dagon and
to make merry. They said,

"Our god has delivered into our
power
Samson our enemy."

25 When their spirits were high, they
said, "Call Samson that he may amuse
us." So they called Samson from the
prison, and he played the buffoon before
them. 24 When the people saw him, they
praised their god. For they said,

"Our god has delivered into our
power
our enemy, the ravager of our
land,
the one who has multiplied our
slain."

Then they stationed him between the
columns. 26 Samson said to the attendant
who was holding his hand, "Put me
where I may touch the columns that sup-
port the temple and may rest against
them." 27 The temple was full of men and
women: all the lords of the Philistines
were there, and from the roof about
three thousand men and women looked
on as Samson provided amusement.
28 Samson cried out to the LORD and
said, "O Lord GOD, remember me!
Strengthen me, O God, this last time that
for my two eyes I may avenge myself
once and for all on the Philistines."
29 Samson grasped the two middle col-
umns on which the temple rested and
braced himself against them, one at his
right hand, the other at his left. 30 And
Samson said, "Let me die with the Phi-
listines!" He pushed hard, and the tem-
ple fell upon the lords and all the people
who were in it. Those he killed at his
death were more than those he had
killed during his lifetime.
31* All his family and kinsmen went
down and bore him up for burial in the
grave of his father Manoah between Zo-
rah and Eshtaol. He had judged Israel
for twenty years.

III: THE TRIBES OF DAN AND BENJAMIN IN THE DAYS OF THE JUDGES

CHAPTER 17

Micah and the Levite. 1 There was a
man in the mountain region of Ephraim
whose name was Micah. 2 He said to his
mother, "The eleven hundred shekels of
silver over which you pronounced a
curse in my hearing when they were
taken from you, are in my possession.
It was I who took them; so now I will
restore them to you." 3*† When he re-
stored the eleven hundred shekels of sil-
ver to his mother, she took two hundred
of them and gave them to the silver-
smith, who made of them a carved idol
overlaid with silver. 4 Then his mother
said, "May the LORD bless my son! I
have consecrated the silver to the LORD
as my gift in favor of my son, by making
a carved idol overlaid with silver." It re-
mained in the house of Micah. 5* Thus
the layman Micah had a sanctuary. He
also made an ephod and household idols,
and consecrated one of his sons, who be-
came his priest. 6* In those days there
was no king in Israel; everyone did what
he thought best.

*

17: 13, 5.
23: 1 Sm 5, 2-5.
31: 15, 20.
17, 3: Ex 20, 4; Lv 19, 4.
5: 18, 14.17.
6: 18, 1; 21, 25.

†

16, 23: Dagon was originally a Mesopotamian deity, whom the Philistines came to worship as their own god of grain.

17, 3: *Idol:* an image, not of a pagan god, but of the Lord. The Mosaic law forbade the making of an image even of the true God.

7 There was a young Levite who had
resided within the tribe of Judah at
Bethlehem of Judah. 8 From that city he
set out to find another place of residence.
On his journey he came to the house of
Micah in the mountain region of
Ephraim. 9 Micah said to him, "Where
do you come from?" He answered him,
"I am a Levite from Bethlehem in Ju-
dah, and am on my way to find some
other place of residence." 10* "Stay with
me," Micah said to him. "Be father and
priest to me, and I will give you ten silver
shekels a year, a set of garments, and
your food." 11 So the young Levite de-
cided to stay with the man, to whom he
became as one of his own sons. 12† Micah
consecrated the young Levite, who be-
came his priest, remaining in his house.
13 Therefore Micah said, "Now I know
that the LORD will prosper me, since the
Levite has become my priest."

CHAPTER 18

Migration of the Danites. 1*† At that
time there was no king in Israel. More-
over the tribe of Danites were in search
of a district to dwell in, for up to that
time they had received no heritage
among the tribes of Israel.
2 So the Danites sent from their clan
a detail of five valiant men of Zorah and
Eshtaol, to reconnoiter the land and
scout it. With their instructions to go and
scout the land, they traveled as far as
the house of Micah in the mountain re-
gion of Ephraim, where they passed the
night. 3*† Near the house of Micah, they
recognized the voice of the young Levite
and turned in that direction. "Who
brought you here and what are you do-
ing here?" they asked him. "What is
your interest here?" 4* "This is how Mi-
cah treats me," he replied to them. "He
pays me a salary and I am his priest."
5 They said to him, "Consult God, that
we may know whether the undertaking
we are engaged in will succeed." 6 The
priest said to them, "Go and prosper: the
LORD is favorable to the undertaking
you are engaged in."
7 So the five men went on and came
to Laish. They saw that the people dwell-
ing there lived securely after the man-
ner of the Sidonians, quiet and trusting,
with no lack of any natural resources.
They were distant from the Sidonians
and had no contact with other people.
8 When the five returned to their kins-
men in Zorah and Eshtaol and were
asked for a report, 9 they replied, "Come,
let us attack them, for we have seen the
land and it is very good. Are you going
to hesitate? Do not be slothful about be-
ginning your expedition to possess the
land. 10 Those against whom you go are
a trusting people, and the land is ample.
God has indeed given it into your power:
a place where no natural resource is
lacking."
11 So six hundred men of the clan of
the Danites, fully armed with weapons
of war, set out from where they were in
Zorah and Eshtaol, 12* and camped in
Judah, up near Kiriath-jearim; hence to
this day the place, which lies west of
Kiriath-jearim, is called Mahaneh-dan.
13 From there they went on to the
mountain region of Ephraim and came
to the house of Micah. 14* The five men
who had gone to reconnoiter the land
of Laish said to their kinsmen, "Do you
know that in these houses there are an
ephod, household idols, and a carved
idol overlaid with silver? Now decide
what you must do!" 15 So turning in that
direction, they went to the house of the
young Levite at the home of Micah and
greeted him. 16 The six hundred men girt
with weapons of war, who were Danites,
stood by the entrance of the gate, and
the priest stood there also. 17 Meanwhile
the five men who had gone to reconnoi-
ter the land went up and entered the
house of Micah. 18 When they had gone
in and taken the ephod, the household
idols, and the carved idol overlaid with
silver, the priest said to them, "What are
you doing?" 19* They said to him, "Be
still: put your hand over your mouth.
Come with us and be our father and
priest. Is it better for you to be priest
for the family of one man or to be priest
for a tribe and a clan in Israel?" 20 The
priest, agreeing, took the ephod, house-
hold idols, and carved idol and went off
in the midst of the band. 21 As they
turned to depart, they placed their little
ones, their livestock, and their goods at
the head of the column.
22 The Danites had already gone some
distance, when those in the houses near
that of Micah took up arms and overtook
them. 23 They called to the Danites, who
turned about and said to Micah, "What
do you want, that you have taken up
arms?" 24 "You have taken my god,
which I made, and have gone off with
my priest as well," he answered. "What
is left for me? How, then, can you ask
me what I want?" 25 The Danites said to
him, "Let us hear no further sound from
you, lest fierce men fall upon you and

*

10: 18, 19.
18, 1: Jos 19, 40-48.
3: 17, 7.
4: 17, 10.
12: 13, 25.
14: 17, 4f.
19: 17, 10.

†

17, 12f: According to Nm 18, 1-7 only those Levites who were descended from Aaron could be consecrated as priests.

18, 1: The tribe of Dan had been assigned a territory with definite limits in central Palestine. However they were unable to gain possession of the better portion of their land (1, 34). So they now seek territory elsewhere in Palestine.

18, 3: *Recognized the voice:* perhaps they noticed the peculiar pronunciation of his south Hebrew dialect.

you and your family lose your lives."
26 The Danites then went on their way,
and Micah, seeing that they were
stronger than he, returned home.
27 Having taken what Micah had
made, and the priest he had had, they
attacked Laish, a quiet and trusting peo-
ple; they put them to the sword and de-
stroyed their city by fire. 28 No one came
to their aid, since the city was far from
Sidon and they had no contact with other
people. The Danites then rebuilt the city,
which was in the valley that belongs to
Beth-rehob, and lived there. 29 They
named it Dan after their ancestor Dan,
son of Israel. However, the name of the
city was formerly Laish. 30† The Danites
set up the carved idol for themselves,
and Jonathan, son of Gershom, son of
Moses, and his descendants were priests
for the tribe of the Danites until the time
of the captivity of the land. 31 They
maintained the carved idol Micah had
made as long as the house of God was
in Shiloh.

CHAPTER 19

The Levite from Ephraim. 1* At that
time, when there was no king in Israel,
there was a Levite residing in remote
parts of the mountain region of Ephraim
who had taken for himself a concubine
from Bethlehem of Judah. 2 His concu-
bine was unfaithful to him and left him
for her father's house in Bethlehem of
Judah, where she stayed for some four
months. 3 Her husband then set out with
his servant and a pair of asses, and went
after her to forgive her and take her
back. She brought him into her father's
house, and on seeing him, the girl's fa-
ther joyfully made him welcome. 4 He
was detained by the girl's father, and
so he spent three days with this father-
in-law of his, eating and drinking and
passing the night there. 5† On the fourth
day they rose early in the morning and
he prepared to go. But the girl's father
said to his son-in-law, "Fortify yourself
with a little food; you can go later on."
6 So they stayed and the two men ate and
drank together. Then the girl's father
said to the husband, "Why not decide
to spend the night here and enjoy your-
self?" 7 The man still made a move to
go, but when his father-in-law pressed
him he went back and spent the night
there.
8 On the fifth morning he rose early
to depart, but the girl's father said,
"Fortify yourself and tarry until the af-
ternoon." When he and his father-in-law
had eaten, 9 and the husband was ready
to go with his concubine and servant, the
girl's father said to him, "It is already
growing dusk. Stay for the night. See,
the day is coming to an end. Spend the
night here and enjoy yourself. Early to-
morrow you can start your journey
home." 10 The man, however, refused to
stay another night; he and his concubine
set out with a pair of saddled asses, and
traveled till they came opposite Jebus,
which is Jerusalem. 11 Since they were
near Jebus with the day far gone, the
servant said to his master, "Come, let
us turn off to this city of the Jebusites
and spend the night in it." 12* But his
master said to him, "We will not turn
off to a city of foreigners, who are not
Israelites, but will go on to Gibeah.
13* Come," he said to his servant, "let
us make for some other place, either
Gibeah or Ramah, to spend the night."
14 So they continued on their way till the
sun set on them when they were abreast
of Gibeah of Benjamin.
15*† There they turned off to enter
Gibeah for the night. The man waited
in the public square of the city he had
entered, but no one offered them the
shelter of his home for the night. 16 In
the evening, however, an old man came
from his work in the field; he was from
the mountain region of Ephraim, though
he lived among the Benjaminite towns-
people of Gibeah. 17 When he noticed the
traveler in the public square of the city,
the old man asked where he was going,
and whence he had come. 18 He said to
him, "We are traveling from Bethlehem
of Judah far up into the mountain region
of Ephraim, where I belong. I have been
to Bethlehem of Judah and am now go-
ing back home; but no one has offered
us the shelter of his house. 19 We have
straw and fodder for our asses, and
bread and wine for the woman and my-
self and for our servant; there is nothing
else we need." 20 "You are welcome," the
old man said to him, "but let me provide
for all your needs, and do not spend the
night in the public square." 21* So he led
them to his house and provided fodder
for the asses. Then they washed their
feet, and ate and drank.
The Outrage at Gibeah. 22*† While
they were enjoying themselves, the men
of the city, who were corrupt, sur-

*

19, 1: 17, 6.
12: 1, 21.
13: Jos 18, 25.
15: 20, 4.
21: Gn 18, 4; 24, 32; 43, 24.
22-25: Gn 19, 4-9.

†

18, 30: *Until . . . land:* about the year 734 B. C., when the Assyrian emperor Tiglath-pileser III subjected northern Palestine.

19, 5-9: Such importuning of guests to prolong their stay at the home of their host is characteristic of Oriental hospitality.

19, 15: Private hospitality was the customary means of providing comfort for travelers where public facilities were so rare.

19, 22: *Who were corrupt:* literally "sons of Belial," indicating extreme perversion; cf Gn 19, 4-8. This crime and its punishment made the name *Gibeah* proverbial as a place of shameful wickedness; cf Hos 9, 9; 10, 9.

rounded the house and beat on the door.
They said to the old man whose house
it was, "Bring out your guest, that we
may abuse him." 23 The owner of the
house went out to them and said, "No,
my brothers; do not be so wicked. Since
this man is my guest, do not commit this
crime. 24 Rather let me bring out my
maiden daughter or his concubine. Rav-
ish them, or do whatever you want with
them; but against the man you must not
commit this wanton crime." 25 When the
men would not listen to his host, the hus-
band seized his concubine and thrust her
outside to them. They had relations with
her and abused her all night until the
following dawn, when they let her go.
26 Then at daybreak the woman came
and collapsed at the entrance of the
house in which her husband was a guest,
where she lay until the morning. 27 When
her husband rose that day and opened
the door of the house to start out again
on his journey, there lay the woman, his
concubine, at the entrance of the house
with her hands on the threshold. 28 He
said to her, "Come, let us go"; but there
was no answer. So the man placed her
on an ass and started out again for
home.

29† On reaching home, he took a knife
to the body of his concubine, cut her into
twelve pieces, and sent them throughout
the territory of Israel. 30* Everyone who
saw this said, "Nothing like this has been
done or seen from the day the Israelites
came up from the land of Egypt to this
day. Take note of it, and state what you
propose to do."

CHAPTER 20

Assembly of Israelites. 1† So all the Is-
raelites came out as one man: from Dan
to Beer-sheba, and from the land of
Gilead, the community was gathered to
the LORD at Mizpah. 2 The leaders of all
the people and all the tribesmen of Is-
rael, four hundred thousand foot sol-
diers who were swordsmen, presented
themselves in the assembly of the people
of God. 3 Meanwhile, the Benjaminites
heard that the Israelites had gone up to
Mizpah. The Israelites asked to be told
how the crime had taken place, 4* and
the Levite, the husband of the murdered
woman, testified: "My concubine and I
went into Gibeah of Benjamin for the
night. 5* But the citizens of Gibeah rose
up against me by night and surrounded
the house in which I was. Me they at-
tempted to kill, and my concubine they
abused so that she died. 6* So I took my
concubine and cut her up and sent her
through every part of the territory of Is-
rael, because of the monstrous crime
they had committed in Israel. 7*† Now
that you are all here, O Israelites, state
what you propose to do." 8 All the people
rose as one man to say, "None of us is
to leave for his tent or return to his
home. 9 Now as for Gibeah, this is what
we will do: We will proceed against it
by lot, 10 taking from all the tribes of Is-
rael ten men for every hundred, a hun-
dred for every thousand, a thousand for
every ten thousand, and procuring sup-
plies for the soldiers who will go to deal
fully and suitably with Gibeah of Ben-
jamin for the crime it committed in
Israel."

11 When, therefore, all the men of Is-
rael without exception were leagued to-
gether against the city, 12† the tribes of
Israel sent men throughout the tribe of
Benjamin to say, "What is this evil which
has occurred among you? 13 Now give
up these corrupt men of Gibeah, that we
may put them to death and thus purge
the evil from Israel." But the Benjamin-
ites refused to accede to the demand of
their brothers, the Israelites. 14 Instead,
the Benjaminites assembled from their
other cities to Gibeah, to do battle with
the Israelites. 15 The number of the Ben-
jaminite swordsmen from the other cit-
ies on that occasion was twenty-six
thousand, in addition to the inhabitants
of Gibeah. 16 Included in this total were
seven hundred picked men who were
left-handed, every one of them able to
sling a stone at a hair without missing.
17 Meanwhile the other Israelites who,
without Benjamin, mustered four hun-
dred thousand swordsmen ready for
battle, 18*† moved on to Bethel and con-
sulted God. When the Israelites asked
who should go first in the attack on the
Benjaminites, the LORD said, "Judah
shall go first." 19 The next day the Israel-
ites advanced on Gibeah with their
forces.

War with Benjamin. 20 On the day the
Israelites drew up in battle array at
Gibeah for the combat with Benjamin,

*

30: Hos 9, 9; 10, 9.
20, 4: 19, 14f.
5: 19, 22-27.
6: 19, 29.
7: 19, 30.
18: 1, 1f.

†

19, 29: A drastic means for arousing the tribes to avenge the unheard of crime of the Benjaminites.

20, 1: *From Dan to Beer-sheba:* from north to south. *The land of Gilead:* all the territory east of the Jordan.

20, 7: The Israelites were asked to decide at once what action to take concerning this crime; cf 2 Sm 16, 20. The Levite undoubtedly addressed the tribal heads who would speak in behalf of the multitude.

20, 12: Before the crime at Gibeah was punished, the Benjaminites were invited to join their brethren, the Israelites, in punishing the crime. Since they failed to respond, special messengers were sent asking them to deliver up the guilty ones. They replied by gathering their forces for combat.

20, 18: *Judah shall go first:* the same response as in 1, 1f, but without the assurance of immediate success. Only after the Israelites were punished at the hands of the Benjaminites for their own grossness, and had performed penance, did they succeed in punishing the latter for their part in the crime of rape and murder, by gaining the victory over them.

21 the Benjaminites came out of the city
and felled twenty-two thousand men of
Israel. 23 Then the Israelites went up and
wept before the LORD until evening.
"Shall I again engage my brother Benja-
min in battle?" they asked the LORD; and
the LORD answered that they should.
22 But though the Israelite soldiers took
courage and again drew up for combat
in the same place as on the previous day,
24 when they met the Benjaminites for
the second time, 25 once again the Ben-
jaminites who came out of Gibeah
against them felled eighteen thousand
Israelites, all of them swordsmen. 26 So
the entire Israelite army went up to
Bethel, where they wept and remained
fasting before the LORD until evening
of that day, besides offering holocausts
and peace offerings before the LORD.
27* When the Israelites consulted the
LORD (for the ark of the covenant of God
was there in those days, 28 and Phinehas,
son of Eleazar, son of Aaron, was minis-
tering to him in those days), and asked,
"Shall I go out again to battle with Ben-
jamin, my brother, or shall I desist?" the
LORD said, "Attack! for tomorrow I will
deliver him into your power." 29*† So Is-
rael set men in ambush around Gibeah.
30 The Israelites went up against the
Benjaminites for the third time and
formed their line of battle at Gibeah as
on other occasions. 31 The Benjaminites
went out to meet them, and in the begin-
ning they killed off about thirty of the
Israelite soldiers in the open field, just
as on the other occasions. 32 Therefore
the Benjaminites thought, "We are de-
feating them as before"; not realizing
that disaster was about to overtake
them. The Israelites, however, had
planned the flight so as to draw them
away from the city onto the highways.
They were drawn away from the city
onto the highways, of which the one led
to Bethel, the other to Gibeon. 33 And
then all the men of Israel rose from their
places. They re-formed their ranks at
Baal-tamar, and the Israelites in am-
bush rushed from their place west of
Gibeah, 34 ten thousand picked men
from all Israel, and advanced against
the city itself. In a fierce battle, 35 the
LORD defeated Benjamin before Israel;
and on that day the Israelites killed
twenty-five thousand one hundred men
of Benjamin, all of them swordsmen.
36 To the Benjaminites it had looked as
though the enemy were defeated, for the
men of Israel gave ground to Benjamin,
trusting in the ambush they had set at
Gibeah. 37 But then the men in ambush
made a sudden dash into Gibeah, over-
ran it, and put the whole city to the
sword. 38 Now, the other Israelites had
agreed with the men in ambush on a
smoke signal they were to send up from
the city. 39 And though the men of Benja-
min had begun by killing off some thirty
of the men of Israel, under the impres-
sion that they were defeating them as
surely as in the earlier fighting, the Isra-
elites wheeled about to resist 40 as the
smoke of the signal column began to rise
up from the city. It was when Benjamin
looked back and saw the whole city in
flames against the sky 41 that the men
of Israel wheeled about. Therefore the
men of Benjamin were thrown into con-
fusion, for they realized the disaster that
had overtaken them. 42 They retreated
before the men of Israel in the direction
of the desert, with the fight being pressed
against them. In their very midst, mean-
while, those who had been in the city
were spreading destruction. 43 The men
of Benjamin had been surrounded, and
were now pursued to a point east of
Gibeah, 44 while eighteen thousand of
them fell, warriors to a man. 45* The rest
turned and fled through the desert to the
rock Rimmon. But on the highways the
Israelites picked off five thousand men
among them, and chasing them up to
Gidom, killed another two thousand of
them there. 46 Those of Benjamin who
fell on that day were in all twenty-five
thousand swordsmen, warriors to a
man. 47 But six hundred others who
turned and fled through the desert
reached the rock Rimmon, where they
remained for four months.
48 The men of Israel withdrew through
the territory of the Benjaminites, putting
to the sword the inhabitants of the cities,
the livestock, and all they chanced upon.
Moreover they destroyed by fire all the
cities they came upon.

CHAPTER 21

Wives for the Survivors. 1† Now the
men of Israel had sworn at Mizpah that
none of them would give his daughter
in marriage to anyone from Benjamin.
2* So the people went to Bethel and re-
mained there before God until evening,
raising their voices in bitter lament.
3 They said, "LORD, God of Israel, why
has it come to pass in Israel that today
one tribe of Israel should be lacking?"
4 Early the next day the people built an
altar there and offered holocausts and
peace offerings. 5* Then the Israelites

* 27: 1 Sm 4, 3f. 29-46: Jos 8, 4-24. 45: 21, 13. 21, 2: 20, 26. 5: 20, 8ff.

† 20, 29-46: This stratagem proved more useful to the Israelites than force, as in the siege of Ai (Jos 8, 3-21). In the parallel accounts the first (vv 29-35) is a summary of the second (vv 36-46).

21, 1-3: The anger of the Israelites led them to destroy their brethren, the Benjaminites. Having realized their goal, however, they were soon filled with dismay, and sought to restore the tribe they had all but exterminated.

asked, "Are there any among all the
tribes of Israel who did not come up to
the LORD for the assembly?" For they
had taken a solemn oath that anyone
who did not go up to the LORD at Mizpah
should be put to death without fail.
6† The Israelites were disconsolate
over their brother Benjamin and said,
"Today one of the tribes of Israel has
been cut off. 7 What can we do about
wives for the survivors, since we have
sworn by the LORD not to give them any
of our daughters in marriage?" 8 And
when they asked whether anyone
among the tribes of Israel had not come
up to the LORD in Mizpah, they found
that none of the men of Jabesh-gilead
had come to the encampment for the as-
sembly. 9 A roll call of the army estab-
lished that none of the inhabitants of
that city were present. 10 The commu-
nity, therefore, sent twelve thousand
warriors with orders to go to Jabesh-
gilead and put those who lived there to
the sword, including the women and
children. 11*† They were told to include
under the ban all males and every
woman who was not still a virgin.
12 Finding among the inhabitants of Ja-
besh-gilead four hundred young virgins,
who had had no relations with men, they
brought them to the camp at Shiloh in
the land of Canaan. 13* Then the whole
community sent a message to the Ben-
jaminites at the rock Rimmon, offering
them peace. 14 When Benjamin returned
at that time, they gave them as wives
the women of Jabesh-gilead whom they
had spared; but these proved to be not
enough for them.
15† The people were still disconsolate
over Benjamin because the LORD had
made a breach among the tribes of Is-
rael. 16 And the elders of the community
said, "What shall we do for wives for the
survivors? For every woman in Benja-
min has been put to death." 17 They said,
"Those of Benjamin who survive must
have heirs, else one of the Israelite tribes
will be wiped out. 18† Yet we cannot give
them any of our daughters in marriage,
because the Israelites have sworn,
'Cursed be he who gives a woman to
Benjamin!' " 19 Then they thought of the
yearly feast of the LORD at Shiloh, north
of Bethel, east of the highway that goes
up from Bethel to Shechem, and south
of Lebonah. 20 And they instructed the
Benjaminites, "Go and lie in wait in the
vineyards. 21 When you see the girls of
Shiloh come out to do their dancing,
leave the vineyards and each of you
seize one of the girls of Shiloh for a wife,
and go to the land of Benjamin. 22 When
their fathers or their brothers come to
complain to us, we shall say to them,
'Release them to us as a kindness, since
we did not take a woman apiece in the
war. Had you yourselves given them
these wives, you would now be guilty.' "
23 The Benjaminites did this; they car-
ried off a wife for each of them from
their raid on the dancers, and went back
to their own territory, where they rebuilt
and occupied the cities. 24 Also at that
time the Israelites dispersed; each of
them left for his own heritage in his own
clan and tribe.
25*† In those days there was no king
in Israel; everyone did what he thought
best.

*

11: Nm 31, 17.
13: 20, 47.
25: 17, 6; 18, 1; 19, 1.

†

21, 6-9: This account is summarized in the parallel passage in vv 2-5.

21, 11: *Under the ban:* see note on Nm 21, 3.

21, 15: *Had made a breach:* what is here attributed to God was in reality the free and deliberate act of the Israelites and happened only by the permissive will of God. The ancients attributed to the first primary cause what is more directly due to secondary causes.

21, 18: Regardless of the serious consequences of their vow, the Israelites considered themselves obliged to fulfill it; cf 11, 31.35f.39.

21, 25: Cf 17, 6; 18, 1; 19, 1. The verse gives the reason why the lawlessness of the period of judges, and the events described herein, were possible.

The Book of

RUTH

The Book of Ruth is named after the Moabite woman who was joined to the Israelite people by her marriage with the influential Boaz of Bethlehem.

The book contains a beautiful example of filial piety, pleasing to the Hebrews especially because of its connection with King David, and useful both to Hebrews and to Gentiles. Its aim is to demonstrate the divine reward for such piety even when practiced by a stranger. Ruth's piety (2, 11), her spirit of self-sacrifice, and her moral integrity were favored by God with the gift of faith and an illustrious marriage whereby she became the ancestress of David and of Christ. In this, the universality of the messianic salvation is foreshadowed.

In the Greek and Latin canons the Book of Ruth is placed just after Judges, to which it is closely related because of the time of its action, and just before Samuel, for which it is an excellent introduction, since it traces the ancestry of the Davidic dynasty. One might characterize the literary form of this book as dramatic, since about two-thirds of it is in dialogue. Yet there is every indication that, as tradition has always held, it contains true history.

There is no certainty about the author of the book. It was written long after the events had passed (4, 7), which took place "in the time of the judges" (1, 1).

CHAPTER 1

Naomi in Moab. 1† Once in the time
of the judges there was a famine in the
land; so a man from Bethlehem of Ju-
dah departed with his wife and two sons
to reside on the plateau of Moab. 2 The
man was named Elimelech, his wife
Naomi, and his sons Mahlon and Chil-
ion; they were Ephrathites from Bethle-
hem of Judah. Some time after their ar-
rival on the Moabite plateau, 3 Elim-
elech, the husband of Naomi, died, and
she was left with her two sons, 4 who
married Moabite women, one named
Orpah, the other Ruth. When they had
lived there about ten years, 5 both Mah-
lon and Chilion died also, and the
woman was left with neither her two
sons nor her husband. 6 She then made
ready to go back from the plateau of
Moab because word reached her there
that the LORD had visited his people and
given them food.

7 She and her two daughters-in-law
left the place where they had been living.
Then as they were on the road back to
the land of Judah, 8† Naomi said to her
two daughters-in-law, "Go back, each
of you, to your mother's house! May the
LORD be kind to you as you were to the
departed and to me! 9 May the LORD
grant each of you a husband and a home
in which you will find rest." She kissed
them good-bye, but they wept with loud
sobs, 10 and told her they would return
with her to her people. 11† "Go back, my
daughters!" said Naomi. "Why should
you come with me? Have I other sons
in my womb who may become your hus-
bands? 12 Go back, my daughters! Go,
for I am too old to marry again. And
even if I could offer any hopes, or if to-
night I had a husband or had borne sons,
13 would you then wait and deprive your-
selves of husbands until those sons grew
up? No, my daughters! my lot is too bit-
ter for you, because the LORD has ex-
tended his hand against me." 14 Again
they sobbed aloud and wept; and Orpah
kissed her mother-in-law good-bye, but
Ruth stayed with her.

15 "See now!" she said, "your sister-in-
law has gone back to her people and her
god. Go back after your sister-in-law!"
16† But Ruth said, "Do not ask me to
abandon or forsake you! for wherever
you go I will go, wherever you lodge I
will lodge, your people shall be my peo-
ple, and your God my God. 17 Wherever
you die I will die, and there be buried.
May the LORD do so and so to me, and
more besides, if aught but death sepa-
rates me from you!" 18 Naomi then

---

†

1, 1f: *In the time of the judges:* three generations before the end of the period of judges; cf 4, 21f. *Bethlehem of Judah:* to distinguish it from the town of the same name in the tribe of Zebulun (Jos 19, 15). *Ephrathites from Bethlehem:* belonging to a Judean clan which settled in Bethlehem; cf 1 Sm 17, 12; 1 Chr 2, 50f; 4, 4.

1, 8: *Mother's house:* the women's part of the dwelling; cf Jgs 4, 17; Sg 3, 4.

1, 11: *Have I other sons . . . husbands?* Naomi insisted that her daughters-in-law remain in their own country only for the sake of posterity. If she had had other sons, the levirate law would have obliged them to marry the widows of her deceased sons to perpetuate the names of the deceased; cf Gn 38, 8; Dt 25, 5f.

1, 16f: An example of heroic fidelity and piety. Ruth's decision, confirmed with an oath, to adhere to her mother-in-law impelled her to abandon her country and its pagan worship.

ceased to urge her, for she saw she was
determined to go with her.

The Return to Bethlehem. 19 So they
went on together till they reached Beth-
lehem. On their arrival there, the whole
city was astir over them, and the women
asked, "Can this be Naomi?" 20*† But
she said to them, "Do not call me Naomi.
Call me Mara, for the Almighty has
made it very bitter for me. 21 I went away
with an abundance, but the LORD has
brought me back destitute. Why should
you call me Naomi, since the LORD has
pronounced against me and the Al-
mighty has brought evil upon me?"
22† Thus it was that Naomi returned with
the Moabite daughter-in-law, Ruth, who
accompanied her back from the plateau
of Moab. They arrived in Bethlehem at
the beginning of the barley harvest.

CHAPTER 2

The Meeting. 1* Naomi had a promi-
nent kinsman named Boaz, of the clan
of her husband Elimelech. 2*† Ruth the
Moabite said to Naomi, "Let me go and
glean ears of grain in the field of anyone
who will allow me that favor." Naomi
said to her, "Go, my daughter," 3 and
she went. The field she entered to glean
after the harvesters happened to be the
section belonging to Boaz of the clan of
Elimelech. 4† Boaz himself came from
Bethlehem and said to the harvesters,
"The LORD be with you!" and they re-
plied, "The LORD bless you!" 5 Boaz
asked the overseer of his harvesters,
"Whose girl is this?" 6* The overseer of
the harvesters answered, "She is the
Moabite girl who returned from the pla-
teau of Moab with Naomi. 7 She asked
leave to gather the gleanings into
sheaves after the harvesters; and ever
since she came this morning she has re-
mained here until now, with scarcely a
moment's rest."

8 Boaz said to Ruth, "Listen, my
daughter! Do not go to glean in anyone
else's field; you are not to leave here.
Stay here with my women servants.
9 Watch to see which field is to be har-
vested, and follow them; I have com-
manded the young men to do you no
harm. When you are thirsty, you may
go and drink from the vessels the young
men have filled." 10 Casting herself pros-
trate upon the ground, she said to him,
"Why should I, a foreigner, be favored
with your notice?" 11* Boaz answered
her: "I have had a complete account of
what you have done for your mother-
in-law after your husband's death; you
have left your father and your mother
and the land of your birth, and have
come to a people whom you did not know
previously. 12 May the LORD reward
what you have done! May you receive
a full reward from the LORD, the God
of Israel, under whose wings you have
come for refuge." 13 She said, "May I
prove worthy of your kindness, my lord:
you have comforted me, your servant,
with your consoling words; would indeed
that I were a servant of yours!" 14 At
mealtime Boaz said to her, "Come here
and have some food; dip your bread in
the sauce." Then as she sat near the
reapers, he handed her some roasted
grain and she ate her fill and had some
left over. 15 She rose to glean, and Boaz
instructed his servants to let her glean
among the sheaves themselves without
scolding her, 16 and even to let drop some
handfuls and leave them for her to glean
without being rebuked.

17 She gleaned in the field until eve-
ning, and when she beat out what she
had gleaned it came to about an ephah
of barley, 18 which she took into the city
and showed to her mother-in-law. Next
she brought out and gave her what she
had left over from lunch. 19 So her
mother-in-law said to her, "Where did
you glean today? Where did you go to
work? May he who took notice of you
be blessed!" Then she told her mother-
in-law with whom she had worked. "The
man at whose place I worked today is
named Boaz," she said. 20*† "May he be
blessed by the LORD, who is ever merci-
ful to the living and to the dead," Naomi
exclaimed to her daughter-in-law; and
she continued, "He is a relative of ours,
one of our next of kin." 21 "He even told
me," added Ruth the Moabite, "that I
should stay with his servants until they
complete his entire harvest." 22 "You
would do well, my dear," Naomi re-
joined, "to go out with his servants; for
in someone else's field you might be in-
sulted." 23 So she stayed gleaning with
the servants of Boaz until the end of the
barley and wheat harvests.

RUTH

*

1, 20: Ex 15, 23.
2, 1: 3, 2.12; 4, 21; Mt 1, 5.
2: Dt 24, 19.
6: 1, 22.
11: 1, 14-17.
20: 3, 9.

†

1, 20f: *Naomi:* "amiable" or "pleasant," suggesting God's favor toward her. *The Almighty has brought evil upon me:* the ancients regarded adversity as a punishment from God for personal sin, as if good and evil were always repaid in a temporal and material manner.

1, 22: *Barley harvest:* early April. This circumstance favored the events of the narrative that follow.

2, 2: *Let me go and glean . . . grain:* even the poor, the widow, the stranger, and the orphan had a right to glean at harvest time; cf Lv 19, 9f; 23, 22; Dt 24, 19-22.

2, 4: *The LORD be with you:* courtesy and religious feeling characterize the salutations of the Hebrews. This greeting is used in the Christian liturgy.

2, 20: *One of our next of kin:* literally "our redeemer," a near relative of the same clan who had the right and duty to restore the land which an impoverished kinsman had alienated (Lv 25, 25-28), and to marry the widow of a relative who had died without male offspring so as to raise up posterity to his name (Dt 25, 5-10).

CHAPTER 3

Ruth Again Presents Herself. 1 When
she was back with her mother-in-law,
Naomi said to her, "My daughter, I must
seek a home for you that will please you.
2* Now is not Boaz, with whose servants
you were, a relative of ours? This eve-
ning he will be winnowing barley at the
threshing floor. 3 So bathe and anoint
yourself; then put on your best attire and
go down to the threshing floor. Do not
make yourself known to the man before
he has finished eating and drinking.
4† But when he lies down, take note of
the place where he does so. Then go, un-
cover a place at his feet, and lie down.
He will tell you what to do." 5 "I will do
whatever you advise," Ruth replied. 6 So
she went down to the threshing floor and
did just as her mother-in-law had in-
structed her.

7 Boaz ate and drank to his heart's
content. Then when he went and lay
down at the edge of the sheaves, she
stole up, uncovered a place at his feet,
and lay down. 8 In the middle of the
night, however, the man gave a start and
turned around to find a woman lying at
his feet. 9† He asked, "Who are you?"
And she replied, "I am your servant
Ruth. Spread the corner of your cloak
over me, for you are my next of kin."
10* He said, "May the LORD bless you,
my daughter! You have been even more
loyal now than before in not going after
the young men, whether poor or rich.
11 So be assured, daughter, I will do for
you whatever you say; all my townspeo-
ple know you for a worthy woman.
12*† Now, though indeed I am closely
related to you, you have another relative
still closer. 13* Stay as you are for to-
night, and tomorrow, if he wishes to
claim you, good! let him do so. But if
he does not wish to claim you, as the
LORD lives, I will claim you myself. Lie
there until morning." 14 So she lay at
his feet until morning, but rose before
men could recognize one another. Boaz
said, "Let it not be known that this
woman came to the threshing floor."
15* Then he said to her, "Take off your
cloak and hold it out." When she did so,
he poured out six measures of barley,
helped her lift the bundle, and left for
the city.

16 Ruth went home to her mother-in-
law, who asked, "How have you fared,
my daughter?" So she told her all the
man had done for her, 17 and concluded,
"He gave me these six measures of bar-
ley because he did not wish me to come
back to my mother-in-law empty-
handed!" 18 Naomi then said, "Wait
here, my daughter, until you learn what
happens, for the man will not rest, but
will settle the matter today."

CHAPTER 4

Boaz Marries Ruth. 1*† Boaz went
and took a seat at the gate; and when
he saw the closer relative of whom he
had spoken come along, he called to him
by name, "Come and sit beside me!"
And he did so. 2† Then Boaz picked out
ten of the elders of the city and asked
them to sit nearby. When they had done
this, 3 he said to the near relative:
"Naomi, who has come back from the
Moabite plateau, is putting up for sale
the piece of land that belonged to our
kinsman Elimelech. 4*† So I thought I
would inform you, bidding you before
those here present, including the elders
of my people, to put in your claim for
it if you wish to acquire it as next of kin.
But if you do not wish to claim it, tell
me so, that I may be guided accordingly,
for no one has a prior claim to yours,
and mine is next." He answered, "I will
put in my claim."

5*† Boaz continued, "Once you ac-
quire the field from Naomi, you must
take also Ruth the Moabite, the widow
of the late heir, and raise up a family
for the departed on his estate." 6 The
near relative replied, "I cannot exercise
my claim lest I depreciate my own es-
tate. Put in a claim yourself in my stead,
for I cannot exercise my claim." 7† Now
it used to be the custom in Israel that,
to make binding a contract of redemp-
tion or exchange, one party would take
off his sandal and give it to the other.
This was the form of attestation in Israel.

---

*

3, 2: 1.
10: Dt 25, 5.
12: 4, 1.
13: 4, 5; Dt 25, 5.
15: 2, 17.
4, 1: 3, 12.
4: Lv 25, 25.
5: 3, 13; Dt 25, 5.

---

†

3, 4: *Uncover a place at his feet, . . .:* confident of the virtue of Ruth and Boaz, Naomi advises this unusual expedient to her daughter-in-law for the purpose of introducing her claim.

3, 9: *Spread the corner of your cloak over me:* be my protector by marrying me according to the duty of a near kinsman; cf Dt 25, 5; Ez 16, 8.

3, 12: *Relative still closer:* who had a prior right and duty to marry Ruth.

4, 1: *Took a seat at the gate:* i.e., of the city, where business affairs were settled.

4, 2: *Ten of the elders:* to serve as judges in legal matters as well as witnesses of the settlement of business affairs; cf Dt 25, 7-9.

4, 4: Poverty had obliged Naomi to sell the land of her deceased husband. The law permitted the nearest kinsman to redeem the land and thus preserve the family patrimony; cf Lv 25, 25.

4, 5f: The heir of Elimelech's field had died without children (1, 5). The nearest of kin could now redeem the land but he must also take Ruth, *the widow of the late heir,* to wife to perpetuate the family of the deceased; cf Dt 25, 5f. The first male child of such a marriage would be the legal son of Mahlon and grandson of Elimelech.

4, 7: *Take off his sandal . . .:* by this act the near relative renounced his legal right, both to the field of Elimelech and to the marriage with Ruth. The custom mentioned in Dt 25, 6 is somewhat different.

8 So the near relative, in saying to Boaz,
"Acquire it for yourself," drew off his
sandal. 9 Boaz then said to the elders and
to all the people, "You are witnesses to-
day that I have acquired from Naomi
all the holdings of Elimelech, Chilion
and Mahlon. 10 I also take Ruth the Mo-
abite, the widow of Mahlon, as my wife,
in order to raise up a family for her late
husband on his estate, so that the name
of the departed may not perish among
his kinsmen and fellow citizens. Do you
witness this today?" 11* All those at the
gate, including the elders, said, "We do
so. May the LORD make this wife come
into your house like Rachel and Leah,
who between them built up the house of
Israel. May you do well in Ephrathah
and win fame in Bethlehem. 12*† With
the offspring the LORD will give you from
this girl, may your house become like
the house of Perez, whom Tamar bore
to Judah."

13 Boaz took Ruth. When they came to-
gether as man and wife, the LORD en-
abled her to conceive and she bore a son.
14 Then the women said to Naomi,
"Blessed is the LORD who has not failed
to provide you today with an heir! May
he become famous in Israel! 15 He will
be your comfort and the support of your
old age, for his mother is the daughter-
in-law who loves you. She is worth more
to you than seven sons!" 16† Naomi took
the child, placed him on her lap, and be-
came his nurse. 17*† And the neighbor
women gave him his name, at the news
that a grandson had been born to Naomi.
They called him Obed. He was the father
of Jesse, the father of David.

18* These are the descendants of
Perez: Perez was the father of Hezron,
19 Hezron was the father of Ram, Ram
was the father of Amminadab, 20* Am-
minadab was the father of Nahshon,
Nahshon was the father of Salmon,
21 Salmon was the father of Boaz, Boaz
was the father of Obed, 22* Obed was the
father of Jesse, and Jesse became the
father of David.

*

11: Gn 29, 31—30, 24; 35, 19.
12: Gn 38, 29.
17: Lk 1, 58.
18-22: 1 Chr 2, 4-15; Mt 1, 3-6.
18: Gn 46, 12; 1 Chr 4, 1.
20: Ex 6, 23; Nm 1, 7.
22: 1 Sm 16, 10-13.

†

4, 12: *Perez, whom Tamar bore to Judah:* the right which Judah unwittingly satisfied for his daughter-in-law Tamar (Gn 38), Boaz willingly rendered to Ruth.

4, 16: *Placed him on her lap:* took him as her own; cf Gn 30, 3; 48, 12; Nm 11, 12.

4, 17: *The father of Jesse, the father of David:* indicating the place of Obed, Jesse and David in the line of Judah and the ancestry of Christ, the Messiah; cf Mt 1, 5f.

THE HISTORICAL BOOKS

The historical books include 1 and 2 Samuel, 1 and 2 Kings, 1 and 2 Chronicles, Ezra, Nehemiah, 1 and 2 Maccabees. To these are added the special literary group of Tobit, Judith, and Esther.

The Books of Tobit, Judith, and 1 and 2 Maccabees, as well as parts of Esther, are called deuterocanonical: they are not contained in the Hebrew canon but have been accepted by the Catholic Church as canonical and inspired.

By means of a series of episodes involving the persons of Samuel, Saul, and David, a century of history unfolds in 1 and 2 Samuel from the close of the period of Judges to the rise and establishment of the monarchy in Israel. Most important is God's promise to David of a lasting dynasty (2 Sm 7), from which royal messianism in the Bible developed.

In 1 and 2 Kings the religious history of Israel extends another four centuries, from the last days of David to the Babylonian captivity and the destruction of Jerusalem (587 B.C.). The various sources for these books are woven into a uniform pattern based on the principle of fidelity to Yahweh for rulers and people alike. The sequence of regnal chronicles in both books is interrupted by a cycle of traditions surrounding the prophets Elijah (1 Kgs) and Elisha (2 Kgs).

Chronicles, Ezra, and Nehemiah form a historical work, uniform in style and basic ideas. Chronicles records the long period from the reign of Saul to the return from exile, not so much with exactitude of detail as with concern for the meaning of the facts which demonstrate God's intervention in history. The Ezra-Nehemiah chronicle constitutes the most important source for the formation of the Jewish religious community after the Babylonian exile; the two persons most responsible for the reorganization of Jewish life were Ezra and Nehemiah.

1 and 2 Maccabees contain independent accounts of partially identical events which accompanied the attempted suppression of Judaism in Palestine in the second century B.C. Vigorous reaction to this attempt established for a time the religious and political independence of the Jews. 1 Maccabees portrays God as the eternal benefactor of the Jews and their unfailing source of help. The people are required to be devoted to his exclusive worship and to observe exactly the law he has given them. 2 Maccabees, besides supplementing the former volume, gives a theological interpretation of the history of the period and contains teaching on the resurrection from the dead, intercession of the saints, and suffrages for the dead.

Tobit, Judith, and Esther are examples of free composition—the religious novel used for purposes of edification and instruction. Interest in whatever historical data these books may contain is merely intensified by the addition of vivid details. Judith is a lesson in Providence: a pious reflection on the annual Passover observance to convey the reassurance that God is still the master of history who saves Israel from her enemies. Esther's purpose is the glorification of the Jewish people and the explanation of the origin, significance, and date of the feast of Purim. It is a literary development of the principle of reversal of fortune through punishment of the prosperous rich and reward for the virtuous who are oppressed.

SAMUEL TO MACCABEES *demonstrates that before as well as during the millennium of history with which it is concerned, Israel was a covenanted people, bound to Yahweh, Lord of the universe, by the ties of faith and obedience. This required observance of the law and worship in his temple, the consequent rewards of which were divine favor and protection. In this way these books anticipate and prepare for the coming of him who would bring type and prophecy to fulfillment, history to term, and holiness to perfection: Christ, the Son of David and the promised Messiah.*

The Books of

SAMUEL

Originally but one book, the scroll of Samuel was early divided into two. The Greek translators called these the first and second Books of Kingdoms, a title St. Jerome later modified to "Kings." The Hebrew title, "Samuel," alludes to the leading figure in the first book, who was responsible for the enthronement of David. It is David's history that the second book recounts.

This sacred work thus comprises the history of about a century, describing the close of the age of the Judges and the beginnings of monarchy in Israel under Saul and David. It is not a complete and continuous history, nor a systematic account of the period, but rather a series of episodes centered around the persons of Samuel, Saul and David, the principal figures leading up to the establishment of the royal dynasty of David.

The final editor is unknown, nor are we certain of the time at which the various strands of the narrative were put together, though one may think of the period, perhaps late in the seventh century B.C., when the other volumes of the "Former Prophets," from Joshua through Kings, were built into a more or less continuous historical corpus. The Samuel-Saul-David narratives clearly depend on several written sources: a Samuel cycle, two sets of stories about Saul and David, and a family history of David. This last (2 Sm 9—20; 1 Kgs 1—2), one of the most vivid historical narratives surviving from ancient times, probably originated early in the reign of Solomon.

One of the most significant theological contributions of the Old Testament is found in 2 Samuel 7, the oracle of Nathan. David is here promised an eternal dynasty, and this becomes the basis for the development of royal messianism throughout the Bible. With this promise to David one should compare 2 Chr 17; Pss 89, 20-38 and 132, 11ff; Acts 2, 30; and Heb 1, 5.

The contents of this work may be divided as follows:

I: History of the Last Judges, Eli and Samuel (1 Sm 1, 1—7, 17)
II: Establishment of the Monarchy in Israel (1 Sm 8, 1—12, 25)
III: Saul and David (1 Sm 13, 1—2 Sm 2, 7)
IV: The Reign of David (2 Sm 2, 8—20, 26)
V: Appendixes (2 Sm 21, 1—24, 25)

THE FIRST BOOK OF SAMUEL

I: HISTORY OF THE LAST JUDGES, ELI AND SAMUEL

CHAPTER 1

Elkanah and His Family at Shiloh.
1* There was a certain man from Rama-
thaim, Elkanah by name, a Zuphite
from the hill country of Ephraim. He
was the son of Jeroham, son of Elihu,
son of Tohu, son of Zuph, an Ephraimite.
2 He had two wives, one named Hannah,
the other Peninnah; Peninnah had
children, but Hannah was childless.
3* This man regularly went on pil-
grimage from his city to worship the
LORD of hosts and to sacrifice to him at
Shiloh, where the two sons of Eli, Hophni
and Phinehas, were ministering as
priests of the LORD. 4 When the day came
for Elkanah to offer sacrifice, he used
to give a portion each to his wife Penin-
nah and to all her sons and daughters,
5* but a double portion to Hannah be-
cause he loved her, though the LORD had
made her barren. 6* Her rival, to upset
her, turned it into a constant reproach
to her that the LORD had left her barren.
7 This went on year after year; each time
they made their pilgrimage to the sanc-
tuary of the LORD, Peninnah would ap-
proach her, and Hannah would weep
and refuse to eat. 8* Her husband Elka-
nah used to ask her: "Hannah, why do
you weep, and why do you refuse to eat?
Why do you grieve? Am I not more to
you than ten sons?"
Hannah's Prayer. 9 Hannah rose after
one such meal at Shiloh, and presented

---

*

1, 1: 1 Chr 6, 19f.
3: Ex 23, 14-17; 34, 23; Dt 16, 16; Jgs 21, 19.
5: Dt 21, 15ff.
6: Gn 16, 4f.
8: Ru 4, 15.

herself before the LORD; at the time, Eli
the priest was sitting on a chair near the
doorpost of the LORD's temple. 10 In her
bitterness she prayed to the LORD, weep-
ing copiously, 11*† and she made a vow,
promising: "O LORD of hosts, if you look
with pity on the misery of your hand-
maid, if you remember me and do not
forget me, if you give your handmaid
a male child, I will give him to the LORD
for as long as he lives; neither wine nor
liquor shall he drink, and no razor shall
ever touch his head." 12 As she remained
long at prayer before the LORD, Eli
watched her mouth, 13 for Hannah was
praying silently; though her lips were
moving, her voice could not be heard.
Eli, thinking her drunk, 14 said to her,
"How long will you make a drunken
show of yourself? Sober up from your
wine!" 15 "It isn't that, my lord," Hannah
answered. "I am an unhappy woman.
I have had neither wine nor liquor; I was
only pouring out my troubles to the
LORD. 16 Do not think your handmaid a
ne'er-do-well; my prayer has been
prompted by my deep sorrow and mis-
ery." 17 Eli said, "Go in peace, and may
the God of Israel grant you what you
have asked of him." 18 She replied,
"Think kindly of your maidservant,"
and left. She went to her quarters, ate
and drank with her husband, and no
longer appeared downcast. 19 Early the
next morning they worshiped before the
LORD, and then returned to their home
in Ramah.

Hannah Bears a Son. When Elkanah
had relations with his wife Hannah, the
LORD remembered her. 20† She con-
ceived, and at the end of her term bore
a son whom she called Samuel, since she
had asked the LORD for him. 21 The next
time her husband Elkanah was going up
with the rest of his household to offer
the customary sacrifice to the LORD and
to fulfill his vows, 22 Hannah did not go,
explaining to her husband, "Once the
child is weaned, I will take him to appear
before the LORD and to remain there for-
ever; I will offer him as a perpetual
nazirite." 23 Her husband Elkanah an-
swered her: "Do what you think best;
wait until you have weaned him. Only,
may the LORD bring your resolve to ful-
fillment!" And so she remained at home
and nursed her son until she had weaned
him.

Samuel Is Offered to God. 24† Once he
was weaned, she brought him up with
her, along with a three-year-old bull, an
ephah of flour, and a skin of wine, and
presented him at the temple of the LORD
in Shiloh. 25 After the boy's father had
sacrificed the young bull, Hannah, his
mother, approached Eli 26 and said:
"Pardon, my lord! As you live my lord,
I am the woman who stood near you
here, praying to the LORD. 27 I prayed
for this child, and the LORD granted my
request. 1:28 Now I, in turn, give him to
the LORD; as long as he lives, he shall
be dedicated to the LORD." She left him
there; 2:1*† and as she worshiped the
LORD, she said:

CHAPTER 2

"My heart exults in the LORD,
my horn is exalted in my God.
I have swallowed up my enemies;
I rejoice in my victory.
2* There is no Holy One like the LORD;
there in no Rock like our God.

3*† "Speak boastfully no longer,
nor let arrogance issue from your mouths.
For an all-knowing God is the LORD,
a God who judges deeds.
4* The bows of the mighty are broken,
while the tottering gird on strength.
5 The well-fed hire themselves out for bread,
while the hungry batten on spoil.
The barren wife bears seven sons,
while the mother of many languishes.

6* "The LORD puts to death and gives life;
he casts down to the nether world;
he raises up again.
7 The LORD makes poor and makes rich,
he humbles, he also exalts.
8* He raises the needy from the dust;
from the ash heap he lifts up the poor,
To seat them with nobles

*

11: Nm 6, 1-5; Jgs 13, 2-5; 16, 17; Lk 1, 15.
2, 1: Dt 33, 17; 2 Sm 22, 3; Ps 18, 2; Is 61, 10; Lk 1, 47.69.
2: 2 Sm 22, 3; Ps 18, 2.
3: Ps 75, 4.
4: Is 40, 29.
6: Dt 32, 39; Tb 4, 19; Jb 5, 11; Ps 30, 4; Wis 16, 13; Lk 1, 52.
8: Jb 9, 6; 38, 6; Ps 104, 5; 121, 3.

†

1, 11: *Give him to the LORD:* some ancient texts call Samuel a *nazir* in this context; see note on Nm 6, 1ff.

1, 20: *Since she had asked:* this explanation would be more directly appropriate for the name Saul, which means "asked"; Samuel means "name of God."

1, 24: *An ephah:* a little more than a bushel.

2, 1-10: A hymn attributed to Hannah, the mother of Samuel, as her thanksgiving to God because she has borne a son despite her previous sterility. She praises God as the helper of the weak (1f), who casts down the mighty and raises up the lowly (3ff), and who alone is the source of true strength (8ff); the hymn ends with a prayer for the king (v 10). This canticle has several points of resemblance with our Lady's *Magnificat.*

2, 1: *Horn:* the symbol of strength; cf Pss 18, 3; 75, 5; 89, 18; 112, 9.

2, 3: *Speak . . . mouths:* addressed to the *enemies* mentioned in v 1.

and make a glorious throne their
heritage.
He gives to the vower his vow,
and blesses the sleep of the just.

"For the pillars of the earth are the
LORD's,
and he has set the world upon
them.
9 He will guard the footsteps of his
faithful ones,
but the wicked shall perish in the
darkness.
For not by strength does man pre-
vail;
10* the LORD's foes shall be shattered.
The Most High in heaven thunders;
the LORD judges the ends of the
earth,
Now may he give strength to his
king,
and exalt the horn of his
anointed!"

11 When Elkanah returned home to Ramah, the child remained in the service of the LORD under the priest Eli.

Wickedness of Eli's Sons. 12 Now the sons of Eli were wicked; they had respect neither for the LORD 13* nor for the priests' duties toward the people. When someone offered a sacrifice, the priest's servant would come with a three-pronged fork, while the meat was still boiling, 14 and would thrust it into the basin, kettle, caldron, or pot. Whatever the fork brought up, the priest would keep. That is how all the Israelites were treated who came to the sanctuary at Shiloh. 15 In fact, even before the fat was burned, the priest's servant would come and say to the man offering the sacrifice, "Give me some meat to roast for the priest. He will not accept boiled meat from you, only raw meat." 16* And if the man protested to him, "Let the fat be burned first as is the custom, then take whatever you wish," he would reply, "No, give it to me now, or else I will take it by force." 17 Thus the young men sinned grievously in the presence of the LORD; they treated the offerings to the LORD with disdain.

The Lord Rewards Hannah. 18† Meanwhile the boy Samuel, girt with a linen apron, was serving in the presence of the LORD. 19 His mother used to make a little garment for him, which she would bring him each time she went up with her husband to offer the customary sacrifice. 20 And Eli would bless Elkanah and his wife, as they were leaving for home. He would say, "May the LORD repay you with children from this woman for the gift she has made to the LORD!" 21* The LORD favored Hannah so that she conceived and gave birth to three more sons and two daughters, while young Samuel grew up in the service of the LORD.

Eli's Futile Rebuke. 22† When Eli was very old, he heard repeatedly how his sons were treating all Israel [and that they were having relations with the women serving at the entry of the meeting tent]. 23 So he said to them: "Why are you doing such things? 24 No, my sons, you must not do these things! It is not a good report that I hear the people of the LORD spreading about you. 25 If a man sins against another man, one can intercede for him with the LORD; but if a man sins against the LORD, who can intercede for him?" But they disregarded their father's warning, since the LORD had decided on their death. 26* Meanwhile, young Samuel was growing in stature and in worth in the estimation of the LORD and of men.

Doom of Eli's House. 27† A man of God came to Eli and said to him: "This is what the LORD says: 'I went so far as to reveal myself to your father's family when they were in Egypt as slaves to the house of Pharaoh. 28*† I chose them out of all the tribes of Israel to be my priests, to go up to my altar, to burn incense, and to wear the ephod before me; and I assigned all the oblations of the Israelites to your father's family. 29 Why do you keep a greedy eye on my sacrifices and on the offerings which I have prescribed? And why do you honor your sons in preference to me, fattening yourselves with the choicest part of every offering of my people Israel?' 30* This, therefore, is the oracle of the LORD, the God of Israel: 'I said in the past that your family and your father's family should minister in my presence forever. But now,' the LORD declares, 'away with this!

*

10: Ps 98, 9.
13-15: Ex 29, 27f; Lv 7, 29-36; Dt 18, 3.
16: Lv 3, 3ff.
21: 3, 19.
26: Lk 2, 52.
28: 23, 9; 30, 7f; Jgs 17, 5.
30f: 2 Sm 22, 26; 1 Kgs 2, 27; Ps 18, 25.

†

2, 18: *Linen apron:* called in Hebrew "ephod," but not the same as the high priest's ephod (Ex 28, 6-14) or the ephod used in divination (v 28). Samuel wore a simple apron such as was worn by the priests (22, 18), and on one occasion also by David (2 Sm 6, 14).

2, 22: The bracketed words, which recall Ex 38, 8, are a gloss in the received text; they are lacking in the oldest Greek translation, and in a Hebrew manuscript from Qumran.

2, 27-36: These verses propose the punishment of Eli from a point of view contemporary with the reform of Josiah (2 Kgs 23, 9; cf v 36); they hint at the events recorded in 22, 18-23 and 1 Kgs 2, 27. The older story of this divine warning is that in 3, 11-14.

2, 28: *Ephod:* a portable container, presumably of cloth, for the lots used in ritual consultation of God during the days of the Judges (Jgs 17, 5; 18, 14-15) and down into the time of David (14, 3ff; 23, 6ff; 30, 7f). The ephod of the high priest described in Ex 28, 6ff becomes a garment upon which a *breastpiece of decision* symbolizes, but no longer serves for, such consultation. The Exodus text codifies a later form of the tradition.

for I will honor those who honor me, but those who spurn me shall be accursed. 31 Yes, the time is coming when I will break your strength and the strength of your father's family, so that no man in your family shall reach old age. 32 You shall witness as a disappointed rival all the benefits enjoyed by Israel, but there shall never be an old man in your family. 33 I will permit some of your family to remain at my altar, to wear out their eyes in consuming greed; but the rest of the men of your family shall die by the sword. 34* You shall have a sign in what will happen to your two sons, Hophni and Phinehas: both shall die on the same day. 35 I will choose a faithful priest who shall do what I have in heart and mind. I will establish a lasting house for him which shall function in the presence of my anointed forever. 36* Then whoever is left of your family will come to grovel before him for a piece of silver or a loaf of bread, and will say: Appoint me, I beg you, to a priestly function, that I may have a morsel of bread to eat.' "

CHAPTER 3

Revelation to Samuel. 1† During the time young Samuel was minister to the LORD under Eli, a revelation of the LORD was uncommon and vision infrequent. 2 One day Eli was asleep in his usual place. His eyes had lately grown so weak that he could not see. 3* The lamp of God was not yet extinguished, and Samuel was sleeping in the temple of the LORD where the ark of God was. 4 The LORD called to Samuel, who answered, "Here I am." 5 He ran to Eli and said, "Here I am. You called me." "I did not call you," Eli said. "Go back to sleep." So he went back to sleep. 6 Again the LORD called Samuel, who rose and went to Eli. "Here I am," he said. "You called me." But he answered, "I did not call you, my son. Go back to sleep." 7 At that time Samuel was not familiar with the LORD, because the LORD had not revealed anything to him as yet. 8 The LORD called Samuel again, for the third time. Getting up and going to Eli, he said, "Here I am. You called me." Then Eli understood that the LORD was calling the youth. 9 So he said to Samuel, "Go to sleep, and if you are called, reply, 'Speak, LORD, for your servant is listening.' " When Samuel went to sleep in his place, 10 the LORD came and revealed his presence, calling out as before, "Samuel, Samuel!" Samuel answered, "Speak, for your servant is listening."

11 The LORD said to Samuel: "I am about to do something in Israel that will cause the ears of everyone who hears it to ring. 12 On that day I will carry out in full against Eli everything I threatened against his family. 13* I announce to him that I am condemning his family once and for all, because of this crime: though he knew his sons were blaspheming God, he did not reprove them. 14 Therefore, I swear to the family of Eli that no sacrifice or offering will ever expiate its crime." 15 Samuel then slept until morning, when he got up early and opened the doors of the temple of the LORD. He feared to tell Eli the vision, 16 but Eli called to him, "Samuel, my son!" He replied, "Here I am." 17† Then Eli asked, "What did he say to you? Hide nothing from me! May God do thus and so to you if you hide a single thing he told you." 18 So Samuel told him everything, and held nothing back. Eli answered, "He is the LORD. He will do what he judges best."

Samuel Acknowledged as Prophet. 19* Samuel grew up, and the LORD was with him, not permitting any word of his to be without effect. 20* Thus all Israel from Dan to Beer-sheba came to know that Samuel was an accredited prophet of the LORD. 21 The LORD continued to appear at Shiloh; he manifested himself to Samuel at Shiloh through his word, 1 and Samuel spoke to all Israel.

CHAPTER 4

Defeat of the Israelites. At that time, the Philistines gathered for an attack on Israel. Israel went out to engage them in battle and camped at Ebenezer, while the Philistines camped at Aphek. 2 The Philistines then drew up in battle formation against Israel. After a fierce struggle Israel was defeated by the Philistines, who slew about four thousand men on the battlefield. 3 When the troops retired to the camp, the elders of Israel said, "Why has the LORD permitted us to be defeated today by the Philistines? Let us fetch the ark of the LORD from Shiloh that it may go into battle among us and save us from the grasp of our enemies."

Loss of the Ark. 4*† So the people sent

---

*

34: 4, 11.
36: 2 Kgs 23, 9.
3, 3: Ex 25, 22; 27, 20f; Lv 24, 2.4; 2 Chr 13, 11.
13: 2, 27-36.
19: 2, 21.
20: Jgs 20, 1.
4, 4: Ex 25, 22.

†

3, 1: *Uncommon:* prophetic communications from God were almost unknown.

3, 17: *May God do thus and so to you:* the Biblical writers avoid repeating for us the specific terms of a curse as the speaker would have uttered it.

4, 4: *Enthroned upon the cherubim:* this title of the Lord seems to have originated in the sanctuary at Shiloh; it represents the divine Majesty as seated upon a throne on which he can be borne through the heaven by winged creatures somewhat as in the visions of Ez 1 and 10.

to Shiloh and brought from there the ark
of the LORD of hosts, who is enthroned
upon the cherubim. The two sons of Eli,
Hophni and Phinehas, were with the ark
of God. 5 When the ark of the LORD ar-
rived in the camp, all Israel shouted so
loudly that the earth resounded. 6 The
Philistines, hearing the noise of shout-
ing, asked, "What can this loud shouting
in the camp of the Hebrews mean?" On
learning that the ark of the LORD had
come into the camp, 7 the Philistines
were frightened. They said, "Gods have
come to their camp." They said also,
"Woe to us! This has never happened
before. 8† Woe to us! Who can deliver us
from the power of these mighty gods?
These are the gods that struck the Egyp-
tians with various plagues and with pes-
tilence. 9 Take courage and be manly,
Philistines; otherwise you will become
slaves to the Hebrews, as they were your
slaves. So fight manfully!" 10* The Phi-
listines fought and Israel was defeated;
every man fled to his own tent. It was
a disastrous defeat, in which Israel lost
thirty thousand foot soldiers. 11* The ark
of God was captured, and Eli's two sons,
Hophni and Phinehas, were among the
dead.

Death of Eli. 12* A Benjaminite fled
from the battlefield and reached Shiloh
that same day, with his clothes torn and
his head covered with dirt. 13 When he
arrived, Eli was sitting in his chair be-
side the gate, watching the road, for he
was troubled at heart about the ark of
God. The man, however, went into the
city to divulge his news, which put the
whole city in an uproar. 14 Hearing the
outcry of the men standing near him,
Eli inquired, "What does this commo-
tion mean?" 15 (Eli was ninety-eight
years old, and his eyes would not focus,
so that he could not see.) 16 The man
quickly came up to Eli and said, "It is
I who have come from the battlefield; I
fled from there today." He asked, "What
happened, my son?" 17 And the messen-
ger answered: "Israel fled from the Phi-
listines; in fact, the troops suffered
heavy losses. Your two sons, Hophni and
Phinehas, are among the dead, and the
ark of God has been captured." 18 At this
mention of the ark of God, Eli fell back-
ward from his chair into the gateway;
since he was an old man and heavy, he
died of a broken neck. He had judged
Israel for forty years.

19 His daughter-in-law, the wife of
Phinehas, was with child and at the point
of giving birth. When she heard the news
concerning the capture of the ark and
the deaths of her father-in-law and her
husband, she was seized with the pangs
of labor, and gave birth. 20* She was
about to die when the women standing
around her said to her, "Never fear! You
have given birth to a son." Yet she nei-
ther answered nor paid any attention.
21 [She named the child Ichabod, saying,
"Gone is the glory from Israel," with ref-
erence to the capture of the ark of God
and to her father-in-law and her hus-
band.] 22* She said, "Gone is the glory
from Israel," because the ark of God had
been captured.

CHAPTER 5

The Ark in the Temple of Dagon.
1* The Philistines, having captured the
ark of God, transferred it from Ebenezer
to Ashdod. 2 They then took the ark of
God and brought it into the temple of
Dagon, placing it beside Dagon. 3 When
the people of Ashdod rose early the next
morning, Dagon was lying prone on the
ground before the ark of the LORD. So
they picked Dagon up and replaced him.
4 But the next morning early, when they
arose, Dagon lay prone on the ground
before the ark of the LORD, his head and
hands broken off and lying on the
threshold, his trunk alone intact. 5 For
this reason, neither the priests of Dagon
nor any others who enter the temple of
Dagon tread on the threshold of Dagon
in Ashdod to this very day; they always
step over it.

The Ark Is Carried About. 6*† Now
the LORD dealt severely with the people
of Ashdod. He ravaged and afflicted the
city and its vicinity with hemorrhoids;
he brought upon the city a great and
deadly plague of mice that swarmed in
their ships and overran their fields. 7 On
seeing how matters stood, the men of
Ashdod decided, "The ark of the God
of Israel must not remain with us, for
he is handling us and our god Dagon se-
verely." 8 So they summoned all the
Philistine lords and inquired of them,
"What shall we do with the ark of the
God of Israel?" The men of Gath replied,
"Let them move the ark of the God of
Israel on to us." 9 So they moved the ark
of the God of Israel to Gath! But after
it had been brought there, the LORD
threw the city into utter turmoil: he af-
flicted its inhabitants, young and old,
and hemorrhoids broke out on them.
10 The ark of God was next sent to Ekron;

1 SAMUEL

*

10: Ps 78, 61.
11: 2, 34.
12: Jos 7, 6; 2 Sm 1, 2; Jer 7, 12.
20: 14, 3; Gn 35, 16ff.
22: Ps 78, 61.
5, 1-5: Jgs 16, 23-30; Is 45, 5f.20f.
6: Ps 78, 66.

†

4, 8: *These mighty gods:* the Philistines, who were polytheists, are represented as supposing the Israelites honored several gods.

5, 6: *Hemorrhoids . . . mice:* a double calamity fell upon them—a plague of mice or rats, and a severe epidemic of pestilential tumors, probably the bubonic plague.

but as it entered that city, the people
there cried out, "Why have they brought
the ark of the God of Israel here to kill
us and our kindred?" 11 Then they, too,
sent a summons to all the Philistine lords
and pleaded: "Send away the ark of the
God of Israel. Let it return to its own
place, that it may not kill us and our kin-
dred." A deadly panic had seized the
whole city, since the hand of God had
been very heavy upon it. 12 Those who
escaped death were afflicted with
hemorrhoids, and the outcry from the
city went up to the heavens.

CHAPTER 6

The Ark To Be Returned. 1 The ark of
the LORD had been in the land of the
Philistines seven months 2 when they
summoned priests and fortune-tellers to
ask, "What shall we do with the ark of
the LORD? Tell us what we should send
back with it." 3† They replied: "If you
intend to send away the ark of the God
of Israel, you must not send it alone, but
must, by all means, make amends to him
through a guilt offering. Then you will
be healed, and will learn why he contin-
ues to afflict you." 4 When asked further,
"What guilt offering should be our
amends to him?", they replied:
"Five golden hemorrhoids and five
golden mice to correspond to the num-
ber of Philistine lords, since the same
plague has struck all of you and your
lords. 5 Therefore, make images of the
hemorrhoids and of the mice that are
infesting your land and give them as a
tribute to the God of Israel. Perhaps then
he will cease to afflict you, your gods,
and your land. 6* Why should you be-
come stubborn, as the Egyptians and
Pharaoh were stubborn? Was it not after
he had dealt ruthlessly with them that
the Israelites were released and de-
parted? 7* So now set to work and make
a new cart. Then take two milch cows
that have not borne the yoke; hitch them
to the cart, but drive their calves indoors
away from them. 8 You shall next take
the ark of the LORD and place it on the
cart, putting in a box beside it the golden
articles that you are offering, as amends
for your guilt. Start it on its way, and
let it go. 9 Then watch! If it goes to Beth-
shemesh along the route to his own terri-
tory, he has brought this great calamity
upon us; if not, we will know it was not
he who struck us, but that an accident
happened to us."
The Ark in Beth-shemesh. 10 They
acted upon this advice. Taking two
milch cows, they hitched them to the
cart but shut up their calves indoors.
11 Then they placed the ark of the LORD
on the cart, along with the box contain-
ing the golden mice and the images of
the hemorrhoids. 12 The cows went
straight for the route to Beth-shemesh
and continued along this road, mooing
as they went, without turning right or
left. The Philistine lords followed them
as far as the border of Beth-shemesh.
13 The people of Beth-shemesh were har-
vesting the wheat in the valley. When
they looked up and spied the ark, they
greeted it with rejoicing. 14* The cart
came to the field of Joshua the Beth-
shemite and stopped there. At a large
stone in the field, the wood of the cart
was split up and the cows were offered
as a holocaust to the LORD. 15 The Le-
vites, meanwhile, had taken down the
ark of God and the box beside it, in
which the golden articles were, and had
placed them on the great stone. The men
of Beth-shemesh also offered other holo-
causts and sacrifices to the LORD that
day. 16 After witnessing this, the five
Philistine lords returned to Ekron the
same day.
Guilt Offering. 17 The golden hemor-
rhoids the Philistines sent back as a guilt
offering to the LORD were as follows: one
for Ashdod, one for Gaza, one for Ash-
kelon, one for Gath, and one for Ekron.
18 The golden mice, however, corre-
sponded to the number of all the cities
of the Philistines belonging to the five
lords, including fortified cities and open
villages. The large stone on which the
ark of the LORD was placed is still in the
field of Joshua the Beth-shemite at the
present time.
Penalty for Irreverence. 19 The de-
scendants of Jeconiah did not join in the
celebration with the inhabitants of Beth-
shemesh when they greeted the ark of
the LORD, and seventy of them were
struck down. The people went into
mourning at this great calamity with
which the LORD had afflicted them.
20 The men of Beth-shemesh asked,
"Who can stand in the presence of this
Holy One? To whom shall he go from
us?" 21 They then sent messengers to the
inhabitants of Kiriath-jearim, saying,
"The Philistines have returned the ark
of the LORD; come down and get it."

CHAPTER 7

1 So the inhabitants of Kiriath-jearim
came for the ark of the LORD and

*

6, 6: Ex 7, 14; 8, 15; 9, 34.
7: Nm 19, 2; Dt 21, 3; 2 Sm 6, 3.
14: 2 Sm 24, 21ff.

†

6, 3: *A guilt offering:* a propitiatory offering customary after unwitting transgression of the ordinances of God regarding holy things or property rights; cf Lv 6, 1ff.

brought it into the house of Abinadab
on the hill, appointing his son Eleazar
as guardian of the ark of the LORD.

Religious Reform. 2 From the day the
ark came to rest in Kiriath-jearim a long
time—twenty years—elapsed, and the
whole Israelite population turned to the
LORD. 3* Samuel said to them: "If you
wish with your whole heart to return to
the LORD, put away your foreign gods
and your Ashtaroth, devote yourselves
to the LORD, and worship him alone.
Then he will deliver you from the power
of the Philistines." 4 So the Israelites put
away their Baals and Ashtaroth, and
worshiped the LORD alone. 5* Samuel
then gave orders, "Gather all Israel to
Mizpah, that I may pray to the LORD for
you." 6*† When they were gathered at
Mizpah, they drew water and poured it
out on the ground before the LORD, and
they fasted that day, confessing, "We
have sinned against the LORD." It was
at Mizpah that Samuel began to judge
the Israelites.

Rout of the Philistines. 7 When the
Philistines heard that the Israelites had
gathered at Mizpah, their lords went up
against Israel. Hearing this, the Israel-
ites became afraid of the Philistines
8* and said to Samuel, "Implore the
LORD our God unceasingly for us, to save
us from the clutches of the Philistines."
9* Samuel therefore took an unweaned
lamb and offered it entire as a holocaust
to the LORD. He implored the LORD for
Israel, and the LORD heard him. 10 While
Samuel was offering the holocaust, the
Philistines advanced to join battle with
Israel. That day, however, the LORD
thundered loudly against the Philistines,
and threw them into such confusion that
they were defeated by Israel. 11 There-
upon the Israelites sallied forth from
Mizpah and pursued the Philistines,
harrying them down beyond Beth-car.
12† Samuel then took a stone and placed
it between Mizpah and Jeshanah; he
named it Ebenezer, explaining, "To this
point the LORD helped us." 13* Thus were
the Philistines subdued, never again to
enter the territory of Israel, for the LORD
was severe with them as long as Samuel
lived. 14 The cities from Ekron to Gath
which the Philistines had taken from Is-
rael were restored to them. Israel also
freed the territory of these cities from
the dominion of the Philistines. More-
over there was peace between Israel and
the Amorites.

15 Samuel judged Israel as long as he
lived. 16 He made a yearly journey, pass-
ing through Bethel, Gilgal and Mizpah
and judging Israel at each of these sanc-
tuaries. 17* Then he used to return to Ra-
mah, for that was his home. There, too,
he judged Israel and built an altar to the
LORD.

II: ESTABLISHMENT OF THE MONARCHY IN ISRAEL

CHAPTER 8

Request for a King. 1† In his old age
Samuel appointed his sons judges over
Israel. 2 His first-born was named Joel,
his second son, Abijah; they judged at
Beer-sheba. 3* His sons did not follow
his example but sought illicit gain and
accepted bribes, perverting justice.
4 Therefore all the elders of Israel came
in a body to Samuel at Ramah 5* and
said to him, "Now that you are old, and
your sons do not follow your example,
appoint a king over us, as other nations
have, to judge us."

God Grants the Request. 6 Samuel
was displeased when they asked for a
king to judge them. He prayed to the
LORD, however, 7* who said in answer:
"Grant the people's every request. It is
not you they reject, they are rejecting
me as their king. 8 As they have treated
me constantly from the day I brought
them up from Egypt to this day, desert-
ing me and worshiping strange gods, so
do they treat you too. 9 Now grant their
request; but at the same time, warn them
solemnly and inform them of the rights
of the king who will rule them."

The Rights of a King. 10 Samuel deliv-
ered the message of the LORD in full to
those who were asking him for a king.
11* He told them: "The rights of the king
who will rule you will be as follows: He
will take your sons and assign them to
his chariots and horses, and they will
run before his chariot. 12* He will also
appoint from among them his com-
manders of groups of a thousand and
of a hundred soldiers. He will set them

*

7, 3: 12, 10.20.24; Jos 24,23; Jgs 6, 6-10; 10, 10-16.
5: 10, 17; Jgs 20, 1.
6: Jgs 20, 26; Ps 22, 14; Lam 2, 19.
8: Ex 17, 9-13.
9f: 2 Sm 22, 14f; Sir 46, 16ff.
13: Jgs 3, 30; 8, 28; 11, 33.
17: 9, 12; 14, 35.
8, 3: Ex 23, 8; Dt 16, 19; Prv 17, 23.
5f: Dt 17, 14f; Hos 13, 10; Acts 13, 21.
7f: 12, 1.12f; Jgs 8, 22f; 10, 13; 1 Kgs 9, 9.
11: 10, 25; Dt 17, 14-20; 1 Kgs 12.
12: 2 Sm 15, 1; 1 Kgs 1, 5.

†

7, 6: *Poured it out on the ground:* for the symbolism, cf 2 Sm 14, 14.

7, 12: *Ebenezer:* or *eben ha-ezer,* means "stone of help."

8, 1: From this chapter on, the First Book of Samuel gives us two and sometimes three viewpoints on most of the events with which it is concerned, such as the appointment of Saul as king, the reasons for his downfall, his relationship with David, even the circumstances of Saul's death (1 Sm 31; 2 Sm 1). The choice of Saul as king is seen, in ch 8, followed by 10, 17-24 and ch 12, as motivated by the people's defection from the proper service of God; this later editorial approach incorporates not only narratives with which it is consistent, but also early traditions (9, 1-10.16; ch 11) which portray the events and their motivation quite differently.

to do his plowing and his harvesting, and
to make his implements of war and the
equipment of his chariots. 13 He will use
your daughters as ointment-makers, as
cooks, and as bakers. 14* He will take the
best of your fields, vineyards, and olive
groves, and give them to his officials.
15 He will tithe your crops and your vine-
yards, and give the revenue to his eu-
nuchs and his slaves. 16 He will take your
male and female servants, as well as
your best oxen and your asses, and use
them to do his work. 17* He will tithe
your flocks and you yourselves will be-
come his slaves. 18 When this takes
place, you will complain against the king
whom you have chosen, but on that day
the LORD will not answer you."

Persistent Demand. 19* The people,
however, refused to listen to Samuel's
warning and said, "Not so! There must
be a king over us. 20 We too must be like
other nations, with a king to rule us and
to lead us in warfare and fight our bat-
tles." 21 When Samuel had listened to all
the people had to say, he repeated it to
the LORD, 22 who then said to him,
"Grant their request and appoint a king
to rule them." Samuel thereupon said to
the men of Israel, "Each of you go to
his own city."

CHAPTER 9

1* There was a stalwart man from
Benjamin named Kish, who was the son
of Abiel, son of Zeror, son of Becorath,
son of Aphiah, a Benjaminite. 2* He had
a son named Saul, who was a handsome
young man. There was no other Israelite
handsomer than Saul; he stood head and
shoulders above the people.

The Lost Asses. 3 Now the asses of
Saul's father, Kish, had wandered off.
Kish said to his son Saul, "Take one of
the servants with you and go out and
hunt for the asses." 4 Accordingly they
went through the hill country of
Ephraim, and through the land of Sha-
lishah. Not finding them there, they con-
tinued through the land of Shaalim
without success. They also went through
the land of Benjamin, but they failed to
find the animals. 5 When they came to
the land of Zuph, Saul said to the servant
who was with him, "Come, let us turn
back, lest my father forget about the
asses and become anxious about us."
6 The servant replied, "Listen! There is
a man of God in this city, a man held
in high esteem; all that he says is sure
to come true. Let us go there now! Per-
haps he can tell us how to accomplish
our errand." 7* But Saul said to his ser-
vant, "If we go, what can we offer the
man? There is no bread in our bags, and
we have no present to give the man of
God. What have we?" 8† Again the ser-
vant answered Saul, "I have a quarter
of a silver shekel. If I give that to the
man of God, he will tell us our way."
10 Saul then said to his servant, "Well
said! Come on, let us go!" And they
went to the city where the man of God
lived.

Quest for Samuel's Aid. 11* As they
were going up the ascent to the city, they
met some girls coming out to draw water
and inquired of them, "Is the seer in
town?" 9*† (In former times in Israel,
anyone who went to consult God used
to say, "Come, let us go to the seer." For
he who is now called prophet was for-
merly called seer.) 12*† The girls an-
swered, "Yes, there—straight ahead.
Hurry now; just today he came to the
city, because the people have a sacrifice
today on the high place. 13 When you en-
ter the city, you may reach him before
he goes up to the high place to eat. The
people will not eat until he arrives; only
after he blesses the sacrifice will the in-
vited guests eat. Go up immediately, for
you should find him right now."

Samuel's Revelation about Saul. 14 So
they went up to the city. As they entered
it, Samuel was coming toward them on
his way to the high place. 15* The day
before Saul's arrival, the LORD had
given Samuel the revelation: 16* "At this
time tomorrow I will send you a man
from the land of Benjamin whom you
are to anoint as commander of my peo-
ple Israel. He shall save my people from
the clutches of the Philistines, for I have
witnessed their misery and accepted
their cry for help." 17 When Samuel
caught sight of Saul, the LORD assured
him, "This is the man of whom I told
you; he is to govern my people." 18 Saul
met Samuel in the gateway and said,
"Please tell me where the seer lives."
19 Samuel answered Saul: "I am the seer.
Go up ahead of me to the high place and
eat with me today. In the morning,
before dismissing you, I will tell you
whatever you wish. 20 As for the asses
you lost three days ago, do not worry
about them, for they have been found.
Whom does Israel desire ardently

---

*

14: 22, 7; 1 Kgs 21, 1-24; Ez 46, 18.
17: 1 Kgs 12, 4.
19: 10, 19.
9, 1: 14, 51; 1 Chr 8, 33.
2: 10, 23.
7f: Nm 22, 7; 1 Kgs 14, 3; 2 Kgs 4, 42; 5, 15; 8, 8f.
11: Gn 24, 11ff; Ex 2, 16.
9: Sir 46, 15.
12: 7, 17; 16, 2.5; 20, 6.29; Dt 12, 13; 1 Kgs 3, 2.4.
15: Acts 13, 21.
16: 10, 1.

---

†

9, 8: *A quarter of a silver shekel:* about a tenth of an ounce of silver.

9, 9: This verse is a later explanation of the term *seer,* first used in the text in 9, 11.

9, 12: *On the high place:* the local sanctuary on the top of a hill, where the sacrifice was offered and the sacrificial meal eaten.

if not you and your father's family?"
21* Saul replied: "Am I not a Benjamin-
ite, of one of the smallest tribes of Israel,
and is not my clan the least among the
clans of the tribe of Benjamin? Why say
such things to me?"
22 Samuel then took Saul and his ser-
vant and brought them to the room,
where he placed them at the head of the
guests, of whom there were about thirty.
23 He said to the cook, "Bring the portion
I gave you and told you to put aside."
24† So the cook took up the leg and what
went with it, and placed it before Saul.
Samuel said: "This is a reserved portion
that has been set before you. Eat, for it
was kept for you until your arrival; I ex-
plained that I was inviting some guests."
Thus Saul dined with Samuel that day.
25 When they came down from the high
place into the city, a mattress was
spread for Saul on the roof, 26 and he
slept there.
Saul's Anointing. At daybreak Sam-
uel called to Saul on the roof, "Get up,
and I will start you on your journey."
Saul rose, and he and Samuel went out-
side the city together. 27 As they were
approaching the edge of the town, Sam-
uel said to Saul, "Tell the servant to go
on ahead of us, but stay here yourself
for the moment, that I may give you a
message from God."

CHAPTER 10

1* Then, from a flask he had with him,
Samuel poured oil on Saul's head; he
also kissed him, saying: "The LORD
anoints you commander over his heri-
tage. You are to govern the LORD's peo-
ple Israel, and to save them from the
grasp of their enemies round about.
"This will be the sign for you that the
LORD has anointed you commander over
his heritage: 2*† When you leave me to-
day, you will meet two men near Ra-
chel's tomb at Zelzah in the territory of
Benjamin, who will say to you, 'The
asses you went to look for have been
found. Your father is no longer worried
about the asses, but is anxious about you
and says, What shall I do about my son?'
3 Farther on, when you arrive at the ter-
ebinth of Tabor, you will be met by three
men going up to God at Bethel; one will
be bringing three kids, another three
loaves of bread, and the third a skin of
wine. 4 They will greet you and offer you
two wave offerings of bread, which you
will take from them. 5*† After that you
will come to Gibeath-elohim, where
there is a garrison of the Philistines. As
you enter that city, you will meet a band
of prophets, in a prophetic state, coming
down from the high place preceded by
lyres, tambourines, flutes and harps.
6* The spirit of the LORD will rush upon
you, and you will join them in their
prophetic state and will be changed into
another man. 7 When you see these signs
fulfilled, do whatever you judge feasible,
because God is with you. 8*† Now go
down ahead of me to Gilgal, for I shall
come down to you, to offer holocausts
and to sacrifice peace offerings. Wait
seven days until I come to you; I shall
then tell you what you must do."
Fulfillment of the Signs. 9 As Saul
turned to leave Samuel, God gave him
another heart. That very day all these
signs came to pass. . . . 10*† When they
were going from there to Gibeah, a band
of prophets met him, and the spirit of
God rushed upon him, so that he joined
them in their prophetic state. 11* When
all who had known him previously saw
him in a prophetic state among the
prophets, they said to one another,
"What has happened to the son of Kish?
Is Saul also among the prophets?" 12 And
someone from that district added, "And
who is their father?" Thus the proverb
arose, "Is Saul also among the proph-
ets?" 13 When he came out of the pro-
phetic state, he went home.
Silence about the Kingship. 14 Saul's
uncle inquired of him and his servant,
"Where have you been?" Saul replied,
"To look for the asses. When we could
not find them, we went to Samuel."
15 Then Saul's uncle said, "Tell me, then,
what Samuel said to you." 16 Saul said
to his uncle, "He assured us that the
asses had been found." But he men-

*

21: 15, 17.
10, 1: 9, 16f; 24, 7; Jgs 9, 9; 1 Kgs 1, 39; Acts 13, 21.
2: Jer 31, 15; Mk 14, 13.
5f: 13, 3; 16, 13; 19, 20f.
6: 11, 6; 16, 13; Jgs 14, 6.19; 15, 14; 2 Kgs 3, 15.
8: 13, 8; Lv 3, 1.
10: 19, 20-24; Nm 11. 25.
11: 19, 24.

†

9, 24: *And what went with it:* a slight change would give "and the fatty tail" as perhaps the original reading. Sheep in the Near East are exceptionally fat-tailed, and such a portion would be thought a special delicacy by the Hebrews. However, the ritual legislation as we know it (Lv 3, 9) would require that the fat tail be burned on the altar. If this general rule was later than the time of Samuel, the present text may have been retouched so as not to seem to contravene it. A Qumran text has "the festive (leg)" here.

10, 2: Here, as in Jer 31, 15, Rachel's tomb is placed north of Jerusalem. Later tradition understood Gn 35, 19f in the sense given by Mt 2, 16ff, and placed the tomb at Bethlehem, farther south.

10, 5: *A garrison of the Philistines:* the Hebrew word for "garrison" has been explained alternatively to mean a pillar erected to mark the Philistine occupation, or an inspector or officer for the collection of taxes. *In a prophetic state:* in an ecstatic condition due to strong feelings of religious enthusiasm induced by a communal observance, possibly accompanied by music and dancing.

10, 8: By inserting this verse, with its *seven days,* an editor has prepared for one narrative of the rejection of Saul (13, 8-15) in the very context of Saul's anointing.

10, 10: The story has here been abridged by omitting the fulfillment of the first two signs given by Samuel (10, 2ff).

tioned nothing to him of what Samuel
had said about the kingship.
Saul Chosen King by Lot. 17* Samuel
called the people together to the LORD
at Mizpah 18* and addressed the Israel-
ites: "Thus says the LORD, the God of
Israel, 'It was I who brought Israel up
from Egypt and delivered you from the
power of the Egyptians and from the
power of all the kingdoms that op-
pressed you.' 19* But today you have re-
jected your God, who delivers you from
all your evils and calamities, by saying
to him, 'Not so, but you must appoint a
king over us.' Now, therefore, take your
stand before the LORD according to
tribes and families." 20 So Samuel had
all the tribes of Israel come forward, and
the tribe of Benjamin was chosen.
21 Next he had the tribe of Benjamin
come forward in clans, and the clan of
Matri was chosen, and finally Saul, son
of Kish, was chosen. But they looked for
him in vain. 22* Again they consulted the
LORD, "Has he come here?" The LORD
answered, "He is hiding among the bag-
gage." 23* They ran to bring him from
there; and when he stood among the
people, he was head and shoulders
above all the crowd. 24* Samuel said to
all the people, "Do you see the man
whom the LORD has chosen? There is
none like him among all the people!"
Then all the people shouted, "Long live
the king!"
25*† Samuel next explained to the peo-
ple the law of royalty and wrote it in a
book, which he placed in the presence
of the LORD. This done, Samuel dis-
missed the people, each to his own place.
26 Saul also went home to Gibeah, ac-
companied by warriors whose hearts the
LORD had touched. 27* But certain
worthless men said, "How can this fel-
low save us?" They despised him and
brought him no present.

CHAPTER 11

Defeat of the Ammonites. 1*† About a
month later, Nahash the Ammonite
went up and laid siege to Jabesh-gilead.
All the men of Jabesh begged Nahash,
"Make a treaty with us, and we will be
your subjects." 2 But Nahash the Am-
monite replied, "This is my condition for
a treaty with you: I must gouge out every
man's right eye, that I may thus bring
ignominy on all Israel." 3 The elders of
Jabesh said to him: "Give us seven days
to send messengers throughout the ter-
ritory of Israel. If no one rescues us, we
will surrender to you." 4 When the mes-
sengers arrived at Gibeah of Saul, they
related the news to the people, all of
whom wept aloud.
5 Just then Saul came in from the field,
behind his oxen. "Why are the people
weeping?" he asked. The message of the
inhabitants of Jabesh was repeated to
him. 6* As he listened to this report, the
spirit of God rushed upon him and he
became very angry. 7* Taking a yoke of
oxen, he cut them into pieces, which he
sent throughout the territory of Israel
by couriers with the message, "If any-
one does not come out to follow Saul
[and Samuel], the same as this will be
done to his oxen!" In dread of the LORD,
the people turned out to a man. 8 When
he reviewed them in Bezek, there were
three hundred thousand Israelites and
seventy thousand Judahites.
9 To the messengers who had come he
said, "Tell the inhabitants of Jabesh-
gilead that tomorrow, while the sun is
hot, they will be rescued." The messen-
gers came and reported this to the in-
habitants of Jabesh, who were jubilant,
10 and said to Nahash, "Tomorrow we
will surrender to you, and you may do
whatever you please with us." 11 On the
appointed day, Saul arranged his troops
in three companies and invaded the
camp during the dawn watch. They
slaughtered Ammonites until the heat of
the day; by then the survivors were so
scattered that no two were left together.
Saul Accepted as King. 12*† The peo-
ple then said to Samuel: "Who ques-
tioned whether Saul should rule over us?
Hand over the men and we will put them
to death." 13* But Saul broke in to say,
"No man is to be put to death this day,
for today the LORD has saved Israel."
14 Samuel said to the people, "Come, let
us go to Gilgal to inaugurate the king-
dom there." 15 So all the people went to
Gilgal, where, in the presence of the
LORD, they made Saul king. They also
sacrificed peace offerings there before
the LORD, and Saul and all the Israelites
celebrated the occasion with great
joy.

---

*

17: 7, 5.
18: Ex 20, 2; Lv 11, 45; 25, 38; Nm 15, 41; Dt 5, 6; Jgs 6, 8f.
19: 8, 19.
22: 30, 24.
23: 9, 2; 16, 7.
24: 2 Sm 16, 16; 1 Kgs 1, 25; 2 Kgs 11, 12.
25: 8, 11; Dt 17, 14-20.
27: 11, 12.
11, 1: 12, 12; 31, 11.
6: 16, 13; Jgs 14, 6.19.
7: 1 Kgs 11, 30; 2 Kgs 13, 18.
12: 10, 27.
13: 2 Sm 19, 23.

---

†

10, 25: *The law of royalty:* the charter defining the rights of the king.

11, 1: *About a month later:* there is ancient evidence for a longer introduction to this campaign. The time indication here may refer to its earlier stages rather than to the events of ch 10.

11, 12-14: With these verses, an editor has harmonized the account of the acknowledgment of Saul as king at Mizpah (10, 17-24) with the public acclamation at Gilgal (11, 15) after the defeat of the Ammonites (11, 1-11). The Greek text of 11, 15 reads "and Samuel anointed Saul as king," instead of *they made Saul king.*

CHAPTER 12

Samuel's Integrity. 1* Samuel addressed all Israel: "I have granted your request in every respect," he said. "I have set a king over you 2 and now the king is your leader. As for me, I am old and gray, and have sons among you. I have lived with you from my youth to the present day. 3* Here I stand! Answer me in the presence of the LORD and of his anointed. Whose ox have I taken? Whose ass have I taken? Whom have I cheated? Whom have I oppressed? From whom have I accepted a bribe and overlooked his guilt? I will make restitution to you." 4 They replied, "You have neither cheated us, nor oppressed us, nor accepted anything from anyone." 5 So he said to them, "The LORD is witness against you this day, and his anointed as well, that you have found nothing in my possession." "He is witness," they agreed.

Samuel Upbraids the People. 6* Continuing, Samuel said to the people: "The LORD is witness, who appointed Moses and Aaron, and who brought your fathers up from the land of Egypt. 7 Now, therefore, take your stand, and I shall arraign you before the LORD, and shall recount for you all the acts of mercy the LORD has done for you and your fathers. 8* When Jacob and his sons went to Egypt and the Egyptians oppressed them, your fathers appealed to the LORD, who sent Moses and Aaron to bring them out of Egypt, and he gave them this place to live in. 9* But they forgot the LORD their God; and he allowed them to fall into the clutches of Sisera, the captain of the army of Jabin, king of Hazor, into the grasp of the Philistines, and into the grip of the king of Moab, who made war against them. 10* Each time they appealed to the LORD and said, 'We have sinned in forsaking the LORD and worshiping Baals and Ashtaroth; but deliver us now from the power of our enemies, and we will worship you.' 11* Accordingly, the LORD sent Jerubbaal, Barak, Jephthah, and Samuel; he delivered you from the power of your enemies on every side, so that you were able to live in security. 12* Yet, when you saw Nahash, king of the Ammonites, advancing against you, you said to me, 'Not so, but a king must rule us,' even though the LORD your God is your king.

Warnings for People and King. 13* "Now you have the king you want, a king the LORD has given you. 14 If you fear the LORD and worship him, if you are obedient to him and do not rebel against the LORD's command, if both you and the king who rules you follow the LORD your God—well and good. 15 But if you do not obey the LORD and if you rebel against his command, the LORD will deal severely with you and your king, and destroy you. 16 Now then, stand ready to witness the great marvel the LORD is about to accomplish before your eyes. 17* Are we not in the harvest time for wheat? Yet I shall call to the LORD, and he will send thunder and rain. Thus you will see and understand how greatly the LORD is displeased that you have asked for a king." 18 Samuel then called to the LORD, and the LORD sent thunder and rain that day.

Assistance Promised. As a result, all the people dreaded the LORD and Samuel. 19 They said to Samuel, "Pray to the LORD your God for us, your servants, that we may not die for having added to all our other sins the evil of asking for a king." 20 "Do not fear," Samuel answered them. "It is true you have committed all this evil; still, you must not turn from the LORD, but must worship him with your whole heart. 21* Do not turn to meaningless idols which can neither profit nor save; they are nothing. 22* For the sake of his own great name the LORD will not abandon his people, since the LORD himself chose to make you his people. 23* As for me, far be it from me to sin against the LORD by ceasing to pray for you and to teach you the good and right way. 24 But you must fear the LORD and worship him faithfully with your whole heart; keep in mind the great things he has done among you. 25 If instead you continue to do evil, both you and your king shall perish."

III: SAUL AND DAVID

CHAPTER 13

1† [Saul was . . . years old when he became king and he reigned . . . (two) years over Israel.]

Saul Offers Sacrifice. 2 Saul chose three thousand men of Israel, of whom two thousand remained with him in Michmash and in the hill country of Bethel, and one thousand were with Jonathan in Gibeah of Benjamin. He sent the rest of the people back to their

*

12, 1: 8, 7.9.22.
3: Ex 20, 17; 23, 8; Nm 16, 15; Dt 16, 19; Sir 46, 19.
6: Mi 6, 4.
8: Gn 46, 5; Ex 1, 11; 2, 23ff.
9: Jgs 3, 12ff; 4, 2f; 10, 7; 13, 1.
10: 7, 3f.
11: Jgs 6, 14.32; 11, 1.
12: 8, 6f.19;11, 1f; Jgs 8, 23.
13: 8, 7.
17: Ex 9, 23.28ff; 1 Kgs 18, 1.
21: Dt 32, 37ff.
22: Jer 14, 21; Ez 20, 9; Dn 3, 34.
23: Ex 32, 11.

†

13, 1: A formula like that of 2 Sm 5, 4 was introduced here at some time; but the age of Saul when he became king remains a blank, and the *two years* assigned for his reign in the received text cannot be correct. Tradition (Acts 13, 21) offers the round number, "forty years."

tents. 3*† Now Jonathan overcame the Philistine garrison which was in Gibeah, and the Philistines got word of it. Then Saul sounded the horn throughout the land, with a proclamation, "Let the Hebrews hear!" 4 Thus all Israel learned that Saul had overcome the garrison of the Philistines and that Israel had brought disgrace upon the Philistines; and the soldiers were called up to Saul in Gilgal.

5 The Philistines also assembled for battle, with three thousand chariots, six thousand horsemen, and foot soldiers as numerous as the sands of the seashore. Moving up against Israel, they encamped in Michmash, east of Beth-aven. 6* Some Israelites, aware of the danger and of the difficult situation, hid themselves in caves, in thickets, among rocks, in caverns, and in cisterns, 7† and other Hebrews passed over the Jordan into the land of Gad and Gilead. Saul, however, held out at Gilgal, although all his followers were seized with fear. 8* He waited seven days—the time Samuel had determined. When Samuel did not arrive at Gilgal, the men began to slip away from Saul. 9 He then said, "Bring me the holocaust and peace offerings," and he offered up the holocaust.

King Saul Reproved. 10 He had just finished this offering when Samuel arrived. Saul went out to greet him, 11 and Samuel asked him, "What have you done?" Saul replied: "When I saw that the men were slipping away from me, since you had not come by the specified time, and with the Philistines assembled at Michmash, 12 I said to myself, 'Now the Philistines will come down against me at Gilgal, and I have not yet sought the LORD's blessing.' So in my anxiety I offered up the holocaust." 13 Samuel's response was: "You have been foolish! Had you kept the command the LORD your God gave you, the LORD would now establish your kingship in Israel as lasting; 14* but as things are, your kingdom shall not endure. The LORD has sought out a man after his own heart and has appointed him commander of his people, because you broke the LORD's command."

Philistine Invasion. 15* Then Samuel set out from Gilgal and went his own way; but the rest of the people went up after Saul to meet the soldiers, going from Gilgal to Gibeah of Benjamin. Saul then numbered the soldiers he had with him, who were about six hundred. 16 Saul, his son Jonathan, and the soldiers they had with them were now occupying Geba of Benjamin, and the Philistines were encamped at Michmash. 17* Meanwhile, raiders left the camp of the Philistines in three bands. One band took the Ophrah road toward the district of Shual; 18 another turned in the direction of Beth-horon; and the third took the road for Geba that overlooks the Valley of the Hyenas toward the desert.

Disarmament of Israel. 19* Not a single smith was to be found in the whole land of Israel, for the Philistines had said, "Otherwise the Hebrews will make swords or spears." 20 All Israel, therefore, had to go down to the Philistines to sharpen their plowshares, mattocks, axes, and sickles. 21 The price for the plowshares and mattocks was two-thirds of a shekel, and a third of a shekel for sharpening the axes and for setting the ox-goads. 22 And so on the day of battle neither sword nor spear could be found in the possession of any of the soldiers with Saul or Jonathan. Only Saul and his son Jonathan had them.

Jonathan's Exploit. 23* An outpost of the Philistines had pushed forward to the pass of Michmash.

CHAPTER 14

1*† One day Jonathan, son of Saul, said to his armor-bearer, "Come let us go over to the Philistine outpost on the other side." But he did not inform his father. 2 (Saul's command post was under the pomegranate tree near the threshing floor on the outskirts of Geba; those with him numbered about six hundred men. 3* Ahijah, son of Ahitub, brother of Ichabod, who was the son of Phinehas, son of Eli, the priest of the LORD at Shiloh, was wearing the ephod.) Nor did the soldiers know that Jonathan had gone. 4 Flanking the ravine through which Jonathan intended to get over to the Philistine outpost there was a rocky crag on each side, one called Bozez, the other Seneh. 5 One crag was to the north, toward Michmash, the other to the south, toward Geba. 6* Jonathan said to his armor-bearer: "Come let us go over to that outpost of the uncircumcised. Perhaps the LORD will help us, because it is no more difficult for the LORD to grant victory through a few than through many."

*

13, 3: 14, 1-15; Jgs 3, 27; 6, 34; 2 Sm 20, 1f.
6: 14, 22.
8: 10, 8.
14: 25, 30; 2 Sm 7, 15f; Ps78, 70; Acts 13, 22.
15: 14, 2.
17: 14, 15.
19: Jgs 5, 8.
23: 14, 15.
14, 1: 13, 3.
3: 2, 28; 4, 21; 14, 18; 23, 9; 30, 7.
6: 17, 26.36.47; Sir 39, 18; 1 Mc 3, 19.

†

13, 3-4: *The Philistine garrison:* see note on 10, 5. *Let the Hebrews hear:* a different reading of these verses, based on the Greek, would yield: "And the Philistines heard that the Hebrews (*or:* the slaves) had revolted. Saul in the meantime sounded the trumpet throughout all the land (v 4), and all Israel heard that Saul. . . ."

13, 7-15: These verses, like 10, 8, anticipate the rejection of Saul; a different occasion and motivation for this are given in ch 15, resumed in 28, 17f.

7 His armor-bearer replied, "Do what-
ever you are inclined to do; I will match
your resolve." 8 Jonathan continued:
"We shall go over to those men and show
ourselves to them. 9 If they say to us,
'Stay there until we can come to you,'
we shall stop where we are; we shall not
go up to them. 10 But if they say, 'Come
up to us,' we shall go up, because the
LORD has delivered them into our grasp.
That will be our sign." 11 Accordingly,
the two of them appeared before the out-
post of the Philistines, who said, "Look,
some Hebrews are coming out of the
holes where they have been hiding."
12 The men of the outpost called to Jona-
than and his armor-bearer. "Come up
here," they said, "and we will teach you
a lesson." So Jonathan said to his ar-
mor-bearer, "Climb up after me, for the
LORD has delivered them into the grasp
of Israel." 13 Jonathan clambered up
with his armor-bearer behind him; as
the Philistines turned to flee him, he cut
them down, and his armor-bearer fol-
lowed him and finished them off. 14 In
this first exploit Jonathan and his ar-
mor-bearer slew about twenty men
within half a furlong. 15 Then panic
spread to the army and to the country-
side, and all the soldiers, including the
outpost and the raiding parties, were
terror-stricken. The earth also shook, so
that the panic was beyond human en-
durance.

Rout of the Philistines. 16 The lookouts
of Saul in Geba of Benjamin saw that
the enemy camp had scattered and were
running about in all directions. 17 Saul
said to those around him, "Count the
troops and find out if any of us are miss-
ing." When they had investigated, they
found Jonathan and his armor-bearer
missing. 18† Saul then said to Ahijah,
"Bring the ephod here." (Ahijah was
wearing the ephod in front of the Israel-
ites at that time.) 19 While Saul was
speaking to the priest, the tumult in the
Philistine camp kept increasing. So he
said to the priest, "Withdraw your
hand." 20* And Saul and all his men
shouted and rushed into the fight, where
the Philistines, wholly confused, were
thrusting swords at one another. 21* In
addition, the Hebrews who had previ-
ously sided with the Philistines and had
gone up with them to the camp, turned
to join the Israelites under Saul and Jon-
athan. 22* Likewise, all the Israelites
who were hiding in the hill country of
Ephraim, on hearing that the Philis-
tines were fleeing, pursued them in the
rout. 23† Thus the LORD saved Israel that
day.

Saul's Oath. The battle continued past
Beth-horon; 24 the whole people, about
ten thousand combatants, were with
Saul, and there was scattered fighting
in every town in the hill country of
Ephraim. And Saul swore a very rash
oath that day, putting the people under
this ban: "Cursed be the man who takes
food before evening, before I am able
to avenge myself on my enemies." So
none of the people tasted food. 25 Indeed,
there was a honeycomb lying on the
ground, 26 and when the soldiers came
to the comb the swarm had left it; yet
no one would raise a hand to his mouth
from it, because the people feared the
oath.

Violation of the Oath. 27 Jonathan,
who had not heard that his father had
put the people under oath, thrust out the
end of the staff he was holding and
dipped in into the honey. Then he raised
it to his mouth and his eyes lit up. 28 At
this one of the soldiers spoke up: "Your
father put the people under a strict oath,
saying, 'Cursed be the man who takes
food this day!' As a result the people are
weak." 29 Jonathan replied: "My father
brings trouble to the land. Look how
bright my eyes are from this small taste
of honey I have had. 30 What is more,
if the people had eaten freely today of
their enemy's booty when they came
across it, would not the slaughter of the
Philistines by now have been the greater
for it?"

Use of Flesh with Blood Forbidden.
31 After the Philistines were routed that
day from Michmash to Aijalon, the peo-
ple were completely exhausted. 32* So
they pounced upon the spoil and took
sheep, oxen and calves, slaughtering
them on the ground and eating the flesh
with blood. 33 Informed that the people
were sinning against the LORD by eating
the flesh with blood, Saul said: "You
have broken faith. Roll a large stone
here for me." 34 He continued: "Mingle
with the people and tell each of them
to bring his ox or his sheep to me.
Slaughter it here and then eat, but you
must not sin against the LORD by eating
the flesh with blood." So everyone
brought to the LORD whatever ox he had
seized, and they slaughtered them there;
35* and Saul built an altar to the LORD—
this was the first time he built an altar
to the LORD.

Jonathan in Danger of Death. 36 Then
Saul said, "Let us go down in pursuit of
the Philistines by night, to plunder

*

20: Jgs 7, 22.
21: 29, 4.
22: 13, 6.
32: 15, 19.21; Lv 3, 17; 7, 26f; 17, 10-14; Acts 15, 20.29.
35: 7, 17; Jgs 6, 24.

†

14, 18: *Ephod:* to be used in consulting God; see note on v 41, and that on 2, 28 above.

14, 23: *Past Beth-horon:* this is a textual correction influenced by 13, 18; the received Hebrew text refers to Bethel (Beth-aven), but the effect of the victory would seem to have been that the main ridge of mountains in the territories of Benjamin and Ephraim was cleared of Philistines.

among them until daybreak and to kill
them all off." They replied, "Do what
you think best." But the priest said, "Let
us consult God." 37* So Saul inquired of
God: "Shall I go down in pursuit of the
Philistines? Will you deliver them into
the power of Israel?" But he received no
answer on this occasion. 38 Saul then
said, "Come here, all officers of the
army. We must investigate and find out
how this sin was committed today. 39 As
the LORD lives who has given victory to
Israel, even if my son Jonathan has
committed it, he shall surely die!" But
none of the people answered him. 40* So
he said to all Israel, "Stand on one side,
and I and my son Jonathan will stand
on the other." The people responded,
"Do what you think best." 41*† And Saul
said to the LORD, the God of Israel: "Why
did you not answer your servant this
time? If the blame for this resides in me
or my son Jonathan, LORD, God of Is-
rael, respond with Urim; but if this guilt
is in your people Israel, respond with
Thummim." Jonathan and Saul were
designated, and the people went free.
42 Saul then said, "Cast lots between me
and my son Jonathan." And Jonathan
was designated. 43 Saul said to Jonathan,
"Tell me what you have done." Jona-
than replied, "I only tasted a little honey
from the end of the staff I was holding.
Am I to die for this?" 44* Saul said, "May
God do thus and so to me if you do not
indeed die, Jonathan!"

Rescue of Jonathan. 45*† But the
army said to Saul: "Is Jonathan to die,
though it was he who brought Israel this
great victory? This must not be! As the
LORD lives, not a single hair of his head
shall fall to the ground, for God was with
him in what he did today!" Thus the sol-
diers were able to rescue Jonathan from
death. 46 After that Saul gave up the pur-
suit of the Philistines, who returned to
their own territory.

Wars and Victories. 47* After taking
over the kingship of Israel, Saul waged
war on all their surrounding enemies—
Moab, the Ammonites, Aram, Beth-re-
hob, the king of Zobah, and the Philis-
tines. Wherever he turned, he was
successful 48 and fought bravely. He de-
feated Amalek and delivered Israel
from the hands of those who were plun-
dering them.

Saul's Family. 49*† The sons of Saul
were Jonathan, Ishvi, and Malchishua;
his two daughters were named, the
elder, Merob, and the younger, Michal.
50 Saul's wife, who was named Ahinoam,
was the daughter of Ahimaaz. The name
of his general was Abner, son of Saul's
uncle, Ner; 51* Kish, Saul's father,
and Ner, Abner's father, were sons of
Abiel.

52 An unremitting war was waged
against the Philistines during Saul's life-
time. When Saul saw any strong or
brave man, he took him into his service.

CHAPTER 15

1 Samuel said to Saul: "It was I the
LORD sent to anoint you king over his
people Israel. Now, therefore, listen to
the message of the LORD. 2* This is what
the LORD of hosts has to say: 'I will pun-
ish what Amalek did to Israel when he
barred his way as he was coming up
from Egypt. 3*† Go, now, attack Ama-
lek, and deal with him and all that he
has under the ban. Do not spare him,
but kill men and women, children and
infants, oxen and sheep, camels and
asses.' "

Disobedience of Saul. 4† Saul alerted
the soldiers, and at Telaim reviewed two
hundred thousand foot soldiers and ten
thousand men of Judah. 5 Saul went to
the city of Amalek, and after setting an
ambush in the wadi, 6* warned the Ken-
ites: "Come! Leave Amalek and with-
draw, that I may not have to destroy you
with them, for you were kind to the Isra-
elites when they came up from Egypt."
After the Kenites left, 7* Saul routed
Amalek from Havilah to the approaches
of Shur, on the frontier of Egypt. 8 He
took Agag, king of Amalek, alive, but on
the rest of the people he put into effect
the ban of destruction by the sword. 9 He
and his troops spared Agag and the best
of the fat sheep and oxen, and the lambs.
They refused to carry out the doom on
anything that was worthwhile, dooming
only what was worthless and of no ac-
count.

*

37: 28, 6.15.
40: Jos 7, 13ff.
41: 28, 6; Ex 28, 30; Dt 33, 8.
44: 3, 17; Ru 1, 17.
45: 2 Sm 14, 11; 1 Kgs 1, 52.
47: 2 Sm 1, 22; 8, 2-5.
49: 18, 20.25; 31, 2;1 Chr 8, 33; 9, 39; 10, 2.
51: 9, 1.
15, 2: Ex 17, 8-10.16; Dt 25, 17ff.
3: 27, 8; 30, 17; Ex 17, 16; Nm 24, 20.
6: Nm 24, 21.
7: 27, 8.

†

14, 41: The *Urim* and *Thummim,* or sacred lots, were a device for ascertaining the will of God; they ceased to be used after the time of David. The material and the shape of these objects, and the manner in which they were used, are unknown. They gave a "yes" or "no" answer to specific questions.

14, 45: *Rescue:* the Hebrew word used is that for the "redemption" of the first-born (Ex 13, 13ff).

14, 49: *Ishvi:* known also as Ishbaal, in 2 Sm 2, 8 and elsewhere. The name may once have read "Ishyo" here.

15, 3: *Under the ban:* in such wars of extermination, all things (men, cities, beasts, etc.) were to be blotted out; nothing could be reserved for private use. The interpretation of God's will here attributed to Samuel is in keeping with the abhorrent practices of blood revenge prevalent among pastoral, seminomadic peoples such as the Hebrews had recently been. The slaughter of the innocent has never been in conformity with the will of God.

15, 4: The numbers here are not realistic; compare 14, 24 above.

Saul Is Reproved. 10 Then the LORD
spoke to Samuel: 11† "I regret having
made Saul king, for he has turned from
me and has not kept my command." At
this Samuel grew angry and cried out
to the LORD all night. 12 Early in the
morning he went to meet Saul, but was
informed that Saul had gone to Carmel,
where he erected a trophy in his own
honor, and that on his return he had
passed on and gone down to Gilgal.
13 When Samuel came to him, Saul
greeted him: "The LORD bless you! I
have kept the command of the LORD."
14 But Samuel asked, "What, then, is the
meaning of this bleating of sheep that
comes to my ears, and the lowing of oxen
that I hear?" 15 Saul replied: "They were
brought from Amalek. The men spared
the best sheep and oxen to sacrifice to
the LORD, your God; but we have carried
out the ban on the rest." 16 Samuel said
to Saul: "Stop! Let me tell you what the
LORD said to me last night." "Speak!"
he replied. 17* Samuel then said:
"Though little in your own esteem, are
you not leader of the tribes of Israel? The
LORD anointed you king of Israel 18* and
sent you on a mission, saying, 'Go and
put the sinful Amalekites under a ban
of destruction. Fight against them until
you have exterminated them.' 19* Why
then have you disobeyed the LORD? You
have pounced on the spoil, thus displeas-
ing the LORD." 20 Saul answered Samuel:
"I did indeed obey the LORD and fulfill
the mission on which the LORD sent me.
I have brought back Agag, and I have
destroyed Amalek under the ban. 21* But
from the spoil the men took sheep and
oxen, the best of what had been banned,
to sacrifice to the LORD their God in Gil-
gal."

22*† But Samuel said:

"Does the LORD so delight in holocausts and sacrifices
as in obedience to the command of the LORD?
Obedience is better than sacrifice,
and submission than the fat of rams.
23 For a sin like divination is rebellion,
and presumption is the crime of idolatry.
Because you have rejected the command of the LORD,
he, too, has rejected you as ruler."

Saul Asks Forgiveness. 24* Saul re-
plied to Samuel: "I have sinned, for I
have disobeyed the command of the
LORD and your instructions. In my fear
of the people, I did what they said.
25 Now forgive my sin, and return with
me, that I may worship the LORD."
26* But Samuel said to Saul, "I will not
return with you, because you rejected
the command of the LORD and the LORD
rejects you as king of Israel." 27* As
Samuel turned to go, Saul seized a loose
end of his mantle, and it tore off. 28* So
Samuel said to him: "The LORD has torn
the kingdom of Israel from you this day,
and has given it to a neighbor of yours,
who is better than you. 29* The Glory of
Israel neither retracts nor repents, for
he is not man that he should repent."
30 But he answered: "I have sinned, yet
honor me now before the elders of my
people and before Israel. Return with
me that I may worship the LORD your
God." 31 And so Samuel returned with
him, and Saul worshiped the LORD.

Agag Is Cut Down. 32 Afterward Sam-
uel commanded, "Bring Agag, king of
Amalek, to me." Agag came to him
struggling and saying, "So it is bitter
death!" 33* And Samuel said,

"As your sword has made women childless,
so shall your mother be childless among women."

Then he cut Agag down before the LORD
in Gilgal.

34 Samuel departed for Ramah, while
Saul went up to his home in Gibeah of
Saul. 35* Never again, as long as he lived,
did Samuel see Saul. Yet he grieved over
Saul, because the LORD regretted having
made him king of Israel.

CHAPTER 16

Samuel Sent to Bethlehem. 1*† The
LORD said to Samuel: "How long will you
grieve for Saul, whom I have rejected
as king of Israel? Fill your horn with oil,
and be on your way. I am sending you
to Jesse of Bethlehem, for I have chosen
my king from among his sons." 2 But
Samuel replied: "How can I go? Saul will
hear of it and kill me." To this the LORD
answered: "Take a heifer along and say,
'I have come to sacrifice to the LORD.'
3 Invite Jesse to the sacrifice, and I my-
self will tell you what to do; you are to

*

17: 9, 21.
18: 28, 18.
19: 14, 32.
21: Lv 27, 28.
22: Prv 21, 3; Hos 6, 6; Am 5, 21-25; Zec 10, 2; Mt 9, 13; 12, 7; Heb 10, 9.
24: 26, 21.
26: 1 Kgs 11, 11.30f.
27: 24, 6.
28: 28, 17; 2 Sm 7, 15f.
29: Nm 23, 19.
33: Ex 21, 23.
35: Gn 6, 6.
16, 1: 1 Kgs 1, 39; Ru 4, 17-22; 1 Chr 11, 3; Is 11, 1; Lk 2, 4.

†

15, 11: *I regret:* God manifests "regret" when, offended by men, he takes away his benefits, graces and favors. It is not God, but men, who change, to their own detriment.

15, 22: Samuel is disapproving, not of sacrifices in general, but of merely external sacrifices offered in defiance of God's commandment and without heartfelt obedience.

16, 1: The anointing here prepared for is unknown to David's brother Eliab in the next chapter (17, 28), and David is twice anointed after Saul's death (2 Sm 2, 4; 5, 3).

anoint for me the one I point out to you."
4 Samuel did as the LORD had com-
manded him. When he entered Bethle-
hem, the elders of the city came
trembling to meet him and inquired, "Is
your visit peaceful, O seer?" 5* He re-
plied: "Yes! I have come to sacrifice to
the LORD. So cleanse yourselves and join
me today for the banquet." He also had
Jesse and his sons cleanse themselves
and invited them to the sacrifice. 6 As
they came, he looked at Eliab and
thought, "Surely the LORD's anointed is
here before him." 7* But the LORD said
to Samuel: "Do not judge from his ap-
pearance or from his lofty stature, be-
cause I have rejected him. Not as man
sees does God see, because man sees the
appearance but the LORD looks into the
heart." 8* Then Jesse called Abinadab
and presented him before Samuel, who
said, "The Lord has not chosen him."
9 Next Jesse presented Shammah, but
Samuel said, "The LORD has not chosen
this one either." 10 In the same way Jesse
presented seven sons before Samuel, but
Samuel said to Jesse, "The LORD has not
chosen any one of these." 11* Then Sam-
uel asked Jesse, "Are these all the sons
you have?" Jesse replied, "There is still
the youngest, who is tending the sheep."
Samuel said to Jesse, "Send for him; we
will not begin the sacrificial banquet un-
til he arrives here." 12* Jesse sent and
had the young man brought to them. He
was ruddy, a youth handsome to behold
and making a splendid appearance. The
LORD said, "There—anoint him, for this
is he!" 13* Then Samuel, with the horn
of oil in hand, anointed him in the midst
of his brothers; and from that day on,
the spirit of the LORD rushed upon
David. When Samuel took his leave, he
went to Ramah.

Saul's Spirit of Melancholy. 14*† The
spirit of the LORD had departed from
Saul, and he was tormented by an evil
spirit sent by the LORD. 15 So the servants
of Saul said to him: "Please! An evil
spirit from God is tormenting you. 16 If
your lordship will order it, we, your
servants here in attendance on you, will
look for a man skilled in playing the
harp. When the evil spirit from God
comes over you, he will play and you
will feel better." 17 Saul then told his
servants, "Find me a skillful harpist and
bring him to me." 18*† A servant spoke
up to say: "I have observed that one of
the sons of Jesse of Bethlehem is a skill-
ful harpist. He is also a stalwart soldier,
besides being an able speaker, and
handsome. Moreover, the LORD is with
him."

David Made Armor-bearer. 19 Ac-
cordingly, Saul dispatched messengers
to ask Jesse to send him his son David,
who was with the flock. 20* Then Jesse
took five loaves of bread, a skin of wine,
and a kid, and sent them to Saul by his
son David. 21* Thus David came to Saul
and entered his service. Saul became
very fond of him, made him his armor-
bearer, 22 and sent Jesse the message,
"Allow David to remain in my service,
for he meets with my approval."
23 Whenever the spirit from God seized
Saul, David would take the harp and
play, and Saul would be relieved and feel
better, for the evil spirit would leave
him.

CHAPTER 17

The Challenge of Goliath. 1 The Philis-
tines rallied their forces for battle at So-
coh in Judah and camped between
Socoh and Azekah at Ephes-dammim.
2 Saul and the Israelites also gathered
and camped in the Vale of the Terebinth,
drawing up their battle line to meet the
Philistines. 3 The Philistines were sta-
tioned on one hill and the Israelites on
an opposite hill, with a valley between
them.
4 A champion named Goliath of Gath
came out from the Philistine camp; he
was six and a half feet tall. 5 He had a
bronze helmet on his head and wore a
bronze corselet of scale armor weighing
five thousand shekels, 6† and bronze
greaves, and had a bronze scimitar
slung from a baldric. 7*† The shaft of his
javelin was like a weaver's heddle-bar,
and its iron head weighed six hundred
shekels. His shield-bearer went before
him. 8 He stood and shouted to the ranks
of Israel: "Why come out in battle for-
mation? I am a Philistine, and you are
Saul's servants. Choose one of your men,

*

5: 9, 12f; 20, 26; Ex 19, 10; Jb 1, 5.
7: 10, 23f; 1 Chr 28, 9; Prv 15, 11; Jer 17, 10; 20, 12; Lk 16, 15; Acts 1, 24.
8ff: 17, 12f; 1 Chr 2, 13ff.
11: 17, 15.28.34; 2 Sm 7, 8.
12: 9, 2.
13: 10, 6; 11, 6; Jgs 3, 10; 9, 9; Sir 46, 13.
14: 18, 10f.
18: 2 Sm 17, 8.
20: 9, 7f; 10, 4.27; 16, 1; 17, 27ff.
21: 18, 2.
17, 7: 2 Sm 21, 19; 1 Chr 11, 23; 20, 5.

†

16, 14: *An evil spirit sent by the LORD:* the Lord permitted Saul to be tormented with violent fits of rage.

16, 18: Of the two traditions which describe the coming of David into Saul's service, the oldest Greek translation retains only the one comprised in 16, 14-23; 17, 1-11.32-54. This effort at consistency is not in accord with the character of the rest of the book; see note on 8, 1. Though square brackets are used in this edition to indicate the passages lacking in the oldest translation, this is meant only to help the reader follow one account at a time. Both are equally a part of the inspired text, as are also the various amplifications and retouchings of the narrative given within brackets in chs 18 and 19.

17, 6: *Scimitar:* the Hebrew word for this is rather rare, and the nature of the weapon was in doubt until recent years. It is not the same as the *sword* of v 45.

17, 7: *Six hundred shekels:* over 15 pounds.

and have him come down to me. 9 If he
beats me in combat and kills me, we will
be your vassals; but if I beat him and
kill him, you shall be our vassals and
serve us." 10 The Philistine continued: "I
defy the ranks of Israel today. Give me
a man and let us fight together." 11 Saul
and all the men of Israel, when they
heard this challenge of the Philistine,
were dismayed and terror-stricken.

David Comes to the Camp.
12*† [David was the son of an Ephrathite
named Jesse, who was from Bethlehem
in Judah. He had eight sons, and in the
days of Saul was old and well on in
years. 13 The three oldest sons of Jesse
had followed Saul to war; these three
sons who had gone off to war were
named, the first-born Eliab, the second
son Abinadab, and the third Shammah.
14 David was the youngest. While the
three oldest had joined Saul, 15* David
would go and come from Saul to tend
his father's sheep at Bethlehem.

16 [Meanwhile the Philistine came for-
ward and took his stand morning and
evening for forty days.

17 [Now Jesse said to his son David:
"Take this ephah of roasted grain and
these ten loaves for your brothers, and
bring them quickly to your brothers in
the camp. 18 Also take these ten cheeses
for the field officer. Greet your brothers
and bring home some token from them.
19 Saul, and they, and all Israel are fight-
ing against the Philistines in the Vale
of the Terebinth." 20* Early the next
morning, having left the flock with a
shepherd, David set out on his errand,
as Jesse had commanded him. He
reached the barricade of the camp just
as the army, on their way to the battle-
ground, were shouting their battle cry.
21 The Israelites and the Philistines drew
up opposite each other in battle array.
22* David entrusted what he had
brought to the keeper of the baggage and
hastened to the battle line, where he
greeted his brothers. 23 While he was
talking with them, the Philistine cham-
pion, by name Goliath of Gath, came up
from the ranks of the Philistines and
spoke as before, and David listened.
24 When the Israelites saw the man, they
all retreated before him, very much
afraid. 25* The Israelites had been say-
ing: "Do you see this man coming up?
He comes up to insult Israel. If anyone
should kill him, the king would give him
great wealth, and his daughter as well,
and would grant exemption to his fa-
ther's family in Israel." 26* David now
said to the men standing by: "What will
be done for the man who kills this Philis-
tine and frees Israel of the disgrace?
Who is this uncircumcised Philistine in
any case, that he should insult the ar-
mies of the living God?" 27 They re-
peated the same words to him and said,
"That is how the man who kills him will
be rewarded." 28 When Eliab, his oldest
brother, heard him speaking with the
men, he grew angry with David and
said: "Why did you come down? With
whom have you left those sheep in the
desert meanwhile? I know your arro-
gance and your evil intent. You came
down to enjoy the battle!" 29 David re-
plied, "What have I done now?—I was
only talking." 30 Yet he turned from him
to another and asked the same question;
and everyone gave him the same answer
as before. 31 The words that David had
spoken were overheard and reported to
Saul, who sent for him.]

David Fights Goliath. 32 Then David
spoke to Saul: "Let your majesty not lose
courage. I am at your service to go and
fight this Philistine." 33 But Saul an-
swered David, "You cannot go up
against this Philistine and fight with
him, for you are only a youth, while he
has been a warrior from his youth."
34* Then David told Saul: "Your servant
used to tend his father's sheep, and
whenever a lion or bear came to carry
off a sheep from the flock, 35 I would go
after it and attack it and rescue the prey
from its mouth. If it attacked me, I would
seize it by the jaw, strike it, and kill it.
36 Your servant has killed both a lion and
a bear, and this uncircumcised Philis-
tine will be as one of them, because he
has insulted the armies of the living
God."

37* David continued: "The LORD, who
delivered me from the claws of the lion
and the bear, will also keep me safe from
the clutches of this Philistine." Saul an-
swered David, "Go! the LORD will be
with you."

Preparation for the Encounter.
38 Then Saul clothed David in his own
tunic, putting a bronze helmet on his
head and arming him with a coat of
mail. 39 David also girded himself with
Saul's sword over the tunic. He walked
with difficulty, however, since he had
never tried armor before. He said to
Saul, "I cannot go in these, because I
have never tried them before." So he
took them off. 40 Then, staff in hand,
David selected five smooth stones from
the wadi and put them in the pocket of
his shepherd's bag. With his sling also

*

12: 16, 1.10; Ru 1, 2.
15: 18, 2; 2 Sm 7, 8.
20: 26, 5.
22: 25, 13.
25: 18, 17; Jos 15, 16.
26: 18, 25; Jgs 15, 18; 2 Kgs 19, 4; Is 37, 4.
34f: Jgs 14, 6; Sir 47, 3.
37: Prv 28, 1.

†

17, 12-31: An alternative account of how David came to undertake the combat with the Philistine is here inserted; it is continued in 17, 55—18, 6. See note on 16, 18.

ready to hand, he approached the Phi-
listine.
David's Victory. 41 With his shield-
bearer marching before him, the Philis-
tine also advanced closer and closer to
David. 42 When he had sized David up,
and seen that he was youthful, and
ruddy, and handsome in appearance, he
held him in contempt. 43 The Philistine
said to David, "Am I a dog that you come
against me with a staff?" Then the Phi-
listine cursed David by his gods 44* and
said to him, "Come here to me, and I
will leave your flesh for the birds of the
air and the beasts of the field." 45 David
answered him: "You come against me
with sword and spear and scimitar, but
I come against you in the name of the
LORD of hosts, the God of the armies of
Israel that you have insulted. 46 Today
the LORD shall deliver you into my hand;
I will strike you down and cut off your
head. This very day I will leave your
corpse and the corpses of the Philistine
army for the birds of the air and the
beasts of the field; thus the whole land
shall learn that Israel has a God. 47* All
this multitude, too, shall learn that it is
not by sword or spear that the LORD
saves. For the battle is the LORD's, and
he shall deliver you into our hands."
48 The Philistine then moved to meet
David at close quarters, while David ran
quickly toward the battle line in the di-
rection of the Philistine. 49 David put his
hand into the bag and took out a stone,
hurled it with the sling, and struck the
Philistine on the forehead. The stone
embedded itself in his brow, and he fell
prostrate on the ground. 50* [Thus David
overcame the Philistine with sling and
stone; he struck the Philistine mortally,
and did it without a sword.] 51* Then
David ran and stood over him; with the
Philistine's own sword [which he drew
from its sheath] he dispatched him and
cut off his head.
Flight of the Philistines. When they
saw that their hero was dead, the Philis-
tines took to flight. 52 Then the men of
Israel and Judah, with loud shouts, went
in pursuit of the Philistines to the ap-
proaches of Gath and to the gates of Ek-
ron, and Philistines fell wounded along
the road from Shaaraim as far as Gath
and Ekron. 53 On their return from the
pursuit of the Philistines, the Israelites
looted their camp. 54*† David took the
head of the Philistine and brought it to
Jerusalem; but he kept Goliath's armor
in his own tent.
David Presented to Saul. 55 [When
Saul saw David go out to meet the Philis-
tine, he asked his general Abner, "Ab-
ner, whose son is that youth?" Abner
replied, "As truly as your majesty is
alive, I have no idea." 56 And the king
said, "Find out whose son the lad is."
57 So when David returned from slaying
the Philistine, Abner took him and pre-
sented him to Saul. David was still hold-
ing the Philistine's head. 58 Saul then
asked him, "Whose son are you, young
man?" David replied, "I am the son of
your servant Jesse of Bethlehem."

CHAPTER 18

David and Jonathan. 1* [By the time
David finished speaking with Saul, Jon-
athan had become as fond of David as
if his life depended on him; he loved him
as he loved himself. 2* Saul laid claim
to David that day and did not allow him
to return to his father's house. 3 And
Jonathan entered into a bond with
David, because he loved him as himself.
4* Jonathan divested himself of the
mantle he was wearing and gave it to
David, along with his military dress, and
his sword, his bow and his belt. 5 David
then carried out successfully every mis-
sion on which Saul sent him. So Saul put
him in charge of his soldiers, and this
was agreeable to the whole army, even
to Saul's own officers.]
Saul's Jealousy. 6* At the approach of
Saul and David (on David's return after
slaying the Philistine), women came out
from each of the cities of Israel to meet
King Saul, singing and dancing, with
tambourines, joyful songs, and sistrums.
7* The women played and sang:

"Saul has slain his thousands,
and David his ten thousands."

8 Saul was very angry and resentful of
the song, for he thought: "They give
David ten thousands, but only thousands
to me. All that remains for him is the
kingship." 9 [And from that day on, Saul
was jealous of David.
10* [The next day an evil spirit from
God came over Saul, and he raged in
his house. David was in attendance,
playing the harp as at other times, while
Saul was holding his spear. 11 Saul
poised the spear, thinking to nail David
to the wall, but twice David escaped
him.] 12 Saul then began to fear David,
[because the LORD was with him, but
had departed from Saul himself.]
13 Accordingly, Saul removed him from

*

44: Dt 28, 26; Is 18, 6; Jer 15, 3.
47: 14, 6; Ps 33, 16.
50: Sir 47, 4; 1 Mc 4, 30.
51: 21, 10.
54: 31, 9.
18, 1: 19, 1-7; 20, 17; 23, 16; 2 Sm 1, 26; 9, 1.
2: 16, 21; 17, 15.
4: 2 Sm 1, 22.
6: Ex 15, 20f; Jgs 11, 34; Jdt 15, 12.
7: 21, 12; 29, 5; Sir 47, 6f.
10f: 16, 14; 19, 9f; 20, 33; 22, 6; 26, 8.

†

17, 54: At the time supposed by this narrative, Jerusalem was still Jebusite, and David had no military tent of his own; the verse is a later gloss.

his presence by appointing him a field
officer. So David led the people on their
military expeditions, 14 and prospered in
all his enterprises, for the LORD was with
him. 15 Seeing how successful he was,
Saul conceived a fear of David: 16* on
the other hand, all Israel and Judah
loved him, since he led them on their
expeditions.
17* [Saul said to David, "There is my
older daughter, Merob, whom I will give
you in marriage if you become my
champion and fight the battles of the
LORD." Saul had in mind, "I shall not
touch him; let the Philistines strike
him." 18 But David answered Saul: "Who
am I? And who are my kin or my fa-
ther's clan in Israel that I should become
the king's son-in-law?" 19* However,
when it was time for Saul's daughter
Merob to be given to David, she was
given in marriage to Adriel the Meho-
lathite instead.]
20* Now Saul's daughter Michal loved
David, and it was reported to Saul, who
was pleased at this, 21 for he thought, "I
will offer her to him to become a snare
for him, so that the Philistines may
strike him." [Thus for the second time
Saul said to David, "You shall become
my son-in-law today."] 22 Saul then or-
dered his servants to speak to David pri-
vately and to say: "The king is fond of
you, and all his officers love you. You
should become the king's son-in-law."
23 But when Saul's servants mentioned
this to David, he said: "Do you think it
easy to become the king's son-in-law?
I am poor and insignificant." 24 When his
servants reported to him the nature of
David's answer, 25* Saul commanded
them to say this to David: "The king de-
sires no other price for the bride than
the foreskins of one hundred Philistines,
that he may thus take vengeance on his
enemies." Saul intended in this way to
bring about David's death through the
Philistines. 26 When the servants re-
ported this offer to David, he was
pleased with the prospect of becoming
the king's son-in-law. [Before the year
was up,] 27 David made preparations
and sallied forth with his men and slew
two hundred Philistines. He brought
back their foreskins and counted them
out before the king, that he might thus
become the king's son-in-law. So Saul
gave him his daughter Michal in mar-
riage. 28 Saul thus came to recognize that
the LORD was with David; besides, his
own daughter Michal loved David.
29 Therefore Saul feared David all the
more [and was his enemy ever after].
30 [The Philistine chiefs continued to
make forays, but each time they took
the field, David was more successful
against them than any other of Saul's
officers, and as a result acquired great
fame.]

CHAPTER 19

Persecution of David. 1* Saul dis-
cussed his intention of killing David with
his son Jonathan and with all his ser-
vants. But Saul's son Jonathan, who was
very fond of David, 2 told him: "My fa-
ther Saul is trying to kill you. Therefore,
please be on your guard tomorrow
morning; get out of sight and remain in
hiding. 3 I, however, will go out and
stand beside my father in the country-
side where you are, and will speak to
him about you. If I learn anything, I will
let you know."
4 Jonathan then spoke well of David
to his father Saul, saying to him: "Let
not your majesty sin against his servant
David, for he has committed no offense
against you, but has helped you very
much by his deeds. 5* When he took his
life in his hands and slew the Philistine,
and the LORD brought about a great vic-
tory for all Israel through him, you were
glad to see it. Why, then, should you be-
come guilty of shedding innocent blood
by killing David without cause?" 6 Saul
heeded Jonathan's plea and swore, "As
the LORD lives, he shall not be killed."
7 So Jonathan summoned David and re-
peated the whole conversation to him.
Jonathan then brought David to Saul,
and David served him as before.
8 When war broke out again, David
went out to fight against the Philistines
and inflicted a great defeat upon them,
putting them to flight. 9* Then an evil
spirit from the LORD came upon Saul as
he was sitting in his house with spear
in hand and David was playing the harp
nearby. 10 Saul tried to nail David to the
wall with the spear, but David eluded
Saul, so that the spear struck only the
wall, and David got away safe.
11† The same night, Saul sent messen-
gers to David's house to guard it, that
he might kill him in the morning.
David's wife Michal informed him, "Un-
less you save yourself tonight, tomorrow
you will be killed." 12* Then Michal let
David down through a window, and he
made his escape in safety. 13* Michal
took the household idol and laid it in the
bed, putting a net of goat's hair at its
head and covering it with a spread.

*

16: 2 Sm 5, 2.
17: 14, 49; 17, 25.
19: 21, 8; 24, 16.
20: 14, 49; 25, 44; 26, 23; 2 Sm 3, 13.
25: 17, 26; Gn 34, 12.
19, 1: 18, 1; 20, 1 ff.
5: Dt 19, 10; Ps 119, 109.
9f: 16, 14; 18, 10f.
12: Jos 2, 15; Acts 9, 25; 2 Cor 11, 33.
13: Gn 31, 19; Jgs 17, 5; 18, 14. 18.20.

†

19, 11: This story in all probability orignially followed 18, 29, placing the episode of David's escape on the night of his marriage with Michal.

14 When Saul sent messengers to arrest
David, she said, "He is sick." 15 Saul,
however, sent the messengers back to
see David and commanded them,
"Bring him up to me in the bed, that I
may kill him." 16 But when the messen-
gers entered, they found the household
idol in the bed, with the net of goat's hair
at its head. 17 Saul therefore asked Mi-
chal: "Why did you play this trick on
me? You have helped my enemy to get
away!" Michal answered Saul: "He
threatened me, 'Let me go or I will kill
you.' "

David and Samuel in Ramah. 18 Thus
David got safely away; he went to Sam-
uel in Ramah, informing him of all that
Saul had done to him. Then he and Sam-
uel went to stay in the sheds. 19 When
Saul was told that David was in the
sheds near Ramah, 20* he sent messen-
gers to arrest David. But when they saw
the band of prophets, presided over by
Samuel, in a prophetic frenzy, they too
fell into the prophetic state. 21 Informed
of this, Saul sent other messengers,
who also fell into the prophetic state.
For the third time Saul sent messen-
gers, but they too fell into the prophetic
state.

Saul among the Prophets. 22 Saul then
went to Ramah himself. Arriving at the
cistern of the threshing floor on the bare
hilltop, he inquired, "Where are Samuel
and David?", and was told, "At the
sheds near Ramah." 23 As he set out
from the hilltop toward the sheds, the
spirit of God came upon him also, and
he continued on in a prophetic condition
until he reached the spot. At the sheds
near Ramah 24* he, too, stripped himself
of his garments and he, too, remained
in the prophetic state in the presence of
Samuel; all that day and night he lay
naked. That is why they say, "Is Saul
also among the prophets?"

CHAPTER 20

David Consults with Jonathan.
1* David fled from the sheds near Ra-
mah, and went to Jonathan. "What have
I done?" he asked him. "What crime or
what offense does your father hold
against me that he seeks my life?"
2 Jonathan answered him: "Heaven for-
bid that you should die! My father does
nothing, great or small, without disclos-
ing it to me. Why, then, should my father
conceal this from me? This cannot be
so!" 3 But David replied: "Your father is
well aware that I am favored with your
friendship, so he has decided, 'Jonathan
must not know of this lest he be grieved.'
Nevertheless, as the LORD lives and as
you live, there is but a step between me
and death." 4 Jonathan then said to
David, "I will do whatever you wish."
5* David answered: "Tomorrow is the
new moon, when I should in fact dine
with the king. Let me go and hide in the
open country until evening. 6 If it turns
out that your father misses me, say,
'David urged me to let him go on short
notice to his city Bethlehem, because his
whole clan is holding its seasonal sacri-
fice there.' 7 If he says, 'Very well,' your
servant is safe. But if he becomes quite
angry, you can be sure he has planned
some harm. 8* Do this kindness for your
servant because of the LORD's bond be-
tween us, into which you brought me:
if I am guilty, kill me yourself! Why
should you give me up to your father?"
9 But Jonathan answered: "Not I! If ever
I find out that my father is determined
to inflict injury upon you, I will certainly
let you know." 10 David then asked Jona-
than, "Who will tell me if your father
gives you a harsh answer?"

Mutual Agreement. 11 [Jonathan re-
plied to David, "Come, let us go out into
the field." When they were out in the
open country together, 12 Jonathan said
to David: "As the LORD, the God of Is-
rael, lives, I will sound out my father
about this time tomorrow. Whether he
is well disposed toward David or not, I
will send you the information. 13* Should
it please my father to bring any injury
upon you, may the LORD do thus and
so to Jonathan if I do not apprise you
of it and send you on your way in peace.
May the LORD be with you even as he
was with my father. 14 Only this: if I am
still alive, may you show me the kind-
ness of the LORD. But if I die, 15 never
withdraw your kindness from my house.
And when the LORD exterminates all the
enemies of David from the surface of the
earth, 16 the name of Jonathan must
never be allowed by the family of David
to die out from among you, or the LORD
will make you answer for it." 17 And in
his love for David, Jonathan renewed his
oath to him, because he loved him as
his very self.]

18 Jonathan then said to him: "Tomor-
row is the new moon; and you will be
missed, since your place will be vacant.
19* On the following day you will be
missed all the more. Go to the spot where
you hid on the other occasion and wait
near the mound there. 20 On the third
day of the month I will shoot arrows, as
though aiming at a target. 21 I will then
send my attendant to go and recover the
arrows. If in fact I say to him, 'Look,
the arrow is this side of you; pick it up,'
come, for you are safe. As the LORD
lives, there will be nothing to fear. 22 But
if I say to the boy, 'Look, the arrow is

---

*

20: 10, 5f. 10; Nm 11, 25.
24: 10, 10ff.
20, 1: 19, 1-7. 11-17.
5: Nm 10, 10; 28, 11-15.
8f: 23, 17f.
13-16: 24, 22f; 2 Sm 9, 1-13; 21, 7.
19: 19, 1-7.

beyond you,' go, for the LORD sends you
away. 23 However, in the matter which
you and I have discussed, the LORD shall
be between you and me forever." 24 So
David hid in the open country.

On the day of the new moon, when the
king sat at table to dine, 25 taking his
usual place against the wall, Jonathan
sat facing him, while Abner sat at the
king's side, and David's place was va-
cant. 26*† Saul, however, said nothing
that day, for he thought, "He must have
become unclean by accident, and not yet
have been cleansed." 27 On the next day,
the second day of the month, David's
place was vacant. Saul inquired of his
son Jonathan, "Why has the son of Jesse
not come to table yesterday or today?"
28 Jonathan answered Saul: "David ur-
gently asked me to let him go to his city,
Bethlehem. 29 'Please let me go,' he
begged, 'for we are to have a clan sacri-
fice in our city, and my brothers insist
on my presence. Now, therefore, if you
think well of me, give me leave to visit
my brothers.' That is why he has not
come to the king's table." 30 But Saul was
extremely angry with Jonathan and said
to him: "Son of a rebellious woman, do
I not know that, to your own shame and
to the disclosure of your mother's
shame, you are the companion of Jesse's
son? 31* Why, as long as the son of Jesse
lives upon the earth, you cannot make
good your claim to the kingship! So send
for him, and bring him to me, for he is
doomed." 32 But Jonathan asked his fa-
ther Saul: "Why should he die? What has
he done?" 33* At this Saul brandished his
spear to strike him, and thus Jonathan
learned that his father was resolved to
kill David. 34 Jonathan sprang up from
the table in great anger and took no food
that second day of the month, for he was
grieved on David's account, since his fa-
ther had railed against him.

Jonathan's Farewell. 35 The next
morning Jonathan went out into the field
with a little boy for his appointment with
David. 36 There he said to the boy, "Run
and fetch the arrow." And as the boy
ran, he shot an arrow beyond him in the
direction of the city. 37 When the boy
made for the spot where Jonathan had
shot the arrow, Jonathan called after
him, "The arrow is farther on!" 38 Again
he called to his lad, "Hurry, be quick,
don't delay!" Jonathan's boy picked up
the arrow and brought it to his master.
39 The boy knew nothing; only Jonathan
and David knew what was meant.
40 Then Jonathan gave his weapons to
this boy of his and said to him, "Go, take
them to the city." 41 When the boy had
left, David rose from beside the mound
and prostrated himself on the ground
three times before Jonathan in homage.
They kissed each other and wept aloud
together. 42* At length Jonathan said to
David, "Go in peace, in keeping with
what we two have sworn by the name
of the LORD: 'The LORD shall be between
you and me, and between your posterity
and mine forever.' "

CHAPTER 21

1 Then David departed on his way, while
Jonathan went back into the city.

The Holy Bread. 2* David went to
Ahimelech, the priest of Nob, who came
trembling to meet him and asked, "Why
are you alone? Is there no one with you?"
3 David answered the priest: "The king
gave me a commission and told me to
let no one know anything about the busi-
ness on which he sent me or the commis-
sion he gave me. For that reason I have
arranged a meeting place with my men.
4* Now what have you on hand? Give me
five loaves, or whatever you can find."
5† But the priest replied to David, "I
have no ordinary bread on hand, only
holy bread; if the men have abstained
from women, you may eat some of that."
6 David answered the priest: "We have
indeed been segregated from women as
on previous occasions. Whenever I go on
a journey, all the young men are conse-
crated—even for a secular journey. All
the more so today, when they are con-
secrated at arms!" 7* So the priest gave
him holy bread, for no other bread was
on hand except the showbread which
had been removed from the LORD's
presence and replaced by fresh bread
when it was taken away. 8 One of Saul's
servants was there that day, detained
before the LORD; his name was Doeg the
Edomite, and he was Saul's chief hench-
man.

The Sword of Goliath. 9 David then
asked Ahimelech: "Do you have a spear
or a sword on hand? I brought along nei-
ther my sword nor my weapons, because
the king's business was urgent." 10* The
priest replied: "The sword of Goliath the
Philistine, whom you killed in the Vale
of the Terebinth, is here [wrapped in a
mantle] behind an ephod. If you wish
to take that, take it; there is no sword
here except that one." David said:

1 SAMUEL

*

26: 16, 5; Lv 7, 20f; 15, 1ff.
31: 2 Sm 12, 5.
33: 18, 11.
42: 2 Sm 9, 1; 21, 7.
21, 2: Is 10, 32; Mk 2, 26.
4: Lv 24, 5. 9.
7: 22, 9; Lv 24, 5–9; Mt 12, 3f; Mk 2, 26; Lk 6, 3ff.
10: 17, 51. 54.

†

20, 26: The meal on the first day of the month would have religious overtones, and a ritual impurity (Lv 15, 16; Dt 23, 10ff) would bar David from sharing in it.

21, 5f: *From women:* the high priest, willing to distribute the holy bread to David and his men, requires that they be free from ritual uncleanness, associated in Old Testament times (Lv 15, 18) with the marriage act. David's answer supposes the discipline of a military campaign under the conditions of "holy war" (Dt 23, 10).

"There is none to match it. Give it to
me!"
David a Fugitive. 11* That same day
David took to flight from Saul, going to
Achish, king of Gath. 12* But the ser-
vants of Achish said, "Is this not David,
the king of the land? During their dances
do they not sing,

> 'Saul has slain his thousands,
> but David his ten thousands'?"

13 David took note of these remarks and
became very much afraid of Achish,
king of Gath. 14 So, as they watched, he
feigned insanity and acted like a mad-
man in their hands, drumming on the
doors of the gate and drooling onto his
beard. 15 Finally Achish said to his ser-
vants: "You see the man is mad. Why
did you bring him to me? 16 Do I not have
enough madmen, that you bring in this
one to carry on in my presence? Should
this fellow come into my house?"

CHAPTER 22

1* David left Gath and escaped to the
cave of Adullam. When his brothers and
the rest of his family heard about it, they
came down to him there. 2 He was joined
by all those who were in difficulties or
in debt, or who were embittered, and he
became their leader. About four hun-
dred men were with him.
3 From there David went to Mizpeh of
Moab and said to the king of Moab, "Let
my father and mother stay with you, un-
til I learn what God will do for me." 4† He
left them with the king of Moab, and they
stayed with him as long as David re-
mained in the refuge.
5 But the prophet Gad said to David:
"Do not remain in the refuge. Leave, and
go to the land of Judah." And so David
left and went to the forest of Hereth.
Doeg Betrays Ahimelech. 6* Now Saul
heard that David and his men had been
located. At the time he was sitting in
Gibeah under a tamarisk tree on the
high place, holding his spear, while all
his servants were standing by. 7* So he
said to them: "Listen, men of Benjamin!
Will the son of Jesse give all of you fields
and vineyards? Will he make each of
you an officer over a thousand or a hun-
dred men, 8 that you have all conspired
against me and no one tells me that my
son has made an agreement with the son
of Jesse? None of you shows sympathy
for me or discloses to me that my son
has stirred up my servant to be an en-
emy against me, as is the case today."
9* Then Doeg the Edomite, who was
standing with the officers of Saul, spoke
up: "I saw the son of Jesse come to
Ahimelech, son of Ahitub, in Nob. 10 He
consulted the LORD for him and gave
him supplies, and the sword of Goliath
the Philistine as well."
Slaughter of the Priests. 11 At this the
king sent a summons to Ahimelech the
priest, son of Ahitub, and to all his family
who were priests in Nob; and they all
came to the king. 12 Then Saul said, "Lis-
ten, son of Ahitub!" He replied, "Yes, my
lord." 13 Saul asked him, "Why did you
conspire against me with the son of
Jesse by giving him food and a sword
and by consulting God for him, that he
might rebel against me and become
my enemy, as is the case today?"
14 Ahimelech answered the king: "And
who among all your servants is as loyal
as David, the king's son-in-law, captain
of your bodyguard, and honored in your
own house? 15 Is this the first time I have
consulted God for him? No indeed! Let
not the king accuse his servant or any-
one in my family of such a thing. Your
servant knows nothing at all, great or
small, about the whole matter." 16 But
the king said, "You shall die, Ahimelech,
with all your family." 17* The king then
commanded his henchmen standing by:
"Make the rounds and kill the priests
of the LORD, for they assisted David.
They knew he was a fugitive and yet
failed to inform me." But the king's
servants refused to lift a hand to strike
the priests of the LORD.
18 The king therefore commanded
Doeg, "You make the rounds and kill the
priests!" So Doeg the Edomite went
from one to the next and killed the
priests himself, slaying on that day
eighty-five who wore the linen ephod.
19 Saul also put the priestly city of Nob
to the sword, including men and women,
children and infants, and oxen, asses
and sheep.
Abiathar Escapes. 20* One son of
Ahimelech, son of Ahitub, named Abia-
thar, escaped and fled to David. 21 When
Abiathar told David that Saul had slain
the priests of the LORD, 22 David said
to him: "I knew that day, when Doeg the
Edomite was there, that he would surely
tell Saul. I am responsible for the death
of all your family. 23 Stay with me. Fear
nothing; he that seeks your life must
seek my life also. You are under my pro-
tection."

CHAPTER 23

Keilah Liberated. 1* David received
information that the Philistines were at-
tacking Keilah and plundering the

*

11: 27, 2; 29, 5.
12: 18, 7; 29, 5.
22, 1: 2 Sm 23, 13; Ps 63; Mi 1, 15.
6: Ps 52.
7: 8, 14.
9f: 21, 2–10.
17: 2, 31. 33; 21, 7.
20: 23, 6; 30, 7; 1 Kgs 2, 26f.
23, 1: Jos 15, 44.

†

22, 4–5: *Refuge:* seemingly connected with the cave complex spoken of in v 1.

threshing floors. 2* So he consulted the LORD, inquiring, "Shall I go and defeat these Philistines?" The LORD answered, "Go, for you will defeat the Philistines and rescue Keilah." 3 But David's men said to him: "We are afraid here in Judah. How much more so if we go to Keilah against the forces of the Philistines!" 4 Again David consulted the LORD, who answered, "Go down to Keilah, for I will deliver the Philistines into your power." 5 David then went with his men to Keilah and fought with the Philistines. He drove off their cattle and inflicted a severe defeat on them, and thus rescued the inhabitants of Keilah.

6* Abiathar, son of Ahimelech, who had fled to David, went down with David to Keilah, taking the ephod with him.

Flight from Keilah. 7 When Saul was told that David had entered Keilah, he said: "God has put him in my grip. Now he has shut himself in, for he has entered a city with gates and bars." 8 Saul then called all the people to war, in order to go down to Keilah and besiege David and his men. 9* When David found out that Saul was planning to harm him, he said to the priest Abiathar, "Bring forward the ephod." 10 David then said: "O LORD God of Israel, your servant has heard a report that Saul plans to come to Keilah, to destroy the city on my account. 11 Will they hand me over? And now: will Saul come down as your servant has heard? O LORD God of Israel, tell your servant." The LORD answered, "He will come down." 12 David then asked, "Will the citizens of Keilah deliver me and my men into the grasp of Saul?" And the LORD answered, "Yes." 13 So David and his men, about six hundred in number, left Keilah and wandered from place to place. When Saul was informed that David had escaped from Keilah, he abandoned the expedition.

David and Jonathan in Horesh. 14 David now lived in the refuges in the desert, or in the barren hill country near Ziph. Though Saul sought him continually, the LORD did not deliver David into his grasp. 15 David was apprehensive because Saul had come out to seek his life; but while he was at Horesh in the barrens near Ziph, 16* Saul's son, Jonathan, came down there to David and strengthened his resolve in the LORD. 17 He said to him: "Have no fear, my father Saul shall not lay a hand to you. You shall be king of Israel and I shall be second to you. Even my father Saul knows this." 18* They made a joint agreement before the LORD in Horesh, where David remained, while Jonathan returned to his home.

Treachery of the Ziphites. 19* Some of the Ziphites went up to Saul in Gibeah and said, "David is hiding among us, now in the refuges, and again at Horesh, or on the hill of Hachilah, south of the wasteland. 20 Therefore, whenever the king wishes to come down, let him do so. It will be our task to deliver him into the king's grasp." 21* Saul replied: "The LORD bless you for your sympathy toward me. 22 Go now and make sure once more! Take note of the place where he sets foot" (for he thought, perhaps they are playing some trick on me). 23 "Look around and learn in which of all the various hiding places he is holding out. Then come back to me with sure information, and I will go with you. If he is in the region, I will search him out among all the families of Judah." 24* So they went off to Ziph ahead of Saul. At this time David and his men were in the desert below Maon, in the Arabah south of the wasteland.

Escape from Saul. 25 When Saul and his men came looking for him, David got word of it and went down to the gorge in the desert below Maon. Saul heard of this and pursued David into the desert below Maon. 26 As Saul moved along one rim of the gorge, David and his men took to the other. David was in anxious flight to escape Saul, and Saul and his men were attempting to outflank David and his men in order to capture them, 27 when a messenger came to Saul, saying, "Come quickly, because the Philistines have invaded the land." 28 Saul interrupted his pursuit of David and went to meet the Philistines. This is how that place came to be called the Gorge of Divisions.

CHAPTER 24

David Spares Saul. 1 David then went up from there and stayed in the refuges behind Engedi. 2 And when Saul returned from the pursuit of the Philistines, he was told that David was in the desert near Engedi. 3 So Saul took three thousand picked men from all Israel and went in search of David and his men in the direction of the wild goat crags. 4* When he came to the sheepfolds along the way, he found a cave, which he entered to ease nature. David and his men were occupying the inmost recesses of the cave.

5 David's servants said to him, "This is the day of which the LORD said to you, 'I will deliver your enemy into your grasp; do with him as you see fit.'" So David moved up and stealthily cut off an end of Saul's mantle. 6* Afterward, however, David regretted that he had

---

*

2: 28, 6.
6: 22, 20; 30, 7.
9: 2, 28.
16: 18, 1.
18: 18, 3; 20, 8.
19: 26, 1-3; Ps 54.
21: 2 Sm 2, 5.
24: 25, 2.
24, 4: Ps 57.
6: 15, 27.

cut off an end of Saul's mantle. 7* He said to his men, "The LORD forbid that I should do such a thing to my master, the LORD's anointed, as to lay a hand on him, for he is the Lord's anointed." 8 With these words David restrained his men and would not permit them to attack Saul. Saul then left the cave and went on his way. 9 David also stepped out of the cave, calling to Saul, "My lord the king!" When Saul looked back, David bowed to the ground in homage 10 and asked Saul: "Why do you listen to those who say, 'David is trying to harm you'? 11 You see for yourself today that the LORD just now delivered you into my grasp in the cave. I had some thought of killing you, but I took pity on you instead. I decided, 'I will not raise a hand against my lord, for he is the LORD's anointed and a father to me.' 12* Look here at this end of your mantle which I hold. Since I cut off an end of your mantle and did not kill you, see and be convinced that I plan no harm and no rebellion. I have done you no wrong, though you are hunting me down to take my life. 13 The LORD will judge between me and you, and the LORD will exact justice from you in my case. I shall not touch you. 14 The old proverb says, 'From the wicked comes forth wickedness.' So I will take no action against you. 15 Against whom are you on campaign, O king of Israel? Whom are you pursuing? A dead dog, or a single flea! 16* The LORD will be the judge; he will decide between me and you. May he see this, and take my part, and grant me justice beyond your reach!"

Saul's Remorse. 17 When David finished saying these things to Saul, Saul answered, "Is that your voice, my son David?" And he wept aloud. 18 Saul then said to David: "You are in the right rather than I; you have treated me generously, while I have done you harm. 19 Great is the generosity you showed me today, when the LORD delivered me into your grasp and you did not kill me. 20 For if a man meets his enemy, does he send him away unharmed? May the LORD reward you generously for what you have done this day. 21* And now, since I know that you shall surely be king and that sovereignty over Israel shall come into your possession, 22* swear to me by the LORD that you will not destroy my descendants and that you will not blot out my name and family." 23 David gave Saul his oath and Saul returned home, while David and his men went up to the refuge.

CHAPTER 25

Death of Samuel. 1* Samuel died, and all Israel gathered to mourn him; they buried him at his home in Ramah.

Nabal and Abigail. Then David went down to the desert of Maon. 2* There was a man of Maon who had property in Carmel; he was very wealthy, owning three thousand sheep and a thousand goats. At this time he was present for the shearing of his flock in Carmel. 3* The man was named Nabal, his wife, Abigail. The woman was intelligent and attractive, but Nabal himself, a Calebite, was harsh and ungenerous in his behavior. 4 When David heard in the desert that Nabal was shearing his flock, 5 he sent ten young men, instructing them: "Go up to Carmel. Pay Nabal a visit and greet him in my name. 6 Say to him, 'Peace be with you, my brother, and with your family, and with all who belong to you. 7 I have just heard that shearers are with you. Now, when your shepherds were with us, we did them no injury, neither did they miss anything all the while they were in Carmel. 8 Ask your servants and they will tell you so. Look kindly on these young men, since we come at a festival time. Please give your servants and your son David whatever you can manage.' "

9 When David's young men arrived, they delivered this message fully to Nabal in David's name, and then waited. 10 But Nabal answered the servants of David: "Who is David? Who is the son of Jesse? Nowadays there are many servants who run away from their masters. 11 Must I take my bread, my wine, my meat that I have slaughtered for my own shearers, and give them to men who come from I know not where?" 12 So David's young men retraced their steps and on their return reported to him all that had been said. 13 Thereupon David said to his men, "Let everyone gird on his sword." And so everyone, David included, girded on his sword. About four hundred men went up after David, while two hundred remained with the baggage.

14 But Nabal's wife Abigail was informed of this by one of the servants, who said: "David sent messengers from the desert to greet our master, but he flew at them screaming. 15 Yet these men were very good to us. We were done no injury, neither did we miss anything all the while we were living among them during our stay in the open country. 16 For us they were like a rampart night and day the whole time we were pasturing the sheep near them. 17 Now, see

---

*

7: 10, 1; 31, 4; 2 Sm 1, 14.
12: Rom 12, 19.
16: 18, 19.31; 26, 19; Pss 35, 1ff; 43, 1.
21: 26, 25.
22: 2 Sm 9, 1ff.
25, 1: 28, 3; Sir 46, 13-20.
2: 23, 24; Jos 15, 55.
3: 27, 3; Jos 14, 6; 1 Chr 2, 42.45.

what you can do, for you must realize that otherwise evil is in store for our master and for his whole family. He is so mean that no one can talk to him." 18 Abigail quickly got together two hundred loaves, two skins of wine, five dressed sheep, five seahs of roasted grain, a hundred cakes of pressed raisins, and two hundred cakes of pressed figs, and loaded them on asses. 19 She then said to her servants, "Go on ahead; I will follow you." But she did not tell her husband Nabal.

20 As she came down through a mountain defile riding on an ass, David and his men were also coming down from the opposite direction. When she met them, 21 David had just been saying: "Indeed, it was in vain that I guarded all this man's possessions in the desert, so that he missed nothing. He has repaid good with evil. 22* May God do thus and so to David, if by morning I leave a single male alive among all those who belong to him." 23 As soon as Abigail saw David, she dismounted quickly from the ass and, falling prostrate on the ground before David, did him homage. 24 As she fell at his feet she said:

"My lord, let the blame be mine. Please let your handmaid speak to you, and listen to the words of your handmaid. 25† Let not my lord pay attention to that worthless man Nabal, for he is just like his name. Fool is his name, and he acts the fool. I, your handmaid, did not see the young men whom my lord sent. 26† Now, therefore, my lord, as the LORD lives, and as you live, it is the LORD who has kept you from shedding blood and from avenging yourself personally. May your enemies and those who seek to harm my lord become as Nabal! 27 Accept this present, then, which your maidservant has brought for my lord, and let it be given to the young men who follow my lord. 28 Please forgive the transgression of your handmaid, for the LORD shall certainly establish a lasting dynasty for my lord, because your lordship is fighting the battles of the LORD, and there is no evil to be found in you your whole life long. 29*† If anyone rises to pursue you and to seek your life, may the life of my lord be bound in the bundle of the living in the care of the LORD your God; but may he hurl out the lives of your enemies as from the hollow of a sling. 30* And when the LORD carries out for my lord the promise of success he has made concerning you, and appoints you as commander over Israel, 31 you shall not have this as a qualm or burden on your conscience, my lord, for having shed innocent blood or for having avenged yourself personally. When the LORD confers this benefit on your lordship, remember your handmaid."

32 David said to Abigail: "Blessed be the LORD, the God of Israel, who sent you to meet me today. 33 Blessed be your good judgment and blessed be you yourself, who this day have prevented me from shedding blood and from avenging myself personally. 34 Otherwise, as the LORD, the God of Israel, lives, who has restrained me from harming you, if you had not come so promptly to meet me, by dawn Nabal would not have had a single man or boy left alive." 35 David then took from her what she had brought him and said to her: "Go up to your home in peace! See, I have granted your request as a personal favor."

Nabal's Death. 36 When Abigail came to Nabal, there was a drinking party in his house like that of a king, and Nabal was merry because he was very drunk. So she told him nothing at all before daybreak the next morning. 37 But then, when Nabal had become sober, his wife told him what had happened. At this his courage died within him, and he became like a stone. 38 About ten days later the LORD struck him and he died. 39 On hearing that Nabal was dead, David said: "Blessed be the LORD, who has requited the insult I received at the hand of Nabal, and who restrained his servant from doing evil, but has punished Nabal for his own evil deeds."

David Marries Abigail and Ahinoam. David then sent a proposal of marriage to Abigail. 40 When David's servants came to Abigail in Carmel, they said to her, "David has sent us to you that he may take you as his wife." 41 Rising and bowing to the ground, she answered, "Your handmaid would become a slave to wash the feet of my lord's servants." 42* She got up immediately, mounted an ass, and followed David's messengers, with her five maids following in attendance upon her. She became his wife, 43* and David also married Ahinoam of Jezreel. Thus both of them were his wives; but Saul gave David's wife Michal, Saul's own daughter, to Palti, son of Laish, who was from Gallim.

*

22: 1 Kgs 16, 11; 21, 21; 2 Kgs 9, 8.
29: Ps 69, 28.
30: 13, 14; 2 Sm 3, 10.
42: 27, 3.
43: 18, 20; 27, 3; 30, 5; 2 Sm 3, 2.13ff; 1 Chr 3, 1.

†

25, 25: *Fool is his name:* Nabal in Hebrew means "a fool."

25, 26: Abigail anticipates that some misfortune will shortly overtake Nabal, as in fact it does (vv 37-38).

25, 29: *The bundle of the living:* the figure is perhaps taken from the practice of tying up valuables in a kerchief or bag for safekeeping. Abigail desires that David enjoy permanent peace and security, but that his enemies be subject to constant agitation and humiliation like a stone whirled about, cast out of the sling, and thereafter disregarded.

CHAPTER 26

Saul's Life Again Spared. 1* Men from Ziph came to Saul in Gibeah, reporting that David was hiding on the hill of Hachilah at the edge of the wasteland. 2 So Saul went off down to the desert of Ziph with three thousand picked men of Israel, to search for David in the desert of Ziph. 3 Saul camped beside the road on the hill of Hachilah, at the edge of the wasteland. David, who was living in the desert, saw that Saul had come into the desert after him 4 and sent out scouts, who confirmed Saul's arrival. 5* David himself then went to the place where Saul was encamped and examined the spot where Saul and Abner, son of Ner, the general, had their sleeping quarters. Saul's were within the barricade, and all his soldiers were camped around him. 6* David asked Ahimelech the Hittite, and Abishai, son of Zeruiah and brother of Joab, "Who will go down into the camp with me to Saul?" Abishai replied, "I will." 7 So David and Abishai went among Saul's soldiers by night and found Saul lying asleep within the barricade, with his spear thrust into the ground at his head and Abner and his men sleeping around him.

8* Abishai whispered to David: "God has delivered your enemy into your grasp this day. Let me nail him to the ground with one thrust of the spear; I will not need a second thrust!" 9 But David said to Abishai, "Do not harm him, for who can lay hands on the LORD's anointed and remain unpunished? 10 As the LORD lives," David continued, "it must be the LORD himself who will strike him, whether the time comes for him to die, or he goes out and perishes in battle. 11 But the LORD forbid that I touch his anointed! Now take the spear which is at his head and the water jug, and let us be on our way." 12 So David took the spear and the water jug from their place at Saul's head, and they got away without anyone's seeing or knowing or awakening. All remained asleep, because the LORD had put them into a deep slumber.

David Taunts Abner. 13 Going across to an opposite slope, David stood on a remote hilltop at a great distance from Abner, son of Ner, and the troops. 14 He then shouted, "Will you not answer, Abner?" And Abner answered, "Who is it that calls me?" 15 David said to Abner: "Are you not a man whose like does not exist in Israel? Why, then, have you not guarded your lord the king when one of his subjects went to kill the king, your lord? 16 This is no creditable service you have performed. As the LORD lives, you people deserve death because you have not guarded your lord, the LORD's anointed. Go, look: where are the king's spear and the water jug that was at his head?"

Saul Admits His Guilt. 17 Saul recognized David's voice and asked, "Is that your voice, my son David?" David answered, "Yes, my lord the king." 18 He continued: "Why does my lord pursue his servant? What have I done? What evil do I plan? 19*† Please, now, let my lord the king listen to the words of his servant. If the LORD has incited you against me, let an offering appease him; but if men, may they be cursed before the LORD, because they have exiled me so that this day I have no share in the LORD's inheritance, but am told: 'Go serve other gods!' 20 Do not let my blood flow to the ground far from the presence of the LORD. For the king of Israel has come out to seek a single flea as if he were hunting partridge in the mountains." 21 Then Saul said: "I have done wrong. Come back, my son David, I will not harm you again, because you have held my life precious today. Indeed, I have been a fool and have made a serious mistake." 22 But David answered: "Here is the king's spear. Let an attendant come over to get it. 23* The LORD will reward each man for his justice and faithfulness. Today, though the LORD delivered you into my grasp, I would not harm the LORD's anointed. 24 As I valued your life highly today, so may the LORD value my life highly and deliver me from all difficulties." 25* Then Saul said to David: "Blessed are you, my son David! You shall certainly succeed in whatever you undertake." David went his way, and Saul returned to his home.

CHAPTER 27

Refuge among Philistines. 1 But David said to himself: "I shall perish some day at the hand of Saul. I have no choice but to escape to the land of the Philistines; then Saul will give up his continual search for me throughout the land of Israel, and I shall be out of his reach." 2* Accordingly, David departed with his six hundred men and went over to Achish, son of Maoch, king of Gath. 3* David and his men lived in Gath with Achish; each one had his family, and David had his two wives, Ahinoam from Jezreel and Abigail, the widow of Nabal from Carmel. 4 When Saul was told that

*

26, 1f: 23, 19f; Ps 54.
5: 17, 20.
6: 1 Chr 2, 16.
8: 18, 11; 19, 10.
19: 24, 16.
23: 18, 20.
25: 24, 21.
27, 2: 21, 11-16.
3: 25, 3.44; 30, 3ff; 2 Sm 2, 3.

†

26, 19: *The Lord's inheritance:* the land of Israel (Dt 32, 8f), under the Lord's special protection, where he could be freely worshiped.

David had fled to Gath, he no longer
searched for him.
In Ziklag. 5 David said to Achish: "If
I meet with your approval, let me have
a place to live in one of the country
towns. Why should your servant live
with you in the royal city?" 6*† That
same day Achish gave him Ziklag,
which has, therefore, belonged to the
kings of Judah up to the present time.
7* In all, David lived a year and four
months in the country of the Philistines.
Raids on Israel's Foes. 8* David and
his men went up and made raids on the
Geshurites, Girzites, and Amalekites—
peoples living in the land between
Telam, on the approach to Shur, and the
land of Egypt. 9 In attacking the land
David would not leave a man or woman
alive, but would carry off sheep, oxen,
asses, camels, and clothes. On his return
he brought these to Achish, 10* who
asked, "Whom did you raid this time?"
And David answered, "The Negeb of Ju-
dah," or "The Negeb of Jerahmeel," or
"The Negeb of the Kenites." 11 But David
would not leave a man or woman alive
to be brought to Gath, fearing that they
would betray him by saying, "This is
what David did." This was his custom
as long as he lived in the country of the
Philistines. 12 And Achish trusted David,
thinking, "He must certainly be detested
by his people Israel. I shall have him as
my vassal forever."

CHAPTER 28

1 In those days the Philistines mus-
tered their military forces to fight
against Israel. So Achish said to David,
"You realize, of course, that you and
your men must go out on campaign with
me to Jezreel." 2 David answered
Achish, "Good! Now you shall learn
what your servant can do." Then Achish
said to David, "I shall appoint you my
permanent bodyguard."
3* Now Samuel had died and, after be-
ing mourned by all Israel, was buried
in his city, Ramah. Meanwhile Saul had
driven mediums and fortune-tellers out
of the land.
Saul in Dismay. 4 The Philistine levies
advanced to Shunem and encamped.
Saul, too, mustered all Israel; they
camped on Gilboa. 5 When Saul saw the
camp of the Philistines, he was dis-
mayed and lost heart completely. 6* He
therefore consulted the LORD; but the
LORD gave no answer, whether in
dreams or by the Urim or through
prophets. 7* Then Saul said to his ser-
vants, "Find me a woman who is a me-
dium, to whom I can go to seek counsel
through her." His servants answered
him, "There is a woman in Endor who
is a medium."
The Witch of Endor. 8* So he dis-
guised himself, putting on other clothes,
and set out with two companions. They
came to the woman by night, and Saul
said to her, "Tell my fortune through a
ghost; conjure up for me the one I ask
you to." 9 But the woman answered him,
"You are surely aware of what Saul has
done, in driving the mediums and for-
tune-tellers out of the land. Why, then,
are you laying snares for my life, to have
me killed?" 10 But Saul swore to her by
the LORD, "As the LORD lives, you shall
incur no blame for this." 11 Then the
woman asked him, "Whom do you want
me to conjure up?" and he answered,
"Samuel."
Samuel Appears. 12† When the
woman saw Samuel, she shrieked at the
top of her voice and said to Saul, "Why
have you deceived me? You are Saul!"
13 But the king said to her, "Have no fear.
What do you see?" The woman an-
swered Saul, "I see a preternatural be-
ing rising from the earth." 14 "What does
he look like?" asked Saul. And she re-
plied, "It is an old man who is rising,
clothed in a mantle." Saul knew that it
was Samuel, and so he bowed face to
the ground in homage.
Saul's Doom. 15* Samuel then said to
Saul, "Why do you disturb me by conjur-
ing me up?" Saul replied: "I am in great
straits, for the Philistines are waging
war against me and God has abandoned
me. Since he no longer answers me
through prophets or in dreams, I have
called you to tell me what I should do."
16* To this Samuel said: "But why do you
ask me, if the LORD has abandoned you
and is with your neighbor? 17 The LORD
has done to you what he foretold through
me: he has torn the kingdom from your
grasp and has given it to your neighbor
David.
18* "Because you disobeyed the
LORD's directive and would not carry out
his fierce anger against Amalek, the

*

6: 30, 1.
7: 29, 3.
8: 15, 3.7.
10: 30, 14.29; 1 Chr 2, 9.25.42.
28, 3: 25, 1; Sir 46, 20.
6: 14, 37.41; Ex 28, 30; Lv 8, 8.
7: Lv 19, 31; 20, 27; Dt 18, 10ff; 1 Chr 10, 13f; Acts 16, 16.
8: 1 Kgs 14, 2.
15: Sir 46, 20.
16: 15, 27f.
18: 15, 18f.26.

†

27, 6: *Has . . . belonged to the kings of Judah:* as a personal holding, outside the system of tribal lands; Jerusalem, when taken by David, had a similar status (2 Sm 5, 7-9).

28, 12: Human beings cannot communicate at will with the souls of the dead. God may, however, permit a departed soul to appear to the living and even to disclose things unknown to them. Saul's own prohibition of necromancy and divination (v 3) was in keeping with the consistent teaching of the Old Testament. If we are to credit the reality of the apparition to Saul, it was due, not to the summons of the witch, but to God's will; the woman merely furnished the occasion.

LORD has done this to you today.
19* Moreover, the LORD will deliver Is-
rael, and you as well, into the clutches
of the Philistines. By tomorrow you and
your sons will be with me, and the LORD
will have delivered the army of Israel
into the hands of the Philistines."
Saul's Despair. 20 Immediately Saul
fell full length on the ground, for he was
badly shaken by Samuel's message.
Moreover, he had no bodily strength left,
since he had eaten nothing all that day
and night. 21 Then the woman came to
Saul, and seeing that he was quite ter-
ror-stricken, said to him: "Remember,
your maidservant obeyed you: I took my
life in my hands and fulfilled the request
you made of me. 22 Now you, in turn,
please listen to your maidservant. Let
me set something before you to eat, so
that you may have strength when you
go on your way." 23 But he refused, say-
ing, "I will not eat." However, when his
servants joined the woman in urging
him, he listened to their entreaties, got
up from the ground, and sat on a couch.
24 The woman had a stall-fed calf in the
house, which she now quickly slaugh-
tered. Then taking flour, she kneaded it
and baked unleavened bread. 25 She set
the meal before Saul and his servants,
and they ate. Then they stood up and
left the same night.

CHAPTER 29

David's Aid Rejected. 1* Now the
Philistines had mustered all their forces
in Aphek, and the Israelites were en-
camped at the spring of Harod near
Jezreel. 2 As the Philistine lords were
marching their groups of a hundred and
a thousand, David and his men were
marching in the rear guard with Achish.
3* The Philistine chiefs asked, "What are
those Hebrews doing here?" And Achish
answered them: "Why, that is David, the
officer of Saul, king of Israel. He has
been with me now for a year or two, and
I have no fault to find with him from
the day he came over to me until the
present." 4* But the Philistine chiefs
were angered at this and said to him:
"Send that man back! Let him return
to the place you picked out for him. He
must not go down into battle with us, lest
during the battle he become our enemy.
For how else can he win back his mas-
ter's favor, if not with the heads of these
men of ours? 5* Is this not the David of
whom they sing during their dances,

'Saul has slain his thousands,
but David his ten thousands'?"

6 So Achish summoned David and said
to him: "As the LORD lives, you are hon-
est, and I should be pleased to have you
active with me in the camp, for I have
found nothing wrong with you from the
day of your arrival to this day. But you
are not welcome to the lords. 7 Withdraw
peaceably, now, and do nothing that
might displease the Philistine lords."
8 But David said to Achish: "What have
I done? Or what have you against your
servant from the first day I have been
with you to this day, that I cannot go
to fight against the enemies of my lord
the king?" 9 "You know," Achish an-
swered David, "that you are acceptable
to me. But the Philistine chiefs have de-
termined you are not to go up with us
to battle. 10 So the first thing tomorrow,
you and your lord's servants who came
with you, go to the place I picked out
for you. Do not decide to take umbrage
at this; you are as acceptable to me as
an angel of God. But make an early
morning start, as soon as it grows light,
and be on your way." 11 So David and
his men left early in the morning to re-
turn to the land of the Philistines. The
Philistines, however, went on up to
Jezreel.

CHAPTER 30

Ziklag in Ruins. 1* Before David and
his men reached Ziklag on the third day,
the Amalekites had raided the Negeb
and Ziklag, had stormed the city, and
had set it on fire. 2 They had taken cap-
tive the women and all who were in the
city, young and old, killing no one; they
had carried them off when they left.
3 David and his men arrived at the city
to find it burned to the ground and their
wives, sons and daughters taken cap-
tive. 4 Then David and those who were
with him wept aloud until they could
weep no more. 5* David's two wives,
Ahinoam of Jezreel and Abigail, the
widow of Nabal from Carmel, had also
been carried off with the rest. 6 Now
David found himself in great difficulty,
for the men spoke of stoning him, so bit-
ter were they over the fate of their sons
and daughters. But with renewed trust
in the LORD his God, 7* David said to
Abiathar, the priest, son of Ahimelech,
"Bring me the ephod!" When Abiathar
brought him the ephod, 8 David inquired
of the LORD, "Shall I pursue these raid-
ers? Can I overtake them?" The LORD
answered him, "Go in pursuit, for you
shall surely overtake them and effect a
rescue."
Raid of the Amalekites. 9 So David
went off with his six hundred men and
came as far as the Wadi Besor, where
those who were to remain behind halted.

19: 31, 2-6; Sir 46, 20.
29, 1: 4, 1.
3: 27, 7.
4: 1 Chr 12, 19f.
5: 18, 6f; 21, 11.
30, 1: 27, 6.10; 1 Chr 12, 21.
5: 25, 42; 27, 3; 30, 5.
7f: 2, 28; 23, 6; Ex 28, 30.

10 David continued the pursuit with four
hundred men, but two hundred were too
exhausted to cross the Wadi Besor and
remained behind. 11 An Egyptian was
found in the open country and brought
to David. He was provided with food,
which he ate, and given water to drink;
12 a cake of pressed figs and two cakes
of pressed raisins were also offered to
him. When he had eaten, he revived; he
had not taken food nor drunk water for
three days and three nights. 13 Then
David asked him, "To whom do you be-
long, and where do you come from?" He
replied: "I am an Egyptian, the slave of
an Amalekite. My master abandoned
me because I fell sick three days ago to-
day. 14* We raided the Negeb of the
Cherethites, the territory of Judah, and
the Negeb of Caleb; and we set Ziklag
on fire." 15 David then asked him, "Will
you lead me down to this raiding party?"
He answered, "Swear to me by God that
you will not kill me or deliver me to my
master, and I will lead you to the raiding
party." 16 He did lead them, and there
were the Amalekites scattered all over
the ground, eating, drinking, and in a
festive mood because of all the rich
booty they had taken from the land of
the Philistines and from the land of Ju-
dah.

The Booty Recovered. 17* From dawn
to sundown David attacked them, put-
ting them under the ban so that none
escaped except four hundred young
men, who mounted their camels and
fled. 18 David recovered everything the
Amalekites had taken, and rescued his
two wives. 19 Nothing was missing, small
or great, booty or sons or daughters, of
all that the Amalekites had taken. David
brought back everything. 20 Moreover,
David took all the sheep and oxen, and
as they drove these before him, they
shouted, "This is David's spoil!"

Division of the Spoils. 21 When David
came to the two hundred men who had
been too exhausted to follow him, and
whom he had left behind at the Wadi
Besor, they came out to meet David and
the men with him. On nearing them
David greeted them. 22 But all the stingy
and worthless men among those who
had accompanied David spoke up to say,
"Since they did not accompany us, we
will not give them anything from the
booty, except to each man his wife and
children. Let them take those along and
be on their way." 23 But David said: "You
must not do this, my brothers, after what
the LORD has given us. He has protected
us and delivered into our grip the band
that came against us. 24* Who could
agree with this proposal of yours?
Rather, the share of the one who goes
down to battle and that of the one who
remains with the baggage shall be the
same; they shall share alike." 25* And
from that day forward he made it a law
and a custom in Israel, as it still is today.

David's Gifts to Judah. 26 When David
came to Ziklag, he sent part of the spoil
to the elders of Judah, city by city, say-
ing, "This is a gift to you from the spoil
of the enemies of the LORD": 27 to those
in Bethel, to those in Ramoth-negeb, to
those in Jattir, 28 to those in Aroer, to
those in Siphmoth, to those in Eshtemoa,
29* to those in Racal, to those in the Je-
rahmeelite cities, to those in the Kenite
cities, 30 to those in Hormah, to those in
Borashan, to those in Athach, 31 to those
in Hebron, and to all the places fre-
quented by David and his men.

CHAPTER 31

Death of Saul and His Sons. 1* As they
pressed their attack on Israel, with the
Israelites fleeing before them and falling
mortally wounded on Mount Gilboa,
2* the Philistines pursued Saul and his
sons closely, and slew Jonathan, Abina-
dab, and Malchishua, sons of Saul. 3 The
battle raged around Saul, and the ar-
chers hit him; he was pierced through
the abdomen. 4* Then Saul said to his
armor-bearer, "Draw your sword and
run me through, lest these uncircum-
cised come and make sport of me." But
his armor-bearer, badly frightened, re-
fused to do it. So Saul took his own sword
and fell upon it. 5*† When the armor-
bearer saw that Saul was dead, he too
fell upon his sword and died with him.
6 Thus Saul, his three sons, and his ar-
mor-bearer died together on that same
day.

7 When the Israelites on the slope of
the valley and those along the Jordan
saw that the men of Israel had fled and
that Saul and his sons were dead, they
too abandoned their cities and fled. Then
the Philistines came and lived in those
cities.

8 The day after the battle the Phi-
listines came to strip the slain, and found
Saul and his three sons lying on Mount
Gilboa. 9* They cut off Saul's head and
stripped him of his armor, and then sent
the good news throughout the land of the
Philistines to their idols and to the peo-
ple. 10 They put his armor in the temple

*

14: 27, 10; Ez 25, 16.
17: 15, 3; Jos 6, 17; Jgs 7, 12.
24: 17, 22; 25, 13.
25: Nm 31, 27.
29: 27, 10.
31, 1-13: 1 Chr 10, 1-12; 2 Sm 1, 1-16; 4, 4.
2: 14, 49; 28, 19; 1 Chr 10, 2f.
4: 24, 7; Jgs 9, 54; 1 Chr 10, 4.
5: 10, 1; 26, 9; 2 Mc 14, 42.
9: 17, 54; 2 Sm 1, 20; 2 Mc 15, 35.

†

31, 5: This report of the suicidal act of Saul is presented as a part of his downfall, to be judged accordingly.

of Astarte, but impaled his body on the
wall of Bethshan.
Burial of Saul. 11* When the inhabit-
ants of Jabesh-gilead heard what the
Philistines had done to Saul, 12† all their
warriors set out, and after marching
throughout the night, removed the bod-
ies of Saul and his sons from the wall
of Beth-shan, and brought them to Ja-
besh, where they cremated them.
13 Then they took their bones and buried
them under the tamarisk tree in Jabesh,
and fasted for seven days.

THE SECOND BOOK OF SAMUEL

CHAPTER 1

Report of Saul's Death. 1* After the
death of Saul, David returned from his
defeat of the Amalekites and spent two
days in Ziklag. 2 On the third day a man
came from Saul's camp, with his clothes
torn and dirt on his head. Going to
David, he fell to the ground in homage.
3 David asked him, "Where do you come
from?" He replied, "I have escaped from
the Israelite camp." 4 "Tell me what
happened," David bade him. He an-
swered that the soldiers had fled the bat-
tle and that many of them had fallen and
were dead, among them Saul and his son
Jonathan. 5 Then David said to the youth
who was reporting to him, "How do you
know that Saul and his son Jonathan are
dead?" 6* The youthful informant re-
plied: "It was by chance that I found my-
self on Mount Gilboa and saw Saul
leaning on his spear, with chariots and
horsemen closing in on him. 7 He turned
around and, seeing me, called me to
him. When I said, 'Here I am,' 8 he asked
me, 'Who are you?' and I replied, 'An
Amalekite.' 9 Then he said to me, 'Stand
up to me, please, and finish me off, for
I am in great suffering, yet fully alive.'
10 So I stood up to him and dispatched
him, for I knew that he could not survive
his wound. I removed the crown from
his head and the armlet from his arm
and brought them here to my lord."
11* David seized his garments and rent
them, and all the men who were with
him did likewise. 12* They mourned and
wept and fasted until evening for Saul
and his son Jonathan, and for the sol-
diers of the LORD of the clans of Israel,
because they had fallen by the sword.
13 Then David said to the young man
who had brought him the information,
"Where are you from?" He replied, "I
am the son of an Amalekite immigrant."
14* David said to him, "How is it that you
were not afraid to put forth your hand
to desecrate the LORD's anointed?"
15 David then called one of the atten-
dants and said to him, "Come, strike him
down"; and the youth struck him a mor-
tal blow. 16 Meanwhile David said to him,
"You are responsible for your own
death, for you testified against yourself
when you said, 'I dispatched the LORD's
anointed.' "
Elegy for Saul and Jonathan. 17 Then
David chanted this elegy for Saul and
his son Jonathan, 18* which is recorded
in the Book of Jashar to be taught to the
Judahites. He sang:

19 "Alas! the glory of Israel, Saul,
slain upon your heights;
how can the warriors have fallen!

20* "Tell it not in Gath,
herald it not in the streets of Ash-
kelon,
Lest the Philistine maidens rejoice,
lest the daughters of the strangers
exult!
21*† Mountains of Gilboa,
may there be neither dew nor rain
upon you,
nor upsurgings of the deeps!
Upon you lie begrimed the warriors'
shields,
the shield of Saul, no longer
anointed with oil.

22* "From the blood of the slain,
from the bodies of the valiant,
The bow of Jonathan did not turn
back,
or the sword of Saul return un-
stained.
23 Saul and Jonathan, beloved and
cherished,
separated neither in life nor in
death,
swifter than eagles, stronger than
lions!
24 Women of Israel, weep over Saul,
who clothed you in scarlet and in
finery,
who decked your attire with orna-
ments of gold.

25 "How can the warriors have fallen—
in the thick of the battle,
slain upon your heights!

*

11ff: 11, 1-11; 2 Sm 2, 4-7.
1, 1: 1 Sm 30, 17-20; 31, 1-13.
6-10: 4, 10; 1 Sm 31, 1-4; 1 Chr 10, 1-4.
11: 13, 31.
12: 1 Sm 31, 13.
14: 1 Sm 10, 1; 24, 7; Ps 105, 15.
18: Jos 10, 13.
20: Jgs 16, 23; 1 Sm 31, 9; Mi 1, 10.
21: Gn 27, 28.
22: 1 Sm 14, 47.

†

31, 12: *Cremated them:* cremation was not normally practiced in Israel, though it was known in the country from pre-Israelite times.

1, 21: *Upsurgings of the deeps:* this reading attempts to recover from an unintelligible Hebrew phrase the poetic parallel to dew and rain. The sense would be a wish that the mountain should have neither moisture from above nor water from springs or wells.

26* “I grieve for you, Jonathan my brother!
most dear have you been to me;
More precious have I held love for you
than love for women.

27 “How can the warriors have fallen,
the weapons of war have perished!”

CHAPTER 2

David Anointed King. 1 After this
David inquired of the LORD, “Shall I go
up into one of the cities of Judah?” The
LORD replied to him, “Yes.” Then David
asked, “Where shall I go?” He replied,
“To Hebron.” 2* So David went up there
accompanied by his two wives, Ahinoam
of Jezreel and Abigail, the widow of Na-
bal of Carmel. 3 David also brought up
his men with their families, and they
dwelt in the cities near Hebron. 4* Then
the men of Judah came there and
anointed David king of the Judahites.
A report reached David that the men
of Jabesh-gilead had buried Saul. 5 So
David sent messengers to the men of Ja-
besh-gilead and said to them: “May you
be blessed by the LORD for having done
this kindness to your lord Saul in bury-
ing him. 6 And now may the LORD be
kind and faithful to you. I, too, will be
generous to you for having done this.
7 Take courage, therefore, and prove
yourselves valiant men, for though your
lord Saul is dead, the Judahites have
anointed me their king.”

IV: THE REIGN OF DAVID

Ishbaal King of Israel. 8* Abner, son
of Ner, Saul’s general, took Ishbaal, son
of Saul, and brought him over to Maha-
naim, 9 where he made him king over
Gilead, the Ashurites, Jezreel, Ephraim,
Benjamin, and the rest of Israel.
10 Ishbaal, son of Saul, was forty years
old when he became king over Israel,
and he reigned for two years. The Ju-
dahites alone followed David. 11* In all,
David spent seven years and six months
in Hebron as king of the Judahites.
Combat near Gibeon. 12 Now Abner,
son of Ner, and the servants of Ishbaal,
Saul’s son, left Mahanaim for Gibeon.
13 Joab, son of Zeruiah, and David’s
servants also set out and met them at
the pool of Gibeon. And they sat down,
one group on one side of the pool and
the other on the opposite side. 14 Then
Abner said to Joab, “Let the young men
rise and perform for us.” Joab replied,
“All right!” 15 So they rose and were
counted off: twelve of the Benjaminites
of Ishbaal, son of Saul, and twelve of
David’s servants. 16† Then each one
grasped his opponent’s head and thrust
his sword into his opponent’s side, and
all fell down together. And so that place,
which is in Gideon, was named the Field
of the Sides.
Death of Asahel. 17 After a very fierce
battle that day, Abner and the men of
Israel were defeated by David’s ser-
vants. 18* The three sons of Zeruiah were
there—Joab, Abishai, and Asahel. Asa-
hel, who was as fleet of foot as a gazelle
in the open field, 19* set out after Abner,
turning neither right nor left in his pur-
suit. 20 Abner turned around and said,
“Is that you, Asahel?” He replied, “Yes.”
21 Abner said to him, “Turn right or left;
seize one of the young men and take
what you can strip from him.” But Asa-
hel would not desist from his pursuit.
22* Once more Abner said to Asahel:
“Stop pursuing me! Why must I strike
you to the ground? How could I face your
brother Joab?” 23 Still he refused to stop.
So Abner struck him in the abdomen
with the heel of his javelin, and the
weapon protruded from his back. He fell
there and died on the spot. And all who
came to the place where Asahel had
fallen and died, came to a halt. 24 Joab
and Abishai, however, continued the
pursuit of Abner. The sun had gone
down when they came to the hill of Am-
mah which lies east of the valley toward
the desert near Geba.
Truce between Joab and Abner.
25 Here the Benjaminites rallied around
Abner, forming a single group, and
made a stand on the hilltop. 26 Then Ab-
ner called to Joab and said: “Must the
sword destroy to the utmost? Do you not
know that afterward there will be bitter-
ness? How much longer will you refrain
from ordering the people to stop the pur-
suit of their brothers?” 27 Joab replied,
“As God lives, if you had not spoken,
the soldiers would not have been with-
drawn from the pursuit of their brothers
until morning.” 28 Joab then sounded the
horn, and all the soldiers came to a halt,
pursuing Israel no farther and fighting
no more. 29 Abner and his men marched
all night long through the Arabah,
crossed the Jordan, marched all through
the morning, and came to Mahanaim.
30 Joab, after interrupting the pursuit of
Abner, assembled all the men. Besides
Asahel, nineteen other servants of David
were missing. 31 But David’s servants
had fatally wounded three hundred and

---

*

26: 1 Sm 18, 1; 1 Mc 9, 21.
2, 2: 1 Sm 25, 42f.
4: 1 Sm 31, 11ff.
8: 1 Sm 14, 50.
11: 5, 5; 1 Kgs 2, 11.
18: 23, 24; 1 Chr 2, 16.
19: 1 Chr 27, 7.
22: 3, 27f.30.

†

2, 16: The nature of this gruesome game is not clear, and the place name is variously given in the older texts.

sixty men of Benjamin, followers of Ab-
ner. 32 They took up Asahel and buried
him in his father's tomb in Bethlehem.
Joab and his men made an all-night
march, and dawn found them in Hebron.

CHAPTER 3

1 There followed a long war between
the house of Saul and that of David, in
which David grew stronger, but the
house of Saul weaker.

Sons Born in Hebron. 2* Sons were
born to David in Hebron: his first-born,
Amnon, of Ahinoam from Jezreel; 3* the
second, Chileab, of Abigail the widow of
Nabal of Carmel; the third, Absalom, son
of Maacah the daughter of Talmai, king
of Geshur; 4* the fourth, Adonijah, son
of Haggith; the fifth, Shephatiah, son of
Abital; 5 and the sixth, Ithream, of
David's wife Eglah. These were born to
David in Hebron.

Ishbaal and Abner Quarrel. 6 During
the war between the house of Saul and
that of David, Abner was gaining power
in the house of Saul. 7* Now Saul had
had a concubine, Rizpah, the daughter
of Aiah. And Ishbaal, son of Saul, said
to Abner, "Why have you been intimate
with my father's concubine?" 8 Enraged
at the words of Ishbaal, Abner said, "Am
I a dog's head in Judah? At present I
am doing a kindness to the house of your
father Saul, to his brothers and his
friends, by keeping you out of David's
clutches; yet this day you charge me
with a crime involving a woman! 9* May
God do thus and so to Abner if I do not
carry out for David what the LORD swore
to him— 10* that is, take away the king-
dom from the house of Saul and estab-
lish the throne of David over Israel and
over Judah from Dan to Beer-sheba."
11 In his fear of Abner, Ishbaal was no
longer able to say a word to him.

Abner and David Reconciled. 12 Then
Abner sent messengers to David in
Telam, where he was at the moment, to
say, "Make an agreement with me, and
I will aid you by bringing all Israel over
to you." 13* He replied, "Very well, I will
make an agreement with you. But one
thing I require of you. You must not ap-
pear before me unless you bring back
Michal, Saul's daughter, when you come
to present yourself to me." 14 At the
same time David sent messengers to
Ishbaal, son of Saul, to say, "Give me
my wife Michal, whom I espoused by
paying a hundred Philistine foreskins."
15* Ishbaal sent for her and took her
away from her husband Paltiel, son of
Laish, 16 who followed her weeping as far
as Bahurim. But Abner said to him, "Go
back!" And he turned back.

17 Abner then said in discussion with
the elders of Israel: "For a long time you
have been seeking David as your king.
18 Now take action, for the LORD has said
of David, 'By my servant David I will
save my people Israel from the grasp
of the Philistines and from the grasp of
all their enemies.' " 19 Abner also spoke
personally to Benjamin, and then went
to make his own report to David in He-
bron concerning all that would be agree-
able to Israel and to the whole house of
Benjamin. 20 When Abner, accompanied
by twenty men, came to David in He-
bron, David prepared a feast for Abner
and for the men who were with him.
21 Then Abner said to David, "I will now
go to assemble all Israel for my lord the
king, that they may make an agreement
with you; you will then be king over all
whom you wish to rule." So David bade
Abner farewell, and he went away in
peace.

Death of Abner. 22 Just then David's
servants and Joab were coming in from
an expedition, bringing much plunder
with them. Abner, having been dis-
missed by David, was no longer with him
in Hebron but had gone his way in peace.
23 When Joab and the whole force he had
with him arrived, he was informed, "Ab-
ner, son of Ner, came to David; he has
been sent on his way in peace." 24 So
Joab went to the king and said: "What
have you done? Abner came to you. Why
did you let him go peacefully on his way?
25 Are you not aware that Abner came
to deceive you and to learn the ins and
outs of all that you are doing?"

26 Joab then left David, and without
David's knowledge sent messengers
after Abner, who brought him back from
the cistern of Sirah. 27* When Abner re-
turned to Hebron, Joab took him aside
within the city gate as though to speak
with him privately. There he stabbed
him in the abdomen, and he died in re-
venge for the killing of Joab's brother
Asahel. 28* Later David heard of it and
said: "Before the LORD; I and my king-
dom are forever innocent. 29 May the full
responsibility for the death of Abner, son
of Ner, be laid to Joab and to all his fam-
ily. May the men of Joab's family never
be without one suffering from a dis-
charge, or a leper, or one unmanly, one
falling by the sword, or one in need of
bread!" 30 [Joab and his brother Abishai
had lain in wait for Abner because he
killed their brother Asahel in battle at
Gibeon.]

David Mourns Abner. 31* Then David
said to Joab and to all the people who

3, 2-5: 1 Chr 3, 14.
3: 13, 37; 15, 8.
4: 1 Kgs 1, 5.
7: 21, 8ff.
9: Ru 1, 17.
10: 5, 2; 1 Sm 25, 30.
13: 1 Sm 18, 20-27.
15: 1 Sm 25, 44.
27: 1 Kgs 2, 5.32.
28.30: 2, 22f.
31: 21, 10.

were with him, "Rend your garments,
gird yourselves with sackcloth, and
mourn over Abner." King David himself
followed the bier. 32 When they had bur-
ied Abner in Hebron, the king wept
aloud at the grave of Abner, and the peo-
ple also wept. 33 And the king sang this
elegy over Abner:

"Would Abner have died like a fool?
34 Your hands were not bound with
chains,
nor your feet placed in fetters;
as men fall before the wicked, you
fell."

And all the people continued to weep for
him. 35* Then they went to console David
with food while it was still day. But
David swore, "May God do thus and so
to me if I eat bread or anything else be-
fore sunset." 36 All the people noted this
with approval, just as they were pleased
with everything that the king did. 37 So
on that day all the people and all Israel
came to know that the king had no part
in the killing of Abner, son of Ner. 38 The
king then said to his servants: "You must
recognize that a great general has fallen
today in Israel. 39* Although I am the
anointed king, I am weak this day, and
these men, the sons of Zeruiah, are too
ruthless for me. May the LORD requite
the evildoer in accordance with his evil
deed."

CHAPTER 4

Death of Ishbaal. 1 When Ishbaal, son
of Saul, heard that Abner had died in
Hebron, he ceased to resist and all Israel
was alarmed. 2* Ishbaal, son of Saul, had
two company leaders named Baanah
and Rechab, sons of Rimmon the Beer-
othite, of the tribe of Benjamin. [Beer-
oth, too, was ascribed to Benjamin:
3* the Beerothites fled to Gittaim, where
they have been resident aliens to this
day. 4*† Jonathan, son of Saul, had a son
named Meribbaal with crippled feet. He
was five years old when the news about
Saul and Jonathan came from Jezreel,
and his nurse took him up and fled. But
in their hasty flight, he fell and became
lame.] 5 The sons of Rimmon the Beer-
othite, Rechab and Baanah, came into
the house of Ishbaal during the heat of
the day, while he was taking his siesta.
6 The portress of the house had dozed
off while sifting wheat, and was asleep.
So Rechab and his brother Baanah
slipped past 7 and entered the house
while Ishbaal was lying asleep in his
bedroom. They struck and killed him,
and cut off his head. Then, taking the
head, they traveled on the Arabah road
all night long.

The Murder Avenged. 8 They brought
the head of Ishbaal to David in Hebron
and said to the king: "This is the head
of Ishbaal, son of your enemy Saul, who
sought your life. Thus has the LORD this
day avenged my lord the king on Saul
and his posterity." 9 But David replied
to Rechab and his brother Baanah, sons
of Rimmon the Beerothite: "As the LORD
lives, who rescued me from all difficulty,
10* in Ziklag I seized and put to death
the man who informed me of Saul's
death, thinking himself the bearer of
good news for which I ought to give him
a reward. 11 How much more now, when
wicked men have slain an innocent man
in bed at home, must I hold you respon-
sible for his death and destroy you from
the earth!" 12* So at a command from
David, the young men killed them and
cut off their hands and feet, hanging
them up near the pool in Hebron. But
he took the head of Ishbaal and buried
it in Abner's grave in Hebron.

CHAPTER 5

David King of Israel. 1* All the tribes
of Israel came to David in Hebron and
said: "Here we are, your bone and your
flesh. 2* In days past, when Saul was our
king, it was you who led the Israelites
out and brought them back. And the
LORD said to you, 'You shall shepherd
my people Israel and shall be com-
mander of Israel.' " 3 When all the elders
of Israel came to David in Hebron, King
David made an agreement with them
there before the LORD, and they
anointed him king of Israel. 4 David was
thirty years old when he became king,
and he reigned for forty years: 5* seven
years and six months in Hebron over Ju-
dah, and thirty-three years in Jerusa-
lem over all Israel and Judah.

Capture of Zion. 6*† Then the king
and his men set out for Jerusalem
against the Jebusites who inhabited the
region. David was told, "You cannot en-
ter here: the blind and the lame will
drive you away!" which was their way
of saying, "David cannot enter here."

*

35: Ru 1, 17.
39: Ps 28, 4; Is 3, 11.
4, 2: 9, 3; Jos 9, 17f.
3: Jos 18, 25.
4: 9, 3; 19, 25.
10: 1, 6-10.14.16.
12: Dt 21, 22f; 1 Sm 31, 10.
5, 1ff: 1 Chr 11, 1ff.
2: 3, 10; Dt 17, 15; 1 Sm 18, 16.
5: 2, 11; 1 Kgs 2, 11; 1 Chr 3, 4.
6-10: 1 Chr 11, 4-9.
6: Jos 15, 63; Jgs 1, 19. 21; Is 29, 3.

†

4, 4: Saul's grandson Meribbaal is the subject of ch 9. The text of this verse may owe its present place to the fact that pre-Christian copies of the Books of Samuel tended to confuse his name with that of his uncle Ishbaal, Saul's son and successor, a principal figure in chs 2-4.

5, 6-12: David's most important military exploit, the taking of Jerusalem, is here presented before his battles with the Philistines, vv 17-25, which were earlier in time. The sense of vv 6 and 8 is in doubt.

7 But David did take the stronghold of
Zion, which is the City of David. 8* On
that day David said: "All who wish to
attack the Jebusites must strike at them
through the water shaft. The lame and
the blind shall be the personal enemies
of David." That is why it is said, "The
blind and the lame shall not enter the
palace."
9* David then dwelt in the stronghold,
which was called the City of David; he
built up the area from Millo to the pal-
ace. 10* David grew steadily more pow-
erful, for the LORD of hosts was with him.
11* Hiram, king of Tyre, sent ambassa-
dors to David; he furnished cedar wood,
as well as carpenters and masons, who
built a palace for David. 12 And David
knew that the LORD had established him
as king of Israel and had exalted his rule
for the sake of his people Israel.

David's Family in Jerusalem.
13* David took more concubines and
wives in Jerusalem after he had come
from Hebron, and more sons and
daughters were born to him in Jerusa-
lem. 14 These are the names of those who
were born to him in Jerusalem: Sham-
mua, Shobab, Nathan, Solomon,
15 Ibhar, Elishua, Nepheg, Japhia,
16 Elishama, Baaliada, and Eliphelet.

Rout of the Philistines. 17† When the
Philistines heard that David had been
anointed king of Israel, they all took the
field in search of him. On hearing this,
David went down to the refuge. 18† The
Philistines came and overran the valley
of Rephaim. 19 David inquired of the
LORD, "Shall I attack the Philistines—
will you deliver them into my grip?" The
LORD replied to David, "Attack, for I will
surely deliver the Philistines into your
grip." 20† David then went to Baal-pera-
zim, where he defeated them. He said,
"The LORD has scattered my enemies
before me like waters that have broken
free." That is why the place is called
Baal-perazim. 21 They abandoned their
gods there, and David and his men car-
ried them away. 22 But the Philistines
came up again and overran the valley
of Rephaim. 23 So David inquired of the
LORD, who replied: "You must not attack
frontally, but circle their rear and meet
them before the mastic trees. 24† When
you hear a sound of marching in the tops
of the mastic trees, act decisively, for
the LORD will have gone forth before you
to attack the camp of the Philistines."
25 David obeyed the LORD's command
and routed the Philistines from Gibeon
as far as Gezer.

CHAPTER 6

The Ark Brought to Jerusalem.
1* David again assembled all the picked
men of Israel, thirty thousand in num-
ber. 2* Then David and all the people
who were with him set out for Baala of
Judah to bring up from there the ark
of God, which bears the name of the
LORD of hosts enthroned above the cher-
ubim. 3* The ark of God was placed on
a new cart and taken away from the
house of Abinadab on the hill. Uzzah and
Ahio, sons of Abinadab, guided the cart,
4 with Ahio walking before it, 5* while
David and all the Israelites made merry
before the LORD with all their strength,
with singing and with citharas, harps,
tambourines, sistrums and cymbals.
6 When they came to the threshing floor
of Nodan, Uzzah reached out his hand
to the ark of God and steadied it, for the
oxen were making it tip. 7 But the LORD
was angry with Uzzah; God struck him
on that spot, and he died there before
God. 8* David was disturbed because the
LORD had vented his anger on Uzzah.
(The place has been called Perez-uzzah
down to the present day.) 9 David feared
the LORD that day and said, "How can
the ark of the LORD come to me?" 10 So
David would not have the ark of the
LORD brought to him in the City of
David, but diverted it to the house of
Obed-edom the Gittite.
11* The ark of the LORD remained in
the house of Obed-edom the Gittite for
three months, and the LORD blessed
Obed-edom and his whole house.
12* When it was reported to King David
that the LORD had blessed the family of
Obed-edom and all that belonged to him,
David went to bring up the ark of God
from the house of Obed-edom into the
City of David amid festivities. 13 As soon
as the bearers of the ark of the LORD
had advanced six steps, he sacrificed an
ox and a fatling. 14* Then David, girt
with a linen apron, came dancing before
the LORD with abandon, 15 as he and all
the Israelites were bringing up the ark
of the LORD with shouts of joy and to

---

*

8: Lv 21, 18; Mt 21, 14f.
9: 1 Kgs 3, 1; 11, 27.
10: Pss 78, 70ff. 89; 132, 13.
11-25: 1 Chr 14, 1-16.
11f: 1 Kgs 5, 15; 1 Chr 14, 1f.
13-16: 1 Chr 3, 5-8; 14, 3-7.
6, 1-11: 1 Chr 13, 1-14.
2: Ex 25, 10; Jos 15, 9; Ps 132, 8ff; 1 Chr 1, 4.
3: 1 Sm 4, 3f; 6, 7f; 7, 1; Dn 3, 55.
5: Pss 68, 25f; 150, 3.5.
8: 1 Kgs 8, 1.
11: 1 Chr 26, 4.
12-23: 1 Chr 15, 1-29; Ps 24, 7-10.
14: 1 Sm 2, 18.

---

†

5, 17: *Refuge:* probably near Adullam (1 Sm 22, 1-5).

5, 18-25: The successive defeats of the Philistines in the *valley of Rephaim* southwest of Jerusalem had the effect of blocking their access to the mountain ridge near *Gibeon,* and confining them to their holdings on the coast and in the foothills beyond Gezer to the west and south.

5, 20: *Baal-perazim:* means approximately "the lord of scatterings."

5, 24: *Sound of marching:* the wind in the treetops suggestive of the Lord's footsteps.

the sound of the horn. 16 As the ark of
the LORD was entering the City of David,
Saul's daughter Michal looked down
through the window and saw King David
leaping and dancing before the LORD,
and she despised him in her heart.
17* The ark of the LORD was brought in
and set in its place within the tent David
had pitched for it. Then David offered
holocausts and peace offerings before
the LORD. 18 When he finished making
these offerings, he blessed the people in
the name of the LORD of hosts. 19 He then
distributed among all the people, to each
man and each woman in the entire mul-
titude of Israel, a loaf of bread, a cut
of roast meat, and a raisin cake. With
this, all the people left for their homes.
20* When David returned to bless his
own family, Saul's daughter Michal
came out to meet him and said, "How
the king of Israel has honored himself
today, exposing himself to the view of
the slave girls of his followers, as a com-
moner might do!" 21* But David replied
to Michal: "I was dancing before the
LORD. As the LORD lives, who preferred
me to your father and his whole family
when he appointed me commander of
the LORD's people, Israel, not only will
I make merry before the LORD, 22 but I
will demean myself even more. I will be
lowly in your esteem, but in the esteem
of the slave girls you spoke of I will be
honored." 23 And so Saul's daughter Mi-
chal was childless to the day of her
death.

CHAPTER 7

David's Concern for the Ark. 1* When
King David was settled in his palace,
and the LORD had given him rest from
his enemies on every side, 2* he said to
Nathan the prophet, "Here I am living
in a house of cedar, while the ark of God
dwells in a tent!" 3* Nathan answered
the king, "Go, do whatever you have in
mind, for the LORD is with you." 4 But
that night the LORD spoke to Nathan and
said: 5* "Go, tell my servant David,
'Thus says the LORD: Should you build
me a house to dwell in? 6 I have not dwelt
in a house from the day on which I led
the Israelites out of Egypt to the present,
but I have been going about in a tent
under cloth. 7 In all my wanderings ev-
erywhere among the Israelites, did I
ever utter a word to any one of the
judges whom I charged to tend my peo-
ple Israel, to ask: Why have you not built
me a house of cedar?'

The Lord's Promises. 8*† "Now then,
speak thus to my servant David, 'The
LORD of hosts has this to say: It was I
who took you from the pasture and from
the care of the flock to be commander
of my people Israel. 9* I have been with
you wherever you went, and I have de-
stroyed all your enemies before you.
And I will make you famous like the
great ones of the earth. 10 I will fix a place
for my people Israel; I will plant them
so that they may dwell in their place
without further disturbance. Neither
shall the wicked continue to afflict them
as they did of old, 11* since the time I
first appointed judges over my people
Israel. I will give you rest from all your
enemies. The LORD also reveals to you
that he will establish a house for you.
12* And when your time comes and you
rest with your ancestors, I will raise up
your heir after you, sprung from your
loins, and I will make his kingdom firm.
13 It is he who shall build a house for my
name. And I will make his royal throne
firm forever. 14 I will be a father to him,
and he shall be a son to me. And if he
does wrong, I will correct him with the
rod of men and with human chastise-
ments; 15* but I will not withdraw my fa-
vor from him as I withdrew it from your
predecessor Saul, whom I removed from
my presence. 16* Your house and your
kingdom shall endure forever before
me; your throne shall stand firm for-
ever.'" 17 Nathan reported all these
words and this entire vision to David.

King David's Prayer. 18* Then King
David went in and sat before the LORD
and said, "Who am I, Lord GOD, and who
are the members of my house, that you
have brought me to this point? 19† Yet

*

17ff: Lv 1, 1-17; 3, 1-17; 1 Chr 16, 1ff.
20: 1 Chr 16, 43.
21: 1 Sm 13, 14; 15, 28.
7, 1-29: 1 Chr 17, 1-27.
1: 1 Kgs 5, 4.
2: Dt 12, 10; 25, 19.
3: Ps 132, 1-5.
5: 1 Kgs 5, 17; 8, 16.27; 1 Chr 22, 8; 28, 3; Is 66, 1; Acts 7, 48.
8: 1 Sm 16, 13; 17, 15-20; Ps 78, 70f; Am 7, 14.
9: Ps 89, 27.
11: 23, 5; 1 Kgs 2, 4-24.
12ff: 1 Kgs 5, 19; 8, 19; 1 Chr 22, 10; 2 Chr 7, 18; Ps 89, 5.27f.30.37f; Lk 1, 32; Heb 1, 5.
15: 23, 5; 1 Sm 13, 14; 15, 26.28; 2 Kgs 19, 34; 1 Chr 17, 11-14; Ps 89, 34.
16: 23, 5; Dn 2, 45; 1 Mc 2, 57; Mk 11, 10; Lk 1, 32f; Heb 1, 8.
18: 1 Chr 17, 16.

†

7, 8-16: The prophecy to David contained in these verses is cited again, in poetic form, in Ps 89, 20-38, and alluded to in Ps 132. The promise regarding the people of Israel, vv 10-11, is a part of the promise to David at least as old as the composition of this chapter of Samuel, where it is anticipated in vv 6-7, and alluded to in David's thanksgiving, vv 23-24; it applies to the people an expression used of David in Ps 89, 23.

The prophecy to David is the basis for Jewish expectation of a Messiah, son of David, which Jesus Christ fulfilled in a transcendent way; cf Acts 2, 30; Heb 1, 5.

7, 19: *This too you have shown to man:* the text as transmitted has, rather, "and this is instruction for (*or:* the law of) mankind." The author of Chronicles (1 Chr 17, 17) saw approximately the same phrase, which he endeavored to fit into the context in a quite different sense. The above is conjectural; cf Dt 5, 24.

even this you see as too little, Lord GOD;
you have also spoken of the house of
your servant for a long time to come:
this too you have shown to man, Lord
GOD! 20 What more can David say to
you? You know your servant, Lord GOD!
21 For your servant's sake and as you
have had at heart, you have brought
about this entire magnificent disclosure
to your servant. 22* And so—
"Great are you, Lord GOD! There is
none like you and there is no God but
you, just as we have heard it told.
23* What other nation on earth is there
like your people Israel, which God has
led, redeeming it as his people; so that
you have made yourself renowned by
doing this magnificent deed, and by do-
ing awe-inspiring things as you cleared
nations and their gods out of the way
of your people, which you redeemed for
yourself from Egypt? 24* You have es-
tablished for yourself your people Israel
as yours forever, and you, LORD, have
become their God. 25 And now, LORD
God, confirm for all time the prophecy
you have made concerning your servant
and his house, and do as you have prom-
ised. 26 Your name will be forever great,
when men say, 'The LORD of hosts is God
of Israel,' and the house of your servant
David stands firm before you. 27 It is you,
LORD of hosts, God of Israel, who said
in a revelation to your servant, 'I will
build a house for you.' Therefore your
servant now finds the courage to make
this prayer to you. 28* And now, Lord
GOD, you are God and your words are
truth; you have made this generous
promise to your servant. 29 Do, then,
bless the house of your servant that it
may be before you forever; for you, Lord
GOD, have promised, and by your bless-
ing the house of your servant shall be
blessed forever."

CHAPTER 8

Summary of David's Wars. 1*† After
this David attacked the Philistines and
conquered them, wresting . . . from the
Philistines. 2† He also defeated Moab
and then measured them with a line,
making them lie down on the ground.
He told off two lengths of line for execu-
tion, and a full length to be spared. Thus
the Moabites became tributary to David.
3* Next David defeated Hadadezer, son
of Rehob, king of Zobah, when he went
to reestablish his dominion at the Eu-
phrates River. 4* David captured from
him one thousand seven hundred horse-
men and twenty thousand foot soldiers.
And he hamstrung all the chariot
horses, preserving only enough for a
hundred chariots. 5 When the Arameans
of Damascus came to the aid of Had-
adezer, king of Zobah, David slew
twenty-two thousand of them. 6 David
then placed garrisons in Aram of Da-
mascus, and the Arameans became sub-
jects, tributary to David. The LORD
brought David victory in all his under-
takings. 7 David also took away the
golden shields used by Hadadezer's
servants and brought them to Jerusa-
lem. [These Shishak, king of Egypt, took
away when he came to Jerusalem in the
days of Rehoboam, son of Solomon.]
8 From Tebah and Berothai, towns of
Hadadezer, King David removed a very
large quantity of bronze. 9 When Toi,
king of Hamath, heard that David had
defeated all the forces of Hadadezer,
10 he sent his son Hadoram to King
David to greet him and to congratulate
him for his victory over Hadadezer in
battle, because Toi had been in many
battles with Hadadezer. Hadoram also
brought with him articles of silver, gold,
and bronze. 11 These, too, King David
consecrated to the LORD, together with
the silver and gold he had taken from
every nation he had conquered: 12 from
Edom and Moab, from the Ammonites,
from the Philistines, from the Amalek-
ites, and from the plunder of Hadadezer,
son of Rehob, king of Zobah.
13*† On his return, David became fa-
mous for having slain eighteen thousand
Edomites in the Salt Valley; 14 after
which he placed garrisons in Edom.
Thus all the Edomites became David's
subjects, and the LORD brought David
victory in all his undertakings.
David's Officials. 15* David reigned
over all Israel, judging and administer-
ing justice to all his people. 16 Joab, son
of Zeruiah, was in command of the
army. Jehoshaphat, son of Ahilud, was
chancellor. 17 Zadok, son of Ahitub, and
Ahimelech, son of Abiathar, were
priests. Shawsha was scribe. 18* Be-
naiah, son of Jehoiada, was in command

*

22: Ex 15, 11; Is 45, 5.
23: Dt 4, 7.34.
24f: Ex 6, 7; Dt 7, 6; 26, 17; 29, 12.
28: Nm 23, 19; Jn 17, 17.
8, 1-18: 1 Chr 18, 1-17.
3-8: 10, 15-19.
3: 10, 6; 1 Kgs 11, 23.
4: Jos 11, 6.9.
13: 2 Kgs 14, 7.
15-18: 20, 23-26; 1 Kgs 4, 1-6; 1 Chr 18, 14-17.
18: 15, 18; 20, 7.23; 23, 20.

†

8, 1: *Wresting . . . :* the Hebrew text here gives "the bridle of the cubit"; 1 Chr 18, 1 understood "Gath and its dependent villages"; others implausibly read "dominion of the capital city."

8, 2: *Two lengths . . . a full length:* usually taken to mean that two-thirds of them were executed; but it could mean that two-thirds were spared, if the line was used full length in their case but doubled on itself to make "two lines" for those to be put to death.

8, 13: *On his return:* possibly to Jerusalem, after the revolt of Absalom, a circumstance which this catalogue of victories would avoid mentioning. 1 Chr 18, 13 attributes the defeat of the Edomites to Abishai.

of the Cherethites and Pelethites. And
David's sons were priests.

CHAPTER 9

David and Meribbaal. 1* David asked,
"Is there any survivor of Saul's house
to whom I may show kindness for the
sake of Jonathan?" 2* Now there was a
servant of the family of Saul named
Ziba. He was summoned to David, and
the king asked him, "Are you Ziba?" He
replied, "Your servant." 3* Then the
king inquired, "Is there any survivor of
Saul's house to whom I may show God's
kindness?" Ziba answered the king,
"There is still Jonathan's son, whose feet
are crippled." 4* The king said to him,
"Where is he?" and Ziba answered, "He
is in the house of Machir, son of Ammiel,
in Lodebar." 5 So King David sent for
him and had him brought from the
house of Machir, son of Ammiel, in
Lodebar. 6 When Meribbaal, son of Jon-
athan, son of Saul, came to David, he
fell prostrate in homage. David said,
"Meribbaal," and he answered, "Your
servant." 7 "Fear not," David said to
him, "I will surely be kind to you for the
sake of your father Jonathan. I will re-
store to you all the lands of your grand-
father Saul, and you shall always eat at
my table." 8* Bowing low, he answered,
"What is your servant that you should
pay attention to a dead dog like me?"
9 The king then called Ziba, Saul's at-
tendant, and said to him: "I am giving
your lord's son all that belonged to Saul
and to all his family. 10 You and your
sons and servants must till the land for
him. You shall bring in the produce,
which shall be food for your lord's fam-
ily to eat. But Meribbaal, your lord's son,
shall always eat at my table." Ziba, who
had fifteen sons and twenty servants,
11* said to the king, "Your servant shall
do just as my lord the king has com-
manded him." And so Meribbaal ate at
David's table like one of the king's sons.
12* Meribbaal had a young son whose
name was Mica; and all the tenants of
Ziba's family worked for Meribbaal.
13* But Meribbaal lived in Jerusalem,
because he always ate at the king's table.
He was lame in both feet.

CHAPTER 10

Insult of the Ammonites. 1*† Some
time later the king of the Ammonites
died, and his son Hanun succeeded him
as king. 2 David thought, "I will be kind
to Hanun, son of Nahash, as his father
was kind to me." So David sent his ser-
vants with condolences to Hanun for the
loss of his father. But when David's ser-
vants entered the country of the Am-
monites, 3 the Ammonite princes said to
their lord Hanun: "Do you think that
David is honoring your father by send-
ing men with condolences? Is it not
rather to explore the city, to spy on it,
and to overthrow it, that David has sent
his messengers to you?" 4* Hanun,
therefore, seized David's servants and,
after shaving off half their beards and
cutting away the lower halves of their
garments at the buttocks, sent them
away. 5 When he was told of it, King
David sent out word to them, since the
men were quite ashamed. "Stay in Jeri-
cho until your beards grow," he said,
"and then come back."

Ammonites Defeated. 6*† In view of
the offense they had given to David, the
Ammonites sent for and hired twenty
thousand Aramean foot soldiers from
Beth-rehob and Zobah, as well as the
king of Maacah with one thousand men,
and twelve thousand men from Tob.
7* On learning this, David sent out Joab
with the entire levy of trained soldiers.
8 The Ammonites came out and drew up
in battle formation at the entrance of
their city gate, while the Arameans of
Zobah and Rehob and the men of Tob
and Maacah remained apart in the open
country. 9 When Joab saw the battle lines
drawn up against him, both front and
rear, he made a selection from all the
picked troops of Israel and arrayed
them against the Arameans. 10 He
placed the rest of the soldiers under the
command of his brother Abishai, who
arrayed them against the Ammonites.
11 Joab said, "If the Arameans are
stronger than I, you shall help me. But
if the Ammonites are stronger than you,
I will come to help you. 12 Be brave; let
us prove our valor for the sake of our
people and the cities of our God; the
LORD will do what he judges best."
13 When Joab and the soldiers who were
with him approached the Arameans for
battle, they fled before him. 14 The Am-
monites, seeing that the Arameans had
fled, also fled from Abishai and with-
drew into the city. Joab then ceased his

*

9, 1: 21, 7; 1 Sm 18, 1-4; 20, 8ff.15f.42.
2: 16, 1-4; 19, 27.
3: 4, 4.
4: 17, 27.
8: 1 Sm 24, 15.
11: 19, 29.
12: 1 Chr 8, 34.
13: 21, 7.
10, 1-19: 1 Chr 19, 1-19.
4: Is 20, 4.
6: 8, 3; 1 Sm 14, 47.
7: 11, 1.

†

10, 1: *Some time later:* early in the reign of David, since Hanun's father had been ruling in Ammon at the beginning of Saul's reign (1 Sm 11) and Solomon was as yet unborn (2 Sm 11, 1; 12, 24).

10, 6-9: A Hebrew text from Qumran (4Q Sam[a]) comes closer in these verses to what is given in 1 Chr 19, 6-9. The scene of the conflict is more likely Rabbath-Ammon, with Josephus (Ant., vii, 123), than Madeba, as in 1 Chr; compare ch 11.

attack on the Ammonites and returned
to Jerusalem.

Arameans Defeated. 15* Then the Ar-
ameans responded to their defeat by Is-
rael with a full mustering of troops;
16 Hadadezer sent for and enlisted Ara-
means from beyond the Euphrates.
They came to Helam, with Shobach,
general of Hadadezer's army, at their
head. 17 On receiving this news, David
assembled all Israel, crossed the Jordan,
and went to Helam. The Arameans drew
up in formation against David and
fought with him. 18 But the Arameans
gave way before Israel, and David's men
killed seven hundred charioteers and
forty thousand of the Aramean foot sol-
diers. Shobach, general of the army, was
struck down and died on the field. 19 All
of Hadadezer's vassal kings, in view of
their defeat by Israel, then made peace
with the Israelites and became their sub-
jects. And the Arameans were afraid to
give further aid to the Ammonites.

CHAPTER 11

David's Sin. 1*† At the turn of the
year, when kings go out on campaign,
David sent out Joab along with his offi-
cers and the army of Israel, and they
ravaged the Ammonites and besieged
Rabbah. David, however, remained in
Jerusalem. 2 One evening David rose
from his siesta and strolled about on the
roof of the palace. From the roof he saw
a woman bathing, who was very beauti-
ful. 3* David had inquiries made about
the woman and was told, "She is
Bathsheba, daughter of Eliam, and wife
of [Joab's armor-bearer] Uriah the Hit-
tite." 4* Then David sent messengers
and took her. When she came to him,
he had relations with her, at a time when
she was just purified after her monthly
period. She then returned to her house.
5 But the woman had conceived, and
sent the information to David, "I am
with child."

6 David therefore sent a message to
Joab, "Send me Uriah the Hittite." So
Joab sent Uriah to David. 7 When he
came, David questioned him about Joab,
the soldiers, and how the war was going,
and Uriah answered that all was well.
8 David then said to Uriah, "Go down to
your house and bathe your feet." Uriah
left the palace, and a portion was sent
out after him from the king's table. 9 But
Uriah slept at the entrance of the royal
palace with the other officers of his lord,
and did not go down to his own house.
10 David was told that Uriah had not
gone home. So he said to Uriah, "Have
you not come from a journey? Why,
then, did you not go down to your
house?" 11* Uriah answered David,
"The ark and Israel and Judah are
lodged in tents, and my lord Joab and
your majesty's servants are encamped
in the open field. Can I go home to eat
and to drink and to sleep with my wife?
As the LORD lives and as you live, I will
do no such thing." 12 Then David said
to Uriah, "Stay here today also, I shall
dismiss you tomorrow." So Uriah re-
mained in Jerusalem that day. On the
day following, 13 David summoned him,
and he ate and drank with David, who
made him drunk. But in the evening he
went out to sleep on his bed among his
lord's servants, and did not go down to
his home. 14 The next morning David
wrote a letter to Joab which he sent by
Uriah. 15 In it he directed: "Place Uriah
up front, where the fighting is fierce.
Then pull back and leave him to be
struck down dead." 16 So while Joab was
besieging the city, he assigned Uriah to
a place where he knew the defenders
were strong. 17 When the men of the city
made a sortie against Joab, some offi-
cers of David's army fell, and among
them Uriah the Hittite died.

18 Then Joab sent David a report of all
the details of the battle, 19 instructing the
messenger, "When you have finished
giving the king all the details of the bat-
tle, 20 the king may become angry and
say to you: 'Why did you go near the
city to fight? Did you not know that they
would shoot from the wall above?
21* Who killed Abimelech, son of Jerub-
baal? Was it not a woman who threw a
millstone down on him from the wall
above, so that he died in Thebez? Why
did you go near the wall?' Then you in
turn shall say, 'Your servant Uriah the
Hittite is also dead.' " 22† The messenger
set out, and on his arrival he relayed to
David all the details as Joab had in-
structed him. 23 He told David: "The men
had us at a disadvantage and came out
into the open against us, but we pushed
them back to the entrance of the city
gate. 24 Then the archers shot at your
servants from the wall above, and some
of the king's servants died, among them
your servant Uriah." 25 David said to the
messenger: "This is what you shall con-
vey to Joab: 'Do not be chagrined at this,
for the sword devours now here and now
there. Strengthen your attack on the city
and destroy it.' Encourage him."

*

15-19: 8, 3-8; 1 Chr 9, 16-19.
11, 1: 10, 7; 1 Chr 20, 1.
3: 23, 39.
4: Lv 15, 19.
11: 1 Sm 4, 3f.
21: Jgs 9, 50-54.

†

11, 1: *At the turn of the year:* in the spring.

11, 22: After this verse, the Greek text, which is here the older form, has David, angry with Joab, repeat exactly the questions Joab had foreseen in vv 20f. In v 24 of our oldest Greek text, the messenger specifies that about eighteen men were killed.

26 When the wife of Uriah heard that
her husband had died, she mourned her
lord. 27 But once the mourning was over,
David sent for her and brought her into
his house. She became his wife and bore
him a son. But the LORD was displeased
with what David had done.

CHAPTER 12

Nathan's Parable. 1*† The LORD sent
Nathan to David, and when he came to
him, he said: "Judge this case for me!
In a certain town there were two men,
one rich, the other poor. 2 The rich man
had flocks and herds in great numbers.
3 But the poor man had nothing at all
except one little ewe lamb that he had
bought. He nourished her, and she grew
up with him and his children. She shared
the little food he had and drank from
his cup and slept in his bosom. She was
like a daughter to him. 4 Now, the rich
man received a visitor, but he would not
take from his own flocks and herds to
prepare a meal for the wayfarer who
had come to him. Instead he took the
poor man's ewe lamb and made a meal
of it for his visitor." 5 David grew very
angry with that man and said to Nathan:
"As the LORD lives, the man who has
done this merits death! 6* He shall
restore the ewe lamb fourfold be-
cause he has done this and has had no
pity."

David's Punishment. 7* Then Nathan
said to David: "You are the man! Thus
says the LORD God of Israel: 'I anointed
you king of Israel. I rescued you from
the hand of Saul. 8 I gave you your lord's
house and your lord's wives for your
own. I gave you the house of Israel and
of Judah. And if this were not enough,
I could count up for you still more. 9 Why
have you spurned the LORD and done
evil in his sight? You have cut down
Uriah the Hittite with the sword; you
took his wife as your own, and him you
killed with the sword of the Ammonites.
10* Now, therefore, the sword shall never
depart from your house, because you
have despised me and have taken the
wife of Uriah to be your wife.' 11* Thus
says the LORD: 'I will bring evil upon you
out of your own house. I will take your
wives while you live to see it, and will
give them to your neighbor. He shall lie
with your wives in broad daylight. 12 You
have done this deed in secret, but I
will bring it about in the presence of
all Israel, and with the sun looking
down.'"

David's Repentance. 13* Then David
said to Nathan, "I have sinned against
the LORD." Nathan answered David:
"The LORD on his part has forgiven your
sin: you shall not die. 14 But since you
have utterly spurned the LORD by this
deed, the child born to you must surely
die." 15 Then Nathan returned to his
house.

The LORD struck the child that the wife
of Uriah had borne to David, and it be-
came desperately ill. 16 David besought
God for the child. He kept a fast, retiring
for the night to lie on the ground clothed
in sackcloth. 17 The elders of his house
stood beside him urging him to rise from
the ground; but he would not, nor would
he take food with them. 18 On the seventh
day, the child died. David's servants,
however, were afraid to tell him that the
child was dead, for they said: "When the
child was alive, we spoke to him, but he
would not listen to what we said. How
can we tell him the child is dead? He
may do some harm!" 19 But David no-
ticed his servants whispering among
themselves and realized that the child
was dead. He asked his servants, "Is the
child dead?" They replied, "Yes, he is."
20 Rising from the ground, David washed
and anointed himself, and changed his
clothes. Then he went to the house of the
LORD and worshiped. He returned to his
own house, where at his request food
was set before him, and he ate. 21 His
servants said to him: "What is this you
are doing? While the child was living,
you fasted and wept and kept vigil; now
that the child is dead, you rise and take
food." 22 He replied: "While the child was
living, I fasted and wept, thinking, 'Per-
haps the LORD will grant me the child's
life.' 23* But now he is dead. Why should
I fast? Can I bring him back again? I
shall go to him, but he will not return
to me." 24 Then David comforted his wife
Bathsheba. He went and slept with her;
and she conceived and bore him a son,
who was named Solomon. The LORD
loved him 25 and sent the prophet Na-
than to name him Jedidiah, on behalf
of the LORD.

Ammonite War Ends. 26* Joab fought
against Rabbah of the Ammonites and
captured this royal city. 27 He sent mes-
sengers to David with the word: "I have
fought against Rabbah and have taken
the water-city. 28 Therefore, assemble
the rest of the soldiers, join the siege
against the city and capture it, lest it be
I that capture the city and it be credited
to me." 29 So David assembled the rest
of the soldiers and went to Rabbah.
When he had fought against it and cap-

*

12, 1: Sir 47, 1.
6: Ex 21, 37; Lk 19, 8.
7: 1 Sm 16, 13.
10: 13, 28f; 18, 14.
11: 16, 11.22.
13: 1 Kgs 21, 29; Pss 32, 5; 50, 6; Sir 47, 11.
23: Jb 7, 9.
26-31: 1 Chr 20, 1-3.

†

12, 1-4: This utterance of Nathan is in regular lines in Hebrew, resembling English blank verse.

tured it, [30]† he took the crown from Milcom's head. It weighed a talent, of gold and precious stones; it was placed on David's head. He brought out immense booty from the city, [31] and also led away the inhabitants, whom he assigned to work with saws, iron picks, and iron axes, or put to work at the brickmold. This is what he did to all the Ammonite cities. David and all the soldiers then returned to Jerusalem.

CHAPTER 13

The Crime of Amnon. [1]* Some time later the following incident occurred. David's son Absalom had a beautiful sister named Tamar, and David's son Amnon loved her. [2] He was in such straits over his sister Tamar that he became sick; since she was a virgin, Amnon thought it impossible to carry out his designs toward her. [3]* Now Amnon had a friend named Jonadab, son of David's brother Shimeah, who was very clever. [4] He asked him, "Prince, why are you so dejected morning after morning? Why not tell me?" So Amnon said to him, "I am in love with Tamar, my brother Absalom's sister." [5] Then Jonadab replied, "Lie down on your bed and pretend to be sick. When your father comes to visit you, say to him, 'Please let my sister Tamar come and encourage me to take food. If she prepares something appetizing in my presence, for me to see, I will eat it from her hand.' " [6] So Amnon lay down and pretended to be sick. When the king came to visit him, Amnon said to the king, "Please let my sister Tamar come and prepare some fried cakes before my eyes, that I may take nourishment from her hand."

[7] David then sent home a message to Tamar, "Please go to the house of your brother Amnon and prepare some nourishment for him." [8] Tamar went to the house of her brother Amnon, who was in bed. Taking dough and kneading it, she twisted it into cakes before his eyes and fried the cakes. [9] Then she took the pan and set out the cakes before him. But Amnon would not eat; he said, "Have everyone leave me." When they had all left him, [10] Amnon said to Tamar, "Bring the nourishment into the bedroom, that I may have it from your hand." So Tamar picked up the cakes she had prepared and brought them to her brother Amnon in the bedroom. [11] But when she brought them to him to eat, he seized her and said to her, "Come! Lie with me, my sister!" [12]* But she answered him, "No my brother! Do not shame me! That is an intolerable crime in Israel. Do not commit this insensate deed. [13]* Where would I take my shame? And you would be a discredited man in Israel. So please, speak to the king; he will not keep me from you."

[14] Not heeding her plea, he overpowered her; he shamed her and had relations with her. [15] Then Amnon conceived an intense hatred for her, which far surpassed the love he had had for her. "Get up and leave," he said to her. [16] She replied, "No, brother, because to drive me out would be far worse than the first injury you have done me." He would not listen to her, [17] but called the youth who was his attendant and said, "Put her outside, away from me, and bar the door after her." [18] Now she had on a long tunic, for that is how maiden princesses dressed in olden days. When his attendant put her out and barred the door after her, [19] Tamar put ashes on her head and tore the long tunic in which she was clothed. Then, putting her hands to her head, she went away crying loudly. [20] Her brother Absalom said to her: "Has your brother Amnon been with you? Be still now, my sister; he is your brother. Do not take this affair to heart." But Tamar remained grief-stricken and forlorn in the house of her brother Absalom. [21] King David, who got word of the whole affair, became very angry. He did not, however, spark the resentment of his son Amnon, whom he favored because he was his first-born. [22] Absalom, moreover, said nothing at all to Amnon, although he hated him for having shamed his sister Tamar.

Absalom's Plot. [23] After a period of two years, Absalom had shearers in Baal-hazor near Ephraim, and he invited all the princes. [24] Absalom went to the king and said: "Your servant is having shearers. Please, your majesty, come with all your retainers to your servant." [25] But the King said to Absalom, "No, my son, all of us should not go lest we be a burden to you." And though Absalom urged him, he refused to go and began to bid him good-bye. [26] Absalom then said, "If you will not come yourself, please let my brother Amnon come to us." The king asked him, "Why should he go to you?" [27] At Absalom's urging, however, he sent Amnon and all the other princes with him. Absalom prepared a banquet fit for royalty. [28]* But he had instructed his servants: "Now watch! When Amnon is merry with wine and I say to you, 'Kill

*

13, 1: 3, 2f; 1 Chr 3, 9.
3: 21, 21.
12: Lv 18, 9; 20, 17; Dt 27, 22.
13: Gn 34, 7.
28f: 12, 10.

†

12, 30: *Weighed a talent:* since this would be more than 75 pounds, some commentators picture the idol's crown as displaying a single precious stone of large size, which David took to wear; but the text does not say this.

Amnon,' put him to death. Do not be
afraid, for it is I who order you to do
it. Be resolute and act manfully."
Death of Amnon. 29 When the ser-
vants did to Amnon as Absalom had
commanded, all the other princes rose,
mounted their mules, and fled. 30 While
they were still on the road, a report
reached David that Absalom had killed
all the princes and that not one of them
had survived. 31* The king stood up, rent
his garments, and then lay on the
ground. All his servants standing by him
also rent their garments. 32 But Jonadab,
son of David's brother Shimeah, spoke
up: "Let not my lord think that all the
young princes have been killed! Amnon
alone is dead, for Absalom was deter-
mined on this ever since Amnon shamed
his sister Tamar. 33 So let not my lord
the king put faith in the report that all
the princes are dead. Amnon alone is
dead." 34 Meanwhile, Absalom had
taken flight. Then the servant on watch
looked about and saw a large group
coming down the slope from the direc-
tion of Bahurim. He came in and re-
ported this, telling the king that he had
seen some men coming down the moun-
tainside from the direction of Bahurim.
35 So Jonadab said to the king: "There!
The princes have come. It is as your
servant said." 36 No sooner had he fin-
ished speaking than the princes came
in, weeping aloud. The king, too, and all
his servants wept very bitterly. 37* But
Absalom, who had taken flight, went to
Talmai, son of Ammihud, king of
Geshur, 38 and stayed in Geshur for
three years.
Efforts for Absalom's Return. 39 The
king continued during all that time to
mourn over his son; but his longing
reached out for Absalom as he became
reconciled to the death of Amnon.

CHAPTER 14

1 When Joab, son of Zeruiah, observed
how the king felt toward Absalom, 2 he
sent to Tekoa and brought from there
a gifted woman, to whom he said: "Pre-
tend to be in mourning. Put on mourning
apparel and do not anoint yourself with
oil, that you may appear to be a woman
who has been long in mourning for a de-
parted one. 3 Then go to the king and
speak to him in this manner." And Joab
instructed her what to say.
4 So the woman of Tekoa went to the
king and fell prostrate to the ground in
homage, saying, "Help, your majesty!"
5* The king said to her, "What do you
want?" She replied: "Alas, I am a widow;
my husband is dead. 6 Your servant had
two sons, who quarreled in the field.
There being no one to part them, one
of them struck his brother and killed
him. 7*† Then the whole clan confronted
your servant and demanded: 'Give up
the one who killed his brother. We must
put him to death for the life of his brother
whom he has slain; we must extinguish
the heir also.' Thus they will quench my
remaining hope and leave my husband
neither name nor posterity upon the
earth." 8 The king then said to the
woman: "Go home. I will issue a com-
mand on your behalf." 9 The woman of
Tekoa answered him, "Let me and my
family be to blame, my lord king; you
and your throne are innocent." 10 Then
the king said, "If anyone says a word
to you, have him brought to me, and he
shall not touch you again." 11 But she
went on to say, "Please, your majesty,
keep in mind the LORD your God, that
the avenger of blood may not go too far
in destruction and that my son may not
be done away with." He replied, "As the
LORD lives, not a hair of your son shall
fall to the ground."
12 The woman continued, "Please let
your servant say still another word to
my lord the king." He replied, "Speak."
13 So the woman said: "Why, then, do
you think of this same kind of thing
against the people of God? In pronounc-
ing as he has, the king shows himself
guilty, for not bringing back his own
banished son. 14*† We must indeed die;
we are then like water that is poured out
on the ground and cannot be gathered
up. Yet, though God does not bring back
life, he does take thought how not to ban-
ish anyone from him. 15 And now, if I
have presumed to speak of this matter
to your majesty, it is because the people
have given me cause to fear. And so your
servant thought: 'Let me speak to the
king. Perhaps he will grant the petition
of his maidservant. 16 For the king must
surely consent to free his servant from
the grasp of one who would seek to de-
stroy me and my son as well from God's
inheritance.' " 17*† And the woman con-
cluded: "Let the word of my lord the
king provide a resting place; indeed, my
lord the king is like an angel of God,
evaluating good and bad. The LORD your
God be with you."
18 The king answered the woman,
"Now do not conceal from me anything

*

31: 1, 11.
37: 3, 3; 15, 8.
14, 5f: 2 Kgs 6, 26f.
7: Nm 35, 19.
14: Jb 7, 9; 14, 7-12; Ps 88, 5.11ff.
17.20: 1 Sm 29, 9.

†

14, 7: *Hope:* literally, "glowing coal." The image is similar to that of the lighted lamp, e.g., Ps 89, 17, to keep alive the ancestral name.

14, 14: *How not to banish:* a possible allusion to the religious institution of cities of refuge for involuntary murderers; see Nm 35, 9-15.

14, 17: *A resting place:* cf Ps 95, 11; Heb 3, 7—4, 11. The reference here is to a return home for Absalom to Israel.

I may ask you!" The woman said, "Let
my lord the king speak." 19 So the king
asked, "Is Joab involved with you in all
this?" And the woman answered: "As
you live, my lord the king, it is just as
your majesty has said, and not other-
wise. It was your servant Joab who in-
structed me and told your servant all
these things she was to say. 20 Your ser-
vant Joab did this to come at the issue
in a roundabout way. But my lord is as
wise as an angel of God, so that he knows
all things on earth."
Absalom's Return. 21 Then the king
said to Joab: "I hereby grant this re-
quest. Go, therefore, and bring back
young Absalom." 22 Falling prostrate to
the ground in homage and blessing the
king, Joab said, "This day I know that
I am in good favor with you, my lord
the king, since the king has granted the
request of his servant." 23 Joab then
went off to Geshur and brought Absalom
to Jerusalem. 24 But the king said, "Let
him go to his own house; he shall not
appear before me." So Absalom went off
to his house and did not appear before
the king.
25 In all Israel there was not a man who
could so be praised for his beauty as Ab-
salom, who was without blemish from
the sole of his foot to the crown of his
head. 26 When he shaved his head—
which he used to do at the end of every
year, because his hair became too heavy
for him—the hair weighed two hundred
shekels according to the royal standard.
27* Absalom had three sons born to him,
besides a daughter named Tamar, who
was a beautiful woman.
Absalom Is Pardoned. 28 Absalom
lived in Jerusalem for two years without
appearing before the king. 29 Then he
summoned Joab to send him to the king,
but Joab would not come to him. Al-
though he summoned him a second
time, Joab refused to come. 30* He there-
fore instructed his servants: "You see
Joab's field that borders mine, on which
he has barley. Go, set it on fire." And
so Absalom's servants set the field on
fire. Joab's farmhands came to him with
torn garments and reported to him what
had been done. 31 At this, Joab went to
Absalom in his house and asked him,
"Why have your servants set my field
on fire?" 32 Absalom answered Joab: "I
was summoning you to come here, that
I may send you to the king to say: 'Why
did I come back from Geshur? I would
be better off if I were still there!' Now,
let me appear before the king. If I am
guilty, let him put me to death." 33 Joab
went to the king and reported this. The
king then called Absalom, who came to
him and in homage fell on his face to
the ground before the king. Then the
king kissed him.

CHAPTER 15

Absalom's Plot. 1* After this Absalom
provided himself with chariots, horses,
and fifty henchmen. 2 Moreover, Absa-
lom used to rise early and stand along-
side the road leading to the gate. If
someone had a lawsuit to be decided by
the king, Absalom would call to him and
say, "From what city are you?" And
when he replied, "Your servant is of
such and such a tribe of Israel,"
3 Absalom would say to him, "Your suit
is good and just, but there is no one to
hear you in the king's name." 4 And he
would continue: "If only I could be ap-
pointed judge in the land! Then every-
one who has a lawsuit to be decided
might come to me and I would render
him justice." 5 Whenever a man ap-
proached him to show homage, he would
extend his hand, hold him, and kiss him.
6 By behaving in this way toward all the
Israelites who came to the king for judg-
ment, Absalom was stealing away the
loyalties of the men of Israel.
Conspiracy in Hebron. 7 After a pe-
riod of four years, Absalom said to the
king: "Allow me to go to Hebron and ful-
fill a vow I made to the LORD. 8* For
while living in Geshur in Aram, your
servant made this vow: 'If the LORD ever
brings me back to Jerusalem, I will wor-
ship him in Hebron.' " 9 The king wished
him a safe journey, and he went off to
Hebron. 10 Then Absalom sent spies
throughout the tribes of Israel to say,
"When you hear the sound of the horn,
declare Absalom king in Hebron."
11 Two hundred men had accompanied
Absalom from Jerusalem. They had
been invited and went in good faith,
knowing nothing of the plan. 12* Absa-
lom also sent to Ahithophel the Gilonite,
David's counselor, an invitation to come
from his town, Giloh, for the sacrifices
he was about to offer. So the conspiracy
gained strength, and the people with Ab-
salom increased in numbers.
David Flees Jerusalem. 13* An infor-
mant came to David with the report,
"The Israelites have transferred their
loyalty to Absalom." 14 At this, David
said to all his servants who were with
him in Jerusalem: "Up! Let us take
flight, or none of us will escape from Ab-
salom. Leave quickly, lest he hurry and
overtake us, then visit disaster upon us
and put the city to the sword." 15 The
king's officers answered him, "Your
servants are ready, whatever our lord
the king chooses to do." 16* Then the
king set out, accompanied by his entire

*

27: 18, 18.
30: Jgs 15, 4f.
15, 1: 1 Sm 8, 11; 1 Kgs 1, 5.
8: 3, 3; 13, 37.
12: 16, 23.
13: Ps 3.
16: 16, 21f; 20, 3.

household, except for ten concubines
whom he left behind to take care of the
palace. 17 As the king left the city, with
all his officers accompanying him, they
halted opposite the ascent of the Mount
of Olives, at a distance, 18* while the
whole army marched past him.

David and Ittai. As all the Cherethites
and Pelethites, and the six hundred men
of Gath who had accompanied him from
that city, were passing in review before
the king, 19 he said to Ittai the Gittite:
"Why should you also go with us? Go
back and stay with the king, for you are
a foreigner and you, too, are an exile
from your own country. 20 You came
only yesterday, and shall I have you
wander about with us today, wherever
I have to go? Return and take your
brothers with you, and may the LORD be
kind and faithful to you." 21* But Ittai
answered the king, "As the LORD lives,
and as my lord the king lives, your ser-
vant shall be wherever my lord the king
may be, whether for death or for life."
22 So the king said to Ittai, "Go, then,
march on." And Ittai the Gittite, with all
his men and all the dependents that
were with him, marched on. 23 Everyone
in the countryside wept aloud as the last
of the soldiers went by, and the king
crossed the Kidron Valley with all the
soldiers moving on ahead of him by way
of the Mount of Olives, toward the de-
sert.

David and the Priests. 24 Zadok, too
[with all the Levite bearers of the ark
of the covenant of God], and Abiathar
brought the ark of God to a halt until
the soldiers had marched out of the city.
25 Then the king said to Zadok: "Take
the ark of God back to the city. If I find
favor with the LORD, he will bring me
back and permit me to see it and its
lodging. 26* But if he should say, 'I am
not pleased with you,' I am ready; let
him do to me as he sees fit." 27 The king
also said to the priest Zadok: "See to it
that you and Abiathar return to the city
in peace, and both your sons with you,
your own son Ahimaaz, and Abiathar's
son Jonathan. 28 Remember, I shall be
waiting at the fords near the desert until
I receive information from you." 29 So
Zadok and Abiathar took the ark of
God back to Jerusalem and remained
there.

30* As David went up the Mount of Ol-
ives, he wept without ceasing. His head
was covered, and he was walking bare-
foot. All those who were with him also
had their heads covered and were weep-
ing as they went. 31* When David was
informed that Ahithophel was among
the conspirators with Absalom, he said,
"O LORD, turn the counsel of Ahithophel
to folly!"

David and Hushai. 32* When David
reached the top, where men used to wor-
ship God, Hushai the Archite was there
to meet him, with rent garments and dirt
upon his head. 33 David said to him: "If
you come with me, you will be a burden
to me. 34* But if you return to the city
and say to Absalom, 'Let me be your
servant, O king; I was formerly your fa-
ther's servant, but now I will be yours,'
you will undo for me the counsel of
Ahithophel. 35 You will have the priests
Zadok and Abiathar there with you. If
you hear anything from the royal pal-
ace, you shall report it to the priests Za-
dok and Abiathar, 36 who have there
with them both Zadok's son Ahimaaz
and Abiathar's son Jonathan. Through
them you shall send on to me whatever
you hear." 37 So David's friend Hushai
went into the city of Jerusalem as Absa-
lom was about to enter it.

CHAPTER 16

David and Ziba. 1* David had gone a
little beyond the top when Ziba, the ser-
vant of Meribbaal, met him with saddled
asses laden with two hundred loaves of
bread, an ephah of cakes of pressed rai-
sins, an ephah of summer fruits, and a
skin of wine. 2 The king said to Ziba,
"What do you plan to do with these?"
Ziba replied: "The asses are for the
king's household to ride on. The bread
and summer fruits are for your servants
to eat, and the wine for those to drink
who are weary in the desert." 3* Then
the king said, "And where is your lord's
son?" Ziba answered the king, "He is
staying in Jerusalem, for he said, 'Now
the Israelites will restore to me my fa-
ther's kingdom.'" 4* The king therefore
said to Ziba, "So! Everything Meribbaal
had is yours." Then Ziba said: "I pay
you homage, my lord the king. May I
find favor with you!"

David and Shimei. 5* As David was
approaching Bahurim, a man named
Shimei, the son of Gera of the same clan
as Saul's family, was coming out of the
place, cursing as he came. 6 He threw
stones at David and at all the king's offi-
cers, even though all the soldiers, in-
cluding the royal guard, were on David's
right and on his left. 7 Shimei was saying
as he cursed: "Away, away, you mur-
derous and wicked man! 8† The LORD

*

18: 8, 18.
21: Ru 1, 16.
26: 16, 10.
30: 19, 5; Mi 1, 8.
31: 16, 23; 17, 14.23.
32: 16, 16.
34: 16, 19.
16, 1: 4, 4; 9, 1-13; 19, 18.25.
3: 19, 26f.
4: 19, 30.
5: 3, 16; 19, 17.22f; 1 Kgs 2, 8.

†

16, 8: *Bloodshed . . . Saul:* refers to the episode recounted in 21, 1-14.

has requited you for all the bloodshed
in the family of Saul, in whose stead you
became king, and the LORD has given
over the kingdom to your son Absalom.
And now you suffer ruin because you are
a murderer." 9* Abishai, son of Zeruiah,
said to the king: "Why should this dead
dog curse my lord the king? Let me go
over, please, and lop off his head."
10* But the king replied: "What business
is it of mine or of yours, sons of Zeruiah,
that he curses? Suppose the LORD has
told him to curse David; who then will
dare to say, 'Why are you doing this?' "
11* Then the king said to Abishai and to
all his servants: "If my own son, who
came forth from my loins, is seeking my
life, how much more might this Benja-
minite do so! Let him alone and let him
curse, for the LORD has told him to.
12 Perhaps the LORD will look upon my
affliction and make it up to me with ben-
efits for the curses he is uttering this
day." 13* David and his men continued
on the road, while Shimei kept abreast
of them on the hillside, all the while curs-
ing and throwing stones and dirt as he
went. 14 The king and all the soldiers
with him arrived at the Jordan tired out,
and stopped there for a rest.

Absalom's Counselors. 15 In the
meantime Absalom, accompanied by
Ahithophel, entered Jerusalem with all
the Israelites. 16* When David's friend
Hushai the Archite came to Absalom, he
said to him: "Long live the king! Long
live the king!" 17 But Absalom asked
Hushai: "Is this your devotion to your
friend? Why did you not go with your
friend?" 18 Hushai replied to Absalom:
"On the contrary, I am his whom the
LORD and all this people and all Israel
have chosen, and with him I will stay.
19* Furthermore, as I was in attendance
upon your father, so will I be before you.
Whom should I serve, if not his son?"
20 Then Absalom said to Ahithophel,
"Offer your counsel on what we should
do." 21* Ahithophel replied to Absalom:
"Have relations with your father's con-
cubines, whom he left behind to take
care of the palace. When all Israel hears
how odious you have made yourself to
your father, all your partisans will take
courage." 22* So a tent was pitched on
the roof for Absalom, and he visited his
father's concubines in view of all Israel.

Counsel of Ahithophel. 23* Now the
counsel given by Ahithophel at that time
was as though one had sought divine
revelation. Such was all his counsel both
to David and to Absalom.

CHAPTER 17

1 Ahithophel went on to say to Absalom:
"Please let me choose twelve thousand
men, and be off in pursuit of David to-
night. 2 If I come upon him when he is
weary and discouraged, I shall cause
him panic. When all the people with him
flee, I shall strike down the king alone.
3 Then I can bring back the rest of the
people to you, as a bride returns to her
husband. It is the death of only one man
you are seeking; then all the people will
be at peace." 4 This plan was agreeable
to Absalom and to all the elders of Israel.

Counsel of Hushai. 5 Then Absalom
said, "Now call Hushai the Archite also;
let us hear what he too has to say."
6 When Hushai came to Absalom, Absa-
lom said to him: "This is what Ahitho-
phel proposed. Shall we follow his
proposal? If not, speak up." 7 Hushai
replied to Absalom, "This time Ahitho-
phel has not given good counsel." 8* And
he went on to say: "You know that your
father and his men are warriors, and
that they are as fierce as a bear in the
wild robbed of her cubs. Moreover, since
your father is skilled in warfare, he will
not spend the night with the people.
9 Even now he lies hidden in one of the
caves or in some other place. And if
some of our soldiers should fall at the
first attack, whoever hears of it will say,
'Absalom's followers have been slaugh-
tered.' 10 Then even the brave man with
the heart of a lion will lose courage. For
all Israel knows that your father is a
warrior and that those who are with him
are brave.

11 "This is what I counsel: Let all Israel
from Dan to Beer-sheba, who are as nu-
merous as the sands by the sea, be called
up for combat; and go with them your-
self. 12 We can then attack him wherever
we find him, settling down upon him as
dew alights on the ground. None shall
survive—neither he nor any of his fol-
lowers. 13 And if he retires into a city,
all Israel shall bring ropes to that city
and we can drag it into the gorge, so that
not even a pebble of it can be found."
14* Then Absalom and all the Israelites
pronounced the counsel of Hushai the
Archite better than that of Ahithophel.
For the LORD had decided to undo
Ahithophel's good counsel, in order thus
to bring Absalom to ruin.

David Told of the Plan. 15 Then
Hushai said to the priests Zadok and
Abiathar: "This is the counsel Ahitho-
phel gave Absalom and the elders of Is-
rael, and this is what I counseled. 16 So
send a warning to David immediately,
not to spend the night at the fords near
the desert, but to cross over without fail.

---

*

9: 19, 23.29; 1 Sm 24, 15; 26, 6.
10: 15, 25f; 19, 23.
11: 12, 11.
13: 19, 19-24.
16: 15, 32-37.
19: 15, 34.
21: 15, 16; 20, 3.
22: 12, 11f.
23: 15, 12.31; 17, 23.
17, 8: Hos 13, 8.
14: 15, 31.

Otherwise the king and all the people
with him will be destroyed." 17 Now Jon-
athan and Ahimaaz were staying at En-
rogel, since they could not risk being
seen entering the city. A maidservant
was to come with information for them,
and they in turn were to go and report
to King David. 18 But an attendant saw
them and informed Absalom. They sped
on their way and reached the house of
a man in Bahurim who had a cistern in
his courtyard. They let themselves down
into this, 19 and the housewife took the
cover and spread it over the cistern,
strewing ground grain on the cover so
that nothing could be noticed. 20 When
Absalom's servants came to the woman
at the house, they asked, "Where are
Ahimaaz and Jonathan?" The woman
replied, "They went by a short while ago
toward the water." They searched, but
found no one, and so returned to Jerusa-
lem. 21 As soon as they left, Ahimaaz and
Jonathan came up out of the cistern and
went on to inform King David. They said
to him: "Leave! Cross the water at once,
for Ahithophel has given the following
counsel in regard to you." 22 So David
and all his people moved on and crossed
the Jordan. By daybreak, there was no
one left who had not crossed.

23* When Ahithophel saw that his
counsel was not acted upon, he saddled
his ass and departed, going to his home
in his own city. Then, having left orders
concerning his family, he hanged him-
self. And so he died and was buried in
his father's tomb.

24 Now David had gone to Mahanaim
when Absalom crossed the Jordan ac-
companied by all the Israelites. 25* Ab-
salom had put Amasa in command of
the army in Joab's place. Amasa was
the son of an Ishmaelite named Ithra,
who had married Abigail, daughter of
Jesse and sister of Joab's mother Zer-
uiah. 26 Israel and Absalom encamped
in the territory of Gilead.

27* When David came to Mahanaim,
Shobi, son of Nahash from Rabbah of
the Ammonites, Machir, son of Ammiel
from Lodebar, and Barzillai, the Gilead-
ite from Rogelim, 28* brought couches,
coverlets, basins and earthenware, as
well as wheat, barley, flour, roasted
grain, beans, lentils, 29 honey, butter and
cheese from the flocks and herds, for
David and those who were with him to
eat; for they said, "The people have been
hungry and tired and thirsty in the
desert."

CHAPTER 18

Preparation for Battle. 1 After mus-
tering the troops he had with him, David
placed officers in command of groups of
a thousand and groups of a hundred.
2 David then put a third part of the sol-
diers under Joab's command, a third
under command of Abishai, son of
Zeruiah and brother of Joab, and a third
under command of Ittai the Gittite. The
king then said to the soldiers, "I intend
to go out with you myself." 3 But they
replied: "You must not come out with
us. For if we should flee, we shall not
count; even if half of us should die, we
shall not count. You are equal to ten
thousand of us. Therefore it is better that
we have you to help us from the city."
4 So the king said to them, "I will do what
you think best"; and he stood by the gate
as all the soldiers marched out in units
of a hundred and of a thousand. 5 But
the king gave this command to Joab,
Abishai and Ittai: "Be gentle with young
Absalom for my sake." All the soldiers
heard the king instruct the various lead-
ers with regard to Absalom.

Defeat of Absalom. 6 David's army
then took the field against Israel, and
a battle was fought in the forest near
Mahanaim. 7 The forces of Israel were
defeated by David's servants, and the
casualties there that day were heavy—
twenty thousand men. 8 The battle
spread out over that entire region, and
the thickets consumed more combatants
that day than did the sword.

Death of Absalom. 9 Absalom unex-
pectedly came up against David's ser-
vants. He was mounted on a mule, and,
as the mule passed under the branches
of a large terebinth, his hair caught fast
in the tree. He hung between heaven and
earth while the mule he had been riding
ran off. 10 Someone saw this and re-
ported to Joab that he had seen Absalom
hanging from a terebinth. 11 Joab said
to his informant: "If you saw him, why
did you not strike him to the ground on
the spot? Then it would have been my
duty to give you fifty pieces of silver and
a belt." 12 But the man replied to Joab:
"Even if I already held a thousand
pieces of silver in my two hands, I would
not harm the king's son, for the king
charged you and Abishai and Ittai in our
hearing to protect the youth Absalom for
his sake. 13 Had I been disloyal and killed
him, the whole matter would have come
to the attention of the king, and you
would stand aloof." 14* Joab replied, "I
will not waste time with you in this way."
And taking three pikes in hand, he
thrust for the heart of Absalom, still
hanging from the tree alive. 15 Next, ten
of Joab's young armor-bearers closed in
on Absalom, and killed him with further
blows. 16* Joab then sounded the horn,
and the soldiers turned back from the

*
23: 15, 31; 16, 23.
25: 19, 14; 20, 4-13.
27: 9, 4; 19, 32; 1 Kgs 2, 7.
28: 19, 32; Ezr 2, 61.
18, 14: 12, 10; 13, 28f.
16: 20, 23-26.

pursuit of the Israelites, because Joab
called on them to halt. 17* Absalom was
taken up and cast into a deep pit in the
forest, and a very large mound of stones
was erected over him. And all the Israel-
ites fled to their own tents.
18* During his lifetime Absalom had
taken a pillar and erected it for himself
in the King's Valley, for he said, "I have
no son to perpetuate my name." The pil-
lar which he named for himself is called
Yadabshalom to the present day.
David Told of Absalom's Death.
19 Then Ahimaaz, son of Zadok, said,
"Let me run to take the good news to
the king that the LORD has set him free
from the grasp of his enemies." 20 But
Joab said to him: "You are not the man
to bring the news today. On some other
day you may take the good news, but
today you would not be bringing good
news, for in fact the king's son is dead."
21 Then Joab said to a Cushite, "Go, tell
the king what you have seen." The Cush-
ite bowed to Joab and sped away. 22 But
Ahimaaz, son of Zadok, said to Joab
again, "Come what may, permit me also
to run after the Cushite." Joab replied:
"Why do you want to run, my son? You
will receive no reward." 23 But he in-
sisted, "Come what may, I want to run."
Joab said to him, "Very well." Ahimaaz
sped off by way of the Jordan plain and
outran the Cushite.
24 Now David was sitting between the
two gates, and a lookout mounted to the
roof of the gate above the city wall,
where he looked about and saw a man
running all alone. 25 The lookout shouted
to inform the king, who said, "If he is
alone, he has good news to report." As
he kept coming nearer, 26 the lookout
spied another runner. From his place
atop the gate he cried out, "There is an-
other man running by himself." And the
king responded, "He, too, is bringing
good news." 27* Then the lookout said,
"I notice that the first one runs like
Ahimaaz, son of Zadok." The king re-
plied, "He is a good man; he comes with
good news." 28 Then Ahimaaz called out
and greeted the king. With face to the
ground he paid homage to the king and
said, "Blessed be the LORD your God,
who has delivered up the men who re-
belled against my lord the king." 29 But
the king asked, "Is the youth Absalom
safe?" And Ahimaaz replied, "I saw a
great disturbance when the king's ser-
vant Joab sent your servant on, but I
do not know what it was." 30 The king
said, "Step aside and remain in attend-
ance here." So he stepped aside and re-
mained there. 31 When the Cushite came
in, he said, "Let my lord the king receive
the good news that this day the LORD
has taken your part, freeing you from
the grasp of all who rebelled against
you." 32 But the king asked the Cushite,
"Is young Absalom safe?" The Cushite
replied, "May the enemies of my lord
the king and all who rebel against you
with evil intent be as that young man!"

CHAPTER 19

1 The king was shaken, and went up
to the room over the city gate to weep.
He said as he wept, "My son Absalom!
My son, my son Absalom! If only I had
died instead of you, Absalom, my son,
my son!"
Joab Reproves David. 2 Joab was told
that the king was weeping and mourning
for Absalom; 3 and that day's victory
was turned into mourning for the whole
army when they heard that the king was
grieving for his son. 4 The soldiers stole
into the city that day like men shamed
by flight in battle. 5* Meanwhile the king
covered his face and cried out in a loud
voice, "My son Absalom! Absalom! My
son, my son!" 6 Then Joab went to his
residence and said: "Though they saved
your life and your sons' and daughters'
lives, also the lives of your wives and
those of your concubines, you have put
all your servants to shame today 7 by
loving those who hate you and hating
those who love you. For you have shown
today that officers and servants mean
nothing to you. Indeed I am now certain
that if Absalom were alive today and all
of us dead, you would think that more
suitable. 8 Now then, get up! Go out and
speak kindly to your servants. I swear
by the LORD that if you do not go out,
not a single man will remain with you
overnight, and this will be a far greater
disaster for you than any that has af-
flicted you from your youth until now."
9 So the king stepped out and sat at the
gate. When all the people were informed
that the king was sitting at the gate, they
came into his presence.
The Reconciliation. Now the Israelites
had fled to their separate tents, 10 but
throughout the tribes of Israel all the
people were arguing among themselves,
saying to one another: "The king deliv-
ered us from the clutches of our ene-
mies, and it was he who rescued us from
the grip of the Philistines. But now he
has fled from the country before Absa-
lom, 11 and Absalom, whom we anointed
over us, died in battle. Why, then, should
you remain silent about restoring the
king to his palace?" When the talk of all
Israel reached the king, 12 David sent
word to the priests Zadok and Abiathar:
"Say to the elders of Judah: 'Why should
you be last to restore the king to his pal-
ace? 13 You are my brothers, you are my

17: Jos 7, 26; 8, 29; 10, 27.
18: 14, 27.
27: 2 Kgs 9, 20.
19, 5: 15, 30.

bone and flesh. Why should you be last
to restore the king?' 14* Also say to
Amasa: 'Are you not my bone and flesh?
May God do thus and so to me, if you
do not become my general permanently
in place of Joab.' " 15 He won over all the
Judahites as one man, and so they sum-
moned the king to return, with all his
servants.

David and Shimei. 16 When the king,
on his return, reached the Jordan, Ju-
dah had come to Gilgal to meet him and
to escort him across the Jordan.
17* Shimei, son of Gera, the Benjaminite
from Bahurim, hurried down with the
Judahites to meet King David, 18* ac-
companied by a thousand men from
Benjamin. Ziba, too, the servant of the
house of Saul, accompanied by his fif-
teen sons and twenty servants, hastened
to the Jordan before the king. 19* They
crossed over the ford to bring the king's
household over and to do whatever he
wished. When Shimei, son of Gera,
crossed the Jordan, he fell down before
the king 20 and said to him: "May my
lord not hold me guilty, and may he not
remember and take to heart the wrong
that your servant did the day my lord
the king left Jerusalem. 21 For your ser-
vant knows that he has done wrong. Yet
realize that I have been the first of the
whole house of Joseph to come down to-
day to meet my lord the king." 22 But
Abishai, son of Zeruiah, countered:
"Shimei must be put to death for this.
He cursed the LORD's anointed."
23* David replied: "What has come be-
tween you and me, sons of Zeruiah, that
you would create enmity for me this
day? Should anyone die today in Israel?
Am I not aware that today I am king
of Israel?" 24 Then the king said to
Shimei, "You shall not die." And the
king gave him his oath.

David and Meribbaal. 25 Meribbaal,
son of Saul, also went down to meet the
king. He had not washed his feet nor
trimmed his mustache nor washed his
clothes from the day the king left until
he returned safely. 26* When he came
from Jerusalem to meet the king, the
king asked him, "Why did you not go
with me, Meribbaal?" 27* He replied:
"My lord the king, my servant betrayed
me. For your servant, who is lame, said
to him, 'Saddle the ass for me, that I may
ride on it and go with the king.' 28 But
he slandered your servant before my
lord the king. But my lord the king is
like an angel of God. Do what you judge
best. 29* For though my father's entire
house deserved only death from my lord
the king, yet you placed your servant
among the guests at your table. What
right do I still have to make further ap-
peal to the king?" 30* But the king said
to him: "Why do you go on talking? I
say, 'You and Ziba shall divide the prop-
erty.' " 31 Meribbaal answered the king,
"Indeed let him have it all, now that my
lord the king has returned safely to his
palace."

David and Barzillai. 32* Barzillai the
Gileadite also came down from Rogelim
and escorted the king to the Jordan for
his crossing, taking leave of him there.
33 It was Barzillai, a very old man of
eighty and very wealthy besides, who
had provisioned the king during his stay
in Mahanaim. 34 The king said to Barzil-
lai, "Cross over with me, and I will pro-
vide for your old age as my guest in
Jerusalem." 35 But Barzillai answered
the king: "How much longer have I to
live, that I should go up to Jerusalem
with the king? 36 I am now eighty years
old. Can I distinguish between good and
bad? Can your servant taste what he eats
and drinks, or still appreciate the voices
of singers and songstresses? Why should
your servant be any further burden to
my lord the king? 37 In escorting the king
across the Jordan, your servant is doing
little enough! Why should the king give
me this reward? 38 Please let your ser-
vant go back to die in his own city by
the tomb of his father and mother. Here
is your servant Chimham. Let him cross
over with my lord the king. Do for him
whatever you will." 39 Then the king said
to him, "Chimham shall come over with
me, and I will do for him as you would
wish. And anything else you would like
me to do for you, I will do." 40 Then all
the people crossed over the Jordan but
the king remained; he kissed Barzillai
and bade him Godspeed as he returned
to his own district. 41 Finally the king
crossed over to Gilgal, accompanied by
Chimham.

Israel and Judah Quarrel. All the peo-
ple of Judah and half of the people of
Israel had escorted the king across.
42 But all these Israelites began coming
to the king and saying, "Why did our
brothers the Judahites steal you away
and escort the king and his household
across the Jordan, along with all David's
men?" 43 All the Judahites replied to the
men of Israel: "Because the king is our
relative. Why are you angry over this
affair? Have we had anything to eat at
the king's expense? Or have portions
from his table been given to us?" 44* The
Israelites answered the Judahites: "We
have ten shares in the king. Also, we are
the first-born rather than you. Why do

2 SAMUEL

---

*

14: 17, 25; 20, 4.
17: 16, 5-13.
18: 16, 1-4; 19, 25-31.
19ff: 16, 13; Ex 22, 27; 1 Kgs 2, 8.
23: 16, 9f; 1 Sm 11, 13; 1 Kgs 2, 8.38.46.
26: 16, 3.
27: 9, 2-13; Dt 21, 12f.
29: 9, 9ff.
30: 16, 4.
32: 17, 27ff; 1 Kgs 2, 7; Ezr 2, 61.
44: 1 Kgs 11, 31.

you slight us? Were we not first to speak
of restoring the king?" Then the Judah-
ites in turn spoke even more fiercely
than the Israelites.

CHAPTER 20

Sheba's Rebellion. 1* Now a rebellious
individual from Benjamin named
Sheba, the son of Bichri, happened to be
there. He sounded the horn and cried
out,

"We have no portion in David,
nor any share in the son of Jesse.
Every man to his tent, O Israel!"

2 So all the Israelites left David for
Sheba, son of Bichri. But from the Jor-
dan to Jerusalem the Judahites re-
mained loyal to their king. 3* When King
David came to his palace in Jerusalem,
he took the ten concubines whom he had
left behind to take care of the palace and
placed them in confinement. He pro-
vided for them, but had no further rela-
tions with them. And so they remained
in confinement to the day of their death,
lifelong widows.

Amasa's Death. 4* Then the king said
to Amasa: "Summon the Judahites for
me within three days. Then present
yourself here." 5 Accordingly Amasa set
out to summon Judah, but delayed be-
yond the time set for him by David.
6 Then David said to Abishai: "Sheba,
son of Bichri, may now do us more harm
than Absalom did. Take your lord's
servants and pursue him, lest he find
fortified cities and take shelter while we
look on." 7* So Joab and the Cherethites
and Pelethites and all the warriors
marched out behind Abishai from Jeru-
salem to campaign in pursuit of Sheba,
son of Bichri. 8*† They were at the great
stone in Gibeon when Amasa met them.
Now Joab had a belt over his tunic, from
which was slung, in its sheath near his
thigh, a sword that could be drawn with
a downward movement. 9 And Joab
asked Amasa, "How are you, my
brother?" With his right hand Joab held
Amasa's beard as if to kiss him. 10* And
since Amasa was not on his guard
against the sword in Joab's other hand,
Joab stabbed him in the abdomen with
it, so that his entrails burst forth to the
ground, and he died without receiving
a second thrust. Then Joab and his
brother Abishai pursued Sheba, son of
Bichri. 11 One of Joab's attendants stood
by Amasa and said, "Let him who favors
Joab and is for David follow Joab."
12 Amasa lay covered with blood in the
middle of the highroad, and the man no-
ticed that all the soldiers were stopping.
So he removed Amasa from the road to
the field and placed a garment over him,
because all who came up to him were
stopping. 13 When he had been removed
from the road, everyone went on after
Joab in pursuit of Sheba, son of Bichri.

Joab Pursues Sheba. 14 Sheba passed
through all the tribes of Israel to Abel
Beth-maacah. Then all the Bichrites as-
sembled and they too entered the city
after him. 15 So David's servants came
and besieged him in Abel Beth-maacah.
They threw up a mound against the city,
and all the soldiers who were with Joab
began battering the wall to throw it
down. 16 Then a wise woman from the
city stood on the outworks and called
out, "Listen, listen! Tell Joab to come
here, that I may speak with him."
17 When Joab had come near her, the
woman said, "Are you Joab?" And he
replied, "Yes." She said to him, "Listen
to what your maidservant has to say."
He replied. "I am listening." 18*† Then
she went on to say: "There is an ancient
saying, 'Let them ask if they will in Abel
19 or in Dan whether loyalty is finished
or ended in Israel.' You are seeking to
beat down a city that is a mother in Is-
rael. Why do you wish to destroy the in-
heritance of the LORD?" 20 Joab
answered, "Not at all, not at all! I do not
wish to destroy or to ruin anything.
21 That is not the case at all. A man
named Sheba, son of Bichri, from the
hill country of Ephraim has rebelled
against King David. Surrender him
alone, and I will withdraw from the
city." Then the woman said to Joab, "His
head shall be thrown to you across the
wall." 22 She went to all the people with
her advice, and they cut off the head of
Sheba, son of Bichri, and threw it out
to Joab. He then sounded the horn, and
they scattered from the city to their own
tents, while Joab returned to Jerusalem
to the king.

David's Officials. 23* Joab was in com-
mand of the whole army of Israel. Ben-
aiah, son of Jehoiada, was in command
of the Cherethites and Pelethites.
24 Adoram was in charge of the forced
labor. Jehoshaphat, son of Ahilud, was
the chancellor. 25* Shawsha was the
scribe. Zadok and Abiathar were priests.
26 Ira the Jairite was also David's priest.

V: APPENDIXES

CHAPTER 21

Gibeonite Vengeance. 1* During Da-
vid's reign there was a famine for three
successive years. David had recourse to

*

20, 1: 1 Kgs 12, 16.
3: 15, 16; 16, 20ff.
4: 17, 25; 19, 14.
7: 8, 18.
8: 2, 13.
10: 1 Kgs 2, 5.
18: Gn 49, 16.
23: 8, 16ff; 23, 20.
25: 8, 17f.
21, 1: 24, 13.

†

20, 8: The text of this verse is quite uncertain.
20, 18f: The proverbial expression here has been poorly transmitted, and its sense is doubtful.

the LORD, who said, "There is bloodguilt
on Saul and his family because he put
the Gibeonites to death." 2* So the king
called the Gibeonites and spoke to them.
(Now the Gibeonites were not Israelites,
but survivors of the Amorites; and al-
though the Israelites had given them
their oath, Saul had attempted to kill
them off in his zeal for the men of Israel
and Judah.) 3 David said to the Gibeon-
ites, "What must I do for you and how
must I make atonement, that you may
bless the inheritance of the LORD?" 4 The
Gibeonites answered him, "We have no
claim against Saul and his house for sil-
ver or gold, nor is it our place to put any
man to death in Israel." Then he said,
"I will do for you whatever you pro-
pose." 5 They said to the king, "As for
the man who was exterminating us and
who intended to destroy us that we
might have no place in all the territory
of Israel, 6 let seven men from among
his descendants be given to us, that we
may dismember them before the LORD
in Gibeon, on the LORD's mountain." The
king replied, "I will give them up."
7* The king, however, spared Meribbaal,
son of Jonathan, son of Saul, because of
the LORD's oath that formed a bond be-
tween David and Saul's son Jonathan.
8* But the king took Armoni and Merib-
baal, the two sons that Aiah's daughter
Rizpah had borne to Saul, and the five
sons of Saul's daughter Merob that she
had borne to Adriel, son of Barzillai the
Meholathite, 9 and surrendered them to
the Gibeonites. They then dismembered
them on the mountain before the LORD.
The seven fell at the one time; they were
put to death during the first days of the
harvest—that is, at the beginning of the
barley harvest.

10* Then Rizpah, Aiah's daughter,
took sackcloth and spread it out for her-
self on the rock from the beginning of
the harvest until rain came down on
them from the sky, fending off the birds
of the sky from settling on them by day,
and the wild animals by night. 11 When
David was informed of what Rizpah, Ai-
ah's daughter, the concubine of Saul,
had done, 12* he went and obtained the
bones of Saul and of his son Jonathan
from the citizens of Jabesh-gilead, who
had carried them off secretly from the
public square of Beth-shan, where the
Philistines had hanged them at the time
they killed Saul on Gilboa. 13 When he
had brought up from there the bones of
Saul and of his son Jonathan, the bones
of those who had been dismembered
were also gathered up. 14* Then the
bones of Saul and of his son Jonathan
were buried in the tomb of his father
Kish at Zela in the territory of Benjamin.
After all that the king commanded had
been carried out, God granted relief to
the land.

Exploits in Philistine Wars. 15 There
was another battle between the Philis-
tines and Israel. David went down with
his servants and fought the Philistines,
but David grew tired. 16 Dadu, one of the
Rephaim, whose bronze spear weighed
three hundred shekels, was about to take
him captive. Dadu was girt with a new
sword and planned to kill David, 17* but
Abishai, son of Zeruiah, came to his as-
sistance and struck and killed the Philis-
tine. Then David's men swore to him,
"You must not go out to battle with us
again, lest you quench the lamp of Is-
rael."

18* After this there was another battle
with the Philistines in Gob. On that occa-
sion Sibbecai, from Husha, killed Saph,
one of the Rephaim. 19* There was an-
other battle with the Philistines in Gob,
in which Elhanan, son of Jair from Beth-
lehem, killed Goliath of Gath, who had
a spear with a shaft like a weaver's hed-
dle-bar. 20 There was another battle at
Gath in which there was a man of large
stature with six fingers on each hand
and six toes on each foot—twenty-four
in all. He too was one of the Rephaim.
21* And when he insulted Israel, Jona-
than, son of David's brother Shimei,
killed him. 22 These four were Rephaim
in Gath, and they fell at the hands of
David and his servants.

CHAPTER 22

Song of Thanksgiving. 1*† David sang
the words of this song to the LORD when
the LORD had rescued him from the
grasp of all his enemies and from the
hand of Saul. 2* This is what he sang:

A

I

"O LORD, my rock, my fortress, my
deliverer,

*

2: Jos 9, 3-27.
7: 9, 13; 1 Sm 18, 3; 20, 8ff.15f.42.
8: 3, 7.
10: 3, 31; 12, 16.
12: 1 Sm 31, 10-13.
14: 24, 25.
17: 1 Kgs 11, 36; 15, 4; 2 Kgs 8, 19.
18-22: 1 Chr 20, 4-8.
18: 23, 27.
19f: 1 Sm 17, 4.7.
21: 13, 3.
22, 1: Ps 18, 1.
2-51: Ps 18, 3-51.

†

22, 1-51: This song of thanksgiving is also given, with a few small variants, in Ps 18. In both places it is attributed to David. Two main sections can be distinguished. In the first part, after an introductory stanza of praise to God (2-4), David describes the peril he was in (5-7), and then poetically depicts, under the form of a theophany, God's intervention in his behalf (8-20), concluding with an acknowledgment of God's justice (21-31). In the second part, God is praised for having prepared the psalmist for war (32-35), given him victory over his enemies (36-39), whom he put to flight (40-43), and bestowed on him dominion over many peoples (44-46). The entire song ends with a paean of grateful praise (47-51).

3*† my God, my rock of refuge!
My shield, the horn of my salvation,
my stronghold, my refuge,
my savior, from violence you keep me safe.
4 'Praised be the LORD,' I exclaim,
and I am safe from my enemies.

II
5† "The breakers of death surged round about me,
the floods of perdition overwhelmed me;
6 The cords of the nether world enmeshed me,
the snares of death overtook me.
7† In my distress I called upon the LORD
and cried out to my God;
From his temple he heard my voice,
and my cry reached his ears.

III
8† "The earth swayed and quaked;
the foundations of the heavens trembled
and shook when his wrath flared up.
9 Smoke rose from his nostrils,
and a devouring fire from his mouth;
he kindled coals into flame.
10* He inclined the heavens and came down,
with dark clouds under his feet.
11*† He mounted a cherub and flew,
borne on the wings of the wind.
12 He made darkness the shelter about him,
with spattering rain and thickening clouds.
13 From the brightness of his presence
coals were kindled to flame.

14 "The LORD thundered from heaven;
the Most High gave forth his voice.
15* He sent forth arrows to put them to flight;
he flashed lightning and routed them.
16 Then the wellsprings of the sea appeared,
the foundations of the earth were laid bare,
At the rebuke of the LORD,
at the blast of the wind of his wrath.

17* "He reached out from on high and grasped me;
he drew me out of the deep waters.
18 He rescued me from my mighty enemy,
from my foes, who were too powerful for me.
19 They attacked me on my day of calamity,
but the LORD came to my support.
20 He set me free in the open,
and rescued me, because he loves me.

IV
21 "The LORD rewarded me according to my justice;
according to the cleanness of my hands he requited me.
22 For I kept the ways of the LORD
and was not disloyal to my God.
23 For his ordinances were all present to me,
and his statutes I put not from me;
24 But I was wholehearted toward him,
and I was on my guard against guilt.
25 And the LORD requited me according to my justice,
according to my innocence in his sight.

26*† "Toward the faithful you are faithful;
toward the wholehearted you are wholehearted;
27 Toward the sincere you are sincere;
but toward the crooked you are astute.
28 You save lowly people,
though on the lofty your eyes look down.
29† You are my lamp, O LORD!
O my God, you brighten the darkness about me.
30 For with your aid I run against an armed band,
and by the help of my God I leap over a wall.
31* God's way is unerring;
the promise of the LORD is fire-tried;
he is a shield to all who take refuge in him."

*
3: 1 Sm 2, 1f.
10: Ps 144, 5.
11: Ex 25, 18.
15: Ps 144, 6.
17: Ps 144, 7.
26f: 1 Sm 2, 30.
31: Prv 30, 5.

†
22, 3: *The horn of my salvation:* my strong savior. The horn, the dreadful weapon of an enraged bull, was a symbol of strength; cf Lk 1, 69.

22, 5f: These verses are to be understood figuratively.

22, 7: *His temple:* his heavenly abode.

22, 8ff: God's intervention is graphically portrayed under the figures of an earthquake (vv 8. 16) and a thunderstorm (vv 9-15); cf Jgs 5, 4f; Pss 29; 97, 2-6; Hb 3.

22, 11: *He mounted a cherub:* since God makes the winds his messengers, or "angels" (Ps 104, 4), he is spoken of poetically as riding on the clouds, or on the angelic creatures called "cherubim." His earthly throne above the ark of the covenant was likewise associated with two winged cherubim; cf Ex 37, 7ff. In both senses the Lord is enthroned upon the cherubim; cf Pss 79, 2; 99, 1.

22, 26f: Men are treated by God in the same way they treat him and their fellow men.

22, 29: *My lamp:* a figure of life and happiness; cf 1 Kgs 11, 36.

B

I

32 "For who is God except the LORD?
Who is a rock save our God?
33 The God who girded me with strength
and kept my way unerring;
34† Who made my feet swift as those of hinds
and set me on the heights;
35 Who trained my hands for war
till my arms could bend a bow of brass.

II

36 "You have given me your saving shield,
and your help has made me great.
37 You made room for my steps;
unwavering was my stride.
38 I pursued my enemies and destroyed them,
nor did I turn again till I made an end of them.
39 I smote them and they did not rise;
they fell beneath my feet.

III

40 "You girded me with strength for war;
you subdued my adversaries beneath me.
41 My enemies you put to flight before me
and those who hated me I destroyed.
42 They cried for help—but no one saved them;
to the LORD—but he answered them not.
43 I ground them fine as the dust of the earth;
like the mud in the streets I trampled them down.

IV

44 "You rescued me from the strife of my people;
you made me head over nations.
A people I had not known became my slaves;
45 as soon as they heard me, they obeyed.
46 The foreigners fawned and cringed before me;
they staggered forth from their fortresses."

C

47 "The LORD live! And blessed be my Rock!
Extolled be my God, rock of my salvation.
48 O God, who granted me vengeance,
who made peoples subject to me
49 and helped me escape from my enemies,
Above my adversaries you exalt me
and from the violent man you rescue me.
50* Therefore will I proclaim you, O LORD, among the nations,
and I will sing praise to your name,
51 You who gave great victories to your king
and showed kindness to your anointed,
to David and his posterity forever."

CHAPTER 23

The Last Words of David

1*† These are the last words of David:

"The utterance of David, son of Jesse;
the utterance of the man God raised up,
Anointed of the God of Jacob,
favorite of the Mighty One of Israel.
2* The spirit of the LORD spoke through me;
his word was on my tongue.
3* The God of Israel spoke;
of me the Rock of Israel said,
'He that rules over men in justice,
that rules in the fear of God,
4* Is like the morning light at sunrise
on a cloudless morning,
making the greensward sparkle after rain.'
5* Is not my house firm before God?
He has made an eternal covenant with me,
set forth in detail and secured.
Will he not bring to fruition
all my salvation and my every desire?
6* But the wicked are all like thorns to be cast away;
they cannot be taken up by hand.
7 He who wishes to touch them
must arm himself with iron and the shaft of a spear,
and they must be consumed by fire."

*

50: Ps 22, 23; Rom 15, 9.
23, 1: 1 Kgs 2, 3–9; Sir 47, 8.
2: Is 59, 21; Jer 1, 9.
3: Ps 72, 1–4.
4: Jgs 5, 31; Ps 72, 6.
5: 7, 11. 15f; Ps 89, 30; Is 55, 3.
6: Dt 13, 14.

†

22, 34: *The heights:* a natural stronghold safe from attack; cf Ps 62, 3; Hb 3, 19.

23, 1–7: The text of this short composition in the spirit of the wisdom writers (Prv 30, 1–6) is difficult in places; it views David's career in retrospect.

2 SAMUEL

David's Warriors. 8*† These are the names of David's warriors. Ishbaal, son of Hachamoni, was the first of the Three. It was he who brandished his battle-ax over eight hundred slain in a single encounter. 9* Next to him, among the Three warriors, was Eleazar, son of Dodo the Ahohite. He was with David at Ephes-dammim when the Philistines assembled there for battle. The Israelites had retreated, 10 but he stood his ground and fought the Philistines until his hand grew tired and became cramped, holding fast to the sword. The LORD brought about a great victory on that day; the soldiers turned back after Eleazar, but only to strip the slain. 11* Next to him was Shammah, son of Agee the Hararite. The Philistines had assembled at Lehi, where there was a plot of land full of lentils. When the soldiers fled from the Philistines, 12 he took his stand in the middle of the plot and defended it. He slew the Philistines, and the LORD brought about a great victory. Such were the deeds of the Three warriors.

13* During the harvest three of the Thirty went down to David in the cave of Adullam, while a Philistine clan was encamped in the Vale of Rephaim. 14 At that time David was in the refuge, and there was a garrison of Philistines in Bethlehem. 15 Now David had a strong craving and said, "Oh, that someone would give me a drink of water from the cistern that is by the gate of Bethlehem!" 16 So the Three warriors broke through the Philistine camp and drew water from the cistern that is by the gate of Bethlehem. But when they brought it to David he refused to drink it, and instead poured it out to the LORD, 17 saying: "The LORD forbid that I do this! Can I drink the blood of these men who went at the risk of their lives?" So he refused to drink it.

18 Abishai, brother of Joab, son of Zeruiah, was at the head of the Thirty. It was he who brandished his spear over three hundred slain. He was listed among the Thirty 19 and commanded greater respect than the Thirty, becoming their leader. However, he did not attain to the Three.

20* Benaiah, son of Jehoiada, a stalwart from Kabzeel, was a man of great achievements. It was he who slew the two lions in Moab. He also went down and killed the lion in the cistern at the time of the snow. 21 It was he, too, who slew an Egyptian of large stature. Although the Egyptian was armed with a spear, he went against him with a club and wrested the spear from the Egyptian's hand, then killed him with his own spear. 22 Such were the deeds performed by Benaiah, son of Jehoiada. He was listed among the Thirty warriors 23* and commanded greater respect than the Thirty. However, he did not attain to the Three. David put him in command of his bodyguard. 24*† Asahel, brother of Joab. . . .

Among the Thirty were: Elhanan, son of Dodo, from Bethlehem; 25 Shammah from En-harod; Elika from En-harod; 26 Helez from Beth-pelet; Ira, son of Ikkesh, from Tekoa; 27* Abiezer from Anathoth; Sibbecai from Hushah; 28 Zalmon from Ahoh; Maharai from Netophah; 29 Heled, son of Baanah, from Netophah; Ittai, son of Ribai, from Gibeah of the Benjaminites; 30 Benaiah from Pirathon; Hiddai from Nahale-gaash; 31 Abibaal from Beth-arabah; Azmaveth from Bahurim; 32 Eliahba from Shaalbon; Jashen the Gunite; Jonathan, 33 son of Shammah the Hararite; Ahiam, son of Sharar the Hararite; 34 Eliphelet, son of Ahasbai, from Beth-maacah; Eliam, son of Ahithophel, from Gilo; 35 Hezrai from Carmel; Paarai the Arbite; 36 Igal, son of Nathan, from Zobah; Bani the Gadite; 37 Zelek the Ammonite; Naharai from Beeroth, armor-bearer of Joab, son of Zeruiah; 38 Ira from Jattir; Gareb from Jattir; 39* Uriah the Hittite—thirty-seven in all.

CHAPTER 24

Census of the People. 1*† The LORD's anger against Israel flared again, and he incited David against the Israelites by prompting him to number Israel and Judah. 2 Accordingly the king said to Joab and the leaders of the army who were with him, "Tour all the tribes in Israel from Dan to Beer-sheba and register the people, that I may know their number." 3 But Joab said to the king: "May the LORD your God increase the number of people a hundredfold for your royal majesty to see it with his own eyes. But why does it please my lord the king to order a thing of this kind?" 4 The king,

*

8-39: 1 Chr 11-41; 27, 1-15.
9: 1 Sm 17, 1.
11: Jgs 15, 9.
13: 1 Sm 22, 1; Mi 1, 15.
20: 8, 18; 20, 23; Jgs 14, 6; 1 Kgs 2, 29f.
23: 1 Sm 22, 14.
24: 2, 18-23.
27: 21, 18.
39: 11, 3f.
24, 1-25: 1 Chr 21, 1-27.

†

23, 8ff: There are thirty-seven warriors in all mentioned in this list. First there are the Three warriors most noted for single-handed exploits (vv 8-12). Then comes the story of a daring adventure by three unnamed members of the larger group (vv 13-17). Next come the commanders of the king's bodyguard, Abishai (vv 18-19) and Benaiah (vv 20-23), with whom must be counted Asahel (v 24) and Joab (vv 18.24.37), and finally the group of the Thirty (vv 24-39).

23, 24: A more complete notice about Asahel, who died early in his career (2 Sm 2, 16-23), is to be presumed lost at this point. Elhanan is the first of the Thirty.

24, 1ff: This story was probably joined at one time to 21, 1-14.

however, overruled Joab and the leaders
of the army, so they left the king's pres-
ence in order to register the people of
Israel. 5 Crossing the Jordan, they began
near Aroer, south of the city in the wadi,
and went in the direction of Gad toward
Jazer. 6 They continued on to Gilead and
to the district below Mount Hermon.
Then they proceeded to Dan; from there
they turned toward Sidon, 7 going to the
fortress of Tyre and to all the cities of
the Hivites and Canaanites, and ending
up at Beer-sheba in the Negeb of Judah.
8 Thus they toured the whole country,
reaching Jerusalem again after nine
months and twenty days. 9 Joab then re-
ported to the king the number of people
registered: in Israel, eight hundred
thousand men fit for military service; in
Judah, five hundred thousand.

The Pestilence. 10*† Afterward, how-
ever, David regretted having numbered
the people, and said to the LORD: "I have
sinned grievously in what I have done.
But now, LORD, forgive the guilt of your
servant, for I have been very foolish."
11 When David rose in the morning, the
LORD had spoken to the prophet Gad,
David's seer, saying: 12 "Go and say to
David, 'This is what the LORD says: I of-
fer you three alternatives; choose one of
them, and I will inflict it on you.' "
13* Gad then went to David to inform
him. He asked: "Do you want a three
years' famine to come upon your land,
or to flee from your enemy three months
while he pursues you, or to have a three
days' pestilence in your land? Now con-
sider and decide what I must reply to
him who sent me." 14 David answered
Gad: "I am in very serious difficulty. Let
us fall by the hand of God, for he is most
merciful; but let me not fall by the hand
of man." 15 Thus David chose the pesti-
lence. Now it was the time of the wheat
harvest when the plague broke out
among the people. [The LORD then sent
a pestilence over Israel from morning
until the time appointed, and seventy
thousand of the people from Dan to
Beer-sheba died.] 16* But when the an-
gel stretched forth his hand toward Je-
rusalem to destroy it, the LORD regretted
the calamity and said to the angel caus-
ing the destruction among the people,
"Enough now! Stay your hand." The an-
gel of the LORD was then standing at the
threshing floor of Araunah the Jebusite.
17† When David saw the angel who was
striking the people, he said to the LORD:
"It is I who have sinned; it is I, the shep-
herd, who have done wrong. But these
are sheep; what have they done? Punish
me and my kindred."

Sacrifice of Atonement. 18 On the
same day Gad went to David and said
to him, "Go up and build an altar to the
LORD on the threshing floor of Araunah
the Jebusite." 19 Following Gad's bid-
ding, David went up as the LORD had
commanded. 20 Now Araunah looked
down and noticed the king and his ser-
vants coming toward him while he was
threshing wheat. So he went out and
paid homage to the king, with face to
the ground. 21 Then Araunah asked,
"Why does my lord the king come to his
servant?" David replied, "To buy the
threshing floor from you, to build an al-
tar to the LORD, that the plague may be
checked among the people." 22* But
Araunah said to David: "Let my lord the
king take and offer up whatever he may
wish. Here are oxen for holocausts, and
threshing sledges and the yokes of the
oxen for wood. 23 All this does Araunah
give to the king." Araunah then said to
the king, "May the LORD your God ac-
cept your offering." 24 The king, how-
ever, replied to Araunah, "No, I must
pay you for it, for I cannot offer to the
LORD my God holocausts that cost noth-
ing." So David bought the threshing
floor and the oxen for fifty silver shekels.
25 Then David built an altar there to the
LORD, and offered holocausts and peace
offerings. The LORD granted relief to the
country, and the plague was checked in
Israel.

*

10: 1 Sm 24, 6; 1 Chr 21, 7.
13: 21, 1.
16: Ex 12, 23; 2 Kgs 19, 35.
22f: 1 Sm 6, 14; 1 Kgs 19, 21.

†

24, 10: The narrative supposes that since the people belonged to the Lord rather than to the king, only the Lord should know their exact number.

24, 17: Before this verse a Qumran manuscript (4Q Sam[a]) gives the fuller text of 1 Chr 21, 16, an alternative to the words *When David saw the angel who was striking the people.*

The Books of

KINGS

The two Books of Kings were originally, like 1 and 2 Samuel, a single historical work. In conjunction with the Books of Samuel, they extend the consecutive history of Israel from the birth of Samuel to the destruction of Jerusalem in 587 B.C. This combined work is designed as a religious history; hence in Kings the temple, which is the chosen site for the worship of Yahweh, occupies the center of attention.

The Books of Kings show clearly the theological bent of a Deuteronomic editor. In them, as already in Judges, material from various sources, such as the "book of the acts of Solomon" (1 Kgs 11, 41) and the "book of the chronicles of the kings of Israel" (1 Kgs 14, 19), is forged into structural unity by an editor whose principal interest is in the fidelity to Yahweh of rulers and people. The reigns of individual kings are adapted to an editorial framework consisting of a presentation and an obituary notice for each, in stereotyped formulas. In between, the achievements of the king are reported—above all, his fidelity or lack of fidelity to Yahweh. The faithful prosper; the unfaithful pay for their defections. Since this is basically a narrative of sin and retribution, it would not be inappropriate to entitle the Books of Kings "The Rise and Fall of the Israelite Monarchy."

Without minimizing the complexity of the process by which this material was transmitted for many centuries, one may speak of two editions of the Books: the first at some time between 621 B.C. and 597 B.C., and the second, final edition during the Exile; probably shortly after Jehoiachin was released from his Babylonian prison (561 B.C.).

1 Kings carries the history of Israel from the last days and death of David to the accession in Samaria of Ahaziah, son of Ahab, near the end of the reign of Jehoshaphat, king of Judah. Judgment is passed on Ahaziah's reign but the details are given only later, in 2 Kings. We should note the two large cycles of traditions which grew up around the great prophetic figures of Elijah and Elisha, the former in 1 Kings and the latter chiefly in 2 Kings. These cycles, which interrupt the sequence of regnal chronicles, were very probably preserved and transmitted by the prophetic communities to which there are references in the same traditions. The Elijah cycle is the more important since it dramatically underscores Israel's critical struggle with the religion of Canaan.

The principal divisions of the Books of Kings are:

I: The Reign of Solomon (1 Kgs 1, 1—11, 43)
II: Judah and Israel to the Time of Ahab (1 Kgs 12, 1—16, 34)
III: Stories of the Prophets (1 Kgs 17, 1—22, 54)
IV: The Kingdoms of Israel and Judah (2 Kgs 1, 1—17, 41)
V: The Kingdom of Judah after 721 B.C. (2 Kgs 18, 1—25, 30)

THE FIRST BOOK OF KINGS

I: THE REIGN OF SOLOMON

CHAPTER 1

1 When King David was old and ad-
vanced in years, though they spread
covers over him he could not keep
warm. 2 His servants therefore said to
him, "Let a young virgin be sought to
attend you, lord king, and to nurse you.
If she sleeps with your royal majesty,
you will be kept warm." 3 So they sought
for a beautiful girl throughout the terri-
tory of Israel, and found Abishag the
Shunamite, whom they brought to the
king. 4 The maiden, who was very beau-
tiful, nursed the king and cared for him,
but the king did not have relations with
her.

Ambition of Adonijah. 5 Adonijah, son
of Haggith, began to display his ambi-
tion to be king. He acquired chariots,
drivers, and fifty henchmen. 6 Yet his fa-
ther never rebuked him or asked why
he was doing this. Adonijah was also
very handsome, and next in age to Ab-
salom by the same mother. 7 He con-
ferred with Joab, son of Zeruiah, and
with Abiathar the priest, and they sup-
ported him. 8 However, Zadok the priest,

Benaiah, son of Jehoiada, Nathan the
prophet, and Shimei and his compan-
ions, the pick of David's army, did not
side with Adonijah. 9† When he slaugh-
tered sheep, oxen, and fatlings at the
stone Zoheleth, near En-rogel, Adonijah
invited all his brothers, the king's sons,
and all the royal officials of Judah. 10 But
he did not invite the prophet Nathan, or
Benaiah, or the pick of the army, or his
brother Solomon.

Solomon Proclaimed King. 11 Then
Nathan said to Bathsheba, Solomon's
mother: "Have you not heard that Ado-
nijah, son of Haggith, has become king
without the knowledge of our lord
David? 12 Come now, let me advise you
so that you may save your life and that
of your son Solomon. 13 Go, visit King
David, and say to him, 'Did you not, lord
king, swear to your handmaid: Your son
Solomon shall be king after me and shall
sit upon my throne? Why, then, has Ado-
nijah become king?' 14 And while you are
still there speaking to the king, I will
come in after you and confirm what you
have said."

15 So Bathsheba visited the king in his
room, while Abishag the Shunamite was
attending him because of his advanced
age. 16 Bathsheba bowed in homage to
the king, who said to her, "What do you
wish?" 17 She answered him: "My lord,
you swore to me your handmaid by the
LORD, your God, that my son Solomon
should reign after you and sit upon your
throne. 18 But now Adonijah has become
king, and you, my lord king, do not know
it. 19 He has slaughtered oxen, fatlings,
and sheep in great numbers; he has in-
vited all the king's sons, Abiathar the
priest, and Joab, the general of the
army, but not your servant Solomon.
20† Now, my lord king, all Israel is wait-
ing for you to make known to them who
is to sit on the throne after your royal
majesty. 21 If this is not done, when my
lord the king sleeps with his fathers, I
and my son Solomon will be considered
criminals."

22 While she was still speaking to the
king, the prophet Nathan came in.
23 When he had been announced, the
prophet entered the king's presence
and, bowing to the floor, did him hom-
age. 24 Then Nathan said: "Have you de-
cided, my lord king, that Adonijah is to
reign after you and sit on your throne?
25 He went down today and slaughtered
oxen, fatlings, and sheep in great num-
bers; he invited all the king's sons, the
commanders of the army, and Abiathar
the priest, and they are eating and
drinking in his company and saying,
'Long live King Adonijah!' 26 But me,
your servant, he did not invite; nor Za-
dok the priest, nor Benaiah, son of Jehoi-
ada, nor your servant Solomon. 27 Was
this done by my royal master's order
without my being told who was to suc-
ceed to your majesty's kingly throne?"

28 King David answered, "Call
Bathsheba here." When she re-entered
the king's presence and stood before
him, 29 the king swore, "As the LORD
lives, who has delivered me from all dis-
tress, 30 this very day I will fulfill the oath
I swore to you by the LORD, the God of
Israel, that your son Solomon should
reign after me and should sit upon my
throne in my place." 31 Bowing to the
floor in homage to the king, Bathsheba
said, "May my lord, King David, live
forever!" 32 Then King David summoned
Zadok the priest, Nathan the prophet,
and Benaiah, son of Jehoiada. When
they had entered the king's presence,
33 he said to them: "Take with you the
royal attendants. Mount my son Solo-
mon upon my own mule and escort him
down to Gihon. 34 There Zadok the priest
and Nathan the prophet are to anoint
him king of Israel, and you shall blow
the horn and cry, 'Long live King Solo-
mon!' 35 When you come back in his
train, he is to go in and sit upon my
throne and reign in my place. I desig-
nate him ruler of Israel and of Judah."
36 In answer to the king, Benaiah, son
of Jehoiada, said: "So be it! May the
LORD, the God of my lord the king, so
decree! 37 As the LORD has been with
your royal majesty, so may he be with
Solomon, and exalt his throne even more
than that of my lord, King David!"

38† So Zadok the priest, Nathan the
prophet, Benaiah, son of Jehoiada, and
the Cherethites and Pelethites went
down, and mounting Solomon on King
David's mule, escorted him to Gihon.
39 Then Zadok the priest took the horn
of oil from the tent and anointed Solo-
mon. They blew the horn and all the peo-
ple shouted, "Long live King Solomon!"
40 Then all the people went up after him,
playing flutes and rejoicing so much as
to split open the earth with their shout-
ing.

41 Adonijah and all the guests who
were with him heard it, just as they
ended their banquet. When Joab heard
the sound of the horn, he asked, "What
does this uproar in the city mean?" 42 As
he was speaking, Jonathan, son of Abi-
athar the priest, arrived. "Come," said
Adonijah, "you are a man of worth and

1, 9: *En-rogel:* the modern Job's Well southeast of Jerusalem. It marked the ancient boundary between the tribes of Benjamin and Judah (Jos 15, 7; 18, 16). Here David's men sought information about Absalom's revolt (2 Sm 17, 17).

1, 20: At this time, neither law nor the right of primogeniture, but the will of the ruling monarch, determined succession to the throne.

1, 38: *Cherethites and Pelethites:* mercenaries in David's bodyguard. They became part of his retinue after he defeated the Philistines and established himself in Jerusalem; cf 2 Sm 8, 18; 15, 18; 20, 23.

must bring good news." 43 "On the con-
trary!" Jonathan answered him. "Our
lord, King David, has made Solomon
king. 44 The king sent with him Zadok
the priest, Nathan the prophet, Benaiah,
son of Jehoiada, and the Cherethites and
Pelethites, and they mounted him upon
the king's own mule. 45 Zadok the priest
and Nathan the prophet anointed him
king at Gihon, and they went up from
there rejoicing, so that the city is in an
uproar. That is the noise you heard.
46 Besides, Solomon took his seat on the
royal throne, 47 and the king's servants
went in and paid their respects to our
lord, King David, saying, 'May God
make Solomon more famous than you
and exalt his throne more than your
own!' And the king in his bed worshiped
God, 48 and this is what he said: 'Blessed
be the LORD, the God of Israel, who has
this day seated one of my sons upon my
throne, so that I see it with my own
eyes.' "

49 All the guests of Adonijah left in ter-
ror, each going his own way. 50† Ado-
nijah, in fear of Solomon, also left; he
went and seized the horns of the altar.
51 It was reported to Solomon that Ado-
nijah, in his fear of King Solomon, had
seized the horns of the altar and said,
"Let King Solomon first swear that he
will not kill me, his servant, with the
sword." 52 Solomon answered, "If he
proves himself worthy, not a hair shall
fall from his head. But if he is found
guilty of crime, he shall die." 53 King Sol-
omon sent to have him brought down
from the altar, and he came and paid
homage to the king. Solomon then said
to him, "Go to your home."

CHAPTER 2

David's Last Instructions and Death.
1† When the time of David's death drew
near, he gave these instructions to his
son Solomon: 2 "I am going the way of
all mankind. Take courage and be a
man. 3* Keep the mandate of the LORD,
your God, following his ways and ob-
serving his statutes, commands, ordi-
nances, and decrees as they are written
in the law of Moses, that you may suc-
ceed in whatever you do, wherever you
turn, 4* and the LORD may fulfill the
promise he made on my behalf when he
said, 'If your sons so conduct themselves
that they remain faithful to me with
their whole heart and with their whole
soul, you shall always have someone of
your line on the throne of Israel.' 5* You
yourself know what Joab, son of Zeru-
iah, did to me when he slew the two gen-
erals of Israel's armies, Abner, son of
Ner, and Amasa, son of Jether. He took
revenge for the blood of war in a time
of peace, and put bloodshed without
provocation on the belt about my waist
and the sandal on my foot. 6 Act with
the wisdom you possess; you must not
allow him to go down to the grave in
peaceful old age.

7* "But be kind to the sons of Barzillai
the Gileadite, and have them eat at your
table. For they received me kindly when
I was fleeing your brother Absalom.

8* "You also have with you Shimei, son
of Gera, the Benjaminite of Bahurim,
who cursed me balefully when I was go-
ing to Mahanaim. Because he came
down to meet me at the Jordan, I swore
to him by the LORD that I would not put
him to the sword. 9 But you must not let
him go unpunished. You are a prudent
man and will know how to deal with him
to send down his hoary head in blood
to the grave."

10* David rested with his ancestors
and was buried in the City of David.
11* The length of David's reign over Is-
rael was forty years: he reigned seven
years in Hebron and thirty-three years
in Jerusalem.

The Kingdom Made Secure. 12 When
Solomon was seated on the throne of his
father David, with his sovereignty firmly
established, 13 Adonijah, son of Haggith,
went to Bathsheba, the mother of Solo-
mon. "Do you come as a friend?" she
asked. "Yes," he answered, 14 and
added, "I have something to say to you."
She replied, "Say it." 15 So he said: "You
know that the kingdom was mine, and
all Israel expected me to be king. But
the kingdom escaped me and became
my brother's, for the LORD gave it to
him. 16 But now there is one favor I would
ask of you. Do not refuse me." And she
said, "Speak on." 17† He said, "Please
ask King Solomon, who will not refuse
you, to give me Abishag the Shunamite
for my wife." 18 "Very well," replied

*

2, 3: Dt 17, 19.
4: 2 Sm 7, 11-16; Ps 132, 11f.
5: 2 Sm 3, 27; 20, 10.
7: 2 Sm 19, 33ff.
8: 2 Sm 16, 5; 19, 19.
10: Acts 2, 29.
11: 1 Chr 29, 27.

†

1, 50: *Horns of the altar:* the protuberances on each of the four corners of the altar were surrounded with a special degree of holiness (Ex 27, 2; 29, 12), and constituted a place of asylum for transgressors of the law (Ex 21, 13f; 1 Kgs 2, 28).

2, 1-6.8-9: Solomon is expected to remove from his father's family the imputation of blood guilt brought upon it by Joab in the unwarranted killings of Abner (2 Sm 3, 27-29) and Amasa (2 Sm 19, 9-10); and likewise to punish Shimei for his curse, the effects of which David had pledged himself not to avenge in person (2 Sm 19, 21-23). The standards of morality presumed in these verses are far from the Christian ones.

2, 17.22-25: *Abishag* had been the concubine of King David (1, 4). His successor, Solomon, inherited his father's harem. When Adonijah requested Abishag as his wife, he was subtly undermining the security of Solomon's throne and exposing himself to the suspicion of insurrection that would cost him his life; cf 2 Sm 3, 6-11; 16, 22.

Bathsheba, "I will speak to the king for you."

19 Then Bathsheba went to King Solomon to speak to him for Adonijah, and the king stood up to meet her and paid her homage. Then he sat down upon his throne, and a throne was provided for the king's mother, who sat at his right. 20 "There is one small favor I would ask of you," she said. "Do not refuse me." "Ask it, my mother," the king said to her, "for I will not refuse you." 21 So she said, "Let Abishag the Shunamite be given to your brother Adonijah for his wife." 22 "And why do you ask Abishag the Shunamite for Adonijah?" King Solomon answered his mother. "Ask the kingdom for him as well, for he is my elder brother and has with him Abiathar the priest and Joab, son of Zeruiah." 23 And King Solomon swore by the LORD: "May God do thus and so to me, and more besides, if Adonijah has not proposed this at the cost of his life. 24 And now, as the LORD lives, who has seated me firmly on the throne of my father David and made of me a dynasty as he promised, this day shall Adonijah be put to death." 25 Then King Solomon sent Benaiah, son of Jehoiada, who struck him dead.

26 The king said to Abiathar the priest: "Go to your land in Anathoth. Though you deserve to die, I will not put you to death this time, because you carried the ark of the Lord GOD before my father David and shared in all the hardships my father endured." 27* So Solomon deposed Abiathar from his office of priest of the LORD, thus fulfilling the prophecy which the LORD had made in Shiloh about the house of Eli.

28 When the news came to Joab, who had sided with Adonijah, though not with Absalom, he fled to the tent of the LORD and seized the horns of the altar. 29 King Solomon was told that Joab had fled to the tent of the LORD and was at the altar. He sent Benaiah, son of Jehoiada, with the order, "Go, strike him down." 30 Benaiah went to the tent of the LORD and said to him, "The king says, 'Come out.'" But he answered, "No! I will die here." Benaiah reported to the king, "This is what Joab said to me in reply." 31 The king answered him: "Do as he has said, Strike him down and bury him, and you will remove from me and from my family the blood which Joab shed without provocation. 32* The LORD will hold him responsible for his own blood, because he struck down two men better and more just than himself, and slew them with the sword without my father David's knowledge: Abner, son of Ner, general of Israel's army, and Amasa, son of Jether, general of Judah's army. 33 Joab and his descendants shall be responsible forever for their blood. But there shall be the peace of the LORD forever for David, and his descendants, and his house, and his throne." 34 Benaiah, son of Jehoiada, went back, struck him down and killed him; he was buried in his house in the desert. 35 The king appointed Benaiah, son of Jehoiada, over the army in his place, and put Zadok the priest in place of Abiathar.

36 Then the king summoned Shimei and said to him: "Build yourself a house in Jerusalem and live there. Do not go anywhere else. 37 For if you leave, and cross the Kidron Valley, be certain you shall die without fail. You shall be responsible for your own blood." 38 Shimei answered the king: "I accept. Your servant will do just as the king's majesty has said." So Shimei stayed in Jerusalem for a long time. 39 But three years later, two of Shimei's servants ran away to Achish, son of Maacah, king of Gath, and Shimei was informed that his servants were in Gath. 40 So Shimei rose, saddled his ass, and went to Achish in Gath in search of his servants, whom he brought back. 41 When Solomon was informed that Shimei had gone from Jerusalem to Gath, and had returned, 42 the king summoned Shimei and said to him: "Did I not have you swear by the LORD to your clear understanding of my warning that, if you left and went anywhere else, you should die without fail? And you answered, 'I accept and obey.' 43 Why, then, have you not kept the oath of the LORD and the command that I gave you?" 44 And the king said to Shimei: "You know in your heart the evil that you did to my father David. Now the LORD requites you for your own wickedness. 45 But King Solomon shall be blessed, and David's throne shall endure before the LORD forever." 46 The king then gave the order to Benaiah, son of Jehoiada, who struck him dead as he left.

CHAPTER 3

Wisdom of Solomon. 1* With the royal power firmly in his grasp, Solomon allied himself by marriage with Pharaoh, king of Egypt. The daughter of Pharaoh, whom he married, he brought to the City of David, until he should finish building his palace, and the temple of the LORD, and the wall around Jerusalem.

2 However, the people were sacrificing on the high places, for up to that time no temple had been built to the name of the LORD. 3 Solomon loved the LORD, and obeyed the statutes of his father David; yet he offered sacrifice and burned incense on the high places.

27: 1 Sm 2, 31.
32: 2 Sm 3, 27; 20, 10.
3, 1: 7, 8; 2 Chr 1, 1.

4 The king went to Gibeon to sacrifice
there, because that was the most re-
nowned high place. Upon its altar Solo-
mon offered a thousand holocausts. 5 In
Gibeon the LORD appeared to Solomon
in a dream at night. God said, "Ask
something of me and I will give it to
you." 6 Solomon answered: "You have
shown great favor to your servant, my
father David, because he behaved faith-
fully toward you, with justice and an up-
right heart; and you have continued this
great favor toward him, even today,
seating a son of his on his throne. 7 O
LORD, my God, you have made me, your
servant, king to succeed my father
David; but I am a mere youth, not know-
ing at all how to act. 8 I serve you in the
midst of the people whom you have cho-
sen, a people so vast that it cannot be
numbered or counted. 9* Give your ser-
vant, therefore, an understanding heart
to judge your people and to distinguish
right from wrong. For who is able to gov-
ern this vast people of yours?"

10 The LORD was pleased that Solomon
made this request. 11 So God said to him:
"Because you have asked for this—not
for a long life for yourself, nor for riches,
nor for the life of your enemies, but for
understanding so that you may know
what is right—12 I do as you requested.
I give you a heart so wise and under-
standing that there has never been any-
one like you up to now, and after you
there will come no one to equal you.
13* In addition, I give you what you have
not asked for, such riches and glory that
among kings there is not your like.
14 And if you follow me by keeping my
statutes and commandments, as your
father David did, I will give you a long
life."

15 When Solomon awoke from his
dream, he went to Jerusalem, stood be-
fore the ark of the covenant of the LORD,
offered holocausts and peace offerings,
and gave a banquet for all his servants.

Solomon's Judgment. 16 Later, two
harlots came to the king and stood be-
fore him. 17 One woman said: "By your
leave, my lord, this woman and I live
in the same house, and I gave birth in
the house while she was present. 18 On
the third day after I gave birth, this
woman also gave birth. We were alone
in the house; there was no one there but
us two. 19 This woman's son died during
the night; she smothered him by lying
on him. 20 Later that night she got up and
took my son from my side, as I, your
handmaid, was sleeping. Then she laid
him in her bosom, after she had laid her
dead child in my bosom. 21 I rose in the
morning to nurse my child, and I found
him dead. But when I examined him in
the morning light, I saw it was not the
son whom I had borne."

22 The other woman answered, "It is
not so! The living one is my son, the dead
one is yours." But the first kept saying,
"No, the dead one is your child, the liv-
ing one is mine!" Thus they argued be-
fore the king.

23 Then the king said: "One woman
claims, 'This, the living one, is my child,
and the dead one is yours.' The other
answers, 'No! The dead one is your child;
the living one is mine.'" 24 The king con-
tinued, "Get me a sword." When they
brought the sword before him, 25 he said,
"Cut the living child in two, and give half
to one woman and half to the other."
26 The woman whose son it was, in the
anguish she felt for it, said to the king,
"Please, my lord, give her the living
child—please do not kill it!" The other,
however, said, "It shall be neither mine
nor yours. Divide it!" 27 The king then
answered, "Give the first one the living
child! By no means kill it, for she is the
mother."

28 When all Israel heard the judgment
the king had given, they were in awe of
him, because they saw that the king had
in him the wisdom of God for giving
judgment.

CHAPTER 4

Chief Officers of the Kingdom. 1 Sol-
omon was king over all Israel, 2 and
these were the officials he had in his
service:

Azariah, son of Zadok, priest;
3 Elihoreph and Ahijah, sons of Shisha, scribes;
Jehoshaphat, son of Ahilud, chancellor;
4 [Benaiah, son of Jehoiada, commander of the army;
Zadok and Abiathar, priests;]
5 Azariah, son of Nathan, chief of the commissaries;
Zabud, son of Nathan, companion to the king;
6 Ahishar, major-domo of the palace; and
Adoniram, son of Abda, superintendent of the forced labor.

Solomon's Royal State. 7† Solomon
had twelve commissaries for all Israel
who supplied food for the king and his
household, each having to provide for
one month in the year. 8 Their names
were:

the son of Hur in the hill country of Ephraim;
9 the son of Deker in Makaz, Shaal-

* 9: 2 Chr 1, 10.
13: Wis 7, 11; Mt 6, 29.

† 4, 7-19: The administration of the kingdom thus initiated by Solomon continued in its main features for the duration of the monarchy in Israel and Judah.

bim, Beth-shemesh, Elon and Beth-hanan;
10 the son of Hesed in Arubboth, as well as in Socoh and the whole region of Hepher;
11 the son of Abinadab, who was married to Solomon's daughter Taphath, in all the Naphath-dor;
12 Baana, son of Ahilud, in Taanach and Megiddo, and beyond Jokmeam, and in all Beth-shean, and in the country around Zarethan below Jezreel from Beth-shean to Abel-meholah;
13 the son of Geber in Ramoth-gilead, having charge of the villages of Jair, son of Manasseh, in Gilead; and of the district of Argob in Bashan—sixty large walled cities with gates barred with bronze;
14 Ahinadab, son of Iddo, in Mahanaim;
15 Ahimaaz, who was married to Basemath, another daughter of Solomon, in Naphtali;
16 Baana, son of Hushai, in Asher and along the rocky coast;
17 Jehoshaphat, son of Paruah, in Issachar;
18 Shimei, son of Ela, in Benjamin;
19† Geber, son of Uri, in the land of Gilead, the land of Sihon, king of the Amorites, and of Og, king of Bashan.

There was one prefect besides, in the king's own land.

CHAPTER 5

7 These commissaries, one for each
month, provided food for King Solomon
and for all the guests at the royal table.
They left nothing unprovided. 8 For the
chariot horses and draft animals also,
each brought his quota of barley and
straw to the required place.

20† Judah and Israel were as numer-
ous as the sands by the sea; they ate and
drank and made merry.

1* Solomon ruled over all the king-
doms from the River to the land of the
Philistines, down to the border of Egypt;
they paid Solomon tribute and were his
vassals as long as he lived.

2 Solomon's supplies for each day were
thirty kors of fine flour, sixty kors of
meal, 3 ten fatted oxen, twenty pasture-
fed oxen, and a hundred sheep, not
counting harts, gazelles, roebucks, and
fatted fowl.

4 He ruled over all the land west of the
Euphrates, from Tiphsah to Gaza, and
over all its kings, and he had peace on
all his borders round about. 5 Thus Ju-
dah and Israel lived in security, every
man under his vine or under his fig tree
from Dan to Beer-sheba, as long as Solo-
mon lived.

6* Solomon had four thousand stalls
for his twelve thousand chariot horses.

9* Moreover, God gave Solomon wis-
dom and exceptional understanding and
knowledge, as vast as the sand on the
seashore. 10 Solomon surpassed all the
Cedemites and all the Egyptians in wis-
dom. 11 He was wiser than all other
men—than Ethan the Ezrahite, or He-
man, Chalcol, and Darda, the musi-
cians—and his fame spread throughout
the neighboring nations. 12* Solomon
also uttered three thousand proverbs,
and his songs numbered a thousand and
five. 13 He discussed plants, from the ce-
dar on Lebanon to the hyssop growing
out of the wall, and he spoke about
beasts, birds, reptiles, and fishes. 14 Men
came to hear Solomon's wisdom from
all nations, sent by all the kings of the
earth who had heard of his wisdom.

Preparations for the Temple. 15 When
Hiram, king of Tyre, heard that Solomon
had been anointed king in place of his
father, he sent an embassy to him; for
Hiram had always been David's friend.
16 Solomon sent back this message to
Hiram: 17 "You know that my father
David, because of the enemies sur-
rounding him on all sides, could not
build a temple in honor of the LORD, his
God, until such a time as the LORD
should put these enemies under the soles
of his feet. 18 But now the LORD, my God,
has given me peace on all sides. There
is no enemy or threat of danger. 19* So
I purpose to build a temple in honor of
the LORD, my God, as the LORD pre-
dicted to my father David when he said:
'It is your son whom I will put upon your
throne in your place who shall build the
temple in my honor.' 20 Give orders,
then, to have cedars from the Lebanon
cut down for me. My servants shall ac-
company yours, since you know that
there is no one among us who is skilled
in cutting timber like the Sidonians, and
I will pay you whatever you say for your
servants' salary."

21 When he had heard the words of Sol-
omon, Hiram was pleased and said,
"Blessed be the LORD this day, who has
given David a wise son to rule this nu-
merous people." 22 Hiram then sent
word to Solomon, "I agree to the pro-
posal you sent me, and I will provide all
the cedars and fir trees you wish. 23 My

*

5, 1: Sir 47, 15f; 2 Chr 9, 26.
6: 2 Chr 9, 25f.
9-14: Sir 47, 16f.
12: 3, 12.
19: 2 Sm 7, 13; 1 Chr 22, 10.

†

4, 19: *One prefect . . . in the king's own land:* the royal territory of Judah had its own peculiar administration different from that of the twelve districts which had to supply the king and his household with a month's provisions of food each year (v 7).

5, 20: this verse belongs to ch 4.

servants shall bring them down from the
Lebanon to the sea, and I will arrange
them into rafts in the sea and bring them
wherever you say. There I will break up
the rafts, and you shall take the lumber.
You, for your part, shall furnish the
provisions I desire for my household."
24 So Hiram continued to provide Solo-
mon with all the cedars and fir trees he
wished; 25 while Solomon every year
gave Hiram twenty thousand kors of
wheat to provide for his household, and
twenty thousand measures of pure oil.
26 The LORD, moreover, gave Solomon
wisdom as he promised him, and there
was peace between Hiram and Solomon,
since they were parties to a treaty.
27 King Solomon conscripted thirty
thousand workmen from all Israel. 28 He
sent them to the Lebanon each month
in relays of ten thousand, so that they
spent one month in the Lebanon and two
months at home. Adoniram was in
charge of the draft. 29 Solomon had sev-
enty thousand carriers and eighty thou-
sand stonecutters in the mountain, 30 in
addition to three thousand three hun-
dred overseers, answerable to Solo-
mon's prefects for the work, directing
the people engaged in the work. 31 By or-
der of the king, fine, large blocks were
quarried to give the temple a foundation
of hewn stone. 32 Solomon's and Hiram's
builders, along with the Gebalites,
hewed them out, and prepared the wood
and stones for building the temple.

CHAPTER 6

Building of the Temple. 1*† In the four
hundred and eightieth year from the de-
parture of the Israelites from the land
of Egypt, in the fourth year of Solomon's
reign over Israel, in the month of Ziv,
which is the second month, the construc-
tion of the temple of the LORD was be-
gun.
2 The temple which King Solomon built
for the LORD was sixty cubits long,
twenty wide, and twenty-five high. 3 The
porch in front of the temple was twenty
cubits from side to side, along the width
of the nave, and ten cubits deep in front
of the temple. 4 Splayed windows with
trellises were made for the temple, 5 and
adjoining the wall of the temple, which
enclosed the nave and the sanctuary, an
annex of several stories was built. 6 Its
lowest story was five cubits wide, the
middle one six cubits wide, the third
seven cubits wide, because there were
offsets along the outside of the temple
so that the beams would not be fastened
into the walls of the temple. 7 (The tem-
ple was built of stone dressed at the
quarry, so that no hammer, axe, or iron
tool was to be heard in the temple during
its construction.) 8 The entrance to the
lowest floor of the annex was at the right
side of the temple, and stairs with inter-
mediate landings led up to the middle
story and from the middle story to the
third. 9 When the temple was built to its
full height, it was roofed in with rafters
and boards of cedar. 10 The annex, with
its lowest story five cubits high, was built
all along the outside of the temple, to
which it was joined by cedar beams.
11† This word of the LORD came to Sol-
omon: 12* "As to this temple you are
building—if you observe my statutes,
carry out my ordinances, keep and obey
all my commands, I will fulfill toward
you the promise I made to your father
David. 13* I will dwell in the midst of the
Israelites and will not forsake my people
Israel."
14 When Solomon finished building the
temple, 15 its walls were lined from floor
to ceiling beams with cedar paneling,
and its floor was laid with fir planking.
16 At the rear of the temple a space of
twenty cubits was set off by cedar parti-
tions from the floor to the rafters, enclos-
ing the sanctuary, the holy of holies.
17 The nave, or part of the temple in front
of the sanctuary, was forty cubits long.
18 The cedar in the interior of the temple
was carved in the form of gourds and
open flowers; all was of cedar, and no
stone was to be seen.
19† In the innermost part of the temple
was located the sanctuary to house the
ark of the LORD's covenant, 20† twenty
cubits long, twenty wide, and twenty
high. 21 Solomon overlaid the interior of
the temple with pure gold. He made in
front of the sanctuary a cedar altar,
overlaid it with gold, and looped it with
golden chains. 22 The entire temple was
overlaid with gold so that it was com-
pletely covered with it; the whole altar
before the sanctuary was also overlaid

*

6, 1: 2 Chr 3, 1. 12: 2 Sm 7, 13. 13: 1 Chr 22, 9f.

†

6, 1: *Construction of the temple of the LORD* is here paralleled in importance with the founding of the nation after the departure from Egypt. In both, God is the central figure who chose Israel as his people, and now chooses the place where his temple should be built (Dt 12, 4-18.26). The year is given in a round number, 480, which corresponds to twelve generations. The *fourth year of Solomon's reign:* c. 968 B.C.

6, 11ff: *The word of the LORD . . . my people Israel:* the oracle, which came as a climax at the completion of the work, was an expression of God's acceptance and approval. Nevertheless the fulfillment of God's promises to David and his royal descendants will depend on their observance of his ordinances and commands.

6, 19: *The innermost part of the temple:* the sanctuary or holy of holies reserved exclusively for the Lord. Here through his presence he dwelt as on a throne between the cherubim above the ark of the covenant (23-28; 2 Chr 3, 10-13). See note on Ex 25, 18ff.

6, 20: *Twenty (cubits) high:* it is usually supposed that the holy of holies was of this height because it had a raised floor, five cubits above the floor level of the nave, rather than a dropped ceiling. The building was twenty-five cubits high (v 2) according to the reading here followed.

with gold. 23 In the sanctuary were two
cherubim, each ten cubits high, made
of olive wood. 24 Each wing of a cherub
measured five cubits so that the space
from wing tip to wing tip of each was
ten cubits. 25 The cherubim were identi-
cal in size and shape, 26 and each was
exactly ten cubits high. 27 The cherubim
were placed in the inmost part of the
temple, with their wings spread wide, so
that one wing of each cherub touched
a side wall while the other wing, pointing
toward the middle of the room, touched
the corresponding wing of the second
cherub. 28 The cherubim, too, were over-
laid with gold.

29 The walls on all sides of both the in-
ner and the outer rooms had carved fig-
ures of cherubim, palm trees, and open
flowers. 30 The floor of both the inner and
the outer rooms was overlaid with gold.
31 At the entrance of the sanctuary,
doors of olive wood were made; the
doorframes had beveled posts. 32 The
two doors were of olive wood, with
carved figures of cherubim, palm trees,
and open flowers. The doors were over-
laid with gold, which was also molded
to the cherubim and the palm trees.
33 The same was done at the entrance
to the nave, where the doorposts of olive
wood were rectangular. 34 The two doors
were of fir wood; each door was banded
by a metal strap, front and back, 35 and
had carved cherubim, palm trees, and
open flowers, over which gold was
evenly applied.

36 The inner court was walled off by
means of three courses of hewn stones
and one course of cedar beams.

37 The foundations of the LORD's tem-
ple were laid in the month of Ziv 38 in
the fourth year, and it was completed
in all particulars, exactly according to
plan, in the month of Bul, the eighth
month, in the eleventh year. Thus it took
Solomon seven years to build it.

CHAPTER 7

Building of the Palace. 1* His own pal-
ace Solomon completed after thirteen
years of construction. 2 He built the hall
called the Forest of Lebanon one hun-
dred cubits long, fifty wide, and thirty
high; it was supported by four rows of
cedar columns, with cedar capitals upon
the columns. 3 Moreover, it had a ceiling
of cedar above the beams resting on the
columns; these beams numbered forty-
five, fifteen to a row. 4 There were three
window frames at either end, with win-
dows in strict alignment. 5 The posts of
all the doorways were rectangular, and
the doorways faced each other, three at
either end. 6 The porch of the columned
hall he made fifty cubits long and thirty
wide. The porch extended the width of
the columned hall, and there was a can-
opy in front. 7 He also built the vestibule
of the throne where he gave judgment—
that is, the tribunal; it was paneled with
cedar from floor to ceiling beams. 8* His
living quarters were in another court, set
in deeper than the tribunal and of the
same construction. A palace like this tri-
bunal was built for Pharaoh's daughter,
whom Solomon had married.

9 All these buildings were of fine
stones, hewn to size and trimmed front
and back with a saw, from the founda-
tion to the bonding course. 10 (The foun-
dation was made of fine, large blocks,
some ten cubits and some eight cubits.
11 Above were fine stones hewn to size,
and cedar wood.) 12 The great court was
enclosed by three courses of hewn stones
and a bonding course of cedar beams.
So also were the inner court of the tem-
ple of the LORD and the temple porch.

Furnishing of the Temple. 13 King Sol-
omon had Hiram brought from Tyre.
14 He was a bronze worker, the son of a
widow from the tribe of Naphtali; his fa-
ther had been from Tyre. He was en-
dowed with skill, understanding, and
knowledge of how to produce any work
in bronze. He came to King Solomon and
did all his metal work.

15*† Two hollow bronze columns were
cast, each eighteen cubits high and
twelve cubits in circumference; their
metal was of four fingers' thickness.
16 There were also two capitals cast in
bronze, to place on top of the columns,
each of them five cubits high. 17 Two
pieces of network with a chainlike mesh
were made to cover the (nodes of the)
capitals on top of the columns, one for
each capital. 18 Four hundred pome-
granates were also cast; two hundred of
them in a double row encircled the piece
of network on each of the two capitals.
19 The capitals on top of the columns
were finished wholly in a lotus pattern
20 above the level of the nodes and their
enveloping network. 21 The columns
were then erected adjacent to the porch
of the temple, one to the right, called Ja-
chin, and the other to the left, called
Boaz. 22 Thus the work on the columns
was completed.

23*† The sea was then cast; it was
made with a circular rim, and measured
ten cubits across, five in height, and

*

7, 1: 1 Kgs 9, 10.
8: 3, 1.
15: Jer 52, 21.
23: 2 Chr 4, 2.

†

7, 15-21: The *two hollow bronze columns,* Jachin and Boaz (2 Chr 3, 17), stood free to the right and left of the temple porch. The names are related to God's power *(Boaz)* founding *(Jachin)* the temple and his people.

7, 23-26: *The sea . . . rested on twelve oxen:* this was a large circular tank containing about twelve thousand gallons of water.

thirty in circumference. 24 Under the brim, gourds encircled it, ten to the cubit all the way around; the gourds were in two rows and were cast in one mold with the sea. 25 This rested on twelve oxen, three facing north, three facing west, three facing south, and three facing east, with their haunches all toward the center, where the sea was set upon them. 26 It was a handbreadth thick, and its brim resembled that of a cup, being lily-shaped. Its capacity was two thousand measures.

27 Ten stands were also made of bronze, each four cubits long, four wide, and three high. 28 When these stands were constructed, panels were set within the framework. 29 On the panels between the frames there were lions, oxen, and cherubim; and on the frames likewise, above and below the lions and oxen, there were wreaths in relief.

30 Each stand had four bronze wheels and bronze axles. 32 The four wheels were below the paneling, and the axletrees of the wheels and the stand were of one piece. Each wheel was a cubit and a half high. 33 The wheels were constructed like chariot wheels; their axles, fellies, spokes, and hubs were all cast.

The four legs of each stand had cast braces, which were under the basin; they had wreaths on each side. 34 These four braces, extending to the corners of each stand, were of one piece with the stand.

35 On top of the stand there was a raised collar half a cubit high, with supports and panels which were of one piece with the top of the stand. 31 This was surmounted by a crown one cubit high within which was a rounded opening to provide a receptacle a cubit and a half in depth. There was carved work at the opening, on panels that were angular, not curved. 36 On the surfaces of the supports and on the panels, wherever there was a clear space, cherubim, lions, and palm trees were carved, as well as wreaths all around. 37 This was how the ten stands were made, all of the same casting, the same size, the same shape. 38 Ten bronze basins were then made, each four cubits in diameter with a capacity of forty measures, one basin for the top of each of the ten stands. 39 The stands were placed, five on the south side of the temple and five on the north. The sea was placed off to the southeast from the south side of the temple.

40 When Hiram made the pots, shovels, and bowls, he therewith completed all his work for King Solomon in the temple of the LORD: 41 two columns, two nodes for the capitals on top of the columns, two pieces of network covering the nodes for the capitals on top of the columns, 42 four hundred pomegranates in double rows on both pieces of network that covered the two nodes of the capitals where they met the columns, 43 ten stands, ten basins on the stands, 44 one sea, twelve oxen supporting the sea, 45 pots, shovels, and bowls. All these articles which Hiram made for King Solomon in the temple of the LORD were of burnished bronze. 46 The king had them cast in the neighborhood of the Jordan, in the clayey ground between Succoth and Zarethan. 47 Solomon did not weigh all the articles because they were so numerous; the weight of the bronze, therefore, was not determined.

48 Solomon had all the articles made for the interior of the temple of the LORD: the golden altar; the golden table on which the showbread lay; 49 the lampstands of pure gold, five to the right and five to the left before the sanctuary, with their flowers, lamps, and tongs of gold; 50 basins, snuffers, bowls, cups, and fire pans of pure gold; and hinges of gold for the doors of the inner room, or holy of holies, and for the doors of the outer room, the nave.

51* When all the work undertaken by King Solomon in the temple of the LORD was completed, he brought in the dedicated offerings of his father David, putting the silver, gold, and other articles in the treasuries of the temple of the LORD.

CHAPTER 8

Dedication of the Temple. 1* At the order of Solomon, the elders of Israel and all the leaders of the tribes, the princes in the ancestral houses of the Israelites, came to King Solomon in Jerusalem, to bring up the ark of the LORD's covenant from the city of David [which is Zion]. 2 All the men of Israel assembled before King Solomon during the festival in the month of Ethanim (the seventh month). 3 When all the elders of Israel had arrived, the priests took up the ark; 4 they carried the ark of the LORD and the meeting tent with all the sacred vessels that were in the tent. (The priests and Levites carried them.)

5 King Solomon and the entire community of Israel present for the occasion sacrificed before the ark sheep and oxen too many to number or count. 6† The priests brought the ark of the covenant

* 51: 2 Chr 5, 1. 8, 1: 2 Chr 5, 2.

† 8, 6-9: The transfer of the ark of the covenant into the newly constructed temple building, and the oracle of God's acceptance (9, 3-9), and his act of possession (8, 10-13), constituted the temple's solemn dedication, and made of it the abiding dwelling of God among his people for which David had hoped (2 Sm 6, 12-15; 7, 1-3). The concurrence of the feast of Booths marks an appropriate transition of God's dwelling among nomadic tribes to his permanent abode among a settled people.

of the LORD to its place beneath the
wings of the cherubim in the sanctuary,
the holy of holies of the temple. 7 The
cherubim had their wings spread out
over the place of the ark, sheltering the
ark and its poles from above. 8 The poles
were so long that their ends could be
seen from that part of the holy place ad-
joining the sanctuary; however, they
could not be seen beyond. (They have
remained there to this day.) 9* There
was nothing in the ark but the two stone
tablets which Moses had put there at
Horeb, when the LORD made a covenant
with the Israelites at their departure
from the land of Egypt.

10 When the priests left the holy place,
the cloud filled the temple of the LORD
11 so that the priests could no longer min-
ister because of the cloud, since the
LORD's glory had filled the temple of the
LORD. 12* Then Solomon said, "The
LORD intends to dwell in the dark cloud;
13 I have truly built you a princely house,
a dwelling where you may abide for-
ever."

14 The king turned and greeted the
whole community of Israel as they
stood. 15 He said to them: "Blessed be the
LORD, the God of Israel, who with his
own mouth made a promise to my father
David and by his hand has brought it
to fulfillment. It was he who said,
16 'Since the day I brought my people Is-
rael out of Egypt, I have not chosen a
city out of any tribe of Israel for the
building of a temple to my honor; but I
choose David to rule my people Israel.'
17* When my father David wished to
build a temple to the honor of the LORD,
the God of Israel, 18 the LORD said to him,
'In wishing to build a temple to my
honor, you do well. 19 It will not be you,
however, who will build the temple; but
the son who will spring from you, he
shall build the temple to my honor.'
20 And now the LORD has fulfilled the
promise that he made: I have succeeded
my father David and sit on the throne
of Israel, as the LORD foretold, and I
have built this temple to honor the LORD,
the God of Israel. 21 I have provided in
it a place for the ark in which is the
covenant of the LORD, which he made
with our fathers when he brought them
out of the land of Egypt."

Solomon's Prayer. 22 Solomon stood
before the altar of the LORD in the pres-
ence of the whole community of Israel,
and stretching forth his hands toward
heaven, 23 he said, "LORD, God of Israel,
there is no God like you in heaven above
or on earth below; you keep your cove-
nant of kindness with your servants who
are faithful to you with their whole heart.
24 You have kept the promise you made
to my father David, your servant. You
who spoke that promise, have this day,
by your own power, brought it to fulfill-
ment. 25* Now, therefore, LORD, God of
Israel, keep the further promise you
made to my father David, your servant,
saying, 'You shall always have someone
from your line to sit before me on the
throne of Israel, provided only that your
descendants look to their conduct so that
they live in my presence, as you have
lived in my presence.' 26 Now, LORD, God
of Israel, may this promise which you
made to my father David, your servant,
be confirmed.

27 "Can it indeed be that God dwells
among men on earth? If the heavens and
the highest heavens cannot contain you,
how much less this temple which I have
built! 28 Look kindly on the prayer and
petition of your servant, O LORD, my
God, and listen to the cry of supplication
which I, your servant, utter before you
this day. 29 May your eyes watch night
and day over this temple, the place
where you have decreed you shall be
honored; may you heed the prayer
which I, your servant, offer in this place.
30 Listen to the petitions of your servant
and of your people Israel which they of-
fer in this place. Listen from your heav-
enly dwelling and grant pardon.

31 "If a man sins against his neighbor
and is required to take an oath sanc-
tioned by a curse, when he comes and
takes the oath before your altar in this
temple, 32 listen in heaven; take action
and pass judgment on your servants.
Condemn the wicked and punish him for
his conduct, but acquit the just and es-
tablish his innocence.

33† "If your people Israel sin against
you and are defeated by an enemy, and
if then they return to you, praise your
name, pray to you, and entreat you in
this temple, 34 listen in heaven and for-
give the sin of your people Israel, and
bring them back to the land you gave
their fathers.

35 "If the sky is closed, so that there
is no rain, because they have sinned
against you and you afflict them, and if
then they repent of their sin, and pray,
and praise your name in this place,
36 listen in heaven and forgive the sin of
your servant and of your people Israel,
teaching them the right way to live and
sending rain upon this land of yours
which you have given to your people as
their heritage.

37 "If there is famine in the land or pes-
tilence; or if blight comes, or mildew, or
a locust swarm, or devouring insects; if

*

9: Ex 34, 27; Heb 9, 4.
12: 2 Chr 6, 1.
17: 2 Sm 7, 5.
25: 2 Sm 7, 12.

†

8, 33-34.46-53: These references to deportation of Israelites to *a hostile land* are an expansion of Solomon's prayer dating from the Babylonian exile four centuries later.

an enemy of your people besieges them in one of their cities; whatever plague or sickness there may be, 38 if then any one [of your entire people Israel] has remorse of conscience and offers some prayer or petition, stretching out his hands toward this temple, 39 listen from your heavenly dwelling place and forgive. You who alone know the hearts of all men, render to each one of them according to his conduct; knowing their hearts, so treat them 40 that they may fear you as long as they live on the land you gave our fathers.

41 "To the foreigner, likewise, who is not of your people Israel, but comes from a distant land to honor you 42 (since men will learn of your great name and your mighty hand and your outstretched arm), when he comes and prays toward this temple, 43 listen from your heavenly dwelling. Do all that the foreigner asks of you, that all the peoples of the earth may know your name, may fear you as do your people Israel, and may acknowledge that this temple which I have built is dedicated to your honor.

44 "Whatever the direction in which you may send your people forth to war against their enemies, if they pray to you, O LORD, toward the city you have chosen and the temple I have built in your honor, 45 listen in heaven to their prayer and petition, and defend their cause.

46* "When they sin against you (for there is no man who does not sin), and in your anger against them you deliver them to the enemy, so that their captors deport them to a hostile land, far or near, 47 may they repent in the land of their captivity and be converted. If then they entreat you in the land of their captors and say, 'We have sinned and done wrong; we have been wicked'; 48 if with their whole heart and soul they turn back to you in the land of the enemies who took them captive, pray to you toward the land you gave their fathers, the city you have chosen, and the temple I have built in your honor, 49 listen from your heavenly dwelling. 50 Forgive your people their sins and all the offenses they have committed against you, and grant them mercy before their captors, so that these will be merciful to them. 51 For they are your people and your inheritance, whom you brought out of Egypt, from the midst of an iron furnace.

52 "Thus may your eyes be open to the petition of your servant and to the petition of your people Israel. Hear them whenever they call upon you, 53 because you have set them apart among all the peoples of the earth for your inheritance, as you declared through your servant Moses when you brought our fathers out of Egypt, O Lord GOD."

54 When Solomon finished offering this entire prayer of petition to the LORD, he rose from before the altar of the LORD, where he had been kneeling with his hands outstretched toward heaven. 55 He stood and blessed the whole community of Israel, saying in a loud voice: 56 "Blessed be the LORD who has given rest to his people Israel, just as he promised. Not a single word has gone unfulfilled of the entire generous promise he made through his servant Moses. 57 May the LORD, our God, be with us as he was with our fathers and may he not forsake us nor cast us off. 58 May he draw our hearts to himself, that we may follow him in everything and keep the commands, statutes, and ordinances which he enjoined on our fathers. 59 May this prayer I have offered to the LORD, our God, be present to him day and night, that he may uphold the cause of his servant and of his people Israel as each day requires, 60 that all the peoples of the earth may know the LORD is God and there is no other. 61 You must be wholly devoted to the LORD, our God, observing his statutes and keeping his commandments, as on this day."

62 The king and all Israel with him offered sacrifices before the LORD. 63 Solomon offered as peace offerings to the LORD twenty-two thousand oxen and one hundred twenty thousand sheep. Thus the king and all the Israelites dedicated the temple of the LORD. 64 On that day the king consecrated the middle of the court facing the temple of the LORD; he offered there the holocausts, the cereal offerings, and the fat of the peace offerings, because the bronze altar before the LORD was too small to hold these offerings.

65 On this occasion Solomon and all the Israelites, who had assembled in large numbers from Labo of Hamath to the Wadi of Egypt, celebrated the festival before the LORD, our God, for seven days. 66 On the eighth day he dismissed the people, who bade the king farewell and went to their homes, rejoicing and happy over all the blessings the LORD had given to his servant David and to his people Israel.

CHAPTER 9

Promise and Warning to Solomon. 1 After Solomon finished building the temple of the LORD, the royal palace, and everything else that he had planned, 2* the LORD appeared to him a second time, as he had appeared to him in Gibeon. 3 The LORD said to him: "I have heard the prayer of petition which you

---

46: 2 Chr 6, 36; Eccl 7, 20; 1 Jn 1, 8.

9, 2: 3, 5; 11, 9; 2 Chr 7, 12.

offered in my presence. I have conse-
crated this temple which you have built;
I confer my name upon it forever, and
my eyes and my heart shall be there al-
ways. 4 As for you, if you live in my pres-
ence as your father David lived,
sincerely and uprightly, doing just as I
have commanded you, keeping my stat-
utes and decrees, 5* I will establish your
throne of sovereignty over Israel for-
ever, as I promised your father David
when I said, 'You shall always have
someone from your line on the throne
of Israel.' 6 But if you and your descen-
dants ever withdraw from me, fail to
keep the commandments and statutes
which I set before you, and proceed to
venerate and worship strange gods, 7 I
will cut off Israel from the land I gave
them and repudiate the temple I have
consecrated to my honor. Israel shall
become a proverb and a byword among
all nations, 8* and this temple shall be-
come a heap of ruins. Every passerby
shall catch his breath in amazement,
and ask, 'Why has the LORD done this
to the land and to this temple?' 9 Men
will answer: 'They forsook the LORD,
their God, who brought their fathers out
of the land of Egypt; they adopted
strange gods which they worshiped and
served. That is why the LORD has
brought down upon them all this evil.' "

Other Acts of the King. 10 After the
twenty years during which Solomon
built the two houses, the temple of the
LORD and the palace of the king—
11 Hiram, king of Tyre, supplying Solo-
mon with all the cedar wood, fir wood,
and gold he wished—King Solomon gave
Hiram twenty cities in the land of Gali-
lee. 12 Hiram left Tyre to see the cities
Solomon had given him, but was not sat-
isfied with them. 13 So he said, "What are
these cities you have given me, my
brother?" And he called them the land
of Cabul, as they are called to this day.
14† Hiram, however, had sent king Solo-
mon one hundred and twenty talents of
gold.

15† This is an account of the forced la-
bor which King Solomon levied in order
to build the temple of the LORD, his pal-
ace, Millo, the wall of Jerusalem, Hazor,
Megiddo, Gezer 16 (Pharaoh, king of
Egypt, had come up and taken Gezer
and, after destroying it by fire and slay-
ing all the Canaanites living in the city,
had given it as dowry to his daughter,
Solomon's wife; 17 Solomon then rebuilt
Gezer), Lower Beth-horon, 18 Baalath,
Tamar in the desert of Judah, 19 all his
cities for supplies, cities for chariots and
for horses, and whatever else Solomon
decided should be built in Jerusalem, in
Lebanon, and in the entire land under
his dominion. 20 All the non-Israelite
people who remained in the land, de-
scendants of the Amorites, Hittites, Per-
izzites, Hivites, and Jebusites 21 whose
doom the Israelites had been unable to
accomplish, Solomon conscripted as
forced laborers, as they are to this day.
22 But Solomon enslaved none of the Is-
raelites, for they were his fighting force,
his ministers, commanders, adjutants,
chariot officers, and charioteers. 23 The
supervisors of Solomon's works who po-
liced the people engaged in the work
numbered five hundred and fifty.

24 As soon as Pharaoh's daughter went
up from the City of David to her palace,
which he had built for her, Solomon built
Millo.

25 Three times a year Solomon used to
offer holocausts and peace offerings on
the altar which he had built to the LORD,
and to burn incense before the LORD;
and he kept the temple in repair.

26† King Solomon also built a fleet at
Ezion-geber, which is near Elath on the
shore of the Red Sea in the land of
Edom. 27 In this fleet Hiram placed his
own expert seamen with the servants of
Solomon. 28 They went to Ophir, and
brought back four hundred and twenty
talents of gold to King Solomon.

CHAPTER 10

Visit of the Queen of Sheba. 1*† The
queen of Sheba, having heard of Solo-
mon's fame, came to test him with subtle
questions. 2 She arrived in Jerusalem
with a very numerous retinue, and with
camels bearing spices, a large amount
of gold, and precious stones. She came
to Solomon and questioned him on every
subject in which she was interested.
3 King Solomon explained everything
she asked about, and there remained
nothing hidden from him that he could
not explain to her.

4 When the queen of Sheba witnessed
Solomon's great wisdom, the palace he
had built, 5 the food at his table, the seat-
ing of his ministers, the attendance and
garb of his waiters, his banquet service,
and the holocausts he offered in the tem-

*

5: 2 Sm 7, 12-16.
8: Dt 29, 23; Jer 22, 8.
10, 1: 2 Chr 9, 1; Mt 12, 42; Lk 11, 31.

†

9, 14: *One hundred and twenty talents of gold:* approximately three million six hundred thousand dollars.

9, 15: *Millo:* probably means a filling, and may refer to an artificial earthwork or platform of stamped ground south of the temple area. It was begun by David (2 Sm 5, 9); cf 9, 24; 11, 27.

9, 26: *Ezion-geber . . . Edom:* the first mention of maritime commerce in the Israelite kingdom (to which the land of Edom was subject after its conquest by King David; cf 2 Sm 8, 14).

10, 1: *Queen of Sheba:* women rulers among the Arabs are recorded in eighth-century-B.C. Assyrian inscriptions. Sheba was for centuries the leading principality in what is now the Yemen.

ple of the LORD, she was breathless.
6 "The report I heard in my country
about your deeds and your wisdom is
true," she told the king. 7 "Though I did
not believe the report until I came and
saw with my own eyes, I have discov-
ered that they were not telling me the
half. Your wisdom and prosperity sur-
pass the report I heard. 8 Happy are your
men, happy these servants of yours, who
stand before you always and listen to
your wisdom. 9 Blessed be the LORD,
your God, whom it has pleased to place
you on the throne of Israel. In his endur-
ing love for Israel, the LORD has made
you king to carry out judgment and
justice." 10 Then she gave the king one
hundred and twenty gold talents, a
very large quantity of spices, and pre-
cious stones. Never again did anyone
bring such an abundance of spices
as the queen of Sheba gave to King
Solomon.

11† Hiram's fleet, which used to bring
gold from Ophir, also brought from
there a large quantity of cabinet wood
and precious stones. 12 With the wood the
king made supports for the temple of the
LORD and for the palace of the king, and
harps and lyres for the chanters. No
more such wood was brought or seen to
the present day.

13 King Solomon gave the queen of
Sheba everything she desired and asked
for, besides such presents as were given
her from Solomon's royal bounty. Then
she returned with her servants to her
own country.

Solomon's Wealth. 14 The gold that
Solomon received every year weighed
six hundred and sixty-six gold talents,
15 in addition to what came from the
Tarshish fleet, from the traffic of mer-
chants, and from all the kings of Arabia
and the governors of the country.

16* Moreover, King Solomon made two
hundred shields of beaten gold (six hun-
dred gold shekels went into each shield)
17 and three hundred bucklers of beaten
gold (three minas of gold went into each
buckler); and he put them in the hall of
the Forest of Lebanon. 18 The king also
had a large ivory throne made, and
overlaid it with refined gold. 19 The
throne had six steps, a back with a round
top, and an arm on each side of the seat.
Next to each arm stood a lion; 20 and
twelve other lions stood on the steps, two
to a step, one on either side of each step.
Nothing like this was produced in any
other kingdom. 21 In addition, all King
Solomon's drinking vessels were of gold,
and all the utensils in the hall of the For-
est of Lebanon were of pure gold. There
was no silver, for in Solomon's time it
was considered worthless. 22† The king
had a fleet of Tarshish ships at sea with
Hiram's fleet. Once every three years
the fleet of Tarshish ships would come
with a cargo of gold, silver, ivory, apes,
and monkeys.

23 Thus King Solomon surpassed in
riches and wisdom all the kings of the
earth. 24 And the whole world sought au-
dience with Solomon, to hear from him
the wisdom which God had put in his
heart. 25 Each one brought his yearly
tribute: silver or gold articles, garments,
weapons, spices, horses and mules.

26* Solomon collected chariots and
drivers; he had one thousand four hun-
dred chariots and twelve thousand driv-
ers; these he allocated among the
chariot cities and to the king's service
in Jerusalem. 27 The king made silver as
common in Jerusalem as stones, and ce-
dars as numerous as the sycamores of
the foothills. 28 Solomon's horses were
imported from Cilicia, where the king's
agents purchased them. 29 A chariot im-
ported from Egypt cost six hundred
shekels, a horse one hundred and fifty
shekels; they were exported at these
rates to all the Hittite and Aramean
kings.

CHAPTER 11

The Sins of Solomon. 1*† King Solo-
mon loved many foreign women besides
the daughter of Pharaoh (Moabites,
Ammonites, Edomites, Sidonians, and
Hittites), 2* from nations with which the
LORD had forbidden the Israelites to in-
termarry, "because," he said, "they will
turn your hearts to their gods." But Solo-
mon fell in love with them. 3 He had
seven hundred wives of princely rank
and three hundred concubines, and his
wives turned his heart.

4 When Solomon was old his wives had
turned his heart to strange gods, and his
heart was not entirely with the LORD, his
God, as the heart of his father David had
been. 5 By adoring Astarte, the goddess
of the Sidonians, and Milcom, the idol

*

16: 14, 26
26: 2 Chr 1, 14.
11, 1: Dt 17, 17; Sir 47, 19f.
2: Ex 34, 16.

†

10, 11f: *Cabinet:* an unknown wood, probably fragrant.

10, 22: *Tarshish ships:* large, strong vessels for long voyages. *Tarshish* was the ancient Tartessus, a Phoenician colony in southern Spain, the name of which denotes a center for smelting metallic ore.

11, 1-3.7: The glorious rise of Solomon, his piety and wisdom, administrative skill and wealth, the extension of his kingdom, his prestige among neighboring rulers, his reign of peace, above all his friendship with God—these are now eclipsed by his sins of intermarriage with great numbers of pagan wives and the consequent forbidden worship of their gods (Ex 34, 11-16; Dt 7, 1-5). His construction of temples in their honor merited the punishment of loss of a united kingdom to his posterity, and the opposition of adversaries to himself (vv 14.23-37). Hadad the Edomite rebelled against Solomon at the beginning of his reign (v 25). Rezon of Syria established a new kingdom in Damascus; Jeroboam of Israel constituted the greatest threat because of his revolt from within. This threefold threat culminated in the breakup of Solomon's kingdom.

of the Ammonites, 6 Solomon did evil in
the sight of the LORD; he did not follow
him unreservedly as his father David
had done. 7 Solomon then built a high
place to Chemosh, the idol of Moab, and
to Molech, the idol of the Ammonites,
on the hill opposite Jerusalem. 8 He did
the same for all his foreign wives who
burned incense and sacrificed to their
gods. 9* The LORD, therefore, became
angry with Solomon, because his heart
was turned away from the LORD, the
God of Israel, who had appeared to him
twice 10 (for though the LORD had forbid-
den him this very act of following
strange gods, Solomon had not obeyed
him).

11 So the LORD said to Solomon: "Since
this is what you want, and you have not
kept my covenant and my statutes
which I enjoined on you, I will deprive
you of the kingdom and give it to your
servant. 12* I will not do this during your
lifetime, however, for the sake of your
father David; it is your son whom I will
deprive. 13 Nor will I take away the whole
kingdom. I will leave your son one tribe
for the sake of my servant David and
of Jerusalem, which I have chosen."

14 The LORD then raised up an adver-
sary to Solomon: Hadad the Edomite,
who was of the royal line in Edom.
15* Earlier, when David had conquered
Edom, Joab, the general of the army,
while going to bury the slain, put to
death every male in Edom. 16 Joab and
all Israel remained there six months un-
til they had killed off every male in
Edom. 17 Meanwhile, Hadad, who was
only a boy, fled toward Egypt with some
Edomite servants of his father. 18 They
left Midian and passing through Paran,
where they picked up additional men,
they went into Egypt to Pharaoh, king
of Egypt, who gave Hadad a house, ap-
pointed him rations, and assigned him
land.

19 Hadad won great favor with Pha-
raoh, so that he gave him in marriage
the sister of Queen Tahpenes, his own
wife. 20 Tahpenes' sister bore Hadad a
son, Genubath. After his weaning, the
queen kept him in Pharaoh's palace,
where he then lived with Pharaoh's own
sons. 21 When Hadad in Egypt heard
that David rested with his ancestors and
that Joab, the general of the army, was
dead, he said to Pharaoh, "Give me
leave to return to my own country."
22 Pharaoh said to him, "What do you
lack with me, that you are seeking to
return to your own country?" "Noth-
ing," he said, "but please let me go!"

23 God raised up against Solomon an-
other adversary, in Rezon, the son of
Eliada, who had fled from his lord,
Hadadezer, king of Zobah, 24 when
David defeated them with slaughter.
Rezon gathered men about him and be-
came leader of a band, went to Damas-
cus, settled there, and became king in
Damascus. 25 He was an enemy of Israel
as long as Solomon lived; this added to
the harm done by Hadad, who made a
rift in Israel by becoming king over
Edom.

26* Solomon's servant Jeroboam, son
of Nebat, an Ephraimite from Zeredah
with a widowed mother, Zeruah, also re-
belled against the king. 27 This is why he
rebelled. King Solomon was building
Millo, closing up the breach of his fa-
ther's City of David. 28 Jeroboam was a
man of means, and when Solomon saw
that he was also an industrious young
man, he put him in charge of the entire
labor force of the house of Joseph. 29* At
that time Jeroboam left Jerusalem, and
the prophet Ahijah the Shilonite met him
on the road. The two were alone in the
area, and the prophet was wearing a
new cloak. 30 Ahijah took off his new
cloak, tore it into twelve pieces, 31* and
said to Jeroboam:

"Take ten pieces for yourself; the
LORD, the God of Israel, says: 'I will tear
away the kingdom from Solomon's
grasp and will give you ten of the tribes.
32 One tribe shall remain to him for the
sake of David my servant, and of Jeru-
salem, the city I have chosen out of all
the tribes of Israel. 33 The ten I will give
you because he has forsaken me and has
worshiped Astarte, goddess of the Sido-
nians, Chemosh, god of Moab, and Mil-
com, god of the Ammonites; he has not
followed my ways or done what is pleas-
ing to me according to my statutes and
my decrees, as his father David did.
34 Yet I will not take any of the kingdom
from Solomon himself, but will keep him
a prince as long as he lives for the sake
of my servant David, whom I chose, who
kept my commandments and statutes.
35 But I will take the kingdom from his
son and will give it to you—that is, the
ten tribes. 36 I will give his son one tribe,
that my servant David may always have
a lamp before me in Jerusalem, the city
in which I choose to be honored. 37 I will
take you; you shall reign over all that
you desire and shall become king of Is-
rael. 38 If, then, you heed all that I com-
mand you, follow my ways, and please
me by keeping my statutes and my com-
mandments like my servant David, I will
be with you. I will establish for you, as
I did for David, a lasting dynasty; I will
give Israel to you. 39 I will punish David's
line for this, but not forever.' "

40 When Solomon tried to have Jero-
boam killed for his rebellion, he escaped

9: 9, 2.
12: 12, 15.
15: 2 Sm 8, 14.
26: 2 Chr 13, 6.
29: 14, 2; 2 Chr 10, 15.
31: 12, 15.

to King Shishak, in Egypt, where he remained until Solomon's death.

41 The rest of the acts of Solomon, with all his deeds and his wisdom, are recorded in the book of the chronicles of Solomon. 42 The time that Solomon reigned in Jerusalem over all Israel was forty years. 43 Solomon rested with his ancestors; he was buried in his father's City of David, and his son Rehoboam succeeded him as king.

II: JUDAH AND ISRAEL TO THE TIME OF AHAB

CHAPTER 12

Secession of Israel. 1*† Rehoboam went to Shechem, where all Israel had come to proclaim him king. 3 They said to Rehoboam: 4 "Your father put on us a heavy yoke. If you now lighten the harsh service and the heavy yoke your father imposed on us, we will serve you." 5 "Come back to me in three days," he answered them. When the people had departed, 6 King Rehoboam consulted the elders who had been in his father's service while he was alive, and asked, "What answer do you advise me to give this people?" 7 They replied, "If today you will be the servant of this people and submit to them, giving them a favorable answer, they will be your servants forever." 8 But he ignored the advice the elders had given him, and consulted the young men who had grown up with him and were in his service. 9 He said to them, "What answer do you advise me to give this people, who have asked me to lighten the yoke my father imposed on them?" 10 The young men who had grown up with him replied, "This is what you must say to this people who have asked you to lighten the yoke your father put on them: 'My little finger is thicker than my father's body. 11 Whereas my father put a heavy yoke on you, I will make it heavier. My father beat you with whips, but I will beat you with scorpions.' "

12 On the third day all Israel came back to King Rehoboam, as he had instructed them to do. 13 Ignoring the advice the elders had given him, the king gave the people a harsh answer. 14 He said to them, as the young men had advised: "My father put on you a heavy yoke, but I will make it heavier. My father beat you with whips, but I will beat you with scorpions." 15* The king did not listen to the people, for the LORD brought this about to fulfill the prophecy he had uttered to Jeroboam, son of Nebat, through Ahijah the Shilonite.

16† When all Israel saw that the king did not listen to them, the people answered the king:

"What share have we in David?
We have no heritage in the son of
 Jesse.
To your tents, O Israel!
Now look to your own house, David."

So Israel went off to their tents, 17 but Rehoboam reigned over the Israelites who lived in the cities of Judah. 18 King Rehoboam then sent out Adoram, superintendent of the forced labor, but all Israel stoned him to death. Rehoboam managed to mount his chariot to flee to Jerusalem, 19 and Israel went into rebellion against David's house to this day. 2 Jeroboam, son of Nebat, who was still in Egypt, where he had fled from King Solomon, returned from Egypt as soon as he learned this. 20 When all Israel heard that Jeroboam had returned, they summoned him to an assembly and made him king over all Israel. None remained loyal to David's house except the tribe of Judah alone.

21 On his arrival in Jersusalem, Rehoboam gathered together all the house of Judah and the tribe of Benjamin—one hundred and eighty thousand seasoned warriors—to fight against the house of Israel, to restore the kingdom to Rehoboam, son of Solomon. 22* However, the LORD spoke to Shemaiah, a man of God: 23 "Say to Rehoboam, son of Solomon, king of Judah, and to the house of Judah and to Benjamin, and to the rest of the people: 24 'Thus says the LORD: You must not march out to fight against your brother Israelites. Let every man return home, for I have brought this about.' " They accepted this message of the LORD and gave up the expedition accordingly.

25 Jeroboam built up Shechem in the hill country of Ephraim and lived there. Then he left it and built up Penuel.

Religious Rebellion. 26† Jeroboam thought to himself: "The kingdom will return to David's house. 27 If now this people go up to offer sacrifices in the

---

*

12, 1: 2 Chr 10, 1. 22-24: 2 Chr 11, 2ff.
15: 11, 12.31.

†

12, 1: *Shechem:* chief city of the northern tribes, where a covenant of fidelity had previously been made between the Lord and his people and a stone of witness had been erected in memory of the event (Jos 24, 25ff).

12, 16: *What share have we in David:* even in David's time the northern tribes seemed ready to withdraw from Judah (2 Sm 20, 1). The unreasonable attitude of Rehoboam toward them intensified the discontent caused by the oppression of Solomon (v 4) and thus precipitated the establishment of a rival monarchy (v 20).

12, 26-32: *Jeroboam* feared reunification of the divided kingdom through worship in the single temple in Jerusalem. To prevent this he encouraged shrines on the high places, and appointed false priests to supplement those of levitical descent. The golden bullocks he installed in two of his sanctuaries, though probably intended as bearers of the invisible Divine Majesty, quickly became occasions for idolatry. Thus Jeroboam caused Israel to sin, and sealed his doom and that of his royal house (13, 34; 14, 7-14).

temple of the LORD in Jerusalem, the
hearts of this people will return to their
master, Rehoboam, king of Judah, and
they will kill me." 28* After taking coun-
sel, the king made two calves of gold and
said to the people: "You have been going
up to Jerusalem long enough. Here is
your God, O Israel, who brought you up
from the land of Egypt." 29† And he put
one in Bethel, the other in Dan. 30 This
led to sin, because the people frequented
these calves in Bethel and in Dan. 31* He
also built temples on the high places and
made priests from among the people
who were not Levites. 32 Jeroboam es-
tablished a feast in the eighth month on
the fifteenth day of the month to dupli-
cate in Bethel the pilgrimage feast of Ju-
dah, with sacrifices to the calves he had
made; and he stationed in Bethel priests
of the high places he had built.

Message of the Prophet from Judah.
33 Jeroboam ascended the altar he built
in Bethel on the fifteenth day of the
eighth month, the month in which he ar-
bitrarily chose to establish a feast for the
Israelites; he was going to offer sacrifice.

CHAPTER 13

1 A man of God came from Judah to
Bethel by the word of the LORD, while
Jeroboam was standing at the altar to
offer sacrifice. 2* He cried out against
the altar the word of the LORD: "O altar,
altar, the LORD says, 'A child shall be
born to the house of David, Josiah by
name, who shall slaughter upon you the
priests of the high places who offer sac-
rifice upon you, and he shall burn hu-
man bones upon you.' " 3 He gave a sign
that same day and said: "This is the sign
that the LORD has spoken: The altar shall
break up and the ashes on it shall be
strewn about."

4 When King Jeroboam heard what the
man of God was crying out against the
altar, he stretched forth his hand from
the altar and said, "Seize him!" But the
hand he stretched forth against him
withered, so that he could not draw it
back. 5 Moreover, the altar broke up and
the ashes from it were strewn about—
the sign the man of God had given as
the word of the LORD. 6 Then the king
appealed to the man of God. "Entreat
the LORD, your God," he said, "and in-
tercede for me that I may be able to
withdraw my hand." So the man of God
entreated the LORD, and the king re-
covered the normal use of his hand.
7 "Come home with me for some refresh-
ment," the king invited the man of God,
"and I will give you a present." 8 "If you
gave me half your kingdom," the man
of God said to the king, "I would not go
with you, nor eat bread or drink water
in this place. 9 For I was instructed by
the word of the LORD not to eat bread
or drink water and not to return by the
way I came." 10 So he departed by an-
other road and did not go back the way
he had come to Bethel.

11 There was an old prophet living in
the city, whose sons came and told him
all that the man of God had done that
day in Bethel. When they repeated to
their father the words he had spoken to
the king, 12 the father asked them,
"Which way did he go?" And his sons
pointed out to him the road taken by the
man of God who had come from Judah.
13 Then he said to his sons, "Saddle the
ass for me." When they had saddled it,
he mounted 14 and followed the man of
God, whom he found seated under a ter-
ebinth. When he asked him, "Are you
the man of God who came from Judah?"
he answered, "Yes." 15 Then he said,
"Come home with me and have some
bread." 16 "I cannot go back with you,
and I cannot eat bread or drink water
with you in this place," he answered,
17 "for I was told by the word of the LORD
neither to eat bread nor drink water
here, and not to go back the way I
came." 18 But he said to him, "I, too, am
a prophet like you, and an angel told me
in the word of the LORD to bring you back
with me to my house and to have you
eat bread and drink water." He was ly-
ing to him, however.

19 So he went back with him, and ate
bread and drank water in his house.
20 But while they were sitting at table,
the LORD spoke to the prophet who had
brought him back, 21 and he cried out to
the man of God who had come from Ju-
dah: "The LORD says, 'Because you re-
belled against the command of the LORD
and did not keep the command which
the LORD, your God, gave you, 22 but re-
turned and ate bread and drank water
in the place where he told you to do nei-
ther, your corpse shall not be brought
to the grave of your ancestors.' "

23 After he had eaten bread and drunk
water, the ass was saddled for him, and
he again 24 set out. But a lion met him
on the road, and killed him. His corpse
lay sprawled on the road, and the ass
remained standing by it, and so did the
lion. 25 Some passers-by saw the body ly-
ing in the road, with the lion standing
beside it, and carried the news to the city
where the old prophet lived. 26 On hear-
ing it, the prophet who had brought him
back from his journey said: "It is the

*

28: Tb 1, 5; Ex 32, 8.
31: 2 Chr 11, 15.
13, 2: 2 Kgs 23, 16.

†

12, 29: *Bethel and Dan:* at the southern and northern boundaries of the separate kingdom of Israel, where sanctuaries had existed in the past (Gn 12, 8; 13, 3; 18, 10-22; 25, 1-16; Jgs 18, 1-31).

man of God who rebelled against the command of the LORD. He has delivered him to a lion, which mangled and killed him, as the LORD predicted to him." 27 Then he said to his sons, "Saddle the ass for me." When they had saddled it, 28 he went off and found the body lying in the road with the ass and the lion standing beside it. The lion had not eaten the body nor had it harmed the ass. 29 The prophet lifted up the body of the man of God and put it on the ass, and brought it back to the city to mourn over it and to bury it. 30 He laid the man's body in his own grave, and they mourned over it: "Alas, my brother!" 31 After he had buried him, he said to his sons, "When I die, bury me in the grave where the man of God is buried. Lay my remains beside his. 32 For the word of the LORD which he proclaimed against the altar in Bethel and against all the shrines on the high places in the cities of Samaria shall certainly come to pass."

33 Jeroboam did not give up his evil ways after this event, but again made priests for the high places from among the common people. Whoever desired it was consecrated and became a priest of the high places. 34 This was a sin on the part of the house of Jeroboam for which it was to be cut off and destroyed from the earth.

CHAPTER 14

Death of Abijah. 1 At that time Abijah, son of Jeroboam, took sick. 2* So Jeroboam said to his wife, "Get ready and disguise yourself so that none will recognize you as Jeroboam's wife. Then go to Shiloh, where you will find the prophet Ahijah. It was he who predicted my reign over this people. 3 Take along ten loaves, some cakes, and a jar of preserves, and go to him. He will tell you what will happen to the child." 4 The wife of Jeroboam obeyed. She made the journey to Shiloh and entered the house of Ahijah who could not see because age had dimmed his sight.

5 The LORD had said to Ahijah: "Jeroboam's wife is coming to consult you about her son, for he is sick. This is what you must tell her. When she comes, she will be in disguise." 6 So Ahijah, hearing the sound of her footsteps as she entered the door, said, "Come in, wife of Jeroboam. Why are you in disguise? I have been commissioned to give you bitter news. 7 Go, tell Jeroboam, 'This is what the LORD, the God of Israel, says: I exalted you from among the people and made you ruler of my people Israel. 8 I deprived the house of David of the kingdom and gave it to you. Yet you have not been like my servant David, who kept my commandments and followed me with his whole heart, doing only what pleased me. 9 You have done worse than all who preceded you: you have gone and made for yourself strange gods and molten images to provoke me; but me you have cast behind your back. 10* Therefore, I am bringing evil upon the house of Jeroboam: I will cut off every male in Jeroboam's line, whether slave or freeman in Israel, and will burn up the house of Jeroboam completely, as though dung were being burned. 11* When one of Jeroboam's line dies in the city, dogs will devour him; when one of them dies in the field, he will be devoured by the birds of the sky. For the LORD has spoken!' 12 So leave; go home! As you step inside the city, the child will die, 13 and all Israel will mourn him and bury him, for he alone of Jeroboam's line will be laid in the grave, since in him alone of Jeroboam's house has something pleasing to the LORD, the God of Israel, been found. 14 Today, at this very moment, the LORD will raise up for himself a king of Israel who will destroy the house of Jeroboam. 15 The LORD will strike Israel like a reed tossed about in the water and will pluck out Israel from this good land which he gave their fathers, scattering them beyond the River, because they made sacred poles for themselves and thus provoked the LORD. 16 He will give up Israel because of the sins Jeroboam has committed and caused Israel to commit."

17 So Jeroboam's wife started back; when she reached Tirzah and crossed the threshold of her house, the child died. 18 He was buried with all Israel mourning him, as the LORD had prophesied through his servant the prophet Ahijah.

19 The rest of the acts of Jeroboam, with his warfare and his reign, are recorded in the book of the chronicles of the kings of Israel. 20 The length of Jeroboam's reign was twenty-two years. He rested with his ancestors, and his son Nadab succeeded him as king.

Reign of Rehoboam. 21* Rehoboam, son of Solomon, reigned in Judah. He was forty-one years old when he became king, and he reigned seventeen years in Jerusalem, the city in which, out of all the tribes of Israel, the LORD chose to be honored. His mother was the Ammonite named Naamah.

22 Judah did evil in the sight of the LORD, and by their sins angered him even more than their fathers had done. 23 They, too, built for themselves high places, pillars, and sacred poles, upon every high hill and under every green

---

14, 2: 11, 29.
10: 15, 29.
11: 16, 4.
21: 2 Chr 12, 13.

tree. 24 There were also cult prostitutes
in the land. Judah imitated all the abom-
inable practices of the nations whom the
LORD had cleared out of the Israelites'
way.
25† In the fifth year of King Rehoboam,
Shishak, king of Egypt, attacked Jeru-
salem. 26* He took everything, including
the treasures of the temple of the LORD
and those of the royal palace, as well
as all the gold shields made under Solo-
mon. 27 To replace them, King Reho-
boam had bronze shields made, which
he entrusted to the officers of the guard
on duty at the entrance of the royal pal-
ace. 28 Whenever the king visited the
temple of the LORD, those on duty would
carry the shields, and then return them
to the guardroom.
29 The rest of the acts of Rehoboam,
with all that he did, are recorded in the
book of the chronicles of the kings of
Judah. 30 There was constant warfare
between Rehoboam and Jeroboam.
31 Rehoboam rested with his ancestors;
he was buried with them in the City of
David. His mother was the Ammonite
named Naamah. His son Abijam suc-
ceeded him as king.

CHAPTER 15

Reign of Abijam. 1* In the eighteenth
year of King Jeroboam, son of Nebat,
Abijam became king of Judah; 2 he
reigned three years in Jerusalem. His
mother's name was Maacah, daughter
of Abishalom. 3 He imitated all the sins
his father had committed before him,
and his heart was not entirely with the
LORD, his God, like the heart of his
grandfather David. 4 Yet for David's
sake the LORD, his God, gave him a lamp
in Jerusalem, raising up his son after
him and permitting Jerusalem to en-
dure; 5* because David had pleased the
LORD and did not disobey any of his
commands as long as he lived, except
in the case of Uriah the Hittite.
7* The rest of Abijam's acts, with all
that he did, are written in the book of
the chronicles of the kings of Judah.
6 There was war between Abijam and
Jeroboam. 8 Abijam rested with his an-
cestors; he was buried in the City of
David, and his son Asa succeeded him
as king.
Reign of Asa. 9 In the twentieth year
of Jeroboam, king of Israel, Asa, king
of Judah, began to reign; 10 he reigned
forty-one years in Jerusalem. His
grandmother's name was Maacah,
daughter of Abishalom. 11 Asa pleased
the LORD like his forefather David,
12 banishing the temple prostitutes from
the land and removing all the idols his
father had made. 13 He also deposed his
grandmother Maacah from her position
as queen mother, because she had made
an outrageous object for Asherah. Asa
cut down this object and burned it in the
Kidron Valley. 14 The high places did not
disappear; yet Asa's heart was entirely
with the LORD as long as he lived. 15 He
brought into the temple of the LORD his
father's and his own votive offerings of
silver, gold, and various utensils.
16 There was war between Asa and
Baasha, king of Israel, as long as they
both reigned. 17* Baasha, king of Israel,
attacked Judah and fortified Ramah to
prevent communication with Asa, king
of Judah. 18† Asa then took all the silver
and gold remaining in the treasuries of
the temple of the LORD and of the royal
palace. Entrusting them to his ministers,
King Asa sent them to Ben-hadad, son
of Tabrimmon, son of Hezion, king of
Aram, resident in Damascus. He said:
19 "There is a treaty between you and
me, as there was between your father
and my father. I am sending you a pres-
ent of silver and gold. Go, break your
treaty with Baasha, king of Israel, that
he may withdraw from me." 20 Ben-ha-
dad agreed with King Asa and sent the
leaders of his troops against the cities
of Israel. They attacked Ijon, Dan, Abel-
beth-maacah, and all Chinnereth, be-
sides all the land of Naphtali. 21 When
Baasha heard of it, he left off fortifying
Ramah, and stayed in Tirzah. 22 Then
King Asa summoned all Judah without
exception, and they carried away the
stones and beams with which Baasha
was fortifying Ramah. With them King
Asa built Geba of Benjamin and Mizpeh.
23 The rest of the acts of Asa, with all
his valor and accomplishments, and the
cities he built, are written in the book
of the chronicles of the kings of Judah.
In his old age, Asa had an infirmity in
his feet. 24* He rested with his ancestors;
he was buried in his forefather's City of
David, and his son Jehoshaphat suc-
ceeded him as king.
Reign of Nadab. 25 In the second year
of Asa, king of Judah, Nadab, son of Jer-
oboam, became king of Israel; he
reigned over Israel two years. 26 He did

*

26: 10, 16.
15, 1: 2 Chr 13, 1f.
5: 2 Sm 11, 4.
7: 2 Chr 13, 2.
17: 2 Chr 16, 1.
24: 2 Chr 17, 1.

†

14, 25: *In the fifth year . . . Shishak, king of Egypt, attacked Jerusalem:* c. 926 B. C. According to 2 Chr 12, 1-12, the repentance of King Rehoboam and of the princes of Israel after the warning of the prophet Shemaiah diverted the actual attack on Jerusalem. Shishak, however, *carried off the treasures of the temple of the LORD and of the king's palace* (2 Chr 12, 9). A bas-relief of this Pharaoh in the temple of Amon at Karnak commemorates his conquest of some hundred and fifty Palestinian and Transjordanian cities and towns.

15, 18: *Ben-hadad . . . king of Aram:* Ben-hadad I, third successor of Rezon, who had thrown off the yoke of the Israelites during the reign of Solomon and become king of Aram (11, 23f).

evil in the LORD's sight, imitating his fa-
ther's conduct and the sin which he had
caused Israel to commit. 27 Baasha, son
of Ahijah, of the house of Issachar, plot-
ted against him and struck him down
at Gibbethon of the Philistines, which
Nadab and all Israel were besieging.
28 Baasha killed him in the third year of
Asa, king of Judah, and reigned in his
stead. 29* Once he was king, he killed off
the entire house of Jeroboam, not leav-
ing a single soul to Jeroboam but de-
stroying him utterly, according to the
warning which the LORD had pro-
nounced through his servant, Ahijah the
Shilonite, 30 because of the sins Jero-
boam committed and caused Israel to
commit, by which he provoked the
LORD, the God of Israel, to anger.
31 The rest of the acts of Nadab, with
all that he did, are written in the book
of the chronicles of the kings of Israel.
32 [There was war between Asa and Ba-
asha, king of Israel, as long as they
lived.]
Reign of Baasha. 33 In the third year
of Asa, king of Judah, Baasha, son of
Ahijah, began his twenty-four-year
reign over Israel in Tirzah. 34 He did evil
in the LORD's sight, imitating the con-
duct of Jeroboam and the sin he had
caused Israel to commit.

CHAPTER 16

1 The LORD spoke against Baasha to
Jehu, son of Hanani, and said: 2 "In-
asmuch as I lifted you up from the dust
and made you ruler of my people Israel,
but you have imitated the conduct of
Jeroboam and have caused my people
Israel to sin, provoking me to anger by
their sins, 3* I will destroy you, Baasha,
and your house; 4* I will make your
house like that of Jeroboam, son of Ne-
bat. If anyone of Baasha's line dies in
the city, dogs shall devour him; if he dies
in the field, he shall be devoured by the
birds of the sky."
5* The rest of the acts of Baasha, with
all his valor and accomplishments, are
written in the book of the chronicles of
the kings of Israel. 6 Baasha rested with
his ancestors; he was buried in Tirzah,
and his son Elah succeeded him as king.
7 [Through the prophet Jehu, son of
Hanani, the LORD had threatened Ba-
asha and his house, because of all the
evil Baasha did in the sight of the LORD,
provoking him to anger by his evil
deeds, so that he became like the house
of Jeroboam; and because he killed Na-
dab.]
Reign of Elah. 8 In the twenty-sixth
year of Asa, king of Judah, Elah, son
of Baasha, began his two-year reign
over Israel in Tirzah. 9 His servant
Zimri, commander of half his chariots,
plotted against him. As he was in Tirzah,
drinking to excess in the house of Arza,
superintendent of his palace in Tirzah,
10* Zimri entered; he struck and killed
him in the twenty-seventh year of Asa,
king of Judah, and reigned in his place.
11 Once he was seated on the royal
throne, he killed off the whole house of
Baasha, not sparing a single male rela-
tive or friend of his. 12 Zimri destroyed
the entire house of Baasha, as the LORD
had prophesied to Baasha through the
prophet Jehu, 13 because of all the sins
which Baasha and his son Elah commit-
ted and caused Israel to commit, pro-
voking the LORD, the God of Israel, to
anger by their idols.
14 The rest of the acts of Elah, with all
that he did, are written in the book of
the chronicles of the kings of Israel.
Reign of Zimri. 15 In the twenty-sev-
enth year of Asa, king of Judah, Zimri
reigned seven days in Tirzah. The army
was besieging Gibbethon of the Philis-
tines 16 when they heard that Zimri had
formed a conspiracy and had killed the
king. So that day in the camp all Israel
proclaimed Omri, general of the army,
king of Israel. 17 Omri marched up from
Gibbethon, accompanied by all Israel,
and laid siege to Tirzah. 18 When Zimri
saw the city was captured, he entered
the citadel of the royal palace and
burned down the palace over him. He
died 19 because of the sins he had com-
mitted, doing evil in the sight of the LORD
by imitating the sinful conduct of Jero-
boam, thus causing Israel to sin.
20 The rest of the acts of Zimri, with
the conspiracy he carried out, are writ-
ten in the book of the chronicles of the
kings of Israel.
21 At that time the people of Israel were
divided, half following Tibni, son of Gi-
nath, to make him king, and half for
Omri. 22 The partisans of Omri prevailed
over those of Tibni, son of Ginath. Tibni
died and Omri became king.
Reign of Omri. 23 In the thirty-first
year of Asa, king of Judah, Omri became
king; he reigned over Israel twelve
years, the first six of them in Tirzah.
24 He then bought the hill of Samaria
from Shemer for two silver talents and
built upon the hill, naming the city he
built Samaria after Shemer, the former
owner. 25 But Omri did evil in the LORD's
sight beyond any of his predecessors.
26 He closely imitated the sinful conduct
of Jeroboam, son of Nebat, causing Is-
rael to sin and to provoke the LORD, the
God of Israel, to anger by their idols.
27 The rest of the acts of Omri, with
all his valor and accomplishments, are

*

29: 14, 10; 21, 22.
16, 3: 21, 22.
4: 14, 11.
5: 2 Chr 16, 1.
10: 2 Kgs 9, 31.

written in the book of the chronicles of
the kings of Israel. 28 Omri rested with
his ancestors; he was buried in Sa-
maria, and his son Ahab succeeded him
as king.
Reign of Ahab. 29 In the thirty-eighth
year of Asa, king of Judah, Ahab, son
of Omri, became king of Israel; he
reigned over Israel in Samaria for
twenty-two years. 30 Ahab, son of Omri,
did evil in the sight of the LORD more
than any of his predecessors. 31 It was
not enough for him to imitate the sins
of Jeroboam, son of Nebat. He even
married Jezebel, daughter of Ethbaal,
king of the Sidonians, and went over to
the veneration and worship of Baal.
32 Ahab erected an altar to Baal in the
temple of Baal which he built in Sa-
maria, 33 and also made a sacred pole.
He did more to anger the LORD, the God
of Israel, than any of the kings of Israel
before him.
34* During his reign, Hiel from Bethel
rebuilt Jericho. He lost his first-born son,
Abiram, when he laid the foundation,
and his youngest son, Segub, when he
set up the gates, as the LORD had fore-
told through Joshua, son of Nun.

III: STORIES OF THE PROPHETS

CHAPTER 17

Drought Predicted by Elijah.
1*† Elijah the Tishbite, from Tishbe in
Gilead, said to Ahab: "As the LORD, the
God of Israel, lives, whom I serve, dur-
ing these years there shall be no dew
or rain except at my word." 2 The LORD
then said to Elijah: 3 "Leave here, go
east and hide in the Wadi Cherith, east
of the Jordan. 4 You shall drink of the
stream, and I have commanded ravens
to feed you there." 5 So he left and did
as the LORD had commanded. He went
and remained by the Wadi Cherith, east
of the Jordan. 6 Ravens brought him
bread and meat in the morning, and
bread and meat in the evening, and he
drank from the stream.
Elijah and the Widow. 7 After some
time, however, the brook ran dry, be-
cause no rain had fallen in the land. 8 So
the LORD said to him: 9 "Move on to
Zarephath of Sidon and stay there. I
have designated a widow there to pro-
vide for you." 10* He left and went to
Zarephath. As he arrived at the en-
trance of the city, a widow was gathering
sticks there; he called out to her, "Please
bring me a small cupful of water to
drink." 11 She left to get it, and he called
out after her, "Please bring along a bit
of bread." 12 "As the LORD, your God,
lives," she answered, "I have nothing
baked; there is only a handful of flour
in my jar and a little oil in my jug. Just
now I was collecting a couple of sticks,
to go in and prepare something for my-
self and my son; when we have eaten
it, we shall die." 13 "Do not be afraid,"
Elijah said to her. "Go and do as you
propose. But first make me a little cake
and bring it to me. Then you can prepare
something for yourself and your son.
14 For the LORD, the God of Israel, says,
'The jar of flour shall not go empty, nor
the jug of oil run dry, until the day when
the LORD sends rain upon the earth.'"
15 She left and did as Elijah had said.
She was able to eat for a year, and he
and her son as well; 16 The jar of flour
did not go empty, nor the jug of oil run
dry, as the LORD had foretold through
Elijah.
17 Some time later the son of the mis-
tress of the house fell sick, and his sick-
ness grew more severe until he stopped
breathing. 18 So she said to Elijah, "Why
have you done this to me, O man of God?
Have you come to me to call attention
to my guilt and to kill my son?" 19 "Give
me your son," Elijah said to her. Taking
him from her lap, he carried him to the
upper room where he was staying, and
laid him on his own bed. 20 He called out
to the LORD: "O LORD, my God, will you
afflict even the widow with whom I am
staying by killing her son?" 21 Then he
stretched himself out upon the child
three times and called out to the LORD:
"O LORD, my God, let the life breath re-
turn to the body of this child." 22 The
LORD heard the prayer of Elijah; the life
breath returned to the child's body and
he revived. 23 Taking the child, Elijah
brought him down into the house from
the upper room and gave him to his
mother. "See!" Elijah said to her, "your
son is alive." 24 "Now indeed I know that
you you are a man of God," the woman
replied to Elijah. "The word of the LORD
comes truly from your mouth."

CHAPTER 18

Elijah and the Prophets of Baal.
1 Long afterward, in the third year, the
LORD spoke to Elijah, "Go, present your-
self to Ahab," he said, "that I may send
rain upon the earth." 2 So Elijah went
to present himself to Ahab.
3 Now the famine in Samaria was bit-

*

34: Jos 6, 26.
17, 1: Sir 48, 3; 5, 17.
10: Lk 4, 26.

†

17, 1: *Elijah the Tishbite:* one of the most important figures in Old Testament history. As his name indicates ("Yahweh is my God"), Elijah was the successful leader in the struggle to preserve the knowledge and worship of Yahweh against the encroaching worship of Baal introduced into Israel by Jezebel, the Tyrian wife of Ahab. The Elijah cycle of narratives includes, besides the above struggle, miracle stories, denunciations of kings, and a preparation for the prophet's role as eschatological forerunner of the "great day of the Lord"; cf Mal 3, 23-24; Mt 17; 10-13; Lk 1, 17.

ter, 4 and Ahab had summoned Obadiah,
his vizier, who was a zealous follower
of the LORD. When Jezebel was murder-
ing the prophets of the LORD, Obadiah
took a hundred prophets, hid them away
fifty each in two caves, and supplied
them with food and drink. 5 Ahab said
to Obadiah, "Come, let us go through the
land to all sources of water and to all
the streams. We may find grass and save
the horses and mules, so that we shall
not have to slaughter any of the beasts."
6 Dividing the land to explore between
them, Ahab went one way by himself,
Obadiah another way by himself.

7 As Obadiah was on his way, Elijah
met him. Recognizing him, Obadiah fell
prostrate and asked, "Is it you, my lord
Elijah?" 8 "Yes," he answered. "Go tell
your master, 'Elijah is here!' " 9 But
Obadiah said, "What sin have I commit-
ted, that you are handing me over to
Ahab to have me killed? 10 As the LORD,
your God, lives, there is no nation or
kingdom where my master has not sent
in search of you. When they replied, 'He
is not here,' he made each kingdom and
nation swear they could not find you.
11 And now you say, 'Go tell your master:
Elijah is here!' 12 After I leave you, the
spirit of the LORD will carry you to some
place I do not know, and when I go to
inform Ahab and he does not find you,
he will kill me. Your servant has revered
the LORD from his youth. 13 Have you not
been told, my lord, what I did when Jez-
ebel was murdering the prophets of the
LORD—that I hid a hundred of the
prophets of the LORD, fifty each in two
caves, and supplied them with food and
drink? 14 And now you say, 'Go tell your
master: Elijah is here!' He will kill me!"
15 Elijah answered, "As the LORD of
hosts lives, whom I serve, I will present
myself to him today."

16 So Obadiah went to meet Ahab and
informed him. Ahab came to meet Eli-
jah, 17 and when he saw Elijah, said to
him, "Is it you, you disturber of Israel?"
18 "It is not I who disturb Israel," he an-
swered, "but you and your family, by
forsaking the commands of the LORD
and following the Baals. 19 Now summon
all Israel to me on Mount Carmel, as well
as the four hundred and fifty prophets
of Baal and the four hundred prophets
of Asherah who eat at Jezebel's table."
20 So Ahab sent to all the Israelites and
had the prophets assemble on Mount
Carmel.

21 Elijah appealed to all the people and
said, "How long will you straddle the is-
sue? If the LORD is God, follow him; if
Baal, follow him." The people, however,
did not answer him. 22 So Elijah said to
the people, "I am the only surviving
prophet of the LORD, and there are four
hundred and fifty prophets of Baal.
23 Give us two young bulls. Let them
choose one, cut it into pieces, and place
it on the wood, but start no fire. I shall
prepare the other and place it on the
wood, but shall start no fire. 24 You shall
call on your gods, and I will call on the
LORD. The God who answers with fire
is God." All the people answered,
"Agreed!"

25 Elijah then said to the prophets of
Baal, "Choose one young bull and pre-
pare it first, for there are more of you.
Call upon your gods, but do not start the
fire." 26 Taking the young bull that was
turned over to them, they prepared it
and called on Baal from morning to
noon, saying, "Answer us, Baal!" But
there was no sound, and no one answer-
ing. And they hopped around the altar
they had prepared. 27 When it was noon,
Elijah taunted them: "Call louder, for he
is a god and may be meditating, or may
have retired, or may be on a journey.
Perhaps he is asleep and must be awak-
ened." 28 They called out louder and
slashed themselves with swords and
spears, as was their custom, until blood
gushed over them. 29 Noon passed and
they remained in a prophetic state until
the time for offering sacrifice. But there
was not a sound; no one answered, and
no one was listening.

30 Then Elijah said to all the people,
"Come here to me." When they had done
so, he repaired the altar of the LORD
which had been destroyed. 31 He took
twelve stones, for the number of tribes
of the sons of Jacob, to whom the LORD
had said, "Your name shall be Israel."
32 He built an altar in honor of the LORD
with the stones, and made a trench
around the altar large enough for two
seahs of grain. 33 When he had arranged
the wood, he cut up the young bull and
laid it on the wood. 34 "Fill four jars with
water," he said, "and pour it over the
holocaust and over the wood." "Do it
again," he said, and they did it again.
"Do it a third time," he said, and they
did it a third time. 35 The water flowed
around the altar, and the trench was
filled with the water.

36 At the time for offering sacrifice, the
prophet Elijah came forward and said,
"LORD, God of Abraham, Isaac, and Is-
rael, let it be known this day that you
are God in Israel and that I am your
servant and have done all these things
by your command. 37 Answer me, LORD!
Answer me, that this people may know
that you, LORD, are God and that you
have brought them back to their
senses." 38 The LORD's fire came down
and consumed the holocaust, wood,
stones, and dust, and it lapped up the
water in the trench. 39 Seeing this, all the
people fell prostrate and said, "The
LORD is God! The LORD is God!" 40 Then
Elijah said to them, "Seize the prophets
of Baal. Let none of them escape!" They

were seized, and Elijah had them brought down to the brook Kishon and there he slit their throats.

41 Elijah then said to Ahab, "Go up, eat and drink, for there is the sound of a heavy rain." 42 So Ahab went up to eat and drink, while Elijah climbed to the top of Carmel, crouched down to the earth, and put his head between his knees. 43 "Climb up and look out to sea," he directed his servant, who went up and looked, but reported, "There is nothing." Seven times he said, "Go look again!" 44 And the seventh time the youth reported, "There is a cloud as small as a man's hand rising from the sea." Elijah said, "Go and say to Ahab, 'Harness up and leave the mountain before the rain stops you.' " 45 In a trice, the sky grew dark with clouds and wind, and a heavy rain fell. Ahab mounted his chariot and made for Jezreel. 46 But the hand of the LORD was on Elijah, who girded up his clothing and ran before Ahab as far as the approaches to Jezreel.

CHAPTER 19

Flight to Horeb. 1 Ahab told Jezebel all that Elijah had done—that he had put all the prophets to the sword. 2 Jezebel then sent a messenger to Elijah and said, "May the gods do thus and so to me if by this time tomorrow I have not done with your life what was done to each of them." 3 Elijah was afraid and fled for his life, going to Beer-sheba of Judah. He left his servant there 4 and went a day's journey into the desert, until he came to a broom tree and sat beneath it. He prayed for death: "This is enough, O LORD! Take my life, for I am no better than my fathers." 5 He lay down and fell asleep under the broom tree, but then an angel touched him and ordered him to get up and eat. 6 He looked and there at his head was a hearth cake and a jug of water. After he ate and drank, he lay down again, 7 but the angel of the LORD came back a second time, touched him, and ordered, "Get up and eat, else the journey will be too long for you!" 8 He got up, ate and drank; then strengthened by that food, he walked forty days and forty nights to the mountain of God, Horeb.

9 There he came to a cave, where he took shelter. But the word of the LORD came to him, "Why are you here, Elijah?" 10 He answered: "I have been most zealous for the LORD, the God of hosts, but the Israelites have forsaken your covenant, torn down your altars, and put your prophets to the sword. I alone am left, and they seek to take my life." 11† Then the LORD said, "Go outside and stand on the mountain before the LORD; the LORD will be passing by." A strong and heavy wind was rending the mountains and crushing rocks before the LORD—but the LORD was not in the wind. After the wind there was an earthquake—but the LORD was not in the earthquake. 12 After the earthquake there was fire—but the LORD was not in the fire. After the fire there was a tiny whispering sound. 13 When he heard this, Elijah hid his face in his cloak and went and stood at the entrance of the cave. A voice said to him, "Elijah, why are you here?" 14* He replied, "I have been most zealous for the LORD, the God of hosts. But the Israelites have forsaken your covenant, torn down your altars, and put your prophets to the sword. I alone am left, and they seek to take my life." 15† "Go, take the road back to the desert near Damascus," the LORD said to him. "When you arrive, you shall anoint Hazael as king of Aram. 16* Then you shall anoint Jehu, son of Nimshi, as king of Israel, and Elisha, son of Shaphat of Abel-meholah, as prophet to succeed you. 17 If anyone escapes the sword of Hazael, Jehu will kill him. If he escapes the sword if Jehu, Elisha will kill him. 18* Yet I will leave seven thousand men in Israel—all those who have not knelt to Baal or kissed him."

Call of Elisha. 19† Elijah set out, and came upon Elisha, son of Shaphat, as he was plowing with twelve yoke of oxen; he was following the twelfth. Elijah went over to him and threw his cloak over him. 20 Elisha left the oxen, ran after Elijah, and said, "Please, let me kiss my father and mother good-bye, and I will follow you." "Go back!" Elijah answered. "Have I done anything to you?" 21 Elisha left him and, taking the yoke of oxen, slaughtered them; he used the plowing equipment for fuel to boil their

*

19, 14: Rom 11, 3. 18: Rom 11, 4.
16: 2 Kgs 9, 2.

†

19, 11ff: Compare these divine manifestations to Elijah with those to Moses (Ex 19, 1-23; 33, 21ff; 34, 5) on the same Mount Horeb (Sinai) (Dt 4, 10-15). Though various phenomena, such as wind, storms, earthquakes, fire (Ex 19, 18f), herald the divine presence, they do not constitute the presence itself which, like the *tiny whispering sound,* is imperceptible and bespeaks the spirituality of God. It was fitting that Elijah, whose mission it was to re-establish the covenant and restore the pure faith, should have returned to Horeb where the covenant was revealed to Moses and through him to the Israelite people (Ex 3, 1-4.17; 33, 18-34, 9). Moses and Elijah appeared with Christ at the time of his transfiguration (Mt 17, 1-9; Mk 9, 1-7; Lk 9, 28-36).

19, 15-17: Elijah himself carried out only the third of the commissions entrusted to him (vv 19-21); Elisha was deputed to perform the first in person (2 Kgs 8, 7-19), and the second through one of his followers (2 Kgs 9, 1-10).

19, 19-21: Elijah's act of throwing his mantle over the shoulders of Elisha expressed the divine call to share the prophetic mission. Elisha's prompt response through destruction of his plow and oxen is an example of total obedience and detachment from his former manner of living in order to promote the glory of God.

flesh, and gave it to his people to eat. Then he left and followed Elijah as his attendant.

CHAPTER 20

Ahab's Victories over Ben-hadad. 1 Ben-hadad, king of Aram, gathered all his forces, and accompanied by thirty-two kings with horses and chariotry, proceeded to invest and attack Samaria. 2 He sent couriers to Ahab, king of Israel, within the city, 3 and said to him, "This is Ben-hadad's message: 'Your silver and gold are mine, and your wives and your promising sons are mine.' " 4 The king of Israel answered, "As you say, my lord king, I and all I have are yours." 5 But the couriers came again and said, "This is Ben-hadad's message: 'I sent you word to give me your silver and gold, your wives and your sons. 6 Now, however, at this time tomorrow I will send my servants to you, and they shall ransack your house and the houses of your servants. They shall seize and take away whatever they consider valuable.' "

7 The king of Israel then summoned all the elders of the land and said: "Understand clearly that this man wants to ruin us. When he sent to me for my wives and sons, my silver and my gold, I did not refuse him." 8 All the elders and all the people said to him, "Do not listen. Do not give in." 9 Accordingly he directed the couriers of Ben-hadad, "Say to my lord the king, 'I will do all that you demanded of your servant the first time. But this I cannot do.' " The couriers left and reported this. 10 Ben-hadad then sent him the message, "May the gods do thus and so to me if there is enough dust in Samaria to make handfuls for all my followers." 11 The king of Israel replied, "Tell him, 'It is not for the man who is buckling his armor to boast as though he were taking it off.' " 12 Ben-hadad was drinking in the pavilions with the kings when he heard this reply. "Prepare the assault," he commanded his servants; and they made ready to storm the city.

13 Then a prophet came up to Ahab, king of Israel and said: "The LORD says, 'Do you see all this huge army? When I deliver it up to you today, you will know that I am the LORD.' " 14 But Ahab asked, "Through whom will it be delivered up?" He answered, "The LORD says, 'Through the retainers of the governors of the provinces.' " Then Ahab asked, "Who is to attack?" He replied, "You are." 15 So Ahab called up the retainers of the governors of the provinces, two hundred thirty-two of them. Behind them he mustered all the Israelite soldiery, who numbered seven thousand. 16 They marched out at noon, while Ben-hadad was drinking heavily in the pavilions with the thirty-two kings who were his allies. 17 When the retainers of the governors of the provinces marched out first, Ben-hadad received word that some men had marched out of Samaria. 18 He answered, "Whether they have come out for peace or for war, in any case take them alive." 19 But when these had come out of the city—the soldiers of the governors of the provinces with the army following them—20 each of them struck down his man. The Arameans fled with Israel pursuing them, while Ben-hadad, king of Aram, escaped on a chariot steed. 21 The king of Israel went out, took the horses and chariots, and inflicted a severe defeat on Aram.

22† Then the prophet went up to the king of Israel and said to him: "Go, regroup your forces. Mark well what you do, for at the beginning of the year the king of Aram will attack you." 23 On the other hand, the servants of the king of Aram said to him: "Their gods are gods of mountains. That is why they defeated us. But if we fight them on level ground, we shall be sure to defeat them. 24 This is what you must do: Take the kings from their posts and put prefects in their places. 25 Mobilize an army as large as the army that has deserted you, horse for horse, chariot for chariot. Let us fight them on level ground, and we shall surely defeat them." He took their advice and did this.

26 At the beginning of the year, Ben-hadad mobilized Aram and went up to Aphek to fight against Israel. 27 The Israelites, too, were called to arms and supplied with provisions; then they went out to engage the foe. The Israelites, encamped opposite them, seemed like a couple of small flocks of goats, while Aram covered the countryside. 28 A man of God came up and said to the king of Israel: "The LORD says, 'Because Aram has said the LORD is a god of mountains, not a god of plains, I will deliver up to you all this large army, that you may know I am the LORD.' " 29 They were encamped opposite each other for seven days. On the seventh day battle was joined, and the Israelites struck down one hundred thousand foot soldiers of Aram in one day. 30 The survivors, twenty-seven thousand of them, fled into the city of Aphek, and there the wall collapsed. Ben-hadad, too, fled, and took refuge within the city, in an inside room.

31 His servants said to him: "We have heard that the kings of the land of Israel are merciful kings. Allow us, therefore, to garb ourselves in sackcloth, with

---

† 20, 22: *At the beginning of the year:* in the spring.

cords around our heads, and go out to the king of Israel. Perhaps he will spare your life." 32 So they dressed in sackcloth girded at the waist, and wearing cords around their heads, they went to the king of Israel. "Your servant Ben-hadad pleads for his life," they said. "Is he still alive?" the king asked. "He is my brother." 33 Hearing this as a good omen, the men quickly took him at his word and said, "Ben-hadad is your brother." He answered, "Go and get him." When Ben-hadad came out to him, the king had him mount his chariot. 34 Ben-hadad said to him, "I will restore the cities which my father took from your father, and you may make yourself bazaars in Damascus, as my father did in Samaria." "On these terms," Ahab replied, "I will set you free." So he made an agreement with him and then set him free.

35 One of the guild prophets was prompted by the LORD to say to his companion, "Strike me." But he refused to strike him. 36 Then he said to him, "Since you did not obey the voice of the LORD, a lion will kill you when you leave me." When they parted company, a lion came upon him and killed him. 37 The prophet met another man and said, "Strike me." The man struck him a blow and wounded him. 38 The prophet went on and waited for the king on the road, having disguised himself with a bandage over his eyes. 39 As the king was passing, he called out to the king and said: "Your servant went into the thick of the battle, and suddenly someone turned and brought me a man and said, 'Guard this man. If he is missing, you shall have to pay for his life with your life or pay out a talent of silver.' 40 But while your servant was looking here and there, the man disappeared." The king of Israel said to him, "That is your sentence. You have decided it yourself." 41 He immediately removed the bandage from his eyes, and the king of Israel recognized him as one of the prophets. 42* He said to him: "The LORD says, 'Because you have set free the man I doomed to destruction, your life shall pay for his life, your people for his people.' " 43 Disturbed and angry, the king of Israel went off homeward and entered Samaria.

CHAPTER 21

Seizure of Naboth's Vineyard. 1 Some time after this, as Naboth the Jezreelite had a vineyard in Jezreel next to the palace of Ahab, king of Samaria, 2 Ahab said to Naboth, "Give me your vineyard to be my vegetable garden, since it is close by, next to my house. I will give you a better vineyard in exchange, or, if you prefer, I will give you its value in money." 3 "The LORD forbid," Naboth answered him, "that I should give you my ancestral heritage." 4 Ahab went home disturbed and angry at the answer Naboth the Jezreelite had made to him: "I will not give you my ancestral heritage." Lying down on his bed, he turned away from food and would not eat.

5 His wife Jezebel came to him and said to him, "Why are you so angry that you will not eat?" 6 He answered her, "Because I spoke to Naboth the Jezreelite and said to him, 'Sell me your vineyard, or, if you prefer, I will give you a vineyard in exchange.' But he refused to let me have his vineyard." 7 "A fine ruler over Israel you are indeed!" his wife Jezebel said to him. "Get up. Eat and be cheerful. I will obtain the vineyard of Naboth the Jezreelite for you."

8 So she wrote letters in Ahab's name and, having sealed them with his seal, sent them to the elders and to the nobles who lived in the same city with Naboth. 9 This is what she wrote in the letters: "Proclaim a fast and set Naboth at the head of the people. 10 Next, get two scoundrels to face him and accuse him of having cursed God and king. Then take him out and stone him to death." 11 His fellow citizens—the elders and the nobles who dwelt in his city—did as Jezebel had ordered them in writing, through the letters she had sent them. 12 They proclaimed a fast and placed Naboth at the head of the people. 13 Two scoundrels came in and confronted him with the accusation, "Naboth has cursed God and king." And they led him out of the city and stoned him to death. 14 Then they sent the information to Jezebel that Naboth had been stoned to death.

15 When Jezebel learned that Naboth had been stoned to death, she said to Ahab, "Go on, take possession of the vineyard of Naboth the Jezreelite which he refused to sell you, because Naboth is not alive, but dead." 16 On hearing that Naboth was dead, Ahab started off on his way down to the vineyard of Naboth the Jezreelite, to take possession of it.

17 But the LORD said to Elijah the Tishbite: 18 "Start down to meet Ahab, king of Israel, who rules in Samaria. He will be in the vineyard of Naboth, of which he has come to take possession. 19*† This is what you shall tell him, 'The LORD

*

20, 42: 22, 35. 21, 19: 22, 38.

†

21, 19: The response of Ahab to this divine judgment is described in v 27, and the consequences are given in vv 28-29, and in 2 Kgs 9, 21-26.

says: After murdering, do you also take
possession? For this, the LORD says: In
the place where the dogs licked up the
blood of Naboth, the dogs shall lick up
your blood, too.' " 20† "Have you found
me out, my enemy?" Ahab said to Eli-
jah. "Yes," he answered. "Because you
have given yourself up to doing evil in
the LORD's sight, 21* I am bringing evil
upon you: I will destroy you and will cut
off every male in Ahab's line, whether
slave or freeman, in Israel. 22* I will
make your house like that of Jeroboam,
son of Nebat, and like that of Baasha,
son of Ahijah, because of how you have
provoked me by leading Israel into sin."
23* (Against Jezebel, too, the LORD de-
clared, "The dogs shall devour Jezebel
in the district of Jezreel.") 24 "When one
of Ahab's line dies in the city, dogs will
devour him; when one of them dies in
the field, the birds of the sky will devour
him." 25 Indeed, no one gave himself up
to the doing of evil in the sight of the
LORD as did Ahab, urged on by his wife
Jezebel. 26 He became completely abom-
inable by following idols, just as the Am-
orites had done, whom the LORD drove
out before the Israelites.

27 When Ahab heard these words, he
tore his garments and put on sackcloth
over his bare flesh. He fasted, slept in
the sackcloth, and went about subdued.
28 Then the LORD said to Elijah the Tish-
bite, 29* "Have you seen that Ahab has
humbled himself before me? Since he
has humbled himself before me, I will
not bring the evil in his time. I will bring
the evil upon his house during the reign
of his son."

CHAPTER 22

Campaign against Ramoth-gilead.
1* Three years passed without war be-
tween Aram and Israel. 2 In the third
year, however, King Jehoshaphat of Ju-
dah came down to the king of Israel,
3 who said to his servants, "Do you not
know that Ramoth-gilead is ours and we
are doing nothing to take it from the king
of Aram?" 4 He asked Jehoshaphat,
"Will you come with me to fight against
Ramoth-gilead?" Jehoshaphat an-
swered the king of Israel, "You and I
are as one, and your people and my peo-
ple, your horses and my horses as well."
5 Jehoshaphat also said to the king of Is-
rael, "Seek the word of the LORD at
once."

6 The king of Israel gathered together
the prophets, about four hundred of
them, and asked, "Shall I go to attack
Ramoth-gilead or shall I refrain?" "Go
up," they answered. "The LORD will de-
liver it over to the king." 7 But Jehosha-
phat said, "Is there no other prophet of
the LORD here whom we may consult?"
8 The king of Israel answered, "There is
one other through whom we might con-
sult the LORD, Micaiah, son of Imlah; but
I hate him because he prophesies not
good but evil about me." Jehoshaphat
said, "Let not your majesty speak of evil
against you."

9 So the king of Israel called an official
and said to him, "Get Micaiah, son of
Imlah, at once." 10 The king of Israel and
King Jehoshaphat of Judah were seated,
each on his throne, clothed in their robes
of state on a threshing floor at the en-
trance of the gate of Samaria, and all
the prophets were prophesying before
them. 11 Zedekiah, son of Chenaanah,
made himself horns of iron and said,
"The LORD says, 'With these you shall
gore Aram until you have destroyed
them.' " 12 The other prophets prophe-
sied in a similar vein, saying: "Go up
to Ramoth-gilead; you shall succeed.
The LORD will deliver it over to the
king."

13 The messenger who had gone to call
Micaiah said to him, "Look now, the
prophets are unanimously predicting
good for the king. Let your word be the
same as any of theirs; predict good."
14 "As the LORD lives," Micaiah an-
swered, "I shall say whatever the LORD
tells me."

15 When he came to the king, the king
said to him, "Micaiah, shall we go to
fight against Ramoth-gilead, or shall we
refrain?" "Go up," he answered, "you
shall succeed! The LORD will deliver it
over to the king." 16 But the king an-
swered him, "How many times must I
adjure you to tell me nothing but the
truth in the name of the LORD?" 17 So
Micaiah said:

"I see all Israel
scattered on the mountains,
like sheep without a shepherd,
and the LORD saying, 'These have
no master!
Let each of them go back home in
peace.' "

18 The king of Israel said to Jehosha-
phat, "Did I not tell you he prophesies

*

21: 2 Kgs 9, 8.
22: 15, 29; 16, 3.
23: 2 Kgs 9, 36.
29: 2 Kgs 9, 26.
22, 1: 2 Chr 18, 1.

†

21, 20-26: In these verses the Judean editor of the Books of Kings substitutes, for the message of Elijah prepared for in v 19, a sweeping and definitive judgment against the whole family of Ahab in the same terms as were used against the families of Jeroboam I (14, 9-11) and Baasha (16, 2-4). This judgment is the fruit of later theological reflection; it is not occasioned directly by the crime against Naboth, but by the idolatry of Ahab and Jezebel. The judgment on Jezebel herself (v 23) may have been uttered by Elijah during the Naboth episode; it finds its fulfillment in 2 Kgs 9, 36-37. Still another theological explanation for the death of Ahab is given by the North Israelite writer of 20, 35-42 above.

not good but evil about me?" [19]† Micaiah
continued: "Therefore hear the word of
the LORD: I saw the LORD seated on his
throne, with the whole host of heaven
standing by to his right and to his left.
[20] The LORD asked, 'Who will deceive
Ahab, so that he will go up and fall at
Ramoth-gilead?' And one said this, an-
other that, [21] until one of the spirits came
forth and presented himself to the LORD,
saying, 'I will deceive him.' The LORD
asked, 'How?' [22] He answered, 'I will go
forth and become a lying spirit in the
mouths of all his prophets.' The LORD
replied, 'You shall succeed in deceiving
him. Go forth and do this.' [23] So now, the
LORD has put a lying spirit in the mouths
of all these prophets of yours, but the
LORD himself has decreed evil against
you."
[24] Thereupon Zedekiah, son of Che-
naanah, came up and slapped Micaiah
on the cheek, saying, "Has the spirit of
the LORD, then, left me to speak with
you?" [25] "You shall find out," Micaiah
replied, "on that day when you retreat
into an inside room to hide." [26] The king
of Israel then said, "Seize Micaiah and
take him back to Amon, prefect of the
city, and to Joash, the king's son, [27] and
say, 'This is the king's order: Put this
man in prison and feed him scanty ra-
tions of bread and water until I return
in safety.'" [28]† But Micaiah said, "If
ever you return in safety, the LORD has
not spoken through me."
[29] The king of Israel and King Je-
hoshaphat of Judah went up to Ramoth-
gilead, [30] and the king of Israel said to
Jehoshaphat, "I will disguise myself and
go into battle, but you put on your own
clothes." So the king of Israel disguised
himself and entered the fray. [31] In the
meantime the king of Aram had given
his thirty-two chariot commanders the
order, "Do not fight with anyone at all
except the king of Israel." [32] When the
chariot commanders saw Jehoshaphat,
they cried out, "That must be the king
of Israel!" and shifted to fight him. But
Jehoshaphat shouted his battle cry,
[33] and the chariot commanders, aware
that he was not the king of Israel, gave
up pursuit of him. [34] Someone, however,
drew his bow at random, and hit the king
of Israel between the joints of his breast-
plate. He ordered his charioteer, "Rein
about and take me out of the ranks, for
I am disabled." [35]* The battle grew fierce
during the day, and the king, who was
propped up in his chariot facing the Ara-
means, died in the evening. The blood
from his wound flowed to the bottom of
the chariot. [36] At sunset a cry went
through the army, "Every man to his
city, every man to his land, [37] for the
king is dead!" So they went to Samaria,
where they buried the king. [38]* When the
chariot was washed at the pool of Sa-
maria, the dogs licked up his blood and
harlots bathed there, as the LORD had
prophesied.
[39] The rest of the acts of Ahab, with
all that he did, including the ivory palace
and all the cities he built, are recorded
in the book of the chronicles of the kings
of Israel. [40] Ahab rested with his ances-
tors, and his son Ahaziah succeeded him
as king.
Reign of Jehoshaphat. [41] Jehosha-
phat, son of Asa, began to reign over Ju-
dah in the fourth year of Ahab, king of
Israel. [42] Jehoshaphat was thirty-five
years old when he began to reign, and
he reigned twenty-five years in Jerusa-
lem. His mother's name was Azubah,
daughter of Shilhi. [43] He followed all the
ways of his father Asa unswervingly, do-
ing what was right in the LORD's sight.
[44] Nevertheless, the high places did not
disappear, and the people continued to
sacrifice and to burn incense on the high
places. [45] Jehoshaphat also made peace
with the king of Israel. [46] The rest of the
acts of Jehoshaphat, with his prowess,
what he did and how he fought, are re-
corded in the book of the chronicles of
the kings of Judah.
[47] He removed from the land the rest
of the cult prostitutes who had remained
in the reign of his father Asa. [48] There
was no king in Edom, but an appointed
regent. [49] Jehoshaphat made Tarshish
ships to go to Ophir for gold; but in fact
the ships did not go, because they were
wrecked at Ezion-geber. [50] Then Aha-
ziah, son of Ahab, said to Jehoshaphat,
"Let my servants accompany your ser-
vants in the ships." But Jehoshaphat
would not agree. [51] Jehoshaphat rested
with his ancestors; he was buried in his
forefathers' City of David. His son Jeho-
ram succeeded him as king.
Reign of Ahaziah. [52]† Ahaziah, son of
Ahab, began to reign over Israel in Sa-
maria in the seventeenth year of Je-
hoshaphat, king of Judah; he reigned
two years over Israel. [53] He did evil in
the sight of the LORD, behaving like his
father, his mother, and Jeroboam, son
of Nebat, who caused Israel to sin. [54] He
served and worshiped Baal, thus pro-
voking the LORD, the God of Israel, just
as his father had done.

*

35: 20, 42. 38: 21, 19.

†

22, 19-23: The prophet Micaiah uses as a last resort to deter Ahab from his foolhardy design of fighting against Ramoth-gilead the literary device of describing false prophets as messengers of a lying spirit which God, after holding counsel with his angels, permits to deceive them.

22, 28: A note in the Hebrew text after this verse attributes to Micaiah ben Imlah the first words of the book of a different Micaiah, the minor prophet of Moreshet.

22, 52: *Seventeenth year:* so the present Hebrew text. More consistent with 2 Kgs 1, 17 would be a date in the twenty-fourth year of Jehoshaphat for Ahab's death; see note on 2 Kgs 3, 1.

THE SECOND BOOK OF KINGS

IV: THE KINGDOMS OF ISRAEL AND JUDAH

CHAPTER 1

Ahaziah Consults Baalzebub. [1]* After
Ahab's death, Moab rebelled against Is-
rael. [2]† Ahaziah had fallen through the
lattice of his roof terrace at Samaria and
had been injured. So he sent out messen-
gers with the instructions: "Go and in-
quire of Baalzebub, the god of Ekron,
whether I shall recover from this in-
jury."
[3] Meanwhile, the angel of the LORD
said to Elijah the Tishbite: "Go, intercept
the messengers of Samaria's king, and
ask them, 'Is it because there is no God
in Israel that you are going to inquire
of Baalzebub, the god of Ekron?' [4] For
this, the LORD says: 'You shall not leave
the bed upon which you lie; instead, you
shall die.' " And with that, Elijah de-
parted. [5] The messengers then returned
to Ahaziah, who asked them. "Why have
you returned?" [6] "A man came up to us,"
they answered, "who said to us, 'Go back
to the king who sent you and tell him:
The LORD says, Is it because there is no
God in Israel that you are sending to in-
quire of Baalzebub, the god of Ekron?
For this you shall not leave the bed upon
which you lie; instead, you shall die.' "
[7] The king asked them, "What was the
man like who came up to you and said
these things to you?" [8]*† "Wearing a
hairy garment," they replied, "with a
leather girdle about his loins." "It is Eli-
jah the Tishbite!" he exclaimed.
Death of Two Captains. [9] Then the
king sent a captain with his company
of fifty men after Elijah. The prophet
was seated on a hilltop when he found
him. "Man of God," he ordered, "the
king commands you to come down."
[10]* "If I am a man of God," Elijah an-
swered the captain, "may fire come
down from heaven and consume you
and your fifty men." And fire came
down from heaven and consumed him
and his fifty men. [11] Ahaziah sent an-
other captain with his company of fifty
men after Elijah. "Man of God," he
called out to Elijah, "the king com-
mands you to come down immediately."
[12]† "If I am a man of God," Elijah an-
swered him, "may fire come down from
heaven and consume you and your fifty
men." And divine fire came down from
heaven, consuming him and his fifty
men.
Death of the King. [13] Again, for the
third time, Ahaziah sent a captain with
his company of fifty men. When the third
captain arrived, he fell to his knees be-
fore Elijah, pleading with him. "Man of
God," he implored him, "let my life and
the lives of these fifty men, your ser-
vants, count for something in your sight!
[14] Already fire has come down from
heaven, consuming two captains with
their companies of fifty men. But now,
let my life mean something to you!"
[15] Then the angel of the LORD said to Eli-
jah, "Go down with him; you need not
be afraid of him."
[16]* So Elijah left and went down with
him and stated to the king: "Thus says
the LORD: 'Because you sent messengers
to inquire of Baalzebub, the god of Ek-
ron, you shall not leave the bed upon
which you lie; instead you shall die.' "
[17]† Ahaziah died in fulfillment of the
prophecy of the LORD spoken by Elijah.
Since he had no son, his brother Joram
succeeded him as king, in the second
year of Jehoram, son of Jehoshaphat,
king of Judah. [18] The rest of the acts of
Ahaziah are recorded in the book of
chronicles of the kings of Israel.

CHAPTER 2

Elijah and Elisha. [1]† When the LORD
was about to take Elijah up to heaven
in a whirlwind, he and Elisha were on
their way from Gilgal. [2] "Stay here,
please," Elijah said to Elisha. "The
LORD has sent me on to Bethel." "As the
LORD lives, and as you yourself live,"
Elisha replied, "I will not leave you." So
they went down to Bethel, [3] where the
guild prophets went out to Elisha and
asked him, "Do you know that the LORD
will take your master from over you to-

*

1, 1: 3, 4-27:
8: Zec 13, 4.
10: Lv 10, 2; Sir 48, 3f; Lk 9, 54f.
16: Sir 48, 6.

†

1, 2: *Baalzebub:* in this form, "Baal of flies." The name in the Hebrew text is a derisive alteration of Baalzebul, "Prince Baal." The best New Testament evidence supports the latter form in Mt 10, 25; Lk 11, 15. Later associations with Aramaic *beeldebaba,* "enemy," gave the ancient name its connotation of "devil."

1, 8: *Hairy garment:* a sign of ascetical and prophetic calling, imitated by John the Baptizer; see Mt 3, 4; Mk 1, 6.

1, 12: *Divine fire:* literally, "fire of God," which in Hebrew sounds quite like *man of God.* The play on words is the basis for Elijah's alleged retort. This story was told among the people to enhance the dignity of the prophet and to reflect the power of God whom he served. The mercy which God extends even to the wicked is described in Wis 11, 17—12, 22, and the prophet Elijah was well aware of it (1 Kgs 21, 28f).

1, 17: *Joram:* in the Second Book of Kings the name Joram (yoram), alternately Jehoram *(yehoram),* appears in numerous passages to designate both the king of Judah, son and successor of Jehoshaphat (848-841 B.C.), and the contemporary king of Israel, son of Ahab (852-841 B.C.). For the convenience of the reader in distinguishing these two kings, the longer form, Jehoram, is used to designate the king of Judah and the shorter form, Joram, to designate the king of Israel. See note on 3, 1.

2, 1: *Gilgal:* commonly identified with Jiljulieh, about seven miles north of Bethel, and different from the Gilgal in Dt 11, 30 near Shechem, and that in Jos 4 and 5, passim, near Jericho.

day?" "Yes, I know it," he replied.
"Keep still."
4 Then Elijah said to him, "Stay here,
please, Elisha, for the LORD has sent me
on to Jericho." "As the LORD lives, and
as you yourself live," Elisha replied, "I
will not leave you." 5 They went on to
Jericho, where the guild prophets ap-
proached Elisha and asked him, "Do
you know that the LORD will take your
master from over you today?" "Yes, I
know it," he replied. "Keep still."
6 Elijah said to Elisha, "Please stay
here; the LORD has sent me on to the
Jordan." "As the LORD lives, and as you
yourself live," Elisha replied, "I will not
leave you." And so the two went on to-
gether. 7 Fifty of the guild prophets fol-
lowed, and when the two stopped at the
Jordan, stood facing them at a distance.
8* Elijah took his mantle, rolled it up and
struck the water, which divided, and
both crossed over on dry ground.
Elisha Succeeds Elijah. 9† When they
had crossed over, Elijah said to Elisha,
"Ask for whatever I may do for you, be-
fore I am taken from you." Elisha an-
swered, "May I receive a double portion
of your spirit." 10* "You have asked
something that is not easy," he replied.
"Still, if you see me taken up from you,
your wish will be granted; otherwise
not." 11* As they walked on conversing,
a flaming chariot and flaming horses
came between them, and Elijah went up
to heaven in a whirlwind. 12*† When Eli-
sha saw it happen he cried out, "My
father! my father! Israel's chariots and
drivers!" But when he could no longer
see him, Elisha gripped his own garment
and tore it in two.
13* Then he picked up Elijah's mantle
which had fallen from him, and went
back and stood at the bank of the Jor-
dan. 14 Wielding the mantle which had
fallen from Elijah, he struck the water
in his turn and said, "Where is the LORD,
the God of Elijah?" When Elisha struck
the water it divided and he crossed over.
15 The guild prophets in Jericho, who
were on the other side, saw him and said,
"The spirit of Elijah rests on Elisha."
They went to meet him, bowing to the
ground before him. 16* "Among your
servants are fifty brave men," they said.
"Let them go in search of your master.
Perhaps the spirit of the LORD has car-
ried him away to some mountain or
some valley." "Do not send them," he
answered. 17 However, they kept urging
him, until he was embarrassed and said,
"Send them." So they sent the fifty men,
who searched for three days without
finding him. 18 When they returned to
Elisha in Jericho, where he was staying,
he said to them, "Did I not tell you not
to go?"
Healing of the Water. 19 Once the in-
habitants of the city complained to Eli-
sha, "The site of the city is fine indeed,
as my lord can see, but the water is bad
and the land unfruitful." 20 "Bring me
a new bowl," Elisha said, "and put salt
into it." When they had brought it to him,
21 he went out to the spring and threw
salt into it, saying, "Thus says the LORD,
'I have purified this water. Never again
shall death or miscarriage spring from
it.' " 22 And the water has stayed pure
even to this day, just as Elisha prophe-
sied.
The Prophet's Curse. 23† From there
Elisha went up to Bethel. While he was
on the way, some small boys came out
of the city and jeered at him. "Go up,
baldhead," they shouted, "go up, bald-
head!" 24 The prophet turned and saw
them, and he cursed them in the name
of the LORD. Then two she-bears came
out of the woods and tore forty-two of
the children to pieces.
25 From there he went to Mount Car-
mel, and thence he returned to Samaria.

CHAPTER 3

Campaign of Joram against Moab.
1† Joram, son of Ahab, became king of

*

2, 8: Ex 14, 16. 22.
10: Nm 11, 17.25.
11: Gn 5, 24; 1 Mc 2, 58; Acts 1, 9.
12: 13, 14; Sir 48, 9. 12.
13: 1 Kgs 19, 19.
16: 1 Kgs 18, 12.

†

2, 9: *Double portion of your spirit:* as the first-born son inherited a double portion of his father's property (Dt 21, 17), so Elisha asks to inherit from Elijah his spirit of prophecy in the degree befitting his principal disciple. In Nm 11, 17. 25, God bestows some of the spirit of Moses on others.

2, 12: *My father:* a religious title accorded prophetic leaders; cf 6, 21; 8, 9. *Israel's chariots and drivers:* Elijah was worth more than a whole army in defending Israel and the true religion. King Joash of Israel uses the same phrase of Elisha himself (13, 14).

2, 23f: This story, like the one about Elijah and the captains (ch 1), is preserved for us in Scripture to convey a popular understanding of the dignity of the prophet. Told in popular vein, it becomes a caricature, in which neither Elisha nor the bears behave in character. See note on 1, 12 and the contrasting narrative in ch 4.

3, 1: The sequence of the reigns between Ahab and Jehu of Israel may be reconstructed as follows: Jehoshaphat of Judah outlived Ahab by a short time, so that Ahaziah of Israel was his contemporary. Jehoram of Judah succeeded his father Jehoshaphat while Ahaziah of Israel was still alive. Jehoram (Joram) of Israel became king, following his brother Ahaziah, in the second year of Jehoram of Judah (2 Kgs 1, 17); this is one datum on which the earliest Greek evidence and the standard Hebrew text are in agreement.

The two Jehorams were contemporary for much of their reigns; Jehoram of Judah was succeeded by Ahaziah something more than a year before Jehu did away with the rulers of both kingdoms (2 Kgs 9, 1-29).

The Moabite campaign of 2 Kgs 3, 4-27 is thus best placed under the two Kings Jehoram, before the Edomite rebellion mentioned in 2 Kgs 8, 20. In the received Hebrew text, Jehoshaphat has been made the Judahite protagonist in the campaign against Moab as a tribute to his piety; this assimilates the story of 2 Kgs 3 to that of 1 Kgs 22, but creates difficulties in the chronology which the extant data leave partly unresolved. An older practice for stories of the Israelite kings was to leave them and their fellow kings without identification by name; cf 2 Kgs 6, 8-7, 20. The name of Jehoshaphat has been omitted from a number of places in 2 Kgs 3-8, in this translation; cf 1 Kgs 22, 51.

Israel in Samaria [in the eighteenth year
of Jehoshaphat, king of Judah, and he
reigned for twelve years]. 2 He did evil
in the LORD's sight, though not as much
as his father and mother. He did away
with the pillar of Baal, which his father
had made, 3 but he still clung to the sin
to which Jeroboam, son of Nebat, had
lured Israel; this he did not give up.
4 Now Mesha, king of Moab, who
raised sheep, used to pay the king of Is-
rael as tribute a hundred thousand
lambs and the wool of a hundred thou-
sand rams. 5 But when Ahab died, the
king of Moab had rebelled against the
king of Israel. 6 Joram as king mustered
all Israel, and when he set out on a cam-
paign from Samaria, 7* he sent the king
of Judah the message: "The king of
Moab is in rebellion against me. Will you
join me in battle against Moab?" "I will,"
he replied. "You and I shall be as one,
your people and mine, and your horses
and mine as well." 8 They discussed
the route for their attack, and settled
upon the route through the desert of
Edom.
9 So the king of Israel set out, accom-
panied by the king of Judah and the king
of Edom. After their roundabout jour-
ney of seven days the water gave out
for the army and for the animals with
them. 10 "Alas!" exclaimed the king of
Israel. "The LORD has called together
these three kings to put them in the
grasp of Moab." 11* But the king of Ju-
dah asked, "Is there no prophet of the
LORD here through whom we may in-
quire of the LORD?" One of the officers
of the king of Israel replied, "Elisha, son
of Shaphat, who poured water on the
hands of Elijah, is here." 12 "He has the
word of the LORD," the king of Judah
agreed. So the kings of Israel, Judah,
and Edom went down to Elisha.
13 "What do you want with me?" Elisha
asked the king of Israel. "Go to the
prophets of your father and to the
prophets of your mother." "No," the
king of Israel replied. "The LORD has
called these three kings together to put
them in the grasp of Moab." 14* Then
Elisha said, "As the LORD of hosts lives,
whom I serve, were it not that I respect
the king of Judah, I should neither look
at you nor notice you at all. 15 Now get
me a minstrel."
When the minstrel played, the power
of the LORD came upon Elisha 16 and he
announced: "Thus says the LORD, 'Pro-
vide many catch basins in this wadi.'
17 For the LORD says, 'Though you will
see neither wind nor rain, yet this wadi
will be filled with water for you, your
livestock, and your pack animals to
drink.' 18 And since the LORD does not
consider this enough, he will also deliver
Moab into your grasp. 19* You shall de-
stroy every fortified city, fell every fruit
tree, stop up all the springs, and ruin
every fertile field with stones."
20* In the morning, at the time of the
sacrifice, water came from the direc-
tion of Edom and filled the land.
21 Meanwhile, all Moab heard that the
kings had come to give them battle; ev-
ery man capable of bearing arms was
called up and stationed at the border.
22† Early that morning, when the sun
shone on the water, the Moabites saw
the water at a distance as red as blood.
23 "This is blood!" they exclaimed. "The
kings have fought among themselves
and killed one another. Quick! To the
spoils, Moabites!" 24 But when they
reached the camp of Israel, the Israel-
ites rose up and attacked the Moabites,
who fled from them. They ranged
through the countryside striking down
the Moabites, and 25*† destroying the
cities; each of them cast stones onto ev-
ery fertile field till they had loaded it
down; all the springs they stopped up
and every useful tree they felled. Finally
only Kir-hareseth was left behind its
stone walls, and the slingers had sur-
rounded it and were attacking it.
26 When he saw that he was losing the
battle, the king of Moab took seven hun-
dred swordsmen to break through to the
king of Aram, but he failed. 27*† So he
took his first-born, his heir apparent,
and offered him as a holocaust upon the
wall. The wrath against Israel was so
great that they gave up the siege and
returned to their own land.

CHAPTER 4

The Widow's Oil. 1*† A certain
woman, the widow of one of the guild
prophets, complained to Elisha: "My
husband, your servant, is dead. You
know that he was a God-fearing man,
yet now his creditor has come to take
my two children as his slaves." 2 "How
can I help you?" Elisha answered her.
"Tell me what you have in the house."
"This servant of yours has nothing in
the house but a jug of oil," she replied.
3 "Go out," he said, "borrow vessels
from all your neighbors—as many

*

3, 7: 1 Kgs 22, 4.
11: 1 Kgs 22, 7.
14: 1 Kgs 18, 15.
19: Dt 20, 19.
20: 1 Kgs 18, 29.
25: Jb 5, 23.
27: Jgs 11, 30f.
4, 1: 1 Kgs 17, 8-16.

†

3, 22: *Red as blood:* possibly caused by the red sandstone of the Wadi Zered (Dt 2, 13), south of Moab.

3, 25: *Kir-hareseth:* modern Kerak, east of the Dead Sea; cf Is 16, 7.11; Jer 48, 31.36.

3, 27: *The wrath against Israel:* probably the wrath of Chemosh, the Moabite god to whom the child was offered. He was feared by the Israelites who lost heart on foreign soil.

4, 1: *His creditor . . . slaves:* Hebrew law permitted the selling of wife and children as chattels for debt; cf Ex 21, 7; Am 2, 6; 8, 6; Is 50.

empty vessels as you can. 4 Then come
back and close the door on yourself and
your children; pour the oil into all the
vessels, and as each is filled, set it aside."
5 She went and did so, closing the door
on herself and her children. As they
handed her the vessels, she would pour
in oil. 6 When all the vessels were filled,
she said to her son, "Bring me another
vessel." "There is none left," he an-
swered her. And then the oil stopped.
7 She went and told the man of God, who
said, "Go and sell the oil to pay off your
creditor; with what remains, you and
your children can live."

Elisha and the Shunammite. 8 One
day Elisha came to Shunem, where
there was a woman of influence, who
urged him to dine with her. Afterward,
whenever he passed by, he used to stop
there to dine. 9 So she said to her hus-
band, "I know that he is a holy man of
God. Since he visits us often, 10 let us ar-
range a little room on the roof and fur-
nish it for him with a bed, table, chair,
and lamp, so that when he comes to us
he can stay there." 11 Sometime later
Elisha arrived and stayed in the room
overnight. 12 Then he said to his servant
Gehazi, "Call this Shunammite woman."
He did so, and when she stood before
Elisha, 13 he told Gehazi, "Say to her,
'You have lavished all this care on us;
what can we do for you? Can we say a
good word for you to the king or to the
commander of the army?' " She replied,
"I am living among my own people."
14 Later Elisha asked, "Can something
be done for her?" "Yes!" Gehazi an-
swered. "She has no son, and her hus-
band is getting on in years." 15 "Call
her," said Elisha. When she had been
called, and stood at the door, 16* Elisha
promised, "This time next year you will
be fondling a baby son." "Please, my
lord," she protested, "you are a man of
God; do not deceive your servant." 17 Yet
the woman conceived, and by the same
time the following year she had given
birth to a son, as Elisha had promised.

18* The day came when the child was
old enough to go out to his father among
the reapers. 19 "My head hurts!" he com-
plained to his father. "Carry him to his
mother," the father said to a servant.
20 The servant picked him up and car-
ried him to his mother; he stayed with
her until noon, when he died in her lap.
21 The mother took him upstairs and laid
him on the bed of the man of God. Clos-
ing the door on him, she went out 22 and
called to her husband, "Let me have a
servant and a donkey. I must go quickly
to the man of God, and I will be back."
23 "Why are you going to him today?"
he asked. "It is neither the new moon
nor the sabbath." But she bade him
good-bye, 24 and when the donkey was
saddled, said to her servant: "Lead on!
Do not stop my donkey unless I tell you
to." 25 She kept going till she reached the
man of God on Mount Carmel. When he
spied her at a distance, the man of God
said to his servant Gehazi: "There is the
Shunammite! 26† Hurry to meet her, and
ask if all is well with her, with her hus-
band, and with the boy." "Greetings,"
she replied. 27 But when she reached
the man of God on the mountain, she
clasped his feet. Gehazi came near to
push her away, but the man of God said:
"Let her alone, she is in bitter anguish;
the LORD hid it from me and did not let
me know." 28 "Did I ask my lord for a
son?" she cried out. "Did I not beg you
not to deceive me?" 29† "Gird your
loins," Elisha said to Gehazi, "take my
staff with you and be off; if you meet
anyone, do not greet him, and if anyone
greets you, do not answer. Lay my staff
upon the boy." 30 But the boy's mother
cried out: "As the LORD lives and as you
yourself live, I will not release you." So
he started to go back with her.

31* Meanwhile, Gehazi had gone on
ahead and had laid the staff upon the
boy, but there was no sound or sign of
life. He returned to meet Elisha and in-
formed him that the boy had not awak-
ened. 32 When Elisha reached the house,
he found the boy lying dead. 33* He went
in, closed the door on them both, and
prayed to the LORD. 34 Then he lay upon
the child on the bed, placing his mouth
upon the child's mouth, his eyes upon
the eyes, and his hands upon the hands.
As Elisha stretched himself over the
child, the body became warm. 35* He
arose, paced up and down the room, and
then once more lay down upon the boy,
who now sneezed seven times and
opened his eyes. 36 Elisha summoned
Gehazi and said, "Call the Shunam-
mite." She came at his call, and Elisha
said to her, "Take your son." 37 She came
in and fell at his feet in gratitude; then
she took her son and left the room.

The Poisoned Stew. 38 When Elisha
returned to Gilgal, there was a famine
in the land. Once, when the guild proph-
ets were seated before him, he said to
his servant, "Put the large pot on, and
make some vegetable stew for the guild
prophets." 39 Someone went out into the
field to gather herbs and found a wild
vine, from which he picked a clothful of
wild gourds. On his return he cut them

---

*

16: Gn 18, 10. 33: 1 Kgs 17, 21-23.
18: 1 Kgs 17, 17-24. 35: Heb 11, 35.
31-36: Acts 20, 10ff.

†

4, 26: *Greetings:* the conventional answer to Gehazi's question, which tells him nothing.

4, 29: *Do not greet him:* the profuse exchange of compliments among Orientals meeting and greeting one another consumed time. Urgency necessitated their omission, as our Lord counseled his disciples (Lk 10, 4).

up into the pot of vegetable stew without anybody's knowing it. 40 The stew was poured out for the men to eat, but when they began to eat it, they exclaimed, "Man of God, there is poison in the pot!" And they could not eat it. 41 "Bring some meal," Elisha said. He threw it into the pot and said, "Serve it to the people to eat." And there was no longer anything harmful in the pot.

Multiplication of Loaves. 42 A man came from Baal-shalishah bringing the man of God twenty barely loaves made from the first fruits, and fresh grain in the ear. "Give it to the people to eat," Elisha said. 43 But his servant objected, "How can I set this before a hundred men?" "Give it to the people to eat," Elisha insisted. "For thus says the LORD, 'They shall eat and there shall be some left over.' " 44 And when they had eaten, there was some left over, as the LORD had said.

CHAPTER 5

Cure of Naaman. 1 Naaman, the army commander of the king of Aram, was highly esteemed and respected by his master, for through him the LORD had brought victory to Aram. But valiant as he was, the man was a leper. 2 Now the Arameans had captured from the land of Israel in a raid a little girl, who became the servant of Naaman's wife. 3 "If only my master would present himself to the prophet in Samaria," she said to her mistress, "he would cure him of his leprosy." 4 Naaman went and told his lord just what the slave girl from the land of Israel had said. 5 "Go," said the king of Aram. "I will send along a letter to the king of Israel." So Naaman set out, taking along ten silver talents, six thousand gold pieces, and ten festal garments. 6 To the king of Israel he brought the letter, which read: "With this letter I am sending my servant Naaman to you, that you may cure him of his leprosy."

7* When he read the letter, the king of Israel tore his garments and exclaimed: "Am I a god with power over life and death, that this man should send someone to me to be cured of leprosy? Take note! You can see he is only looking for a quarrel with me!" 8 When Elisha, the man of God, heard that the king of Israel had torn his garments, he sent word to the king: "Why have you torn your garments? Let him come to me and find out that there is a prophet in Israel."

9 Naaman came with his horses and chariots and stopped at the door of Elisha's house. 10* The prophet sent him the message: "Go and wash seven times in the Jordan, and your flesh will heal, and you will be clean." 11 But Naaman went away angry, saying, "I thought that he would surely come out and stand there to invoke the LORD his God, and would move his hand over the spot, and thus cure the leprosy. 12† Are not the rivers of Damascus, the Abana and the Pharpar, better than all the waters of Israel? Could I not wash in them and be cleansed?" With this, he turned about in anger and left.

13 But his servants came up and reasoned with him. "My father," they said, "if the prophet had told you to do something extraordinary, would you not have done it? All the more now, since he said to you, 'Wash and be clean,' should you do as he said." 14* So Naaman went down and plunged into the Jordan seven times at the word of the man of God. His flesh became again like the flesh of a little child, and he was clean.

15 He returned with his whole retinue to the man of God. On his arrival he stood before him and said, "Now I know that there is no God in all the earth, except in Israel. Please accept a gift from your servant."

16 "As the LORD lives whom I serve, I will not take it," Elisha replied; and despite Naaman's urging, he still refused. 17† Naaman said: "If you will not accept, please let me, your servant, have two mule-loads of earth, for I will no longer offer holocaust or sacrifice to any other god except to the LORD. 18 But I trust the LORD will forgive your servant this: when my master enters the temple of Rimmon to worship there, then I, too, as his adjutant, must bow down in the temple of Rimmon. May the LORD forgive your servant this." 19† "Go in peace," Elisha said to him.

Naaman had gone some distance 20 when Gehazi, the servant of Elisha, the man of God, thought to himself: "My master was too easy with this Aramean Naaman, not accepting what he brought. As the LORD lives, I will run after him and get something out of him." 21 So Gehazi hurried after Naaman. Aware that someone was running after him, Naaman alighted from his chariot to wait for him. "Is everything all right?" he asked. 22 "Yes," Gehazi replied, "but

---

*

5, 7: Gn 30, 2; 1 Sm 2, 6; Jn 5, 21.
10: Jn 9, 7.
14: Lk 4, 27.

†

5, 12: *Wash in them and be cleansed:* typical of the ambiguity in ritual healing or cleanliness. The muddy waters of the Jordan are no match hygienically for the mountain spring waters of Damascus; ritually, it is the other way around.

5, 17: *Two mule-loads of earth:* Israelite earth on which to erect in Aram an altar to the God of Israel.

5, 19: *Go in peace:* Elisha understands and approves the situation of Naaman who, though a proselyte as regards belief in and worship of the God of Israel, is required by his office to assist his master, the king, worshiping in the pagan temple of Rimmon.

my master sent me to say, 'Two young
men have just come to me, guild proph-
ets from the hill country of Ephraim.
Please give them a talent of silver and
two festal garments.' " 23 "Please take
two talents," Naaman said, and pressed
them upon him. He tied up these silver
talents in bags and gave them, with the
two festal garments, to two of his ser-
vants, who carried them before Gehazi.
24 When they reached the hill, Gehazi
took what they had, carried it into the
house, and sent the men on their way.
25 He went in and stood before Elisha
his master, who asked him, "Where
have you been, Gehazi?" He answered,
"Your servant has not gone anywhere."
26 But Elisha said to him: "Was I not
present in spirit when the man alighted
from his chariot to wait for you? Is this
a time to take money or to take gar-
ments, olive orchards or vineyards,
sheep or cattle, male or female ser-
vants? 27* The leprosy of Naaman shall
cling to you and your descendants for-
ever." And Gehazi left Elisha, a leper
white as snow.

CHAPTER 6

Recovery of the Lost Ax. 1 The guild
prophets once said to Elisha: "There is
not enough room for us to continue to
live here with you. 2 Let us go to the Jor-
dan, where by getting one beam apiece
we can build ourselves a place to live."
"Go," Elisha said. 3 "Please agree to ac-
company your servants," one of them
requested. "Yes, I will come," he replied.
4 So he went with them, and when they
arrived at the Jordan they began to fell
trees. 5 While one of them was felling a
tree trunk, the iron axhead slipped into
the water. "O master," he cried out, "it
was borrowed!" 6 "Where did it fall?"
asked the man of God. When he pointed
out the spot, Elisha cut off a stick, threw
it into the water, and brought the iron
to the surface. 7 "Pick it up," he said.
And the man reached down and grasped
it.

Aramean Ambush. 8 When the king of
Aram was waging war on Israel, he
would make plans with his servants to
attack a particular place. 9 But the man
of God would send word to the king of
Israel, "Be careful! Do not pass by this
place, for Aram will attack there." 10 So
the king of Israel would send word to
the place which the man of God had in-
dicated, and alert it; then they would be
on guard. This happened several times.
11 Greatly disturbed over this, the king
of Aram called together his officers.
"Will you not tell me," he asked them,
"who among us is for the king of Israel?"
12 "No one, my lord king," answered one
of the officers. "The Israelite prophet
Elisha can tell the king of Israel the very
words you speak in your bedroom."
13 "Go, find out where he is," he said, "so
that I may take him captive."

Blinded Aramean Soldiers. Informed
that Elisha was in Dothan, 14 he sent
there a strong force with horses and
chariots. They arrived by night and sur-
rounded the city. 15 Early the next
morning, when the attendant of the man
of God arose and went out, he saw the
force with its horses and chariots sur-
rounding the city. "Alas!" he said to Eli-
sha. "What shall we do, my lord?" 16 "Do
not be afraid," Elisha answered. "Our
side outnumbers theirs." 17* Then he
prayed, "O LORD, open his eyes, that he
may see." And the LORD opened the eyes
of the servant, so that he saw the moun-
tainside filled with horses and fiery
chariots around Elisha.

18 When the Arameans came down to
get him, Elisha prayed to the LORD,
"Strike this people blind, I pray you."
And in answer to the prophet's prayer
the LORD struck them blind. 19 Then Eli-
sha said to them: "This is the wrong
road, and this is the wrong city. Follow
me! I will take you to the man you want."
And he led them to Samaria. 20 When
they entered Samaria, Elisha prayed,
"O LORD, open their eyes that they may
see." The LORD opened their eyes, and
they saw that they were inside Samaria.
21 When the king of Israel saw them, he
asked, "Shall I kill them, my father?"
22† "You must not kill them," replied
Elisha. "Do you slay those whom you
have taken captive with your sword or
bow? Serve them bread and water. Let
them eat and drink, and then go back
to their master." 23 The king spread a
great feast for them. When they had
eaten and drunk he sent them away, and
they went back to their master. No more
Aramean raiders came into the land of
Israel.

Siege of Samaria. 24 After this, Ben-
hadad, king of Aram, mustered his
whole army and laid siege to Samaria.
25 Because of the siege the famine in Sa-
maria was so severe that an ass's head
sold for eighty pieces of silver, and a
fourth of a kab of wild onion for five
pieces of silver.

26 One day, as the king of Israel was
walking on the city wall, a woman cried
out to him, "Help, my lord king!"
27 "No," he replied, "the LORD help you!
Where could I find help for you: from

2 KINGS

*

27: Ex 4, 6; Nm 12, 10. 6, 17: 7, 6; Ps 67, 18.

†

6, 22: *With your sword or bow:* since the king would not slay prisoners who had surrendered to his power, much less should he slay prisoners captured by God's power. By oriental custom they became guests within Samaria's walls.

the threshing floor or the winepress?"
28* Then the king asked her, "What
is your trouble?" She replied: "This
woman said to me, 'Give up your son
that we may eat him today; then tomor-
row we will eat my son.' 29 So we boiled
my son and ate him. The next day I said
to her, 'Now give up your son that we
may eat him.' But she hid her son."
30* When the king heard the woman's
words, he tore his garments. And as he
was walking on the wall, the people saw
that he was wearing sackcloth under-
neath, next to his skin.
31 "May God do thus and so to me,"
the king exclaimed, "if the head of Eli-
sha, son of Shaphat, stays on him to-
day!" 32 Meanwhile, Elisha was sitting
in his house in conference with the el-
ders. The king had sent a man ahead
before he himself should come to him.
Elisha had said to the elders: "Do you
know that this son of a murderer is send-
ing someone to cut off my head? When
the messenger comes, see that you close
the door and hold it fast against him.
His master's footsteps are echoing be-
hind him." 33 While Elisha was still
speaking, the king came down to him
and said, "This evil is from the LORD.
Why should I trust in the LORD any
longer?"

CHAPTER 7

1† Elisha said: "Hear the word of the
LORD! Thus says the LORD, 'At this time
tomorrow a seah of fine flour will sell
for a shekel, and two seahs of barley for
a shekel, in the market of Samaria.' "
2* But the adjutant on whose arm the
king leaned, answered the man of God,
"Even if the LORD were to make win-
dows in heaven, how could this hap-
pen?" "You shall see it with your own
eyes," Elisha said, "but you shall not eat
of it."
The Lepers at the Gate. 3* At the city
gate were four lepers who were deliber-
ating, "Why should we sit here until we
die? 4 If we decide to go into the city,
we shall die there, for there is famine
in the city. If we remain here, we shall
die too. Come, let us desert to the camp
of the Arameans. If they spare us, we
live; if they kill us, we die." 5 At twilight
they left for the Arameans; but when
they reached the edge of the camp, no
one was there. 6*† The LORD had caused
the army of the Arameans to hear the
sound of chariots and horses, the din of
a large army, and they had reasoned
among themselves, "The king of Israel
has hired the kings of the Hittites and
the kings of the borderlands to fight us."
7 Then in the twilight they fled, abandon-
ing their tents, their horses, and their
asses, the whole camp just as it was, and
fleeing for their lives.
8 After the lepers reached the edge of
the camp, they went first into one tent,
ate and drank, and took silver, gold, and
clothing from it, and went out and hid
them. Back they came into another tent,
took things from it, and again went out
and hid them. 9 Then they said to one
another: "We are not doing right. This
is a day of good news, and we are keep-
ing silent. If we wait until morning
breaks, we shall be blamed. Come, let
us go and inform the palace."
10 They came and summoned the city
gatekeepers. "We went to the camp of
the Arameans," they said, "but no one
was there—not a human voice, only the
horses and asses tethered, and the tents
just as they were left." 11 The gatekeep-
ers announced this and it was reported
within the palace. 12 Though it was night,
the king got up; he said to his servants:
"Let me tell you what the Arameans
have done to us. Knowing that we are
in famine, they have left their camp to
hide in the field, hoping to take us alive
and enter our city when we leave it."
13 One of his servants, however, sug-
gested: "Since those who are left in the
city are no better off than all the throng
that has perished, let some of us take
five of the abandoned horses and send
scouts to investigate."
End of the Siege. 14 They took two
chariots, and horses, and the king sent
them to reconnoiter the Aramean army.
"Go and find out," he ordered. 15 They
followed the Arameans as far as the Jor-
dan, and the whole route was strewn
with garments and other objects that the
Arameans had thrown away in their
haste. The messengers returned and
told the king.
16 The people went out and plundered
the camp of the Arameans; and then a
seah of fine flour sold for a shekel and
two seahs of barley for a shekel, as the
LORD had said.
17 The king put in charge of the gate
the officer who was his adjutant; but the
people trampled him to death at the
gate, just as the man of God had pre-
dicted when the king visited him. 18 Thus
was fulfilled the prophecy of the man of
God to the king, "Two seahs of barley
will sell for a shekel, and one seah of
fine flour for a shekel at this time tomor-
row at the gate of Samaria." 19 The adju-
tant had answered the man of God,

*

28: Dt 28, 53-57.
30: 1 Kgs 20, 31; 21, 27.
7, 2: 7, 17; Ps 78, 23; Is 24, 18.
3: Lv 13, 46.
6f: 6, 17; 19, 35f; 2 Sm 5, 24.

†

7, 1: *Market:* literally "gate," the principal place of trading in ancient walled cities in time of peace.

7, 6: *Kings of the borderlands:* from Musur in Anatolia rather than Egypt.

"Even if the LORD were to make win-
dows in heaven, how could this hap-
pen?" And Elisha had replied, "You
shall see it with your own eyes, but you
shall not eat of it." 20 And that is what
happened to him, for the people tram-
pled him to death at the gate.

CHAPTER 8

Prediction of Famine. 1* Elisha once
said to the woman whose son he had re-
stored to life: "Get ready! Leave with
your family and settle wherever you
can, because the LORD has decreed a
seven-year famine which is coming
upon the land." 2 The woman got ready
and did as the man of God said, setting
out with her family and settling in the
land of the Philistines for seven years.
3 At the end of the seven years, the
woman returned from the land of the
Philistines and went out to the king to
claim her house and her field. 4 The king
was talking with Gehazi, the servant of
the man of God. "Tell me," he said, "all
the great things that Elisha has done."
5 Just as he was relating to the king how
his master had restored a dead person
to life, the very woman whose son Elisha
had restored to life came to the king to
claim her house and field. "My lord
king," Gehazi said, "this is the woman,
and this is that son of hers whom Elisha
restored to life." 6† The king questioned
the woman, and she told him her story.
With that the king placed an official at
her disposal, saying, "Restore all her
property to her, with all that the field
produced from the day she left the land
until now."

Death of Ben-hadad Foretold. 7 Eli-
sha came to Damascus at a time when
Ben-hadad, king of Aram, lay sick.
When he was told that the man of God
had come there, 8 the king said to Haz-
ael, "Take a gift with you and go call
on the man of God. Have him consult
the LORD as to whether I shall recover
from this sickness." 9 Hazael went to
visit him, carrying a present, and with
forty camel loads of the best goods of
Damascus. On his arrival, he stood be-
fore the prophet and said, "Your son
Ben-hadad, king of Aram, has sent me
to ask you whether he will recover from
his sickness." 10 "Go and tell him," Eli-
sha answered, "that he will surely re-
cover. However, the LORD has showed
me that he will in fact die." 11 Then he
stared him down until Hazael became
ill at ease. The man of God wept, 12* and
Hazael asked, "Why are you weeping,
my lord?" Elisha replied, "Because I
know the evil that you will inflict upon
the Israelites. You will burn their for-
tresses, you will slay their youth with the
sword, you will dash their little children
to pieces, you will rip open their preg-
nant women."
13*† Hazael exclaimed, "How can a
dog like me, your servant, do anything
so important?" "The LORD has showed
you to me as king over Aram," replied
Elisha.
14 Hazael left Elisha and returned to
his master. "What did Elisha tell you?"
asked Ben-hadad. "He told me that you
would surely recover," replied Hazael.
15 The next day, however, Hazael took
a cloth, dipped it in water, and spread
it over the king's face, so that he died.
And Hazael reigned in his stead.

Reign of Jehoram of Judah. 16† In the
fifth year of Joram, son of Ahab, king
of Israel, Jehoram, son of Jehoshaphat,
king of Judah, became king. 17* He was
thirty-two years old when he began to
reign, and he reigned eight years in Je-
rusalem. 18 He conducted himself like
the kings of Israel of the line of Ahab,
since the sister of Ahab was his wife; and
he did evil in the LORD's sight. 19* Even
so, the LORD was unwilling to destroy
Judah, because of his servant David.
For he had promised David that he
would leave him a lamp in the LORD's
presence for all time. 20 During Jeho-
ram's reign, Edom revolted against the
sovereignty of Judah and chose a king
of its own. 21 Thereupon Jehoram with
all his chariots crossed over to Zair. He
arose by night and broke through the
Edomites when they had surrounded
him and the commanders of his chari-
ots. Then his army fled homeward.
22* To this day Edom has been in revolt
against the rule of Judah. Libnah also
revolted at that time. 23 The rest of the
acts of Jehoram, with all that he did, are
recorded in the book of the chronicles
of the kings of Judah. 24 Jehoram rested
with his ancestors and was buried with
them in the City of David. His son Aha-
ziah succeeded him as king.

Accession of Ahaziah. 25† Ahaziah,
son of Jehoram, king of Judah, became
king in the twelfth year of Joram, son
of Ahab, king of Israel. 26 He was twenty-

*

8, 1: 4, 36.
12: 13, 7.
13: 15, 16; 1 Kgs 19, 15.
17ff: 2 Chr 21, 5ff.
19: 2 Sm 7, 11-16; 21, 17; 1 Kgs 11, 36; 15, 4; 2 Chr 21, 7.
22: Gn 27, 40; 2 Chr 21, 8ff.

†

8, 6: *An official:* literally "eunuch," and perhaps actually so in this instance.

8, 13: *A dog . . . your servant:* Hazael feigns humility (1 Sm 24, 14; 2 Sm 9, 8), without attending to the crimes he would commit after usurping the royal power as the prophet predicts. *Anything so important:* literally "a great deed" for a patriotic Syrian.

8, 16: *Jehoram* of Judah succeeded his father Jehoshaphat during the reign of Ahaziah of Israel. See note on 3, 1.

8, 25: *Twelfth year of Joram:* i.e., of Israel, who probably reigned only eight years.

two years old when he began his reign, and he reigned one year in Jerusalem. His mother's name was Athaliah; she was daughter of Omri, king of Israel. 27 He conducted himself like the house of Ahab, doing evil in the LORD's sight as they did, since he was related to them by marriage. 28* He joined Joram, son of Ahab, in battle against Hazael, king of Aram, at Ramoth-gilead, where the Arameans wounded Joram. 29 King Joram returned to Jezreel to be healed of the wounds which the Arameans had inflicted on him at Ramah in his battle against Hazael, king of Aram. Then Ahaziah, son of Jehoram, king of Judah, went down to Jezreel to visit him there in his illness.

CHAPTER 9

Anointing of Jehu. 1* The prophet Elisha called one of the guild prophets and said to him: "Gird your loins, take this flask of oil with you, and go to Ramoth-gilead. 2* When you get there, look for Jehu, son of Jehoshaphat, son of Nimshi. Enter and take him away from his companions into an inner chamber. 3* From the flask you have, pour oil on his head, and say, 'Thus says the LORD: I anoint you king over Israel.' Then open the door and flee without delay." 4 The young man (the guild prophet) went to Ramoth-gilead. 5 When he arrived, the commanders of the army were in session. "I have a message for you, commander," he said. "For which one of us?" asked Jehu. "For you, commander," he answered. 6 Jehu got up and went into the house. Then the young man poured the oil on his head and said, "Thus says the LORD, the God of Israel: 'I anoint you king over the people of the LORD, over Israel. 7† You shall destroy the house of Ahab your master; thus will I avenge the blood of my servants the prophets, and the blood of all the other servants of the LORD shed by Jezebel, 8* and by all the rest of the family of Ahab. I will cut off every male in Ahab's line, whether slave or freeman in Israel. 9 I will deal with the house of Ahab as I dealt with the house of Jeroboam, son of Nebat, and with the house of Baasha, son of Ahijah. 10 Dogs shall devour Jezebel at the confines of Jezreel, so that no one can bury her.' " Then he opened the door and fled.

11 When Jehu rejoined his master's servants, they asked him, "Is all well? Why did that madman come to you?" You know that kind of man and his talk, he replied. 12 But they said, "Not at all! Come, tell us." So he told them what the young man had said to him, and finally, "Thus says the LORD: 'I anoint you king over Israel.' " 13* At once each took his garment, spread it under Jehu on the bare steps, blew the trumpet, and cried out, "Jehu is king!"

14* Thus Jehu, son of Jehoshaphat, son of Nimshi, formed a conspiracy against Joram. Joram, with all Israel, had been besieging Ramoth-gilead against Hazael, king of Aram, 15 but had returned to Jezreel to be healed of the wounds the Arameans had inflicted on him in the battle against Hazael, king of Aram.

Murder of Joram. "If you are truly with me," Jehu said, "see that no one escapes from the city to report in Jezreel." 16 Then Jehu mounted his chariot and drove to Jezreel, where Joram lay ill and Ahaziah, king of Judah, had come to visit him.

17 The watchman standing on the tower in Jezreel saw the troop of Jehu coming and reported, "I see chariots." "Get a driver," Joram said, "and send him to meet them and to ask whether all is well." 18 So a driver went out to meet him and said, "The king asks whether all is well." "What does it matter to you how things are?" Jehu said. "Get behind me." The watchman reported to the king, "The messenger has reached them, but is not returning."

19 Joram sent a second driver, who went to them and said, "The king asks whether all is well." "What does it matter to you how things are?" Jehu replied. "Get behind me."

20 The watchman reported, "The messenger has reached them, but is not returning. The driving is like that of Jehu, son of Nimshi, in its fury." 21 "Prepare my chariot," said Joram. When they had done so, Joram, king of Israel, and Ahaziah, king of Judah, set out, each in his own chariot, to meet Jehu. They reached him near the field of Naboth the Jezreelite. 22† When Joram recognized Jehu, he asked, "Is all well, Jehu?" "How can all be well," Jehu replied, "as long as the many fornications and witchcrafts of your mother Jezebel continue?" 23 Joram reined about and fled, crying to Ahaziah, "Treason, Ahaziah!" 24 But Jehu drew his bow and shot Joram between the shoulders, so that the arrow went through his heart and he collapsed in his chariot. 25* Then Jehu said to his

*

28: 9, 14f.
9, 1: 1 Kgs 21, 29; Hos 1, 4.
2: 1 Kgs 19, 16.
3: 1 Kgs 19, 16.
8ff: 1 Kgs 14, 10f; 16, 3f; 21, 21-24.
13: Mt 21, 8.
14f: 8, 28f; 1 Kgs 22, 3f.
25f: 1 Kgs 21, 9-16.

†

9, 7-10: The editors of the Books of Kings have here added to the prophet's message the same type of indictment and sanctions against *the family of Ahab* as were invoked against the dynasties of *Jeroboam* (1 Kgs 14, 10f), *Baasha* (1 Kgs 16, 3f), and *Ahab* on a previous occasion (1 Kgs 21, 21-24).

9, 22: *Fornications and witchcrafts:* the worship of foreign gods.

adjutant Bidkar, "Take him and throw
him into the field of Naboth the Jezreel-
ite. For I remember that when we were
driving teams behind his father Ahab,
the LORD delivered this oracle against
him: [26] 'As surely as I saw yesterday the
blood of Naboth and the blood of his
sons,' says the LORD, 'I will repay you
for it in that very plot of ground, says
the LORD.' So now take him into this plot
of ground, in keeping with the word of
the LORD."

Death of Ahaziah. [27]* Seeing what
was happening, Ahaziah, king of Judah,
fled toward Beth-haggan. Jehu pursued
him, shouting, "Kill him too!" And they
pierced him as he rode through the pass
of Gur near Ibleam. He continued his
flight as far as Megiddo and died there.
[28] His servants brought him in a chariot
to Jerusalem and buried him in the tomb
of his ancestors in the City of David.
[29] Ahaziah had become king of Judah
in the eleventh year of Joram, son of
Ahab.

Death of Jezebel. [30] When Jezebel
learned that Jehu had arrived in Jezreel,
she shadowed her eyes, adorned her
hair, and looked down from her window.
[31]* As Jehu came through the gate, she
cried out, "Is all well, Zimri, murderer
of your master?" [32] Jehu looked up to the
window and shouted, "Who is on my
side? Anyone?" At this, two or three
eunuchs looked down toward him.
[33] "Throw her down," he ordered. They
threw her down, and some of her blood
spurted against the wall and against the
horses. Jehu rode in over her body
[34] and, after eating and drinking, he
said: "Attend to that accursed woman
and bury her; after all, she was a king's
daughter." [35] But when they went to
bury her, they found nothing of her but
the skull, the feet, and the hands.
[36]* They returned to Jehu, and when
they told him, he said, "This is the
sentence which the LORD pronounced
through his servant Elijah the Tishbite:
'In the confines of Jezreel dogs shall eat
the flesh of Jezebel. [37] The corpse of Jez-
ebel shall be like dung in the field in the
confines of Jezreel, so that no one can
say: This was Jezebel.' "

CHAPTER 10

Killing of Ahab's Descendants.
[1]* Ahab had seventy descendants in Sa-
maria. Jehu prepared letters and sent
them to the city rulers, to the elders, and
to the guardians of Ahab's descendants
in Samaria. [2] "Since your master's sons
are with you," he wrote, "and you have
the chariots, the horses, a fortified city,
and the weapons, when this letter
reaches you [3] decide which is the best
and the fittest of your master's offspring,
place him on his father's throne, and
fight for your master's house." [4] They
were overcome with fright and said, "If
two kings could not withstand him, how
can we?" [5] So the vizier and the ruler
of the city, along with the elders and the
guardians, sent this message to Jehu:
"We are your servants, and we will do
everything you tell us. We will proclaim
no one king; do whatever you think
best." [6] So Jehu wrote them a second let-
ter: "If you are on my side and will obey
me, count the heads of your master's
sons and come to me in Jezreel at this
time tomorrow." [The seventy princes
were in the care of prominent men of
the city, who were rearing them.]

[7] When the letter arrived, they took the
princes and slew all seventy of them, put
their heads in baskets, and sent them
to Jehu in Jezreel. [8] "They have brought
the heads of the princes," a messenger
came in and told him. "Pile them in two
heaps at the entrance of the city until
morning," he ordered. [9] Going out in the
morning, he stopped and said to all the
people: "You are not responsible, and al-
though I conspired against my lord and
slew him, yet who killed all these?
[10]* Know that not a single word which
the LORD has spoken against the house
of Ahab shall go unfulfilled. The LORD
has accomplished all that he fore-
told through his servant Elijah."
[11]* Thereupon Jehu slew all who were
left of the family of Ahab in Jezreel, as
well as all his powerful supporters, inti-
mates, and priests, leaving him no survi-
vor.

Ahaziah's Kinsmen. [12]* Then he set
out for Samaria, and at Beth-eked-ha-
roim on the way, [13] he came across kins-
men of Ahaziah, king of Judah. "Who
are you?" he asked. "We are kinsmen
of Ahaziah," they replied. "We are going
down to visit the princes and the family
of the queen mother." [14] "Take them
alive," Jehu ordered. They were taken
alive, forty-two in number, then slain at
the pit of Beth-eked. Not one of them
was spared.

Jehu in Samaria. [15]* When he had left
there, Jehu met Jehonadab, son of Re-
chab, on the road. He greeted him and
asked, "Are you sincerely disposed to-
ward me, as I am toward you?" "Yes,"
replied Jehonadab. "If you are," contin-
ued Jehu, "give me your hand." Jehona-
dab gave him his hand, and Jehu drew
him up into his chariot. [16] "Come with
me," he said, "and see my zeal for the

*

27ff: 2 Chr 22, 7ff.
31: 1 Kgs 16, 9ff.
36: 1 Kgs 21, 23.
10, 1: Jgs 9, 5; 1 Kgs 15, 29; 16, 11.
10: 1 Kgs 21, 17-24, 29.
11: Hos 1, 4.
12ff: 2 Chr 22, 8f.
15: 1 Chr 2, 55; Jer 35, 1-11.

LORD." And he took him along in his own
chariot.
17 When he arrived in Samaria, Jehu
slew all who remained there of Ahab's
line, doing away with them completely
and thus fulfilling the prophecy which
the LORD had spoken to Elijah.
Baal's Temple Destroyed. 18* Jehu
gathered all the people together and said
to them: "Ahab served Baal to some ex-
tent, but Jehu will serve him yet more.
19 Now summon for me all Baal's proph-
ets, all his worshipers, and all his priests.
See that no one is absent, for I have a
great sacrifice for Baal. Whoever is ab-
sent shall not live." This Jehu did as a
ruse, so that he might destroy the wor-
shipers of Baal. 20 Jehu said further,
"Proclaim a solemn assembly in honor
of Baal." They did so, 21 and Jehu sent
word of it throughout the land of Israel.
All the worshipers of Baal without ex-
ception came into the temple of Baal,
which was filled to capacity. 22* Then
Jehu said to the custodian of the ward-
robe, "Bring out the garments for all the
worshipers of Baal." When he had
brought out the garments for them,
23 Jehu, with Jehonadab, son of Rechab,
entered the temple of Baal and said to
the worshipers of Baal, "Search and be
sure that there is no worshiper of the
LORD here with you, but only worshipers
of Baal." 24 Then they proceeded to offer
sacrifices and holocausts. Now Jehu had
stationed eighty men outside with this
warning, "If one of you lets anyone es-
cape of those whom I shall deliver into
your hands, he shall pay life for life."
25 As soon as he finished offering the ho-
locaust, Jehu said to the guards and offi-
cers, "Go in and slay them. Let no one
escape." So the guards and officers put
them to the sword and cast them out.
Afterward they went into the inner
shrine of the temple of Baal, 26 took out
the stele of Baal, and burned the shrine.
27 Then they smashed the stele of Baal,
tore down the building, and turned it into
a latrine, as it remains today.
28 Thus Jehu rooted out the worship of
Baal from Israel. 29* However, he did not
desist from the sins which Jeroboam,
son of Nebat, had caused Israel to com-
mit, as regards the golden calves at
Bethel and at Dan. 30* The LORD said to
Jehu, "Because you have done well what
I deem right, and have treated the house
of Ahab as I desire, your sons to the
fourth generation shall sit upon the
throne of Israel." 31 But Jehu was not
careful to observe wholeheartedly the
law of the LORD, the God of Israel, since
he did not desist from the sins which
Jeroboam caused Israel to commit.
32* At that time the LORD began to dis-
member Israel. Hazael defeated the Is-
raelites throughout their territory 33 east
of the Jordan (all the land of Gilead, of
the Gadites, Reubenites and Manasseh-
ites), from Aroer on the river Arnon up
through Gilead and Bashan.
34 The rest of the acts of Jehu, his valor
and all his accomplishments, are written
in the book of the chronicles of the kings
of Israel. 35 Jehu rested with his ances-
tors and was buried in Samaria. His son
Jehoahaz succeeded him as king. 36 The
length of Jehu's reign over Israel in Sa-
maria was twenty-eight years.

CHAPTER 11

Rule of Athaliah. 1* When Athaliah,
the mother of Ahaziah, saw that her son
was dead, she began to kill off the whole
royal family. 2† But Jehosheba, daugh-
ter of King Jehoram and sister of Aha-
ziah, took Joash, his son, and spirited
him away, along with his nurse, from
the bedroom where the princes were
about to be slain. She concealed him
from Athaliah, and so he did not die.
3 For six years he remained hidden in
the temple of the LORD, while Athaliah
ruled the land.
4* But in the seventh year, Jehoiada
summoned the captains of the Carians
and of the guards. He had them come
to him in the temple of the LORD, exacted
from them a sworn commitment, and
then showed them the king's son. 5 He
gave them these orders: "This is what
you must do: the third of you who come
on duty on the sabbath shall guard the
king's palace; 6 another third shall be at
the gate Sur; and the last third shall be
at the gate behind the guards. 7 The two
of your divisions who are going off duty
that week shall keep guard over the tem-
ple of the LORD for the king. 8 You shall
surround the king, each with drawn
weapons, and if anyone tries to ap-
proach the cordon, kill him; stay with
the king, whatever he may do."
9* The captains did just as Jehoiada
the priest commanded. Each one with
his men, both those going on duty for
the sabbath and those going off duty that
week, came to Jehoiada the priest.
10* He gave the captains King David's
spears and shields, which were in the
temple of the LORD. 11 And the guards,
with drawn weapons, lined up from the
southern to the northern limit of the en-
closure, surrounding the altar and the

*

18: 1 Kgs 16, 30ff.
22: 1 Kgs 16, 32.
29: 1 Kgs 12, 28f.
30: 15, 12ff.
32: Am 1, 3.
11, 1: Jgs 9, 5.
4-8: 2 Chr 23, 1-7.
9-12: 2 Chr 23, 8-11.
10ff: 2 Sm 8, 7; 1 Kgs 1, 33f.

†

11, 2: *Jehosheba* was the wife of Jehoida, the high priest; cf 2 Chr 22, 11.

temple on the king's behalf. [12]* Then Jehoiada led out the king's son and put the crown and the insignia upon him. They proclaimed him king and anointed him, clapping their hands and shouting, "Long live the king!"

[13]* Athaliah heard the noise made by the people, and appeared before them in the temple of the LORD. [14]† When she saw the king standing by the pillar, as was the custom, and the captains and trumpeters near him, with all the people of the land rejoicing and blowing trumpets, she tore her garments and cried out, "Treason, treason!" [15] Then Jehoiada the priest instructed the captains in command of the force: "Bring her outside through the ranks. If anyone follows her," he added, "let him die by the sword." He had given orders that she should not be slain in the temple of the LORD. [16] She was led out forcibly to the horse gate of the royal palace, where she was put to death.

[17]* Then Jehoiada made a covenant between the LORD as one party and the king and the people as the other, by which they would be the LORD's people; and another covenant, between the king and the people. [18] Thereupon all the people of the land went to the temple of Baal and demolished it. They shattered its altars and images completely, and slew Mattan, the priest of Baal, before the altars. After appointing a detachment for the temple of the LORD, Jehoiada [19] with the captains, the Carians, the guards, and all the people of the land, led the king down from the temple of the LORD through the guards' gate to the palace, where Joash took his seat on the royal throne. [20] All the people of the land rejoiced and the city was quiet, now that Athaliah had been slain with the sword at the royal palace.

CHAPTER 12

Reign of Joash. [1]* Joash was seven years old when he became king. [2] Joash began to reign in the seventh year of Jehu, and he reigned forty years in Jerusalem. His mother, who was named Zibiah, was from Beer-sheba. [3] Joash did what was pleasing to the LORD as long as he lived, because the priest Jehoiada guided him. [4] Still, the high places did not disappear; the people continued to sacrifice and to burn incense there.

[5]* For the priests Joash made this rule: "All the funds for sacred purposes that are brought to the temple of the LORD—the census tax, personal redemption money, and whatever funds are freely brought to the temple of the LORD—[6] the priests may take for themselves, each from his own clients. However, they must make whatever repairs on the temple may prove necessary." [7] Nevertheless, as late as the twenty-third year of the reign of King Joash, the priests had not made needed repairs on the temple. [8] Accordingly, King Joash summoned the priest Jehoiada and the other priests. "Why do you not repair the temple?" he asked them. "You must no longer take funds from your clients, but you shall turn them over for the repairs." [9]* So the priests agreed that they would neither take funds from the people nor make the repairs on the temple.

[10] The priest Jehoiada then took a chest, bored a hole in its lid, and set it beside the stele, on the right as one entered the temple of the LORD. The priests who guarded the entry would put into it all the funds that were brought to the temple of the LORD. [11] When they noticed that there was a large amount of silver in the chest, the royal scribe [and the priest] would come up, and they would melt down all the funds that were in the temple of the LORD, and weigh them. [12] The amount thus realized they turned over to the master workmen in the temple of the LORD. They in turn would give it to the carpenters and builders working in the temple of the LORD, [13] and to the lumbermen and stone cutters, and for the purchase of the wood and hewn stone used in repairing the breaches, and for any other expenses that were necessary to repair the temple. [14] None of the funds brought to the temple of the LORD were used there to make silver cups, snuffers, basins, trumpets, or any gold or silver article. [15] Instead, they were given to the workmen, and with them they repaired the temple of the LORD. [16] Moreover, no reckoning was asked of the men who were provided with the funds to give to the workmen, because they held positions of trust. [17] The funds from guilt-offerings and from sin-offerings, however, were not brought to the temple of the LORD; they belonged to the priests.

[18]* Then King Hazael of Aram mounted a siege against Gath. When he had taken it, Hazael decided to go on to attack Jerusalem. [19] But King Jehoash of Judah took all the dedicated offerings presented by his forebears, Jehoshaphat, Jehoram, and Ahaziah, kings of

*

12: 2 Sm 1, 10.
13-16: 2 Chr 23, 12-15.
17-20: 2 Chr 23, 16-21.
12, 1f: 2 Chr 24, 1f.
5-8: 2 Chr 24, 5-10.
9-16: 2 Chr 24, 11-14.
18: 8, 12.
18-22: 2 Chr 24, 23-27.

†

11, 14: *By the pillar:* see note on 2 Chr 23, 13.

Judah, as well as his own, and all the
gold there was in the treasuries of the
temple and the palace, and sent them
to King Hazael of Aram, who then led
his forces away from Jerusalem. 20 The
rest of the acts of Joash, with all that
he did, are recorded in the book of the
chronicles of the kings of Judah.
21 Certain of his officials entered into a
plot against him and killed him at Beth-
millo. 22 Jozacar, son of Shimeath, and
Jehozabad, son of Shomer, were the offi-
cials who killed him. He was buried in
his forefathers' City of David, and his
son Amaziah succeeded him as king.

CHAPTER 13

Reign of Jehoahaz of Israel. 1 In the
twenty-third year of Joash, son of Aha-
ziah, king of Judah, Jehoahaz, son of
Jehu, began his seventeen-year reign
over Israel in Samaria. 2 He did evil in
the LORD's sight, conducting himself like
Jeroboam, son of Nebat, and not re-
nouncing the sin he had caused Israel
to commit. 3 The LORD was angry with
Israel and for a long time left them in
the power of Hazael, king of Aram, and
of Ben-hadad, son of Hazael. 4* Then Je-
hoahaz entreated the LORD, who heard
him, since he saw the oppression to
which the king of Aram had subjected
Israel. 5† So the LORD gave Israel a sav-
ior, and the Israelites, freed from the
power of Aram, dwelt in their own
homes as formerly. 6*† Nevertheless,
they did not desist from the sins which
the house of Jeroboam had caused Israel
to commit, but persisted in them. The
sacred pole also remained standing in
Samaria. 7 No soldiers were left to Je-
hoahaz, except fifty horsemen with ten
chariots and ten thousand foot soldiers,
since the king of Aram had destroyed
them and trampled them like dust. 8 The
rest of the acts of Jehoahaz, with all his
valor and accomplishments, are re-
corded in the book of the chronicles of
the kings of Israel. 9 Jehoahaz rested
with his ancestors and was buried in Sa-
maria. His son Joash succeeded him as
king.

Reign of Joash of Israel. 10 In the
thirty-seventh year of Joash, king of Ju-
dah, Jehoash, son of Jehoahaz, began
his sixteen-year reign over Israel in Sa-
maria. 11 He did evil in the sight of the
LORD; he did not desist from any of the
sins which Jeroboam, son of Nebat, had
caused Israel to commit, but persisted
in them. 12*† [The rest of the acts of
Joash, the valor with which he fought
against Amaziah, king of Judah, and all
his accomplishments, are recorded in
the book of the chronicles of the kings
of Israel. 13 Joash rested with his ances-
tors, and Jeroboam occupied the throne.
Joash was buried with the kings of Israel
in Samaria.]

14*† When Elisha was suffering from
the sickness of which he was to die, King
Joash of Israel went down to visit him.
"My father, my father!" he exclaimed,
weeping over him. "Israel's chariots and
horsemen!" 15 "Take a bow and some ar-
rows," Elisha said to him. When he had
done so, 16† Elisha said to the king of Is-
rael, "Put your hand on the bow." As
the king held the bow, Elisha placed his
hands over the king's hands 17 and said,
"Open the window toward the east."
He opened it. Elisha said, "Shoot," and
he shot. The prophet exclaimed, "The
LORD's arrow of victory! The arrow of
victory over Aram! You will completely
conquer Aram at Aphec."

18 Then he said to the king of Israel,
"Take the arrows," which he did. Elisha
said to him, "Strike the ground!" He
struck the ground three times and
stopped. 19 Angry with him, the man of
God said: "You should have struck five
or six times; you would have defeated
Aram completely. Now, you will defeat
Aram only three times."

20 Elisha died and was buried. At the
time, bands of Moabites used to raid the
land each year. 21* Once some people
were burying a man, when suddenly
they spied such a raiding band. So they
cast the dead man into the grave of Eli-
sha, and everyone went off. But when
the man came in contact with the bones
of Elisha, he came back to life and rose
to his feet.

22 King Hazael of Aram oppressed Is-
rael during the entire reign of Jehoahaz.
23* But the LORD was merciful with Is-
rael and looked on them with compas-
sion because of his covenant with
Abraham, Isaac, and Jacob. He was un-
willing to destroy them or to cast them
out from his presence. 24 So when King
Hazael of Aram died and his son Ben-
hadad succeeded him as king, 25 Joash,
son of Jehoahaz, took back from Ben-
hadad, son of Hazael, the cities which
Hazael had taken in battle from his fa-
ther Jehoahaz. Joash defeated Ben-ha-
dad three times, and thus recovered the
cities of Israel.

*

13, 4: 14, 26f.
6: Ex 34, 13.
12: 14, 8-16.
14: 2, 12.
21: Sir 48, 14.
23: Dt 9, 27.

†

13, 5: *A savior:* by this language, typical of the Book of Judges (3, 9.15), Jeroboam II of Israel is meant; cf 14, 27.

13, 6: *Sacred pole:* see note on Ex 34, 13.

13, 12f: The conclusion to the reign of Joash is given again in 14, 15f, where it is more appropriate.

13, 14: *My father, my father:* the king expresses here the same sentiments as those with which Elisha addressed Elijah.

13, 16-19: Symbolic acts similar to these are seen in Ex 17, 8ff; Jos 8, 18ff; Ez 4, 1ff.

CHAPTER 14

Amaziah of Judah. 1† In the second
year of Joash, son of Jehoahaz, king of
Israel, Amaziah, son of Joash, king of
Judah, began to reign. 2* He was twenty-
five years old when he became king, and
he reigned twenty-nine years in Jerusa-
lem. His mother, whose name was Jeho-
addin, was from Jerusalem. 3 He pleased
the LORD, yet not like his forefather
David, since he did just as his father
Joash had done. 4 Thus the high places
did not disappear, but the people contin-
ued to sacrifice and to burn incense on
them. 5* When Amaziah had the king-
dom firmly in hand, he slew the officials
who had murdered the king, his father.
6* But the children of the murderers he
did not put to death, obeying the LORD's
command written in the book of the law
of Moses, "Fathers shall not be put to
death for their children, nor shall chil-
dren be put to death for their fathers;
each one shall die for his own sin."

7* Amaziah slew ten thousand Edom-
ites in the Salt Valley, and took Sela in
battle. He renamed it Joktheel, the name
it has to this day.

8* Then Amaziah sent messengers to
Jehoash, son of Jehoahaz, son of Jehu,
king of Israel, with this challenge,
"Come, let us meet face to face." 9 King
Jehoash of Israel sent this reply to the
king of Judah: "The thistle of Lebanon
sent word to the cedar of Lebanon, 'Give
your daughter to my son in marriage,'
but an animal of Lebanon passed by and
trampled the thistle underfoot. 10 You
have indeed conquered Edom, and you
have become ambitious. Enjoy your
glory, but stay at home! Why involve
yourself and Judah with you in misfor-
tune and failure?"

11 But Amaziah would not listen. King
Jehoash of Israel then advanced, and he
and King Amaziah of Judah met in bat-
tle at Beth-shemesh of Judah. 12 Judah
was defeated by Israel, and all the Ju-
dean soldiery fled homeward. 13 King
Jehoash of Israel captured Amaziah,
son of Jehoash, son of Ahaziah, king of
Judah, at Beth-shemesh. He went on to
Jerusalem where he tore down four hun-
dred cubits of the city wall, from the
Gate of Ephraim to the Corner Gate.
14 He took all the gold and silver and all
the utensils there were in the temple of
the LORD and the treasuries of the pal-
ace, and hostages as well. Then he re-
turned to Samaria. 15* The rest of the
acts of Jehoash, his valor, and how he
fought Amaziah, king of Judah, are re-
corded in the book of the chronicles of
the kings of Israel. 16 Jehoash rested
with his ancestors; he was buried in
Samaria with the kings of Israel. His
son Jeroboam succeeded him as king.

17† Amaziah, son of Joash, king of Ju-
dah, survived Jehoash, son of Jehoahaz,
king of Israel, by fifteen years. 18 The
rest of the acts of Amaziah are written
in the book of the chronicles of the kings
of Judah. 19 When a conspiracy was
formed against him in Jerusalem, he
fled to Lachish. But he was pursued to
Lachish and killed there. 20 He was
brought back on horses and buried with
his ancestors in the City of David in Je-
rusalem. 21*† Thereupon all the people
of Judah took the sixteen-year-old Aza-
riah and proclaimed him king to suc-
ceed his father Amaziah. 22 It was
Azariah who rebuilt Elath and restored
it to Judah, after King Amaziah rested
with his ancestors.

Jeroboam II of Israel. 23 In the fif-
teenth year of Amaziah, son of Joash,
king of Judah, Jeroboam, son of Joash,
king of Israel, began his forty-one-year
reign in Samaria. 24 He did evil in the
sight of the LORD; he did not desist from
any of the sins which Jeroboam, son of
Nebat, had caused Israel to commit.
25† He restored the boundaries of Israel
from Labo-of-Hamath to the sea of the
Arabah, just as the LORD, the God of Is-
rael, had prophesied through his ser-
vant, the prophet Jonah, son of Amittai,
from Gath-hepher. 26* For the LORD saw
the very bitter affliction of Israel, where
there was neither slave nor freeman, no
one at all to help Israel. 27 Since the LORD
had not determined to blot out the name
of Israel from under the heavens, he
saved them through Jeroboam, son of
Joash. 28 The rest of the acts of Jero-
boam, his valor and all his accomplish-
ments, how he fought with Damascus
and turned back Hamath from Israel,
are recorded in the book of the chroni-
cles of the kings of Israel. 29 Jeroboam

*

14, 2f: 2 Chr 25, 1f.
5f: 2 Chr 25, 3f.
6: Dt 24, 16; Ez 18, 20.
7: 2 Sm 8, 13f; 2 Chr 25, 11.
8: 13, 12; Jgs 9, 8-15.
15: 13, 12f.
21: 2 Chr 26, 1f.
26: 13, 4f; 1 Kgs 14, 10.

†

14, 1f: *In the second year . . . twenty-nine years in Jerusalem:* the reigns of the kings of Judah between Athaliah and Ahaz are assigned too many years in all to correspond to the reigns in Israel from Jehu to the fall of Samaria. It seems probable that Amaziah was murdered as soon as his son Azariah was old enough to rule, and that Amaziah's reign was nearer nineteen than twenty-nine years. The correlation, in 15, 1, of the beginning of Azariah's reign with the 27th year of Jeroboam II can hardly be correct; and the sixteen-year reign of Jotham of Judah (15, 33) consisted for the most part of a regency during the illness of his father (15, 5).

14, 17: See note on 14, 1f.

14, 21: *Azariah:* also called Uzziah in many texts.

14, 25: *Sea of the Arabah:* the Dead Sea. *Jonah:* see note on Jon 1, 1.

rested with his ancestors, the kings of Israel, and his son Zechariah succeeded him as king.

CHAPTER 15

Azariah of Judah. 1*† Azariah, son of Amaziah, king of Judah, became king in the twenty-seventh year of Jeroboam, king of Israel. 2 He was sixteen years old when he began to reign, and he reigned fifty-two years in Jerusalem. His mother, whose name was Jecholiah, was from Jerusalem. 3 He pleased the LORD just as his father Amaziah had done. 4 Yet the high places did not disappear; the people continued to sacrifice and to burn incense on them. 5* The LORD afflicted the king, and he was a leper to the day of his death. He lived in a house apart, while Jotham, the king's son, was vizier and regent for the people of the land. 6 The rest of the acts of Azariah, and all his accomplishments, are recorded in the book of the chronicles of the kings of Judah. 7 Azariah rested with his ancestors, and was buried with them in the City of David. His son Jotham succeeded him as king.

Zechariah of Israel. 8 In the thirty-eighth year of Azariah, king of Judah, Zechariah, son of Jeroboam, was king of Israel in Samaria for six months. 9 He did evil in the sight of the LORD as his fathers had done, and did not desist from the sins which Jeroboam, son of Nebat, had caused Israel to commit. 10 Shallum, son of Jabesh, conspired against Zechariah, attacked and killed him at Ibleam, and reigned in his place. 11 The rest of the acts of Zechariah are recorded in the book of the chronicles of the kings of Israel. 12* Thus the LORD's promise to Jehu, "Your descendants to the fourth generation shall sit upon the throne of Israel," was fulfilled.

Shallum of Israel. 13 Shallum, son of Jabesh, became king in the thirty-ninth year of Uzziah, king of Judah; he reigned one month in Samaria. 14 Menahem, son of Gadi, came up from Tirzah to Samaria, where he attacked and killed Shallum, son of Jabesh, and reigned in his place. 15 The rest of the acts of Shallum, and the fact of his conspiracy, are recorded in the book of the chronicles of the kings of Israel. 16 At that time, Menahem punished Tappuah, all the inhabitants of the town and of its whole district, because on his way from Tirzah they did not let him in. He punished them even to ripping open all the pregnant women.

Menahem of Israel. 17 In the thirty-ninth year of Azariah, king of Judah, Menahem, son of Gadi, began his ten-year reign over Samaria. 18 He did evil in the sight of the LORD, not desisting from the sins which Jeroboam, son of Nebat, had caused Israel to commit. During his reign, 19† Pul, king of Assyria, invaded the land, and Menahem gave him a thousand talents of silver to have his assistance in strengthening his hold on the kingdom. 20 Menahem secured the money to give to the king of Assyria by exacting it from all the men of substance in the country, fifty silver shekels from each. The king of Assyria did not remain in the country but withdrew. 21 The rest of the acts of Menahem, and all his accomplishments, are recorded in the book of the chronicles of the kings of Israel. 22 Menahem rested with his ancestors, and his son Pekahiah succeeded him as king.

Pekahiah of Israel. 23 In the fiftieth year of Azariah, king of Judah, Pekahiah, son of Menahem, began his two-year reign over Israel in Samaria. 24 He did evil in the sight of the LORD, not desisting from the sins which Jeroboam, son of Nebat, had caused Israel to commit. 25 His adjutant Pekah, son of Remaliah, who had with him fifty men from Gilead, conspired against him, killed him within the palace stronghold in Samaria, and reigned in his place. 26 The rest of the acts of Pekahiah, and all his accomplishments, are recorded in the book of the chronicles of the kings of Israel.

Pekah of Israel. 27† In the fifty-second year of Azariah, king of Judah, Pekah, son of Remaliah, began his twenty-year reign over Israel in Samaria. 28 He did evil in the sight of the LORD, not desisting from the sins which Jeroboam, son of Nebat, had caused Israel to commit. 29 During the reign of Pekah, king of Israel, Tiglath-pileser, king of Assyria, came and took Ijon, Abel-beth-maacah, Janoah, Kedesh, Hazor, all the territory of Naphtali, Gilead, and Galilee, deporting the inhabitants to Assyria. 30 Hoshea, son of Elah, conspired against Pekah, son of Remaliah; he attacked and killed him, and reigned in his place [in the twentieth year of Jotham, son of Uzziah]. 31 The rest of the acts of Pekah, and all his accomplishments, are recorded in the book of the chronicles of the kings of Israel.

Jotham of Judah. 32* In the second

*

15, 1ff: 2 Chr 26, 3f.
5ff: 2 Chr 26, 21ff.
12: 10, 30.
32-38: 2 Chr 27, 1-4.7-9.

†

15, 1: *Twenty-seventh year:* see note on 14, 1f.

15, 19: *Pul:* The Babylonian throne name of the Assyrian Tiglath-pileser III; cf 15, 29.

15, 27: The twenty years here ascribed to *Pekah* are an impossibility; the calculation which made his reign, of five years at most, appear so long may have been based on the attempt to give Jotham of Judah a full sixteen-year reign independently of his regency. See 16, 1 and the note on 14, 1f.

year of Pekah, son of Remaliah, king of
Israel, Jotham, son of Uzziah, king of
Judah, began to reign. 33 He was twenty-
five years old when he became king, and
he reigned sixteen years in Jerusalem.
His mother's name was Jerusha, daugh-
ter of Zadok. 34 He pleased the LORD,
just as his father Uzziah had done.
35† Nevertheless the high places did not
disappear and the people continued to
sacrifice and to burn incense on them.
It was he who built the Upper Gate of
the temple of the LORD. 36 The rest of the
acts of Jotham, and all his accomplish-
ments, are recorded in the book of the
chronicles of the kings of Judah. 37 It was
at that time that the LORD first loosed
Rezin, king of Aram, and Pekah, son of
Remaliah, against Judah. 38 Jotham
rested with his ancestors and was buried
with them in his forefather's City of
David. His son Ahaz succeeded him as
king.

CHAPTER 16

Ahaz of Judah. 1* In the seventeenth
year of Pekah, son of Remaliah, Ahaz,
son of Jotham, king of Judah, began to
reign. 2 Ahaz was twenty years old when
he became king, and he reigned sixteen
years in Jerusalem. He did not please
the LORD, his God, like his forefather
David, 3* but conducted himself like the
kings of Israel, and even immolated his
son by fire, in accordance with the
abominable practice of the nations
whom the LORD had cleared out of the
way of the Israelites. 4* Further, he sac-
rificed and burned incense on the high
places, on hills, and under every leafy
tree.

5* Then Rezin, king of Aram, and
Pekah, son of Remaliah, king of Israel,
came up to Jerusalem to attack it. Al-
though they besieged Ahaz, they were
unable to conquer him. 6* At the same
time the king of Edom recovered Elath
for Edom, driving the Judeans out of it.
The Edomites then entered Elath, which
they have occupied until the present.

7* Meanwhile, Ahaz sent messengers
to Tiglath-pileser, king of Assyria, with
the plea: "I am your servant and your
son. Come up and rescue me from the
clutches of the king of Aram and the
king of Israel, who are attacking me."
8* Ahaz took the silver and gold that
were in the temple of the LORD and in
the palace treasuries and sent them as
a present to the king of Assyria, 9† who
listened to him and moved against Da-
mascus, which he captured. He deported
its inhabitants to Kir and put Rezin to
death.

10 King Ahaz went to Damascus to
meet Tiglath-pileser, king of Assyria.
When he saw the altar in Damascus,
King Ahaz sent to Uriah the priest a
model of the altar and a detailed design
of its construction. 11 Uriah the priest
built an altar according to the plans
which King Ahaz sent him from Damas-
cus, and had it completed by the time
the king returned home. 12 On his arrival
from Damascus, the king inspected this
altar, then went up to it and offered sac-
rifice on it, 13* burning his holocaust and
cereal-offering, pouring out his libation,
and sprinkling the blood of his peace-
offerings on the altar. 14 The bronze altar
that stood before the LORD he brought
from the front of the temple—that is,
from the space between the new altar
and the temple of the LORD—and set it
on the north side of his altar. 15*† "Upon
the large altar," King Ahaz commanded
Uriah the priest, "burn the morning ho-
locaust and the evening cereal offering,
the royal holocaust and cereal offering,
as well as the holocausts, cereal offer-
ings, and libations of the people. You
must also sprinkle on it all the blood of
holocausts and sacrifices. But the old
bronze altar shall be mine for consulta-
tion." 16 Uriah the priest did just as King
Ahaz had commanded. 17* King Ahaz
detached the frames from the bases and
removed the lavers from them; he also
took down the bronze sea from the
bronze oxen that supported it, and set
it on a stone pavement. 18† In deference
to the king of Assyria he removed from
the temple of the LORD the emplacement
which had been built in the temple for
a throne, and the outer entrance for the
king. 19* The rest of the acts of Ahaz are
recorded in the book of the chronicles
of the kings of Judah. 20 Ahaz rested with
his ancestors and was buried with them

*

16, 1-4: 2 Chr 28, 1-4.
3: Lv 18, 21.
4: Dt 12, 2.
5: 2 Chr 28, 5f.
6: 2 Chr 28, 17.
7: 2 Chr 28, 16.
8: 2 Chr 28, 21.
13: 2 Chr 28, 23.
15: Ex 29, 38f; Nm 28, 3f.
17: 2 Chr 28, 24.
19: 2 Chr 28, 26f.

†

15, 35: *The Upper Gate:* also the Gate of Benjamin; cf Jer 20, 2; Ez 9, 2.

16, 9: Firmly dated events bearing on chapters 16 through 20 are: the fall of Damascus (16, 9) in 732 B.C., the fall of Samaria (18, 9-11) in 721 B.C., and Sennacherib's invasion of Judah (18, 13) in 701 B.C., which is equated both in Kgs and in Is 36, 1 with the 14th year of Hezekiah. These data make it necessary to credit Ahaz with at least a twenty-year reign, between 735 and c. 715 B.C., and to exclude the correlations between Hoshea of Israel and Hezekiah in chapter 18.

If the 14th-year correspondence for 701 B.C. is given up, other arrangements are possible. The alleged ages of Jotham (15, 33), Ahaz (16, 2), and Hezekiah (18, 2) at their successive accessions to the throne do not argue for an early date for Hezekiah; but one or more of these may be artificial. Azariah (15, 1-7; Is 6, 1) was still on the throne of Judah in 743 B.C.

16, 15: *For consultation:* perhaps the introduction into Judah of the Babylonian practice of omen sacrifices; cf Ez 21, 16.

16, 18: *Emplacement . . . for a throne, and the outer entrance for the king:* signs of sovereignty for the Hebrew kings.

in the City of David. His son Hezekiah succeeded him as king.

CHAPTER 17

Hoshea of Israel. 1 In the twelfth year of Ahaz, king of Judah, Hoshea, son of Elah, began his nine-year reign over Israel in Samaria. 2 He did evil in the sight of the LORD, yet not to the extent of the kings of Israel before him. 3*† Shalmaneser, king of Assyria, advanced against him, and Hoshea became his vassal and paid him tribute. 4 But the king of Assyria found Hoshea guilty of conspiracy for sending envoys to the king of Egypt at Sais, and for failure to pay the annual tribute to his Assyrian overlord. 5 For this, the king of Assyria arrested and imprisoned Hoshea; he then occupied the whole land and attacked Samaria, which he besieged for three years. 6*† In the ninth year of Hoshea, the king of Assyria took Samaria, and deported the Israelites to Assyria, settling them in Halah, at the Habor, a river of Gozan, and in the cities of the Medes.

7 This came about because the Israelites sinned against the LORD, their God, who had brought them up from the land of Egypt, from under the domination of Pharaoh, king of Egypt, and because they venerated other gods. 8 They followed the rites of the nations whom the LORD had cleared out of the way of the Israelites [and the kings of Israel whom they set up]. 9 They adopted unlawful practices toward the LORD, their God. They built high places in all their settlements, the watchtowers as well as the walled cities. 10* They set up pillars and sacred poles for themselves on every high hill and under every leafy tree. 11 There, on all the high places, they burned incense like the nations whom the LORD had sent into exile at their coming. They did evil things that provoked the LORD, 12 and served idols, although the LORD had told them, "You must not do this."

13* And though the LORD warned Israel and Judah by every prophet and seer, "Give up your evil ways and keep my commandments and statutes, in accordance with the entire law which I enjoined on your fathers and which I sent you by my servants the prophets," 14 they did not listen, but were as stiff-necked as their fathers, who had not believed in the LORD, their God. 15* They rejected his statutes, the covenant which he had made with their fathers, and the warnings which he had given them. The vanity they pursued, they themselves became: they followed the surrounding nations whom the LORD had commanded them not to imitate. 16* They disregarded all the commandments of the LORD, their God, and made for themselves two molten calves; they also made a sacred pole and worshiped all the host of heaven, and served Baal. 17* They immolated their sons and daughters by fire, practiced fortune-telling and divination, and sold themselves into evil doing in the LORD's sight, provoking him 18 till, in his great anger against Israel, the LORD put them away out of his sight. Only the tribe of Judah was left.

19 Even the people of Judah, however, did not keep the commandments of the LORD, their God, but followed the rites practiced by Israel. 20 So the LORD rejected the whole race of Israel. He afflicted them and delivered them over to plunderers, finally casting them out from before him. 21* When he tore Israel away from the house of David, they made Jeroboam, son of Nebat, king; he drove the Israelites away from the LORD, causing them to commit a great sin. 22 The Israelites imitated Jeroboam in all the sins he committed, nor would they desist from them. 23* Finally, the LORD put Israel away out of his sight as he had foretold through all his servants, the prophets; and Israel went into exile from their native soil to Assyria, an exile lasting to the present.

24 The king of Assyria brought people from Babylon, Cuthah, Avva, Hamath, and Sepharvaim, and settled them in the cities of Samaria in place of the Israelites. They took possession of Samaria and dwelt in its cities. 25 When they first settled there, they did not venerate the LORD, so he sent lions among them that killed some of their number. 26 A report reached the king of Assyria: "The nations whom you deported and settled in the cities of Samaria do not know how to worship the God of the land, and he has sent lions among them that are killing them, since they do not know how to worship the God of the land." 27 The king of Assyria gave the order, "Send back one of the priests whom I deported, to go there and settle, to teach them how to worship the God of the land." 28 So one of the priests who had been deported from Samaria returned and settled in Bethel, and taught them how to venerate the LORD.

*

17, 3: 18, 9; Tb 1, 2.
6: 18, 10f.
10: Ex 23, 24; 34, 13; Dt 12, 2.
13: Jer 25, 5; Dt 9, 13.
15: Jer 2, 5.
16: 1 Kgs 12, 28; Ex 34, 13; Dt 4, 19; 17, 2f.
17: Lv 18, 21; Dt 18, 10.
21: 1 Kgs 12, 19f; 12, 26-33.
23: Jer 25, 9.

†

17, 3: *Shalmaneser:* son and successor of Tiglath-pileser.

17, 6: *The king of Assyria:* Shalmaneser's successor and usurper, Sargon II.

29* But these peoples began to make
their own gods in the various cities in
which they were living; in the shrines
on the high places which the Samarians
had made, each people set up gods.
30 Thus the Babylonians made Marduk
and his consort; the men of Cuth made
Nergal; the men of Hamath made
Ashima; 31 the men of Avva made Nib-
haz and Tartak; and the men of Sephar-
vaim immolated their children by fire
to their city gods, King Hadad and his
consort Anath. 32* They also venerated
the LORD, choosing from their number
priests for the high places, who offici-
ated for them in the shrines on the
high places. 33 But, while venerating the
LORD, they served their own gods, fol-
lowing the worship of the nations from
among whom they had been deported.
34*† To this day they worship accord-
ing to their ancient rites. [They did not
venerate the LORD nor observe the stat-
utes and regulations, the law and com-
mandments, which the LORD enjoined
on the descendants of Jacob, whom he
had named Israel. 35* When he made
a covenant with them, he commanded
them: "You must not venerate other
gods, nor worship them, nor serve them,
nor offer sacrifice to them. 36 The LORD,
who brought you up from the land
of Egypt with great power and out-
stretched arm: him shall you venerate,
him shall you worship, and to him shall
you sacrifice. 37 You must be careful to
observe forever the statutes and regula-
tions, the law and commandment, which
he wrote for you, and you must not ven-
erate other gods. 38 The covenant which
I made with you, you must not forget;
you must not venerate other gods. 39 But
the LORD, your God, you must venerate;
it is he who will deliver you from the
power of all your enemies." 40 They did
not listen, however, but continued in
their earlier manner.] 41 Thus these na-
tions venerated the LORD, but also
served their idols. And their sons and
grandsons, to this day, are doing as their
fathers did.

V: THE KINGDOM OF JUDAH AFTER 721 B.C.

CHAPTER 18

Hezekiah. 1* In the third year of Ho-
shea, son of Elah, king of Israel, Heze-
kiah, son of Ahaz, king of Judah, began
to reign. 2 He was twenty-five years old
when he became king, and he reigned
twenty-nine years in Jerusalem. His
mother's name was Abi, daughter of
Zechariah. 3 He pleased the LORD, just
as his forefather David had done. 4* It
was he who removed the high places,
shattered the pillars, and cut down the
sacred poles. He smashed the bronze
serpent called Nehushtan which Moses
had made, because up to that time the
Israelites were burning incense to it. 5 He
put his trust in the LORD, the God of Is-
rael; and neither before him nor after
him was there anyone like him among
all the kings of Judah. 6 Loyal to the
LORD, Hezekiah never turned away
from him, but observed the command-
ments which the LORD had given Moses.
7 The LORD was with him, and he pros-
pered in all that he set out to do. He re-
belled against the king of Assyria and
did not serve him. 8 He also subjugated
the watchtowers and walled cities of the
Philistines, all the way to Gaza and its
territory.
9† In the fourth year of King Hezekiah,
which was the seventh year of Hoshea,
son of Elah, king of Israel, Shalmaneser,
king of Assyria, attacked Samaria, laid
siege to it, 10* and after three years cap-
tured it. In the sixth year of Hezekiah,
the ninth year of Hoshea, king of Israel,
Samaria was taken. 11 The king of As-
syria then deported the Israelites to As-
syria and settled them in Halah, at the
Habor, a river of Gozan, and in the cities
of the Medes. 12* This came about be-
cause they had not heeded the warning
of the LORD, their God, but violated his
covenant, not heeding and not fulfilling
the commandments of Moses, the ser-
vant of the LORD.

Invasion of Sennacherib. 13*† In the
fourteenth year of King Hezekiah, Sen-
nacherib, king of Assyria, went on an
expedition against all the fortified cit-
ies of Judah and captured them.
14 Hezekiah, king of Judah, sent this
message to the king of Assyria at La-
chish: "I have done wrong. Leave me,
and I will pay whatever tribute you im-
pose on me." The king of Assyria ex-
acted three hundred talents of silver and
thirty talents of gold from Hezekiah,
king of Judah. 15 Hezekiah paid him all
the funds there were in the temple of
the LORD and in the palace treasuries.

*

29: Jn 4, 9.
32: 1 Kgs 12, 31.
34: Gn 32, 29.
35: Ex 20, 3ff.
18, 1ff: 2 Chr 28, 27; 29, 1f.
4: Ex 23, 24; 34, 13; Nm 21, 9; Dt 12, 2; 2 Chr 31, 1; Wis 16, 6; Jn 3, 14.
10f: 17, 6; Tb 1, 2.
12: 17, 7-18.
13: 2 Chr 32, 1ff; Sir 48, 18; Is 36, 1.

†

17, 34-40: *They did not . . . earlier manner:* this passage is an adaptation of language denouncing the Israelites to make it applicable to the later Samaritan sect of postexilic times. The original bearing of the discourse [13-15] can be seen by reading it between 22 and 23. Cf also 18, 12.

18, 9: See note on 16, 9.

18, 13: *Sennacherib* succeeded Sargon II as king of Assyria. His Judean campaign was waged in 701 B.C. See note on 16, 9.

18, 13—20, 11: Duplication of Is 36, 1—38, 8.21.22.

16* He broke up the door panels and the
uprights of the temple of the LORD which
he himself had ordered to be overlaid
with gold, and gave the gold to the king
of Assyria.
17*† The king of Assyria sent the gen-
eral, the lord chamberlain, and the com-
mander from Lachish with a great army
to King Hezekiah at Jerusalem. They
went up, and on their arrival in Jerusa-
lem, stopped at the conduit of the upper
pool on the highway of the fuller's field.
18* They called for the king, who sent out
to them Eliakim, son of Hilkiah, the
master of the palace; Shebnah the
scribe; and the herald Joah, son of
Asaph. 19 The commander said to them,
"Tell Hezekiah, 'Thus says the great
king, the king of Assyria: On what do
you base this confidence of yours? 20 Do
you think mere words substitute for
strategy and might in war? On whom,
then, do you rely, that you rebel against
me? 21* This Egypt, the staff on which
you rely, is in fact a broken reed which
pierces the hand of anyone who leans
on it. That is what Pharaoh, king of
Egypt, is to all who rely on him. 22 But
if you say to me, We rely on the LORD,
our God, is not he the one whose high
places and altars Hezekiah has re-
moved, commanding Judah and Jeru-
salem to worship before this altar in
Jerusalem?'
23 "Now, make a wager with my lord,
the king of Assyria: I will give you two
thousand horses if you can put riders
on them. 24 How then can you repulse
even one of the least servants of my lord,
relying as you do on Egypt for chariots
and horsemen? 25 Was it without the
LORD's will that I have come up to de-
stroy this place? The LORD said to me,
'Go up and destroy that land!' "
26 Then Eliakim, son of Hilkiah, and
Shebnah and Joah said to the com-
mander: "Please speak to your servants
in Aramaic; we understand it. Do not
speak to us in Judean within earshot of
the people who are on the wall."
27 But the commander replied: "Was
it to your master and to you that my lord
sent me to speak these words? Was it
not rather to the men sitting on the wall,
who, with you, will have to eat their
own excrement and drink their urine?"
28 Then the commander stepped forward
and cried out in a loud voice in Judean,
"Listen to the words of the great king,
the king of Assyria. 29 Thus says the
king: 'Do not let Hezekiah deceive you,
since he cannot deliver you out of my
hand. 30 Let not Hezekiah induce you to
rely on the LORD, saying, The LORD will
surely save us; this city will not be
handed over to the king of Assyria. 31 Do
not listen to Hezekiah, for the king of
Assyria says: Make peace with me and
surrender! Then each of you will eat of
his own vine and of his own fig-tree, and
drink the water of his own cistern,
32 until I come to take you to a land like
your own, a land of grain and wine, of
bread and orchards, of olives, oil and
fruit syrup. Choose life, not death. Do
not listen to Hezekiah when he would se-
duce you by saying, The LORD will res-
cue us. 33 Has any of the gods of the
nations ever rescued his land from the
hand of the king of Assyria? 34* Where
are the gods of Hamath and Arpad?
Where are the gods of Sepharvaim,
Hena, and Avva? Where are the gods
of the land of Samaria? 35 Which of the
gods for all these lands ever rescued his
land from my hand? Will the LORD then
rescue Jerusalem from my hand?' "
36 But the people remained silent and did
not answer him one word, for the king
had ordered them not to answer him.
37 Then the master of the palace, Eli-
akim, son of Hilkiah, Shebnah the
scribe, and the herald Joah, son of
Asaph, came to Hezekiah with their gar-
ments torn, and reported to him what
the commander had said.

CHAPTER 19

Hezekiah and Isaiah. 1* When King
Hezekiah heard this, he tore his gar-
ments, wrapped himself in sackcloth,
and went into the temple of the LORD.
2 He sent Eliakim, the master of the pal-
ace, Shebnah the scribe, and the elders
of the priests, wrapped in sackcloth, to
tell the prophet Isaiah, son of Amoz,
3† "Thus says Hezekiah: 'This is a day
of distress, of rebuke, and of disgrace.
Children are at the point of birth, but
there is no strength to bring them forth.
4 Perhaps the LORD, your God, will hear
all the words of the commander, whom
his master, the king of Assyria, sent to
taunt the living God, and will rebuke him
for the words which the LORD, your God,
has heard. So send up a prayer for the
remnant that is here.' " 5 When the ser-
vants of King Hezekiah had come to
Isaiah, 6* he said to them, "Tell this to
your master: 'Thus says the LORD: Do
not be frightened by the words you have
heard, with which the servants of the
king of Assyria have blasphemed
me. 7 I am about to put in him such a
spirit that, when he hears a certain re-

*

16: 1 Kgs 6, 20-22.
17: 2 Chr 32, 9; Is 36, 1ff.
18: Is 22, 13-25.
21: Is 30, 1-7; 31, 1-3; Ez 29, 6-7.
34: 17, 24.
19, 1-7: Is 37, 1-7.
6: Is 10, 5-19.

†

18, 17: *General, the lord chamberlain . . . commander:* the text lists three major functionaries by their Assyrian titles, of which only the first, more nearly "lord lieutenant," is military in origin; the *commander* was technically the king's chief butler.
19, 3: See note on Is 37, 3.

port, he will return to his own land, and
there I will cause him to fall by the
sword.' "
8 When the commander, on his return,
heard that the king of Assyria had with-
drawn from Lachish, he found him be-
sieging Libnah. 9 The king of Assyria
heard a report that Tirhakah, king of
Ethiopia, had come out to fight against
him. Again he sent envoys to Hezekiah
with this message: 10 "Thus shall you say
to Hezekiah, king of Judah: 'Do not let
your God on whom you rely deceive you
by saying that Jerusalem will not be
handed over to the king of Assyria.
11 You have heard what the kings of As-
syria have done to all other countries:
they doomed them! Will you, then, be
saved? 12* Did the gods of the nations
whom my fathers destroyed save them?
Gozan, Haran, Rezeph, or the Edenites
in Telassar? 13* Where are the king of
Hamath, the king of Arpad, or the kings
of the cities Sepharvaim, Hena and
Avva?' "
14* Hezekiah took the letter from the
hand of the messengers and read it; then
he went up to the temple of the LORD,
and spreading it out before him, 15* he
prayed in the LORD's presence: "O LORD,
God of Israel, enthroned upon the cher-
ubim! You alone are God over all the
kingdoms of the earth. You have made
the heavens and the earth. 16 Incline
your ear, O LORD, and listen! Open your
eyes, O LORD, and see! Hear the words
of Sennacherib which he sent to taunt
the living God. 17 Truly, O LORD, the
kings of Assyria have laid waste the na-
tions and their lands, 18* and cast their
gods into the fire; they destroyed them
because they were not gods, but the work
of human hands, wood and stone.
19* Therefore, O LORD, our God, save us
from the power of this man, that all the
kingdoms of the earth may know that
you alone, O LORD, are God."
Punishment of Sennacherib. 20 Then
Isaiah, son of Amoz, sent this message
to Hezekiah: "Thus says the LORD, the
God of Israel, in answer to your prayer
for help against Sennacherib, king of
Assyria: I have listened! 21† This is the
word the LORD has spoken concerning
him:

" 'She despises you, laughs you to
scorn,
the virgin daughter Zion!
Behind you she wags her head,
daughter Jerusalem.
22 Whom have you insulted and blas-
phemed,
against whom have you raised
your voice
And lifted up your eyes on high?
Against the Holy One of Israel!
23 Through your servants you have in-
sulted the LORD.
You said: With my many chariots
I climbed the mountain heights,
the recesses of Lebanon;
I cut down its lofty cedars,
its choice cypresses;
I reached the remotest heights,
its forest park.
24 I dug wells and drank water in for-
eign lands;
I dried up with the soles of my feet
all the rivers of Egypt.

25 " 'Have you not heard?
Long ago I prepared it,
From days of old I planned it.
Now I have brought it to pass:
That you should reduce fortified cit-
ies
into heaps of ruins,
26 While their inhabitants, shorn of
power,
are dismayed and ashamed,
Becoming like the plants of the field,
like the green growth,
like the scorched grass on the
housetops.
27* I am aware whether you stand or
sit;
I know whether you come or go,
28 and also your rage against me.
Because of your rage against me
and your fury which has reached
my ears,
I will put my hook in your nose
and my bit in your mouth,
and make you return the way you
came.

29 " 'This shall be a sign for you:
this year you shall eat the after-
growth,
next year, what grows of itself;
But in the third year, sow and reap,
plant vineyards and eat their
fruit!
30 The remaining survivors of the
house of Judah
shall again strike root below
and bear fruit above.
31 For out of Jerusalem shall come a
remnant,
and from Mount Zion, survivors.
The zeal of the LORD of hosts shall
do this.'

32 "Therefore, thus says the LORD con-
cerning the king of Assyria: 'He shall not
reach this city, nor shoot an arrow at
it, nor come before it with a shield, nor
cast up siege-works against it. 33 He shall

*

12: 17, 6.
13: 18, 34.
14-19: 2 Chr 32, 20; Is 37, 14-20.
15: Ex 25, 18.
18: Jer 10, 3.
19: 1 Kgs 18, 24.
27: Ps 139, 2f.

†

19, 21-31: vv 21-28 are addressed to Sennacherib, vv 29-31 to Judah.

return by the same way he came, without entering the city, says the LORD. [34]* I will shield and save this city for my own sake, and for the sake of my servant David.' "

[35]* That night the angel of the LORD went forth and struck down one hundred and eighty-five thousand men in the Assyrian camp. Early the next morning, there they were, all the corpses of the dead. [36] So Sennacherib, the king of Assyria, broke camp, and went back home to Nineveh.

[37] When he was worshiping in the temple of his god Nisroch, his sons Adrammelech and Sharezer slew him with the sword and fled into the land of Ararat. His son Esarhaddon reigned in his stead.

CHAPTER 20

Hezekiah's Illness. [1]* In those days, when Hezekiah was mortally ill, the prophet Isaiah, son of Amoz, came and said to him: "Thus says the LORD: 'Put your house in order, for you are about to die; you shall not recover.' " [2] He turned his face to the wall and prayed to the LORD: [3] "O LORD, remember how faithfully and wholeheartedly I conducted myself in your presence, doing what was pleasing to you!" And Hezekiah wept bitterly.

[4] Before Isaiah had left the central courtyard, the word of the LORD came to him: [5] "Go back and tell Hezekiah, the leader of my people: 'Thus says the LORD, the God of your forefather David: I have heard your prayer and seen your tears. I will heal you. In three days you shall go up to the LORD's temple; [6] I will add fifteen years to your life. I will rescue you and this city from the hand of the king of Assyria; I will be a shield to this city for my own sake, and for the sake of my servant David.' "

[7] Isaiah then ordered a poultice of figs to be brought and applied to the boil, that he might recover. [8] Then Hezekiah asked Isaiah, "What is the sign that the LORD will heal me and that I shall go up to the temple of the LORD on the third day?" [9] Isaiah replied, "This will be the sign for you from the LORD that he will do what he has promised: Shall the shadow go forward or back ten steps?"

[10] "It is easy for the shadow to advance ten steps," Hezekiah answered. "Rather, let it go back ten steps." [11] So the prophet Isaiah invoked the LORD, who made the shadow retreat the ten steps it had descended on the staircase to the terrace of Ahaz.

[12]*† At that time, when Merodach-baladan, son of Baladan, king of Babylon, heard that Hezekiah had been ill, he sent letters and gifts to him. [13] Hezekiah was pleased at this, and therefore showed the messengers his whole treasury, his silver, gold, spices and fine oil, his armory, and all that was in his storerooms; there was nothing in his house or in all his realm that Hezekiah did not show them.

[14] Then Isaiah the prophet came to King Hezekiah and asked him: "What did these men say to you? Where did they come from?" "They came from a distant land, from Babylon," replied Hezekiah. [15] "What did they see in your house?" the prophet asked. "They saw everything in my house," answered Hezekiah. "There is nothing in my storerooms that I did not show them."

[16] Then Isaiah said to Hezekiah: "Hear the word of the LORD: [17] The time is coming when all that is in your house, and everything that your fathers have stored up until this day, shall be carried off to Babylon; nothing shall be left, says the LORD. [18] Some of your own bodily descendants shall be taken and made servants in the palace of the king of Babylon."

[19] Hezekiah replied to Isaiah, "The word of the LORD which you have spoken is favorable." For he thought, "There will be peace and security in my lifetime."

[20]*† The rest of the acts of Hezekiah, all his valor, and his construction of the pool and conduit by which water was brought into the city, are written in the book of the chronicles of the kings of Judah. [21] Hezekiah rested with his ancestors and his son Manasseh succeeded him as king.

CHAPTER 21

Reign of Manasseh. [1]* Manasseh was twelve years old when he began to reign, and he reigned fifty-five years in Jerusalem. His mother's name was Hephzibah. [2] He did evil in the sight of the LORD, following the abominable practices of the nations whom the LORD had cleared out of the way of the Israelites. [3]* He rebuilt the high places which his father Hezekiah had destroyed. He erected altars to Baal, and also set up a sacred pole, as Ahab, king of Israel, had done. He worshiped and served the whole host

*

34: 2 Sm 7, 12; Hos 1, 7.
35: Sir 48, 21; 2 Chr 32, 21f; Is 37, 36-38; 1 Mc 7, 41; 2 Mc 8, 19.
20, 1-9: 2 Chr 32, 24; Is 38, 1-8.
12f: Is 39, 1f; 2 Chr 32, 27ff.
20: 2 Chr 32, 30; Sir 48, 17.
21, 1-10: 2 Chr 33, 1-10.
3: 17, 16; 1 Kgs 18, 4; 16, 32f.

†

20, 12-19: Duplication of Is 39, 1-8.
20, 20: *Pool and conduit:* Hezekiah's tunnel; cf 2 Chr 32, 30.

of heaven. 4 He built altars in the temple
of the LORD, about which the LORD had
said, "I will establish my name in Jeru-
salem"— 5* altars for the whole host of
heaven, in the two courts of the temple.
6 He immolated his son by fire. He
practiced soothsaying and divination,
and reintroduced the consulting of
ghosts and spirits. He did much evil in
the LORD's sight and provoked him to
anger.
7* The Asherah idol he had made, he
set up in the temple, of which the LORD
had said to David and to his son Solo-
mon: "In this temple and in Jerusalem,
which I have chosen out of all the tribes
of Israel, I shall place my name forever.
8 I will not in future allow Israel to be
driven off the land I gave their fathers,
provided that they are careful to observe
all I have commanded them, the entire
law which my servant Moses enjoined
upon them." 9 But they did not listen,
and Manasseh misled them into doing
even greater evil than the nations whom
the LORD had destroyed at the coming
of the Israelites.
10 Then the LORD spoke through his
servants the prophets: 11* "Because Ma-
nasseh, king of Judah, has practiced
these abominations and has done
greater evil than all that was done by
the Amorites before him, and has led Ju-
dah into sin by his idols, 12 therefore thus
says the LORD, the God of Israel: 'I will
bring such evil on Jerusalem and Judah
that, whenever anyone hears of it, his
ears shall ring. 13* I will measure Jeru-
salem with the same cord as I did Sa-
maria, and with the plummet I used for
the house of Ahab. I will wipe Jerusalem
clean as one wipes a dish, wiping it in-
side and out. 14 I will cast off the survi-
vors of my inheritance and deliver them
into enemy hands, to become a prey and
a booty for all their enemies, 15 because
they have done evil in my sight and pro-
voked me from the day their fathers
came forth from Egypt until today.'"
16 In addition to the sin which he
caused Judah to commit, Manasseh did
evil in the sight of the LORD, shedding
so much innocent blood as to fill the
length and breadth of Jerusalem.
17* The rest of the acts of Manasseh, the
sin he committed and all that he did, are
written in the book of the chronicles of
the kings of Judah. 18 Manasseh rested
with his ancestors and was buried in his
palace garden, the garden of Uzza. His
son Amon succeeded him as king.
Reign of Amon. 19* Amon was twenty-
two years old when he began to reign,
and he reigned two years in Jerusa-
lem. His mother's name was Meshul-
lemeth, daughter of Haruz of Jotbah.
20 He did evil in the sight of the LORD,
as his father Manasseh had done. 21 He
followed exactly the path his father had
trod, serving and worshiping the idols
his father had served. 22 He abandoned
the LORD, the God of his fathers, and
did not follow the path of the LORD.
23 Subjects of Amon conspired against
him and slew the king in his palace,
24 but the people of the land then slew
all who had conspired against King
Amon, and proclaimed his son Josiah
king in his stead. 25 The rest of the acts
that Amon did are written in the book
of the chronicles of the kings of Judah.
26 He was buried in his own grave in the
garden of Uzza, and his son Josiah suc-
ceeded him as king.

CHAPTER 22

Reign of Josiah. 1* Josiah was eight
years old when he began to reign, and
he reigned thirty-one years in Jerusa-
lem. His mother's name was Jedidah,
daughter of Adaiah of Bozkath. 2 He
pleased the LORD and conducted himself
unswervingly just as his ancestor David
had done.
3*† In his eighteenth year, King Josiah
sent the scribe Shaphan, son of Azaliah,
son of Meshullam, to the temple of the
LORD with orders to 4* go to the high
priest Hilkiah and have him smelt down
the precious metals that had been do-
nated to the temple of the Lord, which
the doorkeepers had collected from the
people. 5 They were to be consigned to
the master workmen in the temple of the
LORD, who should then pay them out to
the carpenters, builders, and lumber-
men making repairs on the temple, 6 and
for the purchase of wood and hewn stone
for the temple repairs. 7 No reckoning
was asked of them regarding the funds
consigned to them, because they held
positions of trust.
The Book of the Law. 8 The high priest
Hilkiah informed the scribe Shaphan, "I
have found the book of the law in the
temple of the LORD." Hilkiah gave the
book to Shaphan, who read it. 9 Then the
scribe Shaphan went to the king and re-
ported, "Your servants have smelted
down the metals available in the temple
and have consigned them to the master
workmen in the temple of the LORD."
10 The scribe Shaphan also informed the

*

5: Lv 18, 21.
7: 2 Sm 7, 13; 1 Kgs 8, 16; 9, 3.
11: 1 Kgs 21, 26; Jer 15, 4.
13: Is 34, 11; Am 7, 7-9; Lam 2, 8.
17: 2 Chr 33, 18ff.
19-26: 2 Chr 33, 21-25.
22, 1f: 2 Chr 34, 1f.
3-13: 2 Chr 34, 8-21.
4-7: 12, 11-16.

†

22, 3: *Shaphan:* head of a prominent family in the reign of Josiah, secretary to the king, bearer and reader of the newfound book of the law (3-13; 2 Chr 34, 8f.15-20). He and his sons favored the reform of King Josiah and supported the prophet Jeremiah; cf Jer 26, 24.

king that the priest Hilkiah had given him a book, and then read it aloud to the king. 11* When the king had heard the contents of the book of the law, he tore his garments 12 and issued this command to Hilkiah the priest, Ahikam, son of Shaphan, Achbor, son of Micaiah, the scribe Shaphan, and the king's servant Asaiah: 13 "Go, consult the LORD for me, for the people, for all Judah, about the stipulations of this book that has been found, for the anger of the LORD has been set furiously ablaze against us, because our fathers did not obey the stipulations of this book, nor fulfill our written obligations."

14 So Hilkiah the priest, Ahikam, Achbor, Shaphan, and Asaiah betook themselves to the Second Quarter in Jerusalem, where the prophetess Huldah resided. She was the wife of Shallum, son of Tikvah, son of Harhas, keeper of the wardrobe. When they had spoken to her, 15 she said to them, "Thus says the LORD, the God of Israel: 'Say to the man who sent you to me, 16 Thus says the LORD: I will bring upon this place and upon its inhabitants all the evil that is threatened in the book which the king of Judah has read. 17 Because they have forsaken me and have burned incense to other gods, provoking me by everything to which they turn their hands, my anger is ablaze against this place and it cannot be extinguished.'

18 "But to the king of Judah who sent you to consult the LORD, give this response: 'Thus says the LORD, the God of Israel: As for the threats you have heard, 19 because you were heartsick and have humbled yourself before the LORD when you heard my threats that this place and its inhabitants would become a desolation and a curse; because you tore your garments and wept before me; I in turn have listened, says the LORD. 20 I will therefore gather you to your ancestors; you shall go to your grave in peace, and your eyes shall not see all the evil I will bring upon this place.' " This they reported to the king.

CHAPTER 23

1* The king then had all the elders of Judah and of Jerusalem summoned together before him. 2 The king went up to the temple of the LORD with all the men of Judah and all the inhabitants of Jerusalem: priests, prophets, and all the people, small and great. He had the entire contents of the book of the covenant that had been found in the temple of the LORD, read out to them. 3 Standing by the column, the king made a covenant before the LORD that they would follow him and observe his ordinances, statutes and decrees with their whole hearts and souls, thus reviving the terms of the covenant which were written in this book. And all the people stood as participants in the covenant.

4* Then the king commanded the high priest Hilkiah, his vicar, and the doorkeepers to remove from the temple of the LORD all the objects that had been made for Baal, Asherah, and the whole host of heaven. He had these burned outside Jerusalem on the slopes of the Kidron and their ashes carried to Bethel. 5* He also put an end to the pseudo-priests whom the kings of Judah had appointed to burn incense on the high places in the cities of Judah and in the vicinity of Jerusalem, as well as those who burned incense to Baal, to the sun, moon, and signs of the Zodiac, and to the whole host of heaven. 6* From the temple of the LORD he also removed the sacred pole, to the Kidron Valley, outside Jerusalem; there he had it burned and beaten to dust, which was then scattered over the common graveyard. 7*† He tore down the apartments of the cult prostitutes which were in the temple of the LORD, and in which the women wove garments for the Asherah.

8* He brought in all the priests from the cities of Judah, and then defiled, from Geba to Beer-sheba, the high places where they had offered incense. He also tore down the high place of the satyrs, which was at the entrance of the Gate of Joshua, governor of the city, to the left as one enters the city gate. 9 The priests of the high places could not function at the altar of the LORD in Jerusalem; but they, along with their relatives, ate the unleavened bread.

10*† The king also defiled Topheth in the Valley of Ben-hinnom, so that there would no longer be an immolation of sons or daughters by fire in honor of Molech. 11† He did away with the horses which the kings of Judah had dedicated to the sun; these were at the entrance of the temple of the LORD, near the chamber of Nathan-melech the eunuch, which was in the large building. The chariots of the sun he destroyed by fire. 12* He also demolished the altars made by the kings of Judah on the roof (the

*

11-20: 2 Chr 34, 19-28.
23, 1-5: 2 Chr 34, 29-33.
4: 2 Chr 34, 3-5; Sir 49, 3.
5: Dt 17, 3ff.
6: Dt 16, 21; 1 Kgs 14, 23.
7: 1 Kgs 14, 24; Dt 23, 18f.
8: Dt 12, 2f.
10: Lv 18, 21.
12: 21, 5.

†

23, 7: *Cult prostitutes:* of both sexes; cf 1 Kgs 14, 24.

23, 10: *Topheth . . . by fire:* condemned by Deuteronomic law and denounced by Jeremiah (Dt 12, 31; Jer 7, 29ff; Jer 19).

23, 11: *Large building:* to the west of the temple area (1 Chr 26, 18), named in the Hebrew by an Egyptian name for a similar construction.

roof terrace of Ahaz), and the altars
made by Manasseh in the two courts of
the temple of the LORD. He pulverized
them and threw the dust into the Kidron
Valley. 13*† The king defiled the high
places east of Jerusalem, south of the
Mount of Misconduct, which Solomon,
king of Israel, had built in honor of Astarte, the Sidonian horror, of Chemosh,
the Moabite horror, and of Milcom, the
idol of the Ammonites. 14* He broke to
pieces the pillars, cut down the sacred
poles, and filled the places where they
had been with human bones. 15* Likewise the altar which was at Bethel, the
high place built by Jeroboam, son of Nebat, who caused Israel to sin—this same
altar and high place he tore down,
breaking up the stones and grinding
them to powder, and burning the Asherah.

16 When Josiah turned and saw the
graves there on the mountainside, he ordered the bones taken from the graves
and burned on the altar, and thus defiled
it in fulfillment of the word of the LORD
which the man of God had proclaimed
as Jeroboam was standing by the altar
on the feast day. When the king looked
up and saw the grave of the man of God
who had proclaimed these words, 17 he
asked, "What is that tombstone I see?"
The men of the city replied, "It is the
grave of the man of God who came from
Judah and predicted the very things you
have done to the altar of Bethel."
18*† "Let him be," he said, "let no one
move his bones." So they left his bones
undisturbed together with the bones of
the prophet who had come from Samaria.

19* Josiah also removed all the shrines
on the high places near the cities of Samaria which the kings of Israel had
erected, thereby provoking the LORD; he
did the very same to them as he had
done in Bethel. 20 He slaughtered upon
the altars all the priests of the high
places that were at the shrines, and
burned human bones upon them. Then
he returned to Jerusalem.

21* The king issued a command to all
the people to observe the Passover of the
LORD, their God, as it was prescribed in
that book of the covenant. 22 No Passover such as this had been observed during the period when the Judges ruled
Israel, or during the entire period of the
kings of Israel and the kings of Judah,
23 until the eighteenth year of king Josiah, when this Passover of the LORD
was kept in Jerusalem.

24*† Further, Josiah did away with the
consultation of ghosts and spirits, with
the household gods, idols, and all the
other horrors to be seen in the land of
Judah and in Jerusalem, so that he
might carry out the stipulations of the
law written in the book that the priest
Hilkiah had found in the temple of the
LORD.

25* Before him there had been no king
who turned to the LORD as he did, with
his whole heart, his whole soul, and his
whole strength, in accord with the entire
law of Moses; nor could any after him
compare with him.

26 Yet, because of all the provocations
that Manasseh had given, the LORD did
not desist from his fiercely burning anger against Judah. 27* The LORD said:
"Even Judah will I put out of my sight
as I did Israel. I will reject this city, Jerusalem, which I chose, and the temple of
which I said, 'There shall my name be.' "

28* The rest of the acts of Josiah, with
all that he did, are written in the book
of the chronicles of the kings of Judah.
29* In his time Pharaoh Neco, king of
Egypt, went up toward the river Euphrates to the king of Assyria. King Josiah set out to confront him, but was
slain at Megiddo at the first encounter.
30† His servants brought his body on a
chariot from Megiddo to Jerusalem,
where they buried him in his own grave.
Then the people of the land took Jehoahaz, son of Josiah, anointed him, and
proclaimed him king to succeed his father.

Reign of Jehoahaz. 31* Jehoahaz was
twenty-three years old when he began
to reign, and he reigned three months
in Jerusalem. His mother, whose name
was Hamutal, daughter of Jeremiah,
was from Libnah. 32 He did evil in the
sight of the LORD, just as his forebears
had done. 33† Pharaoh Neco took him
prisoner at Riblah in the land of Hamath, thus ending his reign in Jerusalem. He imposed a fine upon the land
of a hundred talents of silver and a talent
of gold. 34 Pharaoh Neco then appointed
Eliakim, son of Josiah, king in place of
his father Josiah; he changed his name

*

13: 1 Kgs 11, 7.
14: Dt 16, 21f; 1 Kgs 14, 23.
15: 1 Kgs 12, 31f; 13, 32.
18: 1 Kgs 13, 31.
19: 2 Chr 34, 6f.
21: Dt 16, 1-8; 2 Chr 35, 1ff.18f.
24: 21, 6; Gn 31, 19; Dt 18, 11; Jgs 18, 14.
25: Dt 6, 5.
27: 24, 2.
28: 2 Chr 35, 26f.
29: 2 Chr 35, 20-24.
31: 2 Chr 36, 2f.

†

23, 13: *Mount of Misconduct:* a paranomasia on "Mount of Olives" (in Hebrew *Maschit/mishcheh*) as suggested by the Targum. Cf Vulgate, "Mount of Offense." *Horror . . . idol:* in all three phrases here the Hebrew uses a pejorative designation meaning "abomination."

23, 18: *From Samaria:* more narrowly, from Bethel; cf 1 Kgs 13, 31f.

23, 24: *Household gods, idols:* teraphim. See note on Gn 31, 19.

23, 30.35: *People of the land:* in this period, the phrase referred to "landed gentry"; in later times it meant "the poor." Cf 24, 14.

23, 33: *A talent of gold:* some manuscripts of the Greek and Syriac texts have "ten talents."

to Jehoiakim. Jehoahaz he took away
with him to Egypt, where he died.
35 Jehoiakim gave the silver and gold to
Pharaoh, but taxed the land to raise the
amount Pharaoh demanded. He exacted
the silver and gold from the people of
the land, from each proportionately, to
pay Pharaoh Neco.
Reign of Jehoiakim. 36* Jehoiakim
was twenty-five years old when he be-
gan to reign, and he reigned eleven
years in Jerusalem. His mother's name
was Zebidah, daughter of Pedaiah, from
Rumah. 37 He did evil in the sight of the
LORD, just as his forebears had done.

CHAPTER 24

1* During his reign Nebuchadnezzar,
king of Babylon, moved against him,
and Jehoiakim became his vassal for
three years. Then Jehoiakim turned and
rebelled against him. 2* The LORD loosed
against him bands of Chaldeans, Ara-
means, Moabites, and Ammonites; he
loosed them against Judah to destroy it,
as the LORD had threatened through his
servants the prophets. 3 This befell Ju-
dah because the LORD had stated that
he would inexorably put them out of his
sight for the sins Manasseh had commit-
ted in all that he did; 4* and especially
because of the innocent blood he shed,
with which he filled Jerusalem, the LORD
would not forgive.
5* The rest of the acts of Jehoiakim,
with all that he did, are written in the
book of the chronicles of the kings of Ju-
dah. 6 Jehoiakim rested with his ances-
tors, and his son Jehoiachin succeeded
him as king. 7 The king of Egypt did not
again leave his own land, for the king
of Babylon had taken all that belonged
to the king of Egypt from the Wadi of
Egypt to the Euphrates River.
Reign of Jehoiachin. 8† Jehoiachin
was eighteen years old when he began
to reign, and he reigned three months
in Jerusalem. His mother's name was
Nehushta, daughter of Elnathan of Je-
rusalem. 9 He did evil in the sight of the
LORD, just as his forebears had done.
10* At that time the officials of Nebu-
chadnezzar, king of Babylon, attacked
Jerusalem, and the city came under
siege. 11 Nebuchadnezzar, king of Baby-
lon, himself arrived at the city while his
servants were besieging it. 12 Then Je-
hoiachin, king of Judah, together with
his mother, his ministers, officers, and
functionaries, surrendered to the king of
Babylon, who, in the eighth year of his
reign, took him captive. 13* He carried
off all the treasures of the temple of the
LORD and those of the palace, and broke
up all the gold utensils that Solomon,
king of Israel, had provided in the tem-
ple of the LORD, as the LORD had fore-
told. 14 He deported all Jerusalem: all the
officers and men of the army, ten thou-
sand in number, and all the craftsmen
and smiths. None were left among the
people of the land except the poor. 15* He
deported Jehoiachin to Babylon, and
also led captive from Jerusalem to Bab-
ylon the king's mother and wives, his
functionaries, and the chief men of the
land. 16 The king of Babylon also led cap-
tive to Babylon all seven thousand men
of the army, and a thousand craftsmen
and smiths, all of them trained soldiers.
17 In place of Jehoiachin, the king of
Babylon appointed his uncle Mattaniah
king, and changed his name to Zede-
kiah.
Reign of Zedekiah. 18* Zedekiah was
twenty-one years old when he became
king, and he reigned eleven years in Je-
rusalem. His mother's name was Hamu-
tal, daughter of Jeremiah of Libnah.
19 He also did evil in the sight of the
LORD, just as Jehoiakim had done.
20* The LORD's anger befell Jerusalem
and Judah till he cast them out from his
presence. Thus Zedekiah rebelled
against the king of Babylon.

CHAPTER 25

1*† In the tenth month of the ninth
year of Zedekiah's reign, on the tenth
day of the month, Nebuchadnezzar, king
of Babylon, and his whole army ad-
vanced against Jerusalem, encamped
around it, and built siege walls on every
side. 2 The siege of the city continued un-
til the eleventh year of Zedekiah. 3 On
the ninth day of the fourth month, when
famine had gripped the city, and the
people had no more bread, 4 the city
walls were breached. Then the king and
all the soldiers left the city by night
through the gate between the two walls
which was near the king's garden. Since
the Chaldeans had the city surrounded,
they went in the direction of the Arabah.
5 But the Chaldean army pursued the
king and overtook him in the desert near
Jericho, abandoned by his whole army.
6 The king was therefore arrested and
brought to Riblah to the king of Babylon,
who pronounced sentence on him. 7 He
had Zedekiah's sons slain before his
eyes. Then he blinded Zedekiah, bound

*

36f: 2 Chr 36, 4f.
24, 1-5: 2 Chr 36, 6ff.
2: 23, 27.
4: 21, 16.
5: 2 Chr 36, 8.
10: 2 Chr 36, 10; Dn 1, 1f.
13: 20, 17; Is 39, 6.
15: Est A, 3; 2, 6.
18: 2 Chr 36, 9; Jer 37, 1f; 52, 1ff.
20: 22, 17; 23, 27.
25, 1-21: Jer 39, 1-10; 52, 4-28.

†

24, 8: *He reigned three months:* in the year 597 B.C.
25, 1-30: This chapter parallels Jer 39 and 52; see notes to those parts of Jeremiah.

him with fetters, and had him brought to Babylon.

8 On the seventh day of the fifth month (this was in the nineteenth year of Nebuchadnezzar, king of Babylon), Nebuzaradan, captain of the bodyguard, came to Jerusalem as the representative of the king of Babylon. 9* He burned the house of the LORD, the palace of the king, and all the houses of Jerusalem; every large building was destroyed by fire. 10 Then the Chaldean troops who were with the captain of the guard tore down the walls that surrounded Jerusalem.

11† Then Nebuzaradan, captain of the guard, led into exile the last of the people remaining in the city, and those who had deserted to the king of Babylon, and the last of the artisans. 12 But some of the country's poor, Nebuzaradan, captain of the guard, left behind as vinedressers and farmers.

13* The bronze pillars that belonged to the house of the LORD, and the wheeled carts and the bronze sea in the house of the LORD, the Chaldeans broke into pieces; they carried away the bronze to Babylon. 14* They took also the pots, the shovels, the snuffers, the bowls, the pans and all the bronze vessels used for service. 15 The fire-holders and the bowls which were of gold or silver the captain of the guard also carried off. 16 The weight in bronze of the two pillars, the bronze sea, and the wheeled carts, all of them furnishings which Solomon had made for the house of the LORD, was never calculated. 17* Each of the pillars was eighteen cubits high; a bronze capital five cubits high surmounted each pillar, and a network with pomegranates encircled the capital, all of bronze; and so for the other pillar, as regards the network.

18 The captain of the guard also took Seraiah the high priest, Zephaniah the second priest, and the three keepers of the entry. 19 And from the city he took one courtier, a commander of soldiers, five men in the personal service of the king who were still in the city, the scribe of the army commander, who mustered the people of the land, and sixty of the common people still remaining in the city. 20 The captain of the guard, Nebuzaradan, arrested these and brought them to the king of Babylon at Riblah; 21 the king had them struck down and put to death in Riblah, in the land of Hamath. Thus was Judah exiled from her land.

Governorship of Gedaliah. 22* As for the people whom he had allowed to remain in the land of Judah, Nebuchadnezzar, king of Babylon, appointed as their governor Gedaliah, son of Ahikam, son of Shaphan. 23 Hearing that the king of Babylon had appointed Gedaliah governor, all the army commanders with their men came to him at Mizpah: Ishmael, son of Nethaniah, Johanan, son of Kareah, Seraiah, son of Tanhumeth the Netophathite, and Jaazaniah, from Beth-maacah. 24 Gedaliah gave the commanders and their men his oath. "Do not be afraid of the Chaldean officials," he said to them. "Remain in the country and serve the king of Babylon, and all will be well with you."

25 But in the seventh month Ishmael, son of Nethaniah, son of Elishama, of royal descent, came with ten men, attacked Gedaliah and killed him, along with the Jews and Chaldeans who were in Mizpah with him. 26 Then all the people, great and small, left with the army commanders and went to Egypt for fear of the Chaldeans.

Release of Jehoiachin. 27* In the thirty-seventh year of the exile of Jehoiachin, king of Judah, on the twenty-seventh day of the twelfth month, Evil-merodach, king of Babylon, in the inaugural year of his own reign, raised up Jehoiachin, king of Judah, from prison. 28 He spoke kindly to him and gave him a throne higher than that of the other kings who were with him in Babylon. 29 Jehoiachin took off his prison garb and ate at the king's table as long as he lived. 30 The allowance granted him by the king was a perpetual allowance, in fixed daily amounts, for as long as he lived.

*

9: 2 Chr 36, 19; Ps 74, 7.
13: 16, 17; 1 Kgs 7, 15-39; 2 Chr 3, 15; 36, 18; Jer 27, 19.
14: 1 Kgs 7, 48ff.
17: 1 Kgs 7, 15; Jer 52, 21ff.
22-26: Jer 40, 5.7—41, 3.
27-30: Jer 52, 31-34.

†

25, 11: *Those who had deserted:* perhaps on the advice of Jeremiah; cf Jer 38, 2f.

The First Book of

CHRONICLES

Originally the two books of Chronicles formed, with the Books of Ezra and Nehemiah, a single historical work, uniform in style and basic ideas. The Greek title, paraleipomena, *means "things omitted, or passed over (in Samuel and Kings)." The Books of Chronicles, however, are more than a supplement to Samuel and Kings; a comparison of the two histories discloses striking differences in scope and purpose. The Books of Chronicles record in some detail the lengthy span from the reign of Saul to the return from the Exile. Unlike the exact science of history today, wherein factual accuracy and impartiality of judgment are the standards for estimating what is of permanent worth, ancient biblical history, with rare exceptions, was less concerned with reporting in precise detail all the facts of a situation than with explaining the meaning of those facts. Such history was primarily interpretative and, in the Old Testament, its purpose was to disclose the action of the living God in the affairs of men. For this reason we speak of it as "sacred history"; its writer's first concern was to bring out the divine or supernatural dimension in history.*

This is apparent when we examine the primary objective of the Chronicler in compiling his work. In view of the situation which confronted the Jewish people at this time (the end of the fifth century B.C.), the Chronicler realized that Israel's political greatness was a thing of the past. It would be a people under God, or nothing. Yet Israel's past held the key to her future. The Chronicler proposed to establish and defend the legitimate claims of the Davidic monarchy in Israel's history, and to underscore the place of Jerusalem and its divinely established temple worship as the center of religious life for the Jewish community of his day. If Judaism was to survive and prosper, it would have to heed the lessons of the past and devoutly serve Yahweh in the place where he had chosen to dwell, the temple of Jerusalem. From the Chronicler's point of view, David's reign was the ideal to which all subsequent rule in Judah must aspire.

The Chronicler was much more interested in David's religious and cultic influence than in his political power. There is little of royal messianism in his book. He apparently regarded as something of the distant past the prophet Zechariah's abortive attempt to have the Davidic kingdom reestablished in the time of Zerubbabel at the end of the sixth century B.C. (Zec 6, 9-15). He saw David's primary importance as deriving from the establishment of Jerusalem and its temple as the center of the true worship of the Lord. Furthermore, he presented David as the one who had authorized the elaborate ritual (which, in point of fact, only gradually evolved in the temple built by Zerubbabel) and who had also appointed Levites to supervise the liturgical services there.

There are good reasons for believing that originally the Books of Ezra and Nehemiah formed the last part of a single literary work that began with 1 and 2 Chronicles. Some authors even regard Ezra himself as having been the anonymous Chronicler. In any case, the Chronicler's Hebrew as well as his religious and political outlook points to c. 400 B.C. as the time of composition of this work.

The Chronicler used sources in writing his history. Besides the canonical Books of Genesis, Exodus, Numbers, Joshua and Ruth, and especially the Books of Samuel and Kings, he cites the titles of many other works no longer extant. "The books of the kings of Israel," or "the books of the kings of Israel and Judah," "the history of Samuel the seer," "the history of Nathan the prophet," "the history of Gad the seer," "the commentary on the Books of Kings," are some of the documents mentioned as historical sources.

In addition, the Chronicler's work contains early preexilic material not found in the Books of Kings. At one time scholars discounted the value of this material, but modern research has shown that, even though the Chronicler may have at times treated the material rather freely, he derived it from authentic and reliable sources.

The principal divisions of 1 Chronicles are as follows:
I: Genealogical Tables (1, 1—9, 34)
II: The History of David (9, 35—29, 30)

I: GENEALOGICAL TABLES

CHAPTER 1

From Adam to Abraham. 1*† Adam,
Seth, Enosh, 2* Kenan, Mahalalel,
Jared, 3* Enoch, Methuselah, Lamech,
4* Noah, Shem, Ham, and Japheth.
5* The descendants of Japheth were
Gomer, Magog, Madai, Javan, Tubal,
Meshech, and Tiras. 6 The descendants
of Gomer were Ashkenaz, Riphath, and
Togarmah. 7 The descendants of Javan
were Elishah, Tarshish, the Kittim, and
the Rodanim.
8* The descendants of Ham were
Cush, Mesraim, Put, and Canaan. 9 The
descendants of Cush were Seba, Havi-
lah, Sabta, Raama, and Sabteca. The
descendants of Raama were Sheba and
Dedan. 10 Cush became the father of
Nimrod, who was the first to be a con-
queror on the earth. 11* Mesraim be-
came the father of the Ludim, Anamim,
Lehabim, Naphtuhim, 12 Pathrusim,
Casluhim, and Caphtorim, from whom
the Philistines sprang. 13 Canaan be-
came the father of Sidon, his first-born,
and Heth, 14 and the Jebusite, the Amo-
rite, the Girgashite, 15 the Hivite, the
Arkite, the Sinite, 16 the Arvadite, the
Zemarite, and the Hamathite.
17* The descendants of Shem were
Elam, Asshur, Arpachshad, Lud, and
Aram. The descendants of Aram were
Uz, Hul, Gether, and Mash. 18 Ar-
pachshad became the father of Shelah,
and Shelah became the father of Eber.
19 Two sons were born to Eber; the first
was named Peleg (for in his time the
world was divided), and his brother was
Joktan. 20 Joktan became the father of
Almodad, Sheleph, Hazarmaveth,
Jerah, 21 Hadoram, Uzal, Diklah,
22 Ebal, Abimael, Sheba, 23 Ophir, Havi-
lah, and Jobab; all these were the sons
of Joktan.
24* Shem, Arpachshad, Shelah,
25 Eber, Peleg, Reu, 26 Serug, Nahor,
Terah, 27* Abram, who was Abraham.
From Abraham to Jacob. 28* The sons
of Abraham were Isaac and Ishmael.
29* These were their descendants:
Nebaioth, the first-born of Ishmael,
then Kedar, Adbeel, Mibsam,
30 Mishma, Dumah, Massa, Hadad,
Tema, 31 Jetur, Naphish, and Kedemah.
These were the descendants of Ishmael.
32* The descendants of Keturah, Abra-
ham's concubine: she bore Zimran, Jok-
shan, Medan, Midian, Ishbak, and
Shuah. The sons of Jokshan were Sheba
and Dedan. 33 The descendants of Mid-
ian were Ephah, Epher, Hanoch, Abida,
and Eldaah. All these were the descen-
dants of Keturah.
34* Abraham became the father of
Isaac. The sons of Isaac were Esau and
Israel.
35* The sons of Esau were Eliphaz,
Reuel, Jeush, Jalam, and Korah. 36 The
sons of Eliphaz were Teman, Omar, Ze-
phi, Gatam, Kenaz, [Timna,] and Ama-
lek. 37 The sons of Reuel were Nahath,
Zerah, Shammah, and Mizzah.
38*† The descendants of Seir were Lo-
tan, Shobal, Zibeon, Anah, Dishon, Ezer,
and Dishan. 39 The sons of Lotan were
Hori and Homam; Timna was the sister
of Lotan. 40 The sons of Shobal were
Alian, Manahath, Ebal, Shephi, and
Onam. The sons of Zibeon were Aiah and
Anah. 41 The sons of Anah: Dishon. The
sons of Dishon were Hemdan, Eshban,
Ithran, and Cheran. 42 The sons of Ezer
were Bilhan, Zaavan, and Jaakan. The
sons of Dishan were Uz and Aran.
43* The kings who reigned in the land
of Edom before they had Israelite kings
were the following: Bela, son of Beor, the
name of whose city was Dinhabah.
44* When Bela died, Jobab, son of Zerah,
from Bozrah, succeeded him. 45* When
Jobab died, Husham, from the land of
the Temanites, succeeded him. 46 Hu-

*

1, 1: 4, 25f; Gn 5, 3.6.9.
2ff: Gn 5, 9-32; 10, 2ff.
3: Gn 4, 25.
4: Gn 5, 32; 6, 10; 9, 18.
5ff: Gn 10, 2ff.
8f: Gn 10, 8.
11-16: Gn 10, 13-18.
17-23: Gn 10, 22-29; 11, 10-18.
24-27: Gn 11, 10-26; Lk 3, 34ff.
27: Gn 17, 5; Neh 9, 7.
28: Gn 16, 11.15; 21, 2f; Gal 4, 22f; Heb 11, 11.
29ff: Gn 25, 13-16.
32f: Gn 25, 1-4.
34: Gn 21, 2f; 25, 19.25f; 32, 28f; Mt 1, 2; Lk 3, 34.
35ff: Gn 36, 4f.10-13.15ff.
38-42: Gn 36, 20-28.
43-54: Gn 36, 31-43.
44: Is 34, 6; 63, 1; Jer 49, 13.22.
45: Gn 36, 11; Jb 2, 11; Jer 49, 7.20.

†

1, 1-9, 34: The Chronicler set as his task the retelling, from his particular viewpoint, of the story of God's people from the beginning to his own day. Since his primary interest was the history of David and the Davidic dynasty of Judah, he presents through mere genealogical lists a summary of what preceded the reign of Saul, David's predecessor in the kingdom. The sources for these genealogies are mostly the canonical Hebrew Scriptures that were already in their present form in his time. The cross references in this book indicate in each case the scriptural sources used.

1, 38: *Seir:* another name for *Esau* (v 35) or *Edom* (v 43).

sham died and Hadad, son of Bedad,
succeeded him. He overthrew the Midi-
anites on the Moabite plateau, and the
name of his city was Avith. 47 Hadad
died and Samlah of Masrekah suc-
ceeded him. 48 Samlah died and Shaul
from Rehoboth-han-nahar succeeded
him. 49 When Shaul died, Baal-hanan,
son of Achbor, succeeded him. 50 Baal-
hanan died and Hadad succeeded him.
The name of his city was Pai, and his
wife's name was Mehetabel. She was
the daughter of Matred, who was the
daughter of Mezahab. 51* After Hadad
died. . . .

These were the chiefs of Edom: the
chiefs of Timna, Aliah, Jetheth, 52 Ohol-
ibamah, Elah, Pinon, 53 Kenaz, Teman,
Mibzar, 54 Magdiel, and Iram were the
chiefs of Edom.

CHAPTER 2

1* These were the sons of Israel: Reu-
ben, Simeon, Levi, Judah, Issachar,
Zebulun, 2* Dan, Joseph, Benjamin,
Naphtali, Gad, and Asher.

Judah. 3*† The sons of Judah were:
Er, Onan, and Shelah; these three were
born to him of Bathshua, a Canaanite
woman. But Judah's first-born, Er, was
wicked in the sight of the LORD, so he
killed him. 4* Judah's daughter-in-law
Tamar bore him Perez and Zerah, so
that he had five sons in all.

5* The sons of Perez were Hezron and
Hamul. 6* The sons of Zerah were Zimri,
Ethan, Heman, Calcol, and Darda—five
in all. 7* The sons of Zimri: Carmi. The
sons of Carmi: Achar, who brought trou-
ble upon Israel by violating the ban.
8 The sons of Ethan: Azariah. 9*† The
sons born to Hezron were Jerahmeel,
Ram, and Chelubai.

10*† Ram became the father of Am-
minadab, and Amminadab became the
father of Nahshon, a prince of the Ju-
dahites. 11* Nahshon became the father
of Salmah. Salmah became the father
of Boaz. 12 Boaz became the father of
Obed. Obed became the father of Jesse.
13* Jesse became the father of Eliab, his
first-born, of Abinadab, the second son,
Shimea, the third, 14 Nethanel, the
fourth, Raddai, the fifth, 15 Ozem, the
sixth, and David, the seventh. 16* Their
sisters were Zeruiah and Abigail. Zeru-
iah had three sons: Abishai, Joab, and
Asahel. 17* Abigail bore Amasa, whose
father was Jether the Ishmaelite.

18*† By his wife Azubah, Caleb, son of
Hezron, became the father of a daugh-
ter, Jerioth. Her sons were Jesher, Sho-
bab, and Ardon. 19* When Azubah died,
Caleb married Ephrath, who bore him
Hur. 20* Hur became the father of Uri,
and Uri became the father of Bezalel.
21* Then Hezron had relations with the
daughter of Machir, the father of Gilead,
having married her when he was sixty
years old. She bore him Segub. 22* Segub
became the father of Jair, who pos-
sessed twenty-three cities in the land of
Gilead. 23* Geshur and Aram took from
them the villages of Jair, that is, Kenath
and its towns, sixty cities in all, which
had belonged to the sons of Machir, the
father of Gilead. 24* After the death of
Hezron, Caleb had relations with Ephra-
thah, the widow of his father Hezron,
and she bore him Ashhur, the father of
Tekoa.

25*† The sons of Jerahmeel, the first-
born of Hezron, were Ram, the first-
born, then Bunah, Oren, and Ozem, his
brothers. 26 Jerahmeel also had another
wife, Atarah by name, who was the
mother of Onam. 27 The sons of Ram, the
first-born of Jerahmeel, were Maaz, Ja-
min, and Eker. 28 The sons of Onam were
Shammai and Jada. The sons of Sham-
mai were Nadab and Abishur. 29 Abi-
shur's wife, who was named Abihail,
bore him Ahban and Molid. 30 The sons
of Nadab were Seled and Appaim. Seled
died without sons. 31* The sons of Ap-
paim: Ishi. The sons of Ishi: Sheshan.
The sons of Sheshan: Ahlai. 32 The sons
of Jada, the brother of Shammai, were

*

51-54: Gn 36, 40-43.
2, 1: Gn 29, 32-35; 30, 18.20; 35, 23.
2: Gn 30, 6.8.11.13. 24; 35, 18.24ff.
3: 4, 21; Gn 38, 1-5; 46, 12.
4: Gn 38, 7.13-30; 46, 12; Rv 4, 12.18; Mt 1, 3.
5: Gn 46, 12.
6: 1 Kgs 5, 11.
7: Jos 7, 1.18ff.24f; 22, 20.
9: Rv 4, 19; Mt 1, 3.
10: Rv 4, 19; Mt 1, 4.
11f: Nm 1, 7; Rv 4, 20f; Mt 1, 4f.
13: 2 Chr 11, 18.
13ff: 1 Sm 16, 6-13; 17, 13f.
16: 2 Sm 2, 18.
17: 2 Sm 17, 25; 19, 14; 20, 4-13.
18: 2, 24.
19: 2, 24.
20: Ex 24, 14; 31, 2; 35, 30; 2 Chr 1, 5.
21: Nm 26, 29; 27, 1; 32, 39; Jos 13, 31; Jgs 5, 14.
22: Nm 32, 41; 1 Kgs 4, 13.
23: Dt 3, 14; Jos 13, 30; Jgs 10, 4.
24: 2, 19; 2 Sm 14, 2; 2 Chr 11, 6.
25: 1 Sm 27, 10; 30, 29; Jb 32, 2.
31: 4, 20.

†

2, 3—4, 23: For two reasons, the Chronicler places the genealogy of the tribe of Judah before that of the other tribes, giving it also at greater length than the others: because of his interest in David and because in the Chronicler's time the people of God were almost exclusively Jews. Both David and the Jews were of the tribe of Judah.

2, 9: *Chelubai:* a variant form of the name *Caleb* (vv 18.42), distinct from *Chelub* of 4, 11.

2, 10-17: Immediate ancestors of David. A similar list is given in Ru 4, 19-22; each list, independent of the other, derives from a common source.

2, 18-24: Descendants of Caleb. In 4, 15, as is often the case in the Pentateuch (Nm 13, 6; 14, 6.30; 26, 65; etc.), Caleb is called *son of Jephunneh.* Here he is called *son of Hezron,* perhaps because the Calebites were reckoned as part of the clan of the Hezronites.

2, 25-41: The Jerahmeelites were a clan in the Negeb of Judah.

Jether and Jonathan. Jether died with-
out sons. 33 The sons of Jonathan were
Peleth and Zaza. These were the descen-
dants of Jerahmeel. 34 Sheshan, who had
no sons, only daughters, had an Egyp-
tian slave named Jarha. 35 Sheshan gave
his daughter in marriage to his slave
Jarha, and she bore him Attai. 36 Attai
became the father of Nathan. Nathan
became the father of Zabad. 37 Zabad be-
came the father of Ephlal. Ephlal be-
came the father of Obed. 38 Obed became
the father of Jehu. Jehu became the fa-
ther of Azariah. 39 Azariah became the
father of Helez. Helez became the father
of Eleasah. 40 Eleasah became the father
of Sismai. Sismai became the father of
Shallum. 41 Shallum became the father
of Jekamiah. Jekamiah became the fa-
ther of Elishama.

42† The descendants of Caleb, the
brother of Jerahmeel: [Mesha] his first-
born, who was the father of Ziph. Then
the sons of Mareshah, who was the fa-
ther of Hebron. 43 The sons of Hebron
were Korah, Tappuah, Rekem, and
Shema. 44 Shema became the father of
Raham, who was the father of Jorkeam.
Rekem became the father of Shammai.
45 The son of Shammai: Maon, who was
the father of Beth-zur. 46 Ephah, Caleb's
concubine, bore Haran, Moza, and Ga-
zez. Haran became the father of Gazez.
47 The sons of Jahdai were Regem, Jo-
tham, Geshan, Pelet, Ephah, and Sha-
aph. 48 Maacah, Caleb's concubine, bore
Sheber and Tirhanah. 49* She also bore
Shaaph, the father of Madmannah,
Sheva, the father of Machbenah, and the
father of Gibea. Achsah was Caleb's
daughter.

50† These were descendants of Caleb,
sons of Hur, the first-born of Ephrathah:
Shobal, the father of Kiriath-jearim,
51 Salma, the father of Bethlehem, and
Hareph, the father of Bethgader. 52 The
sons of Shobal, the father of Kiriath-
jearim, were Reaiah, half the Mana-
hathites, 53* and the clans of Kiriath-
jearim: the Ithrites, the Puthites, the
Shumathites, and the Mishraites. From
these the people of Zorah and the Esh-
taolites derived. 54 The descendants of
Salma were Bethlehem, the Netopha-
thites, Atroth-beth-Joab, half the Mana-
hathites, and the Zorites. 55* The clans
of the Sopherim dwelling in Jabez were
the Tirathites, the Shimeathites, and the
Sucathites. They were the Kenites, who
came from Hammath of the ancestor of
the Rechabites.

CHAPTER 3

1*† The following were the sons of
David who were born to him in Hebron:
the first-born, Amnon, by Ahinoam of
Jezreel; the second, Daniel, by Abigail
of Carmel; 2 the third, Absalom, son of
Maacah, who was the daughter of Tal-
mai, king of Geshur; the fourth, Adoni-
jah, son of Haggith; 3 the fifth, Sheph-
atiah, by Abital; the sixth, Ithream, by
his wife Eglah. 4* Six in all were born
to him in Hebron, where he reigned
seven years and six months. Then he
reigned thirty-three years in Jerusalem,
5*† where the following were born to
him: Shimea, Shobab, Nathan, Solo-
mon—four by Bathsheba, the daughter
of Ammiel; 6 Ibhar, Elishua, Eliphelet,
7 Nogah, Nepheg, Japhia, 8 Elishama,
Eliada, and Eliphelet—nine. 9* All these
were sons of David, in addition to other
sons by concubines; and Tamar was
their sister.

10*† The son of Solomon was Reho-
boam, whose son was Abijah, whose son
was Asa, whose son was Jehoshaphat,
11* whose son was Joram, whose son was
Ahaziah, whose son was Joash,
12* whose son was Amaziah, whose son
was Azariah, whose son was Jotham,
13* whose son was Ahaz, whose son was
Hezekiah, whose son was Manasseh,
14* whose son was Amon, whose son was
Josiah. 15*† The sons of Josiah were: the
first-born Johanan; the second, Je-
hoiakim; the third, Zedekiah; the fourth,
Shallum. 16* The sons of Jehoiakim
were: Jeconiah, his son; Zedekiah, his
son.

17*† The sons of Jeconiah the captive

---

*

49: Jos 15, 16; Jgs 1, 12.
53: Jgs 18, 2.
55: Nm 24, 21; Jgs 1, 16; 4, 11; 1 Sm 15, 6.
3, 1-4: 2 Sm 3, 2-5.
4: 2 Sm 2, 11; 5, 5.
5-8: 2 Sm 5, 14ff.
5: 2 Sm 5, 5.
9: 2 Sm 13, 1f.
10-17: Mt 1, 7-12.
10: 1 Kgs 11, 43; 14, 31; 15, 1.8.24; 2 Chr 9, 31; 12, 16; 13, 23; 17, 1.
11: 1 Kgs 22, 51; 2 Chr 21, 1; 22, 1; 24, 1.27.
12: 2 Kgs 12, 21; 14, 21; 15, 7; 2 Chr 25, 1; 26, 1.23; 27, 1.
13: 2 Kgs 15, 38; 16, 20; 20, 21; 2 Chr 28, 1.27; 32, 33.
14: 2 Kgs 21, 18.26; 2 Chr 33, 20.25.
15: 2 Kgs 23, 34; 24, 17; 2 Chr 36, 4.10.
16: 2 Kgs 24, 6.17; 2 Chr 36, 8.10.
17.19: Ezr 2, 2; 3, 2.8; 5, 2; Sir 49, 11; Hg 1, 1.12.14; Mt 1, 12f; Lk 3, 27.

---

†

2, 42-49: Another list, dating from preexilic times, of the Calebites, a clan that inhabited the south of Judah.

2, 50-55: The Hurites, a clan dwelling to the south and west of Jerusalem and related to the Calebites.

3, 1-9: David's sons.

3, 1: *Daniel:* called *Chileab* in 2 Sm 3, 3.

3, 5: *Shimea:* called *Shammua* in 2 Sm 5, 14. *Ammiel:* called *Eliam* in 2 Sm 11, 3.

3, 10-16: The kings of Judah from Solomon to the destruction of Jerusalem by the Babylonians.

3, 15: *Shallum:* the same as Jehoahaz, Josiah's successor; cf Jer 22, 11.

3, 17-24: The descendants of King *Jechoniah* up to the time of the Chronicler. If twenty-five years are allowed to each generation, the ten generations between *Jechoniah* and *Anani* (the last name on the list) would bring the birth of the latter to about 405 B.C.—an important item in establishing the approximate date of the Chronicler.

were: Shealtiel, 18† Malchiram, Pedaiah,
Shenazzar, Jekamiah, Shama, and Ned-
abiah. 19† The sons of Pedaiah were Ze-
rubbabel and Shimei. The sons of
Zerubbabel were Meshullam and Hana-
niah; Shelomith was their sister. 20 The
sons of Meshullam were Hashubah,
Ohel, Berechiah, Hasadiah, Jushab-
hesed—five. 21 The sons of Hananiah
were Pelatiah, Jeshaiah, Rephaiah, Ar-
nan, Obadiah, and Shecaniah. 22* The
sons of Shecaniah were Shemiah, Hat-
tush, Igal, Bariah, Neariah, Shaphat—
six. 23 The sons of Neariah were Elioe-
nai, Hizkiah, and Azrikam—three.
24 The sons of Elioenai were Hodaviah,
Eliashib, Pelaiah, Akkub, Johanan, Del-
aiah, and Anani—seven.

CHAPTER 4

1*† The descendants of Judah were:
Perez, Hezron, Carmi, Hur, and Shobal.
2 Reaiah, the son of Shobal, became the
father of Jahath, and Jahath became the
father of Ahumai and Lahad. These
were the clans of the Zorathites.

3 These were the descendants of Ha-
reph, the father of Etam: Jezreel, Ishma,
and Idbash; their sister was named Haz-
zelelponi. 4 Penuel was the father of Ge-
dor, and Ezer the father of Hushah.
These were the descendants of Hur, the
first-born of Ephrathah, the father of
Bethlehem.

5* Ashhur, the father of Tekoa, had
two wives, Helah and Naarah. 6 Naarah
bore him Ahuzzam, Hepher, the Teme-
nites and the Ahashtarites. These were
the descendants of Naarah. 7 The sons
of Helah were Zereth, Izhar, Ethnan,
and Koz. 8 Koz became the father of
Anub and Zobebah, as well as of the
clans of Aharhel, son of Harum. 9 Jabez
was the most distinguished of the broth-
ers. His mother had named him Jabez,
saying, "I bore him with pain." 10 Jabez
prayed to the God of Israel: "Oh, that
you may truly bless me and extend my
boundaries! Help me and make me free
of misfortune, without pain!" And God
granted his prayer.

11 Chelub, the brother of Shuhah, be-
came the father of Mehir, who was the
father of Eshton. 12 Eshton became the
father of Bethrapha, Paseah, and Tehin-
nah, the father of the city of Nahash.
These were the men of Recah.

13* The sons of Kenaz were Othniel
and Seraiah. The sons of Othniel were
Hathath and Meonothai; 14 Meonothai
became the father of Ophrah. Seraiah
became the father of Joab, the father of
Geharashim, so called because they
were craftsmen. 15* The sons of Caleb,
son of Jephunneh, were Ir, Elah, and
Naam. The sons of Elah were . . . and
Kenaz.

16 The sons of Jehallelel were Ziph, Zi-
phah, Tiria, and Asarel. 17* The sons of
Ezrah were Jether, Mered, Epher, and
Jalon. Jether became the father of
Miriam, Shammai, and Ishbah, the fa-
ther of Eshtemoa. [. . . . . .] 18 His
(Mered's) Egyptian wife bore Jared, the
father of Gedor, Heber, the father of
Soco, and Jekuthiel, the father of Za-
noah. These were the sons of Bithiah,
the daughter of Pharaoh, whom Mered
married. 19 The sons of his Jewish wife,
the sister of Naham, the father of Keilah,
were Shimon the Garmite and Ishi the
Maacathite. 20 The sons of Shimon were
Amnon, Rinnah, Benhanan, and Tilon.
The son of Ishi was Zoheth and the son
of Zoheth. . . .

21* The descendants of Shelah, son of
Judah, were: Er, the father of Lecah;
Laadah, the father of Mareshah; the
clans of the linen weavers' guild in
Bethashbea; 22 Jokim; the men of
Cozeba; and Joash and Saraph, who held
property in Moab, but returned to Beth-
lehem. [These are events of old.] 23 They
were potters and inhabitants of Netaim
and Gederah, where they lived in the
king's service.

Simeon. 24* The sons of Simeon were
Nemuel, Jamin, Jachin, Zerah, and
Shaul, 25 whose son was Shallum, whose
son was Mibsam, whose son was
Mishma. 26 The descendants of Mishma
were his son Hammuel, whose son was
Zaccur, whose son was Shimei. 27 Shimei
had sixteen sons and six daughters.
His brothers, however, did not have
many sons, and as a result all their
clans did not equal the number of the
Judahites.

28* They dwelt in Beer-sheba, Mola-
dah, Hazar-shual, 29 Bilhah, Ezem, To-
lad, 30 Bethuel, Hormah, Ziklag, 31 Beth-
marcaboth, Hazar-susim, Bethbiri, and
Shaaraim. Until David came to reign,
these were their cities 32 and their vil-
lages. Etam, also, and Ain, Rimmon, To-

*

22: Neh 3, 29.
4, 1: 2, 4f.7.9.50; Gn 38, 29; 46, 12; Mt 1, 3.
5: 2, 24.
13: Jos 15, 17; Jgs 1, 13; 3, 9.11.
15: Nm 13, 6; 14, 6; 32, 12; Jos 14, 6.14.
17: 1 Sm 30, 28.
21: 2, 3; Gn 38, 5; 46, 12; Nm 26, 20.
24: Gn 46, 10; Ex 6, 15; Nm 26, 12f.
28-32: Jos 19, 2-8.

†

3, 18: *Shenazzar:* presumably the same as *Sheshbazzar* of Ezr 1, 8.11; 5, 14ff, the prince of Judah who was the first Jewish governor of Judah after the exile. Both forms of the name probably go back to the Babylonian name Sin-ab-ussar signifying, "O [god] Sin, protect [our] father!"

3, 19: *Zerubbabel:* here called the son of *Pedaiah,* though elsewhere (Hg 1, 12.14; 2, 2.23; Ezr 3, 2.8; 5, 2; Neh 12, 1) called *son of Shealtiel.* The latter term may merely mean that Zerubbabel succeeded Shealtiel as head of the house of David.

4, 1-43: The southern tribes.

chen, and Ashan—five cities, 33 together
with all their outlying villages as far as
Baal. Here is where they dwelt, and so
it was inscribed of them in their family
records.
34 Meshobab, Jamlech, Joshah, son of
Amaziah, 35 Joel, Jehu, son of Joshibiah,
son of Seraiah, son of Asiel, 36 Elioenai,
Jaakobath, Jeshohaiah, Asaiah, Adiel,
Jesimiel, Benaiah, 37 Ziza, son of Shiphi,
son of Allon, son of Jedaiah, son of
Shimri, son of Shemaiah—38* these just
named were princes in their clans, and
their ancestral houses spread out to such
an extent 39† that they went to the ap-
proaches of Gedor, east of the valley,
seeking pasture for their flocks. 40 They
found abundant and good pastures, and
the land was spacious, quiet, and peace-
ful. 41* They who have just been listed
by name set out during the reign of
Hezekiah, king of Judah, and attacked
the tents of Ham (for Hamites dwelt
there formerly) and also the Meunites
who were there. They pronounced
against them the ban that is still in force
and dwelt in their place because they
found pasture there for their flocks.
42 Five hundred of them (the Simeon-
ites) went to Mount Seir under the lead-
ership of Pelatiah, Neariah, Rephaiah,
and Uzziel, sons of Ishi. 43* They at-
tacked the surviving Amalekites who
had escaped, and have resided there to
the present day.

CHAPTER 5

Reuben. 1*† The sons of Reuben, the
first-born of Israel. (He was indeed the
first-born, but because he disgraced the
couch of his father his birthright was
given to the sons of Joseph, son of Is-
rael, so that he is not listed in the fam-
ily records according to birthright.
2* Judah, in fact, became powerful
among his brothers, so that the ruler
came from him, though the birthright
had been Joseph's.) 3* The sons of Reu-
ben, the first-born of Israel, were Ha-
noch, Pallu, Hezron, and Carmi. 4 His
son was Joel, whose son was Shemaiah,
whose son was Gog, whose son was
Shimei, 5 whose son was Micah, whose
son was Reaiah, whose son was Baal,
6* whose son was Beerah, whom Tig-
lath-pileser, the king of Assyria, took
into exile; he was a prince of the Reuben-
ites. 7 His brothers who belonged to his
clans, when they were listed in the fam-
ily records according to their descen-
dants, were: Jeiel, the chief, and
Zechariah, 8* and Bela, son of Azaz, son
of Shema, son of Joel. The Reubenites
lived in Aroer and as far as Nebo and
Baal-meon; 9* toward the east they
dwelt as far as the desert which extends
from the Euphrates River, for they had
much livestock in the land of Gilead.
10* During the reign of Saul they waged
war with the Hagrites, and when they
had defeated them they occupied their
tents throughout the region east of Gil-
ead.
Gad. 11* The Gadites lived alongside
them in the land of Bashan as far as
Salecah. 12* Joel was chief, Shapham
was second in command, and Janai was
judge in Bashan. 13 Their brothers, cor-
responding to their ancestral houses,
were: Michael, Meshullam, Sheba, Jorai,
Jacan, Zia, and Eber—seven. 14 These
were the sons of Abihail, son of Huri,
son of Jaroah, son of Gilead, son of Mi-
chael, son of Jeshishai, son of Jahdo, son
of Buz. 15 Ahi, son of Abdiel, son of Guni,
was the head of their ancestral houses.
16 They dwelt in Gilead, in Bashan and
its towns, and in all the pasture lands
of Sirion to the borders. 17 All were listed
in the family records in the time of Jo-
tham, king of Judah, and of Jeroboam,
king of Israel.
18 The Reubenites, Gadites, and half-
tribe of Manasseh were warriors, men
who bore shield and sword and who
drew the bow, trained in warfare—forty-
four thousand seven hundred and sixty
men fit for military service. 19* When
they waged war against the Hagrites
and against Jetur, Naphish, and Nodab,
20* they received help so that they mas-
tered the Hagrites and all who were with
them. For during the battle they called
on God, and he heard them because they
had put their trust in him. 21 Along with
one hundred thousand men they also
captured their livestock: fifty thousand
camels, two hundred fifty thousand
sheep, and two thousand asses. 22* Many
had fallen in battle, for victory is from
God; and they took over their dwelling
place until the time of the exile.
East Manasseh. 23 The numerous
members of the half-tribe of Manasseh
lived in the land of Bashan as far as
Baal-hermon, Senir, and Mount Her-
mon. 24 The following were the heads of
their ancestral houses: Epher, Ishi,

*

38: Nm 1, 2.
41: 2 Kgs 18, 1f; 2 Chr 29, 1.
43: Ex 17, 8.14; Dt 25, 17ff; 1 Sm 14, 48; 15, 3.7f; 2 Sm 8, 12.
5, 1: Gn 35, 22; 48, 5.15-22; 49, 3f; Dt 33, 6.
2: 28, 4; Gn 49, 8ff.
3: Gn 46, 9; Ex 6, 14; Nm 26, 5f.
6: 2 Kgs 15, 29.
8: Jos 13, 9.16f; Nm 32, 3.38.
9: Jos 22, 9.
10: Ps 83, 6.
11: Jos 13, 11.24-28.
12: Gn 46, 16.
19: 1, 31; 5, 10; Gn 25, 15; Ps 83, 6.
20: Dt 33, 20f.
22: Nm 32, 39; Dt 3, 8ff; Jgs 3, 3.

†

4, 39: *Gedor:* in the Greek, Gerar, no doubt correct.
5, 1-26: The Transjordan tribes.

Eliel, Azriel, Jeremiah, Hodaviah, and
Jahdiel—men who were warriors, fa-
mous men, and heads over their ances-
tral houses.
25* However, they offended the God of
their fathers by lusting after the gods
of the natives of the land, whom God had
cleared out of their way. 26*† Therefore
the God of Israel incited against them
the anger of Pul, king of Assyria, and
of Tiglath-pileser, king of Assyria, who
deported the Reubenites, the Gadites,
and the half-tribe of Manasseh and
brought them to Halah, Habor, and
Hara, and to the river Gozan, where they
have remained to this day.
Levi. 27*† The sons of Levi were Ger-
shon, Kohath, and Merari. 28* The sons
of Kohath were Amram, Izhar, Hebron,
and Uzziel. 29* The children of Amram
were Aaron, Moses, and Miriam. The
sons of Aaron were Nadab, Abihu, Elea-
zar, and Ithamar. 30† Eleazar became
the father of Phinehas. Phinehas be-
came the father of Abishua. 31 Abishua
became the father of Bukki. Bukki be-
came the father of Uzzi. 32 Uzzi became
the father of Zerahiah. Zerahiah became
the father of Meraioth. 33 Meraioth be-
came the father of Amariah. Amariah
became the father of Ahitub. 34 Ahitub
became the father of Zadok. Zadok be-
came the father of Ahimaaz. 35 Ahimaaz
became the father of Azariah. Azariah
became the father of Johanan. 36 Jo-
hanan became the father of Azariah,
who served as priest in the temple Solo-
mon built in Jerusalem. 37 Azariah be-
came the father of Amariah. Amariah
became the father of Ahitub. 38 Ahitub
became the father of Zadok. Zadok be-
came the father of Shallum. 39 Shallum
became the father of Hilkiah. Hilkiah
became the father of Azariah. 40 Azariah
became the father of Seraiah. Seraiah
became the father of Jehozadak.
41 Jehozadak was one of those who went
into the exile which the LORD inflicted
on Judah and Jerusalem through Nebu-
chadnezzar.

CHAPTER 6

1* The sons of Levi were Gershon, Ko-
hath, and Merari. 2* The sons of Ger-
shon were named Libni and Shimei.
3* The sons of Kohath were Amram,
Izhar, Hebron, and Uzziel. 4* The sons
of Merari were Mahli and Mushi.
The following were the clans of Levi,
distributed according to their ancestors:
5 of Gershon: his son Libni, whose son
was Jahath, whose son was Zimmah,
6 whose son was Joah, whose son was
Iddo, whose son was Zerah, whose son
was Jetherai.
7 The descendants of Kohath were: his
son Amminadab, whose son was Korah,
whose son was Assir, 8 whose son was
Elkanah, whose son was Ebiasaph,
whose son was Assir, 9 whose son was
Tahath, whose son was Uriel, whose son
was Uzziah, whose son was Shaul. 10 The
sons of Elkanah were Amasai and Ahi-
moth, 11 whose son was Elkanah, whose
son was Zophai, whose son was Nahath,
12 whose son was Eliab, whose son was
Jeroham, whose son was Elkanah,
whose son was Samuel. 13 The sons of
Samuel were Joel, the first-born, and
Abijah, the second.
14* The descendants of Merari were
Mahli, whose son was Libni, whose son
was Shimei, whose son was Uzzah,
15 whose son was Shimea, whose son was
Haggiah, whose son was Asaiah.
16† The following were entrusted by
David with the choir services in the
LORD's house from the time when the
ark had obtained a permanent resting
place. 17 They served as singers before
the Dwelling of the meeting tent until
Solomon built the temple of the LORD in
Jerusalem, and they performed their
services in an order prescribed for them.
18 Those who so performed are the
following, together with their descen-
dants.
Among the Kohathites: Heman, the
chanter, son of Joel, son of Samuel,
19 son of Elkanah, son of Jeroham, son
of Eliel, son of Toah, 20 son of Zuth, son
of Elkanah, son of Mahath, son of
Amasi, 21 son of Elkanah, son of Joel, son
of Azariah, son of Zaphaniah, 22* son of
Tahath, son of Assir, son of Ebiasaph,
son of Korah, 23 son of Izhar, son of Ko-
hath, son of Levi, son of Israel.
24 His brother Asaph stood at his right
hand. Asaph was the son of Berechiah,
son of Shimea, 25 son of Michael, son of
Baaseiah, son of Malchijah, 26 son of

*

25: Ex 34, 14ff; 2 Kgs 17, 7.
26: 2 Kgs 15, 9.29; 17, 6.
27: 6, 1; 23, 6; Gn 46, 11; Ex 6, 16; Nm 26, 57.
28: 6, 3; Ex 6, 18.
29: Ex 6, 20; Nm 26, 59f.
6, 1: 5, 27; 23, 6; Gn 46, 11; Ex 6, 16; Nm 26, 57.
2: Ex 6, 17.
3: Ex 6, 18; Nm 3, 19; 26, 59.
4: 6, 14; Ex 6, 19; Nm 3, 20; 26, 58.
14: 6, 4; Ex 6, 19; Nm 3, 20; 26, 58.
22: Ex 6, 24.

†

5, 26: *Pul:* the name which the Assyrian king *Tiglath-pileser* III (745-727 B.C.) took as king of Babylon.

5, 27—6, 66: The tribe of Levi. The list gives special prominence to Levi's son *Kohath,* from whom were descended both the Aaronite priests (5, 28-41) and the leading group of temple singers (6, 18-23).

5, 30-41: The line of preexilic priests. The list seems to be confused in vv 36ff, which repeat the names, mostly in inverse order, that occur in vv 34f. A similar but shorter list is given, with variations, in Ezr 7, 1-5.

6, 16-32: The origin of the *choir services* performed by the levitical families in the postexilic temple at the time of the Chronicler is here attributed to David, somewhat as all the laws in the Pentateuch are attributed to Moses.

Ethni, son of Zerah, son of Adaiah,
27* son of Ethan, son of Zimmah, son of
Shimei, 28 son of Jahath, son of Gershon,
son of Levi.
29 Their brothers, the Merarites, stood
at the left: Ethan, son of Kishi, son of
Abdi, son of Malluch, 30 son of Hasha-
biah, son of Amaziah, son of Hilkiah,
31 son of Amzi, son of Bani, son of
Shemer, 32* son of Mahli, son of Mushi,
son of Merari, son of Levi.
33* Their brother Levites were ap-
pointed to all the other services of the
Dwelling of the house of God.
34* However, it was Aaron and his de-
scendants who burnt the offerings on the
altar of holocausts and on the altar of
incense; they alone had charge of the
holy of holies and of making atonement
for Israel, as Moses, the servant of God,
had ordained.
35 These were the descendants of
Aaron: his son Eleazar, whose son was
Phinehas, whose son was Abishua,
36 whose son was Bukki, whose son was
Uzzi, whose son was Zerahiah, 37 whose
son was Meraioth, whose son was Ama-
riah, whose son was Ahitub, 38 whose son
was Zadok, whose son was Ahimaaz.
39† The following were their dwelling
places to which their encampment was
limited. To the descendants of Aaron
who belonged to clan of the Kohathites,
since the first lot fell to them, 40 was as-
signed Hebron with its adjacent pasture
lands in the land of Judah, 41 although
the open country and the villages be-
longing to the city had been given to
Caleb, the son of Jephunneh. 42 There
were assigned to the descendants of
Aaron: Hebron a city of asylum, Libnah
with its pasture lands, Jattir with its pas-
ture lands, Eshtemoa with its pasture
lands, 43 Holon with its pasture lands,
Debir with its pasture lands, 44 Ashan
with its pasture lands, Jetta with its pas-
ture lands, and Beth-shemesh with its
pasture lands. 45 Also from the tribe of
Benjamin: Gibeon with its pasture lands,
Geba with its pasture lands, Almon with
its pasture lands, Anathoth with its pas-
ture lands. In all, they had thirteen cities
with their pasture lands. 49 The Israelites
assigned these cities with their pasture
lands to the Levites, 50 designating them
by name and assigning them by lot from
the tribes of the Judahites, Simeonites,
and Benjaminites.
46 The other Kohathites obtained ten
cities by lot for their clans from the tribe
of Ephraim, from the tribe of Dan, and
from the half-tribe of Manasseh. 47 The
clans of the Gershonites obtained thir-
teen cities from the tribes of Issachar,
Asher, and Naphtali, and from the half-
tribe of Manasseh in Bashan. 48 The
clans of the Merarites obtained twelve
cities by lot from the tribes of Reuben,
Gad, and Zebulun.
51 The clans of the Kohathites obtained
cities by lot from the tribe of Ephraim.
52 They were assigned: Shechem in the
mountain region of Ephraim, a city of
asylum, with its pasture lands, Gezer
with its pasture lands, 53 Kibzaim with
its pasture lands, and Beth-horon with
its pasture lands. 54 From the tribe of
Dan: Elteke with its pasture lands, Gib-
bethon with its pasture lands, Aijalon
with its pasture lands, and Gath-rim-
mon with its pasture lands. 55 From the
half-tribe of Manasseh: Taanach with its
pasture lands and Ibleam with its pas-
ture lands. These belonged to the rest
of the Kohathite clan.
56 The clans of the Gershonites re-
ceived from the half-tribe of Manasseh:
Golan in Bashan with its pasture lands
and Ashtaroth with its pasture lands.
57 From the tribe of Issachar: Kedesh
with its pasture lands, Daberath with its
pasture lands, 58 Ramoth with its pasture
lands, and Engannim with its pasture
lands. 59 From the tribe of Asher: Mashal
with its pasture lands, Abdon with its
pasture lands, 60 Hilkath with its pasture
lands, and Rehob with its pasture lands.
61 From the tribe of Naphtali: Kedesh in
Galilee with its pasture lands, Hammon
with its pasture lands, and Kiriathaim
with its pasture lands.
62 The rest of the Merarites received
from the tribe of Zebulun: Jokneam with
its pasture lands, Kartah with its pasture
lands, Rimmon with its pasture lands,
and Tabor with its pasture lands.
63 Across the Jordan at Jericho [that is,
east of the Jordan] they received from
the tribe of Reuben: Bezer in the desert
with its pasture lands, Jahzah with its
pasture lands, 64 Kedemoth with its pas-
ture lands, and Mephaath with its pas-
ture lands. 65 From the tribe of Gad:
Ramoth in Gilead with its pasture lands,
Mahanaim with its pasture lands,
66 Heshbon with its pasture lands, and
Jazer with its pasture lands.

CHAPTER 7

Issachar. 1*† The sons of Issachar
were Tola, Puah, Jashub, and Shimron:
four. 2* The sons of Tola were Uzzi,
Rephaiah, Jeriel, Jahmai, Ibsam, and
Shemuel, warrior heads of the ancestral
houses of Tola. Their kindred numbered
twenty-two thousand six hundred in the

*

27: 6, 2.5.
32: Ex 6, 19; Nm 26, 58.
33: 15, 17.19; 16, 41f; 2 Chr 5, 12.
34: 16, 39f.
7, 1: Gn 46, 13.
2: Nm 26, 23f; Jgs 10, 1.

†

6, 39-66: Regarding the nature of the rights of Levites in the cities assigned to them, see note on Jos 21, 1.
7, 1-40: The northern tribes.

time of David. 3 The sons of Uzzi: Izarahiah. The sons of Izarahiah were Michael, Obadiah, Joel, and Isshiah. All five of these were chiefs. 4 Their kindred, by ancestral houses, numbered thirty-six thousand men in organized military troops, since they had more wives and sons 5 than their fellow tribesmen. In all the clans of Issachar there was a total of eighty-seven thousand warriors in their family records.

Benjamin. 6* The sons of Benjamin were Bela, Becher, and Jediael—three. 7 The sons of Bela were Ezbon, Uzzi, Uzziel, Jerimoth, and Iri—five. They were heads of their ancestral houses and warriors. Their family records listed twenty-two thousand and thirty-four. 8* The sons of Becher were Zemirah, Joash, Eliezer, Elioenai, Omri, Jeremoth, Abijah, Anathoth, and Alemeth—all these were sons of Becher. 9 Their family records listed twenty thousand two hundred of their kindred who were heads of their ancestral houses and warriors. 10 The sons of Jediael: Bilhan. The sons of Bilhan were Jeush, Benjamin, Ehud, Chenaanah, Zethan, Tarshish, and Ahishahar. 11* All these were descendants of Jediael, heads of ancestral houses and warriors. They numbered seventeen thousand two hundred men fit for military service . . . Shupham and Hupham.

Dan, Naphtali and Manasseh. 12* The sons of Dan: Hushim. 13 The sons of Naphtali were Jahziel, Guni, Jezer, and Shallum. These were descendants of Bilhah. 14*The sons of Manasseh, whom his Aramean concubine bore: she bore Machir, the father of Gilead. 15* Machir took a wife whose name was Maacah; his sister's name was Molecheth. Manasseh's second son was named Zelophehad, but to Zelophehad only daughters were born. 16 Maacah, Machir's wife, bore a son whom she named Peresh. He had a brother named Sheresh, whose sons were Ulam and Rakem. 17 The sons of Ulam: Bedan. These were the descendants of Gilead, the son of Machir, the son of Manasseh. 18 His sister Molecheth bore Ishhod, Abiezer, and Mahlah. 19 The sons of Shemida were Ahian, Shechem, Likhi, and Aniam.

Ephraim. 20* The sons of Ephraim: Shuthelah, whose son was Bered, whose son was Tahath, whose son was Eleadah, whose son was Tahath, 21 whose son was Zabad. Ephraim's son Shuthelah, and Ezer and Elead, who were born in the land, were slain by the inhabitants of Gath because they had gone down to take away their livestock. 22 Their father Ephraim mourned a long time, but after his kinsmen had come and comforted him, 23* he visited his wife, who conceived and bore a son whom he named Beriah, since evil had befallen his house. 24 He had a daughter, Sheerah, who built lower and upper Beth-horon and Uzzen-sheerah. 25 Zabad's son was Rephah, whose son was Resheph, whose son was Telah, whose son was Tahan, 26* whose son was Ladan, whose son was Ammihud, whose son was Elishama, 27 whose son was Nun, whose son was Joshua.

28* Their property and their dwellings were in Bethel and its towns, Naaran to the east, Gezer and its towns to the west, and also Shechem and its towns as far as Ayyah and its towns. 29* Manasseh, however, had possession of Beth-shean and its towns, Taanach and its towns, Megiddo and its towns, and Dor and its towns. In these dwelt the descendants of Joseph, the son of Israel.

Asher. 30* The sons of Asher were Imnah, Iishvah, Ishvi, and Beriah; their sister was Serah. 31 Beriah's sons were Heber and Malchiel, who was the father of Birzaith. 32 Heber became the father of Japhlet, Shomer, Hotham, and their sister Shua. 33 The sons of Japhlet were Pasach, Bimhal, and Ashvath; these were the sons of Japhlet. 34 The sons of Shomer were Ahi, Rohgah, Jehubbah, and Aram. 35 The sons of his brother Hotham were Zophah, Imna, Shelesh, and Amal. 36 The sons of Zophah were Suah, Harnepher, Shual, Beri, Imrah, 37 Bezer, Hod, Shamma, Shilshah, Ithran, and Beera. 38 The sons of Jether were Jephunneh, Pispa, and Ara. 39 The sons of Ulla were Arah, Hanniel, and Rizia. 40 All these were descendants of Asher, heads of ancestral houses, distinguished men, warriors, and chiefs among the princes. Their family records numbered twenty-six thousand men fit for military service.

CHAPTER 8

Benjamin. 1*† Benjamin became the father of Bela, his first-born, Ashbel, the second son, Aharah, the third, 2 Nohah, the fourth, and Rapha, the fifth. 3 The sons of Bela were Addar and Gera, the father of Ehud. 4* The sons of Ehud were Abishua, Naaman, Ahoah, 5 Gera, She-

*

6: 7, 6; Gn 46, 21; Nm 26, 38.
8: 7, 8.
11: Nm 26, 39.
12f: Gn 46, 24; Nm 26, 48f.
14-19: Nm 26, 29-32.
14: Nm 26, 29; Jos 17, 1.
15: Nm 26, 33; Jos 17, 3.
20: Nm 26, 35.
23: 8, 13.
26: Nm 1, 10; 2, 18; 7, 48; 10, 22.
28: Gn 12, 8; 1 Kgs 9, 16.
29: Jos 17, 11.
30: Gn 46, 17; Nm 26, 44ff.
8, 1: 7, 6; Gn 46, 21; Nm 26, 38ff.
4: Jgs 3, 15.

†

8, 1-40: A second, variant list of the Benjaminites, with special prominence given to Saul's family (vv 33-40).

phuphan, and Huram. 6 These were the
sons of Ehud, family heads over those
who dwelt in Geba and were deported
to Manahath. 7 Also Naaman, Ahijah,
and Gera. The last, who led them into
exile, became the father of Uzza and
Ahihud. 8 Shaharaim became a father
on the Moabite plateau after he had put
away his wives Hushim and Baara. 9 By
his wife Hodesh he became the father
of Jobab, Zibia, Mesha, Malcam, 10 Jeuz,
Sachia, and Mirmah. These were his
sons, family heads. 11 By Hushim he be-
came the father of Abitub and Elpaal.
12* The sons of Elpaal were Eber, Mi-
sham, Shemed, who built Ono and Lod
with its nearby towns, 13 Beriah, and
Shema. They were family heads of those
who dwelt in Aijalon, and they put the
inhabitants of Gath to flight. 14 Their
brethren were Elpaal, Shashak, and
Jeremoth. 15 Zebadiah, Arad, Eder,
16 Michael, Ishpah, and Joha were the
sons of Beriah. 17 Zebadiah, Meshullam,
Hizki, Heber, 18 Ishmerai, Izliah, and Jo-
bab were the sons of Elpaal. 19 Jakim,
Zichri, Zabdi, 20 Elienai, Zillethai, Eliel,
21 Adaiah, Beraiah, and Shimrath were
the sons of Shimei. 22 Ishpan, Eber, Eliel,
23 Abdon, Zichri, Hanan, 24 Hananiah,
Elam, Anthothijah, 25 Iphdeiah, and
Penuel were the sons of Shashak.
26 Shamsherai, Shehariah, Athaliah,
27 Jaareshiah, Elijah, and Zichri were
the sons of Jeroham. 28 These were fam-
ily heads over their kindred, chiefs who
dwelt in Jerusalem.

29* In Gibeon dwelt Jeiel, the founder
of Gibeon, whose wife's name was Maa-
cah; 30 also his first-born son, Abdon,
and Zur, Kish, Baal, Ner, Nadab,
31 Gedor, Ahio, Zecher, and Mikloth.
32 Mikloth became the father of Shim-
eah. These, too, dwelt with their relatives
in Jerusalem, opposite their fellow
tribesmen. 33* Ner became the father of
Kish, and Kish became the father of
Saul. Saul became the father of Jona-
than, Malchishua, Abinadab, and Esh-
baal. 34* The son of Jonathan was
Meribbaal, and Meribbaal became the
father of Micah. 35 The sons of Micah
were Pithon, Melech, Tarea, and Ahaz.
36* Ahaz became the father of Jehoad-
dah, and Jehoaddah became the father
of Alemeth, Azmaveth, and Zimri. Zimri
became the father of Moza. 37* Moza be-
came the father of Binea, whose son was
Raphah, whose son was Eleasah, whose
son was Azel. 38 Azel had six sons, whose
names were Azrikam, his first-born,
Ishmael, Sheariah, Azariah, Obadiah,
and Hanan; all these were the sons of
Azel. 39 The sons of Eshek, his brother,
were Ulam, his first-born, Jeush, the
second son, and Eliphelet, the third.
40 The sons of Ulam were combat ar-
chers, and many were their sons and
grandsons: one hundred and fifty. All
these were the descendants of Benja-
min.

CHAPTER 9

1* Thus all Israel was inscribed in its
family records which are recorded in
the book of the kings of Israel.

Now Judah had been carried in cap-
tivity to Babylon because of its rebellion.
2*† The first to settle again in their cities
and dwell there were certain lay Israel-
ites, the priests, the Levites, and the
temple slaves.

Jerusalemites. 3 In Jerusalem lived
Judahites and Benjaminites; also
Ephraimites and Manassehites.
4 Among the Judahites was Uthai, son
of Ammihud, son of Omri, son of Imri,
son of Bani, one of the descendants of
Perez, son of Judah. 5 Among the She-
lanites were Asaiah, the first-born, and
his sons. 6 Among the Zerahites were
Jeuel and six hundred and ninety of
their brethren. 7 Among the Benjamin-
ites were Sallu, son of Meshullam, son
of Hodaviah, son of Hassenuah;
8 Ibneiah, son of Jeroham; Elah, son of
Uzzi, son of Michri; Meshullam, son of
Shephatiah, son of Reuel, son of Ibnijah.
9 Their kindred of various families were
nine hundred and fifty-six. All those
named were heads of their ancestral
houses.

10 Among the priests were Jedaiah; Je-
hoiarib; Jachin; 11 Azariah, son of Hil-
kiah, son of Meshullam, son of Zadok,
son of Meraioth, son of Ahitub, the ruler
of the house of God; 12 Adaiah, son of
Jeroham, son of Pashhur, son of Mal-
chijah; Maasai, son of Adiel, son of
Jahzerah, son of Meshullam, son of
Meshillemith, son of Immer. 13 Their
brethren, heads of their ancestral
houses, were one thousand seven hun-
dred and sixty, valiant for the work of
the service of the house of God.

14 Among the Levites were Shemaiah,
son of Hasshub, son of Azrikam, son of
Hashabiah, one of the descendants of
Merari; 15 Bakbakkar; Heresh; Galal;
Mattaniah, son of Mica, son of Zichri,
a descendant of Asaph; 16 Obadiah, son
of Shemaiah, son of Galal, a descendant
of Jeduthun; and Berechiah, son of Asa,

*

12: Neh 11, 35.
29-32: 9, 35-38.
33-38: 9, 39-44.
33: 10, 2; 1 Sm 9, 1; 14, 49.51; 31, 2.
34: 2 Sm 4, 4; 9, 6.10.12.
36: 9, 42.
37: 9, 43.
9, 1: 2 Chr 16, 11; 20, 34; 25, 26; 27, 7; 33, 18; 36, 8.
2-22: Neh 11, 3-19.
2: Ezr 2, 70; 7, 7; Neh 11, 3.

†

9, 2-34: The inhabitants of Jerusalem after the exile. A similar list, with many variants in the names, is given in Neh 11, 3-24.

son of Elkanah, whose family lived in the villages of the Netophathites.

17 The gatekeepers were Shallum, Akkub, Talmon, Ahiman, and their brethren; Shallum was the chief. 18 Previously they had stood guard at the king's gate on the east side; now they became gatekeepers for the encampments of the Levites. 19 Shallum, son of Kore, son of Ebiasaph, a descendant of Korah, and his brethren of the same ancestral house of the Korahites had as their assigned task the guarding of the threshold of the tent, just as their fathers had guarded the entrance to the encampment of the LORD. 20* Phinehas, son of Eleazar, had been their chief in times past—the LORD be with him! 21* Zechariah, son of Meshelemiah, guarded the gate of the meeting tent. 22 In all, those who were chosen for gatekeepers at the threshold were two hundred and twelve. They were inscribed in the family records of their villages. David and Samuel the seer had established them in their position of trust. 23 Thus they and their sons kept guard over the gates of the house of the LORD, the house which was then a tent. 24* The gatekeepers were stationed at the four sides, to the east, the west, the north, and the south. 25* Their kinsmen who lived in their own villages took turns in assisting them for seven-day periods, 26 while the four chief gatekeepers were on constant duty. These were the Levites who also had charge of the chambers and treasures of the house of God. 27 At night they lodged about the house of God, for it was in their charge and they had the duty of opening it each morning.

28 Some of them had charge of the liturgical equipment, tallying it as it was brought in and taken out. 29 Others were appointed to take care of the utensils and all the sacred vessels, as well as the fine flour, the wine, the oil, the frankincense, and the spices. 30* It was the sons of priests, however, who mixed the spiced ointments. 31* Mattithiah, one of the Levites, the first-born of Shallum the Koreite, was entrusted with preparing the cakes. 32* Benaiah the Kohathite, one of their brethren, was in charge of setting out the showbread each sabbath.

33 These were the chanters and the gatekeepers, family heads over the Levites. They stayed in the chambers when free of duty, for day and night they had to be ready for service. 34 These were the levitical family heads over their kindred, chiefs who dwelt in Jerusalem.

II: THE HISTORY OF DAVID

Genealogy of Saul. 35* In Gibeon dwelt Jeiel, the founder of Gibeon, whose wife's name was Maacah. 36 His first-born son was Abdon; then came Zur, Kish, Baal, Ner, Nadab, 37 Gedor, Ahio, Zechariah, and Mikloth. 38 Mikloth became the father of Shimeam. These, too, with their brethren, dwelt opposite their brethren in Jerusalem. 39 Ner became the father of Kish, and Kish became the father of Saul. Saul became the father of Jonathan, Malchishua, Abinadab, and Eshbaal. 40 The son of Jonathan was Meribbaal, and Meribbaal became the father of Micah. 41 The sons of Micah were Pithon, Melech, Tahrea, and Ahaz. 42 Ahaz became the father of Jehoaddah, and Jehoaddah became the father of Alemeth, Azmaveth, and Zimri. Zimri became the father of Moza. 43 Moza became the father of Binea, whose son was Rephaiah, whose son was Eleasah, whose son was Azel. 44 Azel had six sons, whose names were Azrikam, his first-born, Ishmael, Sheariah, Azariah, Obadiah, and Hanan; these were the sons of Azel.

CHAPTER 10

His Death and Burial. 1* Now the Philistines were at war with Israel; the Israelites fled before the Philistines, and a number of them fell, slain on Mount Gilboa. 2 The Philistines pressed hard after Saul and his sons. When the Philistines had killed Jonathan, Abinadab, and Malchishua, sons of Saul, 3 the whole fury of the battle descended upon Saul. Then the archers found him, and wounded him with their arrows.

4 Saul said to his armor-bearer, "Draw your sword and thrust me through with it, that these uncircumcised may not come and maltreat me." But the armor-bearer, in great fear, refused. So Saul took his own sword and fell on it; 5 and seeing him dead, the armor-bearer also fell on his sword and died. 6 Thus, with Saul and his three sons, his whole house died at one time. 7 When all the Israelites who were in the valley saw that Saul and his sons had died in the rout, they left their cities and fled; thereupon the Philistines came and occupied them.

8 On the following day, when the Philistines came to strip the slain, they found Saul and his sons where they had fallen on Mount Gilboa. 9 They stripped him, cut off his head, and took his armor; these they sent throughout the land of the Philistines to convey the good news to their idols and their people. 10 His armor they put in the house of their gods,

*

20: Ex 6, 25; Nm 25, 7.11; Jgs 20, 28.
21: 26, 2.14.
24: 26, 13.
25: 2 Chr 23, 4f.
30: Ex 30, 22-33.
31f: 23, 29; Lv 2, 1ff; 6, 13ff; 7, 11.
32: Ex 25, 30; Lv 24, 5-8.
35-44: 8, 29-38.
10, 1-12: 1 Sm 31, 1-13.

but his skull they impaled on the temple
of Dagon.
11 When all the inhabitants of Jabesh-
gilead had heard what the Philistines
had done to Saul, 12* its warriors rose
to a man, recovered the bodies of Saul
and his sons, and brought them to Ja-
besh. They buried their bones under the
oak of Jabesh, and fasted seven days.
13*† Thus Saul died because of his re-
bellion against the LORD in disobeying
his command, and also because he
had sought counsel of a necromancer,
14* and had not rather inquired of the
LORD. Therefore the LORD slew him, and
transferred his kingdom to David, the
son of Jesse.

CHAPTER 11

David Is Made King. 1* Then all Israel
gathered about David in Hebron, and
they said: "Surely, we are of the same
bone and flesh as you. 2* Even formerly,
when Saul was still the king, it was you
who led Israel in all its battles. And now
the LORD, your God, has said to you,
'You shall shepherd my people Israel
and be ruler over them.' " 3* Then all the
elders of Israel came to the king at He-
bron, and there David made a covenant
with them in the presence of the LORD;
and they anointed him king over Israel,
in accordance with the word of the LORD
as revealed through Samuel.
Jerusalem Captured. 4* Then David
and all Israel went to Jerusalem, that
is, Jebus, where the natives of the land
were called Jebusites. 5 The inhabitants
of Jebus said to David, "You shall not
enter here." David nevertheless cap-
tured the fortress of Zion, which is the
City of David. 6* David said, "Whoever
strikes the Jebusites first shall be made
the chief commander." Joab, the son of
Zeruiah, was the first to go up; and so
he became chief. 7 David took up his res-
idence in the fortress, which thenceforth
was called the City of David. 8* He re-
built the city on all sides, from the Millo
all the way around, while Joab restored
the rest of the city. 9 David became more
and more powerful, for the LORD of hosts
was with him.
David's Warriors. 10* These were
David's chief warriors who, together
with all Israel, supported him in his
reign in order to make him true king,
even as the LORD had commanded con-
cerning Israel. 11† Here is the list of
David's warriors:
Ishbaal, the son of Hachamoni, chief
of the Three. He brandished his spear
against three hundred, whom he slew in
a single encounter.
12* Next to him Eleazar, the son of
Dodo the Ahohite, one of the Three war-
riors. 13* He was with David at Pas-
dammim, where the Philistines had
massed for battle. The plow-land was
fully planted with barley, but its defend-
ers were retreating before the Philis-
tines. 14 He made a stand on the sown
ground, kept it safe, and cut down the
Philistines. Thus the LORD brought
about a great victory.
15* Three of the Thirty chiefs went
down to the rock, to David, who was in
the cave of Adullam while the Philistines
were encamped in the valley of Reph-
aim. 16 David was then in the stronghold,
and a Philistine garrison was at Bethle-
hem. 17 David expressed a desire: "Oh,
that someone would give me a drink
from the cistern that is by the gate at
Bethlehem!" 18 Thereupon the Three
broke through the encampment of the
Philistines, drew water from the cistern
by the gate at Bethlehem, and carried
it back to David. But David refused to
drink it. Instead, he poured it out as a
libation to the LORD, 19 saying, "God for-
bid that I should do such a thing! Could
I drink the blood of these men who
risked their lives?" For at the risk of
their lives they brought it; and so he re-
fused to drink it. Such deeds as these
the Three warriors performed.
20*† Abishai, the brother of Joab. He
was the chief of the Thirty; he bran-
dished his spear against three hundred,
and slew them. Thus he had a reputation
like that of the Three. 21 He was twice
as famous as any of the Thirty and be-
came their commander, but he did not
attain to the Three.
22 Benaiah, son of Jehoiada, a valiant
man of mighty deeds, from Kabzeel. He
killed the two sons of Ariel of Moab, and
also, on a snowy day, he went down and
killed the lion in the cistern. 23 He like-
wise slew the Egyptian, a huge man five
cubits tall. The Egyptian carried a spear

*

12: 2 Sm 2, 5.
13: Dt 18, 10ff; 1 Sm 13, 13f; 15, 3.11. 26.
14: 1 Sm 15, 28; 2 Sm 3, 9f.
11, 1-9: 2 Sm 5, 1-10.
2: 1 Sm 18, 5.13-16.30; 19, 8.
3: 1 Sm 16, 1.13; 2 Sm 2, 4.
4: Jos 15, 8; Jgs 1, 21; 19, 10f.
6: 2 Sm 2, 13ff; 8, 16.
8: 1 Kgs 9, 15.24; 11, 27; 2 Chr 32, 5.
10-41: 2 Sm 23, 8-39.
12: 27, 4.
13: 1 Sm 17, 1.
15: 14, 9; 2 Sm 5, 18.22.
20f: 2 Sm 23, 18f.
20: 18, 12; 1 Sm 26, 6ff; 2 Sm 16, 9; 18, 2; 21, 17.

†

10, 13f: The Chronicler's comment on why Saul met his tragic end: he had disobeyed the Lord's command given through the prophet Samuel (1 Sm 15, 3-9), and *had sought counsel of a necromancer* (1 Sm 28, 6-19), contrary to the Mosaic law against necromancy (Dt 18, 10f).

11, 11f: *The Three:* the Chronicler names only two of them: *Ishbaal* and *Eleazar.* According to 2 Sm 23, 8-12, the Three were *Ishbaal, Eleazar,* and *Shammah.*

11, 20: *The Thirty:* listed by name in vv 26-47. The list given in 2 Sm 23, 8-39 often differs in names and spellings; for the numbers, see the note there.

that was like a weaver's heddle-bar,
but he came against him with a staff,
wrested the spear from the Egyptian's
hand, and killed him with his own spear.
24 Such deeds as these of Benaiah, the
son of Jehoiada, gave him a reputation
like that of the Three. 25* He was more
famous than any of the Thirty, but he
did not attain to the Three. David put
him in charge of his bodyguard.
26* Also these warriors: Asahel, the
brother of Joab; Elhanan, son of Dodo,
from Bethlehem; 27 Shammoth, from
En-harod; Helez, from Palti; 28 Ira, son
of Ikkesh, from Tekoa; Abiezer, from
Anathoth; 29* Sibbecai, from Husha; Ilai,
from Ahoh; 30* Maharai, from Neto-
phah; Heled, son of Baanah, from Neto-
phah; 31* Ithai, son of Ribai, from
Gibeah of Benjamin; Benaiah, from
Pirathon; 32 Hurai, from the valley of
Gaash; Abiel, from Beth-arabah;
33 Azmaveth, from Bahurim; Eliahba,
from Shaalbon; 34 Jashen the Gunite;
Jonathan, son of Shagee, from En-
harod; 35 Ahiam, son of Sachar, from
En-harod; Elipheleth, son of 36 Ahasabi,
from Beth-maacah; Ahijah, from Gilo;
37 Hezro, from Carmel; Naarai, the son
of Ezbai; 38 Joel, brother of Nathan, from
Rehob, the Gadite; 39 Zelek the Ammon-
ite; Naharai, from Beeroth, the armor-
bearer of Joab, son of Zeruiah; 40 Ira,
from Jattir; Gareb, from Jattir; 41 Uriah
the Hittite; Zabad, son of Ahlai, 42 and,
in addition to the Thirty, Adina, son of
Shiza, the Reubenite, chief of the tribe
of Reuben; 43 Hanan, from Beth-maa-
cah; Joshaphat the Mithnite; 44 Uzzia,
from Ashterath; Shama and Jeiel, sons
of Hotham, from Aroer; 45 Jediael, son
of Shimri, and Joha, his brother, the Ti-
zite; 46 Eliel the Mahavite; Jeribai and
Joshaviah, sons of Elnaam; Ithmah,
from Moab; 47 Eliel, Obed, and Jaasiel
the Mezobian.

CHAPTER 12

David's Early Followers. 1* The fol-
lowing men came to David in Ziklag
while he was still under banishment
from Saul, son of Kish; they, too, were
among the warriors who helped him in
his battles. 2 They were archers who
could use either the right or the left
hand, both in slinging stones and in
shooting arrows with the bow. They were
some of Saul's kinsmen, from Benjamin.
3* Ahiezer was their chief, along with
Joash, both sons of Shemaah of Gibeah;
also Jeziel and Pelet, sons of Azmaveth;
Beracah; Jehu, from Anathoth;
4 Ishmaiah the Gibeonite, a warrior on
the level of the Thirty, and in addition
to their number; 5 Jeremiah; Jahaziel;
Johanan; Jozabad from Gederah;
6 Eluzai; Jerimoth; Bealiah; Shemariah;
Shephatiah the Haruphite; 7 Elkanah,
Isshiah, Azarel, Joezer, and Ishbaal,
who were Korahites; 8 Joelah, finally,
and Zebadiah, sons of Jeroham, from
Gedor.
9* Some of the Gadites also went over
to David when he was at the stronghold
in the wilderness. They were valiant
warriors, experienced soldiers equipped
with shield and spear, who bore them-
selves like lions, and were as swift as
the gazelles on the mountains. 10 Ezer
was their chief, Obadiah was second,
Eliab third, 11 Mishmannah fourth, Jere-
miah fifth, 12 Attai sixth, Eliel seventh,
13 Johanan eighth, Elzabad ninth,
14 Jeremiah tenth, and Machbannai
eleventh. 15 These Gadites were army
commanders, the lesser placed over
hundreds and the greater over thou-
sands. 16 It was they who crossed over
the Jordan when it was overflowing both
its banks in the first month, and dis-
persed all who were in the valleys to the
east and to the west.
17 Some Benjaminites and Judahites
also came to David at the stronghold.
18 David went out to meet them and ad-
dressed them in these words: "If you
come peacefully, to help me, I am of a
mind to have you join me. But if you
have come to betray me to my enemies
though my hands have done no wrong,
may the God of our fathers see and pun-
ish you."
19 Then spirit enveloped Amasai, the
chief of the Thirty, who spoke:

"We are yours, O David,
 we are with you, O son of Jesse.
Peace, peace to you,
 and peace to him who helps you;
 your God it is who helps you."

So David received them and placed
them among the leaders of his troops.
20 Men from Manasseh also deserted
to David when he came with the Philis-
tines to battle against Saul. However, he
did not help the Philistines, for their
lords took counsel and sent him home,
saying, "At the cost of our heads he will
desert to his master Saul." 21 As he was
returning to Ziklag, therefore, these de-
serted to him from Manasseh: Adnah,
Jozabad, Jediael, Michael, Jozabad,
Elihu, and Zillethai, chiefs of thousands
of Manasseh. 22 They helped David by
taking charge of his troops, for they
were all warriors and became com-
manders of his army. 23 And from day
to day men kept coming to David's help
until there was a vast encampment, like
an encampment of angels.

---

*
25: 2 Sm 8, 18; 20, 23.
26: 2, 16; 27, 7.
29: 27, 11.
30: 27, 13.
31: 27, 14.
12, 1: 1 Sm 27, 1-7.
3: 27, 12.
9: Dt 33, 20.

The Assembly at Hebron. 24 This is the muster of the detachments of armed troops that came to David at Hebron to transfer to him Saul's kingdom, as the LORD had ordained. 25† Judahites bearing shields and spears: six thousand eight hundred armed troops. 26 Of the Simeonites, warriors fit for battle: seven thousand one hundred. 27 Of the Levites: four thousand six hundred, 28 along with Jehoiada, leader of the line of Aaron, with another three thousand seven hundred, 29 and Zadok, a young warrior, with twenty-two princes of his father's house. 30 Of the Benjaminites, the brethren of Saul: three thousand—until this time, most of them had held their allegiance to the house of Saul. 31 Of the Ephraimites: twenty thousand eight hundred warriors, men renowned in their ancestral houses. 32 Of the half-tribe of Manasseh: eighteen thousand, designated by name to come and make David king. 33 Of the Issacharites, their chiefs who were endowed with an understanding of the times and who knew what Israel had to do: two hundred chiefs, together with all their brethren under their command. 34 From Zebulun, men fit for military service, set in battle array with every kind of weapon for war: fifty thousand men rallying with a single purpose. 35 From Naphtali: one thousand captains, and with them, armed with shield and lance, thirty-seven thousand men. 36 Of the Danites, set in battle array: twenty-eight thousand six hundred. 37 From Asher, fit for military service and set in battle array: forty thousand. 38 From the other side of the Jordan, of the Reubenites, Gadites, and the half-tribe of Manasseh, men equipped with every kind of weapon of war: one hundred and twenty thousand.

39 All these soldiers, drawn up in battle order, came to Hebron with the resolute intention of making David king over all Israel. The rest of Israel was likewise of one mind to make David king. 40 They remained with David for three days, feasting and drinking, for their brethren had prepared for them. 41 Moreover, their neighbors from as far as Issachar, Zebulun, and Naphtali came bringing food on asses, camels, mules, and oxen—provisions in great quantity of meal, pressed figs, raisins, wine, oil, oxen, and sheep. For there was rejoicing in Israel.

CHAPTER 13

Transfer of the Ark. 1* After David had taken counsel with his commanders of thousands and of hundreds, that is to say, with every one of his leaders, 2* he said to the whole assembly of Israel: "If it seems good to you, and is so decreed by the LORD our God, let us summon the rest of our brethren from all the districts of Israel, and also the priests and the Levites from their cities with pasture lands, that they may join us; 3 and let us bring the ark of our God here among us, for in the days of Saul we did not visit it." 4 And the whole assembly agreed to do this, for the idea was pleasing to all the people.

5*† Then David assembled all Israel, from Shihor of Egypt to Labo of Hamath, to bring the ark of God from Kiriath-jearim. 6* David and all Israel went up to Baalah, that is, to Kiriath-jearim, of Judah, to bring back the ark of God, which was known by the name "LORD enthroned upon the cherubim." 7 They transported the ark of God on a new cart from the house of Abinadab; Uzzah and Ahio were guiding the cart, 8 while David and all Israel danced before God with great enthusiasm, amid songs and music on lyres, harps, tambourines, cymbals, and trumpets.

9† As they reached the threshing floor of Chidon, Uzzah stretched out his hand to steady the ark, for the oxen were upsetting it. 10 Then the LORD became angry with Uzzah and struck him; he died there in God's presence, because he had laid his hand on the ark. 11† David was disturbed because the LORD's anger had broken out against Uzzah. Therefore that place has been called Perez-uzza even to this day.

12 David was now afraid of God, and he said, "How can I bring the ark of God with me?" 13 Therefore he did not take the ark back with him to the City of David, but he took it instead to the house of Obed-edom the Gittite. 14* The ark of God remained in the house of Obed-edom with his family for three months, and the LORD blessed Obed-edom's household and all that he possessed.

CHAPTER 14

David in Jerusalem. 1* Hiram, king of Tyre, sent envoys to David along with

1 CHRONICLES

*

13, 1-14: 2 Sm 6, 1-11.
2: Nm 35, 1ff; Jos 14, 4; 21, 2ff.
5: 15, 3; Jos 13, 3.5; 1 Sm 6, 21; 7, 1f; 2 Sm 6, 1-11.
6: Jos 15, 9; 18, 14; 1 Sm 4, 4; 7, 1.
14: 26, 4f.
14, 1-16: 2 Sm 5, 11-25.
1: 1 Kgs 5, 1; 2 Chr 2, 3.

†

12, 25-38: The Chronicler fills out the pageantry of joyous occasions in keeping with his much later appreciation of the significance of the event in the history of God's people: the numbers in attendance at David's crowning in Hebron (cf 2 Sm 5, 1ff) are recounted in the same spirit of enthusiasm which in v 23 compares David's band of desert freebooters to a numerous encampment of angels.

13, 5: *Shihor of Egypt:* the eastern branch of the Nile delta. *Labo of Hamath:* in southern Syria.

13, 9: *Chidon:* in 2 Sm 6, 6, *Nodan.*

13, 11: *Perez-uzza:* a Hebrew term meaning "the breaking out against Uzza."

masons and carpenters, and cedar wood
to build him a house. 2 David now under-
stood that the LORD had truly confirmed
him as king over Israel, for his kingdom
was greatly exalted for the sake of his
people Israel. 3* David took other wives
in Jerusalem and became the father of
more sons and daughters. 4 These are
the names of those who were born to him
in Jerusalem: Shammua, Shobab, Na-
than, Solomon, 5 Ibhar, Elishua, Elpelet,
6 Nogah, Nepheg, Japhia, 7 Elishama,
Beeliada, and Eliphelet.
The Philistine Wars. 8 When the Phi-
listines had heard that David was
anointed king over all Israel, they went
up in unison to seek him out. But when
David heard of this, he marched out
against them. 9* Meanwhile the Philis-
tines had come and raided the valley of
Rephaim. 10 David inquired of God,
"Shall I advance against the Philistines,
and will you deliver them into my
power?" The LORD answered him, "Ad-
vance, for I will deliver them into your
power." 11 They advanced, therefore, to
Baal-perazim, and David defeated them
there. Then David said, "God has used
me to break through my enemies just
as water breaks through a dam." There-
fore that place was called Baal-perazim.
12* The Philistines had left their gods
there, and David ordered them to be
burnt.
13 Once again the Philistines raided the
valley, 14 and again David inquired of
God. But God answered him: "Do not
try to pursue them, but go around them
and come upon them from the direction
of the mastic trees. 15 When you hear the
sound of marching in the tops of the
mastic trees, then go forth to battle, for
God has already gone before you to
strike the army of the Philistines."
16 David did as God commanded him,
and they routed the Philistine army
from Gibeon to Gezer.
17 Thus David's fame was spread
abroad through every land, and the
LORD made all the nations fear him.

CHAPTER 15

The Ark Brought to Jerusalem.
1 David built houses for himself in the
City of David and prepared a place for
the ark of God, pitching a tent for it
there. 2* At that time he said, "No one
may carry the ark of God except the
Levites, for the LORD chose them to
carry the ark of the LORD and to minister
to him forever." 3* Then David assem-
bled all Israel in Jerusalem to bring the
ark of the LORD to the place which he
had prepared for it. 4 David also called
together the sons of Aaron and the Le-
vites: 5 of the sons of Kohath, Uriel, their
chief, and one hundred and twenty of
his brethren; 6 of the sons of Merari,
Asaiah, their chief, and two hundred
and twenty of his brethren; 7 of the sons
of Gershon, Joel, their chief, and one
hundred and thirty of his brethren; 8 of
the sons of Elizaphan, Shemaiah, their
chief, and two hundred of his brethren;
9 of the sons of Hebron, Eliel, their chief,
and eighty of his brethren; 10 of the sons
of Uzziel, Amminadab, their chief, and
one hundred and twelve of his brethren.
11* David summoned the priests Za-
dok and Abiathar, and the Levites Uriel,
Asaiah, Joel, Shemaiah, Eliel, and Am-
minadab, 12* and said to them: "You, the
heads of the levitical families, must
sanctify yourselves along with your
brethren and bring the ark of the LORD,
the God of Israel, to the place which I
have prepared for it. 13* Because you
were not with us the first time, the wrath
of the LORD our God burst upon us, for
we did not seek him aright." 14 Ac-
cordingly, the priests and the Levites
sanctified themselves to bring up the
ark of the LORD, the God of Israel.
15* The Levites bore the ark of God on
their shoulders with poles, as Moses had
ordained according to the word of the
LORD.
16* David commanded the chiefs of the
Levites to appoint their brethren as
chanters, to play on musical instru-
ments, harps, lyres, and cymbals, to
make a loud sound of rejoicing.
17* Therefore the Levites appointed He-
man, son of Joel, and, among his breth-
ren, Asaph, son of Berechiah; and
among the sons of Merari, their breth-
ren, Ethan, son of Kushaiah; 18 and, to-
gether with these, their brethren of the
second rank: the gatekeepers Zecha-
riah, Uzziel, Shemiramoth, Jehiel, Unni,
Eliab, Benaiah, Maaseiah, Mattithiah,
Eliphelehu, Mikneiah, Obed-edom, and
Jeiel. 19 The chanters, Heman, Asaph,
and Ethan, sounded brass cymbals.
20† Zechariah, Uzziel, Shemiramoth,
Jehiel, Unni, Eliab, Maaseiah, and Be-
naiah played on harps set to "Alamoth."
21 But Mattithiah, Eliphelehu, Mikneiah,

*

3-7: 3, 5-8; 2 Sm 5, 13-16.
9: 11, 15.
12: Dt 7, 5.25.
15, 2: Nm 1, 50; 7, 9; Dt 10, 8; 31, 25; 1 Sm 6, 15; Jos 3, 8.
3: 13, 5; 2 Sm 6, 15.17.
11: 16, 39; 2 Sm 8, 17; 15, 29.35.
12: 2 Chr 29, 5.15.34; 30, 3.15.24.
13: 13, 3.
15: Ex 25, 13ff; Nm 1, 50; 7, 9; 2 Chr 35, 3.
16: 13, 8; 16, 5; 2 Chr 5, 12; 29, 25; Neh 12, 27.
17: 6, 31-47; 25, 1-8.

†

15, 20: *Alamoth:* a musical term (literally, "young women") of uncertain meaning, occurring also in Ps 46, 1, where it is rendered as *virgins.* Perhaps it may mean something like "soprano," whereas the term "eighth" (Hebrew *sheminith,* v 21) may then mean "bass"; cf Pss 6, 1; 12, 1.

Obed-edom, and Jeiel led the chant on
lyres set to "the eighth." 22* Chenaniah
was the chief of the Levites in the chant-
ing; he directed the chanting, for he was
skillful. 23 Berechiah and Elkanah were
gatekeepers before the ark. 24* The
priests, Shebaniah, Joshaphat, Ne-
thanel, Amasai, Zechariah, Benaiah, and
Eliezer, sounded the trumpets before the
ark of God. Obed-edom and Jeiel were
also gatekeepers before the ark.
25* Thus David, the elders of Israel,
and the commanders of thousands went
to bring up the ark of the covenant of
the LORD with joy from the house of
Obed-edom. 26* While the Levites, with
God's help, were bearing the ark of the
covenant of the LORD, seven bulls and
seven rams were sacrificed. 27* David
was clothed in a robe of fine linen, as
were all the Levites who carried the ark,
the singers, and Chenaniah, the leader
of the chant; David was also wearing a
linen ephod. 28 Thus all Israel brought
back the ark of the covenant of the LORD
with joyful shouting, to the sound of
horns, trumpets, and cymbals, and the
music of harps and lyres. 29* But as the
ark of the covenant of the LORD was en-
tering the City of David, Michal, daugh-
ter of Saul, looked down from her
window, and when she saw King David
leaping and dancing, she despised him
in her heart.

CHAPTER 16

1* They brought in the ark of God and
set it within the tent which David had
pitched for it. Then they offered up holo-
causts and peace offerings to God.
2 When David had finished offering up
the holocausts and peace offerings, he
blessed the people in the name of the
LORD, 3 and distributed to every Israel-
ite, to every man and every woman, a
loaf of bread, a piece of meat, and a rai-
sin cake.

The Ministering Levites. 4* He now
appointed certain Levites to minister be-
fore the ark of the LORD, to celebrate,
thank, and praise the LORD, the God of
Israel. 5 Asaph was their chief, and sec-
ond to him were Zechariah, Uzziel, She-
miramoth, Jehiel, Mattithiah, Eliab,
Benaiah, Obed-edom, and Jeiel. These
were to play on harps and lyres, while
Asaph was to sound the cymbals, 6 and
the priests Benaiah and Jahaziel were
to be the regular trumpeters before the
ark of the covenant of God.
7 Then, on that same day, David ap-
pointed Asaph and his brethren to sing
for the first time these praises of the
LORD:

8*† Give thanks to the LORD, invoke his name;
make known among the nations his deeds.
9 Sing to him, sing his praise,
proclaim all his wondrous deeds.
10 Glory in his holy name;
rejoice, O hearts that seek the LORD!
11 Look to the LORD in his strength;
seek to serve him constantly.
12 Recall the wondrous deeds that he has wrought,
his portents, and the judgments he has uttered,
13 You descendants of Israel, his servants,
sons of Jacob, his chosen ones!

14 He, the LORD, is our God;
throughout the earth his judgments prevail.
15 He remembers forever his covenant
which he made binding for a thousand generations—
16 Which he entered into with Abraham
and by his oath to Isaac;
17 Which he established for Jacob by statute,
for Israel as an everlasting covenant,
18 Saying, "To you will I give the land of Canaan
as your allotted inheritance."

19 When they were few in number,
a handful, and strangers there,
20 Wandering from nation to nation,
from one kingdom to another people,
21 He let no one oppress them,
and for their sake he rebuked kings:
22 "Touch not my anointed,
and to my prophets do no harm."

23* Sing to the LORD, all the earth,
announce his salvation, day after day
24 Tell his glory among the nations;
among all peoples, his wondrous deeds.
25 For great is the LORD and highly to be praised;
and awesome is he, beyond all gods.

*
22: 26, 29.
24: Nm 10, 8; Jos 6, 4ff.
25-29: 2 Sm 6, 12-16.
26: 2 Sm 6, 17; 2 Chr 29, 21.
27: 1 Sm 2, 18; 2 Sm 6, 14.
29: 2 Sm 6, 20ff.
16, 1-3: 2 Sm 6, 17ff.
1: 15, 1.
4: Sir 47, 9.
8-22: Ps 105, 1-15.
23-33: Ps 96, 1-13.

†
16, 8-36: A hymn composed of parts, with textual variants, from several Psalms: vv 8-22 = Ps 105, 1-15; vv 23-33 = Ps 96, 1-13; vv 34-36 = Ps 106, 1.47f.

26 For all the gods of the nations are
things of nought,
but the LORD made the heavens.
27 Splendor and majesty go before
him;
praise and joy are in his holy
place.

28 Give to the LORD, you families of na-
tions,
give to the LORD glory and praise;
29 Give to the LORD the glory due his
name!
Bring gifts, and enter his presence;
worship the LORD in holy attire.
30 Tremble before him, all the earth;
he has made the world firm, not
to be moved.

31 Let the heavens be glad and the
earth rejoice;
let them say among the nations:
The LORD is king.
32 Let the sea and what fills it resound;
let the plains rejoice and all that
is in them!
33 Then shall all the trees of the forest
exult
before the LORD, for he comes:
he comes to rule the earth.

34* Give thanks to the LORD, for he is
good,
for his kindness endures forever;
35 And say, "Save us, O God, our sav-
ior,
gather us and deliver us from the
nations,
That we may give thanks to your
holy name
and glory in praising you."

36 Blessed be the LORD, the God of Is-
rael, through all eternity!
Let all the people say, Amen! Alle-
luia.

37 Then David left Asaph and his
brethren there before the ark of the
covenant of the LORD to minister before
the ark regularly according to the daily
ritual; 38* he also left there Obed-edom
and sixty-eight of his brethren, includ-
ing Obed-edom, son of Jeduthun, and
Hosah, to be gatekeepers.
39* But the priest Zadok and his
priestly brethren he left before the
Dwelling of the LORD on the high place
at Gibeon, 40* to offer holocausts to the
LORD on the altar of holocausts regu-
larly, morning and evening, and to do
all that is written in the law of the LORD
which he has decreed for Israel. 41* With
them were Heman and Jeduthun and
the others who were chosen and desig-
nated by name to give thanks to the
LORD, "because his kindness endures
forever," 42* with trumpets and cymbals
for accompaniment, and instruments
for the sacred chant. The sons of Jedu-
thun kept the gate.
43* Then all the people departed, each
to his own home, and David returned
to bless his household.

1 CHRONICLES

CHAPTER 17

The Oracle of Nathan. 1* After David
had taken up residence in his house, he
said to Nathan the prophet, "See, I am
living in a house of cedar, but the ark
of the covenant of the LORD dwells under
tentcloth." 2 Nathan replied to David,
"Do, therefore, whatever you desire, for
God is with you."
3 But that same night the word of God
came to Nathan: 4* "Go and tell my
servant David, Thus says the LORD: It
is not you who are to build a house for
me to dwell in. 5 For I have never dwelt
in a house, from the time when I led Is-
rael onward, even to this day, but I have
been lodging in tent or pavilion 6 as long
as I have wandered about with all of Is-
rael. Did I ever say a word to any of
the judges of Israel whom I commanded
to guide my people, such as, 'Why have
you not built me a house of cedar?'
7* Therefore, tell my servant David,
Thus says the LORD of hosts: I took you
from the pasture, from following the
sheep, that you might become ruler over
my people Israel. 8 I was with you wher-
ever you went, and I cut down all your
enemies before you. I will make your
name great like that of the greatest on
the earth. 9 I will assign a place for my
people Israel and I will plant them in it
to dwell there henceforth undisturbed;
nor shall wicked men ever again oppress
them, as they did at first, 10 and during
all the time when I appointed judges
over my people Israel. And I will subdue
all your enemies. Moreover, I declare to
you that I, the LORD, will build you a
house; 11* so that when your days have
been completed and you must join your
fathers, I will raise up your offspring
after you who will be one of your own
sons, and I will establish his kingdom.
12* He it is who shall build me a house,
and I will establish his throne forever.
13* I will be a father to him, and he shall
be a son to me, and I will not withdraw
my favor from him as I withdrew it from
him who preceded you; 14 but I will
maintain him in my house and in my

34ff: Ps 106, 1.47f.
38: 15, 24.
39: 1 Kgs 3, 4.
40: Ex 29, 38-42; Lv 6, 9; Nm 28, 3.6; 2 Chr 13, 11.
41: 2 Chr 5, 12; 7, 3.6; 20, 21; Ezr 3, 11.
42: 2 Chr 29, 27.
43: 2 Sm 6, 19f.
17, 1-27: 2 Sm 7, 1-29.
1: 15, 1; 2 Sm 5, 11.
4: 28, 3; 1 Kgs 8, 19.
7: 1 Sm 16, 11.
11: 2 Sm 7, 12f.
12: 22, 10; 28, 6.10.
13: 2 Sm 7, 14.

kingdom forever, and his throne shall
be firmly established forever."
15 All these words and this whole vision
Nathan related exactly to David.
David's Thanksgiving. 16 Then David
came in and sat in the LORD's presence,
saying: "Who am I, O LORD God, and
what is my family, that you should have
brought me as far as I have come?
17* And yet, even this you now consider
too little, O God! For you have made a
promise regarding your servant's fam-
ily reaching into the distant future, and
you have looked on me as henceforth
the most notable of men, O LORD God.
18 What more can David say to you? You
know your servant. 19 O LORD, for your
servant's sake and in keeping with your
purpose, you have done this great thing.
20* O LORD, there is no one like you and
there is no God but you, just as we have
always understood.
21* "Is there, like your people Israel,
whom you redeemed from Egypt, an-
other nation on earth whom a god went
to redeem as his people? You won for
yourself a name for great and awesome
deeds by driving out the nations before
your people. 22 You made your people Is-
rael your own forever, and you, O LORD,
became their God. 23 Therefore, O LORD,
may the promise that you have uttered
concerning your servant and his house
remain firm forever. Bring about what
you have promised, 24 that your renown
as LORD of hosts, God of Israel, may be
great and abide forever, while the house
of David, your servant, is established in
your presence.
25* "Because you, O my God, have re-
vealed to your servant that you will build
him a house, your servant has made
bold to pray before you. 26 Since you, O
LORD, are truly God and have promised
this good thing to your servant, 27* and
since you have deigned to bless the
house of your servant, so that it will re-
main forever—since it is you, O LORD,
who blessed it, it is blessed forever."

CHAPTER 18

David's Victories. 1* After this, David
defeated the Philistines and subdued
them; and he took Gath and its towns
away from the control of the Philistines.
2 He also defeated Moab, and the Moab-
ites became his subjects, paying tribute.
3 David then defeated Hadadezer,
king of Zobah toward Hamath, when the
latter was on his way to set up his victory
stele at the river Euphrates. 4* David
took from him twenty thousand foot sol-
diers, one thousand chariots, and seven
thousand horsemen. Of the chariot
horses, David hamstrung all but one
hundred. 5 The Arameans of Damascus
came to the aid of Hadadezer, king of
Zobah, but David also slew twenty-two
thousand of their men. 6 Then David set
up garrisons in the Damascus region of
Aram, and the Arameans became his
subjects, paying tribute. Thus the LORD
made David victorious in all his cam-
paigns.
7 David took the golden shields that
were carried by Hadadezer's attendants
and brought them to Jerusalem. 8* He
likewise took away from Tibhath and
Cun, cities of Hadadezer, large quanti-
ties of bronze, which Solomon later used
to make the bronze sea and the pillars
and the vessels of bronze.
9 When Tou, king of Hamath, heard
that David had defeated the entire army
of Hadadezer, king of Zobah, 10* he sent
his son Hadoram to wish King David
well and to congratulate him on having
waged a victorious war against Had-
adezer; for Hadadezer had been at war
with Tou. He also sent David gold, silver
and bronze utensils of every sort.
11 These also King David consecrated to
the LORD along with all the silver and
gold that he had taken from the nations:
from Edom, Moab, the Ammonites, the
Philistines, and Amalek.
12* Abishai, the son of Zeruiah, also
slew eighteen thousand Edomites in the
Valley of Salt. 13 He set up garrisons in
Edom, and all the Edomites became
David's subjects. Thus the LORD made
David victorious in all his campaigns.
David's Officials. 14* David reigned
over all Israel and dispensed justice and
right to all his people. 15* Joab, son of
Zeruiah, was in command of the army;
Jehoshaphat, son of Ahilud, was herald;
16*† Zadok, son of Ahitub, and Ahime-
lech, son of Abiathar, were priests;
Shavsha was scribe; 17*† Benaiah, son of

*

17: 2 Sm 7, 19.
20: Sir 36, 4.
21: Dt 4, 7; 2 Sm 7, 23.
25: 2 Sm 7, 27.
27: Nm 22, 6.
18, 1-13: 2 Sm 8, 1-14.
4: 2 Sm 8, 14; Jos 11, 6.9.
8: 2 Sm 8, 8; 1 Kgs 7, 15.23.27.
10: 2 Sm 8, 10.
12: 2 Sm 8, 13; 2 Kgs 14, 7.
14-17: 2 Sm 8, 15-18.
15: 11, 6; 2 Sm 8, 16; 1 Kgs 4, 3.
16: 24, 3.6.31; 2 Sm 8, 17.
17: 11, 22; 2 Sm 8, 18; 1 Kgs 1, 38.44.

†

18, 16: *Zadok . . . and Ahimelech, son of Abiathar, were priests:* as in the Chronicler's source, 2 Sm 8, 17. But according to 2 Sm 15, 24.29.35; 17, 15; 19, 11; 20, 25, and even 1 Chr 15, 11, it was Abiathar who shared the priestly office with Zadok, and he remained in this office even during the early years of Solomon's reign (1 Kgs 2, 26; 4, 4). Moreover, according to 1 Sm 22, 20; 23, 6; 30, 7, Ahimelech was the father, not the son, of Abiathar. If the text *Ahimelech, son of Abiathar,* is not due to a scribal change, one must assume that Abiathar had a son who was named after his grandfather and who shared the priestly office with his father during the last years of David's reign.

18, 17: *David's sons were the chief assistants to the king:* in the parallel passage, 2 Sm 8, 18, which was the Chronicler's source, *David's sons were priests.* The change is characteristic of the Chronicler, for whom only Aaron's descendants could be priests.

Jehoiada, was in command of the Cher-
ethites and the Pelethites; and David's
sons were the chief assistants to the
king.

CHAPTER 19

Campaigns against Ammon. 1* Af-
terward Nahash, king of the Ammon-
ites, died and his son succeeded him as
king. 2 David said, "I will show kindness
to Hanun, the son of Nahash, for his fa-
ther treated me with kindness." There-
fore he sent envoys to him to comfort
him over the death of his father. But
when David's servants had entered the
land of the Ammonites to comfort
Hanun, 3 the Ammonite princes said to
Hanun, "Do you think David is doing
this—sending you these consolers—to
honor your father? Have not his ser-
vants rather come to you to explore the
land, spying it out for its overthrow?"
4 Thereupon Hanun seized David's ser-
vants and had them shaved and their
garments cut off half-way at the hips.
Then he sent them away. 5 When David
was informed of what had happened to
his men, he sent messengers to meet
them, for the men had been greatly dis-
graced. "Remain at Jericho," the king
told them, "until your beards have
grown again; and then you may come
back here."
6 When the Ammonites realized that
they had put themselves in bad odor
with David, Hanun and the Ammonites
sent a thousand talents of silver to hire
chariots and horsemen from Aram Na-
haraim, from Aram-maacah, and from
Zobah. 7 They hired thirty-two thousand
chariots along with the king of Maacah
and his army, who came and encamped
before Medeba. The Ammonites also as-
sembled from their cities and came out
for war.
8 When David heard of this, he sent
Joab and his whole army of warriors
against them. 9 The Ammonites
marched out and lined up for a battle
at the gate of the city, while the kings
who had come to their help remained
apart in the open field. 10* When Joab
saw that there was a battle line both in
front of and behind him, he chose some
of the best fighters among the Israelites
and set them in array against the Ara-
means; 11* the rest of the army, which
he placed under the command of his
brother Abishai, then lined up to oppose
the Ammonites. 12 And he said: "If the
Arameans prove too strong for me, you
must come to my help; and if the Am-
monites prove too strong for you, I will
save you. 13 Hold steadfast and let us
show ourselves courageous for the sake
of our people and the cities of our God;
then may the LORD do what seems best
to him." 14 Joab therefore advanced with
his men to engage the Arameans in
battle; but they fled before him. 15 And
when the Ammonites saw that the Ara-
means had fled, they also took to flight
before his brother Abishai, and reen-
tered the city. Joab then returned to Je-
rusalem.
16 Seeing themselves vanquished by
Israel, the Arameans sent messengers
to bring out the Arameans from the
other side of the River, with Shophach,
the general of Hadadezer's army, at
their head. 17 When this was reported to
David, he gathered all Israel together,
crossed the Jordan, and met them. With
the army of David drawn up to fight the
Arameans, they gave battle. 18 But the
Arameans fled before Israel, and David
slew seven thousand of their chariot
fighters and forty thousand of their foot
soldiers; he also killed Shophach, the
general of the army. 19 When the vassals
of Hadadezer saw themselves van-
quished by Israel, they made peace with
David and became his subjects. After
this, the Arameans refused to come to
the aid of the Ammonites.

CHAPTER 20

1 At the beginning of the following
year, the time when kings go to war,
Joab led the army out in force, laid waste
the land of the Ammonites, and went
on to besiege Rabbah, while David him-
self remained in Jerusalem. When Joab
had attacked Rabbah and destroyed it,
2* David took the crown of Milcom from
the idol's head. It was found to weigh
a talent of gold; and it contained pre-
cious stones, which David wore on his
own head. He also brought out a great
amount of booty from the city. 3 He de-
ported the people of the city and set
them to work with saws, iron picks,
and axes. Thus David dealt with all
the cities of the Ammonites. Then he
and his whole army returned to Jerusa-
lem.

Victories over the Philistines. 4* Af-
terward there was another battle with
the Philistines, at Gezer. At that time,
Sibbecai the Hushathite slew Sippai, one
of the descendants of the Raphaim, and
the Philistines were subdued. 5*† Once

*

19, 1-19: 2 Sm 10, 1-19.
10: 20, 23; 1 Kgs 2, 28.34.
11: 23, 18f.
20, 2f: 2 Sm 12, 30f.
4-8: 2 Sm 21, 18-22.
4: 11, 29; 27, 11.
5: 11, 26; 1 Sm 17, 4.23.

†

20, 5: *Elhanan . . . slew Lahmi, the brother of Goliath:* the Chronicler thus solves the difficulty of the apparent contradiction between 1 Sm 17, 49ff (David killed Goliath) and 2 Sm 21, 19 *(Elhanan killed Goliath).*

again there was war with the Philistines, and Elhanan, the son of Jair, slew Lahmi, the brother of Goliath of Gath, whose spear shaft was like a weaver's heddle-bar.

6 In still another battle, at Gath, they encountered a giant, also a descendant of the Raphaim, who had six fingers to each hand and six toes to each foot; twenty-four in all. 7 He defied Israel, and Jonathan, the son of Shimea, David's brother, slew him. 8 These were the descendants of the Raphaim of Gath who died at the hands of David and his servants.

CHAPTER 21

David's Census; the Plague. 1*† A satan rose up against Israel, and he enticed David into taking a census of Israel. 2 David therefore said to Joab and to the other generals of the army, "Go, find out the number of the Israelites from Beer-sheba to Dan, and report back to me that I may know their number." 3 But Joab replied: "May the LORD increase his people a hundredfold! My lord king, are not all of them my lord's subjects? Why does my lord seek to do this thing? Why will he bring guilt upon Israel?" 4 However, the king's command prevailed over Joab, who departed and traversed all of Israel, and then returned to Jerusalem. 5 Joab reported the result of the census to David: of men capable of wielding a sword, there were in all Israel one million one hundred thousand, and in Judah four hundred and seventy thousand. 6* Levi and Benjamin, however, he did not include in the census, for the king's command was repugnant to Joab. 7 This command displeased God, who began to punish Israel. 8 Then David said to God, "I have sinned greatly in doing this thing. Take away your servant's guilt, for I have acted very foolishly."

9* Then the LORD spoke to Gad, David's seer, in these words: 10 "Go, tell David: Thus says the LORD: I offer you three alternatives; choose one of them, and I will inflict it on you." 11 Accordingly, Gad went to David and said to him; "Thus says the LORD: Decide now— 12 will it be three years of famine; or three months of fleeing your enemies, with the sword of your foes ever at your back; or three days of the LORD's own sword, a pestilence in the land, with the LORD's destroying angel in every part of Israel? Therefore choose: What answer am I to give him who sent me?" 13 Then David said to Gad: "I am in dire straits. But I prefer to fall into the hand of the LORD, whose mercy is very great, than into the hands of men."

14 Therefore the LORD sent pestilence upon Israel, and seventy thousand men of Israel died. 15* God also sent an angel to destroy Jerusalem; but as he was on the point of destroying it, the LORD saw and decided against the calamity, and said to the destroying angel, "Enough now! Stay your hand!"

Ornan's Threshing Floor. The angel of the LORD was then standing by the threshing floor of Ornan the Jebusite. 16 When David raised his eyes, he saw the angel of the LORD standing between earth and heaven, with a naked sword in his hand stretched out against Jerusalem. David and the elders, clothed in sackcloth, prostrated themselves face to the ground, 17 and David prayed to God: "Was it not I who ordered the census of the people? I am the one who sinned, I did this wicked thing. But these sheep, what have they done? O LORD, my God, strike me and my father's family, but do not afflict your people with this plague!"

18* Then the angel of the LORD commanded Gad to tell David to go up and erect an altar to the LORD on the threshing floor of Ornan the Jebusite. 19 David went up at Gad's command, given in the name of the LORD. 20 While Ornan was threshing wheat, he turned around and saw the king, and his four sons who were with him, without recognizing them. 21 But as David came on toward him, he looked up and saw that it was David. Then he left the threshing floor and bowed down before David, his face to the ground. 22 David said to Ornan: "Sell me the ground of this threshing floor, that I may build on it an altar to the LORD. Sell it to me at its full price, that the plague may be stayed from the people." 23 But Ornan said to David: "Take it as your own, and let my lord the king do what seems best to him. See, I also give you the oxen for the holocausts, the threshing sledges for the wood, and the wheat for the cereal offering. I give it all to you." 24 But King David replied to Ornan: "No! I will buy it from you properly, at its full price. I will not take what is yours for the LORD, nor offer up holo-

*

21, 1-7: 2 Sm 24, 1-25.
1: Zec 3, 1f.
6: 27, 24; Nm 1, 49.
9: 29, 29; 1 Sm 9, 9; 2 Chr 29, 25.
15: Gn 6, 6; Ex 32, 14; 2 Sm 24, 16; Jon 3, 10.
18: 2 Chr 3, 1.

†

21,1: *A satan:* in the parallel passage of 2 Sm 24, 1 *the Lord's anger*. The change in the term reflects the changed theological outlook of postexilic Israel, when evil could no longer be attributed directly to God. At an earlier period the Hebrew word *satan* ("adversary," or, especially in a court of law, "accuser"), when not used of men, designated an angel who accused men before God (Jb 1, 6-12; 2, 1-7; Zec 3, 1f). Here, as in later Judaism (Wis 2, 24) and in the New Testament, *satan,* or the "devil" (from the Greek translation of the word), designates an evil spirit who tempts men to wrongdoing.

causts that cost me nothing." 25† So
David paid Ornan six hundred shekels
of gold for the place.

Altar of Holocausts. 26* David then
built an altar there to the LORD, and of-
fered up holocausts and peace offerings.
When he called upon the LORD, he an-
swered him by sending down fire from
heaven upon the altar of holocausts.
27 Then the LORD gave orders to the an-
gel to return his sword to its sheath.

28 Once David saw that the LORD had
heard him on the threshing floor of Or-
nan the Jebusite, he continued to offer
sacrifices there. 29* The Dwelling of the
LORD, which Moses had built in the
desert, and the altar of holocausts were
at that time on the high place at Gibeon.
30 But David could not go there to wor-
ship God, for he was fearful of the sword
of the angel of the LORD. 1* Therefore
David said, "This is the house of the
LORD God, and this is the altar of holo-
causts for Israel."

CHAPTER 22

Material for the Temple. 2*† David
then ordered that all the aliens who lived
in the land of Israel be brought together,
and he appointed them stonecutters to
hew out stone blocks for building the
house of God. 3* He also laid up large
stores of iron to make nails for the doors
of the gates, and clamps, together with
so much bronze that it could not be
weighed, 4* and cedar trees without
number. The Sidonians and Tyrians
brought great stores of cedar logs to
David, 5* who said: "My son Solomon is
young and immature; but the house that
is to be built for the LORD must be made
so magnificent that it will be renowned
and glorious in all countries. Therefore
I will make preparations for it." Thus
before his death David laid up materials
in abundance.

Charge to Solomon. 6 Then he called
for his son Solomon and commanded
him to build a house for the LORD, the
God of Israel. 7* David said to Solomon:
"My son, it was my purpose to build a
house myself for the honor of the LORD,
my God. 8 But this word of the LORD
came to me: 'You have shed much blood,
and you have waged great wars. You
may not build a house in my honor, be-
cause you have shed too much blood
upon the earth in my sight. 9*† However,
a son is to be born to you. He will be a
peaceful man, and I will give him rest
from all his enemies on every side. For
Solomon shall be his name, and in his
time I will bestow peace and tranquillity
on Israel. 10* It is he who shall build a
house in my honor; he shall be a son to
me, and I will be a father to him, and I
will establish the throne of his kingship
over Israel forever.' 11 Now, my son, the
LORD be with you, and may you succeed
in building the house of the LORD your
God, as he has said you shall. 12 May the
LORD give you prudence and discern-
ment when he brings you to rule over
Israel, so that you keep the law of the
LORD, your God. 13* Only then shall you
succeed, if you are careful to observe the
precepts and decrees which the LORD
gave Moses for Israel. Be brave and
steadfast; do not fear or lose heart.
14*† See, with great effort I have laid up
for the house of the LORD a hundred
thousand talents of gold, a million tal-
ents of silver, and bronze and iron in
such great quantities that they cannot
be weighed. I have also stored up wood
and stones, to which you must add.
15 Moreover, you have available an un-
limited supply of workmen, stonecut-
ters, masons, carpenters, and every
kind of craftsman 16 skilled in gold, sil-
ver, bronze, and iron. Set to work, there-
fore, and the LORD be with you!"

Charge to the Leaders. 17 David also
commanded all of Israel's leaders to
help his son Solomon: 18* "Is not the
LORD your God with you? Has he not
given you rest on every side? Indeed, he
has delivered the occupants of the land
into my power, and the land is subdued
before the LORD and his people.
19* Therefore, devote your hearts and

*

26: Lv 9, 24; Jgs 6, 21; 1 Kgs 18, 38; 2 Chr 7, 1; 2 Mc 2, 10ff.
29: 16, 39; 1 Kgs 3, 4; 2 Chr 1, 3.
22, 1: 21, 18.26.28;2 Chr 3, 1.
2: 1 Kgs 5, 31f; 9, 20f; 2 Chr 2, 16f.
3: 18, 8; 1 Kgs 7, 47.
4: 10, 27; Ezr 3, 7.
5: 29, 1.
7-10: 17, 1-14; 28, 2-7; 2 Sm 7, 1-16; 1 Kgs 5, 3ff; 8, 17-21.
9: 2 Sm 12, 24.
10: Heb 1, 5.
13: 28, 7.20; Dt 31, 6.23; Jos 1, 6f.9; 1 Kgs 2, 2f.
14: 29, 2ff.
18: 23, 25; Jos 21, 44; 23, 1; 2 Sm 7, 1.
19: 1 Kgs 8, 6.21; 2 Chr 5, 7; 6, 11.

†

21, 25: *Six hundred shekels of gold:* about 10,000 dollars. According to 2 Sm 24, 24, David paid 50 shekels of silver, about 20 dollars, for Ornan's threshing floor; but for the Chronicler the site of the temple was much more precious than that.

22, 2ff: According to 1 Kgs 5, 15-32, it was Solomon who made the material preparations for building the temple, even though David had wished to do so (1 Kgs 5, 17ff). The Chronicler, however, sought to have David, who was Israel's ideal king, more closely connected with Israel's most sacred sanctuary, the temple of Jerusalem.

22, 9: The Hebrew word for peace, *shalom,* is reflected in the name Solomon, in Hebrew, *Shelomo.* A contrast is drawn here between Solomon, the *peaceful man,* and David, who *waged great wars* (v 8). David was prevented from building the temple, not only because all his time was taken up in waging war (1 Kgs 5, 17), but also, because he *shed much blood* (v 8), and in the eyes of the Chronicler this made him ritually unfit for the task.

22, 14: *A hundred thousand talents of gold:* about 3,775 tons of gold. *A million talents of silver:* about 37,750 tons of silver. The fantastically exaggerated figures are intended merely to stress the inestimable value of the temple as the center of Israelite worship. More modest figures are given in 1 Kgs 9, 14.28; 10, 10.14.

souls to seeking the LORD your God. Pro-
ceed to build the sanctuary of the LORD
God, that the ark of the covenant of the
LORD and God's sacred vessels may be
brought into the house built in honor of
the LORD."

CHAPTER 23

The Levitical Classes. 1* When David
had grown old and was near the end of
his days, he made his son Solomon king
over Israel. 2 He then gathered together
all the leaders of Israel, together with
the priests and the Levites.
3* The Levites thirty years old and
above were counted, and their total
number was found to be thirty-eight
thousand men. 4 Of these, twenty-four
thousand were to direct the service of
the house of the LORD, six thousand were
to be officials and judges, 5* four thou-
sand were to be gatekeepers, and four
thousand were to praise the LORD with
the instruments which David had de-
vised for praise. 6* David divided them
into classes according to the sons of
Levi: Gershon, Kohath, and Merari.
7 To the Gershonites belonged Ladan
and Shimei. 8* The sons of Ladan: Jehiel
the chief, then Zetham and Joel; three
in all. 9 The sons of Shimei were Shelo-
moth, Haziel, and Haran; three. These
were the heads of the families of Ladan.
10 The sons of Shimei were Jahath, Zi-
zah, Jeush, and Beriah; these were the
sons of Shimei, four in all. 11 Jahath was
the chief and Zizah was second to him;
but Jeush and Beriah had not many
sons, and therefore they were classed as
a single family, fulfilling a single office.
12* The sons of Kohath: Amram, Izhar,
Hebron, and Uzziel; four in all. 13* The
sons of Amram were Aaron and Moses.
Aaron was set apart to be consecrated
as most holy, he and his sons forever,
to offer sacrifice before the LORD, to
minister to him, and to bless his name
forever. 14 As for Moses, however, the
man of God, his sons were counted as
part of the tribe of Levi. 15* The sons of
Moses were Gershom and Eliezer.
16* The sons of Gershom: Shubael the
chief. 17 The sons of Eliezer were Reha-
biah the chief—Eliezer had no other
sons, but the sons of Rehabiah were very
numerous. 18 The sons of Izhar: Shelo-
mith the chief. 19* The sons of Hebron:
Jeriah, the chief, Amariah, the second,
Jahaziel, the third, and Jekameam, the
fourth. 20* The sons of Uzziel: Micah, the
chief, and Isshiah, the second.
21* The sons of Merari: Mahli and Mu-
shi. The sons of Mahli: Eleazar and Kish.
22* Eleazar died leaving no sons, only
daughters; the sons of Kish, their kins-
men, married them. 23* The sons of Mu-
shi: Mahli, Eder, and Jeremoth; three
in all.
24* These were the sons of Levi ac-
cording to their ancestral houses, the
family heads as they were enrolled one
by one according to their names. They
performed the work of the service of the
house of the LORD from twenty years of
age upward, 27 for David's final orders
were to enlist the Levites from the time
they were twenty years old.
25* David said: "The LORD, the God of
Israel, has given rest to his people, and
has taken up his dwelling in Jerusalem.
26* Henceforth the Levites need not
carry the Dwelling or any of its furnish-
ings or equipment. 28 Rather, their duty
shall be to assist the sons of Aaron in
the service of the house of the LORD,
having charge of the courts, the cham-
bers, and the preservation of everything
holy: they shall take part in the service
of the house of God. 29* They shall also
have charge of the showbread, of the fine
flour for the cereal offering, of the wafers
of unleavened bread, and of the baking
and mixing, and of all measures of
quantity and size. 30* They must be pres-
ent every morning to offer thanks and
to praise the LORD, and likewise in the
evening; 31* and at every offering of ho-
locausts to the LORD on sabbaths, new
moons, and feast days, in such numbers
as are prescribed, they must always be
present before the LORD. 32* They shall
observe what is prescribed for them
concerning the meeting tent, the sanctu-
ary, and the sons of Aaron, their breth-
ren, in the service of the house of the
LORD."

CHAPTER 24

The Priestly Classes. 1* The descen-
dants of Aaron also were divided into
classes. The sons of Aaron were Nadab,
Abihu, Eleazar, and Ithamar. 2* Nadab
and Abihu died before their father, leav-
ing no sons; therefore only Eleazar and
Ithamar served as priests. 3* David,
with Zadok, a descendant of Eleazar,

*

23, 1: 28, 5; 1 Kgs 1, 30.
3: Nm 4, 3.23.30.35.39.43.47; 8, 23-26; 2 Chr 31, 17.
5: 9, 22.
6: 6, 1.16-30; 26, 1-19; Ex 6, 16; Nm 3, 17; 26, 57.
8: 26, 21f; 29, 8.
12: 26, 23; Ex 6, 18; Nm 3, 19; 26, 23ff.
13: 6, 49; Ex 6, 20; 28, 1; Nm 6, 23.
15: Ex 2, 22; 18, 3f.
16: 26, 24.
19: 24, 23.
20: 24, 24f.
21: 6, 29; 24, 26.28f; Ex 6, 19; Nm 3, 20, 33.
22: 24, 28f.
23: 6, 47; 24, 30.
24: 2 Chr 31, 17; Ezr 3, 8.
25: 22, 18; Ps 132, 13.
26: 15, 15; 2 Chr 35, 3.
29: 9, 29.31f; Lv 2, 1.4f; 24, 5-8.
30: Nm 28, 3-8.
31: Nm 28, 2-29, 39.
32: Nm 3, 6-9; 18, 2-5.
24, 1: Ex 6, 23; Nm 3, 2ff; 26, 60.
2: Lv 10, 1-7.12; Nm 3, 2.4.
3: 18, 16; 2 Sm 8, 17; 2 Chr 8, 14.

and Ahimelech, a descendant of Itha-
mar, assigned the functions for the
priestly service. 4 But since the descen-
dants of Eleazar were found to be more
numerous than those of Ithamar, the
former were divided into sixteen groups,
and the latter into eight groups, each un-
der its family head. 5 Their functions
were assigned impartially by lot, for
there were officers of the holy place, and
officers of the divine presence, de-
scended both from Eleazar and from
Ithamar. 6*† The scribe Shemaiah, son
of Nethanel, a Levite, made a record of
it in the presence of the king, and of the
leaders, of Zadok the priest, and of
Ahimelech, son of Abiathar, and of the
heads of the ancestral houses of the
priests and of the Levites, listing two
successive family groups from Eleazar
before each one from Ithamar.
7* The first lot fell to Jehoiarib, the sec-
ond to Jedaiah, 8 the third to Harim, the
fourth to Seorim, 9 the fifth to Malchijah,
the sixth to Mijamin, 10* the seventh to
Hakkoz, the eighth to Abijah, 11 the ninth
to Jeshua, the tenth to Shecaniah, 12 the
eleventh to Eliashib, the twelfth to
Jakim, 13 the thirteenth to Huppah, the
fourteenth to Ishbaal, 14 the fifteenth to
Bilgah, the sixteenth to Immer, 15 the
seventeenth to Hezir, the eighteenth to
Happizzez, 16 the nineteenth to Petha-
hiah, the twentieth to Jehezkel, 17 the
twenty-first to Jachin, the twenty-sec-
ond to Gamul, 18 the twenty-third to
Delaiah, the twenty-fourth to Maaziah.
19* This was the appointed order of their
service when they functioned in the
house of the LORD in keeping with the
precepts given them by Aaron, their fa-
ther, as the LORD, the God of Israel, had
commanded him.

Other Levites. 20* Of the remaining
Levites, there were Shubael, of the de-
scendants of Amram, and Jehdeiah, of
the descendants of Shubael; 21 Isshiah,
the chief, of the descendants of Reha-
biah; 22 Shelomith of the Izharites, and
Jahath of the descendants of Shelomith.
23 The descendants of Hebron were Je-
riah, the chief, Amariah, the second, Ja-
haziel, the third, Jekameam, the fourth.
24 The descendants of Uzziel were Mi-
cah; Shamir, of the descendants of Mi-
cah; 25 Isshiah, the brother of Micah; and
Zechariah, a descendant of Isshiah.
26 The descendants of Merari were
Mahli, Mushi, and the descendants of his
son Uzziah. 27 The descendants of Me-
rari through his son Uzziah: Shoham,
Zaccur, and Ibri. 28 Descendants of
Mahli were Eleazar, who had no sons,
29 and Jerahmeel, of the descendants of
Kish. 30 The descendants of Mushi were
Mahli, Eder, and Jerimoth.

These were the descendants of the
Levites according to their ancestral
houses. 31* They too, in the same man-
ner as their relatives, the descendants
of Aaron, cast lots in the presence of
King David, Zadok, Ahimelech, and the
heads of the priestly and levitical fami-
lies; the more important family did so
in the same way as the less important
one.

CHAPTER 25

The Singers. 1* David and the leaders
of the liturgical cult set apart for service
the descendants of Asaph, Heman, and
Jeduthun, as singers of inspired songs
to the accompaniment of lyres and
harps and cymbals.

This is the list of those who performed
this service: 2† Of the sons of Asaph:
Zaccur, Joseph, Nethaniah, and Asha-
relah, sons of Asaph, under the direction
of Asaph, who sang inspired songs un-
der the guidance of the king. 3 Of Jedu-
thun, these sons of Jeduthun: Gedaliah,
Zeri, Jeshaiah, Shimei, Hashabiah, and
Mattithiah; six, under the direction of
their father Jeduthun, who sang in-
spired songs to the accompaniment of
a lyre, to give thanks and praise to the
LORD. 4 Of Heman, these sons of Heman:
Bukkiah, Mattaniah, Uzziel, Shubael,
and Jerimoth; Hananiah, Hanani, Eli-
athah, Giddalti, Romamti-ezer, Josh-
bekashah, Mallothi, Hothir, and
Mahazioth. 5* All these were the sons of
Heman, the king's seer in divine mat-
ters; to enhance his prestige, God gave
Heman fourteen sons and three daugh-
ters. 6* All these, whether of Asaph, Je-
duthun, or Heman, were under their
fathers' direction in the singing in the
house of the LORD to the accompaniment
of cymbals, harps and lyres, serving in
the house of God, under the guidance
of the king. 7 Their number, together
with that of their brethren who were
trained in singing to the LORD, all of
them skilled men, was two hundred and
eighty-eight. 8* They cast lots for their
functions equally, young and old, mas-
ter and pupil alike.

*

6: 18, 16; 2 Sm 8, 17.
7-10: 9, 10ff; Ezr 2, 36ff; Neh 7, 39ff; 11, 10ff.
10: Lk 1, 5.
19: 2 Chr 23, 8.
20-31: 23, 7-23.
31: 25, 8; 26, 13.
25, 1: 6, 31ff; 15, 16f.19; 16, 37; 2 Chr 5, 12; 35, 15; Neh 12, 27.45.
5: 2 Chr 35, 15.
6: 15, 16.
8: 24, 31.

†

24, 6: *Ahimelech, son of Abiathar:* see note on 18, 16.

25, 2-31: This list of twenty-four classes of temple singers balances the list of the twenty-four classes of priests (24, 4-19). The last nine names in 25, 4, which seem to form a special group, appear to have been originally fragments or *incipits* of hymns. With some slight changes in the vocalization, the names would mean: "Have mercy on me, O LORD," "Have mercy on me," "You are my God," "I magnify," "I extol the help of . . . ," "Sitting in adversity," "I have fulfilled," "He made abundant," and "Visions."

9 The first lot fell to Asaph, the family
of Joseph; he and his sons and his breth-
ren were twelve. Gedaliah was the sec-
ond; he and his brethren and his sons
were twelve. 10 The third was Zaccur, his
sons, and his brethren: twelve. 11 The
fourth fell to Izri, his sons, and his breth-
ren: twelve. 12 The fifth was Nethaniah,
his sons, and his brethren: twelve. 13 The
sixth was Bukkiah, his sons, and his
brethren: twelve. 14 The seventh was
Jesarelah, his sons, and his brethren:
twelve. 15 The eighth was Jeshaiah, his
sons, and his brethren: twelve. 16 The
ninth was Mattaniah, his sons, and his
brethren: twelve. 17 The tenth was
Shimei, his sons, and his brethren:
twelve. 18 The eleventh was Uzziel, his
sons, and his brethren: twelve. 19 The
twelfth fell to Hashabiah, his sons, and
his brethren: twelve. 20 The thirteenth
was Shubael, his sons, and his brethren:
twelve. 21 The fourteenth was Matti-
thiah, his sons, and his brethren: twelve.
22 The fifteenth fell to Jeremoth, his sons,
and his brethren: twelve. 23 The six-
teenth fell to Hananiah, his sons, and his
brethren: twelve. 24 The seventeenth fell
to Joshbekashah, his sons, and his
brethren: twelve. 25 The eighteenth fell
to Hanani, his sons, and his brethren:
twelve. 26 The nineteenth fell to Mallothi,
his sons, and his brethren: twelve. 27 The
twentieth fell to Eliathah, his sons, and
his brethren: twelve. 28 The twenty-first
fell to Hothir, his sons, and his brethren:
twelve. 29 The twenty-second fell to Gid-
dalti, his sons, and his brethren: twelve.
30 The twenty-third fell to Mahazioth, his
sons, and his brethren: twelve. 31 The
twenty-fourth fell to Romamti-ezer, his
sons, and his brethren: twelve.

CHAPTER 26

Classes of Gatekeepers. 1* As for the
classes of gatekeepers. Of the Korahites
was Meshelemiah, the son of Kore, one
of the sons of Abiasaph. 2 Meshelemiah's
sons: Zechariah, the first-born, Jediael,
the second son, Zebadiah, the third,
Jathniel, the fourth, 3 Elam, the fifth, Je-
hohanan, the sixth, Eliehoenai, the sev-
enth. 4 Obed-edom's sons: Shemaiah,
the first-born, Jehozabad, a second son,
Joah, the third, Sachar, the fourth,
Nethanel, the fifth, 5 Ammiel, the sixth,
Issachar, the seventh, Peullethai, the
eighth, for God blessed him. 6 To his son
Shemaiah were born sons who ruled
over their family, for they were war-
riors. 7 The sons of Shemaiah were
Othni, Rephael, Obed, and Elzabad; also
his brethren who were men of might,
Elihu and Semachiah. 8 All these were
the sons of Obed-edom, who, together
with their sons and their brethren, were
mighty men, fit for the service. Of Obed-
edom, sixty-two. 9 Of Meshelemiah,
eighteen sons and brethren, mighty
men.

10* Hosah, a descendant of Merari,
had these sons: Shimri, the chief (for
though he was not the first-born, his fa-
ther made him chief), 11 Hilkiah, the sec-
ond son, Tebaliah, the third, Zechariah,
the fourth. All the sons and brethren of
Hosah were thirteen.

12 To these classes of gatekeepers, un-
der their chief men, were assigned
watches in the service of the house of
the LORD, for each group in the same
way. 13 They cast lots for each gate, the
small and the large families alike.
14* When the lot was cast for the east
side, it fell to Meshelemiah. Then they
cast lots for his son Zechariah, a prudent
counselor, and the north side fell to his
lot. 15 To Obed-edom fell the south side,
and to his sons the storehouse. 16 To
Hosah fell the west side with the Shalle-
cheth gate at the ascending highway.
For each family, watches were estab-
lished. 17 On the east, six watched each
day, on the north, four each day, on the
south, four each day, and at the store-
house they were two and two; 18† as for
the large building on the west, there
were four at the highway and two at the
large building. 19 These were the classes
of the gatekeepers, descendants of Kore
and Merari.

Treasurers. 20* Their brother Levites
superintended the stores for the house
of God and the stores of votive offerings.
21* Among the descendants of Ladan the
Gershonite, the family heads were de-
scendants of Jehiel: the descendants of
Jehiel, 22* Zetham and his brother Joel,
who superintended the treasures of the
house of the LORD. 23 From the Amram-
ites, Izharites, Hebronites, and Uzziel-
ites, 24 Shubael, son of Gershon, son of
Moses, was chief superintendent over
the treasures. 25* His associate per-
tained to Eliezer, whose son was Reha-
biah, whose son was Jeshaiah, whose
son was Joram, whose son was Zichri,
whose son was Shelomith. 26* This She-
lomith and his brethren superintended
all the stores of the votive offerings dedi-
cated by King David, the heads of the
families, the commanders of thousands
and of hundreds, and the commanders
of the army, 27 from the booty they had
taken in the wars, for the enhancement

*

26, 1: 9, 19; 2 Chr 8, 14; 23, 19; 35, 15; Neh 12, 45.
10: 16, 38.
14: 9, 24.
20: 28, 12; 1 Kgs 7, 51.
21: 23, 7f; 29, 8.
22ff: 23, 8.12.16.
25: 23, 17f; 24, 21.
26: 2 Sm 8, 11.

†

26, 18: *The large building* (in the Hebrew text *Parbar*): see note on 2 Kgs 23, 11.

of the house of the LORD. 28 Also, whatever Samuel the seer, Saul, son of Kish, Abner, son of Ner, Joab, son of Zeruiah, and all others had consecrated, was under the charge of Shelomith and his brethren.

Magistrates. 29* Among the Izharites, Chenaniah and his sons were in charge of Israel's civil affairs as officials and judges. 30* Among the Hebronites, Hashabiah and his brethren, one thousand seven hundred police officers, had the administration of Israel on the western side of the Jordan in all the work of the LORD and in the service of the king. 31* Among the Hebronites, Jerijah was their chief according to their family records. In the fortieth year of David's reign search was made, and there were found among them outstanding officers at Jazer of Gilead. 32 His brethren were also police officers, two thousand seven hundred heads of families. King David appointed them to the administration of the Reubenites, the Gadites, and the half-tribe of Manasseh in everything pertaining to God and to the king.

CHAPTER 27

Army Commanders. 1† This is the list of the Israelite family heads, commanders of thousands and of hundreds, and other officers who served the king in all that pertained to the divisions, of twenty-four thousand men each, that came and went month by month throughout the year.

2 Over the first division for the first month was Ishbaal, son of Zabdiel, and in his division were twenty-four thousand men; 3 a descendant of Perez, he was chief over all the commanders of the army for the first month. 4* Over the division of the second month was Eleazar, son of Dodo, from Ahoh, and in his division were twenty-four thousand men. 5* The third army commander, chief for the third month, was Benaiah, son of Jehoiada the priest, and in his division were twenty-four thousand men. 6 This Benaiah was a warrior among the Thirty and over the Thirty. His son Ammizabad was over his division. 7* Fourth, for the fourth month, was Asahel, brother of Joab, and after him his son Zebadiah, and in his division were twenty-four thousand men. 8 Fifth, for the fifth month, was the commander Shamhuth, a descendant of Zerah, and in his division were twenty-four thousand men. 9 Sixth, for the sixth month, was Ira, son of Ikkesh, from Tekoa, and in his division were twenty-four thousand men. 10 Seventh, for the seventh month, was Hellez, from Beth-phelet, of the sons of Ephraim, and in his division were twenty-four thousand men. 11* Eighth, for the eighth month, was Sibbecai the Hushathite, a descendant of Zerah, and in his division were twenty-four thousand men. 12 Ninth, for the ninth month, was Abiezer from Anathoth, of Benjamin, and in his division were twenty-four thousand men. 13 Tenth, for the tenth month, was Maharai from Netophah, a descendant of Zerah, and in his division were twenty-four thousand men. 14 Eleventh, for the eleventh month, was Benaiah the Pirathonite, of Ephraim, and in his division were twenty-four thousand men. 15 Twelfth, for the twelfth month, was Heldai the Netophathite, of the family of Othniel, and in his division were twenty-four thousand men.

Tribal Heads. 16 Over the tribes of Israel, for the Reubenites the leader was Eliezer, son of Zichri; for the Simeonites, Shephatiah, son of Maacah; 17 for Levi, Hashabiah, son of Kemuel; for Aaron, Zadok; 18* for Judah, Eliab, one of David's brothers; for Issachar, Omri, son of Michael; 19 for Zebulun, Ishmaiah, son of Obadiah; for Naphtali, Jeremoth, son of Azriel; 20 for the sons of Ephraim, Hoshea, son of Azaziah; for the half-tribe of Manasseh, Joel, son of Pedaiah; 21 for the half-tribe of Manasseh in Gilead, Iddo, son of Zechariah; for Benjamin, Jaasiel, son of Abner; 22 for Dan, Azarel, son of Jeroham. These were the commanders of the tribes of Israel.

23* David did not count those who were twenty years of age or younger, for the LORD had promised to multiply Israel like the stars of the heavens. 24* Joab, son of Zeruiah, began to take the census, but he did not complete it, for because of it wrath fell upon Israel. Therefore the number did not enter into the book of chronicles of King David.

Overseers. 25* Over the treasures of the king was Azmaveth, the son of Adiel. Over the stores in the country, the cities, the villages, and the towers was Jonathan, son of Uzziah. 26 Over the farm workers who tilled the soil was Ezri, son of Chelub. 27 Over the vineyards was Shimei from Ramah, and over their produce for the wine cellars was Zabdi

*

29: 23, 4.
30: 27, 17; Neh 11, 15f.
31: 23, 19; 29, 27; Jos 13, 25.
27, 4: 9, 37; 11, 12; 2 Sm 23, 9.
5f: 11, 22ff; 18, 17; 2 Sm 23, 20ff.
7: 2 Sm 2, 18; 23, 24.
11: 11, 29; 20, 4; 2 Sm 21, 18.
18: 2, 13.
23: 22, 17.
24: 2 Sm 24, 10.
25: 2 Sm 23, 31.

†

27, 1-15: This list of army commanders is similar to, but distinct from, the list of David's warriors as given in 11, 10-47. The schematic enumeration of the soldiers as presented here is, no doubt, artificial and grossly exaggerated (12 × 24,000 = 288,000 men!), unless the Hebrew word *(eleph)* for *thousand* is understood as designating a military unit of much smaller size; see note on 12, 25-38.

the Shiphmite. 28 Over the olive trees and
sycamores of the foothills was Baal-
hanan the Gederite, and over the stores
of oil was Joash. 29 Over the cattle that
grazed in Sharon was Shitrai the Shar-
onite, and over the cattle in the valleys
was Shaphat, the son of Adlai; 30 over
the camels was Obil the Ishmaelite; over
the she-asses was Jehdeiah the Me-
ronothite; 31 and over the flocks was
Jaziz the Hagrite. All these were the
overseers of King David's possessions.

David's Court. 32 Jonathan, David's
uncle and a man of intelligence, was
counselor and scribe; he and Jehiel, the
son of Hachmoni, were tutors of the
king's sons. 33* Ahithophel was also the
king's counselor, and Hushai the Archite
was the king's confidant. 34† After
Ahithophel came Jehoiada, the son of
Benaiah, and Abiathar. The commander
of the king's army was Joab.

CHAPTER 28

The Assembly at Jerusalem. 1* David
assembled at Jerusalem all the leaders
of Israel, the heads of the tribes, the
commanders of the divisions who were
in the service of the king, the command-
ers of thousands and of hundreds, the
overseers of all the king's estates and
possessions, and his sons, together with
the courtiers, the warriors, and every
important man. 2*† King David rose to
his feet and said: "Hear me, my breth-
ren and my people. It was my purpose
to build a house of repose myself for the
ark of the covenant of the LORD, the foot-
stool for the feet of our God; and I was
preparing to build it. 3 But God said to
me, 'You may not build a house in my
honor, for you are a man who fought
wars and shed blood.' 4* However, the
LORD, the God of Israel, chose me from
all my father's family to be king over
Israel forever. For he chose Judah as
leader, then one family of Judah, that
of my father; and finally, among all the
sons of my father, it pleased him to
make me king over all Israel. 5* And of
all my sons—for the LORD has given me
many sons—he has chosen my son Solo-
mon to sit on the LORD's royal throne
over Israel. 6* For he said to me: 'It is
your son Solomon who shall build my
house and my courts, for I have chosen
him for my son, and I will be a father
to him. 7 I will establish his kingdom for-
ever, if he perseveres in keeping my
commandments and decrees as he
keeps them now.' 8* Therefore, in the
presence of all Israel, the assembly of
the LORD, and in the hearing of our God,
I exhort you to keep and to carry out
all the commandments of the LORD,
your God, that you may continue to pos-
sess this good land and afterward leave
it as an inheritance to your children for-
ever.

9* "As for you, Solomon, my son, know
the God of your father and serve him
with a perfect heart and a willing soul,
for the LORD searches all hearts and un-
derstands all the mind's thoughts. If you
seek him, he will let himself be found
by you; but if you abandon him, he will
cast you off forever. 10 See, then! The
LORD has chosen you to build a house
as his sanctuary. Take courage and set
to work."

Temple Plans Given to Solomon.
11* Then David gave to his son Solomon
the pattern of the portico and of the
building itself, with its storerooms, its
upper rooms and inner chambers, and
the room with the propitiatory. 12 He
provided also the pattern for all else that
he had in mind by way of courts for the
house of the LORD, with the surrounding
compartments for the stores for the
house of God and the stores of the votive
offerings, 13 as well as for the divisions
of the priests and Levites, for all the
work of the service of the house of the
LORD, and for all the liturgical vessels
of the house of the LORD. 14 He specified
the weight of gold to be used in the
golden vessels for the various services
and the weight of silver to be used in
the silver vessels for the various ser-
vices; 15* likewise for the golden lamp-
stands and their lamps he specified the
weight of gold for each lampstand and
its lamps, and for the silver lampstands
he specified the weight of silver for each
lampstand and its lamps, depending on
the use to which each lampstand was to
be put. 16 He specified the weight of gold
for each table to hold the showbread,
and the silver for the silver tables; 17 the
pure gold to be used for the forks and

1 CHRONICLES

*

33: 2 Sm 15, 12.32-37; 16, 16-19.23; 17, 5-16.23.
28, 1: 27, 2-22.25-31; 11, 10ff.
2f: 17, 4; 22, 7ff; 2 Sm 7, 5; 1 Kgs 5, 3; Ps 132, 3-7.
4: 17, 23; Gn 49, 8ff; 1 Sm 16, 6-13.
5: 3, 1-9; 14, 3-7; 22, 9; 23, 1; Wis 9, 7.
6: 17, 11ff; 22, 9f; 2 Sm 7, 12f.
8: Dt 4, 5.
9: 29, 17; 2 Chr 15, 2; 1 Kgs 8, 61.
11: Ex 25, 9.40; 26, 30.
15: Ex 25, 31-37.

†

27, 34: After *Ahithophel:* after his suicide (2 Sm 17, 23). Jehoiada then succeeded him as the king's counselor. *Abiathar:* the priest. The Chronicler does not mention his office because he regards only the Zadokites as legitimate high priests.

28, 2: *The ark . . . , the footstool . . . of our God:* the Lord, who was invisibly entroned upon the cherubim that were associated with the ark of the covenant at Shiloh and later in the Jerusalem temple, had the ark as his footstool; cf Pss 99, 5; 132, 7. The *propitiatory* (28, 11) and the *chariot throne* (28, 18) reflect the different circumstances of the postexilic community, for whom only the place of the ark was a focal point of worship, though the ark itself was no longer present.

pitchers; the amount of gold for each golden bowl and the silver for each silver bowl; 18*† the refined gold, and its weight, to be used for the altar of incense; and, finally, gold for what would suggest a chariot throne: the cherubim that spread their wings and covered the ark of the covenant of the LORD. 19 He had successfully committed to writing the exact specifications of the pattern, because the hand of the LORD was upon him.

20* Then David said to his son Solomon: "Be firm and steadfast; go to work without fear or discouragement, for the LORD God, my God, is with you. He will not fail you or abandon you before you have completed all the work for the service of the house of the LORD. 21* The classes of the priests and Levites are ready for all the service of the house of God; they will help you in all your work with all those who are eager to show their skill in every kind of craftsmanship. Also the leaders and all the people will do everything that you command."

CHAPTER 29

Offerings for the Temple. 1* King David then said to the whole assembly: "My son Solomon, whom alone God has chosen, is still young and immature; the work, however, is great, for this castle is not intended for man, but for the LORD God. 2* For this reason I have stored up for the house of my God, as far as I was able, gold for what will be made of gold, silver for what will be made of silver, bronze for what will be made of bronze, iron for what will be made of iron, wood for what will be made of wood, onyx stones and settings for them, carnelian and mosaic stones, every other kind of precious stone, and great quantities of marble. 3 But now, because of the delight I take in the house of my God, in addition to all that I stored up for the holy house, I give to the house of my God my personal fortune in gold and silver: 4* three thousand talents of Ophir gold, and seven thousand talents of refined silver, for overlaying the walls of the rooms, 5* for the various utensils to be made of gold and silver, and for every work that is to be done by artisans. Now, who else is willing to contribute generously this day to the LORD?"

6* Then the heads of the families, the leaders of the tribes of Israel, the commanders of thousands and of hundreds, and the overseers of the king's affairs came forward willingly 7* and contributed for the service of the house of God five thousand talents and ten thousand darics of gold, ten thousand talents of silver, eighteen thousand talents of bronze, and one hundred thousand talents of iron. 8* Those who had precious stones gave them into the keeping of Jehiel the Gershonite for the treasury of the house of the LORD. 9* The people rejoiced over these free-will offerings, which had been contributed to the LORD wholeheartedly. King David also rejoiced greatly.

David's Prayer. 10 Then David blessed the LORD in the presence of the whole assembly, praying in these words:

"Blessed may you be, O LORD,
God of Israel our father,
from eternity to eternity.

11 "Yours, O LORD, are grandeur and power,
majesty, splendor, and glory.
For all in heaven and on earth is yours;
yours, O LORD, is the sovereignty;
you are exalted as head over all.

12* "Riches and honor are from you,
and you have dominion over all.
In your hand are power and might;
it is yours to give grandeur and strength to all.
13 Therefore, our God, we give you thanks
and we praise the majesty of your name."

14 "But who am I, and who are my people, that we should have the means to contribute so freely? For everything is from you, and we only give you what we have received from you. 15* For we stand before you as aliens: we are only your guests, like all our fathers. Our life on earth is like a shadow that does not abide. 16 O LORD our God, all this wealth that we have brought together to build you a house in honor of your holy name comes from you and is entirely yours. 17 I know, O my God, that you put hearts to the test and that you take pleasure in uprightness. With a sincere heart I have willingly given all these things, and now with joy I have seen your people here present also giving to you generously. 18* O LORD, God of our fathers Abraham, Isaac, and Israel, keep such

1 CHRONICLES

*

18: Ex 25, 18-22; 30, 1-10; 1 Kgs 6, 23-28.
20: 22, 13.16; Jos 1, 5.
21: Ex 36, 1-5.
29, 1: 22, 5; 28, 5.
2: 22, 14.
4: 2 Chr 9, 10; 1 Kgs 9, 28; 10, 11.
5: Ex 25, 2; 35, 5f.
6: 27, 1.25-31; 28, 1.
7: Ezr 2, 69; 8, 27; Neh 7, 70ff.
8: 23, 8; 26, 21.
9: 2 Kgs 12, 4.
12: 2 Chr 20, 6; Wis 6, 3.
15: Lv 25, 23; Wis 2, 5; 5, 9.
18: Ex 3, 6.15f; 4, 5; 1 Kgs 18, 36.

†

28, 18: *Chariot throne:* probably suggested by Ez 1, 4-24; 10, 1-22.

thoughts in the hearts and minds of your
people forever, and direct their hearts
toward you. 19 Give to my son Solomon
a wholehearted desire to keep your com-
mandments, precepts, and statutes, that
he may carry out all these plans and
build the castle for which I have made
preparation."
20 Then David besought the whole as-
sembly, "Now bless the LORD your
God!" And the whole assembly blessed
the LORD, the God of their fathers, bow-
ing down and prostrating themselves
before the LORD and before the king.
21 On the following day they offered sac-
rifices and holocausts to the LORD, a
thousand bulls, a thousand rams, and a
thousand lambs, together with their li-
bations and many other sacrifices for all
Israel; 22† and on that day they ate and
drank in the LORD's presence with great
rejoicing.

Solomon Anointed. Then for a second
time they proclaimed David's son Solo-
mon king, and they anointed him as the
LORD's prince, and Zadok as priest.
23* Thereafter Solomon sat on the throne
of the LORD as king in place of his father
David; he prospered, and all Israel
obeyed him. 24 All the leaders and war-
riors, and also all the other sons of King
David, swore allegiance to King Solo-
mon. 25* And the LORD exalted Solomon
greatly in the eyes of all Israel, giving
him a glorious reign such as had not
been enjoyed by any king over Israel be-
fore him.

Death of David. 26 Thus David, the son
of Jesse, had reigned over all Israel.
27* The time that he reigned over Israel
was forty years: in Hebron he reigned
seven years, and in Jerusalem thirty-
three. 28* He died at a ripe old age, rich
in years and wealth and glory, and his
son Solomon succeeded him as king.
29* Now the deeds of King David, first
and last, can be found written in the his-
tory of Samuel the seer, the history of
Nathan the prophet, and the history of
Gad the seer, 30 together with the partic-
ulars of his reign and valor, and of the
events that affected him and all Israel
and all the kingdoms of the surrounding
lands.

*

23: 28, 5; 2 Chr 9, 8; 1 Kgs 2, 10ff.
25: 2 Chr 1, 12; 1 Kgs 3, 13.
27: 2 Sm 5, 5; 1 Kgs 2, 11.
28: 23, 1.
29: 21, 9; 1 Sm 22, 5.

†

29, 22: *For a second time:* the first time is referred to in 23, 1. Here there is a solemn public ratification of David's earlier appointment of Solomon as his successor.

The Second Book of

CHRONICLES

The Second Book of Chronicles takes up the history of the monarchy where the First Book breaks off. It begins with the account of the reign of Solomon from the special viewpoint of the Chronicler. The portrait of Solomon is an idealized one; he appears as second only to David. The great achievement of the building of the temple and the magnificence of Solomon's court are described in detail while the serious defects of his reign are passed over without comment. All this is in keeping with the Chronicler's purpose of stressing the supreme importance of the temple and its worship. He wishes to impress on his readers the splendor of God's dwelling and the magnificence of the liturgy of sacrifice, prayer and praise offered there. Judah's kings are judged by their attitude toward the temple and its cult. To this ideal of one people, united in the worship of the one true God at the temple of Jerusalem founded by David and Solomon, the restored community would have to conform.

In treating the period of divided monarchy, the Chronicler gives practically all his attention to the kingdom of Judah. His omission of the northern Israelite kings is significant. In his view, the northern tribes of Israel were in religious schism as long as they worshiped Yahweh in a place other than the temple of Jerusalem. The Chronicler makes no mention of the important sanctuaries of Yahweh at Dan and Bethel—as though they had never existed. Nevertheless he retains the ancient ideal of "all Israel" (a phrase occuring forty-one times in Chronicles) as the people of God. The condition he places for a united people is that "the whole congregation of Israel" worship the Lord only in his temple at Jerusalem. This explains his praise of Kings Hezekiah and Josiah for striving, after the fall of Samaria, to unite the remnants of the northern tribes of Israel into the kingdom of Judah.

At the end of the fifth century B.C., during the Chronicler's own time, "the people of the land" were the descendants of the people of all the tribes (including Judah) who had not gone into exile. These had become intermingled with aliens and had evolved a religion of Yahweh very different from the Judaism that developed during the Babylonian exile. Thus, religious and political cooperation between the returned exiles and these "people of the land" was out of the question for the Chronicler. This he clearly shows in the last part of his work, the Books of Ezra and Nehemiah.

The Second Book of Chronicles is divided as follows:

I: The Reign of Solomon (1, 1—9, 31)
II: The Monarchy before Hezekiah (10, 1—27, 9)
III: Reforms of Hezekiah and Josiah (28, 1—36, 1)
IV: End of the Kingdom (36, 2-23)

I: THE REIGN OF SOLOMON

CHAPTER 1

Solomon at Gibeon. 1 Solomon, son of
David, strengthened his hold on the
kingdom, for the LORD, his God, was
with him, constantly making him more
renowned. 2 He sent a summons to all
Israel, to the commanders of thousands
and of hundreds, the judges, the princes
of all Israel, and the family heads;
3* and, accompanied by the whole as-
sembly, he went to the high place at
Gibeon, because the meeting tent of God,
made in the desert by Moses, the LORD's
servant, was there. 4 (The ark of God,
however, David had brought up from
Kiriath-jearim to Jerusalem, where he
had provided a place and pitched a tent
for it.) 5*† The bronze altar made by
Bezalel, son of Uri, son of Hur, he put

*

1, 3-12: 1 Kgs 3, 4-15; 1 Chr 21, 29.

5: Ex 27, 1f; 31, 2; 1 Chr 2, 20.

†

1, 5: *The bronze altar . . . the LORD's Dwelling:* the Chronicler justifies Solomon's worship at the high place of Gibeon. He pictures *the LORD's Dwelling,* i.e., the Mosaic meeting tent, and *the bronze altar* made at Moses' command (Ex 31, 1-9) as still at Gibeon after David had removed the ark of the covenant from there to a new tent in Jerusalem (1 Chr 15, 1.25; 16, 1). The altar made by Bezalel is described as being of acacia wood plated with bronze (Ex 27, 1f). Solomon later made an all-bronze altar for the temple in Jerusalem (2 Chr 4, 1).

in front of the LORD's Dwelling on the
high place. There Solomon and the as-
sembly consulted the LORD, 6 and Solo-
mon offered sacrifice in the LORD's
presence on the bronze altar at the
meeting tent; he offered a thousand ho-
locausts upon it.
7 That night God appeared to Solomon
and said to him, "Make a request of me,
and I will grant it to you." 8 Solomon an-
swered God: "You have shown great fa-
vor to my father David, and you have
allowed me to succeed him as king.
9 Now, LORD God, may your promise to
my father David be fulfilled, for you
have made me king over a people as nu-
merous as the dust of the earth. 10 Give
me, therefore, wisdom and knowledge
to lead this people, for otherwise who
could rule this great people of yours?"
11 God then replied to Solomon: "Since
this has been your wish and you have
not asked for riches, treasures and
glory, nor for the life of those who hate
you, nor even for a long life for yourself,
but have asked for wisdom and knowl-
edge in order to rule my people over
whom I have made you king, 12 wisdom
and knowledge are given you; but I will
also give you riches, treasures and
glory, such as kings before you never
had, nor will those have them who come
after you."
Solomon's Wealth. 13 Solomon re-
turned to Jerusalem from the high place
at Gibeon, from the meeting tent, and
became king over Israel. 14* He gath-
ered together chariots and drivers, so
that he had one thousand four hundred
chariots and twelve thousand drivers he
could station in the chariot cities and
with the king in Jerusalem. 15* The king
made silver and gold as common in Je-
rusalem as stones, while cedars became
as numerous as the sycamores of the
foothills. 16*† Solomon also imported
horses from Egypt and Cilicia. The
king's agents would acquire them by
purchase from Cilicia, 17* and would
then bring up chariots from Egypt and
export them at six hundred silver shek-
els, with the horses going for a hundred
and fifty shekels. At these rates they
served as middlemen for all the Hittite
and Aramean kings.
Preparations for the Temple. 18 Solo-
mon gave orders for the building of a
house to honor the LORD and also of a
house for his own royal estate.

CHAPTER 2

1* He conscripted seventy thousand
men to carry stone and eighty thousand
to cut the stone in the mountains, and
over these he placed three thousand six
hundred overseers. 2* Moreover, Solo-
mon sent this message to Huram, king
of Tyre: "As you dealt with my father
David, sending him cedars to build a
house for his dwelling, so deal with me.
3* I intend to build a house for the honor
of the LORD, my God, and to consecrate
it to him, for the burning of fragrant in-
cense in his presence, for the perpetual
display of the showbread, for holocausts
morning and evening, and for the sab-
baths, new moons, and festivals of the
LORD, our God: such is Israel's perpetual
obligation. 4 And the house I intend to
build must be large, for our God is
greater than all other gods. 5* Yet who
is really able to build him a house, since
the heavens and even the highest heav-
ens cannot contain him? And who am
I that I should build him a house, unless
it be to offer incense in his presence?
6 Now, send me men skilled at work in
gold, silver, bronze and iron, in purple,
crimson, and violet fabrics, and who
know how to do engraved work, to join
the craftsmen who are with me in Judah
and Jerusalem, whom my father David
appointed. 7 Also send me boards of ce-
dar, cypress and cabinet wood from
Lebanon, for I realize that your servants
know how to cut the wood of the Leba-
non. My servants will labor with yours
8 in order to prepare for me a great
quantity of wood, since the house I in-
tend to build must be lofty and wonder-
ful. 9* I will furnish as food for your
servants, the hewers who cut the wood,
twenty thousand kors of wheat, twenty
thousand kors of barley, twenty thou-
sand measures of wine, and twenty
thousand measures of oil."
10 Huram, king of Tyre, wrote an an-
swer which he sent to Solomon: "Be-
cause the LORD loves his people, he has
placed you over them as king." 11* He
added: "Blessed be the LORD, the God
of Israel, who made heaven and earth,
for having given King David a wise son
of intelligence and understanding, who
will build a house for the LORD and also
a house for his royal estate. 12* I am now
sending you a craftsman of great skill,
Huram-abi, 13† son of a Danite woman

*

14: 9, 25; 10, 26-29.
15: 1 Kgs 10, 27.
16: 1 Kgs 10, 28.
17: 1 Kgs 10, 29.
2, 1: 2, 17; 5, 29f.
2-9: 1 Kgs 5, 15-20; 1 Chr 14, 1.
3: Lv 24, 5-8; Nm 28-29.
5: 6, 18.
9: 1 Kgs 5, 25; Ezr 3, 7.
11: 1 Kgs 5, 21.
12f: 1 Kgs 7, 13f; Ex 31, 1-5.

†

1, 16f: *Egypt . . . Cilicia:* it seems likely that the horses came from Cilicia and the chariots from Egypt. Some read the source of these data in 1 Kgs 10, 28f as containing the name (Musur) of a mountain district north of Cilicia, rather than of Egypt; but the author of Chronicles surely understood *Egypt;* cf 9, 28.

2, 13: *A Danite woman:* a widow of the tribe of Naphtali (1 Kgs 7, 14). The Danites had settled in the northern section of Naphtali's territory (Jgs 18, 27ff). Bezalel's fellow craftsman was of the tribe of Dan (Ex 31, 6).

and of a father from Tyre; he knows how
to work with gold, silver, bronze and
iron, with stone and wood, with purple,
violet, fine linen and crimson, and also
how to do all kinds of engraved work
and to devise every type of artistic work
that may be given him and your crafts-
men and the craftsmen of my lord David
your father. 14* And now, let my lord
send to his servants the wheat, barley,
oil and wine which he has promised.
15* For our part, we will cut trees on
Lebanon, as many as you need, and float
them down to you at the port of Joppa,
whence you may take them up to Jeru-
salem."

16* Thereupon Solomon took a census
of all the alien men who were in the land
of Israel (following the census David his
father had taken of them), who were
found to number one hundred fifty-three
thousand six hundred. 17* Of these he
made seventy thousand carriers and
eighty thousand cutters in the moun-
tains, and three thousand six hundred
overseers to keep the people working.

CHAPTER 3

Building of the Temple. 1*† Then Sol-
omon began to build the house of the
LORD in Jerusalem on Mount Moriah,
which had been pointed out to his father
David, on the spot which David had se-
lected, the threshing floor of Ornan the
Jebusite. 2 He began to build in the sec-
ond month of the fourth year of his
reign. 3* These were the specifications
laid down by Solomon for building the
house of God: the length was sixty cubits
according to the old measure, and the
width was twenty cubits; 4*† the porch
which lay before the nave along the
width of the house was also twenty cu-
bits, and it was twenty cubits high. He
overlaid its interior with pure gold.
5* The nave he overlaid with cypress
wood which he covered with fine gold,
embossing on it palms and chains. 6 He
also decorated the building with pre-
cious stones. 7 The house, its beams and
thresholds, as well as its walls and its
doors, he overlaid with gold, and he en-
graved cherubim upon the walls. (The
gold was from Parvaim.) 8* He also
made the room of the holy of holies. Its
length corresponded to the width of the
house, twenty cubits, and its width was
also twenty cubits. He overlaid it with
fine gold to the amount of six hundred
talents. 9 The weight of the nails was fifty
gold shekels. The upper chambers he
likewise covered with gold.

10* For the room of the holy of holies
he made two cherubim of carved work-
manship, which were then overlaid with
gold. 11 The wings of the cherubim
spanned twenty cubits: 12 one wing of
each cherub, five cubits in length, ex-
tended to a wall of the building, while
the other wing, also five cubits in length,
touched the corresponding wing of the
second cherub. 13 The combined wing-
spread of the two cherubim was thus
twenty cubits. They stood upon their
own feet, facing toward the nave. 14*† He
made the veil of violet, purple, crimson
and fine linen, and had cherubim em-
broidered upon it.

15* In front of the building he set two
columns thirty-five cubits high; the cap-
ital topping each was of five cubits. 16 He
worked out chains in the form of a collar
with which he encircled the capitals of
the columns, and he made a hundred
pomegranates which he set on the
chains. 17 He set up the columns to corre-
spond with the nave, one for the right
side and the other for the left, and he
called the one to the right Jachin and
the one to the left Boaz.

CHAPTER 4

1* Then he made a bronze altar twenty
cubits long, twenty cubits wide and ten
cubits high. 2* He also made the molten
sea. It was perfectly round, ten cubits
in diameter, five in depth, and thirty in
circumference; 3† below the rim a ring
of figures of oxen encircled the sea, ten
to the cubit, all the way around; there
were two rows of these cast in the same
mold with the sea. 4 It rested on twelve
oxen, three facing north, three west,
three south, and three east, with their

*

14f: 1 Kgs 5, 22-26.
15: Ezr 3, 7.
16f: 1 Chr 22, 2.
17: 2, 1.
3, 1f: Gn 22, 2; 1 Kgs 6, 1; 1 Chr 21, 22-26.
3: 1 Kgs 6, 2; Ez 40, 5.
4: 1 Kgs 6, 3; Ez 40, 48.
5: 1 Kgs 6, 15; Ez 41, 1.
8: 1 Kgs 6, 16f.20; Ez 41, 3.
10-13: 1 Kgs 6, 23-27.
14: Mt 27, 51.
15ff: 1 Kgs 7, 15-22; Ez 40, 49.
4, 1: Ez 43, 13-17.
2-5: 1 Kgs 7, 23-26; Ez 43, 13.

†

3, 1: *Mount Moriah:* the *height* in *the land of Moriah* (Gn 22, 2). This is the only place in the Bible where the temple mount is identified with the site where Abraham was to sacrifice Isaac.

3, 4: *The porch . . . twenty cubits high:* this measurement, not given in the Books of Kings, is here based on a variant Greek text that may be a later revision. The received Hebrew text says, "one hundred and twenty cubits high." The height of the two free-standing columns adjacent to the porch (1 Kgs 7, 15-16) is nearly doubled by the Chronicler (3, 15).

3, 14: *The veil:* at the entrance of the holy of holies, as also in the Mosaic meeting tent (Ex 26, 31f). Solomon's temple had doors at this place (1 Kgs 6, 31). Apparently there was a veil here in the temple of the Chronicler's time as there was also in Herod's temple (Mt 27, 51; Mk 15, 38; Lk 23, 45).

4, 3: *Oxen:* in 1 Kgs 7, 24 this double row of ornaments is described as being gourds. The text of Kings available to the Chronicler may have been faulty on this point as the words are similar in sound. In 4, 16 the *forks* correspond in a similar way to *bowls* in the text of 1 Kgs (7, 40).

haunches all toward the center; the sea rested on their backs. 5† It was a handbreadth thick, and its brim was made like that of a cup, being lily-shaped. It had a capacity of three thousand measures.

6* Then he made ten basins for washing, placing five of them to the right and five to the left. Here were cleansed the victims for the holocausts; but the sea was for the priests to wash in.

7* He made the lampstands of gold, ten of them as was prescribed, and placed them in the nave, five to the right and five to the left. 8* He made ten tables and had them set in the nave, five to the right and five to the left; and he made a hundred golden bowls. 9* He made the court of the priests and the great courtyard and the gates of the courtyard; the gates he overlaid with bronze. 10* The sea was placed off to the southeast from the right side of the temple.

11* Huram also made the pots, the shovels and the bowls. Huram thus completed the work he had to do for King Solomon in the house of God: 12 two columns, two nodes for the capitals topping these two columns, and two networks covering the nodes of the capitals topping the columns; 13 also four hundred pomegranates for the two networks, with two rows of pomegranates to each network, to cover the two nodes of the capitals topping the columns. 14 He made the stands, and the basins on the stands; 15 one sea, and the twelve oxen under it; 16 likewise the pots, the shovels and the forks. Huram-abi made all these articles for King Solomon from polished bronze for the house of the LORD. 17 The king had them cast in the Jordan region, in the clayey ground between Succoth and Zeredah. 18 Solomon made all these vessels, so many in number that the weight of the bronze was not ascertained.

19 Solomon had all these articles made for the house of God: the golden altar, the tables on which the showbread lay, 20 the lampstands and their lamps of pure gold which were to burn according to prescription before the sanctuary, 21 flowers, lamps and gold tongs [this was the purest gold], 22 snuffers, bowls, cups and firepans of pure gold. As for the entry to the house, its inner doors to the holy of holies, as well as the doors to the nave, were of gold.

CHAPTER 5

Dedication of the Temple. 1* When all the work undertaken by Solomon for the temple of the LORD had been completed, he brought in the dedicated offerings of his father David, putting the silver, the gold and all the other articles in the treasuries of the house of God. 2 At Solomon's order the elders of Israel and all the leaders of the tribes, the princes of the Israelite ancestral houses, came to Jerusalem to bring up the ark of the LORD's covenant from the City of David (which is Zion). 3 All the men of Israel assembled before the king during the festival of the seventh month. 4*† When all the elders of Israel had arrived, the Levites took up the ark, 5 and they carried the ark and the meeting tent with all the sacred vessels that were in the tent; it was the levitical priests who carried them.

6 King Solomon and the entire community of Israel gathered about him before the ark were sacrificing sheep and oxen so numerous that they could not be counted or numbered. 7 The priests brought the ark of the covenant of the LORD to its place beneath the wings of the cherubim in the sanctuary, the holy of holies of the temple. 8 The cherubim had their wings spread out over the place of the ark, sheltering the ark and its poles from above. 9† The poles were long enough so that their ends could be seen from that part of the holy place nearest the sanctuary; however, they could not be seen beyond. The ark has remained there to this day. 10 There was nothing in it but the two tablets which Moses put there on Horeb, the tablets of the covenant which the LORD made with the Israelites at their departure from Egypt.

11 When the priests came out of the holy place (all the priests who were present had purified themselves without reference to the rotation of their various classes), 12 the Levites who were singers, all who belonged to Asaph, Heman, Jeduthun, and their sons and brothers, clothed in fine linen, with cymbals, harps and lyres, stood east of the altar, and with them a hundred and twenty priests blowing trumpets.

13 When the trumpeters and singers were heard as a single voice praising and giving thanks to the LORD, and when they raised the sound of the trumpets, cymbals and other musical instruments

*

6: 1 Kgs 7, 38f; Ez 40, 38.
7: 1 Kgs 7, 49.
8: 1 Kgs 7, 50; 1 Chr 28, 16.
9: 1 Kgs 7, 12.
10: 1 Kgs 7, 39.
11-22: 1 Kgs 7, 40-51.
5, 1-14: 1 Kgs 7, 51—8, 13.
4f: 35, 3.

†

4, 5: *Three thousand measures:* according to 1 Kgs 7, 26, *two thousand measures.*

5, 4: *The Levites:* The parallel passage in 1 Kgs 8, 3 has *the priests;* but see 2 Chr 5, 5, where the Deuteronomic term *levitical priests* is used, as also in 23, 18; 30, 27.

5, 9: *The ark has remained there to this day:* the Chronicler must have copied this from his source (1 Kgs 8, 8) without reflecting that the ark was lost in the Babylonian destruction of Jerusalem; cf 2 Mc 2, 4-8.

to "give thanks to the LORD, for he is
good, for his mercy endures forever,"
the building of the LORD's temple was
filled with a cloud. 14* The priests could
not continue to minister because of the
cloud, since the LORD's glory filled the
house of God.

CHAPTER 6

1* Then Solomon said: "The LORD in-
tends to dwell in the dark cloud. 2 I have
truly built you a princely house and
dwelling, where you may abide for-
ever." 3* Turning about, the king
greeted the whole community of Israel
as they stood. 4 He said: "Blessed be the
LORD, the God of Israel, who with his
own mouth made a promise to my father
David and by his own hands brought it
to fulfillment. He said: 5 'Since the day
I brought my people out of the land of
Egypt, I have not chosen any city from
among all the tribes of Israel for the
building of a temple to my honor, nor
have I chosen any man to be com-
mander of my people Israel; 6 but now
I choose Jerusalem, where I shall be
honored, and I choose David to rule my
people Israel.' 7 My father David wished
to build a temple to the honor of the
LORD, the God of Israel, 8 but the LORD
said to him: 'In wishing to build a temple
to my honor, you do well. 9 However, you
shall not build the temple; rather, your
son whom you will beget shall build the
temple to my honor.'

10 "Now the LORD has fulfilled the
promise that he made. I have succeeded
my father David and have taken my seat
on the throne of Israel, as the LORD fore-
told, and I have built the temple to the
honor of the LORD, the God of Israel.
11 And I have placed there the ark, in
which abides the covenant of the LORD
which he made with the Israelites."

Solomon's Prayer. 12* Solomon then
took his place before the altar of the
LORD in the presence of the whole com-
munity of Israel and stretched forth his
hands. 13† He had made a bronze plat-
form five cubits long, five cubits wide,
and three cubits high, which he had
placed in the middle of the courtyard.
Having ascended it, Solomon knelt in the
presence of the whole of Israel and
stretched forth his hands toward
heaven. 14 Thus he prayed: "LORD, God
of Israel, there is no god like you in
heaven or on earth; you keep your cov-
enant and show kindness to your ser-
vants who are wholeheartedly faithful
to you. 15 You have kept the promise you
made to my father David, your servant.
With your own mouth you spoke it, and
by your own hand you have brought it
to fulfillment this day. 16 Now, therefore,
LORD, God of Israel, keep the further
promise you made to my father David,
your servant, when you said, 'You shall
always have someone from your line to
sit before me on the throne of Israel, pro-
vided only that your descendants look
to their conduct so as always to live ac-
cording to my law, even as you have
lived in my presence.' 17 Now, LORD, God
of Israel, may this promise which you
made to your servant David be con-
firmed.

18 "Can it indeed be that God dwells
with mankind on earth? If the heavens
and the highest heavens cannot contain
you, how much less this temple which
I have built! 19 Look kindly on the prayer
and petition of your servant, O LORD, my
God, and listen to the cry of supplication
your servant makes before you. 20 May
your eyes watch day and night over this
temple, the place where you have de-
creed you shall be honored; may you
heed the prayer which I your servant
offer toward this place. 21 Listen to the
petitions of your servant and of your
people Israel which they direct toward
this place. Listen from your heavenly
dwelling, and when you have heard,
pardon.

22 "When any man sins against his
neighbor and is required to take an oath
of execration against himself, and when
he comes for the oath before your altar
in this temple, 23 listen from heaven: take
action and pass judgment on your ser-
vants, requiting the wicked man and
holding him responsible for his conduct,
but absolving the innocent and reward-
ing him according to his virtue. 24 When
your people Israel have sinned against
you and are defeated by the enemy, but
afterward they return and praise your
name, and they pray to you and entreat
you in this temple, 25 listen from heaven
and forgive the sin of your people Israel,
and bring them back to the land which
you gave them and their fathers.
26 When the sky is closed so that there
is no rain, because they have sinned
against you, but then they pray toward
this place and praise your name, and
they withdraw from sin because you af-
flict them, 27 listen in heaven and forgive
the sin of your servants and of your peo-
ple Israel. But teach them the right way
to live, and send rain upon your land
which you gave your people as their her-
itage. 28 When there is famine in the
land, when there is pestilence, or blight,

*

14: 7, 2; 1 Kgs 8, 10f.
6, 1f: 1 Kgs 8, 12f.
3-11: 1 Kgs 8, 14-21.
12-41: 1 Kgs 8, 22-53.

†

6, 13: This verse is not found in the Chronicler's source; cf 1 Kgs 8, 22f. He has Solomon praying on *a bronze platform . . . in the middle of the courtyard* because at the time of the Chronicler only the priests prayed before the altar.

or mildew, or locusts, or caterpillars;
when their enemies besiege them at any
of their gates; whenever there is a plague
or sickness of any kind; 29 when any Is-
raelite of all your people offers a prayer
or petition of any kind, and in awareness
of his affliction and pain, stretches out
his hands toward this temple, 30 listen
from your heavenly dwelling place, and
forgive. Knowing his heart, render to ev-
eryone according to his conduct, for you
alone know the hearts of men. 31 So may
they fear you and walk in your ways as
long as they live on the land you gave
our fathers.

32 "For the foreigner, too, who is not
of your people Israel, when he comes
from a distant land to honor your great
name, your mighty power, and your out-
stretched arm, when they come in
prayer to this temple, 33 listen from your
heavenly dwelling place, and do what-
ever the foreigner entreats you, that all
the peoples of the earth may know your
name, fearing you as do your people Is-
rael, and knowing that this house which
I have built is dedicated to your honor.

34 "When your people go forth to war
against their enemies, wherever you
send them, and pray to you in the direc-
tion of this city and of the house I have
built to your honor, 35 listen from heaven
to their prayer and petition, and defend
their cause. 36 When they sin against you
(for there is no man who does not sin),
and in your anger against them you de-
liver them to the enemy, so that their
captors deport them to another land, far
or near, 37 when they repent in the land
where they are captive and are con-
verted, when they entreat you in the
land of their captivity and say, 'We have
sinned and done wrong; we have been
wicked,' 38 and with their whole heart
and with their whole soul they turn back
to you in the land of those who hold them
captive, when they pray in the direction
of their land which you gave their fa-
thers, and of the city you have chosen,
and of the house which I have built to
your honor, 39 listen from your heavenly
dwelling place, hear their prayer and
petitions, and uphold their cause. For-
give your people who have sinned
against you. 40 My God, may your eyes
be open and your ears attentive to the
prayer of this place. 41 And now,

"Advance, LORD God, to your resting place,
 you and the ark of your majesty.
May your priests, LORD God, be clothed with salvation,
 may your faithful ones rejoice in good things.
42 LORD God, reject not the plea of your anointed,
 remember the devotion of David, your servant."

CHAPTER 7

1* When Solomon had ended his
prayer, fire came down from heaven
and consumed the holocaust and the
sacrifices, and the glory of the LORD
filled the house. 2* But the priests could
not enter the house of the LORD, for the
glory of the LORD had filled the house
of the LORD. 3 All the Israelites looked
on while the fire came down and the
glory of the LORD was upon the house,
and they fell down upon the pavement
with their faces to the earth and adored,
praising the LORD, "for he is good, for
his mercy endures forever." 4* The king
and all the people were offering sacri-
fices before the LORD. 5* King Solomon
offered as sacrifice twenty-two thousand
oxen, and one hundred twenty thousand
sheep.

End of the Dedication. 6* Thus the
king and all the people dedicated the
house of God. The priests were standing
at their stations, as were the Levites,
with the musical instruments of the
LORD which King David had made for
"praising the LORD, for his mercy en-
dures forever," when David used them
to accompany the hymns. Across from
them the priests blew the trumpets and
all Israel stood.

7* Then Solomon consecrated the mid-
dle part of the court which lay before
the house of the LORD; there he offered
the holocausts and the fat of the peace
offerings, since the bronze altar which
Solomon had made could not hold the
holocausts, the cereal offerings and the
fat.

8* On this occasion Solomon and with
him all Israel, who had assembled in
very large numbers from Labo of Ha-
math to the Wadi of Egypt, celebrated
the festival for seven days. 9*† On the
eighth day they held a special meeting,
for they had celebrated the dedication
of the altar for seven days and the feast
for seven days. 10 On the twenty-third
day of the seventh month he sent the
people back to their tents, rejoicing and
glad at heart at the good things the LORD

*

7, 1-10: 1 Kgs 8, 54-66; Jgs 6, 21; 1 Chr 21, 26; 2 Mc 2, 10.
2: 5, 14; Ex 24, 16; 1 Kgs 8, 10f.
4: 5, 13; 1 Kgs 8, 62; Ps 136, 1.
5: 1 Kgs 8, 62f.
6: Nm 10, 8. 10; Ps 136, 1.
7: 1 Kgs 8, 64.
8: 1 Kgs 8, 65.
9f: 1 Kgs 8, 66.

†

7, 9f: *The feast:* of Booths, celebrated on the fifteenth day of the seventh month and followed by a solemn octave lasting through the twenty-second day (Lv 23, 33-36; Nm 29, 12-35); the people are therefore sent home on the twenty-third day (v 10). The festival (v 8) for *the dedication of the altar* and of the temple lasted for seven days before the feast of Booths, from the seventh to the fourteenth day. According to 1 Kgs 8, 65f, the people are dismissed at the end of these seven days.

had done for David, for Solomon, and
for his people Israel. 11* Solomon com-
pleted the house of the LORD and the
royal palace; he successfully accom-
plished everything he had planned to do
in regard to the house of the LORD and
his own house.

God's Promise to Solomon. 12 The
LORD appeared to Solomon during the
night and said to him: "I have heard
your prayer, and I have chosen this
place for my house of sacrifice. 13 If I
close heaven so that there is no rain, if
I command the locust to devour the land,
if I send pestilence among my people,
14 and if my people, upon whom my
name has been pronounced, humble
themselves and pray, and seek my pres-
ence and turn from their evil ways, I will
hear them from heaven and pardon
their sins and revive their land. 15 Now
my eyes shall be open and my ears at-
tentive to the prayer of this place. 16 And
now I have chosen and consecrated this
house that my name may be there for-
ever; my eyes and my heart also shall
be there always.

17 "As for you, if you live in my pres-
ence as your father David did, doing all
that I have commanded you and keep-
ing my statutes and ordinances, 18 I will
establish your royal throne as I cove-
nanted with your father David when I
said, 'There shall never be lacking
someone of yours as ruler in Israel.'
19 But if you turn away and forsake my
statutes and commands which I placed
before you, if you proceed to venerate
and worship strange gods, 20 then I will
uproot the people from the land I gave
them; I will cast from my sight this
house which I have consecrated to my
honor, and I will make it a proverb and
a byword among all peoples. 21 This tem-
ple which is so exalted—everyone pass-
ing by it will be amazed and ask: 'Why
has the LORD done this to this land and
to this house?' 22 And men will answer:
'They forsook the LORD, the God of their
fathers, who brought them out of the
land of Egypt, and they adopted strange
gods and worshiped them and served
them. That is why he has brought down
upon them all this evil.' "

CHAPTER 8

Public Works. 1* After the twenty
years during which Solomon built the
house of the LORD and his own house,
2† he built up the cities which Huram
had given him, and settled Israelites
there. 3 Then Solomon went to Hamath
of Zoba and conquered it. 4† He built
Tadmor in the desert region and all the
supply cities, which he built in Hamath.
5* He built Upper Beth-horon and Lower
Beth-horon, fortified cities with walls,
gates and bars; 6 also Baalath, all the
supply cities belonging to Solomon, and
all the cities for the chariots, the cities
for the horsemen, and whatever else
Solomon decided should be built in Jeru-
salem, in the Lebanon, and in the entire
land under his dominion. 7 All the people
that remained of the Hittites, Amorites,
Perizzites, Hivites, and Jebusites, who
were not of Israel—8 that is, their de-
scendants remaining in the land, whom
the Israelites had not destroyed—Solo-
mon subjected to forced labor, as they
continue to this day. 9 But Solomon did
not enslave the Israelites for his works.
They became soldiers, commanders of
his warriors, and commanders of his
chariots and his horsemen. 10 They were
also King Solomon's two hundred and
fifty overseers who had charge of the
people.

Solomon's Piety. 11 Solomon brought
the daughter of Pharaoh up from the
City of David to the palace which he had
built for her, for he said, "No wife of
mine shall dwell in the house of David,
king of Israel, for the places where the
ark of the LORD has come are holy."

12 In those times Solomon offered holo-
causts to the LORD upon the altar of the
LORD which he had built in front of the
porch, 13* as was required day by day
according to the command of Moses,
and in particular on the sabbaths, at the
new moons, and on the fixed festivals
three times a year: on the feast of the
Unleavened Bread, the feast of Weeks
and the feast of Booths.

14* And according to the ordinance of
his father David he appointed the vari-
ous classes of the priests for their ser-
vice, and the Levites according to their
functions of praise and ministry along-
side the priests, as the daily duty re-
quired. The gatekeepers of the various
classes stood guard at each gate, since
such was the command of David, the
man of God. 15 There was no deviation
from the king's command in any respect
relating to the priests and Levites or the
treasuries. 16 All of Solomon's work was
carried out successfully from the day
the foundation of the house of the
LORD was laid until the house of the

*

11-22: 1 Kgs 9, 1-9.
8, 1f: 1 Kgs 9, 10f.
5-12: 1 Kgs 9, 18-25.
13: 1 Kgs 9, 25; Ex 23, 14; Nm 28-29.
14: 1 Chr 23-26; Neh 12, 46.

†

8, 2: *The cities which Huram had given him:* according to 1 Kgs 9, 10-14, Solomon had ceded the cities as payment for the timber and gold received from Tyre. But since Huram was dissatisfied, he may have returned the cities to Solomon.

8, 4: *Tadmor:* later known as Palmyra, an important caravan city in the Syrian desert. The parallel passage in 1 Kgs 9, 18 has *Tamar,* in southern Judah; cf Ez 47, 19; 48, 28. But Solomon may well have fortified Tadmor against the Arameans.

LORD had been completed in every de-
tail.
Glories of the Court. 17* In those times
Solomon went to Ezion-geber and to
Elath on the seashore of the land of
Edom. 18* Huram, through his servants,
sent him ships and crewmen acquainted
with the sea, who accompanied Solo-
mon's servants to Ophir and brought
back from there four hundred and fifty
talents of gold to King Solomon.

CHAPTER 9

1* When the queen of Sheba heard of
Solomon's fame, she came to Jerusalem
to test him with subtle questions, accom-
panied by a very numerous retinue and
by camels bearing spices, much gold,
and precious stones. She came to Solo-
mon and questioned him on every sub-
ject in which she was interested.
2 Solomon explained to her everything
she asked about, and there remained
nothing hidden from Solomon that he
could not explain to her.
3 When the queen of Sheba witnessed
Solomon's wisdom, the palace he had
built, 4 the food at his table, the seating
of his ministers, the attendance of his
servants and their dress, his cupbearers
and their dress, and the holocausts he
offered in the house of the LORD, it took
her breath away. 5 "The account I heard
in my country about your deeds and
your wisdom is true," she told the king.
6 "Yet I did not believe the report until
I came and saw with my own eyes. I
have discovered that they did not tell me
the half of your great wisdom; you have
surpassed the stories I heard. 7 Happy
are your men, happy these servants of
yours, who stand before you always and
listen to your wisdom. 8 Blessed be the
LORD, your God, who has been so
pleased with you as to place you on his
throne as king for the LORD, your God.
Because your God has so loved Israel
as to will to make it last forever, he has
appointed you over them as king to ad-
minister right and justice." 9 Then she
gave the king one hundred and twenty
gold talents and a very large quantity
of spices, as well as precious stones.
There was no other spice like that which
the queen of Sheba gave to King Solo-
mon.
10 The servants of Huram and of Solo-
mon who brought gold from Ophir also
brought cabinet wood and precious
stones. 11 With the cabinet wood the king
made stairs for the temple of the LORD
and the palace of the king; also lyres and
harps for the chanters. The like of these
had not been seen before in the land of
Judah.
12 King Solomon gave the queen of
Sheba everything she desired and asked
him for, more than she had brought to
the king. Then she returned to her own
country with her servants.
13* The gold that Solomon received
each year weighed six hundred and
sixty-six gold talents, 14 in addition to
what was collected from travelers and
what the merchants brought. All the
kings of Arabia also, and the governors
of the country, brought gold and silver
to Solomon.
15 Moreover, King Solomon made two
hundred large shields of beaten gold, six
hundred shekels of beaten gold going
into each shield, 16 and three hundred
bucklers of beaten gold, three hundred
shekels of gold going into each buckler;
these the king put in the hall of the For-
est of Lebanon.
17 King Solomon also made a large
ivory throne which he overlaid with fine
gold. 18 The throne had six steps; a foot-
stool of gold was fastened to it, and there
was an arm on each side of the seat, with
two lions standing beside the arms.
19 Twelve other lions also stood there,
one on either side of each step. Nothing
like this had ever been produced in any
other kingdom. 20 Furthermore, all of
King Solomon's drinking vessels were of
gold, and all the utensils in the hall of
the Forest of Lebanon were of pure gold;
silver was not considered of value in Sol-
omon's time. 21 For the king had ships
that went to Tarshish with the servants
of Huram. Once every three years the
fleet of Tarshish would return with a
cargo of gold and silver, ivory, apes and
monkeys. 22 Thus King Solomon sur-
passed all the other kings of the earth
in riches as well as in wisdom.
23 All the kings of the earth sought au-
dience with Solomon, to hear from him
the wisdom which God had put in his
heart. 24 Year in and year out, each one
would bring his tribute—silver and gold
articles, garments, weapons, spices,
horses and mules. 25 Solomon also had
four thousand stalls of horses, chariots,
and twelve thousand horsemen, which
he assigned to the chariot cities and to
the king in Jerusalem. 26 He was ruler
over all the kings from the River to the
land of the Philistines and down to the
border of Egypt. 27 The king made silver
as common in Jerusalem as stones,
while cedars became as numerous as the
sycamores of the foothills. 28† Horses
were imported for Solomon from Egypt
and from all the lands.
The Death of Solomon. 29* The rest of

*

17: 1 Kgs 9, 26; Mt 12, 42; Lk 11, 31.
18: 1 Kgs 9, 27f.
9, 1: 1 Kgs 10, 1f; Mt 12, 42; Lk 11, 31.
13-28: 1 Kgs 10, 14-28.
29ff: 1 Kgs 11, 41ff.

†

9, 28: See note on 1, 16f.

the acts of Solomon, first and last, are written, as is well known, in the acts of Nathan the prophet, in the prophecy of Ahijah the Shilonite, and in the visions of Iddo the seer which concern Jeroboam, son of Nebat. 30 Solomon reigned in Jerusalem over all Israel for forty years. 31 He rested with his ancestors; he was buried in his father's City of David, and his son Rehoboam succeeded him as king.

II: THE MONARCHY BEFORE HEZEKIAH

CHAPTER 10

Division of the Kingdom. 1*† Rehoboam went to Shechem, for all Israel had come to Shechem to proclaim him king. 2 When Jeroboam, son of Nebat, heard of this in Egypt where he had fled from King Solomon, he returned from Egypt. 3 Jeroboam was summoned to the assembly, and he and all Israel said to Rehoboam: 4 "Your father laid a heavy yoke upon us. If you now lighten the harsh service and the heavy yoke that your father imposed on us, we will serve you." 5 "In three days," he answered them, "come back to me."

When the people had departed, 6 King Rehoboam consulted the elders who had been in the service of his father during Solomon's lifetime, asking, "What answer do you advise me to give this people?" 7 They replied, "If you will deal kindly with this people and give in to them, acceding to their request, they will be your servants forever." 8 But he ignored the advice the elders had given him and consulted the young men who had grown up with him and were in his service. 9 He said to them, "What answer do you advise me to give this people, who have asked me to lighten the yoke my father imposed on them?" 10 The young men who had grown up with him replied: "This is the answer you should give to this people who have said to you, 'Your father laid a heavy yoke upon us, but do you lighten our yoke'; this you should say to them: 'My little finger is thicker than my father's body. 11 Whereas my father put a heavy yoke on you, I will make it heavier! My father beat you with whips, but I will beat you with scorpions!' "

12 On the third day, Jeroboam and all the people came back to King Rehoboam as he had instructed them to do. 13 Ignoring the advice the elders had given him, the king gave them a harsh answer, 14 speaking to them according to the advice of the young men: "My father laid a heavy yoke on you, but I will make it heavier. My father beat you with whips, but I will beat you with scorpions." 15* The king would not listen to the people, for this turn of events was divinely ordained to fulfill the prophecy the LORD had uttered to Jeroboam, the son of Nebat, through Ahijah the Shilonite.

16* When all Israel saw that the king would not listen to them, the people answered the king.

"What share have we in David?
We have no heritage in the son of Jesse.
Everyone to your tents, O Israel!
Now look to your own house, David!"

So all Israel went off to their tents. 17 Rehoboam, therefore, reigned over only those Israelites who lived in the cities of Judah. 18 King Rehoboam then sent out Hadoram, who was superintendent of the forced labor, but the Israelites stoned him to death. Rehoboam himself managed to mount his chariot and flee to Jerusalem. 19 Thus Israel has been in rebellion against David's house to this day.

CHAPTER 11

1* On his arrival in Jerusalem Rehoboam gathered together the house of Judah and Benjamin, a hundred and eighty thousand seasoned warriors, to have them fight against Israel and restore the kingdom to him. 2 However, the word of the LORD came to Shemaiah, a man of God: 3 "Say to Rehoboam, son of Solomon, king of Judah, and to all the Israelites in Judah and Benjamin: 4 'Thus says the LORD: You must not march out to fight against your brothers. Let every man return home, for what has occurred I have brought about.' " They obeyed this message of the LORD and gave up the expedition against Jeroboam.

Rehoboam's Works. 5† Rehoboam took up residence in Jerusalem and built fortified cities in Judah. 6 He built up Bethlehem, Etam, Tekoa, 7 Beth-zur, Soco, Adullam, 8 Gath, Mareshah, Ziph, 9 Adoraim, Lachish, Azekah, 10 Zorah, Aijalon, and Hebron; these were fortified cities in Judah and Benjamin. 11 Then he strengthened the fortifications and put commanders in them, with supplies of

---

*

10, 1-14: 1 Kgs 12, 1-14. 15: 1 Kgs 11, 29-39; 12, 15. 16-19: 1 Kgs 12, 16-19. 11, 1-4: 1 Kgs 12, 21-24.

---

†

10, 1: *All Israel:* as in the original source (1 Kgs 12, 1), the northern tribes, distinct from Judah and Benjamin. Contrast the Chronicler's own terms, *those Israelites who lived in the cities of Judah* (v 17), and *all the Israelites* [literally, all Israel] *in Judah* and *Benjamin* (11, 3).

11, 5-12: These verses, though not found in 1 Kgs, are apparently based on a reliable, ancient source.

food, oil and wine. 12 In every city were shields and spears, and he made them very strong. Thus Judah and Benjamin remained his.

Refugees from the North. 13 Now the priests and Levites throughout Israel presented themselves to him from all parts of their land, 14* for the Levites left their assigned pasture lands and their holdings and came to Judah and Jerusalem, because Jeroboam and his sons repudiated them as priests of the LORD. 15* In their place, he himself appointed priests for the high places and satyrs and calves he had made. 16 After them, all those of the Israelite tribes who firmly desired to seek the LORD, the God of Israel, came to Jerusalem to sacrifice to the LORD, the God of their fathers. 17 Thus they strengthened the kingdom of Judah and made Rehoboam, son of Solomon, prevail for three years; for they walked in the way of David and Solomon three years.

Rehoboam's Family. 18 Rehoboam took to himself as wife Mahalath, daughter of Jerimoth, son of David and of Abihail, daughter of Eliab, son of Jesse. 19 She bore him sons: Jehush, Shemariah and Zaham. 20* After her, he married Maacah, daughter of Absalom, who bore him Abijah, Attai, Ziza and Shelomith. 21 Rehoboam loved Maacah, daughter of Absalom, more than all his other wives and concubines; he had taken eighteen wives and sixty concubines, and he fathered twenty-eight sons and sixty daughters. 22 Rehoboam constituted Abijah, son of Maacah, commander among his brothers, for he intended to make him king. 23 He acted prudently, distributing various of his sons throughout all the districts of Judah and Benjamin, in all the fortified cities; and he furnished them with copious provisions and sought an abundance of wives for them.

CHAPTER 12

His Apostasy. 1* After Rehoboam had consolidated his rule and had become powerful, he abandoned the law of the LORD, he and all Israel with him. 2* Thus it happened that in the fifth year of King Rehoboam, Shishak, king of Egypt, attacked Jerusalem, for they had been unfaithful to the LORD. 3† He came up with twelve hundred chariots and sixty thousand horsemen, and there was no counting the army that came with him from Egypt—Libyans, Sukkites and Ethiopians. 4 They captured the fortified cities of Judah and came as far as Jerusalem. 5* Then Shemaiah the prophet came to Rehoboam and the commanders of Judah who had gathered at Jerusalem because of Shishak, and said to them: "Thus says the LORD: 'You have abandoned me, and therefore I have abandoned you to the power of Shishak.'"

6 However, the commanders of Israel and the king humbled themselves saying, "The LORD is just." 7 When the LORD saw that they had humbled themselves, the word of the LORD came to Shemaiah: "Because they have humbled themselves, I will not destroy them; I will give them some deliverance, and my wrath shall not be poured out upon Jerusalem through Shishak. 8 But they shall be his servants, that they may know what it is to serve me and what it is to serve earthly kingdoms." 9* Therefore Shishak, king of Egypt, attacked Jerusalem and carried off the treasures of the temple of the LORD and of the king's palace. He took everything, including the gold bucklers that Solomon had made. 10 (To replace them, King Rehoboam made bronze bucklers, which he entrusted to the officers of the guard on duty at the entrance of the royal palace. 11 Whenever the king visited the temple of the LORD, the troops would come bearing them, and then they would return them to the guardroom.) 12 Because he had humbled himself, the anger of the LORD turned from him so that it did not destroy him completely; and in Judah, moreover, good deeds were found.

13* King Rehoboam consolidated his power in Jerusalem and continued to rule; he was forty-one years old when he became king, and he reigned seventeen years in Jerusalem, the city in which, out of all the tribes of Israel, the LORD chose to be honored. Rehoboam's mother was named Naamah, an Ammonite. 14 He did evil, for he had not truly resolved to seek the LORD. 15* The acts of Rehoboam, first and last, are written, as is well known, in the history of Shemaiah the prophet and of Iddo the seer [his family record]. There was war continually between Rehoboam and Jeroboam. 16 Rehoboam rested with his ancestors; he was buried in the City of David. His son Abijah succeeded him as king.

CHAPTER 13

War between Abijah and Jeroboam. 1* In the eighteenth year of King Jeroboam, Abijah became king of Judah; 2 he reigned three years in Jerusalem. His

*

14: 1 Kgs 12, 32.
15: 1 Kgs 12, 32; Lv 17, 7.
20: 1 Kgs 15, 2.
12, 1: 1 Kgs 11, 4; 14, 22.
2: 1 Kgs 14, 25.
5: 11, 2.
9ff: 1 Kgs 14, 25-28.
13: 1 Kgs 14, 21.
15f: 1 Kgs 14, 29ff.
13, 1f: 1 Kgs 15, 1f.

†

12, 3: *Sukkites:* foreign mercenaries in the Egyptian army.

mother was named Michaiah, daughter of Uriel of Gibeah. There was war between Abijah and Jeroboam.

3 Abijah joined battle with a force of four hundred thousand picked warriors, while Jeroboam lined up against him in battle with eight hundred thousand picked and valiant warriors. 4† Abijah stood on Mount Zemariam, which is in the highlands of Ephraim, and said: "Listen to me, Jeroboam and all Israel! 5 Do you not know that the LORD, the God of Israel, has given the kingdom of Israel to David forever, to him and to his sons, by a covenant made in salt? 6* Yet Jeroboam, son of Nebat, the servant of Solomon, son of David, has stood up and rebelled against his lord! 7 Worthless men, scoundrels, joined him and overcame Rehoboam, son of Solomon, when Rehoboam was young and unthinking, and no match for them. 8 But now, do you think you are a match for the kingdom of the LORD commanded by the sons of David, simply because you are a huge multitude and have with you the golden calves which Jeroboam made you for gods?

9 "Have you not expelled the priests of the LORD, the sons of Aaron, and the Levites, and made for yourselves priests like the peoples of foreign lands? Everyone who comes to consecrate himself with a young bull and seven rams becomes a priest of no-gods. 10 But as for us, the LORD is our God, and we have not forsaken him. The priests ministering to the LORD are sons of Aaron, and the Levites also have their offices. 11 They burn holocausts to the LORD and fragrant incense morning after morning and evening after evening; they display the showbread on the pure table, and the lamps of the golden lampstand burn evening after evening; for we observe our duties to the LORD, our God, but you have abandoned him. 12 See, God is with us, at our head, and his priests are here with trumpets to sound the attack against you. Do not battle against the LORD, the God of your fathers, O Israelites, for you will not succeed!"

13 But Jeroboam had an ambush go around them to come at them from the rear; so that while his army faced Judah, his ambush lay behind them. 14 When Judah turned and saw that they had to battle on both fronts, they cried out to the LORD and the priests sounded the trumpets. 15 Then the men of Judah shouted; and when they did so, God defeated Jeroboam and all Israel before Abijah and Judah. 16 The Israelites fled before Judah, and God delivered them into their hands. 17 Abijah and his people inflicted a severe defeat upon them; five hundred thousand picked men of Israel fell slain. 18 The Israelites were subdued on that occasion and the Judahites were victorious because they relied on the LORD, the God of their fathers. 19 Abijah pursued Jeroboam and took cities from him: Bethel and its dependencies, Jeshanah and its dependencies, and Ephron and its dependencies. 20 Jeroboam did not regain power during the time of Abijah; the LORD struck him down and he died, 21 while Abijah continued to grow stronger. He took to himself fourteen wives and fathered twenty-two sons and sixteen daughters.

Death of Abijah. 22* The rest of Abijah's acts, his deeds and his words, are written in the midrash of the prophet Iddo. 23 Abijah rested with his ancestors; they buried him in the City of David. His son Asa succeeded him as king. During his time, ten years of peace began in the land.

CHAPTER 14

Asa the Reformer. 1* Asa did what was good and pleasing to the LORD, his God, 2 removing the heathen altars and the high places, breaking to pieces the sacred pillars, and cutting down the sacred poles. 3 He commanded Judah to seek the LORD, the God of their fathers, and to observe the law and its commands. 4 He removed the high places and incense stands from all the cities of Judah, and under him the kingdom had peace. 5 He built fortified cities in Judah, for the land had peace and no war was waged against him during these years, because the LORD had given him peace. 6 He said to Judah: "Let us build these cities and surround them with walls, towers, gates and bars. The land is still ours, for we have sought the LORD, our God; we sought him, and he has given us rest on every side." So they built and prospered.

The Ethiopian Invasion. 7† Asa had an army of three hundred thousand shield- and lance-bearers from Judah, and two hundred and eighty thousand from Benjamin who carried bucklers and were archers, all of them valiant warriors. 8* Zerah the Ethiopian moved against them with a force of one million men and three hundred chariots, and he came as far as Mareshah. 9 Asa went out to meet him and set himself in battle ar-

*

6: 1 Kgs 11, 26.
22f: 12, 15; 1 Kgs 15, 7ff.
14, 1f: 33, 15; Ex 23, 24; 34, 13; 1 Kgs 15, 11f.
8: 16, 8.

†

13, 4-12: This is a free composition of the Chronicler to show that this was a religious, rather than a political, war.

14, 7-14: An Ethiopian invasion of Judah is mentioned only in 1 Chronicles. This account may be a legend contrived to show how the pious King Asa was rewarded through divine assistance. There may, however, have been an incursion of nomads from the Negeb at this time; cf vv 13f.

ray in the valley of Zephathah, near Mareshah. 10* Asa called upon the LORD, his God, praying: "O LORD, there is none like you to help the powerless against the strong. Help us, O LORD, our God, for we rely on you, and in your name we have come against this multitude. You are the LORD, our God; let no man prevail against you." 11* And so the LORD defeated the Ethiopians before Asa and Judah, and they fled. 12 Asa and those with him pursued them as far as Gerar, and the Ethiopians fell until there were no survivors, for they were crushed before the LORD and his army, which carried away enormous spoils. 13 Then the Judahites conquered all the cities around Gerar, for the fear of the LORD was upon them; they despoiled all the cities, for there was much booty in them. 14 They attacked also the tents of the cattle-herders and carried off a great number of sheep and camels. Then they returned to Jerusalem.

CHAPTER 15

Cult Reform. 1 Upon Azariah, son of Oded, came the spirit of God. 2* He went forth to meet Asa and said to him: "Hear me, Asa and all Judah and Benjamin! The LORD is with you when you are with him, and if you seek him he will be present to you; but if you abandon him, he will abandon you. 3 For a long time Israel had no true God, no priest-teacher and no law, 4* but when in their distress they turned to the LORD, the God of Israel, and sought him, he was present to them. 5 In that former time there was no peace for anyone to go or come, but there were many terrors upon the inhabitants of the lands. 6* Nation crushed nation and city crushed city, for God destroyed them by every kind of adversity. 7* But as for you, be strong and do not relax, for your work shall be rewarded."

8 When Asa heard these words and the prophecy [Oded the prophet], he was encouraged to remove the detestable idols from the whole land of Judah and Benjamin and from the cities he had taken in the highlands of Ephraim, and to restore the altar of the LORD which was before the vestibule of the LORD. 9 Then he convened all Judah and Benjamin, together with those of Ephraim, Manasseh and Simeon who sojourned with them; for many had fled to him from Israel when they saw that the LORD, his God, was with him. 10† They gathered at Jerusalem in the third month of the fifteenth year of Asa's reign, 11 and sacrificed to the LORD at that time seven hundred oxen and seven thousand sheep of the booty they had brought. 12 They entered into a covenant to seek the LORD, the God of their fathers, with all their heart and soul; 13* and everyone who would not seek the LORD, the God of Israel, was to be put to death, whether small or great, whether man or woman. 14 They swore to the LORD with a loud voice, with shouting and with trumpets and horns. 15* All Judah rejoiced over the oath, for they had sworn with their whole heart and sought him with complete desire, so that he was present to them. And the LORD gave them rest on every side.

16* Maacah, the mother of King Asa, he deposed as queen mother because she had made an outrageous object for Asherah; Asa cut this down, smashed it, and burnt it in the Kidron Valley. 17 Although the high places did not disappear from Israel, yet Asa's heart was undivided as long as he lived. 18 He brought into the house of God his father's votive offerings and his own: silver, gold, and various utensils. 19 There was no war until the thirty-fifth year of Asa's reign.

CHAPTER 16

Asa's Infidelity. 1* In the thirty-sixth year of Asa's reign, Baasha, king of Israel, attacked Judah and fortified Ramah to prevent any communication with Asa, king of Judah. 2 Asa then brought out silver and gold from the treasuries of the temple of the LORD and of the royal palace and sent them to Ben-hadad, king of Aram, who lived in Damascus, with this message: 3 "There is a treaty between you and me, as there was between your father and my father. See, I am sending you silver and gold. Go, break your treaty with Baasha, king of Israel, that he may withdraw from me." 4 Ben-hadad agreed to King Asa's request and sent the leaders of his troops against the cities of Israel. They attacked Ijon, Dan, Abel-maim, and all the store cities of Naphtali. 5 When Baasha heard of it, he left off fortifying Ramah; he stopped his work. 6 Then King Asa commandeered all of Judah to carry away the stone and wood with which Baasha had been fortifying Ramah, and with them he fortified Geba and Mizpah.

*

10: 32, 8.
11: Pss 20, 7f; 60, 11f.
15, 2: Jer 29, 13f; Hos 3, 4f.
4: Dt 4, 29f.
6: Is 19, 2.
7: Is 7, 4; Jer 31, 16.
13: Neh 10, 30.
15: Dt 4, 29.
16ff: 1 Kgs 15, 13ff.
16, 1-6: 1 Kgs 15, 16-21.

†

15, 10ff: With this description of a covenant ceremony in the *third month* of a year beginning in the spring, the Chronicler lays a foundation for celebrating the ancient feast of Pentecost (Weeks) as the time for a solemn renewal of the people's covenant with God on Mount Sinai; see Ex 19, 1ff; Lv 23, 16 and the note there. This is also the background for Pentecost as the "birthday of the Church."

7† At that time Hanani the seer came
to Asa, king of Judah, and said to him:
"Because you relied on the king of Aram
and did not rely on the LORD, your God,
the army of the king of Aram has es-
caped your hand. 8* Were not the Ethio-
pians and Libyans a vast army, with
great numbers of chariots and drivers?
And yet, because you relied on the LORD,
he delivered them into your power.
9* The eyes of the LORD roam over the
whole earth, to encourage those who are
devoted to him wholeheartedly. You
have acted foolishly in this matter, for
from now on you will have wars." 10 But
Asa became angry with the seer and im-
prisoned him in the stocks, so greatly
was he enraged at him over this. Asa
also oppressed some of his people at this
time.

11* Now the acts of Asa, first and last,
can be found recorded in the book of the
kings of Judah and Israel. 12 In the
thirty-ninth year of his reign, Asa con-
tracted a serious disease in his feet. But
even in his sickness he did not seek the
LORD, but only the physicians. 13 Asa
rested with his ancestors; he died in the
forty-first year of his reign. 14 They bur-
ied him in the tomb he had hewn for
himself in the City of David, having laid
him upon a couch which was filled with
spices and various kinds of aromatics
compounded into an ointment. They also
burned a very great funeral pyre for
him.

CHAPTER 17

Zeal of Jehoshaphat for the Law.
1* His son Jehoshaphat succeeded him
as king and strengthened his hold
against Israel. 2 He placed armed forces
in all the fortified cities of Judah, and
put garrisons in the land of Judah and
in the cities of Ephraim which his father
Asa had taken. 3† The LORD was with
Jehoshaphat, for he walked in the ways
his father had pursued in the beginning,
and he did not consult the Baals.
4 Rather, he sought the God of his father
and observed his commands, and not
the practices of Israel. 5 As a result, the
LORD made his kingdom secure, and all
Judah gave Jehoshaphat gifts, so that
he enjoyed great wealth and glory.
6* Thus he was encouraged to follow the
LORD's ways, and again he removed the
high places and the sacred poles from
Judah.

7 In the third year of his reign he sent
his leading men, Ben-hail, Obadiah,
Zechariah, Nethanel and Micaiah, to
teach in the cities of Judah. 8* With them
he sent the Levites Shemaiah, Netha-
niah, Zebadiah, Asahel, Shemiramoth,
Jehonathan, Adonijah and Tobijah, to-
gether with the priests Elishama and Je-
horam. 9* They taught in Judah, having
with them the book containing the law
of the LORD; they traveled through all
the cities of Judah and taught among
the people.

His Power. 10 Now the fear of the LORD
was upon all the kingdoms of the coun-
tries surrounding Judah, so that they did
not war against Jehoshaphat. 11 Some of
the Philistines brought Jehoshaphat
gifts and a tribute of silver; and the Ar-
abs also brought him a flock of seven
thousand seven hundred rams and
seven thousand seven hundred he-
goats.

12 Jehoshaphat grew steadily greater.
He built strongholds and store cities in
Judah. 13 He carried out many works in
the cities of Judah, and he had soldiers,
valiant warriors, in Jerusalem. 14 This
was their mustering according to their
ancestral houses. Of Judah, the com-
manders of thousands: Adnah the com-
mander, and with him three hundred
thousand valiant warriors. 15 Next to
him, Jehohanan the commander, and
with him two hundred eighty thousand.
16 Next to him, Amasiah, son of Zichri,
who offered himself to the LORD, and
with him two hundred thousand valiant
warriors. 17 From Benjamin: Eliada, a
valiant warrior, and with him two hun-
dred thousand armed with bow and
buckler. 18 Next to him, Jozabad, and
with him one hundred and eighty thou-
sand equipped for war. 19 These were at
the service of the king; in addition were
those whom the king had placed in the
fortified cities throughout all Judah.

CHAPTER 18

Alliance with Israel. 1* Jehoshaphat
therefore had wealth and glory in abun-
dance; but he became related to Ahab
by marriage. 2 After some years he went
down to Ahab at Samaria; Ahab offered
numerous sheep and oxen for him and
the people with him, and persuaded him
to go up against Ramoth-gilead. 3 Ahab,
king of Israel, asked Jehoshaphat, king
of Judah, "Will you come with me to Ra-
moth-gilead?" "You and I are as one,"
was his answer; "your people and my
people as well. We will be with you in
the battle." 4 But Jehoshaphat also said

*

8: 14, 8-14.
9: Ps 33, 13ff.
11-14: 1 Kgs 15, 23f.
17, 1: 1 Kgs 15, 24.
6: 20, 33; Ex 34, 13.
8: 19, 8.
9: Ezr 7, 25.
18, 1-34: 1 Kgs 22, 1-35.

†

16, 7: *The king of Aram . . . escaped:* according to the Lucianic recension, "the king of Israel escaped": this may well be the original reading; Asa was friendly with Aram.

17, 3: *The Lord was with Jehoshaphat:* along with Hezekiah and Josiah, Jehoshaphat was one of the Chronicler's favorite kings.

to the king of Israel, "Seek the word of the LORD at once."

The Prophets. 5 The king of Israel gathered his prophets, four hundred in number, and asked them, "Shall we go to attack Ramoth-gilead, or shall I refrain?" "Go up," they answered. "God will deliver it over to the king." 6 But Jehoshaphat said, "Is there no other prophet of the LORD here whom we may consult?" 7 The king of Israel answered Jehoshaphat, "There is still another through whom we may consult the LORD, but I hate him, for he prophesies not good but always evil about me. That is Micaiah, son of Imlah." Jeshoshaphat said, "Let not your Majesty speak of evil against you." 8 So the king of Israel called an official, to whom he said, "Get Micaiah, son of Imlah, at once." 9 The king of Israel and King Jehoshaphat of Judah were seated each on his throne, clothed in their robes of state on a threshing floor at the entrance of the gate of Samaria, and all the prophets were prophesying before them.

10 Zedekiah, son of Chenaanah, made iron horns for himself and said: "The LORD says, 'With these you shall gore Aram until you have destroyed them.' " 11 The other prophets prophesied in the same vein, saying: "Go up to Ramoth-gilead. You shall succeed; the LORD will deliver it over to the king." 12† The messenger who had gone to call Micaiah said to him: "Look now, the prophets unanimously predict good for the king. Let your word, like each of theirs, predict good." 13 "As the LORD lives," Micaiah answered, "I will say what my God tells me."

14 When he came to the king, the king said to him, "Micaiah, shall we go to fight against Ramoth-gilead, or shall I refrain?" "Go up," he answered, "and succeed; they will be delivered into your power." 15 But the king said to him, "How many times must I adjure you to tell me nothing but the truth in the name of the LORD?" 16 Then Micaiah answered:

"I see all Israel
scattered on the mountains,
like sheep without a shepherd,
and the LORD saying, 'These have no master!
Let each of them go back home in peace.' "

17 The king of Israel said to Jehoshaphat, "Did I not tell you that he prophesies no good about me, but only evil?" 18 But Micaiah continued:

"Therefore hear the word of the LORD: I saw the LORD seated on his throne, with the whole host of heaven standing by to his right and to his left. 19 The LORD asked, 'Who will deceive Ahab, king of Israel, so that he will go up and fall at Ramoth-gilead?' And one said this, another that, 20 until a spirit came forward and presented himself to the LORD, saying, 'I will deceive him.' The LORD asked, 'How?' 21 He answered, 'I will go forth and become a lying spirit in the mouths of all his prophets.' The LORD agreed: 'You shall succeed in deceiving him. Go forth and do this.' 22 So now the LORD has put a lying spirit in the mouths of these your prophets, but the LORD himself has decreed evil against you."

23 Thereupon Zedekiah, son of Chenaanah, came up and slapped Micaiah on the cheek, saying, "Which way did the spirit of the LORD go when he left me to speak to you?" 24 "You shall find out," Micaiah replied, "on that day when you enter an innermost chamber to hide." 25 The king of Israel then said: "Seize Micaiah and take him back to Amon, prefect of the city, and to Joash the king's son, 26 and say, 'This is the king's order: Put this man in prison and feed him scanty rations of bread and water until I return in safety!' " 27† But Micaiah said, "If ever you return in safety, the LORD has not spoken through me." And he said, "Hear, O peoples, all of you!"

Ahab's Death. 28 The king of Israel and King Jehoshaphat of Judah went up to Ramoth-gilead 29 and the king of Israel said to Jehoshaphat, "I will go into battle disguised, but you put on your own clothes." So the king of Israel disguised himself and they entered the fray. 30 Meanwhile, the king of Aram had given his chariot commanders the order, "Fight with no one, small or great, except the king of Israel." 31 When the commanders saw Jehoshaphat, they exclaimed, "That must be the king of Israel!" and shifted to fight him. But Jehoshaphat cried out and the LORD helped him; God induced them to leave him. 32 The chariot commanders became aware that he was not the king of Israel and gave up their pursuit of him. 33* Someone, however, drew his bow at random and hit the king of Israel between the joints of his breastplate. He ordered his charioteer, "Rein about and take me out of the ranks, for I am disabled." 34 The battle grew fierce during the day, and the king of Israel braced himself up on his chariot facing the Arameans until evening. He died as the sun was setting.

*

33: 35, 23; 1 Kgs 22, 34.

†

18, 12-22: See note on 1 Kgs 22, 19-23.

18, 27: *"Hear, O peoples, all of you!"*: this quotation, which appears in some texts of 1 Kgs 22, 28, ascribes to the prophet Micaiah ben Imlah the opening words of the prophetic utterance of Micah of Moresheth (Mi 1, 2), a century later.

CHAPTER 19

Jehoshaphat Rebuked. 1 King Jehoshaphat of Judah returned in safety to his house in Jerusalem. 2† Jehu the seer, son of Hanani, met King Jehoshaphat and said to him: "Should you help the wicked and love those who hate the LORD? For this reason, wrath is upon you from the LORD. 3 Yet some good things are to be found in you, since you have removed the sacred poles from the land and have been determined to seek God."

Judges Appointed. 4 Jehoshaphat dwelt in Jerusalem; but he went out again among the people from Beer-sheba to the highlands of Ephraim and brought them back to the LORD, the God of their fathers. 5 He appointed judges in the land, in all the fortified cities of Judah, city by city, 6* and he said to them: "Take care what you do, for you are judging, not on behalf of man, but on behalf of the LORD; he judges with you. 7* And now, let the fear of the LORD be upon you. Act carefully, for with the LORD, our God there is no injustice, no partiality, no bribe-taking." 8* In Jerusalem also, Jehoshaphat appointed some Levites and priests and some of the family heads of Israel to judge in the name of the LORD and to settle quarrels among the inhabitants of Jerusalem. 9 He gave them this command: "You shall act faithfully and wholeheartedly in the fear of the LORD. 10* And in every dispute that your brethren living in their cities bring to you, whether it concerns bloodguilt or questions of law, command, statutes, or judgments, warn them lest they become guilty before the LORD and his wrath come upon you and your brethren. Do that and you shall be guiltless. 11 See now, Amariah is high priest over you in everything that pertains to the LORD, and Zebadiah, son of Ishmael, is leader of the house of Judah in all that pertains to the king; and the Levites will be your officials. Act firmly, and the LORD will be with the good."

CHAPTER 20

Invasion from Edom. 1† After this the Moabites, the Ammonites, and with them some Meunites came to fight against Jehoshaphat. 2 The message was brought to Jehoshaphat: "A great multitude is coming against you from across the sea, from Edom; they are already in Hazazon-tamar" (which is En-gedi). 3 Jehoshaphat was frightened, and he hastened to consult the LORD. He proclaimed a fast for all Judah. 4* Then Judah gathered to seek help from the LORD; from every one of the cities of Judah they came to seek the LORD.

Prayer of Jehoshaphat. 5 Jehoshaphat stood up in the assembly of Judah and Jerusalem in the house of the LORD before the new court, 6* and he said: "LORD, God of our fathers, are you not the God in heaven, and do you not rule over all the kingdoms of the nations? In your hand is power and might, and no one can withstand you. 7* Was it not you, our God, who drove out the inhabitants of this land before your people Israel and gave it forever to the descendants of Abraham, your friend? 8 They have dwelt in it and they built in it a sanctuary to your honor, saying, 9 'When evil comes upon us, the sword of judgment, or pestilence, or famine, we will stand before this house and before you, for your name is in this house, and we will cry out to you in our affliction, and you will hear and save!' 10* And now, see the Ammonites, Moabites, and those of Mount Seir whom you did not allow Israel to invade when they came from the land of Egypt, but instead they passed them by and did not destroy them. 11 See how they are now repaying us by coming to drive us out of the possession you have given us. 12 O our God, will you not pass judgment on them? We are powerless before this vast multitude that comes against us. We are at a loss what to do, hence our eyes are turned toward you."

Victory Prophesied. 13 All Judah was standing before the LORD, with their little ones, their wives, and their young sons. 14 And the spirit of the LORD came upon Jahaziel, son of Zechariah, son of Benaiah, son of Jeiel, son of Mattaniah, a Levite of the clan of Asaph, in the midst of the assembly, 15 and he said: "Listen, all of Judah, inhabitants of Jerusalem, and King Jehoshaphat! The LORD says to you: 'Do not fear or lose heart at the sight of this vast multitude, for the battle is not yours but God's. 16 Go down against them tomorrow. You will see them coming up by the ascent of Ziz, and you will come upon them at the end of the wadi which opens on the wilderness of Jeruel. 17* You will not have to fight in this encounter. Take your places,

*

19, 6: Dt 1, 16ff; 16, 19f.
7: Dt 10, 17.
8: 17, 8f; Dt 17, 8-13; Ps 122, 3ff.
10: Nm 35, 19.
20, 4: Jer 36, 6; Jb 1, 14.
6: 32, 7; Dt 4, 39.
7: Dn 3, 35.
10: Dt 2, 4f. 9f. 18f.
17: Is 8, 10.

†

19, 2: *Jehu the seer, son of Hanani:* hardly the same seer as Jehu, son of Hanani, who prophesied against Baasha almost fifty years earlier (1 Kgs 16, 1).

20, 1-30: Although the account here seems to be a free composition of the Chronicler, there is probably a basis in fact for it; there could well have been a raid of nomads against Judah in the reign of Jehoshaphat, similar to Zerah's attack on Asa (14, 8-14). The story may also, in some way, be connected with the campaign of Israel and Judah against Moab through the territory of Edom (2 Kgs 3, 4-27).

stand firm, and see how the LORD will
be with you to deliver you, Judah and
Jerusalem. Do not fear or lose heart. To-
morrow go out to meet them, and the
LORD will be with you.' " 18 Then Je-
hoshaphat knelt down with his face to
the ground, and all Judah and the inhab-
itants of Jerusalem fell down before the
LORD in worship. 19 Levites from among
the Kohathites and Korahites rose to
sing the praises of the LORD, the God
of Israel, in a resounding chorus.
The Invaders Destroyed. 20* In the
early morning they hastened out to the
wilderness of Tekoa. As they were going
out, Jehoshaphat halted and said: "Lis-
ten to me, Judah and inhabitants of Je-
rusalem! Trust in the LORD, your God,
and you will be found firm. Trust in his
prophets and you will succeed."
21* † After consulting with the people, he
appointed some to sing to the LORD and
some to praise the holy Appearance as
it went forth at the head of the army.
They sang: "Give thanks to the LORD,
for his mercy endures forever." 22 At the
moment they began their jubilant hymn,
the LORD laid an ambush against the
Ammonites, Moabites, and those of
Mount Seir who were coming against
Judah, so that they were vanquished.
23* For the Ammonites and Moabites set
upon the inhabitants of Mount Seir and
completely exterminated them. And
when they had finished with the inhabit-
ants of Seir, they began to destroy each
other.
24 When Judah came to the watch-
tower of the desert and looked toward
the throng, they saw only corpses fallen
on the ground, with no survivors.
25 Jehoshaphat and his people came to
take plunder, and they found an abun-
dance of cattle and personal property,
garments and precious vessels. They
took so much that they were unable to
carry it all; they were three days taking
the spoil, so great was it. 26† On the
fourth day they held an assembly in the
Valley of Beracah—for there they
blessed the LORD; therefore that place
has ever since been called the Valley of
Beracah. 27 Then all the men of Judah
and Jerusalem, with Jehoshaphat at
their head, turned back toward Jerusa-
lem celebrating the joyful victory the
LORD had given them over their ene-
mies. 28 They came to Jerusalem, to the
house of the LORD, with harps, lyres and
trumpets. 29 And the fear of God came
upon all the kingdoms of the surround-
ing lands when they heard how the LORD
had fought against the enemies of Israel.
30 Thereafter Jehoshaphat's kingdom
enjoyed peace, for his God gave him rest
on every side.
Jehoshaphat's Other Deeds. 31* Thus
Jehoshaphat reigned over Judah. He
was thirty-five years old when he be-
came king, and he reigned twenty-five
years in Jerusalem. His mother was
named Azubah, daughter of Shilhi. 32 He
followed the path of his father Asa un-
swervingly, doing what was right in the
LORD's sight. 33 But the high places were
not removed, nor as yet had the people
fixed their hearts on the God of their fa-
thers.
34 The rest of the acts of Jehoshaphat,
first and last, can be found written in
the chronicle of Jehu, son of Hanani,
which is inserted in the book of the kings
of Israel. 35 After this, King Jehoshaphat
of Judah allied himself with King Aha-
ziah of Israel, who did evil. 36* He joined
with him in building ships to sail to
Tarshish; the fleet was built at Ezion-ge-
ber. 37 But Eliezer, son of Dodavahu
from Mareshah, prophesied against Je-
hoshaphat, saying, "Because you have
joined with Ahaziah, the LORD will shat-
ter your work." And the ships were
wrecked and were unable to sail to
Tarshish.

CHAPTER 21

1* Jehoshaphat rested with his ances-
tors; he was buried with them in the City
of David. Jehoram, his son, succeeded
him as king. 2 His brothers, sons of Je-
hoshaphat, were Azariah, Jehiel, Zecha-
riah, Azariah, Michael and Shephatiah;
all these were sons of King Jehoshaphat
of Judah. 3 Their father gave them nu-
merous gifts of silver, gold and precious
objects, together with fortified cities in
Judah, but the kingship he gave to Jeho-
ram because he was the first-born.
Evil Deeds of Jehoram. 4 When Jeho-
ram had come into his father's kingdom
and had consolidated his power, he put
to the sword all his brothers and also
some of the princes of Israel. 5* Jehoram
was thirty-two years old when he be-
came king, and he reigned eight years
in Jerusalem. 6† He conducted himself
like the kings of Israel of the line of
Ahab, because one of Ahab's daughters
was his wife. He did evil in the sight of
the LORD, 7* but the LORD would not de-
stroy the house of David because of the
covenant he had made with David and

*

20: Is 7, 9.
21: Ps 136, 1.
23: Jos 6, 17; Ez 38, 21.
31-34: 1 Kgs 22, 41-45.
36f: 1 Kgs 22, 48f.
21, 1: 1 Kgs 22, 51.
5ff: 2 Kgs 8, 17ff.
7: 1 Kgs 11, 36; 2 Kgs 8, 19.

†

20, 21: *Holy Appearance:* the Lord, who is with the Israelite army (v 17), manifests himself (the same language is in Ps 29, 2) in bringing Israel the victory (Ex 14, 14. 24).

20, 26: *Beracah:* the Hebrew word for "blessing."

21, 6: *One of Ahab's daughters:* Athaliah. In 22, 2 (and its source, 2 Kgs 8, 26) she is called Omri's daughter; but this should probably be understood in the sense of grand-daughter.

because of his promise to give him and
his sons a lamp for all time.
8* During his time Edom revolted
against the sovereignty of Judah; they
chose a king of their own. 9 Thereupon
Jehoram crossed over with his officers
and all the chariots he had. He arose by
night and broke through the Edomites
when they had surrounded him and the
commanders of his chariots. 10 However,
Edom has continued in revolt against
the sovereignty of Judah down to the
present time. Libnah also revolted at
that time against Jehoram's sovereignty
because he had forsaken the LORD, the
God of his fathers. 11 He also set up high
places in the mountains of Judah; he led
the inhabitants of Jerusalem into idola-
try and seduced Judah.
Retribution. 12† He received a letter
from the prophet Elijah with this mes-
sage: "Thus says the LORD, the God of
your ancestor David: 'Because you have
not followed the path of your father Je-
hoshaphat, nor of Asa, king of Judah,
13 but instead have walked in the way
of the kings of Israel and have led Judah
and the inhabitants of Jerusalem into
idolatry, as did the house of Ahab, and
also because you have murdered your
brothers of your father's house who were
better than you, 14 the LORD will strike
your people, your children, your wives,
and all that is yours with a great plague;
15 and you shall have severe pains from
a disease in your bowels, while your
bowels issue forth because of the dis-
ease, day after day.' "
16 Then the LORD stirred up against Je-
horam the animosity of the Philistines
and of the Arabs who bordered on the
Ethiopians. 17 They came up against Ju-
dah, invaded it, and carried away all the
wealth found in the king's palace, along
with his sons and his wives; there was
left to him only one son, Jehoahaz, his
youngest. 18 After these events, the LORD
afflicted him with an incurable disease
of the bowels. 19 As time went on until
a period of two years had elapsed, his
bowels issued forth because of the dis-
ease and he died in great pain. His peo-
ple did not made a pyre for him like that
of his fathers. 20* He was thirty-two
years old when he became king, and he
reigned eight years in Jerusalem. He de-
parted unloved and was buried in the
City of David, but not in the tombs of
the kings.

CHAPTER 22

Ahaziah. 1* Then the inhabitants of
Jerusalem made Ahaziah, his youngest
son, king in his stead, since all the older
sons had been slain by the band that had
come into the fort with the Arabs. Thus
Ahaziah, son of Jehoram, reigned as the
king of Judah. 2 He was twenty-two
years old when he became king, and he
reigned one year in Jerusalem. His
mother was named Athaliah, daughter
of Omri. 3 He, too, followed the ways of
the house of Ahab, because his mother
counseled him to act sinfully. 4 To his
own destruction, he did evil in the sight
of the LORD, as did the house of Ahab,
since they were his counselors after the
death of his father.
5 He was also following their counsel
when he accompanied Jehoram, son of
Ahab, king of Israel, to battle against
Hazael, king of Aram, at Ramoth-gil-
ead. There Jehoram was wounded by
the Arameans. 6 He returned to Jezreel
to be healed of the wounds he had re-
ceived at Rama in his battle against
Hazael, king of Aram. Because of this
illness, Ahaziah, son of Jehoram, king
of Judah, went down to visit Jehoram,
son of Ahab, in Jezreel. 7* Now it was
willed by God for Ahaziah's downfall
that he should join Jehoram, for after
his arrival he rode out with Jehoram to
Jehu, son of Nimshi, whom the LORD had
anointed to cut down the house of Ahab.
8* While Jehu was executing judgment
on the house of Ahab, he also encoun-
tered the princes of Judah and the neph-
ews of Ahaziah who were his attendants,
and he slew them. 9*† Then he looked
for Ahaziah himself. They caught him
where he was hiding in Samaria and
brought him to Jehu, who put him to
death. They buried him, for they said,
"He was the grandson of Jehoshaphat,
who sought the LORD with his whole
heart." There remained in Ahaziah's
house no one powerful enough to wield
the kingship.
Usurpation of Athaliah. 10* When Ath-
aliah, mother of Ahaziah, learned that
her son was dead, she proceeded to kill
off all the royal offspring of the house
of Judah. 11 But Jehosheba, a royal prin-
cess, secretly took Ahaziah's son Joash
from among the king's sons who were
about to be slain, and put him and his
nurse in a bedroom. In this way Je-
hosheba, who was the daughter of King
Jehoram, a sister of Ahaziah, and wife
of Jehoiada the priest, hid the child from
Athaliah's sight, so that she did not put

*

8ff: Gn 27, 40; 2 Kgs 8, 20ff.
20: 2 Kgs 8, 24.
22, 1-6: 2 Kgs 8, 24-29.
7: 2 Kgs 9, 21; 10, 12ff.
8: 2 Kgs 10, 12ff.
9: 2 Kgs 9, 27f.
10ff: 2 Kgs 11, 1ff.

†

21, 12: *Elijah:* the only mention by the Chronicler of this prophet of the northern kingdom of Israel. It is doubtful that Elijah was still living in the reign of Jehoram of Judah; in any case, the attribution of the letter to him is most likely an imaginative filling out of the narration.

22, 9: This account of the death of Ahaziah of Judah is not derived from 2 Kgs 9, 27f, with which it is at variance.

him to death. 12 For six years he remained hidden with them in the house of God, while Athaliah ruled over the land.

CHAPTER 23

Athaliah Overthrown. 1* In the seventh year, Jehoiada took courage and entered a conspiracy with certain captains: Azariah, son of Jehoram; Ishmael, son of Jehohanan; Azariah, son of Obed; Masseiah, son of Adaiah; and Elishaphat, son of Zichri. 2 They journeyed about Judah, gathering the Levites from all the cities of Judah and also the heads of the Israelite families. When they had come to Jerusalem, 3 the whole assembly made a covenant with the king in the house of God. Jehoiada said to them: "Here is the king's son who must reign, as the LORD promised concerning the sons of David. 4 This is what you must do: a third of your number, both priests and Levites, who come in on the sabbath must guard the thresholds, 5 another third must be at the king's palace, and the final third at the Foundation Gate, when all the people will be in the courts of the LORD's temple. 6 Let no one enter the LORD's house except the priests and those Levites who are ministering. They may enter because they are holy; but all the other people must observe the prescriptions of the LORD. 7 The Levites shall surround the king on all sides, each with his weapon drawn. Whoever tries to enter the house must be slain. Stay with the king wherever he goes."

8* The Levites and all Judah did just as Jehoiada the priest commanded. Each brought his men, those who were to come in on the sabbath as well as those who were to depart on the sabbath, since Jehoiada the priest had not dismissed any of the divisions. 9 Jehoiada the priest gave the captains the spears, shields and bucklers of King David which were in the house of God. 10 He stationed all the people, each with his spear in hand, from the southern to the northern extremity of the enclosure, around the altar and the temple on the king's behalf. 11 Then they brought out the king's son, set the crown and the insignia upon him, and made him king. Jehoiada and his sons anointed him, and they cried, "Long live the king!"

12 When Athaliah heard the din of the people running and acclaiming the king, she went to the people in the temple of the LORD. 13† She looked, and there was the king standing beside his pillar at the entrance, the officers and the trumpeters around him, and all the people of the land rejoicing and blowing trumpets, while the singers with their musical instruments were leading the acclaim. Athaliah tore her garments and cried out, "Treason! treason!" 14 Then Jehoiada the priest sent out the captains who were in command of the army; he said to them: "Take her outside through the ranks, and if anyone tries to follow her, let him die by the sword. For," the priest continued, "you must not put her to death in the LORD's temple." 15 So they seized her, and when she arrived at the entrance to the Horse Gate of the palace, they put her to death there.

16 Then Jehoiada made a covenant between himself and all the people and the king, that they should be the LORD's people. 17 And all the people went to the temple of Baal and tore it down. They smashed its altars and images, and they slew Mattan, the priest of Baal, before the altars. 18* Then Jehoiada gave the charge of the LORD's temple into the hands of the levitical priests, to whom David had assigned turns in the temple for offering the holocausts of the LORD, as is written in the law of Moses, with rejoicing and song, as David had provided. 19 Moreover, he stationed guards at the gates of the LORD's temple so that no one unclean in any respect might enter. 20 Then he took the captains, the nobles, the rulers among the people, and all the people of the land, and led the king out of the LORD's house. When they had come within the upper gate of the king's house, they seated the king upon the royal throne. 21 All the people of the land rejoiced and the city was quiet, now that Athaliah had been put to death by the sword.

CHAPTER 24

The Temple Restored. 1* Joash was seven years old when he became king, and he reigned forty years in Jerusalem. His mother, named Zibiah, was from Beer-sheba. 2 Joash did what was pleasing to the LORD as long as Jehoiada the priest lived. 3 Jehoiada provided him with two wives, and he became the father of sons and daughters.

4 After some time, Joash decided to restore the LORD's temple. 5† He called to-

*

23, 1-17.
19ff: 2 Kgs 11, 4-20.
8: 2 Kgs 11, 9;
1 Chr 24, 19.
18: 1 Chr 23, 13.
24, 1-14: 2 Kgs 12, 1-13.

†

23, 13: *Beside his pillar:* the king had a special place in the eastern gateway of the temple court that contained the altar of holocausts. He occupied this place on feasts and sabbaths at the time of the statutory offerings, or when he made free-will offerings of his own; cf 2 Kgs 11, 4 and also Ez 46, 1-8 for a later reflection of this.

24, 5: *Collect money:* according to 2 Kgs 12, 5, the people themselves brought the money to the temple; it consisted, at least in part, of voluntary contributions. At the time of the Chronicler (see Neh 10, 32) there was a fixed head tax for the upkeep of the temple (2 Chr 34, 9), based on Ex 30, 12-16. This was still in force in New Testament times (Mt 17, 24f).

gether the priests and Levites and said
to them: "Go out to all the cities of Judah
and collect money from all Israel that
you may repair the house of your God
over the years. You must hasten this af-
fair." But the Levites did not hasten.
6* Then the king summoned Jehoiada,
who was in charge, and said to him:
"Why have you not required the Levites
to bring in from Judah and Jerusalem
the tax levied by Moses, the servant of
the LORD, and by the assembly of Israel,
for the tent of the testimony?" 7 For the
wicked Athaliah and her sons had dam-
aged the house of God and had even
turned over to the Baals the dedicated
resources of the LORD's temple.

8* At the king's command, therefore,
they made a chest, which they put out-
side the gate of the LORD's temple.
9* They had it proclaimed throughout
Judah and Jerusalem that the tax which
Moses, the servant of God, had imposed
on Israel in the desert should be brought
to the LORD. 10 All the princes and the
people rejoiced; they brought what was
asked and cast it into the chest until it
was filled. 11 Whenever the chest was
brought to the royal officials by the Le-
vites and they saw that it contained
much money, the royal scribe and an
overseer for the high priest came, emp-
tied the chest, then took it back and re-
turned it to its place. This they did day
after day until they had collected a large
sum of money. 12 Then the king and Je-
hoiada gave it to the workmen in charge
of the labor on the LORD's temple, who
hired masons and carpenters to restore
the temple, and also iron- and bronze-
smiths to repair it. 13 The workmen la-
bored, and the task of restoration pro-
gressed under their hands. They
restored the house of God according to
its original form, and reinforced it.
14 After they had finished, they brought
the rest of the money to the king and
to Jehoiada, who had it made into uten-
sils for the LORD's temple, utensils for
the service and the holocausts, and ba-
sins and other gold and silver utensils.
They offered holocausts in the LORD's
temple continually throughout the life-
time of Jehoiada. 15 Jehoiada lived to a
ripe old age; he was a hundred and thirty
years old when he died. 16 He was buried
in the City of David with the kings, be-
cause he had done good in Israel, in par-
ticular with respect to God and his
temple.

Apostasy of King Joash. 17 After the
death of Jehoiada, the princes of Judah
came and paid homage to the king, and
the king then listened to them. 18* They
forsook the temple of the LORD, the God
of their fathers, and began to serve the
sacred poles and the idols; and be-
cause of this crime of theirs, wrath came
upon Judah and Jerusalem. 19 Although
prophets were sent to them to convert
them to the LORD, the people would not
listen to their warnings. 20 Then the spirit
of God possessed Zechariah, son of Je-
hoiada the priest. He took his stand
above the people and said to them: "God
says, 'Why are you transgressing the
LORD's commands, so that you cannot
prosper? Because you have abandoned
the LORD, he has abandoned you.'"
21 But they conspired against him, and
at the king's order they stoned him to
death in the court of the LORD's temple.
22 Thus King Joash was unmindful of the
devotion shown him by Jehoiada, Zech-
ariah's father, and slew his son. And as
he was dying, he said, "May the LORD
see and avenge."

Retribution. 23* At the turn of the year
a force of Arameans came up against
Joash. They invaded Judah and Jerusa-
lem, did away with all the princes of the
people, and sent all their spoil to the king
of Damascus. 24* Though the Aramean
force came with few men, the LORD sur-
rendered a very large force into their
power, because Judah had abandoned
the LORD, the God of their fathers. So
punishment was meted out to Joash.
25* After the Arameans had departed
from him, leaving him in grievous suf-
fering, his servants conspired against
him because of the murder of the son
of Jehoiada the priest. They killed him
on his sickbed. He was buried in the City
of David, but not in the tombs of the
kings.

26 These conspired against him: Za-
bad, son of Shimeath from Ammon, and
Jehozabad, son of Shimrith from Moab.
27* Of his sons, and the great tribute im-
posed on him, and of his rebuilding of
the house of God, there is a written ac-
count in the midrash of the book of the
kings. His son Amaziah succeeded him
as king.

CHAPTER 25

Campaign in Edom. 1* Amaziah was
twenty-five years old when he became
king, and he reigned twenty-nine years
in Jerusalem. His mother, named Jeho-
addan, was from Jerusalem. 2 He did
what was pleasing in the sight of the
LORD, though not wholeheartedly.
3 After he had strengthened his hold on
the kingdom, he slew those of his ser-
vants who had killed the king, his father;
4* but he did not put their children to
death, for he acted according to what
is written in the law, in the Book of Mo-

6: Ex 25, 1-9; Neh 10, 33.
8: 34, 9.
9: Ex 30, 13.
18: Ex 34, 13.
23: 2 Kgs 12, 17f.
24: Dt 32, 30.
25f: 2 Kgs 12, 21f.
27: 2 Kgs 12, 19.22.
25, 1-4: 2 Kgs 14, 1-6.
4: Dt 24, 16; 2 Kgs 14, 5f; Ez 18, 20.

ses, as the LORD commanded: "Fathers
shall not be put to death for their chil-
dren, nor children for their fathers; but
only for his own guilt shall a man be put
to death."
5 Amaziah mustered Judah and
placed them, out of all Judah and Benja-
min according to their ancestral houses,
under leaders of thousands and of hun-
dreds. When he had counted those of
twenty years and over, he found them
to be three hundred thousand picked
men fit for war, capable of handling
lance and shield. 6 He also hired a hun-
dred thousand valiant warriors from Is-
rael for a hundred talents of silver. 7 But
a man of God came to him and said: "O
king, let not the army of Israel go with
you, for the LORD is not with Israel, with
any Ephraimite. 8 Instead, go on your
own, strongly prepared for the conflict;
otherwise the LORD will defeat you in the
face of the enemy. It is God who has
the power to reinforce or to defeat."
9 Amaziah answered the man of God,
"But what is to be done about the hun-
dred talents that I paid for the troops
of Israel?" The man of God replied, "The
LORD can give you much more than
that." 10 Amaziah then disbanded the
troops that had come to him from
Ephraim, and sent them home. They,
however, became furiously angry with
Judah, and returned home blazing with
resentment.
11* Amaziah now assumed command
of his army. They proceeded to the Val-
ley of Salt, and there they killed ten
thousand men of Seir. 12 The Judahites
also brought back another ten thousand
alive, whom they led to the summit of
the Rock and then cast down, so that
they were all crushed. 13 Meanwhile, the
mercenaries whom Amaziah had dis-
missed from battle service with him
raided the cities of Judah from Samaria
to Beth-horon. They killed three thou-
sand of the inhabitants and took away
much booty.

Infidelity of Amaziah. 14 When Ama-
ziah returned from his conquest of the
Edomites he brought back with him the
gods of the people of Seir, which he set
up as his own gods; he bowed down be-
fore them and offered sacrifice to them.
15 Then the anger of the LORD blazed out
against Amaziah, and he sent a prophet
to him who said: "Why have you had
recourse to this people's gods that could
not save their own people from your
hand?" 16 While he was still speaking,
however, the king said to him: "Have
you been made the king's counselor? Be
silent! Why should it be necessary to kill
you?" Therefore the prophet desisted. "I
know, however," he said, "that God has
let you take counsel to your own destruc-
tion, because you have done this thing
and have refused to hear my counsel."

Retribution. 17* Having taken coun-
sel, King Amaziah of Judah sent mes-
sengers to Joash, son of Jehoahaz, son
of Jehu, the king of Israel, saying,
"Come, let us meet each other face to
face." 18* King Joash of Israel sent this
reply to King Amaziah of Judah: "The
thistle of the Lebanon sent a message
to the cedar of the Lebanon, saying,
'Give your daughter to my son for his
wife.' But the wild beasts of the Lebanon
passed by and trampled the thistle
down. 19 You are thinking, 'See, I have
beaten Edom!', and thus ambition
makes you proud. Remain at home. Why
involve yourself, and Judah with you, in
misfortune and failure?" 20 But Amaziah
would not listen, for God had deter-
mined to hand them over because they
had had recourse to the gods of Edom.
21 Therefore King Joash of Israel ad-
vanced and he and King Amaziah met
in battle at Beth-shemesh of Judah.
22 There Judah was defeated by Israel,
and all the Judean soldiers fled home-
ward. 23 King Joash of Israel captured
Amaziah, king of Judah, son of Joash,
son of Jehoahaz, at Beth-shemesh and
brought him to Jerusalem. Then he tore
down the wall of Jerusalem from the
Ephraim Gate to the Corner Gate, a dis-
tance of four hundred cubits. 24† He took
away all the gold and silver and all the
vessels he found in the house of God with
Obed-edom, together with the treasures
of the palace, and hostages as well. Then
he returned to Samaria.
25* Amaziah, son of Joash, king of Ju-
dah, survived Joash, son of Jehoahaz,
king of Israel, by fifteen years. 26 The
rest of the acts of Amaziah, first and last,
can be found written, as is well known,
in the book of the kings of Judah and
Israel. 27 Now from the time that Ama-
ziah ceased to follow the LORD, a con-
spiracy was formed against him in
Jerusalem; hence he fled to Lachish. But
they pursued him to Lachish and put
him to death there. 28† They brought him
back on horses and buried him with his
ancestors in the City of Judah.

CHAPTER 26

The Works of Uzziah. 1* All the people
of Judah chose Uzziah, though he was

*

11: 2 Kgs 14, 7.
17-24: 2 Kgs 14, 8-14.
18: Jgs 9, 7-15; 2 Kgs 14, 9.
25-28: 2 Kgs 14, 17-20.
26, 1-4: 2 Kgs 14, 21f; 15, 1ff.

†

25, 24: *With Obed-edom:* possibly a reference to the priest of an Edomite false worship (cf v 14), if not to a levitical family of gatekeepers; cf 1 Chr 15, 18; 26, 12-15.

25, 28: *The City of Judah:* in the parallel passage of 2 Kgs 14, 20, *the City of David.* The Chronicler is referring, by this term, to the capital of Judah, Jerusalem.

but sixteen years of age, and proclaimed
him king to succeed his father Amaziah.
2 He rebuilt Elath and restored it to Ju-
dah; this was after King Amaziah had
gone to rest with his ancestors. 3 Uzziah
was sixteen years old when he became
king, and he reigned fifty-two years in
Jerusalem. His mother, named Jecoliah,
was from Jerusalem. 4 He pleased the
LORD, just as his father Amaziah had
done.
5*† He was prepared to seek God as
long as Zechariah lived, who taught him
to fear God; and as long as he sought
the LORD, God made him prosper. 6* He
went out and fought the Philistines and
razed the walls of Gath, Jabneh and
Ashdod [and built cities in the district
of Ashdod and in Philistia]. 7 God helped
him against the Philistines, against the
Arabs who dwelt in Gurbaal, and against
the Meunites. 8 The Ammonites paid
tribute to Uzziah and his fame spread
as far as Egypt, for he grew stronger
and stronger. 9 Moreover, Uzziah built
towers in Jerusalem at the Corner Gate,
at the Valley Gate, and at the Angle, and
he fortified them. 10 He built towers in
the desert and dug numerous cisterns,
for he had many cattle. He had plowmen
in the foothills and the plains, and vine-
dressers in the highlands and the garden
land. He was a lover of the soil.
11 Uzziah also had a standing army of
fit soldiers divided into bands according
to the number in which they were mus-
tered by Jeiel the scribe and Maaseiah
the recorder, under the command of
Hananiah, one of the king's officials.
12 The entire number of family heads
over these valiant warriors was two
thousand six hundred, 13 and at their
disposal was a mighty army of three
hundred seven thousand five hundred
fighting men of great valor to help the
king against his enemies. 14 Uzziah pro-
vided for them—for the entire army—
bucklers, lances, helmets, breastplates,
bows and slingstones. 15 He also built
machines in Jerusalem, devices con-
trived to stand on the towers and at the
angles of the walls to shoot arrows and
cast large stones. His fame spread far
and wide, and his power was ascribed
to the marvelous help he had received.
Pride and Fall. 16 But after he had be-
come strong, he became proud to his
own destruction and broke faith with the
LORD, his God. He entered the temple
of the LORD to make an offering on the
altar of incense. 17 But Azariah the
priest, and with him eighty other priests
of the LORD, courageous men, followed
him. 18* They opposed King Uzziah, say-
ing to him: "It is not for you, Uzziah,
to burn incense to the LORD, but for the
priests, the sons of Aaron, who have
been consecrated for this purpose.
Leave the sanctuary, for you have bro-
ken faith and no longer have a part in
the glory that comes from the LORD
God." 19* Uzziah, who was holding a
censer for burning the incense, became
angry, but at the moment he showed his
anger to the priests, while they were
looking at him in the house of the LORD
beside the altar of incense, leprosy broke
out on his forehead. 20 Azariah the chief
priest and all the other priests examined
him, and when they saw that his fore-
head was leprous, they expelled him
from the temple. He himself fled will-
ingly, for the LORD had afflicted him.
21* King Uzziah remained a leper to the
day of his death. As a leper he dwelt in
a segregated house, for he was excluded
from the house of the LORD. Therefore
his son Jotham was regent of the palace
and ruled the people of the land.
22 The prophet Isaiah, son of Amos,
wrote the rest of the acts of Uzziah, first
and last. 23 Uzziah rested with his ances-
tors; he was buried with them in the field
adjoining the royal cemetery, for they
said, "He was a leper." His son Jotham
succeeded him as king.

CHAPTER 27

Jotham. 1* Jotham was twenty-five
years old when he became king, and he
reigned sixteen years in Jerusalem. His
mother was named Jerusha, daughter of
Zadok. 2 He pleased the LORD just as his
father Uzziah had done, though he did
not enter the temple of the LORD; the
people, however, continued to act sin-
fully.
3 He built the upper gate of the LORD's
house and had much construction done
on the wall of Ophel. 4 Moreover, he built
cities in the hill country of Judah, and
in the forest land he set up fortresses
and towers. 5 He fought with the king of
the Ammonites and conquered them.
That year the Ammonites paid him one
hundred talents of silver, together with
ten thousand kors of wheat and ten thou-
sand of barley. They brought the same
to him also in the second and in the third
year. 6 Thus Jotham continued to grow
strong because he lived resolutely in the
presence of the LORD, his God. 7* The
rest of the acts of Jotham, his wars and
his activities, can be found written in the
book of the kings of Israel and Judah.
8 He was twenty-five years old when he

*

5: 24, 2.
6: Am, 1 8.
18: Ex 30, 7.
19: Nm 12, 10.
21ff: 2 Kgs 15, 5ff; Lv 13, 46; Nm 19, 20.
27, 1-3: 2 Kgs 15, 32-35.
7-9: 2 Kgs 15, 36ff.

†

26, 5: *Zechariah:* this person, not otherwise identified, is referred to in language suggesting a pious layman rather than a priest or prophet; cf 29, 1.

became king, and he reigned sixteen years in Jerusalem. 9 Jotham rested with his ancestors and was buried in the City of David, and his son Ahaz succeeded him as king.

III: REFORMS OF HEZEKIAH AND JOSIAH

CHAPTER 28

Impiety of Ahaz. 1* Ahaz was twenty years old when he became king, and he reigned sixteen years in Jerusalem. He did not please the LORD as his forefather David had done, 2 but conducted himself like the kings of Israel and even made molten idols of the Baals. 3* Moreover, he offered sacrifice in the Valley of Ben-hinnom, and immolated his sons by fire according to the abominable practice of the nations which the LORD had cleared out before the Israelites. 4 He offered sacrifice and incense on the high places, on hills, and under every leafy tree.

Retribution. 5* Therefore the LORD, his God, delivered him into the power of the king of Aram. The Arameans defeated him and carried away captive a large number of his people, whom they brought to Damascus. He was also delivered into the power of the king of Israel, who defeated him with great slaughter. 6 For Pekah, son of Remaliah, slew one hundred and twenty thousand of Judah in a single day, all of them valiant men, because they had abandoned the LORD, the God of their fathers. 7 Zichri, an Ephraimite warrior, killed Maaseiah, the king's son, and Azrikam, the master of the palace, and also Elkanah, who was second to the king. 8 The Israelites took away as captives two hundred thousand of their brethren's wives, sons and daughters; they also took from them much plunder, which they brought to Samaria.

The Prophecy of Oded. 9 In Samaria there was a prophet of the LORD by the name of Oded. He went out to meet the army returning to Samaria and said to them: "It was because the LORD, the God of your fathers, was angry with Judah that he delivered them into your hands. You, however, have slaughtered them with a fury that has reached up to heaven. 10 And now you are planning to make the children of Judah and Jerusalem your slaves and bondwomen. Are not you yourselves, therefore, guilty of a crime against the LORD, your God? 11 Now listen to me: send back the captives you have carried off from among your brethren, for the burning anger of the LORD is upon you."

12 At this, some of the Ephraimite leaders, Azariah, son of Johanan, Berechiah, son of Meshillemoth, Jehizkiah, son of Shallum, and Amasa, son of Hadlai, themselves stood up in opposition to those who had returned from the war. 13 They said to them: "Do not bring the captives here, for what you propose will make us guilty before the LORD and increase our sins and our guilt. Our guilt is already great, and there is a burning anger upon Israel." 14 Therefore the soldiers left their captives and the plunder before the princes and the whole assembly. 15* Then the men just named proceeded to help the captives. All of them who were naked they clothed from the booty; they clothed them, put sandals on their feet, gave them food and drink, anointed them, and all who were weak they set on asses. They brought them to Jericho, the city of palms, to their brethren. Then they returned to Samaria.

Further Sins of Ahaz. 16* At that time King Ahaz sent an appeal for help to the kings of Assyria. 17* The Edomites had returned, attacked Judah, and carried off captives. 18 The Philistines too had raided the cities of the foothills and the Negeb of Judah; they captured Beth-shemesh, Aijalon, Gederoth, Soco and its dependencies, Timnah and its dependencies, and Gimzo and its dependencies, and occupied them. 19† For the LORD had brought Judah low because of Ahaz, king of Israel, who let Judah go its own way and proved utterly faithless to the LORD. 20* Tilgath-pilneser, king of Assyria, did indeed come to him, but to oppress him rather than to help him. 21* Though Ahaz plundered the LORD's house and the houses of the king and the princes to make payment to the king of Assyria, it availed him nothing.

22 While he was already in distress, the same King Ahaz became even more unfaithful to the LORD. 23* He sacrificed to the gods of Damascus who had defeated him, saying, "Since it was the gods of the kings of Aram who helped them, I will sacrifice to them that they may help me also." However, they only caused further disaster to him and to all Israel. 24* Ahaz gathered up the utensils of God's house and broke them in pieces. He closed the doors of the LORD's house and had altars made for himself in every corner of Jerusalem. 25 In every city throughout Judah he set up high places

*

28, 1-4: 2 Kgs 16, 1-4.
3: 2 Kgs 16, 3; Lv 18, 21.
5: 2 Kgs 16, 5; Is 7, 1-9.
15: Lk 10, 25-37.
16: 2 Kgs 16, 7.
17: 2 Kgs 16, 6.
20: 2 Kgs 16, 10; Is 7, 17-20; 8, 5-8.
21: 2 Kgs 16, 8.
23: 2 Kgs 16, 12f; Is 10, 20.
24: 29, 3; 30, 14; 2 Kgs 16, 17.

†

28, 19: *Ahaz, king of Israel:* in the period of the divided kingdom the term *king of Israel* would elsewhere mean "king of the northern kingdom of Israel."

to offer sacrifice to other gods. Thus he angered the LORD, the God of his fathers.

26* The rest of his deeds and his activities, first and last, can be found written in the book of the kings of Judah and Israel. 27 Ahaz rested with his ancestors and was buried in Jerusalem—in the city, for they did not bring him to the tombs of the kings of Israel. His son Hezekiah succeeded him as king.

CHAPTER 29

Reforms of Hezekiah. 1* Hezekiah was twenty-five years old when he became king, and he reigned twenty-nine years in Jerusalem. His mother was named Abia, daughter of Zechariah. 2 He pleased the LORD just as his forefather David had done. 3* It was he who, in the first month of the first year of his reign, opened the doors of the LORD's house and repaired them. 4 He summoned the priests and Levites, gathered them in the open space to the east, 5 and said to them: "Listen to me, you Levites! Sanctify yourselves now and sanctify the house of the LORD, the God of your fathers, and clean out the filth from the sanctuary. 6 Our fathers acted faithlessly and did evil in the eyes of the LORD, our God. They abandoned him, turned away their faces from the LORD's dwelling, and turned their backs on him. 7* They also closed the doors of the vestibule, extinguished the lamps, and refused to burn incense and offer holocausts in the sanctuary to the honor of the God of Israel. 8* Therefore the anger of the LORD has come upon Judah and Jerusalem; he has made them an object of terror, astonishment and mockery, as you see with your own eyes. 9 For our fathers, as you know, fell by the sword, and our sons, our daughters and our wives have been taken captive because of this. 10 Now, I intend to make a covenant with the LORD, the God of Israel, that his burning anger may withdraw from us. 11 My sons, be not negligent any longer, for it is you whom the LORD has chosen to stand before him, to minister to him, to be his ministers and to offer incense."

12 Then the Levites arose: Mahath, son of Amasai, and Joel, son of Azariah, descendants of the Kohathites; of the sons of Merari: Kish, son of Abdi, and Azariah, son of Jehallel; of the Gershonites: Joah, son of Zimmah, and Eden, son of Joah; 13 of the sons of Elizaphan: Shimri and Jeuel; of the sons of Asaph: Zechariah and Mattaniah; 14 of the sons of Heman: Jehuel and Shimei; of the sons of Jeduthun: Shemiah and Uzziel. 15 They gathered their brethren together and sanctified themselves; then they came as the king had ordered, to cleanse the LORD's house in keeping with his words.

16 The priests entered the interior of the LORD's house to cleanse it; and whatever they found in the LORD's temple that was unclean they brought out to the court of the LORD's house, where the Levites took it from them and carried it out to the Kidron Valley. 17 They began the work of consecration on the first day of the first month, and on the eighth day of the month they arrived at the vestibule of the LORD; they consecrated the LORD's house during eight days, and on the sixteenth day of the first month, they had finished.

18 Then they went inside to King Hezekiah and said: "We have cleansed the entire house of the LORD, the altar of holocausts with all its utensils, and the table for the showbread with all its utensils. 19 All the articles which King Ahaz during his reign had thrown away because of his apostasy, we have restored and consecrated, and they are now before the LORD's altar."

The Rite of Expiation. 20 Then King Hezekiah hastened to convoke the princes of the city and went up to the LORD's house. 21 Seven bulls, seven rams, seven lambs and seven he-goats were brought for a sin offering for the kingdom, for the sanctuary, and for Judah, and he ordered the sons of Aaron, the priests, to offer them on the altar of the LORD. 22 They slaughtered the bulls, and the priests collected the blood and cast it on the altar. Then they slaughtered the rams and cast the blood on the altar; then they slaughtered the lambs and cast the blood on the altar. 23 Then the he-goats for the sin offering were led before the king and the assembly, who laid their hands upon them. 24 The priests then slaughtered them and offered their blood on the altar to atone for the sin of all Israel; for "The holocaust and the sin offering," the king had said, "is for all Israel."

25 He stationed the Levites in the LORD's house with cymbals, harps and lyres according to the prescriptions of David, of Gad the king's seer, and of Nathan the prophet; for the prescriptions were from the LORD through his prophets. 26 The Levites were stationed with the instruments of David, and the priests with the trumpets. 27 Then Hezekiah ordered the holocaust to be sacrificed on the altar, and in the same instant that the holocaust began, they also began the song of the LORD, to the accompaniment of the trumpets and the instruments of David, king of Israel. 28 The entire as-

---

26f: 2 Kgs 16, 19f.
29, 1ff: 2 Kgs 18, 1ff.
3: 28, 24.
7: 2 Kgs 16, 15.
8f: Lv 26, 32f; Dt 28, 25; Jer 25, 18.

sembly prostrated itself, and they con-
tinued to sing the song and to sound the
trumpets until the holocaust had been
completed. 29 As the holocaust was com-
pleted, the king and all who were with
him knelt and prostrated themselves.
30 King Hezekiah and the princes then
commanded the Levites to sing the
praises of the LORD in the words of
David and of Asaph the seer. They sang
praises till their joy was full, then fell
down and prostrated themselves.
31 Hezekiah now spoke out this com-
mand: "You have undertaken a work for
the LORD. Approach, and bring forward
the sacrifices and thank offerings for the
house of the LORD." Then the assembly
brought forward the sacrifices and
thank offerings and all the holocausts
which were free-will offerings. 32 The
number of holocausts that the assembly
brought forward was seventy oxen, one
hundred rams, and two hundred lambs:
all of these as a holocaust to the LORD.
33 As consecrated gifts there were six
hundred oxen and three thousand
sheep. 34* Since the priests were too few
in number to be able to skin all the vic-
tims for the holocausts, their brethren
the Levites assisted them until the task
was completed and the priests had sanc-
tified themselves; the Levites, in fact,
were more willing than the priests to
sanctify themselves. 35 Also, the holo-
causts were many, along with the fat of
the peace offerings and the libations for
the holocausts. Thus the service of the
house of the LORD was reestablished.
36 Hezekiah and all the people rejoiced
over what God had reestablished for the
people, and at how suddenly this had
been done.

CHAPTER 30

Invitation to the Passover. 1* Heze-
kiah sent a message to all Israel and Ju-
dah, and even wrote letters to Ephraim
and Manasseh saying that they should
come to the house of the LORD in Jerusa-
lem to celebrate the Passover in honor
of the LORD, the God of Israel. 2* The
king, his princes, and the entire assem-
bly in Jerusalem had agreed to celebrate
the Passover during the second month,
3 for they could not celebrate it at the
time of the restoration: the priests had
not sanctified themselves in sufficient
numbers, and the people were not gath-
ered at Jerusalem. 4 When this proposal
had been approved by the king and the
entire assembly, 5 they issued a decree
to be proclaimed throughout all Israel
from Beer-sheba to Dan, that everyone
should come to Jerusalem to celebrate
the Passover in honor of the LORD, the
God of Israel; for not many had kept it
in the manner prescribed. 6 Accordingly
the couriers, with the letters written by
the king and his princes, traversed all
Israel and Judah, and at the king's com-
mand they said: "Israelites, return to the
LORD, the God of Abraham, Isaac and
Israel, that he may return to you, the
remnant left from the hands of the Assy-
rian kings. 7* Be not like your fathers
and your brethren who proved faithless
to the LORD, the God of their fathers, so
that he delivered them over to desola-
tion, as you yourselves now see. 8 Be not
obstinate, as your fathers were; extend
your hands to the LORD and come to his
sanctuary that he has consecrated for-
ever, and serve the LORD, your God, that
he may turn away his burning anger
from you. 9* For when you return to the
LORD, your brethren and your children
will find mercy with their captors and
return to this land; for merciful and
compassionate is the LORD, your God,
and he will not turn away his face from
you if you return to him."
10 So the couriers passed from city to
city in the land of Ephraim and Manas-
seh and as far as Zebulun, but they were
derided and scoffed at. 11 Nevertheless,
some from Asher, Manasseh and Zebu-
lun humbled themselves and came to
Jerusalem. 12 In Judah, however, the
power of God brought it about that the
people were of one mind to carry out the
command of the king and the princes
in accordance with the word of the LORD.
13 Thus many people gathered in Jerusa-
lem to celebrate the feast of Unleavened
Bread in the second month; it was a very
great assembly.
The Passover Celebrated. 14* They
proceeded to take down the altars that
were in Jerusalem; also they removed
all the altars of incense and cast them
into the Kidron Valley. 15 They slaugh-
tered the Passover on the fourteenth day
of the second month. The priests and
Levites, touched with shame, sanctified
themselves and brought holocausts into
the house of the LORD. 16 They stood in
the places prescribed for them accord-
ing to the law of Moses, the man of God.
The priests sprinkled the blood given
them by the Levites; 17* for many in the
assembly had not sanctified themselves,
and the Levites were in charge of
slaughtering the Passover victims for all
who were unclean and therefore could
not consecrate them to the LORD. 18 The
greater part of the people, in fact, chiefly
from Ephraim, Manasseh, Issachar and
Zebulun, had not cleansed themselves.
Nevertheless they ate the Passover, con-
trary to the prescription; for Hezekiah
prayed for them, saying, "May the

2 CHRONICLES

*

34: 1 Chr 15, 12.
30, 1: Ex 12, 1-28.
2ff: Nm 9, 6-13.
7: Acts 7, 51.
9: 1 Kgs 8, 50.
14: 28, 24f.
17: 35, 6.

LORD, who is good, grant pardon to [19] everyone who has resolved to seek God, the LORD, the God of his fathers, though he be not clean as holiness requires." [20] The LORD heard Hezekiah and spared the people.

[21] Thus the Israelites who were in Jerusalem celebrated the feast of Unleavened Bread with great rejoicing for seven days, and the Levites and the priests sang the praises of the LORD day after day with all their strength. [22] Hezekiah spoke encouragingly to all the Levites who had shown themselves well skilled in the service of the LORD. And when they had completed the seven days of festival, slaying peace offerings and singing praises to the LORD, the God of their fathers, [23] the whole assembly agreed to celebrate another seven days. With joy, therefore, they continued the festivity seven days longer. [24] King Hezekiah of Judah had contributed a thousand bulls and seven thousand sheep to the assembly, and the princes had contributed to the assembly a thousand bulls and ten thousand sheep. The priests sanctified themselves in great numbers, [25] and the whole assembly of Judah rejoiced, together with the priests and Levites and the rest of the assembly that had come from Israel, as well as the sojourners from the land of Israel and those that lived in Judah. [26] There was great rejoicing in Jerusalem, for since the days of Solomon, son of David, king of Israel, there had not been the like in the city. [27] Then the levitical priests rose and blessed the people; their voice was heard and their prayer reached heaven, God's holy dwelling.

CHAPTER 31

Liturgical Reform. [1*] After all this was over, those Israelites who had been present went forth to the cities of Judah and smashed the sacred pillars, cut down the sacred poles, and tore down the high places and altars throughout Judah, Benjamin, Ephraim and Manasseh, until all were destroyed. Then the Israelites returned to their various cities, each to his own possession.

[2] Hezekiah reestablished the classes of the priests and the Levites according to their former classification, assigning to each priest and Levite his proper service, whether in regard to holocausts or peace offerings, thanksgiving or praise, or ministering in the gates of the encampment of the LORD. [3*] From his own wealth the king allotted a portion for holocausts, those of morning and evening and those on sabbaths, new moons and festivals, as prescribed in the law of the LORD. [4] He also commanded the people living in Jerusalem to provide the support of the priests and Levites, that they might devote themselves entirely to the law of the LORD.

[5*] As soon as the order was promulgated, the Israelites brought, in great quantities, the best of their grain, wine, oil and honey, and all the produce of the fields; they gave a generous tithe of everything. [6*] Israelites and Judahites living in other cities of Judah also brought in tithes of oxen, sheep, and things that had been consecrated to the LORD, their God; these they brought in and set out in heaps. [7†] It was in the third month that they began to establish these heaps, and they completed them in the seventh month. [8] When Hezekiah and the princes had come and seen the heaps, they blessed the LORD and his people Israel. [9] Then Hezekiah questioned the priests and the Levites concerning the heaps, [10*] and the priest Azariah, head of the house of Zadoc, answered him, "Since they began to bring the offerings to the house of the LORD, we have eaten to the full and have had much left over, for the LORD has blessed his people. This great supply is what was left over."

[11] Hezekiah then gave orders that chambers be constructed in the house of the LORD. When this had been done, [12] the offerings, tithes and consecrated things were deposited there in safekeeping. The overseer of these things was Conaniah the Levite, and his brother Shimei was second in charge. [13] Jehiel, Azaziah, Nahath, Asahel, Jerimoth, Jozabad, Eliel, Ismachiah, Mahath and Benaiah were supervisors subject to Conaniah and his brother Shimei by appointment of King Hezekiah and of Azariah, the prefect of the house of God. [14] Kore, the son of Imnah, a Levite and the keeper of the eastern gate, was in charge of the free-will gifts made to God; he distributed the offerings made to the LORD and the most holy of the consecrated things. [15] Under him in the priestly cities were Eden, Miniamin, Jeshua, Shemaiah, Amariah and Shecaniah, who faithfully made the distribution to their brethren, great and small alike, according to their classes.

[16*] There was also a register by ancestral houses of males thirty years of age and over, for all priests who were eligible to enter the house of the LORD according

---

31, 1: 34, 3f; 2 Kgs 18, 4.
3: 1 Chr 29, 3; Ez 45, 17; Nm 28-29.
5: Nm 18, 8-24; Dt 14, 22f.
6: Nm 12, 44-47; 13, 10-13.
10: Lv 25, 19-22.
16: 1 Chr 23, 3f.

31, 7: *Third month . . . seventh month:* between the feast of Pentecost and that of Booths, an interval without rain in Palestine, at the end of which the problem of storage (v 11) would become more urgent.

to the daily rule to fulfill their service in the order of their classes. 17* The priests were inscribed in their family records according to their ancestral houses, and the Levites of twenty years and over according to their various offices and classes. 18 A distribution was also made to all who were inscribed in the family records, for their little ones, wives, sons and daughters—thus for the entire assembly, since they were to sanctify themselves by sharing faithfully in the consecrated things. 19 The sons of Aaron, the priests who lived on the lands attached to their cities, had in every city men designated by name to distribute portions to every male among the priests and to every Levite listed in the family records.

20 This Hezekiah did in all Judah. He did what was good, upright and faithful before the LORD, his God. 21* Everything that he undertook, for the service of the house of God or for the law and the commandments, was to do the will of his God. He did this wholeheartedly, and he prospered.

CHAPTER 32

Invasion of Sennacherib. 1* But after he had proved his fidelity by such deeds, Sennacherib, king of Assyria, came. He invaded Judah, besieged the fortified cities, and proposed to take them by storm. 2 When Hezekiah saw that Sennacherib was coming with the intention of attacking Jerusalem, 3 he decided in counsel with his princes and warriors to stop the waters of the springs outside the city. When they had pledged him their support, 4* a large crowd was gathered which stopped all the springs and also the running stream in the valley nearby. For they said, "Why should the kings of Assyria come and find an abundance of water?" 5* He then looked to his defenses: he rebuilt the wall where it was broken down, raised towers upon it, and built another wall outside. He strengthened the Millo of the City of David and had a great number of spears and shields prepared. 6 Then he appointed army commanders over the people. He gathered them together in his presence in the open space at the gate of the city and encouraged them with these words: 7* "Be brave and steadfast; do not be afraid or dismayed because of the king of Assyria and all the throng that is coming with him, for there is more with us than with him. 8* For he has only an arm of flesh, but we have the LORD, our God, to help us and to fight our battles." And the people took confidence from the words of King Hezekiah of Judah.

Threat of Sennacherib. 9* After this, while Sennacherib, king of Assyria, himself remained at Lachish with all his forces, he sent his officials to Jerusalem with this message for King Hezekiah of Judah, and all the Judahites who were in Jerusalem: 10 "King Sennacherib of Assyria has this to say: On what are you relying, while you remain under siege in Jerusalem? 11 Has not Hezekiah deceived you, delivering you over to a death of famine and thirst, by his claim that 'the LORD, our God, will save us from the grasp of the king of Assyria'? 12 Has not this same Hezekiah removed his high places and altars and commanded Judah and Jerusalem, 'You shall prostrate yourselves before one altar only, and on it alone you shall offer incense'? 13 Do you not know what my fathers and I have done to all the peoples of other lands? Were the gods of the nations in those lands able to save their lands from my hand? 14 Who among all the gods of those nations which my fathers put under the ban was able to save his people from my hand? Will your god, then, be able to save you from my hand? 15 Let not Hezekiah mislead you further and deceive you in any such way. Do not believe him! Since no other god of any other nation or kingdom has been able to save his people from my hand or the hands of my fathers, how much the less shall your god save you from my hand!"

16 His officials said still more against the LORD God and against his servant Hezekiah, 17* for he had written letters to deride the LORD, the God of Israel, speaking of him in these terms: "As the gods of the nations in other lands have not saved their people from my hand, neither shall Hezekiah's god save his people from my hand." 18 In a loud voice they shouted in the Judean language to the people of Jerusalem who were on the wall, to frighten and terrify them so that they might capture their city. 19 They spoke of the God of Israel as though he were one of the gods of the other peoples of the earth, a work of human hands. 20* But because of this, King Hezekiah and the prophet Isaiah, son of Amos, prayed and called out to heaven.

Defeat of Sennacherib. 21* Then the LORD sent an angel, who destroyed every valiant warrior, leader and commander in the camp of the Assyrian king, so that he had to return shamefaced to his own country. And when he entered the temple of his god, some of his own offspring struck him down there

---

17: 1 Chr 23, 6-24.
21: Ps 119, 2f.
32, 1: 2 Kgs 18, 13.
4: Is 22, 9.11.
5: Neh 2, 17f.
7: 14, 10; 20, 6-12.
8: Is 31, 3.
9-20: 2 Kgs 18, 17-37; Is 36, 1-22.
17: 2 Kgs 19, 9-13; Is 37, 9-13.
20: 2 Kgs 19, 14-19; Is 37, 14-20.
21: 2 Kgs 19, 35ff; Is 37, 36ff.

with the sword. 22 Thus the LORD saved
Hezekiah and the inhabitants of Jerusa-
lem from the hand of Sennacherib, king
of Assyria, as from every other power;
he gave them rest on every side.
23* Many brought gifts for the LORD to
Jerusalem and costly objects for King
Hezekiah of Judah, who thereafter was
exalted in the eyes of all the nations.

Hezekiah's Other Deeds. 24* In those
days Hezekiah became mortally ill. He
prayed to the LORD, who answered him
by giving him a sign. 25 Hezekiah, how-
ever, did not then discharge his debt of
gratitude, for he had become proud.
Therefore anger descended upon him
and upon Judah and Jerusalem. 26* But
then Hezekiah humbled himself for his
pride—both he and the inhabitants of Je-
rusalem; and therefore the LORD did not
vent his anger on them during the time
of Hezekiah.

27* Hezekiah possessed very great
wealth and glory. He had treasuries
made for his silver, gold, precious
stones, spices, jewels, and other precious
things of all kinds; 28 also storehouses for
the harvest of grain, for wine and oil,
and barns for the various kinds of cattle
and for the flocks. 29 He built cities for
himself, and he acquired sheep and oxen
in great numbers, for God gave him very
great riches. 30* This same Hezekiah
stopped the upper outflow of water from
Gihon and led it underground westward
to the City of David. Hezekiah prospered
in all his undertakings. 31 Nevertheless,
in respect to the ambassadors [princes]
sent to him from Babylon to investigate
the sign that had occurred in the land,
God forsook him to test him, that he
might know all that was in his heart.

32 The rest of Hezekiah's acts, includ-
ing his pious works, can be found written
in the Vision of the Prophet Isaiah, son
of Amos, and in the book of the kings
of Judah and Israel. 33† Hezekiah rested
with his ancestors; he was buried at the
approach to the tombs of the descen-
dants of David. All Judah and the inhab-
itants of Jerusalem paid him honor at
his death. His son Manasseh succeeded
him as king.

CHAPTER 33

Impiety of Manasseh. 1* Manasseh
was twelve years old when he became
king, and he reigned fifty-five years in
Jerusalem. 2 He did evil in the sight of
the LORD, following the abominable
practices of the nations whom the LORD
had cleared out of the way of the Israel-
ites. 3 He rebuilt the high places which
his father Hezekiah had torn down,
erected altars for the Baals, made sa-
cred poles, and prostrated himself be-
fore the whole host of heaven and
worshiped them. 4 He even built altars
in the temple of the LORD, of which the
LORD had said, "In Jerusalem shall my
name be forever": 5 he built altars to the
whole host of heaven in the two courts
of the LORD's house. 6 It was he, too, who
immolated his sons by fire in the Valley
of Ben-hinnom. He practiced augury,
divination and magic, and appointed
necromancers and diviners of spirits, so
that he provoked the LORD with the great
evil that he did in his sight. 7 He placed
an idol that he had carved in the house
of God, of which God had said to David
and his son Solomon: "In this house and
in Jerusalem which I have chosen from
all the tribes of Israel I shall place my
name forever. 8 I will not again allow Is-
rael's feet to leave the land which I as-
signed to your fathers, provided they are
careful to observe all that I commanded
them, keeping the whole law and the
statutes and the ordinances given by
Moses." 9 Manasseh misled Judah and
the inhabitants of Jerusalem into doing
even greater evil than the nations which
the LORD had destroyed at the coming
of the Israelites. 10 The LORD spoke to
Manasseh and his people, but they paid
no attention.

His Conversion. 11*† Therefore the
LORD brought against them the army
commanders of the Assyrian king; they
took Manasseh with hooks, shackled
him with chains, and transported him
to Babylon. 12 In this distress, he began
to appease the LORD, his God. He hum-
bled himself abjectly before the God of
his fathers 13† and prayed to him. The
LORD let himself be won over: he heard
his prayer and restored him to his king-
dom in Jerusalem. Then Manasseh un-
derstood that the LORD is indeed God.

14 Afterward he built an outer wall for
the City of David to the west of Gihon
in the valley, extending to the Fish Gate
and encircling Ophel; he built it very
high. He stationed army officers in all
the fortified cities of Judah. 15* He re-
moved the foreign gods and the idol

*

23: 14, 6.
24: 2 Kgs 20, 1-11; Is 38, 1-8.
26.31: 2 Kgs 20, 12-19; Is 39, 1-8.
27f: 2 Kgs 20, 13; Is 39, 2.
30: 2 Kgs 20, 20f.
33, 1-10: 2 Kgs 21, 1-9.
11: Jb 36, 7f; Ez 19, 9.
15: 14, 2.

†

32, 33: *The approach to the tombs:* literally, "the ascent of the tombs," which may mean "the upper section of the tombs," their most prominent and honored place.

33, 11: There is no evidence elsewhere for an imprisonment of King Manasseh in Babylon. However, according to the Assyrian inscriptions, he paid tribute to the Assyrian kings Esarhaddon (680-669 B.C.) and Asshurbanipal (668-627 B.C.). He may well have been obliged to go to Nineveh to take the oath of allegiance as vassal to the king of Assyria.

33, 13: *And prayed to him:* these words led an unknown writer to compose the apocryphal "Prayer of Manasseh," which is added as an appendix to many editions of the Vulgate Bible and is used in the public prayers of the Church.

from the LORD's house and all the altars
he had built on the mount of the LORD's
house and in Jerusalem, and he cast
them outside the city. 16 He restored the
altar of the LORD, and sacrificed on it
peace offerings and thank offerings, and
commanded Judah to serve the LORD,
the God of Israel. 17 Though the people
continued to sacrifice on the high places,
they now did so to the LORD, their God.
18* The rest of the acts of Manasseh,
his prayer to his God, and the words of
the seers who spoke to him in the name
of the LORD, the God of Israel, can be
found written in the chronicles of the
kings of Israel. 19 His prayer and how
his supplication was heard, all his sins
and his infidelity, the sites where he built
high places and erected sacred poles
and carved images before he humbled
himself, all can be found written down
in the history of his seers. 20 Manasseh
rested with his ancestors and was buried
in his own palace. His son Amon suc-
ceeded him as king.
Amon. 21* Amon was twenty-two
years old when he became king, and he
reigned two years in Jerusalem. 22 He
did evil in the sight of the LORD, just as
his father Manasseh had done. Amon of-
fered sacrifice to all the idols which his
father Manasseh had made, and wor-
shiped them. 23 Moreover, he did not
humble himself before the LORD as his
father Manasseh had done; on the con-
trary, Amon only increased his guilt.
24 His servants conspired against him
and put him to death in his own house.
25 But the people of the land slew all
those who had conspired against King
Amon, and then they, the people of the
land, made his son Josiah king in his
stead.

CHAPTER 34

Reforms of Josiah. 1* Josiah was
eight years old when he became king,
and he reigned thirty-one years in Jeru-
salem. 2 He pleased the LORD, following
the path of his ancestor David. 3*† In the
eighth year of his reign, while he was
still a youth, he began to seek after the
God of his forefather David, and in his
twelfth year he began to purge Judah
and Jerusalem of the high places, the
sacred poles and the carved and molten
images. 4 In his presence, the altars of
the Baals were destroyed; the incense
stands erected above them were torn
down; the sacred poles and the carved
and molten images were shattered and
beaten into dust, which was strewn over
the tombs of those who had sacrificed
to them; 5 and the bones of the priests
he burned upon their altars. Thus he
purged Judah and Jerusalem. 6 He did
likewise in the cities of Manasseh,
Ephraim, Simeon, and in the ruined vil-
lages of the surrounding country as far
as Naphtali; 7 he destroyed the altars,
broke up the sacred poles and carved
images and beat them into dust, and tore
down the incense stands throughout the
land of Israel. Then he returned to Jeru-
salem.
The Temple Restored. 8* In the eigh-
teenth year of his reign, in order to
cleanse the temple as well as the land,
he sent Shaphan, son of Azaliah, Maa-
seiah, the ruler of the city, and Joah, son
of Joahaz, the chamberlain, to restore
the house of the LORD, his God. 9* They
came to Hilkiah the high priest and
turned over the money brought to the
house of God which the Levites, the
guardians of the threshold, had col-
lected from Manasseh, Ephraim, and all
the remnant of Israel, as well as from
all of Judah, Benjamin, and the inhabit-
ants of Jerusalem. 10 They turned it over
to the master workmen in the house of
the LORD, and these in turn used it to
pay the workmen in the LORD's house
who were restoring and repairing the
temple. 11 They also gave it to the car-
penters and the masons to buy hewn
stone and timber for the tie beams and
rafters of the buildings which the kings
of Judah had allowed to fall into ruin.
12 The men worked faithfully at their
task; their overseers were Jahath and
Obadiah, Levites of the line of Merari,
and Zechariah and Meshullam, of the
Kohathites, who directed them. All those
Levites who were skillful with musical
instruments 13 were in charge of the men
who carried the burdens, and they di-
rected all the workers in every kind of
labor. Some of the other Levites were
scribes, officials and gatekeepers.
The Finding of the Law. 14* When
they brought out the money that had
been deposited in the house of the LORD,
Hilkiah the priest found the book of the
law of the LORD given through Moses.
15 He reported this to Shaphan the
scribe, saying, "I have found the book
of the law in the house of the LORD." Hil-
kiah gave the book to Shaphan, 16 who
brought it to the king at the same time
that he was making his report to him.

*

18.20: 2 Kgs 21, 17f.
21-25: 2 Kgs 21, 19-26.
34, 1f: 2 Kgs 22, 1f.
3-7: 14, 1-4; 31, 1; 2 Kgs 23, 4-20.
8-13: 2 Kgs 22, 3-7.
9: 24, 8f.
14-28: 2 Kgs 22, 8-20.

†

34, 3: *In his twelfth year:* c. 628 B.C., the year after Asshurbanipal's death, when Judah could free itself from Assyrian domination. From 2 Kgs 22, 1—23, 25 alone, one might think that Josiah's reform began only after the discovery of the book of the law in the temple, in the eighteenth year of his reign. But the Chronicler is no doubt right in placing the beginning of the reform at an earlier period. The very repair of the temple, which led to the finding of the book of the law, must have been occasioned by a cultic reform.

He said, "Your servants are doing everything that has been entrusted to them; 17 they have turned into bullion the metals deposited in the LORD's house and have handed it over to the overseers and the workmen." 18 Then Shaphan the scribe announced to the king, "Hilkiah the priest has given me a book." And Shaphan read from it before the king.

19 When the king heard the words of the law, he tore his garments 20 and issued this command to Hilkiah, to Ahikam, son of Shaphan, to Abdon, son of Michah, to Shaphan the scribe, and to Asaiah, the king's servant: 21 "On behalf of myself and those who are left in Israel and Judah, go, consult the LORD concerning the words of the book that has been found. For the anger of the LORD has been set furiously ablaze against us, since our fathers have not kept the word of the LORD and have not done all that is written in this book." 22 Then Hilkiah and the other men from the king went to the prophetess Huldah, the wife of Shallum, son of Tokhath, son of Hasrah, the guardian of the wardrobe; she dwelt in Jerusalem, in the new quarter. They spoke to her as they had been instructed, 23 and she said to them: "Thus says the LORD, the God of Israel: 'Tell the one who sent you to me, 24 The LORD says: I am prepared to bring evil upon this place and upon its inhabitants, all the curses written in the book that has been read before the king of Judah. 25 Because they have abandoned me and have offered incense to other gods, provoking me by every deed that they have performed, my anger is ablaze against this place and cannot be extinguished.'

26 "But to the king of Judah who sent you to consult the LORD, give this response: 'Thus says the LORD, the God of Israel, concerning the threats you have heard: 27 Because you were heartsick and have humbled yourself before God on hearing his words spoken against this place and its inhabitants; because you have humbled yourself before me, have torn your garments, and have wept before me, I in turn have listened—so declares the LORD. 28 I will gather you to your ancestors and you shall be taken to your grave in peace. Your eyes shall not see all the evil I will bring upon this place and upon its inhabitants.'"

They brought back this message to the king.

Renewal of the Covenant. 29* The king now convened all the elders of Judah and Jerusalem. 30 He went up to the house of the LORD with all the men of Judah and the inhabitants of Jerusalem, the priests, the Levites, and all the people, great and small; and he had read aloud to them the entire text of the book of the covenant that had been found in the house of the LORD. 31† Standing at his post, the king made a covenant before the LORD to follow the LORD and to keep his commandments, decrees, and statutes with his whole heart and soul, thus observing the terms of the covenant written in this book. 32 He thereby committed all who were of Jerusalem and Benjamin, and the inhabitants of Jerusalem conformed themselves to the covenant of God, the God of their fathers. 33* Josiah removed every abominable thing from all the territory belonging to the Israelites, and he obliged all who were in Israel to serve the LORD, their God. During his lifetime they did not desert the LORD, the God of their fathers.

CHAPTER 35

The Passover. 1* Josiah celebrated in Jerusalem a Passover to honor the LORD; the Passover sacrifice was slaughtered on the fourteenth day of the first month. 2 He reappointed the priests to their duties and encouraged them in the service of the LORD's house. 3* He said to the Levites who were to instruct all Israel, and who were consecrated to the LORD: "Put the holy ark in the house built by Solomon, son of David, king of Israel. It shall no longer be a burden on your shoulders. Serve now the LORD, your God, and his people Israel. 4 Prepare yourselves in your ancestral houses and your classes according to the prescriptions of King David of Israel and his son Solomon. 5* Stand in the sanctuary according to the divisions of the ancestral houses of your brethren, the common people, so that the distribution of the Levites and the families may be the same. 6* Slay the Passover sacrifice, sanctify yourselves, and be at the disposition of your brethren, that all may be carried out according to the word of the LORD given through Moses."

7* Josiah contributed to the common people a flock of lambs and kids, thirty thousand in number, each to serve as a Passover victim for any who were present, and also three thousand oxen; these were from the king's property. 8* His princes also gave a free-will gift to the people, the priests and the Levites. Hilkiah, Zechariah and Jehiel, prefects of the house of God, gave to the priests two thousand six hundred Passover vic-

*

29-32: 2 Kgs 23, 1ff.
33: 2 Kgs 23, 4-20.
35, 1-19: 2 Kgs 23, 21ff.
1: Ex 12, 1-28; 2 Kgs 23, 21.
3: 5, 4; 1 Chr 15, 12.15.
5: 1 Chr 24-26.
6: 30, 17.
7: Ex 12, 5.
8: Nm 7, 1-83.

†

34, 31: *Standing at his post:* see note on 23, 13.

tims together with three hundred oxen. 9 Conaniah and his brothers Shemaiah, Nethanel, Hashabiah, Jehiel and Jozabad, the rulers of the Levites, contributed to the Levites five thousand Passover victims, together with five hundred oxen.

10 When the service had been arranged, the priests took their places, as did the Levites in their classes according to the king's command. 11 The Passover sacrifice was slaughtered, whereupon the priests sprinkled some of the blood and the Levites proceeded to the skinning. 12 They separated what was destined for the holocaust and gave it to various groups of the ancestral houses of the common people to offer to the LORD, as is prescribed in the book of Moses. They did the same with the oxen. 13* They cooked the Passover on the fire as prescribed, and also cooked the sacred meals in pots, caldrons and pans, then brought them quickly to all the common people. 14 Afterward they prepared the Passover for themselves and for the priests. Indeed the priests, the sons of Aaron, were busy offering holocausts and the fatty portions until night; therefore the Levites prepared for themselves and for the priests, the sons of Aaron. 15 The singers, the sons of Asaph, were at their posts as prescribed by David: Asaph, Heman and Jeduthun, the king's seer. The gatekeepers were at every gate; there was no need for them to leave their stations, for their brethren, the Levites, prepared for them. 16 Thus the entire service of the LORD was arranged that day so that the Passover could be celebrated and the holocausts offered on the altar of the LORD, as King Josiah had commanded. 17 The Israelites who were present on that occasion kept the Passover and the feast of the Unleavened Bread for seven days. 18* No such Passover had been observed in Israel since the time of the prophet Samuel, nor had any king of Israel kept a Passover like that of Josiah, the priests and Levites, all of Judah and Israel that were present, and the inhabitants of Jerusalem. 19 It was in the eighteenth year of Josiah's reign that this Passover was observed.

Josiah's Reign Ends. 20 After Josiah had done all this to restore the temple, Neco, king of Egypt, came up to fight at Carchemish on the Euphrates, and Josiah went out to intercept him. 21 Neco sent messengers to him, saying: "What quarrel is between us, king of Judah? I have not come against you this day, for my war is with another kingdom, and God has told me to hasten. Do not interfere with God who is with me, as otherwise he will destroy you." 22 But Josiah would not withdraw from him, for he had sought a pretext for fighting with him. Therefore he would not listen to the words of Neco that came from the mouth of God, but went out to fight in the plain of Megiddo. 23* Then the archers shot King Josiah, who said to his servants, "Take me away, for I am seriously wounded." 24 His servants removed him from his own chariot, placed him in another he had in reserve, and brought him to Jerusalem, where he died. He was buried in the tombs of his ancestors, and all Judah and Jerusalem mourned him. 25† Jeremiah also composed a lamentation over Josiah, which is recited to this day by all the male and female singers in their lamentations over Josiah. These have been made obligatory for Israel, and can be found written in the Lamentations.

26* The rest of the chronicle of Josiah, his pious deeds in regard to what is written in the law of the LORD, and his acts, first and last, can be found written in the book of the kings of Israel and Judah.

CHAPTER 36

1* The people of the land took Jehoahaz, son of Josiah, and made him king in Jerusalem in his father's stead.

IV: END OF THE KINGDOM

Jehoahaz. 2 Jehoahaz was twenty-three years old when he became king, and he reigned three months in Jerusalem. 3 The king of Egypt deposed him in Jerusalem and fined the land one hundred talents of silver and a talent of gold. 4 Then the king of Egypt made his brother Eliakim king over Judah and Jerusalem, and changed his name to Jehoiakim. Neco took his brother Jehoahaz away and brought him to Egypt.

Jehoiakim. 5* Jehoiakim was twenty-five years old when he became king, and he reigned eleven years in Jerusalem. He did evil in the sight of the LORD, his God. 6*† Nebuchadnezzar, king of Babylon, came up against him and bound him

*

13: Nm 12, 8f.
18f: 2 Kgs 23, 22f.
23: 18, 33f.
26: 2 Kgs 23, 28.
36, 1-4: 2 Kgs 23, 30-34; 1 Chr 3, 15f.
5: 2 Kgs 23, 36f; Jer 22, 18f.
6: 2 Kgs 24, 1f.

†

35, 25: The reference to a *lamentation over Josiah* composed by Jeremiah is not found either in 2 Kgs or Jer; but see note on Zec 12, 11. *Their lamentations:* probably a reference to the canonical Book of Lamentations.

36, 6: *Nebuchadnezzar . . . bound him with chains to take him to Babylon:* the Chronicler does not say that Jehoiakim was actually taken to Babylon. According to 2 Kgs 24, 1-6, Jehoiakim revolted after being Nebuchadnezzar's vassal for three years; he died in Jerusalem before the Babylonian king could reach the city. However, Dn 1, 1f, apparently based on 2 Chr 36, 6f, speaks of Jehoiakim's deportation to Babylon.

with chains to take him to Babylon. 7 Nebuchadnezzar also carried away to Babylon some of the vessels of the house of the LORD and put them in his palace in Babylon. 8* The rest of the acts of Jehoiakim, the abominable things that he did, and what therefore happened to him, can be found written in the book of the kings of Israel and Judah. His son Jehoiachin succeeded him as king.

Jehoiachin. 9* Jehoiachin was eighteen years old when he became king, and he reigned three months [and ten days] in Jerusalem. He did evil in the sight of the LORD. 10*† At the turn of the year, King Nebuchadnezzar sent for him and had him brought to Babylon, along with precious vessels from the temple of the LORD. He made his brother Zedekiah king over Judah and Jerusalem.

Zedekiah. 11* Zedekiah was twenty-one years old when he became king, and he reigned eleven years in Jerusalem. 12* He did evil in the sight of the LORD, his God, and he did not humble himself before the prophet Jeremiah, who spoke the word of the LORD. 13* He also rebelled against King Nebuchadnezzar, who had made him swear by God. He became stiff-necked and hardened his heart rather than return to the LORD, the God of Israel. 14 Likewise all the princes of Judah, the priests and the people added infidelity to infidelity, practicing all the abominations of the nations and polluting the LORD's temple which he had consecrated in Jerusalem.

Dissolution of Judah. 15* Early and often did the LORD, the God of their fathers, send his messengers to them, for he had compassion on his people and his dwelling place. 16* But they mocked the messengers of God, despised his warnings, and scoffed at his prophets, until the anger of the LORD against his people was so inflamed that there was no remedy. 17* Then he brought up against them the king of the Chaldeans, who slew their young men in their own sanctuary building, sparing neither young man nor maiden, neither the aged nor the decrepit; he delivered all of them over into his grip. 18* All the utensils of the house of God, the large and the small, and the treasures of the LORD's house and of the king and his princes, all these he brought to Babylon. 19* They burnt the house of God, tore down the walls of Jerusalem, set all its palaces afire, and destroyed all its precious objects. 20 Those who escaped the sword he carried captive to Babylon, where they became his and his sons' servants until the kingdom of the Persians came to power. 21 All this was to fulfill the word of the LORD spoken by Jeremiah: "Until the land has retrieved its lost sabbaths, during all the time it lies waste it shall have rest while seventy years are fulfilled."

Decree of Cyrus. 22*† In the first year of Cyrus, king of Persia, in order to fulfill the word of the LORD spoken by Jeremiah, the LORD inspired King Cyrus of Persia to issue this proclamation throughout his kingdom, both by word of mouth and in writing: 23 "Thus says Cyrus, king of Persia: 'All the kingdoms of the earth the LORD, the God of heaven, has given to me, and he has also charged me to build him a house in Jerusalem, which is in Judah. Whoever, therefore, among you belongs to any part of his people, let him go up, and may his God be with him!' "

*

8: 2 Kgs 24, 5.
9: 2 Kgs 24, 8f.
10: 2 Kgs 24, 10-16.
11: 2 Kgs 24, 18ff; Jer 52, 1ff.
12: Jer 37, 1ff.
13: 2 Kgs 25, 1; Jer 52, 4; Ez 17, 13-16.
15: Jer 7, 25; Heb 1, 1.
16: Mt 23, 34ff.
17: Lam 1, 15; 5, 11-14.
18: 2 Kgs 25, 14f.
19: 2 Kgs 25, 9f; Lam 2, 8.
22: Ezr 1, 1ff.

†

36, 10: *His brother Zedekiah:* Zedekiah was actually the brother of Jehoiakim and the uncle of *Jehoiachin* (2 Kgs 24, 17; Jer 37, 1), though scarcely older than his nephew (2 Kgs 24, 8.18; 2 Chr 36, 9.11).

36, 22f: The words of these verses are identical with those of Ezr 1, 1-3a. Originally Ezra-Nehemiah formed the last part of the single work of the Chronicler, of which 1 and 2 Chronicles formed the first part. But when Ezra-Nehemiah was regarded as a natural sequence to the Books of Samuel and of Kings, it was separated from 1 and 2 Chronicles and placed before them. Thus, 1 and 2 Chronicles became the last part of the Hebrew Bible. To prevent this work from ending on a note of doom, Ezr 1, 1-3a was repeated as 2 Chr 36, 22f.

The Book of

EZRA

The last four books of the Hebrew canon are Ezra, Nehemiah, 1 and 2 Chronicles, in that order. Originally, however, Ezra and Nehemiah followed the Books of Chronicles, and formed with them a unified historical work so homogeneous in spirit that one usually speaks of a single author for the four books. He is called "the Chronicler." The treatment of Ezra-Nehemiah as a single book by the earliest chroniclers was undoubtedly due to the fact that in ancient times the two books were put under the one name—Ezra. The combined work Ezra-Nehemiah is our most important literary source for the formation of the Jewish religious community after the Babylonian exile. This is known as the period of the Restoration, and the two men most responsible for the reorganization of Jewish life at this time were Ezra and Nehemiah.

In the present state of the Ezra-Nehemiah text, there are several dislocations of large sections so that the chronological or logical sequence is disrupted. The major instances are pointed out in the footnotes. Although Ezra appears before Nehemiah in this work, it seems probable that Nehemiah's activity preceded his.

What is known of Ezra and his work is due almost exclusively to Ezra 7—10 (the "Ezra Memoirs") and to Neh 8—9. Strictly speaking, the term "Ezra Memoirs" should be used only of that section in which Ezra speaks in the first person, i.e., 7, 27—9, 15. Compare the "Nehemiah Memoirs" in Neh 1, 1—7, 72a; 11, 1f; 12, 27-43; 13, 4-31. The Chronicler combined this material with other sources at his disposal. The personality of Ezra is less known than that of Nehemiah. Ben Sirach, in his praise of the fathers, makes no mention of Ezra. The genealogy of Ezra (7, 1-5) traces his priesthood back to Aaron, brother of Moses. This was the accepted way of establishing the legality of one's priestly office. He is also called a scribe, well-versed in the law of Moses *(7, 6), indicating Ezra's dedication to the study of the Torah, which he sought to make the basic rule of life in the restored community. It was in religious and cultic reform rather than in political affairs that Ezra made his mark as a postexilic leader. Jewish tradition holds him in great honor; the Talmud even regards him as a second Moses, claiming that the Torah would have been given to Israel through Ezra had not Moses preceded him.*

Ezra is sometimes accused of having been a mere legalist who gave excessive attention to the letter of the law. His work, however, should be seen and judged within a specific historical context. He gave to his people a cohesion and spiritual unity which prevented the disintegration of the small Jewish community. Had it not been for the intransigence of Ezra and of those who adopted his ideal, it is doubtful that Judaism would have so effectively resisted Hellenism, then or in later centuries. Ezra set the tone of the postexilic community, and it was characterized by fidelity to the Torah, Judaism's authentic way of life. It is in this light that we can judge most fairly the work of Ezra during the Restoration.

The Book of Ezra is divided as follows:

I: The Return from Exile (1, 1—6, 22)
II: The Deeds of Ezra (7, 1—10, 44)

The following list of the kings of Persia, with the dates of their reigns, will be useful for dating the events mentioned in Ezra-Nehemiah:

Cyrus	*538-529 B.C.*
Cambyses	*529-521 B.C.*
Darius I	*521-485 B.C.*
Xerxes	*485-464 B.C.*
Artaxerxes I	*464-423 B.C.*
Darius II	*423-404 B.C.*

Artaxerxes II . . . . 404-358 B.C.
Artaxerxes III. . . . . 358-337 B.C.
End of the Persian Empire (Defeat of Darius III). . . . . . . 331 B.C.

I: THE RETURN FROM EXILE

CHAPTER 1

The Decree of Cyrus. 1*† In the first year of Cyrus, king of Persia, in order to fulfill the word of the LORD spoken by Jeremiah, the LORD inspired King Cyrus of Persia to issue this proclamation throughout his kingdom, both by word of mouth and in writing: 2 "Thus says Cyrus, king of Persia: 'All the kingdoms of the earth the LORD, the God of heaven, has given to me, and he has also charged me to build him a house in Jerusalem, which is in Judah. 3 Whoever, therefore, among you belongs to any part of his people, let him go up, and may his God be with him! 4 Let everyone who has survived, in whatever place he may have dwelt, be assisted by the people of that place with silver, gold, goods, and cattle, together with free-will offerings for the house of God in Jerusalem.' "

5 Then the family heads of Judah and Benjamin and the priests and Levites—everyone, that is, whom God had inspired to do so—prepared to go up to build the house of the LORD in Jerusalem. 6* All their neighbors gave them help in every way, with silver, gold, goods, and cattle, and with many precious gifts besides all their free-will offerings. 7 King Cyrus, too, had the utensils of the house of the LORD brought forth which Nebuchadnezzar had taken away from Jerusalem and placed in the house of his god. 8† Cyrus, king of Persia, had them brought forth by the treasurer Mithredath, and counted out to Sheshbazzar, the prince of Judah. 9 This was the inventory: sacks of goldware, thirty; sacks of silverware, one thousand and twenty-nine; 10 golden bowls, thirty; silver bowls, four hundred and ten; other ware, one thousand pieces. 11† Total of the gold- and silver ware: five thousand four hundred pieces. All these Sheshbazzar took with him when the exiles were brought back from Babylon to Jerusalem.

CHAPTER 2

Census of the Province. 1*† These are the inhabitants of the province who returned from the captivity of the exiles, whom Nebuchadnezzar, king of Babylon, had carried away to Babylon, and who came back to Jerusalem and Judah, each man in his own city 2 (those who returned with Zerubbabel, Jeshua, Nehemiah, Seraiah, Reelaiah, Mordecai, Bilshan, Mispereth, Bigvai, Rehum, and Baanah):

The census of the men of Israel: 3 sons of Parosh, two thousand one hundred and seventy-two; 4 sons of Shephatiah, three hundred and seventy-two; 5 sons of Arah, seven hundred and seventy-five; 6 sons of Pahath-moab, who were sons of Jeshua and Joab, two thousand eight hundred and twelve; 7 sons of Elam, one thousand two hundred and fifty-four; 8 sons of Zattu, nine hundred and forty-five; 9 sons of Zaccai, seven hundred and sixty; 10 sons of Bani, six hundred and forty-two; 11 sons of Bebai, six hundred and twenty-three; 12 sons of Azgad, one thousand two hundred and twenty-two; 13 sons of Adonikam, six hundred and sixty-six; 14 sons of Bigvai, two thousand and fifty-six; 15 sons of Adin, four hundred and fifty-four; 16 sons of Ater, who were sons of Hezekiah, ninety-eight; 17 sons of Bezai, three hundred and twenty-three; 18 sons of Jorah, one hundred and twelve; 19 sons of Hashum, two hundred and twenty-three; 20 sons of Gibeon, ninety-five; 21 sons of Bethlehem, one hundred and twenty-three; 22 men of Netophah, fifty-six; 23 men of Anathoth, one hundred and twenty-eight; 24 men of Beth-azmaveth, forty-two; 25 men of Kiriath-jearim, Chephirah, and Beeroth, seven hundred and forty-three; 26 men of Ramah and Geba, six hundred and twenty-one; 27 men of Michmas, one hundred and twenty-two; 28 men of Bethel and Ai, two hundred and twenty-three; 29 sons of Nebo, fifty-two; 30 sons of Magbish, one hundred and fifty-six; 31 sons of the

*

1, 1ff: 36, 22f; Jer 25, 11f; 29, 10; Zec 1, 12.
6: Ex 3, 22; 11, 2; 12, 35.
2, 1: Neh 7, 6-67.

†

1, 1: *In the first year of Cyrus:* as sovereign over the world empire which began with his conquest of Babylon; that is, 538 B.C.

1, 8: *Sheshbazzar:* very probably the fourth son of Jehoiachin, king of Judah, taken captive to Babylon in 598 B.C., listed in 1 Chr 3, 18 as Senneser; if so, he was the uncle of Zerubbabel (3, 2ff); see note on 1 Chr 3, 18.

1, 11: *Total . . . five thousand four hundred pieces:* either this figure or the figures given for one or more of the items listed (vv 9f) have been corrupted in the transmission of the text.

2, 1-67: As it now stands, this list is an expanded form of the lists of returned captives from the sixth century B.C.; see Neh 7, 6-72, where it reappears.

other Elam, one thousand two hundred
and fifty-four; 32 sons of Harim, three
hundred and twenty; 33 sons of Lod, Ha-
did, and Ono, seven hundred and
twenty-five; 34 sons of Jericho, three
hundred and forty-five; 35 sons of Sen-
aah, three thousand six hundred and
thirty.

36 The priests: sons of Jedaiah, who
were of the house of Jeshua, nine hun-
dred and seventy-three; 37 sons of Im-
mer, one thousand and fifty-two; 38 sons
of Pashhur, one thousand two hundred
and forty-seven; 39 sons of Harim, one
thousand and seventeen.

40* The Levites: sons of Jeshua, Kad-
miel, Binnui, and Hodaviah, seventy-
four.

41 The singers: sons of Asaph, one hun-
dred and twenty-eight.

42 The gatekeepers: sons of Shallum,
sons of Ater, sons of Talmon, sons of Ak-
kub, sons of Hatita, sons of Shobai, one
hundred and thirty-nine in all.

43 The temple slaves: sons of Ziha, sons
of Hasupha, sons of Tabbaoth, 44 sons of
Keros, sons of Siaha, sons of Padon,
45 sons of Lebanah, sons of Hagabah,
sons of Akkub, 46 sons of Hagab, sons of
Shamlai, sons of Hanan, 47 sons of Gid-
del, sons of Gahar, sons of Reaiah,
48 sons of Rezin, sons of Nekoda, sons
of Gazzam, 49 sons of Uzza, sons of Pa-
seah, sons of Besai, 50 sons of Asnah,
sons of the Meunites, sons of the Nephu-
sites, 51 sons of Bakbuk, sons of Haku-
pha, sons of Harhur, 52 sons of Bazluth,
sons of Mehida, sons of Harsha, 53 sons
of Barkos, sons of Sisera, sons of Temah,
54 sons of Neziah, sons of Hatipha.

55 Descendants of the slaves of Solo-
mon: sons of Sotai, sons of Hassophe-
reth, sons of Peruda, 56 sons of Jaalah,
sons of Darkon, sons of Giddel, 57 sons
of Shephatiah, sons of Hattil, sons of Po-
chereth-hazzebaim, sons of Ami. 58 The
total of the temple slaves and the de-
scendants of the slaves of Solomon was
three hundred and ninety-two.

59 The following who returned from
Tel-melah, Tel-harsha, Cherub, Addan,
and Immer were unable to prove that
their ancestral houses and their descent
were Israelite: 60 sons of Delaiah, sons
of Tobiah, sons of Nekoda, six hundred
and fifty-two. 61* Also, of the priests:
sons of Habaiah, sons of Hakkoz, sons
of Barzillai (he had married one of the
daughters of Barzillai the Gileadite and
became known by his name). 62 These
men searched their family records, but
their names could not be found written
there; hence they were degraded from
the priesthood, 63† and His Excellency
ordered them not to partake of the most
holy foods until there should be a priest
bearing the Urim and Thummim.

64 The entire assembly taken together
came to forty-two thousand three hun-
dred and sixty, 65 not counting their
male and female slaves, who were seven
thousand three hundred and thirty-
seven. They also had two hundred male
and female singers. 66 Their horses were
seven hundred and thirty-six, their
mules two hundred and forty-five,
67 their camels four hundred and thirty-
five, their asses six thousand seven hun-
dred and twenty.

68 When they arrived at the house of
the LORD in Jerusalem, some of the fam-
ily heads made free-will offerings for the
house of God, to rebuild it in its place.
69 According to their means they con-
tributed to the treasury for the temple
service: sixty-one thousand drachmas
of gold, five thousand minas of silver,
and one hundred garments for the
priests. 70 The priests, the Levites, and
some of the common people took up resi-
dence in Jerusalem; but the singers, the
gatekeepers, and the temple slaves
dwelt in their cities. Thus all the Israel-
ites dwelt in their cities.

CHAPTER 3

Restoration of the Altar. 1*† Now
when the seventh month came, after the
Israelites had settled in their cities, the
people gathered at Jerusalem as one
man. 2 Then Jeshua, son of Jozadak, to-
gether with his brethren the priests, and
Zerubbabel, son of Shealtiel, together
with his brethren, set about rebuilding
the altar of the God of Israel in order
to offer on it the holocausts prescribed
in the law of Moses, the man of God.
3* Despite their fear of the peoples of the
land, they replaced the altar on its foun-
dations and offered holocausts to the
LORD on it, both morning and evening.
4* They also kept the feast of Booths in
the manner prescribed, and they offered
the daily holocausts in the proper num-
ber required for each day. 5 Thereafter

*

40: Neh 12, 24.
61: 2 Sm 17, 27; 19, 32f; 1 Kgs 2, 7.
3, 1: Neh 7, 73—8, 1.
3: 1 Kgs 8, 64; Dn 9, 25.
4: Ex 23, 16; Nm 28, 3-8.

†

2, 63: *His Excellency:* the deputy of the Persian government; from the context, he was one of the Jewish exile leaders. Nehemiah as governor receives the same title (Neh 8, 9; 10, 2). *Urim and Thummin:* see note on Ex 28, 30.

3, 1f: *The seventh month:* Tishri (September-October), apparently of 538 B.C.; cf 1, 1; 4, 5. In this case, it was Sheshbazzar who erected the first altar, since he began the work on the foundations of the temple in Jerusalem; cf 5, 16. It was in the second year of Darius I, i.e., in 520 B.C., that *Jeshua* and *Zerubbabel* resumed the work on the temple that had been temporarily interrupted (4, 24—5, 1; Hg 1, 1; 2, 1). The Chronicler or a later editor of the text here attributes to them the beginning of the work which, in reality, they merely completed. *Shealtiel:* the eldest son of King Jehoiachin of Judah and the brother of Sheshbazzar (1 Chr 3, 18f); Zerubbabel was therefore the grandson of Jehoiachin; see note on 1, 8.

they offered the established holocaust, the sacrifices prescribed for the new moons and all the festivals sacred to the LORD, and those which anyone might offer as a freewill gift to the LORD. [6] From the first day of the seventh month they began to offer holocausts to the LORD, though the foundation of the temple of the LORD had not yet been laid.

Founding of the Temple. [7]* Then they hired stonecutters and carpenters, and sent food and drink and oil to the Sidonians and Tyrians that they might ship cedar trees from the Lebanon to the port of Joppa, as Cyrus, king of Persia, had authorized. [8] In the year after their coming to the house of God in Jerusalem, in the second month, Zerubbabel, son of Shealtiel, and Jeshua, son of Jozadak, together with the rest of their brethren, the priests and Levites and all who had come from the captivity to Jerusalem, began by appointing the Levites twenty years of age and over to supervise the work on the house of the LORD. [9] Jeshua and his sons and brethren, with Kadmiel and Binnui, son of Henadad, and their sons and their brethren, the Levites, stood as one man to supervise those who were engaged in the work on the house of God. [10]* When the builders had laid the foundation of the LORD's temple, the vested priests with the trumpets and the Levites, sons of Asaph, were stationed there with the cymbals to praise the LORD in the manner laid down by David, king of Israel. [11]* They alternated in songs of praise and thanksgiving to the LORD, "for he is good, for his kindness to Israel endures forever"; and all the people raised a great shout of joy, praising the LORD because the foundation of the LORD's house had been laid. [12]* Many of the priests, Levites, and family heads, the old men who had seen the former house, cried out in sorrow as they watched the foundation of the present house being laid. Many others, however, lifted up their voices in shouts of joy, [13]* and no one could distinguish the sound of the joyful shouting from the sound of those who were weeping; for the people raised a mighty clamor which was heard afar off.

CHAPTER 4

Samaritan Interference. [1] When the enemies of Judah and Benjamin heard that the exiles were building a temple for the LORD, the God of Israel, [2] they approached Zerubbabel and the family heads and said to them, "Let us build with you, for we seek your God just as you do, and we have sacrificed to him since the days of Esarhaddon, king of Assyria, who had us brought here." [3] But Zerubbabel, Jeshua, and the rest of the family heads of Israel answered them, "It is not your responsibility to build with us a house for our God, but we alone must build it for the LORD, the God of Israel, as King Cyrus of Persia has commanded us." [4] Thereupon the people of the land set out to intimidate and dishearten the people of Judah so as to keep them from building. [5]† They also suborned counselors to work against them and thwart their plans during the remaining years of Cyrus, king of Persia, and until the reign of Darius, king of Persia.

Later Hostility. [6] Also at the beginning of the reign of Ahashuerus they prepared a written accusation against the inhabitants of Judah and Jerusalem.

[7]† Again, in the time of Artaxerxes, Mithredath wrote in concert with Tabeel and the rest of his fellow officials to Artaxerxes, king of Persia. The document was written in Aramaic and was accompanied by a translation. [Aramaic:]

[8]† Then Rehum, the governor, and Shimshai, the scribe, wrote the following letter against Jerusalem to King Artaxerxes: [9] "Rehum, the governor, Shimshai, the scribe, and their fellow judges, officials, and agents from among the Persian, Urukian, Babylonian, Susian (that is Elamite), [10] and the other peoples whom the great and illustrious Assurbanipal transported and settled in the city of Samaria and elsewhere in the province West-of-Euphrates, as follows. . . ." [11] This is a copy of the letter that they sent to him:

"To King Artaxerxes, your servants, the men of West-of-Euphrates, as follows: [12] Let it be known to the king that the Jews who came up from you to us have arrived at Jerusalem and are now rebuilding this rebellious and evil city. They are raising up its walls, and the foundations have already been laid. [13] Now let it be known to the king that if this city is rebuilt and its walls are raised up again, they will no longer pay

*

7: 1 Chr 22, 4; 2 Chr 2, 9.
10: 2, 41.
11: Pss 100, 5; 136; Jer 33, 11.
12: Hg 2, 3.
13: Tb 14, 5.

†

4, 5: *Darius:* Darius I (521-485 B.C.). The temple-building narrative continues in 4, 24. In between (4, 6-23) is a series of notes about the opposition to the returned exiles voiced at the Persian court in the early fifth century B.C., after the temple had been reestablished.

4, 7: *Aramaic:* this word in the original text seems to be a note indicating a change of language from Hebrew to Aramaic, which in fact takes place here. The Aramaic section ends with 6, 18, but again in 7, 12-26 a royal letter is cited in Aramaic.

4, 8-23: The central question here is the rebuilding of the fortification walls of Jerusalem, not the building of the temple. The interruption of work on the city wall some time before 445 B.C. was the occasion for the coming of Nehemiah to Palestine (Neh 1, 1-4; 2, 1-5). *Artaxerxes:* Artaxerxes I (464-423 B.C.).

taxes, tributes, or tolls; thus it can only
result in harm to the throne. 14 Now,
since we partake of the salt of the palace,
we ought not simply to look on while the
king is being dishonored. Therefore we
have sent this message to inform you,
O king, 15 so that inquiry may be made
in the historical records of your fathers.
In the historical records you can dis-
cover and verify that this city is a rebel-
lious city which has proved fatal to kings
and provinces, and that sedition has
been fostered there since ancient times.
For that reason this city was destroyed.
16 We inform you, O king, that if this city
is rebuilt and its walls are raised up
again, by that very fact you will no
longer own any part of West-of-Eu-
phrates."

17 The king sent this answer: "To Re-
hum, the governor, Shimshai, the scribe,
and their fellow officials living in Sa-
maria and elsewhere in the province
West-of-Euphrates, greetings and the
following: 18 The communication which
you sent us has been read plainly in my
presence. 19 When at my command in-
quiry was made, it was verified that
from ancient times this city has risen
up against kings and that rebellion and
sedition have been fostered there.
20 Powerful kings were once in Jerusa-
lem who ruled over all West-of-Eu-
phrates, and taxes, tributes, and tolls
were paid to them. 21 Give orders, there-
fore, that will stop the work of these men.
This city may not be rebuilt until a fur-
ther decree has been issued by me.
22 Take care that you do not neglect this
matter, lest the evil grow to the detri-
ment of the throne."

23* As soon as a copy of King Arta-
xerxes' letter had been read before Re-
hum, the governor, Shimshai, the scribe,
and their fellow officials, they went in
all haste to the Jews in Jerusalem and
stopped their work by force of arms.

Rebuilding of the Temple. 24† Thus it
was that the work on the house of God
in Jerusalem was halted. This inaction
lasted until the second year of the reign
of Darius, king of Persia.

CHAPTER 5

1*† Then the prophets Haggai and
Zechariah, son of Iddo, began to
prophesy to the Jews in Judah and Jeru-
salem in the name of the God of Israel.
2 Thereupon Zerubbabel, son of Sheal-
tiel, and Jeshua, son of Jozadak, began
again to build the house of God in Jeru-
salem, with the prophets of God giving
them support. 3 At that time there came
to them Tattenai, governor of West-of-
Euphrates, and Shethar-bozenai, and
their fellow officials, who asked of them:
"Who issued the decree for you to build
this house and raise this edifice? 4 What
are the names of the men who are build-
ing this structure?" 5 But their God
watched over the elders of the Jews so
that they were not hindered, until a re-
port could go to Darius and then a writ-
ten order be sent back concerning this
matter.

6 A copy of the letter sent to King Da-
rius by Tattenai, governor of West-of-
Euphrates, and Shethar-bozenai, and
their fellow officials from West-of-
Euphrates; 7 they sent him a report in
which was written the following:

"To King Darius, all good wishes! 8 Let
it be known to the king that we have vis-
ited the province of Judah and the house
of the great God: it is being rebuilt of
cut stone and the walls are being rein-
forced with timber; the work is being
carried on diligently and is making good
progress under their hands. 9 We then
questioned the elders, addressing to
them the following words: 'Who issued
the decree for you to build this house
and raise this edifice?' 10 We also asked
them their names, to report them to you
in a list of the men who are their leaders.
11 This was their answer to us: 'We are
the servants of the God of heaven and
earth, and we are rebuilding the house
built here long years ago, which a great
king of Israel built and finished. 12 But
because our fathers provoked the wrath
of the God of heaven, he delivered them
into the power of the Chaldean, Nebu-
chadnezzar, king of Babylon, who de-
stroyed this house and led the people
captive to Babylon. 13 However, in the
first year of Cyrus, king of Babylon, King
Cyrus issued a decree for the rebuilding
of this house of God. 14 Moreover, the
gold and silver utensils of the house of
God which Nebuchadnezzar had taken
from the temple in Jerusalem and car-
ried off to the temple in Babylon, King
Cyrus ordered to be removed from the
temple in Babylon and consigned to a
certain Sheshbazzar, whom he named
governor. 15 And he commanded him:
Take these utensils and deposit them in
the temple of Jerusalem, and let the
house of God be rebuilt on its former site.
16 Then this same Sheshbazzar came
and laid the foundations of the house of
God in Jerusalem. Since that time the
building has been going on, and it is not
yet completed.' 17 Now, if it please the

*

4, 23: Neh 1, 3. Zec 4, 9.
5, 1: Hg 1, 14—2, 9;

†

4, 24: *The second year . . . of Darius:* that is, 520 B.C.; it marks the beginning of the successful restoration of the temple, which was accomplished within the five years following (5, 1—16, 8).

5, 1: *The prophets Haggai and Zechariah:* two of the Minor Prophets, whose books record their role in the encouragement of this work.

king, let a search be made in the royal archives of Babylon to discover whether a decree really was issued by King Cyrus for the rebuilding of this house of God in Jerusalem. And may the king's pleasure in this matter be communicated to us."

CHAPTER 6

The Decree of Darius. 1 Thereupon King Darius issued an order to search the archives in which the Babylonian records were stored away; 2* and in Ecbatana, the stronghold in the province of Media, a scroll was found containing the following text: "Memorandum. 3 In the first year of King Cyrus, King Cyrus issued a decree: The house of God in Jerusalem. The house is to be rebuilt as a place for offering sacrifices and bringing burnt offerings. Its height is to be sixty cubits and its width sixty cubits. 4 It shall have three courses of cut stone for each one of timber. The costs are to be borne by the royal palace. 5 Also, the gold and silver utensils of the house of God which Nebuchadnezzar took from the temple of Jerusalem and brought to Babylon are to be sent back: to be returned to their place in the temple of Jerusalem and deposited in the house of God.

6 "Now, therefore, Tattenai, governor of West-of-Euphrates, and Shethar-bozenai, and you, their fellow officials in West-of-Euphrates, do not interfere in that place. 7 Let the governor and the elders of the Jews continue to work on that house of God; they are to rebuild it on its former site. 8 I also issue this decree concerning your dealing with these elders of the Jews in the rebuilding of that house of God: From the royal revenue, the taxes of West-of-Euphrates, let these men be repaid for their expenses, in full and without delay. 9 Whatever else is required—young bulls, rams, and lambs for holocausts to the God of heaven, wheat, salt, wine, and oil, according to the requirements of the priests who are in Jerusalem—is to be delivered to them day by day without fail, 10 that they may continue to offer sacrifices of pleasing odor to the God of heaven and pray for the life of the king and his sons. 11 I also issue this decree: If any man violates this edict, a beam is to be taken from his house, and he is to be lifted up and impaled on it; and his house is to be reduced to rubble for this offense. 12 And may the God who causes his name to dwell there overthrow every king or people who may undertake to alter this or to destroy this house of God in Jerusalem. I, Darius, have issued this decree; let it be carefully executed."

13 Then Tattenai, the governor of West-of-Euphrates, and Shethar-bozenai, and their fellow officials carried out fully the instructions King Darius had sent them. 14 The elders of the Jews continued to make progress in the building, supported by the message of the prophets, Haggai and Zechariah, son of Iddo. They finished the building according to the command of the God of Israel and the decrees of Cyrus and Darius [and of Artaxerxes, king of Persia]. 15 They completed this house on the third day of the month Adar, in the sixth year of the reign of King Darius. 16 The Israelites—priests, Levites, and the other returned exiles—celebrated the dedication of this house of God with joy. 17 For the dedication of this house of God, they offered one hundred bulls, two hundred rams, and four hundred lambs, together with twelve he-goats as a sin-offering for all Israel, in keeping with the number of the tribes of Israel. 18 Finally, they set up the priests in their classes and the Levites in their divisions for the service of God in Jerusalem, as is prescribed in the book of Moses.

The Passover. 19* The exiles kept the Passover on the fourteenth day of the first month. 20 The Levites, every one of whom had purified himself for the occasion, sacrificed the Passover for the rest of the exiles, for their brethren the priests, and for themselves. 21* The Israelites who had returned from the exile partook of it together with all those who had separated themselves from the uncleanness of the peoples of the land to join them in seeking the LORD, the God of Israel. 22† They joyfully kept the feast of Unleavened Bread for seven days, for the LORD had filled them with joy by making the king of Assyria favorable to them, so that he gave them help in their work on the house of God, the God of Israel.

II: THE DEEDS OF EZRA

CHAPTER 7

Ezra the Scribe. 1† After these events, during the reign of Artaxerxes, king of

---

*

6, 2-12: 1, 4-11. 21: Ps 47, 9.
19-22: Ex 12, 1-20.

†

6, 22: *Assyria:* used here in a broad sense for the Persian Empire.

7, 1-8: The date of Ezra's journey to Palestine is not known with certainty. The *seventh year* of King Artaxerxes I would be 458 B.C., and the present order of the text suggests that date. The narratives of Ezra and Nehemiah make it seem to many, however, that the arrival of Nehemiah in 445 B.C. should precede that of Ezra. If so, Ezra may be thought to have come in 398 B.C., the seventh year of King Artaxerxes II. Others argue for the thirty-seventh year of Artaxerxes I, that is, 428 B.C.; this would suppose that the date given in the text has suffered in transmission.

Persia, Ezra, son of Seraiah, son of Azariah, son of Hilkiah, 2 son of Shallum, son of Zadok, son of Ahitub, 3 son of Amariah, son of Azariah, son of Meraioth, 4 son of Zerahiah, son of Uzzi, son of Bukki, 5 son of Abishua, son of Phinehas, son of Eleazar, son of the high priest Aaron—6* this Ezra came up from Babylon. He was a scribe, well-versed in the law of Moses which was given by the LORD, the God of Israel. Because the hand of the LORD, his God, was upon him, the king granted him all that he requested.

7 Some of the Israelites and some priests, Levites, singers, gatekeepers, and temple slaves also came up to Jerusalem in the seventh year of King Artaxerxes. 8 Ezra came to Jerusalem in the fifth month of that seventh year of the king. 9 On the first day of the first month he resolved on the journey up from Babylon, and on the first day of the fifth month he arrived at Jerusalem, for the favoring hand of his God was upon him. 10* Ezra had set his heart on the study and practice of the law of the LORD and on teaching statutes and ordinances in Israel.

The Decree of Artaxerxes. 11 This is a copy of the rescript which King Artaxerxes gave to Ezra the priest-scribe, the scribe of the text of the LORD's commandments and statutes for Israel:

12* "Artaxerxes, king of kings, to Ezra the priest, scribe of the law of the God of heaven (then, after greetings): 13 I have issued this decree, that anyone in my kingdom belonging to the people of Israel, its priests or Levites, who is minded to go up to Jerusalem with you, may do so. 14 You are the envoy from the king and his seven counselors to supervise Judah and Jerusalem in respect of the law of your God which is in your possession, 15 and to bring with you the silver and gold which the king and his counselors have freely contributed to the God of Israel, whose dwelling is in Jerusalem, 16 as well as all the silver and gold which you may receive throughout the province of Babylon, together with the free-will offerings which the people and priests freely contribute for the house of their God in Jerusalem. 17 You must take care, therefore, to use this money to buy bulls, rams, lambs, and the cereal offerings and libations proper to these, and to offer them on the altar of the house of your God in Jerusalem. 18 You and your brethren may do whatever seems best to you with the remainder of the silver and gold, conformably to the will of your God. 19 The utensils consigned to you for the service of the house of your God you are to deposit before the God of Jerusalem. 20 Whatever else you may be required to supply for the needs of the house of your God, you may draw from the royal treasury. 21 I, Artaxerxes the king, issue this decree to all the treasurers of West-of-Euphrates: Whatever Ezra the priest, scribe of the law of the God of heaven, requests of you, dispense to him accurately, 22 within these limits: silver, one hundred talents; wheat, one hundred kors; wine, one hundred baths; oil, one hundred baths; salt, without limit. 23 Let everything that is ordered by the God of heaven be carried out exactly for the house of the God of heaven, that wrath may not come upon the realm of the king and his sons. 24 We also inform you that it is not permitted to impose taxes, tributes, or tolls on any priest, Levite, singer, gatekeeper, temple slave, or any other servant of that house of God.

25*† "As for you, Ezra, in accordance with the wisdom of your God which is in your possession, appoint magistrates and judges to administer justice to all the people in West-of-Euphrates, to all, that is, who know the laws of your God. Instruct those who do not know these laws. 26 Whoever does not obey the law of your God and the law of the king, let strict judgment be executed upon him, whether death, or corporal punishment, or a fine on his goods, or imprisonment."

Ezra and His Companions. 27 Blessed be the LORD, the God of our fathers, who thus disposed the mind of the king to glorify the house of the LORD in Jerusalem, 28* and who let me find favor with the king, with his counselors, and with all the most influential royal officials. I therefore took courage and, with the hand of the LORD, my God, upon me, I gathered together Israelite family heads to make the return journey with me.

CHAPTER 8

1 This is the list of the family heads who returned with me from Babylon during the reign of King Artaxerxes:

2 Of the sons of Phinehas, Gershon; of the sons of Ithamar, Daniel; of the sons of David, Hattush, 3 son of Shecaniah; of the sons of Parosh, Zechariah, and with him one hundred and fifty males were enrolled; 4 of the sons of Pahath-moab, Eliehoenai, son of Zerahiah, and with him two hundred males; 5 of the sons of Zattu, Shecaniah, son of Jahaziel, and with him three hundred males; 6 of the sons of Adin, Ebed, son of Jonathan, and with him fifty males; 7 of the

*

7, 6: 7, 28; 8, 18; Neh 2, 8. 18.
10: Ps 119, 45.
12-17: 1, 2ff.
25: 2 Chr 17, 9.
28: 7, 6

†

7, 25: *The wisdom of your God:* the Mosaic law; cf vv 6, 14.

sons of Elam, Jeshaiah, son of Athaliah, and with him seventy males; 8 of the sons of Shephatiah, Zebadiah, son of Michael, and with him eighty males; 9 of the sons of Joab, Obadiah, son of Jehiel, and with him two hundred and eighteen males; 10 of the sons of Bani, Shelomith, son of Josiphiah, and with him one hundred and sixty males; 11 of the sons of Bebai, Zechariah, son of Bebai, and with him twenty-eight males; 12 of the sons of Azgad, Johanan, son of Hakkatan, and with him one hundred and ten males; 13 of the sons of Adonikam, younger sons, whose names were Eliphelet, Jeiel, and Shemaiah, and with them sixty males; 14 of the sons of Bigvai, Uthai, son of Zakkur, and with him seventy males.

The Journey to Jerusalem. 15† I had them assemble by the river that flows toward Ahava, where we made camp for three days. There I perceived that both laymen and priests were present, but I could not discover a single Levite. 16 Therefore I sent Eliezer, Ariel, Shemaiah, Jarib, Elnathan, Nathan, Zechariah, and Meshullam, wise leaders, 17 with a command for Iddo, the leader in the place Casiphia, instructing them what to say to Iddo and his brethren, and to the temple slaves in Casiphia, in order to procure for us ministers for the house of our God. 18* They sent to us—for the favoring hand of our God was upon us—a well-instructed man, one of the sons of Mahli, son of Levi, son of Israel, namely Sherebiah, with his sons and brethren, eighteen men. 19 They also sent us Hashabiah, and with him Jeshaiah, sons of Merari, and their brethren and their sons, twenty men. 20* Of the temple slaves (those whom David and the princes appointed to serve the Levites) there were two hundred and twenty. All these men were enrolled by name.

21 Then I proclaimed a fast, there by the river of Ahava, that we might humble ourselves before our God to petition from him a safe journey for ourselves, our children, and all our possessions. 22* For I would have been ashamed to ask the king for troops and horsemen to protect us against enemies along the way, since we had said to the king, "The favoring hand of our God is upon all who seek him, but his mighty wrath is against all who forsake him." 23 So we fasted, and prayed to our God for this, and our petition was granted. 24 Next I selected twelve of the priestly leaders along with Sherebiah, Hashabiah, and ten of their brethren, 25 and I weighed out before them the silver and the gold and the utensils offered for the house of our God by the king, his counselors, his officials, and all the Israelites of that region. 26 I consigned it to them in these amounts: silver, six hundred and fifty talents; silver utensils, one hundred; gold, one hundred talents; 27 twenty golden bowls valued at a thousand darics; two vases of excellent polished bronze, as precious as gold. 28 I addressed them in these words: "You are consecrated to the LORD, and the utensils are also consecrated; the silver and the gold are a free-will offering to the LORD, the God of your fathers. 29 Keep good watch over them till you weigh them out in Jerusalem in the presence of the chief priests and Levites and the family leaders of Israel, in the chambers of the house of the LORD." 30 The priest and the Levites then took over the silver, the gold, and the utensils that had been weighed out, to bring them to Jerusalem, to the house of our God.

31 We set out for Jerusalem from the river of Ahava on the twelfth day of the first month. The hand of our God remained upon us, and he protected us from enemies and bandits along the way. 32 Thus we arrived in Jerusalem, where we first rested for three days. 33 On the fourth day, the silver, the gold, and the utensils were weighed out in the house of our God and consigned to the priest Meremoth, son of Uriah, who was assisted by Eleazar, son of Phinehas; they were assisted by the Levites Jozabad, son of Jeshua, and Noadiah, son of Binnui. 34 Everything was in order as to number and weight, and the total weight was registered. At that same time, 35 those who had returned from the captivity, the exiles, offered as holocausts to the God of Israel twelve bulls for all Israel, ninety-six rams, seventy-seven lambs, and twelve goats as sin-offerings: all these as a holocaust to the LORD. 36† Finally, the orders of the king were presented to the king's satraps and to the governors in West-of-Euphrates, who gave their support to the people and to the house of God.

CHAPTER 9

Denunciation of Mixed Marriages. 1* When these matters had been concluded, the leaders approached me with this report: "Neither the Israelite laymen nor the priests nor the Levites have kept themselves aloof from the peoples of the land and their abominations [Ca-

*

8, 18: 7, 6.
20: 2, 43.
22: Neh 2, 9.
9, 1f: Dt 7, 1; Neh 9, 2.

†

8, 15: *Ahava:* a town at an unidentified site in Babylonia. The river that flowed toward it was probably a branch or canal of the Euphrates.

8, 36: The story of Ezra's mission is seemingly continued from this point by Neh 7, 72b—8, 18, which may be read before Ezr 9, 1.

naanites, Hittites, Perizzites, Jebusites, Ammonites, Moabites, Egyptians, and Amorites]; [2] for they have taken some of their daughters as wives for themselves and their sons, and thus they have desecrated the holy race with the peoples of the land. Furthermore, the leaders and rulers have taken a leading part in this apostasy!"

Ezra's Exhortation. [3]* When I had heard this thing, I tore my cloak and my mantle, plucked hair from my head and beard, and sat there stupefied. [4]* Around me gathered all who were in dread of the sentence of the God of Israel on this apostasy of the exiles, while I remained motionless until the evening sacrifice. [5] Then, at the time of the evening sacrifice, I rose in my wretchedness, and with cloak and mantle torn I fell on my knees, stretching out my hands to the LORD my God.

[6]* I said: "My God, I am too ashamed and confounded to raise my face to you, O my God, for our wicked deeds are heaped up above our heads and our guilt reaches up to heaven. [7]† From the time of our fathers even to this day great has been our guilt, and for our wicked deeds we have been delivered over, we and our kings and our priests, to the will of the kings of foreign lands, to the sword, to captivity, to pillage, and to disgrace, as is the case today.

[8]* "And now, but a short time ago, mercy came to us from the LORD our God, who left us a remnant and gave us a stake in his holy place; thus our God has brightened our eyes and given us relief in our servitude. [9]* For slaves we are, but in our servitude our God has not abandoned us; rather, he has turned the good will of the kings of Persia toward us. Thus he has given us new life to raise again the house of our God and restore its ruins, and has granted us a fence in Judah and Jerusalem. [10] But now, O our God, what can we say after all this? For we have abandoned your commandments, [11]* which you gave through your servants the prophets: the land which you are entering to take as your possession is a land unclean with the filth of the peoples of the land, with the abominations with which they have filled it from one end to the other in their uncleanness. [12]* Do not, then, give your daughters to their sons in marriage, and do not take their daughters for your sons. Never promote their peace and prosperity; thus you will grow strong, enjoy the produce of the land, and leave it as an inheritance to your children forever.

[13] "After all that has come upon us for our evil deeds and our great guilt—though you, our God, have made less of our sinfulness than it deserved and have allowed us to survive as we do—[14] shall we again violate your commandments by intermarrying with these abominable peoples? Would you not become so angered with us as to destroy us without remnant or survivor? [15] O LORD, God of Israel, you are just; yet we have been spared, the remnant we are today. Here we are before you in our sins. Because of all this, we can no longer stand in your presence."

CHAPTER 10

The People's Response. [1] While Ezra prayed and acknowledged their guilt, weeping and prostrate before the house of God, a very large assembly of Israelites gathered about him, men, women, and children; and the people wept profusely. [2] Then Shecaniah, the son of Jehiel, one of the sons of Elam, made this appeal to Ezra: "We have indeed betrayed our God by taking as wives foreign women of the peoples of the land. Yet even now there remains a hope for Israel. [3] Let us therefore enter into a covenant before our God to dismiss all our foreign wives and the children born of them, in keeping with what you, my lord, advise, and those who fear the commandments of our God. Let the law be observed! [4] Rise, then, for this is your duty! We will stand by you, so have courage and take action!"

[5] Ezra rose to his feet and demanded an oath from the chiefs of the priests, from the Levites and from all Israel that they would do as had been proposed; and they swore it. [6]† Then Ezra retired from his place before the house of God and entered the chamber of Johanan, son of Eliashib, where he spent the night neither eating food nor drinking water, for he was in mourning over the betrayal by the exiles. [7] A proclamation was made throughout Judah and Jerusalem that all the exiles should gather together in Jerusalem, [8] and that whoever failed to appear within three days would, according to the judgment of the leaders and elders, suffer the confiscation of all his possessions, and himself be ex-

*

3: Ps 119, 136.
4: Is 66, 2.
6: Ps 38, 4.
8: Is 4, 3.
9: Ps 106, 46.
11: Lv 18, 24f; Ez 36, 17.
12: Dt 7, 3.

†

9, 7: After this verse, the next part of the prayer attributed to Ezra is perhaps to be found in Neh 9, 6-37, which may be read as leading up to Ezr 9, 8-15.

10, 6: *Johanan, son of Eliashib:* actually, the grandson of Eliashib; the father of Johanan was Eliashib's son Joiada (Neh 12, 10f.22). Since Eliashib was high priest at the time of Nehemiah (Neh 3, 1.20f; 13, 4.7) and Johanan, if not yet high priest, was at least old enough to have his own separate quarters (*chamber*) in the temple at the time of Ezra, it is practically certain that Nehemiah's activity in Jerusalem must have preceded that of Ezra.

cluded from the assembly of the exiles.
9† All the men of Judah and Benjamin
gathered together in Jerusalem within
the three-day period: it was in the ninth
month, on the twentieth day of the
month. All the people, standing in the
open place before the house of God, were
trembling both over the matter at hand
and because it was raining. 10 Then Ezra,
the priest, stood up and said to them:
"Your unfaithfulness in taking foreign
women as wives has added to Israel's
guilt. 11* But now, give praise to the
LORD, the God of your fathers, and do
his will: separate yourselves from the
peoples of the land and from these for-
eign women." 12 In answer, the whole as-
sembly cried out with a loud voice: "Yes,
it is our duty to do as you say! 13 But
the people are numerous and it is the
rainy season, so that we cannot remain
out-of-doors; besides, this is not a task
that can be performed in a single day
or even two, for those of us who have
sinned in this regard are many. 14 Let
our leaders represent the whole assem-
bly; then let all those in our cities who
have taken foreign women for wives ap-
pear at appointed times, accompanied
by the elders and magistrates of each
city in question, till we have turned away
from us our God's burning anger over
this affair." 15 Only Jonathan, son of As-
ahel, and Jahzeiah, son of Tikvah, were
against this proposal, with Meshullam
and Shabbethai the Levite supporting
them.

The Guilty. 16† The exiles did as
agreed. Ezra appointed as his assistants
men who were family heads, one for
each family, all of them designated by
name. They held sessions to examine the
matter, beginning with the first day of
the tenth month. 17 By the first day of
the first month they had passed judg-
ment on all the men who had taken for-
eign women for wives.
18 Among the priests, the following
were found to have taken foreign women
for wives: Of the sons of Jeshua, son of
Jozadak, and his brethren: Maaseiah,
Eliezer, Jarib, and Gedaliah. 19 They
pledged themselves to dismiss their
wives, and as a guilt-offering for their
guilt they gave a ram from the flock.
20 Of the sons of Immer: Hanani and
Zebadiah; 21 of the sons of Harim: Maa-
seiah, Elijah, Shemaiah, Jehiel, and
Uzziah; 22 of the sons of Pashhur: Elioe-
nai, Maaseiah, Ishmael, Nethanel, Joza-
bad, and Elasah.
23* Of the Levites: Jozabad, Shimei,
Kelaiah (also called Kelita), Pethahiah,
Judah and Eliezer.
24 Of the singers: Eliashib and Zakkur;
of the gatekeepers: Shallum, Telem, and
Uri.
25 Among the other Israelites: Of the
sons of Parosh: Ramiah, Izziah, Malchi-
jah, Mijamin, Eleazar, Malchijah, and
Benaiah; 26 of the sons of Elam: Matta-
niah, Zechariah, Jehiel, Abdi, Jeremoth,
and Elijah; 27 of the sons of Zattu: Elioe-
nai, Eliashib, Mattaniah, Jeremoth, Za-
bad, and Aziza; 28 of the sons of Bebai:
Jehohanan, Hananiah, Zabbai, and Ath-
lai; 29 of the sons of Bani: Meshullam,
Malluch, Adaiah, Jashub, Sheal, and
Jeremoth; 30 of the sons of Pahath-
moab: Adna, Chelal, Benaiah, Maaseiah,
Mattaniah, Bezalel, Binnui, and Manas-
seh; 31 of the sons of Harim: Eliezer,
Isshijah, Malchijah, Shemaiah, Shim-
eon, 32 Benjamin, Malluch, Shemariah;
33 of the sons of Hashum: Mattenai, Mat-
tattah, Zabad, Eliphelet, Jeremai, Ma-
nasseh, Shimei; 34 of the sons of Begui:
Maadai, Amram, Uel, 35 Benaiah, Be-
deiah, Cheluhi, 36 Vaniah, Meremoth,
Eliashib, 37 Mattaniah, Mattenai, and
Jaasu; 38 of the sons of Binnui: Shimei,
39 Shelemiah, Nathan, and Adaiah; 40 of
the sons of Zachai: Shashai, Sharai,
41 Azarel, Shelemiah, Shemariah,
42 Shallum, Amariah, Joseph; 43 of the
sons of Nebo: Jeiel, Mattithiah, Zabad,
Zebina, Jaddai, Joel, Benaiah.
44† All these had taken foreign wives;
but they sent them away, both the
women and their children.

---

*

10, 11: Neh 9, 2. 23: Neh 8, 7; 10, 11.

---

†

10, 9: *Ninth month:* Chislev (November-December), during the "early rains" in Palestine. Since the assembly took place *in the open . . . all the people . . . were trembling . . . because it was raining.*

10, 16f: The work of the committee lasted three months, from *the first day of the tenth month,* Tebet (December-January), to *the first day of the first month,* Nisan (March-April), of the following Jewish year.

10, 44: The account of the problem of mixed marriages at the time of Ezra is continued in Neh 9, 1-5; this may be read immediately after Ezr 10, 44, though the date given in Neh 9, 1 fits more precisely after Ezr 10, 15; cf Hg 2, 10-14.

The Book of

NEHEMIAH

Problems common to the combined Books Ezra-Nehemiah have been pointed out in the Introduction to the Book of Ezra. The achievements of the two men were complementary; each helped to make it possible for Judaism to maintain its identity during the difficult days of the Restoration. Nehemiah was the man of action who rebuilt the walls of Jerusalem and introduced necessary administrative reforms. Ezra in turn was the great religious reformer who succeeded in establishing the Torah as the constitution of the returned community.

The biblical sources for Nehemiah's life and work are the autobiographical portions scattered through the book. They are called the "Memoirs of Nehemiah," and have been used more extensively and effectively by "the Chronicler" than the "Memoirs of Ezra." No competent scholar questions the authenticity of Nehemiah's memoirs. From these and other sources, the picture emerges of a man dedicated to the single purpose of the welfare of his people. Despite temperamental shortcomings, Nehemiah was a man of good practical sense combined with deep faith in God. In view of his selfless service to a community capable of severely testing any leader, we can be indulgent toward his numerous appeals to God to credit him with the work he had done. Nehemiah was a layman, and his generous dedication of talents to the service of God and of God's people remains an example of undiminished force for laymen today.

The Book of Nehemiah is divided as follows:

I: The Deeds of Nehemiah (1, 1—7, 72)
II: Promulgation of the Law (8, 1—13, 31)

I: THE DEEDS OF NEHEMIAH

CHAPTER 1

Nehemiah's Vocation. 1† The words of
Nehemiah, the son of Hacaliah.
In the month Chislev of the twentieth
year, I was in the citadel of Susa 2 when
Hanani, one of my brothers, came with
other men from Judah. I asked them
about the Jews, the remnant preserved
after the captivity, and about Jerusalem,
3 and they answered me: "The survivors
of the captivity there in the province are
in great distress and under reproach.
Also, the wall of Jerusalem lies
breached, and its gates have been gutted
with fire." 4 When I heard this report, I
began to weep and continued mourning
for several days; I fasted and prayed be-
fore the God of heaven.
5* I prayed: "O LORD, God of heaven,
great and awesome God, you who pre-
serve your covenant of mercy toward
those who love you and keep your com-
mandments, 6* may your ear be atten-
tive, and your eyes open, to heed the
prayer which I, your servant, now offer
in your presence day and night for your
servants the Israelites, confessing the
sins which we of Israel have committed
against you, I and my father's house in-
cluded. 7* Grievously have we offended
you, not keeping the commandments,
the statutes, and the ordinances which
you committed to your servant Moses.
8* But remember, I pray, the promise
which you gave through Moses, your
servant, when you said: 'Should you
prove faithless, I will scatter you among
the nations; 9 but should you return to
me and carefully keep my command-
ments, even though your outcasts have
been driven to the farthest corner of the
world, I will gather them from there, and
bring them back to the place which I
have chosen as the dwelling place for
my name.' 10* They are your servants,
your people, whom you freed by your
great might and your strong hand.
11*† O Lord, may your ear be attentive
to my prayer and that of all your willing
servants who revere your name. Grant

---

*

1, 5: Dt 7, 9.12; Dn 9, 4.
6: 2 Chr 6, 40.
7: Dn 3, 29f.
8f: Dt 30, 1-5.
10: Dt 9, 29.
11: Ps 118, 25.

---

†

1, 1: The first mission of Nehemiah, from the *twentieth year* of Artaxerxes I, lasted from the spring (2, 1) of 445 B. C. until 433 B. C. (5, 14). It is recounted in Neh 1, 1—6, 15; 12, 27-43; 6, 16—7, 5; 11, 1-21, which may be read in that order.

1, 11: *Cupbearer to the king:* an important official in the royal household. Because Nehemiah could appear in the queen's presence (2, 6), it is commonly presumed that he was a eunuch; but this is not necessarily so.

success to your servant this day, and let him find favor with this man"—for I was cupbearer to the king.

CHAPTER 2

Appointment by the King. 1 In the month Nisan of the twentieth year of King Artaxerxes, when the wine was in my charge, I took some and offered it to the king. As I had never before been sad in his presence, 2 the king asked me, "Why do you look sad? If you are not sick, you must be sad at heart." Though I was seized with great fear, 3 I answered the king: "May the king live forever! How could I not look sad when the city where my ancestors are buried lies in ruins, and its gates have been eaten out by fire?" 4 The king asked me, "What is it, then, that you wish?" I prayed to the God of heaven 5 and then answered the king: "If it please the king, and if your servant is deserving of your favor, send me to Judah, to the city of my ancestors' graves, to rebuild it." 6 Then the king, and the queen seated beside him, asked me how long my journey would take and when I would return. I set a date that was acceptable to him, and the king agreed that I might go.

7 I asked the king further: "If it please the king, let letters be given to me for the governors of West-of-Euphrates, that they may afford me safe-conduct till I arrive in Judah; 8* also a letter for Asaph, the keeper of the royal park, that he may give me wood for timbering the gates of the temple-citadel and for the city wall and the house that I shall occupy." The king granted my requests, for the favoring hand of my God was upon me. 9* Thus I proceeded to the governors of West-of-Euphrates and presented the king's letters to them. The king also sent with me army officers and cavalry.

10† When Sanballat the Horonite and Tobiah the Ammonite slave had heard of this, they were very much displeased that someone had come to seek the welfare of the Israelites.

Circuit of the City. 11 When I had arrived in Jerusalem, I first rested there for three days. 12 Then I set out by night with only a few other men (for I had not told anyone what my God had inspired me to do for Jerusalem) and with no other animals but my own mount. 13† I rode out at night by the Valley Gate, passed by the Dragon Spring, and came to the Dung Gate, observing how the walls of Jerusalem lay in ruins and its gates had been eaten out by fire. 14 Then I passed over to the Spring Gate and to the King's Pool. Since there was no room here for my mount to pass with me astride, 15 I continued on foot up the wadi by night, inspecting the wall all the while till I once more reached the Valley Gate, by which I went back in. 16 The magistrates knew nothing of where I had gone or what I was doing, for as yet I had disclosed nothing to the Jews, neither to the priests, nor to the nobles, nor to the magistrates, nor to the others who would be concerned about the matter.

Rebuilding Jerusalem's Walls. 17 Afterward I said to them: "You see the evil plight in which we stand: how Jerusalem lies in ruins and its gates have been gutted by fire. Come, let us rebuild the wall of Jerusalem, so that we may no longer be an object of derision!" 18* Then I explained to them how the favoring hand of my God had rested upon me, and what the king had said to me. They replied, "Let us be up and building!" And they undertook the good work with vigor.

19 On hearing of this, Sanballat the Horonite, Tobiah the Ammonite slave, and Geshem the Arab mocked us and ridiculed us. "What is this that you are about?" they asked. "Are you rebelling against the king?" 20† My answer to them was this: "It is the God of heaven who will grant us success. We, his servants, shall set about the rebuilding; but for you there is to be neither share nor claim nor memorial in Jerusalem."

*

2, 8: Ezr 7, 6.
9: Ezr 8, 22.
18: Ezr 7, 6.

†

2, 10: *Sanballat the Horonite:* the governor of the province of Samaria (3, 33f), apparently a native of one of the Beth-horons. A letter from the Jews living at Elephantine in southern Egypt, dated 408-407 B. C., mentions "Delayah and Shelemyah, the sons of Sanballat, the governor of Samaria." Although his own name was Babylonian—*Sin-uballit,* i.e., "Sin (the moon god) has given life"—his two sons had names referring to Yahweh. *Tobiah, the Ammonite slave:* the governor of the province of Ammon in Transjordan. His honorary title, "servant" (in Hebrew, *ebed*), i.e., of the king, could also be understood as *slave,* and Nehemiah no doubt meant it in this derogatory sense. The Tobiads remained a powerful family even in Maccabean times (2 Mc 3, 11). Sanballat and Tobiah, together with Geshem the Arab (2, 19; 6, 1f), who was probably in charge of Edom and the regions to the south and southeast of Judah, opposed the rebuilding of Jerusalem's walls on political grounds; the city was the capital of a rival province.

2, 13ff: Nehemiah left Jerusalem by *the Valley Gate* near the northwestern end of the old City of David and went south down the Tyropoean Valley toward *the Dragon Spring* (or the En-rogel of Jos 15, 7; 18, 16; 2 Sm 17, 17; 1 Kgs 1, 9, now known as Job's Well) at the juncture of the Valley of Hinnom and the Kidron Valley; he then turned north at *the Dung Gate* (or *the Potsherd Gate* of Jer 19, 2) at the southern end of the city and proceeded up *the wadi,* that is, the Kidron Valley, passing *the Spring Gate* (at the Spring of Gihon) and *the King's Pool* (unidentified); finally he turned west and then south to his starting point.

2, 20: *Neither share nor claim nor memorial:* although Sanballat and Tobiah were Yahwist, Nehemiah would not let them participate in any of the rights of the religious community in Jerusalem.

CHAPTER 3

List of Workers. 1*† Eliashib the high priest and his priestly brethren took up the task of rebuilding the Sheep Gate. They timbered it and set up its doors, its bolts, and its bars, then continued the rebuilding to the Tower of Hananel. 2 At their side the men of Jericho were rebuilding, and next to them was Zaccur, son of Imri. 3* The Fish Gate was rebuilt by the sons of Hassenaah; they timbered it and set up its doors, its bolts, and its bars. 4 At their side Meremoth, son of Uriah, son of Hakkoz, carried out the work of repair; next to him was Meshullam, son of Berechiah, son of Meshezabel; and next to him was Zadok, son of Baana. 5 Next to him the Tekoites carried out the work of repair; however, some of their outstanding men would not submit to the labor asked by their lords.

6 The New City Gate was repaired by Joiada, son of Paseah; and Meshullam, son of Besodeiah; they timbered it and set up its doors, its bolts, and its bars. 7 At their side were Melatiah the Gibeonite, Jadon the Meronothite, and the men of Gibeon and of Mizpah, who were under the jurisdiction of the governor of West-of-Euphrates. 8† Next to them the work of repair was carried out by Uzziel, son of Harhaiah, a member of the goldsmiths' guild, and at his side was Hananiah, one of the perfumers' guild. They restored Jerusalem as far as the wall of the public square. 9 Next to them the work of repair was carried out by Rephaiah, son of Hur, leader of half the district of Jerusalem, 10 and at his side was Jedaiah, son of Harumaph, who repaired opposite his own house. Next to him Hattush, son of Hashabneiah, carried out the work of repair. 11 The adjoining sector, as far as the Oven Tower, was repaired by Malchijah, son of Harim, and Hasshub, of Pahath-moab. 12 At their side the work of repair was carried out by Shallum, son of Hallohesh, leader of half the district of Jerusalem, by himself and his daughters. 13 The Valley Gate was repaired by Hanun and the inhabitants of Zanoah; they rebuilt it and set up its doors, its bolts, and its bars. They also repaired a thousand cubits of the wall up to the Dung Gate. 14 The Dung Gate was repaired by Malchijah, son of Rechab, leader of the district of Beth-haccherem; he rebuilt it and set up its doors, its bolts, and its bars. 15 The Spring Gate was repaired by Shallum, son of Colhozeh, leader of the district of Mizpah; he rebuilt it, roofed it over, and set up its doors, its bolts, and its bars. He also repaired the wall of the Aqueduct Pool near the king's garden as far as the steps that lead down from the City of David. 16 After him, the work of repair was carried out by Nehemiah, son of Azbuk, leader of half the district of Beth-zur, to a place opposite the tombs of David, as far as the artificial pool and the barracks.

17 After him, the Levites carried out the work of repair: Rehum, son of Bani. Next to him, for his own district, was Hashabiah, leader of half the district of Keilah. 18 After him, their brethren carried out the work of repair: Binnui, son of Henadad, leader of half the district of Keilah; 19 next to him Ezer, son of Jeshua, leader of Mizpah, who repaired the adjoining sector, the Corner, opposite the ascent to the arsenal. 20 After him, Baruch, son of Zabbai, repaired the adjoining sector from the Corner to the entrance of the house of Eliashib, the high priest. 21 After him, Meremoth, son of Uriah, son of Hakkoz, repaired the adjoining sector from the entrance of Eliashib's house to the end of the house.

22 After him, the work of repair was carried out by the priests, men of the surrounding country. 23 After them, Benjamin and Hasshub carried out the repair in front of their houses; after them, Azariah, son of Maaseiah, son of Ananiah, made the repairs alongside his house. 24 After him, Binnui, son of Henadad, repaired the adjoining sector from the house of Azariah to the Corner [that is, to the Angle]. 25 After him, Palal, son of Uzai, carried out the work of repair opposite the Corner and the tower projecting from the Upper Palace at the quarters of the guard. After him, Pedaiah, son of Parosh, carried out the work of repair 26 to a point opposite the Water Gate on the east, and the projecting tower. 27 After him, the Tekoites repaired the adjoining sector opposite the great projecting tower, to the wall of Ophel [the temple slaves were dwelling on Ophel].

28 Above the Horse Gate the priests carried out the work of repair, each before his own house. 29* After them Zadok, son of Immer, carried out the repair before his house, and after him the repair was carried out by Shemaiah, son of Shecaniah, keeper of the East Gate. 30 After him, Hananiah, son of Shelemiah, and Hanun, the sixth son of Za-

*

3, 1: Jer 31, 38.
3: Ezr 2, 35; Zep 1, 10.
29: Ezr 40, 6.

†

3, 1-32: The construction work on the gates and walls of the city is described in counterclockwise direction, beginning and ending at *the Sheep Gate* (to the north of the temple). The exact sites of many of the topographical points mentioned are uncertain.

3, 8: *Wall of the public square:* that is, the section of wall bounding the place of assembly outside the Gate of Ephraim, or New City Gate; cf 3, 6; 8, 16.

laph, repaired the adjoining sector; after
them, Meshullam, son of Berechiah, re-
paired the place opposite his own lodg-
ing. 31 After him, Malchijah, a member
of the goldsmiths' guild, carried out the
work of repair as far as the quarters of
the temple slaves and the merchants,
before the Gate of Inspection and as far
as the upper chamber of the Angle.
32 Between the upper chamber of the An-
gle and the Sheep Gate, the goldsmiths
and the merchants carried out the work
of repair.
Opposition from Judah's Foes.
33 When Sanballat heard that we were
rebuilding the wall, it roused his anger
and he became very much incensed. He
ridiculed the Jews, 34 saying in the pres-
ence of his brethren and the troops of
Samaria: "What are these miserable
Jews trying to do? Will they complete
their restoration in a single day? Will
they recover these stones, burnt as they
are, from the heaps of dust?" 35 Tobiah
the Ammonite was beside him, and he
said: "It is a rubble heap they are build-
ing. Any fox that attacked it would
breach their wall of stones!" 36 Take
note, O our God, how we were mocked!
Turn back their derision upon their own
heads and let them be carried away to
a land of captivity! 37* Hide not their
crime and let not their sin be blotted out
in your sight, for they insulted the build-
ers to their face! 38 We, however, contin-
ued to build the wall, which was soon
filled in and completed up to half its
height. The people worked with a will.

CHAPTER 4

1 When Sanballat, Tobiah, the Arabs,
the Ammonites, and the Ashdodites
heard that the restoration of the walls
of Jerusalem was progressing—for the
gaps were beginning to be closed up—
they became extremely angry. 2 There-
upon they all plotted together to come
and fight against Jerusalem and thus
to throw us into confusion. 3 We prayed
to our God and posted a watch against
them day and night for fear of what
they might do. 4 Meanwhile the Judah-
ites were saying:

"Slackened is the bearers' strength,
 there is no end to the rubbish;
Never shall we be able
 the wall to rebuild."

5 Our enemies thought, "Before they are
aware of it or see us, we shall come into
their midst, kill them, and put an end
to the work."
6 When the Jews who lived near them
had come to us from one place after an-
other, and had told us ten times over that
they were about to attack us, 7 I sta-
tioned guards down below, behind the
wall, near the exposed points, assigning
them by family groups with their
swords, their spears, and their bows. 8 I
made an inspection, then addressed
these words to the nobles, the magis-
trates, and the rest of the people: "Have
no fear of them! Keep in mind the LORD,
who is great and to be feared, and fight
for your brethren, your sons and daugh-
ters, your wives and your homes."
9 When our enemies became aware that
we had been warned and that God had
upset their plan, we all went back, each
to his own task at the wall.
10* From that time on, however, only
half my able men took a hand in the
work, while the other half, armed with
spears, bucklers, bows, and breast-
plates, stood guard behind the whole
house of Judah 11 as they rebuilt the wall.
The load carriers, too, were armed; each
did his work with one hand and held a
weapon with the other. 12 Every builder,
while he worked, had his sword girt at
his side. Also, a trumpeter stood beside
me, 13 for I had said to the nobles, the
magistrates, and the rest of the people:
"Our work is scattered and extensive,
and we are widely separated from one
another along the wall; 14 wherever you
hear the trumpet sound, join us there;
our God will fight with us." 15 Thus we
went on with the work, half of the men
with spears at the ready, from daybreak
till the stars came out.
16 At the same time I told the people
to spend the nights inside Jerusalem,
each man with his own attendant, so that
they might serve as a guard by night
and a working force by day. 17 Neither
I, nor my kinsmen, nor any of my at-
tendants, nor any of the bodyguard that
accompanied me took off his clothes; ev-
eryone kept his weapon at his right
hand.

CHAPTER 5

Antisocial Conduct. 1* Then there
rose a great outcry of the common peo-
ple and their wives against certain of
their fellow Jews. 2 Some said: "We are
forced to pawn our sons and daughters
in order to get grain to eat that we may
live." 3 Others said: "We are forced to
pawn our fields, our vineyards, and our
houses, that we may have grain during
the famine." 4 Still others said: "To pay
the king's tax we have borrowed money
on our fields and our vineyards. 5* And
though these are our own kinsmen and
our children are as good as theirs, we
have had to reduce our sons and daugh-

37: Jer 18:23.
4, 10: Ps 149, 6.
5, 1f: Jer 34, 8-22.
5: Ex 21, 7; Lv 25, 39.

ters to slavery, and violence has been done to some of our daughters! Yet we can do nothing about it, for our fields and our vineyards belong to others."

Nehemiah's Action. 6 I was extremely angry when I heard the reasons they had for complaint. 7† After some deliberation, I called the nobles and magistrates to account, saying to them, "You are exacting interest from your own kinsmen!" I then rebuked them severely, 8* saying to them: "As far as we were able, we bought back our fellow Jews who had been sold to Gentiles; you, however, are selling your own brothers, to have them bought back by us." They remained silent, for they could find no answer. 9 I continued: "What you are doing is not good. Should you not walk in the fear of our God, and put an end to the derision of our Gentile enemies? 10 I myself, my kinsmen, and my attendants have lent the people money and grain without charge. Let us put an end to this usury! 11 I ask that you return to them this very day their fields, their vineyards, their olive groves, and their houses, together with the interest on the money, the grain, the wine, and the oil that you have lent them." 12 They answered: "We will return everything and exact nothing further from them. We will do just what you ask." Then I called for the priests and had them administer an oath to these men that they would do as they had promised. 13 I also shook out the folds of my garment, saying, "Thus may God shake from his home and his fortune every man who fails to keep this promise, and may he thus be shaken out and emptied!" And the whole assembly answered, "Amen," and praised the LORD. Then the people did as they had promised.

Nehemiah's Lack of Self-interest. 14 Moreover, from the time that King Artaxerxes appointed me governor in the land of Judah, from his twentieth to his thirty-second year—during these twelve years neither I nor my brethren lived from the governor's allowance. 15 The earlier governors, my predecessors, had laid a heavy burden on the people, taking from them each day forty silver shekels for their food; then too, their men oppressed the people. But I, because I feared God, did not act thus. 16 Moreover, though I had acquired no land of my own, I did my part in this work on the wall, and all my men were gathered there for the work. 17 Though I set my table for a hundred and fifty persons, Jews and magistrates, as well as those who came to us from the nations round about, 18 and though the daily preparations were made at my expense—one beef, six choice muttons, poultry—besides all kinds of wine in abundance every ten days, despite this I did not claim the governor's allowance, for the labor lay heavy upon this people. 19 Keep in mind, O my God, in my favor all that I did for this people.

CHAPTER 6

Plots against Nehemiah. 1 When it had been reported to Sanballat, Tobiah, Geshem the Arab, and our other enemies that I had rebuilt the wall and that there was no breach left in it (though up to that time I had not yet set up the doors in the gates), 2 Sanballat and Geshem sent me this message: "Come, let us hold council together at Caphirim in the plain of Ono." They were planning to do me harm. 3 However, I sent messengers to them with this reply: "I am engaged in a great enterprise and am unable to come down; why should the work stop, while I leave it to come down to you?" 4 Four times they sent me this same proposal, and each time I gave the same reply. 5 Then, the fifth time, Sanballat sent me the same message by one of his servants, who bore an unsealed letter 6 containing this text: "Among the nations it has been reported—Geshem is witness to this—that you and the Jews are planning a rebellion; that for this reason you are rebuilding the wall; and that you are to be their king"—and so on. 7 "Also, that you have set up prophets in Jerusalem to proclaim you king of Judah. Now, since matters like these must reach the ear of the king, come, let us hold council together." 8 I sent him this answer: "Nothing of what you report has taken place; rather, it is the invention of your own mind." 9 They were all trying to frighten us, thinking, "Their hands will slacken in the work, and it will never be completed." But instead, I now redoubled my efforts.

10 I went to the house of Shemaiah, son of Delaiah, son of Mehetabel, who was unable to go about, and he said:

"Let us meet in the house of God,
inside the temple building;
let us lock the doors of the temple.
For men are coming to kill you;
by night they are coming to kill
you."

11 My answer was: "A man like me take flight? Can a man like me enter the temple to save his life? I will not go!" 12 For on consideration it was plain to me that God had not sent him; rather, because Tobiah and Sanballat had bribed him, he voiced this prophecy concerning me

N E H E M I A H

* 8: Lv 25, 48.

† 5, 7: *You are exacting interest from your own kinsmen!:* contrary to the Mosaic law (Dt 23, 20).

[13] that I might act on it out of fear and commit this sin. Then they would have had a shameful story with which to discredit me. [14]* Keep in mind Tobiah and Sanballat, O my God, because of these things they did; keep in mind as well Noadiah the prophetess and the other prophets who were trying to frighten me.

Conclusion of the Work. [15]† The wall was finished on the twenty-fifth day of Elul; it had taken fifty-two days. [16]* When all our enemies had heard of this, and all the nations round about had taken note of it, our enemies lost much face in the eyes of the nations, for they knew that it was with our God's help that this work had been completed. [17]† At that same time, however, many letters were going to Tobiah from the nobles of Judah, and Tobiah's letters were reaching them, [18] for many in Judah were in league with him, since he was the son-in-law of Shecaniah, son of Arah, and his son Jehohanan had married the daughter of Meshullam, son of Berechiah. [19] Thus they would praise his good deeds in my presence and relate to him whatever I said; and Tobiah sent letters trying to frighten me.

CHAPTER 7

[1] When the wall had been rebuilt, I had the doors set up, and the gatekeepers [and the singers and the Levites] were put in charge of them. [2] Over Jerusalem I placed Hanani, my brother, and Hananiah, the commander of the citadel, who was a more trustworthy and God-fearing man than most. [3] I said to them: "The gates of Jerusalem are not to be opened until the sun is hot, and while the sun is still shining they shall shut and bar the doors. Appoint as watchmen the inhabitants of Jerusalem, some at their watch posts, and others before their own houses."

Census of the Province. [4] Now the city was quite wide and spacious, but its population was small, and none of the houses had been rebuilt. [5] When my God had put it into my mind to gather together the nobles, the magistrates, and the common people, and to examine their family records, I came upon the family list of those who had returned in the earliest period. There I found the following written:

[6]*† These are the inhabitants of the province who returned from the captivity of the exiles whom Nebuchadnezzar, king of Babylon, had carried away, and who came back to Jerusalem and Judah, each man to his own city [7] (those who returned with Zerubbabel, Jeshua, Nehemiah, Azariah, Raamiah, Nahamani, Mordecai, Bilshan, Mispereth, Bigvai, Nehum, and Baanah).

The census of the men of Israel: [8] sons of Parosh, two thousand one hundred and seventy-two; [9] sons of Shephatiah, three hundred and seventy-two; [10] sons of Arah, six hundred and fifty-two; [11] sons of Pahath-moab who were sons of Jeshua and Joab, two thousand eight hundred and eighteen; [12] sons of Elam, one thousand two hundred and fifty-four; [13] sons of Zattu, eight hundred and forty-five; [14] sons of Zaccai, seven hundred and sixty; [15] sons of Binnui, six hundred and forty-eight; [16] sons of Bebai, six hundred and twenty-eight; [17] sons of Azgad, two thousand three hundred and twenty-two; [18] sons of Adonikam, six hundred and sixty-seven; [19] sons of Bigvai, two thousand and sixty-seven; [20] sons of Adin, six hundred and fifty-five; [21] sons of Ater who were sons of Hezekiah, ninety-eight; [22] sons of Hashum, three hundred and twenty-eight; [23] sons of Bezai, three hundred and twenty-four; [24] sons of Hariph, one hundred and twelve; [25] sons of Gibeon, ninety-five; [26] men of Bethlehem and Netophah, one hundred and eighty-eight; [27] men of Anathoth, one hundred and twenty-eight; [28] men of Beth-azmaveth, forty-two; [29] men of Kiriath-jearim, Chephirah, and Beeroth, seven hundred and forty-three; [30] men of Ramah and Geba, six hundred and twenty-one; [31] men of Michmas, one hundred and twenty-two; [32] men of Bethel and Ai, one hundred and twenty-three; [33] men of Nebo, fifty-two; [34] sons of another Elam, one thousand two hundred and fifty-four; [35] sons of Harim, three hundred and twenty; [36] sons of Jericho, three hundred and forty-five; [37] sons of Lod, Hadid, and Ono, seven hundred and twenty-one; [38] sons of Senaah, three thousand nine hundred and thirty.

[39] The priests: sons of Jedaiah who were of the house of Jeshua, nine hundred and seventy-three; [40] sons of Immer, one thousand and fifty-two; [41] sons of Pashhur, one thousand two hundred and forty-seven; [42] sons of Harim, one thousand and seventeen.

[43] The Levites: sons of Jeshua, Kadmiel, Binnui, Hodeviah, seventy-four.

[44] The singers: sons of Asaph, one hundred and forty-eight.

[45] The gatekeepers: sons of Shallum,

*

6, 14: Jer 23, 9-40; Zec 13, 3.
16: Pss 118, 22f; 127, 1.
7, 6-72: Ezr 2, 1-70.

†

6, 15: *Elul:* the sixth month (August-September). *Fifty-two days:* according to Josephus (*Antiquities* XI, v 8), the rebuilding of the walls of Jerusalem by Nehemiah took two years and four months, which seems more probable.

6, 17ff: These verses should be read immediately after v 14.

7, 6-72a: See note on Ezr 2, 1-67.

sons of Ater, sons of Talmon, sons of Akkub, sons of Hatita, sons of Shobai, one hundred and thirty-eight.

46 The temple slaves: sons of Ziha, sons of Hasupha, sons of Tabbaoth, 47 sons of Keros, sons of Sia, sons of Padon, 48 sons of Lebana, sons of Hagaba, sons of Shalmai, 49 sons of Hanan, sons of Giddel, sons of Gahar, 50 sons of Reaiah, sons of Rezin, sons of Nekoda, 51 sons of Gazzam, sons of Uzza, sons of Paseah, 52 sons of Besai, sons of the Meunites, sons of the Nephusites, 53 sons of Bakbuk, sons of Hakupha, sons of Harhur, 54 sons of Bazlith, sons of Mehida, sons of Harsha, 55 sons of Barkos, sons of Sisera, sons of Temah, 56 sons of Neziah, sons of Hatipha.

57 Descendants of the slaves of Solomon: sons of Sotai, sons of Sophereth, sons of Perida, 58 sons of Jaala, sons of Darkon, sons of Giddel, 59 sons of Shephatiah, sons of Hattil, sons of Pochereth-hazzebaim, sons of Amon. 60 The total of the temple slaves and the descendants of the slaves of Solomon was three hundred and ninety-two.

61 The following who returned from Tel-melah, Tel-harsha, Cherub, Addon, and Immer were unable to prove that their ancestral houses and their descent were Israelite: 62 sons of Delaiah, sons of Tobiah, sons of Nekoda, six hundred and forty-two. 63 Also, of the priests: sons of Hobaiah, sons of Hakkoz, sons of Barzillai (he had married one of the daughters of Barzillai the Gileadite and became known by his name). 64 These men searched their family records, but their names could not be found written there; hence they were degraded from the priesthood, 65† and His Excellency ordered them not to partake of the most holy foods until there should be a priest bearing the Urim and Thummim.

66 The entire assembly taken together came to forty-two thousand three hundred and sixty, 67 not counting their male and female slaves, who were seven thousand three hundred and thirty-seven. They also had two hundred male and female singers. Their horses were seven hundred and thirty-six, their mules two hundred and forty-five, 68 their camels four hundred and thirty-five, their asses six thousand seven hundred and twenty.

69 Certain of the family heads contributed to the service. His Excellency put into the treasury one thousand drachmas of gold, fifty basins, thirty garments for priests, and five hundred minas of silver. 70 Some of the family heads contributed to the treasury for the temple service: twenty thousand drachmas of gold and two thousand two hundred minas of silver. 71 The contributions of the rest of the people amounted to twenty thousand drachmas of gold, two thousand minas of silver, and sixty-seven garments for priests.

72† The priests, the Levites, the gatekeepers, the singers, the temple slaves, and all Israel took up residence in their cities.

II: PROMULGATION OF THE LAW

CHAPTER 8

Ezra Reads the Law. 1* Now when the seventh month came, the whole people gathered as one man in the open space before the Water Gate, and they called upon Ezra the scribe to bring forth the book of the law of Moses which the LORD prescribed for Israel. 2 On the first day of the seventh month, therefore, Ezra the priest brought the law before the assembly, which consisted of men, women, and those children old enough to understand. 3 Standing at one end of the open place that was before the Water Gate, he read out of the book from daybreak till midday, in the presence of the men, the women, and those children old enough to understand; and all the people listened attentively to the book of the law. 4 Ezra the scribe stood on a wooden platform that had been made for the occasion; at his right side stood Mattithiah, Shema, Anaiah, Uriah, Hilkiah, and Maaseiah, and on his left Pedaiah, Mishael, Malchijah, Hashum, Hashbaddanah, Zechariah, Meshullam. 5 Ezra opened the scroll so that all the people might see it (for he was standing higher up than any of the people); and, as he opened it, all the people rose. 6 Ezra blessed the LORD, the great God, and all the people, their hands raised high, answered, "Amen, amen!" Then they bowed down and prostrated themselves before the LORD, their faces to the ground. 7* [The Levites Jeshua, Bani, Sherebiah, Jamin, Akkub, Shabbethai, Hodiah, Maaseiah, Kelita, Azariah, Jozabad, Hanan, and Pelaiah explained the law to the people, who remained in their places.] 8* Ezra read plainly from the book of the law of God, interpreting it so that all could understand what was read. 9 Then [Nehemiah, that is, His Excellency, and] Ezra the priest-scribe [and the Levites who were instructing the people] said to all the people: "Today is holy to the LORD your God. Do not

*

8, 1: Ezr 3, 1. 8: Ezr 7, 6.
7: 10, 11.

†

7, 65.69: *His Excellency:* see note on Ezr 2, 63.

7, 72b—8, 18: to be read after Ezr 8, 36. The gloss mentioning *Nehemiah* in v 9 was inserted in this Ezra section after the dislocation of several parts of Ezra-Nehemiah had occurred. There is no clear evidence of a simultaneous presence of Nehemiah and Ezra in Jerusalem; Neh 12, 26 and 12, 36 are also scribal glosses.

be sad, and do not weep"—for all the
people were weeping as they heard the
words of the law. 10* He said further:
"Go, eat rich foods and drink sweet
drinks, and allot portions to those who
had nothing prepared; for today is holy
to our LORD. Do not be saddened this
day, for rejoicing in the LORD must be
your strength!" 11 [And the Levites qui-
eted all the people, saying, "Hush, for
today is holy, and you must not be sad-
dened."] 12 Then all the people went to
eat and drink, to distribute portions, and
to celebrate with great joy, for they un-
derstood the words that had been ex-
pounded to them.

The Feast of Booths. 13 On the second
day, the family heads of the whole peo-
ple and also the priests and the Levites
gathered around Ezra the scribe and ex-
amined the words of the law more
closely. 14* They found it written in the
law prescribed by the LORD through Mo-
ses that the Israelites must dwell in
booths during the feast of the seventh
month; 15* and that they should have
this proclamation made throughout
their cities and in Jerusalem: "Go out
into the hill country and bring in
branches of olive trees, oleasters, myr-
tle, palm, and other leafy trees, to make
booths, as the law prescribes." 16 The
people went out and brought in branches
with which they made booths for them-
selves, on the roof of their houses, in
their courtyards, in the courts of the
house of God, and in the open spaces
of the Water Gate and the Gate of
Ephraim. 17 Thus the entire assembly of
the returned exiles made booths and
dwelt in them. Now the Israelites had
done nothing of this sort from the days
of Jeshua, son of Nun, until this occa-
sion; therefore there was very great joy.
18 Ezra read from the book of the law
of God day after day, from the first day
to the last. They kept the feast for seven
days, and the solemn assembly on the
eighth day, as was required.

CHAPTER 9

Confession of the People. 1*† On the
twenty-fourth day of this month, the Is-
raelites gathered together fasting and in
sackcloth, their heads covered with
dust. 2* Those of Israelite descent sepa-
rated themselves from all who were of
foreign extraction, then stood forward
and confessed their sins and the guilty
deeds of their fathers. 3 When they had
taken their places, they read from the
book of the law of the LORD their God,
for a fourth part of the day, and during
another fourth part they made their
confession and prostrated themselves
before the LORD their God. 4 Standing on
the platform of the Levites were Jeshua,
Binnui, Kadmiel, Shebaniah, Bunni,
Sherebiah, Bani, and Chenani, who cried
out to the LORD their God, with a loud
voice. 5* The Levites Jeshua, Kadmiel,
Bani, Hashabneiah, Sherebiah, Hodiah,
Shebaniah, and Pethahiah said,

"Arise, bless the LORD, your God,
from eternity to eternity!"

The Israelites answered with the bless-
ing,

"Blessed is your glorious name,
and exalted above all blessing and
praise."

6† Then Ezra said: "It is you, O LORD,
you are the only one; you made the
heavens, the highest heavens and all
their host, the earth and all that is upon
it, the seas and all that is in them. To
all of them you give life, and the heav-
enly hosts bow down before you.
7* "You, O LORD, are the God who
chose Abram, who brought him out from
Ur of the Chaldees, and named him
Abraham. 8* When you had found his
heart faithful in your sight, you made
the covenant with him to give to him and
his posterity the land of the Canaanites,
Hittites, Amorites, Perizzites, Jebusites,
and Girgashites. These promises of
yours you fulfilled, for you are just.

9* "You saw the affliction of our fathers
in Egypt,
you heard their cry by the Red
Sea;
10* You worked signs and wonders
against Pharaoh,
against all his servants and the
people of his land,
Because you knew of their insolence
toward them;
thus you made for yourself a
name even to this day.
11* The sea you divided before them,
on dry ground they passed
through the midst of the sea;
Their pursuers you hurled into the
depths,
like a stone into the mighty
waters.
12* With a column of cloud you led them
by day,
and by night with a column of fire,

*

10: Est 9, 19.
14: Ex 23, 14; Lv 23, 33-36.
15: Ps 118, 27.
9, 1: Dn 9, 3.
2: Ezr 9, 1f; 10, 11.
5: Dn 2, 20; 3, 52.
7: Gn 12, 1; 17, 5.
8: Gn 15, 18f.
9: Ex 2, 23f.
10: Ex 7—11; 14.
11: Ex 15, 5.10.
12: Ex 13, 21f.

†

9, 1-5: This is a continuation of the account concerning the problem of mixed marriages at the time of Ezra; it should be read immediately after Ezr 10, 44.

9, 6-37: The prayer of Ezra which began in Ezr 9, 6f is here continued; see note on Ezr 9, 7.

To light the way of their journey,
the way in which they must travel.
13* On Mount Sinai you came down,
you spoke with them from heaven;
You gave them just ordinances, firm
laws,
good statutes, and command-
ments;
14* Your holy sabbath you made known
to them,
commandments, statutes, and law
you prescribed for them,
by the hand of Moses your ser-
vant.
15* Food from heaven you gave them
in their hunger,
water from a rock you sent them
in their thirst.
You bade them enter and occupy the
land
which you had sworn with up-
raised hand to give them.

16 "But they, our fathers, proved to be
insolent; they held their necks stiff and
would not obey your commandments.
17* They refused to obey and no longer
remembered the miracles you had
worked for them. They stiffened their
necks and turned their heads to return
to their slavery in Egypt. But you are
a God of pardons, gracious and compas-
sionate, slow to anger and rich in mercy;
you did not forsake them. 18* Though
they made for themselves a molten calf,
and proclaimed, 'Here is your God who
brought you up out of Egypt,' and were
guilty of great effronteries, 19 yet in your
great mercy you did not forsake them
in the desert. The column of cloud did
not cease to lead them by day on their
journey, nor did the column of fire by
night cease to light for them the way by
which they were to travel.
20* "Your good spirit you bestowed on
them, to give them understanding; your
manna you did not withhold from their
mouths, and you gave them water in
their thirst. 21* Forty years in the desert
you sustained them: they did not want;
their garments did not become worn,
and their feet did not become swollen.
22* You gave them kingdoms and peo-
ples, which you divided up among them
as border lands. They possessed the land
of Sihon, king of Heshbon, and the land
of Og, king of Bashan.
23* "You made their children as nu-
merous as the stars of the heavens, and
you brought them into the land which
you had commanded their fathers to en-
ter and possess. 24 The sons went in to
take possession of the land, and you
humbled before them the Canaanite in-
habitants of the land and delivered them
over into their power, their kings as well
as the peoples of the land, to do with
them as they would. 25* They captured
fortified cities and fertile land; they took
possession of houses filled with all good
things, cisterns already dug, vineyards,
olive groves, and fruit trees in abun-
dance. They could eat and have their fill,
fatten and feast themselves on your im-
mense good gifts.
26* "But they were contemptuous and
rebellious: they cast your law behind
their backs, they slew your prophets who
bore witness against them in order to
bring them back to you, and they were
guilty of great effronteries. 27* Therefore
you delivered them into the power of
their enemies, who oppressed them. But
in the time of their oppression they
would cry out to you, and you would hear
them from heaven, and according to
your great mercy give them saviors to
deliver them from the power of their en-
emies.
28 "As soon as they had relief, they
would go back to doing evil in your sight.
Then again you abandoned them to the
power of their enemies, who crushed
them. Then they cried out to you, and
you heard them from heaven and deliv-
ered them according to your mercy,
many times over. 29* You bore witness
against them, in order to bring them
back to your law. But they were insolent
and would not obey your command-
ments; they sinned against your ordi-
nances, from which men draw life when
they practice them. They turned stub-
born backs, stiffened their necks, and
would not obey. 30 You were patient with
them for many years, bearing witness
against them through your spirit, by
means of your prophets; still they would
not listen. Thus you delivered them over
into the power of the peoples of the
lands. 31 Yet in your great mercy you did
not completely destroy them and you
did not forsake them, for you are a kind
and merciful God.
32* "Now, therefore, O our God, great,
mighty, and awesome God, you who in
your mercy preserve the covenant, take
into account all the disasters that have
befallen us, our kings, our princes, our
priests, our prophets, our fathers, and
your entire people, from the time of the
kings of Assyria until this day! 33* In all
that has come upon us you have been
just, for you kept faith while we have
done evil. 34 Yes, our kings, our princes,

NEHEMIAH

---
*

13: Ex 19—20.
14: Ex 20, 8.
15: Ex 16, 4; 17, 1f.
17: Nm 14, 1-4; Ex 34, 6; Dn 9, 9.
18: Ex 32, 4.
20: Dt 2, 7.
21: Dt 8, 4.
22: Nm 21, 21—35; Dt 1, 4; 2, 26—3, 11.
23: Dt 1, 10.
25: Dt 3, 5; 6, 10f; 11, 11; 32, 15.
26: Wis 2, 10-20.
27: Dn 9, 19.
29: Lv 18, 5; 30, 16; 32, 47.
32: Lam 5.
33: Dn 3, 27; 9, 14.

our priests, and our fathers have not
kept your law; they paid no attention to
your commandments and the obliga-
tions of which you reminded them.
35 While they were yet in their kingdom,
in the midst of the many good things that
you had given them and in the wide and
fertile land that you had spread out be-
fore them, they did not serve you nor
did they turn away from their evil deeds.
36 But, see, we today are slaves; and as
for the land which you gave our fathers
that they might eat its fruits and good
things—see, we have become slaves
upon it! 37 Its rich produce goes to the
kings whom you set over us because of
our sins, who rule over our bodies and
our cattle as they please. We are in great
distress!"

CHAPTER 10

Agreement of the People. 1*† In view
of all this, we are entering into a firm
pact, which we are putting into writing.
On the sealed document appear the
names of our princes, our Levites, and
our priests.

2 On the sealed document: His Excel-
lency Nehemiah, son of Hacaliah, and
Zedekiah.

3 Seraiah, Azariah, Jeremiah, 4 Pash-
hur, Amariah, Malchijah, 5 Hattush,
Shebaniah, Malluch, 6 Harim, Mere-
moth, Obadiah, 7 Daniel, Ginnethon,
Baruch, 8 Meshullam, Abijah, Mijamin,
9 Maaziah, Bilgai, Shemaiah: these are
the priests.

10 The Levites: Jeshua, son of Azaniah;
Binnui, of the sons of Henadad; Kad-
miel; 11* and their brethren Shebaniah,
Hodiah, Kelita, Pelaiah, Hanan, 12 Mica,
Rehob, Hashabiah, 13 Zaccur, Shere-
biah, Shebaniah, 14 Hodiah, Bani, Be-
ninu.

15 The leaders of the people: Parosh,
Pahath-moab, Elam, Zattu, Bani,
16 Bunni, Azgad, Bebai, 17 Adonijah, Big-
vai, Adin, 18 Ater, Hezekiah, Azzur,
19 Hodiah, Hashum, Bezai, 20 Hariph,
Anathoth, Nebai, 21 Magpiash, Meshul-
lam, Hezir, 22 Meshezabel, Zadok,
Jaddua, 23 Pelatiah, Hanan, Anaiah,
24 Hoshea, Hananiah, Hasshub, 25 Hal-
lohesh, Pilha, Shobek, 26 Rehum, Ha-
shabnah, Maaseiah, 27 Ahiah, Hanan,
Anan, 28 Malluch, Harim, Baanah.

Provisions of the Pact. 29 The rest of
the people, priests, Levites, gatekeepers,
singers, temple slaves, and all others
who have separated themselves from
the peoples of the lands in favor of the
law of God, with their wives, their sons,
their daughters, all who are of the age
of discretion, 30* join with their brethren
who are their princes, and with the sanc-
tion of a curse take this oath to follow
the law of God which was given through
Moses, the servant of God, and to ob-
serve carefully all the commandments
of the LORD, our LORD, his ordinances
and his statutes.

31* Agreed, that we will not marry our
daughters to the peoples of the land, and
that we will not take their daughters for
our sons.

32* When the peoples of the land bring
in merchandise or any kind of grain for
sale on the sabbath day, we will not buy
from them on the sabbath or on any
other holyday. We will forgo the seventh
year, as well as every kind of debt.

33* We impose these commandments
on ourselves: to give a third of a shekel
each year for the service of the house
of our God, 34 for the showbread, for the
daily cereal offering, for the daily holo-
caust, for the sabbaths, new moons, and
festivals, for the holy offerings, for sin
offerings to make atonement for Israel,
and for every service of the house of our
God. 35* We, priests, Levites, and people,
have determined by lot concerning the
procurement of wood: it is to be brought
to the house of our God by each of our
family houses at stated times each year,
to be burnt on the altar of the LORD, our
God, as the law prescribes. 36* We have
agreed to bring each year to the house
of the LORD the first fruits of our fields
and of our fruit trees, of whatever kind;
37 also, as is prescribed in the law, to
bring to the house of our God, to the
priests who serve in the house of our
God, the first-born of our children and
our animals, including the first-born of
our flocks and herds. 38* The first batch
of our dough, and our offerings of the
fruit of every tree, of wine and of oil,
we will bring to the priests, to the cham-
bers of the house of our God. The tithe
of our fields we will bring to the Levites;
they, the Levites, shall take the tithe in
all the cities of our service. 39 An Aaron-
ite priest shall be with the Levites when
they take the tithe, and the Levites shall
bring the tithe of the tithes to the house
of our God, to the chambers of the trea-
sury. 40 For to these chambers the Isra-
elites and Levites bring the offerings of
grain, wine, and oil; there also are
housed the utensils of the sanctuary, and

*

10, 1: 12, 12-26.
11: Ezr 10, 23.
30: 13, 23-27.
31: 13, 15-22.
32: 5, 1-13; Ex 20, 8; Lv 25, 2-7.
33: 2 Chr 24, 6.9f; Lv 24, 5-9.
35: 13, 31.
36f: Ex 13, 1.11ff; Dt 26, 1.
38: 13, 10-14; Nm 18, 21.24ff.

†

10, 1-40: This section belongs to the Nehemiah narrative rather than to that of Ezra. It is best read after Neh 13, 31. *In view of all this:* considering the situation described in Neh 13, 4-31.

the ministering priests, the gatekeepers,
and the singers. We will not neglect the
house of our God.

CHAPTER 11

Repeopling of Jerusalem. 1*† The
leaders of the people took up residence
in Jerusalem, and the rest of the people
cast lots to bring one man in ten to reside
in Jerusalem, the holy city, while the
other nine would remain in the other cit-
ies. 2 The people applauded all those
men who willingly agreed to take up res-
idence in Jerusalem.
The Residents of Jerusalem. 3* These
are the heads of the province who took
up residence in Jerusalem. (In the cities
of Judah dwelt lay Israelites, priests,
Levites, temple slaves, and the descen-
dants of the slaves of Solomon, each
man on the property he owned in his own
city.)
4 In Jerusalem dwelt both Judahites
and Benjaminites. Of the Judahites:
Athaiah, son of Uzziah, son of Zecha-
riah, son of Amariah, son of Shephatiah,
son of Mehallalel, of the sons of Perez;
5 Maaseiah, son of Baruch, son of Colho-
zeh, son of Hazaiah, son of Adaiah, son
of Joiarib, son of Zechariah, a son of the
Shelanites. 6 The total of the sons of
Perez who dwelt in Jerusalem was four
hundred and sixty-eight valiant men.
7 These were the Benjaminites: Sallu,
son of Meshullam, son of Joed, son of
Pedaiah, son of Kolaiah, son of Maa-
seiah, son of Ithiel, son of Jeshaiah, 8 and
his brethren, warriors, nine hundred
and twenty-eight in number. 9 Joel, son
of Zichri, was their commander, and Ju-
dah, son of Hassenuah, was second in
charge of the city.
10 Among the priests were: Jedaiah;
Joiarib; Jachin; 11 Seraiah, son of Hil-
kiah, son of Meshullam, son of Zadok,
son of Meraioth, son of Ahitub, the ruler
of the house of God, 12 and their brethren
who carried out the temple service, eight
hundred and twenty-two; Adaiah, son of
Jeroham, son of Pelaliah, son of Amzi,
son of Zechariah, son of Pashhur, son
of Malchijah, 13 and his brethren, family
heads, two hundred and forty-two; and
Amasai, son of Azarel, son of Ahzai, son
of Meshillemoth, son of Immer, 14 and
his brethren, warriors, one hundred and
twenty-eight. Their commander was
Zabdiel, son of Haggadol.
15 Among the Levites were Shemaiah,
son of Hasshub, son of Azrikam, son of
Hashabiah, son of Bunni; 16 Shabbethai
and Jozabad, levitical chiefs who were
placed over the external affairs of the
house of God; 17 Mattaniah, son of Mi-
cah, son of Zabdi, son of Asaph, director
of the psalms, who led the thanksgiving
at prayer; Bakbukiah, second in rank
among his brethren; and Abda, son of
Shammua, son of Galal, son of Jedu-
thun. 18 The total of the Levites in the
holy city was two hundred and eighty-
four.
19 The gatekeepers were Akkub, Tal-
mon, and their brethren, who kept watch
over the gates; one hundred and sev-
enty-two in number.
20 The rest of Israel, including priests
and Levites, were in all the other cities
of Judah, each man in his inheritance.
21 The temple slaves lived on Ophel.
Ziha and Gishpa were in charge of the
temple slaves.
22* The prefect of the Levites in Jeru-
salem was Uzzi, son of Bani, son of
Hashabiah, son of Mattaniah, son of Mi-
cah; he was one of the sons of Asaph,
the singers appointed to the service of
the house of God—23 for they had been
appointed by royal decree, and there
was a fixed schedule for the singers as-
signing them their daily duties.
24 Pethahiah, son of Meshezabel, a
descendant of Zerah, son of Judah, was
royal deputy in all affairs that concerned
the people.
The Other Cities. 25 As concerns their
villages in the country: Judahites lived
in Kiriath-arba and its dependencies, in
Dibon and its dependencies, in Jekab-
zeel and its villages, 26 in Jeshua, Mol-
adah, Beth-pelet, 27 in Hazarshual, in
Beer-sheba and its dependencies, 28 in
Ziklag, in Meconah and its dependen-
cies, 29 in En-rimmon, Zorah, Jarmuth,
30 Zanoah, Adullam, and their villages,
Lachish and its countryside, Azekah
and its dependencies. They were settled
from Beer-sheba to Ge-hinnom.
31 Benjaminites were in Geba, Mich-
mash, Aija, Bethel and its dependencies,
32 Anathoth, Nob, Ananiah, 33 Hazor,
Ramah, Gittaim, 34 Hadid, Zeboim, Ne-
ballat, 35 Lod, Ono, and the Valley of the
Artisans.
36 Some sections of the Levites from
Judah settled in Benjamin.

CHAPTER 12

***Priests and Levites under Zerubba-
bel.*** 1* The following are the priests and
Levites who returned with Zerubbabel,
son of Shealtiel, and Jeshua: Seraiah,
Jeremiah, Ezra, 2 Amariah, Malluch,
Hattush, 3 Shecaniah, Rehum, Mere-
moth, 4 Iddo, Ginnethon, Abijah, 5 Mij-

*

11, 1: 7, 4. 22: 2 Chr 20, 14.
3-19: 1 Chr 9, 2-34. 12, 1-6: 12, 12-22.

†

11, 1-19: This list of the family heads who lived in Jerusalem at the time of Nehemiah is best read after 7, 72a. It is basically the same as that given in 1 Chr 9, 2-17, but there are many differences between the two lists.

amin, Maadiah, Bilgah, 6 Shemaiah, and Joiarib, Jedaiah, 7 Sallu, Amok, Hilkiah, Jedaiah. These were the priestly heads and their brethren in the days of Jeshua.

8 The Levites were Jeshua, Binnui, Kadmiel, Sherebiah, Judah, Mattaniah; the last-mentioned, together with his brethren, was in charge of the hymns, 9 while Bakbukiah and Unno and their brethren ministered opposite them by turns.

High Priests. 10† Jeshua became the father of Joiakim, Joiakim became the father of Eliashib, and Eliashib became the father of Joiada. 11 Joiada became the father of Johanan, and Johanan became the father of Jaddua.

Priests and Levites under Joiakim. 12* In the days of Joiakim these were the priestly family heads: for Seraiah, Meraiah; for Jeremiah, Hananiah; 13 for Ezra, Meshullam; for Amariah, Jehohanan; 14 for Malluchi, Jonathan; for Shebaniah, Joseph; 15 for Harim, Adna; for Meremoth, Helkai; 16 for Iddo, Zechariah; for Ginnethon, Meshullam; 17 for Abijah, Zichri; for Miamin, . . . ; for Maadiah, Piltai; 18 for Bilgah, Shammua; for Shemaiah, Jehonathan; 19 and for Joiarib, Mattenai; for Jedaiah, Uzzi; 20 for Sallu, Kallai; for Amok, Eber; 21 for Hilkiah, Hashabiah; for Jedaiah, Nethanel.

22 In the time of Eliashib, Joiada, Johanan, and Jaddua, the family heads of the priests were written down in the Book of Chronicles, up until the reign of Darius the Persian. 23 The sons of Levi: the family heads were written down in the Book of Chronicles, up until the time of Johanan, the son of Eliashib.

24* The heads of the Levites were Hashabiah, Sherebiah, Jeshua, Binnui, Kadmiel. Their brethren who stood opposite them to sing praises and thanksgiving in fulfillment of the command of David, the man of God, one section opposite the other, 25* were Mattaniah, Bakbukiah, Obadiah.

Meshullam, Talmon, and Akkub were gatekeepers. They kept watch over the storerooms at the gates.

26 All these lived in the time of Joiakim, son of Jeshua, son of Jozadak [and in the time of Nehemiah the governor and of Ezra the priest-scribe].

Dedication of the City Wall. 27† At the dedication of the wall of Jerusalem, the Levites were sought out wherever they lived and were brought to Jerusalem to celebrate a joyful dedication with thanksgiving hymns and the music of cymbals, harps, and lyres. 28 The levitical singers gathered together from the region about Jerusalem, from the villages of the Netophathites, 29 from Bethgilgal, and from the plains of Geba and Azmaveth (for the singers had built themselves settlements about Jerusalem). 30 The priests and Levites first purified themselves, then they purified the people, the gates, and the wall.

31 I had the princes of Judah mount the wall, and I arranged two great choirs. The first of these proceeded to the right, along the top of the wall, in the direction of the Dung Gate, 32 followed by Hoshaiah and half the princes of Judah, 33 along with Azariah, Ezra, Meshullam, 34 Judah, Benjamin, Shemaiah, and Jeremiah, 35 priests with the trumpets, and also Zechariah, son of Jonathan, son of Shemaiah, son of Mattaniah, son of Micaiah, son of Zaccur, son of Asaph, 36 and his brethren Shemaiah, Azarel, Milalai, Gilalai, Maai, Nethanel, Judah, and Hanani, with the musical instruments of David, the man of God. [Ezra the scribe was at their head.] 37 At the Spring Gate they went straight up by the steps of the City of David and continued along the top of the wall above the house of David until they came to the Water Gate on the east.

38 The second choir proceeded to the left, followed by myself and the other half of the princes of the people, along the top of the wall past the Oven Tower as far as the Broad Wall, 39 then past the Ephraim Gate [the New City Gate], the Fish Gate, the Tower of Hananel, and the Hundred Tower, as far as the Sheep Gate [and they came to a halt at the Prison Gate].

40 The two choirs took up a position in the house of God; I, too, who had with me half the magistrates, 41 the priests Eliakim, Maaseiah, Minjamin, Micaiah, Elioenai, Zechariah, Hananiah, with the trumpets, 42 and Maaseiah, Shemaiah, Eleazar, Uzzi, Jehohanan, Malchijah, Elam, and Ezer. The singers were heard under the leadership of Jezrahiah. 43 Great sacrifices were offered on that day, and there was rejoicing over the great feast of the LORD in which they shared. The women and the children

NEHEMIAH

---

*

12-22: 10, 3-9; 12, 1-6. 25: 11, 17.
24: Ezr 2, 40.

†

12, 10f: *Jeshua,* the high priest when Zerubbabel was governor, i.e., the last decades of the sixth century B.C. (Hg 1, 1.12.14; 2, 2.4). He was the grandfather of *Eliashib,* the high priest at least in the early period of Nehemiah's governorship, i.e., 445-433 B.C. (Ezr 10, 6; Neh 3, 1.20f; 13, 4.7). Eliashib, in turn, was the grandfather of *Johanan,* a grown man, if not yet a high priest, at the time of Ezra, i.e., c. 400 B.C. (Ezr 10, 6; and note). According to Josephus *(Antiquites XI, v),* whose testimony here is doubtful, *Jaddua,* son of Johanan, died as an old man about the time that Alexander the Great died, i.e., 323 B.C. If this list of the postexilic high priests, at least as far as Johanan, comes, as seems probable (cf v 23), from the Chronicler himself and not from a later scribe, it is of prime importance for dating the Chronicler's work in the first decades of the fourth century B.C.

12, 27-43: *The dedication of the wall of Jerusalem* took place, no doubt, soon after the restoration of the wall and its gates had been completed. Therefore, this section is best read after 6, 15.

joined in, and the rejoicing at Jerusalem
could be heard from afar off.
Offerings for Priests and Levites.
44*† At that time men were appointed
over the chambers set aside for stores,
offerings, first fruits, and tithes; in them
they were to collect from the fields of
the various cities the portions legally as-
signed to the priests and Levites. For Ju-
dah rejoiced in its appointed priests and
Levites 45 who carried out the ministry
of their God and the ministry of puri-
fication (as did the singers and the
gatekeepers) in accordance with the
prescriptions of David and of Solomon,
his son. 46* For the heads of the families
of the singers and the hymns of praise
and thanksgiving to God came down
from the days of David and Asaph in
times of old. 47* Thus all Israel, in the
days of Zerubbabel [and in the days of
Nehemiah], gave the singers and the
gatekeepers their portions, according to
their daily needs. They made their con-
secrated offering to the Levites, and the
Levites made theirs to the sons of Aaron.

CHAPTER 13

Separation from Aliens. 1*† At that
time, when there was reading from the
book of Moses in the hearing of the peo-
ple, it was found written there that "no
Ammonite or Moabite may ever be ad-
mitted into the assembly of God; 2* for
they would not succor the Israelites with
food and water, but they hired Balaam
to curse them, though our God turned
the curse into a blessing." 3* When they
had heard the law, they separated from
Israel every foreign element.
Reform in the Temple. 4† Before this,
the priest Eliashib, who had been placed
in charge of the chambers of the house
of our God and who was an associate
of Tobiah, 5* had set aside for the latter's
use a large chamber in which had previ-
ously been stored the cereal offerings,
incense and utensils, the tithes in grain,
wine, and oil allotted to the Levites, sing-
ers, and gatekeepers, and the offerings
due the priests. 6† During all this time
I had not been in Jerusalem, for in the
thirty-second year of Artaxerxes, king
of Babylon, I had gone back to the king.
After due time, however, I asked leave
of the king 7 and returned to Jerusalem,
where I discovered the evil thing that
Eliashib had done for Tobiah, in setting
aside for him a chamber in the courts
of the house of God. 8 This displeased me
very much, and I had all of Tobiah's
household goods thrown outside the
chamber. 9 Then I gave orders to purify
the chambers, and I had them replace
there the utensils of the house of God,
the cereal offerings, and the incense.
10 I learned, too, that the portions due
the Levites were no longer being given,
so that the Levites and the singers who
should have been carrying out the ser-
vices had deserted, each man to his own
field. 11 I took the magistrates to task,
demanding, "Why is the house of God
abandoned?" Then I brought the Levites
together and had them resume their sta-
tions. 12* All Judah once more brought
in the tithes of grain, wine, and oil to
the storerooms; 13 and in charge of the
storerooms I appointed the priest Shele-
miah, Zadok the scribe, and Pedaiah,
one of the Levites, together with Hanan,
son of Zaccur, son of Mattaniah, as their
assistant; for these men were held to be
trustworthy. It was their duty to make
the distribution to their brethren.
14 Remember this to my credit, O my
God! Let not the devotion which I
showed for the house of my God and its
services be forgotten!
Sabbath Observance. 15* In those
days I perceived that men in Judah were
treading the winepresses on the sabbath;
that they were bringing in sheaves of
grain, loading them on their asses, to-
gether with wine, grapes, figs, and every
other kind of burden, and bringing them
to Jerusalem on the sabbath day. I
warned them to sell none of these vic-
tuals. 16 In Jerusalem itself the Tyrians
who were resident there were importing
fish and every other kind of merchan-
dise and selling it to the Judahites on
the sabbath. 17 I took the nobles of Judah
to task, demanding of them: "What is
this evil thing that you are doing, pro-
faning the sabbath day? 18 Did not your
fathers act in this same way, with the
result that our God has brought all this
evil upon us and upon this city? Would
you add to the wrath against Israel by
once more profaning the sabbath?"

*

44f: 1 Chr 23-26; 2 Chr 8, 14.
46: 2 Chr 29, 30; 35, 15.
47: 13, 10f; 10, 39; Nm 18, 26.
13, 1ff: Dt 23, 3-6.
2: Nm 22-24.
3: 13, 23-28.
5: 12, 44.
12: 10, 38f; 12, 44f.47; 2 Chr 31, 6.
15: 10, 32; Ex 20, 8.

†

12, 44-47: This account of the provisions made for the temple services is apparently a composition of the Chronicler. *At that time:* a mere connective; no particular time is meant, but the account fits best after that of the restoration of the temple (Ezr 6, 13-18) in the days of Zerubbabel (v 47). The gloss mentioning Nehemiah is not in the ancient Greek version.

13, 1ff: These verses were composed by the Chronicler to serve as an introduction to the reforms that Nehemiah instituted during his second mission in Jerusalem (vv 4-31). The part of *the book of Moses* read to the people is freely quoted here from Dt 23, 3-6.

13, 4-31: This is part of the "Memoirs of Nehemiah"; it is continued in 10, 1-40.

13, 6: *After due time:* It is not known when Nehemiah returned to Jerusalem or how long his second period of activity there lasted, but it probably ended before Ezra came to Palestine; see note on Ezr 7, 1-8.

19 When the shadows were falling on
the gates of Jerusalem before the sab-
bath, I ordered the doors to be closed
and forbade them to be reopened till
after the sabbath. I posted some of my
own men at the gates so that no burden
might enter on the sabbath day. 20 The
merchants and sellers of various kinds
of merchandise spent the night once or
twice outside Jerusalem, 21 but then I
warned them, saying to them: "Why do
you spend the night alongside the wall?
If you keep this up, I will lay hands on
you!" From that time on, they did not
return on the sabbath. 22 Then I ordered
the Levites to purify themselves and to
go and watch the gates, so that the sab-
bath day might be kept holy. This, too,
remember in my favor, O my God, and
have mercy on me in accordance with
your great mercy!

Mixed Marriages. 23* Also in those
days I saw Jews who had married Ash-
dodite, Ammonite, or Moabite wives.
24† Of their children, half spoke Ash-
dodite, and none of them knew how to
speak Jewish; and so it was in regard
to the languages of the various other
peoples. 25 I took them to task and cursed
them; I had some of them beaten and
their hair pulled out; and I adjured them
by God: "You shall not marry your
daughters to their sons nor take any of
their daughters for your sons or for
yourselves! 26* Did not Solomon, the
king of Israel, sin because of them?
Though among the many nations there
was no king like him, and though he was
beloved of his God and God had made
him king over all Israel, yet even he was
made to sin by foreign women. 27 Must
it also be heard of you that you have
done this same very great evil, betray-
ing our God by marrying foreign
women?"

28* One of the sons of Joiada, son of
Eliashib the high priest, was the son-in-
law of Sanballat the Horonite! I drove
him from my presence. 29 Remember
against them, O my God, how they de-
filed the priesthood and the covenant of
the priesthood and the Levites!

30 Thus I cleansed them of all foreign
contamination. I established the various
functions for the priests and Levites, so
that each had his appointed task. 31* I
also provided for the procurement of
wood at stated times and for the first
fruits. Remember this in my favor, O my
God!

*

23: 10, 31; 13, 1ff; Dt 23, 3.
26: 1 Kgs 11, 1-13.
28: 2, 10; 13, 4f.7ff.
31: 10, 35f.

†

13, 24: *Ashdodite:* the language spoken at Ashdod, more likely an Aramaic rather than a Philistine dialect. *Jewish:* Hebrew as spoken in postexilic Judah.

The Book of

TOBIT

The Book of Tobit, named after its principal hero, combines specifically Jewish piety and morality with oriental folklore in a fascinating story that has enjoyed wide popularity in both Jewish and Christian circles. Prayers, psalms, and words of wisdom, as well as the skillfully constructed story itself, provide valuable insights into the faith and the religious milieu of its unknown author. The book was probably written early in the second century B.C.; it is not known where.

Tobit, a devout and wealthy Israelite living among the captives deported to Nineveh from the northern kingdom of Israel in 721 B.C., suffers severe reverses and is finally blinded. Because of his misfortunes he begs the Lord to let him die. But recalling the large sum he had formerly deposited in far-off Media, he sends his son Tobiah there to bring back the money. In Media, at this same time, a young woman, Sarah, also prays for death, because she has lost seven husbands, each killed in turn on his wedding night by the demon Asmodeus. God hears the prayers of Tobit and Sarah, and sends the angel Raphael in disguise to aid them both.

Raphael makes the trip to Media with Tobiah. When Tobiah is attacked by a large fish as he bathes, Raphael orders him to seize it and to remove its gall, heart, and liver because they make "useful medicines." Later, at Raphael's urging, Tobiah marries Sarah, and uses the the fish's heart and liver to drive Asmodeus from the bridal chamber. Returning to Nineveh with his wife and his father's money, Tobiah rubs the fish's gall into his father's eyes and cures them. Finally, Raphael reveals his true identity and returns to heaven. Tobit then utters his beautiful hymn of praise. Before dying, Tobit tells his son to leave Nineveh because God will destroy that wicked city. After Tobiah buries his father and mother, he and his family depart for Media, where he later learns that the destruction of Nineveh has taken place.

The inspired author of the book used the literary form of religious novel (as in Jonah and Judith) for the purpose of instruction and edification. There may have been a historical nucleus around which the story was composed, but this possibility has nothing to do with the teaching of the book. The seemingly historical data—names of kings, cities, etc.—are used merely as vivid details to create interest and charm.

Although the Book of Tobit is usually listed with the historical books, it more correctly stands midway between them and the wisdom literature. It contains numerous maxims like those found in the wisdom books (cf 4, 3-19.21; 12, 6-10; 14, 7.9) as well as the customary sapiential themes: fidelity to the law, the intercessory function of angels, piety toward parents, the purity of marriage, reverence for the dead, and the value of almsgiving, prayer, and fasting. The book makes Tobit a relative of Ahiqar, *a hero of ancient Near Eastern folklore.*

Written in Aramaic, the original of the book was lost for centuries. The Greek translation, existing in three different recensions, is our primary source. In 1955, fragments of the book in Aramaic and in Hebrew were recovered from Cave IV at Qumran. These texts are in substantial agreement with the Greek recension that has served as the basis for the present translation.

The divisions of the Book of Tobit are:

- *I: Tobit's Ordeals (1, 3—3, 6)*
- *II: Sarah's Plight (3, 7-17)*
- *III: Tobiah's Journey and Marriage to Sarah (4, 1—9, 6)*
- *IV: Tobiah's Return; Cure of Tobit's Blindness (10, 1—11, 18)*
- *V: Raphael Reveals His Identity (12, 1-22)*
- *VI: Tobit's Song of Praise (13, 1-18)*
- *VII: Epilogue (14, 1-15)*

CHAPTER 1

Tobit. [1]† This book tells the story of Tobit, son of Tobiel, son of Hananiel, son of Aduel, son of Gabael of the family of Asiel, of the tribe of Naphtali, [2]*† who during the reign of Shalmaneser, king of Assyria, was taken captive from Thisbe, which is south of Kedesh Naphtali in upper Galilee, above and to the west of Asser, north of Phogor.

I: TOBIT'S ORDEALS

His Virtue. [3] I, Tobit, have walked all the days of my life on the paths of truth and righteousness. I performed many charitable works for my kinsmen and my people who had been deported with me to Nineveh, in Assyria. [4] When I lived as a young man in my own country, Israel, the entire tribe of my forefather Naphtali had broken away from the house of David and from Jerusalem. This city had been singled out of all Israel's tribes, so that they all might offer sacrifice in the place where the temple, God's dwelling, had been built and consecrated for all generations to come. [5]*† All my kinsmen, like the rest of the tribe of my forefather Naphtali, used to offer sacrifice on all the mountains of Galilee as well as to the young bull which Jeroboam, king of Israel, had made in Dan.

[6]*† I, for my part, would often make the pilgrimage alone to Jerusalem for the festivals, as is prescribed for all Israel by perpetual decree. Bringing with me the first fruits of the field and the firstlings of the flock, together with a tenth of my income and the first shearings of the sheep, I would hasten to Jerusalem [7]* and present them to the priests, Aaron's sons, at the altar. To the Levites who were doing service in Jeusalem I would give the tithe of grain, wine, olive oil, pomegranates, figs, and other fruits. And except for sabbatical years, I used to give a second tithe in money, which each year I would go and disburse in Jerusalem. [8] The third tithe I gave to orphans and widows, and to converts who were living with the Israelites. Every third year I would bring them this offering, and we ate it in keeping with the decree of the Mosaic law and the commands of Deborah, the mother of my father Tobiel; for when my father died, he left me an orphan.

[9] When I reached manhood, I married Anna, a woman of our own lineage. By her I had a son whom I named Tobiah. [10]* Now, after I had been deported to Nineveh, all my brothers and relatives ate the food of heathens, [11] but I refrained from eating that kind of food. [12] Because of this wholehearted service of God, [13]* the Most High granted me favor and status with Shalmaneser, so that I became purchasing agent for all his needs. [14]† Every now and then until his death I would go to Media to buy goods for him. I also deposited several pouches containing a great sum of money with my kinsman Gabael, son of Gabri, who lived at Rages, in Media. [15]† But when Shalmaneser died and his son Sennacherib succeeded him as king, the roads to Media became unsafe, so I could no longer go there.

Courage in Burying the Dead. [16] During Shalmaneser's reign I performed many charitable works for my kinsmen and my people. [17]*† I would give my bread to the hungry and my clothing to the naked. If I saw one of my people who had died and been thrown outside the walls of Nineveh, I would bury him. [18] I also buried anyone whom Sennacherib slew when he returned as a fugitive from Judea during the days of judgment decreed against him by the heavenly King because of the blasphemies he had uttered. In his rage he killed many Israelites, but I used to take their bodies by stealth and bury them; so when Sennacherib looked for them, he could not find them. [19] But a

*

1, 2: 2 Kgs 17, 3; 18, 9ff.
5: 1 Kgs 12, 26-32.
6: Ex 23, 14f. 17; 34, 23; Dt 16, 16.
7f: Nm 18, 12f.24; Dt 14, 22-29; 18, 4f.
10: Lv 11; Dt 14, 3-21; Acts 15, 29; 1 Cor 8, 7ff.
13: Dn 2, 48f.
17: Jb 31, 16-20.

†

1, 1: *Tobit:* in the fragments of the book found at Qumran, is given as *Tôbî,* an abbreviated form of *Tôbîyāh* (v 9; Ezr 2, 60) or of *Tôbîyāhû* (2 Chr 17, 8), a name which means "Yahweh is good." *Tobiel,* "God is good"; *Hananiel,* "God is merciful." The book abounds in theophoric names.

1, 2: *Shalmaneser* (V) (727-722 B.C.): began the siege of Samaria; the inhabitants of the northern kingdom were taken into captivity by his successor, Sargon II (722-705). *Thisbe* and *Phogor:* towns of Galilee that have not been identified; Thisbe in Gilead was perhaps the birthplace of Elijah. *Kedesh:* cf Jos 20, 7. *Asser:* Hazor (Jos 11, 1).

1, 5: Jeroboam established sanctuaries in Dan and Bethel so that the people would no longer go to Jerusalem for the festivals. The gold statues of bulls which he placed in the sanctuaries were considered the throne of Yahweh; but the people soon came to worship the images themselves. Jeroboam also encouraged the high places or hilltop shrines (1 Kgs 12, 26-33).

1, 6ff: *Perpetual decree:* Dt 12, 11.13-14. Refusing to worship at Jeroboam's shrines, the faithful Tobit continued to bring his offerings to Jerusalem; see 2 Chr 11, 16. For the various tithes, cf Nm 18, 20-32; 2 Chr 31, 4-6; Dt 14, 22-29; 26, 12f.

1, 14: *A great sum of money:* literally, "ten silver talents," about ten thousand dollars. *Rages:* modern Rai, about five miles southeast of Teheran. *Media:* the northwestern part of modern Iran.

1, 15: *Sennacherib* (705-681 B.C.): the son of Sargon (722-705 B.C.); neither was descended from Shalmaneser. Inconsistencies such as this point to the fact that the Book of Tobit is a religious novel (see Introduction; also notes on 5, 6 and 14, 15).

1, 17-18: Tobit risked his own life to bury the dead. Deprivation of burial was viewed with horror by the Jews. Cf 4, 3-4; 6, 15; 14, 12-13.

So she retorted: "Where are your charitable deeds now? Where are your virtuous acts? See! Your true character is finally showing itself!"

CHAPTER 3

1 Grief-stricken in spirit, I groaned and wept aloud. Then with sobs I began to pray:

Tobit's Prayer for Death

2* "You are righteous, O Lord,
and all your deeds are just;
All your ways are mercy and truth;
you are the judge of the world.
3* And now, O Lord, may you be mindful of me,
and look with favor upon me.
Punish me not for my sins,
nor for my inadvertent offenses,
nor for those of my fathers.

"They sinned against you,
4* and disobeyed your commandments.
So you handed us over to plundering, exile, and death,
till we were an object lesson, a byword, a reproach
in all the nations among whom you scattered us.

5 "Yes, your judgments are many and true
in dealing with me as my sins
and those of my fathers deserve.
For we have not kept your commandments,
nor have we trodden the paths of truth before you.

6*† "So now, deal with me as you please,
and command my life breath to be taken from me,
that I may go from the face of the earth into dust.
It is better for me to die than to live,
because I have heard insulting calumnies,
and I am overwhelmed with grief.

"Lord, command me to be delivered from such anguish;
let me go to the everlasting abode;
Lord, refuse me not.
For it is better for me to die
than to endure so much misery in life,
and to hear these insults!"

II: SARAH'S PLIGHT

Sarah Falsely Accused. 7† On the
same day, at Ecbatana in Media, it so
happened that Raguel's daughter Sarah
also had to listen to abuse, from one of
her father's maids. 8† For she had been
married to seven husbands, but the
wicked demon Asmodeus killed them off
before they could have intercourse with
her, as it is prescribed for wives. So the
maid said to her: "You are the one who
strangles your husbands! Look at you!
You have already been married seven
times, but you have had no joy with any
one of your husbands. 9 Why do you beat
us? Because your husbands are dead?
Then why not join them! May we never
see a son or daughter of yours!"
10* That day she was deeply grieved
in spirit. She went in tears to an upstairs
room in her father's house with the intention of hanging herself. But she reconsidered, saying to herself: "No! People would level this insult against my father: 'You had only one beloved daughter, but she hanged herself because of ill fortune!' And thus would I cause my father in his old age to go down to the nether world laden with sorrow. It is far better for me not to hang myself, but to beg the Lord to have me die, so that I need no longer live to hear such insults."
11*† At that time, then, she spread out
her hands, and facing the window,
poured out this prayer:

Sarah's Prayer for Death

"Blessed are you, O Lord, merciful God!
Forever blessed and honored is your holy name;

---

*

3, 2: Pss 25, 10; 119, 137; Dn 3, 27.
3: Ex 34, 7.
4: Dt 28, 15; Bar 1, 16-22; 2, 4f; 3, 8; Dn 9, 5f.
6: Nm 11, 15; 1 Kgs 19, 4; Jb 7, 15; Jon 4, 3.8.
10: 6, 15; Gn 37, 35; 42, 38; 44, 29.31.
11: 1 Kgs 8, 44.48; Pss 28, 2; 134, 2; Dn 6, 11.

†

3, 6: *It is better for me to die than to live:* in his distress Tobit uses the words of the petulant Jonah (Jon 4, 3.8), who wished to die because God did not destroy the hated Ninevites. In similar circumstances, Moses (Nm 11, 15), Elijah (1 Kgs 19, 4), and Job (Jb 7, 15) also prayed for death. *Everlasting abode:* a reference to Sheol, the dismal abode of the dead from which no one returns (Jb 7, 9-10; 14, 12; Is 26, 14). The revelation of a blessed immortality had not yet been made. See note on 4, 6.

3, 7: From here on, the story is told in the third person. V 7 relates one of the several marvelous coincidences which the story teller uses to heighten interest; see also vv 16.17; 4, 1; 5, 4. *Ecbatana: Hamadan* in modern Iran; this was the capital of ancient Media. *Raguel:* "friend of God."

3, 8: *Asmodeus:* in Persian *aeshma daeva,* "demon of wrath," adopted into Aramaic with the sense of "the Destroyer." He will be subdued (8, 3) by Raphael (v 17), "God heals."

3, 11: *Facing the window:* that is, looking toward Jerusalem; cf Dn 6, 11: *Blessed are you* and "Blessed be God" are traditional openings of Jewish prayers (8, 5.15; 11, 14; 13, 1).

certain citizen of Nineveh informed the
king that it was I who buried the dead.
When I found out that the king knew all
about me and wanted to put me to death,
I went into hiding; then in my fear I took
to flight. 20 Afterward, all my property
was confiscated; I was left with nothing.
All that I had was taken to the king's
palace, except for my wife Anna and my
son Tobiah.

21*† But less than forty days later the
king was assassinated by two of his sons,
who then escaped into the mountains of
Ararat. His son Esarhaddon, who suc-
ceeded him as king, placed Ahiqar, my
brother Anael's son, in charge of all the
accounts of his kingdom, so that he took
control over the entire administration.
22 Then Ahiqar interceded on my behalf,
and I was able to return to Nineveh. For
under Sennacherib, king of Assyria,
Ahiqar had been chief cupbearer,
keeper of the seal, administrator, and
treasurer; and Esarhaddon reappointed
him. He was a close relative—in fact, my
nephew.

CHAPTER 2

1*† Thus under King Esarhaddon I re-
turned to my home, and my wife Anna
and my son Tobiah were restored to me.
Then on our festival of Pentecost, the
feast of Weeks, a fine dinner was pre-
pared for me, and I reclined to eat.
2† The table was set for me, and when
many different dishes were placed be-
fore me, I said to my son Tobiah: "My
son, go out and try to find a poor man
from among our kinsmen exiled here
in Nineveh. If he is a sincere worshiper
of God, bring him back with you, so
that he can share this meal with me.
Indeed, son, I shall wait for you to come
back."

3 Tobiah went out to look for some poor
kinsman of ours. When he returned he
exclaimed, "Father!" I said to him,
"What is it, son?" He answered, "Father,
one of our people has been murdered!
His body lies in the market place where
he was just strangled!" 4 I sprang to my
feet, leaving the dinner untouched; and
I carried the dead man from the street
and put him in one of the rooms, so
that I might bury him after sunset.
5*† Returning to my own quarters, I
washed myself and ate my food in sor-
row. 6* I was reminded of the oracle pro-
nounced by the prophet Amos against
Bethel:

> "Your festivals shall be turned into
> mourning,
> And all your songs into lamenta-
> tion."

7 And I wept. Then at sunset I went out,
dug a grave, and buried him.

8 The neighbors mocked me, saying to
one another: "Will this man never learn!
Once before he was hunted down for ex-
ecution because of this very thing; yet
now that he has escaped, here he is
again burying the dead!"

Tobit's Blindness. 9 That same night I
bathed, and went to sleep next to the wall
of my courtyard. Because of the heat I
left my face uncovered. 10† I did not
know there were birds perched on the
wall above me, till their warm droppings
settled in my eyes, causing cataracts. I
went to see some doctors for a cure, but
the more they anointed my eyes with
various salves, the worse the cataracts
became, until I could see no more. For
four years I was deprived of eyesight,
and all my kinsmen were grieved at my
condition. Ahiqar, however, took care of
me for two years, until he left for Ely-
mais.

11 At that time my wife Anna worked
for hire at weaving cloth, the kind of
work women do. 12† When she sent back
the goods to their owners, they would
pay her. Late in winter she finished the
cloth and sent it back to the owners.
They paid her the full salary, and also
gave her a young goat for the table. 13 On
entering my house the goat began to
bleat. I called to my wife and said:
"Where did this goat come from? Per-
haps it was stolen! Give it back to its
owners; we have no right to eat stolen
food!" 14*† But she said to me, "It was
given to me as a bonus over and above
my wages." Yet I would not believe her,
and told her to give it back to its owners.
I became very angry with her over this.

*

21: 2 Kgs 19, 37; 2 Chr 32, 21; Sir 48, 21; Is 37, 38; 2 Mc 8, 19.
2, 1: Lv 23, 15-21; Nm 28, 26-31; Dt 16, 9-12.
5: Nm 19, 11-22.
6: Am 8, 10; 1 Mc 1, 39.
14: Jb 2, 9.

†

1, 21: *Esarhaddon:* 681-669 B.C. *Ahiqar:* a hero of ancient folklore, known for his outstanding wisdom. The *Story* (or *Wisdom*) *of Ahiqar* was very popular in antiquity and is extant in many different forms: Aramaic, Syriac, Armenian, Arabic *(Arabian Nights)*, Greek (*Aesop's Fables*), Slavonic, Ethiopic, and Romanian. The sacred author makes Tobit the uncle of the famous Ahiqar in order to enhance Tobit's own prestige. See note on 14, 10.

2, 1: *The feast of Weeks:* also called by its Greek name *Pentecost,* was celebrated fifty days after the Passover. Cf Lv 23, 15-21; Dt 16, 9-12.

2, 2: Almsgiving and charity to the poor are important virtues taught by the book (4, 7-11.16f; 12, 8f; 14, 10f).

2, 5: *I washed myself:* because of ritual defilement from touching a corpse (Nm 19, 11-13).

2, 10: *Cataracts:* literally, "white scales, or films." *Elymais:* the Greek name of ancient Elam, a district northeast of the head of the Persian Gulf.

2, 12: *Late in winter:* literally, "seventh of Dystros," the Macedonian month which corresponds to the Jewish month of Shebat (January-February). *For the table:* literally, "for the hearth"; the gift had probably been made in view of some springtime festival like the Jewish Purim.

2, 14: Anna's sharp rebuke calls to mind the words of Job's wife (Jb 2, 9).

may all your works forever bless
you.
12 And now, O Lord, to you I turn my
face
and raise my eyes.
13 Bid me to depart from the earth,
never again to hear such insults.

14 "You know, O Master, that I am in-
nocent
of any impure act with a man,
15 And that I have never defiled my
own name
or my father's name in the land
of my exile.

"I am my father's only daughter,
and he has no other child to make
his heir,
Nor does he have a close kinsman
or other relative
whom I might bide my time to
marry.
I have already lost seven husbands;
why then should I live any longer?
But if it please you, Lord, not to slay
me,
look favorably upon me and have
pity on me;
never again let me hear these in-
sults!"

An Answer to Prayer. 16 At that very
time, the prayer of these two suppliants
was heard in the glorious presence of
Almighty God. 17*† So Raphael was sent
to heal them both: to remove the cata-
racts from Tobit's eyes, so that he might
again see God's sunlight; and to marry
Raguel's daughter Sarah to Tobit's son
Tobiah, and then drive the wicked de-
mon Asmodeus from her. For Tobiah
had the right to claim her before any
other who might wish to marry her.
In the very moment that Tobit re-
turned from the courtyard to his house,
Raguel's daughter Sarah came down-
stairs from her room.

III: TOBIAH'S JOURNEY AND MARRIAGE TO SARAH

CHAPTER 4

A Father's Instruction. 1 That same
day Tobit remembered the money he
had deposited with Gabael at Rages in
Media, and he thought, 2 "Now that I
have asked for death, why should I not
call my son Tobiah and let him know
about this money before I die?" 3*† So
he called his son Tobiah; and when he
came, he said to him: "My son, when I
die, give me a decent burial. Honor your
mother, and do not abandon her as long
as she lives. Do whatever pleases her,
and do not grieve her spirit in any way.
4 Remember, my son, that she went
through many trials for your sake while
you were in her womb. And when she
dies, bury her in the same grave with
me.
5 "Through all your days, my son, keep
the Lord in mind, and suppress every
desire to sin or to break his command-
ments. Perform good works all the days
of your life, and do not tread the paths
of wrongdoing. 6*† For if you are stead-
fast in your service, your good works will
bring success, not only to you, but also
to all those who live uprightly.
7 "Give alms from your possessions.
Do not turn your face away from any
of the poor, and God's face will not be
turned away from you. 8 Son, give alms
in proportion to what you own. If you
have great wealth, give alms out of your
abundance; if you have but little, distrib-
ute even some of that. But do not hesitate
to give alms; 9* you will be storing up a
goodly treasure for yourself against the
day of adversity. 10 Almsgiving frees one
from death, and keeps one from going
into the dark abode. 11* Alms are a wor-
thy offering in the sight of the Most High
for all who give them.
12* "Be on your guard, son, against ev-
ery form of immorality, and above all,
marry a woman of the lineage of your
forefathers. Do not marry a stranger
who is not of your father's tribe, because
we are sons of the prophets. My boy,
keep in mind Noah, Abraham, Isaac,
and Jacob, our fathers from of old: all
of them took wives from among their
own kinsmen and were blessed in their
children. Remember that their posterity
shall inherit the land. 13 Therefore, my
son, love your kinsmen. Do not be so
proudhearted toward your kinsmen, the
sons and daughters of your people, as
to refuse to take a wife for yourself from
among them. For in such arrogance

*

17: 4, 12f; 6, 12f; Gn 24, 3f.
4, 3: Ex 20, 12; Prv 23, 22; Sir 7, 27.
6: 13, 6; Jn 3, 21; Eph 4, 15.
7f: 12, 8ff; Dt 15, 7f.11; Prv 19, 17; Sir 4, 1-6; 14, 13; Lk 14, 13; 1 Jn 3, 17.
9: Mt 6, 20f.
11: Sir 3, 30; 29, 12.
12: 3, 15.17; 6, 12; Gn 11, 29.31; 25, 20; 28, 1-4; 29, 15-30; Ex 34, 16; Dt 7, 3; Jgs 14, 3.

†

3, 17: *Tobiah had the right:* according to the patriarchal custom of marriage within the family group. Tobiah was Sarah's closest eligible relative (6, 12). Cf 4, 12-13; Gn 24.

4, 3-19: A collection of maxims which parallel those in the wisdom literature, especially Prv and Sir (see Introduction): duties toward parents (3-4); cf also 14, 13; perseverance in virtue and avoidance of evil (5-6.14b); necessity and value of almsgiving and charity (7-11.16-17); marriage to a kinsman (12-13a); industry (13b); prompt payment of wages (14a); the golden rule (15a); temperance (15b); docility (18); prayer (19).

4, 6: Before the revelation of retribution for all men in the afterlife—a doctrine taught in the Book of Wisdom—Old Testament man believed that virtue guaranteed earthly prosperity, and sin earthly disaster (cf Dt 28).

there is ruin and great disorder. Like-
wise, in worthlessness there is decay and
dire poverty, for worthlessness is the
mother of famine.
14* "Do not keep with you overnight
the wages of any man who works for
you, but pay him immediately. If you
thus behave as God's servant, you will
receive your reward. Keep a close watch
on yourself, my son, in everything you
do, and discipline yourself in all your
conduct. 15* Do to no one what you your-
self dislike. Do not drink wine till you
become drunk, nor let drunkenness ac-
company you on your way.
16* "Give to the hungry some of your
bread, and to the naked some of your
clothing. Whatever you have left over,
give away as alms; and do not begrudge
the alms you give. 17*† Be lavish with
your bread and wine at the burial of the
virtuous, but do not share them with sin-
ners.
18 "Seek counsel from every wise man,
and do not think lightly of any advice
that can be useful. 19*† At all times bless
the Lord God, and ask him to make all
your paths straight and to grant success
to all your endeavors and plans. For no
pagan nation possesses good counsel,
but the Lord himself gives all good
things. If the Lord chooses, he raises a
man up; but if he should decide other-
wise, he casts him down to the deepest
recesses of the nether world. So now, my
son, keep in mind my commandments,
and never let them be erased from your
heart.
20 "And now, son, I wish to inform you
that I have deposited a great sum of
money with Gabri's son Gabael at Rages
in Media. 21* Do not be discouraged, my
child, because of our poverty. You will
be a rich man if you fear God, avoid all
sin, and do what is right before the Lord
your God."

CHAPTER 5

The Angel Raphael. 1 Then Tobiah
replied to his father Tobit: "Everything
that you have commanded me, father,
I will do. 2 But how shall I be able to ob-
tain the money from him, since he does
not know me nor do I know him? What
can I show him to make him recognize
me and trust me, so that he will give me
the money? I do not even know which
roads to take for the journey into Me-
dia!" 3† Tobit answered his son Tobiah:
"We exchanged signatures on a docu-
ment written in duplicate; I divided it
into two parts, and each of us kept one;
his copy I put with the money. Think of
it, twenty years have already passed
since I deposited that money! So now,
my son, find yourself a trustworthy man
who will make the journey with you. We
will, of course, give him a salary when
you return; but get back that money
from Gabael."
4*† Tobiah went to look for someone
acquainted with the roads who would
travel with him to Media. As soon as he
went out, he found the angel Raphael
standing before him, though he did not
know that this was an angel of God.
5 Tobiah said to him, "Who are you,
young man?" He replied "I am an Isra-
elite, one of your kinsmen. I have come
here to work." Tobiah said, "Do you
know the way to Media?" 6† The other
replied: "Yes, I have been there many
times. I know the place well and I know
all the routes. I have often traveled to
Media; I used to stay with our kinsman
Gabael, who lives at Rages in Media. It
is a good two days' travel from Ecbat-
ana to Rages, for Rages is situated at
the mountains, Ecbatana out on the
plateau." 7* Tobiah said to him, "Wait
for me, young man, till I go back
and tell my father; for I need you to
make the journey with me. I will, of
course, pay you." 8 Raphael replied,
"Very well, I will wait for you; but do
not be long."
9 Tobiah went back to tell his father
Tobit what had happened. He said to
him, "I have just found a man who is
one of our own Israelite kinsmen!" Tobit
said, "Call the man, so that I may find
out what family and tribe he comes
from, and whether he is trustworthy
enough to travel with you, son." Tobiah
went out to summon the man, saying,
"Young man, my father would like to
see you."

*

14: Lv 19, 13; Dt 24, 15.
15: Mt 7, 12; Lk 6, 31.
16: Dt 15, 10; Is 58, 7; Mt 25, 35f; 2 Cor 9, 7.
17: Jer 16, 7; Lk 14, 13.
19: Dt 4, 6; Ps 119, 10.
21: 1 Tm 6, 6ff.
5, 4: Heb 13, 2.
7: 12, 2.

†

4, 17: Tobit counsels his son either to give alms in honor of the dead, or, more probably, to give the "bread of consolation" to the family of the deceased. Cf Jer 16, 7; Ez 24, 17.

4, 19: Prayer is the foundation of a moral life.

5, 3: *Document:* in Greek *cheirographon.* In the Middle Ages, notably in England, a deed and its duplicate were written on one piece of parchment, with the Latin word *chirographum* inscribed across the top of the sheet or between the two copies of the text. The document was then cut in two in either a straight or a wavy line, the parts being given to the persons concerned. Perhaps this procedure derived from the present verse of Tobit. Duplicate documents, usually one open and the other sealed, are well known from the ancient Near East.

5, 4: *He did not know:* the theme of an angel in disguise occurs frequently in folklore as well as in the Old Testament (Gn 18; cf Heb 13, 2).

5, 6: *It is a good two days' travel from Ecbatana to Rages:* Alexander's army took eleven days in forced marches to cover this distance, about 180 miles. The author is merely using popular impressions about faraway places; he is not teaching geography. (See notes on 1, 15; 3, 7 and Introduction.)

[10]† When Raphael entered the house, Tobit greeted him first. Raphael said, "Hearty greetings to you!" Tobit replied: "What joy is left for me any more? Here I am, a blind man who cannot see God's sunlight, but must remain in darkness, like the dead who no longer see the light! Though alive, I am among the dead. I can hear a man's voice, but I cannot see him." Raphael said, "Take courage! God has healing in store for you; so take courage!" Tobit then said: "My son Tobiah wants to go to Media. Can you go with him to show him the way? I will of course pay you, brother." Raphael answered: "Yes, I can go with him, for I know all the routes. I have often traveled to Media and crossed all its plains and mountains; so I know every road well." [11] Tobit asked, "Brother, tell me, please, what family and tribe are you from?" [12]* Raphael said: "Why? Do you need a tribe and a family? Or are you looking for a hired man to travel with your son?" Tobit replied, "I wish to know truthfully whose son you are, brother, and what your name is."

[13]† Raphael answered, "I am Azariah, son of Hananiah the elder, one of your own kinsmen." [14] Tobit exclaimed: "Welcome! God save you, brother! Do not be provoked with me, brother, for wanting to learn the truth about your family. So it turns out that you are a kinsman, and from a noble and good line! I knew Hananiah and Nathaniah, the two sons of Shemaiah the elder; with me they used to make the pilgrimage to Jerusalem, where we would worship together. No, they did not stray from the right path; your kinsmen are good men. You are certainly of good lineage, and welcome!"

[15]† Then he added: "For each day you are away I will give you the normal wages, plus expenses for you and for my son. If you go with my son, [16] I will even add a bonus to your wages!" Raphael replied: "I will go with him; have no fear. In good health we shall leave you, and in good health we shall return to you, for the way is safe." [17] Tobit said, "God bless you, brother." Then he called his son and said to him: "My son, prepare whatever you need for the journey, and set out with your kinsman. May God in heaven protect you on the way and bring you back to me safe and sound; and may his angel accompany you for safety, my son."

Before setting out on his journey, Tobiah kissed his father and mother. Tobit said to him, "Have a safe journey." [18] But his mother began to weep. She said to Tobit: "Why have you decided to send my child away? Is he not the staff to which we cling, ever there with us in all that we do? [19] I hope more money is not your chief concern! Rather let it be a ransom for our son! [20] What the Lord has given us to live on is certainly enough for us." [21] Tobit reassured her: "Have no such thought. Our son will leave in good health and come back to us in good health. Your own eyes will see the day when he returns to you safe and sound. [22]† So, no such thought; do not worry about them, my love. For a good angel will go with him, his journey will be successful, and he will return unharmed." [1] Then she stopped weeping.

CHAPTER 6

Journey to Rages. [2] When the boy left home, accompanied by the angel, the dog followed Tobiah out of the house and went with them. The travelers walked till nightfall, and made camp beside the Tigris River. [3] Now when the boy went down to wash his feet in the river, a large fish suddenly leaped out of the water and tried to swallow his foot. He shouted in alarm. [4] But the angel said to him, "Take hold of the fish and don't let it get away!" The boy seized the fish and hauled it up on the shore. [5]† The angel then told him: "Cut the fish open and take out its gall, heart, and liver, and keep them with you; but throw away the entrails. Its gall, heart, and liver make useful medicines." [6] After the lad had cut the fish open, he put aside the gall, heart, and liver. Then he broiled and ate part of the fish; the rest he salted and kept for the journey.

Raphael's Instructions. [7] Afterward they traveled on together till they were near Media. The boy asked the angel this question: "Brother Azariah, what medicinal value is there in the fish's heart, liver, and gall?" [8] He answered: "As regards the fish's heart and liver, if you burn them so that the smoke surrounds a man or a woman who is afflicted by a demon or evil spirit, the affliction will leave him completely, and no demons will ever return to him again. [9] And as for the gall, if you rub it on the eyes of a man who has cataracts, blowing into

---

* 12: Jgs 13, 17f.

---

† 5, 10: *Hearty greetings* and *what joy* form a wordplay on the Greek verb *chairein,* "to greet" and "to be joyful."

5, 13-14: *Azariah,* "Yahweh helps"; *Hananiah,* "Yahweh is merciful"; *Nathaniah,* "Yahweh gives"; *Shemaiah,* "Yahweh hears."

5, 15: *The normal wages:* literally, "a drachma," about seventeen cents, a day's wage for a workingman.

5, 22: *My love:* literally, "sister," a term of endearment applied to one's wife; cf 7, 11.15; 8, 4.21; 10, 6.13; Sg 4, 9.10.12; 5, 1f. *A good angel:* a reference to the guardian angel, though Tobit does not know, of course, that Raphael himself, disguised as Azariah, is the good angel in this case.

6, 5: *Its gall . . . medicines:* belief in the healing power of these organs was common among even the physicians of antiquity.

his eyes right on the cataracts, his sight
will be restored."
[10] When they had entered Media and
were getting close to Ecbatana,
[11] Raphael said to the boy, "Brother To-
biah!" He answered, "Yes, what is it?"
Raphael continued: "Tonight we must
stay with Raguel, who is a relative of
yours. He has a daughter named Sarah,
[12*] but no other child. Since you are Sa-
rah's closest relative, you before all
other men have the right to marry her.
Also, her father's estate is rightfully
yours to inherit. Now the girl is sensible,
courageous, and very beautiful; and her
father loves her dearly." [13†] He contin-
ued: "Since you have the right to marry
her, listen to me, brother. Tonight I will
ask the girl's father to let us have her
as your bride. When we return from
Rages, we will hold the wedding feast
for her. I know that Raguel cannot keep
her from you or let her become engaged
to another man; that would be a capital
crime according to the decree in the
Book of Moses, and he knows that it is
your right, before all other men, to
marry his daughter. So heed my words,
brother; tonight we must speak for the
girl, so that we may have her engaged
to you. And when we return from Rages,
we will take her and bring her back with
us to your house."
[14] Tobiah objected, however: "Brother
Azariah, I have heard that this woman
has already been married seven times,
and that her husbands died in their
bridal chambers. On the very night they
approached her, they dropped dead.
And I have heard it said that it was a
demon who killed them. [15*] So now I too
am afraid of this demon. Because he
loves her, he does not harm her; but he
does slay any man who wishes to come
close to her. I am my father's only child.
If I should die, I would bring my father
and mother down to their grave in sor-
row over me. And they have no other
son to bury them!"
[16] Raphael said to him: "Do you not
remember your father's orders? He
commanded you to marry a woman
from your own family. So now listen to
me, brother; do not give another thought
to this demon, but marry Sarah. I know
that tonight you shall have her for your
wife! [17] When you go into the bridal
chamber, take the fish's liver and heart,
and place them on the embers for the
incense. [18†] As soon as the demon smells
the odor they give off, he will flee and
never again show himself near her.
Then when you are about to have inter-
course with her, both of you first rise up
to pray. Beg the Lord of heaven to show
you mercy and grant you deliverance.
But do not be afraid, for she was set
apart for you before the world existed.
You will save her, and she will go with
you. And I suppose that you will have
children by her, who will take the place
of brothers for you. So do not worry."
When Tobiah heard Raphael say that
she was his kinswoman, of his own fami-
ly's lineage, he fell deeply in love with
her, and his heart became set on her.

CHAPTER 7

At the House of Raguel. [1] When they
entered Ecbatana, Tobiah said,
"Brother Azariah, lead me straight to
our kinsman Raguel." So he brought
him to the house of Raguel, whom they
found seated by his courtyard gate.
They greeted him first. He said to them,
"Greetings to you too, brothers! Good
health to you, and welcome!" When he
brought them into his home, [2] he said to
his wife Edna, "This young man looks
just like my kinsman Tobit!" [3] So Edna
asked them, "Who are you, brothers?"
They answered, "We are of the exiles
from Naphtali at Nineveh." [4] She said,
"Do you know our kinsman Tobit?"
They answered, "Indeed we do!" She
asked, "Is he well?" [5] They answered,
"Yes, he is alive and well." Then Tobiah
exclaimed, "He is my father!" [6] Raguel
sprang up and kissed him, shedding
tears of joy. [7] But when he heard that
Tobit had lost his eyesight, he was
grieved and wept aloud. He said to To-
biah: "My child, God bless you! You are
the son of a noble and good father. But
what a terrible misfortune that such a
righteous and charitable man should be
afflicted with blindness!" He continued
to weep in the arms of his kinsman To-
biah. [8] His wife Edna also wept for Tobit;
and even their daughter Sarah began to
weep.
Marriage of Tobiah and Sarah. [9] Af-
terward, Raguel slaughtered a ram from
the flock and gave them a cordial recep-
tion. When they had bathed and reclined
to eat, Tobiah said to Raphael, "Brother
Azariah, ask Raguel to let me marry my
kinswoman Sarah." [10] Raguel overheard
the words; so he said to the boy: "Eat
and drink and be merry tonight, for no
man is more entitled to marry my
daughter Sarah than you, brother. Be-
sides, not even I have the right to give
her to anyone but you, because you are
my closest relative. But I will explain the
situation to you very frankly. [11] I have
given her in marriage to seven men, all

*

6, 12: 4, 12f; Nm 36, 8. 15: 3, 10.

†

6, 13: *Raguel . . . Book of Moses:* Nm 36, 6-8 prescribed marriage within the ancestral tribe, but no death penalty is mentioned.

6, 18: *Rise up to pray:* prayer is needed to drive out the demon.

of whom were kinsmen of ours, and all
died on the very night they approached
her. But now, son, eat and drink. I am
sure the Lord will look after you both."
Tobiah answered, "I will eat or drink
nothing until you set aside what belongs
to me."

Raguel said to him: "I will do it. She
is yours according to the decree of the
Book of Moses. Your marriage to her has
been decided in heaven! Take your kins-
woman; from now on you are her love,
and she is your beloved. She is yours to-
day and ever after. And tonight, son,
may the Lord of heaven prosper you
both. May he grant you mercy and
peace." 12* Then Raguel called his
daughter Sarah, and she came to him.
He took her by the hand and gave her
to Tobiah with the words: "Take her ac-
cording to the law. According to the de-
cree written in the Book of Moses she
is your wife. Take her and bring her
back safely to your father. And may the
God of heaven grant both of you peace
and prosperity." 13* He then called her
mother and told her to bring a scroll,
so that he might draw up a marriage
contract stating that he gave Sarah to
Tobiah as his wife according to the de-
cree of the Mosaic law. Her mother
brought the scroll, and he drew up the
contract, to which they affixed their
seals.

14 Afterward they began to eat and
drink. 15 Later Raguel called his wife
Edna and said, "My love, prepare the
other bedroom and bring the girl there."
16 She went and made the bed in the
room, as she was told, and brought the
girl there. After she had cried over her,
she wiped away the tears and said:
17 "Be brave, my daughter. May the
Lord of heaven grant you joy in place
of your grief. Courage, my daughter."
Then she left.

CHAPTER 8

Expulsion of the Demon. 1 When they
had finished eating and drinking, the
girl's parents wanted to retire. They
brought the young man out of the dining
room and led him into the bedroom.
2† At this point Tobiah, mindful of Ra-
phael's instructions, took the fish's liver
and heart from the bag which he had
with him, and placed them on the em-
bers for the incense. 3† The demon, re-
pelled by the odor of the fish, fled into
Upper Egypt; Raphael pursued him
there and bound him hand and foot.
Then Raphael returned immediately.

4 When the girl's parents left the bed-
room and closed the door behind them,
Tobiah arose from bed and said to his
wife, "My love, get up. Let us pray and
beg our Lord to have mercy on us and
to grant us deliverance." 5* She got up,
and they started to pray and beg that
deliverance might be theirs. He began
with these words:

"Blessed are you, O God of our fathers;
praised be your name forever and ever.
Let the heavens and all your creation
praise you forever.
6* You made Adam and you gave him his wife Eve
to be his help and support;
and from these two the human race descended.
You said, 'It is not good for the man to be alone;
let us make him a partner like himself.'
7 Now, Lord, you know that I take this wife of mine
not because of lust,
but for a noble purpose.
Call down your mercy on me and on her,
and allow us to live together to a happy old age."

8 They said together, "Amen, amen,"
9 and went to bed for the night.

But Raguel got up and summoned his
servants. With him they went out to dig
a grave, 10 for he said, "I must do this,
because if Tobiah should die, we would
be subjected to ridicule and insult."
11 When they had finished digging the
grave, Raguel went back into the house
and called his wife, 12 saying, "Send one
of the maids in to see whether Tobiah
is alive or dead, so that if necessary we
may bury him without anyone's know-
ing about it." 13 She sent the maid, who
lit a lamp, opened the bedroom door,
went in, and found them sound asleep
together. 14 The maid went out and told
the girl's parents that Tobiah was alive,
and that there was nothing wrong.
15 Then Raguel praised the God of
heaven in these words:

"Blessed are you, O God, with every holy and pure blessing!
Let all your chosen ones praise you;
let them bless you forever!

*

7, 12: Gn 24, 50f.
13: 6, 12.
8, 5: Dn 3, 26.
6: Gn 2, 18-23.

†

8, 2f: The manner of coping with demonic influences among the ancients seems quaint to us. However, the fish here is part of the story, and not a recipe for exorcism. It is clear that the author places primary emphasis on the value of prayer to God (6, 18; 8, 4-8), on the role of the angel as God's agent, and on the pious disposition of Tobiah.

8, 3: *Into Upper Egypt:* to the desert there. The desert was considered the dwelling place of demons. Cf Is 13, 21; 34, 14; Mt 4, 1; 12, 43.

16 Blessed are you, who have made me glad;
what I feared did not happen.
Rather you have dealt with us
according to your great mercy.
17 Blessed are you, for you were merciful
toward two only children.
Grant them, Master, mercy and deliverance,
and bring their lives to fulfillment
with happiness and mercy."

18 Then he told his servants to fill in the
grave before dawn.
Wedding Feast. 19 He asked his wife
to bake many loaves of bread; he himself
went out to the herd and picked out two
steers and four rams which he ordered
to be slaughtered. So the servants began
to prepare the feast. 20† He summoned
Tobiah and made an oath in his presence, saying: "For fourteen days you
shall not stir from here, but shall remain
here eating and drinking with me; and
you shall bring joy to my daughter's sorrowing spirit.
21 Take, to begin with, half
of whatever I own when you go back in
good health to your father; the other half
will be yours when I and my wife die.
Be of good cheer, my son! I am your father, and Edna is your mother; and we
belong to you and to your beloved now
and forever. So be happy, son!"

CHAPTER 9

The Money Recovered. 1 Then Tobiah
called Raphael and said to him:
2 "Brother Azariah, take along with you
four servants and two camels and travel
to Rages. Go to Gabael's house and give
him this bond. Get the money and then
bring him along with you to the wedding
celebration.
4 For you know that my father is counting the days. If I should delay my return by a single day, I would
cause him intense grief.
3 You witnessed
the oath that Raguel has sworn; I cannot
violate his oath."
5 So Raphael, together
with the four servants and two camels,
traveled to Rages in Media, where they
stayed at Gabael's house. Raphael gave
Gabael his bond and told him about Tobit's son Tobiah, and that he had married and was inviting him to the wedding
celebration. Gabael promptly checked
over the sealed moneybags, and they
placed them on the camels.
6 The following morning they got an
early start and traveled to the wedding
celebration. When they entered Raguel's
house, they found Tobiah reclining at table. He sprang up and greeted Gabael,
who wept and blessed him, exclaiming:
"O noble and good child, son of a noble
and good, upright and charitable man,
may the Lord grant heavenly blessing
to you and to your wife, and to your
wife's father and mother. Blessed be
God, because I have seen the very image
of my cousin Tobit!"

IV: TOBIAH'S RETURN; CURE OF TOBIT'S BLINDNESS

CHAPTER 10

Anxiety of the Parents. 1 Meanwhile,
day by day, Tobit was keeping track of
the time Tobiah would need to go and
to return. When the number of days was
reached and his son did not appear,
2 he
said, "I wonder what has happened.
Perhaps he has been detained there; or
perhaps Gabael is dead, and there is no
one to give him the money."
3 And he
began to worry.
4 His wife Anna said,
"My son has perished and is no longer
among the living!" And she began to
weep aloud and to wail over her son:
5 "Alas, my child, light of my eyes, that
I let you make this journey!"
6 But Tobit
kept telling her: "Hush, do not think
about it, my love; he is safe! Probably
they have to take care of some unexpected business there. The man who is
traveling with him is trustworthy, and
is one of our own kinsmen. So do not
worry over him, my love. He will be here
soon."
7* But she retorted, "Stop it, and
do not lie to me! My child has perished!"
She would go out and keep watch all day
at the road her son had taken, and she
ate nothing. At sunset she would go back
home to wail and cry the whole night
through, getting no sleep at all.
Departure from Ecbatana. Now at the
end of the fourteen-day wedding celebration which Raguel had sworn to hold
for his daughter, Tobiah went to him and
said: "Please let me go, for I know that
my father and mother do not believe
they will ever see me again. So I beg you,
father, let me go back to my father. I
have already told you how I left him."
8 Raguel said to Tobiah: "Stay, my child,
stay with me. I am sending messengers
to your father Tobit, and they will give
him news of you."
9 But Tobiah insisted,
"No, I beg you to let me go back to my
father."
10 Raguel then promptly handed over
to Tobiah Sarah his wife, together with
half of all his property: male and female
slaves, oxen and sheep, asses and camels, clothing, money, and household
goods.
11 Bidding them farewell, he let
them go. He embraced Tobiah and said
to him: "Good-bye, my son. Have a safe

*

10, 7: Gn 45, 26.

†

8, 20: *For fourteen days:* because of the happy, and unexpected, turn of events, Raguel doubles the time of the wedding feast. When Tobiah returns home, the usual seven-day feast is held (11, 18). Cf Jgs 14, 12.

journey. May the Lord of heaven grant
prosperity to you and to your wife Sarah.
And may I see children of yours before
I die!" 12 Then he kissed his daughter
Sarah and said to her: "My daughter,
honor your father-in-law and your
mother-in-law, because from now on
they are as much your parents as the
ones who brought you into the world. Go
in peace, my daughter; let me hear good
reports about you as long as I live." Fi-
nally he said good-bye to them and sent
them away.
13 Then Edna said to Tobiah: "My child
and beloved kinsman, may the Lord
bring you back safely, and may I live
long enough to see children of you and
of my daughter Sarah before I die. Be-
fore the Lord, I entrust my daughter to
your care. Never cause her grief at any
time in your life. Go in peace, my child.
From now on I am your mother, and
Sarah is your beloved. May all of us be
prosperous all the days of our lives." She
kissed them both and sent them away
in peace.
14 When Tobiah left Raguel, he was full
of happiness and joy, and he blessed the
Lord of heaven and earth, the King of
all, for making his journey so successful.
Finally he said good-bye to Raguel and
his wife Edna, and added, "May I honor
you all the days of my life!"

CHAPTER 11

Homeward Journey. 1 Then they left
and began their return journey. When
they were near Kaserin, just before
Nineveh, 2 Raphael said: "You know
how we left your father. 3 Let us hurry
on ahead of your wife to prepare the
house while the rest of the party are still
on the way." 4 So they both went on
ahead and Raphael said to Tobiah,
"Have the gall in your hand!" And the
dog ran along behind them.
5 Meanwhile, Anna sat watching the
road by which her son was to come.
6 When she saw him coming, she ex-
claimed to his father, "Tobit, your son
is coming, and the man who traveled
with him!"
7 Raphael said to Tobiah before he
reached his father: "I am certain that
his eyes will be opened. 8 Smear the fish
gall on them. This medicine will make
the cataracts shrink and peel off from
his eyes; then your father will again be
able to see the light of day."
Sight Restored. 9* Then Anna ran up
to her son, threw her arms around him,
and said to him, "Now that I have seen
you again, son, I am ready to die!" And
she sobbed aloud. 10 Tobit got up and
stumbled out through the courtyard
gate. Tobiah went up to him 11 with the
fish gall in his hand, and holding him
firmly, blew into his eyes. "Courage, fa-
ther," he said. 12 Next he smeared the
medicine on his eyes, 13 and it made
them smart. Then, beginning at the cor-
ners of Tobit's eyes, Tobiah used both
hands to peel off the cataracts. When To-
bit saw his son, he threw his arms
around him 14 and wept. He exclaimed,
"I can see you, son, the light of my eyes!"
Then he said:

"Blessed be God,
and praised be his great name,
and blessed be all his holy angels.
May his holy name be praised
throughout all the ages,
15* Because it was he who scourged me,
and it is he who has had mercy
on me.
Behold, I now see my son Tobiah!"

Then Tobit went back in, rejoicing and
praising God with full voice. Tobiah told
his father that his journey had been a
success; that he had brought back the
money; and that he had married Ragu-
el's daughter Sarah, who would arrive
shortly, for she was approaching the
gate of Nineveh.
16 Rejoicing and praising God, Tobit
went out to the gate of Nineveh to meet
his daughter-in-law. When the people of
Nineveh saw him walking along briskly,
with no one leading him by the hand,
they were amazed. 17 Before them all To-
bit proclaimed how God had mercifully
restored sight to his eyes. When Tobit
reached Sarah, the wife of his son To-
biah, he greeted her: "Welcome, my
daughter! Blessed be your God for
bringing you to us, daughter! Blessed
are your father and your mother.
Blessed is my son Tobiah, and blessed
are you, daughter! Welcome to your
home with blessing and joy. Come in,
daughter!" That day there was joy for
all the Jews who lived in Nineveh.
18 Ahiqar and his nephew Nadab also
came to rejoice with Tobit. They cele-
brated Tobiah's wedding feast for seven
happy days, and he received many gifts.

V: RAPHAEL REVEALS HIS IDENTITY

CHAPTER 12

Raphael's Wages. 1† When the wed-
ding celebration came to an end, Tobit
called his son Tobiah and said to him,
"Son, see to it that you give what is due
to the man who made the journey with

*

11, 9: Gn 33, 4; 45, 14; 46, 29f; Lk 15, 20.

15: 13, 2; Dt 32, 39; 1 Sm 2, 6; Tb 13, 2.

†

12, 1-5: Tobit and his son generously agree to give Azariah far more than the wages agreed upon in 5, 15-16.

you; give him a bonus too." 2* Tobiah
said: "Father, how much shall I pay
him? It would not hurt me at all to give
him half of all the wealth he brought
back with me. 3 He led me back safe and
sound; he cured my wife; he brought the
money back with me; and he cured you.
How much of a bonus should I give
him?" 4 Tobit answered, "It is only fair,
son, that he should receive half of all that
he brought back." 5 So Tobiah called Raphael and said, "Take as your wages
half of all that you have brought back,
and go in peace."

Exhortation. 6† Raphael called the
two men aside privately and said to
them: "Thank God! Give him the praise
and the glory. Before all the living, acknowledge the many good things he has
done for you, by blessing and extolling
his name in song. Before all men, honor
and proclaim God's deeds, and do not
be slack in praising him. 7 A king's secret
it is prudent to keep, but the works of
God are to be declared and made known.
Praise them with due honor. Do good,
and evil will not find its way to you.
8*† Prayer and fasting are good, but better than either is almsgiving accompanied by righteousness. A little with
righteousness is better than abundance
with wickedness. It is better to give alms
than to store up gold; 9* for almsgiving
saves one from death and expiates every
sin. Those who regularly give alms shall
enjoy a full life; 10 but those habitually
guilty of sin are their own worst enemies.

Raphael's Identity. 11 "I will now tell
you the whole truth; I will conceal nothing at all from you. I have already said
to you, 'A king's secret it is prudent to
keep, but the works of God are to be
made known with due honor.' 12*† I can
now tell you that when you, Tobit, and
Sarah prayed, it was I who presented
and read the record of your prayer before the Glory of the Lord; and I did the
same thing when you used to bury the
dead. 13 When you did not hesitate to get
up and leave your dinner in order to go
and bury the dead, 14† I was sent to put
you to the test. At the same time, however, God commissioned me to heal you
and your daughter-in-law Sarah. 15* I
am Raphael, one of the seven angels who
enter and serve before the Glory of the
Lord."

16 Stricken with fear, the two men fell
to the ground. 17 But Raphael said to
them: "No need to fear; you are safe.
Thank God now and forever. 18 As for
me, when I came to you it was not out
of any favor on my part, but because it
was God's will. So continue to thank him
every day; praise him with song. 19 Even
though you watched me eat and drink.
I did not really do so; what you were seeing was a vision. 20* So now get up from
the ground and praise God. Behold, I am
about to ascend to him who sent me;
write down all these things that have
happened to you." 21 When Raphael ascended they rose to their feet and could
no longer see him. 22 They kept thanking
God and singing his praises; and they
continued to acknowledge these marvelous deeds which he had done when the
angel of God appeared to them.

VI: TOBIT'S SONG OF PRAISE

CHAPTER 13

1*† Then Tobit composed this joyful
prayer:

Blessed be God who lives forever,
because his kingdom lasts for all ages.
2* For he scourges and then has mercy;
he casts down to the depths of the nether world,
and he brings up from the great abyss.
No one can escape his hand.

3 Praise him, you Israelites, before the Gentiles,
for though he has scattered you among them,
4 he has shown you his greatness even there.
Exalt him before every living being,
because he is the Lord our God,
our Father and God forever.

5* He scourged you for your iniquities,

*

12, 2: 5, 3.7.15f.
8: 4, 7-11; Sir 29, 8-13.
9: Dn 4, 24.
12: Jb 33, 23f; Acts 10, 4; Rv 8, 3f.
15: Lk 1, 19; Rv 8, 2.
20: Jgs 13, 20.
13, 1: 3, 11; 8, 5.15; 1 Chr 29, 10; Dn 3, 26.
2: 11, 15; 13, 9; Dt 32, 39; 1 Sm 2, 6; Wis 16, 13.
5: Dt 30, 3; Neh 1, 9.

†

12, 6-10: In the fashion of a wisdom teacher, Raphael gives the two men a short exhortation similar to the one Tobit gave his son in 4, 3-19.

12, 6f: The Jews considered the duty of praising God their most esteemed privilege. Without praise of God, life was meaningless. Cf Is 38, 16-20.

12, 8: *Prayer . . . fasting . . . almsgiving . . . righteousness:* these, together with the proper attitude toward wealth, are treated in great detail by Christ our Lord in the Sermon on the Mount (Mt 6).

12, 12.15: Raphael is one of the seven specially designated intercessors who present man's prayers to God. Angelology was developing in this period. The names of two other angels are given in the Bible: Gabriel (Dn 8, 16; 9, 21; Lk 1, 19.26) and Michael (Dn 10, 13.21; 12, 1; Jude 9; Rv 12, 7).

12, 14: *I was sent . . . test:* God often sends trials to purify his faithful servants further. Cf Jb 1—2.

13, 1-18: Tobit's hymn of praise (cf Ex 15, 1-18; Jdt 16, 1-17) is divided into two parts. The first part (vv 1-8) is a song of praise that echoes themes from the hymns and psalms of the kingdom; the second (vv 9-18) is addressed to Jerusalem in the style of the prophets who spoke of a new and ideal Jerusalem (Is 60); cf Rv 21.

but will again have mercy on you all.
He will gather you from all the Gentiles
among whom you have been scattered.
6* When you turn back to him with all your heart,
to do what is right before him,
Then he will turn back to you,
and no longer hide his face from you.

So now consider what he has done for you,
and praise him with full voice.
Bless the Lord of righteousness,
and exalt the King of the ages.

In the land of my exile I praise him,
and show his power and majesty to a sinful nation.
"Turn back, you sinners! do the right before him:
perhaps he may look with favor upon you
and show you mercy.
7 "As for me, I exalt my God,
and my spirit rejoices in the King of heaven.
8 Let all men speak of his majesty,
and sing his praises in Jerusalem."

9*† O Jerusalem, holy city,
he scourged you for the works of your hands,
but will again pity the children of the righteous.
10* Praise the Lord for his goodness,
and bless the King of the ages,
so that his tent may be rebuilt in you with joy.

May he gladden within you all who were captives;
all who were ravaged may he cherish within you
for all generations to come.
11* A bright light will shine to all parts of the earth;
many nations shall come to you from afar,
And the inhabitants of all the limits of the earth,
drawn to you by the name of the Lord God,
Bearing in their hands their gifts for the King of heaven.
Every generation shall give joyful praise in you,
and shall call you the chosen one,
through all ages forever.
12* Accursed are all who speak a harsh word against you;
accursed are all who destroy you
and pull down your walls,
And all who overthrow your towers
and set fire to your homes;
but forever blessed are all those who build you up.
13 Go, then, rejoice over the children of the righteous,
who shall all be gathered together
and shall bless the Lord of the ages.
14* Happy are those who love you,
and happy those who rejoice in your prosperity.

Happy are all the men who shall grieve over you,
over all your chastisements,
For they shall rejoice in you
as they behold all your joy forever.
15 My spirit blesses the Lord, the great King;
16* Jerusalem shall be rebuilt as his home forever.
Happy for me if a remnant of my offspring survive
to see your glory and to praise the King of heaven!
The gates of Jerusalem shall be built with sapphire and emerald,
and all your walls with precious stones.
The towers of Jerusalem shall be built with gold,
and their battlements with pure gold.
17 The streets of Jerusalem shall be paved
with rubies and stones of Ophir;
18 The gates of Jerusalem shall sing hymns of gladness,
and all her houses shall cry out, "Alleluia!

"Blessed be God who has raised you up!
may he be blessed for all ages!"
For in you they shall praise his holy name forever.

The end of Tobit's hymn of praise.

VII: EPILOGUE

CHAPTER 14

Parting Advice. 1 Tobit died peacefully at the age of a hundred and twelve, and received an honorable burial in

TOBIT

*

6: Dt 30, 2.
9: 11, 15; Mi 7, 19; Rv 21.
10: Is 44, 26.28; Am 9, 11; Zec 1, 16.
11: Is 2, 3f; 9, 1; 49, 6; 60, 1; Mi 4, 2; Zec 8, 22.
12: Bar 4, 31f.
14: Ps 122, 6; Is 66, 10.
16: 14, 5; Is 54, 11-13; 62, 2; Rv 21, 10-21.

†

13, 9: *Works of your hands:* idols.

Nineveh. 2 He was sixty-two years old
when he lost his eyesight, and after he
recovered it he lived in prosperity, giv-
ing alms and continually blessing God
and praising the divine Majesty.
3* Just before he died, he called his son
Tobiah and Tobiah's seven sons, and
gave him this command: "Son, take your
children 4*† and flee into Media, for I be-
lieve God's word which was spoken by
Nahum against Nineveh. It shall all hap-
pen, and shall overtake Assyria and
Nineveh; indeed, whatever was said by
Israel's prophets, whom God commis-
sioned, shall occur. Not one of all the
oracles shall remain unfulfilled, but ev-
erything shall take place in the time ap-
pointed for it. So it will be safer in Media
than in Assyria or Babylon. For I know
and believe that whatever God has
spoken will be accomplished. It shall
happen, and not a single word of the
prophecies shall prove false.
"As for our kinsmen who dwell in Is-
rael, they shall all be scattered and led
away into exile from the Good Land. The
entire country of Israel shall become
desolate; even Samaria and Jerusalem
shall become desolate! God's temple
there shall be burnt to the ground and
shall be desolate for a while. 5*† But God
will again have mercy on them and
bring them back to the land of Israel.
They shall rebuild the temple, but it will
not be like the first one, until the era
when the appointed times shall be com-
pleted. Afterward all of them shall re-
turn from their exile, and they shall
rebuild Jerusalem with splendor. In her
the temple of God shall also be rebuilt;
yes, it will be rebuilt for all generations
to come, just as the prophets of Israel
said of her. 6*† All the nations of the
world shall be converted and shall offer
God true worship; all shall abandon their
idols which have deceitfully led them
into error, 7* and shall bless the God of
the ages in righteousness. Because all
the Israelites who are to be saved in
those days will truly be mindful of God,
they shall be gathered together and
go to Jerusalem; in security shall they
dwell forever in the land of Abraham,
which will be given over to them. Those
who sincerely love God shall rejoice,
but those who become guilty of sin
shall completely disappear from the
land.
9 "Now, children, I give you this com-
mand: serve God faithfully and do what
is right before him; you must tell your
children to do what is upright and to give
alms, to be mindful of God and at all
times to bless his name sincerely and
with all their strength.
8 "Now, as for you, my son, depart
from Nineveh; do not remain here.
10*† The day you bury your mother next
to me, do not even stay overnight within
the confines of the city. For I see that
people here shamelessly commit all
sorts of wickedness and treachery.
Think, my son, of all that Nadab did to
Ahiqar, the very one who brought him
up: Ahiqar went down alive into the
earth! Yet God made Nadab's disgrace-
ful crime rebound against him. Ahiqar
came out again into the light, but Nadab
went into the everlasting darkness, for
he had tried to kill Ahiqar. Because Ahi-
qar had given alms to me, he escaped
from the deadly trap Nadab had set for
him. But Nadab himself fell into the
deadly trap, and it destroyed him. 11 So,
my children, note well what almsgiving
does, and also what wickedness does—
it kills! But now my spirit is about to
leave me."
Death of Tobit and Tobiah. They
placed him on his bed and he died; and
he received an honorable burial.
12* When Tobiah's mother died, he bur-
ied her next to his father. He then de-
parted with his wife and children for
Media, where he settled in Ecbatana
with his father-in-law Raguel. 13 He took
respectful care of his aging father-in-
law and mother-in-law; and he buried
them at Ecbatana in Media. Then he in-
herited Raguel's estate as well as that
of his father Tobit. 14 He died at the ven-
erable age of a hundred and seventeen.
15† But before he died, he heard of the
destruction of Nineveh and saw its ef-

*

14, 3: Gn 47, 29f.
4: Na 2, 2—3, 19.
5: Neh 12, 27; Jer 31, 38.
6: 45, 14; Is 60, 1-4.
7: Is 60, 21; Jer 32, 37; Ez 34, 28; 37, 25; 39, 26.
10: 1, 21f.
12: 4, 4.

†

14, 4f: *Nahum:* one of the minor prophets, whose book contains oracles of doom against Nineveh. Here, in keeping with the period to which he assigns his story, the sacred author makes Tobit speak as if the punishment of Nineveh, the destruction of Jerusalem (587 B. C.), the exile from Judah and the return, would all take place in the future. The technique of using the facts of past history as seemingly future predictions, is a frequent device of apocalyptic writers. *The Good Land:* a favorite name for the promised land. Cf Dt 1, 35; 3, 25; 4, 21.22.

14, 5: *Until the era . . . completed:* a reference to the advent of Messianic times, in which a new, more perfect temple was to be expected. Cf Heb 9, 1-14.

14, 6: Conversion of the Gentiles is also to come in the Messianic era.

14, 10: *Nadab:* In the *Story of Ahiqar,* the hero Ahiqar, chancellor under the Assyrian kings Sennacherib and Esarhaddon, adopts his nephew Nadab and prepares him to become his successor. But Nadab treacherously plots to have his uncle put to death. Ahiqar hides in a friend's house, and is finally vindicated (*came out again into the light*) when Nadab's scheme is discovered. Thereupon Nadab is thrown into a dungeon where he dies (*went into everlasting darkness*). It was Ahiqar's almsgiving that delivered him from death; see note on 2, 2.

14, 15: *Cyaxares:* Nabopolassar, king of Babylon, and Cyaxares conquered and destroyed Nineveh in 612 B. C.; see note on 1, 15.

fects. He witnessed the exile of the city's inhabitants when Cyaxares, king of Media, led them captive into Media. Tobiah praised God for all that he had done against the citizens of Nineveh and Assyria. Before dying he rejoiced over Nineveh's destruction, and he blessed the Lord God forever and ever. Amen.

The Book of

JUDITH

The Book of Judith is a vivid story relating how, in a grave crisis, God delivered the Jewish people through the instrumentality of a woman. The unknown author composed this edifying narrative of divine providence at the end of the second or the beginning of the first century B.C. The original was almost certainly written in Hebrew, but the Greek text shows so much freedom in adapting from the Septuagint the language of older biblical books that it must be regarded as having a literary character of its own. It is this Greek form of the book, accepted as canonical by the Catholic Church, which is translated here. St. Jerome, who prepared (with some reluctance) a Latin text of Judith, based his work on a secondary Aramaic text available to him in Palestine, combined with an older Latin rendering from the Greek. The long hymn of chapter 16 he took in its entirety from that earlier Latin text.

Since it is no longer possible to determine with any precision the underlying events which may have given rise to this narrative, it is enough to note that the author sought to strengthen the faith of his people in God's abiding presence among them. The Book of Judith is a tract for difficult times; the reader, it was hoped, would take to heart the lesson that God was still the Master of history, who could save Israel from her enemies. Note the parallel with the time of the Exodus: as God had delivered his people by the hand of Moses, so he could deliver them by the hand of the pious widow Judith (see note on 2, 12).

The story can be divided into two parts. In the first (cc 1—7), Holofernes, commander-in-chief of the armies of Nebuchadnezzar, leads an overwhelming Assyrian force in a punitive campaign against the vassals who refused to help in the Assyrian war against the Medes. The Jewish people stubbornly resist the enemy at Bethulia, guarding the route of access to Jerusalem. Despite the warning of Achior that the Jews cannot be conquered unless they sin against God, the proud general lays siege to the town and cuts off its water supply. After a siege of thirty-four days, the exhausted defenders are desperate and ready to surrender.

At this point, the climax of the story, Judith (the name means "Jewess") appears and promises to defeat the Assyrians. The rest of the story is too well known to repeat in detail. Having fasted and prayed, Judith dresses in her finest garments and proceeds to the Assyrian camp, where she succeeds in killing Holofernes while he lies in a drunken stupor. The Assyrians panic when they discover this, and the Jews are able to rout and slaughter them. The beautiful hymn of the people honoring Judith (15, 9-10) is often applied to Mary in the liturgy.

Any attempt to read the book directly against the backdrop of Jewish history in relation to the empires of the ancient world is bound to fail. The story was written as a pious reflection on the meaning of the yearly Passover observance. It draws its inspiration from the Exodus narrative (especially Ex 14, 31) and from the texts of Isaiah and the Psalms portraying the special intervention of God for the preservation of Jerusalem. The theme of God's hand as the agent of this providential activity, reflected of old in the hand of Moses and now in the hand of Judith, is again exemplified at a later time in Jewish synagogue art. God's hand reaching down from heaven appears as part of the scene at Dura-Europos (before A.D. 256) in paintings of the Exodus, of the sacrifice of Isaac (Gn 22), and of Ezekiel's valley of dry bones (Ez 37).

The Book of Judith is divided as follows:

I: Peril of the Jews (1, 1—7, 32)
II: Deliverance of the Jews (8, 1—14, 10)
III: Victory (14, 11—16, 25)

I: PERIL OF THE JEWS

CHAPTER 1

War against the Medes. 1 It was the
twelfth year of the reign of Nebuchad-
nezzar, king of the Assyrians in the great
city of Nineveh. At that time Arphaxad
ruled over the Medes in Ecbatana.
2 Around this city he built a wall of
blocks of stone, each three cubits in
height and six in length. He made the
wall seventy cubits high and fifty thick.
3 At the gates he raised towers of a hun-
dred cubits, with a thickness of sixty cu-
bits at the base. 4 The gateway he built
to a height of seventy cubits, with an
opening forty cubits wide for the pas-
sage of his chariot forces and the mar-
shaling of his infantry. 5 Then King
Nebuchadnezzar waged war against
King Arphaxad in the vast plain, in the
district of Ragae. 6† To him there rallied
all the inhabitants of the mountain re-
gion, all who dwelt along the Euphrates,
the Tigris, and the Hydaspes, and King
Arioch of the Elamites, in the plain.
Thus many nations came together to re-
sist the people of Cheleoud.
Ultimatum to the West. 7 Now Nebu-
chadnezzar, king of the Assyrians, sent
messengers to all the inhabitants of Per-
sia, and to all those who dwelt in the
West: to the inhabitants of Cilicia and
Damascus, Lebanon and Anti-Lebanon,
to all who dwelt along the seacoast, 8 to
the peoples of Carmel, Gilead, Upper
Galilee, and the vast plain of Esdraelon,
9 to all those in Samaria and its cities,
and west of the Jordan as far as Jerusa-
lem, Bethany, Chelous, Kadesh, and the
River of Egypt; to Tahpanhes, Raamses,
all the land of Goshen, 10 Tanis, Mem-
phis and beyond, and to all the inhabit-
ants of Egypt as far as the borders of
Ethiopia.
11 But the inhabitants of all that land
disregarded the summons of Nebuchad-
nezzar, king of the Assyrians, and would
not go with him to the war. They were
not afraid of him but regarded him as
a lone individual opposed to them, and
turned away his envoys empty-handed,
in disgrace. 12† Then Nebuchadnezzar
fell into a violent rage against all that
land, and swore by his throne and his
kingdom that he would avenge himself
on all the territories of Cilicia and Da-
mascus and Syria, and also destroy with
his sword all the inhabitants of Moab,
Ammon, the whole of Judea, and those
living anywhere in Egypt as far as the
borders of the two seas.
Defeat of Arphaxad. 13 In the seven-
teenth year he proceeded with his army
against King Arphaxad, and was victo-
rious in his campaign. He routed the
whole force of Arphaxad, his entire cav-
alry and all his chariots, 14 and took pos-
session of his cities. He pressed on to Ec-
batana and took its towers, sacked its
marketplaces, and turned its glory into
shame. 15 Arphaxad himself he overtook
in the mountains of Ragae, ran him
through with spears, and utterly de-
stroyed him. 16* Then he returned home
with all his numerous, motley horde of
warriors; and there he and his army re-
laxed and feasted for a hundred and
twenty days.

CHAPTER 2

Council of War against the West. 1 In
the eighteenth year, on the twenty-sec-
ond day of the first month, there was a
discussion in the palace of Nebuchad-
nezzar, king of the Assyrians, about tak-
ing revenge on the whole world, as he
had threatened. 2 He summoned all his
ministers and nobles, laid before them
his secret plan, and urged the total de-
struction of those countries. 3 They de-
cided to do away with all those who had
refused to comply with the order he had
issued.
4 When he had completed his plan,
Nebuchadnezzar, king of the Assyrians,
summoned Holofernes, general in chief
of his forces, second to himself in com-
mand, and said to him:
5* "Thus says the great king, the lord
of all the earth: Go forth from my pres-
ence, take with you men of proven valor,
a hundred and twenty thousand infantry
and twelve thousand cavalry, 6 and pro-
ceed against all the land of the West, be-
cause they did not comply with the order
I issued. 7† Tell them to have earth and
water ready, for I will come against
them in my wrath; I will cover all the
land with the feet of my soldiers, to
whom I will deliver them as spoils.
8 Their slain shall fill their ravines and
wadies, the swelling torrent shall be
choked with their dead; 9 and I will de-
port them as exiles to the very ends of
the earth.
10 "You go before me and take posses-
sion of all their territories for me. If they
surrender to you, guard them for me till
the day of their punishment. 11 As for
those who resist, show them no quarter,
but deliver them up to slaughter and
plunder in each country you occupy.

* 1, 16: Est 1, 3f. 2, 5f: Est 3, 8f.

† 1, 6: *Cheleoud:* probably the Chaldeans are meant.

1, 12: *The two seas:* the ancient rulers in Mesopotamia often designated the limits of their realm as extending from the Upper Sea (the Mediterranean) to the Lower Sea (the Persian Gulf).

2, 7: *Earth and water:* in the Persian period, the offering of these to a conqueror was a symbolic gesture of unconditional surrender.

12† For as I live, and by the strength of my kingdom, what I have spoken I will accomplish by my power. 13 Do not disobey a single one of the orders of your lord; fulfill them exactly as I have commanded you, and do it without delay."

Campaign of Holofernes. 14 So Holofernes left the presence of his lord, and summoned all the princes, and the generals and officers of the Assyrian army. 15 He mustered a hundred and twenty thousand picked troops, as his lord had commanded, and twelve thousand mounted archers, 16 and grouped them into a complete combat force. 17 He took along a very large number of camels, asses, and mules for their baggage; innumerable sheep, cattle, and goats for their food supply; 18 abundant provisions for each man, and much gold and silver from the royal palace.

19 Then he and his whole army proceeded on their expedition in advance of King Nebuchadnezzar, to cover all the western region with their chariots and cavalry and regular infantry. 20* A huge, irregular force, too many to count, like locusts or the dust of the earth, went along with them.

21 After a three-day march from Nineveh, they reached the plain of Bectileth, and from Bectileth they next encamped near the mountains to the north of Upper Cilicia. 22 From there Holofernes took his whole force, the infantry, cavalry, and chariots, and marched into the mountain region. 23† He devastated Put and Lud, and plundered all the Rassisites and the Ishmaelites on the border of the desert toward the south of Chaldea.

24 Then, following the Euphrates, he went through Mesopotamia, and battered down every fortified city along the Wadi Abron, until he reached the sea. 25 He seized the territory of Cilicia, and cut down everyone who resisted him. Then he proceeded to the southern borders of Japheth, toward Arabia. 26 He surrounded all the Midianites, burned their tents, and plundered their sheepfolds. 27 Descending to the plain of Damascus at the time of the wheat harvest, he set fire to all their fields, destroyed their flocks and herds, despoiled their cities, devastated their plains, and put all their youths to the sword.

28 The fear and dread of him fell upon all the inhabitants of the coastland, upon those in Sidon and Tyre, and those who dwelt in Sur and Ocina, and the inhabitants of Jamnia. Those in Azotus and Ascalon also feared him greatly.

CHAPTER 3

Submission of the West. 1 They therefore sent messengers to him to sue for peace in these words: 2 "We, the servants of Nebuchadnezzar the great king, lie prostrate before you; do with us as you will. 3 Our dwellings and all our wheat fields, our flocks and herds, and all our encampments are at your disposal; make use of them as you please. 4 Our cities and their inhabitants are also at your service; come and deal with them as you see fit."

5 After the spokesmen had reached Holofernes and given him this message, 6 he went down with his army to the seacoast, and stationed garrisons in the fortified cities; from them he impressed picked troops as auxiliaries. 7 The people of these cities and all the inhabitants of the countryside received him with garlands and dancing to the sound of timbrels. 8* Nevertheless, he devastated their whole territory and cut down their sacred groves, for he had been commissioned to destroy all the gods of the earth, so that every nation might worship Nebuchadnezzar alone, and every people and tribe invoke him as a god. 9 At length Holofernes reached Esdraelon in the neighborhood of Dothan, the approach to the main ridge of the Judean mountains; 10† he set up his camp between Geba and Scythopolis, and stayed there a whole month to refurbish all the equipment of his army.

CHAPTER 4

Israelite Defense. 1 When the Israelites who dwelt in Judea heard of all that Holofernes, commander-in-chief of Nebuchadnezzar, king of the Assyrians, had done to the nations, and how he had despoiled all their temples and destroyed them, 2 they were in extreme dread of him, and greatly alarmed for Jerusalem and the temple of the Lord, their God. 3† Now, they had lately returned from exile, and only recently had all the people of Judea been gathered together, and the vessels, the altar, and

---

* 20: Jgs 7, 12. 3, 8: Ex 34, 13.

---

† 2, 12: *As I live:* in the Old Testament, an oath proper to divinity; cf Dt 32, 40. Nebuchadnezzar is making himself equal to God; see 6, 2. *By my power:* literally "by my hand." The hand of Nebuchadnezzar raised in opposition to God and to his people is the occasion for Judith's intervention *by a woman's hand;* cf 9, 9f; Is 10, 5-14.

2, 23: *Put and Lud:* the same as the "Put and Lud" mentioned in Ez 30, 5 as allies of Egypt, and in Ez 27, 10 as supplying mercenary soldiers to Tyre. Here they seem inserted to embellish the narrative with assonance and prophetic associations rather than to indicate definite localities.

3, 10: *Geba:* perhaps originally "Gelboe," the mountain range near the eastern end of which lay *Scythopolis,* the Greek name for ancient Beth-shean (Jos 17, 11).

4, 3: *Returned from exile . . . profanation:* these allusions are variously attributed—to the Persian period (538-323 B.C.), or even to a condition in the days of Antiochus Epiphanes (175-164 B.C.).

the temple been purified from profanation. 4 So they sent word to the whole region of Samaria, to Kona, Beth-horon, Belmain, and Jericho, to Choba and Aesora, and to the valley of Salem. 5 The people there posted guards on all the summits of the high mountains, fortified their villages, and since their fields had recently been harvested, stored up provisions in preparation for war.

6† Joakim, who was high priest in Jerusalem in those days, wrote to the inhabitants of Bethulia [and Betomesthaim], which is on the way to Esdraelon, facing the plain near Dothan, 7 and instructed them to keep firm hold of the mountain passes, since these offered access to Judea. It would be easy to ward off the attacking forces, as the defile was only wide enough for two abreast. 8† The Israelites carried out the orders given them by Joakim, the high priest, and the senate of the whole people of Israel, which met in Jerusalem.

Prayer and Penance. 9 All the men of Israel cried to God with great fervor and did penance— 10*† they, along with their wives, and children, and domestic animals. All their resident aliens, hired laborers, and slaves also girded themselves with sackcloth. 11† And all the Israelite men, women and children who lived in Jerusalem prostrated themselves in front of the temple building, with ashes strewn on their heads, displaying their sackcloth covering before the Lord. 12* The altar, too, they draped in sackcloth; and with one accord they cried out fervently to the God of Israel not to allow their children to be seized, their wives to be taken captive, the cities of their inheritance to be ruined, or the sanctuary to be profaned and mocked for the nations to gloat over.

13* The Lord heard their cry and had regard for their distress. For the people observed a fast of many days' duration throughout Judea, and before the sanctuary of the Lord Almighty in Jerusalem. 14 The high priest Joakim, and all the priests in attendance on the Lord who served his altar, were also girded with sackcloth as they offered the daily holocaust, the votive offerings, and the freewill offerings of the people. 15 With ashes upon their turbans, they cried to the Lord with all their strength to look with favor on the whole house of Israel.

CHAPTER 5

Council against the Israelites. 1 It was reported to Holofernes, commander-in-chief of the Assyrian army, that the Israelites were ready for battle, and had blocked the mountain passes, fortified the summits of all the higher peaks, and placed roadblocks in the plains. 2 In great anger he summoned all the rulers of the Moabites, the generals of the Ammonites, and all the satraps of the seacoast 3 and said to them: "Now tell me, you Canaanites, what sort of people is this that dwells in the mountains? Which cities do they inhabit? How large is their army? In what does their power and strength consist? Who has set himself up as their king and the leader of their army? 4 Why have they refused to come out to meet me along with all the other inhabitants of the West?"

Achior's Speech. 5* Then Achior, the leader of all the Ammonites said to him: "My lord, hear this account from your servant; I will tell you the truth about this people that lives near you [that inhabits this mountain region]; no lie shall escape your servant's lips.

6† "These people are descendants of the Chaldeans. 7* They formerly dwelt in Mesopotamia, for they did not wish to follow the gods of their forefathers who were born in the land of the Chaldeans. 8 Since they abandoned the way of their ancestors, and acknowledged with divine worship the God of heaven, their forefathers expelled them from the presence of their gods. So they fled to Mesopotamia and dwelt there a long time. 9* Their God bade them leave their abode and proceed to the land of Canaan. Here they settled, and grew very rich in gold, silver, and a great abundance of livestock. 10* Later, when famine had gripped the whole land of Canaan, they went down into Egypt. They stayed there as long as they found sustenance, and grew into such a great multitude that the number of their race could not be counted. 11* The king of Egypt, however, rose up against them, shrewdly forced them to labor at brickmaking, oppressed and enslaved them. 12 But they cried to their God, and he

*

4, 10f: Jon 3, 7f.
12: Est 4, 1f.
13: Est 4, 16.
5, 5: 11, 9-19.
7: Gn 11, 31.
9: Gn 11, 31—12, 5.
10: Gn 42, 1-5; 46, 1-7; Ex 1, 7.
11f: Ex 5, 4-21; 7, 1-9.

†

4, 6: *Joakim, who was high priest:* see Bar 1, 7 and the footnote on Bar 1, 8f; this name for a high priest cannot be used in dating the events in Jdt.

4, 8: The organization of the Jewish nation as subject to a *high priest* and a *senate,* or council of elders, was proper to the Greek period (after 323 B.C.), and is reflected in the coinage of John Hyrcanus (135-104 B.C.).

4, 10: *Domestic animals:* see note on Jon 3, 8.

4, 11: *Prostrated themselves in front of the temple building:* for a parallel to this ceremony of entreaty, see Jl 1, 13f; 2, 15ff, and the note on Jl 2, 17.

5, 6-9: Achior outlines the early history of the Hebrews, whose forefather, Abraham, first lived in Ur of the *Chaldeans* (Gn 11, 28) and then migrated to Haran (Gn 11, 31) in Aram Naharaim (Gn 24, 10), which was called *Mesopotamia* by the Greeks. *The gods of their forefathers* were the pagan deities worshiped by Abraham's relatives (Jos 24, 2).

struck the land of Egypt with plagues
for which there was no remedy. When
the Egyptians expelled them, 13* God
dried up the Red Sea before them, 14 and
led them along the route to Sinai and
Kadesh-barnea. First they drove out all
the inhabitants of the desert; 15* then
they settled in the land of the Amorites,
destroyed all the Heshbonites by main
force, crossed the Jordan, and took pos-
session of the whole mountain region.
16* They expelled the Canaanites, the
Perizzites, the Jebusites, the Shechem-
ites, and all the Gergesites; and they
lived in these mountains a long time.
17* "As long as the Israelites did not
sin in the sight of their God, they pros-
pered, for their God, who hates wicked-
ness, was with them. 18* But when they
deviated from the way he prescribed for
them, they were ground down steadily,
more and more, by frequent wars, and
finally taken as captives into foreign
lands. The temple of their God was razed
to the ground, and their cities were occu-
pied by their enemies. 19 But now that
they have returned to their God, they
have come back from the Dispersion
wherein they were scattered, and have
repossessed Jerusalem, where their
sanctuary is, and have settled again in
the mountain region which was unoccu-
pied.
20* "So now, my lord and master, if
these people are at fault, and are sinning
against their God, and if we verify this
offense of theirs, then we shall be able
to go up and conquer them. 21 But if they
are not a guilty nation, then your lord-
ship should keep his distance; otherwise
their Lord and God will shield them, and
we shall become the laughing stock of
the whole world."
22 Now when Achior had concluded his
recommendation, all the people stand-
ing round about the tent murmured; and
the officers of Holofernes and all the in-
habitants of the seacoast and of Moab
alike said he should be cut to pieces.
23 "We are not afraid of the Israelites,"
they said, "for they are a powerless peo-
ple, incapable of a strong defense.
24* Let us therefore attack them; your
great army, Lord Holofernes, will swal-
low them up."

CHAPTER 6

Holofernes' Answer. 1 When the noise
of the crowd surrounding the council
had subsided, Holofernes, commander-
in-chief of the Assyrian army, said to
Achior, in the presence of the whole
throng of coastland peoples, of the Mo-
abites, and of the Ammonite mercenar-
ies: 2* "Who are you, Achior, to proph-
esy among us as you have done today,
and to tell us not to fight against the Isra-
elites because their God protects them?
What god is there beside Nebuchadnez-
zar? He will send his force and destroy
them from the face of the earth. Their
God will not save them; 3* but we, the
servants of Nebuchadnezzar, will strike
them down as one man, for they will be
unable to withstand the force of our cav-
alry. 4* We will overwhelm them with it,
and the mountains shall be drunk with
their blood, and their plains filled with
their corpses. Not a trace of them shall
survive our attack: they shall utterly
perish, says King Nebuchadnezzar, lord
of all the earth; for he has spoken, and
his words shall not remain unfulfilled.
5 As for you, Achior, you Ammonite
mercenary, for saying these things in a
moment of perversity you shall not see
my face after today, until I have taken
revenge on this race of people from
Egypt. 6* Then at my return, the sword
of my army or the spear of my servants
will pierce your sides, and you shall fall
among their slain. 7 My servants will
now conduct you to the mountain region,
and leave you at one of the towns along
the ascent. 8 You shall not die till you are
destroyed together with them. 9 If you
still cherish the hope that they will not
be taken, then there is no need for you
to be downcast. I have spoken, and my
words shall not prove false in any re-
spect."
Achior in Bethulia. 10 Then Holofernes
ordered the servants who were standing
by in his tent to seize Achior, conduct
him to Bethulia, and hand him over to
the Israelites. 11 So the servants took him
in custody and brought him out of the
camp into the plain. From there they led
him into the mountain region till they
reached the springs below Bethulia.
12 When the men of the city saw them,
they seized their weapons and ran out
of the city to the crest of the ridge; and
all the slingers blocked the ascent of
Holofernes' servants by hurling stones
upon them. 13 So they took cover below
the mountain, where they bound Achior
and left him lying at the foot of the
mountain; then they returned to their
lord.
14 The Israelites came down to him
from their city, loosed him, and brought
him into Bethulia. They haled him be-
fore the rulers of the city, 15 who in those
days were Uzziah, son of Micah of the
tribe of Simeon, Chabris, son of Gotho-
niel, and Charmis, son of Melchiel.
16 They then convened all the elders of

13f: Ex 14, 21f.29.
15: Nm 21, 21-32; Jos 2, 10.
16: Dt 7, 1.
17f: Dt 28—30; Ps 106, 40-46; Is 59, 2.
18: 2 Kgs 25.
20f: 8, 18ff; 11, 10.
24: 6, 2; 9, 7; 16, 2.
6, 2: 3, 8; 9, 7.
3: Is 36, 18ff.
4: 6, 17.
6: 5, 22.

the city; and all their young men, as well
as the women, gathered in haste at the
place of assembly. They placed Achior
in the center of the throng, and Uzziah
questioned him about what had hap-
pened. 17 He replied by giving them an
account of what was said in the council
of Holofernes, and of all his own words
among the Assyrian officers, and of all
the boasting threats of Holofernes
against the house of Israel.

18 At this the people fell prostrate and
worshiped God; and they cried out:
19† "Lord, God of heaven, behold their
arrogance! Have pity on the lowliness
of our people, and look with favor this
day on those who are consecrated to
you." 20 Then they reassured Achior and
praised him highly. 21 Uzziah brought
him from the assembly to his home,
where he gave a banquet for the elders.
That whole night they called upon the
God of Israel for help.

CHAPTER 7

Siege of Bethulia. 1 The following day
Holofernes ordered his whole army, and
all the allied troops that had come to his
support, to move against Bethulia, seize
the mountain passes, and engage the Is-
raelites in battle. 2 That same day all
their fighting men went into action.
Their forces numbered a hundred and
seventy thousand infantry and twelve
thousand horsemen, not counting the
baggage train or the men who accompa-
nied it on foot—a very great army.
3 They encamped at the spring in the
valley near Bethulia, and spread out in
breadth toward Dothan as far as Bal-
baim, and in length from Bethulia to
Cyamon, which faces Esdraelon.

4 When the Israelites saw how many
there were, they said to one another in
great dismay: "Soon they will devour the
whole country. Neither the high moun-
tains nor the valleys and hills can sup-
port the mass of them." 5† Yet they all
seized their weapons, lighted fires on
their bastions, and kept watch through-
out the night.

6 On the second day Holofernes led out
all his cavalry in the sight of the Israel-
ites who were in Bethulia. 7 He reconnoi-
tered the approaches to their city and
located their sources of water; these he
seized, stationing armed detachments
around them, while he himself returned
to his troops.

8 All the commanders of the Edomites
and all the leaders of the Ammonites,
together with the generals of the sea-
coast, came to Holofernes and said:
9 "Sir, listen to what we have to say, that
there may be no losses among your
troops. 10* These Israelites do not rely
on their spears, but on the height of the
mountains where they dwell; it is not
easy to reach the summit of their moun-
tains. 11 Therefore, sir, do not attack
them in regular formation; thus not a
single one of your troops will fall. 12 Stay
in your camp, and spare all your sol-
diers. Have some of your servants keep
control of the source of water that flows
out at the base of the mountain, 13* for
that is where the inhabitants of Bethulia
get their water. Then thirst will begin to
carry them off, and they will surrender
their city. Meanwhile, we and our men
will go up to the summits of the nearby
mountains, and encamp there to guard
against anyone's leaving the city.
14 They and their wives and children will
languish with hunger, and even before
the sword strikes them they will be laid
low in the streets of their city. 15 Thus
you will render them dire punishment
for their rebellion and their refusal to
meet you peacefully."

16 Their words pleased Holofernes and
all his ministers, and he ordered their
proposal to be carried out. 17 Thereupon
the Moabites moved camp, together with
five thousand Assyrians. They en-
camped in the valley, and held the water
supply and the springs of the Israelites.
18 The Edomites and the Ammonites
went up and encamped in the mountain
region opposite Dothan; and they sent
some of their men to the south and to
the east opposite Egrebel, near Chusi,
which is on Wadi Mochmur. The rest of
the Assyrian army was encamped in the
plain, covering the whole countryside.
Their enormous store of tents and equip-
ment was spread out in profusion every-
where.

19* The Israelites cried to the Lord,
their God, for they were disheartened,
since all their enemies had them sur-
rounded, and there was no way of slip-
ping through their lines. 20 The whole
Assyrian camp, infantry, chariots, and
cavalry, kept them thus surrounded for
thirty-four days. All the reservoirs of
water failed the inhabitants of Bethulia,
21 and the cisterns ran dry, so that on
no day did they have enough to drink,
but their drinking water was rationed.
22 Their children fainted away, and the

*

7, 10: 1 Kgs 20, 23.28. 19: Ps 106, 6.
13: Ex 5, 21.

†

6, 19: The Latin Vulgate (6, 15) has a longer form of this prayer: "Lord, God of heaven and earth, behold their arrogance; regard our lowliness and look with favor on your holy ones; show that you do not abandon those who trust in you, but that you humble those who trust in themselves and glory in their own strength."

7, 5: *Lighted fires on their bastions:* to serve as signals for alerting the neighboring towns. Reference to fire signals in time of siege is made in the Lachish ostraca at the beginning of the sixth century B.C. *Kept watch throughout the night:* to prevent a surprise attack.

women and youths were consumed with
thirst and were collapsing in the streets
and gateways of the city, with no
strength left in them.
23 All the people, therefore, including
youths, women, and children, went in a
crowd to Uzziah and the rulers of the
city. They set up a great clamor and said
before the elders: 24 "God judge between
you and us! You have done us grave in-
justice in not making peace with the As-
syrians. 25 There is no help for us now!
Instead, God has sold us into their power
by laying us prostrate before them in
thirst and utter exhaustion. 26 Therefore,
summon them and deliver the whole city
as booty to the troops of Holofernes and
to all his forces; 27 we would be better
off to become their prey. We should in-
deed be made slaves, but at least we
should live, and not have to behold our
little ones dying before our eyes and our
wives and children breathing out their
souls. 28 We adjure you by heaven and
earth, and by our God, the Lord of our
forefathers, who is punishing us for our
sins and those of our forefathers, to do
as we have proposed, this very day."
29 All in the assembly with one accord
broke into shrill wailing and loud cries
to the Lord their God. 30 But Uzziah said
to them, "Courage, my brothers! Let us
wait five days more for the Lord our
God, to show his mercy toward us; he
will not utterly forsake us. 31 But if those
days pass without help coming to us, I
will do as you say." 32 Then he dispersed
the men to their posts, and they returned
to the walls and towers of the city; the
women and children he sent to their
homes. Throughout the city they were
in great misery.

II: DELIVERANCE OF THE JEWS

CHAPTER 8

Judith. 1† Now in those days Judith,
daughter of Merari, son of Joseph, son
of Oziel, son of Elkiah, son of Ananias,
son of Gideon, son of Raphain, son of
Ahitob, son of Elijah, son of Hilkiah, son
of Eliab, son of Nathanael, son of Sala-
miel, son of Sarasadai, son of Simeon,
son of Israel, heard of this. 2 Her hus-
band, Manasseh, of her own tribe and
clan, had died at the time of the barley
harvest. 3 While he was in the field su-
pervising those who bound the sheaves,
he suffered sunstroke; and he died of this
illness in Bethulia, his native city. He
was buried with his forefathers in the
field between Dothan and Balamon.
4 The widowed Judith remained three
years and four months at home,
5† where she set up a tent for herself on
the roof of her house. She put sackcloth
about her loins and wore widow's weeds.
6* She fasted all the days of her widow-
hood, except sabbath eves and sabbaths,
new moon eves and new moons, feast-
days and holidays of the house of Israel.
7 She was beautifully formed and lovely
to behold. Her husband, Manasseh, had
left her gold and silver, servants and
maids, livestock and fields, which she
was maintaining. 8 No one had a bad
word to say about her, for she was a very
God-fearing woman.

Her Words to the Elders. 9 When Ju-
dith, therefore, heard of the harsh words
which the people, discouraged by their
lack of water, had spoken against their
ruler, and of all that Uzziah had said to
them in reply, swearing that he would
hand over the city to the Assyrians at
the end of five days, 10 she sent the maid
who was in charge of all her things to
ask Uzziah, Chabris, and Charmis, the
elders of the city, to visit her. 11 When
they came, she said to them: "Listen to
me, you rulers of the people of Bethulia.
What you said to the people today is not
proper. When you promised to hand
over the city to our enemies at the end
of five days unless within that time the
Lord comes to our aid, you interposed
between God and yourselves this oath
which you took. 12* Who are you, then,
that you should have put God to the test
this day, setting yourselves in the place
of God in human affairs? 13 It is the Lord
Almighty for whom you are laying down
conditions; will you never understand
anything? 14* You cannot plumb the
depths of the human heart or grasp the
workings of the human mind; how then
can you fathom God, who has made all
these things, discern his mind, and un-
derstand his plan?
"No, my brothers, do not anger the
Lord our God. 15 For if he does not wish
to come to our aid within the five days,
he has it equally within his power to pro-
tect us at such time as he pleases, or to
destroy us in the face of our enemies.
16 It is not for you to make the Lord our
God give surety for his plans.

"God is not man that he should be
moved by threats,
nor human, that he may be given
an ultimatum.

17 "So while we wait for the salvation
that comes from him, let us call upon
him to help us, and he will hear our cry

*

8, 6: Lk 2, 37.
12: Jb 38, 2; 40, 2.7f; 42, 3.
14: Jb 41, 3; Prv 14, 10; Wis 9, 13; Is 40, 13; Rom 11, 33f; 1 Cor 2, 11.

†

8, 1: *Salamiel, son of Sarasadai:* head of the tribe of *Simeon* during the wanderings of the Israelites in the desert (Nm 1, 6).

8, 5: *A tent:* erected by Judith on the roof of her house (v 5); it was here that the elders came to confer with her (v 11).

if it is his good pleasure. 18* For there
has not risen among us in recent genera-
tions, nor does there exist today, any
tribe, or clan, or town, or city of ours
that worships gods made by hands, as
happened in former days. 19* It was for
such conduct that our forefathers were
handed over to the sword and to pillage,
and fell with great destruction before
our enemies. 20 But since we acknowl-
edge no other god but the Lord, we hope
that he will not disdain us or any of our
people. 21 If we are taken, all Judea will
fall, our sanctuary will be plundered,
and God will make us pay for its profa-
nation with our life's blood. 22 For the
slaughter of our kinsmen, for the taking
of exiles from the land, and for the dev-
astation of our inheritance, he will lay
the guilt on our heads. Wherever we
shall be enslaved among the nations, we
shall be a mockery and a reproach in
the eyes of our masters. 23 Our enslave-
ment will not be turned to our benefit,
but the Lord our God, will maintain it
to our disgrace.

24 "Therefore, my brothers, let us set
an example for our kinsmen. Their lives
depend on us, and the defense of the
sanctuary, the temple, and the altar
rests with us. 25* Besides all this, we
should be grateful to the Lord our God,
for putting us to the test, as he did our
forefathers. 26 Recall how he dealt with
Abraham, and how he tried Isaac, and
all that happened to Jacob in Syrian
Mesopotamia while he was tending the
flocks of Laban, his mother's brother.
27* Not for vengeance did the Lord put
them in the crucible to try their hearts,
nor has he done so with us. It is by way
of admonition that he chastises those
who are close to him."

Uzziah's Response. 28 Then Uzziah
said to her: "All that you have said was
spoken with good sense, and no one can
gainsay your words. 29 Not today only
is your wisdom made evident, but from
your earliest years all the people have
recognized your prudence, which corre-
sponds to the worthy dispositions of your
heart. 30 The people, however, were so
tortured with thirst that they forced us
to speak to them as we did, and to bind
ourselves by an oath that we cannot
break. 31 But now, God-fearing woman
that you are, pray for us that the Lord
may send rain to fill up our cisterns, lest
we be weakened still further."

32 Then Judith said to them: "Listen to
me! I will do something that will go down
from generation to generation among
the descendants of our race. 33 Stand at
the gate tonight to let me pass through
with my maid; and within the days you
have specified before you will surrender
the city to our enemies, the Lord will res-
cue Israel by my hand. 34 You must not
inquire into what I am doing, for I will
not tell you until my plan has been ac-
complished." 35 Uzziah and the rulers
said to her, "Go in peace, and may the
Lord God go before you to take ven-
geance upon our enemies!" 36 Then they
withdrew from the tent and returned to
their posts.

CHAPTER 9

The Prayer of Judith. 1* Judith threw
herself down prostrate, with ashes
strewn upon her head, and wearing
nothing over her sackcloth. While the in-
cense was being offered in the temple
of God in Jerusalem that evening, Judith
prayed to the Lord with a loud voice:
2*† "Lord, God of my forefather Sim-
eon! You put a sword into his hand to
take revenge upon the foreigners who
had immodestly loosened the maiden's
girdle, shamefully exposed her thighs,
and disgracefully violated her body.
This they did, though you forbade it.
3† Therefore you had their rulers
slaughtered; and you covered with their
blood the bed in which they lay deceived,
the same bed that had felt the shame
of their own deceiving. You smote the
slaves together with their princes, and
the princes together with their servants.
4 Their wives you handed over to plun-
der, and their daughters to captivity;
and all the spoils you divided among
your favored sons, who burned with zeal
for you, and in their abhorrence of the
defilement of their kinswoman, called on
you for help.

5* "O God, my God, hear me also, a
widow. It is you who were the author of
those events and of what preceded and
followed them. The present, also, and
the future you have planned. Whatever
you devise comes into being; 6* the
things you decide on come forward and
say, 'Here we are!' All your ways are
in readiness, and your judgment is made
with foreknowledge.

7* "Here are the Assyrians, a vast
force, priding themselves on horse and
rider, boasting of the power of their in-
fantry, trusting in shield and spear, bow
and sling. They do not know that

---

*

18: 5, 20f; 11, 10.
19: Pss 78, 56f; 106, 13f; Jer 7, 16-20; 14, 7.
25f: Gn 22, 1-12; 29, 22-30.
27: Dt 4, 7.
9, 1: Ex 30, 7f; Ps 141, 2.
2: Gn 34.
5: Is 44, 7.
6: Jb 38, 35; Is 46, 9-13; Bar 3, 35.
7f: 5, 23; 6, 2; 16, 2.

†

9, 2: *The maiden:* Dinah, Jacob's daughter, who was violated by Shechem, the Hivite (Gn 34, 2).

9, 3: Because Shechem had deceived and violated Dinah, her brothers, Simeon and Levi, tricked Shechem and the men of his city into being circumcised, and then slew them while they were confined to bed from the circumcision; cf Gn 34, 13-29.

8 " 'You, the Lord, crush warfare;
Lord is your name.'

"Shatter their strength in your might,
and crush their force in your wrath; for
they have resolved to profane your
sanctuary, to defile the tent where your
glorious name resides, and to overthrow
with iron the horns of your altar. 9* See
their pride, and send forth your wrath
upon their heads. Give me, a widow, the
strong hand to execute my plan. 10 With
the guile of my lips, smite the slave to-
gether with the ruler, the ruler together
with his servant; crush their pride by the
hand of a woman.
11 "Your strength is not in numbers,
nor does your power depend upon stal-
wart men; but you are the God of the
lowly, the helper of the oppressed, the
supporter of the weak, the protector of
the forsaken, the savior of those without
hope.
12 "Please, please, God of my forefa-
ther, God of the heritage of Israel, Lord
of heaven and earth, Creator of the
waters, King of all you have created,
hear my prayer! 13* Let my guileful
speech bring wound and wale on those
who have planned dire things against
your covenant, your holy temple, Mount
Zion, and the homes your children have
inherited. 14 Let your whole nation and
all the tribes know clearly that you are
the god of all power and might, and that
there is no other who protects the people
of Israel but you alone."

CHAPTER 10

Judith's Departure. 1 As soon as Ju-
dith had thus concluded, and ceased her
invocation to the God of Israel, 2 she rose
from the ground. She called her maid
and they went down into the house,
which she used only on sabbaths and
feast days. 3* She took off the sackcloth
she had on, laid aside the garments of
her widowhood, washed her body with
water, and anointed it with rich oint-
ment. She arranged her hair and bound
it with a fillet, and put on the festive at-
tire she had worn while her husband,
Manasseh, was living. 4* She chose san-
dals for her feet, and put on her anklets,
bracelets, rings, earrings, and all her
other jewelry. Thus she made herself
very beautiful, to captivate the eyes of
all the men who should see her.
5* She gave her maid a leather flask
of wine and a cruse of oil. She filled a
bag with roasted grain, fig cakes, bread
and cheese; all these provisions she
wrapped up and gave to the maid to
carry.
6 Then they went out to the gate of the
city of Bethulia and found Uzziah and
the elders of the city, Chabri and Char-
mis, standing there. 7 When these men
saw Judith transformed in looks and dif-
ferently dressed, they were very much
astounded at her beauty and said to her,
8 "May the God of our fathers bring you
to favor, and make your undertaking a
success, for the glory of the Israelites
and the exaltation of Jerusalem."
Judith bowed down to God. Then she
said to them, 9 "Order the gate of the city
opened for me, that I may go to carry
out the business we discussed." So they
ordered the youths to open the gate
for her as she requested. 10 When they
did so, Judith and her maid went out.
The men of the city kept her in view
as she went down the mountain and
crossed the valley; then they lost sight
of her.
Judith Captured. 11 As Judith and her
maid walked directly across the valley,
they encountered the Assyrian outpost.
12† The men took her in custody and
asked her, "To what people do you be-
long? Where do you come from, and
where are you going?" She replied: "I
am a daughter of the Hebrews, and I
am fleeing from them, because they are
about to be delivered up to you as prey.
13* I have come to see Holofernes, the
general in chief of your forces, to give
him a trustworthy report; I will show
him the route by which he can ascend
and take possession of the whole moun-
tain district without a single one of his
men suffering injury or loss of life."
14 When the men heard her words and
gazed upon her face, which appeared
wondrously beautiful to them, they said
to her, 15 "By coming down thus
promptly to see our master, you have
saved your life. Now go to his tent; some
of our men will accompany you to pre-
sent you to him. 16 When you stand be-
fore him, have no fear in your heart; give
him the report you speak of, and he will
treat you well." 17 So they detailed a hun-
dred of their men as an escort for her
and her maid, and these conducted
them to the tent of Holofernes.
18 When the news of her arrival spread
among the tents, a crowd gathered in
the camp. They came and stood around
her as she waited outside the tent of Hol-
ofernes, while he was being informed
about her. 19 They marveled at her
beauty, regarding the Israelites with
wonder because of her, and they said
to one another, "Who can despise this

*

9: Ps 33, 16.
13: 10, 4; 11, 20.23; 16, 6.9.
10, 3: 8, 6ff.
4: 9, 13.
5: 12, 2.
13: 11, 5f.

†

10, 12f: The deceitful means used by Judith against Holofernes, here and in 11, 5-19, are to be judged in the light of the moral concepts of Old Testament times; cf Gn 27, 1-25; 34, 13-29; 37, 32ff; Jos 2, 1-7; Jgs 4, 17-22.

people that has such women among
them? It is not wise to leave one man
of them alive, for if any were to be
spared they could beguile the whole
world."

Judith Meets Holofernes. 20 The guard
of Holofernes and all his servants came
out and ushered her into the tent. 21 Now
Holofernes was reclining on his bed un-
der a canopy with a netting of crimson
and gold, emeralds and other precious
stones. 22 When they announced her to
him, he came out to the antechamber,
preceded by silver lamps; 23 and when
Holofernes and his servants beheld Ju-
dith, they all marveled at the beauty of
her face. She threw herself down pros-
trate before him, but his servants raised
her up.

CHAPTER 11

1 Then Holofernes said to her: "Take
courage, lady; have no fear in your
heart! Never have I harmed anyone who
chose to serve Nebuchadnezzar, king of
all the earth. 2 Nor would I have raised
my spear against your people who dwell
in the mountain region, had they not de-
spised me and brought this upon them-
selves. 3 But now tell me why you fled
from them and came to us. In any case,
you have come to safety. Take courage!
Your life is spared tonight and for the
future. 4 No one at all will harm you.
Rather, you will be well treated, as are
all the servants of my lord, King Nebu-
chadnezzar."

5* Judith answered him: "Listen to the
words of your servant, and let your
handmaid speak in your presence! I will
tell no lie to my lord this night, 6 and if
you follow out the words of your hand-
maid, God will give you complete suc-
cess, and my lord will not fail in any of
his undertakings. 7* By the life of Nebu-
chadnezzar, king of all the earth, and
by the power of him who has sent you
to set all creatures aright! not only do
men serve him through you; but even
the wild beasts and the cattle and the
birds of the air, because of your
strength, will live for Nebuchadnezzar
and his whole house. 8 Indeed, we have
heard of your wisdom and sagacity, and
all the world is aware that throughout
the kingdom you alone are competent,
rich in experience, and distinguished in
military strategy.

9* "As for Achior's speech in your
council, we have heard of it. When the
men of Bethulia spared him, he told
them all he had said to you. 10* So then,
my lord and master, do not disregard
his word, but bear it in mind, for it is
true. For our people are not punished,
nor does the sword prevail against them,
except when they sin against their God.
11 But now their guilt has caught up with
them, by which they bring the wrath of
their God upon them whenever they do
wrong; so that my lord will not be re-
pulsed and fail, but death will overtake
them. 12 Since their food gave out and
all their water ran low, they decided to
kill their animals, and determined to
consume all the things which God in his
laws forbade them to eat. 13 They de-
creed that they would use up the first
fruits of grain and the tithes of wine and
oil which they had sanctified and re-
served for the priests who minister in
the presence of our God in Jerusalem:
things which no layman should even
touch with his hands. 14 They have sent
messengers to Jerusalem to bring back
to them authorization from the council
of the elders; for the inhabitants there
have also done these things. 15 On the
very day when the response reaches
them and they act upon it, they will be
handed over to you for destruction.

16 "As soon as I, your handmaid,
learned all this, I fled from them. God
has sent me to perform with you such
deeds that people throughout the world
will be astonished on hearing of them.
17 Your handmaid is, indeed, a God-
fearing woman, serving the God of
heaven night and day. Now I will remain
with you, my lord; but each night your
handmaid will go out to the ravine and
pray to God. He will tell me when the
Israelites have committed their crimes.
18 Then I will come and let you know,
so that you may go out with your whole
force, and not one of them will be able
to withstand you. 19 I will lead you
through Judea, till you come to Jerusa-
lem, and there I will set up your judg-
ment seat. You will drive them like sheep
that have no shepherd, and not even a
dog will growl at you. This was told me,
and announced to me in advance, and
I in turn have been sent to tell you."

20* Her words pleased Holofernes and
all his servants; they marveled at her
wisdom and exclaimed, 21 "No other
woman from one end of the world to the
other looks so beautiful and speaks so
wisely!" 22 Then Holofernes said to her:
"God has done well in sending you
ahead of your people, to bring victory
to our arms, and destruction to those
who have despised my lord. 23* You are
fair to behold, and your words are well
spoken. If you do as you have said, your
God will be my God; you shall dwell in
the palace of King Nebuchadnezzar, and
shall be renowned throughout the
earth."

11, 5f: 10, 13.
7: Jer 27, 6; Bar 3, 16f; Dn 2, 38.
9f: 5, 5.
10: 5, 21; 8, 18.
20: 9, 13.
23: 9, 13.

CHAPTER 12

Judith's Conduct. 1 Then he ordered
them to lead her into the room where
his silverware was kept, and bade them
set a table for her with his own delicacies
to eat and his own wine to drink. 2* But
Judith said, "I will not partake of them,
lest it be an occasion of sin; but I shall
be amply supplied from the things I
brought with me." 3 Holofernes asked
her: "But if your provisions give out,
where shall we get more of the same to
provide for you? None of your people are
with us." 4 Judith answered him, "As
surely as you, my lord, live, your hand-
maid will not use up her supplies till the
Lord accomplishes by my hand what he
has determined."

5 Then the servants of Holofernes led
her into the tent, where she slept till mid-
night. In the night watch just before
dawn, she rose 6 and sent this message
to Holofernes, "Give orders, my lord, to
let your handmaid go out for prayer."
7 So Holofernes ordered his bodyguard
not to hinder her. Thus she stayed in the
camp three days. Each night she went
out to the ravine of Bethulia, where she
washed herself at the spring of the
camp. 8 After bathing, she besought the
Lord, the God of Israel, to direct her way
for the triumph of his people. 9 Then she
returned purified to the tent, and re-
mained there until her food was brought
to her toward evening.

Holofernes' Banquet. 10† On the fourth
day Holofernes gave a banquet for his
servants alone, to which he did not invite
any of the officers. 11 And he said to Ba-
goas, the eunuch in charge of his house-
hold: "Go and persuade this Hebrew
woman in your care to come and to eat
and drink with us. 12 It would be a dis-
grace for us to have such a woman with
us without enjoying her company. If we
do not entice her, she will laugh us to
scorn."

13 So Bagoas left the presence of Holo-
fernes, and came to Judith and said, "So
fair a maiden should not be reluctant to
come to my lord to be honored by him,
to enjoy drinking wine with us, and to
be like one of the Assyrian women who
live in the palace of Nebuchadnezzar."
14 She replied, "Who am I to refuse my
lord? Whatever is pleasing to him I will
promptly do. This will be a joy for me
till the day of my death."

15 Thereupon she proceeded to put on
her festive garments and all her femi-
nine adornments. Meanwhile her maid
went ahead and spread out on the
ground for her in front of Holofernes the
fleece Bagoas had furnished for her
daily use in reclining at her dinner.
16 Then Judith came in and reclined on
it. The heart of Holofernes was in rap-
ture over her, and his spirit was shaken.
He was burning with the desire to pos-
sess her, for he had been biding his time
to seduce her from the day he saw her.
17 Holofernes said to her, "Drink and be
merry with us!" 18 Judith replied, "I will
gladly drink, my lord, for at no time
since I was born have I ever enjoyed life
as much as I do today." 19 She then took
the things her maid had prepared, and
ate and drank in his presence.
20 Holofernes, charmed by her, drank a
great quantity of wine, more than he had
ever drunk on one single day in his life.

CHAPTER 13

1 When it grew late, his servants
quickly withdrew. Bagoas closed the
tent from the outside and excluded the
attendants from their master's pres-
ence. They went off to their beds, for
they were all tired from the prolonged
banquet. 2 Judith was left alone in the
tent with Holofernes, who lay prostrate
on his bed, for he was sodden with wine.
3 She had ordered her maid to stand out-
side the bedroom and wait, as on the
other days, for her to come out; she said
she would be going out for her prayer.
To Bagoas she had said this also.

Beheading of Holofernes. 4 When all
had departed, and no one, small or
great, was left in the bedroom, Judith
stood by Holofernes' bed and said within
herself: "O Lord, God of all might, in this
hour look graciously on my undertaking
for the exaltation of Jerusalem; 5 now is
the time for aiding your heritage and for
carrying out my design to shatter the
enemies who have risen against us."
6 She went to the bedpost near the head
of Holofernes, and taking his sword
from it, 7 drew close to the bed, grasped
the hair of his head, and said,
"Strengthen me this day, O God of Is-
rael!" 8* Then with all her might she
struck him twice in the neck and cut off
his head. 9 She rolled his body off the bed
and took the canopy from its supports.
Soon afterward, she came out and
handed over the head of Holofernes to
her maid, 10 who put it into her food
pouch; and the two went off together as
they were accustomed to do for prayer.

The Return to Bethulia. They passed
through the camp, and skirting the ra-
vine, reached Bethulia on the mountain.
As they approached its gates, 11 Judith
shouted to the guards from a distance:
"Open! Open the gate! God, our God, is
with us. Once more he has made mani-

*

12, 2: 10, 5; Dn 1, 8. 13, 8: Jgs 4, 21.

†

12, 10: *Banquet for his servants alone . . . officers:* Holofernes invited the officials of his household, but not the officers of his army, who were needed for military duty.

fest his strength in Israel and his power against our enemies; he has done it this very day." 12 When the citizens heard her voice, they quickly descended to their city gate and summoned the city elders. 13 All the people, from the least to the greatest, hurriedly assembled, for her return seemed unbelievable. They opened the gate and welcomed the two women. They made a fire for light; and when they gathered around the two, 14 Judith urged them with a loud voice: "Praise God, praise him! Praise God, who has not withdrawn his mercy from the house of Israel, but has shattered our enemies by my hand this very night." 15* Then she took the head out of the pouch, showed it to them, and said: "Here is the head of Holofernes, general in charge of the Assyrian army, and here is the canopy under which he lay in his drunkenness. The Lord struck him down by the hand of a woman. 16 As the Lord lives, who has protected me in the path I have followed, I swear that it was my face that seduced Holofernes to his ruin, and that he did not sin with me to my defilement or disgrace."

17 All the people were greatly astonished. They bowed down and worshiped God, saying with one accord, "Blessed are you, our God, who today have brought to nought the enemies of your people." 18* Then Uzziah said to her: "Blessed are you, daughter, by the Most High God, above all the women on earth; and blessed be the Lord God, the creator of heaven and earth, who guided your blow at the head of the chief of our enemies. 19 Your deed of hope will never be forgotten by those who tell of the might of God. 20 May God make this redound to your everlasting honor, rewarding you with blessings, because you risked your life when your people were being oppressed, and you averted our disaster, walking uprightly before our God." And all the people answered, "Amen! Amen!"

CHAPTER 14

Judith's Counsel. 1 Then Judith said to them: "Listen to me, my brothers. Take this head and hang it on the parapet of your wall. 2 At daybreak, when the sun rises on the earth, let each of you seize his weapons, and let all the able-bodied men rush out of the city under command of a captain, as if about to go down into the plain against the advance guard of the Assyrians, but without going down. 3 They will seize their armor and hurry to their camp to awaken the generals of the Assyrian army. When they run to the tent of Holofernes and do not find him, panic will seize them, and they will flee before you. 4 Then you and all the other inhabitants of the whole territory of Israel will pursue them and strike them down in their tracks. 5 But before doing this, summon for me Achior the Ammonite, that he may see and recognize the one who despised the house of Israel and sent him here to meet his death."

Achior Summoned. 6† So they called Achior from the house of Uzziah. When he came and saw the head of Holofernes in the hand of one of the men in the assembly of the people, he fell forward in a faint. 7 Then, after they lifted him up, he threw himself at the feet of Judith in homage, saying: "Blessed are you in every tent of Judah; and in every foreign nation, all who hear of you will be struck with terror. 8 But now, tell me all that you did during these days." So Judith told him, in the presence of the people, all that she had been doing from the day she left till the time she began speaking to them. 9 When she finished her account, the people cheered loudly, and their city resounded with shouts of joy. 10 Now Achior, seeing all that the God of Israel had done, believed firmly in him. He had the flesh of his foreskin circumcised, and he has been united with the house of Israel to the present day.

III: VICTORY

Consternation in the Camp. 11 At daybreak they hung the head of Holofernes on the wall. Then all the Israelite men took up their arms and went to the slopes of the mountain. 12 When the Assyrians saw them, they notified their captains; these, in turn, went to the generals and division leaders and all their other commanders. 13 They came to the tent of Holofernes and said to the one in charge of all his things, "Waken our master, for the slaves have dared come down to give us battle, to their utter destruction."

14 Bagoas went in, and knocked at the entry of the tent, presuming that he was sleeping with Judith. 15 As no one answered, he parted the curtains, entered the bedroom, and found him lying on the floor, a headless corpse. 16 He broke into a loud clamor of weeping, groaning, and howling, and rent his garments. 17 Then he entered the tent where Judith had her quarters; and, not finding her, he rushed out to the troops and cried: 18* "The slaves have duped us! A single Hebrew

*

15: 14, 18.
18: Jgs 5, 24; Lk 1, 28.42.
14, 18: 13, 15; 16, 5-9; Jgs 9, 54.

†

14, 6-10: In recognizing the head of Holofernes, whom he had known personally, Achior was so overcome with the evidence of the Lord's power exerted through a woman that he believed in the God of Israel.

woman has brought disgrace on the
house of King Nebuchadnezzar. Here is
Holofernes headless on the ground!"
19 When the commanders of the As-
syrian army heard these words, they
rent their tunics and were seized with
consternation. Loud screaming and
howling arose in the camp.

CHAPTER 15

1 On hearing what had happened, those
still in their tents were amazed, 2 and
overcome with fear and trembling. No
one kept ranks any longer; they scat-
tered in all directions, and fled along ev-
ery road, both through the valley and
in the mountains. 3 Those also who were
stationed in the mountain district
around Bethulia took to flight. Then all
the Israelite warriors overwhelmed
them.
Pursuit. 4 Uzziah sent messengers to
Betomasthaim, to Choba and Kona, and
to the whole country of Israel to report
what had happened, that all might fall
upon the enemy and destroy them. 5 On
hearing this, all the Israelites, with one
accord, attacked them and cut them
down as far as Choba. Even those from
Jerusalem and the rest of the mountain
region took part in this, for they too had
been notified of the happenings in the
camp of their enemies. The Gileadites
and the Galileans struck the enemy's
flanks with great slaughter, even beyond
Damascus and its territory. 6 The re-
maining inhabitants of Bethulia swept
down on the camp of the Assyrians,
plundered it, and acquired great riches.
7* The Israelites who returned from the
slaughter took possession of what was
left, till the towns and villages in the
mountains and on the plain were
crammed with the enormous quantity of
booty they had seized.
8* The high priest Joakim and the el-
ders of the Israelites, who dwelt in Jeru-
salem, came to see for themselves the
good things that the Lord had done for
Israel, and to meet and congratulate Ju-
dith. 9† When they had visited her, all
with one accord blessed her, saying:

"You are the glory of Jerusalem,
the surpassing joy of Israel;
You are the splendid boast of our
people.
10 With your own hand you have done
all this;
You have done good to Israel,
and God is pleased with what you
have wrought.
May you be blessed by the Lord Al-
mighty
forever and ever!"

And all the people answered, "Amen!"
11 For thirty days the whole populace
plundered the camp, giving Judith the
tent of Holofernes, with all his silver, his
couches, his dishes, and all his furniture,
which she accepted. She harnessed her
mules, hitched her wagons to them, and
loaded these things on them.
12* All the women of Israel gathered
to see her; and they blessed her and per-
formed a dance in her honor. She took
branches in her hands and distributed
them to the women around her, 13 and
she and the other women crowned
themselves with garlands of olive leaves.
At the head of all the people, she led the
women in the dance, while the men of
Israel followed in their armor, wearing
garlands and singing hymns.
Hymn of Praise. 14 Judith led all Israel
in this song of thanksgiving, and the
people swelled this hymn of praise:

CHAPTER 16

1* "Strike up the instruments,
a song to my God with timbrels,
chant to the Lord with cymbals;
Sing to him a new song,
exalt and acclaim his name.
2* For the Lord is God; he crushes war-
fare,
and sets his encampment among
his people;
he snatched me from the hands
of my presecutors.

3 "The Assyrian came from the
mountains of the north,
with the myriads of his forces he
came;
Their numbers blocked the torrents,
their horses covered the hills.
4 He threatened to burn my land,
put my youths to the sword,
Dash my babes to the ground,
make my children a prey,
and seize my virgins as spoil.

5* "But the Lord Almighty thwarted
them,
by a woman's hand he con-
founded them.
6* Not by youths was their mighty one
struck down,
nor did titans bring him low,
nor huge giants attack him;
But Judith, the daughter of Merari,

*

15, 7: Est 9, 5.16.
8: Est 9, 10.
12: Ex 15, 20f; Jgs 11, 34; 1 Sm 18, 6: Jer 31, 4.13.
16, 1: Pss 81, 2f; 135, 1ff; 149, 1ff.
2: 5, 23; 6, 2; 9, 7f; Ex 15, 3; Ps 46, 10.
5: 14, 8.
6: 9, 13.

†

15, 9: *You are the glory of Jerusalem, the surpassing joy of Israel; you are the splendid boast of our people:* these words are used in the liturgy of the church in regard to the Blessed Virgin Mary.

by the beauty of her countenance
disabled him.
7 She took off her widow's garb
to raise up the afflicted in Israel.
She anointed her face with fragrant
oil;
8 with a fillet she fastened her
tresses,
and put on a linen robe to beguile
him.
9* Her sandals caught his eyes,
and her beauty captivated his
mind.
The sword cut through his neck.

10 "The Persians were dismayed at her
daring,
the Medes appalled at her boldness.
11 When my lowly ones shouted, they
were terrified;
when my weaklings cried out,
they trembled;
at the sound of their war cry, they
took to flight.
12 Sons of slave girls pierced them
through;
the supposed sons of rebel mothers
cut them down;
they perished before the ranks of
my Lord.

13* "A new hymn I will sing to my God.
O Lord, great are you and glorious,
wonderful in power and unsurpassable.
14* Let your every creature serve you;
for you spoke, and they were
made,
You sent forth your spirit, and they
were created;
no one can resist your word.
15* The mountains to their bases, and
the seas, are shaken;
the rocks, like wax, melt before
your glance.
"But to those who fear you,
you are very merciful.

16* Though the sweet odor of every sacrifice
is a trifle,
and the fat of all holocausts but
little in your sight,
one who fears the Lord is forever
great.

17*†"Woe to the nations that rise against
my people!
the Lord Almighty will requite
them;
in the day of judgment he will
punish them:
He will send fire and worms into
their flesh,
and they shall burn and suffer forever."

Thanksgiving. 18 The people then
went to Jerusalem to worship God; when
they were purified, they offered their
holocausts, freewill offerings, and gifts.
19* Judith dedicated, as a votive offering
to God, all the things of Holofernes that
the people had given her, as well as the
canopy that she herself had taken from
his bedroom. 20 For three months the
people continued their celebration in Jerusalem
before the sanctuary, and Judith
remained with them.

Judith's Renown. 21 When those days
were over, each one returned to his inheritance.
Judith went back to Bethulia
and remained on her estate. For the rest
of her life she was renowned throughout
the land. 22 Many wished to marry her,
but she gave herself to no man all the
days of her life from the time of the
death and burial of her husband, Manasseh.
23* She lived to be very old in
the house of her husband, reaching the
advanced age of a hundred and five. She
died in Bethulia, where they buried her
in the tomb of her husband, Manasseh;
24 and the house of Israel mourned her
for seven days. Before she died, she distributed
her goods to the relatives of her
husband, Manasseh, and to her own relatives;
and to the maid she gave her
freedom.
25*† During the life of Judith and for
a long time after her death, no one again
disturbed the Israelites.

*

9: 9, 13.
13: Ps 144, 9.
14: Pss 33, 9; 104, 30; 148, 5.
15: Jgs 5, 5; Ps 97, 5.
16: Ps 86, 11; Sir 34, 13-17.
17: Is 66, 24.
19: Nm 31, 48-54; Dt 13, 13-18; Jos 6, 18f.
23: Gn 23, 19; 49, 29-32.
25: Jgs 3, 11.30; 5, 31; 8, 28.

†

16, 17: *Fire and worms into their flesh:* see footnote on Is 66, 24.

16, 25: The Vulgate adds: "The feast day of this victory was adopted by the Hebrews into the calendar of their holy days, and has been celebrated by the Jews from that time to the present." However, there is no other evidence of such a festivity; and it is the ancient feast of Passover to which the narrative is especially suited.

The Book of

ESTHER

The Book of Esther is named after its Jewish heroine. It tells the story of the plot of Haman the Agagite, jealous and powerful vizier of King Xerxes (Ahasuerus) of Persia (485-464 B.C.), to destroy in a single day all the Jews living in the Persian Empire. He is moved to this out of hatred for the Jewish servant Mordecai, who for religious motives refuses to render him homage. The day of the proposed massacre is determined by lot. Meanwhile Esther, niece and adopted daughter of Mordecai, is chosen queen by King Xerxes in place of Vashti. She averts the pogrom planned against her people and has the royal decree of extermination reversed against Haman and the enemies of the Jews. Mordecai replaces Haman, and together with Esther, works for the welfare of their people. The event is celebrated with feasting and great joy, and the memory of it is to be perpetuated by the annual observance of the feast of Purim (lots), when the lot of destruction for the Jews was reversed for one of deliverance and triumph by Queen Esther and her uncle Mordecai.

The purpose of the book is didactic: the glorification of the Jewish people and the explanation of the origin, significance and date of the feast of Purim on the fourteenth and fifteenth of Adar (February-March). The book was intended as a consolation for Israel, a reminder that God's providence continually watches over them, never abandoning them when they serve him faithfully or turn to him in sincere repentance. There is no justification for interpreting the story in mythological or cultic terms, as though Mordecai and Esther represented Marduk and Ishtar in their mythological triumph over two Elamite deities.

The Hebrew text of Esther is found in the Hebrew Bible, where it is the last of the five megilloth *(scrolls) read on special feasts of the Jewish liturgical year.*

The book is a free composition—not a historical document, despite the Achaemenian coloring of the narrative. Its time of composition may well have been at the end of the Persian Empire, toward the close of the fourth century B.C. The author shows skill in developing his story and in using the art of contrast for instruction and edification. The solution to the difficulties of the book is to be found in its literary presentation rather than in a forced attempt to square detailed data of the narrative with facts. The evident literary motif of the reversal of fortune of the prosperous wicked and the oppressed virtuous through eventual punishment of the former and triumph of the latter, finds parallels in the story of Joseph (Gn 37; 39—45) and of Judith (8—16). The book is vindictive, but it should be remembered that the precept of love of enemies had not yet been taught by the word and example of Christ.

The text of Esther, written originally in Hebrew, was transmitted in two forms: a short Hebrew form and a longer Greek version. The latter contains 107 additional verses, inserted at appropriate places within the Hebrew form of the text. A few of these seem to have a Hebrew origin while the rest are Greek in original composition. It is possible that the Hebrew form of the text is original throughout. If it systematically omits reference to God and his Providence over Israel, this is perhaps due to fear of irreverent response (see note on 4, 14). The Greek text with the above-mentioned additions is probably a later literary paraphrase in which the author seeks to have the reader share his sentiments. This standard Greek text is pre-Christian in origin. The church has accepted the additions as equally inspired with the rest of the book.

In the present translation, the portions preceded by the letters A through F indicate the underlying Greek additions referred to above. The regular chapter numbers apply to the Hebrew text.

The book may be divided as follows:

I: Prologue (A, 1-17)
II: Elevation of Esther (1, 1—2, 23)
III: Haman's Plot against the Jews (3, 1-13; B, 1-7; 3, 14—4, 8; B, 8; 4, 9-16; C, 1—D, 16; 5, 1-14)

IV: Vindication of the Jews (6, 1—8, 12; E, 1-24; 8, 13—10, 3)
V: Epilogue (F, 1-11)

The order of the Vulgate text in relation to the order of the Greek text is as follows:

Vulg. 11, 2—12, 6 = A, 1—17 at the beginning of the book.
13, 1-7 = B, 1—7 after 3, 13.
13, 8—15, 3-19 = C, 1—D, 16 after 4, 16.
15, 1-2 = B, 8.9 after 4, 8.
16, 1-24 = E, 1-24 after 8, 12.
10, 4—10, 13 = F, 1-10 after 10, 3.

I: PROLOGUE

CHAPTER A

Dream of Mordecai. 1*† In the second year of the reign of the great King Ahasuerus, on the first day of Nisan, Mordecai, son of Jair, son of Shimei, son of Kish, of the tribe of Benjamin, had a dream. 2 He was a Jew residing in the city of Susa, a prominent man who served at the king's court, 3* and one of the captives whom Nebuchadnezzar, king of Babylon, had taken from Jerusalem with Jeconiah, king of Judah.

4*† This was his dream. There was noise and tumult, thunder and earthquake—confusion upon the earth. 5 Two great dragons came on, both poised for combat. They uttered a mighty cry, 6 and at their cry every nation prepared for war, to fight against the race of the just. 7 It was a dark and gloomy day. Tribulation and distress, evil and great confusion, lay upon the earth. 8 The whole race of the just were dismayed with fear of the evils to come upon them, and were at the point of destruction. 9* Then they cried out to God, and as they cried, there appeared to come forth a great river, a flood of water from a little spring. 10 The light of the sun broke forth; the lowly were exalted and they devoured the nobles.

11 Having seen this dream and what God intended to do, Mordecai awoke. He kept it in mind, and tried in every way, until night, to understand its meaning.

The Plot Discovered. 12* Mordecai lodged at the court with Bagathan and Thares, two eunuchs of the king who were court guards. 13 He overheard them plotting, investigated their plans, and discovered that they were preparing to lay hands on King Ahasuerus. So he informed the king about them, 14 and the king had the two eunuchs questioned and, upon their confession, put to death. 15 Then the king had these things recorded; Mordecai, too, put them into writing. 16*† The king also appointed Mordecai to serve at the court, and rewarded him for his actions.

17*† Haman, however, son of Hammedatha the Agagite, who was in high honor with the king, sought to harm Mordecai and his people because of the two eunuchs of the king.

II: ELEVATION OF ESTHER

CHAPTER 1

The Banquet of Ahasuerus. 1† During the reign of Ahasuerus—this was the Ahasuerus who ruled over a hundred and twenty-seven provinces from India to Ethiopia—2† while he was occupying the royal throne in the stronghold of Susa, 3* in the third year of his reign, he presided over a feast for all his officers and ministers: the Persian and Median aristocracy, the nobles, and the governors of the provinces. 4 For as many as a hundred and eighty days, he displayed the glorious riches of his king-

---

*

A, 1: 2, 5.
3: 2, 6; 2 Kgs 24, 15; 2 Chr 36, 9f; Jer 22, 24ff; 24, 1; 29, 1f.
4ff: F, 2. 4ff.
9f: F, 3.
12-15: 2, 21ff; 6, 1ff.
16: 6, 3.
17: 3, 1-15; B, 1-7; E, 13.
1, 3: Jdt 1, 16.

---

†

A, 1: *King Ahasuerus:* Xerxes I (486-465 B.C.).
Mordecai: a Babylonian name, after the god Marduk. The genealogy of Mordecai is designed to reflect opposition to Israel's enemy, as narrated in 1 Sm 15, 7ff, where Saul (whose father's name was *Kish, of the Tribe of Benjamin*) conquered Agag the Amalekite; in A, 17 Haman is said to be the son of an Agagite. Further emphasis on the Benjaminite-Agagite opposition can be seen in *Shimei,* the Benjaminite who reviled David (2 Sm 16, 5ff). Jair appears to be the minor Judge, a Transjordanian Manassehite (Jgs 10, 3). The chronology of the book would make Mordecai well over one hundred years old, since he was deported with Jehoiachin about 598 B.C.; cf 2, 5f.

A, 4: The interpretation of this dream is given in F, 1-6.

A, 16: *Rewarded him:* this reward comes only later; see the sequence of events from the Hebrew text of Esther at 2, 22f, and 6, 3 below.

A, 17: *Haman . . . the Agagite:* opposed Mordecai the Benjaminite, by whom, however, he was overcome (7, 9f), just as King Agag, the Amalekite, was conquered by King Saul, ancestor of Mordecai (1 Sm 15, 7ff).

1, 1: *From India to Ethiopia:* from western India to Upper Egypt, the greatest extent of the Persian Empire achieved under Darius the Great, father of Ahasuerus.

1, 2: *Susa:* ancient capital of Elam (Gn 14, 1); under the Achamenid kings, one of the two capitals of the Persian Empire. The other was Persepolis, the summer palace of the kings.

dom and the resplendent wealth of his royal estate.

[5] At the end of this time the king gave a feast of seven days in the garden court of the royal palace for all the people, great and small, who were in the stronghold of Susa. [6] There were white cotton draperies and violet hangings, held by cords of crimson byssus from silver rings on marble pillars. Gold and silver couches were on the pavement, which was of porphyry, marble, mother-of-pearl, and colored stones. [7] Liquor was served in a variety of golden cups, and the royal wine flowed freely, as befitted the king's munificence. [8] By ordinance of the king the drinking was unstinted, for he had instructed all the stewards of his household to comply with the good pleasure of everyone.

[9]† Queen Vashti also gave a feast for the women inside the royal palace of King Ahasuerus.

Deposal of Vashti. [10]* On the seventh day, when the king was merry with wine, he instructed Mehuman, Biztha, Harbona, Bigtha, Abagtha, Zethar, and Carkas, the seven eunuchs who attended King Ahasuerus, [11] to bring Queen Vashti into his presence wearing the royal crown, that he might display her beauty to the populace and the officials, for she was lovely to behold. [12] But Queen Vashti refused to come at the royal order issued through the eunuchs. At this the king's wrath flared up, and he burned with fury. [13] He conferred with the wise men versed in the law, because the king's business was conducted in general consultation with lawyers and jurists. [14]* He summoned Carshena, Shethar, Admatha, Tarshish, Meres, Marsena and Memucan, the seven Persian and Median officials who were in the king's personal service and held first rank in the realm, [15] and asked them, "What is to be done by law with Queen Vashti for disobeying the order of King Ahasuerus issued through the eunuchs?"

[16] In the presence of the king and of the officials, Memucan answered: "Queen Vashti has not wronged the king alone, but all the officials and the populace throughout the provinces of King Ahasuerus. [17] For the queen's conduct will become known to all the women, and they will look with disdain upon their husbands when it is reported, 'King Ahasuerus commanded that Queen Vashti be ushered into his presence, but she would not come.' [18] This very day the Persian and Median ladies who hear of the queen's conduct will rebel against all the royal officials, with corresponding disdain and rancor. [19]*† If it please the king, let an irrevocable royal decree be issued by him and inscribed among the laws of the Persians and Medes, forbidding Vashti to come into the presence of King Ahasuerus and authorizing the king to give her royal dignity to one more worthy than she. [20] Thus, when the decree which the king will issue is published throughout his realm, vast as it is, all wives will honor their husbands, from the greatest to the least."

[21] This proposal found acceptance with the king and the officials, and the king acted on the advice of Memucan. [22]† He sent letters to all the royal provinces, to each province in its own script and to each people in its own language, to the effect that every man should be lord in his own home.

CHAPTER 2

Esther Made Queen. [1] After this, when King Ahasuerus' wrath had cooled, he thought over what Vashti had done and what had been decreed against her. [2] Then the king's personal attendants suggested: "Let beautiful young virgins be sought for the king. [3] Let the king appoint commissaries in all the provinces of his realm to bring together all beautiful young virgins to the harem in the stronghold of Susa. Under the care of the royal eunuch Hegai, custodian of the women, let cosmetics be given them. [4] Then the girl who pleases the king shall reign in place of Vashti." This suggestion pleased the king, and he acted accordingly.

[5] There was in the stronghold of Susa a certain Jew named Mordecai, son of Jair, son of Shimei, son of Kish, a Benjaminite, [6]* who had been exiled from Jerusalem with the captives taken with Jeconiah, king of Judah, whom Nebuchadnezzar, king of Babylon, had deported. [7]*† He was foster father to Hadassah, that is, Esther, his cousin; for she had lost both father and mother. The girl was beautifully formed and lovely to behold. On the death of her father and mother, Mordecai had taken her as his own daughter.

*

1, 10: Dn 5, 1.
14: Ezr 7, 14.
19: 8, 5.8; Dn 6, 8f.
2, 6: A, 3; 2 Kgs 24, 15; 2 Chr 36, 9f; Jer 22, 24ff; 24, 1; 29, 1f.
7: 2, 15.

†

1, 9: *Queen Vashti:* Herodotus (*Histories* 7, 61) relates that the wife of Ahasuerus was Amestris.

1, 19: *Irrevocable royal decree:* the historian Siculus indicates that such a concept of *irrevocable* laws existed in the time of Darius III (335-331 B.C.), the last of the Persian kings; cf 8, 8.

1, 22: *To each province . . . script and to each people . . . language:* many languages were spoken in the Persian Empire, the principal ones being Persian, Elamite, Babylonian, Aramaic, Phoenician, Egyptian, and Greek. Each of them had its own script.

2, 7: *Hadassah* (the feminine form of *hadas,* myrtle), was the name by which this woman would be known among her Jewish compatriots. *Esther* is a variant of the name of the Babylonian goddess Ishtar.

8 When the king's order and decree
had been obeyed and many maidens
brought together to the stronghold of
Susa under the care of Hegai, Esther
also was brought in to the royal palace
under the care of Hegai, custodian of the
women. 9 The girl pleased him and won
his favor. So he promptly furnished her
with cosmetics and provisions. Then
picking out seven maids for her from the
royal palace, he transferred both her
and her maids to the best place in the
harem. 10 Esther did not reveal her na-
tionality or family, for Mordecai had
commanded her not to do so.
11 Day by day Mordecai would walk
about in front of the court of the harem,
to learn how Esther was faring and what
was to become of her.
12 Each girl went in turn to visit King
Ahasuerus after the twelve months'
preparation decreed for the women. Of
this period of beautifying treatment, six
months were spent with oil of myrrh,
and the other six months with perfumes
and cosmetics. 13 Then, when the girl
was to visit the king, she was allowed
to take with her from the harem to the
royal palace whatever she chose. 14* She
would go in the evening and return in
the morning to a second harem under
the care of the royal eunuch Shaashgaz,
custodian of the concubines. She could
not return to the king unless he was
pleased with her and had her summoned
by name.
15 As for Esther, daughter of Abihail
and adopted daughter of his nephew
Mordecai, when her turn came to visit
the king, she did not ask for anything
but what the royal eunuch Hegai, custo-
dian of the women, suggested. Yet she
won the admiration of all who saw her.
16 Esther was led to King Ahasuerus in
his palace in the tenth month, Tebeth,
in the seventh year of his reign. 17 The
king loved Esther more than all other
women, and of all the virgins she won
his favor and benevolence. So he placed
the royal diadem on her head and made
her queen in place of Vashti. 18† Then
the king gave a great feast in honor of
Esther to all his officials and ministers,
granting a holiday to the provinces and
bestowing gifts with royal bounty.
The Plot Discovered. 19*† [To resume:
From the time the virgins had been
brought together, and while Mordecai
was passing his time at the king's gate,
20 Esther had not revealed her family or
nationality, because Mordecai had told
her not to; and Esther continued to fol-
low Mordecai's instructions, just as she
had when she was being brought up by
him. 21*† And during the time that Mor-
decai spent at the king's gate, Bagathan
and Thares, two of the royal eunuchs
who guarded the entrance, had plotted
in anger to lay hands on King Ahas-
uerus. 22 When the plot became known
to Mordecai, he told Queen Esther, who
in turn informed the king for Mordecai.
23† The matter was investigated and
verified, and both of them were hanged
on a gibbet. This was written in the an-
nals for the king's use.]

III: HAMAN'S PLOT AGAINST THE JEWS

CHAPTER 3

Mordecai Refuses to Honor Haman.
1* After these events King Ahasuerus
raised Haman, son of Hammedatha the
Agagite, to high rank, seating him above
all his fellow officials. 2*† All the king's
servants who were at the royal gate
would kneel and bow down to Haman,
for that is what the king had ordered
in his regard. Mordecai, however, would
not kneel and bow down. 3* The king's
servants who were at the royal gate said
to Mordecai, "Why do you disobey the
king's order?" 4 When they had re-
minded him day after day and he would
not listen to them, they informed Ha-
man, to see whether Mordecai's expla-
nation was acceptable, since he had told
them that he was a Jew.
Haman's Reprisal. 5 When Haman
observed that Mordecai would not kneel
and bow down to him, he was filled with
anger. 6 Moreover, he thought it was not
enough to lay hands on Mordecai alone.
Since they had told Haman of Morde-
cai's nationality, he sought to destroy all
the Jews, Mordecai's people, throughout
the realm of King Ahasuerus. 7*† In the
first month, Nisan, in the twelfth year
of King Ahasuerus, the *pur,* or lot, was
cast in Haman's presence to determine
the day and the month for the destruc-
tion of Mordecai's people on a single
day, and the lot fell on the thirteenth day
of the twelfth month, Adar.
Decree against the Jews. 8* Then Ha-

*

14: 2, 19f; 4, 11. 16.
19f: 2, 14.
21ff: A, 12-15; 6, 1ff.
3, 1: B, 3; 5, 11; E, 11.
2: C, 5; 5, 9. 13; 6, 10. 12.
3: 4, 16.
7: 9, 24ff; F, 10.
8: 3, 13; B, 4; E, 24; Dn 3, 8-12; Wis 2, 14f.

†

2.18: *A holiday:* or perhaps, "a remission of taxes."

2, 19-23: This is a resumption, in a slightly different form, of the story already told in A, 12-15.

2, 21: *Mordecai . . . at the king's gate:* to exercise watchful care for Esther. Some understand this to mean that Mordecai was stationed at the gate to render royal service; cf A, 2.

2, 23: *Hanged on a gibbet:* impaled, perhaps, after the Babylonian manner.

3, 2: *Mordecai . . . would not kneel and bow down:* in order not to render to man the homage which he regarded as belonging to God alone; cf C, 5ff.

3, 7: *Pur:* a Babylonian word which the Hebrew translates as *goral,* "lot." This word is preserved in the text because its plural, *purim,* became the name of the feast of Purim commemorating the deliverance of the Jews; cf 9, 24. 26.

man said to King Ahasuerus: "Dis-
persed among the nations throughout
the provinces of your kingdom, there is
a certain people living apart, with laws
differing from those of every other peo-
ple. They do not obey the laws of the
king, and so it is not proper for the king
to tolerate them. [9]* If it please the king,
let a decree be issued to destroy them;
and I will deliver to the procurators ten
thousand silver talents for deposit in the
royal treasury." [10]*† The king took the
signet ring from his hand and gave it
to Haman, son of Hammedatha the
Agagite, the enemy of the Jews. [11] "The
silver you may keep," the king said to
Haman, "but as for this people, do with
them whatever you please."

[12] So the royal scribes were sum-
moned; and on the thirteenth day of the
first month they wrote, at the dictation
of Haman, an order to the royal satraps,
the governors of every province, and the
officials of every people, to each prov-
ince in its own script and to each people
in its own language. It was written in
the name of King Ahasuerus and sealed
with the royal signet ring. [13]* Letters
were sent by couriers to all the royal
provinces, that all the Jews, young and
old, including women and children,
should be killed, destroyed, wiped out
in one day, the thirteenth day of the
twelfth month, Adar, and that their
goods should be seized as spoil.

CHAPTER B

[1] This is a copy of the letter:
"The great King Ahasuerus writes to
the satraps of the hundred and twenty-
seven provinces from India to Ethiopia,
and the governors subordinate to them,
as follows: [2]* When I came to rule many
peoples and to hold sway over the whole
world, I determined not to be carried
away with the sense of power, but al-
ways to deal fairly and with clemency;
to provide for my subjects a life of com-
plete tranquillity; and by making my
government humane and effective as far
as the borders, to restore the peace de-
sired by all men. [3]* When I consulted my
counselors as to how this might be ac-
complished, Haman, who excels among
us in wisdom, who is outstanding for
constant devotion and steadfast loyalty,
and who has gained the second rank in
the kingdom, [4]* brought it to our atten-
tion that, mixed in with all the races
throughout the world, there is one people
of bad will, which by its laws is opposed
to every other people and continually
disregards the decrees of kings, so that
the unity of empire blamelessly de-
signed by us cannot be established.

[5] "Having noted, therefore, that this
most singular people is continually at
variance with all men, lives by divergent
and alien laws, is inimical to our inter-
ests, and commits the worst crimes, so
that stability of government cannot be
obtained, [6]*† we hereby decree that all
those who are indicated to you in the let-
ters of Haman, who is in charge of the
administration and is a second father to
us, shall, together with their wives and
children, be utterly destroyed by the
swords of their enemies, without any
pity or mercy, on the fourteenth day of
the twelfth month, Adar, of the current
year; [7] so that when these people, whose
present ill will is of long standing, have
gone down into the nether world by a
violent death on a single day, they may
at last leave our affairs stable and undis-
turbed for the future."

[3, 14] A copy of the decree to be promul-
gated as law in every province was pub-
lished to all the peoples, that they might
be prepared for that day. [15] The couriers
set out in haste at the king's command;
meanwhile, the decree was promulgated
in the stronghold of Susa. The king and
Haman then sat down to feast, but the
city of Susa was thrown into confusion.

CHAPTER 4

Esther's Aid Sought by Mordecai.

[1]* When Mordecai learned all that was
happening, he tore his garments, put on
sackcloth and ashes, and walked
through the city crying out loudly and
bitterly, [2] till he came before the royal
gate, which no one clothed in sackcloth
might enter. [3] (Likewise in each of the
provinces, wherever the king's legal en-
actment reached, the Jews went into
deep mourning, with fasting, weeping,
and lament; they all slept on sackcloth
and ashes.)

[4] Queen Esther's maids and eunuchs
came and told her. Overwhelmed with
anguish, she sent garments for Morde-
cai to put on, so that he might take off
his sackcloth; but he refused. [5] Esther
then summoned Hathach, one of the
king's eunuchs whom he had placed at
her service, and commanded him to find
out what this action of Mordecai meant
and the reason for it. [6] So Hathach went
out to Mordecai in the public square in

---

*

9: 7, 4.
10: Gn 41, 42.
13: B, 6; 7, 4.
B, 2: E, 8f.
3: 3, 1; 5, 11; E, 11.
4: 3, 8; E, 24.
6: 3, 13; 7, 4; E, 11ff.
4, 1: Jdt 4, 12.

---

†

3, 10: *Signet ring:* a ring containing a seal which was impressed on documents to authenticate them. By giving this ring to Haman, the king bestowed on him the power to authenticate royal decrees.

B, 6: *Fourteenth day:* the Hebrew text, as in 2, 13 above, and the Greek text here translated do not agree on the day of the month specified by the king; in fact, a two-day celebration is decreed in chapter 9, and the 13th, 14th and 15th of Adar are all mentioned; see 9, 15. 18.

front of the royal gate, 7 and Mordecai told him all that had happened, as well as the exact amount of silver Haman had promised to pay to the royal treasury for the slaughter of the Jews. 8 He also gave him a copy of the written decree for their destruction which had been promulgated in Susa, to show and explain to Esther. He was to instruct her to go to the king; she was to plead and intercede with him in behalf of her people. **B:**8 "Remember the days of your lowly estate," Mordecai had him say, "when you were brought up in my charge; for Haman, who is second to the king, has asked for our death. 4, 9 Invoke the Lord and speak to the king for us: save us from death."

Hathach returned to Esther and told her what Mordecai had said. 10 Then Esther replied to Hathach and gave him this message for Mordecai: 11* "All the servants of the king and the people of his provinces know that any man or woman who goes to the king in the inner court without being summoned, suffers the automatic penalty of death, unless the king extends to him the golden scepter, thus sparing his life. Now as for me, I have not been summoned to the king for thirty days."

12 When Esther's words were reported to Mordecai, 13 he had this reply brought to her: "Do not imagine that because you are in the king's palace, you alone of all the Jews will escape. 14† Even if you now remain silent, relief and deliverance will come to the Jews from another source; but you and your father's house will perish. Who knows but that it was for a time like this that you obtained the royal dignity?"

15 Esther sent back to Mordecai the response: 16* "Go and assemble all the Jews who are in Susa; fast on my behalf, all of you, not eating or drinking, night or day, for three days. I and my maids will also fast in the same way. Thus prepared, I will go to the king, contrary to the law. If I perish, I perish!"

CHAPTER C

Prayer of Mordecai. Mordecai went away and did exactly as Esther had commanded. 1 Recalling all that the Lord had done, he prayed to him 2 and said: "O Lord God, almighty King, all things are in your power, and there is no one to oppose you in your will to save Israel. 3 You made heaven and earth and every wonderful thing under the heavens. 4 You are Lord of all, and there is no one who can resist you, Lord. 5* You know all things. You know, O Lord, that it was not out of insolence or pride or desire for fame that I acted thus in not bowing down to the proud Haman. 6 Gladly would I have kissed the soles of his feet for the salvation of Israel. 7 But I acted as I did so as not to place the honor of man above that of God. I will not bow down to anyone but you, my Lord. It is not out of pride that I am acting thus. 8 And now, Lord God, King, God of Abraham, spare your people, for our enemies plan our ruin and are bent upon destroying the inheritance that was yours from the beginning. 9 Do not spurn your portion, which you redeemed for yourself out of Egypt. 10 Hear my prayer; have pity on your inheritance and turn our sorrow into joy: thus we shall live to sing praise to your name, O Lord. Do not silence those who praise you."

11 All Israel, too, cried out with all their strength, for death was staring them in the face.

Prayer of Esther. 12* Queen Esther, seized with mortal anguish, likewise had recourse to the Lord. 13 Taking off her splendid garments, she put on garments of distress and mourning. In place of her precious ointments she covered her head with dirt and ashes. She afflicted her body severely; all her festive adornments were put aside, and her hair was wholly disheveled.

14 Then she prayed to the Lord, the God of Israel, saying: "My Lord, our King, you alone are God. Help me, who am alone and have no help but you, 15* for I am taking my life in my hand. 16* As a child I was wont to hear from the people of the land of my forefathers that you, O Lord, chose Israel from among all peoples, and our fathers from among all their ancestors, as a lasting heritage, and that you fulfilled all your promises to them. 17 But now we have sinned in your sight, and you have delivered us into the hands of our enemies, 18 because we worshiped their gods. You are just, O Lord. 19 But now they are not satisfied with our bitter servitude, but have undertaken 20 to do away with the decree you have pronounced, and to destroy your heritage; to close the mouths of those who praise you, and to extinguish the glory of your temple and your altar; 21 to open the mouths of the heathen to acclaim their false gods, and to extol an earthly king forever.

22 "O Lord, do not relinquish your scepter to those that are nought. Let them not gloat over our ruin, but turn

*

11: 2, 14; 4, 12; D, 12.
16: C, 12f.
C, 5ff: 3, 2; 5, 9.
12f: 4, 16.
15: 4, 16.
16: Dt 4, 20; 7, 6; 9, 29, 14, 2; 26, 18; 32, 9.

†

4, 14: *From another source:* very probably Mordecai refers to divine aid; the Greek additions (C) are explicit about this.

their own counsel against them and
make an example of our chief enemy.
23 Be mindful of us, O Lord. Manifest
yourself in the time of our distress and
give me courage, King of gods and Ruler
of every power. 24 Put in my mouth per-
suasive words in the presence of the lion,
and turn his heart to hatred for our en-
emy, so that he and those who are in
league with him may perish. 25 Save us
by your power, and help me, who am
alone and have no one but you, O Lord.
"You know all things. 26 You know that
I hate the glory of the pagans, and abhor
the bed of the uncircumcised or of any
foreigner. 27 You know that I am under
constraint, that I abhor the sign of gran-
deur which rests on my head when I ap-
pear in public; abhor it like a polluted
rag, and do not wear it in private. 28† I,
your handmaid, have never eaten at the
table of Haman, nor have I graced the
banquet of the king or drunk the wine
of libations. 29 From the day I was
brought here till now, your handmaid
has had no joy except in you, O Lord,
God of Abraham. 30 O God, more power-
ful than all, hear the voice of those
in despair. Save us from the power of
the wicked, and deliver me from my
fear."

CHAPTER D

Esther Is Received by the King. 1 On
the third day, putting an end to her
prayers, she took off her penitential gar-
ments and arrayed herself in her royal
attire. 2 In making her state appearance,
after invoking the all-seeing God and
savior, she took with her two maids; 3 on
the one she leaned gently for support,
4 while the other followed her, bearing
her train. 5 She glowed with the perfec-
tion of her beauty and her countenance
was as joyous as it was lovely, though
her heart was shrunk with fear. 6 She
passed through all the portals till she
stood face to face with the king, who was
seated on his royal throne, clothed in full
robes of state, and covered with gold and
precious stones, so that he inspired great
awe. 7 As he looked up, his features
ablaze with the height of majestic anger,
the queen staggered, changed color, and
leaned weakly against the head of the
maid in front of her. 8 But God changed
the king's anger to gentleness. In great
anxiety he sprang from his throne, held
her in his arms until she recovered, and
comforted her with reassuring words.
9 "What is it, Esther?" he said to her.
"I am your brother. Take courage!
10 You shall not die because of this gen-
eral decree of ours. 11 Come near!"
12* Raising the golden scepter, he
touched her neck with it, embraced her,
and said, "Speak to me."
13 She replied: "I saw you, my lord, as
an angel of God, and my heart was trou-
bled with fear of your majesty. 14 For
you are awesome, my lord, though your
glance is full of kindness." 15 As she said
this, she fainted. 16 The king became
troubled and all his attendants tried to
revive her.

CHAPTER 5

1† [Now on the third day, Esther put
on her royal garments and stood in the
inner courtyard, looking toward the
royal palace, while the king was seated
on his royal throne in the audience
chamber, facing the palace doorway.
2 He saw Queen Esther standing in the
courtyard, and made her welcome by
extending toward her the golden staff
which he held. She came up to him, and
touched the top of the staff.]
3* Then the king said to her, "What is
it, Queen Esther? What is your request?
Even if it is half of my kingdom, it shall
be granted you." 4 "If it please your maj-
esty," Esther replied, "come today with
Haman to a banquet I have prepared."
5 And the king ordered, "Have Haman
make haste to fulfill the wish of Esther."
First Banquet of Esther. So the king
went with Haman to the banquet Esther
had prepared. 6* During the drinking of
the wine, the king said to Esther, "What-
ever you ask for shall be granted, and
whatever request you make shall be
honored, even if it is for half my king-
dom." 7 Esther replied: "This is my peti-
tion and request: 8 if I have found favor
with the king and if it pleases your maj-
esty to grant my petition and honor my
request, come with Haman tomorrow to
a banquet which I shall prepare for you;
and then I will do as you ask."
Haman's Plot Against Mordecai.
9* That day Haman left happy and in
good spirits. But when he saw that Mor-
decai at the royal gate did not rise, and
showed no fear of him, he was filled with
anger toward him. 10 Haman restrained
himself, however, and went home,
where he summoned his friends and
his wife Zeresh. 11* He recounted the
greatness of his riches, the large num-
ber of his sons, and just how the king
had promoted him and placed him
above the officials and royal servants.
12 "Moreover," Haman added, "Queen
Esther invited no one but me to the ban-

*

D, 12: 4, 11.
5, 3: 5, 6; 7, 2; 9, 12.
6: 5, 3.
9: 3, 2f; C, 5ff; 6, 10.12.
11: 3, 1; B, 3; E, 11; 9, 6-10.

†

C, 28: *Wine of libations:* offered in sacrifice to the gods.
5, 1f: The Hebrew text here translated is a short form of the account already given in Greek.

quet with the king; again tomorrow I am
to be her guest, with the king. 13* Yet
none of this satisfies me as long as I con-
tinue to see the Jew Mordecai sitting at
the royal gate." 14* His wife Zeresh and
all his friends said to him, "Have a gib-
bet set up, fifty cubits in height, and in
the morning ask the king to have Morde-
cai hanged on it. Then go to the banquet
with the king in good cheer." This sug-
gestion pleased Haman, and he had the
gibbet erected.

IV: VINDICATION OF THE JEWS

CHAPTER 6

Mordecai's Reward from the King.
1 That night the king, unable to sleep,
asked that the chronicle of notable
events be brought in. While this was be-
ing read to him, 2* the passage occurred
in which Mordecai reported Bagathan
and Teresh, two of the royal eunuchs
who guarded the entrance, for seeking
to lay hands on King Ahasuerus. 3* The
king asked, "What was done to reward
and honor Mordecai for this?" The
king's attendants replied, "Nothing was
done for him."
4* "Who is in the court?" the king
asked. Now Haman had entered the
outer court of the king's palace to sug-
gest to the king that Mordecai should be
hanged on the gibbet he had raised for
him. 5 The king's servants answered
him, "Haman is waiting in the court."
"Let him come in," the king said. 6 When
Haman entered, the king said to him,
"What should be done for the man whom
the king wishes to reward?" Now Ha-
man thought to himself, "Whom would
the king more probably wish to reward
than me?" 7 So he replied to the king:
"For the man whom the king wishes to
reward 8 there should be brought the
royal robe which the king wore and the
horse on which the king rode when the
royal crown was placed on his head.
9* The robe and the horse should be con-
signed to one of the noblest of the king's
officials, who must clothe the man the
king wishes to reward, have him ride on
the horse in the public square of the city,
and cry out before him, 'This is what is
done for the man whom the king wishes
to reward!'" 10* Then the king said to
Haman: "Hurry! Take the robe and
horse as you have proposed, and do this
for the Jew Mordecai, who is sitting at
the royal gate. Do not omit anything you
proposed." 11 So Haman took the robe
and horse, clothed Mordecai, had him
ride in the public square of the city, and
cried out before him, "This is what is
done for the man whom the king wishes
to reward!"
12* Mordecai then returned to the
royal gate, while Haman hurried home,
his head covered in grief. 13 When he told
his wife Zeresh and all his friends every-
thing that had happened to him, his ad-
visers and his wife Zeresh said to him,
"If Mordecai, before whom you are be-
ginning to decline, is of the Jewish race,
you will not prevail against him, but will
surely be defeated by him."
Esther's Second Banquet. 14 While
they were speaking with him, the king's
eunuchs arrived and hurried Haman off
to the banquet Esther had prepared.

CHAPTER 7

1 So the king and Haman went to the
banquet with Queen Esther. 2* Again, on
this second day, during the drinking of
the wine, the king said to Esther, "What-
ever you ask, Queen Esther, shall be
granted you. Whatever request you
make shall be honored, even for half the
kingdom." 3 Queen Esther replied: "If I
have found favor with you, O king, and
if it pleases your majesty, I ask that my
life be spared, and I beg that you spare
the lives of my people. 4* For my people
and I have been delivered to destruction,
slaughter, and extinction. If we were to
be sold into slavery I would remain si-
lent, but as it is, the enemy will be unable
to compensate for the harm done to the
king." 5* "Who and where," said King
Ahasuerus to Queen Esther, "is the man
who has dared to do this?" 6 Esther re-
plied, "The enemy oppressing us is this
wicked Haman." At this, Haman was
seized with dread of the king and queen.
7 The king left the banquet in anger
and went into the garden of the palace,
but Haman stayed to beg Queen Esther
for his life, since he saw that the king
had decided on his doom. 8 When the
king returned from the garden of the
palace to the banquet hall, Haman had
thrown himself on the couch on which
Esther was reclining; and the king ex-
claimed, "Will he also violate the queen
while she is with me in my own house!"
Scarcely had the king spoken when the
face of Haman was covered over.
Punishment of Haman. 9* Harbona,
one of the eunuchs who attended the
king, said, "At the house of Haman
stands a gibbet fifty cubits high. Haman
prepared it for Mordecai, who gave the
report that benefited the king." The king
answered, "Hang him on it." 10 So they
hanged Haman on the gibbet which he
had made ready for Mordecai, and the
anger of the king abated.

13: 3, 2f; 6, 10.12.
14: 6, 4; 7, 9f.
6, 2: A, 12ff; 2, 21ff.
3: A, 16.
4: 5, 14; 7, 9f.
9: Gn 41, 42f; 1 Kgs 1, 33; Dn 5, 29.
10: 2, 21; 3, 2f; 5, 9.13.
12: 2, 21; 3, 2f; 5, 9.13.
7, 2: 5, 3.
4: 3, 13; B, 6.
5: 3, 8f.
9f: 5, 14; 6, 4.

CHAPTER 8

1* That day King Ahasuerus gave the
house of Haman, enemy of the Jews, to
Queen Esther; and Mordecai was admit-
ted to the king's presence, for Esther
had revealed his relationship to her.
2* The king removed his signet ring
from Haman, and transferred it into the
keeping of Mordecai; and Esther put
Mordecai in charge of the house of Ha-
man.

The Second Royal Decree. 3 In an-
other audience with the king, Esther fell
at his feet and tearfully implored him
to revoke the harm done by Haman the
Agagite, and the plan he had devised
against the Jews. 4 The king stretched
forth the golden scepter to Esther. So
she rose and, standing in his presence,
5* said: "If it pleases your majesty and
seems proper to you, and if I have found
favor with you and you love me, let a
document be issued to revoke the letters
which that schemer Haman, son of
Hammedatha the Agagite, wrote for the
destruction of the Jews in all the royal
provinces. 6 For how can I witness the
evil that is to befall my people, and how
can I behold the destruction of my
race?"

7 King Ahasuerus then said to Queen
Esther and to the Jew Mordecai: "Now
that I have given Esther the house of
Haman, and they have hanged him on
the gibbet because he attacked the Jews,
8*† you in turn may write in the king's
name what you see fit concerning the
Jews and seal the letter with the royal
signet ring." For whatever is written
in the name of the king and sealed
with the royal signet ring cannot be re-
voked.

9 At that time, on the twenty-third day
of the third month, Sivan, the royal
scribes were summoned. Exactly as
Mordecai dictated, they wrote to the
Jews and to the satraps, governors, and
officials of the hundred and twenty-
seven provinces from India to Ethiopia:
to each province in its own script and
to each people in its own language, and
to the Jews in their own script and lan-
guage. 10 These letters, which he wrote
in the name of King Ahasuerus and
sealed with the royal signet ring, he sent
by mounted couriers riding thorough-
bred royal steeds. 11* In these letters the
king authorized the Jews in each and ev-
ery city to group together and defend
their lives, and to kill, destroy, wipe out,
along with their wives and children, ev-
ery armed group of any nation or prov-
ince which should attack them, and to
seize their goods as spoil 12 throughout
the provinces of King Ahasuerus, on a
single day, the thirteenth of the twelfth
month, Adar.

CHAPTER E

1 The following is a copy of the letter:
"King Ahasuerus the Great to the gov-
ernors of the provinces in the hundred
and twenty-seven satrapies from India
to Ethiopia, and to those responsible for
our interests: Greetings!

2 "Many have become the more ambi-
tious the more they were showered with
honors through the bountiful generosity
of their patrons. 3 Not only do they seek
to do harm to our subjects; incapable of
bearing such greatness, they even begin
plotting against their own benefactors.
4 Not only do they drive out gratitude
from among men; with the arrogant
boastfulness of those to whom goodness
has no meaning, they suppose they will
escape the vindictive judgment of the
all-seeing God.

5 "Often, too, the fair speech of friends
entrusted with the administration of af-
fairs has induced many placed in au-
thority to become accomplices in the
shedding of innocent blood, and has in-
volved them in irreparable calamities
6 by deceiving with malicious slander
the sincere good will of rulers. 7 This can
be verified in the ancient stories that
have been handed down to us, but more
fully when one considers the wicked
deeds perpetrated in your midst by the
pestilential influence of those undeserv-
ing of authority. 8* We must provide for
the future, so as to render the kingdom
undisturbed and peaceful for all men,
9 taking advantage of changing condi-
tions and deciding always with equitable
treatment matters coming to our atten-
tion.

10† "For instance, Haman, son of
Hammedatha, a Macedonian, certainly
not of Persian blood, and very different
from us in generosity, was hospitably re-
ceived by us. 11* He so far enjoyed the
good will which we have toward all peo-
ples that he was proclaimed 'father of
the king,' before whom everyone was to
bow down; he attained the rank second

---

*

8, 1: 9, 1; Prv 11, 8; 26, 27; Mt 7, 2.
2: Prv 13, 22; Dn 2, 48f.
5: 1, 19.
8: 1, 19.
11f: 9, 1-4.
E, 8f: B, 2.
11: B, 3.6.

---

†

8, 8: *Whatever is written . . . cannot be revoked:* the king cannot directly grant Esther's request (v 5) to revoke the previous decree against the Jews because of the irrevocable character of the laws of the Medes and Persians (1, 19; Dn 6, 9); but he empowers Esther to issue a new decree in his name which renders the earlier decree without effect; cf 3, 12f.

E, 10: *Macedonian:* a redactor of the book in the Hellenistic period used the designation *Macedonian,* here and in v 14, to express, after Macedonia's conquest of Persia, the most odious kind of man that a Persian ruler could be supposed to think of; the Hebrew text, for a similar reason, called Haman an Agagite. See note on A, 17.

to the royal throne. 12 But, unequal to this
dignity, he strove to deprive us of king-
dom and of life; 13* and by weaving intri-
cate webs of deceit, he demanded the
destruction of Mordecai, our savior and
constant benefactor, and of Esther, our
blameless royal consort, together with
their whole race. 14 For by such mea-
sures he hoped to catch us defenseless
and to transfer the rule of the Persians
to the Macedonians. 15 But we find that
the Jews, who were doomed to extinction
by this archcriminal, are not evildoers,
but rather are governed by very just
laws 16 and are the children of the Most
High, the living God of majesty, who has
maintained the kingdom in a flourishing
condition for us and for our forebears.
17 "You will do well, then, to ignore the
letter sent by Haman, son of Hamme-
datha, 18* for he who composed it has
been hanged, together with his entire
household, before the gates of Susa.
Thus swiftly has God, who governs all,
brought just punishment upon him.
19 "You shall exhibit a copy of this let-
ter publicly in every place, to certify that
the Jews may follow their own laws,
20 and that you may help them on the
day set for their ruin, the thirteenth day
of the twelfth month, Adar, to defend
themselves against those who attack
them. 21 For God, the ruler of all, has
turned that day for them from one of
destruction of the chosen race into one
of joy. 22 Therefore, you too must cele-
brate this memorable day among your
designated feasts with all rejoicing, 23 so
that both now and in the future it may
be, for us and for loyal Persians, a cele-
bration of victory, and for those who plot
against us a reminder of destruction.
24* "Every city and province, without
exception, that does not observe this de-
cree shall be ruthlessly destroyed with
fire and sword, so that it will be left not
merely untrodden by men, but even
shunned by wild beasts and birds for-
ever."

CHAPTER 8

13† A copy of the letter to be pro-
mulgated as law in each and every prov-
ince was published among all the
peoples, so that the Jews might be pre-
pared on that day to avenge themselves
on their enemies. 14 Couriers mounted on
royal steeds sped forth in haste at the
king's order, and the decree was pro-
mulgated in the stronghold of Susa.
15* Mordecai left the king's presence
clothed in a royal robe of violet and of
white cotton, with a large crown of gold
and a cloak of crimson byssus. The city
of Susa shouted with joy, 16 and there
was splendor and merriment for the
Jews, exultation and triumph. 17* In
each and every province and in each
and every city, wherever the king's or-
der arrived, there was merriment and
exultation, banqueting and feasting for
the Jews. And many of the peoples of
the land embraced Judaism, for they
were seized with a fear of the Jews.

CHAPTER 9

Victory of the Jews. 1* When the day
arrived on which the order decreed by
the king was to be carried out, the thir-
teenth day of the twelfth month, Adar,
on which the enemies of the Jews had
expected to become masters of them, the
situation was reversed: the Jews became
masters of their enemies. 2 The Jews
mustered in their cities throughout the
provinces of King Ahasuerus to attack
those who sought to do them harm, and
no one could withstand them, but all
peoples were seized with a fear of them.
3 Moreover, all the officials of the prov-
inces, the satraps, governors, and royal
procurators supported the Jews from
fear of Mordecai; 4 for Mordecai was
powerful in the royal palace, and the re-
port was spreading through all the prov-
inces that he was continually growing
in power.
5* The Jews struck down all their ene-
mies with the sword, killing and destroy-
ing them; they did to their enemies as
they pleased. 6* In the stronghold of
Susa, the Jews killed and destroyed five
hundred men. 7 They also killed Par-
shandatha, Dalphon, Aspatha, 8 Pora-
thai, Adalia, Aridatha, 9 Parmashta,
Arisai, Aridai, and Vaizatha, 10*† the ten
sons of Haman, son of Hammedatha, the
foe of the Jews. However, they did not
engage in plundering.
11 On the same day, when the number
of those killed in the stronghold of Susa
was reported to the king, 12 he said to
Queen Esther: "In the stronghold of
Susa the Jews have killed and destroyed
five hundred men, as well as the ten sons
of Haman. What must they have done
in the other royal provinces! You shall
again be granted whatever you ask, and
whatever you request shall be honored."
13 So Esther said, "If it pleases your maj-
esty, let the Jews in Susa be permitted
again tomorrow to act according to to-

*

13: A, 17.
18: 7, 10; 9, 14.
24: 3, 8f: B, 4.
8, 15: Dn 5, 7.
17: 9, 27.
9, 1f: 8, 11f.
5: Jdt 15, 6.
6-10: 5, 11; B, 3; E, 11.
10: 9, 15; Jdt 15, 7.11.

†

8, 13: *Avenge themselves on their enemies:* partly in self-defense (E, 20), and partly to express the fact that the extreme cruelty designed against the Jews by their enemies now recoiled upon the latter as a punishment. Cf 9, 1f.

9, 10: *They did not engage in plundering:* in contrast to the Israelites who fought Agag (1 Sm 15, 9); cf also vv 15f.

day's decree, and let the ten sons of Haman be hanged on gibbets." 14* The king then gave an order to this effect, and the decree was published in Susa. So the ten sons of Haman were hanged, 15*† and the Jews in Susa mustered again on the fourteenth of the month of Adar and killed three hundred men in Susa. However, they did not engage in plundering.

16*† The other Jews, who dwelt in the royal provinces, also mustered and defended themselves, and obtained rest from their enemies. They killed seventy-five thousand of their foes, without engaging in plunder, 17 on the thirteenth day of the month of Adar. On the fourteenth of the month they rested, and made it a day of feasting and rejoicing.

18 (The Jews in Susa, however, mustered on the thirteenth and fourteenth of the month. But on the fifteenth they rested, and made it a day of feasting and rejoicing.) 19 That is why the rural Jews, who dwell in villages, celebrate the fourteenth of the month of Adar as a day of rejoicing and feasting, a holiday on which they send gifts of food to one another.

The Feast of Purim. 20 Mordecai recorded these events and sent letters to all the Jews, both near and far, in all the provinces of King Ahasuerus. 21 He ordered them to celebrate every year both the fourteenth and the fifteenth of the month of Adar 22 as the days on which the Jews obtained rest from their enemies and as the month which was turned for them from sorrow into joy, from mourning into festivity. They were to observe these days with feasting and gladness, sending food to one another and gifts to the poor. 23* The Jews took upon themselves for the future this observance which they instituted at the written direction of Mordecai.

24* Haman, son of Hammedatha the Agagite, the foe of all the Jews, had planned to destroy them and had cast the *pur,* or lot, for the time of their defeat and destruction. 25* Yet, when Esther entered the royal presence, the king ordered in writing that the wicked plan Haman had devised against the Jews should instead be turned against Haman and that he and his sons should be hanged on gibbets. 26 And so these days have been named Purim after the word *pur.*

Thus, because of all that was contained in this letter, and because of what they had witnessed and experienced in this affair, 27* the Jews established and took upon themselves, their descendants, and all who should join them, the inviolable obligation of celebrating these two days every year in the manner prescribed by this letter, and at the time appointed. 28 These days were to be commemorated and kept in every generation, by every clan, in every province, and in every city. These days of Purim were never to fall into disuse among the Jews, nor into oblivion among their descendants.

29† Queen Esther, daughter of Abihail and of Mordecai the Jew, wrote to confirm with full authority this second letter about Purim, 30* when Mordecai sent documents concerning peace and security to all the Jews in the hundred and twenty-seven provinces of Ahasuerus' kingdom. 31† Thus were established, for their appointed time, these days of Purim which Mordecai the Jew and Queen Esther had designated for the Jews, just as they had previously enjoined upon themselves and upon their race the duty of fasting and supplication. 32 The command of Esther confirmed these prescriptions for Purim and was recorded in the book.

CHAPTER 10

1 King Ahasuerus laid tribute on the land and on the islands of the sea. 2 All the acts of his power and valor, as well as a detailed account of the greatness of Mordecai, whom the king promoted, are recorded in the chronicles of the kings of Media and Persia. 3* The Jew Mordecai was next in rank to King Ahasuerus, in high standing among the Jews, and was regarded with favor by his many brethren, as the promoter of his people's welfare and the herald of peace for his whole race.

V: EPILOGUE

CHAPTER F

Mordecai's Dream Fulfilled. 1* Then Mordecai said: "This is the work of God.

*

14: 7, 10; E, 18.
15: 9, 10.
16: Jdt 15, 6.
23: 9, 29.
24ff: 3, 7; F, 10.
25: 6, 5-13.
27: 8, 12.17.
30: 9, 23-26.
10, 3: 2 Mc 15, 14.
F, 1-6: A, 4-10.

†

9, 15: This second slaughter explains the two dates (13th and 14th) of the Purim celebration by Jews in Susa (v 18).

9, 16: *Seventy-five thousand:* according to the Greek text this number was fifteen thousand.

9, 29: *Queen Esther, daughter of Abihail and of Mordecai:* the natural offspring of Abihail and adopted daughter of Mordecai; cf 2, 15. *This second letter:* for the burden of this letter see 9, 20ff. It was endorsed by Queen Esther. The first letter, written in the king's name, is referred to in 8, 9.

9, 31: *Fasting and supplication:* as the Jews had previously undertaken the duty of fasting and supplication to prevent the impending disaster, they now observe days of festival to commemorate their deliverance—in both cases (cf 4, 3.15f) at the request of Mordecai and Esther.

2 I recall the dream I had about these
very things, and not a single detail has
been left unfulfilled—3 the tiny spring
that grew into a river, the light of the
sun, the many waters. The river is
Esther, whom the king married and
made queen. 4 The two dragons are my-
self and Haman. 5 The nations are those
who assembled to destroy the name of
the Jews, 6 but my people is Israel, who
cried to God and was saved.
"The LORD saved his people and deliv-
ered us from all these evils. God worked
signs and great wonders, such as have
not occurred among the nations. 7† For
this purpose he arranged two lots: one
for the people of God, the second for all
the other nations. 8 These two lots were
fulfilled in the hour, the time, and the
day of judgment before God and among
all the nations. 9 God remembered his
people and rendered justice to his inher-
itance.
10*† "Gathering together with joy and
happiness before God, they shall cele-
brate these days on the fourteenth and
fifteenth of the month Adar throughout
all future generations of his people Is-
rael."

* 10: 3, 7; 9, 17f.21.24-28.

† F, 7: *Two lots:* in this passage of the Greek text, which gives a more religious interpretation of the feast, the *two lots* are drawn by God to determine, respectively, the destiny of Israel and that of the nations. In 3, 7 above, translated from the Hebrew text, the feast is called *Purim* because of the lots which Aman cast to determine the day for the extinction of the Jews.

F, 10: The Greek text of Esther contains a postscript as follows:

In the fourth year of the reign of Ptolemy and Cleopatra, Dositheus, who said he was a priest and Levite, and his son Ptolemy brought the present letter of Purim, saying that it was genuine and that Lysimachus, son of Ptolemy, of the community of Jerusalem, had translated it.

The date referred to in this postscript is most probably 78-77 B.C., in the reign of Ptolemy XII and Cleopatra V.

The First Book of

MACCABEES

The name Maccabee, probably meaning "hammer," is actually applied in the Books of Maccabees to only one man, Judas, third son of the priest Mattathias and first leader of the revolt against the Seleucid kings who persecuted the Jews (1 Mc 2, 4.66; 2 Mc 8, 5.16; 10, 1.16). Traditionally the name has come to be applied to the brothers of Judas, his supporters, and even to other Jewish heroes of the period, such as the seven brothers (2 Mc 7).

The two Books of Maccabees, placed last in the Douai version of the Old Testament, contain independent accounts of events in part identical which accompanied the attempted suppression of Judaism in Palestine in the second century B.C. The vigorous reaction to this attempt established for a time the religious and political independence of the Jews.

1 Maccabees was written about 100 B.C., in Hebrew, but the original has not come down to us. Instead, we have an early, pre-Christian, Greek translation full of Hebrew idioms. The author, probably a Palestinian Jew, is unknown. He was familiar with the traditions and sacred books of his people and had access to much reliable information on their recent history (from 175 to 134 B.C.). He may well have played some part in it himself in his youth. His purpose in writing is to record the salvation of Israel which God worked through the family of Mattathias (5, 62)—especially through his three sons, Judas, Jonathan, and Simon, and his grandson, John Hyrcanus. Implicitly the writer compares their virtues and their exploits with those of the ancient heroes, the Judges, Samuel, and David.

There are seven poetic sections in the book which imitate the style of classical Hebrew poetry: four laments (1, 25-28.36-40; 2, 8-13; 3, 45), and three hymns of praise of "our fathers" (2, 51-64), of Judas (3, 3-9), and of Simon (14, 4-15).

The doctrine expressed in the book is the customary belief of Israel, without the new developments which appear in 2 Maccabees and Daniel. The people of Israel have been specially chosen by the one true God as his covenant-partner, and they alone are privileged to know him and worship him. He is their eternal benefactor and their unfailing source of help. The people, in turn, must be loyal to his exclusive worship and must observe exactly the precepts of the law he has given them.

There is no doctrine of individual immortality except in the survival of one's name and fame, nor does the book express any messianic expectation, though messianic images are applied historically to "the days of Simon" (14, 4-17). In true deuteronomic tradition, the author insists on fidelity to the law as the expression of Israel's love for God. The contest which he describes is a struggle, not simply between Jew and Gentile, but between those who would uphold the law and those, Jews or Gentiles, who would destroy it. His severest condemnation goes, not to the Seleucid politicians, but to the lawless apostates among his own people, adversaries of Judas and his brothers, who are models of faith and loyalty.

1 Maccabees has importance also for the New Testament. Salvation is paralleled with Jewish national aspirations (1 Mc 4, 46—14, 41), in contrast to the universal reign of God taught by Christ in the Gospel (Mt 13, 47-50; 22, 1-14). Also, destruction of the wall of the temple separating Jew from Gentile is an act of desecration in 1 Mc 9, 54 but in Eph 2, 14, an act of redemption and unification of both through Christ. On the other hand, association, in 1 Mc 2, 52, of Abraham's offering up of Isaac (Gn 22) with his justification by God (Gn 15, 6) is reflected in Jn 2, 21f, just as the Scriptures are regarded as a source of consolation in 1 Mc 12, 9 and in Rom 15, 4.

The Books of Maccabees, though regarded by Jews and Protestants as apocryphal, i.e., not inspired Scripture, because not contained in the Palestinian Canon or list of books drawn up at the end of the first century A.D., have nevertheless always been accepted by the Catholic Church as inspired, on the basis of apostolic tradition.

1 Maccabees is divided as follows:
- *I: Introduction: Hellenism in Asia Minor (1, 1-9)*
- *II: The Maccabean Revolt (1, 10—2, 70)*
- *III: Leadership of Judas Maccabeus (3, 1—9, 22)*
- *IV: Leadership of Jonathan (9, 23—12, 54)*
- *V: Simon, High Priest and Ethnarch (13, 1—16, 24)*

I: INTRODUCTION: HELLENISM IN ASIA MINOR

CHAPTER 1

Conquests and Death of Alexander.
1* † After Alexander the Macedonian,
Philip's son, who came from the land of
Kittim, had defeated Darius, king of the
Persians and Medes, he became king in
his place, having first ruled in Greece.
2 He fought many campaigns, captured
fortresses, and put kings to death. 3 He
advanced to the ends of the earth, gath-
ering plunder from many nations; the
earth fell silent before him, and his heart
became proud and arrogant. 4 He col-
lected a very strong army and con-
quered provinces, nations, and rulers,
and they became his tributaries. 5 But
after all this he took to his bed, realizing
that he was going to die. 6 He therefore
summoned his officers, the nobles, who
had been brought up with him from his
youth, to divide his kingdom among
them while he was still alive. 7† Alex-
ander had reigned twelve years when
he died.
8 So his officers took over his kingdom,
each in his own territory, 9 and after his
death they all put on royal crowns, and
so did their sons after them for many
years, causing much distress over the
earth.

II: THE MACCABEAN REVOLT

Pact between Jews and Gentiles.
10* † There sprang from these a sinful
offshoot, Antiochus Epiphanes, son of
King Antiochus, once a hostage at
Rome. He became king in the year one
hundred and thirty-seven of the king-
dom of the Greeks.
11* In those days there appeared in Is-
rael men who were breakers of the law,
and they seduced many people, saying:
"Let us go and make an alliance with
the Gentiles all around us; since we sep-
arated from them, many evils have
come upon us." 12 The proposal was
agreeable; 13* some from among the
people promptly went to the king, and
he authorized them to introduce the
way of living of the Gentiles. 14† There-
upon they built a gymnasium in Jeru-
salem according to the Gentile custom.
15* They covered over the mark of their
circumcision and abandoned the holy
covenant; they allied themselves with
the Gentiles and sold themselves to
wrongdoing.
Egyptian Campaign of Antiochus.
16 When his kingdom seemed secure,
Antiochus proposed to become king of
Egypt, so as to rule over both kingdoms.
17*† He invaded Egypt with a strong
force, with chariots and elephants, and
with a large fleet, 18 to make war on Ptol-
emy, king of Egypt. Ptolemy was fright-
ened at his presence and fled, leaving
many casualties. 19 The fortified cities in
the land of Egypt were captured, and
Antiochus plundered the land of Egypt.
Persecution of the Jews. 20*† After
Antiochus had defeated Egypt in the
year one hundred and forty-three, he
returned and went up to Israel and to
Jerusalem with a strong force. 21 He in-
solently invaded the sanctuary and took
away the golden altar, the lampstand for
the light with all its fixtures, 22 the offer-
ing table, the cups and the bowls, the

---

*

1, 1-10: Dn 8, 20ff; 11, 3f.21.
10: 2 Mc 4, 7.
11: 2 Mc 4, 9-17.
13 ff: 2 Mc 4, 7-17.
15: 1 Cor 7, 18.
17: 2 Mc 5, 1; Dn 11, 25-28.
20–24: 2 Mc 5, 11-21.

†

1,1: *Land of Kittim:* Greece. The name referred originally to inhabitants of Kiti, capital of the isle of Cyprus, then to any Cypriots (Is 23, 1; Jer 2, 10), later to Greeks in general, and finally even to Romans. See note on Dn 11, 30. *Darius:* Darius III, Codoman (336-331 B.C.).

1, 7: *Twelve years:* 336-323 B.C.

1, 10: *The year one hundred and thirty-seven:* Antiochus IV seized the throne in September, 175 B.C. Dates are given in this book according to the Seleucid era, which however was reckoned in two different ways. Antiochians considered this date to be October, 312 B.C. (Syrian calendar), while Babylonians and Jewish priests accepted April, 311 B.C. as the commencement of the era (temple calendar). The author of 1 Mc dates political events by the Syrian calendar but religious events by the temple calendar. Accordingly, the civil New Year occurred variously in September or October, the religious New Year in March or April.

1, 14: *Gymnasium:* symbol and center of athletic and intellectual life, it was the chief instrument of Hellenistic propaganda. Jewish youth were attracted by sports and encouraged to join youth clubs. They received training in military skills and in the duties of citizens. Through participation in the intellectual life, many were gradually won over to paganism.

1, 17: *Elephants:* an important part of Seleucid armament. About 300 B.C. Seleucus I, founder of the dynasty, procured five hundred of them from India; cf 6, 34-37.

1, 20: *Defeated Egypt in the year one hundred and forty-three:* 169 B.C. No mention is made in 1 Mc of the second expedition to Egypt a year later, described in 2 Mc 5, 1.11. Dn 11, 25.19 records both.

golden censers, the curtain, the crowns, and the golden ornament on the façade of the temple. He stripped off everything, 23 and took away the gold and silver and the precious vessels; he also took all the hidden treasures he could find. 24 Taking all this, he went back to his own country, after he had spoken with great arrogance and shed much blood.

25 And there was great mourning for Israel, in every place where they dwelt,
26 and the rulers and the elders groaned.
Virgins and young men languished, and the beauty of the women was disfigured.
27 Every bridegroom took up lamentation,
she who sat in the bridal chamber mourned,
28 And the land was shaken on account of its inhabitants,
and all the house of Jacob was covered with shame.

29* Two years later, the king sent the Mysian commander to the cities of Judah, and he came to Jerusalem with a strong force. 30 He spoke to them deceitfully in peaceful terms, and won their trust. Then he attacked the city suddenly, in a great onslaught, and destroyed many of the people in Israel. 31 He plundered the city and set fire to it, demolished its houses and its surrounding walls, 32 took captive the women and children, and seized the cattle. 33*† Then they built up the City of David with a high, massive wall and strong towers, and it became their citadel. 34 There they installed a sinful race, perverse men, who fortified themselves inside it, 35 storing up weapons and provisions, and depositing there the plunder they had collected from Jerusalem. And they became a great threat.

36 The citadel became an ambush against the sanctuary,
and a wicked adversary to Israel at all times.
37 And they shed innocent blood around the sanctuary;
they defiled the sanctuary.
38 Because of them the inhabitants of Jerusalem fled away,
and she became the abode of strangers.
She became a stranger to her own offspring,
and her children forsook her.
39* Her sanctuary was as desolate as a wilderness;
her feasts were turned into mourning,
Her sabbaths to shame,
her honor to contempt.
40 Her dishonor was as great as her glory had been,
and her exalation was turned into mourning.

Prohibitions against Religion. 41 Then the king wrote to his whole kingdom that all should be one people, 42 each abandoning his particular customs. All the Gentiles conformed to the command of the king, 43 and many Israelites were in favor of his religion; they sacrificed to idols and profaned the sabbath.

44* The king sent messengers with letters to Jerusalem and to the cities of Judah, ordering them to follow customs foreign to their land; 45 to prohibit holocausts, sacrifices, and libations in the sanctuary, to profane the sabbaths and feast days, 46* to desecrate the sanctuary and the sacred ministers, 47 to build pagan altars and temples and shrines, to sacrifice swine and unclean animals, 48 to leave their sons uncircumcised, and to let themselves be defiled with every kind of impurity and abomination, 49 so that they might forget the law and change all their observances. 50* Whoever refused to act according to the command of the king should be put to death.

51 Such were the orders he published throughout his kingdom. He appointed inspectors over all the people, and he ordered the cities of Judah to offer sacrifices, each city in turn. 52 Many of the people, those who abandoned the law, joined them and committed evil in the land. 53 Israel was driven into hiding, wherever places of refuge could be found.

54*† On the fifteenth day of the month Chislev, in the year one hundred and forty-five, the king erected the horrible abomination upon the altar of holocausts, and in the surrounding cities of Judah they built pagan altars. 55 They also burnt incense at the doors of houses and in the streets. 56† Any scrolls of the

*

29-32: 2 Mc 5, 24ff.
33: 6, 18.
39 f: Tb 2, 6; Am 8, 10.
44-63: 2 Mc 6, 1-11.
46: 2 Mc 6, 2; Dn 9, 27.
50: 2 Mc 6, 18—7, 41.
54: 6, 7; Dn 9, 27; 11, 31.

†

1, 33: *City of David:* not Mount Zion on the eastern hill of Jerusalem, which David captured from the Jebusites (2 Sm 5, 7), but a new fortress built on the western hill and overlooking the temple and its courts on Mount Zion. It was occupied for twenty-six years by the Syro-Macedonian garrison, together with apostate Jews, and was a continual threat to the temple and the Jewish people (v 36); cf 13, 49ff.

1, 54: *Fifteenth day of the month Chislev, in the year one hundred and forty-five:* December 6, 167 B.C. *Horrible abomination:* in the original Hebrew, a contemptuous pun on the title "Lord of heaven" given to the god Zeus Olympios, to whom an image or perhaps an altar was erected *upon the altar of holocausts* in the temple of Jerusalem; cf Dn 9, 27; 11, 31.

1, 56f: *Scrolls of the law:* one or more of the first five books of the Old Testament.

law which they found they tore up and
burnt. 57* Whoever was found with a
scroll of the covenant, and whoever ob-
served the law, was condemned to death
by royal decree. 58 So they used their
power against Israel, against those who
were caught, each month, in the cities.
59 On the twenty-fifth day of each month
they sacrificed on the altar erected over
the altar of holocausts. 60* Women who
had had their children circumcised were
put to death, in keeping with the decree,
61 with the babies hung from their necks;
their families also and those who had
circumcised them were killed. 62 But
many in Israel were determined and re-
solved in their hearts not to eat anything
unclean; 63* they preferred to die rather
than to be defiled with unclean food or
to profane the holy covenant; and they
did die. Terrible affliction was upon Is-
rael.

CHAPTER 2

Mattathias and His Sons. 1† In those
days Mattathias, son of John, son of
Simeon, a priest of the family of Joarib,
left Jerusalem and settled in Modein.
2* He had five sons: John, who was
called Gaddi; 3 Simon, who was called
Thassi; 4 Judas, who was called Macca-
beus; 5 Eleazar, who was called Avaran;
and Jonathan, who was called Apphus.
6 When he saw the sacrileges that were
being committed in Judah and in Jeru-
salem, 7 he said: "Woe is me! Why was
I born to see the ruin of my people and
the ruin of the holy city, and to sit idle
while it is given into the hands of ene-
mies, and the sanctuary into the hands
of strangers?

8 "Her temple has become like a man
disgraced,
9* her glorious ornaments have been
carried off as spoils,
Her infants have been murdered in
her streets,
her young men by the sword of
the enemy.
10 What nation has not taken its share
of her realm,
and laid its hand on her posses-
sions?
11 All her adornment has been taken
away.
From being free, she has become
a slave.
12 We see our sanctuary and our
beauty
and our glory laid waste,
And the Gentiles have defiled them!
13 Why are we still alive?"

14 Then Mattathias and his sons tore
their garments, put on sackcloth, and
mourned bitterly.
Pagan Worship Refused. 15 The offi-
cers of the king in charge of enforcing
the apostasy came to the city of Modein
to organize the sacrifices. 16 Many of Is-
rael joined them, but Mattathias and his
sons gathered in a group apart. 17 Then
the officers of the king addressed Mat-
tathias: "You are a leader, an honorable
and great man in this city, supported by
sons and kinsmen. 18† Come now, be the
first to obey the king's command, as all
the Gentiles and the men of Judah and
those who are left in Jerusalem have
done. Then you and your sons shall be
numbered among the King's Friends,
and shall be enriched with silver and
gold and many gifts." 19 But Mattathias
answered in a loud voice: "Although all
the Gentiles in the king's realm obey
him, so that each forsakes the religion
of his fathers and consents to the king's
orders, 20 yet I and my sons and my
kinsmen will keep to the covenant of our
fathers. 21 God forbid that we should for-
sake the law and the commandments.
22 We will not obey the words of the king
nor depart from our religion in the
slightest degree."
23 As he finished saying these words,
a certain Jew came forward in the sight
of all to offer sacrifice on the altar in Mo-
dein according to the king's order.
24 When Mattathias saw him, he was
filled with zeal; his heart was moved and
his just fury was aroused; he sprang for-
ward and killed him upon the altar. 25 At
the same time, he also killed the messen-
ger of the king who was forcing them
to sacrifice, and he tore down the altar.
26* Thus he showed his zeal for the law,
just as Phinehas did with Zimri, son of
Salu.
27 Then Mattathias went through the
city shouting, "Let everyone who is zeal-
ous for the law and who stands by the
covenant follow after me!" 28* There-
upon he fled to the mountains with his
sons, leaving behind in the city all their
possessions. 29† Many who sought to live
according to righteousness and religious
custom went out into the desert to settle
there, 30 they and their sons, their wives
and their cattle, because misfortunes
pressed so hard on them.
31 It was reported to the officers and

*

57: 2 Mc 2, 14.
60f: 2 Mc 6, 10.
63: 2 Mc 6, 10.
2, 2: 1 Chr 24, 7.
9: Lam 2, 11.21.
26: 2, 54; Nm 25, 6-14.
28: 2 Mc 5, 27.

†

2, 1: *Modein:* a village twenty miles northwest of Jerusalem.

2, 18: *The King's Friends:* a regular order of nobility at Hellenistic courts. The various grades are frequently mentioned in this book: Friends, Chief Friends, Kinsmen.

2, 29: *The desert:* the sparsely inhabited mountain country southward from Jerusalem and west of the Dead Sea. It was an arid region with some perennial springs and a fair amount of rain in winter.

soldiers of the king who were in the City
of David, in Jerusalem, that certain men
who had flouted the king's order had
gone out to the hiding places in the
desert. 32* Many hurried out after them,
and having caught up with them,
camped opposite and prepared to attack
them on the sabbath. 33 "Enough of
this!" the pursuers said to them. "Come
out and obey the king's command, and
your lives will be spared." 34 But they
replied, "We will not come out, nor will
we obey the king's command to profane
the sabbath." 35 Then the enemy at-
tacked them at once; 36 but they did not
retaliate; they neither threw stones, nor
blocked up their own hiding places.
37 They said, "Let us all die without re-
proach; heaven and earth are our wit-
nesses that you destroy us unjustly."
38 So the officers and soldiers attacked
them on the sabbath, and they died with
their wives, their children and their cat-
tle, to the number of a thousand persons.

39 When Mattathias and his friends
heard of it, they mourned deeply for
them. 40 "If we all do as our kinsmen
have done," they said to one another,
"and do not fight against the Gentiles
for our lives and our traditions, they will
soon destroy us from the earth." 41 On
that day they came to this decision: "Let
us fight against anyone who attacks us
on the sabbath, so that we may not all
die as our kinsmen died in the hiding
places."

42† Then they were joined by a group
of Hasideans, valiant Israelites, all of
them devout followers of the law. 43 And
all those who were fleeing from the di-
saster joined them and supported them.
44* They gathered an army and struck
down sinners in their anger and law-
breakers in their wrath, and the survi-
vors fled to the Gentiles for safety.
45 Mattathias and his friends went about
and tore down the pagan altars; 46 they
also enforced circumcision for any un-
circumcised boys whom they found in
the territory of Israel. 47 They put to
flight the arrogant, and the work pros-
pered in their hands. 48 They saved the
law from the hands of the Gentiles and
of the kings and did not let the sinner
triumph.

Death of Mattathias. 49 When the time
came for Mattathias to die, he said to
his sons: "Arrogance and scorn have
now grown strong; it is a time of disaster
and violent anger. 50 Therefore, my sons,
be zealous for the law and give your lives
for the covenant of our fathers.

51 "Remember the deeds that our fa-
thers did in their times,
and you shall win great glory and
an everlasting name.
52* Was not Abraham found faithful in
trial,
and it was reputed to him as up-
rightness?
53* Joseph, when in distress, kept the
commandment,
and he became master of Egypt.
54* Phinehas our father, for his burning
zeal,
received the covenant of an ever-
lasting priesthood.
55* Joshua, for executing his commis-
sion,
became a judge in Israel.
56* Caleb, for bearing witness before the
assembly,
received an inheritance in the
land.
57* David, for his piety,
received as a heritage a throne of
everlasting royalty.
58* Elijah, for his burning zeal for the
law,
was taken up to heaven.
59* Hananiah, Azariah and Mishael, for
their faith,
were saved from the fire.
60* Daniel, for his innocence,
was delivered from the jaws of
lions.
61 And so, consider this from genera-
tion to generation,
that none who hope in him shall
fail in strength.
62 Do not fear the words of a sinful
man,
for his glory ends in corruption
and worms.
63 Today he is exalted, and tomorrow
he is not to be found,
because he has returned to his
dust,
and his schemes have perished.
64 Children! be courageous and strong
in keeping the law,
for by it you shall be glorified.

65 "Here is your brother Simeon who I
know is a wise man; listen to him always,
and he will be a father to you. 66 And
Judas Maccabeus, a warrior from his
youth, shall be the leader of your army
and direct the war against the nations.
67 You shall also gather about you all who
observe the law, and you shall avenge
the wrongs of your people. 68 Pay back

*

32-38: 2 Mc 6, 11.
44: Is 63, 3.
52: Gn 15, 6; 22, 1ff.
53: Gn 39, 7-10; 41, 39-43.
54: Nm 25, 10-13; Sir 45, 28ff.
55: Jos 1, 2.5.
56: Nm 13, 30; 14, 6-9.24; Jos 14, 14.
57: 2 Sm 2, 4; 7, 16.
58: 1 Kgs 19, 10.14; 2 Kgs 2, 11.
59: Dn 3, 50.
60: Dn 6, 23; 14, 31-42.

†

2, 42: *Hasideans:* in Hebrew *hasidim,* "pious ones," a religious group devoted to the strict observance of the law. They were the forerunners of both the Pharisees and the Essenes. They first supported the Maccabean movement, but subsequently opposed it, regarding it as too political.

the Gentiles what they deserve, and observe the precepts of the law."

69 Then he blessed them, and he was united with his fathers. 70† He died in the year one hundred and forty-six, and was buried in the tombs of his fathers in Modein, and all Israel mourned him greatly.

III: LEADERSHIP OF JUDAS MACCABEUS

CHAPTER 3

Defeat of Apollonius and Seron. 1 Then his son Judas, who was called Maccabeus, took his place. 2 All his brothers and all who had joined his father supported him, and they carried on Israel's war joyfully.

3* He spread abroad the glory of his people,
and put on his breastplate like a giant.
He armed himself with weapons of war;
he planned battles and protected the camp with his sword.
4 In his actions he was like a lion,
like a young lion roaring for prey.
5 He pursued the wicked, hunting them out,
and those who troubled his people he destroyed by fire.
6 The lawbreakers were cowed by fear of him,
and all evildoers were dismayed.
By his hand redemption was happily achieved,
7 and he afflicted many kings;
He made Jacob glad by his deeds,
and his memory is blessed forever.
8 He went about the cities of Judah
destroying the impious there.
He turned away wrath from Israel
9 and was renowned to the ends of the earth;
he gathered together those who were perishing.

10† Then Apollonius gathered the Gentiles, together with a large army from Samaria, to fight against Israel. 11 When Judas learned of it, he went out to meet him and defeated and killed him. Many fell wounded, and the rest fled. 12 Their possessions were seized and the sword of Apollonius was taken by Judas, who fought with it the rest of his life.

13 But Seron, commander of the Syrian army, heard that Judas had gathered many about him, an assembly of faithful men ready for war. 14 So he said, "I will make a name for myself and win glory in the kingdom by defeating Judas and his followers, who have despised the king's command." 15 And again a large company of renegades advanced with him to help him take revenge on the Israelites. 16† When he reached the ascent of Beth-horon, Judas went out to meet him with a few men. 17 But when they saw the army coming against them, they said to Judas: "How can we, few as we are, fight such a mighty host as this? Besides, we are weak today from fasting." 18 But Judas said: "It is easy for many to be overcome by a few; in the sight of Heaven there is no difference between deliverance by many or by few; 19* for victory in war does not depend upon the size of the army, but on strength that comes from Heaven. 20 With great presumption and lawlessness they come against us to destroy us and our wives and children and to despoil us; 21 but we are fighting for our lives and our laws. 22† He himself will crush them before us; so do not be afraid of them." 23 When he finished speaking, he rushed suddenly upon Seron and his army, who were crushed before him. 24*† He pursued Seron down the descent of Beth-horon into the plain. About eight hundred of their men fell, and the rest fled to the country of the Philistines. 25 Then Judas and his brothers began to be feared, and dread fell upon the Gentiles about them. 26 His fame reached the king, and all the Gentiles talked about the battles of Judas.

Regency of Lysias. 27 When Antiochus heard about these events, he was angry; so he ordered a muster of all the forces of his kingdom, a very strong army. 28 He opened his treasure chests, gave his soldiers a year's pay, and commanded them to be prepared for anything. 29 He then found that this exhausted the money in his treasury; moreover the income from the province was small, because of the dissension and distress he had brought upon the land by abolishing the laws which had been in effect from of old. 30 He feared that, as had happened more than once, he would not have enough for his expenses

*

3, 3: 2 Mc 8, 5. 24: Jos 10, 10.
19: 1 Sm 14, 6.

†

2, 70: *In the year one hundred and forty-six:* 166 B.C.

3, 10: *Apollonius:* the Mysian commander mentioned in 1, 29 and in 2 Mc 5, 24.

3, 16: *Beth-horon:* the famous pass leading up from the coastal plain to the Judean hill country. Here Joshua won an important battle (Jos 10, 10f), and in 66 A.D. a Roman force under Cestius was trapped and massacred.

3, 22: *He himself:* out of reverence for God, the author of 1 Mc prefers to use this and other expressions, such as "Heaven," instead of the divine name. Cf 1 Mc 3, 50.

3, 24: *About eight hundred:* the figures given in this book for strength of armies and number of casualties are not to be taken literally. In accordance with biblical usage, they indicate rather the importance of the battle described or the greatness of the victory.

and for the gifts that he had previously
given with a more liberal hand than the
preceding kings. 31 Greatly perplexed,
he decided to go to Persia and levy trib-
ute on those provinces, and so raise a
large sum of money. 32 He left Lysias,
a nobleman of royal blood, in charge of
the king's affairs from the Euphrates
River to the frontier of Egypt, 33 and
commissioned him to take care of his
son Antiochus until his own return. 34 He
entrusted to him half of the army, and
the elephants, and gave him instructions
concerning everything he wanted done.
As for the inhabitants of Judea and Je-
rusalem, 35 Lysias was to send an army
against them to crush and destroy the
power of Israel and the remnant of Jeru-
salem and efface their memory from the
land. 36 He was to settle foreigners in all
their territory and distribute their land
by lot.

37† The king took the remaining half
of the army and set out from Antioch,
his capital, in the year one hundred and
forty-seven; he crossed the Euphrates
River and advanced inland.

The Victories of Judas. 38*† Lysias
chose Ptolemy, son of Dorymenes, and
Nicanor and Gorgias, capable men
among the King's Friends, 39 and with
them he sent forty thousand men and
seven thousand cavalry to invade the
land of Judah and ravage it according
to the king's orders. 40† Setting out with
all their forces, they came and pitched
their camp near Emmaus in the plain.
41 When the merchants of the country
heard of their fame, they came to the
camp, bringing fetters and a large sum
of silver and gold, to buy the Israelites
as slaves. A force from Idumea and
from Philistia joined with them.

42 Judas and his brothers saw that the
situation had become critical now that
armies were encamped within their ter-
ritory; they knew of the orders which the
king had given to destroy and utterly
wipe out the people. 43 So they said to
one another, "Let us restore our people
from their ruined estate, and fight for
our people and our sanctuary!"

44 The assembly gathered together to
prepare for battle and to pray and im-
plore mercy and compassion.

45 Jerusalem was uninhabited, like a desert;
not one of her children entered or came out.
The sanctuary was trampled on,
and foreigners were in the citadel;
it was a habitation of Gentiles.
Joy had disappeared from Jacob,
and the flute and the harp were silent.

46*† Thus they assembled and went to
Mizpah near Jerusalem, because there
was formerly at Mizpah a place of
prayer for Israel. 47 That day they fasted
and wore sackcloth; they sprinkled
ashes on their heads and tore their
clothes. 48† They unrolled the scroll of
the law, to learn about the things for
which the Gentiles consulted the images
of their idols. 49*† They brought with
them the priestly vestments, the first
fruits, and the tithes; and they brought
forward the nazirites who had com-
pleted the time of their vows. 50 And they
cried aloud to Heaven: "What shall we
do with these men, and where shall we
take them? 51 For your sanctuary has
been trampled on and profaned, and
your priests are in mourning and humil-
iation. 52 Now the Gentiles are gathered
together against us to destroy us. You
know what they plot against us. 53 How
shall we be able to resist them unless
you help us?" 54 Then they blew the
trumpets and cried out loudly.

55 After this Judas appointed officers
among the people, over thousands, over
hundreds, over fifties, and over tens.
56* He proclaimed that those who were
building houses, or were just married,
or were planting vineyards, and those
who were afraid, could each return to
his home, according to the law. 57 Then
the army moved off, and they camped
to the south of Emmaus. 58 Judas said:
"Arm yourselves and be brave; in the
morning be ready to fight these Gentiles
who have assembled against us to de-
stroy us and our sanctuary. 59* It is bet-
ter for us to die in battle than to witness
the ruin of our nation and our sanctuary.
Whatever Heaven wills, he will do."

CHAPTER 4

1 Now Gorgias took five thousand in-
fantry and a thousand picked cavalry,
and this detachment set out at night 2 in
order to attack the camp of the Jews and
take them by surprise. Some men from

*

38-44: 2 Mc 8, 8-15.
38f: 7, 26; 2 Mc 4, 45; 8, 8 f; 10, 14.
46ff: 1 Sm 7, 5 f; 2 Mc 8, 16-23.
49: Nm 6, 2-5.
56: Dt 20, 5-8; Jgs 7, 3.
59: 2, 21f.

†

3, 37: This expedition, in the spring of 165 B.C., resulted in failure; cf ch 6.

3, 38: *Nicanor:* the leader of another attack against the Jews four years later. He was finally killed by Judas; cf 7, 26-46.

3, 40: *Emmaus:* probably not the village mentioned in Lk 24, 13, but a settlement about twenty miles west of Jerusalem at the edge of the hill country.

3, 46: . . . *Mizpah a place of prayer for Israel:* a holy place established of old eight miles north and slightly west of Jerusalem. It was here that Samuel began to judge the Israelites (1 Sm 7, 5-11; 10, 17).

3, 48: *To learn . . . idols:* favorable omens for the coming battle. A contrast is intended between the idol worship of the pagans and the consultation of the word of God by the Jews; cf 2 Mc 8, 23.

3, 49: *Nazirites:* see note on Nm 6, 1ff.

the citadel were their guides. 3 Judas heard of it, and himself set out with his soldiers to attack the king's army at Emmaus, 4 while the latter's forces were still scattered away from the camp. 5 During the night Gorgias came into the camp of Judas, and found no one there; so he began to hunt for them in the mountains, saying, "They are fleeing from us."

6 But at daybreak Judas appeared in the plain with three thousand men, who lacked such armor and swords as they would have wished. 7 They saw the army of the Gentiles, strong and breastplated, flanked with cavalry, and made up of expert soldiers. 8 Judas said to the men with him: "Do not be afraid of their numbers or dread their attack. 9* Remember how our fathers were saved in the Red Sea, when Pharaoh pursued them with an army. 10* So now let us cry to Heaven in the hope that he will favor us, remember his covenant with our fathers, and destroy this army before us today. 11 All the Gentiles shall know that there is One who redeems and delivers Israel."

12 When the foreigners looked up and saw them marching toward them, 13 they came out of their camp for battle, and the men with Judas blew the trumpet. 14 The battle was joined and the Gentiles were defeated and fled toward the plain. 15† Their whole rearguard fell by the sword, and they were pursued as far as Gazara and the plains of Judea, to Azotus and Jamnia. About three thousand of their men fell.

16 When Judas and the army returned from the pursuit, 17 he said to the people: "Do not be greedy for the plunder, for there is a fight ahead of us, 18 and Gorgias and his army are near us on the mountain. But now stand firm against our enemies and overthrow them. Afterward you can freely take the plunder."

19 As Judas was finishing this speech, a detachment appeared, looking down from the mountain. 20 They saw that their army had been put to flight and their camp was being burned. The smoke that could be seen indicated what had happened. 21 When they realized this, they were terrified; and when they also saw the army of Judas in the plain ready to attack, 22† they all fled to Philistine territory.

23 Then Judas went back to plunder the camp, and his men collected much gold and silver, violet and crimson cloth, and great treasure. 24* As they returned, they were singing hymns and glorifying Heaven, "for he is good, for his mercy endures forever." 25 Thus Israel had a great deliverance that day.

Victory over Lysias. 26* But those of the foreigners who had escaped went and told Lysias all that had occurred. 27 When he heard it he was disturbed and discouraged, because things in Israel had not turned out as he intended and as the king had ordered.

28 So the following year he gathered together sixty thousand picked men and five thousand cavalry, to subdue them. 29† They came into Idumea and camped at Beth-zur, and Judas met them with ten thousand men. 30* Seeing that the army was strong, he prayed thus:

"Blessed are you, O Savior of Israel, who broke the rush of the mighty one by the hand of your servant David and delivered the camp of the Philistines into the hand of Jonathan, the son of Saul, and his armor-bearer. 31 Give this army into the hands of your people Israel; make them ashamed of their troops and their cavalry. 32 Strike them with fear, weaken the boldness of their strength, and let them tremble at their own destruction. 33 Strike them down by the sword of those who love you, that all who know your name may hymn your praise."

34 Then they engaged in battle, and about five thousand of Lysias' men fell in hand-to-hand fighting. 35† When Lysias saw his ranks beginning to give way, and the increased boldness of Judas, whose men were ready either to live or to die bravely, he withdrew to Antioch and began to recruit mercenaries so as to return to Judea with greater numbers.

Purification of the Temple. 36*† Then Judas and his brothers said, "Now that our enemies have been crushed, let us go up to purify the sanctuary and rededicate it." 37 So the whole army assembled, and went up to Mount Zion. 38* They found the sanctuary desolate, the altar desecrated, the gates burnt, weeds growing in the courts as in a forest or on some mountain, and the priests' chambers demolished. 39 Then they tore their clothes and made great lamentation; they sprinkled their heads with ashes 40 and fell with their faces to the

*

4, 9: Ex 14, 21ff.
10: 2, 21.
24: Ps 118, 1ff.29.
26-35: 2 Mc 11, 1-12.
30: 1 Sm 17, 48ff.
36-59: 2 Mc 10, 1-8.
38: Ps 74, 2-7.

†

4, 15: *Gazara: Gezer* of the Hebrew Bible, five miles northwest of Emmaus; *Azotus,* Hebrew *Ashdod,* lay to the southwest; and *Jamnia,* Hebrew *Jabneel* (Jos 15, 11) or *Jabneh* (2 Chr 26, 6), to the west of Gazara.

4, 22: *Philistine territory:* the coastal cities of southern Palestine, traditionally hostile to Jerusalem. Jamnia in particular was an important base for the Seleucid power.

4, 29: *Beth-zur:* an important frontier city in the mountain area, fifteen miles south of Jerusalem. Its inhabitants were sympathetic to the Maccabees and refused to receive Lysias.

4, 35: According to 2 Mc 11, 13-15, peace negotiations followed between Lysias and Judas.

4, 36: *The sanctuary:* the whole temple area with its walls, courts and outbuildings, to be distinguished from the temple proper, the oblong edifice with porch, main room and inner shrine.

ground. And when the signal was given with trumpets, they cried out to Heaven.

41 Judas appointed men to attack those in the citadel, while he purified the sanctuary. 42 He chose blameless priests, devoted to the law; 43 these purified the sanctuary and carried away the stones of the Abomination to an unclean place. 44* They deliberated what ought to be done with the altar of holocausts that had been desecrated. 45* The happy thought came to them to tear it down, lest it be a lasting shame to them that the Gentiles had defiled it; so they tore down the altar. 46 They stored the stones in a suitable place on the temple hill, until a prophet should come and decide what to do with them. 47* Then they took uncut stones, according to the law, and built a new altar like the former one. 48 They also repaired the sanctuary and the interior of the temple and purified the courts. 49* They made new sacred vessels and brought the lampstand, the altar of incense, and the table into the temple. 50* Then they burned incense on the altar and lighted the lamps on the lampstand, and these illuminated the temple. 51 They also put loaves on the table and hung up curtains. Thus they finished all the work they had undertaken.

52† Early in the morning on the twenty-fifth day of the ninth month, that is, the month of Chislev, in the year one hundred and forty-eight, 53* they arose and offered sacrifice according to the law on the new altar of holocausts that they had made. 54 On the anniversary of the day on which the Gentiles had defiled it, on that very day it was reconsecrated with songs, harps, flutes, and cymbals. 55 All the people prostrated themselves and adored and praised Heaven, who had given them success.

56 For eight days they celebrated the dedication of the altar and joyfully offered holocausts and sacrifices of deliverance and praise. 57 They ornamented the façade of the temple with gold crowns and shields; they repaired the gates and the priests' chambers and furnished them with doors. 58 There was great joy among the people now that the disgrace of the Gentiles was removed. 59*† Then Judas and his brothers and the entire congregation of Israel decreed that the days of the dedication of the altar should be observed with joy and gladness on the anniversary every year for eight days, from the twenty-fifth day of the month Chislev.

60 At that time they built high walls and strong towers around Mount Zion, to prevent the Gentiles from coming and trampling over it as they had done before. 61 Judas also placed a garrison there to protect it, and likewise fortified Beth-zur, that the people might have a stronghold facing Idumea.

CHAPTER 5

Punishment of Hostile Acts. 1*† When the Gentiles round about heard that the altar had been rebuilt and the sanctuary consecrated as before, they were very angry. 2 So they decided to destroy the descendants of Jacob who were among them, and they began to massacre and persecute the people. 3*† Then Judas attacked the sons of Esau at Akrabattene in Idumea, because they were blockading Israel; he defeated them heavily, overcame and despoiled them. 4† He also remembered the malice of the sons of Baean, who had become a snare and a stumbling block to the people by ambushing them along the roads. 5 He forced them to take refuge in towers, which he besieged; he vowed their annihilation and burned down the towers along with all the persons in them. 6† Then he crossed over to the Ammonites, where he found a strong army and a large body of people with Timothy as their leader. 7 He fought many battles with them, routed them, and struck them down. 8 After seizing Jazer and its villages, he returned to Judea.

Liberation of Galilean Jews. 9 The Gentiles in Gilead assembled to attack and destroy the Israelites who were in their territory; these then fled to the stronghold of Dathema. 10 They sent a letter to Judas and his brothers saying: "The Gentiles around us have combined against us to destroy us, 11 and they are preparing to come and seize this stronghold to which we have fled. Timothy is the leader of their army. 12 Come at once and rescue us from them, for many of us have fallen. 13* All our kinsmen who were among the Tobiads have been killed; the Gentiles have carried away their wives and children and their goods,

*

44: 1 Kgs 8, 64.
45: 6, 7.
47: Ex 20, 25.
49: Ex 25, 23-39; 30, 1-6.
50: Ex 30, 7ff.
53.56: Ex 30, 10; Ez 43, 18-27.
59: Jn 10, 22.
5, 1f: 13, 6.
3ff: 2 Mc 10, 15-23.
13: 2 Mc 12, 17.

†

4, 52: *Twenty-fifth day of the ninth month . . . in the year one hundred and forty-eight:* December 14, 164 B.C.

4, 59: *Days of the dedication . . . Chislev:* institution of the feast of Hannukah, also called the feast of Dedication (Jn 10, 22). Josephus Flavius calls it the feast of Lights.

5, 1: The events of this chapter occurred within the year 163 B.C.

5, 3: *Akrabattene:* a district southwest of the Dead Sea.

5, 4: *Sons of Baean:* 2 Mc 10, 15-23 calls them simply Idumeans.

5, 6ff: This summary anticipates the order of events and would fit better between vv 36 and 37. It corresponds to 2 Mc 12, 17-23. The action was probably a reprisal for the massacre referred to in v 13. Timothy was the Seleucid governor of Transjordan. *Jazer:* a town on the road from the Jordan to Amman.

and they have slain there about a thousand men."

14 While they were reading this letter, suddenly other messengers, in torn clothes, arrived from Galilee to deliver a similar message: 15† that the inhabitants of Ptolemais, Tyre, and Sidon, and the whole of Gentile Galilee had joined forces to destroy them. 16 When Judas and the people heard this, a great assembly convened to consider what they should do for their unfortunate kinsmen who were being attacked by enemies.

17 Judas said to his brother Simon: "Choose men for yourself, and go, rescue your kinsmen in Galilee; I and my brother Jonathan will go to Gilead."

18 In Judea he left Joseph, son of Zechariah, and Azariah, leader of the people, with the rest of the army to guard it. 19 "Take charge of these people," he commanded them, "but do not fight against the Gentiles until we return." 20 Three thousand men were allotted to Simon, to go into Galilee, and eight thousand men to Judas, for Gilead.

21 Simon went into Galilee and fought many battles with the Gentiles. They were crushed before him, 22 and he pursued them to the very gate of Ptolemais. About three thousand men of the Gentiles fell, and he gathered their spoils. 23 He took with him the Jews who were in Galilee and in Arbatta, with their wives and children and all that they had, and brought them to Judea with great rejoicing.

Rescue in Gilead. 24* Judas Maccabeus and his brother Jonathan crossed the Jordan and marched for three days through the desert. 25† There they met some Nabateans, who received them peacefully and told them all that had happened to the Jews in Gilead: 26 "Many of them have been imprisoned in Bozrah, in Bosor near Alema, in Chaspho, Maked, and Carnaim"—all of these are large, fortified cities—27 "and some have been imprisoned in other cities of Gilead. Tomorrow their enemies plan to attack the strongholds and to seize and destroy all these people in one day."

28 Thereupon Judas suddenly changed direction with his army, marched across the desert to Bozrah, and captured the city. He slaughtered all the male population, took all their possessions, and set fire to the city. 29 He led his army from that place by night, and they marched toward the stronghold of Dathema. 30 When morning came, they looked ahead and saw a countless multitude of people, with ladders and devices for capturing the stronghold, and beginning to attack the people within. 31 When Judas perceived that the struggle had begun and that the noise of the battle was resounding to heaven with trumpet blasts and loud shouting, 32 he said to the men of his army, "Fight for our kinsmen today."

33 He came up behind them with three columns blowing their trumpets and shouting in prayer. 34 When the army of Timothy realized that it was Maccabeus, they fell back before him, and he inflicted on them a crushing defeat. About eight thousand of their men fell that day. 35 Then he turned toward Alema and attacked and captured it; he killed all the male population, plundered the place, and burned it down. 36 From there he moved on and took Chaspho, Maked, Bosor, and the other cities of Gilead.

37* After these events Timothy assembled another army and camped opposite Raphon, on the other side of the stream. 38 Judas sent men to spy on the camp, and they reported to him: "All the Gentiles around us have rallied to him, making a very large force; 39 they have also hired Arabs to help them, and have camped beyond the stream, ready to attack you." So Judas went forward to attack them.

40* As Judas and his army were approaching the running stream, Timothy said to the officers of his army: "If he crosses over to us first, we shall not be able to resist him; he will certainly defeat us. 41 But if he is afraid and camps on the other side of the river, we will cross over to him and defeat him."

42 But when Judas reached the running stream, he stationed the officers of the people beside the stream and gave them this order: "Do not allow any man to pitch a tent; all must go into battle." 43 He was the first to cross to the attack, with all the people behind him, and the Gentiles were crushed before them; they threw away their arms and fled to the temple enclosure at Carnaim. 44* The Jews captured that city and burnt the enclosure with all who were in it. So Carnaim was subdued, and Judas met with no more resistance.

45 Then he assembled all the Israelites, great and small, who were in Gilead, with their wives and children and their goods, a great crowd of people, to go into the land of Judah. 46*† When they reached Ephron, a large and strongly

*

24-36: 2 Mc 12, 10ff.
37-44: 2 Mc 12, 20-26.
40: 1 Sm 14, 9f.
44: 2 Mc 12, 21.
46-54: 2 Mc 12, 27-31.

†

5, 15: *Ptolemais:* Hebrew *Acco* (Jgs 1, 31), modern Acre, on the coast north of Haifa.

5, 25: *Nabateans:* an Arab people who acquired wealth and power as caravan merchants in the final two centuries B.C. They settled down, established Petra as their capital, and for a time controlled all of Transjordan, even as far as Damascus. It was from a Nabatean governor that St. Paul escaped about 38 A.D. (2 Cor 11, 32f).

5, 46: *Ephron:* a city in Transjordan opposite Beth-shan, about five miles east of the Jordan River. Situated on a height, it dominated the valleys of the two tributaries of the Jordan.

fortified city along the way, they found
it impossible to encircle it on either the
right or the left; they would have to
march right through it. 47* But the men
in the city shut them out and blocked
up the gates with stones. 48 Then Judas
sent them this peaceful message: "We
wish to cross your territory in order to
reach our own; no one will harm you;
we will only march through." But they
would not open to him.

49 So Judas ordered a proclamation to
be made in the camp that everyone
make an attack from the place where
he was. 50 When the men of the army
took up their positions, he assaulted the
city all that day and night, and it was
delivered to him. 51 He slaughtered ev-
ery male, razed and plundered the city,
and passed through it over the slain.

52 Then they crossed the Jordan to the
great plain in front of Beth-shan; 53 and
Judas kept rounding up the stragglers
and encouraging the people the whole
way, until he reached the land of Judah.
54 They ascended Mount Zion in joy and
gladness and offered holocausts, be-
cause not one of them had fallen; they
had returned in safety.

Joseph and Azariah Defeated.
55 During the time that Judas and Jona-
than were in the land of Gilead, and Si-
mon his brother was in Galilee opposite
Ptolemais, 56 Joseph, son of Zechariah,
and Azariah, the leaders of the army,
heard about the brave deeds and the
fighting that they were doing. 57 They
said, "Let us also make a name for our-
selves by going out and fighting against
the Gentiles around us."

58 They gave orders to the men of their
army who were with them, and marched
toward Jamnia. 59 But Gorgias and his
men came out of the city to meet them
in battle. 60 Joseph and Azariah were
beaten, and were pursued to the fron-
tiers of Judea, and about two thousand
Israelites fell that day. 61 It was a bad
defeat for the people, because they had
not obeyed Judas and his brothers,
thinking that they would do brave deeds.
62 But they did not belong to the family
of those men to whom it was granted
to achieve Israel's salvation. 63 The val-
iant Judas and his brothers were greatly
renowned in all Israel and among all the
Gentiles, wherever their name was
heard; 64 and men gathered about them
and praised them.

65† Then Judas and his brothers went
out and attacked the sons of Esau in the
country toward the south; he took He-
bron and its villages, and he destroyed
its strongholds and burned the towers
around it. 66 He then set out for the land
of the Philistines and passed through
Marisa. 67 At that time some priests fell
in battle who had gone out rashly to fight
in their desire to distinguish themselves.
68 Judas then turned toward Azotus in
the land of the Philistines. He destroyed
their altars and burned the statues of
their gods; and after plundering their
cities he returned to the land of Ju-
dah.

CHAPTER 6

Defeat and Death of Antiochus IV.
1*† As King Antiochus was traversing
the inland provinces, he heard that in
Persia there was a city called Elymais,
famous for its wealth in silver and gold,
2 and that its temple was very rich, con-
taining gold helmets, breastplates, and
weapons left there by Alexander, son of
Philip, king of Macedon, the first king
of the Greeks. 3 He went therefore and
tried to capture and pillage the city. But
he could not do so, because his plan be-
came known to the people of the city
4 who rose up in battle against him. So
he retreated and in great dismay with-
drew from there to return to Baby-
lon.

5 While he was in Persia, a messenger
brought him news that the armies sent
into the land of Judah had been put to
flight; 6 that Lysias had gone at first with
a strong army and been driven back by
the Israelites; that they had grown
strong by reason of the arms, men, and
abundant possessions taken from the
armies they had destroyed; 7* that they
had pulled down the Abomination which
he had built upon the altar in Jerusalem;
and that they had surrounded with high
walls both the sanctuary, as it had been
before, and his city of Beth-zur.

8 When the king heard this news, he
was struck with fear and very much
shaken. Sick with grief because his de-
signs had failed, he took to his bed.
9 There he remained many days, over-
whelmed with sorrow, for he knew he
was going to die.

10 So he called in all his Friends and
said to them: "Sleep has departed from
my eyes, for my heart is sinking with
anxiety. 11 I said to myself: 'Into what
tribulation have I come, and in what
floods of sorrow am I now! 12 Yet I was
kindly and beloved in my rule.' But I
now recall the evils I did in Jerusalem,
when I carried away all the vessels of
gold and silver that were in it, and for
no cause gave orders that the inhabit-

*

47: Nm 20, 17-21; 21, 21-25.
6, 1-13: 2 Mc 1, 12-17; 9, 1-29.
7: 1, 54; 4, 41ff.60f.

†

5, 65: *Sons of Esau:* Idumeans.
6, 1: *Elymais:* the mountainous region of Elam, north of the Persian Gulf. This section continues the story from 3, 37 and pertains to events preceding those in 4, 37ff.

ants of Judah be destroyed. 13 I know that this is why these evils have overtaken me; and now I am dying, in bitter grief, in a foreign land."

14 Then he summoned Philip, one of his Friends, and put him in charge of his whole kingdom. 15 He gave him his crown, his robe, and his signet ring, so that he might guide the king's son Antiochus and bring him up to be king. 16† King Antiochus died in Persia in the year one hundred and forty-nine.

The Citadel Besieged. 17*† When Lysias learned that the king was dead, he set up the king's son Antiochus, whom he had reared as a child, to be king in his place; and he gave him the title Eupator.

18* The men in the citadel were hemming in Israel around the sanctuary, continually trying to harm them and to strengthen the Gentiles. 19 But Judas planned to destroy them, and called all the people together to besiege them. 20† So in the year one hundred and fifty they assembled and stormed the citadel, for which purpose he constructed catapults and other devices. 21 Some of the besieged escaped, joined by impious Israelites; 22 they went to the king and said:

"How long will you fail to do justice and avenge our kinsmen? 23 We agreed to serve your father and to follow his orders and obey his edicts. 24 And for this the sons of our people have become our enemies; they have put to death as many of us as they could find and have plundered our estates. 25 They have acted aggressively not only against us, but throughout their whole territory. 26 Look! They have now besieged the citadel in Jerusalem in order to capture it, and they have fortified the sanctuary and Beth-zur. 27 Unless you quickly forestall them, they will do even worse things than these, and you will not be able to stop them."

Campaign against Judas. 28* When the king heard this he was angry, and he called together all his Friends, the officers of his army, and the commanders of the cavalry. 29 Mercenary forces also came to him from other kingdoms and from the islands of the seas. 30 His army numbered a hundred thousand foot-soldiers, twenty thousand cavalry, and thirty-two elephants trained for war. 31 They passed through Idumea and camped before Beth-zur. For many days they attacked it; they constructed siege-devices, but the besieged made a sortie and burned these, and they fought bravely.

32 Then Judas marched away from the citadel and moved his camp to Beth-zechariah, on the way to the king's camp. 33 The king, rising before dawn, moved his force hastily along the road to Beth-zechariah; and the armies prepared for battle, while the trumpets sounded. 34 They showed the elephants the juice of grapes and mulberries to provoke them to fight. 35 The beasts were distributed along the phalanxes, each elephant having assigned to it a thousand men in coats of mail, with bronze helmets, and five hundred picked cavalry. 36 These anticipated the beast wherever it was; and wherever it moved, they moved too and never left it. 37 A strong wooden tower covering each elephant, and fastened to it by a harness, held, besides the Indian mahout, three soldiers who fought from it. 38 The remaining cavalry were stationed on one or the other of the two flanks of the army, to harass the enemy and to be protected from the phalanxes. 39 When the sun shone on the gold and bronze shields, the mountains gleamed with their brightness and blazed like flaming torches. 40 Part of the king's army extended over the heights, while some were on low ground, but they marched forward steadily and in good order. 41 All who heard the noise of their numbers, the tramp of their marching, and the clashing of the arms, trembled; for the army was very great and strong.

42 Judas with his army advanced to fight, and six hundred men of the king's army fell. 43* Eleazar, called Avaran, saw one of the beasts bigger than any of the others and covered with royal armor, and he thought the king must be on it. 44 So he gave up his life to save his people and win an everlasting name for himself. 45 He dashed up to it in the middle of the phalanx, killing men right and left, so that they fell back from him on both sides. 46 He ran right under the elephant and stabbed it in the belly, killing it. The beast fell to the ground on top of him, and he died there.

47 When the Jews saw the strength of the royal army and the ardor of its forces, they retreated from them. 48* A part of the king's army went up to Jerusalem to attack them, and the king established camps in Judea and at Mount

*

17: 2 Mc 10, 10f.
18: 1, 33ff.
28-54: 2 Mc 13, 1-23.
28ff: 2 Mc 13, 1f.
43: 2 Mc 13, 15.
48f: 2 Mc 13, 22-23.

†

6, 16: *The year one hundred and forty-nine:* September 22, 164, to October 9, 163 B.C. A Babylonian list of the Seleucid kings indicates that Antiochus died in November or early December of 164.

6, 17: *The king's son Antiochus:* Antiochus V Eupator, then about nine years old. He was in Antioch, still in the charge of Lysias, who proceeded to govern and wage wars in his name. Both were put to death two years later, when Demetrius, brother of Antiochus IV, arrived to claim the kingship; cf 7, 1ff.

6, 20: *The year one hundred and fifty:* October, 163, to September, 162 B.C.

Zion. 49*† He made peace with the men of Beth-zur, and they evacuated the city, because they had no food there to enable them to stand a siege, for that was a sabbath year in the land. 50 The king took Beth-zur and stationed a garrison there to hold it. 51 For many days he besieged the sanctuary, setting up artillery and machines, fire-throwers, catapults and mechanical bows for shooting arrows and slingstones. 52 The Jews countered by setting up machines of their own, and kept up the fight a long time. 53 But there were no provisions in the storerooms, because it was the seventh year, and the tide-over provisions had been eaten up by those who had been rescued from the Gentiles and brought to Judea. 54 Few men remained in the sanctuary; the rest scattered, each to his own home, for the famine was too much for them.

Peace Treaty. 55* Lysias heard that Philip, whom King Antiochus, before his death, had appointed to train his son Antiochus to be king, 56 had returned from Persia and Media with the army that accompanied the king, and that he was seeking to take over the government. 57* So he hastily resolved to withdraw. He said to the king, the leaders of the army, and the soldiers: "We are growing weaker every day, our provisions are scanty, the place we are besieging is strong, and it is our duty to take care of the affairs of the kingdom. 58 Therefore let us now come to terms with these men, and make peace with them and all their nation. 59 Let us grant them freedom to live according to their own laws as formerly; it was on account of their laws, which we abolished, that they became angry and did all these things."

60 The proposal found favor with the king and the leaders; 61 he sent peace terms to the Jews, and they accepted. So the king and the leaders swore an oath to them, and on these terms they evacuated the fortification. 62 But when the king entered Mount Zion and saw how the place was fortified, he broke the oath he had sworn and gave orders for the encircling wall to be destroyed. 63 Then he departed in haste and returned to Antioch, where he found Philip in possession of the city. He fought against him and took the city by force.

CHAPTER 7

Expedition of Bacchides and Alcimus. 1*† In the year one hundred and fifty-one, Demetrius, son of Seleucus, set out from Rome, arrived with a few men in a city on the seacoast, and began to rule there. 2 As he was preparing to enter the royal palace of his ancestors, the soldiers seized Antiochus and Lysias to bring them to him. 3 When he was informed of this, he said, "Do not show me their faces." 4 So the soldiers killed them, and Demetrius sat on the royal throne.

5† Then all the lawless and impious men of Israel came to him. They were led by Alcimus, who desired to be high priest. 6 They made this accusation to the king against the people: "Judas and his brothers have destroyed all your friends and have driven us out of our country. 7 So now, send a man whom you trust to go and see all the havoc Judas has done to us and to the king's land, and let him punish them and all their supporters."

8 Then the king chose Bacchides, one of the King's Friends, governor of West-of-Euphrates, a great man in the kingdom, and faithful to the king. 9* He sent him and the impious Alcimus, to whom he granted the high priesthood, with orders to take revenge on the Israelites. 10 They set out and, on arriving in the land of Judah with a great army, sent messengers who spoke deceitfully to Judas and his brothers in peaceful terms. 11 But these paid no attention to their words, seeing that they had come with a great army. 12 A group of scribes, however, gathered about Alcimus and Bacchides to ask for a just agreement. 13* The Hasideans were the first among the Israelites to seek peace with them, 14 for they said, "A priest of the line of Aaron has come with the army, and he will not do us any wrong." 15 He spoke with them peacefully and swore to them, "We will not try to injure you or your friends." 16 So they trusted him. But he arrested sixty of them and killed them in one day, according to the text of Scripture:

17* "The flesh of your saints they have
strewn,

*
49: Lv 25, 2.
55-63: 2 Mc 13, 23-26.
57: 2 Mc 11, 13ff.
7, 1-7: 2 Mc 14, 1-11.
9ff: 2 Mc 14, 46.
13f: 2, 42.
17: Ps 79, 1ff.

†
6, 49: *A sabbath year in the land:* when sowing and reaping were prohibited (Ex 23, 10f; Lv 25, 2-7). The year without a harvest (autumn of 164 to autumn of 163) was followed by a food shortage.

7, 1ff: *The year one hundred and fifty-one:* the spring of 161 B.C. *Demetrius,* son of Seleucus, was the lawful heir to the kingdom; but when only nine years old, he was taken as a hostage at Rome in place of his uncle, who ruled as Antiochus IV Epiphanes. At the age of twenty-five Demetrius fled secretly from Rome and, with the support of the Syrians, overcame his rival Antiochus V and put him to death. *The royal palace:* at Antioch.

7, 5f: *Alcimus:* a renegade Jew hostile to the Maccabees, who became high priest after the death of Menelaus (2 Mc 14, 3). He received confirmation in his office from the new King Demetrius (v 9), and brought malicious charges against *Judas and his brothers* and the people (v 6). He wrought more evils on the Israelites than the Gentiles had done (v 23).

and their blood they have shed
round about Jerusalem,
and there was no one to bury
them."

18 Then fear and dread of them came
upon all the people, who said: "There is
no truth or justice among them; they vio-
lated the agreement and the oath that
they swore."
19† Bacchides withdrew from Jerusa-
lem and pitched his camp in Beth-zaith.
He had many of the men arrested who
deserted to him, throwing them into the
great pit. 20 He handed the province over
to Alcimus, leaving troops to help him,
while he himself returned to the king.
21 Alcimus spared no pains to maintain
his high priesthood, 22 and all those who
were disturbing their people gathered
about him. They took possession of the
land of Judah and caused great distress
in Israel. 23 When Judas saw all the evils
that Alcimus and his men were bringing
upon the Israelites, more than even the
Gentiles had done, 24 he went about all
the borders of Judea and took revenge
on the men who had deserted, prevent-
ing them from going out into the coun-
try. 25 But when Alcimus saw that Judas
and his followers were gaining strength
and realized that he could not oppose
them, he returned to the king and ac-
cused them of grave crimes.
Defeat of Nicanor. 26* Then the king
sent Nicanor, one of his famous officers,
who was a bitter enemy of Israel, with
orders to destroy the people. 27† Nicanor
came to Jerusalem with a large force
and deceitfully sent to Judas and his
brothers this peaceable message: 28 "Let
there be no fight between me and you.
I will come with a few men to meet you
peaceably."
29 So he came to Judas, and they
greeted one another peaceably. But Ju-
das' enemies were prepared to seize
him. 30* When he became aware that Ni-
canor had come to him with treachery
in mind, Judas was afraid and would not
meet him again. 31† When Nicanor saw
that his plan had been discovered, he
went out to fight Judas near Caphar-
salama. 32 About five hundred men of
Nicanor's army fell; the rest fled to the
City of David.
33* After this, Nicanor went up to
Mount Zion. Some of the priests from
the sanctuary and some of the elders of
the people came out to greet him peace-
ably and to show him the holocaust that
was being offered for the king. 34† But
he mocked and ridiculed them, defiled
them, and spoke disdainfully. 35 In a
rage he swore: "If Judas and his army
are not delivered to me at once, when
I return victorious I will burn this temple
down." He went away in great anger.
36* The priests, however, went in and
stood before the altar and the sanctuary.
They wept and said: 37 "You have chosen
this house to bear your name, to be a
house of prayer and petition for your
people. 38 Take revenge on this man and
his army, and let them fall by the sword.
Remember their blasphemies, and do
not let them continue."
39 Nicanor left Jerusalem and pitched
his camp at Beth-horon, where the Syr-
ian army joined him. 40† But Judas
camped in Adasa with three thousand
men. Here Judas uttered this prayer:
41* "When they who were sent by the
king blasphemed, your angel went out
and killed a hundred and eighty-five
thousand of them. 42* In the same way,
crush this army before us today, and let
the rest know that Nicanor spoke wick-
edly against your sanctuary; judge him
according to his wickedness."
43* The armies met in battle on the
thirteenth day of the month Adar. Nica-
nor's army was crushed, and he himself
was the first to fall in the battle. 44 When
his army saw that Nicanor was dead,
they threw down their arms and fled.
45 The Jews pursued them a day's jour-
ney, from Adasa to near Gazara, blow-
ing the trumpets behind them as signals.
46 From all the surrounding villages of
Judea people came out and closed in on
them. They hemmed them in, and all the
enemies fell by the sword; not a single
one escaped.
47 Then the Jews collected the spoils
and the booty; they cut off Nicanor's
head and his right arm, which he had
lifted up so arrogantly. These they
brought to Jerusalem and displayed
there. 48 The people rejoiced greatly, and
observed that day as a great festival.
49† They decreed that it should be ob-
served every year on the thirteenth of
Adar. 50† And for a short time the land
of Judah was quiet.

*

26f: 3, 38; 2 Mc 8, 9; 14, 12f.
30: 2 Mc 14, 30.
33-38: 2 Mc 14, 31-36.
36: Jl 2, 17.
41f: 2 Mc 8, 19; 15, 22f.
42: Is 37, 36ff.
43: 2 Mc 15, 25-35.

†

7, 19: *Beth-zaith:* about three miles north of Beth-zur and twelve miles south of Jerusalem.

7, 27: *Nicanor . . . deceitfully sent to Judas:* a more favorable picture of Nicanor, as an honest man who became a personal friend of Judas, is given in 2 Mc 14, 17-25. Their friendship was broken by the intrigues of Alcimus (2 Mc 14, 26-30).

7, 31: *Caphar-salama:* a village seven miles north-northwest of Jerusalem, on the road leading to Beth-horon.

7, 34: *Defiled them:* spitting on the priests caused them to become legally defiled.

7, 40: *Adasa:* a village southeast of Caphar-salama.

7, 49: *The thirteenth of Adar:* March 27, 160 B.C. This day in the Jewish calendar was called the "Day of Nicanor" (2 Mc 15, 36), but it was not long celebrated by the Jews.

7, 50: *A short time:* about one month following the death of Nicanor. After that began the attack of Bacchides resulting in the death of Judas (9, 1-18).

CHAPTER 8

Treaty with the Romans. 1† Judas had heard of the reputation of the Romans. They were valiant fighters and acted amiably to all who took their side. They established a friendly alliance with all who applied to them. 2† He was also told of their battles and the brave deeds that they had performed against the Gauls, conquering them and forcing them to pay tribute. 3 They had gotten possession of the silver and gold mines in Spain, 4 and by planning and persistence had conquered the whole country, although it was very remote from their own. They had crushed the kings who had come against them from the far corners of the earth and had inflicted on them severe defeat, and the rest paid tribute to them every year. 5† Philip and Perseus, king of the Macedonians, and the others who opposed them in battle had been overwhelmed and subjugated. 6† Antiochus the Great, king of Asia, who had fought against them with a hundred and twenty elephants and with cavalry and chariots and a very great army, had been defeated by them. 7 They had taken him alive and obliged him and the kings who succeeded him to pay a heavy tribute, to give hostages and a section of 8† Lycia, Mysia, and Lydia from among their best provinces. The Romans took these from him and gave them to King Eumenes. 9† When the men of Greece had planned to come and destroy them, 10 the Romans discovered it, and sent against the Greeks a single general who made war on them. Many were wounded and fell, and the Romans took their wives and children captive. They plundered them, took possession of their land, tore down their strongholds and reduced them to slavery even to this day. 11 All the other kingdoms and islands that had ever opposed them they destroyed and enslaved; 12 with their friends, however, and those who relied on them, they maintained friendship. They had conquered kings both far and near, and all who heard of their fame were afraid of them. 13 In truth, those whom they desired to help to a kingdom became kings, and those whom they wished to depose they deposed; and they were greatly exalted. 14 Yet with all this, none of them put on a crown or wore purple as a display of grandeur. 15 They had made for themselves a senate house, and every day three hundred and twenty men took counsel, deliberating on all that concerned the people and their well-being. 16† They entrusted their government to one man every year, to rule over their entire country, and they all obeyed that one, and there was no envy or jealousy among them.

17* So Judas chose Eupolemus, son of John, son of Accos, and Jason, son of Eleazar, and sent them to Rome to establish an alliance of friendship with them. 18 He did this to get rid of the yoke, for it was obvious that the kingdom of the Greeks was subjecting Israel to slavery. 19 After making a very long journey to Rome, the envoys entered the senate and spoke as follows: 20 "Judas, called Maccabeus, and his brothers, with the Jewish people, have sent us to you to make a peaceful alliance with you, and to enroll ourselves among your allies and friends." 21 The proposal pleased the Romans, 22*† and this is a copy of the reply they inscribed on bronze tablets and sent to Jerusalem, to remain there with the Jews as a record of peace and alliance:

*

8, 17: 12, 1f; 15, 15-22. 22: 14, 18.

†

8, 1: This chapter contains the account of the embassy which Judas sent to Rome, probably before the death of Nicanor, to conclude a treaty of alliance between Rome and the Jewish nation. Without precise chronology, the pertinent data are gathered into a unified theme.

The image of the Roman Republic greatly impressed the smaller Eastern peoples seeking support against their overlords (1-16), because of Roman success in war (2-11) and effective aid to their allies (12-13). Numerous interventions by Rome in the politics of the Near East bear witness to its power and prestige in the second century B.C. Cf 1 Mc 1, 10; 7, 2; 12, 3; 15, 15-24; 2 Mc 11, 34. With the Roman control of Palestine in 63 B.C., the Republic and later the Empire became heartily detested. The eulogy of Rome in this chapter is one of the reasons why 1 Maccabees was not preserved by the Palestinian Jews of the century that followed.

8, 2: *Gauls:* probably the Celts of northern Italy and southern France, subdued by the Romans in 222 B.C., and again in 200-191 B.C.; but perhaps also those in Asia Minor (the Galatians), whom the Romans defeated in 189 B.C.

8, 5: *Phillip:* Phillip V of Macedonia, defeated by a Graeco-Roman alliance at Cynoscephalae in 197 B.C. *Perseus,* his son, was defeated at Pydna in 168 B.C., and died a prisoner. With this, the kingdom of Macedonia came to an end.

8, 6: *Antiochus:* Antiochus III, greatest of the Seleucid kings. He was defeated at Magnesia in 190 B.C. By the Treaty of Apamea in 189, he was obliged to pay Rome a crushing indemnity of 15,000 talents. It was the weakening of Antiochene power and the growing military and economic influence of Rome that led Antiochus IV to adopt the policy of political, religious and cultural unification of Syria and Palestine.

8, 8: *Lycia, Mysia:* regions in western Asia Minor. These names are restored here by conjectural emendation; the Greek text has "India, Media," most likely through scribal error. *Eumenes:* Eumenes II (197-158), king of Pergamum, an ally of Rome who benefited greatly from Antiochus' losses.

8, 9f: The revolt of the Achaean League, inserted here, occurred in 146 B.C., after Judas' time. It was crushed by the Roman consul Lucius Mummius and marked the end of Greek independence. The author regards all Greeks as the enemies of God.

8, 16: *They entrusted their government to one man:* actually the Roman Republic always had two consuls as joint heads of the government. Presumably, a single one dealt with embassies and answered letters, hence the impression the Jews received; cf 15, 16.

8, 22: *The reply . . . on bronze tablets and sent to Jerusalem:* The decree of the Senate would be inscribed on bronze and kept in the Roman Capitol, with only a copy in letter form sent to Jerusalem. The translation of the decree into Hebrew and then into Greek, as found here in 1 Mc, may have occasioned this error.

23 “May it be well with the Romans and
the Jewish nation at sea and on land for-
ever; may sword and enemy be far from
them. 24 But if war is first made on Rome,
or any of its allies in any of their domin-
ions, 25 the Jewish nation will help them
wholeheartedly, as the occasion shall
demand; 26 and to those who wage war
they shall not give nor provide grain,
arms, money, or ships; this is Rome’s
decision. They shall fulfill their obliga-
tions without receiving any recompense.
27 In the same way, if war is made first
on the Jewish nation, the Romans will
help them willingly, as the occasion shall
demand, 28 and to those who are attack-
ing them there shall not be given grain,
arms, money, or ships; this is Rome’s
decision. They shall fulfill their obliga-
tions without deception. 29 On these
terms the Romans have made an agree-
ment with the Jewish people. 30 But if
both parties hereafter decide to add or
take away anything, they shall do as
they choose, and whatever they shall
add or take away shall be valid.

31 “Moreover, concerning the wrongs
that King Demetrius has done to them,
we have written to him thus: ‘Why have
you made your yoke heavy upon our
friends and allies the Jews? 32 If they
complain about you again, we will do
them justice and make war on you by
land and sea.’ ”

CHAPTER 9

Invasion of Judah. 1 When Demetrius
heard that Nicanor and his army had
fallen in battle, he again sent Bacchi-
des and Alcimus into the land of Judah,
along with the right wing of his army.
2† They took the road to Galilee, and
camping opposite the ascent at Arbela,
they captured it and killed many people.
3† In the first month of the year one hun-
dred and fifty-two, they encamped
against Jerusalem. 4 Then they set out
for Berea with twenty thousand men and
two thousand cavalry. 5 Judas, with
three thousand picked men, had
camped at Elasa. 6 When his men saw
the great number of the troops, they
were very much afraid, and many
slipped away from the camp, until only
eight hundred men remained.

7 As Judas saw that his army was
melting away just when the battle was
imminent, he was panic-stricken, be-
cause he had no time to gather them
together. 8 But in spite of his discourage-
ment, he said to those who remained:
“Let us go forward to meet our enemies;
perhaps we can put up a good fight
against them.” 9 They tried to dissuade
him, saying: “We certainly cannot. Let
us save our lives now, and come back
with our kinsmen, and then fight against
them. Now we are too few.” 10 But Judas
said: “Far be it from me to do such a
thing as to flee from them! If our time
has come, let us die bravely for our kins-
men and not leave a stain upon our
glory!”

Death of Judas. 11 Then the army of
Bacchides moved out of camp and took
its position for combat. The cavalry were
divided into two squadrons, and the
slingers and the archers came on ahead
of the army, and all the valiant men
were in the front line. 12 Bacchides was
on the right wing. Flanked by the two
squadrons, the phalanx attacked as they
blew their trumpets. Those who were on
Judas’ side also blew their trumpets.
13 The earth shook with the noise of the
armies, and the battle raged from morn-
ing until evening. 14 Seeing that Bac-
chides was on the right, with the main
force of his army, Judas, with all the
most stouthearted rallying to him,
15† drove back the right wing and pur-
sued them as far as the mountain slopes.
16 But when the men on the left wing saw
that the right wing was driven back, they
turned and followed Judas and his men,
taking them in the rear. 17 The battle was
fought desperately, and many on both
sides fell wounded. 18 Then Judas fell,
and the rest fled.

19 Jonathan and Simon took their
brother Judas and buried him in the
tomb of their fathers at Modein. 20 All
Israel bewailed him in great grief. They
mourned for him many days, and they
said, 21* “How the mighty one has fallen,
the savior of Israel!” 22 The other acts
of Judas, his battles, the brave deeds he
performed, and his greatness have not
been recorded; but they were very
many.

IV: LEADERSHIP OF JONATHAN

Bacchides and Jonathan. 23 After the
death of Judas, the transgressors of the
law raised their heads in every part of
Israel, and all kinds of evildoers ap-
peared. 24 In those days there was a very

*

9, 21: 2 Sm 1, 27.

†

9, 2: *They took the road . . . Arbela, they captured it:* This passage is restored, in part, by conjectural emendation. The present Greek text could be translated, “They took the road to Gilgal, and camping opposite Mesaloth at Arbela, they captured it.” But Arbela (modern Khirbet Irbid) was in Galilee—on a high hill overlooking the western shore of the Sea of Galilee. Gilgal, on the contrary, was in the Jordan valley near Jericho. “Mesaloth” is probably a corrupt form of a Hebrew word meaning “steps, ascent.”

9, 3: *The first month of the year one hundred and fifty-two:* April/May 160 B.C., by the temple calendar.

9, 15: *As far as the mountain slopes:* conjectural emendation. The Greek text has “as far as Mount Azotus”; this is most unlikely. Apparently the Greek translator mistook the Hebrew word *ashdôt,* “slopes,” *for ašdôd,* “Azotus.”

great famine, and the country deserted
to them. 25 Bacchides chose impious men
and made them masters of the country.
26 These sought out and hunted down the
friends of Judas and brought them to
Bacchides, who punished and derided
them. 27 There had not been such great
distress in Israel since the time prophets
ceased to appear among the people.

28 Then all the friends of Judas came
together and said to Jonathan: 29 "Since
your brother Judas died, there has been
no one like him to oppose our enemies,
Bacchides and those who are hostile to
our nation. 30 Now therefore we have
chosen you today to be our ruler and
leader in his place, and to fight our bat-
tle." 31 From that moment Jonathan ac-
cepted the leadership, and took the place
of Judas his brother.

32 When Bacchides learned of it, he
sought to kill him. 33† But Jonathan and
his brother Simon and all the men with
him discovered this, and they fled to the
desert of Tekoa and camped by the
waters of the pool of Asphar.†

35*† Jonathan sent his brother as
leader of the convoy to ask permission
of his friends, the Nabateans, to deposit
with them their great quantity of bag-
gage. 36† But the sons of Jambri from
Medaba made a raid and seized and car-
ried off John and everything he had.
37 After this, word was brought to Jona-
than and his brother Simon: "The sons
of Jambri are celebrating a great wed-
ding, and with a large escort they are
bringing the bride, the daughter of one
of the great princes of Canaan, from
Nadabath." 38 Remembering the blood
of John their brother, they went up and
hid themselves under cover of the moun-
tain. 39 They watched, and suddenly
saw a noisy crowd with baggage; the
bridegroom and his friends and kins-
men had come out to meet the bride's
party with tambourines and musicians
and much equipment. 40 The Jews rose
up against them from their ambush and
killed them. Many fell wounded, and af-
ter the survivors fled toward the moun-
tain, all their spoils were taken. 41 Thus
the wedding was turned into mourn-
ing, and the sound of music into lamen-
tation. 42 Having taken their revenge
for the blood of their brother, the Jews
returned to the marshes of the Jordan.

43 When Bacchides heard of it, he
came on the sabbath to the banks of the
Jordan with a large force. 44 Then Jona-
than said to his companions, "Let us get
up now and fight for our lives, for today
is not like yesterday and the day before.
45† The battle is before us, and behind
us are the waters of the Jordan on one
side, marsh and thickets on the other,
and there is no way of escape. 46 Cry out
now to Heaven for deliverance from our
enemies." 47 When they joined battle,
Jonathan raised his arm to strike Bac-
chides, but Bacchides backed away
from him. 48 Jonathan and his men
jumped into the Jordan and swam
across to the other side, but the enemy
did not pursue them across the Jordan.
49 A thousand men on Bacchides' side
fell that day.

50† On returning to Jerusalem, Bac-
chides built strongholds in Judea: the
Jericho fortress, as well as Emmaus,
Beth-horon, Bethel, Timnath, Phara-
thon, and Tephon, with high walls and
gates and bars. 51 In each he put a garri-
son to oppose Israel. 52 He fortified the
city of Beth-zur, Gazara and the citadel,
and put soldiers in them and stores of
provisions. 53* He took as hostages the
sons of the leaders of the country and
put them in custody in the citadel at Je-
rusalem.

54† In the year one hundred and fifty-
three, in the second month, Alcimus or-
dered the wall of the inner court of the
sanctuary to be torn down, thus destroy-
ing the work of the prophets. But he only
began to tear it down. 55 Just at that time
he had a stroke, and his work was inter-
rupted; his mouth was closed and he was
paralyzed, so that he could no longer ut-
ter a word to give orders concerning his
house. 56 Finally he died in great agony.
57 Seeing that Alcimus was dead, Bac-
chides returned to the king, and the land
of Judah was quiet for two years.

58 Then all the transgressors of the law
held a council and said: "Jonathan and
his companions are living in peace and
security. Now then, let us have Bac-
chides return, and he will capture all of
them in a single night." 59 So they went
and took counsel with him. 60 When Bac-
chides was setting out with a large force,
he sent letters secretly to all his allies
in Judea, telling them to seize Jonathan
and his companions. They were not able
to do this, however, because their plot
became known. 61 In fact, Jonathan's
men seized about fifty of the men of the
country who were ringleaders in the
mischief and put them to death. 62† Then
Jonathan and Simon and their compan-

*

35: 5, 25. 53: 10, 9.

†

9, 33: *Tekoa:* home of the prophet Amos in the wild country above the Dead Sea, southeast of Jerusalem.

9, 34: Omitted, it is a dittography of verse 43.

9, 35: *Jonathan sent his brother:* this was John who was called Gaddi (1 Mc 2, 2; cf 9, 36.38).

9, 36: *Medaba:* northeast of the Dead Sea.

9, 45: Jonathan's force was apparently trapped in one of the many oxbows of the lower Jordan. Bacchides had crossed and caught them still on the east bank.

9, 50: These sites constitute a ring on the edges of the province of Judea.

9, 54: *In the year . . . second month:* May, 159 B.C.

9, 62: *Bethbasi:* two miles east of Bethlehem and six miles north of Tekoa.

ions withdrew to Bethbasi in the desert;
they rebuilt and strengthened its fortifi-
cations that had been demolished.
63 When Bacchides learned of this, he
gathered together his whole force and
sent word to those who were in Judea.
64 He came and pitched his camp before
Bethbasi, and constructing siege-ma-
chines, he fought against it for many
days.

65 Leaving his brother Simon in the
city, Jonathan, accompanied by a small
group of men, went out into the field.
66 He struck down Odomera and his
kinsmen and the sons of Phasiron in
their encampment; these men had set
out to go up to the siege with their forces.
67 Simon and his men then sallied forth
from the city and set fire to the ma-
chines. 68 They fought against Bac-
chides, and he was beaten. This caused
him great distress. Because the enter-
prise he had planned came to nought,
69 he was angry with the lawless men
who had advised him to invade the prov-
ince. He killed many of them and re-
solved to return to his own country.

70 Jonathan learned of this and sent
ambassadors to make peace with him
and to obtain the release of the prison-
ers. 71 He agreed to do as Jonathan had
asked. He swore an oath to him that he
would never try to injure him for the rest
of his life; 72 and he released the prison-
ers he had previously taken from the
land of Judah. He returned to his own
country and never came into their terri-
tory again.

73† Then the sword ceased in Israel.
Jonathan settled in Michmash; he began
to judge the people and he destroyed the
impious in Israel.

CHAPTER 10

Revolt of Alexander. 1† In the year
one hundred and sixty, Alexander, who
was called Epiphanes, son of Antiochus,
came up and took Ptolemais. He was ac-
cepted and began to reign there. 2 When
King Demetrius heard of it, he mustered
a very large army and marched out to
engage him in combat. 3 Demetrius sent
a letter to Jonathan written in peaceful
terms, to pay him honor; 4 for he said:
"Let us be the first to make peace with
him, before he makes peace with Alex-
ander against us, 5 since he will remem-
ber all the wrongs we have done to him,
his brothers, and his nation."

6 So Demetrius authorized him to
gather an army and procure arms as his
ally; and he ordered that the hostages
in the citadel be released to him.
7 Accordingly Jonathan went up to Jeru-
salem and read the letter to all the peo-
ple. The men in the citadel 8 were struck
with fear when they heard that the king
had given him authority to gather an
army. 9* They released the hostages to
Jonathan, and he gave them back to
their parents. 10 Thereafter Jonathan
dwelt in Jerusalem, and began to build
and restore the city. 11 He ordered the
workmen to build the walls and encircle
Mount Zion with square stones for its
fortification, which they did. 12 The for-
eigners in the strongholds that Bac-
chides had built, took flight; 13 each one
of them left his place and returned to
his own country. 14 Only in Beth-zur did
some remain of those who had aban-
doned the law and the commandments,
for they used it as a place of refuge.

Jonathan Supports Alexander.
15 King Alexander heard of the promises
that Demetrius had made to Jonathan;
he was also told of the battles and valiant
deeds of Jonathan and his brothers and
the troubles that they had endured. 16 He
said, "Shall we ever find another man
like him? Let us now make him our
friend and ally." 17 So he sent Jonathan
a letter written in these terms: 18 "King
Alexander sends greetings to his brother
Jonathan. 19 We have heard of you, that
you are a mighty warrior and worthy
to be our friend. 20* We have therefore
appointed you today to be high priest of
your nation; you are to be called the
King's Friend, and you are to look after
our interests and preserve amity with
us." He also sent him a purple robe and
a crown of gold.

21† Jonathan put on the sacred vest-
ments in the seventh month of the year
one hundred and sixty at the feast of
Booths, and he gathered an army and
procured many arms. 22 When Deme-
trius heard of these things, he was dis-
tressed and said: 23 "Why have we
allowed Alexander to get ahead of us by
gaining the friendship of the Jews and
thus strengthening himself? 24 I too will
write them conciliatory words and offer
dignities and gifts, so that they may be
an aid to me."

1 MACCABEES

*

10, 9: 9, 53. 20: 2, 18.

†

9, 73: *Began to judge:* exercise the governing authority as in the book of Judges. With Jerusalem and the garrison towns (v 50) firmly in Seleucid hands, Jonathan's freedom of action was greatly restricted. *Michmash,* southeast of Bethel, famous for the exploit of the former Jonathan, son of Saul; cf 1 Sm 14.

10, 1: *The year one hundred and sixty:* 152 B.C. *Alexander . . . Antiochus:* Alexander Balas claimed to be a son of Antiochus IV. He had the backing of the Romans, who had never forgiven Demetrius for becoming king without their permission. The latter meanwhile had become unpopular with his own people as well as with the Jews.

10, 21: *Jonathan . . . feast of Booths:* Jonathan began to discharge the office of high priest October 23-30, 152 B.C. For seven years after the death of Alcimus there had been no high priest in Jerusalem. It was taken for granted that the king, though a Gentile, had the power to appoint one. The Maccabees, though a priestly family, were not of the line of Zadok, and some in Israel regarded Jonathan's tenure as a usurpation.

25 So he sent them this message: "King Demetrius sends greetings to the Jewish nation. 26 We have heard how you have kept the treaty with us and continued in our friendship and not gone over to our enemies, and we are glad. 27 Continue, therefore, to keep faith with us, and we will reward you with favors in return for what you do in our behalf. 28 We will grant you many exemptions and will bestow gifts on you.

29* "I now free you, as I also exempt all the Jews, from the tribute, the salt tax, and the crown levies. 30*† Instead of collecting the third of the grain and the half of the fruit of the trees that should be my share, I renounce the right from this day forward: Neither now nor in the future will I collect them from the land of Judah or from the three districts annexed from Samaria. 31 Let Jerusalem and her territory, her tithes and her tolls, be sacred and free from tax. 32 I also yield my authority over the citadel in Jerusalem, and I transfer it to the high priest, that he may put in it such men as he shall choose to guard it. 33 Every one of the Jews who has been carried into captivity from the land of Judah into any part of my kingdom I set at liberty without ransom; and let all their taxes, even those on their cattle, be canceled. 34 Let all feast days, sabbaths, new moon festivals, appointed days, and the three days that precede each feast day, and the three days that follow, be days of immunity and exemption for every Jew in my kingdom. 35 Let no man have authority to exact payment from them or to molest any of them in any matter.

36 "Let thirty thousand Jews be enrolled in the king's army and allowances be given them, as is due to all the king's soldiers. 37 Let some of them be stationed in the king's principal strongholds, and of these let some be given positions of trust in the affairs of the kingdom. Let their superiors and their rulers be taken from among them, and let them follow their own laws, as the king has commanded in the land of Judah.

38 "Let the three districts that have been added to Judea from the province of Samaria be incorporated with Judea so that they may be under one man and obey no other authority than the high priest. 39 Ptolemais and its confines I give as a present to the sanctuary in Jerusalem for the necessary expenses of the sanctuary. 40 I make a yearly personal grant of fifteen thousand silver shekels out of the royal revenues, from appropriate places. 41 All the additional funds that the officials did not hand over as they had done in the first years, shall henceforth be handed over for the services of the temple. 42 Moreover, the dues of five thousand silver shekels that used to be taken from the revenue of the sanctuary every year shall be canceled, since these funds belong to the priests who perform the services. 43 Whoever takes refuge in the temple of Jerusalem or in any of its precincts, because of money he owes the king, or because of any other debt, shall be released, together with all the goods he possesses in my kingdom. 44 The cost of rebuilding and restoring the structures of the sanctuary shall be covered out of the royal revenue. 45 Likewise the cost of building the walls of Jerusalem and fortifying it all around, and of building walls in Judea, shall be donated from the royal revenue."

46 When Jonathan and the people heard these words, they neither believed nor accepted them, for they remembered the great evil that Demetrius had done in Israel, and how sorely he had afflicted them. 47 They therefore decided in favor of Alexander, for he had been the first to address them peaceably, and they remained his allies for the rest of his life.

48 King Alexander gathered together a large army and encamped opposite Demetrius. 49 The two kings joined battle, and when the army of Demetrius fled, Alexander pursued him, and overpowered his soldiers. 50 He pressed the battle hard until sunset, and Demetrius fell that day.

Treaty of Ptolemy and Alexander. 51 Alexander sent ambassadors to Ptolemy, king of Egypt, with this message: 52 "Now that I have returned to my realm, taken my seat on the throne of my fathers, and established my rule by crushing Demetrius and gaining control of my country—53 for I engaged him in battle, defeated him and his army, and recovered the royal throne—54 let us now establish friendship with each other. Give me your daughter for my wife; and as your son-in-law, I will give to you and to her gifts worthy of you."

55 King Ptolemy answered in these words: "Happy the day on which you returned to the land of your fathers and took your seat on their royal throne! 56 I will do for you what you have written; but meet me in Ptolemais, so that we may see each other, and I will become your father-in-law as you have proposed."

57† So Ptolemy with his daughter Cleo-

---

* 29: 11, 28f.35. 30: 11, 28.34.

---

† 10, 30: *The three districts annexed from Samaria:* mentioned by name in 11, 34. The present Greek text, by a scribal error, has added "and Galilee" after "Samaria."

10, 57: *Cleopatra:* Cleopatra Thea, then about fifteen years old. She later married Demetrius II, and later still, his brother Antiochus VII. *The year one hundred and sixty-two:* 151/150 B.C.

patra set out from Egypt and came to
Ptolemais in the year one hundred and
sixty-two. 58 There King Alexander met
him, and Ptolemy gave him his daughter
Cleopatra in marriage. Their wedding
was celebrated at Ptolemais with great
splendor according to the custom of
kings.
59 King Alexander also wrote to Jona-
than to come and meet him. 60* So he
went with pomp to Ptolemais, where he
met the two kings and gave them and
their friends silver and gold and many
gifts and thus won their favor. 61 Some
pestilent Israelites, transgressors of the
law, united against him to accuse him,
but the king paid no heed to them. 62 He
ordered Jonathan to be divested of his
ordinary garments and to be clothed in
royal purple; and so it was done. 63 The
king also had him seated at his side. He
said to his magistrates: "Go with him to
the center of the city and make a procla-
mation that no one is to bring charges
against him on any grounds or be trou-
blesome to him in any way."
64* When his accusers saw the honor
paid to him in the proclamation, and the
purple with which he was clothed, they
all fled. 65 The king also honored him by
numbering him among his Chief Friends
and made him military commander and
governor of the province. 66 So Jonathan
returned in peace and happiness to Je-
rusalem.

Victory over Appollonius. 67† In the
year one hundred and sixty-five, Deme-
trius, son of Demetrius, came from Crete
to the land of his fathers. 68 When King
Alexander heard of it he was greatly
troubled, and returned to Antioch.
69 Demetrius appointed Apollonius gov-
ernor of Coelesyria. Having gathered a
large army, Appollonius pitched his
camp at Jamnia. From there he sent this
message to Jonathan the high priest:
70 "You are the only one who resists
us. I am laughed at and put to shame
on your account. Why are you display-
ing power against us in the mountains?
71 If you have confidence in your forces,
come down now to us in the plain, and
let us test each other's strength there;
the city forces are on my side. 72 Inquire
and learn who I am and who the others
are who are helping me. Men say that
you cannot make a stand against us be-
cause your fathers were twice put to
flight in their own land. 73 Now you too
will be unable to withstand our cavalry
and such a force as this in the plain,
where there is not a stone or a pebble
or a place to flee."
74 When Jonathan heard the message
of Apollonius, he was roused. Choosing
ten thousand men, he set out from Jeru-
salem, and Simon his brother joined him
to help him. 75 He pitched camp near
Joppa, but the men in the city shut him
out because Apollonius had a garrison
there. When the Jews besieged it, 76† the
men of the city became afraid and
opened the gates, and so Jonathan took
possession of Joppa.
77 When Apollonius heard of it, he
drew up three thousand horsemen and
an innumerable infantry. He marched
on Azotus as though he were going on
through the country, but at the same
time he advanced into the plain, because
he had such a large number of horsemen
to rely on. 78 Jonathan followed him to
Azotus, and they engaged in battle.
79 Apollonius, however, had left a thou-
sand cavalry in hiding behind them.
80 When Jonathan discovered that there
was an ambush behind him, his army
was surrounded. From morning until
evening they showered his men with ar-
rows. 81 But his men held their ground,
as Jonathan had commanded, whereas
the enemy's horses became tired out.
82 When the horsemen were exhausted,
Simon attacked the phalanx, over-
whelmed it and put it to flight. 83 The
horsemen too were scattered over the
plain. The enemy fled to Azotus and en-
tered Beth-dagon, the temple of their
idol, to save themselves. 84* But Jona-
than burned and plundered Azotus with
its neighboring towns, and destroyed by
fire both the temple of Dagon and the
men who had taken refuge in it. 85 Those
who fell by the sword, together with
those who were burned alive, came to
about eight thousand men. 86 Then Jona-
than left there and pitched his camp at
Ashkalon, and the people of that city
came out to meet him with great pomp.
87 He and his men then returned to Jeru-
salem, laden with much booty.
88 When King Alexander heard of
these events, he accorded new honors
to Jonathan. 89† He sent him a gold
buckle, such as is usually given to King's
Kinsmen; he also gave him Ekron and
all its territory as a possession.

CHAPTER 11

Alliance of Demetrius and Ptolemy.
1 The king of Egypt gathered his forces,
as numerous as the sands of the sea-
shore, and many ships; and he sought
by deceit to take Alexander's kingdom
and add it to his own. 2 He entered Syria
with peaceful words, and the people in

*

60: 2, 18.
64f: 2, 18; 11, 27.
84: 11, 4; 1 Sm 5, 2-5.

†

10, 67: *The year one hundred and sixty-five:* 147 B.C. *Demetrius:* Demetrius II Nicator.

10, 76: *Joppa:* about forty miles northwest of Jerusalem. For the first time the Maccabees took possession of a seaport; nominally it was on behalf of King Alexander.

10, 89: *Kinsmen:* a class higher than Chief Friends.

the cities opened their gates to welcome him, as King Alexander had ordered them to do, since Ptolemy was his father-in-law. 3 But when Ptolemy entered the cities, he stationed garrison troops in each one. 4* When he reached Azotus, he was shown the temple of Dagon destroyed by fire, Azotus and its suburbs demolished, corpses lying about, and the charred bodies of those burned by Jonathan in the war and stacked up along his route. 5 To prejudice the king against Jonathan, he was told what the latter had done; but the king said nothing. 6 Jonathan met the king with pomp at Joppa, and they greeted each other and spent the night there. 7† Jonathan accompanied the king as far as the river called Eleutherus and then returned to Jerusalem.

8† Plotting evil against Alexander, King Ptolemy took possession of the cities along the seacoast as far as Seleucia-by-the-Sea. 9 He sent ambassadors to King Demetrius, saying: "Come, let us make a pact with each other; I will give you my daughter whom Alexander has married, and you shall reign over your father's kingdom. 10† I regret that I gave him my daughter, for he has sought to kill me." 11 His real reason for accusing Alexander, however, was that he coveted Alexander's kingdom. 12 After taking his daughter away and giving her to Demetrius, Ptolemy broke with Alexander; their enmity became open. 13 Then Ptolemy entered Antioch and assumed the crown of Asia; he thus wore two crowns on his head, that of Egypt and that of Asia.

Deaths of Alexander and Ptolemy. 14 King Alexander was in Cilicia at that time, because the people of that region had revolted. 15 When Alexander heard the news, he came to challenge Ptolemy in battle. Ptolemy marched out and met him with a strong force and put him to flight. 16 Alexander fled to Arabia to seek protection. King Ptolemy's triumph was complete 17 when the Arab Zabdiel cut off Alexander's head and sent it to Ptolemy. 18 But three days later King Ptolemy himself died, and his men in the fortified cities were killed by the inhabitants of the strongholds. 19† Thus Demetrius became king in the year one hundred and sixty-seven.

Pact with Demetrius. 20 At that time Jonathan gathered together the men of Judea to attack the citadel in Jerusalem, and they set up many machines against it. 21 Some transgressors of the law, enemies of their own nation, went to the king and informed him that Jonathan was besieging the citadel. 22 When Demetrius heard this, he was furious, and set out immediately for Ptolemais. He wrote to Jonathan to discontinue the siege and to meet him for a conference at Ptolemais as soon as possible. 23 On hearing this, Jonathan ordered the siege to continue. He selected some elders and priests of Israel and exposed himself to danger 24 by going to the king at Ptolemais. He brought with him silver, gold apparel, and many other presents, and found favor with the king. 25 Although some impious men of his own nation brought charges against him, 26 the king treated him just as his predecessors had done and showed him great honor in the presence of all his Friends. 27 He confirmed him in the high priesthood and in all the honors he had previously held, and had him enrolled among his Chief Friends.

28* Jonathan asked the king to exempt Judea and the three districts of Samaria from tribute, promising him in return three hundred talents. 29 The king agreed and wrote the following letter to Jonathan about all these matters:

30*† "King Demetrius sends greetings to his brother Jonathan and to the Jewish nation. 31† We are sending you, for your information, a copy of the letter that we wrote to Lasthenes our kinsman concerning you. 32 " 'King Demetrius sends greetings to his father Lasthenes. 33 Because of the good will they show us, we have decided to bestow benefits on the Jewish nation, who are our friends and who observe their obligations to us. 34*† Therefore we confirm their possession, not only of the territory of Judea, but also of the three districts of Aphairema, Lydda, and Ramathaim. These districts, together with all their dependencies, were transferred from Samaria to Judea in favor of all those who offer sacrifices for us in Jerusalem

*

11, 4: 10, 84. 28: 10, 29; 11, 34. 30-37: 10, 26-45 34f: 10, 29; 11, 28.

†

11, 7: *Eleutherus:* modern Nahr el-Kebir, the northern border of modern Lebanon; in the second century B.C. the northern limit of Coelesyria.

11, 8: *Seleucia-by-the-Sea:* at the mouth of the Orontes, the port city of Antioch.

11, 10: *I regret . . . to kill me:* according to Josephus, Ammonius, a friend of Alexander, had tried to assassinate Ptolemy, and the latter claimed that Alexander was the instigator, thus calumniating him to gain his kingdom (v 11).

11, 19: *The year one hundred and sixty-seven:* 146/145 B.C. The two deaths (vv 17-18) occurred in the summer of 145 B.C.

11, 30: *Brother:* this title and *father* in v 32 are honorific titles used of the Kinsmen.

11, 31: *Lasthenes:* leader of the mercenary troops who had come with Demetrius from Crete. He was now the young king's chief minister and was apparently responsible for the disastrous policy (v 38) of disbanding the national army.

11, 34: *Aphairema:* the Ophrah of Jos 18, 23; 1 Sm 23, 6; the Ephron of 2 Chr 13, 19; and the Ephraim of Jn 11, 54—modern et-Taiyibeh, five miles northeast of Bethel. *Lydda:* the Lod of the postexilic Jews (Ez 2, 33; Neh 11, 35) and the hometown of Aeneas, who was cured by Peter (Acts 9, 32ff). It is ten miles southeast of Joppa. *Ramathaim:* the Ramathaim-zophim of 1 Sm 1, 1, and the Arimathea of Mt 27, 57—modern Rentis, nine miles northeast of Lydda.

instead of paying the royal taxes that formerly the king received from them each year from the produce of the soil and the fruit of the trees. 35 From this day on we grant them release from payment of all other things that would henceforth be due to us, that is, of tithes and tribute and of the tax on the salt pans and the crown tax. 36 Henceforth none of these provisions shall ever be revoked. 37 Be sure, therefore, to have a copy of these instructions made and given to Jonathan, that it may be displayed in a conspicuous place on the holy hill.' "

The Intrigue of Trypho. 38 When King Demetrius saw that the land was peaceful under his rule and that he had no opposition, he dismissed his entire army, every man to his home, except the foreign troops which he had hired from the islands of the nations. So all the soldiers who had served under his predecessors hated him. 39* When a certain Trypho, who had previously belonged to Alexander's party, saw that all the troops were grumbling at Demetrius, he went to Imalkue the Arab, who was bringing up Alexander's young son Antiochus. 40 Trypho kept urging Imalkue to hand over the boy to him, that he might make him king in his father's place. During his stay there of many days, he told him of all that Demetrius had done and of the hatred that his soldiers had for him.

Jonathan Aids Demetrius. 41 Meanwhile Jonathan sent the request to King Demetrius to withdraw his troops from the citadel of Jerusalem and from the other strongholds, for they were constantly hostile to Israel. 42 Demetrius, in turn, sent this word to Jonathan: "I will not only do this for you and your nation, but I will greatly honor you and your nation when I find the opportunity. 43 Do me the favor, therefore, of sending men to fight for me, because all my troops have revolted."

44 So Jonathan sent three thousand good fighting men to him at Antioch. When they came to the king, he was delighted over their arrival, 45 for the populace, one hundred and twenty thousand strong, had massed in the center of the city in an attempt to kill him. 46 But he took refuge in the palace, while the populace gained control of the main streets and began to fight. 47 So the king called the Jews to his aid. They all rallied around him and spread out through the city. On that day they killed about a hundred thousand men in the city, 48 which, at the same time, they set on fire and plundered on a large scale. Thus they saved the king's life. 49 When the populace saw that the Jews held the city at their mercy, they lost courage and cried out to the king in supplication, 50 "Give us your terms and let the Jews stop attacking us and our city." So they threw down their arms and made peace. 51 The Jews thus gained glory in the eyes of the king and all his subjects, and they became renowned throughout his kingdom. Finally they returned to Jerusalem with much spoil.

52 But when King Demetrius was sure of his royal throne, and the land was peaceful under his rule, 53 he broke all his promises and became estranged from Jonathan. Instead of rewarding Jonathan for all the favors he had received from him, he caused him much trouble.

Alliance with Trypho. 54* After this, Trypho returned and brought with him the young boy Antiochus, who became king and wore the royal crown. 55 All the soldiers whom Demetrius had discharged rallied around Antiochus and fought against Demetrius, who was routed and fled. 56 Trypho captured the elephants and occupied Antioch. 57 Then young Antiochus wrote to Jonathan: "I confirm you in the high priesthood and appoint you ruler over the four districts and wish you to be one of the King's Friends." 58* He also sent him gold dishes and a dinner service, gave him the right to drink from gold cups, to dress in royal purple, and to wear a gold buckle. 59† Likewise, he made Jonathan's brother Simon governor of the region from the Ladder of Tyre to the frontier of Egypt.

60† Jonathan set out and traveled through West-of-Euphrates and its cities, and all the forces of Syria espoused his cause as allies. When he arrived at Ashkalon, the citizens welcomed him with pomp. 61 But when he set out for Gaza, the people of Gaza locked their gates against him. So he besieged it and burned and plundered its suburbs. 62 Then the people of Gaza appealed to him for mercy, and he granted them peace. He took the sons of their chief men as hostages and sent them to Jerusalem. He then traveled on through the province as far as Damascus.

War with Demetrius. 63 Jonathan heard that the generals of Demetrius had come with a strong force to Kadesh in Galilee, intending to remove him from office. 64 So he went to meet them, leaving his brother Simon in the province.

*

39: 12, 39. 58: 2, 18.
54: 11, 39; 12, 39.

†

11, 59: *Ladder of Tyre:* modern Rās en-Nāqūrah, on the border between Lebanon and Israel, where the mountains reach the sea, so that the coastal road must ascend in a series of steps.

11, 60: *West-of-Euphrates:* refers here to the territory of Palestine and Coelesyria, but not Upper Syria; cf 3, 32; 7, 8.

65 Simon besieged Beth-zur, attacked it for many days, and blockaded the inhabitants. 66 When they sued for peace, he granted it to them. He expelled them from the city, took possession of it, and put a garrison there.

67† Meanwhile, Jonathan and his army pitched their camp near the waters of Gennesaret, and at daybreak they went to the plain of Hazor. 68 There, in front of him on the plain, was the army of the foreigners. This army attacked him in the open, having first detached an ambush against him in the mountains. 69 Then the men in ambush rose out of their places and joined in the battle. 70 All of Jonathan's men fled; no one stayed except the army commanders Mattathias, son of Absalom, and Judas, son of Chalphi. 71 Jonathan tore his clothes, threw earth on his head, and prayed. 72 Then he went back to the combat and so overwhelmed the enemy that they took to flight. 73 Those of his men who were running away saw it and returned to him; and with him they pursued the enemy as far as their camp in Kadesh, where they pitched their own camp. 74 Three thousand of the foreign troops fell on that day. Then Jonathan returned to Jerusalem.

CHAPTER 12

Alliances with Rome and Sparta. 1* When Jonathan saw that the times favored him, he sent selected men to Rome to confirm and renew his friendship with the Romans. 2 He also sent letters to Sparta and other places for the same purpose.

3 After reaching Rome, the men entered the senate chamber and said, "The high priest Jonathan and the Jewish people have sent us to renew the earlier friendship and alliance between you and them." 4 The Romans gave them letters addressed to the authorities in the various places, requesting them to provide the envoys with safe conduct to the land of Judah.

5 This is a copy of the letter that Jonathan wrote to the Spartans: 6 "Jonathan the high priest, the senate of the nation, the priests, and the rest of the Jewish people send greetings to their brothers the Spartans. 7*† Long ago a letter was sent to the high priest Onias from Arius, who then reigned over you, stating that you are our brothers, as the attached copy shows. 8 Onias welcomed the envoy with honor and received the letter, which clearly referred to alliance and friendship. 9*† Though we have no need of these things, since we have for our encouragement the sacred books that are in our possession, 10 we have ventured to send word to you for the renewal of brotherhood and friendship, so as not to become strangers to you altogether; a long time has passed since your mission to us. 11 We, on our part, have never ceased to remember you in the sacrifices and prayers that we offer on our feasts and other appropriate days, as it is right and proper to remember brothers. 12 We likewise rejoice in your renown. 13 But many hardships and wars have beset us, and the kings around us have attacked us. 14 We did not wish to be troublesome to you and to the rest of our allies and friends in these wars; 15 with the help of Heaven for our support, we have been saved from our enemies, and they have been humbled. 16* So we have chosen Numenius, son of Antiochus, and Antipater, son of Jason, and we have sent them to the Romans to renew our former friendship and alliance with them. 17 We have also ordered them to come to you and greet you, and to deliver to you our letter about the renewal of our brotherhood. 18 Therefore kindly send us an answer on this matter."

19 This is a copy of the letter that was sent to Onias: 20* "Arius, king of the Spartans, sends greetings to Onias the high priest. 21 A document has been found stating that the Spartans and the Jews are brothers; both nations descended from Abraham. 22 Now that we have learned this, kindly write to us about your welfare. 23 We, on our part, are informing you that your cattle and your possessions are ours, and ours are yours. We have, therefore, given orders that you should be told of this."

Demetrius Repelled. 24 Jonathan heard that the generals of Demetrius had returned to attack him with a stronger army than before. 25† He set out from Jerusalem and went into the country of Hamath to meet them, giving them no time to enter his province. 26 The spies he had sent into their camp came back and reported that the enemy had made ready to attack the Jews that very night. 27 Therefore, when the sun set, Jonathan ordered his men to be on guard and to remain armed, ready for combat, throughout the night. He also

*

12, 1: 8, 17.
7: 12, 20-23.
9: Rom 15, 4.
16: 14, 22; 15, 15.
20-23: 12, 6f.

†

11, 67: *Plain of Hazor:* the site of the ancient Canaanite city (Jos 11, 10), ten miles north of the Lake of Gennesaret.

12, 7: *Onias:* Onias I, high priest from 323-300 or 290 B.C. *Arius:* Arius I, king from 309 to 265 B.C. The letter was sent *long ago*, i.e., a century and a half before.

12, 9: *The sacred books . . . in our possession:* a reference to "the law, the prophets and other books," as mentioned in the Prologue to Sirach (v 1), after 132 B.C.

12, 25: *Country of Hamath:* the Seleucid territory of Upper Syria northeast of Coelesyria and separated from it by the Eleutherus River. The latter territory was under the command of Jonathan (11, 59f).

set outposts all around the camp.
[28] When the enemy heard that Jonathan
and his men were ready for battle, their
hearts sank with fear and dread. They
lighted fires and then withdrew. [29] But
because Jonathan and his men were
watching the lights burning, they did not
know what had happened until morning.
[30] Then Jonathan pursued them, but he
could not overtake them, for they had
crossed the river Eleutherus.

[31] So Jonathan turned aside against
the Arabs who are called Zabadeans,
overwhelming and plundering them.
[32] Then he marched on to Damascus and
traversed that whole region.

[33] Simon also set out and went as far
as Ashkalon and its neighboring strong-
holds. He then turned to Joppa and oc-
cupied it, [34] for he heard that its men had
intended to hand over this stronghold to
the supporters of Demetrius. He left a
garrison there to guard it.

[35] When Jonathan returned, he assem-
bled the elders of the people, and with
them he made plans for building strong-
holds in Judea, [36] for making the walls
of Jerusalem still higher, and for erect-
ing a high barrier between the citadel
and the city, that would isolate the cita-
del and so prevent its garrison from
commerce with the city. [37] The people
therefore worked together on building
up the city, for part of the east wall above
the ravine had collapsed. The quarter
called Chaphenatha was also repaired.
[38] Simon likewise built up Adida in the
Shephelah, and strengthened its fortifi-
cations by providing them with gates
and bars.

Capture of Jonathan. [39]* Trypho was
determined to become king of Asia, as-
sume the crown, and do away with King
Antiochus. [40] But he was afraid that Jon-
athan would not permit him, but would
fight against him. Looking for a way to
seize and kill him, he set out and reached
Beth-shan. [41] Jonathan marched out
against him with forty thousand picked
fighting men and came to Beth-shan.
[42] But when Trypho saw that Jonathan
had arrived with a large army he was
afraid to offer him violence. [43] Instead,
he received him with honor, introduced
him to all his friends, and gave him pres-
ents. He also ordered his friends and sol-
diers to obey him as they would himself.
[44] Then he said to Jonathan: "Why have
you put all your soldiers to so much trou-
ble when we are not at war? [45] Pick out
a few men to stay with you, send the rest
back home, and then come with me to
Ptolemais. I will hand it over to you to-
gether with other strongholds and their
garrisons, as well as the officials, then
I will leave and go home. That is why I
came here."

[46] Jonathan believed him and did as
he said. He dismissed his troops, and
they returned to the land of Judah. [47] But
he kept with him three thousand men,
of whom he sent two thousand to Galilee
while one thousand accompanied him.
[48] Then as soon as Jonathan had entered
Ptolemais, the men of the city closed the
gates and seized him; all who had en-
tered with him, they killed with the
sword.

[49]† Trypho sent soldiers and cavalry
to Galilee and the Great Plain to destroy
all Jonathan's men. [50] These, upon
learning that Jonathan had been cap-
tured and his companions killed, en-
couraged one another and went out in
compact body ready to fight. [51] As their
pursuers saw that they were ready to
fight for their lives, they turned back.
[52] Thus all these men of Jonathan came
safely into the land of Judah. They
mourned over Jonathan and his men,
and were in great fear, and all Israel fell
into deep mourning.

[53]* All the nations round about sought
to destroy them. They said, "Now that
they have no leader to help them, let us
make war on them and wipe out their
memory from among men."

V: SIMON, HIGH PRIEST AND ETHNARCH

CHAPTER 13

Simon, Leader of the Jews. [1] When Si-
mon heard that Trypho was gathering
a large army to invade and ravage the
land of Judah, [2] and saw that the people
were in dread and terror, he went up
to Jerusalem. There he assembled the
people [3] and exhorted them in these
words: "You know what I, my brothers,
and my father's house have done for the
laws and the sanctuary; what battles
and disasters we have been through. [4] It
was for the sake of these, for the sake
of Israel, that all my brothers have per-
ished, and I alone am left. [5] Far be it
from me, then, to save my own life in
any time of distress, for I am not better
than my brothers. [6]* Rather will I
avenge my nation and the sanctuary, as
well as your wives and children, for all
the nations out of hatred have united to
destroy us."

[7] As the people heard these words,
their spirit was rekindled. [8] They
shouted in reply: "You are our leader
in place of your brothers Judas and Jon-
athan. [9] Fight our battles, and we will
do everything that you tell us." [10] So Si-

*

39: 11, 39f.54f. 13, 6: 5, 2; 12, 53.
53: 5, 2; 13, 6.

†

12, 49: *The Great Plain:* of Beth-shan (v 41), where Jonathan's disbanded troops remained.

mon mustered all the men able to fight,
and quickly completing the walls of Je-
rusalem, fortified it on every side. 11 He
sent Jonathan, son of Absalom, to Joppa
with a large force; Jonathan drove out
the occupants and remained there.

Deceit and Treachery of Trypho.
12 Then Trypho moved from Ptolemais
with a large army to invade the land of
Judah, bringing Jonathan with him as
a prisoner. 13 But Simon pitched his
camp at Adida, facing the plain. 14 When
Trypho learned that Simon had suc-
ceeded his brother Jonathan, and that
he intended to fight him, he sent envoys
to him with this message: 15 "We have
detained your brother Jonathan on ac-
count of the money that he owed the
royal treasury in connection with the of-
fices that he held. 16 Therefore, if you
send us a hundred talents of silver, and
two of his sons as hostages to guarantee
that when he is set free he will not revolt
against us, we will release him."

17 Although Simon knew that they
were speaking deceitfully to him, he
gave orders to get the money and the
boys, for fear of provoking much hostil-
ity among the people, who might say
18 that Jonathan perished because Si-
mon would not send Trypho the money
and the boys. 19 So he sent the boys and
the hundred talents; but Trypho broke
his promise and would not let Jonathan
go. 20† Next he began to invade and rav-
age the country. His troops went around
by the road that leads to Adora, but Si-
mon and his army moved along opposite
him everywhere he went. 21 The men in
the citadel sent messengers to Trypho,
urging him to come to them by way of
the desert, and to send them provisions.
22 Although Trypho got all his cavalry
ready to go, there was a heavy fall of
snow that night, and he could not go. So
he left for Gilead. 23† When he was ap-
proaching Baskama, he had Jonathan
killed and buried there. 24 Then Trypho
returned to his own country.

Jonathan's Tomb. 25 Simon sent for
the remains of his brother Jonathan,
and buried him in Modein, the city of
his fathers. 26 All Israel bewailed him
with solemn lamentation, mourning
over him for many days. 27 Then Simon
erected over the tomb of his father and
his brothers a monument of stones, pol-
ished front and back, and raised high
enough to be seen at a distance. 28 He
set up seven pyramids facing one an-
other for his father and his mother and
his four brothers. 29 For the pyramids he
devised a setting of big columns, on
which he carved suits of armor as a per-
petual memorial, and next to the armor
he placed carved ships, which could be
seen by all who sailed the sea. 30 This
tomb which he built at Modein is there
to the present day.

Pact between Simon and Demetrius.
31 Trypho dealt treacherously with the
young King Antiochus. He killed him
32 and assumed the kingship in his place,
putting on the crown of Asia. Thus he
brought much evil on the land. 33 Simon,
on his part, built up the strongholds of
Judea, strengthening their fortifications
with high towers, thick walls, and gates
with bars, and he stored up provisions
in the fortresses. 34 Simon also sent cho-
sen men to King Demetrius with the re-
quest that he grant the land a release
from taxation, for all that Trypho did
was to plunder the land. 35 In reply, King
Demetrius sent him the following let-
ter:

36 "King Demetrius sends greetings to
Simon the high priest, the friend of
kings, and to the elders and the Jewish
people. 37 We have received the gold
crown and the palm branch that you
sent. We are willing to be on most peace-
ful terms with you and to write to our
official to grant you release from tribute.
38 Whatever we have guaranteed to you
remains in force, and the strongholds
that you have built shall remain yours.
39 We remit any oversights and defaults
incurred up to now, as well as the crown
tax that you owe. Any other tax that may
have been collected in Jerusalem shall
no longer be collected there. 40 If any of
you are qualified for enrollment in our
service, let them be enrolled. Let there
be peace between us."

41† Thus in the year one hundred and
seventy, the yoke of the Gentiles was re-
moved from Israel, 42 and the people be-
gan to write in their records and
contracts, "In the first year of Simon,
high priest, governor, and leader of the
Jews."

Capture of Gazara and the Citadel.
43*† In those days Simon besieged Ga-
zara and surrounded it with troops. He
made a siege machine, pushed it up
against the city, and attacked and cap-
tured one of the towers. 44 The men who
had been on the siege machine jumped
down into the city and caused a great
tumult there. 45 The men of the city,
joined by their wives and children, went
up on the wall, with their garments rent,
and cried out in loud voices, begging Si-
mon to grant them peace. 46 "Do not

*

43: 2 Mc 10, 32-38.

†

13, 20f: The invaders made a wide flanking; movement to invade Judea from the south. *Adora* was a few miles southwest of Beth-zur. They would avoid Beth-zur itself and other strongholds of the Maccabees by following the *way of the desert.*

13, 23: *Bashama:* northeast of the Sea of Galilee.

13, 41: *The year one hundred and seventy:* March, 142, to April, 141 B.C., by the temple calendar.

13, 43: *Gazara:* a key position in the Shephelah, fortified by Bacchides in 160 B.C.; cf 9, 52.

treat us according to our evil deeds,"
they said, "but according to your
mercy."
47 So Simon came to terms with them
and did not destroy them. He made
them leave the city, however, and he pu-
rified the houses in which there were
idols. Then he entered the city with
hymns and songs of praise. 48 After re-
moving from it everything that was im-
pure, he settled there men who observed
the law. He improved its fortifications
and built himself a residence.
49 The men in the citadel in Jerusalem
were prevented from going out into the
country and back for the purchase of
food; they suffered greatly from hunger,
and many of them died of starvation.
50 They finally cried out to Simon for
peace, and he gave them peace. He ex-
pelled them from the citadel and
cleansed it of impurities. 51*† On the
twenty-third day of the second month,
in the year one hundred and seventy-
one, the Jews entered the citadel with
shouts of jubilation, waving of palm
branches, the music of harps and cym-
bals and lyres, and the singing of hymns
and canticles, because a great enemy of
Israel had been destroyed. 52 Simon de-
creed that this day should be celebrated
every year with rejoicing. He also
strengthened the fortifications of the
temple hill alongside the citadel, and he
and his companions dwelt there.
53† Seeing that his son John was now a
grown man, Simon made him com-
mander of all his soldiers, with his resi-
dence in Gazara.

CHAPTER 14

Capture of Demetrius. 1† In the year
one hundred and seventy-two, King
Demetrius assembled his army and
marched into Media to obtain help so
that he could fight Trypho. 2† When Ar-
saces, king of Persia and Media, heard
that Demetrius had invaded his terri-
tory, he sent one of his generals to take
him alive. 3 The general went forth and
defeated the army of Demetrius; he cap-
tured him and brought him to Arsaces,
who put him in prison.

Glory of Simon

4* The land was at rest all the days of Simon,
who sought the good of his nation.
His people were delighted with his power
and his magnificence throughout his reign.
5 As his crowning glory he captured the port of Joppa
and made it a gateway to the isles of the sea.
6* He enlarged the borders of his nation
and gained control of the country.
7 He took many enemies prisoners of war
and made himself master of Gazara, Beth-zur, and the citadel.
He cleansed the citadel of its impurities;
there was no one to withstand him.
8* The people cultivated their land in peace;
the land yielded its produce
and the trees of the field their fruit.
9* Old men sat in the squares,
all talking about the good times,
while the young men wore the glorious apparel of war.
10 He supplied the cities with food
and equipped them with means of defense,
till his glorious name reached the ends of the earth.
11* He brought peace to the land,
and Israel was filled with happiness.
12* Every man sat under his vine and his fig tree,
with no one to disturb him.
13 No one was left to attack them in their land;
the kings in those days were crushed.
14 He strengthened all the lowly among his people
and was zealous for the law;
he suppressed all the lawless and the wicked.
15 He made the temple splendid
and enriched its equipment.

Alliance with Rome and Sparta.
16† When people heard in Rome and
even in Sparta that Jonathan had died,
they were deeply grieved. 17 But when
the Romans heard that his brother Si-
mon had been made high priest in his

*
51: 1, 36.
14, 4: 3, 3-9.
6: Ex 34, 24.
8: Zec 8, 12.
9: Zec 8, 4f.
11: Lv 26, 6.
12: Mi 4, 4; Zec 3, 10.

†
13, 51: *The twenty-third day of the second month:* June 3, 141 B.C.

13, 53: *John:* John Hyrcanus, who was to succeed his father as ruler and high priest; cf 16, 23f.

14, 1: *The year one hundred and seventy-two:* 141-140 B.C. The expedition began most probably in the spring of 140.

14, 2: *Arsaces:* Arsaces VI, also called Mithridates I, the Parthian king (171-138 B.C.). Parthians had overrun Persia and now held Babylonia, both of which had hitherto belonged to the Seleucid empire. The Greeks and Macedonians in these countries had appealed to Demetrius for help.

14, 16: The embassy to Rome and Sparta was sent soon after Simon's accession to power, and the replies were received before Demetrius' expedition (vv 1-3)—probably in 142 B.C.

place and was master of the country and the cities, 18* they sent him inscribed tablets of bronze to renew with him the friendship and alliance that they had established with his brothers Judas and Jonathan. 19 These were read before the assembly in Jerusalem.

20 This is a copy of the letter that the Spartans sent: "The rulers and the citizens of Sparta send greetings to Simon the high priest, the elders, the priests, and the rest of the Jewish people, our brothers. 21 The envoys you sent to our people have informed us of your glory and fame, and we were happy that they came. 22* In accordance with what they said we have recorded the following in the public decrees: Since Numenius, son of Antiochus, and Antipater, son of Jason, envoys of the Jews, have come to us to renew their friendship with us, 23 the people have voted to receive the men with honor, and to deposit a copy of their words in the public archives, so that the people of Sparta may have a record of them. A copy of this decree has been made for Simon the high priest."

24* After this, Simon sent Numenius to Rome with a great gold shield weighing a thousand minas, to confirm the alliance with the Romans.

Decree of Honor. 25 When the people heard of these things, they said, "How can we thank Simon and his sons? 26 He and his brothers and his father's house have stood firm and repulsed Israel's enemies. They have thus preserved its liberty." So they made an inscription on bronze tablets, which they affixed to pillars on Mount Zion. 27† The following is a copy of the inscription:

"On the eighteenth day of Elul, in the year one hundred and seventy-two, that is, the third year under Simon the high priest in Asaramel, 28 in a great assembly of priests, people, rulers of the nation, and elders of the country, the following proclamation was made:

29 " 'Since there have often been wars in our country, Simon, son of the priest Mattathias, descendant of Joarib, and his brothers have put themselves in danger and resisted the enemies of their nation, so that their sanctuary and law might be maintained, and they have thus brought great glory to their nation. 30 After Jonathan had rallied his nation and become their high priest, he was gathered to his kinsmen. 31 When the enemies of the Jews sought to invade and devastate their country and to lay hands on their temple, 32 Simon rose up and fought for his nation, spending large sums of his own money to equip the men of his nation's armed forces and giving them their pay. 33 He fortified the cities of Judea, especially the frontier city of Beth-zur, where he stationed a garrison of Jewish soldiers, and where previously the enemy's arms had been stored. 34 He also fortified Joppa by the sea and Gazara on the border of Azotus, a place previously occupied by the enemy; these cities he resettled with Jews, and furnished them with all that was necessary for their restoration. 35 When the Jewish people saw Simon's loyalty and the glory he planned to bring to his nation, they made him their leader and high priest because of all he had accomplished and the loyalty and justice he had shown his nation. In every way he sought to exalt his people.

36 " 'In his time and under his guidance they succeeded in driving the Gentiles out of their country, especially those in the City of David in Jerusalem, who had built for themselves a citadel from which they used to sally forth to defile the environs of the temple and inflict grave injury on its purity. 37 In this citadel he stationed Jewish soldiers, and he strengthened its fortifications for the defense of the land and the city, while he also raised the wall of Jerusalem to a greater height. 38 Consequently, King Demetrius confirmed him in the high priesthood, 39* made him one of his Friends, and conferred the highest honors on him. 40 He had indeed heard that the Romans had addressed the Jews as friends, allies, and brothers and that they had received Simon's envoys with honor.

41 " 'The Jewish people and their priest have, therefore, made the following decisions. Simon shall be their permanent leader and high priest until a true prophet arises. 42 He shall act as governor general over them, and shall have charge of the temple, to make regulations concerning its functions and concerning the country, its weapons and strongholds, 43 he shall be obeyed by all. All contracts made in the country shall be dated by his name. He shall have the right to wear royal purple and gold ornaments. 44 It shall not be lawful for any of the people or priests to nullify any of these decisions, or to contradict the orders given by him, or to convene an assembly in the country without his consent, to be clothed in royal purple or wear an official gold brooch. 45 Whoever acts otherwise or violates any of these prescriptions shall be liable to punishment.

46 " 'All the people approved of granting Simon the right to act in accord with

*

18: 8, 22.
22: 12, 16; 15, 15.
24: 12, 16; 15, 15.
39f: 2, 18.

†

14, 27: *Eighteenth day of Elul:* September 13, 140 B.C. *Asaramel:* a Hebrew name meaning "court of the people of God."

these decisions, 47† and Simon accepted
and agreed to act as high priest, gover-
nor general, and ethnarch of the Jewish
people and priests and to exercise su-
preme authority over all.' "
48 It was decreed that this inscription
should be engraved on bronze tablets,
to be set up in a conspicuous place in
the precincts of the temple, 49 and that
copies of it should be deposited in the
treasury, where they would be available
to Simon and his sons.

CHAPTER 15

Letter of Antiochus. 1† Antiochus, son
of King Demetrius, sent a letter from the
islands of the sea to Simon, the priest
and ethnarch of the Jews, and to all the
nation, 2 which read as follows:
"King Antiochus sends greetings to Si-
mon, the priest and ethnarch, and to the
Jewish nation. 3 Whereas certain villains
have gained control of the kingdom of
my ancestors, I intend to reclaim it, that
I may restore it to its former state. I have
recruited a large number of mercenary
troops and equipped warships 4 to make
a landing in my country and take re-
venge on those who have ruined it and
laid waste many cities in my realm.
5 "Now, therefore, I confirm to you all
the tax exemptions that the kings before
me granted you and whatever other
privileges they conferred on you. 6 I au-
thorize you to coin your own money, as
legal tender in your country. 7 Jeru-
salem and its temple shall be free. All
the weapons you have prepared and all
the strongholds you have built and now
occupy shall remain in your possession.
8 All debts, present or future, due to the
royal treasury shall be canceled for
you, now and for all time. 9 When we
recover our kingdom, we will greatly
honor you and your nation and the tem-
ple, so that your glory will be manifest
in all the earth."
10† In the year one hundred and sev-
enty-four Antiochus invaded the land of
his ancestors, and all the troops rallied
to him, so that few were left with Trypho.
11† Pursued by Antiochus, Trypho fled
to Dor, by the sea, 12 realizing what a
mass of troubles had come upon him
now that his soldiers had deserted him.
13 Antiochus encamped before Dor with
a hundred and twenty thousand infantry
and eight thousand horsemen. 14 While
he invested the city, his ships closed in
along the coast, so that he blockaded it
by land and sea and let no one go in or
out.
Roman Alliance Renewed. 15* Mean-
while, Numenius and his companions
left Rome with letters such as this ad-
dressed to various kings and countries:
16† "Lucius, Consul of the Romans,
sends greetings to King Ptolemy.
17 Certain envoys of the Jews, our friends
and allies, have come to us to renew
their earlier alliance of friendship. They
had been sent by Simon the high priest
and the Jewish people, 18* and they
brought with them a gold shield worth
a thousand minas. 19 Therefore we have
decided to write to various kings and
countries, that they are not to harm
them, or wage war against them or their
cities or their country, and are not to as-
sist those who fight against them. 20 We
have also decided to accept the shield
from them. 21 If, then, any troublemak-
ers from their country take refuge with
you, hand them over to Simon the high
priest, so that he may punish them ac-
cording to their law."
22† The consul sent similar letters to
Kings Demetrius, Attalus, Ariarthes and
Arsaces; 23 to all the countries—Samp-
sames, Sparta, Delos, Myndos, Sicyon,
Caria, Samos, Pamphylia, Lycia, Hali-
carnassus, Rhodes, Phaselis, Cos, Side,
Aradus, Gortyna, Cnidus, Cyprus, and
Cyrene. 24 A copy of the letter was also
sent to Simon the high priest.
Hostility of Antiochus. 25 When King
Antiochus was encamped before Dor, he
assaulted it continuously both with
troops and with the siege machines he
had made. He blockaded Trypho by pre-
venting anyone from going in or out.
26 Simon sent to Antiochus' support two
thousand elite troops, together with gold
and silver and much equipment. 27 But
he refused to accept the aid; in fact, he
broke all the agreements he had previ-
ously made with Simon and became
hostile toward him.
28 He sent Athenobius, one of his
Friends, to confer with Simon and say:
"You are occupying Joppa and Gazara
and the citadel of Jerusalem; these are
cities of my kingdom. 29 You have laid
waste their territories, done great
harm to the land, and taken posses-
sion of many districts in my realm.
30 Therefore, give up the cities you have
seized and the tribute money of the dis-

*

15, 15: 8, 17; 12, 16; 14, 22.24. 18: 14, 24.

†

14, 47: *Ethnarch:* a subaltern ruler over a racial group whose office needed confirmation by a higher authority within the empire.

15, 1: *Antiochus:* Antiochus VII Sidetes, son of Demetrius I, and younger brother of Demetrius II, now a prisoner of the Parthians. At the age of twenty he set out from the island of Rhodes to take his brother's place and drive out the usurper Trypho.

15, 10: *The year one hundred and seventy-four:* 138 B.C.

15, 11: *Dor, by the sea:* a fortress on the Palestinian coast, fifteen miles south of Carmel.

15, 16: *Lucius:* Perhaps Lucius Caecilius Metellus, consul in 142 B.C., or Lucius Calpurnicus Piso, consul in 140-139 B.C. This document pertains to Simon's first years as leader.

15, 22: *Attalus:* Attalus II of Pergamum, reigned 159-138 B.C. *Ariarthes:* Ariarthes V of Cappadocia, reigned 162-130 B.C. *Arsaces:* see note on 14, 2.

tricts outside the territory of Judea of which you have taken possession; 31 or instead, pay me five hundred talents of silver for the devastation you have caused and five hundred talents more for the tribute money of the cities. If you do not do this, we will come and make war on you."

32 So Athenobius, the king's Friend, came to Jerusalem and on seeing the splendor of Simon's court, the gold and silver plate on the sideboard, and the rest of his rich display, he was amazed. When he gave him the king's message, 33 Simon said to him in reply:

"We have not seized any foreign land; what we took is not the property of others, but our ancestral heritage which for a time had been unjustly held by our enemies. 34 Now that we have the opportunity, we are holding on to the heritage of our ancestors. 35 As for Joppa and Gazara, which you demand, the men of these cities were doing great harm to our people and laying waste our country; however, we are willing to pay you a hundred talents for these cities."

36 Athenobius made no reply, but returned to the king in anger. When he told him of Simon's words, of his splendor, and of all he had seen, the king fell into a violent rage.

Victory over Cendebeus. 37† Trypho had gotten aboard a ship and escaped to Orthosia. 38 Then the king appointed Cendebeus commander-in-chief of the seacoast, and gave him infantry and cavalry forces. 39† He ordered him to move his troops against Judea and to fortify Kedron and strengthen its gates, so that he could launch attacks against the Jewish people. Meanwhile the king went in pursuit of Trypho. 40 When Cendebeus came to Jamnia, he began to harass the people and to make incursions into Judea, where he took people captive or massacred them. 41 As the king ordered, he fortified Kedron and stationed horsemen and infantry there, so that they could go out and patrol the roads of Judea.

CHAPTER 16

1 John then went up from Gazara and told his father Simon what Cendebeus was doing. 2 Simon called his two oldest sons, Judas and John, and said to them: "I and my brothers and my father's house have fought the battles of Israel from our youth until today, and many times we succeeded in saving Israel. 3 I have now grown old, but you, by the mercy of Heaven, have come to man's estate. Take my place and my brother's, and go out and fight for our nation; and may the help of Heaven be with you!"

4 John then mustered in the land twenty thousand warriors and horsemen. Setting out against Cendebeus, they spent the night at Modein, 5 rose early, and marched into the plain. There, facing them, was an immense army of foot soldiers and horsemen, and between the two armies was a stream. 6 John and his men took their position against the enemy. Seeing that his men were afraid to cross the stream, John crossed first. When his men saw this, they crossed over after him. 7 Then he divided his infantry into two corps and put his cavalry between them, for the enemy's horsemen were very numerous. 8 They blew the trumpets, and Cendebeus and his army were put to flight; many of them fell wounded, and the rest fled toward the stronghold. 9 It was then that John's brother Judas fell wounded; but John pursued them until Cendebeus reached Kedron, which he had fortified. 10 Some took refuge in the towers on the plain of Azotus, but John set fire to these, and about two thousand of the enemy perished. He then returned to Judea in peace.

Murder of Simon and His Sons. 11 Ptolemy, son of Abubus, had been appointed governor of the plain of Jericho, and he had much silver and gold, 12 being the son-in-law of the high priest. 13 But he became ambitious and sought to get control of the country. So he made treacherous plans to do away with Simon and his sons. 14† As Simon was inspecting the cities of the country and providing for their needs, he and his sons Mattathias and Judas went down to Jericho in the year one hundred and seventy-seven, in the eleventh month (that is, the month Shebat). 15† The son of Abubus gave them a deceitful welcome in the little stronghold called Dok which he had built. While serving them a sumptuous banquet, he had his men hidden there. 16 Then, when Simon and his sons had drunk freely, Ptolemy and his men sprang up, weapons in hand, rushed upon Simon in the banquet hall, and killed him, his two sons, and some of his servants. 17 By this vicious act of treason he repaid good with evil.

18 Then Ptolemy wrote an account of this and sent it to the king, asking that troops be sent to help him and that the country be turned over to him. 19 He sent other men to Gazara to do away with John. To the army officers he sent letters inviting them to come to him so that he

---

15, 37: *Orthosia:* a port between Tripoli and the Eleutherus River.

15, 39: *Kedron:* a few miles southeast of Jamnia and facing the fortress of Gazara held by John Hyrcanus.

16, 14: *In the year one hundred and seventy-seven, in the eleventh month:* January-February, 134 B.C., by the temple calendar.

16, 15: *Dok:* a fortress built on a cliff three miles northwest of Jericho, near modern Ain Duq.

might present them with silver, gold,
and gifts. 20 He also sent others to seize
Jerusalem and the mount of the temple.
21 But someone ran ahead and brought
word to John at Gazara that his father
and his brothers had perished, and that
Ptolemy had sent men to kill him also.
22 On hearing this, John was utterly as-
tounded. When the men came to kill him,
he had them arrested and put to death,
for he knew what they meant to do.
23† Now the rest of the history of John,
his wars and the brave deeds he per-
formed, his rebuilding of the walls, and
his other achievements—24 these things
are recorded in the chronicle of his pon-
tificate, from the time that he succeeded
his father as high priest.

†

16, 23f: John Hyrcanus was ruler and high priest from 134 B.C. till his death in 104 B.C. These verses suggest that the book was written, or at least completed, only after he died.

The Second Book of

MACCABEES

Although this book, like the preceding one, receives its title from its protagonist, Judas Maccabee (or Maccabeus), it is not a sequel to 1 Maccabees. The two differ in many respects. Whereas the first covers the period from the beginning of the reign of Antiochus IV (175 B.C.) to the accession of John Hyrcanus I (134 B.C.), this present book treats of the events in Jewish history from the time of the high priest Onias III and King Seleucus IV (c. 180 B.C.) to the defeat of Nicanor's army (161 B.C.).

The author of 2 Maccabees states (2, 23) that his one-volume work is an abridgment of a certain five-volume work by Jason of Cyrene; but since this latter has not survived, it is difficult to determine its relationship to the present epitome. One does not know how freely the anonymous epitomizer may have rewritten his shorter composition, or how closely he may have followed the wording of the original in the excerpts he made. Some parts of the text here, clearly not derived from Jason's work, are the Preface (2, 19-32), the Epilogue (15, 37-39), and probably also certain moralizing reflections (e. g., 5, 17-20; 6, 12-17). It is certain, however, that both works were written in Greek, which explains why the Second Book of Maccabees was not included in the canon of the Hebrew Bible.

The book is not without genuine historical value in supplementing I Maccabees, and it contains some apparently authentic documents (11, 16-38). Its purpose, whether intended by Jason himself or read into it by the compiler, is to give a theological interpretation to the history of the period. There is less interest, therefore, in the actual exploits of Judas Maccabeus than in God's marvelous interventions. These direct the course of events, both to punish the sacriligeous and blashphemous pagans, and to purify God's holy temple and restore it to his faithful people. The author sometimes effects his purpose by transferring events from their proper chronological order, and giving exaggerated figures for the size of armies and the numbers killed in battle; he also places long, edifying discourses and prayers in the mouths of his heroes, and inclines to elaborate descriptions of celestial apparitions (3, 24-34; 5, 2ff; 10, 29f; 15, 11-16). He is the earliest known composer of stories that glorify God's holy martyrs (6, 18—7, 42; 14, 37-46).

Of theological importance are the author's teachings on the resurrection of the just on the last day (7, 9.11.14.23; 14, 46), the intercession of the saints in heaven for people living on earth (15, 11-16), and the power of the living to offer prayers and sacrifices for the dead (12, 39-46).

The beginning of 2 Maccabees consists of two letters sent by the Jews of Jerusalem to their coreligionists in Egypt. They deal with the observance of the feast commemorating the central event of the book, the purification of the temple. It is uncertain whether the author or a later scribe prefixed these letters to the narrative proper. If the author is responsible for their insertion, he must have written his book some time after 124 B.C., the date of the more recent of the two letters. In any case, Jason's five-volume work very likely continued the history of the Jews well into the Hasmonean period, so that 2 Maccabees would probably not have been produced much before the end of the second century B.C.

The main divisions of 2 Maccabees are:

- *I: Letters to the Jews in Egypt (1, 1—2, 18)*
- *II: Author's Preface (2, 19-32)*
- *III: Heliodorus' Attempt To Profane the Temple (3, 1-40)*
- *IV: Profanation and Persecution (4, 1—7, 42)*
- *V: Victories of Judas and Purification of the Temple (8, 1—10, 8)*
- *VI: Renewed Persecution (10, 9—15, 36)*
- *VII: Epilogue (15, 37-39)*

I: LETTERS TO THE JEWS IN EGYPT

CHAPTER 1

First Letter 124 B.C. 1 The Jews in Je-
rusalem and in the land of Judea send
greetings to their brethren, the Jews in
Egypt, and wish them true peace! 2 May
God bless you and remember his cov-
enant with his faithful servants, Abra-
ham, Isaac and Jacob. 3 May he give to
all of you a heart to worship him and
to do his will readily and generously.
4 May he open your heart to his law and
his commandments and grant you
peace. 5 May he hear your prayers, and
be reconciled to you, and never forsake
you in time of adversity. 6 Even now we
are praying for you here.
7*† In the reign of Demetrius, the year
one hundred and sixty-nine, we Jews
wrote to you during the trouble and vio-
lence that overtook us in those years
after Jason and his followers had re-
volted against the holy land and the
kingdom, 8*† setting fire to the gate-
house and shedding innocent blood. But
we prayed to the Lord, and our prayer
was heard; we offered sacrifices and fine
flour; we lighted the lamps and set out
the loaves of bread. 9† We are now re-
minding you to celebrate the feast of
Booths in the month of Chislev. 10† Dated
in the year one hundred and eighty-
eight.
Festival Letter 164 B.C. The people of
Jerusalem and Judea, the senate, and
Judas send greetings and good wishes
to Aristobulus, counselor of King Ptol-
emy and member of the family of the
anointed priests, and to the Jews in
Egypt. 11† Since we have been saved by
God from grave dangers, we give him
great thanks for having fought on our
side against the king; 12* it was he who
drove out those who fought against the
holy city. 13† When their leader arrived
in Persia with his seemingly irresistible
army, they were cut to pieces in the tem-
ple of the goddess Nanea through a de-
ceitful stratagem employed by Nanea's
priests. 14† On the pretext of marrying
the goddess, Antiochus with his Friends
had come to the place to get its great
treasures by way of dowry. 15 When the
priests of the Nanaeon had displayed the
treasures, Antiochus with a few atten-
dants came to the temple precincts. As
soon as he entered the temple, the
priests locked the doors. 16 Then they
opened a hidden trapdoor in the ceiling,
hurled stones at the leader and his com-
panions and struck them down. They
dismembered the bodies, cut off their
heads and tossed them to the people out-
side. 17 Forever blessed be our God, who
has thus punished the wicked!
18† We shall be celebrating the purifi-
cation of the temple on the twenty-fifth
day of the month Chislev, so we thought
it right to inform you, that you too may
celebrate the feast of Booths and of the
fire that appeared when Nehemiah, the
rebuilder of the temple and the altar, of-
fered sacrifices. 19† When our fathers
were being exiled to Persia, devout
priests of the time took some of the fire
from the altar and hid it secretly in the
hollow of a dry cistern, making sure that
the place would be unknown to anyone.
20 Many years later, when it so pleased
God, Nehemiah, commissioned by the
king of Persia, sent the descendants of
the priests who had hidden the fire to
look for it. 21 When they informed us that
they could not find any fire, but only
muddy water, he ordered them to scoop
some out and bring it. After the material
for the sacrifices had been prepared,
Nehemiah ordered the priests to sprin-
kle with the water the wood and what
lay on it. 22 When this was done and in
time the sun, which had been clouded
over, began to shine, a great fire blazed
up, so that everyone marveled. 23 While
the sacrifice was being burned, the
priests recited a prayer, and all present
joined in with them, Jonathan leading
and the rest responding with Nehemiah.
24 The prayer was as follows: "Lord,
Lord God, creator of all things, awesome
and strong, just and merciful, the only

*

1, 7: 4, 7-20.
8: 1 Mc 4, 38.
12-17: 9, 1-29; 1 Mc 6, 1-13.

†

1, 7: *Demetrius:* Demetrius II, king of Syria (145-139, 129-125 B.C.). *The year one hundred and sixty-nine* of the Seleucid era, 143 B.C. Regarding the dates in 1 and 2 Mc, see note on 1 Mc 1, 10. On the troubles caused by *Jason* and his revolt against *the kingdom,* i.e., the rule of the legitimate high priest, see 4, 7-22.

1, 8: *Our prayer was heard:* in the ultimate victory of the Maccabees.

1, 9: *Feast of Booths in the month of Chislev:* really the feast of the Dedication of the temple (10, 1-8), celebrated on the twenty-fifth of Chislev (Nov.-Dec.). Its solemnity resembles that of the true feast of Booths (Lv 23, 33-43), celebrated on the fifteenth of Tishri (Sept.-Oct.); cf 1, 18.

1, 10: 124 B.C. The date pertains to the preceding, not the following letter.

1, 10: *King Ptolemy:* Ptolemy VI Philometor, ruler of Egypt from 180 to 145 B.C.; he is mentioned also in 1 Mc 1, 18; 10, 51-59.

1, 11f: *The king:* Antiochus IV of Syria, the bitter persecutor of the Jews, who, as *leader* of the Syrian army that invaded Persia, perished there in 164 B.C.

1, 13: *Nanea:* an oriental goddess comparable to Artemis of the Greeks.

1, 14-17: A different account of the death of Antiochus IV is given in 9, 1-29, and another variant account in 1 Mc 6, 1-16. The writer of this letter had probably heard a distorted rumor of the king's death. This fact and other indications show that the letter was written very soon after Antiochus IV died, hence in 164 B.C.

1, 18-36: This purely legendary account of Nehemiah's miraculous fire is incorporated in the letter because of its connection with the temple and its rededication.

1, 18: *Nehemiah, the rebuilder of the temple:* he rebuilt the walls of Jerusalem, but the temple had been rebuilt by Zerubbabel almost a century before.

1, 19: *Persia:* actually Babylonia, which later became part of the Persian Empire.

king and benefactor, 25 who alone are
gracious, just, almighty, and eternal, Is-
rael's savior from all evil, who chose
our forefathers and sanctified them:
26 accept this sacrifice on behalf of all
your people Israel and guard and sanc-
tify your heritage. 27 Gather together our
scattered people, free those who are the
slaves of the Gentiles, look kindly on
those who are despised and detested,
and let the Gentiles know that you are
our God. 28 Punish those who tyrannize
over us and arrogantly mistreat us.
29* Plant your people in your holy place,
as Moses promised."
30 Then the priests began to sing
hymns. 31 After the sacrifice was burned,
Nehemiah ordered the rest of the liquid
to be poured upon large stones. 32 As
soon as this was done, a flame blazed
up, but its light was lost in the brilliance
cast from a light on the altar. 33 When
the event became known and the king
of the Persians was told that, in the very
place where the exiled priests had hid-
den the fire, a liquid was found with
which Nehemiah and his people had
burned the sacrifices, 34 the king, after
verifying the fact, fenced the place off
and declared it sacred. 35 To those on
whom the king wished to bestow favors
he distributed the large revenues he re-
ceived there. 36† Nehemiah and his com-
panions called the liquid nephthar,
meaning purification, but most people
named it naphtha.

CHAPTER 2

1† You will find in the records, not only
that Jeremiah the prophet ordered the
deportees to take some of the aforemen-
tioned fire with them, 2* but also that the
prophet, in giving them the law, admon-
ished them not to forget the command-
ments of the Lord or be led astray in
their thoughts, when seeing the gold and
silver idols and their ornaments. 3 With
other similar words he urged them not
to let the law depart from their hearts.
4*† The same document also tells how
the prophet, following a divine revela-
tion, ordered that the tent and the ark
should accompany him and how he went
off to the mountain which Moses climbed
to see God's inheritance. 5 When Jere-
miah arrived there, he found a room in
a cave in which he put the tent, the ark,
and the altar of incense; then he blocked
up the entrance. 6 Some of those who fol-
lowed him came up intending to mark
the path, but they could not find it.
7 When Jeremiah heard of this, he re-
proved them: "The place is to remain
unknown until God gathers his people
together again and shows them mercy.
8*† Then the Lord will disclose these
things, and the glory of the Lord will be
seen in the cloud, just as it appeared in
the time of Moses and when Solomon
prayed that the Place might be glori-
ously sanctified."
9 It is also related how Solomon in his
wisdom offered a sacrifice at the dedica-
tion and the completion of the temple.
10* Just as Moses prayed to the Lord and
fire descended from the sky and con-
sumed the sacrifices, so Solomon also
prayed and fire came down and burned
up the holocausts. 11*† Moses had said,
"Because it had not been eaten, the sin
offering was burned up." 12 Solomon also
celebrated the feast in the same way for
eight days.
13† Besides these things, it is also told
in the records and in Nehemiah's Mem-
oirs how he collected the books about the
kings, the writings of the prophets and
of David, and the royal letters about sa-
cred offerings. 14* In like manner Judas
also collected for us the books that had
been scattered because of the war, and
we now have them in our possession. 15 If
you need them, send messengers to get
them for you.
16 As we are about to celebrate the
feast of the purification of the temple,
we are writing to you requesting you also
to please celebrate the feast. 17 It is God
who has saved all his people and has re-
stored to all of them their heritage, the
kingdom, the priesthood, and the sacred
rites, 18* as he promised through the law.
We trust in God, that he will soon have
mercy on us and gather us together from
everywhere under the heavens to his
holy Place, for he has rescued us from
great perils and has purified his Place.

II: AUTHOR'S PREFACE

19 This is the story of Judas Maccabeus
and his brothers, of the purification of
the great temple, the dedication of the
altar, 20† the campaigns against Antio-

*

29: 2, 18; Dt 30, 3ff.
2, 2: Bar 6, 3-72.
4f: Dt 32, 49; 34, 1; Rv 11, 19.
8: 1 Kgs 8, 11.
10: Lv 9, 23f; 2 Chr 7, 1.
11: Lv 10, 16-20.
14: 1 Mc 1, 57.
18: Dt 30, 3ff.

†

1, 36: By a play on words, the Greek term *naphtha* (petroleum) is assimilated to some Semitic word, perhaps *nephthar,* meaning "loosened."

2, 1-8: This legendary account of how Jeremiah hid the sacred tent (which was not mentioned after the time of Solomon!), the ark, and the altar is given for the purpose of explaining why the postexilic temple was the legitimate place of worship even without these sacred objects.

2, 4: *The mountain:* Nebo; cf Dt 34, 1.

2, 8: *The Place:* the temple of Jerusalem.

2, 11: The statement attributed here to Moses seems to be based on Lv 10, 16-20.

2, 13: *Nehemiah's Memoirs:* a lost apocryphal work.

2, 20: For the *account of the campaigns against Antiochus IV Epiphanes,* see 4, 7—10, 9; and for the account of those against *his son* Antiochus V *Eupator,* see 10, 10—13, 26.

chus Epiphanes and his son Eupator,
21 and of the heavenly manifestations
accorded to the heroes who fought
bravely for Judaism, so that, few as they
were, they seized the whole land, put to
flight the barbarian hordes, 22 regained
possession of the world-famous temple,
liberated the city, and reestablished the
laws that were in danger of being abol-
ished, while the Lord favored them with
all his generous assistance. 23 All this,
which Jason of Cyrene set forth in detail
in five volumes, we will try to condense
into a single book.

Purpose and Method. 24 In view of the
flood of statistics, and the difficulties en-
countered by those who wish to plunge
into historical narratives where the ma-
terial is abundant, 25 we have aimed to
please those who prefer simple reading,
as well as to make it easy for the studious
who wish to commit things to memory,
and to be helpful to all. 26 For us who
have taken upon ourselves the labor of
making this digest, the task, far from
being easy, is one of sweat and of sleep-
less nights, 27 just as the preparation of
a festive banquet is no light matter for
one who thus seeks to give enjoyment
to others. Similarly, to win the gratitude
of many we will gladly endure these in-
conveniences, 28 while we leave the re-
sponsibility for exact details to the
original author, and confine our efforts
to giving only a summary outline. 29 As
the architect of a new house must give
his attention to the whole structure,
while the man who undertakes the deco-
ration and the frescoes has only to con-
cern himself with what is needed for
ornamentation, so I think it is with us.
30 To enter into questions and examine
them thoroughly from all sides is the
task of the professional historian; 31 but
the man who is making an adaptation
should be allowed to aim at brevity of
expression and to omit detailed treat-
ment of the matter. 32 Here, then, we
shall begin our account without further
ado; it would be nonsense to write a long
preface to a story and then abbreviate
the story itself.

III: HELIODORUS' ATTEMPT TO PROFANE THE TEMPLE

CHAPTER 3

Treachery of Simon. 1*† While the
holy city lived in perfect peace and the
laws were strictly observed because of
the piety of the high priest Onias and
his hatred of evil, 2 the kings themselves
honored the Place and glorified the tem-
ple with the most magnificent gifts.
3† Thus Seleucus, king of Asia, defrayed
from his own revenues all the expenses
necessary for the sacrificial services.
4*† But a certain Simon, of the priestly
course of Bilgah, who had been ap-
pointed superintendent of the temple,
had a quarrel with the high priest about
the supervision of the city market.
5 Since he could not prevail against
Onias, he went to Apollonius of Tarsus,
who at that time was governor of Coele-
syria and Phoenicia, 6 and reported to
him that the treasury in Jerusalem was
so full of untold riches that the total sum
of money was incalculable and out of all
proportion to the cost of the sacrifices,
and that it would be possible to bring it
all under the control of the king.

Mission of Heliodorus. 7 When Apollo-
nius had an audience with the king, he
informed him about the riches that had
been reported to him. The king chose his
minister Heliodorus and sent him with
instructions to expropriate the aforesaid
wealth. 8 So Heliodorus immediately set
out on his journey, ostensibly to visit the
cities of Coelesyria and Phoenicia, but
in reality to carry out the king's purpose.
9 When he arrived in Jerusalem and had
been graciously received by the high
priest of the city, he told him about the
information that had been given, and
explained the reason for his presence,
and he asked if these things were really
true. 10* The high priest explained that
part of the money was a care fund for
widows and orphans, 11† and a part was
the property of Hyrcanus, son of Tobias,
a man who occupied a very high posi-
tion. Contrary to the calumnies of the
impious Simon, the total amounted to
four hundred talents of silver and two
hundred of gold. 12 He added that it was
utterly unthinkable to defraud those
who had placed their trust in the sanctity
of the Place and in the sacred inviolabil-
ity of a temple venerated all over the
world. 13 But because of the orders he
had from the king, Heliodorus said that
in any case the money must be confis-
cated for the royal treasury. 14 So on the
day he had set he went in to take an in-
ventory of the funds.

Anguish of the Faithful. There was
great distress throughout the city.

*

3, 1ff: 4, 19f; 15, 12. 4: 4, 23. 10: Dt 14, 29.

†

3, 1-40: This legendary episode about Heliodorus is recounted here for the purpose of stressing the inviolability of the temple of Jerusalem; its later profanation was allowed by God because of the people's sins; cf 5, 17f.

3, 1: *The high priest Onias:* Onias III, who was high priest from 196 to 175 B.C., and died in 171 B.C. He was the son of Simon, whose praises are sung in Sir 50, 1-21.

3, 3: *Seleucus:* Seleucus IV Philopator, who reigned from 187 to 175 B.C.

3, 4: *Bilgah:* a priestly family mentioned in Neh 12, 5.18.

3, 11: *Son of Tobias:* a member of the Tobiad family of Transjordan (Neh 2, 10; 6, 17ff; 13, 4-8). Hyrcanus' father was Joseph, whose mother was the sister of the high priest Onias II.

15 Priests prostrated themselves in their
priestly robes before the altar, and
loudly begged him in heaven who had
given the law about deposits to keep the
deposits safe for those who had made
them. 16 Whoever saw the appearance of
the high priest was pierced to the heart,
for the changed color of his face mani-
fested the anguish of his soul. 17 The ter-
ror and bodily trembling that had come
over the man clearly showed those who
saw him the pain that lodged in his
heart. 18 People rushed out of their
houses in crowds to make public suppli-
cation, because the Place was in danger
of being profaned. 19 Women, girded
with sackcloth below their breasts, filled
the streets; maidens secluded indoors
ran together, some to the gates, some
to the walls, others peered through the
windows, 20 all of them with hands raised
toward heaven, making supplication.
21 It was pitiful to see the populace vari-
ously prostrated in prayer and the high
priest full of dread and anguish.

Divine Intervention. 22 While they
were imploring the almighty Lord to
keep the deposits safe and secure for
those who had placed them in trust,
23 Heliodorus went on with his plan.
24 But just as he was approaching the
treasury with his bodyguards, the Lord
of spirits who holds all power manifested
himself in so striking a way that those
who had been bold enough to follow He-
liodorus were panic-stricken at God's
power and fainted away in terror.
25 There appeared to them a richly ca-
parisoned horse, mounted by a dreadful
rider. Charging furiously, the horse at-
tacked Heliodorus with its front hoofs.
The rider was seen to be wearing golden
armor. 26 Then two other young men, re-
markably strong, strikingly beautiful,
and splendidly attired, appeared before
him. Standing on each side of him, they
flogged him unceasingly until they had
given him innumerable blows. 27 Sud-
denly he fell to the ground, enveloped
in great darkness. Men picked him up
and laid him on a stretcher. 28 The man
who a moment before had entered
that treasury with a great retinue and
his whole bodyguard was carried away
helpless, having clearly experienced the
sovereign power of God. 29 While he lay
speechless and deprived of all hope of
aid, due to an act of God's power, 30 the
Jews praised the Lord who had marvel-
ously glorified his holy Place; and the
temple, charged so shortly before with
fear and commotion, was filled with joy
and gladness, now that the almighty
Lord had manifested himself.

31 Soon some of the companions of He-
liodorus begged Onias to invoke the
Most High, praying that the life of the
man who was about to expire might be
spared. 32 Fearing that the king might
think that Heliodorus had suffered some
foul play at the hands of the Jews, the
high priest offered a sacrifice for the
man's recovery. 33 While the high priest
was offering the sacrifice of atonement,
the same young men in the same cloth-
ing again appeared and stood before He-
liodorus. "Be very grateful to the high
priest Onias," they told him. "It is for
his sake that the Lord has spared your
life. 34 Since you have been scourged by
Heaven, proclaim to all men the majesty
of God's power." When they had said
this, they disappeared.

Testimony of Heliodorus. 35 After He-
liodorus had offered a sacrifice to the
Lord and made most solemn vows to
him who had spared his life, he bade
Onias farewell, and returned with his
soldiers to the king. 36 Before all men he
gave witness to the deeds of the most
high God that he had seen with his own
eyes. 37 When the king asked Heliodorus
who would be a suitable man to be sent
to Jerusalem next, he answered: 38 "If
you have an enemy or a plotter against
the government, send him there, and
you will receive him back well-flogged,
if indeed he survives at all; for there is
certainly some special divine power
about the Place. 39 He who has his dwell-
ing in heaven watches over that Place
and protects it, and he strikes down and
destroys those who come to harm it."
40 This was how the matter concerning
Heliodorus and the preservation of the
treasury turned out.

IV: PROFANATION AND PERSECUTION

CHAPTER 4

Onias Appeals to the King. 1 The Si-
mon mentioned above as the informer
about the funds against his own country,
made false accusation that it was Onias
who threatened Heliodorus and insti-
gated the whole miserable affair. 2 He
dared to brand as a plotter against the
government the man who was a bene-
factor of the city, a protector of his com-
patriots, and a zealous defender of the
laws. 3 When Simon's hostility reached
such a point that murders were being
committed by one of his henchmen,
4 Onias saw that the opposition was seri-
ous and that Apollonius, son of Menes-
theus, the governor of Coelesyria and
Phoenicia, was abetting Simon's wick-
edness. 5 So he had recourse to the king,
not as an accuser of his countrymen, but
as a man looking to the general and par-
ticular good of all the people. 6 He saw
that, unless the king intervened, it would
be impossible to have a peaceful govern-
ment, and that Simon would not desist
from his folly.

Jews Led by Jason to Apostatize.
7*† But Seleucus died, and when Antio-
chus surnamed Epiphanes succeeded
him on the throne, Onias' brother Jason
obtained the high priesthood by corrupt
means: 8 in an interview, he promised
the king three hundred and sixty talents
of silver, as well as eighty talents from
another source of income. 9† Besides this
he agreed to pay a hundred and fifty
more, if he were given authority to es-
tablish a gymnasium and a youth club
for it and to enroll men in Jerusalem as
Antiochians.

10 When Jason received the king's ap-
proval and came into office, he immedi-
ately initiated his countrymen into the
Greek way of life. 11*† He set aside the
royal concessions granted to the Jews
through the mediation of John, father
of Eupolemus (that Eupolemus who
would later go on an embassy to the Ro-
mans to establish a treaty of friendship
with them); he abrogated the lawful
institutions and introduced customs
contrary to the law. 12*† He quickly es-
tablished a gymnasium at the very foot
of the acropolis, where he induced the
noblest young men to wear the Greek
hat. 13 The craze for Hellenism and for-
eign customs reached such a pitch,
through the outrageous wickedness of
the ungodly pseudo-high-priest Jason,
14 that the priests no longer cared about
the service of the altar. Disdaining the
temple and neglecting the sacrifices,
they hastened, at the signal for the dis-
cus-throwing, to take part in the unlaw-
ful exercises on the athletic field. 15 They
despised what their ancestors had re-
garded as honors, while they highly
prized what the Greeks esteemed as
glory. 16 Precisely because of this, they
found themselves in serious trouble: the
very people whose manner of life they
emulated, and whom they desired to im-
itate in everything, became their ene-
mies and oppressors. 17 It is no light
matter to flout the laws of God, as the
following period will show.

18 When the quinquennial games were
held at Tyre in the presence of the king,
19 the vile Jason sent envoys as repre-
sentatives of the Antiochians of Jerusa-
lem, to bring there three hundred silver
drachmas for the sacrifice to Hercules.
But the bearers themselves decided that
the money should not be spent on a sac-
rifice, as that was not right, but should
be used for some other purpose. 20† So
the contribution destined by the sender
for the sacrifice to Hercules was in fact
applied, by those who brought it, to the
construction of triremes.

21† When Apollonius, son of Menes-
theus, was sent to Egypt for the coro-
nation of King Philometor, Antiochus
learned that the king was opposed to his
policies; so he took measures for his own
security. 22 After going to Joppa, he pro-
ceeded to Jerusalem. There he was re-
ceived with great pomp by Jason and
the people of the city, who escorted him
with torchlights and acclamations; fol-
lowing this, he led his army into Phoeni-
cia.

Menelaus Supplants Jason. 23† Three
years later Jason sent Menelaus, brother
of the aforementioned Simon, to deliver
the money to the king, and to obtain de-
cisions on some important matters.
24 When he had been introduced to the
king, he flattered him with such an air
of authority that he secured the high
priesthood for himself, outbidding Jason
by three hundred talents of silver. 25 He
returned with the royal commission, but
with nothing that made him worthy of
the high priesthood; he had the temper
of a cruel tyrant and the rage of a wild
beast. 26 Then Jason, who had cheated
his own brother and now saw himself
cheated by another man, was driven out
as a fugitive to the country of the Am-
monites.

27 Although Menelaus had obtained
the office, he did not make any payments
of the money he had promised to the
king, 28 in spite of the demand of Sostra-
tus, the commandant of the citadel,
whose duty it was to collect the taxes.
For this reason, both were summoned
before the king. 29 Menelaus left his
brother Lysimachus as his substitute in
the high priesthood, while Sostratus left
Crates, commander of the Cypriots, as
his substitute.

Murder of Onias. 30† While these
things were taking place, the people of
Tarsus and Mallus rose in revolt, be-
cause their cities had been given as a

*

4, 7: 1, 7; 1 Mc 1, 10. 11: 1 Mc 8, 17. 12: 1 Mc 1, 14.

†

4, 7: *Seleucus died:* he was murdered by Heliodorus. *Antiochus Epiphanes* was his younger brother. Onias' brother showed his love for *the Greek way of life* (v 10) by changing his Hebrew name Joshua, or Jesus, to the Greek name *Jason.*

4, 9: *Youth club:* an educational institution in which young men were trained both in Greek intellectual culture and in physical fitness. *Antiochians:* honorary citizens of Antioch, a Hellenistic city of the Seleucid Kingdom that had a corporation of such Antiochians, who enjoyed certain political and commercial privileges.

4, 11: *Eupolemus:* one of the two envoys sent to Rome by Judas Maccabeus (1 Mc 8, 17).

4, 12: Since the *gymnasium,* where the youth exercised naked (Greek *gymnos*), lay in the Tyropoeon Valley to the east of the citadel, it was directly next to the temple on its eastern side. *The Greek hat:* a wide-brimmed hat, traditional headgear of Hermes, the patron god of athletic contests; it formed part of the distinctive costume of the members of the "youth club."

4, 20: *Triremes:* war vessels with three banks of oars.

4, 21: *Philometor:* Ptolemy VI, king of Egypt, c. 172 to c. 145 B.C.

4, 23: *Menelaus:* Jewish high priest from c. 172 to his execution in 162 B.C. (13, 3-8).

4, 30: *Mallus:* a city of Cilicia (v 36) in southeastern Asia Minor, about thirty miles east of *Tarsus.*

gift to Antiochis, the king's mistress.
31 The king, therefore, went off in haste
to settle the affair, leaving Andronicus,
one of his nobles, as his deputy. 32 Then
Menelaus, thinking this a good opportu-
nity, stole some gold vessels from the
temple and presented them to Androni-
cus; he had already sold some other ves-
sels in Tyre and in the neighboring
cities. 33 When Onias had clear evidence
of the facts, he made a public pro-
test, after withdrawing to the inviolable
sanctuary at Daphne, near Antioch.
34 Thereupon Menelaus approached An-
dronicus privately and asked him to lay
hands on Onias. So Andronicus went to
Onias, and by treacherously reassuring
him through sworn pledges with right
hands joined, persuaded him, in spite of
his suspicions, to leave the sanctuary.
Then, without any regard for justice, he
immediately put him to death.

35 As a result, not only the Jews, but
many people of other nations as well,
were indignant and angry over the un-
just murder of the man. 36† When the
king returned from the region of Cilicia,
the Jews of the city, together with the
Greeks who detested the crime, went to
see him about the murder of Onias.
37 Antiochus was deeply grieved and full
of pity; he wept as he recalled the pru-
dence and noble conduct of the de-
ceased. 38 Inflamed with anger, he
immediately stripped Andronicus of his
purple robe, tore off his other garments,
and had him led through the whole city
to the very place where he had commit-
ted the outrage against Onias; and there
he put the murderer to death. Thus the
Lord rendered him the punishment he
deserved.

Riot against Lysimachus. 39† Many
sacrilegious thefts had been committed
by Lysimachus in the city with the con-
nivance of Menelaus. When word was
spread that a large number of gold ves-
sels had been stolen, the people assem-
bled in protest against Lysimachus. 40 As
the crowds, now thoroughly enraged,
began to riot, Lysimachus launched an
unjustified attack against them with
about three thousand armed men under
the leadership of Auranus, a man as ad-
vanced in folly as he was in years.
41 Reacting against Lysimachus' attack,
the people picked up stones or pieces of
wood or handfuls of the ashes lying there
and threw them in wild confusion at Ly-
simachus and his men. 42 As a result,
they wounded many of them and even
killed a few, while they put all the rest
to flight. The sacrilegious thief himself
they slew near the treasury.

43 Charges about this affair were
brought against Menelaus. 44† When the
king came to Tyre, three men sent by
the senate presented to him the justice
of their cause. 45* But Menelaus, seeing
himself on the losing side, promised
Ptolemy, son of Dorymenes, a substan-
tial sum of money if he would win the
king over. 46 So Ptolemy retired with the
king under a colonnade, as if to get some
fresh air, and persuaded him to change
his mind. 47 Menelaus, who was the
cause of all the trouble, the king acquit-
ted of the charges, while he condemned
to death those poor men who would have
been declared innocent even if they had
pleaded their case before Scythians.
48 Thus, those who had prosecuted the
case for the city, for the people, and for
the sacred vessels, quickly suffered un-
just punishment. 49 For this reason, even
some Tyrians were indignant over the
crime and provided sumptuously for
their burial. 50 But Menelaus, thanks to
the covetousness of the men in power,
remained in office, where he grew in
wickedness and became the chief plotter
against his fellow citizens.

CHAPTER 5

Sedition and Death of Jason.
1*† About this time Antiochus sent his
second expedition into Egypt. 2* It then
happened that all over the city, for
nearly forty days, there appeared
horsemen charging in midair, clad in
garments interwoven with gold—com-
panies fully armed with lances 3 and
drawn swords; squadrons of cavalry
in battle array, charges and counter-
charges on this side and that, with brand-
ished shields and bristling spears, flights
of arrows and flashes of gold ornaments,
together with armor of every sort.
4 Therefore all prayed that this vision
might be a good omen.

5† But when a false rumor circulated
that Antiochus was dead, Jason gath-
ered fully a thousand men and suddenly
attacked the city. As the defenders on
the walls were forced back and the city
was finally being taken, Menelaus took
refuge in the citadel. 6 Jason then
slaughtered his fellow citizens without

*

45: 8, 8; 1 Mc 3, 38.
5, 1: 1 Mc 1, 17.
2f: 3, 24ff; 10, 29f; 11, 8.

†

4, 36: *The city:* Antioch. But some understand the Greek to mean "each city."

4, 39: *The city:* Jerusalem. *Menelaus* was still in Syria.

4, 44: *The senate:* the council of Jewish elders at Jerusalem; cf 1 Mc 12, 6.

5, 1: *Second expedition:* the first invasion of Egypt by Antiochus in 169 B.C. (1 Mc 1, 16-20) is not mentioned in 2 Mc, unless the coming of the Syrian army to Palestine (2 Mc 4, 21f) is regarded as the first invasion. The author of 2 Mc apparently combines the first pillage of Jerusalem in 169 B.C. after Antiochus' first invasion of Egypt (1 Mc 1, 20-28; cf 2 Mc 5, 5ff) with the second pillage of the city two years later (167 B.C.), following the king's second invasion of Egypt in 168 B.C. (1 Mc 1, 29-35; cf 2 Mc 5, 24ff).

5, 5: *Jason:* brother of Onias III, was claimant of the high priesthood (4, 7-10). Later he was supplanted by Menelaus who drove him into Transjordan (4, 26).

mercy, not realizing that triumph over one's own kindred was the greatest failure, but imagining that he was winning a victory over his enemies, not his fellow countrymen. 7 Even so, he did not gain control of the government, but in the end received only disgrace for his treachery, and once again took refuge in the country of the Ammonites. 8† At length he met a miserable end. Called to account before Aretas, king of the Arabs, he fled from city to city, hunted by all men, hated as a transgressor of the laws, abhorred as the butcher of his country and his countrymen. After being driven into Egypt, 9 he crossed the sea to the Spartans, among whom he hoped to find protection because of his relations with them. There he who had exiled so many from their country perished in exile; 10 and he who had cast out so many to lie unburied went unmourned himself with no funeral of any kind or any place in the tomb of his ancestors.

The City Ravaged. 11* When these happenings were reported to the king, he thought that Judea was in revolt. Raging like a wild animal, he set out from Egypt and took Jerusalem by storm. 12 He ordered his soldiers to cut down without mercy those whom they met and to slay those who took refuge in their houses. 13 There was a massacre of young and old, a killing of women and children, a slaughter of virgins and infants. 14 In the space of three days, eighty thousand were lost, forty thousand meeting a violent death, and the same number being sold into slavery. 15 Not satisfied with this, the king dared to enter the holiest temple in the world; Menelaus, that traitor both to the laws and to his country, served as guide. 16 He laid his impure hands on the sacred vessels and gathered up with profane hands the votive offerings made by other kings for the advancement, the glory, and the honor of the Place. 17* Puffed up in spirit, Antiochus did not realize that it was because of the sins of the city's inhabitants that the Lord was angry for a little while and hence disregarded the holy Place. 18 If they had not become entangled in so many sins, this man, like Heliodorus, who was sent by King Seleucus to inspect the treasury, would have been flogged and turned back from his presumptuous action as soon as he approached. 19*† The Lord, however, had not chosen the people for the sake of the Place, but the Place for the sake of the people. 20 Therefore, the Place itself, having shared in the people's misfortunes, afterward participated in their good fortune; and what the Almighty had forsaken in his anger was restored in all its glory, once the great Sovereign became reconciled.

21* Antiochus carried off eighteen hundred talents from the temple, and hurried back to Antioch. In his arrogance he planned to make the land navigable and the sea passable on foot, so carried away was he with pride. 22† But he left governors to harass the nation: at Jerusalem, Philip, a Phrygian by birth, and in character more cruel than the man who appointed him; 23† at Mount Gerizim, Andronicus; and besides these, Menelaus, who lorded it over his fellow citizens worse than the others did. Out of hatred for the Jewish citizens, 24*† the king sent Appollonius, commander of the Mysians, at the head of an army of twenty-two thousand men, with orders to kill all the grown men and sell the women and young men into slavery. 25 When this man arrived in Jerusalem, he pretended to be peacefully disposed and waited until the holy day of the sabbath; then, finding the Jews refraining from work, he ordered his men to parade fully armed. 26 All those who came out to watch, he massacred, and running through the city with armed men, he cut down a large number of people.

27* But Judas Maccabeus and about nine others withdrew to the wilderness, where he and his companions lived like wild animals in the hills, continuing to eat what grew wild to avoid sharing the defilement.

CHAPTER 6

The Temple Desecrated. 1* Not long after this the king sent an Athenian senator to force the Jews to abandon the customs of their ancestors and live no longer by the laws of God; 2*† also to profane the temple in Jerusalem and dedicate it to Olympian Zeus, and that on Mount Gerizim to Zeus the Hospitable, as the inhabitants of the place requested. 3 This intensified the evil in an intolerable and utterly disgusting way.

*

11-21: 1 Mc 1, 20-24.
17: 6, 12-16; 7, 16-19.32-38.
19f: 3, 1ff; 1 Chr 17, 9; Mk 2, 27.
21: 1 Mc 1, 23f.
24ff: 1 Mc 1, 29f.
27: 1 Mc 2, 28.
6, 1-11: 1 Mc 1, 44-63.
2: 1 Mc 1, 46; Dn 9, 27.

†

5, 8: *Aretas:* King Aretas I of the Nabateans; cf 1 Mc 5, 25.

5, 19: Man is more important than even the most sacred institutions; cf Mk 2, 27.

5, 22: *Philip, a Phrygian by birth:* the Philip of 6, 11 and 8, 8, but probably not the same as Philip the regent of 9, 29 and 1 Mc 6, 14.

5, 23: *Mount Gerizim:* the sacred mountain of the Samaritans at Shechem; cf 6, 2.

5, 24: *Apollonius:* the *Mysian commander* of 1 Mc 1, 29; mentioned also in 2 Mc 3, 5; 4, 4.

6, 2: *Olympian Zeus:* equated with the Syrian Baal Shamen ("the lord of the heavens"), a term which the Jews rendered as "Shiqqus shomem," *horrible abomination* (Dn 9, 27; 11, 31; 12, 11; 1 Mc 1, 54).

4† The Gentiles filled the temple with debauchery and revelry; they amused themselves with prostitutes and had intercourse with women even in the sacred court. They also brought into the temple things that were forbidden, 5 so that the altar was covered with abominable offerings prohibited by the laws.

Abolition of the Law. 6 A man could not keep the sabbath or celebrate the traditional feasts, nor even admit that he was a Jew. 7† Moreover, at the monthly celebration of the king's birthday the Jews had, from bitter necessity, to partake of the sacrifices, and when the festival of Dionysus was celebrated, they were compelled to march in his procession, wearing wreaths of ivy.

8 At the suggestion of the citizens of Ptolemais, a decree was issued ordering the neighboring Greek cities to act in the same way against the Jews: oblige them to partake of the sacrifices, 9 and put to death those who would not consent to adopt the customs of the Greeks. It was obvious, therefore, that disaster impended. 10* Thus, two women who were arrested for having circumcised their children were publicly paraded about the city with their babies hanging at their breasts and then thrown down from the top of the city wall. 11* Others, who had assembled in nearby caves to observe the sabbath in secret, were betrayed to Philip and all burned to death. In their respect for the holiness of that day, they had scruples about defending themselves.

Purpose of Divine Judgment. 12* Now I beg those who read this book not to be disheartened by these misfortunes, but to consider that these chastisements were meant not for the ruin but for the correction of our nation. 13 It is, in fact, a sign of great kindness to punish sinners promptly instead of letting them go for long. 14* Thus, in dealing with other nations, the Lord patiently waits until they reach the full measure of their sins before he punishes them; but with us he has decided to deal differently, 15 in order that he may not have to punish us more severely later, when our sins have reached their fullness. 16 He never withdraws his mercy from us. Although he disciplines us with misfortunes, he does not abandon his own people. 17 Let these words suffice for recalling this truth. Without further ado we must go on with our story.

Martyrdom of Eleazar. 18*† Eleazar, one of the foremost scribes, a man of advanced age and noble appearance, was being forced to open his mouth to eat pork. 19 But preferring a glorious death to a life of defilement, he spat out the meat, and went forward of his own accord to the instrument of torture, 20 as men ought to do who have the courage to reject the food which it is unlawful to taste even for love of life. 21 Those in charge of that unlawful ritual meal took the man aside privately, because of their long acquaintance with him, and urged him to bring meat of his own providing, such as he could legitimately eat, and to pretend to be eating some of the meat of the sacrifice prescribed by the king; 22 in this way he would escape the death penalty, and be treated kindly because of their old friendship with him. 23 But he made up his mind in a noble manner, worthy of his years, the dignity of his advanced age, the merited distinction of his gray hair, and of the admirable life he had lived from childhood; and so he declared that above all he would be loyal to the holy laws given by God.

He told them to send him at once to the abode of the dead, explaining: 24 "At our age it would be unbecoming to make such a pretense; many young men would think the ninety-year-old Eleazar had gone over to an alien religion. 25 Should I thus dissimulate for the sake of a brief moment of life, they would be led astray by me, while I would bring shame and dishonor on my old age. 26 Even if, for the time being, I avoid the punishment of men, I shall never, whether alive or dead, escape the hands of the Almighty. 27 Therefore, by manfully giving up my life now, I will prove myself worthy of my old age, 28 and I will leave to the young a noble example of how to die willingly and generously for the revered and holy laws."

He spoke thus, and went immediately to the instrument of torture. 29 Those who shortly before had been kindly disposed, now became hostile toward him because what he had said seemed to them utter madness. 30 When he was about to die under the blows, he groaned and said: "The Lord in his holy knowledge knows full well that, although I could have escaped death, I am not only enduring terrible pain in my body from this scourging, but also suffering it with joy in my soul because of my devotion to him." 31 This is how he died, leaving

*

10: 1 Mc 1, 60f.
11: 1 Mc 2, 32-38.
12-16: 5, 17; 7, 16-19.32-38.
14: Wis 11, 9f; 12, 2.22.
18: Lv 11, 7f; Heb 11, 35.

†

6, 4: *Amused themselves with prostitutes:* as in the fertility cults of the ancient Near East; see notes on Bar 6, 10.42f.

6, 7: *Dionysus:* called also Bacchus, the god of the grape harvest and of wine; *ivy* was one of his symbols.

6, 18—7, 42: The stories of Eleazar and of the mother and her seven sons, among the earliest models of "martyrology," were understandably popular among the Christians of the early centuries. Written originally to encourage God's people in times of persecution, they add gruesome details to the record of tortures, and place long speeches in the mouths of the martyrs.

in his death a model of courage and an
unforgettable example of virtue not only
for the young but for the whole nation.

CHAPTER 7

***Martyrdom of a Mother and Her
Sons.*** 1* It also happened that seven
brothers with their mother were ar-
rested and tortured with whips and
scourges by the king, to force them to
eat pork in violation of God's law. 2 One
of the brothers, speaking for the others,
said: "What do you expect to achieve by
questioning us? We are ready to die
rather than transgress the laws of our
ancestors." 3 At that the king, in a fury,
gave orders to have pans and caldrons
heated. 4 While they were being quickly
heated, he commanded his executioners
to cut out the tongue of the one who had
spoken for the others, to scalp him and
cut off his hands and feet, while the rest
of his brothers and his mother looked
on. 5 When he was completely maimed
but still breathing, the king ordered
them to carry him to the fire and fry
him. As a cloud of smoke spread from
the pan, the brothers and their mother
encouraged one another to die bravely,
saying such words as these: 6* "The
Lord God is looking on, and he truly has
compassion on us, as Moses declared in
his canticle, when he protested openly
with the words, 'And he will have pity
on his servants.' "

7 When the first brother had died in
this manner, they brought the second to
be made sport of. After tearing off the
skin and hair of his head, they asked
him, "Will you eat the pork rather than
have your body tortured limb by limb?"
8 Answering in the language of his fore-
fathers, he said, "Never!" So he too in
turn suffered the same tortures as the
first. 9*† At the point of death he said:
"You accursed fiend, you are depriving
us of this present life, but the King of
the world will raise us up to live again
forever. It is for his laws that we are dy-
ing."

10 After him the third suffered their
cruel sport. He put out his tongue at once
when told to do so, and bravely held out
his hands, 11* as he spoke these noble
words: "It was from Heaven that I re-
ceived these; for the sake of his laws I
disdain them; from him I hope to receive
them again." 12 Even the king and his
attendants marveled at the young man's
courage, because he regarded his suf-
ferings as nothing.

13 After he had died, they tortured and
maltreated the fourth brother in the
same way. 14 When he was near death,
he said, "It is my choice to die at the
hands of men with the God-given hope
of being restored to life by him; but for
you, there will be no resurrection to life."

15 They next brought forward the fifth
brother and maltreated him. Looking at
the king, 16* he said: "Since you have
power among men, mortal though you
are, do what you please. But do not think
that our nation is forsaken by God.
17 Only wait, and you will see how his
great power will torment you and your
descendants."

18 After him they brought the sixth
brother. When he was about to die, he
said: "Have no vain illusions. We suffer
these things on our own account, be-
cause we have sinned against our God;
that is why such astonishing things have
happened to us. 19* Do not think, then,
that you will go unpunished for having
dared to fight against God."

20 Most admirable and worthy of ever-
lasting remembrance was the mother,
who saw her seven sons perish in a sin-
gle day, yet bore it courageously be-
cause of her hope in the Lord. 21 Filled
with a noble spirit that stirred her wom-
anly heart with manly courage, she ex-
horted each of them in the language of
their forefathers with these words: 22 "I
do not know how you came into exis-
tence in my womb; it was not I who gave
you the breath of life, nor was it I who
set in order the elements of which each
of you is composed. 23 Therefore, since
it is the Creator of the universe who
shapes each man's beginning, as he
brings about the origin of everything, he,
in his mercy, will give you back both
breath and life, because you now disre-
gard yourselves for the sake of his law."

24 Antiochus, suspecting insult in her
words, thought he was being ridiculed.
As the youngest brother was still alive,
the king appealed to him, not with mere
words, but with promises on oath, to
make him rich and happy if he would
abandon his ancestral customs: he
would make him his Friend and entrust
him with high office. 25 When the youth
paid no attention to him at all, the king
appealed to the mother, urging her to
advise her boy to save his life. 26 After
he had urged her for a long time, she
went through the motions of persuading
her son. 27 In derision of the cruel tyrant,
she leaned over close to her son and said
in their native language: "Son, have pity
on me, who carried you in my womb for
nine months, nursed you for three years,
brought you up, educated and supported

*

7, 1: Jer 15, 9.
6: Dt 32, 36.
9: 12, 44; 14, 46.
11: 12, 43ff.
16-19: 5, 17; 6, 12-16.
19: Acts 5, 39.

†

7, 9: *The King of the world will raise us up:* here, and in vv 11.14.23.29.36, belief in the future resurrection of the body, at least for the just, is clearly stated; cf also 12, 44; 14, 46; Dn 12, 2.

you to your present age. [28]† I beg you, child, to look at the heavens and the earth and see all that is in them; then you will know that God did not make them out of existing things; and in the same way the human race came into existence. [29] Do not be afraid of this executioner, but be worthy of your brothers and accept death, so that in the time of mercy I may receive you again with them."

[30] She had scarcely finished speaking when the youth said: "What are you waiting for? I will not obey the king's command. I obey the command of the law given to our forefathers through Moses. [31] But you, who have contrived every kind of affliction for the Hebrews, will not escape the hands of God. [32]* We, indeed, are suffering because of our sins. [33] Though our living Lord treats us harshly for a little while to correct us with chastisements, he will again be reconciled with his servants. [34] But you, wretch, vilest of all men! do not, in your insolence, concern yourself with unfounded hopes, as you raise your hand against the children of Heaven. [35] You have not yet escaped the judgment of the almighty and all-seeing God. [36] My brothers, after enduring brief pain, have drunk of never-failing life, under God's covenant, but you, by the judgment of God, shall receive just punishments for your arrogance. [37] Like my brothers, I offer up my body and my life for our ancestral laws, imploring God to show mercy soon to our nation, and by afflictions and blows to make you confess that he alone is God. [38] Through me and my brothers, may there be an end to the wrath of the Almighty that has justly fallen on our whole nation." [39] At that, the king became enraged and treated him even worse than the others, since he bitterly resented the boy's contempt. [40]* Thus he too died undefiled, putting all his trust in the Lord. [41] The mother was last to die, after her sons.

[42] Enough has been said about the sacrificial meals and the excessive cruelties.

V: VICTORIES OF JUDAS AND PURIFICATION OF THE TEMPLE

CHAPTER 8

Judas Maccabeus. [1]* Judas Maccabeus and his companions entered the villages, secretly, summoned their kinsmen, and by also enlisting others who remained faithful to Judaism, assembled about six thousand men. [2] They implored the Lord to look kindly upon his people, who were being oppressed on all sides; to have pity on the temple, which was profaned by godless men; [3] to have mercy on the city, which was being destroyed and about to be leveled to the ground; to hearken to the blood that cried out to him; [4] to remember the criminal slaughter of innocent children and the blasphemies uttered against his name; and to manifest his hatred of evil. [5]* Once Maccabeus got his men organized, the Gentiles could not withstand him, for the Lord's wrath had now changed to mercy. [6] Coming unexpectedly upon towns and villages, he would set them on fire. He captured strategic positions, and put to flight a large number of the enemy. [7] He preferred the nights as being especially helpful for such attacks. Soon the fame of his valor spread everywhere.

First Victory over Nicanor. [8]*† When Philip saw that Judas was gaining ground little by little and that his successful advances were becoming more frequent, he wrote to Ptolemy, governor of Coelesyria and Phoenicia, to come to the aid of the king's government. [9]* Ptolemy promptly selected Nicanor, son of Patroclus, one of the Chief Friends, and sent him at the head of at least twenty thousand armed men of various nations to wipe out the entire Jewish race. With him he associated Gorgias, a professional military commander, well-versed in the art of war. [10] Nicanor planned to raise the two thousand talents of tribute owed by the king to the Romans by selling captured Jews into slavery. [11] So he immediately sent word to the coastal cities, inviting them to buy Jewish slaves and promising to deliver ninety slaves for a talent—little did he dream of the punishment that was to fall upon him from the Almighty.

[12] When Judas learned of Nicanor's advance and informed his companions about the approach of the army, [13] the cowardly and those who lacked faith in God's justice deserted and got away. [14] But the others sold everything they had left, and at the same time besought the Lord to deliver those whom the ungodly Nicanor had sold before even meeting them. [15] They begged the Lord to do this, if not for their sake, at least for the sake of the covenants made with their forefathers, and because they themselves bore his holy, glorious name.

*

7, 32.38: 5, 17; 6, 12-16; 17, 16-19.
40f: Heb 11, 35.
8, 1-7: 5, 27; 1 Mc 3, 10-26.
5ff: 1 Mc 3, 3-9.
8: 4, 45; 1 Mc 3, 38.
9: 1 Mc 7, 26.

†

7, 28: *God did not make them out of existing things:* that is, God made all things solely by his omnipotent will and his creative word; cf Heb 11, 3.

8, 8-29.34ff: This account of the campaign of Nicanor and Gorgias against Judas is paralleled, with certain differences, in 1 Mc 3, 38—4, 24.

16 Maccabeus assembled his men, six
thousand strong, and exhorted them not
to be panic-stricken before the enemy,
nor to fear the large number of the Gen-
tiles attacking them unjustly, but to fight
courageously, 17 keeping before their
eyes the lawless outrage perpetrated by
the Gentiles against the holy Place and
the affliction of the humiliated city, as
well as the subversion of their ancestral
way of life. 18 "They trust in weapons
and acts of daring," he said, "but we
trust in almighty God, who can by a
mere nod destroy not only those who at-
tack us, but the whole world." 19* He
went on to tell them of the times when
help had been given their ancestors:
both the time of Sennacherib, when a
hundred and eighty-five thousand of his
men were destroyed, 20 and the time of
the battle in Babylonia against the Gala-
tians, when only eight thousand Jews
fought along with four thousand Mace-
donians; yet when the Macedonians
were hard pressed, the eight thousand
routed one hundred and twenty thou-
sand and took a great quantity of booty,
because of the help they received from
Heaven. 21 With such words he encour-
aged them and made them ready to die
for their laws and their country.

Then Judas divided his army into four,
22† placing his brothers, Simon, Joseph,
and Jonathan, each over a division, as-
signing to each fifteen hundred men.
23* (There was also Eleazar.) After
reading to them from the holy book and
giving them the watchword, "The Help
of God," he himself took charge of the
first division and joined in battle with
Nicanor. 24 With the Almighty as their
ally, they killed more than nine thou-
sand of the enemy, wounded and dis-
abled the greater part of Nicanor's
army, and put all of them to flight.
25 They also seized the money of those
who had come to buy them as slaves.
When they had pursued the enemy for
some time, 26 they were obliged to return
by reason of the late hour, it was the day
before the sabbath, and for that reason
they could not continue the pursuit.
27 They collected the enemy's arms and
stripped them of their spoils, and then
observed the sabbath with fervent praise
and thanks to the Lord who kept them
safe for that day on which he let descend
on them the first dew of his mercy.
28 After the sabbath, they gave a share
of the booty to the persecuted and to
widows and orphans; the rest they di-
vided among themselves and their
children. 29 When this was done, they
made supplication in common, implor-
ing the merciful Lord to be completely
reconciled with his servants.

Timothy and Bacchides Defeated.
30 They also challenged the forces of
Timothy and Bacchides, killed more
than twenty thousand of them, and cap-
tured some very high fortresses. They
divided the enormous plunder, allotting
half to themselves and the rest to the
persecuted, to orphans, widows, and the
aged. 31 They collected the enemies'
weapons and carefully stored them in
suitable places; the rest of the spoils they
carried to Jerusalem. 32 They also killed
the commander of Timothy's forces, a
most wicked man, who had done great
harm to the Jews. 33 While celebrating
the victory in their ancestral city, they
burned both those who had set fire to
the sacred gates and Callisthenes, who
had taken refuge in a little house; so he
received the reward his wicked deeds
deserved.

Humiliation of Nicanor. 34* The ac-
cursed Nicanor, who had brought the
thousand slave dealers to buy the Jews,
35 after being humbled through the
Lord's help by those whom he had
thought of no account, laid aside his fine
clothes and fled alone across country
like a runaway slave, until he reached
Antioch. He was eminently successful in
destroying his own army. 36 So he who
had promised to provide tribute for the
Romans by the capture of the people of
Jerusalem testified that the Jews had a
champion, and that they were invulner-
able for the very reason that they fol-
lowed the laws laid down by him.

CHAPTER 9

***Punishment and Death of Antio-
chus.*** 1*† About that time Antiochus re-
treated in disgrace from the region of
Persia. 2 He had entered the city called
Persepolis and attempted to rob the
temple and gain control of the city.
Thereupon the people had swift recourse
to arms, and Antiochus' men were
routed, so that in the end Antiochus was
put to flight by the natives and forced
to beat a shameful retreat. 3 On his
arrival in Ecbatana, he learned what

*

19: 15, 22; 2 Kgs 19, 35; Is 37, 36.
23: 1 Mc 3, 48.
34f: 8, 23f; 1 Mc 7, 26.
9, 1-29: 1, 12-17; 1 Mc 6, 1-13.

†

8, 22: *Joseph:* called John in 1 Mc 2, 2; 9, 36.38; this paragraph interrupts the story of Nicanor's defeat, which is resumed in v 34. The purpose of the author apparently is to group together the defeats suffered by the Syrians on various occasions. Battles against Timothy are recounted in 1 Mc 5, 37-44 and 2 Mc 12, 10-25; against Bacchides, in 1 Mc 7, 8-20.

9, 1-28: In order to keep together the various accounts of God's punishment of the persecutors of his people, the author places here the stories of Antiochus' illness and death (in actuality the king died only after the purification of the temple; cf 1 Mc 4, 36-59; 6, 1-16; 2 Mc 10, 1-8); of Judas' campaigns in Idumea and Transjordan; cf 1 Mc 5, 1-51; 2 Mc 10, 14-38; and of the first expedition of Lysias (1 Mc 4, 26-35; 2 Mc 11, 1-15).

had happened to Nicanor and to Timothy's forces. 4 Overcome with anger, he planned to make the Jews suffer for the injury done by those who had put him to flight. Therefore he ordered his charioteer to drive without stopping until he finished the journey.

Yet the condemnation of Heaven rode with him, since he said in his arrogance, "I will make Jerusalem the common graveyard of the Jews as soon as I arrive there." 5* So the all-seeing Lord, the God of Israel, struck him down with an unseen but incurable blow; for scarcely had he uttered those words when he was seized with excruciating pains in his bowels and sharp internal torment, 6 a fit punishment for him who had tortured the bowels of others with many barbarous torments. 7 Far from giving up his insolence, he was all the more filled with arrogance. Breathing fire in his rage against the Jews, he gave orders to drive even faster. As a result he hurtled from the dashing chariot, and every part of his body was racked by the violent fall. 8* Thus he who previously, in his superhuman presumption, thought he could command the waves of the sea, and imagined he could weigh the mountaintops in his scales, was now thrown to the ground and had to be carried on a litter, clearly manifesting to all the power of God. 9* The body of this impious man swarmed with worms, and while he was still alive in hideous torments, his flesh rotted off, so that the entire army was sickened by the stench of his corruption. 10 Shortly before, he had thought that he could reach the stars of heaven, and now, no one could endure to transport the man because of this intolerable stench.

11 At last, broken in spirit, he began to give up his excessive arrogance, and to gain some understanding, under the scourge of God, for he was racked with pain unceasingly. 12 When he could no longer bear his own stench, he said, "It is right to be subject to God, and not to think one's mortal self divine." 13 Then this vile man vowed to the Lord, who would no longer have mercy on him, 14 that he would set free the holy city, toward which he had been hurrying with the intention of leveling it to the ground and making it a common graveyard; 15 he would put on perfect equality with the Athenians all the Jews, whom he had judged not even worthy of burial, but fit only to be thrown out with their children to be eaten by vultures and wild animals; 16 he would adorn with the finest offerings the holy temple which he had previously despoiled; he would restore all the sacred vessels many times over; and would provide from his own revenues the expenses required for the sacrifices. 17 Besides all this, he would become a Jew himself and visit every inhabited place to proclaim there the power of God. 18 But since God's punishment had justly come upon him, his sufferings were not lessened, so he lost hope for himself and wrote the following letter to the Jews in the form of a supplication. It read thus:

19† "To my esteemed Jewish citizens, Antiochus, their king and general, sends hearty greetings and best wishes for their health and happiness. 20 If you and your children are well and your affairs are going as you wish, I thank God very much, for my hopes are in heaven. 21 Now that I am ill, I recall with affection the esteem and good will you bear me. On returning from the regions of Persia, I fell victim to a troublesome illness; so I thought it necessary to form plans for the general welfare of all. 22 Actually, I do not despair about my health, since I have great hopes of recovering from my illness. 23 Nevertheless, I know that my father, whenever he went on campaigns in the hinterland, would name his successor, 24 so that, if anything unexpected happened or any unwelcome news came, the people throughout the realm would know to whom the government had been entrusted, and so not be disturbed. 25† I am also bearing in mind that the neighboring rulers, especially those on the borders of our kingdom, are on the watch for opportunities and waiting to see what will happen. I have therefore appointed as king my son Antiochus, whom I have often before entrusted and commended to most of you, when I made hurried visits to the outlying provinces. I have written to him the letter copied below. 26 Therefore I beg and entreat each of you to remember the general and individual benefits you have received, and to continue to show good will toward me and my son. 27 I am confident that, following my policy, he will treat you with mildness and kindness in his relations with you."

28 So this murderer and blasphemer, after extreme sufferings, such as he had inflicted on others, died a miserable death in the mountains of a foreign land. 29 His foster brother Philip brought the body home; but fearing Antiochus' son,

*

5: Acts 12, 20-23.
8: Jb 38, 8-11; Ps 65, 6f; Is 40, 12.
9: Acts 12, 23.

†

9, 19-27: Despite the statement in v 18, this letter is not really a *supplication.* It is rather a notification to all the king's subjects of the appointment of his son as his successor and a request that they be loyal to the new king. Apparently the same letter, which has every appearance of being authentic, was sent to the various peoples throughout the kingdom, with only a few words of address changed for each group.

9, 25: *The letter copied below:* not included in the text of 2 Mc.

he later withdrew into Egypt, to Ptolemy Philometor.

CHAPTER 10

Purification of Temple and City. 1* When Maccabeus and his companions, under the Lord's leadership, had recovered the temple and the city, 2 they destroyed the altars erected by the Gentiles in the marketplace and the sacred enclosures. 3† After purifying the temple, they made a new altar. Then, with fire struck from flint, they offered sacrifice for the first time in two years, burned incense, and lighted lamps. They also set out the showbread. 4 When they had done this, they prostrated themselves and begged the Lord that they might never again fall into such misfortunes, and that if they should sin at any time, he might chastise them with moderation and not hand them over to blasphemous and barbarous Gentiles. 5 On the anniversary of the day on which the temple had been profaned by the Gentiles, that is, the twenty-fifth of the same month Chislev, the purification of the temple took place.

6 The Jews celebrated joyfully for eight days as on the feast of Booths, remembering how, a little while before, they had spent the feast of Booths living like wild animals in caves on the mountains. 7 Carrying rods entwined with leaves, green branches and palms, they sang hymns of grateful praise to him who had brought about the purification of his own Place. 8 By public edict and decree they prescribed that the whole Jewish nation should celebrate these days every year.

VI: RENEWED PERSECUTION

Death of Ptolemy. 9* Such was the end of Antiochus surnamed Epiphanes. 10 Now we shall relate what happened under Antiochus Eupator, the son of that godless man, and shall give a summary of the chief evils caused by the wars. 11 When Eupator succeeded to the kingdom, he put a certain Lysias in charge of the government as commander-in-chief of Coelesyria and Phoenicia. 12† Ptolemy, surnamed Macron, had taken the lead in treating the Jews fairly because of the previous injustice that had been done them, and he endeavored to have peaceful relations with them. 13 As a result, he was accused before Eupator by the King's Friends. In fact, on all sides he heard himself called a traitor for having abandoned Cyprus, which Philometor had entrusted to him, and for having gone over to Antiochus Epiphanes. Since he could not command the respect due to his high office, he ended his life by taking poison.

Victory over the Idumeans. 14† When Gorgias became governor of the region, he employed foreign troops and used every opportunity to attack the Jews. 15* At the same time the Idumeans, who held some important strongholds, were harassing the Jews; they welcomed fugitives from Jerusalem and endeavored to continue the war. 16 Maccabeus and his companions, after public prayers asking God to be their ally, moved quickly against the strongholds of the Idumeans. 17 Attacking vigorously, they gained control of the places, drove back all who manned the walls, and cut down those who opposed them, killing as many as twenty thousand men. 18 When at least nine thousand took refuge in two very strong towers, containing everything necessary to sustain a siege, 19 Maccabeus left Simon and Joseph, along with Zacchaeus and his men, in sufficient numbers to besiege them, while he himself went off to places where he was more urgently needed. 20 But some of the men in Simon's force who were money lovers let themselves be bribed by some of the men in the towers; on receiving seventy thousand drachmas, they allowed a number of them to escape. 21 When Maccabeus was told what had happened, he assembled the rulers of the people and accused those men of having sold their kinsmen for money by setting their enemies free to fight against them. 22 So he put them to death as traitors, and without delay captured the two towers. 23 As he was successful at arms in all his undertakings, he destroyed more than twenty thousand men in the two strongholds.

Victory over Timothy. 24† Timothy, who had previously been defeated by the Jews, gathered a tremendous force of foreign troops and collected a large number of cavalry from Asia; then he appeared in Judea, ready to conquer it by force. 25 At his approach, Maccabeus and his men made supplication to God, sprinkling earth upon their heads and girding their loins in sackcloth. 26* Lying prostrate at the foot of the altar, they begged him to be gracious to them, and to be an enemy to their enemies, and a foe to their foes, as the law declares.

27 After the prayer, they took up their

*

10, 1-8: 1 Mc 4, 36-59.
9: 2, 21; 1 Mc 6, 17.
15-23: 1 Mc 5, 3ff.
26: Ex 23, 22.

†

10, 3: *Two years:* three years according to 1 Mc 1, 54 and 4, 52.

10, 12: *Ptolemy Macron:* son of Dorymenes (4, 45), was formerly hostile to the Jews (6, 8).

10, 14-23: Probably the same campaign of Judas against the Idumeans that is mentioned in 1 Mc 5, 1-3.

10, 24: *Timothy . . . previously . . . defeated by the Jews:* as recounted in 8, 30ff.

arms and advanced a considerable distance from the city, halting when they were close to the enemy. 28† As soon as dawn broke, the armies joined battle, the one having as pledge of success and victory not only their valor but also their reliance on the Lord, and the other taking fury as their leader in the fight.

29* In the midst of the fierce battle, there appeared to the enemy from the heavens five majestic men riding on golden-bridled horses, who led the Jews on. 30 They surrounded Maccabeus, and shielding him with their own armor, kept him from being wounded. They shot arrows and hurled thunderbolts at the enemy, who were bewildered and blinded, thrown into confusion and routed. 31 Twenty-five hundred of their foot soldiers and six hundred of their horsemen were slain. 32* Timothy, however, fled to a well-fortified stronghold called Gazara, where Chaereas was in command. 33 For four days Maccabeus and his men eagerly besieged the fortress. 34 Those inside, relying on the strength of the place, kept repeating outrageous blasphemies and uttering abominable words. 35 When the fifth day dawned, twenty young men in the army of Maccabeus, angered over such blasphemies, bravely stormed the wall and with savage fury cut down everyone they encountered. 36 Others who climbed up the same way swung around on the defenders, taking the besieged in the rear; they put the towers to the torch, spread the fire and burned the blasphemers alive. Still others broke down the gates and let in the rest of the troops, who took possession of the city. 37† Timothy had hidden in a cistern, but they killed him, along with his brother Chaereas, and Apollophanes. 38 On completing these exploits, they blessed, with hymns of grateful praise, the Lord who shows great kindness to Israel and grants them victory.

CHAPTER 11

Defeat of Lysias. 1*† Very soon afterward, Lysias, guardian and kinsman of the king and head of the government, being greatly displeased at what had happened, 2 mustered about eighty thousand infantry and all his cavalry and marched against the Jews. His plan was to make Jerusalem a Greek settlement; 3 to levy tribute on the temple, as he did on the sanctuaries of the other nations; and to put the high priesthood up for sale every year. 4 He did not take God's power into account at all, but felt exultant confidence in his myriads of foot soldiers, his thousands of horsemen, and his eighty elephants.

5 So he invaded Judea, and when he reached Beth-zur, a fortified place about twenty miles from Jerusalem, launched a strong attack against it. 6* When Maccabeus and his men learned that Lysias was besieging the strongholds, they and all the people begged the Lord with lamentations and tears to send a good angel to save Israel. 7 Maccabeus himself was the first to take up arms, and he exhorted the others to join him in risking their lives to help their kinsmen. Then they resolutely set out together. 8* Suddenly, while they were still near Jerusalem, a horseman appeared at their head, clothed in white garments and brandishing gold weapons. 9 Then all of them together thanked God for his mercy, and their hearts were filled with such courage that they were ready to assault not only men, but the most savage beasts, yes, even walls of iron. 10 Now that the Lord had shown his mercy toward them, they advanced in battle order with the aid of their heavenly ally. 11 Hurling themselves upon the enemy like lions, they laid low eleven thousand foot soldiers and sixteen hundred horsemen, and put all the rest to flight. 12 Most of those who got away were wounded and stripped of their arms, while Lysias himself escaped only by shameful flight.

Peace with the Syrians. 13* But Lysias was not a stupid man. He reflected on the defeat he had suffered, and came to realize that the Hebrews were invincible because the mighty God was their ally. He therefore sent a message 14 persuading them to settle everything on just terms, and promising to persuade the king also, and to induce him to become their friend. 15 Maccabeus, solicitous for the common good, agreed to all that Lysias proposed; and the king, on his part, granted in behalf of the Jews all the written requests of Maccabeus to Lysias.

Official Letters. 16 These are the terms of the letter which Lysias wrote to the Jews: "Lysias sends greetings to the Jewish people. 17 John and Absalom, your envoys, have presented your signed communication and asked about the matters contained in it. 18 Whatever had to be referred to the king I called

*

29f: 3, 24ff; 5, 2f; 10, 29f; 11, 8.
32: 1 Mc 13, 43-48.
11, 1-12: 1 Mc 4, 26-35.
6: Ex 23, 20.
8: 3, 24ff; 5, 2f; 10, 29f.
13-33: 1 Mc 6, 57-61.

†

10, 28: *As soon as dawn broke:* the same battle at dawn as in 1 Mc 5, 30-34.

10, 37: *Timothy . . . they killed:* apparently, the same Timothy is still alive in 12, 2.18-25. The present passage is not in chronological order; Gazara, v 32 (Gezer) was not captured by the Jews until much later (cf 1 Mc 9, 50ff; 13, 53).

11, 1-12: The defeat of Lysias at Beth-zur probably occurred before the purification of the temple; cf 1 Mc 4, 26-35.

to his attention, and the things that were
acceptable he has granted. [19] If you
maintain your loyalty to the govern-
ment, I will endeavor to further your in-
terests in the future. [20] On the details of
these matters I have authorized my rep-
resentatives, as well as your envoys, to
confer with you. [21]† Farewell." The year
one hundred and forty-eight, the
twenty-fourth of Dioscorinthius.
[22] The king's letter read thus: "King
Antiochus sends greetings to his brother
Lysias. [23] Now that our father has taken
his place among the gods, we wish the
subjects of our kingdom to be undis-
turbed in conducting their own affairs.
[24] We understand that the Jews do not
agree with our father's policy concern-
ing Greek customs but prefer their own
way of life. They are petitioning us to
let them retain their own customs.
[25] Since we desire that this people too
should be undisturbed, our decision is
that their temple be restored to them
and that they live in keeping with the
customs of their ancestors. [26] Accord-
ingly, please send them messengers to
give them our assurances of friendship,
so that, when they learn of our deci-
sion, they may have nothing to worry
about but may contentedly go about
their own business."
[27] The king's letter to the people was
as follows: "King Antiochus sends greet-
ings to the Jewish senate and to the rest
of the Jews. [28] If you are well, it is what
we desire. We too are in good health.
[29] Menelaus has told us of your wish to
return home and attend to your own af-
fairs. [30] Therefore, those who return by
the thirtieth of Xanthicus will have our
assurance of full permission [31] to ob-
serve their dietary laws and other laws,
just as before, and none of the Jews
shall be molested in any way for faults
committed through ignorance. [32] I have
also sent Menelaus to reassure you.
[33]† Farewell." In the year one hundred
and forty-eight, the fifteenth of Xanthi-
cus.
[34] The Romans also sent them a let-
ter as follows: "Quintus Memmius and
Titus Manius, legates of the Romans,
send greetings to the Jewish people.
[35] Whatever Lysias, kinsman of the king,
has granted you, we also approve. [36] But
the matters on which he passed judg-
ment should be submitted to the king.
As soon as you have considered them,
send someone to us with your decisions
so that we may present them to your ad-
vantage, for we are on our way to Anti-
och. [37] Make haste, then, to send us those
who can inform us of your intentions.
[38]† Farewell." In the year one hundred
and forty-eight, the fifteenth of Xanthi-
cus.

CHAPTER 12

Persecution Renewed. [1] After these
agreements were made, Lysias returned
to the king, and the Jews went about
their farming. [2]† But some of the local
governors, Timothy and Apollonius, son
of Gennaeus, as also Hieronymus and
Demophon, to say nothing of Nicanor,
the commander of the Cyprians, would
not allow them to live in peace.
[3] Some people of Joppa also commit-
ted this outrage: they invited the Jews
who lived among them, together with
their wives and children, to embark on
boats which they had provided. There
was no hint of enmity toward them; [4] this
was done by public vote of the city. When
the Jews, not suspecting treachery and
wishing to live on friendly terms, ac-
cepted the invitation, the people of
Joppa took them out to sea and drowned
at least two hundred of them.
Activity of Judas. [5] As soon as Judas
heard of the barbarous deed perpetrated
against his countrymen, he summoned
his men; [6] and after calling upon God,
the just judge, he marched against the
murderers of his kinsmen. In a night at-
tack he set the harbor on fire, burnt the
boats, and put to the sword those who
had taken refuge there. [7] When the gates
of the town were shut, he withdrew, in-
tending to come back later and wipe out
the entire population of Joppa.
[8] On hearing that the men of Jamnia
planned to give like treatment to the
Jews who lived among them, [9] he at-
tacked the Jamnian populace by night,
setting fire to the harbor and the fleet,
so that the glow of the flames was visible
as far as Jerusalem, thirty miles away.
[10]*† When the Jews had gone about a
mile from there in the campaign against
Timothy, they were attacked by Arabs
numbering at least five thousand foot
soldiers, and five hundred horsemen.
[11] After a hard fight, Judas and his com-
panions, with God's help, were victori-
ous. The defeated nomads begged Judas

*

12, 10-16: 1 Mc 5, 24-36.

†

11, 21: *The year one hundred and forty-eight:* 164 B.C. The reading of the name of the month and its position in the calendar are uncertain.

11, 33: The date, which is the same as the date of the Romans' letter (v 38), cannot be correct. The king's letter must be connected with the peace treaty of the year 149 of the Seleucid era, i. e., 163 B.C. Perhaps the mention of the month of Xanthicus in the body of the letter (v 30) caused the date of the Romans' letter to be transferred to this one.

11, 38: The date is March 12, 164 B.C.

12, 2: *Apollonius, son of Gennaeus:* not the Apollonius who was the son of Menestheus (4, 21). *Nicanor:* probably distinct from the Nicanor of 14, 2.

12, 10: *From there:* not from the aforesaid Jamnia (vv 8f) or Joppa (vv 3-7), but from a place in Transjordan; vv 10-26 parallel the account given in 1 Mc 5, 9-13.24-54 of Judas' campaign in northern Transjordan.

to make friends with them and promised
to supply the Jews with cattle and to help
them in every other way. 12 Realizing
that they could indeed be useful in many
respects, Judas agreed to make peace
with them. After the pledge of friendship
had been exchanged, the Arabs with-
drew to their tents.
13 He also attacked a certain city called
Caspin, fortified with earthworks and
ramparts and inhabited by a mixed pop-
ulation of Gentiles. 14 Relying on the
strength of their walls and their supply
of provisions, the besieged treated Judas
and his men with contempt, insulting
them and even uttering blasphemies
and profanity. 15* But Judas and his men
invoked the aid of the great Sovereign
of the world, who, in the day of Joshua,
overthrew Jericho without battering-
ram or siege machine; then they furi-
ously stormed the ramparts. 16 Cap-
turing the city by the will of God, they
inflicted such indescribable slaughter
on it that the adjacent pool, which was
about a quarter of a mile wide, seemed
to be filled with the blood that flowed
into it.
17*† When they had gone on some
ninety miles, they reached Charax,
where there were certain Jews known
as Toubiani. 18 But they did not find
Timothy in that region, for he had al-
ready departed from there without hav-
ing done anything except to leave
behind in one place a very strong garri-
son. 19 But Dositheus and Sosipater, two
of Maccabeus' captains, marched out
and destroyed the force of more than
ten thousand men that Timothy had left
in the stronghold. 20 Meanwhile, Macca-
beus divided his army into cohorts, with
a commander over each cohort, and
went in pursuit of Timothy, who had a
force of a hundred and twenty thousand
foot soldiers and twenty-five hundred
horsemen. 21 When Timothy learned of
the approach of Judas, he sent on ahead
of him the women and children, as well
as the baggage, to a place called Kar-
nion, which was hard to besiege and
even hard to reach because of the diffi-
cult terrain of that region. 22 But when
Judas' first cohort appeared, the enemy
was overwhelmed with fear and terror
at the manifestation of the All-seeing.
Scattering in every direction, they
rushed away in such headlong flight that
in many cases they wounded one an-
other, pierced by the swords of their own
men. 23 Judas pressed the pursuit vigor-
ously, putting the sinners to the sword
and destroying as many as thirty thou-
sand men.
24 Timothy himself fell into the hands
of the men under Dositheus and Sosipa-
ter; but with great cunning, he asked
them to spare his life and let him go,
because he had in his power the parents
and relatives of many of them, and could
make these suffer. 25 When he had fully
confirmed his solemn pledge to restore
them unharmed, they let him go for the
sake of saving their brethren.
Further Successes. 26† Judas then
marched to Karnion and the shrine of
Atargatis, where he killed twenty-five
thousand people. 27* After the defeat
and destruction of these, he moved his
army to Ephron, a fortified city inhab-
ited by people of many nationalities. Ro-
bust young men took up their posts in
defense of the walls, from which they
fought valiantly; inside were large sup-
plies of machines and missiles. 28 But the
Jews, invoking the Sovereign who forci-
bly shatters the might of his enemies,
got possession of the city and slaugh-
tered twenty-five thousand of the people
in it. 29† Then they set out from there
and hastened on to Scythopolis, sev-
enty-five miles from Jerusalem. 30 But
when the Jews who lived there testified
to the good will shown by the Scythopoli-
tans and to their kind treatment even
in times of adversity, 31 Judas and his
men thanked them and exhorted them
to be well disposed to their race in the
future also. Finally they arrived in Jeru-
salem, shortly before the feast of Weeks.
32 After this feast called Pentecost,
they lost no time in marching against
Gorgias, governor of Idumea, 33 who op-
posed them with three thousand foot sol-
diers and four hundred horsemen. 34 In
the ensuing battle, a few of the Jews
were slain. 35† A man called Dositheus,
a powerful horseman and one of Bace-
nor's men, caught hold of Gorgias,
grasped his military cloak and dragged
him along by main strength, intending
to capture the vile wretch alive, when
a Thracian horseman attacked Dosith-
eus and cut off his arm at the shoulder.
Then Gorgias fled to Marisa. 36 After Es-
dris and his men had been fighting for
a long time and were weary, Judas
called upon the Lord to show himself
their ally and leader in the battle.
37 Then, raising a battle cry in his an-
cestral language, and with songs, he
charged Gorgias' men when they were
not expecting it and put them to flight.
Expiation for the Dead. 38 Judas ral-
lied his army and went to the city of

*

15: Jos 6, 1-21. 17: 1 Mc 5, 13.
17-26: 1 Mc 5, 37-44. 27-31: 5, 45-54.

†

12, 17: *Certain Jews known as Toubiani:* because they lived "in the land of Tob" (1 Mc 5, 13).

12, 26: *Atargatis:* a Syrian goddess, represented by the body of a fish.

12, 29: *Scythopolis:* the Greek name of the city of Beth-shan; cf 1 Mc 5, 52.

12, 35: *One of Bacenor's men:* certain ancient witnesses to the text have "one of the Toubiani"; cf v 17.

Adullam. As the week was ending, they
purified themselves according to custom
and kept the sabbath there. 39 On the fol-
lowing day, since the task had now be-
come urgent, Judas and his men went
to gather up the bodies of the slain and
bury them with their kinsmen in their
ancestral tombs. 40* But under the tunic
of each of the dead they found amulets
sacred to the idols of Jamnia, which the
law forbids the Jews to wear. So it was
clear to all that this was why these men
had been slain. 41 They all therefore
praised the ways of the Lord, the just
judge who brings to light the things that
are hidden. 42† Turning to supplication,
they prayed that the sinful deed might
be fully blotted out. The noble Judas
warned the soldiers to keep themselves
free from sin, for they had seen with
their own eyes what had happened be-
cause of the sin of those who had fallen.
43 He then took up a collection among
all his soldiers, amounting to two thou-
sand silver drachmas, which he sent to
Jerusalem to provide for an expiatory
sacrifice. In doing this he acted in a very
excellent and noble way, inasmuch as
he had the resurrection of the dead in
view; 44 for if he were not expecting the
fallen to rise again, it would have been
useless and foolish to pray for them in
death. 45 But if he did this with a view
to the splendid reward that awaits those
who had gone to rest in godliness, it was
a holy and pious thought. 46 Thus he
made atonement for the dead that they
might be freed from this sin.

CHAPTER 13

The Syrians Invade Judea. 1† In the
year one hundred and forty-nine, Judas
and his men learned that Antiochus Eu-
pator was invading Judea with a large
force, 2*† and that with him was Lysias,
his guardian, who was in charge of the
government. They led a Greek army of
one hundred and ten thousand foot sol-
diers, fifty-three hundred horsemen,
twenty-two elephants, and three hun-
dred chariots armed with scythes.
Death of Menelaus. 3 Menelaus also
joined them, and with great duplicity
kept urging Antiochus on, not for the
welfare of his country, but in the hope
of being established in office. 4*† But the
King of kings aroused the anger of An-
tiochus against the scoundrel. When the
king was shown by Lysias that Menelaus
was to blame for all the trouble, he or-
dered him to be taken to Beroea and ex-
ecuted there in the customary local
method. 5† There is at that place a tower
seventy-five feet high, full of ashes, with
a circular rim sloping down steeply on
all sides toward the ashes. 6 A man guilty
of sacrilege or notorious for certain
other crimes is brought up there and
then hurled down to destruction. 7 In
such a manner was Menelaus, the trans-
gressor of the law, fated to die; he was
deprived even of decent burial. 8 It was
altogether just that he who had commit-
ted so many sins against the altar with
its pure fire and ashes should meet his
death in ashes.
Skirmish near Modein. 9 The king was
advancing, his mind full of savage plans
for inflicting on the Jews worse things
than those they suffered in his father's
time. 10 When Judas learned of this, he
urged the people to call upon the LORD
night and day, to help them now, if ever,
11 when they were about to be deprived
of their law, their country, and their holy
temple; and not to allow this nation,
which had just begun to revive, to be
subjected again to blasphemous Gen-
tiles. 12 When they had all joined in doing
this, and had implored the merciful
LORD continuously with weeping and
fasting and prostrations for three days,
Judas encouraged them and told them
to stand ready. 13 After a private meet-
ing with the elders, he decided that, be-
fore the king's army could invade Judea
and take possession of the city, the Jews
should march out and settle the matter
with God's help. 14 Leaving the outcome
to the Creator of the world, and ex-
horting his followers to fight nobly to
death for the laws, the temple, the
city, the country, and the government,
he pitched his camp near Modein.
15*† Giving his men the battle cry "God's
Victory," he made a night attack on the
king's pavilion with a picked force of the
bravest young men and killed about two
thousand in the camp. They also slew
the lead elephant and its rider.
16† Finally they withdrew in triumph,
having filled the camp with terror and

*

40: Dt 7, 25.
13, 2: 1 Mc 6, 30.
4: 1 Tm 6, 15; Rv
17, 14; 19, 16.
15: 1 Mc 6, 43–46.

†

12, 42-46: This is the earliest statement of the doctrine that prayers (v 42) and sacrifices (v 43) for the dead are efficacious. The statement is made here, however, only for the purpose of proving that Judas believed in the resurrection of the just (7, 9.14.23.36). That is, he believed that expiation could be made for certain sins of otherwise good men—soldiers who had given their lives for God's cause. Thus, they could share in the resurrection. His belief was similar to, but not quite the same as, the Catholic doctrine of purgatory.

13, 1: *In the year one hundred and forty-nine:* 163-162 B.C.

13, 2: *They led:* the Greek means literally "Each (of them) led," but it is unlikely that the author meant the already immense numbers to be doubled; the numbers are similar to those in 1 Mc 6, 30.

13, 4: *Beroea:* the Greek name of Aleppo.

13, 5: *Ashes:* probably smoldering ashes; the *tower* resembles the ancient Persian fire towers.

13, 15: *Slew:* literally "stabbed"; the deed was done by Eleazar (1 Mc 6, 43–46).

13, 16: *They withdrew in triumph:* according to 1 Mc 6, 47 they fled.

confusion. 17 Day was just breaking
when this was accomplished with the
help and protection of the LORD.

Treaty with Antiochus V. 18* The
king, having had a taste of the Jews'
daring, tried to take their positions by
a stratagem. 19 So he marched against
Beth-zur, a strong fortress of the Jews;
but he was driven back, checked, and
defeated. 20 Judas then sent supplies to
the men inside, 21† but Rhodocus, of the
Jewish army, betrayed military secrets
to the enemy. He was found out, ar-
rested, and imprisoned. 22 The king
made a second attempt by negotiating
with the men of Beth-zur. After giving
them his pledge and receiving theirs, he
withdrew 23 and attacked Judas and his
men. But he was defeated. Next he
heard that Philip, who was left in charge
of the government in Antioch had re-
belled. Dismayed, he parleyed with the
Jews, submitted to their terms, and
swore to observe their rights. Having
come to this agreement, he offered a
sacrifice, and honored the temple with
a generous donation. 24† He approved of
Maccabeus and left him as military and
civil governor of the territory from
Ptolemais to the region of the Gerrenes.
25 When he came to Ptolemais, the peo-
ple of that city were angered by the
peace treaty; in fact they were so indig-
nant that they wanted to annul its provi-
sions. 26 But Lysias took the platform,
defended the treaty as well as he could
and won them over by persuasion. After
calming them and gaining their good
will, he returned to Antioch.

That is how the king's attack and with-
drawal went.

CHAPTER 14

Antagonism of Alcimus. 1*† Three
years later, Judas and his men learned
that Demetrius, son of Seleucus, had
sailed into the port of Tripolis with a
powerful army and a fleet, 2 and that he
had occupied the country, after doing
away with Antiochus and his guardian
Lysias.

3 A certain Alcimus, a former high
priest, who had willfully incurred defile-
ment at the time of the revolt, realized
that there was no way for him to salvage
his position and regain access to the holy
altar. 4* So he went to King Demetrius
in the year one hundred and fifty-one
and presented him with a gold crown
and a palm branch, as well as some of
the customary olive branches from the
temple. On that occasion he kept quiet.
5 But he found an opportunity to further
his mad scheme when he was invited to
the council by Demetrius and ques-
tioned about the dispositions and inten-
tions of the Jews. He replied: 6 "Those
Jews called Hasideans, led by Judas
Maccabeus, are warmongers, who stir
up sedition and keep the kingdom from
enjoying peace and quiet. 7 For this rea-
son, now that I am deprived of my an-
cestral dignity, that is to say, the high
priesthood, I have come here—8 first, out
of my genuine concern for the king's in-
terests, and secondly, out of consider-
ation for my own countrymen, since our
entire nation is suffering great affliction
from the unreasonable conduct of the
people just mentioned. 9 When you have
informed yourself in detail on these
matters, O king, act in the interest of our
country and its hard-pressed people
with the same gracious consideration
that you show toward all. 10 As long as
Judas is around, it is impossible for the
state to enjoy peace." 11 When he had
said this, the other Friends who were
hostile to Judas quickly added fuel to
Demetrius' indignation.

Dealings with Nicanor. 12* The king
immediately chose Nicanor, who had
been in command of the elephants, and
appointed him governor of Judea. He
sent him off 13 with orders to put Judas
to death, to disperse his followers, and
to set up Alcimus as high priest of the
great temple. 14† The Gentiles from Ju-
dea, who would have banished Judas,
came flocking to Nicanor, thinking that
the misfortunes and calamities of the
Jews would mean prosperity for them-
selves. 15* When the Jews heard of Nica-
nor's coming, and that the Gentiles were
rallying to him, they sprinkled them-
selves with earth and prayed to him who
established his people forever, and who
always comes to the aid of his heritage.
16 At their leader's command, they set
out at once and came upon the enemy
at the village of Adasa. 17 Judas' brother
Simon had engaged Nicanor, but be-
cause of the sudden appearance of the
enemy suffered a slight repulse.
18 However, when Nicanor heard of the
valor of Judas and his men, and the
great courage with which they fought for
their country, he shrank from deciding
the issue by bloodshed. 19 So he sent
Posidonius, Theodotus and Mattathias

*

18–23: 1 Mc 6, 48–53. 12f: 8, 9; 1 Mc 3, 38f.
14, 1–11: 1 Mc 7, 1–7. 15–19: 1 Mc 7, 26–32.
4: 1 Mc 7, 7.25.

†

13, 21: *Military secrets:* probably about the lack of provisions in the besieged city; cf 1 Mc 6, 49.

13, 24: The Greek text is uncertain and may be rendered: "He approved of Maccabeus, then left Hegemonides as governor of the territory. . . ." *Gerrenes:* probably the inhabitants of Gerar, southeast of Gaza.

14, 1: *Three years later:* actually, *Demetrius* (I Soter), *son of Seleucus* (IV), landed at *Tripolis* in the year 151 of the Seleucid era (v 4), i.e., 162–161 B.C.; cf 1 Mc 7, 1–7.

14, 14: *Who would have banished Judas:* the meaning of the Greek is uncertain; some render it: "who had fled before Judas."

to arrange an agreement. [20] After a long discussion of the terms, each leader communicated them to his troops; and when general agreement was expressed, they assented to the treaty. [21] A day was set on which the leaders would meet by themselves. From each side a chariot came forward and thrones were set in place. [22] Judas had posted armed men in readiness at suitable points for fear that the enemy might suddenly carry out some treacherous plan. But the conference was held in the proper way. [23] Nicanor stayed on in Jerusalem, where he did nothing out of place. He got rid of the throngs of ordinary people who gathered around him; [24] but he always kept Judas in his company, for he had a cordial affection for the man. [25] He urged him to marry and have children; so Judas married, settled down, and shared the common life.

Threats against Judas. [26] When Alcimus saw their friendship for each other, he took the treaty that had been made, went to Demetrius, and said that Nicanor was plotting against the state, and that he had appointed Judas, the conspirator against the kingdom, to be his successor. [27] Stirred up by the villain's calumnies, the king became enraged. He wrote to Nicanor, stating that he was displeased with the treaty, and ordering him to send Maccabeus as a prisoner to Antioch without delay. [28] When this message reached Nicanor he was dismayed, for he hated to break his agreement with a man who had done no wrong. [29] However, there was no way of opposing the king, so he watched for an opportunity to carry out this order by a stratagem. [30] But Maccabeus noticed that Nicanor was becoming cool in his dealings with him, and acting with unaccustomed rudeness when they met; he concluded that this coldness betokened no good. So he gathered together a large number of his men, and went into hiding from Nicanor.

[31]* When Nicanor realized that he had been disgracefully outwitted by the man, he went to the great and holy temple, at a time when the priests were offering the customary sacrifices, and ordered them to surrender Judas. [32] As they declared under oath that they did not know where the wanted man was, [33] he raised his right hand toward the temple and swore this oath: "If you do not hand Judas over to me as prisoner, I will level this shrine of God to the ground; I will tear down the altar, and erect here a splendid temple to Dionysus." [34] With these words he went away. The priests stretched out their hands toward heaven, calling upon the unfailing defender of our nation in these words: [35]* "Lord of all, though you are in need of nothing, you have approved of a temple for your dwelling place among us. [36] Therefore, O holy One, Lord of all holiness, preserve forever undefiled this house, which has been so recently purified."

The Story of Razis. [37]† A certain Razis, one of the elders of Jerusalem, was denounced to Nicanor as a patriot. A man highly regarded, he was called a father of the Jews because of his love for them. [38] In the early days of the revolt, he had been convicted of Judaism, and had risked body and life in his ardent zeal for it. [39] Nicanor, to show his detestation of the Jews, sent more than five hundred soldiers to arrest him. [40] He thought that by arresting such a man he would deal the Jews a hard blow. [41] But when these troops, on the point of capturing the tower, were forcing the outer gate and calling for fire to set the door ablaze, Razis, now caught on all sides, turned his sword against himself, [42] preferring to die nobly rather than fall into the hands of vile men and suffer outrages unworthy of his noble birth. [43] In the excitement of the struggle he failed to strike exactly. So while the troops rushed in through the doors, he gallantly ran up to the top of the wall and with manly courage threw himself down into the crowd. [44] But as they quickly drew back and left an opening, he fell into the middle of the empty space. [45] Still breathing, and inflamed with anger, he got up and ran through the crowd, with blood gushing from his frightful wounds. [46]* Then, standing on a steep rock, as he lost the last of his blood, he tore out his entrails and flung them with both hands into the crowd, calling upon the Lord of life and of spirit to give these back to him again. Such was the manner of his death.

CHAPTER 15

Nicanor's Blasphemy. [1] When Nicanor learned that Judas and his companions were in the territory of Samaria, he decided to attack them in all safety on the day of rest. [2] The Jews who were forced to follow him pleaded, "Do not massacre them in that way, like a savage barbarian, but show respect for the day which the All-seeing has exalted with holiness above all other days." [3]* At this the thrice-sinful wretch asked if there was a ruler in heaven who prescribed the keeping of the sabbath day.

*

31–36: 1 Mc 7, 33–38. 46: 7, 9ff.
35: Act 17, 25. 15, 3: 1 Mc 7, 34.

†

14, 37–46: The story of *Razis* belongs to the "martyrology" class of literature; it is similar to the stories in 6, 18—7, 42.

4 When they replied that there was indeed such a ruler in heaven, the living LORD himself, who commanded the observance of the sabbath day, 5 he said, "I, on my part, am ruler on earth, and my orders are that you take up arms and carry out the king's business." Nevertheless he did not succeed in carrying out his cruel plan.

Fresh Hope. 6† In his utter boastfulness and arrogance Nicanor had determined to erect a public monument of victory over Judas and his men. 7 But Maccabeus remained confident, fully convinced that he would receive help from the LORD. 8 He urged his men not to fear the enemy, but mindful of the help they had received from Heaven in the past, to expect that now, too, victory would be given them by the Almighty. 9† By encouraging them with words from the law and the prophets, and by reminding them of the battles they had already won, he filled them with fresh enthusiasm. 10 Having stirred up their courage, he gave his orders and pointed out at the same time the perfidy of the Gentiles and their violation of oaths. 11 When he had armed each of them, not so much with the safety of shield and spear as with the encouragement of noble words, he cheered them all by relating a dream, a kind of vision, worthy of belief.

12*† What he saw was this: Onias, the former high priest, a good and virtuous man, modest in appearance, gentle in manners, distinguished in speech, and trained from childhood in every virtuous practice, was praying with outstretched arms for the whole Jewish community. 13 Then in the same way another man appeared, distinguished by his white hair and dignity, and with an air about him of extraordinary, majestic authority. 14† Onias then said of him, "This is God's prophet Jeremiah, who loves his brethren and fervently prays for his people and their holy city." 15 Stretching out his right hand, Jeremiah presented a gold sword to Judas. As he gave it to him he said, 16 "Accept this holy sword as a gift from God; with it you shall crush your adversaries."

Defeat and Death of Nicanor. 17 Encouraged by Judas' noble words, which had power to instill valor and stir young hearts to courage, the Jews determined not to delay, but to charge gallantly and decide the issue by hand-to-hand combat with the utmost courage, since their city and its temple with the sacred vessels were in danger. 18* They were not so much concerned about their wives and children or their brothers and kinsmen; their first and foremost fear was for the consecrated sanctuary. 19 Those who remained in the city suffered a like agony, anxious as they were about the battle in the open country.

20 Everyone now awaited the decisive moment. The enemy were already drawing near with their troops drawn up in battle line, their elephants placed in strategic positions, and their cavalry stationed on the flanks. 21 Maccabeus, contemplating the hosts before him, their elaborate equipment, and the fierceness of their elephants, stretched out his hands toward heaven and called upon the LORD who works miracles; for he knew that it is not through arms but through the LORD's decision that victory is won by those who deserve it. 22* He prayed to him thus: "You, O LORD, sent your angel in the days of King Hezekiah of Judea, and he slew a hundred and eighty-five thousand men of Sennacherib's army. 23 Sovereign of the heavens, send a good angel now to spread fear and dread before us. 24 By the might of your arm may those be struck down who have blasphemously come against your holy people!" With this he ended his prayer.

25* Nicanor and his men advanced to the sound of trumpets and battle songs. 26 But Judas and his men met the army with supplication and prayers. 27 Fighting with their hands and praying to God with their hearts, they laid low at least thirty-five thousand, and rejoiced greatly over this manifestation of God's power. 28 When the battle was over and they were joyfully departing, they discovered Nicanor lying there in all his armor; 29 so they raised tumultuous shouts in their native tongue in praise of the divine Sovereign.

30 Then Judas, who was ever in body and soul the chief defender of his fellow citizens, and had maintained from youth his affection for his countrymen, ordered Nicanor's head and whole right arm to be cut off and taken to Jerusalem. 31† When he arrived there, he assembled his countrymen, stationed the priests before the altar, and sent for those in

*

12: 3, 1ff.
18: 1 Mc 4, 36.
22f: 8, 19; 2 Kgs 19, 35; Is 37, 36; 1 Mc 7, 40f.
25–36: 8, 39–50.

†

15, 6: *Public monument of victory:* a heap of stones covered with the arms and armor of the fallen enemy.

15, 9: *The law and the prophets:* the first of the three parts of the Hebrew Scriptures, called *the sacred books* (1 Mc 12, 9).

15, 12: *Onias, the former high priest:* Onias III (3, 1–40). Evidently the author believed that the departed just were in some way alive even before the resurrection.

15, 14: *Jeremiah:* regarded by the postexilic Jews as one of the greatest figures in their history; cf 2, 1; Mt 16, 14. *Who. . . prays for his people:* a clear belief in the intercession of the saints.

15, 31: *Those in the citadel:* presumably Jewish soldiers; actually, the citadel was still in the possession of the Syrians.

the citadel. 32 He showed them the vile Nicanor's head and the wretched blasphemer's arm that had been boastfully stretched out against the holy dwelling of the Almighty. 33 He cut out the tongue of the godless Nicanor, saying he would feed it piecemeal to the birds and would hang up the other wages of his folly opposite the temple. 34 At this, everyone looked toward heaven and praised the Lord who manifests his divine power, saying, "Blessed be he who has kept his own Place undefiled!"

35* Judas hung up Nicanor's head on the wall of the citadel, a clear and evident proof to all of the Lord's help. 36*† By public vote it was unanimously decreed never to let this day pass unobserved, but to celebrate it on the thirteenth day of the twelfth month, called Adar in Aramaic, the eve of Mordecai's Day.

VII: EPILOGUE

Author's Apology. 37 Since Nicanor's doings ended in this way, with the city remaining in possession of the Hebrews from that time on, I will bring my own story to an end here too. 38 If it is well written and to the point, that is what I wanted; if it is poorly done and mediocre, that is the best I could do. 39 Just as it is harmful to drink wine alone or water alone, whereas mixing wine with water makes a more pleasant drink that increases delight, so a skillfully composed story delights the ears of those who read the work. Let this, then, be the end.

*

35: 1 Sm 31, 9f. 36: 1 Mc 7, 49.

†

15, 36: *Mordecai's Day:* the feast of Purim, celebrated on the fourteenth and fifteenth days of Adar (Est 9, 17–22).

THE WISDOM BOOKS

The Books of Job, Psalms, Proverbs, Ecclesiastes, the Song of Songs, Wisdom, and Sirach, are all versified by the skillful use of parallelism, that is, of the balanced and symmetrical phrases peculiar to Hebrew poetry. With the exception of the Psalms, the majority of which are devotional lyrics, and the Song of Songs, a nuptial hymn, these books belong to the general class of wisdom or didactic literature, strictly so called because their chief purpose is instruction.

The wisdom literature of the Bible is the fruit of a movement among ancient oriental people to gather, preserve and express, usually in aphoristic style, the results of human experience as an aid toward understanding and solving the problems of life. In Israel especially, the movement concerned itself with such basic and vital problems as man's origin and destiny, his quest for happiness, the problem of suffering, of good and evil in human conduct, of death, and the state beyond the grave. Originating with oral tradition, these formulations found their way into the historical books of the Old Testament in the shape of proverbs, odes, chants, epigrams, and also into those psalms intended for instruction.

The developed compositions of this literature form the sapiential books. The Book of Proverbs is a collection of sentences or practical norms for moral conduct. The Book of Job is an artistic dialogue skillfully handling the problem of suffering though only from the standpoint of temporal life. Ecclesiastes examines a wide range of human experience only to conclude that all things are vanity except the fear of the Lord and observance of his commandments, and that God requites man in his own good time. Sirach gathers and presents the fruits of past experience, thus preparing for the Book of Wisdom, which sees for the just man seeking happiness the full hope of immortality (Wis 3, 4).

Those who cultivated wisdom were called sages. Men of letters, scribes, skilled in the affairs of government, and counselors to rulers, they were instructors of the people, especially of youth (Sir 51, 13-30). In times of crisis they guided the people by revaluating tradition, thus helping to preserve unity, peace and good will. The most illustrious of the sages, and the originator of wisdom literature in Israel, was Solomon. Because of his fame, some of the wisdom books of which he was not the author bear his name.

Despite numerous resemblances, sometimes exaggerated, between the sapiential literature of pagan nations and the wisdom books of the Bible, the former are often replete with vagaries and abound in polytheistic conceptions; the latter remained profoundly human, universal, fundamentally moral, and essentially religious and monotheistic. Under the influence of the Law and the Prophets, wisdom became piety and virtue; impiety and vice were folly. The teachers of wisdom were regarded as men of God, and their books were placed beside the Law and the Prophets. The highest wisdom became identified with the spirit of God through which the world was created and preserved (Prv 8, 22-31), and mankind was enlightened.

The limitations of Old Testament wisdom served to crystalize the problems of human life and destiny, thus preparing for their solution through New Testament revelation. Ecclesiastes' vain search for success and happiness on earth ends when the Savior assures these things to his followers, not in this world but in the bliss of heaven. The anxiety in the Book of Job over reconciling God's justice and wisdom with the suffering of the innocent is relieved by the account of the Crucified and Risen Redeemer in the Gospel. By fulfilling all that the Psalms foretold concerning him, Jesus makes the Psalter his prayer book and that of the Church for all time. The love of God for the chosen people which underlies the Song of Songs is perfected in the union of Christ with his Church. The personification of the wisdom of Proverbs, Wisdom and Sirach shines forth in resplendent reality in the Word who was with God, and who was God, and who became incarnate to dwell among us; cf Jn 1, 2.14.

The Book of

JOB

The Book of Job, named after its protagonist, is an exquisite dramatic poem which treats of the problem of the suffering of the innocent, and of retribution. The contents of the book, together with its artistic structure and elegant style, place it among the literary masterpieces of all time.

Job, an oriental chieftain, pious and upright, richly endowed in his own person and in domestic prosperity, suffers a sudden and complete reversal of fortune. He loses his property and his children; a loathsome disease afflicts his body; and sorrow oppresses his soul. Nevertheless, Job does not complain against God. When some friends visit him to condole with him, Job protests his innocence and does not understand why he is afflicted. He curses the day of his birth and longs for death to bring an end to his sufferings. The debate which ensues consists of three cycles of speeches. Job's friends insist that his plight can only be a punishment for personal wrongdoing and an invitation from God to repentance. Job rejects their inadequate explanation and calls for a response from God himself. At this point the speeches of a youth named Elihu (chs 32—37) interrupt the development.

In response to Job's plea that he be allowed to see God and hear from him the cause of his suffering, God answers, not by justifying his action before men, but by referring to his own omniscience and almighty power. Job is content with this. He recovers his attitude of humility and trust in God, which is deepened now and strengthened by his experience of suffering.

The author of the book is not known; it was composed some time between the seventh and fifth centuries B.C. Its literary form, with speeches, prologue and epilogue disposed according to a studied plan, indicates that the purpose of the writing is didactic. The lesson is that even the just may suffer here, and their sufferings are a test of their fidelity. They shall be rewarded in the end. Man's finite mind cannot probe the depths of the divine omniscience that governs the world. The problems we encounter can be solved by a broader and deeper awareness of God's power, presence (42, 5) and wisdom.

The divisions of the Book of Job are as follows:

I: Prologue (1, 1—2, 13)
II: First Cycle of Speeches (3, 1—14, 22)
III: Second Cycle of Speeches (15, 1—21, 34)
IV: Third Cycle of Speeches (22, 1—28, 28)
V: Job's Final Summary of His Cause (29, 1—31, 37)
VI: Elihu's Speeches (32, 1—37, 24)
VII: The Lord's Speech (38, 1—42, 6)
VIII: Epilogue (42, 7—17)

I: PROLOGUE

CHAPTER 1

Job's Wealth and Piety. 1*† In the
land of Uz there was a blameless and
upright man named Job, who feared
God and avoided evil. 2† Seven sons and
three daughters were born to him; 3† and
he had seven thousand sheep, three
thousand camels, five hundred yoke of
oxen, five hundred she-asses, and a
great number of work animals, so that
he was greater than any of the men of
the East. 4 His sons used to take turns
giving feasts, sending invitations to their
three sisters to eat and drink with them.
5 And when each feast had run its
course, Job would send for them and
sanctify them, rising early and offering
holocausts for every one of them. For
Job said, "It may be that my sons have

* 1, 1: 2, 3.

† 1, 1: *Uz:* somewhere in Edom or Arabia. *Job:* a not uncommon name in ancient Semitic circles; its original meaning was "enemy."

1, 2 f: The numbers mentioned here indicate Job's great wealth and happiness, external proof of God's friendship.

1, 3: *Men of the East:* that is, east of Palestine.

sinned and blasphemed God in their hearts." This Job did habitually.

6*† One day, when the sons of God came to present themselves before the LORD, Satan also came among them. 7* And the LORD said to Satan, "Whence do you come?" Then Satan answered the LORD and said, "From roaming the earth and patrolling it." 8 And the LORD said to Satan, "Have you noticed my servant Job, and that there is no one on earth like him, blameless and upright, fearing God and avoiding evil?" 9 But Satan answered the LORD and said, "Is it for nothing that Job is God-fearing? 10 Have you not surrounded him and his family and all that he has with your protection? You have blessed the work of his hands, and his livestock are spread over the land. 11* But now put forth your hand and touch anything that he has, and surely he will blaspheme you to your face." 12 And the LORD said to Satan, "Behold, all that he has is in your power; only do not lay a hand upon his person." So Satan went forth from the presence of the LORD.

The First Trial. 13 And so one day, while his sons and his daughters were eating and drinking wine in the house of their eldest brother, 14 a messenger came to Job and said, "The oxen were plowing and the asses grazing beside them, 15† and the Sabeans carried them off in a raid. They put the herdsmen to the sword, and I alone have escaped to tell you." 16† While he was yet speaking, another came and said, "Lightning has fallen from heaven and struck the sheep and their shepherds and consumed them; and I alone have escaped to tell you." 17 While he was yet speaking, another came and said, "The Chaldeans formed three columns, seized the camels, carried them off, and put those tending them to the sword, and I alone have escaped to tell you." 18 While he was yet speaking, another came and said, "Your sons and daughters were eating and drinking wine in the house of their eldest brother, 19 when suddenly a great wind came across the desert and smote the four corners of the house. It fell upon the young people and they are dead; and I alone have escaped to tell you." 20 Then Job began to tear his cloak and cut off his hair. He cast himself prostrate upon the ground, 21*† and said,

"Naked I came forth from my mother's womb,
and naked shall I go back again.
The LORD gave and the LORD has taken away;
blessed be the name of the LORD!"

22* In all this Job did not sin, nor did he say anything disrespectful of God.

CHAPTER 2

The Second Trial. 1* Once again the sons of God came to present themselves before the LORD, and Satan also came with them. 2 And the LORD said to Satan, "Whence do you come?" And Satan answered the LORD and said, "From roaming the earth and patrolling it." 3* And the LORD said to Satan, "Have you noticed my servant Job, and that there is no one on earth like him, faultless and upright, fearing God and avoiding evil? He still holds fast to his innocence although you incited me against him to ruin him without cause." 4† And Satan answered the LORD and said, "Skin for skin! All that a man has will he give for his life. 5* But now put forth your hand and touch his bone and his flesh, and surely he will blaspheme you to your face." 6 And the LORD said to Satan, "He is in your power; only spare his life." 7 So Satan went forth from the presence of the LORD and smote Job with severe boils from the soles of his feet to the crown of his head. 8 And he took a potsherd to scrape himself, as he sat among the ashes. 9*† Then his wife said to him, "Are you still holding to your innocence? Curse God and die." 10* But he said to her, "Are even you going to speak as senseless women do? We accept good things from God; and should we not accept evil?" Through all this, Job said nothing sinful.

Job's Three Friends. 11† Now when three of Job's friends heard of all the misfortune that had come upon him, they set out each one from his own place: Eliphaz from Teman, Bildad from Shuh, and Zophar from Naamath. They met and journeyed together to give him sympathy and comfort. 12 But when, at a distance, they lifted up their eyes and did not recognize him, they began to weep aloud; they tore their cloaks and threw dust upon their heads. 13 Then they sat

*

6 ff: 2, 1 ff.
6: Gn 6, 2.4; Zec 3, 1; Lk 22, 31; Rv 12, 9.
7: 1 Pt 5, 8.
11: 2, 5.
21: Eccl 5, 14; 1 Tm 6, 7.
22: 2, 10; Jas 5, 11.
2, 1: 1, 6.
3: 1, 1.
5: 1, 11.
9: 19, 17.
10: 1, 22; Sir 2, 4; Jas 5, 11.

†

1, 6: *Sons of God:* angels. *Satan:* literally, "adversary."
1, 15: *Sabeans:* from southern Arabia.
1, 16: *Lightning:* literally, "God's fire."
1, 21: *Go back again:* to the earth; cf Gn 2, 7; Sir 40, 1.
2, 4: *Skin for skin:* an expression which, as applied to Job, means that he has borne his suffering patiently thus far only because he seeks to avoid greater suffering and to receive greater favors from God.
2, 9: *Curse God and die:* you have nothing to hope for from God and therefore nothing to live for.
2, 11: The names of Job's friends suggest Edomite origin. The Edomites (Ob 8f) and more specifically the Temanites (Jer 49, 7) enjoyed a reputation for wisdom.

down upon the ground with him seven days and seven nights, but none of them spoke a word to him; for they saw how great was his suffering.

II: FIRST CYCLE OF SPEECHES

CHAPTER 3

Job's Plaint

1 After this, Job opened his mouth and cursed his day. 2 Job spoke out and said:

3* Perish the day on which I was born,
the night when they said, "The child is a boy!"
4 May that day be darkness:
let not God above call for it,
nor light shine upon it!
5 May darkness and gloom claim it,
clouds settle upon it,
the blackness of night affright it!
6 May obscurity seize that day;
let it not occur among the days of the year,
nor enter into the count of the months!

7 May that night be barren;
let no joyful outcry greet it!
8† Let them curse it who curse the sea,
the appointed disturbers of Leviathan!
9 May the stars of its twilight be darkened;
may it look for daylight, but have none,
nor gaze on the eyes of the dawn,
10 Because it kept not shut the doors of the womb
to shield my eyes from trouble!

11* Why did I not perish at birth,
come forth from the womb and expire?
16† Or why was I not buried away like an untimely birth,
like babes that have never seen the light?
12 Wherefore did the knees receive me?
or why did I suck at the breasts?

13 For then I should have lain down and been tranquil;
had I slept, I should then have been at rest
14 With kings and counselors of the earth
who built where now there are ruins
15 Or with princes who had gold
and filled their houses with silver.

17† There the wicked cease from troubling,
there the weary are at rest.
18 There the captives are at ease together,
and hear not the voice of the slave driver.
19 Small and great are there the same,
and the servant is free from his master.

20 Why is light given to the toilers,
and life to the bitter in spirit?
21 They wait for death and it comes not;
they search for it rather than for hidden treasures,
22 Rejoice in it exultingly,
and are glad when they reach the grave:
23 Men whose path is hidden from them,
and whom God has hemmed in!

24 For sighing comes more readily to me than food,
and my groans well forth like water.
25 For what I fear overtakes me,
and what I shrink from comes upon me.
26 I have no peace nor ease;
I have no rest, for trouble comes!

CHAPTER 4

Eliphaz's First Speech

1 Then spoke Eliphaz the Temanite, who said:

2 If someone attempts a word with you, will you mind?
For how can anyone refrain from speaking?
3 Behold, you have instructed many,
and have made firm their feeble hands.
4 Your words have upheld the stumbler;
you have strengthened his faltering knees.
5 But now that it comes to you, you are impatient;
when it touches yourself, you are dismayed.
6 Is not your piety a source of confidence,

*

3, 3: Jer 20, 14. 11: 10, 18f.

†

3, 8: *Leviathan:* in 40, 25, the crocodile; here the reference is probably to a mythological sea monster symbolizing primeval chaos. Cf 9, 13; 26, 13; Pss 74, 13f; 104, 26; Is 27, 1.

3, 16: This verse has been placed between vv 11 and 12 where it probably stood originally. There is reason to believe that here, as well as in several other places in Job, the original order of the poetic lines was accidentally disturbed in the early transmission of the text; so in chapters 12-15; 19-21; 24-31; 34; 36; 38-42. The verse numbers given in such cases are always those of the current Hebrew text, though the arrangement may differ. The footnotes will advise the reader of the difficulties and provide him with further indications for following the progress of thought in the book.

3, 17: *There:* in death.

and your integrity of life your hope?
7* Reflect now, what innocent person perishes?
Since when are the upright destroyed?
8 As I see it, those who plow for mischief
and sow trouble, reap the same.
9* By the breath of God they perish,
and by the blast of his wrath they are consumed.
10† Though the lion roars, though the king of beasts cries out,
yet the teeth of the young lions are broken;
11 The old lion perishes for lack of prey,
and the cubs of the lioness are scattered.

12† For a word was stealthily brought to me,
and my ear caught a whisper of it.
13* In my thoughts during visions of the night,
when deep sleep falls on men,
14 Fear came upon me, and shuddering,
that terrified me to the bones.
15 Then a spirit passed before me,
and the hair of my flesh stood up.
16 It paused, but its likeness I could not discern;
a figure was before my eyes,
and I heard a still voice:

17* "Can a man be righteous as against God?
Can a mortal be blameless against his Maker?
18* Lo, he puts no trust in his servants,
and with his angels he can find fault.
19 How much more with those that dwell in houses of clay,
whose foundation is in the dust,
who are crushed more easily than the moth!
20 Morning or evening they may be shattered;
with no heed paid to it, they perish forever.
21 The pegs of their tent are plucked up;
they die without knowing wisdom."

CHAPTER 5

1 Call now! Will anyone respond to you?
To which of the holy ones will you appeal?
2 Nay, impatience kills the fool
and indignation slays the simpleton.
3* I have seen a fool spreading his roots,
but his household suddenly decayed.
4† His children shall be far from safety;
they shall be crushed at the gate without a rescuer.
5 What they have reaped the hungry shall eat up;
[or God shall take it away by blight;]
and the thirsty shall swallow their substance.
6 For mischief comes not out of the earth,
nor does trouble spring out of the ground;
7† But man himself begets mischief,
as sparks fly upward.

8 In your place, I would appeal to God,
and to God I would state my plea.
10† He gives rain upon the earth
and sends water upon the fields;
11* He sets up on high the lowly,
and those who mourn he exalts to safety.
12 He frustrates the plans of the cunning,
so that their hands achieve no success;
13* He catches the wise in their own ruses,
and the designs of the crafty are routed.

14 They meet with darkness in the daytime,
and at noonday they grope as though it were night.
15 But the poor from the edge of the sword
and from the hand of the mighty, he saves.
16 Thus the unfortunate have hope,
and iniquity closes her mouth.

17 Happy is the man whom God reproves!
The Almighty's chastening do not reject.
18* For he wounds, but he binds up;

---

*

4, 7: Ps 37, 25.
9: Ps 18, 16; Is 11, 4; 2 Thes 2, 8.
13: 33, 15.
17: 9, 2; 15, 14ff; 25, 4; Pss 130, 3; 143, 2.
18: 15, 15; 2 Pt 2, 4; Jude 6.
5, 3: Ps 37, 35f.
11: 1 Sm 2, 7f; Ps 113, 7; Lk 1, 52.
13: 1 Cor 3, 19.
18: Hos 6, 1f.

---

†

4, 10: *The lion:* used figuratively here for the violent, rapacious sinner who cannot prevail against God.

4, 12-21: A dramatic presentation of the idea of man's nothingness in contrast to God's greatness.

5, 4: *At the gate:* of the city, where justice was administered.

5, 7: *Sparks:* in Hebrew, "sons of resheph," which the ancient versions took as the name of a bird.

5,9: Omitted here; it is a duplicate of 9, 10.

he smites, but his hands give healing.
19† Out of six troubles he will deliver you,
and at the seventh no evil shall touch you.
20 In famine he will deliver you from death,
and in war from the threat of the sword;
21 From the scourge of the tongue you shall be hidden,
and shall not fear approaching ruin.

22 At destruction and want you shall laugh;
the beasts of the earth you need not dread.
23 You shall be in league with the stones of the field,
and the wild beasts shall be at peace with you.
24 And you shall know that your tent is secure;
taking stock of your household, you shall miss nothing.
25 You shall know that your descendants are many,
and your offspring as the grass of the earth.
26 You shall approach the grave in full vigor,
as a shock of grain comes in at its season.
27 Lo, this we have searched out; so it is!
This we have heard, and you should know.

CHAPTER 6

Job's First Reply

1 Then Job answered and said:

2 Ah, could my anguish but be measured
and my calamity laid with it in the scales,
3 They would now outweigh the sands of the sea!
Because of this I speak without restraint.
4* For the arrows of the Almighty pierce me,
and my spirit drinks in their poison;
the terrors of God are arrayed against me.
5† Does the wild ass bray when he has grass?
Does the ox low over his fodder?
6 Can a thing insipid be eaten without salt?
Is there flavor in the white of an egg?
7 I refuse to touch them;
they are loathsome food to me.
8 Oh, that I might have my request,
and that God would grant what I long for:
9 Even that God would decide to crush me,
that he would put forth his hand and cut me off!
10 Then I should still have consolation
and could exult through unremitting pain,
because I have not transgressed the commands of the Holy One.
11 What strength have I that I should endure,
and what is my limit that I should be patient?
12 Have I the strength of stones,
or is my flesh of bronze?
13* Have I no helper,
and has advice deserted me?
14 A friend owes kindness to one in despair,
though he have forsaken the fear of the Almighty.

15 My brethren are undependable as a brook,
as watercourses that run dry in the wadies;
16 Though they may be black with ice,
and with snow heaped upon them,
17 Yet once they flow, they cease to be;
in the heat, they disappear from their place.
18 Caravans turn aside from their routes;
they go into the desert and perish.
19† The caravans of Tema search,
the companies of Sheba have hopes;
20 They are disappointed, though they were confident;
they come there and are frustrated.

21 It is thus that you have now become for me;
you see a terrifying thing and are afraid.
22 Have I asked you to give me anything,
to offer a gift for me from your possessions,
23 Or to deliver me from the enemy,
or to redeem me from oppressors?
24 Teach me, and I will be silent;

JOB

*

6, 4: Ps 88, 17. 13: 19, 14f.

†

5, 19: *Six . . . the seventh:* proverbial expression for any large number; cf Prv 24, 16; Lk 17, 4.

6, 5f: Job would not complain if his life were as pleasant to him as fodder to a hungry animal; but his life is as disagreeable as insipid food. *White of an egg:* thus the obscure Hebrew has been understood in Jewish tradition; some render it "mallow juice."

6, 19: *Tema:* in northwest Arabia. *Sheba:* see note on 1, 15.

prove to me wherein I have erred.
25 How agreeable are honest words;
yet how unconvincing is your argument!
26 Do you consider your words as proof,
but the sayings of a desperate man as wind?
27 You would even cast lots for the orphan,
and would barter away your friend!
28 Come, now, give me your attention;
surely I will not lie to your face.
29 Think it over; let there be no injustice.
Think it over; I still am right.
30 Is there insincerity on my tongue,
or cannot my taste discern falsehood?

CHAPTER 7

1*† Is not man's life on earth a drudgery?
Are not his days those of a hireling?
2 He is a slave who longs for the shade,
a hireling who waits for his wages.
3 So I have been assigned months of misery,
and troubled nights have been told off for me.

4 If in bed I say, "When shall I arise?"
then the night drags on;
I am filled with restlessness until the dawn.
5* My flesh is clothed with worms and scabs;
my skin cracks and festers;
6 My days are swifter than a weaver's shuttle;
they come to an end without hope.
7* Remember that my life is like the wind;
I shall not see happiness again.
8 The eye that now sees me shall no more behold me;
as you look at me, I shall be gone.
9* As a cloud dissolves and vanishes,
so he who goes down to the nether world shall come up no more.
10 He shall not again return to his house;
his place shall know him no more.

11 My own utterance I will not restrain;
I will speak in the anguish of my spirit;
I will complain in the bitterness of my soul.
12† Am I the sea, or a monster of the deep,
that you place a watch over me?
Why have you set me up as an object of attack;
or why should I be a target for you?
13 When I say, "My bed shall comfort me,
my couch shall ease my complaint,"
14 Then you affright me with dreams
and with visions terrify me,
15 So that I should prefer choking
and death rather than my pains.
16* I waste away: I cannot live forever;
let me alone, for my days are but a breath.
17 What is man, that you make much of him,
or pay him any heed?
18* You observe him with each new day
and try him at every moment!
19 How long will it be before you look away from me,
and let me alone long enough to swallow my spittle?
20 Though I have sinned, what can I do to you,
O watcher of men?
21 Why do you not pardon my offense,
or take away my guilt?
For soon I shall lie down in the dust;
and should you seek me I shall then be gone.

CHAPTER 8
Bildad's First Speech

1 Bildad the Shuhite spoke out and said:
2 How long will you utter such things?
The words from your mouth are like a mighty wind!
3* Does God pervert judgment,
and does the Almighty distort justice?
4 If your children have sinned against him
and he has left them in the grip of their guilt,
5 Still, if you yourself have recourse to God
and make supplication to the Almighty,
6 Should you be blameless and upright,
surely now he will awake for you

---

*

7, 1: 14, 14.
5: 2, 7f.
7: Pss 8, 5; 144, 3.
9f: 10, 21; 14, 10ff; 2 Sm 12, 23; 14, 14; Wis 2, 1.
16: 14, 1ff.5.
18: Ps 17, 3.
8, 3: 34, 10ff.

†

7, 1: *Drudgery:* taken by some to refer to military service; cf also 14, 14.

7, 12: An allusion in poetic imagery to primeval chaos as a monstrous ocean vanquished by God at the world's creation.

7, 12-21: Job now speaks, not to his friend, but to God.

and restore your rightful domain;
7 Your former state will be of little moment,
for in time to come you will flourish indeed.

8* If you inquire of the former generations,
and give heed to the experience of the fathers
9* (As we are but of yesterday and have no knowledge,
because our days on earth are but a shadow),
10 Will they not teach you and tell you
and utter their words of understanding?
11† Can the papyrus grow up without mire?
Can the reed grass flourish without water?
12 While it is yet green and uncut,
it withers quicker than any grass.
13 So is the end of everyone who forgets God,
and so shall the hope of the godless man perish.

14 His confidence is but a gossamer thread
and his trust is a spider's web.
15 He shall rely upon his family, but it shall not last;
he shall cling to it, but it shall not endure.
16 He is full of sap before sunrise,
and beyond his garden his shoots go forth;
17 About a heap of stones are his roots entwined;
among the rocks he takes hold.
18 Yet if one tears him from his place,
it will disown him: "I have never seen you!"
19 There he lies rotting beside the road,
and out of the soil another sprouts.
20 Behold, God will not cast away the upright;
neither will he take the hand of the wicked.
21 Once more will he fill your mouth with laughter,
and your lips with rejoicing.
22 They that hate you shall be clothed with shame,
and the tent of the wicked shall be no more.

CHAPTER 9

Job's Second Reply

1 Then Job answered and said:

2 I know well that it is so;
but how can a man be justified before God?
3 Should one wish to contend with him,
he could not answer him once in a thousand times.
4 God is wise in heart and mighty in strength;
who has withstood him and remained unscathed?

5 He removes the mountains before they know it;
he overturns them in his anger.
6* He shakes the earth out of its place,
and the pillars beneath it tremble.
7 He commands the sun, and it rises not;
he seals up the stars.

8* He alone stretches out the heavens
and treads upon the crests of the sea.
9 He made the Bear and Orion,
the Pleiades and the constellations of the south;
10 He does great things past finding out,
marvelous things beyond reckoning.

11 Should he come near me, I see him not;
should he pass by, I am not aware of him;
12 Should he seize me forcibly, who can say him nay?
Who can say to him, "What are you doing?"

13† He is God and he does not relent;
the helpers of Rahab bow beneath him.
14 How much less shall I give him any answer,
or choose out arguments against him!
15* Even though I were right, I could not answer him,
but should rather beg for what was due me.

16 If I appealed to him and he answered my call,
I could not believe that he would hearken to my words;
17 With a tempest he might overwhelm me,
and multiply my wounds without cause;
18 He need not suffer me to draw breath,
but might fill me with bitter griefs.

JOB

---

*

8: Dt 4, 32; 32, 7.
9: 14, 2; Pss 102, 12; 109, 23; 144, 4; Wis 2, 5.
9, 6: 26, 11.
8: Ps 104, 2; Is 40, 22.
15: 10, 15.

†

8, 11ff: As marsh plants need water, so man needs God. These verses are taken by some as a quotation from the teaching of the forefathers; cf v 10.

9, 13: *Rehab:* cf 26, 12. See note on Ps 89, 11.

19 If it be a question of strength, he is mighty;
and if of judgment, who will call him to account?
20* Though I were right, my own mouth might condemn me;
were I innocent, he might put me in the wrong.
21 Though I am innocent, I myself cannot know it;
I despise my life.

JOB

22* It is all one! therefore I say:
Both the innocent and the wicked he destroys.
23 When the scourge slays suddenly, he laughs at the despair of the innocent.
24 The earth is given into the hands of the wicked;
he covers the faces of its judges.
If it is not he, who then is it?

25* My days are swifter than a runner,
they flee away; they see no happiness;
26 They shoot by like skiffs of reed, like an eagle swooping upon its prey.
27 If I say: I will forget my complaining,
I will lay aside my sadness and be of good cheer,
28† Then I am in dread of all my pains;
I know that you will not hold me innocent.

29 If I must be accounted guilty,
why then should I strive in vain?
30 If I should wash myself with snow
and cleanse my hands with lye,
31 Yet you would plunge me in the ditch,
so that my garments would abhor me.

32 For he is not a man like myself, that I should answer him,
that we should come together in judgment.
33 Would that there were an arbiter between us,
who could lay his hand upon us both
34 and withdraw his rod from me.
Would that his terrors did not frighten me;
35 that I might speak without being afraid of him.
Since this is not the case with me,

CHAPTER 10

10, 1*† I loathe my life.
I will give myself up to complaint;
I will speak from the bitterness of my soul.
2 I will say to God: Do not put me in the wrong!
Let me know why you oppose me.
3 Is it a pleasure for you to oppress,
to spurn the work of your hands,
and smile on the plan of the wicked?
4 Have you eyes of flesh?
Do you see as man sees?
5* Are your days as the days of a mortal,
and are your years as a man's lifetime,
6 That you seek for guilt in me
and search after my sins,
7* Even though you know that I am not wicked,
and that none can deliver me out of your hand?

8 Your hands have formed me and fashioned me;
will you then turn and destroy me?
9* Oh, remember that you fashioned me from clay!
Will you then bring me down to dust again?
10 Did you not pour me out as milk,
and thicken me like cheese?
11 With skin and flesh you clothed me,
with bones and sinews knit me together.
12 Grace and favor you granted me,
and your providence has preserved my spirit.

13 Yet these things you have hidden in your heart;
I know that they are your purpose:
14 If I should sin, you would keep a watch against me,
and from my guilt you would not absolve me.
15 If I should be wicked, alas for me!
if righteous, I dare not hold up my head,
filled with ignominy and sodden with affliction!
16 Should it lift up, you hunt me like a lion:
repeatedly you show your wondrous power against me,
17 You renew your attack upon me
and multiply your harassment of me;

*

20: 15, 6.
22: Eccl 9, 2.
25: 7, 6.
10, 1: 9, 21.
5: 36, 26.
7: 2, 3.9; Dt 32, 39; Wis 16, 15.
9: 4, 19; 33, 6; Gn 2, 7; 3, 19; Ps 146, 4.

†

9, 28-31: *You:* refers to God.
10, 1: *I loathe my life:* this is the first verse of ch 10.

in waves your troops come against me.

18* Why then did you bring me forth from the womb?
I should have died and no eye have seen me.
19 I should be as though I had never lived;
I should have been taken from the womb to the grave.
20 Are not the days of my life few?
Let me alone, that I may recover a little
21* Before I go whence I shall not return,
to the land of darkness and of gloom,
22 The black, disordered land
where darkness is the only light.

CHAPTER 11

Zophar's First Speech

1 And Zophar the Naamathite spoke out and said:

2 Should not the man of many words be answered,
or must the garrulous man necessarily be right?
3 Shall your babblings keep men silent,
and shall you deride and no one give rebuke?
4 Shall you say: "My teaching is pure,
and I am clean in your sight"?
5 But oh, that God would speak,
and open his lips against you,
6 And tell you that the secrets of wisdom
are twice as effective:
So you might learn that God
will make you answer for your guilt.

7* Can you penetrate the designs of God?
Dare you vie with the perfection of the Almighty?
8 It is higher than the heavens; what can you do?
It is deeper than the nether world; what can you know?
9 It is longer than the earth in measure,
and broader than the sea.
10 If he seize and imprison
or call to judgment, who then can say him nay?
11 For he knows the worthlessness of men
and sees iniquity; will he then ignore it?
12* Will empty man then gain understanding,
and the wild jackass be made docile?

13 If you set your heart aright
and stretch out your hands toward him,
14 If you remove all iniquity from your conduct,
and let not injustice dwell in your tent,
15 Surely then you may lift up your face in innocence;
you may stand firm and unafraid.
16 For then you shall forget your misery,
or recall it like waters that have ebbed away.
17 Then your life shall be brighter than the noonday;
its gloom shall become as the morning,
18* And you shall be secure, because there is hope;
you shall look round you and lie down in safety,
19 and you shall take your rest with none to disturb.

Many shall entreat your favor,
20 but the wicked, looking on, shall be consumed with envy.
Escape shall be cut off from them,
they shall wait to expire.

CHAPTER 12

Job's Third Reply

1 Then Job replied and said:

2 No doubt you are the intelligent folk,
and with you wisdom shall die!
3* But I have intelligence as well as you;
for who does not know such things as these?
4*† I have become the sport of my neighbors:
"The one whom God answers when he calls upon him,
the just, the perfect man," is a laughingstock;
5 The undisturbed esteem my downfall a disgrace
such as awaits unsteady feet;
6 Yet the tents of robbers are prosperous,
and those who provoke God are secure.

7 But now ask the beasts to teach you,
and the birds of the air to tell you;

*

18: 3. 3.11.
21: 7, 9f; 16, 22.
11, 7: Rom 11, 33.
12: 39, 5-8.
18: Lv 26, 6; Ps 4, 9.
12, 3: 13, 2; 15, 9.
4: 21, 3; 30, 1.

†

12, 4f: The Hebrew is somewhat obscure, but the general sense is that the wicked mock at the pious when the latter appear to be abandoned by God; cf Ps 22, 7ff; Mt 27, 39-43.

8 Or the reptiles on earth to instruct you,
and the fish of the sea to inform you.
9 Which of all these does not know
that the hand of God has done this?
10* In his hand is the soul of every living thing,
and the life breath of all mankind.
11* Does not the ear judge words
as the mouth tastes food?
12* So with old age is wisdom,
and with length of days understanding.

13 With him are wisdom and might;
his are counsel and understanding.
14* If he breaks a thing down, there is no rebuilding;
if he imprisons a man, there is no release.
15* He holds back the waters and there is drought;
he sends them forth and they overwhelm the land.
18† He loosens the bonds imposed by kings
and leaves but a waistcloth to bind the king's own loins.
21 He breaks down the barriers of the streams
19 and lets their never-failing waters flow away.

16 With him are strength and prudence;
the misled and the misleaders are his.
17 He sends counselors away barefoot,
and of judges he makes fools.
20 He silences the trusted adviser,
and takes discretion from the aged.
22 The recesses of the darkness he discloses,
and brings the gloom forth to the light.
23 He makes nations great and he destroys them;
he spreads peoples abroad and he abandons them.
24 He takes understanding from the leaders of the land,
25 till they grope in the darkness without light;
he makes them stagger like drunken men.

CHAPTER 13

1 Lo, all this my eye has seen;
my ear has heard and perceived it.
2* What you know, I also know;
I fall not short of you.
3* But I would speak with the Almighty;
I wish to reason with God.
4 You are glossing over falsehoods
and offering vain remedies, every one of you!
5 Oh, that you would be altogether silent!
This for you would be wisdom.

6 Hear now the rebuke I shall utter
and listen to the reproof from my lips.
7 Is it for God that you speak falsehood?
Is it for him that you utter deceit?
8 Is it for him that you show partiality?
Do you play advocate on behalf of God?
9 Will it be well when he shall search you out?
Would you impose on him as one does on men?

10 He will openly rebuke you
if even in secret you show partiality.
11 Surely will his majesty affright you
and the dread of him fall upon you.

12 Your reminders are ashy maxims,
your fabrications are mounds of clay.
13 Be silent, let me alone! that I may speak
and give vent to my feelings.
14† I will carry my flesh between my teeth,
and take my life in my hand.
15* Slay me though he might, I will wait for him;
I will defend my conduct before him.
16 And this shall be my salvation,
that no impious man can come into his presence.

17 Pay careful heed to my speech,
and give my statement a hearing.
18* Behold, I have prepared my case,
I know that I am in the right.

*

10: Acts 17, 28.
11: 34, 3.
12: 32, 7.
14: Rv 3, 7.
15: Gn 7, 11-24.
13, 2: 12, 3; 15, 9.
3: 23, 4.
15: 27, 5.
18: 33, 9.

†

12, 18: *Waistcloth . . . loins:* he reduces kings to the condition of slaves, who wear only a cloth wrapped about the waist.

13, 14: The second half of the verse is a common biblical expression for risking one's life; cf Jgs 12, 3; 1 Sm 19, 5; 28, 21; Ps 119, 109; the first half of the verse must have a similar meaning. Job is so confident of his innocence that he is willing to risk his life by going to judgment with God.

19 If anyone can make a case against me,
then I shall be silent and die.
20† These things only do not use against me,
then from your presence I need not hide:
21 Withdraw your hand far from me,
and let not the terror of you frighten me.
22 Then call me, and I will respond;
or let me speak first, and answer me.

23 What are my faults and my sins?
My misdeeds and my sins make known to me!
24* Why do you hide your face
and consider me your enemy?
25 Will you harass a wind-driven leaf,
or pursue a withered straw?
26 For you draw up bitter indictments against me,
and punish in me the faults of my youth.
27 You put my feet in the stocks;
you watch all my paths
and trace out all my footsteps.

CHAPTER 14

1* Man born of woman
is short-lived and full of trouble,
2* Like a flower that springs up and fades,
swift as a shadow that does not abide.
3 Upon such a one will you cast your eyes
so as to bring him into judgment before you,
13:28† Though he wears out like a leather bottle,
like a garment that the moth has consumed?

14:4* Can a man be found who is clean of defilement?
There is none, 5 however short his days.
You know the number of his months;
you have fixed the limit which he cannot pass.
6 Look away from him and let him be,
while, like a hireling, he completes his day.

7 For a tree there is hope,
if it be cut down, that it will sprout again
and that its tender shoots will not cease.
8 Even though its root grow old in the earth,
and its stump die in the dust,
9 Yet at the first whiff of water it may flourish again
and put forth branches like a young plant.
10* But when a man dies, all vigor leaves him;
when man expires, where then is he?
11 As when the waters of a lake fail,
or a stream grows dry and parches,
12* So men lie down and rise not again.
Till the heavens are no more, they shall not awake,
nor be roused out of their sleep.

13 Oh, that you would hide me in the nether world
and keep me sheltered till your wrath is past;
would fix a time for me, and then remember me!
14* When a man has died, were he to live again,
all the days of my drudgery I would wait,
until my relief should come.
15 You would call, and I would answer you;
you would esteem the work of your hands.
16* Surely then you would count my steps,
and not keep watch for sin in me.
17† My misdeeds would be sealed up in a pouch,
and you would cover over my guilt.

18 But as a mountain falls at last
and its rock is moved from its place,
19 As waters wear away the stones
and floods wash away the soil of the land,
so you destroy the hope of man.
20 You prevail once for all against him
and he passes on;
with changed appearance you send him away.
21 If his sons are honored, he is not aware of it;
if they are in disgrace, he does not know about them.
22 Only his own flesh pains him, and his soul grieves for him.

JOB

*

24: 19, 11; 33, 10.
14, 1: 10, 20; 15, 14; Pss 39, 5f; 89, 46; Wis 2, 1.
2: 8, 9; Pss 90, 6; 102, 12; 103, 15; 109, 23; 144, 4; Is 40, 6f; Jas 1, 10.
4: Ps 51, 4.7.
10: 20, 7.
12: 7, 10.
14: 7, 1.
16: 31, 4; 34, 21.

†

13, 20: From here to the end of chapter 14, Job pleads his case, addressing God rather than his three friends.
14, 28: This verse has been transposed from ch 13.
14, 17: *Sealed up in a pouch:* hidden away and forgotten.

III: SECOND CYCLE OF SPEECHES

CHAPTER 15

Second Speech of Eliphaz

1 Then Eliphaz the Temanite spoke and said:

2 Should a wise man answer with airy opinions,
or puff himself up with wind?
3 Should he argue in speech which does not avail,
and in words which are to no profit?
4 You in fact do away with piety,
and you lessen devotion toward God,
5 Because your wickedness instructs your mouth,
and you choose to speak like the crafty.
6* Your own mouth condemns you, not I;
your own lips refute you.

7 Are you indeed the first-born of mankind,
or were you brought forth before the hills?
8* Are you privy to the counsels of God,
and do you restrict wisdom to yourself?
9* What do you know that we do not know?
What intelligence have you which we have not?
10 There are gray-haired old men among us
more advanced in years than your father.
11 Are the consolations of God not enough for you,
and speech that deals gently with you?

12 Why do your notions carry you away,
and why do your eyes blink,
13 So that you turn your anger against God
and let such words escape your mouth!
14* What is a man that he should be blameless,
one born of woman that he should be righteous?
15* If in his holy ones God places no confidence,
and if the heavens are not clean in his sight,
16 How much less so is the abominable, the corrupt:
man, who drinks in iniquity like water!

17 I will show you, if you listen to me;
what I have seen I will tell—
18 What wise men relate
and have not contradicted since the days of their fathers,
19 To whom alone the land was given,
when no foreigner moved among them.

20 The wicked man is in torment all his days,
and limited years are in store for the tyrant;
21 The sound of terrors is in his ears;
when all is prosperous, the spoiler comes upon him.
22 He despairs of escaping the darkness,
and looks ever for the sword;
23 A wanderer, food for the vultures,
he knows that his destruction is imminent.
24 By day the darkness fills him with dread;
distress and anguish overpower him.

25 Because he has stretched out his hand against God
and bade defiance to the Almighty,
26 One shall rush sternly upon him
with the stout bosses of his shield,
like a king prepared for the charge.
27 Because he has blinded himself with his crassness,
padding his loins with fat,
28 He shall dwell in ruinous cities,
in houses that are deserted,
That are crumbling into clay
29 with no shadow to lengthen over the ground.

He shall not be rich, and his possessions shall not endure;
31 for vain shall be his bartering.
30 A flame shall wither him up in his early growth,
and with the wind his blossoms shall disappear.
32 His stalk shall wither before its time,
and his branches shall be green no more.
33 He shall be like a vine that sheds its grapes unripened,
and like an olive tree casting off its bloom.
34* For the breed of the impious shall be sterile,
and fire shall consume the tents of extortioners.

15, 6: 9, 20.
8: 11, 7; Wis 9, 13; Jer 23, 18; Rom 11, 34; 1 Cor 2, 11.16.
9: 12, 3; 13, 2.
14ff: 25, 4ff.
14: 14, 4.
15: 4, 18f.
34: Wis 3, 11.18.

35*† They conceive malice and bring
forth emptiness;
they give birth to failure.

CHAPTER 16
Job's Fourth Reply

1 Then Job answered and said:

2* I have heard this sort of thing many
times.
Wearisome comforters are you
all!
3 Is there no end to windy words?
Or what sickness have you that
you speak on?
4 I also could talk as you do,
were you in my place.
I could declaim over you,
or wag my head at you;
5 I could strengthen you with talk,
or shake my head with silent lips.
6 If I speak, this pain I have will not
be checked;
if I leave off, it will not depart from
me.

7 But now that I am exhausted and
stunned,
all my company has closed in on
me.
8 As a witness there rises up
my traducer, speaking openly
against me;
9 I am the prey his wrath assails,
he gnashes his teeth against me.
My enemies lord it over me;
10 their mouths are agape to bite me.
They smite me on the cheek insult-
ingly;
they are all enlisted against me.
11 God has given me over to the impi-
ous;
into the clutches of the wicked he
has cast me.
12 I was in peace, but he dislodged me;
he seized me by the neck and
dashed me to pieces.

He has set me up for a target;
13 his arrows strike me from all di-
rections,
He pierces my sides without mercy,
he pours out my gall upon the
ground.
14 He pierces me with thrust upon
thrust;
he attacks me like a warrior.
15 I have fastened sackcloth over my
skin,
and have laid my brow in the dust.
16 My face is inflamed with weeping
and there is darkness over my
eyes,
17 Although my hands are free from
violence,
and my prayer is sincere.

18† O earth, cover not my blood,
nor let my outcry come to rest!
19† Even now, behold, my witness is in
heaven,
and my spokesman is on high.
20 My friends it is who wrong me;
before God my eyes drop tears,
21 That he may do justice for a mortal
in his presence
and decide between a man and his
neighbor.
22 For my years are numbered now,
and I am on a journey from which
I shall not return.
17, 1 My spirit is broken, my lamp of life
extinguished;
my burial is at hand.
2 I am indeed mocked,
and, as their provocation mounts,
my eyes grow dim.

3† Grant me one to offer you a pledge
on my behalf:
who is there that will give surety
for me?
4 You darken their minds to knowl-
edge;
therefore they do not understand.
5 My lot is described as evil,
6* and I am made a byword of the
people;
their object lesson I have become.
7 My eye has grown blind with an-
guish,
and all my frame is shrunken to
a shadow.
8 Upright men are astonished at this,
and the innocent aroused against
the wicked.
9 Yet the righteous shall hold to his
way,
and he who has clean hands in-
crease in strength.

10 But turn now, and come on again;
for I shall not find a wise man
among you!
11 My days are passed away, my plans
are at an end,
the cherished purposes of my
heart.
12 Such men change the night into day;

*

35: Ps 7, 15; Is 59, 4. 16, 2: 12, 3. 17, 6: 30, 9.

†

15, 35: *They give birth to failure:* their wicked plans yield nothing but futile results. Cf Ps 7, 15; Is 59.4.

16, 18: As the blood of those who were unjustly slain cries to heaven for vengeance (Gn 4, 10; Ez 24, 6-9), so Job's sufferings demand redress.

16, 19: *Witness:* refers either to God or, more probably, to Job's prayer.

17, 3: Addressed to God; v 10 to Job's friends.

where there is darkness they talk
of approaching light.
13 If I look for the nether world as my
dwelling,
if I spread my couch in the darkness,
14 If I must call corruption "my father,"
and the maggot "my mother" and
"my sister,"
15 Where then is my hope,
and my prosperity, who shall see?
16 Will they descend with me into the
nether world?
Shall we go down together into the
dust?

JOB

CHAPTER 18

Bildad's Second Speech

1 Then Bildad the Shuhite replied and said:

2 When will you put an end to words?
Reflect, and then we can have discussion.
3 Why are we accounted like the
beasts,
their equals in your sight?
4† You who tear yourself in your anger,
shall the earth be neglected on
your account
[or the rock be moved out of its
place]?

5 Truly, the light of the wicked is extinguished;
no flame brightens his hearth.
6* The light is darkened in his tent;
in spite of him, his lamp goes out.
7 His vigorous steps are hemmed in,
and his own counsel casts him
down.

8 For he rushes headlong into a net,
and he wanders into a pitfall.
9 A trap seizes him by the heel,
and a snare lays hold of him.
10 A noose for him is hid on the ground,
and the toils for him on the way.

11* On every side terrors affright him;
they harry him at each step.
12 Disaster is ready at his side,
13† the first-born of death consumes
his limbs.
14† Fiery destruction lodges in his tent,
and marches him off to the king
of terrors.

He is plucked from the security of
his tent;
15 over his abode brimstone is scattered.
16 Below, his roots dry up,
and above, his branches wither.
17* His memory perishes from the land,
and he has no name on the earth.
18 He is driven from light into darkness,
and banished out of the world.
19 He has neither son nor grandson
among his people,
nor any survivor where once he
dwelt.
20 They who come after shall be appalled at his fate;
they who went before are struck
with horror.

21 So is it then with the dwelling of the
impious man,
and such is the place of him who
knows not God!

CHAPTER 19

Job's Fifth Reply

1 Then Job answered and said:

2 How long will you vex my soul,
grind me down with words?
3 These ten times you have reviled
me,
have assailed me without shame!
4 Be it indeed that I am at fault
and that my fault remains with
me,
5 Even so, if you would vaunt yourselves against me
and cast up to me any reproach,
6 Know then that God has dealt unfairly with me,
and compassed me round with his
net.

7* If I cry out "Injustice!" I am not
heard.
I cry for help, but there is no redress.
8 He has barred my way and I cannot
pass;
he has veiled my path in darkness;
9 He has stripped me of my glory,
and taken the diadem from my
brow.
10 He breaks me down on every side,
and I am gone;
my hope he has uprooted like a
tree.
11* His wrath he has kindled against
me;
he counts me among his enemies.

*

18, 6: 21, 17; Prv 13, 9; 24, 20.
11: 15, 20-24; 27, 20.
17: Ps 34, 17; Prv 2, 22; 10, 7.
19, 7: 30, 20.
11: 13, 24; 33, 10.

†

18, 4: Job himself is portrayed as having the heedless rage of wild beasts, despite which God does not forsake the usual course of Divine Providence.

18, 13: *First-born of death:* that is, disease, plague.

18, 14: *The king of terrors:* of the nether world, death; however, the Hebrew is obscure.

12 His troops advance as one man;
they build up their road to attack me,
and they encamp around my tent.

13* My brethren have withdrawn from me,
and my friends are wholly estranged.
14 My kinsfolk and companions neglect me,
and my guests have forgotten me.
15 Even my handmaids treat me as a stranger;
I am an alien in their sight.
16 I call my servant, but he gives no answer,
though in my speech I plead with him.
17* My breath is abhorred by my wife;
I am loathsome to the men of my family.

18 The young children, too, despise me;
when I appear, they speak against me.
19* All my intimate friends hold me in horror;
those whom I loved have turned against me!
20† My bones cleave to my skin,
and I have escaped with my flesh between my teeth.
21 Pity me, pity me, O you my friends,
for the hand of God has struck me!
22† Why do you hound me as though you were divine,
and insatiably prey upon me?

23*† Oh, would that my words were written down!
Would that they were inscribed in a record:
24 That with an iron chisel and with lead
they were cut in the rock forever!
25*† But as for me, I know that my Vindicator lives,
and that he will at last stand forth upon the dust;
27 Whom I myself shall see:
my own eyes, not another's, shall behold him,
26 And from my flesh I shall see God;
my inmost being is consumed with longing.

28 But you who say, "How shall we persecute him,
seeing that the root of the matter is found in him?"
29 Be afraid of the sword for yourselves,
for these crimes deserve the sword;
that you may know that there is a judgment.

CHAPTER 20

Zophar's Second Speech

1 Then Zophar the Naamathite spoke and said:

3 A rebuke which puts me to shame I hear,
2 and because of this I am disturbed.
So now my thoughts provide me with an answer,
and from my understanding a spirit gives me a reply.

4 Do you not know this from olden time,
since man was placed upon the earth,
5* That the triumph of the wicked is short
and the joy of the impious but for a moment?
6 Though his pride mount up to the heavens
and his head reach to the clouds,
7* Yet he perishes forever like the fuel of his fire,
and the onlookers say, "Where is he?"
8 Like a dream he takes flight and is not found again;
he fades away like a vision of the night.
9 The eye which saw him does so no more;
nor shall his dwelling again behold him.

11 Though his frame is full of youthful vigor,
this shall lie with him in the dust.
12 Though wickedness is sweet in his mouth,
and he hides it under his tongue,
13 Though he retains it and will not let it go
but keeps it still within his mouth,

*

13: 6, 13.
17: 2, 9.
19: Sir 6, 8.
23: 31, 35.
25ff: Phil 3, 20; Ti 2, 13.
20, 5: 21, 13; Ps 37, 35f, 10.36.
7: 14, 10; Ps 37, 10.36.

†

19, 20: *With my flesh between my teeth:* meaning perhaps that Job has been reduced to such an extremity that he scarcely has thin lips over his teeth. But the current Hebrew text of this line is probably corrupt.

19, 22: *Divine:* possessing God's attributes of judgment and authority to punish.

19, 23f: Job regards what he is about to say as so important that he wishes it recorded in a permanent manner.

19, 25.27: The meaning of this passage is obscure because the original text has been poorly preserved and the ancient versions do not agree among themselves. It is certain that Job expresses his belief in a future vindication by God (called here in the Hebrew "Goel"), but the time and manner of this vindication are undefined. In the Vulgate Job is made to indicate a belief in physical resurrection after death, but the Hebrew and the other ancient versions are less specific.

14 Yet in his stomach the food shall turn;
it shall be venom of asps inside him.
15 The riches he swallowed he shall disgorge;
God shall compel his belly to disown them.
16 The poison of asps he shall drink in;
the viper's fangs shall slay him.

17† He shall see no streams of oil,
no torrents of honey or milk.

18 Restoring his gains, he shall not enjoy them;
though his wealth increases, he shall not rejoice.
19 Because he has oppressed the poor,
and stolen a patrimony he had not built up,
21 Therefore his prosperity shall not endure,
10* and his hands shall yield up his riches.
20* Though he has known no quiet in his greed,
his treasures shall not save him.
22* When he abounds to overflowing, he shall be brought into straits,
and nought shall be left of his goods.

23 God shall send against him the fury of his wrath
and rain down his missiles of war upon him.
24 Should he escape the iron weapon,
the bow of bronze shall pierce him through;
25 The dart shall come out of his back;
terrors shall fall upon him.
26* Complete darkness is in store for him;
the fire which shall consume him needs not to be fanned.
27 The heavens shall reveal his guilt,
and the earth shall rise up against him.
28 The flood shall sweep away his house
with the waters that run off in the day of God's anger.

29* This is the portion of a wicked man,
and the heritage appointed him by God.

CHAPTER 21

Job's Sixth Reply

1 Then Job said in reply:

2* At least listen to my words,
and let that be the consolation you offer.
3 Bear with me while I speak;
and after I have spoken, you can mock!
4 Is my complaint toward man?
And why should I not be impatient?
5 Look at me and be astonished,
put your hands over your mouths.
6 When I think of it, I am dismayed,
and horror takes hold on my flesh.

7* Why do the wicked survive,
grow old, become mighty in power?
8 Their progeny is secure in their sight;
they see before them their kinsfolk and their offspring.
9 Their homes are safe and without fear,
nor is the scourge of God upon them.
10 Their bulls gender without fail;
their cows calve and do not miscarry.
11 These folk have infants numerous as lambs,
and their children dance.
12 They sing to the timbrel and harp,
and make merry to the sound of the flute.

13* They live out their days in prosperity,
and tranquilly go down to the nether world.
14* Yet they say to God, "Depart from us,
for we have no wish to learn your ways!
15* What is the Almighty that we should serve him?
And what gain shall we have if we pray to him?"
16* If their happiness is not in their own hands
and if the counsel of the wicked is repulsive to God,
17 How often is the lamp of the wicked put out?
How often does destruction come upon them,
the portion he allots in his anger?

18 Let them be like straw before the wind,
and like chaff which the storm snatches away!
19 May God not store up the man's misery for his children;

*

10: 27, 14.
20: Eccl 5, 9; Lk 12, 20.
22: 15, 20-35.
26: Dt 32, 22.
29: 27, 13.
21, 2: 13, 17.
7: 12, 6; Pss 37, 35; 73, 3; Eccl 8, 14; Jer 12, 1f; Mal 3, 14f.
13: 34, 20.
14: 22, 17.
15: Mal 3, 14.
16: 22, 18.

†

20, 17: *Oil:* olive oil, one of the main agricultural products of Palestine, a land proverbially rich in *honey* and *milk.*

let him requite the man himself
so that he feels it,
20 Let his own eyes see the calamity,
and the wrath of the Almighty let
him drink!
21 For what interest has he in his family after him,
when the number of his months
is finished?
23 One dies in his full vigor,
wholly at ease and content;
24 His figure is full and nourished,
and his bones are rich in marrow.
25 Another dies in bitterness of soul,
having never tasted happiness.
26 Alike they lie down in the dust,
and worms cover them both.

27 Behold, I know your thoughts,
and the arguments you rehearse
against me.
28 For you say, "Where is the house of
the magnate,
and where the dwelling place of
the wicked?"
29 Have you not asked the wayfarers
and do you not recognize their
monuments?

30 Nay, the evil man is spared calamity
when it comes;
32 and on the day he is carried to the
grave
31 Who will charge him with his conduct to his face,
and for what he has done who will
repay him?
33 Sweet to him are the clods of the valley,
and over him the funeral mound
keeps watch,
While all the line of mankind follows
him,
and the countless others who have
gone before.
34 How then can you offer me vain
comfort,
while in your answers perfidy remains?

IV: THIRD CYCLE OF SPEECHES

CHAPTER 22

Eliphaz's Third Speech

1 Then Eliphaz the Temanite answered and said:
2* Can a man be profitable to God?
Though to himself a wise man be
profitable!
21:22†Can anyone teach God knowledge,
seeing that he judges those on
high?
22:3* Is it of advantage to the Almighty
if you are just?
Or is it a gain to him if you make
your ways perfect?
4 Is it because of your piety that he
reproves you—
that he enters with you into judgment?
5 Is not your wickedness manifold?
Are not your iniquities endless?
6*† You have unjustly kept your kinsmen's goods in pawn,
left them stripped naked of their
clothing.
7 To the thirsty you have given no
water to drink,
and from the hungry you have
withheld bread;
8 As if the land belonged to the man
of might,
and only the privileged were to
dwell in it.
9* You have sent widows away empty-handed,
and the resources of orphans you
have destroyed.
10* Therefore snares are round about
you,
and a sudden terror causes you
dismay,
11 Or darkness, in which you cannot
see;
a deluge of waters covers you.

12* Does not God, in the heights of the
heavens,
behold the stars, high though they
are?
13* Yet you say, "What does God know?
Can he judge through the thick
darkness?
14 Clouds hide him so that he cannot
see;
he walks upon the vault of the
heavens!"

15 Do you indeed keep to the ancient
way
trodden by worthless men,
16 Who were snatched away before
their time;
whose foundations a flood swept
away?
17 These men said to God, "Depart
from us!"
and, "What can the Almighty do
to us?"
18*† [Yet he had filled their houses with
good things!

---

* 22, 2: 9, 2.
3: 35, 7.
6: 24, 3; Dt 24, 6.17; Ez 18, 12.16.
9: Dt 24, 17; 27, 19.
10: 18, 8ff.
12: 11, 8.
13f: Pss 10, 11; 73, 11; 94, 7; Is 29, 15; Ez 8, 12; 9, 9.
18: 21, 16.

---

† 21, 22: *Those on high:* the angels.
22, 6ff: This criticism of Job by Eliphaz is altogether untrue, but it is made to dramatize the latter's argument that God always acts justly when he causes someone to suffer. V 8 is misplaced.
22, 18: A gloss, taken partly from 21, 16.

But far be from me the mind of the impious!]
19* The just look on and are gladdened,
and the innocent deride them:
20 "Truly these have been destroyed where they stood,
and such as were left, fire has consumed!"

21 Come to terms with him to be at peace.
In this shall good come to you:
22 Receive instruction from his mouth,
and lay up his words in your heart.
23 If you return to the Almighty, you will be restored;
if you put iniquity far from your tent,
24† And treat raw gold like dust,
and the fine gold of Ophir as pebbles from the brook,
25 Then the Almighty himself shall be your gold
and your sparkling silver.

26 For then you shall delight in the Almighty
and you shall lift up your face toward God.
27* You shall entreat him and he will hear you,
and your vows you shall fulfill.
28 When you make a decision, it shall succeed for you,
and upon your ways the light shall shine.
29* For he brings down the pride of the haughty,
but the man of humble mien he saves.
30* God delivers him who is innocent;
you shall be delivered through cleanness of hands.

CHAPTER 23

Job's Seventh Reply

1 Again Job answered and said:

2 Though I know my complaint is bitter,
his hand is heavy upon me in my groanings.
3 Oh, that today I might find him,
that I might come to his judgment seat!
4 I would set out my cause before him,
and fill my mouth with arguments;
5 I would learn the words with which he would answer,
and understand what he would reply to me.
6 Even should he contend against me with his great power,
yet, would that he himself might heed me!
7 There the upright man might reason with him,
and I should once and for all preserve my rights.

8 But if I go to the east, he is not there;
or to the west, I cannot perceive him;
9 Where the north enfolds him, I behold him not;
by the south he is veiled, and I see him not.
10* Yet he knows my way;
if he proved me, I should come forth as gold.
11 My foot has always walked in his steps;
his way I have kept and have not turned aside.
12 From the commands of his lips I have not departed;
the words of his mouth I have treasured in my heart.
13* But he had decided, and who can say him nay?
What he desires, that he does.
14 For he will carry out what is appointed for me;
and many such things may yet be in his mind.

15 Therefore am I dismayed before him;
when I take thought, I fear him.
16 Indeed God has made my courage fail;
the Almighty has put me in dismay.
17 Yes, would that I had vanished in darkness,
and that thick gloom were before me to conceal me.

CHAPTER 24

1† Why are not times set by the Almighty,
and why do his friends not see his days?
2 The wicked remove landmarks;
they steal away herds and pasture them.
3 The asses of orphans they drive away;

*

19: Ps 107, 42.
27: 33, 26.
29: Ps 138, 6; Prv 29, 23; Mt 23, 12; Lk 1, 52; Jas 4, 10; 1 Pt 5, 5.
30: 17, 9; Ps 18, 21.25.
23, 10: Ps 66, 10; Prv 17, 3; Mal 3, 3; 1 Pt 1, 7.
13: 42, 2; Pss 115, 3; 135, 6.

†

22, 24: *Ophir:* cf note to Ps 45, 10.
24, 1: Why does not God favor his friends by the speedy punishment of his enemies? (The text and order of verses in this chapter are not certain; note the omission of v 9 which duplicates words of vv 2-4.)

they take the widow's ox for a pledge.

4 They force the needy off the road;
all the poor of the land are driven into hiding.
5 Like wild asses in the desert, these go forth
to their task of seeking food;
The steppe provides food for the young among them;
6 they harvest at night in the untilled land.
7 They pass the night naked, without clothing,
for they have no covering against the cold;
8 They are drenched with the rain of the mountains,
and for want of shelter they cling to the rock.
11 Between the rows they press out the oil;
they glean in the the vineyard of the wicked.
They tread the wine presses, yet suffer thirst,
10 and famished are those who carry the sheaves.

12 From the dust the dying groan,
and the souls of the wounded cry out
[yet God does not treat it as unseemly].

13* There are those who are rebels against the light;
they know not its ways;
they abide not in its paths.
14 When there is no light the murderer rises,
to kill the poor and needy.
15* The eye of the adulterer watches for the twilight;
he says, "No eye will see me."
In the night the thief roams about,
and he puts a mask over his face;
16 in the dark he breaks into houses.
By day they shut themselves in;
none of them know the light,
17† for daylight they regard as darkness.

* * *

18 Their portion in the land is accursed,
20 and wickedness is splintered like wood.
19. 21 . . . .
22 To him who rises without assurance of his life
23 he gives safety and support.
He sustains the mighty by his strength,
and his eyes are on their ways.
24 They are exalted for a while, and then they are gone;
they are laid low and, like all others, are gathered up;
like ears of grain they shrivel.

* * *

25 If this be not so, who will confute me,
and reduce my argument to nought?

CHAPTER 25

Bildad's Third Speech

1 Then Bildad the Shuhite answered and said:

2 Dominion and awesomeness are his
who brings about harmony in his heavens.
3† Is there any numbering of his troops?
Yet to which of them does not his light extend?
4* How can a man be just in God's sight,
or how can any woman's child be innocent?
5 Behold, even the moon is not bright
and the stars are not clear in his sight.
6* How much less man, who is but a maggot,
the son of man, who is only a worm?

CHAPTER 26

Job's Reply

1† Then Job spoke again and said:

2 What help you give to the powerless,
what strength to the feeble arm!
3 How you counsel, as though he had no wisdom;
how profuse is the advice you offer!

JOB

*

24, 13: Jn 3, 19f.
15: Prv 7, 9f.
25, 4: 4, 17ff; 9, 2.
6: 4, 19; 15, 16.

†

24, 17: The asterisks which follow this verse mark off a passage (vv 18-24) which cannot be ascribed to Job with certainty. Vv 17-24 are in general poorly preserved; and much of vv 18-21 has not been translated because these verses are obscure. St. Jerome renders them as follows: (18) "He is light upon the face of the water, cursed be his portion on the earth; let him not walk by the way of vineyards. (19) Let him pass from the snow waters to excessive heat, and his sin even to hell. (20) Let mercy forget him; may worms be his sweetness; let him be remembered no more, but be broken in pieces as an unfruitful tree. (21) For he has fed the barren that bears not, and to the widow he has done no good."

25, 3: *His troops:* the heavenly hosts, the stars or the angels. *His light:* compare the wording in 24, 13: *those who are rebels against the light.*

26, 1-14: Probably to be read as Job's reply to Bildad's short speech. Some, however, would make it the reply to Zophar (27, 13-21); it would thus lead up to the poem of ch 28.

4* With whose help have you uttered those words,
and whose is the breath that comes forth from you?
5*† The shades beneath writhe in terror,
the waters, and their inhabitants.
6*† Naked before him is the nether world,
and Abaddon has no covering.

7† He stretches out the North over empty space,
and suspends the earth over nothing at all;
8 He binds up the waters in his clouds,
yet the cloud is not rent by their weight;
9 He holds back the appearance of the full moon
by spreading his clouds before it.

10*† He has marked out a circle on the surface of the deep
as the boundary of light and darkness.
11* The pillars of the heavens tremble
and are stunned at his thunderous rebuke;
12† By his power he stirs up the sea,
and by his might he crushes Rahab;
13*† With his angry breath he scatters the water.
22† and he hurls the lightning against them relentlessly;
His hand pierces the fugitive dragon
as from his hand it strives to flee.

14 Lo, these are but the outlines of his ways,
and how faint is the word we hear!

CHAPTER 27
Job's Reply

11 I will teach you the manner of God's dealings,
and the way of the Almighty I will not conceal.
2*† As God lives, who withholds my deserts,
the Almighty, who has made bitter my soul,
3 So long as I still have life in me
and the breath of God is in my nostrils,
4 My lips shall not speak falsehood,
nor my tongue utter deceit!
5* Far be it from me to account you right;
till I die I will not renounce my innocence.
6 My justice I maintain and I will not relinquish it;
my heart does not reproach me for any of my days.
7 Let my enemy be as the wicked
and my adversary as the unjust!
8 For what can the impious man expect when he is cut off,
when God requires his life?
9 Will God then attend to his cry
when calamity comes upon him?
10 Will he then delight in the Almighty
and call upon him constantly?
12 Behold, you yourselves have all seen it;
why then do you spend yourselves in idle words!

* * *

13*† This is the portion of a wicked man from God,
the inheritance an oppressor receives from the Almighty:
14 Though his children be many, the sword is their destiny.
His offspring shall not be filled with bread.
15 His survivors, when they die, shall have no burial,
and their widows shall not be mourned.

16 Though he heap up silver like dust
and store away mounds of clothing,
17 What he has stored the just man shall wear,
and the innocent shall divide the silver.
18 He builds his house as of cobwebs,
or like a booth put up by the vinekeeper.

19* He lies down a rich man, one last time;
he opens his eyes and nothing remains to him.

*

26, 4: Gn 2, 7.
5: Prv 9, 18.
6: Ps 139, 7-12.
10: 38, 8-11; Prv 8, 29.
11: 9, 6.
13: Is 27, 1.
27, 2: 34, 5.
5: 2, 3.9; 13, 15; 33, 9.
13: 20, 4-29.
19: Pss 49, 18; 76, 6.

†

26, 5: *Shades:* the dead in Sheol, the nether world; cf Pss 6, 6; 88, 11.

26, 6: *Nether world:* cf note to Ps 6, 6. *Abaddon:* Hebrew for "(place of) destruction," a synonym for *nether world;* cf 28, 22; Rv 9, 11.

26, 7: *The North:* used here as a synonym for the firmament, the heavens; cf Is 14, 13.

26, 10: *Circle:* the horizon of the ocean which serves as the boundary for the activity of light and darkness.

26, 12: *Rahab:* cf 9, 13; see note on Ps 89, 11.

26, 13: *The fugitive dragon:* the same term occurs in Is 27, 1 in apposition to Leviathan; see note on 3, 8. This is actually Jb 27, 22.

27, 2-12: This is probably to be read as Job's reply to Zophar's speech of 27, 13-21. In the current Hebrew text the heading for this chapter (27, 1, here omitted) is identical with 29, 1; we should expect rather such a heading as in 21, 1; 23, 1; 26, 1.

27, 13-21: This is probably to be read as Zophar's third speech. The asterisks are present to indicate it is not likely that the sacred writer intended these words to be ascribed to Job.

20 Terrors rush upon him by day;
at night the tempest carries him off.
21† The storm wind seizes him and he disappears;
it sweeps him out of his place.

* * *

CHAPTER 28

The Inaccessibility of Wisdom

1† There is indeed a mine for silver,
and a place for gold which men refine.
2 Iron is taken from the earth,
and copper is melted out of stone.
4 . . . .
5 The earth, though out of it comes forth bread,
is in fiery upheaval underneath.
6 Its stones are the source of sapphires,
and there is gold in its dust.

12* But whence can wisdom be obtained,
and where is the place of understanding?
13 Man knows nothing to equal it,
nor is it to be had in the land of the living.
15* Solid gold cannot purchase it,
nor can its price be paid with silver.
16† It cannot be bought with gold of Ophir,
with the precious onyx or the sapphire.
17 Gold or crystal cannot equal it,
nor can golden vessels reach its worth.
18 Neither coral nor jasper should be thought of;
it surpasses pearls and 19 Arabian topaz.
20 Whence, then, comes wisdom,
and where is the place of understanding?
21 It is hid from the eyes of any beast;
from the birds of the air it is concealed.
7 The path to it no bird of prey knows,
nor has the hawk's eye seen that path.
8 The proud beasts have not trodden it,
nor has the lion gone that way.
14 The abyss declares, "It is not in me";
and the sea says, "I have it not."
22† Abaddon and Death say,
"Only by rumor have we heard of it."

23* God knows the way to it;
it is he who is familiar with its place.
24 For he beholds the ends of the earth
and sees all that is under the heavens.
3 He has set a boundary for the darkness;
to the farthest confines he penetrates.
9 He sets his hand to the flinty rock,
and overturns the mountains at their foundations.
10 He splits channels in the rocks;
his eyes behold all that is precious.
11 He probes the wellsprings of the streams,
and brings hidden things to light.

25 He has weighed out the wind,
and fixed the scope of the waters;
26* When he made rules for the rain
and a path for the thunderbolts,
27 Then he saw wisdom and appraised it,
gave it its setting, knew it through and through.
28* And to man he said:
Behold, the fear of the LORD is wisdom;
and avoiding evil is understanding.

V: JOB'S FINAL SUMMARY OF HIS CAUSE

CHAPTER 29

1 Job took up his theme anew and said;

2* Oh, that I were as in the months past!
as in the days when God watched over me,
3 While he kept his lamp shining above my head,
and by his light I walked through darkness;
4 As I was in my flourishing days,
when God sheltered my tent;

JOB

*

28, 12: Eccl 7, 24f; Bar 3, 14f.29-33.
15: Prv 3, 14; 8, 10f. 19; 16, 16; Wis 7, 7-11.
23-27: Prv 8, 22-31.
23: Prv 2, 6; Sir 1, 1; Jas 1, 5.
26: 38, 25; Prv 3, 20.
28: Ps 111, 10; Prv 1, 7; 9, 10; Sir 1, 16.
29, 2: 1, 10.

†

27, 21: The Hebrew has two more verses: v 22 (read above with 26, 13); and v 23, which is a variant form of v 21.

28, 1-28: Note the changed order of verses; v 4 is uncertain.

This chapter contains a beautifully vivid description of that Wisdom which is beyond the attainment of creatures; known only to God, it is reflected in the order and majesty of his creation. Man, however, can, in a way, participate in this Wisdom by fearing the LORD and avoiding evil. Scholars are not agreed regarding the authorship of this poem, though it is altogether worthy of the author of the Book of Job. Used here as a counterpoise to ch 3 at the beginning of the dialogue, it may have been first conceived as an independent poem.

28, 16: *Ophir:* cf note to Ps 45, 10.

28, 22: *Abaddon:* cf note to 26, 6.

5 When the Almighty was yet with me,
and my children were round about me;
6† When my footsteps were bathed in milk,
and the rock flowed with streams of oil;
7 When I went forth to the gate of the city
and set up my seat in the square—
8 Then the young men saw me and withdrew,
while the elders rose up and stood;
9* The chief men refrained from speaking
and covered their mouths with their hands;
10 The voice of the princes was silenced,
and their tongues stuck to the roofs of their mouths.

21 For me they listened and waited;
they were silent for my counsel.
22 Once I spoke, they said no more,
but received my pronouncement drop by drop.
23 They waited for me as for the rain;
they drank in my words like the spring rains.
24 When I smiled on them they were reassured;
25 mourners took comfort from my cheerful glance.
I chose out their way and presided;
I took a king's place in the armed forces.
11 Whoever heard of me blessed me;
those who saw me commended me.
12 For I rescued the poor who cried out for help,
the orphans, and the unassisted;
13 The blessing of those in extremity came upon me,
and the heart of the widow I made joyful.
14 I wore my honesty like a garment;
justice was my robe and my turban.

15 I was eyes to the blind,
and feet to the lame was I;
16 I was a father to the needy;
the rights of the stranger I studied,
17 And I broke the jaws of the wicked man;
from his teeth I forced the prey.
18† Then I said: "In my own nest I shall grow old;
I shall multiply years like the phoenix.
19 My root is spread out to the waters;
the dew rests by night on my branches.
20 My glory is fresh within me,
and my bow is renewed in my hand!"

CHAPTER 30

1* But now they hold me in derision
who are younger in years than I;
Whose fathers I should have disdained
to rank with the dogs of my flock.
2 Such strength as they had, to me meant nought;
they were utterly destitute.

3* In want and hunger was their lot,
they who fled to the parched wastelands:
4† They plucked saltwort and shrubs;
the roots of the broom plant were their food.
5 They were banished from among men,
with an outcry like that against a thief—

6 To dwell on the slopes of the wadies,
in caves of sand and stone;
7 Among the bushes they raised their raucous cry;
under the nettles they huddled together.
8 Irresponsible, nameless men,
they were driven out of the land.

9* Yet now they sing of me in mockery;
I am become a byword among them.
10 They abhor me, they stand aloof from me,
they do not hesitate to spit in my face!
11 Indeed, they have loosed their bonds; they lord it over me,
and have thrown off restraint in my presence.

12 To subvert my paths they rise up;
they build their approaches for my ruin.
13 To destroy me, they attack with none to stay them;
14 as through a wide breach they advance.
Amid the uproar they come on in waves;
15 over me rolls the terror.

*

9: Wis 8, 10ff.
30, 1: 12, 4; 19, 18.
3-8: 24, 5f.
9: 17, 6.

†

29, 6: Hyperbole to express abundance; see note on 20, 17.

29, 18: *Phoenix:* a legendary bird which, after several centuries of life, consumed itself in fire, then rose from its ashes in youthful freshness. This meaning, originally intended in the Greek, later came to mean "palm tree." Some render the Hebrew as "sand."

30, 4: *Saltwort:* found in salt marshes and very sour to the taste; eaten by the extremely poor as a cooked vegetable. *Broom plant:* the juniper or brushwood; cf Ps 120, 4; a figure of bitterness and poverty, because of its bitter-tasting roots which are practically inedible.

My dignity is borne off on the wind,
and my welfare vanishes like a cloud.
18† One with great power lays hold of my clothing;
by the collar of my tunic he seizes me:
19 He has cast me into the mire;
I am leveled with the dust and ashes.

20* I cry to you, but you do not answer me;
you stand off and look at me,
21 Then you turn upon me without mercy
and with your strong hand you buffet me.
22 You raise me up and drive me before the wind;
I am tossed about by the tempest.

23* Indeed I know you will turn me back in death
to the destined place of everyone alive.
24 Yet should not a hand be held out
to help a wretched man in his calamity?
25* Or have I not wept for the hardships of others;
was not my soul grieved for the destitute?
26 Yet when I looked for good, then evil came;
when I expected light, then came darkness.

16 My soul ebbs away from me;
27 days of affliction have overtaken me.
17 My frame takes no rest by night;
my inward parts seethe and will not be stilled.
28 I go about in gloom, without the sun;
I rise up in public to voice my grief.

29 I have become the brother of jackals,
companion to the ostrich.
30 My blackened skin falls away from me;
the heat scorches my very frame.
31 My harp is turned to mourning,
and my reed pipe to sounds of weeping.

CHAPTER 31

2 But what is man's lot from God above,
his inheritance from the Almighty on high?
3 Is it not calamity for the unrighteous,
and woe for evildoers?
4* Does he not see my ways,
and number all my steps?
6* Let God weigh me in the scales of justice;
thus will he know my innocence!

5† If I have walked in falsehood
and my foot has hastened to deceit;
7 If my steps have turned out of the way,
and my heart has followed my eyes,
or any stain clings to my hands,
8 Then may I sow, but another eat of it,
or may my planting be rooted up!

38 If my land has cried out against me
till its very furrows complained;
39 If I have eaten its produce without payment
and grieved the hearts of its tenants;
40 Then let the thistles grow instead of wheat
and noxious weeds instead of barley!
1† If I have made an agreement with my eyes
and entertained any thoughts against a maiden;
9 If my heart has been enticed toward a woman,
and I have lain in wait at my neighbor's door;
10 Then may my wife grind for another,
and may others cohabit with her!
11* For that would be heinous,
a crime to be condemned;
12* A fire that should burn down to the abyss
till it consumed all my possessions to the roots.

13 Had I refused justice to my manservant
or to my maid, when they had a claim against me,
14 What then should I do when God rose up;
what could I answer when he demanded an account?
15 Did not he who made me in the womb make him?

JOB

*

20: 19, 7.
23: Heb 9, 27.
25: 29, 12-16.
31, 4: 14, 16; 34, 21; Ps 139, 3; Prv 5, 21.
6: 23, 10.
11: Ex 20, 14; Lv 20, 10; Dt 22, 22.
12: Sir 9, 8f.

†

30, 18-23: Job here refers to God's stern treatment of him.
31, 5-34: Job's final protestation of his innocence.
31, 1.9: Note the gradation: avoidance of sinful glances and thoughts against a maiden; desire for another's wife.

Did not the same One fashion us before our birth?

16* If I have denied anything to the poor,
or allowed the eyes of the widow to languish
17 While I ate my portion alone,
with no share in it for the fatherless,
18 Though like a father God has reared me from my youth,
guiding me even from my mother's womb—

19 If I have seen a wanderer without clothing,
or a poor man without covering,
20 Whose limbs have not blessed me when warmed with the fleece of my sheep;
21† If I have raised my hand against the innocent
because I saw that I had supporters at the gate—

22 Then may my arm fall from the shoulder,
my forearm be broken at the elbow!
23 For the dread of God will be upon me,
and his majesty will overpower me.
24 Had I put my trust in gold
or called fine gold my security;
25 Or had I rejoiced that my wealth was great,
or that my hand had acquired abundance—
26*† Had I looked upon the sun as it shone,
or the moon in the splendor of its progress,
27 And had my heart been secretly enticed
to waft them a kiss with my hand;
28* This too would be a crime for condemnation,
for I should have denied God above.

29* Had I rejoiced at the destruction of my enemy
or exulted when evil fell upon him,
30 Even though I had not suffered my mouth to sin
by uttering a curse against his life—

31† Had not the men of my tent exclaimed,
"Who has not been fed with his meat!"
32 Because no stranger lodged in the street,
but I opened my door to wayfarers—
33† Had I, out of human weakness, hidden my sins
and buried my guilt in my bosom
34 Because I feared the noisy multitude
and the scorn of the tribes terrified me—
then I should have remained silent, and not come out of doors!

35* Oh, that I had one to hear my case,
and that my accuser would write out his indictment!
36† Surely, I should wear it on my shoulder
or put it on me like a diadem;
37† Of all my steps I should give him an account;
like a prince I should present myself before him.

This is my final plea; let the Almighty answer me!

The words of Job are ended.

VI: ELIHU'S SPEECHES

CHAPTER 32

1* Then the three men ceased to an-
swer Job, because he was righteous in
his own eyes. 2*† But the anger of Elihu,
son of Barachel the Buzite, of the family
of Ram, was kindled. He was angry with
Job for considering himself rather than
God to be in the right. 3* He was angry
also with the three friends because they
had not found a good answer and had
not condemned Job. 4 But since these
men were older than he, Elihu bided his
time before addressing Job. 5 When,
however, Elihu saw that there was no
reply in the mouths of the three men,
his wrath was inflamed. 6 So Elihu, son

*

16-23: 29, 12-16.
26f: Dt 4, 19.
28: Dt 17, 2-7.
29: Prv 24, 17.
35: 19, 23; 23, 3-7.
32, 1: 33, 9.
2: 13, 18; 27, 6; 34, 5; 35, 2.
3: 22, 5.

†

31, 21: *Gate:* cf notes on Jb 5, 4; Ru 4, 1.

31, 26ff: Job never sinned by worshiping the sun or the moon; *waft them a kiss:* an act of idolatrous worship.

31, 31: The members of his household will testify to his hospitality.

31, 33f: Job's present protest is made, not in spite of hidden sins which he had been unwilling to disclose, but out of genuine innocence.

31, 36: *On my shoulder:* i.e., boldly, proudly.

31, 37: *Like a prince:* not as a frightened criminal. *Final plea:* literally, "tau," the last letter of the Hebrew alphabet; in the current Hebrew text this line is in v 35, while the following one ends v 40.

32, 2: *Elihu* means "My God is he." This speaker was from Buz, which, according to Jer 25, 23, was near Tema and Dedan. A young man, he impetuously and impatiently upbraids Job for his boldness toward God, and the three friends for not successfully answering Job. He undertakes to defend God's absolute justice and to explain more clearly why there is suffering. While fundamentally his position is the same as that of the three friends, he does locate more definitely, though not perfectly, the place of suffering in the divine plan.

of Barachel the Buzite, spoke out and said:

I am young and you are very old;
therefore I held back and was afraid
to declare to you my knowledge.
7* Days should speak, I thought,
and many years teach wisdom!
8* But it is a spirit in man,
the breath of the Almighty, that gives him understanding.
9 It is not those of many days who are wise,
nor the aged who understand the right.
10 Therefore I say, hearken to me;
let me too set forth my knowledge!

11 Behold, I have waited for your discourses,
and have given ear to your arguments.
12 Yes, I followed you attentively
as you searched out what to say;
And behold, there is none who has convicted Job,
not one of you who could refute his statements.
13† Yet do not say, "We have met wisdom.
God may vanquish him but not man!"
14 For had he addressed his words to me,
I should not then have answered him as you have done.

15 They are dismayed, they make no more reply;
words fail them.
16 Must I wait? Now that they speak no more,
and have ceased to make reply,
17 I too will speak my part;
I also will show my knowledge!

18 For I am full of matters to utter;
the spirit within me compels me.
19 Like a new wineskin with wine under pressure,
my bosom is ready to burst.
20 Let me speak and obtain relief;
let me open my lips, and make reply.
21 I would not be partial to anyone,
nor give flattering titles to any.
22 For I know nought of flattery;
if I did, my Maker would soon take me away.

CHAPTER 33

1 Therefore, O Job, hear my discourse,
and hearken to all my words.
2 Behold, now I open my mouth;
my tongue and my voice form words.
3 I will state directly what is in my mind,
my lips shall utter knowledge sincerely;
4* For the spirit of God has made me,
the breath of the Almighty keeps me alive.
5 If you are able, refute me;
draw up your arguments and stand forth.
6* Behold I, like yourself, have been taken
from the same clay by God.
7 Therefore no fear of me should dismay you,
nor should my presence weigh heavily upon you.

8 But you have said in my hearing,
as I listened to the sound of your words:
9* "I am clean and without transgression;
I am innocent; there is no guilt in me.
10* Yet he invents pretexts against me
and reckons me as his enemy.
11* He puts my feet in the stocks;
he watches all my ways!"
12 In this you are not just, let me tell you;
for God is greater than man.
13* Why, then, do you make complaint against him
that he gives no account of his doings?
14 For God does speak, perhaps once,
or even twice, though one perceive it not.

15 In a dream, in a vision of the night,
[when deep sleep falls upon men]
as they slumber in their beds,
16 It is then he opens the ears of men
and as a warning to them, terrifies them;
17 By turning man from evil
and keeping pride away from him,
18 He withholds his soul from the pit
and his life from passing to the grave.

19 Or a man is chastened on his bed by pain
and unceasing suffering within his frame,

JOB

*

7: 12, 12.
8: 33, 4.
33, 4: 32, 8.
6: 31, 15.
9: 10, 7; 13, 18; 27, 5f; 29, 14; 32, 1; 34, 5.
10: 13, 24; 19, 11.
11: 13, 27; 31, 4.
13: 31, 35.

†

32, 13: *Met wisdom:* in Job's arguments.

20* So that to his appetite food becomes repulsive,
and his senses reject the choicest nourishment.
21 His flesh is wasted so that it cannot be seen,
and his bones, once invisible, appear;
22 His soul draws near to the pit,
his life to the place of the dead.

23† If then there be for him an angel,
one out of a thousand, a mediator,
To show him what is right for him
and bring the man back to justice,
24 He will take pity on him and say,
"Deliver him from going down to the pit;
I have found him a ransom."

25 Then his flesh shall become soft as a boy's;
he shall be again as in the days of his youth.
26* He shall pray and God will favor him;
he shall see God's face with rejoicing.
27 He shall sing before men and say,
"I sinned and did wrong,
yet he has not punished me accordingly.
28 He delivered my soul from passing to the pit,
and I behold the light of life."

29 Lo, all these things God does,
twice, or thrice, for a man,
30 Bringing back his soul from the pit
to the light, in the land of the living.
31 Be attentive, O Job; listen to me!
Be silent and I will speak.
32 If you have aught to say, then answer me.
Speak out! I should like to see you justified.
33 If not, then do you listen to me;
be silent while I teach you wisdom.

CHAPTER 34

1 Then Elihu continued and said:

2 Hear, O wise men, my discourse,
and you that have knowledge, hear me!
3* For the ear tests words,
as the taste does food.
4 Let us discern for ourselves what is right;
let us learn between us what is good.
5* For Job has said, "I am innocent,
but God has taken what is my due.
6* Notwithstanding my right I am set at nought;
in my wound the arrow rankles,
sinless though I am."

7 What man is like Job?
He drinks in blasphemies like water,
8 Keeps company with evildoers
and goes along with wicked men,
9* When he says, "It profits a man nought
that he is pleasing to God."
10* Therefore, men of understanding, hearken to me:
far be it from God to do wickedness;
far from the Almighty to do wrong!
11* Rather, he requites men for their conduct,
and brings home to a man his way of life.
12* Surely, God cannot act wickedly,
the Almighty cannot violate justice.
13* Who gave him government over the earth,
or who else set all the land in its place?
14 If he were to take back his spirit to himself,
withdraw to himself his breath,
15* All flesh would perish together,
and man would return to the dust.

16 Now, do you, O Job, hear this!
Hearken to the words I speak!
17 Can an enemy of justice indeed be in control,
or will you condemn the supreme Just One,
18 Who says to a king, "You are worthless!"
and to nobles, "You are wicked!"
19* Who neither favors the person of princes,
nor respects the rich more than the poor?
For they are all the work of his hands;
20* in a moment they die, even at midnight.
He brings on nobles, and takes them away,

*
20: 6, 7.
26: 22, 26-29.
34, 3: 12, 11.
5: 33, 9f.
6: 9, 20.
9: 9, 22f.30f; 21, 15; 35, 3.
10: 36, 23.
11: Ps 62, 13; Prv 24, 12; Mt 16, 27; Rom 2, 6; 2 Cor 5, 10; Rv 22, 12.
12: 8, 3.
13: 38, 4-7.
15: 10, 9.
19: Dt 10, 17; 2 Chr 19, 7; Wis 6, 7; Acts 10, 34; Rom 2, 11; Eph 6, 9; Col 3, 25; 1 Pt 1, 17.
20: 21, 3.

†
33, 23: *Angel:* one of the thousands who stand between God and man as intermediaries, reminding man of his duties and giving God an account of their fulfillment.

removing the powerful without lifting a hand;
21 For his eyes are upon the ways of man,
and he beholds all his steps.

22 There is no darkness so dense
that evildoers can hide in it.
25 Therefore he discerns their works;
he turns at night and crushes them.
23 For he forewarns no man of his time
to come before God in judgment.
24* Without a trial he breaks the mighty,
and sets others in their stead,
27 Because they turned away from him
and heeded none of his ways,
28 But caused the cries of the poor to reach him,
so that he heard the plea of the afflicted.

29† If he remains tranquil, who then can condemn?
If he hides his face, who then can behold him?
30 . . . .
31 When anyone says to God,
"I was misguided; I will offend no more.
32 Teach me wherein I have sinned;
if I have done wrong, I will do so no more,"
33 Would you then say that God must punish,
since you reject what he is doing?
It is you who must choose, not I;
speak, therefore, what you know.

34 Men of understanding will say to me,
every wise man who hears my views:
35* "Job speaks without intelligence,
and his words are without sense."
36 Let Job be tried to the limit,
since his answers are those of the impious;
37 For he is adding rebellion to his sin
by brushing off our arguments
and addressing many words to God.

CHAPTER 35

1 Then Elihu proceeded and said:
2* Do you think it right to say,
"I am just rather than God?"
3* To say, "What does it profit me;
what advantage have I more than if I had sinned?"
4† I have words for a reply to you
and your three companions as well.
5 Look up to the skies and behold;
regard the heavens high above you.
6 If you sin, what injury do you do to God?
Even if your offenses are many,
how do you hurt him?
7* If you are righteous, what do you give him,
or what does he receive from your hand?
8 Your wickedness can affect only a man like yourself;
and your justice only a fellow human being.
9 In great oppression men cry out;
they call for help because of the power of the mighty,
10 Saying, "Where is God, my Maker,
who has given visions in the night,
11 Taught us rather than the beasts of the earth,
and made us wise rather than the birds of the heavens?"
12 Though thus they cry out, he answers not
against the pride of the wicked.

13 But it is idle to say God does not hear
or that the Almighty does not take notice.
14† Even though you say that you see him not,
the case is before him; with trembling should you wait upon him.
15 But now that you have done otherwise, God's anger punishes,
nor does he show concern that a man will die.
16* Yet Job to no purpose opens his mouth,
and without knowledge multiplies words.

CHAPTER 36

1 Elihu proceeded further and said:
2 Wait yet a little and I will instruct you,
for there are still words to be said on God's behalf.
3 I will bring my knowledge from afar,
and to my Maker I will accord the right.
4 For indeed, my theme cannot fail me:
the one perfect in knowledge I set before you.

JOB

*

24: Ps 2, 9.
35: 35, 16; 38, 2; 42, 3.
35, 2: 32, 2.
3: 34, 9.
7: 22, 3; 41, 2; Lk 17, 10; Rom 11, 35.
16: 34, 35; 38, 2; 42, 3.

†

34, 26.29f: The extant Hebrew text of these verses contains several added phrases which either represent duplication or are very obscure.

35, 4: *A reply to you:* Elihu refers to Job's statement that the innocent suffer as much as the wicked, and especially to Eliphaz's words in 22, 2f.

35, 14f: The text here is uncertain. It seems to indicate that Job should have realized God's indifference is only apparent, and that, because he has not done so, God will punish him.

5† Behold, God rejects the obstinate in heart;
he preserves not the life of the wicked.
6* He withholds not the just man's rights,
but grants vindication to the oppressed,
7* And with kings upon thrones
he sets them, exalted forever.

JOB

8 Or if they are bound with fetters
and held fast by bonds of affliction,
9 Then he makes known to them what they have done
and their sins of boastful pride.
10 He opens their ears to correction
and exhorts them to turn back from evil.
11 If they obey and serve him,
they spend their days in prosperity,
their years in happiness.
12† But if they obey not, they perish;
they die for lack of knowledge.

13 The impious in heart lay up anger for themselves;
they cry not for help when he enchains them;
14† Therefore they expire in youth,
and perish among the reprobate.
15 But he saves the unfortunate through their affliction,
and instructs them through distress.
16–20† . . . .
21 Take heed, turn not to evil;
for you have preferred carousal to affliction.

22 Behold, God is sublime in his power.
What teacher is there like him?
23* Who prescribes for him his conduct,
or who can say, "You have done wrong"?
24 Remember, you should extol his work,
which men have praised in song.
25 All men contemplate it;
man beholds it from afar.

26 Lo, God is great beyond our knowledge;
the number of his years is past searching out.
27 He holds in check the waterdrops
that filter in rain through his mists,
28 Till the skies run with them
and the showers rain down on mankind.
31† For by these he nourishes the nations,
and gives them food in abundance.
29.30† Lo! he spreads the clouds in layers
as the carpeting of his tent.
32 In his hands he holds the lightning,
and he commands it to strike the mark.
33 His thunder speaks for him
and incites the fury of the storm.

CHAPTER 37

1 At this my heart trembles
and leaps out of its place,
2† To hear his angry voice
as it rumbles forth from his mouth!
3 Everywhere under the heavens he sends it,
with his lightning, to the ends of the earth.
4 Again his voice roars—
the majestic sound of his thunder.

5 He does great things beyond our knowing;
wonders past our searching out.
6 For he says to the snow, "Fall to the earth";
likewise to his heavy, drenching rain.
7 He shuts up all mankind indoors;
8 the wild beasts take to cover
and remain quietly in their dens.
9† Out of its chamber comes forth the tempest;
from the north winds, the cold.
10* With his breath God brings the frost,
and the broad waters become congealed.
11 With hail, also, the clouds are laden,
as they scatter their flashes of light.

*

36, 6: Ps 72, 4.12f. 23: 34, 10; Is 40, 13.
7: Ps 113, 7f. 37, 10: Ps 148, 17.

†

36, 5-21: Perhaps this section should be read between vv 6 and 7 of chapter 34.
36, 12: *Knowledge:* practical wisdom in serving God, which they lack because they refused it when warned (cf v 10).
36, 14: *Reprobate:* cf Dt 23, 18f.
36, 16-20: The Hebrew text here is in disorder. The Vulgate has: "(16) Therefore he will give you most ample salvation from the narrow mouth which has no foundations beneath it; but the repose of your table will be filled with fatness. (17) Your case has been judged as that of the wicked; case and judgment you will receive. (18) Let no wrath, then, overcome you, that you oppress anyone; nor let numerous gifts mislead you. (19) Lay down your greatness without tribulation, and all who are mighty in strength. (20) Do not draw out the night, that people may go in place of them."
36, 31: *These:* refers to *the showers* of v 28, if the verse order indicated above is correct.
36, 29f: Because of the uncertainty of the text, no translation of these verses has received unanimous approval from exegetes.
37, 2: *Voice:* the thunder.
37, 9: *Chamber:* where it was popularly believed storms were kept enclosed.

12† He it is who changes their rounds,
according to his plans,
in their task upon the surface of
the earth,
13 whether for punishment or
mercy, as he commands.

14 Hearken to this, O Job!
Stand and consider the wondrous
works of God!
15 Do you know how God lays his commands upon them,
and makes the light shine forth
from his clouds?
16 Do you know how the clouds are
banked,
the wondrous work of him who is
perfect in knowledge?
17 You, whom the streams of water fail
when a calm from the south
comes over the land,
18† Do you spread out with him the firmament of the skies,
hard as a brazen mirror?
19 Teach us then what we shall say to
him;
we cannot, for the darkness, make
our plea.
20† Will he be told about it when I speak,
or when a man says he is being
destroyed?
21† Nay, rather, it is as the light which
men see not
while it is obscured among the
clouds,
till the wind comes by and sweeps
the clouds away.

22† From the North the splendor comes,
surrounding God's awesome majesty!
23 The Almighty! we cannot discover
him,
pre-eminent in power and judgment;
his great justice owes no one an
accounting.
24 Therefore men revere him,
though none can see him, however
wise their hearts.

VII: THE LORD'S SPEECH

CHAPTER 38

1† Then the LORD addressed Job out
of the storm and said:

2 Who is this that obscures divine
plans
with words of ignorance?
3*† Gird up your loins now, like a man;
I will question you, and you tell
me the answers!
4 Where were you when I founded the
earth?
Tell me, if you have understanding.
5 Who determined its size; do you
know?
Who stretched out the measuring
line for it?
6 Into what were its pedestals sunk,
and who laid the cornerstone,
7† While the morning stars sang in
chorus
and all the sons of God shouted
for joy?

8* And who shut within doors the sea,
when it burst forth from the
womb;
9 When I made the clouds its garment
and thick darkness its swaddling
bands?
10 When I set limits for it
and fastened the bar of its door,
11 And said: Thus far shall you come
but no farther,
and here shall your proud waves
be stilled!

12 Have you ever in your lifetime commanded the morning
and shown the dawn its place
13 For taking hold of the ends of the
earth,
till the wicked are shaken from its
surface?
14 The earth is changed as is clay by
the seal,
and dyed as though it were a garment;
15 But from the wicked the light is
withheld,
and the arm of pride is shattered.

16 Have you entered into the sources
of the sea,
or walked about in the depths of
the abyss?

JOB

*

38, 3: 40, 2. 8: Gn 1, 9.

†

37, 12: *Their rounds:* of *rain* (36, 27), of *clouds* (36, 29f), of *lightning* and *thunder* (36, 32f), of *snow* (37, 6), of *winds* (37, 9).

37, 18: *The firmament . . . mirror:* the ancients thought of the sky as a ceiling above which were the "upper waters" (cf Gn 1, 6f; 7, 11); when this ceiling became as hard as metal, the usual rain failed to fall on the earth (cf Lv 26, 19; Dt 28, 23).

37, 20: Will an angel bring this to God's attention?

37, 21: Even though God seems not to know our circumstances, he does know them, just as surely as the sun shines, unseen by man, behind the clouds.

37, 22: Now the storms of doubt and ignorance disappear, and *from the North,* used here as a symbol for God's mysterious abode, comes *the splendor* of the manifestation of God's majestic ways.

38, 1: Now the LORD enters the debate and addresses two discourses (38—39 and 40—41) to Job, in which he speaks of his wisdom and power, which are altogether beyond the capacity of Job, who therefore should never dare to demand a reason for the divine actions. *Out of the storm:* frequently the background of the appearances of the LORD in the Old Testament; cf Pss 18; 50; Na 1, 3; Hb 3.

38, 3: *Gird up your loins:* prepare for combat—figuratively, be ready to defend yourself in debate.

38, 7: *Sons of God:* angels; cf 1, 6.

JOB

17 Have the gates of death been shown to you,
or have you seen the gates of darkness?
18 Have you comprehended the breadth of the earth?
Tell me, if you know all:
19 Which is the way to the dwelling place of light,
and where is the abode of darkness,
20 That you may take them to their boundaries
and set them on their homeward paths?
21† You know, because you were born before them,
and the number of your years is great!

22† Have you entered the storehouse of the snow,
and seen the treasury of the hail
23 Which I have reserved for times of stress,
for the days of war and of battle?
24 Which way to the parting of the winds,
whence the east wind spreads over the earth?

25 Who has laid out a channel for the downpour
and for the thunderstorm a path
26 To bring rain to no man's land,
the unpeopled wilderness;
27 To enrich the waste and desolate ground
till the desert blooms with verdure?

28 Has the rain a father;
or who has begotten the drops of dew?
29 Out of whose womb comes the ice,
and who gives the hoarfrost its birth in the skies,
30 When the waters lie covered as though with stone
that holds captive the surface of the deep?

31† Have you fitted a curb to the Pleiades,
or loosened the bonds of Orion?
32 Can you bring forth the Mazzaroth in their season,
or guide the Bear with its train?
33 Do you know the ordinances of the heavens;
can you put into effect their plan on the earth?

34† Can you raise your voice among the clouds,
or veil yourself in the waters of the storm?
35† Can you send forth the lightnings on their way,
or will they say to you, "Here we are"?
37 Who counts the clouds in his wisdom?
Or who tilts the water jars of heaven
38 So that the dust of earth is fused into a mass
and its clods made solid?

39 Do you hunt the prey for the lioness
or appease the hunger of her cubs,
40 While they crouch in their dens,
or lie in wait in the thicket?
36† Who puts wisdom in the heart,
and gives the cock its understanding?
41* Who provides nourishment for the ravens
when their young ones cry out to God,
and they rove abroad without food?

CHAPTER 39

1 Do you know about the birth of the mountain goats,
watch for the birth pangs of the hinds,
2 Number the months that they must fulfill,
and fix the time of their bringing forth?
3 They crouch down and bear their young;
they deliver their progeny in the desert.
4 When their offspring thrive and grow,
they leave and do not return.

5 Who has given the wild ass his freedom,
and who has loosed him from bonds?
6 I have made the wilderness his home
and the salt flats his dwelling.
7 He scoffs at the uproar of the city,
and hears no shouts of a driver.
8 He ranges the mountains for pasture,
and seeks out every patch of green.

*

41: Ps 147, 9.

†

38, 21: Divine irony.

38, 22f: *Hail . . . of war:* thus God used a hailstorm to rout Joshua's foes in the battle of Gibeon; cf Jos 10, 11; Sir 46, 5.

38, 31f: *Pleiades . . . Orion . . . Bear:* cf 9, 9. *Mazzaroth:* It is uncertain what astronomical group is meant by this Hebrew word; perhaps a southern constellation (cf 9, 9).

38, 34: *Veil yourself . . . storm:* wrap yourself in a cloud, as God comes in a theophany; cf Ps 18, 12.

38, 35: *Here we are:* at your service.

38, 36: *Understanding:* the reflection of divine Wisdom discernible in the created animal instincts of the *cock.*

9 Will the wild ox consent to serve you,
and to pass the nights by your manger?
10 Will a rope bind him in the furrow,
and will he harrow the valleys after you?
11 Will you trust him for his great strength
and leave to him the fruits of your toil?
12 Can you rely on him to thresh out your grain
and gather in the yield of your threshing floor?

13† The wings of the ostrich beat idly;
her plumage is lacking in pinions.
14† When she leaves her eggs on the ground
and deposits them in the sand,
15 Unmindful that a foot may crush them,
that the wild beasts may trample them,
16 She cruelly disowns her young
and ruthlessly makes nought of her brood;
17 For God has withheld wisdom from her
and has given her no share in understanding.
18 Yet in her swiftness of foot
she makes sport of the horse and his rider.

19† Do you give the horse his strength,
and endow his neck with splendor?
20 Do you make the steed to quiver
while his thunderous snorting spreads terror?
21 He jubilantly paws the plain
and rushes in his might against the weapons.
22 He laughs at fear and cannot be deterred;
he turns not back from the sword.
23 Around him rattles the quiver,
flashes the spear and the javelin.
24 Frenzied and trembling he devours the ground;
he holds not back at the sound of the trumpet,
25 but at each blast he cries, "Aha!"
Even from afar he scents the battle,
the roar of the chiefs and the shouting.

26 Is it by your discernment that the hawk soars,
that he spreads his wings toward the south?
27 Does the eagle fly up at your command
to build his nest aloft?
28 On the cliff he dwells and spends the night,
on the spur of the cliff or the fortress.
29 From thence he watches for his prey;
his eyes behold it afar off.
30* His young ones greedily drink blood;
where the slain are, there is he.

CHAPTER 40

1 The LORD then said to Job:

2* Will we have arguing with the Almighty by the critic?
Let him who would correct God give answer!

3 Then Job answered the LORD and
said:

4 Behold, I am of little account; what can I answer you?
I put my hand over my mouth.
5 Though I have spoken once, I will not do so again;
though twice, I will do so no more.

6 Then the LORD addressed Job out of
the storm and said:

7 Gird up your loins now, like a man.
I will question you, and you tell me the answers!
8 Would you refuse to acknowledge my right?
Would you condemn me that you may be justified?

9 Have you an arm like that of God,
or can you thunder with a voice like his?
10 Adorn yourself with grandeur and majesty,
and array yourself with glory and splendor.
11 Let loose the fury of your wrath;
12 tear down the wicked and shatter them.
Bring down the haughty with a glance;
13 bury them in the dust together;
in the hidden world imprison them.
14 Then will I too acknowledge
that your own right hand can save you.

15† See, besides you I made Behemoth,
that feeds on grass like an ox.
16 Behold the strength in his loins,

JOB

*

39, 30: Mt 24, 28; Lk 17, 37. 40, 2: 38, 3.

†

39, 13: *The wings of the ostrich* cannot raise her from the ground, but they help her to run swiftly.
39, 14ff: It was popularly believed that, because the ostrich laid her eggs on the sand, she was thereby cruelly abandoning them; cf Lam 4, 3.
39, 19-25: The famous description of a war horse.
40, 15: *Behemoth:* the hippopotamus.

and his vigor in the sinews of his belly.
17 He carries his tail like a cedar;
the sinews of his thighs are like cables.
18 His bones are like tubes of bronze;
his frame is like iron rods.
19 He came at the beginning of God's ways,
and was made the taskmaster of his fellows;
20 For the produce of the mountains is brought to him,
and of all wild animals he makes sport.
21 Under the lotus trees he lies,
in coverts of the reedy swamp.
22 The lotus trees cover him with their shade;
all about him are the poplars on the bank.
23 If the river grows violent, he is not disturbed;
he is tranquil though the torrent surges about his mouth.
24† Who can capture him by his eyes,
or pierce his nose with a trap?

25† Can you lead about Leviathan with a hook,
or curb his tongue with a bit?
26 Can you put a rope into his nose,
or pierce through his cheek with a gaff?
27 Will he then plead with you, time after time,
or address you with tender words?
28 Will he make an agreement with you
that you may have him as a slave forever?
29 Can you play with him, as with a bird?
Can you put him in leash for your maidens?
30† Will the traders bargain for him?
Will the merchants divide him up?

31 Can you fill his hide with barbs,
or his head with fish spears?
32 Once you but lay a hand upon him,
no need to recall any other conflict!

CHAPTER 41

2† Is he not relentless when aroused;
who then dares stand before him?
1 Whoever might vainly hope to do so
need only see him to be overthrown.
3 Who has assailed him and come off safe—
Who under all the heavens?

4 I need hardly mention his limbs,
his strength, and the fitness of his armor.
5 Who can strip off his outer garment,
or penetrate his double corselet?
6 Who can force open the doors of his mouth,
close to his terrible teeth?
7 Rows of scales are on his back,
tightly sealed together;
8 They are fitted each so close to the next
that no space intervenes;
9 So joined one to another
that they hold fast and cannot be parted.

10 When he sneezes, light flashes forth;
his eyes are like those of the dawn.
11 Out of his mouth go forth firebrands;
sparks of fire leap forth.
12 From his nostrils issues steam,
as from a seething pot or bowl.
13 His breath sets coals afire;
a flame pours from his mouth.
14 Strength abides in his neck,
and terror leaps before him.

15.16 His heart is hard as stone;
his flesh, as the lower millstone.
17† When he rises up, the mighty are afraid;
the waves of the sea fall back.
18 Should the sword reach him, it will not avail;
nor will the spear, nor the dart, nor the javelin.
19 He regards iron as straw,
and bronze as rotten wood.
20 The arrow will not put him to flight;
slingstones used against him are but straws.
21 Clubs he esteems as splinters;
he laughs at the crash of the spear.

22 His belly is sharp as pottery fragments;
he spreads like a threshing sledge upon the mire.
23 He makes the depths boil like a pot;
the sea he churns like perfume in a kettle.
24 Behind him he leaves a shining path;
you would think the deep had the hoary head of age.
25 Upon the earth there is not his like,
intrepid he was made.
26 All, however lofty, fear him;
he is king over all proud beasts.

40, 24: *Eyes . . . nose:* the only exposed parts of the submerged beast.

40, 25: *Leviathan* here is the crocodile. But cf 3, 8.

40, 30: *Merchants:* literally, "Canaanites," whose reputation for trading was so widespread that their name came to be used for merchants; cf Prv 31, 24. The meaning of this verse is that the crocodile is too powerful a creature to be sold like a common fish.

41, 2: *Before him:* some read, "before me," i.e., God; also in v 3.

41, 17: The text here is uncertain.

CHAPTER 42

1 Then Job answered the LORD and
said:

2† I know that you can do all things,
and that no purpose of yours can
be hindered.
3* I have dealt with great things that
I do not understand;
things too wonderful for me,
which I cannot know.
5 I had heard of you by word of mouth,
but now my eye has seen you.
6 Therefore I disown what I have said,
and repent in dust and ashes.

VIII: EPILOGUE

Job's Restoration. 7† And it came to
pass after the LORD had spoken these
words to Job, that the LORD said to Eli-
phaz the Temanite, "I am angry with
you and with your two friends; for you
have not spoken rightly concerning me,
as has my servant Job. 8† Now, there-
fore, take seven bullocks and seven
rams, and go to my servant Job, and of-
fer up a holocaust for yourselves; and
let my servant Job pray for you; for his
prayer I will accept, not to punish you
severely. For you have not spoken
rightly concerning me, as has my ser-
vant Job." 9 Then Eliphaz the Temanite,
and Bildad the Shuhite, and Zophar the
Naamathite, went and did as the LORD
had commanded them. And the LORD
accepted the intercession of Job.
10 Also, the LORD restored the prosper-
ity of Job, after he had prayed for his
friends; the LORD even gave to Job twice
as much as he had before. 11† Then all
his brethren and his sisters came to him,
and all his former acquaintances, and
they dined with him in his house. They
condoled with him and comforted him
for all the evil which the LORD had
brought upon him; and each one gave
him a piece of money and a gold ring.
12* Thus the LORD blessed the latter
days of Job more than his earlier ones.
For he had fourteen thousand sheep, six
thousand camels, a thousand yoke of
oxen, and a thousand she-asses. 13 And
he had seven sons and three daughters,
14† of whom he called the first Jemimah,
the second Keziah, and the third Keren-
happuch. 15† In all the land no other
women were as beautiful as the daugh-
ters of Job; and their father gave them
an inheritance among their brethren.
16*† After this, Job lived a hundred and
forty years; and he saw his children, his
grandchildren, and even his great-
grandchildren. 17 Then Job died, old and
full of years.

JOB

*

42, 3: 34, 35; 35, 16; 38, 2.
12: 1, 3.
16: 5, 25f.

†

42, 2-6: In the current Hebrew text, this final utterance of Job is interrupted by words ascribed to God (vv 3f) which are in large part a duplication of 38, 2f.

42, 7: The three friends of Job (Elihu is ignored in the Epilogue) are criticized by the LORD because they had (even though in good faith) leveled false charges against him.

42, 8: Job becomes the intercessor for his friends, as were other great Old Testament characters, e.g., Abraham and Moses, and as our Lord would be, whom he prefigured. *Seven:* a symbolic number.

42, 11: *A piece of money:* the term is the same as that used in Gn 33, 19; Jos 24, 32. *Gold ring:* for the nose or ear.

42, 14: Job's daughters had names symbolic of their charms: *Jemimah,* dove; *Keziah,* precious perfume (cf Ps 45, 9); *Kerenhappuch,* cosmetic jar—more precisely, a container for a black powder that was used like modern mascara.

42, 15: Ordinarily daughters did not inherit property unless there were no sons; cf Nm 27, 1-11.

42, 16: As his other rewards were *twice as much as he had before* (v 10) so Job's *hundred and forty years* were double the expected span of human life; cf Ps 90, 10.

The Book of

PSALMS

The Hebrew Psalter numbers 150 songs. The corresponding number in the LXX differs because of a different division of certain psalms. Hence the numbering in the Greek Psalter (which was followed by the Latin Vulgate) is usually one digit behind the Hebrew. In the New American Bible the numbering of the verses follows the Hebrew numbering; many of the traditional English translations are often a verse number behind the Hebrew because they do not count the superscriptions as a verse.

The superscriptions derive from pre-Christian Jewish tradition, and they contain technical terms, many of them apparently liturgical, which are no longer known to us. Seventy-three psalms are attributed to David, but there is no sure way of dating any psalm. Some are pre-exilic (before 587 B.C.), and others are post-exilic (after 539 B.C.), but not as late as the Maccabean period (ca. 165 B.C.). The psalms are the product of many individual collections (e.g., Songs of Ascents, Pss 120—134), which were eventually combined into the present work in which one can detect five "books," because of the doxologies which occur at 41, 14; 72, 18-19; 89, 53; 106, 48.

Two important features of the psalms deserve special notice. First, the majority were composed originally precisely for liturgical worship. This is shown by the frequent indication of liturgical leaders interacting with the community (e.g., 118, 1-4). Secondly, they follow certain distinct patterns or literary forms. Thus, the hymn is a song of praise, in which a community is urged joyfully to sing out the praise of God. Various reasons are given for this praise (often introduced by "for" or "because"): the divine work of creation and sustenance (Pss 8; 104), or the divine acts in Israel's favor (Pss 135, 1-12; 136). Some of the hymns have received a more specific classification, based on content. The "Songs of Zion" are so called because they exalt Zion, the city in which God dwells among the people (Pss 46; 48). Others are termed "enthronement" psalms because they reenact or re-present in the liturgy the kingship of the Lord (Pss 47; 96—99). Characteristic of the songs of praise is the joyful summons to get involved in the activity; Ps 104 is an exception to this, although it remains universal in its thrust.

Another type of psalm is similar to the hymn: the thanksgiving psalm. This too is a song of praise acknowledging the Lord as the rescuer of the psalmist from a desperate situation. Very often the psalmist will give a flashback, recounting the past distress, and the plea that was uttered (Pss 30; 116). The setting for such prayers seems to have been the offering of a todah *(a "praise" sacrifice) with friends in the Temple.*

There are more psalms of lament than of any other type. They may be individual (e.g., Pss 3—7; 22) or communal (e.g., Ps 44). Although they usually begin with a cry for help, they develop in various ways. The description of the distress is couched in the broad imagery typical of the Bible (one is in Sheol, the Pit, or is afflicted by enemies or wild beasts, etc.)—in such a way that one cannot pinpoint the exact nature of the psalmist's plight. However, Ps 51 (cf. also Ps 130) seems to refer clearly to deliverance from sin. Several laments end on a note of certainty that the Lord has heard the prayer (cf. Ps 7, but contrast Ps 88), and the Psalter has been characterized as a movement from lament to praise. If this is somewhat of an exaggeration, it serves at least to emphasize the frequent expressions of trust which characterize the lament. In some cases it would seem as if the theme of trust has been lifted out to form a literary type all its own; cf. Pss 23; 62; 91. Among the communal laments can be counted Pss 74 and 79. They complain to the Lord about some national disaster, and try to motivate God to intervene in favor of the suffering people.

Other psalms are clearly classified on account of content, and they may be in themselves laments or psalms of thanksgiving. Among the "royal" psalms, that deal directly with the currently reigning king, are Pss 20, 21, and 72. Many of the royal psalms were given a messianic interpretation by Christians. In Jewish tradition they were preserved, even after kingship had disappeared, because they were read in the light of the Davidic covenant reported in 2 Samuel 7. Certain psalms are called wisdom psalms because they seem to betray the influence of the concerns of the sages (cf. Pss 37; 49), but there is no general agreement as to the number of these prayers. Somewhat related to the wisdom psalms are the "torah" psalms, in which the torah *(instruction or law) of the Lord is glorified (Pss 1; 19, 8-14; 119). Pss 78, 105 and 106 can be considered as "historical" psalms. Although the majority of the psalms have a liturgical setting, there are certain prayers that may be termed "liturgies," so clearly does their structure reflect a liturgical incident (e.g., Pss 15; 24).*

It is obvious that not all of the psalms can be pigeonholed into neat classifications, but even a brief sketch of these types helps us to catch the structure and spirit of the psalms we read. It has been rightly said that the psalms are "a school of prayer." They not only provide us with models to follow, but inspire us to voice our own deepest feelings and aspirations.

FIRST BOOK—Psalms 1-41

PSALM 1†

True Happiness in God's Law

I

1† Happy those who do not follow
the counsel of the wicked,
Nor go the way of sinners,
nor sit in company with scoffers.*
2† Rather, the law of the LORD is their joy;
God's law they study day and night.*
3 They are like a tree*
planted near streams of water,
that yields its fruit in season;
Its leaves never wither;
whatever they do prospers.

II

4† But not the wicked!
They are like chaff driven by the wind.*
5 Therefore the wicked will not survive judgment,
nor will sinners in the assembly of the just.
6 The LORD watches over the way of the just,*
but the way of the wicked leads to ruin.

PSALM 2†

A Psalm for a Royal Coronation

1 Why do the nations protest
and the peoples grumble in vain?*
2† Kings on earth rise up
and princes plot together
against the LORD and his anointed:*
3 "Let us break their shackles
and cast off their chains!"*
4 The one enthroned in heaven laughs;
the Lord derides them,*
5 Then speaks to them in anger,
terrifies them in wrath:
6 "I myself have installed my king
on Zion, my holy mountain."
7 I will proclaim the decree of the LORD,
who said to me, "You are my son;
today I am your father.*
8 Only ask it of me,
and I will make your inheritance the nations,

---

*

1, 1: Pss 26, 4-5; 40, 5.
2: Jos 1, 8; Ps 119; Sir 39, 1.
3: Pss 52, 10; 92, 13-15; Jer 17, 8.
4: Pss 35, 5; 83, 14-16; Jb 21, 18.
6: Ps 37, 18.
2, 1: Rv 11, 18.
2: Ps 83, 6.
3: Ps 149, 8.
4: Pss 37, 13; 59, 9; Wis 4, 18.
7: Pss 89, 27; 110, 2-3; Is 49, 1.

---

†

Ps 1: A preface to the whole Book of Psalms, contrasting with striking similes the destiny of the good and the wicked. The psalm views life as activity, as choosing either the good or the bad. Each "way" brings its inevitable consequences. The wise through their good actions will experience rootedness and life, and the wicked, rootlessness and death.

1, 1: *Those*: literally, "the man." That word is used here and in many of the Psalms as typical, and therefore is translated "they." *The way*: a common biblical term for manner of living or moral conduct (Pss 32, 8; 101, 2. 6; Prv 2, 20; 1 Kgs 8, 36).

1, 2: *The law of the LORD*: either the Torah, the first five books of the Bible, or, more probably, divine teaching or instruction.

1, 4: *The wicked*: those who by their actions distance themselves from God's life-giving presence.

Ps 2: A royal psalm. To rebellious kings (1-3) God responds vigorously (4-6). A speaker proclaims the divine decree (in the legal adoption language of the day), making the Israelite king the earthly representative of God (7-9) and warning kings to obey (10-11). The psalm has a messianic meaning for the Church; the New Testament understands it of Christ (Acts 4, 25-27; 13, 33; Heb 1, 5).

2, 2: *Anointed*: in Hebrew *mashiah*, "anointed"; in Greek *christos*, whence English Messiah and Christ. In Israel kings (Jgs 9, 8; 1 Sm 9, 16; 16, 12-13) and high priests (Lv 8, 12; Nm 3, 3) received the power of their office through anointing.

your possession the ends of the earth.
9 With an iron rod you shall shepherd them,
like a clay pot you will shatter them."*
10 And now, kings, give heed;
take warning, rulers on earth.
11 Serve the LORD with fear;
with trembling bow down in homage,
Lest God be angry and you perish from the way
in a sudden blaze of anger.
Happy are all who take refuge in God!*

PSALMS

PSALM 3†

Threatened but Trusting

1† *A psalm of David, when he fled from his son Absalom.**

I

2 How many are my foes, LORD!
How many rise against me!
3† How many say of me,
"God will not save that one."*
Selah
4 But you, LORD, are a shield around me;
my glory, you keep my head high.*

II

5 Whenever I cried out to the LORD,
I was answered from the holy mountain. *Selah*
6 Whenever I lay down and slept,
the LORD preserved me to rise again.*
7 I do not fear, then, thousands of people
arrayed against me on every side.

III

8 Arise, LORD! Save me, my God!
You will shatter the jaws of all my foes;
you will break the teeth of the wicked.*
9 Safety comes from the LORD!
Your blessing for your people!*
Selah

PSALM 4†

Trust in God

1† *For the leader; with stringed instruments. A psalm of David.*

I

2 Answer when I call, my saving God.
In my troubles, you cleared a way;
show me favor; hear my prayer.*

II

3 How long will you people mock my honor,
love what is worthless, chase after lies?* *Selah*
4 Know that the LORD works wonders for the faithful;
the LORD hears when I call out.
5† Tremble and do not sin;
upon your beds ponder in silence.*
6 Offer fitting sacrifice
and trust in the LORD.*

III

7 Many say, "May we see better times!
LORD, show us the light of your face!"* *Selah*
8 But you have given my heart more joy
than they have when grain and wine abound.
9 In peace I shall both lie down and sleep,*
for you alone, LORD, make me secure.

PSALM 5†

Prayer for Divine Help

1 *For the leader; with wind instruments. A psalm of David.*

*

9: Rv 2, 27; 12, 5; 19, 15.
11: Pss 34, 9; 146, 5; Prv 16, 20.
3, 1: 2 Sm 15, 13ff.
3: Ps 71, 11.
4: Pss 7, 11; 18, 3; 62, 7-8; Dt 33, 29; Is 60, 19.
6: Ps 4, 9; Prv 3, 24.
8: Ps 58, 7.
9: Ps 28, 9; Jon 2, 10.
4, 2: Ps 118, 5.
3: Ps 62, 4.
5: Eph 4, 26.
6: Ps 51, 19.
7: Pss 31, 17; 44, 4; 67, 1; 80, 4; Jb 13, 24; Nm 6, 25; Dn 9, 17.
9: Ps 3, 6.

†

Ps 3: An individual lament complaining of enemies who deny that God will come to the rescue (2-3). Despite such taunts the psalmist hopes for God's protection even in sleep (4-7). The psalm prays for an end to the enemies' power to speak maliciously (8) and closes peacefully with an expression of trust (9).

3, 1: The superscription, added later, relates the psalm to an incident in the life of David.

3, 3. 5. 9: *Selah*: the term is generally considered a direction to the cantor or musicians but its exact meaning is not known. It occurs 71 times in 39 psalms.

Ps 4: An individual lament emphasizing trust in God. The petition is based upon the psalmist's vivid experience of God as savior (2). That experience of God is the basis for the warning to the wicked: revere God who intervenes on the side of the faithful (3-6). The faithful psalmist exemplifies the blessings given to the just (7-9).

4, 1: *For the leader*: many psalm headings contain this rubric. Its exact meaning is unknown but may signify that such psalms once stood together in a collection of "the choirmaster." Cf 1 Chr 15, 21.

4, 5: *Tremble*: be moved deeply with religious awe. The Greek translation understood the emotion to be anger, and it is so cited in Eph 4, 26.

Ps 5: A lament contrasting the security of the house of God (8-9. 12-13) with the danger of the company of evildoers (5-7. 10-11). The psalmist therefore prays that God will hear (2-4) and grant the protection and joy of the temple.

I

2 Hear my words, O LORD;
listen to my sighing.*
3 Hear my cry for help,
my king, my God!
To you I pray, O LORD;
4 at dawn you will hear my cry;
at dawn I will plead before you and wait.*

II

5 You are not a god who delights in evil;
no wicked person finds refuge with you;
6 the arrogant cannot stand before you.
You hate all who do evil;
7 you destroy all who speak falsely.*
Murderers and deceivers
the LORD abhors.

III

8 But I can enter your house
because of your great love.
I can worship in your holy temple
because of my reverence for you, LORD.*
9 Guide me in your justice because of my foes;
make straight your way before me.*

IV

10† For there is no sincerity in their mouths;
their hearts are corrupt.
Their throats are open graves;*
on their tongues are subtle lies.
11 Declare them guilty, God;
make them fall by their own devices.*
Drive them out for their many sins;
they have rebelled against you.

V

12 Then all who take refuge in you will be glad
and forever shout for joy.*
Protect them that you may be the joy
of those who love your name.
13 For you, LORD, bless the just;
you surround them with favor like a shield.

PSALM 6†

Prayer in Distress

1† *For the leader; with stringed instruments, "upon the eighth." A psalm of David.*

I

2 Do not reprove me in your anger, LORD,
nor punish me in your wrath.*
3 Have pity on me, LORD, for I am weak;
heal me, LORD, for my bones are trembling.*
4† In utter terror is my soul—
and you, LORD, how long . . . ?*
5† Turn, LORD, save my life;
in your mercy rescue me.
6† For who among the dead remembers you?
Who praises you in Sheol?*

II

7 I am wearied with sighing;
all night long tears drench my bed;
my couch is soaked with weeping.
8 My eyes are dimmed with sorrow,
worn out because of all my foes.*

III

9 Away from me, all who do evil! *
The LORD has heard my weeping.
10 The LORD has heard my prayer;
the LORD takes up my plea.
11 My foes will be terrified and disgraced;
all will fall back in sudden shame.*

*

5, 2: Pss 86, 6; 130, 1-2.
4: Wis 16, 28.
7: Ps 101, 7; Wis 14, 9; Hb 1, 13.
8: Ps 138, 2; Jon 2, 5.
9: Ps 23, 3; Prv 4, 11; Is 26, 7.
10: Rom 3, 13.
11: Ps 141, 10.
12: Ps 64, 11.
6, 2: Ps 38, 2.
3: Jer 17, 14-15.
4: Pss 13, 2-3; 74, 10; 89, 47.
6: Pss 30, 10; 88, 11; 115, 17; Is 38, 18.
8: Pss 31, 10; 38, 11; 40, 13.
9: Ps 119, 115; Mt 7, 23; Lk 13, 27.
11: Pss 35, 4. 26; 40, 15; 71, 13.

†

5, 10: *Their throats*: their speech brings harm to their hearers (cf Jer 5, 16). The verse mentions four parts of the body, each a source of evil to the innocent.

Ps 6: The first of the seven Penitential Psalms (Pss 6, 32, 38, 51, 102, 130, 143), a designation dating from the seventh century A.D. for psalms suitable to express repentance. The psalmist does not, as in many laments, claim to be innocent but appeals to God's mercy (5). Sin here, as often in the Bible, is both the sinful act and its injurious consequences; here it is physical sickness (3-4. 7-8) and the attacks of enemies (8. 9. 11). The psalmist prays that the effects of personal and social sin be taken away.

6, 1: *Upon the eighth*: apparently a musical notation, now lost.

6, 4: *How long?*: elliptical for "How long will it be before you answer my prayer?" Cf Ps 13, 2-3.

6, 5: *mercy*: Heb. *hesed*, translated as "mercy" or "love," describes God's affectionate fidelity to human beings, which is rooted in divine and not human integrity.

6, 6: A motive for God to preserve the psalmist from death: in the shadowy world of the dead no one offers you praise. Sheol is the biblical term for the underworld where the insubstantial souls of dead human beings dwelt. It was similar to the Hades of Greek and Latin literature. In the second century B.C., biblical books begin to speak positively of life with God after death (Dn 12, 1-3; Wis 3).

PSALM 7†

God the Vindicator

1 *A plaintive song of David, which he sang to the* LORD *concerning Cush, the Benjaminite.*

I

2 LORD my God, in you I take refuge;
rescue me; save me from all who pursue me,*
3 Lest they maul me like lions,
tear me to pieces with none to save.

II

4† LORD my God, if I am at fault in this,
if there is guilt on my hands,
5 If I have repaid my friend with evil—
I spared even those who hated me without cause—
6 Then let my enemy pursue and overtake me,
trample my life to the ground,
and leave me dishonored in the dust.* *Selah*

III

7 Rise up, LORD, in your anger;
rise against the fury of my foes.*
Wake to judge as you have decreed.
8 Have the assembly of the peoples gather about you;
sit on your throne high above them,
9 O LORD, judge of the nations.
Grant me justice, LORD, for I am blameless,
free of any guilt.
10 Bring the malice of the wicked to an end;
uphold the innocent,
O God of justice,
who tries hearts and minds.*

IV

11 A shield before me is God
who saves the honest heart.*
12 God is a just judge,
who rebukes in anger every day.
13 If sinners do not repent,
God sharpens his sword,
strings and readies the bow,*
14 Prepares his deadly shafts,
makes arrows blazing thunderbolts.*

V

15 Sinners conceive iniquity;
pregnant with mischief,
they give birth to failure.*
16 They open a hole and dig it deep,
but fall into the pit they have dug.*
17 Their mischief comes back upon themselves;
their violence falls on their own heads.

VI

18 I praise the justice of the LORD;
I celebrate the name of the LORD Most High.*

PSALM 8†

Divine Majesty and Human Dignity

1† *For the leader; "upon the* gittith.*"*
A psalm of David.

2 O LORD, our Lord,
how awesome is your name through all the earth!
You have set your majesty above the heavens!
3† Out of the mouths of babes* and infants
you have drawn a defense against your foes,
to silence enemy and avenger.
4 When I see your heavens, the work of your fingers,
the moon and stars that you set in place—
5† What are humans that you are mindful of them,*
mere mortals that you care for them?*

---

*

7, 2: Pss 6, 5; 22, 21.
6: Ps 143, 3.
7: Pss 9, 4; 19, 20.
10: Pss 17, 3; 26, 2; 35, 24; 43, 1; 139, 23; Jer 17, 10; 20, 12.
11: Ps 3, 4.
13: Ps 11, 2.
14: Is 50, 11.
15: Jb 15, 35; Is 59, 4.
16: Pss 9, 16; 35, 8; 57, 7; Prv 26, 27; Eccl 10, 8; Sir 27, 26.
18: Pss 18, 50; 30, 5; 135, 3; 146, 2.
8, 3: Mt 21, 16; Wis 10, 21.
5: Ps 144, 3; Jb 7, 17. • Heb 2, 6ff.

---

†

Ps 7: An individual lament. The psalmist flees to God's presence in the sanctuary for justice and protection (2-3) and takes an oath that only the innocent can swear (4-6). The innocent psalmist can thus hope for the just God's protection (7-14) and be confident that the actions of the wicked will come back upon their own heads (15-17). The justice of God leads the psalmist to praise (18).

7, 4: *At fault in this*: in the accusation the enemies have made against the psalmist.

Ps 8: While marvelling at the limitless grandeur of God (2-3), the psalmist is struck first by the smallness of human beings in creation (4-5), and then by the royal dignity and power that God has graciously bestowed upon them (6-10).

8, 1: *Upon the gittith*: probably the title of the melody to which the psalm was to be sung or a musical instrument.

8, 3: *Babes and infants*: the text is obscure. Some join this line to the last line of 2 (itself obscure) to read: "(you) whose majesty is exalted above the heavens / by the mouths of babes and infants." *Drawn a defense*: some prefer the Septuagint's "fashioned praise," which is quoted in Mt 21, 16. *Enemy and avenger*: probably cosmic enemies. The primeval powers of watery chaos are often personified in poetic texts (Pss 74, 13-14; 89, 11; Jb 9, 13; 26, 12-13; Is 51, 9).

8, 5: *Humans . . . mere mortals*: literally, "(mortal) person" . . . "son of man (in sense of a human being, Hebrew *'adam*)." The emphasis is on the fragility and mortality of human beings to whom God has given great dignity.

6† Yet you have made them little less than a god,
crowned them with glory and honor.
7 You have given them rule over the works of your hands,*
put all things at their feet:
8 All sheep and oxen,
even the beasts of the field,
9 The birds of the air, the fish of the sea,
and whatever swims the paths of the seas.
10 O LORD, our Lord,
how awesome is your name through all the earth!

PSALMS 9-10†

Thanksgiving for Victory and Prayer for Justice

1† *For the leader; according to* Muth Labben. *A psalm of David.*

A

I

2 I will praise you, LORD, with all my heart;
I will declare all your wondrous deeds.
3 I will delight and rejoice in you;
I will sing hymns to your name, Most High.
4 For my enemies turn back;
they stumble and perish before you.

II

5 You upheld my right and my cause,
seated on your throne, judging justly.
6 You rebuked the nations, you destroyed the wicked;
their name you blotted out for all time.*
7 The enemies have been ruined forever;
you destroyed their cities;
their memory has perished.

III

8 The LORD rules forever,
has set up a throne for judgment.
9 It is God who governs the world with justice,*
who judges the peoples with fairness.
10 The LORD is a stronghold for the oppressed,
a stronghold in times of trouble.*
11 Those who honor your name trust in you;
you never forsake those who seek you, LORD.

IV

12 Sing hymns to the LORD enthroned on Zion;
proclaim God's deeds among the nations!
13 For the avenger of bloodshed remembers,
does not forget the cry of the afflicted.*

V

14 Have mercy on me, LORD;
see how my foes afflict me!
You alone can raise me from the gates of death.*
15† Then I will declare all your praises,
sing joyously of your salvation
in the gates of daughter Zion.

VI

16 The nations fall into the pit they dig;
in the snare they hide, their own foot is caught.
17† The LORD is revealed in this divine rule:
by the deeds they do the wicked are trapped.* *Higgaion. Selah*

VII

18 To Sheol the wicked will depart,
all the nations that forget God.
19 The needy will never be forgotten,
nor will the hope of the afflicted ever fade.*
20 Arise, LORD, let no mortal prevail;
let the nations be judged in your presence.

PSALMS

* 7ff: Gn 1, 26. 28; Wis 9, 2; 1 Cor 15, 27.
9-10, 6: Jb 18, 17.
9: Pss 96, 10; 98, 9.
10: Ps 37, 39; Is 25, 4.
13: Jb 16, 18.
14: Wis 16, 13.
17: Sir 27, 26.
19: Prv 23, 18.

† 8, 6: *Little less than a god*: Hebrew *'elohim*, the ordinary word for "God" or "the gods" or members of the heavenly court. The Greek version translated *'elohim* by "angel, messenger"; several ancient and modern versions so translate. The meaning seems to be that God created human beings almost at the level of the beings in the heavenly world. Heb 2, 9 finds the eminent fulfillment of this verse in Jesus Christ, who was humbled before being glorified. Cf also 1 Cor 15, 27, where St. Paul applies to Christ the closing words of v 7.

Pss 9-10: Pss 9 and 10 in the Hebrew text have been transmitted as separate poems but they actually form a single acrostic poem and are so transmitted in the Greek and Latin tradition. Each verse of the two psalms begins with a successive letter of the Hebrew alphabet (though several letters have no corresponding stanza). The psalm states loosely connected themes: the rescue of the helpless poor from their enemies, God's worldwide judgment and rule over the nations, the psalmist's own concern for rescue (14-15).

9, 1: *Muth Labben*: probably the melodic accompaniment of the psalm, now lost.

9, 15: *Daughter Zion*: an ancient Near Eastern city could sometimes be personified as a woman or a queen, the spouse of the god of the city.

9, 17: *The Lord is revealed in this divine rule*: God has so made the universe that the wicked are punished by the very actions they perform.

21 Strike them with terror, LORD;
show the nations they are mere mortals. *Selah*

B

I

1 Why, LORD, do you stand at a distance
and pay no heed to these troubled times?
2 Arrogant scoundrels pursue the poor;
they trap them by their cunning schemes.*

II

3 The wicked even boast of their greed;
these robbers curse and scorn the LORD.*
4 In their insolence the wicked boast:
"God doesn't care, doesn't even exist."*
5 Yet their affairs always succeed;
they ignore your judgment on high;
they sneer at all who oppose them.
6 They say in their hearts, "We will never fall;
never will we see misfortune."
7 Their mouths are full of oaths, violence, and lies;
discord and evil are under their tongues.*
8 They wait in ambush near towns;
their eyes watch for the helpless,
to murder the innocent in secret.*
9 They lurk in ambush like lions in a thicket,
hide there to trap the poor,
snare them and close the net.*
10 The helpless are crushed, laid low;
they fall into the power of the wicked,
11 Who say in their hearts, "God pays no attention,
shows no concern, never bothers to look."*

III

12 Rise up, LORD God! Raise your arm!
Do not forget the poor!
13 Why should the wicked scorn God,
say in their hearts, "God doesn't care"?
14 But you do see;
you do observe this misery and sorrow;*
you take the matter in hand.
To you the helpless can entrust their cause;
you are the defender of orphans.*
15 Break the arms of the wicked and depraved;
make them account for their crimes;
let none of them survive.

IV

16 The LORD is king forever;*
the nations have vanished from God's land.
17 You listen, LORD, to the needs of the poor;
you encourage them and hear their prayers.
18 You win justice for the orphaned and oppressed;*
no one on earth will cause terror again.

PSALM 11†

Confidence in the Presence of God

1 *For the leader. Of David.*

I

In the LORD I take refuge;
how can you say to me,
"Flee like a bird to the mountains!*
2 See how the wicked string their bows,
fit their arrows to the string
to shoot from the shadows at the upright.*
3† When foundations are being destroyed,
what can the upright do?"

II

4 The LORD is in his holy temple;
the LORD's throne is in heaven.*
God's eyes keep careful watch;
they test all peoples.
5 The LORD tests the good and the bad,
hates those who love violence,
6† And rains upon the wicked
fiery coals and brimstone,

---

*

B, 2: Is 32, 7.
3: Ps 36, 2.
4: Ps 14, 1; Jb 22, 13; Is 29, 15; Jer 5, 12; Zep 1, 12.
7: Is 32, 7; Rom 3, 14.
8: Ps 11, 2; Jb 24, 14.
9: Ps 17, 12; Prv 1, 11; Jer 5, 26.
11: Pss 44, 25; 64, 6; 73, 11; 94, 7; Ez 9, 9.
14: Pss 31, 8; 56, 9; 2 Kgs 20, 5; Is 25, 8; Rv 7, 17. • Ex 22, 21-22.
16: Ps 145, 13; Jer 10, 10.
18: Dt 10, 18.
11, 1: Pss 55, 7; 91, 4.
2: Pss 7, 13; 37, 14; 57, 5; 64, 4.
4: Pss 14, 2; 102, 20; Hb 2, 20; Dt 26, 15; Is 66, 1; Mt 5, 34.

---

†

Ps 11: A song of trust. Though friends counsel flight to the mountain country (a traditional hideout) to escape trouble (1-3), the innocent psalmist reaffirms confidence in God, who protects those who seek asylum in the temple (4-7).

11, 3: *Foundations*: usually understood of public order. Cf Ps 82, 5.

11, 6: *Their allotted cup*: the cup that God gives people to drink is a common figure for their destiny. Cf Pss 16, 5; 75, 9; Mt 20, 22; 26, 39; Rv 14, 10.

a scorching wind their allotted cup.*
7 The LORD is just and loves just deeds;
the upright shall see his face.

PSALM 12†

Prayer against Evil Tongues

1 *For the leader; "upon the eighth." A psalm of David.*

I

2 Help, LORD, for no one loyal remains;
the faithful have vanished from the human race.*
3 Those who tell lies to one another
speak with deceiving lips and a double heart.*

II

4 May the LORD cut off all deceiving lips,
and every boastful tongue,
5 Those who say, "By our tongues we prevail;
when our lips speak, who can lord it over us?"*

III

6 "Because they rob the weak, and the needy groan,
I will now arise," says the LORD;
"I will grant safety to whoever longs for it."*

IV

7† The promises of the LORD are sure,
silver refined in a crucible,
silver purified seven times.*
8 LORD, protect us always;
preserve us from this generation.
9 On every side the wicked strut;
the shameless are extolled by all.

PSALM 13†

Prayer in Time of Illness

1 *For the leader. A psalm of David.*

I

2 How long, LORD? Will you utterly forget me?
How long will you hide your face from me?*
3 How long must I carry sorrow in my soul,
grief in my heart day after day?
How long will my enemy triumph over me?

II

4 Look upon me, answer me, LORD, my God!
Give light to my eyes lest I sleep in death,
5 Lest my enemy say, "I have prevailed,"
lest my foes rejoice at my downfall.*

III

6 I trust in your faithfulness.
Grant my heart joy in your help,
That I may sing of the LORD,
"How good our God has been to me!"*

PSALM 14†

A Lament over Widespread Corruption

1† *For the leader. Of David.*

I

Fools say in their hearts,
"There is no God."*
Their deeds are loathsome and corrupt;
not one does what is right.
2 The LORD looks down from heaven
upon the human race,*
To see if even one is wise,*
if even one seeks God.
3 All have gone astray;
all alike are perverse.

---

* 6: Pss 120, 4; 140, 11; Prv 16, 27; Ez 38, 22; Rv 8, 5; 20, 10.
12, 2: Pss 14, 3; 116, 11; Is 59, 15; Mi 7, 2.
3: Pss 28, 3; 55, 22; Is 59, 3-4; Jer 9, 7.
5: Sir 5, 3.
6: Is 33, 10.
7: Pss 18, 31; 19, 8; Prv 30, 5.
13, 2: Pss 6, 4; 44, 25; 77, 8; 79, 5; 89, 47; 94, 3; Lam 5, 20.
5: Ps 38, 17.
6: Ps 116, 7.
14, 1: Pss 10, 4; 36, 2; Is 32, 6; Jer 5, 12.
2: Pss 11, 4; 102, 20.
2b-3: Rom 3, 11-12.

---

† Ps 12: A lament. The psalmist, thrown into a world where lying and violent people persecute the just (2-3), prays that the wicked be punished (4-5). The prayer is not simply for vengeance but arises from a desire to see God's justice appear on earth. V 6 preserves the word of assurance spoken by the priest to the lamenter; it is not usually transmitted in such psalms. In vv 7-9 the psalmist affirms the intention to live by the word of assurance.

12, 7: *A crucible*: literally "in a crucible in the ground." The crucible was placed in the ground for support.

Ps 13: A lament in which the psalmist, seriously ill (4), expresses fear that enemies will interpret his or her death as a divine judgment. Hence the heartfelt prayer (2-3) is for healing that will signal to those enemies that the psalmist enjoys God's favor (4-5). The poem ends with a confession of trust in God and a statement of praise (6).

Ps 14: The lament (duplicated in Ps 53) depicts the world as consisting of two types of people: "the fools" (= the wicked, 1-3) and "the company of the just" (4-6; also called "my people," and "the poor"). The wicked persecute the just, but the psalm expresses the hope that God will punish the wicked and reward the good.

14, 1: *Fools*: literally, "the fool." The singular is used typically, hence the plural translation.

Not one does what is right,
not even one.*

II

4 Will these evildoers never learn?
They devour my people as they devour bread;*
they do not call upon the LORD.*
5 They have good reason, then, to fear;
God is with the company of the just.
6 They would crush the hopes of the poor,
but the poor have the LORD as their refuge.

III

7† Oh, that from Zion might come
the deliverance of Israel,
That Jacob may rejoice, and Israel be glad
when the LORD restores his people!*

PSALM 15†
The Righteous Israelite

1† *A psalm of David.*

I

LORD, who may abide in your tent?
Who may dwell on your holy mountain?*

II

2 Whoever walks without blame,*
doing what is right,
speaking truth from the heart;
3 Who does not slander a neighbor,
does no harm to another,
never defames a friend;
4 Who disdains the wicked,
but honors those who fear the LORD;
Who keeps an oath despite the cost,
5† lends no money at interest,
accepts no bribe against the innocent.*

III

Whoever acts like this
shall never be shaken.

PSALM 16†
God the Supreme Good

1† *A* miktam *of David.*

I

Keep me safe, O God;
in you I take refuge.*
2 I say to the LORD,
you are my Lord,
you are my only good.
3 Worthless are all the false gods of the land.
Accursed are all who delight in them.
4† They multiply their sorrows
who court other gods.
Blood libations to them I will not pour out,
nor will I take their names upon my lips.
5 LORD, my allotted portion and my cup,
you have made my destiny secure.*
6† Pleasant places were measured out for me;
fair to me indeed is my inheritance.

II

7 I bless the LORD who counsels me;
even at night my heart exhorts me.
8 I keep the LORD always before me;
with the Lord at my right, I shall never be shaken.*
9 Therefore my heart is glad, my soul rejoices;
my body also dwells secure,
10† For you will not abandon me to Sheol,

---

*

3: Ps 12, 1.
4: Ps 27, 2; Is 9, 11. • Ps 79, 6.
7: Ps 85, 2.
15, 1: Is 56, 7.
2: Ps 119, 1.
5: Ex 22, 24; 23, 8.
16, 1: Ps 25, 20.
5: Pss 23, 5; 73, 26; Nm 18, 20; Lam 3, 24.
8: Pss 73, 23; 121, 5. 8-12; Acts 2, 25-28.

---

†

14, 7: *Israel . . . Jacob . . . his people*: the righteous poor are identified with God's people.

Ps 15: The psalm records a liturgical scrutiny at the entrance to the temple court (cf Ps 24, 3-6; Is 33, 14b-16). The Israelite wishing to be admitted had to ask the temple official what conduct was appropriate to God's precincts. Note the emphasis on virtues relating to one's neighbor.

15, 1: *Your tent . . . your holy mountain*: the temple could be referred to as "tent" (Ps 61, 5; Is 33, 20), a reference to the tent of the wilderness period and the tent of David (2 Sm 6, 17; 7, 2), predecessors of the temple. *Holy mountain*: a venerable designation of the divine abode (Pss 2, 6; 3, 5; 43, 3; 48, 2, etc.).

15, 5: *Lends no money at interest*: lending money in the Old Testament was often seen as assistance to the poor in their distress, not as an investment; making money off the poor by charging interest was thus forbidden (Ex 22, 24; Lv 25, 36-37; Dt 23, 20).

Ps 16: In the first section, the psalmist rejects the futile worship of false gods (2-5), preferring Israel's God (1), the giver of the land (6). The second section reflects on the wise and life-giving presence of God (7-11).

16, 1: *Miktam*: a term occurring six times in psalm superscriptions, always with "David." Its meaning is unknown.

16, 4: *Take their names*: to use the gods' names in oaths and hence to affirm them as one's own gods.

16, 6: *Pleasant places were measured out for me*: the psalmist is pleased with the plot of land measured out to the family, which was to be passed on to succeeding generations ("my inheritance").

16, 10: *Nor let your faithful servant see the pit*: Hebrew *shahath* means here the pit, a synonym for Sheol, the underworld. The Greek translation derives the word here and elsewhere from the verb *shahath*, "to be corrupt." On the basis

nor let your faithful servant see
the pit.*
11 You will show me the path to life,
abounding joy in your presence,
the delights at your right hand
forever.

PSALM 17†

Prayer for Rescue from Persecutors

1 *A prayer of David.*

I

Hear, LORD, my plea for justice;
pay heed to my cry;
Listen to my prayer
spoken without guile.
2 From you let my vindication come;
your eyes see what is right.
3 You have tested my heart,
searched it in the night.*
You have tried me by fire,
but find no malice in me.
My mouth has not transgressed
4 as humans often do.
As your lips have instructed me,
I have kept the way of the law.
5 My steps have kept to your paths;
my feet have not faltered.*

II

6 I call upon you; answer me, O God.
Turn your ear to me; hear my
prayer.
7 Show your wonderful love,
you who deliver with your right
arm
those who seek refuge from their
foes.
8† Keep me as the apple of your eye;
hide me in the shadow of your
wings
9 from the violence of the wicked.*

III

My ravenous enemies press upon
me;*
10† they close their hearts,
they fill their mouths with proud
roaring.
11 Their steps even now encircle me;
they watch closely, keeping low
to the ground,
12 Like lions eager for prey,
like young lions lurking in am-
bush.
13 Rise, O LORD, confront and cast
them down;
rescue me so from the wicked.
14 Slay them with your sword;
with your hand, LORD, slay them;
snatch them from the world in
their prime.
Their bellies are being filled with
your friends;
their children are satisfied too,
for they share what is left with
their young.
15† I am just—let me see your face;
when I awake, let me be filled with
your presence.*

PSALM 18†

A King's Thanksgiving for Victory

1 *For the leader. Of David, the ser-
vant of the LORD, who sang to
the LORD the words of this song
after the LORD had rescued him
from the clutches of all his ene-
mies and from the hand of Saul.*
2 *He said:*

I

I love you, LORD, my strength,
3† LORD, my rock, my fortress, my
deliverer,*
My God, my rock of refuge,
my shield, my saving horn, my
stronghold!*
4 Praised be the LORD, I exclaim!
I have been delivered from my en-
emies.

*

10: Pss 28, 1; 30, 4; 49, 16; 86, 13; Jon 2, 7; Acts 13, 35.
17, 3: Pss 26, 2; 139, 23.
5: Ps 18, 36; Jb 23, 11-12.
9: Pss 36, 8; 57, 2; 61, 5; 63, 8; 91, 4; Dt 32, 10; Ru 2, 12; Zec 2, 12; Mt 23, 37.
9b-12: Pss 10, 9; 22, 14. 22; 35, 17; 58, 7; Jb 4, 10-11.
15: Pss 4, 7; 31, 17; 67, 2; 80, 4; Nm 6, 25; Dn 9, 17.
18, 2-51: 2 Sm 22, 2-51.
3: Pss 3, 4; 31, 3-4; 42, 10; Gn 49, 24; Dt 32, 4.

†

of the Greek, Acts 2, 25-32 and 13, 35-37 apply the verse to Christ's resurrection, "Nor will you suffer your holy one to see corruption."

Ps 17: A lament of an individual unjustly attacked who has taken refuge in the temple. Confident of being found innocent, the psalmist cries out for God's just judgment (1-5) and requests divine help against enemies (6-9a). Those ravenous lions (9b-12) should be punished (13-14). The psalm ends with a serene statement of praise (15). The Hebrew text of vv 3-4 and 14 is uncertain.

17, 8: *Apple of your eye . . . shadow of your wings*: images of God's special care. Cf Dt 32, 10; Prv 7, 2; Is 49, 2.

17, 10-12. 14: An extended metaphor: the enemies are lions.

17, 15: *When I awake*: probably the psalmist has spent the night in the sanctuary (cf 3) and hopes to wake to an oracle assuring God's protective presence.

Ps 18: A royal thanksgiving for a military victory, duplicated in 2 Sm 22. Thanksgiving psalms are in essence reports of divine rescue. The psalm has two parallel reports of rescue, the first told from a heavenly perspective (5-20), and the second from an earthly perspective (36-46). The first report adapts old mythic language of a cosmic battle between sea and rainstorm in order to depict God's rescue of the Israelite king from his enemies. Each report has a short hymnic introduction (2-4. 32-35) and conclusion (21-31. 47-51).

18, 3: *My saving horn*: my strong savior. The horn referred to is the weapon of a bull and the symbol of fertility. Cf 1 Sm 2, 10; Ps 132, 17; Lk 1, 69.

II

5 The breakers of death surged round about me;
the menacing floods terrified me.
6† The cords of Sheol tightened;
the snares of death lay in wait for me.*
7† In my distress I called out: LORD!
I cried out to my God.*
From his temple he heard my voice;
my cry to him reached his ears.
8† The earth rocked and shook;
the foundations of the mountains trembled;
they shook as his wrath flared up.*
9 Smoke rose in his nostrils,
a devouring fire poured from his mouth;
it kindled coals into flame.
10 He parted the heavens and came down,
a dark cloud under his feet.*
11† Mounted on a cherub he flew,
borne along on the wings of the wind.
12 He made darkness the cover about him;
his canopy, heavy thunderheads.
13 Before him scudded his clouds,
hail and lightning too.*
14 The LORD thundered from heaven;
the Most High made his voice resound.*
15† He let fly his arrows and scattered them;
shot his lightning bolts and dispersed them.*
16 Then the bed of the sea appeared;
the world's foundations lay bare,*
At the roar of the LORD,
at the storming breath of his nostrils.
17 He reached down from on high and seized me;
drew me out of the deep waters.*
18 He rescued me from my mighty enemy,
from foes too powerful for me.
19 They attacked me on a day of distress,
but the LORD came to my support.
20 He set me free in the open;
he rescued me because he loves me.

III

21 The LORD acknowledged my righteousness,
rewarded my clean hands.*
22 For I kept the ways of the LORD;
I was not disloyal to my God.
23 His laws were all before me,
his decrees I did not cast aside.
24 I was honest toward him;
I was on guard against sin.
25 So the LORD rewarded my righteousness,
the cleanness of my hands in his sight.
26 Toward the faithful you are faithful;
to the honest you are honest;*
27 Toward the sincere, sincere;
but to the perverse you are devious.
28 Humble people you save;
haughty eyes you bring low.*
29 You, LORD, give light to my lamp;
my God brightens the darkness about me.*
30 With you I can rush an armed band,
with my God to help I can leap a wall.
31 God's way is unerring;
the LORD's promise is tried and true;
he is a shield for all who trust in him.*

IV

32 Truly, who is God except the LORD?
Who but our God is the rock?*
33 This God who girded me with might,
kept my way unerring,
34 Who made my feet swift as a deer's,
set me safe on the heights,*
35† Who trained my hands for war,
my arms to bend even a bow of bronze.*

V

36 You have given me your protecting shield;
your right hand has upheld me;
you stooped to make me great.

---

*

6: Pss 88, 8; 93, 3-4; 116, 3-4.
7: Jon 2, 3.
8: Pss 97, 3-4; 99, 1; Jgs 5, 4-5; Is 64, 1; Hab 3, 9-11.
10: Pss 104, 3; 144, 5; Is 63, 19.
13: Ex 13, 21; 19, 16.
14: Pss 29; 77, 19; Ex 19, 19; Jb 37, 3-4.
15: Ps 144, 6; Wis 5, 21.
16: Ps 77, 17; Zec 9, 14.
17: Ps 144, 7.
21: Ps 26; 1 Sm 26, 23.
26: Ps 125, 4.
28: Jb 22, 29; Prv 3, 34.
29: Pss 27, 1; 36, 10; 43, 3; 119, 105; Jb 29, 3; Mi 7, 8.
31: Pss 12, 6; 77, 13; Prv 30, 5.
32: Is 44, 8; 45, 21.
34: Hb 3, 19.
35: Ps 144, 1.

---

†

18, 6: *Cords*: hunting imagery, the cords of a snare.

18, 7: *His temple*: his heavenly abode.

18, 8-16: God appears in the storm, which in Palestine comes from the west. The introduction to the theophany (vv 8-9) is probably a description of a violent, hot, and dry east-wind storm. In the fall transition period from the rainless summer to the rainy winter such storms regularly precede the rains. Cf Ex 14, 21-22.

18, 11: *Cherub*: a winged creature, derived from myth, in the service of the deity (Gn 3, 24; Ex 25, 18-20; 37, 6-9). Cherubim were the throne bearers of the deity (Pss 80, 2; 99, 1; 1 Kgs 6, 23-28; 8, 6-8).

18, 15: *Arrows*: lightning.

18, 35: *Bow of bronze*: hyperbole for a bow difficult to bend and therefore capable of propelling an arrow with great force.

37 You gave me room to stride;
my feet never stumbled.*
38 I pursued my enemies and overtook them;
I did not turn back till I destroyed them.
39 I struck them down; they could not rise;
they fell dead at my feet.
40 You girded me with strength for war,
subdued adversaries at my feet.
41 My foes you put to flight before me;
those who hated me I destroyed.
42 They cried for help, but no one saved them;
cried to the LORD but got no answer.
43 I ground them fine as dust in the wind;
like mud in the streets I trampled them down.
44 You rescued me from the strife of peoples;
you made me head over nations.
A people I had not known became my slaves;
45 as soon as they heard of me they obeyed.
Foreigners cringed before me;
46 their courage failed;
they came trembling from their fortresses.*

VI

47 The LORD lives! Blessed be my rock!*
Exalted be God, my savior!
48 O God who granted me vindication,
made peoples subject to me,*
49 and preserved me from my enemies,
Truly you have exalted me above my adversaries,
from the violent you have rescued me.
50 Thus I will proclaim you, LORD, among the nations;
I will sing the praises of your name.*
51 You have given great victories to your king,
and shown kindness to your anointed,
to David and his posterity forever.*

PSALM 19†

God's Glory in the Heavens and in the Law

1 *For the leader. A psalm of David.*

I

2 The heavens declare the glory of God;
the sky proclaims its builder's craft.*
3 One day to the next conveys that message;
one night to the next imparts that knowledge.
4† There is no word or sound;
no voice is heard;
5† Yet their report goes forth through all the earth,
their message, to the ends of the world.
God has pitched there a tent for the sun;
6 it comes forth like a bridegroom from his chamber,
and like an athlete joyfully runs its course.
7 From one end of the heavens it comes forth;
its course runs through to the other;
nothing escapes its heat.

II

8 The law of the LORD is perfect,
refreshing the soul.
The decree of the LORD is trustworthy,
giving wisdom to the simple.*
9 The precepts of the LORD are right,
rejoicing the heart.
The command of the LORD is clear,
enlightening the eye.
10 The fear of the LORD is pure,
enduring forever.
The statutes of the LORD are true,
all of them just;
11 More desirable than gold,
than a hoard of purest gold,
Sweeter also than honey
or drippings from the comb.*
12† By them your servant is instructed;
obeying them brings much reward.

*

37: Ps 17, 5.
46: Mi 7, 17.
47: Ps 144, 1.
48: Ps 144, 2.
50: Pss 7, 18; 30, 5; 57, 9; 135, 3; 146, 2; Rom 15, 9.
51: Pss 89, 28-37; 144, 10; 1 Sm 2, 10.
19, 2: Pss 8, 1; 50, 6; 97, 6.
8: Pss 12, 7; 119.
11: Sir 24, 19.

†

Ps 19: The heavenly elements of the world, now beautifully arranged, bespeak the power and wisdom of their creator (2-7). The creator's wisdom is available to human beings in the law (8-11), toward which the psalmist prays to be open (12-15). The themes of light and speech unify the poem.

19, 4: *No word or sound*: the regular functioning of the heavens and the alternation of day and night inform humans without words of the creator's power and wisdom.

19, 5: *The sun*: in other religious literature the sun is a judge and lawgiver since it sees all in its daily course; 5b-7 form a transition to the law in 8-11. The six synonyms for God's revelation (8-11) are applied to the sun in comparable literature.

19, 12: *Instructed*: the Hebrew verb means both to shine and to teach. Cf Dn 12, 3.

III

13 Who can detect heedless failings?
Cleanse me from my unknown faults.
14 But from willful sins keep your servant;
let them never control me.
Then shall I be blameless,
innocent of grave sin.
15 Let the words of my mouth meet with your favor,
keep the thoughts of my heart before you,
LORD, my rock and my redeemer.

PSALM 20†

Prayer for the King in Time of War

1 *For the leader. A psalm of David.*

I

2 The LORD answer you in time of distress;
the name of the God of Jacob defend you!
3 May God send you help from the temple,
from Zion be your support.*
4† May God remember your every offering,
graciously accept your holocaust, *Selah*
5 Grant what is in your heart,
fulfill your every plan.
6† May we shout for joy at your victory,
raise the banners in the name of our God.
The LORD grant your every prayer!

II

7 Now I know victory is given
to the anointed of the LORD.*
God will answer him from the holy heavens
with a strong arm that brings victory.
8 Some rely on chariots, others on horses,
but we on the name of the LORD our God.*
9 They collapse and fall,
but we stand strong and firm.*
10 LORD, grant victory to the king;
answer when we call upon you.

PSALM 21†

Thanksgiving and Assurances for the King

1 *For the leader. A psalm of David.*

I

2 LORD, the king finds joy in your power;*
in your victory how greatly he rejoices!
3 You have granted him his heart's desire;
you did not refuse the prayer of his lips. *Selah*
4 For you welcomed him with goodly blessings;
you placed on his head a crown of pure gold.
5 He asked life of you;
you gave it to him,
length of days forever.*
6 Great is his glory in your victory;
majesty and splendor you confer upon him.
7 You make him the pattern of blessings forever,
you gladden him with the joy of your presence.
8 For the king trusts in the LORD,
stands firm through the love of the Most High.

II

9 Your hand will reach all your enemies;
your right hand will reach your foes!
10 At the time of your coming
you will drive them into a furnace.
Then the LORD's anger will consume them,
devour them with fire.
11 Even their descendants you will wipe out from the earth,
their offspring from the human race.
12 Though they intend evil against you,
devising plots, they will not succeed,
13 For you will put them to flight;
you will aim at them with your bow.

---

* 20, 3: Pss 128, 5; 134, 3.
7: Ps 18, 51; 144, 10; 1 Sm 2, 10.
8: Ps 147, 10-11; 2 Chr 14, 10; Prv 21, 31; 1 Sm 17, 45; Is 31, 1; 36, 9.
9: Is 40, 30.
21, 2: Ps 63, 12.
5: 1 Kgs 3, 14.

---

† Ps 20: The people pray for the king before battle. The people ask for divine help (2-6) and express confidence that such help will be given (7-10). A solemn assurance of divine help may well have been given between the two sections in the liturgy, something like the promises of Pss 12, 6 and 21, 9-13. The final verse (10) echoes the opening verse.

20, 4: *Remember*: God's remembering implies readiness to act. Cf Gn 8, 1; Ex 2, 24.

20, 6: *Victory*: the Hebrew root is often translated "salvation," "to save," but in military contexts it can have the specific meaning of "victory."

Ps 21: The first part of this royal psalm is a thanksgiving (2-8), and the second is a promise that the king will triumph over his enemies (9-14). The king's confident prayer (3. 5) and trust in God (8) enable him to receive the divine gifts of vitality, peace, and military success. V 14 reprises v 1. When kings ceased in Israel after the sixth century B.C., the psalm was sung of a future Davidic king.

III

14 Arise, LORD, in your power!*
We will sing and chant the praise of your might.

PSALM 22†

The Prayer of an Innocent Person

1† *For the leader; according to "The deer of the dawn." A psalm of David.*

I

2 My God, my God, why have you abandoned me?
Why so far from my call for help, from my cries of anguish?*
3 My God, I call by day, but you do not answer;
by night, but I have no relief.*
4 Yet you are enthroned as the Holy One;
you are the glory of Israel.*
5 In you our ancestors trusted;
they trusted and you rescued them.
6 To you they cried out and they escaped;
in you they trusted and were not disappointed.*
7† But I am a worm, hardly human,
scorned by everyone, despised by the people.*
8 All who see me mock me;
they curl their lips and jeer;
they shake their heads at me:*
9 "You relied on the LORD—let him deliver you;
if he loves you, let him rescue you."*
10 Yet you drew me forth from the womb,
made me safe at my mother's breast.
11 Upon you I was thrust from the womb;
since birth you are my God.*
12 Do not stay far from me,
for trouble is near,
and there is no one to help.*

II

13† Many bulls surround me;
fierce bulls of Bashan encircle me.
14 They open their mouths against me,
lions that rend and roar.*
15 Like water my life drains away;
all my bones grow soft.
My heart has become like wax,
it melts away within me.
16† As dry as a potsherd is my throat;
my tongue sticks to my palate;
you lay me in the dust of death.
17 Many dogs surround me;
a pack of evildoers closes in on me.
So wasted are my hands and feet
18 that I can count all my bones.*
They stare at me and gloat;
19 they divide my garments among them;
for my clothing they cast lots.*
20 But you, LORD, do not stay far off;
my strength, come quickly to help me.
21 Deliver me from the sword,
my forlorn life from the teeth of the dog.
22 Save me from the lion's mouth,
my poor life from the horns of wild bulls.*

III

23† Then I will proclaim your name to the assembly;
in the community I will praise you:*
24 "You who fear the LORD, give praise!
All descendants of Jacob, give honor;
show reverence, all descendants of Israel!

PSALMS

*

14: Nm 10, 35.
22, 2: Is 49, 14; 54, 7; Mt 27, 46; Mk 15, 34.
3: Sir 2, 10.
4: Is 6, 3.
6: Ps 25, 3; Is 49, 23; Dn 3, 40.
7: Is 53, 3.
8: Ps 109, 25; Mt 27, 39; Mk 15, 29; Lk 23, 35.
9: Ps 71, 11; Wis 2, 18-20; Mt 27, 43.
11: Ps 71, 6; Is 44, 2; 46, 3.
12: Pss 35, 22; 38, 22; 71, 12.
14: Ps 17, 12; Jb 4, 10; 1 Pt 5, 8.
18: Ps 109, 24.
19: Mt 27, 35; Mk 15, 24; Lk 23, 34; Jn 19, 24.
22: Pss 7, 2-3; 17, 12; 35, 17; 57, 5; 58, 7; 2 Tm 4, 17.
23: Pss 26, 12; 35, 18; 40, 10; 109, 30; 149, 1; 2 Sm 22, 50; Heb 2, 12.

†

Ps 22: A lament unusual in structure and in intensity of feeling. The psalmist's present distress is contrasted with God's past mercy in vv 2-12. In vv 13-22 enemies surround the psalmist. The last third is an invitation to praise God (23-27), becoming a universal chorus of praise (28-32). The psalm is important in the New Testament. Its opening words occur on the lips of the crucified Jesus (Mk 15, 34; Mt 27, 46), and several other verses are quoted, or at least alluded to, in the accounts of Jesus' passion (Mt 27, 35. 43; Jn 19, 24).

22, 1: *The deer of the dawn*: apparently the title of the melody.

22, 7: *I am a worm, hardly human*: the psalmist's sense of isolation and dehumanization, an important motif of Ps 22, is vividly portrayed here.

22, 13-14: *Bulls*: the enemies of the psalmist are also portrayed in less-than-human form, as wild animals (cf 17. 21-22). *Bashan*: a grazing land east of the Jordan, famed for its cattle. Cf Dt 32, 14; Ez 39, 18; Am 4, 1.

22, 16: *The dust of death*: the netherworld, the domain of the dead.

22, 23: *In the community I will praise you*: the person who offered a thanksgiving sacrifice in the temple recounted to the other worshipers the favor received from God and invited them to share in the sacrificial banquet. The final section (24-32) may be a summary or a citation of the psalmist's poem of praise.

25† For God has not spurned or disdained
the misery of this poor wretch,
Did not turn away from me,
but heard me when I cried out.
26 I will offer praise in the great assembly;
my vows I will fulfill before those who fear him.
27† The poor will eat their fill;
those who seek the LORD will offer praise.
May your hearts enjoy life forever!"*

IV

28 All the ends of the earth
will worship and turn to the LORD;
All the families of nations
will bow low before you.*
29 For kingship belongs to the LORD,
the ruler over the nations.*
30† All who sleep in the earth
will bow low before God;
All who have gone down into the dust
will kneel in homage.
31 And I will live for the LORD;
my descendants will serve you.
32 The generation to come will be told of the Lord,
that they may proclaim to a people yet unborn
the deliverance you have brought.*

PSALM 23†

The Lord, Shepherd and Host

1† *A psalm of David.*

I

The LORD is my shepherd;
there is nothing I lack.*
2 In green pastures you let me graze;
to safe waters you lead me;
3† you restore my strength.
You guide me along the right path
for the sake of your name.*
4† Even when I walk through a dark valley,*
I fear no harm for you are at my side;
your rod and staff give me courage.

II

5† You set a table before me
as my enemies watch;
You anoint my head with oil;*
my cup overflows.*
6† Only goodness and love will pursue me
all the days of my life;
I will dwell in the house of the LORD*
for years to come.

PSALM 24†

The Glory of God in Procession to Zion

1 *A psalm of David.*

I

The earth is the LORD's and all it holds,*
the world and those who live there.
2 For God founded it on the seas,
established it over the rivers.*

II

3 Who may go up the mountain of the LORD?*
Who can stand in his holy place?
4† "The clean of hand and pure of heart,
who are not devoted to idols,
who have not sworn falsely.
5 They will receive blessings from the LORD,

---

* 27: Pss 23, 5; 69, 33.
28: Ps 86, 9; Tb 13, 11; Is 45, 22; 52, 10; Zec 14, 16.
29: Ps 103, 19; Ob 21; Zec 14, 9.
32: Pss 48, 14-15; 71, 18; 78, 6; 102, 19; Is 53, 10.
23, 1: Pss 80, 2; 95, 7; 100, 3; Dt 2, 7.
3: Prv 4, 11.
4: Jb 10, 21-22; Is 50, 10.
5: Ps 92, 11. • Ps 16, 5.
6: Ps 27, 4.
24, 1: Pss 50, 12; 89, 12; Dt 10, 14; 1 Cor 10, 26.
2: Ps 136, 6; Is 42, 5.
3: Ps 15, 1.

---

† 22, 25: *Turn away*: literally, "hides his face from me," an important metaphor for God withdrawing from someone, e.g., Mi 3, 4; Is 8, 17; Pss 27, 9; 69, 18; 88, 15.

22, 27: *The poor*: originally the poor, who were dependent on God; the term (*'anawim*) came to include the religious sense of "humble, pious, devout."

22, 30: Hebrew unclear. The translation assumes that all on earth (28-29) and under the earth (30) will worship God.

Ps 23: God's loving care for the psalmist is portrayed under the figures of a shepherd for the flock (1-4) and a host's generosity toward a guest (5-6). The imagery of both sections is drawn from traditions of the exodus (Is 40, 11; 49, 10; Jer 31, 10).

23, 1: *My shepherd*: God as good shepherd is common in both the Old Testament and the New Testament (Ez 34, 11-16 and Jn 10, 11-18).

23, 3: *The right path*: connotes "right way" and "way of righteousness."

23, 4: *A dark valley*: a different division of the Hebrew consonants yields the translation "the valley of the shadow of death."

23, 5: *You set a table before me*: this expression occurs in an exodus context in Ps 78, 19. *As my enemies watch*: my enemies see that I am God's friend and guest. *Oil*: a perfumed ointment made from olive oil, used especially at banquets (Ps 104, 15; Mt 26, 7; Lk 7, 37. 46; Jn 12, 2).

23, 6: *Goodness and love*: the blessings of God's covenant with Israel.

Ps 24: The psalm apparently accompanied a ceremony of the entry of God (invisibly enthroned upon the ark), followed by the people, into the temple. The temple commemorated the creation of the world (1-2). The people had to affirm their fidelity before being admitted into the sanctuary (3-6; cf Ps 15). A choir identifies the approaching God and invites the very temple gates to bow down in obeisance (7-10).

24, 4-5: Literally, "the one whose hands are clean." The singular is used for the entire class of worshipers, hence the plural translation.

and justice from their saving God.
6 Such are the people that love the LORD,
that seek the face of the God of Jacob." *Selah*

III

7† Lift up your heads, O gates;
rise up, you ancient portals,
that the king of glory may enter.*
8 Who is this king of glory?
The LORD, a mighty warrior,
the LORD, mighty in battle.
9 Lift up your heads, O gates;
rise up, you ancient portals,
that the king of glory may enter.
10 Who is this king of glory?
The LORD of hosts is the king of glory. *Selah*

PSALM 25†

Confident Prayer for Forgiveness and Guidance

1 *Of David.*

I

I wait for you, O LORD;
I lift up my soul 2 to my God.*
In you I trust; do not let me be disgraced;*
do not let my enemies gloat over me.
3 No one is disgraced who waits for you,*
but only those who lightly break faith.
4 Make known to me your ways, LORD;
teach me your paths.*
5† Guide me in your truth and teach me,
for you are God my savior.
For you I wait all the long day,
because of your goodness, LORD.
6 Remember your compassion and love, O LORD;
for they are ages old.*
7 Remember no more the sins of my youth;*
remember me only in light of your love.

II

8 Good and upright is the LORD,
who shows sinners the way,
9 Guides the humble rightly,
and teaches the humble the way.
10 All the paths of the LORD are faithful love
toward those who honor the covenant demands.
11 For the sake of your name, LORD,
pardon my guilt, though it is great.
12 Who are those who fear the LORD?
God shows them the way to choose.*
13 They live well and prosper,
and their descendants inherit the land.*
14 The counsel of the LORD belongs to the faithful;
the covenant instructs them.
15 My eyes are ever upon the LORD,
who frees my feet from the snare.*

III

16 Look upon me, have pity on me,
for I am alone and afflicted.*
17 Relieve the troubles of my heart;
bring me out of my distress.
18 Put an end to my affliction and suffering;
take away all my sins.
19 See how many are my enemies,
see how fiercely they hate me.
20 Preserve my life and rescue me;
do not let me be disgraced, for I trust in you.
21 Let honesty and virtue preserve me;
I wait for you, O LORD.
22† Redeem Israel, God,
from all its distress!

PSALM 26†

Prayer of Innocence

1 *Of David.*

*

7: Ps 118, 19-20.
25, 1: Pss 86, 4; 143, 8. • Ps 71, 1.
3: Ps 22, 6; Is 49, 23; Dn 3, 40.
4: Pss 27, 11; 86, 11; 119, 12. 35; 143, 8. 10.
6: Sir 51, 8.
7: Jb 13, 26; Is 64, 8.
12: Prv 19, 23.
13: Ps 37, 9. 29.
15: Pss 123, 1. 2; 141, 8.
16: Pss 86, 16; 119, 132.

†

24, 7. 9: *Lift up your heads, O gates . . . you ancient portals*: the literal meaning is impossible since the portcullis (a gate that moves up and down) was unknown in the ancient world. Extra-biblical parallels suggest a full personification of the circle of gate towers: they are like a council of elders, bowed down and anxious, awaiting the return of the army and the Great Warrior gone to battle.

Ps 25: A lament. Each verse begins with a successive letter of the Hebrew alphabet. Such acrostic psalms are often a series of statements only loosely connected. The psalmist mixes ardent pleas (1-2. 16-22) with expressions of confidence in God who forgives and guides.

25, 5: *Because of your goodness, LORD*: these words have been transposed from the end of 7 to preserve the pattern of two lines per letter of the Hebrew alphabet in the acrostic poem.

25, 22: A final verse beginning with the Hebrew letter *pe* is added to the normal 22-letter alphabet. Thus the letters *aleph*, *lamed*, and *pe* open the first, middle (v 11), and last lines of the psalm. Together, they spell *aleph*, the first letter of the alphabet.

Ps 26: Like a priest washing before approaching the altar (Ex 30, 17-21), the psalmist seeks God's protection upon entering the temple. 1-3, matched by 11-12, remind God of past integrity while asking for purification; 4-5, matched by 9-10, pray for inclusion among the just; 6-8, the center of the poem, express the joy in God at the heart of all ritual.

I
Grant me justice, LORD!
I have walked without blame.*
In the LORD I have trusted;
I have not faltered.
2 Test me, LORD, and try me;
search my heart and mind.*
3 Your love is before my eyes;
I walk guided by your faithfulness.*

II
4 I do not sit with deceivers,
nor with hypocrites do I mingle.
5 I hate the company of evildoers;
with the wicked I do not sit.
6† I will wash my hands in innocence*
and walk round your altar, LORD,
7 Lifting my voice in thanks,
recounting all your wondrous deeds.
8 LORD, I love the house where you dwell,
the tenting-place of your glory.*

III
9 Do not take me away with sinners,
nor my life with the violent.*
10 Their hands carry out their schemes;
their right hands are full of bribes.
11 But I walk without blame;*
redeem me, be gracious to me!*
12† My foot stands on level ground;
in assemblies I will bless the LORD.*

PSALM 27†

Trust in God

1 *Of David.*

A

I
The LORD is my light and my salvation;*
whom do I fear?
The LORD is my life's refuge;
of whom am I afraid?
2† When evildoers come at me
to devour my flesh,*
These my enemies and foes
themselves stumble and fall.
3 Though an army encamp against me,
my heart does not fear;
Though war be waged against me,
even then do I trust.

II
4 One thing I ask of the LORD;
this I seek:
To dwell in the LORD's house
all the days of my life,
To gaze on the LORD's beauty,
to visit his temple.*
5 For God will hide me in his shelter
in time of trouble,*
Will conceal me in the cover of his tent;
and set me high upon a rock.
6 Even now my head is held high
above my enemies on every side!
I will offer in his tent
sacrifices with shouts of joy;
I will sing and chant praise to the LORD.

B

I
7 Hear my voice, LORD, when I call;
have mercy on me and answer me.
8† "Come," says my heart, "seek God's face";
your face, LORD, do I seek!*
9 Do not hide your face from me;
do not repel your servant in anger.
You are my help; do not cast me off;
do not forsake me, God my savior!
10 Even if my father and mother forsake me,
the LORD will take me in.*

II
11 LORD, show me your way;
lead me on a level path
because of my enemies.*
12 Do not abandon me to the will of my foes;
malicious and lying witnesses
have risen against me.

26, 1: Ps 7, 9.
2: Pss 17, 3; 139, 23.
3: Ps 86, 11.
6: Ps 73, 13.
8: Pss 29, 9; 63, 3; Ex 24, 16; 25, 8.
9: Ps 28, 3.
11: Ps 101, 6. • Ps 25, 16.
12: Pss 22, 23; 35, 18; 149, 1.
27, 1: Pss 18, 29; 36, 10; 43, 3; Is 10, 17; Mi 7, 8.
2: Ps 14, 4.
4: Pss 23, 6; 61, 5.
5: Ps 31, 21.
8: Ps 24, 6; Hos 5, 15.
10: Is 49, 15.
11: Pss 25, 4; 86, 11.

26, 6: *I will wash my hands*: the washing of hands was a liturgical act (Ex 30, 19. 21; 40, 31-32), symbolic of inner as well as outer cleanness. Cf Is 1, 16.

26, 12: *On level ground*: in safety, where there is no danger of tripping and falling. *In assemblies*: at the temple. Having walked around the altar, the symbol of God's presence, the psalmist blesses God.

Ps 27: Tradition has handed down the two sections of the psalm (1-6 and 7-14) as one psalm, though each part could be understood as complete in itself. Asserting boundless hope that God will bring rescue (1-3), the psalmist longs for the presence of God in the temple, protection from all enemies (4-6). In part B there is a clear shift in tone (7-12); the climax of the poem comes with "I believe" (13), echoing "I trust" (3).

27, 2: *To devour my flesh*: the psalmist's enemies are rapacious beasts (Pss 7, 3; 17, 12; 22, 14. 17).

27, 8: *Seek God's face* (literally: "to seek his face"): to commune with God in the temple. The idiom is derived from the practice of journeying to sacred places. Cf Hos 5, 15; 2 Sm 21, 1; Ps 24, 6.

13† But I believe I shall enjoy the LORD's goodness
in the land of the living.*
14 Wait for the LORD, take courage;
be stouthearted, wait for the LORD!

PSALM 28†

Petition and Thanksgiving

1† *Of David.*

I

To you, LORD, I call;
my Rock, do not be deaf to me.*
If you fail to answer me,
I will join those who go down to the pit.*
2† Hear the sound of my pleading when I cry to you,
lifting my hands toward your holy place.*
3 Do not drag me off with the wicked,
with those who do wrong,*
Who speak peace to their neighbors
though evil is in their hearts.*
4 Repay them for their deeds,
for the evil that they do.
For the work of their hands repay them;
give them what they deserve.*
5 They pay no heed to the LORD's works,
to the deeds of God's hands.*
God will tear them down,
never to be rebuilt.

II

6† Blessed be the LORD,
who has heard the sound of my pleading.
7 The LORD is my strength and my shield,
in whom my heart trusted and found help.
So my heart rejoices;
with my song I praise my God.

III

8† LORD, you are the strength of your people,
the saving refuge of your anointed king.
9 Save your people, bless your inheritance;
feed and sustain them forever!

PSALM 29†

The Lord of Majesty Acclaimed as King of the World

1† *A psalm of David.*

I

Give to the LORD, you heavenly beings,
give to the LORD glory and might;
2 Give to the LORD the glory due God's name.
Bow down before the LORD's holy splendor!*

II

3† The voice of the LORD is over the waters;
the God of glory thunders,
the LORD, over the mighty waters.
4 The voice of the LORD is power;
the voice of the LORD is splendor.*
5 The voice of the LORD cracks the cedars;
the LORD splinters the cedars of Lebanon,
6† Makes Lebanon leap like a calf,
and Sirion like a young bull.
7 The voice of the LORD strikes with fiery flame;
8† the voice of the LORD rocks the desert;

PSALMS

---

* 13: Ps 116, 9; Is 38, 11.
28, 1: Ps 18, 2. • Pss 30, 4; 88, 5; 143, 7; Prv 1, 12.
2: Ps 134, 2.
3: Ps 26, 9. • Pss 12, 2; 55, 22; 62, 5; Prv 26, 24-28.
4: 2 Sm 3, 39.
5: Is 5, 12.
29, 2: Pss 68, 35; 96, 7-9.
4: Pss 46, 7; 77, 18-19; Jb 37, 4; Is 30, 30.

---

†

27, 13: *In the land of the living*: or "in the land of life," an epithet of the Jerusalem temple (Pss 52, 7; 116, 9; Is 38, 11), where the faithful had access to the life-giving presence of God.

Ps 28: A lament asking that the psalmist, who has taken refuge in the temple (2), not be punished with the wicked, who are headed inevitably toward destruction (1. 3-5). The statement of praise is exceptionally lengthy and vigorous (6-7). The psalm ends with a prayer (8-9).

28, 1: *The pit*: a synonym for Sheol, the shadowy place of the dead.

28, 2: *Your holy place*: the innermost part of the temple, the holy of holies, containing the ark. Cf 1 Kgs 6, 16. 19-23; 8, 6-8.

28, 6: The psalmist shifts to fervent thanksgiving, probably responding to a priestly or prophetic oracle in 5cd (not usually transmitted) assuring the worshiper that the prayer has been heard.

28, 8: *Your people . . . your anointed king*: salvation is more than individual, affecting all the people and their God-given leader.

Ps 29: The hymn invites the members of the heavenly court to acknowledge God's supremacy by ascribing glory and might to God alone (1-2a. 9b). Divine glory and might are dramatically visible in the storm (3-9a). The storm apparently comes from the Mediterranean onto the coast of Syria-Palestine and then moves inland. In 10 the divine beings acclaim God's eternal kingship. The psalm concludes with a prayer that God will impart the power just displayed to the Israelite king and through the king to Israel.

29, 1: *You heavenly beings*: literally "sons of God," i.e., members of the heavenly court who served Israel's God in a variety of capacities.

29, 3: *The voice of the LORD*: the sevenfold repetition of the phrase imitates the sound of crashing thunder and may allude to God's primordial slaying of Leviathan, the seven-headed sea monster of Canaanite mythology.

29, 6: *Sirion*: the Phoenician name for Mount Hermon. Cf Dt 3, 9.

29, 8: *The desert of Kadesh*: probably north of Palestine in the neighborhood of Lebanon and Hermon.

the LORD rocks the desert of Kadesh.
9† The voice of the LORD twists the oaks
and strips the forests bare.
All in his palace say, "Glory!"

III
10† The LORD sits enthroned above the flood!*
The LORD reigns as king forever!
11† May the LORD give might to his people;
may the LORD bless his people with peace!*

PSALM 30†

Thanksgiving for Deliverance

1† *A psalm. A song for the dedication of the temple. Of David.*

I
2 I praise you, LORD, for you raised me up
and did not let my enemies rejoice over me.
3† O LORD, my God,
I cried out to you and you healed me.
4† LORD, you brought me up from Sheol;
you kept me from going down to the pit.*

II
5 Sing praise to the LORD, you faithful;
give thanks to God's holy name.
6 For divine anger lasts but a moment;
divine favor lasts a lifetime.
At dusk weeping comes for the night;
but at dawn there is rejoicing.

III
7† Complacent, I once said,
"I shall never be shaken."
8 LORD, when you showed me favor
I stood like the mighty mountains.
But when you hid your face
I was struck with terror.*
9 To you, LORD, I cried out;
with the Lord I pleaded for mercy:
10† "What gain is there from my lifeblood,
from my going down to the grave?
Does dust give you thanks
or declare your faithfulness?
11 Hear, O LORD, have mercy on me;
LORD, be my helper."

IV
12 You changed my mourning into dancing;
you took off my sackcloth
and clothed me with gladness.*
13 With my whole being I sing
endless praise to you.
O LORD, my God,
forever will I give you thanks.

PSALM 31†

Prayer in Distress and Thanksgiving for Escape

1 *For the leader. A psalm of David.*

I
2 In you, LORD, I take refuge;*
let me never be put to shame.
In your justice deliver me;
3 incline your ear to me;
make haste to rescue me!
Be my rock of refuge,
a stronghold to save me.
4 You are my rock and my fortress;*
for your name's sake lead and guide me.
5 Free me from the net they have set for me,
for you are my refuge.
6† Into your hands I commend my spirit;*
you will redeem me, LORD, faithful God.

---

* 10: Bar 3, 3. 11: Ps 68, 36. 30, 4: Ps 28, 1; Jon 2, 7. 8: Ps 104, 29. 12: Is 61, 3; Jer 31, 13. 31, 2-4: Ps 71, 1-3. 4: Ps 18, 2. 6: Lk 23, 46; Acts 7, 59.

---

† 29, 9b-10: Having witnessed God's supreme power (3-9a), the gods acknowledge the glory that befits the king of the divine and human world.

29, 10: *The flood*: God defeated the primordial waters and made them part of the universe. Cf Pss 89, 10-13 and 93, 3-4.

29, 11: *His people*: God's people, Israel.

Ps 30: An individual thanksgiving in four parts: praise and thanks for deliverance and restoration (2-4); an invitation to others to join in (5-6); a flashback to the time before deliverance (7-11); a return to praise and thanks (12-13). Two sets of images recur: 1) going down, death, silence; 2) coming up, life, praising. God has delivered the psalmist from one state to the other.

30, 1: *For the dedication of the temple*: a later adaptation of the psalm to celebrate the purification of the temple in 164 B.C. during the Maccabean Revolt.

30, 3: *Healed*: for God as healer, see also Pss 103, 3; 107, 20; Hos 6, 1; 7, 1; 11, 3; 14, 5.

30, 4: *Sheol . . . pit*: the shadowy underworld residence of the spirits of the dead, here a metaphor for near death.

30, 7: *Complacent*: untroubled existence is often seen as a source of temptation to forget God. Cf Dt 8, 10-18; Hos 13, 6; Prv 30, 9.

30, 10: in the stillness of Sheol no one gives you praise; let me live and be among your worshipers. Cf Pss 6, 6; 88, 11-13; 115, 17; Is 38, 18.

Ps 31: A lament (2-19) with a strong emphasis on trust (4. 6. 15-16), ending with an anticipatory thanksgiving (20-25). As is usual in laments, the affliction is couched in general terms. The psalmist feels overwhelmed by evil people but trusts in the "faithful God" (6).

31, 6: *Into your hands I commend my spirit*: in Lk 23, 46 Jesus breathes his last with this psalm verse. Stephen in Acts 7, 59 alludes to these words as he is attacked by enemies. The verse is used as an antiphon in the Divine Office at Compline, the last prayer of the day.

7 You hate those who serve worthless idols,
but I trust in the LORD.
8 I will rejoice and be glad in your love,
once you have seen my misery,
observed my distress.*
9 You will not abandon me into enemy hands,
but will set my feet in a free and open space.

II
10 Be gracious to me, LORD, for I am in distress;
with grief my eyes are wasted,
my soul and body spent.
11 My life is worn out by sorrow,
my years by sighing.
My strength fails in affliction;
my bones are consumed.*
12 To all my foes I am a thing of scorn,
to my neighbors, a dreaded sight,
a horror to my friends.
When they see me in the street,
they quickly shy away.*
13† I am forgotten, out of mind like the dead;
I am like a shattered dish.
14† I hear the whispers of the crowd;
terrors are all around me.
They conspire against me;
they plot to take my life.
15 But I trust in you, LORD;
I say, "You are my God."*
16 My times are in your hands;
rescue me from my enemies,
from the hands of my pursuers.
17 Let your face shine on your servant;*
save me in your kindness.
18 Do not let me be put to shame,
for I have called to you, LORD.
Put the wicked to shame;
reduce them to silence in Sheol.
19 Strike dumb their lying lips,
proud lips that attack the just
in contempt and scorn.*

III
20 How great is your goodness, Lord,
stored up for those who fear you.
You display it for those who trust you,
in the sight of all the people.
21 You hide them in the shelter of your presence,
safe from scheming enemies.
You keep them in your abode,
safe from plotting tongues.*
22 Blessed be the LORD,
who has shown me wondrous love,
and been for me a city most secure.
23 Once I said in my anguish,
"I am shut out from your sight."*
Yet you heard my plea,
when I cried out to you.
24 Love the LORD, all you faithful.
The LORD protects the loyal,
but repays the arrogant in full.
25 Be strong and take heart,
all you who hope in the LORD.

PSALM 32†

Remission of Sin

1 *Of David. A* maskil.

I
Happy the sinner whose fault is removed,
whose sin is forgiven.*
2 Happy those to whom the LORD imputes no guilt,
in whose spirit is no deceit.

II
3† As long as I kept silent, my bones wasted away;
I groaned all the day.*
4 For day and night your hand was heavy upon me;
my strength withered as in dry summer heat. *Selah*
5 Then I declared my sin to you;
my guilt I did not hide.*
I said, "I confess my faults to the LORD,"
and you took away the guilt of my sin. *Selah*
6† Thus should all your faithful pray
in time of distress.
Though flood waters threaten,
they will never reach them.*
7 You are my shelter; from distress you keep me;
with safety you ring me round. *Selah*

PSALMS

---

* 8: Ps 10, 14.
11: Pss 32, 3; 38, 10-11.
12: Jb 19, 13-19.
15: Ps 140, 7; Is 25, 1.
17: Ps 67, 1; Nm 6, 24.
19: Ps 12, 4.
21: Ps 27, 5.
23: Jon 2, 5.
32, 1: Is 1, 18; Ps 65, 3; Rom 4, 7-8.
3: Ps 31, 11.
5: Pss 38, 19; 51, 5.
6: Ps 18, 5.

---

† 31, 13: *Like a shattered dish*: a common comparison for something ruined and useless. Cf Is 30, 14; Jer 19, 11; 22, 28.

31, 14: *Terrors are all around*: a cry used in inescapable danger. Cf Jer 6, 25; 20, 10; 46, 5; 49, 29.

Ps 32: An individual thanksgiving and the second of the seven Penitential Psalms (cf Ps 6). The opening declaration—the forgiven are blessed (1-2)—arises from the psalmist's own experience. At one time the psalmist was stubborn and closed, a victim of sin's power (3-4), and then became open to the forgiving God (5-7). Sin here, as often in the Bible, is not only the personal act of rebellion against God but also the consequences of that act—frustration and waning of vitality. Having been rescued, the psalmist can teach others the joys of justice and the folly of sin (8-11).

32, 3: *I kept silent*: did not confess the sin before God.

32, 6: *Flood waters*: the untamed waters surrounding the earth, a metaphor for danger.

III

8 I will instruct you and show you the way you should walk,
give you counsel and watch over you.
9 Do not be senseless like horses or mules;
with bit and bridle their temper is curbed,
else they will not come to you.

IV

10 Many are the sorrows of the wicked,
but love surrounds those who trust in the LORD.
11 Be glad in the LORD and rejoice, you just;
exult, all you upright of heart.*

PSALM 33†

Praise of God's Power and Providence

I

1 Rejoice, you just, in the LORD;
praise from the upright is fitting.*
2 Give thanks to the LORD on the harp;
on the ten-stringed lyre offer praise.*
3 Sing to God a new song;
skillfully play with joyful chant.
4 For the LORD's word is true;
all his works are trustworthy.
5 The LORD loves justice and right
and fills the earth with goodness.*

II

6† By the LORD's word the heavens were made;
by the breath of his mouth all their host.*
7† The waters of the sea were gathered as in a bowl;
in cellars the deep was confined.*

III

8 Let all the earth fear the LORD;
let all who dwell in the world show reverence.
9 For he spoke, and it came to be,
commanded, and it stood in place.*
10 The LORD foils the plan of nations,
frustrates the designs of peoples.
11 But the plan of the LORD stands forever,
wise designs through all generations.*
12 Happy the nation whose God is the LORD,
the people chosen as his very own.*

IV

13 From heaven the LORD looks down
and observes the whole human race,*
14 Surveying from the royal throne
all who dwell on earth.
15 The one who fashioned the hearts of them all
knows all their works.

V

16 A king is not saved by a mighty army,
nor a warrior delivered by great strength.
17 Useless is the horse for safety;
its great strength, no sure escape.
18 But the LORD's eyes are upon the reverent,
upon those who hope for his gracious help,
19 Delivering them from death,
keeping them alive in times of famine.

VI

20 Our soul waits for the LORD,
who is our help and shield.*
21 For in God our hearts rejoice;
in your holy name we trust.
22 May your kindness, LORD, be upon us;
we have put our hope in you.

PSALM 34†

Thanksgiving to God Who Delivers the Just

1† *Of David, when he feigned madness before Abimelech, who forced him to depart.*

* 11: Ps 33, 1.
33, 1: Pss 32, 11; 147, 1.
2: Pss 92, 4; 144, 9.
5: Ps 119, 64.
6: Gn 2, 1.
7: Ps 78, 13; Gn 1, 9-10; Ex 15, 8.
9: Ps 148, 5; Gn 1, 3f; Jdt 16, 14.
11: Prv 19, 21; Is 40, 8.
12: Ps 144, 15; Ex 19, 6; Dt 7, 6.
13: Jb 34, 21; Sir 15, 19; Jer 16, 17; 32, 19.
20: Ps 115, 9.

† Ps 33: A hymn in which the just are invited (1-3) to praise God, who by a mere word (4-5) created the three-tiered universe of the heavens, the cosmic waters, and the earth (6-9). Human words, in contrast, effect nothing (10-11). The greatness of human beings consists in God's choosing them as a special people and their faithful response (12-22).

33, 6: *All their host*: the stars of the sky are commonly viewed as a vast army, e.g., Neh 9, 6; Is 40, 26; 45, 12; Jer 33, 22.

33, 7: *The waters . . . as in a bowl*: ancients sometimes attributed the power keeping the seas from overwhelming land to a primordial victory of the storm-god over personified Sea. God confines the seas as easily as one puts water in a bowl.

Ps 34: A thanksgiving in acrostic form, each line beginning with a successive letter of the Hebrew alphabet. In this psalm one letter is missing and two are in reverse order. The psalmist, fresh from the experience of being rescued (5. 7), can teach the "poor," those who are defenseless, to trust in God alone (4. 12). God will make them powerful (5-11) and give them protection (12-23).

34, 1: *Abimelech*: a scribal error for Achish. In 1 Sm 21, 13-16, David feigned madness before Achish, not Abimelech.

I

2 I will bless the LORD at all times;
praise shall be always in my mouth.*
3 My soul will glory in the LORD
that the poor may hear and be glad.
4 Magnify the LORD with me;
let us exalt his name together.

II

5 I sought the LORD, who answered me,
delivered me from all my fears.
6 Look to God that you may be radiant with joy
and your faces may not blush for shame.
7 In my misfortune I called,
the LORD heard and saved me from all distress.
8 The angel of the LORD, who encamps with them,
delivers all who fear God.*
9 Learn to savor how good the LORD is;
happy are those who take refuge in him.*
10 Fear the LORD, you holy ones;
nothing is lacking to those who fear him.*
11† The powerful grow poor and hungry,
but those who seek the LORD lack no good thing.

III

12† Come, children, listen to me;*
I will teach you the fear of the LORD.
13 Who among you loves life,*
takes delight in prosperous days?
14 Keep your tongue from evil,
your lips from speaking lies.
15 Turn from evil and do good;*
seek peace and pursue it.
16 The LORD has eyes for the just*
and ears for their cry.
17 The LORD's face is against evildoers
to wipe out their memory from the earth.
18 When the just cry out, the LORD hears
and rescues them from all distress.
19 The LORD is close to the brokenhearted,
saves those whose spirit is crushed.
20 Many are the troubles of the just,
but the LORD delivers from them all.
21 God watches over all their bones;
not a one shall be broken.*
22 Evil will slay the wicked;
those who hate the just are condemned.
23 The LORD redeems loyal servants;
no one is condemned whose refuge is God.

PSALM 35†

Prayer for Help against Unjust Enemies

1† *Of David.*

I

Oppose, LORD, those who oppose me;
war upon those who make war upon me.
2 Take up the shield and buckler;
rise up in my defense.
3 Brandish lance and battle-ax
against my pursuers.
Say to my heart,
"I am your salvation."
4 Let those who seek my life
be put to shame and disgrace.
Let those who plot evil against me*
be turned back and confounded.
5 Make them like chaff before the wind,*
with the angel of the LORD driving them on.
6 Make their way slippery and dark,
with the angel of the LORD pursuing them.

II

7 Without cause they set their snare for me;
without cause they dug a pit for me.
8 Let ruin overtake them unawares;
let the snare they have set catch them;

PSALMS

*

34, 2: Ps 145, 2.
8: Ex 14, 19.
9: Ps 2, 12.
10: Prv 3, 7.
12: Prv 1, 8; 4, 1.
13-17: 1 Pt 3, 10-12.
15: Ps 37, 27.
16: Ps 33, 18.
21: Jn 19, 36.
35, 4: Pss 40, 15; 71, 13.
5: Pss 1, 4; 83, 14; Jb 21, 18.

†

34, 11: *The powerful*: literally, "lions." Fierce animals were sometimes metaphors for influential people.

34, 12: *Children*: the customary term for students in Wisdom literature.

Ps 35: A lament of a person betrayed by friends. The psalmist prays that the evildoers be publicly exposed as unjust (1-8), and gives thanks in anticipation of vindication (9-10). Old friends are the enemies (11-16). May their punishment come quickly (17-21)! The last part (22-26) echoes the opening in praying for the destruction of the psalmist's persecutors. The psalm may appear vindictive, but one must keep in mind that the psalmist is praying for *public* redress now of a *public* injustice. There is at this time no belief in an afterlife in which justice will be redressed.

35, 1-6: The mixture of judicial, martial, and hunting images shows that the language is figurative. The actual injustice is false accusation of serious crimes (11. 15. 20-21). The psalmist seeks lost honor through a trial before God.

let them fall into the pit they have
dug.*
9 Then I will rejoice in the LORD,
exult in God's salvation.
10 My very bones shall say,
"O LORD, who is like you,*
Who rescue the afflicted from the
powerful,
the afflicted and needy from the
despoiler?"

III
11 Malicious witnesses come forward,
accuse me of things I do not know.
12 They repay me evil for good
and I am all alone.*
13† Yet I, when they were ill, put on
sackcloth,
afflicted myself with fasting,
sobbed my prayers upon my bo-
som.
14 I went about in grief as for my
brother,
bent in mourning as for my
mother.
15 Yet when I stumbled they gathered
with glee,
gathered against me like strang-
ers.
They slandered me without ceasing;
16 without respect they mocked me,
gnashed their teeth against me.

IV
17 Lord, how long will you look on?
Save me from roaring beasts,
my precious life from lions!*
18 Then I will thank you in the great
assembly;
I will praise you before the mighty
throng.*
19 Do not let lying foes smirk at me,
my undeserved enemies wink
knowingly.*
20 They speak no words of peace,
but against the quiet in the land
they fashion deceitful speech.*
21 They open wide their mouths
against me.
They say, "Aha! Good!
Our eyes relish the sight!"*
22 You see this, LORD; do not be silent;*
Lord, do not withdraw from me.
23 Awake, be vigilant in my defense,
in my cause, my God and my
Lord.
24 Defend me because you are just,
LORD;
my God, do not let them gloat over
me.
25 Do not let them say in their hearts,
"Aha! Just what we wanted!"
Do not let them say,
"We have devoured that one!"
26 Put to shame and confound
all who relish my misfortune.
Clothe with shame and disgrace
those who lord it over me.
27 But let those who favor my just
cause
shout for joy and be glad.
May they ever say, "Exalted be the
LORD
who delights in the peace of his
loyal servant."
28 Then my tongue shall recount your
justice,
declare your praise, all the day
long.*

PSALM 36†

Human Wickedness and Divine Providence

1 *For the leader. Of David, the ser-
vant of the LORD.*

I
2 Sin directs the heart of the wicked;
their eyes are closed to the fear
of God.*
3† For they live with the delusion:
their guilt will not be known and
hated.
4 Empty and false are the words of
their mouth;
they have ceased to be wise and
do good.
5 In their beds they hatch plots;
they set out on a wicked way;
they do not reject evil.*

II
6† LORD, your love reaches to heaven;
your fidelity, to the clouds.*
7 Your justice is like the highest
mountains;
your judgments, like the mighty
deep;

*

8: Pss 7, 16; 9, 16; 57, 7; Prv 26, 27; Eccl 10, 8; Sir 27, 26.
10: Ps 86, 8; 89, 7. 9; Ex 15, 11.
12: Pss 27, 12; 38, 20-21; 109, 5; Jer 18, 20.
17: Pss 17, 12; 22, 22; 58, 7.
18: Pss 22, 23; 26, 12; 35, 18; 40, 10; 149, 1.
19: Ps 38, 17.
20: Ps 120, 6-7.
21: Ps 40, 16; Lam 2, 16.
22: Pss 22, 12; 38, 21; 109, 1.
28: Ps 71, 15-16.
36, 2: Rom 3, 18.
5: Mi 2, 1.
6: Pss 57, 11; 71, 19.

†

35, 13. 15-17: The Hebrew is obscure.

Ps 36: A psalm with elements of wisdom (2-5), the hymn (6-10), and the lament (11-13). The rule of sin over the wicked (2-5) is contrasted with the rule of divine love and mercy over God's friends (6-10). The psalm ends with a prayer that God's guidance never cease (11-13).

36, 3: *Hated*: punished by God.

36, 6-7: *Love . . . judgments*: God actively controls the entire world.

all living creatures you sustain,
LORD.
8† How precious is your love, O God!
We take refuge in the shadow of your wings.*
9 We feast on the rich food of your house;
from your delightful stream * you give us drink.
10 For with you is the fountain of life,*
and in your light we see light.*
11 Continue your kindness toward your friends,
your just defense of the honest heart.
12 Do not let the foot of the proud overtake me,
nor the hand of the wicked disturb me.
13 There make the evildoers fall;
thrust them down, never to rise.

PSALM 37†

The Fate of Sinners and the Reward of the Just

1 *Of David.*

Aleph

Do not be provoked by evildoers;
do not envy those who do wrong.*
2 Like grass they wither quickly;
like green plants they wilt away.*

Beth

3† Trust in the LORD and do good
that you may dwell in the land and live secure.*
4 Find your delight in the LORD
who will give you your heart's desire.*

Gimel

5 Commit your way to the LORD;
trust that God will act*
6 And make your integrity shine like the dawn,
your vindication like noonday.*

Daleth

7 Be still before the LORD;
wait for God.
Do not be provoked by the prosperous,
nor by malicious schemers.

He

8 Give up your anger, abandon your wrath;
do not be provoked; it brings only harm.
9 Those who do evil will be cut off,
but those who wait for the LORD will possess the land.*

Waw

10 Wait a little, and the wicked will be no more;
look for them and they will not be there.
11 But the poor will possess the land,*
will delight in great prosperity.

Zayin

12 The wicked plot against the just
and grind their teeth at them;
13 But the LORD laughs at them,*
knowing their day is coming.

Heth

14 The wicked draw their swords;
they string their bows
To fell the poor and oppressed,
to slaughter those whose way is honest.*
15 Their swords will pierce their own hearts;
their bows will be broken.

Teth

16 Better the poverty of the just
than the great wealth of the wicked.*
17 The arms of the wicked will be broken;
the LORD will sustain the just.

Yodh

18 The LORD watches over the days of the blameless;

PSALMS

* 8: Ps 17, 8. 9: Gn 2, 8. 10. 10: Is 55, 1; Jn 4, 14. • Ps 80, 4. 8. 20. 37, 1: Prv 3, 31; 23, 17; 24, 1. 19. 2: Pss 90, 5-6; 102, 12; 103, 15-16; Jb 14, 2; Is 40, 7. 3: Ps 128, 2. 4: Prv 10, 24. 5: Ps 55, 23; Prv 3, 5; 16, 3. 6: Wis 5, 6; Is 58, 10. 9: Ps 25, 13; Prv 2, 21; Is 57, 13. 11: Mt 5, 4. 13: Pss 2, 4; 59, 9; Wis 4, 18. 14: Pss 11, 2; 57, 5; 64, 4. 16: Prv 15, 16; 16, 8.

† 36, 8: *The shadow of your wings*: metaphor for divine protection. It probably refers to the winged cherubim in the holy of holies in the temple. Cf 1 Kgs 6, 23-28. 32; 2 Chr 3, 10-13; Ez 1, 4-9.

Ps 37: The psalm responds to the problem of evil, which the Old Testament often expresses as a question: why do the wicked prosper and the good suffer? The psalm answers that the situation is only temporary. God will reverse things, rewarding the good and punishing the wicked here on earth. The perspective is concrete and earthbound: people's very actions place them among the ranks of the good or wicked. Each group or "way" has its own inherent dynamism—eventual frustration for the wicked, eventual reward for the just. The psalm is an acrostic, i.e., each section begins with a successive letter of the Hebrew alphabet. Each section has its own imagery and logic.

37, 3. 9. 11. 22. 27. 29. 34: *The land*: the promised land, Israel, which became for later interpreters a type or figure of heaven. Cf Heb 11, 9-10. 13-16. The New Testament Beatitudes (Mt 5, 3-12; Lk 6, 20-26) have been influenced by the psalm, especially their total reversal of the present and their interpretation of the happy future as possession of the land.

their heritage lasts forever.
19 They will not be disgraced when times are hard;
in days of famine they will have plenty.

Kaph

20 The wicked perish,
the enemies of the LORD;
Like the beauty of meadows they vanish;
like smoke they disappear.*

Lamedh

21 The wicked borrow but do not repay;
the just are generous in giving.
22 For those blessed by the Lord will possess the land,
but those accursed will be cut off.

Mem

23 Those whose steps are guided by the LORD;*
whose way God approves,
24 May stumble, but they will never fall,
for the LORD holds their hand.

Nun

25 Neither in my youth, nor now in old age
have I ever seen the just abandoned*
or their children begging bread.
26 The just always lend generously,
and their children become a blessing.

Samekh

27 Turn from evil and do good,
that you may inhabit the land forever.*
28 For the LORD loves justice
and does not abandon the faithful.

Ayin

When the unjust are destroyed,
and the children of the wicked cut off,
29 The just will possess the land
and live in it forever.*

Pe

30 The mouths of the just utter wisdom;*
their tongues speak what is right.
31 God's teaching is in their hearts;*
their steps do not falter.

Sadhe

32 The wicked spy on the just
and seek to kill them.
33 But the LORD does not leave the just in their power,
nor let them be condemned when tried.

Qoph

34 Wait eagerly for the LORD,
and keep to the way;*
God will raise you to possess the land;
you will gloat when the wicked are cut off.

Resh

35 I have seen ruthless scoundrels,
strong as flourishing cedars.*
36 When I passed by again, they were gone;
though I searched, they could not be found.

Shin

37 Observe the honest, mark the upright;
those at peace with God have a future.*
38 But all sinners will be destroyed;
the future of the wicked will be cut off.

Taw

39 The salvation of the just is from the LORD,
their refuge in time of distress.*
40 The LORD helps and rescues them,
rescues and saves them from the wicked,
because in God they take refuge.

PSALM 38†

Prayer of an Afflicted Sinner

1 *A psalm of David. For remembrance.*

I

2 LORD, punish me no more in your anger;
in your wrath do not chastise me!*
3 Your arrows have sunk deep in me;*
your hand has come down upon me.

*

20: Wis 5, 14.
23: Prv 20, 24.
25: Jb 4, 7; Sir 2, 10.
27: Ps 34, 14-15; Am 5, 14.
29: Ps 25, 13; Prv 2, 21; Is 57, 13.
30: Prv 10, 31.
31: Ps 40, 9; Dt 6, 6; Is 51, 7; Jer 31, 33.
34: Ps 31, 24.
35: Ps 92, 8-9; Is 2, 13; Ez 31, 10-11.
37: Prv 23, 18; 24, 14.
39: Ps 9, 10; Is 25, 4.
38, 2: Ps 6, 2.
3: Jb 6, 4; Lam 3, 12; Pss 31, 11; 64, 7.

†

Ps 38: In this lament, one of the Penitential Psalms (cf Ps 6), the psalmist acknowledges the sin that has brought physical and mental sickness and social ostracism. There is no one to turn to for help; only God can undo the past and restore the psalmist.

4 My flesh is afflicted because of your anger;
my frame aches because of my sin.*
5 My iniquities overwhelm me,
a burden beyond my strength.*

II
6 Foul and festering are my sores
because of my folly.
7 I am stooped and deeply bowed;*
all day I go about mourning.
8 My loins burn with fever;
my flesh is afflicted.
9 I am numb and utterly crushed;
I wail with anguish of heart.*
10 My Lord, my deepest yearning is before you;
my groaning is not hidden from you.
11 My heart shudders, my strength forsakes me;
the very light of my eyes has failed.*
12 Friends and companions shun my pain;
my neighbors stand far off.
13 Those who seek my life lay snares for me;
they seek my misfortune, they speak of ruin;
they plot treachery all the day.

III
14 But I am like the deaf, hearing nothing,
like the dumb, saying nothing,
15 Like someone who does not hear,
who has no answer ready.
16 LORD, I wait for you;
O Lord, my God, answer me.*
17 For I fear they will gloat,
exult over me if I stumble.

IV
18 I am very near to falling;
my pain is with me always.
19 I acknowledge my guilt
and grieve over my sin.*
20 But many are my foes without cause,
a multitude of enemies without reason,
21 Repaying me evil for good,
harassing me for pursuing good.*
22 Forsake me not, O LORD;
my God, be not far from me!*
23 Come quickly to help me,*
my Lord and my salvation!

PSALM 39†

The Vanity of Life

1 *For the leader, for Jeduthun.* A psalm of David.*

I
2 I said, "I will watch my ways,
lest I sin with my tongue;
I will set a curb on my mouth."
3 Dumb and silent before the wicked,
I refrained from any speech.
But my sorrow increased;
4 my heart smoldered within me.*
In my thoughts a fire blazed up,
and I broke into speech:

II
5 LORD, let me know my end, the number of my days,
that I may learn how frail I am.
6 You have given my days a very short span;
my life is as nothing before you.
All mortals are but a breath.*
Selah
7 Mere phantoms, we go our way;
mere vapor, our restless pursuits;
we heap up stores without knowing for whom.
8 And now, Lord, what future do I have?
You are my only hope.
9 From all my sins deliver me;
let me not be the taunt of fools.

III
10 I was silent and did not open my mouth
because you were the one who did this.
11 Take your plague away from me;
I am ravaged by the touch of your hand.
12 You rebuke our guilt and chasten us;
you dissolve all we prize like a cobweb.
All mortals are but a breath.
Selah
13 Listen to my prayer, LORD, hear my cry;
do not be deaf to my weeping!
I sojourn with you like a passing stranger,
a guest, like all my ancestors.*

PSALMS

* 4: Is 1, 5-6. 5: Ps 40, 13; Ezr 9, 6. 7: Ps 35, 14. 9: Ps 102, 4-6. 11: Pss 6, 8; 31, 10. 16: Ps 13, 4. 19: Pss 32, 5; 51, 5. 21: Ps 109, 5. 22: Pss 22, 2. 12. 20; 35, 22. 23: Ps 40, 14. 39, 1: 1 Chr 16, 41; Pss 62, 1; 77, 1. 3: Jer 20, 9. 6: Pss 62, 10; 90, 9-10; 144, 4; Jb 7, 6. 16; 14, 1. 5; Eccl 6, 12; Wis 2, 5. 13: Ps 119, 19; Gn 23, 4; Heb 11, 13; 1 Pt 2, 11.

† Ps 39: The lament of a mortally ill person who at first had resolved to remain silently submissive (2-4). But the grief was too much and now the psalmist laments the brevity and vanity of life (5-7), yet remaining hopeful (8-10). The psalmist continues to express both acceptance of the illness and hope for healing in 11-14.

14 Turn your gaze from me, that I may
find peace
before I depart to be no more.

PSALM 40†

Gratitude and Prayer for Help

1 *For the leader. A psalm of David.*

A

I

2 I waited, waited for the LORD;
who bent down and heard my
cry,*
3 Drew me out of the pit of de-
struction,
out of the mud of the swamp,*
Set my feet upon rock,
steadied my steps,
4† And put a new song in my mouth,*
a hymn to our God.
Many shall look on in awe
and they shall trust in the LORD.

II

5 Happy those whose trust is the
LORD,
who turn not to idolatry
or to those who stray after false-
hood.*
6 How numerous, O LORD, my God,
you have made your wondrous
deeds!
And in your plans for us
there is none to equal you.*
Should I wish to declare or tell them,
too many are they to recount.*

III

7† Sacrifice and offering you do not
want;*
but ears open to obedience you
gave me.
Holocausts and sin-offerings you do
not require;
8 so I said, "Here I am;
your commands for me are writ-
ten in the scroll.
9 To do your will is my delight;
my God, your law is in my
heart!"*
10 I announced your deed to a great
assembly;
I did not restrain my lips;
you, LORD, are my witness.*
11 Your deed I did not hide within my
heart;
your loyal deliverance I have pro-
claimed.
I made no secret of your enduring
kindness
to a great assembly.

B

I

12 LORD, do not withhold your compas-
sion from me;
may your enduring kindness ever
preserve me.*
13 For all about me are evils beyond
count;
my sins so overcome me I cannot
see.
They are more than the hairs of my
head;
my courage fails me.*

II

14 LORD, graciously rescue me!*
Come quickly to help me,
LORD!
15 Put to shame and confound
all who seek to take my life.
Turn back in disgrace
those who desire my ruin.*
16 Let those who say "Aha!"*
know dismay and shame.
17 But may all who seek you
rejoice and be glad in you.
May those who long for your
help
always say, "The LORD be glori-
fied."*
18 Though I am afflicted and poor,
the Lord keeps me in mind.
You are my help and deliverer;
my God, do not delay!

*

40, 2: Lam 3, 25.
3: Pss 28, 1; 30, 4; 69, 3. 15-16; 88, 5; Prv 1, 12; Jon 2, 7.
4: Ps 33, 3.
5: Ps 1, 1; Prv 16, 20; Jer 17, 7.
6: Ps 35, 10. • Pss 71, 15; 139, 17-18.
7-9: Heb 10, 5-7; Ps 51, 18-19; Am 5, 22; Hos 6, 6; Is 1, 11-15.
9: Ps 37, 31.
10: Pss 22, 23; 26, 12; 35, 18; 149, 1.
12: Ps 89, 34.
13: Ps 38, 5. 11; Ezr 9, 6.
14-18: Pss 70, 2-6; 71, 12.
15: Ps 35, 4. 26.
16: Ps 35, 21. 25.
17: Ps 35, 27.

†

Ps 40: A thanksgiving (2-13) has been combined with a lament (14-18), that appears also in Ps 70. The psalmist describes the rescue in spatial terms—being raised up from the swampy underworld to firm earth where one can praise God (2-4). All who trust God will experience like protection (5-6)! The psalm stipulates the precise mode of thanksgiving: not animal sacrifice but open and enthusiastic proclamation of the salvation just experienced (7-11). A prayer for protection concludes (12-18).

40, 4: *A new song*: a song in response to the new action of God (cf Pss 33, 3; 96, 1; 144, 9; 149, 1; Is 42, 10). Giving thanks is not purely a human response but is itself a divine gift.

40, 7-9: Obedience is better than sacrifice (cf 1 Sm 15, 22; Is 1, 10-20; Hos 6, 6; Am 5, 22-25; Mi 6, 6-8; Act 7, 42-43 [quoting Am 5, 25-26 LXX]). Heb 10, 5-9 quotes the somewhat different Greek version and interprets it as Christ's self-oblation.

PSALM 41†
Thanksgiving after Sickness

1 *For the leader. A psalm of David.*

I

2† Happy those concerned for the lowly and poor;
when misfortune strikes, the LORD delivers them.*
3 The LORD keeps and preserves them,
makes them happy in the land,
and does not betray them to their enemies.
4 The LORD sustains them on their sickbed,
allays the malady when they are ill.

II

5 Once I prayed, "LORD, have mercy on me;
heal me, I have sinned against you.
6 My enemies say the worst of me:
'When will that one die and be forgotten?'
7 When people come to visit me,
they speak without sincerity.
Their hearts store up malice;
they leave and spread their vicious lies.*
8 My foes all whisper against me;
they imagine the worst about me:
9 I have a deadly disease, they say;
I will never rise from my sickbed.
10† Even the friend who had my trust,
who shared my table, has scorned me.*
11† But you, LORD, have mercy and raise me up
that I may repay them as they deserve."

III

12 By this I know you are pleased with me,
that my enemy no longer jeers at me.
13 For my integrity you have supported me
and let me stand in your presence forever.

* * *

14† Blessed be the LORD, the God of Israel,
from all eternity and forever.
Amen. Amen.*

SECOND BOOK—Psalms 42-72

PSALMS 42-43†
Longing for God's Presence in the Temple

1† *For the leader. A* maskil *of the Korahites.*

I

2 As the deer longs for streams of water,*
so my soul longs for you, O God.
3† My being thirsts for God, the living God.
When can I go and see the face of God?*
4 My tears have been my food day and night,*
as they ask daily, "Where is your God?"*
5 Those times I recall
as I pour out my soul,*
When I went in procession with the crowd,
I went with them to the house of God,
Amid loud cries of thanksgiving,

PSALMS

*
41, 2: Tb 4, 7-11.
7: Pss 31, 12; 38, 12-13; 88, 8; Jb 19, 13-19; Jer 20, 10.
10: Ps 55, 14-15; Jn 13, 18.
14: Neh 9, 5.
42-43,
2-3: Pss 63, 2; 84, 3; 143, 6; Is 26, 9.
3: Ps 27, 4.
4: Pss 80, 6; 102, 10. • Ps 79, 10; Jl 2, 17.
5: Lam 3, 20.

†
Ps 41: A thanksgiving for rescue from illness (4. 5. 9). Many people, even friends, have interpreted the illness as a divine punishment for sin and have ostracized the psalmist (5-11). The healing shows the return of God's favor and rebukes the psalmist's detractors (12-13).

41, 2: *Happy those concerned for the lowly and poor*: other psalms use the same formula ("Happy those") for those whom God favors. Cf Pss 32, 1-2; 34, 9; 40, 5; 65, 5. The psalmist's statement about God's love of the poor is based on the experience of being rescued (1-3).

41, 10: *Even the friend . . . has scorned me:* Jn 13, 18 cites this verse to characterize Judas as a false friend. *Scorned me*: an interpretation of the unclear Hebrew, "made great the heel against me."

41, 11: *That I may repay them as they deserve*: the healing itself is an act of judgment through which God decides for the psalmist and against the false friends. The prayer is not necessarily for strength to punish enemies.

41, 14: The doxology, not part of the psalm, marks the end of the first of the five books of the Psalter. Compare Pss 72, 18-20; 89, 53; 106, 48.

Pss 42-43: Pss 42-43 form a single lament of three sections, each section ending in an identical refrain (42, 6. 12; 43, 5). The psalmist is in the extreme north of Israel, far from Jerusalem, and longs for the divine presence that Israel experienced in the temple liturgy. Despite sadness, the psalmist hopes once again to join the worshiping crowds.

42, 1: *The Korahites:* a major guild of temple singers (2 Chr 20, 19) whose name appears in the superscriptions of Pss 42; 44-49; 84-85; 87-88.

42, 3: *See the face of God*: "face" designates a personal presence (Gn 33, 10; Ex 10, 28-29; 2 Sm 17, 11). The expressions "see God/God's face" occur elsewhere (Pss 11, 7; 17, 15; 63, 3; cf Ex 24, 10; 33, 7-11; Jb 33, 26) for the presence of God in the temple.

with the multitude keeping festival.*
6 Why are you downcast, my soul;
why do you groan within me?
Wait for God, whom I shall praise again,
my savior and my God.

II

7† My soul is downcast within me;
therefore I will remember you
From the land of the Jordan and Hermon,
from the land of Mount Mizar.*
8† Here deep calls to deep in the roar of your torrents.
All your waves and breakers sweep over me.*
9 At dawn may the LORD bestow faithful love
that I may sing praise through the night,
praise to the God of my life.
10 I say to God, "My rock,
why do you forget me?*
Why must I go about mourning
with the enemy oppressing me?"
11 It shatters my bones, when my adversaries reproach me.
They say to me daily: "Where is your God?"
12 Why are you downcast, my soul,
why do you groan within me?
Wait for God, whom I shall praise again,
my savior and my God.

III

1 Grant me justice, God;
defend me from a faithless people;
from the deceitful and unjust rescue me.*
2 You, God, are my strength.
Why then do you spurn me?
Why must I go about mourning,
with the enemy oppressing me?
3† Send your light and fidelity,
that they may be my guide*
And bring me to your holy mountain,
to the place of your dwelling,*
4 That I may come to the altar of God,
to God, my joy, my delight.
Then I will praise you with the harp,
O God, my God.
5 Why are you downcast, my soul?
Why do you groan within me?
Wait for God, whom I shall praise again,
my savior and my God.

PSALM 44†

God's Past Favor and Israel's Present Need

1 *For the leader. A* maskil *of the Korahites.*

I

2 O God, we have heard with our own ears;
our ancestors have told us*
The deeds you did in their days,
with your own hand in days of old:
3 You rooted out nations to plant them,*
crushed peoples to make room for them.
4 Not with their own swords did they conquer the land,*
nor did their own arms bring victory;
It was your right hand, your own arm,
the light of your face, for you favored them.*
5 You are my king and my God,*
who bestows victories on Jacob.
6 Through you we batter our foes;
through your name, trample our adversaries.
7 Not in my bow do I trust,
nor does my sword bring me victory.
8 You have brought us victory over our enemies,
shamed those who hate us.
9 In God we have boasted all the day long;
your name we will praise forever.
Selah

II

10 But now you have rejected and disgraced us;*
you do not march out with our armies.*

*

5: Ps 122, 5.
7: Ps 43, 3.
8: Pss 18, 5; 32, 6; 69, 2; 88, 8; Jon 2, 4.
10: Pss 18, 2; 31, 3-4.
III, 1: Ps 119, 154.
3: Pss 18, 29; 27, 1; 36, 10; Mi 7, 8. • Ps 122, 1.
44, 2: Ps 78, 3.
3: Pss 78, 55; 80, 9f.
4: Dt 8, 17f; Jos 24, 12. • Pss 4, 7; 31, 17; 67, 2; 80, 4; Nm 6, 25; Dn 9, 17.
5: Ps 145, 1.
10-27: Ps 89, 39-52.
10: Ps 60, 12.

†

42, 7: *From the land of the Jordan*: the sources of the Jordan are in the foothills of Mount Hermon in present-day southern Lebanon. Mount Mizar is presumed to be a mountain in the same range.

42, 8: *Here deep calls to deep*: to the psalmist, the waters arising in the north are overwhelming and far from God's presence, like the waters of chaos (Pss 18, 5; 69, 2-3. 15; Jon 2, 3-6).

43, 3: *Your light and fidelity*: a pair of divine attributes personified as guides for the pilgrimage. The psalmist seeks divine protection for the journey to Jerusalem.

Ps 44: In this lament the community reminds God of past favors which it has always acknowledged (2-9). But now God has abandoned Israel to defeat and humiliation (10-17), though the people are not conscious of any sin against the covenant (18-23). They struggle with being God's special people amid divine silence; yet they continue to pray (24-27).

11† You make us retreat before the foe;
those who hate us plunder us at will.*
12 You hand us over like sheep to be slaughtered,
scatter us among the nations.*
13 You sell your people for nothing;
you make no profit from their sale.*
14 You make us the reproach of our neighbors,*
the mockery and scorn of those around us.
15 You make us a byword among the nations;
the peoples shake their heads at us.
16 All day long my disgrace is before me;
shame has covered my face
17 At the sound of those who taunt and revile,
at the sight of the spiteful enemy.

III

18 All this has come upon us,
though we have not forgotten you,
nor been disloyal to your covenant.
19† Our hearts have not turned back,
nor have our steps strayed from your path.
20† Yet you have left us crushed,
desolate in a place of jackals;*
you have covered us with darkness.
21 If we had forgotten the name of our God,
stretched out our hands to another god,
22 Would not God have discovered this,
God who knows the secrets of the heart?
23 For you we are slain all the day long,
considered only as sheep to be slaughtered.*

IV

24 Awake! Why do you sleep, O Lord?
Rise up! Do not reject us forever!*
25 Why do you hide your face;*
why forget our pain and misery?
26 We are bowed down to the ground;*
our bodies are pressed to the earth.
27 Rise up, help us!
Redeem us as your love demands.

PSALM 45†

Song for a Royal Wedding

1 *For the leader; according to "Lilies."* A maskil *of the Korahites. A love song.*

I

2 My heart is stirred by a noble theme,
as I sing my ode to the king.
My tongue is the pen of a nimble scribe.

II

3 You are the most handsome of men;
fair speech has graced your lips,
for God has blessed you forever.*
4 Gird your sword upon your hip, mighty warrior!
In splendor and majesty ride on triumphant!*
5 In the cause of truth and justice
may your right hand show you wondrous deeds.
6 Your arrows are sharp;
peoples will cower at your feet;
the king's enemies will lose heart.
7† Your throne, O god, stands forever;*
your royal scepter is a scepter for justice.
8 You love justice and hate wrongdoing;
therefore God, your God, has anointed you
with the oil of gladness above your fellow kings.
9† With myrrh, aloes, and cassia
your robes are fragrant.
From ivory-paneled palaces
stringed instruments bring you joy.

*

11: Lv 26, 17; Dt 28, 25.
12: Lv 26, 33; Dt 28, 64.
13: Dt 32, 30; Is 52, 3.
14-17: Pss 79, 4; 80, 7; 123, 3-4; Jb 12, 4; Dn 9, 16.
20: Jer 9, 10.
23: Rom 8, 36.
24: Pss 10, 1; 74, 1; 77, 8; 79, 5; 83, 2.
25: Pss 10, 11; 89, 47; Jb 13, 24.
26: Ps 119, 25.
45, 3: Song 5, 10-16.
4: Ps 21, 5.
7-8: Heb 1, 8-9.

†

44, 11: *You make us retreat*: the corollary of v 4. Defeat, like victory, is God's doing; neither Israel nor its enemies can claim credit (23).

44, 19: *Our hearts have not turned back*: Israel's defeat was not caused by its lack of fidelity.

44, 20: *A place of jackals*: following Israel's defeat and exile (11-12), the land lies desolate, inhabited only by jackals. Cf Is 13, 22; Jer 9, 10; 10, 22. Others take *tannim* as "sea monster" (cf Ez 29, 3; 32, 2) and render: "you crushed us as you did the sea monster."

Ps 45: A song for the Davidic king's marriage to a foreign princess from Tyre in Phoenicia. The court poet sings (2. 18) of God's choice of the king (3. 8), of his role in establishing divine rule (4-8), and of his splendor as he waits for his bride (9-10). The woman is to forget her own house when she becomes wife to the king (11-13). Her majestic beauty today is a sign of the future prosperity of the royal house (14-18). The psalm was retained in the collection when there was no reigning king, and came to be applied to the king who was to come, the messiah.

45, 7: *O god*: the king, in courtly language, is called "god," i.e., more than human, representing God to the people. Heb 1, 8-9 applies 7-8 to Christ.

45, 9: *Ivory-paneled palaces*: literally, "palaces of ivory." Ivory paneling and furniture decoration have been found in Samaria and other ancient Near Eastern cities. Cf Am 3, 15.

10† Daughters of kings are your lovely wives;
a princess arrayed in Ophir's gold comes to stand at your right hand.

III

11† Listen, my daughter, and understand;
pay me careful heed.
Forget your people and your father's house,
12 that the king might desire your beauty.
He is your lord;
13 honor him, daughter of Tyre.
Then the richest of the people will seek your favor with gifts.*
14 All glorious is the king's daughter as she enters,*
her raiment threaded with gold;
15 In embroidered apparel she is led to the king.
The maids of her train are presented to the king.
16 They are led in with glad and joyous acclaim;
they enter the palace of the king.

IV

17 The throne of your fathers your sons will have;
you shall make them princes through all the land.*
18 I will make your name renowned through all generations;
thus nations shall praise you forever.*

PSALM 46†

God, the Protector of Zion

1† *For the leader. A song of the Korahites. According to* alamoth.

I

2 God is our refuge and our strength,
an ever-present help in distress.*
3† Thus we do not fear, though earth be shaken
and mountains quake to the depths of the sea,
4† Though its waters rage and foam
and mountains totter at its surging.*
The LORD of hosts is with us;
our stronghold is the God of Jacob. *Selah*

II

5† Streams of the river gladden the city of God,
the holy dwelling of the Most High.*
6 God is in its midst; it shall not be shaken;
God will help it at break of day.*
7 Though nations rage and kingdoms totter,
God's voice thunders and the earth trembles.*
8 The LORD of hosts is with us;
our stronghold is the God of Jacob. *Selah*

III

9 Come and see the works of the LORD,
who has done fearsome deeds on earth;*
10 Who stops wars to the ends of the earth,
breaks the bow, splinters the spear,
and burns the shields with fire;*
11 Who says:
"Be still and confess that I am God!
I am exalted among the nations,
exalted on the earth."*
12 The LORD of hosts is with us;
our stronghold is the God of Jacob. *Selah*

PSALM 47†

The Ruler of All the Nations

1 *For the leader. A psalm of the Korahites.*

*

13: Ps 72, 10-11; Is 60, 5f.
14-16: Ez 16, 10-13.
17: Gn 17, 6.
18: Is 60, 15.
46, 2: Ps 48, 4; Is 33, 2.
3: Ps 93, 3-4; Jb 9, 5-6; Is 24, 18-20; 54, 10.
5: Pss 48, 2-3; 76, 3.
6: Is 7, 14.
7: Pss 2, 1-5; 48, 5-8; 76, 7-9; Is 17, 12-14.
9: Ps 48, 9-10.
10: Ps 76, 4.
11: Ps 48, 11.

†

45, 10: *Ophir's gold*: uncertain location, possibly a region on the coast of southern Arabia or eastern Africa, famous for its gold. Cf 1 Kgs 9, 28; 10, 11; Jb 22, 24.

45, 11: *Forget your people and your father's house*: the bride should no longer consider herself a daughter of her father's house, but the wife of the king—the queen.

Ps 46: A song of confidence in God's protection of Zion with close parallels to Ps 48. The dominant note in Ps 46 is sounded by the refrain, *The LORD of hosts is with us* (4. 8. 12). The first strophe (2-4) sings of the security of God's presence even in utter chaos; the second (5-8), of divine protection of the city from its enemies; the third (9-12), of God's imposition of imperial peace.

46, 1: *Alamoth:* the melody of the psalm, now lost.

46, 3-4: Figurative ancient Near Eastern language to describe social and political upheavals.

46, 4b: The first line of the refrain is similar in structure and meaning to Isaiah's name for the royal child, Immanuel, *With us is God* (Is 7, 14; 8, 8. 10).

46, 5: Jerusalem is not situated on a river. This description derives from mythological descriptions of the divine abode and symbolizes the divine presence as the source of all life (cf Is 33, 21; Ez 47, 1-12; Jl 4, 18; Zec 14, 8; Rv 22, 1-2).

Ps 47: A hymn calling on the nations to acknowledge the universal rule of Israel's God (2-5) who is enthroned as king over Israel and the nations (6-10).

I

2 All you peoples, clap your hands;
shout to God with joyful cries.*
3 For the LORD, the Most High, inspires awe,
the great king over all the earth,*
4 Who made people subject to us,
brought nations under our feet,*
5† Who chose a land for our heritage,
the glory of Jacob, the beloved.*
Selah

II

6† God mounts the throne amid shouts of joy;
the LORD, amid trumpet blasts.*
7 Sing praise to God, sing praise;
sing praise to our king, sing praise.

III

8 God is king over all the earth;*
sing hymns of praise.
9 God rules over the nations;
God sits upon his holy throne.
10 The princes of the peoples assemble
with the people of the God of Abraham.
For the rulers of the earth belong to God,
who is enthroned on high.*

PSALM 48†

The Splendor of the Invincible City

1† *A psalm of the Korahites. A song.*

I

2 Great is the LORD and highly praised
in the city of our God:*
The holy mountain,
3† fairest of heights,
the joy of all the earth,*
Mount Zion, the heights of Zaphon,*
the city of the great king.

II

4 God is its citadel,
renowned as a stronghold.
5 See! The kings assembled,
together they invaded.
6† When they looked they were astounded;
terrified, they were put to flight!*
7 Trembling seized them there,
anguish, like a woman's labor,*
8† As when the east wind wrecks
the ships of Tarshish!

III

9† What we had heard we now see
in the city of the LORD of hosts,
In the city of our God,
founded to last forever. *Selah*

10 O God, within your temple
we ponder your steadfast love.
11 Like your name, O God,
your praise reaches the ends of the earth.*
Your right hand is fully victorious.
12 Mount Zion is glad!
The cities of Judah rejoice
because of your saving deeds!*

IV

13 Go about Zion, walk all around it,
note the number of its towers.
14 Consider the ramparts, examine its citadels,
that you may tell future generations:*
15† "Yes, so mighty is God,
our God who leads us always!"

PSALMS

---

* 47, 2: Ps 89, 16; Zep 3, 14.
3: Ps 95, 3; Ex 15, 18; Is 24, 23; 52, 7.
4: Ps 2, 8.
5: Is 58, 14.
6: Pss 24, 8. 10; 68, 18-19; 98, 6.
8-9: Pss 72, 11; 93, 1; 96, 10; 97, 1; 99, 1; Jer 10, 7.
10: Ps 89, 19; Ex 3, 6; Is 2, 2-4.
48, 2: Pss 96, 4; 145, 3.
3: Ps 50, 2; Lam 2, 15. • Is 14, 13.
6: Jgs 5, 19.
7: Ex 15, 14; Jer 4, 31.
11: Mal 1, 11.
12: Ps 97, 8.
14: Pss 22, 31-32; 71, 18.

---

† 47, 5: *Our heritage . . . the glory*: the land of Israel (cf Is 58, 14), which God has given Israel in an act of sovereignty.

47, 6: *God mounts the throne*: "has gone up to the throne," according to the context (9). Christian liturgical tradition has applied the verse to the ascension of Christ.

Ps 48: A Zion hymn, praising the holy city as the invincible dwelling place of God. Unconquerable, it is an apt symbol of God who has defeated all enemies. After seven epithets describing the city (2-3), the psalm describes the victory by the Divine Warrior over hostile kings (4-8). The second half proclaims the dominion of the God of Zion over all the earth (9-12) and invites pilgrims to announce that God is eternally invincible like Zion itself (13-15).

48, 1: *Korahites:* see note on Ps 42, 1.

48, 3: *The heights of Zaphon*: the mountain abode of the Canaanite storm-god Baal in comparable texts. To speak of Zion as if it were Zaphon was to claim for Israel's God what Canaanites claimed for Baal. Though topographically speaking Zion is only a hill, viewed religiously it towers over other mountains as the home of the supreme God (cf Ps 68, 16-17).

48, 6: *When they looked*: the kings are stunned by the sight of Zion, touched by divine splendor. The language is that of holy war, in which the enemy panics and flees at the sight of divine glory.

48, 8: *The ships of Tarshish*: large ships, named after the distant land or port of Tarshish, probably ancient Tartessus in southern Spain, although other identifications have been proposed. Cf Is 2, 16; 60, 9; Jon 1, 3.

48, 9: *What we had heard we now see*: the glorious things that new pilgrims had heard about the holy city—its beauty and awesomeness—they now see with their own eyes. The seeing here contrasts with the seeing of the hostile kings in 6.

48, 15: *So mighty is God*: Israel's God is like Zion in being eternal and invincible. The holy city is therefore a kind of "sacrament" of God.

PSALM 49†

Confidence in God rather than in Riches

1† *For the leader. A psalm of the Korahites.*

2 Hear this, all you peoples!
Give ear, all who inhabit the world,
3 You of lowly birth or high estate,
rich and poor alike.
4 My mouth shall speak wisdom,
my heart shall offer insight.*
5† I will turn my attention to a problem,
expound my question to the music of a lyre.

I

6 Why should I fear in evil days,
when my wicked pursuers ring me round,
7 Those who trust in their wealth
and boast of their abundant riches?*
8† One cannot redeem oneself,
pay to God a ransom.*
9 Too high the price to redeem a life;
one would never have enough
10 To stay alive forever
and never see the pit.
11 Anyone can see that the wisest die,
the fool and the senseless pass away too,*
and must leave their wealth to others.*
12 Tombs are their homes forever,
their dwellings through all generations,
though they gave their names to their lands.
13 For all their riches
mortals do not abide;
they perish like the beasts.*

II

14 This is the destiny of those who trust in folly,
the end of those so pleased with their wealth. *Selah*
15 Like sheep they are herded into Sheol,
where death will be their shepherd.
Straight to the grave they descend,
where their form will waste away,
Sheol will be their palace.
16† But God will redeem my life, *Selah*
will take me from the power of Sheol.*
17 Do not fear when others become rich,
when the wealth of their houses grows great.
18 When they die they will take nothing with them,
their wealth will not follow them down.*
19 When living, they congratulate themselves and say:
"All praise you, you do so well."
20 But they will join the company of their forebears,
never again to see the light.*
21 For all their riches,
if mortals do not have wisdom,
they perish like the beasts.

PSALM 50†

The Acceptable Sacrifice

1 *A psalm of Asaph.*

I

The LORD, the God of gods,
has spoken and summoned the earth
from the rising of the sun to its setting.*
2 From Zion God shines forth,*
perfect in beauty.
3 Our God comes and will not be silent!
Devouring fire precedes,
storming fiercely round about.*
4 God summons the heavens above

*

49, 4: Ps 78, 2; Mt 13, 35.
7: Jb 31, 24.
8: Prv 10, 15; 11, 4; Ez 7, 19; Mt 16, 26.
11: Eccl 2, 16. • Ps 39, 7; Sir 11, 18-19.
13: Eccl 3, 18-21.
16: Pss 16, 10; 86, 13; 103, 4; 116, 8.
18: Sir 11, 18-19; Eccl 5, 15; 1 Tm 6, 7.
20: Jb 10, 21-22.
50, 1: Dt 10, 17; Jos 22, 22.
2: Ps 48, 2.
3: Ps 97, 3; Dn 7, 10.

†

Ps 49: The psalm affirms confidence in God (cf Pss 23; 27, 1-6; 62) in the face of the apparent good fortune of the unjust rich. Cf Pss 37; 73. Reliance on wealth is misplaced (8-10) for it is of no avail in the face of death (18-20). After inviting all to listen to this axiom of faith (2-5), the psalmist depicts the self-delusion of the ungodly (6-13), whose destiny is to die like ignorant beasts (13. 18; cf Prv 7, 21-23). Their wealth should occasion no alarm, for they will come to nought, whereas God will save the just (14-21).

49, 1: *Korahites*: see note on Ps 42, 1.

49, 5: *Problem*: the psalmist's personal solution to the perennial biblical problem of the prosperity of the wicked. *Question*: parallel in meaning to *problem*; in Wisdom literature it means the mysterious way of how the world works.

49, 8: *One cannot redeem oneself*: an axiom. For the practice of redemption, cf Jb 6, 21-23. A play on the first Hebrew word of v 8 and v 16 relates the two verses.

49, 16: *Will take me*: the same Hebrew verb is used of God "taking up" a favored servant: Enoch in Gn 5, 24; Elijah in 2 Kgs 2, 11-12; the righteous person in Ps 73, 24. The verse apparently states the hope that God will rescue the faithful psalmist in the same manner.

Ps 50: A covenant lawsuit stating that the sacrifice God really wants is the sacrifice of praise accompanied by genuine obedience (cf Mi 6, 1-8). It begins with a theophany and the summoning of the court (1-6). Then in direct address God explains what is required of the faithful (7-15), rebukes the hypocritical worshiper (16-21), and concludes with a threat and a promise (22-23; cf Is 1, 19-20).

and the earth to the judgment of his people:
5 "Gather my faithful ones before me, those who made a covenant with me by sacrifice."
6 The heavens proclaim divine justice,
for God alone is the judge.* *Selah*

II

7 "Listen, my people, I will speak;
Israel, I will testify against you;
God, your God, am I.
8 Not for your sacrifices do I rebuke you,
nor for your holocausts, set before me daily.
9 I need no bullock from your house,
no goats from your fold.*
10 For every animal of the forest is mine,
beasts by the thousands on my mountains.
11 I know every bird of the heavens;
the creatures of the field belong to me.
12 Were I hungry, I would not tell you,
for mine is the world and all that fills it.*
13 Do I eat the flesh of bulls
or drink the blood of goats?
14 Offer praise as your sacrifice to God;*
fulfill your vows to the Most High.
15 Then call on me in time of distress;*
I will rescue you, and you shall honor me."

III

16 But to the wicked God says:
"Why do you recite my commandments
and profess my covenant with your lips?
17 You hate discipline;
you cast my words behind you!
18 When you see thieves, you befriend them;
with adulterers you throw in your lot.
19 You give your mouth free rein for evil;
you harness your tongue to deceit.
20 You sit maligning your own kin,
slandering the child of your own mother.
21 When you do these things should I be silent?
Or do you think that I am like you?
I accuse you, I lay the charge before you.

IV

22 "Understand this, you who forget God,
lest I attack you with no one to rescue.
23 Those who offer praise as a sacrifice honor me;
to the obedient I will show the salvation of God."*

PSALM 51†

The Miserere: Prayer of Repentance

1 *For the leader. A psalm of David,*
2 *when Nathan the prophet came to him after his affair with Bathsheba.**

I

3 Have mercy on me, God, in your goodness;
in your abundant compassion blot out my offense.
4 Wash away all my guilt;
from my sin cleanse me.
5 For I know my offense;
my sin is always before me.*
6 Against you alone have I sinned;
I have done such evil in your sight
That you are just in your sentence,
blameless when you condemn.*
7† True, I was born guilty,
a sinner, even as my mother conceived me.*
8 Still, you insist on sincerity of heart;
in my inmost being teach me wisdom.
9† Cleanse me with hyssop, that I may be pure;

PSALMS

*

6: Pss 19, 2; 97, 6.
9: Ps 69, 32; Am 5, 21-22.
12: Pss 24, 1; 89, 12; Dt 10, 14; 1 Cor 10, 26.
14: Heb 13, 15.
15: Ps 77, 3.
23: Ps 91, 16.
51, 1: 2 Sm 12.
5: Pss 32, 5; 38, 19; Is 59, 12.
6: Rom 3, 4.
7: Jb 14, 4.

†

Ps 51: A lament, the most famous of the seven Penitential Psalms, prays for the removal of the personal and social disorders that sin has brought. The poem has two parts of approximately equal length: 3-10 and 11-19, and a conclusion in 20-21. The two parts interlock by repetition of "blot out" in the first verse of each section (3. 11), of "wash (away)" just after the first verse of each section (4) and just before the last verse (9) of the first section, and of "heart," "God," and "spirit" in 12 and 19. The first part (3-10) asks deliverance from sin, which is not just a past act but its emotional, physical, and social consequences. The second part (11-19) seeks something more profound than wiping the slate clean: nearness to God, living by the spirit of God (12-13), like the relation between God and people described in Jer 31, 33-34. Nearness to God brings joy and the authority to teach sinners (15-16). Such proclamation is better than offering sacrifice (17-19). The last two verses ask for the rebuilding of Jerusalem (20-21).

51, 7: *A sinner, even as my mother conceived me*: literally, "In iniquity was I conceived," an instance of hyperbole: at no time was the psalmist ever without sin. Cf Ps 88, 16, "I am mortally afflicted since youth," i.e., I have always been afflicted. The verse does not imply that the sexual act of conception is sinful.

51, 9: *Hyssop*: a small bush whose many woody twigs make a natural sprinkler. It was prescribed in the Mosaic law as an instrument for sprinkling sacrificial blood or lustral water for cleansing. Cf Ex 12, 22; Lv 14, 4; Nm 19, 18.

wash me, make me whiter than snow.*
10 Let me hear sounds of joy and gladness;
let the bones you have crushed rejoice.

II
11 Turn away your face from my sins;
blot out all my guilt.
12 A clean heart create for me, God;
renew in me a steadfast spirit.*
13 Do not drive me from your presence,
nor take from me your holy spirit.*
14 Restore my joy in your salvation;
sustain in me a willing spirit.
15 I will teach the wicked your ways,
that sinners may return to you.
16 Rescue me from death, God, my saving God,
that my tongue may praise your healing power.*
17 Lord, open my lips;
my mouth will proclaim your praise.
18† For you do not desire sacrifice;
a burnt offering you would not accept.*
19 My sacrifice, God, is a broken spirit;
God, do not spurn a broken, humbled heart.

III
20† Make Zion prosper in your good pleasure;
rebuild the walls of Jerusalem.*
21 Then you will be pleased with proper sacrifice,
burnt offerings and holocausts;
then bullocks will be offered on your altar.

PSALM 52†

The Deceitful Tongue

1 *For the leader. A* maskil *of David,*
2 *when Doeg the Edomite went and told Saul, "David went to the house of Ahimelech."**

I
3 Why do you glory in evil,
you scandalous liar?
All day long 4 you plot destruction;
your tongue is like a sharpened razor,
you skillful deceiver.*
5 You love evil rather than good,
lies rather than honest speech.* *Selah*
6 You love any word that destroys,
you deceitful tongue.*

II
7 Now God will strike you down,
leave you crushed forever,
Pluck you from your tent,
uproot you from the land of the living.* *Selah*
8 The righteous will look on with awe;
they will jeer and say:*
9 "That one did not take God as a refuge,
but trusted in great wealth,
relied on devious plots."*

III
10† But I, like an olive tree in the house of God,*
trust in God's faithful love forever.
11 I will praise you always
for what you have done.
I will proclaim before the faithful*
that your name is good.

PSALM 53†

A Lament over Widespread Corruption

1 *For the leader; according to* Mahalath. *A* maskil *of David.*

I
2 Fools say in their hearts,*
"There is no God."*

*

9: Jb 9, 30; Is 1, 18; Ez 36, 25.
12: Ez 11, 19.
13: Wis 1, 5; 9, 17; Is 63, 11; Hg 2, 5; Rom 8, 9.
16: Ps 30, 10.
18: Ps 40, 7; 50, 8; Am 5, 21-22; Hos 6, 6; Is 1, 11-15; Heb 10, 5-7.
20: Jer 31, 4; Ez 36, 33.
52, 1: 1 Sm 21, 8; 22, 6ff.
3: Pss 12, 3; 59, 8; 120, 2-3; Sir 51, 3.
5: Jer 4, 22; Jn 3, 19-20.
6: Jer 9, 4.
7: Pss 27, 13; 28, 5; 56, 14; Jb 18, 14; Prv 2, 22; Is 38, 11.
8: Pss 44, 14; 64, 9.
9: Jb 31, 24; Prv 11, 28.
10: Pss 1, 3; 92, 12-14; Jer 11, 16; 17, 8.
11: Pss 22, 23; 26, 12; 35, 18; 149, 1.
53, 2-6a: Ps 14, 1-5a.
2: Pss 10, 4; 36, 2; Is 32, 6; Jer 5, 12.

†

51, 18: *For you do not desire sacrifice*: the mere offering of the ritual sacrifice apart from good dispositions is not acceptable to God. Cf Ps 50.

51, 20-21: Most scholars think that these verses were added to the psalm some time after the destruction of the temple in 587 B.C. The verses assume that the rebuilt temple will be an ideal site for national reconciliation.

Ps 52: A condemnation of the powerful and arrogant (3-6), who bring down upon themselves God's judgment (7). The just, those who trust in God alone, are gladdened and strengthened by the downfall of their traditional enemies (8-11).

52, 10: *Like a green olive tree*: the righteous will flourish in the house of God like a well-watered olive tree. Cf Pss 92, 14; 128, 3.

Ps 53: A lament of an individual, duplicated in Ps 14, except that "God" is used for "the Lord," and v 6 is different. See under Ps 14.

Their deeds are loathsome and corrupt;
not one does what is right.
3 God looks down from heaven
upon the human race,*
To see if even one is wise,*
if even one seeks God.
4 All have gone astray;
all alike are perverse.
Not one does what is right, not even one.*

II

5 Will these evildoers never learn?
They devour my people as they devour bread;*
they do not call upon God.*
6 They have good reason to fear,
though now they do not fear.
For God will certainly scatter
the bones of the godless.
They will surely be put to shame,
for God has rejected them.

III

7 Oh, that from Zion might come
the deliverance of Israel,
That Jacob may rejoice and Israel be glad*
when God restores the people!

PSALM 54†

Confident Prayer in Great Peril

1 *For the leader. On stringed instruments. A* maskil *of David,* 2 *when the Ziphites came and said to Saul, "David is hiding among us."**

I

3† O God, by your name save me.
By your strength defend my cause.
4 O God, hear my prayer.
Listen to the words of my mouth.
5 The arrogant have risen against me;
the ruthless seek my life;
they do not keep God before them.* *Selah*

II

6 God is present as my helper;*
the Lord sustains my life.
7 Turn back the evil upon my foes;
in your faithfulness, destroy them.*
8 Then I will offer you generous sacrifice
and praise your gracious name, LORD,
9 Because it has rescued me from every trouble,
and my eyes look down on my foes.*

PSALM 55†

A Lament over Betrayal

1 *For the leader. On stringed instruments. A* maskil *of David.*

I

2 Listen, God, to my prayer;*
do not hide from my pleading;
3 hear me and give answer.
I rock with grief; I groan
4 at the uproar of the enemy,
the clamor of the wicked.
They heap trouble upon me,
savagely accuse me.
5 My heart pounds within me;
death's terrors fall upon me.
6 Fear and trembling overwhelm me;
shuddering sweeps over me.
7 I say, "If only I had wings like a dove
that I might fly away and find rest.*
8 Far away I would flee;
I would stay in the desert.*
Selah
9 I would soon find a shelter
from the raging wind and storm."

II

10 Lord, check and confuse their scheming.
I see violence and strife in the city
11 making rounds on its walls day and night.
Within are mischief and evil;
12 treachery is there as well;
oppression and fraud never leave its streets.*

---

* 3: Pss 11, 4; 102, 20.
2b-3: Rom 3, 11-12.
4: Ps 12, 2.
5: Ps 27, 2; Is 9, 11. • Ps 79, 6.
7: Ps 85, 2.
54, 1: 1 Sm 23, 19; 26, 1.
5: Ps 86, 14.
6: Ps 118, 7.
7: Ps 143, 12.
9: Pss 59, 11; 91, 8; 92, 12.
55, 2-3: Pss 5, 2-3; 86, 6; 130, 1-2; Lam 3, 56; Jon 2, 3.
7: Ps 11, 1.
8: Jer 9, 1; Rv 12, 6.
12: Jer 5, 1; 6, 6; Ez 22, 2; Hb 1, 3; Zep 3, 1.

---

† Ps 54: A lament in which the person under attack calls directly upon God for help (3-5). Refusing to despair, the psalmist hopes in God, who is active in history and just (6-7). The psalm ends with a serene promise to return thanks (8-9).

54, 3: *By your name*: one is present in one's name, hence God as revealed to humans.

Ps 55: The psalmist, betrayed by intimate friends (14-15, 21-22), prays that God punish those oath breakers and thus be acknowledged as the protector of the wronged. The sufferings of the psalmist include both ostracism (4) and mental turmoil (5-6), culminating in the wish to flee society (7-9). The wish for a sudden death for one's enemies (16) occurs elsewhere in the psalms; an example of such a death is the earth opening under the wicked Dathan and Abiram (Nm 16, 31-32). The psalmist, confident of vindication, exhorts others to a like trust in the God of justice (23-24). The psalm is not so much for personal vengeance as for a public vindication of God's righteousness now. There was no belief in an afterlife where such vindication could take place.

PSALMS

13 If an enemy had reviled me,
that I could bear;
If my foe had viewed me with contempt,
from that I could hide.
14 But it was you, my other self,
my comrade and friend,*
15 You, whose company I enjoyed,
at whose side I walked
in procession in the house of God.

III

16 Let death take them by surprise;
let them go down alive to Sheol,*
for evil is in their homes and hearts.
17 But I will call upon God,
and the LORD will save me.
18 At dusk, dawn, and noon
I will grieve and complain,
and my prayer will be heard.*
19 God will give me freedom and peace
from those who war against me,
though there are many who oppose me.
20 God, who sits enthroned forever,*
will hear me and humble them.
For they will not mend their ways;
they have no fear of God.
21 They strike out at friends
and go back on their promises.
22 Softer than butter is their speech,
but war is in their hearts.
Smoother than oil are their words,
but they are unsheathed swords.*
23 Cast your care upon the LORD,
who will give you support.
God will never allow
the righteous to stumble.*
24 But you, God, will bring them down
to the pit of destruction.*
These bloodthirsty liars
will not live half their days,
but I put my trust in you.*

PSALM 56†

Trust in God

1† *For the director. According to* Yonath elem rehoqim. *A* miktam *of David, when the Philistines seized him at Gath.**

I

2 Have mercy on me, God,
for I am treated harshly;
attackers press me all the day.
3 My foes treat me harshly all the day;
yes, many are my attackers.
O Most High, 4 when I am afraid,
in you I place my trust.
5 God, I praise your promise;
in you I trust, I do not fear.*
What can mere flesh do to me?*

II

6 All the day they foil my plans;
their every thought is of evil against me.
7 They hide together in ambush;
they watch my every step;
they lie in wait for my life.*
8 They are evil; watch them, God!
Cast the nations down in your anger!
9† My wanderings you have noted;
are my tears not stored in your vial,
recorded in your book?*
10 My foes turn back when I call on you.
This I know: God is on my side.
11 God, I praise your promise;
12 in you I trust, I do not fear.
What can mere mortals do to me?

III

13 I have made vows to you, God;
with offerings I will fulfill them,*
14 Once you have snatched me from death,
kept my feet from stumbling,
That I may walk before God
in the light of the living.

PSALM 57†

Confident Prayer for Deliverance

1† *For the director. Do not destroy. A* miktam *of David, when he fled from Saul into a cave.**

---

* 14: Ps 41, 10; Jer 9, 3; Mt 26, 21-24 par.
16: Ps 49, 15; Nm 16, 33; Prv 1, 2; Is 5, 14.
18: Dn 6, 11.
20: Pss 29, 10; 93, 2; Bar 3, 3.
22: Pss 12, 3; 28, 3; 57, 5; 62, 5; 64, 4; Prv 26, 24-28; Jer 9, 7.
23: Ps 37, 5; Prv 3, 5; 16, 3; 1 Pt 5, 7.
24: Pss 28, 1; 30, 4; 40, 3; 88, 5; 143, 7; Prv 1, 12; Jon 2, 7. • Pss 25, 2; 56, 4; 130, 5.
56, 1: 1 Sm 21, 10.
5: Ps 130, 5. • Ps 118, 6; Heb 13, 6.
7: Ps 140, 5-6.
9: Ps 10, 14; 2 Kgs 20, 5; Is 25, 8; Rv 7, 17.
13: Nm 30, 3.
57, 1: 1 Sm 22, 1.

---

† Ps 56: Beset physically (2-3) and psychologically (6-7), the psalmist maintains a firm confidence in God (5. 9-10). Nothing will prevent the psalmist from keeping the vow to give thanks for God's gift of life (13-14). A refrain (5. 11-12) divides the psalm in two equal parts.

56, 1: *Yonath elem rehoqim*: Hebrew words probably designating the melody to which the psalm was to be sung.

56, 9: *Are my tears not stored in your vial*: a unique saying in the Old Testament. The context suggests that the tears are saved because they are precious; God puts a high value on each of the psalmist's troubles.

Ps 57: Each of the two equal strophes contains a prayer for rescue from enemies, accompanied by joyful trust in God (2-5, 7-11). The refrain prays that God be manifested as saving (6, 12). Ps 108 is nearly identical to part of this psalm (57, 8-12 = 108, 2-6).

57, 1: *Do not destroy*: probably the title of the melody to which the psalm was to be sung.

I

2† Have mercy on me, God,
have mercy on me.
In you I seek shelter.
In the shadow of your wings I seek shelter
till harm pass by.*
3 I call to God Most High,
to God who provides for me.
4 May God send help from heaven to save me,
shame those who trample upon me.
May God send fidelity and love.
Selah
5 I must lie down in the midst of lions
hungry for human prey.*
Their teeth are spears and arrows;
their tongue, a sharpened sword.*
6 Show yourself over the heavens, God;
may your glory appear above all the earth.*

II

7 They have set a trap for my feet;
my soul is bowed down;
They have dug a pit before me.
May they fall into it themselves!*
Selah
8 My heart is steadfast, God,
my heart is steadfast.
I will sing and chant praise.*
9† Awake, my soul;
awake, lyre and harp!
I will wake the dawn.*
10 I will praise you among the peoples, Lord;
I will chant your praise among the nations.*
11 For your love towers to the heavens;
your faithfulness, to the skies.*
12 Show yourself over the heavens, God;
may your glory appear above all the earth.

PSALM 58†

The Dethroning of Unjust Rulers

1† *For the leader. Do not destroy. A* miktam *of David.*

I

2† Do you indeed pronounce justice, O gods;
do you judge mortals fairly?*
3 No, you freely engage in crime;
your hands dispense violence to the earth.

II

4 The wicked have been corrupt since birth;
liars from the womb, they have gone astray.
5† Their poison is like the poison of a snake,
like that of a serpent stopping its ears,*
6 So as not to hear the voice of the charmer
who casts such cunning spells.

III

7 O God, smash the teeth in their mouths;
break the jaw-teeth of these lions, LORD!*
8 Make them vanish like water flowing away;*
trodden down, let them wither like grass.*
9† Let them dissolve like a snail that oozes away,
like an untimely birth that never sees the sun.*
10 Suddenly, like brambles or thistles,
have the whirlwind snatch them away.*
11 Then the just shall rejoice to see the vengeance
and bathe their feet in the blood of the wicked.*
12 Then it will be said:
"Truly there is a reward for the just;

*

2: Pss 17, 8; 36, 8.
5: Pss 17, 11-12; 22, 22; 58, 7. • Pss 11, 2; 64, 4.
6: Ps 72, 19; Nm 14, 21.
7: Pss 7, 15; 140, 5-6.
8: Ps 108, 2.
9: Jb 38, 12.
10: Pss 9, 12; 18, 50.
11: Pss 36, 6; 71, 19.
58, 2: Ps 82, 2; Dt 16, 19.
5: Pss 64, 4; 140, 3; Rom 3, 13.
7: Ps 3, 7.
8: Wis 16, 29. • Ps 37, 2.
9: Jb 3, 16.
10: Jb 21, 18; Hos 13, 3; Na 1, 10.
11: Ps 68, 24; Is 63, 1-6.

†

57, 2: *The shadow of your wings*: probably refers to the wings of the cherubim (powerful winged animals) whose wings spread over the ark in the inner chamber of the temple (1 Kgs 6, 23-28).

57, 9: *I will wake the dawn*: by a bold figure the psalmist imagines the sound of music and singing will waken a new day.

Ps 58: A lament expressing trust in God's power to dethrone all powers obstructing divine rule of the world. First condemned are "the gods," the powers that were popularly imagined to control human destinies (2-3), then "the wicked," the human instruments of these forces (4-6). The psalmist prays God to prevent them from harming the just (7-10). The manifestation of justice will gladden the just; they will see that their God is with them (11-12). The psalm is less concerned with personal vengeance than with public vindication of God's justice now.

58, 1: *Do not destroy*: probably the title of the melody to which the psalm was to be sung.

58, 2: *Gods*: the Bible sometimes understands pagan gods to be lesser divine beings who are assigned by Israel's God to rule the foreign nations. Here they are accused of injustice, permitting the human judges under their patronage to abuse the righteous. Cf Ps 82.

58, 5-6: The image is that of a poisonous snake that is controlled by the voice or piping of its trainer.

58, 9: *A snail that oozes away*: empty shells suggested to ancients that snails melted away as they left a slimy trail.

there is a God who is judge on
earth!"

PSALM 59†

Complaint Against Bloodthirsty Enemies

1† *For the director. Do not destroy. A* miktam *of David, when Saul sent people to watch his house and kill him.**

I

2 Rescue me from my enemies, my God;
lift me out of reach of my foes.
3 Deliver me from evildoers;
from the bloodthirsty save me.
4 They have set an ambush for my life;
the powerful conspire against me.
For no offense or misdeed of mine, LORD,
5 for no fault they hurry to take up arms.
Come near and see my plight!
6 You, LORD of hosts, are the God of Israel!
Awake! Punish all the nations.
Have no mercy on these worthless traitors. *Selah*
7 Each evening they return,
growling like dogs, prowling the city.*
8† Their mouths pour out insult;
sharp words are on their lips.
They say: "Who is there to hear?"
9 You, LORD, laugh at them;
you deride all the nations.*
10 My strength, for you I watch;
you, God, are my fortress, 11 my loving God.

II

May God go before me,
and show me my fallen foes.
12 Slay them, God,
lest they deceive my people.
Shake them by your power;
Lord, our shield, bring them down.
13 For the sinful words of their mouths and lips
let them be caught in their pride.
For the lies they have told under oath*
14 destroy them in anger,
destroy till they are no more.
Then people will know God rules over Jacob,
yes, even to the ends of the earth.* *Selah*
15 Each evening they return,
growling like dogs, prowling the city.
16 They roam about as scavengers;
if they are not filled, they howl.

III

17 But I shall sing of your strength,
extol your love at dawn,
For you are my fortress,
my refuge in time of trouble.
18 My strength, your praise I will sing;
you, God, are my fortress, my loving God.

PSALM 60†

Lament after Defeat in Battle

1 *For the leader; according to "The Lily of. . . ." A* miktam *of David (for teaching),* 2 *when he fought against Aram-Naharaim and Aram-Zobah; and Joab, coming back, killed twelve thousand Edomites in the Valley of Salt.**

I

3 O God, you rejected us, broke our defenses;
you were angry but now revive us.
4 You rocked the earth, split it open;*
repair the cracks for it totters.
5 You made your people go through hardship,
made us stagger from the wine you gave us.*
6 Raise up a flag for those who revere you,
a refuge for them out of bowshot. *Selah*
7† Help with your right hand and answer us
that your loved ones may escape.

*

59, 1: 1 Sm 19, 11.
7: Ps 55, 11.
9: Pss 2, 4; 37, 13; Wis 4, 18.
13: Prv 12, 13; 18, 7.
14: Ps 83, 18-19; Ez 5, 13.
60, 1: 2 Sm 8, 2. 3. 13; 1 Chr 18, 2. 3. 12.
3: Ps 75, 4; Is 24, 19.
5: Ps 75, 9; Is 51, 17. 21-22; Jer 25, 15.

†

Ps 59: A lament in two parts (2-9, 11b-17), each ending in a refrain (10, 18). Both parts alternate prayer for vindication (2-3, 5b-6; 11b-14) with vivid depictions of the psalmist's enemies (4-5a. 7-8. 15-16). The near curse in 12-13 is not a crude desire for revenge but a wish that God's just rule over human affairs be recognized now.

59, 1: *Do not destroy*: probably the title of the melody to which the psalm was to be sung.

59, 8: *Who is there to hear?*: a sample of the enemies' godless reflection. The answer is that God hears their blasphemies.

Ps 60: The community complains that God has let the enemy win the battle (3-5) and asks for an assurance of victory (6-7). In the oracle God affirms ownership of the land; the invasion of other nations is not permanent and will be reversed ultimately (8-10). With renewed confidence, the community resolves to fight again (11). The opening lament is picked up again (12-14), but this time with new awareness of God's power and human limitation.

60, 7-14: These verses occur again as the second half of Ps 108.

II

8† In the sanctuary God promised:
"I will exult, will apportion Shechem;
the valley of Succoth I will measure out.
9† Gilead is mine, mine is Manasseh;
Ephraim is the helmet for my head,
Judah, my own scepter.
10† Moab is my washbowl;
upon Edom I cast my sandal.*
I will triumph over Philistia."

III

11† Who will bring me to the fortified city?
Who will lead me into Edom?
12 Was it not you who rejected us, God?
Do you no longer march with our armies?*
13 Give us aid against the foe;
worthless is human help.
14 We will triumph with the help of God,
who will trample down our foes.

PSALM 61†

Prayer of the King in Time of Danger

1 *For the leader; with stringed instruments. Of David.*

I

2 Hear my cry, O God,
listen to my prayer!
3† From the brink of Sheol I call;
my heart grows faint.
Raise me up, set me on a rock,
4 for you are my refuge,
a tower of strength against the foe.*
5 Then I will ever dwell in your tent,
take refuge in the shelter of your wings.* *Selah*

II

6† O God, when you accept my vows
and hear the plea of those
who revere your name in prayer:
7 "Add to the days of the king's life;
may his years be many generations;*
8 May he reign before God forever;*
may your love and fidelity preserve him"—*
9† Then I will sing your name forever,
fulfill my vows day after day.

PSALM 62†

Trust in God Alone

1† *For the leader;* 'al Jeduthun. *A psalm of David.*

I

2 My soul rests in God alone,*
from whom comes my salvation.
3 God alone is my rock and salvation,
my secure height; I shall never fall.
4 How long will you set upon people,
all of you beating them down,
As though they were a sagging fence
or a battered wall?
5 Even from my place on high
they plot to dislodge me.
They delight in lies;
they bless with their mouths,
but inwardly they curse.* *Selah*

II

6 My soul, be at rest in God alone,
from whom comes my hope.
7 God alone is my rock and my salvation,
my secure height; I shall not fall.
8 My safety and glory are with God,*
my strong rock and refuge.
9 Trust God at all times, my people!
Pour out your hearts to God our refuge! *Selah*

III

10† Mortals are a mere breath,
the powerful but an illusion;*

PSALMS

*

10: Ru 4, 7-8.
12: Ps 44, 10.
61, 4: Ps 46, 2.
5: Pss 17, 8; 36, 8; 57, 2.
7: Ps 21, 5.
8: Pss 72, 5; 89, 5. 30. 37. • Pss 85, 11; 89, 15. 25; Prv 20, 28.
62, 2-3.
6-7: Pss 18, 3; 31, 3-4; 42, 10; 118, 8; 146, 3.
5: Pss 12, 3; 28, 3; 55, 22; Prv 26, 24-25.
8: Ps 3, 3; Is 26, 4; 60, 19.
10: Pss 39, 6-7; 144, 4; Jb 7, 16; Wis 2, 5.

†

60, 8: *I will apportion . . . measure out*: God lays claim to these places. *The valley of Succoth*: probably the lower stretch of the Jabbok valley.

60, 9: *Judah, my own scepter*: an allusion to the Testament of Jacob, Gn 49, 10.

60, 10: *Moab is my washbowl*: Moab borders the Dead Sea, hence a metaphor for the country. *Upon Edom I cast my sandal*: an ancient legal gesture of taking possession of land.

60, 11: *The fortified city*: perhaps Bozrah, the fortified capital of Edom. Cf Is 34, 6; 63, 1; Am 1, 12.

Ps 61: A lament of the king who feels himself at the brink of death (3) and cries out for the strong and saving presence of God (3b-5). The king cites the prayer being made for him (7-8), and promises to give thanks to God.

61, 3: *Brink of Sheol*: literally, "edge of the earth," "earth" being taken in its occasional meaning "the underworld." Cf Jon 2, 3.

61, 6: *In prayer*: added for sense. Vv 7-8 express *the plea* of v 6.

61, 9: *Then*: Hebrew "just as," i.e., in accord with the vows referred to in v 6.

Ps 62: A song of trust displaying serenity from experiencing God's power (the refrains of 2-3 and 6-7) and anger toward unjust enemies (4-5). From the experience of being rescued, the psalmist can teach others to trust in God (10-13).

62, 1: *'Al Jeduthun*: apparently the Hebrew name for the melody.

62, 10: *On a balance they rise*: precious objects were weighed by balancing two pans suspended from a beam. The lighter pan rises.

On a balance they rise;
together they are lighter than air.
11 Do not trust in extortion;
in plunder put no empty hope.
Though wealth increase,
do not set your heart upon it.*
12† One thing God has said;
two things I have heard:*
Power belongs to God;
13 so too, Lord, does kindness,
And you render to each of us
according to our deeds.*

PSALMS

PSALM 63†

Ardent Longing for God

1 *A psalm of David, when he was in the wilderness of Judah.**

I

2 O God, you are my God—
for you I long!
For you my body yearns;
for you my soul thirsts,
Like a land parched, lifeless,
and without water.*
3 So I look to you in the sanctuary
to see your power and glory.
4† For your love is better than life;
my lips offer you worship!

II

5 I will bless you as long as I live;
I will lift up my hands, calling on your name.
6 My soul shall savor the rich banquet of praise,
with joyous lips my mouth shall honor you!
7 When I think of you upon my bed,
through the night watches I will recall
8 That you indeed are my help,
and in the shadow of your wings I shout for joy.*
9 My soul clings fast to you;
your right hand upholds me.

III

10 But those who seek my life will come to ruin;
they shall go down to the depths of the earth!
11 They shall be handed over to the sword
and become the prey of jackals!
12† But the king shall rejoice in God;
all who swear by the Lord shall exult,
for the mouths of liars will be shut!*

PSALM 64†

Treacherous Conspirators Punished by God

1 *For the leader. A psalm of David.*

I

2 O God, hear my anguished voice;
from the foes I dread protect my life.
3 Hide me from the malicious crowd,
the mob of evildoers.
4 They sharpen their tongues like swords,
ready their bows for arrows of poison words.*
5† They shoot at the innocent from ambush,
shoot without risk, catch them unawares.
6 They resolve on their wicked plan;
they conspire to set snares;
they say: "Who will see us?"
7 They devise wicked schemes,
conceal the schemes they devise;
the designs of their hearts are hidden.*

II

8 But God will shoot arrows at them
and strike them unawares.*
9 They will be brought down by their own tongues;
all who see them will shake their heads.*
10 Then all will fear and proclaim God's deed,
pondering what has been done.
11† The just will rejoice and take refuge in the LORD;

*

11: Jb 31, 25; Eccl 5, 9; Jer 17, 11; Mt 6, 19-21. 24.
12: Jb 40, 5.
13: Pss 28, 4; 31, 24; 2 Sm 3, 39; Jb 34, 11; Jer 17, 10; Mt 16, 27; Rom 2, 6; 2 Tm 4, 14.
63, 1: 1 Sm 24.
2: Pss 42, 2; 143, 6; Is 26, 9.
8: Pss 17, 8; 36, 8.
12: Ps 107, 42.
64, 4: Pss 11, 2; 37, 14; 55, 22; 57, 5.
7: Ps 140, 3; Prv 6, 14.
8: Pss 7, 13-14; 38, 3; Dt 32, 42.
9: Pss 5, 11; 44, 14; 52, 6.

†

62, 12: *One thing . . . two things*: parallelism of numbers for the sake of variation, a common device in Semitic poetry. One should not literally add up the numbers. Cf Am 1, 3; Prv 6, 16-19; 30, 15. 18. 21.

Ps 63: A psalm expressing the intimate relationship between God and the worshiper. Separated from God (2), the psalmist longs for the divine life given in the temple (3-6), which is based on a close relationship with God (7-9). May all my enemies be destroyed and God's true worshipers continue in giving praise (10-12)!

63, 4: *For your love is better than life*: only here in the Old Testament is anything prized above life—in this case God's love.

63, 12: *All who swear by the Lord*: to swear by a particular god meant that one was a worshiper of that god (Is 45, 23; 48, 1; Zep 1, 5).

Ps 64: A lament of a person overwhelmed by the malice of the wicked who are depicted in the psalms as the enemies of the righteous (2-7). When people see God bringing upon the wicked the evil they intended against others, they will know who is the true ruler of the world (8-10). The final verse is a vow of praise (11).

64, 5: *Catch them unawares*: literally, "suddenly," i.e., "unexpectedly."

all the upright will glory in their
God.*

PSALM 65†

Thanksgiving for God's Blessings

1 *For the leader. A psalm of David.*
A song.

I

2† To you we owe our hymn of praise,
O God on Zion;
To you our vows must be fulfilled,
3† you who hear our prayers.
To you all flesh must come*
4 with its burden of wicked deeds.
We are overcome by our sins;
only you can pardon them.*
5 Happy the chosen ones you bring
to dwell in your courts.
May we be filled with the good things
of your house,
the blessings of your holy temple!

II

6† You answer us with awesome deeds
of justice,
O God our savior,
The hope of all the ends of the earth
and of far distant islands.*
7 You are robed in power,
you set up the mountains by your
might.
8 You still the roaring of the seas,*
the roaring of their waves,
the tumult of the peoples.*
9 Distant peoples stand in awe of your
marvels;
east and west you make resound
with joy.
10†† You visit the earth and water it,
make it abundantly fertile.*
God's stream is filled with water;
with it you supply the world with
grain.
Thus do you prepare the earth:
11 you drench plowed furrows,
and level their ridges.
With showers you keep the ground
soft,
blessing its young sprouts.
12† You adorn the year with your
bounty;
your paths drip with fruitful rain.
13 The untilled meadows also drip;
the hills are robed with joy.
14 The pastures are clothed with flocks,
the valleys blanketed with grain;
they cheer and sing for joy.*

PSALM 66†

Praise of God, Israel's Deliverer

1 *For the leader. A song; a psalm.*

I

Shout joyfully to God, all you on
earth;
2 sing of his glorious name;
give him glorious praise.*
3 Say to God: "How awesome your
deeds!
Before your great strength your
enemies cringe.
4 All on earth fall in worship before
you;*
they sing of you, sing of your
name!" *Selah*

II

5† Come and see the works of God,
awesome in the deeds done for us.
6 He changed the sea to dry land;
through the river they passed on
foot.*
Therefore let us rejoice in him,
7 who rules by might forever,
Whose eyes are fixed upon the na-
tions.
Let no rebel rise to challenge!
Selah
8 Bless our God, you peoples;
loudly sound his praise,
9 Who has kept us alive
and not allowed our feet to slip.*
10 You tested us, O God,
tried us as silver tried by fire.*
11 You led us into a snare;

PSALMS

*

11: Pss 36, 8; 57, 2.
65, 3: Is 66, 23.
4: Pss 32, 1-2; 78, 38; Is 1, 18.
6: Is 66, 19.
8: Pss 89, 10; 107, 29; Jb 38, 11; Mt 8, 26. • Is 17, 12.
10: Lv 26, 4; Is 30, 23. 25; Jl 2, 22-23.
14: Is 44, 23.
66, 2: Ps 65, 14; Is 44, 23.
3-4: Ps 18, 45; Mi 7, 17.
6: Pss 74, 15; 114, 3; Ex 14, 21f; Jos 3, 14ff; Is 44, 27; 50, 2.
9: Pss 91, 12; 121, 3; 1 Sm 2, 9; Prv 3, 23.
10: Is 48, 10.

†

Ps 65: The community, aware of its unworthiness (3-4), gives thanks for divine bounty (5), a bounty resulting from God's creation victory (6-9). At God's touch the earth comes alive with vegetation and flocks (10-14).

65, 2: *Vows*: the Israelites were accustomed to promising sacrifices in the temple if their prayers were heard.

65, 3: *To you all flesh must come*: all must have recourse to God's mercy.

65, 6: *Awesome deeds*: the acts of creating—installing mountains, taming seas, restraining nations (7-8)—that are visible worldwide (6. 9).

65, 10-14: Apparently a description of the agricultural year, beginning with the first fall rains that soften the hard sun-baked soil (10-11).

65, 10: *God's stream*: the fertile waters of the earth derive from God's fertile waters in the heavenly world.

65, 12: *Paths*: probably the tracks of God's storm chariot dropping rain upon earth.

Ps 66: In the first part (1-12), the community praises God for powerful acts for Israel, both in the past (the exodus from Egypt and the entry into the land [6]) and in the present (deliverance from a recent but unspecified calamity [8-12]). In the second part (13-20), an individual from the rescued community fulfills a vow to offer a sacrifice of thanksgiving. As often in thanksgivings, the rescued person steps forward to teach the community what God has done (16-20).

66, 5-6: Cf the events described in Ex 14, 1-15, 21; Jos 3, 11-4, 24, and Ps 114.

you bound us at the waist as captives.
12† You let captors set foot on our neck;
we went through fire and water;
then you led us out to freedom.*

III
13† I will bring holocausts to your house;
to you I will fulfill my vows,
14 The vows my lips pronounced
and my mouth spoke in distress.
15 Holocausts of fatlings I will offer you
and burnt offerings of rams;
I will sacrifice oxen and goats.
Selah
16 Come and hear, all you who fear God,
while I recount what has been done for me.
17 I called to the Lord with my mouth;
praise was upon my tongue.
18 Had I cherished evil in my heart,
the Lord would not have heard.
19 But God did hear
and listened to my voice in prayer.
20 Blessed be God, who did not refuse me
the kindness I sought in prayer.

PSALM 67†

Harvest Thanks and Petition

1 *For the leader; with stringed instruments. A psalm; a song.*

I
2† May God be gracious to us and bless us;
may God's face shine upon us.*
Selah
3 So shall your rule be known upon the earth,
your saving power among all the nations.*
4 May the peoples praise you, God;
may all the peoples praise you!

II
5 May the nations be glad and shout for joy;
for you govern the peoples justly,
you guide the nations upon the earth.*
Selah
6 May the peoples praise you, God;
may all the peoples praise you!

III
7 The earth has yielded its harvest;
God, our God, blesses us.*
8 May God bless us still;
that the ends of the earth may revere our God.

PSALM 68†

The Exodus and Conquest, Pledge of Future Help

1 *For the leader. A psalm of David; a song.*

I
2† God will arise for battle;
the enemy will be scattered;
those who hate God will flee.*
3 The wind will disperse them like smoke;
as wax is melted by fire,
so the wicked will perish before God.*
4 Then the just will be glad;
they will rejoice before God;
they will celebrate with great joy.

II
5† Sing to God, praise the divine name;
exalt the rider of the clouds.

*

12: Is 43, 2.
67, 2: Pss 4, 7; 31, 17; 44, 4; 80, 4; Dn 9, 17.
3: Jer 33, 9.
5: Ps 98, 9.
7: Ps 85, 13; Lv 26, 4; Ez 34, 27; Hos 2, 23-24.
68, 2: Nm 10, 35.
3: Ps 97, 5; Jdt 16, 15; Wis 5, 14; Mi 1, 4.

†

66, 12: *You let captors set foot on our neck*: literally, "you let men mount our head." Conquerors placed their feet on the neck of their enemies as a sign of complete defeat. Cf Jos 10, 24. A ceremonial footstool of the Egyptian king Tutankhamen portrays bound and prostrate bodies of enemies ready for the king's feet on their heads, and one of Tutankhamen's ceremonial chariots depicts the king as a sphinx standing with paw atop the neck of an enemy.

66, 13: *Holocausts*: wholly burnt offerings. Cf Lv 1, 3-13; 6, 1-4; 22, 17-20.

Ps 67: A petition for a bountiful harvest (7), made in the awareness that Israel's prosperity will persuade the nations to worship its God.

67, 2: *May God be gracious to us*: the people's petition echoes the blessing pronounced upon them by the priests. Cf Nm 6, 22-27.

Ps 68: The psalm is extremely difficult because the Hebrew text is badly preserved and the ceremony that it describes is uncertain. The translation assumes the psalm accompanied the early autumn Feast of Tabernacles (Sukkoth), which included a procession of the tribes (25-28). Israel was being oppressed by a foreign power, perhaps Egypt (31-32)—unless Egypt stands for any oppressor. The psalm may have been composed from segments of ancient poems, which would explain why the transitions are implied rather than explicitly stated. At any rate, v 2 is based on Nm 10, 35-36, and vv 8-9 are derived from Jgs 5, 4-5.

The argument develops in nine stanzas (each of three to five poetic lines): 1. confidence that God will destroy Israel's enemies (2-4); 2. call to praise God as savior (5-7); 3. God's initial rescue of Israel from Egypt (8), the Sinai encounter (9), and the settlement in Canaan (10-11); 4. the defeat of the Canaanite kings (12-15); 5. the taking of Jerusalem, where Israel's God will rule the world (16-19); 6. praise for God's past help and for the future interventions that will be modeled on the ancient exodus-conquest (20-24); 7. procession at the Feast of Tabernacles (25-28); 8. prayer that the defeated enemies bring tribute to the temple (29-32); 9. invitation for all kingdoms to praise Israel's God (33-36).

68, 2: The opening line alluding to Nm 10, 35 makes clear that God's assistance in the period of the exodus and conquest is the model and assurance of all future divine help.

68, 5: *Exalt the rider of the clouds*: God's intervention is in the imagery of Canaanite myth in which the storm-god

Rejoice before this God
whose name is the LORD.*
6 Father of the fatherless, defender of widows*—
this is the God whose abode is holy,
7† Who gives a home to the forsaken,
who leads prisoners out to prosperity,
while rebels live in the desert.

III

8 God, when you went forth before your people,*
when you marched through the desert, *Selah*
9 The earth quaked, the heavens shook,
before God, the One of Sinai,
before God, the God of Israel.
10-11 You claimed a land as your own, O God;
your people settled there.
There you poured abundant rains, God,
graciously given to the poor in their need.

IV

12a †The Lord announced the news of victory:
13a "The kings and their armies are in desperate flight.*
12b All you people so numerous,
14a will you stay by the sheepfolds?*
13b Every household will share the booty,
14b perhaps a dove sheathed with silver,
14c its wings covered with yellow gold."
15† When the Almighty routed the kings there,
the spoils were scattered like snow on Zalmon.

V

16 You high mountains of Bashan,
you rugged mountains of Bashan,
17† You rugged mountains, why look with envy
at the mountain where God has chosen to dwell,
where the LORD resides forever?*
18 God's chariots were myriad, thousands upon thousands;
from Sinai the Lord entered the holy place.
19 You went up to its lofty height;
you took captives, received slaves as tribute.*
No rebels can live in the presence of God.

VI

20 Blessed be the Lord day by day,
God, our salvation, who carries us.* *Selah*
21 Our God is a God who saves;
escape from death is in the LORD God's hands.
22 God will crush the skulls of the enemy,
the hairy heads of those who walk in sin.*
23† The Lord has said:
"Even from Bashan I will fetch them,
fetch them even from the depths of the sea.
24 You will wash your feet in your enemy's blood;
the tongues of your dogs will lap it up."*

VII

25† Your procession comes into view, O God,
your procession into the holy place, my God and king.
26 The singers go first, the harpists follow;
in their midst girls sound the timbrels.*
27 In your choirs, bless God;
bless the LORD, you from Israel's assemblies.
28 In the lead is Benjamin, few in number;
there the princes of Judah, a large throng,
the princes of Zebulun, the princes of Naphtali, too.*

---

* 5: Pss 18, 10; 104, 3; Dt 33, 26; Is 19, 1.
6-7: Pss 103, 6; 146, 7. 9; Ex 22, 20-22; Bar 6, 37.
8-9: Pss 44, 10; 114, 4. 7; Jgs 5, 4-5; Heb 12, 26.
13a: Jgs 5, 19. 22.
14a: Jgs 5, 16.
17: Ps 132, 13-14; Ez 43, 7.
19: Ps 47, 8; Eph 4, 8-10.
20: Pss 34, 2; 145, 2; Is 46, 3-4; 63, 9.
22: Dt 32, 42.
24: Pss 58, 11; 1 Kgs 21, 19; 22, 38; Is 63, 1-6.
26: Pss 81, 2-3; 87, 7; 149, 3; 150, 3-5; 2 Sm 6, 5.
28: Is 8, 23.

---

† mounted the storm clouds to ride to battle. Such theophanies occur throughout the psalm: 2-3. 8-10. 12-15. 18-19. 22-24. 29-32. 34-35. See Dt 33, 26; Ps 18, 8-16; Is 19, 1.

68, 7: *While rebels live in the desert*: rebels must live in the arid desert, whereas God's people will live in the well-watered land (vv 8-11).

68, 12-15: The Hebrew text upon which the translation is based has apparently suffered dislocation and has been substantially rearranged for sense. The version of the defeat of the kings differs from that in the book of Joshua, where the people play a significant role. Here God alone is responsible for the victory (though the actual battle is not described); Israel only gathers the spoils. God alone is the source of Israel's success; human effort is not important.

68, 15: *Zalmon*: generally taken as the name of a mountain where snow is visible in winter, perhaps to be located in the Golan Heights or in the mountains of Bashan or Hauran east of the Sea of Galilee.

68, 17: *The mountain*: Mount Zion, the site of the temple.

68, 23: *Even from Bashan . . . from the depths of the sea*: the heights and the depths, the farthest places where enemies might flee.

68, 25-28: *Your procession*: the procession renews God's original taking up of residence on Zion, described in 16-19.

VIII

29 Summon again, O God, your power,
the divine power you once showed for us.
30 Show it from your temple on behalf of Jerusalem,
that kings may bring you tribute.
31†† Roar at the wild beast of the reeds,
the herd of mighty bulls, the lords of nations;
scatter the nations that delight in war.
32 Exact rich tribute from lower Egypt,*
from upper Egypt, gold and silver;
make Ethiopia extend its hands to God.*

IX

33 You kingdoms of the earth, sing to God;*
chant the praises of the Lord, *Selah*
34 Who rides the heights of the ancient heavens,
whose voice is thunder, mighty thunder.
35 Confess the power of God,
whose majesty protects Israel,
whose power is in the sky.
36 Awesome is God in his holy place,
the God of Israel,
who gives power and strength to his people.*
Blessed be God!

PSALM 69†

A Cry of Anguish in Great Distress

1† *For the leader; according to "Lilies." Of David.*

I

2† Save me, God,
for the waters have reached my neck.*
3 I have sunk into the mire of the deep,
where there is no foothold.
I have gone down to the watery depths;
the flood overwhelms me.*
4 I am weary with crying out;
my throat is parched.
My eyes have failed,
looking for my God.*
5† More numerous than the hairs of my head
are those who hate me without cause.*
Too many for my strength
are my treacherous enemies.
Must I now restore
what I did not steal?

II

6 God, you know my folly;
my faults are not hidden from you.
7 Let those who wait for you, LORD of hosts,
not be shamed through me.
Let those who seek you, God of Israel,*
not be disgraced through me
8 For your sake I bear insult,
shame covers my face.*
9 I have become an outcast to my kin,
a stranger to my mother's children.*
10† Because zeal for your house consumes me,
I am scorned by those who scorn you.*
11 I have wept and fasted,*
but this led only to scorn.
12 I clothed myself in sackcloth;
I became a byword for them.
13 They who sit at the gate gossip about me;
drunkards make me the butt of their songs.

III

14 But I pray to you, LORD,
for the time of your favor.

*

32: Ez 29, 2ff, • Is 18, 7; 45, 14.
33: Ps 138, 4.
36: Pss 28, 8; 29, 11.
69, 2: Pss 18, 5; 93, 3-4; Jb 22, 11.
3: Pss 40, 2; 124, 4-5.
4: Pss 25, 15; 119, 82; 123, 2; 141, 8; Is 38, 14.
5: Ps 40, 13; Lam 3, 52; Jn 15, 25.
7: Ps 40, 17.
8: Jer 15, 15.
9: Jb 19, 13-15.
10: Ps 119, 139; Jn 2, 17; Rom 15, 3.
11-13: Ps 109, 24-25; Jb 30, 9; Lam 3, 14.

†

68, 31: *The wild beast of the reeds*: probably the Nile crocodile, a symbol for Egypt; see 32 and Ez 29, 2-5.

68, 31-32: *Lower Egypt* is the delta area north of Cairo. *Upper Egypt* is the Nile Valley from Cairo to Aswan. *Ethiopia* is still further south.

Ps 69: A lament complaining of suffering in language both metaphorical (2-3 and 15-16, the waters of chaos) and literal (4. 5. 9. 11-13, exhaustion, alienation from family and community, false accusation). In the second part the psalmist prays with special emphasis that the enemies be punished for all to see (23-29). Despite the pain, the psalmist does not lose hope that all be set right, and promises public praise (30-37). The psalm, which depicts the suffering of the innocent just person vividly, is cited often by the New Testament especially in the passion accounts, e.g., v 5 in Jn 15, 25; v 22 in Mk 15, 23. 36 and parallels and in Jn 19, 29. The psalm prays not so much for personal vengeance as for public vindication of God's justice. There was, at this time, no belief in an afterlife where such vindication could take place. Redress had to take place now, in the sight of all.

69, 1: *"Lilies"*: apparently the name of the melody.

69, 2: *Waters*: the waters of chaos from which God created the world are a common metaphor for extreme distress. Cf Pss 18, 5; 42, 8; 88, 8; Jon 2, 3-6.

69, 5: *What I did not steal*: the psalmist, falsely accused of theft, is being forced to make restitution.

69, 10: *Zeal for your house consumes me*: the psalmist's commitment to God's cause brings only opposition. Cf Jn 2, 17. *I am scorned by those who scorn you*: Rom 15, 3 uses the verse as an example of Jesus' unselfishness.

God, in your great kindness answer me
with your constant help.*
15 Rescue me from the mire;*
do not let me sink.
Rescue me from my enemies
and from the watery depths.
16 Do not let the floodwaters overwhelm me,
nor the deep swallow me,
nor the mouth of the pit close over me.
17 Answer me, LORD, in your generous love;
in your great mercy turn to me.
18 Do not hide your face from your servant;
in my distress hasten to answer me.*
19 Come and ransom my life;
because of my enemies redeem me.
20 You know my reproach, my shame, my disgrace;
before you stand all my foes.
21 Insult has broken my heart, and I am weak;
I looked for compassion, but there was none,
for comforters, but found none.*
22 Instead they put gall in my food;
for my thirst they gave me vinegar.*

IV

23 Make their own table a snare for them,
a trap for their friends.*
24 Make their eyes so dim they cannot see;
keep their backs ever feeble.
25 Pour out your wrath upon them;
let the fury of your anger overtake them.
26 Make their camp desolate,
with none to dwell in their tents.*
27 For they pursued the one you struck,
added to the pain of the one you wounded.
28 Add that to their crimes;
let them not attain to your reward.
29 Strike them from the book of the living;
do not count them among the just!*

V

30 But I am afflicted and in pain;
let your saving help protect me, God,
31† That I may praise God's name in song
and glorify it with thanksgiving.
32 My song will please the LORD more than oxen,
more than bullocks with horns and hooves:*
33 "See, you lowly ones, and be glad;
you who seek God, take heart!*
34 For the LORD hears the poor,
does not spurn those in bondage.
35 Let the heavens and the earth sing praise,
the seas and whatever moves in them!"

VI

36 God will rescue Zion,
rebuild the cities of Judah.*
God's servants shall dwell in the land and possess it;
37 it shall be the heritage of their descendants;
those who love God's name shall dwell there.*

PSALM 70†

Prayer for Divine Help

1 *For the leader; of David. For remembrance.*

2 Graciously rescue me, God!*
Come quickly to help me, LORD!*
3 Confound and put to shame
those who seek my life.*
Turn back in disgrace
those who desire my ruin.
4 Let those who say "Aha!"*
turn back in their shame.
5 But may all who seek you
rejoice and be glad in you.
May those who long for your help
always say, "God be glorified!"*
6 Here I am, afflicted and poor.
God, come quickly!
You are my help and deliverer.
LORD, do not delay!

---

* 14: Is 49, 8.
15-16: Pss 28, 1; 30, 4; 32, 6; 40, 3; 88, 5; Prv 1, 12.
18: Pss 102, 3; 143, 7.
21: Lam 1, 2.
22: Lam 3, 15; Mt 27, 34. 48; Mk 15, 23.
23: Rom 11, 9-10.
26: Acts 1, 20.
29: Ps 139, 16; Ex 32, 32; Is 4, 3; Dn 12, 1; Mal 3, 16; Rv 3, 5.
32: Pss 40, 7; 50, 8-9. 14; 51, 18; Is 1, 11-15; Hos 6, 6; Am 5, 21-22; Heb 10, 5-8.
33: Pss 22, 27; 35, 27; 70, 5.
36: Is 44, 26; Ez 36, 10.
37: Ps 102, 29; Is 65, 9.
70, 2-6: Ps 40, 14-18.
2: Ps 71, 12.
3: Ps 35, 4. 26.
4: Ps 35, 21. 25.
5: Ps 35, 27.

---

† 69, 31: *That I may praise God's name in song*: the actual song is cited in 33-35, the word "praise" in 35 referring back to "praise" in 31.

Ps 70: A lament of a poor and afflicted person (6) who has no resource except God, and who cries out to be saved from the enemy. The psalm is almost identical to Ps 40, 14-18.

PSALM 71†
Prayer in Time of Old Age

I

1 In you, LORD, I take refuge;*
let me never be put to shame.*
2 In your justice rescue and deliver me;
listen to me and save me!
3 Be my rock and refuge,
my secure stronghold;
for you are my rock and fortress.*
4 My God, rescue me from the power of the wicked,
from the clutches of the violent.*
5 You are my hope, Lord;
my trust, GOD, from my youth.
6 On you I depend since birth;
from my mother's womb you are my strength;*
my hope in you never wavers.
7† I have become a portent to many,
but you are my strong refuge!
8 My mouth shall be filled with your praise,
shall sing your glory every day.

II

9 Do not cast me aside in my old age;
as my strength fails, do not forsake me.
10 For my enemies speak against me;
they watch and plot against me.*
11 They say, "God has abandoned that one
Pursue, seize the wretch!
No one will come to the rescue!"
12 God, do not stand far from me;
my God, hasten to help me.*
13 Bring to a shameful end
those who attack me;
Cover with contempt and scorn
those who seek my ruin.*
14 I will always hope in you
and add to all your praise.
15 My mouth shall proclaim your just deeds,
day after day your acts of deliverance,
though I cannot number them all.*
16 I will speak of the mighty works of the Lord;
O GOD, I will tell of your singular justice.

III

17 God, you have taught me from my youth;
to this day I proclaim your wondrous deeds.
18 Now that I am old and gray,*
do not forsake me, God,
That I may proclaim your might
to all generations yet to come,*
Your power
19 and justice, God,
to the highest heaven.
You have done great things;*
O God, who is your equal?*
20 You have sent me many bitter afflictions,
but once more revive me.
From the watery depths of the earth
once more raise me up.
21 Restore my honor;
turn and comfort me,
22 That I may praise you with the lyre
for your faithfulness, my God,
And sing to you with the harp,
O Holy One of Israel!
23 My lips will shout for joy as I sing your praise;
my soul, too, which you have redeemed.
24 Yes, my tongue shall recount
your justice day by day.
For those who sought my ruin
will have been shamed and disgraced.

PSALM 72†
A Prayer for the King

1† *Of Solomon.*

I

O God, give your judgment to the king;
your justice to the son of kings;*
2 That he may govern your people with justice,
your oppressed with right judgment,*
3 That the mountains may yield their bounty for the people,
and the hills great abundance,*

* 71, 1-3: Ps 31, 2-4. 1: Ps 25, 2. 3: Ps 18, 3. 4: Ps 140, 2. 6: Ps 22, 11. 10: Pss 3, 2; 22, 8. 12: Ps 22, 20. 13: Pss 35, 4; 40, 15; 70, 3. 15: Ps 35, 28. 18: Is 46, 3-4. • Pss 22, 31-32; 48, 14-15; 145, 4. 19: Ps 72, 18. • Ps 86, 8. 72, 1: Ps 99, 4; Jer 23, 5. 2: Prv 31, 8-9. 3: Is 52, 7; 55, 12.

† Ps 71: A lament of an old person (9. 18) whose afflictions are interpreted by enemies as a divine judgment (11). The first part of the psalm pleads for help (1-4) on the basis of a hope learned from a lifetime's experience of God; the second part describes the menace (9-13) yet remains buoyant (14-16); the third develops the theme of hope and praise.

71, 7: *A portent to many*: the afflictions of the sufferer are taken as a manifestation of God's anger. Cf Dt 28, 46; Ps 31, 12.

Ps 72: A royal psalm in which the Israelite king, as the representative of God, is the instrument of divine justice (1-4. 12-14) and blessing (5-7. 15-17) for the whole world. The king is human, giving only what he has received from God. Hence intercession must be made for him. The extravagant language is typical of oriental royal courts.

72, 1: *The king . . . the son of kings*: the crown prince is the king's son; the prayer envisages the dynasty.

4 That he may defend the oppressed among the people,
save the poor and crush the oppressor.

II

5 May he live as long as the sun endures,
like the moon, through all generations.*
6 May he be like rain coming down upon the fields,
like showers watering the earth,*
7 That abundance may flourish in his days,
great bounty, till the moon be no more.

III

8† May he rule from sea to sea,
from the river to the ends of the earth.*
9 May his foes kneel before him,
his enemies lick the dust.*
10† May the kings of Tarshish and the islands bring tribute,
the kings of Arabia and Seba offer gifts.*
11 May all kings bow before him,
all nations serve him.*
12 For he rescues the poor when they cry out,
the oppressed who have no one to help.
13 He shows pity to the needy and the poor*
and saves the lives of the poor.
14† From extortion and violence he frees them,
for precious is their blood in his sight.

IV

15 Long may he live, receiving gold from Arabia,
prayed for without cease, blessed day by day.
16† May wheat abound in the land,
flourish even on the mountain heights.
May his fruit increase like Lebanon's,
his wheat like the grasses of the land.*
17† May his name be blessed forever;
as long as the sun, may his name endure.*
May the tribes of the earth give blessings with his name;
may all the nations regard him as favored.*

* * *

18† Blessed be the LORD, the God of Israel,
who alone does wonderful deeds.*
19 Blessed be his glorious name forever;
may all the earth be filled with the LORD's glory.*
Amen and amen.
20 The end of the psalms of David, son of Jesse.

THIRD BOOK—Psalms 73-89

PSALM 73†

The Trial of the Just

1 *A psalm of Asaph.*

How good God is to the upright,
the Lord, to those who are clean of heart!

I

2 But, as for me, I lost my balance;
my feet all but slipped,
3 Because I was envious of the arrogant
when I saw the prosperity of the wicked.*
4 For they suffer no pain;
their bodies are healthy and sleek.
5 They are free of the burdens of life;
they are not afflicted like others.

PSALMS

*

5: Ps 89, 37-38; Jer 31, 35.
6: Dt 32, 2; Is 45, 8; Hos 6, 3.
8: Dt 11, 24; Zec 9, 10.
9: Is 49, 23; Mi 7, 17.
10: Ps 68, 30; Is 60, 5-6; 1 Kgs 10, 1ff.
11: Pss 47, 8.
13: Prv 31, 9.
16: Is 27, 6; Hos 14, 6-8; Am 9, 13.
17: Ps 21, 7. • Gn 12, 3; Zec 8, 13.
18: Pss 41, 14; 89, 53; 106, 48; 136, 4.
19: Ps 57, 5; Nm 14, 21.
73, 3: Ps 37, 1; Jb 21, 13.

†

72, 8: *From sea to sea . . . the ends of the earth*: the boundaries of the civilized world known at the time: from the Mediterranean Sea (the western sea) to the Persian Gulf (the eastern sea), and from the Euphrates (the river) to the islands and lands of southwestern Europe, "the ends of the earth." The words may also have a mythic nuance—the earth surrounded by cosmic waters, hence everywhere.

72, 10: *Tarshish and the islands*: the far west (Ps 48, 6); *Arabia and Seba*: the far south (1 Kgs 10, 1).

72, 14: *Their blood*: cf Ps 116, 15.

72, 16: The translation of the difficult Hebrew is tentative.

72, 17: *May the tribes of the earth give blessing with his name*: an echo of the promise to the ancestors (Gn 12, 3; 26, 4; 28, 14), suggesting that the monarchy in Israel fulfilled the promise to Abraham, Isaac, and Jacob.

72, 18-19: A doxology marking the end of Book II of the Psalter.

Ps 73: The opening verse of this probing poem (cf Pss 37, 49) is actually the psalmist's hard-won conclusion from personal experience: God is just and good! The psalmist describes near loss of faith (2-3), occasioned by observing the wicked who blasphemed God with seeming impunity (4-12). Feeling abandoned despite personal righteousness, the psalmist could not bear the injustice until an experience of God's nearness in the temple made clear how deluded the wicked were. Their sudden destruction shows their impermanence (13-20). The just can thus be confident, for, as the psalmist now knows, their security is from God (1. 23-28).

6 Thus pride adorns them as a necklace;
violence clothes them as a robe.
7 Out of their stupidity comes sin;
evil thoughts flood their hearts.*
8 They scoff and spout their malice;
from on high they utter threats.*
9† They set their mouths against the heavens,
their tongues roam the earth.
10† So my people turn to them
and drink deeply of their words.
11 They say, "Does God really know?"
"Does the Most High have any knowledge?"*
12 Such, then, are the wicked,
always carefree, increasing their wealth.

II

13 Is it in vain that I have kept my heart clean,
washed my hands in innocence?*
14 For I am afflicted day after day,
chastised every morning.
15 Had I thought, "I will speak as they do,"
I would have betrayed your people.
16 Though I tried to understand all this,
it was too difficult for me,
17† Till I entered the sanctuary of God
and came to understand their end.

III

18 You set them, indeed, on a slippery road;
you hurl them down to ruin.
19 How suddenly they are devastated;
undone by disasters forever!
20 They are like a dream after waking, Lord,
dismissed like shadows when you arise.*

IV

21 Since my heart was embittered
and my soul deeply wounded,
22 I was stupid and could not understand;
I was like a brute beast in your presence.
23 Yet I am always with you;
you take hold of my right hand.*
24† With your counsel you guide me,
and at the end receive me with honor.
25 Whom else have I in the heavens?
None beside you delights me on earth.
26 Though my flesh and my heart fail,
God is the rock of my heart, my portion forever.
27 But those who are far from you perish;
you destroy those unfaithful to you.
28 As for me, to be near God is my good,
to make the Lord GOD my refuge.
I shall declare all your works
in the gates of daughter Zion.

PSALM 74†

Prayer at the Destruction of the Temple

1† *A maskil of Asaph.*

I

Why, God, have you cast us off forever?*
Why does your anger burn against the sheep of your pasture?*
2 Remember your flock that you gathered of old,
the tribe you redeemed as your very own.
Remember Mount Zion where you dwell.*
3 Turn your steps toward the utter ruins,
toward the sanctuary devastated by the enemy.
4 Your foes roared triumphantly in your shrine;
they set up their own tokens of victory.

*

7: Jb 15, 27.
8: Ps 17, 10.
11: Ps 10, 11; Jb 22, 13.
13: Ps 26, 6; Mal 3, 14.
20: Jb 20, 8.
23: Ps 121, 5.
74, 1: Pss 10, 1; 44, 24; 77, 8. • Ps 80, 5.
2: Pss 68, 17; 132, 13; Ex 15, 17; Jer 10, 16; 51, 19.

†

73, 9: *They set their mouths against the heavens*: in an image probably derived from mythic stories of half-divine giants, the monstrous speech of the wicked is likened to enormous jaws gaping wide, devouring everything in sight.

73, 10: The Hebrew is obscure.

73, 17: *And came to understand their end*: the psalmist receives a double revelation in the temple: 1) the end of the wicked comes unexpectedly (18-20); 2) God is with me.

73, 24: *And at the end receive me with honor*: a perhaps deliberately enigmatic verse. It is understood by some commentators as reception into heavenly glory, hence the traditional translation, "receive me into glory." The Hebrew verb can indeed refer to mysterious divine elevation of a righteous person into God's domain: Enoch in Gn 5, 24; Elijah in 2 Kgs 2, 11- 12; the righteous psalmist in Ps 49, 16. Personal resurrection in the Old Testament, however, is clearly attested only in the second century B.C. The verse is perhaps best left unspecified as a reference to God's nearness and protection.

Ps 74: A communal lament sung when the enemy invaded the temple; it would be especially appropriate at the destruction of Jerusalem in 587 B.C. Israel's God is urged to look upon the ruined sanctuary and remember the congregation who worshiped there (1-11). People and sanctuary are bound together; an attack on Zion is an attack on Israel. In the second half of the poem, the community brings before God the story of their origins—their creation (12-17)—in order to move God to reenact that deed of creation now. Will God allow a lesser power to destroy the divine project (18-23)?

74, 1: *Forever*: the word implies that the disaster is already of long duration. Cf 74, 9 and note.

5 They hacked away like foresters gathering boughs,
swinging their axes in a thicket of trees.
6 They smashed all your engraved work,
pounded it with hammer and pick.
7 They set your sanctuary on fire;
the abode of your name they razed and profaned.*
8 They said in their hearts, "Destroy them all!
Burn all the shrines of God in the land!"
9† Now we see no signs,
we have no prophets,*
no one who knows how long.
10 How long, O God, shall the enemy jeer?*
Shall the foe revile your name forever?
11 Why draw back your right hand,
why keep it idle beneath your cloak?

II

12† Yet you, God, are my king from of old,
winning victories throughout the earth.
13 You stirred up the sea in your might;*
you smashed the heads of the dragons on the waters.*
14 You crushed the heads of Leviathan,*
tossed him for food to the sharks.
15 You opened up springs and torrents,
brought dry land out of the primeval waters.
16 Yours the day and yours the night;
you set the moon and sun in place.
17 You fixed all the limits of the earth;
summer and winter you made.*
18 Remember how the enemy has jeered, O LORD,
how a foolish people has reviled your name.
19 Do not surrender to beasts those who praise you;
do not forget forever the life of your afflicted.
20 Look to your covenant,
for the land is filled with gloom;
the pastures, with violence.
21 Let not the oppressed turn back in shame;
may the poor and needy praise your name.
22 Arise, God, defend your cause;
remember the constant jeers of the fools.
23 Do not ignore the clamor of your foes,
the unceasing uproar of your enemies.

PSALM 75†

God the Judge of the World

1 *For the leader. Do not destroy! A psalm of Asaph; a song.*

I

2† We thank you, God, we give thanks;
we call upon your name,
declare your wonderful deeds.
You said:
3 "I will choose the time;
I will judge fairly.
4 The earth and all its inhabitants will quake,
but I have firmly set its pillars."*
Selah

II

5† So I say to the boastful: "Do not boast!"*
to the wicked: "Do not raise your horns!
6 Do not raise your horns against heaven!
Do not speak arrogantly against the Rock!"*
7 For judgment comes not from east or from west,
not from the desert or from the mountains,*
8 But from God who decides,
who brings some low and raises others high.*

PSALMS

*

7: Is 64, 10; Ps 79, 1.
9: Lam 2, 9.
10: Ps 89, 47.
13: Ps 89, 10. • Is 51, 9-10.
14: Jb 3, 8; 40, 25; Is 27, 1.
16-17: Gn 1.
75, 4: Pss 46, 3; 60, 4; 93, 1; 96, 10; 104, 5; 1 Sm 2, 8; Is 24, 19.
5: 1 Sm 2, 3; Zec 2, 1-4.
6: Jb 15, 25.
7: Mt 24, 23-27.
8: Jb 5, 11; 1 Sm 2, 7.

†

74, 9: *Now we see no signs*: ancients often asked prophets to say for how long a divine punishment was to last. Cf 2 Sm 24, 13. Here no prophet has arisen to indicate the duration.

74, 12-17: Comparable Canaanite literature describes the storm-god's victory over all-encompassing Sea and its allies (dragons and Leviathan) and the subsequent peaceful arrangement of the universe, sometimes through the placement of paired cosmic elements (day and night, sun and moon). Cf Ps 89, 12-13. The psalm apparently equates the enemies attacking the temple with the destructive cosmic forces already tamed by God. Why then are those forces now raging untamed against your own people?

Ps 75: The psalmist gives thanks and rejoices (2. 10) for the direct intervention of God, which is promised in two oracles (3-4. 11). Expecting that divine intervention, the psalmist warns evildoers to repent (5-9).

75, 2: *You said*: supplied for clarity here and in v 11. The translation assumes in both places that the psalmist is citing an oracle of God.

75, 5: *Do not raise your horns!*: the horn is the symbol of strength; to raise one's horn is to exalt one's own power as v 6 explains.

9† Yes, a cup is in the LORD's hand,
foaming wine, fully spiced.
When God pours it out,
they will drain it even to the dregs;
all the wicked of the earth must drink.*
10 But I will rejoice forever;
I will sing praise to the God of Jacob,
11 Who has said:
"I will break off all the horns of the wicked,
but the horns of the just shall be lifted up."*

PSALM 76†

God Defends Zion

1 *For the leader; a psalm with stringed instruments. A song of Asaph.*

I

2 Renowned in Judah is God,*
whose name is great in Israel.
3† On Salem is God's tent, a shelter on Zion.
4 There the flashing arrows were shattered,
shield, sword, and weapons of war.* *Selah*

II

5† Terrible and awesome are you,
stronger than the ancient mountains.
6 Despoiled are the bold warriors;
they sleep their final sleep;
the hands of all the mighty have failed.*
7 At your roar, O God of Jacob,
chariots and steeds lay still.
8 So terrible and awesome are you;
who can stand before you and your great anger?*
9 From the heavens you pronounced sentence;
the earth was terrified and reduced to silence,
10 When you arose, O God, for judgment
to deliver the afflicted of the land. *Selah*
11† Even wrathful Edom praises you;
the remnant of Hamath keeps your feast.

III

12 Make and keep vows to the LORD your God.*
May all present bring gifts to this awesome God,
13 Who checks the pride of princes,
inspires awe among the kings of earth.

PSALM 77†

Confidence in God during National Distress

1 *For the leader;* 'al Jeduthun. *A psalm of Asaph.*

I

2 I cry aloud to God,
cry to God to hear me.
3 On the day of my distress I seek the Lord;
by night my hands are raised unceasingly;*
I refuse to be consoled.
4 When I think of God, I groan;
as I ponder, my spirit grows faint.* *Selah*
5 My eyes cannot close in sleep;
I am troubled and cannot speak.
6 I consider the days of old;
the years long past 7 I remember.*
In the night I meditate in my heart;
I ponder and my spirit broods:
8 "Will the Lord reject us forever,*
never again show favor?
9 Has God's love ceased forever?
Has the promise failed for all ages?
10 Has God forgotten mercy,
in anger withheld compassion?" *Selah*

9: Ps 60, 5; Jb 21, 20; Is 51, 17.21-22; Jer 25, 15ff.; Hb 2, 16.
11: Ps 92, 11.
76, 2: Hb 3, 2.
4: Pss 46, 10; 122, 6-9.
6: 2 Kgs 19, 35; Jer 51, 39; Na 3, 18.
8: Dt 7, 21; 1 Sm 6, 20; Na 1, 6; Mal 3, 2.
12: Nm 30, 3.
77, 3: Pss 50, 15; 88, 2.
4: Jon 2, 8.
7: Ps 143, 5; Dt 32, 7.
8-10: Pss 13, 2; 44, 24; 74, 1; 80, 5; 89, 47; Lam 3, 31.

---

†

75, 9: *A cup*: "the cup of God's wrath" is the punishment inflicted on the wicked. Cf Is 51, 17; Jer 25, 15-29; 49, 12; Ez 23, 31-33. *Spiced*: literally, "a mixed drink"; spices or drugs were added to wine. Cf Prv 9, 2. 5.

Ps 76: A song glorifying Zion, the mountain of Jerusalem where God destroyed Israel's enemies. Zion is thus the appropriate site to celebrate the victory (3-4), a victory described in parallel scenes (5-7. 8-11). Israel is invited to worship its powerful patron deity (12-13).

76, 3: *Salem*: an ancient name for Jerusalem, used here perhaps on account of its allusion to the Hebrew word for peace, *shalom*. Cf Gn 14, 18; Heb 7, 1-3.

76, 5: *Ancient mountains*: conjectural translation of a difficult Hebrew phrase on the basis of Gn 49, 26. The mountains are part of the structure of the universe (Ps 89, 12-13).

76, 11: *Edom . . . Hamath*: conjectural translation. Israel's neighbors to the southeast and north.

Ps 77: A community lament in which the speaker ("I") describes the anguish of Israel at God's silence when its very existence is at stake (2-11). In response the speaker recites the story of how God brought the people into existence (12-21). The question is thus posed to God: Will you allow the people you created to be destroyed?

11† I conclude: "My sorrow is this,
the right hand of the Most High
has left us."*

II

12† I will remember the deeds of the
LORD;
yes, your wonders of old I will remember.*
13 I will recite all your works;
your exploits I will tell.
14 Your way, O God, is holy;
what god is as great as our God?*
15 You alone are the God who did
wonders;
among the peoples you revealed
your might.*
16 With your arm you redeemed your
people,
the descendants of Jacob and Joseph.* *Selah*
17 The waters saw you, God;
the waters saw you and lashed
about,
trembled even to their depths.*
18 The clouds poured down their rains;
the thunderheads rumbled;
your arrows flashed back and
forth.*
19 The thunder of your chariot wheels
resounded;
your lightning lit up the world;
the earth trembled and quaked.*
20 Through the sea was your path;
your way, through the mighty waters,
though your footsteps were unseen.*
21 You led your people like a flock
under the care of Moses and
Aaron.*

PSALM 78†

A New Beginning in Zion and David

1 *A maskil of Asaph.*

I

Attend, my people, to my teaching;
listen to the words of my mouth.
2† I will open my mouth in story,
drawing lessons from of old.*
3 We have heard them, we know them;
our ancestors have recited them
to us.*
4 We do not keep them from our
children;
we recite them to the next generation,
The praiseworthy and mighty deeds
of the LORD,
the wonders that he performed.*
5 God set up a decree in Jacob,
established a law in Israel:*
What he commanded our ancestors,
they were to teach their children;
6 That the next generation might
come to know,
children yet to be born.*
In turn they were to recite them to
their children,
7 that they too might put their trust
in God,
And not forget the works of God,
keeping his commandments.
8 They were not to be like their
ancestors,
a rebellious and defiant generation,*
A generation whose heart was not
constant,*
whose spirit was not faithful to
God,
9† Like the ranks of Ephraimite
archers,
who retreated on the day of battle.
10 They did not keep God's covenant;
they refused to walk by his law.
11 They forgot his works,

*

11: Ex 15, 6. 12; Pss 17, 7; 18, 36.
12: Ps 143, 5.
14: Ps 18, 31; Ex 15, 11.
15: Pss 86, 10; 89, 6.
16: Gn 46, 26-27; Neh 1, 10.
17: Pss 18, 16; 114, 3; Na 1, 4.
18: Pss 18, 14-15; 29; 144, 6; Jb 37, 3-4; Wis 5, 21; Hb 3, 10-11; Zec 9, 14.
19: Pss 18, 8; 97, 4; 99, 1; Ex 19, 16; Jgs 5, 4-5.
20: Neh 9, 11; Wis 14, 3; Is 51, 10; Hb 3, 15.
21: Ps 78, 52; Is 63, 11-14; Hos 12, 14; Mi 6, 4.
78, 2: Ps 49, 5; Mt 13, 35.
3: Ps 44, 2.
4: Ex 10, 2; Dt 4, 9; Jb 8, 8.
5: Ps 147, 19; Dt 33, 4.
6: Ps 22, 31-32; Dt 4, 9; 6, 7.
8: Dt 31, 27; 32, 5. • Ps 95, 10.

†

77, 11: *I conclude*: literally, "I said." The psalmist, after pondering the present distress and God's promises to Israel, has decided that God has forgotten the people.

77, 12: *I will remember*: the verb sometimes means to make present the great deeds of Israel's past by reciting them. Cf Pss 78, 42; 105, 5; 106, 7.

Ps 78: A recital of history to show that past generations did not respond to God's gracious deeds and were punished by God making the gift into a punishment. Will Israel now fail to appreciate God's new act—the choosing of Zion and of David? The tripartite introduction invites Israel to learn the lessons hidden in its traditions (1-4. 5-7. 8-11); each section ends with the mention of God's acts. There are two distinct narratives of approximately equal length: the wilderness events (12-39) and the movement from Egypt to Canaan (40-72). The structure of both is parallel: gracious act (12-16. 40-55), rebellion (17-20. 56-58), divine punishment (21-31. 59-64), God's readiness to forgive and begin anew (32-39. 65-72). The psalm may reflect the reunification program of either King Hezekiah (late eighth century) or King Josiah (late seventh century) in that the Northern Kingdom (Ephraim, Joseph) is especially invited to accept Zion and the Davidic king.

78, 2: *Story*: Hebrew *mashal* literally means "comparison" and can signify a story with a hidden meaning. Mt 13, 35 cites the verse to explain Jesus' use of parables.

78, 9: *Ephraimite archers*: Ephraim was the most important tribe of the Northern Kingdom. Its military defeat (here unspecified) demonstrates its infidelity to God, who otherwise would have protected it.

the wondrous deeds he had shown them.

II

A

12† In the sight of their ancestors God did wonders,
in the land of Egypt, the plain of Zoan.*
13 He split the sea and led them across,*
piling up the waters rigid as walls.*
14 God led them with a cloud by day,
all night with the light of fire.*
15 He split rock in the desert,
gave water to drink, abounding as the deep.*
16 He made streams flow from crags,
drew out rivers of water.

B

17 But they went on sinning against him,
rebelling against the Most High in the desert.*
18 They tested God in their hearts,
demanding the food they craved.*
19 They spoke against God, and said,
"Can God spread a table in the desert?*
20 True, when he struck the rock,
water gushed forth,
the wadis flooded.
But can he also provide bread,
give meat to his people?"

C

21 The LORD heard and grew angry;*
fire blazed up against Jacob;
anger flared up against Israel.
22 For they did not believe in God,
did not trust in his saving power.
23† So he commanded the skies above;
the doors of heaven he opened.
24 God rained manna upon them for food;
bread from heaven he gave them.*
25 All ate a meal fit for heroes;
food he sent in abundance.
26 He stirred up the east wind in the heavens;
by his power God brought on the south wind.
27 He rained meat upon them like dust,
winged fowl like the sands of the sea,
28 Brought them down in the midst of the camp,
round about their tents.
29 They ate and were well filled;
he gave them what they had craved.
30 But while they still wanted more,
and the food was still in their mouths,
31 God's anger attacked them,
killed their best warriors,
laid low the youth of Israel.*
32 In spite of all this they went on sinning,
they did not believe in his wonders.

D

33 God ended their days abruptly,
their years in sudden death.
34 When he slew them, they began to seek him;
they again inquired of their God.*
35† They remembered that God was their rock,
God Most High, their redeemer.
36 But they deceived him with their mouths,
lied to him with their tongues.
37 Their hearts were not constant toward him;
they were not faithful to his covenant.*
38† But God is merciful and forgave their sin;
he did not utterly destroy them.
Time and again he turned back his anger,
unwilling to unleash all his rage.*
39 He was mindful that they were flesh,
a breath that passes and does not return.

---

*

12: Ps 106, 7.
13-14: Ex 14-15; Ps 136, 13.
13: Ex 14, 22; 15, 8.
14: Ps 105, 39; Ex 13, 21; Wis 18, 3.
15: Pss 105, 41; 114, 8; Ex 17, 1-7; Nm 20, 2-13; Dt 8, 15; Wis 11, 4; Is 48, 21.
17: Dt 9, 7; Ez 20, 13.
18: Ps 106, 14; Ex 16, 2-36.
19: Ps 23, 5.
21f: Nm 11; Dt 32, 22.
24: Ps 105, 40; Ex 16, 4. 14; Dt 8, 3; Wis 16, 20; Jn 6, 31.
31: Nm 14, 29.
34: Dt 32, 15. 18; Is 26, 16.
37: Ps 95, 10; Is 29, 13.
38: Ps 85, 4; Ex 32, 14; Is 48, 9; Ez 20, 22.

---

†

78, 12. 43: *Zoan*: a city on the arm of the Nile, a former capital of Egypt.

78, 23-31: On the manna and the quail, see Ex 16 and Nm 11. Unlike Ex 16, here both manna and quail are instruments of punishment, showing that a divine gift can become deadly because of Israel's apostasy.

78, 35: *Remembered*: invoked God publicly in worship. Their words were insincere (36).

78, 38: God is always ready to forgive and begin anew, as in choosing Zion and David (65-72).

III

A

40 How often they rebelled against God in the desert,
grieved him in the wasteland.
41 Again and again they tested God,
provoked the Holy One of Israel.
42 They did not remember his power,
the day he redeemed them from the foe,*
43† When he displayed his wonders in Egypt,
his marvels in the plain of Zoan.*
44 God changed their rivers to blood;
their streams they could not drink.
45 He sent insects that devoured them,*
frogs that destroyed them.
46 He gave their harvest to the caterpillar,
the fruits of their labor to the locust.
47 He killed their vines with hail,*
their sycamores with frost.
48 He exposed their flocks to deadly hail,
their cattle to lightning.*
49 He unleashed against them his fiery breath,
roar, fury, and distress,
storming messengers of death.
50 He cleared a path for his anger;
he did not spare them from death;
he delivered their beasts to the plague.
51 He struck all the firstborn of Egypt,*
love's first child in the tents of Ham.
52 God led forth his people like sheep;
he guided them through the desert like a flock.*
53 He led them on secure and unafraid,
but the sea enveloped their enemies.*
54 He brought them to his holy land,
the mountain his right hand had won.*
55 God drove out the nations before them,
apportioned them a heritage by lot,
settled the tribes of Israel in their tents.

B

56 But they tested, rebelled against God Most High,
his decrees they did not observe.
57 They turned back, deceitful like their ancestors;
they proved false like a bow with no tension.
58 They enraged him with their high places;
with their idols they goaded him.*

C

59 God heard and grew angry;
he rejected Israel completely.
60† He forsook the shrine at Shiloh,*
the tent where he dwelt with humans.
61 He gave up his might into captivity,
his glorious ark into the hands of the foe.*
62 God abandoned his people to the sword;
he was enraged against his heritage.
63 Fire consumed their young men;
their young women heard no wedding songs.*
64 Their priests fell by the sword;
their widows made no lamentation.

D

65 Then the Lord awoke as from sleep,
like a warrior from the effects of wine.
66 He put his enemies to flight;
everlasting shame he dealt them.
67 He rejected the tent of Joseph,
chose not the tribe of Ephraim.
68† God chose the tribe of Judah,
Mount Zion which he favored.*
69 He built his shrine like the heavens,
like the earth which he founded forever.
70 He chose David his servant,
took him from the sheepfold.*
71 From tending sheep God brought him,
to shepherd Jacob, his people,
Israel, his heritage.*

PSALMS

*

42: Ps 106, 21.
43f: Pss 105, 27-36; 135, 9; Ex 7, 14-11, 10; 12, 29-36; Wis 16-18.
45: Ex 8, 17.
47: Wis 16, 16.
48: Ex 9, 3.
51: Pss 105, 36; 136, 10; Ex 12, 29.
52: Ps 77, 21.
53: Ex 14, 26-28.
54: Ex 15, 17.
58: Dt 32, 16. 21.
60: Jos 18, 1; 1 Sm 1, 3; Jer 7, 12; 26, 6.
61: 1 Sm 4, 11. 22.
63: Dt 32, 25; Jer 7, 34.
68: Pss 48, 2; 50, 2; Lam 2, 15.
70: Ps 89, 21; Ez 34, 23; 37, 24; 2 Chr 6, 6.
71: 1 Sm 16, 11-13; 2 Sm 7, 8.

†

78, 43-55: Ex 7-12 records ten plagues. Here there are six divine attacks upon Egypt; the seventh climactic act is God's bringing Israel to the holy land.

78, 60: *Shiloh*: an important shrine in the north prior to Jerusalem. Despite its holy status, it was destroyed (60-64; cf Jer 7, 12. 14).

78, 68. 70: God's ultimate offer of mercy to the sinful helpless people is Zion and the Davidic king.

72 He shepherded them with a pure
heart;
with skilled hands he guided
them.

PSALM 79†

A Prayer for Jerusalem

1 *A psalm of Asaph.*

I

O God, the nations have invaded
your heritage;
they have defiled your holy tem-
ple,
have laid Jerusalem in ruins.*
2 They have left the corpses of your
servants
as food for the birds of the heav-
ens,
the flesh of your faithful for the
beasts of the earth.*
3 They have spilled their blood like
water
all around Jerusalem,
and no one is left to bury them.*
4 We have become the reproach of our
neighbors,
the scorn and derision of those
around us.*

II

5 How long, LORD? Will you be angry
forever?
Will your rage keep burning like
fire?*
6 Pour out your wrath on nations that
reject you,
on kingdoms that do not call on
your name,*
7 For they have devoured Jacob,
laid waste his home.
8 Do not hold past iniquities against
us;
may your compassion come
quickly,
for we have been brought very
low.*

III

9 Help us, God our savior,
for the glory of your name.
Deliver us, pardon our sins
for your name's sake.*
10 Why should the nations say,
"Where is their God?"*
Before our eyes make clear to the
nations
that you avenge the blood of your
servants.*

IV

11 Let the groans of prisoners come be-
fore you;
by your great power free those
doomed to death.*
12 Lord, inflict on our neighbors
sevenfold
the disgrace they inflicted on
you.*
13 Then we, your people, the sheep of
your pasture,
will give thanks to you forever;
through all ages we will declare
your praise.

PSALM 80†

Prayer To Restore God's Vineyard

1† *For the leader; according to "Lil-
ies."* Eduth. *A psalm of Asaph.*

I

2 Shepherd of Israel, listen,
guide of the flock of Joseph!
From your throne upon the cheru-
bim reveal yourself*
3 to Ephraim, Benjamin, and Ma-
nasseh.
Stir up your power, come to save
us.
4 O LORD of hosts, restore us;
Let your face shine upon us,
that we may be saved.*

II

5 LORD of hosts,
how long will you burn with anger
while your people pray?*

---

* 79, 1: 2 Kgs 25, 9-10; Lam 1, 10.
2: Jer 7, 33.
3: 1 Mc 7, 17; Jer 14, 16.
4: Pss 44, 14; 80, 7; 123, 3-4; Jb 12, 4; Dn 9, 16; Zep 2, 8.
5: Pss 13, 2; 44, 24; 89, 47; Dt 4, 24.
6: Ps 14, 4; Jer 10, 25.
8: Ps 142, 7.
9: Ez 20, 44; 36, 22.
10: Pss 42, 4; 115, 2; Jl 2, 17. • Jl 4, 21.
11: Ps 102, 21.
12: Ps 89, 51-52.
80, 2: Pss 23, 1-3; 95, 7; 100, 3; Gn 48, 15; Ex 25, 22; 1 Sm 4, 4; 2 Sm 6, 2; Mi 7, 14.
4. 8. 20: Pss 4, 7; 31, 17; 67, 2; 85, 5; Nm 6, 25; Dn 9, 17.
5: Pss 13, 2; 44, 24; 74, 1; 79, 5; 89, 47; Dt 4, 24.

---

† Ps 79: A communal lament complaining that the nations have defiled the temple and murdered the holy people, leaving their corpses unburied (1-4). The occasion is probably the destruction of Jerusalem by the Babylonian army in 587 B.C. The people ask how long the withdrawal of divine favor will last (5), pray for action now (6-7), and admit that their own sins have brought about the catastrophe (8-9). They seek to persuade God to act for reasons of honor: the nations who do not call upon the Name are running amok (6); the divine honor is compromised (1. 10. 12); God's own servants suffer (2-4. 11).

Ps 80: A community lament in time of military defeat. Using the familiar image of Israel as a vineyard, the people complain that God has broken down the wall protecting the once splendid vine brought from Egypt (9-14). They pray that God will again turn to them and use the Davidic king to lead them to victory (15-20).

80, 1: *Lilies . . . . Eduth*: the first term is probably the title of the melody to which the psalm was to be sung; the second is unexplained.

6 You have fed them the bread of tears,
made them drink tears in abundance.*
7 You have left us to be fought over by our neighbors;
our enemies deride us.*
8 O LORD of hosts, restore us;
let your face shine upon us,
that we may be saved.

III

9† You brought a vine out of Egypt;
you drove away the nations and planted it.
10 You cleared the ground;
it took root and filled the land.
11 The mountains were covered by its shadow,
the cedars of God by its branches.
12† It sent out boughs as far as the sea,
shoots as far as the river.
13 Why have you broken down the walls,
so that all who pass by pluck its fruit?*
14 The boar from the forest strips the vine;
the beast of the field feeds upon it.*
15 Turn again, LORD of hosts;
look down from heaven and see;
Attend to this vine,
16 the shoot your right hand has planted.
17 Those who would burn or cut it down—
may they perish at your rebuke.
18† May your help be with the man at your right hand,
with the one whom you once made strong.
19 Then we will not withdraw from you;
revive us, and we will call on your name.
20 LORD of hosts, restore us;
let your face shine upon us,
that we may be saved.

PSALM 81†

An Admonition to Fidelity

1† *For the leader; "upon the* gittith." *Of Asaph.*

I

2 Sing joyfully to God our strength;*
shout in triumph to the God of Jacob!
3 Take up a melody, sound the timbrel,
the sweet-sounding harp and lyre.
4† Blow the trumpet at the new moon,
at the full moon, on our solemn feast.*
5 For this is a law in Israel,
an edict of the God of Jacob,*
6† Who made it a decree for Joseph
when he came out of the land of Egypt.

II

I hear a new oracle:
7† "I relieved their shoulders of the burden;
their hands put down the basket.*
8† In distress you called and I rescued you;
unseen, I spoke to you in thunder;
At the waters of Meribah I tested you and said:* *Selah*
9 'Listen, my people, I give you warning!
If only you will obey me, Israel!*
10† There must be no foreign god among you;*
you must not worship an alien god.
11 I, the LORD, am your God,
who brought you up from the land of Egypt.

*

6: Pss 42, 4; 102, 10.
7: Pss 44, 14; 79, 4; 123, 3-4; Jb 12, 4; Dn 9, 16; Zep 2, 8.
13: Ps 89, 41.
14: Hos 2, 14.
81, 2: Pss 43, 4; 68, 26; 149, 3; 150, 3-4; Jdt 16, 1.
4: Lv 23, 24; Nm 29, 1.
5: Ex 23, 14ff.
7: Ex 1, 14; 6, 6.
8: Ps 95, 8; Ex 2, 23ff; 17, 7; 19, 16; Nm 20, 13; 27, 14.
9: Ex 15, 26; Is 55, 2-3.
10-11: Ex 20, 2-6; Dt 5, 6-10.

†

80, 9: *A vine*: a frequent metaphor for Israel. Cf Is 5, 1-7; 27, 2-5; Jer 2, 21; Hos 10, 1; Mt 21, 33.

80, 12: *The sea*: the Mediterranean. *The river*: the Euphrates. Cf Gn 15, 18; 1 Kgs 5, 1. The terms may also have a mythic nuance—the seas that surround the earth; sea and river are sometimes paralleled in poetry.

80, 18: *The man at your right hand . . . the one*: the Davidic king who will lead the army in battle.

Ps 81: At a pilgrimage feast, probably harvest in the fall, the people assemble in the temple in accord with the Sinai ordinances (2-6a). They hear a divine word (mediated by a temple speaker) telling how God rescued them from slavery in Egypt (7-9), gave them the fundamental commandment of fidelity (9-11), which would bring punishment if they refused to obey (12-13). But if Israel repents, God will be with them once again, bestowing protection and fertility (14-17).

81, 1: *Upon the gittith*: probably the title of the melody to which the psalm was to be sung or a musical instrument.

81, 4: *New moon . . . full moon*: the pilgrimage feast of harvest began with a great assembly (Lv 23, 24; Nm 29, 1), used the new moon as a sign (Nm 29, 6), and included trumpets (Lv 23, 24).

81, 6: *I hear a new oracle*: literally, "a tongue I do not know I hear." A temple official speaks the word of God (6b-17), which is authoritative and unlike merely human words (cf Nm 24, 4. 16).

81, 7: *I relieved their shoulders of the burden*: literally, "his [Israel's] shoulder," hence the plural translation. A reference to the liberation of Israel from slavery in Egypt. *The basket*: for carrying clay to make bricks. Cf Ex 1, 14.

81, 8: *Meribah*: place of rebellion in the wilderness; cf Ex 17, 7; Nm 20, 13.

81, 10: *There must be no foreign god among you*: as in Pss 50 and 95, Israel is challenged to obey the first commandment of fidelity to God after the proclamation of the exodus.

Open wide your mouth that I may fill it.'
12 But my people did not listen to my words;
Israel did not obey me.
13 So I gave them over to hardness of heart;
they followed their own designs.*
14 But even now if my people would listen,
if Israel would walk in my paths,*
15 In a moment I would subdue their foes,
against their enemies unleash my hand.*
16 Those who hate the LORD would tremble,
their doom sealed forever.
17 But Israel I would feed with the finest wheat,
satisfy them with honey from the rock."*

PSALM 82†
The Downfall of Unjust Gods

1 *A psalm of Asaph.*

I

God rises in the divine council,
gives judgment in the midst of the gods.*
2 "How long will you judge unjustly
and favor the cause of the wicked?* *Selah*
3 Defend the lowly and fatherless;
render justice to the afflicted and needy.
4 Rescue the lowly and poor;
deliver them from the hand of the wicked."*

II

5† The gods neither know nor understand,
wandering about in darkness,
and all the world's foundations shake.
6† I declare: "Gods though you be,
offspring of the Most High all of you,
7 Yet like any mortal you shall die;
like any prince you shall fall."
8† Arise, O God, judge the earth,
for yours are all the nations.

PSALM 83†
Prayer against a Hostile Alliance

1 *A song; a psalm of Asaph.*

I

2 God, do not be silent;
God, be not still and unmoved!*
3 See how your enemies rage;
your foes proudly raise their heads.
4 They conspire against your people,
plot against those you protect.*
5 They say, "Come, let us wipe out their nation;
let Israel's name be mentioned no more!"
6 They scheme with one mind,
in league against you:*
7† The tents of Ishmael and Edom,
the people of Moab and Hagar,*
8 Gebal, Ammon, and Amalek,*
Philistia and the inhabitants of Tyre.*
9 Assyria, too, in league with them
gives aid to the descendants of Lot. *Selah*

II

10† Deal with them as with Midian;
as with Sisera and Jabin at the torrent Kishon,*
11 Those destroyed at Endor,
who became dung for the ground.*
12 Make their nobles like Oreb and Zeeb,

---

*

13: Jer 3, 17; 7, 24.
14: Is 48, 18.
15: Lv 26, 7-8.
17: Ps 147, 14; Dt 32, 13-14.
82, 1: Is 3, 13-14.
2: Ps 58, 2.
4: Dt 1, 17.
83, 2: Pss 10, 1; 44, 24; 109, 1.
4: Jer 11, 9.
6: Ps 2, 2.
7: Nm 20, 23; 1 Chr 5, 10. 19.
8: Ex 17, 8. • Jos 13, 2.
10: Ex 2, 15; Is 9, 3; 10, 26.
11: Jer 8, 2.

---

†

Ps 82: As in Ps 58, the pagan gods are seen as subordinate divine beings to whom Israel's God had delegated oversight of the foreign countries in the beginning (Dt 32, 8-9 LXX). Now God arises in the heavenly assembly (1) to rebuke the unjust "gods" (2-4), who are stripped of divine status and reduced in rank to mortals (5-7). They are accused of misruling the earth by not upholding the poor. A short prayer for universal justice concludes the psalm (8).

82, 5: The gods are blind and unable to declare what is right. Their misrule shakes earth's foundations (cf Pss 11, 3; 75, 4), which God made firm in creation (Ps 96, 10).

82, 6: *I declare: "Gods though you be"*: in Jn 10, 34 Jesus uses the verse to prove that those to whom the word of God is addressed can fittingly be called "gods."

82, 8: *Judge the earth*: according to Dt 32, 8-9 LXX, Israel's God had originally assigned jurisdiction over the foreign nations to the subordinate deities, keeping Israel as a personal possession. Now God will directly take over the rulership of the whole world.

Ps 83: The community lament complains to God of the nations' attempts to wipe out the name of Israel (2-9). The psalmist sees all Israel's enemies throughout its history united in a conspiracy (3-9). May God destroy the current crop of enemies as the enemies of old were destroyed (10-13), and may they be pursued until they acknowledge the name of Israel's God (14-19).

83, 7-9: Apart from the Assyrians, all the nations listed here were neighbors of Israel. *The people of . . . Hagar*: a tribe of the desert regions east of *Ammon* and *Moab* (1 Chr 5, 10. 19-22). *Gebal* is the Phoenician city of Byblos or perhaps a mountain region south of the Dead Sea. *The descendants of Lot* are Moab and Edom (Gn 19, 36-38 and Dt 2, 9). These nations were never united against Israel in the same period; the psalm has lumped them all together.

83, 10-13: For the historical events, see Jgs 4—8.

all their princes like Zebah and
Zalmunna,
13 Who made a plan together,
"Let us seize the pastures of God."
14 My God, turn them into withered
grass,
into chaff flying before the wind.*
15 As a fire raging through a forest,
a flame setting mountains
ablaze,*
16 Pursue them with your tempest;
terrify them with your storm.*
17 Cover their faces with shame,
till they pay you homage, LORD.
18 Let them be dismayed and shamed
forever;
let them perish in disgrace.
19 Show them you alone are the LORD,
the Most High over all the earth.*

PSALM 84†

Prayer of a Pilgrim to Jerusalem

1 *For the leader; "upon the* gittith." *A psalm of the Korahites.*

I

2 How lovely your dwelling,
O LORD of hosts!*
3 My soul yearns and pines
for the courts of the LORD.*
My heart and flesh cry out
for the living God.
4† As the sparrow finds a home
and the swallow a nest to settle
her young,
My home is by your altars,
LORD of hosts, my king and my
God!*
5 Happy are those who dwell in your
house!
They never cease to praise you.
Selah

II

6 Happy are those who find refuge in
you,
whose hearts are set on pilgrim
roads.
7† As they pass through the Baca
valley,
they find spring water to drink.
Also from pools the Lord provides
water
for those who lose their way.
8 They pass through outer and inner
wall
and see the God of gods on Zion.

III

9 LORD of hosts, hear my prayer;
listen, God of Jacob. *Selah*
10† O God, look kindly on our shield;
look upon the face of your
anointed.*

IV

11 Better one day in your courts
than a thousand elsewhere.
Better the threshold of the house of
my God
than a home in the tents of the
wicked.
12 For a sun and shield is the LORD God,
bestowing all grace and glory.
The LORD withholds no good thing
from those who walk without re-
proach.
13 O LORD of hosts,
happy are those who trust in you!

PSALM 85†

Prayer for Divine Favor

1 *For the leader. A psalm of the Korahites.*

I

2 You once favored, LORD, your land,
restored the good fortune of Ja-
cob.*
3 You forgave the guilt of your people,
pardoned all their sins. *Selah*
4 You withdrew all your wrath,
turned back your burning anger.*

II

5 Restore us once more, God our
savior;
abandon your wrath against us.*
6 Will you be angry with us forever,
drag out your anger for all gener-
ations?*

*

14: Pss 1, 4; 35, 5; 58, 10; Is 5, 24; 10, 17; 17, 13; 29, 5; Ez 21, 3.
15: Ps 50, 3.
16: Jb 25, 32; 27, 21.
19: Ps 97, 9; Dt 4, 39; Dn 3, 45.
84, 2: Pss 43, 3-4; 122, 1.
3: Pss 42, 2-3; 63, 2-3; 143, 6; Is 26, 9.
4: Ps 5, 3.
10: Ps 89, 19.
85, 2: Pss 14, 7; 126, 4.
4: Ps 78, 38; Ex 32, 14; Is 48, 9.
5: Ps 80, 4.
6: Pss 79, 5; 89, 47.

†

Ps 84: Israelites celebrated three pilgrimage feasts in Jerusalem annually. The psalm expresses the sentiments of the pilgrims eager to enjoy the divine presence.

84, 4: The desire of a restless bird for a secure home is an image of the desire of a pilgrim for the secure house of God. Cf Ps 42, 2-3, where the image for the desire of the pilgrim is the thirst of the deer for water.

84, 7: *Baca valley*: Hebrew obscure; probably a valley on the way to Jerusalem.

84, 10: *Our shield . . . your anointed*: the king had a role in the liturgical celebration. For the king as shield, cf Ps 89, 19.

Ps 85: A national lament reminding God of past favors and forgiveness (2-4) and begging for forgiveness and grace now (5-8). A speaker represents the people who wait humbly with open hearts (9-10): God will be active on their behalf (11-14). The situation suggests the conditions of Judea during the early postexilic period, the fifth century B.C.; the thoughts are similar to those of postexilic prophets (Hg 1, 5-11; 2, 6-9).

7 Please give us life again,
that your people may rejoice in you.
8 Show us, LORD, your love;
grant us your salvation.

III
9† I will listen for the word of God;
surely the LORD will proclaim peace
To his people, to the faithful,
to those who trust in him.
10 Near indeed is salvation for the loyal;
prosperity will fill our land.
11† Love and truth will meet;
justice and peace will kiss.*
12 Truth will spring from the earth;
justice will look down from heaven.*
13 The LORD will surely grant abundance;
our land will yield its increase.*
14 Prosperity will march before the Lord,
and good fortune will follow behind.

PSALMS

PSALM 86†

Prayer in Time of Distress

1 *A prayer of David.*

I
Hear me, LORD, and answer me,
for I am poor and oppressed.
2 Preserve my life, for I am loyal;
save your servant who trusts in you.
3 You are my God; pity me, Lord;
to you I call all the day.
4 Gladden the soul of your servant;
to you, Lord, I lift up my soul.*
5 Lord, you are kind and forgiving,
most loving to all who call on you.*
6 LORD, hear my prayer;
listen to my cry for help.*
7 In this time of trouble I call,
for you will answer me.

II
8 None among the gods can equal you, O Lord;
nor can their deeds compare to yours.*
9 All the nations you have made shall come
to bow before you, Lord,
and give honor to your name.*
10 For you are great and do wondrous deeds;
and you alone are God.

III
11 Teach me, LORD, your way
that I may walk in your truth,*
single-hearted and revering your name.
12 I will praise you with all my heart,
glorify your name forever, Lord my God.
13 Your love for me is great;
you have rescued me from the depths of Sheol.*
14 O God, the arrogant have risen against me;
a ruthless band has sought my life;
to you they pay no heed.
15 But you, Lord, are a merciful and gracious God,
slow to anger, most loving and true.*
16 Turn to me, have pity on me;
give your strength to your servant;
save this child of your handmaid.*
17 Give me a sign of your favor:
make my enemies see, to their confusion,
that you, LORD, help and comfort me.

PSALM 87†

Zion the True Birthplace of Diaspora Pilgrims

1 *A psalm of the Korahites. A song.*

I
The LORD loves the city*
founded on holy mountains,
2† Loves the gates of Zion
more than any dwelling in Jacob.

---

*
11: Pss 89, 15; 97, 2.
12: Is 45, 8.
13: Ps 67, 7; Lv 26, 4; Ez 34, 27; Hos 2, 23-24; Zec 8, 12.
86, 4: Pss 25, 1; 143, 8.
5: Jl 2, 13.
6: Pss 5, 2; 130, 1-2.
8: Pss 35, 10; 89, 9; Ex 15, 11; Dt 3, 24; Jer 10, 6.
9: Ps 22, 28; Zec 14, 16; Rv 15, 4.
11: Pss 25, 4; 26, 3; 27, 11; 119, 12. 35; 143, 8. 10.
13: Pss 30, 4; 40, 3; Jon 2, 7.
15: Pss 103, 8; 130, 7; 145, 8; Ex 34, 6.
16: Pss 25, 16; 116, 16; Wis 9, 5.
87, 1-2: Pss 76, 2-3; 78, 68-69.

---

†
85, 9: The prophet listens to God's revelation. Cf Hb 2, 1.
85, 11-14: Divine activity is personified as pairs of virtues.
Ps 86: An individual lament. The psalmist, "poor and oppressed" (1), "devoted" (2), "your servant" (2. 4. 16), "rescued from the depths of Sheol" (13), attacked by the ruthless (14), desires only God's protection (1-7. 11-17).
Ps 87: A song of Zion, like Psalms 46, 48, 76, and 132. After the Exile of the sixth century B.C., diaspora Jews from all over the world (4) made the long pilgrimage to Jerusalem, the city of God (1-3). Such Jews may have hailed from distant lands, but the psalm sees them as children of Zion (5-7). The original occasion may have been Pentecost, which always attracted a large number of diaspora Jews.
87, 2: *The gates*: the city itself, a common Hebrew idiom.

3 Glorious things are said of you,
O city of God! *Selah*

II

4 From Babylon and Egypt I count
those who acknowledge the LORD.
Philistia, Ethiopia, Tyre,
of them it can be said:
"This one was born there."
5† But of Zion it must be said:
"They all were born here."*
The Most High confirms this;*
6 the Lord notes in the register of
the peoples:
"This one was born here."*
Selah
7 So all sing in their festive dance:
"Within you is my true home."*

PSALM 88†

A Despairing Lament

1 *A song; a psalm of the Korahites. For the leader; according to* Mahalath. *For singing; a* maskil *of Heman the Ezrahite.*

I

2 LORD, my God, I call out by day;
at night I cry aloud in your presence.*
3 Let my prayer come before you;
incline your ear to my cry.*
4† For my soul is filled with troubles;*
my life draws near to Sheol.
5 I am reckoned with those who go
down to the pit;
I am weak, without strength.
6 My couch is among the dead,
with the slain who lie in the grave.
You remember them no more;
they are cut off from your care.
7 You plunged me into the bottom of
the pit,
into the darkness of the abyss.
8 Your wrath lies heavy upon me;
all your waves crash over me.*
Selah
9 Because of you my friends shun me;
you make me loathsome to them;*
Caged in, I cannot escape;
10 my eyes grow dim from trouble.

II

All day I call on you, LORD;
I stretch out my hands to you.
11† Do you work wonders for the dead?
Do the shades arise and praise
you?* *Selah*
12 Is your love proclaimed in the grave,
your fidelity in the tomb?
13 Are your marvels declared in the
darkness,
your righteous deeds in the land
of oblivion?

III

14 But I cry out to you, LORD;
in the morning my prayer comes
before you.
15 Why do you reject me, LORD?
Why hide your face from me?
16 I am mortally afflicted since youth;
lifeless, I suffer your terrible
blows.
17 Your wrath has swept over me;
your terrors have reduced me to
silence.*
18 All the day they surge round like a
flood;
from every side they close in on
me.
19 Because of you companions shun
me;*
my only friend is darkness.

PSALM 89†

A Lament over God's Promise to David

1 *A* maskil *of Ethan the Ezrahite.*

I

2 The promises of the LORD I will sing
forever,*
proclaim your loyalty through all
ages.
3† For you said, "My love is established
forever;

PSALMS

*

5: Gal 4, 26. • Ps 48, 9.
6: Is 4, 3.
7: Pss 68, 26; 149, 3.
88, 2: Ps 77, 3.
3: Ps 119, 170.
4-7: Pss 28, 1; 30, 4; 40, 3; 86, 13; 143, 7; Nm 16, 33; Jb 17, 1; Jon 2, 7.
8: Pss 18, 5; 32, 6; 42, 8; 69, 2; Jon 2, 4.
9: Pss 38, 12; 79, 4; 80, 7; 123, 3-4; 142, 8; Jb 12, 4; 19, 13; Lam 3, 7; Dn 9, 16.
11: Pss 6, 6; 30, 10; 38, 18; 115, 17.
17: Jb 6, 4; 20, 25.
19: Jb 19, 13.
89, 2: Is 63, 7.

†

87, 5-6: The bond between the exile and the holy city was so strong as to override the exile's citizenship of lesser cities.

Ps 88: A lament in which the psalmist prays for rescue from the alienation of approaching death. Each of the three stanzas begins with a call to God (2. 10b. 14) and complains of the death that separates one from God. The tone is persistently grim.

88, 4-8: In imagination the psalmist already experiences the alienation of Sheol.

88, 11-13: The psalmist seeks to persuade God to act out of concern for divine honor: the shades give you no worship, so keep me alive to offer you praise.

Ps 89: The community laments the defeat of the Davidic king, to whom God promised kingship as enduring as the heavens (2-5). The psalm narrates how God became king of the divine beings (6-9) and how the Davidic king became king of earthly kings (20-38). Since the defeat of the king calls into question God's promise, the community ardently prays God to be faithful to the original promise to David (39-52).

89, 3-5: David's dynasty is to be as long-lasting as the heavens, a statement reinforced by using the same verbs (establish, stand) both of the divine love and loyalty and of the Davidic dynasty and throne. Cf 29-30.

my loyalty will stand as long as the heavens.
4 I have made a covenant with my chosen one;
I have sworn to David my servant:
5 I will make your dynasty stand forever
and establish your throne through all ages."* *Selah*

II

6 The heavens praise your marvels, LORD,
your loyalty in the assembly of the holy ones.*
7† Who in the skies ranks with the LORD?
Who is like the LORD among the gods?*
8 A God dreaded in the council of the holy ones,
greater and more awesome than all who sit there!
9 LORD, God of hosts, who is like you?
Mighty LORD, your loyalty is always present.
10 You rule the raging sea;*
you still its swelling waves.
11† You crushed Rahab with a mortal blow;
your strong arm scattered your foes.
12 Yours are the heavens, yours the earth;
you founded the world and everything in it.*
13† Zaphon and Amanus you created;
Tabor and Hermon rejoice in your name.
14 Mighty your arm, strong your hand,
your right hand is ever exalted.
15 Justice and judgment are the foundation of your throne;
love and loyalty march before you.*
16 Happy the people who know you, LORD,
who walk in the radiance of your face.
17 In your name they sing joyfully all the day;
at your victory they raise the festal shout.*
18† You are their majestic strength;
by your favor our horn is exalted.*
19 Truly the LORD is our shield,
the Holy One of Israel, our king!*

III

20 Once you spoke in vision;*
to your faithful ones you said:
"I have set a leader over the warriors;
I have raised up a hero from the army.
21 I have chosen David, my servant;
with my holy oil I have anointed him.
22 My hand will be with him;*
my arm will make him strong.
23 No enemy shall outwit him,
nor shall the wicked defeat him.
24 I will crush his foes before him,
strike down those who hate him.
25 My loyalty and love will be with him;
through my name his horn will be exalted.
26† I will set his hand upon the sea,
his right hand upon the rivers.
27 He shall cry to me, 'You are my father,*
my God, the Rock that brings me victory!'
28† I myself make him firstborn,
Most High over the kings of the earth.
29 Forever I will maintain my love for him;*
my covenant with him stands firm.
30 I will establish his dynasty forever,
his throne as the days of the heavens.
31 If his descendants forsake my law,*
do not follow my decrees,
32 If they fail to observe my statutes,
do not keep my commandments,

*

5: Pss 61, 7-8; 132, 11; 2 Sm 7, 8-16.
6: Pss 29, 1; 82, 1; Jb 1, 6; 5, 1.
7-9: Pss 35, 10; 86, 8; 113, 5; Ex 15, 11; Jer 10, 6.
10-11: Pss 65, 8; 74, 13-15; 107, 29; Jb 7, 12; Is 51, 9-10.
12: Pss 24, 1-2; 50, 12; Dt 10, 14; 1 Cor 10, 26.
15: Pss 85, 11-12; 97, 2.
17: Ps 47, 2; Zep 3, 14.
18: Pss 112, 9; 148, 14.
19: Pss 47, 9; 96, 10; 97, 1; 99, 1; Is 6, 3.
20-21: Pss 78, 70; 132, 11-12; 2 Sm 7, 4. 8-16; 1 Chr 17, 3. 7-14; Is 42, 1; Acts 13, 22
22-25: 1 Sm 2, 9-10.
27-28: Pss 2, 7; 110, 2-3; 2 Sm 7, 9. 14; Col 1, 15. 18; Rv 1, 5.
29-30: Pss 18, 51; 61, 8; 144, 10; 2 Sm 7, 11; Is 55, 3.
31-33: Lv 26, 14-33.

†

89, 7: *The gods*: literally, "the sons of gods," "the holy ones" and "courtiers" of 6 and 8. These heavenly spirits are members of God's court.

89, 11: *Rahab*: a mythological sea monster whose name is used in the Bible mainly as a personification of primeval chaos. Cf Jb 9, 13; 26, 12; Ps 74, 13-14; Is 51, 9.

89, 13: *Zaphon and Amanus*: two sacred mountains in northern Syria. *Tabor*: a high hill in the valley of Jezreel in northern Israel. *Hermon*: a mountain in Lebanon, forming the southern spur of the Anti-Lebanon range.

89, 18. 25: *Horn*: a concrete noun for an abstract quality; horn is a symbol of strength.

89, 26: *The sea . . . the rivers*: geographically the limits of the Davidic Empire (the Mediterranean and the Euphrates); mythologically, the traditional forces of chaos. See note on v 11.

89, 28: *Most High*: a divine title, which is here extended to David as God's own king. Cf Ps 2, 7-9; Is 9, 5. As God rules over the members of the heavenly council (6-9), so David, God's surrogate, rules over earthly kings.

33 I will punish their crime with a rod
and their guilt with lashes.
34 But I will not take my love from him,
nor will I betray my bond of loyalty.*
35 I will not violate my covenant;
the promise of my lips I will not alter.*
36 By my holiness I swore once for all:*
I will never be false to David.
37† His dynasty will continue forever,*
his throne, like the sun before me.
38 Like the moon it will stand eternal,
forever firm like the sky!" *Selah*

IV

39 But now you have rejected and spurned,*
been enraged at your anointed.
40 You renounced the covenant with your servant,
defiled his crown in the dust.
41 You broke down all his defenses,*
left his strongholds in ruins.
42 All who pass through seize plunder;
his neighbors deride him.
43 You have exalted the right hand of his foes,
have gladdened all his enemies.*
44 You turned back his sharp sword,
did not support him in battle.
45 You brought to an end his splendor,
hurled his throne to the ground.
46 You cut short the days of his youth,
covered him with shame. *Selah*
47 How long, LORD?
Will you stay hidden forever?
Must your wrath smolder like fire?*
48 Remember how brief is my life,
how frail the race you created!*
49 What mortal can live and not see death?
Who can escape the power of Sheol?* *Selah*
50 Where are your promises of old, Lord,
the loyalty sworn to David?
51 Remember, Lord, the insults to your servants,
how I bear all the slanders of the nations.*
52 Your enemies, LORD, insult your anointed;
they insult my every endeavor.

* * *

53† Blessed be the LORD forever! Amen and amen!*

FOURTH BOOK—Psalms 90-106

PSALM 90†

God's Eternity and Human Frailty

1 *A prayer of Moses, the man of God.*

I

Lord, you have been our refuge
through all generations.
2 Before the mountains were born,
the earth and the world brought forth,
from eternity to eternity you are God.*
4† A thousand years in your eyes
are merely a yesterday,*
3† But humans you return to dust,
saying, "Return, you mortals!"*
4c Before a watch passes in the night,
5† you have brought them to their end;*
They disappear like sleep at dawn;
they are like grass that dies.
6† It sprouts green in the morning;
by evening it is dry and withered.*

II

7 Truly we are consumed by your anger,
filled with terror by your wrath.
8 You have kept our faults before you,
our hidden sins exposed to your sight.*

PSALMS

*

34: Ps 40, 12; Sir 47, 22.
35: Jer 33, 20-21.
36: Am 4, 2.
37-38: Pss 61, 8; 72, 5; Sir 43, 6.
39-47: Ps 44, 10-25.
41-42: Ps 80, 13-14.
43: Lam 1, 5.
47: Pss 13, 2; 44, 25; 74, 10; 79, 5; Dt 4, 24.
48: Pss 39, 5-6; 62, 10; 90, 9-10; 144, 4; Jb 7, 6. 16; 14, 1.5; Eccl 6, 12; Wis 2, 5.
49: Ps 90, 3.
51: Ps 79, 12.
53: Pss 41, 14; 72, 18; 106, 48.
90, 2: Pss 48, 15; 55, 20; 93, 2; 102, 13; Hb 1, 12.
4: 2 Pt 3, 8.
3: Pss 103, 14; 104, 29; 146, 4; Gn 3, 19; 1 Mc 2, 63; Jb 34, 14-15; Eccl 3, 20; 12, 7; Sir 40, 11.
5: Ps 89, 48.
6: Pss 37, 2; 102, 11; 103, 15-16; Jb 14, 1-2; Is 40, 6-8.
8: Ps 109, 14-15; Hos 7, 2.

†

89, 37-38: *Like the sun before me . . . like the sky*: as enduring as the heavenly lights. Cf 2-5 and Ps 72, 5. 17.

89, 53: The doxology at the end of the third book of the Psalms; it is not part of Ps 89.

Ps 90: A communal lament that describes only in general terms the cause of the community's distress. After confidently invoking God (1), the psalm turns to a complaint contrasting God's eternity with the brevity of human life (2-6) and sees in human suffering the punishment for sin (7-12). The psalm concludes with a plea for God's intervention (13-17).

90, 3: *Return*: one word of God is enough to return mortals to the dust from which they were created. Humans were created from earth in Gn 2, 7; 3, 19.

90, 4: The translation reverses the order of the difficult Hebrew verses 3 and 4 to get the probable original order. *A watch in the night*: the night was divided into three sentry periods or watches. Cf Jgs 7, 19.

90, 5: *You have brought them to their end*: an interpretation of the unclear Hebrew.

90, 6: *It is dry and withered*: the transitory nature of the grass under the scorching sun was proverbial. Cf Ps 129, 6; Is 40, 6-8.

9 Our life ebbs away under your wrath;*
our years end like a sigh.
10 Seventy is the sum of our years,
or eighty, if we are strong;
Most of them are sorrow and toil;
they pass quickly, we are all but gone.
11 Who comprehends your terrible anger?
Your wrath matches the fear it inspires.
12 Teach us to count our days aright,
that we may gain wisdom of heart.
13 Relent, O LORD! How long?
Have pity on your servants!
14 Fill us at daybreak with your love,*
that all our days we may sing for joy.
15 Make us glad as many days as you humbled us,
for as many years as we have seen trouble.*
16 Show your deeds to your servants,
your glory to their children.
17 May the favor of the Lord our God be ours.*
Prosper the work of our hands!
Prosper the work of our hands!

PSALM 91†

Security Under God's Protection

I

1† You who dwell in the shelter of the Most High,
who abide in the shadow of the Almighty,
2 Say to the LORD, "My refuge and fortress,
my God in whom I trust."*
3 God will rescue you from the fowler's snare,
from the destroying plague,
4 Will shelter you with pinions,
spread wings that you may take refuge;*
God's faithfulness is a protecting shield.
5 You shall not fear the terror of the night
nor the arrow that flies by day,*
6 Nor the pestilence that roams in darkness,
nor the plague that ravages at noon.*
7 Though a thousand fall at your side,
ten thousand at your right hand,
near you it shall not come.
8 You need simply watch;
the punishment of the wicked you will see.*
9 You have the LORD for your refuge;
you have made the Most High your stronghold.
10 No evil shall befall you,
no affliction come near your tent.*
11† For God commands the angels*
to guard you in all your ways.*
12 With their hands they shall support you,
lest you strike your foot against a stone.*
13 You shall tread upon the asp and the viper,
trample the lion and the dragon.*

II

14 Whoever clings to me I will deliver;
whoever knows my name I will set on high. *
15 All who call upon me I will answer;*
I will be with them in distress;*
I will deliver them and give them honor.
16 With length of days I will satisfy them
and show them my saving power.*

PSALM 92†

A Hymn of Thanksgiving for God's Fidelity

1 *A psalm. A sabbath song.*

---

*

9-10: Pss 39, 5-7; 62, 10; 102, 24-25; 144, 4; Gn 6, 3; Jb 7, 6. 16; 14, 5; Prv 10, 27; Eccl 6, 12; Wis 2, 5; Sir 18, 8; Is 65, 20.
14: Ps 17, 15.
15: Nm 14, 34; Jer 31, 13.
17: Ps 33, 22.
91, 2: Pss 18, 3; 31, 3-4; 42, 10; 142, 6; 2 Sm 22, 3.
4: Pss 17, 8; 36, 8; 57, 2; 63, 8; Dt 32, 11; Ru 2, 12; Mt 23, 37.
5: Prv 3, 25; Song 3, 8.
6: Dt 32, 24.
8: Ps 92, 12.
10: Prv 12, 21; Dt 7, 15.
11-12: Mt 4, 6; Lk 4, 10f.
11: Heb 1, 14.
12: Ps 121, 3; Prv 3, 23.
13: Is 11, 8; Lk 10, 19.
14: Pss 9, 11; 119, 132.
15: Jer 33, 3; Zec 13, 9. • Is 43, 2.
16: Prv 3, 2.

---

†

Ps 91: A prayer of someone who has taken refuge in the security of the temple (1-2). The psalmist is confident that God's presence will protect the people in every dangerous situation (3-13). The final verses are an oracle of salvation promising salvation to those who trust in God (14-16).

91, 1: *The shelter of the Most High*: basically "hiding place" but in the psalms a designation for the protected temple precincts. Cf Pss 27, 5; 31, 21; 61, 5. *The shadow of the Almighty*: literally, "the shadow of the wings of the Almighty." Cf Pss 17, 8; 36, 8; 57, 2; 63, 8. V 4 makes clear that the shadow is an image of the safety afforded by the outstretched wings of the cherubim in the holy of holies.

91, 11-12: The words are cited in Lk 4, 10-11; Mt 4, 6, as Jesus' reply to Satan in the desert.

Ps 92: A hymn of praise and thanks for God's faithful deeds (2-5). The wicked, deluded by their prosperity (6-9), are punished (10), whereas the psalmist has already experienced God's protection (11-16).

I

2 It is good to give thanks to the LORD,
to sing praise to your name, Most High,*
3 To proclaim your love in the morning,
your faithfulness in the night,
4 With the ten-stringed harp,
with melody upon the lyre.*
5 For you make me jubilant, LORD, by your deeds;
at the works of your hands I shout for joy.

II

6 How great are your works, LORD!*
How profound your purpose!
7 A senseless person cannot know this;
a fool cannot comprehend.
8 Though the wicked flourish like grass
and all sinners thrive,*
They are destined for eternal destruction;
9 for you, LORD, are forever on high.
10 Indeed your enemies, LORD,
indeed your enemies shall perish;
all sinners shall be scattered.*

III

11 You have given me the strength of a wild bull;*
you have poured rich oil upon me.*
12 My eyes look with glee on my wicked enemies;
my ears delight in the fall of my foes.*
13 The just shall flourish like the palm tree,
shall grow like a cedar of Lebanon.*
14† Planted in the house of the LORD,
they shall flourish in the courts of our God.
15 They shall bear fruit even in old age,
always vigorous and sturdy,
16 As they proclaim: "The LORD is just;
our rock, in whom there is no wrong."*

PSALM 93†

God is a Mighty King

1† The LORD is king, robed with majesty;
the LORD is robed, girded with might.*
The world will surely stand in place,
never to be moved.*
2 Your throne stands firm from of old;
you are from everlasting, LORD.*
3† The flood has raised up, LORD;
the flood has raised up its roar;
the flood has raised its pounding waves.
4 More powerful than the roar of many waters,
more powerful than the breakers of the sea,
powerful in the heavens is the LORD.
5 Your decrees are firmly established;
holiness belongs to your house, LORD,
for all the length of days.

PSALM 94†

A Prayer for Deliverance from the Wicked

I

1 LORD, avenging God,
avenging God, shine forth!*
2 Rise up, judge of the earth;
give the proud what they deserve.*

II

3 How long, LORD, shall the wicked,
how long shall the wicked glory?*

PSALMS

---

*

92, 2: Pss 33, 1; 147, 1.
4: Pss 33, 2; 144, 9.
6-7: Pss 131, 1; 139, 6. 17; Wis 13, 1; 17, 1.
8: Ps 37, 35.
10: Pss 68, 1-2; 125, 5.
11: Ps 75, 10; Dt 33, 17. • Ps 23, 5.
12: Ps 91, 8.
13: Pss 1, 3; 52, 10; Jer 17, 8.
16: Dt 32, 4.
93, 1: Pss 47, 8; 96, 10; 97, 1; 99, 1. • Pss 75, 2-3; 104, 5.
2: Pss 55, 20; 90, 2; 102, 13; Hb 1, 12.
94, 1: Na 1, 2.
2: Jer 51, 56; Lam 3, 64.
3: Pss 13, 2; 75, 5; Jer 12, 1.

---

†

92, 14: *Planted*: the just are likened to trees growing in the sacred precincts of the temple, which is often seen as the source of life and fertility because of God's presence. Cf Ps 36, 9. 10; Ez 47, 1-12.

Ps 93: A hymn celebrating the kingship of God, who created the world (1-2) by defeating the sea (3-4). In the ancient myth that is alluded to here, Sea completely covered the land, making it impossible for the human community to live. Sea, or Flood, roars in anger against God, who is personified in the storm. God's utterances or decrees are given authority by the victory over Sea (5).

93, 1: *The LORD is king*: literally, "the LORD reigns." This psalm, and Pss 47 and 96-99, are sometimes called enthronement psalms. They may have been used in a special liturgy during which God's ascent to the throne was ritually reenacted. They have also been interpreted eschatologically, pointing to the coming of God as king at the end-time.

93, 3: *The flood*: the primordial sea was tamed by God in the act of creation. It is a figure of chaos and rebellion. Cf Ps 46, 4.

Ps 94: A lament of an individual who is threatened by wicked people. The danger affects the whole community. Calling upon God as judge (1-2), the psalm complains about oppression of the holy community by people within (3-7). Bold declarations of faith follow: denunciation of evildoers (8-11) and assurance to the just (12-15). The psalm continues with further lament (16-19) and ends with strong confidence in God's response (20-23).

4 How long will they mouth haughty speeches,
go on boasting, all these evildoers?*
5 They crush your people, LORD,
torment your very own.
6 They kill the widow and alien;
the fatherless they murder.*
7 They say, "The LORD does not see;
the God of Jacob takes no notice."*

III

8 Understand, you stupid people!
You fools, when will you be wise?*
9 Does the one who shaped the ear not hear?
The one who formed the eye not see?*
10 Does the one who guides nations not rebuke?
The one who teaches humans not have knowledge?
11 The LORD does know human plans;
they are only puffs of air.*

IV

12 Happy those whom you guide, LORD,*
whom you teach by your instruction.
13 You give them rest from evil days,
while a pit is being dug for the wicked.
14 You, LORD, will not forsake your people,
nor abandon your very own.*
15 Judgment shall again be just,
and all the upright of heart will follow it.

V

16 Who will rise up for me against the wicked?
Who will stand up for me against evildoers?
17 If the LORD were not my help,
I would long have been silent in the grave.*
18 When I say, "My foot is slipping,"
your love, LORD, holds me up.*
19 When cares increase within me,
your comfort gives me joy.

VI

20 Can unjust judges be your allies,
those who create burdens in the name of law,
21 Those who conspire against the just
and condemn the innocent to death?
22 No, the LORD is my secure height,
my God, the rock where I find refuge,
23 Who will turn back their evil upon them*
and destroy them for their wickedness.
Surely the LORD our God will destroy them!*

PSALM 95†

A Call to Praise and Obedience

I

1 Come, let us sing joyfully to the LORD;
cry out to the rock of our salvation.*
2 Let us greet him with a song of praise,
joyfully sing out our psalms.
3 For the LORD is the great God,
the great king over all gods,*
4 Whose hand holds the depths of the earth;
who owns the tops of the mountains.
5 The sea and dry land belong to God,
who made them, formed them by hand.*

II

6 Enter, let us bow down in worship;
let us kneel before the LORD who made us.
7 For this is our God,
whose people we are,
God's well-tended flock.*

III

Oh, that today you would hear his voice:*
8† Do not harden your hearts as at Meribah,
as on the day of Massah in the desert.
9 There your ancestors tested me;

---

* 4: Ps 73; Mal 2, 17; 3, 14. 6: Ex 22, 21-22; Dt 24, 17-22. 7: Pss 10, 11; 64, 6; 73, 11; Jb 22, 13-14; Ez 9, 9. 8: Prv 1, 22; 8, 5. 9: Ex 4, 11; Prv 20, 12. 11: Ps 33, 15; 1 Cor 3, 20. 12: Ps 119, 71; Jb 5, 17. 14: 1 Sm 12, 22; Sir 47, 22. 17: Ps 115, 17. 18: Ps 145, 14. 23: Pss 7, 16; 9, 16; 35, 8; 57, 7; Prv 26, 27; Eccl 10, 8; Sir 27, 26. • Ps 107, 42. 95, 1: Dt 32, 15. 3: Pss 47, 2; 135, 5. 5: Ps 24, 1-2. 7: Pss 23, 1-3; 100, 3; Mi 7, 14. 7c-11: Pss 81, 8; 106, 32; Heb 3, 7-11. 15; 4, 3. 5. 7.

---

† Ps 95: Twice the psalm calls the people to praise and worship God (1-2. 6), the king of all creatures (3-5) and shepherd of the flock (7ab). The last strophe warns the people to be more faithful than were their ancestors in the journey to the promised land (7c-11). This invitation to praise God regularly opens the Church's official prayer, the Liturgy of the Hours.

95, 8: *Meribah*: literally, "contention"; the place where the Israelites quarreled with God. *Massah*: "testing," the place where they put God to the trial. Cf Ex 17, 7; Nm 20, 13.

they tried me though they had
seen my works.*
10 Forty years I loathed that generation;
I said: "This people's heart goes astray;
they do not know my ways."*
11† Therefore I swore in my anger:
"They shall never enter my rest."

PSALM 96†

God of the Universe

I

1 Sing to the LORD a new song;*
sing to the LORD, all the earth.
2 Sing to the LORD, bless his name;
announce his salvation day after day.
3 Tell God's glory among the nations;
among all peoples, God's marvelous deeds.*

II

4† For great is the LORD and highly to be praised,
to be feared above all gods.*
5 For the gods of the nations all do nothing,
but the LORD made the heavens.*
6 Splendor and power go before him;
power and grandeur are in his holy place.

III

7 Give to the LORD, you families of nations,
give to the LORD glory and might;
8 give to the LORD the glory due his name!*
Bring gifts and enter his courts;
9 bow down to the LORD, splendid in holiness.
Tremble before God, all the earth;
10 say among the nations: The LORD is king.*
The world will surely stand fast,
never to be moved.
God rules the peoples with fairness.

IV

11 Let the heavens be glad and the earth rejoice;
let the sea and what fills it resound;*
12 let the plains be joyful and all that is in them.
Then let all the trees of the forest rejoice
13 before the LORD who comes,
who comes to govern the earth,*
To govern the world with justice
and the peoples with faithfulness.

PSALM 97†

The Divine Ruler of All

I

1 The LORD is king; let the earth rejoice;
let the many islands be glad.*
2 Cloud and darkness surround the Lord;
justice and right are the foundation of his throne.*
3 Fire goes before him;
everywhere it consumes the foes.
4 Lightning illumines the world;
the earth sees and trembles.*
5 The mountains melt like wax before the LORD,
before the Lord of all the earth.*
6 The heavens proclaim God's justice;
all peoples see his glory.*

II

7† All who serve idols are put to shame,
who glory in worthless things;
all gods bow down before you.*
8 Zion hears and is glad,
and the cities of Judah rejoice
because of your judgments, O LORD.*
9 You, LORD, are the Most High over all the earth,*
exalted far above all gods.
10 The LORD loves those who hate evil,
protects the lives of the faithful,*

*

9: Nm 14, 22; 20, 2-13; Dt 6, 16; 33, 8.
10: Ps 78, 8; Nm 14, 34; Dt 32, 5.
96, 1: Ps 98, 1; Is 42, 10.
3: Pss 98, 4; 105, 1.
4: Pss 48, 2; 95, 3; 145, 3.
5: Ps 97, 7; Is 40, 17; 1 Cor 8, 4.
7: Ps 29, 2.
10: Pss 75, 4; 93, 1.
11: Ps 98, 7.
13: Ps 98, 9.
97, 1: Pss 75, 4; 93, 1; 96, 10.
2: Pss 85, 11; 89, 15; Ex 19, 6; Dt 4, 11; 5, 22; 1 Kgs 8, 12.
4: Pss 18, 8; 50, 3; 77, 18; 99, 1; Jgs 5, 4-5.
5: Jdt 16, 15; Mi 1, 4.
6: Ps 50, 6.
7: Ps 96, 5.
8: Ps 48, 12.
9: Ps 83, 19.
10: Ps 121, 7.

†

95, 11: *My rest*: the promised land as in Dt 12, 9. Heb 4 applies the verse to the eternal rest of heaven.

Ps 96: A hymn inviting all humanity to praise the glories of Israel's God (1-3), who is the sole God (4-6). To the just ruler of all belongs worship (7-10); even inanimate creation is to offer praise (11-13). This psalm has numerous verbal and thematic contacts with Is 40-55, as does Ps 98. Another version of the psalm is 1 Chr 16, 23-33.

96, 4: For references to other gods, see comments on Pss 58 and 82.

Ps 97: The hymn begins with God appearing in a storm, a traditional picture of some ancient Near Eastern gods (1-6); cf Ps 18, 8-16; Mi 1, 3-4; Hb 3, 3-15. Israel rejoices in the overthrowing of idol worshipers and their gods (7-9) and the rewarding of the faithful righteous (10-12).

97, 7: *All gods*: divine beings thoroughly subordinate to Israel's God. The Greek translates "angels," an interpretation adopted by Heb 1, 6.

rescues them from the hand of the
wicked.
11 Light dawns for the just;
gladness, for the honest of heart.*
12 Rejoice in the LORD, you just,
and praise his holy name.*

PSALM 98†
The Coming of God

1† *A psalm.*

I

Sing a new song to the LORD,
who has done marvelous deeds,*
Whose right hand and holy arm
have won the victory.*
2 The LORD has made his victory
known;
has revealed his triumph for the
nations to see,
3 Has remembered faithful love
toward the house of Israel.
All the ends of the earth have
seen
the victory of our God.

II

4 Shout with joy to the LORD, all the
earth;
break into song; sing praise.
5 Sing praise to the LORD with the
harp,
with the harp and melodious
song.
6 With trumpets and the sound of the
horn
shout with joy to the King, the
LORD.*

III

7 Let the sea and what fills it re-
sound,*
the world and those who dwell
there.
8 Let the rivers clap their hands,
the mountains shout with them for
joy,*
9 Before the LORD who comes,
who comes to govern the earth,*
To govern the world with justice
and the peoples with fairness.*

PSALM 99†
The Holy King

I

1† The LORD is king, the peoples trem-
ble;
God is enthroned on the cheru-
bim, the earth quakes.*
2 The LORD is great on Zion,
exalted above all the peoples.
3 Let them praise your great and awe-
some name:
Holy is God!*

II

4 O mighty king, lover of justice,
you alone have established fair-
ness;
you have created just rule in Ja-
cob.*
5† Exalt the LORD, our God;
bow down before his footstool;*
holy is God!

III

6 Moses and Aaron were among his
priests,
Samuel among those who called
on God's name;
they called on the LORD, who an-
swered them.*
7 From the pillar of cloud God spoke
to them;
they kept the decrees, the law
they received.*
8 O LORD, our God, you answered
them;
you were a forgiving God,
though you punished their of-
fenses.*
9 Exalt the LORD, our God;
bow down before his holy moun-
tain;
holy is the LORD, our God.

*

11: Ps 112, 4.
12: Ps 30, 5.
98, 1: Ps 96, 1; Is 42, 10. • Is 59, 16; 63, 5.
6: Ps 47, 6-7.
7: Ps 96, 11.
8: Is 44, 23; 55, 12.
9: Ps 96, 13. • Ps 67, 5.
99, 1: Pss 18, 8-11; 80, 2; 93, 1; Ex 25, 22; 1 Sm 4, 4; 2 Sm 6, 2.
3: Is 6, 3.
4: Pss 72, 1; 99, 4; Jer 23, 5.
5: Ps 132, 7.
6: Jer 15, 1.
7: Ex 33, 9; Nm 12, 5.
8: Ex 32, 11; Nm 20, 12.

†

Ps 98: A hymn, similar to Ps 96, extolling God for Israel's victory (1-3). All nations (4-6) and even inanimate nature (7-8) are summoned to welcome God's coming to rule over the world (9).

98, 1: *Marvelous deeds . . . victory*: the conquest of all threats to the peaceful existence of Israel, depicted in the psalms variously as a cosmic force such as Sea, or nations bent on Israel's destruction, or evildoers seemingly triumphant. *Whose right hand and holy arm*: God is pictured as a powerful warrior.

Ps 99: A hymn to God as the king whose grandeur is most clearly seen on Mount Zion (2) and in the laws given to Israel (4). Israel is special because of God's word of justice, which was mediated by the revered speakers, Moses, Aaron, and Samuel (6-8). The poem is structured by the threefold statement that God is holy (3. 5. 9) and by the twice-repeated command to praise (5. 9).

99, 1: *Enthroned on the cherubim*: cherubim were composite beings with animal and human features, common in ancient Near Eastern art. Two cherubim were placed on the ark (or box) of the covenant in the holy of holies. Upon them God was believed to dwell invisibly. Cf Ex 25, 20-22; 1 Sm 4, 4; 2 Sm 6, 2; Ps 80, 2.

99, 5: *Footstool*: a reference to the ark. Cf 1 Chr 28, 2; Ps 132, 7.

PSALM 100†

Processional Hymn

1 *A psalm of thanksgiving.*

Shout joyfully to the LORD, all you lands;
2 worship the LORD with cries of gladness;
come before him with joyful song.
3† Know that the LORD is God,
our maker to whom we belong,
whose people we are, God's well-tended flock.*
4 Enter the temple gates with praise,
its courts with thanksgiving.
Give thanks to God, bless his name;*
5 good indeed is the LORD,
Whose love endures forever,
whose faithfulness lasts through every age.

PSALM 101†

Norm of Life for Rulers

1 *A psalm of David.*

I

I sing of love and justice;
to you, LORD, I sing praise.
2† I follow the way of integrity;*
when will you come to me?
I act with integrity of heart
within my royal court.*
3 I do not allow into my presence
anyone who speaks perversely.
Whoever acts shamefully I hate;
no such person can be my friend.*
4 I shun the devious of heart;
the wicked I do not tolerate.
5 Whoever slanders another in secret
I reduce to silence.*
Haughty eyes and arrogant hearts*
I cannot endure.

II

6† I look to the faithful of the land;
they alone can be my companions.
Those who follow the way of integrity,*
they alone can enter my service.
7 No one who practices deceit
can hold a post in my court.
No one who speaks falsely
can be among my advisors.*
8† Each morning I clear the wicked from the land,
and rid the LORD's city of all evildoers.

PSALM 102†

Prayer in Time of Distress

1 *The prayer of one afflicted and wasting away whose anguish is poured out before the LORD.*

I

2 LORD, hear my prayer;
let my cry come to you.
3 Do not hide your face from me
now that I am in distress.*
Turn your ear to me;
when I call, answer me quickly.
4 For my days vanish like smoke;*
my bones burn away as in a furnace.
5 I am withered, dried up like grass,
too wasted to eat my food.
6 From my loud groaning
I become just skin and bones.
7 I am like a desert owl,
like an owl among the ruins.
8 I lie awake and moan,
like a lone sparrow on the roof.
9† All day long my enemies taunt me;
in their rage, they make my name a curse.
10 I eat ashes like bread,
mingle my drink with tears.*
11 Because of your furious wrath,
you lifted me up just to cast me down.
12 My days are like a lengthening shadow;*
I wither like the grass.*

*

100, 3: Pss 23, 1; 95, 7; Mi 7, 14; Is 64, 7.
4-5: Pss 106, 1; 107, 1; 118, 1; 136, 1; 138, 8; Jer 33, 11.
101, 2: Ps 26, 11. • 1 Kgs 9, 4; Is 33, 15.
3: Prv 11, 20.
5: Prv 17, 20; 30, 10. • Prv 21, 4.
6: Ps 26, 11; Prv 20, 7.
7: Ps 5, 5; Prv 25, 5.
102, 3: Pss 69, 18; 143, 7.
4-6: Ps 38, 7-9.
10: Pss 42, 4; 80, 6.
12: Pss 109, 23; 144, 4; Jb 8, 9; 14, 2; Eccl 6, 12; Wis 2, 5. • Ps 90, 5-6.

†

Ps 100: A hymn inviting the people to enter the temple courts with thank offerings for the God who created them.

100, 3: Although the people call on all the nations of the world to join in their hymn, they are conscious of being the chosen people of God.

Ps 101: The king, grateful at being God's chosen (1), promises to be a ruler after God's own heart (2-3), allowing into the royal service only the God-fearing (3-8).

101, 2: *Within my royal court*: the king promises to make his own household a model for Israel, banning all officials who abuse their power.

101, 6: *I look to the faithful of the land*: the king seeks companions only among those faithful to God.

101, 8: *Each morning*: the normal time for the administration of justice (2 Sm 15, 2; Jer 21, 12) and for the arrival of divine aid (Pss 59, 17; 143, 8; Is 33, 2). *I clear the wicked from the land*: the king, as God's servant, is responsible for seeing that divine justice is carried out.

Ps 102: A lament, one of the Penitential Psalms. The psalmist, experiencing psychic and bodily disintegration (4-12), cries out to God (1-3). In the temple precincts where God has promised to be present, the psalmist recalls God's venerable promises to save the poor (13-23). The final part (24-29) restates the original complaint and prayer, and emphasizes God's eternity.

102, 9: *They make my name a curse*: enemies use the psalmist's name in phrases such as, "May you be as wretched as this person!"

II

13 But you, LORD, are enthroned forever;
your renown is for all generations.*
14 You will again show mercy to Zion;
now is the time for pity;
the appointed time has come.
15 Its stones are dear to your servants;
its dust moves them to pity.
16 The nations shall revere your name, LORD,
all the kings of the earth, your glory,*
17 Once the LORD has rebuilt Zion
and appeared in glory,
18 Heeding the plea of the lowly,
not scorning their prayer.
19 Let this be written for the next generation,
for a people not yet born,
that they may praise the LORD:*
20† "The LORD looked down from the holy heights,
viewed the earth from heaven,*
21 To attend to the groaning of the prisoners,
to release those doomed to die."*
22 Then the LORD's name will be declared on Zion,
the praise of God in Jerusalem,
23 When all peoples and kingdoms gather
to worship the LORD.*

III

24 God has shattered my strength in mid-course,
has cut short my days.
25† I plead, O my God,
do not take me in the midst of my days.*
Your years last through all generations.
26 Of old you laid the earth's foundations;*
the heavens are the work of your hands.
27 They perish, but you remain;
they all wear out like a garment;
Like clothing you change them and they are changed,
28 but you are the same, your years have no end.
29 May the children of your servants live on;
may their descendants live in your presence.*

PSALM 103†
Praise of Divine Goodness

1 *Of David.*

I

Bless the LORD, my soul;
all my being, bless his holy name!
2 Bless the LORD, my soul;
do not forget all the gifts of God,
3 Who pardons all your sins,
heals all your ills,
4 Delivers your life from the pit,*
surrounds you with love and compassion,
5† Fills your days with good things;
your youth is renewed like the eagle's.

II

6 The LORD does righteous deeds,
brings justice to all the oppressed.*
7 His ways were revealed to Moses,
mighty deeds to the people of Israel.
8 Merciful and gracious is the LORD,
slow to anger, abounding in kindness.*
9 God does not always rebuke,
nurses no lasting anger,
10 Has not dealt with us as our sins merit,
nor requited us as our deeds deserve.

III

11 As the heavens tower over the earth,
so God's love towers over the faithful.*
12 As far as the east is from the west,
so far have our sins been removed from us.
13 As a father has compassion on his children,
so the LORD has compassion on the faithful.
14 For he knows how we are formed,
remembers that we are dust.*
15 Our days are like the grass;
like flowers of the field we blossom.*

---

* 13: Pss 55, 20; 90, 2; 93, 2; 102, 13; 135, 13; 145, 13; Lam 5, 19; Hb 1, 12.
16: Is 59, 19; 66, 18.
19: Ps 22, 31-32.
20: Pss 11, 4; 14, 2.
21: Ps 79, 11.
23: Is 60, 3-4; Zec 2, 15; 8, 22.
25: Pss 39, 5; 90, 10; Jb 14, 5.
26-28: Heb 1, 10-12.
29: Ps 69, 36-37.
103, 4: Pss 28, 1; 30, 4; 40, 3; 69, 16; 88, 5; 143, 7; Prv 1, 12; Jon 2, 7.
6: Ps 146, 6-7.
8: Pss 86, 15; 145, 8; Ex 34, 6-7; Nm 14, 18; Jer 3, 12; Jl 2, 13; Jon 4, 2.
11: Is 55, 9.
14: Ps 90, 3.
15: Pss 37, 2; 90, 5-6; Is 40, 7.

---

† 102, 20-23: Both 20-21 and 22-23 depend on 19.

102, 25: *In the midst of my days*: when the normal span of life is but half completed. Cf Is 38, 10; Jer 17, 11.

Ps 103: The speaker in this hymn begins by praising God for personal benefits (1-5), then moves on to God's mercy toward all the people (6-18). Even sin cannot destroy that mercy (11-13), for the eternal God is well aware of the people's human fragility (14-18). The psalmist invites the heavenly beings to join in praise (19-22).

103, 5: *Your youth is renewed like the eagle's*: because of the eagle's long life it was a symbol of perennial youth and vigor. Cf Is 40, 31.

16 The wind sweeps over us and we are gone;
our place knows us no more.
17 But the LORD's kindness is forever,
toward the faithful from age to age.
He favors the children's children
18 of those who keep his covenant,
who take care to fulfill its precepts.

IV
19 The LORD's throne is established in heaven;
God's royal power rules over all.
20 Bless the LORD, all you angels,*
mighty in strength and attentive,
obedient to every command.
21 Bless the LORD, all you hosts,
ministers who do God's will.
22 Bless the LORD, all creatures,
everywhere in God's domain.
Bless the LORD, my soul!

PSALM 104†

Praise of God the Creator

I
1 Bless the LORD, my soul!
LORD, my God, you are great indeed!
You are clothed with majesty and glory,
2 robed in light as with a cloak.
You spread out the heavens like a tent;*
3† you raised your palace upon the waters.
You make the clouds your chariot;
you travel on the wings of the wind.
4 You make the winds your messengers;
flaming fire, your ministers.*

II
5† You fixed the earth on its foundation,
never to be moved.
6 The ocean covered it like a garment;
above the mountains stood the waters.
7 At your roar they took flight;
at the sound of your thunder they fled.*
8 They rushed up the mountains, down the valleys
to the place you had fixed for them.
9 You set a limit they cannot pass;
never again will they cover the earth.*

III
10 You made springs flow into channels
that wind among the mountains.
11 They give drink to every beast of the field;*
here wild asses quench their thirst.
12 Beside them the birds of heaven nest;
among the branches they sing.
13 You water the mountains from your palace;
by your labor the earth abounds.
14 You raise grass for the cattle
and plants for our beasts of burden.
You bring bread from the earth,
15 and wine to gladden our hearts,
Oil to make our faces gleam,
food to build our strength.
16† The trees of the LORD drink their fill,
the cedars of Lebanon, which you planted.
17 There the birds build their nests;
junipers are the home of the stork.*
18 The high mountains are for wild goats;
the rocky cliffs, a refuge for badgers.

IV
19 You made the moon to mark the seasons,*
the sun that knows the hour of its setting.
20 You bring darkness and night falls,
then all the beasts of the forest roam abroad.
21 Young lions roar for prey;
they seek their food from God.*
22 When the sun rises, they steal away
and rest in their dens.
23 People go forth to their work,
to their labor till evening falls.

PSALMS

*

20: Ps 148, 2; Dn 3, 58.
104, 2: Prv 8, 27-28; Jb 9, 8; Is 40, 22; Gn 1, 6-7; Am 9, 6.
4: Heb 1, 7.
7: Ps 29, 3.
9: Jer 5, 22; Gn 9, 11-15.
11-14: Ps 147, 8-9.
17: Ez 31, 6.
19: Sir 43, 6.
21: Jb 38, 39.

†

Ps 104: A hymn praising God who easily and skillfully made rampaging waters and primordial night into a world vibrant with life. The psalmist describes God's splendor in the heavens (1-4), how the chaotic waters were tamed to fertilize and feed the world (5-18), and how primordial night was made into a gentle time of refreshment (19-23). The picture is like Gn 1, 1-2: a dark and watery chaos is made dry and lighted so that creatures might live. The psalmist reacts to the beauty of creation with awe (24-34). May sin not deface God's work (35)!

104, 3: *Your palace upon the waters*: God's heavenly dwelling above the upper waters of the sky. Cf Gn 1, 6-7; Ps 29, 10.

104, 5-9: God places the gigantic disk of the earth securely on its foundation and then, as a warrior, chases away the enveloping waters and confines them under, above, and around the earth.

104, 16-18: Even the exotic flora and fauna of the high mountains of the Lebanon range receive adequate water.

V

24 How varied are your works, LORD!
In wisdom you have wrought them all;
the earth is full of your creatures.*
25 Look at the sea, great and wide!
It teems with countless beings,
living things both large and small.*
26† Here ships ply their course;
here Leviathan, your creature, plays.*

VI

27 All of these look to you
to give them food in due time.*
28 When you give to them, they gather;
when you open your hand, they are well filled.
29† When you hide your face, they are lost.
When you take away their breath, they perish
and return to the dust from which they came.*
30 When you send forth your breath, they are created,
and you renew the face of the earth.

VII

31 May the glory of the LORD endure forever;
may the LORD be glad in these works!
32 If God glares at the earth, it trembles;
if God touches the mountains, they smoke!*
33 I will sing to the LORD all my life;
I will sing praise to my God while I live.*
34 May my theme be pleasing to God;
I will rejoice in the LORD.
35† May sinners vanish from the earth,
and the wicked be no more.
Bless the LORD, my soul! Hallelujah!

PSALM 105†

God's Fidelity to the Promise

I

1 Give thanks to the LORD, invoke his name;*
make known among the peoples his deeds!*
2 Sing praise, play music;
proclaim all his wondrous deeds!
3 Glory in his holy name;
rejoice, O hearts that seek the LORD!
4 Rely on the mighty LORD;
constantly seek his face.*
5 Recall the wondrous deeds he has done,
his signs and his words of judgment,
6 You descendants of Abraham his servant,
offspring of Jacob the chosen one!

II

7 The LORD is our God
who rules the whole earth.
8 He remembers forever his covenant,
the pact imposed for a thousand generations,
9 Which was made with Abraham,
confirmed by oath to Isaac,*
10 And ratified as binding for Jacob,
an everlasting covenant for Israel:
11 "To you I give the land of Canaan,
your own allotted heritage."*

III

12 When they were few in number,*
a handful, and strangers there,
13 Wandering from nation to nation,
from one kingdom to another,
14† He let no one oppress them;
for their sake he rebuked kings:
15† "Do not touch my anointed,
to my prophets do no harm."

IV

16 Then he called down a famine on the land,
destroyed the grain that sustained them.*

* ———

24: Ps 92, 6; Sir 39, 16.
25: Sir 43, 26.
26: Jb 3, 8; 40, 25.
27: Pss 136, 25; 145, 15-16.
29: Jb 34, 14-15; Eccl 3, 20; Ps 90, 3.
32: Ps 144, 5.
33: Ps 146, 2.
105, 1-15: 1 Chr 16, 8-22.
1: Pss 18, 50; 96, 3; 145, 5; Is 12, 4-5.
4: Pss 24, 6; 27, 8.
9: Gn 15, 1ff; 26, 3.
11: Gn 12, 7; 15, 18.
12-13: Dt 4, 27; 26, 5.
16: Gn 41, 54. 57.

† ———

104, 26: *Leviathan*: a sea monster symbolizing primeval chaos. Cf Ps 74, 14; Is 27, 1; Jb 40, 25. God does not destroy chaos but makes it part of the created order.

104, 29-30: On one level, the spirit (or wind) of God is the fall and winter rains that provide food for all creatures. On another, it is the breath (or spirit) of God that makes beings live.

104, 35: *Hallelujah*: a frequent word in the last third of the Psalter. The word combines the plural imperative of praise (*hallelu*) with an abbreviated form of the divine name Yah(weh).

Ps 105: A hymn to God who promised the land of Canaan to the holy people. Cf Pss 78; 106; 136. Israel is invited to praise and seek the presence of God (1-6), who is faithful to the promise of land to the ancestors (7-11). In every phase of the national story—the ancestors in the land of Canaan (12-15), Joseph in Egypt (16-22), Israel in Egypt (23-38), Israel in the desert on the way to Canaan (39-45)—God remained faithful, reiterating the promise of the land to successive servants.

105, 14: *Kings*: Pharaoh and Abimelech of Gerar. Cf Gn 12, 17; 20, 6-7.

105, 15: *My anointed . . . my prophets*: the patriarchs Abraham, Isaac, and Jacob, who were "anointed" in the sense of being consecrated and recipients of God's revelation.

PSALMS

17 He had sent a man ahead of them,
Joseph, sold as a slave.*
18 They shackled his feet with chains;
collared his neck in iron,*
19 Till his prediction came to pass,
and the word of the LORD proved
him true.*
20 The king sent and released him;
the ruler of peoples set him free.*
21 He made him lord over his palace,
ruler over all his possessions,*
22 To instruct his princes by his word,
to teach his elders wisdom.

V

23† Then Israel entered Egypt;*
Jacob lived in the land of Ham.
24 God greatly increased his people,
made them too many for their
foes.*
25 He turned their hearts to hate his
people,
to treat his servants unfairly.*
26 He sent his servant Moses,
Aaron whom he had chosen.*
27† They worked his signs in Egypt*
and wonders in the land of Ham.
28 He sent darkness and it grew dark,
but they rebelled against his
word.
29 He turned their waters into blood
and killed all their fish.
30 Their land swarmed with frogs,
even the chambers of their kings.
31 He spoke and there came swarms
of flies,
gnats through all their country.
32 For rain he gave them hail,
flashes of lightning throughout
their land.
33 He struck down their vines and fig
trees,
shattered the trees of their coun-
try.
34 He spoke and the locusts came,
grasshoppers without number.*
35 They devoured every plant in the
land;
they ravaged the crops of their
fields.
36 He struck down every firstborn in
the land,
the first fruits of all their vigor.
37 He brought his people out,
laden with silver and gold;*
no stragglers among the tribes.
38 Egypt rejoiced when they left,
for panic had seized them.

VI

39 He spread a cloud as a cover,
and made a fire to light up the
night.*
40 They asked and he brought them
quail;
with bread from heaven he filled
them.*
41 He split the rock and water gushed
forth;
it flowed through the desert like
a river.*
42 For he remembered his sacred word
to Abraham his servant.
43 He brought his people out with joy,
his chosen ones with shouts of tri-
umph.
44 He gave them the lands of the
nations,
the wealth of the peoples to own,*
45 That they might keep his laws
and observe his teachings.*
Hallelujah!

PSALMS

PSALM 106†

Israel's Confession of Sin

1 Hallelujah!

A

Give thanks to the LORD, who is
good,
whose love endures forever.*
2 Who can tell the mighty deeds of the
LORD,
proclaim in full God's praise?

---

* 17: Gn 37, 28. 36; 45, 5.
18: Gn 39, 20.
19: Gn 40-41.
20: Gn 41, 14.
21: Gn 41, 41-44.
23: Gn 46, 1-47, 12; Acts 7, 15.
24: Ex 1, 7; Acts 7, 17.
25: Ex 1, 8-14.
26: Ex 3, 10; 4, 27.
27-36: Ps 78, 43-51; Ex 7-12.
34: Jl 1, 4.
37: Ex 12, 33-36.
39: Ps 78, 14; Ex 13, 21-22; Wis 18, 3.
40: Ps 78, 24-28; Ex 16, 13-15; Nm 11, 31ff; Wis 16, 20.
41: Ps 78, 15-16; Ex 17, 1-7; Nm 20, 11.
44: Dt 4, 37-40.
45: Dt 6, 20-25; 7, 8-11.
106, 1: Pss 100, 5; 107, 1; 1 Chr 16, 34; Jer 33, 11; Dn 3, 89.

---

† 105, 23. 27: *The land of Ham*: a synonym for Egypt. Cf Gn 10, 6.

105, 27-38: This psalm and Ps 78, 43-51 have an account of the plagues differing in number or in order from Ex 7, 14-12, 30. Several versions of the exodus story were current.

Ps 106: Israel is invited to praise the God whose mercy has always tempered judgment of Israel (1-3). The speaker, on behalf of all, seeks solidarity with the people, who can always count on God's fidelity despite their sin (4-5). Confident of God's mercy, the speaker invites national repentance (6) by reciting from Israel's history eight instances of sin, judgment, and forgiveness. The sins are the rebellion at the Red Sea (6-12; see Ex 14-15), the craving for meat in the desert (13-15; see Nm 11), the challenge to Moses' authority (16-18; see Nm 16), the golden calf episode (19-23; see Ex 32-34), the refusal to take Canaan by the southern route (24-27; see Nm 13-14 and Dt 1-2), the rebellion at Baal-Peor (28-31; see Nm 25, 1-10), the anger of Moses (32-33; see Nm 20, 1-13), and mingling with the nations (34-47). The last, as suggested by its length and generalized language, may be the sin that invites the repentance of the present generation. The text gives the site of each sin: Egypt (7), the desert (14), the camp (16), Horeb (19), in their tents (25), Baal-Peor (28), the waters of Meribah (32), Canaan (38).

3 Happy those who do what is right,
whose deeds are always just.*
4 Remember me, LORD, as you favor your people;
come to me with your saving help,*
5 That I may see the prosperity of your chosen,
rejoice in the joy of your people,
and glory with your heritage.

B

6 We have sinned like our ancestors;*
we have done wrong and are guilty.

I

7 Our ancestors in Egypt
did not attend to your wonders.
They did not remember your great love;
they defied the Most High at the Red Sea.
8 Yet he saved them for his name's sake
to make his power known.*
9 He roared at the Red Sea and it dried up.
He led them through the deep as through a desert.*
10 He rescued them from hostile hands,
freed them from the power of the enemy.
11 The waters covered their oppressors;
not one of them survived.
12 Then they believed his words
and sang songs of praise.*

II

13 But they soon forgot all he had done;
they had no patience for his plan.
14 In the desert they gave way to their cravings,
tempted God in the wasteland.*
15 So he gave them what they asked
and sent among them a wasting disease.*

III

16 In the camp they challenged Moses*
and Aaron, the holy one of the LORD.
17 The earth opened and swallowed Dathan,
it closed on the followers of Abiram.
18 Against that company the fire blazed;
flames consumed the wicked.

IV

19 At Horeb they fashioned a calf,*
worshiped a metal statue.
20 They exchanged their glorious God
for the image of a grass-eating bull.
21 They forgot the God who saved them,
who did great deeds in Egypt,*
22 Amazing deeds in the land of Ham,
fearsome deeds at the Red Sea.
23† He would have decreed their destruction,
had not Moses, the chosen leader,
Withstood him in the breach
to turn back his destroying anger.*

V

24 Next they despised the beautiful land;*
they did not believe the promise.
25 In their tents they complained;
they did not obey the LORD.
26 So with raised hand he swore
to destroy them in the desert,
27 To scatter their descendants among the nations,
disperse them in foreign lands.

VI

28 They joined in the rites of Baal of Peor,*
ate food sacrificed to dead gods.
29 They provoked him by their actions,
and a plague broke out among them.
30 Then Phinehas rose to intervene,
and the plague was brought to a halt.
31 This was counted for him as a righteous deed
for all generations to come.

VII

32† At the waters of Meribah they angered God,*

*

3: Is 56, 1-2.
4: Ps 25, 7; Neh 5, 19.
6-7: Ps 78, 11-17; Ex 14, 11; Lv 26, 40; 1 Kgs 8, 47; Bar 2, 12; Dn 9, 5.
8: Ez 36, 20-22.
9: Ex 14, 21-31; Is 50, 2; 63, 11-14; Na 1, 4.
12: Ex 15, 1-21.
14: Ps 78, 18; Ex 15, 24; 16, 3; Nm 11, 1-6.
15: Ps 78, 26-31; Nm 11, 33.
16-18: Nm 16; Dt 11, 6; Is 26, 11.
19-20: Ex 32; Dt 9, 8-21; Jer 2, 11; Acts 7, 41; Rom 1, 23.
21: Ps 78, 42-58; Dt 32, 18; Jer 2, 32.
23: Ex 32, 11; Dt 9, 25; Ez 22, 30.
24-27: Lv 26, 33; Nm 14; Dt 1, 25-36; Ez 20, 15. 23.
28-31: Nm 25; Dt 26, 14; Sir 45, 23-24.
32-33: Ps 95, 8-9; Ex 17, 1-7; Nm 20, 2-13; Dt 6, 16; 33, 8.

†

106, 23: *Withstood him in the breach*: the image is that of Moses standing in a narrow break made in the wall to keep anyone from entering.

106, 32: *Moses suffered because of them*: Moses was not allowed to enter the promised land because of his rash words (Nm 20, 12). According to Dt 1, 37, Moses was not allowed to cross because of the people's sin, not his own.

and Moses suffered because of them.
33 They so embittered his spirit
that rash words crossed his lips.

VIII

34 They did not destroy the peoples
as the LORD had commanded them,*
35 But mingled with the nations
and imitated their ways.*
36 They worshiped their idols
and were ensnared by them.*
37† They sacrificed to the gods
their own sons and daughters,
38 Shedding innocent blood,
the blood of their own sons and daughters,
Whom they sacrificed to the idols of Canaan,
desecrating the land with bloodshed.
39 They defiled themselves by their actions,
became adulterers by their conduct.
40 So the LORD grew angry with his people,
abhorred his own heritage.
41 He handed them over to the nations,
and their adversaries ruled them.*
42 Their enemies oppressed them,
kept them under subjection.
43 Many times did he rescue them,
but they kept rebelling and scheming
and were brought low by their own guilt.*
44 Still God had regard for their affliction
when he heard their wailing.
45 For their sake he remembered his covenant
and relented in his abundant love,*
46 Winning for them compassion
from all who held them captive.

C

47 Save us, LORD, our God;
gather us from among the nations
That we may give thanks to your holy name
and glory in praising you.*

* * *

48† Blessed be the LORD, the God of Israel,
from everlasting to everlasting!
Let all the people say, Amen!*
Hallelujah!

FIFTH BOOK—Psalms 107-150

PSALM 107†

God the Savior of Those in Distress

1 "Give thanks to the LORD who is good,
whose love endures forever!"*
2 Let that be the prayer of the LORD's redeemed,
those redeemed from the hand of the foe,*
3 Those gathered from foreign lands,
from east and west, from north and south.*

I

4 Some had lost their way in a barren desert;
found no path toward a city to live in.
5 They were hungry and thirsty;
their life was ebbing away.*
6 In their distress they cried to the LORD,
who rescued them in their peril,
7 Guided them by a direct path*
so they reached a city to live in.*
8 Let them thank the LORD for such kindness,
such wondrous deeds for mere mortals.
9 For he satisfied the thirsty,
filled the hungry with good things.*

II

10 Some lived in darkness and gloom,
in prison, bound with chains,

PSALMS

*

34: Dt 7, 1; Jgs 2, 1-5.
35: Lv 18, 3; Jgs 1, 27-35; 3, 5.
36-38: Lv 18, 21; Nm 35, 33; Dt 32, 17; Jgs 2, 11-13. 17. 19; 2 Kgs 16, 3; Bar 4, 7; 1 Cor 10, 20.
41: Jgs 2, 14-23.
43: Is 63, 7-9.
45: Lv 26, 42.
47: 1 Chr 16, 35.
48: Pss 41, 14; 72, 18; 89, 53; 1 Chr 16, 36; Neh 9, 5.
107, 1: Pss 100, 4-5; 106, 1; Jer 33, 11.
2: Is 63, 12.
3: Is 43, 5-6; 49, 12; Zec 8, 7.
5: Dt 8, 15; 32, 10; Is 49, 10.
7: Is 35, 8; 40, 3; 43, 19. • Dt 6, 10.
9: Lk 1, 53.

†

106, 37: *The gods*: Hebrew *shedim*, customarily translated "demons," occurs in parallelism with "gods" in an important inscription from Transjordan and hence is translated "gods."

106, 48: A doxology ending Book IV of the Psalter. It is not part of the psalm.

Ps 107: A hymn inviting those who have been rescued by God to give praise (1-3). Four archetypal divine rescues are described, each ending in thanksgiving: from the sterile desert (4-9), from imprisonment in gloom (10-16), from mortal illness (17-22), and from the angry sea (23-32). The number four connotes totality, all the possible varieties of rescue. The same saving activity of God is shown in Israel's history (33-41); whenever the people were endangered God rescued them. The last verses invite people to ponder the persistent saving acts of God (42-43).

11 Because they rebelled against God's word,
scorned the counsel of the Most High,*
12 Who humbled their hearts through hardship;
they stumbled with no one to help.*
13 In their distress they cried to the LORD,
who saved them in their peril,
14 Led them forth from darkness and gloom
and broke their chains asunder.*
15 Let them thank the LORD for such kindness,
such wondrous deeds for mere mortals.
16 For he broke down the gates of bronze
and snapped the bars of iron.

III

17 Some fell sick from their wicked ways,
afflicted because of their sins.
18 They loathed all manner of food;*
they were at the gates of death.
19 In their distress they cried to the LORD,
who saved them in their peril,
20 Sent forth the word to heal them,*
snatched them from the grave.
21 Let them thank the LORD for such kindness,
such wondrous deeds for mere mortals.
22 Let them offer a sacrifice in thanks,
declare his works with shouts of joy.

IV

23 Some went off to sea in ships,
plied their trade on the deep waters.*
24 They saw the works of the LORD,
the wonders of God in the deep.
25 He spoke and roused a storm wind;
it tossed the waves on high.*
26 They rose up to the heavens, sank to the depths;
their hearts trembled at the danger.
27 They reeled, staggered like drunkards;
their skill was of no avail.*
28 In their distress they cried to the LORD,
who brought them out of their peril,
29 Hushed the storm to a murmur;
the waves of the sea were stilled.*
30 They rejoiced that the sea grew calm,
that God brought them to the harbor they longed for.
31 Let them thank the LORD for such kindness,
such wondrous deeds for mere mortals.
32 Let them praise him in the assembly of the people,
give thanks in the council of the elders.

V

33† God changed rivers into desert,
springs of water into thirsty ground,*
34 Fruitful land into a salty waste,
because of the wickedness of its people.*
35 He changed the desert into pools of water,
arid land into springs of water,*
36 And settled the hungry there;
they built a city to live in.*
37 They sowed fields and planted vineyards,
brought in an abundant harvest.*
38 God blessed them, they became very many,
and their livestock did not decrease.*
40 But he poured out contempt on princes,
made them wander the trackless wastes,*
39 Where they were diminished and brought low
through misery and cruel oppression,
41 While the poor were released from their affliction;
their families increased like their flocks.*
42 The upright saw this and rejoiced;*
all wickedness shut its mouth.
43 Whoever is wise will take note of these things,*
will ponder the merciful deeds of the LORD.

*

11: Is 42, 7. 22; Jb 36, 8-9; Prv 1, 25.
12: Ps 106, 43.
14: Is 42, 7; 49, 9; 51, 14.
18: Jb 6, 6-7; 33, 20.
20: Ps 147, 15; Wis 16, 12; Is 55, 11; Mt 8, 8.
23: Sir 43, 25.
25: Jon 1, 4.
27: Is 29, 9.
29: Pss 65, 8; 89, 10; Mt 8, 26 par.
33: Is 35, 7; 42, 15; 50, 2.
34: Gn 19, 23-28; Dt 29, 22; Sir 39, 23.
35: Ps 114, 8; Is 41, 8.
36: Ez 36, 35.
37: Is 65, 21; Jer 31, 5.
38: Dt 7, 13-14.
40: Jb 12, 23-25.
41: Ps 113, 7.
42: Pss 58, 11; 63, 12.
43: Hos 14, 10.

†

107, 33-41: God destroyed Sodom and Gomorrah in Gn 18-19, which the psalm sees as the destruction of the wicked inhabitants of Canaan to prepare the way for Israel (33-34). God then led Israel through the desert to give them a fertile land (35-38) and protected them from every danger (39-41).

PSALM 108†

Prayer for Victory

1 *A song; a psalm of David*

I

2 My heart is steadfast, God;*
my heart is steadfast.
I will sing and chant praise.
3 Awake, my soul; awake, lyre and harp!
I will wake the dawn.*
4 I will praise you among the peoples, LORD;
I will chant your praise among the nations.*
5 For your love towers to the heavens;
your faithfulness, to the skies.*
6 Appear on high over the heavens, God;
may your glory appear above all the earth.
7 Help with your right hand and answer us
that your loved ones may escape.

II

8 God promised in the sanctuary:*
"I will exult, I will apportion Shechem;
the valley of Succoth I will measure out.
9 Gilead is mine, mine is Manasseh;
Ephraim is the helmet for my head,
Judah, my own scepter.
10 Moab is my washbowl;
upon Edom I cast my sandal;*
I will triumph over Philistia."

III

11 Who will bring me to the fortified city?
Who will lead me into Edom?
12 Was it not you who rejected us, God?
Do you no longer march with our armies?*
13 Give us aid against the foe;
worthless is human help.
14 We will triumph with the help of God,
who will trample down our foes.

PSALM 109†

Prayer of a Person Falsely Accused

1 *For the leader. A psalm of David.*

I

O God, whom I praise, do not be silent,*
2 for wicked and treacherous mouths attack me.
They speak against me with lying tongues;
3 with hateful words they surround me,
attacking me without cause.
4 In return for my love they slander me,
even though I prayed for them.
5 They repay me evil for good,
hatred for my love.*

II

My enemies say of me:
6† "Find a lying witness,
an accuser to stand by his right hand,
7 That he may be judged and found guilty,
that his plea may be in vain.
8 May his days be few;
may another take his office.*
9 May his children be fatherless,
his wife, a widow.*
10 May his children be vagrant beggars,
driven from their hovels.
11 May the usurer snare all he owns,
strangers plunder all he earns.
12 May no one treat him kindly
or pity his fatherless children.
13 May his posterity be destroyed,*
his name cease in the next generation.
14 May the LORD remember his fathers' guilt;
his mother's sin not be canceled.*
15 May their guilt be always before the LORD,*
till their memory is banished from the earth,*
16 For he did not remember to show kindness,

PSALMS

*

108, 2-6: Ps 57, 8-12.
3: Jb 38, 12.
4: Pss 9, 12; 18, 50; 148, 13.
5: Pss 36, 6; 71, 19.
8-14: Ps 60, 8-14.
10: Ru 4, 7-8.
12: Ps 44, 10.
109, 1: Pss 35, 22; 83, 1.
5: Pss 35, 12; 38, 21; Prv 17, 13; Jer 18, 20.
8: Acts 1, 20.
9: Ex 22, 23; Jer 18, 21.
13: Ps 21, 11; Prv 10, 7.
14: Ex 20, 5.
15: Ps 90, 8. • Ps 34, 16.

†

Ps 108: A prayer compiled from two other psalms: 2-6 are virtually the same as Ps 57, 8-12; 7-14 are the same as Ps 60, 7-14. An old promise of salvation (8-10) is combined with a confident assurance (1-6. 14) and petition (7. 12-13).

Ps 109: A lament notable for the length and vehemence of its prayer against evildoers (6-20); the cry to God (1) and the complaint (22-25) are brief in comparison. The psalmist is apparently the victim of a slander campaign, potentially devastating in a society where reputation and honor are paramount. In the emotional perspective of the psalm, there are only two types of people: the wicked and their poor victims. The psalmist is a poor victim (22. 31) and by that fact a friend of God and enemy of the wicked. The psalmist seeks vindication not on the basis of personal virtue but because of God's promise to protect the poor.

109, 6: *An accuser*: Hebrew *satan*, a word occurring in Jb 1-2 and Zec 3, 1-2. In the latter passage Satan stands at the right hand of the high priest to bring false accusations against him before God. Here the accuser is human.

but hounded the wretched poor
and brought death to the broken-hearted.
17 He loved cursing; may it come upon him;
he hated blessing; may none come to him.
18 May cursing clothe him like a robe;
may it enter his belly like water,
seep into his bones like oil.
19 May it be near as the clothes he wears,
as the belt always around him."

III

20† May the LORD bring all this upon my accusers,
upon those who speak evil against me.
21 But you, LORD, my God,
deal kindly with me for your name's sake;
in your great mercy rescue me.
22 For I am sorely in need;
my heart is pierced within me.
23 Like a lengthening shadow I near my end,
all but swept away like the locust.
24 My knees totter from fasting;*
my flesh has wasted away.
25 I have become a mockery to them;
when they see me, they shake their heads.
26 Help me, LORD, my God;
save me in your kindness.
27 Make them know this is your hand,
that you, LORD, have acted.
28 Though they curse, may you bless;
shame my foes, that your servant may rejoice.
29 Clothe my accusers with disgrace;
make them wear shame like a mantle.
30 I will give fervent thanks to the LORD;
before all I will praise my God.*
31 For God stands at the right hand of the poor
to defend them against unjust accusers.

PSALM 110†

God Appoints the King both King and Priest

1† *A psalm of David.*

The LORD says to you, my lord:
"Take your throne at my right hand,
while I make your enemies your footstool."*
2 The scepter of your sovereign might
the LORD will extend from Zion.
The LORD says: "Rule over your enemies!
3† Yours is princely power from the day of your birth.
In holy splendor before the daystar,
like the dew I begot you."*
4† The LORD has sworn and will not waver:
"Like Melchizedek you are a priest forever."*
5 At your right hand is the Lord,
who crushes kings on the day of wrath,*
6 Who, robed in splendor, judges nations,
crushes heads across the wide earth,
7† Who drinks from the brook by the wayside
and thus holds high the head.*

PSALM 111†

Praise of God for Goodness to Israel

1† Hallelujah!

I will praise the LORD with all my heart*

*

24-25: Ps 69, 11-13.
30: Ps 111, 1.
110, 1: Mt 22, 44; Acts 2, 34-35; 1 Cor 15, 25; Heb 1, 13; 8, 1; 10, 12-13; 1 Pt 3, 22.
3: Pss 2, 7; 89, 27; Is 49, 1.
4: Pss 89, 35; 132, 11; Gn 14, 18; Heb 5, 6; 7, 21.
5: Ps 2, 9; Rv 2, 27; 12, 5; 19, 15.
7: Ps 3, 4.
111, 1: Ps 138, 1.

†

109, 20: *May the LORD bring all this*: the psalmist prays that God ratify the curses of 6-19 and bring them upon the wicked.

Ps 110: A royal psalm in which a court singer recites three oracles in which God assures the king that his enemies are conquered (1-2), makes the king "son" in traditional adoption language (3), gives priestly status to the king and promises to be with him in future military ventures (4-7).

110, 1: *The LORD says to you, my lord*: literally, "The LORD says to my lord," a polite form of address of an inferior to a superior. Cf 1 Sm 25, 25; 2 Sm 1, 10. The court singer refers to the king. Jesus in the synoptic gospels (Mt 22, 41-46 and parallels) takes the psalmist to be David and hence "my lord" refers to the messiah, who must be someone greater than David. *Your footstool*: in ancient times victorious kings put their feet on the prostrate bodies of their enemies.

110, 3: *Like the dew I begot you*: an adoption formula as in Pss 2, 7; 89, 27-28. *Before the daystar*: possibly an expression for before the world began (Prv 8, 22).

110, 4: *Like Melchizedek*: Melchizedek was the ancient king of Salem (Jerusalem) who blessed Abraham (Gn 14, 18-20); like other kings of the time he performed priestly functions. Heb 7 sees in Melchizedek a type of Christ.

110, 7: *Who drinks from the brook by the wayside*: the meaning is uncertain. Some see an allusion to a rite of royal consecration at the Gihon spring (cf 1 Kgs 1, 33. 38). Others find here an image of the divine warrior (or king) pursuing enemies so relentlessly that he does not stop long enough to eat and drink.

Ps 111: A temple singer (1) tells how God is revealed in Israel's history (2-10). The deeds reveal God's very self, powerful, merciful, faithful. The poem is an acrostic, each verse beginning with a successive letter of the Hebrew alphabet.

111, 1: *In the assembled congregation of the upright*: in the temple. Cf Ps 149, 1.

in the assembled congregation of
the upright.
2 Great are the works of the LORD,
to be treasured for all their de-
lights.
3† Majestic and glorious is your work,
your wise design endures forever.
4 You won renown for your wondrous
deeds;
gracious and merciful is the
LORD.*
5† You gave food to those who fear
you,
mindful of your covenant forever.
6† You showed powerful deeds to your
people,
giving them the lands of the na-
tions.
7 The works of your hands are right
and true,
reliable all your decrees,
8 Established forever and ever,
to be observed with loyalty and
care.
9 You sent deliverance to your people,
ratified your covenant forever;
holy and awesome is your name.
10† The fear of the LORD is the beginning
of wisdom;*
prudent are all who live by it.
Your praise endures forever.

PSALM 112†

The Blessings of the Just

1† Hallelujah!

Happy are those who fear the LORD,
who greatly delight in God's com-
mands.*
2 Their descendants shall be mighty
in the land,
a generation upright and blessed.
3† Wealth and riches shall be in their
homes;
their prosperity shall endure for-
ever.
4 They shine through the darkness, a
light for the upright;*
they are gracious, merciful, and
just.
5 All goes well for those gracious in
lending,
who conduct their affairs with jus-
tice.
6 They shall never be shaken;
the just shall be remembered for-
ever.*
7 They shall not fear an ill report;
their hearts are steadfast, trust-
ing the LORD.
8 Their hearts are tranquil, without
fear,
till at last they look down on their
foes.
9† Lavishly they give to the poor;
their prosperity shall endure for-
ever;*
their horn shall be exalted in
honor.
10 The wicked shall be angry to see
this;
they will gnash their teeth and
waste away;
the desires of the wicked come to
nothing.

PSALM 113†

Praise of God's Care of the Poor

1 Hallelujah!

I

Praise, you servants of the LORD,
praise the name of the LORD.*
2 Blessed be the name of the LORD
both now and forever.
3 From the rising of the sun to its
setting
let the name of the LORD be
praised.

II

4 High above all nations is the LORD;
above the heavens God's glory.*
5 Who is like the LORD,
our God enthroned on high,
6 looking down on heaven and
earth?*

*

4: Ps 103, 8; 112, 4.
10: Prv 1, 7; 9, 10; Sir 1, 16.
112, 1: Pss 1, 1-2; 119, 1-2; 128, 1.
4: Pss 37, 6; 97, 11; Prv 13, 9; Is 58, 10.
6: Prv 10, 7; Wis 8, 13.
9: Prv 22, 9; 2 Cor 9, 9.
113, 1: Ps 135, 1.
4: Ps 148, 13.
6: Ps 89, 7-9.

†

111, 3: *Your*: the psalm refers to God in the third person throughout; the shift to the second person is for the sake of inclusive language.

111, 5: *Food to those who fear you*: probably a reference to the manna in the desert, which elsewhere is seen as a type of the Eucharist. Cf Jn 6, 31-33. 49-51.

111, 6: *Lands*: literally, "inheritance, heritage."

111, 10: *The fear of the LORD*: reverence for God, the Hebrew term for religion.

Ps 112: An acrostic poem detailing the blessings received by those who remain close to God by obedience to the commandments. Among their blessings are children (2), wealth that enables them to be magnanimous (3. 5. 9), and virtue by which they encourage others (4). The just person is an affront to the wicked, whose hopes remain unfulfilled (10). The logic resembles Pss 1 and 111.

112, 1: *Happy are those*: literally, "Happy the person." "Person" is used typically, hence the plural translation.

112, 3: *Prosperity*: literally, "justice." In the Second Temple Period the word acquired the nuance of liberality and almsgiving. Cf Sir 3, 30; 7, 10; Mt 6, 1-4.

112, 9: *Their horn*: the symbol for vitality and honor.

Ps 113: A hymn exhorting the congregation to praise God's name, i.e., the way in which God is present in the world; the name is mentioned three times in 1-3. The divine name is especially honored in the temple (1) but its recognition is not limited by time (2) and space (3), for God is everywhere active (4-5) especially in rescuing the lowly faithful (7-9).

7 The LORD raises the needy from the dust,
lifts the poor from the ash heap,*
8 Seats them with princes,
the princes of the people,
9 Gives the childless wife a home,
the joyful mother of children.*
Hallelujah!

PSALM 114†

The Lord's Wonders at the Exodus

1 When Israel came forth from Egypt,
the house of Jacob from an alien people,
2 Judah became God's holy place,
Israel, God's domain.*
3† The sea beheld and fled;
the Jordan turned back.*
4 The mountains skipped like rams;
the hills, like lambs of the flock.*
5 Why was it, sea, that you fled?
Jordan, that you turned back?
6 You mountains, that you skipped like rams?
You hills, like lambs of the flock?
7 Tremble, earth, before the Lord,*
before the God of Jacob,
8† Who turned rock into pools of water,
stone into flowing springs.*

PSALM 115†

The Greatness of the True God

I

1 Not to us, LORD, not to us
but to your name give glory
because of your faithfulness and love.*
2† Why should the nations say,
"Where is their God?"*
3 Our God is in heaven;
whatever God wills is done.*

II

4 Their idols are silver and gold,*
the work of human hands.*
5 They have mouths but do not speak,
eyes but do not see.
6 They have ears but do not hear,
noses but do not smell.
7 They have hands but do not feel,
feet but do not walk,
and no sound rises from their throats.
8 Their makers shall be like them,
all who trust in them.

III

9† The house of Israel trusts in the LORD,*
who is their help and shield.*
10 The house of Aaron trusts in the LORD,
who is their help and shield.
11 Those who fear the LORD trust in the LORD,
who is their help and shield.
12 The LORD remembers us and will bless us,
will bless the house of Israel,
will bless the house of Aaron,
13 Will bless those who fear the LORD,
small and great alike.
14 May the LORD increase your number,
you and your descendants.
15 May you be blessed by the LORD,
who made heaven and earth.
16† The heavens belong to the LORD,
but the earth is given to us.*
17† The dead do not praise the LORD,
all those gone down into silence.*
18 It is we who bless the LORD,
both now and forever.
Hallelujah!

---

*

7: Ps 107, 41; 1 Sm 2, 7-8.
9: 1 Sm 2, 5; Is 54, 1.
114, 2: Ex 19, 6.
3: Ex 14, 21f; Jos 3, 14ff; Pss 66, 6; 74, 15.
4: Ps 29, 6; Wis 19, 9.
7: Ps 68, 9.
8: Ex 17, 6; Nm 20, 11.
115, 1: Ez 36, 22-23.
2: Ps 79, 10.
3: Ps 135, 6.
4-10: Ps 135, 15-19; Wis 15, 15-16; Is 44, 9f; Jer 10, 1-5.
4: Is 40, 19.
9: Ps 118, 2-4.•Ps 33, 20.
16: Gn 1, 28.
17: Pss 6, 6; 88, 11ff; Sir 17, 22f; Is 38, 18.

---

†

Ps 114: A hymn celebrating Israel's escape from Egypt, journey through the wilderness, and entry into the promised land, and the miracles of nature that bore witness to God's presence in their midst. In the perspective of the psalm, the people proceed directly from Egypt into the promised land (1-2). Sea and Jordan, which stood like soldiers barring the people from their land, flee before the mighty God as the earth recoils from the battle (3-4). The poet taunts the natural elements as one taunts defeated enemies (5-6).

114, 3-4: Pairs of cosmic elements such as sea and rivers, mountains and hills, are sometimes mentioned in creation accounts. Personified here as warriors, the pairs tremble in fear before the Divine Warrior. The quaking also recalls the divine appearance in the storm at Sinai (Ex 19, 16-19) and elsewhere (Jgs 5, 4-5; Ps 18, 8-16).

114, 8: The miracles of giving drink to the people in the arid desert. Cf Ex 17, 1-7; Is 41, 17-18.

Ps 115: A response to the enemy taunt, "Where is your God?" This hymn to the glory of Israel's God (1-3) ridicules the lifeless idols of the nations (4-8), expresses in a litany the trust of the various classes of the people in God (9-11), invokes God's blessing on them as they invoke the divine name (12-15), and concludes as it began with praise of God. Ps 135, 15-18 similarly mocks the Gentile gods and has a similar litany and hymn (Ps 135, 19-21).

115, 2: *Where is their God?*: implies that God cannot help them.

115, 9-11: *The house of Israel . . . the house of Aaron . . . those who fear the LORD*: the laity of Israelite birth, the priests, and the converts to Judaism. Cf Pss 118, 2-4; 135, 19-21. In the New Testament likewise "those who fear the Lord" means converts to Judaism (cf Act 10, 2. 22. 35; 13, 16. 26).

115, 16: *The heavens*: literally "the heaven of heavens" or "the highest heavens," i.e., above the firmament. See note on Ps 148, 4.

115, 17: See note on Ps 6, 6.

PSALM 116†

Thanksgiving to God Who Saves from Death

I

1 I love the LORD, who listened
to my voice in supplication,
2 Who turned an ear to me
on the day I called.
3† I was caught by the cords of death;*
the snares of Sheol had seized me;
I felt agony and dread.
4 Then I called on the name of the LORD,
"O LORD, save my life!"

II

5 Gracious is the LORD and just;
yes, our God is merciful.*
6 The LORD protects the simple;
I was helpless, but God saved me.
7 Return, my soul, to your rest;
the LORD has been good to you.*
8 For my soul has been freed from death,
my eyes from tears, my feet from stumbling.*
9† I shall walk before the LORD
in the land of the living.*

III

10† I kept faith, even when I said,
"I am greatly afflicted!"*
11 I said in my alarm,
"No one can be trusted!"*
12 How can I repay the LORD
for all the good done for me?
13† I will raise the cup of salvation
and call on the name of the LORD.
14 I will pay my vows to the LORD
in the presence of all his people.
15† Too costly in the eyes of the LORD
is the death of his faithful.*
16 LORD, I am your servant,
your servant, the child of your maidservant;*
you have loosed my bonds.
17 I will offer a sacrifice of thanksgiving
and call on the name of the LORD.*
18 I will pay my vows to the LORD*
in the presence of all his people,
19 In the courts of the house of the LORD,
in your midst, O Jerusalem.
Hallelujah!

PSALM 117†

The Nations Called To Praise

1 Praise the LORD, all you nations!
Give glory, all you peoples!*
2 The LORD's love for us is strong;
the LORD is faithful forever.
Hallelujah!

PSALM 118†

Hymn of Thanksgiving

I

1 Give thanks to the LORD, who is good,*
whose love endures forever.
2 Let the house of Israel say:
God's love endures forever.
3 Let the house of Aaron say,
God's love endures forever.
4 Let those who fear the LORD say,*
God's love endures forever.

II

5 In danger I called on the LORD;
the LORD answered me and set me free.
6 The LORD is with me; I am not afraid;
what can mortals do against me?*
7 The LORD is with me as my helper;
I shall look in triumph on my foes.
8 Better to take refuge in the LORD*
than to put one's trust in mortals.

PSALMS

*

116, 3: Ps 18, 5; Jon 2, 3.
5: Ex 34, 6.
7: Ps 13, 6.
8: Ps 56, 14; Is 25, 8; Rv 21, 4.
9: Pss 27, 13; 56, 14; Is 38, 11.
10: 2 Cor 4, 13.
11: Ps 12, 2.
15: Ps 72, 14; Is 43, 4.
16: Pss 86, 16; 143, 12; Wis 9, 5.
17: Lv 7, 12ff.
18: Jon 2, 10.
117, 1: Rom 15, 11.
118, 1: Pss 100, 5; 136, 1f.
4: Ps 115, 9-11.
6: Ps 27, 1; Heb 13, 6.
8f: Ps 146, 3.

†

Ps 116: A thanksgiving in which the psalmist responds to divine rescue from mortal danger (3-4) and from near despair (10-11) with vows and temple sacrifices (13-14. 17-19). The Greek and Latin versions divide the psalm into two parts: 1-9 and 10-19, corresponding to its two major divisions.

116, 3: *The cords of death*: death is personified here; it attempts to capture the psalmist with snares and nets. Cf Ps 18, 6.

116, 9: *The land of the living*: the phrase elsewhere is an epithet of the Jerusalem Temple (cf Pss 27, 13; 52, 7; Is 38, 11). Hence the psalmist probably refers to being present to God in the temple.

116, 10: *I kept faith, even when I said*: even in the days of despair, the psalmist did not lose all hope.

116, 13: *The cup of salvation*: probably the libation of wine poured out in gratitude for rescue. Cf Ex 25, 29; Nm 15, 5. 7. 10.

116, 15: *Too costly in the eyes of the LORD*: the meaning is that the death of God's faithful is grievous to God, not that God is pleased with the death. Cf Ps 72, 14. In Wis 3, 5-6 God accepts the death of the righteous as a sacrificial burnt offering

Ps 117: This shortest of hymns calls on the nations to acknowledge God's supremacy. The supremacy of Israel's God has been demonstrated to them by the people's secure existence, which is owed entirely to God's gracious fidelity.

Ps 118: A thanksgiving liturgy accompanying a victory procession of the king and the people into the temple precincts. After an invocation in the form of a litany (1-4), the psalmist (very likely speaking in the name of the community) describes how the people confidently implored God's help (5-9) when hostile peoples threatened its life (10-14); vividly God's rescue is recounted (15-18). Then follows a dialogue at the temple gates between the priests and the psalmist as the latter enters to offer the thanksgiving sacrifice (19-25). Finally, the priests impart their blessing (26-27), and the psalmist sings in gratitude (28-29).

9 Better to take refuge in the LORD
than to put one's trust in princes.

III

10 All the nations surrounded me;
in the LORD's name I crushed them.
11 They surrounded me on every side;
in the LORD's name I crushed them.
12 They surrounded me like bees;*
they blazed like fire among thorns;
in the LORD's name I crushed them.
13 I was hard pressed and falling,
but the LORD came to my help.*
14 The LORD, my strength and might,
came to me as savior.*

IV

15 The joyful shout of deliverance
is heard in the tents of the victors:
"The LORD's right hand strikes with power;
16 the LORD's right hand is raised;
the LORD's right hand strikes with power."
17 I shall not die but live
and declare the deeds of the LORD.
18 The LORD chastised me harshly,
but did not hand me over to death.

V

19 Open the gates of victory;
I will enter and thank the LORD.*
20† This is the LORD's own gate,
where the victors enter.
21 I thank you for you answered me;
you have been my savior.
22† The stone the builders rejected
has become the cornerstone.*
23 By the LORD has this been done;
it is wonderful in our eyes.
24 This is the day the LORD has made;
let us rejoice in it and be glad.
25† LORD, grant salvation!
LORD, grant good fortune!

VI

26 Blessed is he
who comes in the name of the LORD.*
We bless you from the LORD's house.
27 The LORD is God and has given us light.
Join in procession with leafy branches
up to the horns of the altar.

VII

28 You are my God, I give you thanks;
my God, I offer you praise.
29 Give thanks to the LORD, who is good,
whose love endures forever.

PSALM 119†

A Prayer to God, the Lawgiver

Aleph

1 Happy those whose way is blameless,
who walk by the teaching of the LORD.*
2 Happy those who observe God's decrees,
who seek the LORD with all their heart.*
3 They do no wrong;
they walk in God's ways.
4 You have given them the command
to keep your precepts with care.
5 May my ways be firm
in the observance of your laws!
6 Then I will not be ashamed
to ponder all your commands.
7 I will praise you with sincere heart
as I study your just edicts.
8 I will keep your laws;
do not leave me all alone.

Beth

9 How can the young walk without fault?

---

* 12: Dt 1, 44.
13: Ps 129, 1-2.
14: Ex 15, 2; Is 12, 2.
19: Is 26, 2.
22: Mt 21, 42; Lk 20, 17; Acts 4, 11; Rom 9, 33; 1 Pt 2, 7.
26: Mt 21, 9; 23, 39.
119, 1: Pss 1, 1-2; 15, 2; 112, 1.
2: Dt 4, 29.

---

† 118, 20: *Where the victors enter*: their victory has demonstrated that God favors them; they are "just" in the biblical sense.

118, 22: *The stone the builders rejected*: a proverb: what is insignificant to human beings has become great through divine election. The "stone" may originally have meant the foundation stone or capstone of the temple. The New Testament interpreted the verse as referring to the death and resurrection of Christ (Mt 21, 42; Acts 4, 11; cf Is 28, 16 and Rom 9, 33; 1 Pt 2, 7).

118, 25: *Grant salvation*: the Hebrew for this cry has come into English as "Hosanna." This cry and the words in 26 were used in the gospels to welcome Jesus entering the temple on Palm Sunday (Mk 11, 9-10).

Ps 119: This psalm, the longest by far in the psalter, praises God for giving such splendid laws and instruction for people to live by. The author glorifies and thanks God for the Torah, prays for protection from sinners enraged by others' fidelity to the law, laments the cost of obedience, delights in the law's consolations, begs for wisdom to understand the precepts, and asks for the rewards of keeping them. Several expected elements do not appear in the psalm: Mount Sinai with its story of God's revelation and gift to Israel of instruction and commandments, the temple and other institutions related to revelation and laws (frequent in other psalms). The psalm is fascinated with God's word directing and guiding human life.

The poem is an acrostic; its twenty-two stanzas (of eight verses each) are in the order of the Hebrew alphabet. Each of the eight verses within a stanza begins with the same letter. Each verse contains one word for "instruction." The translation here given attempts to translate each Hebrew word for "instruction" with the same English word. There are, however, nine words for "instruction," not eight, so the principle of a different word for "instruction" in each verse cannot be maintained with perfect consistency. The nine words for "instruction" in the translation are: law, edict, command, precept, word, utterance, way, decree, and teaching.

Only by keeping your words.
10 With all my heart I seek you;
do not let me stray from your commands.
11 In my heart I treasure your promise,
that I may not sin against you.
12 Blessed are you, O LORD;
teach me your laws.*
13 With my lips I recite
all the edicts you have spoken.
14 I find joy in the way of your decrees
more than in all riches.
15 I will ponder your precepts
and consider your paths.
16 In your laws I take delight;
I will never forget your word.

Gimel

17 Be kind to your servant that I may live,
that I may keep your word.
18 Open my eyes to see clearly
the wonders of your teachings.
19† I am a sojourner in the land;*
do not hide your commands from me.
20 At all times my soul is stirred
with longing for your edicts.
21 With a curse you rebuke the proud
who stray from your commands.
22 Free me from disgrace and contempt,
for I observe your decrees.
23 Though princes meet and talk against me,
your servant studies your laws.
24 Your decrees are my delight;
they are my counselors.

Daleth

25 I lie prostrate in the dust;*
give me life in accord with your word.
26 I disclosed my ways and you answered me;
teach me your laws.
27 Make me understand the way of your precepts;
I will ponder your wondrous deeds.
28 I weep in bitter pain;
in accord with your word to strengthen me.
29 Lead me from the way of deceit;
favor me with your teaching.
30 The way of loyalty I have chosen;
I have set your edicts before me.
31 I cling to your decrees, LORD;
do not let me come to shame.
32† I will run the way of your commands,
for you open my docile heart.

He

33 LORD, teach me the way of your laws;
I shall observe them with care.*
34 Give me insight to observe your teaching,
to keep it with all my heart.
35 Lead me in the path of your commands,*
for that is my delight.
36 Direct my heart toward your decrees
and away from unjust gain.
37 Avert my eyes from what is worthless;
by your way give me life.
38 For your servant fulfill your promise
made to those who fear you.
39 Turn away from me the taunts I dread,
for your edicts bring good.
40 See how I long for your precepts;
in your justice give me life.

Waw

41 Let your love come to me, LORD,
salvation in accord with your promise.
42 Let me answer my taunters with a word,
for I trust in your word.
43 Do not take the word of truth from my mouth,
for in your edicts is my hope.
44 I will keep your teachings always,
for all time and forever.
45 I will walk freely in an open space
because I cherish your precepts.
46 I will speak openly of your decrees
without fear even before kings.
47 I delight in your commands,
which I dearly love.
48† I lift up my hands to your commands;
I study your laws, which I love.

Zayin

49 Remember your word to your servant
by which you give me hope.
50 This is my comfort in affliction,
your promise that gives me life.
51 Though the arrogant utterly scorn me,
I do not turn from your teaching.
52 When I recite your edicts of old
I am comforted, LORD.

PSALMS

*

12: Pss 25, 4; 27, 11; 86, 11; 143, 8. 10.
19: Ps 39, 13.
25: Ps 44, 26.
33: Ps 19, 12.
35: Pss 25, 4; 27, 11; 86, 11; 143, 8. 10.

†

119, 19: *A sojourner in the land*: like someone without the legal protection of a native inhabitant, the psalmist has a special need for the guidance of God's teaching.
119, 32: *For you open my docile heart*: literally, "you make broad my heart."
119, 48: *I lift up my hands to your commands*: to lift up the hands was an ancient gesture of reverence to God. Here the picture is applied to God's law.

53 Rage seizes me because of the wicked;
they forsake your teaching.
54 Your laws become my songs
wherever I make my home.
55 Even at night I remember your name
in observance of your teaching, LORD.
56 This is my good fortune,
for I have observed your precepts.

Heth

57 My portion is the LORD;
I promise to keep your words.
58 I entreat you with all my heart:
have mercy on me in accord with your promise.
59 I have examined my ways
and turned my steps to your decrees.
60 I am prompt, I do not hesitate
in keeping your commands.
61 Though the snares of the wicked surround me,
your teaching I do not forget.
62 At midnight I rise to praise you
because your edicts are just.
63 I am the friend of all who fear you,
of all who keep your precepts.
64 The earth, LORD, is filled with your love;*
teach me your laws.

Teth

65 You have treated your servant well,
according to your word, O LORD.
66 Teach me wisdom and knowledge,
for in your commands I trust.
67 Before I was afflicted I went astray,
but now I hold to your promise.
68 You are good and do what is good;
teach me your laws.
69 The arrogant smear me with lies,
but I observe your precepts with all my heart.
70 Their hearts are gross and fat;*
as for me, your teaching is my delight.
71 It was good for me to be afflicted,
in order to learn your laws.
72 Teaching from your lips is more precious to me
than heaps of silver and gold.

Yodh

73 Your hands made me and fashioned me;
give me insight to learn your commands.
74 Those who fear you rejoice to see me,
because I hope in your word.
75 I know, LORD, that your edicts are just;
though you afflict me, you are faithful.
76 May your love comfort me
in accord with your promise to your servant.
77 Show me compassion that I may live,
for your teaching is my delight.
78 Shame the proud for oppressing me unjustly,
that I may study your precepts.
79 Let those who fear you turn to me,
those who acknowledge your decrees.
80 May I be wholehearted toward your laws,
that I may not be put to shame.

Kaph

81 My soul longs for your salvation;
I put my hope in your word.*
82 My eyes long to see your promise.*
When will you comfort me?
83 I am like a wineskin shriveled by smoke,*
but I have not forgotten your laws.
84 How long can your servant survive?
When will your edict doom my foes?
85 The arrogant have dug pits for me;
defying your teaching.
86 All your commands are steadfast.
Help me! I am pursued without cause.
87 They have almost ended my life on earth,
but I do not forsake your precepts.
88 In your kindness give me life,
to keep the decrees you have spoken.

Lamedh

89† Your word, LORD, stands forever;*
it is firm as the heavens.
90 Through all generations your truth endures;
fixed to stand firm like the earth.
91 By your edicts they stand firm to this day,
for all things are your servants.
92 Had your teaching not been my delight,
I would have perished in my affliction.
93 I will never forget your precepts;
through them you give me life.
94 I am yours; save me,
for I cherish your precepts.
95 The wicked hope to destroy me,
but I pay heed to your decrees.
96 I have seen the limits of all perfection,

64: Ps 33, 5.
69: Pss 17, 10; 73, 7; Jb 15, 27.
81: Ps 130, 6.
82: Pss 25, 15; 123, 1-2; 141, 8.
83: Jb 30, 30.
89: Is 40, 8.

---

† 119, 89-91: God's word creates the world, which manifests that word by its permanence and reliability.

but your command is without bounds.

Mem

97 How I love your teaching, Lord!
I study it all day long.
98 Your command makes me wiser than my foes,
for it is always with me.
99 I have more understanding than all my teachers,
because I ponder your decrees.
100 I have more insight than my elders,
because I observe your precepts.*
101 I keep my steps from every evil path,
that I may obey your word.
102 From your edicts I do not turn,
for you have taught them to me.
103 How sweet to my tongue is your promise,
sweeter than honey to my mouth!*
104 Through your precepts I gain insight;
therefore I hate all false ways.

Nun

105 Your word is a lamp for my feet,
a light for my path.*
106 I make a solemn vow
to keep your just edicts.
107 I am very much afflicted, LORD;
give me life in accord with your word.
108 Accept my freely offered praise;*
LORD, teach me your decrees.
109 My life is always at risk,
but I do not forget your teaching.
110 The wicked have set snares for me,
but from your precepts I do not stray.
111 Your decrees are my heritage forever;
they are the joy of my heart.
112 My heart is set on fulfilling your laws;
they are my reward forever.

Samekh

113 I hate every hypocrite;
your teaching I love.
114 You are my refuge and shield;
in your word I hope.
115 Depart from me, you wicked,*
that I may observe the commands of my God.
116 Sustain me by your promise that I may live;
do not disappoint me in my hope.
117 Strengthen me that I may be safe,
ever to contemplate your laws.
118 You reject all who stray from your laws,
for vain is their deceit.
119 Like dross you regard all the wicked on earth;
therefore I love your decrees.
120 My flesh shudders with dread of you;
I hold your edicts in awe.

Ayin

121 I have fulfilled your just edict;
do not abandon me to my oppressors.
122 Guarantee your servant's welfare;
do not let the arrogant oppress me.
123 My eyes long to see your salvation
and the justice of your promise.
124 Act with kindness toward your servant;
teach me your laws.
125 I am your servant; give me discernment
that I may know your decrees.
126 It is time for the LORD to act;
they have disobeyed your teaching.
127 Truly I love your commands
more than the finest gold.
128 Thus I follow all your precepts;
every wrong way I hate.

Pe

129 Wonderful are your decrees;
therefore I observe them.
130 The revelation of your words sheds light,
gives understanding to the simple.
131 I sigh with open mouth,
yearning for your commands.
132 Turn to me and be gracious,*
your edict for lovers of your name.
133 Steady my feet in accord with your promise;
do not let iniquity lead me.
134 Free me from human oppression,
that I may keep your precepts.
135 Let your face shine upon your servant;
teach me your laws.
136 My eyes shed streams of tears
because your teaching is not followed.

Sadhe

137 You are righteous, LORD,
and just are your edicts.*
138 You have issued your decrees in justice
and in surpassing faithfulness.
139 I am consumed with rage,
because my foes forget your words.
140 Your servant loves your promise;
it has been proved by fire.

PSALMS

* 100: Jb 32, 6; Wis 4, 8-9.
103: Ps 19, 11.
105: Ps 18, 29; Prv 6, 23.
108: Ps 50, 14. 23; Heb 13, 15.
115: Pss 6, 9; 139, 19; Jb 21, 14.
132: Pss 25, 16; 86, 16.
137: Tb 3, 2.

141 Though belittled and despised,
I do not forget your precepts.
142 Your justice is forever right,
your teaching forever true.
143 Though distress and anguish come upon me,
your commands are my delight.
144 Your decrees are forever just;
give me discernment that I may live.

Qoph

145 I call with all my heart, O LORD;
answer me that I may observe your laws.
146 I call to you to save me
that I may keep your decrees.
147 I rise before dawn and cry out;
I put my hope in your words.
148 My eyes greet the night watches
as I meditate on your promise.*
149 Hear my voice in your love, O LORD;
by your edict give me life.
150 Malicious persecutors draw near me;
they are far from your teaching.
151 You are near, O LORD;
reliable are all your commands.
152 Long have I known from your decrees
that you have established them forever.

Resh

153 Look at my affliction and rescue me,
for I have not forgotten your teaching.
154 Take up my cause and redeem me;*
for the sake of your promise give me life.
155 Salvation is far from sinners
because they do not cherish your laws.
156 Your compassion is great, O LORD;
in accord with your edicts give me life.
157 Though my persecutors and foes are many
I do not turn from your decrees.
158 I view the faithless with loathing,*
because they do not heed your promise.
159 See how I love your precepts, LORD;
in your kindness give me life.
160 Your every word is enduring;
all your just edicts are forever.

Shin

161 Princes persecute me without reason,
but my heart reveres only your word.
162 I rejoice at your promise,
as one who has found rich spoil.
163 Falsehood I hate and abhor;
your teaching I love.
164 Seven times a day I praise you
because your edicts are just.
165 Lovers of your teaching have much peace;*
for them there is no stumbling block.
166 I look for your salvation, LORD,
and I fulfill your commands.
167 I observe your decrees;
I love them very much.
168 I observe your precepts and decrees;
all my ways are before you.

Taw

169 Let my cry come before you, LORD;*
in keeping with your word give me discernment.
170 Let my prayer come before you;
rescue me according to your promise.
171 May my lips pour forth your praise,
because you teach me your laws.
172 May my tongue sing of your promise,
for all your commands are just.
173 Keep your hand ready to help me,
for I have chosen your precepts.
174 I long for your salvation, LORD;
your teaching is my delight.
175 Let me live to praise you;
may your edicts give me help.
176 I have wandered like a lost sheep;
seek out your servant,
for I do not forget your commands.*

PSALM 120†

Prayer of a Returned Exile

1† *A song of ascents.*

I

The LORD answered me
when I called in my distress:*
2 LORD, deliver me from lying lips,
from treacherous tongues.*

148: Pss 63, 7; 77, 7.
154: Ps 43, 1.
158: Ps 139, 22.
165: Ps 72, 7.
169: Ps 88, 3.
176: Is 53, 6; Jer 50, 6; Lk 15, 1-7.
120, 1: Jon 2, 3.
2: Ps 12, 3-5; Sir 51, 3.

Ps 120: A thanksgiving, reporting divine rescue (1) yet with fervent prayer for further protection against lying attackers (2-4). The psalmist is acutely conscious of living away from God's own land where divine peace prevails (5-7).

120, 1: *Song of ascents*: Pss 120—134 all begin with this superscription. Most probably these fifteen psalms once formed a collection of psalms sung when pilgrims went to Jerusalem, since one "ascended" to Jerusalem (1 Kgs 12, 28; Pss 24, 3; 122, 4; Lk 2, 42) or to the house of God or to an altar (1 Kgs 12, 33; 2 Kgs 23, 2; Ps 24, 3). Less probable is the explanation that these psalms were sung by the exiles when they "ascended" to Jerusalem from Babylonia (cf Ezr 7, 9). The idea, found in the Mishnah, that the fifteen steps on which the Levites sang corresponded to these fifteen psalms (*Middot* 2, 5) must underlie the Vulgate translation *canticum graduum*, "song of the steps" or "gradual song."

II

3† What will the Lord inflict on you,
O treacherous tongue,
and what more besides?
4† A warrior's sharpened arrows
and fiery coals of brushwood!*

III

5† Alas, I was an alien in Meshech,
I lived near the tents of Kedar!
6 Too long did I live
among those who hated peace.
7 When I spoke of peace,
they were for war.*

PSALM 121†
The Lord My Guardian

1† *A song of ascents.*

I

I raise my eyes toward the mountains.
From where will my help come?*
2 My help comes from the LORD,
the maker of heaven and earth.*

II

3 God will not allow your foot to slip;*
your guardian does not sleep.
4 Truly, the guardian of Israel
never slumbers nor sleeps.
5† The LORD is your guardian;
the LORD is your shade
at your right hand.*
6 By day the sun cannot harm you,
nor the moon by night.*
7 The LORD will guard you from all evil,
will always guard your life.*
8 The LORD will guard your coming and going
both now and forever.*

PSALM 122†
A Pilgrim's Prayer for Jerusalem

1 *A song of ascents. Of David.*

I

I rejoiced when they said to me,
"Let us go to the house of the LORD."*
2 And now our feet are standing
within your gates, Jerusalem.
3† Jerusalem, built as a city,
walled round about.*
4 Here the tribes have come,
the tribes of the LORD,
As it was decreed for Israel,
to give thanks to the name of the LORD.*
5 Here are the thrones of justice,
the thrones of the house of David.

II

6 For the peace of Jerusalem pray:
"May those who love you prosper!
7 May peace be within your ramparts,
prosperity within your towers."*
8 For family and friends I say,
"May peace be yours."
9 For the house of the LORD, our God,
I pray,
"May blessings be yours."

PSALM 123†
Reliance on the Lord

1 *A song of ascents.*

To you I raise my eyes,
to you enthroned in heaven.*
2 Yes, like the eyes of a servant
on the hand of his master,
Like the eyes of a maid
on the hand of her mistress,

*

4: Pss 11, 6; 140, 11; Prv 16, 27.
7: Pss 35, 20; 140, 3-4.
121, 1: Jer 3, 23.
2: Pss 124, 8; 146, 6.
3: Pss 66, 9; 91, 12; 1 Sm 2, 9; Prv 3, 23.
5: Pss 16, 8; 73, 23.
6: Wis 18, 3; Is 25, 4; 49, 10.
7: Ps 97, 10.
8: Dt 28, 6.
122, 1: Pss 43, 3-4; 84, 2-5.
3: Ps 48, 13-14.
4: Dt 16, 16.
7: Ps 128, 5.
123, 1: Pss 25, 15; 119, 82; 141, 8.

†

120, 3: *More besides*: a common curse formula in Hebrew was "May the Lord do such and such evils to you [the evils being specified], and add *still more* to them." Cf 1 Sm 3, 17; 14, 44; 25, 22. Here the psalmist is at a loss for a suitable malediction.

120, 4: *Coals of brushwood*: coals made from the stalk of the broom plant burn with intense heat. The psalmist thinks of lighted coals cast at his enemies.

120, 5: *Meshech* was in the far north (Gn 10, 2) and *Kedar* was a tribe of the north Arabian desert (Gn 25, 13). The psalmist may be thinking generally of all aliens living among inhospitable peoples.

Ps 121: A blessing given to someone embarking on a dangerous journey, whether a soldier going on a campaign or a pilgrim returning home from the temple. People look anxiously at the wooded hills. Will God protect them on their journey (1)? The speaker declares that God is not confined to a place or a time (2), that every step is guarded (3-4); night and day (5-6) God watches over their every movement (7-8).

121, 1: *The mountains*: possibly Mount Zion, the site of the temple and hence of safety, but more probably mountains as a place of dangers, causing anxiety to the psalmist.

121, 5-6: The image of shade, a symbol of protection, is apt: God as shade protects from the harmful effects that ancients believed were caused by the sun and moon.

Ps 122: A song of Zion, sung by pilgrims obeying the law to visit Jerusalem three times on a journey. The singer anticipates joining the procession into the city (1-3). Jerusalem is a place of encounter, where the people praise God (4) and hear the divine justice mediated by the king (5). The very buildings bespeak God's power (cf Ps 48, 13-15). May the grace of this place transform the people's lives (6-9)!

122, 3: *Walled round about*: literally, "which is joined to it," probably referring both to the density of the buildings and to the dense population.

Ps 123: A lament that begins as a prayer of an individual (1), who expresses by a touching comparison exemplary confidence in God (2). The psalm ends in prayer that God relieve the people's humiliation at the hands of the arrogant (3-4).

So our eyes are on the LORD our God,
till we are shown favor.
3 Show us favor, LORD, show us favor,
for we have our fill of contempt.*
4 We have our fill of insult from the insolent,
of disdain from the arrogant.

PSALM 124†

God, the Rescuer of the People

1 *A song of ascents. Of David.*

I

Had not the LORD been with us,
let Israel say,*
2 Had not the LORD been with us,
when people rose against us,
3 They would have swallowed us alive,*
for their fury blazed against us.
4 The waters would have engulfed us,
the torrent overwhelmed us;*
5 seething waters would have drowned us.

II

6 Blessed be the LORD, who did not leave us
to be torn by their fangs.
7 We escaped with our lives
like a bird from the fowler's snare;
the snare was broken and we escaped.
8† Our help is the name of the LORD,
the maker of heaven and earth.*

PSALM 125†

Israel's Protector

1 *A song of ascents.*

I

Like Mount Zion are they
who trust in the LORD,
unshakable, forever enduring.*
2 As mountains surround Jerusalem,
the LORD surrounds his people
both now and forever.*

II

3† The scepter of the wicked will not prevail
in the land given to the just,
Lest the just themselves
turn their hands to evil.

III

4 Do good, LORD, to the good,
to those who are upright of heart.*
5 But those who turn aside to crooked ways
may the LORD send down with the wicked.*
Peace upon Israel!*

PSALM 126†

The Reversal of Zion's Fortunes

1 *A song of ascents.*

I

When the LORD restored the fortunes of Zion,*
then we thought we were dreaming.
2 Our mouths were filled with laughter;
our tongues sang for joy.*
Then it was said among the nations,
"The LORD had done great things for them."
3 The LORD has done great things for us;
Oh, how happy we were!
4† Restore again our fortunes, LORD,
like the dry stream beds of the Negeb.

II

5 Those who sow in tears
will reap with cries of joy.*
6 Those who go forth weeping,
carrying sacks of seed,
Will return with cries of joy,
carrying their bundled sheaves.

*

3: Ps 44, 13-14; Jb 12, 4.
124, 1: Ps 129, 1.
3: Prv 1, 12.
4: Pss 18, 5; 69, 2.
8: Pss 121, 2; 146, 6.
125, 1: Prv 10, 25.
2: Dt 32, 11.
4: Ps 18, 25ff.
5: Prv 3, 32. • Ps 128, 6.
126, 1: Ps 14, 7.
2: Jb 8, 21.
5: Bar 4, 23; Is 65, 19.

†

Ps 124: A thanksgiving which teaches that Israel's very existence is owed to God who rescues them. In the first part Israel's enemies are compared to the mythic sea dragon (2b-3a; cf Jer 51, 34) and Flood (3b-5; cf Is 51, 9-10). The psalm heightens the malice of human enemies by linking them to the primordial enemies of God's creation. Israel is a bird freed from the trapper's snare (6-8)—freed originally from Pharaoh and now from the current danger.

124, 8: *Our help is the name*: for the idiom, see Ex 18, 4.

Ps 125: In response to exilic anxieties about the ancient promises of restoration, the psalm expresses confidence that God will surround the people as the mountains surround Zion (1-2). The just will not be contaminated by the wicked (3). May God judge between the two groups (4-5).

125, 3: *The land given to the just*: literally, "the lot of the just." The promised land was divided among the tribes of Israel by lot (Nm 26, 55; Jos 18). *The just* are the members of the people who are obedient to God. If the domination of the wicked were to continue in the land, even the just would be infected by their evil attitudes.

Ps 126: A lament probably sung shortly after Israel's return from exile. The people rejoice that they are in Zion (1-3) but mere presence in the holy city is not enough; they must pray for the prosperity and the fertility of the land (4). The last verses are probably an oracle of promise: the painful work of sowing will be crowned with life (5-6).

126, 4: *Like the dry stream beds of the Negeb*: the psalmist prays for rain in such abundance that the dry riverbeds will run.

PSALM 127†

The Need of God's Blessing

1 *A song of ascents. Of Solomon.*

I

Unless the LORD build the house,
they labor in vain who build.
Unless the LORD guard the city,
in vain does the guard keep watch.
2 It is vain for you to rise early
and put off your rest at night,
To eat bread earned by hard toil—
all this God gives to his beloved in sleep.*

II

3 Children too are a gift from the LORD,
the fruit of the womb, a reward.*
4 Like arrows in the hand of a warrior
are the children born in one's youth.
5† Blessed are they whose quivers are full.
They will never be shamed
contending with foes at the gate.

PSALM 128†

The Happy Home of the Just

1† *A song of ascents.*

I

Happy are all who fear the LORD,
who walk in the ways of God.*
2 What your hands provide you will enjoy;
you will be happy and prosper:*
3 Like a fruitful vine
your wife within your home,
Like olive plants
your children around your table.*
4 Just so will they be blessed
who fear the LORD.

II

5 May the LORD bless you from Zion,
all the days of your life*
That you may share Jerusalem's joy
6 and live to see your children's children.*
Peace upon Israel!*

PSALM 129†

Against Israel's Enemies

1 *A song of ascents.*

I

Much have they oppressed me from my youth,
now let Israel say.*
2 Much have they oppressed me from my youth,*
yet they have not prevailed.
3 Upon my back the plowers plowed,
as they traced their long furrows.*
4† But the just LORD cut me free
from the ropes of the yoke of the wicked.

II

5 May they be scattered in disgrace,
all who hate Zion.
6† May they be like grass on the rooftops
withered in early growth,*
7 Never to fill the reaper's hands,
nor the arms of the binders of sheaves,
8† With none passing by to call out:
"The blessing of the LORD be upon you!
We bless you in the name of the LORD!"*

PSALMS

*

127, 2: Eccl 2, 24.
3: Pss 115, 14; 128, 3; Dt 28, 11; Prv 17, 6.
128, 1: Ps 112, 1.
2: Ps 112, 3.
3: Jb 29, 5; Ps 144, 12.
5: Pss 20, 3; 134, 3.
6: Jb 42, 16; Prv 17, 6. • Ps 125, 5.
129, 1: Ps 124, 1.
2: Ps 118, 13.
3: Is 51, 23.
6: Is 37, 27.
8: Ps 118, 26.

†

Ps 127: The psalm puts together two proverbs (1-2 and 3-5) on God establishing "houses" or families. The prosperity of human groups is not the work of humans but the gift of God.

127, 5: *At the gate*: the reference is not to enemies besieging the walls of a city but to adversaries in litigation. Lawcourts functioned in the open area near the main city gate. The more adult sons a man had, the more forceful he would appear in disputes. Cf Prv 31, 23.

Ps 128: A statement that the ever-reliable God will bless the reverent (1). God's blessing is concrete: satisfaction and prosperity, a fertile spouse and abundant children (2-4). The perspective is that of the adult male, ordinarily the ruler and representative of the household to the community. The last verses extend the blessing to all the people for generations to come (5-6).

128, 1: *All who fear the LORD*: literally, singular: "the one fearing," is used in a typical sense and so is translated by the plural.

Ps 129: A psalm giving thanks for God's many rescues of Israel over the long course of their history (1-4); the people pray that their oppressors never know the joy of harvest (5-8).

129, 4: *The ropes of the yoke of the wicked*: usually understood as the rope for yoking animals to the plow. If it is severed, the plowing (cf 3) comes to a halt.

129, 6: *Like grass on the rooftops*: after the spring rains, grass would sprout from the coat of mud with which the flat roofs of simple houses were covered, but when the dry summer began there was no moisture in the thin roof-covering to sustain the grass.

129, 8: *The blessing of the LORD be upon you*: harvesters greeted one another with such blessings. Cf Ru 2, 4.

PSALM 130†
Prayer for Pardon and Mercy

1† *A song of ascents.*

I
Out of the depths I call to you, LORD;
2 Lord, hear my cry!
May your ears be attentive
to my cry for mercy.*
3 If you, LORD, mark our sins,
Lord, who can stand?*
4† But with you is forgiveness
and so you are revered.

II
5 I wait with longing for the LORD,
my soul waits for his word.*
6 My soul looks for the Lord
more than sentinels for daybreak.*
More than sentinels for daybreak,
7 let Israel look for the LORD,
For with the LORD is kindness,
with him is full redemption,*
8 And God will redeem Israel
from all their sins.*

PSALM 131†
Humble Trust in God

1 *A song of ascents. Of David.*

LORD, my heart is not proud;
nor are my eyes haughty.
I do not busy myself with great matters,
with things too sublime for me.*
2 Rather, I have stilled my soul,
hushed it like a weaned child.
Like a weaned child on its mother's lap,
so is my soul within me.*
3 Israel, hope in the LORD,
now and forever.

PSALM 132†
The Covenant between David and God

1† *A song of ascents.*

I
LORD, remember David
and all his anxious care;
2† How he swore an oath to the LORD,
vowed to the Mighty One of Jacob:
3 "I will not enter the house where I live,*
nor lie on the couch where I sleep;
4 I will give my eyes no sleep,
my eyelids no rest,
5 Till I find a home for the LORD,
a dwelling for the Mighty One of Jacob."
6† "We have heard of it in Ephrathah;
we have found it in the fields of Jaar.
7 Let us enter God's dwelling;
let us worship at God's footstool."*

8 "Arise, LORD, come to your resting place,*
you and your majestic ark.
9 Your priests will be clothed with justice;
your faithful will shout for joy."
10 For the sake of David your servant,
do not reject your anointed.

II
11 The LORD swore an oath to David,
a pledge never to be broken:*
"Your own offspring* I will set upon your throne.
12 If your sons observe my covenant,
the laws I shall teach them,
Their sons, in turn,
shall sit forever on your throne."
13 Yes, the LORD has chosen Zion,
desired it for a dwelling:
14 "This is my resting place forever;
here I will dwell, for I desire it.
15 I will bless Zion with meat;
its poor I will fill with bread.

*

130, 2: Pss 5, 2-3; 55, 2-3; 86, 6; Lam 3, 55-56; Jon 2, 3.
3: Na 1, 6.
5: Ps 119, 81.
6: Is 21, 11; 26, 9.
7: Pss 86, 15; 100, 5; 103, 8.
8: Ps 25, 22; Mt 1, 21.
131, 1: Ps 139, 6.
2: Is 66, 12-13.
132, 3: 2 Sm 7; 1 Chr 28, 2.
7: Ps 99, 5.
8-10: Pss 2, 2; 89, 21; 95, 11; Nm 10, 35; 2 Chr 6, 41-42; Sir 24, 7.
11: Ps 110, 4; 2 Sm 7, 12.
11-14: Ps 68, 17; 1 Kgs 8, 13; Sir 24, 7.

†

Ps 130: This lament, a Penitential Psalm, is the *De profundis* used in liturgical prayers for the faithful departed. In deep sorrow the psalmist cries to God (1-2), asking for mercy (3-4). The psalmist's trust (5-6) becomes a model for the people (7-8).

130, 1: *The depths*: Sheol here is a metaphor of total misery. Deep anguish makes the psalmist feel "like those descending to the pit" (Ps 143, 7).

130, 4: *And so you are revered*: the experience of God's mercy leads one to a greater sense of God.

Ps 131: A song of trust, in which the psalmist gives up self-sufficiency (1), like a babe enjoying the comfort of its mother's lap (2), thus providing a model for Israel's faith (3).

Ps 132: A song for a liturgical ceremony in which the ark, the throne of Israel's God, was carried in procession to the temple. The singer asks that David's care for the proper housing of the ark be regarded with favor (1-5), and tells how it was brought to Jerusalem (6-10). There follows God's promise of favor to the Davidic dynasty (11-12) and to Zion (13-17). The transfer of the ark to the tent in Jerusalem is described in 2 Sm 6.

132, 1: *All his anxious care*: to build the temple. Cf 2 Sm 7, 1-17 and 1 Kgs 8, 17.

132, 2. 5: *Mighty One of Jacob*: one of the titles of Israel's God. Cf Gn 49, 24; Is 49, 26; 60, 16.

132, 6: *Ephrathah*: the homeland of David. Cf Ru 4, 11. *The fields of Jaar*: poetic for Kiriath-jearim, a town west of Jerusalem, where the ark remained for several generations. Cf 1 Sm 7, 1-2 ; 2 Sm 6, 2; 1 Chr 13, 5-6.

16 I will clothe its priests with blessing;
its faithful shall shout for joy.*
17† There I will make a horn sprout for David's line;*
I will set a lamp for my anointed.
18 His foes I will clothe with shame,
but on him my crown shall gleam."

PSALM 133†

A Vision of a Blessed Community

1† *A song of ascents. Of David.*

How good it is, how pleasant,
where the people dwell as one!
2† Like precious ointment on the head,*
running down upon the beard,
Upon the beard of Aaron,
upon the collar of his robe.
3† Like dew of Hermon coming down
upon the mountains of Zion.*
There the LORD has lavished blessings,
life for evermore!*

PSALM 134†

Exhortation to the Night Watch To Bless God

1† *A song of ascents.*

Come, bless the LORD,
all you servants of the LORD
Who stand in the house of the LORD
through the long hours of night.*
2 Lift up your hands toward the sanctuary,*
and bless the LORD.
3 May the LORD who made heaven and earth*
bless you from Zion.

PSALM 135†

Praise of God, the Ruler and Benefactor of Israel

1 Hallelujah!

I

Praise the name of the LORD!
Praise, you servants of the LORD,*
2 Who stand in the house of the LORD,
in the courts of the house of our God!*
3 Praise the LORD; the LORD is good!
Sing to God's name; it is gracious!
4† For the LORD has chosen Jacob,
Israel as a treasured possession.*

II

5 I know that the LORD is great,
our Lord is greater than all gods.*
6 Whatever the LORD wishes
he does in heaven and on earth,
in the seas and in all the deeps.*
7 He raises storm clouds from the end of the earth,
makes lightning and rain,
brings forth wind from the storehouse.*

III

8 He struck down Egypt's firstborn,*
human and beast alike,
9 And sent signs and portents against you, Egypt,
against Pharaoh and all his servants.
10 The Lord struck down many nations,*
slew mighty kings—
11 Sihon, king of the Amorites,
Og, king of Bashan,
all the kings of Canaan—

PSALMS

*

16: 2 Chr 6, 41; Is 61, 10.
17: Is 11, 1; Jer 33, 15; Ez 29, 21; Zec 3, 8; Lk 1, 69.
133, 2: Ex 30, 25. 30.
3: Hos 14, 6. • Dt 28, 8; 30, 20.
134, 1: Ps 135, 1-2; 1 Chr 9, 33.
2: Pss 28, 2; 141, 2.
3: Pss 20, 3; 128, 5; Nm 6, 24.
135, 1: Ps 113, 1.
2: Ps 134, 1.
4: Pss 33, 12; 144, 15; Ex 19, 6; Dt 7, 6.
5: Ps 95, 3; Ex 18, 11.
6: Ps 115, 3.
7: Ps 148, 8; Jer 10, 13; 51, 16; Jb 37, 9.
8-9: Pss 78, 51; 105, 27. 36; 136, 10; Ex 12, 29.
10-12: Nm 21, 21-35; Dt 2, 24-3, 17; Ps 136, 17-22.

†

132, 17: *A horn sprout for David's line*: the image of the horn, a symbol of strength, is combined with that of a "sprout," a term used for the Davidic descendant (cf Jer 23, 5; 33, 15; Zec 3, 8; 6, 12). Early Christians referred the latter designation to Christ as son of David (Lk 1, 69).

Ps 133: A benediction over a peaceful community, most probably the people Israel, but appropriate too for Israelite families (1). The history of Israel, whether of its ancestors in the book of Genesis or of later periods, was a history of distinct groups struggling to live in unity. Here that unity is declared blessed, like the holy oils upon the priest Aaron or the dew of the rainless summer that waters the crops (2-3).

133, 1: *The people*: literally, "brothers," i.e., male and female members of a kin group or people—most probably, the people Israel.

133, 2: *Ointment*: oil was used at the consecration of the high priest (Ex 30, 22-33).

133, 3: *Dew*: dew was an important source of moisture in the dry climate (Gn 27, 28; Hos 14, 6). *Hermon*: the majestic snow-capped mountain visible in the north of Palestine.

Ps 134: A brief liturgy exhorting the temple singers to acknowledge the great deeds of God at a night service (cf Is 30, 29). Mount Zion is the place from which blessings affect the lives of humans, for there Israel's God dwells.

134, 1: *Servants of the LORD*: priests and Levites. Cf Dt 10, 8; Pss 113, 1; 135, 1; Dn 3, 84-85.

Ps 135: The hymn begins and ends with an invitation to praise God (1-3, 19-20) for the great act of choosing Israel (4). The story of Israel's emergence as a people is told in 5-14; God created and redeemed the people, easily conquering all opposition. God's defeat of hostile powers means that the powers themselves and their images are useless (15-18). The last three verses appear also in Ps 115, 4-8.

135, 4: Though all nations are God's, Israel has a special status as God's "treasured" people: Ex 19, 5; Dt 7, 6; 14, 2; 26, 18; Mal 3, 17.

12 And made their land a heritage,
a heritage for Israel his people.
13 O LORD, your name is forever,
your renown, from age to age!*
14 For the LORD defends his people,
shows mercy to his servants.*

IV

15 The idols of the nations are silver
and gold,*
the work of human hands.
16 They have mouths but speak not;
they have eyes but see not;
17 They have ears but hear not;
no breath is in their mouths.
18 Their makers shall be like them,
all who trust in them.

V

19 House of Israel, bless the LORD!*
House of Aaron, bless the LORD!
20 House of Levi, bless the LORD!
You who fear the LORD, bless the
LORD!
21 Blessed from Zion be the LORD,
who dwells in Jerusalem!
Hallelujah!

PSALM 136†

Hymn of Thanksgiving for God's Everlasting Love

I

1 Praise the LORD, who is so good;*
God's love endures forever;
2 Praise the God of gods;
God's love endures forever;
3 Praise the Lord of lords;
God's love endures forever;

II

4 Who alone has done great wonders,*
God's love endures forever;
5 Who skillfully made the heavens,*
God's love endures forever;
6 Who spread the earth upon the
waters,*
God's love endures forever;
7 Who made the great lights,
God's love endures forever;
8 The sun to rule the day,
God's love endures forever;
9 The moon and stars to rule the
night,*
God's love endures forever;

III

10 Who struck down the firstborn of
Egypt, *
God's love endures forever;
11 And led Israel from their midst,
God's love endures forever;
12 With mighty hand and outstretched
arm,*
God's love endures forever;
13 Who split in two the Red Sea,
God's love endures forever;
14 And led Israel through,
God's love endures forever;
15 But swept Pharaoh and his army
into the Red Sea,*
God's love endures forever;
16 Who led the people through the
desert,*
God's love endures forever;

IV

17 Who struck down great kings,*
God's love endures forever;
18 Slew powerful kings,
God's love endures forever;
19 Sihon, king of the Amorites,
God's love endures forever;
20 Og, king of Bashan,
God's love endures forever;
21 And made their lands a heritage,
God's love endures forever;
22† A heritage for Israel, God's servant,
God's love endures forever.

V

23 The LORD remembered us in our
misery,
God's love endures forever;
24 Freed us from our foes,
God's love endures forever;
25 And gives food to all flesh,
God's love endures forever.

VI

26 Praise the God of heaven,
God's love endures forever.

PSALM 137†

Sorrow and Hope in Exile

I

1 By the rivers of Babylon
we sat mourning and weeping
when we remembered Zion.*

---

*
13: Ps 102, 13; Ex 3, 15.
14: Dt 32, 36.
15-18: Ps 115, 4-6. 8.
19-20: Ps 118, 2-4.
136, 1: Pss 100, 5; 118, 1.
4: Ps 72, 18.
5: Gn 1, 9-19.
6: Ps 24, 2.
9: Jer 31, 35.
10: Ex 12, 29. 51; 14, 22. 27; 15, 22; Pss 78, 51-52; 135, 8.
12: Dt 4, 34.
15: Ex 14, 21f.
16: Dt 8, 2. 15.
17-22: Ps 135, 10-12.
137, 1: Ez 3, 15; Lam 3, 48.

---

†
Ps 136: The hymn praises Israel's God ("the God of gods," 2), who has created the world in which Israel lives. The refrain occurring after every line suggests that a speaker and chorus sang the psalm in antiphonal fashion. A single act of God is described in 4-25: God arranges the heavens and the earth as the environment for human community, and then creates the community by freeing them and giving them land. In the final section (23-25) God, who created the people and gave them land, continues to protect and nurture them.

136, 22: *A heritage for Israel*: the land was given to Israel by God to be handed on to future generations.

Ps 137: A temple singer refuses to sing the people's sacred songs in an alien land despite demands from Babylonian

2† On the poplars of that land
we hung up our harps.*
3 There our captors asked us
for the words of a song;
Our tormentors, for a joyful song:
"Sing for us a song of Zion!"
4 But how could we sing a song of the LORD
in a foreign land?

II

5 If I forget you, Jerusalem,
may my right hand wither.*
6 May my tongue stick to my palate
if I do not remember you,
If I do not exalt Jerusalem
beyond all my delights.

III

7 Remember, LORD, against Edom
that day at Jerusalem.
They said: "Level it, level it
down to its foundations!"*
8 Fair Babylon, you destroyer,
happy those who pay you back
the evil you have done us!*
9† Happy those who seize your children
and smash them against a rock.*

PSALM 138†
Hymn of a Grateful Heart

1† *Of David.*

I

I thank you, LORD, with all my heart;*
before the gods to you I sing.
2 I bow low toward your holy temple;
I praise your name for your fidelity and love.
For you have exalted over all
your name and your promise.
3 When I cried out, you answered;
you strengthened my spirit.

II

4 All the kings of earth will praise you, LORD,
when they hear the words of your mouth.
5 They will sing of the ways of the LORD:
"How great is the glory of the LORD!"
6 The LORD is on high, but cares for the lowly*
and knows the proud from afar.
7 Though I walk in the midst of dangers,
you guard my life when my enemies rage.
You stretch out your hand;
your right hand saves me.
8 The LORD is with me to the end.
LORD, your love endures forever.
Never forsake the work of your hands!

PSALM 139†
The All-knowing and Ever-present God

1 *For the leader. A psalm of David.*

I

LORD, you have probed me, you know me:
2† you know when I sit and stand;*
you understand my thoughts from afar.
3 My travels and my rest you mark;
with all my ways you are familiar.
4 Even before a word is on my tongue,
LORD, you know it all.
5 Behind and before you encircle me
and rest your hand upon me.
6 Such knowledge is beyond me,
far too lofty for me to reach.*

II

7 Where can I hide from your spirit?
From your presence, where can I flee?
8 If I ascend to the heavens, you are there;

*

2: Is 24, 8; Lam 5, 14.
3: Jer 51, 50.
7: Jer 49, 7; Lam 4, 21-22; Ez 25, 12-14.
8: Is 47, 1-3; Jer 50-51.
9: Hos 14, 1.
138, 1: Ps 9, 1.
6: Lk 1, 51-52.
139, 2: 2 Kgs 19, 27; Jb 12, 13.
6: Ps 131, 1.

†

captors (1-4). The singer swears an oath by what is most dear to a musician—hands and tongue—to exalt Jerusalem always (5-6). The psalm ends with a prayer that the old enemies of Jerusalem, Edom and Babylon, be destroyed (7-9).

137, 2: *Poplars*: sometimes incorrectly translated "willow." The Euphrates poplar is a high tree common on riverbanks in the Orient.

137, 9: *Happy those who seize your children and smash them against a rock*: the infants represent the future generations, and so must be destroyed if the enemy is truly to be eradicated.

Ps 138: A thanksgiving to God, who came to the rescue of the psalmist. Divine rescue was not the result of the psalmist's virtues but of God's loving fidelity (1-3). The act is not a private transaction but a public act that stirs the surrounding nations to praise God's greatness and care for the people (4-6). The psalmist, having experienced salvation, trusts that God will always be there in moments of danger (7-8).

138, 1: *Before the gods*: i.e., heavenly beings, who were completely subordinate to Israel's God. The earthly temple represents the heavenly palace of God.

Ps 139: A hymnic meditation on God's omnipresence and omniscience. The psalmist is keenly aware of God's all-knowing gaze (1-6), of God's presence in every part of the universe (7-12), and of God's control over the psalmist's very self (13-16). Summing up 1-16, 17-18 express wonder. There is only one place hostile to God's rule—wicked people. The psalmist prays to be removed from their company (19-24).

139, 2: *When I sit and stand*: in all my physical movement.

if I lie down in Sheol, you are there
too.*
9† If I fly with the wings of dawn
and alight beyond the sea,
10 Even there your hand will guide me,
your right hand hold me fast.
11† If I say, "Surely darkness shall hide
me,
and night shall be my light" —
12 Darkness is not dark for you,
and night shines as the day.
Darkness and light are but one.*

III

13 You formed my inmost being;
you knit me in my mother's
womb.*
14 I praise you, so wonderfully you
made me;
wonderful are your works!
My very self you knew;
15† my bones were not hidden from
you,
When I was being made in secret,
fashioned as in the depths of the
earth.
16 Your eyes foresaw my actions;
in your book all are written
down;*
my days were shaped, before one
came to be.

IV

17 How precious to me are your de-
signs, O God;
how vast the sum of them!
18 Were I to count, they would outnum-
ber the sands;
to finish, I would need eternity.*
19 If only you would destroy the
wicked, O God,
and the bloodthirsty would depart
from me!*
20 Deceitfully they invoke your name;
your foes swear faithless oaths.
21 Do I not hate, LORD, those who hate
you?
Those who rise against you, do I
not loathe?*
22 With fierce hatred I hate them,
enemies I count as my own.

V

23 Probe me, God, know my heart;
try me, know my concerns.*
24† See if my way is crooked,
then lead me in the ancient paths.

PSALM 140†

Prayer for Deliverance from the Wicked

1 *For the leader. A psalm of David.*

I

2 Deliver me, LORD, from the wicked;
preserve me from the violent,*
3 From those who plan evil in their
hearts,
who stir up conflicts every day,
4† Who sharpen their tongues like
serpents,
venom of asps upon their lips.*
Selah

II

5 Keep me, LORD, from the clutches
of the wicked;
preserve me from the violent,
who plot to trip me up.*
6† The arrogant have set a trap for me;
villains have spread a net,
laid snares for me by the wayside.
Selah
7 I say to the LORD: You are my God;*
listen, LORD, to the words of my
prayer.
8 My revered LORD, my strong helper,
my helmet on the day of battle.
9 LORD, do not grant the desires of the
wicked;
do not let their plots succeed.
Selah
10 Around me they raise their proud
heads;
may the mischief they threaten
overwhelm them.
11 May God rain burning coals upon
them,*
cast them into the grave never
more to rise.

III

12 Slanderers will not survive on earth;
evil will quickly entrap the vio-
lent.

*

8: Jb 23, 8-9; Jer 23, 23-24.
12: Jb 12, 22.
13: Wis 7, 1; Eccl 11, 5; Jb 1, 21.
16: Mal 3, 16.
18: Jb 11, 7.
19: Jb 21, 14.
21: Ps 119, 158.
23: Pss 17, 3; 26, 2.
140, 2: Ps 71, 4.
4: Ps 64, 4; Rom 3, 13.
5: Jer 18, 22; Pss 56, 7; 57, 7.
7: Ps 31, 15.
11: Pss 11, 6; 120, 4; Gn 19, 24.

†

139, 9: *Fly with the wings of dawn*: go to the extremities of the east. *Beyond the sea*: uttermost bounds of the west; the sea is the Mediterranean.

139, 11: *Night shall be my light*: night to me is what day is to others.

139, 15: *The depths of the earth*: figurative language for the womb, stressing the hidden and mysterious operations that occur there.

139, 24: *My way . . . the ancient paths*: the manner of living of our ancestors, who were faithful to God's will. Cf Jer 6, 16.

Ps 140: A lament seeking rescue from violent and treacherous foes (2-6). The psalmist remains trusting (7-8), vigorously praying that the plans of the wicked recoil upon themselves (9-12). A serene statement of praise ends the psalm (13-14). The psalmist is content to be known as one of "the needy," "the poor," "the just," "the upright" (13-14), a class of people expecting divine protection.

140, 4: Similar metaphors for a wicked tongue are used in Pss 52, 4; 55, 22; 58, 5.

140, 6: *Have set a trap . . . have spread a net*: the same figure, of hunters setting traps, occurs in Pss 9, 16; 31, 5; 35, 7; 64, 6. Cf Mt 22, 15; Lk 11, 54.

13 For I know the LORD will secure
justice for the needy, their rights
for the poor.
14 Then the just will give thanks to your
name;
the upright will dwell in your
presence.*

PSALM 141†

Prayer for Deliverance from the Wicked

1 *A psalm of David.*

LORD, I call to you;
come quickly to help me;
listen to my plea when I call.
2† Let my prayer be incense before
you;
my uplifted hands an evening
sacrifice.*
3 Set a guard, LORD, before my mouth,
a gatekeeper at my lips.*
4 Do not let my heart incline to evil,
or yield to any sin.
I will never feast upon
the fine food of evildoers.
5† Let the just strike me; that is
kindness;
let them rebuke me; that is oil for
my head.*
All this I shall not refuse,
but will pray despite these trials.
6 When their leaders are cast over the
cliff,
all will learn that my prayers were
heard.
7 As when a farmer plows a field into
broken clods,
so their bones will be strewn at
the mouth of Sheol.
8 My eyes are upon you, O GOD, my
Lord;*
in you I take refuge; do not strip
me of life.
9 Guard me from the trap they have
set for me,
from the snares of evildoers.*
10 Into their own nets let all the wicked
fall,
while I make good my own escape.

PSALM 142†

A Prayer in Time of Trouble

1† *A* maskil *of David, when he was in
the cave. A prayer.*

2 With full voice I cry to the LORD;
with full voice I beseech the LORD.
3 Before God I pour out my complaint,
lay bare my distress.
4 My spirit is faint within me,*
but you know my path.*
Along the way I walk
they have hidden a trap for me.*
5 I look to my right hand,*
but no friend is there.
There is no escape for me;
no one cares for me.
6 I cry out to you, LORD,
I say, You are my refuge,*
my portion in the land of the liv-
ing.*
7 Listen to my cry for help,
for I am brought very low.*
Rescue me from my pursuers,
for they are too strong for me.
8† Lead me out of my prison,
that I may give thanks to your
name.
Then the just shall gather around
me
because you have been good to
me.

PSALM 143†

A Prayer in Distress

1 *A psalm of David.*

LORD, hear my prayer;
in your faithfulness listen to my
pleading;
answer me in your justice.

*

14: Pss 11, 7; 16, 11; 17, 15.
141, 2: Ps 134, 2; Ex 30, 8.
3: Sir 22, 27.
5: Prv 9, 8; 25, 12.
8: Pss 25, 15; 123, 1-2.
9: Ps 142, 4.
142, 4: Ps 143, 4. • Ps 139, 24. • Ps 141, 9.
5: Pss 16, 8; 73, 23; 121, 5.
6: Ps 91, 2. 9. • Pss 16, 5; 27, 13; 116, 9; Is 38, 11.
7: Ps 79, 8.

†

Ps 141: A lament of an individual (1-2) who is keenly aware that only the righteous can worship God properly and who therefore prays to be protected from the doomed wicked (3-10).

141, 2: *Incense*: literally, "smoke," i.e., the fragrant fumes arising from the altar at the burning of sacrificial animals or of aromatic spices; also used in Rv 5, 8 as a symbol of prayer. *My uplifted hands*: the gesture of supplication. Cf Pss 28, 2; 63, 5; 88, 10; 119, 48; 134, 2; 143, 6.

141, 5-7: the Hebrew text is obscure.

Ps 142: In this lament imploring God for help (2-4b), the psalmist tells how enemies have set a trap (4c-5), and prays for rescue (6-8). The speaker feels utterly alone (5), exhausted (7), and may even be imprisoned (8a). Prison is possibly a metaphor for general distress. The last two verses are the vow of praise, made after receiving an assurance of divine help (8cd).

142, 1: *In the cave*: cf 1 Sm 22, 1; 24, 1-3; Ps 57, 1.

142, 8: *Then the just shall gather around me*: in the temple, when the psalmist offers a thanksgiving sacrifice.

Ps 143: One of the Church's seven Penitential Psalms, this lament is a prayer to be freed from death-dealing enemies. The psalmist addresses God, aware that there is no equality between God and humans; salvation is a gift (1-2). Victimized by evil people (3-4), the psalmist recites ("remembers") God's past actions on behalf of the innocent (5-6). The psalm continues with fervent prayer (7-9) and a strong desire for guidance and protection (10-12).

2 Do not enter into judgment with your servant;
before you no living being can be just.*
3† The enemy has pursued me;
they have crushed my life to the ground.*
They have left me in darkness
like those long dead.*
4 My spirit is faint within me;
my heart is dismayed.*
5 I remember the days of old;
I ponder all your deeds;
the works of your hands I recall.*
6 I stretch out my hands to you;
I thirst for you like a parched land.* *Selah*
7 Hasten to answer me, LORD;
for my spirit fails me.
Do not hide your face from me,
lest I become like those descending to the pit.*
8 At dawn let me hear of your kindness,
for in you I trust.
Show me the path I should walk,
for to you I entrust my life.*
9 Rescue me, LORD, from my foes,
for in you I hope.
10 Teach me to do your will,
for you are my God.
May your kind spirit guide me
on ground that is level.
11 For your name's sake, LORD, give me life;
in your justice lead me out of distress.
12 In your kindness put an end to my foes;
destroy all who attack me,
for I am your servant.*

PSALM 144†

A Prayer for Victory and Prosperity

1† *Of David.*

I

Blessed be the LORD, my rock,
who trains my hands for battle,
my fingers for war;
2 My safeguard and my fortress,
my stronghold, my deliverer,
My shield, in whom I trust,
who subdues peoples under me.

II

3† LORD, what are mortals that you notice them;
human beings, that you take thought of them?*
4† They are but a breath;
their days are like a passing shadow.*
5† LORD, incline your heavens and come;
touch the mountains and make them smoke.*
6 Flash forth lightning and scatter my foes;
shoot your arrows and rout them.
7 Reach out your hand from on high;
deliver me from the many waters;
rescue me from the hands of foreign foes.
8† Their mouths speak untruth;
their right hands are raised in lying oaths.
9 O God, a new song I will sing to you;
on a ten-stringed lyre I will play for you.*
10 You give victory to kings;
you delivered David your servant.*
From the menacing sword 11 deliver me;
rescue me from the hands of foreign foes.
Their mouths speak untruth;
their right hands are raised in lying oaths.

III

12 May our sons be like plants*
well nurtured from their youth,
Our daughters, like carved columns,
shapely as those of the temple.
13 May our barns be full
with every kind of store.
May our sheep increase by thousands,
by tens of thousands in our fields;
may our oxen be well fattened.

*

143, 2: Eccl 7, 20; Jb 4, 17; Rom 3, 20.
3: Ps 7, 6. • Lam 3, 6.
4: Ps 142, 4; Jb 17, 1.
5: Ps 77, 6. 12.
6: Pss 42, 2; 63, 2.
7: Pss 28, 1; 30, 4; 88, 5; Prv 1, 12.
8: Pss 25, 4; 27, 11; 86, 11; 119, 12. 35.
12: Ps 116, 16.
144, 3: Jb 7, 17.
4: Pss 62, 10; 90, 9-10; Jb 7, 16; Eccl 6, 12; Wis 2, 5.
5: Is 63, 19.
9: Ps 33, 2-3.
10: Ps 18, 51.
12: Ps 128, 3.

†

143, 3: *They have crushed*: literally, "he crushed"; the singular is used typically, hence the plural translation.

Ps 144: The psalm may reflect a ceremony in which the king, as leader of the army, asked God's help (1-8). In 9 the poem shifts abruptly from pleading to thanksgiving, and (except for 11) shifts again to prayer for the people. The first section (1-2) is a prayer of thanks for victory; the second (3-7a), a humble acknowledgment of human nothingness and a supplication that God show forth saving power; the third (9-11), a promise of future thanksgiving; the fourth (12-15), a wish for prosperity and peace. A prayer for deliverance from treacherous foes serves as a refrain after the second and third sections (7b-8. 11). Except for its final section, the psalm is made up almost entirely of verses from other psalms.

144, 1-2: Composed of phrases from Ps 18, 3. 35. 47-48.

144, 3: Similar to Ps 8, 5.

144, 4: Composed of phrases from Pss 39, 6; 102, 12.

144, 5-7: Adapted in large part from Pss 18, 10. 15. 17; 104, 32.

144, 8b. 11b: *Their right hands are raised in lying oaths*: the psalmist's enemies give false testimony.

14 May there be no breach in the walls,
no exile, no outcry in our streets.*
15 Happy the people so blessed;
happy the people whose God is the LORD.*

PSALM 145†

The Greatness and Goodness of God

1 *Praise. Of David.*

I will extol you, my God and king;
I will bless your name forever.
2 Every day I will bless you;
I will praise your name forever.*
3 Great is the LORD and worthy of high praise; *
God's grandeur is beyond understanding.
4 One generation praises your deeds to the next
and proclaims your mighty works.*
5 They speak of the splendor of your majestic glory,
tell of your wonderful deeds.*
6 They speak of your fearsome power
and attest to your great deeds.*
7 They publish the renown of your abounding goodness
and joyfully sing of your justice.
8 The LORD is gracious and merciful,
slow to anger and abounding in love.*
9 The LORD is good to all,
compassionate to every creature.*
10 All your works give you thanks, O LORD
and your faithful bless you.*
11 They speak of the glory of your reign
and tell of your great works,
12 Making known to all your power,
the glorious splendor of your rule.
13 Your reign is a reign for all ages,
your dominion for all generations.*
The LORD is trustworthy in every word,
and faithful in every work.
14 The LORD supports all who are falling
and raises up all who are bowed down.*
15 The eyes of all look hopefully to you;
you give them their food in due season.*
16 You open wide your hand
and satisfy the desire of every living thing.
17 You, LORD, are just in all your ways,
faithful in all your works.*
18 You, LORD, are near to all who call upon you,
to all who call upon you in truth.*
19 You satisfy the desire of those who fear you;
you hear their cry and save them.*
20 You, LORD, watch over all who love you,
but all the wicked you destroy.*
21 My mouth will speak your praises, LORD;
all flesh will bless your holy name forever.*

PSALM 146†

Trust in God the Creator and Redeemer

1 Hallelujah!

2 Praise the LORD, my soul;
I shall praise the LORD all my life,
sing praise to my God while I live.*

I

3 Put no trust in princes,
in mere mortals powerless to save.*
4 When they breathe their last, they return to the earth;
that day all their planning comes to nothing.*

II

5 Happy those whose help is Jacob's God,
whose hope is in the LORD, their God,

---

* 14: Is 65, 19.
15: Ps 33, 12.
145, 2: Ps 34, 2.
3: Pss 48, 2; 95, 3; 96, 4; Jb 36, 26.
4: Pss 22, 31-32; 48, 14-15; 71, 18; 78, 4; Ex 10, 2; Dt 4, 9.
5: Pss 96, 3; 105, 2.
6: Ps 66, 3.
8: Pss 86, 5. 15; 103, 8; Ex 34, 6; Sir 2, 11.
9: Ps 103, 13; Wis 11, 24.
10: Dn 3, 57.
13: Pss 10, 16; 102, 13; 146, 10; Lam 5, 19; Dn 3, 100; Rv 11, 15.
14: Pss 94, 18; 146, 8.
15: Pss 136, 25; 104, 27-28; Mt 6, 25-26.
17: Dt 32, 4.
18: Dt 4, 7; Is 55, 6; 58, 9.
19: Ps 34, 18.
20: Jgs 5, 31.
21: Sir 40, 35.
146, 2: Pss 103, 1; 104, 33.
3: Ps 118, 8-9.
4: Pss 90, 3; 104, 29; 1 Mc 2, 63; Jb 34, 14-15; Eccl 3, 20; 12, 7; Sir 40, 11; Is 2, 22.

---

† Ps 145: A hymn in acrostic form; every verse begins with a successive letter of the Hebrew alphabet. Acrostic poems usually do not develop ideas but consist rather of loosely connected statements. The singer invites all to praise God (1-3. 21). The "works of God" make God present and invite human praise (4-7); they climax in a confession (8-9). God's mighty acts show forth divine kingship (10-20), a major theme in the literature of early Judaism and in Christianity.

Ps 146: A hymn of someone who has learned there is no other source of strength except the merciful God. Only God, not mortal humans (3-4), can help vulnerable and oppressed people (5-9). The first of the five hymns that conclude the Psalter.

PSALMS

6 The maker of heaven and earth,
the seas and all that is in them,*
Who keeps faith forever,
7 secures justice for the oppressed,*
gives food to the hungry.
The LORD sets prisoners free;*
8 the LORD gives sight to the blind.
The LORD raises up those who are bowed down;*
the LORD loves the righteous.
9 The LORD protects the stranger,
sustains the orphan and the widow,*
but thwarts the way of the wicked.
10 The LORD shall reign forever,
your God, Zion, through all generations!*
Hallelujah!

PSALM 147†

God's Word Restores Jerusalem

1 Hallelujah!

I

How good to celebrate our God in song;
how sweet to give fitting praise.*
2 The LORD rebuilds Jerusalem,
gathers the dispersed of Israel,*
3 Heals the brokenhearted,
binds up their wounds,*
4 Numbers all the stars,
calls each of them by name.*
5 Great is our Lord, vast in power,
with wisdom beyond measure.*
6 The LORD sustains the poor,
but casts the wicked to the ground.*

II

7 Sing to the LORD with thanksgiving;
with the lyre celebrate our God,*
8† Who covers the heavens with clouds,
provides rain for the earth,
makes grass sprout on the mountains,*
9 Who gives animals their food
and ravens what they cry for.*
10† God takes no delight in the strength of horses,
no pleasure in the runner's stride.*
11 Rather the LORD takes pleasure in the devout,
those who await his faithful care.

III

12 Glorify the LORD, Jerusalem;
Zion, offer praise to your God,
13 Who has strengthened the bars of your gates,
blessed your children within you,*
14 Brought peace to your borders,
and filled you with finest wheat.*
15† The LORD sends a command to earth;
his word runs swiftly!*
16 Thus snow is spread like wool,
frost is scattered like ash,*
17 Hail is dispersed like crumbs;
before such cold the waters freeze.
18 Again he sends his word and they melt;
the wind is unleashed and the waters flow.
19 The LORD also proclaims his word to Jacob,
decrees and laws to Israel.*
20 God has not done this for other nations;
of such laws they know nothing.
Hallelujah!

PSALM 148†

All Creation Summoned To Praise

1 Hallelujah!

I

Praise the LORD from the heavens;
give praise in the heights.
2 Praise him, all you angels;
give praise, all you hosts.*

---

* 6: Ex 20, 11; Pss 121, 2; 124, 8; Acts 14, 15; Rv 14, 7.
7: Ps 103, 6. • Ps 68, 7; Is 49, 9; 61, 1.
8: Ps 145, 14.
9: Ps 68, 6; Dt 10, 18.
10: Ps 145, 13; Lam 5, 19.
147, 1: Pss 33, 1; 92, 2.
2: Is 11, 12; 56, 8; Jer 31, 10.
3: Jb 5, 18; Is 30, 26; 61, 1; Jer 33, 6.
4: Is 40, 26.
5: Jdt 16, 13; Jer 51, 15.
6: Ps 146, 9; 1 Sm 2, 7-8.
7: Ps 71, 22.
8: Ps 104, 13f; Jb 5, 10; Jer 14, 22; Jl 2, 23.
9: Jb 38, 41; Mt 6, 26.
10: Pss 20, 8; 33, 16-18.
13: Ps 48, 14.
14: Ps 81, 17.
15: Ps 33, 9.
16: Jb 6, 16; 37, 10; 38, 22.
19: Ps 78, 5; Bar 3, 37; Dt 4, 7-8.
148, 2: Dn 3, 58-63; Ps 103, 20f.

---

† Ps 147: The hymn is divided into three sections by the calls to praise in 1, 7, and 12. The first section praises the powerful creator who restores exiled Judah (1-6); the second section, the creator who provides food to animals and humans; the third and climactic section exhorts the holy city to recognize it has been re-created and made the place of disclosure for God's word, a word as life-giving as water.

147, 8-9: God clothes the fields and feeds the birds. Cf Mt 6, 26. 30.

147, 10-11: Acknowledging one's dependence upon God rather than claiming self-sufficiency pleases God. Cf Pss 20, 8; 33, 16-19.

147, 15-19: God speaks through the thunder of nature and the word of revealed law. Cf Is 55, 10-11. The weather phenomena are well known in Jerusalem: a blizzard of snow and hail followed by a thunderstorm that melts the ice.

Ps 148: A hymn inviting the beings of heaven (1-6) and of earth (7-14) to praise God. The hymn does not distinguish between inanimate and animate (and rational) nature.

3 Praise him, sun and moon;
give praise, all shining stars.
4† Praise him, highest heavens,
you waters above the heavens.
5 Let them all praise the LORD's name;
for the LORD commanded and they were created,*
6 Assigned them duties forever,
gave them tasks that will never change.

II

7 Praise the LORD from the earth,
you sea monsters and all deep waters;*
8 You lightning and hail, snow and clouds,
storm winds that fulfill his command;
9 You mountains and all hills,
fruit trees and all cedars;*
10 You animals wild and tame,
you creatures that crawl and fly;*
11 You kings of the earth and all peoples,
princes and all who govern on earth;
12 Young men and women too,
old and young alike.
13 Let them all praise the LORD's name,
for his name alone is exalted,
majestic above earth and heaven.*
14† The LORD has lifted high the horn of his people;
to the glory of all the faithful,
of Israel, the people near to their God.
Hallelujah!

PSALM 149†

Praise God with Song and Sword

1 Hallelujah!

Sing to the LORD a new song,
a hymn in the assembly of the faithful.*
2 Let Israel be glad in their maker,
the people of Zion rejoice in their king.
3† Let them praise his name in festive dance,
make music with tambourine and lyre. *
4 For the LORD takes delight in his people,
honors the poor with victory.
5† Let the faithful rejoice in their glory,
cry out for joy at their banquet,
6 With the praise of God in their mouths,
and a two-edged sword in their hands,*
7 To bring retribution on the nations,
punishment on the peoples,*
8 To bind their kings with chains,
shackle their nobles with irons,
9† To execute the judgments decreed for them—
such is the glory of all God's faithful.
Hallelujah!

PSALM 150†

Final Doxology

1† Hallelujah!

Praise God in his holy sanctuary;*
give praise in the mighty dome of heaven.
2 Give praise for his mighty deeds,*
praise him for his great majesty.
3 Give praise with blasts upon the horn,*
praise him with harp and lyre.

PSALMS

*

5: Ps 33, 9; Gn 1, 3f; Jdt 16, 14.
7: Gn 1, 21; Ps 135, 6.
9: Is 44, 23.
10: Gn 1, 21. 24f; Ps 30, 5. Dt 4, 7.
13: Ps 30, 5; Dt 4, 7.
149, 1: Pss 22, 23; 26, 12; 35, 18; 40, 10; Jdt 16, 1.
3: Pss 68, 26; 81, 2-3; 87, 7; 150, 3-4.
6: Neh 4, 10-12; 2 Mc 15, 27.
7: Wis 3, 8.
150, 1: Dn 3, 53.
2: Dt 3, 24.
3ff: Pss 81, 3-4; 149, 3; 2 Sm 6, 5; 1 Chr 13, 8; 16, 5. 42; 2 Chr 5, 12-13; 7, 6.

†

148, 4: *Highest heavens*: literally, "the heavens of the heavens," i.e., the space above the firmament, where the "upper waters" are stored. Cf Gn 1, 6-7; Dt 10, 14; 1 Kgs 8, 27; Ps 104, 3. 13.

148, 14: *The LORD has lifted high the horn of his people*: horn = strength, the concrete noun for the abstract. Of all peoples God has chosen Israel to return praise and thanks in a special way.

Ps 149: A hymn inviting the people of Israel to celebrate their God in song and festive dance (1-3. 5) because God has chosen them and given them victory (4). The exodus and conquest are the defining acts of Israel; the people must be ready to do again those acts in the future at the divine command (6-9).

149, 3: *Make music with tambourine and lyre*: the verse recalls the great exodus hymn of Ex 15, 20.

149, 5: *At their banquet*: literally, "upon their couches." The people reclined to banquet.

149, 9: *The glory*: what brings honor to the people is their readiness to carry out the divine will, here conceived as punishing injustice done by the nations.

Ps 150: The psalm is a closing doxology both for the fifth book of the Psalms (107-149) and for the Psalter as a whole. Temple musicians and dancers are called to lead all beings on earth and in heaven in praise of God. The psalm proclaims to whom praise shall be given, and where (1); what praise shall be given, and why (2); how praise shall be given (3-5), and by whom (6).

150, 1: *His holy sanctuary*: God's temple on earth. *The mighty dome of heaven*: literally, "[God's] strong vault"; heaven is here imagined as a giant plate separating the inhabited world from the waters of the heavens.

4 Give praise with tambourines and dance,
praise him with flutes and strings.*
5 Give praise with crashing cymbals,
praise him with sounding cymbals.
6 Let everything that has breath
give praise to the LORD!*
Hallelujah!

4: Ps 68, 26; Ex 15, 20.
6: Rv 5, 13.

PSALMS

The Book of

PROVERBS

The first word of this book, Mishle, *has provided the title by which it is generally designated in Jewish and Christian circles. The name "Proverbs," while not an exact equivalent of* Mishle, *describes the main contents satisfactorily, even though it is hardly an adequate designation for such parts as 1, 1—9, 18 or 31, 10-31. Among some early Christian writers the book was also known by the name of "Wisdom," and in the Roman Missal it was referred to as a "Book of Wisdom."*

The Book of Proverbs is an anthology of didactic poetry forming part of the sapiential literature of the Old Testament. Its primary purpose, indicated in the first sentence (1, 2f), is to teach wisdom. It is thus directed particularly to the young and inexperienced (1, 4); but also to those who desire advanced training in wisdom (1, 5f). The wisdom which the book teaches, covers a wide field of human and divine activity, ranging from matters purely secular to most lofty moral and religious truths, such as God's omniscience (5, 21; 15, 3-11), power (19, 21; 21, 30), providence (20, 1-24), goodness (15, 29), and the joy and strength resulting from abandonment to him (3, 5; 16, 20; 18, 10). The teaching of the entire book is placed on a firm religious foundation by the principle that "the fear of the Lord *is the beginning of knowledge" (1, 7; cf 9, 10).*

To Solomon are explicitly ascribed parts II and V of the book; he is the patron of Hebrew wisdom. Of Agur (part VI) and Lemuel (part VIII), nothing further is known. Parts III and IV are attributed to "the wise." The remaining parts are anonymous.

The manner of compilation is conjectural. Parts II and V may have circulated first as independent collections, compiled before the fall of Jerusalem, as the references to Solomon (10, 1) and Hezekiah (25, 1) suggest. Parts III, IV and VII would seem to belong together as a third collection of a similar kind. The author of the first nine chapters, a religious sage familiar with the earlier sacred books, was the editor of the whole as we have it, probably in the early part of the fifth century B.C.

Christ and the Apostles often expressly quoted the Proverbs (Jn 7, 38; Rom 12, 20; Jas 4, 6) or repeated their teaching; compare Lk 10, 14, and Prv 25, 7; 1 Pt 4, 8; Jas 5, 20 and Prv 10, 12. The book has an important place in the Latin and Greek liturgies.

On the basis of titles, subject matter, and poetic structure the Book of Proverbs may be divided as follows:

I: Introduction: The Value of Wisdom (1, 1—9, 18)
II: First Collection of the Proverbs of Solomon (10, 1—22, 16)
III: Sayings of the Wise (22, 17—24, 22)
IV: Other Sayings of the Wise (24, 23-34)
V: Second Collection of the Proverbs of Solomon (25, 1—29, 27)
VI: The Words of Agur (30, 1-6)
VII: Numerical Proverbs (30, 7-33)
VIII: The Words of Lemuel (31, 1-9)
IX: The Ideal Wife (31, 10-31)

I: INTRODUCTION: THE VALUE OF WISDOM

CHAPTER 1

Purpose of the Proverbs of Solomon†

1* The Proverbs of Solomon, the son of
David,
king of Israel:
2† That men may appreciate wisdom
and discipline,

* 1, 1: 10, 1; 25, 1; 1 Kgs 4, 32.

† 1, 1-6: This prologue explains the purpose of the book: to educate the inexperienced in knowledge and right conduct, and to increase the learning of the wise man by proverbs, parables and riddles.

1, 2: *Discipline:* education or formation which dispels ignorance and corrects vice.

may understand words of intelligence;
3 May receive training in wise conduct,
in what is right, just and honest;
4† That resourcefulness may be imparted to the simple,
to the young man knowledge and discretion.
5 A wise man by hearing them will advance in learning,
an intelligent man will gain sound guidance,
6 That he may comprehend proverb and parable,
the words of the wise and their riddles.

7*† The fear of the LORD is the beginning of knowledge;
wisdom and instruction fools despise.

The Path of the Wicked: Greed and Violence†

8 Hear, my son, your father's instruction,
and reject not your mother's teaching;
9 A graceful diadem will they be for your head;
a torque for your neck.
10 My son, should sinners entice you,
11 and say,
"Come along with us!
Let us lie in wait for the honest man,
let us, unprovoked, set a trap for the innocent;
12 Let us swallow them up, as the nether world does, alive,
in the prime of life, like those who go down to the pit!
13 All kinds of precious wealth shall we gain,
we shall fill our houses with booty;
14 Cast in your lot with us,
we shall all have one purse!"—

15 My son, walk not in the way with them,
hold back your foot from their path!
16* [For their feet run to evil,
they hasten to shed blood.]
17† It is in vain that a net is spread
before the eyes of any bird—
18 These men lie in wait for their own blood,
they set a trap for their own lives.
19 This is the fate of everyone greedy of loot:
unlawful gain takes away the life of him who acquires it.

Wisdom in Person Gives Warning†

20* Wisdom cries aloud in the street,
in the open squares she raises her voice;
21 Down the crowded ways she calls out,
at the city gates she utters her words:
22 "How long, you simple ones, will you love inanity,
23 how long will you turn away at my reproof?
Lo! I will pour out to you my spirit,
I will acquaint you with my words.

24* "Because I called and you refused,
I extended my hand and no one took notice;
25 Because you disdained all my counsel,
and my reproof you ignored—
26 I, in my turn, will laugh at your doom;
I will mock when terror overtakes you;
27 When terror comes upon you like a storm,
and your doom approaches like a whirlwind;
when distress and anguish befall you.

28† "Then they call me, but I answer not;
they seek me, but find me not;
29 Because they hated knowledge,
and chose not the fear of the LORD;
30 They ignored my counsel,
they spurned all my reproof;
And in their arrogance they preferred arrogance,
and like fools they hated knowledge:
31† "Now they must eat the fruit of their own way,
and with their own devices be glutted.
32 For the self-will of the simple kills them,

*

7: 9, 10; Jb 28, 28; Ps 111, 10; Sir 1, 16.
16: Is 59, 7.
20: 8, 1-3; 9, 3.
24: Is 65, 2.12; 66, 4; Jer 7, 13.

†

1, 4: *Simple:* immature and inexperienced, hence easily influenced for good or evil.

1, 7: *Fear of the LORD:* reverential fear and respect for God on account of his sovereignty, goodness and justice toward men. This is the foundation of religion.

1, 8-19: A warning against association with the greedy and the violent who seek to destroy the honest man and to steal his possessions (11-14). The trap which the wicked set for the innocent (11), in the end (19) takes away the life of the wicked themselves.

1, 17: Instructed by the wise man, the youth (of v 4) will recognize the invitation of the wicked (11-14) as a *net* spread before him, and he will thus, like the *bird*, be protected against falling into it.

1, 20-33: Wisdom is here personified; with divine authority she sets forth and proclaims the moral order, instructing and threatening (24-33) the multitudes in the streets and places of assembly.

1, 28: Overtaken by doom, the foolish seek wisdom, but in vain because they do so too late. Cf Jn 7, 34; 8, 21.

1, 31: Sinners are punished by the bad fruits which their sins produce. Cf Wis 11, 16.

the smugness of fools destroys them.
33* But he who obeys me dwells in security,
in peace, without fear of harm."

CHAPTER 2†

The Blessings of Wisdom†

1 My son, if you receive my words
and treasure my commands,
2† Turning your ear to wisdom,
inclining your heart to understanding;
3 Yes, if you call to intelligence,
and to understanding raise your voice;
4 If you seek her like silver,
and like hidden treasures search her out:

5 Then will you understand the fear of the LORD;
the knowledge of God you will find;
6* For the LORD gives wisdom,
from his mouth come knowledge and understanding;
7 He has counsel in store for the upright,
he is the shield of those who walk honestly,
8 Guarding the paths of justice,
protecting the way of his pious ones.

9 Then you will understand rectitude and justice,
honesty, every good path;
10 For wisdom will enter your heart,
knowledge will please your soul,
11 Discretion will watch over you,
understanding will guard you;

12 Saving you from the way of evil men,
from men of perverse speech,
13 Who leave the straight paths
to walk in the way of darkness,
14 Who delight in doing evil,
rejoice in perversity;
15 Whose ways are crooked,
and devious their paths;

16* Saving you from the wife of another,
from the adulteress with her smooth words,
17 Who forsakes the companion of her youth
and forgets the pact with her God;
18* For her path sinks down to death,
and her footsteps lead to the shades;
19 None who enter thereon come back again,
or gain the paths of life.
20 Thus you may walk in the way of good men,
and keep to the paths of the just.
21* For the upright will dwell in the land,
the honest will remain in it;
22 But the wicked will be cut off from the land,
the faithless will be rooted out of it.

CHAPTER 3

Attitude toward the Lord†

1 My son, forget not my teaching,
keep in mind my commands;
2* For many days, and years of life,
and peace, will they bring you.

3 Let not kindness and fidelity leave you;
bind them around your neck;
4 Then will you win favor and good esteem
before God and man.
5 Trust in the LORD with all your heart,
on your own intelligence rely not;
6 In all your ways be mindful of him,
and he will make straight your paths.

7* Be not wise in your own eyes,
fear the LORD and turn away from evil;
8 This will mean health for your flesh
and vigor for your bones.
9* Honor the LORD with your wealth,
with first fruits of all your produce;

PROVERBS

*

33: 8, 33f.
2, 6: Jb 32, 8; Wis 7, 25; Sir 1, 1; Jas 1, 5.
16: 5, 3.20; 6, 24; 7, 5; 22, 14.
18: 5, 5f; 7, 27.
21f: 10, 7.30; Jb 18, 17; Pss 21, 9-13; 37, 22.28.
3, 2: 4, 10; 9, 11; 10, 27.
7: Rom 11, 25; 12, 16.
9: Ex 34, 26; Lv 27, 30; Dt 26, 2; Sir 7, 31; 35, 7.

†

2—7: These chapters form an ordered discourse in seven "columns" of twenty-two verses each. Chapter 2 introduces the four topics about which the sage instructs his pupil: the service of God (3, 1-12.25-34), the search for wisdom (3, 13-24.35; 4, 1-9), the avoidance of evil companions among men (4, 10-27; 5, 21-23), and among women (5, 1-20; 6, 20—7, 27). The last topic is treated at a length equal to the first three because the discourse is meant especially for youths (cf 1, 4).

2, 1-22: The search for wisdom (1-4) leads to the protection of God (5-8) and of wisdom herself (9ff; cf 1, 20-33) and to deliverance from evil men (12-15) and evil women (16-19), and so to lasting happiness (20ff).

2, 2f: *Wisdom, understanding, intelligence:* various names or aspects of the same gift.

3, 1-12: Many are the rewards for fidelity and trust in God, and for diffidence of self (1-8). Cf Dt 30, 20; Is 38, 19. The offering of material things for divine worship is blessed by an increase of such goods (9f). Even correction and chastisement are a mark of God's love and favor (11f).

10 Then will your barns be filled with grain,
with new wine your vats will overflow.
11* The discipline of the LORD, my son, disdain not;
spurn not his reproof;
12* For whom the LORD loves he reproves,
and he chastises the son he favors.

The Value of Wisdom†

13* Happy the man who finds wisdom,
the man who gains understanding!
14 For her profit is better than profit in silver,
and better than gold is her revenue;
15*† She is more precious than corals,
and none of your choice possessions can compare with her.

16 Long life is in her right hand,
in her left are riches and honor;
17 Her ways are pleasant ways,
and all her paths are peace;

18*† She is a tree of life to those who grasp her,
and he is happy who holds her fast.
19 The LORD by wisdom founded the earth,
established the heavens by understanding;
20† By his knowledge the depths break open,
and the clouds drop down dew.
21 My son, let not these slip out of your sight:
keep advice and counsel in view;
22 So will they be life to your soul,
and an adornment for your neck.
23 Then you may securely go your way;
your foot will never stumble;
24 When you lie down, you need not be afraid,
when you rest, your sleep will be sweet.
35 Honor is the possession of wise men,
but fools inherit shame.

Attitude toward Fellow Men†

25† Be not afraid of sudden terror,
of the ruin of the wicked when it comes;
26 For the LORD will be your confidence,
and will keep your foot from the snare.

27 Refuse no one the good on which he has a claim
when it is in your power to do it for him.
28 Say not to your neighbor, "Go, and come again,
tomorrow I will give," when you can give at once.

29 Plot no evil against your neighbor,
against him who lives at peace with you.
30 Quarrel not with a man without cause,
with one who has done you no harm.
31* Envy not the lawless man
and choose none of his ways:
32 To the LORD the perverse man is an abomination,
but with the upright is his friendship.

33 The curse of the LORD is on the house of the wicked,
but the dwelling of the just he blesses;
34* When he is dealing with the arrogant, he is stern,
but to the humble he shows kindness.

CHAPTER 4

Wisdom: the Supreme Guide of Men†

1 Hear, O children, a father's instruction,
be attentive, that you may gain understanding!
2 Yes, excellent advice I give you;
my teaching do not forsake.
3 When I was my father's child,
frail, yet the darling of my mother,
4* He taught me, and said to me:

*

11: Heb 12, 5f.
12: Jdt 8, 27; Rv 3, 19.
13: 8, 34f.
15: 8, 11.19; Wis 7, 8-11.
18: 4, 13; 8, 35; 11, 30; Gn 2, 9; 3, 22.
31: 23, 17; 24, 1.19; Ps 37, 1.
34: 1, 26.
4, 4: 1 Kgs 2, 2ff.

†

3, 13-24: Wisdom, or understanding, is more valuable than silver and gold. Its fruit is long life, riches, honor and happiness (13-18). Even the creation of the universe and its adornment (Gn 1) were not done without wisdom (19f). It is the life of the soul and gives security in work and in repose (21-24).

3, 15: *Corals:* some precious stone may be intended.

3, 18: *A tree of life:* cf 11, 30; 13, 12; Gn 2, 9.

3, 20: For the Hebrews, *the depths* enclosed the great subterranean ocean; the rain and dew descended from the celestial ocean above the firmament; cf Gn 1, 6-10; Jb 26, 8.12; Pss 18, 16; 24, 2.

3, 25-34: Serving God with confidence in him (25f) requires serving one's neighbor through kindness (27f), peace with the good (29ff), no envy of the wicked (31), because the Lord's friendship and kindness are with the just; his curse is with the wicked.

3, 25: *The ruin of the wicked:* i.e., the ruin that comes upon the wicked.

4, 1-9: The sage speaks as a father admonishing his children to secure wisdom at any cost.

"Let your heart hold fast my words:
keep my commands, that you may live!
5 "Get wisdom, get understanding!
Do not forget or turn aside from the words I utter.
6 Forsake her not, and she will preserve you;
love her, and she will safeguard you;
7 The beginning of wisdom is: get wisdom;
at the cost of all you have, get understanding.
8 Extol her, and she will exalt you;
she will bring you honors if you embrace her;
9 She will put on your head a graceful diadem;
a glorious crown will she bestow on you."

The Good and the Evil Way†

10* Hear, my son, and receive my words,
and the years of your life shall be many.
11 On the way of wisdom I direct you,
I lead you on straightforward paths.
12 When you walk, your step will not be impeded,
and should you run, you will not stumble.
13 Hold fast to instruction, never let her go;
keep her, for she is your life.

14 The path of the wicked enter not,
walk not on the way of evil men;
15 Shun it, cross it not,
turn aside from it, and pass on.
16 For they cannot rest unless they have done evil;
to have made no one stumble steals away their sleep.
17 For they eat the bread of wickedness
and drink the wine of violence.
19 The way of the wicked is like darkness;
they know not on what they stumble.
18† But the path of the just is like shining light,
that grows in brilliance till perfect day.

20 My son, to my words be attentive,
to my sayings incline your ear;
21 Let them not slip out of your sight,
keep them within your heart;
22* For they are life to those who find them,
to man's whole being they are health.
23 With closest custody, guard your heart,
for in it are the sources of life.
24 Put away from you dishonest talk,
deceitful speech put far from you.
25 Let your eyes look straight ahead
and your glance be directly forward.
26 Survey the path for your feet,
and let all your ways be sure.
27 Turn neither to right nor to left,
keep your foot far from evil.

CHAPTER 5

Warning against Adultery†

1 My son, to my wisdom be attentive,
to my knowledge incline your ear,
2 That discretion may watch over you,
and understanding may guard you.
3* The lips of an adulteress drip with honey,
and her mouth is smoother than oil;
4 But in the end she is as bitter as wormwood,
as sharp as a two-edged sword.
5* Her feet go down to death,
to the nether world her steps attain;
6 Lest you see before you the road to life,
her paths will ramble, you know not where.
7 So now, O children, listen to me,
go not astray from the words of my mouth.
8* Keep your way far from her,
approach not the door of her house,
9*† Lest you give your honor to others,
and your years to a merciless one;
10 Lest strangers have their fill of your wealth,
your hard-won earnings go to an alien's house;

PROVERBS

---

*

10: 3, 2.
22: 8, 35.
5, 3: 7, 5.
5: 2, 18; 7, 27.
8: 7, 25.
9f: Sir 9, 6.

---

†

4, 10-27: The way of wisdom leads directly to life (10-13); it is a light that grows brighter (18). The wise man is bound to shun (14-17) the dark and violent path of the wicked (19). Singleness of purpose and right conduct proceed from the heart of a wise man as from the source of life (23-26); they save him from destruction on evil paths (4, 27; 5, 21ff).

4, 18: *Till perfect day:* literally, "till the day is established"; this may refer to full daylight or to noonday.

5, 1-20: Understanding and discretion guard a man against the wiles of an adulteress, which lead astray and beget bitterness, bloodshed and death (1-6). They destroy honor, waste the years of life, despoil hard-earned wealth, consume the flesh, and bring remorse in the end (7-14). Conjugal fidelity and love for one wife only bring happiness and security (15-20). Cf 6, 20—7, 27.

5, 9: *Honor:* the words "life" and "wealth" have also been read in this place. *A merciless one:* the offended husband; cf 6, 34f.

11 And you groan in the end,
when your flesh and your body are consumed;
12 And you say, "Oh, why did I hate instruction,
and my heart spurn reproof!
13 Why did I not listen to the voice of my teachers,
nor to my instructors incline my ear!
14 I have all but come to utter ruin,
condemned by the public assembly!"

15 Drink water from your own cistern,
running water from your own well.
16 How may your water sources be dispersed abroad,
streams of water in the streets?
17 Let your fountain be yours alone,
not one shared with strangers;
18 And have joy of the wife of your youth,
19† your lovely hind, your graceful doe.
Her love will invigorate you always,
through her love you will flourish continually,
6:22 When you lie down she will watch over you,
and when you wake, she will share your concerns;
wherever you turn, she will guide you.
5:20 Why then, my son, should you go astray for another's wife
and accept the embraces of an adulteress?
21*†For each man's ways are plain to the LORD's sight;
all their paths he surveys;
22 By his own iniquities the wicked man will be caught,
in the meshes of his own sin he will be held fast;
23 He will die from lack of discipline,
through the greatness of his folly he will be lost.

CHAPTER 6

Miscellaneous Proverbs†

1* My son, if you have become surety to your neighbor,
given your hand in pledge to another,
2 You have been snared by the utterance of your lips,
caught by the words of your mouth;
3 So do this, my son, to free yourself,
since you have fallen into your neighbor's power:
Go, hurry, stir up your neighbor!
4 Give no sleep to your eyes,
nor slumber to your eyelids;
5 Free yourself as a gazelle from the snare,
or as a bird from the hand of the fowler.

6* Go to the ant, O sluggard,
study her ways and learn wisdom;
7 For though she has no chief,
no commander or ruler,
8 She procures her food in the summer,
stores up her provisions in the harvest.
9 How long, O sluggard, will you rest?
when will you rise from your sleep?
10† A little sleep, a little slumber,
a little folding of the arms to rest—
11 Then will poverty come upon you like a highway man,
and want like an armed man.

12 A scoundrel, a villain, is he
who deals in crooked talk.
13 He winks his eyes,
shuffles his feet,
makes signs with his fingers;
14 He has perversity in his heart,
is always plotting evil,
sows discord.
15 Therefore suddenly ruin comes upon him;
in an instant he is crushed beyond cure.
16† There are six things the LORD hates,
yes, seven are an abomination to him;
17 Haughty eyes, a lying tongue,
and hands that shed innocent blood;
18 A heart that plots wicked schemes,
feet that run swiftly to evil,
19 The false witness who utters lies,
and he who sows discord among brothers.

Warning against Adultery†

20 Observe, my son, your father's bidding,

*

21: Jb 14, 16; 31, 4; 34, 21. Sir 8, 13; 29, 19.
6, 1f: 11, 15; 22, 26; 6: 30, 25.

†

5, 19: *Lovely hind . . . graceful doe:* oriental symbols of feminine beauty and charm; cf Sg 2, 7.9.17.

5, 21-23: These verses are best read after 4, 27.

6, 1-19: These verses interrupt the discourse of chapters 2-7, which should be read apart from them; they contain four shorter proverbs akin to those in chapter 30.

6, 1: *Given your hand in pledge:* literally, "struck your hands"; this was probably the legal method for closing a contract.

6, 10: This verse may be regarded as the sluggard's reply or as a continuation of the remonstrance.

6, 16-19: The seven vices symbolized for the most part by bodily organs are pride, lying, murder, intrigue, readiness to do evil, false witness, and the stirring up of discord.

6, 20—7, 27: Parental training and the love of wisdom are an invaluable and constant help for the young (6, 20-23; 7, 1-4). They are the best defense against adultery (6, 24; 7, 5.24f), which involves the guilty in many dangers and punishments (6, 26-35; 7, 6-27). Cf 5, 1-20.

and reject not your mother's
teaching;
21 Keep them fastened over your heart
always,
put them around your neck;
23 For the bidding is a lamp, and the
teaching a light,
and a way to life are the reproofs
of discipline;
24* To keep you from your neighbor's
wife,
from the smooth tongue of the
adulteress.

25* Lust not in your heart after her
beauty,
let her not captivate you with her
glance!
26† For the price of a loose woman
may be scarcely a loaf of bread,
But if she is married,
she is a trap for your precious life.
27 Can a man take fire to his bosom,
and his garments not burned?
28 Or can a man walk on live coals,
and his feet not be scorched?
29* So with him who goes in to his neighbor's
wife—
none who touches her shall go unpunished.

30 Men despise not the thief if he steals
to satisfy his appetite when he is
hungry;
31 Yet if he be caught he must pay back
sevenfold;
all the wealth of his house he may
yield up.
32 But he who commits adultery is a
fool;
he who would destroy himself
does it.
33 A degrading beating will he get,
and his disgrace will not be wiped
away;
34 For vindictive is the husband's
wrath,
he will have no pity on the day of
vengeance;
35 He will not consider any restitution,
nor be satisfied with the greatest
gifts.

CHAPTER 7

1 My son, keep my words,
and treasure my commands.
2 Keep my commands and live,
my teaching as the apple of your
eye;
3* Bind them on your fingers,
write them on the tablet of your
heart.
4 Say to Wisdom, "You are my sister!"
call Understanding, "Friend!"
5* That they may keep you from another's
wife,
from the adulteress with her
smooth words.
6 For at the window of my house,
through my lattice I looked out—
7 And I saw among the simple ones,
I observed among the young men,
a youth with no sense,
8 Going along the street near the corner,
then walking in the direction of
her house—
9 In the twilight, at dusk of day,
at the time of the dark of night.
10 And lo! the woman comes to meet
him,
robed like a harlot, with secret designs—
11 She is fickle and unruly,
in her home her feet cannot rest;
12 Now she is in the streets, now in the
open squares,
and at every corner she lurks in
ambush—
13 When she seizes him, she kisses him,
and with an impudent look says
to him:

14† "I owed peace offerings,
and today I have fulfilled my
vows;
15 So I came out to meet you,
to look for you, and I have found
you!
16 With coverlets I have spread my
couch,
with brocaded cloths of Egyptian
linen;
17 I have sprinkled my bed with myrrh,
with aloes, and with cinnamon.

18 "Come, let us drink our fill of love,
until morning, let us feast on love!
19 For my husband is not at home,
he has gone on a long journey;
20 A bag of money he took with him,
not till the full moon will he return
home."

21* She wins him over by her repeated
urging,
with her smooth lips she leads him
astray;

PROVERBS

*

24: 2, 16; 7, 5.
25: Ex 20, 17; Dt 5, 21; Sir 9, 8; 25, 20; Mt 5, 28.
29: Sir 9, 9.
7, 3: Dt 6, 8.
5: 2, 16; 6, 24;
21: 5, 3; 6, 24.

†

6, 26: Some interpret the verse in a progressive sense, i.e., to satisfy the increasing demands of a courtesan a man is reduced to poverty; if the woman is married, even his very life is endangered.

7, 14: *"Peace offerings . . . vows":* a portion of the sacrifice reverted to the donor and had to be eaten on the same day at a family festival (Lv 7, 11-15). In this figure, the adulteress offers to share with the foolish young man the deadly feast of her sensuality.

22 He follows her stupidly,
like an ox that is led to slaughter;
Like a stag that minces toward the net,
23 till an arrow pierces its liver;
Like a bird that rushes into a snare,
unaware that its life is at stake.

24 So now, O children, listen to me,
be attentive to the words of my mouth!
25 Let not your heart turn to her ways,
go not astray in her paths;
26 For many are those she has struck down dead,
numerous, those she has slain.
27* Her house is made up of ways to the nether world,
leading down into the chambers of death.

PROVERBS

CHAPTER 8

The Discourse of Wisdom†

1* Does not Wisdom call,
and Understanding raise her voice?
2 On the top of the heights along the road,
at the crossroads she takes her stand;
3 By the gates at the approaches of the city,
in the entryways she cries aloud:
4 "To you, O men, I call;
my appeal is to the children of men.
5† You simple ones, gain resource,
you fools, gain sense.

6 "Give heed! for noble things I speak;
honesty opens my lips.
7† Yes, the truth my mouth recounts,
but the wickedness my lips abhor.
8 Sincere are all the words of my mouth,
no one of them is wily or crooked;
9 All of them are plain to the man of intelligence,
and right to those who attain knowledge.
10 Receive my instruction in preference to silver,
and knowledge rather than choice gold.
11* [For Wisdom is better than corals,
and no choice possessions can compare with her.]

12 "I, Wisdom, dwell with experience,
and judicious knowledge I attain.
13* [The fear of the LORD is to hate evil;]
Pride, arrogance, the evil way,
and the perverse mouth I hate.
14† Mine are counsel and advice;
Mine is strength; I am understanding.
15 By me kings reign,
and lawgivers establish justice;
16 By me princes govern,
and nobles; all the rulers of earth.

17 "Those who love me I also love,
and those who seek me find me.
18* With me are riches and honor,
enduring wealth and prosperity.
19* My fruit is better than gold, yes, than pure gold,
and my revenue than choice silver.
20 On the way of duty I walk,
along the paths of justice,
21 Granting wealth to those who love me,
and filling their treasuries.

22* "The LORD begot me, the first-born of his ways,
the forerunner of his prodigies of long ago;
23*† From of old I was poured forth,
at the first, before the earth.
24† When there were no depths I was brought forth,
when there were no fountains or springs of water;
25 Before the mountains were settled into place,
before the hills, I was brought forth;
26 While as yet the earth and the fields were not made,
nor the first clods of the world.

27* "When he established the heavens I was there,

*

27: 2, 18ff; 5, 5.
8, 1: 1, 20f; 9, 3.
11: 3, 15; Wis 7, 8.
13: 6, 16f; 16, 5.
18: 3, 16.
19: 3, 14.
22: Wis 9, 9; Sir 1, 1; 24, 9.
23: Sir 1, 4.
27: 3, 19; Sir 24, 4f.

†

8, 1-36: Wisdom is here personified as in 1, 20-33, to confirm the words of the teacher of wisdom. She exalts her grandeur and origin, and invites all (1-11) to be attentive to her salutary influence in human society (12-21), for she was privileged to be present at the creation of the world (22-31). Finally, she promises life and the favor of God to those who find her, death to those who despise her.

8, 5: *Simple ones . . . fools:* see note on 1, 4.

8, 7f: The truth and sincerity of wisdom are absolute because they are divine. They can neither deceive nor tolerate deception. An intelligent man understands and accepts them.

8, 14: What is here predicated of wisdom is elsewhere attributed to God (Jb 12, 13-16).

8, 22-31: Wisdom is of divine origin. It is here represented as a being which existed before all things (22-26) and concurred with God when he planned and executed the creation of the universe, adorned it with beauty and variety, and established its wonderful order (27-30). Here that plurality of divine Persons is foreshadowed which was afterward to be fully revealed when Wisdom in the Person of Jesus Christ became incarnate.

8, 23: *Poured forth:* the exact meaning of the Hebrew is uncertain; the expression must imply the equivalent of "born." The Hebrews liken the movement of air and of spirit to that of liquids.

8, 24-26: The formless mass from which God created the heavens and the earth; cf Gn 1, 1f; 2, 4ff.

when he marked out the vault
over the face of the deep;
28 When he made firm the skies above,
when he fixed fast the foundations
of the earth;
29 When he set for the sea its limit,
so that the waters should not
transgress his command;
30*† Then was I beside him as his craftsman,
and I was his delight day by day,
Playing before him all the while,
31 playing on the surface of his earth;
and I found delight in the sons of
men.

32 "So now, O children, listen to me;
33 instruction and wisdom do not reject!
Happy the man who obeys me,
and happy those who keep my
ways,
34 Happy the man watching daily at
my gates,
waiting at my doorposts;
35* For he who finds me finds life,
and wins favor from the LORD;
36 But he who misses me harms himself;
all who hate me love death."

CHAPTER 9

The Two Banquets†

1 Wisdom has built her house,
she has set up her seven columns;
2 She has dressed her meat, mixed
her wine,
yes, she has spread her table.
3*† She has sent out her maidens; she
calls
from the heights out over the city:
4 "Let whoever is simple turn in here;
to him who lacks understanding,
I say,
5 Come, eat of my food,
and drink of the wine I have
mixed!
6 Forsake foolishness that you may
live;
advance in the way of understanding.
11* For by me your days will be multiplied
and the years of your life increased."

7 He who corrects an arrogant man
earns insult;
and he who reproves a wicked
man incurs opprobrium.
8* Reprove not an arrogant man, lest
he hate you;
reprove a wise man, and he will
love you.
9 Instruct a wise man, and he becomes still wiser;
teach a just man, and he advances
in learning.
10* The beginning of wisdom is the fear
of the LORD,
and knowledge of the Holy One is
understanding.
12 If you are wise, it is to your own advantage;
and if you are arrogant, you alone
shall bear it.

13* The woman Folly is fickle,
she is inane, and knows nothing.
14 She sits at the door of her house
upon a seat on the city heights,
15 Calling to passers-by
as they go on their straight way:
16 "Let whoever is simple turn in here,
or who lacks understanding; for
to him I say,
17† Stolen water is sweet,
and bread gotten secretly is pleasing!"
18† Little he knows that the shades are
there,
that in the depths of the nether
world are her guests!

II: FIRST COLLECTION OF THE PROVERBS OF SOLOMON†

CHAPTER 10

1* The Proverbs of Solomon:

A wise son makes his father glad,
but a foolish son is a grief to his
mother.

2* Ill-gotten treasures profit nothing,
but virtue saves from death.

PROVERBS

---

*

30: Wis 9, 9.
35: 3, 13-18; 4, 22.
9, 3: 8, 1f.
8: Sir 10, 7.
10: 1, 7; Jb 28, 28; Ps 111, 10; Sir 1, 16.
11: 3, 2.16; 4, 10; 10, 27.
13-18: 7, 7-27.
10, 1: 1, 1; 15, 20; 17, 25; 19, 13; 25, 1; 29, 15.
2: 11, 4.6.

---

†

8, 30: *His craftsman:* furnishing God with the plan, as it were, for the creation of all things; cf Jb 38, 1f; Wis 7, 22—8, 1. *I was his delight:* the ever-present object of God's complacency.

9, 1-6.13-18: Wisdom and folly are represented as matrons, each inviting people to her banquet. Wisdom offers the food and drink of divine doctrine and virtue which give life (1-6). Unstable and senseless folly furnishes the stolen bread and water of deceit and vice which bring death to her guests.

9, 3: *She calls:* i.e., indirectly, through her maidens; but the text could also mean that wisdom herself publicly proclaims her invitation.

9, 17: The secrecy implies wrongdoing.

9, 18: The banquet chamber of folly is a tomb from which no one who enters it is released.

10, 1—22, 16: The varied contents of this first collection of Solomon's proverbs apply mostly to individual life. Each of its three hundred and seventy-five proverbs is meant to be distinct from the others, developing one idea through contrasting parallelism in chapters 10-15, and a climactic treatment in 16-22.

3 The LORD permits not the just to hunger,
but the craving of the wicked he thwarts.

4* The slack hand impoverishes,
but the hand of the diligent enriches.

5 A son who fills the granaries in summer is a credit;
a son who slumbers during harvest, a disgrace.

6 Blessings are for the head of the just,
but a rod for the back of the fool.

7 The memory of the just will be blessed,
but the name of the wicked will rot.

8 A wise man heeds commands,
but a prating fool will be overthrown.

9 He who walks honestly walks securely,
but he whose ways are crooked will fare badly.

10 He who winks at a fault causes trouble,
but he who frankly reproves promotes peace.

11 A fountain of life is the mouth of the just,
but the mouth of the wicked conceals violence.

12*†Hatred stirs up disputes,
but love covers all offenses.

13 On the lips of the intelligent is found wisdom,
[but the mouth of the wicked conceals violence].

14 Wise men store up knowledge,
but the mouth of a fool is imminent ruin.

15† The rich man's wealth is his strong city;
the ruination of the lowly is their poverty.

16* The just man's recompense leads to life,
the gains of the wicked, to sin.

17* A path to life is his who heeds admonition,
but he who disregards reproof goes astray.

18 It is the lips of the liar that conceal hostility;
but he who spreads accusations is a fool.

19* Where words are many, sin is not wanting;
but he who restrains his lips does well.

20 Like choice silver is the just man's tongue;
the heart of the wicked is of little worth.

21 The just man's lips nourish many,
but fools die for want of sense.

22*†It is the LORD's blessing that brings wealth,
and no effort can substitute for it.

23 Crime is the entertainment of the fool;
so is wisdom for the man of sense.

24 What the wicked man fears will befall him,
but the desire of the just will be granted.

25 When the tempest passes, the wicked man is no more;
but the just man is established forever.

26 As vinegar to the teeth, and smoke to the eyes,
is the sluggard to those who use him as a messenger.

27* The fear of the LORD prolongs life,
but the years of the wicked are brief.

28 The hope of the just brings them joy,
but the expectation of the wicked comes to nought.

29 The LORD is a stronghold to him who walks honestly,
but to evildoers, their downfall.

30 The just man will never be disturbed,

PROVERBS

*

4: 6, 11, 12, 24; 13, 4; 20, 13; 28, 19.
12: 1 Cor 13, 4-7; 1 Pt 4, 8.
16: 11, 18f.
17: 15, 10.
19: 17, 27; Sir 20, 17; Jas 1, 19.
22: Sir 11, 22.
27: 3, 2; 4, 10; 9, 11; 14, 27.

†

10, 12: *Love covers all offenses:* a favorite maxim of the Apostles; cf 1 Cor 13, 7; Jas 5, 20; 1 Pt 4, 8; also Prv 17, 9.

10, 15: The inspired author reflects upon the reality of the power of money and the defeat of poverty, without approving these things.

10, 22: The blessing of God rather than our own industry crowns our efforts with success; cf Ps 127, 1f; Mt 6, 25-34.

but the wicked will not abide in the land.

31 The mouth of the just yields wisdom,
but the perverse tongue will be cut off.

32 The lips of the just know how to please,
but the mouth of the wicked, how to pervert.

CHAPTER 11

1* False scales are an abomination to the LORD,
but a full weight is his delight.

2 When pride comes, disgrace comes;
but with the humble is wisdom.

3 The honesty of the upright guides them;
the faithless are ruined by their duplicity.

4*† Wealth is useless on the day of wrath,
but virtue saves from death.

5* The honest man's virtue makes his way straight,
but by his wickedness the wicked man falls.

6 The virtue of the upright saves them,
but the faithless are caught in their own intrigue.

7* When a wicked man dies his hope perishes,
and what is expected from strength comes to nought.

8 The just man escapes trouble,
and the wicked man falls into it in his stead.

9* With his mouth the impious man would ruin his neighbor,
but through their knowledge the just make their escape.

10* When the just prosper, the city rejoices;
and when the wicked perish, there is jubilation.

11 Through the blessing of the righteous the city is exalted,
but through the mouth of the wicked it is overthrown.

12 He who reviles his neighbor has no sense,
but the intelligent man keeps silent.

13* A newsmonger reveals secrets,
but a trustworthy man keeps a confidence.

14* For lack of guidance a people falls;
security lies in many counselors.

15* He is in a bad way who becomes surety for another,
but he who hates giving pledges is safe.

16 A gracious woman wins esteem,
but she who hates virtue is covered with shame.

[The slothful become impoverished,
but the diligent gain wealth.]

17 A kindly man benefits himself,
but a merciless man harms himself.

18* The wicked man makes empty profits,
but he who sows virture has a sure reward.

19 Virtue directs toward life,
but he who pursues evil does so to his death.

20 The depraved in heart are an abomination to the LORD,
but those who walk blamelessly are his delight.

21 Truly the evil man shall not go unpunished,
but those who are just shall escape.

22 Like a golden ring in a swine's snout
is a beautiful woman with a rebellious disposition.

23 The desire of the just ends only in good;
the expectation of the wicked is wrath.

24 One man is lavish yet grows still richer;
another is too sparing, yet is the poorer.

25 He who confers benefits will be amply enriched,

*

11, 1: 16, 11; 20, 10; Lv 19, 35f.
4: 10, 2.
5: 28, 18.
7: 10, 28; Wis 3, 18.
9: 29, 5.
10: 28, 12; 29, 2.
13: 20, 19.
14: 15, 22; 20, 18; 24, 6.
15: 6, 1f.
18: 10,16.

†

11, 4: *Wealth . . . death:* not what a man is worth but what he is, counts before God.

PROVERBS

and he who refreshes others will
himself be refreshed.

26 Him who monopolizes grain, the
people curse—
but blessings upon the head of him
who distributes it!

27 He who seeks the good commands
favor,
but he who pursues evil will have
evil befall him.

28* He who trusts in his riches will fall,
but like green leaves the just
flourish.

29 He who upsets his household has
empty air for a heritage;
and the fool will become slave to
the wise man.

30 The fruit of virtue is a tree of life,
but violence takes lives away.

31* If the just man is punished on earth,
how much more the wicked and
the sinner!

PROVERBS

CHAPTER 12

1* He who loves correction loves
knowledge,
but he who hates reproof is stupid.

2 The good man wins favor from the
LORD,
but the schemer is condemned by
him.

3 No man is built up by wickedness,
but the root of the just will never
be disturbed.

4* A worthy wife is the crown of her
husband,
but a disgraceful one is like rot in
his bones.

5 The plans of the just are legitimate;
the designs of the wicked are de-
ceitful.

6 The words of the wicked are a
deadly ambush,
but the speech of the upright saves
them.

7 The wicked are overthrown and are
no more,
but the house of the just stands
firm.

8 According to his good sense a man
is praised,
but one with a warped mind is de-
spised.

9* Better a lowly man who supports
himself
than one of assumed importance
who lacks bread.

10 The just man takes care of his beast,
but the heart of the wicked is mer-
ciless.

11* He who tills his own land has food
in plenty,
but he who follows idle pursuits is
a fool.

12 The stronghold of evil men will be
demolished,
but the root of the just is enduring.

13 In the sin of his lips the evil man is
ensnared,
but the just comes free of trouble.

14*† From the fruit of his words a man
has his fill of good things,
and the work of his hands comes
back to reward him.

15 The way of the fool seems right in
his own eyes,
but he who listens to advice is
wise.

16 The fool immediately shows his an-
ger,
but the shrewd man passes over
an insult.

17* He tells the truth who states what
he is sure of,
but a lying witness speaks deceit-
fully.

18 The prating of some men is like
sword thrusts,
but the tongue of the wise is heal-
ing.

19 Truthful lips endure forever,
the lying tongue, for only a mo-
ment.

20 Deceit is in the hands of those who
plot evil,
but those who counsel peace have
joy.

21 No harm befalls the just,
but the wicked are overwhelmed
with misfortune.

*

28: Ps 52, 9f.
31: 1 Pt 4, 18.
12, 1: 15, 5.10; 29, 1; Sir 19, 5; 21, 6.
4: Sir 26, 1.16.
9: Sir 10, 26.
11: 28, 19; Sir 20, 27.
14: 13, 2; 18, 20.
17: 14, 5.

†

12, 14: Cf Mt 7, 17; Gal 6, 8.

22* Lying lips are an abomination to the LORD,
but those who are truthful are his delight.

23 A shrewd man conceals his knowledge,
but the hearts of fools gush forth folly.

24* The diligent hand will govern,
but the slothful will be enslaved.

25* Anxiety in a man's heart depresses it,
but a kindly word makes it glad.

26 The just man surpasses his neighbor,
but the way of the wicked leads them astray.

27 The slothful man catches not his prey,
but the wealth of the diligent man is great.

28 In the path of justice there is life,
but the abominable way leads to death.

CHAPTER 13

1 A wise son loves correction,
but the senseless one heeds no rebuke.

2* From the fruit of his words a man eats good things,
but the treacherous one craves violence.

3* He who guards his mouth protects his life;
to open wide one's lips brings downfall.

4 The soul of the sluggard craves in vain,
but the diligent soul is amply satisfied.

5 Anything deceitful the just man hates,
but the wicked brings shame and disgrace.

6* Virtue guards one who walks honestly,
but the downfall of the wicked is sin.

7 One man pretends to be rich, yet has nothing;
another pretends to be poor, yet has great wealth.

8 A man's riches serve as ransom for his life,
but the poor man heeds no rebuke.

9*† The light of the just shines gaily,
but the lamp of the wicked goes out.

10 The stupid man sows discord by his insolence,
but with those who take counsel is wisdom.

11* Wealth quickly gotten dwindles away,
but amassed little by little, it grows.

12 Hope deferred makes the heart sick,
but a wish fulfilled is a tree of life.

13† He who despises the word must pay for it,
but he who reveres the commandment will be rewarded.

14 The teaching of the wise is a fountain of life,
that a man may avoid the snares of death.

15 Good sense brings favor,
but the way of the faithless is their ruin.

16 The shrewd man does everything with prudence,
but the fool peddles folly.

17 A wicked messenger brings on disaster,
but a trustworthy envoy is a healing remedy.

18 Poverty and shame befall the man who disregards correction,
but he who heeds reproof is honored.

19 Lust indulged starves the soul,
but fools hate to turn from evil.

20* Walk with wise men and you will become wise,
but the companion of fools will fare badly.

PROVERBS

*

22: 6, 17.
24: 10, 4; 13, 4.
25: 15, 13; 17, 22.
13, 2: 12, 14; 18, 20.
3: 18, 7; 21, 23.
6: 11, 3.5f.
9: 24, 20.
11: 28, 20.22.
20: Sir 6, 34; 8, 8.17.

†

13, 9: *Light . . . lamp:* symbols of life and prosperity; cf 4, 18f.
13, 13: *Word:* advice, or God's law.

21 Misfortune pursues sinners,
but the just shall be recompensed with good.

22 The good man leaves an inheritance to his children's children,
but the wealth of the sinner is stored up for the just.

23 A lawsuit devours the tillage of the poor,
but some men perish for lack of a law court.

24* He who spares his rod hates his son,
but he who loves him takes care to chastise him.

25 When the just man eats, his hunger is appeased;
but the belly of the wicked suffers want.

PROVERBS

CHAPTER 14

1 Wisdom builds her house,
but Folly tears hers down with her own hands.

2 He who walks uprightly fears the LORD,
but he who is devious in his ways spurns him.

3 In the mouth of the fool is a rod for his back,
but the lips of the wise preserve them.

4 Where there are no oxen, the crib remains empty;
but the large crops come through the strength of the bull.

5* A truthful witness does not lie,
but a false witness utters lies.

6 The senseless man seeks in vain for wisdom,
but knowledge is easy to the man of intelligence.

7 To avoid the foolish man, take steps!
But knowing lips one meets with by surprise.

8 The shrewd man's wisdom gives him knowledge of his way,
but the folly of fools is their deception.

9 Guilt lodges in the tents of the arrogant,
but favor in the house of the just.

10 The heart knows its own bitterness,
and in its joy no one else shares.

11* The house of the wicked will be destroyed,
but the tent of the upright will flourish.

12* Sometimes a way seems right to a man,
but the end of it leads to death!

13 Even in laughter the heart may be sad,
and the end of joy may be sorrow.

14 The scoundrel suffers the consequences of his ways,
and the good man reaps the fruit of his paths.

15 The simpleton believes everything,
but the shrewd man measures his steps.

16 The wise man is cautious and shuns evil;
the fool is reckless and sure of himself.

17 The quick-tempered man makes a fool of himself,
but the prudent man is at peace.

18 The adornment of simpletons is folly,
but shrewd men gain the crown of knowledge.

19 Evil men must bow down before the good,
and the wicked, at the gates of the just.

20* Even by his neighbor the poor man is hated,
but the friends of the rich are many.

21 He sins who despises the hungry;
but happy is he who is kind to the poor!

22 Do not those who plot evil go astray?
But those intent on good gain kindness and constancy.

23 In all labor there is profit,
but mere talk tends only to penury.

24 The crown of the wise is resourcefulness;
the diadem of fools is folly.

---

* 24: 19, 18; 22, 15; 23, 13f; 29, 15; Sir 30, 1.8-13.
14, 5: 12, 17.
11: 3,33; 12, 7; 15, 25.
12: 16, 25.
20: 19, 4.7; Sir 6, 8.12.

25 The truthful witness saves lives,
but he who utters lies is a betrayer.

26 In the fear of the LORD is a strong defense;
even for one's children he will be a refuge.

27 The fear of the LORD is a fountain of life,
that a man may avoid the snares of death.

28 In many subjects lies the glory of the king;
but if his people are few, it is the prince's ruin.

29* The patient man shows much good sense,
but the quick-tempered man displays folly at its height.

30 A tranquil mind gives life to the body,
but jealousy rots the bones.

31* He who oppresses the poor blasphemes his Maker,
but he who is kind to the needy glorifies him.

32 The wicked man is overthrown by his wickedness,
but the just man finds a refuge in his honesty.

33 In the heart of the intelligent wisdom abides,
but in the bosom of fools it is unknown.

34 Virtue exalts a nation,
but sin is a people's disgrace.

35 The king favors the intelligent servant,
but the worthless one incurs his wrath.

CHAPTER 15

1* A mild answer calms wrath,
but a harsh word stirs up anger.

2 The tongue of the wise pours out knowledge,
but the mouth of fools spurts forth folly.

3 The eyes of the LORD are in every place,
keeping watch on the evil and the good.

4 A soothing tongue is a tree of life,
but a perverse one crushes the spirit.

5* The fool spurns his father's admonition,
but prudent is he who heeds reproof.

6 In the house of the just there are ample resources,
but the earnings of the wicked are in turmoil.

7 The lips of the wise disseminate knowledge,
but the heart of fools is perverted.

8* The sacrifice of the wicked is an abomination to the LORD,
but the prayer of the upright is his delight.

9* The way of the wicked is an abomination to the LORD,
but he loves the man who pursues virtue.

10 Severe punishment is in store for the man who goes astray;
he who hates reproof will die.

11† The nether world and the abyss lie open before the LORD;
how much more the hearts of men!

12 The senseless man loves not to be reproved;
to wise men he will not go.

13* A glad heart lights up the face,
but by mental anguish the spirit is broken.

14 The mind of the intelligent man seeks knowledge,
but the mouth of fools feeds on folly.

15 Every day is miserable for the depressed,
but a lighthearted man has a continual feast.

16† Better a little with fear of the LORD
than a great fortune with anxiety.

17 Better a dish of herbs where love is
than a fatted ox and hatred with it.

*

29: 16, 32; 19, 11; Jas 1, 19.
31: 17, 5.
15, 1: 25, 15; Sir 6, 5.
5: 12, 1; 13, 18.
8: 21, 27; Eccl 4, 17; Sir 34, 18ff; Is 1, 11-15.
9: 11, 20; 21, 21.
13: 12, 25; 17, 22; Sir 30, 22.

†

15, 11: *Nether world . . . abyss:* the abode of the dead, signifying the profound obscurity which is open nevertheless to the sight and power of God.

15, 16f: Not the amount of temporal goods but the virtue of their possessor makes them a source of happiness.

18* An ill-tempered man stirs up strife,
but a patient man allays discord.

19 The way of the sluggard is hemmed in as with thorns,
but the path of the diligent is a highway.

20* A wise son makes his father glad,
but a fool of a man despises his mother.

21 Folly is joy to the senseless man,
but the man of understanding goes the straight way.

22* Plans fail when there is no counsel,
but they succeed when counselors are many.

23* There is joy for a man in his utterance;
a word in season, how good it is!

24 The path of life leads the prudent man upward,
that he may avoid the nether world below.

25 The LORD overturns the house of the proud,
but he preserves intact the widow's landmark.

26* The wicked man's schemes are an abomination to the LORD,
but the pure speak what is pleasing to him.

27 He who is greedy of gain brings ruin on his own house,
but he who hates bribes will live.

28 The just man weighs well his utterance,
but the mouth of the wicked pours out evil.

29 The LORD is far from the wicked,
but the prayer of the just he hears.

30 A cheerful glance brings joy to the heart;
good news invigorates the bones.

31* He who listens to salutary reproof
will abide among the wise.

32 He who rejects admonition despises his own soul,
but he who heeds reproof gains understanding.

33* The fear of the LORD is training for wisdom,
and humility goes before honors.

CHAPTER 16

1† Man may make plans in his heart,
but what the tongue utters is from the LORD.

2* All the ways of a man may be pure in his own eyes,
but it is the LORD who proves the spirit.

3 Entrust your works to the LORD,
and your plans will succeed.

4† The LORD has made everything for his own ends,
even the wicked for the evil day.

5* Every proud man is an abomination to the LORD;
I assure you that he will not go unpunished.

6 By kindness and piety guilt is expiated,
and by the fear of the LORD man avoids evil.

7 When the LORD is pleased with a man's ways,
he makes even his enemies be at peace with him.

8 Better a little with virtue,
than a large income with injustice.

9* In his mind a man plans his course,
but the LORD directs his steps.

10† The king's lips are an oracle;
no judgment he pronounces is false.

11* Balance and scales belong to the LORD;
all the weights used with them are his concern.

12* Kings have a horror of wrongdoing,
for by righteousness the throne endures.

13* The king takes delight in honest lips,
and the man who speaks what is right he loves.

*
18: 26, 21; 29, 22; Sir 28, 11.
20: 10, 1; 29, 3.
22: 11, 14.
23: 25, 11; Sir 20, 6.
26: 6, 18.
31: 25, 12.
33: 1, 7; Sir 1, 24.
16, 2: 21, 2.
5: 6, 16f; 8, 13.
9: 19, 21; 20, 24.
11: 11, 1.
12: 25, 5.
13: 14, 35; 22, 11.

†
16, 1: Words, like actions, often produce results different from those which were planned.

16, 4: Even the wicked, in their punishment, cannot escape glorifying God's justice.

16, 10: Decisions of supreme judicial authority were presumed disinterested and correct.

14* The king's wrath is like messengers of death,
but a wise man can pacify it.

15 In the light of the king's countenance is life,
and his favor is like a rain cloud in spring.

16* How much better to acquire wisdom than gold!
To acquire understanding is more desirable than silver.

17 The path of the upright avoids misfortune;
he who pays attention to his way safeguards his life.

18* Pride goes before disaster,
and a haughty spirit before a fall.

19 It is better to be humble with the meek
than to share plunder with the proud.

20 He who plans a thing will be successful;
happy is he who trusts in the LORD!

21 The wise man is esteemed for his discernment,
yet pleasing speech increases his persuasiveness.

22 Good sense is a fountain of life to its possessor,
but folly brings chastisement on fools.

23 The mind of the wise man makes him eloquent,
and augments the persuasiveness of his lips.

24 Pleasing words are a honeycomb,
sweet to the taste and healthful to the body.

25* Sometimes a way seems right to a man,
but the end of it leads to death!

26* The laborer's appetite labors for him,
for his mouth urges him on.

27 A scoundrel is a furnace of evil,
and on his lips there is a scorching fire.

28* An intriguer sows discord,
and a talebearer separates bosom friends.

29 A lawless man allures his neighbor,
and leads him into a way that is not good.

30 He who winks his eye is plotting trickery;
he who compresses his lips has mischief ready.

31* Gray hair is a crown of glory;
it is gained by virtuous living.

32* A patient man is better than a warrior,
and he who rules his temper, than he who takes a city.

33† When the lot is cast into the lap,
its decision depends entirely on the LORD.

CHAPTER 17

1 Better a dry crust with peace
than a house full of feasting with strife.

2† An intelligent servant will rule over a worthless son,
and will share the inheritance with the brothers.

3 The crucible for silver, and the furnace for gold,
but the tester of hearts is the LORD.

4† The evil man gives heed to wicked lips,
and listens to falsehood from a mischievous tongue.

5* He who mocks the poor blasphemes his Maker;
he who is glad at calamity will not go unpunished.

6 Grandchildren are the crown of old men,
and the glory of children is their parentage.

7 Fine words are out of place in a fool;
how much more, lying words in a noble!

P R O V E R B S

*

14: 19, 12; 20, 2.
16: 8, 10f.19.
18: 11, 2.
25: 14, 12.
26: 10, 4.
28: 6, 14.19; 17, 9; 26, 22; Sir 28, 15.
31: 20, 29.
32: 14, 29.
17, 5: 14, 31.

†

16, 33: The favorable or unfavorable result of chance depends on God. Deciding strifes and doubts by lot was practiced by the ancient Hebrews; cf Ex 28, 15-30; Lv 16, 8; Jos 7, 14; 1 Sm 10, 20f.

17, 2: Intelligence and ability are esteemed more highly than nobility of blood.

17, 4: To justify his own evil ways, a wicked man judges evil of others. Cf Mt 7, 1-5.

8 A man who has a bribe to offer rates it a magic stone;
at every turn it brings him success.

9 He who covers up a misdeed fosters friendship,
but he who gossips about it separates friends.

10 A single reprimand does more for a man of intelligence
than a hundred lashes for a fool.

11 On rebellion alone is the wicked man bent,
but a merciless messenger will be sent against him.

12 Face a bear robbed of her cubs,
but never a fool in his folly!

13* If a man returns evil for good,
from his house evil will not depart.

14 The start of strife is like the opening of a dam;
therefore, check a quarrel before it begins!

15* He who condones the wicked, he who condemns the just,
are both an abomination to the LORD.

16 Of what use in the fool's hand are the means
to buy wisdom, since he has no mind for it?

17* He who is a friend is always a friend,
and a brother is born for the time of stress.

18* Senseless is the man who gives his hand in pledge,
who becomes surety for his neighbor.

19*†He who loves strife loves guilt;
he who builds his gate high courts disaster.

20 He who is perverse in heart finds no good,
and a double-tongued man falls into trouble.

21 To be a fool's parent is grief for a man;
the father of a numskull has no joy.

22* A joyful heart is the health of the body,
but a depressed spirit dries up the bones.

23 The wicked man accepts a concealed bribe
to pervert the course of justice.

24* The man of intelligence fixes his gaze on wisdom,
but the eyes of a fool are on the ends of the earth.

25* A foolish son is vexation to his father,
and bitter sorrow to her who bore him.

26 It is wrong to fine an innocent man,
but beyond reason to scourge princes.

27* He who spares his words is truly wise,
and he who is chary of speech is a man of intelligence.

28 Even a fool, if he keeps silent, is considered wise;
if he closes his lips, intelligent.

CHAPTER 18

1 In estrangement one seeks pretexts:
with all persistence he picks a quarrel.

2 The fool takes no delight in understanding,
but rather in displaying what he thinks.

3 With wickedness comes contempt,
and with disgrace comes scorn.

4* The words from a man's mouth are deep waters,
but the source of wisdom is a flowing brook.

5* It is not good to be partial to the guilty,
and so to reject a rightful claim.

6 The fool's lips lead him into strife,
and his mouth provokes a beating.

7* The fool's mouth is his ruin;
his lips are a snare to his life.

*

13: Mt 5, 39; Rom 12, 17; 1 Thes 5, 15; 1 Pt 3, 9.
15: 24, 24; Is 5, 23.
17: 18, 24.
18: 6, 1f; 11, 15.
19: 15, 18.
22: 12, 25; 15, 13.
24: Eccl 8, 1.
25: 10, 1; 29, 15.
27: 10, 19; Sir 1, 21; Jas 1, 19.
18, 4: 20, 5; Jn 7, 38.
5: 24, 23; 28, 21.
7: 10, 14; 12, 13; 13, 3; Eccl 10, 12.

†

17, 19: *Builds . . . high:* a symbol of arrogance.

8* The words of a talebearer are like dainty morsels
that sink into one's inmost being.

9 The man who is slack in his work
is own brother to the man who is destructive.

10† The name of the LORD is a strong tower;
the just man runs to it and is safe.

11* The rich man's wealth is his strong city;
he fancies it a high wall.

12*† Before his downfall a man's heart is haughty,
but humility goes before honors.

13*† He who answers before he hears—
his is the folly and the shame.

14 A man's spirit sustains him in infirmity—
but a broken spirit who can bear?

15 The mind of the intelligent gains knowledge,
and the ear of the wise seeks knowledge.

16* A man's gift clears the way for him,
and gains him access to great men.

17 The man who pleads his case first seems to be in the right;
then his opponent comes and puts him to the test.

18† The lot puts an end to disputes,
and is decisive in a controversy between the mighty.

19 A brother is a better defense than a strong city,
and a friend is like the bars of a castle.

20*† From the fruit of his mouth a man has his fill;
with the yield of his lips he sates himself.

21* Death and life are in the power of the tongue;
those who make it a friend shall eat its fruit.

22* He who finds a wife finds happiness;
it is a favor he receives from the LORD.

23 The poor man implores,
but the rich man answers harshly.

24* Some friends bring ruin on us,
but a true friend is more loyal than a brother.

CHAPTER 19

1* Better a poor man who walks in his integrity
than he who is crooked in his ways and rich.

2 Without knowledge even zeal is not good;
and he who acts hastily, blunders.

3 A man's own folly upsets his way,
but his heart is resentful against the LORD.

4* Wealth adds many friends,
but the friend of the poor man deserts him.

5* The false witness will not go unpunished,
and he who utters lies will not escape.

6 Many curry favor with a noble;
all are friends of the man who has something to give.

7 All the poor man's brothers hate him;
how much more do his friends shun him!

8 He who gains intelligence is his own best friend;
he who keeps understanding will be successful.

9 The false witness will not go unpunished,
and he who utters lies will perish.

10 Luxury is not befitting a fool;
much less should a slave rule over princes.

11 It is good sense in a man to be slow to anger,
and it is his glory to overlook an offense.

PROVERBS

*

8: 26, 22.
11: 10, 15.
12: 11, 2; 16, 18; Sir 10, 15.
13: Sir 11, 8.
16: 21, 14.
20: 12, 14; 13, 2.
21: Sir 37, 18.
22: 12, 4; 19, 14; Sir 7, 26.
24: 17, 17.
19, 1: 28, 6.
4: 14, 20; Sir 13, 20ff.
5: Dt 19, 16-20; Dn 13, 61.

†

18, 10f: Religion is a strong support and sure refuge in the struggle of life. The rich foolishly rely on their wealth for such support.

18, 12: Compare the Savior's words: "Whoever exalts himself will be humbled; but whoever humbles himself will be exalted" (Mt 23, 12).

18, 13: To speak without first listening is characteristic of a fool; cf 10, 14; Sir 11, 8.

18, 18: See note on 16, 33.

18, 20f: Everyone must accept the consequences, of benefit or harm to himself, which his words produce.

12* The king's wrath is like the roaring of a lion,
but his favor, like dew on the grass.

13* The foolish son is ruin to his father,
and the nagging of a wife is a persistent leak.

14* Home and possessions are an inheritance from parents,
but a prudent wife is from the LORD.

15* Laziness plunges a man into deep sleep,
and the sluggard must go hungry.

16* He who keeps the precept keeps his life,
but the despiser of the word will die.

17*†He who has compassion on the poor lends to the LORD,
and he will repay him for his good deed.

18* Chastise your son, for in this there is hope;
but do not desire his death.

19 The man of violent temper pays the penalty;
even if you rescue him, you will have it to do again.

20 Listen to counsel and receive instruction,
that you may eventually become wise.

21* Many are the plans in a man's heart,
but it is the decision of the LORD that endures.

22 From a man's greed comes his shame;
rather be a poor man than a liar.

23 The fear of the LORD is an aid to life;
one eats and sleeps without being visited by misfortune.

24* The sluggard loses his hand in the dish;
he will not even lift it to his mouth.

25* If you beat an arrogant man, the simple learn a lesson;
if you rebuke an intelligent man, he gains knowledge.

26* He who mistreats his father, or drives away his mother,
is a worthless and disgraceful son.

27 If a son ceases to hear instruction,
he wanders from words of knowledge.

28 An unprincipled witness perverts justice,
and the mouth of the wicked pours out iniquity.

29* Rods are prepared for the arrogant,
and blows for the backs of fools.

CHAPTER 20

1* Wine is arrogant, strong drink is riotous;
none who goes astray for it is wise.

2* The dread of the king is as when a lion roars;
he who incurs his anger forfeits his life.

3 It is honorable for a man to shun strife,
while every fool starts a quarrel.

4 In seedtime the sluggard plows not;
when he looks for the harvest, it is not there.

5* The intention in the human heart is like water far below the surface,
but the man of intelligence draws it forth.

6 Many are declared to be men of virtue:
but who can find one worthy of trust?

7 When a man walks in integrity and justice,
happy are his children after him!

8 A king seated on the throne of judgment
dispels all evil with his glance.

9*†Who can say, "I have made my heart clean,
I am cleansed of my sin"?

10* Varying weights, varying measures,
are both an abomination to the LORD.

---

*

12: 20, 2.
13: 10, 1; 17, 25.
14: 18, 22.
15: 6, 9ff.
16: 13, 13; 16, 17.
17: 14, 21; 22, 9; 28, 27.
18: 13, 24; 23, 13f.
21: 16, 9.
24: 26, 15.
25: 17, 10; 21, 11.
26: Sir 3, 16.
29: 26, 3.
20, 1: 23, 29-35.
2: 19, 12.
5: 18, 4.
9: 1 Kgs 8, 46; 2 Chr 6, 36; Eccl 7, 20; 1 Jn 1, 8.
10: 11, 1; 20, 23.

---

†

19, 17: Cf Mt 25, 34-40.
20, 9: Man can be free of sin only by the power of God. Cf 1 Kgs 8, 46ff; Jb 4, 17; 14, 4; Pss 51, 2ff; 130, 3f; Rom 3, 23f; 1 Jn 1, 8.

11 Even by his manners the child betrays
whether his conduct is innocent and right.

12 The ear that hears, and the eye that sees—
the LORD has made them both.

13 Love not sleep, lest you be reduced to poverty;
eyes wide open mean abundant food.

14† "Bad, bad!" says the buyer;
but once he has gone his way, he boasts.

15 Like gold or a wealth of corals,
wise lips are a precious ornament.

16*†Take his garment who becomes surety for another,
and for strangers yield it up!

17 The bread of deceit is sweet to a man,
but afterward his mouth will be filled with gravel.

18 Plans made after advice succeed;
so with wise guidance wage your war.

19 A newsmonger reveals secrets;
so have nothing to do with a babbler!

20*†If one curses his father or mother,
his lamp will go out at the coming of darkness.

21 Possessions gained hastily at the outset
will in the end not be blessed.

22* Say not, "I will repay evil!"
Trust in the LORD and he will help you.

23* Varying weights are an abomination to the LORD,
and false scales are not good.

24*†Man's steps are from the LORD;
how, then, can a man understand his way?

25† Rashly to pledge a sacred gift is a trap for a man,
or to regret a vow once made.

26 A wise king winnows the wicked,
and threshes them under the cartwheel.

27 A lamp from the LORD is the breath of man;
it searches through all his inmost being.

28* Kindness and piety safeguard the king,
and he upholds his throne by justice.

29* The glory of young men is their strength,
and the dignity of old men is gray hair.

30 Evil is cleansed away by bloody lashes,
and a scourging to the inmost being.

CHAPTER 21

1 Like a stream is the king's heart in the hand of the LORD;
wherever it pleases him, he directs it.

2* All the ways of a man may be right in his own eyes,
but it is the LORD who proves hearts.

3*†To do what is right and just
is more acceptable to the LORD than sacrifice.

4 Haughty eyes and a proud heart—
the tillage of the wicked is sin.

5 The plans of the diligent are sure of profit,
but all rash haste leads certainly to poverty.

6 He who makes a fortune by a lying tongue
is chasing a bubble over deadly snares.

*

16: 27, 13.
20: 30, 11.17; Ex 21, 17; Lv 20, 9; Mt 15, 4.
22: 24, 29; Sir 28, 1; Mt 5, 39; Rom 12, 17.19; 1 Thes 5, 15; 1 Pt 3, 9.
23: 11, 1; 20, 10.
24: 16, 9.
28: 16, 12.
29: 16, 31.
21, 2: 16, 2.
3: 1 Sm 15, 22; Hos 6, 6.

†

20, 14: What one wishes to buy is valued cheaply in order that it may be obtained at a low price; once purchased, it is deemed more valuable.

20, 16: Caution is again advised in the matter of becoming surety; cf 6, 1ff.

20, 20: *His lamp will go out:* misfortune, even death, awaits him; cf 13, 9; Ex 21, 17.

20, 24: Man is dependent upon God and cannot fully foresee his own course.

20, 25: This verse cautions against making vows without proper reflection; cf Dt 23, 22ff; Eccl 5, 4f.

21, 3: External rites or sacrifices do not please God unless accompanied by internal worship and right moral conduct; cf 15, 8; 21, 27; Is 1, 11-15; Am 5, 22; Mal 1, 12.

7 The oppression of the wicked will sweep them away,
because they refuse to do what is right.

8 The way of the culprit is crooked,
but the conduct of the innocent is right.

9* It is better to dwell in a corner of the housetop
than in a roomy house with a quarrelsome woman.

10 The soul of the wicked man desires evil;
his neighbor finds no pity in his eyes.

11* When the arrogant man is punished, the simple are the wiser;
when the wise man is instructed, he gains knowledge.

12 The just man appraises the house of the wicked:
there is one who brings down the wicked to ruin.

13 He who shuts his ear to the cry of the poor
will himself also call and not be heard.

14 A secret gift allays anger,
and a concealed present, violent wrath.

15* To practice justice is a joy for the just,
but terror for evildoers.

16† The man who strays from the way of good sense
will abide in the assembly of the shades.

17 He who loves pleasure will suffer want;
he who loves wine and perfume will not be rich.

18*† The wicked man serves as ransom for the just,
and the faithless man for the righteous.

19 It is better to dwell in a wilderness
than with a quarrelsome and vexatious wife.

20 Precious treasure remains in the house of the wise,
but the fool consumes it.

21 He who pursues justice and kindness
will find life and honor.

22 The wise man storms a city of the mighty,
and overthrows the stronghold in which it trusts.

23* He who guards his mouth and his tongue
keeps himself from trouble.

24 Arrogant is the name for the man of overbearing pride
who acts with scornful effrontery.

25 The sluggard's propensity slays him,
for his hands refuse to work.

26 Some are consumed with avarice all the day,
but the just man gives unsparingly.

27* The sacrifice of the wicked is an abomination,
the more so when they offer it with a bad intention.

28* The false witness will perish,
but he who listens will finally have his say.

29 The wicked man is brazenfaced,
but the upright man pays heed to his ways.

30 There is no wisdom, no understanding,
no counsel, against the LORD.

31 The horse is equipped for the day of battle,
but victory is the LORD's.

CHAPTER 22

1* A good name is more desirable than great riches,
and high esteem, than gold and silver.

2* Rich and poor have a common bond:
the LORD is the maker of them all.

3* The shrewd man perceives evil and hides,

*

9: 21, 19; 25, 24; 27, 15; Sir 25, 23.
11: 19, 25.
15: 10, 29.
18: 11, 8.
23: 13, 3.
27: 15, 8; Sir 34, 18ff.
28: 19, 5.9.
22, 1: Eccl 7, 1.
2: 29, 13.
3: 27, 12.

†

21, 16: *Assembly of the shades:* cf note on Jb 26, 5.

21, 18: *Wicked . . . ransom for the just:* exemplified in the history of God's chosen people whom he ransomed from Egypt at the cost of the life of Pharaoh and his army (Ex 14, 23-31), and from Babylon by giving to Cyrus, the Persian conqueror, Egypt, Ethiopia and Seba, the richest lands of the world (Is 43, 1ff).

while simpletons continue on and
suffer the penalty.

4 The reward of humility and fear of
the LORD
is riches, honor and life.

5 Thorns and snares are on the path
of the crooked;
he who would safeguard his life
will shun them.

6 Train a boy in the way he should go;
even when he is old, he will not
swerve from it.

7 The rich rule over the poor,
and the borrower is the slave of
the lender.

8* He who sows iniquity reaps calamity,
and the rod destroys his labors.

9 The kindly man will be blessed,
for he gives of his sustenance to
the poor.

10 Expel the arrogant man and discord
goes out;
strife and insult cease.

11* The LORD loves the pure of heart;
the man of winning speech has the
king for his friend.

12 The eyes of the LORD safeguard
knowledge,
but he defeats the projects of the
faithless.

13*†The sluggard says, "A lion is outside;
in the streets I might be slain."

14* The mouth of the adulteress is a
deep pit;
he with whom the LORD is angry
will fall into it.

15 Folly is close to the heart of a child,
but the rod of discipline will drive
it far from him.

16† He who oppresses the poor to enrich
himself
will yield up his gains to the rich
as sheer loss.

III: SAYINGS OF THE WISE

17*†The sayings of the wise:

Incline your ear, and hear my
words,
and apply your heart to my doctrine;

18 For it will be well if you keep them
in your bosom,
if they all are ready on your lips.

19† That your trust may be in the LORD,
I make known to you the words
of Amen-em-Ope.

20 Have I not written for you the
"Thirty,"
with counsels and knowledge,

21 To teach you truly
how to give a dependable report
to one who sends you?

22 Injure not the poor because they are
poor,
nor crush the needy at the gate;

23*†For the LORD will defend their
cause,
and will plunder the lives of those
who plunder them.

24 Be not friendly with a hotheaded
man,
nor the companion of a wrathful
man,

25 Lest you learn his ways,
and get yourself into a snare.

26* Be not one of those who give their
hand in pledge,
of those who become surety for
debts;

27 For if you have not the means to pay,
your bed will be taken from under
you.

28* Remove not the ancient landmark
which your fathers set up.

29 You see a man skilled at his work?
He will stand in the presence of
kings;

*

8: Jb 4, 8; Sir 7, 3; Hos 8, 7.
11: Mt 5, 8.
13: 26, 13.
14: 23, 27.
17: 5, 1.
23: 23, 11.
26: 6, 1f; 11, 15; 17, 18.
28: 23, 10; Dt 19, 14; 27, 17.

†

22, 13: To avoid the effort required for doing good, *the sluggard* exaggerates the difficulties that must be overcome.

22, 16: Money gained by exploiting the poor is in turn lost to those who are more wealthy.

22, 17—24, 22: This collection of proverbs, introduced as *sayings of the wise*, is given in the more intimate and personal form of an address to a pupil called the *son* and is arranged in strophes instead of couplets.

22, 17—23, 35: The maxims warn against: oppression of the poor and defenseless (22, 22f), anger (24f), giving surety for debts (26f), bad manners at a king's table (23, 1f), anxiety for riches (4f), a grudging host (6ff), intemperance in food and drink (19ff.29-35), and adultery (26ff). They exhort to: careful workmanship (22, 29), respect for the rights of orphans (23, 10f), correction of the young (13f), filial piety (15f.22-25), and fear of the LORD (17f).

22, 19f: *Amen-em-Ope:* an Egyptian scribe to whom is attributed a collection of maxims in *Thirty* chapters (v 20) composed for the instruction of his children and addressed to a young man who wishes to enter upon a career. The inspired editor of Proverbs does not translate these, but uses their materials in constructing a similar collection of proverbs.

he will not stand in the presence
of obscure men.

CHAPTER 23

1 When you sit down to dine with a ruler,
keep in mind who is before you;
2† And put a knife to your throat
if you have a ravenous appetite.
3 Do not desire his delicacies;
they are deceitful food.

4 Toil not to gain wealth,
cease to be concerned about it;
5 While your glance flits to it, it is gone!
for assuredly it grows wings,
like the eagle that flies toward heaven.

6 Do not take food with a grudging man,
and do not desire his dainties;
7 For in his greed he is like a storm.
"Eat and drink," he says to you,
though his heart is not with you;
8 The little you have eaten you will vomit up,
and you will have wasted your agreeable words.

9* Speak not for the fool's hearing;
he will despise the wisdom of your words.

10* Remove not the ancient landmark,
nor invade the fields of orphans;
11* For their redeemer is strong;
he will defend their cause against you.

12 Apply your heart to instruction,
and your ears to words of knowledge.

13* Withhold not chastisement from a boy;
if you beat him with the rod, he will not die.
14* Beat him with the rod,
and you will save him from the nether world.

15 My son, if your heart be wise,
my own heart also will rejoice;
16 And my inmost being will exult,
when your lips speak what is right.

17* Let not your heart emulate sinners,
but be zealous for the fear of the LORD always;
18* For you will surely have a future,
and your hope will not be cut off.

19 Hear, my son, and be wise,
and guide your heart in the right way.
20 Consort not with winebibbers,
nor with those who eat meat to excess;
21 For the drunkard and the glutton come to poverty,
and torpor clothes a man in rags.

22 Listen to your father who begot you,
and despise not your mother when she is old.
23 Get the truth, and sell it not—
wisdom, instruction and understanding.
24* The father of a just man will exult with glee;
he who begets a wise son will have joy in him.
25 Let your father and mother have joy;
let her who bore you exult.

26 My son, give me your heart,
and let your eyes keep to my ways.
27 For the harlot is a deep ditch,
and the adulteress a narrow pit;
28* Yes, she lies in wait like a robber,
and increases the faithless among men.

29† Who scream? Who shriek?
Who have strife? Who have anxiety?
Who have wounds for nothing?
Who have black eyes?
30* Those who linger long over wine,
those who engage in trials of blended wine.
31 Look not on the wine when it is red,
when it sparkles in the glass.
It goes down smoothly;
32 but in the end it bites like a serpent,
or like a poisonous adder.
33 Your eyes behold strange sights,
and your heart utters disordered thoughts;
34 You are like one now lying in the depths of the sea,
now sprawled at the top of the mast.
35† "They struck me, but it pained me not;
They beat me, but I felt it not;
When shall I awake
to seek wine once again?"

*

23, 9: 9, 7.
10: 22, 28.
11: 22, 23.
13: 13, 24; 19, 18; Sir 30, 1.
14: 29, 15.17.
17: 3, 31; 24, 1.19.
18: 24, 14.
24: 10, 1.
28: 7, 10-27.
30: 20, 1; Sir 19, 2; Hos 4, 11.

†

23, 2: *Put a knife to your throat:* a metaphor for self-restraint.

23, 29-35: A vivid description of the evil effects, physical and psychological, of drunkenness.

23, 35: Wine makes the drunkard insensible to bodily and moral harm. His one desire is to indulge again.

CHAPTER 24

1*†Be not emulous of evil men,
and desire not to be with them;
2 For their hearts plot violence,
and their lips speak of foul play.

3 By wisdom is a house built,
by understanding is it made firm;
4 And by knowledge are its rooms filled
with every precious and pleasing possession.

5* A wise man is more powerful than a strong man,
and a man of knowledge than a man of might;
6* For it is by wise guidance that you wage your war,
and the victory is due to a wealth of counselors.
7*†For a fool, to be silent is wisdom;
not to open his mouth at the gate.

8 He who plots evil doing—
men call him an intriguer.
9 Beyond intrigue and folly and sin,
it is arrogance that men find abominable.

10† If you remain indifferent in time of adversity,
your strength will depart from you.
11† Rescue those who are being dragged to death,
and from those tottering to execution withdraw not.
12* If you say, "I know not this man!"
does not he who tests hearts perceive it?
He who guards your life knows it,
and he will repay each one according to his deeds.

13 If you eat honey, my son, because it is good,
if virgin honey is sweet to your taste;
14* Such, you must know, is wisdom to your soul.
If you find it, you will have a future,
and your hope will not be cut off.

15 Lie not in wait against the home of the just man,
ravage not his dwelling place;
16† For the just man falls seven times and rises again,
but the wicked stumble to ruin.

17 Rejoice not when your enemy falls,
and when he stumbles, let not your heart exult,
18 Lest the LORD see it, be displeased with you,
and withdraw his wrath from your enemy.

19 Be not provoked with evildoers,
nor envious of the wicked;
20* For the evil man has no future,
the lamp of the wicked will be put out.

21† My son, fear the LORD and the king;
have nothing to do with those who rebel against them;
22 For suddenly arises the destruction they send,
and the ruin from either one, who can measure?

IV: OTHER SAYINGS OF THE WISE

23*†These also are sayings of the wise:

To show partiality in judgment is not good.
24 He who says to the wicked man, "You are just"—
men will curse him, people will denounce him;
25 But those who convict the evildoer will fare well,
and on them will come the blessing of prosperity.
26† He gives a kiss on the lips
who makes an honest reply.

27† Complete your outdoor tasks,
and arrange your work in the field;
afterward you can establish your house.

PROVERBS

*

24, 1: 3, 31; 23, 17.
5: 21, 22.
6: 20, 18.
7: Sir 6, 21.
12: Ps 62, 13; Sir 16, 12; Mt 16, 27; Rom 2, 6.
14: 23, 18.
20: 13, 9.
23: 18, 5; 28, 21; Lv 19, 15; Dt 1, 17; 16, 19.

†

24, 1-22: These verses continue an exhortation to wisdom (vv 3-7.13f), and against: violence (1f), pride and intrigue (8f), callousness (10-12), injustice (15f), joy in the failure of others (17f) or scandal at their success (19f), and rebellion against authority (21f).

24, 7: *At the gate:* of the city, where justice was administered and public affairs discussed; see note on Ru 4, 1. Cf also Pss 69, 13; 127, 5; Prv 22, 22; 31, 23.31.

24, 10: *Indifferent:* to those who suffer unjustly.

24, 11: *Rescue . . . death:* most probably refers to the legal rescue of those unjustly condemned to death.

24, 16: *The just man* overcomes every misfortune which oppresses him. *Seven times:* i.e., an indefinite number; cf Mt 18, 21f; Lk 17, 4.

24, 21f: One owes obedience to God and to supreme civil authority (Mt 22, 21; Rom 13, 1ff; 1 Pt 2, 13f). The punishments for failure in either duty transcend the limits of private justice.

24, 23-34: This collection of sayings continues in the same vein as the preceding: it instructs in fairness (23-26) and preparation for the future (27); and warns against vengeance (28f) and slothfulness (30-34).

24, 26: *He gives a kiss on the lips:* shows himself a true friend.

24, 27: This verse is commonly interpreted as advocating careful and practical preparation for marriage.

28* Be not a witness against your neighbor without just cause,
thus committing folly with your lips.

29*† Say not, "As he did to me, so will I do to him;
I will repay the man according to his deeds."

30 I passed by the field of the sluggard,
by the vineyard of the man without sense;
31 And behold! it was all overgrown with thistles;
its surface was covered with nettles,
and its stone wall broken down.
32 And as I gazed at it, I reflected;
I saw and learned the lesson:
33* A little sleep, a little slumber,
a little folding of the arms to rest—
34 Then will poverty come upon you like a highwayman,
and want like an armed man.

PROVERBS

V: SECOND COLLECTION OF THE PROVERBS OF SOLOMON

CHAPTER 25

1*† These also are proverbs of Solomon. The men of Hezekiah, king of Judah, transmitted them.

2 God has glory in what he conceals,
kings have glory in what they fathom.

3 As the heavens in height, and the earth in depth,
the heart of kings is unfathomable.

4 Remove the dross from silver,
and it comes forth perfectly purified;
5 Remove the wicked from the presence of the king,
and his throne is made firm through righteousness.

6† Claim no honor in the king's presence,
nor occupy the place of great men;
7* For it is better that you be told, "Come up closer!"
than that you be humbled before the prince.

8 What your eyes have seen
bring not forth hastily against an opponent;
For what will you do later on
when your neighbor puts you to shame?
9 Discuss your case with your neighbor,
but another man's secret do not disclose;
10 Lest, hearing it, he reproach you,
and your ill repute cease not.

11 Like golden apples in silver settings
are words spoken at the proper time.

12 Like a golden earring, or a necklace of fine gold,
is a wise reprover to an obedient ear.

13 Like the coolness of snow in the heat of the harvest
is a faithful messenger for the one who sends him.
[He refreshes the soul of his master.]

14 Like clouds and wind when no rain follows
is the man who boastfully promises what he never gives.

15* By patience is a ruler persuaded,
and a soft tongue will break a bone.

16 If you find honey, eat only what you need,
lest you become glutted with it and vomit it up.

17 Let your foot be seldom in your neighbor's house,
lest he have more than enough of you, and hate you.

18 Like a club, or a sword, or a sharp arrow,
is the man who bears false witness against his neighbor.

19 Like an infected tooth or an unsteady foot
is [dependence on] a faithless man in time of trouble.

20* Like a moth in clothing, or a maggot in wood,
sorrow gnaws at the human heart.

---

*

28: 19, 5; 25, 18.
29: 20, 22.
33f: 6, 10f.
25, 1: 1, 1.
7: Lk 14, 8ff.
15: 15, 1.4.
20: Sir 30, 24.

---

†

24, 29: This verse indicates great progress from the principle of the law of Talion (see note on Ex 21, 23ff) toward the teaching found in Rom 12, 17ff. Cf also Prv 25, 21ff.

25, 1: *The men of Hezekiah:* literary men at the royal court of Hezekiah who are represented as transcribing the proverbs from other collections. Hezekiah was a reformer of national religious life (2 Chr 29, 25-30).

25, 6f: Compare the lesson on humility which was taught by Christ (Lk 14, 7-11).

21*† If your enemy be hungry, give him food to eat,
if he be thirsty, give him to drink;
22 For live coals you will heap on his head,
and the LORD will vindicate you.

23 The north wind brings rain,
and a backbiting tongue an angry countenance.

24* It is better to dwell in a corner of the housetop
than in a roomy house with a quarrelsome woman.

25 Like cool water to one faint from thirst
is good news from a far country.

26 Like a troubled fountain or a polluted spring
is a just man who gives way before the wicked.

27† To eat too much honey is not good;
nor to seek honor after honor.

28 Like an open city with no defenses
is the man with no check on his feelings.

CHAPTER 26†

1 Like snow in summer, or rain in harvest,
honor for a fool is out of place.

2 Like the sparrow in its flitting, like the swallow in its flight,
a curse uncalled-for arrives nowhere.

3* The whip for the horse, the bridle for the ass,
and the rod for the back of fools.

4† Answer not the fool according to his folly,
lest you too become like him.

5 Answer the fool according to his folly,
lest he become wise in his own eyes.

6 He cuts off his feet, he drinks down violence,
who sends messages by a fool.

7† A proverb in the mouth of a fool
hangs limp, like crippled legs.

8 Like one who entangles the stone in the sling
is he who gives honor to a fool.

9 Like a thorn stick brandished by the hand of a drunkard
is a proverb in the mouth of fools.

10 Like an archer wounding all who pass by
is he who hires a drunken fool.

11* As the dog returns to his vomit,
so the fool repeats his folly.

12 You see a man wise in his own eyes?
There is more hope for a fool than for him.

13* The sluggard says, "There is a lion in the street,
a lion in the middle of the square!"

14 The door turns on its hinges,
the sluggard, on his bed!

15* The sluggard loses his hand in the dish;
he is too weary to lift it to his mouth.

16 The sluggard imagines himself wiser
than seven men who answer with good sense.

17 Like the man who seizes a passing dog by the ears
is he who meddles in a quarrel not his own.

18 Like a crazed archer
scattering firebrands and deadly arrows
19 Is the man who deceives his neighbor,
and then says, "I was only joking."

20 For lack of wood, the fire dies out;
and when there is no talebearer, strife subsides.

21* What a bellows is to live coals, what wood is to fire,

PROVERBS

*

21: Rom 12, 20.
24: 21, 9.
26, 3: 19, 29; Sir 33, 25.
11: 2 Pt 2, 22.
13: 22, 13.
15: 19, 24.
21: 15, 18; 29, 22.

†

25, 21f: Charity is invaluable in resolving enmities and restoring peace. *Live coals:* i.e., either remorse and embarrassment for the harm done, or increased punishment for refusing reconciliation. Cf Mt 5, 44; Rom 12, 20.

25, 27: *Nor . . . honor after honor:* the text is uncertain.

26, 1-28: Concrete images describe the vices of fools (1-12), of sluggards (13-16), of meddlers (17-19), of talebearers (20ff), and of flatterers (23-28).

26, 4f: There is no contradiction between these two proverbs. In any answer the wise man gives he must protect his own interest against the fool.

26, 7ff: The fool abuses whatever knowledge he possesses.

such is a contentious man in enkindling strife.

22* The words of a talebearer are like dainty morsels
that sink into one's inmost being.

23 Like a glazed finish on earthenware are smooth lips with a wicked heart.

24 With his lips an enemy pretends,
but in his inmost being he maintains deceit;

25*† When he speaks graciously, trust him not,
for seven abominations are in his heart.

26 A man may conceal hatred under dissimulation,
but his malice will be revealed in the assembly.

27* He who digs a pit falls into it;
and a stone comes back upon him who rolls it.

28 The lying tongue is its owner's enemy,
and the flattering mouth works ruin.

PROVERBS

CHAPTER 27

1 Boast not of tomorrow,
for you know not what any day may bring forth.

2 Let another praise you—not your own mouth;
Someone else—not your own lips.

3* Stone is heavy, and sand a burden,
but a fool's provocation is heavier than both.

4 Anger is relentless, and wrath overwhelming—
but before jealousy who can stand?

5 Better is an open rebuke
than a love that remains hidden.

6 Wounds from a friend may be accepted as well meant,
but the greetings of an enemy one prays against.

7 One who is full, tramples on virgin honey;
but to the man who is hungry, any bitter thing is sweet.

8 Like a bird that is far from its nest
is a man who is far from his home.

9 Perfume and incense gladden the heart,
but by grief the soul is torn asunder.

10 Your own friend and your father's friend forsake not;
but if ruin befalls you, enter not a kinsman's house.
Better is a neighbor near at hand
than a brother far away.

11 If you are wise, my son, you will gladden my heart,
and I will be able to rebut him who taunts me.

12* The shrewd man perceives evil and hides;
simpletons continue on and suffer the penalty.

13*† Take his garment who becomes surety for another,
and for the sake of a stranger, yield it up!

14† When one greets his neighbor with a loud voice in the early morning,
a curse can be laid to his charge.

15* For a persistent leak on a rainy day
the match is a quarrelsome woman.

16 He who keeps her stores up a stormwind;
he cannot tell north from south.

17 As iron sharpens iron,
so man sharpens his fellow man.

18 He who tends a fig tree eats its fruit,
and he who is attentive to his master will be enriched.

19 As one face differs from another,
so does one human heart from another.

20* The nether world and the abyss are never satisfied;
so too the eyes of men.

21 As the crucible tests silver and the furnace gold,
so a man is tested by the praise he receives.

*

22: 18, 8.
25: Sir 12, 10; 27, 23.
27: Eccl 10, 8; Sir 27, 25f.
27, 3: Sir 22, 14f.
12: 22, 3.
13: 20, 16.
15: 21, 9; 25, 24.
20: 30, 16; Eccl 4, 8.

†

26, 25: *Seven abominations:* many evil intentions.
27, 13: See note on 20, 16.
27, 14: The *loud voice* suggests hypocrisy in the greeting.

22 Though you should pound the fool to bits
with the pestle, amid the grits in a mortar,
his folly would not go out of him.

23† Take good care of your flocks,
give careful attention to your herds;
24 For wealth lasts not forever,
nor even a crown from age to age.
25 When the grass is taken away and the aftergrowth appears,
and the mountain greens are gathered in,
26 The lambs will provide you with clothing,
and the goats will bring the price of a field,
27 And there will be ample goat's milk to supply you,
to supply your household,
and maintenance for your maidens.

CHAPTER 28

1 The wicked man flees although no one pursues him;
but the just man, like a lion, feels sure of himself.

2† If a land is rebellious, its princes will be many;
but with a prudent man it knows security.

3 A rich man who oppresses the poor
is like a devastating rain that leaves no food.

4† Those who abandon the law praise the wicked man,
but those who keep the law war against him.

5 Evil men understand nothing of justice,
but those who seek the LORD understand all.

6* Better a poor man who walks in his integrity
than he who is crooked in his ways and rich.

7 He who keeps the law is a wise son,
but the gluttons' companion disgraces his father.

8† He who increases his wealth by interest and overcharge
gathers it for him who is kind to the poor.

9*† When one turns away his ear from hearing the law,
even his prayer is an abomination.

10 He who seduces the upright into an evil way
will himself fall into his own pit.
[And blameless men will gain prosperity.]

11 The rich man is wise in his own eyes,
but a poor man who is intelligent sees through him.

12 When the just are triumphant, there is great jubilation;
but when the wicked gain preeminence, people hide.

13 He who conceals his sins prospers not,
but he who confesses and forsakes them obtains mercy.

14 Happy the man who is always on his guard;
but he who hardens his heart will fall into evil.

15 Like a roaring lion or a ravenous bear
is a wicked ruler over a poor people.

16 The less prudent the prince, the more his deeds oppress.
He who hates ill-gotten gain prolongs his days.

17 Though a man burdened with human blood
were to flee to the grave, none should support him.

18 He who walks uprightly is safe,
but he whose ways are crooked falls into the pit.

19* He who cultivates his land will have plenty of food,
but from idle pursuits a man has his fill of poverty.

20* The trustworthy man will be richly blessed;
he who is in haste to grow rich will not go unpunished.

*

28, 6: 19, 1. 19: 12, 11.
9: 21, 27. 20: 13, 11.

†

27, 23-27: The land of Palestine was very suitable for flocks and herds, which formed the principal source of wealth for their owners.

28, 2: The meaning of this poorly preserved verse seems to be that frequent changes of rulers often result from moral corruption and political disorder.

28, 4: *The law:* religious and moral teaching.

28, 8: *Interest and overcharge* were strictly forbidden in the old law among Israelites because it was presumed that the borrower was in distress; cf Ex 22, 25; Lv 25, 35ff; Dt 23, 19; Ps 15, 5; Ez 18, 8. Civil and divine law will take the offender's wealth from him.

28, 9: Prayers offered in bad faith are displeasing to God.

21* To show partiality is never good:
for even a morsel of bread a man may do wrong.

22 The avaricious man is perturbed about his wealth,
and he knows not when want will come upon him.

23 He who rebukes a man gets more thanks in the end
than one with a flattering tongue.

24* He who defrauds father or mother and calls it no sin,
is a partner of the brigand.

25 The greedy man stirs up disputes,
but he who trusts in the LORD will prosper.

26 He who trusts in himself is a fool,
but he who walks in wisdom is safe.

27* He who gives to the poor suffers no want,
but he who ignores them gets many a curse.

28 When the wicked gain pre-eminence, other men hide;
but at their fall the just flourish.

CHAPTER 29

1 The man who remains stiff-necked and hates rebuke
will be crushed suddenly beyond cure.

2* When the just prevail, the people rejoice;
but when the wicked rule, the people groan.

3* He who loves wisdom makes his father glad,
but he who consorts with harlots squanders his wealth.

4 By justice a king gives stability to the land;
but he who imposes heavy taxes ruins it.

5 The man who flatters his neighbor
is spreading a net under his feet.

6 The wicked man steps into a snare,
but the just man runs on joyfully.

7 The just man has a care for the rights of the poor;
the wicked man has no such concern.

8* Arrogant men set the city ablaze,
but wise men calm the fury.

9 If a wise man disputes with a fool,
he may rage or laugh but can have no peace.

10 Bloodthirsty men hate the honest man,
but the upright show concern for his life.

11* The fool gives vent to all his anger;
but by biding his time, the wise man calms it.

12 If a ruler listens to lying words,
his servants all become wicked.

13*†The poor and the oppressor have a common bond:
the LORD gives light to the eyes of both.

14 If a king is zealous for the rights of the poor,
his throne stands firm forever.

15* The rod of correction gives wisdom,
but a boy left to his whims disgraces his mother.

16 When the wicked prevail, crime increases;
but their downfall the just will behold.

17 Correct your son, and he will bring you comfort,
and give delight to your soul.

18 Without prophecy the people become demoralized;
but happy is he who keeps the law.

19* By words no servant can be trained;
for he understands what is said, but obeys not.

20* Do you see a man hasty in his words?
More can be hoped for from a fool!

21 If a man pampers his servant from childhood,
he will turn out to be stubborn.

22* An ill-tempered man stirs up disputes,

*

21: 24, 23.
24: Mk 7, 11ff.
27: 19, 17; Sir 4, 3-8.
29, 2: 11, 10.
3: 5, 10; 10, 1.
8: 11, 11.
11: 12, 16; 25, 28; Sir 21, 26.
13: 22, 2.
15: 13, 24, 22, 15; 23, 13f; Sir 22, 6; 30, 1.
19: Sir 33, 25f.
20: Eccl 5, 1.
22: 15, 18; 26, 21.

†

29, 13: God gives life to all classes of people; cf 22, 2.

and a hotheaded man is the cause
of many sins.

23* Man's pride causes his humiliation,
but he who is humble of spirit obtains honor.

24† The accomplice of a thief is his own enemy:
he hears himself put under a curse, yet discloses nothing.

25 The fear of man brings a snare,
but he who trusts in the LORD is safe.

26 Many curry favor with the ruler,
but the rights of each are from the LORD.

27 The evildoer is an abomination to the just,
and he who walks uprightly is an abomination to the wicked.

VI: THE WORDS OF AGUR

CHAPTER 30

1† The words of Agur, son of Jakeh the Massaite:

The pronouncement of mortal man:
"I am not God;
I am not God, that I should prevail.
2 Why, I am the most stupid of men,
and have not even human intelligence;
3 Neither have I learned wisdom,
nor have I the knowledge of the Holy One.
4 Who has gone up to heaven and come down again—
who has cupped the wind in his hands?
Who has bound up the waters in a cloak—
who has marked out all the ends of the earth?
What is his name, what is his son's name,
if you know it?"
5* Every word of God is tested;
he is a shield to those who take refuge in him.
6* Add nothing to his words,
lest he reprove you, and you be exposed as a deceiver.

VII: NUMERICAL PROVERBS

7 Two things I ask of you,
deny them not to me before I die:
8 Put falsehood and lying far from me,
give me neither poverty nor riches;
[provide me only with the food I need;]
9 Lest, being full, I deny you,
saying, "Who is the LORD?"
Or, being in want, I steal,
and profane the name of my God.

10 Slander not a servant to his master,
lest he curse you, and you have to pay the penalty.
11*† There is a group of people that curses its father,
and blesses not its mother.
12 There is a group that is pure in its own eyes,
yet is not purged of its filth.
13 There is a group—how haughty their eyes!
how overbearing their glance!
14 There is a group whose incisors are swords,
whose teeth are knives,
Devouring the needy from the earth,
and the poor from among men.

15† The two daughters of the leech are, "Give, Give."
Three things are never satisfied,
four never say, "Enough!"
16* The nether world, and the barren womb;
the earth, that is never saturated with water,
and fire, that never says, "Enough!"

17 The eye that mocks a father,
or scorns an aged mother,
Will be plucked out by the ravens in the valley;
the young eagles will devour it.

18† Three things are too wonderful for me,

*

23: 11, 2; 16, 18; 18, 12; Jb 22, 29.
30, 5: Ps 12, 7.
6: Dt 4, 2.
11: 20, 20.
16: 27, 20.

†

29, 24: *Is his own enemy:* because he not only incurs guilt as an accomplice but, by his silence, brings down on himself the curse invoked on the unknown guilty partner.

30, 1: *Agur:* an unknown person. *Massaite:* from Massa in northern Arabia, elsewhere referred to as an encampment of the Ishmaelites (Gn 25, 14). But the word may not be intended as a place name; it might signify "an oracle," "a prophecy."

30, 1ff: Agur wishes to stress man's insignificance when he is compared to God; cf Jb 38—39.

30, 11-14: Perverted people are here classified as unfilial (11), self-righteous (12), proud (13) and rapacious (14).

30, 15ff: *The two daughters . . . "Give, Give":* the text is obscure but the sense seems to be that *the leech* is insatiable in its desire for blood, just as desire for blood, just as are *the nether world* for victims, *the barren womb* for offspring, the parched *earth* for *water,* and *fire* for fuel (16).

30, 18f: The soaring flight of the eagle, the mysterious movement upon a rock of the serpent which has no feet, the path of the ship through the trackless deep, and the marvelous procreation of human life, excite great wonderment.

yes, four I cannot understand:
19 The way of an eagle in the air,
the way of a serpent upon a rock,
The way of a ship on the high seas,
and the way of a man with a maiden.

20† Such is the way of an adulterous woman:
she eats, wipes her mouth,
and says, "I have done no wrong."

21 Under three things the earth trembles,
yes, under four it cannot bear up:
22* Under a slave when he becomes king,
and a fool when he is glutted with food;
23 Under an odious woman when she is wed,
and a maidservant when she displaces her mistress.

24 Four things are among the smallest on the earth,
and yet are exceedingly wise:
25 Ants—a species not strong,
yet they store up their food in the summer;
26† Rock-badgers—a species not mighty,
yet they make their home in the crags;
27 Locusts—they have no king,
yet they migrate all in array;
28 Lizards—you can catch them with your hands,
yet they find their way into king's palaces.

29 Three things are stately in their stride,
yes, four are stately in their carriage:
30 The lion, mightiest of beasts,
who retreats before nothing;
31 The strutting cock, and the he-goat,
and the king at the head of his people.

32† If you have foolishly been proud
or presumptuous—put your hand on your mouth;
33 For the stirring of milk brings forth curds,
and the stirring of anger brings forth blood.

VIII: THE WORDS OF LEMUEL

CHAPTER 31

1 The words of Lemuel, king of Massa.
The advice which his mother gave him:

2 What, my son, my first-born!
what, O son of my womb;
what, O son of my vows!
3* Give not your vigor to women,
nor your strength to those who ruin kings.
4* It is not for kings, O Lemuel,
not for kings to drink wine;
strong drink is not for princes!
5 Lest in drinking they forget what the law decrees,
and violate the rights of all who are in need.
6 Give strong drink to one who is perishing,
and wine to the sorely depressed;
7 When they drink, they will forget their misery,
and think no more of their burdens.
8 Open your mouth in behalf of the dumb,
and for the rights of the destitute;
9 Open your mouth, decree what is just,
defend the needy and the poor!

IX: THE IDEAL WIFE

10* When one finds a worthy wife,
her value is far beyond pearls.
11 Her husband, entrusting his heart to her,
has an unfailing prize.
12† She brings him good, and not evil,
all the days of her life.
13 She obtains wool and flax
and makes cloth with skillful hands.
14† Like merchant ships,
she secures her provisions from afar.
15 She rises while it is still night,
and distributes food to her household.
16 She picks out a field to purchase;
out of her earnings she plants a vineyard.
17 She is girt about with strength,
and sturdy are her arms.
18† She enjoys the success of her dealings;
at night her lamp is undimmed.
19 She puts her hands to the distaff,
and her fingers ply the spindle.

*

22: 19, 10; Eccl 10, 6f. 4: 20, 1.
31, 3: 5, 9. 10-31: Sir 26, 1ff. 13-18.

†

30, 20: This verse portrays the indifference of an adulterous woman who thinks there is no trace of her wicked act.

30, 26: *Rock-badgers:* cf note to Ps 104, 18.

30, 32f: The anger aroused by overweening pride threatens an awesome punishment.

31, 12: *Good, and not evil:* i.e., prosperity, not adversity.

31, 14: *Merchant:* literally, "Canaanite" (cf v 24), probably because the merchant class had been composed chiefly of Canaanites.

31, 18: *Her lamp is undimmed:* indicates abundance of productive work and its accompanying prosperity; cf 20, 20; Jb 18, 6.

20 She reaches out her hands to the poor,
and extends her arms to the needy.
21 She fears not the snow for her household;
all her charges are doubly clothed.
22 She makes her own coverlets;
fine linen and purple are her clothing.
23 Her husband is prominent at the city gates
as he sits with the elders of the land.
24 She makes garments and sells them,
and stocks the merchants with belts.
25† She is clothed with strength and dignity,
and she laughs at the days to come.
26 She opens her mouth in wisdom,
and on her tongue is kindly counsel.
27 She watches the conduct of her household,
and eats not her food in idleness.
28 Her children rise up and praise her;
her husband, too, extols her:
29 "Many are the women of proven worth,
but you have excelled them all."
30† Charm is deceptive and beauty fleeting;
the woman who fears the LORD is to be praised.
31 Give her a reward of her labors,
and let her works praise her at the city gates.

†

31, 25: Laughs at the days to come: anticipates the future with gladness free from anxiety.

31, 30: The true charm of the ideal wife is her religious spirit, for she *fears the LORD;* cf note on 1, 7.

The Book of

ECCLESIASTES

The title Ecclesiastes given to this book is the Greek translation of the Hebrew name Qoheleth meaning, perhaps, "one who convokes an assembly." The book, however, does not consist of public addresses, but is a treatise, more or less logically developed, on the vanity of all things. Reflections in prose and aphorisms in verse are intermingled in Ecclesiastes, which contains, besides, an introduction and an epilogue.

The book is concerned with the purpose and value of human life. While admitting the existence of a divine plan, it considers such a plan to be hidden from man, who seeks happiness without ever finding it here below (3, 11; 8, 7.17). Ecclesiastes applies his "Vanity of vanities" to everything "under the sun," even to that wisdom which seeks to find at last a semblence of good in the things of the world. Merit does not yield happiness for it is often tried by suffering. Riches and pleasures do not avail. Existence is monotonous, enjoyment fleeting and vain; darkness quickly follows. Life, then, is an enigma beyond human ability to solve.

While Ecclesiastes concedes that there is an advantage for man in the enjoyment of certain legitimate pleasures lest he lapse into pessimism and despair, he nevertheless considers this indulgence also vanity unless man returns due thanks to the Creator who has given him all. Under this aspect, earthly wisdom would rise to the higher level of true spiritual wisdom. This true wisdom is not found "under the sun" but is perceived only by the light of faith, inasmuch as it rests with God, who is the final Judge of the good and the bad, and whose reign endures forever. The Epilogue gives the clue to this thought (12, 13f).

The moral teaching of the book is imperfect, like the Old Testament itself (Heb 7, 19), yet it marks an advance in the development of the doctrine of divine retribution. While rejecting the older solution of earthly rewards and punishments, Ecclesiastes looks forward to a more lasting one. The clear answer to the problem was to come with the light of Christ's teaching concerning future life.

The author of the book was a teacher of popular wisdom (12, 9). Qoheleth was obviously only his literary name. Because he is called "David's son, king in Jerusalem," it was commonly thought that he was King Solomon. Such personation, however, was but a literary device to lend greater dignity and authority to the book—a circumstance which does not in any way impugn its inspired character. The Epilogue seems to have been written by an editor, probably a disciple of Qoheleth. The entire work differs considerably in language and style from earlier books of the Old Testament. It reflects a late period of Hebrew, and was probably written about three centuries before Christ.

ECCLESIASTES

CHAPTER 1

1*† The words of David's son, Qoheleth, king in Jerusalem:

Vanity of Toil without Profit

2*† Vanity of vanities, says Qoheleth,
vanity of vanities! All things are vanity!
3*† What profit has man from all the labor
which he toils at under the sun?
4 One generation passes and another comes,
but the world forever stays.
5 The sun rises and the sun goes down;
then it presses on to the place where it rises.
6 Blowing now toward the south, then toward the north,
the wind turns again and again, resuming its rounds.
7 All rivers go to the sea,
yet never does the sea become full.
To the place where they go,
the rivers keep on going.

*

1, 1: 7, 27; 12, 8f.
2: 12, 8.
3: 2, 11.22; 3, 9; 5, 15.

†

1, 1: *Qoheleth:* see Introduction.
1, 2: *Vanity of vanities:* a Hebrew superlative expressing the supreme degree of futility and emptiness.
1, 3: *Under the sun:* used throughout this book to signify "on the earth."

8*† All speech is labored;
there is nothing man can say.
The eye is not satisfied with seeing
nor is the ear filled with hearing.

9* What has been, that will be; what
has been done, that will be done. Nothing
is new under the sun. 10* Even the thing
of which we say, "See, this is new!" has
already existed in the ages that pre-
ceded us. 11*† There is no remembrance
of the men of old; nor of those to come
will there be any remembrance among
those who come after them.

I: QOHELETH'S INVESTIGATION OF LIFE

Twofold Introduction. 12 I, Qoheleth,
was king over Israel in Jerusalem,
13* and I applied my mind to search and
investigate in wisdom all things that are
done under the sun.

A thankless task God has appointed
for men to be busied about.

14*† I have seen all things that are done
under the sun, and behold, all is vanity
and a chase after wind.

15 What is crooked cannot be made straight,
and what is missing cannot be supplied.

16* Though I said to myself, "Behold,
I have become great and stored up wis-
dom beyond all who were before me in
Jerusalem, and my mind has broad ex-
perience of wisdom and knowledge";
17* yet when I applied my mind to know
wisdom and knowledge, madness and
folly, I learned that this also is a chase
after wind.

18 For in much wisdom there is much sorrow,
and he who stores up knowledge stores up grief.

CHAPTER 2

Study of Pleasure-seeking. 1*† I said
to myself, "Come, now, let me try you
with pleasure and the enjoyment of good
things." But behold, this too was vanity.
2 Of laughter I said: "Mad!" and of
mirth: "What good does this do?" 3† I
thought of beguiling my senses with
wine, though my mind was concerned
with wisdom, and of taking up folly, until
I should understand what is best for men
to do under the heavens during the lim-
ited days of their life.
4 I undertook great works; I built my-
self houses and planted vineyards; 5 I
made gardens and parks, and set out in
them fruit trees of all sorts. 6 And I con-
structed for myself reservoirs to water
a flourishing woodland. 7 I acquired
male and female slaves, and slaves were
born in my house. I also had growing
herds of cattle and flocks of sheep, more
than all who had been before me in Jeru-
salem. 8 I amassed for myself silver and
gold, and the wealth of kings and prov-
inces. I got for myself male and female
singers and all human luxuries. 9 I be-
came great, and I stored up more than
all others before me in Jerusalem; my
wisdom, too, stayed with me. 10* Nothing
that my eyes desired did I deny them,
nor did I deprive myself of any joy, but
my heart rejoiced in the fruit of all my
toil. This was my share for all my toil.
11* But when I turned to all the works
that my hands had wrought, and to the
toil at which I had taken such pains, be-
hold! all was vanity and a chase after
wind, with nothing gained under the sun.
12 For what will the man do who is to
come after the king? What men have al-
ready done!
Study of Wisdom and Folly. I went on
to the consideration of wisdom, madness
and folly. 13 And I saw that wisdom has
the advantage over folly as much as
light has the advantage over darkness.

14* The wise man has eyes in his head,
but the fool walks in darkness.

Yet I knew that one lot befalls both of
them. 15 So I said to myself, if the fool's
lot is to befall me also, why then should
I be wise? Where is the profit for me?
And I concluded in my heart that this
too is vanity. 16* Neither of the wise man
nor of the fool will there be an abiding
remembrance, for in days to come both
will have been forgotten. How is it that
the wise man dies as well as the fool!
17 Therefore I loathed life, since for me
the work that is done under the sun is
evil; for all is vanity and a chase after
wind.

Study of the Fruits of Toil

To Others the Profits. 18 And I de-
tested all the fruits of my labor under

*

8: 8, 17.
9: 3, 15; 6, 10.
10: 3, 15.
11: 2, 16.
13: 8, 9.
14: 2, 11.17.
16: 2, 9.
17: 2, 3; 7, 25.
2, 1: Wis 2, 6.
10: 3, 22; 5, 18.
11: 1, 17; Sir 44, 9.
14f: 6, 8; 9, 2f.
16: 1, 11; Wis 2, 4.

†

1, 8: *All speech . . . man can say:* or "All things are wearisome beyond man's power to tell."

1, 11: Men remember nothing long, God never forgets.

1, 14: *Chase after wind:* futility, like an attempt to corral the winds. Cf Hos 12, 2. The ancient versions understood "affliction of spirit." These words are used to conclude sections of the discourse, as far as 6, 9.

2, 1-11: The author here assumes the role of Solomon.

2, 3: *Though my mind . . . wisdom:* while indulging in pleasure the author hopes to discover wherein man's true happiness consists.

the sun, because I must leave them to
a man who is to come after me. 19 And
who knows whether he will be a wise
man or a fool? Yet he will have control
over all the fruits of my wise labor under
the sun. This also is vanity. 20 So my feel-
ings turned to despair of all the fruits
of my labor under the sun. 21 For here
is a man who has labored with wisdom
and knowledge and skill, and to another,
who has not labored over it, he must
leave his property. This also is vanity
and a great misfortune. 22* For what
profit comes to a man from all the toil
and anxiety of heart with which he has
labored under the sun? 23 All his days
sorrow and grief are his occupation;
even at night his mind is not at rest. This
also is vanity.

24*† There is nothing better for man
than to eat and drink and provide him-
self with good things by his labors. Even
this, I realized, is from the hand of God.
25 For who can eat or drink apart from
him? 26* For to whatever man he sees
fit he gives wisdom and knowledge and
joy; but to the sinner he gives the task
of gathering possessions to be given to
whatever man God sees fit. This also is
vanity and a chase after wind.

CHAPTER 3

Man Cannot Hit on the Right Time To Act

1 There is an appointed time for everything,
and a time for every affair under the heavens.
2 A time to be born, and a time to die;
a time to plant, and a time to uproot the plant.
3 A time to kill, and a time to heal;
a time to tear down, and a time to build.
4 A time to weep, and a time to laugh;
a time to mourn, and a time to dance.
5 A time to scatter stones, and a time to gather them;
a time to embrace, and a time to be far from embraces.
6 A time to seek, and a time to lose;
a time to keep, and a time to cast away.
7 A time to rend, and a time to sew;
a time to be silent, and a time to speak.
8 A time to love, and a time to hate;
a time of war, and a time of peace.

9* What advantage has the worker from
his toil? 10 I have considered the task
which God has appointed for men to be
busied about. 11* He has made every-
thing appropriate to its time, and has put
the timeless into their hearts, without
men's ever discovering, from beginning
to end, the work which God has done.
12 I recognized that there is nothing bet-
ter than to be glad and to do well during
life. 13* For every man, moreover, to eat
and drink and enjoy the fruit of all his
labor is a gift of God. 14 I recognized that
whatever God does will endure forever;
there is no adding to it, or taking from
it. Thus has God done that he may be
revered. 15*† What now is has already
been; what is to be, already is; and God
restores what would otherwise be dis-
placed.

The Problem of Retribution. 16* And
still under the sun in the judgment place
I saw wickedness, and in the seat of jus-
tice, iniquity. 17* And I said to myself,
both the just and the wicked God will
judge, since there is a time for every af-
fair and on every work a judgment. 18 I
said to myself: As for the children of
men, it is God's way of testing them and
of showing that they are in themselves
like beasts. 19 For the lot of man and of
beast is one lot; the one dies as well as
the other. Both have the same life-
breath, and man has no advantage over
the beast; but all is vanity. 20* Both go
to the same place; both were made from
the dust, and to the dust they both re-
turn. 21* Who knows if the life-breath of
the children of men goes upward and
the life-breath of beasts goes earth-
ward? 22* And I saw that there is nothing
better for a man than to rejoice in his
work; for this is his lot. Who will let him
see what is to come after him?

CHAPTER 4

Vanity of Toil. 1* Again I considered
all the oppressions that take place under
the sun: the tears of the victims with
none to comfort them! From the hand
of their oppressors comes violence, and
there is none to comfort them! 2* And
those now dead, I declared more fortu-
nate in death than are the living to be
still alive. 3 And better off than both is
the yet unborn, who has not seen the
wicked work that is done under the sun.
4 Then I saw that all toil and skillful work
is the rivalry of one man for another.

*

22: 1, 3.
24: 3, 12f.22; 5, 17f; 8, 15.
26: Prv 13, 22.
3, 9: 1, 3.
11: 8, 17; 11, 5; Gn 1, 31.
13: 2, 24.
15: 1, 9.
16: 4, 1.
17: 12, 14.
20: 12, 7; Gn 2, 7; 3, 19; Ps 103, 14; Wis 2, 3; Sir 10, 9; 17, 1; 40, 11.
21: Wis 2, 2.
22: 8, 7; 10, 14.
4, 1: 5, 7.
2: 7, 2.

†

2, 24: Unrestrained indulgence is not advocated here, but legitimate pleasure and the cheerfulness it begets.

3, 15: *God restores:* the meaning is probably that God allows no part of his creation to drop out of existence.

This also is vanity and a chase after
wind.

5† "The fool folds his arms
and consumes his own flesh"—
6 Better is one handful with tranquility
than two with toil and a chase after wind!

Companions and Successors. 7 Again
I found this vanity under the sun: 8 a soli-
tary man with no companion; with nei-
ther son nor brother. Yet there is no end
to all his toil, and riches do not satisfy
his greed. "For whom do I toil and de-
prive myself of good things?" This also
is vanity and a worthless task. 9 Two are
better than one: they get a good wage
for their labor. 10 If the one falls, the
other will lift up his companion. Woe to
the solitary man! For if he should fall,
he has no one to lift him up. 11 So also,
if two sleep together, they keep each
other warm. How can one alone keep
warm? 12 Where a lone man may be
overcome, two together can resist. A
three-ply cord is not easily broken.
13 Better is a poor but wise youth than
an old but foolish king who no longer
knows caution; 14† for from a prison
house one comes forth to rule, since even
in his royalty he was poor at birth.
15† Then I saw all those who are to live
and move about under the sun with the
heir apparent who will succeed to his
place. 16 There is no end to all these peo-
ple, to all over whom he takes prece-
dence; yet the later generations will not
applaud him. This also is vanity and a
chase after wind.
Vanity of Many Words. 17*† Guard
your step when you go to the house of
God. Let your approach be obedience,
rather than the fools' offering of sacri-
fice; for they know not how to keep from
doing evil.

CHAPTER 5

1 Be not hasty in your utterance and
let not your heart be quick to make a
promise in God's presence. God is in
heaven and you are on earth; therefore
let your words be few.

2† For nightmares come with many cares,
and a fool's utterance with many words.

3* When you make a vow to God, delay
not its fulfillment. For God has no plea-
sure in fools; fulfill what you have
vowed. 4 You had better not make a vow
than make it and not fulfill it. 5 Let not
your utterances make you guilty, and
say not before his representative, "It
was a mistake," lest God be angered by
such words and destroy the works of
your hands. 6* Rather, fear God!
Gain and Loss of Goods. 7* If you see
oppression of the poor, and violation of
rights and justice in the realm, do not
be shocked by the fact, for the high offi-
cial has another higher than he watch-
ing him and above these are others
higher still—. 8† Yet an advantage for a
country in every respect is a king for
the arable land.
9* The covetous man is never satisfied
with money, and the lover of wealth
reaps no fruit from it; so this too is van-
ity. 10 Where there are great riches,
there are also many to devour them. Of
what use are they to the owner except
to feast his eyes upon? 11 Sleep is sweet
to the laboring man, whether he eats lit-
tle or much, but the rich man's abun-
dance allows him no sleep.
12* This is a grievous evil which I have
seen under the sun: riches kept by their
owner to his hurt. 13 Should the riches
be lost through some misfortune, he may
have a son when he is without means.
14* As he came forth from his mother's
womb, so again shall he depart, naked
as he came, having nothing from his la-
bor that he can carry in his hand. 15 This
too is a grievous evil, that he goes just
as he came. What then does it profit him
to toil for wind? 16 All the days of his life
are passed in gloom and sorrow, under
great vexation, sickness and wrath.
17* Here is what I recognize as good:
it is well for a man to eat and drink and
enjoy all the fruits of his labor under the
sun during the limited days of the life
which God gives him; for this is his lot.
18 Any man to whom God gives riches
and property, and grants power to par-
take of them, so that he receives his lot
and finds joy in the fruits of his toil, has
a gift from God. 19† For he will hardly
dwell on the shortness of his life, because
God lets him busy himself with the joy
of his heart.

ECCLESIASTES

*

17: 1 Sm 15, 22; Hos 6, 6.
5, 3: Nm 30, 3; Dt 23, 23; Ps 50, 14.
6: 12, 13; Dt 10, 12.
7: 3, 16; 4, 1.
9: Prv 28, 22.
12: Jb 20, 20.
14: Jb 1, 21; 1 Tm 6, 7.
17f: 2, 24.

†

4, 5: *Consumes his own flesh:* refuses to work for the necessities of life and consequently suffers hunger and impairs his bodily health.

4, 14: *Prison house:* probably his mother's womb, from which the king issues without possessions. Cf 5, 14.

4, 15: The king is no sooner dead than the people transfer their allegiance to his successor.

4, 17: *The fools' . . . sacrifice:* unacceptable to God because of their disobedience; cf 1 Sm 15, 22; Hos 6, 6.

5, 2: *Nightmares:* literally, "dreams."

5, 8: The wording of this verse has perhaps never been adequately explained.

5, 19: The meaning is that the joys of life, though temporary, keep a man from dwelling on the ills which afflict humanity.

CHAPTER 6

Limited Worth of Enjoyment. 1 There
is another evil which I have seen under
the sun, and it weighs heavily upon man:
2* there is the man to whom God gives
riches and property and honor, so that
he lacks none of all the things he craves;
yet God does not grant him power to
partake of them, but a stranger devours
them. This is vanity and a dire plague.
3† Should a man have a hundred chil-
dren and live many years, no matter to
what great age, still if he has not the full
benefit of his goods, or if he is deprived
of burial, of this man I proclaim that the
child born dead is more fortunate than
he. 4 Though it came in vain and goes
into darkness and its name is enveloped
in darkness; 5 though it has not seen or
known the sun, yet the dead child is at
rest rather than such a man. 6† Should
he live twice a thousand years and not
enjoy his goods, do not both go to the
same place?

7† All man's toil is for his mouth, yet
his desire is not fulfilled. 8 For what ad-
vantage has the wise man over the fool,
or what advantage has the poor man in
knowing how to conduct himself in life?
9† "What the eyes see is better than what
the desires wander after." This also is
vanity and a chase after wind.

II: QOHELETH'S CONCLUSIONS

10† Whatever is, was long ago given its
name, and the nature of man is known,
and that he cannot contend in judgment
with one who is stronger than he. 11 For
though there are many sayings that
multiply vanity, what profit is there for
a man? 12* For who knows what is good
for a man in life, the limited days of his
vain life (which God has made like a
shadow)? Because—who is there to tell
a man what will come after him under
the sun?

A. Man Cannot Find Out What Is Good for Him To Do

CHAPTER 7

Critique of Sages on the Day of Adversity

1*† A good name is better than good
ointment,
and the day of death than the day
of birth.
2* It is better to go to the house of
mourning
than to the house of feasting,
For that is the end of every man,
and the living should take it to
heart.
3 Sorrow is better than laughter,
because when the face is sad the
heart grows wiser.
4 The heart of the wise is in the house
of mourning,
but the heart of fools is in the
house of mirth.
5 It is better to hearken to the wise
man's rebuke
than to hearken to the song of
fools;
6 For as the crackling of thorns under
a pot,
so is the fool's laughter.

This also is vanity,
7 For oppression can make a fool of
a wise man,
and a bribe corrupts the heart.
8 Better is the end of speech than its
beginning;
better is the patient spirit than the
lofty spirit.
9 Do not in spirit become quickly dis-
contented,
for discontent lodges in the bosom
of a fool.

10 Do not say: How is it that former times
were better than these? For it is not in
wisdom that you ask about this.

11 Wisdom and an inheritance are
good,
and an advantage to those that see
the sun.

12 For the protection of wisdom is as the
protection of money; and the advantage
of knowledge is that wisdom preserves
the life of its owner.
13 Consider the work of God. Who
can make straight what he has made
crooked? 14 On a good day enjoy good
things, and on an evil day consider: Both
the one and the other God has made,
so that man cannot find fault with him
in anything.

Critique of Sages on Justice and Wickedness

15 I have seen all manner of things in
my vain days: a just man perishing in

*

6, 2: 2, 18f.
12: Jb 8, 9; 14, 2; Ps 102, 12.
7, 1: 4, 2; Prv 22, 1; Sir 41, 13.
2: 4, 2.

†

6, 3: A large family, a long life, an honorable burial, all were highly esteemed by the Hebrews, and it was considered a great misfortune to be deprived of them.
6, 6: *Same place:* the grave.
6, 7: *Mouth:* appetite, and therefore, body.
6, 9: *Better . . . wander after:* the good that is present to us is better than that which is absent and, perhaps, unattainable.
6, 10: The one who is stronger than man is God.
7, 1: *Ointment:* applied to the child at birth; *a good name* remains even after death.

his justice, and a wicked one surviving
in his wickedness. 16*† "Be not just to
excess, and be not overwise, lest you be
ruined. 17† Be not wicked to excess, and
be not foolish. Why should you die before
your time?" 18† It is good to hold to this
rule, and not to let that one go; but he
who fears God will win through at all
events.
19 Wisdom is a better defense for the
wise man than would be ten princes in
the city, 20*† yet there is no man on earth
so just as to do good and never sin. 21* Do
not give heed to every word that is spo-
ken lest you hear your servant speaking
ill of you, 22 for you know in your heart
that you have many times spoken ill of
others.
23 All these things I probed in wisdom.
I said, "I will acquire wisdom"; but it
was beyond me. 24 What exists is far-
reaching; it is deep, very deep: who can
find it out? 25* I turned my thoughts to-
ward knowledge; I sought and pursued
wisdom and reason, and I recognized
that wickedness is foolish and folly is
madness.
Critique of Sages on Women. 26* More
bitter than death I find the woman who
is a hunter's trap, whose heart is a snare
and whose hands are prison bonds. He
who is pleasing to God will escape her,
but the sinner will be entrapped by her.
27 Behold, this have I found, says Qohe-
leth, adding one thing to another that I
might discover the answer 28† which my
soul still seeks and has not found: One
man out of a thousand have I come upon,
but a woman among them all I have not
found. 29† Behold, only this have I found
out: God made mankind straight, but
men have had recourse to many calcu-
lations.

CHAPTER 8

Critique of Sages on the Wise Man and the King

1 Who is like the wise man,
and who knows the explanation of things?
A man's wisdom illumines his face,
but an impudent look is resented.

2 Observe the precept of the king, and
in view of your oath to God, 3 be not
hasty to withdraw from the king; do not
join in with a base plot, for he does what-
ever he pleases, 4 because his word is
sovereign, and who can say to him,
"What are you doing?"
5 "He who keeps the commandment
experiences no evil, and the wise man's
heart knows times and judgments; 6 for
there is a time and a judgment for ev-
erything."—Yet it is a great affliction for
man 7* that he is ignorant of what is to
come; for who will make known to him
how it will be? 8 There is no man who
is master of the breath of life so as to
retain it, and none has mastery of the
day of death. There is no exemption
from the struggle, nor are the wicked
saved by their wickedness. 9* All these
things I considered and I applied my
mind to every work that is done under
the sun, while one man tyrannizes over
another to his hurt.
The Problem of Retribution. 10† Mean-
while I saw wicked men approach and
enter; and as they left the sacred place,
they were praised in the city for what
they had done. This also is vanity.
11 Because the sentence against evil-
doers is not promptly executed, there-
fore the hearts of men are filled with the
desire to commit evil—12 because the
sinner does evil a hundred times and
survives. Though indeed I know that it
shall be well with those who fear God,
for their reverence toward him; 13† and
that it shall not be well with the wicked
man, and he shall not prolong his shad-
owy days, for his lack of reverence to-
ward God.
14 This is a vanity which occurs on
earth: there are just men treated as
though they had done evil and wicked
men treated as though they had done
justly. This, too, I say is vanity.
15*† Therefore I commend mirth, be-
cause there is nothing good for man un-
der the sun except eating and drinking
and mirth: for this is the accompani-
ment of his toil during the limited days
of the life which God gives him under
the sun.
16* When I applied my heart to know
wisdom and to observe what is done on

ECCLESIASTES

*

16f: 8, 12ff.
20: Jb 25, 4; Prv 20, 9; 1 Kgs 8, 46; Rom 3, 23; Jas 3, 2; 1 Jn 1, 8.
21f: 1 Kgs 8, 46.
25: 1, 17.
26: Prv 5, 4.
8, 7: 3, 22; 10, 14.
9: 1, 13f.
15: 2, 24; 9, 7.
16: 1, 13; 3, 10.

†

7, 16: St. Jerome explains the warning against excessive justice in reference to the self-righteous man who is so stern that he is never willing to forgive sin in others; cf vv 20ff.

7, 17: Untimely death was traditionally recognized as a divine punishment of the wicked; cf 1 Sm 2, 31-34; Jer 17, 11; Ps 55, 24; Prv 10, 27. This warning against presumptuous wickedness is not an endorsement of any lesser degree of misconduct.

7, 18: *This rule . . . that one:* the sayings cited in vv 16f. Others refer *this* and *that* to riches and wisdom (cf 7, 12), justice and wisdom, or justice and wickedness. This last supposition makes the author's thought hard to follow.

7, 20: This is to be understood in the sense of Rom 5, 12. See note there.

7, 28: The author found sincerity rare among men, but among women still more rare.

7, 29: *Calculations:* the many vain attempts and schemes of men to attain happiness by their own efforts.

8, 10: The text is obscure. The Latin has "wicked men buried, who, while still alive, were in the holy place and were praised in the city as if their works were just."

8, 13: *Shadowy:* perhaps an addition here; cf 6, 12.

8, 15: See notes on 2, 24; 5, 19.

earth, 17* I recognized that man is un-
able to find out all God's work that is
done under the sun, even though neither
by day nor by night do his eyes find rest
in sleep. However much man toils in
searching, he does not find it out; and
even if the wise man says that he knows,
he is unable to find it out.

B. Man Does Not Know What Is To Come

CHAPTER 9

1† All this I have kept in mind and rec-
ognized: the just, the wise, and their
deeds are in the hand of God. Love from
hatred man cannot tell; both appear
equally vain, 2* in that there is the same
lot for all, for the just and the wicked,
for the good and the bad, for the clean
and the unclean, for him who offers sac-
rifice and him who does not. As it is for
the good man, so it is for the sinner; as
it is for him who swears rashly, so it is
for him who fears an oath. 3 Among all
the things that happen under the sun,
this is the worst, that things turn out the
same for all. Hence the minds of men
are filled with evil, and madness is in
their hearts during life; and afterward
they go to the dead.
4 Indeed, for any among the living
there is hope; a live dog is better off than
a dead lion. 5* For the living know that
they are to die, but the dead no longer
know anything. There is no further rec-
ompense for them, because all memory
of them is lost. 6 For them, love and ha-
tred and rivalry have long since per-
ished. They will never again have part
in anything that is done under the
sun.
7* Go, eat your bread with joy and
drink your wine with a merry heart, be-
cause it is now that God favors your
works. 8 At all times let your garments
be white, and spare not the perfume for
your head. 9 Enjoy life with the wife
whom you love, all the days of the fleet-
ing life that is granted you under the sun.
This is your lot in life, for the toil of your
labors under the sun. 10 Anything you
can turn your hand to, do with what
power you have; for there will be no
work, nor reason, nor knowledge, nor
wisdom in the nether world where you
are going.
The Evil Time Not Known. 11 Again I
saw under the sun that the race is not
won by the swift, nor the battle by the
valiant, nor a livelihood by the wise, nor
riches by the shrewd, nor favor by the
experts; for a time of calamity comes
to all alike. 12† Man no more knows his
own time than fish taken in the fatal net,
or birds trapped in the snare; like these
the children of men are caught when the
evil time falls suddenly upon them.

The Uncertain Future and the Sages

13 On the other hand I saw this wise
deed under the sun, which I thought sub-
lime. 14 Against a small city with few
men in it advanced a mighty king, who
surrounded it and threw up great siege-
works about it. 15 But in the city lived a
man who, though poor, was wise, and
he delivered it through his wisdom. Yet
no one remembered this poor man.
16* Though I had said, "Wisdom is better
than force," yet the wisdom of the poor
man is despised and his words go un-
heeded.

17 "The quiet words of the wise are better heeded
than the shout of a ruler of fools"—!

18 "A fly that dies can spoil the perfumer's ointment,
and a single slip can ruin much that is good."

CHAPTER 10

1 More weighty than wisdom or wealth is a little folly!
2† The wise man's understanding turns him to his right;
the fool's understanding turns him to his left.

3 When the fool walks through the
street, in his lack of understanding he
calls everything foolish.
4 Should the anger of the ruler burst
upon you, forsake not your place; for
mildness abates great offenses.
5 I have seen under the sun another
evil, like a mistake that proceeds from
the ruler: 6 a fool put in lofty position
while the rich sit in lowly places. 7 I have
seen slaves on horseback, while princes
walked on the ground like slaves.

8 He who digs a pit may fall into it,
and he who breaks through a wall may be bitten by a serpent.
9* He who moves stones may be hurt by them,

ECCLESIASTES

*

17: 3, 11.
9, 2: 2, 14.
5: 1, 11.
7: 2, 1.24; 8, 15; 11, 9.
16: Prv 24, 5.
10, 9f: Pr 26, 27; Sir 27, 29.

†

9, 1-10: These statement are based on a very imperfect concept of life beyond the grave. With Christian revelation about the future life came the only satisfactory solution of the problem which so perplexed the author.

9, 1: *Love from hatred:* divine favor or disfavor.

9, 12: *His own time:* the time of death or sudden disaster.

10, 2: It is doubtful whether the author is endorsing either direction; cf Prv 4, 25ff.

and he who chops wood is in danger from it.

10 If the iron becomes dull, though at first he made easy progress, he must increase his efforts; but the craftsman has the advantage of his skill.

11 If the serpent bites because it has not been charmed,
then there is no advantage for the charmer.

12* Words from the wise man's mouth win favor,
but the fool's lips consume him.
13 The beginning of his words is folly,
and the end of his talk is utter madness;
14* yet the fool multiplies words.
Man knows not what is to come,
for who can tell him what is to come after him?
15† When will the fool be weary of his labor,
he who knows not the way to the city?

MAN DOES NOT KNOW WHAT EVIL WILL COME

16 Woe to you, O land, whose king was a servant,
and whose princes dine in the morning!
17 Blessed are you, O land, whose king is of noble birth,
and whose princes dine at the right time
(for vigor and not in drinking bouts).
18 When hands are lazy, the rafters sag;
when hands are slack, the house leaks.
19 Bread and oil call forth merriment
and wine makes the living glad,
but money answers for everything.
20 Even in your thoughts do not make light of the king,
nor in the privacy of your bedroom revile the rich.
Because the birds of the air may carry your voice,
a winged creature may tell what you say.

CHAPTER 11

1† Cast your bread upon the waters;
after a long time you may find it again.
2† Make seven or eight portions;
you know not what misfortune may come upon the earth.

MAN DOES NOT KNOW WHAT GOOD WILL COME

3 When the clouds are full,
they pour out rain upon the earth.
Whether a tree falls to the south or to the north,
wherever it falls, there shall it lie.
4 One who pays heed to the wind will not sow,
and one who watches the clouds will never reap.
5* Just as you know not how the breath of life
fashions the human frame in the mother's womb,
So you know not the work of God
which he is accomplishing in the universe.
6 In the morning sow your seed,
and at evening let not your hand be idle:
For you know not which of the two will be successful,
or whether both alike will turn out well.

Poem on Youth and Old Age. 7 Light
is sweet! and it is pleasant for the eyes
to see the sun. 8 However many years
a man may live, let him, as he enjoys
them all, remember that the days of
darkness will be many. All that is to
come is vanity.

9 Rejoice, O young man, while you are young
and let your heart be glad in the days of your youth.
Follow the ways of your heart,
the vision of your eyes;
Yet understand that as regards all this
God will bring you to judgment.
10† Ward off grief from your heart
and put away trouble from your presence,
though the dawn of youth is fleeting.

CHAPTER 12

1 Remember your Creator in the days of your youth,
before the evil days come
And the years approach of which you will say,
I have no pleasure in them;
2† Before the sun is darkened.

*

12: Sir 21, 19. 14: 5, 2; 8, 7. 11, 5: 8, 17.

†

10, 15: *He who . . . city:* perhaps a proverbial expression for supreme stupidity.

11, 1: This may refer to a spirit of adventure in business or to generosity in almsgiving. *Waters:* of the ocean, which sometimes carry lost treasures to the shore.

11, 2: This verse refers either to almsgiving or to the wisdom of not putting all one's cargo into a single vessel.

11, 10: *Dawn . . . fleeting:* literally, "youth and the dawn [of life] are vanity."

12, 2: *The sun . . . return:* the cloudy and rainy Palestinian winter, a natural symbol of old age.

and the light, and the moon, and the stars,
while the clouds return after the rain;
3† When the guardians of the house tremble,
and the strong men are bent,
And the grinders are idle because they are few,
and they who look through the windows grow blind;
4† When the doors to the street are shut,
and the sound of the mill is low;
When one waits for the chirp of a bird,
but all the daughters of song are suppressed;
5† And one fears heights,
and perils in the street;
When the almond tree blooms,
and the locust grows sluggish
and the caper berry is without effect,
Because man goes to his lasting home,
and mourners go about the streets;
6† Before the silver cord is snapped
and the golden bowl is broken,
And the pitcher is shattered at the spring,
and the broken pulley falls into the well,
7* And the dust returns to the earth as it once was,
and the life breath returns to God who gave it.

8* Vanity of vanities, says Qoheleth,
all things are vanity!

Epilogue. 9 Besides being wise, Qoheleth taught the people knowledge, and weighed, scrutinized and arranged many proverbs. 10 Qoheleth sought to find pleasing sayings, and to write down true sayings with precision. 11† The sayings of the wise are like goads; like fixed spikes are the topics given by one collector. 12* As to more than these, my son, beware. Of the making of many books there is no end, and in much study there is weariness for the flesh.

13*† The last word, when all is heard: Fear God and keep his commandments, for this is man's all; 14* because God will bring to judgment every work, with all its hidden qualities, whether good or bad.

*

12, 7: 3, 20f; Jb 34, 15.
8: 1, 2.
12: 1, 18.
13: 5, 6.
14: 11, 9.

†

12, 3: *Guardians:* the arms; *strong men:* the legs; *grinders:* the teeth; *they who . . . windows:* the eyes.

12, 4: *Doors:* the tightly compressed lips; *sound of the mill:* perhaps the sound of mastication; *daughters of song:* the voice.

12, 5: *The almond tree blooms:* resembling the white hair of age. *The locust . . . sluggish:* an image of the stiffness in movement of the aged. *The caper berry:* a stimulant for appetite.

12, 6: *The golden bowl* suspended by the *silver cord* was a symbol of life; the snapping of the cord and the breaking of the bowl, a symbol of death. *The pitcher . . . the broken pulley:* another pair of metaphors for life and its ending.

12, 11: *Goads . . . one collector:* the *sayings* were stimulants to thought and also *spikes* or centers around which to group correlated pronouncements *of the wise.*

12, 13: *Man's all:* St. Jerome explains: "Unto this is every man born that, knowing his Maker, he may revere him in fear, honor, and the observance of his commandments."

The Song of

SONGS

The Song of Songs, meaning the greatest of songs (1, 1), contains in exquisite poetic form the sublime portrayal and praise of the mutual love of the Lord and his people. The Lord is the Lover and his people are the beloved. Describing this relationship in terms of human love, the author simply follows Israel's tradition. Isaiah (5, 1-7; 54, 4-8), Jeremiah (2, 2f.32), and Ezekiel (16; 23) all characterize the covenant between the Lord and Israel as a marriage. Hosea the prophet sees the idolatry of Israel in the adultery of Gomer (1—3). He also represents the Lord speaking to Israel's heart (2, 16) and changing her into a new spiritual people, purified by the Babylonian captivity and betrothed anew to her divine Lover "in justice and uprightness, in love and mercy" (2, 21).

The author of the Song, using the same literary figure, paints a beautiful picture of the ideal Israel, the chosen people of the Old and New Testaments, whom the Lord led by degrees to an exalted spiritual union with himself in the bond of perfect love. When the Song is thus interpreted there is no reason for surprise at the tone of the poem, which employs in its descriptions the courtship and marriage customs of the author's time. Moreover, the poem is not an allegory in which each remark, e. g., in the dialogue of the lovers, has a higher meaning. It is a parable in which the true meaning of mutual love comes from the poem as a whole.

While the Song is thus commonly understood by most Catholic scholars, it is also possible to see in it an inspired portrayal of ideal human love. Here we would have from God a description of the sacredness and the depth of married union.

Although the poem is attributed to Solomon in the traditional title (1, 1), the language and style of the work, among other considerations, point to a time after the end of the Babylonian Exile (538 B.C.) as that in which an unknown poet composed this masterpiece. The structure of the Song is difficult to analyze; here it is regarded as a lyric dialogue, with dramatic movement and interest.

The use of marriage as a symbol, characteristic of the Song, is found extensively also in the New Testament (Mt 9, 15; 25, 1-13; Jn 3, 29; 2 Cor 11, 2; Eph 5, 23-32; Rv 19, 7ff; 21, 9ff). In Christian tradition, the Song has been interpreted in terms of the union between Christ and the Church and, particularly by St. Bernard, of the union between Christ and the individual soul. Throughout the liturgy, especially in the Little Office, there is a consistent application of the Song of Songs to the Blessed Virgin Mary.

THE SONG OF SONGS BY SOLOMON†

CHAPTER 1

Love's Desires

2 *B**† Let him kiss me with kisses of his mouth!
More delightful is your love than wine!
3 Your name spoken is a spreading perfume—
that is why the maidens love you.
4* Draw me!—
D We will follow you eagerly!
B Bring me, O king, to your chambers.
D With you we rejoice and exult,
we extol your love; it is beyond wine:
how rightly you are loved!

Love's Boast

5 *B*† I am as dark—but lovely,
O daughters of Jerusalem—
As the tents of Kedar,
as the curtains of Salma.

---

* 1, 2f: 4, 10. 4: 4, 10.

---

† 1, 1: This title is actually the first verse of chapter 1.

1, 2ff: The marginal letters indicate the speaker of the verses: *B*—Bride; *D*—Daughters of Jerusalem; *G*—Bridegroom. In vv 2-7 the bride and the daughters address the bridegroom who appears here as a king, but more often in the poem as a shepherd. King and shepherd are familiar figures of the Lord in the Sacred Scriptures. Cf Ps 23, 1; Is 40, 11; Jn 10, 1-16.

1, 5: *Daughters of Jerusalem:* the chorus whom the bride addresses and who ask her questions (5, 9; 6, 1), thus developing action within the poem. *Kedar:* a Syrian desert region whose name suggests blackness; tents were often made of black goat hair. *Curtains:* tent coverings of *Salma,* a region close to Kedar.

6† Do not stare at me because I am swarthy,
because the sun has burned me.
My brothers have been angry with me;
they charged me with the care of the vineyards:
my own vineyard I have not cared for.

Love's Inquiry

7B† Tell me, you whom my heart loves,
where you pasture your flock,
where you give them rest at midday,
Lest I be found wandering
after the flocks of your companions.

8G If you do not know,
O most beautiful among women,
Follow the tracks of the flock
and pasture the young ones
near the shepherds' camps.

Love's Vision

9G† To the steeds of Pharaoh's chariots
would I liken you, my beloved:
10 Your cheeks lovely in pendants,
your neck in jewels.
11 We will make pendants of gold for you,
and silver ornaments.

Love's Union

12B† For the king's banquet
my nard gives forth its fragrance.
13† My lover is for me a sachet of myrrh
to rest in my bosom.
14† My lover is for me a cluster of henna
from the vineyards of Engedi.

15G*† Ah, you are beautiful, my beloved,
ah, you are beautiful; your eyes are doves!

16B† Ah, you are beautiful, my lover— yes,
you are lovely.
Our couch, too, is verdant;
17 the beams of our house are cedars,
our rafters, cypresses.

CHAPTER 2

1† I am a flower of Sharon,
a lily of the valley.

2G As a lily among thorns,
so is my beloved among women.
3B As an apple tree among the trees of the woods,
so is my lover among men.

I delight to rest in his shadow,
and his fruit is sweet to my mouth.
4*† He brings me into the banquet hall
and his emblem over me is love.
5* Strengthen me with raisin cakes,
refresh me with apples,
for I am faint with love.
6* His left hand is under my head
and his right arm embraces me.
7*† I adjure you, daughters of Jerusalem,
by the gazelles and hinds of the field,
Do not arouse, do not stir up love
before its own time.

A Tryst in the Spring

8B† Hark! my lover— here he comes
springing across the mountains,
leaping across the hills.
9 My lover is like a gazelle
or a young stag.
Here he stands behind our wall,
gazing through the windows,
peering through the lattices.
10 My lover speaks; he says to me,
"Arise, my beloved, my beautiful one,
and come!
11 "For see, the winter is past,
the rains are over and gone.
12 The flowers appear on the earth,
the time of pruning the vines has come,
and the song of the dove is heard in our land.
13 The fig tree puts forth its figs,
and the vines, in bloom, give forth fragrance.

---

*

1, 15: 4, 1.7. 6: 8, 3.
2, 4: 1, 4. 7: 3, 5; 8, 4.
5: 5, 8.

†

1, 6: *Swarthy:* tanned by the sun from working in her brothers' vineyards. *My own vineyard:* the bride herself; cf Is 5, 1-7, where Israel is designated as the vineyard and the Lord is the Lover.

1, 7: Here and elsewhere in the Song (3, 1; 5, 8; 6, 1), the bride expresses her desire to be in the company of her lover. These verses point to a certain tension in the poem. Only at the end (8, 5ff) does mutual possession of the lovers become final.

1, 9ff: The bridegroom compares the girl's beauty to the rich adornment of the royal chariot of Pharaoh.

1, 12: *Nard:* a precious perfume, a figure of the bride; cf 4, 14.

1, 13: *Myrrh:* produced from aromatic resin of balsam or roses.

1, 14: *Henna:* a plant which bears white scented flowers.

1, 15: *Doves:* suggesting innocence and charm.

1, 16f: Though the meeting place of the lovers is but a shepherd's hut of green branches, it becomes a palace with beams of cedar and rafters of cypress when adorned with their love.

2, 1: *Flower of Sharon:* probably the narcissus, which grows in the fertile Plain of Sharon lying between Mount Carmel and Jaffa on the Mediterranean coast.

2, 4ff: *The banquet hall:* the sweet things of the table, the embrace of the bride and bridegroom, express the delicacy of their affection and the intimacy of their love.

2, 7: *By the gazelles and hinds:* the swiftness of these animals and the luster and soft expression of their eyes are suggestive of love; cf Prv 5, 19.

2, 8ff: In this sudden change of scene, the bride pictures her lover hastening toward her dwelling until his voice is heard bidding her come to him.

SONG OF SONGS

Arise, my beloved, my beautiful one,
and come!

14† "O my dove in the clefts of the rock,
in the secret recesses of the cliff,
Let me see you,
let me hear your voice,
For your voice is sweet,
and you are lovely."

15B† Catch us the foxes, the little foxes
that damage the vineyards; for
our vineyards are in bloom!

16* My lover belongs to me and I to him;
he browses among the lilies.
17*† Until the day breathes cool and the
shadows lengthen,
roam, my lover,
Like a gazelle or a young stag
upon the mountains of Bether.

CHAPTER 3

Loss and Discovery

1B*† On my bed at night I sought him
whom my heart loves—
I sought him but I did not find him.
2 I will rise then and go about the city;
in the streets and crossings I will
seek
Him whom my heart loves.
I sought him but I did not find him.
3 The watchmen came upon me
as they made their rounds of the
city:
Have you seen him whom my
heart loves?
4* I had hardly left them
when I found him whom my heart
loves.
I took hold of him and would not let
him go
till I should bring him to the home
of my mother,
to the room of my parent.
5* I adjure you, daughters of Jerusa-
lem,
by the gazelles and hinds of the
field,
Do not arouse, do not stir up love
before its own time.

Regal State of the Bridegroom

6D*† What is this coming up from the
desert,
like a column of smoke
Laden with myrrh, with frank-
incense,
and with the perfume of every ex-
otic dust?
7 Ah, it is the litter of Solomon;
sixty valiant men surround it,
of the valiant men of Israel:
8 All of them expert with the sword,
skilled in battle,
Each with his sword at his side
against danger in the watches of
the night.
9 King Solomon made himself a car-
riage
of wood from Lebanon.
10 He made its columns of silver,
its roof of gold,
Its seat of purple cloth,
its framework inlaid with ivory.
11 Daughters of Jerusalem, come forth
and look upon King Solomon
In the crown with which his mother
has crowned him
on the day of his marriage,
on the day of the joy of his heart.

CHAPTER 4

The Charms of the Beloved

1G* Ah, you are beautiful, my beloved,
ah, you are beautiful!
Your eyes are doves
behind your veil.
Your hair is like a flock of goats
streaming down the mountains of
Gilead.
2† Your teeth are like a flock of ewes
to be shorn,
which come up from the washing,
All of them big with twins,
none of them thin and barren.
3† Your lips are like a scarlet strand;
your mouth is lovely.
Your cheek is like a half-pome-
granate
behind your veil.

4*† Your neck is like David's tower
girt with battlements;
A thousand bucklers hang upon it,
all the shields of valiant men.
5* Your breast are like twin fawns,
the young of a gazelle
that browse among the lilies.

SONG OF SONGS

*

16: 6, 3; 7, 10.
17: 4, 6; 8, 14.
3, 1ff: 5, 2ff.
4: 8, 2.
5: 2, 7; 8, 4.
6: 6, 10; 8, 5.
4, 1: 1, 15.
1ff: 6, 5ff.
4: 7, 5.
5: 7, 4.

†

2, 14: The bride is addressed as though she were a dove in a mountain fastness out of sight and reach.

2, 15: A snatch of song in answer to the request of v 14; cf 8, 13f. *Foxes:* all who threaten to disturb the security of love symbolized by the vineyard; cf v 16.

2, 17: *Breathes cool:* in the evening when the sun is going down. Cf Gn 3, 8. *Bether:* a very obscure word; some interpret it in the sense of ruggedness; others, of spices; still others, of sacrifice (Gn 15, 10).

3, 1ff: See the parallel in 5, 2-8.

3, 6ff: The lover is portrayed as King Solomon, escorted by sixty armed men, coming in royal procession to meet his bride.

4, 2: *Teeth:* praised for whiteness and regularity.

4, 3: *Pomegranate:* a fruit somewhat like an orange, with a firm skin and deep red color. The girl's cheek is compared, in roundness and tint, to a half-pomegranate.

4, 4: The ornaments about her neck are compared to the trophies on the city walls. Cf 1 Kgs 10, 10; 14, 26ff; Ez 27, 10.

6*† Until the day breathes cool and the shadows lengthen,
I will go to the mountain of myrrh, to the hill of incense.
7† You are all-beautiful, my beloved, and there is no blemish in you.

8† Come from Lebanon, my bride, come from Lebanon, come!
Descend from the top of Amana, from the top of Senir and Hermon,
From the haunts of lions, from the leopards' mountains.
9*† You have ravished my heart, my sister, my bride;
you have ravished my heart with one glance of your eyes,
with one bead of your necklace.
10* How beautiful is your love, my sister, my bride,
how much more delightful is your love than wine,
and the fragrance of your ointments than all spices!
11† Your lips drip honey, my bride, sweetmeats and milk are under your tongue;
And the fragrance of your garments is the fragrance of Lebanon.

The Lover and His Garden

12G*† You are an enclosed garden, my sister, my bride,
an enclosed garden, a fountain sealed.
13 You are a park that puts forth pomegranates,
with all choice fruits;
14† Nard and saffron, calamus and cinnamon,
with all kinds of incense;
Myrrh and aloes,
with all the finest spices.
15 You are a garden fountain, a well of water
flowing fresh from Lebanon.
16† Arise, north wind! Come, south wind!
blow upon my garden
that its perfumes may spread abroad.
B Let my lover come to his garden
and eat its choice fruits.

CHAPTER 5

1G*† I have come to my garden, my sister, my bride;
I gather my myrrh and my spices,
I eat my honey and my sweetmeats,
I drink my wine and my milk.

D Eat, friends; drink! Drink freely of love!

A Fruitless Search

2B*† I was sleeping, but my heart kept vigil;
I heard my lover knocking:
"Open to me, my sister, my beloved, my dove, my perfect one!
For my head is wet with dew,
my locks with the moisture of the night."
3† I have taken off my robe,
am I then to put it on?
I have bathed my feet,
am I then to soil them?

4 My lover put his hand through the opening;
my heart trembled within me,
and I grew faint when he spoke.
5 I rose to open to my lover,
with my hands dripping myrrh:
With my fingers dripping choice myrrh
upon the fittings of the lock.
6*† I opened to my lover—
but my lover had departed, gone.
I sought him but I did not find him;
I called to him but he did not answer me.

7*† The watchmen came upon me
as they made their rounds of the city;
They struck me, and wounded me,
and took my mantle from me,
the guardians of the walls.
8* I adjure you, daughters of Jerusalem,
if you find my lover—
What shall you tell him?—
that I am faint with love.

---

*
6: 2, 17.
9: 6, 5.
10: 1, 2f.
12: 6, 2.11.
5, 1: 6, 2.
2ff: 3, 1f.
6: 3, 1.
7: 3, 3.
8: 2, 5.

---

†
4, 6: *Mountain of myrrh. . . hill of incense:* spoken figuratively of the bride; cf 8, 14.
4, 7: Cf St. Paul's description of the Church in Eph 5, 27. This verse is also applied to Our Lady, especially in the Liturgy of the feast of the Immaculate Conception.
4, 8: *Amana . . . Senir and Hermon:* these rugged heights symbolize obstacles that would separate the lovers; cf 2, 14.
4, 9: *Sister:* a term of endearment; it forms part of the conventional language of love used in this canticle.
4, 11: *Honey:* sweet words. Cf Prv 5, 3.
4, 12: *Enclosed garden . . . fountain sealed:* reserved for the bridegroom alone. The bride's fidelity is implied. Cf Prv 5, 15-19.
4, 14: These plants are all known for their sweet scent.
4, 16: The last two lines of the verse are spoken by the girl, inviting her lover to herself, the *garden.*
5, 1: *Eat, friends; drink!:* the lovers are encouraged to enjoy the delights of their love, symbol of Christ's union with the Church.
5, 2-8: A trial similar to that in 3, 1ff.
5, 3f: The bride's hesitation is due, not to levity, but to strong emotion.
5, 6: The disappearance of the lover seems to be a deliberate trial and test inflicted on the girl.
5, 7: *The watchmen* do not know the reason for the girl's appearance in the city streets; cf 3, 2ff.

The Charms of the Lost Lover

9D How does your lover differ from any other,
O most beautiful among women?
How does your lover differ from any other,
that you adjure us so?

10B† My lover is radiant and ruddy;
he stands out among thousands.
11 His head is pure gold;
his locks are palm fronds,
black as the raven.
12 His eyes are like doves
beside running waters,
His teeth would seem bathed in milk,
and are set like jewels.
13 His cheeks are like beds of spice
with ripening aromatic herbs.
His lips are red blossoms;
they drip choice myrrh.

14 His arms are rods of gold
adorned with chrysolites.
His body is a work of ivory
covered with sapphires.
15 His legs are columns of marble
resting on golden bases.
His stature is like the trees on Lebanon,
imposing as the cedars.
16 His mouth is sweetness itself;
he is all delight.
Such is my lover, and such my friend,
O daughters of Jerusalem.

CHAPTER 6

Discovery

1D† Where has your lover gone,
O most beautiful among women?
Where has your lover gone
that we may seek him with you?

2B*† My lover has come down to his garden,
to the beds of spice,
To browse in the garden
and to gather lilies.
3* My lover belongs to me and I to him;
he browses among the lilies.

The Charms of the Beloved

4G† You are as beautiful as Tirzah, my beloved,
as lovely as Jerusalem,
as awe-inspiring as bannered troops.
5* Turn your eyes from me,
for they torment me.
Your hair is like a flock of goats
streaming down from Gilead.
6* Your teeth are like a flock of ewes
which come up from the washing,
All of them big with twins,
none of them thin and barren.
7 Your cheek is like a half-pomegranate
behind your veil.

8 There are sixty queens, eighty concubines,
and maidens without number—
9 One alone is my dove, my perfect one,
her mother's chosen,
the dear one of her parent.
The daughters saw her and declared her fortunate,
the queens and concubines, and they sang her praises;

10D* Who is this that comes forth like the dawn,
as beautiful as the moon, as resplendent as the sun,
as awe-inspiring as bannered troops?

Love's Meeting

11B* I came down to the nut garden
to look at the fresh growth of the valley,
To see if the vines were in bloom.
if the pomegranates had blossomed.
12† Before I knew it, my heart had made me
the blessed one of my kinswomen.

CHAPTER 7

The Beauty of the Bride

1D† Turn, turn, O Shulammite,
turn, turn, that we may look at you!

*

6, 2: 4, 12; 5, 1.
3: 2, 16; 7, 11.
5: 4, 9.
6f: 4, 1ff.
10: 3, 6; 8, 5.
11: 4, 12ff; 7, 13.

†

5, 10f: In answer to the question of v 9, the girl sings her lover's praises (vv 10-16). *Gold:* indicates how precious the lover is. *Palm fronds:* his thick, luxuriant growth of hair.

6, 1: The daughters of Jerusalem are won by this description of the lover and offer their aid in seeking him.

6, 2f: Determined to share her lover with no one, the girl refuses the aid offered by the daughters in seeking him. She implies that she had never really lost him, for he *has come down to his garden.*

6, 4-9: The lover again celebrates her beauty. *Tirzah:* probably meaning "pleasant"; it was the early capital of the northern kingdom of Israel (1 Kgs 16).

6, 12: The text is obscure in Hebrew and in the ancient versions. The Vulgate reads: "I did not know; my soul disturbed me because of the chariots of Aminadab."

7, 1: *Shulammite:* so called either because the girl is considered to be from Shulam in the plain of Esdraelon (cf 1 Kgs 1, 3) or because the name may mean "the peaceful one," and thus recall the name of Solomon. *As at the dance of the two companies:* the meaning is uncertain. The question in this verse could be construed as a refusal to dance; more probably, however, the girl accedes, as the following verses suggest.

B Why would you look at the Shulam-
mite
as at the dance of the two compa-
nies?

2D† How beautiful are your feet in san-
dals,
O prince's daughter!
Your rounded thighs are like jewels,
the handiwork of an artist.
3 Your navel is a round bowl
that should never lack for mixed
wine.
Your body is a heap of wheat
encircled with lilies.
4* Your breasts are like twin fawns,
the young of a gazelle.
5*† Your neck is like a tower of ivory.
Your eyes are like the pools in
Heshbon
by the gate of Bath-rabbim.
Your nose is like the tower on Leba-
non
that looks toward Damascus.
6 You head rises like Carmel;
your hair is like draperies of pur-
ple;
a king is held captive in its tresses.

Love's Desires

7G How beautiful you are, how pleas-
ing,
my love, my delight!
8† Your very figure is like a palm tree,
your breasts are like clusters.
9 I said: I will climb the palm tree,
I will take hold of its branches.
Now let your breasts be like clusters
of the vine
and the fragrance of your breath
like apples,
10† And your mouth like an excellent
wine—

Love's Union

B that flows smoothly for my lover,
spreading over the lips and the
teeth.
11*† I belong to my lover
and for me he yearns.
12 Come, my lover, let us go forth to
the fields
and spend the night among the
villages.
13* Let us go early to the vineyards, and
see
if the vines are in bloom,
If the buds have opened,
if the pomegranates have blos-
somed;
There will I give you my love.
14† The mandrakes give forth fra-
grance,
and at our doors are all choice
fruits;
Both fresh and mellowed fruits, my
lover,
I have kept in store for you.

CHAPTER 8

1 Oh, that you were my brother,
nursed at my mother's breasts!
If I met you out of doors, I would
kiss you
and none would taunt me.
2* I would lead you, bring you in
to the home of my mother.
There you would teach me to give
you
spiced wine to drink and pome-
granate juice.

3* His left hand is under my head
and his right arm embraces me.
4* I adjure you, daughters of Jerusa-
lem,
by the gazelles and hinds of the
field,
Do not arouse, do not stir up love,
before its own time.

Homecoming

5D*† Who is this coming up from the de-
sert, leaning upon her lover?

G Under the apple tree I awakened
you;
it was there that your mother con-
ceived you,
it was there that your parent con-
ceived.

True Love

6B† Set me as a seal on your heart,
as a seal on your arm;

*

7, 4: 4, 5.
5: 4, 4.
11: 2, 16; 6, 3.
13: 6, 11.
8, 2: 3, 4.
3: 2, 6.
4: 2, 7; 3, 5.
5: 3, 6; 6, 10.

†

7, 2-6: A flattering description of the girl's charms. *Rounded . . . jewels:* the meaning of these Hebrew words is not certain. *Wine* and *wheat* are symbolic of fertility; they are here associated with parts of the body which have a close relation to fruitfulness.

7, 5: The comparison emphasizes the stateliness and whiteness of the neck, and the limpidity of the eyes. *Bath-rabbim:* a proper name which occurs only here; there was a city of Rabbah northeast of *Heshbon* in Transjordan. Cf Jer 49, 3.

7, 8f: *Palm tree:* a figure of stateliness. The bridegroom is eager to enjoy the possession of his bride.

7, 10: The bride delicately turns his compliment into an expression of the love and tenderness she feels for him.

7, 11-14: The girl's answer assures him of her affection and invites him to return with her to the rural delights which are associated with their love and which recall the meeting described in 6, 11f.

7, 14: *Mandrakes:* herbs believed to have power to arouse love and promote fertility; cf Gn 30, 14ff.

8, 5: The lovers are pictured walking homeward, enjoying the fulfillment of the desire which the girl expressed in vv 1f. The groom speaks of their first meeting.

8, 6f: *Seal:* this could be worn bound to the arm, as here, or suspended at the neck, or as a ring (Jer 22, 24). It was used for identification and signatures. *Stern . . . relentless:* in human experience, death and the nether world are inevitable, unrelenting; in the end they always triumph. Love, which is just as certain of its victory, matches its strength against the natural enemies of life; waters cannot extinguish it nor floods carry it away. It is more priceless than all riches.

For stern as death is love,
relentless as the nether world is devotion;
its flames are a blazing fire.
7 Deep waters cannot quench love,
nor floods sweep it away.
Were one to offer all he owns to purchase love,
he would be roundly mocked.

Chastity and Its Welcome

8† "Our sister is little
and she has no breasts as yet.
What shall we do for our sister
when her courtship begins?
9 If she is a wall,
we will build upon it a silver parapet;
If she is a door,
we will reinforce it with a cedar plank."

10 I am a wall,
and my breasts are like towers.
So now in his eyes I have become
one to be welcomed.

The Bride and Her Dowry

11*B*† Solomon had a vineyard at Baal-hamon;
he gave over the vineyard to caretakers.
For its fruit one would have to pay
a thousand silver pieces.

12 My vineyard is at my own disposal;
the thousand pieces are for you, O Solomon,
and two hundred for the caretakers of its fruit.

Life Together

13*G*† O garden-dweller,
my friends are listening for your voice,
let me hear it!

14*B** Be swift, my lover,
like a gazelle or a young stag
on the mountains of spices!

---

* 14: 2, 9.17; 4, 6.

---

† 8, 8ff: The bride affirms her chastity. In 8, 9 she quotes the course of action which her elder brothers had decided on. While she is yet immature, they will shelter her in view of eventual marriage. If she is virtuous, she will be honored; if she is unchaste, she will be kept under strict vigilance. In reply to this she proclaims her virtue and boasts of having found welcome from her lover.

8, 11f: These enigmatic verses have been variously interpreted. In v 11 the girl alludes to a vineyard of great value which is compared to her own self in v 12. Her enormous dowry, *a thousand silver pieces,* is in keeping with her intrinsic worth. She has been the generous lover, giving herself and a dowry to her lover, referred to as *Solomon,* and also smaller gifts to her brothers, *the caretakers* (cf vv 8ff).

8, 13f: As in 2, 14f, her lover asks for a word or a song and she replies in words similar to those found in 2, 17.

The Book of
WISDOM

The Book of Wisdom was written about a hundred years before the coming of Christ. Its author, whose name is not known to us, was a member of the Jewish community at Alexandria, in Egypt. He wrote in Greek, in a style patterned on that of Hebrew verse. At times he speaks in the person of Solomon, placing his teachings on the lips of the wise king of Hebrew tradition in order to emphasize their value. His profound knowledge of the earlier Old Testament writings is reflected in almost every line of the book, and marks him, like Ben Sira, as an outstanding representative of religious devotion and learning among the sages of postexilic Judaism.

The primary purpose of the sacred author was the edification of his co-religionists in a time when they had experienced suffering and oppression, in part at least at the hands of apostate fellow Jews. To convey his message he made use of the most popular religious themes of his time, namely the splendor and worth of divine wisdom (6, 22—11, 1), the glorious events of the Exodus (11, 2-16; 12, 23-27; 15, 18—19, 22), God's mercy (11, 17—12, 22), the folly of idolatry (13, 1—15, 17), and the manner in which God's justice is vindicated in rewarding or punishing the individual soul (1, 1—6, 21). The first ten chapters especially form a preparation for the fuller teachings of Christ and his Church. Many passages from this section of the book, notably 3, 1-8, are used by the Church in her liturgy.

The principal divisions of the Book of Wisdom are:

I: Reward of Justice (1, 1—6, 21)
II: Praise of Wisdom by Solomon (6, 22—11, 1)
III: Special Providence of God during the Exodus (11, 2-16; 12, 23-27; 15, 18—19, 22) with digressions on God's mercy (11, 17—12, 22) and on the folly and shame of idolatry (13, 1—15, 17)

I: THE REWARD OF JUSTICE

CHAPTER 1

Exhortation to Justice, the Key to Life

1*† Love justice, you who judge the earth;
think of the LORD in goodness,
and seek him in integrity of heart;
2* Because he is found by those who test him not,
and he manifests himself to those who do not disbelieve him.
3* For perverse counsels separate a man from God,
and his power, put to the proof, rebukes the foolhardy;
4* Because into a soul that plots evil wisdom enters not,
nor dwells she in a body under debt of sin.
5*† For the holy spirit of discipline flees deceit
and withdraws from senseless counsels;
and when injustice occurs it is rebuked.
6* For wisdom is a kindly spirit,
yet she acquits not the blasphemer of his guilty lips;
Because God is the witness of his inmost self
and the sure observer of his heart
and the listener to his tongue.
7*† For the spirit of the LORD fills the world,
is all-embracing, and knows what man says.
8* Therefore no one who utters wicked things can go unnoticed,
nor will chastising condemnation pass him by.
9 For the devices of the wicked man shall be scrutinized,

---

*

1, 1: 1 Chr 29, 17; Ps 2, 10; Is 26, 9.
1f: Sir 1, 25.
2: 1 Chr 28, 9.
3: Is 59, 2.
4: Sir 15, 7f; Rom 7, 14.
5: Is 63, 10.
6: Jer 17, 10.
6f: Jer 23, 24f.
7: 12, 1.
8: Prv 19, 5.

†

1, 1: *Justice:* not merely the cardinal virtue of that name (cf 8, 7), but the universal moral quality which is the application of Wisdom to moral conduct.

1, 5: *Discipline:* here and elsewhere, another name for Wisdom; *injustice:* the opposite of the virtue in 1, 1.

1, 7: This verse is applied to the Holy Spirit in the liturgy at Pentecost.

and the sound of his words shall
reach the LORD,
for the chastisement of his transgressions;
10* Because a jealous ear hearkens to
everything,
and discordant grumblings are no
secret.
11† Therefore guard against profitless
grumbling,
and from calumny withhold your
tongues;
For a stealthy utterance does not go
unpunished,
and a lying mouth slays the soul.
12 Court not death by your erring way
of life,
nor draw to yourselves destruction by the works of your hands.
13* Because God did not make death,
nor does he rejoice in the destruction of the living.
14 For he fashioned all things that they
might have being;
and the creatures of the world are
wholesome,
And there is not a destructive drug
among them
nor any domain of the nether
world on earth,
15* For justice is undying.

The Wicked Reject Immortality and Justice Alike

16* It was the wicked who with hands
and words invited death,
considered it a friend, and pined
for it,
and made a covenant with it,
Because they deserve to be in its
possession,

CHAPTER 2

1* they who said among themselves,
thinking not aright:
"Brief and troublous is our lifetime;
neither is there any remedy for
man's dying,
nor is anyone known to have come
back from the nether world.
2 For haphazard were we born,
and hereafter we shall be as
though we had not been;
Because the breath in our nostrils is
a smoke
and reason is a spark at the beating of our hearts,
3* And when this is quenched, our body
will be ashes
and our spirit will be poured
abroad like unresisting air.
4 Even our name will be forgotten in
time,
and no one will recall our deeds.
So our life will pass away like the
traces of a cloud,
and will be dispersed like a mist
Pursued by the sun's rays
and overpowered by its heat.
5* For our lifetime is the passing of a
shadow;
and our dying cannot be deferred
because it is fixed with a seal; and
no one returns.
6* Come, therefore, let us enjoy the
good things that are real,
and use the freshness of creation
avidly.
7 Let us have our fill of costly wine
and perfumes,
and let no springtime blossom
pass us by;
8 let us crown ourselves with rosebuds ere they wither.
9*† Let no meadow be free from our
wantonness;
everywhere let us leave tokens of
our rejoicing,
for this our portion is, and this our
lot.
10* Let us oppress the needy just man;
let us neither spare the widow
nor revere the old man for his hair
grown white with time.
11 But let our strength be our norm of
justice;
for weakness proves itself useless.
12*† Let us beset the just one, because he
is obnoxious to us;
he sets himself against our doings,
Reproaches us for transgressions of
the law
and charges us with violations of
our training.
13* He professes to have knowledge of
God
and styles himself a child of the
LORD.
14* To us he is the censure of our
thoughts;
merely to see him is a hardship
for us,
15 Because his life is not like other
men's,
and different are his ways.
16* He judges us debased;

*

10f: Nm 14, 27f.
13f: Ez 18, 32; 33, 11; 2 Pt 3, 9.
15: Is 51, 6ff.
16: Is 28, 15.
2, 1: Jb 14, 1; 7, 9.
3: Jb 7, 9; Jas 4, 14.
5: Ps 144, 4.
6: Is 22, 13; 1 Cor 15, 32.
9: Jer 13, 25.
10: Ex 22, 22ff; Lv 19, 32.
12: Hos 8, 1.
13: Mt 27, 43; Jn 8, 55; 10, 36-39.
14: Mt 9, 4.
16: Jer 6, 30.

†

1, 11: *Calumny:* speech against God and his providence is meant.

2, 9: *Let no meadow . . . wantonness:* the extant Greek Mss have "Let none of us be without part in our wanton doings." Most Latin Mss have both forms of this line.

2, 12-20: Often applied to the Passion of our Lord; many have understood these verses as a direct prophecy. Cf Mt 27, 41-44.

2, 12: *Law:* the law of Moses; *training* has the same meaning.

he holds aloof from our paths as
from things impure.
He calls blest the destiny of the just
and boasts that God is his Father.
17* Let us see whether his words be true;
let us find out what will happen
to him.
18* For if the just one be the son of God,
he will defend him
and deliver him from the hand of
his foes.
19 With revilement and torture let us
put him to the test
that we may have proof of his gen-
tleness
and try his patience.
20* Let us condemn him to a shameful
death;
for according to his own words,
God will take care of him."
21* These were their thoughts, but they
erred;
for their wickedness blinded
them,
22* And they knew not the hidden coun-
sels of God;
neither did they count on a recom-
pense of holiness
nor discern the innocent souls' re-
ward.
23* For God formed man to be imper-
ishable;
the image of his own nature he
made him.
24* But by the envy of the devil, death
entered the world,
and they who are in his possession
experience it.

CHAPTER 3

The Hidden Counsels of God:

A. ON SUFFERING

1*† But the souls of the just are in the
hand of God,
and no torment shall touch them.
2 They seemed, in the view of the fool-
ish, to be dead;
and their passing away was
thought an affliction
3* and their going forth from us, ut-
ter destruction.
But they are in peace.
4 For if before men, indeed, they be
punished,
yet is their hope full of immortal-
ity;
5* Chastised a little, they shall be
greatly blessed,
because God tried them
and found them worthy of him-
self.
6*† As gold in the furnace, he proved
them,
and as sacrificial offerings he took
them to himself.
7*† In the time of their visitation they
shall shine,
and shall dart about as sparks
through stubble;
8* They shall judge nations and rule
over peoples,
and the LORD shall be their King
forever.
9* Those who trust in him shall under-
stand truth,
and the faithful shall abide with
him in love:
Because grace and mercy are with
his holy ones,
and his care is with the elect.
10† But the wicked shall receive a
punishment to match their
thoughts,
since they neglected justice and
forsook the LORD.
11* For he who despises wisdom and in-
struction is doomed.
Vain is their hope, fruitless are their
labors,
and worthless are their works.
12* Their wives are foolish and their
children wicked;
accursed is their brood.

B. ON CHILDLESSNESS

13† Yes, blessed is she who, childless
and undefiled,
knew not transgression of the
marriage bed;
she shall bear fruit at the visita-
tion of souls.
14*† So also the eunuch whose hand
wrought no misdeed,
who held no wicked thoughts
against the LORD—
For he shall be given fidelity's choice
reward

*

17: Gn 37, 20.
18: Ps 22, 9; Is 42, 1; Mt 27, 43; Jn 5, 18.
20: Jas 5, 6.
21: Rom 1, 21.
22: Ps 18, 24f; Prv 11, 18; Mt 11, 25.
23: Gn 1, 26f; Is 54, 16 LXX.
24: Gn 3, 1-24; Rom 5, 12.
3, 1: Jb 12, 10; 5, 19.
3: Is 57, 2.
5: Tb 12, 13; 2 Cor 4, 17; 1 Pt 1, 6f.
6: Ps 51, 19; Prv 17, 3; Sir 2, 5; Is 48, 10.
7: Dn 12, 3; Ob 18; Mal 3, 3; Mt 13, 43.
8: 8, 14; Prv 8, 16; Dn 7, 22; 1 Cor 6, 2; Rv 20, 4.
9: 4, 15; Jb 10, 12; Jn 15, 10.
11: Prv 1, 7.
11f: Sir 41, 8.
12: Dt 28, 18ff.
14: Is 56, 2-5.

†

3, 1-8: Verses frequently applied to the martyrs.

3, 6: *Offerings:* the image is that of the holocaust, in which the victim is completely consumed by fire.

3, 7: *Visitation:* God's loving judgment of those who have been faithful to him; the same word is used in 14, 11 for the punishment of the wicked at God's final judgment. Cf also 3, 13.

3, 10: *To match their thoughts:* a fate as empty as that which they describe; cf 2, 1-5.

3, 13: *Visitation of souls:* that is, the last judgment. Cf 3, 7-9.

3, 14: *Fidelity's choice reward:* cf Is 56, 1-8. *More gratifying:* better than sons and daughters; cf Is 56, 5.

and a more gratifying heritage in
the LORD's temple.
15* For the fruit of noble struggles is a
glorious one;
and unfailing is the root of under-
standing.
16* But the children of adulterers will
remain without issue,
and the progeny of an unlawful
bed will disappear.
17 For should they attain long life, they
will be held in no esteem,
and dishonored will their old age
be at last;
18 While should they die abruptly, they
have no hope
nor comfort in the day of scrutiny;
19* for dire is the end of the wicked
generation.

CHAPTER 4

1*† Better is childlessness with virtue;
for immortal is its memory:
because both by God is it acknowl-
edged, and by men.
2 When it is present men imitate it,
and they long for it when it is
gone;
And forever it marches crowned in
triumph,
victorious in unsullied deeds of
valor.
3* But the numerous progeny of the
wicked shall be of no avail;
their spurious offshoots shall not
strike deep root
nor take firm hold.
4* For even though their branches
flourish for a time,
they are unsteady and shall be
rocked by the wind
and, by the violence of the winds,
uprooted;
5 Their twigs shall be broken off un-
timely,
and their fruit be useless, unripe
for eating,
and fit for nothing.
6 For children born of lawless unions
give evidence of the wickedness
of their parents, when they are
examined.

c. On Early Death

7* But the just man, though he die
early, shall be at rest.
8* For the age that is honorable comes
not with the passing of time,
nor can it be measured in terms
of years.
9 Rather, understanding is the hoary
crown for men,
and an unsullied life, the attain-
ment of old age.
10*† He who pleased God was loved;
he who lived among sinners was
transported—
11* Snatched away, lest wickedness
pervert his mind
or deceit beguile his soul;
12* For the witchery of paltry things ob-
scures what is right
and the whirl of desire transforms
the innocent mind.
13 Having become perfect in a short
while, he reached the fullness of
a long career;
14* for his soul was pleasing to the
LORD,
therefore he sped him out of the
midst of wickedness.
But the people saw and did not un-
derstand,
nor did they take this into ac-
count.†
16* Yes, the just man dead condemns
the sinful who live,
and youth swiftly completed
condemns the many years of the
wicked man grown old.
17 For they see the death of the wise
man
and do not understand what the
LORD intended for him,
or why he made him secure.
18* They see, and hold him in contempt;
but the LORD laughs them to
scorn.
19* And they shall afterward become
dishonored corpses
and an unceasing mockery
among the dead.
For he shall strike them down
speechless and prostrate
and rock them to their founda-
tions;
They shall be utterly laid waste
and shall be in grief
and their memory shall perish.

The Final Judgment of the Wicked

20† Fearful shall they come, at the
counting up of their sins,
and their lawless deeds
shall convict them to their face.

---

* 15: Sir 1, 18.
16: 2 Sm 12, 14.
19: Ps 34, 22.
4, 1: Sir 16, 1ff; Prv 3, 3f.
3: Sir 23, 25.
4: Sir 40, 15; Is 40, 24.
7: 3, 3.
8f: Jb 12, 12; 32, 9; Sir 25, 4ff.
10: Gn 5, 24; Sir 44, 16; Heb 11, 5.
11: Is 57, 1f.
12: 2, 21; Dn 13, 9.
14: Gn 19, 22.29; 2 Pt 2, 7.
16: Mt 12, 41f.
18: Ps 37, 13.
19: Neh 1, 10 LXX; Ps 18, 8; Is 14, 19; Jer 23, 39f; 2 Mc 3, 29.

---

† 4, 1: The Latin form of this line, "Oh, how fair is the chaste generation in its glory!" is a later adaptation which is applied in the liturgy to the splendor of virginity.

4, 10f: There are allusions here to Enoch (Gn 5, 21-24), who was young by patriarchal standards, and to Lot (Gn 19, 10f; 2 Pt 2, 7f). Cf also is 57, 1f.

4, 15: The verse here omitted repeats the last two lines of 3, 9.

4, 20: *Counting up:* the last judgment.

CHAPTER 5

1* Then shall the just one with great assurance confront
his oppressors who set at nought his labors.
2 Seeing this, they shall be shaken with dreadful fear,
and amazed at the unlooked-for salvation.
3 They shall say among themselves, rueful
and groaning through anguish of spirit:
"This is he whom once we held as a laughingstock
and as a type for mockery, 4 fools that we were!
His life we accounted madness,
and his death dishonored.
5* See how he is accounted among the sons of God;
how his lot is with the saints!
6* We, then, have strayed from the way of truth,
and the light of justice did not shine for us,
and the sun did not rise for us.
7 We had our fill of the ways of mischief and of ruin;
we journeyed through impassable deserts,
but the way of the LORD we knew not.
8* What did our pride avail us?
What have wealth and its boastfulness afforded us?
9* All of them passed like a shadow
and like a fleeting rumor;
10 Like a ship traversing the heaving water,
of which, when it has passed, no trace can be found,
no path of its keel in the waves.
11 Or like a bird flying through the air;
no evidence of its course is to be found—
But the fluid air, lashed by the beat of pinions,
and cleft by the rushing force
Of speeding wings, is traversed:
and afterward no mark of passage can be found in it.
12 Or as, when an arrow has been shot at a mark,
the parted air straightway flows together again
so that none discerns the way it went through—
13* Even so we, once born, abruptly came to nought
and held no sign of virtue to display,
but were consumed in our wickedness."
14* Yes, the hope of the wicked is like thistledown borne on the wind,
and like fine, tempest-driven foam;
Like smoke scattered by the wind,
and like the passing memory of the nomad camping for a single day.
15* But the just live forever,
and in the LORD is their recompense,
and the thought of them is with the Most High.
16* Therefore shall they receive the splendid crown,
the beauteous diadem, from the hand of the LORD—
For he shall shelter them with his right hand,
and protect them with his arm.
17* He shall take his zeal for armor
and he shall arm creation to requite the enemy;
18 He shall don justice for a breastplate
and shall wear sure judgment for a helmet;
19* He shall take invincible rectitude as a shield
20 and whet his sudden anger for a sword,
And the universe shall war with him against the foolhardy.
21* Well-aimed shafts of lightnings shall go forth
and from the clouds as from a well-drawn bow shall leap to the mark;
22* and as from his sling, wrathful hailstones shall be hurled.
The water of the sea shall be enraged against them
and the streams shall abruptly overflow;
23* A mighty wind shall confront them
and a tempest winnow them out;
Thus lawlessness shall lay the whole earth waste
and evildoing overturn the thrones of potentates.

CHAPTER 6

Exhortation To Seek Wisdom

1* Hear, therefore, kings, and understand;
learn, you magistrates of the earth's expanse!

5, 1f: 2 Thes 1, 6f.
1: Col 2, 15.
5: Acts 26, 18; Col 1, 12.
6: Prv 4, 18f; Jn 12, 35.
6f: Is 59, 6-14.
8: Ps 49, 7; Prv 10, 2.
9ff: 1 Chr 20, 15; Ps 144, 4; Jb 9, 25f LXX.
13: Ez 33, 10.
14: Jb 21, 18; Pss 1, 4; 37, 20; Is 17, 13.
15: Is 62, 11; Ez 18, 9.
16: Ex 33, 22; Is 62, 3; 2 Tm 4, 8; 1 Pt 5, 4.
17: Is 59, 16.
19f: Dt 32, 40ff.
21: Hb 3, 9ff.
22: Dt 11, 4.
23: 11, 20; Sir 10, 13f.
6, 1f: 1, 1; Sir 33, 19; Mi 3, 1.9.

2 Hearken, you who are in power over the multitude
and lord it over throngs of peoples!
3* Because authority was given you by the LORD
and sovereignty by the Most High,
who shall probe your works and scrutinize your counsels!
4† Because, though you were ministers of his kingdom, you judged not rightly,
and did not keep the law,
nor walk according to the will of God,
5 Terribly and swiftly shall he come against you,
because judgment is stern for the exalted—
6* For the lowly may be pardoned out of mercy
but the mighty shall be mightily put to the test.
7* For the Lord of all shows no partiality,
nor does he fear greatness,
Because he himself made the great as well as the small,
and he provides for all alike;
8 but for those in power a rigorous scrutiny impends.
9* To you, therefore, O princes, are my words addressed
that you may learn wisdom and that you may not sin.
10† For those who keep the holy precepts hallowed shall be found holy,
and those learned in them will have ready a response.
11 Desire therefore my words;
long for them and you shall be instructed.
12* Resplendent and unfading is Wisdom,
and she is readily perceived by those who love her,
and found by those who seek her.
13* She hastens to make herself known in anticipation of men's desire;
14 he who watches for her at dawn shall not be disappointed,
for he shall find her sitting by his gate.
15 For taking thought of her is the perfection of prudence,
and he who for her sake keeps vigil shall quickly be free from care;
16* Because she makes her own rounds, seeking those worthy of her,
and graciously appears to them in the ways,
and meets them with all solicitude.
17* For the first step toward discipline is a very earnest desire for her;
then, care for discipline is love of her;
18 love means the keeping of her laws;
To observe her laws is the basis for incorruptibility;
19 and incorruptibility makes one close to God;
20 thus the desire for Wisdom leads up to a kingdom.
21 If, then, you find pleasure in throne and scepter, you princes of the peoples,
honor Wisdom, that you may reign as kings forever.

II: PRAISE OF WISDOM BY SOLOMON

Introduction

22* Now what wisdom is, and how she came to be I shall relate;
and I shall hide no secrets from you,
But from the very beginning I shall search out
and bring to light knowledge of her,
nor shall I diverge from the truth.
23* Neither shall I admit consuming jealousy to my company,
because that can have no fellowship with Wisdom.
24* A great number of wise men is the safety of the world,
and a prudent king, the stability of his people;
25 so take instruction from my words, to your profit.

CHAPTER 7

Solomon Is Like All Other Men

1*† I too am a mortal man, the same as all the rest,
and a descendant of the first man formed on earth.
And in my mother's womb I was molded into flesh

*

3: 2 Chr 36, 23; Prv 8, 15f; Jn 19, 11; Rom 13, 1ff.
6ff: Lk 12, 48.
7: Dt 1, 17; Prv 22, 2.
9ff: Dt 4, 10; Ps 2, 12; Sir 32, 14; 1 Jn 3, 7.
12: 7, 10; Prv 8, 17; Jer 29, 13.
13ff: Prv 8, 3.17.34.
16: Prv 8, 20f; Sir 15, 1ff.
17-21: Ps 2, 10ff; Prv 4, 4-9; 7, 1-4; 8, 15f; Dn 7, 27; Jn 14, 15.21; 1 Jn 5, 3.
22: Tb 12, 7.11; Mt 13, 11; Jn 15, 15.
23: 7, 13; Jas 3, 14f.
24: Prv 24, 6; 29, 4; Sir 10, 1ff.
7, 1f: 10, 1; Gn 2, 7; Jb 10, 9-12; 33, 6; 1 Cor 15, 47ff.

†

6, 4: *Law:* that of Moses; cf v 10; 2, 12.
6, 10: *Response:* a suitable plea before the great Judge. Cf Prv 22, 21; Jb 31, 14; Hb 2, 1; Sir 8, 9.
7, 1: *First man formed on earth:* Adam. The author omits throughout the book the proper names of the characters in sacred history of whom he speaks; see especially chapter 10.

2† in a ten-months' period—body and blood,
from the seed of man, and the pleasure that accompanies marriage.
3 And I too, when born, inhaled the common air,
and fell upon the kindred earth;
wailing, I uttered that first sound common to all.
4 In swaddling clothes and with constant care I was nurtured.
5 For no king has any different origin or birth,
6* but one is the entry into life for all; and in one same way they leave it.

Solomon Prayed and Wisdom and Riches Came to Him

7* Therefore I prayed, and prudence was given me;
I pleaded and the spirit of Wisdom came to me.
8* I preferred her to scepter and throne,
And deemed riches nothing in comparison with her,
9 nor did I liken any priceless gem to her;
Because all gold, in view of her, is a little sand,
and before her, silver is to be accounted mire.
10* Beyond health and comeliness I loved her,
And I chose to have her rather than the light,
because the splendor of her never yields to sleep.
11* Yet all good things together came to me in her company,
and countless riches at her hands;
12* And I rejoiced in them all, because Wisdom is their leader,
though I had not known that she is the mother of these.

Solomon Prays for Help To Speak of Wisdom

13* Simply I learned about her, and ungrudgingly do I share—
her riches I do not hide away;
14† For to men she is an unfailing treasure;
those who gain this treasure win the friendship of God,
to whom the gifts they have from discipline commend them.
15 Now God grant I speak suitably
and value these endowments at their worth:
For he is the guide of Wisdom
and the director of the wise.
16* For both we and our words are in his hand,
as well as all prudence and knowledge of crafts.
17 For he gave me sound knowledge of existing things,
that I might know the organization of the universe and the force of its elements,
18 The beginning and the end and the midpoint of times,
the changes in the sun's course and the variations of the seasons.
19 Cycles of years, positions of the stars,
20 natures of animals, tempers of beasts,
Powers of the winds and thoughts of men,
uses of plants and virtues of roots—
21 Such things as are hidden I learned and such as are plain;
22* for Wisdom, the artificer of all, taught me.

Nature and Incomparable Dignity of Wisdom

For in her is a spirit
intelligent, holy, unique,
Manifold, subtle, agile,
clear, unstained, certain,
Not baneful, loving the good, keen,
unhampered, beneficent, 23 kindly,
Firm, secure, tranquil,
all-powerful, all-seeing,
And pervading all spirits,
though they be intelligent, pure and very subtle.
24* For Wisdom is mobile beyond all motion,
and she penetrates and pervades all things by reason of her purity.
25 For she is an aura of the might of God
and a pure effusion of the glory of the Almighty;
therefore nought that is sullied enters into her.
26* For she is the refulgence of eternal light,

---

*

6: Jb 1, 21; 1 Tm 6, 7f.
7: 1 Kgs 3, 5-15; Prv 2, 3-11.
8f: 8, 5; 1 Kgs 10, 21; Prv 3, 14ff; 8, 10.18f; Jb 28, 15-19.
10: Prv 6, 23.
11: Prv 8, 21.
12: Prv 8, 14f.
13: 6, 23.
16: 3, 1.
22: 14, 2; Prv 8, 30.
22f: Heb 4, 12f; Jas 3, 17.
24: 8, 1.
26: 2 Cor 4, 4; Col 1, 15; Heb 1, 3.

---

†

7, 2: *In a ten-months' period:* thus the ancients were accustomed to reckon the period of pregnancy.
7, 14: *Discipline:* cf note on 1, 5.

the spotless mirror of the power of God,
the image of his goodness.
27* And she, who is one, can do all things,
and renews everything while herself perduring;
And passing into holy souls from age to age,
she produces friends of God and prophets.
28 For there is nought God loves, be it not one who dwells with Wisdom.
29* For she is fairer than the sun
and surpasses every constellation of the stars.
Compared to light, she takes precedence;
30 for that, indeed, night supplants,
but wickedness prevails not over Wisdom.

CHAPTER 8

1*† Indeed, she reaches from end to end mightily
and governs all things well.

Solomon Sought Wisdom, the Source of Blessings

2* Her I loved and sought after from my youth;
I sought to take her for my bride
and was enamored of her beauty.
3 She adds to nobility the splendor of companionship with God;
even the LORD of all loved her.
4* For she is instructress in the understanding of God,
the selector of his works.
5* And if riches be a desirable possession in life,
what is more rich than Wisdom, who produces all things?
6* And if prudence renders service,
who in the world is a better craftsman than she?
7† Or if one loves justice,
the fruits of her works are virtues;
For she teaches moderation and prudence,
justice and fortitude,
and nothing in life is more useful for men than these.
8* Or again, if one yearns for copious learning,
she knows the things of old, and infers those yet to come.
She understands the turns of phrases and the solutions of riddles;
signs and wonders she knows in advance
and the outcome of times and ages.

Solomon Sought Wisdom as His Counselor and Comfort

9 So I determined to take her to live with me,
knowing that she would be my counselor while all was well,
and my comfort in care and grief.
10* For her sake I should have glory among the masses,
and esteem from the elders, though I be but a youth.
11 I should become keen in judgment,
and should be a marvel before rulers.
12† They would abide my silence and attend my utterance;
and as I spoke on further,
they would place their hands upon their mouths.
13* For her sake I should have immortality
and leave to those after me an everlasting memory.
14* I should govern peoples, and nations would be my subjects—
15 terrible princes, hearing of me, would be afraid;
in the assembly I should appear noble, and in war courageous.
16* Within my dwelling, I should take my repose beside her;
For association with her involves no bitterness
and living with her no grief,
but rather joy and gladness.

Solomon Realizes That Wisdom Is a Gift of God

17* Thinking thus within myself,
and reflecting in my heart
That there is immortality in kinship with Wisdom,
18 and good pleasure in her friendship,
and unfailing riches in the works of her hands,

*

27: Ex 33, 11; Jb 42, 2; Ps 104, 29; Jl 3, 1.
29f: Sg 6, 3.9.
8, 1: 7, 24; 15, 1.
2: 1 Kgs 3, 7ff; Ps 45, 12; Prv 5, 18; 8, 17.
4: Prv 8, 27-31.
5: Prv 8, 18f.
6f: Prv 8, 14f.
8: Prv 1, 6; Sir 39, 1ff; 42, 19f; Dn 2, 21.
10ff: 1 Kgs 3, 28; Jb 29, 8ff.21f.
13: Sir 15, 6; 41, 12f; Is 56, 5.
14: 3, 8; Pss 18, 48; 47, 4.
16: Prv 29, 6; Sir 15, 6; Bar 3, 38.
17: Prv 3, 18.

†

8, 1: *End to end:* from one end of the heavens to the other.

8, 7: *Moderation . . . fortitude:* what are now known as the cardinal virtues.

8, 12: *Hands upon their mouths:* an oft-mentioned sign of respect among the ancients for unanswerable wisdom; cf Jb 40, 4.

And that in frequenting her society
there is prudence,
and fair renown in sharing her
discourses,
I went about seeking to take her
for my own.
19† Now, I was a well-favored child,
and I came by a noble nature;
20 or rather, being noble, I attained
an unsullied body.
21*†And knowing that I could not otherwise possess her except God
gave it—
and this, too, was prudence, to
know whose is the gift—
I went to the LORD and besought
him,
and said with all my heart:

CHAPTER 9

Solomon's Prayer

1* God of my fathers, LORD of mercy.
you who have made all things by
your word
2* And in your wisdom have established man
to rule the creatures produced by
you,
3* To govern the world in holiness and
justice,
and to render judgment in integrity of heart:
4* Give me Wisdom, the attendant at
your throne,
and reject me not from among
your children;
5* For I am your servant, the son of
your handmaid,
a man weak and short-lived
and lacking in comprehension of
judgment and of laws.
6* Indeed, though one be perfect
among the sons of men,
if Wisdom, who comes from you,
be not with him,
he shall be held in no esteem.
7* You have chosen me king over your
people
and magistrate for your sons and
daughters.
8* You have bid me build a temple on
your holy mountain
and an altar in the city that is your
dwelling place,
a copy of the holy tabernacle
which you had established from
of old.
9* Now with you is Wisdom, who knows
your works
and was present when you made
the world;
Who understands what is pleasing
in your eyes
and what is conformable with
your commands.
10* Send her forth from your holy heavens
and from your glorious throne
dispatch her
That she may be with me and work
with me,
that I may know what is your
pleasure.
11* For she knows and understands all
things,
and will guide me discreetly in my
affairs
and safeguard me by her glory;
12* Thus my deeds will be acceptable,
and I shall judge your people
justly
and be worthy of my father's
throne.
13* For what man knows God's counsel,
or who can conceive what our
LORD intends?
14 For the deliberations of mortals are
timid,
and unsure are our plans.
15* For the corruptible body burdens
the soul
and the earthen shelter weighs
down the mind that has many
concerns.
16* And scarce do we guess the things
on earth,
and what is within our grasp we
find with difficulty;
but when things are in heaven,
who can search them out?
17* Or who ever knew your counsel, except you had given Wisdom
and sent your holy spirit from on
high?
18* And thus were the paths of those on
earth made straight,
and men learned what was your
pleasure,
and were saved by Wisdom.

---

*

21: 1 Kgs 3, 9; 4, 29; Prv 2, 6; Jas 1, 5.
9, 1: Ps 86, 15.
1f: Gn 1; Ps 33, 6; Prv 3, 19; Jer 10, 12; Jn 1, 3.10.
2: Ps 8, 7ff; Sir 17, 2ff.
3: 1 Kgs 3, 6; 9, 4f; Ps 9, 8f.
4: 2 Chr 1, 10.
5: 1 Kgs 3, 7; Ps 116, 16.
6: 3, 17; 1 Kgs 11, 4; 1 Cor 3, 18ff.
7: 1 Chr 28, 5.
8: Ex 25, 8f; 2 Sm 7, 13; 1 Chr 28, 5; 2 Chr 6, 1f; 7, 7; Tb 1, 4; Pss 15, 1; 48, 2f.
9: Dt 6, 17f; Prv 8, 22-31; Jn 1, 1ff.10.
10: 18, 15; Mt 5, 34; Jn 3, 17; 20, 21.
11: 8, 8.
12: 1 Kgs 3, 6-9.
13: Is 40, 13; Bar 3, 31.
15: Jb 4, 19.
16: Sir 1, 3; Jn 3, 12.
17: Jn 14, 26.
18: 10, 9; Prv 28, 26.

---

†

8, 19f: Here the sacred writer mentions first bodily, then spiritual, excellence. To make it plain that the latter is the governing factor in the harmonious development of the human person, he then reverses the order.

8, 21: *Possess her:* in the Latin, "be continent." Though this verse has often been cited in connection with the virtue of chastity, the original must certainly mean "be possessed of Wisdom."

WISDOM

CHAPTER 10†

Wisdom Preserves Her Followers

1*† She preserved the first-formed father of the world
when he alone had been created;
And she raised him up from his fall,
2* and gave him power to rule all things.
3*† But when the unjust man withdrew from her in his anger,
he perished through his fratricidal wrath.
4*† When on his account the earth was flooded, Wisdom again saved it,
piloting the just man on frailest wood.
5*† She, when the nations were sunk in universal wickedness,
knew the just man, kept him blameless before God,
and preserved him resolute against pity for his child.
6*† She delivered the just man from among the wicked who were being destroyed,
when he fled as fire descended upon Pentapolis—
7*† Where as a testimony to its wickedness,
there yet remain a smoking desert,
Plants bearing fruit that never ripens,
and the tomb of a disbelieving soul, a standing pillar of salt.
8 For those who forsook Wisdom
first were bereft of knowledge of the right,
And then they left mankind a memorial of their folly—
so that they could not even be hidden in their fall.
9* But Wisdom delivered from tribulations those who served her.
10*† She, when the just man fled from his brother's anger,
guided him in direct ways,
Showed him the kingdom of God
and gave him knowledge of holy things;
She prospered him in his labors
and made abundant the fruit of his works,
11* Stood by him against the greed of his defrauders,
and enriched him;
12*† She preserved him from foes,
and secured him against ambush,
And she gave him the prize for his stern struggle
that he might know that devotion to God is mightier than all else.
13*† She did not abandon the just man when he was sold,
but delivered him from sin.
14 She went down with him into the dungeon,
and did not desert him in his bonds,
Until she brought him the scepter of royalty
and authority over his oppressors,
Showed those who had defamed him false,
and gave him eternal glory.
15* The holy people and blameless race—it was she
who delivered them from the nation that oppressed them.
16*† She entered the soul of the LORD's servant,
and withstood fearsome kings with signs and portents;
17* she gave the holy ones the recompense of their labors,
Conducted them by a wondrous road,
and became a shelter for them by day
and a starry flame by night.
18 She took them across the Red Sea
and brought them through the deep waters—
19† But their enemies she overwhelmed,
and cast them up from the bottom of the depths.
20* Therefore the just despoiled the wicked;
and they sang, O LORD, your holy name
and praised in unison your conquering hand—

WISDOM

*

10, 1-16: Heb 11, 17-27.
1: 7, 1.
2: Gn 1, 28.
3: Gn 4, 1-16.
4: 14, 5f; Gn 6, 5-9.
5: Gn 22, 7-10.
6: Gn 18, 22-33; 19, 15-25; 2 Pt 2, 6f.
7: Gn 19, 26; Lk 17, 32.
9: 16, 8.
10: Gn 27, 43ff; 28, 12-15.
11: Gn 30, 29f; 31, 5-12.
12: Gn 32, 24-29; 1 Tm 4, 8.
13f: Gn 37-45.
13: Gn 39, 7-10.
15: Ex 3, 9; 14, 30; 19, 6.
16: 1, 4; 7, 27; Ex 4, 10; Ps 76, 13.
17ff: 14, 3; 19, 7; Ex 13, 21f; 14-15; Pss 77, 20f; 78, 13.53; Is 4, 5f.
20: Ex 12, 35f; 15, 1-21.

†

10, 1-21: This chapter prepares for the following section (11, 2—19, 22) on the history of Israel in the Exodus, by reviewing the dealings of Wisdom with the patriarchs. It has a parallel in Sir 44—50; cf also Wis 18, 9.

10, 1f: Adam.

10, 3: Cain.

10, 4: Noah.

10, 5: Abraham.

10, 6: Lot. *Pentapolis:* the five cities, including Sodom; cf Gn 14, 2.

10, 7: Disbelieving soul: Lot's wife; cf Gn 19, 26.

10, 10ff: Jacob.

10, 12: *Devotion to God:* in the Greek this signifies "piety" or "religion," and is the equivalent of the Hebrew "fear of the LORD"; cf Prv 1, 7.

10, 13f: Joseph.

10, 16: Moses.

10, 19: *Cast them up:* their bodies, on the shore.

21* Because Wisdom opened the mouths of the dumb,
and gave ready speech to infants.

CHAPTER 11

1* She made their affairs prosper through the holy prophet.

III: SPECIAL PROVIDENCE OF GOD DURING THE EXODUS

Introduction

2*† They journeyed through the uninhabited desert,
and in solitudes they pitched their tents;
3* they withstood enemies and took vengeance on their foes.
4 When they thirsted, they called upon you,
and water was given them from the sheer rock,
assuagement for their thirst from the hard stone.
5* For by the things through which their foes were punished
they in their need were benefited.

First Example: Water Punishes the Egyptians and Benefits the Israelites

6*† Instead of a spring, when the perennial river
was troubled with impure blood
7 as a rebuke to the decree for the slaying of infants,
You gave them abundant water in an unhoped-for way,
8 once you had shown by the thirst they then had
how you punished their adversaries.
9* For when they had been tried, though only mildly chastised,
they recognized how the wicked, condemned in anger, were being tormented.
11* Both those afar off and those close by were afflicted:
10 the latter you tested, admonishing them as a father;
the former as a stern king you probed and condemned.
12* For a twofold grief took hold of them
and a groaning at the remembrance of the ones who had departed.
13 For when they heard that the cause of their own torments
was a benefit to these others, they recognized the Lord.
14* Him who of old had been cast out in exposure they indeed mockingly rejected;
but in the end of events, they marveled at him,
since their thirst proved unlike that of the just.

Second Example: Animals Punish the Egyptians and Benefit the Israelites

15*† And in return for their senseless, wicked thoughts,
which misled them into worshiping dumb serpents and worthless insects,
You sent upon them swarms of dumb creatures for vengeance;
16* that they might recognize that a man is punished by the very things through which he sins.

Digression on God's Mercy

17* For not without means was your almighty hand,
that had fashioned the universe from formless matter,
to send upon them a drove of bears or fierce lions,
18 Or new-created, wrathful, unknown beasts
to breathe forth fiery breath,
Or pour out roaring smoke,
or flash terrible sparks from their eyes.
19 Not only could these attack and completely destroy them;
even their frightful appearance itself could slay.
20* Even without these, they could have been killed at a single blast,
pursued by retribution
and winnowed out by your mighty spirit;
But you have disposed all things by measure and number and weight.
21* For with you great strength abides always;

*

21: Ex 4, 10-15; Ps 8, 3; Mt 11, 25.
11, 1: Dt 2, 7; Hos 12, 14.
2ff: Ex 17, 2-6; Nm 20, 1-13; Pss 63, 2; 107, 4-7; Jer 2, 6.
3: Ex 17, 8-16; Nm 21, 1ff; 21-35; 31, 1-12; Ps 118, 10ff.
5: 16, 1f.
6ff: 18, 5; Ex 1, 22; 7, 17-24.
9ff: 3, 5; 16, 3f; Dt 8, 2-5; Ps 6, 2; Prv 3, 12; 2 Mc 6, 12-16.
11: Ps 6, 2.
12f: 16, 8; Ex 14, 4.18.
14: Ex 2, 3.
15: 12, 23f; 15, 18—16, 1; Ex 7, 26ff.
16: 12, 23.27; Ex 10, 16; Prv 1, 31f; 26, 27.
17ff: 12, 8f; 16, 1.5; Gn 1, 1f; Dt 32, 24; 2 Kgs 17, 25f; Hos 13, 4-8.
20: Jb 4, 9.
21: 12, 12; 2 Chr 20, 6.

†

11, 2ff: Few verses in these later chapters can be fully understood without consulting the passages in the Mosaic books which are indicated in the cross references. The theme of this part of the book is expressed in 11, 5, and is illustrated in the following chapters by five examples drawn from Exodus events.

11, 6ff: *The perennial river:* the Nile; the contrast is between the first plague of Egypt (Ex 7, 17-24) and the water drawn from the rock in Horeb (Ex 17, 5-7; Nm 20, 8-11).

11, 15: *Dumb:* that is, irrational.

who can resist the might of your
arm?
22*†Indeed, before you the whole universe is as a grain from a balance,
or a drop of morning dew come down upon the earth.
23* But you have mercy on all, because you can do all things;
and you overlook the sins of men that they may repent.
24* For you love all things that are
and loathe nothing that you have made;
for what you hated, you would not have fashioned.
25* And how could a thing remain, unless you willed it;
or be preserved, had it not been called forth by you?
26* But you spare all things, because they are yours, O LORD and lover of souls,

CHAPTER 12

1* for your imperishable spirit is in all things!
2 Therefore you rebuke offenders little by little,
warn them, and remind them of the sins they are committing,
that they may abandon their wickedness and believe in you, O LORD!
3* For truly, the ancient inhabitants of your holy land,
4 whom you hated for deeds most odious—
Works of witchcraft and impious sacrifices;
5† a cannibal feast of human flesh and of blood, from the midst of . . .—
These merciless murderers of children,
6* and parents who took with their own hands defenseless lives,
You willed to destroy by the hands of our fathers,
7* that the land that is dearest of all to you
might receive a worthy colony of God's children.
8* But even these, as they were men, you spared,
and sent wasps as forerunners of your army
they they might exterminate them by degrees.
9* Not that you were without power to have the wicked vanquished in battle by the just,
or wiped out at once by terrible beasts or by one decisive word;
10* But condemning them bit by bit, you gave them space for repentance.
You were not unaware that their race was wicked
and their malice ingrained,
And that their dispositions would never change;
11* for they were a race accursed from the beginning.
Neither out of fear for anyone
did you grant amnesty for their sins.
12* For who can say to you, "What have you done?"
or who can oppose your decree?
Or when peoples perish, who can challenge you, their maker;
or who can come into your presence as vindicator of unjust men?
13* For neither is there any god besides you who have the care of all,
that you need show you have not unjustly condemned;
14* Nor can any king or prince confront you on behalf of those you have punished.
15* But as you are just, you govern all things justly;
you regard it as unworthy of your power
to punish one who has incurred no blame.
16* For your might is the source of justice;
your mastery over all things makes you lenient to all.
17*†For you show your might when the perfection of your power is disbelieved;
and in those who know you, you rebuke temerity.
18 But though you are master of might,

WISDOM

*

22: Hos 13, 3.
23: 12, 10; Dt 9, 27; Acts 17, 30; Rom 2, 4; 11, 32; 2 Pt 3, 9.
24: Ps 145, 9.
25: Is 41, 4.
26: 12, 16; Is 63, 9.
12, 1: 1, 7.
3ff: 14, 23; Dt 18, 9-12; Pss 5, 6; 106, 28.34-39; Jer 19, 4f; Ez 16, 3.20f.36.
6: Nm 33, 52.
7: Dt 11, 12.
8: Ex 23, 28ff; Dt 7, 17-24.
9: 11, 18; 18, 15; Nm 16, 21.
10: 11, 23; Ps 55, 20; Sir 16, 9.
11: Gn 9, 25.
12: 2 Sm 16, 10; Eccl 8, 4; Sir 46, 19; Is 45, 9; Dn 4, 32; Rom 9, 19ff.
13: 6, 7; Dt 3, 24; 32, 39; Is 44, 6.8.
14: Jer 49, 19; 50, 44.
15: Gn 18, 23ff; Dt 32, 4.
16: 2, 11; 11, 26; Ps 103, 19.
17: 15, 2f; Ex 9, 16.

†

11, 22: *Grain from a balance:* a tiny particle used for weighing on sensitive scales.

12, 5: *And of blood, from the midst of . . .:* this line is obscure in the current Greek text and in all extant translations. Either one or two words would complete it. The horrible crimes here spoken of (cf 14, 23) were not unheard of in the ancient pagan world.

12, 17: The brunt of God's anger and vindictive justice is borne by those who know him and yet defy his authority and might. Cf 1, 2; 15, 2, but also 12, 27; 18, 13.

you judge with clemency,
and with much lenience you govern us;
for power, whenever you will, attends you.
19* And you taught your people, by these deeds,
that those who are just must be kind;
And you gave your sons good ground for hope
that you would permit repentance for their sins.
20 For these were enemies of your servants, doomed to death;
yet, while you punished them with such solicitude and pleading,
granting time and opportunity to abandon wickedness,
21* With what exactitude you judged your sons,
to whose fathers you gave the sworn covenants of goodly promises!
22 Us, therefore, you chastise and our enemies with a thousand blows you punish,
that we may think earnestly of your goodness when we judge,
and, when being judged, may look for mercy.

Second Example Resumed

23* Hence those unjust also, who lived a life of folly,
you tormented through their own abominations.
24* For they went far astray in the paths of error,
taking for gods the worthless and disgusting among beasts,
deceived like senseless infants.
25* Therefore as though upon unreasoning children,
you sent your judgment on them as a mockery;
26 But they who took no heed of punishment which was but child's play
were to experience a condemnation worthy of God.
27* For in the things through which they suffered distress,
since they were tortured by the very things they deemed gods,
They saw and recognized the true God
whom before they had refused to know;
with this, their final condemnation came upon them.

CHAPTER 13

Digression on False Worship

A. Nature Worship

1*† For all men were by nature foolish who were in ignorance of God,
and who from the good things seen did not succeed in knowing him who is,
and from studying the works did not discern the artisan;
2*† But either fire, or wind, or the swift air,
or the circuit of the stars, or the mighty water,
or the luminaries of heaven, the governors of the world, they considered gods.
3* Now if out of joy in their beauty they thought them gods,
let them know how far more excellent is the Lord than these;
for the original source of beauty fashioned them.
4* Or if they were struck by their might and energy,
let them from these things realize how much more powerful is he who made them.
5 For from the greatness and the beauty of created things
their original author, by analogy, is seen.
6† But yet, for these the blame is less;
For they indeed have gone astray perhaps,
though they seek God and wish to find him.
7 For they search busily among his works,
but are distracted by what they see, because the things seen are fair.
8 But again, not even these are pardonable.
9 For if they so far succeeded in knowledge
that they could speculate about the world,
how did they not more quickly find its LORD?

B. Idolatry

10* But doomed are they, and in dead things are their hopes,

---

*

19f: 11, 23; Sir 17, 24.
21: 18, 22; Gn 50, 24; Dt 7, 6-14; Ps 105, 8ff.
23: 11, 16; 16, 1.
24: Dt 11, 28; Jer 5, 28; Rom 1, 23.
25: Jer 4, 22.
27: 16, 16; Ex 14, 4.28.
13, 1: Acts 14, 17; Eph 4, 17ff.
2: Gn 1, 14-19; Dt 4, 19; Jb 31, 26ff.
3: Ps 8, 4.
4: Jer 10, 2; Bar 6, 39.
10: 3, 11; 15, 5.17; Dt 4, 25-28; 7, 25; 27, 15; Ps 115, 4; Hos 14, 4; Acts 17, 29.

†

13, 1: *Him who is:* the Hebrew sacred name of God; cf Ex 3, 14.

13, 2: *Luminaries of heaven:* the Latin interprets, "sun and moon"; *governors:* cf Gn 1, 16.

13, 6: *The blame is less:* the greater blame is incurred by those mentioned in 13, 10 and 15, 14ff.

who termed gods things made by human hands:
Gold and silver, the product of art, and likenesses of beasts,
or useless stone, the work of an ancient hand.

The Carpenter and Wooden Idols

11* A carpenter may saw out a suitable tree
and skillfully scrape off all its bark,
And deftly plying his art,
produce something fit for daily use,
12 and use up the refuse from his handiwork
in preparing his food, and have his fill;
13* Then the good-for-nothing refuse from these remnants,
crooked wood grown full of knots,
he takes and carves to occupy his spare time.
This wood he models with listless skill,
and patterns it on the image of a man
14* or makes it resemble some worthless beast.
When he has daubed it with red and crimsoned its surface with red stain,
and daubed over every blemish in it,
15* He makes a fitting shrine for it
and puts it on the wall, fastening it with a nail.
16* Thus lest it fall down he provides for it,
knowing that it cannot help itself;
for, truly, it is an image and needs help.
17* But when he prays about his goods or marriage or children,
he is not ashamed to address the thing without a soul.
And for vigor he invokes the powerless;
18 and for life he entreats the dead;
And for aid he beseeches the wholly incompetent,
and about travel, something that cannot even walk.
19 And for profit in business and success with his hands
he asks facility of a thing with hands completely inert.

CHAPTER 14

1* Again, one preparing for a voyage and about to traverse the wild waves
cries out to wood more unsound than the boat that bears him.
2 For the urge for profits devised this latter,
and Wisdom the artificer produced it.
3* But your providence, O Father! guides it,
for you have furnished even in the sea a road,
and through the waves a steady path,
4* Showing that you can save from any danger,
so that even one without skill may embark.
5* But you will that the products of your Wisdom be not idle;
therefore men trust their lives even to frailest wood,
and have been safe crossing the surge on a raft.
6*† For of old, when the proud giants were being destroyed,
the hope of the universe, who took refuge on a raft,
left to the world a future for his race, under the guidance of your hand.
7† For blest is the wood through which justice comes about;
8* but the handmade idol is accursed, and its maker as well:
he for having produced it, and it, because though corruptible, it was termed a god.
9 Equally odious to God are the evildoer and his evil deed;
10 and the thing made shall be punished with its contriver.
11* Therefore upon even the idols of the nations shall a visitation come,
since they have become abominable amid God's works,
Snares for the souls of men
and a trap for the feet of the senseless.

The Origin and Evils of Idolatry

12* For the source of wantoness is the devising of idols;
and their invention was a corruption of life.
13* For in the beginning they were not,
nor shall they continue forever;

*
11-19: Is 44, 9-20.
11: 15, 7; Bar 6, 58.
13: Dt 4, 16.
14: Jer 10, 9.
15: Is 40, 20; 41, 7; 44, 13.
16: 1 Sm 5, 3ff; Bar 6, 57.
17ff: 15, 15.
14, 1: Is 46, 7.
3: Ps 107, 23-30; Is 43, 16.
4: 16, 8.
5: 10, 4.
6: Gn 6, 4; 17, 1ff.21f.
8: Rom 1, 23.
11: 3, 7; 23, 33; Nm 33, 4; Jos 23, 13; Ps 115, 4; Jer 6, 15; 10, 15; 46, 25; Hos 9, 15.
12: Rom 1, 23ff.
13: Is 2, 18.

†
14, 6: Noah.
14, 7: Often applied to the Cross of our Lord.

14 for by the vanity of men they
came into the world,
and therefore a sudden end is devised for them.
15 For a father, afflicted with untimely
mourning,
made an image of the child so
quickly taken from him,
And now honored as a god what was
formerly a dead man
and handed down to his subjects
mysteries and sacrifices.
16* Then, in time, the impious practice
gained strength and was observed as law,
and graven things were worshiped by princely decrees.
17 Men who lived so far away that they
could not honor him in his presence
copied the appearance of the distant king
And made a public image of him
they wished to honor,
out of zeal to flatter him when absent, as though present.
18 And to promote this observance
among those to whom it was
strange,
the artisan's ambition provided a
stimulus.
19* For he, mayhap in his determination to please the ruler,
labored over the likeness to the
best of his skill;
20* And the masses, drawn by the
charm of the workmanship,
soon thought he should be worshiped who shortly before was
honored as a man.
21 And this became a snare for mankind,
that men enslaved to either grief
or tyranny
conferred the incommunicable
Name on stocks and stones.
22* Then it was not enough for them to
err in their knowledge of God;
but even though they live in a
great war of ignorance,
they call such evils peace.
23* For while they celebrate either
child-slaying sacrifices or clandestine mysteries,
or frenzied carousals in unheard-of rites,
24 They no longer safeguard either
lives or pure wedlock;
but each either waylays and kills
his neighbor, or aggrieves him
by adultery.
25* And all is confusion—blood and
murder, theft and guile,
corruption, faithlessness, turmoil,
perjury,
26 Disturbance of good men, neglect of
gratitude,
besmirching of souls, unnatural
lust,
disorder in marriage, adultery
and shamelessness.
27* For the worship of infamous idols
is the reason and source and extremity of all evil.
28* For they either go mad with enjoyment, or prophesy lies,
or live lawlessly or lightly forswear themselves.
29 For as their trust is in soulless idols,
they expect no harm when they
have sworn falsely.
30*† But on both counts shall justice overtake them:
because they thought ill of God
and devoted themselves to
idols,
and because they deliberately
swore false oaths, despising piety.
31† For not the might of those that are
sworn by
but the retribution of sinners
ever follows upon the transgression of the wicked.

CHAPTER 15

1* But you, our God, are good and true,
slow to anger, and governing all
with mercy.
2* For even if we sin, we are yours, and
know your might;
but we will not sin, knowing that
we belong to you.
3* For to know you well is complete justice,
and to know your might is the root
of immortality.
4* For neither did the evil creation of
men's fancy deceive us,
nor the fruitless labor of painters,
A form smeared with varied colors,
5 the sight of which arouses yearning in the senseless man,
till he longs for the inanimate
form of a dead image.
6* Lovers of evil things, and worthy of
such hopes
are they who make them and long
for them and worship them.

*

16: Dn 3, 4ff; 1 Mc 1, 47-50.
19: Is 44, 12f LXX.
20: 15, 4.
22-31: Jer 2, 20; 3, 1-25; Hos 4, 1f.9-19; Rom 1, 26-31; Gal 5, 19ff; 1 Tm 1, 9f.
22: Jer 6, 14; Ez 13, 10.
23: 12, 4f; 14, 15; Is 57, 5.
25f: Jer 7, 8f; 22, 17.
27: Ex 23, 13.
28: Jer 5, 31; 29, 26.
30: 1, 1.8; 11, 20; Jer 5, 2.7.
15, 1: Ex 34, 6f; Pss 86, 5.15; 145, 8.9.14.
2: Jb 10, 14f LXX.
3: 3, 15; Jn 17, 3.
4: 13, 14.
6: Ps 115, 8.

†

14, 30: *Piety:* the sanctity of oaths.

14, 31: Perjury is a form of deceit which calls for punishment even though it be practiced in the name of a lifeless idol.

The Potter's Clay Idols

7* For truly the potter, laboriously working the soft earth,
molds for our service each several article:
Both the vessels that serve for clean purposes
and their opposites, all alike;
As to what shall be the use of each vessel of either class
the worker in clay is the judge.
8* And with misspent toil he molds a meaningless god from the selfsame clay;
though he himself shortly before was made from the earth
And after a little, is to go whence he was taken,
when the life that was lent him is demanded back.
9* But his concern is not that he is to die
nor that his span of life is brief;
Rather, he vies with goldsmiths and silversmiths
and emulates molders of bronze,
and takes pride in modeling counterfeits.
10* Ashes his heart is! more worthless than earth is his hope,
and more ignoble than clay his life;
11* Because he knew not the one who fashioned him,
and breathed into him a quickening soul,
and infused a vital spirit.
12* Instead, he esteemed our life a plaything,
and our span of life a holiday for gain;
"For one must," says he, "make profit every way, be it even out of evil."
13 For this man more than any knows that he is sinning,
when out of earthen stuff he creates fragile vessels and idols alike.
14* But all quite senseless, and worse than childish in mind,
are the enemies of your people who enslaved them.
15* For they esteemed all the idols of the nations gods,
which have no use of the eyes for vision,
nor nostrils to snuff the air,
Nor ears to hear,
nor fingers on their hands for feeling;
even their feet are useless to walk with.
16* For a man made them;
one whose spirit has been lent him fashioned them.
For no man succeeds in fashioning a god like himself;
17 being mortal, he makes a dead thing with his lawless hands.
For he is better than the things he worships;
he at least lives, but never they.

Second Example Resumed

18*† And besides, they worship the most loathsome beasts—
for compared as to folly, these are worse than the rest,
19* Nor for their looks are they good or desirable beasts,
but they have escaped both the approval of God and his blessing.

CHAPTER 16

1*† Therefore they were fittingly punished by similar creatures,
and were tormented by a swarm of insects.
2* Instead of this punishment, you benefited your people
with a novel dish, the delight they craved,
by providing quail for their food;
3* That those others, when they desired food,
since the creatures sent to plague them were so loathsome,
should be turned from even the craving of necessities,
While these, after a brief period of privation, partook of a novel dish.
4* For upon those oppressors, inexorable want had to come;
but these needed only be shown how their enemies were being tormented.
5* For when the dire venom of beasts came upon them
and they were dying from the bite of crooked serpents,

*

7: 13, 11; Jer 18, 3f; Rom 9, 21; 2 Tm 2, 20f.
8: Gn 3, 19; Eccl 12, 7.
9: Bar 6, 46.
10: Jb 13, 12 LXX.
11: Gn 2, 7; Zec 12, 1.
12: Jas 4, 13f.
14: Ex 1, 13.
15: 14, 11; Dt 4, 28; Pss 115, 4-7; 135, 15ff.
16f: 13, 10.
18: 11, 15; 12, 24.
19: Gn 1, 25; 3, 14.
16, 1: 11, 15f; 12, 23.27; Ex 7, 27; 8, 12.17.
2: 11, 13; 19, 11f; Ex 16, 13; Nm 11, 31f; Ps 105, 40.
3: 11, 15; Ex 8, 10; 16, 3.
4: 11, 8f.
5f: Nm 21, 4-9; Dt 32, 24; Jer 8, 17 LXX.

†

15, 18ff: The author here returns to the main theme of chapters 11—19, which was interrupted by the digression 13, 1—15, 17.

15, 18: *For . . . rest:* this may mean that the creatures worshiped by the Egyptians (e.g., crocodiles, serpents, scarabs, etc.) were more patently lacking in intelligence than the general run of beasts; cf 11, 15; 12, 24.

16, 1: *They:* the Egyptian idolaters.

your anger endured not to the end.
6† But as a warning, for a short time
they were terrorized,
though they had a sign of salvation, to remind them of the precept of your law.
7 For he who turned toward it was
saved, not by what he saw,
but by you, the savior of all.
8* And by this also you convinced our
foes
that you are he who delivers from
all evil.
9* For the bites of locusts and of flies
slew them,
and no remedy was found to save
their lives
because they deserved to be punished by such means;
10* But not even the fangs of poisonous
reptiles overcame your sons,
for your mercy brought the antidote to heal them.
11* For as a reminder of your injunctions, they were stung,
and swiftly they were saved,
Lest they should fall into deep forgetfulness
and become unresponsive to your
beneficence.
12* For indeed, neither herb nor application cured them,
but your all-healing word, O
LORD!
13* For you have dominion over life and
death;
you lead down to the gates of the
nether world, and lead back.
14† Man, however, slays in his malice,
but when the spirit has come
away, it does not return,
nor can he bring back the soul
once it is confined.
15 But your hand none can escape.

Third Example: A Rain of Manna for Israel instead of the Plague of Storms

16* For the wicked who refused to know
you
were punished by the might of
your arm,
Pursued by unwonted rains and
hailstorms and unremitting
downpours,
and consumed by fire.
17* For against all expectation, in water
which quenches anything,
the fire grew more active;
For the universe fights on behalf of
the just.
18* For now the flame was tempered
so that the beasts might not be
burnt up that were sent upon the
wicked,
but that these might see and know
they were struck by the judgment of God;
19 And again, even in the water, fire
blazed beyond its strength
so as to consume the produce of
the wicked land.
20* Instead of this, you nourished your
people with food of angels
and furnished them bread from
heaven, ready to hand, untoiled-for,
endowed with all delights and
conforming to every taste.
21* For this substance of yours revealed
your sweetness toward your
children,
and serving the desire of him who
received it,
was blended to whatever flavor
each one wished.
22*† Yet snow and ice withstood fire and
were not melted,
that they might know that their
enemies' fruits
Were consumed by a fire that blazed
in the hail
and flashed lightning in the rain.
23* But this fire, again, that the just
might be nourished,
forgot even its proper strength;
24* For your creation, serving you, its
maker,
grows tense for punishment
against the wicked,
but is relaxed in benefit for those
who trust in you.
25 Therefore at that very time, transformed in all sorts of ways,
it was serving your all-nourishing
bounty
according to what they needed
and desired;
26* That your sons whom you loved
might learn, O LORD,
that it is not the various kinds of
fruits that nourish man,
but it is your word that preserves
those who believe you!
27* For what was not destroyed by fire,
when merely warmed by a momentary sunbeam, melted;
28* So that men might know that one

*

8: Gn 48, 16; 2 Mc 1, 24f.
9: Ex 8, 16-28; 10, 4-19; Pss 78, 45f; 105, 31.34; Rv 9, 1-11.
10: Dt 32, 33.
11: Ps 78, 11.
12: Ex 15, 26.
13ff: Dt 32, 39; 1 Sm 2, 6; Tb 13, 2; Ps 78, 34.39; Eccl 8, 8; Dn 5, 19; 2 Mc 6, 26; 7, 23.
16: 11, 21; 12, 27; Ex 5, 2; 9, 29-34.
17: 10, 20; 19, 20; Ex 9, 23-28; 2 Mc 8, 36; 14, 34.
18f: 19, 20f.
20: Ex 16, 4; Nm 11, 8; Ps 78, 24f; Jn 6, 31.
21: Ps 34, 9.
22: Ex 9, 25-31; 10, 12; Ps 148, 8.
23: 19, 21.
24: 5, 17.20; 19, 6; Sir 39, 25ff.
26: Dt 8, 3; Mt 4, 4.
27: Ex 16, 21.
28: Pss 57, 9f; 92, 3.

†

16, 6: *Sign:* the brazen serpent; cf Nm 21, 9.
16, 14: *Confined:* in the nether world, in limbo.
16, 22: *Snow and ice:* the manna; cf 16, 27; 19, 21.

WISDOM

must give you thanks before the sunrise,
and turn to you at daybreak.
29* For the hope of the ingrate melts like a wintry frost
and runs off like useless water.

CHAPTER 17

Fourth Example: Darkness Afflicts the Egyptians, While the Israelites Have Light

1* For great are your judgments, and hardly to be described;
therefore the unruly souls were wrong.
2* For when the lawless thought to enslave the holy nation,
shackled with darkness, fettered by the long night,
they lay confined beneath their own roofs as exiles from the eternal providence.
3* For they who supposed their secret sins were hid
under the dark veil of oblivion
Were scattered in fearful trembling, terrified by apparitions.
4 For not even their inner chambers kept them fearless,
for crashing sounds on all sides terrified them,
and mute phantoms with somber looks appeared.
5* No force, even of fire, was able to give light,
nor did the flaming brilliance of the stars
succeed in lighting up that gloomy night.
6*† But only intermittent, fearful fires flashed through upon them;
And in their terror they thought beholding these was worse
than the times when that sight was no longer to be seen.
7* And mockeries of the magic art were in readiness,
and a jeering reproof of their vaunted shrewdness.
8 For they who undertook to banish fears and terrors from the sick soul
themselves sickened with a ridiculous fear.
9* For even though no monstrous thing frightened them,
they shook at the passing of insects and the hissing of reptiles,
10 And perished trembling,
reluctant to face even the air that they could nowhere escape.
11* For wickedness, of its nature cowardly, testifies in its own condemnation,
and because of a distressed conscience, always magnifies misfortunes.
12 For fear is nought but the surrender of the helps that come from reason;
13 and the more one's expectation is of itself uncertain,
the more one makes of not knowing the cause that brings on torment.
14† So they, during that night, powerless though it was,
that had come upon them from the recesses of a powerless nether world,
while all sleeping the same sleep,
15* Were partly smitten by fearsome apparitions
and partly stricken by their souls' surrender,
for fear came upon them, sudden and unexpected.
16* Thus, then, whoever was there fell into that unbarred prison and was kept confined.
17 For whether one was a farmer, or a shepherd,
or a worker at tasks in the wasteland,
Taken unawares, he served out the inescapable sentence;
18* for all were bound by the one bond of darkness.
And were it only the whistling wind,
or the melodious song of birds in the spreading branches,
Or the steady sound of rushing water,
19 or the rude crash of overthrown rocks,
Or the unseen gallop of bounding animals,
or the roaring cry of the fiercest beasts,
Or an echo resounding from the hollow of the hills,
these sounds, inspiring terror, paralyzed them.
20* For the whole world shone with brilliant light
and continued its works without interruption;
21 Over them alone was spread oppressive night,

*
29: 5, 14; 2 Sm 14, 14.
17, 1: Ex 6, 6 LXX.
2: 18, 4; Ex 1, 13f; 19, 6.10, 21ff.
3f: 1, 7f; 10, 8; 18, 17.
5: 10, 17; Jer 23, 24 LXX.
6: Ex 9, 23f.
7: 12, 25f; Ex 7, 11f.22; 8, 3; 9, 11; 10, 2.
9: 16, 1; Jer 26, 22 LXX.
11: 4, 6; 10, 7; Rom 2, 15.
15: Ex 11, 9f.
16: 18, 4; Ex 10, 23.
18f: Lv 26, 36.
20f: Ex 10, 23; Is 9, 1; 60, 1ff; 2 Pt 2, 17.

†
17, 6: *Fires:* that is, lightnings.
17, 14: *Powerless:* the nether world, the home of darkness, has no power against God, nor even against such men as do not submit to it of themselves; cf 1, 14ff.

an image of the darkness that next
should come upon them;
yet they were to themselves more
burdensome than the darkness.

CHAPTER 18

1 But your holy ones had very great
light;
And those others, who heard their
voices but did not see their
forms,
since now they themselves had
suffered, called them blest;
2† And because they who formerly had
been wronged did not harm
them, they thanked them,
and pleaded with them, for the
sake of the difference between
them.
3* Instead of this, you furnished the
flaming pillar
which was a guide on the unknown way,
and the mild sun for an honorable
migration.
4* For those deserved to be deprived
of light and imprisoned by
darkness,
who had kept your sons confined
through whom the imperishable
light of the law was to be given
to the world.

Fifth Example: Death of the Egyptian First-born; the Israelites Are Spared

5*† When they determined to put to
death the infants of the holy
ones,
and when a single boy had been
cast forth but saved,
As a reproof you carried off their
multitude of sons
and made them perish all at once
in the mighty water.
6* That night was known beforehand
to our fathers,
that, with sure knowledge of the
oaths in which they put their
faith, they might have courage.
7* Your people awaited
the salvation of the just and the
destruction of their foes.
8* For when you punished our adversaries,
in this you glorified us whom you
had summoned.
9*† For in secret the holy children of the
good were offering sacrifice
and putting into effect with one
accord the divine institution,
That your holy ones should share
alike the same good things and
dangers,
having previously sung the
praises of the fathers.
10* But the discordant cry of their enemies responded,
and the piteous wail of mourning
for children was borne to them.
11* And the slave was smitten with the
same retribution as his master;
even the plebeian suffered the
same as the king.
12* And all alike by a single death
had countless dead;
For the living were not even sufficient for the burial,
since at a single instant their nobler offspring were destroyed.
13*† For though they disbelieved at every
turn on account of sorceries,
at the destruction of the first-born
they acknowledged that the
people was God's son.
14 For when peaceful stillness compassed everything
and the night in its swift course
was half spent,
15* Your all-powerful word from heaven's royal throne
bounded, a fierce warrior, into the
doomed land,
16* bearing the sharp sword of your
inexorable decree.
And as he alighted, he filled every
place with death;
he still reached to heaven, while
he stood upon the earth.
17* Then, forthwith, visions in horrible
dreams perturbed them
and unexpected fears assailed
them;
18 And cast half-dead, one here, another there,
each was revealing the reason for
his dying.
19 For the dreams that disturbed them
had proclaimed this beforehand,
lest they perish unaware of why
they suffered ill.
20* But the trial of death touched at one
time even the just,
and in the desert a plague struck
the multitude;

*

18, 3: Ex 13, 21.
4: 17, 2; Ps 119, 105; Is 2, 3.5.
5: 11, 7.14; Ex 1, 16.22; 2, 3.6-10; 15, 10; Neh 9, 11.
6: 12, 21; Ex 6, 8; 13, 5.
7: Ex 14, 13.
8: 19, 22; Ex 3, 18; Is 43, 3f.
9: Ex 12, 21-28; Sir 44—50.
10: Ex 12, 30; Jer 9, 17.19.
11: Ex 11, 5; 12, 29.
12: Nm 33, 4.
13: 17, 7; Ex 4, 22f; 12, 12.29; 13, 2.13.15.
15: 9, 10; Ex 15, 3.
16: 1 Chr 21, 16; Heb 4, 12; Rv 1, 16.
17ff: 17, 3f.
20: 16, 5; Nm 17, 9-15.

†

18, 2: *The difference between them:* God's distinctive manner of treating the Israelites and the Egyptians according to their respective merits.
18, 5: *Single boy:* Moses.
18, 9: *Praises of the fathers:* cf Sir 44—50; Wis 10.
18, 13: *People:* the Hebrews.

Yet not for long did the anger last.
21*†For the blameless man hastened to be their champion,
bearing the weapon of his special office,
prayer and the propitiation of incense;
He withstood the wrath and put a stop to the calamity,
showing that he was your servant.
22*†And he overcame the bitterness not by bodily strength, not by force of arms;
But by word he overcame the smiter,
recalling the sworn covenants with their fathers.
23* For when corpses had already fallen one on another in heaps,
he stood in the midst and checked the anger,
and cut off the way to the living.
24*†For on his full-length robe was the whole world,
and the glories of the fathers were carved in four rows upon the stones,
and your grandeur was on the crown upon his head.
25* To these names the destroyer yielded, and these he feared;
for the mere trial of anger was enough.

CHAPTER 19

1*†But the wicked, merciless wrath assailed until the end.
For he knew beforehand what they were yet to do:
2*†That though they themselves had agreed to the departure
and had anxiously sent them on their way,
they would regret it and pursue them.
3*†For while they were still engaged in funeral rites
and were mourning at the burials of the dead,
They adopted another senseless plan;
and those whom they had sent away with entreaty,
they pursued as fugitives.
4 For a compulsion suited to this ending drew them on,
and made them forgetful of what had befallen them,
That they might fill out the torments of their punishment,
5† and your people might experience a glorious journey
while those others met an extraordinary death.
6* For all creation, in its several kinds,
was being made over anew,
serving its natural laws,
that your children might be preserved unharmed.
7* The cloud overshadowed their camp;
and out of what had before been water, dry land was seen emerging:
Out of the Red Sea an unimpeded road,
and a grassy plain out of the mighty flood.
8 Over this crossed the whole nation sheltered by your hand,
after they beheld stupendous wonders.
9* For they ranged about like horses,
and bounded about like lambs,
praising you, O LORD! their deliverer.
10* For they were still mindful of what had happened in their sojourn:
how instead of the young of animals the land brought forth gnats,
and instead of fishes the river swarmed with countless frogs.
11* And later they saw also a new kind of bird
when, prompted by desire, they asked for pleasant foods;
12 For to appease them quail came to them from the sea.
13*†And the punishments came upon the sinners
only after forewarnings from the violence of the thunderbolts.
For they justly suffered for their own misdeeds,
since indeed they treated their guests with the more grievous hatred.
14* For those others did not receive unfamiliar visitors,
but these were enslaving beneficent guests.

WISDOM

21: Nm 16, 7ff.
22: 12, 21; Ex 32, 12f; Ps 20, 8.
23: Nm 14, 29f.
24: Ex 28, 15-21.31-38; Sir 45, 8-12; 50, 11.
25: 1 Chr 21, 15.
19, 1: Ex 14, 4.
2: Ex 12, 33; 14,5.8.
3: 18, 10.12; Ex 12, 30ff.
6: 5, 17; 16, 24.
7: Ex 14, 21-29.
9: 10, 20; 16, 8; Ex 15, 1-18; Ps 114, 4-6.
10: Ex 7, 27ff; 8, 12-15; Ps 105, 30f.
11f: 16, 2; Ps 78, 18.
13: 2 Mc 7, 18.32.
14f: Gn 15, 13; Ex 2, 22.

18, 21: *Blameless man:* Aaron, acting according to his office of high priest and intercessor.
18, 22: *Smiter:* the destroying angel; cf v 25.
18, 24: *Glories . . . grandeur:* the name of God and the names of the tribes were inscribed on the high priest's apparel.
19, 1: *He:* i.e., God.
19, 2: *Them:* the Hebrews.
19, 3: *They:* the Egyptians.
19, 5: *Glorious:* more precisely, "wondrous," but the word reflects *glorified* in 18, 8 and 19, 22.
19, 13: *More grievous:* than that of the people of Sodom; cf Gn 19.

15† And not that only; but what punishment was to be theirs
since they received strangers unwillingly!
16* Yet these, after welcoming them with festivities,
oppressed with awful toils
those who now shared with them the same rights.
17* And they were struck with blindness,
as those others had been at the portals of the just—
When, surrounded by yawning darkness,
each sought the entrance of his own gate.
18 For the elements, in variable harmony among themselves,
like strings of the harp, produce new melody,
while the flow of music steadily persists.
And this can be perceived exactly from a review of what took place.
19 For land creatures were changed into water creatures,
and those that swam went over on to the land.
20* Fire in water maintained its own strength,
and water forgot its quenching nature;
21 Flames, by contrast, neither consumed the flesh
of the perishable animals that went about in them,
nor melted the icelike, quick-melting kind of ambrosial food.
22* For every way, O LORD! you magnified and glorified your people;
unfailing, you stood by them in every time and circumstance.

*

16: Gn 45, 17-20; 47, 4ff; Ex 1, 11.
17: 17, 2; Gn 19, 11.
20f: 16, 17ff. 22f. 27.
22: 18, 8; Lv 26, 44; Ps 126, 3.

†

19, 15: *Theirs:* the people of Sodom.

The Book of

SIRACH

(Ecclesiasticus)

The Book of Sirach derives its name from the author, Jesus, son of Eleazar, son of Sirach *(50, 27). Its earliest title seems to have been "Wisdom of the Son of Sirach." The designation "Liber Ecclesiasticus," meaning "Church Book," appended to some Greek and Latin manuscripts was due to the extensive use which the church made of this book in presenting moral teaching to catechumens and to the faithful.*

The author, a sage who lived in Jerusalem, was thoroughly imbued with love for the law, the priesthood, the temple, and divine worship. As a wise and experienced observer of life he addressed himself to his contemporaries with the motive of helping them to maintain religious faith and integrity through study of the holy books, and through tradition.

The book contains numerous maxims formulated with care, grouped by affinity, and dealing with a variety of subjects such as the individual, the family, and the community in their relations with one another and with God. It treats of friendship, education, poverty and wealth, the law, religious worship, and many other matters which reflect the religious and social customs of the time.

Written in Hebrew between 200 and 175 B.C., the text was translated into Greek sometime after 132 B.C. by the author's grandson, who also wrote a Foreword which contains information about the book, the author, and the translator himself. Until the close of the nineteenth century Sirach was known only in translations, of which this Greek rendering was the most important. From it the Latin version was made. Between 1896 and 1900, again in 1931, and several times since 1956, manuscripts were discovered containing in all about two thirds of the Hebrew text, which agrees substantially with the Greek. One such text, from Masada, is pre-Christian in date.

Though not included in the Hebrew Bible after the first century A.D., nor accepted by Protestants, the Book of Sirach has always been recognized by the Catholic Church as divinely inspired and canonical. The Foreword, though not inspired, is placed in the Bible because of its antiquity and importance.

The contents of Sirach are of a discursive nature, not easily divided into separate parts. Chapters 1—43 deal largely with moral instruction; chapters 44, 1—50, 24 contain a eulogy of the heroes of Israel and some of the patriarchs. There are two appendices in which the author expresses his gratitude to God, and appeals to the unlearned to acquire true wisdom.

The Church uses the Book of Sirach extensively in her liturgy.

Foreword

Many important truths have been handed down to us through the law, the prophets, and the later authors; and for these the instruction and wisdom of Israel merit praise. Now, those who are familiar with these truths must not only understand them themselves but, as lovers of wisdom, be able, in speech and in writing, to help others less familiar. Such a one was my grandfather, Jesus, who, having devoted himself for a long time to the diligent study of the law, the prophets, and the rest of the books† of our ancestors, and having developed a thorough familiarity with them, was moved to write something himself in the nature of instruction and wisdom, in order that those who love wisdom might, by acquainting themselves with what he too had written, make even greater progress in living in conformity with the divine law.

You therefore are now invited to read it in a spirit of attentive good will, with indulgence for any apparent failure on our part, despite earnest efforts, in the interpretation of particular passages. For words spoken originally in Hebrew are not as effective when they are translated into another language. That is true not only of this book but of the law itself, the prophets and the rest of the books, which differ no little when they are read in the original.

† *The law, the prophets, and the rest of the books:* the Sacred Scriptures of the Old Testament written before the time of Sirach, according to the threefold division of the present Hebrew Bible.

I arrived in Egypt in the thirty-eighth year of the reign of King Euergetes,†and while there, I found a reproduction of our valuable teaching.† I therefore considered myself in duty bound to devote some diligence and industry to the translation of this book. Many sleepless hours of close application have I devoted in the interval to finishing the book for publication, for the benefit of those living abroad who wish to acquire wisdom and are disposed to live their lives according to the standards of the law.

The Wisdom of Sirach

CHAPTER 1

Praise of Wisdom†

1*† All wisdom comes from the LORD
and with him it remains forever.
2 The sand of the seashore, the drops of rain,
the days of eternity: who can number these?
3 Heaven's height, earth's breadth,
the depths of the abyss: who can explore these?
4 Before all things else wisdom was created;
and prudent understanding, from eternity.
5* To whom has wisdom's root been revealed?
Who knows her subtleties?
6 There is but one, wise and truly awe-inspiring,
seated upon his throne:
7* It is the LORD; he created her,
has seen her and taken note of her.
8 He has poured her forth upon all his works,
upon every living thing according to his bounty;
he has lavished her upon his friends.

9† Fear of the LORD is glory and splendor,
gladness and a festive crown.
10 Fear of the LORD warms the heart,
giving gladness and joy and length of days.
11 He who fears the LORD will have a happy end;
even on the day of his death he will be blessed.
12* The beginning of wisdom is fear of the LORD,
which is formed with the faithful in the womb.
13 With devoted men was she created from of old,
and with their children her beneficence abides.
14* Fullness of wisdom is fear of the LORD;
she inebriates men with her fruits.
15 Her entire house she fills with choice foods,
her granaries with her harvest.
16* Wisdom's garland is fear of the LORD,
with blossoms of peace and perfect health.
17 Knowledge and full understanding she showers down;
she heightens the glory of those who possess her.
18 The root of wisdom is fear of the LORD;
her branches are length of days.

19† One cannot justify unjust anger;
anger plunges a man to his downfall.
20 A patient man need stand firm but for a time,
and then contentment comes back to him.
21 For a while he holds back his words,
then the lips of many herald his wisdom.
22 Among wisdom's treasures is the paragon of prudence;
but fear of the LORD is an abomination to the sinner.
23 If you desire wisdom, keep the commandments,
and the LORD will bestow her upon you;
24 For fear of the LORD is wisdom and culture;
loyal humility is his delight.
25† Be not faithless to the fear of the LORD,

*

1, 1: 1 Kgs 3, 9.
5: Bar 3, 15.
7: Jb 28, 27.
12: Jb 28, 28; Ps 111, 10; Prv 1, 7; 9, 10.
14: Eccl 12, 13.
16: 21, 11.

†

Thirty-eighth . . . Euergetes: 132 B.C. The reference is to Ptolemy VII, Physkon Euergetes II (170–163; 145–117 B.C.).

Reproduction . . . teaching: may refer to the Septuagint (Greek) translation of Hebrew wisdom writings predating Sirach.

1, 1-8: The Lord is the source and preserver of wisdom (1); he created her from eternity, *before all things else* (4-7); all his works reflect wisdom (2f.8).

1,1: *Wisdom:* here the author speaks of true wisdom, namely God's external revelation of himself. Throughout the book he describes in great detail just what wisdom is; sometimes it is divine; sometimes it is a synonym for God's law; sometimes it is human. But the author makes clear that even human wisdom, properly understood, comes from God.

1, 9-18: Here are described the spiritual and temporal blessings that come during the lifetime of him who fears the Lord, i.e., practices true religion.

1,9: *Fear of the Lord:* see note on Ps 111, 10.

1, 19-22: The disciple of wisdom shuns *unjust anger* which brings *downfall.* By patience and self-control he preserves calm, recovers *contentment,* and receives public praise. The sinner, on the contrary, despises the restraints which religion imposes.

1, 25-29: Infidelity to religion, or the use of it for any but the single purpose of serving God, is hypocrisy and self-exaltation, deserving of public disgrace.

nor approach it with duplicity of heart.
26 Play not the hypocrite before men;
over your lips keep watch.
27 Exalt not yourself lest you fall
and bring upon you dishonor;
28 For then the LORD will reveal your secrets
and publicly cast you down,
29 Because you approached the fear of the LORD
with your heart full of guile.

CHAPTER 2

Duties toward God

1*† My son, when you come to serve the LORD,
prepare yourself for trials.
2 Be sincere of heart and steadfast,
undisturbed in time of adversity.
3 Cling to him, forsake him not;
thus will your future be great.
4 Accept whatever befalls you,
in crushing misfortune be patient;
5* For in fire gold is tested,
and worthy men in the crucible of humiliation.
6 Trust God and he will help you;
make straight your ways and hope in him.

7 You who fear the LORD, wait for his mercy,
turn not away lest you fall.
8 You who fear the LORD, trust him,
and your reward will not be lost.
9 You who fear the LORD, hope for good things,
for lasting joy and mercy.
10* Study the generations long past and understand;
has anyone hoped in the LORD and been disappointed?
Has anyone persevered in his fear and been forsaken?
has anyone called upon him and been rebuffed?
11 Compassionate and merciful is the LORD;
he forgives sins, he saves in time of trouble.

12† Woe to craven hearts and drooping hands,
to the sinner who treads a double path!
13 Woe to the faint of heart who trust not,
who therefore will have no shelter!
14 Woe to you who have lost hope!
what will you do at the visitation of the LORD?
15* Those who fear the LORD disobey not his words;
those who love him keep his ways.
16 Those who fear the LORD seek to please him,
those who love him are filled with his law.
17 Those who fear the LORD prepare their hearts
and humble themselves before him.
18* Let us fall into the hands of the LORD
and not into the hands of men,
For equal to his majesty
is the mercy that he shows.

CHAPTER 3

Duties toward Parents†

1 Children, pay heed to a father's right;
do so that you may live.
2 For the LORD sets a father in honor over his children;
a mother's authority he confirms over her sons.
3 He who honors his father atones for sins;
4 he stores up riches who reveres his mother.
5 He who honors his father is gladdened by children,
and when he prays he is heard.
6 He who reveres his father will live a long life;
he obeys the LORD who brings comfort to his mother.
7 He who fears the LORD honors his father,
and serves his parents as rulers.
8* In word and deed honor your father
that his blessing may come upon you;
9* For a father's blessing gives a family firm roots,
but a mother's curse uproots the growing plant.

*

2, 1: 2 Tm 3, 12.
5: Prv 17, 3; Wis 3, 6; 1 Pt 1, 7.
10: Pss 31, 2; 145, 18f.
15: Jn 14, 23.
18: 18, 3.
3, 8: Ex 20, 12; Dt 5, 16; Mt 15, 4; Mk 7, 10; Eph 6, 2.
9: Gn 27, 29; 49, 2-27.

†

2, 1-11: Serving God is not without its trials (1); moreover, it must be done with sincerity, steadfastness and fidelity (2f). Misfortune and humiliation merely purify man and prove his worth (4f). Patience and unwavering trust in God are always rewarded with the benefits of God's mercy and of *lasting joy* (6-11).

2, 12-18: A warning to those who compromise their religion in time of affliction; they fail in courage and trust and therefore have no security (12ff). But those who fear the Lord through obedience, reverence, love and humility find his *mercy equal to his majesty* (15-18).

3, 1-16: Besides the virtues that must characterize our conduct toward God, special duties toward our neighbor are enjoined, such as honor and respect toward parents, with corresponding blessings (1-9). Even to old and infirm parents this respect is due (10-13); through it, the sins of children are pardoned (14f). Failure to render respect is blasphemy and merits a curse from God (16). Cf Ex 20, 12; Eph 6, 2f.

10 Glory not in your father's shame,
for his shame is no glory to you!
11 His father's honor is a man's glory;
disgrace for her children, a mother's shame.
12* My son, take care of your father when he is old;
grieve him not as long as he lives.
13 Even if his mind fail, be considerate with him;
revile him not in the fullness of your strength.
14 For kindness to a father will not be forgotten,
it will serve as a sin offering—it will take lasting root.
15 In time of tribulation it will be recalled to your advantage,
like warmth upon frost it will melt away your sins.
16* A blasphemer is he who despises his father;
accursed of his Creator, he who angers his mother.

Humility†

17 My son, conduct your affairs with humility,
and you will be loved more than a giver of gifts.
18* Humble yourself the more, the greater you are,
and you will find favor with God.
19† For great is the power of God;
by the humble he is glorified.
20* What is too sublime for you, seek not,
into things beyond your strength search not.
21 What is committed to you, attend to;
for what is hidden is not your concern.
22 With what is too much for you meddle not,
when shown things beyond human understanding.
23 Their own opinion has misled many,
and false reasoning unbalanced their judgment.
24 Where the pupil of the eye is missing, there is no light,
and where there is no knowledge, there is no wisdom.

25 A stubborn man will fare badly in the end,
and he who loves danger will perish in it.
26 A stubborn man will be burdened with sorrow;
a sinner will heap sin upon sin.
27* For the affliction of the proud man there is no cure;
he is the offshoot of an evil plant.
28 The mind of a sage appreciates proverbs,
and an attentive ear is the wise man's joy.

Alms for the Poor†

29* Water quenches a flaming fire,
and alms atone for sins.
30 He who does a kindness is remembered afterward;
when he falls, he finds a support.

CHAPTER 4

1*† My son, rob not the poor man of his livelihood;
force not the eyes of the needy to turn away.
2 A hungry man grieve not,
a needy man anger not;
3 Do not exasperate the downtrodden;
delay not to give to the needy.
4 A beggar in distress do not reject;
avert not your face from the poor.
5 From the needy turn not your eyes,
give no man reason to curse you;
6 For if in the bitterness of his soul he curse you,
his Creator will hear his prayer.
7 Endear yourself to the assembly;
before a ruler bow your head.
8 Give a hearing to the poor man,
and return his greeting with courtesy;
9 Deliver the oppressed from the hand of the oppressor;
let not justice be repugnant to you.
10 To the fatherless be as a father,
and help their mother as a husband would;
Thus will you be like a son to the Most High,
and he will be more tender to you than a mother.

The Rewards of Wisdom†

11 Wisdom instructs her children
and admonishes those who seek her.

*

12: Prv 23, 22.
16: Prv 19, 26; 30, 11.14.17.
18: Mt 23, 12.
20: Ps 131, 1.
27: Dt 32, 32; Wis 12, 10.
29: Dn 4, 27.
4, 1: Tb 4, 7-11.

†

3, 17-27: Humility gives a true estimate of self (17ff). Through it a man performs duty, avoids what is beyond his understanding and strength (20ff). Pride, however, begets false greatness, misjudgment, stubbornness, sorrow, affliction and perdition (23-27).

3, 19: An alternate or additional line would read: "For though many have been great in the course of time, it is to the humble he reveals his secrets." Cf Mt 11, 25f; 1 Cor 1, 26-29.

3, 29—4, 10: Mercy and kindness toward those in misfortune atone for sin and endear a man to God and to his fellow men.

4, 1: *Eyes of the needy:* when they look for help; cf 18, 17.

4, 11-19: The Hebrew text presents wisdom speaking in the first person, as in ch 24. The precious fruits of wisdom: life, favor, glory, blessings, God's love, are intended to arouse desire for her (11-14). Her disciples are like priests (14) and judges (15), even partners who possess her for themselves and their descendants (16). They enjoy happiness and penetrate her profound secrets after surviving her tests (17f). Those who fail her are abandoned to destruction (19).

12 He who loves her loves life;
those who seek her out win her favor.
13 He who holds her fast inherits glory;
wherever he dwells, the LORD bestows blessings.
14* Those who serve her serve the Holy One;
those who love her the LORD loves.
15 He who obeys her judges nations;
he who hearkens to her dwells in her inmost chambers.
16 If one trusts her, he will possess her;
his descendants too will inherit her.
17 She walks with him as a stranger,
and at first she puts him to the test;
Fear and dread she brings upon him
and tries him with her discipline;
With her precepts she puts him to the proof,
until his heart is fully with her.
18 Then she comes back to bring him happiness
and reveal her secrets to him.
19 But if he fails her, she will abandon him
and deliver him into the hands of despoilers.

Sincerity and Justice†

20 Use your time well; guard yourself from evil,
and bring upon yourself no shame.
21 There is a sense of shame laden with guilt,
and a shame that merits honor and respect.
22 Show no favoritism to your own discredit;
let no one intimidate you to your own downfall.
23 Refrain not from speaking at the proper time,
and hide not away your wisdom;
24 For it is through speech that wisdom becomes known,
and knowledge through the tongue's rejoinder.
25 Never gainsay the truth,
and struggle not against the rushing stream.
26 Be not ashamed to acknowledge your guilt,
but of your ignorance rather be ashamed.
27 Do not abase yourself before an impious man,
nor refuse to do so before rulers.
28 Even to the death fight for truth,
and the LORD your God will battle for you.
29 Be not surly in your speech,
nor lazy and slack in your deeds.
30 Be not a lion at home,
nor sly and suspicious at work.
31 Let not your hand be open to receive
and clenched when it is time to give.

CHAPTER 5

Against Presumption†

1* Rely not on your wealth;
say not: "I have the power."
2 Rely not on your strength
in following the desires of your heart.
3 Say not: "Who can prevail against me?"
for the LORD will exact the punishment.
4 Say not: "I have sinned, yet what has befallen me?"
for the LORD bides his time.
5 Of forgiveness be not overconfident,
adding sin upon sin.
6 Say not: "Great is his mercy;
my many sins he will forgive."
7 For mercy and anger alike are with him;
upon the wicked alights his wrath.
8 Delay not your conversion to the LORD,
put it not off from day to day;
9 For suddenly his wrath flames forth;
at the time of vengeance, you will be destroyed.
10* Rely not upon deceitful wealth,
for it will be no help on the day of wrath.

Sincerity in Speech

11† Winnow not in every wind,
and start not off in every direction.
12† Be consistent in your thoughts;
steadfast be your words.
13* Be swift to hear,
but slow to answer.
14 If you have the knowledge, answer your neighbor;

SIRACH

*

14: Wis 7, 28.
5, 1: Lk 12, 19.
10: Prv 10, 2; 11, 4.
28.
13: Prv 29, 20; Jas 1, 19.

†

4, 20-31: Besides the interior trials of discipline and precept, the disciple of wisdom is warned against external dangers to his sincerity and justice, namely evil, human respect (20f), compromise of liberty in speech and action (22-25), false shame, and ignorance (26). He must fight for the truth (28), and avoid cynicism and laziness (29), and inconsistency in his conduct (30).

5, 1-10: The vices of the rich are pride and independence (1f), presumption (3), false security (4-7), and impenitence (8), which cannot escape the divine wrath (9f). Cf Prv 18, 23; 19, 1; 28, 6.

5, 11: A proverbial expression condemning inconstancy and advocating sincerity and honesty.

5, 12—6, 1: Proper use of the tongue requires constancy in speech (5, 12), prudence (13f), reserve (15), charity (6, 1), as well as the avoidance of detraction, *calumny* (16), and double talk, which bring shame and disgrace (5, 17; 6, 1).

if not, put your hand over your mouth.
15 Honor and dishonor through talking!
A man's tongue can be his downfall.
16 Be not called a detractor;
use not your tongue for calumny;
17 For shame has been created for the thief,
and the reproach of his neighbor for the double-tongued.

CHAPTER 6

1† Say nothing harmful, small or great;
be not a foe instead of a friend;
A bad name and disgrace will you acquire:
"That for the evil man with double tongue!"

2* Fall not into the grip of desire,
lest, like fire, it consume your strength;
3 Your leaves it will eat, your fruits destroy,
and you will be left a dry tree,
4 For contumacious desire destroys its owner
and makes him the sport of his enemies.

True Friendship†

5 A kind mouth multiplies friends,
and gracious lips prompt friendly greetings.
6 Let your acquaintances be many,
but one in a thousand your confidant.
7* When you gain a friend, first test him,
and be not too ready to trust him
8 For one sort of friend is a friend when it suits him,
but he will not be with you in time of distress.
9 Another is a friend who becomes an enemy,
and tells of the quarrel to your shame.
10 Another is a friend, a boon companion,
who will not be with you when sorrow comes.
11 When things go well, he is your other self,
and lords it over your servants;
12 But if you are brought low, he turns against you
and avoids meeting you.
13 Keep away from your enemies;
be on your guard with your friends.
14 A faithful friend is a sturdy shelter;
he who finds one finds a treasure.
15 A faithful friend is beyond price,
no sum can balance his worth.
16 A faithful friend is a life-saving remedy,
such as he who fears God finds;
17 For he who fears God behaves accordingly,
and his friend will be like himself.

Blessings of Wisdom†

18 My son, from your youth embrace discipline;
thus will you find wisdom with graying hair.
19 As though plowing and sowing, draw close to her;
then await her bountiful crops.
20 For in cultivating her you will labor but little,
and soon you will eat of her fruits.
21 How irksome she is to the unruly!
The fool cannot abide her.
22 She will be like a burdensome stone to test him,
and he will not delay in casting her aside.

23† For discipline is like her name,
she is not accessible to many.
24 Listen, my son, and heed my advice;
refuse not my counsel.
25 Put your feet into her fetters,
and your neck under her yoke.
26 Stoop your shoulders and carry her
and be not irked at her bonds.
27 With all your soul draw close to her;
with all your strength keep her ways.
28 Search her out, discover her; seek her and you will find her.
Then when you have her, do not let her go;
29 Thus will you afterward find rest in her,
and she will become your joy.
30 Her fetters will be your throne of majesty;
her bonds, your purple cord.
31*†You will wear her as your robe of glory,
bear her as your splendid crown.

---

*

6, 2-3: 9, 8; 23, 17; Jb 31, 12; Is 56, 3.
7ff: 12, 8f; 37, 1-5; Prv 19, 4.
31: Is 62, 3.

---

†

6, 1: *"That. . . double tongue!"*: people will say this against the man whose deceitful tongue has brought him to disgrace.

6, 5-17: True friends are discerned not by prosperity (11), but through the trials of adversity: distress, quarrels (9), sorrow (10) and misfortune (12). Such friends are rare and their value is beyond estimation, a gift from God (14-17).

6, 18-37: The various figures in each of the three strophes urge the search for wisdom through patience (19-23), docility (32-37), and perseverance in trials (25ff), promising rich rewards (28-31). Cf 4, 11-19.

6, 23: *Discipline* (*musar*, in the sense of wisdom) is a perfect homonym for *musar*, "removed, withdrawn"; thus the path of *discipline* is inaccessible to many.

6, 31: Some forms of the text speak also of the "yoke" of wisdom under the imagery of golden ornaments.

32 My son, if you wish, you can be taught;
if you apply yourself, you will be shrewd.
33 If you are willing to listen, you will learn;
if you give heed, you will be wise.
34 Frequent the company of the elders;
whoever is wise, stay close to him.
35* Be eager to hear every godly discourse;
let no wise saying escape you.
36 If you see a man of prudence, seek him out;
let your feet wear away his doorstep!
37* Reflect on the precepts of the LORD,
let his commandments be your constant meditation;
Then he will enlighten your mind,
and the wisdom you desire he will grant.

CHAPTER 7

Conduct in Public Life†

1 Do no evil, and evil will not overtake you;
2 avoid wickedness, and it will turn aside from you.
3* Sow not in the furrows of injustice,
lest you harvest it sevenfold.
4 Seek not from the LORD authority,
nor from the king a place of honor.
5* Parade not your justice before the Lord,
and before the king flaunt not your wisdom.
6 Seek not to become a judge
if you have not strength to root out crime,
Or you will show favor to the ruler
and mar your integrity.
7 Be guilty of no evil before the city's populace,
nor disgrace yourself before the assembly.
8 Do not plot to repeat a sin;
not even for one will you go unpunished.
9* Say not: "He will appreciate my many gifts;
the Most High will accept my offerings."
10 Be not impatient in prayers,
and neglect not the giving of alms.
11† Laugh not at an embittered man;
be mindful of him who exalts and humbles.
12 Plot no mischief against your brother,
nor against your friend and companion.
13 Delight not in telling lie after lie,
for it never results in good.
14*† Thrust not yourself into the deliberations of princes,
and repeat not the words of your prayer.
15* Hate not laborious tasks,
nor farming, which was ordained by the Most High.
16 Do not esteem yourself better than your fellows;
remember, his wrath will not delay.
17* More and more, humble your pride;
what awaits man is worms.

Duties of Family Life, Religion and Charity†

18† Barter not a friend for money,
nor a dear brother for the gold of Ophir.
19 Dismiss not a sensible wife;
a gracious wife is more precious than corals.
20* Mistreat not a servant who faithfully serves,
nor a laborer who devotes himself to his task.
21† Let a wise servant be dear to you as your own self;
refuse him not his freedom.
22 If you have livestock, look after them;
if they are dependable, keep them.
23*† If you have sons, chastise them;
bend their necks from childhood.
24* If you have daughters, keep them chaste,
and be not indulgent to them.
25* Giving your daughter in marriage ends a great task;
but give her to a worthy man.

*

35: 8, 9.
37: Ps 1, 2.
7, 3: Prv 22, 8.
5: Jb 9, 2; Ps 143, 2; Prv 25, 6; 1 Cor 4, 4.
9: 34, 18; 35, 12.
14: 32, 7ff; Mt 6, 7.
15: Gn 2, 15; 3, 17.
17: Is 66, 24.
20: Lv 19, 13; Dt 24, 14f; Jas 5, 4.
23: 30, 8-13; Prv 13, 24.
24: 42, 9ff.
25: 1 Cor 7, 36ff.

†

7, 1-17: In the conduct of social relations wisdom forbids *evil* and *injustice* (1ff), pride (5.15ff), ambition and human respect (4.6), public disorder (7), presumption and impatience toward God (9f), ridicule (11), *mischief* and deceit toward one's neighbor (8. 12f).

7, 11: *Him who exalts and humbles:* God; cf 1 Sm 2, 7; Ps 75, 8; Lk 1, 52.

7, 14: *Repeat not . . . prayer:* brevity of speech in dealings with superiors and more especially with God is a sign of reverence and respect; cf Eccl 5, 1; Mt 6, 7.

7, 18-36: The duties of respect and appreciation, justice and kindness should characterize relations toward members of the household (18-28), and also toward God and his priests (29ff), the poor and afflicted, the living and the dead (32-36).

7, 18: *Ophir* was the port, at present unidentified, to which the ships of Solomon sailed and from which they brought back gold and silver; cf note on Ps 44 (45), 10.

7, 21: After six years of service a Hebrew slave was entitled to freedom, cf Ex 21, 2; Dt 15, 12-15.

7, 23: *Bend their necks:* keep them from rebellious pride; so with the Greek. Cf 30, 12. The present Hebrew text, which is probably not original here, reads: "Choose wives for them while they are young."

26 If you have a wife, let her not seem odious to you;
but where there is ill-feeling, trust her not.
27* With your whole heart honor your father;
your mother's birthpangs forget not.
28 Remember, of these parents you were born;
what can you give them for all they gave you?
29 With all your soul, fear God,
revere his priests.
30 With all your strength, love your Creator,
forsake not his ministers.
31*† Honor God and respect the priest;
give him his portion as you have been commanded:
First fruits and contributions,
due sacrifices and holy offerings.
32 To the poor man also extend your hand,
that your blessing may be complete;
33† Be generous to all the living,
and withhold not your kindness from the dead.
34* Avoid not those who weep,
but mourn with those who mourn;
35* Neglect not to visit the sick—
for these things you will be loved.
36 In whatever you do, remember your last days,
and you will never sin.

CHAPTER 8

Prudence in Dealing with Other Men†

1 Contend not with an influential man,
lest you fall into his power.
2* Quarrel not with a rich man,
lest he pay out the price of your downfall;
For gold has dazzled many,
and perverts the character of princes.
3* Dispute not with a man of railing speech,
heap no wood upon his fire.
4 Be not too familiar with an unruly man,
lest he speak ill of your forebears.
5*† Shame not a repentant sinner;
remember, we all are guilty.
6 Insult no man when he is old,
for some of us, too, will grow old.
7 Rejoice not when a man dies;
remember, we are all to die.
8* Spurn not the discourse of the wise,
but acquaint yourself with their proverbs;
From them you will acquire the training
to serve in the presence of princes.
9 Reject not the tradition of old men
which they have learned from their fathers;
From it you will obtain the knowledge
how to answer in time of need.
10 Kindle not the coals of a sinner,
lest you be consumed in his flaming fire.
11† Let not the impious man intimidate you;
it will set him in ambush against you.
12* Lend not to one more powerful than yourself;
and whatever you lend, count it as lost.
13 Go not surety beyond your means;
think any pledge a debt you must pay.
14 Contend not at law with a judge,
for he will settle it according to his whim.
15 Travel not with a ruthless man,
lest he weigh you down with calamity;
For he will go his own way straight,
and through his folly you will perish with him.
16 Provoke no quarrel with a quick-tempered man,
nor ride with him through the desert,
For bloodshed is nothing to him;
when there is no one to help you,
he will destroy you.
17 Take no counsel with a fool,
for he can keep nothing to himself.
18* Before a stranger do nothing that should be kept secret,
for you know not what it will engender.
19 Open your heart to no man,
and banish not your happiness.

*

27: Ex 20, 12.
31: Lv 7, 31; Nm 18, 18.
34: Rom 12, 15.
35: Mt 25, 36.
8, 2: 31, 6; Dt 16, 19.
3: Prv 26, 20.
5: 1 Kgs 8, 46; 1 Jn 1, 8.
8f: 6, 35.
12: 29, 4-7; Prv 17, 18.
18: Prv 25, 9f.

†

7, 31: *First fruits . . . holy offerings:* cf Ex 29, 27; Lv 7, 31-34; Nm 18, 8-20; Dt 18, 1-5.

7, 33: This seems to refer to the observances ordained toward the dead, that is, proper mourning and burial. Cf 2 Sm 21, 12ff; Tb 1, 20; 12, 12. When this verse is read in the light of later teaching, prayers for the souls of the deceased would also be recommended. Cf 2 Mc 12, 43ff.

8, 1-19: A prudent man will be circumspect, avoiding conflict with the powerful, the rich and insolent, the impious, the irascible, and with judges (1ff.10ff.14.16). He will seek friendship not with the undisciplined (4.12f) and the ruthless (15), nor with fools and strangers (17ff), but with the wise and the ancients of the people (8f).

8, 5: *We all are guilty:* cf 1 Kgs 8, 46; 2 Chr 6, 36; Eccl 7, 20; Rom 3, 9f; 1 Jn 1, 8.

8, 11: To give in to the wicked in one instance becomes an occasion of sin for the future.

CHAPTER 9

Advice concerning Women†

1 Be not jealous of the wife of your bosom,
lest you teach her to do evil against you.
2* Give no woman power over you
to trample upon your dignity.
3 Be not intimate with a strange woman,
lest you fall into her snares.
4 With a singing girl be not familiar,
lest you be caught in her wiles.
5† Entertain no thoughts against a virgin,
lest you be enmeshed in damages for her.
6* Give not yourself to harlots,
lest you surrender your inheritance.
7 Gaze not about the lanes of the city
and wander not through its squares;
8* Avert your eyes from a comely woman;
gaze not upon the beauty of another's wife—
Through woman's beauty many perish,
for lust for it burns like fire.
9 With a married woman dine not,
recline not at table to drink by her side,
Lest your heart be drawn to her
and you go down in blood to the grave.

Choice of Friends†

10 Discard not an old friend,
for the new one cannot equal him.
A new friend is like new wine
which you drink with pleasure only when it has aged.
11 Envy not a sinner's fame,
for you know not what disaster awaits him.
12 Rejoice not at a proud man's success;
remember he will not reach death unpunished.
13 Keep far from the man who has power to kill,
and you will not be filled with the dread of death.
But if you approach him, offend him not,
lest he take away your life;
Know that you are stepping among snares
and walking over a net.
14 As best you can, take your neighbors' measure,
and associate with the wise.
15 With the learned be intimate;
let all your conversation be about the law of the LORD.
16 Have just men for your table companions;
in the fear of God be your glory.

Concerning Rulers†

17 Skilled artisans are esteemed for their deftness;
but the ruler of his people is the skilled sage.
18 Feared in the city is the man of railing speech,
and he who talks rashly is hated.

CHAPTER 10

1* A wise magistrate lends stability to his people,
and the government of a prudent man is well ordered.
2* As the people's judge, so are his ministers;
as the head of a city, its inhabitants.
3* A wanton king destroys his people,
but a city grows through the wisdom of its princes.
4 Sovereignty over the earth is in the hand of God,
who raises up on it the man of the hour;
5 Sovereignty over every man is in the hand of God,
who imparts his majesty to the ruler.

The Sin of Pride†

6* No matter the wrong, do no violence to your neighbor,
and do not walk the path of arrogance.

SIRACH

*

9, 2: 25, 21.
6: Prv 5, 3-11; 6, 24; 29, 3.
8: 25, 20; 41, 21.
10, 1: Wis 6, 24.
2f: Prv 29, 12.
3: Prv 29, 4.8.
6: Lv 19, 18.

†

9, 1-9: Prudence and reserve in dealing with women are the best defense of morality. To preserve the liberty and dignity of his person and the integrity of his possessions, a man must avoid jealousy toward his own wife and familiarity toward all other women. Cf 25, 12—26, 18.

9, 1: Unjust suspicions often engender hatred between husband and wife and may prompt a wife to commit those faults *of* which heretofore she had been innocent.

9, 5: Cf Ex 22, 15f: Dt 22, 28f; Jb 31, 1.

9, 10-16: In social relations, adherence to *the law of the Lord* should serve as a guide (15). Associate with true friends (10), with the just and the learned (14ff); avoid the company of the mighty and of sinners doomed to punishment (11ff). Cf 8, 1-19.

9, 17—10, 5: Public office as conducted justly or unjustly benefits or destroys the people, according to the axiom, "as the prince, so the people." Cf Is 24, 2. God, however, has sovereignty over both.

10, 6-18: Glory displayed through arrogance and pride is false and displeasing to God and men, because founded on *dust and ashes* (6-11). It is the denial of the glory due to God, and therefore the source of all sin (12f). Even the memory of the proud is destroyed and God transfers their power to the lowly (14-18).

7 Odious to the LORD and to men is arrogance,
and the sin of oppression they both hate.
8 Dominion is transferred from one people to another
because of the violence of the arrogant.
9† Why are dust and ashes proud?
even during life man's body decays;
10 A slight illness—the doctor jests,
a king today—tomorrow he is dead.
11* When a man dies, he inherits corruption;
worms and gnats and maggots.
12 The beginning of pride is man's stubbornness
in withdrawing his heart from his Maker;
13* For pride is the reservoir of sin,
a source which runs over with vice;
Because of it God sends unheard-of afflictions
and brings men to utter ruin.
14 The thrones of the arrogant God overturns
and establishes the lowly in their stead.
15 The roots of the proud God plucks up,
to plant the humble in their place:
16 He breaks down their stem to the level of the ground,
then digs their roots from the earth.
17 The traces of the proud God sweeps away
and effaces the memory of them from the earth.
18 Insolence is not allotted to a man,
nor stubborn anger to one born of woman.

True Glory†

19 Whose offspring can be in honor?
Those of men.
Which offspring are in honor?
Those who fear God.
Whose offspring can be in disgrace?
Those of men.
Which offspring are in disgrace?
Those who transgress the commandments.
20 Among brethren their leader is in honor;
he who fears God is in honor among his people.
21 Be it tenant or wayfarer, alien or pauper,
his glory is the fear of the LORD.
22* It is not just to despise a man who is wise but poor,
nor proper to honor any sinner.
23 The prince, the ruler, the judge are in honor;
but none is greater than he who fears God.
24* When free men serve a prudent slave,
the wise man does not complain.
25 Flaunt not your wisdom in managing your affairs,
and boast not in your time of need.
26* Better the worker who has plenty of everything
than the boaster who is without bread.

27 My son, with humility have self-esteem;
prize yourself as you deserve.
28 Who will acquit him who condemns himself?
who will honor him who discredits himself?
29 The poor man is honored for his wisdom
as the rich man is honored for his wealth;
30 Honored in poverty, how much more so in wealth!
Dishonored in wealth, in poverty how much the more!

CHAPTER 11

1 The poor man's wisdom lifts his head high
and sets him among princes.
2 Praise not a man for his looks;
despise not a man for his appearance.
3 Least is the bee among winged things,
but she reaps the choicest of all harvests.
4 Mock not the worn cloak
and jibe at no man's bitter day:
For strange are the works of the LORD,
hidden from men his deeds.
5† The oppressed often rise to a throne,
and some that none would consider wear a crown.
6 The exalted often fall into utter disgrace;
the honored are given into enemy hands.

*

11: Jb 17, 14.
13: Prv 18, 12.
22: Jas 2, 1-4.
24: Prv 17, 2.
26: Prv 12, 9.

†

10, 9f: The text is uncertain. Its general implication is that man deteriorates physically even while alive: a slight illness today may be followed by death tomorrow. The uncertainty of life leaves no room for pride.

10, 19—11, 6: Regardless of social barriers, genuine honor among men comes from fear of the Lord and a true estimate of self. The Lord exalts the lowly and oppressed; transgressors of the *commandments* merit dishonor and disgrace.

11, 5: Cf 1 Sm 2, 8; Ps 105, 17-22; Lk 1, 52.

Moderation†

7 Before investigating, find no fault;
examine first, then criticize.
8* Before hearing, answer not,
and interrupt no one in the middle of his speech.
9 Dispute not about what is not your concern;
in the strife of the arrogant take no part.

10 My son, why increase your cares,
since he who is avid for wealth will not be blameless?
Even if you run after it, you will never overtake it;
however you seek it, you will not find it.
11* One may toil and struggle and drive,
and fall short all the more.
12 Another goes his way a weakling and a failure,
with little strength and great misery—
Yet the eyes of the LORD look favorably upon him;
he raises him free of the vile dust,
13 Lifts up his head and exalts him
to the amazement of the many.
14*†Good and evil, life and death,
poverty and riches, are from the LORD.
15† Wisdom and understanding and knowledge of affairs,
love and virtuous paths are from the LORD.
16 Error and darkness were formed with sinners from their birth,
and evil grows old with evildoers.
17 The LORD's gift remains with the just;
his favor brings continued success.
18 A man may become rich through a miser's life,
and this is his allotted reward:
19*†When he says: "I have found rest,
now I will feast on my possessions,"
He does not know how long it will be
till he dies and leaves them to others.

20 My son, hold fast to your duty, busy yourself with it,
grow old while doing your task.
21 Admire not how sinners live,
but trust in the LORD and wait for his light;
For it is easy with the LORD
suddenly, in an instant, to make a poor man rich.
22 God's blessing is the lot of the just man,
and in due time his hopes bear fruit.
23 Say not: "What do I need?
What further pleasure can be mine?"
24 Say not: "I am independent.
What harm can come to me now?"
25* The day of prosperity makes one forget adversity;
the day of adversity makes one forget prosperity.
26† For it is easy with the LORD on the day of death
to repay man according to his deeds.
27 A moment's affliction brings forgetfulness of past delights;
when a man dies, his life is revealed.
28 Call no man happy before his death,
for by how he ends, a man is known.

Care in Choosing Friends

29 Bring not every man into your house,
for many are the snares of the crafty one;
30 Though he seem like a bird confined in a cage,
yet like a spy he will pick out the weak spots.
31 The talebearer turns good into evil;
with a spark he sets many coals afire.
32 The evil man lies in wait for blood,
and plots against your choicest possessions.
33 Avoid a wicked man, for he breeds only evil,
lest you incur a lasting stain.
34 Lodge a stranger with you, and he will subvert your course,
and make a stranger of you to your own household.

SIRACH

CHAPTER 12

1† If you do good, know for whom you are doing it,
and your kindness will have its effect.

*

11, 8: Prv 18, 13.
11: Ps 127, 2; Eccl 4, 8.
14: Jb 1, 21; 2, 10.
19: Eccl 4, 8; 6, 2; Lk 12, 19.
25: 18, 25.

†

11, 7-25: Discretion regulates a man's conduct toward others and their affairs (7ff); as regards his own interests, a man should avoid solicitude for the passing external benefits of life and property (10-14.18f.21.23ff), and cultivate the lasting inward gifts of wisdom and virtue (15.17.20.22).

11, 14: Divine Providence ultimately governs the lives of men. *Evil:* misfortune and calamity sent by God either in punishment or as an incentive to repentance or to greater virtue.

11, 15f: Some ancient witnesses omit these two verses.

11, 19: Cf the parable of the rich man, Lk 12, 16-21.

11, 26ff: Sirach, writing before Christian revelation, did not go beyond the hour of death to find full divine retribution.

12, 1-7: The limitations to the practice of charity here reflected were removed by Christ, who requires that good be done even to enemies and to those who hate, persecute and calumniate us (Mt 5, 43-48).

2 Do good to the just man and reward will be yours,
if not from him, from the LORD.
3† No good comes to him who gives comfort to the wicked,
nor is it an act of mercy that he does.
4* Give to the good man, refuse the sinner;
refresh the downtrodden, give nothing to the proud man.
5 No arms for combat should you give him,
lest he use them against yourself;
6 With twofold evil you will meet
for every good deed you do for him.
7 The Most High himself hates sinners,
and upon the wicked he takes vengeance.

8*† In our prosperity we cannot know our friends;
in adversity an enemy will not remain concealed.
9* When a man is successful even his enemy is friendly;
in adversity even his friend disappears.
10 Never trust your enemy,
for his wickedness is like corrosion in bronze.
11† Even though he acts humbly and peaceably toward you,
take care to be on your guard against him.
Rub him as one polishes a brazen mirror,
and you will find that there is still corrosion.
12 Let him not stand near you,
lest he oust you and take your place.
Let him not sit at your right hand,
lest he then demand your seat,
And in the end you appreciate my advice,
when you groan with regret, as I warned you.
13 Who pities a snake charmer when he is bitten,
or anyone who goes near a wild beast?
14 So is it with the companion of the proud man,
who is involved in his sins:
15 While you stand firm, he makes no bold move;
but if you slip, he cannot hold back.
16 With his lips an enemy speaks sweetly,
but in his heart he schemes to plunge you into the abyss.
Though your enemy has tears in his eyes,
if given the chance, he will never have enough of your blood.
17 If evil comes upon you, you will find him at hand;
feigning to help, he will trip you up,
18 Then he will nod his head and clap his hands
and hiss repeatedly, and show his true face.

CHAPTER 13

Caution Regarding Associates†

1 He who touches pitch blackens his hand;
he who associates with an impious man learns his ways.
2 Bear no burden too heavy for you;
go with no one greater or wealthier than yourself.
How can the earthen pot go with the metal cauldron?
When they knock together, the pot will be smashed:
3 The rich man does wrong and boasts of it,
the poor man is wronged and begs forgiveness.
4 As long as the rich man can use you he will enslave you,
but when you are exhausted, he will abandon you.
5 As long as you have anything he will speak fair words to you,
and with smiles he will win your confidence;
6 When he needs something from you he will cajole you,
then without regret he will impoverish you.
7 While it serves his purpose he will beguile you,
then twice or three times he will terrify you;
When later he sees you he will pass you by,
and shake his head over you.
8 Guard against being presumptuous;
be not as those who lack sense.
9 When invited by a man of influence, keep your distance;
then he will urge you all the more.
10 Be not bold with him lest you be rebuffed,
but keep not too far away lest you be forgotten.

*

12, 4f: Gal 6, 10.
8: Prv 17, 17.
9: Prv 19, 4-7.

†

12, 3ff: The author advises against generosity to those who would abuse it.
12, 8-18: Through adversity friends are distinguished from enemies; to trust the latter or permit them intimacy is to invite disaster. Cf note on 6, 5-17.
12, 11: *Brazen mirror:* see note on Ex 38, 8.
13, 1—14, 2: By means of various figures Sirach indicates the practical impossibility of genuine and sincere companionship between the poor and the proud rich. He lays down the principle of associating with equals (13, 15).

SIRACH

11 Engage not freely in discussion with him,
trust not his many words;
For by prolonged talk he will test you,
and though smiling he will probe you.
12 Mercilessly he will make of you a laughingstock,
and will not refrain from injury or chains.
13 Be on your guard and take care
never to accompany men of violence.

14 Every living thing loves its own kind,
every man a man like himself.
15 Every being is drawn to its own kind;
with his own kind every man associates.
16* Is a wolf ever allied with a lamb?
So it is with the sinner and the just.
17† Can there be peace between the hyena and the dog?
Or between the rich and the poor can there be peace?
18 Lion's prey are the wild asses of the desert;
so too the poor are feeding grounds for the rich.
19 A proud man abhors lowliness;
so does the rich man abhor the poor.
20 When a rich man stumbles he is supported by a friend;
when a poor man trips he is pushed down by a friend.
21 Many are the supporters for a rich man when he speaks;
though what he says is odious, it wins approval.
When a poor man speaks they make sport of him;
he speaks wisely and no attention is paid him.
22 A rich man speaks and all are silent,
his wisdom they extol to the clouds.
A poor man speaks and they say: "Who is that?"
If he slips they cast him down.
23 Wealth is good when there is no sin;
but poverty is evil by the standards of the proud.
24* The heart of a man changes his countenance,
either for good or for evil.
25 The sign of a good heart is a cheerful countenance;
withdrawn and perplexed is the laborious schemer.

CHAPTER 14

1* Happy the man whose mouth brings him no grief,
who is not stung by remorse for sin.
2 Happy the man whose conscience does not reproach him,
who has not lost hope.

The Use of Wealth

3† Wealth ill becomes the mean man;
and to the miser, of what use is gold?
4* What he denies himself he collects for others,
and in his possessions a stranger will revel.
5 To whom will he be generous who is stingy with himself
and does not enjoy what is his own?
6 None is more stingy than he who is stingy with himself;
he punishes his own miserliness.
7 If ever he is generous, it is by mistake;
and in the end he displays his greed.
8 In the miser's opinion his share is too small;
9 he refuses his neighbor and brings ruin on himself.
10 The miser's eye is rapacious for bread,
but on his own table he sets it stale.

11* My son, use freely whatever you have
and enjoy it as best you can;
12 Remember that death does not tarry,
nor have you been told the grave's appointed time.
13* Before you die, be good to your friend,
and give him a share in what you possess.
14 Deprive not yourself of present good things,
let no choice portion escape you.
15 Will you not leave your riches to others,
and your earnings to be divided by lot?
16 Give, take, and treat yourself well,
for in the nether world there are no joys to seek.
17* All flesh grows old, like a garment;

SIRACH

*

13, 16: 2 Cor 6, 14ff.
24: Prv 15, 13.
14, 1: 19, 15; 25, 8; Jas 3, 2.
4: Eccl 6, 2.
11: Prv 3, 9.
13: 4, 1; Tb 4, 7.
17: Ps 103, 14ff; Is 40, 6; Jas 1, 10; 1 Pt 1, 24.

†

13, 17: The hostility between the dogs which guard the flocks at night and the rapacious hyenas is proverbial in Palestine.

14, 3-16: The miser does no good even to himself (3-10); wealth should be wisely used during life, for it must be left behind at death (11-16). In the light of the gospel, generosity has a higher motivation and promise of reward than the Old Testament writer could propose. Cf Mt 6, 19ff; Lk 12, 32ff.

the age-old law is: All must die.
18* As with the leaves that grow on a vigorous tree:
one falls off and another sprouts—
So with the generations of flesh and blood:
one dies and another is born.
19 All man's works will perish in decay,
and his handiwork will follow after him.

The Search for Wisdom and Its Blessings†

20* Happy the man who meditates on wisdom,
and reflects on knowledge;
21 Who ponders her ways in his heart,
and understands her paths;
22 Who pursues her like a scout,
and lies in wait at her entry way;
23 Who peeps through her windows,
and listens at her doors;
24 Who encamps near her house,
and fastens his tent pegs next to her walls;
25 Who pitches his tent beside her,
and lives as her welcome neighbor;
26 Who builds his nest in her leafage,
and lodges in her branches;
27 Who takes shelter with her from the heat,
and dwells in her home.

SIRACH

CHAPTER 15

1 He who fears the LORD will do this;
he who is practiced in the law will come to wisdom.
2 Motherlike she will meet him,
like a young bride she will embrace him,
3* Nourish him with the bread of understanding,
and give him the water of learning to drink.
4 He will lean upon her and not fall,
he will trust in her and not be put to shame.
5 She will exalt him above his fellows;
in the assembly she will make him eloquent.
6* Joy and gladness he will find,
an everlasting name inherit.
7 Worthless men will not attain to her,
haughty men will not behold her.
8 Far from the impious is she,
not to be spoken of by liars.
9 Unseemly is praise on a sinner's lips,
for it is not accorded to him by God.
10 But praise is offered by the wise man's tongue;
its rightful steward will proclaim it.

Man's Free Will

11 Say not: "It was God's doing that I fell away";
for what he hates he does not do.
12* Say not: "It was he who set me astray";
for he has no need of wicked man.
13 Abominable wickedness the LORD hates,
he does not let it befall those who fear him.
14* When God, in the beginning, created man,
he made him subject to his own free choice.
15 If you choose you can keep the commandments;
it is loyalty to do his will.
16 There are set before you fire and water;
to whichever you choose, stretch forth your hand.
17* Before man are life and death,
whichever he chooses shall be given him.
18 Immense is the wisdom of the LORD;
he is mighty in power, and all-seeing.
19* The eyes of God see all he has made;
he understands man's every deed.
20 No man does he command to sin,
to none does he give strength for lies.

CHAPTER 16

God's Punishment of Sinners†

1 Desire not a brood of worthless children,
nor rejoice in wicked offspring.
2 Many though they be, exult not in them
if they have not the fear of the LORD.
3* Count not on their length of life,
have no hope in their future.
For one can be better than a thousand;
rather die childless than have godless children!

---

*

18: Eccl 1, 4.
20: Ps 1, 2.
15, 3: Jn 4, 10; 6, 31ff.
6: 6, 29-32.
12: Jas 1, 13.
14: Gn 1, 27.
17: Dt 30, 15.
19: Pss 33, 18; 34, 16; Heb 4, 13.
16, 3f: Wis 4, 1f.

†

14, 20—15, 20: From his social teaching the sage now turns to consider individual responsibility. Happiness is to be found in the pursuit and possession of wisdom (14, 20—15, 5). Joy and honor are given, not to the sinner (7ff), but to him who fears God and observes his law (1-6.10). The sinner is fully responsible for his conduct because God, who sees all things (18f), is not the author of wickedness (11ff.20): he gives to every man the liberty to choose between good and evil (14-17).

16, 1-21: Sinful offspring are a great misfortune (1-4), for history and experience show how God punishes sin (5-10). He judges everyone according to his deeds (11ff); no one is hidden from him or escapes retribution at his hand (15-21).

4 Through one wise man can a city be peopled;
through a clan of rebels it becomes desolate.
5 Many such things has my eye seen,
even more than these has my ear heard.
6*† Against a sinful band fire is enkindled,
upon a godless people wrath flames out.
7*† He forgave not the leaders of old
who rebelled long ago in their might;
8*† He spared not the neighbors of Lot
whom he detested for their pride;
9† Nor did he spare the doomed people
who were uprooted because of their sin;
10*† Nor the six hundred thousand foot soldiers
who perished for the impiety of their hearts.
11 And had there been but one stiff-necked man,
it were a wonder had he gone unpunished.
For mercy and anger alike are with him
who remits and forgives, though on the wicked alights his wrath.
12 Great as his mercy is his punishment;
he judges men, each according to his deeds.
13 A criminal does not escape with his plunder;
a just man's hope God does not leave unfulfilled.
14 Whoever does good has his reward,
which each receives according to his deeds.
15 Say not: "I am hidden from God;
in heaven who remembers me?
Among so many people I cannot be known;
what am I in the world of spirits?
16 Behold, the heavens, the heaven of heavens,
the earth and the abyss tremble at his visitation;
17 The roots of the mountains, the earth's foundations,
at his mere glance, quiver and quake.
18 Of me, therefore, he will take no thought;
with my ways who will concern himself?
19* If I sin, no eye will see me;
if all in secret I am disloyal, who is to know?
20 Who tells him of just deeds
and what could I expect for doing my duty?"
21 Such are the thoughts of senseless men,
which only the foolish knave will think.

Divine Wisdom Seen in Creation†

22 Hearken to me, my son, take my advice,
apply your mind to my words,
23 While I propose measured wisdom,
and impart accurate knowledge.
24* When at the first God created his works
and, as he made them, assigned their tasks,
25 He ordered for all time what they were to do
and their domains from generation to generation.
They were not to hunger, nor grow weary,
nor ever cease from their tasks.
26 Not one should ever crowd its neighbor,
nor should they ever disobey his word.
27* Then the LORD looked upon the earth,
and filled it with his blessings.
28 Its surface he covered with all manner of life
which must return into it again.

CHAPTER 17

1* The LORD from the earth created man,
and in his own image he made him.
2* Limited days of life he gives him
and makes him return to earth again.
3 He endows man with a strength of his own,
and with power over all things else on earth.
4 He puts the fear of him in all flesh,
and gives him rule over beasts and birds.

*

6: 21, 9.
7: Gn 6, 4; Wis 14, 6; Bar 3, 26ff.
8: Gn 19, 24ff.
10: Nm 14, 29.
19: 23, 18.
24: Gn 1, 4ff.
27: Gn 1, 20ff.
17, 1: Gn 2, 7; 3, 19.
2ff: Gn 1, 26ff; Ps 8, 4-8.

†

16, 6: For Korah and his *band* (6a), see Nm 16, 35; Ps 106, 18; for the disgruntled Israelites (6b), Ps 78, 21f.

16, 7: *The leaders of old:* the "mighty men of old" who were destroyed by the flood: Gn 6, 4; Wis 14, 6; Bar 3, 26ff.

16, 8: The people of Sodom and Gomorrah: Gn 19, 24f; Ez 16, 49f.

16, 9: The Canaanites: Ex 23, 23f.27-31; 33, 2; Dt 7, 1; Wis 12, 3.

16, 10: The Israelites who murmured against Moses: Nm 11, 20; 14, 12.22ff.

16, 22—17, 18: In harmony with Gn 1—2, the author describes God's wisdom in creating the universe and all things in it (22-28), endowing man with a moral nature, with wisdom and knowledge and freedom of will according to his own image (17, 1.6), so that man may govern the earth (3f), praise God's name (8), obey his law (9-12), and render to him an account of his deeds (18). Cf Pss 19; 104.

5 He forms men's tongues and eyes
and ears,
and imparts to them an understanding heart.
6 With wisdom and knowledge he fills
them;
good and evil he shows them.
7 He looks with favor upon their
hearts,
and shows them his glorious
works,
8 That they may describe the wonders
of his deeds
and praise his holy name.
9 He has set before them knowledge,
a law of life as their inheritance;
10† An everlasting covenant he has
made with them,
his commandments he has revealed to them.
11 His majestic glory their eyes beheld,
his glorious voice their ears heard.
12 He says to them, "Avoid all evil";
each of them he gives precepts
about his fellow men.
13 Their ways are ever known to him,
they cannot be hidden from his
eyes.
14*† Over every nation he places a ruler,
but the LORD's own portion is Israel.
15 All their actions are clear as the sun
to him,
his eyes are ever upon their ways.
16 Their wickedness cannot be hidden
from him;
all of their sins are before the
LORD.
17 A man's goodness God cherishes
like a signet ring,
a man's virtue, like the apple of
his eye.
18* Later he will rise up and repay them,
and requite each one of them as
they deserve.

Appeal for a Return to God†

19 But to the penitent he provides a way
back,
he encourages those who are losing hope!
20 Return to the LORD and give up sin,
pray to him and make your offenses few.
21 Turn again to the Most High and
away from sin,
hate intensely what he loathes;
22* Who in the nether world can glorify
the Most High
in place of the living who offer
their praise?
23 No more can the dead give praise
than those who have never
lived;
they glorify the LORD who are
alive and well.
24 How great the mercy of the LORD,
his forgiveness of those who return to him!
25 The like cannot be found in men,
for not immortal is any son of
man.
26† Is anything brighter than the sun?
Yet it can be eclipsed.
How obscure then the thoughts of
flesh and blood!
27 God watches over the hosts of highest heaven,
while all men are dust and ashes.

CHAPTER 18

The Divine Power and Mercy†

1 The Eternal is the judge of all things
without exception;
the LORD alone is just.
2 Whom has he made equal to describing his works,
and who can probe his mighty
deeds?
3 Who can measure his majestic
power,
or exhaust the tale of his mercies?
4 One cannot lessen, nor increase,
nor penetrate the wonders of the
LORD.
5 When a man ends he is only beginning,
and when he stops he is still bewildered.
6 What is man, of what worth is he?
the good, the evil in him, what are
these?
7* The sum of a man's days is great
if it reaches a hundred years:
8 Like a drop of sea water, like a grain
of sand,
so are these few years among the
days of eternity.
9 That is why the LORD is patient with
men

*

14: Ex 19, 5; Dt 4, 19f; 32, 8f; Dn 10, 13-21; 12, 1; Rom 13, 1.
18: Jb 19, 25; Jl 3, 4.
22f: Pss 6, 6; 115, 17; Is 38, 18.
18, 7: Ps 90, 10.

†

17, 10: *An everlasting covenant . . . his commandments:* the various covenants which God entered into with mankind, e.g., Gn 2, 15ff; 17, 1-22, especially on Mount Sinai where the people saw God's glory and heard his voice (Ex 19, 16—24, 18).

17, 14: *Ruler:* this may refer to civil authority or to angels placed over nations as guardians; see note on Dt 32, 8 and the cross references above.

17, 19-27: Exhorting the sinner to return to God (19ff.24ff), the author implies that the Lord will postpone death for a repentant sinner so that he may fulfill his destiny of praising God on earth (22f). In the light of Christian teaching, the gift of final penitence extends this divine purpose into life everlasting. See note on Ps 6, 6; cf also Ez 18, 23; 33, 11-16.

17, 26: *Obscure:* literally, evil; compare Gn 6, 5. Though moral fault is not excluded, the thought here is the inability to understand the merciful designs of God. Cf Wis 9, 14-18.

18, 1-13: Not only are God's justice and power beyond man's understanding (1-5), his mercy also is boundless and surpasses all human compassion (6-13).

and showers upon them his mercy.
10 He sees and understands that their death is grievous,
and so he forgives them all the more.
11 Man may be merciful to his fellow man,
but the LORD's mercy reaches all flesh,
12* Reproving, admonishing, teaching,
as a shepherd guides his flock;
13 Merciful to those who accept his guidance,
who are diligent in his precepts.

The Necessity of Prudence

14† My son, to your charity add no reproach,
nor spoil any gift by harsh words.
15 Like dew that abates a burning wind,
so does a word improve a gift.
16 Sometimes the word means more than the gift;
both are offered by a kindly man.
17* Only a fool upbraids before giving;
a grudging gift wears out the expectant eyes.
18 Be informed before speaking;
before sickness prepare the cure.
19† Before you are judged, seek merit for yourself,
and at the time of visitation you will have a ransom.
20 Before you have fallen, humble yourself;
when you have sinned, show repentance.
21 Delay not to forsake sins,
neglect it not till you are in distress.
22*† Let nothing prevent the prompt payment of your vows;
wait not to fulfill them when you are dying.
23 Before making a vow have the means to fulfill it;
be not one who tries the LORD.
24* Think of wrath and the day of death,
the time of vengeance when he will hide his face.
25* Remember the time of hunger in the time of plenty,
poverty and want in the day of wealth.
26 Between morning and evening the weather changes;
before the LORD all things are fleeting.
27 A wise man is circumspect in all things;
when sin is rife he keeps himself from wrongdoing.
28† Any learned man should make wisdom known,
and he who attains to her should declare her praise;
29 Those trained in her words must show their wisdom,
dispensing sound proverbs like life-giving waters.

Self-Control†

30* Go not after your lusts,
but keep your desires in check.
31 If you satisfy your lustful appetites
they will make you the sport of your enemies.
32 Have no joy in the pleasures of a moment
which bring on poverty redoubled;
33 Become not a glutton and a winebibber
with nothing in your purse.

CHAPTER 19

1 He who does so grows no richer;
he who wastes the little he has will be stripped bare.
2* Wine and women make the mind giddy,
and the companion of harlots becomes reckless.
4 He who lightly trusts in them has no sense,
and he who strays after them sins against his own life.
3 Rottenness and worms will possess him,
for contumacious desire destroys its owner.

The Proper Use of Speech†

5 He who gloats over evil will meet with evil,

SIRACH

---

*

12: Jn 10, 11.
17: 20, 13.
22: Nm 30, 3; Dt 23, 22; Ps 50, 14; Prv 20, 25; Eccl 5, 4.
24: 7, 16.
25: 11, 25.
30: Rom 6, 12; 13, 14.
19, 2: Prv 20, 1; 23, 20ff.

---

†

18, 14-27: The practice of charity is an art which avoids every offense to the recipient (14-18). Prudence directs the changing circumstances of daily life toward the attainment of its reward *at the time of visitation,* i.e., the day of reckoning (19-27).

18, 19: *Merit . . . ransom:* almsgiving is often portrayed in the Bible as a means of approach to the forgiving mercy of God. Cf 3, 29f; 29, 11f; Tb 12, 12f; Dn 4, 24; Lk 16, 9; Acts 10, 31.

18, 22f: The usual object of a vow in Old Testament times was the offering of a bloody sacrifice.

18, 28f: A general statement on the teaching of wisdom, serving either as a conclusion to the preceding section or as an introduction to the following one. The neighbors of the wise man are regarded as the field into which he channels the waters of wisdom to encourage growth. Cf 24, 28-31.

18, 30—19, 4: Inordinate gratification of the senses makes a man unreasonable, the slave of passion, *the sport of* his *enemies.* In the end it destroys him physically and spiritually.

19, 5-16: An excellent commentary on the eighth commandment of the Decalogue, forbidding intemperance in speech through calumny, rash judgment, and detraction (5f), and inculcating discreet silence in defense of self and of neighbor (7-11). Justice requires that an accused neighbor be given a hearing, and charity urges fraternal correction; both together fulfill *the law of the Most High* (12-16); cf Mt 7, 1f; 18, 15f.

and he who repeats an evil report
has no sense.
6* Never repeat gossip,
and you will not be reviled.
7* Tell nothing to friend or foe;
if you have a fault, reveal it not,
8 For he who hears it will hold it against you,
and in time become your enemy.
9 Let anything you hear die within you;
be assured it will not make you burst.
10 When a fool hears something, he is in labor,
like a woman giving birth to a child.
11 Like an arrow lodged in a man's thigh
is gossip in the breast of a fool.
12* Admonish your friend—he may not have done it;
and if he did, that he may not do it again.
13 Admonish your neighbor—he may not have said it;
and if he did, that he may not say it again.
14 Admonish your friend—often it may be slander;
every story you must not believe.
15* Then, too, a man can slip and not mean it;
who has not sinned with his tongue?
16* Admonish your neighbor before you break with him;
thus will you fulfill the law of the Most High.

How to Recognize True Wisdom†

17* All wisdom is fear of the LORD;
perfect wisdom is the fulfillment of the law.
18 The knowledge of wickedness is not wisdom,
nor is there prudence in the counsel of sinners.
19 There is a shrewdness that is detestable,
while the simple man may be free from sin.
20 There are those with little understanding who fear God,
and those of great intelligence who violate the law.
21 There is a shrewdness keen but dishonest,
which by duplicity wins a judgment.
22 There is the wicked man who is bowed in grief,
but is full of guile within;
23 He bows his head and feigns not to hear,
but when not observed, he will take advantage of you:
24 Even though his lack of strength keeps him from sinning,
when he finds the opportunity, he will do harm.
25 One can tell a man by his appearance;
a wise man is known as such when first met.
26 A man's attire, his hearty laughter and his gait,
proclaim him for what he is.

CHAPTER 20

Conduct of the Wise and the Foolish

1† An admonition can be inopportune,
and a man may be wise to hold his peace.
2 It is much better to admonish than to lose one's temper,
for one who admits his fault will be kept from disgrace.
3† Like a eunuch lusting for intimacy with a maiden
is he who does right under compulsion.
4 One man is silent and is thought wise,
another is talkative and is disliked.
5* One man is silent because he has nothing to say;
another is silent, biding his time.
6 A wise man is silent till the right time comes,
but a boasting fool ignores the proper time.
7 He who talks too much is detested;
he who pretends to authority is hated.

8† Some misfortunes bring success;
some things gained are a man's loss.
9† Some gifts do one no good,
and some must be paid back double.

*

6: Prv 25, 10.
7: 8, 18f.
12: Lv 19, 17; Mt 18, 15; Lk 17, 3.
15: 14, 1; Jas 3, 2.
16: Lv 19, 17.
17: 1, 1.12.14; Jb 28, 28; Ps 111, 10; Prv 1, 7; 9, 10.
20, 5: 20, 1; Prv 10, 19; 17, 28.

†

19, 17-26: True and false wisdom as here described are synonymous with virtue and vice, with *the fulfillment of the law* and the violation of it.

20, 1-7: Wisdom indicates the proper times for speech and silence, that is, the occasions when the most benefit can be gained from them.

20, 3: The sense is that violence or force against a person can prevent an external act of sin or compel a good deed without eliminating the internal sin or desire of wrongdoing. Cf 20, 20.

20, 8-16: In a series of paradoxes the author indicates how much true and lasting values differ from apparent ones.

20, 9: *And some . . . double:* or perhaps, "but some are doubly precious."

SIRACH

10 Humiliation can follow fame,
while from obscurity a man can lift up his head.
11 A man may buy much for little,
but pay for it seven times over.
12 A wise man makes himself popular by a few words,
but fools pour forth their blandishments in vain.
13 A gift from a rogue will do you no good,
for in his eyes his one gift is equal to seven.
14 He gives little and criticizes often,
and like a crier he shouts aloud.
He lends today, he asks it back tomorrow;
hateful indeed is such a man.
15 A fool has no friends,
nor thanks for his generosity;
16 Those who eat his bread have an evil tongue.
How many times they laugh him to scorn!

17† A fall to the ground is less sudden than a slip of the tongue;
that is why the downfall of the wicked comes so quickly.
18 Insipid food is the untimely tale;
the unruly are always ready to offer it.
19 A proverb when spoken by a fool is unwelcome,
for he does not utter it at the proper time.
20 A man through want may be unable to sin,
yet in this tranquility he cannot rest.
21 One may lose his life through shame,
and perish through a fool's intimidation.
22 A man makes a promise to a friend out of shame,
and has him for his enemy needlessly.
23 A lie is a foul blot in a man,
yet it is constantly on the lips of the unruly.
24 Better a thief than an inveterate liar,
yet both will suffer disgrace;
25 A liar's way leads to dishonor,
his shame remains ever with him.
26† A wise man advances himself by his words,
a prudent man pleases the great.
27 He who works his land has abundant crops,
he who pleases the great is pardoned his faults.
28* Favors and gifts blind the eyes;
like a muzzle over the mouth they silence reproof.
29 Hidden wisdom and unseen treasure—
of what value is either?
30 Better the man who hides his folly
than the one who hides his wisdom.

CHAPTER 21

Sin Must Be Avoided†

1 My son, if you have sinned, do so no more,
and for your past sins pray to be forgiven.
2 Flee from sin as from a serpent.
that will bite you if you go near it;
Its teeth are lion's teeth,
destroying the souls of men.
3 Every offense is a two-edged sword;
when it cuts, there can be no healing.
4 Violence and arrogance wipe out wealth;
so too a proud man's home is destroyed.
5 Prayer from a poor man's lips is heard at once,
and justice is quickly granted him.
6 He who hates correction walks the sinner's path,
but he who fears the LORD repents in his heart.
7 Widely known is the boastful speaker
but the wise man knows his own faults.
8 He who builds his house with another's money
is collecting stones for his funeral mound.
9* A band of criminals is like a bundle of tow;
they will end in a flaming fire.
10† The path of sinners is smooth stones
that end in the depths of the nether world.

*

20, 28: Ex 23, 8; Dt 16, 19. 21, 9: Ps 21, 9.

†

20, 17-25: The ill-timed speech of *the wicked, the unruly* and *a fool* is repulsive (17ff); human respect exposes one to intimidation, rash promises and enmity (21f); lies bring dishonor and lasting disgrace (23ff).

20, 26-30: Unlike the fool who invites disaster through misuse of his tongue, the sage through prudent speech gains in honor and esteem among the great (26f). He must beware, however, of accepting bribes, lest he share in evil through silence when he should reprove (28ff).

21, 1-10: Under various figures, the consequences of sin are described as destructive of wealth, and even of bodily life, and deserving of death and a place in the depths of the nether world (2ff.6a.8ff). Through prayer, forgiveness can be sought (1), and through fear of the Lord, repentance is achieved (1, 5.6b).

21, 10: *The path of sinners . . . nether world:* eternal retribution is not yet proposed in this reference. It became clearly revealed through the teaching of Christ; cf Mt 7, 13f; 25, 41-46; Lk 16, 19-31.

The Wise and the Foolish Differ†

11 He who keeps the law controls his impulses;
he who is perfect in fear of the LORD has wisdom.
12 He can never be taught who is not shrewd,
but one form of shrewdness is thoroughly bitter.
13* A wise man's knowledge wells up in a flood,
and his counsel, like a living spring;
14 A fool's mind is like a broken jar—
no knowledge at all can it hold.
15 When an intelligent man hears words of wisdom,
he approves them and adds to them;
the wanton hears them with scorn
and casts them behind his back.
16 A fool's chatter is like a load on a journey,
but there is charm to be found upon the lips of the wise.
17 The views of a prudent man are sought in an assembly,
and his words are considered with care.
18 Like a house in ruins is wisdom to a fool;
the stupid man knows it only as inscrutable words.
19 Like fetters on the legs is learning to a fool,
like a manacle on his right hand.
20* A fool raises his voice in laughter,
but the prudent man at the most smiles gently.
21 Like a chain of gold is learning to a wise man,
like a bracelet on his right arm.

22* The fool steps boldly into a house,
while the well-bred man remains outside;
23 A boor peeps through the doorway of a house,
but a cultured man keeps his glance cast down.
24 It is rude for one to listen at a door;
a cultured man would be overwhelmed by the disgrace of it.
25 The lips of the impious talk of what is not their concern,
but the words of the prudent are carefully weighed.
26 Fools' thoughts are in their mouths,
wise men's words are in their hearts.
27† When a godless man curses his adversary
he really curses himself.
28 A slanderer besmirches himself,
and is hated by his neighbors.

CHAPTER 22

On Laziness and Foolishness

1† The sluggard is like a stone in the mud;
everyone hisses at his disgrace.
2 The sluggard is like a lump of dung;
whoever touches him wipes his hands.
3* An unruly child is a disgrace to its father;
if it be a daughter she brings him to poverty.
4 A thoughtful daughter becomes a treasure to her husband,
a shameless one is her father's grief.
5 A hussy shames her father and her husband;
by both she is despised.
6† Like a song in time of mourning is inopportune talk,
but lashes and discipline are at all times wisdom.
7* Teaching a fool is like gluing a broken pot,
or like disturbing a man in the depths of sleep;
8 He talks with a slumberer who talks with a fool,
for when it is over, he will say, "What was that?"
9 Weep over the dead man, for his light has gone out;
weep over the fool, for sense has left him.
10 Weep but a little over the dead man, for he is at rest;
but worse than death is the life of a fool.

*

13: Prv 13, 14; 16, 22.
20: Eccl 7, 6.
22: Prv 25, 17.
22, 3: Prv 17, 21; 19, 13.
7-11: Prv 23, 9.

†

21, 11-28: The mind of the wise man is a fountain of knowledge (13.15); his will is trained to keep the law (11); his words are gracious, valued, carefully weighed, sincere (16f.25f); his conduct is respectful, cultured and restrained (20.22ff). The fool's mind is devoid of knowledge and impenetrable to it (12.14.18f); his will rejects it (15); his talk is burdensome (16), his laughter unrestrained (20), his conversation shallow and meddlesome (25f); his conduct is bold and rude (22ff); his abuse of others redounds on himself (27f).

21, 27: *Adversary:* this can be understood in the sense that, if a man curses one who led him into sin, he implicitly curses himself for having yielded to the sin; or in the sense that the enemy is the man's own sinful nature; or even in the sense that the enemy is the devil, since the Hebrew word used here is *satan.* Cf 1 Chr 21, 1; Zec 3, 2; 2 Pt 2, 12f; Jude 9.

22, 1-15: To Sirach, a lazy person and an unruly child are a cause of shame and disgrace; everyone wishes to be rid of them (1-5). A wicked fool is as senseless as a man asleep or dead, but the grief he causes others lasts a lifetime (7-11). He is like a brute, troublesome and intolerable (12-15).

22, 6: *Like a song . . . is . . . talk:* some understand *talk* in the sense of a rebuke unheeded by the unruly as a joyful song is out of place among mourners. Corporal punishment, however, is always effective.

SIRACH

11* Seven days of mourning for the dead,
but for the wicked fool a whole lifetime.

12 Speak but seldom with the stupid man,
be not the companion of a brute;
13 Beware of him lest you have trouble
and be spattered when he shakes himself;
Turn away from him and you will find rest
and not be wearied by his lack of sense.
14 What is heavier than lead,
and what is its name but "Fool"?
15* Sand and salt and an iron mass
are easier to bear than a stupid man.

16† Masonry bonded with wooden beams
is not loosened by an earthquake;
Neither is a resolve constructed with careful deliberation
shaken in a moment of fear.
17 A resolve that is backed by prudent understanding
is like the polished surface of a smooth wall.
18 Small stones lying on an open height
will not remain when the wind blows;
Neither can a timid resolve based on foolish plans
withstand fear of any kind.

The Preservation of Friendship†

19 One who jabs the eye brings tears:
he who pierces the heart bares its feelings.
20 He who throws stones at birds drives them away,
and he who insults a friend breaks up the friendship.
21 Should you draw a sword against a friend,
despair not, it can be undone.
22 Should you speak sharply to a friend,
fear not, you can be reconciled.
But a contemptuous insult, a confidence broken,
or a treacherous attack will drive away any friend.

23 Make fast friends with a man while he is poor;
thus will you enjoy his prosperity with him.
In time of trouble remain true to him,
so as to share in his inheritance when it comes.
24 Before flames burst forth an oven smokes;
so does abuse come before bloodshed.
25 From a friend in need of support
no one need hide in shame;
26 But from him who brings harm to his friend
all will stand aloof who hear of it.

Prayer†

27* Who will set a guard over my mouth,
and upon my lips an effective seal,
That I may not fail through them,
that my tongue may not destroy me?

CHAPTER 23

1† LORD, Father and Master of my life,
permit me not to fall by them!
2 Who will apply the lash to my thoughts,
to my mind the rod of discipline,
That my failings may not be spared,
nor the sins of my heart overlooked;
3 Lest my failings increase,
and my sins be multiplied;
Lest I succumb to my foes,
and my enemy rejoice over me?
4 LORD, Father and God of my life,
abandon me not into their control!
5 A brazen look allow me not;
ward off passion from my heart,
6 Let not the lustful cravings of the flesh master me,
surrender me not to shameless desires.

The Proper Use of the Tongue†

7 Give heed, my children, to the instruction that I pronounce,
for he who keeps it will not be enslaved.

SIRACH

---

*

11: Gn 50, 10. 27: Ps 141, 3.
15: Prv 27, 3.

†

22, 16ff: A prudent mind firmly resolved is undisturbed by violent and conflicting thoughts, whereas a foolish person is tossed about by the winds of fear, like small stones whipped about by high winds.

22, 19-26: As disputes and violence weaken friendship, and disloyalty and abuse of confidence destroy it utterly (19-22.24.26), so kindness to a poor man in time of poverty and adversity builds up friendship and merits a share in his prosperity and inheritance (23.25).

22, 27—23, 6: The sage implores the divine assistance to preserve him through stern discipline from sins of the tongue (22, 27; 23, 1); ignorance of mind and weakness of will (2f); and inclinations of the senses and the flesh, lest he fall into the hands of his enemies, or become a prey of shameful desires (3-6).

23, 1: *LORD, Father and Master of my life:* these words express the tender personal relationship between the author's soul and God, the need of his assistance, and the truth of his providence.

23, 7-15: A warning against sins of the tongue through misuse of the Holy Name, thoughtless swearing which involves obligation and incurs guilt (7-11), blasphemy (12), talk that is coarse and blundersome (13f), and the incorrigible habit of *abusive language* (15).

8 Through his lips is the sinner ensnared;
the railer and the arrogant man fall thereby.
9* Let not your mouth form the habit of swearing,
or becoming too familiar with the Holy Name.
10† Just as a slave that is constantly under scrutiny
will not be without welts,
So one who swears continually by the Holy Name
will not remain free from sin.
11* A man who often swears heaps up obligations;
the scourge will never be far from his house.
If he swears in error, he incurs guilt;
if he neglects his obligation, his sin is doubly great.
If he swears without reason he cannot be found just,
and all his house will suffer affliction.
12 There are words which merit death;
may they never be heard among Jacob's heirs.
For all such words are foreign to the devout,
who do not wallow in sin.
13 Let not your mouth become used to coarse talk,
for in it lies sinful matter.
14* Keep your father and mother in mind
when you sit among the mighty,
Lest in their presence you commit a blunder
and disgrace your upbringing,
By wishing you had never been born
or cursing the day of your birth.
15 A man who has the habit of abusive language
will never mature in character as long as he lives.

Sins of the Flesh†

16† Two types of men multiply sins,
a third draws down wrath;
For burning passion is a blazing fire,
not to be quenched till it burns itself out:
A man given to sins of the flesh,
who never stops until the fire breaks forth;
17* The rake to whom all bread is sweet
and who is never through till he dies;
18* And the man who dishonors his marriage bed
and says to himself "Who can see me?
Darkness surrounds me, walls hide me;
no one sees me; why should I fear to sin?"
Of the Most High he is not mindful,
19 fearing only the eyes of men;
He does not understand that the eyes of the LORD,
ten thousand times brighter than the sun,
Observe every step a man takes
and peer into hidden corners.
20 He who knows all things before they exist
still knows them all after they are made.
21*† Such a man will be punished in the streets of the city;
when he least expects it, he will be apprehended.

22 So also with the woman who is unfaithful to her husband
and offers as heir her son by a stranger.
23† First, she has disobeyed the law of the Most High;
secondly, she has wronged her husband;
Thirdly, in her wanton adultery
she has borne children by another man.
24† Such a woman will be dragged before the assembly,
and her punishment will extend to her children;
25 Her children will not take root;
her branches will not bring forth fruit.
26 She will leave an accursed memory;
her disgrace will never be blotted out.
27* Thus all who dwell on the earth shall know,
and all who inhabit the world shall understand,
That nothing is better than the fear of the LORD,

*

23, 9: Ex 20, 7; Lv 19, 12; Dt 5, 11; Mt 5, 33ff.
11: Lv 5, 4ff.
14: 7, 27; Ex 20, 12; Dt 5, 16.
17: Prv 9, 17.
18: Is 29, 15.
21f: Lv 20, 10; Dt 22, 21.
27: 1, 10-18.24; Prv 3, 1f.

†

23, 10: *As a slave . . . under scrutiny,* so is he who calls on God to witness the truth of what he says.

23, 16-27: From sins of the tongue the author proceeds to treat of sins of the flesh and their dire consequences. The passion of lust tyrannizes over its victims and, like fire, consumes and utterly destroys them (16f.22-26). The false security of the adulterer serves but to aggravate his inevitable fate (18-21). Only the fear of the Lord and observance of his commandments can assure moral safety (27).

23, 16: *Two types . . . a third:* three kinds of sins of impurity, with increasing degrees of gravity: solitary sins (16), fornication (17) and adultery (18-21).

23, 21: Cf Lv 20, 10; Dt 22, 22.

23, 23: The detailed evil of adultery includes disobedience to God's law (Ex 20, 14), injustice to a partner in marriage, and disgraceful offspring.

23, 24f: The judgment of *the assembly* determined the illegitimacy of children born of adultery or incest and excluded them from the "community of the LORD" (Dt 23, 3). Cf Wis 3, 16-19; 4, 3-6.

nothing more salutary than to
obey his commandments.

CHAPTER 24

Praise of Wisdom

1† Wisdom sings her own praises,
before her own people she proclaims her glory;
2 In the assembly of the Most High she opens her mouth,
in the presence of his hosts she declares her worth:
3* "From the mouth of the Most High I came forth,
and mistlike covered the earth.
4 In the highest heavens did I dwell,
my throne on a pillar of cloud.
5 The vault of heaven I compassed alone,
through the deep abyss I wandered.
6 Over waves of the sea, over all the land,
over every people and nation I held sway.
7 Among all these I sought a resting place;
in whose inheritance should I abide?

8 "Then the Creator of all gave me his command,
and he who formed me chose the spot for my tent,
Saying, 'In Jacob make your dwelling,
in Israel your inheritance.'
9 Before all ages, in the beginning, he created me,
and through all ages I shall not cease to be.
10 In the holy tent I ministered before him,
and in Zion I fixed my abode.
11 Thus in the chosen city he has given me rest,
in Jerusalem is my domain.
12 I have struck root among the glorious people,
in the portion of the LORD, his heritage.

13 "Like a cedar on Lebanon I am raised aloft,
like a cypress on Mount Hermon,
14 Like a palm tree in En-gedi,
like a rosebush in Jericho,
Like a fair olive tree in the field,
like a plane tree growing beside the water.
15*† Like cinnamon, or fragrant balm, or precious myrrh,
I give forth perfume;
Like galbanum and onycha and sweet spices,
like the odor of incense in the holy place.
16 I spread out my branches like a terebinth,
my branches so bright and so graceful.
17 I bud forth delights like the vine,
my blossoms become fruit fair and rich.
18† Come to me, all you that yearn for me,
and be filled with my fruits;
19 You will remember me as sweeter than honey,
better to have than the honeycomb.
20*† He who eats of me will hunger still,
he who drinks of me will thirst for more;
21 He who obeys me will not be put to shame,
he who serves me will never fail."
22*† All this is true of the book of the Most High's covenant,
the law which Moses commanded us
as an inheritance for the community of Jacob.
23* It overflows, like the Pishon, with wisdom—
like the Tigris in the days of the new fruits.
24 It runs over, like the Euphrates, with understanding,
like the Jordan at harvest time.
25† It sparkles like the Nile with knowledge,
like the Gihon at vintage time.
26 The first man never finished comprehending wisdom,
nor will the last succeed in fathoming her.

*

24, 3ff: 1, 1; Prv 2, 6; 8, 22-36; Wis 7, 24f.
15: Ex 30, 22-25.
20: Is 55, 1; Jn 6, 35.
22: Ex 24, 7.
23ff: Gn 2, 11-14.

†

24, 1-27: In this chapter Wisdom speaks in the first person, describing her origin, her dwelling place in Israel, and the reward she gives her followers. As in Prv 8, Wisdom is described as a being who comes from God and is distinct from him. While we do not say with certainty that this description applies to a personal being, it does foreshadow the beautiful doctrine of the Word of God later developed in St. John's Gospel (Jn 1, 1-14). In the liturgy this chapter is applied to the Blessed Virgin because of her constant and intimate association with Christ, the Incarnate Wisdom.

24, 15: These substances were associated with worship, being mentioned in Ex 30, 22f.34 as the ingredients of the anointing oil and the sacred incense. Israel was a priestly nation.

24, 18: Compare the words of the Savior in Mt 11, 28ff.

24, 20: So pleasing is wisdom to man that, far from being satiated, he will always desire more.

24, 22: Here the author begins to speak once more, Wisdom having ended her discourse in the preceding verse. Wisdom and the law of Moses are now identified.

24, 25: *Gihon:* understood by some to have been a name for the Nile: cf Gn 2, 13.

27 For deeper than the sea are her thoughts;
her counsels, than the great abyss.

28† Now I, like a rivulet from her stream,
channeling the waters into a garden,
29 Said to myself, "I will water my plants,
my flower bed I will drench";
And suddenly this rivulet of mine became a river,
then this stream of mine, a sea.
30 Thus do I send my teachings forth shining like the dawn,
to become known afar off.
31 Thus do I pour out instruction like prophecy
and bestow it on generations to come.

CHAPTER 25

Those Who Are Worthy of Praise†

1 With three things I am delighted,
for they are pleasing to the LORD and to men:
Harmony among brethren, friendship among neighbors,
and the mutual love of husband and wife.
2 Three kinds of men I hate;
their manner of life I loathe indeed:
A proud pauper, a rich dissembler,
and an old man lecherous in his dotage.

3 What you have not saved in your youth,
how will you acquire in your old age?
4 How becoming to the gray-haired is judgment,
and a knowledge of counsel to those on in years!
5 How becoming to the aged is wisdom,
understanding and prudence to the venerable!
6 The crown of old men is wide experience;
their glory, the fear of the LORD.

7 There are nine who come to my mind as blessed,
a tenth whom my tongue proclaims:
The man who finds joy in his children,
and he who lives to see his enemies' downfall.
8† Happy is he who dwells with a sensible wife,
and he who plows not like a donkey yoked with an ox.
Happy is he who sins not with his tongue,
and he who serves not his inferior.
9 Happy is he who finds a friend
and he who speaks to attentive ears.
10 He who finds wisdom is great indeed,
but not greater than he who fears the LORD.
11 Fear of the LORD surpasses all else.
its possessor is beyond compare.

Wicked and Virtuous Women†

12 Worst of all wounds is that of the heart,
worst of all evils is that of a woman.
13 Worst of all sufferings is that from one's foes,
worst of all vengeance is that of one's enemies:
14 No poison worse than that of a serpent,
no venom greater than that of a woman.
15 With a dragon or a lion I would rather dwell
than live with an evil woman.
16 Wickedness changes a woman's looks,
and makes her sullen as a female bear.
17 When her husband sits among his neighbors,
a bitter sigh escapes him unawares.

18 There is scarce any evil like that in a woman;
may she fall to the lot of the sinner!
19 Like a sandy hill to aged feet
is a railing wife to a quiet man.
20 Stumble not through woman's beauty,
nor be greedy for her wealth;
21 The man is a slave, in disgrace and shame,
when a wife supports her husband.

†

24, 28-31: Spoken by the author. He had at first drawn a small portion of the water of wisdom for his own private benefit, but finding it so useful, he soon began to let others share in this boon by teaching them the lessons of wisdom.

25, 1-11: While praising brotherly love, love of neighbor, and conjugal love, the sage condemns their opposites in the arrogant pauper who despises his brother, the fraudulent rich man who cheats his neighbor, and the lecherous old man unfaithful to his wife (1f). This last, sensual from his youth, lacks the mature blessings of judgment and wisdom in old age (3-6), and the joy of a peaceful household, where honesty and dignity, friendship, wisdom and fear of God prevail (7-11).

25, 8: *Like a donkey yoked with an ox:* incompatibility between husband and wife.

25, 12-25: Wickedness in a woman is most grievous, painful and bitter to her husband. Through it she becomes vengeful, dangerous and intolerable, jealous, talkative, intemperate and unchaste. Even her very appearance is changed (12-17). The worst of all evils, a source of grief, a snare and a disgrace to her husband, she depresses his mind, saddens and breaks his heart, destroys his strength (18-22). She must not be indulged but made obedient or punished (24f).

22 Depressed mind, saddened face,
broken heart—this from an evil wife.
Feeble hands and quaking knees—
from a wife who brings no happiness to her husband.
23† In woman was sin's beginning,
and because of her we all die.
24 Allow water no outlet,
and be not indulgent to an erring wife.
25 If she walks not by your side,
cut her away from you.

CHAPTER 26

1*† Happy the husband of a good wife,
twice-lengthened are his days;
2† A worthy wife brings joy to her husband,
peaceful and full is his life.
3* A good wife is a generous gift
bestowed upon him who fears the LORD;
4 Be he rich or poor, his heart is content,
and a smile is ever on his face.

5 There are three things at which my heart quakes,
a fourth before which I quail:
Though false charges in public, trial before all the people,
and lying testimony are harder to bear than death,
6† A jealous wife is heartache and mourning
and a scourging tongue like the other three.
7 A bad wife is a chafing yoke;
he who marries her seizes a scorpion.
8 A drunken wife arouses great anger,
for she does not hide her shame.
9 By her eyelids and her haughty stare
an unchaste wife can be recognized.

10* Keep a strict watch over an unruly wife,
lest, finding an opportunity, she make use of it;
11 Follow close if her eyes are bold,
and be not surprised if she betrays you:
12 As a thirsty traveler with eager mouth
drinks from any water that he finds,
So she settles down before every tent peg
and opens her quiver for every arrow.

13 A gracious wife delights her husband,
her thoughtfulness puts flesh on his bones;
14 A gift from the LORD is her governed speech,
and her firm virtue is of surpassing worth.
15 Choicest of blessings is a modest wife,
priceless her chaste person.
16 Like the sun rising in the LORD's heavens,
the beauty of a virtuous wife is the radiance of her home.
17† Like the light which shines above the holy lampstand,
are her beauty of face and graceful figure.
18† Golden columns on silver bases
are her shapely limbs and steady feet.

Dangers to Integrity and Friendship

19* These two bring grief to my heart,
and the third arouses my horror:
A wealthy man reduced to want;
illustrious men held in contempt;
And the man who passes from justice to sin,
for whom the LORD makes ready the sword.

SIRACH

*

26, 1: 25, 8; Prv 18, 22; 31, 10ff.
3: 36, 24.
10: 42, 11.
19: Ez 18, 24ff.

†

25, 23: According to the account in Gn 3, to which Ben Sirach refers, sin, the cause of death, originated in woman: Eve, the first human being to sin, induced Adam to follow her example. But it is through Adam, as head of the race, that original sin and its punishment of spiritual death are presented by St. Paul (Rom 5) as having entered the world, to become the occasion for the redemptive work of Christ our Lord.

26, 1-4.13-18: *A good wife* is as a gift from God, bringing *joy* and peace, happiness and contentment to her husband (1-4) through *her thoughtfulness*, reserve, modesty and chastity, *beauty*, grace and virtue (13-18).

26, 2: *Worthy:* gifted spiritually, mentally and physically. Cf Prv 31, 10.

26, 6-12: A repetition of the thought expressed in 25, 12-25.

26, 17f: *The holy lampstand* and the *golden columns* stood in the holy place of the ancient Tabernacle (Ex 25, 31-40; 26, 32).

26, 18: Among the additions found here in some manuscripts are the following lines:

"My son, take care in the prime of life
not to surrender your strength to strangers;
Single out from the land a goodly field
and there with confidence sow the seed of your increase;
So shall you have your offspring around you,
and in confidence shall they grow up.

"Though a woman for hire be thought of as a trifle,
a married woman is a deadly snare for those who embrace her. [Cf Prv 6, 26.]

"A wife's complaint should be made in meekness,
and show itself in a slight flush;
But a loud-mouthed, scolding wife
is a trumpet signaling for battle:
Any human being who answers that challenge
will spend his life amid the turbulence of war."

20† A merchant can hardly remain upright,
nor a shopkeeper free from sin;

CHAPTER 27

1* For the sake of profit many sin,
and the struggle for wealth blinds the eyes.
2 Like a peg driven between fitted stones,
between buying and selling sin is wedged in.
3 Unless you earnestly hold fast to the fear of the LORD,
suddenly your house will be thrown down.
4 When a sieve is shaken, the husks appear;
so do a man's faults when he speaks.
5* As the test of what the potter molds is in the furnace,
so in his conversation is the test of a man.
6* The fruit of a tree shows the care it has had;
so too does a man's speech disclose the bent of his mind.
7 Praise no man before he speaks,
for it is then that men are tested.
8 If you strive after justice you will attain it,
and put it on like a splendid robe.
9 Birds nest with their own kind,
and fidelity comes to those who live by it.
10 As a lion crouches in wait for prey,
so do sins for evildoers.
11 Ever wise are the discourses of the devout,
but the godless man, like the moon, is inconstant.
12 Limit the time you spend among fools,
but frequent the company of thoughtful men.
13 The conversation of the wicked is offensive,
their laughter is wanton guilt.
14 Their oath-filled talk makes the hair stand on end,
their brawls make one stop one's ears.
15* Wrangling among the haughty ends in bloodshed,
their cursing is painful to hear.

16*† He who betrays a secret cannot be trusted,
he will never find an intimate friend.
17 Cherish your friend, keep faith with him;
but if you betray his confidence, follow him not;
18 For as an enemy might kill a man,
you have killed your neighbor's friendship.
19 Like a bird released from the hand,
you have let your friend go and cannot recapture him;
20 Follow him not, for he is far away,
he has fled like a gazelle from the trap.
21* A wound can be bound up, and an insult forgiven,
but he who betrays secrets does hopeless damage.

Malice, Anger and Vengeance

22 He who has shifty eyes plots mischief
and no one can ward him off;
23* In your presence he uses honeyed talk,
and admires your every word,
But later he changes his tone
and twists your words to your ruin.
24* There is nothing that I hate so much,
and the LORD hates him as well.
25* As a stone falls back on him who throws it up,
so a blow struck in treachery injures more than one.
26 As he who digs a pit falls into it,
and he who lays a snare is caught in it,
27 Whoever does harm will be involved in it
without knowing how it came upon him.

28 Mockery and abuse will be the lot of the proud,
and vengeance lies in wait for them like a lion.
29 The trap seizes those who rejoice in pitfalls,
and pain will consume them before they die;
30 Wrath and anger are hateful things,
yet the sinner hugs them tight.

*

27, 1: 7, 18; 31, 6; Prv 30, 8f.
5: 1 Pt 1, 7.
6: Mt 7, 20.
15: 23, 9-15.
16: Prv 11, 13; 20, 19.
21: 22, 20.
23: Prv 26, 24ff.
24: Prv 6, 13.16.
25f: Ps 7, 16f; Prv 26, 27; Eccl 10, 8.

†

26, 20—27, 15: From proper conduct in family life, the author proceeds to social morality, warning especially against injustice in commerce (26, 20—27, 3), and perversity of speech in business (4-7). The pursuit of *justice* in these matters is all the more meritorious as it is difficult (8ff). The discourses of the devout are marked with wisdom, but the conversations of the wicked, with offense, swearing, *cursing*, quarrels and even *bloodshed* (11-15).

27, 16—28, 11: Betrayal of *confidence* through indiscretion destroys *friendship* and does irreparable harm (16-21); cf 22, 22. False friendship based on hypocrisy and deceit is hateful to God and man (22ff); it soon becomes a victim of its own treachery (25ff). The same fate awaits the malicious and *vengeful* (27, 28—28, 1). They can obtain mercy and forgiveness only by first forgiving their neighbor, being mindful of death and of the commandments of the Most High (28, 2-7). And they must avoid quarrels and *strife* (8-11).

SIRACH

CHAPTER 28

1* The vengeful will suffer the LORD's vengeance,
for he remembers their sins in detail.
2* Forgive your neighbor's injustice;
then when you pray, your own sins will be forgiven.

3* Should a man nourish anger against his fellows
and expect healing from the LORD?
4 Should a man refuse mercy to his fellows,
yet seek pardon for his own sins?
5 If he who is but flesh cherishes wrath,
who will forgive his sins?
6* Remember your last days, set enmity aside;
remember death and decay, and cease from sin!
7 Think of the commandments, hate not your neighbor;
of the Most High's covenant, and overlook faults.

8 Avoid strife and your sins will be fewer,
for a quarrelsome man kindles disputes,
9* Commits the sin of disrupting friendship
and sows discord among those at peace.
10* The more wood, the greater the fire,
the more underlying it, the fiercer the fight;
The greater a man's strength, the sterner his anger,
the greater his power, the greater his wrath.
11 Pitch and resin make fires flare up,
and insistent quarrels provoke bloodshed.

The Evil Tongue†

12 If you blow upon a spark, it quickens into flame,
if you spit on it, it dies out;
yet both you do with your mouth!
13* Cursed be gossips and the double-tongued,
for they destroy the peace of many.
14 A meddlesome tongue subverts many,
and makes them refugees among the peoples;
It destroys walled cities,
and overthrows powerful dynasties.
15 A meddlesome tongue can drive virtuous women from their homes
and rob them of the fruit of their toil;
16 Whoever heeds it has no rest,
nor can he dwell in peace.

17 A blow from a whip raises a welt,
but a blow from the tongue smashes bones;
18* Many have fallen by the edge of the sword,
but not as many as by the tongue.
19 Happy he who is sheltered from it,
and has not endured its wrath;
Who has not borne its yoke
nor been fettered with its chain;
20 For its yoke is a yoke of iron
and its chains are chains of bronze!
21 Dire is the death it inflicts,
besides which even the nether world is a gain;
22 It will not take hold among the just
nor scorch them in its flame,
23 But those who forsake the LORD will fall victims to it,
as it burns among them unquenchably!
It will hurl itself against them like a lion;
like a panther, it will tear them to pieces.
24* As you hedge round your vineyard with thorns,
set barred doors over your mouth;
25 As you seal up your silver and gold,
so balance and weigh your words.
26 Take care not to slip by your tongue
and fall victim to your foe waiting in ambush.

CHAPTER 29

Loans, Alms and Surety†

1* He does a kindness who lends to his neighbor,
and he fulfills the precepts who holds out a helping hand.

---

*
28, 1: Dt 32, 35; Rom 12, 19.
2: Mt 6, 14.
3: Mt 18, 23ff.
6: 7, 36; 38, 20.
9: Prv 15, 18.
10ff: Prv 26, 20f.
13: 5, 16f.
18: Jas 3, 5ff.
24: 22, 27; Ps 141, 3.
29, 1: Dt 15, 8; Ps 112, 5; Prv 19, 17.

---

†
28, 12-26: Further treatment of sins of the tongue and their havoc; cf 5, 12—6, 1; 19, 5-16; 20, 17-25; 23, 7-15. *Gossips and the double-tongued* destroy domestic peace (12-16). The *whip, the sword, chains, even the nether world,* are not so cruel as the suffering inflicted by an evil tongue (17-21). Not *the just* but *those who forsake the LORD* are *victims* of their evil tongues (22f). Therefore, guard your mouth and tongue as you would guard treasure against an enemy (24ff).

29, 1-20: Some practical maxims concerning the use of wealth. Give *to a poor man* (8f), lend to a needy neighbor, but repay *when a loan falls due* lest the lender's burden be increased (1-5) and his kindness abused (6f); through charity build up defense against evil (10-13). *Go surety for your neighbor according to your means, but take care* (20) not to fall, for the shameless play false and bring their protectors and themselves to misfortune and ruin (14-19).

2* Lend to your neighbor in his hour of need,
and pay back your neighbor when a loan falls due;
3 Keep your promise, be honest with him,
and you will always come by what you need.
4 Many a man who asks for a loan
adds to the burdens of those who help him;
5 When he borrows, he kisses the lender's hand
and speaks with respect of his creditor's wealth;
But when payment is due he disappoints him
and says he is helpless to meet the claim.
6 If the lender is able to recover barely half,
he considers this an achievement;
If not, he is cheated of his wealth
and acquires an enemy at no extra charge;
With curses and insults the borrower pays him back,
with abuse instead of honor.
7 Many refuse to lend, not out of meanness,
but from fear of being cheated.

8 To a poor man, however, be generous;
keep him not waiting for your alms;
9* Because of the precept, help the needy,
and in their want, do not send them away empty-handed.

10 Spend your money for your brother and friend,
and hide it not under a stone to perish;
11* Dispose of your treasure as the Most High commands,
for that will profit you more than the gold.
12 Store up almsgiving in your treasure house,
and it will save you from every evil;
13 Better than a stout shield and a sturdy spear
it will fight for you against the foe.

14* A good man goes surety for his neighbor,
and only the shameless would play him false;
15 Forget not the kindness of your backer,
for he offers his very life for you.
16 The wicked turn a pledge on their behalf into misfortune,
and the ingrate abandons his protector;
17* Going surety has ruined many prosperous men
and tossed them about like waves of the sea,
18 Has exiled men of prominence
and sent them wandering through foreign lands.
19 The sinner through surety comes to grief,
and he who undertakes too much falls into lawsuits.
20 Go surety for your neighbor according to your means,
but take care lest you fall thereby.

Frugality and Its Rewards†

21* Life's prime needs are water, bread, and clothing,
a house, too, for decent privacy.
22* Better a poor man's fare under the shadow of one's own roof
than sumptuous banquets among strangers.
23 Be it little or much, be content with what you have,
and pay no heed to him who would disparage your home;
24 A miserable life it is to go from house to house,
for as a guest you dare not open your mouth.
25 The visitor has no thanks for filling the cups;
besides, you will hear these bitter words:
26 "Come here, stranger, set the table,
give me to eat the food you have!
27 Away, stranger, for one more worthy;
for my brother's visit I need the room!"
28 Painful things to a sensitive man
are abuse at home and insults from his creditors.

CHAPTER 30

The Training of Children†

1* He who loves his son chastises him often,

---

*

2: Ex 22, 24ff; Lv 25, 36; Mt 5, 42.
9: 4, 1ff; Lv 19, 9f; 23, 22; Dt 15, 8.
11: 17, 17; Tb 4, 7ff.
14: 8, 13.
17: Prv 6, 1f; 11, 15.
21: 39, 26.
22: 40, 29.
30, 1: Prv 13, 24; 23, 13; 29, 15; Heb 12, 7.

†

29, 21-28: The man who provides his own basic *needs* of food, clothing and dwelling, and is content with what he has, preserves his freedom and self-respect (21ff). But if he lives as a guest, even among the rich, he exposes himself to insult and *abuse* (24-28).

30, 1-13: Sound discipline and careful education of children correct frivolity and stubbornness, prevent remorse and humiliation, and bring to parents lasting joy and delight, prestige among friends, jealousy of enemies, perpetuation and vindication of themselves through their offspring (1-6). Lack of discipline and overindulgence of children bring *sorrow* and disappointment, *terror* and *grief* (7-13).

that he may be his joy when he grows up.
2 He who disciplines his son will benefit from him,
and boast of him among his intimates.
3 He who educates his son makes his enemy jealous,
and shows his delight in him among his friends.
4 At the father's death, he will seem not dead,
since he leaves after him one like himself,
5 Whom he looks upon through life with joy,
and even in death, without regret:
6 The avenger he leaves against his foes,
and the one to repay his friends with kindness.

7 He who spoils his son will have wounds to bandage,
and will quake inwardly at every outcry.
8 A colt untamed turns out stubborn;
a son left to himself grows up unruly.
9 Pamper your child and he will be a terror for you,
indulge him and he will bring you grief.
10 Share not in his frivolity lest you share in his sorrow,
when finally your teeth are clenched in remorse.
11 Give him not his own way in his youth,
and close not your eyes to his follies.
12* Bend him to the yoke when he is young,
thrash his sides while he is still small,
Lest he become stubborn, disobey you,
and leave you disconsolate.
13 Discipline your son, make heavy his yoke,
lest his folly humiliate you.

Health of Soul and Body†

14 Better a poor man strong and robust,
than a rich man with wasted frame.
15 More precious than gold is health and well-being,
contentment of spirit than coral.
16 No treasure greater than a healthy body;
no happiness, than a joyful heart!
17*† Preferable is death to a bitter life,
unending sleep to constant illness.
18* Dainties set before one who cannot eat
are like the offerings placed before a tomb.
19 What good is an offering to an idol
that can neither taste nor smell?
20 So it is with the afflicted man
who groans at the good things his eyes behold!

21* Do not give in to sadness,
torment not yourself with brooding;
22 Gladness of heart is the very life of man,
cheerfulness prolongs his days.
23* Distract yourself, renew your courage,
drive resentment far away from you;
For worry has brought death to many,
nor is there aught to be gained from resentment.
24 Envy and anger shorten one's life,
worry brings on premature old age.
25* One who is cheerful and gay while at table
benefits from his food.

CHAPTER 31

The Proper Attitude toward Riches†

1 Keeping watch over riches wastes the flesh,
and the care of wealth drives away rest.
2† Concern for one's livelihood banishes slumber;
more than a serious illness it disturbs repose.
3 The rich man labors to pile up wealth,
and his only rest is wanton pleasure;
4 The poor man toils for a meager subsistence,
and if ever he rests, he finds himself in want.

SIRACH

*

12: 7, 23.
17: 41, 2.
18: Tb 4, 17.
21: 38, 20; Prv 12, 25; 15, 13; 17, 22.
23: 38, 18f.
25: Prv 15, 15.

†

30, 14-25: Health of mind and body and joy of heart are judged more precious than wealth (14ff); bitterness, *constant illness* and affliction more difficult to bear than *death* (17-20). *Sadness, resentment,* anxiety, *envy and anger shorten . . . life;* they should be dispelled by *cheerfulness* and *gladness of heart,* which help to prolong one's days (21-25).

30, 17: *Preferable is death . . . constant illness:* the true value of human suffering was revealed through the passion and death of Christ. It serves as reparation for sin, and when united with Christ's suffering, as merit for eternal life.

31, 1-11: Solicitude for acquiring wealth and anxiety over preserving it disturb *repose* and easily lead to sin and ruin (1-7). Cf Mt 6, 25-34. A *rich man* who has not sinned or been seduced by wealth is worthy of praise (8-11).

31, 2: The Hebrew adds a verse that seems out of place here: "A faithful comrade drives away reproach, and the friend who keeps secrets is as dear as life."

5 The lover of gold will not be free from sin,
for he who pursues wealth is led astray by it.
6* Many have been ensnared by gold, though destruction lay before their eyes;
7 It is a stumbling block to those who are avid for it,
a snare for every fool.

8*† Happy the rich man found without fault,
who turns not aside after gain!
9 Who is he, that we may praise him?
he, of all his kindred, has done wonders,
10 For he has been tested by gold and come off safe,
and this remains his glory;
He could have sinned but did not,
could have done evil but would not,
11* So that his possessions are secure,
and the assembly recounts his praises.

Table Etiquette†

12 If you are dining with a great man,
bring not a greedy gullet to his table,
Nor cry out, "How much food there is here!"
13* Remember that gluttony is evil.
No creature is greedier than the eye:
therefore it weeps for any cause.
15 Recognize that your neighbor feels as you do,
and keep in mind your own dislikes:
14 Toward what he eyes, do not put out a hand;
nor reach when he does for the same dish.
16 Behave at table like a favored guest,
and be not greedy, lest you be despised.
17* Be the first to stop, as befits good manners;
gorge not yourself, lest you give offense.
18 If there are many with you at table,
be not the first to reach out your hand.
19* Does not a little suffice for a well-bred man?
When he lies down, it is without discomfort.
20 Distress and anguish and loss of sleep,
and restless tossing for the glutton!
Moderate eating ensures sound slumber
and a clear mind next day on rising.
21† If perforce you have eaten too much,
once you have emptied your stomach, you will have relief.
22 Listen to me, my son, and scorn me not;
later you will find my advice good.
In whatever you do, be moderate,
and no sickness will befall you.
23* On a man generous with food, blessings are invoked,
and this testimony to his goodness is lasting;
24 He who is miserly with food is denounced in public,
and this testimony to his stinginess is lasting.
25 Let not wine-drinking be the proof of your strength,
for wine has been the ruin of many.
26 As the furnace probes the work of the smith,
so does wine the hearts of the insolent.
27* Wine is very life to man
if taken in moderation.
Does he really live who lacks the wine
which was created for his joy?
28 Joy of heart, good cheer and merriment
are wine drunk freely at the proper time.
29 Headache, bitterness and disgrace
is wine drunk amid anger and strife.
30 More and more wine is a snare for the fool;
it lessens his strength and multiplies his wounds.
31 Rebuke not your neighbor when wine is served,
nor put him to shame while he is merry;
Use no harsh words with him
and distress him not in the presence of others.

CHAPTER 32

1 If you are chosen to preside at dinner, be not puffed up,

*

31, 6: 8, 2.
8: 5, 1.10.
11: Prv 29, 14.
13: 37, 28ff; Prv 23, 1f.
17: 37, 29.
19: Eccl 5, 11.
23: Prv 22, 9.
27: Ps 104, 15; 1 Tm 5, 23.

†

31, 8ff: The Church in her liturgy applies this passage to holy confessors of the Faith.

31, 12—32, 13: A man observing etiquette at table avoids greed and selfishness (31, 12f), is considerate of a neighbor's likes and dislikes and is *generous* toward him (14f.23f), observes proper manners (16ff), is *moderate* in *eating* and drinking (19-22.25-30). A good host makes himself one with his guests, is solicitous for them (32, 1f), provides conversation and diversion (3-6), is modest in speech (7f.10), is respectful of elders (9), polite in comportment and grateful to God for his *favors* (11ff).

31, 21: *Emptied your stomach:* the practice of induced vomiting, well-known among pagan Romans, and less well-known among the Jews, seems to be referred to here.

but with the guests be as one of themselves;
Take care of them first before you sit down;
2 when you have fulfilled your duty, then take your place,
To share in their joy
and win praise for your hospitality.
3 Being older, you may talk; that is only your right,
but temper your wisdom, not to disturb the singing.
4 When wine is present, do not pour out discourse,
and flaunt not your wisdom at the wrong time.
5 Like a seal of carnelian in a setting of gold
is a concert when wine is served.
6 Like a gold mounting with an emerald seal
is string music with delicious wine.
7* Young man, speak only when necessary,
when they have asked you more than once;
8 Be brief, but say much in those few words,
be like the wise man, taciturn.
9 When among your elders be not forward,
and with officials be not too insistent.
10 Like the lightning that flashes before a storm
is the esteem that shines on modesty.
11 When it is time to leave, tarry not;
be off for home! There take your ease,
12 And there enjoy doing as you wish,
but without sin or words of pride.
13 Above all, give praise to your Creator,
who showers his favors upon you.

The Providence of God†

14* He who would find God must accept discipline;
he who seeks him obtains his request.
15* He who studies the law masters it,
but the hypocrite finds it a trap.
16* His judgment is sound who fears the LORD;
out of obscurity he draws forth a clear plan.
17* The sinner turns aside reproof
and distorts the law to suit his purpose.
18 The thoughtful man will not neglect direction;
the proud and insolent man is deterred by nothing.
19* Do nothing without counsel,
and then you need have no regrets.
20 Go not on a way that is set with snares,
and let not the same thing trip you twice.
21 Be not too sure even of smooth roads,
22 be careful on all your paths.
23 Whatever you do, be on your guard,
for in this way you will keep the commandments.
24 He who keeps the law preserves himself;
and he who trusts in the LORD shall not be put to shame.

CHAPTER 33

1* No evil can harm the man who fears the LORD;
through trials, again and again he is safe.
2 He who hates the law is without wisdom,
and is tossed about like a boat in a storm.
3† The prudent man trusts in the word of the LORD,
and the law is dependable for him as a divine oracle.
4 Prepare your words and you will be listened to;
draw upon your training, and then give your answer.
5† Like the wheel of a cart is the mind of a fool;
his thoughts revolve in circles.
6 A fickle friend is like the stallion
that neighs, no matter who the rider.
7 Why is one day more important than another,
when it is the sun that lights up every day?
8* It is due to the LORD's wisdom that they differ;
it is through him the seasons and feasts come and go.

*

32, 7ff: 7, 14.
14: 4, 13.
15: 2, 16.
16: Ps 37, 6.
17: 21, 6; Prv 12, 1.
19: 37, 16; Tb 4, 18.
33, 1: Ps 91, 10.
8: Gn 1, 14.

†

32, 14—33, 4: God is shown to reveal himself through the discipline of his law, a clear and safe plan of life for the pious Jew of old. *Direction* and *counsel* are aids in following it (14ff.18-24; 33, 1.3f). Sinners and hypocrites, hating *the law* or distorting it, fail in wisdom and are devoid of security (32, 15.17f; 33, 2).

33, 3: *Oracle:* as the answer given through the Urim and Thummim to the high priest is true, so the law proves itself true to him who obeys it. Cf Ex 28, 30; Nm 27, 21.

33, 5-15: Contrasts observable in the physical universe as well as in the moral order serve the purposes of divine wisdom (5-9). All creatures are *like clay. . . in the hands of their Creator*—the fool and the wise man, the sinner, and the just (10-15). This does not imply that man is created to be a sinner: God is not the author of wickedness. Cf Jas 1, 13f.

9* Some he dignifies and sanctifies,
and others he lists as ordinary days.
10* So too, all men are of clay,
for from earth man was formed;
11 Yet with his great knowledge the LORD makes men unlike;
in different paths he has them walk.
12 Some he blesses and makes great,
some he sanctifies and draws to himself.
Others he curses and brings low,
and expels them from their place.
13* Like clay in the hands of a potter,
to be molded according to his pleasure,
So are men in the hands of their Creator,
to be assigned by him their function.
14* As evil contrasts with good, and death with life,
so are sinners in contrast with the just;
15 See now all the works of the Most High:
they come in pairs, the one the opposite of the other.

16† Now I am the last to keep vigil,
like a gleaner after the vintage;
17 Since by the LORD's blessing I have made progress
till like a vintager I have filled my wine press,
18 I would inform you that not for myself only have I toiled,
but for every seeker after wisdom.

SIRACH

Property and Servants†

19* Listen to me, O leaders of the multitude;
O rulers of the assembly, give ear!
20 Let neither son nor wife, neither brother nor friend,
have power over you as long as you live.
21 While breath of life is still in you,
let no man have dominion over you.
Give not to another your wealth,
lest then you have to plead with him;
22 Far better that your children plead with you
than that you should look to their generosity.
23 Keep control over all your affairs;
let no one tarnish your glory.
24 When your few days reach their limit,
at the time of death distribute your inheritance.

25 Fodder and whip and loads for an ass;
the yoke and harness and the rod of his master.
27 Food, correction and work for a slave;
and for a wicked slave, punishment in the stocks.
26* Make a slave work and he will look for his rest;
let his hands be idle and he will seek to be free.
28 Force him to work that he be not idle,
for idleness is an apt teacher of mischief.
29 Put him to work, for that is what befits him;
if he becomes unruly, load him with chains.
30 But never lord it over any human being,
and do nothing unjust.
31* If you have but one slave, treat him like yourself,
for you have acquired him with your life's blood;
32 If you have but one slave, deal with him as a brother,
for you need him as you need your life:
33 If you mistreat him and he runs away,
in what direction will you look for him?

CHAPTER 34

Trust in the Lord and Not in Dreams†

1 Empty and false are the hopes of the senseless,
and fools are borne aloft by dreams.
2 Like a man who catches at shadows or chases the wind,
is the one who believes in dreams.
3 What is seen in dreams is to reality
what the reflection of a face is to the face itself.
4* Can the unclean produce the clean?
can the liar ever speak the truth?

*

9: Ex 20, 11.
10: Gn 2, 7.
13: Wis 15, 7; Jer 18, 1-6; Rom 9, 20f.
14: 42, 25.
19: Wis 6, 1f.
26: Prv 29, 19.
31: 7, 21.
34, 4: Jb 14, 4.

†

33, 16ff: Here the author refers to himself as the most recent of the writers who have endeavored to present true wisdom to their readers.

33, 19-33: Public officials should reject every influence that would restrict their freedom in the management of their affairs. They must make their own household subservient to them rather than be subservient to it (19-24). Slaves are to be given *food* and *work* and *correction* but never to be treated unjustly (25-29). Great care should be taken of good slaves (30-33).

34, 1-17: Confidence placed in *dreams,* divinations and *omens* is false because these are devoid of reality (1-8). True confidence is founded on *knowledge* and *experience* (9-12), and above all on the fear of the Lord, with its accompanying blessings of divine assistance and protection (13-17).

5 Divination, omens and dreams all are unreal;
what you already expect, the mind depicts.
6 Unless it be a vision specially sent by the Most High,
fix not your heart on it;
7 For dreams have led many astray,
and those who believed in them have perished.
8 The law is fulfilled without fail,
and perfect wisdom is found in the mouth of the faithful man.
9 A man with training gains wide knowledge;
a man of experience speaks sense.
10 One never put to the proof knows little,
whereas with travel a man adds to his resourcefulness.
11 I have seen much in my travels,
learned more than ever I could say.
12 Often I was in danger of death,
but by these attainments I was saved.

13 Lively is the courage of those who fear the LORD,
for they put their hope in their savior;
14* He who fears the LORD is never alarmed,
never afraid; for the LORD is his hope.
15 Happy the soul that fears the LORD!
In whom does he trust, and who is his support?
16* The eyes of the LORD are upon those who love him;
he is their mighty shield and strong support,
A shelter from the heat, a shade from the noonday sun,
a guard against stumbling, a help against falling.
17 He buoys up the spirits, brings a sparkle to the eyes,
gives health and life and blessing.

True Worship of God†

18* Tainted his gifts who offers in sacrifice ill-gotten goods!
Mock presents from the lawless win not God's favor.
19 The Most High approves not the gifts of the godless,
nor for their many sacrifices does he forgive their sins.
20 Like the man who slays a son in his father's presence
is he who offers sacrifice from the possessions of the poor.
21* The bread of charity is life itself for the needy;
he who withholds it is a man of blood.
22 He slays his neighbor who deprives him of his living:
he sheds blood who denies the laborer his wages.
23 If one man builds up and another tears down,
what do they gain but trouble?
24 If one man prays and another curses,
whose voice will the LORD hear?
25* If a man again touches a corpse after he has bathed,
what did he gain by the purification?
26 So with a man who fasts for his sins,
but then goes and commits them again:
Who will hear his prayer,
and what has he gained by his mortification?

CHAPTER 35†

1* To keep the law is a great oblation,
and he who observes the commandments sacrifices a peace offering.
2† In works of charity one offers fine flour,
and when he gives alms he presents his sacrifice of praise.
3 To refrain from evil pleases the LORD,
and to avoid injustice is an atonement.
4* Appear not before the LORD empty-handed,
for all that you offer is in fulfillment of the precepts.
5 The just man's offering enriches the altar
and rises as a sweet odor before the Most High.

SIRACH

*

14: Pss 23, 4; 112, 7f; Prv 3, 23ff; 28, 1.
16: Pss 33, 18; 34, 16.
18: 35, 11; Prv 21, 27.
21f: Lv 19, 13; Dt 24, 14f; Tb 4, 14.
25: Nm 19, 11f; Prv 26, 11; 2 Pt 2, 22.
35, 1ff: 1 Sm 15, 22; Ps 51, 18f; Is 1, 11-18; Hos 6, 6; Am 5, 21-24.
4: Ex 23, 15; 34, 20; Dt 16, 16.

†

34, 18-26: To be acts of true religion, sacrifice and penance must be accompanied by the proper moral dispositions. To offer to God goods taken from the poor (18-22), or to practice penance without interior reform, is a mockery, worthless in the sight of God (23-26). Cf Mt 15, 4-7; Mk 7, 9-13.

35, 1-24: Keeping *the commandments* of the law and avoiding *injustice* constitute sacrifice pleasing and acceptable to God (1ff). Offerings also should be made to him, cheerfully and *generously;* these he *repays . . . sevenfold* (4-10). Extortion from widows and orphans is injustice, which God quickly repays (11-18). Punishing the *proud* and the *merciless* and coming to the aid of the distressed, he *requites* all *according to* their *deeds* (19-24).

35, 2: *Fine flour,* together with oil and frankincense, was a prescribed offering to God; cf Lv 2, 1ff.

6 The just man's sacrifice is most pleasing,
nor will it ever be forgotten.
7* In generous spirit pay homage to the LORD,
be not sparing of freewill gifts.
8* With each contribution show a cheerful countenance,
and pay your tithes in a spirit of joy.
9 Give to the Most High as he has given to you,
generously, according to your means.
10* For the LORD is one who always repays,
and he will give back to you sevenfold.
11* But offer no bribes, these he does not accept!
Trust not in sacrifice of the fruits of extortion,
12* For he is a God of justice,
who knows no favorites.
13† Though not unduly partial toward the weak,
yet he hears the cry of the oppressed.
14* He is not deaf to the wail of the orphan,
nor to the widow when she pours out her complaint;

15 Do not the tears that stream down her cheek
cry out against him that causes them to fall?
16 He who serves God willingly is heard;
his petition reaches the heavens.
17 The prayer of the lowly pierces the clouds;
it does not rest till it reaches its goal,
18 Nor will it withdraw till the Most High responds,
judges justly and affirms the right.

19* God indeed will not delay,
and like a warrior, will not be still
20 Till he breaks the backs of the merciless
and wreaks vengeance upon the proud;
21 Till he destroys the haughty root and branch,
and smashes the scepter of the wicked;
22 Till he requites mankind according to its deeds,
and repays men according to their thoughts;
23 Till he defends the cause of his people,
and gladdens them by his mercy.
24 Welcome is his mercy in time of distress
as rain clouds in time of drought.

CHAPTER 36

A Prayer for God's People†

1 Come to our aid, O God of the universe,
and put all the nations in dread of you!
2 Raise your hand against the heathen,
that they may realize your power.
3 As you have used us to show them your holiness,
so now use them to show us your glory.
4 Thus they will know, as we know,
that there is no God but you.

5 Give new signs and work new wonders;
show forth the splendor of your right hand and arm;
6* Rouse your anger, pour out wrath,
humble the enemy, scatter the foe.
7 Hasten the day, bring on the time;
9 crush the heads of the hostile rulers.
8 Let raging fire consume the fugitive,
and your people's oppressors meet destruction.

10 Gather all the tribes of Jacob,
that they may inherit the land as of old,
11* Show mercy to the people called by your name;
Israel, whom you named your first-born.
12* Take pity on your holy city,
Jerusalem, your dwelling place.
13 Fill Zion with your majesty,
your temple with your glory.

14 Give evidence of your deeds of old;
fulfill the prophecies spoken in your name,
15 Reward those who have hoped in you,
and let your prophets be proved true.
16 Hear the prayer of your servants,

*

7: 7, 31.
8: 2 Cor 9, 7.
10: Prv 19, 17.
11: 34, 18f; Prv 21, 27.
12: Dt 10, 17; 2 Chr 19, 7; Jb 34, 19; Wis 6, 7; Acts 10, 34; Rom 2, 11; Gal 2, 6; 1 Pt 1, 17.
14f: Ex 22, 22.
19: Is 42, 13ff; 2 Pt 3, 9.
36, 6: Ps 79, 6.
11: Ex 4, 22.
12: 2 Chr 6, 41; Ps 132, 8.14; Is 2, 1ff; Mi 4, 1ff.

†

35, 13: Cf Lv 19, 15.

36, 1-17: Making an act of faith and hope in the supreme Lord of the universe, the author begs God to continue manifesting his *holiness* and *mercy* through *Israel,* his people (1ff.10-13), and his *power* and justice through the punishment of the nations (2.5-9), that all the earth may acknowledge him *the eternal God* (4.14-17).

SIRACH

for you are ever gracious to your people;
17 Thus it will be known to the very ends of the earth
that you are the eternal God.

Choice of Associates†

18 The throat can swallow any food,
yet some foods are more agreeable than others;
19 As the palate tests meat by its savor,
so does a keen mind insincere words.
20 A deceitful character causes grief,
but an experienced man can turn the tables on him.
21 Though any man may be accepted as a husband,
yet one girl will be more suitable than another:
22* A woman's beauty makes her husband's face light up,
for it surpasses all else that charms the eye;
23 And if, besides, her speech is kindly,
his lot is beyond that of mortal men.
24* A wife is her husband's richest treasure,
a helpmate, a steadying column.
25 A vineyard with no hedge will be overrun;
a man with no wife becomes a homeless wanderer.
26 Who will trust an armed band
that shifts from city to city?
27* Or a man who has no nest,
but lodges where night overtakes him?

CHAPTER 37

1* Every friend declares his friendship,
but there are friends who are friends in name only.
2 Is it not a sorrow unto death
when your bosom companion becomes your enemy?
3 "Alas, my companion! Why were you created
to blanket the earth with deceit?"
4 A false friend will share your joys,
but in time of trouble he stands afar off.
5 A true friend will fight with you against the foe,
against your enemies he will be your shield-bearer.
6 Forget not your comrade during the battle,
and neglect him not when you distribute your spoils.

7 Every counselor points out a way,
but some counsel ways of their own;
8 Be on the alert when one proffers advice,
find out first of all what he wants.
For he may be thinking of himself alone;
why should the profit fall to him?
9 He may tell you how good your way will be,
and then stand by to watch your misfortune.
10 Seek no advice from one who regards you with hostility;
from those who envy you, keep your intentions hidden.
11 Speak not to a woman about her rival,
nor to a coward about war,
to a merchant about business,
to a buyer about value,
to a miser about generosity,
to a cruel man about mercy,
to a lazy man about work,
to a seasonal laborer about the harvest,
to an idle slave about a great task:
pay no attention to any advice they give.
12 Instead, associate with a religious man,
who you are sure keeps the commandments;
Who is like-minded with yourself
and will feel for you if you fall.
13 Then, too, heed your own heart's counsel;
for what have you that you can depend on more?
14 A man's conscience can tell him his situation
better than seven watchmen in a lofty tower.
15 Most important of all, pray to God
to set your feet in the path of truth.

Wisdom and Temperance†

16* A word is the source of every deed;
a thought, of every act.
17 The root of all conduct is the mind;
four branches it shoots forth:
18* Good and evil, death and life,

SIRACH

---

*

22: 26, 13ff.
24: Gn 2, 18; Prv 18, 22.
27: Prv 27, 8.
37, 1: 6, 7ff.
16: 32, 19.
18: Prv 18, 21.

---

†

36, 18—37, 15: In the choice of wife, friend or associate, experience is a discerner of character (18-21). *Beauty* and *kindly speech* make a woman desirable as wife (22f). The good wife becomes *her husband's richest treasure,* his *helpmate* in establishing his household (24-27). *A true friend* fights for his comrade and shares his spoils with him (37, 5f); a false one deceives and abandons him in time of need (1-4). A true counselor and associate should be sought among those who keep the commandments, not among those who break them and seek their own advantage (7-12). In all things *pray to God* for light and follow conscience (13ff).

37, 16-25: Thoughts determine action. Wisdom is the source of *good* and *life;* folly, of *evil* and *death* (16ff). If the fruits of a man's wisdom benefit himself, he may be praised in his own lifetime; if they benefit his people, his praise endures after him, in their lives (19-25).

their absolute mistress is the
tongue.
19 A man may be wise and benefit
many,
yet be of no use to himself.
20 Though a man may be wise, if his
words are rejected
he will be deprived of all enjoyment.
21 When a man is wise to his own advantage,
the fruits of his knowledge are
seen in his own person;
22* When a man is wise to his people's
advantage,
the fruits of his knowledge are enduring:
23 Limited are the days of one man's
life,
but the life of Israel is days without number.
24 One wise for himself has full enjoyment,
and all who see him praise him;
25* One wise for his people wins a heritage of glory,
and his name endures forever.

26† My son, while you are well, govern
your appetite
so that you allow it not what is bad
for you;
27* For not every food is good for everyone,
nor is everything suited to every
taste.
28* Be not drawn after every enjoyment,
neither become a glutton for
choice foods,
29 For sickness comes with overeating,
and gluttony brings on biliousness.
30 Through lack of self-control many
have died,
but the abstemious man prolongs
his life.

SIRACH

CHAPTER 38

Sickness and Death†

1 Hold the physician in honor, for he
is essential to you,
and God it was who established
his profession.
2 From God the doctor has his wisdom,
and the king provides for his
sustenance.
3 His knowledge makes the doctor
distinguished,
and gives him access to those in
authority.
4 God makes the earth yield healing
herbs
which the prudent man should not
neglect;
5* Was not the water sweetened by a
twig
that men might learn his power?
6 He endows men with the knowledge
to glory in his mighty works,
7 Through which the doctor eases
pain
and the druggist prepares his
medicines;
8 Thus God's creative work continues
without cease
in its efficacy on the surface of the
earth.

9* My son, when you are ill, delay not,
but pray to God, who will heal you:
10 Flee wickedness; let your hands be
just,
cleanse your heart of every sin;
11* Offer your sweet-smelling oblation
and petition,
a rich offering according to your
means.
12 Then give the doctor his place
lest he leave; for you need him too.
13 There are times that give him an advantage,
14 and he too beseeches God
That his diagnosis may be correct
and his treatment bring about a
cure.
15 He who is a sinner toward his Maker
will be defiant toward the doctor.

16*†My son, shed tears for one who is
dead
with wailing and bitter lament;
As is only proper, prepare the body,
absent not yourself from his
burial:
17 Weeping bitterly, mourning fully,
pay your tribute of sorrow, as he
deserves,
18 One or two days, to prevent gossip;
then compose yourself after your
grief,
19* For grief can bring on an extremity
and heartache destroy one's
health.

*

22: 15, 1ff.
25: 39, 9; 44, 13f.
27: 1 Cor 6, 12; 10, 23.
28f: 31, 13.16ff.
38, 5: Ex 15, 25.
9: Is 38, 2f.
11: Lv 2, 1ff.
16: 22, 9f.
19: Prv 12, 25; 15, 13; 17, 22.

†

37, 26-30: Temperance and self-control should govern a man's appetite for food, which is intended not to destroy but to preserve life.

38, 1-15: The profession of medicine comes from *God,* who *makes the earth yield healing herbs* and gives the physician knowledge of their virtue (1-8). In illness the sick man should cleanse his soul from sin and petition God for help through an offering of sacrifice; the physician, too, does well to invoke God that he may understand the illness and apply the proper remedy (9-14). The sinner, in contrast, defies both his Maker and the doctor (15).

38, 16-23: A period of mourning for the deceased and care for their burial is becoming (16ff). But grief should not be excessive, for it neither helps the dead, who cannot return, nor fails to harm the living. The mourner's own end will quickly follow, and the time to prepare for it is now (19-23).

20* Turn not your thoughts to him again;
cease to recall him; think rather of the end.
21* Recall him not, for there is no hope of his return;
it will not help him, but will do you harm.
22* Remember that his fate will also be yours;
for him it was yesterday, for you today.
23 With the departed dead, let memory fade;
rally your courage, once the soul has left.

Vocations of the Craftsman and the Scribe†

24 The scribe's profession increases his wisdom;
whoever is free from toil can become a wise man.
25 How can he become learned who guides the plow,
who thrills in wielding the goad like a lance,
Who guides the ox and urges on the bullock,
and whose every concern is for cattle?
26 His care is for plowing furrows,
and he keeps a watch on the beasts in the stalls.

27 So with every engraver and designer
who, laboring night and day,
Fashions carved seals,
and whose concern is to vary the pattern.
His care is to produce a vivid impression,
and he keeps watch till he finishes his design.

28 So with the smith standing near his anvil,
forging crude iron.
The heat from the fire sears his flesh,
yet he toils away in the furnace heat.
The clang of the hammer deafens his ears,
His eyes are fixed on the tool he is shaping.
His care is to finish his work,
and he keeps watch till he perfects it in detail.

29 So with the potter sitting at his labor,
revolving the wheel with his feet.
He is always concerned for his products,
and turns them out in quantity.
30 With his hands he molds the clay,
and with his feet softens it.
His care is for proper coloring,
and he keeps watch on the fire of his kiln.
31 All these men are skilled with their hands,
each one an expert at his own task;
32 Without them no city could be lived in,
and wherever they stay, they need not hunger.
33 They do not occupy the judge's bench,
nor are they prominent in the assembly;
They set forth no decisions or judgments,
nor are they found among the rulers;
34 Yet they maintain God's ancient handiwork,
and their concern is for exercise of their skill.

CHAPTER 39

1 How different the man who devotes himself
to the study of the law of the Most High!
He explores the wisdom of the men of old
and occupies himself with the prophecies;
2 He treasures the discourses of famous men,
and goes to the heart of involved sayings;
3 He studies obscure parables,
and is busied with the hidden meanings of the sages.
4 He is in attendance on the great,
and has entrance to the ruler.
5 He travels among the peoples of foreign lands
to learn what is good and evil among men.
6 His care is to seek the LORD, his Maker,
to petition the Most High,
To open his lips in prayer,
to ask pardon for his sins.

SIRACH

*

20: 7, 36; 18, 24; 30, 21.
21: 2 Sm 12, 23; Wis 2, 1.
22: Jas 4, 13ff.

†

38, 24—39, 11: More excellent than the useful service of craftsmen—farmer, engraver, smith, potter (25-34)—is the profession of the scribe (24), who studies and meditates on *the law of the Most High*, seeks him in prayer of thanksgiving, petition and repentance for sin (39, 1.6f), *explores the wisdom* of the past and present, travels abroad to observe the conduct of many peoples, and attends rulers and great men. Through the spirit of understanding granted by God, he will show forth his wisdom to the glory of God's law, gaining renown for generations to come (2-5.8-11).

Then, if it pleases the LORD Almighty,
he will be filled with the spirit of understanding;
He will pour forth his words of wisdom
and in prayer give thanks to the LORD,
7 Who will direct his knowledge and his counsel,
as he meditates upon his mysteries.
8 He will show the wisdom of what he has learned
and glory in the law of the LORD's covenant.
9* Many will praise his understanding;
his fame can never be effaced;
Unfading will be his memory,
through all generations his name will live;
10 Peoples will speak of his wisdom,
and in assembly sing his praises.
11 While he lives he is one out of a thousand,
and when he dies his renown will not cease.

Praise of God the Creator†

12 Once more I will set forth my theme
to shine like the moon in its fullness!
13 Listen, my faithful children: open up your petals,
like roses planted near running waters;
14 Send up the sweet odor of incense,
break forth in blossoms like the lily.
Send up the sweet odor of your hymn of praise;
bless the LORD for all he has done!
15 Proclaim the greatness of his name,
loudly sing his praises,
With music on the harp and all stringed instruments;
sing out with joy as you proclaim:

16* The works of God are all of them good;
in its own time every need is supplied.
17* At his word the waters become still as in a flask;
he had but to speak and the reservoirs were made.
18 He has but to command and his will is done;
nothing can limit his achievement.
19* The works of all mankind are present to him;
not a thing escapes his eye.
20 His gaze spans all the ages;
to him there is nothing unexpected.
21 No cause then to say: "What is the purpose of this?"
Everything is chosen to satisfy a need.
22 His blessing overflows like the Nile;
like the Euphrates it enriches the surface of the earth.
23* Again, his wrath expels the nations
and turns fertile land into a salt marsh.
24 For the virtuous his paths are level,
to the haughty they are steep;
25 Good things for the good he provided from the beginning,
but for the wicked good things and bad.
26* Chief of all needs for human life
are water and fire, iron and salt,
The heart of the wheat, milk and honey,
the blood of the grape, and oil, and cloth;
27 For the good all these are good,
but for the wicked they turn out evil.
28 There are storm winds created to punish,
which in their fury can dislodge mountains;
When destruction must be, they hurl all their force
and appease the anger of their Maker.
29 In his treasury also, kept for the proper time,
are fire and hail, famine, disease,
30 Ravenous beasts, scorpions, vipers,
and the avenging sword to exterminate the wicked;
31 In doing his bidding they rejoice,
in their assignments they disobey not his command.
32 So from the first I took my stand,
and wrote down as my theme:
33* The works of God are all of them good;
every need when it comes he fills.
34 No cause then to say: "This is not as good as that";
for each shows its worth at the proper time.
35 So now with full joy of heart proclaim
and bless the name of the Holy One.

SIRACH

*

39, 9: 37, 25; 44, 14.
16: Gn 1, 31; Eccl 3, 11.
17: Gn 1, 6-10; Ex 14, 21f; Jos 3, 16.
19: 15, 19; 42, 20.
23: Jos 1, 2-6.
26: 29, 21.
33: 39, 16; Gn 1, 31; Eccl 3, 11.

†

39, 12-35: The sage invites his disciples to join him in joyfully proclaiming his favorite theme: *The works of God are all of them good; in its own time every need is supplied* (12-16.32-35). He describes God's omniscience, supreme power and wisdom, whereby all created things, good in themselves, are ever present to him, obey him, and fulfill their intended purpose (17-21), bringing blessing to the virtuous, but evil and punishment to the wicked who misuse them (22-31). Cf similar hymns of praise, 36, 1-17; 42, 15—43, 35.

CHAPTER 40

Joys and Miseries of Life†

1* A great anxiety has God allotted,
and a heavy yoke, to the sons of men;
From the day one leaves his mother's womb
to the day he returns to the mother of all the living,
2 His thoughts, the fear in his heart,
and his troubled forebodings till the day he dies—
3 Whether he sits on a lofty throne
or grovels in dust and ashes,
4 Whether he bears a splendid crown
or is wrapped in the coarsest of cloaks—
5 Are of wrath and envy, trouble and dread,
terror of death, fury and strife.
Even when he lies on his bed to rest,
his cares at night disturb his sleep.
6 So short is his rest it seems like none,
till in his dreams he struggles as he did by day,
Terrified by what his mind's eye sees,
like a fugitive being pursued;
7 As he reaches safety, he wakes up
astonished that there was nothing to fear.
8 So it is with all flesh, with man and with beast,
but for sinners seven times more.
9* Plague and bloodshed, wrath and the sword,
plunder and ruin, famine and death:
10 For the wicked, these were created evil,
and it is they who bring on destruction.

11† All that is of earth returns to earth,
and what is from above returns above.
12 All that comes from bribes or injustice will be wiped out,
but loyalty remains for ages.
13 Wealth out of wickedness is like a wadi in spate:
like a mighty stream with lightning and thunder,
14* Which, in its rising, rolls along the stones,
but suddenly, once and for all, comes to an end.
15 The offshoot of violence will not flourish,
for the root of the godless is on sheer rock;
16 Or they are like reeds on the riverbank,
withered before all other plants;
17† But goodness will never be cut off,
and justice endures forever.
Wealth or wages can make life sweet,
but better than either is finding a treasure.
18* A child or a city will preserve one's name,
but better than either, attaining wisdom.
19 Sheepfolds and orchards bring flourishing health;
but better than either, a devoted wife;
20* Wine and music delight the soul,
but better than either, conjugal love.
21 The flute and the harp offer sweet melody,
but better than either, a voice that is true.
22* Charm and beauty delight the eye,
but better than either, the flowers of the field.
23 A friend, a neighbor, are timely guides,
but better than either, a prudent wife.
24 A brother, a helper, for times of stress;
but better than either, charity that rescues.
25 Gold and silver make one's way secure,
but better than either, sound judgment.
26 Wealth and vigor build up confidence,
but better than either, fear of God.
Fear of the LORD leaves nothing wanting;
he who has it need seek no other support:
27* The fear of God is a paradise of blessings;
its canopy, all that is glorious.

*

40, 1: Gn 3, 17; Jb 7, 1; 14, 1; Eccl 2, 23.
9: 39, 28ff.
14: 23, 25; Wis 4, 3ff.
18: Prv 19, 14.
20: Ps 104, 15.
22: Mt 6, 28f.
27: Is 4, 5.

†

40, 1-16: The former idyllic description of the universe is contrasted with the picture of the evils afflicting humanity. Every man, high or low, is burdened from birth to death with fears, anxieties and troubles, by day and often by night, the time appointed for rest (1-7). For sinners, the suffering is much greater (8ff). What they gained by violence and injustice is quickly destroyed; but *justice endures forever* (14ff).

40, 1: *Mother of all the living:* the earth from which man was taken. Cf Gn 2, 7; 3, 19f; Jb 1, 21; Ps 139, 15.

40, 11: *All that is of earth . . . returns above:* a reference to bodily mortality and to the divine origin of life from the Spirit of God. Cf 41, 10; Gn 2, 7; 3, 19; Jb 34, 14f; Pss 104, 29f; 146, 4; Eccl 12, 7. The Greek and the Latin render the second half of the verse: "all waters shall return to the sea."

40, 17-27: Of the many treasures making life sweet, such as *health,* children, friends, *music, vigor,* the best are called true *conjugal love, wisdom,* and above all, *fear of God;* cf 25, 6-11.

28† My son, live not the life of a beggar,
better to die than to beg;
29* When one has to look to another's table,
his life is not really a life.
His neighbor's delicacies bring revulsion of spirit
to one who understands inward feelings:
30 In the mouth of the shameless man begging is sweet,
but within him it burns like fire.

CHAPTER 41†

1 O death! how bitter the thought of you
for the man at peace amid his possessions,
For the man unruffled and always successful,
who still can enjoy life's pleasures.
2* O death! how welcome your sentence
to the weak man of failing strength,
Tottering and always rebuffed,
with no more sight, with vanished hope.
3* Fear not death's decree for you;
remember, it embraces those before you, and those after.
4 Thus God has ordained for all flesh;
why then should you reject the will of the Most High?
Whether one has lived a thousand years, a hundred, or ten,
in the nether world he has no claim on life.

5* A reprobate line are the children of sinners,
and witless offspring are in the homes of the wicked.
6 Their dominion is lost to sinners' children,
and reproach abides with their descendants.
7 Children curse their wicked father,
for they suffer disgrace through him.
8 Woe to you, O sinful men,
who forsake the law of the Most High.
9 If you have children, calamity will seize them;
you will beget them only for groaning.
When you stumble, there is lasting joy;
at death, you become a curse.
10* Whatever is of nought returns to nought,
so too the godless from void to void.
11* Man's body is a fleeting thing,
but a virtuous name will never be annihilated.
12* Have a care for your name, for it will stand by you
better than precious treasures in the thousands;
13 The boon of life is for limited days,
but a good name, for days without number.

True and False Shame†

14 My children, heed my instruction about shame;
judge of disgrace only according to my rules,
For it is not always well to be ashamed,
nor is it always the proper thing to blush:
15 Before father and mother be ashamed of immorality,
before master and mistress, of falsehood;
16 Before prince and ruler, of flattery;
before the public assembly, of crime;
17 Before friend and companion, of disloyalty,
and of breaking an oath or agreement.
18 Be ashamed of theft from the people where you settle,
and of stretching out your elbow when you dine;
19 Of refusing to give when asked,
of defrauding another of his appointed share,
20 Of failing to return a greeting,
and of rebuffing a friend;
21* Of gazing at a married woman,
and of entertaining thoughts about another's wife;
Of trifling with a servant girl you have,
and of violating her couch;
22* Of using harsh words with friends,
and of following up your gifts with insults;

---

* 29: 29, 24.
41, 2: 30, 17.
3: 38, 20ff.
5ff: 3, 9ff; Wis 3, 16-19.
10: 40, 11; Wis 4, 19.
11: Prv 10, 7.
12: Prv 22, 1; Eccl 7, 1.
21: 9, 8; Mt 5, 28.
22: 18, 14; 20, 13.

---

† 40, 28ff. Among the Jews, beggary was considered degrading to human dignity; it was agreeable only to the shameless, who had lost their sense of honor. Cf 29, 22f.

41, 1-13: Whether *death* seems *bitter* to one who enjoys *peace,* success and pleasure, or welcome to one who is weak and in despair, it comes to all and must be accepted as the will of God (1-4). As the human body passes away (11), so do those who have sinned through the body and their offspring alike, who, needy and accursed, pass on with their parents as if they had never been (5-10). Only the good name of the virtuous endures (11ff).

41, 13: After this verse many texts repeat 20, 29f.

41, 14—42, 8: The author illustrates the subject of true and false shame with numerous and detailed examples of sin (14-24) and virtue (42, 1-8), following the norm of the commandments.

23* Of repeating what you hear,
and of betraying secrets—
24 These are the things you should rightly avoid as shameful
if you would be looked upon by everyone with favor.

CHAPTER 42

1* But of these things be not ashamed,
lest you sin through human respect:
2 Of the law of the Most High and his precepts,
or of the sentence to be passed upon the sinful;
3 Of sharing the expenses of a business or a journey,
or of dividing an inheritance or property;
4* Of accuracy of scales and balances,
or of tested measures and weights;
5* Of acquiring much or little,
or of bargaining in dealing with a merchant;
Of constant training of children,
or of beating the sides of a disloyal servant;
6 Of a seal to keep an erring wife at home,
or of a lock placed where there are many hands;
7 Of numbering every deposit,
or of recording all that is given or received;
8 Of chastisement of the silly and the foolish,
or of the aged and infirm answering for wanton conduct.
Thus you will be truly cautious
and recognized by all men as discreet.

A Father's Care for His Daughter†

9* A daughter is a treasure that keeps her father wakeful,
and worry over her drives away rest:
Lest she pass her prime unmarried,
or when she is married, lest she be disliked;
10 While unmarried, lest she be seduced,
or, as a wife, lest she prove unfaithful;
Lest she conceive in her father's home,
or be sterile in that of her husband.
11* Keep a close watch on your daughter,
lest she make you the sport of your enemies,
A byword in the city, a reproach among the people,
an object of derision in public gatherings.
See that there is no lattice in her room,
no place that overlooks the approaches to the house.
12* Let her not parade her charms before men,
or spend her time with married women;
13 For just as moths come from garments,
so harm to women comes from women:
14 Better a man's harshness than a woman's indulgence,
and a frightened daughter than any disgrace.

The Works of God in Nature†

15* Now will I recall God's works;
what I have seen, I will describe.
At God's word were his works brought into being;
they do his will as he has ordained for them.
16 As the rising sun is clear to all,
so the glory of the LORD fills all his works;
17 Yet even God's holy ones must fail
in recounting the wonders of the LORD,
Though God has given these, his hosts, the strength
to stand firm before his glory.
18 He plumbs the depths and penetrates the heart;
their innermost being he understands.
The Most High possesses all knowledge,
and sees from of old the things that are to come:
19 He makes known the past and the future,
and reveals the deepest secrets.
20* No understanding does he lack;
no single thing escapes him.
21 Perennial is his almighty wisdom;
he is from all eternity one and the same,
22* With nothing added, nothing taken away;

*

23: 27, 16.
42, 1: Prv 24, 23; Jas 2, 1.
4: Prv 11, 1.
5: 30, 1-13; 33, 25-33.
9: 7, 24f.
11: 26, 10.
12f: 9, 1-9.
15: Ps 77, 12f.
20: 39, 19; Wis 1, 6-10.
22: Is 40, 13; Rom 11, 34.

†

42, 9-14: The author considers a daughter to be a source of anxiety to her father, lest she fail to marry, or *be seduced,* or lest, marrying, she be *disliked, prove unfaithful,* or find herself *sterile* (9f). He is advised to *keep a close watch* on her at home, and on her companionship while abroad, lest he suffer on her account among the people (11-14).

42, 15—43, 35: These verses comprise a new section. In them the author contemplates God's power, beauty and goodness as manifested in the mighty work of creating and preserving the universe (42, 15ff.23.25; 43, 1-27), his omniscience (42, 18ff), his perfect wisdom (21f), his eternity (24). The conclusion is a fervent hymn of praise (43, 28-35). Cf 16, 22—18, 13.

no need of a counselor for him!
23 How beautiful are all his works!
even to the spark and the fleeting vision!
24 The universe lives and abides forever;
to meet each need, each creature is preserved.
25* All of them differ, one from another,
yet none of them has he made in vain,
For each in turn, as it comes, is good;
can one ever see enough of their splendor?

CHAPTER 43

1* The clear vault of the sky shines forth
like heaven itself, a vision of glory.
2 The orb of the sun, resplendent at its rising:
what a wonderful work of the Most High!
3 At noon it seethes the surface of the earth,
and who can bear its fiery heat?
4 Like a blazing furnace of solid metal,
it sets the mountains aflame with its rays;
By its fiery darts the land is consumed;
the eyes are dazzled by its light.
5 Great indeed is the LORD who made it,
at whose orders it urges on its steeds.
6* The moon, too, that marks the changing times,
governing the seasons, their lasting sign,
7 By which we know the feast days and fixed dates,
this light-giver which wanes in its course:
8 As its name says, each month it renews itself;
how wondrous in this change!
9* The beauty, the glory, of the heavens are the stars
that adorn with their sparkling the heights of God,
10 At whose command they keep their place
and never relax in their vigils.
A weapon against the flood waters stored on high,
lighting up the firmament by its brilliance,
11* Behold the rainbow! Then bless its Maker,
for majestic indeed is its splendor;
12 It spans the heavens with its glory,
this bow bent by the mighty hand of God.
13 His rebuke marks out the path for the lightning,
and speeds the arrows of his judgment to their goal.
14 At it the storehouse is opened,
and like vultures the clouds hurry forth.
15 In his majesty he gives the storm its power
and breaks off the hailstones.
16 The thunder of his voice makes the earth writhe;
before his might the mountains quake.
17 A word from him drives on the south wind,
the angry north wind, the hurricane and the storm.
18 He sprinkles the snow like fluttering birds;
it comes to settle like swarms of locusts.
19 Its shining whiteness blinds the eyes,
the mind is baffled by its steady fall.
20 He scatters frost like so much salt;
it shines like blossoms on the thornbush.
21 Cold northern blasts he sends
that turn the ponds to lumps of ice.
He freezes over every body of water,
and clothes each pool with a coat of mail.
22 When the mountain growth is scorched with heat,
and the flowering plains as though by flames,
23 The dripping clouds restore them all,
and the scattered dew enriches the parched land.
24 His is the plan that calms the deep,
and plants the islands in the sea.
25* Those who go down to the sea tell part of its story,
and when we hear them we are thunderstruck;
26 In it are his creatures, stupendous, amazing,
all kinds of life, and the monsters of the deep.
27* For him each messenger succeeds,
and at his bidding accomplishes his will.

28† More than this we need not add;
let the last word be, he is all in all!
29 Let us praise him the more, since we cannot fathom him,
for greater is he than all his works;

*

25: 33, 15.
43, 1ff: Ps 19, 2f.
6: Lv 23, 5; Nm 28, 11-14; Ps 81, 4.
9: Ps 8, 4.
11: Gn 9, 13.
25: Ps 104, 25-30.
27: Ps 33, 6.

†

43, 28: *All in all:* the perfections reflected in creation are found in a transcendent way in God, who alone is their source.

30 Awful indeed is the LORD's majesty,
and wonderful is his power.
31 Lift up your voices to glorify the LORD,
though he is still beyond your power to praise;
32 Extol him with renewed strength,
and weary not, though you cannot reach the end:
33* For who can see him and describe him?
or who can praise him as he is?
34 Beyond these, many things lie hid;
only a few of his works have we seen.
35* It is the LORD who has made all things,
and to those who fear him he gives wisdom.

CHAPTER 44

Praise of Israel's Great Ancestors†

1† Now will I praise those godly men,
our ancestors, each in his own time:
2* The abounding glory of the Most High's portion,
his own part, since the days of old.
Subduers of the land in kingly fashion,
men of renown for their might,
3* Or counselors in their prudence,
or seers of all things in prophecy;
4 Resolute princes of the folk,
and governors with their staves;
Authors skilled in composition,
and forgers of epigrams with their spikes;
5 Composers of melodious psalms,
or discoursers on lyric themes;
6 Stalwart men, solidly established
and at peace in their own estates—
7 All these were glorious in their time,
each illustrious in his day.
8 Some of them have left behind a name
and men recount their praiseworthy deeds;
9 But of others there is no memory,
for when they ceased, they ceased.
And they are as though they had not lived,
they and their children after them.
10 Yet these also were godly men
whose virtues have not been forgotten;
11 Their wealth remains in their families,
their heritage with their descendants;
12 Through God's covenant with them
their family endures,
their posterity, for their sake.
13 And for all time their progeny will endure,
their glory will never be blotted out;
14* Their bodies are peacefully laid away,
but their name lives on and on.
15 At gatherings their wisdom is retold,
and the assembly proclaims their praise.

The Early Patriarchs

16*†[ENOCH walked with the LORD and was taken up,
that succeeding generations might learn by his example.]
17* NOAH, found just and perfect,
renewed the race in the time of devastation.
Because of his worth there were survivors,
and with a sign to him the deluge ended;
18 A lasting agreement was made with him,
that never should all flesh be destroyed.
19* ABRAHAM, father of many peoples,
kept his glory without stain:
20*†He observed the precepts of the Most High,
and entered into an agreement with him;
In his own flesh he incised the ordinance,
and when tested he was found loyal.
21† For this reason, God promised him with an oath
that in his descendants the nations would be blessed,

SIRACH

*

33: Ps 106, 2.
35: Jb 28, 28.
44, 2: Dt 32, 8f.
3: 39, 1.
14: Wis 3, 3.
16: 49, 14; Gn 5, 18-24; Heb 11, 5.
17: Gn 6, 8—9, 29; Heb 11, 7.
19: Gn 12, 1—25, 10; Gal 3, 6; Heb 11, 8-19.
20: Gn 17, 10; 22, 1.

†

44, 1—50, 24: As in the previous section God's wisdom shone forth in the works of nature, so in these chapters it is also revealed through the history of God's people as seen in the lives of their patriarchs, prophets, priests and rulers. The example of these great men, whose virtues are here recalled, constitutes a high point of the author's teaching and illustrates his belief in the canonical Scriptures.

44, 1-15: The reader is here introduced to those men of Israel, later mentioned by name, who through various achievements and beneficial social activities have acquired great renown (1-8.14f); and also to those who, though forgotten, endure through the fruit of their *virtues* and through their families because of *God's covenant with them* (9-13).

44, 16: *Enoch:* because of his friendship with God and also by reason of his unusual disappearance from the earth, this prophet's renown was great among the chosen people, particularly in the two centuries just before the coming of Christ; cf Gn 5, 21-24; Heb 11, 5. The present verse is an expansion of the original text; cf 49, 14.

44, 20: *In his own flesh . . . ordinance:* the covenant of circumcision; cf Gn 17, 10-14. *And when tested . . . loyal:* Abraham's willingness to sacrifice his son Isaac at the Lord's command; cf Gn 22, 9-12.

44, 21: *The River:* the Euphrates; cf Gn 2, 14.

That he would make him numerous as the grains of dust,
and exalt his posterity like the stars;
That he would give them an inheritance from sea to sea,
and from the River to the ends of the earth.
22* And for ISAAC he renewed the same promise
because of Abraham, his father.
The covenant with all his forebears was confirmed,
and the blessing rested upon the head of JACOB.
23 God acknowledged him as the first-born,
and gave him his inheritance.
He fixed the boundaries for his tribes,
and their division into twelve.

CHAPTER 45

Praise of Moses, Aaron and Phinehas†

1* From him was to spring the man
who won the favor of all:
Dear to God and men,
MOSES, whose memory is held in benediction.
2*† God's honor devolved upon him,
and the Lord strengthened him with fearful powers;
3* God wrought swift miracles at his words
and sustained him in the king's presence.
He gave him the commandments for his people,
and revealed to him his glory.
4* For his trustworthiness and meekness
God selected him from all mankind;
5† He permitted him to hear his voice,
and led him into the cloud,
Where, face to face, he gave him the commandments,
the law of life and understanding,
That he might teach his precepts to Jacob,
his judgments and decrees to Israel.

6*† He raised up also, like Moses in holiness,
his brother AARON, of the tribe of Levi.
7† He made him perpetual in his office
when he bestowed on him the priesthood of his people;
He established him in honor
and crowned him with lofty majesty;
8 He clothed him with splendid apparel,
and adorned him with the glorious vestments:
Breeches and tunic and robe
with pomegranates around the hem,
9 And a rustle of bells round about,
through whose pleasing sound at each step
He would be heard within the sanctuary,
and the children of his race would be remembered;
10 The sacred vestments of gold, of violet,
and of crimson, wrought with embroidery;
The breastpiece for decision, the ephod and cincture
11 with scarlet yarn, the work of the weaver;
Precious stones with seal engravings
in golden settings, the work of the jeweler,
To commemorate in incised letters
each of the tribes of Israel;
12 On his turban the diadem of gold,
its plate wrought with the insignia of holiness,
Majestic, glorious, renowned for splendor,
a delight to the eyes, beauty supreme.
13 Before him, no one was adorned with these,
nor may they ever be worn by any
Except his sons and them alone,
generation after generation, for all time.
14 His cereal offering is wholly burnt
with the established sacrifice twice each day;

*

22: Gn 26, 3.5.24; 27, 28f; 28, 14.
45, 1: Ex 2, 2; 11, 3; 33, 11; Nm 12.7.
2: Ex 7, 1—13, 22.
2-5: Ex 7—Dt 34.
3: Ex 4, 17; 7, 1.
4: Nm 12, 3, 7.
6ff: Ex 28f; Wis 18, 24.

†

45, 1-5: *Moses* manifested God's power through miracles (1ff), God's authority through the promulgation of the commandments and the law (5), and God's mercy through the intimacy granted him by the Lord for his own faithfulness and meekness (4f). The very personification of the old covenant, Moses was also a type of Christ, the Prophet and Legislator of the new; cf Dt 18, 15.

45, 2: *God's honor devolved upon him:* Moses was actually God's substitute in dealing with Pharaoh, hence God entrusted his own honor to Moses.

45, 5: *Face to face:* on God's intimacy with Moses, see Ex 33, 11; Nm 12, 8. St. Paul alluded to this in 1 Cor 13, 12.

45, 6-21: The author here expresses his reverence and esteem for the priesthood of the old covenant. He recalls God's choice of *Aaron* and his sons for this sublime office (6f), and describes in detail the beauty of the high priest's vestments (8-13). He relates the ordination of Aaron at the hands of Moses, his brother (15), and describes the priestly functions, of offering sacrifice to God (16), and of blessing (15), teaching, governing and judging the people (17); the *inheritance* of the high priest (20ff); the punishment of those *families* who were *jealous* of Aaron (18f); and the confirmation of the covenant of the priesthood with Aaron's descendants through *Phinehas* (23ff).

45, 7: The *priesthood* of Aaron was superseded by the priesthood of Christ; cf Heb 7, 18-28.

15 For Moses ordained him
and anointed him with the holy oil,
In a lasting covenant with him
and with his family, as permanent as the heavens,
That he should serve God in his priesthood
and bless his people in his name.
16 He chose him from all mankind
to offer holocausts and choice offerings,
To burn sacrifices of sweet odor for a memorial,
and to atone for the people of Israel.
17 He gave to him his laws,
and authority to prescribe and to judge:
To teach the precepts to his people,
and the ritual to the descendants of Israel.
18* Men of other families were inflamed against him,
were jealous of him in the desert,
The followers of Dathan and Abiram,
and the band of Korah in their defiance.
19 But the LORD saw this and became angry,
he destroyed them in his burning wrath.
He brought down upon them a miracle,
and consumed them with his flaming fire.
20* Then he increased the glory of Aaron
and bestowed upon him his inheritance:
The sacred offerings he allotted to him,
with the showbread as his portion;
21 The oblations of the LORD are his food,
a gift to him and his descendants.
22 But he holds no land among the people
nor shares with them their heritage;
For the LORD himself is his portion,
his inheritance in the midst of Israel.

23* PHINEHAS too, the son of Eleazar,
was the courageous third of his line
When, zealous for the God of all,
he met the crisis of his people
And, at the prompting of his noble heart,
atoned for the children of Israel.
24 Therefore on him again God conferred the right,
in a covenant of friendship, to provide for the sanctuary,
So that he and his descendants
should possess the high priesthood forever.
25* For even his covenant with David,
the son of Jesse of the tribe of Judah,
Was an individual heritage through one son alone;
but the heritage of Aaron is for all his descendants.

26 And now bless the LORD
who has crowned you with glory!
May he grant you wisdom of heart
to govern his people in justice,
Lest their welfare should ever be forgotten,
or your authority, throughout all time.

CHAPTER 46

Joshua, Caleb and the Judges†

1* Valiant leader was JOSHUA, son of Nun,
assistant to Moses in the prophetic office,
Formed to be, as his name implies,
the great savior of God's chosen ones,
To punish the enemy
and to win the inheritance for Israel.
2* What glory was his when he raised his arm,
to brandish his javelin against the city!
3† And who could withstand him
when he fought the battles of the LORD?
4* Did he not by his power stop the sun,
so that one day became two?
5 He called upon the Most High God
when his enemies beset him on all sides,
And God Most High gave answer to him
in hailstones of tremendous power,
6 Which he rained down upon the hostile army
till on the slope he destroyed the foe;
That all the doomed nations might know
that the LORD was watching over his people's battles.
And because he was a devoted follower of God

*

18: Nm 16, 1ff.
20f: Nm 18, 11-21; Dt 10, 9.
23: Nm 25, 7-13; Ps 106, 30f; 1 Mc 2, 26.54.
25: 2 Sm 7, 12-16.
46, 1: Ex 17, 9; Nm 27, 18; Dt 34, 9; Jos 1, 1-4.
2: Jos 8, 18.
4: Jos 10, 13.

†

46, 1-6: *Joshua,* whose name means "the Lord is savior" (1), was the instrument through which God delivered his people in miraculous ways (2-6) by destroying their enemies, whose land he gave to the Israelites as an *inheritance* (1).
46, 3: *The battles of the LORD:* cf Jos 6—10.

7*† and in Moses' lifetime showed himself loyal,
He and CALEB, son of Jephunneh,
when they opposed the rebel assembly,
Averted God's anger from the people
and suppressed the wicked complaint—
8* Because of this, they were the only two spared
from the six hundred thousand infantry,
To lead the people into their inheritance,
the land flowing with milk and honey.
9* And the strength he gave to Caleb
remained with him even in his old age
Till he won his way onto the summits of the land;
his family too received an inheritance,
10 That all the people of Jacob might know
how good it is to be a devoted follower of the LORD.
11*†The JUDGES, too, each one of them,
whose hearts were not deceived,
Who did not abandon God:
may their memory be ever blessed,
12 Their bones return to life from their resting place,
and their names receive fresh luster in their children!
13* Beloved of his people, dear to his Maker,
dedicated from his mother's womb,
Consecrated to the LORD as a prophet,
was SAMUEL, the judge and priest.
At God's word he established the kingdom
and anointed princes to rule the people.
14 By the law of the LORD he judged the nation,
when he visited the encampments of Jacob.
15 As a trustworthy prophet he was sought out
and his words proved him true as a seer.
16* He, too, called upon God,
and offered him a suckling lamb;
17* Then the LORD thundered forth from heaven,
and the tremendous roar of his voice was heard.
18 He brought low the rulers of the enemy
and destroyed all the lords of the Philistines.
19* When Samuel approached the end of his life,
he testified before the LORD and his anointed prince,
"No bribe or secret gift have I taken from any man!"
and no one dared gainsay him.
20* Even when he lay buried, his guidance was sought;
he made known to the king his fate,
And from the grave he raised his voice
as a prophet, to put an end to wickedness.

CHAPTER 47

Nathan, David and Solomon

1*† After him came NATHAN
who served in the presence of David.
2* Like the choice fat of the sacred offerings,
so was DAVID in Israel.
3* He made sport of lions as though they were kids,
and of bears, like lambs of the flock.
4* As a youth he slew the giant
and wiped out the people's disgrace,
When his hand let fly the slingstone
that crushed the pride of Goliath.
5 Since he called upon the Most High God,
who gave strength to his right arm
To defeat the skilled warrior
and raise up the might of his people,
6* Therefore the women sang his praises

*

7: Nm 13, 30; 14, 6.
8: Nm 14, 22-38.
9: Jos 14, 6; 15, 13.
11: Jgs 1, 1—16, 31.
13: 1 Sm 1, 10ff; 8, 4ff; 10, 1; 16, 13.
16: 1 Sm 7, 9.
17: 12, 18.
19: 1 Sm 12, 3.
20: 1 Sm 28, 14.
47, 1: 2 Sm 7, 2.
2: 1 Sm 16, 11.
3: 1 Sm 17, 35.
4: 1 Sm 17, 49.
6: 1 Sm 18, 7.

†

46, 7-10: *Caleb,* who with Joshua advised Moses and the people in the desert to conquer Canaan, despite the counsel of their companion scouts and the rebellion of the people, merited to lead the Israelites of the succeeding generation into the Promised Land. Caleb in his old age received as his inheritance a portion of land which he himself had previously conquered; cf Jos 15, 13f.

46, 11-20: Of the *Judges* praised and blessed for their fidelity to God in opposing idolatry, *Samuel,* a man of spotless integrity, was the greatest (11f.19). He was judge of the entire nation, and was also a prophet and priest who through his sacrificial offering obtained victory over the Philistines. He established the kingdom, anointed kings (13-18), and even after his death foretold the king's fate and *put an end to wickedness* (20).

47, 1-11: *David,* a youthful and fearless warrior, the favorite of all Israel, by defeating *Goliath,* the boastful Philistine giant, removed *the people's disgrace* and greatly strengthened their power (1-7). *With his whole being he loved* and praised God, and his devotion to divine worship led him to develop a liturgical cult. David fell into sin, but repenting, received pardon from God and the promise of an everlasting kingdom (8-11).

and ascribed to him tens of thousands.
When he assumed the royal crown, he battled
7* and subdued the enemy on every side.
He destroyed the hostile Philistines
and shattered their power till our own day.
8 With his every deed he offered thanks
to God Most High, in words of praise.
With his whole being he loved his Maker
and daily had his praises sung;
9* He added beauty to the feasts
and solemnized the seasons of each year
With string music before the altar,
providing sweet melody for the psalms
10 So that when the Holy Name was praised,
before daybreak the sanctuary would resound.
11* The LORD forgave him his sins
and exalted his strength forever;
He conferred on him the rights of royalty
and established his throne in Israel.

12*†Because of his merits he had as his successor
a wise son, who lived in security:
13* SOLOMON reigned during an era of peace,
for God made tranquil all his borders.
He built a house to the name of God,
and established a lasting sanctuary.
14* How wise you were when you were young,
overflowing with instruction, like the Nile in flood!
15 Your understanding covered the whole earth,
and, like a sea, filled it with knowledge.
16 Your fame reached distant coasts,
and their peoples came to hear you;
17 With song and story and riddle,
and with your answers, you astounded the nations.
18† You were called by that glorious name
which was conferred upon Israel.
Gold you gathered like so much iron,
you heaped up silver as though it were lead;
19* But you abandoned yourself to women
and gave them dominion over your body.
20 You brought dishonor upon your reputation,
shame upon your marriage,
Wrath upon your descendants,
and groaning upon your domain;
21* Thus two governments came into being,
when in Ephraim kingship was usurped.
22* But God does not withdraw his mercy,
nor permit even one of his promises to fail.
He does not uproot the posterity of his chosen one,
nor destroy the offspring of his friend.
So he gave to Jacob a remnant,
to David a root from his own family.
23*†Solomon finally slept with his fathers,
and left behind him one of his sons,
Expansive in folly, limited in sense,
REHOBOAM, who by his policy made the people rebel;
Until one arose who should not be remembered,
the sinner who led Israel into sin,
Who brought ruin to Ephraim
24 and caused them to be exiled from their land.

Elijah and Elisha

Their sinfulness grew more and more,
25† and they lent themselves to every evil,

*

7: 2 Sm 5, 6-25.
9: 1 Chr 16, 4ff; 23, 2ff; 25, 1-7.
11: 2 Sm 12, 13; 7, 12-16.
12: 1 Kgs 2, 12.
13: 1 Kgs 5, 1.5.
14-18: 1 Kgs 5, 9-14; 10, 14-28.
19: 1 Kgs 11, 1ff.
21: 1 Kgs 12, 1ff.
22: 2 Sm 7, 15; Ps 89, 34ff.
23: 1 Kgs 11, 43; 12, 13.21; 13, 34; 2 Kgs 17, 6ff.

†

47, 12-24: *Solomon,* son and successor of David, inherited peace through his father's conquests. He built the magnificent temple of Jerusalem (12f) and received from God the favor of unparalleled wisdom, through which he obtained great fame (14-17). Luxury and sensuality, however, brought disgrace upon him, and because of his oppressive burdens, he disposed the kingdom for division after his death (19-21.23f). Nevertheless God did not withdraw his promise of establishing his throne in the descendants of David (22).

47, 18: Cf 2 Sm 12, 25, where Solomon is called Jedidiah, "beloved of the Lord." The same term is used of Israel in Jer 11, 15.

47, 23: *Expansive:* the name *Rehoboam* means "the people is expansive," that is, widespread. *The sinner: Jeroboam;* cf 1 Kgs 12, 2.20.26-32.

47, 25—48, 11: The prophetic ministry of *Elijah* amid widespread idolatry is here described as a judgment by fire (47, 25f). Through his preaching, miracles and vengeance against God's enemies within and without Israel, the prophet succeeded for a time in destroying idols and in restoring faith and the worship of the true God (48, 2-8). His miraculous departure from this life gave rise to the belief that he did not die but would return before the end of the world to *put an end to wrath* and restore the tribes of Israel (9ff). Cf Mt 17, 9-13.

CHAPTER 48

1* Till like a fire there appeared the prophet
whose words were as a flaming furnace.
2 Their staff of bread he shattered,
in his zeal he reduced them to straits;
3* By God's word he shut up the heavens
and three times brought down fire.
4 How awesome are you, ELIJAH!
Whose glory is equal to yours?
5* You brought a dead man back to life
from the nether world, by the will of the LORD.
6* You sent kings down to destruction,
and nobles, from their beds of sickness.
7* You heard threats at Sinai,
at Horeb avenging judgments.
8* You anointed kings who should inflict vengeance,
and a prophet as your successor.
9* You were taken aloft in a whirlwind,
in a chariot with fiery horses.
10* You are destined, it is written, in time to come
to put an end to wrath before the day of the LORD,
To turn back the hearts of fathers toward their sons,
and to reestablish the tribes of Jacob.
11 Blessed is he who shall have seen you before he dies,
12*†O Elijah, enveloped in the whirlwind!

Then ELISHA, filled with a twofold portion of his spirit,
wrought many marvels by his mere word.
During his lifetime he feared no one,
nor was any man able to intimidate his will.
13* Nothing was beyond his power;
beneath him flesh was brought back into life.
14 In life he performed wonders,
and after death, marvelous deeds.
15* Despite all this the people did not repent,
nor did they give up their sins,
Until they were rooted out of their land
and scattered all over the earth.
But Judah remained, a tiny people,
with its rulers from the house of David.
16 Some of these did what was right,
but others were extremely sinful.

Hezekiah and Isaiah†

17* HEZEKIAH fortified his city
and had water brought into it;
With iron tools he cut through the rock
and he built reservoirs for water.
18* During his reign Sennacherib led an invasion
and sent his adjutant;
He shook his fist at Zion
and blasphemed God in his pride.
19 The people's hearts melted within them,
and they were in anguish like that of childbirth.
20* But they called upon the Most High God
and lifted up their hands to him;
He heard the prayer they uttered,
and saved them through ISAIAH.
21* God struck the camp of the Assyrians
and routed them with a plague.
22 For Hezekiah did what was right
and held fast to the paths of David,
As ordered by the illustrious prophet
Isaiah, who saw the truth in visions.
23* In his lifetime he turned back the sun
and prolonged the life of the king.
24* By his powerful spirit he looked into the future
and consoled the mourners of Zion;
25 He foretold what should be till the end of time,
hidden things yet to be fulfilled.

---

*

48, 1: 1 Kgs 17, 1.
3: 1 Kgs 17, 1; 2 Kgs 1, 9-14.
5: 1 Kgs 17, 22.
6: 1 Kgs 21, 19; 2 Kgs 1, 17.
7: 1 Kgs 19, 8ff.
8: 1 Kgs 19, 15ff.
9: 2 Kgs 2, 11.
10: Mal 3, 23f; Mt 17, 10.
12: 2 Kgs 2, 9; 3, 13.
13f: 2 Kgs 13, 21.
15: 2 Kgs 15, 29; 18, 11.
17: 2 Kgs 20, 20; 2 Chr 32, 3ff.30.
18: 2 Kgs 18, 13ff; Is 36, 1ff.
20: 2 Kgs 19, 20.
21: 2 Kgs 19, 35; Is 37, 36.
23: 2 Kgs 20, 11; Is 38, 8.
24f: 2 Kgs 20, 17; Is 40, 1ff; 42, 9; 46, 10; 48, 6; 61, 2.

†

48, 12-16: *Elisha* fearlessly continued the work of his predecessor by numerous miracles (12ff), but the obstinacy of the people eventually brought on the destruction of the kingdom of Israel and the dispersion of its subjects. *Judah,* however, survived under the rule of Davidic kings, both good and bad (15f).

48, 17-25: The fidelity, trust and courage of King *Hezekiah* (17.22), the zeal of the prophet *Isaiah,* and the prayer of the people (20) availed with God. The Assyrian oppressors were routed (18f.21), the king's life was prolonged, and consolations were granted the people through Isaiah's prophecies concerning the future (23ff), especially the coming of the Messiah and the establishment of his kingdom; cf Is 7, 14; 9, 6f; 40—65.

CHAPTER 49

Josiah and the Prophets†

1* The name JOSIAH is like blended incense,
made lasting by a skilled perfumer.
Precious is his memory, like honey to the taste,
like music at a banquet.
2 For he grieved over our betrayals,
and destroyed the abominable idols.
3 He turned to God with his whole heart,
and, though times were evil, he practiced virtue.
4 Except for David, Hezekiah and Josiah,
they all were wicked;
They abandoned the Law of the Most High,
these kings of Judah, right to the very end.
5 So he gave over their power to others,
their glory to a foolish foreign nation
6* Who burned the holy city
and left its streets desolate,
As JEREMIAH had foretold; 7* for they had treated him badly
who even in the womb had been made a prophet,
To root out, pull down, and destroy,
and then to build and to plant.
8* EZEKIEL beheld the vision
and described the different creatures of the chariot;
9* He also referred to JOB,
who always persevered in the right path.
10 Then, too, the TWELVE PROPHETS—
may their bones return to life from their resting place!—
Gave new strength to Jacob
and saved him by their faith and hope.

The Heroes after the Exile

11*†How can we fittingly praise ZERUBBABEL,
who was like a signet ring on God's right hand,
12 And Jeshua, Jozadak's son?
In their time they built the house of God;
They erected the holy temple,
destined for everlasting glory.
13* Extolled be the memory of NEHEMIAH!
He rebuilt our ruined walls,
Restored our shattered defenses,
and set up gates and bars.

The Earliest Patriarchs

14*†Few on earth have been made the equal of ENOCH,
for he was taken up bodily.
15* Was ever a man born like JOSEPH?
Even his dead body was provided for.
16* Glorious, too, were SHEM and SETH and ENOS;
but beyond that of any living being was the splendor of ADAM.

CHAPTER 50

Simon, Son of Jochanan

1† The greatest among his brethren, the glory of his people,
was SIMON the priest, son of Jochanan,
In whose time the house of God was renovated,
in whose days the temple was reinforced.
2 In his time also the wall was built
with powerful turrets for the temple precincts;
3 In his time the reservoir was dug,
the pool with a vastness like the sea's.
4 He protected his people against brigands
and strengthened his city against the enemy.
5 How splendid he was as he appeared from the tent,
as he came from within the veil!

*

49, 1: 2 Kgs 22, 1; 2 Chr 34, 1.
6: 2 Kgs 25, 9; 2 Chr 36, 19.
7: Jer 1, 5.10.
8: Ez 1, 4ff.
9: Ez 14, 14.20.
11f: Ezr 3, 2; Hg 1, 12; Zec 3, 1.
13: Neh 1, 1; 3, 1.
14: 44, 16; Gn 5, 18-24.
15: Gn 37—50; Ex 13, 19; Jos 24, 32.
16: Gn 1, 27; 4, 25f.

†

49, 1-10: The author's praise of King *Josiah* (1-3), of the prophets *Jeremiah* and *Ezekiel* and likewise the minor prophets (7-10) derives from their spirit of fidelity to the Lord and his law amid the infidelity of kings and people (4ff.10).

49, 11ff: *Zerubbabel* and *Jeshua,* in rebuilding the temple, and *Nehemiah,* the governor, in repairing the walls of the Holy City also restored what these constructions signify, namely, religious worship and civil authority as prescribed in the law.

49, 14ff: The patriarchs here mentioned were glorious because of their spirit of religion, i.e., their profound reverence for God and obedience to him. *The splendor of Adam,* moreover, was due to his direct origin from God.

50, 1-21: The *son of Jochanan* here mentioned was Simon II, *in whose time* as high priest (219-196 B.C.) great works were accomplished for the benefit of public worship and welfare (1-4). The author, a contemporary of this high priest, describes in great detail and by numerous comparisons the impression of awful majesty received, the lofty joy aroused, at sight of the high priest fully vested entering the sanctuary, ascending the altar (6-11), and, in the presence of the whole assembly of Israel, encircled by assistant priests bearing offerings, sacrificing the burnt offering on the Day of Atonement, while the trumpets blast and the people bow down in adoration of *the Most High* (12-17). The hymnody, the joyful shouts of the multitude, and finally the high priest's blessing, in which he pronounces—once only in the year, on this occasion—the holy name of Yahweh, climax the description of this most solemn Jewish liturgical function (18-21).

6 Like a star shining among the clouds,
like the full moon at the holyday season;
7 Like the sun shining upon the temple,
like the rainbow appearing in the cloudy sky;
8 Like the blossoms on the branches in springtime,
like a lily on the banks of a stream;
Like the trees of Lebanon in summer,
9 like the fire of incense at the sacrifice;
Like a vessel of beaten gold,
studded with precious stones;
10 Like a luxuriant olive tree thick with fruit,
like a cypress standing against the clouds;
11* Vested in his magnificent robes,
and wearing his garments of splendor,
As he ascended the glorious altar
and lent majesty to the court of the sanctuary.

12 When he received the sundered victims from the priests
while he stood before the sacrificial wood,
His brethren ringed him about like a garland,
like a stand of cedars on Lebanon;
13 All the sons of Aaron in their dignity
clustered around him like poplars,
With the offerings to the LORD in their hands,
in the presence of the whole assembly of Israel.
14 Once he had completed the services at the altar
with the arranging of the sacrifices for the Most High,
15* And had stretched forth his hand for the cup,
to offer blood of the grape,
And poured it out at the foot of the altar,
a sweet-smelling odor to the Most High God,
16* The sons of Aaron would sound a blast,
the priests, on their trumpets of beaten metal;
A blast to resound mightily
as a reminder before the Most High.
17 Then all the people with one accord
would quickly fall prostrate to the ground
In adoration before the Most High,
before the Holy One of Israel.

18 Then hymns would re-echo,
and over the throng sweet strains of praise resound.

19 All the people of the land would shout for joy,
praying to the Merciful One,
As the high priest completed the services at the altar
by presenting to God the sacrifice due;
20* Then coming down he would raise his hands
over all the congregation of Israel.
The blessing of the LORD would be upon his lips,
the name of the LORD would be his glory.
21 Then again the people would lie prostrate
to receive from him the blessing of the Most High.

22† And now, bless the God of all,
who has done wondrous things on earth;
Who fosters men's growth from their mother's womb,
and fashions them according to his will!
23 May he grant you joy of heart
and may peace abide among you;
24 May his goodness toward us endure in Israel
as long as the heavens are above.

Epilogue and Canticles†

25† My whole being loathes two nations,
the third is not even a people:
26*†Those who live in Seir and Philistia,
and the degenerate folk who dwell in Shechem.

27† Wise instruction, appropriate proverbs,
I have written in this book,
I, Jesus, son of Eleazar, son of Sirach,
as they gushed forth from my heart's understanding.
28 Happy the man who meditates upon these things,

SIRACH

*

50, 11: 45, 8-12; Ex 28, 2-5; 39, 1-21.
15f: Nm 15, 5; 28, 7.
16: Nm 10, 10.
20: Nm 6, 23-26.
26: 2 Kgs 17, 24; Jn 4. 9.

†

50, 22ff: Praise and thanksgiving are given to God for his wondrous works, and a blessing is invoked on man that he may enjoy peace and gladness of heart and the abiding goodness of the Most High.

50, 25f: The author's abhorrence of the pagan Edomites (Idumeans), Philistines and Samaritans can be understood in the light of Old Testament thinking, which does not always distinguish between hatred of evildoers and hatred of the evil they do.

50, 25: *Not even a people:* the Samaritans.

50, 26: *Seir:* Mount Seir in the territory of the Edomites. *Shechem:* a city in Samaria.

50, 27ff: These verses contain the subscription of the author, *Jesus, son of Eleazar, son of Sirach,* to his long and beautiful treatise on wisdom as applying to all of human life, integrating it under the direction of *the fear of the Lord.*

wise the man who takes them to heart!
29 If he puts them into practice, he can cope with anything,
for the fear of the LORD is his lamp.

CHAPTER 51

1*† I give you thanks, O God of my father;
I praise you, O God my savior!
I will make known your name, refuge of my life;
2* you have been my helper against my adversaries.
You have saved me from death,
and kept back my body from the pit,
From the clutches of the nether world you have snatched my feet;
3* you have delivered me, in your great mercy
From the scourge of a slanderous tongue,
and from lips that went over to falsehood;
From the snare of those who watched for my downfall,
and from the power of those who sought my life;
From many a danger you have saved me,
4* from flames that hemmed me in on every side;
From the midst of unremitting fire,
5 from the deep belly of the nether world;
From deceiving lips and painters of lies,
6* from the arrows of dishonest tongues.
I was at the point of death,
my soul was nearing the depths of the nether world;
7* I turned every way, but there was no one to help me,
I looked for one to sustain me, but could find no one.
8 But then I remembered the mercies of the LORD,
his kindness through ages past;
For he saves those who take refuge in him,
and rescues them from every evil.
9 So I raised my voice from the very earth,
from the gates of the nether world, my cry.
10* I called out: O Lord, you are my father,
you are my champion and my savior;
Do not abandon me in time of trouble,
in the midst of storms and dangers.
11 I will ever praise your name
and be constant in my prayers to you.
Thereupon the LORD heard my voice,
he listened to my appeal;
12† He saved me from evil of every kind
and preserved me in time of trouble.
For this reason I thank him and I praise him;
I bless the name of the LORD.

13*† When I was young and innocent,
I sought wisdom.
14 She came to me in her beauty,

---

* 51, 1: Ps 138, 1.
2: Ps 91, 3.
3: Pss 40, 5; 91, 3.
4: Ps 66, 12.
6: Pss 88, 4; 94, 17.
7: Pss 22, 12; 142, 5.
10: Ps 89, 27.
13: 34, 11.

---

† 51, 1-12: A canticle of praise and thanks to God for delivering the author from slander, dangers, destruction, death, the nether world, and evil of every kind.

51, 12: After this verse the Hebrew text gives the litany of praise contained below. It is similar to Ps 136. Though not found in any versions, and therefore of doubtful authenticity, the litany seems from internal evidence to go back to the time of Sirach:

Give thanks to the Lord, for he is good, for his mercy endures forever;
Give thanks to the God of glory, for his mercy endures forever;
Give thanks to the guardian of Israel, for his mercy endures forever;
Give thanks to the creator of the universe, for his mercy endures forever;
Give thanks to the redeemer of Israel, for his mercy endures forever;
Give thanks to him who gathers the dispersed of Israel, for his mercy endures forever;
Give thanks to him who builds his city and his sanctuary, for his mercy endures forever;
Give thanks to him who makes a horn to sprout forth for the house of David, for his mercy endures forever;
Give thanks to him who has chosen for his priests the sons of Zadok, for his mercy endures forever;
Give thanks to the shield of Abraham, for his mercy endures forever;
Give thanks to the rock of Isaac, for his mercy endures forever;
Give thanks to the mighty one of Jacob, for his mercy endures forever;
Give thanks to him who has chosen Zion, for his mercy endures forever;
Give thanks to the king over kings of kings, for his mercy endures forever.
He has lifted up the horn of his people, be this his praise from all his faithful ones,
From the children of Israel, the people close to him. Alleluia! (Cf Ps 148, 14.)

51, 13-30: An alphabetic canticle describing: a) the approach to wisdom through prayer, persistent study and instruction (13-17), purification from sin, enlightenment and ardent desire; b) the possession of wisdom (18-22). The author concludes with an urgent invitation to men to receive *instruction* in *wisdom* from him, and to live by it, because wisdom gives herself *to those who seek her* (23-26); and for their labor, God will reward them in the end (27-30). Cf Mt 11, 28; Eccl 12, 14.

In the Greek of 13f there is an expansion introducing Solomon as the speaker. This deviates from the original author's intent. It reads: "Publicly, in my prayer, facing the temple, I asked for her."

and until the end I will cultivate her.
15 As the blossoms yielded to ripening grapes,
the heart's joy,
My feet kept to the level path
because from earliest youth I was familiar with her.
16 In the short time I paid heed,
I met with great instruction.
17 Since in this way I have profited,
I will give my teacher grateful praise.
18 I became resolutely devoted to her—
the good I persistently strove for.
19 I burned with desire for her,
never turning back.
I became preoccupied with her,
never weary of extolling her.
My hand opened her gate
and I came to know her secrets.
20* For her I purified my hands;
in cleanness I attained to her.
At first acquaintance with her, I gained understanding
such that I will never forsake her.
21 My whole being was stirred as I learned about her;
therefore I have made her my prize possession.
22 The LORD has granted me my lips as a reward,
and my tongue will declare his praises.
23* Come aside to me, you untutored,
and take up lodging in the house of instruction;
24 How long will you be deprived of wisdom's food,
how long will you endure such bitter thirst?
25* I open my mouth and speak of her:
gain, at no cost, wisdom for yourselves.
26* Submit your neck to her yoke,
that your mind may accept her teaching.
For she is close to those who seek her,
and the one who is in earnest finds her.
27 See for yourselves! I have labored only a little,
but have found much.
28 Acquire but a little instruction;
you will win silver and gold through her.
29 Let your spirits rejoice in the mercy of God,
and be not ashamed to give him praise.
30* Work at your tasks in due season,
and in his own time God will give you your reward.

* 20: Prv 4, 6. 23: Prv 8, 5. 25: 6, 20. 26: 6, 25. 30: 2, 8; Jb 34, 11; Jn 9, 4.

THE PROPHETIC BOOKS

The prophetic books bear the names of the four major and twelve minor prophets, besides Lamentations and Baruch. The terms "major" and "minor" refer merely to the length of the respective compositions and not to any distinction in the prophetic office. Jonah is a story of the mission of the prophet rather than a collection of prophecies. Lamentations and Daniel are listed among the hagiographa in the Hebrew Bible, not among the prophetic books. The former contains a series of elegies on the fate of Jerusalem; the latter is apocalyptic in character. Daniel, who lived far removed from Palestine, was not called by God to preach; yet the book is counted as prophecy. Baruch, though excluded from the Hebrew canon, is found in the Septuagint version, and the Church has always acknowledged it to be sacred and inspired.

The prophetic books, together with the oral preaching of the prophets, were the result of the institution of prophetism, in which a succession of Israelites chosen by God and appointed by him to be prophets received communications from him and transmitted them to the people in his name (Dt 18, 15-20). The prophets were spokesmen of God, intermediaries between him and his people. The communications they received from God came through visions, dreams, and ecstasies and were transmitted to the people through sermons, writings, and symbolic actions.

The office of prophet was due to a direct call from God. It was not the result of heredity, just as it was not a permanent gift but a transient one, subject entirely to the divine will. The prophets preserved and developed revealed religion (1 Sm 12, 6-25), denounced idolatry (1 Kgs 14, 1-13), defended the moral law (2 Sm 12, 1-15), gave counsel in political matters (Is 31, 1ff), and often also in matters of private life (1 Sm 9, 6-9). At times miracles confirmed their preaching, and their predictions of the future intensified the expectation of the Messiah and of his kingdom.

The prophetic literature in this volume contains the substance of the prophets' authentic preaching, résumés, and genuine samples of such preaching. Some parts were recorded by the prophets themselves, some by persons other than the prophets who uttered them.

The prophecies express judgments of the people's moral conduct, on the basis of the Mosaic alliance between God and Israel. They teach sublime truths and lofty morals. They contain exhortations, threats, announcements of punishment, promises of deliverance, made with solemn authority and in highly imaginative language. In the affairs of men, their prime concern is the interests of God, especially in what pertains to the chosen people through whom the Messiah is to come; hence their denunciations of idolatry and of that externalism in worship which excludes the interior spirit of religion. They are concerned also with the universal nature of the moral law, with personal responsibility, with the person and office of the Messiah, and with the conduct of foreign nations.

In content, the literary genre of prophecy uses warning and threat besides exhortation and promise to declare in God's name events of the near and distant future (Is 8—9). In form, the divine source of prophetic declaration appears in: "The word (or oracle) of the Lord," or "Thus says the LORD," followed by the announcement of a coming event and its moral cause (Hos 4, 7-10). Divine exhortation and promise are introduced by such forms as: "Hear this word, O men of Israel, that the LORD pronounces over you" (Am 3, 1). Kindly and persuasive tones pervade the promises of reward and even the threats of punishment (Am 5, 14-15).

Disregard for exact chronological perspective in the prophecies is an additional characteristic. Predictions of the immediate and distant future are often interrelated, not on the basis of years separating the events but on the analogy of the pattern joining present with very distant, though similar, conditions and circumstances. This is prophetic compenetration, idealization in which persons and things of the more immediate present, in the prophet's day, fade into a wider and more perfect order of persons and things of the future; the former are figures and types of the latter. Thus, some details of what the Psalmist said of the kingdom of David and Solomon (Ps 72) went beyond what was fulfilled in these men, as St. Thomas points out, and found their realization only in the kingdom of Christ. St. Jerome before him, and still earlier the apostles themselves—Peter (Acts 2, 14-36) and Paul (Gal

4, 21-31)—taught us that through anticipation in types we discover in Sacred Scripture the truth of things to come.

Thus the universal blessing for mankind, often promised by God through the mouths of his prophets in figures and types, was in time to become personalized and to confer its full benefit on us through the Word made flesh, who became for us the New Covenant through his life, death, and resurrection, as the prophets had foretold.

The Book of

ISAIAH

The greatest of the prophets appeared at a critical moment of Israel's history. The second half of the eighth century B.C. witnessed the collapse of the northern kingdom under the hammerlike blows of Assyria (722), while Jerusalem itself saw the army of Sennacherib drawn up before its walls (701). In the year that Uzziah, king of Judah, died (742), Isaiah received his call to the prophetic office in the Temple of Jerusalem. Close attention should be given to chapter 6, where this divine summons to be the ambassador of the Most High is circumstantially described.

The vision of the Lord enthroned in glory stamps an indelible character on Isaiah's ministry and provides the key to the understanding of his message. The majesty, holiness and glory of the Lord took possession of his spirit and, conversely, he gained a new awareness of human pettiness and sinfulness. The enormous abyss between God's sovereign holiness and man's sin overwhelmed the prophet. Only the purifying coal of the seraphim could cleanse his lips and prepare him for acceptance of the call: "Here I am, send me!"

The ministry of Isaiah may be divided into three periods, covering the reigns of Jotham (742-735), Ahaz (735-715), and Hezekiah (715-687). To the first period belong, for the most part, the early oracles (1—5) which exposed the moral breakdown of Judah and its capital, Jerusalem. With the accession of Ahaz, the prophet became adviser to the king, whose throne was threatened by the Syro-Ephraimite coalition. Rejecting the plea of Isaiah for faith and courage, the weak Ahaz turned to Assyria for help. From this period came the majority of messianic oracles found in the section of Immanuel prophecies (6—12).

Hezekiah succeeded his father and undertook a religious reform which Isaiah undoubtedly supported. But the old intrigues began again, and the king was soon won over to the pro-Egyptian party. Isaiah denounced this "covenant with death" and again summoned Judah to faith in Yahweh as her only hope. But it was too late; the revolt had already begun. Assyria acted quickly and her army, after ravaging Judah, laid siege to Jerusalem (701). "I shut up Hezekiah like a bird in his cage," boasts the famous inscription of Sennacherib. But Yahweh delivered the city, as Isaiah had promised: God is the Lord of history, and Assyria but an instrument in his hands.

Little is known about the last days of this great religious leader, whose oracles, of singular poetic beauty and power, constantly reminded his wayward people of their destiny and the fidelity of Yahweh to his promises.

The complete Book of Isaiah is an anthology of poems composed chiefly by the great prophet, but also by disciples, some of whom came many years after Isaiah. In 1—39 most of the oracles come from Isaiah and faithfully reflect the situation in eighth-century Judah. To disciples deeply influenced by the prophet belong sections such as the Apocalypse of Isaiah (24—27), the oracles against Babylon (13—14), and probably the poems of 34—35.

Chapters 40—55, sometimes called the Deutero-Isaiah, are generally attributed to an anonymous poet who prophesied toward the end of the Babylonian exile. From this section come the great messianic oracles known as the songs of the Servant, whose mysterious destiny of suffering and glorification is fulfilled in the passion and glorification of Christ. Chapters 56—66 contain oracles from a later period and were composed by disciples who inherited the spirit and continued the work of the great prophet.

The principal divisions of the Book of Isaiah are the following:

A: The Book of Judgment

- *I: Indictment of Israel and Judah (1, 1—5, 30)*
- *II: Immanuel Prophecies (6, 1—12, 6)*
- *III: Oracles against the Pagan Nations (13, 1—23, 18)*
- *IV: Apocalypse of Isaiah (24, 1—27, 13)*
- *V: The Lord Alone, Israel's and Judah's Salvation (28, 1—33, 24)*

VI: The Lord, Zion's Avenger (34, 1—35, 10)
VII: Historical Appendix (36, 1—39, 8)

B: The Book of Consolation

I: The Lord's Glory in Israel's Liberation (40, 1—48, 21)
II: Expiation of Sin, Spiritual Liberation of Israel (49, 1—55, 13)
III: Return of the First Captives (56, 1—66, 24)

A: THE BOOK OF JUDGMENT

I: INDICTMENT OF ISRAEL AND JUDAH

CHAPTER 1

Israel's Sinfulness. 1† The vision which Isaiah, son of Amoz, had concerning Judah and Jerusalem in the days of Uzziah, Jotham, Ahaz and Hezekiah, kings of Judah.

2* Hear, O heavens, and listen, O earth,
for the LORD speaks:
Sons have I raised and reared,
but they have disowned me!
3† An ox knows its owner,
and an ass, its master's manger;
But Israel does not know,
my people has not understood.
4*† Ah! sinful nation, people laden with wickedness,
evil race, corrupt children!
They have forsaken the LORD,
spurned the Holy One of Israel,
apostatized.
5† Where would you yet be struck,
you that rebel again and again?
The whole head is sick,
the whole heart faint.
6 From the sole of the foot to the head
there is no sound spot:
Wound and welt and gaping gash,
not drained, or bandaged,
or eased with salve.
7 Your country is waste,
your cities burnt with fire;
Your land before your eyes
strangers devour
[a waste, like Sodom overthrown]—
8† And daughter Zion is left
like a hut in a vineyard,
Like a shed in a melon patch,
like a city blockaded.

9*† Unless the LORD of hosts
had left us a scanty remnant,
We had become as Sodom,
we should be like Gomorrah.
10 Hear the word of the LORD,
princes of Sodom!
Listen to the instruction of our God,
people of Gomorrah!
11*† What care I for the number of your sacrifices?
says the LORD.
I have had enough of whole-burnt rams
and fat of fatlings;
In the blood of calves, lambs and goats
I find no pleasure.

12 When you come in to visit me,
who asks these things of you?
13*† Trample my courts no more!
Bring no more worthless offerings;
your incense is loathsome to me.
New moon and sabbath, calling of assemblies,
octaves with wickedness: these I cannot bear.
14 Your new moons and festivals I detest;
they weigh me down, I tire of the load.
15*† When you spread out your hands,
I close my eyes to you;
Though you pray the more,
I will not listen.
Your hands are full of blood!
16 Wash yourselves clean!
Put away your misdeeds from before my eyes;

*

1, 2: Dt 32, 1.5f.
4: 5, 24; Dt 32, 15.
9: Rom 9, 29.
11: Ps 50, 8-13; Sir 34, 19; Mi 6, 7.
13: Prv 15, 8; Jer 6, 20.
15: Prv 1, 28; Sir 34, 21-25.

†

1, 1: The title of the book: an editorial addition. *Isaiah:* meaning "the salvation of the LORD," or "The LORD is salvation." *Amoz:* not the minor prophet. *Judah:* the southern kingdom of the tribes of Judah and Benjamin. *Uzziah:* also called Azariah; cf 2 Kgs 15, 1; 2 Chr 26, 1.

1, 3: *Israel:* not the northern kingdom, as in 9, 11, exclusively, which Isaiah usually calls "Ephraim" from the tribe bordering on the southern kingdom, but the entire chosen people, cf 8, 14.

1, 4: *Holy One of Israel:* a title used frequently by Isaiah, rarely by other writers.

1, 5-8: Sufferings inflicted upon God's people for their sins.

1, 8: *Daughter Zion:* Jerusalem. *Hut . . . shed:* for the shelter of watchmen and laborers.

1, 9: *LORD of hosts:* God, who is the Creator and Ruler of the heavenly armies of the angels, stars, etc. *Remnant:* St. Paul uses this text in Rom 9, 29, where he speaks of God's saving mercy toward the Jews and Gentiles. *Sodom . . . Gomorrah:* cf Gn 19.

1, 11: *The number of your sacrifices:* however numerous, they are not acceptable without the right dispositions on the part of the worshipers.

1, 13: *Octaves with wickedness:* the solemnity of the feasts marred by evil deeds.

1, 15: *Spread out your hands:* in prayer.

cease doing evil; 17* learn to do
good.
Make justice your aim: redress the
wronged,
hear the orphan's plea, defend the
widow.

18* Come now, let us set things right,
says the LORD:
Though your sins be like scarlet,
they may become white as snow;
Though they be crimson red,
they may become white as wool.
19 If you are willing, and obey,
you shall eat the good things of
the land;
20 But if you refuse and resist,
the sword shall consume you:
for the mouth of the LORD has
spoken!

21*†How has she turned adulteress,
the faithful city, so upright!
Justice used to lodge within her,
but now, murderers.
22 Your silver is turned to dross,
your wine is mixed with water.
23* Your princes are rebels
and comrades of thieves;
Each one of them loves a bribe
and looks for gifts.
The fatherless they defend not,
and the widow's plea does not
reach them.
24* Now, therefore, says the Lord,
the LORD of hosts, the Mighty One
of Israel:
Ah! I will take vengeance on my
foes
and fully repay my enemies!
25 I will turn my hand against you,
and refine your dross in the fur-
nace,
removing all your alloy.
26* I will restore your judges as at first,
and your counselors as in the be-
ginning;
After that you shall be called
city of justice, faithful city.

27† Zion shall be redeemed by judg-
ment,
and her repentant ones by justice.
28 Rebels and sinners alike shall be
crushed,
those who desert the LORD shall
be consumed.
29† You shall be ashamed of the tere-
binths which you prized,
and blush for the groves which
you chose.
30 You shall become like a tree with
falling leaves,
like a garden that has no water.
31 The strong man shall turn to tow,
and his work shall become a
spark;
Both shall burn together,
and there shall be none to quench
the flames.

CHAPTER 2

Zion, the Messianic Capital. 1† This is what Isaiah, son of Amoz, saw concerning Judah and Jerusalem.

2*† In days to come,
The mountain of the LORD's house
shall be established as the highest
mountain
and raised above the hills.
All nations shall stream toward it;
3*† many peoples shall come and say:
"Come, let us climb the LORD's
mountain,
to the house of the God of Jacob,
That he may instruct us in his ways,
and we may walk in his paths."
For from Zion shall go forth instruc-
tion,
and the word of the LORD from Je-
rusalem.
4* He shall judge between the nations,
and impose terms on many peo-
ples.
They shall beat their swords into
plowshares
and their spears into pruning
hooks;
One nation shall not raise the sword
against another,
nor shall they train for war again.

5 O house of Jacob, come,
let us walk in the light of the LORD!

The Lord's Judgment against Idols

6*†You have abandoned your people,
the house of Jacob,

*

17: Ex 23, 6; Dt 24, 17; Sir 4, 9f; Jer 22, 3; Ez 22, 7; Zec 7, 9f.
18: Ps 51, 9.
21: Jer 3, 8; Hos 2, 7.
23: Ex 23, 8; Dt 16, 19.
24: Dt 32, 41.
26: Jer 33, 7ff; Zec 8, 3.
2, 2ff: Mi 4, 1ff.
2: 56, 7.
3: Zec 8, 20-23.
4: 9, 7; 11, 4; Ps 72, 3f; Zec 9, 10.
6: 8, 19; 19, 3.

†

1, 21: A picture of Jerusalem, once so faithful to God. Apostasy from the covenant is often likened by the prophets to unfaithfulness to the marriage vow.

1, 27: This verse is the key to the whole Book of Isaiah. Zion's defiant persistence in sin has demanded a divine *judgment,* by which her survivors will be cleansed and will return to God in *justice;* cf 40, 2.

1, 29: *Terebinths which you prized . . . groves which you chose:* as popular shrines for idolatrous worship.

2, 1: An editorial addition introducing chapters 2-5.

2, 2-4: The messianic destiny which ensures Judah's later restoration. In the messianic kingdom the prophets generally see *the Lord's house* as the seat of authority and the source of clear and certain doctrine; also, its rule willingly accepted by all peoples, maintained by spiritual sanctions, and tending to universal peace. This passage is found substantially unchanged in Mi 4, 1-3; it probably, although not certainly, has Isaiah as its author.

2, 3: *Zion . . . Jerusalem:* types of the earthly center of the messianic kingdom.

2, 6: *Fortune-tellers and soothsayers:* divination was strictly forbidden; cf Dt 18, 9-14.

Because they are filled with fortune-tellers
and soothsayers, like the Philistines;
they covenant with strangers.
7 Their land is full of silver and gold,
and there is no end to their treasures;
Their land is full of horses,
and there is no end to their chariots.
8* Their land is full of idols;
they worship the works of their hands,
that which their fingers have made.

9 But man is abased,
each one brought low.
[Do not pardon them!]
10* Get behind the rocks,
hide in the dust,
From the terror of the LORD
and the splendor of his majesty!
11† The haughty eyes of man will be lowered,
the arrogance of men will be abased,
and the LORD alone will be exalted, on that day.
12 For the LORD of hosts will have his day
against all that is proud and arrogant,
all that is high, and it will be brought low;
13† Yes, against all the cedars of Lebanon
and all the oaks of Bashan,
14 Against all the lofty mountains
and all the high hills,
15 Against every lofty tower
and every fortified wall,
16† Against all the ships of Tarshish
and all stately vessels.
17 Human pride will be abased,
the arrogance of men brought low,
And the LORD alone will be exalted,
on that day.

18 The idols will perish forever.

19 Men will go into caves in the rocks
and into holes in the earth,
From the terror of the LORD
and the splendor of his majesty,
when he arises to overawe the earth.

20 On that day men will throw to the
moles and the bats the idols of silver and
gold which they made for worship.

21 They go into caverns in the rocks
and into crevices in the cliffs,
From the terror of the LORD
and the splendor of his majesty,
when he arises to overawe the earth.

22 As for you, let man alone,
in whose nostrils is but a breath;
for what is he worth?

CHAPTER 3

Judgment of Judah and Jerusalem

1*† The Lord, the LORD of hosts,
shall take away from Jerusalem
and from Judah
support and prop [all supplies of bread and water]:
2 Hero and warrior,
judge and prophet, fortune-teller and elder,
3 The captain of fifty and the nobleman,
counselor, skilled magician, and expert charmer.
4 I will make striplings their princes;
the fickle shall govern them,
5 And the people shall oppress one another,
yes, every man his neighbor.
The child shall be bold toward the elder,
and the base toward the honorable.
6 When a man seizes his brother
in his father's house, saying,
"You have clothes! Be our ruler,
and take in hand this ruin!"—
7 Then shall he answer in that day:
"I will not undertake to cure this,
when in my own house there is no bread or clothing!
You shall not make me ruler of the people."

8 Jerusalem is crumbling, Judah is falling;
for their speech and their deeds are before the LORD,
a provocation in the sight of his majesty.
9 Their very look bears witness against them;
their sin like Sodom they vaunt,
They hide it not. Woe to them!
they deal out evil to themselves.
10 Happy the just, for it will be well with them,
the fruit of their works they will eat.

*

8: 31, 1ff.
10: 2 Thes 1, 9.
3, 1: Lv 26, 26; Ez 4, 16.

†

2, 11: *That day:* the day of the Lord, a day of retribution, often referred to, especially by the minor prophets, and described in terms of natural phenomena: earthquake, fire, storm.

2, 13: *Lebanon:* Mount Lebanon in Syria, famed for its cedars. *Bashan:* the wooded uplands east of the Jordan River.

2, 16: *Tarshish:* cf note on Ps 48, 8.

3, 1-12: Anarchy will reign in Jerusalem and Judah. In the prevailing desperation, even the most unworthy and the least qualified will be sought as rulers.

ISAIAH

11 Woe to the wicked man! All goes ill,
with the work of his hands he will be repaid.
12 My people—a babe in arms will be their tyrant,
and women will rule them!
O my people, your leaders mislead,
they destroy the paths you should follow.

13 The LORD rises to accuse,
standing to try his people.
14 The Lord enters into judgment
with his people's elders and princes:
It is you who have devoured the vineyard;
the loot wrested from the poor is in your houses.
15* What do you mean by crushing my people,
and grinding down the poor when they look to you?
says the Lord, the GOD of hosts.

16* The LORD said:
Because the daughters of Zion are haughty,
and walk with necks outstretched
Ogling and mincing as they go,
their anklets tinkling with every step,
17† The Lord shall cover the scalps of Zion's daughters with scabs,
and the LORD shall bare their heads.

18 On that day the LORD will do away
with the finery of the anklets, sunbursts,
and crescents; 19 the pendants, brace-
lets, and veils; 20 the headdresses, ban-
gles, cinctures, perfume boxes, and
amulets; 21† the signet rings, and the
nose rings; 22 the court dresses, wraps,
cloaks, and purses; 23 the mirrors, linen
tunics, turbans, and shawls.

24 Instead of perfume there will be stench,
instead of the girdle, a rope,
And for the coiffure, baldness;
for the rich gown, a sackcloth skirt.
Then, instead of beauty:
25 Your men will fall by the sword,
and your champions, in war;
26 Her gates will lament and mourn,
as the city sits desolate on the ground.

CHAPTER 4

1† Seven women will take hold of one man
on that day, saying:
"We will eat our own food
and wear our own clothing;
Only let your name be given us,
put an end to our disgrace!"

The Messianic Branch

2*† On that day,
The branch of the LORD will be luster and glory,
and the fruit of the earth will be honor and splendor
for the survivors of Israel.
3*† He who remains in Zion
and he that is left in Jerusalem
Will be called holy:
every one marked down for life in Jerusalem.
4 When the Lord washes away
the filth of the daughters of Zion,
And purges Jerusalem's blood from her midst
with a blast of searing judgment,
5* Then will the LORD create,
over the whole site of Mount Zion
and over her place of assembly,
A smoking cloud by day
and a light of flaming fire by night.
6 For over all, his glory will be shelter and protection:
shade from the parching heat of day,
refuge and cover from storm and rain.

CHAPTER 5

The Vineyard Song

1† Let me now sing of my friend,
my friend's song concerning his vineyard.
My friend had a vineyard
on a fertile hillside;
2 He spaded it, cleared it of stones,
and planted the choicest vines;
Within it he built a watchtower,
and hewed out a wine press.
Then he looked for the crop of grapes,
but what it yielded was wild grapes.

3 Now, inhabitants of Jerusalem and men of Judah,

ISAIAH

*

15: Lv 25, 42.55.
16ff: 32, 11f.
4, 2: 11, 1; Jer 23, 5; 33, 15.
3: 6, 13; 10, 20; Ob 17.
5: Ex 13, 21.

†

3, 17: *Bare their heads:* a mark of social disgrace; cf Nm 5, 18.

3, 21: *Nose rings:* of gold, a feminine ornament in the East; cf note on Gn 24, 22.

4, 1: *Seven women . . . one man:* the disproportion of the sexes due to war leaves the female population almost without male partners. The women are eager to marry, not for support, but to avoid the disgrace of being childless.

4, 2: *Branch of the LORD:* divine blessings in general, which later culminated in the Messiah; cf Jer 23, 5; Zec 3, 8; 6, 12.

4, 3: *Marked down for life:* in God's list of his elect; cf Ex 32, 32.

5, 1: *My friend had a vineyard:* the Lord and his chosen people.

judge between me and my vineyard:
4 What more was there to do for my vineyard
that I had not done?
Why, when I looked for the crop of grapes,
did it bring forth wild grapes?
5 Now, I will let you know
what I mean to do to my vineyard:
Take away its hedge, give it to grazing,
break through its wall, let it be trampled!
6 Yes, I will make it a ruin:
it shall not be pruned or hoed,
but overgrown with thorns and briers;
I will command the clouds
not to send rain upon it.
7† The vineyard of the LORD of hosts
is the house of Israel,
and the men of Judah are his cherished plant;
He looked for judgment, but see, bloodshed!
for justice, but hark, the outcry!

Doom of the Unjust

8*† Woe to you who join house to house,
who connect field with field,
Till no room remains, and you are left to dwell
alone in the midst of the land!
9* In my hearing the LORD of hosts has sworn:
Many houses shall be in ruins,
large ones and fine, with no one to live in them.
10† Ten acres of vineyard
shall yield but one liquid measure,
And a homer of seed
shall yield but an ephah.
17 Lambs shall graze there at pasture,
and kids shall eat in the ruins of the rich.

11 Woe to those who demand strong drink
as soon as they rise in the morning,
And linger into the night
while wine inflames them!
12* With harp and lyre, timbrel and flute,
they feast on wine;
But what the LORD does, they regard not,
the work of his hands they see not.
13 Therefore my people go into exile,
because they do not understand;
Their nobles die of hunger,
and their masses are parched with thirst.
14*† Therefore the nether world enlarges its throat
and opens its maw without limit;
Down go their nobility and their masses,
their throngs and their revelry.
15 Men shall be abased, each one brought low,
and the eyes of the haughty lowered,
16 But the LORD of hosts shall be exalted by his judgment,
and God the Holy shall be shown holy by his justice.

18 Woe to those who tug at guilt with cords of perversity,
and at sin as if with cart ropes!
19* To those who say, "Let him make haste
and speed his work, that we may see it;
On with the plan of the Holy One of Israel!
let it come to pass, that we may know it!"
20 Woe to those who call evil good, and good evil,
who change darkness into light,
and light into darkness,
who change bitter into sweet, and sweet into bitter!
21* Woe to those who are wise in their own sight,
and prudent in their own esteem!
22* Woe to the champions at drinking wine,
the valiant at mixing strong drink!
23* To those who acquit the guilty for bribes,
and deprive the just man of his rights!
24 Therefore, as the tongue of fire licks up stubble,
as dry grass shrivels in the flame,
Even so their root shall become rotten
and their blossom scatter like dust;
For they have spurned the law of the LORD of hosts,
and scorned the word of the Holy One of Israel.
25 Therefore the wrath of the LORD
blazes against his people,
he raises his hand to strike them;

*

5, 8: Mi 2, 2.
9: 6, 12.
12: Am 6, 5f.
14: Hb 2, 5.
19: Jer 5, 12; 2 Pt 3, 4.
21: Prv 3, 7; Rom 12, 16.
22: Sir 31, 3.
23: Ex 23, 8; Prv 17, 15.

†

5, 7: *Judgment . . . bloodshed . . . justice . . . outcry:* in Hebrew, these adversative terms constitute a play on words.
5, 8-10: Land-grabbers who unjustly acquire property will be impoverished instead of enriched.
5, 10: *Ten acres:* a field requiring ten days of plowing by a yoke of oxen. *Liquid measure:* in Hebrew, a "bath," i.e., about ten gallons. *Homer:* a dry measure of about ten bushels. *Ephah:* a dry measure of about one bushel.
5, 14: *Nether world:* cf note on Ps 6, 6.

When the mountains quake,
their corpses shall be like refuse in the streets.
For all this, his wrath is not turned back,
and his hand is still outstretched.

Invasion

26*†* He will give a signal to a far-off nation,
and whistle to them from the ends of the earth;
speedily and promptly will they come.
27 None of them will stumble with weariness,
none will slumber and none will sleep.
None will have his waist belt loose,
nor the thong of his sandal broken.
28 Their arrows are sharp,
and all their bows are bent.
The hoofs of their horses seem like flint,
and their chariot wheels like the hurricane.
29 Their roar is that of the lion,
like the lion's whelps they roar;
They growl and seize the prey,
they carry it off and none will rescue it.
30* [They will roar over it, on that day,
with a roaring like that of the sea.]

II: IMMANUEL PROPHECIES

CHAPTER 6

Call of Isaiah. 1*† In the year King
Uzziah died, I saw the Lord seated on
a high and lofty throne, with the train
of his garment filling the temple.
2 Seraphim were stationed above; each
of them had six wings: with two they
veiled their faces, with two they veiled
their feet, and with two they hovered
aloft.
3* "Holy, holy, holy is the LORD of
hosts!" they cried one to the other. "All
the earth is filled with his glory!" 4*† At
the sound of that cry, the frame of the
door shook and the house was filled with
smoke.
5*† Then I said, "Woe is me, I am
doomed! For I am a man of unclean lips,
living among a people of unclean lips;
yet my eyes have seen the King, the
LORD of hosts!" 6 Then one of the sera-
phim flew to me, holding an ember
which he had taken with tongs from the
altar.
7*† He touched my mouth with it.
"See," he said, "now that this has
touched your lips, your wickedness is re-
moved, your sin purged."
8 Then I heard the voice of the Lord
saying, "Whom shall I send? Who will
go for us?" "Here I am," I said; "send
me!" 9*† And he replied: Go and say to
this people:

Listen carefully, but you shall not understand!
Look intently, but you shall know nothing!
10* You are to make the heart of this people sluggish,
to dull their ears and close their eyes;
Else their eyes will see, their ears hear,
their heart understand,
and they will turn and be healed.

11 "How long, O Lord?" I asked. And
he replied:

Until the cities are desolate,
without inhabitants,
Houses, without a man,
and the earth is a desolate waste.
12† Until the LORD removes men far away,
and the land is abandoned more and more.
13* If there be still a tenth part in it,
then this in turn shall be laid waste;
As with a terebinth or an oak
whose trunk remains when its leaves have fallen.
[Holy offspring is the trunk.]

*

30: 8, 22.
6, 1: Jn 12, 41.
3: Rv 4, 8.
4: 1 Kgs 8, 10f; Rv 15, 8.
5: Gn 32, 3; Ex 20, 19; 33, 20; Jgs 6, 22; 13, 22.
7: Jer 1, 9; Dn 10, 16.
9: Mt 13, 14f; Mk 4, 12; Lk 8, 10; Acts 28, 26f.
10: Jer 5, 21; Jn 12, 40.
13: 10, 22.

†

5, 26-30: A description of the invading Assyrian army, God's instrument for punishing his people.

6, 1: *In the year King Uzziah died:* 742 B.C.

6, 1ff: *Temple:* the holy place, just in front of the holy of holies. *Seraphim:* literally "the burning ones," are celestial beings who surround the throne of God. Each has six wings. Reverence for the divine majesty causes them to veil their faces with two wings; modesty, to veil their extremities in similar fashion; alacrity in God's service, to extend two wings in preparation for flight. *Holy, holy, holy:* God's perfect interior holiness whose exterior manifestation is *his glory.* These words are found in the Roman liturgy just before the Canon of the Mass.

6, 4: *Smoke:* reminiscent of the clouds which surrounded God at Mount Sinai; cf Ex 19, 16-19; Dt 4, 11f.

6, 5: *Doomed:* it was popularly believed that to see God would lead to one's death; cf Gn 32, 31; Ex 33, 20; Jgs 13, 22.

6, 7: *Touched your lips:* Isaiah is thus symbolically purified to be worthy of his vocation as God's prophet. In the Roman liturgy, the celebrant at Mass makes reference to this incident just before he reads the gospel.

6, 9f: The truth that the nation will remain impenitent is vividly foretold, as if its obstinacy would be caused, instead of merely occasioned, by the prophet's warning. Cf Mt 13, 13ff; Mk 4, 12; Lk 8, 10.

6, 12: Several limited deportations in the time of Isaiah would later culminate in the Babylonian exile.

CHAPTER 7

Birth of Immanuel. 1*† In the days of
Ahaz, king of Judah, son of Jotham, son
of Uzziah, Rezin, king of Aram, and
Pekah, king of Israel, son of Remaliah,
went up to attack Jerusalem, but they
were not able to conquer it. 2 When word
came to the house of David that Aram
was encamped in Ephraim, the heart of
the king and heart of the people trem-
bled, as the trees of the forest tremble
in the wind.

3*† Then the LORD said to Isaiah: Go
out to meet Ahaz, you and your son
Shear-jashub, at the end of the conduit
of the upper pool, on the highway of the
fuller's field, 4 and say to him: Take care
you remain tranquil and do not fear; let
not your courage fail before these two
stumps of smoldering brands [the blaz-
ing anger of Rezin and the Arameans,
and of the son of Remaliah], 5 because
of the mischief that Aram [Ephraim and
the son of Remaliah] plots against you,
saying, 6† "Let us go up and tear Judah
asunder, make it our own by force, and
appoint the son of Tabeel king there."

7 Thus says the LORD:
This shall not stand, it shall not be!
8 Damascus is the capital of Aram,
and Rezin the head of Damascus;
Samaria is the capital of Ephraim,
and Remaliah's son the head of Samaria.
9*† But within sixty years and five,
Ephraim shall be crushed, no longer a nation.
Unless your faith is firm
you shall not be firm!

10 Again the LORD spoke to Ahaz:
11† Ask for a sign from the LORD, your
God; let it be deep as the nether world,
or high as the sky! 12† But Ahaz an-
swered, "I will not ask! I will not tempt
the LORD!" 13 Then he said: Listen, O
house of David! Is it not enough for you
to weary men, must you also weary my
God? 14† Therefore the Lord himself will
give you this sign: the virgin shall be
with child, and bear a son, and shall
name him Immanuel. 15† He shall be liv-
ing on curds and honey by the time he
learns to reject the bad and choose the
good. 16 For before the child learns to re-
ject the bad and choose the good, the
land of those two kings whom you dread
shall be deserted.

17 The LORD shall bring upon you and
your people and your father's house
days worse than any since Ephraim se-
ceded from Judah. [This means the king
of Assyria.] 18 On that day

The LORD shall whistle
for the fly that is in the farthest streams of Egypt,
and for the bee in the land of Assyria.
19 All of them shall come and settle
in the steep ravines and in the rocky clefts,
on all thornbushes and in all pastures.

20† On that day the LORD shall shave
with the razor hired from across the
River [with the king of Assyria] the
head, and the hair between the legs. It
shall also shave off the beard.

21 On that day a man shall keep a
heifer or a couple of sheep, 22 and from
their abundant yield of milk he shall live
on curds; curds and honey shall be the
food of all who remain in the land. 23 On
that day every place where there used
to be a thousand vines, worth a thousand
pieces of silver, shall be turned to briers
and thorns. 24 Men shall go there with
bow and arrows; for all the country shall
be briers and thorns. 25 For fear of briers
and thorns you shall not go upon any
mountainside which used to be hoed
with the mattock; they shall be grazing
land for cattle and shall be trampled
upon by sheep.

*

7, 1: 2 Kgs 16, 5; 2 Chr 28, 5-15.
3: 36, 2; 2 Chr 32, 3.
9: 8. 6ff.

†

7, 1: *Days of Ahaz:* who ruled from 735 to 715 B.C. This attack against Jerusalem by the kings of *Aram* (Syria) and *Israel* was occasioned by Ahaz' refusal to enter with them into an anti-Assyrian alliance; cf 2 Kgs 16.

7, 3: *Shear-jashub:* this name means "a remnant will return."

7, 6: *Son of Tabeel:* an adherent of Jerusalem's enemies. His appointment would interrupt the lawful succession from David.

7, 9: *Within sixty years and five:* if the text is correct, its reference is unknown.

7, 11: *Deep . . . sky:* an extraordinary or miraculous sign that would prove God's firm will to save the royal house of David from its oppressors.

7, 12: *Tempt the LORD:* Ahaz expresses in this hypocritical way his preference for depending upon the might of Assyria rather than upon God.

7, 14: The *sign* proposed by Isaiah was concerned with the preservation of Judah in the midst of distress (cf 7, 15.17), but more especially with the fulfillment of God's earlier promise to David (2 Sm 7, 12-16) in the coming of *Immanuel* (meaning, "With us is God") as the ideal king (cf 9, 5-6; 11, 1-5). The Church has always followed St. Matthew in seeing the transcendent fulfillment of this verse in Christ and his Virgin Mother. The prophet need not have known the full force latent in his own words; and some Catholic writers have sought a preliminary and partial fulfillment in the conception and birth of the future King Hezekiah, whose mother, at the time Isaiah spoke, would have been a young, unmarried woman (Hebrew, *almah*). The Holy Spirit was preparing, however, for another Nativity which alone could fulfill the divinely given terms of Immanuel's mission, and in which the perpetual virginity of the Mother of God was to fulfill also the words of this prophecy in the integral sense intended by the divine Wisdom.

7, 15: *Curds and honey:* the restricted diet of those who remain after devastation has changed the once fertile fields of Judah into grazing land; cf 7, 21-25.

7, 20: God will use the Assyrians *from across the River* (the Euphrates) as his instrument (*razor*) to inflict disgrace and suffering upon his people.

CHAPTER 8

The Son of Isaiah. 1† The LORD said
to me: Take a large cylinder-seal, and
inscribe on it in ordinary letters: "Be-
longing to Maher-shalal-hash-baz."
2† And I took reliable witnesses, Uriah
the priest, and Zechariah, son of Jeber-
echiah. 3† Then I went to the prophetess
and she conceived and bore a son. The
LORD said to me: Name him Maher-
shalal-hash-baz, 4 for before the child
knows how to call his father or mother
by name, the wealth of Damascus and
the spoil of Samaria shall be carried off
by the king of Assyria.
5 Again the LORD spoke to me:

6*† Because this people has rejected
the waters of Shiloah that flow gently,
And melts with fear before the loftiness
of Rezin and Remaliah's son,
7 Therefore the LORD raises against them
the waters of the River, great and mighty
[the king of Assyria and all his power].
It shall rise above all its channels,
and overflow all its banks;
8 It shall pass into Judah, and flood it all throughout:
up to the neck it shall reach;
It shall spread its wings
the full width of your land, Immanuel!

9 Know, O peoples, and be appalled!
Give ear, all you distant lands!
Arm, but be crushed! Arm, but be crushed!
10† Form a plan, and it shall be thwarted;
make a resolve, and it shall not be carried out,
for "With us is God!"

Disciples of Isaiah. 11* For thus said
the LORD to me, taking hold of me and
warning me not to walk in the way of
this people:

12 Call not alliance what this people calls alliance,
and fear not, nor stand in awe of what they fear.
13 But with the LORD of hosts make your alliance—
for him be your fear and your awe.
14* Yet he shall be a snare, an obstacle and a stumbling stone
to both the houses of Israel,
A trap and a snare
to those who dwell in Jerusalem;
15 And many among them shall stumble and fall,
broken, snared, and captured.

16† The record is to be folded and the
sealed instruction kept among my disci-
ples. 17 For I will trust in the LORD, who
is hiding his face from the house of Ja-
cob; yes, I will wait for him. 18† Look at
me and the children whom the Lord has
given me: we are signs and portents in
Israel from the LORD of hosts who dwells
on Mount Zion. 19*† And when they say
to you, "Inquire of mediums and for-
tune-tellers (who chirp and mutter!);
should not a people inquire of their gods,
apply to the dead on behalf of the liv-
ing?"—20 then this document will furnish
its instruction. That kind of thing they
will surely say.
The Prince of Peace. 23† First he de-
graded the land of Zebulun and the land
of Naphtali; but in the end he has glori-
fied the seaward road, the land west of
the Jordan, the District of the Gentiles.

Anguish has taken wing, dispelled is darkness:
for there is no gloom where but now there was distress.

CHAPTER 9

1* The people who walked in darkness
have seen a great light;
Upon those who dwelt in the land of gloom
a light has shone.

*

8, 6: Jn 9, 7.11.
11: Ez 3, 14.
14: Rom 9, 33; 1 Pt 2, 8.
19: Lv 19, 31; Dt 18, 10ff.
9, 1f: Mt 4, 15f.

†

8, 1: *Ordinary letters:* easily read by all. *Maher-shalal-hash-baz:* a symbolic name to be given to another son of Isaiah (v 3); it means "quick spoils; speedy plunder," and describes what the Assyrians will do.

8, 2: *Reliable witnesses:* who would testify that Isaiah had indeed prophesied the future destruction. *Uriah the priest:* cf 2 Kgs 16, 10.

8, 3: *The prophetess:* wife of Isaiah.

8, 6ff: *This people:* Judah. *Waters of Shiloah:* the stream that flows into the pool of Shiloah in Jerusalem, its slow current symbolizing the silent, divine protection which Judah has rejected. God will therefore summon the mighty Assyrian army, symbolized by *the River* (Euphrates), to devastate Judah, which, however, will not be entirely destroyed, because it is the land of *Immanuel.*

8, 10: The *plan* of Israel's enemies will be *thwarted* because, as the name "Immanuel" signifies, *With us is God.*

8, 16: *Kept among my disciples:* for preservation and transmission.

8, 18: *Signs:* Isaiah and his sons had symbolic names.

8, 19: *Chirp and mutter:* a mocking reference to the sounds uttered by necromancers, as if the dead were speaking; all such practices were forbidden.

8, 21f: These verses have been transposed and placed within 14, 25, which affords the context in which they can be understood.

8,23: *Zebulun . . . Naphtali:* northern Palestine, which was first to be attacked by the Assyrians; God, however, redeems it, as he redeems all his people. *Seaward road:* from Damascus, across southern Galilee to the Mediterranean Sea. *District of the Gentiles:* northern Galilee, inhabited by pagans; cf Jos 20, 7; Is 9, 1; Mt 4, 15f refers to this, since Jesus began his public mission in Galilee.

2 You have brought them abundant joy
and great rejoicing,
As they rejoice before you as at the harvest,
as men make merry when dividing spoils.
3 For the yoke that burdened them,
the pole on their shoulder,
And the rod of their taskmaster
you have smashed, as on the day of Midian.
4* For every boot that tramped in battle,
every cloak rolled in blood,
will be burned as fuel for flames.
5*† For a child is born to us, a son is given us;
upon his shoulder dominion rests.
They name him Wonder-Counselor, God-Hero,
Father-Forever, Prince of Peace.
6* His dominion is vast
and forever peaceful,
From David's throne, and over his kingdom,
which he confirms and sustains
By judgment and justice,
both now and forever.
The zeal of the LORD of hosts will do this!

Fall of the Northern Kingdom

7 The Lord has sent word against Jacob,
it falls upon Israel;
8 And all the people know it,
Ephraim and those who dwell in Samaria,
those who say in arrogance and pride of heart,
9 "Bricks have fallen,
but we will build with cut stone;
Sycamores are felled,
but we will replace them with cedars."
10 But the LORD raises up their foes against them
and stirs up their enemies to action:
11† Aram on the east and the Philistines on the west
devour Israel with open mouth.
For all this, his wrath is not turned back,
and his hand is still outstretched!

12 The people do not turn to him who struck them,
nor seek the LORD of hosts.
13 So the LORD severs from Israel head and tail,
palm branch and reed in one day.
14 [The elder and the noble are the head,
the prophet who teaches falsehood is the tail.]
15* The leaders of this people mislead them
and those to be led are engulfed.
16 For this reason, the Lord does not spare their young men,
and their orphans and widows he does not pity;
They are wholly profaned and sinful,
and every mouth gives vent to folly.
For all this, his wrath is not turned back,
his hand is still outstretched!

17 For wickedness burns like fire,
devouring brier and thorn;
It kindles the forest thickets,
which go up in columns of smoke.
18 At the wrath of the LORD of hosts the land quakes,
and the people are like fuel for fire;
No man spares his brother,
each devours the flesh of his neighbor.
19 Though they hack on the right, they are hungry;
though they eat on the left, they are not filled.
20† Manasseh devours Ephraim, and Ephraim Manasseh;
together they turn on Judah.
For all this, his wrath is not turned back,
his hand is still outstretched!

CHAPTER 10
Social Injustice

1* Woe to those who enact unjust statutes
and who write oppressive decrees,
2* Depriving the needy of judgment
and robbing my people's poor of their rights,
Making widows their plunder,
and orphans their prey!

ISAIAH

*

4: Sir 39, 9.
5: Ps 72, 7; Lk 2, 11.14.
6: Jer 23, 5; Lk 1, 32f.
15: 28, 7; Jer 2, 8; 5, 31; 20, 6; 23, 13f; 29, 30ff; Ez 13, 1-7; 22, 28; Mi 3, 11.
10, 1: Jer 8, 8.
2: 1, 23.

†

9, 5: *A child:* the Immanuel of Is 7, 14 and 8, 8; cf 11, 1.2.9. In Christian tradition and liturgy, this passage is used to refer to Christ. *Upon his shoulder dominion rests:* authority. *Wonder-Counselor:* remarkable for his wisdom and prudence. *God-Hero:* a warrior and a defender of his people, like God himself. *Father-Forever:* ever devoted to his people. *Prince of Peace:* his reign will be characterized by peace.

9, 11: *Aram:* the Syrian kingdom, with its capital at Damascus.

9, 20: *Manasseh . . . Ephraim:* two of the leading tribes of the northern kingdom.

3 What will you do on the day of punishment,
when ruin comes from afar?
To whom will you flee for help?
Where will you leave your wealth,
4 Lest it sink beneath the captive
or fall beneath the slain?
For all this, his wrath is not turned back,
his hand is still outstretched!

Assyria the Unconscious Instrument of God

5 Woe to Assyria! My rod in anger,
my staff in wrath.
6† Against an impious nation I send him,
and against a people under my wrath I order him
To seize plunder, carry off loot,
and tread them down like the mud of the streets.
7 But this is not what he intends,
nor does he have this in mind;
Rather, it is in his heart to destroy,
to make an end of nations not a few.
8 "Are not my commanders all kings?" he says,
9*† "Is not Calno like Carchemish,
Or Hamath like Arpad,
or Samaria like Damascus?
10 Just as my hand reached out to idolatrous kingdoms
that had more images than Jerusalem and Samaria,
11* Just as I treated Samaria and her idols,
shall I not do to Jerusalem and her graven images?"

12 [But when the LORD has brought to an
end all his work on Mount Zion and in
Jerusalem,

I will punish the utterance
of the king of Assyria's proud heart,
13 and the boastfulness of his haughty eyes. For he says:]

"By my own power I have done it,
and by my wisdom, for I am shrewd.
I have moved the boundaries of peoples,
their treasures I have pillaged,
and, like a giant, I have put down the enthroned.
14 My hand has seized like a nest
the riches of nations;
As one takes eggs left alone,
so I took in all the earth;
No one fluttered a wing,
or opened a mouth, or chirped!"

15 Will the axe boast against him who hews with it?
Will the saw exalt itself above him who wields it?
As if a rod could sway him who lifts it,
or a staff him who is not wood!
16† Therefore the Lord, the LORD of hosts,
will send among his fat ones leanness,
And instead of his glory there will be kindling
like the kindling of fire.
17 The Light of Israel will become a fire,
Israel's Holy One a flame,
That burns and consumes his briers
and his thorns in a single day.
18 His splendid forests and orchards
will be consumed, soul and body;
19 And the remnant of the trees in his forest
will be so few,
Like poles set up for signals,
that any boy can record them.
20 On that day
The remnant of Israel,
the survivors of the house of Jacob,
will no more lean upon him who struck them;
But they lean upon the LORD,
the Holy One of Israel, in truth.
21† A remnant will return, the remnant of Jacob,
to the mighty God.
22* For though your people, O Israel,
were like the sand of the sea,
Only a remnant of them will return;
their destruction is decreed
as overwhelming justice demands.

23 Yes, the destruction he has decreed,
the Lord, the GOD of hosts, will carry
out within the whole land. 24 Therefore
thus says the Lord, the GOD of hosts: O
my people, who dwell in Zion, do not fear
the Assyrian, though he strikes you with
a rod, and raises his staff against you.
25 For only a brief moment more, and
my anger shall be over; but them I will
destroy in wrath. 26* Then the LORD of
hosts will raise against them a scourge
such as struck Midian at the rock of
Oreb; and he will raise his staff over the
sea as he did against Egypt. 27† On that
day,

ISAIAH

*

9: 36, 19; Am 6, 2. 22: Rom 9, 27f.
11: 36, 20. 26: Jgs 7, 25.

†

10, 6f: *Impious nation:* Israel. It was God's intention to use Assyria merely to punish, not to destroy, his people.
10, 9: *Calno . . . Damascus:* cities captured by the Assyrians.
10, 16: *His fat ones:* the strong men of the king of Assyria.
10, 21: *A remnant will return:* in Hebrew, *shear-jashub,* an allusion to the name of Isaiah's son, Shear-jashub; cf 7, 3.
10, 27-32: A poetic description of the progress of the Assyrian army, advancing from the north through Judah to the gates of Jerusalem.

His burden shall be taken from your shoulder,
and his yoke shattered from your neck.

Sennacherib's Invasion

He has come up from the direction of Rimmon,
28 he has reached Aiath, passed through Migron,
at Michmash his supplies are stored.
29 They cross the ravine:
"We will spend the night at Geba."
Ramah is in terror,
Gibeah of Saul has fled.
30 Cry and shriek, O daughter of Gallim!
Hearken, Laishah! Answer her, Anathoth!
31 Madmenah is in flight,
the inhabitants of Gebim seek refuge.
32† Even today he will halt at Nob,
he will shake his fist at the mount of daughter Zion,
the hill of Jerusalem!
33 Behold, the Lord, the LORD of hosts,
lops off the boughs with terrible violence;
The tall of stature are felled,
and the lofty ones brought low;
34 The forest thickets are felled with the axe,
and Lebanon in its splendor falls.

ISAIAH

CHAPTER 11

The Rule of Immanuel

1*† But a shoot shall sprout from the stump of Jesse,
and from his roots a bud shall blossom.
2*† The spirit of the LORD shall rest upon him:
a spirit of wisdom and of understanding,
A spirit of counsel and of strength,
a spirit of knowledge and of fear of the LORD,
3 and his delight shall be the fear of the LORD.
Not by appearance shall he judge,
nor by hearsay shall he decide,
4* But he shall judge the poor with justice,
and decide aright for the land's afflicted.
He shall strike the ruthless with the rod of his mouth,
and with the breath of his lips he shall slay the wicked.
5 Justice shall be the band around his waist,
and faithfulness a belt upon his hips.
6*† Then the wolf shall be a guest of the lamb,
and the leopard shall lie down with the kid;
The calf and the young lion shall browse together,
with a little child to guide them.
7 The cow and the bear shall be neighbors,
together their young shall rest;
the lion shall eat hay like the ox.
8 The baby shall play by the cobra's den,
and the child lay his hand on the adder's lair.
9* There shall be no harm or ruin on all my holy mountain;
for the earth shall be filled with knowledge of the LORD,
as water covers the sea.

Union of Ephraim and Judah

10* On that day,
The root of Jesse,
set up as a signal for the nations,
The Gentiles shall seek out,
for his dwelling shall be glorious.
11*† On that day,
The Lord shall again take it in hand
to reclaim the remnant of his people
that is left from Assyria and Egypt,
Pathros, Ethiopia, and Elam,
Shinar, Hamath, and the isles of the sea.
12 He shall raise a signal to the nations
and gather the outcasts of Israel;
The dispersed of Judah he shall assemble
from the four corners of the earth.
13* The envy of Ephraim shall pass away,
and the rivalry of Judah be removed;

---

*

11, 1: Lk 3, 32.
2: Mt 3, 16; Mk 1, 10.
4: Pss 72, 2.4; 98, 9; 2 Thes 2, 8.
6: 65, 25.
9: Hb 2, 14.
10: 49, 22; Rom 15, 12.
11: 27, 13; Mi 7, 12; Zec 10, 10.
13: Ex 37, 16-17.

---

†

10, 32ff: Just when the enemy is about to capture Jerusalem, God intervenes and destroys the hostile army.

11, 1: *Jesse:* David's father. *Shoot . . . stump:* after the Babylonian Exile only a *stump* of the Davidic dynasty will remain; from it will arise the new *shoot,* the messianic King.

11, 2f: The source of the traditional names of the gifts of the Holy Spirit. The Septuagint and the Vulgate read "piety" for *fear of the LORD* in its first occurence, thus listing seven gifts.

11, 6-9: This picture of the idyllic harmony of paradise is a dramatic symbol of the universal peace and justice of messianic times.

11, 11: *Pathros . . . sea:* where God's people lived in exile. *Pathros:* upper Egypt. *Elam:* east of Babylonia. *Shinar:* Babylonia. *Hamath:* on the Orontes River in Syria. *Isles:* or coastlands, in the Mediterranean.

Ephraim shall not be jealous of Judah,
and Judah shall not be hostile to Ephraim;
14† But they shall swoop down on the foothills
of the Philistines to the west,
together they shall plunder the Kedemites;
Edom and Moab shall be their possessions,
and the Ammonites their subjects.
15*† The LORD shall dry up the tongue of the Sea of Egypt,
and wave his hand over the Euphrates in his fierce anger
And shatter it into seven streamlets,
so that it can be crossed in sandals.
16 There shall be a highway for the remnant of his people
that is left from Assyria,
As there was for Israel
when he came up from the land of Egypt.

CHAPTER 12

Song of Thanksgiving

1† On that day, you will say:
I give you thanks, O LORD;
though you have been angry with me,
your anger has abated, and you have consoled me.
2* God indeed is my savior;
I am confident and unafraid.
My strength and my courage is the LORD,
and he has been my savior.

3 With joy you will draw water
at the fountain of salvation, 4 and say on that day:
Give thanks to the LORD, acclaim his name;
among the nations make known his deeds,
proclaim how exalted is his name.
5* Sing praise to the LORD for his glorious achievement;
let this be known throughout all the earth.
6* Shout with exultation, O city of Zion,
for great in your midst
is the Holy One of Israel!

III: ORACLES AGAINST THE PAGAN NATIONS

CHAPTER 13

Babylon. 1 An oracle concerning Babylon; a vision of Isaiah, son of Amoz.

2*† Upon the bare mountains set up a signal;
cry out to them,
Wave for them to enter
the gates of the volunteers.

3† I have commanded my dedicated soldiers,
I have summoned my warriors,
eager and bold to carry out my anger.
4* Listen! the rumble on the mountains:
that of an immense throng!
Listen! the noise of kingdoms,
nations assembled!
The LORD of hosts is mustering
an army for battle.
5 They come from a far-off country,
and from the end of the heavens,
The LORD and the instruments of his wrath,
to destroy all the land.

6*† Howl, for the day of the LORD is near;
as destruction from the Almighty it comes.
7* Therefore all hands fall helpless,
the bows of the young men fall from their hands.
Every man's heart melts 8* in terror.
Pangs and sorrows take hold of them,
like a woman in labor they writhe;
They look aghast at each other,
their faces aflame.

9 Lo, the day of the LORD comes,
cruel, with wrath and burning anger;
To lay waste the land
and destroy the sinners within it!

10* The stars and constellations of the heavens
send forth no light;

*

15: Ex 14, 29.
12, 2: Ex 15, 2; Ps 118, 14.
5: Ex 15, 1.
6: 41, 14.16; 54, 1; Zep 3, 14; Zec 2, 10.
13, 2: 5, 26.
4: Jer 50, 9.
6: Jer 46, 10; Jl 1, 15.
7: Ez 7, 17.
8: 21, 3; Ps 48, 7; Mi 4, 9.
10: 24, 23.

†

11, 14: *Kedemites:* tribes in the Arabian Desert.

11, 15: *Tongue . . . Egypt:* the body of water between Egypt and Palestine.

12, 1-6: Israel's thanksgiving to the Lord, expressed in language like that of the Psalms.

13, 2: *To them:* the Medes (v 17) and Persians, who would destroy Babylon. *Gates of the volunteers:* the mustering places of Babylon's enemies for war against her.

13, 3: *Dedicated soldiers:* in the sense that they will wage a "holy war" and carry out God's plan.

13, 6ff: *Day of the LORD:* described often in prophetical writings, it generally signified the coming of the Lord in power and majesty to destroy his enemies and inaugurate his kingdom. Here it refers to the overthrow of Babylon. The figures used convey the idea of horror and destruction. Read vv 6-8 with vv 14-16.

The sun is dark when it rises,
and the light of the moon does not shine.
11* Thus I will punish the world for its evil
and the wicked for their guilt.
I will put an end to the pride of the arrogant,
the insolence of tyrants I will humble.
12† I will make mortals more rare than pure gold,
men, than gold of Ophir.
13 For this I will make the heavens tremble
and the earth shall be shaken from its place,
At the wrath of the LORD of hosts
on the day of his burning anger.

14* Like a hunted gazelle,
or a flock that no one gathers,
Every man shall turn to his kindred
and flee to his own land.
15 Everyone who is caught shall be run through;
to a man, they shall fall by the sword.
16* Their infants shall be dashed to pieces in their sight;
their houses shall be plundered
and their wives ravished.

17* I am stirring up against them the Medes,
who think nothing of silver
and take no delight in gold.
18 The fruit of the womb they shall not spare,
nor shall they have eyes of pity for children.
19 And Babylon, the jewel of kingdoms,
the glory and pride of the Chaldeans,
Shall be overthrown by God
like Sodom and like Gomorrah.
20* She shall never be inhabited,
nor dwelt in, from age to age;
The Arab shall not pitch his tent there,
nor shepherds couch their flocks.
21*† But wildcats shall rest there
and owls shall fill the houses;
There ostriches shall dwell,
and satyrs shall dance.
22 Desert beasts shall howl in her castles,
and jackals in her luxurious palaces.
Her time is near at hand
and her days shall not be prolonged.

CHAPTER 14

The King of Babylon. 1* When the
LORD has pity on Jacob and again
chooses Israel and settles them on their
own soil, the aliens will join them and
be counted with the house of Jacob.
2* The house of Israel will take them and
bring them along to its place, and possess them as male and female slaves on
the Lord's soil, making captives of its
captors and ruling over its oppressors.
3* On the day the LORD relieves you of
sorrow and unrest and the hard service
in which you have been enslaved,
4*† you will take up this taunt-song
against the king of Babylon:

How the oppressor has reached his end!
how the turmoil is stilled!
5 The LORD has broken the rod of the wicked,
the staff of the tyrants
6 That struck the peoples in wrath
relentless blows;
That beat down the nations in anger,
with oppression unchecked.
7 The whole earth rests peacefully,
song breaks forth;
8* The very cypresses rejoice over you,
and the cedars of Lebanon:
"Now that you are laid to rest,
there will be none to cut us down."

9 The nether world below is all astir
preparing for your coming;
It awakens the shades to greet you,
all the leaders of the earth;
It has the kings of all nations
rise from their thrones.
10 All of them speak out
and say to you,
"You too have become weak like us,
you are the same as we.
11* Down to the nether world your pomp is brought,
the music of your harps.
The couch beneath you is the maggot,
your covering, the worm."

12† How have you fallen from the heavens,
O morning star, son of the dawn!
How are you cut down to the ground,
you who mowed down the nations!
13*† You said in your heart:

*

11: 2, 17; Jer 50, 32.
14: Jer 50, 16.
16: Na 3, 10.
17: 21, 2; Jer 51, 11.28.
20: Jer 51, 62.
21: 34, 13f; 35, 7.
14, 1: 56, 3; 60, 4; Ps 102, 14; Jer 24, 6; Zec 1, 17.
2: 66, 20.
3: Jer 30, 10.
4: Hb 2, 6.
8: Ez 31, 16.
11: Sir 10, 13.
13: Jer 51, 53; Am 9, 2.

†

13, 12: *Ophir:* cf note to Ps 45, 10.

13, 21: *Satyrs:* in the popular mind, demons of goatlike form dwelling in ruins, symbols of immorality; cf Lv 17, 7.

14, 4-21: This *taunt-song,* or satire, is one of the finest in the Bible.

14, 12: *Morning star:* the king of Babylon. The Vulgate has "Lucifer," a name applied by the Church Fathers to Satan.

14, 13: *Recesses of the North:* see note on Ps 48, 3.

"I will scale the heavens;
Above the stars of God
I will set up my throne;
I will take my seat on the Mount of Assembly,
in the recesses of the North.
14* I will ascend above the tops of the clouds;
I will be like the Most High!"
15 Yet down to the nether world you go
to the recesses of the pit!

16 When they see you they will stare, pondering over you:
"Is this the man who made the earth tremble,
and kingdoms quake?
17 Who made the world a desert,
razed its cities,
and gave his captives no release?
18 All the kings of the nations lie in glory,
each in his own tomb;
19 But you are cast forth without burial,
loathsome and corrupt,
Clothed as those slain at sword-point,
a trampled corpse.
Going down to the pavement of the pit,
20 you will never be one with them in the grave."

For you have ruined your land,
you have slain your people!
Let him not be named forever,
that scion of an evil race!
21 Make ready to slaughter his sons
for the guilt of their fathers;
Lest they rise and possess the earth,
and fill the breadth of the world with tyrants.

22* I will rise up against them, says the
LORD of hosts, and cut off from Babylon
name and remnant, progeny and off-
spring, says the LORD. 23 I will make it
a haunt of hoot owls and a marshland;
I will sweep it with the broom of destruc-
tion, says the LORD of hosts.

Assyria

24 The LORD of hosts has sworn:
As I have resolved,
so shall it be;
As I have proposed,
so shall it stand:
25 I will break the Assyrian in my land
and trample him on my mountains;
8:21† He shall pass through it hard-pressed and hungry,
and in his hunger he shall become enraged,
and curse his king and his gods.
He shall look upward,
but there shall be strict darkness without any dawn;
8:22 He shall gaze at the earth,
but there shall be distress and darkness,
with the light blacked out by its clouds.
14:25 Then his yoke shall be removed from them,
and his burden from their shoulder.
26 This is the plan proposed for the whole earth,
and this the hand outstretched over all nations.
27 The LORD of hosts has planned;
who can thwart him?
His hand is stretched out;
who can turn it back?

Philistia. 28† In the year that King
Ahaz died, there came this oracle:

29† Rejoice not, O Philistia, not a man of you,
that the rod which smote you is broken;
For out of the serpent's root shall come an adder,
its fruit shall be a flying saraph.
30 In my pastures the poor shall eat,
and the needy lie down in safety;
But I will kill your root with famine
that shall slay even your remnant.
31 Howl, O gate; cry out, O city!
Philistia, all of you melts away!
For there comes a smoke from the north,
without a straggler in the ranks.
32* What will one answer the messengers of the nation?
"The LORD has established Zion,
and in her the afflicted of his people find refuge."

CHAPTER 15

Moab

1* Oracle on Moab:
Laid waste in a night,
Ar of Moab is destroyed;
Laid waste in a night,
Kir of Moab is destroyed.
2*† Up goes daughter Dibon
to the high places to weep;

ISAIAH

*
14: Ez 28, 2. 17f; Zep 3, 12.
22: Jer 51, 62. 15, 1: 16, 7.
32: Pss 87, 5; 102, 2: Jer 48, 38f.

†
8, 21-22: *He . . . clouds:* The two verses have been transposed from chapter 8.
14, 28: *The year that King Ahaz died:* 715 B.C.
14, 29: *Rod:* an Assyrian oppressor whose identity is uncertain. *Flying saraph:* a poisonous serpent, distinguished by its speedy movement; cf note on Nm 21, 6.
15, 2: *Every head . . . sheared off:* traditional signs of grief.

Over Nebo and over Medeba
Moab wails.
Every head is shaved,
every beard sheared off.
3 In the streets they wear sackcloth,
lamenting and weeping;
On the rooftops and in the squares
everyone wails.
4* Heshbon and Elealeh cry out,
they are heard as far as Jahaz.
At this the loins of Moab tremble,
his soul quivers within him;
5* The heart of Moab cries out,
his fugitives reach Zoar
[Eglath-shelishiyah].
The ascent of Luhith
they climb weeping;
On the way to Horonaim
they utter rending cries.

6 The waters of Nimrim
have become a waste;
The grass is withered,
new growth is gone,
nothing is green.
7 So now whatever they have acquired
or stored away
they carry across the Gorge of the
Poplars,
8 For the cry has gone round
the land of Moab;
As far as Eglaim the wailing,
and to Beer-elim, the wail.
9† The waters of Dimon are filled with
blood,
but I will bring still more upon Dimon:
Lions for those who are fleeing from
Moab
and for those who remain in the
land!

CHAPTER 16

1 Send them forth, hugging the earth
like reptiles,
from Sela across the desert,
to the mount of daughter Zion.
2† Like flushed birds,
like startled nestlings,
Are the daughters of Moab
at the fords of the Arnon.
3† Offer counsel, take their part:
at high noon let your shadow be
like the night,
To hide the outcasts,
to conceal the fugitives.
4 Let the outcasts of Moab live with
you,
be their shelter from the destroyer.
When the struggle is ended, the ruin
complete,
and they have done with trampling the land,
5* A throne shall be set up in mercy,
and on it shall sit in fidelity
[in David's tent]
A judge upholding right
and prompt to do justice.
6* We have heard of the pride of Moab,
how very proud he is,
With his haughty, arrogant insolence
that his empty words do not
match.
7*† Therefore Moab wails for Moab,
everywhere they wail;
For the raisin cakes of Kir-hareseth
they sigh, stricken with grief.
8† The terraced slopes of Heshbon languish,
the vines of Sibmah,
Whose clusters overpowered
the lords of nations,
While they reached as far as Jazer
and scattered over the desert,
And whose branches spread forth
and extended over the sea.
9* Therefore I weep with Jazer
for the vines of Sibmah;
I water you with tears,
Heshbon and Elealeh;
For on your summer fruits and harvests
the battle cry has fallen.
10* From the orchards are taken away
joy and gladness,
In the vineyards there is no singing,
no shout of joy;
In the wine presses no one treads
grapes,
the vintage shout is stilled.
11* Therefore for Moab
my breast moans like a lyre,
and my heart for Kir-hareseth.
12*† When Moab grows weary on the
high places,
he shall enter his sanctuary to
pray,
but it shall avail him nothing.

13† This is the word the LORD spoke
against Moab in times past. 14 But now

*
4: Jer 48, 34.
5: 16, 9; Jer 48, 3.
16, 5: 32, 1.
6: Jer 48, 29.
7: 15, 3.
9: 15, 5; Jer 48, 32.
10: 24, 8.
11: 15, 5; Jer 48, 36.
12: Jer 48, 13.

†
15, 9: There is in the Hebrew a play on words: *Dimon* and *dam,* the latter signifying "blood."
16, 2: *The Arnon:* principal river of Moab.
16, 3-5: Directed to Jerusalem, which should receive the suffering Moabites with mercy, as befits the city of David's family, who were partly descended from Ruth the Moabite.
16, 7-14: Moab had been prosperous; now it has become a desert.
16, 7: *Raisin cakes:* masses of dried compressed grapes used as food (cf 2 Sm 6, 19; 1 Chr 16, 3; Sg 2, 5), and also in pagan cult (Hos 3, 1).
16, 8: *Desert:* to the east. *Sea:* the Dead Sea.
16, 12: In vain do the Moabites appeal to their god Chemosh.
16, 13f: A prose application of the preceding poetic oracle against Moab (15, 1— 16, 12); cf Jer 4, 8. *Like those of a hireling:* who fulfills his period of service according to the shortest manner of reckoning; cf 21, 16.

the LORD has spoken: In three years, like
those of a hireling, the glory of Moab
shall be degraded despite all its great
multitude; there shall be a remnant,
very small and weak.

CHAPTER 17

Damascus

1*† Oracle on Damascus:
Lo, Damascus shall cease to be a city
and become a ruin;
2 Her cities shall be forever abandoned,
given over to flocks to lie in undisturbed.
3† The fortress shall be lost to Ephraim
and the kingdom to Damascus;
The remnant of Aram shall have the same glory
as the Israelites,
says the LORD of hosts.
4* On that day
The glory of Jacob shall fade,
and his full body grow thin,
5† Like the reaper's mere armful of stalks
when he gathers the standing grain;
Or as when one gleans the ears
in the Valley of Rephaim.
6*† Only a scattering of grapes shall be left!
As when an olive tree has been beaten,
Two or three olives remain at the very top,
four or five on its fruitful branches,
says the LORD, the God of Israel.

7* On that day man shall look to his maker,
his eyes turned toward the Holy One of Israel.
8† He shall not look to the altars, his handiwork,
nor shall he regard what his fingers have made:
the sacred poles or the incense stands.
9* On that day his strong cities shall be
like those abandoned by the Hivites and Amorites
When faced with the children of Israel:
they shall be laid waste.
10*† For you have forgotten God, your savior,
and remembered not the Rock, your strength.
Therefore, though you plant your pagan plants
and set out your foreign vine slips,
11 Though you make them grow the day you plant them
and make your sprouts blossom on the next morning,
The harvest shall disappear on the day of the grievous blow,
the incurable blight.

12† Ah! the roaring of many peoples
that roar like the roar of the seas!
The surging of nations
that surge like the surging of mighty waves!
13 But God shall rebuke them,
and they shall flee far away;
Windswept, like chaff on the mountains,
like tumbleweed in a storm.
14 In the evening, they spread terror,
before morning, they are gone!
Such is the portion of those who despoil us,
the lot of those who plunder us.

CHAPTER 18

Ethiopia

1† Ah, land of buzzing insects,
beyond the rivers of Ethiopia,
2* Sending ambassadors by sea,
in papyrus boats on the waters!
Go, swift messengers,
to a nation tall and bronzed,
To a people dreaded near and far,
a nation strong and conquering,
whose land is washed by rivers.
3 All you who inhabit the world,
who dwell on earth,
When the signal is raised on the mountain, look!
When the trumpet blows, listen!

4 For thus says the LORD to me:
I will quietly look on from where I dwell,

*

17, 1: Jer 49, 23.
4: 10, 16.
6: 24, 13.
7 Mi 5, 12.
9: 27, 10.
10: Jer 2, 32; Hos 8, 14.
18, 2: 18, 7.

†

17, 1: *Damascus:* capital of Syria, destroyed in 732 B.C.

17, 3: *Ephraim:* Israel, leagued with Syria against Assyria and Judah; destroyed in 721 B.C. *Aram:* Syria.

17, 5: *Valley of Rephaim:* a fertile plain to the southwest of Jerusalem; cf Jos 15, 8; 2 Sm 5, 18.

17, 6: Olives not easily picked by hand were knocked from the tree by means of a long stick; cf 24, 13.

17, 8: *Sacred poles:* see note on Ex 34, 13. *Incense stands:* small altars on which incense was burned in idolatrous worship; cf 27, 9; Lv 26, 30.

17, 10: *Pagan plants:* literally "plants of delights," understood by some as planted in honor of the god of fertility.

17, 12f: *Many peoples:* the hordes that accompanied the invading Assyrians, whom God repels just as he vanquished the primeval waters of chaos; see notes on Jb 3, 8; 7, 12; Ps 89, 11.

18, 1: *Land of buzzing insects:* the region of the Upper Nile where these multiplied with great rapidity.

18, 1f: *Papyrus boats:* light and serviceable vessels made of bundles of papyrus stalks and sealed with pitch. Egypt, ruled by a dynasty from *Ethiopia,* had invited Judah to join a coalition against Assyria, but Isaiah bade the *ambassadors* return to their own people.

Like the glowing heat of sunshine,
like a cloud of dew at harvest time.
5 Before the vintage, when the flowering is ended,
and the blooms are succeeded by ripening grapes,
Then comes the cutting of branches with pruning hooks
and the discarding of the lopped-off shoots.
6 They shall all be left to the mountain birds of prey,
and to the beasts in the land;
The birds of prey shall summer on them
and on them all the beasts of the earth shall winter.

7* Then will gifts be brought to the
LORD of hosts from a people tall and
bronzed, from a people dreaded near
and far, a nation strong and conquering,
whose land is washed by rivers—to
Mount Zion where dwells the name of
the LORD of hosts.

CHAPTER 19

Egypt

1 Oracle on Egypt:
See, the LORD is riding on a swift cloud
on his way to Egypt;
The idols of Egypt tremble before him,
the hearts of the Egyptians melt within them.
2 I will rouse Egypt against Egypt:
brother will war against brother,
Neighbor against neighbor,
city against city, kingdom against kindgom.
3* The courage of the Egyptians ebbs away within them,
and I will bring to nought their counsel;
They shall consult idols and charmers,
ghosts and spirits.
4*† I will deliver Egypt
into the power of a cruel master,
A harsh king who shall rule over them,
says the Lord, the LORD of hosts.
5* The waters shall be drained from the sea,
the river shall shrivel and dry up;
6 Its streams shall become foul,
and the canals of Egypt shall dwindle and dry up.
Reeds and rushes shall wither away,
7 and bulrushes on the bank of the Nile;
All the sown land along the Nile
shall dry up and blow away, and be no more.
8 The fishermen shall mourn and lament,
all who cast hook in the Nile;
Those who spread their nets in the water
shall pine away.
9* The linen-workers shall be disappointed,
the combers and weavers shall turn pale;
10 The spinners shall be crushed,
all the hired laborers shall be despondent.

11† Utter fools are the princes of Zoan!
the wisest of Pharaoh's advisers give stupid counsel.
How can you say to Pharaoh,
"I am a disciple of wise men, of ancient kings"?
12 Where then are your wise men?
Let them tell you and make known
What the LORD of hosts has planned against Egypt.
13 The princes of Zoan have become fools,
the princes of Memphis have been deceived.
The chiefs of her tribes
have led Egypt astray.
14 The LORD has prepared among them
a spirit of dizziness,
And they have made Egypt stagger
in whatever she does,
as a drunkard staggers in his vomit.
15*† Egypt shall have no work to do
for head or tail, palm branch or reed.

16* On that day the Egyptians shall be
like women, trembling with fear, be-
cause of the LORD of hosts shaking his
fist at them. 17* And the land of Judah
shall be a terror to the Egyptians. Every
time they remember Judah, they shall
stand in dread because of the plan which
the LORD of hosts has in mind for
them.
18† On that day there shall be five cities
in the land of Egypt speaking the lan-
guage of Canaan and swearing by the
LORD of hosts; one shall be called "City
of the Sun."

*

7: 45, 14; Zep 3, 10; Mal 1, 11.
19, 3: 44, 25.
4: Ez 29, 19; 30, 10.
5: Ez 30, 12; 32, 2.
9: Ez 27, 7.
15: 9, 14.
16: Na 3, 13.
17: Ex 14, 25.

†

19, 4: *Cruel master:* the king of Assyria.

19, 11.13: *Zoan,* later known as Tanis, and *Memphis* (in Hebrew, *Noph*) were the key cities of the Nile Delta.

19, 15: *Head or tail, palm branch or reed:* the leaders or the people; cf 9, 13f.

19, 18: *Five cities:* colonies of Jews living together and speaking their languages, Hebrew and Aramaic; cf Jer 43. *City of the Sun:* the meaning is uncertain, but the reference seems to be to the city known later as Heliopolis.

19 On that day there shall be an altar
to the LORD in the land of Egypt, and
a sacred pillar to the LORD near the
boundary. 20 It shall be a sign and a wit-
ness to the LORD of hosts in the land of
Egypt, when they cry out to the LORD
against their oppressors, and he sends
them a savior to defend and deliver
them. 21* The LORD shall make himself
known to Egypt, and the Egyptians shall
know the LORD in that day; they shall
offer sacrifices and oblations, and fulfill
the vows they make to the LORD.
22 Although the LORD shall smite Egypt
severely, he shall heal them; they shall
turn to the LORD and he shall be won
over and heal them.
23 On that day there shall be a highway
from Egypt to Assyria; the Assyrians
shall enter Egypt, and the Egyptians en-
ter Assyria, and Egypt shall serve As-
syria.
24* On that day Israel shall be a third
party with Egypt and Assyria, a blessing
in the midst of the land, 25 when the LORD
of hosts blesses it: "Blessed be my people
Egypt, and the work of my hands As-
syria, and my inheritance, Israel."

CHAPTER 20

Captivity of Egypt and Ethiopia. 1 In
the year the general sent by Sargon,
king of Assyria, fought against Ashdod
and captured it, 2† the LORD gave a
warning through Isaiah, the son of
Amoz: Go and take off the sackcloth
from your waist, and remove the san-
dals from your feet. This he did, walking
naked and barefoot. 3 Then the LORD
said: Just as my servant Isaiah has gone
naked and barefoot for three years as
a sign and portent against Egypt and
Ethiopia, 4 so shall the king of Assyria
lead away captives from Egypt, and ex-
iles from Ethiopia, young and old, naked
and barefoot, with buttocks uncovered
[the shame of Egypt]. 5* They shall be
dismayed and ashamed because of
Ethiopia, their hope, and because of
Egypt, their boast. 6* The inhabitants
of this coastland shall say on that
day, "Look at our hope! We have fled
here for help and deliverance from
the king of Assyria; where can we flee
now?"

CHAPTER 21
Fall of Babylon

1† Oracle on the wastelands by the sea:
Like whirlwinds sweeping in waves through the Negeb,
there comes from the desert, from the fearful land,
2*† A cruel sight, revealed to me:
the traitor betrays,
the despoiler spoils.
"Go up, Elam; besiege, O Media;
I will put an end to all groaning!"
3* Therefore my loins are filled with anguish,
pangs have seized me like those of a woman in labor;
I am too bewildered to hear,
too dismayed to look.
4 My mind reels,
shuddering assails me;
My yearning for twilight
has turned into dread.

5† They set the table,
spread out the rugs;
they eat, they drink.
Rise up, O princes,
oil the shield!
6 For thus says my Lord to me:
Go, station a watchman,
let him tell what he sees.
7 If he sees a chariot,
a pair of horses,
Someone riding an ass,
someone riding a camel,
Then let him pay heed,
very close heed.
8* Then the watchman cried,
"On the watchtower, O my Lord,
I stand constantly by day;
And I stay at my post
through all the watches of the night.
9* Here he comes now:
a single chariot,
a pair of horses;
He calls out and says,
'Fallen, fallen is Babylon,
And all the images of her gods
are smashed to the ground.' "
10* O my people who have been threshed,
beaten on my threshing floor!
What I have heard
from the LORD of hosts,
The God of Israel,
I have announced to you.

*

21: Zec 14, 16.18.
24: Gn 12, 2.
20, 5: 30, 3.5.
6: 31, 3; 36, 6.
21, 2: 13, 17.
3: Ps 38, 8.
8: Hb 2, 1.
9: 46, 1; Jer 50, 2; 51, 8; Rv 14, 8.
10: 51, 23.

†

20, 2-6: The symbolic act of the prophet conveyed the idea that Assyria would lead captive the Egyptians and Ethiopians. The Judeans and their allies would then realize the folly of having trusted in them.

21, 1: *Wastelands by the sea:* Babylonia. *Negeb:* the desert south of Judah.

21, 2: *Elam. . . Media:* nations which, under the leadership of Cyrus, captured Babylon in 538 B.C. *End to all groaning:* those who were captive of Babylon shall be freed.

21, 5: Babylon is destroyed while its leaders are feasting; cf Dn 5. *Oil the shield:* shields were oiled and greased so as to divert blows more easily.

Edom

11† Oracle on Edom:
They call to me from Seir,
"Watchman, how much longer the night?
Watchman, how much longer the night?"
12 The watchman replies,
"Morning has come, and again night.
If you will ask, ask; come back again."

Arabia

13† Oracle on Arabia:
In the thicket in the nomad country spend the night,
O caravans of Dedanites.
14 Meet the thirsty, bring them water;
you who dwell in the land of Tema,
greet the fugitives with bread.
15 They flee from the sword,
from the whetted sword;
From the taut bow,
from the fury of battle.

16† For thus says the Lord to me: In another year, like those of a hireling, all the glory of Kedar shall come to an end.
17 Few of Kedar's stalwart archers shall remain, for the LORD, the God of Israel, has spoken.

CHAPTER 22

Jerusalem

1† Oracle of the Valley of Vision:
What is the matter with you now,
that you have gone up,
all of you, to the housetops,
2* O city full of noise and chaos,
O wanton town!
Your slain are not slain with the sword,
nor killed in battle.
3* All your leaders fled away together,
fled afar off;
All who were in you were captured together,
captured without the use of a bow.
4* At this I say: Turn away from me,
let me weep bitterly;
Do not try to comfort me
for the ruin of the daughter of my people.
5* It is a day of panic, rout and confusion,
from the Lord, the GOD of hosts,
in the Valley of Vision.
Walls crash;
they cry for help to the mountains.
6† Elam takes up the quivers,
Aram mounts the horses,
and Kir uncovers the shields.
7 Your choice valleys are filled with chariots,
and horses are posted at the gates,
8† and shelter over Judah is removed.

On that day you looked to the weapons in the House of the Forest; 9 you saw that the breaches in the City of David were many; you collected the water of the lower pool. 10 You numbered the houses of Jerusalem, tearing some down to strengthen the wall; 11 you made a reservoir between the two walls for the water of the old pool. But you did not look to the city's Maker, nor did you consider him who built it long ago.

12* On that day the Lord,
the GOD of hosts, called on you
To weep and mourn,
to shave your head and put on sackcloth.
13* But look! you feast and celebrate,
you slaughter oxen and butcher sheep,
You eat meat and drink wine:
"Eat and drink, for tomorrow we die!"
14 This reaches the ears of the LORD of hosts—
You shall not be pardoned this wickedness till you die,
says the Lord, the GOD of hosts.

Shebna and Eliakim

15† Thus says the Lord, the GOD of hosts:
Up, go to that official,
Shebna, master of the palace,
16 Who has hewn for himself a sepulcher on a height
and carved his tomb in the rock:
"What are you doing here, and what people have you here,
that here you have hewn for yourself a tomb?"

*

22, 2: 32, 13.
3: 2 Kgs 25, 4.
4: Jer 6, 26; 9, 1; 14, 17.
5: 37, 3.
12: Jl 2, 17.
13: 56, 12; Wis 2, 6; 1 Cor 15, 32.

†

21, 11f: *Seir:* another name for Edom. The Edomites ask the prophet how much longer they must suffer *(the night of suffering);* he answers ambiguously: "Liberation *(morning)* and further suffering *(night),*" but perhaps they will later receive a more encouraging answer *(ask, come back again).*

21, 13f: *Arabia:* that is, *the nomad country. Dedanites:* an Arab tribe associated with Edom and *Tema,* and living east of the Red Sea; cf Gn 10, 7; 25, 3; Jer 25, 23.

21, 16: *Year . . . of a hireling:* see note on 16, 14. *Kedar:* a nomad tribe in Arabia; cf 42, 11; 60, 7; Ps 120, 5.

22, 1-8: *Valley of Vision:* while the people live in revelry and disorder, the prophet foresees the impending doom of the city.

22, 6: *Elam, Aram, Kir:* all allies of Assyria. *Kir:* perhaps the same people referred to in Am 1, 5.

22, 8-11: Defense measures, in which the inhabitants of Jerusalem placed their trust instead of relying on God. *House of the Forest:* an armory built by Solomon; its columns of wood suggested the trees of a forest; cf 1 Kgs 7, 2; 10, 17.

22, 15: *Shebna:* referred to as the scribe in 36, 3.

17 The LORD shall hurl you down headlong, mortal man!
He shall grip you firmly
18 And roll you up and toss you like a ball
into an open land
To perish there, you and the chariots you glory in,
you disgrace to your master's house!
19 I will thrust you from your office
and pull you down from your station.

20*†On that day I will summon my servant
Eliakim, son of Hilkiah;
21 I will clothe him with your robe,
and gird him with your sash,
and give over to him your authority.
He shall be a father to the inhabitants of Jerusalem,
and to the house of Judah.
22*†I will place the key of the House of David on his shoulder;
when he opens, no one shall shut,
when he shuts, no one shall open.
23 I will fix him like a peg in a sure spot,
to be a place of honor for his family;
24† On him shall hang all the glory of his family:
descendants and offspring,
all the little dishes, from bowls to jugs.

25 On that day, says the LORD of hosts,
the peg fixed in a sure spot shall give
way, break off and fall, and the weight
that hung on it shall be done away with;
for the LORD has spoken.

CHAPTER 23
Tyre and Sidon

1† Oracle on Tyre:
Wail, O ships of Tarshish,
for your port is destroyed;
From the land of the Kittim
the news reaches them.
2 Silence! you who dwell on the coast,
you merchants of Sidon,
Whose messengers crossed the sea
3† over the deep waters.
The grain of Shihor, the harvest of the Nile, was her revenue,
and she the merchant among nations.
4† Shame, O Sidon, fortress on the sea,
for the sea has spoken:
"I have not been in labor, nor given birth,
nor raised young men,
nor reared virgins."
5 When it is heard in Egypt
they shall be in anguish at the news of Tyre.
6 Pass over to Tarshish, wailing,
you who dwell on the coast!
7 Is this your wanton city,
whose origin is from old,
Whose feet have taken her
to dwell in distant lands?
8 Who has planned such a thing
against Tyre, the bestower of crowns,
Whose merchants are princes,
whose traders are the earth's honored men?
9* The LORD of hosts has planned it,
to disgrace all pride of majesty,
to degrade all the earth's honored men.
10 Cross to your own land,
O ship of Tarshish;
the harbor is no more.
11† His hand he stretches out over the sea,
he shakes kingdoms;
The LORD has ordered the destruction
of Canaan's strongholds.
12* You shall exult no more, he says,
you who are now oppressed, virgin daughter Sidon.
Arise, pass over to the Kittim,
even there you shall find no rest.

13*† [This people is the land of the Chal-
deans, not Assyria.]

She whom the impious founded,
setting up towers for her,
Has had her castles destroyed,
and has been turned into a ruin.
14 Lament, O ships of Tarshish,
for your haven is destroyed.

15*† On that day, Tyre shall be forgot-
ten for seventy years. With the days of
another king, at the end of seventy
years, it shall be for Tyre as in the song
about the harlot:

16 Take a harp, go about the city,
O forgotten harlot;
Pluck the strings skillfully, sing many songs,
that they may remember you.

ISAIAH

*

20: 2 Kgs 18, 18.37.
22: Rv 3, 7.
23, 9: Ez 28, 7.
12: Ez 28, 21f.
13: Ez 26, 7.
15: Jer 25, 11.

†

22, 20: *Eliakim:* also referred to in 36, 3; he is described as loyal to God.
22, 22: *Key:* symbol of authority; cf Mt 16, 19; Rv 3, 7.
22, 24f: If Eliakim should anger God, he and his family (compared here to dishes, bowls and jugs) will suffer disaster.
23, 1-4.12ff: These verses refer to Sidon, vv 5-11 to Tyre.
23, 1: *Kittim:* Cyprus.
23, 3: *Shihor:* a synonym for the Nile.
23, 4: *The sea:* brings to distant coasts the news that Sidon must disown her children; her people are dispersed.
23, 11: *Canaan's strongholds:* the fortresses of Phoenicia.
23, 13: The gloss here identifies *she whom the impious founded* with *the land of the Chaldeans.*
23, 15: *Seventy years:* a conventional period of time indicating simply a long disaster; cf Jer 25, 11 and 29, 10.

17* At the end of the seventy years the
LORD shall visit Tyre. She shall return
to her hire and deal with all the world's
kingdoms on the face of the earth.
18† But her merchandise and her hire
shall be sacred to the LORD. It shall not
be stored up or laid away, but from her
merchandise those who dwell before the
LORD shall eat their fill and clothe themselves in choice attire.

IV: APOCALYPSE OF ISAIAH

CHAPTER 24

Devastation of the World: A Remnant Saved

1*† Lo, the LORD empties the land and lays it waste;
he turns it upside down,
scattering its inhabitants:
2 Layman and priest alike,
servant and master,
The maid as her mistress,
the buyer as the seller,
The lender as the borrower,
the creditor as the debtor.
3 The earth is utterly laid waste, utterly stripped,
for the LORD has decreed this thing.
4 The earth mourns and fades,
the world languishes and fades;
both heaven and earth languish.
5† The earth is polluted because of its inhabitants,
who have transgressed laws, violated statutes,
broken the ancient covenant.
6 Therefore a curse devours the earth,
and its inhabitants pay for their guilt;
Therefore they who dwell on earth turn pale,
and few men are left.
7* The wine mourns, the vine languishes,
all the merry-hearted groan.
8* Stilled are the cheerful timbrels,
ended the shouts of the jubilant,
stilled is the cheerful harp.
9 They cannot sing and drink wine;
strong drink is bitter to those who partake of it.
10*† Broken down is the city of chaos,
shut against entry, every house.
11* In the streets they cry out for lack of wine;
all joy has disappeared
and cheer has left the land.
12 In the city nothing remains but ruin;
its gates are battered and desolate.
13* Thus it is within the land,
and among the peoples,
As with an olive tree after it is beaten,
as with a gleaning when the vintage is done.
14† These lift up their voice in acclaim;
from the sea they proclaim the majesty of the LORD:
15* "For this, in the coastlands,
give glory to the LORD!
In the coastlands of the sea,
to the name of the LORD, the God of Israel!"
16 From the end of the earth we hear songs:
"Splendor to the Just One!"
But I said, "I am wasted, wasted away.
Woe is me! The traitors betray:
with treachery have the traitors betrayed!
17* Terror, pit, and trap
are upon you, inhabitant of the earth;
18 He who flees at the sound of terror
will fall into the pit;
He who climbs out of the pit
will be caught in the trap.
For the windows on high will be opened
and the foundations of the earth will shake.
19 The earth will burst asunder,
the earth will be shaken apart,
the earth will be convulsed.
20* The earth will reel like a drunkard,
and it will sway like a hut;
Its rebellion will weigh it down,
until it falls, never to rise again."

21*† On that day the LORD will punish
the host of the heavens in the heavens,
and the kings of the earth on the earth.
22 They will be gathered together
like prisoners into a pit;
They will be shut up in a dungeon,
and after many days they will be punished.
23*† Then the moon will blush
and the sun grow pale,

*

17: Ez 27, 12.
24, 1: 13, 9; Hos 4, 9.
7: Jl 1, 10.
8: Jer 7, 34; Hos 2, 13.
10: 25, 2.
11: Jer 48, 33; Lam 5, 14f.
13: 17, 6; Mi 7, 1.
15: 42, 10.12; Zep 2, 11.
17f: Jer 48, 43f.
20: 9, 14.
21: Ps 76, 13.
23: 13, 10; Jl 3, 3f; 4, 15.

†

23, 18: Describes the conversion of Tyre.

24, 1—27, 13: This section, probably composed at a later date, contains oracles on the day of the Lord, combined with hymns of thanksgiving and of supplication.

24, 5: *Ancient covenant:* God's commandments to all mankind.

24, 10: *City of chaos:* a symbol of godlessness as opposed to Jerusalem, the city of God.

24, 14: *These:* the saved.

24, 21: *Host of the heavens:* the stars, which were regarded by the pagans as gods; cf Dt 4, 19; Jer 8, 2.

24, 23: *His elders:* the heavenly courtiers surrounding the throne of God.

For the LORD of hosts will reign
on Mount Zion and in Jerusalem,
glorious in the sight of his elders.

CHAPTER 25

1*† O LORD, you are my God,
I will extol you and praise your name;
For you have fulfilled your wonderful plans of old,
faithful and true.
2* For you have made the city a heap,
the fortified city a ruin;
The castle of the insolent is a city no more,
nor ever to be rebuilt.
3 Therefore a strong people will honor you,
fierce nations will fear you.
4* For you are a refuge to the poor,
a refuge to the needy in distress;
Shelter from the rain,
shade from the heat.
As with the cold rain,
5 as with the desert heat,
even so you quell the uproar of the wanton.
6† On this mountain the LORD of hosts
will provide for all peoples
A feast of rich food and choice wines,
juicy, rich food and pure, choice wines.
7* On this mountain he will destroy
the veil that veils all peoples,
The web that is woven over all nations;
8 he will destroy death forever.
The Lord GOD will wipe away
the tears from all faces;
The reproach of his people he will remove
from the whole earth; for the LORD has spoken.

9* On that day it will be said:
"Behold our God, to whom we looked to save us!
This is the LORD for whom we looked;
let us rejoice and be glad that he has saved us!"
10*† For the hand of the LORD will rest on this mountain,
but Moab will be trodden down
as a straw is trodden down in the mire.
11* He will stretch forth his hands in Moab
as a swimmer extends his hands to swim;
He will bring low their pride
as his hands sweep over them.
12* The high-walled fortress he will raze,
and strike it down level with the earth, with the very dust.

CHAPTER 26

The Divine Vindicator. 1 On that day they will sing this song in the land of Judah:

"A strong city have we;
he sets up walls and ramparts to protect us.
2* Open up the gates
to let in a nation that is just,
one that keeps faith.
3* A nation of firm purpose you keep in peace;
in peace, for its trust in you."

4* Trust in the LORD forever!
For the LORD is an eternal Rock.
5* He humbles those in high places,
and the lofty city he brings down;
He tumbles it to the ground,
levels it with the dust.
6 It is trampled underfoot by the needy,
by the footsteps of the poor.
7* The way of the just is smooth;
the path of the just you make level.
8 Yes, for your way and your judgments, O LORD,
we look to you;
Your name and your title
are the desire of our souls.
9* My soul yearns for you in the night,
yes, my spirit within me keeps vigil for you;
When your judgment dawns upon the earth,
the world's inhabitants learn justice.
10* The wicked man, spared, does not learn justice;
in an upright land he acts perversely,
and sees not the majesty of the LORD.
11 O LORD, your hand is uplifted,
but they behold it not;
Let them be shamed when they see your zeal for your people:
let the fire prepared for your enemies consume them.
12* O LORD, you mete out peace to us,
for it is you who have accomplished all we have done.

ISAIAH

*

25, 1: Ex 15, 2.
2: Jer 9, 11.
4: 14, 32; 2; Na 1, 7.
7: 60, 1.3; 1 Cor 15, 53ff; Rv 7, 17; 21, 4.
9: 30, 18f.
10: Zep 2, 9f.
11: 16, 6f. 14.
12: 26, 5.
26, 2: Ps 118, 19f.
3: 32, 17f; 54, 13.
4: 30, 29; Ps 62, 8.
5: 25, 12; 32, 19.
7: Ps 23, 3f; Prv 11, 3.5.
9: Ps 94, 15.
10: 5, 12.
12: Jer 29, 11.

†

25, 1-8: Victory in messianic times.
25, 6: *This mountain:* Zion, symbol of the heavenly Jerusalem.
25, 10: *Moab:* symbol of God's enemies.

13 O LORD, our God, other lords than
you have ruled us;
it is from you only that we can call
upon your name.

14 Dead they are, they have no life,
shades that cannot rise;
For you have punished and destroyed them,
and wiped out all memory of
them.
15* You have increased the nation, O
LORD,
increased the nation to your own
glory,
and extended far all the borders
of the land.
16* O LORD, oppressed by your punishment,
we cried out in anguish under
your chastising.
17* As a woman about to give birth
writhes and cries out in her pains,
so were we in your presence, O
LORD.
18 We conceived and writhed in pain,
giving birth to wind;
Salvation we have not achieved for
the earth,
the inhabitants of the world cannot bring it forth.
19*†But your dead shall live, their
corpses shall rise;
awake and sing, you who lie in the
dust.
For your dew is a dew of light,
and the land of shades gives birth.

ISAIAH

Day of the Lord: Reward and Punishment

20 Go, my people, enter your chambers,
and close your doors behind you;
Hide yourselves for a brief moment,
until the wrath is past.
21* See, the LORD goes forth from his
place,
to punish the wickedness of the
earth's inhabitants;
The earth will reveal the blood upon
her,
and no longer conceal her slain.

CHAPTER 27

1*† On that day,
The LORD will punish with his sword
that is cruel, great, and strong,
Leviathan the fleeing serpent,
Leviathan the coiled serpent;
and he will slay the dragon that
is in the sea.

2* On that day—
The pleasant vineyard, sing about it!
3* I, the LORD, am its keeper,
I water it every moment;
Lest anyone harm it,
night and day I guard it.
4* I am not angry,
but if I were to find briers and
thorns,
In battle I should march against
them;
I should burn them all.
8* Expunging and expelling, I should
strive against them,
carrying them off with my cruel
wind in time of storm.

6 In days to come Jacob shall take
root,
Israel shall sprout and blossom,
covering all the world with fruit.
7† Is he to be smitten as his smiter was
smitten?
or slain as his slayer was slain?
5*†Or shall he cling to me for refuge?
He must make peace with me;
peace shall he make with me!
9 This, then, shall be the expiation of
Jacob's guilt,
this the whole fruit of the removal
of his sin:
He shall pulverize all the stones of
the altars
like pieces of chalk;
no sacred poles or incense altars
shall stand.

10*†For the fortified city shall be desolate,
an abandoned pasture, a forsaken
wilderness,
where calves shall browse and lie.
Its boughs shall be destroyed,
11* its branches shall wither and be
broken off,
and women shall come to build a
fire with them.
This is not an understanding people;
therefore their maker shall not
spare them,
nor shall he who formed them
have mercy on them.

*

15: 54, 2f; Neh 9, 23.
16: Hos 6, 1.
17: Mi 4, 10.
19: Ez 37, 5f; Dn 12, 2; Hos 6, 2.
21: Mi 1, 3.
27, 1: Jb 40, 25-32; Ez 32, 2.
2: 5, 1.
3: 5, 2ff; Ps 121, 4f.
4: 10, 17.
8: Jer 18, 17.
5: 37, 31; Rom 11, 12.
10: 6, 11.
11: Jer 4, 22.

†

26, 19: This verse refers to the restoration of Israel in messianic times under the figure of the resurrection of the dead; cf Ez 37.

27, 1: *Leviathan . . . dragon:* symbols of the forces of evil which God vanquishes even as he overcame primeval chaos; cf notes on Jb 3, 8; 7, 12.

27, 5.9: Israel will *make peace with* God and destroy all signs of idolatrous worship.

27, 7 God's people will not be treated as sternly as were their enemies.

27, 10f: *The fortified city:* symbol of the powers of evil; see note on 24, 10.

12† On that day,
The LORD shall beat out the grain between the Euphrates and the Wadi of Egypt,
and you shall be gleaned one by one, O sons of Israel.

13*† On that day,
A great trumpet shall blow,
and the lost in the land of Assyria and the outcasts in the land of Egypt
Shall come and worship the LORD on the holy mountain, in Jerusalem.

V: THE LORD ALONE, ISRAEL'S AND JUDAH'S SALVATION

CHAPTER 28

The Fate of Samaria

1*† Woe to the majestic garland of the drunkard Ephraim,
To the fading blooms of his glorious beauty,
on the head of him who is stupefied with wine.
2*† Behold, the LORD has a strong one and a mighty,
who, like a downpour of hail, a destructive storm,
Like a flood of water, great and overflowing,
levels to the ground with violence;
3 With feet that will trample
the majestic garland of the drunkard Ephraim.
4 The fading blooms of his glorious beauty
on the head of the fertile valley
Will be like an early fig before summer:
when a man sees it,
he picks and swallows it at once.

5 On that day the LORD of hosts
will be a glorious crown
And a brilliant diadem
to the remnant of his people,
6 A spirit of justice
to him who sits in judgment,
And strength to those
who turn back the battle at the gate.

Against Judah

7* But these also stagger from wine
and stumble from strong drink:
Priest and prophet stagger from strong drink,
overpowered by wine;
Led astray by strong drink,
staggering in their visions,
tottering when giving judgment.
8 Yes, all the tables
are covered with filthy vomit,
with no place left clean.

9† "To whom would he impart knowledge?
To whom would he convey the message?
To those just weaned from milk,
those taken from the breast?
10 For he says,
'Command on command, command on command,
rule on rule, rule on rule,
here a little, there a little!' "
11*† Yes, with stammering lips and in a strange language
he will speak to this people
12 to whom he said:
This is the resting place,
give rest to the weary;
Here is repose—
but they would not listen.
13 So for them the word of the LORD shall be:
"Command on command, command on command,
Rule on rule, rule on rule,
here a little, there a little!"
So that when they walk, they stumble backward,
broken, ensnared, and captured.

14 Therefore, hear the word of the LORD, you arrogant,
who rule this people in Jerusalem:
15*† Because you say, "We have made a covenant with death,
and with the nether world we have made a pact;
When the overwhelming scourge passes,
it will not reach us;
For we have made lies our refuge,

*

13: Hos 11, 11.
28, 1: Hos 7, 5; Am 6, 6.
2: 30, 30.
7: 56, 10.12.
11: Jer 5, 15; 1 Cor 14, 21; Dt 28, 49; Bar 4, 15.
15: Wis 1, 16; Jer 5, 12.

†

27, 12: *The Euphrates and the Wadi of Egypt:* the ideal borders of Israel; cf Gn 15, 18; 2 Kgs 24, 7.

27, 13: The triumph of God's people is described in eschatological language; they will gather in Jerusalem from *Assyria* and *Egypt.*

28, 1: *Ephraim:* the northern kingdom. Its capital, Samaria, was built upon a hill, suggestive of a *majestic garland* adorning the head of the drunken kingdom.

28, 2: *A strong one and a mighty:* Assyria.

28, 9f: The words of those who ridicule Isaiah. The Hebrew of v 10, by its very sound, conveys the idea of mocking imitation of what the prophet says, as though he spoke like a stammering child: *SAU LASAU, SAU LASAU, CAU LACAU, CAU LACAU, ZE'ER SHAM, ZE'ER SHAM.* But in v 13 God repeats these words in deadly earnest, putting them in the mouth of the victorious pagan army.

28, 11: God will answer the mockers and defend Isaiah. *Strange language:* spoken by the invading army.

28, 15.18: *A covenant with death, and with the nether world:* an alliance with foreign powers, such as Egypt and Babylon, to prevent death and destruction. *Have made lies . . . a hiding place:* this confidence in human aid proves to be false and deceitful, incapable of averting the dreaded disaster. *Overwhelming scourge:* the flood of the Assyrian invasion; cf 8, 7f.

and in falsehood we have found
a hiding place,"—
16*† Therefore, thus says the Lord GOD:
See, I am laying a stone in Zion,
a stone that has been tested,
A precious cornerstone as a sure
foundation;
he who puts his faith in it shall
not be shaken.
17 I will make of right a measuring
line,
of justice a level.—
Hail shall sweep away the refuge of
lies,
and waters shall flood the hiding
place.
18 Your covenant with death shall be
canceled
and your pact with the nether
world shall not stand.
When the overwhelming scourge
passes,
you shall be trampled down by it.
19 Whenever it passes, it shall take you;
morning after morning it shall
pass,
By day and by night;
terror alone shall convey the mes-
sage.
20 For the bed shall be too short to
stretch out in,
and the cover too narrow to wrap
in.
21*† For the LORD shall rise up as on
Mount Perazim,
bestir himself as in the Valley of
Gibeon,
To carry out his work, his singular
work,
to perform his deed, his strange
deed.
22* Now, be arrogant no more
lest your bonds be tightened,
For I have heard from the Lord, the
GOD of hosts,
the destruction decreed for the
whole earth.
23† Give ear and hear my voice,
pay attention and listen to what
I say:
24 Is the plowman forever plowing,
always loosening and harrowing
his land for planting?
25† When he has leveled the surface,
does he not scatter gith and sow
cumin,
Put in wheat and barley,
with spelt as its border?
26 He has learned this rule,
instructed by his God.
27 Gith is not threshed with a sledge,
nor does a cartwheel roll over
cumin.
But gith is beaten out with a staff,
and cumin crushed for food with
a rod.
28 No, he does not thresh it unendingly,
nor does he crush it
with his noisy cartwheels and
horses.
29 This too comes from the LORD of
hosts;
wonderful is his counsel and great
his wisdom.

CHAPTER 29

The Fall of Jerusalem

1*† Woe to Ariel, Ariel,
the city where David encamped!
Add year to year,
let the feasts come round.
2* But I will bring distress upon Ariel,
with mourning and grief.
You shall be to me like Ariel,
3* I will encamp like David against
you;
I will encircle you with outposts
and set up siege works against
you.
4† Prostrate you shall speak from the
earth,
and from the base dust your
words shall come.
Your voice shall be like a ghost's
from the earth,
and your words like chirping from
the dust.
5* The horde of your arrogant shall be
like fine dust,
the horde of the tyrants like flying
chaff.
Then suddenly, in an instant,
6 you shall be visited by the LORD
of hosts,
With thunder, earthquake, and
great noise,
whirlwind, storm, and the flame
of consuming fire.

*

16: Ps 118, 22; Mt 21, 42; Acts 4, 11; Rom 9, 33; 1 Pt 2, 6.
21: Jos 10, 10; 2 Sm 5, 20; 1 Chr 14, 11.
22: 10, 23.
29, 1: 2 Sm 5, 9.
2: 33, 7.
3: 2 Kgs 25, 1; Ez 4, 2.
5: 17, 13; Ps 18, 43; Jb 21, 18.

†

28, 16: *A stone in Zion:* the true and *sure foundation* of salvation promised by God to the Davidic dynasty (cf 7, 13-16; 9, 1-6), which the Apostles saw fulfilled in Christ the universal Savior; cf 1 Pt 2, 6-8; Rom 9, 33; 10, 9ff. *Cornerstone:* the assurance of salvation rejected by Israel in the prophet's time, is reflected by the psalmist (Ps 118, 22) and fulfilled in the Person of Christ; cf Mt 21, 42; Lk 20, 17; Acts 4, 11; Rom 9, 33; 1 Pt 2, 7.

28, 21: *Mount Perazim . . . Valley of Gibeon:* where David defeated the Philistines; cf 2 Sm 5, 20. 25; 1 Chr 14, 11.16.

28, 23-29: The practical variation of the farmer's work taught him by God reflects God's dealing with his people, wisely adapted to circumstances; he does not crush their weakness altogether; cf ch 29.

28, 25: *Gith . . . cumin:* herbs used in seasoning food. *Spelt:* a variety of wheat.

29, 1f: *Ariel:* variously interpreted to mean "lion of God" or "hearth (altar) of God," a poetic name for Jerusalem; or perhaps to be read as Uru-el, "foundation of God," an archaic name for the Jebusite city of Jerusalem; *like* that *Ariel,* against which *David encamped,* it will be besieged by God.

29, 4: *Chirping:* see note on 8, 19.

7† Then like a dream,
a vision in the night,
Shall be the horde of all the nations
who war against Ariel
with all the earthworks of her besiegers.
8 As when a hungry man dreams he is eating
and awakens with an empty stomach,
Or when a thirsty man dreams he is drinking
and awakens faint and dry,
So shall the horde of all the nations be,
who make war against Zion.

Blindness and Perversity

9*† Be irresolute, stupefied;
blind yourselves and stay blind!
Be drunk, but not from wine,
stagger, but not from strong drink!
10* For the LORD has poured out on you
a spirit of deep sleep.
He has shut your eyes [the prophets]
and covered your heads [the seers].

11* For you the revelation of all this has become like the words of a sealed scroll. When it is handed to one who can read, with the request, "Read this," he replies, "I cannot; it is sealed." 12 When it is handed to one who cannot read, with the request, "Read this," he replies, "I cannot read."

13* The Lord said:
Since this people draws near with words only
and honors me with their lips alone,
though their hearts are far from me,
And their reverence for me has become
routine observance of the precepts of men,
14* Therefore I will again deal with this people
in surprising and wondrous fashion:
The wisdom of its wise men shall perish
and the understanding of its prudent men be hid.
15* Woe to those who would hide their plans
too deep for the LORD!
Who work in the dark, saying,
"Who sees us, or who knows us?"
16* Your perversity is as though the potter
were taken to be the clay:
As though what is made should say
of its maker,
"He made me not!"
Or the vessel should say of the potter,
"He does not understand."

Redemption

17*† But a very little while,
and Lebanon shall be changed
into an orchard,
and the orchard be regarded as
a forest!
18* On that day the deaf shall hear
the words of a book;
And out of gloom and darkness,
the eyes of the blind shall see.
19* The lowly will ever find joy in the LORD,
and the poor rejoice in the Holy One of Israel.
20* For the tyrant will be no more
and the arrogant will have gone;
All who are alert to do evil will be cut off,
21* those whose mere word condemns a man,
Who ensnare his defender at the gate,
and leave the just man with an empty claim.
22*† Therefore thus says the LORD,
the God of the house of Jacob,
who redeemed Abraham:
Now Jacob shall have nothing to be ashamed of,
nor shall his face grow pale.
23 When his children see
the work of my hands in his midst,
They shall keep my name holy;
they shall reverence the Holy One of Jacob,
and be in awe of the God of Israel.
24 Those who err in spirit shall acquire understanding,
and those who find fault shall receive instruction.

ISAIAH

*

9: 19, 14; 28, 7f.
10: 6, 10; Rom 11, 8.
11: Dn 12, 4.
13: Ez 33, 31; Mt 15, 8f; Mk 7, 6f.
14: Jer 49, 7; 1 Cor 1, 19.
15: 30, 1; Ez 8, 12; Jn 3, 19f.
16: 45, 9; Jer 18, 6; Rom 9, 20.
17: 32, 15.
18: 35, 5; 42, 6f.
19: 61, 1.
20: 28, 22.
21: Am 5, 10.12.
22: 45, 17.

†

29, 7f: Just when the Assyrians think their capture of Jerusalem to be certain, the Lord will snatch victory from their hands and save his city.

29, 9-12: Jerusalem in her blindness refuses to believe God's revelation that she will be saved.

29, 17-24: The prophet presents God's plan of redemption in terms of unheard-of natural phenomena as if such changes in nature took place, e.g., the change of the cedars of Lebanon into an orchard (v 17).

29, 22: *Who redeemed Abraham:* by freeing him from the idolatry of his native land.

CHAPTER 30

Futile Alliance with Egypt

1* Woe to the rebellious children,
says the LORD,
Who carry out plans that are not mine,
who weave webs that are not inspired by me,
adding sin upon sin.
2* They go down to Egypt,
but my counsel they do not seek.
They find their strength in Pharaoh's protection
and take refuge in Egypt's shadow;
3* Pharaoh's protection shall be your shame,
and refuge in Egypt's shadow your disgrace.
4* When their princes are at Zoan
and their messengers reach Hanes,
5* All shall be ashamed
of a people that gain them nothing,
Neither help nor benefit,
but only shame and reproach.

6† [Oracle on the Beasts of the Negeb]

Through the distressed and troubled land
of the lioness and roaring lion,
of the viper and flying saraph,
They carry their riches on the backs of asses
and their treasures on the humps of camels
To a people good for nothing,
7† to Egypt whose help is futile and vain.
Therefore I call her
"Rahab quelled."

8*† Now come, write it on a tablet they can keep,
inscribe it in a record;
That it may be in future days
an eternal witness:
9* This is a rebellious people,
deceitful children,
Children who refuse
to obey the law of the LORD.
10* They say to the seers, "Have no visions";
to the prophets, "Do not descry for us what is right;
speak flatteries to us, conjure up illusions.
11* Out of the way! Out of our path!
Let us hear no more
of the Holy One of Israel."

12 Therefore, thus says the Holy One of Israel:
Because you reject this word,
And put your trust in what is crooked and devious,
and depend on it,
13* This guilt of yours shall be
like a descending rift
Bulging out in a high wall
whose crash comes suddenly, in an instant.
14* It crashes like a potter's jar
smashed beyond rescue,
And among its fragments cannot be found
a sherd to scoop fire from the hearth
or dip water from the cistern.
15* For thus said the Lord GOD,
the Holy One of Israel:
By waiting and by calm you shall be saved,
in quiet and in trust your strength lies.
But this you did not wish.
16* "No," you said,
"Upon horses we will flee."
—Very well, flee!
"Upon swift steeds we will ride."
—Not so swift as your pursuers.
17 A thousand shall tremble at the threat of one;
if five threaten you, you shall flee,
Until you are left like a flagstaff on the mountaintop,
like a flag on the hill.
18* Yet the LORD is waiting to show you favor,
and he rises to pity you;
For the LORD is a God of justice:
blessed are all who wait for him!

19* O people of Zion, who dwell in Jerusalem,
no more will you weep;
He will be gracious to you when you cry out,
as soon as he hears he will answer you.
20† The Lord will give you the bread you need
and the water for which you thirst.

*

30, 1: 1, 4.
2: 31, 1; 36, 6.
3: 20, 5; Jer 2, 36f.
4: 19, 11.
5: 36, 6.
8: 8, 1.16; Jer 36, 2; Heb 2, 2.
9: 1, 4; Jer 7, 28.
10: Jer 5, 31.
11: Jb 21, 14f.
13: Ez 13, 14.
14: Jer 19, 11.
15: 7, 4; Mi 7, 7.
16: 31, 3.
18: Ps 34, 9; Jer 17, 7.
19: 58, 9.

†

30, 6: *Flying saraph:* see note on Nm 21, 6.

30, 7: *Rahab:* Egypt, here as elsewhere (cf Ps 87, 4), is compared to the stormy, impetuous sea monster (cf 51, 9; Jb 26, 12; Ps 89, 11), which yet, when asked for aid by Judah, becomes silent, *quelled.*

30, 8: Isaiah will write down his condemnation of the people so that (vv 12-18) its fulfillment may afterward be admitted.

30, 20: *Teacher:* God, who in the past taught in a veiled manner through his prophets, will in future help them to understand his teaching clearly. This was eminently true when the Son of God became Man.

No longer will your Teacher hide
himself,
but with your own eyes you shall
see your Teacher,
21* While from behind, a voice shall
sound in your ears:
"This is the way; walk in it,"
when you would turn to the right
or to the left.
22* And you shall consider unclean your
silver-plated idols
and your gold-covered images;
You shall throw them away like
filthy rags
to which you say, "Begone!"

Zion's Future Prosperity

23* He will give rain for the seed
that you sow in the ground,
And the wheat that the soil produces
will be rich and abundant.
On that day your cattle will graze
in spacious meadows;
24 The oxen and the asses that till the
ground
will eat silage tossed to them
with shovel and pitchfork.
25* Upon every high mountain and lofty
hill
there will be streams of running
water.
On the day of the great slaughter,
when the towers fall,
26* The light of the moon will be like that
of the sun
and the light of the sun will be
seven times greater
[like the light of seven days].
On the day the LORD binds up the
wounds of his people,
he will heal the bruises left by his
blows.

Divine Judgment on Assyria

27† See the name of the LORD coming
from afar
in burning wrath, with lowering
clouds!
His lips are filled with fury,
his tongue is like a consuming fire;
28 His breath, like a flood in a ravine
that reaches suddenly to the neck,
Will winnow the nations with a de-
structive winnowing,
and with repeated winnowings
will he battle against them
[and a bridle on the jaws of the
peoples to send them astray].
30 The LORD will make his glorious
voice heard,
and let it be seen how his arm de-
scends
In raging fury and flame of consum-
ing fire,
in driving storm and hail.
31 When the LORD speaks, Assyria will
be shattered,
as he strikes with the rod;
32 While at every sweep of the rod
which the LORD will bring down
on him in punishment,
29† You will sing
as on a night when a feast is ob-
served,
And be merry of heart,
as one marching along with a flute
Toward the mountain of the LORD,
toward the Rock of Israel,
accompanied by the timbrels and
lyres.
33 For the pyre has long been ready,
prepared for the king;
Broad and deep it is piled
with dry grass and wood in abun-
dance,
And the breath of the LORD, like a
stream of sulphur,
will set it afire.

CHAPTER 31

Against the Egyptian Alliance

1* Woe to those who go down to Egypt
for help,
who depend upon horses;
Who put their trust in chariots be-
cause of their number,
and in horsemen because of their
combined power,
But look not to the Holy One of Israel
nor seek the LORD!
2 Yet he too is wise and will bring dis-
aster;
he will not turn from what he has
threatened to do.
He will rise up against the house of
the wicked
and against those who help evil-
doers.
3* The Egyptians are men, not God,
their horses are flesh, not spirit;
When the LORD stretches forth his
hand,
the helper shall stumble, the one
helped shall fall,
and both of them shall perish to-
gether.

4 Thus says the LORD to me:
As a lion or a lion cub
growling over its prey,
With a band of shepherds
assembled against it,

ISAIAH

*

21: Jer 31, 33f.
22: 31, 7.
23: Lv 26, 3.5.
25: Jl 4, 18.
26: Jer 30, 17.
31, 1: 30, 2; 36, 6.
3: Ps 146, 3ff.

†

30, 27-33: God's punishment of Assyria. *The name of the LORD:* God himself; cf Ps 20, 2.

30, 29-33: *Pyre:* on which the corpse of the king of Assyria is burned. This is the occasion of festal rejoicing for the Israelites, who are now free from his yoke.

Is neither frightened by their shouts
nor disturbed by their noise,
So shall the LORD of hosts come down
to wage war upon the mountain and hill of Zion.
5* Like hovering birds, so the LORD of hosts
shall shield Jerusalem,
To protect and deliver,
to spare and rescue it.

6* Return, O children of Israel, to him
whom you have utterly deserted. 7* On
that day each one of you shall spurn his
sinful idols of silver and gold, which he
made with his hands.

Downfall of Assyria

8* Assyria shall fall by a sword not wielded by man,
no mortal sword shall devour him;
He shall flee before the sword,
and his young men shall be impressed as laborers.
9† He shall rush past his crag in panic,
and his princes shall flee in terror from his standard,
Says the LORD who has a fire in Zion
and a furnace in Jerusalem.

CHAPTER 32

The Kingdom of Justice

1* See, a king will reign justly
and princes will rule rightly.
2* Each of them will be a shelter from the wind,
a retreat from the rain.
They will be like streams of water in a dry country,
like the shade of a great rock in a parched land.
3 The eyes of those who see will not be closed;
the ears of those who hear will be attentive.
4 The flighty will become wise and capable,
and the stutterers will speak fluently and clearly.
5 No more will the fool be called noble,
nor the trickster be considered honorable.
6* For the fool speaks foolishly,
planning evil in his heart:
How to do wickedness,
to speak perversely against the LORD,
To let the hungry go empty
and the thirsty be without drink.
7 And the trickster uses wicked trickery, planning crimes:
How to ruin the poor with lies,
and the needy when they plead their case.
8 But the noble man plans noble things,
and by noble things he stands.

The Women of Jerusalem

9 O complacent ladies, rise up and hear my voice,
overconfident women, give heed to my words.
10* In a little more than a year
you overconfident ones will be shaken;
The vintage will fail,
there will be no harvest.
11* Tremble, you who are complacent!
Shudder, you who are overconfident!
Strip yourselves bare,
with only a loincloth to cover you.
12 Beat your breasts
for the pleasant fields, the fruitful vine,
13* And the soil of my people,
overgrown with thorns and briers;
For all the joyful houses,
the wanton city.
14*† Yes, the castle will be forsaken,
the noisy city deserted;
19 Down it comes, as trees come down in the forest!
The city will be utterly laid low.
Hill and tower will become wasteland forever
for wild asses to frolic in, and flocks to pasture,
15*† Until the spirit from on high
is poured out on us.

Then will the desert become an orchard
and the orchard be regarded as a forest.
16 Right will dwell in the desert
and justice abide in the orchard.
17* Justice will bring about peace;
right will produce calm and security.
18* My people will live in peaceful country,
in secure dwellings and quiet resting places.

*

5: Ps 91, 4.
6: Jer 3, 12.
7: 30, 22.
8: 37, 36.
32, 1: 16, 5; Ps 72, 2ff; Jer 23, 5.
2: 4, 6; 25, 4.
6: Prv 10, 32; Eccl 10, 12f.
10: Zep 1, 13.
11: Jer 4, 8.
13: 7, 23; 34, 13.
14: 27, 10.
15: 35, 1; 44, 3.
17: 54, 13f; Ps 72, 7; Jas 3, 18.
18: Mi 4, 4.

†

31, 9: *Crag:* the king as the rallying point of the princes.

32, 14.19: *The castle:* the citadel of Jerusalem. *Hill and tower:* the fortified hill, in Hebrew *Ophel,* with its stronghold called "the great projecting tower" in Neh 3, 27.

32, 15-18.20: Extraordinary peace and prosperity will come to Israel under just rulers.

20* Happy are you who sow beside every stream,
and let the ox and the ass go freely!

CHAPTER 33

Overthrow of Assyria

1 Woe, O destroyer never destroyed,
O traitor never betrayed!
When you finish destroying, you will be destroyed;
when wearied with betraying, you will be betrayed.
2* O LORD, have pity on us, for you we wait.
Be our strength every morning,
our salvation in time of trouble!
3 At the roaring sound, peoples flee;
when you rise in your majesty, nations are scattered.
4* Men gather spoil as caterpillars are gathered up;
they rush upon it like the onrush of locusts.
5* The LORD is exalted, enthroned on high;
he fills Zion with right and justice.
6* That which makes her seasons lasting,
the riches that save her, are wisdom and knowledge;
the fear of the LORD is her treasure.

7† See, the men of Ariel cry out in the streets,
the messengers of Shalem weep bitterly.
8* The highways are desolate,
travelers have quit the paths,
Covenants are broken, their terms are spurned;
yet no man gives it a thought.
9*† The country languishes in mourning,
Lebanon withers with shame;
Sharon is like the steppe,
Bashan and Carmel are stripped bare.

10 Now will I rise up, says the LORD,
now will I be exalted, now be lifted up.
11 You conceive dry grass, bring forth stubble;
my spirit shall consume you like fire.
12* The peoples shall be as in a limekiln,
like brushwood cut down for burning in the fire.
13 Hear, you who are far off, what I have done;
you who are near, acknowledge my might.
14* On Zion sinners are in dread,
trembling grips the impious:
"Who of us can live with the consuming fire?
who of us can live with the everlasting flames?"
15* He who practices virtue and speaks honestly,
who spurns what is gained by oppression,
Brushing his hands free of contact with a bribe,
stopping his ears lest he hear of bloodshed,
closing his eyes lest he look on evil—
16 He shall dwell on the heights,
his stronghold shall be the rocky fastness,
his food and drink in steady supply.

Restoration of Zion

17† Your eyes will see a king in his splendor,
they will look upon a vast land.
18 Your mind will dwell on the terror:
"Where is he who counted, where is he who weighed?
Where is he who counted the towers?"
19 To the people of alien tongue you will look no more,
the people of obscure speech,
stammering in a language not understood.
20 Look to Zion, the city of our festivals;
let your eyes see Jerusalem
as a quiet abode, a tent not to be struck,
Whose pegs will never be pulled up,
nor any of its ropes severed.
22 Indeed the LORD will be there with us, majestic;
yes, the LORD our judge, the LORD our lawgiver,
the LORD our king, he it is who will save us.
21† In a place of rivers and wide streams
on which no boat is rowed,
where no majestic ship passes,
23 The rigging hangs slack;
it cannot hold the mast in place,
nor keep the sail spread out.

ISAIAH

*

20: 30, 23.
33, 2: 25, 9.
4: 2 Chr 20, 25.
5: 1, 26.
6: Prv 9, 10.
8: Jgs 5, 6.
9: Na 1, 4.
12: 10, 17.
14: Na 1, 6.
15: Pss 15, 2-6; 24, 4f.

†

33, 7: *Ariel . . . Shalem:* Jerusalem; cf 29, 1; Gn 14, 18.
33, 9: *Sharon:* the fertile plain near the Mediterranean.
33, 17: *King:* the messianic king, or God; cf v 22.
33, 21.23: *Boat . . . majestic ship:* of a foreign oppressor.

Then the blind will divide great spoils
and the lame will carry off the loot.
24 No one who dwells there will say, "I am sick";
the people who live there will be forgiven their guilt.

VI: THE LORD, ZION'S AVENGER

CHAPTER 34

Judgment upon Edom

1* Come near, O nations, and hear;
be attentive, O peoples!
Let the earth and what fills it listen,
the world and all it produces.
2 The LORD is angry with all the nations
and is wrathful against all their host;
he has doomed them and given them over to slaughter.
3* Their slain shall be cast out,
their corpses shall send up a stench;
The mountains shall run with their blood,
4* and all the hills shall rot;
The heavens shall be rolled up like a scroll,
and all their host shall wither away,
As the leaf wilts on the vine,
or as the fig withers on the tree.

5* When my sword has drunk its fill in the heavens,
lo, it shall come down in judgment
upon Edom, a people I have doomed.
6* The LORD has a sword filled with blood,
greasy with fat,
With the blood of lambs and goats,
with the fat of rams' kidneys;
For the LORD has a sacrifice in Bozrah,
a great slaughter in the land of Edom.
7 Wild oxen shall be struck down with fatlings,
and bullocks with bulls;
Their land shall be soaked with blood,
and their earth greasy with fat.
8* For the LORD has a day of vengeance,
a year of requital by Zion's defender.
9 Edom's streams shall be changed into pitch
and her earth into sulphur,
and her land shall become burning pitch;
10 Night and day it shall not be quenched,
its smoke shall rise forever.
From generation to generation she shall lie waste,
never again shall anyone pass through her.
11*† But the desert owl and hoot owl shall possess her,
the screech owl and raven shall dwell in her.
The LORD will measure her with line and plummet
to be an empty waste
for satyrs to dwell in.

12* Her nobles shall be no more,
nor shall kings be proclaimed there;
all her princes are gone.
13* Her castles shall be overgrown with thorns,
her fortresses with thistles and briers.
She shall become an abode for jackals
and a haunt for ostriches.
14† Wildcats shall meet with desert beasts,
satyrs shall call to one another;
There shall the lilith repose,
and find for herself a place to rest.
15 There the hoot owl shall nest and lay eggs,
hatch them out and gather them in her shadow;

There shall the kites assemble,
none shall be missing its mate.

16*† Look in the book of the LORD and read:
No one of these shall be lacking,
For the mouth of the LORD has ordered it,
and his spirit shall gather them there.
17 It is he who casts the lot for them,
and with his hands he marks off their shares of her;
They shall possess her forever,
and dwell there from generation to generation.

ISAIAH

*

34, 1: Dt 32, 1.
3: Ez 32, 4.6.
4: 13, 10; Ez 32, 7f; 4, 15.
5: Jer 46, 10.
6f: Jer 49, 12f.
8: 13, 9; 63, 4.
11: 14, 23; Zep 2, 14.
12: Ob 18.
13: 13, 21; Hos 9, 6.
16: Jos 18, 10; Ps 78, 55.

†

34, 11: *Satyrs:* see note on 13, 21; cf 34, 14.

34, 14: *Lilith:* a female demon thought to roam about the desert.

34, 16: *Book of the LORD:* God's list of all his creatures; cf Ps 69, 29, "the book of the living"; Ps 139, 16, "your book."

CHAPTER 35

Israel's Deliverance

1*† The desert and the parched land will exult;
the steppe will rejoice and bloom.
2* They will bloom with abundant flowers,
and rejoice with joyful song.
The glory of Lebanon will be given to them,
the splendor of Carmel and Sharon;
They will see the glory of the LORD,
the splendor of our God.
3* Strengthen the hands that are feeble,
make firm the knees that are weak,
4* Say to those whose hearts are frightened:
Be strong, fear not!
Here is your God,
he comes with vindication;
With divine recompense
he comes to save you.
5* Then will the eyes of the blind be opened,
the ears of the deaf be cleared;
6* Then will the lame leap like a stag,
then the tongue of the dumb will sing.

Streams will burst forth in the desert,
and rivers in the steppe.
7 The burning sands will become pools,
and the thirsty ground, springs of water;
The abode where jackals lurk
will be a marsh for the reed and papyrus.
8 A highway will be there,
called the holy way;
No one unclean may pass over it,
nor fools go astray on it.
9* No lion will be there,
nor beast of prey go up to be met upon it.
It is for those with a journey to make,
and on it the redeemed will walk.
10* Those whom the LORD has ransomed will return
and enter Zion singing,
crowned with everlasting joy;
They will meet with joy and gladness,
sorrow and mourning will flee.

VII: HISTORICAL APPENDIX

CHAPTER 36

Invasion of Sennacherib. 1*† In the
fourteenth year of King Hezekiah, Sen-
nacherib, king of Assyria, went on an
expedition against all the fortified cities
of Judah and captured them. 2 From
Lachish the king of Assyria sent his
commander with a great army to King
Hezekiah in Jerusalem. When he
stopped at the conduit of the upper pool,
on the highway of the fuller's field,
3 there came out to him the master of
the palace, Eliakim, son of Hilkiah, and
Shebna the scribe, and the herald Joah,
son of Asaph. 4 The commander said to
them, "Tell King Hezekiah: Thus says
the great king, the king of Assyria, 'On
what do you base this confidence of
yours? 5 Do you think mere words sub-
stitute for strategy and might in war?
On whom, then, do you rely, that you
rebel against me? 6* This Egypt, the staff
on which you rely, is in fact a broken
reed which pierces the hand of anyone
who leans on it. That is what Pharaoh,
king of Egypt, is to all who rely on him.
7*† But if you say to me: "We rely on
the LORD, our God," is not he the one
whose high places and altars Hezekiah
removed, commanding Judah and Jeru-
salem to worship before this altar?'

8 "Now, make a wager with my lord
the king of Assyria: 'I will give you two
thousand horses, if you can put riders
on them.' 9 How then can you repulse
even one of the least servants of my
lord? And yet you rely on Egypt for
chariots and horsemen! 10* 'Was it with-
out the LORD's will that I have come up
to destroy this land? The LORD said to
me, "Go up and destroy that land!"' "

11† Then Eliakim and Shebna and
Joah said to the commander, "Please
speak to your servants in Aramaic; we
understand it. Do not speak to us in Ju-
dean within earshot of the people who
are on the wall."

12 But the commander replied, "Was
it to you and your master that my lord
sent me to speak these words? Was it

*

35, 1: 55, 12f.
2: 60, 13; Ps 96, 12.
3: Jb 4, 3f; Heb 12, 12.
4: 41, 10; Zec 8, 13.
5: 29, 18; 32, 3.
6: 41, 18; 43, 10.19.
9: 62, 10; Lv 26, 6.
10: 51, 11.
36, 1: 2 Kgs 18, 13; 2 Chr 32, 1.
6: 30, 2.
7: 2 Kgs 18, 4.
10: 10, 5f.

†

35, 1-10: Similar to the description of the return from the exile, as found in chaps. 40—55.

36, 1—39, 8: Except for 38, 9-20, this historical appendix describing the siege, etc., is paralleled in 2 Kgs 18, 13—20, 19, which, however, has certain details proper to itself. The events are also recorded in substantially the same way in the cuneiform inscriptions of Sennacherib.

36, 7: The Assyrians pretend that Hezekiah's removal of the *high places and altars* (illegal sanctuaries) was taken by the Lord as an insult. They declare to Jerusalem's emissaries that the city therefore no longer has a right to the Lord's protection and that they are the ones who truly carry out his will (cf v 10).

36, 11: The Jewish emissaries ask that the conversation be carried on in *Aramaic,* not in *Judean,* for they fear the effect of the Assyrian claims upon the morale of the people.

not rather to the men sitting on the wall,
who, with you, will have to eat their own
excrement and drink their own urine?"
13 Then the commander stepped forward
and cried out in a loud voice in Judean,
"Listen to the words of the great king,
the king of Assyria. 14 Thus says the
king: 'Do not let Hezekiah deceive you,
since he cannot deliver you. 15 Let not
Hezekiah induce you to rely on the
LORD, saying, "The LORD will surely
save us; this city will not be handed over
to the king of Assyria." ' 16* Do not listen
to Hezekiah, for the king of Assyria says:
'Make peace with me and surrender!
Then each of you will eat of his own vine
and of his own fig tree, and drink the
water of his own cistern, 17 until I come
to take you to a land like your own, a
land of grain and wine, of bread and
vineyards. 18* Do not let Hezekiah se-
duce you by saying, "The LORD will save
us." Has any of the gods of the nations
ever rescued his land from the hand of
the king of Assyria? 19* Where are the
gods of Hamath and Arpad? Where are
the gods of Sepharvaim? Where are the
gods of Samaria? Have they saved Sa-
maria from my hand? 20 Which of all the
gods of these lands ever rescued his land
from my hand? Will the LORD then save
Jerusalem from my hand?' " 21 But they
remained silent and did not answer him
one word, for the king had ordered them
not to answer him.

22 Then the master of the palace, Eli-
akim, son of Hilkiah, Shebna the scribe,
and the herald Joah, son of Asaph, came
to Hezekiah with their garments torn,
and reported to him what the com-
mander had said.

CHAPTER 37

1 When King Hezekiah heard this, he
tore his garments, wrapped himself in
sackcloth, and went into the temple of
the LORD. 2 He sent Eliakim, the master
of the palace, and Shebna the scribe, and
the elders of the priests, wrapped in
sackcloth, to tell the prophet Isaiah, son
of Amoz: 3† "Thus says Hezekiah: 'This
is a day of distress, of rebuke, and of
disgrace. Children are at the point of
birth, but there is no strength to bring
them forth. 4 Perhaps the LORD, your
God, will hear the words of the com-
mander, whom his master, the king of
Assyria, sent to taunt the living God, and
will rebuke him for the words which the
LORD, your God, has heard. Send up a
prayer for the remnant that is here.' "
5 When the servants of King Hezekiah
had come to Isaiah, 6* he said to them:
"Tell this to your master: 'Thus says the
LORD: Do not be frightened by the words
you have heard, with which the servants
of the king of Assyria have blasphemed
me. 7 I am about to put in him such a
spirit that, when he hears a certain re-
port, he will return to his own land, and
there I will cause him to fall by the
sword.' "
8 When the commander returned to
Lachish and heard that the king of As-
syria had left there, he found him be-
sieging Libnah. 9† The king of Assyria
heard a report that Tirhakah, king of
Ethiopia, had come out to fight against
him. Again he sent envoys to Hezekiah
with this message: "Thus shall you say
to Hezekiah, king of Judah: 10* 'Do not
let your God on whom you rely deceive
you by saying that Jerusalem will not
be handed over to the king of Assyria.
11 You yourself have heard what the
kings of Assyria have done to all the
countries: They doomed them! Will you,
then, be saved? 12 Did the gods of the na-
tions whom my fathers destroyed save
them? Gozen, Haran, Rezeph, and the
Edenites in Telassar? 13 Where is the
king of Hamath, the king of Arpad, or
a king of the cities of Sepharvaim, Hena
or Ivvah?' "
14 Hezekiah took the letter from the
hand of the messengers and read it; then
he went up to the temple of the LORD,
and spreading it out before him, 15 he
prayed to the LORD: 16† "O LORD of hosts,
God of Israel, enthroned upon the cher-
ubim! You alone are God over all the
kingdoms of the earth. You have made
the heavens and the earth. 17 Incline
your ear, O LORD, and listen! Open your
eyes, O LORD and see! Hear all the words
of the letter that Sennacherib sent to
taunt the living God. 18 Truly, O LORD,
the kings of Assyria have laid waste all
the nations and their lands, 19* and cast
their gods into the fire; they destroyed
them because they were not gods but the
work of human hands, wood and stone.
20 Therefore, O LORD, our God, save us
from his hand, that all the kingdoms of
the earth may know that you, O LORD,
alone are God."
Punishment of Sennacherib. 21 Then
Isaiah, son of Amoz, sent this message

*

16: 1 Kgs 4, 25; Zec 3, 10.
18: 37, 11.
19: 10, 9; 37, 13.
37, 6: 41, 10-14; 51, 7.
10: 36, 14.
19: Jer 16, 20.

†

37, 3: A proverbial expression. In the Bible the pangs of childbirth often typify extreme anguish; cf 13, 8; Jer 6, 24; Mi 4, 9f. In this instance there is reference to the desperate situation of Hezekiah from which he was scarcely able to free himself.

37, 9: *Tirhakah:* may have been general of the Egyptian army in 701 B.C.; later he became king, one of the Ethiopian dynasty of Egyptian kings (c. 690-664 B.C.). Many consider that this account in Isaiah combines features of two originally distinct sieges of Jerusalem by Sennacherib.

37, 16: In contrast to the empty boasting of the Assyrians, Hezekiah proclaims the Lord as *God over all the kingdoms of the earth.*

to Hezekiah: Thus says the LORD, the
God of Israel: In answer to your prayer
for help against Sennacherib, king of
Assyria, 22* this is the word the LORD has
spoken concerning him:

She despises you, laughs you to scorn,
the virgin daughter Zion;
Behind you she wags her head,
daughter Jerusalem.
23* Whom have you insulted and blasphemed,
against whom have you raised your voice
And lifted up your eyes on high?
Against the Holy One of Israel!
24 Through your servants you have insulted the Lord:
You said, "With my many chariots
I climbed the mountain heights,
the recesses of Lebanon;
I cut down its lofty cedars,
its choice cypresses;
I reached the remotest heights,
its forest park.
25 I dug wells and drank water in foreign lands;
I dried up with the soles of my feet
all the rivers of Egypt.

26 Have you not heard?
Long ago I prepared it,
From days of old I planned it,
now I have brought it to pass:
That you should reduce fortified cities
into heaps of ruins,
27 While their inhabitants, shorn of power,
are dismayed and ashamed,
Becoming like the plants of the field,
like the green growth,
like the scorched grass on the housetops.
28 I am aware whether you stand or sit;
I know whether you come or go,
and also your rage against me.
29 Because of your rage against me
and your fury which has reached my ears,
I will put my hook in your nose
and my bit in your mouth,
and make you return the way you came.

30† This shall be a sign for you:
this year you shall eat the aftergrowth,
next year, what grows of itself;
But in the third year, sow and reap,
plant vineyards and eat their fruit!
31* The remaining survivors of the house of Judah
shall again strike root below
and bear fruit above.
32 For out of Jerusalem shall come a remnant,
and from Mount Zion, survivors.
The zeal of the LORD of hosts shall do this.

33 Therefore, thus says the LORD con-
cerning the king of Assyria: He shall not
reach this city, nor shoot an arrow at
it, nor come before it with a shield, nor
cast up siegeworks against it. 34* He
shall return by the same way he came,
without entering the city, says the LORD.
35* I will shield and save this city for my
own sake, and for the sake of my servant
David.
36*† The angel of the LORD went forth
and struck down one hundred and
eighty-five thousand in the Assyrian
camp. Early the next morning, there
they were, all the corpses of the dead.
37* So Sennacherib, the king of Assyria,
broke camp and went back home to
Nineveh.
38† When he was worshiping in the
temple of his god Nisroch, his sons
Adrammelech and Sharezer slew him
with the sword and fled into the land of
Ararat. His son Esarhaddon reigned in
his stead.

CHAPTER 38

Sickness and Recovery of Hezekiah. 1*† In those days, when Hezekiah
was mortally ill, the prophet Isaiah, son
of Amoz, came and said to him: "Thus
says the LORD: Put your house in order,
for you are about to die; you shall not
recover." 2 Then Hezekiah turned his
face to the wall and prayed to the LORD:
3* "O LORD, remember how faithfully
and wholeheartedly I conducted myself

*

22: 2 Kgs 19, 21.
23: 1, 4.
31: 27, 6.
34: 37, 29.
35: 1 Kgs 15, 4f.
36: 10, 12; 17, 14.
37: 2 Kgs 19, 35f.
38, 1: 2 Kgs 20, 1.
3: 2 Kgs 18, 5f.

†

37, 30: *You:* Hezekiah. *A sign:* it is difficult to know the nature of this sign. Either it is merely a proverbial expression to signify that prosperity follows adversity, or it indicates that after two years the normal conditions of life will be resumed.

37, 36: The destruction of Sennacherib's army is also recorded by Herodotus, a Greek historian of the fifth century B.C. It was probably due to the bubonic plague, but the sacred author attributes it to its ultimate cause, God through his angel.

37, 38: The violent death of Sennacherib (681 B.C.) is also mentioned in non-biblical sources. It occurred twenty years after his invasion of Judea.

38, 1—39, 8: The events of this section—sickness and recovery of Hezekiah, embassy of Merodach-baladan—point forward to Babylon (cc 40-66). They occurred prior to the events of 36, 1—37, 38, which point back to Assyria (1, 1—35, 10).

38, 1: *In those days:* a time prior to the siege of Jerusalem in 701 B.C.

in your presence, doing what was pleas-
ing to you!" And Hezekiah wept bitterly.
4 Then the word of the LORD came to
Isaiah: 5† "Go, tell Hezekiah: Thus says
the LORD, the God of your father David:
I have heard your prayer and seen your
tears. I will heal you: in three days you
shall go up to the LORD's temple; I will
add fifteen years to your life. 6* I will
rescue you and this city from the hand
of the king of Assyria; I will be a shield
to this city."
21 Isaiah then ordered a poultice of figs
to be taken and applied to the boil, that
he might recover. 22 Then Hezekiah
asked, "What is the sign that I shall go
up to the temple of the LORD?"
7 [Isaiah answered:] "This will be the
sign for you from the LORD that he will
do what he has promised: 8*† See, I will
make the shadow cast by the sun on the
stairway to the terrace of Ahaz go back
the ten steps it has advanced." So the
sun came back the ten steps it had ad-
vanced.

Hezekiah's Hymn of Thanksgiving.
9 The song of Hezekiah, king of Judah,
after he had been sick and had re-
covered from his illness:

10*† Once I said,
"In the noontime of life I must de-
part!
To the gates of the nether world I
shall be consigned
for the rest of my years."
11† I said, "I shall see the LORD no more
in the land of the living.
No longer shall I behold my fellow
men
among those who dwell in the
world."
12*† My dwelling, like a shepherd's tent,
is struck down and borne away
from me;
You have folded up my life, like a
weaver
who severs the last thread.
Day and night you give me over to
torment;
13 I cry out until the dawn.
Like a lion he breaks all my bones;
[day and night you give me over
to torment].
14 Like a swallow I utter shrill cries;
I moan like a dove.
My eyes grow weak, gazing heaven-
ward:
O Lord, I am in straits; be my
surety!

15† What am I to say or tell him?
He has done it!
I shall go on through all my years
despite the bitterness of my soul.
16† Those live whom the LORD protects;
yours . . . the life of my spirit.
You have given me health and life;
17† thus is my bitterness transformed
into peace.
You have preserved my life
from the pit of destruction,
When you cast behind your back
all my sins.
18*† For it is not the nether world that
gives you thanks,
nor death that praises you;
Neither do those who go down into
the pit
await your kindness.
19 The living, the living give you
thanks,
as I do today.
Fathers declare to their sons,
O God, your faithfulness.
20 The LORD is our savior;
we shall sing to stringed instru-
ments
In the house of the LORD
all the days of our life.

CHAPTER 39

Embassy from Merodach-baladan.
1*† At that time when Merodach-bala-
dan, son of Baladan, king of Babylon,
heard that Hezekiah had recovered
from his sickness, he sent letters and
gifts to him. 2* Hezekiah was pleased at
this, and therefore showed the messen-
gers his treasury, the silver and gold,

*

6: 37, 35.
8: 2 Kgs 20, 9.11.
10: Jb 17, 11; Ps 102, 25.
12: Jb 7, 6.
18: Pss 6, 6; 88, 11-13.
39, 1-8: 2 Kgs 20, 12.
2: 2 Chr 32, 25ff.

†

38, 5: Since Hezekiah died in 687 B.C., this sickness of his seems to have been in 702 B.C., that is, *fifteen years* before.

38, 8: *Stairway to the terrace of Ahaz:* this interpretation is based on a reading of the Hebrew text revised according to the Dead Sea Scroll of Isaiah; cf 2 Kgs 23, 12. Many translate the phrase as "steps of Ahaz" and understand this as referring to a sundial.

38, 10: *In the noontime of life:* long before the end of a full span of life; cf Pss 55, 24; 102, 25.

38, 11: *See the LORD:* go to the Temple and take part in its service.

38, 12: These two metaphors emphasize the suddenness and finality of death.

38, 15: *What am I to say or tell him?:* a rhetorical question, as if the poet were at a loss in giving fitting expression to his gratitude; cf Ps 116, 12. *He has done it:* accomplished the cure. *Despite the bitterness:* even though the one praying was previously so dejected.

38, 16: *Yours . . . the life of my spirit:* the current Hebrew text is corrupt. The revised Latin psalter renders it: "you have revived my soul."

38, 17: *You cast behind your back all my sins:* figurative language to express the divine forgiveness of sins, as if God no longer saw or cared about them. This expression is ordinarily used of men forgetting God; cf 1 Kgs 14, 9; Ez 23, 35; Ps 50, 17.

38, 18f: See note on Ps 6, 6.

39, 1: *Merodach-baladan:* twice king of Babylon, probably from 721 to 710 B.C., and again for nine months, in 704-703. This visit of his messengers, certainly before 701, was in reality a political one. Babylon hoped to lead an anti-Assyrian confederation composed of neighboring states.

the spices and fine oil, his whole armory,
and everything that was in his store-
rooms; there was nothing in his house
or in his whole realm that he did not
show them.
3 Then Isaiah the prophet came to
King Hezekiah and asked him, "What
did these men say to you? Where did
they come from?" Hezekiah answered,
"They came to me from a distant land,
from Babylon." 4 "What did they see in
your house?" he asked. Hezekiah re-
plied, "They saw everything in my
house; there is nothing in my storerooms
that I did not show them."
5 Then Isaiah said to Hezekiah, "Hear
the word of the LORD of hosts:
6*† Behold, the days shall come when
all that is in your house, and everything
that your fathers have stored up until
this day, shall be carried off to Babylon;
nothing shall be left, says the LORD.
7* Some of your own bodily descendants
shall be taken and made servants in
the palace of the king of Babylon."
8*† Hezekiah replied to Isaiah, "The
word of the LORD which you have spoken
is favorable." For he thought, "There
will be peace and security in my life-
time."

B: THE BOOK OF CONSOLATION

I: THE LORD'S GLORY IN ISRAEL'S LIBERATION

CHAPTER 40

Promise of Salvation

1 Comfort, give comfort to my people,
says your God.
2*† Speak tenderly to Jerusalem, and proclaim to her
that her service is at an end,
her guilt is expiated;
Indeed, she has received from the hand of the LORD
double for all her sins.

3*† A voice cries out:
In the desert prepare the way of the LORD!
Make straight in the wasteland a highway for our God!
4 Every valley shall be filled in,
every mountain and hill shall be made low;
The rugged land shall be made a plain,
the rough country, a broad valley.
5 Then the glory of the LORD shall be revealed,
and all mankind shall see it together;
for the mouth of the LORD has spoken.
6* A voice says, "Cry out!"
I answer, "What shall I cry out?"
"All mankind is grass,
and all their glory like the flower of the field.
7 The grass withers, the flower wilts,
when the breath of the LORD blows upon it.
[So then, the people is the grass.]
8 Though the grass withers and the flower wilts,
the word of our God stands forever."

9 Go up onto a high mountain,
Zion, herald of glad tidings;
Cry out at the top of your voice,
Jerusalem, herald of good news!
Fear not to cry out
and say to the cities of Judah:
Here is your God!
10 Here comes with power
the Lord GOD,
who rules by his strong arm;
Here is his reward with him,
his recompense before him.
11* Like a shepherd he feeds his flock;
in his arms he gathers the lambs,
Carrying them in his bosom,
and leading the ewes with care.

Power of the Creator To Save His People

12† Who has cupped in his hand the waters of the sea,
and marked off the heavens with a span?
Who has held in a measure the dust of the earth,
weighed the mountains in scales
and the hills in a balance?
13* Who has directed the spirit of the LORD,

*

6: 2 Kgs 24, 13; 25, 13ff.
7: 2 Chr 33, 11; Dan 1, 2f.
8: 2 Chr 32, 26.
40, 2: 50, 21.
3: Mt 3, 3; Jn 1, 23.
6: Jb 8, 12; 14, 2; Ps 37, 2; Sir 14, 18; Jas 1, 10; 1 Pt 1, 24.
11: 49, 9f; 63, 11; Ez 34, 23; 37, 24; Jn 10, 11.
13: Wis 9, 13; Rom 11, 34; 1 Cor 2, 16; Jb 38, 1ff.

†

39, 6: Because Judah preferred to follow a pro-Babylonian policy, instead of trusting in God, it would later be exiled to Babylon.

39, 8: *Favorable:* for the exile would not occur in his lifetime.

40, 2: *Service:* servitude and exile.

40, 3-5: The figurative language here describes the actual return of the exiles from Babylon to Jerusalem. It is the Lord who leads them; their road is made easy for them. Mt 3, 3 and parallels see in these verses a prophecy of the Baptizer and Christ.

40, 12: *Span:* the distance between the extended little finger and the thumb. *Measure:* literally, "third"; here a small container.

or has instructed him as his counselor?
14 Whom did he consult to gain knowledge?
Who taught him the path of judgment,
or showed him the way of understanding?

15 Behold, the nations count as a drop in the bucket,
as dust on the scales;
the coastlands weigh no more than powder.
16† Lebanon would not suffice for fuel,
nor its animals be enough for holocausts.
17 Before him all the nations are as nought,
as nothing and void he accounts them.

18* To whom can you liken God?
With what equal can you confront him?
19* An idol, cast by a craftsman,
which the smith plates with gold
and fits with silver chains?
20* Mulberry wood, the choice portion
which a skilled craftsman picks out for himself,
Choosing timber that will not rot,
to set up an idol that will not be unsteady?

41:6† One man helps another,
one says to the other, "Keep on!"
41:7† The craftsman encourages the goldsmith,
the one who beats with the hammer, him who strikes on the anvil;
He says the soldering is good,
and he fastens it with nails to steady it.

40:21 Do you not know? Have you not heard?
Was it not foretold you from the beginning?
Have you not understood? Since the earth was founded
22* He sits enthroned above the vault of the earth,
and its inhabitants are like grasshoppers;
He stretches out the heavens like a veil,
spreads them out like a tent to dwell in.
23 He brings princes to nought
and makes the rulers of the earth as nothing.
24 Scarcely are they planted or sown,
scarcely is their stem rooted in the earth,
When he breathes upon them and they wither,
and the stormwind carries them away like straw.

25 To whom can you liken me as an equal?
says the Holy One.
26*† Lift up your eyes on high
and see who has created these:
He leads out their army and numbers them,
calling them all by name.
By his great might and the strength of his power
not one of them is missing!
27† Why, O Jacob, do you say,
and declare, O Israel,
"My way is hidden from the LORD,
and my right is disregarded by my God"?
28 Do you not know
or have you not heard?
The LORD is the eternal God,
creator of the ends of the earth.
He does not faint nor grow weary,
and his knowledge is beyond scrutiny.
29 He gives strength to the fainting;
for the weak he makes vigor abound.
30 Though young men faint and grow weary,
and youths stagger and fall,
31 They that hope in the LORD will renew their strength,
they will soar as with eagles' wings;
They will run and not grow weary,
walk and not grow faint.

CHAPTER 41

The Liberator of Israel

1† Keep silence before me, O coastlands;
you peoples, wait for my words!
Let them draw near and speak;
let us come together for judgment.

2† Who has stirred up from the East
the champion of justice,

---

*

18f: Acts 17, 29.
19: Ps 115, 4-7.
20: 44, 13.
22: Ps 104, 2.
26: Ps 147, 4f.

---

†

40, 16: *Lebanon . . . fuel:* the famed cedars would not be enough to keep the fires of sacrifice burning.

41, 6-7: These two verses have been transposed to chapter 40.

40, 26: *Created:* see note on Gn 1, 1. *By name:* for he is their Creator.

40, 27f: God's people, here called *Jacob* and *Israel,* must not give way to discouragement: their *Lord is the eternal God.*

41, 1-4: It is generally agreed that these verses describe the vocation and victory of Cyrus, whom the Lord used as his instrument to redeem Israel.

41, 2: Cyrus is the *champion of justice* and God's *attendant.*

and summoned him to be his attendant?
To him he delivers the nations
and subdues the kings;
With his sword he reduces them to dust,
with his bow, to driven straw.
3 He pursues them, passing on without loss,
by a path his feet do not even tread.
4* Who has performed these deeds?
He who has called forth the generations since the beginning.
I, the LORD, am the first,
and with the last I will also be.
5 The coastlands see, and fear;
the ends of the earth tremble:
these things are near, they come to pass.
8* But you, Israel, my servant,
Jacob, whom I have chosen,
offspring of Abraham my friend—
9 You whom I have taken from the ends of the earth
and summoned from its far-off places,
You whom I have called my servant,
whom I have chosen and will not cast off—
10 Fear not, I am with you;
be not dismayed; I am your God.
I will strengthen you, and help you,
and uphold you with my right hand of justice.

11 Yes, all shall be put to shame and disgrace
who vent their anger against you;
Those shall perish and come to nought
who offer resistance.
12 You shall seek out, but shall not find,
those who strive against you;
They shall be as nothing at all
who do battle with you.

13 For I am the LORD, your God,
who grasp your right hand;
It is I who say to you, "Fear not,
I will help you."
14† Fear not, O worm Jacob,
O maggot Israel;
I will help you, says the LORD;
your redeemer is the Holy One of Israel.
15 I will make of you a threshing sledge,
sharp, new, and double-edged,
To thresh the mountains and crush them,
to make the hills like chaff.
16 When you winnow them, the wind shall carry them off
and the storm shall scatter them.
But you shall rejoice in the LORD,
and glory in the Holy One of Israel.

17 The afflicted and the needy seek water in vain,
their tongues are parched with thirst.
I, the LORD, will answer them;
I, the God of Israel, will not forsake them.
18 I will open up rivers on the bare heights,
and fountains in the broad valleys;
I will turn the desert into a marshland,
and the dry ground into springs of water.
19 I will plant in the desert the cedar,
acacia, myrtle, and olive;
I will set in the wasteland the cypress,
together with the plane tree and the pine,
20 That all may see and know,
observe and understand,
That the hand of the LORD has done this,
the Holy One of Israel has created it.

21† Present your case, says the LORD;
bring forward your reasons, says the King of Jacob.
22 Let them come near and foretell to us
what it is that shall happen!
What are the things of long ago?
Tell us, that we may reflect on them
And know their outcome;
or declare to us the things to come!
23 Foretell the things that shall come afterward,
that we may know that you are gods!
Do something, good or evil,
that will put us in awe and in fear.
24 Why, you are nothing and your work is nought!
To choose you is an abomination.

25† I have stirred up one from the north,
and he comes;
from the east I summon him by name;
He shall trample the rulers down like red earth,
as the potter treads the clay.
26 Who announced this from the beginning, that we might know;
beforehand, that we might say it is true?

ISAIAH

*

41, 4: 44, 7; 46, 10. 8f: 44, 1f.21; 45, 4.

†

41, 14: *Redeemer:* in Hebrew, *goel,* one who frees another from slavery and avenges his sufferings; cf Lv 25, 48; Dt 19, 6.12.
41, 21-24: An indictment of idols.
41, 25: *I summon him:* Cyrus.

Not one of you foretold it, not one spoke;
no one heard you say,
27 "The first news for Zion: they are coming now,"
or, "For Jerusalem I will pick out a bearer of the glad tidings."
28 When I look, there is not one,
no one of them to give counsel,
to make an answer when I question them.
29 Ah, all of them are nothing,
their works are nought,
their idols are empty wind!

CHAPTER 42

The Servant of the Lord

1*† Here is my servant whom I uphold,
my chosen one with whom I am pleased,
Upon whom I have put my spirit;
he shall bring forth justice to the nations,
2 Not crying out, not shouting,
not making his voice heard in the street.
3† A bruised reed he shall not break,
and a smoldering wick he shall not quench,
4† Until he establishes justice on the earth;
the coastlands will wait for his teaching.

5 Thus says God, the LORD,
who created the heavens and stretched them out,
who spreads out the earth with its crops,
Who gives breath to its people
and spirit to those who walk on it:
6* I, the LORD, have called you for the victory of justice,
I have grasped you by the hand;
I formed you, and set you
as a covenant of the people,
a light for the nations,
7 To open the eyes of the blind,
to bring out prisoners from confinement,
and from the dungeon, those who live in darkness.
8 I am the LORD, this is my name;
my glory I give to no other,
nor my praise to idols.
9 See, the earlier things have come to pass,
new ones I now foretell;
Before they spring into being,
I announce them to you.

The Salvation of Israel Despite Its Sins

10 Sing to the LORD a new song,
his praise from the end of the earth:
Let the sea and what fills it resound,
the coastlands, and those who dwell in them.
11† Let the steppe and its cities cry out,
the villages where Kedar dwells;
Let the inhabitants of Sela exult,
and shout from the top of the mountains.
12 Let them give glory to the LORD,
and utter his praise in the coastlands.

13* The LORD goes forth like a hero,
like a warrior he stirs up his ardor;
He shouts out his battle cry,
against his enemies he shows his might:
14 I have looked away, and kept silence,
I have said nothing, holding myself in;
But now, I cry out as a woman in labor,
gasping and panting.
15* I will lay waste mountains and hills,
all their herbage I will dry up;
I will turn the rivers into marshes,
and the marshes I will dry up.
16* I will lead the blind on their journey;
by paths unknown I will guide them.
I will turn darkness into light before them,
and make crooked ways straight.
These things I do for them,
and I will not forsake them.
17 They shall be turned back in utter shame
who trust in idols;
Who say to molten images,
"You are our gods."
18† You who are deaf, listen,
you who are blind, look and see!
19 Who is blind but my servant,
or deaf like the messenger I send?
20 You see many things without taking note;
your ears are open, but without hearing.

*

42, 1: 45, 6; 49, 6.
6: 45, 13.
13: Ex 14, 3.
15: Ex 9, 25; 10, 15; 14, 21; Ps 105, 33ff.
16: Ex 13, 21.

†

42, 1-4: *Servant:* there are three other "Servant-of-the-Lord" oracles, 49, 1-7; 50, 4-11; 52, 13—53, 12. Many identifications have been proposed, e.g., historical Israel, ideal Israel, an Old Testament historical character before or during the lifetime of the prophet, the prophet himself. The New Testament and Christian tradition, however, have seen a fulfillment of these prophecies in Jesus Christ.

42, 3: A reference to the mercy of Christ.

42, 4: *Coastlands:* the lands of the Mediterranean. In the Old Testament the word often refers to the pagan lands of the west.

42, 11: *Kedar:* cf footnote to 21, 16. *Sela:* Petra, the capital of Edom.

42, 18-20: Because of their unbelief, the Lord rebukes his people, whom he calls his *servant,* his *messenger.*

ISAIAH

21 Though it pleased the LORD in his justice
to make his law great and glorious,
22† This is a people despoiled and plundered,
all of them trapped in holes,
hidden away in prisons.
They are taken as booty, with no one to rescue them,
as spoil, with no one to demand their return.

23 Who of you gives ear to this?
Who listens and pays heed for the time to come?
24† Who was it that gave Jacob to be plundered,
Israel to the despoilers?
Was it not the LORD, against whom we have sinned?
In his ways they refused to walk,
his law they disobeyed.
25 So he poured out wrath upon them,
his anger, and the fury of battle;
It blazed round about them, yet they did not realize,
it burned them, but they took it not to heart.

CHAPTER 43

Promises of Redemption and Restoration

1 But now, thus says the LORD,
who created you, O Jacob, and formed you, O Israel:
Fear not, for I have redeemed you;
I have called you by name: you are mine.
2 When you pass through the water,
I will be with you;
in the rivers you shall not drown.
When you walk through fire, you shall not be burned;
the flames shall not consume you.
3† For I am the LORD, your God,
the Holy One of Israel, your savior.
I give Egypt as your ransom,
Ethiopia and Seba in return for you.
4* Because you are precious in my eyes
and glorious, and because I love you,
I give men in return for you
and peoples in exchange for your life.
5 Fear not, for I am with you;
from the east I will bring back your descendants,
from the west I will gather you.
6* I will say to the north: Give them up!
and to the south: Hold not back!
Bring back my sons from afar,
and my daughters from the ends of the earth:
7 Everyone who is named as mine,
whom I created for my glory,
whom I formed and made.
8 Lead out the people who are blind
though they have eyes,
who are deaf though they have ears.

9† Let all the nations gather together,
let the peoples assemble!
Who among them could have revealed this,
or foretold to us the earlier things?
Let them produce witnesses to prove themselves right,
that one may hear and say, "It is true!"
10 You are my witnesses, says the LORD,
my servants whom I have chosen
To know and believe in me
and understand that it is I.
Before me no god was formed,
and after me there shall be none.

11 It is I, I the LORD;
there is no savior but me.
12 It is I who foretold, I who saved;
I made it known, not any strange god among you;
You are my witnesses, says the LORD.
I am God, 13* yes, from eternity I am He;
There is none who can deliver from my hand:
who can countermand what I do?

14† Thus says the LORD, your redeemer,
the Holy One of Israel:
For your sakes I send to Babylon;
I will lower all the bars,
and the Chaldeans shall cry out in lamentation.
15 I am the LORD, your Holy One,
the creator of Israel, your King.
16* Thus says the LORD,
who opens a way in the sea
and a path in the mighty waters,
17* Who leads out chariots and horsemen,
a powerful army,
Till they lie prostrate together, never to rise,

I S A I A H

*

43, 4: Dt 4, 37; Hos 11, 1.
6: 49, 22; Ez 16, 20.
13: 41, 4.
16: 51, 10f; Ex 14, 21.
17: Ex 15, 4.

†

42, 22: *A people:* Israel in exile.
42, 24: *Despoilers:* the Assyrians and Babylonians.
43, 3f: *Egypt . . . Ethiopia and Seba:* countries which God permitted the Persians to conquer in return for having given Israel its freedom.
43, 9: Only God can know and predict future events; cf 41, 1-5.21-29.
43, 14-17: The destruction of Babylon.

snuffed out and quenched like a wick.
18† Remember not the events of the past,
the things of long ago consider not;
19 See, I am doing something new!
Now it springs forth, do you not perceive it?
In the desert I make a way,
in the wasteland, rivers.
20 Wild beasts honor me,
jackals and ostriches,
For I put water in the desert
and rivers in the wasteland
for my chosen people to drink,
21 The people whom I formed for myself,
that they might announce my praise.

22† Yet you did not call upon me, O Jacob,
for you grew weary of me, O Israel.
23* You did not bring me sheep for your holocausts,
nor honor me with your sacrifices.
I did not exact from you the service of offerings,
nor weary you for frankincense.
24† You did not buy me sweet cane for money,
nor fill me with the fat of your sacrifices;
Instead, you burdened me with your sins,
and wearied me with your crimes.
25 It is I, I, who wipe out,
for my own sake, your offenses;
your sins I remember no more.
26 Would you have me remember,
have us come to trial?
Speak up, prove your innocence!
27† Your first father sinned;
your spokesmen rebelled against me
28 Till I repudiated the holy gates,
put Jacob under the ban,
and exposed Israel to scorn.

ISAIAH

CHAPTER 44

1 Hear then, O Jacob, my servant,
Israel, whom I have chosen.
2† Thus says the LORD who
made you, your help, who formed you from the womb:
Fear not, O Jacob, my servant,
the darling whom I have chosen.
3 I will pour out water upon the thirsty ground,
and streams upon the dry land;
I will pour out my spirit upon your offspring,
and my blessing upon your descendants.
4* They shall spring up amid the verdure
like poplars beside the flowing waters.
5*† One shall say, "I am the LORD's,"
another shall be named after Jacob,
And this one shall write on his hand,
"The LORD's,"
and Israel shall be his surname.

The True God and False Gods

6* Thus says the LORD, Israel's King
and redeemer, the LORD of hosts:
I am the first and I am the last;
there is no God but me.
7 Who is like me? Let him stand up and speak,
make it evident, and confront me with it.
Who of old announced future events?
Let them foretell to us the things to come.
8*† Fear not, be not troubled:
did I not announce and foretell it long ago?
You are my witnesses! Is there a God
or any Rock besides me?

9*† Idol makers all amount to nothing,
and their precious works are of no avail,
as they themselves give witness. To their
shame, they neither see nor know any-
thing; and they are more deaf than men
are. 10 Indeed, all the associates of any-
one who forms a god, or casts an idol
to no purpose, will be put to shame;
11 they will all assemble and stand forth,
to be reduced to fear and shame.
12* The smith fashions an iron image,
works it over the coals, shapes it with
hammers, and forges it with his strong
arm. He is hungry and weak, drinks no
water and becomes exhausted.

*

23: Jer 6, 20.
44, 4: 54, 1ff.
5: 43, 7; 45, 14.
6: 41, 44; 43, 15; 45, 21; 48, 3.12; 51, 15; 54, 5.
8: 43, 10.12; Dt 32, 4.
9: 48, 5.7.
12: Wis 13, 11f.

†

43, 18: No need to think solely of the past wonders of the exodus from Egypt; equally great is the exodus from Babylon.

43, 22-28: The reason for the liberation of the Israelites is not their fidelity but rather God's mercy.

43, 24: *Sweet cane:* a fragrant substance used in making incense and the sacred anointing oil; cf Ex 30, 23; Jer 6, 20.

43, 27: *First father:* Adam or Jacob, or collectively "early ancestors." *Spokesmen:* leaders, priests, prophets.

44, 2: *The darling:* see note on Dt 32, 15; cf also Dt 33, 5.26.

44, 5: *Write on his hand:* an allusion to the Babylonian custom of tatooing the owner's name on the hand of his slave; cf also Rv 13, 16.

44, 8: *Rock:* place of refuge; said of God in Dt 32, 4.18; 1 Sm 2, 2; etc.

44, 9-20: Satire on the makers and worshipers of idols.

13 The carpenter stretches a line and
marks with a stylus the outline of an idol.
He shapes it with a plane and measures
it off with a compass, making it like a
man in appearance and dignity, to oc-
cupy a shrine.
14 He cuts down cedars,
takes a holm or an oak, and lays hold
of other trees of the forest, which the
Lord had planted and the rain made
grow
15 to serve man for fuel. With a part
of their wood he warms himself, or
makes a fire for baking bread; but with
another part he makes a god which he
adores, an idol which he worships.
16 Half of it he burns in the fire, and on
its embers he roasts his meat; he eats
what he has roasted until he is full, and
then warms himself and says, "Ah! I am
warm, I feel the fire."
17 Of what remains
he makes a god, his idol, and prostrate
before it in worship, he implores it,
"Rescue me, for you are my god."

18 The idols have neither knowledge
nor reason; their eyes are coated so that
they cannot see, and their hearts so that
they cannot understand.
19 Yet he does
not reflect, nor have the intelligence and
sense to say, "Half of the wood I burned
in the fire, and on its embers I baked
bread and roasted meat which I ate.
Shall I then make an abomination out
of the rest, or worship a block of wood?"
20† He is chasing ashes—a thing that
cannot save itself when the flame con-
sumes it; yet he does not say, "Is not
this thing in my right hand a fraud?"

21 Remember this, O Jacob,
you, O Israel, who are my servant!
I formed you to be a servant to me;
O Israel, by me you shall never
be forgotten:
22 I have brushed away your offenses
like a cloud,
your sins like a mist;
return to me, for I have redeemed
you.

23 Raise a glad cry, you heavens: the
LORD has done this;
shout, you depths of the earth.
Break forth, you mountains, into
song,
you forest, with all your trees.
For the LORD has redeemed Jacob,
and shows his glory through Is-
rael.

Cyrus, Anointed of the Lord, Liberator of Israel

24* Thus says the LORD, your redeemer,
who formed you from the womb:
I am the LORD, who made all things,
who alone stretched out the heav-
ens;
when I spread out the earth, who
was with me?
25 It is I who bring to nought the omens
of liars,
who make fools of diviners;
I turn wise men back
and make their knowledge foolish.
26 It is I who confirm the words of my
servants,
I carry out the plan announced by
my messengers;
I say to Jerusalem: Be inhabited;
to the cities of Judah: Be rebuilt;
I will raise up their ruins.
27* It is I who said to the deep: Be dry;
I will dry up your wellsprings.
28*† I say of Cyrus: My shepherd,
who fulfills my every wish;
He shall say of Jerusalem, "Let her
be rebuilt,"
and of the temple, "Let its founda-
tions be laid."

CHAPTER 45

1† Thus says the LORD to his anointed,
Cyrus,
whose right hand I grasp,
Subduing nations before him,
and making kings run in his ser-
vice,
Opening doors before him
and leaving the gates unbarred:
2*† I will go before you
and level the mountains;
Bronze doors I will shatter,
and iron bars I will snap.
3 I will give you treasures out of the
darkness,
and riches that have been hidden
away,
That you may know that I am the
LORD,
the God of Israel, who calls you
by your name.

4* For the sake of Jacob, my servant,
of Israel my chosen one,
I have called you by your name,
giving you a title, though you
knew me not.
5 I am the LORD and there is no other,
there is no God besides me.
It is I who arm you, though you know
me not,

*

24: 40, 22; Jb 9, 8.
27: 42, 15; 51, 10.
28: Jer 3, 15; Ez 34, 23.
45, 2: Ps 107, 16.
4: 40, 26.

†

44, 20: *Chasing ashes:* exerting efforts in vain; cf Hos 12, 2; Eccl 1, 14; 2, 11.17.

44, 28: *Cyrus:* king of Persia (559-529 B.C.) and conqueror of Babylon (538 B.C.), who liberated the Jews, permitting them to return to their native land and to rebuild Jerusalem and the Temple.

45, 1: *Anointed:* in Hebrew, *meshiah,* from which the word "Messiah" is derived; from its Greek translation *Christos,* we have the name "Christ." Applied to kings, "anointed" originally referred only to those of Israel, but it is here given to Cyrus because he is the agent of the Lord.

45, 2: *Bronze doors:* of Babylon.

6† so that toward the rising and the setting of the sun
men may know that there is none besides me.
I am the LORD, there is no other;
7† I form the light, and create the darkness,
I make well-being and create woe;
I, the LORD, do all these things.
8*† Let justice descend, O heavens, like dew from above,
like gentle rain let the skies drop it down.
Let the earth open and salvation bud forth;
let justice also spring up!
I, the LORD, have created this.
9*† Woe to him who contends with his Maker;
a potsherd among potsherds of the earth!
Dare the clay say to its modeler, "What are you doing?"
or, "What you are making has no hands"?
10 Woe to him who asks a father, "What are you begetting?"
or a woman, "What are you giving birth to?"

11 Thus says the LORD,
the Holy One of Israel, his maker:
You question me about my children,
or prescribe the work of my hands for me!
12 It was I who made the earth
and created mankind upon it;
It was my hands that stretched out the heavens;
I gave the order to all their host.
13† It was I who stirred up one for the triumph of justice;
all his ways I make level.
He shall rebuild my city
and let my exiles go free
Without price or ransom,
says the LORD of hosts.

14*† Thus says the LORD:
The earnings of Egypt, the gain of Ethiopia,
and the Sabeans, tall of stature,
Shall come over to you and belong to you;
they shall follow you, coming in chains.
Before you they shall fall prostrate, saying in prayer:
"With you only is God, and nowhere else;
the gods are nought.
15*† Truly with you God is hidden,
the God of Israel, the savior!
16 Those are put to shame and disgrace
who vent their anger against him;
Those go in disgrace
who carve images.
17 Israel, you are saved by the LORD,
saved forever!
You shall never be put to shame or disgrace
in future ages."

18† For thus says the LORD,
The creator of the heavens,
who is God,
The designer and maker of the earth
who established it,
Not creating it to be a waste,
but designing it to be lived in:
I am the LORD, and there is no other.
19 I have not spoken from hiding
nor from some dark place of the earth,
And I have not said to the descendants of Jacob,
"Look for me in an empty waste."
I, the LORD, promise justice,
I foretell what is right.

20† Come and assemble, gather together,
you fugitives from among the gentiles!
They are without knowledge who bear wooden idols
and pray to gods that cannot save.
21 Come here and declare
in counsel together:
Who announced this from the beginning
and foretold it from of old?
Was it not I, the LORD,
besides whom there is no other God?
There is no just and saving God but me.

22 Turn to me and be safe,
all you ends of the earth,
for I am God; there is no other!

---

* 8: Pss 72, 6; 85, 11. 9: Jer 18, 6; Rom 9, 20. 14: 43, 3. 15: 55, 8; Prv 25, 2.

---

† 45, 6: The Gentiles will come to know the true God; cf also vv 20-25.

45, 7: *Create woe:* God permits evil for the sake of a greater good.

45, 8: The Vulgate rendering gives a more precise messianic sense to this verse, using "just one" and "savior" in place of *justice* and *salvation.* The Advent liturgy uses the Vulgate form, *Rorate coeli desuper . . .,* to express the world's longing for the coming of Christ.

45, 9: No one may challenge God's freedom of action, exemplified here by the selection of Cyrus as his anointed.

45, 13: *One:* Cyrus, called by God for the deliverance and restoration of Israel.

45, 14: *Egypt . . . Ethiopia . . . Sabeans:* the Egyptians and their allies who, when conquered by Cyrus, are seen as acknowledging the God of Israel to be the one true God; cf 43, 3.

45, 15: *God is hidden:* he dwells invisibly in the holy of holies.

45, 18: *Waste:* an allusion to the beginning of creation, when the earth was *waste and void* (Gn 1, 2), the same Hebrew word, *tohu,* being used in both passages. The further reference here is to Palestine, which God wishes again to be inhabited by the returning exiles.

45, 20: *Who bear wooden idols:* in their religious processions. The gods of the pagans have feet but cannot walk; cf Ps 115, 7; Bar 6, 25.

23* By myself I swear,
uttering my just decree
and my unalterable word:
To me every knee shall bend;
by me every tongue shall swear,
24 Saying, "Only in the LORD
are just deeds and power.
Before him in shame shall come
all who vent their anger against him.
25 In the LORD shall be the vindication
and the glory
of all the descendants of Israel."

CHAPTER 46

The Gods of Babylon

1† Bel bows down, Nebo stoops,
their idols are upon beasts and cattle;
They must be borne up on shoulders,
carried as burdens by the weary.
2 They stoop and bow down together;
unable to save those who bear them,
they too go into captivity.

3* Hear me, O house of Jacob,
all who remain of the house of Israel,
My burden since your birth,
whom I have carried from your infancy.
4 Even to your old age I am the same,
even when your hair is gray I will bear you;
It is I who have done this, I who will continue,
and I who will carry you to safety.

5 Whom would you compare me with,
as an equal,
or match me against, as though we were alike?
6 There are those who pour out gold
from a purse
and weigh out silver on the scales;
Then they hire a goldsmith to make it into a god
before which they fall down in worship.
7 They lift it to their shoulders to carry;
when they set it in place again, it stays,
and does not move from the spot.
Although they cry out to it, it cannot answer;
it delivers no one from distress.

8 Remember this and be firm,
bear it well in mind, you rebels;
remember the former things,
those long ago:
9 I am God, there is no other;
I am God, there is none like me.
10 At the beginning I foretell the outcome;
in advance, things not yet done.
I say that my plan shall stand,
I accomplish my every purpose.
11† I call from the east a bird of prey,
from a distant land, one to carry out my plan.
Yes, I have spoken, I will accomplish it;
I have planned it, and I will do it.
12 Listen to me, you fainthearted,
you who seem far from the victory of justice:
13 I am bringing on my justice, it is not far off,
my salvation shall not tarry;
I will put salvation within Zion,
and give to Israel my glory.

CHAPTER 47

The Fall of Babylon

1† Come down, sit in the dust,
O virgin daughter Babylon;
Sit on the ground, dethroned,
O daughter of the Chaldeans.
No longer shall you be called
dainty and delicate.
2 Take the millstone and grind flour,
remove your veil;
Strip off your train, bare your legs,
pass through the streams.
3 Your nakedness shall be uncovered
and your shame be seen;
I will take vengeance,
I will yield to no entreaty,
says our redeemer,
4 Whose name is the LORD of hosts,
the Holy One of Israel.

5 Go into darkness and sit in silence,
O daughter of the Chaldeans,
No longer shall you be called
sovereign mistress of kingdoms.
6 Angry at my people,
I profaned my inheritance,
And I gave them into your hand;
but you showed them no mercy,
And upon old men
you laid a very heavy yoke.
7* You said, "I shall remain always,
a sovereign mistress forever!"
But you did not lay these things to heart,
you disregarded their outcome.

8* Now hear this, voluptuous one,
enthroned securely,

*

23: Rom 14, 11; Phil 2, 10.
46, 3: 44, 2.
47, 7: 14, 13f.
8: Zep 2, 15; Rv 18, 7.

†

46, 1: *Bel. . . Nebo:* gods of Babylon; their complete helplessness is here contrasted with God's omnipotence.
46, 11: *From the east a bird of prey:* Cyrus; cf 41, 2-4.
47, 1-15: A taunt-song, mocking Babylon, once queen of the nations, now made a slave girl.

Saying to yourself,
"I, and no one else!
I shall never be a widow,
or suffer the loss of my children"—
9† Both these things shall come to you
suddenly, in a single day:
Complete bereavement and widowhood
shall come upon you
For your many sorceries
and the great number of your spells;
10 Because you felt secure in your wickedness,
and said, "No one sees me."
Your wisdom and your knowledge
led you astray,
And you said to yourself,
"I, and no one else!"
11 But upon you shall come evil
you will not know how to predict;
Disaster shall befall you
which you cannot allay.
Suddenly there shall come upon you
ruin which you will not expect.
12 Keep up, now, your spells
and your many sorceries.
Perhaps you can make them avail,
perhaps you can strike terror!

13 You wearied yourself with many consultations,
at which you toiled from your youth;
Let the astrologers stand forth to save you,
the stargazers who forecast at each new moon
what would happen to you.
14 Lo, they are like stubble,
fire consumes them;
They cannot save themselves
from the spreading flames.
This is no warming ember,
no fire to sit before.
15 Thus do your wizards serve you
with whom you have toiled from your youth;
Each wanders his own way,
with none to save you.

ISAIAH

CHAPTER 48
Exhortations to the Exiles

1 Hear this, O house of Jacob
called by the name Israel,
sprung from the stock of Judah,
You who swear by the name of the LORD
and invoke the God of Israel
without sincerity or justice,
2 Though you are named after the holy city
and rely on the God of Israel,
whose name is the LORD of hosts.
3 Things of the past I foretold long ago,
they went forth from my mouth,
I let you hear of them;
then suddenly I took action and they came to be.
4 Because I know that you are stubborn
and that your neck is an iron sinew
and your forehead bronze,
5 I foretold them to you of old;
before they took place I let you hear of them,
That you might not say, "My idol did them,
my statue, my molten image commanded them."
6* Now that you have heard, look at all this;
must you not admit it?

From now on I announce new things to you,
hidden events of which you knew not.
7 Now, not long ago, they are brought into being,
and beforetime you did not hear of them,
so that you cannot claim to have known them;
8* You neither heard nor knew,
they did not reach your ears beforehand.
Yes, I know you are utterly treacherous,
a rebel you were called from birth.
9 For the sake of my name I restrain my anger,
for the sake of my renown I hold it back from you,
lest I should destroy you.
10* See, I have refined you like silver,
tested you in the furnace of affliction.
11 For my sake, for my own sake, I do this;
why should I suffer profanation?
My glory I will not give to another.

12* Listen to me, Jacob,
Israel, whom I named!
I, it is I who am the first,
and also the last am I.
13* Yes, my hand laid the foundations of the earth;
my right hand spread out the heavens.

*

48, 6: 42, 9.
8: 43, 22ff.
10: 1, 25; Jer 6, 29f; Zec 13, 9; Mal 3, 2.
12: 41, 4; 44, 6; 48, 12; Rv 1, 8.17.
13: 40, 22.26; 45 12.18.

†

47, 9-13.15: Babylon was known for its sorcery and astrology.

When I call them,
they stand forth at once.

14† All of you assemble and listen:
Who among you foretold these things?
The LORD's friend shall do his will against Babylon and the progeny of Chaldea.
15 I myself have spoken, I have called him,
I have brought him, and his way succeeds!
16† Come near to me and hear this!
Not from the beginning did I speak it in secret;
At the time it comes to pass, I am present:
"Now the Lord GOD has sent me, and his spirit."
17 Thus says the LORD, your redeemer,
the Holy One of Israel:
I, the LORD, your God,
teach you what is for your good,
and lead you on the way you should go.
18 If you would hearken to my commandments,
your prosperity would be like a river,
and your vindication like the waves of the sea;
19 Your descendants would be like the sand,
and those born of your stock like its grains,
Their name never cut off
or blotted out from my presence.

20 Go forth from Babylon, flee from Chaldea!
With shouts of joy proclaim this, make it known;
Publish it to the ends of the earth, and say,
"The LORD has redeemed his servant Jacob.
21* They did not thirst
when he led them through dry lands;
Water from the rock he set flowing for them;
he cleft the rock, and waters welled forth."
22 [There is no peace for the wicked, says the LORD.]

II: EXPIATION OF SIN, SPIRITUAL LIBERATION OF ISRAEL

CHAPTER 49

The Servant of the Lord

1*† Hear me, O coastlands,
listen, O distant peoples.
The LORD called me from birth,
from my mother's womb he gave me my name.
2† He made of me a sharp-edged sword
and concealed me in the shadow of his arm.
He made me a polished arrow,
in his quiver he hid me.
3† You are my servant, he said to me,
Israel, through whom I show my glory.

4* Though I thought I had toiled in vain,
and for nothing, uselessly, spent my strength,
Yet my reward is with the LORD,
my recompense is with my God.
5 For now the LORD has spoken
who formed me as his servant from the womb,
That Jacob may be brought back to him
and Israel gathered to him;
And I am made glorious in the sight of the LORD,
and my God is now my strength!
6*† It is too little, he says, for you to be my servant,
to raise up the tribes of Jacob,
and restore the survivors of Israel;
I will make you a light to the nations,
that my salvation may reach to the ends of the earth.
7* Thus says the LORD,
the redeemer and the Holy One of Israel,
To the one despised, whom the nations abhor,
the slave of rulers:
When kings see you, they shall stand up,
and princes shall prostrate themselves
Because of the LORD who is faithful,

*

21: Ex 17, 6; Nm 20, 11.
49, 1: 41, 9; 43, 1; 44, 2.24; 46, 3.
4: 40, 27.
6: 42, 1-6; 44, 5; 45, 14; Lk 2, 32; Acts 13, 46f.
7: 49, 23; 55, 5.

†

48, 14: *The LORD's friend:* Cyrus, who carries out God's plans.
48, 16: *"Now the Lord . . . spirit":* said by Cyrus; cf v 14.
49: 1-7: The second of the four "Servant-of-the-Lord" oracles.
49, 1: *Gave me my name:* designated me for a special office (cf Jer 1, 5), or perhaps, made me renowned (cf Ps 45, 18).
49, 2: The Servant was made ready and fit for the preaching of God's word.
49, 3: *Israel:* the Servant is identified with the people of Israel as their ideal representative; however, since vv 5f seem to distinguish the Servant from Israel, some regard the word *Israel* here as a gloss.
49, 6: The Servant's vocation will be not only the restoration of Israel but the conversion of the world; cf Lk 2, 32.

the Holy One of Israel who has
chosen you.

The Liberation and Restoration of Zion

8* Thus says the LORD:
In a time of favor I answer you,
on the day of salvation I help you,
To restore the land
and allot the desolate heritages,
9* Saying to the prisoners: Come out!
To those in darkness: Show yourselves!
Along the ways they shall find pasture,
on every bare height shall their pastures be.
10* They shall not hunger or thirst,
nor shall the scorching wind or the sun strike them;
For he who pities them leads them
and guides them beside springs of water.
11* I will cut a road through all my mountains,
and make my highways level.
12† See, some shall come from afar,
others from the north and the west,
and some from the land of Syene.

13 Sing out, O heavens, and rejoice, O earth,
break forth into song, you mountains.
For the LORD comforts his people
and shows mercy to his afflicted.

14* But Zion said, "The LORD has forsaken me;
my Lord has forgotten me."
15* Can a mother forget her infant,
be without tenderness for the child of her womb?
Even should she forget,
I will never forget you.
16† See, upon the palms of my hands I have written your name;
your walls are ever before me.
17 Your rebuilders make haste,
as those who tore you down and laid you waste
go forth from you;
18 Look about and see,
they are all gathering and coming to you.
As I live, says the LORD,
you shall be arrayed with them all as with adornments,
like a bride you shall fasten them on you.

19 Though you were waste and desolate,
a land of ruins,
Now you shall be too small for your inhabitants,
while those who swallowed you up will be far away.
20 The children whom you had lost
shall yet say to you,
"This place is too small for me,
make room for me to live in."
21* You shall ask yourself:
"Who has borne me these?
I was bereft and barren
[exiled and repudiated];
who has reared them?
I was left all alone;
where then do these come from?"

22* Thus says the Lord GOD:
See, I will lift up my hand to the nations,
and raise my signal to the peoples;
They shall bring your sons in their arms,
and your daughters shall be carried on their shoulders.
23 Kings shall be your foster fathers,
their princesses your nurses;
Bowing to the ground, they shall worship you
and lick the dust at your feet.
Then you shall know that I am the LORD,
and those who hope in me shall never be disappointed.

24 Thus says the LORD:
Can booty be taken from a warrior?
or captives be rescued from a tyrant?
25 Yes, captives can be taken from a warrior,
and booty be rescued from a tyrant;
Those who oppose you I will oppose,
and your sons I will save.
26* I will make your oppressors eat their own flesh,
and they shall be drunk with their own blood
as with the juice of the grape.
All mankind shall know
that I, the LORD, am your savior,
your redeemer, the Mighty One of Jacob.

---

*

8: 2 Cor 6, 2.
9: 42, 7.18ff.
10: 51, 14; Rv 7, 16.
11: 40, 3f.
14: 40, 27.
15: 43, 4; 44, 21; 46, 3f.
21: 54, 1ff.
22: 5, 26; 13, 2.
26: 19, 2; Ez 38, 21; Zec 14, 13.

---

†

49, 12: *Syene:* now called Aswan, at the first cataract of the Nile in southern Egypt.
49, 16: *Upon the palms . . . name:* for continual remembrance; cf Ex 13, 9.16; Dt 6, 6-9.

CHAPTER 50
Salvation Only through the Lord's Servant

1*† Thus says the LORD:
Where is the bill of divorce
with which I dismissed your mother?
Or to which of my creditors
have I sold you?
It was for your sins that you were sold,
for your crimes that your mother was dismissed.

2*† Why was no one there when I came?
Why did no one answer when I called?
Is my hand too short to ransom?
Have I not the strength to deliver?
Lo, with my rebuke I dry up the sea,
I turn rivers into a desert;
Their fish rot for lack of water,
and die of thirst.
3 I clothe the heavens in mourning,
and make sackcloth their vesture.

4† The Lord GOD has given me
a well-trained tongue,
That I might know how to speak to the weary
a word that will rouse them.
Morning after morning
he opens my ear that I may hear;
5† And I have not rebelled,
have not turned back.
6*† I gave my back to those who beat me,
my cheeks to those who plucked my beard;
My face I did not shield
from buffets and spitting.

7* The Lord GOD is my help,
therefore I am not disgraced;
I have set my face like flint,
knowing that I shall not be put to shame.
8 He is near who upholds my right;
if anyone wishes to oppose me,
let us appear together.
Who disputes my right?
Let him confront me.
9* See, the Lord GOD is my help;
who will prove me wrong?
Lo, they will all wear out like cloth,
the moth will eat them up.
10*† Who among you fears the LORD,
heeds his servant's voice,
And walks in darkness
without any light,
Trusting in the name of the LORD
and relying on his God?
11 All of you kindle flames
and carry about you fiery darts;
Walk by the light of your own fire
and by the flares you have burnt!
This is your fate from my hand:
you shall lie down in a place of pain.

CHAPTER 51
Exhortation To Trust in the Lord

1*† Listen to me, you who pursue justice,
who seek the LORD;
Look to the rock from which you were hewn,
to the pit from which you were quarried;
2* Look to Abraham, your father,
and to Sarah, who gave you birth;
When he was but one I called him,
I blessed him and made him many.
3 Yes, the LORD shall comfort Zion
and have pity on all her ruins;
Her deserts he shall make like Eden,
her wasteland like the garden of the LORD;
Joy and gladness shall be found in her,
thanksgiving and the sound of song.

4*† Be attentive to me, my people;
my folk, give ear to me.
For law shall go forth from my presence,
and my judgment, as the light of the peoples.
5 I will make my justice come speedily;
my salvation shall go forth
[and my arm shall judge the nations];
In me shall the coastlands hope,
and my arm they shall await.

*

50, 1: Dt 24, 1-4; Mt 19, 3; Mk 10, 2ff; Is 54, 6ff.
2: Ex 7, 18; Ps 105, 29.
6: 2 Sm 10, 4ff; Mt 26, 67; 27, 30.
7: Ez 3, 9.
9: 51, 6-8; Ps 102, 27.
10: 43, 1f; 44, 1f.
51, 1: Rom 9, 30f.
2: Ez 33, 24; Gn 12, 2ff; 22, 17.
4: 2, 3.

†

50, 1: Responding to the people's complaint of utter abandonment by God, the prophet shows that their sins were responsible for their banishment. Since there was no bill of divorce, the bond between the Lord and his people still exists and he will ultimately save them.

50, 2: Israel's faith in God is weak; she does not answer his call, nor believe in his promises of deliverance.

50, 4-11: The third of the four "Servant-of-the-Lord" oracles; in vv 4-9 the Servant speaks; in vv 10f God reproves the people for not following the Servant.

50, 5: The Servant does not refuse the divine vocation.

50, 6: He willingly submits to insults and beatings. *Plucked my beard:* a grave insult.

50, 10f: Instead of trusting in the Lord and his Servant, the people rely on their own devices, to their own destruction.

51, 1: *Rock . . . pit:* your glorious ancestry.

51, 4f: The conversion of the Gentiles.

6† Raise your eyes to the heavens,
and look at the earth below;
Though the heavens grow thin like smoke,
the earth wears out like a garment
and its inhabitants die like flies,
My salvation shall remain forever
and my justice shall never be dismayed.
7 Hear me, you who know justice,
you people who have my teaching at heart:
Fear not the reproach of men,
be not dismayed at their revilings.
8* They shall be like a garment eaten by moths,
like wool consumed by grubs;
But my justice shall remain forever
and my salvation, for all generations.

9*† Awake, awake, put on strength,
O arm of the LORD!
Awake as in the days of old,
in ages long ago!
Was it not you who crushed Rahab,
you who pierced the dragon?
10† Was it not you who dried up the sea,
the waters of the great deep,
Who made the depths of the sea into a way
for the redeemed to pass over?
11 Those whom the LORD has ransomed will return
and enter Zion singing,
crowned with everlasting joy;
They will meet with joy and gladness,
sorrow and mourning will flee.

ISAIAH

12 I, it is I who comfort you.
Can you then fear mortal man,
who is human only, to be looked upon as grass,
13 And forget the LORD, your maker,
who stretched out the heavens
and laid the foundations of the earth?
All the day you are in constant dread
of the fury of the oppressor;
But when he sets himself to destroy,
what is there of the oppressor's fury?

14 The oppressed shall soon be released;
they shall not die and go down into the pit,
nor shall they want for bread.
15* For I am the LORD, your God,
who stirs up the sea so that its waves roar;
the LORD of hosts by name.
16 I have put my words into your mouth
and shielded you in the shadow of my hand,
I, who stretched out the heavens,
who laid the foundations of the earth,
who say to Zion: You are my people.

The Cup of the Lord

17* Awake, awake!
Arise, O Jerusalem,
You who drank at the LORD's hand
the cup of his wrath;
Who drained to the dregs
the bowl of staggering!
18 She has no one to guide her
of all the sons she bore;
She has no one to grasp her by the hand,
of all the sons she reared!—
19 Your misfortunes are double;
who is there to condole with you?
Desolation and destruction, famine and sword!
Who is there to comfort you?
20 Your sons lie helpless
at every street corner
like antelopes in a net.
They are filled with the wrath of the LORD,
the rebuke of your God.

21* But now, hear this, O afflicted one,
drunk, but not with wine,
22 Thus says the LORD, your Master,
your God, who defends his people:
See, I am taking from your hand
the cup of staggering;
The bowl of my wrath
you shall no longer drink.
23 I will put it into the hands of your tormentors,
those who ordered you
to bow down, that they might walk over you,
While you offered your back like the ground,
like the street for them to walk on.

CHAPTER 52

Let Zion Rejoice

1 Awake, awake!
Put on your strength, O Zion;
Put on your glorious garments,
O Jerusalem, holy city.
No longer shall the uncircumcised
or the unclean enter you.

*
8: 50, 9.
9: Ex 15, 16; Jb 9, 13; 26, 12; Pss 74, 13; 89, 11.
15: Jer 31, 35.
17: Jer 25, 15ff; Ez 23, 32ff.
21: 29, 9.

†
51, 6: God's *salvation* and *justice* are eternal, in contrast to the impermanence of *the heavens and the earth:* cf Mt 24, 35.

51, 9: *Rahab:* see note on 30, 7. *The dragon:* see notes on 27, 1; Ps 74, 13.

51, 10: *Great deep:* another reference to the primeval chaos of Gn 1, 2.

2 Shake off the dust,
ascend to the throne, Jerusalem;
Loose the bonds from your neck,
O captive daughter Zion!
3 For thus says the LORD:
You were sold for nothing,
and without money you shall be redeemed.

4 Thus says the Lord GOD:
To Egypt in the beginning my people went down,
to sojourn there;
Assyria, too, oppressed them for nought.
5 But now, what am I to do here?
says the LORD.
My people have been taken away without redress;
their rulers make a boast of it,
says the LORD;
all the day my name is constantly reviled.
6 Therefore on that day my people shall know my renown,
that it is I who have foretold it.
Here I am!
7*† How beautiful upon the mountains
are the feet of him who brings glad tidings,
Announcing peace, bearing good news,
announcing salvation, and saying to Zion,
"Your God is King!"

8* Hark! Your watchmen raise a cry,
together they shout for joy,
For they see directly, before their eyes,
the LORD restoring Zion.
9 Break out together in song,
O ruins of Jerusalem!
For the LORD comforts his people,
he redeems Jerusalem.
10 The LORD has bared his holy arm
in the sight of all the nations;
All the ends of the earth will behold
the salvation of our God.

11† Depart, depart, come forth from there,
touch nothing unclean!
Out from there! Purify yourselves,
you who carry the vessels of the LORD.
12* Yet not in fearful haste will you come out,
nor leave in headlong flight,
For the LORD comes before you,
and your rear guard is the God of Israel.

Suffering and Triumph of the Servant of the Lord

13† See, my servant shall prosper,
he shall be raised high and greatly exalted.
14* Even as many were amazed at him—
so marred was his look beyond that of man,
and his appearance beyond that of mortals—
15* So shall he startle many nations,
because of him kings shall stand speechless;
For those who have not been told shall see,
those who have not heard shall ponder it.

CHAPTER 53

1* Who would believe what we have heard?
To whom has the arm of the LORD been revealed?
2*† He grew up like a sapling before him,
like a shoot from the parched earth;
There was in him no stately bearing
to make us look at him,
nor appearance that would attract us to him.
3*† He was spurned and avoided by men,
a man of suffering, accustomed to infirmity,
One of those from whom men hide their faces,
spurned, and we held him in no esteem.

4*† Yet it was our infirmities that he bore,
our sufferings that he endured,
While we thought of him as stricken,
as one smitten by God and afflicted.
5* But he was pierced for our offenses,
crushed for our sins,

ISAIAH

*

52, 7: 40, 9; Rom 10, 15.
8: 62, 6.
12: Ex 12, 11.
14: Ps 69, 8.
15: Mi 7, 16.
53, 1: 52, 10; Jn 12, 38; Rom 10, 16.
2: 11, 1.
3: Jb 19, 18; Ps 31, 11ff; Mk 9, 11.
4: Jer 10, 19; Mt 8, 17.
5: 1 Cor 15, 3; 1 Pt 2, 24.

†

52, 7-10: God leads his people back from Babylon to Zion, from whose ruined walls *watchmen . . . shout for joy;* cf Rom 10, 15.

52, 11: *From there:* from Babylon. *Vessels of the LORD:* taken to Babylon by Nebuchadnezzar, now carried back by the exiled priests returning in procession to Zion; cf Ezr 1, 7.

52, 13—53, 12: The last of the four "Servant-of-the-Lord" oracles. An extraordinary description of the sinless Servant, who by his voluntary suffering atones for the sins of his people, and saves them from just punishment at the hands of God. Only in Jesus Christ is the prophecy perfectly fulfilled.

53, 2: Only God appreciated his Servant's true greatness.

53, 3: Because he suffered, he was regarded as a sinner and therefore as one to be *spurned.*

53, 4ff: He did indeed suffer but it was for the sins of mankind, and through his sufferings men are *healed.*

Upon him was the chastisement that
makes us whole,
by his stripes we were healed.
6* We had all gone astray like sheep,
each following his own way;
But the LORD laid upon him
the guilt of us all.

7* Though he was harshly treated, he
submitted
and opened not his mouth;
Like a lamb led to the slaughter
or a sheep before the shearers,
he was silent and opened not his
mouth.
8 Oppressed and condemned, he was
taken away,
and who would have thought any
more of his destiny?
When he was cut off from the land
of the living,
and smitten for the sin of his peo-
ple,
9* A grave was assigned him among
the wicked
and a burial place with evildoers,
Though he had done no wrong
nor spoken any falsehood.
10† [But the LORD was pleased
to crush him in infirmity.]

If he gives his life as an offering for
sin,
he shall see his descendants in a
long life,
and the will of the LORD shall be
accomplished through him.
11 Because of his affliction
he shall see the light in fullness
of days;
Through his suffering, my servant
shall justify many,
and their guilt he shall bear.
12* Therefore I will give him his portion
among the great,
and he shall divide the spoils with
the mighty,
Because he surrendered himself to
death
and was counted among the
wicked;
And he shall take away the sins of
many,
and win pardon for their offenses.

CHAPTER 54

The New Zion

1*† Raise a glad cry, you barren one
who did not bear,
break forth in jubilant song, you
who were not in labor,
For more numerous are the children
of the deserted wife
than the children of her who has
a husband,
says the LORD.
2* Enlarge the space for your tent,
spread out your tent cloths un-
sparingly;
lengthen your ropes and make
firm your stakes.
3 For you shall spread abroad to the
right and to the left;
Your descendants shall dispossess
the nations
and shall people the desolate cit-
ies.

4 Fear not, you shall not be put to
shame;
you need not blush, for you shall
not be disgraced.
The shame of your youth you shall
forget,
the reproach of your widowhood
no longer remember.
5† For he who has become your hus-
band is your Maker;
his name is the LORD of hosts;
Your redeemer is the Holy One of
Israel,
called God of all the earth.

6* The LORD calls you back,
like a wife forsaken and grieved
in spirit,
A wife married in youth and then
cast off,
says your God.
7 For a brief moment I abandoned
you,
but with great tenderness I will
take you back.
8 In an outburst of wrath, for a mo-
ment
I hid my face from you;
But with enduring love I take pity
on you,
says the LORD, your redeemer.

9* This is for me like the days of Noah,
when I swore that the waters of
Noah
should never again deluge the
earth;
So I have sworn not to be angry with
you,
or to rebuke you.

*

6: Lv 16, 21ff.
7: Mt 26, 63; Acts 8, 32.
9: 1 Pt 2, 22f; 1 Jn 3, 5.
12: Mk 15, 28; Lk 22, 37.
54, 1: Gal 4, 27.
2: 49, 20.
6: Mal 2, 14f.
9: Gn 9, 15.

†

53, 10ff: Because he fulfilled the divine will by suffering for the sins of others, the Servant will be rewarded by the Lord. *See the light:* enjoy happiness. This line may originally have read, "he shall drink and eat to the full"—at the thanksgiving sacrifice at which *he shall divide the spoils* (v 12).

54, 1: Jerusalem, pictured as a wife who had been *barren* and *deserted,* now suddenly finds herself with innumerable children (the returning exiles); cf Gal 4, 27 for the application of this text to the Church, the New Zion.

54, 5: *Redeemer:* cf note on 41, 14.

ISAIAH

10* Though the mountains leave their place
and the hills be shaken,
My love shall never leave you
nor my covenant of peace be shaken,
says the LORD, who has mercy on you.

11*† O afflicted one, storm-battered and unconsoled,
I lay your pavements in carnelians,
and your foundations in sapphires;
12 I will make your battlements of rubies,
your gates of carbuncles,
and all your walls of precious stones.
13 All your sons shall be taught by the LORD,
and great shall be the peace of your children.
14 In justice shall you be established,
far from the fear of oppression,
where destruction cannot come near you.
15 Should there be any attack, it shall not be of my making;
whoever attacks you shall fall before you.

16 Lo, I have created the craftsman
who blows on the burning coals
and forges weapons as his work;
It is I also who have created
the destroyer to work havoc.
17 No weapon fashioned against you shall prevail;
every tongue you shall prove false
that launches an accusation against you.
This is the lot of the servants of the LORD,
their vindication from me, says the LORD.

CHAPTER 55

An Invitation to Grace

1*† All you who are thirsty,
come to the water!
You who have no money,
come, receive grain and eat;
Come, without paying and without cost,
drink wine and milk!
2 Why spend your money for what is not bread;
your wages for what fails to satisfy?
Heed me, and you shall eat well,
you shall delight in rich fare.
3* Come to me heedfully,
listen, that you may have life.
I will renew with you the everlasting covenant,
the benefits assured to David.
4 As I made him a witness to the peoples,
a leader and commander of nations,
5* So shall you summon a nation you knew not,
and nations that knew you not shall run to you,
Because of the LORD, your God,
the Holy One of Israel, who has glorified you.

6 Seek the LORD while he may be found,
call him while he is near.
7 Let the scoundrel forsake his way,
and the wicked man his thoughts;
Let him turn to the LORD for mercy;
to our God, who is generous in forgiving.
8 For my thoughts are not your thoughts,
nor are your ways my ways, says the LORD.
9 As high as the heavens are above the earth,
so high are my ways above your ways
and my thoughts above your thoughts.

10 For just as from the heavens
the rain and snow come down
And do not return there
till they have watered the earth,
making it fertile and fruitful,
Giving seed to him who sows
and bread to him who eats,
11 So shall my word be
that goes forth from my mouth;
It shall not return to me void,
but shall do my will,
achieving the end for which I sent it.

12 Yes, in joy you shall depart,
in peace you shall be brought back;
Mountains and hills shall break out in song before you,
and all the trees of the countryside shall clap their hands.

*

10: Pss 76, 5; 46, 3.
11: Rv 21, 18-21.
55, 1: Jn 4, 10ff; 6, 35; 7, 37ff; Rv 21, 6; 22, 17.
3: 2 Sm 7, 12-16.
5: Acts 13, 34.

†

54, 11f: Cf Rv 21. *Afflicted one:* Jerusalem; *carnelians:* reddish quartz, hard and durable, *carbuncles:* another precious stone of red color.

55, 1ff: God's salvation is freely extended to his people and to all nations; through him will *the benefits assured to David* be renewed; cf 12, 3; Jn 7, 37.

13† In place of the thornbush, the cypress shall grow,
instead of nettles, the myrtle.
This shall be to the LORD's renown,
an everlasting imperishable sign.

III: RETURN OF THE FIRST CAPTIVES

CHAPTER 56

The Lord's House Open to All

1† Thus says the LORD:
Observe what is right, do what is just;
for my salvation is about to come,
my justice, about to be revealed.
2 Happy is the man who does this,
the son of man who holds to it;
Who keeps the sabbath free from profanation,
and his hand from any evildoing.
3† Let not the foreigner say,
when he would join himself to the LORD,
"The LORD will surely exclude me from his people";
Nor let the eunuch say,
"See, I am a dry tree."
4* For thus says the LORD:
To the eunuchs who observe my sabbaths
and choose what pleases me
and hold fast to my covenant,
5† I will give, in my house
and within my walls, a monument and a name
Better than sons and daughters;
an eternal, imperishable name will I give them.

6 And the foreigners who join themselves to the LORD,
ministering to him,
Loving the name of the LORD,
and becoming his servants—
All who keep the sabbath free from profanation
and hold to my covenant,
7* Them I will bring to my holy mountain
and make joyful in my house of prayer;
Their holocausts and sacrifices
will be acceptable on my altar,
For my house shall be called
a house of prayer for all peoples.
8 Thus says the Lord GOD,
who gathers the dispersed of Israel:
Others will I gather to him
besides those already gathered.

Blind Leaders

9*† All you wild beasts of the field,
come and eat,
all you beasts in the forest!
10 My watchmen are blind,
all of them unaware;
They are all dumb dogs,
they cannot bark;
Dreaming as they lie there,
loving their sleep.
11 They are relentless dogs,
they know not when they have enough.
These are the shepherds
who know no discretion;
Each of them goes his own way,
every one of them to his own gain:
12* "Come, I will fetch some wine;
let us carouse with strong drink,
And tomorrow will be like today,
or even greater."

CHAPTER 57

1 The just man perishes,
but no one takes it to heart;
Devout men are swept away,
with no one giving it a thought.
Though he is taken away from the presence of evil,
the just man 2 enters into peace;
There is rest on his couch
for the sincere, straightforward man.

Faithless People

3 But you, draw near,
you sons of a sorceress,
adulterous, wanton race!
4 Of whom do you make sport,
at whom do you open wide your mouth,
and put out your tongue?
Are you not rebellious children,
a worthless race;
5* You who are in heat among the terebinths,
under every green tree;
You who immolate children in the wadies,
behind the crevices in the cliffs?

*

56, 4: Wis 3, 14f.
7: 1 Kgs 8, 29f; Mt 21, 13.
9: Ez 34, 5.
12: 28, 7ff; Wis 2, 7.
57, 5: Jer 7, 31; 19, 5; Ez 20, 28.31.

†

55, 13: *Thornbush . . . nettles:* suggestive of the desert and therefore symbolic of suffering and hardship; *cypress, myrtle:* suggestive of fertile land and therefore symbolic of joy and strength.

56, 1-8: Participation in the future messianic salvation is offered to all who believe in the Lord and keep his commandments, regardless of origin or social condition.

56, 3: Eunuchs had originally been excluded from the community of the Lord; cf Dt 23, 2; Wis 3, 14. *Dry tree:* unable to produce the fruit of offspring.

56, 5: *A monument and a name:* a memorial inscription to prevent oblivion for one who had no children; cf 2 Sm 18, 18; Neh 7, 15; 13, 14.

56, 9—57, 13: This section is apparently preexilic, written in the manner of the older prophets who condemned the pagan rites of Baal worship.

56, 9: *Wild beasts:* foreign nations, which are invited to come and ravage Israel.

6† Among the smooth stones of the wadi is your portion,
these are your lot;
To these you poured out libations,
and brought offerings.
Should I decide not to punish these things?
7* Upon a high and lofty mountain
you made your bed,
and there you went up to offer sacrifice.
8 Behind the door and the doorpost
you placed your indecent symbol.
Deserting me, you spread out
your high, wide bed;
And of those whose embraces you love
you carved the symbol and gazed upon it
9† While you approached the king with scented oil,
and multiplied your perfumes;
While you sent your ambassadors far away,
down even to the nether world.
10 Though worn out by your many misdeeds,
you never said, "It is hopeless";
New strength you found,
and so you did not weaken.

11 Of whom were you afraid? Whom did you fear,
that you became false
And did not remember me
or give me any thought?
Was I to remain silent and unseeing,
so that you would not have me to fear?
12† I will expose your justice
and your works;
13† They shall not help you when you cry out,
nor save you in your distress.

All these the wind shall carry off,
the breeze shall bear away;
But he who takes refuge in me shall inherit the land,
and possess my holy mountain.

Comfort for the Afflicted

14* Build up, build up, prepare the way,
remove the stumbling blocks from my people's path.
15* For thus says he who is high and exalted,
living eternally, whose name is the Holy One:
On high I dwell, and in holiness,
and with the crushed and dejected in spirit,
To revive the spirits of the dejected,
to revive the hearts of the crushed.
16 I will not accuse forever,
nor always be angry;
For their spirits would faint before me,
the souls that I have made.
17* Because of their wicked avarice I was angry,
and struck them, hiding myself in wrath,
as they went their own rebellious way.
18 I saw their ways,
but I will heal them and lead them;
I will give full comfort
to them and to those who mourn for them,
19 I, the Creator, who gave them life.

Peace, peace to the far and the near,
says the LORD; and I will heal them.
20 But the wicked are like the tossing sea
which cannot be calmed,
And its waters cast up mud and filth.
21* No peace for the wicked! says my God.

CHAPTER 58

True Fasting

1† Cry out full-throated and unsparingly,
lift up your voice like a trumpet blast;
Tell my people their wickedness,
and the house of Jacob their sins.
2† They seek me day after day,
and desire to know my ways,
Like a nation that has done what is just
and not abandoned the law of their God;
They ask me to declare what is due them,
pleased to gain access to God.
3 "Why do we fast, and you do not see it?
afflict ourselves, and you take no note of it?"

Lo, on your fast day you carry out your own pursuits,
and drive all your laborers.

*

7: Hos 4, 13; Jer 2, 20; Ez 6, 13.
14: 40, 3f.
15: 61, 2f.
17: 56, 11.
21: 48, 21.

†

57, 6: *Smooth stones:* the Hebrew word for this expression has the same consonants as the word for "portion"; instead of making the Lord their portion (cf Ps 16, 5), the people adored slabs of stone which they took from the streambeds in valleys and set up as idols; cf Jer 3, 9. Therefore, it is implied, they will be swept away as by a sudden torrent of waters carrying them down the rocky-bottomed gorge to destruction and death without burial.

57, 9: *The king:* the pagan god Moloch. *Ambassadors:* children sent to him through a sacrificial death.

57, 12: *Justice:* here used ironically.

57, 13: *All these:* the wicked mentioned in 57, 3-10.

58, 1: This command is directed to the prophet.

58, 2-14: Merely external worship does not avail with God; it must be joined to internal sincerity.

4 Yes, your fast ends in quarreling
and fighting,
striking with wicked claw.
Would that today you might fast
so as to make your voice heard
on high!
5* Is this the manner of fasting I wish,
of keeping a day of penance:
That a man bow his head like a reed,
and lie in sackcloth and ashes?
Do you call this a fast,
a day acceptable to the LORD?
6 This, rather, is the fasting that I
wish:
releasing those bound unjustly,
untying the thongs of the yoke;
Setting free the oppressed,
breaking every yoke;
7* Sharing your bread with the hungry,
sheltering the oppressed and the
homeless;
Clothing the naked when you see
them,
and not turning your back on your
own.

8 Then your light shall break forth like
the dawn,
and your wound shall quickly be
healed;
Your vindication shall go before you,
and the glory of the LORD shall be
your rear guard.
9 Then you shall call, and the LORD
will answer,
you shall cry for help, and he will
say: Here I am!
If you remove from your midst op-
pression,
false accusation and malicious
speech;
10 If you bestow your bread on the hun-
gry
and satisfy the afflicted;
Then light shall rise for you in the
darkness,
and the gloom shall become for
you like midday;
11* Then the LORD will guide you always
and give you plenty even on the
parched land.
He will renew your strength,
and you shall be like a watered
garden,
like a spring whose water never
fails.
12* The ancient ruins shall be rebuilt for
your sake,
and the foundations from ages
past you shall raise up;
"Repairer of the breach," they shall
call you,
"Restorer of ruined homesteads."

13 If you hold back your foot on the
sabbath
from following your own pursuits
on my holy day;
If you call the sabbath a delight,
and the LORD's holy day honor-
able;
If you honor it by not following your
ways,
seeking your own interests, or
speaking with malice—
14 Then you shall delight in the LORD,
and I will make you ride on the
heights of the earth;
I will nourish you with the heritage
of Jacob, your father,
for the mouth of the LORD has spo-
ken.

CHAPTER 59

Sin and Confession

1* Lo, the hand of the LORD is not too
short to save,
nor his ear too dull to hear.
2 Rather, it is your crimes
that separate you from your God,
It is your sins that make him hide
his face
so that he will not hear you.
3* For your hands are stained with
blood,
your fingers with guilt;
Your lips speak falsehood,
and your tongue utters deceit.
4† No one brings suit justly,
no one pleads truthfully;
They trust in emptiness and tell lies;
they conceive mischief and bring
forth malice.
5*† They hatch adders' eggs,
and weave spiders' webs:
Whoever eats their eggs will die,
if one of them is pressed, it will
hatch as a viper;
6 Their webs cannot serve as clothing,
nor can they cover themselves
with their works.
Their works are evil works,
and deeds of violence come from
their hands.
7* Their feet run to evil,
and they are quick to shed inno-
cent blood;
Their thoughts are destructive
thoughts,
plunder and ruin are on their
highways.
8 The way of peace they know not,
and there is nothing that is right
in their paths;

*

58, 5: Zec 7, 5.
7: Ez 18, 7. 16; Mt 25, 35.
11: 51, 3; Ps 24.
12: 61, 4.
59, 1: 50, 2; Nm 11, 23.
3: 1, 15.
5: Jb 20, 12-16.
7: Rom 3, 15.

†

59, 4: *Emptiness:* things having no value.
59, 5f: A proverb signifying evil works—*adders' eggs*—and useless devices—*spiders' webs;* the former do positive harm to oneself and others; the latter serve no useful purpose.

ISAIAH

Their ways they have made crooked,
whoever treads them knows no peace.

9† That is why right is far from us
and justice does not reach us.
We look for light, and lo, darkness;
for brightness, but we walk in gloom!
10 Like blind men we grope along the wall,
like people without eyes we feel our way.
We stumble at midday as at dusk,
in Stygian darkness, like the dead.
11* We all growl like bears,
like doves we moan without ceasing.
We look for right, but it is not there;
for salvation, and it is far from us.
12 For our offenses before you are many,
our sins bear witness against us.
Yes, our offenses are present to us,
and our crimes we know:
13 Transgressing, and denying the LORD,
turning back from following our God,
Threatening outrage, and apostasy,
uttering words of falsehood the heart has conceived.
14 Right is repelled,
and justice stands far off;
For truth stumbles in the public square,
uprightness cannot enter.
15 Honesty is lacking,
and the man who turns from evil is despoiled.

The Redeemer in Zion

The LORD saw this, and was aggrieved
that right did not exist.
16 He saw that there was no one,
and was appalled that there was none to intervene;
So his own arm brought about the victory,
and his justice lent him its support.
17* He put on justice as his breastplate,
salvation, as the helmet on his head;
He clothed himself with garments of vengeance,
wrapped himself in a mantle of zeal.
18 He repays his enemies their deserts,
and requites his foes with wrath.

19 Those in the west shall fear the name of the LORD,
and those in the east, his glory;
For it shall come like a pent-up river
which the breath of the LORD drives on.
20* He shall come to Zion a redeemer
to those of Jacob who turn from sin, says the LORD.
21 This is the covenant with them
which I myself have made, says the LORD:
My spirit which is upon you
and my words that I have put into your mouth
Shall never leave your mouth,
nor the mouths of your children
Nor the mouths of your children's children
from now on and forever, says the LORD.

CHAPTER 60

Glory of the New Zion

1† Rise up in splendor! Your light has come,
the glory of the Lord shines upon you.
2 See, darkness covers the earth,
and thick clouds cover the peoples;
But upon you the LORD shines,
and over you appears his glory.
3* Nations shall walk by your light,
and kings by your shining radiance.
4* Raise your eyes and look about;
they all gather and come to you:
Your sons come from afar,
and your daughters in the arms of their nurses.

5 Then you shall be radiant at what you see,
your heart shall throb and overflow,
For the riches of the sea shall be emptied out before you,
the wealth of nations shall be brought to you.
6 Caravans of camels shall fill you,
dromedaries from Midian and Ephah;
All from Sheba shall come
bearing gold and frankincense,
and proclaiming the praises of the LORD.
7 All the flocks of Kedar shall be gathered for you,

ISAIAH

*

11: 38, 14.
17: Wis 5, 17ff; Eph 6, 14; 1 Thes 5, 8.
20: Rom 11, 26f.
60, 3: 42, 6; 45, 14; 49, 6.
4: 49, 18.

†

59, 9-15: Spoken by the people through the mouth of the prophet.
60, 1-6: The Church makes use of these verses for the first reading of the Mass on the feast of Epiphany, for she sees in them symbols of her universality.

the rams of Nebaioth shall be your sacrifices;
They will be acceptable offerings on my altar,
and I will enhance the splendor of my house.

8† What are these that fly along like clouds,
like doves to their cotes?
9 All the vessels of the sea are assembled,
with the ships of Tarshish in the lead,
To bring your children from afar
with their silver and gold,
In the name of the LORD, your God,
the Holy One of Israel, who has glorified you.

10 Foreigners shall rebuild your walls,
and their kings shall be your attendants;
Though I struck you in my wrath,
yet in my good will I have shown you mercy.
11* Your gates shall stand open constantly;
day and night they shall not be closed
But shall admit to you the wealth of nations,
and their kings, in the vanguard.
12 For the people or kingdom shall perish
that does not serve you;
those nations shall be utterly destroyed.
13*†The glory of Lebanon shall come to you:
the cypress, the plane and the pine,
To bring beauty to my sanctuary,
and glory to the place where I set my feet.
14 The children of your oppressors shall come,
bowing low before you;
All those who despised you
shall fall prostrate at your feet.
They shall call you "City of the LORD,"
"Zion of the Holy One of Israel."

15* Once you were forsaken,
hated and unvisited,
Now I will make you the pride of the ages,
a joy to generation after generation.
16 You shall suck the milk of nations,
and be nursed at royal breasts;
You shall know that I, the LORD, am your savior,
your redeemer, the Mighty One of Jacob.
17 In place of bronze I will bring gold,
instead of iron, silver;
In place of wood, bronze,
instead of stones, iron;
I will appoint peace your governor,
and justice your ruler.

18 No longer shall violence be heard of
in your land,
or plunder and ruin within your boundaries.
You shall call your walls "Salvation"
and your gates "Praise."
19* No longer shall the sun
be your light by day,
Nor the brightness of the moon
shine upon you at night;
The LORD shall be your light forever,
your God shall be your glory.
20 No longer shall your sun go down,
or your moon withdraw,
For the LORD will be your light forever,
and the days of your mourning shall be at an end.
21 Your people shall all be just,
they shall always possess the land,
They, the bud of my planting,
my handiwork to show my glory.
22* The smallest shall become a thousand,
the youngest, a mighty nation;
I, the LORD, will swiftly accomplish
these things
when their time comes.

CHAPTER 61

The Mission to the Afflicted

1*†The spirit of the Lord GOD is upon me,
because the LORD has anointed me;
He has sent me to bring glad tidings
to the lowly,
to heal the brokenhearted,
To proclaim liberty to the captives
and release to the prisoners,
2* To announce a year of favor from the LORD
and a day of vindication by our God,
to comfort all who mourn;
3 To place on those who mourn in Zion
a diadem instead of ashes,

*

11: Rv 21, 25.
13: 35, 2.
15: Ez 16.
19: Rv 21, 23; 22, 5.
22: Gn 12, 2; 17, 6.
61, 1: 42, 1; 48, 16; Lk 4, 18f.
2: Mt 5, 5.

†

60, 8f: *Like clouds, like doves:* the white sails of *the ships of Tarshish;* cf note on Ps 48, 8.

60, 13: *Glory of Lebanon:* the cedars, together with *the cypress, the plane and the pine,* all precious, durable wood.

61, 1f: This was spoken by the prophet in regard to the restoration of Zion, but quoted by Christ as referring to his mission; cf Lk 4, 18f. *Year of favor . . . day of vindication:* the time of God's salvation.

To give them oil of gladness in place of mourning,
a glorious mantle instead of a listless spirit.
They will be called oaks of justice,
planted by the LORD to show his glory.

The Reward of Israel

4* They shall rebuild the ancient ruins,
the former wastes they shall raise up
And restore the ruined cities,
desolate now for generations.
5 Strangers shall stand ready to pasture your flocks,
foreigners shall be your farmers and vinedressers.
6 You yourselves shall be named priests of the LORD,
ministers of our God you shall be called.
You shall eat the wealth of the nations
and boast of riches from them.

7* Since their shame was double
and disgrace and spittle were their portion,
They shall have a double inheritance in their land,
everlasting joy shall be theirs.
8* For I, the LORD, love what is right,
I hate robbery and injustice;
I will give them their recompense faithfully,
a lasting covenant I will make with them.
9 Their descendants shall be renowned among the nations,
and their offspring among the peoples;
All who see them shall acknowledge them
as a race the LORD has blessed.

10 I rejoice heartily in the LORD,
in my God is the joy of my soul;
For he has clothed me with a robe of salvation,
and wrapped me in a mantle of justice,
Like a bridegroom adorned with a diadem,
like a bride bedecked with her jewels.
11 As the earth brings forth its plants,
and a garden makes its growth spring up,
So will the Lord GOD make justice and praise
spring up before all the nations.

CHAPTER 62

Jerusalem the Lord's Bride

1 For Zion's sake I will not be silent,
for Jerusalem's sake I will not be quiet,
Until her vindication shines forth like the dawn
and her victory like a burning torch.

2*† Nations shall behold your vindication,
and all kings your glory;
You shall be called by a new name
pronounced by the mouth of the LORD.
3 You shall be a glorious crown in the hand of the LORD,
a royal diadem held by your God.
4* No more shall men call you "Forsaken,"
or your land "Desolate,"
But you shall be called "My Delight,"
and your land "Espoused."
For the LORD delights in you,
and makes your land his spouse.
5 As a young man marries a virgin,
your Builder shall marry you;
And as a bridegroom rejoices in his bride
so shall your God rejoice in you.

Restoration of Zion

6† Upon your walls, O Jerusalem,
I have stationed watchmen;
Never, by day or by night,
shall they be silent.
O you who are to remind the LORD,
take no rest
7 And give no rest to him,
until he re-establishes Jerusalem
And makes of it
the pride of the earth.

8* The LORD has sworn by his right hand
and by his mighty arm:
No more will I give your grain
as food to your enemies;
Nor shall foreigners drink your wine,
for which you toiled.
9* But you who harvest the grain shall eat it,
and you shall praise the LORD;
You who gather the grapes shall drink the wine
in the courts of my sanctuary.

*

4: 58, 12.
7: 40, 2.
8: 55, 3; 59, 21.
62, 2: Rv 2, 17; 3, 12.
4: 49, 15f; 54, 1ff.
8: 52, 10.
9: Dt 12, 17f; 14, 23.

†

62, 2: *New name:* figurative expression for a new state of happiness; cf Rv 2, 17; 3, 12.

62, 6f: *Remind the LORD . . . give no rest to him:* figuratively, as though to make certain that the Lord will remember his pledge to Jerusalem. Cf Lk 11, 7f.

10*†Pass through, pass through the gates,
prepare the way for the people;
Build up, build up the highway,
clear it of stones,
raise up a standard over the nations.
11* See, the LORD proclaims
to the ends of the earth:
Say to daughter Zion,
your savior comes!
Here is his reward with him,
his recompense before him.
12* They shall be called the holy people,
the redeemed of the LORD,
And you shall be called "Frequented,"
a city that is not forsaken.

CHAPTER 63

Punishment of Edom

1† Who is this that comes from Edom,
in crimsoned garments, from Bozrah—
This one arrayed in majesty,
marching in the greatness of his strength?
"It is I, I who announce vindication,
I who am mighty to save."
2* Why is your apparel red,
and your garments like those of the wine presser?

3 "The wine press I have trodden alone,
and of my people there was no one with me.
I trod them in my anger,
and trampled them down in my wrath;
Their blood spurted on my garments;
all my apparel I stained.
4* For the day of vengeance was in my heart,
my year for redeeming was at hand.
5* I looked about, but there was no one to help,
I was appalled that there was no one to lend support;
So my own arm brought about the victory
and my own wrath lent me its support.
6 I trampled down the peoples in my anger,
I crushed them in my wrath,
and I let their blood run out upon the ground."

Prayer for the Return of God's Favor

7*†The favors of the LORD I will recall,
the glorious deeds of the LORD,
Because of all he has done for us;
for he is good to the house of Israel,
He has favored us according to his mercy
and his great kindness.

8 He said: They are indeed my people,
children who are not disloyal;
So he became their savior
9* in their every affliction.
It was not a messenger or an angel,
but he himself who saved them.
Because of his love and pity
he redeemed them himself,
Lifting them and carrying them
all the days of old.
10 But they rebelled, and grieved
his holy spirit;
So he turned on them like an enemy,
and fought against them.

11 Then they remembered the days of old
and Moses, his servant;
Where is he who brought up out of the sea
the shepherd of his flock?
Where is he who put his holy spirit
in their midst;
12 Whose glorious arm
was the guide at Moses' right;
Who divided the waters before them,
winning for himself eternal renown;
13 Who led them without stumbling through the depths
like horses in the open country,
14 Like cattle going down into the plain,
the spirit of the LORD guiding them?
Thus you led your people,
bringing glory to your name.

15* Look down from heaven and regard us
from your holy and glorious palace!
Where is your zealous care and your might,
your surge of pity and your mercy?
O Lord, hold not back,
16 for you are our father.
Were Abraham not to know us,

---

*

10: 58, 14.
11: 40, 10.
12: 62, 4.
63, 2: Rv 19, 13.
4: 34, 8; 61, 2.
5: 59, 16.
7: 26, 15.
9: Dt 4, 37f.
15: Dt 26, 15; Bar 2, 16.

---

†

62, 10: The command is given to the workmen to begin the reconstruction of the city.

63, 1-6: In a dramatic dialogue between God and the prophet, the Lord is portrayed as the sole avenger of justice against his enemies.

63, 7—64, 11: A prayer probably composed toward the end of the exile, in which the prophet, after recalling God's blessings on Israel in its past history (63, 7-10), especially at the Exodus (11-14), begs the Lord to come once more to the aid of his people (63, 15—64, 3), who now humbly confess their sins (4-11).

nor Israel to acknowledge us,
You, LORD, are our father,
our redeemer you are named forever.
17 Why do you let us wander, O LORD, from your ways,
and harden our hearts so that we fear you not?
Return for the sake of your servants,
the tribes of your heritage.
18 Why have the wicked invaded your holy place,
why have our enemies trampled your sanctuary?
19 Too long have we been like those you do not rule,
who do not bear your name.

Oh, that you would rend the heavens and come down,
with the mountains quaking before you,

CHAPTER 64

1 As when brushwood is set ablaze,
or fire makes the water boil!
Thus your name would be made known to your enemies
and the nations would tremble before you,
2 While you wrought awesome deeds we could not hope for,
3* such as they had not heard of from of old.
No ear has ever heard, no eye ever seen,
any God but you
doing such deeds for those who wait for him.
4 Would that you might meet us doing right,
that we were mindful of you in our ways!
Behold, you are angry, and we are sinful;
5 all of us have become like unclean men,
all our good deeds are like polluted rags;
We have all withered like leaves,
and our guilt carries us away like the wind.
6 There is none who calls upon your name,
who rouses himself to cling to you;
For you have hidden your face from us
and have delivered us up to our guilt.
7 Yet, O LORD, you are our father;
we are the clay and you the potter:
we are all the work of your hands.
8 Be not so very angry, LORD,
keep not our guilt forever in mind;
look upon us, who are all your people.
9* Your holy cities have become a desert,
Zion is a desert, Jerusalem a waste.
10 Our holy and glorious temple
in which our fathers praised you
Has been burned with fire;
all that was dear to us is laid waste.
11 Can you hold back, O LORD, after all this?
Can you remain silent, and afflict us so severely?

CHAPTER 65

Necessity of Punishment

1* I was ready to respond to those who asked me not,
to be found by those who sought me not.
I said: Here I am! Here I am!
To a nation that did not call upon my name.

2* I have stretched out my hands all the day
to a rebellious people,
Who walk in evil paths
and follow their own thoughts,
3 People who provoke me
continually, to my face,
Offering sacrifices in the groves
and burning incense on bricks,
4 Living among the graves
and spending the night in caverns,
Eating swine's flesh,
with carrion broth in their dishes,
5† Crying out, "Hold back,
do not touch me; I am too sacred for you!"

These things enkindle my wrath,
a fire that burns all the day.
6 Lo, before me it stands written;
I will not be quiet until I have paid in full
7 Your crimes and the crimes of your fathers as well,
says the LORD.
Since they burned incense on the mountains,
and disgraced me on the hills,
I will at once pour out in full measure
their recompense into their laps.

Fate of the Good and the Bad in Israel

8 Thus says the LORD:
When the juice is pressed from grapes,

*

64, 3: 1 Cor 2, 9.
9: Ps 79, 1.
65, 1: Rom 10, 20.
2: Rom 10, 21.

†

65, 5: *I am too sacred for you:* the uncleanness of pork, obvious to a Semite, is what these people claim has made them sacred! The prophet ridicules them. Some translate: "I will render you sacred," and understand this as referring to the concept of sacredness as something contagious.

ISAIAH

men say, "Do not discard them,
for there is still good in them";
Thus will I do with my servants:
I will not discard them all;
9 From Jacob I will save offspring,
from Judah, those who are to inherit my mountains;
My chosen ones shall inherit the land,
my servants shall dwell there.
10 Sharon shall be a pasture for the flocks
and the valley of Achor a resting place for the cattle
of my people who have sought me.

11† But you who forsake the LORD,
forgetting my holy mountain,
You who spread a table for Fortune
and fill cups of blended wine for Destiny,
12* You I will destine for the sword;
you shall all go down in slaughter.
Since I called and you did not answer,
I spoke and you did not listen,
But did what was evil in my sight
and preferred things which displease me,
13 therefore thus says the Lord GOD:
Lo, my servants shall eat,
but you shall go hungry;
My servants shall drink,
but you shall be thirsty;
My servants shall rejoice,
but you shall be put to shame;
14 My servants shall shout
for joy of heart,
But you shall cry out for grief of heart
and howl for anguish of spirit.
15 The Lord GOD shall slay you,
and the name you leave
Shall be used by my chosen ones for cursing;
but my servants shall be called by another name
16 By which he will be blessed
on whom a blessing is invoked in the land;
He who takes an oath in the land
shall swear by the God of truth;
For the hardships of the past shall be forgotten,
and hidden from my eyes.

The World Renewed

17* Lo, I am about to create new heavens
and a new earth;
The things of the past shall not be remembered
or come to mind.
18 Instead, there shall always be rejoicing and happiness
in what I create;
For I create Jerusalem to be a joy
and its people to be a delight;
19 I will rejoice in Jerusalem
and exult in my people.
No longer shall the sound of weeping be heard there,
or the sound of crying;
20 No longer shall there be in it
an infant who lives but a few days,
or an old man who does not round out his full lifetime;
He dies a mere youth who reaches but a hundred years,
and he who fails of a hundred shall be thought accursed.

21 They shall live in the houses they build,
and eat the fruit of the vineyards they plant;
22 They shall not build houses for others to live in,
or plant for others to eat.
As the years of a tree, so the years of my people;
and my chosen ones shall long enjoy
the produce of their hands.
23 They shall not toil in vain,
nor beget children for sudden destruction;
For a race blessed by the LORD
are they and their offspring.
24 Before they call, I will answer;
while they are yet speaking, I will hearken to them.
25*†The wolf and the lamb shall graze alike,
and the lion shall eat hay like the ox
[but the serpent's food shall be dust].
None shall hurt or destroy
on all my holy mountain, says the LORD.

CHAPTER 66

True and False Worship

1* Thus says the LORD:
The heavens are my throne,
the earth is my footstool.
What kind of house can you build for me;
what is to be my resting place?
2 My hand made all these things
when all of them came to be, says the LORD.

*

12: 66, 4; Prv 1, 24; Jer 7, 13.
17: 66, 22; Rv 21, 1.
25: 11, 6-9.
66, 1: 2 Sm 7, 4ff; 1 Kgs 8, 27; Acts 7, 49; 17, 24.

†

65, 11f: *Destiny:* the Hebrew also has a play on the words: *Destiny* and *destine; menî* and *manîthî.*
65, 25: See note on 11, 6-9.

This is the one whom I approve:
the lowly and afflicted man who trembles at my word.

3* Merely slaughtering an ox is like slaying a man;
sacrificing a lamb, like breaking a dog's neck;
Bringing a cereal offering, like offering swine's blood;
burning incense, like paying homage to an idol.
Since these have chosen their own ways
and taken pleasure in their own abominations,
4*† I in turn will choose ruthless treatment for them
and bring upon them what they fear.

Because, when I called, no one answered,
when I spoke, no one listened;
Because they did what was evil in my sight,
and chose what gave me displeasure,
5 Hear the word of the LORD,
you who tremble at his word:
Your brethren who, because of my name,
hate and reject you, say,
"Let the LORD show his glory
that we may see your joy";
but they shall be put to shame.
6* A sound of roaring from the city,
a sound from the temple,
The sound of the LORD
repaying his enemies their deserts!

Mother Zion

7*† Before she comes to labor,
she gives birth;
Before the pains come upon her,
she safely delivers a male child.
8 Who ever heard of such a thing,
or saw the like?
Can a country be brought forth in one day,
or a nation be born in a single moment?
Yet Zion is scarcely in labor
when she gives birth to her children.
9 Shall I bring a mother to the point of birth,
and yet not let her child be born?
says the LORD;
Or shall I who allow her to conceive,
yet close her womb? says your God.

10 Rejoice with Jerusalem and be glad because of her,
all you who love her;
Exult, exult with her,
all you who were mourning over her!
11 Oh, that you may suck fully
of the milk of her comfort,
That you may nurse with delight
at her abundant breasts!
12 For thus says the LORD:
Lo, I will spread prosperity over her like a river,
and the wealth of the nations like an overflowing torrent.
As nurslings, you shall be carried in her arms,
and fondled in her lap;
13 As a mother comforts her son,
so will I comfort you;
in Jerusalem you shall find your comfort.
14 When you see this, your heart shall rejoice,
and your bodies flourish like the grass;
The LORD's power shall be known to his servants,
but to his enemies, his wrath.
15 Lo, the LORD shall come in fire,
his chariots like the whirlwind,
To wreak his wrath with burning heat
and his punishment with fiery flames.
16 For the LORD shall judge all mankind
by fire and sword.
and many shall be slain by the LORD.

17* They who sanctify and purify
themselves to go to the groves, as follow-
ers of one who stands within, they who
eat swine's flesh, loathsome things and
mice, shall all perish with their deeds
and their thoughts, says the LORD.
Gathering of the Nations. 18† I come
to gather nations of every language;
they shall come and see my glory. 19 I
will set a sign among them; from them
I will send fugitives to the nations: to
Tarshish, Put and Lud, Mosoch, Tubal
and Javan, to the distant coastlands that
have never heard of my fame, or seen
my glory; and they shall proclaim my
glory among the nations. 20 They shall
bring all your brethren from all the na-
tions as an offering to the LORD, on
horses and in chariots, in carts, upon
mules and dromedaries, to Jerusalem,
my holy mountain, says the LORD, just

ISAIAH

*

3: Lv 11, 7.
4: 65, 12; Prv 1, 24; Jer 7, 13.
6: Jl 4, 16; Am 1, 2.
7-9: 49, 18-21; 54, 1.
17: Lv 11, 29.

†

66, 4f: Worship which is merely external is as evil as though it were idolatry.
66, 7-9: The absence of labor in Zion's childbearing is a symbol of the joyful begetting of the new people of God.
66, 18-21: God summons the neighboring nations to Zion and from among them will send some to far distant lands to proclaim his glory. *All your brethren:* Jews in exile.

as the Israelites bring their offering to
the house of the LORD in clean vessels.
21 Some of these I will take as priests and
Levites, says the LORD.

Lasting Reward and Punishment

22* As the new heavens and the new earth
which I will make
Shall endure before me, says the LORD,
so shall your race and your name endure.
23 From one new moon to another,
and from one sabbath to another,
All mankind shall come to worship
before me, says the LORD.
24*† They shall go out and see the corpses
of the men who rebelled against me;
Their worm shall not die,
nor their fire be extinguished;
and they shall be abhorrent to all mankind.

* 22: 65, 17; Rv 21, 1. 24: Mk 9, 45.

† 66, 24: God's enemies lie dead outside the walls of the New Jerusalem; just as in the past, corpses, filth and refuse lay in the Valley of Hinnom outside the city, where huge fires were constantly burning; cf Jos 15, 8; 2 Chr 28, 3; Mk 9, 45-48.

ISAIAH

The Book of

JEREMIAH

The Book of Jeremiah combines history, biography, and prophecy. It portrays a nation in crisis and introduces the reader to an extraordinary leader upon whom the Lord placed the heavy burden of the prophetic office. Jeremiah was born about 650 B.C. of a priestly family from the little village of Anathoth, near Jerusalem. While still very young he was called to his task in the thirteenth year of King Josiah (628), whose reform, begun with enthusiasm and hope, ended with his death on the battlefield of Megiddo (609) as he attempted to stop the northward march of the Egyptian Pharaoh Neco.

The prophet heartily supported the reform of the pious King Josiah, which began in 629 B.C. Nineveh, the capital of Assyria, fell in 612, preparing the way for the new colossus, Babylon, which was soon to put an end to Judean independence.

After the death of Josiah the old idolatry returned. Jeremiah opposed it with all his strength. Arrest, imprisonment, and public disgrace were his lot. Jeremiah saw in the nation's impenitence the sealing of its doom. Nebuchadnezzar captured Jerusalem and carried King Jehoiachin into exile (22, 24).

During the years 598-587, Jeremiah attempted to counsel Zedekiah in the face of bitter opposition. The false prophet Hananiah proclaimed that the yoke of Babylon was broken and a strong pro-Egyptian party in Jerusalem induced Zedekiah to revolt. Nebuchadnezzar took swift and terrible vengeance; Jerusalem was destroyed in 587 and its leading citizens sent into exile. About this time Jeremiah uttered the great oracle of the "New Covenant" (31, 31-34) sometimes called "The Gospel before the Gospel." This passage contains his most sublime teaching and is a landmark in Old Testament theology.

The prophet remained amidst the ruins of Jerusalem, but was later forced into Egyptian exile by a band of conspirators. There, according to an old tradition, he was murdered by his own countrymen. The influence of Jeremiah was greater after his death than before. The exiled community read and meditated on the lessons of the prophet, and his influence can be seen in Ezekiel, certain of the psalms, and the second part of Isaiah. Shortly after the exile, the Book of Jeremiah as we have it today was published in a final edition. It is divided as follows:

I: Oracles in the Days of Josiah (1, 1—6, 30)
II: Oracles Mostly in the Days of Jehoiakim (7, 1—20, 18)
III: Oracles in the Last Years of Jerusalem (21, 1—33, 26)
IV: Fall of Jerusalem (34, 1—45, 5)
V: Oracles against the Nations (46, 1—51, 64)
VI: Historical Appendix (52, 1-34)

I: ORACLES IN THE DAYS OF JOSIAH

CHAPTER 1

1† The words of Jeremiah, son of Hil-
kiah, of a priestly family in Anathoth,
in the land of Benjamin. 2* The word of
the LORD first came to him in the days
of Josiah, son of Amon, king of Judah,
in the thirteenth year of his reign,
3*† and continued through the reign of
Jehoiakim, son of Josiah, king of Judah,
and until the downfall and exile of Jeru-
salem in the fifth month of the eleventh
year of Zedekiah, son of Josiah, king of
Judah.

Call of Jeremiah

4 The word of the LORD came to me
thus:

* 1, 2: 25, 3. 3: 25, 1.

† 1, 1: *Anathoth:* a village about three miles northeast of Jerusalem, where Solomon exiled Abiathar (1 Kgs 2, 26f); it is probable that Jeremiah belonged to the *priestly family* of Abiathar.

1, 3: *Until the downfall:* these words were originally prefixed as a title to a collection of Jeremiah's prophecies which lacked chapters 40-44. The new title in 40, 1 and the oracles that follow clearly show that Jeremiah continued to prophesy after the destruction of Jerusalem in 587 B.C.

5*† Before I formed you in the womb I knew you,
before you were born I dedicated you,
a prophet to the nations I appointed you.
6† "Ah, Lord GOD!" I said,
"I know not how to speak; I am too young."

7 But the LORD answered me,

Say not, "I am too young."
To whomever I send you, you shall go;
whatever I command you, you shall speak.
8 Have no fear before them,
because I am with you to deliver you, says the LORD.

9* Then the LORD extended his hand and touched my mouth, saying,

See, I place my words in your mouth!
10 This day I set you
over nations and over kingdoms,
To root up and to tear down,
to destroy and to demolish,
to build and to plant.

11† The word of the LORD came to me
with the question: What do you see, Jere-
miah? "I see a branch of the watching-
tree," I replied. 12 Then the LORD said
to me: Well have you seen, for I am
watching to fulfill my word. 13*† A sec-
ond time the word of the LORD came to
me with the question: What do you see?
"I see a boiling cauldron," I replied,
"that appears from the north."
14* And from the north, said the LORD
to me, evil will boil over upon all who
dwell in the land.

15* Lo, I am summoning
all the kingdoms of the north, says the LORD;
Each king shall come and set up his throne
at the gateways of Jerusalem,
Opposite her walls all around
and opposite all the cities of Judah.
16* I will pronounce my sentence against them
for all their wickedness in forsaking me,
And in burning incense to strange gods
and adoring their own handiwork.

17 But do you gird your loins;
stand up and tell them
all that I command you.
Be not crushed on their account,
as though I would leave you crushed before them;
18* For it is I this day
who have made you a fortified city,
A pillar of iron, a wall of brass,
against the whole land:
Against Judah's kings and princes,
against its priests and people.
19 They will fight against you, but not prevail over you,
for I am with you to deliver you, says the LORD.

CHAPTER 2

Infidelity of Israel

1† This word of the LORD came to me:
2*† Go, cry out this message for Jerusa-
lem to hear!

I remember the devotion of your youth,
how you loved me as a bride,
Following me in the desert,
in a land unsown.
3*† Sacred to the LORD was Israel,
the first fruits of his harvest;
Should anyone presume to partake of them,
evil would befall him, says the LORD.

4 Listen to the word of the LORD, O house of Jacob!
All you clans of the house of Israel,
5* thus says the LORD:
What fault did your fathers find in me

*

5: 49, 1; Gal 1, 15f.
9: Is 6, 7.
13: Ez 11, 3.7; 24, 3.
14: 4, 6; 6, 1.
15: 6, 22.
16: Is 2, 8.
18: 6, 27; 15, 20; Ez 3, 8.
2, 2: Dt 2, 7; 32, 9-12; Mi 6, 4.
3: 12, 14; Ex 4, 22; Dt 7, 6; 14, 2.
5: Is, 5, 4; Mi 6, 3.

†

1, 5: Jeremiah was destined to the office of prophet before his birth; cf Is 49, 1.5; Lk 1, 15; Gal 1, 15f. *I knew you:* I loved you and chose you. *I dedicated you:* I set you apart to be a prophet. Some Fathers and later theologians understand this to mean that Jeremiah was freed from original sin before his birth. The context does not justify this conclusion. *The nations:* the pagan neighbors of Judah, besides the great world powers—Assyria, Babylonia, Egypt—intimately associated with Judah's destiny.

1, 6: *I am too young:* Jeremiah's youth (he was less than thirty years old) must not be an obstacle to the responsibilities of the prophetic office; God will supply for his human defects (cf vv 7f).

1, 11: *The watching-tree:* the almond tree, which is the first to blossom in the springtime as though it had not slept. The Hebrew name contains a play on words with "I am watching."

1, 13: *Boiling cauldron . . . the north:* symbol of an invasion from the north; cf vv 14f.

2, 1—3, 5: These verses probably contain the earliest of Jeremiah's preachings. The covenant relationship, symbolized by the figure of a marriage, was frequently broken by Israel, seen here as an unfaithful wife unworthy of reconciliation with God (3, 1-5).

2, 2: *Devotion:* Israel's gratitude, fidelity, and love for God.

2, 3: *First fruits:* an offering to God which became his exclusive property, and could therefore not be put to profane use; cf Lv 22, 1.

that they withdrew from me,
Went after empty idols,
and became empty themselves?
6* They did not ask, "Where is the LORD
who brought us up from the land of Egypt,
Who led us through the desert,
through a land of wastes and gullies,
Through a land of drought and darkness,
through a land which no one crosses,
where no man dwells?"

7* When I brought you into the garden land
to eat its goodly fruits,
You entered and defiled my land,
you made my heritage loathsome.
8*† The priests asked not,
"Where is the LORD?"
Those who dealt with the law knew me not:
the shepherds rebelled against me.
The prophets prophesied by Baal,
and went after useless idols.
9* Therefore will I yet accuse you, says the LORD,
and even your children's children I will accuse.
10† Pass over to the coast of the Kittim and see,
send to Kedar and carefully inquire:
Where has the like of this been done?
11* Does any other nation change its gods?—
yet they are not gods at all!
But my people have changed their glory
for useless things.
12 Be amazed at this, O heavens,
and shudder with sheer horror, says the LORD.
13* Two evils have my people done:
they have forsaken me, the source of living waters;
They have dug themselves cisterns,
broken cisterns, that hold no water.

14† Is Israel a slave, a bondman by birth?
Why then has he become booty?
15* Against him lions roar
full-throated cries.
They have made his land a waste;
his cities are charred ruins, without inhabitant.
16† Yes, the people of Memphis and Tahpanhes
shave the crown of your head.
17* Has not the forsaking of the LORD, your God,
done this to you?
18† And now, why go to Egypt,
to drink the waters of the Nile?
Why go to Assyria,
to drink the waters of the Euphrates?
19* Your own wickedness chastises you,
your own infidelities punish you.
Know then, and see, how evil and bitter
is your forsaking the LORD, your God,
And showing no fear of me,
says the Lord, the GOD of hosts.

20*† Long ago you broke your yoke,
you tore off your bonds.
"I will not serve," you said.
On every high hill, under every green tree,
you gave yourself to harlotry.
21* I had planted you, a choice vine
of fully tested stock;
How could you turn out obnoxious to me,
a spurious vine?
22* Though you scour it with soap,
and use much lye,
The stain of your guilt is still before me,
says the Lord GOD.
23† How can you say, "I am not defiled,
I have not gone after the Baals"?
Consider your conduct in the Valley,
recall what you have done:
A frenzied she-camel, coursing near and far,
24 breaking away toward the desert,
Snuffing the wind in her ardor—
who can restrain her lust?

*

6: Ex 20, 2f; Dt 8, 14; Is 63, 11ff.
7: Lv 18, 24f; Dt 8, 7-10; 32, 13f.
8: 8, 8ff; 23, 1.13.
9: Ex 20, 5.
11: 16, 20; Ps 106, 20.
13: 17, 13; Ps 36, 9; Is 1, 4.
15: 9, 11.
17: 4, 18; 30, 15.
19: Prv 5, 22; Hos 5, 5.
20: 3, 6.13; Jgs 10, 6.
21: Ex 15, 17; Ps 80, 9; Is 5, 4.
22: Jb 9, 30.

†

2, 8: *Those who dealt with the law:* the priests. *The shepherds:* the kings and nobles.

2, 10: *Kittim:* a Phoenician colony in Cyprus. *Kedar:* a nomad tribe of the Syrian desert. These two names represent West and East.

2, 14: *Bondman by birth:* a perpetual slave, different from the debt-slave, who was to be freed after six years; cf Ex 21, 2.

2, 16: *Memphis:* the capital of Lower Egypt. *Tahpanhes:* A frontier city of Egypt, east of the Delta. *Shave the crown of your head:* the spoilation of Judah at the hands of the Egyptians.

2, 18: *Egypt* and *Assyria* were the protecting foreign powers favored by rival parties within Judah. The desire for such foreign alliances is a further desertion of the Lord, *the source of living waters* (v 13), in favor of the above-named powers, symbolized by *the Nile* and *the Euphrates* rivers.

2, 20: *Harlotry:* idolatry (because Israel is the bride of God).

2, 23: *The Valley:* of Ben-hinnom, south of Jerusalem, site of the infamous sanctuary of Topheth where children were sacrificed to Molech; cf 7, 31.

No beasts need tire themselves
seeking her;
in her month they will meet her.

25* Stop wearing out your shoes
and parching your throat!
But you say, "No use! no!
I love these strangers,
and after them I must go."
26* As the thief is shamed when caught,
so shall the house of Israel be
shamed:
They, their kings and their princes,
their priests and their prophets;
27 They who say to a piece of wood,
"You are my father,"
and to a stone, "You gave me
birth."
They turn to me their backs, not
their faces;
yet, in their time of trouble they
cry out,
"Rise up and save us!"
28* Where are the gods you made for
yourselves?
Let them rise up!
Will they save you in your time
of trouble?
For as numerous as your cities
are your gods, O Judah!
And as many as the streets of Jerusalem
are the altars you have set up for
Baal.

29 How dare you still plead with me?
You have all rebelled against me,
says the LORD.
30* In vain I struck your children;
the correction they did not take.
Your sword devoured your prophets
like a ravening lion.
31 You, of this generation,
take note of the word of the Lord:
Have I been a desert to Israel,
a land of darkness?
Why do my people say, "We have
moved on,
we will come to you no more"?
32* Does a virgin forget her jewelry,
a bride her sash?
Yet my people have forgotten me
days without number.

33 How well you pick your way
when seeking love!
You who, in your wickedness,
have gone by ways unclean!
34 You, on whose clothing there is
the life-blood of the innocent,
whom you found committing no
burglary;
35 Yet withal you say, "I am innocent;
at least, his anger is turned away
from me."
Behold, I will judge you
on that word of yours, "I have not
sinned."

36* How very base you have become
in changing your course!
By Egypt will you be shamed,
as you were shamed by Assyria.
37* From there also shall you go away
with hands upon your head;
For the LORD has rejected those in
whom you trust,
with them you will have no success.

CHAPTER 3

1*† If a man sends away his wife
and, after leaving him,
she marries another man,
Does the first husband come back
to her?
Would not the land be wholly defiled?
But you have sinned with many lovers,
and yet you would return to me!
says the LORD.

2*† Lift your eyes to the heights, and
see,
where have men not lain with
you?
By the waysides you waited for them
like an Arab in the desert.
You defiled the land
by your wicked harlotry.
3* Therefore the showers were withheld,
the spring rain failed.
But because you have a harlot's
brow,
you refused to blush.

4 Even now do you not call me, "My
father,
you who are the bridegroom of my
youth"?
5 "Will he keep his wrath forever,
will he hold his grudge to the
end?"
This is what you say; yet you do
all the evil you can.

Judah and Israel. 6* The LORD said to
me in the days of King Josiah: See now
what rebellious Israel has done! She has
gone up every high mountain, and under

---

*

25: 18, 12.
26: 48, 27; Rom 6, 21.
28: 11, 13; Dt 32, 38; Jgs 10, 14.
30: 5, 3; Neh 9, 26.
32: 13, 25; Dt 32, 18.
36: 2 Chr 28, 16-21.
37: 2 Sm 13, 19.
3, 1: Dt 24, 1-4.
2: Ez 16, 24f.
3: 6, 15; 8, 12.
6: 2, 20; Dt 12, 2.

---

†

3, 1: Such remarriage of divorced spouses was forbidden by Dt 24, 1-4. Under this figure the prophet sees the presumption of Judah, the unfaithful spouse, who thinks she can return to the Lord after uniting herself to other gods.

3, 2: *An Arab:* a marauding nomad who lay in wait for caravans.

every green tree she has played the har-
lot. 7 And I thought, after she has done
all this she will return to me. But she
did not return. Then, even though her
traitor sister Judah saw 8* that for all
the adulteries rebellious Israel had com-
mitted, I put her away and gave her a
bill of divorce, nevertheless her traitor
sister Judah was not frightened; she too
went off and played the harlot. 9* Eager
to sin, she polluted the land, committing
adultery with stone and wood. 10 With all
this, the traitor sister Judah did not re-
turn to me wholeheartedly, but insin-
cerely, says the LORD.

Restoration of Israel

11* Then the LORD said to me: Rebel
Israel is inwardly more just than trai-
torous Judah. 12* Go, proclaim these
words toward the north, and say:

Return, rebel Israel, says the LORD,
I will not remain angry with you;
For I am merciful, says the LORD,
I will not continue my wrath forever.
13* Only know your guilt:
how you rebelled against the LORD, your God,
How you ran hither and yon to strangers
[under every green tree]
and would not listen to my voice, says the LORD.
14*† Return, rebellious children, says the LORD,
for I am your Master;
I will take you, one from a city, two from a clan,
and bring you to Zion.
15* I will appoint over you shepherds after my own heart,
who will shepherd you wisely and prudently.
16 When you multiply and become fruitful in the land,
says the LORD,
They will in those days no longer say,
"The ark of the covenant of the LORD!"
They will no longer think of it, or remember it,
or miss it, or make another.

17* At that time they will call Jerusa-
lem the LORD's throne; there all nations
will be gathered together to honor the
name of the LORD at Jerusalem, and
they will walk no longer in their hard-
hearted wickedness. 18* In those days
the house of Judah will join the house
of Israel; together they will come from
the land of the north to the land which
I gave to your fathers as a heritage.

Conditions for Forgiveness

19* I had thought:
How I should like to treat you as sons,
And give you a pleasant land,
a heritage most beautiful among the nations!
You would call me, "My Father," I thought,
and never cease following me.
20* But like a woman faithless to her lover,
even so have you been faithless to me,
O house of Israel, says the LORD.
21 A cry is heard on the heights!
the plaintive weeping of Israel's children,
Because they have perverted their ways
and forgotten the LORD, their God.
22* Return, rebellious children,
and I will cure you of your rebelling.
"Here we are, we now come to you
because you are the LORD, our God.
23* Deceptive indeed are the hills,
the thronging mountains;
In the LORD, our God, alone
is the salvation of Israel.
24† The shame-god has devoured
our fathers' toil from our youth,
Their sheep and their cattle,
their sons and their daughters.
25* Let us lie down in our shame,
let our disgrace cover us,
for we have sinned against the LORD, our God,
From our youth to this day, we and our fathers also;
we listened not to the voice of the LORD, our God."

CHAPTER 4

1* If you wish to return, O Israel, says the LORD,
return to me.

JEREMIAH

*

8: 2 Kgs 17, 6.18-23; Ez 23, 11.
9: 2, 27.
11: Ez 16, 51; 23, 11.
12: Dt 4, 29ff.
13: 2, 20.25; Lv 26, 40.
14: 23, 3; Is 10, 21f.
15: Ez 34, 23; Jn 21, 15.
17: Is 2, 2.
18: 30, 3; 31, 8.
19: 31, 9.20; Is 63, 16.
20: 5, 11.
22: Hos 3, 5.
23: 14, 8.
25: 16, 11f; 22, 21.
4, 1: 25, 5.

†

3, 14-18: A remnant of Israel (14) will reunite with Judah (18). The elementary cult of the Lord represented by *the ark of the covenant* will now be replaced by a more deeply spiritual and universal alliance, symbolized by his throne in the ideal Jerusalem around which *all nations will be gathered together* (17).

3, 24: *Shame-god:* literally, shame, a term commonly substituted for Baal, the Canaanite god with many local shrines.

If you put your detestable things out
of my sight,
and do not stray,
2*† Then you can swear, "As the LORD
lives,"
in truth, in judgment, and in justice;
Then shall the nations use his name
in blessing,
and glory in him.

3* For to the men of Judah and to Jerusalem, thus says the LORD:

Till your untilled ground,
sow not among thorns.
4*† For the sake of the LORD, be circumcised,
remove the foreskins of your
hearts,
O men of Judah and citizens of Jerusalem;
Lest my anger break out like fire,
and burn till none can quench it,
because of your evil deeds.

The Invasion from the North

5 Proclaim it in Judah,
make it heard in Jerusalem;
Blow the trumpet through the land,
summon the recruits!
Say, "Fall in, let us march
to the fortified cities."
6 Bear the standard to Zion,
seek refuge without delay!
Evil I bring from the north,
and great destruction.
7* Up comes the lion from his lair,
the destroyer of nations has set
out,
has left his place,
To turn your land into desolation,
till your cities lie waste and empty.
8* So gird yourselves with sackcloth,
mourn and wail:
"The blazing wrath of the LORD
is not turned away from us."

9 In that day, says the LORD,
The king will lose heart, and the
princes;
the priests will be amazed,
and the prophets stunned.
10*† "Alas! Lord GOD," they will say,
"You only deceived us
When you said: Peace shall be yours;
for the sword touches our very
soul."
11 At that time it will be said
of this people and of Jerusalem,
"From the glaring heights through
the desert
a wind comes toward the daughter of my people."
Not to winnow, not to cleanse,
12* does this wind from the heights
come at my bidding;
And I myself now pronounce
sentence upon them.

13 See! like storm clouds he advances,
like a hurricane his chariots;
Swifter than eagles are his steeds:
"Woe to us! we are ruined."
14 Cleanse your heart of evil, O Jerusalem,
that you may be saved.
How long must your pernicious
thoughts
lodge within you?
15 Listen! They proclaim it from Dan,
from Mount Ephraim they announce destruction:
16* "Make this known to the nations,
announce it to Jerusalem:
The besiegers are coming from the
distant land,
shouting their war cry against the
cities of Judah."
17* Like watchmen of the fields they
surround her,
for she has rebelled against me,
says the LORD.
18* Your conduct, your misdeeds, have
done this to you;
how bitter is this disaster of yours,
how it reaches to your very heart!

19† My breast! my breast! how I suffer!
The walls of my heart!
My heart beats wildly,
I cannot be still;
For I have heard the sound of the
trumpet,
the alarm of war.
20* Ruin after ruin is reported;
the whole earth is laid waste.
In an instant my tents are ravaged;
in a flash, my shelters.
21 How long must I see that signal,
hear that trumpet sound!

22* Fools my people are,
they know me not;
Senseless children they are,
having no understanding;

*

2: 12, 16; Dt 10, 20; Is 65, 16.
3: Hos 10, 12; Mt 13, 7.22.
4: 9, 24.
7: 2, 15; 5, 6.
8: 6, 26; Is 5, 25.
10: 6, 14.
12: 1, 16.
16: 5, 15.
17: 6, 3.
18: 2, 17.19.
20: 10, 20.
22: Dt 32, 5f.28.

†

4, 2: *As the LORD lives:* this oath, made sincerely, implies Israel's return to God and loyal adherence to him. Thus the ancient promises are fulfilled; cf Gn 12, 3; 18, 18; 22, 18; 26, 4; Ps 72, 17.

4, 4: The mere external rite of circumcision avails nothing unless accompanied by the removal of blindness and obstinacy of heart; cf Rom 2, 25.29; 1 Cor 7, 19; Gal 5, 6; 6, 13.15.

4, 10: *You only deceived us:* the false prophets blame their deception on God; cf 14, 13-16.

4, 19ff: Probably the prophet's own anguish at the coming destruction of Judah.

They are wise in evil,
but know not how to do good.
23* I looked at the earth, and it was waste and void;
at the heavens, and their light had gone out!
24 I looked at the mountains, and they were trembling,
and all the hills were crumbling!
25 I looked and behold, there was no man;
even the birds of the air had flown away!
26* I looked and behold, the garden land was a desert,
with all its cities destroyed
before the LORD, before his blazing wrath.

27* For thus says the LORD:
Waste shall the whole land be;
I will [not] wholly destroy it.
28* Because of this the earth shall mourn,
the heavens above shall darken;
I have spoken, I will not repent,
I have resolved, I will not turn back.
29 At the shout of horseman and bowman
each city takes to flight;
They shrink into the thickets,
they scale the rocks:
All the cities are abandoned,
and no one dwells in them.
30 You now who are doomed, what do you mean
by putting on purple,
bedecking yourself with gold,
Shading your eyes with cosmetics,
beautifying yourself in vain?
Your lovers spurn you,
they seek your life.
31* Yes, I hear the moaning, as of a woman in travail,
like the anguish of a mother with her first child—
The cry of daughter Zion gasping,
as she stretches forth her hands:
"Ah, woe is me! I sink exhausted
before the slayers!"

CHAPTER 5

Universal Corruption

1 Roam the streets of Jerusalem,
look about and observe,
Search through her public places,
to find even one
Who lives uprightly
and seeks to be faithful,
and I will pardon her!
2 Though they say, "As the LORD lives,"
they swear falsely.
3* O LORD, do your eyes not look for honesty?
You struck them, but they did not cringe;
you laid them low, but they refused correction;
They set their faces harder than stone,
and refused to return to you.
4* It is only the lowly, I thought,
who are foolish;
For they know not the way of the LORD,
their duty to their God.
5* I will go to the great ones
and speak with them;
For they know the way of the LORD,
their duty to their God.
But, one and all, they had broken the yoke,
torn off the harness.
6 Therefore lions from the forest slay them,
wolves of the desert ravage them,
Leopards keep watch round their cities:
all who come out are torn to pieces
For their many crimes
and their numerous rebellions.

7 Why should I pardon you these things?
Your sons have forsaken me,
they swear by gods that are not.
I fed them, but they committed adultery;
to the harlot's house they throng.
8* Lustful stallions they are,
each neighs after another's wife.
9 Shall I not punish them for these things?
says the LORD;
On a nation such as this shall I not take vengeance?
10* Climb to her terraces, and ravage them,
destroy them [not] wholly.
Tear away her tendrils,
they do not belong to the LORD.
11* For they have openly rebelled against me,
both the house of Israel and the house of Judah,
says the LORD.
12*†They denied the LORD,
saying, "Not he—
No evil shall befall us,
neither sword nor famine shall we see.
13 The prophets have become wind,
and the word is not in them.

JEREMIAH

*

23: Is 24, 1.3.
26: Lv 26, 31.
27: 5, 18.
28: Is 24, 4.
31: 6, 24.
5, 3: 2, 30.
4: 8, 7.
5: 6, 13.
8: 13, 27.
10: 2, 21.
11: 3, 20.
12: 14, 13; Is 28, 15.

†

5, 12: *They denied the LORD:* the people act as though God does not exist and will not interfere.

May their threats be carried out
against themselves!"

14 Now, for this that you have said,
says the LORD, the God of hosts—
Behold, I make my words
in your mouth, a fire,
And this people is the wood
that it shall devour!—
15* Beware, I will bring against you
a nation from afar,
O house of Israel, says the LORD;
A long-lived nation, an ancient nation,
a people whose language you know not,
whose speech you cannot understand.
16 Their quivers are like open graves;
all of them are warriors.
17* They will devour your harvest and your bread,
devour your sons and your daughters,
Devour your sheep and cattle,
devour your vines and fig trees;
They will beat flat with the sword
the fortified city in which you trust.

18* Yet even in those days, says the
LORD, I will not wholly destroy you.
19 And when they ask, "Why has the
LORD done all these things to us?" say
to them, "As you have forsaken me to
serve strange gods in your own land, so
shall you serve strangers in a land not
your own."

20 Announce this to the house of Jacob,
proclaim it in Judah:
21* Pay attention to this,
foolish and senseless people
Who have eyes and see not,
who have ears and hear not.
22* Should you not fear me, says the LORD,
should you not tremble before me?
I made the sandy shore the sea's limit,
which by eternal decree it may not overstep.
Toss though it may, it is to no avail;
though its billows roar, they cannot pass.
23 But this people's heart is stubborn
and rebellious;
they turn and go away,
24*† And say not in their hearts,
"Let us fear the LORD, our God,
Who gives us rain
early and late, in its time;
Who watches for us
over the appointed weeks of harvest."
25* Your crimes have prevented these things,
your sins have turned back these
blessings from you.
26* For there are among my people
criminals;
like fowlers they set traps,
but it is men they catch.
27 Their houses are as full of treachery
as a bird-cage is of birds;
Therefore they grow powerful and rich,
28* fat and sleek.
They go their wicked way;
justice they do not defend
By advancing the claim of the fatherless
or judging the cause of the poor.
29 Shall I not punish these things? says
the LORD;
on a nation such as this shall I not
take vengeance?
30 A shocking, horrible thing
has happened in the land:
31* The prophets prophesy falsely,
and the priests teach as they wish;
Yet my people will have it so;
what will you do when the end comes?

CHAPTER 6

The Enemy at the Gates

1* Flee, sons of Benjamin,
out of Jerusalem!
Blow the trumpet in Tekoa,
raise a signal over Beth-haccherem;
For evil threatens from the north,
and mighty destruction.
2 O lovely and delicate
daughter Zion, you are ruined!
3*† Against her, shepherds come with
their flocks;
all around, they pitch their tents,
each one grazes his portion.
4 "Prepare for war against her,
Up! let us rush upon her at midday!
Alas! the day is waning,
evening shadows lengthen;
5* Up! let us rush upon her by night,
destroy her palaces!"

6* For thus says the LORD of hosts:
Hew down her trees,

*

15: Dt 28, 49.
17: Dt 28, 31.
18: 4, 27.
21: Is 6, 9.
22: Jb 38, 10f.
24: Gn 8, 22; Dt 11, 14.
25: 2, 17.19.
26: Prv 1, 11.
28: 12, 1; Is 1, 23.
31: 14, 14; Mi 2, 11.
6, 1: 1, 14f.
3: 4, 17.
5: 2 Chr 36, 19.
6: 32, 24; Zep 3, 1-4.

†

5, 24: *Rain early and late:* autumn and spring rains respectively. *Appointed weeks of harvest:* the seven weeks between the Passover (Dt 16, 9f) and Pentecost, during which it ordinarily did not rain.

6, 3: *Shepherds . . . with their flocks:* foreign invaders with their armies.

throw up a siege mound against
Jerusalem.
Woe to the city marked for punishment;
nought but oppression within her!
7* As the well gushes out its waters,
so she gushes out her wickedness.
Violence and destruction resound in her;
ever before me are wounds and blows.
8 Be warned, O Jerusalem,
lest I be estranged from you;
Lest I turn you into a desert,
a land where no man dwells.

9 Thus says the LORD of hosts:
Glean, glean like a vine
the remnant of Israel;
Pass your hand, like a vintager,
repeatedly over the tendrils.
10* To whom shall I speak?
whom shall I warn, and be heard?
See! their ears are uncircumcised,
they cannot give heed;
See, the word of the LORD has become for them
an object of scorn, which they will not have.
11* Therefore my wrath brims up within me,
I am weary of holding it in;
I will pour it out upon the child in the street,
upon the young men gathered together.
Yes, all will be taken, husband and wife,
graybeard with ancient.
12* Their houses will fall to strangers,
their fields and their wives as well;
For I will stretch forth my hand
against those who dwell in this land, says the LORD.
13* Small and great alike, all are greedy for gain;
prophet and priest, all practice fraud.
14*† They would repair, as though it were nought,
the injury to my people:
"Peace, peace!" they say,
though there is no peace.
15* They are odious; they have done abominable things,
yet they are not at all ashamed,
they know not how to blush.
Hence they shall be among those who fall;
in their time of punishment they shall go down,
says the LORD.

16*† Thus says the LORD:
Stand beside the earliest roads,
ask the pathways of old
Which is the way to good, and walk it;
thus you will find rest for your souls.
But they said, "We will not walk it."
17† When I raised up watchmen for them:
"Hearken to the sound of the trumpet!"
they said, "We will not hearken."
18 Therefore hear, O nations,
and know, O earth,
what I will do with them:
19* See, I bring evil upon this people,
the fruit of their own schemes,
Because they heeded not my words,
because they despised my law.
20* Of what use to me incense that comes from Sheba,
or sweet cane from far-off lands?
Your holocausts find no favor with me,
your sacrifices please me not.
21* Therefore, thus says the LORD:
See, I will place before this people
obstacles to bring them down;
Fathers and sons alike,
neighbors and friends shall perish.

22* Thus says the LORD:
See, a people comes from the land of the north,
a great nation, roused from the ends of the earth.
23 Bow and javelin they wield;
cruel and pitiless are they.
They sound like the roaring sea
as they ride forth on steeds,
Each in his place, for battle
against you, daughter Zion.
24* We hear the report of them;
helpless fall our hands,
Anguish takes hold of us,
throes like a mother's in childbirth.
25 Go not forth into the field,
step not into the street,
Beware of the enemy's sword;
terror on every side!
26* O daughter of my people, gird on sackcloth,
roll in the ashes.

JEREMIAH

*

7: Is 57, 20.
10: 7, 26; 20, 8.
11: Ez 9, 6.
12: 8, 10; Dt 28, 30ff.
13: 8, 10; 23, 11.
14: 8, 11.
15: 3, 3; 8, 12.
16: 7, 23f; 18, 15.
19: Prv 1, 31.
20: Is 1, 11; 43, 24.
21: Is 8, 14f.
22: 1, 15; 5, 15.
24: 4, 31.
26: 25, 34; Am 8, 10.

†

6, 14: *As though it were nought:* the false assurance of well-being given by priest and prophet cannot reduce the harm which universal materialism and corruption have done to the people.

6, 16: *Earliest roads . . . pathways of old:* history and the lessons to be learned from it.

6, 17: *Watchmen:* the prophets who, like Jeremiah, had upheld God's moral law.

Mourn as for an only child
with bitter wailing,
For sudden upon us
comes the destroyer.

27* A tester among my people I have appointed you,
to search and test their way.
28 Arch-rebels are they all,
dealers in slander,
all of them corrupt.
29 The bellows roars,
the lead is consumed by the fire;
In vain has the smelter refined,
the wicked are not drawn off.
30 "Silver rejected" they shall be called,
for the LORD has rejected them.

II: ORACLES MOSTLY IN THE DAYS OF JEHOIAKIM

CHAPTER 7

The Temple Sermon. 1† The following
message came to Jeremiah from the
LORD: 2 Stand at the gate of the house
of the LORD, and there proclaim this
message: Hear the word of the LORD, all
you of Judah who enter these gates to
worship the LORD! 3* Thus says the LORD
of hosts, the God of Israel: Reform your
ways and your deeds, so that I may re-
main with you in this place. 4* Put not
your trust in the deceitful words: "This
is the temple of the LORD! The temple
of the LORD! The temple of the
LORD!" 5 Only if you thoroughly reform
your ways and your deeds; if each of you
deals justly with his neighbor; 6*† if you
no longer oppress the resident alien, the
orphan, and the widow; if you no longer
shed innocent blood in this place, or fol-
low strange gods to your own harm,
7* will I remain with you in this place,
in the land which I gave your fathers
long ago and forever.
8 But here you are, putting your trust
in deceitful words to your own loss!
9* Are you to steal and murder, commit
adultery and perjury, burn incense to
Baal, go after strange gods that you
know not, 10* and yet come to stand be-
fore me in this house which bears my
name, and say: "We are safe; we can
commit all these abominations again"?
11* Has this house which bears my name
become in your eyes a den of thieves?
I too see what is being done, says the
LORD. 12*† You may go to Shiloh, which
I made the dwelling place of my name
in the beginning. See what I did to it be-
cause of the wickedness of my people
Israel. 13 And now, because you have
committed all these misdeeds, says the
LORD, because you did not listen, though
I spoke to you untiringly; because you
did not answer, though I called you, 14* I
will do to this house named after me,
in which you trust, and to this place
which I gave to you and your fathers,
just as I did to Shiloh. 15* I will cast you
away from me, as I cast away all your
brethren, all the offspring of Ephraim.
Abuses in Worship 16* You, now, do
not intercede for this people; raise not
in their behalf a pleading prayer! Do not
urge me, for I will not listen to you. 17 Do
you not see what they are doing in the
cities of Judah, in the streets of Jerusa-
lem? 18*† The children gather wood,
their fathers light the fire, and the
women knead dough to make cakes for
the queen of heaven, while libations are
poured out to strange gods in order to
hurt me. 19* Is it I whom they hurt, says
the LORD; is it not rather themselves, to
their own confusion? 20* See now, says
the Lord GOD, my anger and my wrath
will pour out upon this place, upon man
and beast, upon the trees of the field and
the fruits of the earth; it will burn with-
out being quenched.
21 Thus says the LORD of hosts, the God
of Israel: Heap your holocausts upon
your sacrifices; eat up the flesh! 22† In
speaking to your fathers on the day I
brought them out of the land of Egypt,
I gave them no command concerning
holocaust or sacrifice. 23* This rather is
what I commanded them: Listen to my
voice; then I will be your God and you
shall be my people. Walk in all the ways
that I command you, so that you may
prosper.
24* But they obeyed not, nor did they
pay heed. They walked in the hardness
of their evil hearts and turned their
backs, not their faces, to me. 25* From
the day that your fathers left the land

*

27: 1, 18.
7, 3: 18, 11; 26, 13.
4: Mi 3, 11.
6: Ex 22, 21-24.
7: Dt 4, 40.
9: 44, 17.
10: 32, 34.
11: Mt 21, 13.
12: Jos 18, 1.
14: 26, 9.
15: 1 Kgs 9, 7; 2 Kgs 17, 23.
16: 11, 14; 14, 11.
18: 44, 17.19.
19: Jb 35, 6.
20: 36, 29; 2 Kgs 22, 17.
23: 11, 4; Lv 26, 3.12.
24: 17, 23.
25: 2 Chr 36, 15f; Bar 1, 19.

†

7, 1-15: *The temple of the LORD* will not serve as a place of refuge for the Jews against their enemies if they fail to reform their evil ways.

7, 6: *The resident alien:* specially protected by law; cf Ex 20, 10; Nm 9, 14; 15, 14; Dt 5, 14; 28, 43.

7, 12: *Shiloh:* original place of worship from the time of Joshua to that of Samuel. The sanctuary was later rejected by God and destroyed by the Philistines; cf 1 Sm 1, 9; 4, 3f; Ps 78, 60.68f.

7, 18: *Queen of heaven:* the Assyro-Babylonian Ishtar, goddess of fertility, whose worship was introduced under King Manasseh and was revived after Josiah's death. Cakes shaped like stars (Ishtar was identified with the planet Venus) were offered in her honor.

7, 22: *I gave them no command:* right conduct rather than mere external cult was God's will concerning his people (v 23).

of Egypt even to this day, I have sent
you untiringly all my servants the
prophets. 26* Yet they have not obeyed
me nor paid heed; they have stiffened
their necks and done worse than their
fathers. 27 When you speak all these
words to them, they will not listen to you
either; when you call to them, they will
not answer you. 28 Say to them: This is
the nation which does not listen to the
voice of the LORD, its God, or take cor-
rection. Faithfulness has disappeared;
the word itself is banished from their
speech.

29*†Cut off your dedicated hair and
throw it away!
on the heights intone an elegy;
For the LORD has rejected and cast
off
the generation that draws down
his wrath.

30* The people of Judah have done
what is evil in my eyes, says the LORD.
They have defiled the house which bears
my name by setting up in it their abomi-
nable idols. 31 In the Valley of Ben-hin-
nom they have built the high place of
Topheth to immolate in fire their sons
and their daughters, such a thing as I
never commanded or had in mind.
32* Therefore, beware! days will come,
says the LORD, when Topheth and the
Valley of Ben-hinnom will no longer be
called such, but rather the Valley of
Slaughter. For lack of space, Topheth
will be a burial place. 33* The corpses of
this people will be food for the birds of
the sky and for the beasts of the field,
which no one will drive away. 34* In the
cities of Judah and in the streets of Jeru-
salem I will silence the cry of joy, the
cry of gladness, the voice of the bride-
groom and the voice of the bride; for the
land will be turned to rubble.

CHAPTER 8

1* At that time, says the LORD, the
bones of the kings and princes of Judah,
the bones of the priests and the prophets,
and the bones of the citizens of Jerusa-
lem will be emptied out of their graves
2*† and spread out before the sun and
the moon and the whole army of heaven,
which they loved and served, which they
followed, consulted, and worshiped.
They will not be gathered up for burial,
but will lie like dung upon the ground.
3 Death will be preferred to life by all
the survivors of this wicked race who
remain in any of the places to which I
banish them, says the LORD of hosts.

Israel's Conduct Incomprehensible

4 Tell them: Thus says the LORD:
When someone falls, does he not rise
again?
if he goes astray, does he not turn
back?
5* Why do these people rebel
with obstinate resistance?
Why do they cling to deceptive idols,
refuse to turn back?
6* I listen closely:
they speak what is not true;
No one repents of his wickedness,
saying, "What have I done!"
Everyone keeps on running his
course,
like a steed dashing into battle.
7* Even the stork in the air
knows it seasons;
Turtledove, swallow and thrush
observe their time of return,
But my people do not know
the ordinance of the LORD.

8*† How can you say, "We are wise,
we have the law of the LORD"?
Why, that has been changed into
falsehood
by the lying pen of the scribes!
9* The wise are confounded,
dismayed and ensnared;
Since they have rejected the word
of the LORD,
of what avail is their wisdom?

Shameless in Their Crimes

10* Therefore, I will give their wives to
strangers,
their fields to spoilers.
Small and great alike, all are greedy
for gain,
prophet and priest, all practice
fraud.
11*†They would repair, as though it were
nought,
the injury to the daughter of my
people:
"Peace, peace!" they say,
though there is no peace.
12* They are odious; they have done
abominable things,

*

26: 19, 15; 2 Chr 30, 8.
29: 9, 17-21.
30: 32, 34.
32: 19, 6; 32, 35.
33: 16, 4; 34, 20.
34: 16, 9.
8, 1: Bar 2, 24.
2: Dt 4, 19.
5: 5, 3; 7, 24.26.
6: Jb 34, 31f.
7: Is 1, 3.
8: Mal 2, 8; Rom 2, 17-23.
9: 1 Cor 3, 20.
10: 6, 13; Dt 28, 30.
11: 6, 14.
12: 6, 15.

†

7, 29: *Dedicated hair:* the unshorn hair of the nazirite, regarded as sacred because of a vow, temporary or permanent, to abstain from cutting or shaving the hair, from contact with a corpse, and from all products of the vine; cf Nm 6, 4-8. The cutting of this hair was a sign of extreme mourning.

8, 2: *Army of heaven:* the stars, worshiped by the pagan nations and even by the inhabitants of Jerusalem during the reigns of Manasseh and Amon.

8, 8f: *Lying pen of the scribes:* because the interpretations and ordinances of the scribes ran counter to the *word of the Lord.*

8, 11: *Daughter of my people:* the people itself personified as a woman.

yet they are not at all ashamed,
they know not how to blush.
Hence they shall be among those who fall;
in their time of punishment they shall go down,
says the LORD.

Threats of Punishment

13 I will gather them all in, says the LORD:
no grapes on the vine,
No figs on the fig trees,
foliage withered!
14* Why do we remain here?
Let us form ranks and enter the walled cities,
to perish there;
For the LORD has wrought our destruction,
he has given us poison to drink,
because we have sinned against the LORD.
15* We wait for peace to no avail;
for a time of healing, but terror comes instead.
16 From Dan is heard
the snorting of his steeds;
The neighing of his stallions
shakes the whole land.
They come devouring the land and all it contains,
the city and those who dwell in it.
17* Yes, I will send against you
poisonous snakes,
Against which no charm will work
when they bite you, says the LORD.

The Prophet's Grief over the People's Suffering

18 My grief is incurable,
my heart within me is faint.
19* Listen! the cry of the daughter of my people,
far and wide in the land!
Is the LORD no longer in Zion,
is her King no longer in her midst?
[Why do they provoke me with their idols,
with their foreign nonentities?]
20 "The harvest has passed, the summer is at an end,
and yet we are not safe!"
21* I am broken by the ruin of the daughter of my people.
I am disconsolate; horror has seized me.
22*†Is there no balm in Gilead,
no physician there?
Why grows not new flesh
over the wound of the daughter of my people?
23 Oh, that my head were a spring of water,
my eyes a fountain of tears,
That I might weep day and night
over the slain of the daughter of my people!

CHAPTER 9

The Corruption of the People

1 Would that I had in the desert
a travelers' lodge!
That I might leave my people
and depart from them.
They are all adulterers,
a faithless band.
2 They ready their tongues like a drawn bow;
with lying, and not with truth,
they hold forth in the land.
They go from evil to evil,
but me they know not, says the LORD.
3† Be on your guard, everyone against his neighbor;
put no trust in any brother.
Every brother apes Jacob, the supplanter,
every friend is guilty of slander.
4* Each one deceives the other,
no one speaks the truth.
They have accustomed their tongues to lying,
and are perverse, and cannot repent.
5 Violence upon violence,
deceit upon deceit:
They refuse to recognize me,
says the LORD.

6 Therefore, thus says the LORD of hosts:

I will smelt them and test them;
how else should I deal with their wickedness?
7* A murderous arrow is his tongue,
his mouth utters deceit;
He speaks cordially with his friends,
but in his heart he lays an ambush!
8* For these things, says the LORD,
shall I not punish them?
On a nation such as this
shall I not take vengeance?

Dirge over the Ravaged Land

9* Over the mountains, break out in cries of lamentation,
over the pasture lands, intone a dirge:

*

14: 9, 14; 23, 15.
15: 14, 19.
17: Dt 32, 24.
19: Dt 32, 21; Mi 4, 9.
21: 14, 17.
22: 46, 11.
9, 4: 12, 6.
7: Pss 28, 3; 62, 4.
8: 5, 9.29.
9: 4, 25; 12, 4.

†

8, 22: *Gilead:* noted for its healing balm but unable to heal the moral wound of the people.

9, 3: *Jacob, the supplanter:* in Hebrew, a play on words. Jacob, as his name indicates ("he supplants"), deprived his brother Esau of his birthright; cf Gn 25, 26.33.

They are scorched, and no man crosses them,
unheard is the bleat of the flock;
Birds of the air as well as beasts,
all have fled, and are gone.
10* I will turn Jerusalem into a heap of ruins,
a haunt of jackals;
The cities of Judah I will make into a waste,
where no one dwells.

11* Who is so wise that he can understand this? Let him to whom the mouth of the LORD has spoken make it known:

Why is the land ravaged,
scorched like a wasteland untraversed?

12 The LORD answered: Because they
have abandoned my law, which I set before them, and have not followed it or
listened to my voice, 13* but followed
rather the hardness of their hearts and the Baals, as their fathers had taught
them; 14* therefore, thus says the LORD
of hosts, the God of Israel: See now, I will give them wormwood to eat and poi-
son to drink. 15* I will scatter them
among nations whom neither they nor their fathers have known; I will send the sword to pursue them until I have completely destroyed them.

16 Thus says the LORD of hosts:
Attention! tell the wailing women to come,
summon the best of them;
17* Let them come quickly
and intone a dirge for us,
That our eyes may be wet with weeping,
our cheeks run with tears.
18 The dirge is heard from Zion:
Ruined we are, and greatly ashamed;
We must leave the land,
give up our homes!
19 Hear, you women, the word of the LORD,
let your ears receive his message.
Teach your daughters this dirge,
and each other this lament.
20* Death has come up through our windows,
has entered our palaces;
It cuts down the children in the street,
young people in the squares.
21 The corpses of the slain
lie like dung on a field,
Like sheaves behind the harvester,
with no one to gather them.

True Glory

22* Thus says the LORD:
Let not the wise man glory in his wisdom,
nor the strong man glory in his strength,
nor the rich man glory in his riches;
23 But rather, let him who glories, glory in this,
that in his prudence he knows me,
Knows that I, the LORD, bring about kindness,
justice and uprightness on the earth;
For with such am I pleased, says the LORD.

Circumcision Worthless. 24* See, days
are coming, says the LORD, when I will demand an account of all those circum-
cised in their flesh: 25† Egypt and Judah, Edom and the Ammonites, Moab and the desert dwellers who shave their temples. For all these nations, like the whole house of Israel, are uncircumcised in heart.

CHAPTER 10

The Folly of Idolatry

1 Hear the word which the LORD speaks to you, O house of Israel.
2*† Thus says the LORD:
Learn not the customs of the nations,
and have no fear of the signs of the heavens,
though the nations fear them.
3* For the cult idols of the nations are nothing,
wood cut from the forest,
Wrought by craftsmen with the adze,
4* adorned with silver and gold.
With nails and hammers they are fastened,
that they may not totter.
5* Like a scarecrow in a cucumber field are they,
they cannot speak;
They must be carried about,
for they cannot walk.
Fear them not, they can do no harm,
neither is it in their power to do good.

JEREMIAH

*

10: Is 13, 22.
11: Ps 107, 43; Hos 14, 10.
13: 7, 24; 19, 4f.
14: 23, 15.
15: Lv 26, 33; Dt 28, 36.64.
17: 14, 17.
20: 14, 16.
22: Prv 21, 30.
24: 4, 4.
10, 2: Bar 6, 6.
3: Wis 13, 11; Is 44, 9.
4: Is 40, 19; 41, 7.
5: Ps 115, 4-8; Bar 6, 15.

†

9, 25: *Desert dwellers . . . temples:* Arab tribesmen who cut off their hair and shaved their temples in honor of the pagan god Dushara. This was forbidden the Israelites (Lv 19, 27).

10, 2: *Signs of the heavens:* phenomena in the sky superstitiously regarded by the pagans as dire omens.

6* No one is like you, O LORD,
great are you,
great and mighty is your name.
7* Who would not fear you,
King of the nations,
for it is your due!
Among all the wisest of the nations,
and in all their domain,
there is none like you.

8 One and all they are dumb and senseless,
these idols they teach about are wooden:
9 Silver strips brought from Tarshish,
and gold from Ophir,
The work of the craftsman
and the handiwork of the smelter,
Clothed with violet and purple—
all of them the work of artisans.

11* Thus shall you say of them: Let the gods that did not make heaven and earth perish from the earth, and from beneath these heavens!

10* The LORD is true God,
he is the living God, the eternal King,
Before whose anger the earth quakes,
whose wrath the nations cannot endure:
12* He who made the earth by his power,
established the world by his wisdom,
and stretched out the heavens by his skill.
13 When he thunders, the waters in the heavens roar,
and he brings up clouds from the end of the earth;
He makes the lightning flash in the rain,
and releases stormwinds from their chambers.
14* Every man is stupid, ignorant;
every artisan is put to shame by his idol:
He has molded a fraud,
without breath of life.
15 Nothingness are they, a ridiculous work;
they will perish in their time of punishment.
16* Not like these is the portion of Jacob:
he is the creator of all things;
Israel is his very own tribe,
LORD of hosts is his name.

JEREMIAH

Abandonment of Judah

17 Lift your bundle and leave the land,
O city living in a state of siege!
18 For thus says the LORD:
Behold, this time
I will sling away the inhabitants of the land;
I will hem them in,
that they may be taken.
19 Woe is me! I am undone,
my wound is incurable;
Yet I had thought:
if I make light of my wound, I can bear it.
20* My tent is ruined,
all its cords are severed.
My sons have left me, they are no more:
no one to pitch my tent,
no one to raise its curtains.
21* Yes, the shepherds were stupid as cattle,
the LORD they sought not;
Therefore they had no success,
and all their flocks were scattered.
22 Listen! a noise! it comes closer,
a great uproar from the northern land:
To turn the cities of Judah
into a desert haunt of jackals.

Prayer of Jeremiah

23 You know, O LORD,
that man is not master of his way;
Man's course is not within his choice,
nor is it for him to direct his step.
24 Punish us, O LORD, but with equity,
not in anger, lest you have us dwindle away.
25* Pour out your wrath on the nations
that know you not,
on the tribes that call not upon your name;
For they have devoured Jacob utterly,
and laid waste his dwelling.

CHAPTER 11

Plea for Fidelity to the Covenant.
1 The following message came to Jeremiah from the LORD: 2 Speak to the men
of Judah and to the citizens of Jerusalem, 3* saying to them: Thus says the
LORD, the God of Israel: Cursed be the
man who does not observe the terms of
this covenant, 4* which I enjoined upon
your fathers the day I brought them up
out of the land of Egypt, that iron
foundry, saying: Listen to my voice and
do all that I command you. Then you
shall be my people, and I will be your
God. 5 Thus I will fulfill the oath which
I swore to your fathers, to give them a
land flowing with milk and honey: the

*

6: Ps 86, 8ff.
7: 5, 22; Ps 47, 2.8.
10: Ps 10, 16.
11: Ps 96, 5.
12: Ps 104, 5.
14: Rom 1, 22f.
16: 31, 35.
20: 4, 20.
21: 23, 1; Ez 34, 5f.
25: Ps 79, 6f.
11, 3: Dt 27, 26.
4: Dt 4, 20; 1 Kgs 8, 51.

one you have today. "Amen, LORD," I
answered.
6 Then the LORD said to me: Proclaim
all these words in the cities of Judah and
in the streets of Jerusalem: Hear the
words of this covenant and obey them.
7 Urgently and constantly I warned your
fathers to obey my voice, from the day
I brought them up out of the land of
Egypt even to this day. 8* But they did
not listen or give ear. Each one followed
the hardness of his evil heart, till I
brought upon them all the threats of this
covenant which they had failed to observe as I commanded them.
9 A conspiracy has been found, the
LORD said to me, among the men of Judah and the citizens of Jerusalem.
10* They have returned to the crimes of
their forefathers who refused to obey my
words. They also have followed and
served strange gods; the covenant which
I had made with their fathers, the house
of Israel and the house of Judah have
broken. 11* Therefore, thus says the
LORD: See, I bring upon them misfortune
which they cannot escape. Though they
cry out to me, I will not listen to them.
12* Then the cities of Judah and the citizens of Jerusalem will go and cry out
to the gods to which they have been offering incense. But these gods will give
them no help whatever when misfortune
strikes.

13* For as numerous as your cities
are your gods, O Judah!
And as many as the streets of Jerusalem
are the altars for offering sacrifice
to Baal.

14* Do not intercede on behalf of this
people, nor utter a plea for them. I will
not listen when they call to me at the
time of their misfortune.

Sacrifices of No Avail

15 What right has my beloved in my
house,
while she prepares her plots?
Can vows and sacred meat turn
away
your misfortune from you?
Will you still be jubilant
16 when you hear the great invasion?
A spreading olive tree, goodly to behold,
the LORD has named you;
Now he sets fire to it,
its branches burn.

17* The LORD of hosts who planted you
has decreed misfortune for you because
of the evil done by the house of Israel
and by the house of Judah, who provoked me by sacrificing to Baal.

The Plot against Jeremiah

18 I knew it because the LORD informed
me; at that time you, O LORD, showed
me their doings.

CHAPTER 12

1* You would be in the right, O LORD,
if I should dispute with you;
even so, I must discuss the case
with you.
Why does the way of the godless
prosper,
why live all the treacherous in
contentment?
2* You planted them; they have taken
root,
they keep on growing and bearing
fruit.
You are upon their lips,
but far from their inmost
thoughts.
3*† You, O Lord, know me, you see me,
you have found that at heart I am
with you.
Pick them out like sheep for the
slaughter,
set them apart for the day of carnage.
4 How long must the earth mourn,
the green of the whole countryside
wither?
For the wickedness of those who
dwell in it
beasts and birds disappear,
because they say, "God does not
see our ways."

5 If running against men has wearied
you,
how will you race against horses?
And if in a land of peace you fall
headlong,
what will you do in the thickets of
the Jordan?

6* For even your own brothers, the
members of your father's house, betray
you; they have recruited a force against
you. Do not believe them, even if they
are friendly to you in their words.
11:19*† Yet I, like a trusting lamb led

*

8: 2 Kgs 17, 14.
10: Dt 31, 16; Ez 20, 21-30.
11: 14, 12; Mi 3, 4.
12: Dt 32, 37f.
13: 2, 28; Hos 10, 1.
14: 7, 16; 14, 11.
17: Is 5, 2.
12, 1: Jb 21, 7; Mal 3, 15.
2: Is 29, 13.
3: 17, 18; Jb 23, 10.
6: 9, 4.
11, 19: 18, 18; 20, 10; Wis 2, 20.

†

12, 3: Jeremiah does not seek private vengeance but the punishment of the wicked by the Lord; cf 20, 12. Nevertheless, the prophet's reaction to persecution shows the difference between the spirit of the Old Testament and the New.
12, 19-23: These verses have been transposed from chapter 11.

to slaughter, had not realized that they
were hatching plots against me: "Let us
destroy the tree in its vigor; let us cut
him off from the land of the living, so
that his name will be spoken no more."

20* But, you, O LORD of hosts, O just
 Judge,
 searcher of mind and heart,
Let me witness the vengeance you
 take on them,
 for to you I have entrusted my
 cause!

21* Therefore, thus says the LORD con-
cerning the men of Anathoth who seek
your life, saying, "Do not prophesy in
the name of the LORD; else you shall die
by our hand." 22* Therefore, thus says
the LORD of hosts: I am going to punish
them. The young men shall die by the
sword; their sons and daughters shall
die by famine. 23* None shall be spared
among them, for I will bring misfortune
upon the men of Anathoth, the year of
their punishment.

The Lord's Complaint

12:7* I abandon my house,
 cast off my heritage;
The beloved of my soul I deliver
 into the hand of her foes.
8* My heritage has turned on me
 like a lion in the jungle;
Because she has roared against me,
 I treat her as an enemy.
9* My heritage is a prey for hyenas,
 is surrounded by vultures;
Come, gather together, all you
 beasts of the field,
 come and eat!
10* Many shepherds have ravaged my
 vineyard,
 have trodden my heritage under-
 foot;
The portion that delighted me they
 have turned
 into a desert waste.
11 They have made it a mournful
 waste,
 desolate it lies before me,
Desolate, all the land,
 because no one takes it to heart.
12* Upon every desert height
 brigands have come up.
The LORD has a sword which con-
 sumes
 the land, from end to end:
 no peace for all mankind.
13 They have sown wheat and reaped
 thorns,
 they have tired themselves out to
 no purpose;
They recoil before their harvest,
 the flaming anger of the LORD.

Judah's Neighbors. 14*† Thus says the
LORD against all my evil neighbors who
plunder the heritage which I gave my
people Israel as their own: See, I will
pluck them up from their land; the house
of Judah I will pluck up in their midst.
15* But after plucking them up, I will pity
them again and bring them back, each
to his heritage, each to his land. 16* And
if they carefully learn my people's cus-
tom of swearing by my name, "As the
LORD lives," they who formerly taught
my people to swear by Baal shall be built
up in the midst of my people. 17* But if
they do not obey, I will uproot and de-
stroy that nation entirely, says the LORD.

CHAPTER 13

Judah's Corruption. 1† The LORD said
to me: Go buy yourself a linen loincloth;
wear it on your loins, but do not put it
in water. 2 I bought the loincloth, as the
LORD commanded, and put it on. 3 A sec-
ond time the word of the LORD came to
me thus: 4 Take the loincloth which you
bought and are wearing, and go now to
the Parath; there hide it in a cleft of the
rock. 5 Obedient to the LORD's com-
mand, I went to the Parath and buried
the loincloth. 6 After a long interval, he
said to me: Go now to the Parath and
fetch the loincloth which I told you to
hide there. 7 Again I went to the Parath,
sought out and took the loincloth from
the place where I had hid it. But it was
rotted, good for nothing! 8 Then the mes-
sage came to me from the LORD: 9* Thus
says the LORD: So also I will allow the
pride of Judah to rot, the great pride of
Jerusalem. 10* This wicked people who
refuse to obey my words, who walk in
the stubbornness of their hearts, and fol-
low strange gods to serve and adore
them, shall be like this loincloth which
is good for nothing. 11* For, as close as
the loincloth clings to a man's loins, so
had I made the whole house of Israel
and the whole house of Judah cling to
me, says the LORD; to be my people, my
renown, my praise, my beauty. But they
did not listen.

---

*

20: 15, 15.
21: Am 7, 13. 16.
22: 18, 21f.
23: 23, 12.
12, 7: Ps 78, 62; Lam 2, 1f.
8: Ps 106, 40.
9: 2 Kgs 24, 2; Is 56, 9.
10: 6, 3; Is 63, 18.
12: Is 42, 25; 57, 21.
14: 2 Kgs 24, 2.
15: Am 9, 14.
16: Dt 6, 13.
17: Is 60, 12.
13, 9: Prv 16, 18.
10: 2, 20; 7, 24; 16, 11.
11: Ex 19, 5; Dt 26, 18f.

---

†

12, 14: *My evil neighbors:* nations surrounding Israel, the land belonging to the Lord; cf Is 8, 8.

13, 1-11: This is probably a vision of the prophet symbolizing the religious corruption of Judah at the hands of the Babylonians, represented here by the river *Parath,* the Euphrates; though a spring of the same name, northeast of Anathoth, may be directly meant.

The Broken Wineflask

12 Now speak to them this word: Thus
says the LORD, the God of Israel: Every
wineflask is meant to be filled with wine.
If they reply, "Do we not know that ev-
ery wineflask is meant to be filled with
wine?" 13* say to them: Thus says the
LORD: Beware! I am filling with drunk-
enness all the inhabitants of this land,
the kings who succeed to David's throne,
the priests and prophets, and all the citi-
zens of Jerusalem. 14* I will dash them
against each other, fathers and sons to-
gether, says the LORD; I will show no
compassion, I will not spare or pity, but
will destroy them.

A Last Warning

15 Give ear, listen humbly,
for the LORD speaks.
16* Give glory to the LORD, your God,
before it grows dark;
Before your feet stumble
on darkening mountains;
Before the light you look for turns to darkness,
changes into black clouds.
17* If you do not listen to this in your pride,
I will weep in secret many tears;
My eyes will run with tears
for the LORD's flock, led away to exile.

Exile

18* Say to the king and to the queen mother:
come down from your throne;
From your heads fall
your magnificent crowns.
19 The cities of the Negeb are besieged,
with no one to relieve them;
All Judah is banished
in universal exile.

Jerusalem's Disgrace

20* Lift up your eyes and see
men coming from the north.
Where is the flock entrusted to you,
the sheep that were your glory?
21* What will you say when they place as rulers over you
those whom you taught to be your lovers?
Will not pangs seize you
like those of a woman giving birth?
22* If you ask in your heart
why these things befall you:
For your great guilt your skirts are stripped away
and you are violated.
23* Can the Ethiopian change his skin?
the leopard his spots?
As easily would you be able to do good,
accustomed to evil as you are.
24* I will scatter them like chaff that flies
when the desert wind blows.
25* This is your lot, the portion measured out to you
from me, says the LORD.
Because you have forgotten me,
and trusted in the lying idol,
26* I now will strip off your skirts from you,
so that your shame will appear.
27* Your adulteries, your neighings,
your shameless prostitutions:
On the hills in the highlands
I see these horrible crimes of yours.
Woe to you, Jerusalem, how long will it yet be
before you become clean!

CHAPTER 14

The Great Drought

1* The word of the LORD that came to
Jeremiah concerning the drought:
2* Judah mourns,
her gates are lifeless;
Her people sink down in mourning:
from Jerusalem ascends a cry of anguish.
3* The nobles send their servants for water,
but when they come to the cisterns
They find no water
and return with empty jars.
Ashamed, despairing, they cover their heads
4* because of the stricken soil;
Because there is no rain in the land
the farmers are ashamed, they cover their heads.
5 Even the hind in the field deserts her offspring
because there is no grass.
6 The wild asses stand on the bare heights,
gasping for breath like jackals;
Their eyes grow dim,
because there is no vegetation to be seen.
7* Even though our crimes bear witness against us,
take action, O LORD, for the honor of your name—

JEREMIAH

---

*

13: 25, 15-18; Is 51, 17.
14: 19, 10f.
16: Prv 4, 18f; Is 5, 30; Am 8, 9.
17: 14, 17; Ps 119, 136.
18: 22, 26; 2 Kgs 24, 12.15.
20: 6, 22f.
21: 2 Kgs 16, 7.
22: Is 47, 2f.
23: Ps 55, 20.
24: Pss 1, 4; 83, 14.
25: Jb 20, 29.
26: Ez 16, 32.
27: 2, 20.
14, 1: Lv 26, 19f.
2: Is 3, 26.
3: Am 4, 8.
4: Dt 28, 23.
7: Dn 9, 4-14.

Even though our rebellions are many,
though we have sinned against you.
8 O Hope of Israel, O LORD,
our savior in time of need!
Why should you be a stranger in this land,
like a traveler who has stopped but for a night?
9* Why are you like a man dumbfounded,
a champion who cannot save?
You are in our midst, O LORD,
your name we bear:
do not forsake us!

10* Thus says the LORD of this people:
They so love to wander
that they do not spare their feet.
The LORD has no pleasure in them;
now he remembers their guilt,
and will punish their sins.

11* Then the LORD said to me: Do not
intercede for this people. 12* If they fast,
I will not listen to their supplication. If
they offer holocausts or cereal offerings,
I will not accept them. Rather, I will destroy them with the sword, famine, and
pestilence.
13* Ah! Lord GOD, I replied, it is the
prophets who say to them, "You shall
not see the sword; famine shall not befall
you. Indeed, I will give you lasting peace
in this place."
14* Lies these prophets utter in my
name, the LORD said to me. I did not
send them; I gave them no command
nor did I speak to them. Lying visions,
foolish divination, dreams of their own
imagination, they prophesy to you.
15* Therefore, thus says the LORD: Concerning the prophets who prophesy in
my name, though I did not send them;
who say, "Sword and famine shall not
befall this land": by the sword and famine shall these prophets meet their end.
16* The people to whom they prophesy
shall be cast out into the streets of Jerusalem by famine and the sword. No one
shall bury them, their wives, their sons,
or their daughters, for I will pour out
upon them their own wickedness.
17* Speak to them this word:

Let my eyes stream with tears
day and night, without rest,
Over the great destruction which overwhelms
the virgin daughter of my people,
over her incurable wound.
18 If I walk out into the field,
look! those slain by the sword;
If I enter the city,
look! those consumed by hunger.
Even the prophet and the priest
forage in a land they know not.
19* Have you cast Judah off completely?
Is Zion loathsome to you?
Why have you struck us a blow
that cannot be healed?
We wait for peace, to no avail;
for a time of healing, but terror comes instead.
20* We recognize, O LORD, our wickedness,
the guilt of our fathers;
that we have sinned against you.
21* For your name's sake spurn us not,
disgrace not the throne of your glory;
remember your covenant with us,
and break it not.
22* Among the nations' idols is there
any that gives rain?
Or can the mere heavens send showers?
Is it not you alone, O LORD,
our God, to whom we look?
You alone have done all these things.

CHAPTER 15

1* The LORD said to me: Even if Moses
and Samuel stood before me, my heart
would not turn toward this people. Send
them away from me. 2* If they ask you
where they should go, tell them, Thus
says the LORD: Whoever is marked for
death, to death; whoever is marked for
the sword, to the sword; whoever is
marked for famine, to famine; whoever
is marked for captivity, to captivity.
3* Four kinds of scourge I have decreed
against them, says the LORD: the sword
to slay them; dogs to drag them about;
the birds of the sky and the beasts of
the earth to devour and destroy them.
4* And I will make them an object of
horror to all the kingdoms of the earth
because of what Manasseh, son of Hezekiah, king of Judah, did in Jerusalem.

Scene of Tragedy

5* Who will pity you, Jerusalem,
who will console you?
Who will stop to ask
about your welfare?

9: Is 59, 1f; 63, 19.
10: 2, 25.
11: 11, 14; Ex 32, 10.
12: 6, 20; Is 1, 11.13.
13: 4, 10; 5, 12.
14: 5, 31; 23, 16.
15: 5, 12f.
16: 7, 33; 19, 7.
17: 9, 17.
19: 8, 15; 2 Chr 36, 16.
20: Ps 106, 6; Dn 9, 5.8.
21: 14, 7; Lv 26, 44; Ps 25, 11.
22: 5, 24; Zec 10, 1.
15, 1: Ps 99, 6; Ez 14, 14.16.
2: 14, 12; Ez 5, 12.
3: Ez 14, 21.
4: 24, 9; 2 Kgs 21, 11-16; 23, 26; 24, 3f.
5: Is 51, 19.

6* You have disowned me, says the LORD,
turned your back upon me;
And so I stretched out my hand to destroy you,
I was weary of sparing you.
7* I winnowed them with the fan
in every city gate.
I destroyed my people through bereavement;
they returned not from their evil ways.
8 Their widows were more numerous before me
than the sands of the sea.
I brought against the mother of youths
the spoiler at midday;
Suddenly I struck her
with anguish and terror.
9* The mother of seven swoons away,
gasping out her life;
Her sun sets in full day,
she is disgraced, despairing.
Their survivors I will give to the sword
before their enemies, says the LORD.

Jeremiah's Complaint

10* Woe to me, mother, that you gave me birth!
a man of strife and contention to all the land!
I neither borrow nor lend,
yet all curse me.
11* Tell me, LORD, have I not served you for their good?
Have I not interceded with you
in the time of misfortune and anguish?
15* You know I have.
Remember me, LORD, visit me,
and avenge me on my persecutors.
Because of your long-suffering banish me not;
know that for you I have borne insult.
16 When I found your words, I devoured them;
they became my joy and the happiness of my heart,
Because I bore your name,
O LORD, God of hosts.
17* I did not sit celebrating
in the circle of merrymakers;
Under the weight of your hand I sat alone
because you filled me with indignation.
18*† Why is my pain continuous,
my wound incurable, refusing to be healed?
You have indeed become for me a treacherous brook,
whose waters do not abide!

19 Thus the LORD answered me:
If you repent, so that I restore you,
in my presence you shall stand;
If you bring forth the precious without the vile,
you shall be my mouthpiece.
Then it shall be they who turn to you,
and you shall not turn to them;
20* And I will make you toward this people
a solid wall of brass.
Though they fight against you,
they shall not prevail,
For I am with you,
to deliver and rescue you, says the LORD.
21 I will free you from the hand of the wicked,
and rescue you from the grasp of the violent.

CHAPTER 16

Jeremiah's Life a Warning. 1 This
message came to me from the LORD:
2 Do not marry any woman; you shall
not have sons or daughters in this place,
3 for thus says the LORD concerning the
sons and daughters who will be born in
this place, the mothers who will give
them birth, the fathers who will beget
them in this land: 4* Of deadly disease
they shall die. Unlamented and unburied they will lie like dung on the ground.
Sword and famine will make an end of
them, and their corpses will become food
for the birds of the sky and the beasts
of the field.
5* Go not into a house of mourning, the
LORD continued: go not there to lament
or offer sympathy. For I have withdrawn my friendship from this people,
says the LORD, my kindness and my
pity. 6*† They shall die, the great and
the lowly, in this land, and shall go unburied and unlamented. No one will
gash himself or shave his head for them.
7* They will not break bread with the bereaved to console them in their bereavement; they will not give them the cup
of consolation to drink over the death
of father or mother.

*

6: Am 7, 8.
7: Is 41, 16.
9: 1 Sm 2, 5.
10: 20, 14.
11: 39, 11-14.
15: 11, 20; 12, 3; Ps 69, 8.
17: Ps 25, 4.
18: 14, 19; 30, 15.
20: 1, 18; 6, 27.
16, 4: 7, 33; 22, 18.
5: Ez 24, 16f.
6: Lv 19, 28; Dt 14, 1.
7: Ez 24, 17.

†

15, 12-14: These verses are omitted in the text because v 12 in the Hebrew is a dittography of 17, 1, and vv 13-14 are a dittography of 17, 31.

15, 18: *A treacherous brook:* that dries up when its waters are needed. The prophet complains that he cannot rely on God with unfailing assurance of his assistance.

16, 6f: These verses refer to popular mourning practices, sometimes connected with pagan superstition; cf Dt 14, 1f.

8 Enter not a house where people are
celebrating, to sit with them eating and
drinking. 9* For thus says the LORD of
hosts, the God of Israel: Before your
very eyes and during your lifetime I will
silence from this place the cry of joy and
the cry of gladness, the voice of the
bridegroom and the voice of the bride.
10* When you proclaim all these words
to this people and they ask you: "Why
has the LORD pronounced all these great
evils against us? What is our crime?
What sin have we committed against the
LORD, our God?"—11* you shall answer
them: It is because your fathers have
forsaken me, says the LORD, and fol-
lowed strange gods, which they served
and worshiped; but me they have for-
saken, and my law they have not ob-
served. 12* And you have done worse
than your fathers. Here you are, every
one of you, walking in the hardness of
his evil heart instead of listening to me.
13 I will cast you out of this land into a
land that neither you nor your fathers
have known; there you can serve
strange gods day and night, because I
will not grant you my mercy.
Return from Exile. 14* However, days
will surely come, says the LORD, when
it will no longer be said, "As the LORD
lives, who brought the Israelites out of
Egypt"; 15* but rather, "As the LORD
lives, who brought the Israelites out of
the land of the north and out of all the
countries to which he had banished
them." I will bring them back to the land
which I gave their fathers.
Double Punishment. 16* Look! I will
send many fishermen, says the LORD, to
catch them. After that, I will send many
hunters to hunt them out from every
mountain and hill and from the clefts
of the rocks. 17* For my eyes are upon
all their ways; they are not hidden from
me, nor does their guilt escape my view.
18* I will at once repay them double for
their crime and their sin of profaning
my land with their detestable corpses of
idols, and filling my heritage with their
abominations.

Conversion of the Heathen

19* O LORD, my strength, my fortress,
my refuge in the day of distress!
To you will the nations come
from the ends of the earth, and
say,
"Mere frauds are the heritage of our
fathers,
empty idols of no use."
20* Can man make for himself gods?
These are not gods.
21* Look, then: I will give them knowl-
edge;
this time I will leave them in no
doubt
Of my strength and my power:
they shall know that my name is
LORD.

CHAPTER 17

The Sin of Judah and Its Punishment

1* The sin of Judah is written
with an iron stylus,
Engraved with a diamond point
upon the tablets of their hearts.
[And the horns of their altars, 2 when
their sons remember their altars and
their sacred poles, beside the green
trees, on the high hills, 3 the peaks in the
highland.]
Your wealth and all your treasures
I will give as spoil.
In recompense for all your sins
throughout your borders,
4* You will relinquish your hold on
your heritage
which I have given you.
I will enslave you to your enemies
in a land that you know not:
For a fire has been kindled by my
wrath
that will burn forever.

True Wisdom

5* Thus says the LORD:
Cursed is the man who trusts in hu-
man beings,
who seeks his strength in flesh,
whose heart turns away from the
LORD.
6 He is like a barren bush in the desert
that enjoys no change of season,
But stands in a lava waste,
a salt and empty earth.
7* Blessed is the man who trusts in the
LORD,
whose hope is the LORD.
8* He is like a tree planted beside the
waters
that stretches out its roots to the
stream:
It fears not the heat when it comes,
its leaves stay green;
In the year of drought it shows no
distress,
but still bears fruit.
9 More tortuous than all else is the hu-
man heart,
beyond remedy; who can under-
stand it?

9: 7, 34; 25, 10.
10: 2, 35; 5, 19; 13, 22.
11: 22, 9; Dt 29, 25.
12: 7, 24ff.
14: 23, 7f.
15: 24, 6.
16: 2 Kgs 24, 2; Lam 4, 19.
17: 32, 19; Jb 34, 21.
18: Is 40, 2.
19: 2, 11; Is 2, 2f.
20: 2, 11; Gal 4, 8.
21: Am 5, 8.
17, 1: Jb 19, 24.
4: 5, 19; Dt 32, 22.
5: Ps 146, 2f.
7: Ps 1, 3.
8: Is 58, 11.

10* I, the LORD, alone probe the mind
and test the heart,
To reward everyone according to his
ways,
according to the merit of his
deeds.
11* A partridge that mothers a brood
not her own
is the man who acquires wealth
unjustly:
In midlife it will desert him;
in the end he is only a fool.

The Source of Life

12* A throne of glory, exalted from the
beginning,
such is our holy place.
13* O hope of Israel, O LORD!
all who forsake you shall be in dis-
grace;
The rebels in the land shall be put
to shame;
they have forsaken the source of
living waters
[the LORD].

Prayer for Vengeance

14 Heal me, LORD, that I may be
healed;
save me, that I may be saved,
for it is you whom I praise.
15* See how they say to me,
"Where is the word of the LORD?
Let it come to pass!"
16 Yet I did not press you to send ca-
lamity;
the day without remedy I have not
desired.
You know what passed my lips;
it is present before you.
17* Do not be my ruin,
you, my refuge in the day of mis-
fortune.
18* Let my persecutors, not me, be con-
founded;
let them, not me, be broken.
Bring upon them the day of misfor-
tune,
crush them with repeated de-
struction.

Observance of the Sabbath. 19*† Thus
said the LORD to me: Go, stand at the
Gate of Benjamin, where the kings of Ju-
dah enter and leave, and at the other
gates of Jerusalem. 20 There say to them:
Hear the word of the LORD, you kings
of Judah, and all Judah, and all you citi-
zens of Jerusalem who enter these gates!
21* Thus says the LORD: As you love your
lives, take care not to carry burdens on
the sabbath day, to bring them in
through the gates of Jerusalem.
22* Bring no burden from your homes
on the sabbath. Do no work whatever,
but keep holy the sabbath, as I com-
manded your fathers, 23* though they
did not listen or give ear, but stiffened
their necks so as not to hear or take cor-
rection. 24* If you obey me wholeheart-
edly, says the LORD, and carry no
burden through the gates of this city on
the sabbath, keeping the sabbath holy
and abstaining from all work on it,
25* then, through the gates of this city,
kings who sit upon the throne of David
will continue to enter, riding in their
chariots or upon their horses, along with
their princes, and the men of Judah, and
the citizens of Jerusalem. This city will
remain inhabited forever. 26* To it peo-
ple will come from the cities of Judah
and the neighborhood of Jerusalem,
from the land of Benjamin and from the
foothills, from the hill country and the
Negeb, to bring holocausts and sacri-
fices, cereal offerings and incense and
thank offerings to the house of the LORD.
27* But if you do not obey me and keep
holy the sabbath, if you carry burdens
and come through the gates of Jerusa-
lem on the sabbath, I will set unquench-
able fire to its gates, which will consume
the palaces of Jerusalem.

CHAPTER 18

The Potter's Vessel. 1† This word
came to Jeremiah from the LORD: 2 Rise
up, be off to the potter's house; there I
will give you my message. 3 I went down
to the potter's house and there he was,
working at the wheel. 4* Whenever the
object of clay which he was making
turned out badly in his hand, he tried
again, making of the clay another object
of whatever sort he pleased. 5 Then the
word of the Lord came to me: 6* Can I
not do to you, house of Israel, as this
potter has done? says the LORD. Indeed,
like clay in the hand of the potter, so
are you in my hand, house of Israel.
7* Sometimes I threaten to uproot and
tear down and destroy a nation or a
kingdom. 8* But if that nation which I
have threatened turns from its evil, I
also repent of the evil which I threatened

*

10: 32, 19; 1 Sm 16, 7; Eccl 12, 14.
11: Prv 13, 11; Lk 12, 20.
12: 14, 21.
13: 2, 13.
15: Is 5, 19; 2 Pt 3, 4.
17: 16, 19.
18: 15, 15; 18, 20-23; Ps 35, 5f.
19: 7, 2.
21: Neh 13, 15-19.
22: Ex 20, 8; 23, 12.
23: 5, 3; 7, 24.
24: Is 58, 14.
25: 22, 4.
26: 32, 44.
27: Ez 22, 8.
18, 4: Rom 9, 20f.
6: Wis 15, 7; Is 45, 9.
7: 1, 10.
8: 26, 3; Is 55, 7; Ez 18, 21. 27.

†

17, 19: *The Gate of Benjamin:* probably the northern gate of the temple area and city wall of Jerusalem; cf 20, 2; 37, 12; 38, 7.

18, 1-12: The lesson of the potter is not that God deals arbitrarily with his people, but that he is almighty to destroy or restore, accordingly as they disobey him or fulfill his plans.

to do. 9 Sometimes, again, I promise to
build up and plant a nation or a king-
dom. 10* But if that nation does what is
evil in my eyes, refusing to obey my
voice, I repent of the good with which
I promised to bless it.
11* And now, tell this to the men of Ju-
dah and the citizens of Jerusalem: Thus
says the LORD: Take care! I am fashion-
ing evil against you and making a plan.
Return, each of you, from his evil way;
reform your ways and your deeds.
12* But they will say, "No use! We will
follow our own devices; each one of us
will behave according to the stubborn-
ness of his evil heart!"

Judah's Apostasy Unnatural

13* Therefore thus says the LORD:
Ask among the nations—
who has ever heard the like?
Truly horrible things
has virgin Israel done!
14† Does the snow of Lebanon
desert the rocky heights?
Do the gushing waters dry up
that flow fresh down the mountains?
15* Yet my people have forgotten me:
they burn incense to a thing that does not exist.
They stumble out of their ways,
the paths of old,
To travel on bypaths,
not the beaten track.
16* Their land shall be turned into a desert,
an object of lasting ridicule:
All passers-by will be amazed,
will shake their heads.
17* Like the east wind, I will scatter them
before their enemies;
I will show them my back, not my face,
in their day of disaster.

Another Prayer for Vengeance.
18* "Come," they said, "let us contrive
a plot against Jeremiah. It will not mean
the loss of instruction from the priests,
nor of counsel from the wise, nor of mes-
sages from the prophets. And so, let us
destroy him by his own tongue; let us
carefully note his every word."

19 Heed me, O LORD,
and listen to what my adversaries say.
20* Must good be repaid with evil
that they should dig a pit to take my life?
Remember that I stood before you
to speak in their behalf,
to turn away your wrath from them.
21*† So now, deliver their children to famine,
do away with them by the sword.
Let their wives be made childless
and widows;
let their men die of pestilence,
their young men be slain by the sword in battle.
22 May cries be heard from their homes,
when suddenly you send plunderers against them.
For they have dug a pit to capture me,
they have hid snares for my feet;
23* But you, O LORD, know
all their plans to slay me.
Forgive not their crime,
blot not out their sin in your sight!
Let them go down before you,
proceed against them in the time of your anger.

CHAPTER 19

Symbol of the Potter's Flask. 1 Thus
said the LORD: Go, buy a potter's earthen
flask. Take along some of the elders of
the people and of the priests, 2† and go
out toward the Valley of Ben-hinnom,
at the entrance of the Potsherd Gate;
there proclaim the words which I will
speak to you: 3 Listen to the word of the
LORD, kings of Judah and citizens of Je-
rusalem: Thus says the LORD of hosts,
the God of Israel: I am going to bring
such evil upon this place that all who
hear of it will feel their ears tingle.
4* This is because they have forsaken
me and alienated this place by burning
in it incense to strange gods which nei-
ther they nor their fathers knew; and the
kings of Judah have filled this place with
the blood of the innocent. 5* They have
built high places for Baal to immolate
their sons in fire as holocausts to Baal:
such a thing as I neither commanded
nor spoke of, nor did it ever enter my
mind. 6* Therefore, days will come, says
the LORD, when this place will no longer

---

*

10: Nm 14, 22f.
11: 7, 3; 25, 5; 35, 15.
12: 2, 25; 7, 24.
13: 2, 10f; 5, 30.
15: 2, 13.32.
16: 19, 8; Lv 26, 32; 1 Kgs 9, 8.
17: Prv 1, 24-31.
18: 11, 19; Ps 35, 15f.
20: Ps 35, 12.
21: Ps 109, 9f.
23: Neh 4, 5; Pss 35, 4; 37, 32f.
19, 4: 1, 16; 2 Kgs 21, 16; 24, 4.
5: 7, 31f; 32, 35.
6: 7, 32.

†

18, 14: *Lebanon:* here apparently including Mount Hermon, whose snow-capped peak can be seen from parts of Palestine all year round. The prophet contrasts the certainties of nature with Israel's unnatural desertion of the Lord for idols (v 15).

18, 21: In the Old Testament a man's family was regarded as part of his personality, to be rewarded or punished along with him; cf Jos 7, 24ff.

19, 2: *Potsherd Gate:* in the south wall of Jerusalem, through which potsherds and other refuse were carried to the Valley of Ben-hinnom.

JEREMIAH

be called Topheth, or the Valley of Ben-
hinnom, but rather, the Valley of
Slaughter. 7* In this place I will foil the
plan of Judah and Jerusalem; I will
make them fall by the sword before their
enemies, by the hand of those that seek
their lives. Their corpses I will give as
food to the birds of the sky and the
beasts of the field. 8 I will make this city
an object of amazement and derision.
Because of all its wounds, every passer-
by will be amazed and will catch his
breath. 9* I will have them eat the flesh
of their sons and daughters; they shall
eat one another's flesh during the strict
siege by which their enemies and those
who seek their lives will confine them.
10 And you shall break the flask in the
sight of the men who went with you,
11* and say to them: Thus says the LORD
of hosts: Thus will I smash this people
and this city, as one smashes a clay pot
so that it cannot be repaired. And To-
pheth shall be a burial place, for lack
of place to bury elsewhere. 12* Thus I will
do to this place and to its inhabitants,
says the LORD; I will make this city like
Topheth. 13* And the houses of Jerusa-
lem and the palaces of the kings of Ju-
dah shall be defiled like the place of
Topheth, all the houses upon whose roofs
they burnt incense to the whole host of
heaven and poured out libations to
strange gods.
14* When Jeremiah returned from To-
pheth, where the LORD had sent him to
prophesy, he stood in the court of the
house of God and said to all the people:
15* Thus says the LORD of hosts, the God
of Israel: I will surely bring upon this
city all the evil with which I threatened
it, because they have stiffened their
necks and have not obeyed my words.

CHAPTER 20

1*† Jeremiah was heard prophesying
these things by the priest Pashhur, son
of Immer, chief officer in the house of
the LORD. 2* So he had the prophet
scourged and placed in the stocks at the
upper Gate of Benjamin in the house of
the LORD. 3*† The next morning, after
Pashhur had released Jeremiah from
the stocks, the prophet said to him: In-
stead of Pashhur, the LORD will name
you "Terror on every side." 4† For thus
says the LORD: Indeed, I will deliver you
to terror, you and all your friends. Your
own eyes shall see them fall by the sword
of their enemies. All Judah I will deliver
to the king of Babylon, who shall take
them captive to Babylon or slay them
with the sword. 5* All the wealth of this
city, all it has toiled for and holds dear,
all the treasures of the kings of Judah,
I will give as plunder into the hands of
their foes, who shall seize it and carry
it away to Babylon. 6* You Pashhur, and
all the members of your household shall
go into exile. To Babylon you shall go,
you and all your friends; there you shall
die and be buried, because you have
prophesied lies to them.

Jeremiah's Interior Crisis

7† You duped me, O LORD, and I let myself be duped;
you were too strong for me, and you triumphed.
All the day I am an object of laughter;
everyone mocks me.
8 Whenever I speak, I must cry out,
violence and outrage is my message;
The word of the LORD has brought me
derision and reproach all the day.
9* I say to myself, I will not mention him,
I will speak in his name no more.
But then it becomes like fire burning in my heart,
imprisoned in my bones;
I grow weary holding it in,
I cannot endure it.
10* Yes, I hear the whisperings of many:
"Terror on every side!
Denounce! let us denounce him!"
All those who were my friends
are on the watch for any misstep of mine.
"Perhaps he will be trapped; then we can prevail,
and take our vengeance on him."
11* But the LORD is with me, like a mighty champion:
my persecutors will stumble, they will not triumph.
In their failure they will be put to utter shame,
to lasting, unforgettable confusion.

*

7: 7, 33.
9: Lv 26, 29.
11: 7, 32.
12: 2 Kgs 23, 10.
13: 32, 29.
14: 26, 2.
15: 7, 26; Prv 29, 1.
20, 1: 21, 1.
2: 29, 26.
3: 6, 25.
5: 2 Kgs 20, 17; 24, 12-16.
6: 14, 13f; 28, 15.
9: 6, 11; Jb 32, 18.
10: Jb 19, 19; Ps 31, 13; Lk 20, 20.
11: 1, 8; 15, 20.

†

20, 1: *Chief officer in the house of the LORD:* head of the temple police; cf 29, 26. By entering the temple court (19, 14), Jeremiah had put himself under Pashhur's jurisdiction.

20, 3: *Terror on every side:* Pashhur will share the fate of doomed Jerusalem and will experience personally all that the people as a whole have had to endure.

20, 4: *Babylon:* mentioned here for the first time as the land of exile. The prophecy probably dates from after 605 B.C., when Nebuchadnezzar defeated Egypt and made the Chaldean empire dominant in Syria and Palestine.

20, 7: *You duped me:* to be understood in the light of Jeremiah's intimate dealings with God; cf 15, 18.

12* O LORD of hosts, you who test the just,
who probe mind and heart,
Let me witness the vengeance you take on them,
for to you I have entrusted my cause.
13* Sing to the LORD,
praise the LORD,
For he has rescued the life of the poor
from the power of the wicked!

14*† Cursed be the day
on which I was born!
May the day my mother gave me birth
never be blessed!
15 Cursed be the man who brought the news
to my father, saying,
"A child, a son, has been born to you!"
filling him with great joy.
16* Let that man be like the cities
which the LORD relentlessly overthrew;
Let him hear war cries in the morning,
battle alarms at noonday,
17* because he did not dispatch me in the womb!
Then my mother would have been my grave,
her womb confining me forever.
18* Why did I come forth from the womb,
to see sorrow and pain,
to end my days in shame?

III: ORACLES IN THE LAST YEARS OF JERUSALEM

CHAPTER 21

Fate of Zedekiah and Jerusalem.
1† The message which came to Jeremiah
from the LORD when King Zedekiah sent
him Pashhur, son of Malchiah, and the
priest Zephaniah, son of Maaseiah, with
this request: 2 Inquire for us of the LORD,
because Nebuchadnezzar, king of Baby-
lon, is attacking us. Perhaps the LORD
will deal with us according to all his won-
derful works, so that he will withdraw
from us. 3 But Jeremiah answered them:
This is what you shall report to Zede-
kiah: 4* Thus says the LORD, the God of
Israel: I will turn back in your hands the
weapons with which you intend to fight
the king of Babylon and the Chaldeans
who besiege you outside the walls. These
weapons I will pile up in the midst of
this city, 5* and I myself will fight
against you with outstretched hand and
mighty arm, in anger, and wrath, and
great rage! 6* I will strike the inhabitants
of this city, both man and beast; they
shall die in a great pestilence. 7* After
that, says the LORD, I will hand over
Zedekiah, king of Judah, and his minis-
ters and the people in this city who sur-
vive pestilence, sword, and famine, into
the hand of Nebuchadnezzar, king of
Babylon, into the hands of their enemies
and those who seek their lives. He shall
strike them with the edge of the sword,
without quarter, without pity or mercy.
8* And to this people you shall say:
Thus says the LORD: See, I am giving
you a choice between life and death.
9 Whoever remains in this city shall die
by the sword or famine or pestilence. But
whoever leaves and surrenders to the
besieging Chaldeans shall live and have
his life as booty. 10† For I have turned
against this city, for its woe and not for
its good, says the LORD. It shall be given
into the power of the king of Babylon
who shall burn it with fire.

Oracles regarding the Kings

11† To the royal house of Judah:
Hear the word of the LORD, 12* O house of David!
Thus says the LORD:
Each morning dispense justice,
rescue the oppressed from the hand of the oppressor,
Lest my fury break out like fire
which burns without being quenched,
because of the evil of your deeds.
13† Beware! I am against you, Valley-site,

---

*

12: 11, 20.
13: Pss 35, 9f; 109, 30f.
14: 15, 10; Jb 3, 1-10; 10, 18.
16: Gn 19, 25; Is 13, 19.
17: Jb 3, 10f; 10, 19.
18: Jb 14, 1.
21, 4: 37, 8ff.
5: Is 63, 10; Lam 2, 4f.
6: 16, 4.
7: 24, 8ff; Dt 28, 49f.
8: 21, 9; Dt 30, 15.19.
12: 4, 4; 22, 3; Zec 7, 9.

†

20, 14-18: Deception, sorrow and terror have brought the prophet close to the point of despair; nevertheless he has expressed his utmost confidence in the triumph of God's will (vv 11ff); cf Jb 3, 3-12.

21, 1: *Zedekiah:* brother of Jehoiakim, appointed king by Nebuchadnezzar after he had carried Jehoiachin away to captivity (2 Kgs 24, 17). *Pashhur:* different from the one in 20, 1ff but also one of Jeremiah's enemies; cf 38, 1.4.

21, 10: Jeremiah consistently pointed out the uselessness of resistance to Babylon, since the Lord had delivered Judah to Nebuchadnezzar (27, 6). Because of this the prophet was denounced and imprisoned as a traitor (37, 13f).

21, 11—23, 8: This section contains an editor's collection of Jeremiah's oracles against the kings of Judah. They are placed in the chronological order of the kings, and are prefaced by the oracles against the kings of Judah in general (21, 11—22, 9).

21, 13: *Valley-site, Rock of the Plain:* Mount Zion, surrounded by valleys, was regarded by the royal house as impregnable. Despite this natural fortification, God shows derisively that it is no more than a rock rising from the plain, undefendable against the attack of his fury.

Rock of the Plain, says the LORD.
You who say, "Who will attack us,
who can penetrate our retreats?"
14*†I will punish you, says the LORD,
as your deeds deserve!
I will kindle a fire in its forest
that shall devour all its surroundings.

CHAPTER 22

1 The LORD told me this: Go down to
the palace of the king of Judah and there
deliver this message: 2* You shall say:
Listen to the word of the LORD, king of
Judah, who sit on the throne of David,
you, your ministers, and your people
that enter by these gates! 3* Thus says
the LORD: Do what is right and just. Rescue the victim from the hand of his oppressor. Do not wrong or oppress the
resident alien, the orphan, or the widow,
and do not shed innocent blood in this
place. 4 If you carry out these commands, kings who succeed to the throne
of David will continue to enter the gates
of this palace, riding in chariots or
mounted on horses, with their ministers,
and their people. 5 But if you do not obey
these commands, I swear by myself,
says the LORD: this palace shall become
rubble. 6† For thus says the LORD concerning the palace of the king of Judah:

Though you be to me like Gilead,
like the peak of Lebanon,
I will turn you into a waste,
a city uninhabited.
7* Against you I will send destroyers,
each with his axe:
They shall cut down your choice cedars,
and cast them into the fire.

8* Many people will pass by this city
and ask one another: "Why has the LORD
done this to so great a city?" 9* And the
answer will be given: "Because they
have deserted their covenant with the
LORD, their God, by worshiping and
serving strange gods."

Jehoahaz

10*†Weep not for him who is dead,
mourn not for him!
Weep rather for him who is going away;
never again will he see
the land of his birth.

11† Thus says the LORD concerning
Shallum, son of Josiah, king of Judah,
who succeeded his father as king. He has
left this place never to return. 12 Rather,
he shall die in the place where they exiled him; this land he shall not see again.

Jehoiakim

13*†Woe to him who builds his house on wrong,
his terraces on injustice;
Who works his neighbor without pay,
and gives him no wages.
14 Who says, "I will build myself a spacious house,
with airy rooms,"
Who cuts out windows for it,
panels it with cedar,
and paints it with vermillion.
15*†Must you prove your rank among kings
by competing with them in cedar?
Did not your father eat and drink?
He did what was right and just,
and it went well with him.
16* Because he dispensed justice to the weak and the poor,
it went well with him.
Is this not true knowledge of me?
says the LORD.
17* But your eyes and heart are set on nothing
except on your own gain,
On shedding innocent blood,
on practicing oppression and extortion.

18*† Therefore, thus says the LORD
concerning Jehoiakim, son of Josiah,
king of Judah:

They shall not lament him,
"Alas! my brother"; "Alas! sister."
They shall not lament him,
"Alas, Lord! alas, Majesty!"

*

14: 2 Kgs 25, 9; 2 Chr 36, 19.
22, 2: 17, 20.
3: 21, 12; Ex 22, 21-24; Dt 24, 17.
7: 21, 14.
8: Dt 29, 24ff.
9: 19, 4; 40, 2f.
10: 2 Chr 35, 23ff.
13: Lv 19, 13; Dt 24, 14; Hb 2, 9.12.
15: 2 Kgs 23, 25.
16: Prv 31, 9.
17: Ez 22, 13.27.
18: 16, 4ff; 1 Kgs 13, 30

†

21, 14: *Its forest:* probably the royal palace, built of cedar wood; cf 22, 14; in 1 Kgs 7, 2 the armory of Solomon's palace is called "the house of the forest of Lebanon."

22, 6: *Gilead . . . Lebanon:* both were known for their trees; cf v 7.

22, 10: *Him who is dead:* Josiah. His successor, Jehoahaz, *who is going away,* was deported by Pharaoh Neco to Egypt, where he died (2 Kgs 23, 33f).

22, 11: *Shallum:* Jehoahaz is called this only here. Presumably it was his name at birth, while Jehoahaz was his royal name.

22, 13: *Without pay:* either by forced labor in public works, or inasmuch as workers were defrauded of their hire. Despite the impoverishment caused in Judah by the payment of foreign tribute, Jehoiakim embarked on a program of lavish building in Jerusalem (v 14). Social injustice is the cause of much of the prophetic condemnation of the kings (v 17).

22, 15f: Josiah, the reforming king, prospered materially without oppressing his people; he embodied all the ideals of kingship.

22, 18: *"Alas! my brother"; "Alas! sister":* customary cries of mourning.

19*†The burial of an ass shall he be given,
dragged forth and cast out
beyond the gates of Jerusalem.

Jeconiah

20*†Scale Lebanon and cry out,
in Bashan lift up your voice;
Cry out from Abarim,
for all your lovers are crushed.
21 I spoke to you when you were secure,
but you answered, "I will not listen."
This has been your way from your youth,
not to listen to my voice.
22 The wind shall shepherd all your shepherds,
your lovers shall go into exile.
Surely then you shall be ashamed and confounded
because of all your wickedness.
23 You who dwell on Lebanon,
who nest in the cedars,
How you shall groan when pains come upon you,
like the pangs of a woman in travail!

24† As I live, says the LORD, if you, Co-
niah, son of Jehoiakim, king of Judah,
are a signet ring on my right hand, I
will snatch you from it. 25* I will deliver
you into the hands of those who seek
your life; the hands of those whom you
fear; the hands of Nebuchadnezzar, king
of Babylon, and the Chaldeans. 26*† I
will cast you out, you and the mother
who bore you, into a different land from
the one you were born in; and there you
shall die. 27* Neither of them shall come
back to the land for which they yearn.

28 Is this man Coniah a vessel despised,
to be broken up,
an instrument that no one wants?
Why are he and his descendants cast out?
why thrown into a land they know not?
29 O land, land, land,
hear the word of the LORD—
30*† Thus says the LORD:
Write this man down as one childless,
who will never thrive in his lifetime!
No descendant of his shall achieve
a seat on the throne of David
as ruler again over Judah.

CHAPTER 23

Messianic Reign. 1*† Woe to the shep-
herds who mislead and scatter the flock
of my pasture, says the LORD.
2* Therefore, thus says the LORD, the
God of Israel, against the shepherds who
shepherd my people: You have scattered
my sheep and driven them away. You
have not cared for them, but I will take
care to punish your evil deeds. 3* I my-
self will gather the remnant of my flock
from all the lands to which I have driven
them and bring them back to their
meadow; there they shall increase and
multiply. 4* I will appoint shepherds for
them who will shepherd them so that
they need no longer fear and tremble;
and none shall be missing, says the
LORD.

5* Behold, the days are coming, says the LORD,
when I will raise up a righteous shoot to David;

---

*

19: 36, 30.
20: 30, 14f; Dt 32, 49.
25: 21, 7; 34, 20.
26: 2 Kgs 24, 15.
27: 44, 14.
30: 36, 30; 1 Chr 3, 16f; Mt 1, 12.
23, 1: 22, 22.
2: Ez 34, 4ff; Zec 11, 16f.
3: 29, 14; 32, 37.
4: 3, 15; Ez 34, 11f.
5: 33, 14ff; Is 4, 2; 9, 5f; 11, 1-5.

---

†

22, 19: *The burial of an ass:* no burial at all, except to be cast outside the city as refuse. This prophecy regards the popular feeling toward Jehoiakim rather than the actual circumstances of his burial. According to 2 Kgs 24, 5 he was buried with his fathers in Jerusalem. However, his grave may have been profaned by Nebuchadnezzar.

22, 20-23: The prophet first apostrophizes Jerusalem, which is bidden to scale *Lebanon, Bashan,* and *Abarim,* i.e., the highest surrounding mountains to the north, northeast, and southeast, to gaze on the ruin of its *lovers,* i.e., the false leaders of Judah, called its *shepherds* (22); cf 2, 8. The year is 597 B.C., after Nebuchadnezzar's deportation of Jehoiachin. Jerusalem still stands (23), apparently as secure as the heights of Lebanon, but destruction is to follow (cf v 6).

22, 24: *Coniah:* a shortened form of Jeconiah, the name which Jeremiah gives the king called elsewhere in the Bible Jehoiachin. *A signet ring:* the seal used by important men—in a sense, their most valuable possession—mounted in a ring worn constantly on the hand. The Lord says that even were Jehoiachin such a precious possession, he would reject him. The words in vv 24-30 date from the short three-month reign of Jehoiachin, before he was carried away by Nebuchadnezzar.

22, 26: *You and the mother who bore you:* the queen mother held a special position in the monarchy of Judah, and in the Books of Kings she is invariably mentioned by name along with the king (1 Kgs 15, 2; 2 Kgs 18, 2). Jehoiachin did indeed die in Babylon.

22, 30: *Childless:* Jehoiachin is so considered because none of his descendants will be king. From the Book of Ezekiel, who dates his oracles according to Jehoiachin's fictitious regnal years, it is evident that the people expected Jehoiachin to return. The above prophecy of Jeremiah was uttered to dispel this hope (28, 4). Of the seven sons born to Jehoiachin in exile, none became king. His grandson Zerubbabel presided for a time over the Jewish community after the return from exile, but not as king.

23, 1-8: With the false rulers who have governed his people the Lord contrasts himself, the good shepherd, who will in the times of restoration appoint worthy rulers (1-4). A messianic King will arise from the line of David who will rule over Judah and Israel with the justice of the Lord, fulfilling all the kingly ideals (5f). *"The Lord our justice"* is probably an ironic wordplay on the name of the weak King Zedekiah ("The Lord is justice"); the messianic King will be in reality what Zedekiah's name falsely proclaims him. The final verses, 7-8, were probably added during the exile.

As king he shall reign and govern wisely,
he shall do what is just and right in the land.
6* In his days Judah shall be saved,
Israel shall dwell in security.
This is the name they give him:
"The LORD our justice."

7* Therefore, the days will come, says
the LORD, when they shall no longer say,
"As the LORD lives, who brought the Is-
raelites out of the land of Egypt"; 8 but
rather, "As the LORD lives, who brought
the descendants of the house of Israel
up from the land of the north"—and
from all the lands to which I banished
them; they shall again live on their own
land.

The False Prophets

9† Concerning the prophets:
My heart within me is broken,
my bones all tremble;
I am like a man who is drunk,
overcome by wine,
Because of the LORD,
because of his holy words.
10* With adulterers the land is filled;
on their account the land mourns,
the pasture ranges are seared.
Theirs is an evil course,
theirs is unjust power.
11* Both prophet and priest are godless!
In my very house I find their wickedness,
says the LORD.
12* Hence their way shall become for them
slippery ground.
In the darkness they shall lose their footing,
and fall headlong;
Evil I will bring upon them:
the year of their punishment, says the LORD.
13* Among Samaria's prophets
I saw unseemly deeds:
They prophesied by Baal
and led my people Israel astray.
14* But among Jerusalem's prophets
I saw deeds still more shocking:
Adultery, living in lies,
siding with the wicked,
so that no one turns from evil;
To me they are all like Sodom,
its citizens like Gomorrah.

15* Therefore, thus says the LORD of
hosts against the prophets:

Behold, I will give them wormwood to eat,
and poison to drink;
For from Jerusalem's prophets
ungodliness has gone forth into the whole land.

16* Thus says the LORD of hosts:
Listen not to the words of your prophets,
who fill you with emptiness;
Visions of their own fancy they speak,
not from the mouth of the LORD.
17*† They say to those who despise the word of the LORD,
"Peace shall be yours";
And to everyone who walks in hardness of heart,
"No evil shall overtake you."
18* Now, who has stood in the council of the LORD,
to see him and to hear his word?
Who has heeded his word, so as to announce it?
19* See, the storm of the LORD!
His wrath breaks forth
In a whirling storm
that bursts upon the heads of the wicked.
20 The anger of the LORD shall not abate
until he has done and fulfilled
what he has determined in his heart.
When the time comes,
you shall fully understand.
21* I did not send these prophets,
yet they ran;
I did not speak to them,
yet they prophesied.
22 Had they stood in my council,
and did they but proclaim to my people my words,
They would have brought them back from evil ways
and from their wicked deeds.
23*† Am I a God near at hand only, says the LORD,
and not a God far off?
24 Can a man hide in secret
without my seeing him? says the LORD.

*

6: Dn 9, 24.
7f: 16, 14f.
10: 4, 22; 5, 7f; 9, 2. 10.
11: 6, 13.
12: Ps 35, 6.
13: 1 Kgs 18, 19.
14: 29, 21ff; Is 1, 9f.
15: 8, 14; 9, 14.
16: 14, 14.
17: 5, 12; Ez 13, 10; Mi 3, 11; Zec 10, 2.
18: Jb 15, 8; Is 40, 13; 1 Cor 2, 16.
19: 30, 23.
21: 29, 9.
23: 16, 17; Ps 139, 8.

†

23, 9-40: After the collection of oracles against the kings, the editor of the book placed this collection of oracles against the false prophets. With them are associated the priests, for both have betrayed their trust as instructors in the religion of the Lord; cf 2, 8; 4, 9; 6, 13f.

23, 17-20: Not only are the false prophets personally immoral, but they encourage immorality by prophesying good of those who do evil. The true prophet, on the other hand, sees the inevitable consequences of sin.

23, 23: *Near at hand only . . . far off:* God knows not merely the present but also the future.

Do I not fill
both heaven and earth? says the
LORD.

25 I have heard the prophets who
prophesy lies in my name say, "I had
a dream! I had a dream!" 26 How long
will this continue? Is my name in the
hearts of the prophets who prophesy lies
and their own deceitful fancies? 27* By
their dreams which they recount to each
other, they think to make my people for-
get my name, just as their fathers forgot
my name for Baal. 28*† Let the prophet
who has a dream recount his dream; let
him who has my word speak my word
truthfully!

What has straw to do with the
wheat?
says the LORD.
29 Is not my word like fire, says the
LORD,
like a hammer shattering rocks?

30* Therefore I am against the proph-
ets, says the LORD, who steal my words
from each other. 31 Yes, I am against the
prophets, says the LORD, who borrow
speeches to pronounce oracles. 32* Yes,
I am against the prophets who prophesy
lying dreams, says the LORD, and who
lead my people astray by recounting
their lies and by their empty boasting.
From me they have no mission or com-
mand, and they do this people no good
at all, says the LORD.

33† And when this people, or a prophet
or a priest asks you, "What is the burden
of the LORD?" you shall answer, "You
are the burden, and I cast you off, says
the LORD." 34 If a prophet or a priest or
anyone else mentions "the burden of the
LORD," I will punish that man and his
house. 35 Thus you shall ask, when
speaking to one another, "What answer
did the LORD give?" or, "What did the
LORD say?" 36 But the burden of the
LORD you shall mention no more. For
each man his own word becomes the
burden so that you pervert the words of
the living God, the LORD of hosts, our
God. 37 Thus shall you ask the prophet,
"What answer did the LORD give?" or,
"What did the LORD say?" 38 But if you
ask about "the burden of the LORD,"
then thus says the LORD: Because you
use this phrase, "the burden of the
LORD," though I forbade you to use it,
39 therefore I will lift you on high and
cast you from my presence, you and the
city which I gave to you and your fa-
thers. 40* And I will bring upon you eter-
nal reproach, eternal, unforgettable
shame.

CHAPTER 24

The Two Baskets of Figs. 1*† The
LORD showed me two baskets of figs
placed before the temple of the LORD.—
This was after Nebuchadnezzar, king of
Babylon, had exiled from Jerusalem
Jeconiah, son of Jehoiakim, king of Ju-
dah, and the princes of Judah, the arti-
sans and the skilled workers, and
brought them to Babylon.—2 One basket
contained excellent figs, the early-
ripening kind. But the other basket con-
tained very bad figs, so bad they could
not be eaten. 3* Then the LORD said to
me: What do you see, Jeremiah? "Figs,"
I replied; "the good ones are very good,
but the bad ones very bad, so bad they
cannot be eaten." 4 Thereupon this word
of the LORD came to me: 5* Thus says
the LORD, the God of Israel: Like these
good figs, even so will I regard with favor
Judah's exiles whom I sent away from
this place into the land of the Chaldeans.
6* I will look after them for their good,
and bring them back to this land, to build
them up, not to tear them down; to plant
them, not to pluck them out. 7* I will give
them a heart with which to understand
that I am the LORD. They shall be my
people and I will be their God, for they
shall return to me with their whole heart.
8* And like the figs that are bad, so bad
they cannot be eaten—yes, thus says the
LORD—even so will I treat Zedekiah,
king of Judah, and his princes, the rem-
nant of Jerusalem remaining in this land
and those who have settled in the land
of Egypt. 9* I will make them an object
of horror to all the kingdoms of the
earth, a reproach and a byword, a taunt
and a curse, in all the places to which
I will drive them. 10* I will send upon
them the sword, famine, and pestilence,
until they have disappeared from the
land which I gave them and their fa-
thers.

*

27: Jgs 3, 7; 8, 33.
28: Nm 12, 6.
30: Dt 18, 20.
32: 28, 15ff.
40: 20, 11.
24, 1: Am 8, 1f.
3: 1, 11.
5: 29, 11; Lv 26, 44f.
6: 12, 15; Am 9, 15.
7: 30, 22; 31, 1; 32, 37; Bar 2, 31.
8: 29, 18.
9: 15, 4; Dt 28, 37.
10: 14, 12.

†

23, 28f: *Straw . . . wheat:* such is the contrast between false and true prophecy. True prophecy is like fire (cf 5, 14; 20, 9), producing violent results (v 29); Jeremiah's own life is a testimony of this.

23, 33-40: A wordplay on *massā'*, which means both oracle (usually of woe) and burden. In 34ff it appears that the word *massā'* itself is forbidden the people in the meaning of a divine oracle. Doubtless this was because of some association unknown to us. In Hos 2, 18 it is forbidden to call God "Baal" ("master"), because of the association of this title with the Canaanite god.

24, 1-10: Jeremiah, like Ezekiel, saw that no good could be expected from the people who had been left in Judah under Zedekiah or who had fled into Egypt; good was to be hoped for only from those who would pass through the purifying experience of the exile to form the new Israel.

CHAPTER 25

Seventy Years of Exile. 1*† The word
that came to Jeremiah concerning all
the people of Judah, in the fourth year
of Jehoiakim, son of Josiah, king of Ju-
dah (the first year of Nebuchadnezzar,
king of Babylon). 2 This word the
prophet Jeremiah spoke to all the people
of Judah and all the citizens of Jerusa-
lem: 3* Since the thirteenth year of Jo-
siah, son of Amon, king of Judah, to this
day—these three and twenty years—the
word of the LORD has come to me and
I spoke to you untiringly, but you would
not listen. 4* Though you refused to lis-
ten or pay heed, the LORD has sent you
without fail all his servants the prophets
5 with this message: Turn back, each of
you, from your evil way and from your
evil deeds; then you shall remain in the
land which the LORD gave you and your
fathers, from of old and forever. 6* Do
not follow strange gods to serve and
adore them, lest you provoke me with
your handiwork, and I bring evil upon
you. 7* But you would not listen to me,
says the LORD, and so you provoked me
with your handiwork to your own harm.
8 Hence, thus says the LORD of hosts:
Since you would not listen to my words,
9* lo! I will send for and fetch all the
tribes of the north, says the LORD (and
I will send to Nebuchadnezzar, king of
Babylon, my servant); I will bring them
against this land, against its inhabitants,
and against all these neighboring na-
tions. I will doom them, making them
an object of horror, of ridicule, of ever-
lasting reproach. 10 Among them I will
bring to an end the song of joy and the
song of gladness, the voice of the bride-
groom and the voice of the bride, the
sound of the millstone and the light of
the lamp. 11* This whole land shall be
a ruin and a desert. Seventy years these
nations shall be enslaved to the king of
Babylon; 12* but when the seventy years
have elapsed, I will punish the king of
Babylon and the nation and the land of
the Chaldeans for their guilt, says the
LORD. Their land I will turn into ever-
lasting desert. 13 Against that land I will
fulfill all the words I have spoken against
it [all that is written in this book, which
Jeremiah prophesied against all the na-
tions]. 14* They also shall be enslaved to
great nations and mighty kings, and
thus I will repay them according to their
own deeds and according to their own
handiwork.

***The Cup of Judgment on the Na-
tions.*** 15*† For thus said the LORD, the
God of Israel, to me: Take this cup of
foaming wine from my hand, and have
all the nations to whom I will send you
drink it. 16* They shall drink, and be
convulsed, and go mad, because of the
sword I will send among them. 17 I took
the cup from the hand of the LORD and
gave drink to all the nations to which
the LORD sent me: 18 [Jerusalem, the cit-
ies of Judah, her kings and her princes,
to make them a ruin and a desert, an
object of ridicule and cursing, as they
are today;] 19 Pharaoh, king of Egypt,
and his servants, his princes, all the peo-
ple under him, native 20† and foreign; all
the kings of the land of Uz; all the kings
of the land of the Philistines: Ashkelon,
Gaza, Ekron, and the remnant of Ash-
dod; 21 Edom, Moab, and the Ammon-
ites; 22† all the kings of Tyre, of Sidon,
and of the shores beyond the sea;
23† Dedan and Tema and Buz, all the
desert dwellers who shave their temples;
24 [all the kings of Arabia;] 25 all the
kings of Zimri, of Elam, of the Medes;
26† all the kings of the north, near and
far, one after the other; all the kingdoms
upon the face of the earth [and after
them the king of Sheshach shall drink].

27* Tell them: Thus says the LORD of
hosts, the God of Israel: Drink! become
drunk and vomit; fall, never to rise, be-
fore the sword that I will send among
you! 28* If they refuse to take the cup
from your hand and drink, say to them:
Thus says the LORD of hosts: You must
drink! 29 For since with this city, which
is called by my name, I begin to inflict
evil, how can you possibly be spared?
You shall not be spared! I will call down
the sword upon all who inhabit the earth,
says the LORD of hosts.
30* Prophesy against them all these
things and say to them:

The LORD roars from on high,
from his holy dwelling he raises
his voice;

---

*
25, 1: 36, 1.
3: 1, 2.
4: 2 Chr 36, 15.
6: 7, 6f.
7: 7, 17ff.
9: 1, 15; 43, 10.
11: Lv 26, 32-35.
12: Is 13, 20ff.
14: 27, 7; 50,9.41f; 51, 6.24.
15: Rv 14, 10.
16: 51, 7.
27: Ob 16.
28: 49, 12.
30: 51, 14.

†

25, 1-14: *The fourth year of Jehoiakim:* 605 B.C. Officially, *the first year of Nebuchadnezzar* began the following year; but as early as his victory over Egypt at Carchemish in 605, Nebuchadnezzar was the dominant power in the Near East, in whom Jeremiah now saw the fulfillment of his prophecy of the enemy to come from the north (cf 1, 13; 6, 22ff). In vv 11f occurs for the first time the prophecy of the seventy years' exile; cf 29, 10. This Jeremiah intends as a round number, to signify that the present generation must die out.

25, 15ff: Jeremiah is a prophet to the nations (cf 1, 5) as well as to his own people. All the nations mentioned here appear again in the more extensive collection of Jeremiah's oracles against the nations in chapters 46-51.

25, 20: *Uz:* the homeland of Job, in Edomite or Arabian territory.

25, 22: *The shores beyond the sea:* Phoenician commercial colonies planted throughout the Mediterranean world.

25, 23: *Dedan and Tema and Buz:* North Arabian tribes.

25, 26: *Sheshach:* Babylon. The word is formed from *bābēl* by substituting letters of the Hebrew alphabet in inverse order.

Mightily he roars over the range,
a shout like that of vintagers over the grapes.
31 To all who inhabit the earth to its very ends
the uproar spreads;
For the LORD has an indictment against the nations,
he is to pass judgment upon all mankind:
The godless shall be given to the sword,
says the LORD.
32 Thus says the LORD of hosts:
Lo! calamity stalks
from nation to nation;
A great storm is unleashed
from the ends of the earth.

33* On that day, those whom the LORD
has slain will be strewn from one end
of the earth to the other. None will
mourn them, none will gather them for
burial; they shall lie like dung on the
field.

34 Howl, you shepherds, and wail!
roll in the dust, leaders of the flock!
The time for your slaughter has come;
like choice rams you shall fall.
35* There is no flight for the shepherds,
no escape for the leaders of the flock.
36 Listen! Wailing from the shepherds,
howling by the leaders of the flock!
For the LORD lays waste their grazing place,
37 desolate lie the peaceful pastures;
38* The lion leaves his lair,
and their land is made desolate
By the sweeping sword,
by the burning wrath of the LORD.

CHAPTER 26

Jeremiah Threatened with Death.
1† In the beginning of the reign of Je-
hoiakim, son of Josiah, king of Judah,
this message came from the LORD:
2* Thus says the LORD: Stand in the
court of the house of the LORD and speak
to the people of all the cities of Judah
who come to worship in the house of the
LORD; whatever I command you, tell
them, and omit nothing. 3* Perhaps they
will listen and turn back, each from his
evil way, so that I may repent of the evil
I have planned to inflict upon them for
their evil deeds. 4 Say to them: Thus says
the LORD: If you disobey me, not living
according to the law I placed before you
5* and not listening to the words of my
servants the prophets, whom I send you
constantly though you do not obey them,
6* I will treat this house like Shiloh, and
make this the city which all the nations
of the earth shall refer to when cursing
another.
7 Now the priests, the prophets, and all
the people heard Jeremiah speak these
words in the house of the LORD. 8 When
Jeremiah finished speaking all that the
LORD bade him speak to all the people,
the priests and prophets laid hold of him,
crying, "You must be put to death! 9 Why
do you prophesy in the name of the
LORD: 'This house shall be like Shiloh,'
and 'This city shall be desolate and
deserted'?" And all the people gath-
ered about Jeremiah in the house of the
LORD.
10 When the princes of Judah were in-
formed of these things, they came up
from the king's palace to the house of
the LORD and held court at the New Gate
of the house of the LORD. 11* The priests
and prophets said to the princes and to
all the people, "This man deserves
death; he has prophesied against this
city, as you have heard with your own
ears." 12 Jeremiah gave this answer to
the princes and all the people: "It was
the LORD who sent me to prophesy
against this house and city all that you
have heard. 13* Now, therefore, reform
your ways and your deeds; listen to the
voice of the LORD your God, so that the
LORD will repent of the evil with which
he threatens you. 14 As for me, I am in
your hands; do with me what you think
good and right. 15 But mark well: if you
put me to death, it is innocent blood you
bring on yourselves, on this city and its
citizens. For in truth it was the LORD who
sent me to you, to speak all these things
for you to hear."
16 Thereupon the princes and all the
people said to the priests and the proph-
ets, "This man does not deserve death;
it is in the name of the LORD, our God,
that he speaks to us." 17 At this, some
of the elders of the land came forward
and said to all the people assembled,
18*† "Micah of Moresheth used to
prophesy in the days of Hezekiah, king
of Judah, and he told all the people of
Judah: Thus says the LORD of hosts:

Zion shall become a plowed field,
Jerusalem a heap of ruins,
and the temple mount a forest ridge.

*

33: 8, 2; 16, 4.6.
35: 32, 4.
38: 4, 7.
26, 2: 7, 2.
3: 18, 3.
5: 25, 4.
6: 7, 12.14.
11: 38, 4.
13: 7, 3.
18: Mi 1, 1; 3, 12.

†

26, 1: *The beginning of the reign:* a technical expression for the time between a king's accession to the throne and the beginning of his first official (calendar) year as king. Jehoiakim's first regnal year was 608 B.C.

26, 18: *Micah of Moresheth:* the prophet Micah, who appears among the canonical minor prophets (cf Mi 1, 1).

19* Did Hezekiah, king of Judah, and all
Judah condemn him to death? Did they
not rather fear the LORD and entreat the
favor of the LORD, so that he repented
of the evil with which he had threatened
them? But we are on the point of com-
mitting this great evil to our own undo-
ing."
The Fate of Uriah. 20 There was an-
other man who prophesied in the name
of the LORD, Uriah, son of Shemaiah,
from Kiriath-jearim; he prophesied the
same things against this city and land
as Jeremiah did. 21 When King Je-
hoiakim and all his officers and princes
were informed of his words, the king
sought to kill him. But Uriah heard of
it and fled in fear to Egypt. 22 Thereupon
King Jehoiakim sent Elnathan, son of
Achbor, and others with him into Egypt
23 to bring Uriah back to the king, who
had him slain by the sword and his
corpse cast into the common grave.
24† But Ahikam, son of Shaphan, pro-
tected Jeremiah, so that he was not
handed over to the people to be put to
death.

CHAPTER 27

Serve Babylon or Perish. 1† [In the
beginning of the reign of Jehoiakim, son
of Josiah, king of Judah,] . . . this mes-
sage came to Jeremiah from the LORD:
2 Thus said the LORD to me: Make for
yourself bands and yoke bars and put
them over your shoulders. 3 Send to the
kings of Edom, of Moab, of the Ammon-
ites, of Tyre, and of Sidon, through the
ambassadors who have come to Jerusa-
lem to Zedekiah, king of Judah, 4 and
charge them thus: Tell your masters:
Thus says the LORD of hosts, the God
of Israel: 5* It was I who made the earth,
and man and beast on the face of the
earth, by my great power, with my out-
stretched arm; and I can give them to
whomever I think fit. 6* Now I have
given all these lands into the hand of
Nebuchadnezzar, king of Babylon, my
servant; even the beasts of the field I
have given him for his use. 7* All nations
shall serve him and his son and his
grandson, until the time of his land, too,
shall come. Then it in turn shall serve
great nations and mighty kings.
8* Meanwhile, if any nation or kingdom
will not serve Nebuchadnezzar, king of
Babylon, or will not bend its neck under
the yoke of the king of Babylon, I will
punish that nation with sword, famine,
and pestilence, says the LORD, until I
give them into his hand.
9*† You, however, must not listen to
your prophets, to your diviners and
dreamers, to your soothsayers and sor-
cerers, who say to you, "You need not
serve the king of Babylon." 10* For they
prophesy lies to you, in order to drive
you far from your land, to make me ban-
ish you so that you will perish. 11* The
people that submits its neck to the yoke
of the king of Babylon to serve him I
will leave in peace on its own land, says
the LORD, to till it and dwell in it.
12* To Zedekiah, king of Judah, I spoke
the same words: Submit your necks to
the yoke of the king of Babylon; serve
him and his people, so that you may live.
13* Why should you and your people die
by sword, famine, and pestilence, with
which the LORD has threatened the na-
tion that will not serve the king of
Babylon? 14* Do not listen to the words
of those prophets who say, "You need
not serve the king of Babylon," for they
prophesy lies to you. 15* I did not send
them, says the LORD, but they prophesy
falsely in my name, with the result that
I must banish you, and you will perish,
you and the prophets who are prophesy-
ing to you.
16* To the priests and to all the people
I spoke as follows: Thus says the LORD:
Do not listen to the words of your proph-
ets who prophesy to you: "The vessels
of the house of the LORD will be brought
back from Babylon soon now," for they
prophesy lies to you. 17 Do not listen to
them! Serve the king of Babylon that you
may live; else this city will become a
heap of ruins. 18 If they were prophets,
if the word of the LORD were with them,
they would intercede with the LORD of
hosts, that the vessels which remain in
the house of the LORD and in the palace
of the king of Judah and in Jerusalem
might not be taken to Babylon. 19† For
thus says the LORD of hosts concerning
the pillars, the bronze sea, the stands,
and the rest of the vessels that remain

*

19: 2 Chr 32, 26.
27, 5: 32, 17.
6: 25, 9; 43, 10; Ez 30, 21.25.
7: 25, 11; 2 Chr 36, 20.
8: 25, 9; Bar 2, 22.
9: 29, 8.
10: 14, 13-16.
11: Bar 2, 21.
12: 38, 17.
13: 24, 8ff.
14: 14, 14; 23, 21.
15: 20, 6.
16: 28, 3; 2 Chr 36, 7.10.18.

†

26, 24: *Ahikam, son of Shaphan:* one of Josiah's officials (2 Kgs 22, 12) and father of Gedaliah, Jeremiah's friend, who was governor of Judah after Zedekiah's deportation (cf 39, 14; 40, 5ff).

27, 1—29, 32: A special collection of Jeremiah's prophecies dealing with false prophets. From stylistic peculiarities, quite evident in the Hebrew, it is plain that these three chapters once existed independently of the other prophecies of Jeremiah.

27, 1: [*In the beginning of the reign of Jehoiakim . . . Judah*]: this gloss cannot be correct because according to 28, 1 the time is the fourth year of Zedekiah 594 B.C., the occasion of an embassy of the neighboring states (v 3), doubtless for the purpose of laying plans against Nebuchadnezzar.

27, 9: *Your prophets:* seers and diviners served the Gentile kings as the professional prophets served the kings of Judah.

27, 19-22: This prophecy was fulfilled after Zedekiah's disastrous defeat; cf 2 Kgs 25, 13ff.

in this city, 20 which Nebuchadnezzar, king of Babylon, did not take when he exiled Jeconiah, son of Jehoiakim, king of Judah, from Jerusalem to Babylon, along with all the nobles of Judah and Jerusalem—21* yes, thus says the LORD of hosts, the God of Israel, concerning the vessels that remain in the house of the LORD, in the palace of the king of Judah, and in Jerusalem: 22 To Babylon they shall be brought, and there they shall remain, until the day I look for them, says the LORD; then I will bring them back and restore them to this place.

CHAPTER 28

The Two Yokes. 1 That same year, in [the beginning of] the reign of Zedekiah, king of Judah, in the fifth month of the fourth year, the prophet Hananiah, son of Azzur, from Gibeon, said to me in the house of the LORD in the presence of the priests and all the people: 2 "Thus says the LORD of hosts, the God of Israel: 'I will break the yoke of the king of Babylon. 3 Within two years I will restore to this place all the vessels of the temple of the LORD which Nebuchadnezzar, king of Babylon, took away from this place to Babylon. 4 And I will bring back to this place Jeconiah, son of Jehoiakim, king of Judah, and all the exiles of Judah who went to Babylon,' says the LORD, 'for I will break the yoke of the king of Babylon.' "

5 The prophet Jeremiah answered the prophet Hananiah in the presence of the priests and all the people assembled in the house of the LORD, 6 and said: Amen! thus may the LORD do! May he fulfill the things you have prophesied by bringing the vessels of the house of the LORD and all the exiles back from Babylon to this place! 7 But now, listen to what I am about to state in your hearing and the hearing of all the people. 8 From of old, the prophets who were before you and me prophesied war, woe, and pestilence against many lands and mighty kingdoms. 9* But the prophet who prophesies peace is recognized as truly sent by the LORD only when his prophetic prediction is fulfilled.

10 Thereupon the prophet Hananiah took the yoke from the neck of the prophet Jeremiah, broke it, 11 and said in the presence of all the people: "Thus says the LORD: 'Even so, within two years I will break the yoke of Nebuchadnezzar, king of Babylon, from off the neck of all the nations.' " At that, the prophet Jeremiah went away.

12 Some time after the prophet Hananiah had broken the yoke from off the neck of the prophet Jeremiah, the word of the LORD came to Jeremiah: 13 Go tell Hananiah this: Thus says the LORD: By breaking a wooden yoke, you forge an iron yoke! 14* For thus says the LORD of hosts, the God of Israel: A yoke of iron I will place on the necks of all these nations serving Nebuchadnezzar, king of Babylon, and they shall serve him; even the beasts of the field I give him.

15 To the prophet Hananiah the prophet Jeremiah said: Hear this, Hananiah! The LORD has not sent you, and you have raised false confidence in this people. 16* For this, says the LORD, I will dispatch you from the face of the earth; this very year you shall die, because you have preached rebellion against the LORD. 17 That same year, in the seventh month, Hananiah the prophet died.

CHAPTER 29

Letter to the Exiles in Babylon. 1 This is the contents of the letter which the prophet Jeremiah sent from Jerusalem to the remaining elders among the exiles, to the priests, the prophets, and all the people who were exiled by Nebuchadnezzar from Jerusalem to Babylon. 2* This was after King Jeconiah and the queen mother, the courtiers, the princes of Judah and Jerusalem, the artisans and the skilled workmen had left Jerusalem. 3† Delivered in Babylon by Elasah, son of Shaphan, and by Gemariah, son of Hilkiah, whom Zedekiah, king of Judah, sent to the king of Babylon, the letter read:

4 Thus says the LORD of hosts, the God of Israel, to all the exiles whom I exiled from Jerusalem to Babylon: 5 Build houses to dwell in; plant gardens, and eat their fruits. 6 Take wives and beget sons and daughters; find wives for your sons and give your daughters husbands, so that they may bear sons and daughters. There you must increase in number, not decrease. 7* Promote the welfare of the city to which I have exiled you; pray for it to the LORD, for upon its welfare depends your own.

10* Thus says the LORD: Only after seventy years have elapsed for Babylon will I visit you and fulfill for you my promise to bring you back to this place. 11 For I know well the plans I have in mind for

---

*

21f: 2 Kgs 25, 13-17; 2 Chr 36, 18.22.
28, 9: Dt 18, 22.
14: 27, 6f; Dt 28, 48.
16: Dt 13, 6.
29, 2: 2 Kgs 24, 15.
7: 1 Tm 2, 1f.
10: 25, 11; 2 Chr 36, 21f; Ezr 1, 1; Dn 9, 2; Zec 1, 12; 7, 5.

---

†

29, 3: *Elasah:* possibly the brother of Ahikam (cf 26, 24). *Gemariah:* perhaps the son of the high priest Hilkiah; cf 2 Kgs 22, 4. Zedekiah had dispatched these men to Nebuchadnezzar for some other purpose, possibly the payment of tribute, but Jeremiah took advantage of their mission to send his letter by them.

you, says the LORD, plans for your wel-
fare, not for woe! plans to give you a fu-
ture full of hope. [12]* When you call me,
when you go to pray to me, I will listen
to you. [13] When you look for me, you will
find me. Yes, when you seek me with
all your heart, [14]* you will find me with
you, says the LORD, and I will change
your lot; I will gather you together from
all the nations and all the places to which
I have banished you, says the LORD, and
bring you back to the place from which
I have exiled you.

[16] Thus says the LORD concerning the
king who sits on David's throne, and all
the people who remain in this city, your
brethren who did not go with you into
exile; [17] thus says the LORD of hosts: I
am sending against them sword, famine
and pestilence. I will make them like rot-
ten figs, too bad to be eaten. [18]* I will
pursue them with sword, famine, and
pestilence, and make them an object of
horror to all the kingdoms of the earth,
of malediction, astonishment, ridicule,
and reproach to all the nations among
which I will banish them. [19]* For they
did not listen to my words, says the
LORD, though I kept sending them my
servants the prophets, only to have them
go unheeded, says the LORD.

[20] You, now, listen to the word of the
LORD, all you exiles whom I sent away
from Jerusalem to Babylon. [15] As for
your saying, "The LORD has raised up
for us prophets here in Babylon"—
[8]* thus says the LORD of hosts, the God
of Israel: Do not let yourselves be de-
ceived by the prophets and diviners who
are among you; do not listen to those
among you who dream dreams. [9]* For
they prophesy lies to you in my name;
I did not send them, says the LORD.
[21]* This is what the LORD of hosts, the
God of Israel, has to say about those who
prophesy lies to you in my name, Ahab,
son of Kolaiah, and Zedekiah, son of
Maaseiah: I am handing them over to
Nebuchadnezzar, king of Babylon, who
will slay them before your eyes. [22] All
the exiles of Judah in Babylon will pat-
tern a curse after them: "May the LORD
make you like Zedekiah and Ahab,
whom the king of Babylon roasted in the
flames." [23]* For they are criminals in Is-
rael, committing adultery with their
neighbors' wives, and alleging in my
name things I did not command. I know,
I am witness, says the LORD.

The False Prophet Shemaiah. [24] Say
this to Shemaiah, the Nehelamite:
[25] Thus says the LORD of hosts, the God
of Israel: Because you sent letters on
your own authority to all the people of
Jerusalem, to all the priests and to Zeph-
aniah, the priest, son of Maaseiah, with
this message: [26]† "The LORD has ap-
pointed you priest in place of the priest
Jehoiada, so that there may be police
officers in the house of the LORD, to take
action against all madmen and those
who pose as prophets, by putting them
into the stocks or the pillory. [27] Why,
then, do you not rebuke Jeremiah of An-
athoth who poses as a prophet among
you? [28] For he sent us in Babylon this
message: It will be a long time; build
houses to live in; plant gardens and eat
their fruits. . . ."

[29] When the priest Zephaniah read this
letter to the prophet, [30] the word of the
LORD came to Jeremiah: [31] Send the
message to all the exiles: Thus says the
LORD concerning Shemaiah, the Nehel-
amite: Because Shemaiah prophesies to
you without a mission from me, and
raises false confidence, [32] says the LORD,
I will therefore punish Shemaiah, the
Nehelamite, and his offspring. None of
them shall survive among this people to
see the good I will do to this people, says
the LORD, because he preached rebellion
against the LORD.

CHAPTER 30

The Restoration. [1]† The following
message came to Jeremiah from the
LORD: [2]* Thus says the LORD, the God
of Israel: Write all the words I have spo-
ken to you in a book. [3]* For behold, the
days will come, says the LORD, when I
will change the lot of my people (of Is-
rael and Judah, says the LORD), and
bring them back to the land which I gave
to their fathers; they shall have it as
their possession.

[4] These are the words which the LORD
spoke to Israel and to Judah: [5] thus says
the LORD:

A cry of dismay we hear;
    fear reigns, not peace.
[6]* Inquire, and see:
    since when do men bear children?

JEREMIAH

*

12: 33, 3.
14: 23, 3.8.
18: 15, 4; 24, 9; 34, 17f.
19: 25, 4.
8: 27, 9.14.
9: 5, 31.
21: 14, 14.
23: 23, 14.
30, 2: 36, 2; Hb 2, 2; Rv 1, 11.
3: 29, 14; 31, 8.10.23; 32, 37.44; Ez 39, 25; Am 9, 14.
6: 6, 24; 50, 43.

†

29, 26-29: The words of Jeremiah to the false prophet Shemaiah are not fully preserved in the current Hebrew text, as is seen in the incomplete sentence of this translation (vv 25-28). In his letter to Zephaniah Shemaiah reminds him of his authority, as Pashhur's successor, to imprison Jeremiah. Zephaniah, however, merely reads the letter to Jeremiah but does not imprison him.

30, 1—31, 40: These two chapters do not belong chronologically to those that precede or follow. They contain mainly oracles of salvation which Jeremiah originally uttered on behalf of the conquered remnants of the northern kingdom; then, after Judah began to share Samaria's fate, the oracles were extended to include Judah. Their composition is to be placed early in Jeremiah's ministry, probably after the fall of Nineveh (612 B.C.), when Josiah assumed power over the North; cf 2 Kgs 23, 15ff.

Why, then, do I see all these men,
with their hands on their loins
like women in childbirth?
Why have all their faces turned
deathly pale?
7* How mighty is that day—
none like it!
A time of distress for Jacob,
though he shall be saved from it.

8* On that day, says the LORD of hosts,
"I will break his yoke from off your
necks and snap your bonds." Strangers
shall no longer enslave them; 9*† in-
stead, they shall serve the LORD, their
God, and David, their king, whom I will
raise up for them.

10* But you, my servant Jacob, fear not,
says the LORD,
be not dismayed, O Israel!
Behold, I will deliver you from the
far-off land,
your descendants, from their land
of exile;
Jacob shall again find rest,
shall be tranquil and undisturbed,
11* for I am with you, says the LORD,
to deliver you.
I will make an end of all the nations
among which I have scattered
you;
but of you I will not make an end.
I will chastise you as you deserve,
I will not let you go unpunished.

12* For thus says the LORD:
Incurable is your wound,
grievous your bruise;
13 There is none to plead your cause,
no remedy for your running sore,
no healing for you.
14* All your lovers have forgotten you,
they do not seek you.
I struck you as an enemy would
strike,
punished you cruelly;
15* Why cry out over your wound?
your pain is without relief.
Because of your great guilt,
your numerous sins,
I have done this to you.

16* Yet all who devour you shall be de-
voured,
all your enemies shall go into ex-
ile.
All who plunder you shall be plun-
dered,
all who pillage you I will hand over
to pillage.
17* For I will restore you to health;
of your wounds I will heal you,
says the LORD.
"The outcast" they have called you,
"with no avenger."

18* Thus says the LORD:
See! I will restore the tents of Jacob,
his dwellings I will pity;
City shall be rebuilt upon hill,
and palace restored as it was.
19* From them will resound songs of
praise,
the laughter of happy men.
I will make them not few, but many;
they will not be tiny, for I will glo-
rify them.
20* His sons shall be as of old,
his assembly before me shall
stand firm;
I will punish all his oppressors.
21† His leader shall be one of his own,
and his rulers shall come from his
kin.
When I summon him, he shall ap-
proach me;
how else should one take the
deadly risk
of approaching me? says the
LORD.
22* You shall be my people,
and I will be your God.

23* See, the storm of the LORD!
His wrath breaks forth
In a whirling storm
that bursts upon the heads of the
wicked.
24* The anger of the LORD will not
abate
until he has done and fulfilled
what he has determined in his
heart.
When the time comes,
you will fully understand.

CHAPTER 31

Good News of the Return

1* At that time, says the LORD,
I will be the God of all the tribes
of Israel,
and they shall be my people.

*

7: Am 5, 18; Zep 1, 14f.
8: Is 14, 5f; Ez 34, 27.
9: Ez 34, 23; 37, 24; Hos 3, 5; Lk 1, 69.
10: 46, 27; Is 43, 5.
11: 46, 28; Ez 11, 16f; Am 9, 8f.
12: 10, 19; 14, 17; 15, 18.
14: 22, 22; Lam 1, 19.
15: 15, 18.
16: 2, 3.
17: 33, 6.
18: 33, 7.11; Ezr 6, 3-15; Ez 36, 10.
19: Is 35, 10; 51, 11.
20: Is 49, 26.
22: 24, 7; 31, 1.33; 32, 38; Lv 26, 12; Ez 11, 20; 36, 28.
23: 23, 19.
24: 23, 20.
31, 1: 30, 22.

†

30, 9: *David, their king:* the messianic King of the Davidic line, often called David by the prophets; cf Ez 34, 23f; 37, 24f; Hos 3, 5.

30, 21: *His leader:* probably not the messianic King, but simply any one of the rulers of the restored Israel, who will no longer be foreigners, and with whom the Lord will be on terms of intimacy, as with the whole people. *The deadly risk of approaching me:* to approach God unsummoned brings death; cf Lv 16, 1f.

2† Thus says the LORD:
The people that escaped the sword
have found favor in the desert.
As Israel comes forward to be given
his rest,
3* the LORD appears to him from afar:
With age-old love I have loved you;
so I have kept my mercy toward
you.
4 Again I will restore you, and you
shall be rebuilt,
O virgin Israel;
Carrying your festive tambourines,
you shall go forth dancing with the
merrymakers.
5* Again you shall plant vineyards
on the mountains of Samaria;
those who plant them shall enjoy
the fruits.
6* Yes, a day will come when the
watchmen
will call out on Mount Ephraim:
"Rise up, let us go to Zion,
to the LORD, our God."

The Road of Return

7* For thus says the LORD:
Shout with joy for Jacob,
exult at the head of the nations;
proclaim your praise and say:
The LORD has delivered his people,
the remnant of Israel.
8* Behold, I will bring them back
from the land of the north;
I will gather them from the ends of
the world,
with the blind and the lame in
their midst,
The mothers and those with child;
they shall return as an immense
throng.
9* They departed in tears,
but I will console them and guide
them;
I will lead them to brooks of water,
on a level road, so that none shall
stumble.
For I am a father to Israel,
Ephraim is my first-born.
10 Hear the word of the LORD, O na-
tions,
proclaim it on distant coasts, and
say:
He who scattered Israel, now gath-
ers them together,
he guards them as a shepherd his
flock.
11* The LORD shall ransom Jacob,
he shall redeem him from the
hand of his conqueror.
12* Shouting, they shall mount the
heights of Zion,
they shall come streaming to the
LORD's blessings:
The grain, the wine, and the oil,
the sheep and the oxen;
They themselves shall be like
watered gardens,
never again shall they languish.
13 Then the virgins shall make merry
and dance,
and young men and old as well.
I will turn their mourning into joy,
I will console and gladden them
after their sorrows.
14 I will lavish choice portions upon the
priests,
and my people shall be filled with
my blessings,
says the LORD.

End of Rachel's Mourning

15*† Thus says the LORD:
In Ramah is heard the sound of
moaning,
of bitter weeping!
Rachel mourns her children,
she refuses to be consoled
because her children are no more.
16 Thus says the LORD:
Cease your cries of mourning,
wipe the tears from your eyes.
The sorrow you have shown shall
have its reward,
says the LORD,
they shall return from the ene-
my's land.
17* There is hope for your future, says
the LORD;
your sons shall return to their own
borders.
18* I hear, I hear Ephraim pleading:
You chastised me, and I am chas-
tened;
I was an untamed calf.
If you allow me, I will return,
for you are the LORD, my God.
19* I turn in repentance;
I have come to myself, I strike my
breast;
I blush with shame,
I bear the disgrace of my youth.
20* Is Ephraim not my favored son,
the child in whom I delight?

JEREMIAH

*

3: Dt 7, 8; 10, 15; Is 43, 4; 63, 9; Hos 11, 1.4.
5: Is 65, 21; Am 9, 14.
6: Is 2, 3; 27, 13; Mi 4, 2.
7: Is 12, 6.
8: 3, 18; 23, 3.8; Is 35, 5f.
9: Ex 4, 22.
11: Is 44, 23; 48, 20.
12: Is 58, 11.
15: Mt 2, 18.
17: 29, 10-14.
18: Lv 26, 40ff.
19: Dt 30, 1ff.
20: Hos 11, 8.

†

31, 2: *The people that escaped the sword:* the exiles who were not killed but deported; they *have found favor in the desert,* across which they were driven into captivity. The prophet alludes to the first desert wandering of Israel (Ex 16ff), in which the people found the Lord. *His rest:* the land of promise. The perfect fulfillment of this promised rest is found only in the New Testament (Heb chapters 3 and 4).

31, 15: *Ramah:* a village about five miles north of Jerusalem, where Rachel was buried (1 Sm 10, 2). *Rachel:* said to mourn for her children since she was the ancestress of Ephraim, the chief of the northern tribes. Mt 2, 18 applies this verse to the slaughter of the innocents by Herod.

Often as I threaten him,
I still remember him with favor;
My heart stirs for him,
I must show him mercy, says the
LORD.

Summons To Return Home

21 Set up road markers,
put up guideposts;
Turn your attention to the highway,
the road by which you went.
Turn back, O virgin Israel,
turn back to these your cities.
22† How long will you continue to stray,
rebellious daughter?
The LORD has created a new thing
upon the earth:
the woman must encompass the
man with devotion.

23* Thus says the LORD of hosts, the
God of Israel: When I change their lot
in the land of Judah and her cities, they
shall again repeat this greeting: "May
the LORD bless you, holy mountain,
abode of justice!" 24 Judah and all her
cities, the farmers and those who lead
the flock, shall dwell there together.
25 For I will refresh the weary soul; every
soul that languishes I will replenish.
26† Upon this I awoke and opened my
eyes; but my sleep was sweet to me.
27 The days are coming, says the LORD,
when I will seed the house of Israel and
the house of Judah with the seed of man
and the seed of beast. 28* As I once
watched over them to uproot and pull
down, to destroy, to ruin, and to harm,
so I will watch over them to build and
to plant, says the LORD. 29*† In those
days they shall no longer say,

"The fathers ate unripe grapes,
and the children's teeth are set on
edge,"

30 but through his own fault only shall
anyone die: the teeth of him who eats
the unripe grapes shall be set on edge.
The New Covenant. 31*† The days are
coming, says the LORD, when I will make
a new covenant with the house of Israel
and the house of Judah. 32* It will not
be like the covenant I made with their
fathers the day I took them by the hand
to lead them forth from the land of
Egypt; for they broke my covenant and
I had to show myself their master, says
the LORD. 33* But this is the covenant
which I will make with the house of Is-
rael after those days, says the LORD. I
will place my law within them, and write
it upon their hearts; I will be their God,
and they shall be my people. 34* No
longer will they have need to teach their
friends and kinsmen how to know the
LORD. All, from least to greatest, shall
know me, says the LORD, for I will for-
give their evildoing and remember their
sin no more.

Certainty of God's Promise

35* Thus says the LORD,
He who gives the sun to light the
day,
moon and stars to light the night;
Who stirs up the sea till its waves
roar,
whose name is LORD of hosts:
36* If ever these natural laws give way
in spite of me, says the LORD,
Then shall the race of Israel cease
as a nation before me forever.
37 Thus says the LORD:
If the heavens on high can be mea-
sured,
or the foundations below the earth
be sounded,
Then will I cast off the whole race
of Israel
because of all they have done,
says the LORD.

Rebuilding of Jerusalem. 38*† The
days are coming, says the LORD, when

*

23: 30, 3; Ps 122, 8.
28: 1, 10; 18, 7.
29: Dt 24, 16; Ez 18, 2.
31: 32, 40; Heb 9, 15.
32: Ex 24, 7f; Dt 5, 2.
33: 32, 40; Ez 37, 26; Heb 10, 16.
34: Is 54, 13.
35: Gn 1, 14-18.
36: 33, 20f.
38: Neh 12, 38; Zec 14, 10f.

†

31, 22: *The woman must encompass the man:* the words "with devotion," not in the Hebrew, are added for the sense. No fully satisfactory explanation has been given this text. Among the more probable are these: (a) Formerly the man (the Lord) encompassed the woman (Israel) with mercy and devotion; now in the spiritual religion of Israel which will follow on the restoration, this order will be reversed. (b) So secure will Israel be after the restoration that women will no longer need the natural protection of their husbands, but even weak women can protect men. (c) St. Jerome in his commentary on this verse understood it of Mary's virginal conception of Christ. "The LORD has created a new thing on earth; without seed of man, without carnal union and conception, 'a woman will encompass a man' within her womb—One who, though He will later appear to advance in wisdom and age through the stages of infancy and childhood, yet, while confined for the usual number of months in his mother's womb, will already be perfect man."

31, 26: *I awoke . . . sweet to me:* probably said by the prophet himself.

31, 29: *"The fathers . . . on edge":* a proverb used in Israel, expressing the idea that children suffer for the sins of their parents (cf Ez 18, 2). The Israel of the restoration will be characterized instead by personal responsibility and retribution for one's acts (v 30; cf vv 31-34).

31, 31-34: The *new covenant* to be made with Israel is a common theme of the prophets, beginning with Hosea. According to Jeremiah, the qualities of the new covenant that make it different from the old are: (a) It will not be broken, but will last forever; (b) Its law will be written in the heart, not merely on tablets of stone; (c) The knowledge of God will be so generally shown forth in the life of the people that it will no longer be necessary to put it into words of instruction. In the fullest sense, this prophecy was fulfilled only through the work of Jesus Christ; cf Lk 22, 20; 1 Cor 11, 25.

31, 38: *From the Tower of Hananel to the Corner Gate:* from the northeast to the northwest.

the city shall be rebuilt as the LORD's, from the Tower of Hananel to the Corner Gate. [39] The measuring line shall be stretched from there straight to the hill Gareb and then turn to Goah. [40]† The whole valley of corpses and ashes, all the slopes toward the Kidron Valley, as far as the corner of the Horse Gate at the east, shall be holy to the LORD. Never again shall the city be rooted up or thrown down.

CHAPTER 32

Pledge of Restoration. [1]† This message came to Jeremiah from the LORD in the tenth year of Zedekiah, king of Judah, the eighteenth year of Nebuchadnezzar. [2]* At that time the army of the king of Babylon was besieging Jerusalem, and the prophet Jeremiah was imprisoned in the quarters of the guard, at the king's palace. [3]* Zedekiah, king of Judah, had imprisoned him there, remonstrating: "How dare you prophesy: Thus says the LORD: I am handing over this city to the king of Babylon, who will capture it. [4]* Neither shall Zedekiah, king of Judah, escape the hands of the Chaldeans; rather shall he be handed over to the king of Babylon. They shall meet and speak face to face, [5]* and Zedekiah shall be taken to Babylon. There he shall remain, until I attend to him, says the LORD; in fighting the Chaldeans, you cannot win!"

[6]† This message came to me from the LORD, said Jeremiah: [7]*† Hanamel, son of your uncle Shallum, will come to you with the offer: "Buy for yourself my field in Anathoth, since you, as nearest relative, have the first right of purchase." [8] Then, as the LORD foretold, Hanamel, my uncle's son, came to me to the quarters of the guard and said, "Please buy my field in Anathoth, in the district of Benjamin; as nearest relative, you have the first claim to possess it; make it yours." I knew this was what the LORD meant, [9] so I bought the field in Anathoth from my cousin Hanamel, paying him the money, seventeen silver shekels.

[10] When I had written and sealed the deed, called witnesses and weighed out the silver on the scales, [11]† I accepted the deed of purchase, both the sealed copy, containing title and conditions, and the open one. [12]* This deed of purchase I gave to Baruch, son of Neriah, son of Mahseiah, in the presence of my cousin Hanamel and of the witnesses who had signed the deed, and before all the men of Judah who happened to be in the quarters of the guard.

[13] In their presence I gave Baruch this charge: [14]† Thus says the LORD of hosts, the God of Israel: Take these deeds, both the sealed and the open deed of purchase, and put them in an earthen jar, so that they can be kept there a long time. [15] For thus says the LORD of hosts, the God of Israel: Houses and fields and vineyards shall again be bought in this land.

[16] After giving the deed of purchase to Baruch, son of Neriah, I prayed thus to the LORD: [17]* Ah, Lord GOD, you have made heaven and earth by your great might, with your outstretched arm; nothing is impossible to you. [18]* You continue your kindness through a thousand generations; and you repay the fathers' guilt, even into the lap of their sons who follow them. O God, great and mighty, whose name is LORD of hosts, [19]* great in counsel, mighty in deed, whose eyes are open to all the ways of men, giving to each according to his ways, according to the fruit of his deeds: [20]* you have wrought signs and wonders in the land of Egypt and to this day, both in Israel and among all other men, until now you have gained renown. [21] With strong hand and outstretched arm you brought your people Israel out of the land of Egypt amid signs and wonders and great terror. [22]* This land you gave them, as you had promised their fathers under oath, a land flowing with milk and honey. [23]* They entered and took pos-

*

32, 2: 33, 1; 37, 20; 38, 6; 39, 14.
3: 26, 9; 34, 2; 37, 6-10.
4: 34, 3; 38, 18.23; 39, 4-7.
5: 39, 7; 52, 11.
7: Lv 25, 24-34; Ru 4, 4.
12: 36, 4.
17: 2 Kgs 19, 15; Jb 42, 2.
18: Ex 20, 5f; Dt 5, 9.
19: Jb 34, 21; Ps 33, 13ff.
20: Ex 6, 6; Dt 4, 34; Ps 135, 9.
22: 11, 5; Gn 15, 18; 17, 8; 26, 3.
23: 7, 24ff; Dn 9, 10-14.

†

31, 40: *Valley of corpses and ashes:* the Valley of Ben-hinnom, which joins the Kidron at the southeast of ancient Jerusalem. *The Horse Gate:* in the eastern city wall, at the southeast corner of the temple area.

32, 1-44: This chapter recounts a prophecy "in action." At the Lord's command, Jeremiah fulfills his family duty to purchase the land of his cousin, carrying out all the legal forms, including records, to testify that Judah will be restored and that the life of the past will be resumed.

32, 1: *The tenth year of Zedekiah:* 588 B.C. *The eighteenth year of Nebuchadnezzar:* dating his reign from his victory at Carchemish; see note on 25, 1-14.

32, 6-9: Jeremiah's imprisonment by the weak-willed Zedekiah was a technical custody that did not deprive him of all freedom of action. The siege maintained by the Chaldeans (v 2) was only now beginning (v 24), and could be bypassed by individual persons going to and fro between Jerusalem and nearby Anathoth.

32, 7: *The first right of purchase:* the obligation of the closest relative to redeem the property of one in economic distress, so that the ancestral land might remain within the family (Lv 25, 25-28); see note on Ru 2, 20.

32, 11: *The sealed copy . . . and the open one:* the legal deed of sale was written on a scroll, which was then rolled up and sealed; about it was rolled another scroll, left unsealed, containing a copy or a summary of the first.

32, 14: *In an earthen jar:* the first of the Dead Sea Scrolls were found in such a jar.

session of it, but they did not listen to your voice; by your law they did not live, and what you commanded they failed to do. Hence you let all these evils befall them. 24* See, the siegeworks have arrived at this city to breach it; the city will be handed over to the Chaldeans who are attacking it, amid sword, famine, and pestilence. What you threatened has happened, you see it yourself; 25 and yet you tell me, O Lord GOD: Buy the field with money, call in witnesses. But the city has already been handed over to the Chaldeans!

26 Then this word of the LORD came to Jeremiah: 27 I am the LORD, the God of all mankind! Is anything impossible to me? 28 This now is what the LORD says: I will hand over this city to the Chaldeans, for Nebuchadnezzar, king of Babylon, to take. 29* The Chaldeans who are attacking it shall enter this city and set fire to it, burning it and its houses, on the roofs of which incense was burned to Baal and libations were poured out to strange gods as a provocation to me. 30* The Israelites and the Judeans from their youth have done only what is evil in my eyes; the Israelites did nothing but provoke me with the works of their hands, says the LORD. 31 From the day it was built to this day, this city has excited my anger and wrath, 32* so that I must put it out of my sight for all the wickedness the Israelites and Judeans, with their kings and their princes, their priests and their prophets, the men of Judah and the citizens of Jerusalem, have done to provoke me. 33* They turned their backs to me, not their faces; though I kept teaching them, they would not listen to my correction. 34* They defiled the house named after me by the horrid idols they set up in it. 35*† They built high places to Baal in the Valley of Ben-hinnom, and immolated their sons and daughters to Molech, bringing sin upon Judah; this I never commanded them, nor did it even enter my mind that they should practice such abominations.

36 Now, therefore, thus says the LORD, the God of Israel, concerning this city, which as you say is handed over to the king of Babylon amid sword, famine, and pestilence: 37* Behold, I will gather them together from all the lands to which in anger, wrath, and great rage I banish them; I will bring them back to this place and settle them here in safety. 38* They shall be my people, and I will be their God. 39 One heart and one way I will give them, that they may fear me always, to their own good and that of their children after them. 40* I will make with them an eternal covenant, never to cease doing good to them; into their hearts I will put the fear of me, that they may never depart from me. 41* I will take delight in doing good to them: I will replant them firmly in this land, with all my heart and soul.

42* For thus says the LORD: Just as I brought upon this people all this great evil, so I will bring upon them all the good I promise them. 43* Fields shall again be bought in this land, which you call a desert, without man or beast, handed over to the Chaldeans. 44* Fields shall be bought with money, deeds written and sealed, and witnesses shall be used in the land of Benjamin, in the suburbs of Jerusalem, in the cities of Judah and of the hill country, in the cities of the foothills and of the Negeb, when I change their lot, says the LORD.

CHAPTER 33

Restoration of Jerusalem. 1 The word of the LORD came to Jeremiah a second time while he was still imprisoned in the quarters of the guard: 2 Thus says the LORD who made the earth and gave it form and firmness, whose name is LORD: 3* Call to me, and I will answer you; I will tell to you things great beyond reach of your knowledge. 4* Thus says the LORD, the God of Israel, concerning the houses of this city and the palaces of Judah's kings, which are being destroyed in the face of siegeworks and the sword: 5* men come to battle the Chaldeans, and these houses will be filled with the corpses of those whom I slay in my anger and wrath, when I hide my face from this city for all their wickedness.

6* Behold, I will treat and assuage the city's wounds; I will heal them, and reveal to them an abundance of lasting peace. 7* I will change the lot of Judah and the lot of Israel, and rebuild them as of old. 8* I will cleanse them of all the guilt they incurred by sinning against me; all their offenses by which they sinned and rebelled against me, I will forgive. 9 Then Jerusalem shall be my joy, my praise, my glory, before all the

*

24: 21, 5; 33, 4.
29: 21, 10; 37, 8ff.
30: 3, 25; 44, 8.
32: 2, 26; Is 3, 8.
33: 7, 24.
34: 7, 30; 2 Kgs 21, 4f.
35: 7, 31; 19, 5; Ps 106, 37f.
37: 23, 3; 29, 14; Is 11, 12; Ez 11, 17.
38: 24, 7; 31, 33.
40: 31, 31ff.
41: Dt 30, 9.
42: 33, 10-14; Zec 8, 13.
43: 33, 10.
44: 17, 26; 33, 7.
33, 3: Is 48, 6.
4: 32, 24.
5: 21, 4ff.
6: Is 57, 18.
7: 30, 3; 32, 44.
8: Ez 36, 25.

†

32, 35: *Molech:* the god to whom human sacrifice was offered in the Valley of Ben-hinnom. Here, as in 19, 5, he is given the name *Baal;* see note on Lv 18, 21.

nations of the earth, as they hear of all
the good I will do among them. They
shall be in fear and trembling over all
the peaceful benefits I will give her.
10* Thus says the LORD: In this place
of which you say, "How desolate it is,
without man, without beast!" and in the
cities of Judah, in the streets of Jerusa-
lem that are now deserted, without man,
without citizen, without beast, there
shall yet be heard 11* the cry of joy, the
cry of gladness, the voice of the bride-
groom, the voice of the bride, the sound
of those who bring thank offerings to the
house of the LORD, singing, "Give thanks
to the LORD of hosts, for the LORD is
good; his mercy endures forever." For
I will restore this country as of old, says
the LORD.
12 Thus says the LORD of hosts: In this
place, now desolate, without man or
beast, and in all its cities there shall
again be sheepfolds for the shepherds
to couch their flocks. 13 In the cities of
the hill country, of the foothills, and of
the Negeb, in the land of Benjamin and
the suburbs of Jerusalem, and in the cit-
ies of Judah, flocks will again pass under
the hands of the one who counts them,
says the LORD.
14† The days are coming, says the
LORD, when I will fulfill the promise I
made to the house of Israel and Judah.
15* In those days, in that time, I will raise
up for David a just shoot; he shall do
what is right and just in the land. 16 In
those days Judah shall be safe and Jeru-
salem shall dwell secure; this is what
they shall call her: "The LORD our jus-
tice." 17* For thus says the LORD: Never
shall David lack a successor on the
throne of the house of Israel, 18* nor shall
priests of Levi ever be lacking, to offer
holocausts before me, to burn cereal of-
ferings, and to sacrifice victims.
This word of the LORD also came to
Jeremiah: 19 Thus says the LORD: 20* If
you can break my covenant with day,
and my covenant with night, so that day
and night no longer alternate in se-
quence, 21 then can my covenant with
my servant David also be broken, so that
he will not have a son to be king upon
his throne, and my covenant with the
priests of Levi who minister to me.
22 Like the host of heaven which cannot
be numbered, and the sands of the sea
which cannot be counted, I will multiply
the descendants of my servant David
and the Levites who minister to me.
23 This word of the LORD came to Jere-
miah: 24* Have you not noticed what
these people are saying: "The LORD has
rejected the two tribes which he had
chosen"? They spurn my people as if it
were no longer a nation in their eyes.
25* Thus says the LORD: When I have no
covenant with day and night, and have
given no laws to heaven and earth,
26 then too will I reject the descendants
of Jacob and of my servant David, so
as not to take from his descendants rul-
ers for the race of Abraham, Isaac, and
Jacob. For I will change their lot and
show them mercy.

IV: FALL OF JERUSALEM

CHAPTER 34

Fate of Zedekiah. 1* This word came
to Jeremiah from the LORD while Nebu-
chadnezzar, king of Babylon, and his ar-
mies and the earth's kingdoms subject
to him, as well as the other peoples, were
all attacking Jerusalem and all her cit-
ies: 2* Thus says the LORD, the God of
Israel: Go to Zedekiah, king of Judah,
and tell him: Thus says the LORD: I am
handing this city over to the king of
Babylon; he will destroy it with fire.
3* Neither shall you escape his hand;
rather you will be captured and fall into
his hands. You shall see the king of
Babylon and speak to him face to face.
Then you shall be taken to Babylon.
4 But if you obey the word of the LORD,
Zedekiah, king of Judah, then, says the
LORD to you, you shall not die by the
sword. 5 You shall die in peace, and they
will lament you as their lord, and burn
spices for your burial as they did for
your fathers, the kings who preceded
you from the first; it is I who make this
promise, says the LORD.
6 The prophet Jeremiah told all these
things to Zedekiah, king of Judah, in Je-
rusalem, 7† while the armies of the king
of Babylon were attacking Jerusalem
and the remaining cities of Judah, La-

JEREMIAH

*

10: 32, 43.
11: 1 Chr 16, 34; Ezr 3, 11; Ps 136, 1.
15: 23, 5; Ps 72, 1-4.12ff; Is 11, 1.
17: 2 Sm 7, 16; 1 Kgs 2, 4; Ps 89, 4f.29.36f.
18: Ez 44, 15f.
20f: 31, 36f; Ps 89, 37f.
24: Rom 11, 1f.
25f: 31, 36f; 32, 44.
34, 1: 52, 4; 2 Kgs 25, 1.
2: 21, 10; 32, 3.28.
3: 32, 4; 52, 11.

†

33, 14-26: This is the longest continuous passage in the Book of Jeremiah that is lacking in the Greek. It appears to be the postexilic composition of an inspired writer who used parts of the prophecies of Jeremiah—often, however, in a sense different from the prophet's. The prediction of an eternal Davidic dynasty (14-17) to fulfill the prophecy of Nathan (2 Sm 7, 11-16), and of a perpetual priesthood and sacrifice (18), was not to be realized in the restoration of the Jewish nation. It finds its fulfillment only in Jesus of Nazareth, who combined with his messianic Davidic kingship an eternal priesthood; cf Heb 6, 20; 7, 24f.

34, 7: *Lachish and Azekah:* fortress towns to the southwest of Jerusalem which Nebuchadnezzar besieged to prevent help coming to Jerusalem from Egypt. Between 1935 and 1938, archaeologists found at Lachish several letters written on pottery fragments which date from 598 or 588 B.C., and which mention both Lachish and Azekah.

chish, and Azekah, since these alone were left of the fortified cities of Judah.

The Pact Broken. 8† This is the word that came to Jeremiah from the LORD after King Zedekiah had made an agreement with all the people in Jerusalem to issue an edict of emancipation. 9* Everyone was to free his Hebrew slaves, male and female, so that no one should hold a man of Judah, his brother, in slavery. 10 All the princes and the others who entered the agreement consented to set free their male and female servants, so that they should be slaves no longer. But though they agreed and freed them, 11 afterward they took back their male and female slaves whom they had set free and again forced them into service.

12 Then this word of the LORD came to Jeremiah: 13 Thus says the LORD, the God of Israel: The day I brought your fathers out of the land of Egypt, out of the place where they were slaves, I made this covenant with them: 14 Every seventh year each of you shall set free his Hebrew brother who has sold himself to you; six years he shall serve you, but then you shall let him go free. Your fathers, however, did not heed me or obey me. 15 Today you indeed repented and did what is right in my eyes by proclaiming the emancipation of your brethren and making an agreement before me in the house that is named after me. 16* But then you changed your mind and profaned my name by taking back your male and female slaves to whom you had given their freedom; you forced them once more into slavery. 17 Therefore, thus says the LORD: You did not obey me by proclaiming your neighbors and kinsmen free. I now proclaim you free, says the LORD, for the sword, famine, and pestilence. I will make you an object of horror to all the kingdoms of the earth. 18† The men who violated my covenant and did not observe the terms of the agreement which they made before me, I will make like the calf which they cut in two, between whose two parts they passed. 19 The princes of Judah and of Jerusalem, the courtiers, the priests, and the common people, who passed between the parts of the calf, 20* I will hand over, all of them, to their enemies, to those who seek their lives: their corpses shall be food for the birds of the air and the beasts of the field.

21* Zedekiah, too, king of Judah, and his princes, I will hand over to their enemies, to those who seek their lives, to the soldiers of the king of Babylon who have at present withdrawn from you. 22* I will give the command, says the LORD, and bring them back to this city. They shall attack and capture it, and destroy it with fire; the cities of Judah I will turn into a desert where no man dwells.

JEREMIAH

CHAPTER 35

The Faithful Rechabites. 1 This word came to Jeremiah from the LORD in the days of Jehoiakim, son of Josiah, king of Judah: 2† Approach the Rechabites and speak to them; bring them into the house of the LORD, to one of the rooms, and give them wine to drink. 3 So I went and brought Jaazaniah, son of Jeremiah, son of Habazziniah, his brothers and all his sons, the whole company of the Rechabites, 4† into the house of the LORD, to the room of the sons of Hanan, son of Igdaliah, the man of God, next to the princes' room, above the room of Maaseiah, son of Shallum, keeper of the doorway. 5 I set before these Rechabite men bowls full of wine and offered them cups to drink the wine.

6† "We do not drink wine," they said to me: "Jonadab, Rechab's son, our father, forbade us in these words: 'Neither you nor your children shall ever drink wine. 7 Build no house and sow no seed; neither plant nor own a vineyard. You shall dwell in tents all your life, so that you may live long on the earth where you are wayfarers.' 8 Now we have heeded Jonadab, Rechab's son, our father, in all his prohibitions. All our lives we have not drunk wine, neither we, nor our wives, nor our sons, nor our daughters. 9 We build no houses to live in; we

*

9: Ex 21, 2ff; Lv 25, 39.46; Dt 15, 12-15.
16: Lv 19, 12.
20: 7, 33; 16, 4; 19, 7.
21: 37, 5.11.
22: 37, 8; 52, 7-13; 2 Chr 36, 17.19.

†

34, 8-22: While the Chaldean siege of Jerusalem was in progress, the citizens of Jerusalem made a covenant at Zedekiah's instigation to free their brother Judeans who were in slavery. Doubtless this was both to provide additional free defenders for the city and to offer reparation for past violations of the law, according to which Hebrew slaves were to serve no longer than six years (Dt 15, 12-15). But when the siege was temporarily lifted, probably because of the help promised by Pharaoh Hophra (cf 37, 5), the inhabitants of Jerusalem broke the covenant and once more pressed their brethren into slavery (v 11).

34, 18f: As the Bible (Gn 15, 10-17) and also contemporary inscriptions make clear, agreements were sometimes ratified by walking between the divided pieces of animals while the contracting parties invoked on themselves a fate similar to that of the slaughtered beast if they should fail to keep their word. *The agreement:* that mentioned in vv 10.15.

35, 2: *The Rechabites:* reactionaries who believed that the Lord could not be well served except by maintaining the original nomadic conditions of Israel's life. Without sharing their convictions, the prophet holds up their fidelity to their ideals as an example to put to shame his faithless countrymen. *In the days of Jehoiakim:* probably in 599 or 598 B.C.

35, 4: *The sons of Hanan:* probably the disciples of this *man of God* or prophet. *Maaseiah:* possibly the father of the priest Zephaniah (29, 25; 37, 3). *Keeper of the doorway:* a priestly function of responsibility; cf 52, 24.

35, 6: *Jonadab:* a contemporary of King Jehu; cf 2 Kgs 10, 15ff.

own no vineyards or fields or crops, 10 and we live in tents; we obediently do everything our father Jonadab commanded us. 11† But when Nebuchadnezzar, king of Babylon, invaded this land, we decided to come into Jerusalem to escape the army of the Chaldeans and the army of Aram; that is why we are now living in Jerusalem."

12 Then this word of the LORD came to Jeremiah: 13* Thus says the LORD of hosts, the God of Israel: Go, say to the men of Judah and to the citizens of Jerusalem: Will you not take correction and obey my words? says the LORD. 14* The advice of Jonadab, Rechab's son, by which he forbade his children to drink wine, has been followed: to this day they have not drunk it; they obeyed their father's command. Me, however, you have not obeyed, although I spoke to you untiringly and insistently. 15* I kept sending you all my servants the prophets, telling you to turn back, all of you, from your evil way; to reform your conduct, and not follow strange gods or serve them, if you would remain on the land which I gave you and your fathers; but you did not heed me or obey me. 16 Yes, the children of Jonadab, Rechab's son, observed the command which their father laid on them; but this people does not obey me! 17* Now, therefore, says the LORD God of hosts, the God of Israel: I will bring upon Judah and all the citizens of Jerusalem every evil that I threatened; because when I spoke they did not obey, when I called they did not answer.

18 But to the company of the Rechabites Jeremiah said: Thus says the LORD of hosts, the God of Israel: Since you have obeyed the command of Jonadab, your father, kept all his commands and done everything he commanded you, 19 thus therefore says the LORD of hosts, the God of Israel: Never shall there fail to be a descendant of Jonadab, Rechab's son, standing in my service.

CHAPTER 36

Baruch Writes the Prophecies of Jeremiah. 1 In the fourth year of Jehoiakim, son of Josiah, king of Judah, this word came to Jeremiah from the LORD: 2 Take a scroll and write on it all the words I have spoken to you against Israel, Judah, and all the nations, from the day I first spoke to you, in the days of Josiah, until today. 3* Perhaps, when the house of Judah hears all the evil I have in mind to do to them, they will turn back each from his evil way, so that I may forgive their wickedness and their sin. 4 So Jeremiah called Baruch, son of Neriah, who wrote down on a scroll, as Jeremiah dictated, all the words which the LORD had spoken to him.

9 In the ninth month, in the fifth year of Jehoiakim, son of Josiah, king of Judah, a fast to placate the LORD was proclaimed for all the people of Jerusalem and all who came from Judah's cities to Jerusalem. 5† Then Jeremiah charged Baruch: I cannot go to the house of the LORD; I am prevented from doing so. 6 Do you go on the fast day and read publicly in the LORD's house the LORD's words from the scroll you wrote at my dictation; read them also to all the men of Judah who come up from their cities. 7* Perhaps they will lay their supplication before the LORD and will all turn back from their evil way; for great is the fury of anger with which the LORD has threatened this people.

8 Baruch, son of Neriah, did everything the prophet Jeremiah commanded; from the book-scroll he read the LORD's words in the LORD's house. 10† It was in the room of Gemariah, son of the scribe Shaphan, in the upper court of the LORD's house, at the entrance of the New Temple-Gate, that Baruch publicly read the words of Jeremiah from his book.

11 Now Micaiah, son of Gemariah, son of Shaphan, heard all the words of the LORD read from the book. 12† So he went down to the king's palace, into the scribe's chamber, where the princes were just then in session: Elishama, the scribe, Delaiah, son of Shemaiah, Elnathan, son of Achbor, Gemariah, son of Shaphan, Zedekiah, son of Hananiah, and the other princes. 13 To them Micaiah reported all that he had heard Baruch read publicly from his book. 14 Thereupon the princes sent Jehudi, son of Nethaniah, son of Shelemiah, son of Cushi, to Baruch with the order: "Come, and bring with you the scroll you read publicly to the people." Scroll in hand, Baruch, son of Neriah, went to them. 15 "Sit down," they said to him, "and read it to us." Baruch read it to them, 16 and when they heard all its words, they were frightened and said to

*

35, 13: 32, 33.
14: 7, 13; 25, 3; 2 Chr 36, 15f.
15: 25, 4f.7.
17: 11, 8f.
36, 3: 26, 3; Is 55, 6f.
7: 2 Kgs 22, 13.

†

35, 11: *The army of Aram:* Nebuchadnezzar enlisted the help of Judah's foreign neighbors in his assault on Jerusalem.

36, 5: *I am prevented:* probably because of his temple sermon (7, 1-15), or because of temporary ritual uncleanness.

36, 10: *Gemariah:* member of a family friendly to Jeremiah, which had rights to a room in the fortress of the temple gateway overlooking the court of the temple; from a window in this room Baruch read Jeremiah's prophetic sermon to the people.

36, 12: *The scribe's chamber:* the office of the royal secretary.

one another, "We must certainly tell the
king all these things." 17 Then they asked
Baruch: "Tell us, please, how you came
to write down all these words."
18 "Jeremiah dictated all these words to
me," Baruch answered them, "and I
wrote them down with ink in the book."
19 At this the princes said to Baruch, "Go
into hiding, you and Jeremiah; let no one
know where you are."

20 Leaving the scroll in safekeeping in
the room of Elishama the scribe, they
entered the room where the king was.
When they told him everything that had
happened, 21 he sent Jehudi to fetch the
scroll. Jehudi brought it from the room
of Elishama the scribe, and read it to
the king and to all the princes who were
in attendance on the king. 22 Now the
king was sitting in his winter house,
since it was the ninth month, and fire
was burning in a brazier before him.
23† Each time Jehudi finished reading
three or four columns, the king would
cut off the piece with a scribe's knife and
cast it into the fire in the brazier, until
the entire roll was consumed in the fire.
24 Hearing all these words did not
frighten the king and his ministers or
cause them to rend their garments.
25 And though Elnathan, Delaiah, and
Gemariah urged the king not to burn the
scroll, he would not listen to them, 26 but
commanded Jerahmeel, a royal prince,
and Seraiah, son of Azriel, and Shele-
miah, son of Abdeel, to arrest Baruch,
the secretary, and the prophet Jere-
miah. But the LORD kept them con-
cealed.

27 This word of the LORD came to Jere-
miah, after the king burned the scroll
with the text Jeremiah had dictated to
Baruch: 28 Take another scroll, and write
on it everything that the first scroll con-
tained, which Jehoiakim, king of Judah,
burned up. 29 And against Jehoiakim,
king of Judah, say this: Thus says the
LORD: You burned that scroll, saying,
"Why did you write on it: Babylon's king
shall surely come and lay waste this land
and empty it of man and beast?"
30*† The LORD now says of Jehoiakim,
king of Judah: No descendant of his
shall succeed to David's throne; his
corpse shall be cast out, exposed to the
heat of day, to the cold of night. 31 I will
punish him and his descendants and his
ministers for their wickedness; against
them and the citizens of Jerusalem and
the men of Judah I will fulfill all the
threats of evil which went unheeded.

32 Jeremiah took another scroll, and
gave it to his secretary, Baruch, son of
Neriah; he wrote on it at Jeremiah's dic-
tation all the words contained in the
book which Jehoiakim, king of Judah,
had burned in the fire, and many others
of the same kind in addition.

CHAPTER 37

Jeremiah in the Dungeon. 1* Coniah,
son of Jehoiakim, was succeeded by
King Zedekiah, son of Josiah; he was
made king over the land of Judah by
Nebuchadnezzar, king of Babylon.
2 Neither he, nor his ministers, nor the
people of the land would listen to the
words of the LORD spoken by Jeremiah
the prophet. 3* Yet King Zedekiah sent
Jehucal, son of Shelemiah, and Zepha-
niah, son of Maaseiah the priest, to the
prophet Jeremiah with this request:
"Pray to the LORD, our God, for us."
4† At this time Jeremiah had not yet
been put into prison; he still came and
went freely among the people. 5*† Also,
Pharaoh's army had set out from Egypt,
and when the Chaldeans who were be-
sieging Jerusalem heard this report they
marched away from the city.

6 This word of the LORD then came to
the prophet Jeremiah: 7* Thus says the
LORD, the God of Israel: Give this answer
to the king of Judah who sent you to me
to consult me: Pharaoh's army which
has set out to help you will return to its
own land, Egypt. 8* The Chaldeans shall
return to the fight against this city; they
shall capture it and destroy it with fire.
9 Thus says the LORD: Do not deceive
yourselves with the thought that the
Chaldeans will leave you for good, be-
cause they shall not leave! 10* Even if
you were to defeat the whole Chaldean
army now attacking you, and only the
wounded remained, each in his tent,
these would rise up and destroy the city
with fire.

11* When the Chaldean army lifted the
siege of Jerusalem at the threat of the
army of Pharaoh, 12 Jeremiah set out
from Jerusalem for the district of Benja-
min, to take part with his family in the
division of an inheritance. 13 But when
he reached the Gate of Benjamin, he met
the captain of the guard, a man named
Irijah, son of Shelemiah, son of Hana-
niah; he seized the prophet Jeremiah,
saying, "You are deserting to the Chal-
deans!" 14 "That is a lie!" Jeremiah an-

*

30: 22, 19.
37, 1: 52, 1; 2 Kgs 24, 17; 2 Chr 36, 10.
3: 21, 1.
5: Ez 17, 15; 29, 6f.
7: Ez 17, 17.
8: 34, 22.
10: 21, 4.
11: Zec 14, 10.

†

36, 23: *A scribe's knife:* used to sharpen the reeds which were employed as pens.

36, 30: Jehoiakim's son Jehoiachin was named king, but reigned only three months; he was known better for his thirty-seven-year exile in Babylon. *His corpse shall be cast out:* see note on 22, 19.

37, 4: *Put into prison:* as described in 32, 1ff. Chronologically, the present episode follows 34, 1-7.

37, 5: *Pharaoh's army:* the force sent by Pharaoh Hophra which caused the Chaldeans momentarily to lift the siege of Jerusalem (cf 34, 21).

swered, "I am not deserting to the Chal-
deans." Without listening, Irijah kept
Jeremiah in custody and brought him
to the princes.
15* The princes were enraged, and had
Jeremiah beaten and thrown into prison
in the house of Jonathan the scribe,
which they were using as a jail. 16 And
so Jeremiah entered the vaulted dun-
geon, where he remained a long time.
17* Once King Zedekiah had him
brought to his palace and he asked him
secretly whether there was any message
from the LORD. Yes! Jeremiah an-
swered: you shall be handed over to the
king of Babylon. 18* Jeremiah then
asked King Zedekiah: In what have I
wronged you, or your ministers, or this
people, that you should put me in prison?
19 And where are your own prophets
now, 20 who prophesied to you that the
king of Babylon would not attack you
or this land? Hear now, my lord king,
and grant my petition: do not send me
back into the house of Jonathan the
scribe, or I shall die there.
21* King Zedekiah ordered that Jere-
miah be confined in the quarters of the
guard, and given a loaf of bread each
day from the bakers' shop until all the
bread in the city was eaten up. Thus
Jeremiah remained in the quarters of
the guard.

CHAPTER 38

Jeremiah in the Miry Cistern.
1† Shephatiah, son of Mattan, Gedaliah,
son of Pashhur, Jucal, son of Shelemiah,
and Pashhur, son of Malchiah, heard
Jeremiah speaking these words to all the
people: 2* Thus says the LORD: He who
remains in this city shall die by sword,
or famine, or pestilence; but he who goes
out to the Chaldeans shall live; his life
shall be spared him as booty, and he
shall live. 3 Thus says the LORD: This city
shall certainly be handed over to the
army of the king of Babylon; he shall
capture it.
4*† "This man ought to be put to
death," the princes said to the king; "he
demoralizes the soldiers who are left in
this city, and all the people, by speaking
such things to them; he is not interested
in the welfare of our people, but in their
ruin." 5 King Zedekiah answered: "He is
in your power"; for the king could do
nothing with them. 6* And so they took
Jeremiah and threw him into the cistern
of Prince Malchiah, which was in the
quarters of the guard, letting him down
with ropes. There was no water in the
cistern, only mud, and Jeremiah sank
into the mud.
7† Now Ebed-melech, a Cushite, a
courtier in the king's palace, heard that
they had put Jeremiah into the cistern.
The king happened just then to be at the
Gate of Benjamin, 8 and Ebed-melech
went there from the palace and said to
him, 9* "My lord king, these men have
been at fault in all they have done to
the prophet Jeremiah, casting him into
the cistern. He will die of famine on the
spot, for there is no more food in the
city." 10 Then the king ordered Ebed-
melech the Cushite to take three men
along with him, and draw the prophet
Jeremiah out of the cistern before he
should die. 11 Ebed-melech took the men
along with him, and went first to the
linen closet in the palace, from which
he took some old, tattered rags; these
he sent down to Jeremiah in the cistern,
with ropes. 12 Then he said to Jeremiah,
"Put the old, tattered rags between your
armpits and the ropes." Jeremiah did
so, 13 and they drew him up with the
ropes out of the cistern. But Jeremiah
remained in the quarters of the guard.
14* Once King Zedekiah summoned
the prophet Jeremiah to come to him at
the third entrance to the house of the
LORD. "I have a question to ask you,"
the king said to Jeremiah; "hide nothing
from me." Jeremiah answered Zede-
kiah: 15* If I tell you anything, you will
have me killed, will you not? If I counsel
you, you will not listen to me! 16 But King
Zedekiah swore to Jeremiah secretly:
"As the LORD lives who gave us the
breath of life, I will not kill you; nor will
I hand you over to these men who seek
your life."
17* Thereupon Jeremiah said to Zede-
kiah: Thus says the LORD God of hosts,
the God of Israel: If you surrender to
the princes of Babylon's king, you shall
save your life; this city shall not be de-
stroyed with fire, and you and your fam-
ily shall live. 18* But if you do not
surrender to the princes of Babylon's
king, this city shall fall into the hands
of the Chaldeans, who shall destroy it
with fire, and you shall not escape their
hands.
19* King Zedekiah, however, said to
Jeremiah, "I am afraid of the men of

*

15: 38, 6-13.
17: 21, 7; 32, 3; 34, 21.
18: 26, 19.
21: 32, 2; 38, 28.
38, 2: 21, 9f; 39, 18; 45, 5.
4: 26, 11.
6: 37, 14f.
9: 52, 6.
14: 37, 16.
15: Lk 22, 67f.
17: 27, 12f; 2 Kgs 24, 12.
18: 32, 4.
19: 1 Sm 31, 4.

†

38, 1: Jeremiah enjoyed sufficient liberty *in the quarters of the guard* (37, 21) to speak to the people; cf 32, 6-9. *Gedaliah, son of Pashhur:* the latter is possibly the Pashhur of 20, 1. *Pashhur, son of Malchiah:* mentioned in 21, 1.

38, 4: *He demoralizes the soldiers:* literally, "he weakens their hands." One of the Lachish ostraca (see note on 34, 7) uses the same expression of the princes in Jerusalem.

38, 7: *A Cushite:* an Ethiopian. Ebed-melech evidently held a position of some authority at court.

Judah who have deserted to the Chalde-
ans; I may be handed over to them, and
they will mistreat me." [20]* You will not
be handed over, Jeremiah answered.
Please obey the voice of the LORD and
do as I tell you; then it shall go well with
you, and your life will be spared. [21] But
if you refuse to surrender, this is what
the LORD shows me: [22]* All the women
left in the house of Judah's king shall
be brought out to the princes of Baby-
lon's king, and they shall taunt you thus:

"They betrayed you, outdid you,
your good friends!
Now that your feet are stuck in the
mud,
they slink away."

[23]* All your wives and sons shall be led
forth to the Chaldeans, and you shall not
escape their hands; you shall be handed
over to the king of Babylon, and this city
shall be destroyed with fire.

[24] Then Zedekiah said to Jeremiah,
"Let no one know about this conversa-
tion, or you shall die. [25] If the princes
hear I spoke to you, if they come and
ask you, 'Tell us what you said to the
king; do not hide it from us, or we will
kill you,' or, 'What did the king say to
you?' [26] give them this answer: 'I peti-
tioned the king not to send me back to
Jonathan's house to die there.' " [27] When
all the princes came to Jeremiah, they
questioned him, and he answered them
in the very words the king had com-
manded. They said no more to him, for
nothing had been heard of the earlier
conversation. [28]* Thus Jeremiah stayed
in the quarters of the guard till the day
Jerusalem was taken.

CHAPTER 39

Jeremiah and Gedaliah. When Jeru-
salem was taken. . . . [1]*† In the tenth
month of the ninth year of Zedekiah,
king of Judah, Nebuchadnezzar, king of
Babylon, and all his army marched
against Jerusalem and besieged it. [2]† On
the ninth day of the fourth month, in the
eleventh year of Zedekiah, a breach was
made in the city's defenses. [3] All the
princes of the king of Babylon came and
occupied the middle gate: Nergal-sha-
rezer, of Simmagir, the chief officer,
Nebushazban, the high dignitary, and
all the other princes of the king of Baby-
lon. . . . [4]*† When Zedekiah, king of Ju-
dah, saw them, he and all his warriors
fled by night, leaving the city on the
Royal Garden Road through the gate be-
tween the two walls. He went in the di-
rection of the Arabah, [5]*† but the
Chaldean army pursued them, and
overtook and captured Zedekiah in the
desert near Jericho. He was brought to
Riblah, in the land of Hamath, where
Nebuchadnezzar, king of Babylon, pro-
nounced sentence upon him. [6]* As Zede-
kiah looked on, his sons were slain at
Riblah by order of the king of Babylon,
who slew also all the nobles of Judah.
[7]* He then blinded Zedekiah and bound
him in chains to bring him to Babylon.

[8]* The Chaldeans set fire to the king's
palace and the houses of the people, and
demolished the walls of Jerusalem.
[9]* Nebuzaradan, chief of the bodyguard,
deported to Babylon the rest of the peo-
ple left in the city, those who had de-
serted to him, and the rest of the
workmen. [10]* But some of the poor who
had no property were left in the land of
Judah by Nebuzaradan, chief of the
bodyguard, and were given at the same
time vineyards and farms.

[11] Concerning Jeremiah, Nebuchad-
nezzar, king of Babylon, gave the follow-
ing orders through Nebuzaradan, chief
of the bodyguard: [12]* "Take him and
look after him; let no harm befall him,
but treat him as he himself requests."
[13] Thereupon Nebuzaradan, chief of the
bodyguard, and Nebushazban, the high
dignitary, and Nergal-sharezer, the
chief officer, and all the nobles of the
king of Babylon, [14]* had Jeremiah taken
out of the quarters of the guard, and en-
trusted to Gedaliah, son of Ahikam, son
of Shaphan, to be brought home. And
so he remained among the people.

***A Word of Comfort for Ebed-
melech.*** [15] While Jeremiah was still im-
prisoned in the quarters of the guard,
the word of the LORD came to him:
[16]* Go, tell this to Ebed-melech the
Cushite: Thus says the LORD of hosts, the
God of Israel: Behold, I am now fulfilling
the words I spoke against this city, for
evil and not for good; and this before
your very eyes. [17] But on that day I will
rescue you, says the LORD; you shall not
be handed over to the men of whom you
are afraid. [18]* I will make certain that

*

20: 2 Chr 20, 20.
22: Jb 6, 15; 19, 13f.19.
23: 41, 10.
28: 39, 14.
39, 1f: 52, 4-16; 2 Kgs 25, 1-12; Ez 24, 1.
4: 52, 7.
5: 32, 4f; 38, 18.
6: 34, 21.
7: 32, 4f; Ez 12, 13.
8: 21, 10; 34, 2; 52, 13.
9: 2 Kgs 25, 11.
10: 2 Kgs 25, 12.22.
12: 40, 4.
14: 26, 24; 38, 28.
16: 21, 10; Dn 9, 12.
18: 45, 5; Pss 25, 3; 36, 40.

†

39, 1: *The tenth month of the ninth year:* the month Tebet (mid-December to mid-January) of the year 589/8 B.C.

39, 2: *The ninth day of the fourth month, in the eleventh year:* in July of 587 B.C.

39, 4: *The Royal Garden Road:* along the southeast side of the city; the royal garden was in the Kidron Valley. *The gate between the two walls:* the southernmost city gate, at the end of the Tyropoean Valley. *The Arabah:* the Jordan Valley. Zedekiah was attempting to escape across the Jordan when he was captured near Jericho.

39, 5: *Riblah:* Nebuchadnezzar's headquarters in Syria, which had also been used by Pharaoh Neco (2 Kgs 23, 33).

you escape and do not fall by the sword.
Your life shall be spared as booty, be-
cause you trusted in me, says the LORD.

CHAPTER 40

Jeremiah Still in Judah. 1*† This word
came to Jeremiah from the LORD, after
Nebuzaradan, captain of the bodyguard,
had released him in Ramah, where he
had found him a prisoner in chains,
among the captives of Jerusalem and
Judah who were being exiled to Babylon.
2 When the captain of the bodyguard
took charge of Jeremiah, he said to him,
"The LORD, your God, foretold the ruin
of this place. 3 Now he has brought about
in deed what he threatened; because you
sinned against the LORD and did not
obey his voice, this fate has befallen you.
4* And now, I am freeing you today from
the fetters that bind your hands; if it
seems good to you to come with me to
Babylon, you may come: I will look after
you well. But if it does not please you
to come to Babylon, you need not come.
See, the whole land is before you; go
wherever you think good and proper";
5* and then, before he left—"or go to
Gedaliah, son of Ahikam, son of Sha-
phan, whom the king of Babylon has ap-
pointed ruler over the cities of Judah;
stay with him among the people, or go
wherever you please." The captain of
the bodyguard gave him food and gifts
and let him go. 6*† Jeremiah went to
Gedaliah, son of Ahikam, in Mizpah, and
stayed with him among the people left
in the land.
7 When the army leaders who were still
in the field with all their men heard that
the king of Babylon had given Gedaliah,
son of Ahikam, charge of the land, of
men, women, and children, and of those
poor who had not been led captive to
Babylon, 8† they came with their men to
Gedaliah in Mizpah: Ishmael, son of
Nethaniah; Johanan, son of Kareah;
Seraiah, son of Tanhumeth; the sons of
Ephai of Netophah; and Jezaniah of
Beth-maacah. 9* Gedaliah, son of Ahi-
kam, son of Shaphan, adjured them and
their men not to be afraid to serve the
Chaldeans: to stay in the land and sub-
mit to the king of Babylon, for their own
welfare; 10 saying that he himself would
remain in Mizpah, as their intermediary
with the Chaldeans who should come to
them. They were to collect the wine, the
fruit, and the oil, to store them in jars,
and to settle in the cities they occupied.
11 When the people of Judah in Moab,
those among the Ammonites, those in
Edom, and those in all other lands heard
that the king of Babylon had left a rem-
nant in Judah, and had appointed over
them Gedaliah, son of Ahikam, son of
Shaphan, 12 they all returned to the land
of Judah from the places to which they
had scattered. They went to Gedaliah at
Mizpah and had a rich harvest of wine
and fruit.
Assassination of Gedaliah. 13 Now Jo-
hanan, son of Kareah, and all the lead-
ers of the armies in the field came to
Gedaliah in Mizpah 14*† and asked him
whether he did not know that Baalis, the
king of the Ammonites, had sent Ish-
mael, son of Nethaniah, to assassinate
him. 15 But Gedaliah, son of Ahikam,
would not believe them. Then Johanan,
son of Kareah, said secretly to Gedaliah
in Mizpah: "Let me go and kill Ishmael,
son of Nethaniah; no one will know it.
Why should he be allowed to kill you?
All the Jews who have now rallied to you
will be dispersed and the remnant of Ju-
dah will perish." 16 Nevertheless, Geda-
liah, son of Ahikam, answered Johanan,
son of Kareah, "You shall do nothing of
the kind; you have lied about Ishmael."

CHAPTER 41

1* In the seventh month Ishmael, son
of Nethaniah, son of Elishama, of royal
descent, one of the king's nobles, came
with ten men to Gedaliah, son of Ahi-
kam, at Mizpah. And while they were
together at table in Mizpah, 2 Ishmael,
son of Nethaniah, and the ten who were
with him, rose up and attacked with
swords Gedaliah, son of Ahikam, son of
Shaphan, whom the king of Babylon had
made ruler over the land; and they killed
him. 3 Ishmael also slew all the men of
Judah of military age who were with
Gedaliah and the Chaldean soldiers who
were there.
4 The second day after the murder of
Gedaliah, before anyone knew of it,
5 eighty men with beards shaved off,
clothes in rags, and with gashes on their
bodies came from Shechem, Shiloh, and
Samaria, bringing food offerings and in-
cense for the house of the LORD.

JEREMIAH

*

40, 1: 39, 14.
4: 39, 12.
5: 39, 14; 2 Kgs 25, 22.
6: 39, 14.
9: 27, 12f; 2 Kgs 25, 24.
14: 41, 1ff.10.
41, 1: 40, 14ff; 2 Kgs 25, 25.

†

40, 1: *This word:* actually, no further word of the Lord is recorded until 42, 7ff. This is a title affixed to the following chapters after they were attached to an earlier form of the book ending with chapter 39.

40, 6: *Mizpah:* some five miles northwest of Jerusalem, where Israel chose its first king (1 Sm 10, 17-24). Presumably Jerusalem had been damaged too much by the Chaldean conquest to remain a seat of government.

40, 8: *Jezaniah:* the seal ring of a high official of this name was discovered in 1932 at the site usually identified with Mizpah, Tell en-Nasbe.

40, 14: *The Ammonites:* they resented the survival of their ancient enemy, Judah. *Ishmael:* their willing tool, who doubtless aspired to rule over Judah himself, as he was of the house of David; cf 41, 1.

6 Ishmael son of Nethaniah, went out
from Mizpah to meet them, weeping as
he went. 7 "Come to Gedaliah, son of
Ahikam," he said as he met them. When
they were once inside the city, Ishmael,
son of Nethaniah, and his men slew
them and threw them into the cistern.
8 But there were ten among them who
pleaded with Ishmael: "Do not kill us;
we have stores buried in the field: wheat
and barley, oil and honey." And so he
spared them and did not kill them, as
he had killed their companions. 9* The
cistern into which Ishmael threw all the
corpses of the men he had killed was the
large one made by King Asa to defend
himself against Baasha, king of Israel;
this cistern Ishmael, son of Nethaniah,
filled with the slain.

10† Ishmael, son of Nethaniah, led
away the remnant of the people left in
Mizpah and the princesses, whom Nebu-
zaradan, captain of the bodyguard, had
confided to Gedaliah, son of Ahikam.
With these captives, Ishmael, son of
Nethaniah, set out to make his way to
the Ammonites.

Flight to Egypt. 11 But when Johanan,
son of Kareah, and the other army lead-
ers with him heard of the crimes Ish-
mael, son of Nethaniah, had committed,
12† they took all their men and set out
to attack Ishmael, son of Nethaniah.
They overtook him at the Great Waters
in Gibeon. 13 At the sight of Johanan, son
of Kareah, and the other army leaders,
the people who were Ishmael's captives
rejoiced. 14 All of those whom Ishmael
had brought away from Mizpah went
over to Johanan, son of Kareah. 15 But
Ishmael, son of Nethaniah, escaped
from Johanan and fled to the Ammon-
ites with eight men. 16 Then Johanan,
son of Kareah, and all his army leaders
took charge of the remnant of the peo-
ple, both the soldiers and the women and
children with their guardians, whom
Ishmael, son of Nethaniah, had brought
away from Mizpah after he killed Geda-
liah, son of Ahikim. From Gibeon,
17 they retreated to the lodging place of
Chimham near Bethlehem, where they
stopped, intending to flee into Egypt.
18 They were afraid of the Chaldeans, be-
cause Ishmael, son of Nethaniah, had
slain Gedaliah, son of Ahikam, whom
the king of Babylon had made ruler in
the land of Judah.

CHAPTER 42

1 Then all the army leaders, Johanan,
son of Kareah, Azariah, son of Ho-
shaiah, and all the people, high and low,
approached the prophet Jeremiah 2 and
said, "Grant our petition; pray for us to
the LORD, your God, for all this remnant.
We are now few who once were many,
as you well see. 3 Let the LORD, your God,
show us what way we should take and
what we should do." 4* Very well! the
prophet Jeremiah answered them: I will
pray to the LORD, your God, as you de-
sire; whatever the LORD answers you, I
will tell you; I will withhold nothing from
you. 5* And they said to Jeremiah, "May
the LORD be our witness: we will truly
and faithfully follow all the instructions
the LORD, your God, will send us.
6* Whether it is pleasant or difficult, we
will obey the command of the LORD, our
God, to whom we are sending you, so
that it will go well with us for obeying
the command of the LORD, our God."

7 Ten days passed before the word of
the LORD came to Jeremiah. 8 Then he
called Johanan, son of Kareah, his army
leaders, and all the people, high and low,
9 and said to them: Thus says the LORD,
the God of Israel, to whom you sent me
to offer your prayer: 10* If you remain
quietly in this land I will build you up,
and not tear you down; I will plant you,
not uproot you; for I regret the evil I
have done you. 11* Do not fear the king
of Babylon, before whom you are now
afraid; do not fear him, says the LORD,
for I am with you to save you, to rescue
you from his power. 12* I will grant you
mercy, so that he will be sorry for you
and let you return to your land. 13 But
if you disobey the voice of the LORD,
your God, and decide not to remain in
this land, 14* saying, "No, we will go to
Egypt, where we will see no more of war,
hear the trumpet alarm no longer, nor
hunger for bread; there we will live";
15 then listen to the word of the LORD,
remnant of Judah: Thus says the LORD
of hosts, the God of Israel: If you are
determined to go to Egypt, when you ar-
rive there to stay, 16* the sword you fear
shall reach you in the land of Egypt; the
hunger you dread shall cling to you no
less in Egypt, and there you shall die.
17* All those men who determine to go
to Egypt to stay, shall die by the sword,
famine, and pestilence; not one shall
survive or escape the evil that I will
bring upon them. 18* For thus says the
LORD of hosts, the God of Israel: Just
as my furious anger was poured out

*

9: 1 Kgs 15, 16; 2 Chr 16, 6.
42, 4: 1 Sm 3, 18.
5: Jgs 11, 10.
6: 7, 23; Dt 5, 33; 6, 3.
10: 31, 28; 32, 41.
11: 30, 10f.
12: Ps 106, 45f; Prv 16, 7.
14: Dt 28, 68.
16: 44, 13f.27.
17: 29, 17f; 44, 14.28.
18: 44, 12.

†

41, 10: *The princesses:* of the royal house of Judah. They had not been deported to Babylon with the men of this house.

41, 12: *Gibeon:* today called El-Jib; it is northwest of Jerusalem. The most recent excavations have revealed the extensive dimensions of the city spring and well, called here *the Great Waters:* cf 2 Sm 2, 12ff.

upon the citizens of Jerusalem, so shall my anger be poured out on you when you reach Egypt. You shall become an example of malediction and horror, a curse and a reproach, and you shall never see this place again.

19 It is the LORD who has spoken to you, remnant of Judah; do not go to Egypt! You can never say that I did not warn you this day. 20 At the cost of your lives you have deceived me, sending me to the LORD, your God, saying, "Pray for us to the LORD, our God; make known to us all that the LORD, our God, shall say, and we will do it." 21* Today I proclaim his message, but you obey the voice of the LORD, your God, in nothing that he has commissioned me to make known to you. 22* Have no doubt of this, you shall die by the sword, famine, and pestilence in the place where you wish to go and settle.

CHAPTER 43

1 When Jeremiah finished speaking to the people all these words of the LORD, their God, with which the LORD had sent him to them, 2 Azariah, son of Hoshaiah, Johanan, son of Kareah, and all the insolent men shouted to Jeremiah: "You lie; it was not the LORD, our God, who sent you to tell us not to go to Egypt to settle. 3* It is Baruch, son of Neriah, who stirs you up against us, to hand us over to the Chaldeans to be killed or exiled to Babylon."

4* Johanan, son of Kareah, and the rest of the leaders and the people did not obey the LORD's command to stay in the land of Judah. 5 Instead, Johanan, son of Kareah, and all the army leaders took along the whole remnant of Judah that had been dispersed among the nations and had returned thence to dwell again in the land of Judah: 6* men, women, and children, the princesses and everyone whom Nebuzaradan, captain of the bodyguard, had entrusted to Gedaliah, son of Ahikam, son of Shaphan; also Jeremiah, the prophet, and Baruch, son of Neriah. 7* Against the LORD's command they went to Egypt, and arrived at Tahpanhes. . . .

Jeremiah in Egypt. 8 This word of the LORD came to Jeremiah in Tahpanhes: 9† Take with you large stones and sink them in mortar in the brickyard at the entrance to the royal building in Tahpanhes, while the men of Judah look on, 10* and then say to them: Thus says the LORD of hosts, the God of Israel: I will send for my servant Nebuchadnezzar, king of Babylon, and bring him here. He will set his throne upon these stones which I, Jeremiah, have sunk, and stretch his canopy over them. 11* He shall come and strike the land of Egypt: with death, whoever is marked for death; with exile, everyone destined for exile; with the sword, all who are intended for the sword. 12* He shall set fire to the temples of Egypt's gods, and burn the gods or carry them off. As a shepherd delouses his cloak, he shall delouse the land of Egypt and depart victorious. 13 He shall smash the obelisks of the temple of the sun in the land of Egypt and destroy with fire the temples of the Egyptian gods.

CHAPTER 44

1 This word came to Jeremiah for all the people of Judah who were living in Egypt, at Migdol, Tahpanhes, and Memphis, and in Upper Egypt: 2*† Thus says the LORD of hosts, the God of Israel: You have seen all the evil I brought on Jerusalem and the other cities of Judah. Today they are ruins and uninhabited, 3* because of the evil they did to provoke me, going after strange gods, serving them and sacrificing to them, gods which neither they, nor you, nor your fathers knew. 4 Though I kept sending to you all my servants the prophets, with the plea not to commit this horrible deed which I hate, 5* they would not listen or accept the warning to turn away from the evil of sacrificing to strange gods. 6 Therefore the fury of my anger poured forth in flame over the cities of Judah and the streets of Jerusalem, so that they became the ruinous waste they are today.

7 Now thus says the LORD God of hosts, the God of Israel: Why do you inflict so great an evil upon yourselves? Will you root out from Judah man and wife, child and nursling, and not leave yourselves even a remnant? 8* Will you go on provoking me by the works of your hands, by sacrificing to strange gods here in the land of Egypt where you have come to live? Will you be rooted out and become a curse and a disgrace among all the nations of the earth? 9* Have you forgotten the evil deeds which your fathers,

*

21: Zec 7, 11f.
22: 44, 12; Hos 9, 6.
43, 3: 38, 4.
4: 41, 16.
6: 41, 10.
7: 42, 13f; 44, 1.
10: 27, 6; Ez 29, 19.
11: 46, 13; Ez 30, 10.
12: 46, 25; Ez 30, 13f.
44, 2: 34, 22; Lv 26, 32f.
3: 11, 17; Dt 32, 17.
5: 7, 24.26; 19, 4.
8: 25, 6f.
9: 1 Kgs 11, 1.8; Ezr 9, 7.14.

†

43, 9: *The royal building:* residence of the Egyptian governor.

44, 2-30: Chronologically, this is the last of Jeremiah's prophecies to his countrymen. The narrative leaves him an old man nearing seventy, rejected by his people. According to tradition, he was murdered in Egypt by fellow Judeans.

and the kings of Judah and their wives,
and you yourselves and your wives have
done in the land of Judah and the streets
of Jerusalem? 10* To this day they have
not been crushed; they do not fear or
follow the law and the statutes which I
set before you and your fathers.
11 Hence, thus says the LORD of hosts,
the God of Israel: I have determined evil
against you; and I will uproot all Judah.
12* I will take away the remnant of Ju-
dah who insisted on coming to dwell in
Egypt, so that they shall be wholly de-
stroyed. In the land of Egypt they shall
fall by the sword or be consumed by
hunger. High and low, they shall die by
the sword, or by hunger, and become an
example of malediction, a horror, a
curse and a reproach. 13* Thus will I
punish those who live in Egypt, just as
I punished Jerusalem with sword, hun-
ger, and pestilence. None of the remnant
of Judah that have come to settle in the
land of Egypt shall escape or survive.
14 None shall return to the land of Judah,
though they yearn to return and live
there. Only scattered refugees shall re-
turn.
15 From all the men who knew that
their wives were burning incense to
strange gods, from all the women who
were present in the immense crowd, and
from all the people who lived in Lower
and Upper Egypt, Jeremiah received
this answer: 16* "We will not listen to
what you say in the name of the LORD.
17* Rather will we continue doing what
we had proposed; we will burn incense
to the queen of heaven and pour out liba-
tions to her, as we and our fathers, our
kings and princes have done in the cities
of Judah and the streets of Jerusalem.
Then we had enough food to eat and we
were well off; we suffered no misfortune.
18 But since we stopped burning incense
to the queen of heaven and pouring out
libations to her, we are in need of every-
thing and are being destroyed by the
sword and by hunger. 19* And when we
burned incense to the queen of heaven
and poured out libations to her, was it
without our husbands' consent that we
baked for her cakes in her image and
poured out libations to her?"
20 To all the people, men and women,
who gave him this answer, Jeremiah
said: 21* Was it not this that the LORD
remembered and brought to mind, that
you burned incense in the cities of Judah
and the streets of Jerusalem: you, your
fathers, your kings and princes, and the
people generally? 22* The LORD could no
longer bear your evil deeds, the horrible
things which you were doing; and so
your land became a waste, a desert, a
thing accursed and without inhabitants,
as it is today. 23* Because you burned
incense and sinned against the LORD,
not obeying the voice of the LORD, not
living by his law, his statutes, and his
decrees, this evil has befallen you at the
present day.
24 Jeremiah said further to all the peo-
ple, including the women: Hear the word
of the LORD, all you Judeans in the land
of Egypt: 25 Thus says the LORD of hosts,
the God of Israel: You and your wives
have stated your intentions, and kept
them in fact: "We will continue to fulfill
the vows we have made to burn incense
to the queen of heaven and to pour out
libations to her." Very well! keep your
vows, carry out your resolutions! 26 But
listen then to the word of the LORD, all
you people of Judah who live in Egypt;
I swear by my own great name, says the
LORD, in the whole land of Egypt no man
of Judah shall henceforth pronounce my
name, saying, "As the Lord GOD lives."
27* I am watching over them to do evil,
not good. All the men of Judah in Egypt
shall perish by the sword or famine until
they are utterly destroyed. 28* Those
who escape the sword to return from the
land of Egypt to the land of Judah shall
be few in number. The whole remnant
of Judah who came to settle in Egypt
shall know whose word stands, mine or
theirs.
29 That you may know how surely my
threats of punishment for you shall be
fulfilled, this shall be a sign to you, says
the LORD, that I will punish you in this
place. 30*† Thus says the LORD: See! I
will hand over Pharaoh Hophra, king of
Egypt, to his enemies, to those who seek
his life, just as I handed over Zedekiah,
king of Judah, to his enemy and mortal
foe, Nebuchadnezzar, king of Babylon.

CHAPTER 45

A Message to Baruch. 1*† This is the
message that the prophet Jeremiah gave
to Baruch, son of Neriah, when he wrote
in a book the prophecies that Jeremiah
dictated in the fourth year of Jehoiakim,
son of Josiah, king of Judah: 2 Thus says

*

10: 7, 24.
12: 42, 15.18.22.
13: 43, 11.
16: 6, 16f.
17: 5, 3; 7, 18.
19: 7, 18.
21: 11, 13.
22: 15, 6.
23: 2 Kgs 17, 15; Dn 9, 11f.
27: Ez 7, 3-7.
28: Dt 28, 62; Is 10, 22.
30: 39, 5ff; 46, 25f; Ez 29, 3f; 30, 21.
45, 1: 36, 4.18.32.

†

44, 30: Hophra: killed by his own people. The ruler of Egypt at the time of its conquest by Nebuchadnezzar was Hophra's successor Amasis, who was also slain by his enemies.

45, 1-5: At the conclusion of his narrative, Baruch appends a prophecy given him personally by Jeremiah when he first wrote down Jeremiah's words (cf chap. 36). The future revealed by the prophet had depressed Baruch; this prophecy was to assure him of his personal safety, while repeating the Lord's determination to destroy Judah.

the LORD, God of Israel, to you, Baruch,
3* because you said, "Alas! the LORD
adds grief to my pain; I am weary from
groaning, and can find no rest": 4* say
this to him, says the LORD: What I have
built, I am tearing down; what I have
planted, I am uprooting: even the whole
land. 5* And do you seek great things
for yourself? Seek them not! I am bringing evil on all mankind, says the LORD,
but your life I will leave you as booty,
wherever you may go.

V: ORACLES AGAINST THE NATIONS

CHAPTER 46†

1 This is the word of the LORD that
came to the prophet Jeremiah against
the nations.

Against Egypt. 2† Concerning Egypt.
Against the army of Pharaoh Neco, king of Egypt, which was defeated at Carchemish on the Euphrates by Nebuchadnezzar, king of Babylon, in the fourth year of Jehoiakim, son of Josiah, king of Judah:

3 Prepare shield and buckler!
march to battle!
4 Harness the horses,
mount, charioteers!
Fall in with your helmets;
polish your spears, put on your breastplates.
5* What do I see?
With broken ranks
They fall back;
their heroes are routed,
They flee headlong
without making a stand.
Terror on every side,
says the LORD!
6 The swift cannot flee,
nor the hero escape:
There in the north, on the Euphrates' bank,
they stumble and fall.

7 Who is this that surges forward like the Nile,
like rivers of billowing waters?
8* Egypt surges like the Nile,
like rivers of billowing waters.
"I will surge forward," he says, "and cover the earth,
destroying the city and its people.
9 Forward, horses!
drive madly, chariots!
Set out, warriors,
Cush and Put, bearing your shields,
Men of Lud, stretching your bows!"
10* But this is the day of the Lord GOD of hosts,
a day of vengeance, vengeance on his foes!
The sword devours, is sated, drunk with their blood:
for the Lord GOD of hosts holds a slaughter feast
in the northland, on the Euphrates.

11* Go up to Gilead, and take balm,
O virgin daughter Egypt!
No use to multiply remedies;
for you there is no cure.
12* The nations hear of your shame,
your cries fill the earth.
Warrior trips over warrior,
both fall together.

13*† The message which the LORD
gave to the prophet Jeremiah concerning the advance of Nebuchadnezzar,
king of Babylon, to attack the land of Egypt:

14* Announce it in Egypt, publish it in Migdol,
proclaim it in Memphis and Tahpanhes!
Say: Take your stand, prepare yourselves,
the sword has already devoured your neighbors.
15† Why has Apis fled,
your mighty one failed to stand?
The LORD thrust him down;
16* he stumbled repeatedly, and fell.
They said one to another,
"Up! let us return to our own people,
To the land of our birth,
away from the destroying sword."

17† Call Pharaoh, king of Egypt, by the name
"The noise that let its time go by."
18† As I live, says the King

*

3: Lam 1, 3; 5, 5.
4: 18, 7; Is 5, 5f.
5: 25, 26-29.
46, 5: 6, 25; 49, 29.
8: Ez 29, 3; 32, 2.
10: Dt 32, 42; Is 13, 9; Ez 39, 17-20.
11: 8, 22; 51, 8; Ez 30, 21f.
12: Ez 32, 9-12.
13: 43, 10f; 44, 30; Is 19, 1.
14: 44, 1.
16: Lv 26, 37.

†

46—51: In these chapters most of Jeremiah's oracles against the foreign nations have been gathered together and placed at the end of his book; in the Greek text they appear with the other oracles against the nations, in chap. 25. In general, they are in chronological order: 46, 1—49, 33, from the fourth year of Jehoiakim; 49, 34-39, at the beginning of Zedekiah's reign; 50, 1—51, 64, from the fourth year of Zedekiah.

46, 2: Carchemish on the Euphrates: the western terminus of the Mesopotamian trade route, where Nebuchadnezzar defeated Neco in 605 B.C., thus gaining undisputed control of Syria and Palestine.

46, 13: In 601 B.C. Nebuchadnezzar advanced against Egypt and even entered the country, but finally had to withdraw to Syria.

46, 15: *Apis:* the chief god of Memphis, venerated in the form of a black bull.

46, 17: *"The noise . . . go by":* in Hebrew there is wordplay here on the name Hophra, who still made a pretense of power though his career was at an end.

46, 18: *Tabor. . . Carmel:* outstanding mountains of Palestine, symbols of strength, to which Nebuchadnezzar is compared.

whose name is LORD of hosts,
Like Tabor among the mountains he shall come,
like Carmel above the sea.
19 Pack your baggage for exile,
capital city of daughter Egypt;
Memphis shall become a desert,
an empty ruin.
20 Egypt is a pretty heifer,
from the north a horsefly lights upon her.
21 The mercenaries in her ranks
are like fatted calves;
They too turn and flee together,
stand not their ground,
When the day of their ruin comes upon them,
the time of their punishment.
22 She sounds like a retreating reptile!
Yes, they come in force;
like woodchoppers, they attack her with axes.
23 They cut down her forest, says the LORD,
impenetrable though it be;
More numerous than locusts,
they cannot be counted.
24 Disgraced is daughter Egypt,
handed over to the people of the north.

25*† The LORD of hosts, the God of Israel, has said: See! I will punish Amon of Thebes, and Egypt, her gods and her kings, Pharaoh, and those who trust in him. 26* I will hand them over to those who seek their lives, to Nebuchadnezzar, king of Babylon, and his ministers. But later on Egypt shall be inhabited again, as in times past, says the LORD.

27* But you, my servant Jacob, fear not;
be not dismayed, O Israel.
Behold, I will deliver you from the far-off land,
your descendants, from their land of exile.
Jacob shall again find rest,
shall be tranquil and undisturbed.
28* You, my servant Jacob, never fear,
says the LORD,
for I am with you;
I will make an end of all the nations
to which I have driven you,
But of you I will not make an end:
I will chastise you as you deserve,
I will not let you go unpunished.

CHAPTER 47

Against the Philistines. 1* This is the word that came from the LORD to the prophet Jeremiah concerning the Philistines, before Pharaoh attacked Gaza: 2† Thus says the LORD:

Behold: waters are rising from the north,
a torrent in flood;
It shall flood the land and all that is in it,
the cities and their people.
All the people of the land
set up a wailing cry.
3 They hear the stamping hooves of his steeds,
the rattling chariots, the rumbling wheels.
Fathers turn not to save their children;
their hands fall helpless
4*† Because of the day which has come
to ruin all the Philistines,
And cut off from Tyre and Sidon
the last of their allies.
Yes, the LORD is destroying the Philistines,
the remnant from the coasts of Caphtor.
5*† Gaza is shaved bald,
Ashkelon is reduced to silence;
Ashdod, the remnant of their strength,
how long will you gash yourself?
6† Alas, sword of the LORD!
how long till you find rest?
Return into your scabbard;
stop, be still!
7* How can it find rest
when the LORD has commanded it?
Against Ashkelon and the seashore
he has appointed it.

CHAPTER 48

Against Moab. 1† Concerning Moab, thus says the LORD of hosts, the God of Israel:

Woe to Nebo, it is laid waste;
Kiriathaim is disgraced and captured,
Disgraced and overthrown is the stronghold:

*

25: Ez 30, 15f.
26: 44, 30; Ez 30, 4; 32, 11f.
27: 30, 10; 43, 5.
28: 30, 11.
47, 1: Ez 25, 15f; Zep 2, 4.
4: 25, 22; Ez 25, 16f; Am 1, 8; 9, 7.
5: Am 1, 7.
7: Zep 2, 5f.

†

46, 25: *Amon:* the sun-god worshiped at Thebes, in Upper Egypt.

47, 2-7: This prophecy was fulfilled in 605/4 B.C.

47, 4: *Tyre and Sidon:* Phoenician cities associated commercially with the Philistines, and enemies of Nebuchadnezzar; cf 27, 1-4. Nebuchadnezzar carried out a thirteen-year siege of Tyre which was only partially successful. *Caphtor:* probably the island of Crete, the traditional place of origin of the Philistines; cf Am 9, 7.

47, 5: Of the ancient Philistine cities, neither Gath nor Ekron (25, 20) is mentioned in this period of waning independence of the seacoast.

47, 6: Words of the Philistines.

48, 1-47: Moab was one of the Israelites' bitterest enemies. According to Flavius Josephus, Moab and Ammon were conquered by Nebuchadnezzar in his twenty-third year, 582 B.C., five years after the destruction of Jerusalem.

2 Moab's glory is no more.
Evil they plan against Heshbon:
"Come, let us put an end to her as a people."
You, too, Madmen, shall be reduced to silence;
behind you stalks the sword.
3* Listen! a cry from Horonaim
of ruin and great destruction!
4 Moab is crushed,
their outcry is heard in Zoar.
5 The ascent of Luhith
they climb weeping;
On the descent to Horonaim
the cry of destruction is heard.
6 "Flee, save your lives,
to survive like the wild ass in the desert!"
7*† Because you trusted in your works and your treasures,
you also shall be captured.
Chemosh shall go into exile,
his priests and princes with him.
8 The destroyer comes upon every city,
not a city escapes;
Ruined is the valley,
wasted the plain, as the LORD has said.
9 Set up a memorial for Moab,
for it is an utter wasteland;
Its cities are turned into ruins
where no one dwells.
10 [Cursed be he who does the LORD's work remissly,
cursed he who holds back his sword from blood.]
11* Moab has been tranquil from his youth,
has rested upon his lees;
He was not poured from one flask to another,
he went not into exile.
Thus he kept his taste,
and his scent was not lost.

12 Hence, the days shall come, says the
LORD, when I will send him coopers to
turn him over; they shall empty his
flasks and break his jars. 13* Chemosh
shall disappoint Moab, as Israel was dis-
appointed by Bethel in which they
trusted.

14 How can you say, "We are heroes,
men valiant in war"?
15 The ravager of Moab and his cities advances,
the flower of his youth goes down to be slaughtered,
says the King, the LORD of hosts by name.
16 Near at hand is Moab's ruin,
his disaster hastens apace.
17 Mourn for him, all you his neighbors,
all you who knew him well!
Say: How the strong staff is broken,
the glorious rod!
18* Come down from glory, sit on the ground,
you that dwell in Dibon;
Moab's ravager has come up against you,
he has ruined your strongholds.
19* Stand by the wayside, watch closely,
you that dwell in Aroer;
Ask the man who flees, the woman who tries to escape:
say to them, "What has happened?"
20* Moab is disgraced, yes, destroyed,
howl and cry out;
Publish it at the Arnon,
Moab is ruined!

21* For judgment has come on the land
of the plateau: on Holon, Jahzah, and
Mephaath, 22 on Dibon, Nebo, and Beth-
diblathaim, 23 on Kiriathaim, Beth-
gamul, and Beth-meon, 24 on Kerioth
and on Bozrah: on all the cities of Moab,
far and near.

25 Moab's strength is broken,
his might is shattered, says the LORD.

26 Because he boasted against the
LORD, make Moab drunk so that he
retches and vomits, and he too becomes
a laughingstock. 27* Is Israel a laugh-
ingstock to you? Was she caught among
thieves, that you shake your head when-
ever you speak of her?

28 Leave the cities, dwell in the crags,
you that dwell in Moab.
Be like a dove that nests
out of reach on the edge of a chasm.
29* We have heard of the pride of Moab,
pride beyond bounds:
His loftiness, his pride, his scorn,
his insolence of heart.
30 I know, says the LORD, his arrogance;
liar in boast, liar in deed.
31* And so I wail over Moab,
over all Moab I cry,
over the men of Kir-heres I moan.
32* More than for Jazer I weep over you,
vineyard of Sibmah.
Your tendrils trailed down to the sea,
as far as Jazer they stretched.
Upon your harvest, upon your vintage,
the ravager has fallen.

*

48, 3ff: Is 15, 5.
7: Nm 21, 29.
11: Zep 1, 12.
13: Is 16, 12.
18: Nm 21, 30.
19: Dt 2, 36.
20: Is 16, 7.
21: Is 15, 4.
27: Zep 2, 8ff.
29f: Is 16, 6.
31: Is 16, 7.
32: Is 16, 8f.

†

48, 7: *Chemosh:* chief god of the Moabites.

33 Joy and jubilation are at an end
in the fruit gardens of the land of Moab.
I drain the wine from the wine vats,
the treader treads no more,
the vintage shout is stilled.

34* The cry of Heshbon and Elealeh is
heard as far as Jahaz; they call from
Zoar to Horonaim, and to Eglath-sheli-
shiyah, for even the waters of Nimrim
turn into a desert. 35 I will leave no one
in Moab, says the LORD, to offer a holo-
caust on the high place, or to burn in-
cense to his gods. 36* Hence the wail of
flutes for Moab is in my heart; for the
men of Kir-heres the wail of flutes is in
my heart: the wealth they acquired has
perished. 37* Every head has been made
bald, every beard shaved; every hand
is gashed, and the loins of all are clothed
in sackcloth. 38 On every roof of Moab
and in all his squares there is mourning;
I have shattered Moab like a pot that
no one wants, says the LORD. 39 How ter-
ror seizes Moab, and wailing! How he
turns his back in shame! Moab has be-
come a laughingstock and a horror to
all his neighbors! 40* For thus says the
LORD:

Behold, like an eagle he soars,
spreads his wings over Moab.
41* Cities are taken,
strongholds seized:
On that day the hearts of Moab's heroes
are like the heart of a woman in travail.
42* Moab shall be destroyed, no more a people,
because he boasted against the LORD.
43* Terror, pit, and trap be upon you,
people of Moab, says the LORD.
44 He who flees from the terror
falls into the pit;
He who climbs from the pit
is caught in the trap;
For I will bring these things upon Moab
in the year of their punishment,
says the LORD.
45* In Heshbon's shadow stop short
the exhausted refugees;
For fire breaks forth from Heshbon,
and a blaze from the house of Sihon:
It consumes the brow of Moab,
the skull of the noisemakers.
46 Woe to you, O Moab,
you are ruined, O people of Chemosh!
Your sons are taken into exile,
your daughters into captivity.
47* But I will change the lot of Moab
in the days to come, says the LORD.
Thus far the judgment on Moab.

CHAPTER 49

Against the Ammonites. 1† Concerning the Ammonites, thus says the LORD:

Has Israel no sons?
has he no heir?
Why then has Milcom disinherited Gad,
why have his people settled in Gad's cities?
2*† But the days are coming, says the LORD,
when against Rabbah of the Ammonites
I will sound the battle alarm;
She shall become a mound of ruins,
and her daughter cities shall be destroyed by fire.
Israel shall inherit those who disinherited her,
says the LORD.
3* Howl, Heshbon, for the ravager approaches,
shriek, daughters of Rabbah!
Put on sackcloth and mourn,
run to and fro, gashing yourselves;
For Milcom goes into exile
along with his priests and captains.
4 Why do you glory in your strength,
your ebbing strength, rebellious daughter?
You who trust in your treasures,
saying,
"Who can come against me?"
5* I am bringing terror upon you,
says the Lord GOD of hosts,
from all round about you;
You shall be scattered, each man in headlong flight,
with no one to rally the fugitives.
6 But afterward I will change the lot
of the Ammonites, says the LORD.

Against Edom. 7† Concerning Edom, thus says the LORD of hosts:

Is there no more wisdom in Teman,
has counsel perished from the prudent,

*

34: Is 15, 4f.
36: Is 16, 11.
37: 47, 5; Is 15, 2f; Ez 7, 18.
40: 49, 22.
41: 6, 24; 30, 6.
42: Zep 2, 9f.
43: Is 24, 17f.
45: Nm 21, 28f.
47: 49, 39.
49, 2: Am 1, 14.
3: Is 15, 2ff.
5: 48, 47.

†

49, 1: *Milcom:* chief god of the Ammonites. The Transjordan tribe of Gad bordered on Ammon, and after the collapse of the northern kingdom the Ammonites occupied its territory.

49, 2: *Rabbah of the Ammonites:* or Rabbath-Ammon, capital of the Ammonite kingdom. The modern Amman is the capital of the kingdom of Jordan.

49, 7-22: *Edom:* this implacable enemy from ancient times profited from Judah's downfall; cf Ob 11f.

49, 7: *Teman:* a district of Edom, used here for the whole country; it was famous for its wise men; cf Jb 2, 11.

has their wisdom become corrupt?
8*† Flee, retreat, hide in deep holes,
you who live in Dedan:
For I will bring destruction upon Esau
when I come to punish him.
9* If vintagers came upon you,
they would leave no gleanings;
If thieves by night,
they would destroy as they pleased.
10* So I myself will strip Esau;
I will uncover his retreats so that he cannot hide.
He is ruined: sons, and brothers,
and neighbors, so that he is no more.
11* Leave your orphans behind, I will keep them alive;
your widows, let them trust in me.

12* For thus says the LORD: Even those
not sentenced to drink the cup must
drink it! Shall you then go unpunished?
You shall not go unpunished; you shall
surely drink it. 13*† By my own self I
have sworn, says the LORD: Bozrah shall
become an object of horror and a disgrace, a desolation and a curse; she and
all her cities shall become ruins forever.

14 I have heard a report from the LORD,
a herald has been sent among the nations:
Gather together, move against her,
rise up for battle.
15* Small will I make you among the nations,
despised among men!
16* The terror you spread beguiled you,
and your presumption of heart;
You that live in rocky crags,
that hold the heights of the hill:
Though you build your nest high as the eagle,
from there I will drag you down,
says the LORD.

17 Edom shall become an object of horror. Every passer-by shall be appalled
and catch his breath at all her wounds.
18* As when Sodom, Gomorrah, and
their neighbors were overthrown, says
the LORD, not a man shall dwell there:
no one shall visit there.

19* As when a lion comes up from the thicket of Jordan
to the permanent feeding grounds,
So I, in an instant, will drive men off;
and whom I choose I will establish there!
For who is like me? who can call me to account?
What shepherd can stand against me?
20 Therefore, hear the counsel of the LORD,
which he has taken against Edom;
Hear the plans he has made
against those that live in Teman:
They shall be dragged away, even the smallest sheep,
their own pasture shall be aghast because of them.
21 At the noise of their fall the earth quakes,
to the Red Sea the outcry is heard!
22* See! like an eagle he soars aloft,
and spreads his wings over Bozrah;
On that day the hearts of Edom's heroes shall be
like the heart of a woman in travail.

Against Damascus. Concerning Damascus:

23*† Hamath and Arpad are covered with shame,
they have heard bad news;
Worried, they toss like the sea
which cannot rest.
24 Damascus is weakened, she turns to flee,
panic has seized her.
Distress and pangs take hold of her,
like those of a woman in travail.
25 How can the city of glory be forsaken,
the town of delight!
26 But now her young men shall fall in her streets,
and all her warriors shall be stilled.
On that day, says the LORD of hosts,
27† I will set fire to the wall of Damascus,
and it shall devour the palaces of Ben-hadad.

Against Arabia. 28* Of Kedar and the
kingdoms of Hazor, defeated by Nebuchadnezzar, king of Babylon, thus says
the LORD:

Rise up, attack Kedar,
ravage the Easterners.

JEREMIAH

*

8: Ez 25, 13.
9: Ob 5.
10: Mal 1, 3.
11: Dt 10, 18; Ps 68, 6.
12: 25, 15.28; Lam 4, 21f.
13: Is 34, 6; Ez 35, 3-9; Ob 16.
15: Ob 2.
16: 48, 29f.
18: 50, 40; Dt 29, 23.
19: 12, 5; 25, 9; 50, 44f.
22: 4, 13.
23: Is 36, 19; 37, 13.
28: Is 21, 16.

†

49, 8: *Esau:* Jacob's brother, the traditional ancestor of the Edomites; cf Gn 36.

49, 13: *Bozrah:* capital of Edom, southeast of the Dead Sea.

49, 23: *Hamath and Arpad:* independent Aramean states to the north of Damascus; the invasion is conceived as coming from the north. The situation is of the eighth century B.C. Cf Is 10, 9ff.

49, 27: *The palaces of Ben-hadad:* the royal palaces in Damascus where at least three kings bore this name; cf 1 Kgs 15, 18; 20.

29* Their tents and herds shall be taken away,
their tent curtains and all their goods;
Their camels they shall carry off for themselves,
and shout from upon them, "Terror on every side!"
30 Flee! leave your homes, hide in deep holes,
you that live in Hazor, says the LORD;
For counsel has been taken against you,
a plan has been formed against you
[Nebuchadnezzar, king of Babylon].
31 Rise up! set out against a nation that is at peace,
that lives secure, says the LORD,
That has no gates or bars,
and dwells alone.
32* Their camels shall be your booty,
their many herds your spoil;
I will scatter to the winds those who shave their temples,
from all sides I will bring ruin upon them,
says the LORD.
33 Hazor shall become a haunt of jackals,
a desert forever,
Where no man lives,
no human being stays.

Against Elam. 34† The following word
of the LORD against Elam came to the
prophet Jeremiah at the beginning of the
reign of Zedekiah, king of Judah: 35 Thus
says the LORD of hosts:

Behold, I will break the bow of Elam,
the mainstay of their might.
36 I will bring upon Elam the four winds
from the four ends of the heavens:
I will scatter them to all these winds,
till there is no nation
to which the outcasts of Elam shall not come.
37 I will break Elam before their foes,
before those who seek their life;
I will bring evil upon them,
my burning wrath, says the LORD.
I will send the sword to pursue them
until I have completely made an end of them;
38 My throne I will set up in Elam
and destroy from there king and princes,
says the LORD.
39 But in the days to come I will change
the lot of Elam, says the LORD.

CHAPTER 50

The First Prophecy against Babylon.
1*† The word which the LORD spoke against Babylon, against the land of the Chaldeans, through the prophet Jeremiah:

2† Announce and publish it among the nations;
publish it, hide it not, but say:
Babylon is taken, Bel confounded,
Merodach shattered;
her images are put to shame, her idols shattered.
3* A people from the north advances against her
to turn her land into a desert,
So that no one shall live there,
because man and beast have fled away.
4* In those days, at that time, says the LORD,
the men of Israel and of Judah shall come,
Weeping as they come, to seek the LORD, their God;
5* to their goal in Zion they shall ask the way.
"Come, let us join ourselves to the LORD
with covenant everlasting, never to be forgotten."
6* Lost sheep were my people,
their shepherds misled them,
straggling on the mountains;
From mountain to hill they wandered,
losing the way to their fold.
7* Whoever came upon them devoured them,
and their enemies said, "We incur no guilt,
Because they sinned against the LORD,
the hope of their fathers, their abode of justice."

8* Flee from Babylon, leave the land of the Chaldeans,
be like the rams at the head of the flock.
9* See, I am stirring up against Babylon
a band of great nations from the north;

*

29: 4, 20.
32: 9, 25.
50, 1: 51, 1; Is 13, 1-14; 21, 1-10.
3: 51, 48; Is 13, 17.
4: 3, 18; Ps 126, 6.
5: 31, 31; 32, 40.
6: Is 53, 6; 1 Pt 2, 25.
7: 31, 23.
8: 51, 6.45; Is 48, 20.
9: 51, 27.

†

49, 34: *Elam:* the ancient kingdom to the east of Babylonia.
50, 1—51, 58: a collection of miscellaneous prophecies against Babylon which now stands as the introduction to the story in 51, 59-64. The Greek text of 50, 1 omits *through the prophet Jeremiah,* and it is in fact likely that these oracles are not Jeremiah's, but were composed by other inspired writers after the fall of Jerusalem, who may have used some of Jeremiah's texts. Babylon fell to the Persians in 538 B.C.
50, 2 *Bel:* originally the name of the god of Nippur in Mesopotamia, then identified with *Merodach* (Marduk), chief god of Babylon.

from there they advance, and she shall be taken.
Their arrows are arrows of the skilled warrior;
none shall return without effect.
10 Chaldea shall be their plunder,
and all her plunderers shall be enriched,
says the LORD.
11 Yes, rejoice and exult,
you that plunder my portion;
Frisk like calves on the green,
snort like stallions!
12* Your mother shall be sorely put to shame,
she that bore you shall be abashed;
See, the last of the nations,
a desert, dry and waste.
13* Because of the LORD's wrath she shall be empty,
and become a total desert;
Everyone who passes by Babylon will be appalled
and catch his breath, at all her wounds.
14* Take your posts encircling Babylon,
you who bend the bow;
Shoot at her, spare not your arrows,
15*† raise the war cry against her on all sides.
She surrenders, her bastions fall,
her walls are torn down:
Vengeance of the LORD is this! Take revenge on her,
as she has done, do to her;
for she sinned against the LORD.
16* Cut off from Babylon the sower
and him who wields the sickle in harvest time!
Before the destroying sword,
each of them turns to his own people,
everyone flees to his own land.
17* A stray sheep was Israel
that lions pursued;
Formerly the king of Assyria devoured her,
now Nebuchadnezzar of Babylon gnaws her bones.

18* Therefore, thus says the LORD of hosts, the God of Israel:

I will punish the king of Babylon and his land,
as once I punished the king of Assyria;
19* But I will bring back Israel to her fold,
to feed on Carmel and Bashan,
And on Mount Ephraim and Gilead,
till she has her fill.

20* In those days, at that time, says the LORD:

They shall seek Israel's guilt, but it shall be no more,
and Judah's sins, but these shall no longer be found;
for I will forgive the remnant I preserve.

21† Attack the land of Merathaim,
and those who live in Pekod;
Slaughter and doom them, says the LORD,
do all I have commanded you.
22 Battle alarm in the land,
dire destruction!
23* How has the hammer of the whole earth
been broken and shattered!
What an object of horror
Babylon has become among the nations.
24* You ensnared yourself, and were caught,
O Babylon, before you knew it!
You were discovered and seized,
because you challenged the LORD.
25* The LORD opens his armory
and brings forth the weapons of his wrath;
For the Lord GOD of hosts has work to do
in the land of the Chaldeans.

26 Come upon her from every side,
open her granaries,
Pile up her goods in heaps and doom it,
leave not a remnant.
27 Slay all her oxen,
let them go down to the slaughter;
Woe to them! their day has come,
the time of their punishment.
28* Listen! the fugitives, the escaped
from the land of Babylon:
They announce in Zion
the vengeance of the LORD, our God.
29* Call up against Babylon archers,
all who bend the bow;
Encamp around her,
let no one escape.
Repay her for her deeds;
as she has done, do to her,
For she insulted the LORD,
the Holy One of Israel.

*

12: 51, 43; Is 13, 20ff.
13: 25, 12.
14: 51, 11; Is 21, 2.
15: 51, 11.44.58; Ps 137, 8.
16: Is 13, 14.
17: 2 Kgs 17, 24; 18, 14.
18: Is 10, 12; 14, 24f.
19: 23, 3; Ez 34, 13f.
20: 31, 34; Is 43, 25; Mi 7, 19.
23: 51, 20; Is 14, 6.
24: 51, 57.
25: 51, 11f; Is 13, 5.
28: 51, 10f.
29: 51, 56.

†

50, 15: *Her walls are torn down:* the prophet is not predicting the details of Babylon's downfall, but describing such a downfall in conventional language. Actually, Babylon was surrendered peaceably, without destruction.

50, 21: *Merathaim,* "twice bitter," and *Pekod,* "punishment," are here symbolic terms for Babylonia, though probably they suggest also the names of regions in that country.

30* Therefore her young men shall fall
in her streets,
all her warriors shall perish on
that day,
says the LORD.

31 I am against you, man of insolence,
says the Lord GOD of hosts;
For your day has come,
the time for me to punish you.
32 Insolence stumbles and falls;
there is no one to raise him up.
I will kindle in his cities a fire
that shall devour everything
around him.
33 Thus says the LORD of hosts:
Oppressed are the men of Israel,
and with them the men of Judah;
All their captors hold them fast
and refuse to let them go.
34* Strong is their avenger,
whose name is LORD of hosts;
He will defend their cause with suc-
cess,
and give rest to the earth,
but unrest to those who live in
Babylon.

35 A sword upon the Chaldeans, says
the LORD,
upon Babylon's people, her
princes and wise men!
36 A sword upon the soothsayers,
that they may become fools!
A sword upon her warriors,
that they may tremble;
37* A sword upon her motley throng,
that they may become women!
A sword upon her treasures,
that they may be plundered;
38* A sword upon her waters,
that they may dry up!
For it is a land of idols,
and they shall be made frantic by
fearful things.
39* Hence, wildcats and desert beasts
shall dwell there,
and ostriches shall occupy it;
Never again shall it be peopled, or
lived in,
from age to age.
40* As when God overturned Sodom
and Gomorrah, with their neigh-
bors, says the LORD,
Not a man shall dwell there,
no human being shall tarry there.

41* See! a people comes from the north,
a great nation, and mighty kings
roused from the ends of the earth.
42 Bow and javelin they wield,
cruel and pitiless are they;
They sound like the roaring sea,
as they ride forth on steeds,
Each in his place for battle
against you, daughter Babylon.
43* The king of Babylon hears news of
them,
and helpless fall his hands;
Anguish seizes him,
throes like a mother's in child-
birth.
44* As when a lion comes up from the
Jordan's thicket
to the permanent feeding
grounds,
So I, in one instant, will drive them
off,
and whom I choose I will establish
there;
For who is like me? who calls me
to account?
what shepherd can stand against
me?
45* Therefore hear the counsel of the
LORD
which he has taken against Baby-
lon;
Hear the plans he has made
against the land of the Chalde-
ans:
They shall be dragged away, even
the smallest sheep;
their own pasture shall be aghast
because of them.
46* At the cry "Babylon is captured!"
the earth quakes;
the outcry is heard among the na-
tions.

CHAPTER 51

The Second Prophecy against Babylon

1 Thus says the LORD:
See! I rouse against Babylon,
and against those who live in
Chaldea,
a destroying wind.
2* Against Babylon I will send winnow-
ers
to winnow her and lay waste her
land;
They shall besiege her from all sides
on the day of affliction.
3* Let the bowman draw his bow,
and flaunt his coat of mail;
Spare not her young men,
doom her entire army.
4* The slain shall fall in the land of
Chaldea,
the transfixed, in her streets;
5 For Israel and Judah are not wid-
owed
of their God, the LORD of hosts,
And the Chaldean land is full of guilt

---

*

30: 49, 26; 51, 4.
34: 51, 36.
37: 51, 30; Na 3, 13.
38: 51, 32.36.
39: 51, 37; Is 13, 21f.
40: 51, 43.
41: 51, 27f.
43: Is 13, 7.
44: 49, 19.
45: 51, 12.29.
46: 51, 29.
51, 2: 15, 7; Is 41, 16.
3: 50, 14.29.
4: 50, 30.

to be punished by the Holy One
of Israel.

6* Flee out of Babylon;
let each one save his life,
perish not for her guilt;
This is a time of vengeance for the
LORD,
he pays her her due.
7* Babylon was a golden cup in the
hand of the LORD
which made the whole earth
drunk;
The nations drank its wine,
with this they have become mad.
8* Babylon suddenly falls and is
crushed:
howl over her!
Bring balm for her wounds,
in case she can be healed.
9* "We have tried to heal Babylon,
but she cannot be healed.
Leave her, let us go, each to his
own land."
Her judgment reaches heaven,
it touches the clouds.
10* The LORD has brought to light our
just cause;
come, let us tell in Zion
what the LORD, our God, has done.

11*†Sharpen the arrows,
fill the quivers;
The LORD has stirred up the spirit
of Media's kings;
Babylon he is resolved to destroy.
Yes, it is the vengeance of the LORD,
vengeance for his temple.
12 Against the walls of Babylon raise
a signal,
make strong the watch;
Post sentries,
arrange ambushes!
For the LORD has planned and he
will carry out
his threat against the inhabitants
of Babylon.
13* You who dwell by mighty waters,
rich in treasure,
Your end has come,
the term at which you shall be cut
off!
14 The LORD of hosts has sworn by
himself:
I will fill you with men as numer-
ous as locusts,
who shall raise over you the vin-
tage shout!
15* He has sworn who made the earth
by his power,
and established the world by his
wisdom,
and stretched out the heavens by
his skill.
16 When he thunders, the waters in the
heavens roar,
and he brings up clouds from the
end of the earth;
He makes the lightning flash in the
rain,
and releases stormwinds from
their chambers.
17 Every man is stupid, ignorant;
every artisan is put to shame by
his idol:
He molded a fraud,
without breath of life.
18 Nothingness are they, a ridiculous
work,
that will perish in their time of
punishment.
19 Not like these is the portion of Jacob,
he is the creator of all things;
Israel is his very own tribe,
LORD of hosts is his name.

20 You are my hammer,
my weapon for war;
With you I shatter nations,
with you I destroy kingdoms.
21* With you I shatter horse and rider,
with you I shatter chariot and
driver.
22* With you I shatter man and wife,
with you I shatter old and young,
with you I shatter the youth and
maiden.
23 With you I shatter the shepherd and
his flock,
with you I shatter the farmer and
his team,
with you I shatter satraps and
prefects.
24* Thus will I repay Babylon,
and all who live in Chaldea
All the evil they did to Zion,
as you shall see with your own
eyes, says the LORD.
25* Beware! I am against you,
destroying mountain,
destroyer of the entire earth, says
the LORD;
I will stretch forth my hand against
you,
roll you down over the cliffs,
and make you a burnt mountain:
26* They will not take from you a cor-
nerstone,
or a foundation stone;
Ruins forever shall you be,
says the LORD.

JEREMIAH

*

6: 50, 8.15.29; Is 48, 20.
7: Rv 14, 8; 17, 4.
8: Rv 18, 9-18.
9: Is 13, 14; Rv 18, 5.
10: 50, 28.
11: 2 Kgs 17, 6; Is 13, 17.
13: Na 2, 1.
15: 10, 12.
21: Dn 7, 7.19.23.
22: Is 13, 16.18.
24: 25, 14; 50, 29; Ps 137, 8.
25: Rv 8, 7; 18, 8f.
26: 25, 12; Ps 118, 22.

†

51, 11: *Media's kings:* the Medes dwelt with the Persians in the land now known as Iran. At the time these words were written the Medes were the dominant people of the two, but within a short time the Persians had gained the ascendancy.

27*† Raise a signal on the earth,
blow the trumpet among the nations;
Dedicate peoples to war against her,
summon against her the kingdoms,
Ararat, Minni, and Ashkenaz;
Appoint recruiting officers against her,
send up horses like bristling locusts.
28 Dedicate peoples to war against her:
the king of Media,
Its governors and all its prefects,
every land in his domain.
29 The earth quakes and writhes,
the LORD's plan against Babylon is carried out,
Turning the land of Babylon
into a desert where no one lives.
30 Babylon's warriors have ceased to fight,
they remain in their strongholds;
Dried up is their strength,
they have become women.
Burned are their homes,
and broken their bars.
31* One runner meets another,
herald meets herald,
Telling the king of Babylon
that all his city is taken.
32 The fords have been seized,
and the fortresses set on fire,
while warriors are in panic.

33* For thus says the LORD of hosts, the God of Israel:

Daughter Babylon is like a threshing floor
at the time it is trodden;
Yet a little while,
and the harvest time will come for her.
34† He has consumed me, routed me,
[Nebuchadnezzar, king of Babylon,]
he has left me as an empty vessel;
He has swallowed me like a dragon:
filled his belly with my delights,
and cast me out.
35 My torn flesh be upon Babylon,
says the city on Zion;
My blood upon the people of Chaldea,
says Jerusalem.
36 But now, thus says the LORD:
Surely I will defend your cause,
I will avenge you;
I will dry up her sea,
and drain her fountain.
37* Babylon shall become a heap of ruins,
a haunt of jackals;
A place of horror and ridicule,
where no one lives.
38* They all roar like lions,
growl like lion cubs.
39 When they are parched, I will set a drink before them
to make them drunk, that they may be overcome
with perpetual sleep, never to awaken,
says the LORD.
40 I will bring them down like lambs to the slaughter,
like rams and goats.
41* How has she been seized, made captive,
the glory of the whole world!
What a horror has Babylon become among nations:
42 against Babylon the sea rises,
she is overwhelmed by the roaring waves!
43 Her cities have become a desert,
parched and arid land
Where no man lives,
and no one passes through.
44 I will punish Bel in Babylon,
and make him disgorge what he swallowed;
peoples shall stream to him no more.
The wall of Babylon falls!
45 Leave her, my people, let each one save himself
from the burning wrath of the LORD.

46* Be not discouraged for fear of rumors spread in the land; this year the rumor comes, then violence in the land, tyrant against tyrant. 47 But behold, the days are coming when I will punish the idols of Babylon; her whole land shall be put to shame, and all her slain shall lie fallen within her. 48* Then heaven, and earth, and everything in them shall shout over Babylon with joy, when the destroyers come against her from the north, says the LORD. 49 Babylon, too, must fall, O slain of Israel, as at the hands of Babylon have fallen the slain of all the earth.

50 You who have escaped the sword,
go on, stand not still;
Remember the LORD from afar,
let Jerusalem come to your minds.
51* We are ashamed because we have heard taunts,
confusion covers our faces;
strangers have entered
the holy places of the house of the LORD.

JEREMIAH

*

27: Na 3, 17.
31: 2 Chr 30, 6; Jb 1, 14-18.
33: Rv 14, 15.
37: Is 25, 2.
38: Na 2, 11f.
41: Is 13, 19.
46: Mt 24, 6f.
48: Rv 18, 20.
51: Pss 44, 16f; 78, 1-4.

†

51, 27: *Ararat, Minni, and Ashkenaz:* regions or people in what is now Armenia, subject at this time to Media.
51, 34: *Me, my:* refers to Jerusalem.

52 But behold, the days are coming,
says the LORD,
when I will punish her idols,
and in her whole land the
wounded will groan.
53* Though Babylon scale the heavens,
and make her strong heights inaccessible,
destroyers from me shall reach
her, says the LORD.
54 Hear! loud cries from Babylon,
dire destruction from the land of
the Chaldeans;
55 For the LORD lays Babylon waste,
stills her loud cry,
Though her waves were roaring like
mighty waters,
and their clamor was heard afar.
56* For the destroyer comes upon her,
[Babylon,]
her heroes are captured, their
bows broken;
The LORD is a God who requites,
he will surely repay.

57 I will make her princes and her wise
men drunk, her governors, her prefects,
and her warriors, so that they sleep an
eternal sleep, never to awaken, says the
King, whose name is the LORD of hosts.
58* Thus says the LORD of hosts:

The walls of spacious Babylon shall
be leveled utterly;
her lofty gates shall be destroyed
by fire.
The toil of the nations is for nothing;
for the flames the peoples weary
themselves.

The Prophecy Sent to Babylon.
59† This was the errand given by the
prophet Jeremiah to Seraiah, son of Neriah, son of Mahseiah, when he went to
Babylon for the king in the fourth year
of the reign of Zedekiah; Seraiah was
chief quartermaster. 60† Jeremiah had
written all the misfortune that was to befall Babylon in a single book: all these
words that were written against Babylon. 61* And Jeremiah said to Seraiah:
When you reach Babylon, see that you
read aloud all these words, 62 and then
say: O LORD, you yourself threatened to
destroy this place, so that neither man
nor beast should dwell in it, since it
would remain an everlasting desert.
63* When you have finished reading this
book, tie a stone to it and throw it in the
Euphrates, 64† and say: Thus shall
Babylon sink. Never shall she rise, because of the evil I am bringing upon her.
[To "weary themselves" are the words
of Jeremiah.]

VI: HISTORICAL APPENDIX

CHAPTER 52

Capture of Jerusalem. 1*† Zedekiah
was twenty-one years old when he became king, and he reigned eleven years
in Jerusalem. His mother's name was
Hamutal, daughter of Jeremiah of Libnah. 2 He did what was evil in the eyes
of the LORD, just as Jehoiakim had done.
3 Indeed, what was done in Jerusalem
and in Judah so angered the LORD that
he cast them out from his presence.

Zedekiah rebelled against the king of
Babylon. 4*† In the tenth month of the
ninth year of his reign, on the tenth day
of the month, Nebuchadnezzar, king of
Babylon, and his whole army advanced
against Jerusalem, encamped around it,
and built siege walls on every side. 5 The
siege of the city continued until the eleventh year of King Zedekiah.

6 On the ninth day of the fourth month,
when famine had gripped the city and
the people had no more bread, 7 the city
walls were breached. Then all the soldiers took to flight and left the city by
night through the gate between the two
walls which was near the king's garden.
With the Chaldeans surrounding the
city, they went in the direction of the Arabah. 8 But the Chaldean army pursued
the king and overtook Zedekiah in the
desert near Jericho, while his whole
army fled from him.

9 The king, therefore, was arrested
and brought to Riblah, in the land of
Hamath, to the king of Babylon, who
pronounced sentence on him. 10 As Zedekiah looked on, the king of Babylon
slew his sons as well as all the princes
of Judah at Riblah. 11 Then he blinded
Zedekiah, bound him with fetters, and
had him brought to Babylon and kept
in prison until the day of his death.

Destruction of Jerusalem. 12† On the
tenth day of the fifth month (this was
in the nineteenth year of Nebuchadnezzar, king of Babylon), Nebuzaradan,

*

53: Is 14, 13.
56: Na 1, 2.
58: Hb 2, 13.
61: 50, 1-51.
63: Rv 18, 21.
52, 1-27: 2 Kgs 24, 18—25, 21.
4-16: 39, 1-10.

†

51, 59: *Seraiah:* the brother of Baruch; cf 32, 12. *The king:* Zedekiah. Perhaps Seraiah went to Babylon to explain away the presence of foreign ambassadors in Jerusalem that same year; cf 27, 3.

51, 60: Jeremiah prophesied against Babylon, even as he foretold Judah's release from Babylon's power (3, 14-18; 32, 15; 33, 6-9.12f); but his *book* against Babylon was thrown in the Euphrates (v 63). The preceding oracles were composed by later writers; see note on 50, 1—51, 58.

51, 64: *To "weary themselves" are the words of Jeremiah:* an editorial remark concerning the end of v 58.

52, 1-34: This supplement to the Book of Jeremiah was taken by the final editor from 2 Kgs 24, 18—25, 30 and placed here in order to show the fulfillment of Jeremiah's prophecies. In part this repeats the history given in Jer 39-41; the history of Gedaliah in 2 Kgs 25, 22-26, however, has not been reproduced here.

52, 4: *In the tenth month of the ninth year of his reign, on the tenth day of the month:* January 15, 588 B.C. Cf 39, 1.

52, 12: *On the tenth day of the fifth month . . . nineteenth year:* the tenth of Ab—July/August in 587 B.C.

captain of the bodyguard, came to Jeru-
salem as the representative of the king
of Babylon. 13 He burned the house of the
LORD, the palace of the king, and all the
houses of Jerusalem; every large build-
ing he destroyed with fire. 14 And the
Chaldean troops who were with the cap-
tain of the guard tore down all the walls
that surrounded Jerusalem.
15 Then Nebuzaradan, captain of the
guard, led into exile the rest of the people
left in the city, and those who had de-
serted to the king of Babylon, and the
rest of the artisans. 16 But some of the
country's poor, Nebuzaradan, captain of
the guard, left behind as vinedressers
and farmers.
17 The bronze pillars that belonged to
the house of the LORD, and the wheeled
carts and the bronze sea in the house
of the LORD, the Chaldeans broke into
pieces; they carried away all the bronze
to Babylon. 18 They took also the pots,
the shovels, the snuffers, the bowls, the
pans, and all the bronze vessels used for
service. 19 The basins also, the fire hold-
ers, the bowls, the pots, the lampstands,
the pans, the sacrificial bowls which
were of gold or silver, these too the cap-
tain of the guard carried off, 20 as well
as the two pillars, the one sea, and the
twelve oxen of bronze under the sea, and
the wheeled carts which King Solomon
had made for the house of the LORD. The
bronze of all these furnishings could not
be weighed.
21 Each of the pillars was eighteen cu-
bits high and twelve cubits in diameter;
each was four fingers thick, and hollow
inside. 22 A bronze capital five cubits
high surmounted the one pillar, and a
network with pomegranates encircled
the capital, all of brass; and so for the
other pillar. The pomegranates . . .
23 there were ninety-six pomegranates.
There were a hundred pomegranates, all
around the network.
24 The captain of the guard also took
Seraiah, the high priest, Zephaniah, the
second priest, and the three keepers of
the entry. 25 And from the city he took
one courtier, a commander of soldiers,
and seven men in the personal service
of the king who were present in the city,
and the scribe of the army commander
who mustered the people of the land,
and sixty of the common people who
were in the city. 26 The captain of the
guard, Nebuzaradan, arrested these and
brought them to the king of Babylon at
Riblah, 27 who had them struck down
and put to death in Riblah, in the land
of Hamath.
Thus was Judah exiled from her land.
28† This is the number of the people
whom Nebuchadnezzar led away cap-
tive: in his seventh year, three thousand
and twenty-three people of Judah; 29 in
the eighteenth year of Nebuchadnezzar,
eight hundred and thirty-two persons
from Jerusalem; 30 in the twenty-third
year of Nebuchadnezzar, Nebuzaradan,
captain of the guard, exiled seven hun-
dred and forty-five people of Judah: four
thousand six hundred persons in all.
Favor Shown to Jehoiachin. 31*† In
the thirty-seventh year of the exile of
Jehoiachin, king of Judah, on the
twenty-fifth day of the twelfth month,
Evil-merodach, king of Babylon, in the
inaugural year of his reign, took up the
case of Jehoiachin, king of Judah, and
released him from prison. 32† He spoke
kindly to him and gave him a throne
higher than that of the other kings who
were with him in Babylon. 33 Jehoiachin
took off his prison garb and ate at the
king's table as long as he lived. 34 The
allowance given him by the king of
Babylon was a perpetual allowance, in
fixed daily amounts, all the days of his
life until the day of his death.

*

31-34: 2 Kgs 25, 27-30.

†

52, 28-30: These verses are missing in the Greek text and have not been taken from 2 Kgs 25, but from some other source using a different system of chronology. Besides the deportations of 598 and 587 B.C., mention is made here of a final one that took place in the year 582/1, possibly as a sequel to the murder of Gedaliah; cf 41, 2.

52, 31-34: In the year 561/0 B.C., Jehoiachin was released from prison by Nebuchadnezzar's successor Awel-Marduk (Evil-merodach), who reigned only two years. Babylonian records confirm the fact that Jehoiachin and his family were supported at public expense.

52, 32: *The other kings:* who had also been brought as captives to Babylon.

The Book of

LAMENTATIONS

The sixth century B.C. was an age of crisis, a turning point in the history of Israel. With the destruction of the temple and the interruption of its ritual, the exile of the leaders and loss of national sovereignty, an era came to an end. Not long after the fall of Jerusalem (587) an eyewitness of the national humiliation composed these five laments. They combine confession of sin, grief over the suffering and humiliation of Zion, submission to merited chastisement, and strong faith in the constancy of Yahweh's love and power to restore. The union of poignant grief and unquenchable hope reflects the constant prophetic vision of the weakness of man and the strength of God's love; it also shows how Israel's faith in Yahweh could survive the shattering experience of national ruin.

As a literary work, the Book of Lamentations is carefully constructed according to a familiar structural device. The first four poems are acrostics in which the separate stanzas begin with successive letters of the Hebrew alphabet from the first to the last. Far from destroying the spontaneous pathos of the songs, this literary feature permits a symbolic and disciplined expression of the profound grief, the sinful responsibility, and the enduring hope of the suffering community. The figure of Israel as the bride of Yahweh, familiar from the prophets, appears here again; but now Zion is a desolate widow, the Judaea Capta *of Titus' memorial coins, sustained only by the faith that God's chastisement will eventually give place to his infinite compassion.*

CHAPTER 1

Jerusalem Abandoned and Disgraced

1† How lonely she is now,
the once crowded city!
Widowed is she
who was mistress over nations;
The princess among the provinces
has been made a toiling slave.

2* Bitterly she weeps at night,
tears upon her cheeks,
With not one to console her
of all her dear ones;
Her friends have all betrayed her
and become her enemies.

3* Judah has fled into exile
from oppression and cruel slavery;
Yet where she lives among the nations
she finds no place to rest:
All her persecutors come upon her
where she is narrowly confined.

4* The roads to Zion mourn
for lack of pilgrims going to her feasts;
All her gateways are deserted,
her priests groan,
Her virgins sigh;
she is in bitter grief.

5 Her foes are uppermost,
her enemies are at ease;
The LORD has punished her
for her many sins.
Her little ones have gone away,
captive before the foe.

6 Gone from daughter Zion
is all her glory:
Her princes, like rams
that find no pasture,
Have gone off without strength
before their captors.

7 Jerusalem is mindful of the days
of her wretched homelessness,
When her people fell into enemy hands,
and she had no one to help her;
When her foes gloated over her,
laughed at her ruin.

8* Through the sin of which she is guilty,
Jerusalem is defiled;
All who esteemed her think her vile
now that they see her nakedness;
She herself groans
and turns away.

---

* 1, 2: Jer 30, 14; Ez 16, 37.
3: Dt 28, 65; Jer 45, 3.
4: Jer 14, 2.
8: Is 47, 2; Jer 13, 22.26.

† 1, 1-22: In this poem the poet first describes Jerusalem's miserable state after the destruction wrought by the Chaldeans (vv 1-11a); in v 11b the city itself takes up the lament.

9 Her filth is on her skirt;
she gave no thought how she would end.
Astounding is her downfall,
with no one to console her.
Look, O LORD, upon her misery,
for the enemy has triumphed!

10* The foe stretched out his hand
to all her treasures;
She has seen those nations
enter her sanctuary
Whom you forbade to come
into your assembly.

11* All her people groan,
searching for bread;
They give their treasures for food,
to retain the breath of life.
"Look O LORD, and see
how worthless I have become!

12 "Come, all you who pass by the way,
look and see
Whether there is any suffering like my suffering,
which has been dealt me
When the LORD afflicted me
on the day of his blazing wrath.

13* "From on high he sent fire
down into my very frame;
He spread a net for my feet,
and overthrew me.
He left me desolate,
in pain all the day.

14† "He has kept watch over my sins;
by his hand they have been plaited:
They have settled about my neck,
he has brought my strength to its knees;
The Lord has delivered me into their grip,
I am unable to rise.

15* "All the mighty ones in my midst
the Lord has cast away;
He summoned an army against me
to crush my young men;
The LORD has trodden in the wine press
virgin daughter Judah.

16* "At this I weep,
my eyes run with tears:
Far from me are all who could console me,
any who might revive me;
My sons were reduced to silence
when the enemy prevailed."

17* Zion stretched out her hands,
but there was no one to console her;
The LORD gave orders against Jacob
for his neighbors to be his foes;
Jerusalem has become in their midst
a thing unclean.

18* "The LORD is just;
I had defied his command.
Listen, all you peoples,
and behold my suffering:
My maidens and my youths
have gone into captivity.

19*†"I cried out to my lovers,
but they failed me.
My priests and my elders
perished in the city;
Where they sought food for themselves,
they found it not.

20* "Look, O LORD, upon my distress:
all within me is in ferment,
My heart recoils within me
from my monstrous rebellion.
In the streets the sword bereaves,
at home death stalks.

21 "Give heed to my groaning;
there is no one to console me.
All my enemies rejoice at my misfortune:
it is you who have wrought it.
Bring on the day you have proclaimed,
that they may be even as I.

22*†"Let all their evil come before you;
deal with them
As you have dealt with me
for all my sins;
My groans are many,
and I am sick at heart."

CHAPTER 2

The Lord's Wrath against Zion

1† How the Lord in his wrath
has detested daughter Zion!
He has cast down from heaven to earth
the glory of Israel,

*

10: Jer 51, 51.
11: Jer 52, 6.
13: Ez 12, 13.
15: Jer 8, 16.
16: Jer 13, 17; 14, 17.
17: Ps 74, 7.
18: Dt 28, 41.
19: Jer 30, 14.
20: 2, 11.
22: 3, 64.

†

1, 14: *They have been plaited . . . my neck:* the sins of the people have been bound together and laid as a yoke on their back; cf Mt 23, 4.

1, 19: *My lovers:* Zion's foreign allies, who failed to help her, as the prophets had warned.

1, 22: Zion fully acknowledges her guilt and the justness of divine punishment; nevertheless, she pleads that her enemies also be punished for their guilt.

2, 1: *The glory of Israel:* the temple. *His footstool:* the ark of the covenant (1 Chr 28, 2; Pss 99, 5; 132, 7); or again, the temple (Ez 43, 7).

Unmindful of his footstool
on the day of his wrath.

2 The Lord has consumed without pity
all the dwellings of Jacob;
He has torn down in his anger
the fortresses of daughter Judah;
He has brought to the ground in dishonor
her king and her princes.

3*† He broke off, in fiery wrath,
the horn that was Israel's whole strength;
He withheld the support of his right hand
when the enemy approached;
He blazed up in Jacob like a flaming fire
devouring all about it.

4* Like an enemy he made taut his bow;
with his arrows in his right hand
He took his stand as a foe, and slew
all on whom the eye doted;
Over the tent of daughter Zion
he poured out his wrath like fire.

5 The Lord has become an enemy,
he has consumed Israel:
Consumed all her castles
and destroyed her fortresses;
For daughter Judah he has multiplied
moaning and groaning.

6* He has demolished his shelter like a garden booth,
he has destroyed his dwelling;
In Zion the LORD has made
feast and sabbath to be forgotten;
He has scorned in fierce wrath
both king and priest.

7* The Lord has disowned his altar,
rejected his sanctuary;
The walls of her towers
he has handed over to the enemy,
Who shout in the house of the LORD
as on a feast day.

8*† The LORD marked for destruction
the wall of daughter Zion:
He stretched out the measuring line;
his hand brought ruin, yet he did not relent—
He brought grief on wall and rampart
till both succumbed.

9* Sunk into the ground are her gates;
he has removed and broken her bars.
Her king and her princes are among the pagans;
priestly instruction is wanting,
And her prophets have not received
any vision from the LORD.

10*† On the ground in silence sit
the old men of daughter Zion;
They strew dust on their heads
and gird themselves with sackcloth;
The maidens of Jerusalem
bow their heads to the ground.

11*† Worn out from weeping are my eyes,
within me all is in ferment;
My gall is poured out on the ground
because of the downfall of the daughter of my people,
As child and infant faint away
in the open spaces of the town.

12* They ask their mothers,
"Where is the cereal?"—in vain,
As they faint away like the wounded
in the streets of the city,
And breathe their last
in their mothers' arms.

13* To what can I liken or compare you,
O daughter Jerusalem?
What example can I show you for your comfort,
virgin daughter Zion?
For great as the sea is your downfall;
who can heal you?

14* Your prophets had for you
false and specious visions;
They did not lay bare your guilt,
to avert your fate;
They beheld for you in vision
false and misleading portents.

15* All who pass by
clap their hands at you;
They hiss and wag their heads
over daughter Jerusalem:
"Is this the all-beautiful city,
the joy of the whole earth?"

16* All your enemies
open their mouths against you;
They hiss and gnash their teeth.
They say, "We have devoured her.
This at last is the day we hoped for;
we have lived to see it!"

*

2, 3: 1, 12.
4: Jer 30, 14.
6: 1, 4; Is 1, 13; 5, 5.
7: Ez 24, 21.
8: Jer 52, 13.
9: Dt 28, 36.
10: Is 3, 26.
11: 3, 48.
12: 1, 11.
13: 1, 12.
14: Is 58, 1; Jer 2, 8; 23, 16.
15: Jer 18, 16.
16: 3, 46.

†

2, 3: *Horn:* symbol of power and strength; cf 2, 17; 1 Sm 2, 10; Lk 1, 69; etc.

2, 8: *The measuring line:* used not only in building, but in deciding what must be destroyed; cf Is 34, 11; 2 Kgs 21, 13.

2, 10: *They strew dust:* as a sign of penance; cf Jb 2, 12.

2, 11: *My gall is poured out on the ground:* I am afflicted with bitter sorrow; cf Jb 16, 13.

17* The LORD has done as he decreed:
he has fulfilled the threat
He set forth from days of old;
he has destroyed and had no pity,
Letting the enemy gloat over you
and exalting the horn of your foes.

18 Cry out to the Lord;
moan, O daughter Zion!
Let your tears flow like a torrent
day and night;
Let there be no respite for you,
no repose for your eyes.

19 Rise up, shrill in the night,
at the beginning of every watch;
Pour out your heart like water
in the presence of the Lord;
Lift up your hands to him
for the lives of your little ones
[Who faint from hunger
at the corner of every street].

20*†"Look, O LORD, and consider:
whom have you ever treated thus?
Must women eat their offspring,
their well-formed children?
Are priest and prophet to be slain
in the sanctuary of the LORD?

21* "Dead in the dust of the streets
lie young and old;
My maidens and young men
have fallen by the sword;
You have slain on the day of your wrath,
slaughtered without pity.

22* "You summoned as for a feast day
terrors against me from all sides;
There was not, on the day of your wrath,
either fugitive or survivor;
Those whom I bore and reared
my enemy has utterly destroyed."

CHAPTER 3

Sufferings of the Prophet and His People

1*†I am a man who knows affliction
from the rod of his anger,
2 One whom he has led and forced to walk
in darkness, not in the light;
3 Against me alone he brings back his hand
again and again all the day.
4* He has worn away my flesh and my skin,
he has broken my bones;
5 He has beset me round about
with poverty and weariness;
6* He has left me to dwell in the dark
like those long dead.

7 He has hemmed me in with no escape
and weighed me down with chains;
8* Even when I cry out for help,
he stops my prayer;
9 He has blocked my ways with fitted stones,
and turned my paths aside.

10* A lurking bear he has been to me,
a lion in ambush!
11* He deranged my ways, set me astray,
left me desolate.
12* He bent his bow, and set me up
as the target for his arrow.

13* He pierces my sides
with shafts from his quiver.
14* I have become a laughingstock for all nations,
their taunt all the day long;
15* He has sated me with bitter food,
made me drink my fill of wormwood.

16 He has broken my teeth with gravel,
pressed my face in the dust;
17 My soul is deprived of peace,
I have forgotten what happiness is;
18 I tell myself my future is lost,
all that I hoped for from the LORD.
19 The thought of my homeless poverty
is wormwood and gall;
20 Remembering it over and over
leaves my soul downcast within me.
21 But I will call this to mind,
as my reason to have hope:

22* The favors of the LORD are not exhausted,
his mercies are not spent;
23 They are renewed each morning,
so great is his faithfulness.
24* My portion is the LORD, says my soul;
therefore will I hope in him.

25* Good is the LORD to one who waits for him,
to the soul that seeks him;

---

*

17: Dt 28, 15.
20: 4, 10.
21: 3, 43; 2 Chr 36, 17; Jer 6, 11.
22: Jer 42, 17.
3, 1: Jer 20, 18.
4: Jb 30, 30; Is 38, 13.
6: Ps 143, 3.
8: Ps 22, 2.
10: Jb 10, 16; Hos 13, 8.
11: 1, 13.
12: 2, 4; Jb 16, 12.
13: Jb 6, 4; Ps 38, 3.
14: Jb 30, 9; Ps 69, 13.
15: Jer 9, 14; 23, 15.
22: Neh 9, 31.
24: Pss 16, 5; 73, 26.
25: Ps 130, 6; Is 30, 18.

---

†

2, 20: *Must women eat their offspring:* extreme famine in a besieged city sometimes led to this form of cannibalism; cf 4, 10; 2 Kgs 6, 28f; Bar 2, 3; Ez 5, 10.

3, 1-21: The author identifies Zion's sufferings with his own.

26 It is good to hope in silence
for the saving help of the LORD.
27† It is good for a man to bear
the yoke from his youth.

28 Let him sit alone and in silence,
when it is laid upon him.
29*†Let him put his mouth to the dust;
there may yet be hope.
30* Let him offer his cheek to be struck,
let him be filled with disgrace.

31* For the Lord's rejection
does not last forever;
32* Though he punishes, he takes pity,
in the abundance of his mercies;
33* He has no joy in afflicting
or grieving the sons of men.

34 When anyone tramples underfoot
all the prisoners in the land,
35 When he distorts men's rights
in the very sight of the Most High,
36 When he presses a crooked claim,
the Lord does not look on unconcerned.

37 Who commands so that it comes to pass,
except the Lord ordains it;
38* Except it proceeds from the mouth of the Most High,
whether the thing be good or bad!
39* Why should any living man complain,
any mortal, in the face of his sins?

40* Let us search and examine our ways
that we may return to the LORD!
41 Let us reach out our hearts
toward God in heaven!
42 We have sinned and rebelled;
you have not forgiven us.

43* You veiled yourself in wrath and pursued us,
you slew us and took no pity;
44 You wrapped yourself in a cloud
which prayer could not pierce.
45* You have made us offscourings and refuse
among the nations.

46 All our enemies
have opened their mouths against us;
47* Terror and the pit have been our lot,
desolation and destruction;
48* My eyes run with streams of water
over the downfall of the daughter of my people.

49 My eyes flow without ceasing,
there is no respite,
50 Till the LORD from heaven
looks down and sees.
51 My eyes torment my soul
at the sight of all the daughters of my city.

52 Those who were my enemies without cause
hunted me down like a bird;
53* They struck me down alive in the pit,
and sealed me in with a stone.
54 The waters flowed over my head,
and I said, "I am lost!"

55* I called upon your name, O LORD,
from the bottom of the pit;
56 You heard me call, "Let not your ear
be deaf to my cry for help!"
57 You came to my aid when I called to you;
you said, "Have no fear!"

58 You defended me in mortal danger,
you redeemed my life.
59* You see, O LORD, how I am wronged;
do me justice!
60 You see all their vindictiveness,
all their plots against me.
61 You hear their insults, O LORD,
[all their plots against me],
62 The whispered murmurings of my foes,
against me all the day;
63 Whether they sit or stand,
see, I am their taunt song.

64 Requite them as they deserve, O LORD,
according to their deeds;
65* Give them hardness of heart,
as your curse upon them;
66 Pursue them in wrath and destroy them
from under your heavens!

CHAPTER 4

Miseries of the Besieged City

1 How tarnished is the gold,
how changed the noble metal;
How the sacred stones lie strewn
at every street corner!

2* Zion's precious sons,
fine gold their counterpart,
Now worth no more than earthen jars
made by the hands of a potter!

*

29: Jb 42, 6.
30: Is 50, 6; Mt 5, 39.
31: Ps 103, 9.
32: Is 54, 8f.
33: Heb 12, 10f.
38: Is 45, 7.
39: Prv 19, 3.
40: Jl 2, 12f.
43: 2, 21.
45: 1 Cor 4, 13.
47: Is 24, 17; Jer 48, 43.
48: Ps 119, 136.
53: Jer 37, 16; 38, 6-9.
55f: Ps 130, 1f.
59: Ps 35, 23.
65: Jer 11, 20; 2 Tm 4, 14.
4, 2: Jer 19, 11.

†

3, 27: *To bear the yoke:* to do God's will; cf Jer 2, 20.
3, 29: *Let him put his mouth to the dust:* in humble submission; cf Ps 72, 9.

3*† Even the jackals bare their breasts
and suckle their young;
The daughter of my people has become as cruel
as the ostrich in the desert.

4 The tongue of the suckling cleaves
to the roof of its mouth in thirst;
The babes cry for food,
but there is no one to give it to them.

5* Those accustomed to dainty food
perish in the streets;
Those brought up in purple
now cling to the ash heaps.

6* The punishment of the daughter of my people
is greater than the penalty of Sodom,
Which was overthrown in an instant
without the turning of a hand.

7 Brighter than snow were her princes,
whiter than milk,
More ruddy than coral,
more precious than sapphire.

8* Now their appearance is blacker than soot,
they are unrecognized on the streets;
Their skin shrinks on their bones,
as dry as wood.

9 Better for those who perish by the sword
than for those who die of hunger,
Who waste away, as though pierced through,
lacking the fruits of the field!

10* The hands of compassionate women
boiled their own children,
To serve them as mourners' food
in the downfall of the daughter of my people.

11* The LORD has spent his anger,
poured out his blazing wrath;
He has kindled a fire in Zion
that has consumed her foundations.

12 The kings of the earth did not believe,
nor any of the world's inhabitants,
That enemy or foe could enter
the gates of Jerusalem.

13*† Because of the sins of her prophets
and the crimes of her priests,
Who shed in her midst
the blood of the just!—

14* They staggered blindly in the streets,
soiled with blood,
So that people could not touch
even their garments:

15 "Away you unclean!" they cried to them,
"Away, away, do not draw near!"
If they left and wandered among the nations,
nowhere could they remain.

16 The LORD himself has dispersed them,
he regards them no more;
He does not receive the priests with favor,
nor show kindness to the elders.

17† Our eyes ever wasted away,
looking in vain for aid;
From our watchtower we watched
for a nation that could not save us.

18 Men dogged our steps
so that we could not walk in our streets;
Our end drew near, and came;
our time had expired.

19* Our pursuers were swifter
than eagles in the air,
They harassed us on the mountains
and waylaid us in the desert.

20*† The anointed one of the LORD, our breath of life,
was caught in their snares,
He in whose shadow we thought
we could live on among the nations.

21*† Though you rejoice and are glad, O daughter Edom,
you who dwell in the land of Uz,
To you also shall the cup be passed;
you shall become drunk and naked.

LAMENTATIONS

*

3: Jb 39, 16.
5: Dt 28, 56.
6: Gn 19, 23-29; 2 Pt 2, 6; Jude 1, 7.
8: 3, 4.
10: 2, 20; Dt 28, 56f; 2 Kgs 6, 29.
11: Jer 7, 20; Ez 5, 13.
13: Jer 6, 13.
14: Is 59, 10.
19: Jer 4, 13; Hb 1, 8.
20: 2, 9; Ez 19, 4.8.
21: 1, 21; Jer 25, 15.

†

4, 3: *Cruel as the ostrich:* see note on Jb 39, 14ff. Jerusalem, in her distress, has abandoned her children.

4, 13ff: The priests and the false prophets lulled the people into an illusory security (Jer 2, 8; 5, 31; 6, 13; etc.), condoning and entering into their crimes so that they themselves became unclean.

4, 17: *A nation:* Egypt, which failed to give effective aid against Babylon.

4, 20: *Our breath of life:* the king. This is a royal epithet borrowed from Egyptian usage, while *the anointed one of the LORD* is Israelite. After the disaster of 598 B.C. (2 Kgs 24, 1-17), Jerusalem could have hoped to live in peace amidst her neighbors; but they (vv 21f) as well as Babylon turned against her to ensure her total devastation in 587 B.C.

4, 21: *Uz:* see note on Jer 25, 20.

22* Your chastisement is completed, O daughter Zion,
he will not prolong your exile;
But your wickedness, O daughter Edom, he will punish,
he will lay bare your sins.

CHAPTER 5

The Prophet's Lament and Supplication

1 Remember, O LORD, what has befallen us,
look, and see our disgrace:
2* Our inherited lands have been turned over to strangers,
our homes to foreigners.
3 We have become orphans, fatherless;
widowed are our mothers.
4 The water we drink we must buy,
for our own wood we must pay.
5 On our necks is the yoke of those who drive us;
we are worn out, but allowed no rest.

6† To Egypt we submitted,
and to Assyria, to fill our need of bread.
7† Our fathers, who sinned, are no more;
but we bear their guilt.
8† Slaves rule over us;
there is no one to rescue us from their hands.
9* At the peril of our lives we bring in our sustenance,
in the face of the desert heat;
10* Our skin is shriveled up, as though by a furnace,
with the searing blasts of famine.

11* The wives in Zion were ravished by the enemy,
the maidens in the cities of Judah;
12* Princes were gibbeted by them,
elders shown no respect.
13 The youths carry the millstones,
boys stagger under their loads of wood;
14† The old men have abandoned the gate,
the young men their music.

15* The joy of our hearts has ceased,
our dance has turned into mourning;
16 The garlands have fallen from our heads:
woe to us, for we have sinned!
17 Over this our hearts are sick,
at this our eyes grow dim:
18 That Mount Zion should be desolate,
with jackals roaming there!

19* You, O LORD, are enthroned forever;
your throne stands from age to age.
20* Why, then, should you forget us,
abandon us so long a time?
21* Lead us back to you, O LORD, that we may be restored:
give us anew such days as we had of old.
22* For now you have indeed rejected us,
and in full measure turned your wrath against us.

*

22: Is 40, 2.
5, 2: Ps 79, 1.
9: Jer 6, 25.
10: 4, 8.
11: Zec 14, 2.
12: 4, 16.
15: Jer 16, 9; 25, 10; Am 8, 10.
19: Pss 9, 8; 45, 7; 102, 13.27.
20: Pss 13, 1; 42, 10.
21: Ps 80, 19f.
22: Jer 14, 19.

†

5, 6: In its state of abjection, Judah was forced to depend on its traditional enemies to the west and the east for subsistence. Mesopotamia is here called by the name it had long borne, *Assyria*, though in these times the power of the Assyrians had been superseded by that of the Chaldeans.

5, 7: *Our fathers:* collective responsibility, for good and for evil, was recognized in the Old Testament; cf Jer 31, 29. But the present generation is also personally guilty of sin (v 16).

5, 8: Administrations imposed by foreign powers were notoriously corrupt and inept. The Hebrew word for "slave" is the same as that used for an official (servant of the ruler); the author doubtless intends the double meaning here.

5, 14: *The gate:* the place of assembly, where city decisions were made and judgment given by the elders and other notables; see note on Ru 4, 1.

The Book of

BARUCH

The opening verses of this book ascribe it, or at least its first part, to Baruch, the well-known secretary of the prophet Jeremiah. It contains five very different compositions, the first and the last in prose, the others in poetic form. The prose sections were certainly composed in Hebrew, though the earliest known form of the book is in Greek.

An observance of the feast of Booths with a public prayer of penitence and petition (1, 15—3, 8), such as is supposed by the introduction (1, 1-14), would not have been possible during the lifetime of Baruch after the fall of Jerusalem; this indeed is suggested in the prayer itself (2, 26). The prayer is therefore to be understood as the pious reflection of a later Jewish writer upon the circumstances of the exiles in Babylon as he knew them from the Book of Jeremiah. He expresses in their name sentiments called for by the prophet, and ascribes the wording of these sentiments to the person most intimately acquainted with Jeremiah's teaching, namely, Baruch. The purpose of this literary device is to portray for his own and later generations the spirit of repentance which prompted God to bring the exile to an end.

The lesson thus gained is followed by a hymn in praise of Wisdom (3, 9—4, 4), exalting the law of Moses as the unique gift of God to Israel, the observance of which is the way to life and peace. The ideal city of Jerusalem is then represented (4, 5-29) as the solicitous mother of all exiles, who is assured in the name of God that all her children will be restored to her (4, 30—5, 9).

The final chapter is really a separate work, with a title of its own (6, 1). It is patterned after the earlier letter of Jeremiah (Jer 29), in the spirit of the warnings against idolatry contained in Jer 10 and Is 44. Its earnestness is impressive, but in restating previous inspired teachings at a later day, it does so with no special literary grace.

Thus the principal divisions of the book are seen to be:

- *I: Prayer of the Exiles (1, 1—3, 8)*
- *II: Praise of Wisdom in the Law of Moses (3, 9—4, 4)*
- *III: Jerusalem Bewails and Consoles Her Captive Children (4, 5-29)*
- *IV: Jerusalem Consoled: The Captivity about To End (4, 30—5, 9)*
- *V: The Letter of Jeremiah against Idolatry (6, 1-72)*

I: PRAYER OF THE EXILES

CHAPTER 1

Meeting in Babylon. 1* Now these are
the words of the scroll which Baruch,
son of Neriah, son of Mahseiah, son of
Zedekiah, son of Hasadiah, son of Hil-
kiah, wrote in Babylon, 2*† in the fifth
year [on the seventh day of the month,
at the time when the Chaldeans took Je-
rusalem and burnt it with fire]. 3* And
Baruch read the words of this scroll for
Jeconiah, son of Jehoiakim, king of Ju-
dah, to hear it, as well as all the peo-
ple who came to the reading: 4† the
nobles, the kings' sons, the elders, and
the whole people, small and great alike
—all who lived in Babylon by the river
Sud.
5 They wept and fasted and prayed be-
fore the LORD, 6* and collected such
funds as each could furnish. 7 These they
sent to Jerusalem, to Jehoiakim, son of
Hilkiah, son of Shallum, the priest, and
to the priests and the whole people who

*

1, 1: Jer 32, 12; 36, 4; 45, 1-5.
2: 2 Kgs 25, 8ff.
3: 2 Kgs 24, 8-17; Jer 22, 24-30; 51, 59-64.
3-4: 2 Kgs 23, 1-2.
6: Dt 16, 17.

†

1, 2: *In the fifth year on the seventh day of the month:* Jerusalem fell on the seventh day of the fifth month; cf 2 Kgs 25, 8; Jer 52, 12. Either the text read originally "the fifth month," or it refers to the observance of an anniversary of the fall of Jerusalem in 587 B.C.

1, 4: *The river Sud:* one of the Babylonian canals, not otherwise identified. In ancient non-Biblical Hebrew fragments discovered in 1952, there is reference to a river "Sur" in a similar context.

were with him in Jerusalem. 8† [This
was when he received the vessels of the
house of the Lord that had been re-
moved from the temple, to restore them
to the land of Judah, on the tenth of Si-
van. These silver vessels Zedekiah, son
of Josiah, king of Judah, had had made
9 after Nebuchadnezzar, king of Baby-
lon, carried off Jeconiah, and the
princes, and the skilled workers, and the
nobles, and the people of the land from
Jerusalem, as captives, and brought
them to Babylon.]
10* Their message was: "We send you
funds, with which you are to procure
holocausts, sin offerings, and frankin-
cense, and to prepare cereal offerings;
offer these on the altar of the LORD our
God, 11*† and pray for the life of Nebu-
chadnezzar, king of Babylon, and that
of Belshazzar, his son, that their life-
times may equal the duration of the
heavens above the earth; 12 and that the
LORD may give us strength, and light to
our eyes, that we may live under the pro-
tective shadow of Nebuchadnezzar, king
of Babylon, and that of Belshazzar, his
son, and serve them long, finding favor
in their sight.

Confession of Guilt. 13 "Pray for us
also to the LORD, our God; for we have
sinned against the LORD, our God, and
the wrath and anger of the LORD have
not yet been withdrawn from us at the
present day. 14* And read out publicly
this scroll which we send you, in the
house of the LORD, on the feast day and
during the days of assembly:
15* "Justice is with the LORD, our God;
and we today are flushed with shame,
we men of Judah and citizens of Jerusa-
lem, 16 that we, with our kings and rulers
and priests and prophets, and with our
fathers, 17 have sinned in the LORD's
sight 18 and disobeyed him. We have nei-
ther heeded the voice of the LORD, our
God, nor followed the precepts which the
LORD set before us. 19 From the time the
LORD led our fathers out of the land of
Egypt until the present day, we have
been disobedient to the LORD, our God,
and only too ready to disregard his
voice. 20* And the evils and the curse
which the LORD enjoined upon Moses,
his servant, at the time he led our fathers
forth from the land of Egypt to give us
the land flowing with milk and honey,
cling to us even today. 21 For we did not
heed the voice of the LORD, our God, in
all the words of the prophets whom he
sent us, 22 but each one of us went off
after the devices of our own wicked
hearts, served other gods, and did evil
in the sight of the LORD, our God.

CHAPTER 2

1 "And the LORD fulfilled the warning
he had uttered against us: against our
judges, who governed Israel, against our
kings and princes, and against the men
of Israel and Judah. 2* He brought down
upon us evils so great that there has not
been done anywhere under heaven what
has been done in Jerusalem, as was writ-
ten in the law of Moses: 3† that one after
another of us should eat the flesh of his
son or of his daughter. 4* He has made
us subject to all the kingdoms round
about us, a reproach and a horror
among all the nations round about to
which the LORD has scattered us. 5 We
are brought low, not raised up, because
we sinned against the LORD, our God,
not heeding his voice.
6* "Justice is with the LORD, our God;
and we, like our fathers, are flushed with
shame even today. 7 All the evils of
which the LORD had warned us have
come upon us: 8 and we did not plead
before the LORD, or turn, each from the
figments of his evil heart. 9* And the
LORD kept watch over the evils, and
brought them home to us; for the LORD
is just in all the works he commanded
us to do, 10 but we did not heed his voice,
or follow the precepts of the LORD which
he set before us.

Prayer for Deliverance. 11* "And
now, LORD, God of Israel, you who led
your people out of the land of Egypt with
your mighty hand, with signs and won-
ders and great might, and with your
upraised arm, so that you have made
for yourself a name till the present day:
12* we have sinned, been impious, and
violated, O LORD, our God, all your stat-
utes. 13 Let your anger be withdrawn
from us, for we are left few in number
among the nations to which you scat-
tered us. 14 Hear, O LORD, our prayer of
supplication, and deliver us for your own
sake: grant us favor in the presence of

*

10: Jer 17, 26.
11: Dt 11, 21; Jer 29, 7; Dn 5, 1-2; 1 Tm 2, 1f.
14: Ex 23, 14ff; Lv 23, 35f; Hos 9, 5; Sir 50, 6.
15: 2, 6; 3, 8; Neh 9, 6-37; Ezr 9, 6-15; Dn 9, 4-19.
20: Lv 26, 14-39; Dt 28, 15-68.
2, 2f: 2 Kgs 6, 28f; Jer 19, 9; Lam 2, 20; 4, 10; Ez 5, 10.
4: Jer 29, 18.
6: 1, 15.
9: Jer 1, 12; 31, 28; 44, 27.
11: Dt 6, 21-22.
12: Ps 106, 6.

†

1, 8f: *He:* possibly Baruch; less likely *Jehoiakim . . . the priest* (v 7), a member of the high-priestly family not mentioned elsewhere. The *silver vessels* here described are distinct from the vessels referred to in 2 Kgs 25, 14 and Ezr 1, 7ff. The author of this note may have thought of the *fifth year* (v 1) of Zedekiah, in view of Jer 28, 1; 29, 1ff. A "fifth year," again with no month mentioned, is given in Ez 1, 2 for the inaugural vision of Ezekiel's prophetic career.

1, 11: *Nebuchadnezzar . . . Belshazzar, his son:* as in Dn 5, 1f. Later Jewish tradition seems to have simplified the history of the past by making the last Chaldean ruler of Babylon the son of the conqueror of Jerusalem.

2, 3: *One after another of us should eat:* see note on Lam 2, 20.

our captors, 15* that the whole earth may
know that you are the LORD, our God,
and that Israel and his descendants bear
your name. 16* O LORD, look down from
your holy dwelling and take thought of
us; turn, O LORD, your ear to hear us.
17* Look directly at us, and behold: it is
not the dead in the nether world, whose
spirits have been taken from within
them, who will give glory and vindica-
tion to the LORD. 18* He whose soul is
deeply grieved, who walks bowed and
feeble, with failing eyes and famished
soul, will declare your glory and justice,
LORD!

19 "Not on the just deeds of our fathers
and our kings do we base our plea for
mercy in your sight, O LORD, our God.
20 You have brought your wrath and an-
ger down upon us, as you had warned
us through your servants the prophets:
21* 'Thus says the LORD: Bend your
shoulders to the service of the king of
Babylon, that you may continue in the
land I gave your fathers: 22 for if you do
not hear the LORD's voice so as to serve
the king of Babylon,

23* I will make to cease from the cities of Judah
and from the streets of Jerusalem
The sounds of joy and the sounds of gladness,
the voice of the bridegroom
and the voice of the bride;
And all the land shall be deserted,
without inhabitants.'

24* But we did not heed your voice, or
serve the king of Babylon, and you ful-
filled the threats you had made through
your servants the prophets, to have the
bones of our kings and the bones of our
fathers brought out from their burial
places. 25*† And indeed, they lie exposed
to the heat of day and the frost of night.
They died in dire anguish, by hunger
and the sword and plague. 26*† And you
reduced the house which bears your
name to what it is today, for the wicked-
ness of the kingdom of Israel and the
kingdom of Judah.

God's Promises Recalled. 27 "But with
us, O Lord, our God, you have dealt in
all your clemency and in all your great
mercy. 28 This was your warning
through your servant Moses, the day
you ordered him to write down your law
in the presence of the Israelites: 29 If you
do not heed my voice, surely this great
and numerous throng will dwindle away
among the nations to which I will scatter
them. 30* For I know they will not heed
me, because they are a stiff-necked peo-
ple. But in the land of their captivity they
shall have a change of heart; 31* they
shall know that I, the LORD, am their
God. I will give them hearts, and heedful
ears; 32* and they shall praise me in the
land of their captivity, and shall invoke
my name. 33* Then they shall turn back
from their stiff-necked stubbornness,
and from their evil deeds, because they
shall remember the fate of their fathers
who sinned against the LORD. 34 And I
will bring them back to the land which
with my oath I promised to their fathers,
to Abraham, Isaac and Jacob; and they
shall rule it. I will make them increase;
they shall not then diminish. 35* And I
will establish for them, as an eternal
covenant, that I will be their God, and
they shall be my people; and I will not
again remove my people Israel from the
land I gave them.

CHAPTER 3

1 "LORD Almighty, God of Israel, af-
flicted souls and dismayed spirits call to
you. 2 Hear, O LORD, for you are a God
of mercy; and have mercy on us, who
have sinned against you: 3* for you are
enthroned forever, while we are perish-
ing forever. 4 LORD Almighty, God of Is-
rael, hear the prayer of Israel's few, the
sons of those who sinned against you;
they did not heed the voice of the LORD,
their God, and the evils cling to us.
5 Remember at this time not the mis-
deeds of our fathers, but your own hand
and name: 6 for you are the LORD our
God; and you, O LORD, we will praise!
7* For this, you put into our hearts the
fear of you: that we may call upon your
name, and praise you in our captivity,
when we have removed from our hearts
all the wickedness of our fathers who
sinned against you. 8 Behold us today in
our captivity, where you scattered us,
a reproach, a curse, and a requital for
all the misdeeds of our fathers, who
withdrew from the LORD, our God."

II: PRAISE OF WISDOM IN THE LAW OF MOSES

9* Hear, O Israel, the commandments of life:
listen, and know prudence!

*

15: Sir 36, 11; Jer 14, 9.
16: Dt 26, 15.
17: Ps 6, 6; Is 38, 18.
18: Zep 2, 3.
21: Jer 27, 12.
23: Jer 7, 34.
24: Jer 8, 1f.
25: Jer 7, 34; 14, 12; 31, 30.
26: Jer 7, 10-15.
30: Dt 30, 1f; 31, 27.
31: Jer 24, 7; Ez 36, 26; Ps 40, 7.
32: Tb 13, 7.
33ff: Dt 30, 1-10.
35: Jer 31, 31; Lam 4, 22.
3, 3: Pss 29, 10; 102, 12f.
7: Jer 31, 33.
9: Prv 4, 20ff.

†

2, 25: *They lie exposed:* probably an allusion to Jer 36, 30; see note on Jer 22, 19.

2, 26: *The house which bears your name:* the temple of Jerusalem. *What it is today:* during the exile it lay in ruins.

10 How is it, Israel,
that you are in the land of your foes,
grown old in a foreign land,
Defiled with the dead,
11* accounted with those destined for the nether world?
12* You have forsaken the fountain of wisdom!
13* Had you walked in the way of God,
you would have dwelt in enduring peace.
14* Learn where prudence is,
where strength, where understanding;
That you may know also
where are length of days, and life,
where light of the eyes, and peace.

15* Who has found the place of wisdom,
who has entered into her treasuries?
16* Where are the rulers of the nations,
they who lorded it over the wild beasts of the earth,
17 and made sport of the birds of the heavens:
They who heaped up the silver
and the gold in which men trust;
of whose possessions there was no end?
18 They schemed anxiously for money,
but there is no trace of their work:
19 They have vanished down into the nether world,
and others have risen up in their stead.

20 Later generations have seen the light,
have dwelt in the land,
But the way to understanding they have not known,
21 they have not perceived her paths,
or reached her;
their offspring were far from the way to her.
22*† She has not been heard of in Canaan,
nor seen in Teman.
23 The sons of Hagar who seek knowledge on earth,
the merchants of Midian and Teman,
the phrasemakers seeking knowledge,
These have not known the way to wisdom,
nor have they her paths in mind.

24† O Israel, how vast is the house of God,
how broad the scope of his dominion:
25 Vast and endless,
high and immeasurable!
26* In it were born the giants,
renowned at the first,
stalwarts, skilled in war.
27* Not these did God choose,
nor did he give them the way of understanding;
28* They perished for lack of prudence,
perished through their folly.
29* Who has gone up to the heavens and taken her,
or brought her down from the clouds?
30 Who has crossed the sea and found her,
bearing her away rather than choice gold?
31 None knows the way to her,
nor has any understood her paths.

32 Yet he who knows all things knows her;
he has probed her by his knowledge—
He who established the earth for all time,
and filled it with four-footed beasts;
33 He who dismisses the light, and it departs,
calls it, and it obeys him trembling;
34 Before whom the stars at their posts
shine and rejoice;
35* When he calls them, they answer, "Here we are!"
shining with joy for their Maker.
36 Such is our God;
no other is to be compared to him:
37* He has traced out all the way of understanding,
and has given her to Jacob, his servant,
to Israel, his beloved son.

38* Since then she has appeared on earth,
and moved among men.

CHAPTER 4

1* She is the book of the precepts of God,
the law that endures forever;
All who cling to her will live,
but those will die who forsake her.
2* Turn, O Jacob, and receive her:
walk by her light toward splendor.

*

11: Ps 88, 5.
12: Jer 2.13; Jn 4, 10.14.
13: Is 48, 18.
14: Prv 3, 2; 8, 14.
15ff: Jb 28, 1-28.
16: Jer 27, 6.
22: Jer 49, 7; Ez 28, 4-5; Zec 9, 2; Jb 2, 11.
26: Gn 6, 4; Wis 14, 6.
27: 1 Sm 16, 7-10.
28: Sir 10, 8.
29: Dt 30, 12f; Sir 24, 4; Rom 10, 6f.
35: Jb 38, 7; Ps 147, 4; Is 40, 26.
37: Ps 147, 19; Sir 24, 8-12.
38: Wis 9, 18; Jn 1, 14.
4, 1: Dt 4, 6-8; Prv 8, 35f; Sir 24, 22.
2: Prv 4, 13.19.

†

3, 22f: Despite the renown for wisdom of the peoples of *Canaan* or Phoenicia (Ez 28, 3f), of *Teman* (Jer 49, 7), of *the sons of Hagar* or the Arabians, they did not possess true wisdom, which is found only in the law of God.

3, 24: *The house of God:* here, the created universe.

3 Give not your glory to another,
your privileges to an alien race.
4* Blessed are we, O Israel;
for what pleases God is known to us!

III: JERUSALEM BEWAILS AND CONSOLES HER CAPTIVE CHILDREN

5 Fear not, my people!
Remember, Israel,
6* You were sold to the nations
not for your destruction;
It was because you angered God
that you were handed over to your foes.
7* For you provoked your Maker
with sacrifices to demons, to no-gods;
8 You forsook the Eternal God who nourished you,
and you grieved Jerusalem who fostered you.
9 She indeed saw coming upon you
the anger of God; and she said:

"Hear, you neighbors of Zion!
God has brought great mourning upon me,
10 For I have seen the captivity
that the Eternal God has brought upon my sons and daughters.
11 With joy I fostered them;
but with mourning and lament I let them go.
12* Let no one gloat over me, a widow, bereft of many:
For the sins of my children I am left desolate,
because they turned from the law of God,
13 and did not acknowledge his statutes;
In the ways of God's commandments they did not walk,
nor did they tread the disciplined paths of his justice.

14 "Let Zion's neighbors come,
to take note of the captivity of my sons and daughters,
brought upon them by the Eternal God.
15* He has brought against them a nation from afar,
a nation ruthless and of alien speech,
That has neither reverence for age
nor tenderness for childhood;
16 They have led away this widow's cherished sons,
have left me solitary, without daughters.
17 What can I do to help you?
18* He who has brought this evil upon you
must himself deliver you from your enemies' hands.
19 Farewell, my children, farewell:
I am left desolate.
20* I have taken off the garment of peace,
have put on sackcloth for my prayer of supplication,
and while I live I will cry out to the Eternal God.

21* "Fear not, my children; call upon God,
who will deliver you from oppression at enemy hands.
22 I have trusted in the Eternal God for your welfare,
and joy has come to me from the Holy One
Because of the mercy that will swiftly reach you
from your eternal savior.
23* With mourning and lament I sent you forth,
but God will give you back to me
with enduring gladness and joy.
24* As Zion's neighbors lately saw you taken captive,
so shall they soon see God's salvation come to you,
with great glory and the splendor of the Eternal God.

25*† "My children, bear patiently the anger
that has come from God upon you;
Your enemies have persecuted you,
and you will soon see their destruction
and trample upon their necks.
26* My pampered children have trodden rough roads,
carried off by their enemies like sheep in a raid.
27* Fear not, my children; call out to God!
He who brought this upon you will remember you.
28 As your hearts have been disposed to stray from God,
turn now ten times the more to seek him;
29* For he who has brought disaster upon you

---

*

4: Dt 4, 32-37; 33, 29.
6: Jgs 2, 14; Is 50, 1; 52, 3.
7-8: Dt 32, 13-18; 1 Cor 10, 20.
12: Lam 1, 1.2.7.
15: Dt 28, 49f; Jer 5, 15; 6, 22f.
18: Jer 32, 42.
20: Jdt 9, 1; Est 4, 16.
21: Jer 51, 5.
23: Jer 31, 12f.
24: Is 60, 1ff.
25: Is 51, 23.
26: Lam 2, 22.
27: Is 40, 1.
29: Is 35, 10.

†

4, 25: *Trample upon their necks:* love of enemies was not an Old Testament ideal. The Babylonians are considered here, however, to be God's enemies as well as Israel's.

BARUCH

will, in saving you, bring you back
enduring joy."

IV: JERUSALEM CONSOLED: THE CAPTIVITY ABOUT TO END

30* Fear not, Jerusalem!
He who gave you your name is your encouragement.
31 Fearful are those who harmed you,
who rejoiced at your downfall;
32* Fearful are the cities where your children were enslaved,
fearful the city that took your sons.
33* As that city rejoiced at your collapse,
and made merry at your downfall,
so shall she grieve over her own desolation.
34 I will take from her the joyous throngs,
and her exultation shall be turned to mourning:
35*†For fire shall come upon her
from the Eternal God, for a long time,
and demons shall dwell in her
from that time on.

36* Look to the east, Jerusalem!
behold the joy that comes to you from God.
37 Here come your sons whom you once let go,
gathered in from the east and from the west
By the word of the Holy One,
rejoicing in the glory of God.

CHAPTER 5

1* Jerusalem, take off your robe of mourning and misery;
put on the splendor of glory from God forever:
2* Wrapped in the cloak of justice from God,
bear on your head the mitre
that displays the glory of the eternal name.
3 For God will show all the earth your splendor:
4* you will be named by God forever
the peace of justice, the glory of God's worship.

5 Up, Jerusalem! stand upon the heights;
look to the east and see your children
Gathered from the east and the west
at the word of the Holy One,
rejoicing that they are remembered by God.
6* Led away on foot by their enemies
they left you:
but God will bring them back to you
borne aloft in glory as on royal thrones.
7* For God has commanded
that every lofty mountain be made low,
And that the age-old depths and gorges
be filled to level ground,
that Israel may advance secure in the glory of God.
8* The forests and every fragrant kind of tree
have overshadowed Israel at God's command;
9 For God is leading Israel in joy
by the light of his glory,
with his mercy and justice for company.

V: THE LETTER OF JEREMIAH AGAINST IDOLATRY

CHAPTER 6

1* A copy of the letter which Jeremiah
sent to those who were being led captive
to Babylon by the king of the Babylonians, to convey to them what God had
commanded him:
For the sins you committed before
God, you are being led captive to Babylon by Nebuchadnezzar, king of the
Babylonians. 2† When you reach Babylon you will be there many years, a period seven generations long; after which
I will bring you back from there in peace.
3* And now in Babylon you will see borne
upon men's shoulders gods of silver and
gold and wood, which cast fear upon the
pagans. 4 Take care that you yourselves
do not imitate their alien example and
stand in fear of them, 5 when you see the
crowd before them and behind worshiping them. Rather, say in your hearts,
"You, O LORD, are to be worshiped!";
6* for my angel is with you, and he is
the custodian of your lives.
7* Their tongues are smoothed by

30: Ps 46, 5; Is 60, 14.
32: Jer 51, 43.
33f: Is 13, 20ff; 47, 1-11; Jer 50, 13.
35: Is 34, 9-14.
36: Is 60, 4f.
5, 1: Is 52, 1.
2: Ex 39, 30; Wis 18, 24; Is 61, 10; 62, 3.
4: Is 1, 26; 32, 17; Jer 33, 16.
6: Is 49, 22.
7: Is 40, 3f.
8: Is 41, 19.
6, 1: Jer 29, 1.
3: Is 46, 7; Jer 10, 1-16.
6: Ex 23, 20.
7: Ps 135, 16.

4, 35: Deserts and desolate places were looked upon as the special habitations of *demons;* Tb 8, 3; Lk 11, 24.

6, 2: *Seven generations:* possibly an indication of the date of this composition by an author writing for his contemporaries for whom the conditions of the exile were still realities. He has multiplied the *seventy years* of Jer 29, 10 by three or four.

woodworkers; they are covered with gold and silver—but they are a fraud, and cannot speak. 8 People bring gold, as to a maiden in love with ornament, 9 and furnish crowns for the heads of their gods. Then sometimes the priests take the silver and gold from their gods and spend it on themselves, 10† or give part of it to the harlots on the terrace. They trick them out in garments like men, these gods of silver and gold and wood; 11 but though they are wrapped in purple clothing, they are not safe from corrosion or insects. 12 They wipe their faces clean of the house dust which is thick upon them. 13 Each has a scepter, like the human ruler of a district; but none does away with those that offend against it. 14 Each has in its right hand an axe or dagger, but it cannot save itself from war or pillage. Thus it is known they are not gods; do not fear them.

15 As useless as one's broken tools 16 are their gods, set up in their houses; their eyes are full of dust from the feet of those who enter. 17 Their courtyards are walled in like those of a man brought to execution for a crime against the king; the priests reinforce their houses with gates and bars and bolts, lest they be carried off by robbers. 18 They light more lamps for them than for themselves, yet not one of these can they see. 19 They are like any beam in the house; it is said their hearts are eaten away. Though the insects out of the ground consume them and their garments, they do not feel it. 20 Their faces are blackened by the smoke of the house. 21 Bats and swallows alight on their bodies and on their heads; and cats as well as birds. 22 Know, therefore, that they are not gods, and do not fear them.

23 Despite the gold that covers them for adornment, unless someone wipes away the corrosion, they do not shine; nor did they feel anything when they were molded. 24 They are bought at any price, and there is no spirit in them. 25* Having no feet, they are carried on men's shoulders, displaying their shame to all; and those who worship them are put to confusion 26 because, if they fall to the ground, the worshipers must raise them up. They neither move of themselves if one sets them upright, nor come upright if they fall; but one puts gifts beside them as beside the dead. 27*† Their priests resell their sacrifices for their own advantage. Even their wives cure parts of the meat, but do not share it with the poor and the weak; 28 the menstruous and women in childbed handle their sacrifices. Knowing from this that they are not gods, do not fear them.

29 How can they be called gods? For women bring the offerings to these gods of silver and gold and wood; 30* and in their temples the priests squat with torn tunic and with shaven hair and beard, and with their heads uncovered. 31 They shout and wail before their gods as others do at a funeral banquet. 32 The priests take some of their clothing and put it on their wives and children. 33*† Whether they are treated well or ill by anyone, they cannot requite it; they can neither set up a king nor remove him. 34 Similarly, they cannot give anyone riches or coppers; if one fails to fulfill a vow to them, they cannot exact it of him. 35* They neither save a man from death, nor deliver the weak from the strong. 36 To no blind man do they restore his sight, nor do they save any man in an emergency. 37 They neither pity the widow nor benefit the orphan. 38 These gilded and silvered wooden statues are like stones from the mountains; and their worshipers will be put to shame. 39 How then can it be thought or claimed that they are gods?

40† Even the Chaldeans themselves have no respect for them; for when they see a deaf mute, incapable of speech, they bring forward Bel and ask the god to make noise, as though the man could understand; 41 and they are themselves unable to reflect and abandon these gods, for they have no sense. 42*† And their women, girt with cords, sit by the roads, burning chaff for incense; 43 and whenever one of them is drawn aside by some passer-by who lies with her, she mocks her neighbor who has not been dignified as she has, and has not had her cord broken. 44 All that takes place around these gods is a fraud: how then can it be thought or claimed that they are gods?

45 They are produced by woodworkers and goldsmiths, and they are nothing else than what these craftsmen wish them to be. 46 Even those who produce them are not long-lived; 47 how then can what they have produced be gods? They have left frauds and opprobrium to their successors. 48 For when war or disaster comes upon them, the priests deliberate

*

25: Wis 13, 16.
27: Lv 12, 4; 15, 19f; Dt 14, 28f.
30: Lv 10, 6; 21, 5.10.
33: Dn 2, 21.
35: Pss 68, 6; 146, 7ff.
42-43: Jer 3,2.

†

6, 10: *Harlots on the terrace:* cult prostitutes, common in the idolatrous religions of the Gentiles.

6, 27-31: From the point of view of Jewish ritual law, the practices named here were grotesque and depraved; cf Lv 12, 2ff; 15, 19-23.

6, 33-39: All that the gods cannot do, the true God does; cf 1 Sm 2, 7; Dt 23, 22; Pss 68, 6; 146, 7-9; Is 35, 4f.

6, 40: *Bel:* cf note on Jer 50, 2.

6, 42f: This seems to refer to the obligation of Babylonian women to serve once in their lives as cult prostitutes. The unbroken cord was a sign that this duty had not yet been fulfilled. *Chaff:* burnt as an aphrodisiac or for use in erotic rites.

among themselves where they can hide
with them. 49 How then can one not know
that these are no-gods, which do not
save themselves either from war or from
disaster? 50 They are wooden, gilded and
silvered; they will later be known for
frauds. To all peoples and kings it will
be clear that they are not gods, but hu-
man handiwork; and that God's work is
not in them.

51 Who does not know that they are not
gods? 52 They set no king over the land,
nor do they give men rain. 53 They nei-
ther vindicate their own rights, nor do
they recover what is unjustly taken, for
they are unable; 54 they are like crows
between heaven and earth. For when
fire breaks out in the temple of these
wooden or gilded or silvered gods,
though the priests flee and are safe, they
themselves are burnt up in the fire like
beams. 55 They cannot resist a king, or
enemy forces. 56 How then can it be ad-
mitted or thought that they are gods?

They are safe from neither thieves nor
bandits, these wooden and silvered and
gilded gods; 57 those who seize them strip
off the gold and the silver, and go away
with the clothing that was on them, and
they cannot help themselves. 58* How
much better to be a king displaying his
valor, or a handy tool in a house, the
joy of its owner, than these false gods;
or the door of a house, that keeps safe
those who are within, rather than these
false gods; or a wooden post in a palace,
rather than these false gods! 59 The sun
and moon and stars are bright, and obe-
dient in the service for which they are
sent. 60 Likewise the lightning, when it
flashes, is a goodly sight; and the same
wind blows over all the land. 61 The
clouds, too, when commanded by God
to proceed across the whole world, fulfill
the order; 62 and fire, sent from on high
to burn up the mountains and the for-
ests, does what has been commanded.
But these false gods are not their equal,
whether in beauty or in power; 63 so that
it is unthinkable, and cannot be claimed,
that they are gods. They can neither ex-
ecute judgment, nor benefit man.
64 Know, therefore, that they are not
gods, and do not fear them.

65 Kings they neither curse nor bless.
66 They show the nations no signs in the
heavens, nor are they brilliant like the
sun, nor shining like the moon. 67 The
beasts which can help themselves by
fleeing to shelter are better than they
are. 68 Thus in no way is it clear to us
that they are gods; so do not fear them.
69 For like a scarecrow in a cucumber
patch, that is no protection, are their
wooden, gilded, silvered gods. 70 Just
like a thornbush in a garden on which
perches every kind of bird, or like a
corpse hurled into darkness, are their
silvered and gilded wooden gods.
71 From the rotting of the purple and the
linen upon them, it can be known that
they are not gods; they themselves will
in the end be comsumed, and be a dis-
grace in the land. 72 The better for the
just man who has no idols: he shall be
far from disgrace!

*

58: Wis 13, 10-15; 15, 7ff.

The Book of

EZEKIEL

Ezekiel's complex character makes him one of the most interesting figures in Israelite prophecy. In many ways he resembles the more primitive type of prophet represented by Elijah and Elisha; yet he clearly depends on all his predecessors in prophecy, and his teaching is a development of theirs. His unique contribution to the history of prophetism lies in his manifest interest in the temple and the liturgy, an interest paralleled in no other prophet—not even Jeremiah who, like Ezekiel, was also a priest. Particularly because of this interest, Ezekiel's influence on postexilic religion was enormous, and not without reason has he been called "the father of Judaism." This has resulted in his prophecies reaching us with the evident marks of editing and addition by the post-exilic circles that shared his intense interest. However, we may be sure that in this book we have throughout what is in substance the prophet's own work.

Ezekiel became a prophet in Babylon—the first prophet to receive the call to prophesy outside the Holy Land. As one of the exiles deported by Nebuchadnezzar in 597, his first task was to prepare his fellow countrymen in Babylon for the final destruction of Jerusalem, which they believed to be inviolable. Accordingly, the first part of his book consists of reproaches for Israel's past and present sins and the confident prediction of yet a further devastation of the land of promise and a more general exile. In 587, when Nebuchadnezzar destroyed Jerusalem, Ezekiel was vindicated before his unbelieving compatriots.

After this time, Ezekiel's message changes. From now on his prophecy is characterized by the promise of salvation in a new covenant, and he is anxious to lay down the conditions necessary to obtain it. Even as Jeremiah had believed, Ezekiel thought that the exiles were the hope of Israel's restoration, once God's allotted time for the Exile had been accomplished. His final eight chapters are an utopian vision of the Israel of the future, rid of its past evils and reestablished firmly under the rule of the Lord. The famous vision of the dry bones in chapter 37 expresses his firm belief in a forthcoming restoration, Israel rising to new life from the graveyard of Babylon. But Ezekiel's new covenant, like Jeremiah's, was to see its true fulfillment only in the New Testament.

Perhaps no other prophet has stressed the absolute majesty of God as Ezekiel does. This appears not only in the tremendous vision by the river Chebar with which his prophecy opens, but throughout the book. Ultimately, says Ezekiel, whatever God does to or for man is motivated by zeal for his own holy name. The new heart and the new spirit which must exist under the new covenant cannot be the work of man; they too must be the work of God. By such teachings he helped prepare for the New Testament doctrine of salvation through grace.

The Book of Ezekiel is divided as follows:

I: CALL OF THE PROPHET

CHAPTER 1

The Vision: God on the Cherubim.
1*† In the thirtieth year, on the fifth day
of the fourth month, while I was
among the exiles by the river Chebar,
the heavens opened, and I saw divine
visions.—2† On the fifth day of the

* 1,1: 3, 23; 10, 20; 43, 3.

† 1, 1: *The thirtieth year,* which corresponds to the fifth year of exile (v 2), has never been satisfactorily explained; possibly it refers to the prophet's age. *The river Chebar:* probably a canal near Nippur, southeast of Babylon, one of the sites on which the Jewish exiles were settled.

1, 2: *The fifth day of the fourth month, the fifth year:* July 31, 593 B.C.; cf v 1.

month, the fifth year, that is, of King Je-
hoiachin's exile, 3 the word of the LORD
came to the priest Ezekiel, the son of
Buzi, in the land of the Chaldeans by the
river Chebar.—There the hand of the
LORD came upon me.
4† As I looked, a stormwind came from
the North, a huge cloud with flashing fire
[enveloped in brightness], from the
midst of which [the midst of the fire]
something gleamed like electrum.
5† Within it were figures resembling four
living creatures that looked like this:
their form was human, 6 but each had
four faces and four wings, 7 and their
legs went straight down; the soles of
their feet were round. They sparkled
with a gleam like burnished bronze.
10*† Their faces were like this: each of
the four had the face of a man, but on
the right side was the face of a lion, and
on the left side the face of an ox, and
finally each had the face of an eagle.
9 Their faces [and their wings] looked
out on all their four sides; they did not
turn when they moved, but each went
straight forward. 12 [Each went straight
forward; wherever the spirit wished to
go, there they went; they did not turn
when they moved.]
8 Human hands were under their
wings, and the wings of one touched
those of another. 11 Each had two wings
spread out above so that they touched
one another's, while the other two wings
of each covered his body. 13 In among
the living creatures something like
burning coals of fire could be seen; they
seemed like torches, moving to and fro
among the living creatures. The fire
gleamed, and from it came forth flashes
of lightning.
15 As I looked at the living creatures,
I saw wheels on the ground, one beside
each of the four living creatures. 16 The
wheels had the sparkling appearance of
chrysolite, and all four of them looked
the same: they were constructed as
though one wheel were within another.
17 They could move in any of the four
directions they faced, without veering as
they moved. 18* The four of them had
rims, and I saw that their rims were full
of eyes all around. 19 When the living
creatures moved, the wheels moved with
them; and when the living creatures
were raised from the ground, the wheels
also were raised. 20 Wherever the spirit
wished to go, there the wheels went, and
they were raised together with the living
creatures; for the spirit of the living
creatures was in the wheels.
22† Over the heads of the living crea-
tures, something like a firmament could
be seen, seeming like glittering crystal,
stretched straight out above their heads.
23 Beneath the firmament their wings
were stretched out, one toward the
other. [Each of them had two covering
his body.] 24 Then I heard the sound of
their wings, like the roaring of mighty
waters, like the voice of the Almighty.
When they moved, the sound of the tu-
mult was like the din of an army. [And
when they stood still, they lowered their
wings.]
26† Above the firmament over their
heads something like a throne could be
seen, looking like sapphire. Upon it was
seated, up above, one who had the ap-
pearance of a man. 27 Upward from
what resembled his waist I saw what
gleamed like electrum; downward from
what resembled his waist I saw what
looked like fire; he was surrounded with
splendor. 28 Like the bow which appears
in the clouds on a rainy day was the
splendor that surrounded him. Such was
the vision of the likeness of the glory of
the LORD.

CHAPTER 2

Eating of the Scroll. When I had seen
it, I fell upon my face and heard a voice
that said to me: 1† Son of man, stand up!
I wish to speak with you. 2† As he spoke
to me, spirit entered into me and set me
on my feet, and I heard the one who was
speaking 3 say to me: Son of man, I am
sending you to the Israelites, rebels who
have rebelled against me; they and their
fathers have revolted against me to this
very day. 4 Hard of face and obstinate
of heart are they to whom I am sending
you. But you shall say to them: Thus says
the Lord GOD! 5 And whether they heed
or resist—for they are a rebellious
house—they shall know that a prophet
has been among them. 6† But as for you,
son of man, fear neither them nor their
words when they contradict you and re-
ject you, and when you sit on scorpions.
Neither fear their words nor be dis-
mayed at their looks, for they

---

*

10: Rv 4, 6f. 6.8.
18: 10, 12; Rv 4,

†

1, 4: *The North:* the abode of God; see notes on Jb 37, 22; Ps 48, 3. *Electrum:* an alloy of gold and silver, used here for some undetermined bright metal.

1, 5: *Four living creatures:* identified as cherubim in 10, 20f.

1, 10-22: Note the changed order of the verses and the omission of the textually uncertain verses 14 and 21. Such changes also occur elsewhere in this book.

1, 22f. 26: This symbolic description of God's throne is similar to that in Ex 24, 9f.

1, 26: *One who had the appearance of a man:* God appearing in human form (v 28); cf Ex 33, 18-23.

2, 1: *Son of man:* a formal way of saying simply "man"; God's habitual way of addressing the prophet throughout this book. Probably the title is used to emphasize the separation of the divine and the human.

2, 2: *Spirit:* vital power, coming from God, which enables the prophet to hear the word of God; cf 8, 3; 9, 24; 11, 1.

2, 6: *When you sit on scorpions:* the prophet must be prepared for the bitterest opposition.

are a rebellious house. 7 [But speak my words to them, whether they heed or resist, for they are rebellious.] 8 As for you, son of man, obey me when I speak to you: be not rebellious like this house of rebellion, but open your mouth and eat what I shall give you.

9* It was then I saw a hand stretched out to me, in which was a written scroll 10 which he unrolled before me. It was covered with writing front and back, and written on it was: Lamentation and wailing and woe!

CHAPTER 3

1 He said to me: Son of man, eat what is before you; eat this scroll, then go, speak to the house of Israel. 2 So I opened my mouth and he gave me the scroll to eat. 3*† Son of man, he then said to me, feed your belly and fill your stomach with this scroll I am giving you. I ate it, and it was as sweet as honey in my mouth. He said: 4 Son of man, go now to the house of Israel, and speak my words to them.

5 Not to a people with difficult speech and barbarous language am I sending you, 6 nor to the many peoples [with difficult speech and barbarous language] whose words you cannot understand. If I were to send you to these, they would listen to you; 7 but the house of Israel will refuse to listen to you, since they will not listen to me. For the whole house of Israel is stubborn of brow and obstinate in heart. 8 But I will make your face as hard as theirs, and your brow as stubborn as theirs, 9 like diamond, harder than flint. Fear them not, nor be dismayed at their looks, for they are a rebellious house.

10 Son of man, he said to me, take into your heart all my words that I speak to you; hear them well. 11 Now go to the exiles, to your countrymen, and say to them: Thus says the Lord GOD!—whether they heed or resist!

EZEKIEL

12† Then spirit lifted me up, and I heard behind me the noise of a loud rumbling as the glory of the LORD rose from its place: 13 the noise made by the wings of the living creatures striking one another, and by the wheels alongside them, a loud rumbling. 14 The spirit which had lifted me up seized me, and I went off spiritually stirred, while the hand of the LORD rested heavily upon me. 15† Thus I came to the exiles who lived at Tel-abib by the river Chebar, and for seven days I sat among them distraught.

The Prophet as Watchman. 17*† Thus the word of the LORD came to me: Son of man, I have appointed you a watchman for the house of Israel. When you hear a word from my mouth, you shall warn them for me.

18 If I say to the wicked man, You shall surely die; and you do not warn him or speak out to dissuade him from his wicked conduct so that he may live: that wicked man shall die for his sin, but I will hold you responsible for his death. 19 If, on the other hand, you have warned the wicked man, yet he has not turned away from his evil nor from his wicked conduct, then he shall die for his sin, but you shall save your life.

20 If a virtuous man turns away from virtue and does wrong when I place a stumbling block before him, he shall die. He shall die for his sin, and his virtuous deeds shall not be remembered; but I will hold you responsible for his death if you did not warn him. 21 When, on the other hand, you have warned a virtuous man not to sin, and he has in fact not sinned, he shall surely live because of the warning, and you shall save your own life.

Ezekiel's Dumbness. 22† The hand of the LORD came upon me, and he said to me: Get up and go out into the plain, where I will speak with you. 23* So I got up and went out into the plain, and I saw that the glory of the LORD was in that place, like the glory I had seen by the river Chebar. I fell prone, 24 but then spirit entered into me and set me on my feet, and he spoke with me.

He said to me: Go shut yourself up in your house. 25 [As for you, son of man, they will put cords upon you and bind you with them, so that you cannot go out among them.] 26† I will make your tongue stick to your palate so that you will be dumb and unable to rebuke them for being a rebellious house. 27 Only when I speak with you and open your mouth, shall you say to them: Thus says the Lord GOD! Let him heed who will, and let him resist who will, for they are a rebellious house.

*

2, 9: Rv 5, 1.
3, 3: Rv 10, 9f.
17: 33, 7.
23: 1, 3; 10, 15.20.22; 43, 3.

†

3, 3: *As sweet as honey:* though the prophet must foretell terrible things, the word of God is sweet to him who receives it.

3, 12: *The glory of the LORD:* the divine presence, manifested here in visible form.

3, 15: *Tel-abib:* one of the sites where the exiles were settled, probably near Nippur.

3, 17-21: This passage refers to one of the prophet's most characteristic qualities. It was placed here by an editor, though it properly belongs to a later stage in Ezekiel's ministry; cf chapter 33.

3, 22-27: This passage also belongs to a later period, with 24, 25ff and 33, 21f, during the time of the final siege of Jerusalem, when Ezekiel's prophecies consisted mainly of symbolic actions rather than words.

3, 26: *Dumb:* unwilling to speak to the people in exile while Jerusalem was being besieged; cf 24, 27.

II: BEFORE THE SIEGE OF JERUSALEM

CHAPTER 4

Acts Symbolic of Siege and Exile. 3:16† At the end of seven days. . . . , 1 As for you, son of man, take a clay tablet; lay it in front of you, and draw on it a city [Jerusalem]. 2 Raise a siege against it: build a tower, lay out a ramp, pitch camps, and set up battering-rams all around. 3 Then take an iron griddle and set it up as an iron wall between you and the city. Fix your gaze on it: it shall be in the state of siege, and you shall besiege it. This shall be a sign for the house of Israel. 4 Then you shall lie on your left side, while I place the sins of the house of Israel upon you. As many days as you lie thus, you shall bear their sins. 5† For the years of their sins I allot you the same number of days, three hundred and ninety, during which you will bear the sins of the house of Israel. 6 When you finish this, you are to lie down again, but on your right side, and bear the sins of the house of Judah forty days; one day for each year I have allotted you. 7† Fixing your gaze on the siege of Jerusalem, with bared arm you shall prophesy against it. 8 See, I will bind you with cords so that you cannot turn from one side to the other until you have completed the days of your siege.

9† Again, take wheat and barley, and beans and lentils, and millet and spelt; put them in a single vessel and make bread out of them. Eat it for as many days as you lie upon your side, three hundred and ninety. 10 The food you eat shall be twenty shekels a day by weight; each day the same. 11 And the water you drink shall be the sixth of a hin by measure; each day the same. 16† Then he said to me: Son of man, I am breaking the staff of bread in Jerusalem. They shall eat bread which they have weighed out anxiously, and they shall drink water which they have measured out fearfully, 17 so that, owing to the scarcity of bread and water, everyone shall be filled with terror and waste away because of his sins.

12 For your food you must bake barley loaves over human excrement in their sight, said the LORD. 13* Thus the Israelites shall eat their food unclean among the nations where I scatter them. 14 "Oh no, Lord GOD!" I protested. "Never have I been made unclean, and from my youth till now, never have I eaten carrion flesh or that torn by wild beasts; never has any unclean meat entered my mouth." 15 Very well, he replied, I allow you cow's dung in place of human excrement; bake your bread on that.

CHAPTER 5

1 As for you, son of man, take a sharp sword and use it like a barber's razor, passing it over your head and beard. Then take a set of scales and divide the hair you have cut. 2† Burn a third in the fire, within the city, when the days of your siege are completed; place another third around the city and strike it with the sword; the final third strew in the wind, and pursue it with the sword. 3 [But of the last take a small number and tie them in the hem of your garment. 4 Then take some of these and throw them in the midst of the fire and burn them.]

Say to the whole house of Israel: 5 Thus says the Lord GOD: This is Jerusalem! In the midst of the nations I placed her, surrounded by foreign countries. 6 But she rebelled against my ordinances more wickedly than the nations, and against my statutes more than the foreign countries surrounding her; she has spurned my ordinances and has not lived by my statutes. 7 Therefore thus says the Lord GOD: Because you have been more rebellious than the nations surrounding you, not living by my statutes nor fulfilling my ordinances, but acting according to the ordinances of the surrounding nations; 8† therefore thus says the Lord GOD: See, I am coming at you! I will inflict punishments in your midst while the nations look on. 9 Because of all your abominations I will do with you what I have never done before, the like of which I will never do again. 10† This means that fathers within you shall eat sons, and sons shall eat fathers. I will inflict punishments upon you

*

4, 13: Hos 9, 4.

†

3, 16: *At the end of seven days. . .*: the incomplete sentence probably contained some such words as "the word of the Lord came to me." For *seven days,* see v 15. (This verse has been transposed from chapter 3.)

4, 5f: *Three hundred and ninety days . . . forty days:* symbolically representing the respective lengths of the periods of exile of northern Israelites and Judahites. Northern Israel had already fallen to Assyria in 722 B.C. The letters in the Hebrew phrase for *the days of your siege* (v 8), each of which has its own numerical value, add up to three hundred and ninety. Forty years represent one generation.

4, 7: *Bared arm:* a symbol of unrestrained power.

4, 9-17: This action represents the scarcity of food during the siege of Jerusalem, and the consequent need to eat whatever is at hand. *Twenty shekels:* about nine ounces. *The sixth of a hin:* about one quart.

4, 16: *Breaking the staff of bread:* reducing the supply of bread which sustains the life of man as the walking staff sustains the traveler on his journey; cf 5, 16; 14, 13; Lv 26, 26; Ps 105, 16; Is 3, 1.

5, 2: *The city:* the one drawn on the tablet.

5, 8: *I am coming at you:* an expression borrowed from the language of warfare in which enemies attacked one another with the sword. *You* in vv 8-17 is Jerusalem.

5, 10: *Fathers . . . shall eat sons, and sons . . . fathers:* see note on Lam 2, 20.

and scatter all that remain of your peo-
ple in every direction.
11 Therefore, as I live, says the Lord
GOD, because you have defiled my sanc-
tuary with all your detestable abomina-
tions, I swear to cut you down. I will not
look upon you with pity nor have mercy.
12 A third of your people shall die of pes-
tilence and perish of hunger within you;
another third shall fall by the sword all
around you; and a third I will scatter
in every direction, and I will pursue
them with the sword. 16* When I loose
against you the cruel, destructive ar-
rows of hunger, I will break your staff
of bread; 17 I will send famine against
you, and wild beasts that shall rob you
of your children. Pestilence and
bloodshed shall stalk through you, and
I will bring the sword upon you. I, the
LORD, have spoken!
13 Thus shall my anger spend itself,
and I will wreak my fury upon them till
I am appeased; they shall know that I,
the LORD, have spoken in my jealousy
when I spend my fury upon them. 14 I
will make you a waste and a reproach
among the nations that surround you,
which every passer-by may see. 15 When
I execute judgment upon you in anger
and fury and with furious chastise-
ments, you shall be a reproach and an
object of scorn, a terrible warning to the
nations that surround you. I, the LORD,
have spoken!

CHAPTER 6

Against the Mountains of Israel.
1 Thus the word of the LORD came to me:
2 Son of man, turn toward the mountains
of Israel, and prophesy against them:
3*† Mountains of Israel, hear the word
of the Lord GOD. Thus says the Lord GOD
[to the mountains and hills, the ravines
and valleys]: See, I am bringing a sword
against you, and I will destroy your high
places. 4 Your altars shall be laid waste,
your incense stands shall be broken, and
I will cast down your slain ones before
your idols; 5† I will scatter their bones
all around your altars. 6 In all your
dwelling places cities shall be made des-
olate and high places laid waste, so that
your altars will be made desolate and
laid waste, your idols broken and re-
moved, and your incense stands
smashed to bits. 7 [The slain shall fall
in your midst, and you shall know that
I am the LORD. 8 I have warned you.]
When some of your people have es-
caped to other nations from the sword,
and have been scattered over the foreign
lands, 9 then those who have escaped
will remember me among the nations to
which they have been exiled, after I
have broken their adulterous hearts that
turned away from me [and their eyes
which lusted after idols]. They shall
loathe themselves because of their evil
deeds, all their abominations. 10 Then
they shall know that it was not in vain
that I, the LORD, threatened to inflict this
calamity upon them.
11† Thus says the Lord GOD: Clap your
hands, stamp your feet, and cry "Alas!"
because of all the abominations of the
house of Israel, for which they shall fall
by the sword, by famine, and by pesti-
lence. 12 He that is far off shall die of pes-
tilence, he that is near shall fall by the
sword, and he that is besieged shall per-
ish by famine; so will I spend my fury
upon them. 13† Then shall they know
that I am the LORD, when their slain
shall lie amid their idols, all about their
altars, on every high hill and mountain-
top, beneath every green tree and leafy
oak, wherever they offered appeasing
odors to any of their gods. 14† I will
stretch out my hand against them, and
wherever they live I will make the land
a desolate waste, from the desert to Rib-
lah; thus shall they know that I am the
LORD.

CHAPTER 7

The End Has Come. 1 Thus the word
of the LORD came to me: 2 Son of man,
now say: Thus says the Lord GOD to the
land of Israel: An end! The end has come
upon the four corners of the land! 3 Now
the end is upon you; I will unleash my
anger against you and judge you ac-
cording to your conduct and lay upon
you the consequences of all your abomi-
nations. 4 I will not look upon you with
pity nor have mercy; I will bring your
conduct down upon you, and the conse-
quences of your abominations shall be
in your midst; then shall you know that
I am the LORD.
5 Thus says the Lord GOD: Disaster
upon disaster! See it coming! 6 An end
is coming, the end is coming upon you!
See it coming! 7 The climax has come for
you who dwell in the land! The time has
come, near is the day: a time of conster-
nation, not of rejoicing. 8 Soon now I will
pour out my fury upon you and spend
my anger upon you; I will judge you ac-
cording to your conduct and lay upon

*

5, 16: 4, 16; 14, 13. 6, 3: 36, 1.

†

6, 3: *High places:* the sanctuaries on the mountaintops where illegal worship, whether of the Lord or of Canaanite deities, was performed.

6, 5: *Scatter their bones . . . altars:* dead men's bones defiled a place; cf 2 Kgs 23, 14.

6, 11: *Clap your hands, stamp your feet:* here evidently signs of mourning; in 25, 6, signs of joy.

6, 13: *Every green tree and leafy oak:* sacred groves had a long history in Palestine as places of worship; cf Dt 12, 2; note on Gn 12, 6.

6, 14: *From the desert to Riblah:* the whole land, from the far south to the far north.

you the consequences of all your abomi-
nations. 9 I will not look upon you with
pity nor have mercy; I will deal with you
according to your conduct, and the con-
sequences of your abominations shall be
in your midst; then shall you know that
it is I, the LORD, who strike.
10 See, the day of the LORD! See, the
end is coming! Lawlessness is in full
bloom, insolence flourishes, 11 violence
has risen to support wickedness. It shall
not be long in coming, nor shall it delay.
12† The time has come, the day dawns.
Let not the buyer rejoice nor the seller
mourn, for wrath shall be upon all the
throng. 13 The seller shall not regain
what he sold as long as he lives, for
wrath shall be upon all the throng. Be-
cause of his sins, no one shall preserve
his life. 14 They shall sound the trumpet
and make everything ready, yet no one
shall go to war, for my wrath is upon
all the throng.
15 The sword is outside; pestilence and
hunger are within. He that is in the coun-
try shall die by the sword; pestilence and
famine shall devour those in the city.
16 Even those who escape and flee to the
mountains like the doves of the valleys—
I will put them all to death, each one
for his own sins. 17 All their hands shall
be limp, and all their knees shall run
with water. 18*† They shall put on sack-
cloth, and horror shall cover them;
shame shall be on all their faces and
baldness on all their heads. 19* They
shall fling their silver into the streets,
and their gold shall be considered ref-
use. Their silver and gold cannot save
them on the day of the LORD's wrath.
They shall not be allowed to satisfy their
craving or fill their bellies, for this has
been the occasion of their sin. 20 In the
beauty of their ornaments they put their
pride: they made of them their abomina-
ble images [their idols]. For this reason
I make them refuse. 21 I will hand them
over as booty to foreigners, to be spoiled
and defiled by the wicked of the earth.
22† I will turn away my face from them,
and my treasure shall be profaned: rob-
bers shall enter and profane it.
23 They shall wreak slaughter, for the
land is filled with bloodshed and the city
full of violence. 24 I will bring in the worst
of the nations, who shall take possession
of their houses. I will put an end to their
proud strength, and their sanctuaries
shall be profaned. 25 When anguish
comes they shall seek peace, but there
will be none. 26 There shall be disaster
after disaster, rumor after rumor.
Prophetic vision shall fade; instruction
shall be lacking to the priest, and coun-
sel to the elders, 27 while the prince shall
be enveloped in terror, and the hands
of the common people shall tremble. I
will deal with them according to their
conduct, and according to their judg-
ments I will judge them; thus they shall
know that I am the LORD.

CHAPTER 8

***Vision of Abominations in the Tem-
ple.*** 3*† Spirit lifted me up in the air
and brought me in divine visions to Je-
rusalem, to the entrance of the north
gate, where stood the statue of jealousy
which stirs up jealousy. 5† He said to me:
Son of man, look toward the north! I
looked toward the north and saw north-
ward of the gate the altar of the statue
of jealousy. 6 Son of man, he asked me,
do you see what they are doing? Do you
see the great abominations that the
house of Israel is practicing here, so that
I must depart from my sanctuary? But
you shall see still greater abominations!
7 Then he brought me to the entrance
of the court, where I saw there was a
hole in the wall. 8 Son of man, he or-
dered, dig through the wall. I dug
through the wall and saw a door. 9 Enter,
he said to me, and see the abominable
evils which they are doing here. 10† I en-
tered and saw that all around upon the
wall were pictured the figures of all
kinds of creeping things and loathsome
beasts [all the idols of the house of Is-
rael]. 11 Before these stood seventy of the
elders of the house of Israel, among
whom stood Jaazaniah, son of Shaphan,
each of them with his censer in his hand,
and the fragrance of the incense was ris-
ing upward. 12 Then he said to me: Do
you see, son of man, what each of these
elders of the house of Israel is doing in
his idol room? They think: "The LORD
cannot see us; the LORD has forsaken the
land." 13 He continued: You shall see still
greater abominations that they are
practicing.
14† Then he brought me to the en-

*

7, 18: Is 15, 2; Jer 48, 37.
19: Prv 11, 4; Sir 5, 10; Zep 1, 18.
8, 3: Dn 14, 6.

†

7, 12f: Mundane affairs will cease to have any meaning in view of the disaster that is to come.
7, 18: *Baldness:* shaving the head was a sign of mourning.
7, 22: *My treasure:* the temple of Jerusalem.
8, 3: *The statue of jealousy which stirs up jealousy:* the statue which provokes the Lord's jealousy for his honor. This was probably the statue of the goddess Asherah erected by the wicked King Manasseh (cf 2 Kgs 21, 7; 2 Chr 33, 7.15). Though it had been removed by King Josiah (2 Kgs 23, 6), it had no doubt been set up again in the repaganizing of Jerusalem that followed on Josiah's death.
8, 5: *He:* an angel accompanies Ezekiel in these visions and represents the voice of the Lord; cf 40, 3f.
8, 10: *Creeping things and loathsome beasts:* probably Egyptian deities, which were represented in animal form. During the last days of Jerusalem King Zedekiah was allied with Egypt, trusting in it for protection against the Chaldeans.
8, 14: *Weeping for Tammuz:* the withering of trees and plants in autumn was thought to be due to the descent of *Tammuz,* the Babylonian god of fertility, to the nether world of the dead; this descent was bewailed by the women.

trance of the north gate of the temple,
and I saw sitting there the women who
were weeping for Tammuz. 15 Then he
said to me: Do you see this, son of man?
You shall see other abominations,
greater than these!
16† Then he brought me into the inner
court of the LORD's house, and there at
the door of the LORD's temple, between
the vestibule and the altar, were about
twenty-five men with their backs to the
LORD's temple and their faces toward
the east; they were bowing down to the
sun. 17† Do you see, son of man? he
asked me. Is it such a trivial matter for
the house of Judah to do the abominable
things they have done here—for they
have filled the land with violence, and
again and again they have provoked
me—that now they must also put the
branch to my nose? 18 Therefore I in turn
will act furiously: I will not look upon
them with pity nor will I show mercy.

CHAPTER 9

Slaughter of the Idolaters. 1 Then he
cried loud for me to hear: Come, you
scourges of the city! 2 With that I saw
six men coming from the direction of the
upper gate which faces the north, each
with a destroying weapon in his hand.
In their midst was a man dressed in
linen, with a writer's case at his waist.
They entered and stood beside the
bronze altar. 3 Then he called to the man
dressed in linen with the writer's case
at his waist, 4*† saying to him: Pass
through the city [through Jerusalem]
and mark an X on the foreheads of those
who moan and groan over all the abomi-
nations that are practiced within it. 5 To
the others I heard him say: Pass through
the city after him and strike! Do not look
on them with pity nor show any mercy!
6 Old men, youths and maidens, women
and children—wipe them out! But do not
touch any marked with the X; begin at
my sanctuary. So they began with the
men [the elders] who were in front of
the temple. 7 Defile the temple, he said
to them, and fill the courts with the slain;
then go out and strike in the city.
8 As they began to strike, I was left
alone. I fell prone, crying out, Alas, Lord
GOD! Will you destroy all that is left of
Israel when you pour out your fury on
Jerusalem?" 9 He answered me: The sins
of the house of Israel are great beyond
measure; the land is filled with
bloodshed, the city with lawlessness.
They think that the LORD has forsaken
the land, that he does not see them. 10 I,
however, will not look upon them with
pity, nor show any mercy. I will bring
down their conduct upon their heads.
11 Then I saw the man dressed in linen
with the writing case at his waist make
his report: "I have done as you ordered."
11:24† Spirit lifted me up and brought
me back to the exiles in Chaldea [in a
vision, by God's spirit]. Then the vision
I had seen left me, 11:25 and I told the ex-
iles everything the LORD had shown me.

CHAPTER 10

God's Glory Leaves Jerusalem.
8:1† On the fifth day of the sixth month,
in the sixth year, as I was sitting in my
house, and the elders of Judah sat before
me, the hand of the Lord GOD fell upon
me there. 8:2† I looked up and saw a form
that looked like a man. Downward from
what seemed to be his waist, there was
fire; from his waist upward there
seemed to be a brightness like the sheen
of electrum. He stretched out what ap-
peared to be a hand and seized me by
the hair of my head. . . .
8:4 I saw there the glory of the God of
Israel, like the vision I had seen in the
plain. The cherubim were stationed to
the right of the temple; 20* these were
the living creatures I had seen beneath
the God of Israel by the river Chebar,
whom I now recognized to be cherubim.
21 Each had four faces and four wings;
something like human hands were un-
der their wings. 22 Their faces looked just
like those I had seen by the river Chebar;
each one went straight forward.
14* Each had four faces: the first face
was that of an ox, the second that of a
man, the third that of a lion, and the
fourth that of an eagle. 15 Such were the
living creatures I had seen by the river
Chebar.
9* I also saw four wheels beside them,

*

9, 4: Ex 12, 7; Rv 7, 3.
10, 20: 1, 1.3.
14: 1, 10.
9: 1, 15f.

†

8, 16: *Bowing down to the sun:* sun worship had been made an important part of Judahite idolatry by the impious kings; cf 2 Kgs 23, 11.

8, 17: *Put the branch to my nose:* the meaning is uncertain. Perhaps it refers to an Egyptian practice imported into Judah: the Egyptian sun god Re is pictured with a vine branch at his nose, signifying the transfer of creative power (divine breath) to living things. Such rites were abominable to the Lord.

9, 4: Ezekiel is pre-eminently the prophet of personal retribution; the innocent inhabitants of Jerusalem are to be spared when the idolatrous are punished. *An X:* literally, the Hebrew letter taw, which had the form of a cross.

11, 24f: These verses have been transposed from chapter 11 and placed after 9, 11.

8, 1—11, 25: In these chapters of the current Hebrew text, several visions involving the temple of Jerusalem were combined to form a single continuous vision. The redistribution of verses in this translation is an attempt to separate the original visions. 8, 1.2.4 have been transposed here from chapter 8.

8, 1: *The fifth day of the sixth month, in the sixth year:* September 17, 592 B.C.

8, 2: The dots suppose the omission of some words describing the prophet's being transported in his visions to the court of the temple.

one wheel beside each cherub; the wheels appeared to have the luster of chrysolite stone. 10 All four of them seemed to be made the same, as though they were a wheel within a wheel. 11 When they moved, they went in any one of their four directions without veering as they moved; for in whichever direction they were faced, they went straight toward it without veering as they moved. 12* The rims of the four wheels were full of eyes all around. 13 I heard the wheels given the name "wheelwork." 16* When the cherubim moved, the wheels went beside them; when the cherubim lifted their wings to rise from the earth, even then the wheels did not leave their sides. 17 When they stood still, the wheels stood still; when they rose, the wheels rose with them; for the living creatures' spirit was in them.

1 I looked and saw in the firmament above the cherubim what appeared to be sapphire stone; something like a throne could be seen upon it. 2† He said to the man dressed in linen: Go within the wheelwork under the cherubim; fill both your hands with burning coals from among the cherubim, then scatter them over the city. As I looked on, he entered.

The glory of the God of Israel had gone up from the cherubim, upon which it had been, to the threshold of the temple. 3 As the man entered, the cloud filled the inner court, 4 and the glory of the LORD rose from over the cherubim to the threshold of the temple; the temple was filled with the cloud, and all the court was bright with the glory of the LORD. 5 The noise of the wings of the cherubim could be heard as far as the outer court; it was like the voice of God the Almighty when he speaks.

6 When he had commanded the man dressed in linen to take fire from within the wheelwork, among the cherubim, the man entered and stood by one of the wheels. 7 Thereupon its cherub stretched out his hand toward the fire that was among the cherubim. He took up some of it and put it in the hands of the one dressed in linen, who took it and came out. 8 [Something like human hands could be seen under the wings of the cherubim.]

18 Then the glory of the LORD left the threshold of the temple and rested upon the cherubim. 19 These lifted their wings, and I saw them rise from the earth, the wheels rising along with them. They stood at the entrance of the eastern gate of the LORD's house, and the glory of the God of Israel was up above them. 11:22† Then the cherubim lifted their wings, and the wheels went along with them, while up above them was the glory of the God of Israel. 23 And the glory of the LORD rose from the city and took a stand on the mountain which is to the east of the city.

CHAPTER 11

Judgment of the Princes. 1 Spirit lifted me up and brought me to the east gate of the temple. At the entrance of the gate I saw twenty-five men, among whom were Jaazaniah, son of Azzur, and Pelatiah, son of Benaiah, princes of the people. 2 The LORD said to me: Son of man, these are the men who are planning evil and giving wicked counsel in this city. 3† "Shall we not," they say, "be building houses soon? The city is the kettle, and we are the meat." 4 Therefore prophesy against them, son of man, prophesy! 5 Then the spirit of the LORD fell upon me, and he told me to say: Thus says the LORD: This is the way you talk, house of Israel, and what you are plotting I well know. 6 You have slain many in this city and have filled its streets with your slain. 7 Therefore thus says the Lord GOD: Your slain whom you have placed within it, they are the meat, and the city is the kettle; but you I will take out of it. 8 You fear the sword, but the sword I will bring upon you, says the Lord GOD. 9 I will bring you out of the city, and hand you over to foreigners, and inflict punishments upon you. 10 By the sword you shall fall; at the boundaries of Israel I will judge you; thus you shall know that I am the LORD. 11 The city shall not be a kettle for you, nor shall you be the meat within it. At the boundaries of Israel I will judge you, 12 and you shall know that I am the LORD, by whose statutes you have not lived, and whose ordinances you have not kept; rather, you have acted according to the ordinances of the nations around you.

13 While I was prophesying, Pelatiah, the son of Benaiah, died. I fell prone and cried out in a loud voice: "Alas, Lord GOD! will you utterly wipe out what remains of Israel?"

Restoration of the Exiles. 14 Thus the word of the LORD came to me: 15† Son of man, it is about your kinsmen, your fellow exiles, and the whole house of Is-

*

12: 1, 18. 16: 1, 19.

†

10, 2: *The burning coals* within the wheelwork under God's throne, a sign of the divine presence (cf 28, 14; Ps 18, 13), symbolize the judgment to be visited on the city.

10, 22f: These verses have been transposed from chapter 11.

11, 3: These words reflect the false confidence of the inhabitants of Jerusalem in the face of the Chaldean invasion. Jerusalem, they think, is like an iron kettle protecting the meat within it from harm; but cf 24, 3-6.

11, 15-21: Like Jeremiah (cf chapter 29), Ezekiel knows that no reform is to be expected from the men of Judah who remained in Palestine; but the exiles will be the ones to form the new Israel. The new, spiritual covenant will replace the former covenant; cf Jer 24, 7.

rael that the inhabitants of Jerusalem say, "They are far away from the LORD; to us the land of Israel has been given as our possession." 16 Therefore say: Thus says the Lord GOD: Though I have removed them far among the nations and scattered them over foreign countries—and was for a while their only sanctuary in the countries to which they had gone—17 I will gather you from the nations and assemble you from the countries over which you have been scattered, and I will restore to you the land of Israel. 18 They shall return to it and remove from it all its detestable abominations. 19* I will give them a new heart and put a new spirit within them; I will remove the stony heart from their bodies, and replace it with a natural heart, 20 so that they will live according to my statutes, and observe and carry out my ordinances; thus they shall be my people and I will be their God. 21 But as for those whose hearts are devoted to their detestable abominations, I will bring down their conduct upon their heads, says the Lord GOD.

CHAPTER 12

Acts Symbolic of the Exile. 1 Thus the word of the LORD came to me: 2 Son of man, you live in the midst of a rebellious house; they have eyes to see but do not see, and ears to hear but do not hear, for they are a rebellious house. 3 Now, son of man, during the day while they are looking on, prepare your baggage as though for exile, and again while they are looking on, migrate from where you live to another place; perhaps they will see that they are a rebellious house. 4 You shall bring out your baggage like an exile in the daytime while they are looking on; in the evening, again while they are looking on, you shall go out like one of those driven into exile; 5† while they look on, dig a hole in the wall and pass through it; 6 while they look on, shoulder the burden and set out in the darkness; cover your face that you may not see the land, for I have made you a sign for the house of Israel.

7 I did as I was told. During the day I brought out my baggage as though it were that of an exile, and at evening I dug a hole through the wall with my hand and, while they looked on, set out in the darkness, shouldering my burden.

8 Then, in the morning, the word of the LORD came to me: 9 Son of man, did not the house of Israel, that rebellious house, ask you what you were doing? 10 Tell them: Thus says the Lord GOD: This oracle concerns Jerusalem and the whole house of Israel within it. 11 I am a sign for you: as I have done, so shall it be done to them; as captives they shall go into exile. 12 The prince who is among them shall shoulder his burden and set out in darkness, going through a hole that he has dug in the wall, and covering his face lest he be seen by anyone. 13*† But I will spread my net over him, and he shall be taken in my snare. I will bring him to Babylon, into the land of the Chaldeans—but he shall not see it—and there he shall die. 14 All his retinue, his aides, and his troops I will scatter in every direction, and pursue them with the sword. 15 Then shall they know that I am the LORD, when I disperse them among the nations and scatter them over foreign lands. 16 Yet I will leave a few of them to escape the sword, famine and pestilence, so that they may tell of all their abominations among the nations to which they will come; thus they shall know that I am the LORD.

17 Thus the word of the LORD came to me: 18 Son of man, eat your bread trembling, and drink your water shaking with anxiety. 19 Then say to the people of the land: Thus says the Lord GOD of the inhabitants of Jerusalem [to the land of Israel]: They shall eat their bread in anxiety and drink their water in horror, that their land may be emptied of the violence of all its inhabitants that now fills it. 20 Inhabited cities shall be in ruins, and the land shall be a waste; thus you shall know that I am the LORD.

Prophecy Ridiculed. 21 Thus the word of the LORD came to me: 22† Son of man, what is this proverb that you have in the land of Israel: "The days drag on, and no vision ever comes to anything"? 23 Say to them therefore: Thus says the Lord GOD: I will put an end to this proverb; they shall never quote it again in Israel. Rather, say to them: The days are at hand, and also the fulfillment of every vision. 25 Whatever I speak is final, and it shall be done without further delay. In your days, rebellious house, whatever I speak I will bring about, says the Lord GOD.

24 There shall no longer be any false visions or deceitful divinations within the house of Israel, because it is I, the LORD, who will speak.

26 Thus the word of the LORD came to me: 27 Son of man, listen to the house of Israel saying, "The vision he sees is a long way off; he prophesies of the distant future!" 28 Say to them therefore: Thus

*

11, 19: 36, 26; Jer 31, 33.
12, 13: 17, 20; 32, 3.

†

12, 5: *Dig a hole in the wall:* the exiles are to leave Jerusalem through the broken walls of the ruined city.

12, 13: *But he shall not see it:* Zedekiah was blinded by Nebuchadnezzar before being deported to Babylonia; cf 2 Kgs 25, 7.

12, 22.27: These words were used against Ezekiel because of the apparent failure of his prophecies; cf Jer 20, 7ff.

says the Lord GOD: None of my words shall be delayed any longer; whatever I speak is final, and it shall be done, says the Lord GOD.

CHAPTER 13

Against the Prophets of Peace. 1 Thus the word of the LORD came to me: 2 Son of man, prophesy against the prophets of Israel, prophesy! Say to those who prophesy their own thought: Hear the word of the LORD: 5 You did not step into the breach, nor did you build a wall about the house of Israel that would stand firm against attack on the day of the LORD. 7 Was not the vision you saw false, and your divination lying? 8 Therefore thus says the Lord GOD: Because you have spoken falsehood and have seen lying visions, therefore see! I am coming at you, says the Lord GOD.

10† For the very reason that they led my people astray, saying, "Peace!" when there was no peace, and that, as one built a wall, they would cover it with whitewash, 11 say then to the whitewashers: I will bring down a flooding rain; hailstones shall fall, and a stormwind shall break out. 12 And when the wall has fallen, will you not be asked: Where is the whitewash you spread on?

13 Therefore thus says the Lord GOD: In my fury I will let loose stormwinds; because of my anger there shall be a flooding rain, and hailstones shall fall with destructive wrath. 14 I will tear down the wall that you have whitewashed and level it to the ground, laying bare its foundations. When it falls, you shall be crushed beneath it; thus you shall know that I am the LORD. 15 When I have spent my fury on the wall and its whitewashers, I tell you there shall be no wall, nor shall there be whitewashers—16 those prophets of Israel who prophesied to Jerusalem and saw for it visions of peace when there was no peace, says the Lord GOD.

Against False Prophets in Chaldea. 3* Thus says the Lord GOD: Woe to those prophets who are fools, who follow their own spirit and have seen no vision. 4 Like foxes among ruins are your prophets, O Israel! 6 Their visions are false and their divination lying. They say, "Thus says the LORD!" though the LORD did not send them; then they wait for him to fulfill their word! 9 But I will stretch out my hand against the prophets who have false visions and who foretell lies. They shall not belong to the community of my people, nor be recorded in the register of the house of Israel, nor enter the land of Israel; thus you shall know that I am the LORD.

Against False Prophetesses. 17 Now, son of man, turn toward the daughters of your people who prophesy their own thoughts; against these, prophesy: Thus says the Lord GOD: 22 Because you have disheartened the upright man with lies when I did not wish him grieved, and have encouraged the wicked man not to turn from his evil conduct and save his life; 23 therefore you shall no longer see false visions and practice divination, but I will rescue my people from your power. Thus you shall know that I am the LORD.

Against Sorceresses. 18† Woe to those who sew bands for everyone's wrists and make veils for every size of head so as to entrap their owners. Do you think to entrap the lives of my people, yet keep yourselves alive? 19† You dishonor me before my people with handfuls of barley and crumbs of bread, killing those who should not die and keeping alive those who should not live, lying to my people who willingly hear lies. 20 Therefore thus says the Lord GOD: See! I am coming at those bands of yours in which you entrap men's lives: I will tear them from their arms and set free those you have caught. 21 I will tear off your veils and rescue my people from your power, so that they shall no longer be prey to your hands. Thus you shall know that I am the LORD.

CHAPTER 14

Prophecy Useless for Idolaters. 1 When certain elders of Israel came and sat down before me, 2 the word of the LORD came to me: 3 Son of man, these men have the memory of their idols fresh in their hearts, and they keep the occasion of their sin before them. Why should I allow myself to be consulted by them? 4 Therefore speak with them, and say to them: Thus says the Lord GOD: If anyone of the house of Israel, holding the memory of his idols in his heart and keeping the occasion of his sin before him, has recourse to a prophet, I, the LORD, will be his answer in person because of his many idols. 5 Thus would I bring back to their senses the house of Israel, who have become estranged from me through all their idols.

6 Therefore say to the house of Israel:

*

13, 3: 14, 9; 34, 2; Jer 23, 1.

†

13, 10: To the confidence which the people had in their defenses against the Chaldeans, the false prophets contributed the illusion of security by predictions of peace, like men who whitewash a wall rather than allow its defects to be seen.

13, 18: *Sew bands . . . make veils:* magical practices believed to give to the sorceresses power over those on whom they placed these objects.

13, 19: *Handfuls of barley and crumbs of bread:* used in divination and forecasting the future.

Thus says the Lord GOD: Return and be converted from your idols; turn yourselves away from all your abominations. 7 For if anyone of the house of Israel or any alien resident in Israel is estranged from me, and holds the memory of his idols in his heart and keeps the occasion of his sin before him, yet asks a prophet to consult me for him, I, the LORD, will be his answer in person. 8 I will turn against that man, and make of him an example and a byword. I will cut him off from the midst of my people. Thus you shall know that I am the LORD.

9*† As for the prophet, if he is beguiled into speaking a word, I, the LORD, shall have beguiled that prophet; I will stretch out my hand against him and root him out of my people Israel. 10 Each shall receive punishment for his sin, the inquirer and the prophet shall be punished alike, 11 so that the house of Israel may no longer stray from me and may no longer be defiled by all their sins. Thus they shall be my people, and I will be their God, says the Lord GOD.

Personal Responsibility. 12† Thus the word of the LORD came to me: 13* Son of man, when a land sins against me by breaking faith, I stretch out my hand against it and break its staff of bread, I let famine loose upon it and cut off from it both man and beast; 14† and even if these three men were in it, Noah, Daniel, and Job, they could save only themselves by their virtue, says the Lord GOD. 15 If I were to cause wild beasts to prowl the land, depopulating it so that it became a waste, traversed by none because of the wild beasts, 16 and these three men were in it, as I live, says the Lord GOD, I swear they could save neither sons nor daughters; they alone would be saved, and the land would be a waste. 17 Or if I brought the sword upon this country, commanding the sword to pass through the land cutting off from it man and beast, 18 and these three men were in it, as I live, says the Lord GOD, they would be unable to save either sons or daughters; they alone would be saved. 19 Or if I were to send pestilence into this land, pouring out upon it my bloodthirsty fury, cutting off from it man and beast, 20 even if Noah, Daniel, and Job were in it, as I live, says the Lord GOD, I swear that they could save neither son nor daughter; they would save only themselves by their virtue.

21 Thus says the Lord GOD: Even though I send Jerusalem my four cruel punishments, the sword, famine, wild beasts, and pestilence, to cut off from it man and beast, 22 still some survivors shall be left in it who will bring out sons and daughters; when they come out to you, you shall see their conduct and their actions and be consoled regarding the evil I have brought on Jerusalem [all that I have brought upon it]. 23 They shall console you when you see their conduct and actions, for you shall then know that it was not without reason that I did to it what I did, says the Lord GOD.

CHAPTER 15

Parable of the Vine. 1 Thus the word of the LORD came to me: 2 Son of man, what makes the wood of the vine better than any other wood? That branch among the trees of the forest! 3 Can you use its wood to make anything worthwhile? Can you make even a peg from it, to hang on it any kind of vessel? 4 If you throw it on the fire as fuel and the fire devours both ends and even the middle is scorched, is it still good for anything? 5 Why, even when it was whole it was good for nothing; how much less, when the fire has devoured and scorched it, can it be used for anything! 6 Therefore, thus says the Lord GOD: Like the wood of the vine among the trees of the forest, which I have destined as fuel for the fire, do I make the inhabitants of Jerusalem. 7 I will set my face against them; they have escaped from the fire, but the fire shall devour them. Thus you shall know that I am the LORD, when I turn my face against them. 8 I will make the land a waste, because they have broken faith, says the Lord GOD.

CHAPTER 16

The Faithless Spouse. 1 Thus the word of the LORD came to me: 2 Son of man, make known to Jerusalem her abominations. 3† Thus says the Lord GOD to Jerusalem: By origin and birth you are of the land of Canaan; your father was an Amorite and your mother a Hittite. 4 As for your birth, the day you were born your navel cord was not cut; you were neither washed with water nor anointed, nor were you rubbed with salt, nor swathed in swaddling clothes. 5 No one

*

14, 9: 1 Kgs 22, 23. 13: 4, 16.

†

14, 9: *I, the LORD, shall have beguiled that prophet:* the ancient Israelites attributed to God every action, good or evil; cf 1 Sm 18, 10; 2 Sm 24, 1ff. We would say, rather, that God permitted this deceit.

14, 12-23: The doctrine of personal responsibility before God was not new (cf 3, 16-21; 18; 33, 1-20); but it had not been emphasized by the prophets before the exile, who mostly predicted national retribution and called for national repentance.

14, 14: *Noah, Daniel, and Job:* proverbially virtuous men. The Daniel named here may be the traditional just judge of the ancient past, celebrated in Canaanite literature, who is possibly reflected in Dn 13, but is not the hero of Dn 1-12.

16, 3f: *By origin and birth . . . Canaan . . . Amorite . . . Hittite:* the inhabitants of Jerusalem and Judah absorbed not only pre-Israelite racial strains, but also many elements of the country's pagan cult and customs.

looked on you with pity or compassion
to do any of these things for you. Rather,
you were thrown out on the ground as
something loathsome, the day you were
born.
6 Then I passed by and saw you welter-
ing in your blood. I said to you: Live in
your blood 7 and grow like a plant in the
field. You grew and developed, you came
to the age of puberty; your breasts were
formed, your hair had grown, but you
were still stark naked. 8† Again I passed
by you and saw that you were now old
enough for love. So I spread the corner
of my cloak over you to cover your
nakedness; I swore an oath to you and
entered into a covenant with you; you
became mine, says the Lord GOD. 9 Then
I bathed you with water, washed away
your blood, and anointed you with oil.
10 I clothed you with an embroidered
gown, put sandals of fine leather on your
feet; I gave you a fine linen sash and
silk robes to wear. 11 I adorned you with
jewelry: I put bracelets on your arms,
a necklace about your neck, 12 a ring in
your nose, pendants in your ears, and
a glorious diadem upon your head.
13 Thus you were adorned with gold and
silver; your garments were of fine linen,
silk, and embroidered cloth. Fine flour,
honey, and oil were your food. You were
exceedingly beautiful, with the dignity
of a queen. 14 You were renowned among
the nations for your beauty, perfect as
it was, because of my splendor which I
had bestowed on you, says the Lord
GOD.
15 But you were captivated by your
own beauty, you used your renown to
make yourself a harlot, and you lavished
your harlotry on every passer-by, whose
own you became. 16† You took some of
your gowns and made for yourself
gaudy high places, where you played the
harlot. . . . 17 You took the splendid gold
and silver ornaments that I had given
you and made for yourself male images,
with which also you played the harlot.
18 You took your embroidered gowns to
cover them; my oil and my incense you
set before them; 19 the food that I had
given you, the fine flour, the oil, and the
honey with which I fed you, you set be-
fore them as an appeasing odor, says
the Lord GOD. 20*† The sons and daugh-
ters you had borne me you took and of-
fered as sacrifices to be devoured by
them! Was it not enough that you had
become a harlot? 21* You slaughtered
and immolated my children to them,
making them pass through fire. 22 And
through all your abominations and har-
lotries you remembered nothing of when
you were a girl, stark naked and welter-
ing in your blood.
23 Then after all your evildoing—woe,
woe to you! says the Lord GOD—24† you
raised for yourself a platform and a dais
in every public place. 25* At every street
corner you built a dais for yourself to
use your beauty obscenely, spreading
your legs for every passer-by, playing
the harlot countless times. 26 You played
the harlot with the Egyptians, your lust-
ful neighbors, so many times that I was
provoked to anger. 27 Therefore I
stretched out my hand against you, I di-
minished your allowance and delivered
you over to the will of your enemies, the
Philistines, who revolted at your lewd
conduct. 28 You also played the harlot
with the Assyrians, because you were
not satisfied; and after playing the harlot
with them, you were still not satisfied.
29 Again and again you played the har-
lot, now going to Chaldea, the land of
the traders; but despite this, you were
still not satisfied.
30 How wild your lust! says the Lord
GOD, that you did all these things, acting
like a shameless prostitute, 31 building
your platform at every street corner and
erecting your dais in every public place!
Yet you were unlike a prostitute, since
you disdained payment. 32 The adulter-
ous wife receives, instead of her hus-
band, payment. 33 All harlots receive
gifts. But you rather bestowed your gifts
on all your lovers, bribing them to come
to you from all sides for your harlotry.
34 Thus in your harlotry you were differ-
ent from all other women. No one sought
you out for prostitution. Since you gave
payment instead of receiving it, how dif-
ferent you were!
35 Therefore, harlot, hear the word of
the LORD! 36 Thus says the Lord GOD: Be-
cause you poured out your lust and re-
vealed your nakedness in your harlotry
with your lovers and abominable idols,
and because you sacrificed the life-blood
of your children to them, 37* I will now
gather together all your lovers whom
you tried to please, whether you loved
them or loved them not; I will gather
them against you from all sides and ex-
pose you naked for them to see. 38 I will
inflict on you the sentence of adulter-

*

16, 20: 20, 26. 31; 23, 37ff; Lv 18, 21; 20,2; Dt 12, 31; 18, 10; 2 Kgs 21, 6; 23, 10; 24, 4; Jer 7, 31; 19, 5; 32, 34; Mi 6, 7.
21: 2 Kgs 16, 3; 17, 17; 21, 6; 23, 10.
25: 23, 8; Is 57, 7; Jer 2, 20; 3, 2; 5, 7; 13, 27; Hos 2, 4; 4, 13.
37: 23, 10.

†

16, 8: *I spread the corner of my cloak over you to cover your nakedness:* and also to signify the intention of marriage; cf Ru 3, 9.

16, 16: Fine robes were used to cover a couch for harlotry; cf Prv 7, 16f. In the allegory of this chapter the viewpoint often shifts from the figure (harlotry) to the reality (idolatry).

16, 20f: Human sacrifice was introduced under Judah's impious kings; cf 2 Kgs 16, 3; 17, 17; Jer 7, 31.

16, 24: *A platform and a dais:* associated with ritual prostitution, which the Israelites borrowed from Canaanite practice.

esses and murderesses; I will wreak fury
and jealousy upon you. 39 I will hand you
over to them to tear down your platform
and demolish your dais; they shall strip
you of your garments and take away
your splendid ornaments, leaving you
stark naked. 40 They shall lead an as-
sembly against you to stone you and
hack you with their swords. 41* They
shall burn your apartments with fire and
inflict punishments on you while many
women look on. Thus I will put an end
to your harlotry, and you shall never
again give payment. 42 When I have
wreaked my fury upon you I will cease
to be jealous of you, I will be quiet and
no longer vexed. 43 Because you did not
remember what happened when you
were a girl, but enraged me with all
these things, therefore in return I am
bringing down your conduct upon your
head, says the Lord GOD. For did you
not add lewdness to the rest of your
abominable deeds?

44 See, everyone who is fond of prov-
erbs will say of you, 'Like mother, like
daughter.' 45† Yes, you are the true
daughter of the mother who spurned her
husband and children, and you are a
true sister to those who spurned their
husbands and children—your mother
was a Hittite and your father an Amo-
rite. 46† Your elder sister was Samaria
with her daughters, living to the north
of you; and your younger sister, living
to the south of you, was Sodom with her
daughters. 47 Yet not only in their ways
did you walk, and act as abominably as
they did; in a very short time you be-
came more corrupt in all your ways than
they. 48 As I live, says the Lord GOD, I
swear that your sister Sodom, with her
daughters, has not done as you and your
daughters have done! 49* And look at the
guilt of your sister Sodom: she and her
daughters were proud, sated with food,
complacent in their prosperity, and they
gave no help to the poor and needy.
50 Rather, they became haughty and
committed abominable crimes in my
presence; then, as you have seen, I re-
moved them. 51 Samaria did not commit
half your sins! You have done more
abominable things than they, and have
even made your sisters appear just, with
all the abominable deeds you have done.
52 You, then, bear your shame; you are
an argument in favor of your sisters! In
view of your sinful deeds, more abomi-
nable than theirs, they appear just in
comparison with you. Blush for shame,
and bear the shame of having made
your sisters appear just.

53 I will restore their fortunes, the for-
tune of Sodom and her daughters and
of Samaria and her daughters [and I will
restore your fortune along with them],
54 that you may bear your shame and
be disgraced for all the comfort you
brought them. 55 Yes, your sisters,
Sodom and her daughters, Samaria and
her daughters, shall return to their for-
mer state [you and your daughters shall
return to your former state]. 56 Was not
your sister Sodom kept in bad repute by
you while you felt proud of yourself,
57 before your wickedness became evi-
dent? Now you are like her, reproached
by the Edomites and all your neighbors,
despised on all sides by the Philistines.
58 The penalty of your lewdness and your
abominations—you must bear it all, says
the LORD.

59 For thus speaks the Lord GOD: I will
deal with you according to what you
have done, you who despised your oath,
breaking a covenant. 60 Yet I will re-
member the covenant I made with you
when you were a girl, and I will set up
an everlasting covenant with you.
61 Then you shall remember your con-
duct and be ashamed when I take your
sisters, those older and younger than
you, and give them to you as daughters,
even though I am not bound by my
covenant with you. 62 For I will reestab-
lish my covenant with you, that you may
know that I am the LORD, 63 that you may
remember and be covered with confu-
sion, and that you may be utterly si-
lenced for shame when I pardon you for
all you have done, says the Lord GOD.

CHAPTER 17

The Eagles and the Vine. 1 Thus the
word of the LORD came to me: 2 Son of
man, propose a riddle, and speak this
proverb to the house of Israel: 3 Thus
speaks the Lord GOD:

The great eagle, with great wings,
with long pinions,
with thick plumage, many-hued,
came to Lebanon.
He took the crest of the cedar,
4 tearing off its topmost branch,
And brought it to a land of trades-
men,
set it in a city of merchants.
5 Then he took some seed of the land,
and planted it in a seedbed;
A shoot by plentiful waters,
like a willow he placed it,
6 To sprout and grow up a vine,
dense and low-lying,

*

41: 2 Kgs 25, 9. 49: Gn 19, 24.

†

16, 45: *True daughter of the mother:* Jerusalem has followed in the footsteps of its heathen forebears; cf v 3.

16, 46: *Your elder sister was Samaria:* Samaria can be called an elder sister in view of the relatively greater importance of the northern kingdom, Israel, during most of Old Testament history. Also, the relatively insignificant Sodom of ancient history can be called *your younger sister.*

Its branches turned toward him,
its roots lying under him.
Thus it became a vine, produced branches
and put forth shoots.
7 But there was another great eagle,
great of wing, rich in plumage;
To him this vine bent its roots,
sent out its branches,
That he might water it more freely
than the bed where it was planted.
8 In a fertile field by plentiful waters
it was planted,
to grow branches, bear fruit,
and become a majestic vine.

9 Say: Thus says the Lord GOD: Can
it prosper? Will he not rather tear it out
by the roots and strip off its fruit, so that
all its green growth will wither when he
pulls it up by the roots? [No need of a
mighty arm or many people to do this.]
10 True, it is planted, but will it prosper?
Will it not rather wither, when touched
by the east wind, in the bed where it
grew?

11† Thus the word of the LORD came
to me: 12 Son of man, say now to the re-
bellious house: Do you not understand
what this means? It is this: The king of
Babylon came to Jerusalem and took
away its king and princes with him to
Babylon. 13 Then he selected a man of
the royal line with whom he made a
covenant, binding him under oath, while
removing the nobles of the land, 14 so
that the kingdom would remain a mod-
est one, without aspirations, and would
keep his covenant and obey him. 15 But
this man rebelled against him, sending
envoys to Egypt to obtain horses and a
great army. Can he prosper? Can he who
does such things escape? Can he break
a covenant and still go free? 16 As I live,
says the Lord GOD, in the home of the
king who set him up to rule, whose oath
he spurned, whose covenant with him
he broke, there in Babylon I swear he
shall die! 17 When ramps are cast up and
siege towers are built for the destruction
of many lives, he shall not be saved in
the conflict by Pharaoh with a great
army and numerous troops. 18 He
spurned his oath, breaking his covenant.
Though he gave his hand in pledge, he
did all these things. He shall not escape!

19 Therefore say: Thus says the Lord
GOD: As I live, my oath which he
spurned, my covenant which he broke,
I swear to bring down upon his head.
20* I will spread my net over him, and
he shall be taken in my snare. I will bring
him to Babylon and enter into judgment
with him there over his breaking faith
with me. 21 All the crack troops among
his forces shall fall by the sword, and
the survivors shall be scattered in every
direction. Thus you shall know that I,
the LORD, have spoken.

22† Therefore say: Thus says the Lord
GOD:

I, too, will take from the crest of the cedar,
from its topmost branches tear off a tender shoot,
And plant it on a high and lofty mountain;
23 on the mountain heights of Israel
I will plant it.
It shall put forth branches and bear fruit,
and become a majestic cedar.
Birds of every kind shall dwell beneath it,
every winged thing in the shade of its boughs.
24 And all the trees of the field shall know
that I, the LORD,
Bring low the high tree,
lift high the lowly tree,
Wither up the green tree,
and make the withered tree bloom.

As I, the LORD, have spoken, so will I
do.

CHAPTER 18

Personal Responsibility. 1 Thus the
word of the LORD came to me: Son of
man, 2*† what is the meaning of this
proverb that you recite in the land of
Israel:

"Fathers have eaten green grapes,
thus their children's teeth are on edge"?

3 As I live, says the Lord GOD: I swear
that there shall no longer be anyone
among you who will repeat this proverb
in Israel. 4 For all lives are mine; the life
of the father is like the life of the son,
both are mine; only the one who sins
shall die.

5 If a man is virtuous—if he does what
is right and just, 6† if he does not eat on
the mountains, nor raise his eyes to the
idols of the house of Israel; if he does
not defile his neighbor's wife, nor have

*

17, 20: 12, 13; 32, 3. 18, 2: Jer 13, 1, 29.

†

17, 11-21: These verses explain the foregoing allegory. In 597 B.C., Nebuchadnezzar removed King Jehoiachin and took him into exile; in his place he set Zedekiah, Jehoiachin's uncle, on the throne and received from him the oath of loyalty. But Zedekiah was beguiled into rebellion by Pharaoh Hophra of Egypt, and thereby merited punishment; cf 2 Kgs 24, 10—25, 7.

17, 22f: *I, too, will take from the crest of the cedar . . . plant it:* the Lord will restore Israel under a messianic King from the same Davidic dynasty.

18, 2: *Fathers . . . on edge:* a proverb by which the people claimed that they were being punished for their ancestors' sins rather than for their own; cf Jer 31, 29.

18, 6: *Eat on the mountains:* partake of ritual meals at the heathen high places.

relations with a woman in her menstrual
period; 7* if he oppresses no one, gives
back the pledge received for a debt,
commits no robbery; if he gives food to
the hungry and clothes the naked; 8 if
he does not lend at interest nor exact
usury; if he holds off from evildoing,
judges fairly between a man and his op-
ponent; 9 if he lives by my statutes and
is careful to observe my ordinances, that
man is virtuous—he shall surely live,
says the Lord GOD.

10 But if he begets a son who is a thief,
a murderer, or who does any of these
things 11 (though the father does none
of them), a son who eats on the moun-
tains, defiles the wife of his neighbor,
12 oppresses the poor and needy, com-
mits robbery, does not give back a
pledge, raises his eyes to idols, does
abominable things, 13 lends at interest
and exacts usury—this son certainly
shall not live. Because he practiced all
these abominations, he shall surely die;
his death shall be his own fault.

14 On the other hand, if a man begets
a son who, seeing all the sins his father
commits, yet fears and does not imitate
him; 15 a son who does not eat on the
mountains, or raise his eyes to the idols
of the house of Israel, or defile his neigh-
bor's wife; 16 who does not oppress any-
one, or exact a pledge, or commit
robbery; who gives his food to the hun-
gry and clothes the naked; 17 who holds
off from evildoing, accepts no interest
or usury, but keeps my ordinances and
lives by my statutes—this one shall not
die for the sins of his father, but shall
surely live. 18 Only the father, since he
violated rights, and robbed, and did
what was not good among his people,
shall in truth die for his sins. 19 You ask:
"Why is not the son charged with the
guilt of his father?" Because the son has
done what is right and just, and has been
careful to observe all my statutes, he
shall surely live. 20* Only the one who
sins shall die. The son shall not be
charged with the guilt of his father, nor
shall the father be charged with the guilt
of his son. The virtuous man's virtue
shall be his own, as the wicked man's
wickedness shall be his.

21 But if the wicked man turns away
from all the sins he committed, if he
keeps all my statutes and does what is
right and just, he shall surely live, he
shall not die. 22 None of the crimes he
committed shall be remembered against
him; he shall live because of the virtue
he has practiced. 23* Do I indeed derive
any pleasure from the death of the
wicked? says the Lord GOD. Do I not
rather rejoice when he turns from his
evil way that he may live?

24 And if the virtuous man turns from
the path of virtue to do evil, the same
kind of abominable things that the
wicked man does, can he do this and still
live? None of his virtuous deeds shall be
remembered, because he has broken
faith and committed sin; because of this,
he shall die. 25* You say, "The LORD's
way is not fair!" Hear now, house of Is-
rael: Is it my way that is unfair, or
rather, are not your ways unfair?
26 When a virtuous man turns away from
virtue to commit iniquity, and dies, it is
because of the iniquity he committed
that he must die. 27 But if a wicked man,
turning from the wickedness he has
committed, does what is right and just,
he shall preserve his life; 28 since he has
turned away from all the sins which he
committed, he shall surely live, he shall
not die. 29 And yet the house of Israel
says, "The LORD's way is not fair!" Is
it my way that is not fair, house of Israel,
or rather, is it not that your ways are
not fair?

30* Therefore I will judge you, house
of Israel, each one according to his ways,
says the Lord GOD. Turn and be con-
verted from all your crimes, that they
may be no cause of guilt for you. 31 Cast
away from you all the crimes you have
committed, and make for yourselves a
new heart and a new spirit. Why should
you die, O house of Israel? 32* For I have
no pleasure in the death of anyone who
dies, says the Lord GOD. Return and
live!

CHAPTER 19

1 As for you, son of man, raise a
lamentation over the prince of Israel:

Allegory of the Lions

2† What a lioness was your mother,
a lion of lions!
Among young lions she couched
to rear her whelps.
3 One whelp she raised up,
a young lion he became;
He learned to seize prey,
men he devoured.
4 Then nations raised cries against
him,
in their pit he was caught;
They took him away with hooks
to the land of Egypt.

*

7: Is 58, 7; Mt 25, 35.
20: Dt 24, 16; 2 Kgs 14, 6; 2 Chr 25, 4.
23: 33, 11; 2 Pt 3, 9.
25: 33, 20.
30: Mt 3, 2; Lk 3, 3.
32: 18, 23; 33, 11; 2 Pt 3, 9.

†

19, 2-9: The meaning of this allegory is uncertain. Probably the two *young lions* are Jehoahaz and Zedekiah, sons of the same mother, who were deported to Egypt and Babylonia respectively. Cf 2 Kgs 23, 31-34; 24, 18ff.

5 Then she saw that in vain she had
waited,
her hope was destroyed.
She took another of her whelps,
him she made a young lion.
6 He prowled among the lions,
a young lion he became;
He learned to seize prey,
men he devoured;
7 He ravaged their strongholds,
their cities he wasted.
The land and all in it were appalled
at the noise of his roar.
8 Nations laid out against him
snares all about him;
They spread their net to take him,
in their pit he was caught.
9 They put him in a cage and took him
away
to the king of Babylon,
So that his voice would not be heard
on the mountains of Israel.

Allegory of the Vine Branch

10† Your mother was like a vine
planted by the water;
Fruitful and branchy was she
because of the abundant water.
11 One strong branch she put out
as a royal scepter.
Stately was her height
amid the dense foliage;
Notably tall was she
with her many clusters.
12* But she was torn up in fury
and flung to the ground;
The east wind withered her up,
her fruit was torn off;
Then her strong branch withered up,
fire devoured it.
13 So now she is planted in the desert,
in a land dry and parched,
14 For fire came out of the branch
and devoured her shoots;
She is now without a strong branch,
a ruler's scepter.

This is a lamentation and serves as a lamentation.

CHAPTER 20

Israel's History of Infidelity. 1† In the
seventh year, on the tenth day of the fifth
month, some of the elders of Israel came
to consult the LORD and sat down before
me. 2 Then the word of the LORD came
to me: 3 Son of man, speak with the el-
ders of Israel and say to them: Thus says
the Lord GOD: Have you come to consult
me? As I live! I swear I will not allow
myself to be consulted by you, says the
Lord GOD.

4 Will you judge them? Will you judge,
son of man? Make known to them the
abominations of their ancestors 5 in
these words: Thus speaks the Lord GOD:
The day I chose Israel, I swore to the
descendants of the house of Jacob; in the
land of Egypt I revealed myself to them
and swore: I am the LORD, your God.
6 That day I swore to bring them out of
the land of Egypt to the land I had
scouted for them, a land flowing with
milk and honey, a jewel among all lands.
7 Then I said to them: Throw away, each
of you, the detestable things that have
held your eyes; do not defile yourselves
with the idols of Egypt: I am the LORD,
your God.

8 But they rebelled against me and re-
fused to listen to me; none of them threw
away the detestable things that had held
their eyes, they did not abandon the
idols of Egypt. Then I thought of pouring
out my fury on them and spending my
anger on them there in the land of
Egypt; 9 but I acted for my name's sake,
that it should not be profaned in the sight
of the nations among whom they were,
in whose presence I had made myself
known to them, revealing that I would
bring them out of the land of Egypt.
10 Therefore I led them out of the land
of Egypt and brought them into the
desert. 11* Then I gave them my statutes
and made known to them my ordi-
nances, which everyone must keep, to
have life through them. 12* I also gave
them my sabbaths to be a sign between
me and them, to show that it was I, the
LORD, who made them holy.

13 But the house of Israel rebelled
against me in the desert. They did not
observe my statutes, and they despised
my ordinances that bring life to those
who keep them. My sabbaths, too, they
desecrated grievously. Then I thought
of pouring out my fury on them in the
desert to put an end to them, 14 but I
acted for my name's sake, that it should
not be profaned in the sight of the na-
tions in whose presence I had brought
them out. 15 Nevertheless I swore to
them in the desert not to bring them to
the land I had given them, a land flowing
with milk and honey, a jewel among all
lands. 16 So much were their hearts de-
voted to their idols, they had not lived
by my statutes, but despised my ordi-
nances and desecrated my sabbaths.
17 But I looked on them with pity, not
wanting to destroy them, so I did not put
an end to them in the desert.

18 Then I said to their children in the
desert: Do not observe the statutes of

*

19, 12: Hos 13, 15.
20, 11: Lv 18, 5; Rom 10, 5.
12: Ex 20, 8; 31, 13; Dt 5, 12.

†

19, 10-14: *A vine:* Judah. *One strong branch:* the Davidic king.

20, 1: *The seventh year, on the tenth day of the fifth month:* August 14, 591 B.C.

your parents or keep their ordinances;
do not defile yourselves with their idols.
19 I am the LORD, your God: observe my
statutes and be careful to keep my ordi-
nances; 20 keep holy my sabbaths, as a
sign between me and you to show that
I am the LORD, your God. 21 But their
children rebelled against me: they did
not observe my statutes or keep my or-
dinances that bring life to those who ob-
serve them, and my sabbaths they
desecrated. Then I thought of pouring
out my fury on them, of spending my
anger on them in the desert; 22 but I
stayed my hand, acting for my name's
sake, lest it be profaned in the sight of
the nations in whose presence I brought
them out. 23 Nevertheless I swore to
them in the desert that I would disperse
them among the nations and scatter
them over foreign lands; 24 for they did
not keep my ordinances, but despised
my statutes and desecrated my sab-
baths, with eyes only for the idols of their
fathers. 25† Therefore I gave them stat-
utes that were not good, and ordinances
through which they could not live. 26 I
let them become defiled by their gifts,
by their immolation of every first-born,
so as to make them an object of horror.
27 Therefore speak to the house of Is-
rael, son of man, and tell them: Thus
says the Lord GOD: In this way also your
fathers blasphemed me, breaking faith
with me: 28 when I had brought them to
the land I had sworn to give them, and
they saw all its high hills and leafy trees,
there they offered their sacrifices [there
they brought their offensive offerings],
there they sent up appeasing odors, and
there they poured out their libations. 29 I
asked them: To what sort of high place
do you betake yourselves?—and so they
call it a high place even to the present
day. 30 Therefore say to the house of Is-
rael: Thus says the Lord GOD: Will you
defile yourselves like your fathers? Will
you lust after their detestable idols? 31 By
offering your gifts, by making your
children pass through the fire, you defile
yourselves with all your idols even to this
day. Shall I let myself be consulted by
you, house of Israel? As I live! says the
Lord GOD: I swear I will not let myself
be consulted by you.
32 What you are thinking of shall never
happen: "We shall be like the nations,
like the peoples of foreign lands, serving
wood and stone." 33 As I live, says the
Lord GOD, with a mighty hand and out-
stretched arm, with poured-out wrath,
I swear I will be king over you! 34 With
a mighty hand and outstretched arm,
with poured-out wrath, I will bring you
out from the nations and gather you
from the countries over which you are
scattered; 35† then I will lead you to the
desert of the peoples, where I will enter
into judgment with you face to face.
36 Just as I entered into judgment with
your fathers in the desert of the land of
Egypt, so will I enter into judgment with
you, says the Lord GOD. 37 I will count
you with the staff and bring back but a
small number. 38 I will separate from
you those who have rebelled and trans-
gressed against me; from the land where
they sojourned as aliens I will bring
them out, but they shall not return to
the land of Israel. Thus you shall know
that I am the LORD.
39 As for you, house of Israel, thus says
the Lord GOD: Come, each one of you,
destroy your idols! Then listen to me,
and never again profane my holy name
with your gifts and your idols. 40 For on
my holy mountain, on the mountain
height of Israel, says the Lord GOD,
there the whole house of Israel without
exception shall worship me; there I will
accept them, and there I will claim your
tributes and the first fruits of your offer-
ings, and all that you dedicate. 41 As a
pleasing odor I will accept you, when I
have brought you from among the na-
tions and gathered you out of the coun-
tries over which you were scattered; and
by means of you I will manifest my holi-
ness in the sight of the nations. 42 Thus
you shall know that I am the LORD, when
I bring you back to the land of Israel,
the land which I swore to give to your
fathers. 43 There you shall recall your
conduct and all the deeds by which you
defiled yourselves; and you shall loathe
yourselves because of all the evil things
you did. 44 And you shall know that I am
the LORD when I deal with you thus, for
my name's sake, and not according to
your evil conduct and corrupt actions,
O house of Israel, says the Lord GOD.

CHAPTER 21

The Sword of the Lord. 1 Thus the
word of the LORD came to me: 2† Son of
man, look southward, preach toward the
south, and prophesy against the forest
of the southern land. 3 Hear the word of
the LORD! you shall say to the southern
forest. Thus says the Lord GOD: See! I
am kindling a fire in you that shall de-
vour all trees, the green as well as the
dry. The blazing flame shall not be
quenched, but from south to north every
face shall be scorched by it. 4 Everyone

†

20, 25f: *I gave them statutes that were not good:* the Lord permitted them to adopt pagan practices, including the abominable sacrifice of their newborn infants, which could only merit their destruction. See note on 14, 9.

20, 35-38: Exile in the pagan lands will serve the same purpose as the desert journey after the Exodus from Egypt: the rebellious will be eliminated, and only a remnant will survive.

21, 2ff: The southern kingdom, Judah, is likened to a forest about to be burned; cf Jer 21, 14.

shall see that I, the LORD, have kindled
it, and it shall not be quenched.
5 But I said, "Alas! Lord GOD, they say
to me, 'Is not this the one who is forever
spinning parables?' " 6 Then the word of
the LORD came to me: 7 Son of man, look
toward Jerusalem, preach against their
sanctuary, and prophesy against the
land of Israel, 8† saying to the land of
Israel: Thus says the LORD: See! I am
coming at you; I will draw my sword
from its sheath and cut off from you the
virtuous and the wicked. 9 Thus my
sword shall leave its sheath against ev-
eryone from south to north, 10 and ev-
eryone shall know that I, the LORD, have
drawn my sword from its sheath, and
it shall not be sheathed again.

Act Symbolic of the City's Fall. 11 As
for you, son of man, groan! with shat-
tered strength groan bitterly while they
look on. 12† And when they ask you,
"Why are you groaning?", you shall say:
Because of a report; when it comes every
heart shall fail, every hand shall fall
helpless, every spirit shall be daunted,
and every knee shall run with water.
See, it is coming, it is here! says the Lord
GOD.

Song of the Sword. 13 Thus the word
of the LORD came to me: 14 Son of man,
prophesy! say: Thus says the LORD:

A sword, a sword has been sharp-
ened,
a sword, a sword has been bur-
nished:
15 To work slaughter has it been sharp-
ened,
to flash lightning has it been bur-
nished.
Why should I now withdraw it?
You have spurned the rod and ev-
ery judgment!
16 I have given it over to the burnisher
that he might hold it in his hand,
A sword sharpened and burnished
to be put in the hand of a slayer.
17 Cry out and wail, son of man,
for it is destined for my people;
It is for all the princes of Israel,
victims of the sword with my peo-
ple.

Therefore, slap your thigh, 18† for the
sword has been tested; and why should
it not be so? says the Lord GOD, since
you have spurned the rod.

19 As for you, son of man, prophesy,
brushing one hand against the
other:
While the sword is doubled and tri-
pled,
this sword of slaughter,
This great sword of slaughter
which threatens all around,
20 That every heart may tremble;
for many will be the fallen.
At all their gates
I have appointed the sword for
slaughter,
Fashioned to flash lightning,
burnished for slaughter.
21 Cleave to the right! destroy!
to the left! wherever your edge is
turned.

22† Then, I too, shall brush one hand
against the other and wreak my fury.
I, the LORD, have spoken.

Nebuchadnezzar at the Crossroads.
23 Thus the word of the LORD came to
me: 24 Son of man, make for yourself two
roads over which the sword of the king
of Babylon can come. Both roads shall
lead out from the same land. Then put
a signpost at the head of each road, 25 so
that the sword can come to Rabbah of
the Ammonites or to Judah's capital, Je-
rusalem. 26† For at the fork where the
two roads divide stands the king of
Babylon, divining; he has shaken the
arrows, inquired of the teraphim, in-
spected the liver. 27† In his right hand
is the divining arrow marked "Jerusa-
lem," bidding him to give the order for
slaying, to raise his voice in the battle
cry, to post battering rams at the gates,
to cast up a ramp, to build a siege tower.
28 In their eyes this is but a lying oracle;
yet they are bound by the oaths they
have sworn, and the arrow taken in
hand marks their guilt.
29 Therefore thus says the Lord GOD:
Because you have drawn attention to
your guilt, with your crimes laid bare
and your sinfulness in all your wicked
deeds revealed (because attention has
been drawn to you), you shall be taken
in hand. 30 And as for you, depraved and
wicked prince of Israel, whose day is
coming when your life of crime will be
ended, 31 thus says the Lord GOD: Off
with the turban and away with the
crown! Nothing shall be as it was! Up
with the low and down with the high!
32 Twisted, twisted, twisted will I leave
it; it shall not be the same until he comes
who has the claim against the city; and
to him I will hand it over.

---

†

21, 8: *Cut off from you the virtuous and the wicked:* a more complete devastation of Jerusalem than that described in 9, 6.

21, 12: *A report:* the news of the fall of Jerusalem; cf 33, 21f.

21, 17: *Slap your thigh:* a gesture signifying grief and dread.

21, 22: *Brush one hand against the other:* a gesture signifying the rejection of responsibility; cf 22, 13; Nm 24, 10.

21, 26: Three forms of divination are mentioned: *arrow* divination, consisting in the use of differently marked arrows, extracted or shaken from a case at random; the consultation of the *teraphim* or household idols, and *liver* divination, scrutiny of the configurations of the livers of newly slaughtered animals, a common form of divination in Mesopotamia.

21, 27f: An *arrow marked "Jerusalem"* is picked out, which *marks* the guilt of the city's inhabitants for having broken their oath of allegiance to Nebuchadnezzar.

Against the Ammonites. 33† As for you, son of man, prophesy: Thus says the Lord GOD against the Ammonites and their insults: A sword, a sword is drawn for slaughter, burnished to consume and to flash lightning, 34 because you planned with false visions and lying divinations to lay it on the necks of depraved and wicked men whose day has come when their crimes are at an end. 35 Return it to its sheath! In the place where you were created, in the land of your origin, I will judge you. 36 I will pour out my indignation upon you, breathing my fiery wrath upon you, I will hand you over to ravaging men, artisans of destruction. 37 You shall be fuel for the fire, your blood shall flow throughout the land. You shall not be remembered, for I, the LORD, have spoken.

CHAPTER 22

Crimes of Jerusalem. 1 Thus the word of the LORD came to me: 2 You, son of man, would you judge, would you judge the bloody city? Then make known all her abominations, 3 and say: Thus says the Lord GOD: Woe to the city which sheds blood within herself so that her time has come, and which has made idols for her own defilement. 4 By the blood which you shed you have been made guilty, and with the idols you made you have become defiled; you have brought on your day, so that the end of your years has come. Therefore I make you an object of scorn to the nations and a laughingstock to all foreign lands. 5 Those near you and those far off shall deride you because of your foul reputation and your great perversity. 6 See! the princes of Israel, family by family, are in you only for bloodshed. 7 Within you, father and mother are despised; in your midst, they extort from the resident alien; within you, they oppress orphans and widows. 8 What is holy to me you have spurned, and my sabbaths you have desecrated. 9 There are those in you who slander to cause bloodshed; within you are those who feast on the mountains; in your midst are those who do lewd things. 10 In you are those who uncover the nakedness of their fathers, and in you those who coerce women in their menstrual period. 11* There are those in you who do abominable things with the wives of their neighbors, men who defile their daughters-in-law by incest, men who coerce their sisters, the daughters of their own fathers. 12 There are those in you who take bribes to shed blood. You exact interest and usury; you despoil your neighbors violently; and me you have forgotten, says the Lord GOD.

13 See, I am brushing one hand against the other because of the unjust profits you have made and because of the bloodshed in your midst. 14 Can your heart remain firm, will your hands be strong, in the days when I deal with you? I, the LORD, have spoken, and I will act. 15 I will disperse you among the nations and scatter you over foreign lands, so that I may purge your uncleanness. 16 In you I will allow myself to be profaned in the eyes of the nations; thus you shall know that I am the LORD.

17 Thus the word of the LORD came to me: 18 Son of man, the house of Israel has become dross for me. All of them are bronze and tin, iron and lead [in the midst of a furnace]: dross from silver have they become. 19 Therefore thus says the Lord GOD: Because all of you have become dross, therefore I must gather you together within Jerusalem. 20 Just as silver, bronze, iron, lead, and tin are gathered into a furnace and smelted in the roaring flames, so I will gather you together in my furious wrath, put you in, and smelt you. 21 When I have assembled you, I will blast you with the fire of my anger and smelt you with it. 22 You shall be smelted by it just as silver is smelted in a furnace. Thus you shall know that I, the LORD, have poured out my fury on you.

23 Thus the word of the LORD came to me: 24 Son of man, say to her: You are a land unrained on [that is, not rained on] at the time of my fury. 25 Her princes are like roaring lions that tear prey; they devour people, seizing their wealth and precious things, and make widows of many within her. 26 Her priests violate my law and profane what is holy to me; they do not distinguish between the sacred and the profane, nor teach the difference between the unclean and the clean; they pay no attention to my sabbaths, so that I have been profaned in their midst. 27* Her nobles within her are like wolves that tear prey, shedding blood and destroying lives to get unjust gain. 28 Her prophets cover them with whitewash, pretending to visions that are false and performing lying divinations, saying, "Thus says the Lord GOD," although the LORD has not spoken. 29 The people of the land practice extortion and commit robbery; they afflict the poor and the needy, and oppress the resident alien without justice. 30 Thus I have

*

22, 11: Jer 5, 7f. Zep 3, 3.
27: Mi 3, 11;

†

21, 33-37: In the preceding section Nebuchadnezzar is represented as deciding whether to attack Jerusalem or Rabbath-Ammon. As it happened, Jerusalem was chosen for attack; later, however, the Chaldeans also invaded Ammon. The present oracle against Ammon is inserted here, rather than in chapters 25-32, in order to complement the oracle against Jerusalem.

searched among them for someone who could build a wall or stand in the breach before me to keep me from destroying the land; but I found no one. 31 Therefore I have poured out my fury upon them; with my fiery wrath I have consumed them; I have brought down their conduct upon their heads, says the Lord GOD.

CHAPTER 23

The Two Sisters. 1 Thus the word of the LORD came to me: 2 Son of man, there were two women, daughters of the same mother, 3 who even as young girls played the harlot in Egypt. There the Egyptians caressed their bosoms and fondled their virginal breasts. 4† Oholah was the name of the elder, and the name of her sister was Oholibah. They became mine and bore sons and daughters. [As for their names: Samaria is Oholah, and Jerusalem is Oholibah.] 5 Oholah became a harlot faithless to me; she lusted after her lovers, the Assyrians, warriors 6 dressed in purple, governors and officers, all of them attractive young men, knights mounted on horses. 7 Thus she gave herself as a harlot to them, to all the elite of the Assyrians, and she defiled herself with all those for whom she lusted [with all their idols]. 8 She did not give up the harlotry which she had begun in Egypt, when they had lain with her as a young girl, fondling her virginal breasts and pouring out their impurities on her. 9 Therefore I handed her over to her lovers, the Assyrians for whom she had lusted. 10* They exposed her nakedness, her sons and daughters they took away, and herself they slew with the sword. Thus she became a byword for women, for they punished her grievously.

11 Though her sister Oholibah saw all this, her lust was more depraved than her sister's, and she outdid her in harlotry. 12 She too lusted after the Assyrians, governors and officers, warriors impeccably clothed, knights mounted on horses, all of them attractive young men. 13 I saw that she had defiled herself. Both had gone down the same path, 14 yet she went further in her harlotry. When she saw men drawn on the wall, the images of Chaldeans drawn with vermillion, 15 with sashes girded about their waists, flowing turbans on their heads, all looking like chariot warriors, the portraits of Babylonians, natives of Chaldea, 16 she lusted for them; no sooner had she set eyes on them than she sent messengers to them in Chaldea. 17 Then the Babylonians came to her, to the love couch, and defiled her with their intercourse. As soon as she was defiled by them, she became disgusted with them. 18 Her harlotry was discovered and her shame was revealed, and I became disgusted with her as I had become disgusted with her sister. 19 But she played the harlot all the more, recalling the days of her girlhood, when she had been a harlot in the land of Egypt. 20 She lusted for the lechers of Egypt, whose members are like that of an ass, and whose heat is like that of stallions.

21 You yearned for the lewdness of your girlhood, when the Egyptians fondled your breasts, caressing your bosom. 22 Therefore, Oholibah, thus says the Lord GOD: I will now stir up your lovers against you, those with whom you are disgusted, and I will bring them against you from every side: 23† the men of Babylon and all of Chaldea, Pekod, Shoa and Koa, along with all those of Assyria, attractive young men, all of them governors and officers, charioteers and warriors, all of them horsemen. 24 They shall come against you from the north with chariots and wagons and many peoples. Shields, bucklers, and helmets they shall array against you everywhere. 25 I will leave it to them to judge, and they will judge you by their own ordinances. I will let loose my jealousy against you, so that they shall deal with you in fury, cutting off your nose and ears; and what is left of you shall fall by the sword. They shall take away your sons and daughters, and what is left of you shall be devoured by fire. 26 They shall strip off your clothes and seize your splendid ornaments. 27 I will put an end to your lewdness and to the harlotry you began in Egypt; you shall no longer look toward it, nor shall you remember Egypt again.

28 For thus says the Lord GOD: I am now handing you over to those whom you hate, to those who fill you with disgust. 29 They shall deal with you in hatred, seizing all that you have worked for and leaving you stark naked, so that your indecent nakedness is exposed. Your lewdness and harlotry 30 have brought these things upon you, because you played the harlot with the nations by defiling yourself with their idols.

31 Because you followed in the path of your sister, I will hand you her cup. 32 Thus says the Lord GOD:

> The cup of your sister you shall
> drink,

*

23, 10: 16, 37.

†

23, 4: *Oholah . . . Oholibah:* symbolic names. The first, standing for Samaria, may be read to mean "her own tent"; the latter, standing for Jerusalem, means "my tent is in her." The references seem to be to the schismatic temple and cult of the Lord in Samaria, as opposed to their authentic counterpart in Jerusalem.

23, 23: *Pekod, Shoa and Koa:* peoples living about the Tigris, part of "greater Babylonia."

so wide and deep, which holds so
much,
33 Filled with destruction and grief,
a cup of dismay, the cup of your
sister.

34 You shall drain it dry, and gnaw at
the very sherds of the cup, and you shall
tear out your breasts; for I have spoken,
says the Lord GOD. 35 Therefore thus
says the Lord GOD: Because you have
forgotten me and cast me behind your
back, it is for you to bear the penalty
of your lewdness and harlotry.
36 Then the LORD said to me: Son of
man, would you judge Oholah and Oho-
libah? Then make known to them their
abominations. 37 For they committed
adultery, and blood is on their hands.
They committed adultery with their
idols; to feed them they immolated the
children they had borne me. 38 [This, too,
they did to me: they defiled my sanctu-
ary and desecrated my sabbaths. 39 On
the very day they slew their children for
their idols, they entered my sanctuary
to desecrate it. Thus they acted within
my house.] 40† Moreover, they sent for
men who had to come from afar, to
whom messengers were sent. And so
they came—and for them you bathed
yourself, painted your eyes, and put on
ornaments. 41 You sat on a couch pre-
pared for them, with a table spread be-
fore it, on which you had set my incense
and oil. 42 Then was heard the shout of
a carefree mob in the city, and these
were men brought in from the desert,
who put bracelets on the women's arms
and splendid diadems on their heads.
43 So I said: "Oh, this woman jaded with
adulteries! Now they will commit whore-
dom with her, and as for her. . . ."
44 And indeed they did come to her as
men come to a harlot. Thus they came
to Oholah and Oholibah, the lewd
women. 45 But just men shall punish
them with the sentence meted out to
adulteresses and murderesses, for they
have committed adultery, and blood is
on their hands.
46 Thus says the Lord GOD: Summon
an assembly against them, and deliver
them over to terror and plunder. 47 The
assembly shall stone them and hack
them to pieces with their swords. They
shall slay their sons and daughters, and
burn their houses with fire. 48 Thus I will
put an end to lewdness in the land, and
all the women will be warned not to imi-
tate your lewdness. 49 They shall inflict
on you the penalty of your lewdness, and
you shall pay for your sins of idolatry.
Thus you shall know that I am the LORD.

CHAPTER 24

Allegory of the Pot. 1† On the tenth
day of the tenth month, in the ninth year,
the word of the LORD came to me: 2 Son
of man, write down this date today, for
this very day the king of Babylon has
invested Jerusalem. 3† Propose this par-
able to the rebellious house: Thus says
the Lord GOD:

Set up the pot, set it up,
then pour in some water.
4 Put in it pieces of meat,
all good pieces: thigh and shoul-
der;
Fill it with the choicest joints
5 taken from the pick of the flock.
Then pile the wood beneath it;
bring to a boil these pieces
and the joints that are in it.
6* Take out its pieces, one by one,
without casting lots for it.

Therefore, thus says the Lord GOD: Woe
to the bloody city, a pot containing rust,
whose rust has not been removed. 7† For
the blood she shed is in her midst; she
poured it on the bare rock; she did not
pour it out on the earth, to be covered
with dust. 8 To work up my wrath, to ex-
cite my vengeance, she put her blood on
the bare rock, not to be covered.
9 Therefore, thus says the Lord GOD:

I, too, will heap up a great bonfire,
10 piling on wood and kindling the
fire,
Till the meat has been cooked,
till the broth has boiled.

11 Then I will set the pot empty on the
coals till its metal glows red hot, till the
impurities in it melt, and its rust disap-
pears. 12 Yet not even with fire will its
great rust be removed. 13 Because you
have sullied yourself with lewdness
when I would have purified you, and you
refused to be purified of your unclean-
ness, therefore you shall not be purified
until I wreak my fury on you. 14 I, the
LORD, have spoken; it is coming, for I
will bring it about without fail. I will not
have pity nor repent. By your conduct
and your deeds you shall be judged, says
the Lord GOD.
***Symbol of the Destruction of the
Temple.*** 15 Thus the word of the LORD
came to me: 16 Son of man, by a sudden
blow I am taking away from you the de-

*

24, 6: Na 3, 1; Hb 2, 12.

†

23, 40: *Men who had to come from afar:* ambassadors from Assyria and Babylon. Alliances with these countries aided in the corruption of both Israel and Judah.

24, 1: *The tenth day of the tenth month, in the ninth year:* January 15, 588 B.C. The same date is given in Jer 52, 4.

24, 3ff: This present comparison of the inhabitants of Jerusalem to meat boiled in a pot symbolizes their punishment rather than their supposed protection as in 11, 3.

24, 7: *Blood . . . to be covered with dust:* since blood was sacred to God, it had to be covered with earth (Lv 17, 13); the blood of a murdered man that was left uncovered cried to heaven for vengeance; cf Jb 16, 18; Gn 4, 10.

light of your eyes, but do not mourn or
weep or shed any tears. [17]† Groan in si-
lence, make no lament for the dead, bind
on your turban, put your sandals on your
feet, do not cover your beard, and do
not eat the customary bread. [18] That
evening my wife died, and the next
morning I did as I had been com-
manded. [19] Then the people asked me,
"Will you not tell us what all these things
that you are doing mean for us?" I there-
fore spoke to the people that morning,
[20] saying to them: Thus the word of the
LORD came to me: [21] Say to the house
of Israel: Thus says the Lord GOD: I will
now desecrate my sanctuary, the
stronghold of your pride, the delight of
your eyes, the desire of your soul. The
sons and daughters you left behind shall
fall by the sword. [24] Ezekiel shall be a
sign for you: all that he did you shall
do when it happens. Thus you shall know
that I am the LORD. [22]† You shall do as
I have done, not covering your beards
nor eating the customary bread. [23] Your
turbans shall remain on your heads,
your sandals on your feet. You shall not
mourn or weep, but you shall rot away
because of your sins and groan one to
another.

End of Ezekiel's Dumbness. [25]* As for
you, son of man, truly, on the day I take
away from them their bulwark, their
glorious joy, the delight of their eyes, the
desire of their soul, and the pride of their
hearts, their sons and daughters, [26] that
day the fugitive will come to you, that
you may hear it for yourself; [27] that day
your mouth shall be opened and you
shall be dumb no longer. Thus you shall
be a sign to them, and they shall know
that I am the LORD.

III: PROPHECIES AGAINST FOREIGN NATIONS

CHAPTER 25

Against Ammon. [1] Thus the word of
the LORD came to me: [2] Son of man, turn
toward the Ammonites and prophesy
against them. [3]* Say to the Ammonites:
Hear the word of the LORD! Thus says
the Lord GOD: Because you cried out
your joy over the desecration of my
sanctuary, the devastation of the land
of Israel, and the exile of the house of
Judah, [4]† therefore I will deliver you into
the possession of the Easterners. They
shall set up their encampments among
you and pitch their tents; they shall eat
your fruits and drink your milk. [5] I will
make Rabbah a pasture for camels, and
the villages of the Ammonites a resting
place for flocks. Thus you shall know
that I am the LORD.

[6] For thus says the Lord GOD: Because
you clapped your hands and stamped
your feet, rejoicing most maliciously in
your heart over the land of Israel,
[7] therefore I will stretch out my hand
against you. I will make you plunder for
the nations, I will cut you off from the
peoples, and remove you from the lands.
I will destroy you, and thus you shall
know that I am the LORD.

Against Moab. [8]* Thus says the Lord
GOD: Because Moab said, "See! the
house of Judah is like all other nations,"
[9]† therefore I will clear the shoulder of
Moab totally of its cities, the jewels of
the land: Beth-jesimoth, Baal-meon,
and Kiriathaim. [10] I will hand her over,
along with the Ammonites, into the pos-
session of the Easterners, that she may
not be remembered among the peoples.
[11] Thus I will execute judgment upon
Moab, that they may know that I am the
LORD.

Against Edom. [12]* Thus says the Lord
GOD: Because Edom has taken ven-
geance on the house of Judah and has
made itself grievously guilty by taking
vengeance on them, [13] therefore thus
says the Lord GOD: I will stretch out my
hand against Edom and cut off from it
man and beast. I will make it a waste
from Teman to Dedan; they shall fall by
the sword. [14] My vengeance upon Edom
I will entrust to my people Israel, who
will deal with Edom in accordance with
my anger and my fury; thus they shall
know my vengeance, says the Lord
GOD.

Against the Philistines. [15] Thus says
the Lord GOD: Because the Philistines
have acted revengefully, and have taken
vengeance with destructive malice in
their hearts, with an undying enmity,
[16]† therefore thus says the Lord GOD:
See! I am stretching out my hand
against the Philistines; I will cut off the
Cherethites and wipe out the remnant
on the seacoast. [17] I will execute great
acts of vengeance on them, punishing
them furiously. Thus they shall know
that I am the LORD, when I wreak my
vengeance on them.

*

24, 25ff: 3, 22-27.
25, 3: Jer 40, 14; 41, 10; 49, 2; Am 1, 13ff; Zep 2, 8ff.
8: Sir 50, 26; Is 15, 1-9; 16, 1-14; Jer 48, 1-47; Am 2, 1ff; Zep 2, 8f.
12ff: 35, 1ff; Is 34, 5; Jer 49, 7-22; Jl 4, 19; Am 1, 11f; Ob 1, 1-21.

†

24, 17: *The customary bread:* eaten as a mourning observance; cf Jer 16, 7. The other gestures here forbidden were also popular mourning customs.

24, 22f: The fall of the city will be so sudden and final that the exiles will have no time to go into mourning.

25, 4: *The Easterners:* nomadic tribes to the east of Ammon and Moab.

25, 9: *The shoulder of Moab:* the edge of the Moabite plateau.

25, 16: *Cherethites:* a people forming part of the Philistine nation; cf Zep 2, 5.

CHAPTER 26

Against the City of Tyre. 1 On the first
day of the . . . month in the eleventh
year, the word of the LORD came to me:
2 Son of man, because of what Tyre said
of Jerusalem:

"Aha! it is broken, the gateway to
the peoples;
now that it is ruined, its wealth reverts to me!"
3* therefore thus says the Lord GOD:
See! I am coming at you, Tyre;
I will churn up against you many
nations,
even as the sea churns up its
waves;
4† They shall destroy the walls of Tyre
and raze her towers.
I will scrape the ground from her
and leave her a bare rock;
5 She shall be a drying place for nets
in the midst of the sea.

I have spoken, says the Lord GOD: and
she shall be booty for the nations. 6† And
her daughters on the mainland shall be
slaughtered by the sword; thus they
shall know that I am the LORD.
7 For thus says the Lord GOD: I am
now bringing up against Tyre from the
north Nebuchadnezzar the king of
Babylon, the king of kings, with horses
and chariots, with cavalry and a great
and mighty army.

8 Your daughters on the mainland
he shall slay with the sword;
He shall place a siege tower against
you,
cast up a ramp about you,
and raise his shields against you.
9 He shall pound your walls with battering-rams
and break down your towers with
his weapons.
10 The surge of his horses shall cover
you with dust,
amid the noise of steeds, of wheels
and of chariots.
Your walls shall shake as he enters
your gates,
even as one enters a city that is
breached.
11 With the hoofs of his horses
he shall trample all your streets;
Your people he shall slay by the
sword;
your mighty pillars he shall pull
to the ground.
12 Your wealth shall be plundered,
your merchandise pillaged;
Your walls shall be torn down,
your precious houses demolished;
Your stones, your timber, and your
clay
shall be cast into the sea.
13 I will put an end to the noise of your
songs,
and the sound of your lyres shall
be heard no more.
14 I will make you a bare rock;
a drying place for nets shall you
be.

Never shall you be rebuilt, for I have
spoken, says the Lord GOD.
15 Thus says the Lord GOD to Tyre: At
the noise of your fall, at the groaning
of the wounded, when the sword slays
in your midst, shall not the isles quake?
16† All the princes of the sea shall step
down from their thrones, lay aside their
robes, and strip off their embroidered
garments. They shall be clothed in
mourning and, sitting on the ground,
they shall tremble at every moment and
be horrified at you. 17 Then they shall utter a lament over you:

How have you perished, gone from
the seas,
city most prized!
Once she was mighty on the sea,
she and her dwellers,
Who spread terror into all
that dwelt by the sea.
18 On this, the day of your fall,
the islands quake!

The isles in the sea are terrified at your
passing.
19 For thus says the Lord GOD: When
I make you a city desolate like cities that
are no longer inhabited, when I churn
up the abyss against you, and its mighty
waters cover you, 20† then I will thrust
you down with those who descend into
the pit, those of the bygone age; and I
will make you dwell in the nether lands,
in the everlasting ruins, with those who
go down to the pit, so that you may never
return to take your place in the land of
the living. 21 I will make you a devastation, and you shall be no more; you shall
be sought, but never again found, says
the Lord GOD.

CHAPTER 27

The Ship Tyre. 1 Thus the word of the
LORD came to me: 2 As for you, son of
man, utter a lament over Tyre, 3 and say

*

26, 3: Is 26, 1-21; 47, 4; Jl 4, 4f; Zec 9, 2ff.

†

26, 4f: *A bare rock:* the Tyre of Ezekiel's time was situated on a rocky island just off the Phoenician coast; it was not until the time of Alexander the Great that it was connected by a causeway to the mainland.

26, 6: *Her daughters:* tributary towns and villages on the mainland.

26, 16: *The princes of the sea:* the rulers of the islands and coastal cities leagued commercially with Tyre.

26, 20: *Those who descend into the pit:* the dead, pictured as dwelling in a place or cave of darkness.

to Tyre that is situated at the approaches of the sea, that brought the trade of the peoples to many a coastland: Thus says the Lord GOD:

Tyre, you said, "I am a ship,
perfect in beauty."
4 In the midst of the sea your builders placed you,
perfected your beauty.
5† With cypress from Senir they built for you
all of your decks;
Cedar from Lebanon they took
to make you a mast;
6† From the highest oaks of Bashan
they made your oars;
Your bridge they made of cypress wood
from the coasts of Kittim.
7† Fine embroidered linen from Egypt
became your sail [to serve you as a banner].
Purple and scarlet from the coasts of Elishah
covered your cabin.
8† Citizens of Sidon and Arvad
served as your oarsmen;
Skilled men of Zemer were in you
to be your mariners;
9 The elders and experts of Gebal were in you
to caulk your seams.

Every ship and sailor on the sea came
to you to carry trade. 10 Persia and Lud
and Put were in your army as warriors;
shield and helmet they hung upon you,
increasing your splendor. 11 The men of
Arvad were all about your walls, and the
Gamadites were in your towers; they
hung their bucklers all around on your
walls, and made perfect your beauty.
12 Tarshish traded with you, so great was
your wealth, exchanging silver, iron, tin,
and lead for your wares. 13 Javan, Tubal,
and Meshech were also traders with you,
exchanging slaves and articles of bronze
for your goods. 14 From Beth-togarmah
horses, steeds, and mules were exchanged for your wares. 15 The Rhodanites trafficked with you; many
coastlands traded with you; ivory tusks
and ebony wood they gave you for payment. 16 Edom traded with you, so many
were your products, exchanging garnets, purple, embroidered cloth, fine
linen, coral, and rubies for your wares.
17 Judah and the land of Israel trafficked
with you, exchanging Minnith wheat,
figs, honey, oil, and balm for your goods.
18 Damascus traded with you, so great
was your wealth, exchanging Helbon
wine and Zahar wool. 19 Javan exchanged wrought iron, cassia, and aromatic cane from Uzal for your wares.
20 Dedan traded with you for riding gear.
21 The trade of Arabia and of all the
sheikhs of Kedar belonged to you; they
dealt in lambs, rams, and goats. 22 The
merchants of Sheba and Raamah also
traded with you, exchanging for your
wares the very choicest spices, all kinds
of precious stones, and gold. 23 Haran,
Canneh, and Eden, the merchants of
Sheba, Asshur, and Chilmad 24 traded
with you, marketing with you rich garments, violet mantles, embroidered
cloth, varicolored carpets, and firmly
woven cords. 25 Ships of Tarshish journeyed for you in your merchandising.

You were full and heavily laden
in the heart of the sea.
26 Through the deep waters your oarsmen
brought you home,
But the east wind smashed you
in the heart of the sea.
27 Your wealth, your goods, your wares,
your sailors, and your crew,

[the caulkers of your seams, those who traded for your goods, all your warriors who were in you, and all the great crowd within you]

Sank into the heart of the sea
on the day of your shipwreck.
28 Hearing the shouts of your mariners,
the shores begin to quake.
29 Down from their ships
come all who ply the oar;
The sailors, all the mariners of the sea,
stand on the shore,
30 Making their voice heard on your behalf,
shouting bitter cries,
Strewing dust on their heads,
rolling in the ashes.
31 For you they shave their heads
and put on sackcloth,
For you they weep in anguish,
with bitter lament.
32 In their mourning they utter a lament over you;
thus they wail over you:
Who was ever destroyed like Tyre
in the midst of the sea?
33 With your goods which you drew from the seas
you filled many peoples;
With your great wealth and merchandise
you enriched the kings of the earth.

†

27, 5: *Senir:* another name for Mount Hermon; cf Dt 3, 9.
27, 6: *Bashan:* northern Transjordan, which, like Lebanon, was noted for its great forests. *Kittim:* probably Cyprus.
27, 7: *Elishah:* probably another term for Cyprus.
27, 8f: *Sidon . . . Arvad . . . Zemer . . . Gebal:* Phoenician cities in Tyre's orbit of influence; the last-named is the classical Byblos.

34 Now you are wrecked in the sea,
in the watery depths;
Your wares and all your crew
have gone down with you.
35 All who dwell on the coastlands
are aghast over you,
Their kings are terrified,
their faces convulsed.
36 The traders among the peoples
now hiss at you;
You have become a horror,
and you shall be no more.

CHAPTER 28

The Prince of Tyre. 1 Thus the word
of the LORD came to me: 2 Son of man,
say to the prince of Tyre: Thus says the
Lord GOD:

Because you are haughty of heart,
you say, "A god am I!
I occupy a godly throne
in the heart of the sea!"—
And yet you are a man, and not a
god,
however you may think yourself
like a god.
3† Oh yes, you are wiser than Daniel,
there is no secret that is beyond
you.
4 By your wisdom and your intelligence
you have made riches for yourself;
You have put gold and silver
into your treasuries.
5 By your great wisdom applied to
your trading
you have heaped up your riches;
your heart has grown haughty
from your riches—
6 therefore thus says the Lord
GOD:
Because you have thought yourself
to have the mind of a god,
7 Therefore I will bring against you
foreigners, the most barbarous of
nations.
They shall draw their swords
against your beauteous wisdom,
they shall run them through your
splendid apparel.
8 They shall thrust you down to the
pit, there to die
a bloodied corpse, in the heart of
the sea.
9 Will you then say, "I am a god!"
when you face your murderers?
No, you are a man, not a god,
handed over to those who will slay
you.
10 You shall die the death of the uncircumcised
at the hands of foreigners,
for I have spoken,
says the Lord GOD.

11 Thus the word of the LORD came to
me: 12† Son of man, utter a lament over
the king of Tyre, saying to him: Thus
says the Lord GOD:

You were stamped with the seal of
perfection,
of complete wisdom and perfect
beauty.
13 In Eden, the garden of God, you
were,
and every precious stone was your
covering
[carnelian, topaz, and beryl, chrysolite,
onyx, and jasper, sapphire, garnet, and
emerald];
Of gold your pendants and jewels
were made, on the day you were
created.
14† With the Cherub I placed you;
you were on the holy mountain of
God,
walking among the fiery stones.
15 Blameless you were in your conduct
from the day you were created,
Until evil was found in you,
16 the result of your far-flung trade;
violence was your business, and
you sinned.
Then I banned you from the mountain of God;
the Cherub drove you from among
the fiery stones.
17 You became haughty of heart because of your beauty;
for the sake of splendor you debased your wisdom.
I cast you to the earth, so great was
your guilt;
I made you a spectacle in the sight
of kings.
18 Because of your guilt, your sinful
trade,
I have profaned your sanctuaries,
And I have brought out fire from
your midst
which will devour you.
I have reduced you to dust on the
earth
in the sight of all who should see
you.
19 Among the peoples, all who knew
you
stand aghast at you;
You have become a horror,
you shall be no more.

Against Sidon. 20* Thus the word of
the LORD came to me: 21* Son of man,
look toward Sidon, and prophesy against

EZEKIEL

28, 20: Is 23, 1-18. 21: Jer 47, 4.

28, 3: *Wiser than Daniel:* see note on 14, 14.
28, 12-19: This picture of Tyre and its fall recalls images of the earthly paradise portraying the creation of man in perfection and his fall (Gn, chapters 2-3).
28, 14: *The holy mountain of God:* the residence of God was sometimes designated as a mountain; cf Is 14, 13. *The fiery stones:* associated with the divine presence; cf 1, 13; Ps 18, 13.

it: 22* Thus says the Lord GOD: See! I am coming at you, Sidon; I will be glorified in your midst. Then they shall know that I am the LORD, when I inflict punishments upon it and use it to manifest my holiness.

23 Into it I will send pestilence,
and blood shall flow in its streets.
Within it shall fall those slain
by the sword that comes against
it from every side.

Thus they shall know that I am the LORD. 24 Sidon shall no longer be a tearing thorn for the house of Israel, a brier that scratches them more than all the others about them who despise them; thus they shall know that I am the LORD.

25 Thus says the Lord GOD: When I gather the house of Israel from the peoples among whom they are scattered, then I will manifest my holiness through them in the sight of the nations. Then they shall live on their land which I gave to my servant Jacob; 26 they shall live on it in security, building houses and planting vineyards. They shall dwell secure while I inflict punishments on all their neighbors who despised them; thus they shall know that I, the LORD, am their God.

CHAPTER 29

Egypt the Crocodile. 1† On the twelfth day of the tenth month in the tenth year, the word of the LORD came to me: 2† Son of man, set your face against Pharaoh, king of Egypt, and prophesy against him and against all Egypt. 3† Say this to him: Thus says the Lord GOD:

See! I am coming at you, Pharaoh,
king of Egypt,
Great crouching monster
amidst your Niles:
Who say, "The Niles are mine;
it is I who made them!"

4 I will put hooks in your jaws and make the fish of your Niles stick to your scales, then draw you up from the midst of your Niles along with all the fish of your Niles sticking to your scales.

5 I will cast you into the desert,
you and all the fish of your Niles;
You shall fall upon the open field,
you shall not be taken up or buried;
To the beasts of the earth and the
birds of the air
I give you as food,
6* That all who dwell in Egypt may
know
that I am the LORD.
Because you have been a reed staff
for the house of Israel:
7 When they held you in hand, you
splintered,
throwing every shoulder out of
joint;
When they leaned on you, you broke,
bringing each one of them down
headlong;

8 therefore thus says the Lord GOD: See! I will bring the sword against you, and cut off from you both man and beast. 9 The land of Egypt shall become a desolate waste; thus they shall know that I am the LORD.

Because you said, "The Niles are mine; it is I who made them," 10† therefore see! I am coming at you and against your Niles; I will make the land of Egypt a waste and a desolation from Migdol to Syene, and even to the frontier of Ethiopia. 11 No foot of man or beast shall pass through it; they shall not pass through it, and it will be uninhabited for forty years. 12 I will make the land of Egypt the most desolate of lands, and its cities shall be the most deserted of cities for forty years; and I will scatter the Egyptians among the nations and strew them over foreign lands. 13 Yet thus says the Lord GOD: At the end of forty years I will gather the Egyptians from the peoples among whom they are scattered, 14† and I will restore Egypt's fortune, bringing them back to the land of Pathros, the land of their origin, where it will be the lowliest 15 of kingdoms, never more to set itself above the nations. I will make them few, that they may not dominate the nations. 16 No longer shall they be for the house of Israel to trust in, but the living reminder of its guilt for having turned to follow after them. Thus they shall know that I am the LORD.

The Wages of Nebuchadnezzar. 17† On the first day of the first month in the twenty-seventh year, the word of the LORD came to me: 18† Son of man, Nebuchadnezzar, the king of Babylon, has led

*

22: Jl 4, 4; Zec 9, 2ff. 29, 6: Is 36, 6.

†

29, 1: *The twelfth day of the tenth month in the tenth year:* January 7, 587 B.C. The siege of Jerusalem had begun a year earlier; cf 24, 1.

29, 2: Egypt was allied with Judah against the Chaldeans.

29. 3: *Niles:* the many rivulets of the Nile as it branches out into the Delta.

29, 10: *From Migdol to Syene:* from the northern to the southern extremity of Egypt. *Syene* is the modern Assuan.

29, 14: *Pathros, the land of their origin:* upper Egypt, that is, southern Egypt, where the Egyptians were thought to have originated; Is 11, 11; Jer 44, 1.15.

29, 17: *The first day of the first month in the twenty-seventh year:* April 26, 571 B.C. This is the latest date attached to any prophecy in Ezekiel.

29, 18f: The fulfillment of Ezekiel's prophecy against Tyre (chapters 26-28) was a thirteen-year siege of the city by Nebuchadnezzar (587-574 B.C.). Tyre seems to have been taken, but its resources were exhausted and the booty was small. Therefore Ezekiel now prophesies that Nebuchadnezzar will collect his *wages* as God's instrument in the punishment of Tyre, by plundering Egypt.

his army in an exhausting campaign
against Tyre. Their heads became bald
and their shoulders were galled; but nei-
ther he nor his army received any wages
from Tyre for the campaign he led
against it. [19]* Therefore thus says the
Lord GOD: I am now giving the land of
Egypt to Nebuchadnezzar, king of
Babylon. He shall carry off its riches,
plundering and pillaging it for the wages
of his soldiers, who did it for me; [20] as
payment for his toil I have given him
the land of Egypt, says the Lord GOD.
[21] On that day I will make a horn
sprout for the house of Israel, and I will
cause you to speak out in their midst;
thus they shall know that I am the LORD.

CHAPTER 30

The Day of the Lord against Egypt.
[1] Thus the word of the LORD came to me:
[2] Son of man, speak this prophecy: Thus
says the Lord GOD: Cry, Oh, the day!
[3] for near is the day, near is the day of
the LORD; a day of clouds, doomsday for
the nations shall it be. [4] Then a sword
shall come upon Egypt, and anguish
shall be in Ethiopia, when the slain fall
in Egypt, when her riches are seized and
her foundations are overthrown.
[5] Ethiopia, Put, Lud, all Arabia, Libya,
and people of the allied territory shall
fall by the sword with them. [6] Those who
support Egypt shall fall, and down shall
come her proud strength; from Migdol
to Syene they shall fall there by the
sword, says the Lord GOD. [7] She shall
be the most devastated of lands, and her
cities shall be the most desolate of all.
[8] Then they shall know that I am the
LORD, when I set fire to Egypt and when
all who help her are broken. [9] On that
day messengers shall hasten forth at my
command to terrify unsuspecting Ethio-
pia; they shall be in anguish on the day
of Egypt, which is surely coming.
[10] Thus says the Lord GOD: I will put
an end to the throngs of Egypt by the
hand of Nebuchadnezzar, king of Baby-
lon. [11] He and his people with him, the
most ruthless of nations, shall be
brought in to devastate the land. They
shall draw their swords against Egypt,
and fill the land with the slain. [12] I will
turn the Niles into dry land and sell the
land over to the power of the wicked.
The land and everything in it I will hand
over to foreigners to devastate. I, the
LORD, have spoken.
[13]* Thus says the Lord GOD: I will put
an end to the great ones of Memphis and
the princes of the land of Egypt, that
they may be no more. I will cast fear
into the land of Egypt, and devastate
Pathros. [14] I will set fire to Zoan, and in-
flict punishments on Thebes. [15] I will
pour out my wrath on Pelusium, Egypt's
stronghold, and cut down the crowds in
Memphis. [16] I will set fire to Egypt; Syene
shall writhe in anguish; Thebes shall be
breached and its walls shall be demol-
ished. [17] The young men of On and of
Pibeseth shall fall by the sword, and the
cities themselves shall go into captivity.
[18] In Tehaphnehes the day shall be dark-
ened when I break the scepter of Egypt.
Her haughty pride shall cease from her,
clouds shall cover her, and her daugh-
ters shall go into captivity. [19] Thus will
I inflict punishments on Egypt, that they
may know that I am the LORD.
Pharaoh's Broken Arm. [20]† On the
seventh day of the first month in the
eleventh year, the word of the LORD
came to me: [21]† Son of man, I have bro-
ken the arm of Pharaoh, the king of
Egypt, and see, it has not been bound
up with bandages and healing remedies
that it may be strong enough to hold the
sword. [22] Therefore thus says the Lord
GOD: See! I am coming at Pharaoh, the
king of Egypt. I will break his strong
arm, so that the sword drops from his
hand. [23] I will scatter the Egyptians
among the nations and strew them over
foreign lands. [24] But I will strengthen the
arms of the king of Babylon, and put my
sword in his hand, which he will bring
against Egypt so as to plunder and pil-
lage it. [25] [I will make the arms of the
king of Babylon strong, but the arms of
Pharaoh shall drop.] Then they shall
know that I am the LORD, when I put
my sword in the hand of the king of
Babylon for him to wield against the
land of Egypt. [26] [I will scatter the Egyp-
tians among the nations and strew them
over foreign lands.] Thus they shall
know that I am the LORD.

CHAPTER 31

Allegory of the Cypress. [1]† On the first
day of the third month in the eleventh
year, the word of the LORD came to me:
[2] Son of man, say to Pharaoh, the king
of Egypt, and to his hordes: What are
you like in your greatness?

[3] Behold, a cypress [cedar] in Leba-
non,

---

* 19: Jer 46, 2. 30, 13: Zec 13, 2.

---

† 30, 20: *The seventh day of the first month in the eleventh year:* April 29, 587 B.C.

30, 21-26: This oracle was uttered during the siege of Jerusalem, which had now lasted more than a year (24, 1). Pharaoh Hophra went to the aid of Jerusalem, causing the Chaldeans to lift the siege temporarily; cf Jer 34, 21; 37, 6f. In the prophet's eyes, this was interfering with the divine punishment of Judah that was to be inflicted by the Chaldeans. The Egyptians were routed by the Chaldeans, and were able to offer no more help to Jerusalem; cf chapter 31.

31, 1: *The first day of the third month in the eleventh year:* June 21, 587 B.C.

beautiful of branch, lofty of stature,
amid the very clouds lifted its crest.
4 Waters made it grow, the abyss made it flourish,
sending its rivers round where it was planted,
turning its streams to all the trees of the field.
5 Thus it grew taller than every other tree of the field,
and longer of branch because of the abundant water.
6 In its boughs nested all the birds of the air,
under its branches all beasts of the field gave birth,
in its shade dwelt numerous peoples of every race.
7 It became beautiful and stately in its spread of foliage,
for its roots were turned toward abundant water.
8 The cedars in the garden of God were not its equal,
nor could the fir trees match its boughs,
Neither were the plane trees like it for branches;
no tree in the garden of God matched its beauty.
9 I made it beautiful, with much foliage,
the envy of all Eden's trees in the garden of God.

10 Therefore thus says the Lord GOD: Because it became lofty in stature, raising its crest among the clouds, and because it became proud in heart at its height,
11 I have handed it over to the mightiest of the nations, which has dealt with it in keeping with its wickedness. I humiliated it.
12 Foreigners, the most ruthless of the nations, cut it down and left it on the mountains. Its foliage was brought low in all the valleys, its branches lay broken in all the ravines of the land, and all the peoples of the land withdrew from its shade, abandoning it.

13 On its fallen trunk rested all the birds of the air,
and by its branches were all the beasts of the field.

14 Thus no tree may grow lofty in stature or raise its crest among the clouds; no tree fed by water may stand by itself in its loftiness.

For all of them are destined for death,
for the land below,
For the company of mortals,
those who go down into the pit.

15 Thus says the Lord GOD: On the day
he went down to the nether world I made the abyss close up over him; I stopped its streams so that the deep waters were held back. I cast gloom over Lebanon because of him, so that all the trees in the land drooped on his account.
16 At the crash of his fall I made the nations rock, when I cast him down to the nether world with those who go down into the pit. In the land below, all Eden's trees were consoled, Lebanon's choice and best, all that were fed by water.
17 They too have come down with him to the nether world, to those slain by the sword; those who dwelt in his shade are dispersed among the nations.
18 Which was your equal in glory or size among the trees of Eden? Yet you have been brought down with the trees of Eden to the land below. You shall lie with the uncircumcised, with those slain by the sword. Such are Pharaoh and all his hordes, says the Lord GOD.

CHAPTER 32

Dirge over Pharaoh. 1† On the first day of the twelfth month in the twelfth year, the word of the LORD came to me:
2 Son of man, utter a lament over Pharaoh, the king of Egypt, saying to him: Lion of the nations, you are destroyed.

You were like a monster in the sea,
spouting in your streams,
Stirring the water with your feet
and churning its streams.

3* Thus says the Lord GOD:

I will spread my net over you
[with a host of many nations],
and draw you up in my seine.
4 I will leave you on the land;
on the open field I will cast you.
I will have all the birds of the air alight on you,
and all the beasts of the earth eat their fill of you.
5 I will leave your flesh on the mountains,
and fill the valleys with your carcass.
6 I will water the land with what flows from you,
and the river beds shall be filled with your blood.
7* When I snuff you out I will cover the heavens,
and all their stars I will darken;
The sun I will cover with clouds,

EZEKIEL

*

32, 3: 12, 13; 17, 20. 7: Is 13, 10; Jl 2, 10; 4, 15; Mt 24, 29.

†

32, 1: *The first day of the twelfth month in the twelfth year:* March 3, 585 B.C.

and the moon shall not give its
light.
8 All the shining lights in the heavens
I will darken on your account,
And I will spread darkness over
your land,
says the Lord GOD.

9 I will grieve the hearts of many peo-
ples when I lead you captive among the
nations, to lands which you do not know.
10 Many peoples shall be appalled at you,
and their kings shall shudder over you
in horror when they see me brandish my
sword, and on the day of your downfall
every one of them shall continuously
tremble for his own life. 11 For thus says
the Lord GOD: The sword of the king of
Babylon shall come upon you.

12 I will cut down your horde with the
blades of warriors,
all of them the most ruthless of the
nations;
They shall lay waste the glory of
Egypt,
and all her hordes shall be de-
stroyed.
13 I will have all of her animals perish
beside her abundant waters;
The foot of man shall stir them no
longer,
nor shall the hoof of beast disturb
them.
14 Then will I make their waters clear,
and their streams flow like oil,
says the Lord GOD.

15 When I turn Egypt into a waste, the
land shall be devastated of all that is in
it; when I strike all who live there, they
shall know that I am the LORD. 16 This
is a dirge, and it shall be sung: the
daughters of the nations shall chant it;
over Egypt and all its hordes shall they
chant it, says the Lord GOD.

Dirge over Egypt. 17 On the fifteenth
day of the first month in the twelfth year,
the word of the LORD came to me: 18 Son
of man, lament over the throngs of
Egypt, for the mighty nations have
thrust them down to the bottom of the
earth, with those who go down into the
pit. 20 In the midst of those slain by the
sword shall they fall, and place shall be
made with them for all their hordes.
Then from the midst of the nether world,
the mighty warriors shall speak to
Egypt: 19 "Whom do you excel in beauty?
21 Come down, you and your allies, lie
with the uncircumcised, with those slain
by the sword."

22 There is Assyria with all her com-
pany, all of them slain, 23 whose graves
have been made in the recesses of the
pit; her company is around Egypt's
grave, all of them slain, fallen by the
sword, who spread terror in the land of
the living. 24 There is Elam with all her
throng about Egypt's grave, all of them
slain, fallen by the sword: they have
gone down uncircumcised to the bottom
of the earth, who spread their terror in
the land of the living, and they bear their
disgrace with those who go down into
the pit; 25 in the midst of the slain they
are placed. 26 There are Meshech and
Tubal and all their throng about her
grave, all of them uncircumcised, slain
by the sword, for they spread their ter-
ror in the land of the living.

27† They do not lie with the mighty
men fallen of old, who went down to the
nether world with their weapons of war,
whose swords were placed under their
heads and whose shields were laid over
their bones, though the mighty men
caused terror in the land of the living.
28 But in the midst of the uncircumcised
shall you lie, with those slain by the
sword.

29 There are Edom, her kings, and all
her princes, who despite their might
have been placed with those slain by the
sword; with the uncircumcised they lie,
and with those who go down into the pit.
30 There are all the princes of the north
and all the Sidonians, who have gone
down with the slain, because of the ter-
ror their might inspired; they lie uncir-
cumcised with those slain by the sword
and bear their disgrace with those who
go down to the pit. 31 When Pharaoh sees
these, he shall be comforted for all his
hordes slain by the sword—Pharaoh and
all his army, says the Lord GOD. 32 Since
he spread his terror in the land of the
living, therefore is he laid to rest among
the uncircumcised, with those slain by
the sword—Pharaoh and all his hordes,
says the Lord GOD.

IV: SALVATION FOR ISRAEL

CHAPTER 33

The Prophet a Watchman. 1 Thus the
word of the LORD came to me: 2 Son of
man, speak thus to your countrymen:
When I bring the sword against a coun-
try, and the people of this country select
one of their number to be their watch-
man, 3 and the watchman, seeing the
sword coming against the country,
blows the trumpet to warn the people,
4 anyone hearing but not heeding the
warning of the trumpet and therefore
slain by the sword that comes against
him, shall be responsible for his own
death. 5 He heard the trumpet blast yet
refused to take warning; he is responsi-
ble for his own death, for had he taken
warning he would have escaped with his

---

† 32, 27: *The mighty men fallen of old:* the semilegendary heroes of the prehistoric past, who were thought to have once dominated the world; cf Is 14, 9.

life. 6 But if the watchman sees the sword coming and fails to blow the warning trumpet, so that the sword comes and takes anyone, I will hold the watchman responsible for that person's death, even though that person is taken because of his own sin.

7* You, son of man, I have appointed watchman for the house of Israel; when you hear me say anything, you shall warn them for me. 8 If I tell the wicked man that he shall surely die, and you do not speak out to dissuade the wicked man from his way, he [the wicked man] shall die for his guilt, but I will hold you responsible for his death. 9 But if you warn the wicked man, trying to turn him from his way, and he refuses to turn from his way, he shall die for his guilt, but you shall save yourself.

Individual Retribution. 10 As for you, son of man, speak to the house of Israel: You people say, "Our crimes and our sins weigh us down; we are rotting away because of them. How can we survive?" 11* Answer them: As I live, says the Lord GOD, I swear I take no pleasure in the death of the wicked man, but rather in the wicked man's conversion, that he may live. Turn, turn from your evil ways! Why should you die, O house of Israel?

12 As for you, son of man, tell your countrymen: The virtue which a man has practiced will not save him on the day that he sins; neither will the wickedness that a man has done bring about his downfall on the day that he turns from his wickedness [nor can the virtuous man, when he sins, remain alive]. 13 Though I say to the virtuous man that he shall surely live, if he then presumes on his virtue and does wrong, none of his virtuous deeds shall be remembered; because of the wrong he has done, he shall die. 14 And though I say to the wicked man that he shall surely die, if he turns away from his sin and does what is right and just, 15 giving back pledges, restoring stolen goods, living by the statutes that bring life, and doing no wrong, he shall surely live, he shall not die. 16 None of the sins he committed shall be held against him; he has done what is right and just, he shall surely live.

17 Yet your countrymen say, "The way of the LORD is not fair!"; but it is their way that is not fair. 18 When a virtuous man turns away from what is right and does wrong, he shall die for it. 19 But when a wicked man turns away from wickedness and does what is right and just, because of this he shall live. 20* And still you say, "The way of the LORD is not fair!"? I will judge every one of you according to his ways, O house of Israel.

The Fugitive from Jerusalem. 21† On the fifth day of the tenth month, in the twelfth year of our exile, the fugitive came to me from Jerusalem and said, "The city is taken!" 22 The hand of the LORD had come upon me the evening before the fugitive arrived, and he opened my mouth when the fugitive reached me in the morning. My mouth was opened, and I was dumb no longer.

The Survivors in Judah. 23† Thus the word of the LORD came to me: 24 Son of man, they who live in the ruins on the land of Israel reason thus: "Abraham, though but a single individual, received possession of the land; we, therefore, being many, have as permanent possession the land that has been given to us." 25 Give them this answer: Thus says the Lord GOD: You eat on the mountains, you raise your eyes to your idols, you shed blood—yet you would keep possession of the land? 26 You rely on your sword, you do abominable things, each one of you defiles his neighbor's wife—yet you would keep possession of the land? 27 Tell them this: Thus says the Lord GOD: As I live, those who are in the ruins I swear shall fall by the sword; those who are in the open field I have given to the wild beasts for food; and those who are in fastnesses and in caves shall die by the plague. 28 I will make the land a desolate waste, so that its proud strength will come to an end, and the mountains of Israel shall be so desolate that no one will cross them. 29 Thus they shall know that I am the LORD, when I make the land a desolate waste because of all abominable things they have done.

The Prophet's False Popularity. 30† As for you, son of man, your countrymen are talking about you along the walls and in the doorways of houses. They say to one another, "Come and hear the latest word that comes from the LORD." 31 My people come to you as people always do; they sit down before you and hear your words, but they will not obey them, for lies are on their lips and their desires are fixed on dishonest gain.

*

33, 7: 3, 17. 11: 18, 23-32. 20: 18, 25.

†

33, 21f: January 8, 585 B.C. According to Jeremiah (39, 2), Jerusalem was taken in July, 587. Some MSS read "eleventh" for *twelfth* year (January, 586); even so, there was ample time between the fall of Jerusalem and the arrival of the fugitive from that city to journey to Babylon. However, this is the fugitive sent to fulfill the promise of 24, 25.27, the eye witness who would release Ezekiel from his dumbness; cf 3, 26f.

33, 23-29: News brought by the fugitive furnished the occasion of this prophecy. Like Jeremiah, Ezekiel rejects the idea that the survivors in Judah have any claim to the land. The new Israel is to be formed from the exiles.

33, 30: The fulfillment of Ezekiel's prophecies about Jerusalem was responsible for this temporary enthusiasm among the unstable people.

32 For them you are only a ballad singer, with a pleasant voice and a clever touch. They listen to your words, but they will not obey them. 33 But when it comes—and it is surely coming!—they shall know that there was a prophet among them.

CHAPTER 34

Parable of the Shepherds. 1 Thus the word of the LORD came to me: 2*† Son of man, prophesy against the shepherds of Israel, in these words prophesy to them [to the shepherds]: Thus says the Lord GOD: Woe to the shepherds of Israel who have been pasturing themselves! Should not shepherds, rather, pasture sheep? 3 You have fed off their milk, worn their wool, and slaughtered the fatlings, but the sheep you have not pastured. 4 You did not strengthen the weak nor heal the sick nor bind up the injured. You did not bring back the strayed nor seek the lost, but you lorded it over them harshly and brutally. 5 So they were scattered for lack of a shepherd, and became food for all the wild beasts. My sheep were scattered 6 and wandered over all the mountains and high hills; my sheep were scattered over the whole earth, with no one to look after them or to search for them.

7 Therefore, shepherds, hear the word of the LORD: 8 As I live, says the Lord GOD, because my sheep have been given over to pillage, and because my sheep have become food for every wild beast, for lack of a shepherd; because my shepherds did not look after my sheep, but pastured themselves and did not pasture my sheep; 9 because of this, shepherds, hear the word of the LORD: 10 Thus says the Lord GOD: I swear I am coming against these shepherds. I will claim my sheep from them and put a stop to their shepherding my sheep so that they may no longer pasture themselves. I will save my sheep, that they may no longer be food for their mouths.

11 For thus says the Lord GOD: I myself will look after and tend my sheep. 12 As a shepherd tends his flock when he finds himself among his scattered sheep, so will I tend my sheep. I will rescue them from every place where they were scattered when it was cloudy and dark. 13 I will lead them out from among the peoples and gather them from the foreign lands; I will bring them back to their own country and pasture them upon the mountains of Israel [in the land's ravines and all its inhabited places]. 14 In good pastures will I pasture them, and on the mountain heights of Israel shall be their grazing ground. There they shall lie down on good grazing ground, and in rich pastures shall they be pastured on the mountains of Israel. 15 I myself will pasture my sheep; I myself will give them rest, says the Lord GOD. 16 The lost I will seek out, the strayed I will bring back, the injured I will bind up, the sick I will heal [but the sleek and the strong I will destroy], shepherding them rightly.

Separation of the Sheep. 17 As for you, my sheep, says the Lord GOD, I will judge between one sheep and another, between rams and goats. 18 Was it not enough for you to graze on the best pasture, that you had to trample the rest of your pastures with your feet? Was it not enough for you to drink the clearest water, that you had to foul the remainder with your feet? 19 Thus my sheep had to graze on what your feet had trampled and drink what your feet had fouled. 20 Therefore thus says the Lord GOD: Now will I judge between the fat and the lean sheep. 21 Because you push with side and shoulder, and butt all the weak sheep with your horns until you have driven them out, 22 I will save my sheep so that they may no longer be despoiled, and I will judge between one sheep and another. 23*† I will appoint one shepherd over them to pasture them, my servant David; he shall pasture them and be their shepherd. 24 I, the LORD, will be their God, and my servant David shall be prince among them. I, the LORD, have spoken.

25 I will make a covenant of peace with them, and rid the country of ravenous beasts, that they may dwell securely in the desert and sleep in the forests. 26 I will place them about my hill, sending rain in due season, rains that shall be a blessing to them. 27 The trees of the field shall bear their fruits, and the land its crops, and they shall dwell securely on their own soil. Thus they shall know that I am the LORD when I break the bonds of their yoke and free them from the power of those who enslaved them. 28 They shall no longer be despoiled by the nations or devoured by beasts of the earth, but shall dwell secure, with no one to frighten them. 29 I will prepare for them peaceful fields for planting; they shall no longer be carried off by famine in the land, or bear the reproaches of the nations. 30 Thus they shall know that I, the LORD, am their God, and they are my people, the house of Israel, says the Lord GOD. 31 [You, my sheep, you are the sheep of my pasture, and I am your God, says the Lord GOD.]

EZEKIEL

*

34, 2: 13, 3; Jer 23, 1. 23: Is 40, 21; Hos 3, 5; Jn 10, 11.14.

†

34, 2: *The shepherds of Israel:* the leaders of the people.
34, 23: *One shepherd. . . servant David:* a messianic Davidic King who will rule over the restored Israel (vv 25-31) in the name of the Lord.

CHAPTER 35

Against Edom. 1*† Thus the word of
the LORD came to me: 2 Son of man, set
your face against Mount Seir, and
prophesy against it. 3 Say to it: Thus says
the Lord GOD: See! I am coming at you,
Mount Seir. I will stretch out my hand
against you and make you a desolate
waste. 4 Your cities I will turn into ruins,
and you shall be a waste; thus you shall
know that I am the LORD.

5 Because you never let die your ha-
tred for the Israelites, whom you deliv-
ered over to the power of the sword at
the time of their trouble, when their
crimes came to an end, 6 therefore, as
I live, says the Lord GOD, you have been
guilty of blood, and blood, I swear, shall
pursue you. 7 I will make Mount Seir a
desolate waste, and cut off from it any
traveler. 8 With the slain I will fill your
hills, your valleys, and all your ravines
[in them the slain shall fall by the
sword]: 9 desolate will I make you for-
ever, and leave your cities without in-
habitants; thus you shall know that I am
the LORD.

10† Because you said: The two nations
and the two lands have become mine;
we shall possess them—although the
LORD was there—11 therefore, as I live,
says the Lord GOD, I will deal with you
according to your anger and your envy
which you have exercised [in your ha-
tred] against them. I will make myself
known among you when I judge you,
12 and you shall know that I am the
LORD.

I have heard all the contemptuous
things you have uttered against the
mountains of Israel: "They are desolate,
they have been given us to devour." 13 I
have heard the insolent and wild words
you have spoken against me. 14 Thus
says the Lord GOD: Just as you rejoiced
over my land because it was desolate,
so will I do to you. 15 In keeping with your
glee over the devastation of the inheri-
tance of the house of Israel, so will I treat
you. A waste shall you be, Mount Seir,
you and the whole of Edom. Thus they
shall know that I am the LORD.

CHAPTER 36

Regeneration of the Land. 1* As for
you, son of man, prophesy to the moun-
tains of Israel: Mountains of Israel, hear
the word of the LORD! 2 Thus says the
Lord GOD: Because the enemy has said
of you, "Ha! the everlasting heights have
become our possession" 3 [therefore
prophesy in these words: Thus says the
Lord GOD:]; because you have been ridi-
culed and despised on all sides for hav-
ing become a possession for the rest of
the nations, and have become a byword
and a popular jeer; 4 therefore, moun-
tains of Israel, hear the word of the
LORD: [Thus says the Lord GOD to the
mountains and hills, the ravines and
valleys, the desolate ruins and aban-
doned cities, which have been given over
to the pillage and mockery of the re-
maining nations round about; 5 therefore
thus says the Lord GOD:] Truly, with
burning jealousy I speak against the rest
of the nations [and against all of Edom]
who with wholehearted joy and utter
contempt have considered my land their
possession to be delivered over to plun-
der. 6 [Therefore, prophesy concerning
the land of Israel, and say to the moun-
tains and hills, the ravines and valleys:
Thus says the Lord GOD:] With jealous
fury I speak, because you have borne
the reproach of the nations. 7 Therefore
do I solemnly swear that your neighbor-
ing nations shall bear their own re-
proach.

8 As for you, mountains of Israel, you
shall grow branches and bear fruit for
my people Israel, for they shall soon re-
turn. 9 See, I come to you, it is to you
that I turn; you will be tilled and sown,
10 and I will settle crowds of men upon
you, the whole house of Israel; cities
shall be repeopled, and ruins rebuilt. 11 I
will settle crowds of men and beasts
upon you, to multiply and be fruitful. I
will repeople you as in the past, and be
more generous to you than in the begin-
ning; thus you shall know that I am the
LORD.

12 [My people Israel are the ones
whom I will have walk upon you; they
shall take possession of you, and you
shall be their heritage. Never again shall
you rob them of their children.]

13† Thus says the Lord GOD: Because
they have said of you, "You are a land
that devours men, and you rob your peo-
ple of their children"; 14 therefore, never
again shall you devour men or rob your
people of their children, says the Lord
GOD. 15 No more will I permit you to hear
the reproach of nations, or bear insults
from peoples, or rob your people of their
children, says the Lord GOD.

Regeneration of the People. 16 Thus
the word of the LORD came to me: 17 Son
of man, when the house of Israel lived
in their land, they defiled it by their

*

35, 1ff: 25, 12ff. 36, 1: 6, 3.

†

35, 1-15: After the fall of Jerusalem, Edom assisted the Chaldeans in devastating the land and subduing the population, and ended by occupying part of Judah's former territory. For this reason these oracles against Edom are found in the context of the city's fall.

35, 10: *The two nations and the two lands:* the superseded kingdoms of Israel and Judah and their territories.

36, 13: *A land that devours men:* destroys its own population, as could be seen in its disastrous political history.

conduct and deeds. In my sight their
conduct was like the defilement of
a menstruous woman. 18 Therefore I
poured out my fury upon them [because
of the blood which they poured out on
the ground, and because they defiled it
with idols]. 19 I scattered them among
the nations, dispersing them over for-
eign lands; according to their conduct
and deeds I judged them. 20* But when
they came among the nations [wherever
they came], they served to profane my
holy name, because it was said of them:
"These are the people of the LORD, yet
they had to leave their land." 21 So I have
relented because of my holy name which
the house of Israel profaned among the
nations where they came. 22 Therefore
say to the house of Israel: Thus says the
Lord GOD: Not for your sakes do I act,
house of Israel, but for the sake of my
holy name, which you profaned among
the nations to which you came. 23 I will
prove the holiness of my great name,
profaned among the nations, in whose
midst you have profaned it. Thus the na-
tions shall know that I am the LORD, says
the Lord GOD, when in their sight I prove
my holiness through you. 24 For I will
take you away from among the nations,
gather you from all the foreign lands,
and bring you back to your own land.
25* I will sprinkle clean water upon you
to cleanse you from all your impurities,
and from all your idols I will cleanse you.
26* I will give you a new heart and place
a new spirit within you, taking from your
bodies your stony hearts and giving you
natural hearts. 27* I will put my spirit
within you and make you live by my
statutes, careful to observe my decrees.
28 You shall live in the land I gave your
fathers; you shall be my people, and I
will be your God. 29 I will save you from
all your impurities; I will order the grain
to be abundant, and I will not send fam-
ine against you. 30 I will increase the fruit
on your trees and the crops in your
fields; thus you shall no longer bear
among the nations the reproach of fam-
ine. 31 Then you shall remember your
evil conduct, and that your deeds were
not good; you shall loathe yourselves for
your sins and your abominations. 32 Not
for your sakes do I act, says the Lord
GOD—let this be known to you! Be
ashamed and abashed because of your
conduct, O house of Israel.
33 Thus says the Lord GOD: When I pu-
rify you from all your crimes, I will re-
people the cities, and the ruins shall be
rebuilt; 34 the desolate land shall be
tilled, which was formerly a wasteland
exposed to the gaze of every passer-by.
35 "This desolate land has been made
into a garden of Eden," they shall say.
"The cities that were in ruins, laid waste,
and destroyed are now repeopled and
fortified." 36 Thus the neighboring na-
tions that remain shall know that I, the
LORD, have rebuilt what was destroyed
and replanted what was desolate. I, the
LORD, have promised, and I will do it.
37 Thus says the Lord GOD: This also
I will be persuaded to do for the house
of Israel: to multiply them like sheep.
38 As with sacrificial sheep, the sheep of
Jerusalem on its feast days, the cities
which were in ruins shall be filled with
flocks of men; thus they shall know that
I am the LORD.

CHAPTER 37

Vision of the Dry Bones. 1† The hand
of the LORD came upon me, and he led
me out in the spirit of the LORD and set
me in the center of the plain, which was
now filled with bones. 2 He made me
walk among them in every direction so
that I saw how many they were on the
surface of the plain. How dry they were!
3 He asked me: Son of man, can these
bones come to life? "Lord GOD," I an-
swered, "you alone know that." 4 Then
he said to me: Prophesy over these
bones, and say to them: Dry bones, hear
the word of the LORD! 5 Thus says the
Lord GOD to these bones: See! I will bring
spirit into you, that you may come to
life. 6 I will put sinews upon you, make
flesh grow over you, cover you with skin,
and put spirit in you so that you may
come to life and know that I am the
LORD. 7 I prophesied as I had been told,
and even as I was prophesying I heard
a noise; it was a rattling as the bones
came together, bone joining bone. 8 I saw
the sinews and the flesh come upon
them, and the skin cover them, but there
was no spirit in them. 9 Then he said to
me: Prophesy to the spirit, prophesy, son
of man, and say to the spirit: Thus says
the Lord GOD: From the four winds
come, O spirit, and breathe into these
slain that they may come to life. 10 I
prophesied as he told me, and the spirit
came into them; they came alive and
stood upright, a vast army. 11 Then he
said to me: Son of man, these bones are
the whole house of Israel. They have
been saying, "Our bones are dried up,
our hope is lost, and we are cut off."
12 Therefore, prophesy and say to them:
Thus says the Lord GOD: O my people,
I will open your graves and have you
rise from them, and bring you back to

---

* 20: Is 52, 5; Rom 2, 24.
25: Ps 51, 4; Zec 13, 1; Hb 10, 22; Jn 3, 5.
26: Jer 31, 33.
27: 37, 14; 39, 29; Is 42, 1; 44, 3; 59, 21; Hg 2, 5; Jl 3, 1f.

---

† 37, 1-14: This vision is a prediction of the restoration of Israel under the figure of a resurrection from the dead; it is not concerned with the doctrine of resurrection itself.

the land of Israel. 13 Then you shall know
that I am the LORD, when I open your
graves and have you rise from them, O
my people! 14 I will put my spirit in you
that you may live, and I will settle you
upon your land; thus you shall know that
I am the LORD. I have promised, and I
will do it, says the LORD.

The Two Sticks. 15† Thus the word of
the LORD came to me: 16 Now, son of
man, take a single stick, and write on
it: Judah and those Israelites who are
associated with him. Then take another
stick and write on it: Joseph [the stick
of Ephraim] and all the house of Israel
associated with him. 17 Then join the two
sticks together, so that they form one
stick in your hand. 18 When your coun-
trymen ask you, "Will you not tell us
what you mean by all this?", 19 answer
them: Thus says the Lord GOD: [I will
take the stick of Joseph, which is in the
hand of Ephraim, and of the tribes of
Israel associated with him, and I will join
to it the stick of Judah, making them a
single stick; they shall be one in my
hand. 20 The sticks on which you write
you shall hold up before them to see.
21 Tell them: Thus speaks the Lord GOD:]
I will take the Israelites from among the
nations to which they have come, and
gather them from all sides to bring them
back to their land. 22 I will make them
one nation upon the land, in the moun-
tains of Israel, and there shall be one
prince for them all. Never again shall
they be two nations, and never again
shall they be divided into two kingdoms.

23 No longer shall they defile them-
selves with their idols, their abomina-
tions, and all their transgressions. I will
deliver them from all their sins of apos-
tasy, and cleanse them so that they may
be my people and I may be their God.
24* My servant David shall be prince
over them, and there shall be one shep-
herd for them all; they shall live by my
statutes and carefully observe my de-
crees. 25 They shall live on the land
which I gave to my servant Jacob, the
land where their fathers lived; they shall
live on it forever, they, and their chil-
dren, and their children's children, with
my servant David their prince forever.
26* I will make with them a covenant of
peace; it shall be an everlasting cove-
nant with them, and I will multiply them,
and put my sanctuary among them for-
ever. 27 My dwelling shall be with them;
I will be their God, and they shall be my
people. 28 Thus the nations shall know
that it is I, the LORD, who make Israel
holy, when my sanctuary shall be set up
among them forever.

CHAPTER 38

First Prophecy against Gog. 1† Thus
the word of the LORD came to me:
2*† Son of man, turn toward Gog [the
land of Magog], the chief prince of
Meshech and Tubal, and prophesy
against him: 3 Thus says the Lord GOD:
See! I am coming at you, Gog, chief
prince of Meshech and Tubal. 4 I will
lead you forth with all your army, horses
and riders all handsomely outfitted, a
great horde with bucklers and shields,
all of them carrying swords: 5 Persia,
Cush, and Put with them [all with shields
and helmets], 6 Gomer with all its troops,
Beth-togarmah from the recesses of the
north with all its troops, many peoples
with you. 7 Prepare yourself, be ready,
you and all your horde assembled about
you, and be at my disposal. 8 After many
days you will be mustered [in the last
years you will come] against a nation
which has survived the sword, which has
been assembled from many peoples [on
the mountains of Israel which were long
a ruin], which has been brought forth
from among the peoples and all of whom
now dwell in security. 9 You shall come
up like a sudden storm, advancing like
a cloud to cover the earth, you and all
your troops and the many peoples with
you.

10 Thus says the Lord GOD: At that
time thoughts shall arise in your mind,
and you shall devise an evil scheme: 11 "I
will go up against a land of open villages
and attack the peaceful people who are
living in security, all of them living with-
out walls, having neither bars nor gates,
12† to plunder and pillage, turning my
hand against the ruins that were repeo-
pled and against a people gathered from
the nations, a people concerned with
cattle and goods, who dwell at the navel
of the earth." 13 Sheba and Dedan, the
merchants of Tarshish and all her young
lions shall ask you: "Is it for plunder that
you have come? Is it for pillage that you
have summoned your horde, to carry off

*

37, 24: 34, 23; Jer 23, 5; 33, 15.
26: Ps 110, 4.
38, 2: Rv 20, 7f.

†

37, 15-22: The symbolic action of joining two sticks into one signifies the future union of Israel and Judah under one messianic King.

38, 1—39, 20: These three oracles against Gog may refer either to a specific foreign invasion in the future, or to the apocalyptic struggle between good and evil at the end of time. By some they are ascribed to a later author than Ezekiel, who lived after the exile and the return to Palestine.

38, 2: *Gog:* the name is almost certainly a symbolic one taken from that of Gyges, king of Lydia, whether or not the prophet has a specific person in mind. The gloss *Magog* may be an Akkadian expression, *mat-Gog,* "the land of Gog." *Meshech and Tubal,* as well as *Gomer and Beth-togarmah* (v 6), were countries around the Black Sea, the northernmost countries known to the Hebrews: *the north* (cf also v 15) was the traditional direction from which invasion was expected; cf Jer 1, 13ff.

38, 12: *Who dwell at the navel of the earth:* the people of Israel (cf v 18; also 5, 5). Many ancient peoples spoke of their own homelands as "the navel," that is, the center of the earth.

silver and gold, to take away cattle and
goods, to seize much plunder?"
17 Thus says the Lord GOD: It is of you
that I spoke in ancient times through my
servants, the prophets of Israel, who
prophesied in those days that I would
bring you against them. 18 But on that
day, the day when Gog invades the land
of Israel, says the Lord GOD, my fury
shall be aroused. In my anger 19 and in
my jealousy, in my fiery wrath, I swear:
On that day there shall be a great shak-
ing upon the land of Israel. 20 Before me
shall tremble the fish of the sea and the
birds of the air, the beasts of the field
and all the reptiles that crawl upon the
ground, and all men who are on the land.
Mountains shall be overturned, and
cliffs shall tumble, and every wall shall
fall to the ground. 21 Against him I will
summon every terror, says the Lord
GOD, every man's sword against his
brother. I will hold judgment with him
in pestilence and bloodshed; 22 flooding
rain and hailstones, fire and brimstone,
I will rain upon him, upon his troops,
and upon the many peoples with him.
23 I will prove my greatness and holiness
and make myself known in the sight of
many nations; thus they shall know that
I am the LORD.

Second Prophecy against Gog.
14 Therefore prophesy, son of man, and
say to Gog: Thus says the Lord GOD:
When my people Israel are dwelling in
security, will you not bestir yourself
15 and come from your home in the re-
cesses of the north, you and many peo-
ples with you, all mounted on horses, a
great horde and a mighty army? 16 You
shall come up against my people Israel
like a cloud covering the land. In the last
days I will bring you against my land,
that the nations may know of me, when
in their sight I prove my holiness
through you, O Gog.

CHAPTER 39

Third Prophecy against Gog. 1 Now,
son of man, prophesy against Gog in
these words: Thus says the Lord GOD:
See! I am coming at you, Gog, chief
prince of Meshech and Tubal. 2 I will
turn you about, I will urge you on, and
I will make you come up from the re-
cesses of the north; I will lead you
against the mountains of Israel. 3 Then
I will strike the bow from your left hand,
and make the arrows drop from your
right. 4 Upon the mountains of Israel you
shall fall, you and all your troops and
the peoples who are with you. To birds
of prey of every kind and to the wild
beasts I am giving you to be eaten. 5 On
the open field you shall fall, for I have
decreed it, says the Lord GOD.
6 I will send fire upon Magog and upon
those who live securely in the coast-
lands; thus they shall know that I am
the LORD. 7 I will make my holy name
known among my people Israel; I will
no longer allow my holy name to be pro-
faned. Thus the nations shall know that
I am the LORD, the Holy One in Israel.
8 Yes, it is coming and shall be fulfilled,
says the Lord GOD. This is the day I have
decreed.
9 Then shall those who live in the cities
of Israel go out and burn weapons:
[shields and bucklers,] bows and ar-
rows, clubs and lances; for seven years
they shall make fires with them. 10 They
shall not have to bring in wood from the
fields or cut it down in the forests, for
they shall make fires with the weapons.
Thus they shall plunder those who plun-
dered them and pillage those who pil-
laged them, says the Lord GOD.
11† On that day I will give Gog for his
tomb a well-known place in Israel, the
Valley of Abarim east of the sea [it is
blocked to travelers]. Gog shall be bur-
ied there with all his horde, and it shall
be named "Valley of Hamon-gog." 12 To
purify the land, the house of Israel shall
need seven months to bury them. 13 All
the people of the land shall bury them
and gain renown for it, when I reveal
my glory, says the Lord GOD. 14 Men
shall be permanently employed to pass
through the land burying those who lie
unburied, so as to purify the land. For
seven months they shall keep searching.
15 When they pass through, should they
see a human bone, let them put up a
marker beside it, until others have bur-
ied it in the Valley of Hamon-gog.
16 [Also the name of the city shall be Ha-
monah.] Thus the land shall be purified.
17 As for you, son of man, says the Lord
GOD, say to birds of every kind and to
all the wild beasts: Come together, from
all sides gather for the slaughter I am
about to provide for you, a great slaugh-
ter on the mountains of Israel: you shall
have flesh to eat and blood to drink.
18 You shall eat the flesh of warriors and
drink the blood of the princes of the land
[rams, lambs, and goats, bullocks, fat-
lings of Bashan, all of them]. 19 From the
slaughter which I will provide for you,
you shall eat fat until you are filled and
drink blood until you are drunk. 20 You
shall be filled at my table with horses
and riders, with warriors and soldiers
of every kind, says the Lord GOD.
Israel's Return. 21 Thus I will display
my glory among the nations, and all the
nations shall see the judgment I have
executed and the hand I have laid upon
them. 22 From that day forward the

---

† 39, 11: *The Valley of Abarim:* in the Abarim mountains, east of the Jordan. *Hamon-gog:* means "the horde of Gog."

house of Israel shall know that I am the
LORD, their God. 23 The nations shall
know that because of its sins the house
of Israel went into exile; for they trans-
gressed against me, and I hid my face
from them and handed them over to
their foes, so that all of them fell by the
sword. 24 According to their uncleanness
and their transgressions I dealt with
them, hiding my face from them.
25 Therefore, thus says the Lord GOD:
Now I will restore the fortunes of Jacob
and have pity on the whole house of Is-
rael, and I will be jealous for my holy
name. 26 They shall forget their disgrace
and all the times they broke faith with
me, when they live in security on their
land with no one to frighten them.
27 When I bring them back from among
the peoples, I will gather them from the
lands of their enemies, and will prove
my holiness through them in the sight
of many nations. 28* Thus they shall
know that I, the LORD, am their God,
since I who exiled them among the na-
tions, will gather them back on their
land, not leaving any of them behind.
29 No longer will I hide my face from
them, for I have poured out my spirit
upon the house of Israel, says the Lord
GOD.

V: THE NEW ISRAEL

The New Temple

CHAPTER 40

The Man with a Measure. 1† On the
tenth day of the month beginning the
twenty-fifth year of our exile, fourteen
years after the city was taken, that very
day the hand of the LORD came upon
me and brought me 2 in divine visions
to the land of Israel, where he set me
down on a very high mountain. On it
there seemed to be a city being built be-
fore me. 3 When he had brought me
there, all at once I saw a man whose ap-
pearance was that of bronze; he was
standing in the gate, holding a linen cord
and a measuring rod. 4 The man said to
me, "Son of man, look carefully and lis-
ten intently, and pay strict attention to
all that I will show you, for you have
been brought here so that I might show
it to you. Tell the house of Israel all that
you see." 5† [Then I saw an outer wall
that completely surrounded the temple.
The man was holding a measuring rod
six cubits long, each cubit being a cubit
and a handbreadth; he measured the
width and the height of the structure,
each of which were found to be one rod.]
The East Gate. 6† Then he went to the
gate which faced the east, climbed its
steps, and measured the gate's thresh-
old, which was found to be a rod wide.
7 The cells were a rod long and a rod
wide, and the pilasters between the cells
measured five cubits. The threshold of
the gate adjoining the vestibule of the
gate toward the inside measured one
rod. 8 He measured the vestibule of the
gate, 9 which was eight cubits, and its pi-
lasters, which were two cubits. The ves-
tibule of the gate was toward the inside.
10 The cells of the east gate were three
on either side, of equal size, and the pi-
lasters on either side were also of equal
size. 11 He measured the gate's entrance,
which was ten cubits wide, while the
width of the gate's passage itself was
thirteen cubits. 12 The border before
each of the cells on both sides was one
cubit; the cells themselves were six cu-
bits on either side, from opening to open-
ing. 13 He measured the gate from the
back wall of one cell to the back wall
of the cell on the opposite side: the width
was twenty-five cubits. 14 He measured
the vestibule, which was twenty-five cu-
bits. The pilasters adjoining the court on
either side were six cubits. 15 The length
of the gate from the front entrance to
the front of the vestibule on the inside
was fifty cubits. 16 Within the gateway
on both sides there were splayed win-
dows let into the cells [and into their pi-
lasters]; likewise, within the vestibule on
both sides there were windows. The pi-
lasters were decorated with palms.
The Outer Court. 17† Then he brought
me to the outer court, where there were
chambers and a pavement. The pave-
ment was laid all around the court, and
the chambers, which were on the pave-
ment, were thirty in number. 18 The
pavement lay alongside the gates, as
wide as the gates were long; this was the
lower pavement. 19 He measured the
width of the court from the front of the
lower gate to the front of the inner gate;
it was one hundred cubits between them.
The North Gate. Then he proceeded

*

39, 28: 36, 23.

†

40, 1—48, 35: This lengthy vision of the new Israel is dated (40, 1) April 28, 573 B.C. It is largely concerned with the new temple and the prescriptions to govern it, but other details of the restored commonwealth are included, forming a kind of program for the future. The literary form of the vision has been aptly termed "utopian": it is plain that the prophet did not expect a literal fulfillment of much of what he described. The passage doubtless underwent successive additions, both from the prophet and from later inspired writers.

40, 5: *A cubit and a handbreadth:* the ordinary cubit consisted of six handbreadths; the great cubit, of seven. In measuring the temple, a rod six great cubits long was used. The ordinary cubit was about one and a half feet, or, more exactly, 17.5 inches; the large cubit, 20.4 inches.

40, 6-16: The east gate, leading into the outer court of the temple, is described more fully than the north and south gates, which, however, were of the same dimensions. On the west side of the outer court there was a large building instead of a gate (41, 12).

40, 17: *The outer court:* the court outside the temple area proper, which had its own inner court (vv 28-37).

north, [20] where, on the outer court, there was a gate facing north, whose length and width he measured. [21] Its cells, three on either side, its pilasters, and its vestibule had the same measurements as those of the first gate; it was fifty cubits long and twenty-five cubits wide. [22] Its windows, the windows of its vestibule, and its palm decorations were of the same proportions as those of the gate facing the east. Seven steps led up to it, and its vestibule was toward the inside. [23] The inner court had a gate opposite the north gate, just as at the east gate; he measured one hundred cubits from one gate to the other.

The South Gate. [24] Then he led me south, to where there was a southern gate, whose cells, pilasters, and vestibule he measured; they were the same size as the others. [25] The gate and its vestibule had windows on both sides, like the other windows. It was fifty cubits long and twenty-five cubits wide. [26] It was ascended by seven steps; its vestibule was toward the inside; and it was decorated with palms here and there on its pilasters. [27] The inner court also had a southern gate; from gate to gate he measured one hundred cubits.

Gates of the Inner Court. [28]† Then he brought me to the inner court by the south gate, where he measured the south gate. Its dimensions were the same as the others; [29] its cells, its pilasters, and its vestibule were the same size as the others. The gate and its vestibule had windows on both sides; and it was fifty cubits long and twenty-five cubits wide. [31] But its vestibule was toward the outer court; palms were on its pilasters, and it had a stairway of eight steps. [32] Then he brought me to the gate facing the east, where he measured the gate, whose dimensions were found to be the same. [33] Its cells, its pilasters, and its vestibule were the same size as the others; the gate and its vestibule had windows on both sides; it was fifty cubits long and twenty-five cubits wide. [34] But its vestibule was toward the outer court; palms were on its pilasters here and there, and it had a stairway of eight steps. [35] Then he brought me to the north gate, where he measured the dimensions [36] of its cells, its pilasters, and its vestibule, and found them the same. The gate and its vestibule had windows on both sides; it was fifty cubits long and twenty-five cubits wide. [37] Its vestibule was toward the outer court; palms were on its pilasters here and there, and it had a stairway of eight steps.

Side Rooms. [38] There was a chamber opening off the vestibule of the gate, where the holocausts were rinsed. [39] In the vestibule of the gate there were two tables on either side, on which were slaughtered the sin offerings and guilt offerings. [40] Along the wall of the vestibule, but outside, near the entrance of the north gate, were two tables, and on the other side of the vestibule of the gate there were two tables. [41] There were four tables on either side of the gate [eight tables], on which the sacrifices were slaughtered. [42] There were four tables for holocausts, made of cut stone, one and a half cubits long, one and a half cubits wide, and one cubit high. [43] The ledges, a handbreadth wide, were set on the inside all around, and on them were laid the instruments with which the holocausts were slaughtered. On the tables themselves the flesh was laid. [44] He then led me to the inner court where there were two chambers, one beside the north gate, facing south, and the other beside the south gate, facing north. [45] He said to me, "This chamber which faces south is for the priests who have charge of the temple, [46]† and the chamber which faces north is for the priests who have charge of the altar. These are the Zadokites, the only Levites who may come near to minister to the LORD." [47] Then he measured the court, which was a hundred cubits long and a hundred cubits wide, a perfect square. The altar stood in front of the temple.

The Temple Building. [48]† Then he brought me into the vestibule of the temple and measured the pilasters on each side, which were five cubits. The width of the doorway was fourteen cubits, and the side walls on either side of the door measured three cubits. [49]† The vestibule was twenty cubits wide and twelve cubits deep; ten steps led up to it, and there were columns by the pilasters, one on either side.

CHAPTER 41

[1] Then he brought me to the nave and measured the pilasters, which were six cubits thick on either side. [2] The width of the entrance was ten cubits, and the walls at either side of it measured five cubits each. He measured the length of the nave, which was found to be forty cubits, while its width was twenty.

[3] Then he went in beyond and measured the pilasters flanking that en-

†

40, 28-37: The gates leading into the inner court of the temple area correspond to the gates leading into the outer court, with the exception that their vestibules are on the outer rather than the inner side. (Verse 30, a dittography of v 29, is omitted.)

40, 46: *The Zadokites:* descendants of the priestly line of Zadok; cf 2 Sm 15, 24-29; 1 Kgs 1, 32ff; 2, 35.

40, 48—41, 15: The description of Ezekiel's visionary temple closely follows the description of the temple of Solomon (1 Kgs 6).

40, 49—41, 4: *Vestibule . . . nave . . . holy of holies:* the three divisions of the temple building in progressing order of sanctity. The last is called "the inner sanctuary" in 1 Kgs 6.

trance, which were two cubits; the width
of the entrance was six cubits, and the
walls at either side of it extended seven
cubits each. 4 He measured the space be-
yond the nave, twenty cubits long and
twenty cubits wide, and said to me, "This
is the holy of holies."
5 Then he measured the wall of the
temple, which was six cubits thick; the
side chambers, which extended all the
way around the temple, had a width of
four cubits. 6 There were thirty side
chambers built one above the other in
three stories, and there were offsets in
the outside wall of the temple that en-
closed the side chambers; these served
as supports, so that there were no sup-
ports in the temple wall proper. 7 There
was a broad circular passageway that
led upward to the side chambers, for the
temple was enclosed all the way around
and all the way upward; therefore the
temple had a broad way running up-
ward so that one could pass from the
lowest to the middle and the highest
story. 8 About the temple was a raised
pavement completely enclosing it—the
foundations of the side chambers—a full
rod of six cubits in extent. 9 The width
of the outside wall which enclosed the
side chambers was five cubits. Between
the side chambers of the temple 10 and
the chambers of the court was an open
space twenty cubits wide going all
around the temple. 11 The side chambers
had entrances to the open space, one en-
trance on the north and another on the
south. The width of the wall surrounding
the open space was five cubits. 12† The
building fronting the free area on the
west side was seventy cubits front to
back; the wall of the building was five
cubits thick all around, and it measured
ninety cubits from side to side. 13 He
measured the temple, which was one
hundred cubits long. The free area, to-
gether with the building and its walls,
was a hundred cubits in length. 14 The
façade of the temple, along with the free
area, on the east side, was one hundred
cubits wide. 15 He measured the building
which lay the length of the free area and
behind it, and together with its walls on
both sides it was one hundred cubits.
Interior of the Temple. The inner nave
and the outer vestibule 16 were paneled
with precious wood all around, covered
from the ground to the windows. There
were splayed windows with trellises
about them [facing the threshold]. 17 As
high as the lintel of the door, even into
the interior part of the temple as well
as outside, on every wall on every side
in both the inner and outer rooms were
carved 18 the figures of cherubim and
palmtrees: a palmtree between every
two cherubim. Each cherub had two
faces: 19 a man's face looking at a palm-
tree on one side, and a lion's face looking
at a palmtree on the other; thus they
were figured on every side throughout
the whole temple. 20 From the ground to
the lintel of the door the cherubim and
palmtrees were carved on the walls.
21 The way into the nave was a square
doorframe. In front of the holy place was
something that looked like 22† a wooden
altar, three cubits in height, two cubits
long, and two cubits wide. It had corners,
and its base and sides were of wood. He
said to me, "This is the table which is
before the LORD." 23 The nave had a dou-
ble door, and also the holy place had 24 a
double door. Each door had two mov-
able leaves; two leaves were on one
doorjamb and two on the other.
25 Carved upon them [on the doors of the
nave] were cherubim and palmtrees,
like those carved on the walls. Before
the vestibule outside was a wooden lat-
tice. 26 There were splayed windows
[and palmtrees] on both side walls of the
vestibule, and the side chambers of the
temple. . . .

CHAPTER 42

Other Structures. 1 Then he led me
north to the outer court, bringing me to
some chambers on the north that lay
across the free area and which were also
across from the building. 2 Their length
was a hundred cubits on the north side,
and they were fifty cubits wide. 3 Across
the twenty cubits of the inner court and
the pavement of the outer court, there
were three parallel rows of them on dif-
ferent levels. 4 In front of the chambers,
to the inside, was a walk ten cubits broad
and a wall of one cubit; but the entrances
of the chambers were on the north.
5† The outermost chambers were the
lowest, for the system of levels set them
at a level lower than the closest cham-
bers and those in between; 6 for they
were in three rows and had no founda-
tions to conform with the foundations of
the courts, therefore they were on a
lower terrace of the ground than the
closest and the middle chambers. 7 On
the far side there was a wall running
parallel to the chambers along the outer
court; its length before these chambers
was fifty cubits, 8 for the length of the
chambers belonging to the outer court
was fifty cubits, but along its entire
length the wall measured one hundred
cubits. 9 Below these chambers there
was the way in from the east, so that

†

41, 12: *The building:* the function of this structure lying behind the temple is never specified.

41, 22: *A wooden altar:* the altar of incense, standing in the nave at the entrance to the holy of holies.

42, 5f: The three rows of identical chambers, since they rested on different ground levels, necessarily had roofs on correspondingly different levels.

one could enter from the outer court 10 where the wall of the court began.

To the south along the side of the free area and the building there were also chambers, 11 before which was a passage. These looked like the chambers to the north, just as long and just as wide, with the same exits and plan and entrances. 12 Below the chambers to the south there was an entrance at the beginning of the way which led to the back wall, by which one could enter from the east. 13† He said to me, "The north and south chambers which border on the free area are the sanctuary chambers; here the priests who draw near to the LORD shall eat the most sacred meals, and here they shall keep the most sacred offerings: cereal offerings, sin offerings, and guilt offerings; for it is a holy place. 14 When the priests have once entered, they shall not leave the holy place for the outer court until they have left here the clothing in which they ministered, for it is holy. They shall put on other garments, and then approach the place destined for the people."

Measuring the Outer Court. 15 When he had finished measuring the inner temple area, he brought me out by way of the gate which faces east and measured all the limits of the court. 16 He measured the east side: five hundred cubits by his measuring rod. Then he turned 17 and measured the north side: five hundred cubits by the measuring rod. He turned 18 to the south and measured five hundred cubits by the measuring rod. 19 Then he turned to the west and measured five hundred cubits by the measuring rod. 20 Thus he measured it in the four directions, five hundred cubits long and five hundred cubits wide. It was surrounded by a wall, to separate the sacred from the profane.

Restoration of the Temple

CHAPTER 43

The Return of the Lord. 1 Then he led me to the gate which faces the east, 2 and there I saw the glory of the God of Israel coming from the east. I heard a sound like the roaring of many waters, and the earth shone with his glory. 3* The vision was like that which I had seen when he came to destroy the city, and like that which I had seen by the river Chebar. I fell prone 4 as the glory of the LORD entered the temple by way of the gate which faces the east, 5 but spirit lifted me up and brought me to the inner court. And I saw that the temple was filled with the glory of the LORD. 6 Then I heard someone speaking to me from the temple, while the man stood beside me. 7 The voice said to me: Son of man, this is where my throne shall be, this is where I will set the soles of my feet; here I will dwell among the Israelites forever. Never again shall they and their kings profane my holy name with their harlotries and with the corpses of their kings [their high places]. 8† When they placed their threshold against my threshold and their doorpost next to mine, so that only a wall was between us, they profaned my holy name by their abominable deeds; therefore I consumed them in my wrath. 9 From now on they shall put far from me their harlotry and the corpses of their kings, and I will dwell in their midst forever.

The Law of the Temple. 10 As for you, son of man, describe the temple to the house of Israel [that they may be ashamed of their sins], both its measurements and its design; 11 [and if they are ashamed of all that they have done,] make known to them the form and design of the temple, its exits and entrances, all its statutes and laws; write these down for them to see, that they may carefully observe all its laws and statutes. 12 This is the law of the temple: its whole surrounding area on the mountain top shall be most sacred.

The Altar. 13† These were the measurements of the altar in cubits of one cubit plus a handbreadth. Its base was one cubit high and one cubit deep, with a rim around its edges of one span. The height of the altar itself was as follows: 14 from its base at the bottom up to the lower edge it was two cubits high, and this ledge was one cubit deep; from the lower to the upper ledge it was four cubits high, and this ledge also was one cubit deep; 15 the hearth of the altar was four cubits high, and extending from the top of the hearth were the four horns of the altar. 16 The hearth was a square: twelve cubits long and twelve cubits wide. 17 The upper ledge was also a square: fourteen cubits long and fourteen cubits wide. The lower ledge, likewise a square, was sixteen cubits long and sixteen cubits wide, with a half-cubit rim surrounding it. And there was a base of one cubit all around. The steps of the altar face the east.

18 Then he said to me: Son of man, thus

---

* 43, 3: 1, 1.

---

† 42, 13: The function of these chambers is explained again in 46, 19f.

43, 8: *They placed their threshold against my threshold:* the preexilic temple and the royal palace belonged to the same complex of buildings, and this physical proximity was reflected in the use made of the temple by kings like Ahaz and Manasseh, who treated it as their private chapel for pagan rites. In the new Israel the temple is free, even physically, from civil jurisdiction; cf 45, 7f.

43, 13: *The altar:* of holocausts, standing in the inner court of the temple area; cf 40, 47.

says the Lord GOD: These are the statutes for the altar when it is set up for the offering of holocausts upon it and for the sprinkling of blood against it. [19] Give a young bull as a sin offering to the priests, the Levites who are of the line of Zadok, who draw near me to minister to me, says the Lord GOD. [20] Take some of its blood and put it on the four horns of the altar, and on the four corners of the ledge, and on the rim all around. Thus you shall purify it and make atonement for it. [21] Then take the bull of the sin offering, which is to be burnt in a designated part of the temple, outside the sanctuary. [22] On the second day present an unblemished he-goat as a sin offering, to purify the altar as was done with the bull. [23] When you have finished the purification, bring an unblemished young bull and an unblemished ram from the flock, [24] and present them before the LORD; the priests shall strew salt on them and offer them to the LORD as holocausts. [25] Daily for seven days you shall offer a he-goat as a sin offering, and a young bull and a ram from the flock, all unblemished, shall be offered [26] for seven days. Thus atonement shall be made for the altar, and it shall be purified and dedicated. [27] And when these days are over, from the eighth day on, the priests shall offer your holocausts and peace offerings on the altar. Then I will accept you, says the Lord GOD.

CHAPTER 44

The Closed Gate. [1] Then he brought me back to the outer gate of the sanctuary, facing the east; but it was closed. [2] He said to me: This gate is to remain closed; it is not to be opened for anyone to enter by it; since the LORD, the God of Israel, has entered by it, it shall remain closed. [3]† Only the prince may sit down in it to eat his meal in the presence of the LORD. He must enter by way of the vestibule of the gate, and leave by the same way.

The New Law

Admission to the Temple. [4] Then he brought me by way of the north gate to the façade of the temple, and when I looked I saw the glory of the LORD filling the LORD's temple, and I fell prone. [5] Then he said to me: Son of man, pay strict attention, look carefully, and listen intently to all that I will tell you about the statutes and laws of the LORD's temple; be attentive in regard to those who are to be admitted to the temple and all those who are to be excluded from the sanctuary. [6] Say to that rebellious house, the house of Israel: Thus says the Lord GOD: Enough of all these abominations of yours, O house of Israel! [7]† You have admitted foreigners, uncircumcised both in heart and flesh, to my sanctuary to profane it when you offered me food, fat, and blood; thus you have broken my covenant by all your abominations. [8] Instead of caring for the service of my temple, you have appointed such as these to serve me in my sanctuary in your stead. [9] Thus says the Lord GOD: No foreigners, uncircumcised in heart and in flesh, shall ever enter my sanctuary; none of the foreigners who live among the Israelites.

Levites. [10]† But as for the Levites who departed from me when Israel strayed from me to pursue their idols, they shall bear the consequences of their sin. [11] They shall serve in my sanctuary as gatekeepers and temple servants; they shall slaughter the holocausts and the sacrifices for the people, and they shall stand before the people to minister for them. [12] Because they used to minister for them before their idols, and became an occasion of sin to the house of Israel, therefore I have sworn an oath against them, says the Lord GOD: they shall bear the consequences of their sin. [13] They shall no longer draw near me to serve as my priests, nor shall they touch any of my sacred things, or the most sacred things. Thus they shall bear their disgrace because of all their abominable deeds. [14] But I will set them to the service of the temple, for all its work and for everything that is to be done in it.

Priests. [15] As for the levitical priests, however, the Zadokites who cared for my sanctuary when the Israelites strayed from me, they shall draw near me to minister to me, and they shall stand before me to offer me fat and blood, says the Lord GOD. [16] It is they who shall enter my sanctuary, they who shall approach my table to minister to me, and they who shall carry out my service. [17] Whenever they enter the gates of the inner court, they shall wear linen garments; they shall not put on anything woolen when they minister at the gates of the inner court or within the

EZEKIEL

†

44, 3: The prince stands at the eastern gate of the inner court while his sacrifice is offered up (46, 2); he then goes to the vestibule of the outer court, there to partake of his sacrificial meal. The closed outer gate on the eastern side signifies that the Lord has entered the temple permanently, not to depart again.

44, 7ff: In the preexilic temple various menial services had been performed by foreigners; cf Jos 9, 22-27. In the new temple the Levites will perform these services (vv 10-14).

44, 10-14: Levites other than the Zadokite priesthood of Jerusalem had performed priestly functions at the various sanctuaries and high places in Israel and Judah, where the worship of the Lord had often been corrupted with pagan elements. The demotion of the Levites to menial service in the temple was enforced in the actual restoration after the exile, and explains why relatively few Levites were willing to return; cf Ezr 8, 15ff.

temple. [18]* They shall have linen turbans on their heads and linen drawers on their loins; they shall not gird themselves with anything that causes sweat. [19]*† When they are to go out to the people in the outer court, they shall take off the garments in which they ministered and leave them in the chambers of the sanctuary, putting on other garments; thus they will not transmit holiness to the people with their garments.

[20]* They shall not shave their heads nor let their hair hang loose, but they shall keep their hair carefully trimmed. [21]* No priest shall drink wine when he is to enter the inner court. [22]* They shall not take for their wives either widows or divorced women, but only virgins of the race of Israel; however, they may marry women who are the widows of priests. [23] They shall teach my people to distinguish between the sacred and the profane, and make known to them the difference between the clean and the unclean. [24]* In capital cases they shall stand as judges, judging them according to my decrees. They shall observe my laws and statutes on all my festivals, and keep my sabbaths holy.

[25]* They shall not make themselves unclean by coming near any dead person, unless it be their father, mother, son, daughter, brother, or maiden sister; for these they may make themselves unclean. [26] After a priest has been cleansed, he must wait an additional seven days, [27] and on the day he enters the inner court to minister in the sanctuary, he shall present his sin offering, says the Lord GOD. [28]* They shall have no inheritance, for I am their inheritance; you shall give them no property in Israel, for I am their property. [29]*† They shall eat the cereal offering, the sin offering, and the guilt offering; whatever is under the ban in Israel shall be theirs. [30]* All the choicest first fruits of every kind, and all the best of your offerings of every kind, shall belong to the priests; likewise the best of your dough you shall give to the priests to bring a blessing down upon your house. [31]* The priests shall not eat anything, whether flesh or fowl, that has died of itself or has been killed by wild beasts.

CHAPTER 45

The Sacred Tract. [1] When you apportion the land into inheritances, you shall set apart a sacred tract of land for the LORD, twenty-five thousand cubits long and twenty thousand wide; its whole area shall be sacred. [2] Of this land a square plot, five hundred by five hundred cubits, surrounded by a free space of fifty cubits, shall be assigned to the sanctuary. [3] Also from this sector measure off a strip, twenty-five thousand cubits long and ten thousand wide, within which shall be the sanctuary, the holy of holies. [4] This shall be the sacred part of the land belonging to the priests, the ministers of the sanctuary, who draw near to minister to the LORD; it shall be a place for their homes and pasture land for their cattle. [5] Also there shall be a strip twenty-five thousand cubits long and ten thousand wide as property for the Levites, the ministers of the temple, that they may have cities to live in. [6] As property of the City you shall designate a strip five thousand cubits wide and twenty-five thousand long, parallel to the sacred tract; this shall belong to the whole house of Israel. [7] The prince shall have a section bordering on both sides of the combined sacred tract and City property, extending westward on the western side and eastward on the eastern side, corresponding in length to one of the tribal portions from the western boundary to the eastern boundary [8] of the land. This shall be his property in Israel, so that the princes of Israel will no longer oppress my people, but will leave the land to the house of Israel according to their tribes.

Weights and Measures. [9]† Thus says the Lord GOD: Enough, you princes of Israel! Put away violence and oppression, and do what is right and just! Stop evicting my people! says the Lord GOD. [10]* You shall have honest scales, an honest ephah, and an honest liquid measure. [11] The ephah and the liquid measure shall be of the same size: the liquid measure equal to a tenth of a homer, and the ephah equal to a tenth of a ho-

*

44, 18: Ex 28, 40.42; 29, 9; 38, 28; Lv 6, 3.
19: 42, 13.14.
20: Lv 21, 5.
21: Lv 10, 9.
22: Lv 21, 7.14.
24: Dt 17, 9; 19, 17.
25: Lv 21, 1ff.11.
28: Nm 18, 20; Dt 18, 1.
29: Lv 2, 3.10; 6, 9.22; 7, 9; 10, 12; Nm 18, 9; 18, 14.
30: Ex 34, 26; Dt 18, 4.
31: Lv 22, 8.
45, 10: Lv 19, 35; Dt 25, 13-16; Hos 12, 8; Am 8, 5; Mi 6, 10f.

†

44, 19: *Thus they will not transmit holiness to the people:* holiness was thought of as something physical, as though it were communicable, and therefore not to be brought in contact with unconsecrated persons.

44, 29: *Under the ban:* dedicated to the Lord, withdrawn from profane use.

45, 9-12: Besides the land monopoly fostered by royal greed and collusion with the wealthy (Mi 2, 2; Is 3, 12-15; 5, 8-10), one grave social evil of preexilic Israel was dishonesty in business; cf Hos 12, 8; Am 8, 5. *Ephah:* a dry measure; *liquid measure:* in Hebrew, a "bath," standardized according to the *homer* (a dry measure of about 10 bushels, or 80 gallons). In v 12 reference is made to the change in value of the *mina:* before the exile it was valued at 50 shekels, but afterward, in imitation of Babylonian practice, the 60-shekel mina was adopted. The shekel was a unit of weight slightly less than half an ounce. As a monetary unit, the value obviously differed greatly, depending on whether it was a gold or a silver shekel.

mer; by the homer they shall be deter-
mined. 12* The shekel shall be twenty
gerahs. Twenty shekels, twenty-five
shekels, plus fifteen shekels shall be your
mina.

Offerings. 13 These are the offerings
you shall make: one sixth of an ephah
from each homer of wheat, and one sixth
of an ephah from each homer of barley.
14† The regulation for oil: for every
measure of oil, a tenth of a measure,
computed by the kor of ten liquid mea-
sures [or a homer, for ten liquid mea-
sures make a homer]. 15 One sheep from
the flock for every two hundred from the
pasturage of Israel, for sacrifice—holo-
causts and peace offerings and atone-
ment sacrifices, says the Lord GOD. 16 All
the people of the land shall be bound to
this offering [for the prince in Israel].
17 It shall be the duty of the prince to
provide the holocausts, cereal offerings,
and libations on the feasts, new moons,
and sabbaths, on all the festivals of the
house of Israel. He shall offer the sin of-
ferings, cereal offerings, holocausts, and
peace offerings, to make atonement on
behalf of the house of Israel.

The Passover. 18 Thus says the Lord
GOD: On the first day of the first month
you shall use an unblemished young bull
as a sacrifice to purify the sanctuary.
19 Then the priest shall take some of the
blood from the sin offering and put it on
the doorposts of the temple, on the four
corners of the ledge of the altar, and on
the doorposts of the gates of the inner
court. 20 You shall repeat this on the first
day of the seventh month for those who
have sinned through inadvertence or ig-
norance; thus you shall make atonement
for the temple. 21* On the fourteenth day
of the first month you shall observe the
feast of the Passover; for seven days un-
leavened bread is to be eaten. 22 On that
day the prince shall offer on his own be-
half, and on behalf of all the people of
the land, a bull as a sin offering. 23 On
each of the seven days of the feast he
shall offer as a holocaust to the LORD
seven bulls and seven rams without
blemish, and as a sin offering he shall
offer one male goat each day. 24† As a
cereal offering he shall offer one ephah
for each bull and one ephah for each
ram; and he shall offer one hin of oil for
each ephah.

The Feast of Booths. 25 On the fif-
teenth day of the seventh month, the
feast day, and for seven days, he shall
perform the same rites, making the
same sin offerings, the same holocausts,
the same cereal offerings and offerings
of oil.

CHAPTER 46

Sabbaths. 1 Thus says the Lord GOD:
The gate toward the east of the inner
court shall remain closed throughout the
six working days, but on the sabbath and
on the day of the new moon it shall be
open. 2 The prince shall enter from out-
side by way of the vestibule of the gate
and remain standing at the doorpost of
the gate; then while the priests offer his
holocausts and peace offerings, he shall
worship at the threshold of the gate and
then leave; the gate shall not be closed
until evening. 3 The people of the land
shall worship before the LORD at the
door of this gate on the sabbaths and
new moons. 4* The holocausts which the
prince presents to the LORD on the sab-
bath shall consist of six unblemished
lambs and an unblemished ram,
5 together with a cereal offering of one
ephah for the ram, whatever he pleases
for the lambs, and a hin of oil for each
ephah. 6* On the day of the new moon
he shall provide an unblemished young
bull, also six lambs and a ram without
blemish, 7 with a cereal offering of one
ephah for the bull and one for the ram,
for the lambs as much as he has at hand,
and for each ephah a hin of oil.

Ritual Laws. 8 The prince shall always
enter and depart by the vestibule of the
gate. 9* When the people of the land en-
ter the presence of the LORD to worship
on the festivals, if they enter by the north
gate they shall leave by the south gate,
and if they enter by the south gate they
shall leave by the north gate; no one
shall return by the gate through which
he has entered, but he shall leave by the
opposite gate. 10 The prince shall be in
their midst when they enter, and he shall
also leave with them. 11 On the feasts and
festivals the cereal offering shall be an
ephah for a bull, an ephah for a ram,
but for the lambs as much as one
pleases, and a hin of oil with each ephah.
12 When the prince makes a freewill of-
fering to the LORD, whether holocausts
or peace offerings, the eastern gate shall
be opened for him, and he shall offer his
holocausts or his peace offerings as on
the sabbath; then he shall leave, and the
gate shall be closed after his departure.
13* He shall offer as a daily holocaust to
the LORD an unblemished yearling lamb;
this he shall offer every morning. 14 With
it every morning he shall provide as a
cereal offering one sixth of an ephah,
with a third of a hin of oil to moisten

*

12: Ex 30, 13; Lv 27, 25; Nm 3, 47; 18, 16.
21: Ex 12, 6; Lv 23, 5; Nm 28, 16.
46, 4: Nm 28, 9f.
6: Nm 28, 11-15.
9: Ex 23, 17; 34, 23; Dt 16, 16.
13: Ex 29, 38-42; Nm 28, 3-8.

†

45, 14: *Kor:* both a liquid and a dry measure, corresponding to the homer.

45, 24: *Hin:* a sixth part of the liquid measure called a bath.

the fine flour. This cereal offering to the
LORD is mandatory with the established
holocaust. 15* The lamb, the cereal offer-
ing, and the oil are to be offered every
morning as an established holocaust.

The Prince and the Land. 16 Thus says
the Lord GOD: If the prince makes a gift
of part of his inheritance to any of his
sons, it shall belong to his sons; that
property is theirs by inheritance. 17† But
if he makes a gift of part of his inheri-
tance to one of his servants, it shall be-
long to the latter only until the year of
release, when it shall revert to the
prince. Only the inheritance given to his
sons is permanent. 18 The prince shall
not seize any part of the inheritance of
the people by evicting them from their
property. He shall provide an inheri-
tance for his sons from his own property,
so that none of my people will be driven
from their property.

The Temple Kitchens. 19 Then he
brought me by the entrance which is on
the side of the gate to the chambers [of
the sanctuary, reserved to the priests]
which face the north. There, at their
west end, I saw a place, 20 concerning
which he said to me, "Here the priests
cook the guilt offerings and the sin offer-
ings, and bake the cereal offerings, so
that they do not have to take them into
the outer court at the risk of transmitting
holiness to the people." 21 Then he led
me into the outer court and had me pass
around the four corners of the court, and
I saw that in each corner there was an-
other court: 22 in the four corners of the
court, minor courts, forty cubits long
and thirty wide, all four of them the
same size. 23 A wall of stones surrounded
each of the four, and hearths were built
beneath the stones all the way around.
24 He said to me, "These are the kitchens
where the temple ministers cook the
sacrifices of the people."

CHAPTER 47

The Wonderful Stream. 1*† Then he
brought me back to the entrance of the
temple, and I saw water flowing out from
beneath the threshold of the temple to-
ward the east, for the facade of the tem-
ple was toward the east; the water flowed
down from the southern side of the tem-
ple, south of the altar. 2 He led me out-
side by the north gate, and around to
the outer gate facing the east, where I
saw water trickling from the southern
side. 3 Then when he had walked off to
the east with a measuring cord in his
hand, he measured off a thousand cubits
and had me wade through the water,
which was ankle-deep. 4 He measured
off another thousand and once more had
me wade through the water, which was
now knee-deep. Again he measured off
a thousand and had me wade; the water
was up to my waist. 5 Once more he
measured off a thousand, but there was
now a river through which I could not
wade; for the water had risen so high
it had become a river that could not be
crossed except by swimming. 6 He asked
me, "Have you seen this, son of man?"
Then he brought me to the bank of the
river, where he had me sit. 7 Along the
bank of the river I saw very many trees
on both sides. 8 He said to me, "This
water flows into the eastern district
down upon the Arabah, and empties into
the sea, the salt waters, which it makes
fresh. 9 Wherever the river flows, every
sort of living creature that can multiply
shall live, and there shall be abundant
fish, for wherever this water comes the
sea shall be made fresh. 10† Fishermen
shall be standing along it from En-gedi
to En-eglaim, spreading their nets
there. Its kinds of fish shall be like those
of the Great Sea, very numerous. 11 Only
its marshes and swamps shall not be
made fresh; they shall be left for salt.
12 Along both banks of the river, fruit
trees of every kind shall grow; their
leaves shall not fade, nor their fruit fail.
Every month they shall bear fresh fruit,
for they shall be watered by the flow
from the sanctuary. Their fruit shall
serve for food, and their leaves for medi-
cine."

The New Israel

Boundaries of the Land. 13† Thus says
the Lord GOD: These are the boundaries
within which you shall apportion the
land among the twelve tribes of Israel
[Joseph having two portions]. 14 All of
you shall have a like portion in this land
which I swore to give to your fathers,
that it might fall to you as your inheri-
tance. 15* This is the boundary of the
land on the north side: from the Great
Sea in the direction of Hethlon, past
Labo of Hamath, to Zedad, 16 Berothah,
and Sibraim, along the frontiers of
Hamath and Damascus, to Hazar-enon

*

15: Ex 29, 42.
47, 1: Sir 24, 28f; Jl 4, 18; Zec 13, 1; Rv 22, 1f.
15: Nm 34, 7ff.

†

46, 17: *The year of release:* the jubilee year; cf Lv 25, 23-55.

47, 1-12: The wonderful and superabundant stream flowing from the temple, restoring to fertility traditionally arid ground, is symbolic of the return of the conditions of primeval paradise; cf Gn 2, 10-14. Water signifies great blessings, just as dryness signifies a curse; cf 26, 5.14.

47, 10: *From En-gedi to En-eglaim:* the former was about halfway down the western shore of the Dead Sea, the latter may have been at its northern extremity.

47, 13-20: These boundaries of the restored Israel correspond to those of the Davidic kingdom at its fullest extent, the so-called "ideal boundaries" of the promised land; cf Nm 34, 3-12.

which is on the border of the Hauran.
17 Thus the border shall extend from the
sea to Hazar-enon, with the frontier of
Hamath and Damascus to the north.
This is the northern boundary. 18 The
eastern boundary: between the Hau-
ran—toward Damascus—and Gilead on
the one side, and the land of Israel on
the other side, the Jordan shall form the
boundary down to the eastern sea as far
as Tamar. This is the eastern boundary.
19 The southern boundary: from Tamar
to the waters of Meribath-kadesh,
thence to the Wadi of Egypt, and on to
the Great Sea. This is the southern
boundary. 20 The western boundary: the
Great Sea forms the boundary up to a
point parallel to Labo of Hamath. This
is the western boundary.

The Northern Portions. 21 You shall
distribute this land among yourselves
according to the tribes of Israel. 22* You
shall allot it as inheritances for your-
selves and for the aliens resident in your
midst who have bred children among
you. The latter shall be to you like native
Israelites; along with you they shall re-
ceive inheritances among the tribes of
Israel. 23 In whatever tribe the alien may
be resident, there you shall assign him
his inheritance, says the Lord GOD.

CHAPTER 48

1*† This is the list of the tribes. Dan:
at the northern extremity, adjoining
Hamath, all along from the approaches
to Hethlon through Labo of Hamath to
Hazar-enon, on the northerly border
with Damascus, with his possession
reaching from the eastern to the western
boundary. 2 Asher: on the frontier of
Dan, from the eastern to the western
boundary. 3 Naphtali: on the frontier of
Asher, from the eastern to the western
boundary. 4 Manasseh: on the frontier of
Naphtali, from the eastern to the west-
ern boundary. 5 Ephraim: on the frontier
of Manasseh, from the eastern to the
western boundary. 6 Reuben: on the
frontier of Ephraim, from the eastern
to the western boundary. 7 Judah: on the
frontier of Reuben, from the eastern to
the western boundary.

The Sacred Tract. 8 On the frontier of
Judah, from the eastern to the western
boundary there shall be the tract which
you shall set apart, twenty-five thousand
cubits from north to south, and as wide
as one of the tribal portions from the
eastern to the western boundary. In the
center of the tract shall be the sanctu-
ary. 9The tract that you set aside for the
LORD shall be twenty-five thousand cu-
bits across by twenty thousand north
and south. 10 In this sacred tract the
priests shall have twenty-five thousand
cubits on the north, ten thousand on the
west, ten thousand on the east, and
twenty-five thousand on the south; and
the sanctuary of the LORD shall be in its
center. 11 The consecrated priests, the
Zadokites, who fulfilled my service and
did not stray along with the Israelites
as the Levites did, 12 shall have within
this tract of land their own most sacred
domain, next to the territory of the Le-
vites. 13 The Levites shall have a terri-
tory corresponding to that of the priests,
twenty-five thousand cubits by ten thou-
sand. The whole tract shall be twenty-
five thousand cubits across and twenty
thousand north and south. 14 They may
not sell or exchange or alienate this, the
best part of the land, for it is sacred to
the LORD. 15 The remaining five thou-
sand cubits along the twenty-five-thou-
sand-cubit line are profane land,
assigned to the City for dwellings and
pasture; the City shall be at their center.
16 These are the dimensions of the City:
the north side, forty-five hundred cubits;
the south side, forty-five hundred cubits;
the east side, forty-five hundred cubits;
and the west side, forty-five hundred cu-
bits. 17 The pasture lands of the City shall
extend north two hundred and fifty cu-
bits, south two hundred and fifty cubits,
east two hundred and fifty cubits, and
west two hundred and fifty cubits.
18 There shall remain an area along the
sacred tract, ten thousand cubits to the
east and ten thousand to the west, whose
produce shall provide food for the work-
ers of the City. 19 The workers in the City
shall be taken from all the tribes of Is-
rael. 20 The entire tract shall be twenty-
five thousand by twenty-five thousand
cubits; as a perfect square you shall set
apart the sacred tract together with the
City property.

21 The remainder shall belong to the
prince: the land on both sides of the
sacred tract and the City property, ex-
tending along the twenty-five-thou-
sand-cubit line eastward to the eastern
boundary, and westward along the
twenty-five-thousand-cubit line to the
western boundary, a territory parallel
with the tribal portions for the prince.
The sacred tract and the sanctuary of
the temple shall be in the middle.
22 Thus, except for the property of the
Levites and the City property, which lie
in the midst of the prince's property, the
territory between the portions of Judah
and of Benjamin shall belong to the
prince.

*

22: Ex 12, 48; Lv 19, 34; 24, 22; Nm 9, 14; Jos 8, 33.
48, 1: 47, 15ff.

†

48, 1-29: This distribution of the land among the tribes does not correspond to the geographical realities of Palestine. It is a description of the ideal order, like that in 47, 1-12.

The Southern Portions. 23 These are the remaining tribes. Benjamin: from the eastern to the western boundary. 24 Simeon: on the frontier of Benjamin, from the eastern to the western boundary. 25 Issachar: on the frontier of Simeon, from the eastern to the western boundary. 26 Zebulun: on the frontier of Issachar, from the eastern to the western boundary. 27 Gad: on the frontier of Zebulun, from the eastern to the western boundary. 28 Along the frontier of Gad shall be the southern boundary, which shall extend from Tamar to the waters of Meribath-kadesh, and from there to the Wadi of Egypt, and on to the Great Sea. 29 Such is the land which you shall apportion as inheritances among the tribes of Israel, and these are their portions, says the Lord GOD.

The Gates of the City. 30 These are the exits of the City, the gates of which are named after the tribes of Israel. On the north side, measuring forty-five hundred cubits, 31 there shall be three gates: the gate of Reuben, the gate of Judah, and the gate of Levi. 32 On the east side, measuring forty-five hundred cubits, there shall be three gates: the gate of Joseph, the gate of Benjamin, and the gate of Dan. 33 On the south side, measuring forty-five hundred cubits, there shall be three gates: the gate of Simeon, the gate of Issachar, and the gate of Zebulun. 34 On the west side, measuring forty-five hundred cubits, there shall be three gates: the gate of Gad, the gate of Asher, and the gate of Naphtali. 35 The perimeter of the City is eighteen thousand cubits. The name of the City shall henceforth be "The LORD is here."

The Book of

DANIEL

This Book takes its name, not from the author, who is actually unknown, but from its hero, a young Jew taken early to Babylon, where he lived at least until 538 B.C. Strictly speaking, the book does not belong to the prophetic writings but rather to a distinctive type of literature known as "apocalyptic," of which it is an early specimen. Apocalyptic writing enjoyed its greatest popularity from 200 B.C. to 100 A.D., a time of distress and persecution for Jews, and later, for Christians. Though subsequent in time to the prophetic, apocalyptic literature has its roots in the teaching of the prophets, who often pointed ahead to the day of the Lord, the consummation of history. For both prophet and apocalyptist Yahweh was the Lord of history, and he would ultimately vindicate his people.

This work was composed during the bitter persecution carried on by Antiochus IV Epiphanes (167-164) and was written to strengthen and comfort the Jewish people in their ordeal.

The Book contains stories originating in and transmitted by popular traditions which tell of the trials and triumphs of the wise Daniel and his three companions. The moral is that men of faith can resist temptation and conquer adversity. The characters are not purely legendary but rest on older historical tradition. What is more important than the question of historicity, and closer to the intention of the author, is the fact that a persecuted Jew of the second century B.C. would quickly see the application of these stories to his own plight.

There follows a series of visions promising deliverance and glory to the Jews in the days to come. The great nations of the ancient world have risen in vain against Yahweh; his kingdom shall overthrow existing powers and last forever. Under this apocalyptic imagery are contained some of the best elements of prophetic teaching: the insistence on right conduct, the divine control over events, the certainty that the kingdom of God will ultimately triumph. The arrival of the kingdom is a central theme of the synoptic gospels, and Jesus, in calling himself the "Son of Man," reminds us that he fulfills the destiny of this mysterious figure in the seventh chapter of Daniel.

The added episodes of Susanna, Bel, and the Dragon, found only in the Greek version, are edifying short stories with a didactic purpose.

These three sections constitute the divisions of the Book of Daniel:

I: Daniel and the Kings of Babylon (1, 1—6, 29)
II: Daniel's Visions (7, 1—12, 13)
III: Appendix (13, 1—14, 42)

I: DANIEL AND THE KINGS OF BABYLON

CHAPTER 1

The Food Test. 1* In the third year of
the reign of Jehoiakim, king of Judah,
King Nebuchadnezzar of Babylon came
and laid siege to Jerusalem. 2*† The
Lord handed over to him Jehoiakim,
king of Judah, and some of the vessels
of the temple of God, which he carried
off to the land of Shinar, and placed in
the temple treasury of his god.
3 The king told Ashpenaz, his chief
chamberlain, to bring in some of the Is-
raelites of royal blood and of the nobility,
4 young men without any defect, hand-
some, intelligent and wise, quick to
learn, and prudent in judgment, such as
could take their place in the king's pal-
ace; they were to be taught the language
and literature of the Chaldeans; 5 after
three years' training they were to enter
the king's service. The king allotted
them a daily portion of food and wine
from the royal table. 6 Among these were
men of Judah: Daniel, Hananiah,
Mishael, and Azariah. 7† The chief

*

1, 1: 2 Kgs 24, 1; 2 Chr 36, 6; Jer 25, 1.
2: 5, 2; Gn 10, 10; 2 Kgs 24, 2; 2 Chr 36, 7.

†

1, 2: *Shinar:* ancient name for Babylonia, a deliberate archaism in this text; cf Gn 10, 10; 11, 2.

1, 7: The young men are given Babylonian names as a sign of their adoption by the king.

chamberlain changed their names: Daniel to Belteshazzar, Hananiah to Shadrach, Mishael to Meshach, and Azariah to Abednego.

8† But Daniel was resolved not to defile himself with the king's food or wine; so he begged the chief chamberlain to spare him this defilement. 9 Though God had given Daniel the favor and sympathy of the chief chamberlain, 10 he nevertheless said to Daniel, "I am afraid of my lord the king; it is he who allotted your food and drink. If he sees that you look wretched by comparison with the other young men of your age, you will endanger my life with the king." 11 Then Daniel said to the steward whom the chief chamberlain had put in charge of Daniel, Hananiah, Mishael, and Azariah, 12 "Please test your servants for ten days. Give us vegetables to eat and water to drink. 13 Then see how we look in comparison with the other young men who eat from the royal table, and treat your servants according to what you see." 14 He acceded to this request, and tested them for ten days; 15 after ten days they looked healthier and better fed than any of the young men who ate from the royal table. 16 So the steward continued to take away the food and wine they were to receive, and gave them vegetables.

17 To these four young men God gave knowledge and proficiency in all literature and science, and to Daniel the understanding of all visions and dreams. 18 At the end of the time the king had specified for their preparation, the chief chamberlain brought them before Nebuchadnezzar. 19 When the king had spoken with all of them, none was found equal to Daniel, Hananiah, Mishael, and Azariah; and so they entered the king's service. 20 In any question of wisdom or prudence which the king put to them, he found them ten times better than all the magicians and enchanters in his kingdom. 21*† Daniel remained there until the first year of King Cyrus.

CHAPTER 2

The King's Dream.† 1 In the second year of his reign, King Nebuchadnezzar had a dream which left his spirit no rest and robbed him of his sleep. 2† So he ordered that the magicians, enchanters, sorcerers, and Chaldeans be summoned to interpret the dream for him. When they came and presented themselves to the king, 3 he said to them, "I had a dream which will allow my spirit no rest until I know what it means." 4† The Chaldeans answered the king [Aramaic]: "O king, live forever! Tell your servants the dream and we will give its meaning." 5 The king answered the Chaldeans, "This is what I have decided: unless you tell me the dream and its meaning, you shall be cut to pieces and your houses destroyed. 6 But if you tell me the dream and its meaning, you shall receive from me gifts and presents and great honors. Now tell me the dream and its meaning."

7 Again they answered, "Let the king tell his servants the dream and we will give its meaning." 8 But the king replied: "I know for certain that you are bargaining for time, since you know what I have decided. 9 If you do not tell me the dream, there can be but one decree for you. You have framed a false and deceitful interpretation to present me with till the crisis is past. Tell me the dream, therefore, that I may be sure that you can also give its correct interpretation."

10 The Chaldeans answered the king: "There is not a man on earth who can do what you ask, O king; never has any king, however great and mighty, asked such a thing of any magician, enchanter, or Chaldean. 11 What you demand, O king, is too difficult; there is no one who can tell it to the king except the gods who do not dwell among men." 12 At this the king became violently angry and ordered all the wise men of Babylon to be put to death. 13 When the decree was issued that the wise men should be slain, Daniel and his companions were also sought out.

14 Then Daniel prudently took counsel with Arioch, the captain of the king's guard, who had set out to kill the wise men of Babylon: 15 "O officer of the king," he asked, "what is the reason for this harsh order from the king?" When Arioch told him, 16 Daniel went and asked for time from the king, that he might give him the interpretation.

17 Daniel went home and informed his companions Hananiah, Mishael, and Azariah, 18 that they might implore the

*

21: 6, 28.

†

1, 8: *This defilement:* the bread, meat, and wine of the Gentiles, which were unclean (Hos 9, 3; Tb 1, 12; Jdt 10, 5; 12, 1f) because they might have been offered to idols or prepared over firewood taken from a sacred grove. Only raw vegetables and water were safe from this danger (v 12).

1, 21: *The first year of King Cyrus:* the year of this Persian king's conquest of Babylon, 539/8 B.C.

2, 1-49: The chronology of v 1 is in conflict with that of 1, 5.18, and in v 25 Daniel appears to be introduced to the king for the first time. It seems that the story of this chapter was originally entirely independent of chapter 1, and later retouched slightly to fit its present setting.

2, 2: *Chaldeans:* here probably astrologers, who were so associated with the Chaldeans in the Hebrew mind that in the later language they are sometimes simply called by the name of that people.

2, 4: *Aramaic:* from 2, 4 to 7, 28 the text of Daniel is in Aramaic, not Hebrew, as indicated by this gloss.

mercy of the God of heaven in regard
to this mystery, so that Daniel and his
companions might not perish with the
rest of the wise men of Babylon.
19 During the night the mystery was re-
vealed to Daniel in a vision, and he
blessed the God of heaven:

20 "Blessed be the name of God forever
and ever,
for wisdom and power are his.
21 He causes the changes of the times
and seasons,
makes kings and unmakes them.
He gives wisdom to the wise
and knowledge to those who un-
derstand.
22* He reveals deep and hidden things
and knows what is in the dark-
ness,
for the light dwells with him.
23 To you, O God of my fathers,
I give thanks and praise,
because you have given me wis-
dom and power.
Now you have shown me what we
asked of you,
you have made known to us the
king's dream."

24 So Daniel went to Arioch, whom the
king had appointed to destroy the wise
men of Babylon, and said to him, "Do
not put the wise men of Babylon to
death. Bring me before the king, and I
will tell him the interpretation of the
dream." Arioch quickly brought Daniel
to the king and said, 25 "I have found a
man among the Judean captives who
can give the interpretation to the king."
26 The king asked Daniel, whose name
was Belteshazzar, "Can you tell me the
dream that I had, and its meaning?"
27 In the king's presence Daniel made
this reply:

"The mystery about which the king
has inquired, the wise men, enchanters,
magicians, and astrologers could not ex-
plain to the king. 28 But there is a God
in heaven who reveals mysteries, and
he has shown King Nebuchadnezzar
what is to happen in days to come; this
was the dream you saw as you lay in
bed. 29 To you in your bed there came
thoughts about what should happen in
the future, and he who reveals mysteries
showed you what is to be. 30 To me also
this mystery has been revealed; not that
I am wiser than any other living person,
but in order that its meaning may be
made known to the king, that you may
understand the thoughts in your own
mind.

31 "In your vision, O king, you saw a
statue, very large and exceedingly
bright, terrifying in appearance as it
stood before you. 32 The head of the
statue was pure gold, its chest and arms
were silver, its belly and thighs bronze,
33† the legs iron, its feet partly iron and
partly tile. 34 While you looked at the
statue, a stone which was hewn from a
mountain without a hand being put to
it, struck its iron and tile feet, breaking
them in pieces. 35 The iron, tile, bronze,
silver, and gold all crumbled at once,
fine as the chaff on the threshing floor
in summer, and the wind blew them
away without leaving a trace. But the
stone that struck the statue became a
great mountain and filled the whole
earth.

36† "This was the dream; the interpre-
tation we shall also give in the king's
presence. 37 You, O king, are the king of
kings; to you the God of heaven has
given dominion and strength, power and
glory; 38 men, wild beasts, and birds of
the air, wherever they may dwell, he has
handed over to you, making you ruler
over them all; you are the head of gold.
39 Another kingdom shall take your
place, inferior to yours, then a third
kingdom, of bronze, which shall rule
over the whole earth. 40 There shall be
a fourth kingdom, strong as iron; it shall
break in pieces and subdue all these oth-
ers, just as iron breaks in pieces and
crushes everything else. 41 The feet and
toes you saw, partly of potter's tile and
partly of iron, mean that it shall be a
divided kingdom, but yet have some of
the hardness of iron. As you saw the iron
mixed with clay tile, 42 and the toes
partly iron and partly tile, the kingdom
shall be partly strong and partly fragile.
43 The iron mixed with clay tile means
that they shall seal their alliances by in-
termarriage, but they shall not stay
united, any more than iron mixes with
clay. 44* In the lifetime of those kings the
God of heaven will set up a kingdom that
shall never be destroyed or delivered up
to another people; rather, it shall break
in pieces all these kingdoms and put an
end to them, and it shall stand forever.
45 That is the meaning of the stone you
saw hewn from the mountain without a
hand being put to it, which broke in
pieces the tile, iron, bronze, silver, and
gold. The great God has revealed to the
king what shall be in the future; this is

*

2, 22: Jn 1, 9; 8, 12; 1 Cor 4, 5; 1 Jn 1, 6.

44: Mt 21, 44; Lk 20, 18.

†

2, 33: *Partly tile:* terra cotta tile was much in use among the Babylonians for decoration and for actual construction.

2, 36-45: The four successive kingdoms in this apocalyptic perspective are the Babylonian (gold), the Median (silver), the Persian (bronze), and the Hellenistic (iron). The last, after Alexander's death, was divided among his generals (vv 41f). The two resulting kingdoms, which most affected the Jews, were the dynasty of the Ptolemies in Egypt and that of the Seleucids in Syria, who tried in vain, by war and through intermarriage, to restore the unity of Alexander's empire (v 43). The stone hewn from the mountain is the messianic kingdom awaited by the Jews (vv 44f). Our Lord made this image personal to himself; cf Lk 20, 17f.

exactly what you dreamed, and its meaning is sure."

46 Then King Nebuchadnezzar fell down and worshiped Daniel and ordered sacrifice and incense offered to him. 47 To Daniel the king said, "Truly your God is the God of gods and Lord of kings and a revealer of mysteries; that is why you were able to reveal this mystery." 48 He advanced Daniel to a high post, gave him many generous presents, made him ruler of the whole province of Babylon and chief prefect over all the wise men of Babylon. 49 At Daniel's request the king made Shadrach, Meshach, and Abednego administrators of the province of Babylon, while Daniel himself remained at the king's court.

CHAPTER 3

The Fiery Furnace. 1† King Nebuchadnezzar had a golden statue made, sixty cubits high and six cubits wide, which he set up in the plain of Dura in the province of Babylon. 2† He then ordered the satraps, prefects, and governors, the counselors, treasurers, judges, magistrates and all the officials of the provinces to be summoned to the dedication of the statue which he had set up. 3 The satraps, prefects, and governors, the counselors, treasurers, judges, and magistrates and all the officials of the provinces, all these came together for the dedication and stood before the statue which King Nebuchadnezzar had set up. 4† A herald cried out: "Nations and peoples of every language, when you hear the sound of the trumpet, flute, lyre, harp, psaltery, bagpipe, and all the other musical instruments, 5 you are ordered to fall down and worship the golden statue which King Nebuchadnezzar has set up. 6† Whoever does not fall down and worship shall be instantly cast into a white-hot furnace." 7 Therefore, as soon as they heard the sound of the trumpet, flute, lyre, harp, psaltery, bagpipe, and all the other musical instruments, the nations and peoples of every language all fell down and worshiped the golden statue which King Nebuchadnezzar had set up.

8 At that point, some of the Chaldeans came and accused the Jews 9 to King Nebuchadnezzar: "O king, live forever! 10 O king, you issued a decree that everyone who heard the sound of the trumpet, flute, lyre, harp, psaltery, bagpipe, and all the other musical instruments should fall down and worship the golden statue; 11 whoever did not was to be cast into a white-hot furnace. 12 There are certain Jews whom you have made administrators of the province of Babylon: Shadrach, Meshach, Abednego; these men, O king, have paid no attention to you; they will not serve your god or worship the golden statue which you set up."

13 Nebuchadnezzar flew into a rage and sent for Shadrach, Meshach, and Abednego, who were promptly brought before the king. 14 King Nebuchadnezzar questioned them: "Is it true, Shadrach, Meshach, and Abednego, that you will not serve my god, or worship the golden statue that I set up? 15 Be ready now to fall down and worship the statue I had made, whenever you hear the sound of the trumpet, flute, lyre, harp, psaltery, bagpipe, and all the other musical instruments; otherwise, you shall be instantly cast into the white-hot furnace; and who is the God that can deliver you out of my hands?" 16 Shadrach, Meshach, and Abednego answered King Nebuchadnezzar, "There is no need for us to defend ourselves before you in this matter. 17† If our God, whom we serve, can save us from the white-hot furnace and from your hands, O king, may he save us! 18 But even if he will not, know, O king, that we will not serve your god or worship the golden statue which you set up."

19 Nebuchadnezzar's face became livid with utter rage against Shadrach, Meshach, and Abednego. He ordered the furnace to be heated seven times more than usual 20 and had some of the strongest men in his army bind Shadrach, Meshach, and Abednego and cast them into the white-hot furnace. 21 They were bound and cast into the white-hot furnace with their coats, hats, shoes and other garments, 22 for the king's order was urgent. So huge a fire was kindled in the furnace that the flames devoured the men who threw Shadrach, Meshach, and Abednego into it. 23 But these three fell, bound, into the midst of the white-hot furnace.

24† They walked about in the flames, singing to God and blessing the Lord. 25 In the fire Azariah stood up and prayed aloud:

26 "Blessed are you, and praiseworthy,
O Lord, the God of our fathers,
and glorious forever is your name.

† ——

3, 1: *Dura:* several places in Babylonia bore this name. Probably the present reference is to one a few miles south of Babylon. Colossi of the type mentioned here were not uncommon in antiquity; a cubit was seventeen and a half inches.

3, 2: *Satraps:* the Persian major governors.

3, 4: *Psaltery:* a harplike instrument.

3, 6: Death by fire was not unknown as a punishment in Babylonia; cf Jer 29, 22.

3, 17: *If our God . . . can save us:* the youths do not question the efficacy of the divine power, but whether it will be exercised (v 18).

3, 24-90: These verses are inspired additions to the Aramaic text of Daniel, translated from the Greek form of the book. They were originally composed in Hebrew or Aramaic, which has not been preserved. The Church has always regarded them as part of the canonical Scriptures.

27 For you are just in all you have done;
all your deeds are faultless, all your ways right,
and all your judgments proper.
28 You have executed proper judgments
in all that you have brought upon us
and upon Jerusalem, the holy city of our fathers.
By a proper judgment you have done all this
because of our sins;
29 For we have sinned and transgressed
by departing from you,
and we have done every kind of evil.
30 Your commandments we have not heeded or observed,
nor have we done as you ordered us for our good.
31 Therefore all you have brought upon us,
all you have done to us,
you have done by a proper judgment.
32 You have handed us over to our enemies,
lawless and hateful rebels;
to an unjust king, the worst in all the world.
33 Now we cannot open our mouths;
we, your servants, who revere you,
have become a shame and a reproach.
34 For your name's sake, do not deliver us up forever,
or make void your covenant.
35 Do not take away your mercy from us,
for the sake of Abraham, your beloved,
Isaac your servant, and Israel your holy one,
36 To whom you promised to multiply their offspring
like the stars of heaven,
or the sand on the shore of the sea.
37 For we are reduced, O Lord, beyond any other nation,
brought low everywhere in the world this day
because of our sins.
38 We have in our day no prince, prophet, or leader,
no holocaust, sacrifice, oblation, or incense,
no place to offer first fruits, to find favor with you.
39 But with contrite heart and humble spirit
let us be received;
40 As though it were holocausts of rams and bullocks,
or thousands of fat lambs,
So let our sacrifice be in your presence today
as we follow you unreservedly;
for those who trust in you cannot be put to shame.
41 And now we follow you with our whole heart,
we fear you and we pray to you.
42 Do not let us be put to shame,
but deal with us in your kindness and great mercy.
43 Deliver us by your wonders,
and bring glory to your name, O Lord:
44 Let all those be routed
who inflict evils on your servants;
Let them be shamed and powerless,
and their strength broken;
45 Let them know that you alone are the Lord God,
glorious over the whole world."

46 Now the king's men who had thrown
them in continued to stoke the furnace
with brimstone, pitch, tow, and faggots.
47 The flames rose forty-nine cubits
above the furnace, 48 and spread out,
burning the Chaldeans nearby. 49 But the
angel of the Lord went down into the fur-
nace with Azariah and his companions,
drove the fiery flames out of the furnace,
50 and made the inside of the furnace as
though a dew-laden breeze were blow-
ing through it. The fire in no way touched
them or caused them pain or harm.
51 Then these three in the furnace with
one voice sang, glorifying and blessing
God:

52 "Blessed are you, O Lord, the God of our fathers,
praiseworthy and exalted above all forever;
And blessed is your holy and glorious name,
praiseworthy and exalted above all for all ages.
53 Blessed are you in the temple of your holy glory,
praiseworthy and glorious above all forever.
54 Blessed are you on the throne of your kingdom,
praiseworthy and exalted above all forever.
55 Blessed are you who look into the depths
from your throne upon the cherubim,
praiseworthy and exalted above all forever.
56 Blessed are you in the firmament of heaven,
praiseworthy and glorious forever.
57 Bless the Lord, all you works of the Lord,
praise and exalt him above all forever.
58 Angels of the Lord, bless the Lord,
praise and exalt him above all forever.

59* You heavens, bless the Lord,
praise and exalt him above all forever.
60 All you waters above the heavens, bless the Lord,
praise and exalt him above all forever.
61 All you hosts of the Lord, bless the Lord;
praise and exalt him above all forever.
62 Sun and moon, bless the Lord;
praise and exalt him above all forever.
63 Stars of heaven, bless the Lord;
praise and exalt him above all forever.
64 Every shower and dew, bless the Lord;
praise and exalt him above all forever.
65 All you winds, bless the Lord;
praise and exalt him above all forever.
66 Fire and heat, bless the Lord;
praise and exalt him above all forever.
67 [Cold and chill, bless the Lord;
praise and exalt him above all forever.
68 Dew and rain, bless the Lord;
praise and exalt him above all forever.]
69 Frost and chill, bless the Lord;
praise and exalt him above all forever.
70 Ice and snow, bless the Lord;
praise and exalt him above all forever.
71 Nights and days, bless the Lord;
praise and exalt him above all forever.
72 Light and darkness, bless the Lord;
praise and exalt him above all forever.
73 Lightnings and clouds, bless the Lord;
praise and exalt him above all forever.
74 Let the earth bless the Lord,
praise and exalt him above all forever.
75 Mountains and hills, bless the Lord;
praise and exalt him above all forever.
76 Everything growing from the earth, bless the Lord;
praise and exalt him above all forever.
77 You springs, bless the Lord;
praise and exalt him above all forever.
78 Seas and rivers, bless the Lord;
praise and exalt him above all forever.
79 You dolphins and all water creatures, bless the Lord,
praise and exalt him above all forever.
80 All you birds of the air, bless the Lord;
praise and exalt him above all forever.
81 All you beasts, wild and tame, bless the Lord;
praise and exalt him above all forever.
82 You sons of men, bless the Lord;
praise and exalt him above all forever.
83 O Israel, bless the Lord;
praise and exalt him above all forever.
84 Priests of the Lord, bless the Lord;
praise and exalt him above all forever.
85 Servants of the Lord, bless the Lord;
praise and exalt him above all forever.
86 Spirits and souls of the just, bless the Lord;
praise and exalt him above all forever.
87 Holy men of humble heart, bless the Lord;
praise and exalt him above all forever.
88 Hananiah, Azariah, Mishael, bless the Lord;
praise and exalt him above all forever.
For he has delivered us from the nether world,
and saved us from the power of death;
He has freed us from the raging flame
and delivered us from the fire.
89 Give thanks to the Lord, for he is good,
for his mercy endures forever.
90 Bless the God of gods, all you who fear the Lord;
praise him and give him thanks,
because his mercy endures forever."

Hearing them sing, and astonished at
seeing them alive, 91 King Nebuchad-
nezzar rose in haste and asked his no-
bles, "Did we not cast three men bound
into the fire?" "Assuredly, O king," they
answered. 92† "But," he replied, "I see
four men unfettered and unhurt, walk-
ing in the fire, and the fourth looks like
a son of God." 93 Then Nebuchadnezzar
came to the opening of the white-hot fur-
nace and called to Shadrach, Meshach,
and Abednego: "Servants of the most
high God, come out." Thereupon Sha-
drach, Meshach, and Abednego came
out of the fire. 94 When the satraps, pre-
fects, governors, and nobles of the king

DANIEL

* 3, 59f: Ps 148, 4.

† 3, 92: *A son of God:* an angel; cf Jb 1, 6.

came together, they saw that the fire had
had no power over the bodies of these
men; not a hair of their heads had been
singed, nor were their garments altered;
there was not even a smell of fire about
them. 95 Nebuchadnezzar exclaimed,
"Blessed be the God of Shadrach, Me-
shach, and Abednego, who sent his an-
gel to deliver the servants that trusted
in him; they disobeyed the royal com-
mand and yielded their bodies rather
than serve or worship any god except
their own God. 96 Therefore I decree for
nations and peoples of every language
that whoever blasphemes the God of
Shadrach, Meshach, and Abednego
shall be cut to pieces and his house de-
stroyed. For there is no other God who
can rescue like this." 97 Then the king
promoted Shadrach, Meshach, and
Abednego in the province of Babylon.
Vision of the Great Tree.† 98 King
Nebuchadnezzar to the nations and peo-
ples of every language, wherever they
dwell on earth: abundant peace! 99† It
has seemed good to me to publish the
signs and wonders which the most high
God has accomplished in my regard.

100* How great are his signs, how mighty his wonders;
his kingdom is an everlasting kingdom,
and his dominion endures through all generations.

CHAPTER 4

1 I, Nebuchadnezzar, was at home in
my palace, content and prosperous. 2 I
had a terrifying dream as I lay in bed,
and the images and the visions of my
mind frightened me. 3 So I issued a de-
cree that all the wise men of Babylon
should be brought before me to give the
interpretation of the dream. 4 When the
magicians, enchanters, Chaldeans, and
astrologers had come in, I related the
dream before them; but none of them
could tell me its meaning. 5*† Finally
there came before me Daniel, whose
name is Belteshazzar after the name of
my god, and in whom is the spirit of the
holy God. I repeated the dream to him:
6 "Belteshazzar, chief of the magicians,
I know that the spirit of the holy God
is in you and no mystery is too difficult
for you; tell me the meaning of the vi-
sions that I saw in my dream.

7 "These were the visions I saw while
in bed: I saw a tree of great height at
the center of the world. 8 It was large
and strong, with its top touching the
heavens, and it could be seen to the ends
of the earth. 9 Its leaves were beautiful
and its fruit abundant, providing food
for all. Under it the wild beasts found
shade, in its branches the birds of the
air nested; all men ate of it. 10† In the
vision I saw while in bed, a holy sentinel
came down from heaven, 11† and cried
out:

" 'Cut down the tree and lop off its branches,
strip off its leaves and scatter its fruit;
let the beasts flee its shade, and the birds its branches.

12 But leave in the earth its stump and roots,
fettered with iron and bronze, in the grass of the field.
Let him be bathed with the dew of heaven;
his lot be to eat, among beasts, the grass of the earth.

13 Let his mind be changed from the human;
let him be given the sense of a beast,
till seven years pass over him.

14* By decree of the sentinels is this decided,
by order of the holy ones, this sentence;
That all who live may know
that the Most High rules over the kingdom of men:
He can give it to whom he will,
or set over it the lowliest of men.'

15 "This is the dream that I, King
Nebuchadnezzar, had. Now, Belteshaz-
zar, tell me its meaning. Although none
of the wise men in my kingdom can tell
me the meaning, you can, because the
spirit of the holy God is in you."

16 Then Daniel, whose name was Bel-
teshazzar, was appalled for a while, ter-
rified by his thoughts. "Belteshazzar,"
the king said to him, "let not the dream
or its meaning terrify you." 17† "My
lord," Belteshazzar replied, "this dream

---

* 100: 4, 31; 7, 14. 4, 5: Gn 41, 38. 14: 1 Sm 2, 8; 16, 11; Is 62, 6.

---

† 3, 98—4, 34: This section has the form of a letter written by Nebuchadnezzar to his subjects.

3, 99: *The most high God:* the Jews, especially in the diaspora, used this title to distinguish their God from those of the pagans. On the lips of a polytheist (so also in v 93) it was merely the title of another god. It was an ancient divine name used in Canaan; cf Gn 14, 18.

4, 5: *After the name of my god:* Belteshazzar, the Babylonian name given to Daniel at the king's orders (1, 7), is Balatsu-ussur, "protect his life." In the king's intention, this would be an abbreviation for *Bel-balatsu-ussur.* It would thus include an appeal to the god Bel, originally the name of the city god of Nippur, and later identified with Marduk, the chief god of Babylon. Daniel's use of the name would refer the prayer rather to the true God.

4, 10: *A holy sentinel:* an angel. This term is found in the Bible only in this chapter of Daniel, but it is common in later Jewish literature.

4, 11ff: As the tree is Nebuchadnezzar (v 19), the description passes from metaphor to the reality.

4, 17: *"This dream . . . for your foes":* Daniel speaks as a courtier.

should be for your enemies, and its
meaning for your foes. The large, strong
tree that you saw, with its top touching
the heavens, that could be seen by the
whole earth, [18] which had beautiful fo-
liage and abundant fruit, providing food
for all, under which the wild beasts lived,
and in whose branches the birds of the
air dwelt—[19] you are that tree, O king,
large and strong! Your majesty has be-
come so great as to touch the heavens,
and your rule extends over the whole
earth. [20] As for the king's vision of a holy
sentinel that came down from heaven
and proclaimed: 'Cut down the tree and
destroy it, but leave in the earth its
stump and roots, fettered with iron and
bronze in the grass of the field; let him
be bathed with the dew of heaven, and
let his lot be among wild beasts till seven
years pass over him'—[21] this is its mean-
ing, O king; this is the sentence which
the Most High has passed upon my lord
king: [22]*† You shall be cast out from
among men and dwell with wild beasts;
you shall be given grass to eat like an
ox and be bathed with the dew of
heaven; seven years shall pass over you,
until you know that the Most High rules
over the kingdom of men and gives it
to whom he will. [23] The command that
the stump and roots of the tree are to
be left means that your kingdom shall
be preserved for you, once you have
learned it is heaven that rules.
[24]*† Therefore, O king, take my advice;
atone for your sins by good deeds, and
for your misdeeds by kindness to the
poor; then your prosperity will be
long."

[25] All this happened to King Nebu-
chadnezzar. [26] Twelve months later, as
he was walking on the roof of the royal
palace in Babylon, [27]† the king said,
"Babylon the great! Was it not I, with
my great strength, who built it as a royal
residence for my splendor and maj-
esty?" [28] While these words were still on
the king's lips, a voice spoke from
heaven, "It has been decreed for you,
King Nebuchadnezzar, that your king-
dom is taken from you! [29] You shall be
cast out from among men, and shall
dwell with wild beasts; you shall be given
grass to eat like an ox, and seven years
shall pass over you, until you learn that
the Most High rules over the kingdom
of men and gives it to whom he will."
[30]† At once this was fulfilled. Nebuchad-
nezzar was cast out from among men,
he ate grass like an ox, and his body was
bathed with the dew of heaven, until his
hair grew like the feathers of an eagle,
and his nails like the claws of a bird.

[31]* When this period was over, I,
Nebuchadnezzar, raised my eyes to
heaven; my reason was restored to me,
and I blessed the Most High, I praised
and glorified him who lives forever:

His dominion is an everlasting do-
minion,
and his kingdom endures through
all generations.
32 All who live on the earth are counted
as nothing;
he does as he pleases with the
powers of heaven
as well as with those who live on
the earth.
There is no one who can stay his
hand
or say to him, "What have you
done?"

[33] At the same time my reason re-
turned to me, and for the glory of my
kingdom, my majesty and my splendor
returned to me. My nobles and lords
sought me out; I was restored to my
kingdom, and became much greater
than before. [34] Therefore, I, Nebuchad-
nezzar, now praise and exalt and glorify
the King of heaven, because all his
works are right and his ways just; and
those who walk in pride he is able to
humble.

CHAPTER 5

The Writing on the Wall. [1]† King Bel-
shazzar gave a great banquet for a thou-
sand of his lords, with whom he drank.
[2]† Under the influence of the wine, he
ordered the gold and silver vessels
which Nebuchadnezzar, his father, had
taken from the temple in Jerusalem, to
be brought in so that the king, his lords,
his wives and his entertainers might
drink from them. [3] When the gold and
silver vessels taken from the house of
God in Jerusalem had been brought in,
and while the king, his lords, his wives
and his entertainers were drinking
[4] wine from them, they praised their

*

22: 5, 21.
24: Sir 3, 30; 4, 8.
31: 3, 100; 7, 14.

†

4, 22: The description is of a form of insanity called lycanthropy, in which the patient acts like a wolf.

4, 24: A classic Scriptural text for the efficacy of good works.

4, 27: The words attributed to the king are similar to the boastings in the royal inscriptions by which the Mesopotamian kings testified to their mighty works.

4, 30ff: There is no certainty of any such thing happening to Nebuchadnezzar as is described here. Some scholars think that the Nebuchadnezzar of this chapter is actually Nabonidus, the father of Belshazzar, who was mysteriously absent from Babylon for a number of years. The biblical author's chief interest was not in the historicity of this popular tale, but in the object lesson it contained for the proud "divine" kings of the Seleucid dynasty.

5, 1: *King Belshazzar:* Belshazzar was actually the crown prince, but he had been given royal authority in Babylon by his father Nabonidus.

5, 2: *Nebuchadnezzar, his father:* several kings of Babylon intervened between Nebuchadnezzar and Belshazzar. Either the term *father* is used here in the broad sense of "remote predecessor," or the name *Nebuchadnezzar* is used for "Nabonidus."

gods of gold and silver, bronze and iron, wood and stone.

5 Suddenly, opposite the lampstand, the fingers of a human hand appeared, writing on the plaster of the wall in the king's palace. When the king saw the wrist and hand that wrote, 6 his face blanched; his thoughts terrified him, his hip joints shook, and his knees knocked. 7 The king shouted for the enchanters, Chaldeans, and astrologers to be brought in. "Whoever reads this writing and tells me what it means," he said to the wise men of Babylon, "shall be clothed in purple, wear a golden collar about his neck, and be third in the government of the kingdom." 8 But though all the king's wise men came in, none of them could either read the writing or tell the king what it meant. 9 Then King Belshazzar was greatly terrified; his face went ashen, and his lords were thrown into confusion.

10 When the queen heard of the discussion between the king and his lords, she entered the banquet hall and said, "O king, live forever! Be not troubled in mind, nor look so pale! 11 There is a man in your kingdom in whom is the spirit of the holy God; during the lifetime of your father he was seen to have brilliant knowledge and god-like wisdom. In fact, King Nebuchadnezzar, your father, made him chief of the magicians, enchanters, Chaldeans, and astrologers, 12 because of the extraordinary mind possessed by this Daniel, whom the king named Belteshazzar. He knew and understood how to interpret dreams, explain enigmas, and solve difficulties. Now therefore, summon Daniel to tell you what this means."

13 Then Daniel was brought into the presence of the king. The king asked him, "Are you the Daniel, the Jewish exile, whom my father, the king, brought from Judah? 14 I have heard that the spirit of God is in you, that you possess brilliant knowledge and extraordinary wisdom. 15 Now, the wise men and enchanters were brought in to me to read this writing and tell me its meaning, but they could not say what the words meant. 16 But I have heard that you can interpret dreams and solve difficulties; if you are able to read the writing and tell me what it means, you shall be clothed in purple, wear a gold collar about your neck, and be third in the government of the kingdom."

17 Daniel answered the king: "You may keep your gifts, or give your presents to someone else; but the writing I will read for you, O king, and tell you what it means. 18 The Most High God gave your father Nebuchadnezzar a great kingdom and glorious majesty. 19 Because he made him so great, the nations and peoples of every language dreaded and feared him. Whomever he wished, he killed or let live; whomever he wished, he exalted or humbled. 20 But when his heart became proud and his spirit hardened by insolence, he was put down from his royal throne and deprived of his glory; 21* he was cast out from among men and was made insensate as a beast; he lived with wild asses, and ate grass like an ox; his body was bathed with the dew of heaven, until he learned that the Most High God rules over the kingdom of men and appoints over it whom he will. 22 You, his son, Belshazzar, have not humbled your heart, though you knew all this; 23 you have rebelled against the Lord of heaven. You had the vessels of his temple brought before you, so that you and your nobles, your wives and your entertainers, might drink wine from them; and you praised the gods of silver and gold, bronze and iron, wood and stone, that neither see nor hear nor have intelligence. But the God in whose hand is your life breath and the whole course of your life, you did not glorify. 24 By him were the wrist and hand sent, and the writing set down.

25† "This is the writing that was inscribed: MENE, TEKEL, and PERES. These words mean: 26† MENE, God has numbered your kingdom and put an end to it; 27 TEKEL, you have been weighed on the scales and found wanting; 28 PERES, your kingdom has been divided and given to the Medes and Persians."

29 Then by order of Belshazzar they clothed Daniel in purple, with a gold collar about his neck, and proclaimed him third in the government of the kingdom. 30 The same night Belshazzar, the Chaldean king, was slain:

CHAPTER 6

1† And Darius the Mede succeeded to the kingdom at the age of sixty-two.

In the Lions' Den. 2 Darius decided to appoint over his entire kingdom one

---

* 5, 21: 4, 22.

---

† 5, 25: *Mene, Tekel, and Peres:* these seem to be the Aramaic names of weights and monetary values: the mina, the shekel (the sixtieth part of a mina), and the parsu (a half-mina).

5, 26ff: Daniel interprets these three terms by a play on the words: *Mene,* connected with the verb meaning to number; *Tekel,* with the verb meaning to weigh; *Peres,* with the verb meaning to divide. There is also a play on the last term with the word for Persians.

6, 1: *Darius the Mede:* unknown in profane history. The Median kingdom had already been conquered by Cyrus the Persian, and it was Cyrus who captured Babylon. Evidently the author of Daniel has deliberately adopted an apocalyptic view of history, derived from prophecy (cf Is 13, 17ff; Jer 51, 11.28ff), according to which the Medes formed the second of four world kingdoms preceding the messianic times; see note on 2, 36-45. The character of Darius the Mede has probably been modeled on that of the Persian King Darius the Great (522-486 B.C.), the second successor of Cyrus.

hundred and twenty satraps, to safe-
guard his interests; 3 these were ac-
countable to three supervisors, one of
whom was Daniel. 4 Daniel outshone all
the supervisors and satraps because an
extraordinary spirit was in him, and the
king thought of giving him authority
over the entire kingdom. 5 Therefore the
supervisors and satraps tried to find
grounds for accusation against Daniel
as regards the administration. But they
could accuse him of no wrongdoing; be-
cause he was trustworthy, no fault of
neglect or misconduct was to be found
in him. 6 Then these men said to them-
selves, "We shall find no grounds for ac-
cusation against this Daniel unless by
way of the law of his God." 7 So these
supervisors and satraps went thronging
to the king and said to him, "King Da-
rius, live forever! 8* All the supervisors
of the kingdom, the prefects, satraps,
nobles, and governors are agreed that
the following prohibition ought to be put
in force by royal decree: no one is to ad-
dress any petition to god or man for
thirty days, except to you, O king; other-
wise he shall be cast into a den of lions.
9† Now, O king, issue the prohibition
over your signature, immutable and ir-
revocable under Mede and Persian
law." 10 So King Darius signed the pro-
hibition and made it law.

11 Even after Daniel heard that this
law had been signed, he continued his
custom of going home to kneel in prayer
and give thanks to his God in the upper
chamber three times a day, with the
windows open toward Jerusalem. 12 So
these men rushed in and found Daniel
praying and pleading before his God.
13 Then they went to remind the king
about the prohibition: "Did you not de-
cree, O king, that no one is to address
a petition to god or man for thirty days,
except to you, O king; otherwise he shall
be cast into a den of lions?" The king
answered them, "The decree is absolute,
irrevocable under the Mede and Persian
law." 14 To this they replied, "Daniel, the
Jewish exile, has paid no attention to
you, O king, or to the decree you issued;
three times a day he offers his prayer."
15 The king was deeply grieved at this
news and he made up his mind to save
Daniel; he worked till sunset to rescue
him. 16 But these men insisted. "Keep in
mind, O king," they said, "that under
the Mede and Persian law every royal
prohibition or decree is irrevocable."
17† So the king ordered Daniel to be
brought and cast into the lions' den. To
Daniel he said, "May your God, whom
you serve so constantly, save you." 18 To
forestall any tampering, the king sealed
with his own ring and the rings of the
lords the stone that had been brought
to block the opening of the den.

19 Then the king returned to his palace
for the night; he refused to eat and he
dismissed the entertainers. Since sleep
was impossible for him, 20 the king rose
very early the next morning and has-
tened to the lions' den. 21 As he drew
near, he cried out to Daniel sorrowfully,
"O Daniel, servant of the living God, has
the God whom you serve so constantly
been able to save you from the lions?"
22* Daniel answered the king: "O king,
live forever! 23 My God has sent his angel
and closed the lions' mouths so that they
have not hurt me. For I have been found
innocent before him; neither to you have
I done any harm, O king!" 24 This gave
the king great joy. At his order Daniel
was removed from the den, unhurt be-
cause he trusted in his God. 25 The king
then ordered the men who had accused
Daniel, along with their children and
their wives, to be cast into the lions' den.
Before they reached the bottom of the
den, the lions overpowered them and
crushed all their bones.

26 Then King Darius wrote to the na-
tions and peoples of every language,
wherever they dwell on the earth: "All
peace to you! 27 I decree that throughout
my royal domain the God of Daniel is
to be reverenced and feared:

"For he is the living God, enduring
forever;
his kingdom shall not be de-
stroyed,
and his dominion shall be without
end.
28* He is a deliverer and savior,
working signs and wonders in
heaven and on earth,
and he delivered Daniel from the
lions' power."

29 So Daniel fared well during the reign
of Darius and the reign of Cyrus the Per-
sian.

II: DANIEL'S VISIONS

CHAPTER 7

Vision of the Four Beasts. 1† In the
first year of King Belshazzar of Babylon,

---

*

6, 8: Est 1, 19. 22: 1 Mc 2, 60. 28: 1, 21.

†

6, 9: *Immutable and irrevocable:* the passages in Est 1, 19 and 8, 8 also refer to the immutability of Medo-Persian laws. The historian Diodorus Siculus indicates that such a concept existed in the time of Darius III (335-331 B.C.), the last of the Persian kings. Cf vv 13.16.

6, 17: *The lions' den:* a pit too deep to be easily scaled; its opening was blocked with a stone (v 18).

7, 1-27: The significance of this vision is the same as that of Nebuchadnezzar's dream in chapter 2; see note on 2, 36-45. To the four succeeding world kingdoms, Babylonian, Median, Persian, and Greek, is opposed the messianic kingdom of the people of God. The imagery of this chapter has been used extensively in the Revelation of St. John, where it is applied to the Roman empire, the persecutor of the Church.

Daniel had a dream as he lay in bed,
and was terrified by the visions of his
mind. Then he wrote down the dream;
the account began: 2† In the vision I saw
during the night, suddenly the four
winds of heaven stirred up the great sea,
3 from which emerged four immense
beasts, each different from the others.
4† The first was like a lion, but with ea-
gle's wings. While I watched, the wings
were plucked; it was raised from the
ground to stand on two feet like a man,
and given a human mind. 5† The second
was like a bear; it was raised up on one
side, and among the teeth in its mouth
were three tusks. It was given the order,
"Up, devour much flesh." 6† After this
I looked and saw another beast, like a
leopard; on its back were four wings like
those of a bird, and it had four heads.
To this beast dominion was given.
7† After this, in the visions of the night
I saw the fourth beast, different from all
the others, terrifying, horrible, and of
extraordinary strength; it had great iron
teeth with which it devoured and
crushed, and what was left it trampled
with its feet. 8 I was considering the ten
horns it had, when suddenly another, a
little horn, sprang out of their midst, and
three of the previous horns were torn
away to make room for it. This horn had
eyes like a man, and a mouth that spoke
arrogantly. 9† As I watched,

Thrones were set up
 and the Ancient One took his throne.
His clothing was snow bright,
 and the hair on his head as white as wool;
His throne was flames of fire,
 with wheels of burning fire.
10* A surging stream of fire
 flowed out from where he sat;
Thousands upon thousands were ministering to him,
 and myriads upon myriads attended him.

The court was convened, and the
books were opened. 11 I watched, then,
from the first of the arrogant words
which the horn spoke, until the beast was
slain and its body thrown into the fire
to be burnt up. 12 The other beasts, which
also lost their dominion, were granted
a prolongation of life for a time and a
season. 13† As the visions during the
night continued, I saw

One like a son of man coming,
 on the clouds of heaven;
When he reached the Ancient One
 and was presented before him,
14* He received dominion, glory, and kingship;
 nations and peoples of every language serve him.
His dominion is an everlasting dominion
 that shall not be taken away,
 his kingship shall not be destroyed.

15 I, Daniel, found my spirit anguished
within its sheath of flesh, and I was terri-
fied by the visions of my mind. 16 I ap-
proached one of those present and asked
him what all this meant in truth; in an-
swer, he made known to me the meaning
of the things: 17 "These four great beasts
stand for four kingdoms which shall
arise on the earth. 18 But the holy ones
of the Most High shall receive the king-
ship, to possess it forever and ever."
19 But I wished to make certain about
the fourth beast, so very terrible and dif-
ferent from the others, devouring and
crushing with its iron teeth and bronze
claws, and trampling with its feet what
was left; 20 about the ten horns on its
head, and the other one that sprang up,
before which three horns fell; about the
horn with the eyes and the mouth that
spoke arrogantly, which appeared
greater than its fellows. 21 For, as I
watched, that horn made war against
the holy ones and was victorious 22 until
the Ancient One arrived; judgment was
pronounced in favor of the holy ones of
the Most High, and the time came when
the holy ones possessed the kingdom.

*

7, 10: Rv 5, 11.
14: 3, 100; 4, 31; Mi 4, 7; Lk 1, 32.

†

7, 2: *The great sea:* the primordial ocean beneath the earth, according to primitive cosmology (Gn 7, 11; 49, 25). This was thought to contain various monsters (Is 27, 1; Jb 7, 12), and in particular mythological monsters symbolizing the chaos which God had vanquished in ancient times (Jb 9, 13; 26, 13; etc.).

7, 4: The representation of the Babylonian empire as a winged lion, a common motif in Babylonian art, symbolizes the bestial power hostile to God. The two wings that *were plucked* represent Nebuchadnezzar and Belshazzar. *On two feet like a man . . . a human mind:* contrasts with what is said in 4, 13.30.

7, 5: *A bear:* represents the Median empire, its *three tusks* symbolizing its destructive nature; hence, the command: "*Up, devour much flesh.*"

7, 6: *A leopard:* used to symbolize the swiftness with which Cyrus the Persian established his kingdom. *Four heads:* corresponding to the four Persian kings of 11, 2.

7, 7f: Alexander's empire was *different from all the others* in that it was Western rather than Oriental in inspiration. The *ten horns* represent the kings of the Seleucid dynasty, the only part of the Hellenistic empire that concerned the author. The *little horn* is Antiochus IV Epiphanes (175-163 B.C.), the worst of the Seleucid kings, who usurped the throne.

7, 9f: A vision of the heavenly throne of God *(the Ancient One),* who sits in judgment (symbolized by *fire*) over the nations. Some of the details of the vision, depicting the divine majesty and omnipotence, are to be found in Ez 1.

7, 13f: *One like a son of man:* in contrast to the worldly kingdoms opposed to God, which appear as beasts, the glorified people of God that will form his kingdom on earth is represented in human form (v 18). Just as our Lord applied the figure of the stone hewn from the mountain to himself (2, 36-45), he also made the title "Son of Man" his most characteristic way of referring to himself, as the One in whom and through whom the salvation of God's people came to be realized.

23 He answered me thus:

"The fourth beast shall be a fourth
kingdom on earth,
different from all the others;
It shall devour the whole earth,
beat it down, and crush it.
24 The ten horns shall be ten kings
rising out of that kingdom;
another shall rise up after them,
Different from those before him,
who shall lay low three kings.
25† He shall speak against the Most
High
and oppress the holy ones of the
Most High,
thinking to change the feast days
and the law.
They shall be handed over to him
for a year, two years, and a half-
year.
26 But when the court is convened,
and his power is taken away
by final and absolute destruction,
27 Then the kingship and dominion and
majesty
of all the kingdoms under the
heavens
shall be given to the holy people
of the Most High,
Whose kingdom shall be everlasting:
all dominions shall serve and obey
him."

28† The report concluded: I, Daniel,
was greatly terrified by my thoughts,
and my face blanched, but I kept the
matter to myself.

CHAPTER 8

Vision of the Ram and He-goat.
1† After this first vision, I, Daniel, had
another, in the third year of the reign
of King Belshazzar. 2† In my vision I saw
myself in the fortress of Susa in the
province of Elam; I was beside the river
Ulai. 3 I looked up and saw standing by
the river a ram with two great horns,
the one larger and newer than the other.
4 I saw the ram butting toward the west,
north, and south. No beast could with-
stand it or be rescued from its power;
it did what it pleased and became very
powerful.
5 As I was reflecting, a he-goat with
a prominent horn on its forehead sud-
denly came from the west across the
whole earth without touching the
ground. 6 It approached the two-horned
ram I had seen standing by the river,
and rushed toward it with savage force.
7 I saw it attack the ram with furious
blows when they met, and break both
its horns. It threw the ram, which had
not the force to withstand it, to the
ground, and trampled upon it; and no
one could rescue it from its power.
8 The he-goat became very powerful,
but at the height of its power the great
horn was shattered, and in its place
came up four others, facing the four
winds of heaven. 9† Out of one of them
came a little horn which kept growing
toward the south, the east, and the glori-
ous country. 10† Its power extended to
the host of heaven, so that it cast down
to earth some of the host and some of
the stars and trampled on them. 11 It
boasted even against the prince of the
host, from whom it removed the daily
sacrifice, and whose sanctuary it cast
down, 12 as well as the host, while sin re-
placed the daily sacrifice. It cast truth
to the ground, and was succeeding in its
undertaking.
13† I heard a holy one speaking, and
another said to whichever one it was that
spoke, "How long shall the events of this
vision last concerning the daily sacrifice,
the desolating sin which is placed there,
the sanctuary, and the trampled host?"
14 He answered him, "For two thousand
three hundred evenings and mornings;
then the sanctuary shall be purified."
15 While I, Daniel, sought the meaning
of the vision I had seen, a manlike figure
stood before me, 16† and on the Ulai I
heard a human voice that cried out,
"Gabriel, explain the vision to this
man." 17† When he came near where I
was standing, I fell prostrate in terror.
But he said to me, "Understand, son of
man, that the vision refers to the end
time." 18 As he spoke to me, I fell forward
in a faint; he touched me and made me
stand up. 19 "I will show you," he said,

---

†

7, 25: The reference is to the persecutions of Antiochus IV and his attempt to force the Jews to give up their customs and to adopt Hellenistic ways (1 Mc 1, 33f). *A year, two years, and a half-year:* an indefinite, evil period of time. As seven is the Jewish "perfect" number, half of it signifies great imperfection. Actually, this corresponds fairly accurately to the duration of Antiochus' persecution.

7, 28: This verse ends the Aramaic part of the Book of Daniel.

8, 1-27: This vision repeats the major part of the preceding one, though in a more explicit fashion. As explained in vv 20ff, *the two-horned ram* represents the combined kingdom of the Medes and Persians, destroyed by Alexander's Hellenistic empire originating in the west. Once again the author is interested only in the Seleucid dynasty, which emerged from the dissolution of Alexander's empire after his death in 323 B.C.

8, 2: *The fortress of Susa:* the royal palace of the Persian kings in the ancient territory of Elam, east of Babylonia. *The river Ulai:* a canal along the northern side of Susa.

8, 9: *A little horn,* as in chapter 7, is Antiochus IV. *The glorious country:* Palestine.

8, 10ff: *The host of heaven:* ordinarily meaning the stars, here refers to the people of God; cf 12, 3. *The prince of the host:* God himself, with whose holy religion Antiochus interfered (1 Mc 1, 45).

8, 13: *The desolating sin:* the Hebrew contains a wordplay (*shomem*) on the name Baal Shamem ("lord of the heavens," the Greek Zeus Olympios), referring to the statue with which Antiochus profaned the temple of Jerusalem (2 Mc 6, 2).

8, 16: The angel Gabriel is mentioned here for the first time in the Bible. There is wordplay in the preceding verse on geber—*manlike figure.*

8, 17: *The end time:* the day of the Lord, when God sits in judgment on his enemies (v 19).

“what is to happen later in the period
of wrath; for at the appointed time, there
will be an end.
20 “The two-horned ram you saw rep-
resents the kings of the Medes and Per-
sians. 21 The he-goat is the king of the
Greeks, and the great horn on its fore-
head is the first king. 22 The four that
rose in its place when it was broken are
four kingdoms that will issue from his
nation, but without his strength.

23 “After their reign,
when sinners have reached their measure,
There shall arise a king, impudent and skilled in intrigue.
24 He shall be strong and powerful,
bring about fearful ruin,
and succeed in his undertaking.
He shall destroy powerful peoples;
25 his cunning shall be against the holy ones,
his treacherous conduct shall succeed.
He shall be proud of heart
and destroy many by stealth.
But when he rises against the prince of princes,
he shall be broken without a hand being raised.
26 The vision of the evenings and the mornings
is true, as spoken;
Do you, however, keep this vision undisclosed,
because the days are to be many.”

27 I, Daniel, was weak and ill for some
days; then I arose and took care of the
king’s affairs. But I was appalled at the
vision, which I could not understand.

CHAPTER 9

Gabriel and the Seventy Weeks. 1† It
was the first year that Darius, son of
Ahasuerus, of the race of the Medes,
reigned over the kingdom of the Chalde-
ans; 2*† in the first year of his reign I,
Daniel, tried to understand in the Scrip-
tures the counting of the years of which
the LORD spoke to the prophet Jeremiah:
that for the ruins of Jerusalem seventy
years must be fulfilled.
3 I turned to the Lord God, pleading
in earnest prayer, with fasting, sack-
cloth, and ashes. 4* I prayed to the LORD,
my God, and confessed, “Ah, Lord,
great and awesome God, you who keep
your merciful covenant toward those
who love you and observe your com-
mandments! 5* We have sinned, been
wicked and done evil; we have rebelled
and departed from your command-
ments and your laws. 6 We have not
obeyed your servants the prophets, who
spoke in your name to our kings, our
princes, our fathers, and all the people
of the land. 7 Justice, O Lord, is on your
side; we are shamefaced even to this
day: the men of Judah, the residents of
Jerusalem, and all Israel, near and far,
in all the countries to which you have
scattered them because of their treach-
ery toward you. 8 O LORD, we are shame-
faced, like our kings, our princes, and
our fathers, for having sinned against
you. 9 But yours, O Lord, our God, are
compassion and forgiveness! Yet we re-
belled against you 10 and paid no heed
to your command, O LORD, our God, to
live by the law you gave us through your
servants the prophets. 11* Because all Is-
rael transgressed your law and went
astray, not heeding your voice, the
sworn malediction, recorded in the law
of Moses, the servant of God, was poured
out over us for our sins. 12 You carried
out the threats you spoke against us and
against those who governed us, by
bringing upon us in Jerusalem the great-
est calamity that has ever occurred un-
der heaven. 13† As it is written in the law
of Moses, this calamity came full upon
us. As we did not appease the LORD, our
God, by turning back from our wicked-
ness and recognizing his constancy, 14 so
the LORD kept watch over the calamity
and brought it upon us. You, O LORD,
our God, are just in all that you have
done, for we did not listen to your voice.
15* “Now, O Lord, our God, who led
your people out of the land of Egypt with
a strong hand, and made a name for
yourself even to this day, we have
sinned, we are guilty. 16 O Lord, in keep-
ing with all your just deeds, let your an-
ger and your wrath be turned away from
your city Jerusalem, your holy moun-
tain. On account of our sins and the
crimes of our fathers, Jerusalem and
your people have become the reproach
of all our neighbors. 17 Hear, therefore,
O God, the prayer and petition of your
servant; and for your own sake, O Lord,
let your face shine upon your desolate
sanctuary. 18* Give ear, O my God, and

*

9, 2f: Jer 25, 11; 29, 10.
4: Neh 1, 5.
5: Bar 1, 17.
11: Dt 27, 15.
15: Bar 2, 11; Ex 14, 22.
18: Jer 25, 29.

†

9, 1: *Darius:* see the note on 6, 1.

9, 2: *Seventy years:* the prophet Jeremiah (25, 11; 29, 10) prophesied a Babylonian captivity of seventy years, a round number signifying the complete passing away of the existing generation. Jeremiah’s prophecy was fulfilled in the capture of Babylon by Cyrus and the subsequent return of the Jews to Palestine. However, the author of Daniel, living during the persecution of Antiochus, sees the conditions of the exile still existing; therefore, in his meditation he extends Jeremiah’s number to seventy weeks of years (v 24), i.e., seven times seventy years, to characterize the Jewish victory over the Seleucids as the ultimate fulfillment of the prophecy.

9, 13: *As it is written:* the first time that this formula of Scriptural citation is used in the Bible. The reference (v 11) is to the sanctions of Lv 26, 14ff; Dt 28, 15ff.

listen; open your eyes and see our ruins
and the city which bears your name.
When we present our petition before
you, we rely not on our just deeds, but
on your great mercy. 19 O Lord, hear!
O Lord, pardon! O Lord, be attentive and
act without delay, for your own sake, O
my God, because this city and your peo-
ple bear your name!"

20 I was still occupied with my prayer,
confessing my sin and the sin of my peo-
ple Israel, presenting my petition to the
LORD, my God, on behalf of his holy
mountain—21*† I was still occupied with
this prayer, when Gabriel, the one whom
I had seen before in vision, came to me
in rapid flight at the time of the evening
sacrifice. 22 He instructed me in these
words: "Daniel, I have now come to give
you understanding. 23 When you began
your petition, an answer was given
which I have come to announce, because
you are beloved. Therefore, mark the
answer and understand the vision.

24† "Seventy weeks are decreed
for your people and for your holy city:
Then transgression will stop and sin will end,
guilt will be expiated,
Everlasting justice will be introduced,
vision and prophecy ratified,
and a most holy will be anointed.
25† Know and understand this:
From the utterance of the word
that Jerusalem was to be rebuilt
Until one who is anointed and a leader,
there shall be seven weeks.
During sixty-two weeks
it shall be rebuilt,
With streets and trenches,
in time of affliction.
26† After the sixty-two weeks
an anointed shall be cut down
when he does not possess the city;
And the people of a leader who will come
shall destroy the sanctuary.
Then the end shall come like a torrent;
until the end there shall be war,
the desolation that is decreed.
27*† For one week he shall make
a firm compact with the many;
Half the week
he shall abolish sacrifice and oblation;
On the temple wing shall be the horrible abomination
until the ruin that is decreed
is poured out upon the horror."

CHAPTER 10

Vision of the Hellenistic Wars. 1† In
the third year of Cyrus, king of Persia,
a revelation was given to Daniel, who
had been named Belteshazzar. The rev-
elation was certain: a great war; he un-
derstood it from the vision. 2† In those
days, I, Daniel, mourned three full
weeks. 3 I ate no savory food, I took no
meat or wine, and I did not anoint myself
at all until the end of the three weeks.

4† On the twenty-fourth day of the first
month I was on the bank of the great
river, the Tigris. 5† As I looked up, I saw
a man dressed in linen with a belt of fine
gold around his waist. 6 His body was
like chrysolite, his face shown like light-
ning, his eyes were like fiery torches, his
arms and feet looked like burnished
bronze, and his voice sounded like the
roar of a multitude. 7 I alone, Daniel, saw
the vision; but great fear seized the men
who were with me; they fled and hid
themselves, although they did not see

*

21: Dn 8, 16. 2 Mc 6, 2.
27: Mt 24, 15;

†

9, 21: *At the time of the evening sacrifice:* between three and four in the afternoon.

9, 24: *Seventy weeks:* i.e., of years. Just as Jeremiah's seventy years was an approximation (see note on v 2), the four hundred and ninety years here is not to be taken literally. Similarly, the distribution of the "weeks" in the following verses indicates only relative proportions of the total figure. *A most holy:* an expression used almost always of an object, the altar or the temple, but once (1 Chr 23, 13) of Aaron the high priest. The author sees the definitive establishment of the kingdom of God, realized in the reconsecration of the temple after Antiochus' desecration, or personified in the holy community (like the Son of Man of chapter 7). The Fathers of the Church almost unanimously understood the reference to be to Christ, the final realization of the prophecy.

9, 25: *From the utterance . . . to be rebuilt:* from the time of Jeremiah's prophecy. *One . . . anointed and a leader:* either Cyrus, who was called the anointed of the Lord to end the exile (Is 45, 1), or the high priest Joshua who presided over the rebuilding of the altar of sacrifice after the exile (Ezr 3, 2). *Seven weeks:* forty-nine years, an approximation of the time of the exile. *During sixty-two weeks . . . rebuilt:* a period of 434 years, roughly approximating the interval between the rebuilding of Jerusalem after the exile and the beginning of the Seleucid persecution.

9, 26: *An anointed:* doubtless the high priest Onias III, murdered in 171 B.C., from which the author dates the beginning of the persecution. Onias was in exile when he was killed. *A leader:* Antiochus IV.

9, 27: *One week: the final phase of the period in view,* the time of Antiochus' persecution; *he* is Antiochus himself. *The many:* the faithless Jews who allied themselves with the heathen; cf 1 Mc 1, 11ff. *Half the week:* three and a half years; see note on 7, 25. The temple was desecrated by Antiochus from 167 to 165 B.C. *The temple wing:* probably the main portal. *The horrible abomination:* see note on 8, 13. Perhaps an inscription was placed on the portal of the temple dedicating it to the Olympian Zeus. Our Lord referred to this passage in his own prediction of the destruction of Jerusalem (Mt 24, 15).

10, 1—12, 13: This final vision repeats some of the material contained in the others. It is concerned with history of the worldly kingdoms from the time of Cyrus to the defeat of the tyrant Antiochus.

10, 2: *Mourned:* perhaps the author intends to recall the interruption in the rebuilding of the temple, which occurred during this time (Ezr 4, 1-4).

10, 4: *The first month:* the month Nisan (mid-March to mid-April).

10, 5f: The heavenly person of the vision is probably the angel Gabriel, as in 9, 21. *Chrysolite:* or topaz, a yellowish precious stone.

the vision. 8 So I was left alone, seeing
this great vision. No strength remained
in me; I turned the color of death and
was powerless. 9 When I heard the sound
of his voice, I fell face forward in a faint.
10 But then a hand touched me, raising
me to my hands and knees. 11 "Daniel,
beloved," he said to me, "understand the
words which I am speaking to you; stand
up, for my mission now is to you." When
he said this to me, I stood up trembling.
12 "Fear not, Daniel," he continued;
"from the first day you made up your
mind to acquire understanding and
humble yourself before God, your
prayer was heard. Because of it I started
out, 13† but the prince of the kingdom of
Persia stood in my way for twenty-one
days, until finally Michael, one of the
chief princes, came to help me. I left him
there with the prince of the kings of Per-
sia, 14 and came to make you understand
what shall happen to your people in the
days to come; for there is yet a vision
concerning those days."
15 While he was speaking thus to me,
I fell forward and kept silent. 16 Then
something like a man's hand touched
my lips; I opened my mouth and said
to the one facing me, "My lord, I was
seized with pangs at the vision and I was
powerless. 17 How can my lord's servant
speak with you, my lord? For now no
strength or even breath is left in me."
18 The one who looked like a man
touched me again and strengthened me,
saying, 19 "Fear not, beloved, you are
safe; take courage and be strong."
20 When he spoke to me, I grew strong
and said, "Speak, my lord, for you have
strengthened me." "Do you know," he
asked, "why I have come to you? Soon
I must fight the prince of Persia again.
When I leave, the prince of Greece will
come; 21* but I shall tell you what is writ-
ten in the truthful book. No one supports
me against all these except Michael,
your prince, 11,1† standing as a rein-
forcement and a bulwark for me. 2† Now
I shall tell you the truth.

CHAPTER 11

"Three kings of Persia are yet to come;
and a fourth shall acquire the greatest
riches of all. Strengthened by his riches,
he shall rouse all the kingdom of Greece.
3 But a powerful king shall appear and
rule with great might, doing as he
pleases. 4 No sooner shall he appear than
his kingdom shall be broken and divided
in four directions under heaven; but not
among his descendants or in keeping
with his mighty rule, for his kingdom
shall be torn to pieces and belong to oth-
ers than they.
5† "The king of the south shall grow
strong, but one of his princes shall grow
stronger still and govern a domain
greater than his. 6 After some years they
shall become allies: the daughter of the
king of the south shall come to the king
of the north in the interest of peace. But
her bid for power shall fail: and her line
shall not be recognized, and she shall
be given up, together with those who
brought her, her son and her husband.
But later 7 a descendant of her line shall
succeed to his rank, and shall come
against the rampart and enter the
stronghold of the king of the north, and
conquer them. 8 Even their gods, with
their molten images and their precious
vessels of silver and gold, he shall carry
away as booty into Egypt. For years he
shall have nothing to do with the king
of the north. 9 Then the latter shall in-
vade the land of the king of the south,
and return to his own country.
10 "But his sons shall prepare and as-
semble a great armed host, which shall
advance like a flood, then withdraw.
When it returns and surges around the
stronghold, 11 the king of the south, pro-
voked, shall go out to fight against the
king of the north, whose great host shall
make a stand but shall be given into his
hand 12 and be carried off. In the pride
of his heart, he shall lay low tens of thou-
sands, but he shall not triumph. 13 For
the king of the north shall raise another
army, greater than before; after some
years he shall attack with this large
army and great resources. 14* In those
times many shall resist the king of the
south, and outlaws of your people shall
rise up in fulfillment of vision, but they
shall fail. 15 When the king of the north
comes, he shall set up siegeworks and
take the fortified city by storm. The
power of the south shall not withstand
him, and not even his picked troops shall

*

10, 21: Rv 12, 7. 11, 14: Is 19, 1.

†

10, 13: *The prince of the kingdom of Persia:* the guardian angel of Persia. The later Judaism ascribed protecting angels to various groups of human society, often as little more than personifications. *Michael:* the angel who is the protector of God's people (v 21).

11, 1: *Standing . . . truth:* these are the first two verses of chapter 11.

11, 2-4: The *three kings of Persia* who follow Cyrus are uncertain, since there were more than three Persian kings between Cyrus and the dissolution of the kingdom. The *fourth* is doubtless Xerxes I (486-465 B.C.), the great campaigner against Greece. The *powerful king* is Alexander the Great, who ended the Persian empire by his victory at Issus in 333 B.C.

11, 5-45: These verses describe the dynastic histories of the Ptolemies in Egypt (*the king of the south*) and the Seleucids in Syria (*the king of the north*), the two divisions of the Hellenistic empire that were of interest to the author (v 6). In vv 10-20 is described the struggle between the two kingdoms for the control of Palestine, in which the Seleucids were eventually victorious. The reference in v 20 is to Seleucus IV, who sent Heliodorus to plunder the temple treasure in Jerusalem (2 Mc 3). Finally, vv 21-45 describe the career of Antiochus IV and his persecution, in details that have been seen above.

have the strength to resist. 16 He shall
attack him and do as he pleases, with
no one to withstand him. He shall stop
in the glorious land, dealing destruction.
17 He shall set himself to penetrate the
entire strength of his kingdom. He shall
conclude an agreement with him and
give him a daughter in marriage in or-
der to destroy the kingdom, but this shall
not succeed in his favor. 18 He shall turn
to the coastland and take many, but a
leader shall put an end to his shameful
conduct, so that he cannot renew it
against him. 19 He shall turn to the
strongholds of his own land, but shall
stumble and fall, to be found no more.
20 In his stead one shall arise who will
send a tax collector through the glorious
kingdom, but he shall soon be destroyed,
though not in conflict or in battle.

21 "There shall rise in his place a despi-
cable person, to whom the royal insignia
shall not be given. By stealth and fraud
he shall seize the kingdom. 22 Armed
might shall be completely overwhelmed
by him and crushed, and even the prince
of the covenant. 23 After allying with
him, he shall treacherously rise to power
with a small party. 24 By stealth he shall
enter prosperous provinces and do that
which his fathers or grandfathers never
did; he shall distribute spoil, booty, and
riches among them and devise plots
against their strongholds; but only for
a time. 25 He shall call on his strength
and cleverness to meet the king of the
south with a great army; the king of the
south shall prepare for battle with a very
large and strong army, but he shall not
succeed because of the plots devised
against him. 26 Even his table compan-
ions shall seek to destroy him, his army
shall be overwhelmed, and many shall
fall slain. 27 The two kings, resolved on
evil, shall sit at table together and ex-
change lies, but they shall have no suc-
cess, because the appointed end is not
yet.

28 "He shall turn back toward his land
with great riches, his mind set against
the holy covenant; he shall arrange mat-
ters and return to his land. 29 At the time
appointed he shall come again to the
south, but this time it shall not be as be-
fore. 30† When ships of the Kittim con-
front him, he shall lose heart and
retreat. Then he shall direct his rage and
energy against the holy covenant; those
who forsake it he shall once more single
out. 31 Armed forces shall move at his
command and defile the sanctuary
stronghold, abolishing the daily sacrifice
and setting up the horrible abomination.
32 By his deceit he shall make some who
were disloyal to the covenant apostatize;
but those who remain loyal to their God
shall take strong action. 33 The nation's
wise men shall instruct the many;
though for a time they will become vic-
tims of the sword, of flames, exile, and
plunder. 34 When they fall, few people
shall help them, but many shall join
them out of treachery. 35 Of the wise
men, some shall fall, so that the rest may
be tested, refined, and purified, until the
end time which is still appointed to
come.

36† "The king shall do as he pleases,
exalting himself and making himself
greater than any god; he shall utter
dreadful blasphemies against the God of
gods. He shall prosper only till divine
wrath is ready, for what is determined
must take place. 37 He shall have no re-
gard for the gods of his ancestors or for
the one in whom women delight; for no
god shall he have regard, because he
shall make himself greater than all.
38 Instead, he shall give glory to the god
of strongholds; a god unknown to his fa-
thers he shall glorify with gold, silver,
precious stones, and other treasures.
39 To defend the strongholds he shall sta-
tion a people of a foreign god. Whoever
acknowledges him he shall provide with
abundant honor; he shall make them
rule over the many and distribute the
land as a reward.

40 "At the appointed time the king of
the south shall come to grips with him,
but the king of the north shall over-
whelm him with chariots and horsemen
and a great fleet, passing through the
countries like a flood. 41 He shall enter
the glorious land and many shall fall,
except Edom, Moab, and the chief part
of Ammon, which shall escape from his
power. 42 He shall extend his power over
the countries, and not even the land of
Egypt shall escape. 43 He shall control
the riches of gold and silver and all the
treasures of Egypt; Libya and Ethiopia
shall be in his train. 44 When news from
the east and the north terrifies him, he
shall set out with great fury to slay and
to doom many. 45 He shall pitch the tents
of his royal pavilion between the sea and
the glorious holy mountain, but he shall
come to his end with none to help him.

CHAPTER 12

1*† "At that time there shall arise
Michael, the great prince,

---

* 12, 1: Rv 12, 7.

---

† 11, 30: *Kittim:* originally this word meant Cypriots or other island dwellers. Here it means the Romans, who forced Antiochus to withdraw from Egypt during his second campaign there.

11, 36-39: Instead of venerating Apollo, one of *the gods of his ancestors,* Antiochus venerated, and even identified himself with, Zeus Olympios, whom the Romans equated with the god of their fortress in Rome, Jupiter Capitolinus, *the god of strongholds.*

12, 1: *Written in the book:* the book of God's predestination.

guardian of your people;
It shall be a time unsurpassed in distress
since nations began until that time.
At that time your people shall escape,
everyone who is found written in the book.
2*† Many of those who sleep
in the dust of the earth shall awake;
some shall live forever,
others shall be an everlasting horror and disgrace.
3* But the wise shall shine brightly
like the splendor of the firmament,
And those who lead the many to justice
shall be like the stars forever.

4 "As for you, Daniel, keep secret the
message and seal the book until the end
time; many shall fall away and evil shall
increase."
5 I, Daniel, looked and saw two others,
one standing on either bank of the river.
6 One of them said to the man clothed
in linen, who was upstream, "How long
shall it be to the end of these appalling
things?" 7*† The man clothed in linen,
who was upstream, lifted his right and
left hands to heaven; and I heard him
swear by him who lives forever that it
should be for a year, two years, a half-
year; and that, when the power of the
destroyer of the holy people was brought
to an end, all these things should end.
8 I heard, but I did not understand; so I
asked, "My lord, what follows this?"
9 "Go, Daniel," he said, "because the
words are to be kept secret and sealed
until the end time. 10 Many shall be re-
fined, purified, and tested, but the
wicked shall prove wicked; none of them
shall have understanding, but the wise
shall have it. 11 From the time that the
daily sacrifice is abolished and the hor-
rible abomination is set up, there shall
be one thousand two hundred and ninety
days. 12 Blessed is the man who has pa-
tience and perseveres until the one thou-
sand three hundred and thirty-five
days. 13 Go, take your rest, you shall rise
for your reward at the end of days."

III. APPENDIX

CHAPTER 13

Susanna's Virtue. 1† In Babylon there
lived a man named Joakim, 2 who mar-
ried a very beautiful and God-fearing
woman, Susanna, the daughter of Hil-
kiah; 3 her pious parents had trained
their daughter according to the law of
Moses. 4 Joakim was very rich; he had
a garden near his house, and the Jews
had recourse to him often because he
was the most respected of them all.
5 That year, two elders of the people
were appointed judges, of whom the
Lord said, "Wickedness has come out of
Babylon: from the elders who were to
govern the people as judges." 6 These
men, to whom all brought their cases,
frequented the house of Joakim. 7 When
the people left at noon, Susanna used to
enter her husband's garden for a walk.
8 When the old men saw her enter every
day for her walk, they began to lust for
her. 9 They suppressed their con-
sciences; they would not allow their eyes
to look to heaven, and did not keep in
mind just judgments. 10 Though both
were enamored of her, they did not tell
each other their trouble, 11 for they were
ashamed to reveal their lustful desire to
have her. 12 Day by day they watched
eagerly for her. 13 One day they said to
each other, "Let us be off for home, it
is time for lunch." So they went out and
parted; 14 but both turned back, and
when they met again, they asked each
other the reason. They admitted their
lust, and then they agreed to look for
an occasion when they could meet her
alone.
15 One day, while they were waiting for
the right moment, she entered the gar-
den as usual, with two maids only. She
decided to bathe, for the weather was
warm. 16 Nobody else was there except
the two elders, who had hidden them-
selves and were watching her. 17 "Bring
me oil and soap," she said to the maids,
"and shut the garden doors while I
bathe." 18 They did as she said; they shut
the garden doors and left by the side
gate to fetch what she had ordered, un-
aware that the elders were hidden in-
side.
19 As soon as the maids had left, the
two old men got up and hurried to her.
20 "Look," they said, "the garden doors
are shut, and no one can see us; give
in to our desire, and lie with us. 21 If you
refuse, we will testify against you that
you dismissed your maids because a
young man was here with you."

*

2: Mt 25, 46; Jn 5, 29.
3: Wis 3, 7.
7: Rv 10, 5f.

†

12, 2: The first Israelites who have fallen (11, 33ff) *shall awake,* that is, rise to *live forever.* A resurrection of the wicked as in later, Christian teaching (Jn 5, 28f) is implied here if the *others* are included in the *many;* but cf Is 66, 24.

12, 7: *A year, two years, a half-year:* see note on 7, 25. The author's perspective is the end of Antiochus, and beyond, the final consummation of all things.

13, 1—14, 42: The short stories in these two chapters may have originally been about some other Daniel or Daniels than the hero of the main part of the book. They exist now only in Greek, but probably were first composed in Hebrew or Aramaic. They are excluded from the Jewish canon of Scripture, but the Church has always included them among the inspired writings.

22 "I am completely trapped," Su-
sanna groaned. "If I yield, it will be my
death; if I refuse, I cannot escape your
power. 23 Yet it is better for me to fall
into your power without guilt than to sin
before the Lord." 24 Then Susanna
shrieked, and the old men also shouted
at her, 25 as one of them ran to open the
garden doors. 26 When the people in the
house heard the cries from the garden,
they rushed in by the side gate to see
what had happened to her. 27 At the ac-
cusations by the old men, the servants
felt very much ashamed, for never had
any such thing been said about Susanna.
28 When the people came to her hus-
band Joakim the next day, the two
wicked elders also came, fully deter-
mined to put Susanna to death. Before
all the people they ordered: 29 "Send for
Susanna, the daughter of Hilkiah, the
wife of Joakim." When she was sent for,
30 she came with her parents, children
and all her relatives. 31 Susanna, very
delicate and beautiful, 32 was veiled; but
those wicked men ordered her to un-
cover her face so as to sate themselves
with her beauty. 33 All her relatives and
the onlookers were weeping.
34 In the midst of the people the two
elders rose up and laid their hands on
her head. 35 Through her tears she
looked up to heaven, for she trusted in
the Lord wholeheartedly. 36 The elders
made this accusation: "As we were
walking in the garden alone, this woman
entered with two girls and shut the doors
of the garden, dismissing the girls. 37 A
young man, who was hidden there, came
and lay with her. 38 When we, in a corner
of the garden, saw this crime, we ran
toward them. 39 We saw them lying to-
gether, but the man we could not hold,
because he was stronger than we; he
opened the doors and ran off. 40 Then we
seized this one and asked who the young
man was, 41 but she refused to tell us.
We testify to this." The assembly be-
lieved them, since they were elders and
judges of the people, and they con-
demned her to death.
42 But Susanna cried aloud: "O eternal
God, you know what is hidden and are
aware of all things before they come to
be: 43 you know that they have testified
falsely against me. Here I am about to
die, though I have done none of the
things with which these wicked men
have charged me."
44 The Lord heard her prayer. 45 As she
was being led to execution, God stirred
up the holy spirit of a young boy named
Daniel, 46 and he cried aloud: "I will have
no part in the death of this woman."
47 All the people turned and asked him,
"What is this you are saying?" 48 He
stood in their midst and continued, "Are
you such fools, O Israelites! To condemn
a woman of Israel without examination
and without clear evidence? 49 Return to
court, for they have testified falsely
against her."
50 Then all the people returned in
haste. To Daniel the elders said, "Come,
sit with us and inform us, since God has
given you the prestige of old age." 51 But
he replied, "Separate these two far from
one another that I may examine them."
52 After they were separated one from
the other, he called one of them and said:
"How you have grown evil with age!
Now have your past sins come to term:
53* passing unjust sentences, condemn-
ing the innocent, and freeing the guilty,
although the Lord says, 'The innocent
and the just you shall not put to death.'
54 Now, then, if you were a witness, tell
me under what tree you saw them to-
gether." 55† "Under a mastic tree," he
answered. "Your fine lie has cost you
your head," said Daniel; "for the angel
of God shall receive the sentence from
him and split you in two." 56 Putting him
to one side, he ordered the other one to
be brought. "Offspring of Canaan, not
of Judah," Daniel said to him, "beauty
has seduced you, lust has subverted
your conscience. 57† This is how you
acted with the daughters of Israel, and
in their fear they yielded to you; but a
daughter of Judah did not tolerate your
wickedness. 58 Now, then, tell me under
what tree you surprised them together."
59 "Under an oak," he said. "Your fine
lie has cost you also your head," said
Daniel; "for the angel of God waits with
a sword to cut you in two so as to make
an end of you both."
60 The whole assembly cried aloud,
blessing God who saves those that hope
in him. 61* They rose up against the two
elders, for by their own words Daniel
had convicted them of perjury. Accord-
ing to the law of Moses, they inflicted
on them the penalty they had plotted to
impose on their neighbor: 62 they put
them to death. Thus was innocent blood
spared that day.
63 Hilkiah and his wife praised God for
their daughter Susanna, as did Joakim
her husband and all her relatives, be-
cause she was found innocent of any
shameful deed. 64 And from that day on-
ward Daniel was greatly esteemed by
the people.

*

13, 53: Ex 23, 7. 61f: Dt 19, 18.19.

†

13, 55-59: The contrast between the *mastic tree,* which is small, and the majestic *oak* emphasizes the contradiction between the statements of the two elders. In the Greek text there is a play on words between the names of these two trees and the mortal punishment decreed by Daniel for the elders.

13, 57: Besides the evident moral intent of this story, it appears to have served the purpose of contrasting the northern and the southern kingdoms, Israel and Judah, in favor of the latter.

CHAPTER 14

Bel and the Dragon. 1† After King Astyages was laid with his fathers, Cyrus the Persian succeeded to his kingdom. 2† Daniel was the king's favorite and was held in higher esteem than any of the friends of the king. 3† The Babylonians had an idol called Bel, and every day they provided for it six barrels of fine flour, forty sheep, and six measures of wine. 4 The king worshiped it and went every day to adore it; but Daniel adored only his God. 5 When the king asked him, "Why do you not adore Bel?" Daniel replied, "Because I worship not idols made with hands, but only the living God who made heaven and earth and has dominion over all mankind." 6 Then the king continued, "You do not think Bel is a living god? Do you not see how much he eats and drinks every day?" 7 Daniel began to laugh. "Do not be deceived, O king," he said; "it is only clay inside and bronze outside; it has never taken any food or drink." 8 Enraged, the king called his priests and said to them, "Unless you tell me who it is that consumes these provisions, you shall die. 9 But if you can show that Bel consumes them, Daniel shall die for blaspheming Bel." Daniel said to the king, "Let it be as you say!" 10 There were seventy priests of Bel, besides their wives and children.

When the king went with Daniel into the temple of Bel, 11 the priests of Bel said, "See, we are going to leave. Do you, O king, set out the food and prepare the wine; then shut the door and seal it with your ring. 12 If you do not find that Bel has eaten it all when you return in the morning, we are to die; otherwise Daniel shall die for his lies against us." 13 They were not perturbed, because under the table they had made a secret entrance through which they always came in to consume the food. 14 After they departed the king set the food before Bel, while Daniel ordered his servants to bring some ashes, which they scattered through the whole temple; the king alone was present. Then they went outside, sealed the closed door with the king's ring, and departed. 15 The priests entered that night as usual, with their wives and children, and they ate and drank everything.

16 Early the next morning, the king came with Daniel. 17 "Are the seals unbroken, Daniel?" he asked. And Daniel answered, "They are unbroken, O king." 18 As soon as he had opened the door, the king looked at the table and cried aloud, "Great you are, O Bel; there is no trickery in you." 19 But Daniel laughed and kept the king from entering. "Look at the floor," he said; "whose footprints are these?" 20 "I see the footprints of men, women, and children!" said the king. 21 The angry king arrested the priests, their wives, and their children. They showed him the secret door by which they used to enter to consume what was on the table. 22 He put them to death, and handed Bel over to Daniel, who destroyed it and its temple.

23 There was a great dragon which the Babylonians worshiped. 24 "Look!" said the king to Daniel, "you cannot deny that this is a living god, so adore it." 25 But Daniel answered, "I adore the Lord, my God, for he is the living God. 26 Give me permission, O king, and I will kill this dragon without sword or club." "I give you permission," the king said. 27 Then Daniel took some pitch, fat, and hair; these he boiled together and made into cakes. He put them into the mouth of the dragon, and when the dragon ate them, he burst asunder. "This," he said, "is what you worshiped."

28 When the Babylonians heard this, they were angry and turned against the king. "The king has become a Jew," they said; "he has destroyed Bel, killed the dragon, and put the priests to death." 29 They went to the king and demanded: "Hand Daniel over to us, or we will kill you and your family." 30 When he saw himself threatened with violence, the king was forced to hand Daniel over to them. 31 They threw Daniel into a lions' den, where he remained six days. 32 In the den were seven lions, and two carcasses and two sheep had been given to them daily. But now they were given nothing, so that they would devour Daniel.

33 In Judea there was a prophet, Habakkuk; he mixed some bread in a bowl with the stew he had boiled, and was going to bring it to the reapers in the field, 34 when an angel of the Lord told him, "Take the lunch you have to Daniel in the lions' den at Babylon." 35 But Habakkuk answered, "Babylon, sir, I have never seen, and I do not know the den!" 36* The angel of the Lord seized him by the crown of his head and carried him by the hair; with the speed of the wind, he set him down in Babylon above the den. 37 "Daniel, Daniel," cried Habakkuk, "take the lunch God has sent you." 38 "You have remembered me, O God," said Daniel; "you have not forsaken

*

14, 36: Ez 8, 3.

†

14, 1: *King Astyages:* the last of the Median kings, defeated by Cyrus in 550 B.C. This story preserves the fiction of a successive Median and Persian rule of Babylon.

14, 2: This verse in the Septuagint Greek text reads: "There was once a priest, Daniel by name, the son of Abal, a favorite of the king of Babylon." This may represent an earlier form of the story, before it was attached to the Book of Daniel.

14, 3: *Bel:* see the note on 4, 5.

those who love you." 39 While Daniel be-
gan to eat, the angel of the Lord at once
brought Habakkuk back to his own
place.
40 On the seventh day the king came
to mourn for Daniel. As he came to the
den and looked in, there was Daniel, sit-
ting there! 41 The king cried aloud, "You
are great, O Lord, the God of Daniel, and
there is no other besides you!" 42 Daniel
he took out, but those who had tried to
destroy him he threw into the den, and
they were devoured in a moment before
his eyes.

The Book of

HOSEA

Hosea belonged to the northern kingdom and began his prophetic career in the last years of Jeroboam II (786-746 B.C.). Some believe that he was a priest, others that he was a cult prophet; the prophecy, our only source of information concerning his life, gives us no certain answer in the matter. The collected oracles reveal a very sensitive, emotional man who could pass quickly from violent anger to the deepest tenderness. The prophecy pivots around his own unfortunate marriage to Gomer, a personal tragedy which profoundly influenced his teaching. In fact, his own prophetic vocation and message were immeasurably deepened by the painful experience he underwent in his married life.

Gomer, the adultress, symbolized faithless Israel. And just as Hosea could not give up his wife forever even when she played the harlot, so Yahweh could not renounce Israel, who had been betrothed to him. God would chastise, but it would be the chastisement of the jealous lover, longing to bring back the beloved to the fresh and pure joy of their first love.

Israel's infidelity took the form of idolatry and ruthless oppression of the poor. No amount of mechanically offered sacrifices could atone for her serious sins. Chastisement alone remained; God would have to strip her of the rich ornaments bestowed by her false lovers and thus bring her back to the true lover. A humiliated Israel would again seek Yahweh. The eleventh chapter of Hosea is one of the summits of Old Testament theology; God's love for his people has never been expressed more tenderly. Hosea began the tradition of describing the relation between Yahweh and Israel in terms of marriage. This symbolism appears later on in the Old Testament; and, in the New, both St. John and St. Paul express in the same imagery the union between Christ and his Church.

The Book of Hosea is divided as follows:

I: The Prophet's Marriage and Its Lesson (1, 1—3, 5)
II: Israel's Guilt and Punishment (4, 1—14, 10)

I: THE PROPHET'S MARRIAGE AND ITS LESSON†

CHAPTER 1

Marriage with an Unfaithful Wife.
1 The word of the LORD that came to Hosea, the son of Beeri, in the days of Uzziah, Jotham, Ahaz, Hezekiah, kings of Judah, and in the days of Jeroboam, son of Joash, king of Israel. 2† In the beginning of the LORD's speaking to Hosea, the LORD said to Hosea:

Go, take a harlot wife and harlot's children,
for the land gives itself to harlotry,
turning away from the LORD.

3 So he went and took Gomer, the daughter of Diblaim; and she conceived and bore him a son. 4† Then the LORD said to him:

Give him the name Jezreel,
for in a little while
I will punish the house of Jehu
for the bloodshed at Jezreel
And bring to an end the kingdom
of the house of Israel;
5 On that day I will break the bow of Israel
in the valley of Jezreel.

6† When she conceived again and bore a daughter, the LORD said to him:

†

1—3: This section is ordinarily thought to be biographical, the prophet's personal tragedy figuring as the relation of God to his people Israel. Hosea's marriage to a harlot wife represents Israel's infidelity to her Lord; hence the symbolic names of the children (1, 4-9). In 2, 4-25 the Lord protests this infidelity and decrees its consequences, but promises restoration in return for amendment; his punishments are medicinal. In chapter 3 Hosea once more takes back his wife, but only conditionally, signifying God's long-suffering love for Israel and hope for her return.

1, 2: *A harlot wife:* this does not necessarily mean that Gomer was a harlot when Hosea married her; the verse describes the event in its final consequences.

1, 4: *Jezreel:* the strategic valley in northern Israel where *Jehu* brought the dynasty of Omri to an end through bloodshed (2 Kgs 9-10). Jeroboam II was the last king but one of the house of Jehu; the prophecy in this verse was fulfilled by the murder of his son, who reigned only six months (2 Kgs 15, 8-10).

1, 6: *Lo-ruhama:* "she is not pitied." The "pity" that is here withheld from Israel is God's gratuitous love which inspires his beneficent acts.

Give her the name Lo-ruhama;
I no longer feel pity for the house of Israel:
rather, I abhor them utterly.

7† Yet for the house of Judah I feel pity;
I will save them by the LORD, their God;
But I will not save them by war,
by sword or bow, by horses or horsemen.

8 After she weaned Lo-ruhama, she
conceived and bore a son. 9† Then the
LORD said:

Give him the name Lo-ammi,
for you are not my people,
and I will not be your God.

CHAPTER 2

Israel's Punishment and Restoration

4† Protest against your mother, protest!
for she is not my wife,
and I am not her husband.
Let her remove her harlotry from before her,
her adultery from between her breasts,
5† Or I will strip her naked,
leaving her as on the day of her birth;
I will make her like the desert,
reduce her to an arid land,
and slay her with thirst.
6 I will have no pity on her children,
for they are the children of harlotry.
7† Yes, their mother has played the harlot;
she that conceived them has acted shamefully.
"I will go after my lovers," she said,
"who give me my bread and my water,
my wool and my flax, my oil and my drink."

10 Since she has not known
that it was I who gave her
the grain, the wine, and the oil,
And her abundance of silver,
and of gold, which they used for Baal,
11 Therefore I will take back my grain in its time,
and my wine in its season;
I will snatch away my wool and my flax,
with which she covers her nakedness.
12 So now I will lay bare her shame
before the eyes of her lovers,
and no one can deliver her out of my hand.
13 I will bring an end to all her joy,
her feasts, her new moons, her sabbaths,
and all her solemnities.
14 I will lay waste her vines and fig trees,
of which she said, "These are the hire
my lovers have given me";
I will turn them into rank growth
and wild beasts shall devour them.
15† I will punish her for the days of the Baals,
for whom she burnt incense
While she decked herself out with her rings and her jewels,
and, in going after her lovers,
forgot me, says the LORD.

8† Therefore, I will hedge in her way with thorns
and erect a wall against her,
so that she cannot find her paths.
9 If she runs after her lovers, she shall not overtake them;
if she looks for them she shall not find them.
Then she shall say,
"I will go back to my first husband,
for it was better with me then than now."

16† So I will allure her;
I will lead her into the desert
and speak to her heart.
17 From there I will give her the vineyards she had,
and the valley of Achor as a door of hope.
She shall respond there as in the days of her youth,

†

1, 7: The terrible punishments announced by the prophets were so fully realized that later generations made a point of recalling the same prophets' messages of consolation also, even though it meant taking these from another context. Thus, an editor placed the words of 2, 1ff after the repudiation of Israel in 1, 9; here the more natural order has been restored. The present verse is another example of the same thing. In addition, it may be the work of a later hand, dating from a time when the prophecies of Hosea were circulated in the south, after the dissolution of the northern kingdom that he had prophesied. The second part of the verse emphasizes the power of the Lord, who needs no human agents to fulfill his will. It may refer to the deliverance of Jerusalem from the siege of Sennacherib (2 Kgs 19, 35ff).

1, 9: *Lo-ammi:* "not my people."

2, 4: The Lord speaks of Israel, still using the example of Hosea's wife.

2, 5: *I will strip her naked:* contemporary documents indicate that this was a conventional punishment for adultery.

2,7: *My lovers:* the local fertility deities to whom, rather than to the Lord (v 10), the unfaithful Israelites attributed the produce of the land.

2, 15: *The days of the Baals:* ritual observances held in various local shrines in honor of Baal.

2, 8f: The crop failures, blight, etc., sent by the Lord (vv 11-14) have as their purpose to make Israel see the folly of her ways.

2, 16f: Israel's journey in the desert represents for Hosea the time of Israel's fidelity, before it was corrupted by the ways of Canaan; cf Jer 2, 2-7; Am 5, 25. Thus, he pictures a restoration in terms of a new entry into the promised land.

when she came up from the land
of Egypt.

18† On that day, says the LORD,
She shall call me "My husband,"
and never again "My baal."
19 Then will I remove from her mouth
the names of the Baals,
so that they shall no longer be invoked.
20 I will make a covenant for them on
that day,
with the beasts of the field,
With the birds of the air,
and with the things that crawl or
the ground.
Bow and sword and war
I will destroy from the land,
and I will let them take their rest
in security.

21† I will espouse you to me forever:
I will espouse you in right and in
justice,
in love and in mercy;
22 I will espouse you in fidelity,
and you shall know the LORD.
23 On that day I will respond, says the
LORD;
I will respond to the heavens,
and they shall respond to the
earth;
24 The earth shall respond to the grain,
and wine, and oil,
and these shall respond to Jezreel.
25* I will sow him for myself in the land,
and I will have pity on Lo-ruhama.
I will say to Lo-ammi, "You are my
people,"
and he shall say, "My God!"

CHAPTER 3

Triumph of Love

1† Again the LORD said to me:
Give your love to a woman
beloved of a paramour, an adulteress;
Even as the LORD loves the people
of Israel,
though they turn to other gods
and are fond of raisin cakes.

2† So I bought her for fifteen pieces of
silver and a homer and a lethech of barley.
3 Then I said to her:

"Many days you shall wait for me;
you shall not play the harlot
Or belong to any man;
I in turn will wait for you."

4† For the people of Israel shall remain
many days
without king or prince,
Without sacrifice or sacred pillar,
without ephod or household idols.

5*† Then the people of Israel shall turn
back
and seek the LORD, their God,
and David, their king;
They shall come trembling to the
LORD
and to his bounty, in the last days.

2:1*† The number of the Israelites
shall be like the sand of the sea,
which can be neither measured
nor counted.
Whereas they were called,
"Lo-ammi,"
They shall be called,
"Children of the living God."
2:2 Then the people of Judah and of Israel
shall be gathered together;
They shall appoint for themselves
one head
and come up from other lands,
for great shall be the day of
Jezreel.
2:3 Say to your brothers, "Ammi,"
and to your sisters, "Ruhama."

---

* 25: Rom 9, 25; 1 Pt 2, 10. 3, 5: Ez 34, 23. 2, 1: Rom 9, 26.

---

† 2, 18: *My baal:* the word means "lord, master." It was commonly used by women of their husbands, but it is to be shunned as a title for the Lord because of its association with the pagan god Baal. Probably it had been so used by many Israelites, who saw little if any difference between the worship of the Lord and the worship of Baal.

2, 21f: The Lord will once more espouse Israel; the qualities ascribed to the renewed people are the bridal gift (cf Gn 24, 53) with which he will endow it. *In right and in justice:* two terms dear to Hosea, used by him especially to condemn the popular social injustice and corruption of the legal processes. Here they mean right conduct in general. *Love:* one of the most characteristic words of Hosea's prophecy. It means a dutiful love, based on a social relation; here it refers to the covenant between God and his people. It is a love fulfilled by the performance of mutual obligations. *Mercy:* from the same root as the word translated *pity* in 1, 6; cf v. 25. *And you shall know the LORD:* another characteristic expression of Hosea; cf 4, 1; 5, 4; 6, 3.6. It means not an abstract but a practical knowledge, i.e., acknowledgment of his will, obedience to his law.

3, 1-5: Hosea is instructed to take Gomer back, redeeming her from her paramours. On condition of her amendment, she will be restored to her former position of wife. This in turn signifies God's enduring love for his people. He will put the people through a period of trial—the dissolution of the kingdom—in order that they may return to him wholeheartedly.

3, 1: *Raisin cakes:* offerings to the fertility goddess Ashera, the female counterpart of Baal; cf Jer 7, 18; 44, 19.

3, 2: *Homer:* about ten bushels. *Lethech:* a half-homer.

3, 4: *Sacred pillar:* the stone massebah, originally perhaps a phallic symbol, representing Baal. These were also used, with another signification, in Israelite worship; see notes on Gn 28, 18; Ex 34, 13. *Ephod:* an instrument used in consulting the deity; cf 1 Sm 23, 6-12; 30, 7; see notes on Ex 28, 6. 15-30. *Household idols:* images regarded as the tutelary deities of the household; cf Gn 31, 19; Jgs 17, 5; 18, 14. 17f.

3, 5: *David, their king:* the messianic King of the Davidic line who will restore the kingdom of God's people; cf Jer 23, 5; Ez 34, 23f: *The last days:* the messianic age.

2, 1-3: These verses (The number . . . Ruhama) (transposed from chapter 2) continue the conditional promise of restoration made in 3, 1-5, reversing the dire predictions of chapter 1; the symbolic names now become names of honor: *Jezreel,* "God sows"; *Ammi,* "my people"; *Ruhama,* "she is pitied."

II: ISRAEL'S GUILT AND PUNISHMENT

CHAPTER 4

Crimes of Israel

1 Hear the word of the LORD, O people of Israel,
for the LORD has a grievance
against the inhabitants of the land:
There is no fidelity, no mercy,
no knowledge of God in the land.
2* False swearing, lying, murder, stealing and adultery!
in their lawlessness, bloodshed follows bloodshed.
3 Therefore the land mourns,
and everything that dwells in it languishes:
The beasts of the field,
the birds of the air,
and even the fish of the sea perish.

Guilt of the Priests

4† But let no one protest, let no one complain;
with you is my grievance, O priests!
5 You shall stumble in the day,
and the prophets shall stumble with you at night;
I will destroy your mother.
6 My people perish for want of knowledge!
Since you have rejected knowledge,
I will reject you from my priesthood;
Since you have ignored the law of your God,
I will also ignore your sons.

7 One and all they sin against me,
exchanging their glory for shame.
8 They feed on the sin of my people,
and are greedy for their guilt.
9* The priests shall fare no better than the people:
I will punish them for their ways,
and repay them for their deeds.
10 They shall eat but not be satisfied,
they shall play the harlot but not increase,
Because they have abandoned the LORD
11 to practice harlotry.

Old wine and new
deprive my people of understanding.
12† They consult their piece of wood,
and their wand makes pronouncements for them,
For the spirit of harlotry has led them astray;
they commit harlotry, forsaking their God.
13 On the mountaintops they offer sacrifice
and on the hills they burn incense,
Beneath oak and poplar and terebinth,
because of their pleasant shade.
That is why your daughters play the harlot,
and your daughters-in-law are adulteresses.
14† Am I then to punish your daughters for their harlotry,
your daughters-in-law for their adultery?
You yourselves consort with harlots,
and with prostitutes you offer sacrifice!
So must a people without understanding come to ruin.
15† Though you play the harlot, O Israel,
let not Judah become guilty!
Come not to Gilgal,
nor up to Beth-aven,
to swear, "As the Lord lives!"
16 For Israel is as stubborn as a heifer;
will the LORD now give them broad pastures
as though they were lambs?
17† Ephraim is an associate of idols,
let him alone!
18 When their carousing is over,
they give themselves to harlotry;
in their arrogance they love shame.
19† The wind has bound them up in its pinions;
they shall have only shame from their altars.

---

* 4, 2: Ex 20, 13-17. 9: Is 24, 2.

---

† 4, 4ff; Hosea is particularly severe with the *priests* in the northern kingdom, who had led the way in the general apostasy from God's law. The *prophets* here associated with the priests (v 5) were doubtless cult prophets, who were often unworthy of their pretended calling; cf Jer 2, 8; 4, 9f; 6, 13f; 23, 9-40.

4, 12: *Wood . . . wand:* an idol used in divination.

4, 14: *With prostitutes you offer sacrifice:* the ritual prostitution practiced at the Canaanite shrine was introduced even into sanctuaries dedicated to the Lord. In comparison, the adultery that had become common in Israel was a far less reprehensible crime.

4, 15: *Gilgal:* not the Gilgal of the south (Jos 4, 19f), but a sanctuary north of Bethel where there was an association of cult prophets (2 Kgs 2, 1ff; 4, 38). *Beth-aven:* literally, "house of iniquity," Hosea's nickname for Bethel, or a scribal substitute for Bethel, "house of god," in this context. Bethel was one of the royal shrines of Israel, where there was a schismatic public worship of the Lord; cf 1 Kgs 12, 26-30.

4, 17: *Ephraim:* the heartland of the northern kingdom. During the latter part of Hosea's prophetic career, Ephraim was all that remained of Israel after the Assyrians had overrun Transjordan and Galilee.

4, 19: The Israelites shall be carried from their country as by a whirlwind. To this their idolatry has brought them.

CHAPTER 5

Guilt of the Leaders

1*† Hear this, O priests,
Pay attention, O house of Israel,
O household of the king, give ear!
It is you who are called to judgment.
For you have become a snare at Mizpah,
and a net spread upon Tabor.
2 In their perversity they have sunk into wickedness,
and I am rejected by them all.

3 I know Ephraim,
and Israel is not hidden from me;
Now Ephraim has played the harlot,
Israel is defiled.
4 Their deeds do not allow them
to return to their God;
For the spirit of harlotry is in them,
and they do not recognize the LORD.

5 The arrogance of Israel bears witness against him;
Ephraim stumbles in his guilt,
and Judah stumbles with them.
6 With their flocks and their herds they shall go
to seek the LORD, but they shall not find him;
he has withdrawn himself from them.
7 They have been untrue to the LORD,
for they have begotten illegitimate children;
Now shall the new moon devour them
together with their fields.

Political Upheavals†

8† Blow the horn in Gibeah,
the trumpet in Ramah!
Sound the alarm in Beth-aven:
"Look behind you, O Benjamin!"
9 Ephraim shall become a waste
on the day of chastisement:
Against the tribes of Israel
I announce what is sure to be.
10*† The princes of Judah have become
like those that move a boundary line;
Upon them I will pour out
my wrath like water.

11† Is Ephraim maltreated, his rights violated?
No, he has willingly gone after filth!
12† I am like a moth for Ephraim,
like maggots for the house of Judah.
13† When Ephraim saw his infirmity,
and Judah his sore,
Ephraim went to Assyria,
and Judah sent to the great king.
But he cannot heal you
nor take away your sore.
14 For I am like a lion to Ephraim,
like a young lion to the house of Judah;
It is I who rend the prey and depart,
I carry it away and no one can save it from me.

Insincere Conversion

15† I will go back to my place
until they pay for their guilt
and seek my presence.

CHAPTER 6

† In their affliction, they shall look for me:
1 "Come, let us return to the LORD,
For it is he who has rent, but he will heal us;
he has struck us, but he will bind our wounds.
2*† He will revive us after two days;
on the third day he will raise us up,
to live in his presence.
3 Let us know, let us strive to know the LORD;
as certain as the dawn is his coming,
and his judgment shines forth like the light of day!
He will come to us like the rain,
like spring rain that waters the earth."

*

5, 1: Mi 3, 1. 6, 2: 1 Cor 15, 4.
10: Dt 19, 14; 27, 17.

†

5, 1: *Mizpah:* probably the Mizpah in Transjordan is meant; cf Jos 11, 8. *Tabor:* the mountain that dominates the valley of Jezreel.

5, 8-14: This passage refers to the Syro-Ephraimite war of 735-734 B.C., when a coalition of Arameans and Israelites attempted to dethrone the king of Judah. Judah repulsed the attempt with the aid of Assyria, and the latter devastated both Aram and Israel; cf 2 Kgs 16, 5-9. Hosea condemns both Israel and Judah for the war.

5, 8: A vision of invasion, from *Gibeah* and *Ramah* in northern Judah, into Israel.

5, 10: *Like those that move a boundary line:* comparison of the invaders to a classic case of social injustice; cf Dt 19, 14; 27, 17; Prv 23, 10f.

5, 11: *Gone after filth:* by allying himself with Aram.

5, 12: *Moth . . . maggots:* internal corruption will work the Lord's punishment on both Israel and Judah.

5, 13: *Ephraim went . . . the great king:* in 738 B.C. the Israelite King Manahem had to pay tribute to the Assyrian king Tiglath-pileser III, whose vassal he became (2 Kgs 15, 19f). Under the threat of the Syro-Ephraimite invasion King Ahaz of Judah also submitted himself and his country to Tiglath-pileser (2 Kgs 16, 7-9). "The great king" was the title used by the Assyrian kings.

5, 15: The Lord withdraws himself from Israel, hoping for its repentance.

6, 1: *In . . . me:* this is the last line of ch 5.

6, 2: *After two days; on the third day:* after a short lapse of time.

4† What can I do with you, Ephraim?
What can I do with you, Judah?
Your piety is like a morning cloud,
like the dew that early passes away.
5 For this reason I smote them through the prophets,
I slew them by the words of my mouth;
6* For it is love that I desire, not sacrifice,
and knowledge of God rather than holocausts.
7 But they, in their land, violated the covenant;
there they were untrue to me.
8 Gilead is a city of evildoers,
tracked with blood.
9 As brigands ambush a man,
a band of priests slay on the way to Shechem,
committing monstrous crime.
10 In the house of Israel I have seen a horrible thing:
there harlotry is found in Ephraim,
Israel is defiled.
11† For you also, O Judah,
a harvest has been appointed.

CHAPTER 7

1 When I would bring about the restoration of my people,
when I would heal Israel,
The guilt of Ephraim stands out,
the wickedness of Samaria;
They practice falsehood,
thieves break in, bandits plunder abroad.
2 Yet they do not remind themselves
that I remember all their wickedness.
Even now their crimes surround them,
present to my sight.

Failure of the Monarchy†

3 In their wickedness they regale the king,
the princes too, with their deceits.
4 They are all kindled to wrath
like a blazing oven,
Whose fire the baker desists from stirring
once the dough is kneaded until it has risen.
5 On the day of our king,
the princes are overcome with the heat of wine.
He extends his hand among dissemblers;
6 the plotters approach with hearts like ovens.
All the night their anger sleeps;
in the morning it flares like a blazing fire.
7 They are all heated like ovens,
and consume their rulers.
All their kings have fallen;
none of them calls upon me.

Foreign Alliances

8† Ephraim mingles with the nations,
Ephraim is a hearth cake unturned.
9 Strangers have sapped his strength,
but he takes no notice of it;
Of gray hairs, too, there is a sprinkling,
but he takes no notice of it.
10 The arrogance of Israel bears witness against him;
yet they do not return to the LORD, their God,
nor seek him, for all that.

11 Ephraim is like a dove,
silly and senseless;
They call upon Egypt,
they go to Assyria.
12 Even as they go I will spread my net around them,
like birds in the air I will bring them down.
In an instant I will send them captive from their land.

Perversity of Israel

13 Woe to them, they have strayed from me!
Ruin to them, they have sinned against me!
Though I wished to redeem them,
they spoke lies against me.
14† They have not cried to me from their hearts
when they wailed upon their beds;

---

* 6: 1 Sm 15, 22; Eccl 4, 17; Mt 9, 13; 12, 7.

---

† 6, 4: *Piety:* the word is translated "love" in 2, 21 and in v 6 below.

6, 11: *Harvest:* when the land will reap the consequences of its sins.

7, 3-7: This passage refers to the dynastic upheavals of Israel's declining days. Between the death of Jeroboam II and the fall of Samaria to the Assyrians, a matter of some twenty-five years, there were four separate dynasties on the throne and as many murdered kings. The prophet compares the Israelite nobles who were inflamed with passion to an overheated oven that consumes what it is supposed to bake; thus the land consumes its kings. *Regale:* with wine (v 3). Like fire smoldering through the night and blazing up in the morning, the sleeping anger of plotters soon breaks out in open rebellion; the succession of night and morning suggests the short reigns of the various kings of this troubled period.

7, 8: *A hearth cake unturned:* burnt on one side, half baked on the other, and therefore useless. Israel's decline in power is ascribed to its disastrous meddling in the power politics of the neighboring nations.

7, 14: *They lacerated themselves:* a common oriental practice in prayers of earnest impetration (1 Kgs 18, 28); the practice was forbidden in Israelite religion (Lv 19, 28; Dt 14, 1).

For wheat and wine they lacerated themselves,
while they rebelled against me.
15 Though I trained and strengthened their arms,
yet they devised evil against me.
16 They have again become useless,
like a treacherous bow.
Their princes shall fall by the sword
because of the insolence of their tongues;
thus they shall be mocked in the land of Egypt.

CHAPTER 8

1 A trumpet to your lips,
You who watch over the house of the LORD!
Since they have violated my covenant,
and sinned against my law,
2 While to me they cry out,
"O, God of Israel, we know you!"
3 The men of Israel have thrown away what is good;
the enemy shall pursue them.

4† They made kings, but not by my authority;
they established princes, but without my approval.
With their silver and gold they made idols for themselves, to their own destruction.
5 Cast away your calf, O Samaria!
my wrath is kindled against them;
How long will they be unable to attain
innocence in Israel?
6 The work of an artisan
no god at all,
Destined for the flames—
such is the calf of Samaria!

7 When they sow the wind,
they shall reap the whirlwind;
The stalk of grain that forms no ear
can yield no flour;
Even if it could,
strangers would swallow it.
8 Israel is swallowed up;
he is now among the nations
a thing of no value.
9 They went up to Assyria—
a wild ass off on its own—
Ephraim bargained for lovers.
10 Even though they bargain with the nations,
I will now gather an army;
King and princes shall shortly
succumb under the burden.

11† When Ephraim made many altars to expiate sin,
his altars became occasions of sin.
12 Though I write for him my many ordinances,
they are considered as a stranger's.
13 Though they offer sacrifice,
immolate flesh and eat it,
the LORD is not pleased with them.
He shall still remember their guilt
and punish their sins;
they shall return to Egypt.
14* Israel has forgotten his maker
and built palaces.
Judah, too, has fortified many cities,
but I will send fire upon his cities,
to devour their castles.

CHAPTER 9

Exile without Worship

1† Rejoice not, O Israel,
exult not like the nations!
For you have been unfaithful to your God,
loving a harlot's hire
upon every threshing floor.
2 Threshing floor and wine press shall not nourish them,
the new wine shall fail them.

3 They shall not dwell in the LORD's land;
Ephraim shall return to Egypt,
and in Assyria they shall eat unclean food.
4† They shall not pour libations of wine to the LORD,
or proffer their sacrifices before him.
Theirs will be like mourners' bread,
that makes unclean all who eat of it;
Such food as they have shall be for themselves;
it cannot enter the house of the LORD.

5† What will you do on the festival day,
the day of the LORD's feast?

*

8, 14: Am 2, 5.

†

8, 4-6: Israel's monarchy and separate sanctuary are here associated, as in 1 Kgs 12, 20-33; both were the result of rebellion against the divinely approved Davidic dynasty and the Jerusalem temple with the ark of the covenant. The calf image set up by Jeroboam I in the royal shrines prevented Israel from attaining *innocence* (vv 5f).

8, 11: The very multiplicity of sanctuaries throughout the land was a danger to the purity of worship. The local shrines were speedily assimilated to the cult places used by the Canaanites, and the Lord was identified with the god Baal worshiped there. Thus the Deuteronomic writers, influenced by prophetic ideas, ended by restricting sacrificial worship to the one temple in Jerusalem.

9, 1f: *Upon every threshing floor:* an allusion to harvest festivals in honor of Baal, to whom the Israelites had attributed the fertility of the land; cf 2, 7.

9, 4: *Mourners' bread:* bread eaten at funeral rites; cf Dt 26, 13f. Contact with a corpse made a person ritually unclean, together with everything he touched. Such bread could not be offered to the Lord.

9, 5: *The LORD's feast:* doubtless the autumn feast of Booths, the most important of the Israelite public celebrations; cf Lv 23, 34.

6 When they go from the ruins,
Egypt shall gather them in, Memphis shall bury them.
Weeds shall overgrow their silver treasures,
and thorns invade their tents.

The Prophet Ridiculed

7 They have come, the days of punishment!
they have come, the days of recompense!
Let Israel know it!
"The prophet is a fool,
the man of the spirit is mad!"
Because your iniquity is great,
great, too, is your hostility.

8 A prophet is Ephraim's watchman with God,
yet a fowler's snare is on all his ways,
hostility in the house of his God.
9† They have sunk to the depths of corruption,
as in the days of Gibeah;
He shall remember their iniquity
and punish their sins.

Crime of Baal-peor

10† Like grapes in the desert,
I found Israel;
Like the first fruits of the fig tree in its prime,
I considered your fathers.
When they came to Baal-peor
and consecrated themselves to the Shame,
they became as abhorrent as the thing they loved.
11 The glory of Ephraim flies away like a bird:
no birth, no carrying in the womb, no conception.
Were they to bear children,
I would slay the darlings of their womb.
12 Even though they bring up their children,
I will make them childless, till not one is left.
Woe to them
when I turn away from them!
13 Ephraim, as I saw, was like Tyre,
planted in a beauteous spot;
But Ephraim shall bring out
his children to the slayer.
14† Give them, O LORD!
give them what?
Give them an unfruitful womb,
and dry breasts!

Crime of Gilgal

15*† All their wickedness is in Gilgal;
yes, there they incurred my hatred.
Because of their wicked deeds
I will drive them out of my house.
I will love them no longer;
all their princes are rebels.
16 Ephraim is stricken,
their root is dried up;
they shall bear no fruit.

17 My God will disown them
because they have not listened to him;
they shall be wanderers among the nations.

CHAPTER 10

Punishment of Idolatry

1† Israel is a luxuriant vine
whose fruit matches its growth.
The more abundant his fruit,
the more altars he built;
The more productive his land,
the more sacred pillars he set up.
2 Their heart is false,
now they pay for their guilt;
God shall break down their altars
and destroy their sacred pillars.
3 If they would say,
"We have no king"—
Since they do not fear the LORD,
what can the king do for them?
4† Nothing but make promises,
swear false oaths, and make alliances,
While justice grows wild
like wormwood in a plowed field!

5† The inhabitants of Samaria fear
for the calf of Beth-aven;
The people mourn for it
and its priests wail over it,
because the glory has departed from it.
6 It too shall be carried to Assyria,
as an offering to the great king.
Ephraim shall be taken into captivity,
Israel be shamed by his schemes.

7 The king of Samaria shall disappear,

---

* 15: 1 Sm 8, 5.

---

† 9, 9: *The days of Gibeah:* a reference to the outrage committed at Gibeah in the days of the Judges (Jgs 19, 22-30).

9, 10: At *Baal-peor* (Nm 25, 1-5) the Israelites consecrated themselves to Baal, here called *the Shame.*

9, 14: *An unfruitful womb:* this appears to be a reversal of the ancient blessing of Joseph contained in Gn 49, 25f, in which the increase, hence fruitfulness, promised to the patriarch is even signified by the name of his son Ephraim, on whose descendants the prophet now invokes the curse of extinction.

9, 15: *Gilgal:* see note on 4, 15.

10, 1: *Sacred pillars:* see note on 3, 4.

10, 4: *Justice . . . like wormwood:* the administration of justice, which should have been the mainstay of the people, has in corrupt hands become another instrument of oppression; cf Am 6, 13.

10, 5: *The calf of Beth-aven:* see notes on 4, 15; 8, 4ff.

like foam upon the waters.
8* The high places of Aven shall be destroyed,
the sin of Israel;
thorns and thistles shall overgrow their altars.
Then they shall cry out to the mountains, "Cover us!"
and to the hills, "Fall upon us!"

9* Since the days of Gibeah
you have sinned, O Israel.
There they took their stand;
war was not to reach them in Gibeah.
10*† Against the wanton people I came
and I chastised them;
I gathered troops against them
when I chastised them for their two crimes.

Time To Seek the Lord

11 Ephraim was a trained heifer,
willing to thresh;
I myself laid a yoke
upon her fair neck;
Ephraim was to be harnessed, Judah was to plow,
Jacob was to break his furrows:
12* "Sow for yourselves justice,
reap the fruit of piety;
Break up for yourselves a new field,
for it is time to seek the LORD,
till he come and rain down justice upon you."
13 But you have cultivated wickedness,
reaped perversity,
and eaten the fruit of falsehood.

Because you have trusted in your chariots,
and in your many warriors,
14*† Turmoil shall break out among your tribes
and all your fortresses shall be ravaged
As Salman ravaged Beth-arbel in time of war,
smashing mothers and their children.
15 So shall it be done to you, Bethel,
Because of your utter wickedness:
At dawn the king of Israel
shall perish utterly.

CHAPTER 11

When Israel Was a Child

1*† When Israel was a child I loved him,
out of Egypt I called my son.
2 The more I called them,
the farther they went from me,
Sacrificing to the Baals
and burning incense to idols.
3 Yet it was I who taught Ephraim to walk,
who took them in my arms;
4† I drew them with human cords,
with bands of love;
I fostered them like one
who raises an infant to his cheeks;
Yet, though I stooped to feed my child,
they did not know that I was their healer.

5 He shall return to the land of Egypt,
and Assyria shall be his king;
6 The sword shall begin with his cities
and end by consuming his solitudes.
Because they refused to repent,
their own counsels shall devour them.
7 His people are in suspense about returning to him;
and God, though in unison they cry out to him,
shall not raise them up.

End of the Exile

8*† How could I give you up, O Ephraim,
or deliver you up, O Israel?
How could I treat you as Admah,
or make you like Zeboiim?
My heart is overwhelmed,
my pity is stirred.
9 I will not give vent to my blazing anger,
I will not destroy Ephraim again;
For I am God and not man,
the Holy One present among you;
I will not let the flames consume you.

10 They shall follow the LORD,
who roars like a lion;
When he roars,
his sons shall come frightened from the west,
11 Out of Egypt they shall come trembling, like sparrows,

*

10, 8: Is 2, 19; Lk 23, 30; Rv 6, 16.
9: Jgs 20, 1.
10: Jer 4, 3.
12: Is 45, 8.
14: Jgs 8, 10ff.
11, 1: Mt 2, 15.
8: Gn 19, 24f.

†

10, 10: *Their two crimes:* possibly the outrage described in Jgs 19 is conceived as a double crime, of adultery and murder. Or the prophet regards the proclamation of the monarchy (cf 1 Sm 10, 23f) as a crime.

10, 14: *As Salman ravaged Beth-arbel:* allusion to an invasion not otherwise mentioned in the Bible. Salman may have been the Moabite king of this name mentioned in an inscription of Tiglath-pileser III. There were several Beth-arbels in Palestine; this one was probably in Transjordan.

11, 1: *Out of Egypt:* Hosea, like most of the prophets, dates the real beginning of Israel from the time of Moses and the Exodus. Mt 2, 15 applies this text to the return of the Christ Child from Egypt.

11, 4: *I drew them . . . with bands of love:* not forcing them like draft animals, but drawing them with kindness and affection.

11, 8: *Admah . . . Zeboiim:* cities destroyed with Sodom and Gomorrah (Dt 29, 22).

from the land of Assyria, like doves;
And I will resettle them in their homes,
says the LORD.

CHAPTER 12

Infidelity of Israel

1 Ephraim has surrounded me with lies,
the house of Israel, with deceit;
Judah is still rebellious against God,
against the Holy One, who is faithful.
2† Ephraim chases the wind,
ever pursuing the gale.
His lies and falsehoods are many:
he comes to terms with Assyria,
and carries oil to Egypt.

3† The LORD has a grievance against Israel:
he shall punish Jacob for his conduct,
for his deeds he shall repay him.
4* In the womb he supplanted his brother,
and as a man he contended with God;
5 He contended with the angel and triumphed,
entreating him with tears.
At Bethel he met God
and there he spoke with him:
6 The LORD, the God of hosts,
the LORD is his name!
7 You shall return by the help of your God,
if you remain loyal and do right
and always hope in your God.

8 A merchant who holds a false balance,
who loves to defraud!
9 Though Ephraim says,
"How rich I have become;
I have made a fortune!"
All his gain shall not suffice him
for the guilt of his sin.
10 I am the LORD, your God,
since the land of Egypt;
I will again have you live in tents,
as in that appointed time.
11 I granted many visions
and spoke to the prophets,
through whom I set forth examples.
12 In Gilead is falsehood, they have come to nought,
in Gilgal they sacrifice to bullocks;
Their altars are like heaps of stones
in the furrows of the field.

13* When Jacob fled to the land of Aram,
he served for a wife;
for a wife Israel tended sheep.
14*† By a prophet the LORD brought Israel out of Egypt,
and by a prophet they were protected.
15 Ephraim has exasperated his lord;
therefore he shall cast his bloodguilt upon him
and repay him for his outrage.

CHAPTER 13

1 Ephraim's word caused fear,
for he was exalted in Israel;
but he sinned through Baal and died.

Punishment for Ingratitude

2 Now they continue to sin,
making for themselves molten images,
Silver idols according to their fancy,
all of them the work of artisans.
"To these," they say, "offer sacrifice."
Men kiss calves!
3 Therefore, they shall be like a morning cloud
or like the dew that early passes away,
Like chaff storm-driven from the threshing floor
or like smoke out of the window.

4* I am the LORD, your God,
since the land of Egypt;
You know no God besides me,
and there is no savior but me.
5 I fed you in the desert,
in the torrid land.
6 They ate their fill;
when filled, they became proud of heart
and forgot me.
7 Therefore, I will be like a lion to them,
like a panther by the road I will keep watch.
8 I will attack them like a bear robbed of its young,
and tear their hearts from their breasts;

*

12, 4: Gn 25, 26; 32, 25.
13: Gn 28, 5; 29, 20.
14: Ex 14, 21f.
13, 4: Is 43, 11.

†

12, 2: *He comes . . . Egypt:* allusion to the commercial and military pacts with the great powers, consistently condemned by the prophets as derogatory of the Lord's claim on his people.

12, 3-7: Contemporary Israel and the Israel represented by its ancestor Jacob (Israel) are here alternated, a splendid example of the Hebrew concept of "corporate personality" or easy transition from the individual to the community of which he is part. Hosea recalls the history of Jacob as it now appears in Genesis, but with some differences of detail and order.

12, 14: *A prophet:* Moses.

I will devour them on the spot like
a lion,
as though a wild beast were to
rend them.

9 Your destruction, O Israel!
who is there to help you?
10* Where now is your king,
that he may rescue you in all your
cities?
And your rulers, of whom you said,
"Give me a king and princes"?
11† I give you a king in my anger,
and I take him away in my wrath.

12 The guilt of Israel is wrapped up,
his sin is stored away.
13† The birth pangs shall come for him,
but he shall be an unwise child;
For when it is time he shall not pre-
sent himself
where children break forth.
14*† Shall I deliver them from the power
of the nether world?
shall I redeem them from death?
Where are your plagues, O death!
where is your sting, O nether
world!
My eyes are closed to compassion.

15* Though he be fruitful among his fel-
lows,
an east wind shall come, a wind
from the LORD,
rising from the desert,
That shall dry up his spring,
and leave his fountain dry.
It shall loot his land
of every precious thing.

CHAPTER 14

1 Samaria shall expiate her guilt,
for she has rebelled against her
God.
They shall fall by the sword,
their little ones shall be dashed to
pieces,
their expectant mothers shall be
ripped open.

Sincere Conversion

2 Return, O Israel, to the LORD, your
God;
you have collapsed through your
guilt.
3 Take with you words,
and return to the LORD;
Say to him, "Forgive all iniquity,
and receive what is good, that we
may render
as offerings the bullocks from our
stalls.
4 Assyria will not save us,
nor shall we have horses to mount;
We shall say no more, 'Our god,'
to the work of our hands;
for in you the orphan finds com-
passion."

5 I will heal their defection,
I will love them freely;
for my wrath is turned away from
them.
6 I will be like the dew for Israel:
he shall blossom like the lily;
He shall strike root like the Lebanon
cedar,
7 and put forth his shoots.
His splendor shall be like the olive
tree
and his fragrance like the Leba-
non cedar.
8 Again they shall dwell in his shade
and raise grain;
They shall blossom like the vine,
and his fame shall be like the wine
of Lebanon.

9 Ephraim! What more has he to do
with idols?
I have humbled him, but I will
prosper him.
"I am like a verdant cypress tree"—
Because of me you bear fruit!

* * *

10† Let him who is wise understand
these things;
let him who is prudent know them.
Straight are the paths of the LORD,
in them the just walk,
but sinners stumble in them.

---

*

10: 1 Sm 8, 5. 15: Ex 19, 12.
14: 1 Cor 15, 54.

†

13, 11: *I give you a king . . . in my wrath:* the Lord punishes the people of the northern kingdom by giving them incompetent kings who are soon deposed.

13, 13: Israel's sin is such as to warrant its destruction (v 12), because it refuses to do penance. It will therefore perish as surely as the unborn child which dies in its mother's body because it does not properly employ the only way to safety.

13, 14: *Shall . . . nether world:* a vigorous affirmation of the Lord's determination to destroy Israel. St. Paul cites these words in a different sense (1 Cor 15, 54f), that of the ultimate victory of life over death in the resurrection of the body on the last day, wrought through the merits of Christ's passion and resurrection.

14. 10: A later addition in the style of the wisdom literature.

The Book of

JOEL

This prophecy is rich in apocalyptic imagery and strongly eschatological in tone. It was composed about 400 B.C. Its prevailing theme is the day of the Lord.

A terrible invasion of locusts ravaged Judah. So frightful was the scourge that the prophet visualized it as a symbol of the coming day of the Lord. In the face of this threatening catastrophe, the prophet summoned the people to repent, to turn to the Lord with fasting and weeping. They were ordered to convoke a solemn assembly in which the priests would pray for deliverance. The Lord answered their prayer and promised to drive away the locusts and bless the land with peace and prosperity. To these material blessings would be added an outpouring of the spirit on all flesh. St. Peter, in his first discourse before the people at Pentecost (Acts 2, 16-21), sees in the coming of the Holy Spirit the fulfillment of this promise (1, 1—3, 5).

The concluding poem pictures the nations gathered in the Valley of Jehoshaphat, where the Lord is about to pass judgment. Israel's enemies are summoned to hear the solemn indictment; their evil deeds are at last requited. The tumultuous throng assembled in the valley of decision is made up of the enemies of God and they face inevitable destruction. The oracle changes abruptly from the terrifying image of judgment to a vision of Israel restored and forever secure from her enemies. God is both the vindicator of his people and the source of their blessing (4, 1-21).

CHAPTER 1

The Land Invaded. 1 The word of the LORD which came to Joel, the son of Pethuel.

2 Hear this, you elders!
Pay attention, all you who dwell in the land!
Has the like of this happened in your days,
or in the days of your fathers?
3 Tell it to your children,
and your children to their children,
and their children to the next generation.
4† What the cutter left,
the locust swarm has eaten;
What the locust swarm left,
the grasshopper has eaten;
And what the grasshopper left,
the devourer has eaten.

5 Wake up, you drunkards, and weep;
wail, all you drinkers of wine,
Because the juice of the grape
will be withheld from your mouths.
6† For a people has invaded my land,
mighty and without number;
His teeth are the teeth of a lion,
and his molars those of a lioness.
7 He has laid waste my vine,
and blighted my fig tree;
He has stripped it, sheared off its bark;
its branches are made white.
8 Lament like a virgin girt with sackcloth
for the spouse of her youth.
9 Abolished are offering and libation
from the house of the LORD;
In mourning are the priests,
the ministers of the LORD.
10 The field is ravaged,
the earth mourns,
Because the grain is ravaged,
the must has failed,
the oil languishes.

11 Be appalled, you husbandmen!
wail, you vinedressers!
Over the wheat and the barley,
because the harvest of the field has perished.
12 The vine has dried up,
the fig tree is withered;
The pomegranate, the date palm also, and the apple,
all the trees of the field are dried up;
Yes, joy has withered away
from among mankind.

Call to Penance

13 Gird yourselves and weep, O priests!
wail, O ministers of the altar!

†

1, 4: *Cutter . . . locust . . . grasshopper . . . devourer:* these names refer to various species of locusts; they can only be approximate.

1, 6: *A people:* the locusts compared to an invading army.

Come, spend the night in sackcloth,
O ministers of my God!
The house of your God is deprived
of offering and libation.
14* Proclaim a fast,
call an assembly;
Gather the elders,
all who dwell in the land,
Into the house of the LORD, your God,
and cry to the LORD!

15 Alas, the day!
for near is the day of the LORD,
and it comes as ruin from the Almighty.
16 From before our very eyes
has not the food been cut off;
And from the house of our God,
joy and gladness?
17 The seed lies shriveled under its clods;
the stores are destroyed,
The barns are broken down,
for the grain has failed.
18 How the beasts groan!
The herds of cattle are bewildered!
Because they have no pasturage,
even the flocks of sheep have perished.

19 To you, O LORD, I cry!
for fire has devoured the pastures of the plain,
and flame has enkindled all the trees of the field.
20 Even the beasts of the field
cry out to you;
For the streams of water are dried up,
and fire has devoured the pastures of the plain.

CHAPTER 2

The Day of the Lord

1 Blow the trumpet in Zion,
sound the alarm on my holy mountain!
Let all who dwell in the land tremble,
for the day of the LORD is coming;
2 Yes, it is near, a day of darkness and of gloom,
a day of clouds and somberness!
Like dawn spreading over the mountains,
a people numerous and mighty!
Their like has not been from of old,
nor will it be after them,
even to the years of distant generations.
3 Before them a fire devours,
and after them a flame enkindles;
Like the garden of Eden is the land before them,
and after them a desert waste;
from them there is no escape.
4 Their appearance is that of horses;
like steeds they run.
5 As with the rumble of chariots
they leap on the mountaintops;
As with the crackling of a fiery flame
devouring stubble;
Like a mighty people
arrayed for battle.
6 Before them peoples are in torment,
every face blanches.

7 Like warriors they run,
like soldiers they scale the wall;
They advance, each in his own lane,
without swerving from their paths.
8 No one crowds another,
each advances in his own track;
Though they fall into the ditches,
they are not checked.

9 They assault the city,
they run upon the wall,
they climb into the houses;
In at the windows
they come like thieves.
10* Before them the earth trembles,
the heavens shake;
The sun and the moon are darkened,
and the stars withhold their brightness.

11* The LORD raises his voice
at the head of his army;
For immense indeed is his camp,
yes, mighty, and it does his bidding.
For great is the day of the LORD,
and exceedingly terrible; who can bear it?
12 Yet even now, says the LORD,
return to me with your whole heart,
with fasting, and weeping, and mourning;
13* Rend your hearts, not your garments,
and return to the LORD, your God.
For gracious and merciful is he,
slow to anger, rich in kindness,
and relenting in punishment.
14* Perhaps he will again relent
and leave behind him a blessing,
Offerings and libations
for the LORD, your God.

15* Blow the trumpet in Zion!
proclaim a fast,
call an assembly;
16 Gather the people,
notify the congregation;

1, 14: 2, 15.
2, 10: 4, 15; Is 13, 10; Ez 32, 7f; Mt 24, 29; Mk 13, 24; Lk 21, 25f.
11: Jer 30, 7; Am 5, 18; Zep 1, 15.
13: Ps 86, 5; Jon 4, 2.
14: Jon 3, 9.
15: 1, 14.

Assemble the elders,
gather the children
and the infants at the breast;
Let the bridegroom quit his room,
and the bride her chamber.
17† Between the porch and the altar
let the priests, the ministers of the
LORD, weep,
And say, "Spare, O LORD, your peo-
ple,
and make not your heritage a re-
proach,
with the nations ruling over them!
Why should they say among the
peoples,
'Where is their God?' "

Blessings for God's People. 18 Then
the LORD was stirred to concern for his
land and took pity on his people. 19 The
LORD answered and said to his people:

See, I will send you
grain, and wine, and oil,
and you shall be filled with them;
No more will I make you
a reproach among the nations.
20† No, the northerner I will remove far
from you,
and drive him out into a land arid
and waste,
With his van toward the eastern sea,
and his rear toward the western
sea;
And his foulness shall go up,
and his stench shall go up.

21 Fear not, O land!
exult and rejoice!
for the LORD has done great
things.
22 Fear not, beasts of the field!
for the pastures of the plain are
green;
The tree bears its fruit,
the fig tree and the vine give their
yield.

23*† And do you, O children of Zion, exult
and rejoice in the LORD, your God!
He has given you the teacher of jus-
tice:
he has made the rain come down
for you,
the early and the late rain as be-
fore.
24 The threshing floors shall be full of
grain
and the vats shall overflow with
wine and oil.

25 And I will repay you for the years
which the locust has eaten,
The grasshopper, the devourer, and
the cutter,
my great army which I sent
among you.
26 You shall eat and be filled,
and shall praise the name of the
LORD, your God,
Because he has dealt wondrously
with you;
my people shall nevermore be put
to shame.
27 And you shall know that I am in the
midst of Israel;
I am the LORD, your God, and
there is no other;
my people shall nevermore be put
to shame.

CHAPTER 3

1*† Then afterward I will pour out
my spirit upon all mankind.
Your sons and daughters shall
prophesy,
your old men shall dream dreams,
your young men shall see visions;
2 Even upon the servants and the
handmaids,
in those days, I will pour out my
spirit.

3 And I will work wonders in the heav-
ens and on the earth,
blood, fire, and columns of smoke;
4* The sun will be turned to darkness,
and the moon to blood,
At the coming of the Day of the
LORD,
the great and terrible day.
5* Then everyone shall be rescued
who calls on the name of the LORD;
For on Mount Zion there shall be a
remnant,
as the LORD has said,
And in Jerusalem survivors
whom the LORD shall call.

---

*

23: Hos 10, 12.
3, 1-5: Is 44, 3; Acts 2, 17-21.
4: 2, 10.
5: Rom 10, 13.

---

†

2, 17: The priests stood in the open space between the outdoor altar of holocausts and the temple building, facing the latter in order thereby to look toward God present in the holy of holies.

2, 20: *The northerner:* the locusts, that are compared to an invading army, which in Palestine came from the north; cf Jer 1, 14f; 4, 6; Ez 26, 7; 38, 6.15.

2, 23: *The teacher of justice:* the rain sent by God to show his fidelity to his promises, and to teach his people to be faithful to his commandments; cf Dt 11, 14. There is also a play on words here between the Hebrew word *moreh* (teacher) and the Hebrew word *yoreh* (the early rain). The expression likewise had a messianic connotation; cf Is 30, 20. The founder of the Essene sect of Qumran (second century B.C.) was known as "The Teacher of Justice."

3, 1f: *I will pour out my spirit:* In the Old Testament the *spirit* is the gift of God bestowed on those acting as his agents. The promise of the spirit is quoted by St. Peter in Acts 2, 17-21 as fulfilled in an eminent way by the gift of the Holy Spirit, the Third Person of the Blessed Trinity, bestowed on the Apostles.

CHAPTER 4

Judgment upon the Nations

1 Yes, in those days, and at that time,
when I would restore the fortunes
of Judah and Jerusalem,
2† I will assemble all the nations
and bring them down to the Valley
of Jehoshaphat,
And I will enter into judgment with
them there
on behalf of my people and my in-
heritance, Israel;
Because they have scattered them
among the nations,
and divided my land.
3 Over my people they have cast lots;
they gave a boy for a harlot,
and sold a girl for the wine they
drank.

4 Moreover, what are you to me, Tyre
and Sidon, and all the regions of Philis-
tia? Would you take vengeance upon me
by some action? But if you do take action
against me, swiftly, speedily, I will re-
turn your deed upon your own head.
5 You took my silver and my gold, and
brought my precious treasures into your
temples! 6 You sold the people of Judah
and Jerusalem to the Greeks, removing
them far from their own country! 7 See,
I will rouse them from the place into
which you have sold them, and I will re-
turn your deed upon your own head. 8† I
will sell your sons and your daughters
to the people of Judah, who shall sell
them to the Sabeans, a nation far off.
Indeed, the LORD has spoken.

9 Declare this among the nations:
proclaim a war,
rouse the warriors to arms!
Let all the soldiers
report and march!
10† Beat your plowshares into swords,
and your pruning hooks into
spears;
let the weak man say, "I am a
warrior!"

11† Hasten and come, all you neighbor-
ing peoples,
assemble there!
[Bring down, O Lord, your war-
riors!]
12 Let the nations bestir themselves
and come up
to the Valley of Jehoshaphat;
For there I will sit in judgment
upon all the neighboring nations.

13*† Apply the sickle,
for the harvest is ripe;
Come and tread,
for the wine press is full;
The vats overflow,
for great is their malice.
14 Crowd upon crowd
in the valley of decision;
For near is the day of the LORD
in the valley of decision.
15* Sun and moon are darkened,
and the stars withhold their
brightness.
16* The LORD roars from Zion,
and from Jerusalem raises his
voice;
The heavens and the earth quake,
but the LORD is a refuge to his peo-
ple,
a stronghold to the men of Israel.

Salvation for God's Elect

17 Then shall you know that I, the
LORD, am your God,
dwelling on Zion, my holy moun-
tain;
Jerusalem shall be holy,
and strangers shall pass through
her no more.
18*† And then, on that day,
the mountains shall drip new
wine,
and the hills shall flow with milk;
And the channels of Judah
shall flow with water:
A fountain shall issue from the
house of the LORD,
to water the Valley of Shittim.
19 Egypt shall be a waste,
and Edom a desert waste,
Because of violence done to the peo-
ple of Judah,
because they shed innocent blood
in their land.
20 But Judah shall abide forever,
and Jerusalem for all generations.
21 I will avenge their blood,
and not leave it unpunished.
The LORD dwells in Zion.

*

4, 13: Rv 14, 15. 15: 2, 10; 3, 4. 16: Jer 25, 30; Am 1, 2. 18: Am 9, 13; Ez 47, 1-12; Zec 14, 8.

†

4, 2: *Valley of Jehoshaphat:* a symbolic name of the place of final judgment (v 14). The name Jehoshaphat signifies "Yahweh judges." This place has been popularly identified with the Kidron Valley.

4, 8: *Sabeans:* a south Arabian people known for their commerce.

4, 10: This imagery is used in the reverse sense in Is 2, 4; Mi 4, 3. Here the warlike weapons are made in response to God's summons to armies which he selected to expel forever the unlawful invaders from the land of his chosen people.

4, 11: *Warriors:* the angels; cf Zec 14, 5.

4, 13: Because of their numerous crimes, the nations are ripe for punishment. The use of warlike weapons against them is likened to the onslaught on the fields and vines at harvest time.

4, 18: *The Valley of Shittim,* or "the ravine of the acacia trees": perhaps a part of the Kidron Valley southeast of Jerusalem; the prophetic picture of a stream of water flowing from a fountain in the temple of Jerusalem is to be found in Ez 47, 1. The Shittim east of the Jordan (see note on Nm 25, 1) is hardly referred to here.

The Book of

AMOS

Amos was a shepherd of Tekoa in Judah, who exercised his ministry during the prosperous reign of Jeroboam II (786-746 B.C.). He prophesied in Israel at the great cult center of Bethel, from which he was finally expelled by the priest in charge of this royal sanctuary. The poetry of Amos, who denounces the hollow prosperity of the northern kingdom, is filled with imagery and language taken from his own pastoral background. The book is an anthology of his oracles and was compiled either by the prophet or by some of his disciples.

The prophecy begins with a sweeping indictment of Damascus, Philistia, Tyre, and Edom; but the forthright herdsman saves his climactic denunciation for Israel, whose injustice and idolatry are sins against the light granted to her. Israel could indeed expect the day of Yahweh, but it would be a day of darkness and not light. When Amos prophesied the overthrow of the sanctuary, the fall of the royal house, and the captivity of the people, it was more than Israelite officialdom could bear. The priest of Bethel drove Amos from the shrine—but not before hearing a terrible sentence pronounced upon himself.

Amos is a prophet of divine judgment, and the sovereignty of Yahweh in nature and history dominates his thought. But he was no innovator; his conservatism was in keeping with the whole prophetic tradition calling the people back to the high moral and religious demands of Yahweh's revelation. In common with the other prophets, Amos knew that divine punishment is never completely destructive; it is part of the hidden plan of God to bring salvation to men. The perversity of the human will may retard, but it cannot totally frustrate, this design of a loving God. The last oracle opens up a perspective of restoration under a Davidic king.

The Book of Amos may be divided as follows:

I: Judgment of the Nations (1, 1—2, 16)
II: Words and Woes for Israel (3, 1—6, 14)
III: Symbolic Visions: Threats and Promises (7, 1—9, 8b)
Epilogue: Messianic Perspective (9, 8c-15)

I: JUDGMENT OF THE NATIONS

CHAPTER 1

1*† The words of Amos, a shepherd from Tekoa, which he received in vision concerning Israel, in the days of Uzziah, king of Judah, and in the days of Jeroboam, son of Joash, king of Israel, two years before the earthquake:

2* The LORD will roar from Zion,
and from Jerusalem raise his voice:
The pastures of the shepherds will languish,
and the summit of Carmel wither.

Aram

3† Thus says the LORD:
For three crimes of Damascus, and for four,
I will not revoke my word;
Because they threshed Gilead
with sledges of iron,
4† I will send fire upon the house of Hazael,
to devour the castles of Ben-hadad.
5† I will break the bar of Damascus;

---

* 1, 1: Zec 14, 5. 2: Jer 25, 30; Jl 3, 16.

---

† 1, 1: *The earthquake:* which according to Hebrew tradition marked the crime of Uzziah when he attempted to offer incense in the temple (2 Chr 26, 16-21). Zechariah mentions it several centuries later (Zec 14, 5).

1, 3: *For three crimes . . . four:* crime after crime, an indefinite number; cf 1, 6. The series of judgments on the foreign nations shows that the Lord demands the observance of the moral order everywhere; Israel and Judah, despite their privileged position, are no exception. *I will not revoke my word:* God will not withdraw his threat of punishment against each of these nations. *They threshed Gilead:* the people of Aram under King Hazael had devastated Gilead; cf 2 Kgs 10, 32f.

1, 4: *Fire:* devastation caused by the Assyrians (1, 7.10. 12.14; 2, 2.5); cf 1 Sm 15, 18. *Hazael* and *Ben-hadad:* kings of the Arameans whose captial was *Damascus* (v 5); they fought against Israel (2 Kgs 13, 3), and had long occupied the region of Gilead (v 3) in Transjordan.

1, 5: *Bar of Damascus:* the beam securing the main gate of the city against invaders, symbol of its defenses. *Valley of Aven* ("vale of wickedness") and *Beth-eden* ("house of pleasure"): Aramean territory from southwest to northeast.

I will root out those who live in the
Valley of Aven,
And the sceptered ruler of Beth-eden;
the people of Aram shall be exiled
to Kir,
says the LORD.

Philistia

6 Thus says the LORD:
For three crimes of Gaza, and for four,
I will not revoke my word;
Because they took captive whole groups
to hand over to Edom,
7 I will send fire upon the wall of Gaza,
to devour her castles;
8 I will root out those who live in Ashdod,
and the sceptered ruler of Ashkelon;
I will turn my hand against Ekron,
and the last of the Philistines shall perish,
says the Lord GOD.

Tyre

9† Thus says the LORD:
For three crimes of Tyre, and for four
I will not revoke my word;
Because they delivered whole
groups captive to Edom,
and did not remember the pact of brotherhood,
10 I will send fire upon the wall of Tyre,
to devour her castles.

Edom

11† Thus says the LORD:
For three crimes of Edom, and for four,
I will not revoke my word;
Because he pursued his brother with the sword,
choking up all pity;
Because he persisted in his anger
and kept his wrath to the end,
12† I will send fire upon Teman,
and it will devour the castles of Bozrah.

Ammon

13 Thus says the LORD:
For three crimes of the Ammonites,
and for four,
I will not revoke my word;
Because they ripped open expectant
mothers in Gilead,
while extending their territory,
14† I will kindle a fire upon the wall of
Rabbah,
and it will devour her castles
Amid clamor on the day of battle
and stormwind in a time of tempest.
15 Their king shall go into captivity,
he and his princes with him, says
the LORD.

CHAPTER 2

Moab

1† Thus says the LORD:
For three crimes of Moab, and for four,
I will not revoke my word;
Because he burned to ashes
the bones of Edom's king,
2 I will send fire upon Moab,
to devour the castles of Kerioth;
Moab shall meet death amid uproar
and shouts and trumpet blasts.
3 I will root out the judge from her midst,
and her princes I will slay with
him, says the LORD.

Judah

4† Thus says the LORD:
For three crimes of Judah, and for four,
I will not revoke my word;
Because they spurned the law of the LORD,
and did not keep his statutes;
Because the lies which their fathers followed
have led them astray,
5 I will send fire upon Judah,
to devour the castles of Jerusalem.

Israel†

6† Thus says the LORD:
For three crimes of Israel, and for four,
I will not revoke my word;
Because they sell the just man for silver,

---

†

1, 9: *Pact of brotherhood:* Hiram of Tyre had made a pact with Solomon and called him brother (1 Kgs 5, 12; 9, 13).

1, 11: *Pursued his brother:* the Edomites were descended from Esau, the brother of Jacob (Gn 25-27); nevertheless they constantly nourished enmity against Jacob's descendants, the Israelites.

1, 12: *Teman* and *Bozrah:* two of the chief cities of Edom; cf Jer 49, 20.

1, 14: *Rabbah:* now called Amman, the modern capital of the Hashemite Kingdom of Jordan.

2, 1: Here the prophet stresses the gravity of Moab's violation of the Semitic custom of providing honorable burial for the dead.

2, 4: *The lies:* false gods, who exist only in the minds of their worshipers. The crimes of Judah are infidelity and idolatry, in contrast to the sins for which the surrounding nations are judged.

2, 6-13: The detailed crimes of Israel are placed in strong contrast with the benefits with which the Lord favored his people.

2, 6: *A pair of sandals:* indicating how cheaply the rich regarded the poor.

AMOS

and the poor man for a pair of sandals.
7 They trample the heads of the weak
into the dust of the earth,
and force the lowly out of the way.
Son and father go to the same prostitute,
profaning my holy name.
8† Upon garments taken in pledge
they recline beside any altar;
And the wine of those who have been fined
they drink in the house of their god.

9* Yet it was I who destroyed the Amorites before them,
who were as tall as the cedars,
and as strong as the oak trees.
I destroyed their fruit above,
and their roots beneath.
10* It was I who brought you up from the land of Egypt,
and who led you through the desert for forty years,
to occupy the land of the Amorites:
11† I who raised up prophets among your sons,
and nazirites among your young men.
Is this not so, O men of Israel?
says the LORD.
12 But you gave the nazirites wine to drink,
and commanded the prophets not to prophesy.

13 Beware, I will crush you into the ground
as a wagon crushes when laden with sheaves.
14 Flight shall perish from the swift,
and the strong man shall not retain his strength;
The warrior shall not save his life,
15 nor the bowman stand his ground;
The swift of foot shall not escape,
nor the horseman save his life.
16 And the most stouthearted of warriors
shall flee naked on that day, says the LORD.

II: WORDS AND WOES FOR ISRAEL

CHAPTER 3

First Word. 1 Hear this word, O men of Israel, that the LORD pronounces over you, over the whole family that I brought up from the land of Egypt:

2† You alone have I favored,
more than all the families of the earth;
Therefore I will punish you
for all your crimes.

3 Do two walk together
unless they have agreed?
4 Does a lion roar in the forest
when it has no prey?
Does a young lion cry out from its den
unless it has seized something?
5 Is a bird brought to earth by a snare
when there is no lure for it?
Does a snare spring up from the ground
without catching anything?
6† If the trumpet sounds in a city,
will the people not be frightened?
If evil befalls a city,
has not the LORD caused it?
7 Indeed, the Lord GOD does nothing
without revealing his plan
to his servants, the prophets.

8 The lion roars—
who will not be afraid!
The Lord GOD speaks—
who will not prophesy!

9† Proclaim this in the castles of Ashdod,
in the castles of the land of Egypt:
"Gather about the mountain of Samaria,
and see the great disorders within her,
the oppression in her midst."
10 For they know not how to do what is right,
says the LORD,
Storing up in their castles
what they have extorted and robbed.
11 Therefore, thus says the Lord GOD:
An enemy shall surround the land,
and strip you of your strength,
and pillage your castles,

12 Thus says the LORD:
As the shepherd snatches from the mouth of the lion
a pair of legs or the tip of an ear of his sheep,
So the Israelites who dwell in Samaria shall escape

*

2, 9: Nm 21, 24; Dt 2. 2.14.
10: Ex 14, 21; Dt 8,

†

2, 8: *Upon garments . . . any altar:* usurers kept the garments taken as pledges from the poor; but instead of restoring them to their owners before nightfall (Ex 22, 25; Dt 24, 12), they used them in idolatrous worship. *Wine . . . their god:* under the guise of a religious ceremony they drink the wine obtained through unjust fines.

2, 11: *Nazirites:* see note on Nm 6, 1ff.

3, 2: God's choice of Israel brought its own responsibility.

3, 6: The sufferings which sinful man experiences through the permissive will of God are presented here, as elsewhere in the Old Testament, simply as caused by the Lord.

3, 9: Israel's southern neighbors, beyond Judah, are invited by the prophetic orator to witness the moral disorders of God's people.

with the corner of a couch or a
piece of a cot.

13 Hear and bear witness against the house of Jacob, says the Lord GOD, the God of hosts:

14 On the day when I punish Israel for his crimes,
I will visit also the altars of Bethel:
The horns of the altar shall be broken off
and fall to the ground.
15† Then will I strike the winter house and the summer house;
The ivory apartments shall be ruined,
and their many rooms shall be no more,
says the LORD.

CHAPTER 4
Second Word

1† Hear this word, women of the mountain of Samaria,
you cows of Bashan,
You who oppress the weak
and abuse the needy;
Who say to your lords,
"Bring drink for us!"
2 The Lord GOD has sworn by his holiness:
Truly the days are coming upon you
When they shall drag you away with hooks,
the last of you with fishhooks;
3 You shall go out through the breached walls
each by the most direct way,
And you shall be cast into the mire,
says the LORD.

4† Come to Bethel and sin,
to Gilgal, and sin the more;
Each morning bring your sacrifices,
every third day, your tithes;
5 Burn leavened food as a thanksgiving sacrifice,
proclaim publicly your freewill offerings,
For so you love to do, O men of Israel,
says the Lord GOD.

6 Though I have made your teeth
clean of food in all your cities,
and have made bread scarce in all your dwellings,
Yet you returned not to me,
says the LORD.

7 Though I also withheld the rain from you
when the harvest was still three months away;
I sent rain upon one city
but not upon another;
One field was watered by rain,
but another without rain dried up;
8 Though two or three cities staggered to one city
for water that did not quench their thirst;
Yet you returned not to me,
says the LORD.

9* I struck you with blight and searing wind;
your many gardens and vineyards,
your fig trees and olive trees the locust devoured;
Yet you returned not to me,
says the LORD.

10† I sent upon you a pestilence like that of Egypt,
and with the sword I slew your young men;
Your horses I let be captured,
to your nostrils I brought the stench of your camps;
Yet you returned not to me,
says the LORD.
11* I brought upon you such upheaval
as when God overthrew Sodom and Gomorrah:
you were like a brand plucked from the fire;
Yet you returned not to me,
says the LORD.

12 So now I will deal with you in my own way, O Israel!
and since I will deal thus with you,
prepare to meet your God, O Israel:
13 Him who formed the mountains, and created the wind,
and declares to man his thoughts;
Who made the dawn and the darkness,
and strides upon the heights of the earth:
The LORD, the God of hosts by name.

AMOS

*

4, 9: Hg 2, 17. 11: Gn 19, 24.

†

3, 15: *Ivory apartments:* rooms containing furniture inlaid in ivory, similar to the pieces discovered in the excavations at Samaria.

4, 1: *Bashan:* the region east of the Sea of Galilee, famous for its rich pasture and fattened herds, to which Amos likens the indolent women of Samaria.

4, 4f: This invitation to the sanctuaries of the northern kingdom is ironical. Pilgrimages to the shrines of *Bethel* and *Gilgal* were the more displeasing to God because they were contrary to his will and ineffective toward improvement of morals.

4, 10: *Pestilence like that of Egypt:* plagues were well known in Egypt; cf Dt 7, 15; 28, 27.60. *Stench of your camps:* caused by the unburied bodies.

CHAPTER 5

Third Word

1 Hear this word which I utter over you,
a lament, O house of Israel:
2 She is fallen, to rise no more,
the virgin Israel;
She lies abandoned upon her land,
with no one to raise her up.

3 For thus says the Lord GOD:
The city that marched out with a thousand
shall be left with a hundred,
Another that marched out with a hundred
shall be left with ten,
of the house of Israel.

4 For thus says the LORD
to the house of Israel:
Seek me, that you may live,
5 but do not seek Bethel;
Do not come to Gilgal,
and do not cross to Beer-sheba.
For Gilgal shall be led into exile,
and Bethel shall become nought.
6† Seek the LORD, that you may live,
lest he come upon the house of Joseph like a fire
That shall consume, with none to quench it
for the house of Israel:
8* He who made the Pleiades and Orion,
who turns darkness into dawn,
and darkens day into night;
Who summons the waters of the sea,
and pours them out upon the surface of the earth;
9 Who flashes destruction upon the strong,
and brings ruin upon the fortress;
whose name is LORD.

First Woe

7 Woe to those who turn judgment to wormwood
and cast justice to the ground!
10† They hate him who reproves at the gate
and abhor him who speaks the truth.
11* Therefore, because you have trampled upon the weak
and exacted of them levies of grain,
Though you have built houses of hewn stone,
you shall not live in them!
Though you have planted choice vineyards,
you shall not drink their wine!

12 Yes, I know how many are your crimes,
how grievous your sins:
Oppressing the just, accepting bribes,
repelling the needy at the gate!
13 Therefore the prudent man is silent at this time,
for it is an evil time.

14 Seek good and not evil,
that you may live;
Then truly will the LORD, the God of hosts,
be with you as you claim!
15* Hate evil and love good,
and let justice prevail at the gate;
Then it may be that the LORD, the God of hosts,
will have pity on the remnant of Joseph.

16 Therefore, thus says the LORD,
the God of hosts, the Lord:
In every square there shall be lamentation,
and in every street they shall cry, Alas! Alas!
They shall summon the farmers to wail
and professional mourners to lament,
17 And in every vineyard there shall be lamentation
when I pass through your midst,
says the LORD.

Second Woe

18*† Woe to those who yearn for the day of the LORD!
What will this day of the LORD mean for you?
Darkness and not light!
19 As if a man went to flee from a lion,
and a bear should meet him;
Or as if on entering his house
he were to rest his hand against the wall,
and a snake should bite him.
20 Will not the day of the LORD be darkness and not light,
gloom without any brightness?

---

*

5, 8: Am 9, 6.
11: Zep 1, 13.
15: Ps 97, 10; Rom 12, 9.
18: Jer 30, 7; Jl 2, 11; Zep 1, 15.

†

5, 6: *House of Joseph:* the kingdom of Israel or northern kingdom, the chief tribes of which were descended from Ephraim and Manasseh, the sons of Joseph; cf 5, 15; 6, 6.

5, 10: *At the gate:* see note on Ps 127, 5.

5, 18: *Day of the LORD:* a technical expression which in earliest times referred to God's special intervention in human affairs. Through it his power and justice triumphed in his people. The present passage is the first instance in which it means a day of punishment of sinners. During the exile it assumed the meaning of a time when God would avenge Israel against her oppressors and bring about her restoration (Jer 50, 27; Ez 30, 3ff). Still later it came to mean the day of final judgment of the world when the good will be rewarded and the wicked punished (Mal 3, 19ff; Jl 2, 1ff; Zep 1, 14ff).

21*†I hate, I spurn your feasts,
I take no pleasure in your solemnities;
22 Your cereal offerings I will not accept,
nor consider your stall-fed peace offerings.
23 Away with your noisy songs!
I will not listen to the melodies of your harps.
But if you would offer me holocausts,
24 then let justice surge like water,
and goodness like an unfailing stream.
25*†Did you bring me sacrifices and offerings
for forty years in the desert, O house of Israel?
26† You will carry away Sakkuth, your king,
and Kaiwan, your star god,
the images that you have made for yourselves;
27 For I will exile you beyond Damascus,
say I, the LORD, the God of hosts by name.

CHAPTER 6

Third Woe

1*†Woe to the complacent in Zion,
to the overconfident on the mount of Samaria,
Leaders of a nation favored from the first,
to whom the people of Israel have recourse!
2 Pass over to Calneh and see,
go from there to Hamath the great,
and down to Gath of the Philistines!
Are you better than these kingdoms,
or is your territory wider than theirs?
3 You would put off the evil day,
yet you hasten the reign of violence!
4 Lying upon beds of ivory,
stretched comfortably on their couches,
They eat lambs taken from the flock,
and calves from the stall!
5 Improvising to the music of the harp,
like David, they devise their own accompaniment.
6 They drink wine from bowls
and anoint themselves with the best oils;
yet they are not made ill by the collapse of Joseph!
7 Therefore, now they shall be the first to go into exile,
and their wanton revelry shall be done away with.

8* The Lord GOD has sworn by his very self,
say I, the LORD, the God of hosts:
I abhor the pride of Jacob,
I hate his castles,
and I give over the city with everything in it;
9 Should there remain ten men
in a single house, these shall die.
10 Only a few shall be left
to carry the dead out of the houses;
If one says to a man inside a house,
"Is anyone with you?" and he answers, "No one,"
Then he shall say, "Silence!"
for no one must mention the name of the LORD.
11 Indeed, the LORD has given the command
to shatter the great house to bits,
and reduce the small house to rubble.
12† Can horses run across a cliff?
or can one plow the sea with oxen?
Yet you have turned judgment into gall,
and the fruit of justice into wormwood.
13† You rejoice in Lodebar,
and say, "Have we not, by our own strength,
seized for ourselves Karnaim?"
14† Beware, I am raising up against you,
O house of Israel,
say I, the LORD, the God of hosts,

AMOS

---

*

21: Is 1, 11; Jer 6, 20; Mal 1, 12.
25: Acts 7, 42.
6, 1: Lk 6, 24.
8: Jer 51, 14.

†

5, 21-27: The Lord condemns, not ritual worship in itself, but the cult whose exterior rites and solemnity have no relation to interior morality and justice. The Israelites falsely worshiped him as neighboring nations adored Baal or Chamos, deities which were thought to protect their respective peoples against their enemies in return for ritual observances, without any relation to right conduct.

5, 25: The meaning is not certain; according to some, the idea is that during the forty years' wandering in the desert the simple, rudimentary worship of God was accompanied by the practice of justice, in contrast to the elaborate ritual unaccompanied by works of justice in the prophet's time.

5, 26: *Sakkuth . . . star god:* although the text is uncertain, it seems quite probable that reference is made to the Assyrian deities, Sakkuth, god of war and light, and Kaiwan, the planet Saturn. The people will go into exile, from which these gods have been unable to save them.

6, 1-7: The luxury of the people in Samaria will be punished by exile. They failed to learn the lesson from *Calneh, Hamath* and *Gath* at the approach of the powerful and warlike Assyrians.

6, 1: *The complacent in Zion . . . the overconfident . . . of Samaria:* the proud and self-interested rulers of Judah and Israel.

6, 12: *Can horses . . . oxen?:* one cannot change the course of nature, as the Israelites attempted to do by their sins of injustice.

6, 13: *Lodebar. . . Karnaim:* in Transjordan; they had been captured by the Israelites. Perhaps it is in irony that reference is made to these two cities, for the root of the first suggests "nothing" and that of the second, "horns" or "strength."

6, 14: *A nation:* Assyria.

AMOS

A nation that shall oppress you
from Labo of Hamath even to the
Wadi Arabah.

III: SYMBOLIC VISIONS: THREATS AND PROMISES

CHAPTER 7

Vision of Locusts. 1† This is what the
Lord GOD showed me: He was forming
a locust swarm when the late growth be-
gan to come up (the late growth after
the king's mowing). 2 While they were
eating all the grass in the land, I said:

Forgive, O Lord GOD!
How can Jacob stand?
He is so small!

3 And the LORD repented of this. "It shall
not be," said the Lord GOD.
Visions of Fire. 4† Then the Lord GOD
showed me this: he called for a judgment
by fire. It had devoured the great abyss,
and was consuming the land, 5 when I
said:

Cease, O Lord GOD!
How can Jacob stand?
He is so small!

6 The LORD repented of this. "This also
shall not be," said the Lord GOD.
Visions of the Plummet. 7† Then the
Lord GOD showed me this: he was stand-
ing by a wall, plummet in hand. 8 The
LORD asked me, "What do you see,
Amos?" And when I answered, "A
plummet," the Lord said:

See, I will lay the plummet
in the midst of my people Israel;
I will forgive them no longer.
9 The high places of Isaac shall be laid waste,
and the sanctuaries of Israel made desolate;
I will attack the house of Jeroboam with the sword.

Amos and Amaziah. 10 Amaziah, the
priest of Bethel, sent word to Jeroboam,
king of Israel: "Amos has conspired
against you here within Israel; the coun-
try cannot endure all his words. 11 For
this is what Amos says:

Jeroboam shall die by the sword,
and Israel shall surely be exiled
from its land."

12 To Amos, Amaziah said: "Off with
you, visionary, flee to the land of Judah!
There earn your bread by prophesying,
13 but never again prophesy in Bethel;
for it is the king's sanctuary and a royal
temple." 14† Amos answered Amaziah,
"I was no prophet, nor have I belonged
to a company of prophets; I was a shep-
herd and a dresser of sycamores.
15 The LORD took me from following the
flock, and said to me, Go, prophesy to
my people Israel. 16 Now hear the word
of the LORD!"

You say: prophesy not against Israel,
preach not against the house of Isaac.
17 Now thus says the LORD:
Your wife shall be made a harlot in the city,
and your sons and daughters shall fall by the sword;
Your land shall be divided by measuring line,
and you yourself shall die in an unclean land;
Israel shall be exiled far from its land.

CHAPTER 8

Vision of the Fruit Basket. 1 This is
what the Lord GOD showed me: a basket
of ripe fruit. 2 "What do you see, Amos?"
he asked. I answered, "A basket of ripe
fruit." Then the LORD said to me:

The time is ripe to have done with my people Israel;
I will forgive them no longer.
3 The temple songs shall become wailings on that day,
says the Lord GOD.
Many shall be the corpses,
strewn everywhere. Silence!

Against Greed

4 Hear this, you who trample upon the needy
and destroy the poor of the land!
5† "When will the new moon be over,"
you ask,
"that we may sell our grain,
and the sabbath, that we may display the wheat?
We will diminish the ephah,
add to the shekel,
and fix our scales for cheating!
6 We will buy the lowly man for silver,
and the poor man for a pair of sandals;
even the refuse of the wheat we will sell!"

†

7, 1: *The king's mowing:* the first mowing, a portion of which was payable to the king as a tax.

7, 4: *Fire:* understood by many as a burning drought.

7, 7: *Plummet in hand:* signifying that God is about to withdraw his mercy from his people and that the nation is to be measured for destruction.

7, 14f: Amos denies that he belonged to the class of professional prophets; his vocation is due to the personal intervention of the Lord.

8, 5: *Ephah:* a standard of measure; a little more than a bushel.

7† The LORD has sworn by the pride of Jacob:
Never will I forget a thing they have done!
8† Shall not the land tremble because of this,
and all who dwell in it mourn,
While it rises up and tosses like the Nile,
and settles back like the river of Egypt?

9 On that day, says the Lord GOD,
I will make the sun set at midday
and cover the earth with darkness in broad daylight.
10* I will turn your feasts into mourning
and all your songs into lamentations.
I will cover the loins of all with sackcloth
and make every head bald.
I will make them mourn as for an only son,
and bring their day to a bitter end.

11 Yes, days are coming, says the Lord GOD,
when I will send famine upon the land:
Not a famine of bread, or thirst for water,
but for hearing the word of the LORD.
12 Then shall they wander from sea to sea
and rove from the north to the east
In search of the word of the LORD,
but they shall not find it.

13 On that day, fair virgins and young men
shall faint from thirst;
14† Those who swear by the shameful idol of Samaria,
"By the life of your god, O Dan!"
"By the life of your love, O Beer-sheba!"
those shall fall, never to rise again.

CHAPTER 9

Vision of the Altar. 1† I saw the Lord standing beside the altar, and he said:

Strike the bases, so that the door-jambs totter
till you break them off on the heads of them all!
Those who are left I will slay with the sword;
not one shall flee,
no survivor shall escape.
2* Though they break through to the nether world,
even from there my hand shall bring them out;
Though they climb to the heavens,
I will bring them down;
3† Though they hide on the summit of Carmel,
there too I will hunt them out and take them away;
Though they hide from my gaze
in the bottom of the sea,
I will command the serpent there to bite them;
4* Though they are led into captivity by their enemies,
there will I command the sword to slay them.
I will fix my gaze upon them
for evil, and not for good,
5 I, the Lord GOD of hosts.
I melt the earth with my touch,
so that all who dwell on it mourn,
While it all rises up like the Nile,
and settles back like the river of Egypt;
6* I have built heaven, my upper chamber,
and established my vault over the earth;
I summon the waters of the sea
and pour them upon the surface of the earth,
I, the LORD by name.

7*† Are you not like the Ethiopians to me,
O men of Israel, says the LORD?
Did I not bring the Israelites from the land of Egypt
As I brought the Philistines from Caphtor
and the Arameans from Kir?
8 The eyes of the Lord GOD are on this sinful kingdom;
I will destroy it from off the face of the earth.

Epilogue: Messianic Perspective

But I will not destroy the house of Jacob completely,
says the LORD.

*

8, 10: Tb 2, 6; 1 Mc 1, 41.
9, 2: Ps 139, 8.
4: Jer 44, 11.
6: Am 5, 8.
7: Dt 2, 23; Jer 47, 4.

†

8, 7: *The pride of Jacob:* the sinful pride detested by God (6, 8), in contrast to God himself, who is the true Pride of Jacob.

8, 8: The figure is based on the annual flooding of the river Nile.

8, 14: *Dan* and *Beer-sheba:* the extreme northern and southern limits of the country, where idolatrous worship was offered.

9, 1-8: There will be no escape from God's punishment, symbolized here by the destruction of a building, probably the schismatic temple at Bethel.

9, 3: *Serpent:* the sea monster of familiar legend, subdued by God at the time of creation and lurking still in the ocean depths; cf Ps 89, 10f.

9, 7: *The Ethiopians . . . the Philistines . . . the Arameans:* by nature Israel is not different from any other nation. It was not because of any merit on Israel's part that God delivered them from Egypt. *Caphtor:* the island of Crete.

AMOS

9 For see, I have given the command
to sift the house of Israel among
all the nations,
As one sifts with a sieve,
letting no pebble fall to the
ground.
10 By the sword shall all sinners among
my people die,
those who say, "Evil will not reach
or overtake us."
11*†On that day I will raise up
the fallen hut of David;
I will wall up its breaches,
raise up its ruins,
and rebuild it as in the days of old,
12 That they may conquer what is left
of Edom
and all the nations that shall bear
my name,
say I, the LORD, who will do this.
13* Yes, days are coming,
says the LORD,
When the plowman shall overtake
the reaper,
and the vintager, him who sows
the seed;
The juice of grapes shall drip down
the mountains,
and all the hills shall run with it.
14 I will bring about the restoration of
my people Israel;
they shall rebuild and inhabit
their ruined cities,
Plant vineyards and drink the wine,
set out gardens and eat the fruits.
15 I will plant them upon their own
ground;
never again shall they be plucked
From the land I have given them,
say I, the LORD, your God.

* 11: Acts 15, 16. 13: Jl 3, 18.

† 9, 11f: In Acts 15, 15ff St. James interprets this passage in a messianic sense. *Fallen hut:* the kingdom. *The nations that shall bear my name:* the Gentile peoples who shall be converted to the Lord, that is, conquered by him, and therefore shall bear his name.

The Book of

OBADIAH

The twenty-one verses of this book contain the shortest and sternest prophecy in the Old Testament. Nothing is known of the author, although his oracle against Edom, a long-standing enemy of Israel, indicates a date of composition sometime in the fifth century B.C. During this period the Edomites had been forced to abandon their ancient home near the Gulf of Aqaba and had settled in southern Judah, where they appear among the adversaries of the Jews returning from exile.

The prophecy is a bitter cry for vengeance against Edom for its heinous crimes. The mountain of Esau will be occupied and ravaged by the enemy but Zion shall remain inviolate. Judah and Israel shall again form one nation; and that triumphant refrain of Israelite eschatology will be heard once more: "The Kingdom is the Lord's!" Many of the verses in this prophecy can be paralleled in Jer 49, 7-22, but it is difficult to determine the precise relationship between these similar passages.

Title and Theme

1* The vision of Obadiah.
[Thus says the Lord GOD:]

Of Edom we have heard a message from the LORD,
and a herald has been sent among the nations:
"Up! let us go to war against him!"

Edom Shall Perish

2* See, I make you small among the nations;
you are held in dire contempt.
3 The pride of your heart has deceived you:
you who dwell in the clefts of the rock,
whose abode is in the heights,
Who say in your heart,
"Who will bring me down to earth?"
4 Though you go as high as the eagle,
and your nest be set among the stars,
From there will I bring you down,
says the LORD.
5*† If thieves came to you, if robbers by night,
how could you be thus destroyed:
would they not steal merely till they had enough?
If vintagers came to you,
would they not leave some gleanings?
6 How they search Esau,
seek out his hiding places!
7† To the border they drive you—
all your allies;
They deceive you, they overpower you—
those at peace with you;
Those who eat your bread
lay snares beneath you:
There is no understanding in him!
8*† Shall I not, says the LORD, on that day
make the wise men disappear from Edom,
and understanding from the mount of Esau?
9† Your warriors, O Teman, shall be crushed,
till all on Mount Esau are destroyed.

The Cause

10*† Because of violence to your brother Jacob,
disgrace shall cover you
and you shall be destroyed forever.
11† On the day when you stood by,
on the day when aliens carried off his possessions,
And strangers entered his gates
and cast lots over Jerusalem,
you too were one of them.

*

1, 1: Jer 49, 14.
2ff: Jer 49, 15f.
5: Jer 49, 9.
8: Is 29, 14; 1 Cor 1, 19.
10: Gn 27, 41f.

†

5: Something of value may escape the robber, and the vintager always leaves something for the gleaners, but God's devastation of Edom will be complete.

7: *There is no understanding in him:* Edom's faithless allies assure one another that he does not have sense enough to be able to defend himself.

8: *The wise men:* Edom was proverbial for its wise men; cf Jer 49, 7.

9: *Teman:* one of the names used for the land southeast of Palestine, here synonymous with Edom. *Esau:* here used as the name of the land.

10: *Your brother Jacob:* Esau, also called Edom, and Jacob, the father of Judah, were the sons of Isaac (Gn 25, 24ff).

11: After the devastation of Judah, Edom occupied the southern part of its territory. Edomites also joined the invading Chaldean forces (13) and assisted them in capturing the people of Judah (14).

OBADIAH

12 Gaze not upon the day of your brother,
the day of his disaster;
Exult not over the children of Judah
on the day of their ruin;
Speak not haughtily
on the day of distress!
13 Enter not the gate of my people
on the day of their calamity;
Gaze not, you at least, upon his misfortune
on the day of his calamity;
Lay not hands upon his possessions
on the day of his calamity!
14 Stand not at the crossroads
to slay his refugees;
Betray not his fugitives
on the day of distress!

Judgment upon the Nations

15* For near is the day of the LORD
for all the nations!
As you have done, so shall it be done to you,
your deed shall come back upon your own head;
16† As you have drunk upon my holy mountain,
so shall all the nations drink continually.
Yes, they shall drink and swallow,
and shall become as though they had not been.

Judah Shall Be Restored

17† But on Mount Zion there shall be a portion saved;
the mountain shall be holy,
And the house of Jacob shall take possession
of those that dispossessed them.
18 The house of Jacob shall be a fire,
and the house of Joseph a flame;
The house of Esau shall be stubble,
and they shall set them ablaze and devour them;
Then none shall survive of the house of Esau,
for the LORD has spoken.
19 They shall occupy the Negeb, the mount of Esau,
and the foothills of the Philistines;
And they shall occupy the lands of Ephraim
and the lands of Samaria,
and Benjamin shall occupy Gilead.
20† The captives of the host of the children of Israel
shall occupy the Canaanite land
as far as Zarephath,
And the captives of Jerusalem who are in Sepharad
shall occupy the cities of the Negeb.
21† And saviors shall ascend Mount Zion
to rule the mount of Esau,
and the kingship shall be the LORD's.

---

*

15f: Ps 137, 7ff.

†

16: *As you have drunk:* the Lord addresses the people of Judah. As the people of Jerusalem have drunk the cup of retribution, so shall the nations, and especially Edom (18), suffer punishment. This metaphorical use of drinking the cup of God's wrath is common in the Bible; cf Jb 21, 20; Is 19, 14; Jer 25, 15f.

17ff: The Israelites shall be restored and shall occupy the lands of those who oppressed them. The survivors of Judah shall be rejoined by the returned exiles from northern Israel.

20: *Zarephath:* a town in Phoenicia, north of Tyre; cf 1 Kgs 17, 10. Ezekiel's ideal boundaries of the new Israel (Ez 47, 13ff) extend farther north. *Sepharad:* probably Sardis in western Asia Minor. The later rabbis thought it to be Spain.

21: *Saviors:* the victorious Israelites who will rule over their enemies after the fashion of the ancient Judges; cf Jgs 3, 9.15.31; 10, 1.

The Book of

JONAH

Written in the postexilic era, probably in the fifth century B.C., this book is a didactic story with an important theological message. It concerns a disobedient prophet who attempted to run away from his divine commission, was cast overboard and swallowed by a great fish, rescued in a marvelous manner, and sent on his way to Nineveh, the traditional enemy of Israel. To the surprise of Jonah, the wicked city listened to his message of doom and repented immediately. All, from king to lowliest subject, humbled themselves in sackcloth and ashes. Seeing their repentance, God did not carry out the punishment he had planned for them. Whereupon Jonah complained to God about the unexpected success of his mission; he was bitter because Yahweh, instead of destroying, had led the people to repentance and then spared them.

From this partly humorous story, a very sublime lesson may be drawn. Jonah stands for a narrow and vindictive mentality, all too common among the Jews of that period. Because they were the chosen people, a good many of them cultivated an intolerant nationalism which limited the mercy of God to their nation. It was abhorrent to their way of thinking that nations as wicked as Assyria should escape his wrath.

The prophecy, which is both instructive and entertaining, strikes directly at this viewpoint. It is a parable of mercy, showing that God's threatened punishments are but the expression of a merciful will which moves all men to repent and seek forgiveness. The universality of the story contrasts sharply with the particularistic spirit of many in the postexilic community. The book has also prepared the way for the gospel with its message of redemption for all, both Jew and Gentile.

CHAPTER 1

The First Mission. 1*† This is the word
of the LORD that came to Jonah, son of
Amittai: 2* "Set out for the great city of
Nineveh, and preach against it; their
wickedness has come up before me."
3† But Jonah made ready to flee to
Tarshish away from the LORD. He went
down to Joppa, found a ship going to
Tarshish, paid the fare, and went aboard
to journey with them to Tarshish, away
from the LORD.
4 The LORD, however, hurled a violent
wind upon the sea, and in the furious
tempest that arose the ship was on the
point of breaking up. 5 Then the mari-
ners became frightened and each one
cried to his god. To lighten the ship for
themselves, they threw its cargo into the
sea. Meanwhile, Jonah had gone down
into the hold of the ship, and lay there
fast asleep. 6 The captain came to him
and said, "What are you doing asleep?
Rise up, call upon your God! Perhaps
God will be mindful of us so that we may
not perish."
7 Then they said to one another,
"Come, let us cast lots to find out on
whose account we have met with this
misfortune." So they cast lots, and thus
singled out Jonah. 8 "Tell us," they said,
"what is your business? Where do you
come from? What is your country, and
to what people do you belong?" 9 "I am
a Hebrew," Jonah answered them; "I
worship the LORD, the God of heaven,
who made the sea and the dry land."
10 Now the men were seized with great
fear and said to him, "How could you
do such a thing!"—They knew that he
was fleeing from the LORD, because he
had told them.—11 "What shall we do
with you," they asked, "that the sea may
quiet down for us?" For the sea was
growing more and more turbulent.
12 Jonah said to them, "Pick me up and
throw me into the sea, that it may quiet
down for you; since I know it is because
of me that this violent storm has come
upon you."
13 Still the men rowed hard to regain
the land, but they could not, for the sea
grew ever more turbulent. 14† Then they
cried to the LORD: "We beseech you, O
LORD, let us not perish for taking this

*

1, 1: 2 Kgs 14, 25. 2: 3, 3; 4, 11.

†

1, 1: *Jonah, son of Amittai:* a prophet of this name lived at the time of Jeroboam II (786-746 B.C.).

1, 3: *Tarshish:* identified by many with Tartessus, an ancient Phoenician colony in southwest Spain; precise identification with any particular Phoenician center in the western Mediterranean is uncertain. To the Hebrews it stood for the far west.

1, 14: Since it has pleased the Lord to punish Jonah, the mariners ask that in ridding themselves of him they be not charged with the crime of murder.

man's life; do not charge us with shed-
ding innocent blood, for you, LORD, have
done as you saw fit." [15] Then they took
Jonah and threw him into the sea, and
the sea's raging abated. [16] Struck with
great fear of the LORD, the men offered
sacrifice and made vows to him.

CHAPTER 2

[1]* But the LORD sent a large fish, that
swallowed Jonah; and he remained in
the belly of the fish three days and three
nights. [2] From the belly of the fish Jonah
said this prayer to the LORD, his God:

Psalm of Thanksgiving

[3]* Out of my distress I called to the
LORD,
and he answered me;
From the midst of the nether world
I cried for help,
and you heard my voice.
[4]* For you cast me into the deep, into
the heart of the sea,
and the flood enveloped me;
All your breakers and your billows
passed over me.
[5]* Then I said, "I am banished from
your sight!
yet would I again look upon your
holy temple."
[6]* The waters swirled about me,
threatening my life;
the abyss enveloped me;
seaweed clung about my head.
[7]* Down I went to the roots of the
mountains;
the bars of the nether world
were closing behind me forever,
But you brought my life up from the
pit,
O LORD, my God.
[8]* When my soul fainted within me,
I remembered the LORD;
My prayer reached you
in your holy temple.
[9]* Those who worship vain idols
forsake their source of mercy.
[10]* But I, with resounding praise,
will sacrifice to you;
What I have vowed I will pay:
deliverance is from the LORD.

[11] Then the LORD commanded the fish
to spew Jonah upon the shore.

CHAPTER 3

Conversion of Nineveh. [1] The word of
the LORD came to Jonah a second time:
[2] "Set out for the great city of Nineveh,
and announce to it the message that I
will tell you." [3] So Jonah made ready
and went to Nineveh, according to the
LORD's bidding. Now Nineveh was an
enormously large city; it took three days
to go through it. [4]† Jonah began his jour-
ney through the city, and had gone but
a single day's walk announcing, "Forty
days more and Nineveh shall be de-
stroyed," [5]* when the people of Nineveh
believed God; they proclaimed a fast
and all of them, great and small, put on
sackcloth.
[6] When the news reached the king of
Nineveh, he rose from his throne, laid
aside his robe, covered himself with
sackcloth, and sat in the ashes. [7] Then
he had this proclaimed throughout
Nineveh, by decree of the king and his
nobles: "Neither man nor beast, neither
cattle nor sheep, shall taste anything;
they shall not eat, nor shall they drink
water. [8]† Man and beast shall be covered
with sackcloth and call loudly to God;
every man shall turn from his evil way
and from the violence he has in hand.
[9]* Who knows, God may relent and for-
give, and withhold his blazing wrath, so
that we shall not perish." [10] When God
saw by their actions how they turned
from their evil way, he repented of the
evil that he had threatened to do to them;
he did not carry it out.

CHAPTER 4

Jonah's Anger: God's Reproof. [1]† But
this was greatly displeasing to Jonah,
and he became angry. [2]* "I beseech you,
LORD," he prayed, "is not this what I
said while I was still in my own country?
This is why I fled at first to Tarshish. I
knew that you are a gracious and merci-
ful God, slow to anger, rich in clemency,
loathe to punish. [3]* And now, LORD,
please take my life from me; for it is bet-
ter for me to die than to live." [4] But the
LORD asked, "Have you reason to be an-
gry?"
[5] Jonah then left the city for a place
to the east of it, where he built himself
a hut and waited under it in the shade,
to see what would happen to the city.

---

*

2, 1: Mt 12, 40; 16, 4; Lk 11, 30; 1 Cor 15, 4.
3: Pss 18, 7; 120, 1.
4: Ps 42, 8.
5: Ps 31, 23; Is 38, 11.
6: Pss 18, 5; 69, 2.
7: Pss 16, 10; 30, 4.
8: Pss 5, 8; 18, 7; 88, 3.
9: Ps 31, 7.
10: Ps 50, 14.
3, 5: Mt 12, 41; Lk 11, 32.
9: Jl 2, 14.
4, 2: Ps 86, 5; Jl 2, 13.
3: 1 Kgs 19, 4.

†

3, 4: *Shall be destroyed:* the Hebrew expression reminds the reader of the "overthrowing" of the wicked cities, Sodom and Gomorrah, by a special act of God.

3, 8: *Beast . . . sackcloth:* the animals carried the signs of this repentance, as on occasions of joy they bore garlands.

4, 1: *He became angry:* because of his narrowly nationalistic vindictiveness, Jonah did not wish the Lord to forgive the Ninevites.

6† And when the LORD God provided a
gourd plant, that grew up over Jonah's
head, giving shade that relieved him of
any discomfort, Jonah was very happy
over the plant. 7 But the next morning
at dawn God sent a worm which at-
tacked the plant, so that it withered.
8 And when the sun arose, God sent a
burning east wind; and the sun beat
upon Jonah's head till he became faint.
Then he asked for death, saying, "I
would be better off dead than alive."

9 But God said to Jonah, "Have you
reason to be angry over the plant?" "I
have reason to be angry," Jonah an-
swered, "angry enough to die." 10† Then
the LORD said, "You are concerned over
the plant which cost you no labor and
which you did not raise; it came up in
one night and in one night it perished.
11 And should I not be concerned over
Nineveh, the great city, in which there
are more than a hundred and twenty
thousand persons who cannot distin-
guish their right hand from their left,
not to mention the many cattle?"

†

4, 6: *Gourd plant:* the Hebrew word, *kikayon* means here a wide-leafed plant of the cucumber or castor-bean variety.

4, 10f: Jonah is selfish in bemoaning his personal loss of a shady gourd plant without any concern over the threat of loss of life to the Ninevites through the destruction of their city. If God in his kindness provided the plant for his prophet without the latter's effort or merit, how much more is he disposed to show love and mercy toward all men, Jew and Gentile, when they repent of their sins and implore his pardon! God's providence is also shown here to extend even to animals.

The Book of

MICAH

Micah was a contemporary of Isaiah. Of his personal life and call we know nothing except that he came from the obscure village of Moresheth in the foothills. His were the broad vistas of the Judean lowland and the distant sea on the western horizon. With burning eloquence he attacked the rich exploiters of the poor, fraudulent merchants, venal judges, corrupt priests and prophets. To the man of the countryside the vices of the nation seemed centered in its capitals, for both Samaria and Jerusalem are singled out for judgment. An interesting notice in Jer 26, 17f informs us that the reform of Hezekiah was influenced by the preaching of Micah.

The prophecy may be divided into three parts:

I: The impending judgment of the Lord, followed by an exposition of its causes, Israel's sins. Censure of Judah's leaders for betrayal of their responsibility. (1, 1—3, 12)

II: The glory of the restored Zion. A prince of David's house will rule over a reunited Israel. (St. Matthew's Nativity narrative points to Christ's birth in Bethlehem as the fulfillment of this propehecy.) A remnant shall survive the chastisement of Judah and her adversaries shall be destroyed. (4, 1—5, 14)

III: The case against Israel, in which the Lord is portrayed as the plaintiff who has maintained fidelity to the covenant. The somber picture closes with a prayer for national restoration and a beautiful expression of trust in God's pardoning mercy. (6, 1—7, 20)

It should be noted that each of these three divisions begins with reproach and the threat of punishment, and ends on a note of hope and promise.

I: PUNISHMENT OF ISRAEL'S SINS

CHAPTER 1

Divine Judgment. 1 The word of the LORD which came to Micah of Moresheth in the days of Jotham, Ahaz, and Hezekiah, kings of Judah: that is, the vision he received concerning Samaria and Jerusalem.

2*† Hear, O peoples, all of you,
give heed, O earth, and all that fills you!
Let the Lord GOD be witness against you,
the Lord from his holy temple!
3* For see, the LORD comes forth from his place,
he descends and treads upon the heights of the earth.
4 The mountains melt under him
and the valleys split open,
Like wax before the fire,
like water poured down a slope.
5 For the crime of Jacob all this comes to pass,
and for the sins of the house of Israel.
What is the crime of Jacob?
Is it not Samaria?
And what is the sin of the house of Judah?
Is it not Jerusalem?
6 I will make Samaria a stone heap in the field,
a place to plant for vineyards;
I will throw down into the valley her stones,
and lay bare her foundations.
7*† All her idols shall be broken to pieces,
all her wages shall be burned in the fire,
and all her statues I will destroy.
As the wages of a harlot they were gathered,
and to the wages of a harlot shall they return.

8* For this reason I lament and wail,
I go barefoot and naked;

---

*

1, 2: Dt 32, 1; Is 1, 2.
3f: Is 26, 21; Na 1, 5; Hb 3, 10.
7: Hos 9, 1.
8: Jb 30, 29.

†

1, 2: *His holy temple:* God's heavenly temple; the prophet pictures a theophany (3f).

1, 7: The comparison of the unfaithful people with a prostitute, first found in Hosea, is frequent with the prophets; probably ritual prostitution is meant; cf Am 2, 7f; Hos 4, 14.

I utter lamentation like the jackals,
and mourning like the ostriches.
9 There is no remedy for the blow she has been struck;
rather, it has come even to Judah,
It reaches to the gate of my people,
even to Jerusalem.

10*† Publish it not in Gath,
weep not at all;
In Beth-leaphrah
roll in the dust.
11 Pass by,
you who dwell in Shaphir!
The inhabitants of Zaanan
come not forth from their city.
The lamentation of Beth-ezel
finds in you its grounds.
12 How can the inhabitants of Maroth
hope for good?
For evil has come down from the LORD
to the gate of Jerusalem.
13 Harness steeds to the chariots,
O inhabitants of Lachish;
Lachish, the beginning of sin
for daughter Zion,
Because there were in you
the crimes of Israel.
14 Therefore you shall give parting gifts
to Moresheth-gath;
Beth-achzib is a deception
to the kings of Israel.
15 Yet must I bring to you the conqueror,
O inhabitants of Mareshah;
Even to Adullam shall go
the glory of Israel.

16† Make yourself bald, pluck out your hair,
for the children whom you cherish;
Let your baldness be as the eagle's,
because they are exiled from you.

CHAPTER 2

Social Evils

1 Woe to those who plan iniquity,
and work out evil on their couches;
In the morning light they accomplish it
when it lies within their power.
2† They covet fields, and seize them;
houses, and they take them;
They cheat an owner of his house,
a man of his inheritance.
3 Therefore thus says the LORD:
Behold, I am planning against this race an evil
from which you shall not withdraw your necks;
Nor shall you walk with head high,
for it will be a time of evil.
4 On that day a satire shall be sung over you,
and there shall be a plaintive chant:
"Our ruin is complete,
our fields are portioned out among our captors,
The fields of my people are measured out,
and no one can get them back!"
5† Thus you shall have no one
to mark out boundaries by lot
in the assembly of the LORD.

6† "Preach not," they preach,
"let them not preach of these things!"
The shame will not withdraw.
7 How can it be said, O house of Jacob,
"Is the LORD short of patience,
or are such his deeds?"
Do not my words promise good
to him who walks uprightly?

8 But of late my people has risen up as an enemy:
you have stripped off the mantle covering the tunic
Of those who go their way in confidence,
as though it were spoils of war.
9† The women of my people you drive out
from their pleasant houses;
From their children you take away
forever the honor I gave them.
10† "Up! Be off,
this is no place to rest";
For any trifle you exact
a crippling pledge.

11 If one, acting on impulse, should make the futile claim:

---

* 10: 2 Sm 1, 20.

---

† 1, 10-15: The Judean cities here named were in the vicinity of Moresheth, the region with which Micah was most familiar. They were to experience divine chastisement. In the Hebrew, wordplays on the names of these cities abound. The text is partly obscure.

1, 16: Shaving the head was a sign of mourning; cf Is 3, 24; Am 8, 10.

2, 2: Land monopoly, also denounced by Isaiah, was a chronic vice in Judah. To protect the poor against it, a man's *inheritance,* his ancestral property, was supposed to be inviolate; cf 1 Kgs 21, 1-4; but the wealthy in their greed were enslaving men for their debts and depriving them of their land.

2, 5: *To mark our boundaries by lot:* an allusion to the initial distribution of the land of Palestine among the Israelites; cf Jos 13-21. The appropriate punishment of those greedy for land will be the loss of their land to their enemies (v 4), a loss that will be irrevocable.

2, 6f: The words in quotation marks are the protestations of the people against the prophet's predictions of doom.

2, 9: *The honor I gave them:* their dignity as free Israelites.

2, 10: *A crippling pledge:* Israelite law forbade exacting pledges for loans that would work hardship on the borrower (Ex 22, 25f; Dt 24, 6.10-13.17); but the law was habitually violated.

"I pour you wine and strong drink
as my prophecy,"
then he would be the prophet of
this people.
12† I will gather you, O Jacob, each and
every one,
I will assemble all the remnant of
Israel;
I will group them like a flock in the
fold,
like a herd in the midst of its cor-
ral;
they shall not be thrown into panic
by men.
13 With a leader to break the path
they shall burst open the gate and
go out through it;
Their king shall go through before
them,
and the LORD at their head.

CHAPTER 3

Downfall of Present Leaders

1 And I said:
Hear, you leaders of Jacob,
rulers of the house of Israel!
Is it not your duty to know what is
right,
2* You who hate what is good, and
love evil?
You who tear their skin from them,
and their flesh from their bones!
3 They eat the flesh of my people,
and flay their skin from them,
and break their bones.
They chop them in pieces like flesh
in a kettle,
and like meat in a caldron.
4 When they cry to the LORD,
he shall not answer them;
Rather shall he hide his face from
them at that time,
because of the evil they have done.

5*† Thus says the LORD regarding the
prophets
who lead my people astray;
Who, when their teeth have some-
thing to bite,
announce peace,
But when one fails to put something
in their mouth,
proclaim war against him.
6* Therefore you shall have night, not
vision,
darkness, not divination;
The sun shall go down upon the
prophets,
and the day shall be dark for
them.
7 Then shall the seers be put to shame,
and the diviners confounded;
They shall cover their lips, all of
them,
because there is no answer from
God.
8 But as for me, I am filled with power,
with the spirit of the LORD,
with authority and with might;
To declare to Jacob his crimes
and to Israel his sins.
9 Hear this, you leaders of the house
of Jacob,
you rulers of the house of Israel!
You who abhor what is just,
and pervert all that is right;
10 Who build up Zion with bloodshed,
and Jerusalem with wickedness!
11* Her leaders render judgment for a
bribe,
her priests give decisions for a sal-
ary,
her prophets divine for money,
While they rely on the LORD, saying,
"Is not the LORD in the midst of
us?
No evil can come upon us!"
12* Therefore, because of you,
Zion shall be plowed like a field,
and Jerusalem reduced to rubble,
And the mount of the temple
to a forest ridge.

II: THE NEW ISRAEL

CHAPTER 4

The People To Be Restored

1*† In days to come
the mount of the LORD's house
Shall be established higher than the
mountains;
it shall rise high above the hills,
And peoples shall stream to it:
2 Many nations shall come, and say,
"Come, let us climb the mount of the
LORD,
to the house of the God of Jacob,
That he may instruct us in his ways,
that we may walk in his paths."
For from Zion shall go forth instruc-
tion,
and the word of the LORD from Je-
rusalem.
3 He shall judge between many peo-
ples
and impose terms on strong and
distant nations;
They shall beat their swords into
plowshares,

*

3, 2: Am 2, 7.
5: Ez 13, 10.
6: Jer 15, 9; Am 8, 9; Zec 13, 3.
11: Ez 22, 27; Zep 3, 3.
12: Jer 26, 18.
4, 1ff: Is 2, 2ff.

†

2, 12f: The messianic passage concerning the restoration after the Babylonian exile seems out of place here and is probably a later addition.

3, 5-8: Almost all the prophetic books contain oracles against the false prophets. Here Micah accuses them of prophesying for venal motives and determining the prophecy by the price that is paid them; he contrasts his own disinterested preaching of the word of God.

4, 1ff: See note on Is 2, 2ff.

and their spears into pruning hooks;
One nation shall not raise the sword against another,
nor shall they train for war again.
4* Every man shall sit under his own vine
or under his own fig tree, undisturbed;
for the mouth of the LORD of hosts has spoken.
5 For all the peoples walk
each in the name of its god,
But we will walk in the name of the LORD,
our God, forever and ever.

6 On that day, says the LORD,
I will gather the lame,
And I will assemble the outcasts,
and those whom I have afflicted.
7* I will make of the lame a remnant,
and of those driven far off a strong nation;
And the LORD shall be king over them on Mount Zion,
from now on forever.
8† And you, O Magdal-eder,
hillock of daughter Zion!
Unto you shall it come:
the former dominion shall be restored,
the kingdom of daughter Jerusalem.

9 Now why do you cry out so?
Are you without a king?
Or has your counselor perished,
That you are seized with pains
like a woman in travail?
10† Writhe in pain, grow faint,
O daughter Zion,
like a woman in travail;
For now shall you go forth from the city
and dwell in the fields;
To Babylon shall you go,
there shall you be rescued.
There shall the LORD redeem you
from the hand of your enemies.

11 How many nations are gathered against you!
They say, "Let her be profaned,
let our eyes see Zion's downfall!"
12 But they know not the thoughts of the LORD,
nor understand his counsel,
When he has gathered them
like sheaves on the threshing floor.
13* Arise and thresh, O daughter Zion;
your horn I will make iron
And your hoofs bronze,
that you may crush many peoples;
You shall devote their spoils to the LORD,
and their riches to the Lord of the whole earth.

Restoration through the Messiah

14† Now fence yourself in, Bat-gader!
"They have laid siege against us!"
With the rod they strike on the cheek
the ruler of Israel.

CHAPTER 5

1*† But you, Bethlehem-Ephrathah
too small to be among the clans of Judah,
From you shall come forth for me
one who is to be ruler in Israel;
Whose origin is from of old,
from ancient times.
2*† (Therefore the Lord will give them up, until the time
when she who is to give birth has borne,
And the rest of his brethren shall return
to the children of Israel.)
3 He shall stand firm and shepherd his flock
by the strength of the LORD,
in the majestic name of the LORD, his God;
And they shall remain, for now his greatness
shall reach to the ends of the earth;
4† he shall be peace.

If Assyria invades our country
and treads upon our land,
We shall raise against it seven shepherds,
eight men of royal rank;

*

4: Hos 14, 8; Am 9, 14.
7: Is 6, 13; Dn 7, 14; Zep 3, 19; Lk 1, 32.
13: Is 41, 15; Hos 10, 11.
5, 1: Ru 1, 2; 1 Sm 17, 12; Mt 2, 6; Jn 7, 42.
2f: Is 7, 14; 11, 1f.

†

4, 8: *Magdal-eder:* "tower of the flock," an ancient place name (cf Gn 35, 21), here used symbolically of Jerusalem.

4, 10: *For now . . . your enemies:* probably a later addition to the text, when the prediction of exile had been fulfilled in the Babylonian captivity. The prophet sees the exile as the means whereby God will purify and restore his people.

4, 14: *Bat-gader:* "fenced-in maiden," another symbolic name for Jerusalem, then under siege from the Assyrians.

5, 1: In contrast to Bat-gader (4, 14), where *the ruler of Israel,* the reigning king, is in peril of his life from the Assyrians, is the tiny city and clan of *Bethlehem-Ephrathah,* from which comes the ancient Davidic dynasty *(whose origin is from of old, from ancient times)* with its messianic King, *one who is to be ruler in Israel.*

5, 2: *She who is to give birth:* the mother of the Messiah; cf Is 7, 14.

5, 4f: This passage, expressing confidence in Judah's ability to deliver itself from Assyria, is in contrast with the preceding messianic oracle, which ascribes deliverance to the Lord and his agent. Some believe that here the prophet is quoting the words of the defiant men of Judah. The *shepherds* and *men of royal rank* are one and the same: warriors capable of routing Assyria. The same kind of numerical progression is used by Amos (1, 3), and elsewhere in the Bible.

5† And they shall tend the land of Assyria with the sword,
and the land of Nimrod with the drawn sword;
And we shall be delivered from Assyria,
if it invades our land
and treads upon our borders.

6 The remnant of Jacob shall be
in the midst of many peoples,
Like dew coming from the LORD,
like raindrops on the grass,
Which wait for no man,
nor tarry for the sons of men.
7 And the remnant of Jacob shall be among the nations,
in the midst of many peoples,
Like a lion among beasts of the forest,
like a young lion among flocks of sheep;
When it passes through, it tramples
and tears, and there is none to deliver.
8 Your hand shall be lifted above your foes,
and all your enemies shall be destroyed.

9† On that day, says the LORD,
I will destroy the horses from your midst
and ruin your chariots;
10 I will demolish the cities of your land
and tear down all your fortresses.
11 I will abolish the means of divination from your use,
and there shall no longer be soothsayers among you.
12*† I will abolish your carved images
and the sacred pillars from your midst;
And you shall no longer adore
the works of your hands.
13 I will tear out the sacred poles from your midst,
and destroy your cities.
14 I will wreak vengeance in anger and wrath
upon the nations that have not hearkened.

III: ADMONITION

CHAPTER 6

Accusation and Answer

1* Hear, then, what the LORD says:
Arise, present your plea before the mountains,
and let the hills hear your voice!
2 Hear, O mountains, the plea of the LORD,
pay attention, O foundations of the earth!
For the LORD has a plea against his people,
and he enters into trial with Israel.
3* O my people, what have I done to you,
or how have I wearied you? Answer me!
4* For I brought you up from the land of Egypt,
from the place of slavery I released you;
And I sent before you Moses,
Aaron, and Miriam.
5*† My people, remember what Moab's King Balak planned,
and how Balaam, the son of Beor, answered him
. . . from Shittim to Gilgal,
that you may know the just deeds of the LORD.

6*† With what shall I come before the LORD,
and bow before God most high?
Shall I come before him with holocausts,
with calves a year old?
7† Will the LORD be pleased with thousands of rams,
with myriad streams of oil?
Shall I give my first-born for my crime,
the fruit of my body for the sin of my soul?
8* You have been told, O man, what is good,
and what the LORD requires of you:
Only to do right and to love goodness,
and to walk humbly with your God.

*

12: Hos 3, 4; 10, 1f.
6, 1: Is 6, 2; Ob 1.
3: Jer 2, 5.
4: Ex 15, 20.
5: Nm 22, 23.
6f: Hos 6, 6; 8, 13; Am 5, 21.
8: Dt 26, 16; Zec 7, 9; Mt 23, 23.

†

5, 5: *Nimrod:* the legendary ancestor of the Mesopotamians; cf Gn 10, 10ff.

5, 9-13: Part of the messianic restoration will consist in the removal of everything that has drawn Israel away from the Lord; this includes not only the objects of false worship, but also the armaments in which the idolaters had trusted.

5, 12f: *Sacred pillars . . . sacred poles:* see note on Ex 34, 13.

6, 5: *From Shittim to Gilgal:* from the east to the west side of the Jordan; the events described in Jos 3—5 are meant. The text is defective; however, it is evident that this verse continues the remembrance of God's deeds of mercy to Israel, beginning with the Exodus (v 4) and extending to the conquest, deeds which have provoked so little response from his people.

6, 6ff: The people ask how they shall worship the Lord, proposing the various forms of sacrifice. The prophet replies that sacrifice avails nothing without the true spirit of religion. This is one of the best expressions of the prophetic teaching on religion, the preparation for such New Testament passages as Jas 1, 27.

6, 7: *Shall I give my first-born:* through Canaanite influence the abominable practice of human sacrifice had been introduced under impious kings (cf 2 Kgs 16, 3; 21, 6).

9† Hark! the LORD cries to the city.
[It is wisdom to fear your name!]
Hear, O tribe and city council,
12 You whose rich men are full of violence,
whose inhabitants speak falsehood
with deceitful tongues in their heads!
10 Am I to bear any longer criminal hoarding
and the meager ephah that is accursed?
11 Shall I acquit criminal balances,
bags of false weights?

13 Rather I will begin to strike you
with devastation because of your sins.
15* You shall sow, yet not reap,
tread out the olive, yet pour no oil,
and the grapes, yet drink no wine.
14* You shall eat, without being satisfied,
food that will leave you empty;
What you acquire, you cannot save;
what you do save, I will deliver up to the sword.
16† You have kept the decrees of Omri,
and all the works of the house of Ahab,
and you have walked in their counsels;
Therefore I will deliver you up to ruin,
and your citizens to derision;
and you shall bear the reproach of the nations.

CHAPTER 7

Condemnation and Prayer

1 Alas! I am as when the fruit is gathered,
as when the vines have been gleaned;
There is no cluster to eat,
no early fig that I crave.
2* The faithful are gone from the earth,
among men the upright are no more!
They all lie in wait to shed blood,
each one ensnares the other.
3* Their hands succeed at evil;
the prince makes demands,
The judge is had for a price,
The great man speaks as he pleases,
4 The best of them is like a brier,
the most upright like a thorn hedge.
The day announced by your watchmen!
your punishment has come;
now is the time of your confusion.
5*† Put no trust in a friend,
have no confidence in a companion;
Against her who lies in your bosom
guard the portals of your mouth.
6* For the son dishonors his father,
the daughter rises up against her mother,
The daughter-in-law against her mother-in-law,
and a man's enemies are those of his household.
7* But as for me, I will look to the LORD,
I will put my trust in God my savior;
my God will hear me!

8† Rejoice not over me, O my enemy!
though I have fallen, I will arise;
though I sit in darkness, the LORD is my light.
9 The wrath of the LORD I will endure
because I have sinned against him,
Until he takes up my cause,
and establishes my right.
He will bring me forth to the light;
I will see his justice.
10 When my enemy sees this,
shame shall cover her:
She who said to me,
"Where is the LORD, thy God?"
My eyes shall see her downfall;
now shall she be trampled underfoot,
like the mire in the streets.

11† It is the day for building your walls;
on that day the boundary shall be taken away.
12* It is the day; and they shall come to you
from Assyria and from Egypt,
From Tyre even to the River,
from sea to sea, and from mountain to mountain;
13 And the land shall be a waste
because of its citizens,

MICAH

*

15: Dt 28, 38; Am 5, 11; Hg 1, 6.
14: Hos 4, 10.
7, 2: Is 1, 21; Hos 4, 2.
3: Is 1, 23.
5: Jer 9, 3.
6: Mt 10, 35f.
7: Is 8, 17.
12: Zec 14, 16.

†

6, 9: *The city:* Jerusalem as the embodiment of the crimes of the entire land.

6, 16: Judah has followed the example of the northern kingdom epitomized in the semipaganism of Omri and his son Ahab (1 Kgs 16, 25-34), copying both the corrupted worship and the social injustice of their reigns.

7, 5f: Corresponding to the widespread civil corruption and apostasy from religion is the breakdown of normal human and family relations.

7, 8ff: The unnamed enemy of Judah mentioned in these verses may be Assyria or one of the neighboring countries, such as Edom, which stood by to profit at Judah's downfall.

7, 11ff: This prophecy of restoration and repopulation of the promised land by the Jews now in exile appears to be from the period after the destruction of Jerusalem by the Chaldeans (587 B.C.).

as a result of their deeds.

14† Shepherd your people with your staff,
the flock of your inheritance,
That dwells apart in a woodland,
in the midst of Carmel.
Let them feed in Bashan and Gilead,
as in the days of old;
15 As in the days when you came from the land of Egypt,
show us wonderful signs.

16 The nations shall behold and be put to shame,
in spite of all their strength;
They shall put their hands over their mouths;
their ears shall become deaf.
17 They shall lick the dust like the serpent,
like reptiles on the ground;
They shall come quaking from their fastnesses,
trembling in fear of you [the LORD, our God].

18* Who is there like you, the God who removes guilt
and pardons sin for the remnant of his inheritance;
Who does not persist in anger forever,
but delights rather in clemency,
19 And will again have compassion on us,
treading underfoot our guilt?
You will cast into the depths of the sea
all our sins;
20* You will show faithfulness to Jacob,
and grace to Abraham,
As you have sworn to our fathers
from days of old.

* 18: Jer 10, 6; Acts 10, 43. 20: Ps 105, 6; Is 41, 8; 63, 16.

† 7, 14-17: This prayer appears to be from the time after the return from exile (537 B.C.), when the people, few in number, possessed only a fragment of their former land, and were surrounded by hostile nations.

The Book of

NAHUM

Shortly before the fall of Nineveh in 612 B.C., Nahum uttered his prophecy against the hated city. To understand the prophet's exultant outburst of joy over the impending destruction it is necessary to recall the savage cruelty of Assyria, which had made it the scourge of the ancient Near East for almost three centuries. The royal inscriptions of Assyria afford the best commentary on the burning denunciation of "the bloody city." In the wake of their conquests, mounds of heads, impaled bodies, enslaved citizens, and avaricious looters testified to the ruthlessness of the Assyrians. Little wonder that Judah joined in the general outburst of joy over the destruction of Nineveh!

But Nahum is not a prophet of unrestrained revenge. God's moral government of the world is asserted. Yahweh is the avenger but he is also merciful, a citadel in the day of distress. Nineveh's doom was a judgment on the wicked city. Before many years passed, Jerusalem too was to learn the meaning of such a judgment.

The Book is divided as follows:
The Lord's Coming in Judgment (1, 2—2, 1.3)
The Fall of Nineveh (2, 2—3, 19)

CHAPTER 1

1 Oracle about Nineveh. The book of the vision of Nahum of Elkosh.

The Lord's Coming in Judgment

2† A jealous and avenging God is the LORD,
an avenger is the LORD, and angry;
The LORD brings vengeance on his adversaries,
and lays up wrath for his enemies;
3* The LORD is slow to anger, yet great in power,
and the LORD never leaves the guilty unpunished.
In hurricane and tempest is his path,
and clouds are the dust at his feet;
4*† He rebukes the sea and leaves it dry,
and all the rivers he dries up.
Withered are Bashan and Carmel,
and the bloom of Lebanon fades;
5 The mountains quake before him,
and the hills dissolve;
The earth is laid waste before him,
the world and all who dwell in it.
6*† Before his wrath, who can stand firm,
and who can face his blazing anger?
His fury is poured out like fire,
and the rocks are rent asunder before him.
7 The LORD is good,
a refuge on the day of distress;
He takes care of those who have recourse to him,
8 when the flood rages;
He makes an end of his opponents,
and his enemies he pursues with darkness.

9† What are you imputing to the LORD?
It is he who will make an end!
The enemy shall not rise a second time;
10 As when a tangle of thornbushes is set aflame,
like dry stubble, they shall be utterly consumed.
12† For, says the LORD,
be they ever so many and so vigorous,
still they shall be mown down and disappear.
Though I have humbled you,
I will humble you no more.
13* Now will I break his yoke from off you,
and burst asunder your bonds.

---

*

1, 3: Ex 19, 16ff.
4: Is 33, 9; Hb 3, 6ff.
6: Zep 1, 15; 2, 3.
13: Is 9, 4; 10, 27.

---

†

1, 2-8: A poem written in the style of the alphabetic psalms; cf Pss 9A; 25; 111; 119. Here, however, most of the verses beginning with the letters of the second half of the alphabet are not preserved.

1, 2: *A jealous . . .God:* see note on Ex 20, 5.

1, 4: *Bashan, Carmel* and *Lebanon* were famous for their forests.

1, 6f: The coming of God in judgment has two aspects: to those who oppose him it will be unbearable; to *those who have recourse to him* it will bring strength and consolation.

1, 9: *What are you imputing to the LORD?:* the people of Judah are asked what they think God has in mind.

1, 12f: *They:* the enemies of Judah. *You:* Judah. *His yoke:* the dominion of the Assyrian king over Judah.

11† From you he came
who devised evil against the LORD,
the scoundrel planner.

14† The LORD has commanded regarding you:
no descendant shall come to bear your name;
From your temple I will abolish
the carved and the molten image;
I will make your grave a mockery.

CHAPTER 2

1* See, upon the mountains there advances
the bearer of good news, announcing peace!
Celebrate your feasts, O Judah,
fulfill your vows!
For nevermore shall you be invaded
by the scoundrel; he is completely destroyed.
3 The LORD will restore the vine of Jacob,
the pride of Israel,
Though ravagers have ravaged them
and ruined the tendrils.

The Fall of Nineveh

2† The hammer comes up against you;
guard the rampart,
Keep watch on the road, gird your loins,
marshall all your strength!
4 The shields of his warriors are crimsoned,
the soldiers colored in scarlet;
Fiery steel are the chariots
on the day of his mustering.
The horses are frenzied;
5 the chariots dash madly through the streets
And wheel in the squares,
looking like firebrands,
flashing like lightning bolts.
6† His picked troops are called,
ranks break at their charge;
To the wall they rush,
the mantelet is set up.
7 The river gates are opened,
the palace shudders,
8† Its mistress is led forth captive,
and her handmaids, under guard,
Moaning like doves,
beating their breasts.
9 Nineveh is like a pool
whose waters escape;
"Stop! Stop!"
but none turns back.
10 "Plunder the silver, plunder the gold!"
There is no end to the treasure,
to their wealth in precious things
of every kind!
11* Emptiness, desolation, waste;
melting hearts and trembling knees,
Writhing in every frame,
every face blanched!
12† Where is the lions' cave,
the young lions' den,
Where the lion went in and out,
and the cub, with no one to disturb them?
13 The lion snatched enough for his cubs,
and strangled for his lionesses;
He filled his dens with prey,
and his caves with plunder.
14 I come against you,
says the LORD of hosts;
I will consume in smoke your chariots,
and the sword shall devour your young lions;
Your preying on the land I will bring to an end,
the cry of your lionesses shall be heard no more.

CHAPTER 3

Ruin Imminent and Inevitable

1* Woe to the bloody city, all lies,
full of plunder, whose looting never stops!
2 The crack of the whip, the rumbling sounds of wheels;
horses a-gallop, chariots bounding,
3 Cavalry charging,
The flame of the sword, the flash of the spear,
the many slain, the heaping corpses,
the endless bodies to stumble upon!
4* For the many debaucheries of the harlot,
fair and charming, a mistress of witchcraft,
Who enslaved nations with her harlotries,
and peoples by her witchcraft:
5*† I am come against you,

*

2, 1: Is 52, 7; Rom 10, 15.
11: Jl 2, 6.
3, 1: Hb 2, 12.
4: Mi 1, 7; Rv 17, 1f.
5: Is 47, 3; Jer 13, 26; Hos 2, 12.

†

1, 11: *From you . . . the scoundrel planner:* addressed to Nineveh, the capital city of Sennacherib, king of Assyria, who besieged Jerusalem c. 700 B.C.
1, 14: *You:* the king of Assyria.
2, 2: *The hammer comes up against you:* the enemy is about to crush Nineveh.
2, 6: *Mantelet:* a movable shelter protecting the besiegers.
2, 8: *Mistress . . . and her handmaids:* either the queen of Nineveh with the ladies of her court, or the statue of Ishtar, Nineveh's chief goddess, with her temple prostitutes.
2, 12: *The lion:* the king of Assyria.
3, 5f: The punishment of adulteresses.

and I will strip your skirt from you;
I will show your nakedness to the nations,
to the kingdoms your shame!
6 I will cast filth upon you,
disgrace you and put you to shame;
7 Till everyone who sees you runs from you, saying,
"Nineveh is destroyed; who can pity her?
Where can one find any to console her?"

8*† Are you better than No-amon
that was set among the streams,
Surrounded by waters,
with the flood for her rampart
and water her wall?
9 Ethiopia was her strength, and Egypt,
and others without end;
Put and the Libyans were her auxiliaries.
10 Yet even she went captive into exile,
even her little ones were dashed to pieces
at the corner of every street;
For her nobles they cast lots,
and all her great men were put into chains.
11* You too, shall drink of this till you faint away;
you, too, shall seek a refuge from the foe.
12 All your fortresses are but fig trees,
bearing early figs
That fall, when shaken,
into the hungry mouth.
13* See, the troops are women in your midst;
to your foes the gates of your land are open wide,
fire has consumed their bars.
14† Draw water for the siege,
strengthen your fortresses;
Go down into the mud and tread the clay,
take hold of the brick mold!
15 There the fire shall consume you,
the sword shall cut you down.

Multiply like the grasshoppers,
multiply like the locusts!
16 Make your couriers more numerous than the stars,
17 your garrisons as many as grasshoppers,
And your scribes as locust swarms
gathered on the rubble fences on a cold day!
Yet when the sun warms them,
the grasshoppers will spread their wings and fly,
and vanish, no one knows where.
18 Alas! how your shepherds slumber,
O king of Assyria,
your nobles have gone to rest;
Your people are scattered upon the mountains,
with none to gather them.
19 There is no healing for your hurt,
your wound is mortal.
All who hear this news of you
clap their hands over you;
For who has not been overwhelmed,
steadily, by your malice?

NAHUM

---

*

8: Jer 46, 25. 13: Jer 51, 30.
11: Mi 2, 11.

†

3, 8: *No-amon:* No was the Egyptian name of the capital of Upper Egypt, called Thebes by the Greeks; its tutelary deity was Amon. This great city was destroyed by the Assyrians in 663 B.C.

3, 14: An ironic exhortation to prepare the city for a futile defense. *Go down . . . brick mold:* make bricks for the city walls.

The Book of

HABAKKUK

This prophecy dates from the years 605-597 B.C., or between the great Babylonian victory at Carchemish and Nebuchadnezzar's invasion of Judah which culminated in the capture of Jerusalem. The situation of Judah was desperate at this time, with political intrigue and idolatry widespread in the small kingdom. The first two chapters consist of a dialogue between the prophet and the Lord. For what may be the first time in Israelite literature, a man questions the ways of God, as Habakkuk calls him to account for his government of the world. To this question God replies that he has prepared a chastising rod, Babylon, which will be the avenging instrument in his hand. There is added the divine assurance that the just Israelite will not perish in the calamities about to be visited on the nation.

The third chapter is a magnificent religious lyric, filled with reminiscences of Israel's past and rich in literary borrowings from the poetry of ancient Canaan, though still expressing authentic Israelite faith. God appears in all his majestic splendor and executes vengeance on Judah's enemies. The prophecy ends with a joyous profession of confidence in the Lord, the Savior.

CHAPTER 1

1 The oracle which Habakkuk the prophet received in vision.

The Prophet's Complaint and Its Answer

2† How long, O LORD? I cry for help
but you do not listen!
I cry out to you, "Violence!"
but you do not intervene.
3 Why do you let me see ruin;
why must I look at misery?
Destruction and violence are before me;
there is strife, and clamorous discord.
4 This is why the law is benumbed,
and judgment is never rendered:
Because the wicked circumvent the just;
this is why judgment comes forth perverted.

5*† Look over the nations and see,
and be utterly amazed!
For a work is being done in your days
that you would not have believed, were it told.
6 For see, I am raising up Chaldea,
that bitter and unruly people,
That marches the breadth of the land
to take dwellings not his own.
7 Terrible and dreadful is he,
from himself derive his law and his majesty.
8† Swifter than leopards are his horses,
and keener than wolves at evening.
His horses prance,
his horsemen come from afar:
They fly like the eagle hastening to devour;
9 each comes for the rapine,
Their combined onset is that of a stormwind
that heaps up captives like sand.
10 He scoffs at kings,
and princes are his laughingstock;
He laughs at any fortress,
heaps up a ramp, and conquers it.
11† Then he veers like the wind and is gone—
this culprit who makes his own strength his god!

*

1, 5: Acts 13, 41.

†

1, 2-4: Traditionally, these verses have been taken as the prophet's complaint against the internal evils of Judah; the language used is that employed by Amos, Isaiah, and Jeremiah to condemn the social abuses of their day. In vv 5ff the Lord answers this complaint by indicating the Chaldean empire as his instrument for punishing his people for these sins.

1, 5: *Look over the nations and see:* after Nebuchadnezzar's defeat of Egypt in 605 B.C., there could be little doubt that it was the Chaldean ambition to dominate the entire Near East.

1, 8: *Wolves at evening:* the wolf is apparently thought of as more rabid and vicious in the evening when setting out for prey (Jer 5, 6; Zep 3, 3).

1, 11: *Veers like the wind:* the conquests of the ancient Near East were mainly raiding expeditions to collect tribute. As far as administration of conquered territories was concerned, both the Assyrians and Chaldeans were usually content to install friendly rulers and then depart. *This culprit:* though the Chaldeans were used by God as the agents of his punishment, this did not diminish their own guilt as ruthless marauders.

12† Are you not from eternity, O LORD,
my holy God, immortal?
O LORD you have marked him for judgment,
O Rock, you have readied him for punishment!
13 Too pure are your eyes to look upon evil,
and the sight of misery you cannot endure.
Why, then, do you gaze on the faithless in silence
while the wicked man devours
one more just than himself?
14 You have made man like the fish of the sea,
like creeping things without a ruler.
15† He brings them all up with his hook,
he hauls them away with his net,
He gathers them in his seine;
and so he rejoices and exults.
16† Therefore he sacrifices to his net,
and burns incense to his seine;
For thanks to them his portion is generous,
and his repast sumptuous.
17 Shall he, then, keep on brandishing his sword
to slay peoples without mercy?

CHAPTER 2

1* I will stand at my guard post,
and station myself upon the rampart,
And keep watch to see what he will say to me,
and what answer he will give to my complaint.

2 Then the LORD answered me and said:
Write down the vision
Clearly upon the tablets,
so that one can read it readily.
3 For the vision still has its time,
presses on to fulfillment, and will not disappoint;
If it delays, wait for it,
it will surely come, it will not be late.
4*† The rash man has no integrity;
but the just man, because of his faith, shall live.
Wealth, too, is treacherous:
the proud, unstable man—
5 He who opens wide his throat like the nether world,
and is insatiable as death,
Who gathers to himself all the nations,
and rallies to himself all the peoples—
6 Shall not all these take up a taunt against him,
satire and epigrams about him, to say:
Woe to him who stores up what is not his:
how long can it last!
he loads himself down with debts.
7 Shall not your creditors rise suddenly?
Shall not they who make you tremble awake?
You shall become their spoil!
8 Because you despoiled many peoples
all the rest of the nations shall despoil you;
Because of men's blood shed,
and violence done to the land,
to the city and to all who dwell in it.

9 Woe to him who pursues evil gain for his household,
setting his nest on high
to escape the reach of misfortune!
10 You have devised shame for your household,
cutting off many peoples, forfeiting your own life:
11† For the stone in the wall shall cry out,
and the beam in the woodwork shall answer it!

12* Woe to him who builds a city by bloodshed,
and establishes a town by wickedness!
13*† Is not this from the LORD of hosts:
peoples toil for the flames,

HABAKKUK

---

*

2, 1: Ps 85, 9.
4: Rom 1, 17; Gal 3, 11; Heb 10, 38.
12: Ez 24, 9; Na 3, 1.
13: Jer 51, 58.

†

1, 12—2, 1: It is generally thought that this complaint is directed against the Chaldeans and their terrible destruction. But it may well be a continuation of 1, 2-4, against the wicked Judahites who have merited God's punishment.

1, 12: *O Rock:* an ancient title celebrating the Lord's power; cf Ps 18, 32.

1, 15: The *he* of this and the following verses, to whom is attributed such extensive evil and the destruction of many peoples, may be the wicked of Judah embodied in King Jehoiakim, ally of the powerful Pharaoh Neco of Egypt; the devastation wrought by Jehoiakim and Neco together is condemned.

1, 16: *He sacrifices to his net:* in v 15 the wicked ruler in question is represented as catching men in a net. This verse alludes to some rite involving the sacrificial veneration of the weapons of war.

2, 4: *The just man, because of his faith, shall live:* the faith which here enables the virtuous man to survive the impending doom is both a confident belief in God's justice, and patience in awaiting its execution. St. Paul quotes these words (Rom 1, 17; Gal 3, 11; Heb 10, 38) to confirm his teaching that man receives justification and supernatural life through faith in Christ.

2, 11f: The palaces, built at the expense of gross injustice (vv 6-10), call down vengeance on their builders. This is typical prophetic language for the condemnation of social crimes within Israel and Judah.

2, 13: *Peoples toil for the flames:* they build only to have fire consume their work, when they build contrary to God's will.

and nations grow weary for
nought!
14* But the earth shall be filled
with the knowledge of the LORD's
glory
as water covers the sea.

15 Woe to you who give your neighbors
a flood of your wrath to drink,
and make them drunk, till their
nakedness is seen!
16 You are filled with shame instead of
glory;
drink, you too, and stagger!
On you shall revert the cup from the
LORD's right hand,
and utter shame on your glory.
17† For the violence done to Lebanon
shall cover you,
and the destruction of the beasts
shall terrify you;
Because of men's blood shed,
and violence done to the land,
to the city and to all who dwell in
it.
19 Woe to him who says to wood,
"Awake!"
to dumb stone, "Arise!"
Can such a thing give oracles?
See, it is overlaid with gold and sil-
ver,
but there is no life breath in it.
18† Of what avail is the carved image,
that its maker should carve it?
Or the molten image and lying ora-
cle,
that its very maker should trust
in it,
and make dumb idols?
20* But the LORD is in his holy temple;
silence before him, all the earth!

CHAPTER 3

Canticle

1† *Prayer of Habakkuk, the prophet. To a plaintive tune.*

2† O LORD, I have heard your renown,
and feared, O LORD, your work.
In the course of the years revive it,
in the course of the years make
it known;
in your wrath remember compas-
sion!

3† God comes from Teman,
the Holy One from Mount Paran.
Covered are the heavens with his
glory,
and with his praise the earth is
filled.
4 His splendor spreads like the light;
rays shine forth from beside him,
where his power is concealed.
5 Before him goes pestilence,
and the plague follows in his steps.
6 He pauses to survey the earth;
his look makes the nations trem-
ble.
The eternal mountains are shat-
tered,
the age-old hills bow low
along his ancient ways.

7 I see the tents of Cushan collapse;
trembling are the pavilions of the
land of Midian.
8 Is your anger against the streams,
O LORD?
Is your wrath against the streams,
your rage against the sea,
That you drive the steeds
of your victorious chariot?
9 Bared and ready is your bow,
filled with arrows is your quiver.
Into streams you split the earth;
10 at sight of you the mountains
tremble.
A torrent of rain descends;
the ocean gives forth its roar.
The sun forgets to rise,
11* the moon remains in its shelter,
At the light of your flying arrows,
at the gleam of your flashing
spear.

12 In wrath you bestride the earth,
in fury you trample the nations.
13*† You come forth to save your people,
to save your anointed one.
You crush the heads of the wicked,
you lay bare their bases at the
neck.
14 You pierce with your shafts the
heads of their princes
whose boast would be of devour-
ing
the wretched in their lair.
15 You tread the sea with your steeds
amid the churning of the deep
waters.

*

14: Is 11, 9. 3, 11: Jos 10, 12.
20: Ps 11, 4. 13: Is 51, 9ff.

†

2, 17: *The violence done to Lebanon:* the spoliation of the cedar forests of Lebanon, used in lavish building projects by the great conquerors; cf Is 14, 8; 37, 24. *The destruction of the beasts:* the killing-off of the wild animals through excessive hunting by the same conquerors; cf Bar 3, 16.

2, 18-20: Idolatrous worship is here shown to be folly by contrasting man-made idols with the majesty of the one true God.

3, 1: A later liturgical rubric. So also the end of v 19.

3, 2: *In the course of the years revive it:* renew today your wondrous deeds of the past.

3, 3-15: Cf the theophanies in Dt 33, 2f; Jgs 5, 4f; Pss 18, 8-16; 68, 8f; 77, 17-21; 97, 1-5; Na 1, 3-6, etc. Conventional language is employed to describe the appearance of the Lord, as in Ex 19, 16-19.

3, 3: *Teman:* a region in Edom. *Mount Paran:* in the territory of Edom: or the northern part of the Sinaitic peninsula. The Lord is represented as coming from Sinai, where he had appeared to Moses and given Israel the covenant and the law.

3, 13: *Your anointed one:* the theocratic king, the head of God's people.

16 I hear, and my body trembles;
at the sound, my lips quiver.
Decay invades my bones,
my legs tremble beneath me.
I await the day of distress
that will come upon the people who attack us.

17 For though the fig tree blossom not
nor fruit be on the vines,
Though the yield of the olive fail
and the terraces produce no nourishment,
Though the flocks disappear from the fold
and there be no herd in the stalls,
18* Yet will I rejoice in the LORD
and exult in my saving God.
19 GOD, my Lord, is my strength;
he makes my feet swift as those of hinds
and enables me to go upon the heights.

For the leader; with stringed instruments.

---

* 18f: Ps. 18, 32f; Mi 7, 7.

The Book of

ZEPHANIAH

The title of the prophecy informs us that the ministry of Zephaniah took place during the reign of Josiah (640-609 B.C.). The protest against the worship of false gods, and the condemnation of the pro-Assyrian court ministers who served as regents during Josiah's minority, allow us to place the work in the first decade of the reign. Accordingly, the prophecy of Zephaniah comes rightly before that of Jeremiah, who was probably influenced by it in both language and ideas.

The age of Zephaniah was a time of religious degradation, when the old idolatries reappeared and men worshiped sun, moon, and stars. Rites completely alien to the pure monotheism taught by Moses flourished in Jerusalem. To the corrupt city Zephaniah announced the impending judgment, the day of the Lord. The prophecy may be divided into three sections, corresponding to the three chapters of the book:

The day of the Lord: A day of doom. The last few verses of this oracle give the classic description of the day of the Lord as an overwhelming disaster. The Christian hymn Dies Irae *is based on this passage (1, 2-18)*

The day of the Lord: A day of judgment of the nations, traditional enemies of God's people (2, 1-15)

Reproach and Promise for Jerusalem: Despite Judah's infidelities, the Lord in his mercy will spare a holy remnant, which will finally enjoy peace. The prophecy closes with a hymn of joy sung by the remnant restored to Zion (3, 1-20)

CHAPTER 1

1 The word of the LORD which came to Zephaniah, the son of Cushi, the son of Gedaliah, the son of Amariah, the son of Hezekiah, in the days of Josiah, the son of Amon, king of Judah.

The Day of the Lord: A Day of Doom

2 I will completely sweep away all things
from the face of the earth, says the LORD.
3* I will sweep away man and beast,
I will sweep away the birds of the sky,
and the fishes of the sea.
I will overthrow the wicked;
I will destroy mankind
from the face of the earth, says the LORD.
4 I will stretch out my hand against Judah,
and against all the inhabitants of Jerusalem;
I will destroy from this place the last vestige of Baal,
the very names of his priests.
5*† And those who adore the host of heaven on the roofs,
with those who adore the LORD
but swear by Milcom;
6 And those who have fallen away from the LORD,
and those who do not seek the LORD.

7† Silence in the presence of the Lord GOD!
for near is the day of the LORD,
Yes, the LORD has prepared a slaughter feast,
he has consecrated his guests.
8 On the day of the LORD's slaughter feast
I will punish the princes, and the king's sons,
and all that dress in foreign apparel.
9† I will punish, on that day,
all who leap over the threshold,
Who fill the house of their master
with violence and deceit.
10† On that day, says the LORD,

---

* 1, 3: Hos 4, 3. 5: Jer 8, 2; 19, 13.

---

† 1, 5: *The host of heaven:* the stars, the worship of which was introduced into Judah by the Assyrians. *Milcom:* the god of the Ammonites; cf 1 Kgs 11, 5.7.33; 2 Kgs 23, 13.

1, 7: *He has consecrated his guests:* God has prepared those whom he has invited to share as soldiers in the booty, or as beast and bird scavengers of carrion, on the day of slaughter. Cf Jer 46, 10; Ez 39, 17.

1, 9: *Leap over the threshold:* the reference is to a superstitious custom of the pagans, witnessed to at least in regard to the worship of Dagon (1 Sm 5, 5).

1, 10f: *The New Quarter . . . the Mortar:* sections of Jerusalem (cf 2 Kgs 22, 14).

A cry will be heard from the Fish Gate,
a wail from the New Quarter,
loud crashing from the hills.
11 Wail, O inhabitants of the Mortar!
for all the merchants will be destroyed,
all who weigh out silver, done away with.
12† At that time I will explore Jerusalem with lamps;
I will punish the men who thicken on their lees,
Who say in their hearts,
"Neither good nor evil can the LORD do."
13* Their wealth shall be given to pillage
and their houses to devastation;
They will build houses, but shall not dwell in them,
plant vineyards, but not drink their wine.
14 Near is the great day of the LORD,
near and very swiftly coming,
Hark, the day of the LORD!
bitter, then, the warrior's cry.
15* A day of wrath is that day
a day of anguish and distress,
A day of destruction and desolation,
a day of darkness and gloom,
A day of thick black clouds,
16* a day of trumpet blasts and battle alarm
Against fortified cities,
against battlements on high.
17 I will hem men in
till they walk like the blind,
because they have sinned against the LORD;
And their blood shall be poured out like dust,
and their brains like dung.
18* Neither their silver nor their gold
shall be able to save them
on the day of the LORD's wrath,
When in the fire of his jealousy
all the earth shall be consumed.
For he shall make an end, yes, a sudden end,
of all who live on the earth.

CHAPTER 2

The Day of the Lord: A Day of Judgment

1† Gather, gather yourselves together,
O nation without shame!
2 Before you are driven away,
like chaff that passes on;
Before there comes upon you
the blazing anger of the LORD:
Before there comes upon you
the day of the LORD's anger.
3 Seek the LORD, all you humble of the earth,
who have observed his law;
Seek justice, seek humility;
perhaps you may be sheltered
on the day of the LORD's anger.
4*† For Gaza shall be forsaken,
and Ashkelon shall be a waste,
Ashdod they shall drive out at midday,
and Ekron shall be uprooted.
5† Woe to you who dwell by the seacoast,
to the Cretan folk!
The word of the LORD is against you,
I will humble you, land of the Philistines,
and leave you to perish without an inhabitant!
6 The coastland of the Cretans shall become
fields for shepherds, and folds for flocks.
7 The coast shall belong
to the remnant of the house of Judah;
by the sea they shall pasture.
In the houses of Ashkelon at evening
they shall couch their flocks,
For the LORD their God shall visit them,
and bring about their restoration.

8 I have heard the revilings uttered by Moab,
and the insults of the Ammonites,
When they reviled my people
and made boasts against their territory.
9 Therefore, as I live, says the LORD of hosts,
the God of Israel,
Moab shall become like Sodom,
the land of Ammon like Gomorrah:
A field of nettles and a salt pit
and a waste forever.
The remnant of my people shall plunder them,
the survivors of my nation dispossess them.
10 Such shall be the requital of their pride,
because they reviled and boasted against
the people of the LORD of hosts.

*

13: Am 5, 11.
15: Jer 30, 7; Jl 2, 11; Am 5, 18.
16: Am 2, 2.
18: 3, 8; Ez 7, 19.
2, 4: Am 1, 6ff; Zec 9, 5.

†

1, 12: *The men who thicken on their lees:* those who are overconfident because, like bottles of wine in which the sediment has settled to the bottom, they have remained at peace and undisturbed for a long time.

2, 1: *Nation without shame:* Judah.

2, 4: *Gaza . . . Ashkelon . . . Ashdod . . . Ekron:* four of the five cities of the Philistine confederation. The fifth city, Gath, is not mentioned, perhaps because it was already destroyed.

2, 5: *Cretan folk:* the Philistines, who came from Crete; see note on Dt 2, 23.

11 The LORD shall inspire them with fear
when he makes all the gods of earth to waste away;
Then, each from its own place,
all the coastlands of the nations shall adore him.

12† You too, O Cushites,
shall be slain by the sword of the LORD.
13 He will stretch out his hand against the north,
to destroy Assyria;
He will make Nineveh a waste,
dry as the desert.
14* In her midst shall settle in droves
all the wild life of the hollows;
The screech owl and the desert owl
shall roost in her columns;
Their call shall resound from the window,
the raven's croak from the doorway.
15† Is this the exultant city
that dwelt secure;
That told herself,
"There is no other than I!"
How has she become a waste,
a lair for wild beasts?
Whoever passes by her
hisses, and shakes his fist!

CHAPTER 3

Reproach and Promise for Jerusalem

1 Woe to the city, rebellious and polluted,
to the tyrannical city!
2* She hears no voice,
accepts no correction;
In the LORD she has not trusted,
to her God she has not drawn near.
3* Her princes in her midst
are roaring lions;
Her judges are wolves of the night
that have had no bones to gnaw by morning.
4* Her prophets are insolent,
treacherous men;
Her priests profane what is holy,
and do violence to the law.
5 The LORD within her is just,
who does no wrong;
Morning after morning he renders judgment
unfailingly, at dawn.

6* I have destroyed nations,
their battlements are laid waste;
I have made their streets deserted,
with no one passing through;
Their cities are devastated,
with no man dwelling in them.
7 I said, "Surely now you will fear me,
you will accept correction";
She should not fail to see
all I have visited upon her.
Yet all the more eagerly have they done
all their corrupt deeds.
8* Therefore, wait for me, says the LORD,
against the day when I arise as accuser;
For it is my decision to gather together the nations,
to assemble the kingdoms,
In order to pour out upon them my wrath,
all my blazing anger;
For in the fire of my jealousy
shall all the earth be consumed.
9 For then I will change and purify
the lips of the peoples,
That they all may call upon the name of the LORD,
to serve him with one accord;
10 From beyond the rivers of Ethiopia
and as far as the recesses of the North,
they shall bring me offerings.

11 On that day
You need not be ashamed
of all your deeds,
your rebellious actions against me;
For then will I remove from your midst
the proud braggarts,
And you shall no longer exalt yourself
on my holy mountain.
12* But I will leave as a remnant in your midst
a people humble and lowly,
Who shall take refuge in the name of the LORD;
13* the remnant of Israel.
They shall do no wrong
and speak no lies;
Nor shall there be found in their mouths
a deceitful tongue;
They shall pasture and couch their flocks
with none to disturb them.

14* Shout for joy, O daughter Zion!
sing joyfully, O Israel!
Be glad and exult with all your heart,
O daughter Jerusalem!

---

*

2, 14: Is 34, 11.
3, 2: Jer 2, 30; 7, 28.
3: Ez 22, 27; Mi 3, 11.
4: Jer 23, 32.
6: Jer 2, 15.
8: 1, 18.
12: Hos 14, 4.
13: Mi 4, 4.
14: Zec 9, 9.

---

†

2, 12: *Cushites:* the Egyptians, at this time under a Cushite or Ethiopian dynasty.
2, 15: *The exultant city:* Nineveh.

15 The LORD has removed the judgment against you,
he has turned away your enemies;
The King of Israel, the LORD, is in your midst,
you have no further misfortune to fear.
16* On that day, it shall be said to Jerusalem:
Fear not, O Zion, be not discouraged!
17 The LORD, your God, is in your midst,
a mighty savior;
He will rejoice over you with gladness,
and renew you in his love,
He will sing joyfully because of you,
18 as one sings at festivals.

I will remove disaster from among you,
so that none may recount your disgrace.
19* Yes, at that time I will deal
with all who oppress you;
I will save the lame,
and assemble the outcasts;
I will give them praise and renown
in all the earth, when I bring about their restoration.
20 At that time I will bring you home,
and at that time I will gather you;
For I will give you renown and praise,
among all the peoples of the earth,
When I bring about your restoration
before your very eyes, says the LORD.

16: Mt 14, 27.
19: Mi 4, 6.

The Book of

HAGGAI

Postexilic prophecy begins with Haggai, who received the word of the Lord in the second year of Darius (520 B.C.). The Jews who returned from the exile in Babylonia had encountered formidable obstacles in their efforts to re-establish Jewish life in Judah. The Samaritans had succeeded in blocking the rebuilding of the temple; but after Darius acceded to the throne (522), permission was given to resume the work. At this critical moment, when defeatism and a certain lethargy had overtaken his repatriated countrymen, Haggai came forward with his exhortations to them to complete the great task. The first oracle, an appeal to the Jews, is contained in chapter 1. To this appeal Haggai added a short oracle of encouragement (2, 1-9) for the sake of those who gloomily contrasted the former magnificence of Solomon's temple with the second temple: the Lord would be present in this new abode, and its glory, enhanced by the offerings of the Gentiles, would surpass the ancient splendor.

The prophecy may be divided into five oracles:

The call to rebuild the temple. The economic distress so apparent in Judah is due to the Jews' neglect of the Lord while they provide for their own needs (1, 1-15).

The future glory of the new temple, surpassing that of the old (2, 1-9).

Unworthiness of a people, who may be the Samaritans, to offer sacrifice at the newly restored altar. This oracle is cast in the literary form of a torah, *an instruction given the people by a priest (2, 10-14).*

A promise of immediate blessings, which follows upon the undertaking (chapter 1) to rebuild the temple (2, 15-19).

A pledge to Zerubbabel, descendant of David, repository of the messianic hopes (2, 20-23).

CHAPTER 1

Exhortation to Rebuild the Temple of the Lord. 1*† On the first day of the sixth
month in the second year of King Da-
rius, the word of the LORD came through
the prophet Haggai to the governor of
Judah, Zerubbabel, son of Shealtiel, and
to the high priest Joshua, son of Jehoza-
dak:
2 Thus says the LORD of hosts: This
people says: "Not now has the time come
to rebuild the house of the LORD."
3 (Then this word of the LORD came
through Haggai, the prophet:) 4*† Is it
time for you to dwell in your own pan-
eled houses, while this house lies in
ruins?

5 Now thus says the LORD of hosts:
Consider your ways!
6* You have sown much, but have brought in little;
you have eaten, but have not been satisfied;
You have drunk, but have not been exhilarated;
have clothed yourselves, but not been warmed;
And he who earned wages
earned them for a bag with holes in it.

7 Thus says the LORD of hosts:
Consider your ways!
8 Go up into the hill country;
bring timber, and build the house
That I may take pleasure in it
and receive my glory, says the LORD.
9* You expected much, but it came to little;
and what you brought home, I blew away.
For what cause? says the LORD of hosts.
Because my house lies in ruins,
while each of you hurries to his own house.

---

* 1, 1: Ezr 4, 24; 5, 1; 6, 14.
4: 2 Sm 7, 2.
6: Dt 28, 38ff; Mi 6, 15.
9: 2 Kgs 25, 9.

---

† 1, 1: *The sixth month in the second year:* August/September in 520 B.C.

1, 4: The luxury of the homes of the wealthy with their *paneled houses* contrasts sadly with the ruined state of the Lord's *house.*

10* Therefore the heavens withheld from you their dew,
and the earth her crops.
11 And I called for a drought
upon the land and upon the mountains;
Upon the grain, and upon the wine, and upon the oil,
and upon all that the ground brings forth;
Upon men and upon beasts,
and upon all that is produced by hand.

12† Then Zerubbabel, son of Shealtiel,
and the high priest Joshua, son of Je-
hozadak, and all the remnant of the peo-
ple listened to the voice of the LORD,
their God, and to the words of the
prophet Haggai, because the LORD, their
God, had sent him, and the people
feared because of the LORD. 13 And the
LORD's messenger, Haggai, proclaimed
to the people as the message of the LORD:
I am with you, says the LORD.
14 Then the LORD stirred up the spirit
of the governor of Judah, Zerubbabel,
son of Shealtiel, and the spirit of the high
priest Joshua, son of Jehozadak, and the
spirit of all the remnant of the people,
so that they came and set to work on
the house of the LORD of hosts, their God,
15 on the twenty-fourth day of the sixth
month.

CHAPTER 2

Future Glory of the New Temple. In
the second year of King Darius, 1 on the
twenty-first day of the seventh month,
the word of the LORD came through the
prophet Haggai: 2 Tell this to the gover-
nor of Judah, Zerubbabel, son of Sheal-
tiel, and to the high priest Joshua, son
of Jehozadak, and to the remnant of the
people:

3 Who is left among you
that saw this house in its former glory?
And how do you see it now?
Does it not seem like nothing in your eyes?
4* But now take courage, Zerubbabel, says the LORD,
and take courage, Joshua, high priest, son of Jehozadak,
And take courage, all you people of the land,
says the LORD, and work!
For I am with you, says the LORD of hosts.
5* This is the pact that I made with you when you came out of Egypt,
And my spirit continues in your midst;
do not fear!
6*† For thus says the LORD of hosts:
One moment yet, a little while,
and I will shake the heavens and the earth,
the sea and the dry land.
7* I will shake all the nations,
and the treasures of all the nations will come in,
And I will fill this house with glory,
says the LORD of hosts.
8 Mine is the silver and mine the gold,
says the LORD of hosts.
9* Greater will be the future glory of this house
than the former, says the LORD of hosts;
And in this place I will give you peace,
says the LORD of hosts.

Offerings of the Unclean Rejected.
10 On the twenty-fourth day of the ninth
month, in the second year of King Da-
rius, the word of the LORD came to the
prophet Haggai: 11* Thus says the LORD
of hosts: Ask the priests for a decision:
12† If a man carries sanctified flesh in
the fold of his garment and the fold
touches bread, or pottage, or wine, or
oil, or any other food, do they become
sanctified? "No," the priests answered.
13* Then Haggai said: If a person un-
clean from contact with a corpse touches
any of these, do they become unclean?
The priests answered, "They become
unclean." 14 Then Haggai continued:

So is this people, and so is this nation in my sight, says the LORD:
And so are all the works of their hands;
and what they offer there is unclean.

***Promise of Immediate Blessings.*†**
15 But now, consider from this day for-
ward. Before there was a stone laid upon
a stone in the temple of the LORD, 16* how
did you fare?

HAGGAI

*

10: Gn 27, 28; Am 4, 6-9.
2, 4: Zec 8, 9.
5: Ex 29, 45; Lv 26, 45.
6: Heb 12, 26.
7: Gn 49, 10; Is 60, 5.9.11; Mal 3, 1; Rv 21, 26.
9: Is 2, 2ff; Zec 6, 13.
11: Dt 17, 8-13; Zec 7, 3.
13: Nm 19, 11.13.22.
16: Is 5, 10.

†

1, 12: *The remnant of the people:* a technical term in Haggai and Zechariah for the returned exiles.

2, 6-9: From the later period of Ezekiel's preaching onward, the temple became, as here, one of the dominant messianic themes. *Greater will be the future glory of this house than the former:* because Christ will enter it.

2, 12ff: According to the ritual concepts of the Jews, uncleanness was more contagious than sacredness. Inasmuch as the people were unclean, their offerings became unclean (Nm 19, 22).

2, 15-19: This prophecy is intimately linked with chapter 1, and should be read with it.

When one went to a heap of grain
for twenty measures,
it would yield but ten;
When another went to the vat to
draw fifty measures,
there would be but twenty.
17 I struck you in all the works of your
hands
with blight, searing wind, and
hail,
yet you did not return to me, says
the LORD.

18† [Consider from this day forward:
from the twenty-fourth day of the ninth
month. From the day on which the tem-
ple of the LORD was founded, consider!]

19 Indeed, the seed has not sprouted,
nor have the vine, the fig, the
pomegranate
and the olive tree yet borne.
From this day, I will bless!

Pledge to Zerubbabel. 20† The mes-
sage of the LORD came a second time
to Haggai on the twenty-fourth day of
the month: 21 Tell this to Zerubbabel, the
governor of Judah:

I will shake the heavens and the
earth;
22* I will overthrow the thrones of
kingdoms,
destroy the power of the kingdoms
of the nations.
I will overthrow the chariots and
their riders,
and the riders with their horses
shall go down by one another's
sword.
23*† On that day, says the LORD of
hosts,
I will take you, Zerubbabel,
son of Shealtiel, my servant, says
the LORD,
And I will set you as a signet ring;
for I have chosen you, says the
LORD of hosts.

*

22: Ez 38, 21; Dn 2, 44; Zec 14, 13; Lk 1, 52.

23: Sg 8, 6; Sir 49, 11; Is 42, 1; 44, 1f.

†

2, 18: *The ninth month:* the ordinal *ninth* has been copied incorrectly from 2, 10. This note clearly concerns the *twenty-fourth day of the sixth month, on which the temple of the Lord was founded* (1, 15).

2, 20: *The month:* probably again the sixth month, as in 1, 15 and 2, 18; see note on the latter.

2, 23: This promise to Zerubbabel, reversing the punishment of his grandfather (Jer 22, 24), is a continuation of the messianic hope; cf Zec 6, 11f.

The Book of

ZECHARIAH

Zechariah's initial prophecy is dated to 520 B.C., the same year as that in which Haggai received the prophetic call. The first eight chapters of the Book of Zechariah contain oracles which certainly belong to him while the last six (sometimes called "Deutero-Zechariah") represent the work of one or more unknown authors. In the prophecies proper to Zechariah eight symbolic visions are recorded, all meant to promote the work of rebuilding the temple and to encourage the returned exiles, especially their leaders, Joshua and Zerubbabel. In the final chapter of this first division Zechariah portrays the messianic future under the figure of a prosperous land to which the nations come in pilgrimage, eager to follow the God of Israel.

The second part of Zechariah is divided into two sections, each with its own introductory title. The first (9—11) consists of oracles whose historical background, date and authorship are extremely difficult to determine. With 9, 9 begins the messianic vision of the coming of the Prince of Peace. The verses describing the triumphant appearance of the humble king are taken up by the four Evangelists to describe the entry of Christ into Jerusalem on Palm Sunday. Chapter 12 is introduced by an oracle proclaiming the victory of God's people over the heathen. The prophecy closes by describing in apocalyptic imagery, the final assault of the enemy on Jerusalem, after which the messianic age begins.

CHAPTER 1

Necessity of Conversion. 1*† In the
second year of Darius, in the eighth
month, the word of the LORD came to
the prophet Zechariah, son of Bere-
chiah, son of Iddo: 2 The LORD was in-
deed angry with your fathers . . . 3 and
say to them: Thus says the LORD of hosts:
Return to me, says the LORD of hosts,
and I will return to you, says the LORD
of hosts. 4* Be not like your fathers
whom the former prophets warned:
Thus says the LORD of hosts: Turn from
your evil ways and from your wicked
deeds. But they would not listen or pay
attention to me, says the LORD. 5 Your
fathers, where are they? And the proph-
ets, can they live forever? 6* But my
words and my decrees, which I en-
trusted to my servants the prophets, did
not these overtake your fathers? Then
they repented and admitted: "The LORD
of hosts has treated us according to our
ways and deeds, just as he had deter-
mined he would."

The Four Horsemen. 7† In the second
year of Darius, on the twenty-fourth day
of Shebat, the eleventh month, the word
of the LORD came to the prophet Zecha-
riah, son of Berechiah, son of Iddo, in
the following way: 8*† I had a vision dur-
ing the night. There appeared the driver
of a red horse, standing among myrtle
trees in a shady place, and behind him
were red, sorrel, and white horses.
9 Then I asked, "What are these, my
lord?"; and the angel who spoke with me
answered me, "I will show you what
these are." 10* The man who was stand-
ing among the myrtle trees spoke up and
said, "These are they whom the LORD
has sent to patrol the earth." 11 And they
answered the angel of the LORD who was
standing among the myrtle trees and
said, "We have patrolled the earth; see,
the whole earth is tranquil and at rest!"

12*† Then the angel of the Lord spoke
out and said, "O LORD of hosts, how long
will you be without mercy for Jerusalem
and the cities of Judah that have felt
your anger these seventy years?" 13* To
the angel who spoke with me, the LORD
replied with comforting words.

14* And the angel who spoke with me
said to me, Proclaim: Thus says the
LORD of hosts: I am deeply moved for
the sake of Jerusalem and Zion, 15*† and

---

*

1, 1: Ezr 4, 24; 5, 1; 6, 14.
4: Jer 25, 5; 35, 15; Mal 3, 7.
6: Lam 2, 17; Lv 26, 14ff; Dt 28, 15.
8: Rv 6, 4.
10: 6, 7.
12: 7, 5; Jer 25, 11; Dn 9, 2.
13: Jer 29, 10.
14: 8, 2; Jl 2, 18.
15: Is 47, 6; Ob 10-14.

---

†

1, 1: *The second year . . . eighth month:* October/November, 520 B.C.

1, 7: *The second year . . . eleventh month:* January/February, 519 B.C.

1, 8-11: *The driver of a red horse:* apparently distinct from *the man,* or *angel of the LORD . . . standing among the myrtle trees,* who spoke with the prophet. The four horsemen are sent by God to the four corners of the earth (2, 10), to see if the whole earth is at peace.

1, 12: *These seventy years:* see note on Jer 25, 1-14.

1, 15: *The complacent nations:* the neighbors of Judah; especially Edom, which enjoyed their present prosperity and security at Judah's expense.

I am exceedingly angry with the com-
placent nations; whereas I was but a lit-
tle angry, they added to the harm.
16*† Therefore, says the LORD: I will turn
to Jerusalem in mercy; my house shall
be built in it, says the LORD of hosts, and
a measuring line shall be stretched over
Jerusalem. 17* Proclaim further: Thus
says the LORD of hosts: My cities shall
again overflow with prosperity; the LORD
will again comfort Zion, and again
choose Jerusalem.

CHAPTER 2

Four Horns and Four Blacksmiths.
1† I raised my eyes and looked; there
were four horns. 2 Then I asked the angel
who spoke with me what these were. He
answered me, "These are the horns that
scattered Judah and Israel and Jerusa-
lem."
3 Then the LORD showed me four
blacksmiths. And I asked, "What are
these coming to do?" 4 And he said,
"Here are the horns that scattered Ju-
dah, so that no man raised his head any
more; but these have come to terrify
them: to cast down the horns of the na-
tions that raised their horns to scatter
the land of Judah."
The New Jerusalem. 5* Again I raised
my eyes and looked: there was a man
with a measuring line in his hand.
6* "Where are you going?" I asked. "To
measure Jerusalem," he answered; "to
see how great is its width and how great
its length."
7 Then the angel who spoke with me
advanced, and another angel came out
to meet him, 8*† and said to him, "Run,
tell this to that young man: People will
live in Jerusalem as though in open
country, because of the multitude of men
and beasts in her midst. 9 But I will be
for her an encircling wall of fire, says
the LORD, and I will be the glory in her
midst."
10† Up, up! Flee from the land of the
north, says the LORD; for I scatter you
to the four winds of heaven, says the
LORD. 11 Up, escape to Zion! you who
dwell in daughter Babylon. 12* For thus
said the LORD of hosts (after he had al-
ready sent me) concerning the nations
that have plundered you: Whoever
touches you touches the apple of my eye.
13 See, I wave my hand over them; they
become plunder for their slaves. Thus
you shall know that the LORD of hosts
has sent me.
14* Sing and rejoice, O daughter Zion!
See, I am coming to dwell among you,
says the LORD. 15 Many nations shall join
themselves to the LORD on that day, and
they shall be his people, and he will dwell
among you, and you shall know that the
LORD of hosts has sent me to you. 16 The
LORD will possess Judah as his portion
of the holy land, and he will again choose
Jerusalem. 17 Silence, all mankind, in
the presence of the LORD! for he stirs
forth from his holy dwelling.

CHAPTER 3

Joshua the High Priest. 1* Then he
showed me Joshua the high priest stand-
ing before the angel of the LORD, while
Satan stood at his right hand to accuse
him. 2* And the angel of the LORD said
to Satan, "May the LORD rebuke you,
Satan; may the LORD who has chosen
Jerusalem rebuke you! Is not this man
a brand snatched from the fire?"
3† Now Joshua was standing before
the angel, clad in filthy garments. 4* He
spoke and said to those who were stand-
ing before him, "Take off his filthy gar-
ments, and clothe him in festal
garments." 5 He also said, "Put a clean
miter on his head." And they put a clean
miter on his head and clothed him with
the garments. Then the angel of the
LORD, standing, said, "See, I have taken
away your guilt."
6 The angel of the LORD then gave
Joshua this assurance: 7 "Thus says the
LORD of hosts: If you walk in my ways
and heed my charge, you shall judge my
house and keep my courts, and I will
give you access among these standing
here. 8*† Listen, O Joshua, high priest!
You and your associates who sit before
you are men of good omen. Yes, I will
bring my servant the Shoot. 9*† Look at

*

16: 8, 3; Ezr 6, 14.
17: Is 51, 3.
2, 5: Rv 11, 1.
6: Dt 28, 64.
8: Ez 36, 11.
12: Dt 32, 10; Ps 17, 8.
14: Ez 37, 26.
3, 1: Hg 1, 1; 1 Chr 21, 1.
2: Rom 8, 33; Jude 9.
4: Lk 15, 22.
8: Is 4, 2; 11, 1; Jer 23, 5; 33, 15.
9: 4, 10.

†

1, 16: *Measuring line:* not for devastation, as in Is 34, 11, but for reconstruction.

2, 1-4: *Four horns:* symbolic of the hostile forces which, from the four corners of the earth, invaded and devastated *the land of Judah. Four blacksmiths:* the powers used by God to destroy these enemies of his people.

2, 8: *That young man:* the angel or *man with a measuring line* of v 5.

2, 10: *The land of the north:* Babylonia (v 11).

3, 3: *Filthy garments:* symbolic of mourning for the dead, or of national catastrophe, and implying acknowledgment of guilt (v 5).

3, 8: *Men of good omen:* the restoration of the priesthood is a sign of the coming of the messianic times. *My servant the Shoot:* identified, in the earliest form of 6, 11f as the prophet composed it, with Zerubbabel, direct descendant of King David and rebuilder of the temple; and, as such, a type of the Messiah; cf Jer 23, 5.

3, 9: *One stone with seven facets:* apparently the same as *the select stone* of 4, 10, which seems to be a precious gem. The *seven facets* are explained in 4, 10 as signifying the Lord's vigilance over the world. *I will engrave its inscription:* the same Hebrew verb for *engrave* is used in Ex 28, 9.11 in regard to the inscriptions on the twelve precious stones of the priestly breastpiece.

the stone that I have placed before
Joshua, one stone with seven facets. I
will engrave its inscription, says the
LORD of hosts, and I will take away the
guilt of the land in one day. 10* On that
day, says the LORD of hosts, you will in-
vite one another under your vines and
fig trees."

CHAPTER 4

4 Then I said to the angel who spoke
with me, "What are these things, my
lord?" 5 And the angel who spoke with
me replied, "Do you not know what these
things are?" "No, my lord," I answered.
6 Then he said to me, "This is the LORD's
message to Zerubbabel: Not by an army,
nor by might, but by my spirit, says the
LORD of hosts. 7*† What are you, O great
mountain? Before Zerubbabel you are
but a plain. He shall bring out the cap-
stone amid exclamations of 'Hail, Hail'
to it."
8 This word of the LORD then came to
me: 9* The hands of Zerubbabel have
laid the foundations of this house, and
his hands shall finish it; then you shall
know that the LORD of hosts has sent me
to you. 10* For even they who were
scornful on that day of small beginnings
shall rejoice to see the select stone in the
hands of Zerubbabel. These seven facets
are the eyes of the LORD that range over
the whole earth.
The Lampstand. 1† Then the angel
who spoke with me returned and awak-
ened me, like a man awakened from his
sleep. 2* "What do you see?" he asked
me. "I see a lampstand all of gold, with
a bowl at the top," I replied; "on it are
seven lamps with their tubes, 3* and be-
side it are two olive trees, one on the
right and the other on the left." 11 I then
asked him, "What are these two olive
trees at each side of the lampstand?"
12 And again I asked, "What are the two
olive tufts which freely pour out fresh
oil through the two golden channels?"
13 "Do you not know what these are?"
he said to me. "No, my lord," I answered
him. 14 He said, "These are the two
anointed who stand by the LORD of the
whole earth."

CHAPTER 5

The Flying Scroll. 1*† Then I raised
my eyes again and saw a scroll flying.
2 "What do you see?" he asked me. I an-
swered, "I see a scroll flying; it is twenty
cubits long and ten cubits wide." 3 Then
he said to me: "This is the curse which
is to go forth over the whole earth; in
accordance with it shall every thief be
swept away, and in accordance with it
shall every perjurer be expelled from
here. 4* I will send it forth, says the LORD
of hosts, and it shall come into the house
of the thief, or into the house of him who
perjures himself with my name; it shall
lodge within his house, consuming it,
timber and stones."
The Flying Bushel. 5† Then the angel
who spoke with me came forward and
said to me, "Raise your eyes and see
what this is that comes forth." 6 "What
is it?" I asked. And he answered, "This
is a bushel container coming. This is
their guilt in all the land." 7 Then a
leaden cover was lifted, and there was
a woman sitting inside the bushel.
8 "This is Wickedness," he said; and he
thrust her inside the bushel, pushing the
leaden cover into the opening. 9 Then I
raised my eyes and saw two women
coming forth with a wind ruffling their
wings, for they had wings like the wings
of a stork. As they lifted up the bushel
into the air, 10 I said to the angel who
spoke with me, "Where are they taking
the bushel?" 11* He replied, "To build a
temple for it in the land of Shinar; when
the temple is ready, they will deposit it
there in its place."

CHAPTER 6

Four Chariots. 1† Again I raised my
eyes and saw four chariots coming out
from between two mountains; and the
mountains were of bronze. 2* The first
chariot had red horses, the second char-
iot black horses, 3 the third chariot white
horses, and the fourth chariot spotted
horses—all of them strong horses. 4 I
asked the angel who spoke with me,

*

10: 1 Kgs 4, 25.
4, 7: Ezr 3, 11ff; Ps 118, 22.
9: Ezr 6, 14ff.
10: 3, 9.
4, 2: Rv 1, 12.
3: Rv 11, 4.
5, 1: Ez 2, 9.
4: Lv 19, 12.
11: Gn 11, 2ff.
6, 2: 1, 8; Rv 6, 4.

†

4, 7: *Great mountain:* figure of the obstacles confronting Zerubbabel in building the temple. *A plain:* figure of the ease with which he will overcome these obstacles.

4, 1ff.11-14: *The two anointed:* literally, "the two sons of oil," Joshua, the anointed high priest, and Zerubbabel, the anointed prince. Just as the two olive trees in this imagery supply the sacred seven-branched lampstand (Ex 25, 31-40) with oil (v 12), so these two men, in ministering to the community, *stand by* (serve) *the Lord.*

5, 1-4: The enormous scroll, thirty feet by fifteen (the dimensions in length and breadth of the portico of Solomon's temple, 1 Kgs 6, 3), contains a list of maledictions on sinners, similar to that in Dt 27, 15-26. The *thief* and the *perjurer* represent all sinners, who are expelled from the holy community.

5, 5-11: The *woman* sealed in the *bushel container* is a figure of the general corruption of the people of Judah. She is removed from the Holy Land and transported to *Shinar,* that is, Babylonia, where a dwelling is being prepared for her; this is a symbol of the reign of *Wickedness* in pagan lands, contrasted with the reign of holiness in the Lord's dwelling on Mount Zion.

6, 1-8: The *four chariots* represent the angelic hosts sent by the Lord to the four ends of the earth. The chariot with the *black horses* brings the *spirit,* i.e., anger of the Lord against the land of the north, Babylonia.

"What are these, my lord?" 5* The angel
said to me in reply, "These are the four
winds of the heavens, which are coming
forth after being reviewed by the LORD
of all the earth." 6 The chariot with the
black horses was turning toward the
land of the north, the red and the white
horses went after them, and the spotted
ones went toward the land of the south.
7 As these strong horses emerged, eager
to set about patrolling the earth, he said,
"Go, patrol the earth!" Then, as they pa-
trolled the earth, 8 he called out to me
and said, "See, they that go forth to the
land of the north will make my spirit rest
in the land of the north."

The Coronation. 9 This word of the
LORD then came to me: 10 Take from the
returned captives Heldai, Tobijah, Je-
daiah; and go the same day to the house
of Josiah, son of Zephaniah (these had
come from Babylon). 11† Silver and gold
you shall take, and make a crown; place
it on the head of [Joshua, son of Jehoza-
dak, the high priest] Zerubbabel.
12* And say to him: Thus says the LORD
of hosts: Here is a man whose name is
Shoot, and where he is he shall sprout,
and he shall build the temple of the
LORD. 13* Yes, he shall build the temple
of the LORD, and taking up the royal in-
signia, he shall sit as ruler upon his
throne. The priest shall be put at his
right hand, and between the two of them
there shall be friendly understanding.
14 The crown itself shall be a memorial
offering in the temple of the LORD in fa-
vor of Heldai, Tobijah, Jedaiah, and the
son of Zephaniah. 15* And they who are
from afar shall come and build the tem-
ple of the LORD, and you shall know that
the LORD of hosts has sent me to you.
And if you heed carefully the voice of
the LORD your God. . . .

CHAPTER 7

True Fasting. 1† In the fourth year
of Darius the king [the word of the LORD
came to Zechariah], on the fourth day
of Chislev, the ninth month, 2 Beth-
elsarezer sent Regemmelech and his
men to implore favor of the LORD 3* and
to ask the priests of the house of the
LORD of hosts, and the prophets, "Must
I mourn and abstain in the fifth month
as I have been doing these many years?"
4 Thereupon this word of the LORD of
hosts came to me: 5* Say to all the people
of the land and to the priests: When you
fasted and mourned in the fifth and in
the seventh month these seventy years,
was it really for me that you fasted?
6 And when you were eating and drink-
ing, was it not for yourselves that you
ate, and for yourselves that you drank?
7* Were not these the words which the
LORD spoke through the former proph-
ets, when Jerusalem and the surround-
ing cities were inhabited and at peace,
when the Negeb and the foothills were
inhabited? 8 [This word of the LORD
came to Zechariah: 9* Thus says the
LORD of hosts:] Render true judgment,
and show kindness and compassion to-
ward each other. 10* Do not oppress the
widow or the orphan, the alien or the
poor; do not plot evil against one another
in your hearts. 11* But they refused to
listen; they stubbornly turned their
backs and stopped their ears so as not
to hear. 12* And they made their hearts
diamondhard so as not to hear the
teaching and the message that the LORD
of hosts had sent by his spirit through
the former prophets. 13* Then the LORD
of hosts in his great anger said that, as
they had not listened when he called, so
he would not listen when they called,
14* but would scatter them with a whirl-
wind among all the nations that they did
not know. Thus the land was left desolate
after them with no one traveling to and
fro; they made the pleasant land into a
desert.

CHAPTER 8

In the Days of the Messiah. 1 This
word of the LORD of hosts came: Thus
says the LORD of hosts:

2* I am intensely jealous for Zion,
 stirred to jealous wrath for her.
3* Thus says the LORD:
I will return to Zion,
 and I will dwell within Jerusalem;
Jerusalem shall be called the faith-
 ful city,
 and the mountain of the LORD of
 hosts,
 the holy mountain.

4 Thus says the LORD of hosts: Old men
and old women, each with staff in hand
because of old age, shall again sit in the

*

5: Ps 104, 4.
12: 3, 8; Eph 2, 20; Heb 3, 3.
13: Ps 110, 4; Heb 3, 1.
15: Eph 2, 19f.
7, 3: 8, 19.
5: Is 58, 5; Rom 14, 6.
7: Jer 17, 26.
9: Is 58, 6.
10: Ex 22, 21-24; Dt 24, 17; Is 1, 17; Jer 5, 28.
11: Neh 9, 29; Hos 4, 16.
12: Ez 11, 19; 36, 26; Neh 9, 29.
13: Is 1, 15; Mi 3, 4.
14: Dt, 4, 27.
8, 2: Na 1, 2.
3: Is 2, 2; Jer 31, 23.

†

6, 11: *Make a crown; place it on the head of [Joshua, son of Jehozadak, the high priest] Zerubbabel:* According to the current Hebrew text, Joshua the high priest is to be crowned. However, since the crown is a sign of royalty, the original text must have had the name of Zerubbabel here, not that of Joshua. In 3, 8 Joshua is a different man from the one called *the Shoot,* and in v 12 it is upon *the Shoot* that the crown is to be placed.

7, 1: *The fourth year of Darius . . . the fourth day of Chislev, the ninth month:* November, 518 B.C.

streets of Jerusalem. 5 The city shall be filled with boys and girls playing in her streets. 6 Thus says the LORD of hosts: Even if this should seem impossible in the eyes of the remnant of this people, shall it in those days be impossible in my eyes also, says the LORD of hosts? 7* Thus says the LORD of hosts: Lo, I will rescue my people from the land of the rising sun, and from the land of the setting sun. 8* I will bring them back to dwell within Jerusalem. They shall be my people, and I will be their God, with faithfulness and justice.

9* Thus says the LORD of hosts: Let your hands be strong, you who in these days hear these words spoken by the prophets on the day when the foundation of the house of the LORD of hosts was laid for the building of the temple. 10 For before those days there were no wages for men, or hire for beasts; those who came and went had no security from the enemy, for I set every man against his neighbor. 11 But now I will not deal with the remnant of this people as in former days, says the LORD of hosts, 12 for it is the seedtime of peace: the vine shall yield its fruit, the land shall bear its crops, and the heavens shall give their dew; all these things I will have the remnant of the people possess. 13* Just as you were a curse among the nations, O house of Judah and house of Israel, so will I save you that you may be a blessing; do not fear, but let your hands be strong.

14* Thus says the LORD of hosts: As I determined to harm you when your fathers provoked me to wrath, says the LORD of hosts, and I did not relent, 15 so again in these days I have determined to favor Jerusalem and the house of Judah; do not fear! 16* These then are the things you should do: Speak the truth to one another; let there be honesty and peace in the judgments at your gates, 17* and let none of you plot evil against another in his heart, nor love a false oath. For all these things I hate, says the LORD.

18 This word of the LORD of hosts came to me: 19† Thus says the LORD of hosts: The fast days of the fourth, the fifth, the seventh, and the tenth months shall become occasions of joy and gladness, cheerful festivals for the house of Judah; only love faithfulness and peace. 20 Thus says the LORD of hosts: There shall yet come peoples, the inhabitants of many cities; 21* and the inhabitants of one city shall approach those of another, and say, "Come! let us go to implore the favor of the LORD"; and, "I too will go to seek the LORD." 22* Many peoples and strong nations shall come to seek the LORD of hosts in Jerusalem and to implore the favor of the LORD. 23* Thus says the LORD of hosts: In those days ten men of every nationality, speaking different tongues, shall take hold, yes, take hold of every Jew by the edge of his garment and say, "Let us go with you, for we have heard that God is with you."

CHAPTER 9

Invasion by the Lord†

1 An oracle:
The word of the LORD is upon the land of Hadrach,
and Damascus is its resting place,
For the cities of Aram are the LORD's,
as are all the tribes of Israel,
2* Hamath also, on its border,
Tyre too, and Sidon, however wise they be.
3 Tyre built herself a stronghold,
and heaped up silver like dust,
and gold like the mire of the streets.
4* Lo, the LORD will strip her of her possessions,
and smite her power on the sea,
and she shall be devoured by fire.
5 Ashkelon shall see it and be afraid;
Gaza also: she shall be in great anguish;
Ekron, too, for her hope shall come to nought.
The king shall disappear from Gaza,
and Ashkelon shall not be inhabited,
6*† and the baseborn shall occupy Ashdod.
I will destroy the pride of the Philistine
7† and take from his mouth his bloody meat,
and his abominations from between his teeth:

*

7: Is 11, 11; Jer 30, 18.
8: Jer 4, 2.
9: Ezr 5, 1; Hg 2, 18.
13: Is 19, 24; Jer 42, 18; Hg 2, 19; Zep 3, 20.
14: Jer 31, 28.
16: 7, 9.
17: 7, 10.
21: Is 2, 3.
22: Is 60, 3.
23: Is 66, 23.
9, 2: Jer 49, 23.
4: Is 23, 1-18; Ez 26, 1—28, 26.
6: Am 1, 8.

†

8, 19: The fast day of *the fourth* month recalled the fall of Jerusalem in June, 587 B.C. (2 Kgs 25, 3f); that of *the fifth* month, the burning of the temple by Nebuzaradan in July of the same year (2 Kgs 25, 8f); that of *the seventh* month, the murder of Gedaliah in September of the same year (Jer 41, 1f); that of *the tenth* month, the beginning of the final siege of Jerusalem in January, 588 B.C. (2 Kgs 25, 1).

9, 1-8: Divine judgment is about to fall on the surrounding hostile peoples: *Aram* (Syria), including the cities of *Hadrach* and *Damascus;* Phoenicia, with its cities of *Tyre* and *Sidon;* Philistia, with its cities of *Ashkelon, Gaza, Ekron,* and *Ashdod.*

9, 6: *The baseborn:* people of mixed ancestry.

9, 7: *Remnant:* see note on Hg 1, 12. The *Jebusites:* the pre-Israelite inhabitants of Jerusalem, conquered by David and incorporated into Israel.

ZECHARIAH

He also shall become a remnant for
our God,
and shall be like a family in Judah,
and Ekron shall be like the Jebusites.
8† I will encamp by my house as a
guard
that none may pass to and fro;
No oppressor shall pass over them
again,
for now I have regard for their affliction.

Restoration under the Messiah

9*† Rejoice heartily, O daughter Zion,
shout for joy, O daughter Jerusalem!
See, your king shall come to you;
a just savior is he,
Meek, and riding on an ass,
on a colt, the foal of an ass.
10*† He shall banish the chariot from
Ephraim,
and the horse from Jerusalem;
The warrior's bow shall be banished,
and he shall proclaim peace to the
nations.
His dominion shall be from sea to
sea,
and from the River to the ends of
the earth.
11*† As for you, for the blood of your
covenant with me,
I will bring forth your prisoners
from the dungeon.
12*† In the return to the fortress
of the waiting prisoners,
This very day, I will return you
double for your exile.
13 For I will bend Judah as my bow,
I will arm myself with Ephraim;
I will arouse your sons, O Zion,
[against your sons, O Yavan,]
and I will use you as a warrior's
sword.

14 The LORD shall appear over them,
and his arrow shall shoot forth as
lightning;
The LORD God shall sound the trumpet,
and come in a storm from the
south.
15 The LORD of hosts shall be a shield
over them,
they shall overcome sling stones
and trample them underfoot;
They shall drink blood like wine,
till they are filled with it like libation bowls,
like the corners of the altar.
16* And the LORD, their God, shall save
them on that day,
his people, like a flock.
For they are the jewels in a crown
raised aloft over his land.
17 For what wealth is theirs, and what
beauty!
grain that makes the youths flourish,
and new wine, the maidens!

CHAPTER 10

The New Order of Things

1* Ask of the LORD rain in the spring
season!
It is the LORD who makes storm
clouds.
And sends men the pouring rain;
for everyone, grassy fields.
2*† For the teraphim speak nonsense,
the diviners have false visions:
Deceitful dreams they tell,
empty comfort they offer.
This is why they wander like sheep,
wretched: they have no shepherd.
3 My wrath is kindled against the
shepherds,
and I will punish the leaders;
For the LORD of hosts will visit his
flock,
the house of Judah, and make
them his stately war horse.

4 From him shall come leader and
chief,
from him warrior's bow and every
officer.
5 They shall all be warriors,
trampling the mire of the streets
in battle;
They shall wage war because the
LORD is with them,
and shall put the horsemen to
rout.
6 I will strengthen the house of Judah,
the house of Joseph I will save;

*

9: Is 62, 11; Jer 23, 5; Mt 21, 5; Jn 12, 15.
10: Hos 1, 7.
11: Is 42, 7; Ez 24, 8.
12: Is 61, 7.
16: Is 62, 3.
10, 1: Dt 11, 14; Jer 14, 22.
2: Jer 10, 8; Ez 34, 5.

†

9, 8: *My house:* the Holy Land; cf Hos 8, 1; 9, 15; Jer 12, 7.

9, 9: The Messiah will come, not as a conquering warrior, but in lowliness and peace. Not like the last kings of Judah, who rode in chariots and on horses (Jer 17, 25; 22, 4), but like the princes of old (Gn 49, 11; Jgs 5, 10; 10, 4), the Messiah will ride on an ass. The Evangelists see a literal fulfillment of this prophecy in the Savior's triumphant entry into Jerusalem (Mt 21, 4f; Jn 12, 14f).

9, 10: *The River:* The Euphrates; see note on Ps 72, 8.

9, 11: *The blood of your covenant with me:* the covenant between the Lord and Israel sealed with sacrificial blood (Ex 24, 8).

9, 12: *The waiting prisoners:* the exiles awaiting the return to their country, where they will receive a double compensation for the double punishment they had suffered; cf Is 40, 2; 61, 7.

10, 2: *Teraphim:* household idols, used for divination; cf Gn 31, 19.34f; Jgs 17, 5; 18, 17f.20; Ez 21, 26; Hos 3, 4.

I will bring them back, because I
have mercy on them,
they shall be as though I had
never cast them off,
for I am the LORD, their God, and
I will hear them.
7 Then Ephraim shall be valiant men,
and their hearts shall be cheered
as by wine.
Their children shall see it and be
glad,
their hearts shall rejoice in the
LORD.

8* I will whistle for them to come together,
and when I redeem them
they will be as numerous as before.
9 I sowed them among the nations,
yet in distant lands they remember me;
they shall rear their children and
return.
10* I will bring them back from the land
of Egypt,
and gather them from Assyria.
I will bring them into Gilead and into
Lebanon,
but these shall not suffice them;
11* I will cross over to Egypt
and smite the waves of the sea
and all the depths of the Nile shall
be dried up.
The pride of Assyria shall be cast
down,
and the scepter of Egypt taken
away.
12* I will strengthen them in the LORD,
and they shall walk in his name,
says the LORD.

CHAPTER 11

1 Open your doors, O Lebanon,
that the fire may devour your cedars!
2 Wail, you cypress trees,
for the cedars are fallen,
the mighty have been despoiled.
Wail, you oaks of Bashan,
for the impenetrable forest is cut
down!
3 Hark! the wailing of the shepherds,
their glory has been ruined.
Hark! the roaring of the young lions,
the jungle of the Jordan is laid
waste.

Allegory of the Shepherds.† 4 Thus
said the LORD, my God: Shepherd the
flock to be slaughtered. 5* For they who
buy them slay them with impunity; while
those who sell them say, "Blessed be the
LORD, I have become rich!" Even their
own shepherds do not feel for them.
6 (Nor shall I spare the inhabitants of the
earth any more, says the LORD. Yes, I
will deliver each of them into the power
of his neighbor, or into the power of his
king; they shall crush the earth, and I
will not deliver it out of their power.)
7* So I became the shepherd of the
flock to be slaughtered for the sheep
merchants. I took two staffs, one of
which I called "Favor," and the other,
"Bonds," and I fed the flock. 8 In a single
month I did away with the three shepherds. I wearied of them, and they behaved badly toward me. 9* "I will not
feed you," I said. "What is to die, let it
die; what is to perish, let it perish, and
let those that are left devour one another's flesh."
10 Then I took my staff "Favor" and
snapped it asunder, breaking off the
covenant which I had made with all peoples; 11 that day it was broken off. The
sheep merchants who were watching me
understood that this was the word of the
LORD. 12* I said to them, "If it seems
good to you, give me my wages; but if
not, let it go." And they counted out my
wages, thirty pieces of silver. 13* But the
LORD said to me, "Throw it in the treasury, the handsome price at which they
valued me." So I took the thirty pieces
of silver and threw them into the treasury in the house of the LORD.
14 Then I snapped asunder my other
staff, "Bonds," breaking off the brotherhood between Judah and Israel. 15 The
LORD said to me: This time take the gear
of a foolish shepherd. 16* For I will raise
up a shepherd in the land who will take
no note of those that perish, nor seek the
strays, nor heal the injured, nor feed
what survives—he will eat the flesh of
the fat ones and tear off their hoofs!

17* Woe to my foolish shepherd
who forsakes the flock!
May the sword fall upon his arm
and upon his right eye;
Let his arm wither away entirely,
and his right eye be blind forever!

*

8: Ez 36, 37.
10: Is 11, 11; 49, 20; Hos 11, 11.
11: Is 11, 15; Ez 30, 13.
12: Mi 4, 5.
11, 5: Jer 50, 7.
7: Hos 5, 6.
9: Jer 15, 2.
12: Ex 21, 32; Mt 26, 15.
13: Mt 27, 9f.
16: Ez 34, 2ff.
17: Jn 10, 12.

†

11, 4-17: In this allegory the prophet becomes the good shepherd of God's flock, which is being slaughtered; he is the defender of the people exploited by bad rulers. *The three shepherds,* rulers in general, are to destroy one another in a short time *(a single month).* The service of the good shepherd is contemptuously valued at *thirty pieces of silver,* the legal indemnity (Ex 21, 32) for a gored slave. The prophet is thus a type of Christ, whose mission of salvation to his people was appraised by the Sanhedrists, the false shepherds, at the same base price (Mt 26, 14ff). In the case of the prophet as well as of Christ (Mt 27, 5), the money is thrown into the temple treasury, i. e., paid to God, showing thereby how shamefully his divine love and care are requited.

CHAPTER 12

Jerusalem God's Instrument. † 1* An oracle: the word of the LORD concerning Israel. Thus says the LORD, who spreads out the heavens, lays the foundations of the earth, and forms the spirit of man within him: 2* See, I will make Jerusalem a bowl to stupefy all peoples round about. [Judah will be besieged, even Jerusalem.] 3* On that day I will make Jerusalem a weighty stone for all peoples. All who attempt to lift it shall injure themselves badly, and all the nations of the earth shall be gathered against her. 4 On that day, says the LORD, I will strike every horse with fright, and its rider with madness. I will strike blind all the horses of the peoples, but upon the house of Judah I will open my eyes, 5 and the princes of Judah shall say to themselves, "The inhabitants of Jerusalem have their strength in the LORD of hosts, their God." 6* On that day I will make the princes of Judah like a brazier of fire in the woodland, and like a burning torch among sheaves, and they shall devour right and left all the surrounding peoples; but Jerusalem shall still abide on its own site. 7 The LORD shall save the tents of Judah first, that the glory of the house of David and the glory of the inhabitants of Jerusalem may not be exalted over Judah. 8* On that day, the LORD will shield the inhabitants of Jerusalem, and the weakling among them shall be like David on that day, and the house of David godlike, like an angel of the LORD before them. 9 On that day I will seek the destruction of all nations that come against Jerusalem.

Messianic Jerusalem. 10*† I will pour out on the house of David and on the inhabitants of Jerusalem a spirit of grace and petition; and they shall look on him whom they have thrust through, and they shall mourn for him as one mourns for an only son, and they shall grieve over him as one grieves over a first-born.

11*† On that day the mourning in Jerusalem shall be as great as the mourning of Hadadrimmon in the plain of Megiddo. 12 And the land shall mourn, each family apart: the family of the house of David, and their wives; the family of the house of Nathan, and their wives; 13 the family of the house of Levi, and their wives; the family of Shemei, and their wives; 14 and all the rest of the families, each family apart, and the wives apart.

CHAPTER 13

The End of Falsehood. 1*† On that day there shall be open to the house of David and to the inhabitants of Jerusalem, a fountain to purify from sin and uncleanness. 2* On that day, says the LORD of hosts, I will destroy the names of the idols from the land, so that they shall be mentioned no more; I will also take away the prophets and the spirit of uncleanness from the land. 3* If a man still prophesies, his parents, father and mother, shall say to him, "You shall not live, because you have spoken a lie in the name of the LORD." When he prophesies, his parents, father and mother, shall thrust him through.

4† On that day, every prophet shall be ashamed to prophesy his vision, neither shall he assume the hairy mantle to mislead, 5* but he shall say, "I am no prophet, I am a tiller of the soil, for I have owned land since my youth." 6† And if anyone asks him, "What are these wounds on your chest?" he shall answer, "With these I was wounded in the house of my dear ones."

The Song of the Sword

7*† Awake, O sword, against my shepherd,

---

*

12, 1: Is 42, 5.
2: Is 51, 17; Jer 51, 7.
3: Mt 21, 44.
6: Ob 18.
8: Ex 32, 34.
10: Jer 6, 26; Jn 19, 34; Rv 1, 7.
11: 2 Chr 35, 22-25.
13, 1: Heb 9, 14; 1 Pt 1, 18f; Rv 1, 5.
2: Mi 5, 12; 2 Pt 2, 1.
3: Dt 18, 20; Mi 3, 5ff.
5: Am 7, 14.
7: Mt 26, 31.

†

12, 1-9: Under the image of the deliverance of Judah and Jerusalem from invading enemies, the prophet foretells the ultimate victory of God's people in the messianic age.

12, 10: The divine blessings *(a spirit of grace and petition)* will be poured out on God's people through the intervention of an unnamed sufferer *(him whom they have thrust through)*, similar to the Servant of the Lord in Is 52, 13—53, 12. In Jn 19, 37 the Evangelist sees in this passage a prophecy fulfilled in the piercing of Christ's side.

12, 11: The mourning for the pierced victim in Jerusalem is compared to a lamentation *in the plain of Megiddo* apparently over a certain personage called *Hadadrimmon.* The reference is no longer clear. Both *Hadad* and *Rimmon* were names of the Semitic storm god, often identified with the god Baal. Some see here a reference to the annual mourning by the pagans over the death of the fertility god. According to others, *Hadadrimmon* is the name of a place near Megiddo, and the reference would then be to the mourning over the death of King Josiah, who was killed in battle there; cf 2 Chr 35, 22-25.

13, 1: *A fountain to purify from sin:* in contrast to the lustral water used in ritual purification; cf Nm 19, 9.13.20; 31, 23. The Lord himself is the *fountain of living water* (Jer 2, 13); cf Is 12, 2ff.

13, 4: *Hairy mantle:* worn by prophets as a mark of their calling; cf 2 Kgs 1, 8; Mt 3, 4.

13, 6: *Wounds on your chest:* literally, "wounds between your hands." The false prophets, like the prophets of Baal (1 Kgs 18, 28), apparently inflicted wounds on themselves; to defend himself against the accusation of being a false prophet, a man will deny having inflicted wounds on himself and say instead that he received them at home, *"in the house of my dear ones."* In the liturgy this test is applied to Christ in an accommodated sense.

13, 7: When the shepherd is killed, the sheep are scattered. In Mt 26, 31 the Evangelist quotes from this verse, in somewhat different form, the words, "I will strike the shepherd, and the sheep of the flock will be dispersed," as said by Christ shortly before his arrest in the Garden of Olives and the flight of the Apostles.

against the man who is my associate,
says the LORD of hosts.
Strike the shepherd
that the sheep may be dispersed,
and I will turn my hand against the little ones.
8 In all the land, says the LORD,
two thirds of them shall be cut off and perish,
and one third shall be left.
9* I will bring the one third through fire,
and I will refine them as silver is refined,
and I will test them as gold is tested.
They shall call upon my name,
and I will hear them.
I will say, "They are my people,"
and they shall say, "The LORD is my God."

CHAPTER 14

The Fight for Jerusalem. † 1 Lo, a day
shall come for the LORD when the spoils
shall be divided in your midst. 2 And I
will gather all the nations against Jerusalem for battle: the city shall be taken,
houses plundered, women ravished; half
of the city shall go into exile, but the rest
of the people shall not be removed from
the city. 3 Then the LORD shall go forth
and fight against those nations, fighting
as on a day of battle. 4 That day his feet
shall rest upon the Mount of Olives,
which is opposite Jerusalem to the east.
The Mount of Olives shall be cleft in two
from east to west by a very deep valley,
and half of the mountain shall move to
the north and half of it to the south. 5 And
the valley of the LORD's mountain shall
be filled up when the valley of those two
mountains reaches its edge; it shall be
filled up as it was filled up by the earthquake in the days of King Uzziah of Judah. Then the LORD, my God, shall
come, and all his holy ones with him.
6 On that day there shall no longer be
cold or frost. 7* There shall be one continuous day, known to the LORD, not day
and night, for in the evening time there
shall be light.
8* On that day, living waters shall flow
from Jerusalem, half to the eastern sea,
and half to the western sea, and it shall
be so in summer and in winter. 9* The
LORD shall become king over the whole
earth; on that day the LORD shall be the
only one, and his name the only one.
10* And from Geba to Rimmon in the
Negeb, all the land shall turn into a
plain; but Jerusalem shall remain exalted in its place. From the Gate of Benjamin to the place of the First Gate, to
the Corner Gate; and from the Tower of
Hananel to the king's wine presses,
11* they shall occupy her. Never again
shall she be doomed; Jerusalem shall
abide in security.
12 And this shall be the plague with
which the LORD shall strike all the nations that have fought against Jerusalem: their flesh shall rot while they stand
upon their feet, and their eyes shall rot
in their sockets, and their tongues shall
rot in their mouths.
13 On that day there shall be among
them a great tumult from the LORD: every man shall seize the hand of his
neighbor, and the hand of each shall be
raised against that of his neighbor.
14 Judah also shall fight against Jerusalem. The riches of all the surrounding
nations shall be gathered together, gold,
silver, and garments, in great abundance.
15 Similar to this plague shall be the
plague upon the horses, mules, camels,
asses, and upon all the beasts that are
in those camps.
16* All who are left of all the nations
that came against Jerusalem shall come
up year after year to worship the King,
the LORD of hosts, and to celebrate the
feast of Booths. 17 If any of the families
of the earth does not come up to Jerusalem to worship the King, the LORD of
hosts, no rain shall fall upon them.
18 And if the family of Egypt does not
come up, or enter, upon them shall fall
the plague which the LORD will inflict
upon all the nations that do not come
up to celebrate the feast of Booths.
19 This shall be the punishment of Egypt,
and the punishment of all the nations
that do not come up to celebrate the feast
of Booths.
20 On that day there shall be upon the
bells of the horses, "Holy to the LORD."
The pots in the house of the LORD shall
be as the libation bowls before the altar.
21* And every pot in Jerusalem and in
Judah shall be holy to the LORD of hosts;
and all who come to sacrifice shall take
them and cook in them. On that day
there shall no longer be any merchant
in the house of the LORD of hosts.

*

9: Jer 30, 22; Ps 66, 10.
14, 7: Rv 21, 23.
8: 13, 1; Ez 47, 1-8; Jl 3, 18.
9: Dt 6, 4; Eph 4, 5f; Rv 11, 15.
10: 12, 6: Neh 3, 6; 12, 38.
11: Jer 31, 40; Rv 22, 3.
16: Lv 23, 34.43; Neh 8, 14; Is 60, 6.9.
21: Mt 21, 12; Jn 2, 13-16.

†

14, 1-21: An apocalyptic description of the day of the Lord, in which Jerusalem, the figure of God's elect, after much suffering (siege: vv 1ff; riot: v 13; plague: vv 12.15), is rescued by the Lord (vv 4f) and given great blessings (vv 6-11.14.16-21).

The Book of

MALACHI

This work was composed by an anonymous writer shortly before Nehemiah's arrival in Jerusalem (445 B.C.). Because of the sharp reproaches he was leveling against the priests and rulers of the people, the author probably wished to conceal his identity. To do this he made a proper name out of the Hebrew expression for "My Messenger" (Malachi), which occurs in 1, 1 and 3, 1. The historical value of the prophecy is considerable in that it gives us a picture of life in the Jewish community returned from Babylon, between the period of Haggai and the reform measures of Ezra and Nehemiah. It is likely that the author's trenchant criticism of abuses and religious indifference in the community prepared the way for these necessary reforms.

The chosen people had made a sorry return for divine love. The priests, who should have been leaders, had dishonored God by their blemished sacrifices. In his first chapter, the writer foresees the time when all nations will offer a pure oblation (1, 11)—a prophecy whose fulfillment the Church sees in the Sacrifice of the Mass. The author then turns from priests to people, denouncing their marriages with pagans and their callous repudiation of Israelite wives. Imbued with the rationalist and critical spirit of the times, many had wearied God with the question, "Where is the God of justice?" To this question the prophet replies that the day of the Lord is coming. But first the forerunner must come, who will prepare the soil for repentance and true worship. The Gospel writers point to John the Baptizer, as the forerunner ushering in the messianic age, the true day of the Lord. When the ground is prepared God will appear, measuring out rewards and punishments and purifying the nation in the furnace of judgment. He will create a new order in which the ultimate triumph of good is inevitable.

CHAPTER 1

1 An oracle. The word of the LORD to Israel through Malachi.

Israel Preferred to Edom

2* I have loved you, says the LORD;
but you say, "How have you loved us?"
3*† Was not Esau Jacob's brother? says the LORD:
yet I loved Jacob, but hated Esau;
I made his mountains a waste,
his heritage a desert for jackals.
4* If Edom says, "We have been crushed
but we will rebuild the ruins,"
Thus says the LORD of hosts:
They indeed may build, but I will tear down,
And they shall be called the land of guilt,
the people with whom the LORD is angry forever.
5* Your own eyes shall see it, and you will say,
"Great is the LORD, even beyond the land of Israel."

Sins of the Priests and Levites

6 A son honors his father,
and a servant fears his master;
If then I am a father,
where is the honor due to me?
And if I am a master,
where is the reverence due to me?—
So says the LORD of hosts to you, O priests,
who despise his name.
But you ask, "How have we despised your name?"
7 By offering polluted food on my altar!
Then you ask, "How have we polluted it?"
By saying the table of the LORD may be slighted!
8*† When you offer a blind animal for sacrifice,
is this not evil?

*

1, 2: Dt 7, 6ff; Ez 16; Am 1, 11.
3: Gn 25, 23; Rom 9, 13.
4: Is 34, 5f; 63, 1-6; Jer 49, 7-22; Ob 21.
5: Is 60.
8: Lv 22, 19-25; Dt 15, 21.

†

1, 3ff: The thought passes from the person *Esau* to his descendants, *Edom,* and from the person *Jacob* to his descendants, *Israel. Loved:* preferred; *hated:* rejected; cf Gn 25, 21ff. St. Paul uses this passage as an example of God's freedom of choice in calling the Gentiles to the faith (Rom 9, 13).

1, 8: The offering in sacrifice of a *lame, sick* or *blind animal* was forbidden in the law (Lv 22, 17-25; Dt 17, 1).

When you offer the lame or the sick,
is it not evil?
Present it to your governor; see if he will accept it,
or welcome you, says the LORD of hosts.
9 So now if you implore God for mercy on us,
when you have done the like
Will he welcome any of you?
says the LORD of hosts.

10† Oh, that one among you would shut the temple gates
to keep you from kindling fire on my altar in vain!
I have no pleasure in you, says the LORD of hosts;
neither will I accept any sacrifice from your hands,
11* For from the rising of the sun, even to its setting,
my name is great among the nations;
And everywhere they bring sacrifice to my name,
and a pure offering;
For great is my name among the nations,
says the LORD of hosts.
12 But you behave profanely toward me by thinking
the LORD's table and its offering may be polluted,
and its food slighted.
13 You also say, "What a burden!"
and you scorn it, says the LORD of hosts;
You bring in what you seize, or the lame, or the sick;
yes, you bring it as a sacrifice.
Shall I accept it from your hands?
says the LORD.
14 Cursed is the deceiver, who has in his flock a male,
but under his vow sacrifices to the LORD a gelding;
For a great King am I, says the LORD of hosts,
and my name will be feared among the nations.

CHAPTER 2

1 And now, O priests, this commandment is for you:
If you do not listen,
2* And if you do not lay it to heart,
to give glory to my name, says the LORD of hosts,
I will send a curse upon you
and of your blessing I will make a curse.
Yes, I have already cursed it,
because you do not lay it to heart.
3† Lo, I will deprive you of the shoulder
and I will strew dung in your faces,
The dung of your feasts,
and you will be carried off with it.
4* Then you will know that I sent you this commandment
because I have a covenant with Levi,
says the LORD of hosts.
5* My covenant with him was one of life and peace;
fear I put in him, and he feared me,
and stood in awe of my name.
6* True doctrine was in his mouth,
and no dishonesty was found upon his lips;
He walked with me in integrity and in uprightness,
and turned many away from evil.
7* For the lips of the priest are to keep knowledge,
and instruction is to be sought from his mouth,
because he is the messenger of the LORD of hosts.
8 But you have turned aside from the way,
and have caused many to falter by your instruction;
You have made void the covenant of Levi,
says the LORD of hosts.
9 I, therefore, have made you contemptible
and base before all the people,
Since you do not keep my ways,
but show partiality in your decisions.

Sins of the People

10*† Have we not all the one Father?
Has not the one God created us?

*

11: Ps 113, 3; Is 59, 19.
2, 2: Lv 26, 14-45; Dt 28, 15-68.
4: Nm 25, 12f.
5: Nm 25, 12; Ez 37, 26ff.
6: Dt 33, 8-11.
7: Lv 10, 10f; Dt 17, 9f; Jer 18, 18; Hg 2, 12.
10: Mt 23, 9; Jb 31, 15; Eph 4, 6.

†

1, 10f: The imperfect sacrifices offered without sincerity by the people of Judah are displeasing to the Lord. He will rather be pleased with the offerings of the Gentile nations throughout the world *(from the rising of the sun, even to its setting),* which anticipate the *pure offering* to be sacrificed in messianic times, the universal Sacrifice of the Mass, as we are told by the Council of Trent.

2, 3: *I will deprive you of the shoulder:* this part of a sacrificial animal, allotted by the law (Dt 18, 3) to the priests, will be withheld from them.

2, 10-16: Intermarriage of Israelites with foreigners was forbidden according to Dt 7, 1-4. After the exile this law was strictly enforced (Ezr 9-10). Foreign marriages are here portrayed as a violation of the covenant (v 10), which made the sacrifices offered by the offenders unacceptable to God (v 13). They were all the more reprehensible when accompanied by the divorce of Israelite wives (vv 14ff). This gradual return to the primitive ideal of the indissolubility of marriage was fully realized in New Testament times through the teaching of Christ; cf Mt 19, 3-12.

Why then do we break faith with each other,
violating the covenant of our fathers?
11* Judah has broken faith; an abominable thing
has been done in Israel and in Jerusalem.
Judah has profaned the temple which the LORD loves,
and has married an idolatrous woman.
12 May the LORD cut off from the man who does this
both witness and advocate out of the tents of Jacob,
and anyone to offer sacrifice to the LORD of hosts!

13 This also you do: the altar of the LORD you cover
with tears, weeping and groaning,
Because he no longer regards your sacrifice
nor accepts it favorably from your hand;
14* And you say, "Why is it?"—
Because the LORD is witness
between you and the wife of your youth,
With whom you have broken faith
though she is your companion, your betrothed wife.
15* Did he not make one being, with flesh and spirit:
and what does that one require but godly offspring?
You must then safeguard life that is your own,
and not break faith with the wife of your youth.
16 For I hate divorce,
says the LORD, the God of Israel,
And covering one's garment with injustice,
says the LORD of hosts;
You must then safeguard life that is your own,
and not break faith.

17 You have wearied the LORD with your words,
yet you say, "How have we wearied him?"
By your saying, "Every evildoer
is good in the sight of the LORD,
And he is pleased with him";
or else, "Where is the just God?"

CHAPTER 3

The Messenger of the Covenant

1*† Lo, I am sending my messenger
to prepare the way before me;
And suddenly there will come to the temple
the LORD whom you seek,
And the messenger of the covenant whom you desire.
Yes, he is coming, says the LORD of hosts.
2 But who will endure the day of his coming?
And who can stand when he appears?
For he is like the refiner's fire,
or like the fuller's lye.
3* He will sit refining and purifying [silver],
and he will purify the sons of Levi,
Refining them like gold or like silver
that they may offer due sacrifice to the LORD.
4 Then the sacrifice of Judah and Jerusalem
will please the LORD,
as in days of old, as in years gone by.
5 I will draw near to you for judgment,
and I will be swift to bear witness
Against the sorcerers, adulterers, and perjurers,
those who defraud the hired man of his wages,
Against those who defraud widows and orphans;
those who turn aside the stranger,
and those who do not fear me, says the LORD of hosts.

6† Surely I, the LORD, do not change,
nor do you cease to be sons of Jacob.
7* Since the days of your fathers you have turned aside
from my statutes, and have not kept them.
Return to me, and I will return to you,
says the LORD of hosts.
Yet you say, "How must we return?"
8* Dare a man rob God? Yet you are robbing me!
And you say, "How do we rob you?"
In tithes and in offerings!
9 You are indeed accursed,
for you, the whole nation, rob me.
10*† Bring the whole tithe
into the storehouse,

*

11: Ezr 9, 2, Neh 13, 25.
14: Gn 31, 49f; Prv 5, 18ff.
15: Gn 2, 7.22ff.
3, 1: Is 40, 3; Mt 11, 10; Mk 1, 2; Lk 1, 17; 7, 27.
3: Is 1, 25; Zec 13, 9.
7: Zec 1, 3f; Acts 7, 51.
8: Neh 13, 10-14.
10: 2 Chr 31, 10f; Neh 10, 38; 13, 12; Prv 3, 9f.

†

3, 1: *My messenger . . . before me:* in v 23 this messenger is called Elijah. In Mt 11, 10 these words are quoted by Christ as referring to John the Baptizer, who prepared the way for the coming of the Savior; cf Mt 3, 1ff.11f; 17, 11ff; Mk 1, 2-8; Lk 3, 2-18; Jn 1, 31-34.

3, 6f: God is faithful to his promises. He will not abandon the Israelites, who are still his people.

3, 10: *Storehouse:* the temple treasury.

That there may be food in my house,
and try me in this, says the LORD of hosts:
Shall I not open for you the flood-gates of heaven,
to pour down blessing upon you without measure?
11 For your sake I will forbid the locust to destroy your crops;
And the vine in the field will not be barren,
says the LORD of hosts.

12 Then all nations will call you blessed,
for you will be a delightful land,
says the LORD of hosts.

13 You have defied me in word, says the LORD,
yet you ask, "What have we spoken against you?"
14* You have said, "It is vain to serve God,
and what do we profit by keeping his command,
And going about in penitential dress
in awe of the LORD of hosts?
15 Rather must we call the proud blessed;
for indeed evildoers prosper,
and even tempt God with impunity."
16*† Then they who fear the LORD spoke with one another,
and the LORD listened attentively;
And a record book was written before him
of those who fear the LORD and trust in his name.
17* And they shall be mine, says the LORD of hosts,
my own special possession, on the day I take action.
And I will have compassion on them,
as a man has compassion on his son who serves him.
18 Then you will again see the distinction
between the just and the wicked;
Between him who serves God,
and him who does not serve him.
19* For lo, the day is coming, blazing like an oven,
when all the proud and all evildoers will be stubble,
And the day that is coming will set them on fire,
leaving them neither root nor branch,
says the LORD of hosts.
20* But for you who fear my name, there will arise
the sun of justice with its healing rays;
And you will gambol like calves out of the stall
21 and tread down the wicked;
They will become ashes under the soles of your feet,
on the day I take action, says the LORD of hosts.

22* Remember the law of Moses my servant,
which I enjoined him on Horeb,
The statutes and ordinances
for all Israel.
23*† Lo, I will send you
Elijah, the prophet,
Before the day of the LORD comes,
the great and terrible day,
24† To turn the hearts of the fathers to their children,
and the hearts of the children to their fathers,
Lest I come and strike
the land with doom.

Lo, I will send you
Elijah, the prophet,
Before the day of the LORD comes,
the great and terrible day.

*

14: Jb 21, 14f; 22, 17; Ps 73, 11f.
16: Rv 20, 12.
17: Ex 19, 5; Dt 7, 6; Pss 103, 13; 135, 4.
19: Is 13, 9; 34, 8; Jl 3, 3; Zep 1, 18; 2 Pt 3, 7.
20: Lk 1, 78f.
22: Ex 20; Lv 26; Dt 4, 1.5f.
24: (2, 24) Mt 11, 14; 17, 10; Mk 9, 10ff; Lk 1, 17.

†

3, 16: *Record book:* see note on Ex 32, 32.

3, 23: *Elijah:* described in 2 Kgs 2, 11 as taken heavenward in a fiery chariot. Here his return to earth seems to be foretold. Jewish tradition has interpreted this literally; Christ declared it to be fulfilled in the coming of John the Baptizer (Mt 17, 10-13).

3, 24: The words in fine print, a repetition of v 23a-d, have been added by the scribes so that the collection of the twelve minor prophets will not end with the threat of doom.

THE REVISED NEW TESTAMENT

THE BOOKS OF
THE NEW TESTAMENT
AND
THEIR ABBREVIATIONS

[ ] indicates a gloss

THE NEW AMERICAN BIBLE
THE NEW TESTAMENT
PREFACE TO THE FIRST EDITION

The New Testament translation has been approached with essentially the same fidelity to the thought and individual style of the biblical writers as was applied in the Old Testament. In some cases, however, the problem of marked literary peculiarities had to be met. What by any Western standard are the limited vocabularies and stylistic infelicities of the evangelists cannot be retained in the exact form in which they appear in the originals without displeasing the modern ear. A compromise is here attempted whereby some measure of the poverty of the evangelists' expression is kept and placed at the service of their message in its richness. Similarly, the syntactical shortcomings of Paul, his frequent lapses into anacoluthon, and the like, are rendered as they occur in his epistles rather than "smoothed out." Only thus, the translators suppose, will contemporary readers have some adequate idea of the kind of writing they have before them. When the prose of the original flows more smoothly, as in Luke, Acts, and Hebrews, it is reflected in the translation.

The Gospel according to John comprises a special case. Absolute fidelity to his technique of reiterated phrasing would result in an assault on the English ear, yet the softening of the vocal effect by substitution of other words and phrases would destroy the effectiveness of his poetry. Again, resort is had to compromise. This is not an easy matter when the very repetitiousness which the author deliberately employed is at the same time regarded by those who read and speak English to be a serious stylistic defect. Only those familiar with the Greek originals can know what a relentless tattoo Johannine poetry can produce. A similar observation could be made regarding other New Testament books as well. Matthew and Mark are given to identical phrasing twice and three times in the same sentence. As for the rhetorical overgrowth and mixed figures of speech in the letters of Peter, James, and Jude, the translator must resist a powerful compulsion to tidy them up if only to render these letters intelligibly.

Without seeking refuge in complaints against the inspired authors, however, the translators of *The New American Bible* here state that what they have attempted is a translation rather than a paraphrase. To be sure, all translation can be called paraphrase by definition. Any striving for complete fidelity will shortly end in infidelity. Nonetheless, it must be pointed out that the temptation to improve overladen sentences by the consolidation or elimination of multiplied adjectives, or the simplification of clumsy hendiadys, has been resisted here. For the most part, rhetorically ineffective words and phrases are retained in this translation in some form, even when it is clear that a Western contemporary writer would never have employed them.

The spelling of proper names in *The New American Bible* follows the customary forms found in most English Bibles since the Authorized Version.

Despite the arbitrary character of the divisions into numbered verses (a scheme which in its present form is only four centuries old), the translators have made a constant effort to keep within an English verse the whole verbal content of the Greek verse. At times the effort has not seemed worth the result since it often does violence to the original author's flow of expression, which preceded it by so many centuries. If this translation had been prepared for purposes of public reading only, the editors would have foregone the effort at an early stage. But since they never departed from the threefold objective of preparing a translation suitable for liturgical use, private reading, and the purposes of students, the last-named consideration prevailed. Those familiar with Greek should be able to discover how the translators of the New Testament have rendered any given original verse of scripture, if their exegetical or theological tasks require them to know this. At the same time, the fact should be set down here that the editors did not commit themselves in the synoptic gospels to rendering repeated words or phrases identically.

This leads to a final consideration: the Greek text used for the New Testament. Here, punctuation and verse division are at least as important as variant readings. In general, Nestle-Aland's *Novum Testamentum Graece* (25th edition, 1963) was followed. Additional help was derived from *The Greek New Testament* (Aland, Black, Metzger, Wikgren), produced for the use of translators by the United Bible Societies in 1966. However, the editors did not confine themselves strictly to these texts; at times, they inclined toward readings otherwise attested. The omission of alternative translations does not mean that the translators think them without merit, but only that in every case they had to make a choice.

Poorly attested readings do not occur in this translation. Doubtful readings of some merit appear within brackets; public readers may include such words or phrases, or omit them entirely without any damage to sense. Parentheses are used, as ordinarily in English, as a punctuation device. Material they enclose is in no sense textually doubtful. It is simply thought to be parenthetical in the intention of the biblical author, even though there is no such punctuation mark in Greek. The difficulty in dealing with quotation marks is well known. Since they do not appear in any form in the original text, wherever they occur here they constitute an editorial decision.

PREFACE TO THE REVISED EDITION

The New Testament of *The New American Bible*, a fresh translation from the Greek text, was first published in complete form in 1970, together with the Old Testament translation that had been completed the previous year. Portions of the New Testament had appeared earlier, in somewhat different form, in the provisional Mass lectionary of 1964 and in the *Lectionary for Mass* of 1970.

Since 1970 many different printings of the New Testament have been issued by a number of publishers, both separately and in complete bibles, and the text has become widely known both in the United States and in other English-speaking countries. Most American Catholics have been influenced by it because of its widespread use in the liturgy, and it has received a generally favorable reception from many other Christians as well. It has taken its place among the standard contemporary translations of the New Testament, respected for its fidelity to the original and its attempt to render this into current American English.

Although the scriptures themselves are timeless, translations and explanations of them quickly become dated in an era marked by rapid cultural change to a degree never previously experienced. The explosion of biblical studies that has taken place in our century and the changing nature of our language itself require periodic adjustment both in translations and in the accompanying explanatory materials. The experience of actual use of the New Testament of *The New American Bible*, especially in oral proclamation, has provided a basis for further improvement. Accordingly, it was decided in 1978 to proceed with a thorough revision of the New Testament to reflect advances in scholarship and to satisfy needs identified through pastoral experience.

For this purpose a steering committee was formed to plan, organize, and direct the work of revision, to engage collaborators, and to serve as an editorial board to coordinate the work of the various revisers and to determine the final form of the text and the explanatory materials. Guidelines were drawn up and collaborators selected in 1978 and early 1979, and November of 1980 was established as the deadline for manuscripts. From December 1980 through September 1986 the editorial board met a total of fifty times and carefully reviewed and revised all the material in order to insure accuracy and consistency of approach. The editors also worked together with the bishops' ad hoc committee that was appointed by the National Conference of Catholic Bishops in 1982 to oversee the revision.

The threefold purpose of the translation that was expressed in the preface to the first edition has been maintained in the revision: to provide a version suitable for liturgical proclamation, for private reading, and for purposes of study. Special attention has been given to the first of these purposes, since oral proclamation demands special qualities in a translation, and experience had provided insights and suggestions that could lead to improvement in this area. Efforts have also been made, however, to facilitate devotional reading by providing suitable notes and introductory materials, and to assist the student by achieving greater accuracy and consistency in the translation and supplying more abundant information in the introductions and notes.

The primary aim of the revision is to produce a version as accurate and faithful to the meaning of the Greek original as is possible for a translation. The editors have consequently moved in the direction of a formal-equivalence approach to translation, matching the vocabulary, structure, and even word order of the original as closely as possible in the receptor language. Some other contemporary biblical versions have adopted, in varying degrees, a dynamic-equivalence approach, which attempts to respect the individuality of each language by expressing the meaning of the original in a linguistic structure suited to English, even though this may be very different from the corresponding Greek structure. While this approach often results in fresh and brilliant renderings, it has the disadvantages of more or less radically abandoning traditional biblical and liturgical terminology and phraseology, of expanding the text to include what more properly belongs in notes, commentaries, or preaching, and of tending toward paraphrase. A more formal approach seems better suited to the specific purposes intended for this translation.

At the same time, the editors have wished to produce a version in English that reflects contemporary American usage and is readily understandable to ordinary educated people, but one that will be recognized as dignified speech, on the level of formal rather than colloquial usage. These aims are not in fact contradictory, for there are different levels of language in current use: the language of formal situations is not that of colloquial conversation, though people understand both and may pass from one to the other without adverting to the transition. The liturgy is a formal situation that requires a level of discourse more dignified, formal, and hieratic than the world of business, sport, or informal communication. People readily understand this more formal level even though they may not often use it; our passive vocabulary is much larger than our active vocabulary. Hence this revision, while avoiding archaisms, does not shrink from traditional biblical terms that are easily understood even though not in common use in everyday speech. The level of language consciously aimed at is one appropriate for liturgical proclamation; this may also permit the translation to serve the purposes of devotional reading and serious study.

A particular effort has been made to insure consistency of vocabulary. Always to translate a given Greek word by the same English equivalent would lead to ludicrous results and to infidelity to the meaning of the text. But in passages where a particular Greek term retains the same meaning, it has been rendered in the same way insofar as this has been feasible; this is particularly significant in the case of terms that have a specific theological meaning. The synoptic gospels have been carefully translated so as to reveal both the similarities and the differences of the Greek.

An especially sensitive problem today is the question of discrimination in language. In recent years there has been much discussion about allegations of anti-Jewish expressions in the New Testament and of language that discriminates against various minorities. Above all, however, the question of discrimination against women affects the largest number of people and arouses the greatest degree of interest and concern. At present there is little agreement about these problems or about the best way to deal with them. In all these areas the present translation attempts to display a sensitivity appropriate to the present state of the questions under discussion, which are not yet resolved and in regard to which it is impossible to please everyone, since intelligent and sincere participants in the debate hold mutually contradictory views.

The primary concern in this revision is fidelity to what the text says. When the meaning of the Greek is inclusive of both sexes, the translation seeks to reproduce such inclusivity insofar as this is possible in normal English usage, without resort to inelegant circumlocutions or neologisms that would offend against the dignity of the language. Although the generic sense of *man* is traditional in English, many today reject it; its use has therefore generally been avoided, though it is retained in cases where no fully satisfactory equivalent could be found. English does not possess a gender-inclusive third personal pronoun in the singular, and this translation continues to use the masculine resumptive pronoun after *everyone* or *anyone,* in the traditional way, where this cannot be avoided without infidelity to the meaning.

The translation of the Greek word *adelphos,* particularly in the plural form *adelphoi,* poses an especially delicate problem. While the term literally means *brothers* or other male blood relatives, even in profane Greek the plural can designate two persons, one of either sex, who were born of the same parents. It was adopted by the early Christians to designate, in a figurative sense, the members of the Christian community, who were conscious of a new familial relationship to one another by reason of their adoption as children of God. They are consequently addressed as *adelphoi*. This has traditionally been rendered into English by *brothers* or, more archaically, *brethren*. There has never been any doubt that this designation includes *all* the members of the Christian community, both male and female. Given the absence in English of a corresponding term that explicitly includes both sexes, this translation retains the usage of *brothers,* with the inclusive meaning that has been traditionally attached to it in this biblical context.

Since the New Testament is the product of a particular time and culture, the views expressed in it and the language in which they are expressed reflect a particular cultural conditioning, which sometimes makes them quite different from contemporary ideas and concerns. Discriminatory language should be eliminated insofar as possible whenever it is unfaithful to the meaning of the New Testament, but the text should not be altered in order to adjust it to contemporary concerns. This translation does not introduce any changes, expansions, additions to, or subtractions from the text of scripture. It further retains the traditional biblical ways of speaking about God and about Christ, including the use of masculine nouns and pronouns.

The Greek text followed in this translation is that of the third edition of *The Greek New Testament,* edited by Kurt Aland, Matthew Black, Carlo Martini, Bruce Metzger, and Allen Wikgren, and published by the United Bible Society in 1975. The same text, with a different critical apparatus and variations in punctuation and typography, was published as the twenty-sixth edition of the Nestle-Aland *Novum Testamentum Graece* in 1979 by the Deutsche Bibelstiftung, Stuttgart. This edition has also been consulted. When variant readings occur, the translation, with few exceptions, follows the reading that was placed in the text of these Greek editions, though the occurrence of the principal variants is pointed out in the notes.

The editors of the Greek text placed square brackets around words or portions of words of which the authenticity is questionable because the evidence of textual witnesses is inconclusive. The same has been done in the translation insofar as it is possible to reproduce this convention in English. It should be possible to read the text either with or without the disputed words, but in English it is not always feasible to provide this alternative, and in some passages the bracketed words must be included to make sense. As in the first edition, parentheses do not indicate textual uncertainty, but are simply a punctuation device to indicate a passage that in the editors' judgment appears parenthetical to the thought of the author.

Citations from the Old Testament are placed within quotation marks; longer citations are set off as block quotations in a separate indented paragraph. The sources of such citations, as well as those of many more or less subtle allusions to the Old Testament, are identified in the biblical cross-reference section at the bottom of each page. Insofar as possible, the translation of such Old Testament citations agrees with that of *The New American Bible* Old Testament whenever the underlying Greek agrees with the Hebrew (or, in some cases, the Aramaic or Greek) text from which the Old Testament translation was made. But citations in the New Testament frequently follow the Septuagint or some other version, or were made from memory; hence, in many cases the translation in the New Testament passage will not agree with what appears in the Old Testament. Some of these cases are explained in the notes.

It is a further aim of the revised edition to supply explanatory materials more abundantly than in the first edition. In most cases the introductions and notes have been entirely rewritten and expanded, and the cross-references checked and revised. It is intended that these materials should reflect the present state of sound biblical scholarship and should be presented in such a form that they can be assimilated by the ordinary intelligent reader without specialized biblical training. While they have been written with the ordinary educated Christian in mind, not all technical vocabulary can be entirely dispensed with in approaching the Bible, any more than in any other field. It is the hope of the editors that these materials, even if they sometimes demand an effort, will help the reader to a fuller and more intelligent understanding of the New Testament and a fruitful appropriation of its meaning for personal spiritual growth.

The New American Bible is a Roman Catholic translation. This revision, however, like the first edition, has been accomplished with the collaboration of scholars from other Christian churches, both among the revisers and on the editorial board, in response to the encouragement of Vatican Council II (*Dei Verbum,* 22). The editorial board expresses gratitude to all who have collaborated in the revision: to all the revisers, consultants, and bishops who contributed to it, to reviewers of the first edition, and to those who voluntarily submitted suggestions. May this translation fulfill its threefold purpose, "so that the word of the Lord may speed forward and be glorified" (2 Thes 3, 1).

The Feast of St. Jerome
September 30, 1986

THE GOSPELS

The collection of writings that constitutes the New Testament begins with four gospels. Next comes the Acts of the Apostles, followed by twenty-one letters that are attributed to Paul, James, Peter, John, and Jude. Finally, at the end of the early church's scriptures stands the Revelation to John. Virtually all Christians agree that these twenty-seven books constitute the "canon," a term that means "rule" and designates the list of writings that are regarded as authoritative for Christian faith and life.

It is the purpose of this Introduction to describe those features that are common to the four gospels. A similar treatment of the letters of the New Testament is provided in the two Introductions that appear before the Letter to the Romans and before the Letter of James, respectively. The Acts of the Apostles, a work that is both historical and theological, and Revelation, an apocalyptic work, have no counterparts in the New Testament; the special Introductions prefixed to these books treat of the literary characteristics proper to each of them.

While the New Testament contains four writings called "gospels," there is in reality only one gospel running through all of the Christian scriptures, the gospel of and about Jesus Christ. Our English word "gospel" translates the Greek term euangelion, *meaning "good news." This noun was used in the plural by the Greek translators of the Old Testament to render the Hebrew term for "good news" (2 Sm 4, 10; possibly also 18, 20.25). But it is the corresponding verb* euangelizomai, *"to proclaim good news," that was especially significant in preparing for the New Testament idea of "gospel," since this term is used by Deutero-Isaiah for announcing the great victory of God that was to establish his universal kingship and inaugurate the new age (Is 40, 9; 52, 7; 61, 1).*

Paul used the word euangelion *to designate the message that he and the other apostles proclaimed, the "gospel of God" (Rom 1, 1; 15, 16; 2 Cor 11, 7; 1 Thes 2, 2.8.9). He often referred to it simply as "the gospel" (Rom 1, 16; 10, 16; 11, 28; etc.) or, because of its content and origin, as "the gospel of Christ" (Rom 15, 19; 1 Cor 9, 12; 1 Thes 3, 2; etc.). Because of its personal meaning for him and his own particular manner of telling the story about Jesus Christ and of explaining the significance of his cross and resurrection, Paul also referred to this message as "my gospel" (Rom 2, 16; cf Gal 1, 11; 2, 2) or "our gospel" (2 Cor 4, 3; 1 Thes 1, 5; 2 Thes 2, 14).*

It was Mark, as far as we know, who first applied the term "gospel" to a book telling the story of Jesus; see Mk 1, 1 and the note there. This form of presenting Jesus' life, works, teachings, passion, and resurrection was developed further by the other evangelists; see the Introduction to each gospel. The first three of the canonical gospels, Matthew, Mark, and Luke, are so similar at many points when viewed together, particularly when arranged in parallel columns or lines, that they are called "synoptic" gospels, from the Greek word for such a general view. The fourth gospel, John, often differs significantly from the synoptics in outline and approach. This work never uses the word "gospel" or its corresponding verb; nevertheless, its message concerns the same Jesus, and the reader is urged to believe in him as the Messiah, "that through this belief you may have life in his name" (20, 31).

From the second century onward, the practice arose of designating each of these four books as a "gospel," understood as a title, and of adding a phrase with a name that identified the traditional author, e.g., "The Gospel according to Matthew." The arrangement of the canon that was adopted, with the four gospels grouped together at the beginning followed by Acts, provides a massive focus upon Jesus and allows Acts to serve as a framework for the letters of the New Testament. This order, however, conceals the fact that Luke's two volumes, a gospel and Acts, were intended by their author to go together. It further obscures the point that Paul's letters were written before any of our gospels, though the sayings and deeds of Jesus stand behind all the New Testament writings.

The Gospel According to

MATTHEW

The position of the Gospel according to Matthew as the first of the four gospels in the New Testament reflects both the view that it was the first to be written, a view that goes back to the late second century A.D., and the esteem in which it was held by the church; no other was so frequently quoted in the noncanonical literature of earliest Christianity. Although the majority of scholars now reject the opinion about the time of its composition, the high estimation of this work remains. The reason for that becomes clear upon study of the way in which Matthew presents his story of Jesus, the demands of Christian discipleship, and the breaking-in of the new and final age through the ministry but particularly through the death and resurrection of Jesus.

The gospel begins with a narrative prologue (1, 1—2, 23), the first part of which is a genealogy of Jesus starting with Abraham, the father of Israel (1, 1-17). Yet at the beginning of that genealogy Jesus is designated as "the son of David, the son of Abraham" (1, 1). The kingly ancestor who lived about a thousand years after Abraham is named first, for this is the genealogy of Jesus Christ, the Messiah, the royal anointed one (1, 16). In the first of the episodes of the infancy narrative that follow the genealogy, the mystery of Jesus' person is declared. He is conceived of a virgin by the power of the Spirit of God (1, 18-25). The first of the gospel's fulfillment citations, whose purpose it is to show that he was the one to whom the prophecies of Israel were pointing, occurs here (1, 23): he shall be named Emmanuel, for in him God is with us.

The announcement of the birth of this newborn king of the Jews greatly troubles not only King Herod but all Jerusalem (2, 1-3), yet the Gentile magi are overjoyed to find him and offer him their homage and their gifts (2, 10-11). Thus his ultimate rejection by the mass of his own people and his acceptance by the Gentile nations is foreshadowed. He must be taken to Egypt to escape the murderous plan of Herod. By his sojourn there and his subsequent return after the king's death he relives the Exodus experience of Israel. The words of the Lord spoken through the prophet Hosea, "Out of Egypt I called my son," are fulfilled in him (2, 15); if Israel was God's son, Jesus is so in a way far surpassing the dignity of that nation, as his marvelous birth and the unfolding of his story show (see 3, 17; 4, 1-11; 11, 27; 14, 33; 16, 16; 27, 54). Back in the land of Israel, he must be taken to Nazareth in Galilee because of the danger to his life in Judea, where Herod's son Archelaus is now ruling (2, 22-23). The sufferings of Jesus in the infancy narrative anticipate those of his passion, and if his life is spared in spite of the dangers, it is because his destiny is finally to give it on the cross as "a ransom for many" (20, 28). Thus the word of the angel will be fulfilled, ". . . he will save his people from their sins" (1, 21; cf 26, 28).

In 4, 12 Matthew begins his account of the ministry of Jesus, introducing it by the preparatory preaching of John the Baptist (3, 1-12), the baptism of Jesus that culminates in God's proclaiming him his "beloved Son" (3, 13-17), and the temptation in which he proves his true sonship by his victory over the devil's attempt to deflect him from the way of obedience to the Father (4, 1-11). The central message of Jesus' preaching is the coming of the kingdom of heaven and the need for repentance, a complete change of heart and conduct, on the part of those who are to receive this great gift of God (4, 17). Galilee is the setting for most of his ministry; he leaves there for Judea only in 19, 1, and his ministry in Jerusalem, the goal of his journey, is limited to a few days (21, 1—25, 46).

In this extensive material there are five great discourses of Jesus, each concluding with the formula "When Jesus finished these words" or one closely similar

(7, 28; 11, 1; 13, 53; 19, 1; 26, 1). These are an important structure of the gospel. In every case the discourse is preceded by a narrative section, each narrative and discourse together constituting a "book" of the gospel. The discourses are, respectively, the "Sermon on the Mount" (5, 3—7, 27), the missionary discourse (10, 5-42), the parable discourse (13, 3-52), the "church order" discourse (18, 3-35), and the eschatological discourse (24, 4—25, 46). In large measure the material of these discourses came to Matthew from his tradition, but his work in modifying and adding to what he had received is abundantly evident. No other evangelist gives the teaching of Jesus with such elegance and order as he.

In the "Sermon on the Mount" the theme of righteousness is prominent, and even at this early stage of the ministry the note of opposition is struck between Jesus and the Pharisees, who are designated as "the hypocrites" (6, 2.5.16). The righteousness of his disciples must surpass that of the scribes and Pharisees; otherwise, in spite of their alleged following of Jesus, they will not enter into the kingdom of heaven (5, 20). Righteousness means doing the will of the heavenly Father (7, 21), and his will is proclaimed in a manner that is startling to all who have identified it with the law of Moses. The antitheses of the Sermon (5, 21-48) both accept (5, 21-30.43-48) and reject (5, 31-42) elements of that law, and in the former case the understanding of the law's demands is deepened and extended. The antitheses are the best commentary on the meaning of Jesus' claim that he has come not to abolish but to fulfill the law (5, 17). What is meant by fulfillment of the law is not the demand to keep it exactly as it stood before the coming of Jesus, but rather his bringing the law to be a lasting expression of the will of God, and in that fulfillment there is much that will pass away. Should this appear contradictory to his saying that "until heaven and earth pass away" not even the smallest part of the law will pass (5, 18), that time of fulfillment is not the dissolution of the universe but the coming of the new age, which will occur with Jesus' death and resurrection. While righteousness in the new age will continue to mean conduct that is in accordance with the law, it will be conduct in accordance with the law as expounded and interpreted by Jesus (cf 28, 20, ". . . all that I have commanded you").

Though Jesus speaks harshly about the Pharisees in the Sermon, his judgment is not solely a condemnation of them. The Pharisees are portrayed as a negative example for his disciples, and his condemnation of those who claim to belong to him while disobeying his word is no less severe (7, 21-23.26-27).

In 4, 23 a summary statement of Jesus' activity speaks not only of his teaching and proclaiming the gospel but of his "curing every disease and illness among the people"; this is repeated almost verbatim in 9, 35. The narrative section that follows the Sermon on the Mount (8, 1—9, 38) is composed principally of accounts of those merciful deeds of Jesus, but it is far from being simply a collection of stories about miraculous cures. The nature of the community that Jesus will establish is shown; it will always be under the protection of him whose power can deal with all dangers (8, 23-27), but it is only for those who are prepared to follow him at whatever cost (8, 16-22), not only believing Israelites but Gentiles who have come to faith in him (8, 10-12). The disciples begin to have some insight, however imperfect, into the mystery of Jesus' person. They wonder about him whom "the winds and the sea obey" (8, 27), and they witness his bold declaration of the forgiveness of the paralytic's sins (9, 2). That episode of the narrative moves on two levels. When the crowd sees the cure that testifies to the authority of Jesus, the Son of Man, to forgive sins (9, 6), they glorify God "who had given such authority to human beings" (9, 8). The forgiveness of sins is now not the prerogative of Jesus alone but of "human beings," that is, of the disciples who constitute the community of Jesus, the church. The ecclesial character of this narrative section could hardly be more plainly indicated.

The end of the section prepares for the discourse on the church's mission

(10, 5-42). Jesus is moved to pity at the sight of the crowds who are like sheep without a shepherd (9, 36), and he sends out the twelve disciples to make the proclamation with which his own ministry began, "The kingdom of heaven is at hand" (10, 7; cf 4, 17), and to drive out demons and cure the sick as he has done (10, 1). Their mission is limited to Israel (10, 5-6) as Jesus' own was (15, 24), yet in v 16 that perspective broadens and the discourse begins to speak of the mission that the disciples will have after the resurrection and of the severe persecution that will attend it (10, 18). Again, the discourse moves on two levels: that of the time of Jesus and that of the time of the church.

The narrative section of the third book (11, 2—12, 50) deals with the growing opposition to Jesus. Hostility toward him has already been manifested (8, 10; 9, 3.10-13.34), but here it becomes more intense. The rejection of Jesus comes, as before, from Pharisees, who take "counsel against him to put him to death" (12, 14) and repeat their earlier accusation that he drives out demons because he is in league with demonic power (12, 22-24). But they are not alone in their rejection. Jesus complains of the lack of faith of "this generation" of Israelites (11, 16-19) and reproaches the towns "where most of his mighty deeds had been done" for not heeding his call to repentance (11, 20-24). This dark picture is relieved by Jesus' praise of the Father who has enabled "the childlike" to accept him (11, 25-27), but on the whole the story is one of opposition to his word and blindness to the meaning of his deeds. The whole section ends with his declaring that not even the most intimate blood relationship with him counts for anything; his only true relatives are those who do the will of his heavenly Father (12, 48-50).

The narrative of rejection leads up to the parable discourse (13, 3-52). The reason given for Jesus' speaking to the crowds in parables is that they have hardened themselves against his clear teaching, unlike the disciples to whom knowledge of "the mysteries of the kingdom has been granted" (13, 10-16). In 13, 36 he dismisses the crowds and continues the discourse to his disciples alone, who claim, at the end, to have understood all that he has said (13, 51). But, lest the impression be given that the church of Jesus is made up only of true disciples, the explanation of the parable of the weeds among the wheat (13, 37-43), as well as the parable of the net thrown into the sea "which collects fish of every kind" (13, 47-49), shows that it is composed of both the righteous and the wicked, and that separation between the two will be made only at the time of the final judgment.

In the narrative that constitutes the first part of the fourth book of the gospel (13, 54—17, 27), Jesus is shown preparing for the establishment of his church with its teaching authority that will supplant the blind guidance of the Pharisees (15, 13-14), whose teaching, curiously said to be that of the Sadducees also, is repudiated by Jesus as the norm for his disciples (16, 6.11-12). The church of Jesus will be built on Peter (16, 18), who will be given authority to bind and loose on earth, an authority whose exercise will be confirmed in heaven (16, 19). The metaphor of binding and loosing has a variety of meanings, among them that of giving authoritative teaching. This promise is made to Peter directly after he has confessed Jesus to be the Messiah, the Son of the living God (16, 16), a confession that he has made as the result of revelation given to him by the heavenly Father (16, 17); Matthew's ecclesiology is based on his high christology.

Directly after that confession Jesus begins to instruct his disciples about how he must go the way of suffering and death (16, 21). Peter, who has been praised for his confession, protests against this and receives from Jesus the sharpest of rebukes for attempting to deflect Jesus from his God-appointed destiny. The future rock upon whom the church will be built is still a man of "little faith" (see 14, 31). Both he and the other disciples must know not only that Jesus will have to suffer and die but that they too will have to follow him on the way of the cross if they are truly to be his disciples (16, 24-25).

The discourse following this narrative (18, 1-35) is often called the "church order" discourse, although that title is perhaps misleading since the emphasis is not on the structure of the church but on the care that the disciples must have for one another in respect to guarding each other's faith in Jesus (18, 6-7), to seeking out those who have wandered from the fold (18, 10-14), and to repeated forgiving of their fellow disciples who have offended them (18, 21-35). But there is also the obligation to correct the sinful fellow Christian and, should one refuse to be corrected, separation from the community is demanded (18, 15-18).

The narrative of the fifth book (19, 1—23, 39) begins with the departure of Jesus and his disciples from Galilee for Jerusalem. In the course of their journey Jesus for the third time predicts the passion that awaits him at Jerusalem and also his resurrection (20, 17-19). At his entrance into the city he is hailed as the Son of David by the crowds accompanying him (21, 9). He cleanses the temple (21, 12-17), and in the few days of his Jerusalem ministry he engages in a series of controversies with the Jewish religious leaders (21, 23-27; 22, 15-22.23-33.34-40.41-46), meanwhile speaking parables against them (21, 28-32.33-46), against all those Israelites who have rejected God's invitation to the messianic banquet (22, 1-10), and against all, Jew and Gentile, who have accepted but have shown themselves unworthy of it (22, 11-14). Once again, the perspective of the evangelist includes not only the time of Jesus' ministry but that of the preaching of the gospel after his resurrection. The narrative culminates in Jesus' denunciation of the scribes and Pharisees, reflecting not only his own opposition to them but that of Matthew's church (23, 1-36), and in Jesus' lament over Jerusalem (23, 37-39).

In the discourse of the fifth book (24, 1—25, 46), the last of the great structural discourses of the gospel, Jesus predicts the destruction of the temple and his own final coming. The time of the latter is unknown (24, 36.44), and the disciples are exhorted in various parables to live in readiness for it, a readiness that entails faithful attention to the duties of the interim period (24, 45—25, 30). The coming of Jesus will bring with it the great judgment by which the everlasting destiny of all will be determined (25, 31-46).

The story of Jesus' passion and resurrection (26, 1—28, 20), the climax of the gospel, throws light on all that has preceded. In Mt "righteousness" means both the faithful response to the will of God demanded of all to whom that will is announced and also the saving activity of God for his people (see 3, 15; 5, 6; 6, 33). The passion supremely exemplifies both meanings of that central Matthean word. In Jesus' absolute faithfulness to the Father's will that he drink the cup of suffering (26, 39), the incomparable model for Christian obedience is given; in his death "for the forgiveness of sins" (26, 28), the saving power of God is manifested as never before.

Matthew's portrayal of Jesus in his passion combines both the majestic serenity of the obedient Son who goes his destined way in fulfillment of the scriptures (26, 52-54), confident of his ultimate vindication by God, and the depths of fear and abandonment that he feels in face of death (26, 38-39; 27, 46). These two aspects are expressed by an Old Testament theme that occurs often in the narrative, i.e., the portrait of the suffering Righteous One who complains to God in his misery, but is certain of eventual deliverance from his terrible ordeal.

The passion-resurrection of God's Son means nothing less than the turn of the ages, a new stage of history, the coming of the Son of Man in his kingdom (28, 18; cf 16, 28). That is the sense of the apocalyptic signs that accompany Jesus' death (27, 51-53) and resurrection (28, 2). Although the old age continues, as it will until the manifestation of Jesus' triumph at his parousia, the final age has now begun. This is known only to those who have seen the Risen One and to those, both Jews and Gentiles, who have believed in their announcement of Jesus' triumph and have themselves become his disciples (cf 28, 19). To them he is constantly, though invisibly, present (28, 20), verifying the name Emmanuel, "God is with us" (cf 1, 23).

The questions of authorship, sources, and the time of composition of this gospel have received many answers, none of which can claim more than a greater or lesser degree of probability. The one now favored by the majority of scholars is the following.

The ancient tradition that the author was the disciple and apostle of Jesus named Matthew (see 10, 3) is untenable because the gospel is based, in large part, on the Gospel according to Mark (almost all the verses of that gospel have been utilized in this), and it is hardly likely that a companion of Jesus would have followed so extensively an account that came from one who admittedly never had such an association rather than rely on his own memories. The attribution of the gospel to the disciple Matthew may have been due to his having been responsible for some of the traditions found in it, but that is far from certain.

The unknown author, whom we shall continue to call Matthew for the sake of convenience, drew not only upon the Gospel according to Mark but upon a large body of material (principally, sayings of Jesus) not found in Mk that corresponds, sometimes exactly, to material found also in the Gospel according to Luke. This material, called "Q" (probably from the first letter of the German word Quelle, meaning "source"), represents traditions, written and oral, used by both Matthew and Luke. Mark and Q are sources common to the two other synoptic gospels; hence the name the "Two-Source Theory" given to this explanation of the relation among the synoptics.

In addition to what Matthew drew from Mk and Q, his gospel contains material that is found only there. This is often designated "M," written or oral tradition that was available to the author. Since Mk was written shortly before or shortly after A.D. 70 (see Introduction to Mk), Mt was composed certainly after that date, which marks the fall of Jerusalem to the Romans at the time of the First Jewish Revolt (A.D. 66-70), and probably at least a decade later since Matthew's use of Mk presupposes a wide diffusion of that gospel. The post-A.D. 70 date is confirmed within the text by 22, 7, which refers to the destruction of Jerusalem.

As for the place where the gospel was composed, a plausible suggestion is that it was Antioch, the capital of the Roman province of Syria. That large and important city had a mixed population of Greek-speaking Gentiles and Jews. The tensions between Jewish and Gentile Christians there in the time of Paul (see Gal 2, 1-14) in respect to Christian obligation to observe Mosaic law are partially similar to tensions that can be seen between the two groups in Matthew's gospel. The church of Matthew, originally strongly Jewish Christian, had become one in which Gentile Christians were predominant. His gospel answers the question how obedience to the will of God is to be expressed by those who live after the "turn of the ages," the death and resurrection of Jesus.

The principal divisions of the Gospel according to Matthew are the following:

I: The Infancy Narrative (1, 1—2, 23)
II: The Proclamation of the Kingdom (3, 1—7, 29)
III: Ministry and Mission in Galilee (8, 1—11, 1)
IV: Opposition from Israel (11, 2—13, 53)

V: Jesus, the Kingdom, and the Church (13, 54—18, 35)
VI: Ministry in Judea and Jerusalem (19, 1—25, 46)
VII: The Passion and Resurrection (26, 1—28, 20)

I: THE INFANCY NARRATIVE†

CHAPTER 1

The Genealogy of Jesus. 1*† The book
of the genealogy of Jesus Christ, the son
of David, the son of Abraham.
2* Abraham became the father of
Isaac, Isaac the father of Jacob, Jacob
the father of Judah and his brothers.
3* Judah became the father of Perez
and Zerah, whose mother was Tamar.
Perez became the father of Hezron,
Hezron the father of Ram, 4* Ram the
father of Amminadab. Amminadab be-
came the father of Nahshon, Nahshon
the father of Salmon, 5* Salmon the fa-
ther of Boaz, whose mother was Rahab.
Boaz became the father of Obed, whose
mother was Ruth. Obed became the fa-
ther of Jesse, 6* Jesse the father of Da-
vid the king.
David became the father of Solomon,
whose mother had been the wife of
Uriah. 7*† Solomon became the father
of Rehoboam, Rehoboam the father of
Abijah, Abijah the father of Asaph.
8 Asaph became the father of Jehosha-
phat, Jehoshaphat the father of Joram,
Joram the father of Uzziah. 9 Uzziah be-
came the father of Jotham, Jotham the
father of Ahaz, Ahaz the father of Heze-
kiah. 10† Hezekiah became the father of
Manasseh, Manasseh the father of
Amos, Amos the father of Josiah.
11 Josiah became the father of Jecho-
niah and his brothers at the time of the
Babylonian exile.
12* After the Babylonian exile, Jecho-
niah became the father of Shealtiel,
Shealtiel the father of Zerubbabel,
13 Zerubbabel the father of Abiud. Abiud
became the father of Eliakim, Eliakim
the father of Azor, 14 Azor the father of
Zadok. Zadok became the father of
Achim, Achim the father of Eliud,
15 Eliud the father of Eleazar. Eleazar
became the father of Matthan, Matthan
the father of Jacob, 16 Jacob the father
of Joseph, the husband of Mary. Of her
was born Jesus who is called the Mes-
siah.
17† Thus the total number of genera-
tions from Abraham to David is four-
teen generations; from David to the
Babylonian exile, fourteen generations;
from the Babylonian exile to the Mes-
siah, fourteen generations.

---

*

1, 1: Gn 5, 1 / 1 Chr 17, 11 / Gn 22, 18.
2-17: Lk 3, 23-38.
2: Gn 21, 3; 25, 26; 29, 35; 1 Chr 2, 1.
3: Gn 38, 29-30; Ru 4, 18; 1 Chr 2, 4-9.
4: Ru 4, 19-20; 1 Chr 2, 10-11.
5: Ru 4, 21-22; 1 Chr 2, 11-12.
6: 2 Sm 12, 24; 1 Chr 2, 15; 3, 5.
7-11: 2 Kgs 25, 1-21; 1 Chr 3, 10-15.
12-16: 1 Chr 3, 16-19.

---

†

1, 1—2, 23: The infancy narrative forms the prologue of the gospel. Consisting of a genealogy and five stories, it presents the coming of Jesus as the climax of Israel's history, and the events of his conception, birth, and early childhood as the fulfillment of Old Testament prophecy. The genealogy is probably traditional material that Matthew edited. In its first two sections (1, 2-11) it was drawn from Ru 4, 18-22 and 1 Chr 1—3. Except for Jechoniah, Shealtiel, and Zerubbabel, none of the names in the third section (1, 12-16) is found in any Old Testament genealogy. While the genealogy shows the continuity of God's providential plan from Abraham on, discontinuity is also present. The women Tamar (1, 3), Rahab and Ruth (1, 5), and the wife of Uriah, Bathsheba (1, 6), bore their sons through unions that were in varying degrees strange and unexpected. These "irregularities" culminate in the supreme "irregularity" of the Messiah's birth of a virgin mother; the age of fulfillment is inaugurated by a creative act of God.

Drawing upon both biblical tradition and Jewish stories, Matthew portrays Jesus as reliving the Exodus experience of Israel and the persecutions of Moses. His rejection by his own people and his passion are foreshadowed by the troubled reaction of "all Jerusalem" to the question of the magi who are seeking the "newborn king of the Jews" (2, 2-3), and by Herod's attempt to have him killed. The magi who do him homage prefigure the Gentiles who will accept the preaching of the gospel. The infancy narrative proclaims who Jesus is, the savior of his people from their sins (1, 21), Emmanuel in whom "God is with us" (1, 23), and the Son of God (2, 15).

1, 1: *The Son of David, the son of Abraham:* two links of the genealogical chain are singled out. Although the later, David is placed first in order to emphasize that Jesus is the royal Messiah. The mention of Abraham may be due not only to his being the father of the nation Israel but to Matthew's interest in the universal scope of Jesus' mission; cf Gn 22, 18, ". . . in your descendants all the nations of the earth shall find blessing."

1, 7: The successor of Abijah was not Asaph but Asa (see 1 Chr 3, 10). Some textual witnesses read the latter name; however, *Asaph* is better attested. Matthew may have deliberately introduced the psalmist Asaph into the genealogy (and in v 10 the prophet Amos) in order to show that Jesus is the fulfillment not only of the promises made to David (see 2 Sm 7) but of all the Old Testament.

1, 10: *Amos:* some textual witnesses read *Amon,* who was the actual successor of Manasseh (see 1 Chr 3, 14).

1, 17: Matthew is concerned with fourteen generations, probably because fourteen is the numerical value of the Hebrew letters forming the name of David. In the second section of the genealogy (6b-11), three kings of Judah, Ahaziah, Joash, and Amaziah, have been omitted (see 1 Chr 3, 11-12), so that there are fourteen generations in that section. Yet the third (12-16) apparently has only thirteen. Since Matthew here emphasizes that each section has fourteen, it is unlikely that the thirteen of the last was due to his oversight. Some scholars suggest that *Jesus who is called the Messiah* (16b) doubles the final member of the chain: *Jesus,* born within the family of David, opens up the new age as *Messiah,* so that in fact there are fourteen generations in the third section. This is perhaps too subtle, and the hypothesis of a slip not on the part of Matthew but of a later scribe seems likely. On *Messiah,* see the note on Lk 2, 11.

***The Birth of Jesus.*†** 18† Now this is
how the birth of Jesus Christ came
about. When his mother Mary was be-
trothed to Joseph, but before they lived
together, she was found with child
through the holy Spirit. 19† Joseph her
husband, since he was a righteous man,
yet unwilling to expose her to shame,
decided to divorce her quietly.
20*† Such was his intention when, be-
hold, the angel of the Lord appeared to
him in a dream and said, "Joseph, son
of David, do not be afraid to take Mary
your wife into your home. For it is
through the holy Spirit that this child
has been conceived in her. 21† She will
bear a son and you are to name him
Jesus, because he will save his people
from their sins." 22 All this took place
to fulfill what the Lord had said through
the prophet:

23*†"Behold, the virgin shall be with
child and bear a son,
and they shall name him Emman-
uel,"

which means "God is with us." 24 When
Joseph awoke, he did as the angel of
the Lord had commanded him and took
his wife into his home. 25*† He had no
relations with her until she bore a son,
and he named him Jesus.

CHAPTER 2

***The Visit of the Magi.*†** 1† When Jesus
was born in Bethlehem of Judea, in the
days of King Herod, behold, magi from
the east arrived in Jerusalem,
2*† saying, "Where is the newborn king
of the Jews? We saw his star at its rising
and have come to do him homage."
3 When King Herod heard this, he was
greatly troubled, and all Jerusalem with
him. 4† Assembling all the chief priests
and the scribes of the people, he in-
quired of them where the Messiah was
to be born. 5* They said to him, "In
Bethlehem of Judea, for thus it has been
written through the prophet:

6 'And you, Bethlehem, land of Ju-
dah,
are by no means least among the
rulers of Judah;
since from you shall come a ruler,
who is to shepherd my people Is-
rael.' "

7 Then Herod called the magi secretly
and ascertained from them the time of
the star's appearance. 8 He sent them
to Bethlehem and said, "Go and search
diligently for the child. When you have
found him, bring me word, that I too
may go and do him homage." 9 After
their audience with the king they set
out. And behold, the star that they had
seen at its rising preceded them, until
it came and stopped over the place
where the child was. 10 They were over-
joyed at seeing the star, 11*† and on en-
tering the house they saw the child with
Mary his mother. They prostrated
themselves and did him homage. Then
they opened their treasures and offered
him gifts of gold, frankincense, and
myrrh. 12 And having been warned in

*

20: 2, 13.19; Lk 1, 35.
23: Is 7, 14 LXX.
25: Lk 2, 7.
2, 2: Nm 24, 17.
5-6: Mi 5, 1 / 2 Sm 5, 2.
11: Ps 72, 10-11.15; Is 60, 6.

†

1, 18-25: This first story of the infancy narrative spells out what is summarily indicated in v 16. The virginal conception of Jesus is the work of the Spirit of God. Joseph's decision to divorce Mary is overcome by the heavenly command that he take her into his home and accept the child as his own. The natural genealogical line is broken but the promises to David are fulfilled; through Joseph's adoption the child belongs to the family of David. Matthew sees the virginal conception as the fulfillment of Is 7, 14.

1, 18: *Betrothed to Joseph:* betrothal was the first part of the marriage, constituting a man and woman as husband and wife. Subsequent infidelity was considered adultery. The betrothal was followed some months later by the husband's taking his wife into his home, at which time normal married life began.

1, 19: *A righteous man:* as a devout observer of the Mosaic law, Joseph wished to break his union with someone whom he suspected of gross violation of the law. It is commonly said that the law required him to do so, but the texts usually given in support of that view, e.g., Dt 22, 20-21, do not clearly pertain to Joseph's situation. *Unwilling to expose her to shame:* the penalty for proved adultery was death by stoning; cf Dt 22, 21-23.

1, 20: *The angel of the Lord:* in the Old Testament a common designation of God in communication with a human being. *In a dream:* see 2, 13.19.22. These dreams may be meant to recall the dreams of Joseph, son of Jacob the patriarch (Gn 37, 5-11.19). A closer parallel is the dream of Amram, father of Moses, related by Josephus (*Antiquities* 2, 9, 3 §§212, 215-16).

1, 21: *Jesus:* in first-century Judaism the Hebrew name Joshua (Greek *Iēsous*) meaning "Yahweh helps" was interpreted as "Yahweh saves."

1, 23: *God is with us:* God's promise of deliverance to Judah in Isaiah's time is seen by Matthew as fulfilled in the birth of Jesus, in whom God is with his people. The name Emmanuel is alluded to at the end of the gospel where the risen Jesus assures his disciples of his continued presence, ". . . I am with you always, until the end of the age" (28, 20).

1, 25: *Until she bore a son:* the evangelist is concerned to emphasize that Joseph was not responsible for the conception of Jesus. The Greek word translated "until" does not imply normal marital conduct after Jesus' birth, nor does it exclude it.

2, 1-12: The future rejection of Jesus by Israel and his acceptance by the Gentiles are retrojected into this scene of the narrative.

2, 1: *In the days of King Herod:* Herod reigned from 37 to 4 B.C. *Magi:* originally a designation of the Persian priestly caste, the word became used of those who were regarded as having more than human knowledge. Matthew's magi are astrologers.

2, 2: *We saw his star:* it was a common ancient belief that a new star appeared at the time of a ruler's birth. Matthew also draws upon the Old Testament story of Balaam, who had prophesied that "A star shall advance from Jacob" (Nm 24, 17), though there the star means not an astral phenomenon but the king himself.

2, 4: Herod's consultation with the chief priests and scribes has some similarity to a Jewish legend about the child Moses in which the "sacred scribes" warn Pharaoh about the imminent birth of one who will deliver Israel from Egypt and the king makes plans to destroy him.

2, 11: Cf Ps 72, 10.15; Is 60, 6. These Old Testament texts led to the interpretation of the magi as kings.

a dream not to return to Herod, they
departed for their country by another
way.
***The Flight to Egypt.*†** 13† When they
had departed, behold, the angel of the
Lord appeared to Joseph in a dream
and said, "Rise, take the child and his
mother, flee to Egypt, and stay there
until I tell you. Herod is going to search
for the child to destroy him." 14 Joseph
rose and took the child and his mother
by night and departed for Egypt.
15*† He stayed there until the death of
Herod, that what the Lord had said
through the prophet might be fulfilled,
"Out of Egypt I called my son."
The Massacre of the Infants. 16 When
Herod realized that he had been de-
ceived by the magi, he became furious.
He ordered the massacre of all the boys
in Bethlehem and its vicinity two years
old and under, in accordance with the
time he had ascertained from the magi.
17 Then was fulfilled what had been said
through Jeremiah the prophet:

18*†"A voice was heard in Ramah,
sobbing and loud lamentation;
Rachel weeping for her children,
and she would not be consoled,
since they were no more."

The Return from Egypt. 19 When
Herod had died, behold, the angel of the
Lord appeared in a dream to Joseph in
Egypt 20*† and said, "Rise, take the
child and his mother and go to the land
of Israel, for those who sought the
child's life are dead." 21 He rose, took
the child and his mother, and went to
the land of Israel. 22† But when he heard
that Archelaus was ruling over Judea
in place of his father Herod, he was
afraid to go back there. And because
he had been warned in a dream, he de-
parted for the region of Galilee. 23*† He
went and dwelt in a town called Naza-
reth, so that what had been spoken
through the prophets might be fulfilled,
"He shall be called a Nazorean."

II: THE PROCLAMATION OF THE KINGDOM

CHAPTER 3

***The Preaching of John the Baptist.*†**
1*† In those days John the Baptist ap-
peared, preaching in the desert of Ju-
dea 2*† [and] saying, "Repent, for the
kingdom of heaven is at hand!" 3*† It
was of him that the prophet Isaiah had
spoken when he said:

"A voice of one crying out in the
desert,
'Prepare the way of the Lord,
make straight his paths.' "

---

*

15: Hos 11, 1.
18: Jer 31, 15.
20: Ex 4, 19.
23: 13, 54; Mk 1, 9; Lk 2, 39; 4, 34; Jn 19, 19.
3, 1-12: Mk 1, 2-8; Lk 3, 2-17.
2: 4, 17; 10, 7.
3: Is 40, 3.

---

†

2, 13-23: Biblical and nonbiblical traditions about Moses are here applied to the child Jesus, though the dominant Old Testament type is not Moses but Israel (see v 15).

2, 13: *Flee to Egypt:* Egypt was a traditional place of refuge for those fleeing from danger in Palestine (see 1 Kgs 11, 40; Jer 26, 21), but the main reason why the child is to be taken to Egypt is that he may relive the Exodus experience of Israel.

2, 15: The fulfillment citation is taken from Hos 11, 1. Israel, God's son, was called out of Egypt at the time of the Exodus; Jesus, the Son of God, will similarly be called out of that land in a new exodus. The father-son relationship between God and the nation is set in a higher key. Here the son is not a group adopted as "son of God," but the child who, as conceived by the holy Spirit, stands in unique relation to God. He is son of David and of Abraham, of Mary and of Joseph, but, above all, of God.

2, 18: Jer 31, 15 portrays Rachel, wife of the patriarch Jacob, weeping for her children taken into exile at the time of the Assyrian invasion of the northern kingdom (722-21 B.C.). Bethlehem was traditionally identified with Ephrath, the place near which Rachel was buried (see Gn 35, 19; 48, 7), and the mourning of Rachel is here applied to her lost children of a later age. *Ramah:* about six miles north of Jerusalem. The lamentation of Rachel is so great as to be heard at a far distance.

2, 20: *For those who sought the child's life are dead:* Moses, who had fled from Egypt because the Pharaoh sought to kill him (see Ex 2, 15), was told to return there, "for all the men who sought your life are dead" (Ex 4, 19).

2, 22: With the agreement of the emperor Augustus, Archelaus received half of his father's kingdom, including Judea, after Herod's death. He had the title "ethnarch" (i.e., "ruler of a nation") and reigned from 4 B.C. to A.D. 6.

2, 23: *Nazareth . . . he shall be called a Nazorean:* the tradition of Jesus' residence in Nazareth was firmly established, and Matthew sees it as being in accordance with the foreannounced plan of God. The town of Nazareth is not mentioned in the Old Testament, and no such prophecy can be found there. The vague expression "through the prophets" may be due to Matthew's seeing a connection between Nazareth and certain texts in which there are words with a remote similarity to the name of that town. Some such Old Testament texts are Is 11, 1 where the Davidic king of the future is called "a bud" *(nēṣer)* that shall blossom from the roots of Jesse, and Jgs 13, 5.7 where Samson, the future deliverer of Israel from the Philistines, is called one who shall be consecrated (a *nāzîr*) to God.

3, 1-12: Here Matthew takes up the order of Jesus' ministry found in the gospel of Mark, beginning with the preparatory preaching of John the Baptist.

3, 1: Unlike Luke, Matthew says nothing of the Baptist's origins and does not make him a relative of Jesus. *The desert of Judea:* the barren region west of the Dead Sea extending up the Jordan valley.

3, 2: *Repent:* the Baptist calls for a change of heart and conduct, a turning of one's life from rebellion to obedience toward God. *The kingdom of heaven is at hand:* "heaven" (literally, "the heavens") is a substitute for the name "God" that was avoided by devout Jews of the time out of reverence. The expression "the kingdom of heaven" occurs only in the gospel of Matthew. It means the effective rule of God over his people. In its fullness it includes not only human obedience to God's word, but the triumph of God over physical evils, supremely over death. In the expectation found in Jewish apocalyptic, the kingdom was to be ushered in by a judgment in which sinners would be condemned and perish, an expectation shared by the Baptist. This was modified in Christian understanding where the kingdom was seen as being established in stages, culminating with the parousia of Jesus.

3, 3: See the note on Jn 1, 23.

4*† John wore clothing made of camel's hair and had a leather belt around his waist. His food was locusts and wild honey. 5 At that time Jerusalem, all Judea, and the whole region around the Jordan were going out to him 6† and were being baptized by him in the Jordan River as they acknowledged their sins.

7*† When he saw many of the Pharisees and Sadducees coming to his baptism, he said to them, "You brood of vipers! Who warned you to flee from the coming wrath? 8 Produce good fruit as evidence of your repentance. 9* And do not presume to say to yourselves, 'We have Abraham as our father.' For I tell you, God can raise up children to Abraham from these stones. 10 Even now the ax lies at the root of the trees. Therefore every tree that does not bear good fruit will be cut down and thrown into the fire. 11*† I am baptizing you with water, for repentance, but the one who is coming after me is mightier than I. I am not worthy to carry his sandals. He will baptize you with the holy Spirit and fire. 12*† His winnowing fan is in his hand. He will clear his threshing floor and gather his wheat into his barn, but the chaff he will burn with unquenchable fire."

The Baptism of Jesus. † 13* Then Jesus came from Galilee to John at the Jordan to be baptized by him. 14† John tried to prevent him, saying, "I need to be baptized by you, and yet you are coming to me?" 15 Jesus said to him in reply, "Allow it now, for thus it is fitting for us to fulfill all righteousness." Then he allowed him. 16*† After Jesus was baptized, he came up from the water and behold, the heavens were opened [for him], and he saw the Spirit of God descending like a dove [and] coming upon him. 17*† And a voice came from the heavens, saying, "This is my beloved Son, with whom I am well pleased."

CHAPTER 4

The Temptation of Jesus. † 1* Then Jesus was led by the Spirit into the desert to be tempted by the devil. 2*† He fasted for forty days and forty nights, and afterwards he was hungry. 3 The tempter approached and said to him, "If you are the Son of God, command that these stones become loaves of bread." 4*† He said in reply, "It is written:

*

4: 11, 7-8; 2 Kgs 1, 8; Zec 13, 4.
7: 12, 34; 23, 33; Is 59, 5.
9: Jn 8, 33.39; Rom 9, 7-8; Gal 4, 21-31.
11: Jn 1, 26-27.33; Acts 1, 5.
12: 13, 30; Is 41, 16; Jer 15, 7.
13-17: Mk 1, 9-11; Lk 3, 21-22; Jn 1, 31-34.
16: Is 42, 1.
17: 12, 18; 17, 5; Gn 22, 2; Ps 2, 7; Is 42, 1.
4, 1-11: Mk 1, 12-13; Lk 4, 1-13.
2: Ex 24, 18; Dt 8, 2.
4: Dt 8, 3.

MATTHEW

†

3, 4: The clothing of John recalls the austere dress of the prophet Elijah (2 Kgs 1, 8). The expectation of the return of Elijah from heaven to prepare Israel for the final manifestation of God's kingdom was widespread, and according to Matthew this expectation was fulfilled in the Baptist's ministry (11, 14; 17, 11-13).

3, 6: Ritual washing was practiced by various groups in Palestine between 150 B.C. and A.D. 250. John's baptism may have been related to the purificatory washings of the Essenes at Qumran.

3, 7: *Pharisees and Sadducees:* the former were marked by devotion to the law, written and oral, and the scribes, experts in the law, belonged predominantly to this group. The Sadducees were the priestly aristocratic party, centered in Jerusalem. They accepted as scripture only the first five books of the Old Testament, followed only the letter of the law, rejected the oral legal traditions, and were opposed to teachings not found in the Pentateuch, such as the resurrection of the dead. Matthew links both of these groups together as enemies of Jesus (16, 1.6.11.12; cf Mk 8, 11-13.15). The threatening words that follow are addressed to them rather than to "the crowds" as in Lk 3, 7. *The coming wrath:* the judgment that will bring about the destruction of unrepentant sinners.

3, 11: *Baptize you with the holy Spirit and fire:* the water baptism of John will be followed by an "immersion" of the repentant in the cleansing power of the Spirit of God, and of the unrepentant in the destroying power of God's judgment. However, some see *the holy Spirit* and *fire* as synonymous, and the effect of this "baptism" as either purification or destruction. See the note on Lk 3, 16.

3, 12: The discrimination between the good and the bad is compared to the procedure by which a farmer separates wheat and chaff. The *winnowing fan* was a forklike shovel with which the threshed wheat was thrown into the air. The kernels fell to the ground; the light chaff, blown off by the wind, was gathered and burned up.

3, 13-17: The baptism of Jesus is the occasion on which he is equipped for his ministry by the holy Spirit and proclaimed to be the Son of God.

3, 14-15: This dialogue, peculiar to Matthew, reveals John's awareness of Jesus' superiority to him as the mightier one who is coming and who will baptize with the holy Spirit (11). His reluctance to admit Jesus among the sinners whom he is baptizing with water is overcome by Jesus' response. *To fulfill all righteousness:* in this gospel to *fulfill* usually refers to fulfillment of prophecy, and *righteousness* to moral conduct in conformity with God's will. Here, however, as in 5, 6 and 6, 33, *righteousness* seems to mean the saving activity of God. *To fulfill all righteousness* is to submit to the plan of God for the salvation of the human race. This involves Jesus' identification with sinners; hence the propriety of his accepting John's baptism.

3, 16: *The Spirit . . . coming upon him:* cf Is 42, 1.

3, 17: *This is my beloved Son:* the Marcan address to Jesus (Mk 1, 11) is changed into a proclamation. The Father's voice speaks in terms that reflect Is 42, 1, Ps 2, 7, and Gn 22, 2.

4, 1-11: Jesus, proclaimed Son of God at his baptism, is subjected to a triple temptation. Obedience to the Father is a characteristic of true sonship, and Jesus is tempted by the devil to rebel against God, overtly in the third case, more subtly in the first two. Each refusal of Jesus is expressed in language taken from the Book of Deuteronomy (Dt 8, 3; 6, 13.16). The testings of Jesus resemble those of Israel during the wandering in the desert and later in Canaan, and the victory of Jesus, the true Israel and the true Son, contrasts with the failure of the ancient and disobedient "son," the old Israel. In the temptation account Matthew is almost identical with Luke; both seem to have drawn upon the same source.

4, 2: *Forty days and forty nights:* the same time as that during which Moses remained on Sinai (Ex 24, 18). The time reference, however, seems primarily intended to recall the forty years during which Israel was tempted in the desert (Dt 8, 2).

4, 4: Cf Dt 8, 3. Jesus refuses to use his power for his own benefit and accepts whatever God wills.

'One does not live by bread alone,
but by every word that comes
forth from the mouth of God.' "

5† Then the devil took him to the holy
city, and made him stand on the para-
pet of the temple, 6* and said to him,
"If you are the Son of God, throw your-
self down. For it is written:

'He will command his angels con-
cerning you'
and 'with their hands they will
support you,
lest you dash your foot against a
stone.' "

7* Jesus answered him, "Again it is
written, 'You shall not put the Lord,
your God, to the test.' " 8 Then the devil
took him up to a very high mountain,
and showed him all the kingdoms of
the world in their magnificence, 9† and
he said to him, "All these I shall give
to you, if you will prostrate yourself
and worship me." 10* At this, Jesus
said to him, "Get away, Satan! It is writ-
ten:

'The Lord, your God, shall you wor-
ship
and him alone shall you serve.' "

11 Then the devil left him and, behold,
angels came and ministered to him.
The Beginning of the Galilean
Ministry.† 12* When he heard that John
had been arrested, he withdrew to Gali-
lee. 13* He left Nazareth and went to live
in Capernaum by the sea, in the region
of Zebulun and Naphtali, 14 that what
had been said through Isaiah the
prophet might be fulfilled:

15* "Land of Zebulun and land of
Naphtali,
the way to the sea, beyond the
Jordan,
Galilee of the Gentiles,
16* the people who sit in darkness
have seen a great light,
on those dwelling in a land over-
shadowed by death
light has arisen."

17*† From that time on, Jesus began to
preach and say, "Repent, for the king-
dom of heaven is at hand."
The Call of the First Disciples.†
18* As he was walking by the Sea of Gal-
ilee, he saw two brothers, Simon who
is called Peter, and his brother Andrew,
casting a net into the sea; they were
fishermen. 19 He said to them, "Come af-
ter me, and I will make you fishers of
men." 20† At once they left their nets
and followed him. 21 He walked along
from there and saw two other brothers,
James, the son of Zebedee, and his
brother John. They were in a boat, with
their father Zebedee, mending their
nets. He called them, 22 and immedi-
ately they left their boat and their fa-
ther and followed him.
Ministering to a Great Multitude.†
23*† He went around all of Galilee,
teaching in their synagogues, proclaim-
ing the gospel of the kingdom, and cur-
ing every disease and illness among the
people. 24† His fame spread to all of
Syria, and they brought to him all who
were sick with various diseases and
racked with pain, those who were pos-
sessed, lunatics, and paralytics, and he
cured them. 25*† And great crowds from
Galilee, the Decapolis, Jerusalem, and
Judea, and from beyond the Jordan fol-
lowed him.

*

6: Ps 91, 11-12.
7: Dt 6, 16.
10: 16, 23; Dt 6, 13.
12-13: Mk 1, 14-15; Lk 4, 14.31.
13: Jn 2, 12.
15-16: Is 8, 23 LXX; 9, 1.
16: Lk 1, 79.
17: 3, 2.
18-22: Mk 1, 16-20; Lk 5, 1-11.
23: 9, 35; Mk 1, 39; Lk 4, 15.44.
25: Mk 3, 7-8; Lk 6, 17-19.

†

4, 5-7: The devil supports his proposal by an appeal to the scriptures, Ps 91, 11a.12. Unlike Israel (Dt 6, 16), Jesus refuses to "test" God by demanding from him an extraordinary show of power.

4, 9: The worship of Satan to which Jesus is tempted is probably intended to recall Israel's worship of false gods. His refusal is expressed in the words of Dt 6, 13.

4, 12-17: Isaiah's prophecy of the light rising upon Zebulun and Naphtali (Is 8, 23—9, 1) is fulfilled in Jesus' residence at Capernaum. The territory of these two tribes was the first to be devastated (733-32 B.C.) at the time of the Assyrian invasion. In order to accommodate Jesus' move to Capernaum to the prophecy, Matthew speaks of that town as being "in the region of Zebulun and Naphtali" (13), whereas it was only in the territory of the latter, and he understands the sea of the prophecy, the Mediterranean, as the sea of Galilee.

4, 17: At the beginning of his preaching Jesus takes up the words of John the Baptist (3, 2) although with a different meaning; in his ministry the kingdom of heaven has already begun to be present (12, 28).

4, 18-22: The call of the first disciples promises them a share in Jesus' work and entails abandonment of family and former way of life. Three of the four, Simon, James, and John, are distinguished among the disciples by a closer relation with Jesus (17, 1; 26, 37).

4, 20: Here and in v 22, as in Mark (1, 16-20) and unlike the Lucan account (5, 1-11), the disciples' response is motivated only by Jesus' invitation, an element that emphasizes his mysterious power.

4, 23-25: This summary of Jesus' ministry concludes the narrative part of the first book of Matthew's gospel (chs 3-4). The activities of his ministry are teaching, proclaiming the gospel, and healing; cf 9, 35.

4, 23: *Their synagogues:* Matthew usually designates the Jewish synagogues as *their synagogue(s)* (9, 35; 10, 17; 12, 9; 13, 54) or, in address to Jews, *your synagogues* (23, 34), an indication that he wrote after the break between church and synagogue.

4, 24: *Syria:* the Roman province to which Palestine belonged.

4, 25: *The Decapolis:* a federation of Greek cities in Palestine, originally ten in number, all but one east of the Jordan.

CHAPTER 5

The Sermon on the Mount. † 1† When
he saw the crowds, he went up the
mountain, and after he had sat down,
his disciples came to him. 2 He began
to teach them, saying:

The Beatitudes†

3*†"Blessed are the poor in spirit,
for theirs is the kingdom of
heaven.
4*†Blessed are they who mourn,
for they will be comforted.
5*†Blessed are the meek,
for they will inherit the land.
6† Blessed are they who hunger and
thirst for righteousness,
for they will be satisfied.
7* Blessed are the merciful,
for they will be shown mercy.
8*†Blessed are the clean of heart,
for they will see God.
9 Blessed are the peacemakers,
for they will be called children of
God.
10*†Blessed are they who are perse-
cuted for the sake of righteous-
ness,
for theirs is the kingdom of
heaven.
11* Blessed are you when they insult you
and persecute you and utter every kind
of evil against you [falsely] because of
me. 12*† Rejoice and be glad, for your
reward will be great in heaven. Thus
they persecuted the prophets who were
before you.
The Similes of Salt and Light. †
13*† "You are the salt of the earth. But
if salt loses its taste, with what can it
be seasoned? It is no longer good for
anything but to be thrown out and tram-
pled underfoot. 14* You are the light of
the world. A city set on a mountain can-
not be hidden. 15* Nor do they light a
lamp and then put it under a bushel bas-
ket; it is set on a lampstand, where it
gives light to all in the house. 16* Just
so, your light must shine before others,
that they may see your good deeds and
glorify your heavenly Father.
Teaching about the Law. † 17 "Do not
think that I have come to abolish the
law or the prophets. I have come not
to abolish but to fulfill. 18* Amen, I say
to you, until heaven and earth pass

*

5, 3-12: Lk 6, 20-23.
4: Is 61, 2-3; Rv 21, 4.
5: Gn 13, 15; Ps 37, 11.
7: 18, 33; Jas 2, 13.
8: Pss 24, 4-5; 73, 1.
10: 1 Pt 2, 20; 3, 14; 4, 14.
11: 10, 22; Acts 5, 41.
12: 2 Chr 36, 16; Heb 11, 32-38; Jas 5, 10.
13: Mk 9, 50; Lk 14, 34-35.
14: Jn 8, 12.
15: Mk 4, 21; Lk 8, 16; 11, 33.
16: Jn 3, 21.
18: Lk 16, 17.

†

5, 1—7, 29: The first of the five discourses that are a central part of the structure of this gospel. It is the discourse section of the first book and contains sayings of Jesus derived from Q and from M. The Lucan parallel is in that gospel's "Sermon on the Plain" (Lk 6, 20-49), although some of the sayings in Matthew's "Sermon on the Mount" have their parallels in other parts of Luke. The careful topical arrangement of the sermon is probably not due only to Matthew's editing; he seems to have had a structured discourse of Jesus as one of his sources. The form of that source may have been as follows: four beatitudes (5, 3-4.6.11-12), a section on the new righteousness with illustrations (5, 17.20-24.27-28.33-48), a section on good works (6, 1-6.16-18), and three warnings (7, 1-2.15-21.24-27).

5, 1-2: Unlike Luke's sermon, this is addressed not only to the disciples but to the crowds (see 7, 28).

5, 3-12: The form *Blessed are (is)* occurs frequently in the Old Testament in the Wisdom literature and in the psalms. Although modified by Matthew, the first, second, fourth, and ninth beatitudes have Lucan parallels (5, 3 // Lk 6, 20; 5, 4 // Lk 6, 21b; 5, 6 // Lk 6, 21a; 5, 11-12 // Lk 5, 22-23). The others were added by the evangelist and are probably his own composition. A few manuscripts, Western and Alexandrian, and many versions and patristic quotations give the second and third beatitudes in inverted order.

5, 3: *The poor in spirit:* in the Old Testament, the *poor* (*ʿănāwîm*) are those who are without material possessions and whose confidence is in God (see Is 61, 1; Zep 2, 3; in the NAB the word is translated *lowly* and *humble,* respectively, in those texts). Matthew added *in spirit* in order either to indicate that only the devout poor were meant or to extend the beatitude to all, of whatever social rank, who recognized their complete dependence on God. The same phrase *poor in spirit* is found in the Qumran literature (1QM 14, 7).

5, 4: Cf Is 61, 2, "(The Lord has sent me) . . . to comfort all who mourn." *They will be comforted:* here the passive is a "theological passive" equivalent to the active "God will comfort them"; so also in vv 6 and 7.

5, 5: Cf Ps 37, 11, ". . . the meek shall possess the land." In the psalm "the land" means the land of Palestine; here it means the kingdom.

5, 6: *For righteousness:* a Matthean addition. For the meaning of *righteousness* here, see the note on 3, 14-15.

5, 8: Cf Ps 24, 4. Only one "whose heart is clean" can take part in the temple worship. To be with God in the temple is described in Ps 42, 3 as "beholding his face," but here the promise to *the clean of heart* is that they will *see God* not in the temple but in the coming kingdom.

5, 10: *Righteousness* here, as usually in Matthew, means conduct in conformity with God's will.

5, 12: *The prophets who were before you:* the disciples of Jesus stand in the line of the persecuted prophets of Israel. Some would see the expression as indicating also that Matthew considered all Christian disciples as prophets.

5, 13-16: By their deeds the disciples are to influence the world for good. They can no more escape notice than *a city set on a mountain.* If they fail in good works, they are as useless as flavorless salt or as a lamp whose light is concealed.

5, 13: The unusual supposition of salt losing its flavor has led some to suppose that the saying refers to the salt of the Dead Sea that, because chemically impure, could lose its taste.

5, 17-20: This statement of Jesus' position concerning the Mosaic law is composed of traditional material from Matthew's sermon documentation (see the note on 5, 1—7, 29), other Q material (cf 18 and Lk 16, 17), and the evangelist's own editorial touches. *To fulfill* the law appears at first to mean a literal enforcement of the law in the least detail: *until heaven and earth pass away* nothing of the law *will pass* (18). Yet the "passing away" of heaven and earth is not necessarily the end of the world understood, as in much apocalyptic literature, as the dissolution of the existing universe. The "turning of the ages" comes with the apocalyptic event of Jesus' death and resurrection, and those to whom this gospel is addressed are living in the new and final age, prophesied by Isaiah as the time of "new heavens and a new earth" (Is 65, 17; 66, 22). Meanwhile, during Jesus' ministry when the kingdom is already breaking in, his mission remains within the framework of the law, though with significant anticipation of the age to come, as the following antitheses (vv 21-48) show.

away, not the smallest letter or the
smallest part of a letter will pass from
the law, until all things have taken
place. 19† Therefore, whoever breaks
one of the least of these commandments
and teaches others to do so will be called
least in the kingdom of heaven. But
whoever obeys and teaches these com-
mandments will be called greatest in
the kingdom of heaven. 20 I tell you, un-
less your righteousness surpasses that
of the scribes and Pharisees, you will
not enter into the kingdom of heaven.

Teaching about Anger.† 21*† "You
have heard that it was said to your an-
cestors, 'You shall not kill; and whoever
kills will be liable to judgment.' 22*† But
I say to you, whoever is angry with his
brother will be liable to judgment, and
whoever says to his brother, 'Raqa,' will
be answerable to the Sanhedrin, and
whoever says, 'You fool,' will be liable
to fiery Gehenna. 23* Therefore, if you
bring your gift to the altar, and there
recall that your brother has anything
against you, 24 leave your gift there at
the altar, go first and be reconciled with
your brother, and then come and offer
your gift. 25* Settle with your opponent
quickly while on the way to court with
him. Otherwise your opponent will hand
you over to the judge, and the judge will
hand you over to the guard, and you
will be thrown into prison. 26 Amen, I
say to you, you will not be released until
you have paid the last penny.

Teaching about Adultery. 27*† "You
have heard that it was said, 'You shall
not commit adultery.' 28 But I say to you,
everyone who looks at a woman with
lust has already committed adultery
with her in his heart. 29*† If your right
eye causes you to sin, tear it out and
throw it away. It is better for you to lose
one of your members than to have your
whole body thrown into Gehenna.
30 And if your right hand causes you to
sin, cut it off and throw it away. It is
better for you to lose one of your mem-
bers than to have your whole body go
into Gehenna.

Teaching about Divorce.† 31* "It was
also said, 'Whoever divorces his wife
must give her a bill of divorce.' 32* But
I say to you, whoever divorces his wife
(unless the marriage is unlawful)
causes her to commit adultery, and
whoever marries a divorced woman
commits adultery.

Teaching about Oaths. 33*† "Again
you have heard that it was said to your
ancestors, 'Do not take a false oath, but
make good to the Lord all that you vow.'
34*† But I say to you, do not swear at
all; not by heaven, for it is God's throne;
35 nor by the earth, for it is his footstool;
nor by Jerusalem, for it is the city of
the great King. 36 Do not swear by your
head, for you cannot make a single hair

*

21: Ex 20, 13; Dt 5, 17.
22: Jas 1, 19-20.
23: Mk 11, 25.
25-26: 18, 34-35; Lk 12, 58-59.
27: Ex 20, 14; Dt 5, 18.
29-30: 18, 8-9; Mk 9, 43-47.
31: 19, 3-9; Dt 24, 1.
32: Lk 16, 18; 1 Cor 7, 10-11.
33: Lv 19, 12; Nm 30, 3.
34-37: Ps 48, 3; Sir 23, 9; Is 66, 1; Jas 5, 12.

†

5, 19: Probably *these commandments* means those of the Mosaic law. But this is an interim ethic "until heaven and earth pass away."

5, 21-48: Six examples of the conduct demanded of the Christian disciple. Each deals with a commandment of the law, introduced by *You have heard that it was said to your ancestors* or an equivalent formula, followed by Jesus' teaching in respect to that commandment, *But I say to you;* thus their designation as "antitheses." Three of them accept the Mosaic law but extend or deepen it (21-22; 27-28; 43-44); three reject it as a standard of conduct for the disciples (31-32; 33-37; 38-39).

5, 21: Cf Ex 20, 13; Dt 5, 17. The second part of the verse is not an exact quotation from the Old Testament, but cf Ex 21, 12.

5, 22: Anger is the motive behind murder, as the insulting epithets are steps that may lead to it. They, as well as the deed, are all forbidden. *Raqa:* an Aramaic word *rēqāʾ* or *rēqâ* probably meaning "imbecile," "blockhead," a term of abuse. The ascending order of punishment, *judgment* (by a local council?), trial before *the Sanhedrin,* condemnation to *Gehenna,* points to a higher degree of seriousness in each of the offenses. *Sanhedrin:* the highest judicial body of Judaism. *Gehenna:* in Hebrew *gê-hinnōm,* "Valley of Hinnom," or *gê ben-hinnōm,* "Valley of the son of Hinnom," southwest of Jerusalem, the center of an idolatrous cult during the monarchy in which children were offered in sacrifice (see 2 Kgs 23, 10; Jer 7, 31). In Jos 18, 16 (Septuagint, Codex Vaticanus) the Hebrew is transliterated into Greek as *gaienna,* which appears in the New Testament as *geenna.* The concept of punishment of sinners by fire either after death or after the final judgment is found in Jewish apocalyptic literature (e.g., Enoch 90, 26) but the name *geenna* is first given to the place of punishment in the New Testament.

5, 22-26: Reconciliation with an offended brother is urged in the admonition of vv 23-24 and the parable of vv 25-26 (// Lk 12, 58-59). The severity of the judge in the parable is a warning of the fate of unrepentant sinners in the coming judgment by God.

5, 27: See Ex 20, 14; Dt 5, 18.

5, 29-30: No sacrifice is too great to avoid total destruction in *Gehenna.*

5, 31-32: See Dt 24, 1-5. The Old Testament commandment that a bill of divorce be given to the woman assumes the legitimacy of divorce itself. It is this that Jesus denies. *(Unless the marriage is unlawful):* this "exceptive clause," as it is often called, occurs also in 19, 9, where the Greek is slightly different. There are other sayings of Jesus about divorce that prohibit it absolutely (see Mk 10, 11-12; Lk 16, 18; cf 1 Cor 7, 10.11b), and most scholars agree that they represent the stand of Jesus. Matthew's "exceptive clauses" are understood by some as a modification of the absolute prohibition. It seems, however, that the unlawfulness that Matthew gives as a reason why a marriage must be broken refers to a situation peculiar to his community: the violation of Mosaic law forbidding marriage between persons of certain blood and/or legal relationship (Lv 18, 6-18). Marriages of that sort were regarded as incest (*porneia*), but some rabbis allowed Gentile converts to Judaism who had contracted such marriages to remain in them. Matthew's "exceptive clause" is against such permissiveness for Gentile converts to Christianity; cf the similar prohibition of *porneia* in Acts 15, 20.29. In this interpretation, the clause constitutes no exception to the absolute prohibition of divorce when the marriage is lawful.

5, 33: This is not an exact quotation of any Old Testament text, but see Ex 20, 7, Dt 5, 11, and Lv 19, 12. The purpose of an oath was to guarantee truthfulness by one's calling on God as witness.

5, 34-36: The use of these oath formularies that avoid the divine name is in fact equivalent to swearing by it, for all the things sworn by are related to God.

white or black. 37† Let your 'Yes' mean
'Yes,' and your 'No' mean 'No.' Any-
thing more is from the evil one.
Teaching about Retaliation.†
38* "You have heard that it was said,
'An eye for an eye and a tooth for a
tooth.' 39* But I say to you, offer no re-
sistance to one who is evil. When some-
one strikes you on [your] right cheek,
turn the other one to him as well.
40 If anyone wants to go to law with you
over your tunic, hand him your cloak
as well. 41*† Should anyone press you
into service for one mile, go with him
for two miles. 42* Give to the one who
asks of you, and do not turn your back
on one who wants to borrow.
Love of Enemies.† 43* "You have
heard that it was said, 'You shall love
your neighbor and hate your enemy.'
44 But I say to you, love your enemies,
and pray for those who persecute you,
45 that you may be children of your
heavenly Father, for he makes his sun
rise on the bad and the good, and causes
rain to fall on the just and the unjust.
46† For if you love those who love you,
what recompense will you have? Do not
the tax collectors do the same? 47† And
if you greet your brothers only, what
is unusual about that? Do not the pa-
gans do the same? 48*† So be perfect,
just as your heavenly Father is perfect.

CHAPTER 6

Teaching about Almsgiving.†
1* "[But] take care not to perform righ-
teous deeds in order that people may
see them; otherwise, you will have no
recompense from your heavenly Fa-
ther. 2*† When you give alms, do not
blow a trumpet before you, as the hypo-
crites do in the synagogues and in the
streets to win the praise of others.
Amen, I say to you, they have received
their reward. 3 But when you give alms,
do not let your left hand know what your
right is doing, 4 so that your almsgiving
may be secret. And your Father who
sees in secret will repay you.
Teaching about Prayer. 5 "When you
pray, do not be like the hypocrites, who
love to stand and pray in the syna-
gogues and on street corners so that
others may see them. Amen, I say to
you, they have received their reward.
6 But when you pray, go to your inner
room, close the door, and pray to your
Father in secret. And your Father who
sees in secret will repay you. 7† In pray-
ing, do not babble like the pagans, who
think that they will be heard because
of their many words. 8 Do not be like
them. Your Father knows what you
need before you ask him.
The Lord's Prayer.† 9*† "This is how
you are to pray:

---

*

38: Ex 21, 24; Lv 24, 19-20.
39-42: Lk 6, 29-30.
41: Lam 3, 30.
42: Dt 15, 7-8.
43-48: Lk 6, 27.32-36.
43: Lv 19, 18.
48: Lv 11, 44; 19, 2; Dt 18, 13; Jas 1, 4; 1 Pt 1, 16; 1 Jn 3, 3.
6, 1: 23, 5.
2: Jn 12, 43.
9-13: Lk 11, 2-4.

†

5, 37: *Let your 'Yes,' mean 'Yes,' and your 'No' mean 'No':* literally, "let your speech be 'Yes, yes,' 'No, no.' " Some have understood this as a milder form of oath, permitted by Jesus. In view of v 34, "Do not swear at all," that is unlikely. *From the evil one:* i.e., from the devil. Oath-taking presupposes a sinful weakness of the human race, namely, the tendency to lie. Jesus demands of his disciples a truthfulness that makes oaths unnecessary.

5, 38-42: See Lv 24, 20. The Old Testament commandment was meant to moderate vengeance; the punishment should not exceed the injury done. Jesus forbids even this proportionate retaliation. Of the five examples that follow, only the first deals directly with retaliation for evil; the others speak of liberality.

5, 41: Roman garrisons in Palestine had the right to requisition the property and services of the native population.

5, 43-48: See Lv 19, 18. There is no Old Testament commandment demanding hatred of one's enemy, but the "neighbor" of the love commandment was understood as one's fellow countryman. Both in the Old Testament (Ps 139, 19-22) and at Qumran (1QS 9, 21) hatred of evil persons is assumed to be right. Jesus extends the love commandment to the enemy and the persecutor. His disciples, as children of God, must imitate the example of their Father, who grants his gifts of sun and rain to both the good and the bad.

5, 46: *Tax collectors:* Jews who were engaged in the collection of indirect taxes such as tolls and customs. See the note on Mk 2, 14.

5, 47: Jesus' disciples must not be content with merely usual standards of conduct; see v 20 where the verb "surpass" (Greek *perisseuō*) is cognate with the *unusual* (*perisson*) of this verse.

5, 48: *Perfect:* in the gospels this word occurs only in Matthew, here and in 19, 21. The Lucan parallel (6, 36) demands that the disciples be *merciful.*

6, 1-18: The sermon continues with a warning against doing good in order to be seen and gives three examples, almsgiving (2-4), prayer (5-15), and fasting (16-18). In each, the conduct of *the hypocrites* (2) is contrasted with that demanded of the disciples. The sayings about *reward* found here and elsewhere (5, 12.46; 10, 41-42) show that this is a genuine element of Christian moral exhortation. Possibly to underline the difference between the Christian idea of *reward* and that of *the hypocrites,* the evangelist uses two different Greek verbs to express the rewarding of the disciples and that of *the hypocrites;* in the latter case it is the verb *apechō,* a commercial term for giving a receipt for what has been paid in full (2.5.16).

6, 2: *The hypocrites:* the scribes and Pharisees, see 23, 13.15. 23.25.27.29. The designation reflects an attitude resulting not only from the controversies at the time of Jesus' ministry but from the opposition between Pharisaic Judaism and the church of Matthew. *They have received their reward:* they desire praise and have received what they were looking for.

6, 7-15: Matthew inserts into his basic traditional material an expansion of the material on prayer that includes the model prayer, the "Our Father." That prayer is found in Lk 11, 2-4 in a different context and in a different form.

6, 7: The example of what Christian prayer should be like contrasts it now not with the prayer of the hypocrites but with that of *the pagans.* Their babbling probably means their reciting a long list of divine names, hoping that one of them will force a response from the deity.

6, 9-13: Matthew's form of the "Our Father" follows the liturgical tradition of his church. Luke's less developed form also represents the liturgical tradition known to him, but it is probably closer than Matthew's to the original words of Jesus.

6, 9: *Our Father in heaven:* this invocation is found in many rabbinic prayers of the post-New Testament period. *Hallowed be your name:* though the "hallowing" of the divine name could be understood as reverence done to God by human praise and by obedience to his will, this is more probably a petition that God hallow his own name, i.e., that he manifest his glory by an act of power (cf Ez 36, 23), in this case, by the establishment of his kingdom in its fullness.

Our Father in heaven,
hallowed be your name,
10*† your kingdom come,
your will be done,
on earth as in heaven.
11*† Give us today our daily bread;
12*† and forgive us our debts,
as we forgive our debtors;
13*† and do not subject us to the final
test,
but deliver us from the evil one.

14*† If you forgive others their trans-
gressions, your heavenly Father will
forgive you. 15* But if you do not forgive
others, neither will your Father forgive
your transgressions.
Teaching about Fasting. 16† "When
you fast, do not look gloomy like the
hypocrites. They neglect their appear-
ance, so that they may appear to others
to be fasting. Amen, I say to you, they
have received their reward. 17 But when
you fast, anoint your head and wash
your face, 18 so that you may not appear
to be fasting, except to your Father who
is hidden. And your Father who sees
what is hidden will repay you.
Treasure in Heaven.† 19* "Do not
store up for yourselves treasures on
earth, where moth and decay destroy,
and thieves break in and steal. 20* But
store up treasures in heaven, where nei-
ther moth nor decay destroys, nor
thieves break in and steal. 21 For where
your treasure is, there also will your
heart be.
The Light of the Body.† 22* "The
lamp of the body is the eye. If your eye
is sound, your whole body will be filled
with light; 23 but if your eye is bad, your
whole body will be in darkness. And if
the light in you is darkness, how great
will the darkness be.
God and Money. 24*† "No one can
serve two masters. He will either hate
one and love the other, or be devoted
to one and despise the other. You cannot
serve God and mammon.
Dependence on God.† 25* "Therefore
I tell you, do not worry about your life,
what you will eat [or drink], or about
your body, what you will wear. Is not
life more than food and the body more
than clothing? 26* Look at the birds in
the sky; they do not sow or reap, they
gather nothing into barns, yet your
heavenly Father feeds them. Are not
you more important than they? 27† Can
any of you by worrying add a single mo-
ment to your life-span? 28 Why are you
anxious about clothes? Learn from the
way the wild flowers grow. They do not
work or spin. 29 But I tell you that not
even Solomon in all his splendor was
clothed like one of them. 30† If God so
clothes the grass of the field, which
grows today and is thrown into the oven
tomorrow, will he not much more pro-
vide for you, O you of little faith?
31 So do not worry and say, 'What are
we to eat?' or 'What are we to drink?'
or 'What are we to wear?' 32 All these
things the pagans seek. Your heavenly
Father knows that you need them all.
33† But seek first the kingdom [of God]
and his righteousness, and all these
things will be given you besides. 34 Do
not worry about tomorrow; tomorrow
will take care of itself. Sufficient for a
day is its own evil.

---

*

10: 26, 42.
11: Prv 30, 8-9.
12: 18, 21-22; Sir 28, 2.
13: Jn 17, 15; 2 Thes 3, 3.
14: 18, 35; Sir 28, 1-5; Mk 11, 25.
15: Jas 2, 13.
19: Jas 5, 2-3.
20-21: Lk 12, 33-34.
22-23: Lk 11, 34-36.
24: Lk 16, 13.
25-33: Lk 12, 22-31.
26: Pss 145, 15-16; 147, 9.

---

†

6, 10: *Your kingdom come:* this petition sets the tone of the prayer, and inclines the balance toward divine rather than human action in the petitions that immediately precede and follow it. *Your will be done, on earth as in heaven:* a petition that the divine purpose to establish the kingdom, a purpose present now *in heaven,* be executed *on earth.*

6, 11: *Give us today our daily bread:* the rare Greek word *epiousios,* here *daily,* occurs in the New Testament only here and in Lk 11, 3. A single occurrence of the word outside of these texts and of literature dependent on them has been claimed, but the claim is highly doubtful. The word may mean *daily* or "future" (other meanings have also been proposed). The latter would conform better to the eschatological tone of the whole prayer. So understood, the petition would be for a speedy coming of the kingdom (*today*), which is often portrayed in both the Old Testament and the New under the image of a feast (Is 25, 6; Mt 8, 11; 22, 1-10; Lk 13, 29; 14, 15-24).

6, 12: *Forgive us our debts:* the word *debts* is used metaphorically of sins, "debts" owed to God (see Lk 11, 4). The request is probably for forgiveness at the final judgment.

6, 13: Jewish apocalyptic writings speak of a period of severe trial before the end of the age, sometimes called the "messianic woes." This petition asks that the disciples be spared that *final test.*

6, 14-15: These verses reflect a set pattern called "Principles of Holy Law." Human action now will be met by a corresponding action of God at the final judgment.

6, 16: The only fast prescribed in the Mosaic law was that of the Day of Atonement (Lv 16, 31), but the practice of regular fasting was common in later Judaism; cf *Didache* 9, 1.

6, 19-34: The remaining material of this chapter is taken almost entirely from Q. It deals principally with worldly possessions, and the controlling thought is summed up in v 24: the disciple can serve only one master and must choose between God and wealth (*mammon*). See further the note on Lk 16, 9.

6, 22-23: In this context the parable probably points to the need for the disciple to be enlightened by Jesus' teaching on the transitory nature of earthly riches.

6, 24: *Mammon:* an Aramaic word meaning wealth or property.

6, 25-34: Jesus does not deny the reality of human needs (32), but forbids making them the object of anxious care and, in effect, becoming their slave.

6, 27: *Life-span:* the Greek word can also mean "stature." If it is taken in that sense, the word here translated *moment* (literally, "cubit") must be translated literally as a unit not of time but of spatial measure. The cubit is about eighteen inches.

6, 30: *Of little faith:* except for the parallel in Lk 12, 28, the word translated *of little faith* is found in the New Testament only in Matthew. It is used by him of those who are disciples of Jesus but whose faith in him is not as deep as it should be (see Mt 8, 26; 14, 31; 16, 8 and the cognate noun in 17, 20).

6, 33: *Righteousness:* see the note on 3, 14-15.

CHAPTER 7

Judging Others.† 1*† "Stop judging,
that you may not be judged. 2* For as
you judge, so will you be judged, and
the measure with which you measure
will be measured out to you. 3 Why do
you notice the splinter in your brother's
eye, but do not perceive the wooden
beam in your own eye? 4 How can you
say to your brother, 'Let me remove
that splinter from your eye,' while the
wooden beam is in your eye? 5† You
hypocrite, remove the wooden beam
from your eye first; then you will see
clearly to remove the splinter from your
brother's eye.

Pearls before Swine. 6*† "Do not give
what is holy to dogs, or throw your
pearls before swine, lest they trample
them underfoot, and turn and tear you
to pieces.

The Answer to Prayers. 7* "Ask and
it will be given to you; seek and you will
find; knock and the door will be opened
to you. 8* For everyone who asks, re-
ceives; and the one who seeks, finds;
and to the one who knocks, the door will
be opened. 9† Which one of you would
hand his son a stone when he asks for
a loaf of bread, 10 or a snake when he
asks for a fish? 11* If you then, who are
wicked, know how to give good gifts to
your children, how much more will your
heavenly Father give good things to
those who ask him.

The Golden Rule. 12*† "Do to others
whatever you would have them do to
you. This is the law and the prophets.

The Narrow Gate.† 13*† "Enter
through the narrow gate; for the gate
is wide and the road broad that leads
to destruction, and those who enter
through it are many. 14 How narrow the
gate and constricted the road that leads
to life. And those who find it are few.

False Prophets.† 15* "Beware of false
prophets, who come to you in sheep's
clothing, but underneath are ravenous
wolves. 16* By their fruits you will know
them. Do people pick grapes from
thornbushes, or figs from thistles?
17 Just so, every good tree bears good
fruit, and a rotten tree bears bad fruit.
18 A good tree cannot bear bad fruit, nor
can a rotten tree bear good fruit.
19* Every tree that does not bear good
fruit will be cut down and thrown into
the fire. 20 So by their fruits you will
know them.

The True Disciple.† 21* "Not every-
one who says to me, 'Lord, Lord,' will
enter the kingdom of heaven, but only
the one who does the will of my Father
in heaven. 22* Many will say to me on
that day, 'Lord, Lord, did we not proph-
esy in your name? Did we not drive
out demons in your name? Did we not
do mighty deeds in your name?'
23*† Then I will declare to them sol-
emnly, 'I never knew you. Depart from
me, you evildoers.'

The Two Foundations.†
24* "Everyone who listens to these
words of mine and acts on them will be
like a wise man who built his house on
rock. 25* The rain fell, the floods came,

*

7, 1-5: Lk 6, 37-38.41-42.
1: Rom 2, 1-2; 1 Cor 4, 5.
2: Wis 12, 22; Mk 4, 24.
6: Prv 23, 9.
7-11: Mk 11, 24; Lk 11, 9-13.
7: 18, 19.
8: Lk 18, 1-8; Jn 14, 13.
11: 1 Jn 5, 14-15.
12: Lk 6, 31.
13: Lk 13, 24.
15: 2 Pt 2, 1.
16-17: 12, 33; Lk 6, 43-44.
19: 3, 10.
21: Is 29, 13; Lk 6, 46.
22-23: Lk 13, 26-27.
22: 25, 11-12.
23: Pss 5, 5; 6, 9.
24-27: Lk 6, 47-49.
25-26: Prv 10, 25.

†

7, 1-12: In v 1 Matthew returns to the basic traditional material of the sermon (Lk 6, 37-38.41-42). The governing thought is the correspondence between conduct toward one's fellows and God's conduct toward the one so acting.

7, 1: This is not a prohibition against recognizing the faults of others, which would be hardly compatible with vv 5 and 6, but against passing judgment in a spirit of arrogance, forgetful of one's own faults.

7, 5: *Hypocrite:* the designation previously given to the scribes and Pharisees is here given to the Christian disciple who is concerned with the faults of another and ignores his own more serious offenses.

7, 6: *Dogs* and *swine* were Jewish terms of contempt for Gentiles. This saying may originally have derived from a Jewish Christian community opposed to preaching the gospel (*what is holy, pearls*) to Gentiles. In the light of 28, 19 that can hardly be Matthew's meaning. He may have taken the saying as applying to a Christian dealing with an obstinately impenitent fellow Christian (18, 17).

7, 9-10: There is a resemblance between a stone and a round loaf of bread and between a serpent and the scaleless fish called *barbut.*

7, 12: See Lk 6, 31. This saying, known since the eighteenth century as the "Golden Rule," is found in both positive and negative form in pagan and Jewish sources, both earlier and later than the gospel. *This is the law and the prophets* is an addition probably due to the evangelist.

7, 13-28: The final section of the discourse is composed of a series of antitheses, contrasting two kinds of life within the Christian community, that of those who obey the words of Jesus and that of those who do not. Most of the sayings are from Q and are found also in Luke.

7, 13-14: The metaphor of the "two ways" was common in pagan philosophy and in the Old Testament. In Christian literature it is found also in the *Didache* (1-6) and the *Epistle of Barnabas* (18-20).

7, 15-20: Christian disciples who claimed to speak in the name of God are called *prophets* (15) in 10, 41 and in 23, 34. They were presumably an important group within the church of Matthew. As in the case of the Old Testament prophets, there were both true and false ones, and for Matthew the difference could be recognized by the quality of their deeds, the *fruits* (16). The mention of *fruits* leads to the comparison with trees, some producing good fruit, others bad.

7, 21-23: The attack on the false prophets is continued, but is broadened to include those disciples who perform works of healing and exorcism in the name of Jesus (*Lord*) but live evil lives. Entrance into the kingdom is only for those who do the will of the Father. On the day of judgment (*on that day*) the morally corrupt prophets and miracle workers will be rejected by Jesus.

7, 23: *I never knew you:* cf 10, 33. *Depart from me, you evildoers:* cf Ps 6, 9.

7, 24-27: The conclusion of the discourse (cf Lk 6, 47-49). Here the relation is not between saying and doing as in vv 15-23 but between hearing and doing, and the words of Jesus are applied to every Christian (*everyone who listens*).

and the winds blew and buffeted the house. But it did not collapse; it had been set solidly on rock. 26 And everyone who listens to these words of mine but does not act on them will be like a fool who built his house on sand. 27 The rain fell, the floods came, and the winds blew and buffeted the house. And it collapsed and was completely ruined."

28† When Jesus finished these words, the crowds were astonished at his teaching, 29*† for he taught them as one having authority, and not as their scribes.

III: MINISTRY AND MISSION IN GALILEE†

CHAPTER 8

The Cleansing of a Leper. 1* When Jesus came down from the mountain, great crowds followed him. 2† And then a leper approached, did him homage, and said, "Lord, if you wish, you can make me clean." 3 He stretched out his hand, touched him, and said, "I will do it. Be made clean." His leprosy was cleansed immediately. 4*† Then Jesus said to him, "See that you tell no one, but go show yourself to the priest, and offer the gift that Moses prescribed; that will be proof for them."

The Healing of a Centurion's Servant.† 5*† When he entered Capernaum, a centurion approached him and appealed to him, 6 saying, "Lord, my servant is lying at home paralyzed, suffering dreadfully." 7 He said to him, "I will come and cure him." 8† The centurion said in reply, "Lord, I am not worthy to have you enter under my roof; only say the word and my servant will be healed. 9 For I too am a person subject to authority, with soldiers subject to me. And I say to one, 'Go,' and he goes; and to another, 'Come here,' and he comes; and to my slave, 'Do this,' and he does it." 10† When Jesus heard this, he was amazed and said to those following him, "Amen, I say to you, in no one in Israel have I found such faith. 11*† I say to you, many will come from the east and the west, and will recline with Abraham, Isaac, and Jacob at the banquet in the kingdom of heaven, 12 but the children of the kingdom will be driven out into the outer darkness, where there will be wailing and grinding of teeth." 13 And Jesus said to the centurion, "You may go; as you have believed, let it be done for you." And at that very hour [his] servant was healed.

The Cure of Peter's Mother-in-Law.† 14* Jesus entered the house of Peter, and saw his mother-in-law lying in bed with a fever. 15* He touched her hand, the fever left her, and she rose and waited on him.

Other Healings. 16† When it was evening, they brought him many who were possessed by demons, and he drove out the spirits by a word and cured all the sick, 17*† to fulfill what had been said by Isaiah the prophet:

"He took away our infirmities
and bore our diseases."

*

29: Mk 1, 22; Lk 4, 32.
8, 1-4: Mk 1, 40-44; Lk 5, 12-14.
4: Lv 14, 2-32; Lk 17, 14.
5-13: Lk 7, 1-10; Jn 4, 46-53.
11-12: 13, 42.50; 22, 13; 24, 51; 25, 30; Lk 13, 28-29.
14-16: Mk 1, 29-34; Lk 4, 38-41.
15: 9, 25.
17: Is 53, 4.

†

7, 28-29: *When Jesus finished these words:* this or a similar formula is used by Matthew to conclude each of the five great discourses of Jesus (cf 11, 1; 13, 53; 19, 1; 26, 1).

7, 29: *Not as their scribes:* scribal instruction was a faithful handing down of the traditions of earlier teachers; Jesus' teaching is based on his own authority. *Their scribes:* for the implications of *their*, see the note on 4, 23.

8, 1—9, 38: This narrative section of the second book of the gospel is composed of nine miracle stories, most of which are found in Mark, although Matthew does not follow the Marcan order and abbreviates the stories radically. The stories are arranged in three groups of three, each group followed by a section composed principally of sayings of Jesus about discipleship. Verse 9, 35 is an almost verbatim repetition of 4, 23. Each speaks of Jesus' teaching, preaching, and healing. The teaching and preaching form the content of chs 5-7; the healing, that of chs 8-9. Some scholars speak of a portrayal of Jesus as "Messiah of the Word" in 5-7 and "Messiah of the Deed" in 8-9. That is accurate so far as it goes, but there is also a strong emphasis on discipleship in 8-9; these chapters have not only christological but ecclesiological import.

8, 2: *A leper:* see the note on Mk 1, 40.

8, 4: Cf Lv 14, 2-9. *That will be proof for them:* the Greek can also mean "that will be proof against them." It is not clear whether *them* refers to the priests or the people.

8, 5-13: This story comes from Q (see Lk 7, 1-10) and is also reflected in Jn 4, 46-54. The similarity between the Q story and the Johannine is due to a common oral tradition, not to a common literary source. As in the later story of the daughter of the Canaanite woman (15, 21-28) Jesus here breaks with his usual procedure of ministering only to Israelites and anticipates the mission to the Gentiles.

8, 5: *A centurion:* a military officer commanding a hundred men. He was probably in the service of Herod Antipas, tetrarch of Galilee; see the note on 14, 1.

8, 8-9: Acquainted by his position with the force of a command, the centurion expresses faith in the power of Jesus' mere word.

8, 10: *In no one in Israel:* there is good textual attestation (e.g., Codex Sinaiticus) for a reading identical with that of Lk 7, 9, "not even in Israel." But that seems to be due to a harmonization of Matthew with Luke.

8, 11-12: Matthew inserts into the story a Q saying (see Lk 13, 28-29) about the entrance of Gentiles into the kingdom and the exclusion of those Israelites who, though descended from the patriarchs and members of the chosen nation (*the children of the kingdom*), refused to believe in Jesus. *There will be wailing and grinding of teeth:* the first occurrence of a phrase used frequently in this gospel to describe final condemnation (13, 42.50; 22, 13; 24, 51; 25, 30). It is found elsewhere in the New Testament only in Lk 13, 28.

8, 14-15: Cf Mk 1, 29-31. Unlike Mark, Matthew has no implied request by others for the woman's cure. Jesus acts on his own initiative, and the cured woman rises and waits not on "them" (Mk 1, 31) but on *him*.

8, 16: *By a word:* a Matthean addition to Mk 1, 34; cf 8, 8.

8, 17: This fulfillment citation from Is 53, 4 follows the MT, not the LXX. The prophet speaks of the Servant of the Lord who suffers vicariously for the sins ("infirmities") of others; Matthew takes the *infirmities* as physical afflictions.

The Would-be Followers of Jesus.†
18*† When Jesus saw a crowd around
him, he gave orders to cross to the other
side. 19*† A scribe approached and said
to him, "Teacher, I will follow you
wherever you go." 20† Jesus answered
him, "Foxes have dens and birds of the
sky have nests, but the Son of Man has
nowhere to rest his head." 21 Another
of [his] disciples said to him, "Lord, let
me go first and bury my father."
22† But Jesus answered him, "Follow
me, and let the dead bury their dead."

The Calming of the Storm at Sea.
23*† He got into a boat and his disciples
followed him. 24† Suddenly a violent
storm came up on the sea, so that the
boat was being swamped by waves; but
he was asleep. 25*† They came and
woke him, saying, "Lord, save us! We
are perishing!" 26† He said to them,
"Why are you terrified, O you of little
faith?" Then he got up, rebuked the
winds and the sea, and there was great
calm. 27 The men were amazed and said,
"What sort of man is this, whom even
the winds and the sea obey?"

The Healing of the Gadarene Demoniacs.
28*† When he came to the
other side, to the territory of the Gada-
renes, two demoniacs who were coming
from the tombs met him. They were so
savage that no one could travel by that
road. 29† They cried out, "What have
you to do with us, Son of God? Have
you come here to torment us before the
appointed time?" 30† Some distance
away a herd of many swine was feeding.
31* The demons pleaded with him, "If
you drive us out, send us into the herd
of swine." 32 And he said to them, "Go
then!" They came out and entered the
swine, and the whole herd rushed down
the steep bank into the sea where they
drowned. 33 The swineherds ran away,
and when they came to the town they re-
ported everything, including what had
happened to the demoniacs. 34 There-
upon the whole town came out to meet
Jesus, and when they saw him they
begged him to leave their district.

CHAPTER 9

The Healing of a Paralytic. 1*† He
entered a boat, made the crossing, and
came into his own town. 2* And there
people brought to him a paralytic lying
on a stretcher. When Jesus saw their
faith, he said to the paralytic, "Courage,
child, your sins are forgiven." 3† At
that, some of the scribes said to them-
selves, "This man is blaspheming."
4 Jesus knew what they were thinking,
and said, "Why do you harbor evil
thoughts? 5 Which is easier, to say,
'Your sins are forgiven,' or to say,
'Rise and walk'? 6*† But that you may
know that the Son of Man has authority
on earth to forgive sins"—he then said
to the paralytic, "Rise, pick up your

*

18: Mk 4, 35.
19-22: Lk 9, 57-60.
23-27: Mk 4, 35-40; Lk 8, 22-25.
25-26: Ps 107, 28-29.
28-34: Mk 5, 1-17; Lk 8, 26-37.
31: Lk 4, 34.41.
9, 1-8: Mk 2, 3-12; Lk 5, 18-26.
2: Lk 7, 48.
6: Jn 5, 27.

†

8, 18-22: This passage between the first and second series of miracles about following Jesus is taken from Q (see Lk 9, 57-62). The third of the three sayings found in the source is absent from Matthew.

8, 18: *The other side:* i.e., of the Sea of Galilee.

8, 19: *Teacher:* for Matthew, this designation of Jesus is true, for he has Jesus using it of himself (10, 24.25; 23, 8; 26, 18), yet when it is used of him by others they are either his opponents (9, 11; 12, 38; 17, 24; 22, 16.24.36) or, as here and in 19, 16, well-disposed persons who cannot see more deeply. Thus it reveals an inadequate recognition of who Jesus is.

8, 20: *Son of Man:* see the note on Mk 8, 31. This is the first occurrence in Mt of a term that appears in the New Testament only in sayings of Jesus, except for Acts 7, 56 and possibly 9, 6 (// Mk 2, 10; Lk 5, 24). In Mt it refers to Jesus in his ministry (seven times, as here), in his passion and resurrection (nine times, e.g., 17, 22), and in his glorious coming at the end of the age (thirteen times, e.g., 24, 30).

8, 22: *Let the dead bury their dead:* the demand of Jesus overrides what both the Jewish and the Hellenistic world regarded as a filial obligation of the highest importance. See the note on Lk 9, 60.

8, 23: *His disciples followed him:* the first miracle in the second group (8, 23—9, 8) is introduced by a verse that links it with the preceding sayings by the catchword "follow." In Mk the initiative in entering the boat is taken by the disciples (Mk 4, 35-41); here, Jesus enters first and the disciples follow.

8, 24: *Storm:* literally, "earthquake," a word commonly used in apocalyptic literature for the shaking of the old world when God brings in his kingdom. All the synoptics use it in depicting the events preceding the parousia of the Son of Man (24, 7; Mk 13, 8; Lk 21, 11). Matthew has introduced it here and in his account of the death and resurrection of Jesus (27, 51-54; 28, 2).

8, 25: The reverent plea of the disciples contrasts sharply with their reproach of Jesus in Mk 4, 38.

8, 26: *You of little faith:* see the note on 6, 30. *Great calm:* Jesus' calming the sea may be meant to recall the Old Testament theme of God's control over the chaotic waters (Pss 65, 8; 89, 10; 93, 3-4; 107, 29).

8, 28: *Gadarenes:* this is the reading of Codex Vaticanus, supported by other important textual witnesses. The original reading of Codex Sinaiticus was Gazarenes, later changed to Gergesenes, and a few versions have Gerasenes. Each of these readings points to a different territory connected, respectively, with the cities Gadara, Gergesa, and Gerasa (modern Jerash). There is the same confusion of readings in the parallel texts, Mk 5, 1 and Lk 8, 26; there the best reading seems to be "Gerasenes," whereas "Gadarenes" is probably the original reading in Mt. The town of Gadara was about five miles southeast of the Sea of Galilee, and Josephus (*Life* 9 §42) refers to it as possessing territory that lay on that sea. *Two demoniacs:* Mark (5, 1-20) has one.

8, 29: *What have you to do with us?:* see the note on Jn 2, 4. *Before the appointed time:* the notion that evil spirits were allowed by God to afflict human beings until the time of the final judgment is found in Enoch 16, 1 and Jubilees 10, 7-10.

8, 30: The tending of pigs, animals considered unclean by Mosaic law (Lv 11, 6-7), indicates that the population was Gentile.

9, 1: *His own town:* Capernaum; see 4, 13.

9, 3: *Scribes:* see the note on Mk 2, 6. Matthew omits the reason given in the Marcan story for the charge of blasphemy: "Who but God alone can forgive sins?" (Mk 2, 7).

9, 6: It is not clear whether "But that you may know . . . to forgive sins" is intended to be a continuation of the words of Jesus or a parenthetical comment of the evangelist to those who would hear or read this gospel. In any case, Matthew here follows the Marcan text.

stretcher, and go home." 7 He rose and
went home. 8† When the crowds saw this
they were struck with awe and glorified
God who had given such authority to
human beings.

The Call of Matthew. † 9*† As Jesus
passed on from there, he saw a man
named Matthew sitting at the customs
post. He said to him, "Follow me." And
he got up and followed him. 10*† While
he was at table in his house, many tax
collectors and sinners came and sat
with Jesus and his disciples. 11† The
Pharisees saw this and said to his disci-
ples, "Why does your teacher eat with
tax collectors and sinners?" 12† He
heard this and said, "Those who are
well do not need a physician, but the
sick do. 13*† Go and learn the meaning
of the words, 'I desire mercy, not sacri-
fice.' I did not come to call the righteous
but sinners."

The Question about Fasting. 14* Then
the disciples of John approached him
and said, "Why do we and the Pharisees
fast [much], but your disciples do not
fast?" 15† Jesus answered them, "Can
the wedding guests mourn as long as
the bridegroom is with them? The days
will come when the bridegroom is taken
away from them, and then they will
fast. 16† No one patches an old cloak
with a piece of unshrunken cloth, for
its fullness pulls away from the cloak
and the tear gets worse. 17 People do not
put new wine into old wineskins. Other-
wise the skins burst, the wine spills out,
and the skins are ruined. Rather, they
pour new wine into fresh wineskins, and
both are preserved."

The Official's Daughter and the Woman with a Hemorrhage. †
18*† While he was saying these things
to them, an official came forward, knelt
down before him, and said, "My daugh-
ter has just died. But come, lay your
hand on her, and she will live." 19 Jesus
rose and followed him, and so did his
disciples. 20† A woman suffering hemor-
rhages for twelve years came up behind
him and touched the tassel on his cloak.
21* She said to herself, "If only I can
touch his cloak, I shall be cured."
22 Jesus turned around and saw her, and
said, "Courage, daughter! Your faith
has saved you." And from that hour the
woman was cured.

23 When Jesus arrived at the official's
house and saw the flute players and the
crowd who were making a commo-
tion, 24† he said, "Go away! The girl is
not dead but sleeping." And they ridi-
culed him. 25 When the crowd was put
out, he came and took her by the hand,
and the little girl arose. 26 And news
of this spread throughout all that land.

The Healing of Two Blind Men. †
27*† And as Jesus passed on from there,

---

*

9-13: Mk 2, 14-17; Lk 5, 27-32.
10: 11, 19; Lk 15, 1-2.
13: 12, 7; Hos 6, 6.
14-17: Mk 2, 18-22; Lk 5, 33-39.
18-26: Mk 5, 22-43; Lk 8, 41-56.
21: 14, 36; Nm 15, 37.
27-31: 20, 29-34.
27: 15, 22.

---

†

9, 8: *Who had given such authority to human beings:* a significant difference from Mk 2, 12 ("They . . . glorified God, saying, 'We have never seen anything like this' "). Matthew's extension to *human beings* of the authority to forgive sins points to the belief that such authority was being claimed by Matthew's church.

9, 9-17: In this section the order is the same as that of Mk 2, 13-22.

9, 9: *A man named Matthew:* Mark names this tax collector Levi (2, 14). No such name appears in the four lists of the twelve who were the closest companions of Jesus (10, 2-4; Mk 3, 16-19; Lk 6, 14-16; Acts 1, 13 [eleven, because of the defection of Judas Iscariot]), whereas all four list a Matthew, designated in 10, 3 as "the tax collector." The evangelist may have changed the "Levi" of his source to *Matthew* so that this man, whose call is given special notice, like that of the first four disciples (4, 18-22), might be included among the twelve. Another reason for the change may be that the disciple Matthew was the source of traditions peculiar to the church for which the evangelist was writing.

9, 10: *His house:* it is not clear whether *his* refers to Jesus or Matthew. *Tax collectors:* see the note on 5, 46. Table association with such persons would cause ritual impurity.

9, 11: *Teacher:* see the note on 8, 19.

9, 12: See the note on Mk 2, 17.

9, 13: *Go and learn . . . not sacrifice:* Matthew adds the prophetic statement of Hos 6, 6 to the Marcan account (see also 12, 7). If mercy is superior to the temple sacrifices, how much more to the laws of ritual impurity.

9, 15: Fasting is a sign of mourning and would be as inappropriate at this time of joy, when Jesus is proclaiming the kingdom, as it would be at a marriage feast. Yet the saying looks forward to the time when Jesus will no longer be with the disciples visibly, the time of Matthew's church. *Then they will fast:* see *Didache* 8, 1.

9, 16-17: Each of these parables speaks of the unsuitability of attempting to combine the old and the new. Jesus' teaching is not a patching up of Judaism, nor can the gospel be contained within the limits of Mosaic law.

9, 18-34: In this third group of miracles, the first (18-26) is clearly dependent on Mark (Mk 5, 21-43). Though it tells of two miracles, the cure of the woman had already been included within the story of the raising of the official's daughter, so that the two were probably regarded as a single unit. The other miracles seem to have been derived from Mark and Q respectively, though there Matthew's own editing is much more evident.

9, 18: *Official:* literally, "ruler." Mark calls him "one of the synagogue officials" (Mk 5, 22). *My daughter has just died:* Matthew heightens the Marcan "my daughter is at the point of death" (Mk 5, 23).

9, 20: *Tassel:* possibly "fringe." The Mosaic law prescribed that tassels be worn on the corners of one's garment as a reminder to keep the commandments (see Nm 15, 37-39; Dt 22, 12).

9, 24: *Sleeping:* sleep is a biblical metaphor for death (see Ps 87, 6 LXX; Dn 12, 2; 1 Thes 5, 10). Jesus' statement is not a denial of the child's real death, but an assurance that she will be roused from her sleep of death.

9, 27-31: This story was probably composed by Matthew out of Mark's story of the healing of a blind man named Bartimaeus (Mk 10, 46-52). Mark places the event late in Jesus' ministry, just before his entrance into Jerusalem, and Matthew has followed his Marcan source at that point in his gospel also (see 20, 29-34). In each of the Matthean stories the single blind man of Mark becomes two. The reason why Matthew would have given a double version of the Marcan story and placed the earlier one here may be that he wished to add a story of Jesus' curing the blind at this point in order to prepare for Jesus' answer to the emissaries of the Baptist (11, 4-6) in which Jesus, recounting his works, begins with his giving sight to the blind.

9, 27: *Son of David:* this messianic title is connected once with the healing power of Jesus in Mark (10, 47-48) and Luke (18, 38-39) but more frequently in Matthew (see also 12, 23; 15, 22; 20, 30-31).

two blind men followed [him], crying
out, "Son of David, have pity on us!"
28 When he entered the house, the blind
men approached him and Jesus said
to them, "Do you believe that I can
do this?" "Yes, Lord," they said to
him. 29 Then he touched their eyes
and said, "Let it be done for you ac-
cording to your faith." 30 And their
eyes were opened. Jesus warned
them sternly, "See that no one knows
about this." 31 But they went out and
spread word of him through all that
land.

The Healing of a Mute Person.†
32* As they were going out, a demoniac
who could not speak was brought to
him, 33* and when the demon was
driven out the mute person spoke. The
crowds were amazed and said, "Noth-
ing like this has ever been seen in Is-
rael." 34*† But the Pharisees said, "He
drives out demons by the prince of de-
mons."

The Compassion of Jesus. 35*† Jesus
went around to all the towns and vil-
lages, teaching in their synagogues,
proclaiming the gospel of the king-
dom, and curing every disease and ill-
ness. 36*† At the sight of the crowds,
his heart was moved with pity for them
because they were troubled and aban-
doned, like sheep without a shepherd.
37*† Then he said to his disciples,
"The harvest is abundant but the labor-
ers are few; 38 so ask the master of
the harvest to send out laborers for his
harvest."

CHAPTER 10

The Mission of the Twelve.† 1*† Then
he summoned his twelve disciples and
gave them authority over unclean spir-
its to drive them out and to cure every
disease and every illness. 2† The names
of the twelve apostles are these: first,
Simon called Peter, and his brother
Andrew; James, the son of Zebe-
dee, and his brother John; 3 Philip and
Bartholomew, Thomas and Matthew
the tax collector; James, the son of
Alphaeus, and Thaddeus; 4 Simon the
Cananean, and Judas Iscariot who be-
trayed him.

The Commissioning of the Twelve.†
5* Jesus sent out these twelve after in-
structing them thus, "Do not go into pa-
gan territory or enter a Samaritan town.
6* Go rather to the lost sheep of the
house of Israel. 7* As you go, make this
proclamation: 'The kingdom of heaven
is at hand.' 8† Cure the sick, raise the
dead, cleanse lepers, drive out demons.
Without cost you have received; without
cost you are to give. 9* Do not take gold
or silver or copper for your belts;
10* no sack for the journey, or a second
tunic, or sandals, or walking stick. The
laborer deserves his keep. 11* Whatever
town or village you enter, look for a
worthy person in it, and stay there until
you leave. 12 As you enter a house, wish

*

32-34: 12, 22-24; Lk 11, 14-15.
33: Mk 2, 12; 7, 37.
34: 10, 25; Mk 3, 22.
35: 4, 23; Lk 8, 1.
36: Nm 27, 17; 1 Kgs 22, 17; Jer 50, 6; Ez 34, 5; Mk 6, 34.
37-38: Lk 10, 2; Jn 4, 35.
10, 1-4: Mk 3, 14-19; Lk 6, 13-16; Acts 1, 13.
5-15: Mk 6, 7-13; Lk 9, 1-6.
6: 15, 24.
7: 3, 2; 4, 17.
9-10: Mk 6, 8-9; Lk 9, 3; 10, 4.
10: Lk 10, 7; 1 Cor 9, 14; 2 Tm 5, 18.
11-15: Mk 6, 10-11; Lk 9, 4-5; 10, 5-12.

†

9, 32-34: The source of this story seems to be Q (see Lk 11, 14-15). As in the preceding healing of the blind, Matthew has two versions of this healing, the later in 12, 22-24 and the earlier here.

9, 34: This spiteful accusation foreshadows the growing opposition to Jesus in chs 11 and 12.

9, 35: See the notes on 4, 23-25 and 8, 1—9, 38.

9, 36: See Mk 6, 34; Nm 27, 17; 1 Kgs 22, 17.

9, 37-38: This Q saying (see Lk 10, 2) is only imperfectly related to this context. It presupposes that only God (*the master of the harvest*) can take the initiative in sending out preachers of the gospel, whereas in Matthew's setting it leads into ch 10, where Jesus does so.

10, 1—11, 1: After an introductory narrative (10, 1-4), the second of the discourses of the gospel. It deals with the mission now to be undertaken by the disciples (5-15), but the perspective broadens and includes the missionary activity of the church between the time of the resurrection and the parousia.

10, 1: *His twelve disciples:* although, unlike Mark (3, 13-14) and Luke (6, 12-16), Matthew has no story of Jesus' choosing the Twelve, he assumes that the group is known to the reader. The earliest New Testament text to speak of it is 1 Cor 15, 5. The number probably is meant to recall the twelve tribes of Israel and implies Jesus' authority to call all Israel into the kingdom. While Luke (6, 13) and probably Mark (4, 10.34) distinguish between the Twelve and a larger group also termed disciples, Matthew tends to identify the disciples and the Twelve. *Authority . . . every illness:* activities the same as those of Jesus; see 4, 23; 9, 35; 10, 8. The Twelve also share in his proclamation of the kingdom (10, 7). But although he teaches (4, 23; 7, 28; 9, 35), they do not. Their commission to teach comes only after Jesus' resurrection, after they have been fully instructed by him (28, 20).

10, 2-4: Here, for the only time in Matthew, the Twelve are designated *apostles*. The word "apostle" means "one who is sent," and therefore fits the situation here described. In the Pauline letters, the place where the term occurs most frequently in the New Testament, it means primarily one who has seen the risen Lord and has been commissioned to proclaim the resurrection. With slight variants in Luke and Acts, the names of those who belong to this group are the same in the four lists given in the New Testament (see the note on 9, 9). *Cananean:* this represents an Aramaic word meaning "zealot." The meaning of that designation is unclear (see the note on Lk 6, 15).

10, 5-6: Like Jesus (15, 24), the Twelve are sent only to Israel. This saying may reflect an original Jewish Christian refusal of the mission to the Gentiles, but for Matthew it expresses rather the limitation that Jesus himself observed during his ministry.

10, 8-11: The Twelve have received their own call and mission through God's gift, and the benefits they confer are likewise to be given freely. They are not to take with them money, provisions, or unnecessary clothing; their lodging and food will be provided by those who receive them.

it peace. 13† If the house is worthy, let
your peace come upon it; if not, let your
peace return to you. 14*† Whoever will
not receive you or listen to your words—
go outside that house or town and shake
the dust from your feet. 15* Amen, I say
to you, it will be more tolerable for the
land of Sodom and Gomorrah on the
day of judgment than for that town.

Coming Persecutions. 16* "Behold, I
am sending you like sheep in the midst
of wolves; so be shrewd as serpents and
simple as doves. 17*† But beware of peo-
ple, for they will hand you over to courts
and scourge you in their synagogues,
18 and you will be led before governors
and kings for my sake as a witness be-
fore them and the pagans. 19* When
they hand you over, do not worry about
how you are to speak or what you are
to say. You will be given at that moment
what you are to say. 20 For it will not
be you who speak but the Spirit of your
Father speaking through you.
21*† Brother will hand over brother to
death, and the father his child; children
will rise up against parents and have
them put to death. 22† You will be hated
by all because of my name, but whoever
endures to the end will be saved.
23† When they persecute you in one
town, flee to another. Amen, I say to
you, you will not finish the towns of Is-
rael before the Son of Man comes.
24* No disciple is above his teacher, no
slave above his master. 25† It is enough
for the disciple that he become like
his teacher, for the slave that he be-
come like his master. If they have
called the master of the house Beel-
zebul, how much more those of his
household!

Courage under Persecution.
26*† "Therefore do not be afraid of
them. Nothing is concealed that will not
be revealed, nor secret that will not be
known. 27 What I say to you in the dark-
ness, speak in the light; what you hear
whispered, proclaim on the housetops.
28* And do not be afraid of those who
kill the body but cannot kill the soul;
rather, be afraid of the one who can de-
stroy both soul and body in Gehenna.
29 Are not two sparrows sold for a small
coin? Yet not one of them falls to the
ground without your Father's knowl-
edge. 30 Even all the hairs of your head
are counted. 31 So do not be afraid; you
are worth more than many sparrows.
32† Everyone who acknowledges me be-
fore others I will acknowledge before
my heavenly Father. 33* But whoever
denies me before others, I will deny be-
fore my heavenly Father.

Jesus: A Cause of Division. 34* "Do
not think that I have come to bring
peace upon the earth. I have come to
bring not peace but the sword. 35 For I
have come to set

a man 'against his father,
a daughter against her mother,
and a daughter-in-law against her
mother-in-law;
36 and one's enemies will be those
of his household.'

The Conditions of Discipleship.
37* "Whoever loves father or mother
more than me is not worthy of me, and
whoever loves son or daughter more
than me is not worthy of me; 38† and
whoever does not take up his cross and
follow after me is not worthy of me.
39*† Whoever finds his life will lose it,
and whoever loses his life for my sake
will find it.

*

14: Acts 13, 51; 18, 6.
15: 11, 24; Gn 19, 1-29; Jude 7.
16: Lk 10, 3.
17-22: Mk 13, 9-13; Lk 21, 12-19.
17: Acts 5, 40.
19: Ex 4, 11-12; Jer 1, 6-10; Lk 12, 11-12.
21-22: 24, 9.13.
24-25: Lk 6, 40; Jn 13, 16; 15, 20.
26-33: Lk 12, 2-9.
26: Mk 4, 22; Lk 8, 17; 1 Tm 5, 25.
28: Jas 4, 12.
33: Mk 8, 38; Lk 9, 26; 2 Tm 2, 12; Rv 3, 5.
34-35: Lk 12, 51-53.
37-39: 16, 24-25; Lk 14, 26-27.
39: Mk 8, 35; Lk 9, 24; Jn 12, 25.

†

10, 13: The greeting of peace is conceived of not merely as a salutation but as an effective word. If it finds no worthy recipient, it will return to the speaker.

10, 14: *Shake the dust from your feet:* this gesture indicates a complete disassociation from such unbelievers.

10, 17: The persecutions attendant upon the post-resurrection mission now begin to be spoken of. Here Matthew brings into the discourse sayings found in Mk 13, which deals with events preceding the parousia.

10, 21: See Mi 7, 6, which is cited in vv 35.36.

10, 22: *To the end:* the original meaning was probably "until the parousia." But it is not likely that Matthew expected no missionary disciples to suffer death before then, since he envisages the martyrdom of other Christians (21). For him, *the end* is probably that of the individual's life (see 28).

10, 23: *Before the Son of Man comes:* since the coming of the Son of Man at the end of the age had not taken place when this gospel was written, much less during the mission of the Twelve during Jesus' ministry, Matthew cannot have meant the coming to refer to the parousia. It is difficult to know what he understood it to be: perhaps the "proleptic parousia" of 28, 16-20, or the destruction of the temple in A.D. 70, viewed as a coming of Jesus in judgment on unbelieving Israel.

10, 25: *Beelzebul:* see 9, 34 for the charge linking Jesus with "the prince of demons," who is named *Beelzebul* in 12, 24. The meaning of the name is uncertain; possibly, "lord of the house."

10, 26: The *concealed* and *secret* coming of the kingdom is to be proclaimed by them, and no fear must be allowed to deter them from that proclamation.

10, 32-33: In the Q parallel (Lk 12, 8-9), the Son of Man will acknowledge those who have acknowledged Jesus, and those who deny him will be denied (by the Son of Man) before the angels of God at the judgment. Here Jesus and the Son of Man are identified, and the acknowledgment or denial will be before his heavenly Father.

10, 38: The first mention of the cross in Matthew, explicitly that of the disciple, but implicitly that of Jesus (*and follow after me*). Crucifixion was a form of capital punishment used by the Romans for offenders who were not Roman citizens.

10, 39: One who denies Jesus in order to save one's earthly life will be condemned to everlasting destruction; loss of earthly life for Jesus' sake will be rewarded by everlasting life in the kingdom.

Rewards.† 40* "Whoever receives you receives me, and whoever receives me receives the one who sent me. 41† Whoever receives a prophet because he is a prophet will receive a prophet's reward, and whoever receives a righteous man because he is righteous will receive a righteous man's reward. 42* And whoever gives only a cup of cold water to one of these little ones to drink because he is a disciple—amen, I say to you, he will surely not lose his reward."

CHAPTER 11

1† When Jesus finished giving these commands to his twelve disciples, he went away from that place to teach and to preach in their towns.

IV: OPPOSITION FROM ISRAEL

The Messengers from John the Baptist.† 2*† When John heard in prison of the works of the Messiah, he sent his disciples to him 3† with this question, "Are you the one who is to come, or should we look for another?" 4 Jesus said to them in reply, "Go and tell John what you hear and see: 5*† the blind regain their sight, the lame walk, lepers are cleansed, the deaf hear, the dead are raised, and the poor have the good news proclaimed to them. 6 And blessed is the one who takes no offense at me."

Jesus' Testimony to John.† 7* As they were going off, Jesus began to speak to the crowds about John, "What did you go out to the desert to see? A reed swayed by the wind? 8 Then what did you go out to see? Someone dressed in fine clothing? Those who wear fine clothing are in royal palaces. 9† Then why did you go out? To see a prophet? Yes, I tell you, and more than a prophet. 10* This is the one about whom it is written:

'Behold, I am sending my messenger ahead of you;
he will prepare your way before you.'

11† Amen, I say to you, among those born of women there has been none greater than John the Baptist; yet the least in the kingdom of heaven is greater than he. 12*† From the days of John the Baptist until now, the kingdom of heaven suffers violence, and the violent are taking it by force. 13† All the prophets and the law prophesied up to the time of John. 14* And if you are willing to accept it, he is Elijah, the one who is to come. 15 Whoever has ears ought to hear.

16*† "To what shall I compare this generation? It is like children who sit

---

*

40: Lk 10, 16; Jn 12, 44; 13, 20.
42: 25, 40; Mk 9, 41.
11, 2-11: Lk 7, 18-28.
5: Is 26, 19; 29, 18-19; 35, 5-6; 61, 1.
7: 3, 3.5.
10: Ex 23, 20; Mal 3, 1; Mk 1, 2; Lk 1, 76.
12: Lk 16, 16.
14: 17, 10-13; Mal 3, 23; Lk 1, 17.
16-19: Lk 7, 31-35.

†

10, 40-42: All who receive the disciples of Jesus receive him, and God who sent him, and will be rewarded accordingly.

10, 41: *A prophet:* one who speaks in the name of God; here, the Christian prophets who proclaim the gospel. *Righteous man:* since righteousness is demanded of all the disciples, it is difficult to take the *righteous man* of this verse and *one of these little ones* (42) as indicating different groups within the followers of Jesus. Probably all three designations are used here of Christian missionaries as such.

11, 1: The closing formula of the discourse refers back to the original addressees, the Twelve.

11, 2—12, 50: The narrative section of the third book deals with the growing opposition to Jesus. It is largely devoted to disputes and attacks relating to faith and discipleship and thus contains much sayings-material, drawn in large part from Q.

11, 2: *In prison:* see 4, 12; 14, 1-12. *The works of the Messiah:* the deeds of chs 8-9.

11, 3: The question probably expresses a doubt of the Baptist that Jesus is *the one who is to come* (cf Mal 3, 1) because his mission has not been one of fiery judgment as John had expected (3, 2).

11, 5-6: Jesus' response is taken from passages of Isaiah (26, 19; 29, 18-19; 35, 5-6; 61, 1) that picture the time of salvation as marked by deeds such as those that Jesus is doing. The beatitude is a warning to the Baptist not to disbelieve because his expectations have not been met.

11, 7-19: Jesus' rebuke of John is counterbalanced by a reminder of the greatness of the Baptist's function (7-15) that is followed by a complaint about those who have heeded neither John nor Jesus (16-19).

11, 9-10: In common Jewish belief there had been no prophecy in Israel since the last of the Old Testament prophets, Malachi. The coming of a new prophet was eagerly awaited, and Jesus agrees that John was such. Yet he was *more than a prophet*, for he was the precursor of the one who would bring in the new and final age. The Old Testament quotation is a combination of Mal 3, 1 and Ex 23, 20, with the significant change that the *before me* of Malachi becomes *before you*. The messenger now precedes not God, as in the original, but Jesus.

11, 11: John's preeminent greatness lies in his function of announcing the imminence of the kingdom (3, 1). But to be in the kingdom is so great a privilege that the least who has it is greater than the Baptist.

11, 12: The meaning of this difficult saying is probably that the opponents of Jesus are trying to prevent people from accepting the kingdom and to snatch it away from those who have received it.

11, 13: *All the prophets and the law:* Matthew inverts the usual order, "law and prophets," and says that both have *prophesied*. This emphasis on the prophetic character of the law points to its fulfillment in the teaching of Jesus and to the transitory nature of some of its commandments (see the note on 5, 17-20).

11, 16-19: See Lk 7, 31-35. The meaning of the parable (16-17) and its explanation (18-19b) is much disputed. A plausible view is that the *children* of the parable are two groups, one of which proposes different entertainments to the other that will not agree with either proposal. The first represents John, Jesus, and their disciples; the second those who reject John for his asceticism and Jesus for his table association with those despised by the religiously observant. Verse 19c (*her works*) forms an inclusion with v 2 ("the works of the Messiah"). The original form of the saying is better preserved in Lk 7, 35, ". . . wisdom is vindicated by all her children." There John and Jesus are the children of Wisdom; here the works of Jesus the Messiah are those of divine Wisdom, of which he is the embodiment. Some important textual witnesses, however, have essentially the same reading as in Luke.

in marketplaces and call to one another,
17 'We played the flute for you, but you
did not dance, we sang a dirge but you
did not mourn.' 18* For John came nei-
ther eating nor drinking, and they said,
'He is possessed by a demon.' 19* The
Son of Man came eating and drinking
and they said, 'Look, he is a glutton and
a drunkard, a friend of tax collectors
and sinners.' But wisdom is vindicated
by her works."

Reproaches to Unrepentant Towns.
20* Then he began to reproach the towns
where most of his mighty deeds had
been done, since they had not repented.
21*† "Woe to you, Chorazin! Woe to you,
Bethsaida! For if the mighty deeds done
in your midst had been done in Tyre
and Sidon, they would long ago have
repented in sackcloth and ashes.
22 But I tell you, it will be more tolerable
for Tyre and Sidon on the day of judg-
ment than for you. 23*† And as for you,
Capernaum:

'Will you be exalted to heaven?
You will go down to the nether-
world.'

For if the mighty deeds done in your
midst had been done in Sodom, it would
have remained until this day. 24* But I
tell you, it will be more tolerable for the
land of Sodom on the day of judgment
than for you."

The Praise of the Father. † 25* At that
time Jesus said in reply, "I give praise
to you, Father, Lord of heaven and
earth, for although you have hidden
these things from the wise and the
learned you have revealed them to the
childlike. 26 Yes, Father, such has been
your gracious will. 27* All things have
been handed over to me by my Father.
No one knows the Son except the Fa-
ther, and no one knows the Father ex-
cept the Son and anyone to whom the
Son wishes to reveal him.

The Gentle Mastery of Christ. †
28† "Come to me, all you who labor and
are burdened, and I will give you rest.
29*† Take my yoke upon you and learn
from me, for I am meek and humble of
heart; and you will find rest for your-
selves. 30 For my yoke is easy, and my
burden light."

CHAPTER 12

Picking Grain on the Sabbath. †
1*† At that time Jesus was going
through a field of grain on the sabbath.
His disciples were hungry and began to
pick the heads of grain and eat them.
2 When the Pharisees saw this, they said
to him, "See, your disciples are doing
what is unlawful to do on the sabbath."
3*† He said to them, "Have you not read
what David did when he and his com-
panions were hungry, 4* how he went
into the house of God and ate the bread
of offering, which neither he nor his
companions but only the priests could
lawfully eat? 5*† Or have you not read
in the law that on the sabbath the priests
serving in the temple violate the sab-
bath and are innocent? 6 I say to you,
something greater than the temple is
here. 7*† If you knew what this meant,
'I desire mercy, not sacrifice,' you
would not have condemned these inno-
cent men. 8*† For the Son of Man is
Lord of the sabbath."

*

18: Lk 1, 15.
19: 9, 10-11.
20-24: Lk 10, 12-15.
21: Jl 4, 4-7.
23: Is 14, 13-15.
24: 10, 15.
25-27: Lk 10, 21-22.
27: Jn 3, 35; 6, 46; 7, 28; 10, 15.
29: Sir 51, 26; Jer 6, 16.
12, 1-8: Mk 2, 23-28; Lk 6, 1-5.
1: Dt 23, 26.
3-4: 1 Sm 21, 2-7.
4: Lv 24, 5-9.
5: Lv 24, 8; Nm 28, 9-10.
7: Hos 6, 6.
8: Jn 5, 16-17.

†

11, 21: Tyre and Sidon were pagan cities denounced for their wickedness in the Old Testament; cf Jl 4, 4-7.

11, 23: Capernaum's pride and punishment are described in language taken from the taunt song against the king of Babylon (Is 14, 13-15).

11, 25-27: This Q saying, identical with Lk 10, 21-22 except for minor variations, introduces a joyous note into this section, so dominated by the theme of unbelief. While *the wise and the learned,* the scribes and Pharisees, have rejected Jesus' preaching and the significance of his mighty deeds, *the childlike* have accepted them. Acceptance depends upon the Father's revelation, but this is granted to those who are open to receive it and refused to the arrogant. Jesus can speak of all mysteries because he is *the Son* and there is perfect reciprocity of knowledge between him and the Father; what has been *handed over* to him is revealed only to those whom he wishes.

11, 28-29: These verses are peculiar to Matthew and are similar to Ben Sirach's invitation to learn wisdom and submit to her yoke (Sir 51, 23.26).

11, 28: *Who labor and are burdened:* burdened by the law as expounded by the scribes and Pharisees (23, 4).

11, 29: In place of the yoke of the law, complicated by scribal interpretation, Jesus invites the burdened to take the yoke of obedience to his word, under which they *will find rest;* cf Jer 6, 16.

12, 1-14: Matthew here returns to the Marcan order that he left in 9, 18. The two stories depend on Mk 2, 23-28 and 3, 1-6, respectively, and are the only places in either gospel that deal explicitly with Jesus' attitude toward sabbath observance.

12, 1-2: The picking of the heads of grain is here equated with reaping, which was forbidden on the sabbath (Ex 34, 21).

12, 3-4: See 1 Sm 21, 2-7. In the Marcan parallel (2, 25-26) the high priest is called Abiathar, although in 1 Sm this action is attributed to Ahimelech. The Old Testament story is not about a violation of the sabbath rest; its pertinence to this dispute is that a violation of the law was permissible because of David's men being without food.

12, 5-6: This and the following argument (7) are peculiar to Matthew. The temple service seems to be the changing of the showbread on the sabbath (Lv 24, 8) and the doubling on the sabbath of the usual daily holocausts (Nm 28, 9-10). The argument is that the law itself requires work that breaks the sabbath rest, because of the higher duty of temple service. If temple duties outweigh the sabbath law, how much more does the presence of Jesus, with his proclamation of the kingdom (*something greater than the temple*), justify the conduct of his disciples.

12, 7: See the note on 9, 13.

12, 8: The ultimate justification for the disciples' violation of the sabbath rest is that Jesus, the Son of Man, has supreme authority over the law.

The Man with a Withered Hand.
9* Moving on from there, he went into
their synagogue. 10† And behold, there
was a man there who had a withered
hand. They questioned him, "Is it lawful
to cure on the sabbath?" so that they
might accuse him. 11† He said to them,
"Which one of you who has a sheep that
falls into a pit on the sabbath will not
take hold of it and lift it out? 12 How
much more valuable a person is than a
sheep. So it is lawful to do good on the
sabbath." 13 Then he said to the man,
"Stretch out your hand." He stretched
it out, and it was restored as sound as
the other. 14*† But the Pharisees went
out and took counsel against him to put
him to death.

The Chosen Servant.† 15† When Jesus
realized this, he withdrew from that
place. Many [people] followed him, and
he cured them all, 16 but he warned
them not to make him known. 17 This
was to fulfill what had been spoken
through Isaiah the prophet:

18* "Behold, my servant whom I have chosen,
my beloved in whom I delight;
I shall place my spirit upon him,
and he will proclaim justice to the Gentiles.
19† He will not contend or cry out,
nor will anyone hear his voice in the streets.
20 A bruised reed he will not break,
a smoldering wick he will not quench,
until he brings justice to victory.
21† And in his name the Gentiles will hope."

Jesus and Beelzebul.† 22* Then they
brought to him a demoniac who was
blind and mute. He cured the mute per-
son so that he could speak and see.
23*† All the crowd was astounded, and
said, "Could this perhaps be the Son of
David?" 24*† But when the Pharisees
heard this, they said, "This man drives
out demons only by the power of Beelze-
bul, the prince of demons." 25*† But he
knew what they were thinking and said
to them, "Every kingdom divided
against itself will be laid waste, and no
town or house divided against itself will
stand. 26 And if Satan drives out Satan,
he is divided against himself; how, then,
will his kingdom stand? 27† And if I
drive out demons by Beelzebul, by
whom do your own people drive them
out? Therefore they will be your judges.
28*† But if it is by the Spirit of God that
I drive out demons, then the kingdom
of God has come upon you. 29† How can
anyone enter a strong man's house and
steal his property, unless he first ties up
the strong man? Then he can plunder
his house. 30*† Whoever is not with me
is against me, and whoever does not
gather with me scatters. 31*† Therefore,
I say to you, every sin and blasphemy
will be forgiven people, but blasphemy
against the Spirit will not be forgiven.
32 And whoever speaks a word against
the Son of Man will be forgiven; but

MATTHEW

*

9-15: Mk 3, 1-6; Lk 6, 6-11.
14: Jn 5, 18.
18-21: Is 42, 1-4.
22-24: 9, 32-34; Lk 11, 14-15.
23: 9, 27.
24: 10, 25; Mk 3, 22.
25-29: Mk 3, 23-27; Lk 11, 17-22.
28: Lk 11, 20.
30: Lk 11, 23.
31-32: Mk 3, 28-30; Lk 12, 10.

†

12, 10: Rabbinic tradition later than the gospels allowed relief to be given to a sufferer on the sabbath if life was in danger. This may also have been the view of Jesus' Pharisaic contemporaries. But the case here is not about one in danger of death.

12, 11: Matthew omits the question posed by Jesus in Mk 3, 4 and substitutes one about rescuing a sheep on the sabbath, similar to that in Lk 14, 5.

12, 14: See Mk 3, 6. Here the plan to bring about Jesus' death is attributed to the Pharisees only. This is probably due to the situation of Matthew's church, when the sole opponents were the Pharisees.

12, 15-21: Matthew follows Mk 3, 7-12 but summarizes his source in two verses (15.16) that pick up the withdrawal, the healings, and the command for silence. To this he adds a fulfillment citation from the first Servant Song (Is 42, 1-4) that does not correspond exactly to either the Hebrew or the LXX of that passage. It is the longest Old Testament citation in this gospel, emphasizing the meekness of Jesus, the Servant of the Lord, and foretelling the extension of his mission to the Gentiles.

12, 15: Jesus' knowledge of the Pharisees' plot and his healing *all* are peculiar to Matthew.

12, 19: The servant's not contending is seen as fulfilled in Jesus' withdrawal from the disputes narrated in 1-14.

12, 21: Except for a minor detail, Matthew here follows the LXX, although the meaning of the Hebrew ("the coastlands will wait for his teaching") is similar.

12, 22-32: For the exorcism, see the note on 9, 32-34. The long discussion combines Marcan and Q material (Mk 3, 22-30; Lk 11, 19-20.23; 12, 10). Mk 3, 20-21 is omitted, with a consequent lessening of the sharpness of 12, 48.

12, 23: See the note on 9, 27.

12, 24: See the note on 10, 25.

12, 25-26: Jesus' first response to the Pharisees' charge is that if it were true, Satan would be destroying his own kingdom.

12, 27: Besides pointing out the absurdity of the charge, Jesus asks how the work of Jewish exorcists (*your own people*) is to be interpreted. Are they, too, to be charged with collusion with Beelzebul? For an example of Jewish exorcism see Josephus, *Antiquities* 8, 2, 5 §§42-49.

12, 28: The Q parallel (Lk 11, 20) speaks of the "finger" rather than of the "spirit" of God. While the difference is probably due to Matthew's editing, he retains *the kingdom of God* rather than changing it to his usual "kingdom of heaven." *Has come upon you:* see 4, 17.

12, 29: A short parable illustrates what Jesus is doing. The *strong man* is Satan, whom Jesus has tied up and whose *house* he is plundering. Jewish expectation was that Satan would be chained up in the last days (Rv 20, 2); Jesus' exorcisms indicate that those days have begun.

12, 30: This saying, already attached to the preceding verses in Q (see Lk 11, 23), warns that there can be no neutrality where Jesus is concerned. Its pertinence in a context where Jesus is addressing not the neutral but the bitterly opposed is not clear. The accusation of scattering, however, does fit the situation. Jesus is the shepherd of God's people (2, 6), his mission is to the lost sheep of Israel (15, 24); the Pharisees, who oppose him, are guilty of scattering the sheep.

12, 31: *Blasphemy against the Spirit:* the sin of attributing to Satan (24) what is the work of the Spirit of God (28).

MATTHEW

whoever speaks against the holy Spirit
will not be forgiven, either in this age
or in the age to come.

A Tree and Its Fruits. 33*† "Either
declare the tree good and its fruit is
good, or declare the tree rotten and its
fruit is rotten, for a tree is known by
its fruit. 34*† You brood of vipers, how
can you say good things when you are
evil? For from the fullness of the heart
the mouth speaks. 35 A good person
brings forth good out of a store of good-
ness, but an evil person brings forth evil
out of a store of evil. 36*† I tell you, on
the day of judgment people will render
an account for every careless word they
speak. 37 By your words you will be ac-
quitted, and by your words you will be
condemned."

The Demand for a Sign.† 38*† Then
some of the scribes and Pharisees said
to him, "Teacher, we wish to see a sign
from you." 39† He said to them in reply,
"An evil and unfaithful generation
seeks a sign, but no sign will be given
it except the sign of Jonah the prophet.
40† Just as Jonah was in the belly of the
whale three days and three nights, so
will the Son of Man be in the heart of
the earth three days and three nights.
41† At the judgment, the men of Nineveh
will arise with this generation and con-
demn it, because they repented at the
preaching of Jonah; and there is some-
thing greater than Jonah here. 42* At
the judgment the queen of the south will
arise with this generation and condemn
it, because she came from the ends of
the earth to hear the wisdom of Solo-
mon; and there is something greater
than Solomon here.

The Return of the Unclean Spirit.†
43* "When an unclean spirit goes out of
a person it roams through arid regions
searching for rest but finds none.
44 Then it says, 'I will return to my home
from which I came.' But upon return-
ing, it finds it empty, swept clean, and
put in order. 45 Then it goes and brings
back with itself seven other spirits more
evil than itself, and they move in and
dwell there; and the last condition of
that person is worse than the first. Thus
it will be with this evil generation."

The True Family of Jesus.† 46* While
he was still speaking to the crowds, his
mother and his brothers appeared out-
side, wishing to speak with him.
[47† Someone told him, "Your mother
and your brothers are standing outside,
asking to speak with you."] 48 But he
said in reply to the one who told him,
"Who is my mother? Who are my broth-
ers?" 49 And stretching out his hand to-
ward his disciples, he said, "Here are
my mother and my brothers. 50 For
whoever does the will of my heavenly
Father is my brother, and sister, and
mother."

CHAPTER 13

The Parable of the Sower.† 1* On that
day, Jesus went out of the house and
sat down by the sea. 2 Such large crowds
gathered around him that he got into a
boat and sat down, and the whole crowd

*

33-35: Lk 6, 43-45.
34: 3, 7; 23, 33; 15, 11-12; Lk 3, 7.
36-37: Jas 3, 1-2.
38-42: 16, 1-4; Jon 2, 1; 3, 1-10; Mk 8, 11-12; Lk 11, 29-32.
42: 1 Kgs 10, 1-10.
43-45: Lk 11, 24-26.
46-50: Mk 3, 31-35; Lk 8, 19-21.
13, 1-15: Mk 4, 1-12; Lk 8, 4-10.

†

12, 33: *Declare:* literally, "make." The meaning of this verse is obscure. Possibly it is a challenge to the Pharisees either to declare Jesus and his exorcisms good or both of them bad. A tree is known by its fruit; if the fruit is good, so must the tree be. If the driving out of demons is good, so must its source be.

12, 34: The admission of Jesus' goodness cannot be made by the Pharisees, for they are evil, and the words that proceed from their evil hearts cannot be good.

12, 36-37: If on the day of judgment people will be held accountable for even their *careless* words, the vicious accusations of the Pharisees will surely lead to their condemnation.

12, 38-42: This section is mainly from Q (see Lk 11, 29-32). Mk 8, 11-12, which Matthew has followed in 16, 1-4, has a similar demand for a sign. The scribes and Pharisees refuse to accept the exorcisms of Jesus as authentication of his claims and demand a sign that will end all possibility of doubt. Jesus' response is that no such sign will be given. Because his opponents are evil and see him as an agent of Satan, nothing will convince them.

12, 38: *Teacher:* see the note on 8, 19. In 16, 1 the request is for a sign "from heaven" (Mk 8, 11).

12, 39: *Unfaithful:* literally, "adulterous." The covenant between God and Israel was portrayed as a marriage bond, and unfaithfulness to the covenant as adultery; cf Hos 2, 4-15; Jer 3, 6-10.

12, 40: See Jon 2, 1. While in Q the sign was simply Jonah's preaching to the Ninevites (Lk 11, 30.32), Matthew here adds Jonah's sojourn *in the belly of the whale* for *three days and three nights,* a prefigurement of Jesus' sojourn in the abode of the dead and, implicitly, of his resurrection.

12, 41-42: The Ninevites who *repented* (see Jon 3, 1-10) and *the queen of the south* (i.e., of Sheba; see 1 Kgs 10, 1-13) were pagans who responded to lesser opportunities than have been offered to Israel in the ministry of Jesus, *something greater than Jonah* or *Solomon.* At the final judgment they will condemn the faithless *generation* that has rejected him.

12, 43-45: Another Q passage; cf 11, 24-26. Jesus' ministry has broken Satan's hold over Israel, but the refusal of *this evil generation* to accept him will lead to a worse situation than what preceded his coming.

12, 46-50: See Mk 3, 31-35. Matthew has omitted Mk 3, 20-21, which is taken up in Mk 3, 31 (see the note on 12, 22-32), yet the point of the story is the same in both gospels: natural kinship with Jesus counts for nothing; only one who *does the will of* his *heavenly Father* belongs to his true family.

12, 47: This verse is omitted in some important textual witnesses, including Codex Sinaiticus (original reading) and Codex Vaticanus.

13, 1-53: The discourse in parables is the third great discourse of Jesus in Mt and constitutes the second part of the third book of the gospel. Matthew follows the Marcan outline (Mk 4, 1-35) but has only two of Mark's parables, the five others being from Q and M. In addition to the seven parables, the discourse gives the reason why Jesus uses this type of speech (10-15), declares the blessedness of those who understand his teaching (16-17), explains the parable of the sower (18-23) and of the weeds (36-43), and ends with a concluding statement to the disciples (51-52).

stood along the shore. 3† And he spoke
to them at length in parables, saying:
"A sower went out to sow. 4 And as he
sowed, some seed fell on the path, and
birds came and ate it up. 5 Some fell on
rocky ground, where it had little soil.
It sprang up at once because the soil
was not deep, 6 and when the sun rose
it was scorched, and it withered for lack
of roots. 7 Some seed fell among thorns,
and the thorns grew up and choked it.
8 But some seed fell on rich soil, and
produced fruit, a hundred or sixty or
thirtyfold. 9 Whoever has ears ought to
hear."

The Purpose of Parables. 10 The disci-
ples approached him and said, "Why do
you speak to them in parables?" 11† He
said to them in reply, "Because knowl-
edge of the mysteries of the kingdom
of heaven has been granted to you, but
to them it has not been granted. 12*† To
anyone who has, more will be given and
he will grow rich; from anyone who has
not, even what he has will be taken
away. 13*† This is why I speak to them
in parables, because 'they look but do
not see and hear but do not listen or
understand.' 14* Isaiah's prophecy is
fulfilled in them, which says:

'You shall indeed hear but not un-
derstand,
you shall indeed look but never
see.
15 Gross is the heart of this people,
they will hardly hear with their
ears,
they have closed their eyes,
lest they see with their eyes
and hear with their ears
and understand with their heart
and be converted,
and I heal them.'

The Privilege of Discipleship.†
16* "But blessed are your eyes, because
they see, and your ears, because they
hear. 17 Amen, I say to you, many
prophets and righteous people longed
to see what you see but did not see it,
and to hear what you hear but did not
hear it.

***The Explanation of the Parable of the
Sower.***† 18* "Hear then the parable of
the sower. 19 The seed sown on the path
is the one who hears the word of the
kingdom without understanding it, and
the evil one comes and steals away what
was sown in his heart. 20 The seed sown
on rocky ground is the one who hears
the word and receives it at once with
joy. 21 But he has no root and lasts only
for a time. When some tribulation or
persecution comes because of the word,
he immediately falls away. 22 The seed
sown among thorns is the one who hears
the word, but then worldly anxiety and

*

12: 25, 29; Mk 4, 25; Lk 8, 18; 19, 26.
13: Jn 9, 39.
14-15: Is 6, 9-10; Jn 12, 40; Acts 28, 26-27; Rom 11, 8.
16-17: Lk 10, 23-24; 1 Pt 1, 10-12.
18-23: Mk 4, 13-20; Lk 8, 11-15.

†

13, 3: *In parables:* the word "parable" (Greek *parabolē*) is used in the LXX to translate the Hebrew *māshāl*, a designation covering a wide variety of literary forms such as axioms, proverbs, similitudes, and allegories. In the New Testament the same breadth of meaning of the word is found, but there it primarily designates stories that are illustrative comparisons between Christian truths and events of everyday life. Sometimes the event has a strange element that is quite different from usual experience (e.g., in v 33, the enormous amount of dough in the parable of the yeast); this is meant to sharpen the curiosity of the hearer. If each detail of such a story is given a figurative meaning, the story is an allegory. Those who maintain a sharp distinction between parable and allegory insist that a parable has only one point of comparison, and that while parables were characteristic of Jesus' teaching, to see allegorical details in them is to introduce meanings that go beyond their original intention and even falsify it. However, to exclude any allegorical elements from a parable is an excessively rigid mode of interpretation, now abandoned by many scholars.

13, 3-8: Since in Palestine sowing often preceded ploughing, much of the seed is scattered on ground that is unsuitable. Yet while much is wasted, the seed that falls on good ground bears fruit in extraordinarily large measure. The point of the parable is that, in spite of some failure because of opposition and indifference, the message of Jesus about the coming of the kingdom will have enormous success.

13, 11: Since a parable is figurative speech that demands reflection for understanding, only those who are prepared to explore its meaning can come to know it. To understand is a gift of God, granted to the disciples but not to the crowds. In Semitic fashion, both the disciples' understanding and the crowd's obtuseness are attributed to God. The question of human responsibility for the obtuseness is not dealt with, although it is asserted in v 13. *The mysteries:* as in Lk 8, 10; Mk 4, 11 has "the mystery." The word is used in Dn 2, 18.19.27 and in the Qumran literature (1QpHab 7, 8; 1QS 3, 23; 1QM 3, 9) to designate a divine plan or decree affecting the course of history that can be known only when revealed. *Knowledge of the mysteries of the kingdom of heaven* means recognition that the kingdom has become present in the ministry of Jesus.

13, 12: In the New Testament use of this axiom of practical "wisdom" (see 25, 29; Mk 4, 25; Lk 8, 18; 19, 26), the reference transcends the original level. God gives further understanding to one who accepts the revealed mystery; from the one who does not, he will take it away (note the "theological passive," *more will be given, what he has will be taken away*).

13, 13: *Because 'they look . . . or understand':* Matthew softens his Marcan source, which states that Jesus speaks in parables so that the crowds may not understand (Mk 4, 12), and makes such speaking a punishment given *because* they have not accepted his previous clear teaching. However, his citation of Is 6, 9-10 in v 14 supports the harsher Marcan view.

13, 16-17: Unlike the unbelieving crowds, the disciples have seen that which the *prophets* and the *righteous* of the Old Testament *longed to see* without having their longing fulfilled.

13, 18-23: See Mk 4, 14-20; Lk 8, 11-15. In this explanation of the parable the emphasis is on the various types of soil on which the seed falls, i.e., on the dispositions with which the preaching of Jesus is received. The second and third types particularly are explained in such a way as to support the view held by many scholars that the explanation derives not from Jesus but from early Christian reflection upon apostasy from the faith that was the consequence of persecution and worldliness respectively. Others, however, hold that the explanation may come basically from Jesus even though it was developed in the light of later Christian experience. The four types of persons envisaged are (1) those who never accept *the word of the kingdom* (19); (2) those who believe for a while but fall away because of *persecution* (20-21); (3) those who believe, but in whom *the word* is choked by *worldly anxiety* and the seduction of *riches* (22); (4) those who respond to *the word* and produce *fruit* abundantly (23).

the lure of riches choke the word and
it bears no fruit. 23 But the seed sown
on rich soil is the one who hears the
word and understands it, who indeed
bears fruit and yields a hundred or sixty
or thirtyfold."

***The Parable of the Weeds among the Wheat.*†** 24 He proposed another para-
ble to them. "The kingdom of heaven
may be likened to a man who sowed
good seed in his field. 25† While every-
one was asleep his enemy came and
sowed weeds all through the wheat, and
then went off. 26 When the crop grew
and bore fruit, the weeds appeared as
well. 27 The slaves of the householder
came to him and said, 'Master, did you
not sow good seed in your field? Where
have the weeds come from?' 28 He an-
swered, 'An enemy has done this.' His
slaves said to him, 'Do you want us to
go and pull them up?' 29 He replied, 'No,
if you pull up the weeds you might up-
root the wheat along with them. 30*† Let
them grow together until harvest; then
at harvest time I will say to the harvest-
ers, "First collect the weeds and tie
them in bundles for burning; but gather
the wheat into my barn." ' "

***The Parable of the Mustard Seed.*†**
31* He proposed another parable to
them. "The kingdom of heaven is like
a mustard seed that a person took and
sowed in a field. 32*† It is the smallest
of all the seeds, yet when full-grown it
is the largest of plants. It becomes a
large bush, and the 'birds of the sky
come and dwell in its branches.' "

The Parable of the Yeast. 33*† He
spoke to them another parable. "The
kingdom of heaven is like yeast that a
woman took and mixed with three mea-
sures of wheat flour until the whole
batch was leavened."

The Use of Parables. 34*† All these
things Jesus spoke to the crowds in
parables. He spoke to them only in par-
ables, 35*† to fulfill what had been said
through the prophet:

"I will open my mouth in parables,
I will announce what has lain hid-
den from the foundation
[of the world]."

The Explanation of the Parable of the Weeds. 36† Then, dismissing the
crowds, he went into the house. His dis-
ciples approached him and said, "Ex-
plain to us the parable of the weeds in
the field." 37† He said in reply, "He who
sows good seed is the Son of Man,
38† the field is the world, the good seed
the children of the kingdom. The weeds
are the children of the evil one, 39† and
the enemy who sows them is the devil.
The harvest is the end of the age, and
the harvesters are angels. 40 Just as
weeds are collected and burned [up]
with fire, so will it be at the end of the
age. 41† The Son of Man will send his
angels, and they will collect out of his
kingdom all who cause others to sin and
all evildoers. 42* They will throw them
into the fiery furnace, where there will
be wailing and grinding of teeth.
43*† Then the righteous will shine
like the sun in the kingdom of their
Father. Whoever has ears ought to
hear.

*

30: 3, 12.
31-32: Mk 4, 30-32; Lk 13, 18-19.
32: Ez 17, 23; 31, 6; Dn 4, 7-9.17-19.
33: Lk 13, 20-21.
34-35: Mk 4, 33-34.
35: Ps 78, 2.
42: 8, 12; Rv 21, 8.
43: Dn 12, 3.

†

13, 24-30: This parable is peculiar to Matthew. The comparison in v 24 does not mean that *the kingdom of heaven may be likened* simply to the person in question but to the situation narrated in the whole story. The refusal of *the householder* to allow his *slaves* to separate *the wheat* from *the weeds* while they are still growing is a warning to the disciples not to attempt to anticipate the final judgment of God by a definitive exclusion of sinners from the kingdom. In its present stage it is composed of the good and the bad. The judgment of God alone will eliminate the sinful. Until then there must be patience and the preaching of repentance.

13, 25: *Weeds:* darnel, a poisonous weed that in its first stage of growth resembles wheat.

13, 30: *Harvest:* a common biblical metaphor for the time of God's judgment; cf Jer 51, 33; Jl 4, 13; Hos 6, 11.

13, 31-33: See Mk 4, 30-32; Lk 13, 18-21. The parables of the mustard seed and the yeast illustrate the same point: the amazing contrast between the small beginnings of the kingdom and its marvelous expansion.

13, 32: See Dn 4, 7-9.17-19, where the birds nesting in the tree represent the people of Nebuchadnezzar's kingdom. See also Ez 17, 23 and 31, 6.

13, 33: Except in this Q parable and in 16, 12, *yeast* (or "leaven") is, in New Testament usage, a symbol of corruption (see 16, 6.11-12; Mk 8, 15; Lk 12, 1; 1 Cor 5, 6-8; Gal 5, 9). *Three measures:* an enormous amount, enough to feed a hundred people. The exaggeration of this element of the parable points to the greatness of the kingdom's effect.

13, 34: *Only in parables:* see vv 10-15.

13, 35: *The prophet:* some textual witnesses read "Isaiah the prophet." The quotation is actually from Ps 78, 2; the first line corresponds to the LXX text of the psalm. The psalm's title ascribes it to Asaph, the founder of one of the guilds of temple musicians. He is called "the prophet" (NAB "the seer") in 2 Chr 29, 30, but it is doubtful that Matthew averted to that; for him, any Old Testament text that could be seen as fulfilled in Jesus was prophetic.

13, 36: *Dismissing the crowds:* the return of Jesus to the house marks a break with the crowds, who represent unbelieving Israel. From now on his attention is directed more and more to his disciples and to their instruction. The rest of the discourse is addressed to them alone.

13, 37-43: In the explanation of the parable of the weeds emphasis lies on the fearful end of the wicked, whereas the parable itself concentrates on patience with them until judgment time.

13, 38: *The field is the world:* this presupposes the resurrection of Jesus and the granting to him of "all power in heaven and on earth" (28, 18).

13, 39: *The end of the age:* this phrase is found only in Mt (13, 40.49; 24, 3; 28, 20).

13, 41: *His kingdom:* the *kingdom* of *the Son of Man* is distinguished from that of the Father (43); see 1 Cor 15, 24-25. The church is the place where Jesus' kingdom is manifested, but his royal authority embraces the entire world; see the note on 13, 38.

13, 43: See Dn 12, 3.

More Parables.† 44*† "The kingdom of heaven is like a treasure buried in a field, which a person finds and hides again, and out of joy goes and sells all that he has and buys that field. 45 Again, the kingdom of heaven is like a merchant searching for fine pearls. 46 When he finds a pearl of great price, he goes and sells all that he has and buys it. 47 Again, the kingdom of heaven is like a net thrown into the sea, which collects fish of every kind. 48 When it is full they haul it ashore and sit down to put what is good into buckets. What is bad they throw away. 49 Thus it will be at the end of the age. The angels will go out and separate the wicked from the righteous 50 and throw them into the fiery furnace, where there will be wailing and grinding of teeth.

Treasures New and Old. 51† "Do you understand all these things?" They answered, "Yes." 52† And he replied, "Then every scribe who has been instructed in the kingdom of heaven is like the head of a household who brings from his storeroom both the new and the old." 53 When Jesus finished these parables, he went away from there.

V: JESUS, THE KINGDOM, AND THE CHURCH

The Rejection at Nazareth.† 54*† He came to his native place and taught the people in their synagogue. They were astonished and said, "Where did this man get such wisdom and mighty deeds? 55* Is he not the carpenter's son? Is not his mother named Mary and his brothers James, Joseph, Simon, and Judas? 56 Are not his sisters all with us? Where did this man get all this?" 57* And they took offense at him. But Jesus said to them, "A prophet is not without honor except in his native place and in his own house." 58 And he did not work many mighty deeds there because of their lack of faith.

CHAPTER 14

Herod's Opinion of Jesus.† 1*† At that time Herod the tetrarch heard of the reputation of Jesus 2 and said to his servants, "This man is John the Baptist. He has been raised from the dead; that is why mighty powers are at work in him."

The Death of John the Baptist. 3*† Now Herod had arrested John, bound [him], and put him in prison on account of Herodias, the wife of his brother Philip, 4* for John had said to him, "It is not lawful for you to have her." 5* Although he wanted to kill him,

---

*

44-45: Prv 2, 4; 4, 7.
54-58: Mk 6, 1-6; Lk 4, 16-30.
54: 2, 23; Jn 1, 46; 7, 15.
55: 12, 46; 27, 56; Jn 6, 42.
57: Jn 4, 44.
14, 1-12: Mk 6, 14-29.
1: Lk 3, 1.
1-2: Lk 9, 7-9.
3-4: Lk 3, 19-20.
4: Lv 18, 16; 20, 21.
5: 21, 26.

---

†

13, 44-50: The first two of the last three parables of the discourse have the same point. The *person* who *finds* a buried *treasure* and the *merchant* who finds a *pearl of great price* sell *all* that they have to acquire these finds; similarly, the one who understands the supreme value of the kingdom gives up whatever he must to obtain it. The *joy* with which this is done is made explicit in the first parable, but it may be presumed in the second also. The concluding parable of the fishnet resembles the explanation of the parable of the weeds with its stress upon the final exclusion of evil persons from the kingdom.

13, 44: In the unsettled conditions of Palestine in Jesus' time, it was not unusual to guard valuables by burying them in the ground.

13, 51: Matthew typically speaks of the understanding of the disciples.

13, 52: Since Matthew tends to identify the disciples and the Twelve (see the note on 10, 1), this saying about the Christian *scribe* cannot be taken as applicable to all who accept the message of Jesus. While the Twelve are in many ways representative of all who believe in him, they are also distinguished from them in certain respects. The church of Matthew has leaders among whom are a group designated as "scribes" (23, 34). Like the scribes of Israel, they are teachers. It is the Twelve and these their later counterparts to whom this verse applies. The *scribe . . . instructed in the kingdom of heaven* knows both the teaching of Jesus (*the new*) and the law and prophets (*the old*) and provides in his own teaching *both the new and the old* as interpreted and fulfilled by *the new*. On the translation *head of a household* (for the same Greek word translated *householder* in v 27), see the note on 24, 45-51.

13, 54—17, 27: This section is the narrative part of the fourth book of the gospel.

13, 54-58: After the Sermon on the Mount the crowds are in admiring astonishment at Jesus' teaching (7, 28); here the astonishment is of those who take *offense at him.* Familiarity with his background and family leads them to regard him as pretentious. Matthew modifies his Marcan source (6, 1-6). Jesus is not the carpenter but *the carpenter's son* (55), "and among his own kin" is omitted (57), *he did not work many mighty deeds* in face of such unbelief (58) rather than the Marcan ". . . he was not able to perform any mighty deed there" (6, 5), and there is no mention of his amazement at his townspeople's lack of faith.

14, 1-12: The murder of the Baptist by Herod Antipas prefigures the death of Jesus (see 17, 12). The Marcan source (6, 14-29) is much reduced and in some points changed. In Mk Herod reveres John as a holy man and the desire to kill him is attributed to Herodias (6, 19.20), whereas here that desire is Herod's from the beginning (5).

14, 1: *Herod the tetrarch:* Herod Antipas, son of Herod the Great. When the latter died, his territory was divided among three of his surviving sons, Archelaus who received half of it (2, 23), Herod Antipas who became ruler of Galilee and Perea, and Philip who became ruler of northern Transjordan. Since he received a quarter of his father's domain, Antipas is accurately designated *tetrarch* ("ruler of a fourth [part]"), although in v 9 Matthew repeats the "king" of his Marcan source (6, 26).

14, 3: Herodias was not the wife of Herod's half-brother Philip but of another half-brother, Herod Boethus. The union was prohibited by Lv 18, 16; 20, 21. According to Josephus (*Antiquities* 18, 5, 2 §§116-19), Herod imprisoned and then executed John because he feared that the Baptist's influence over the people might enable him to lead a rebellion.

he feared the people, for they regarded him as a prophet. 6 But at a birthday celebration for Herod, the daughter of Herodias performed a dance before the guests and delighted Herod 7 so much that he swore to give her whatever she might ask for. 8 Prompted by her mother, she said, "Give me here on a platter the head of John the Baptist." 9 The king was distressed, but because of his oaths and the guests who were present, he ordered that it be given, 10 and he had John beheaded in the prison. 11 His head was brought in on a platter and given to the girl, who took it to her mother. 12 His disciples came and took away the corpse and buried him; and they went and told Jesus.

The Return of the Twelve and the Feeding of the Five Thousand.† 13* When Jesus heard of it, he withdrew in a boat to a deserted place by himself. The crowds heard of this and followed him on foot from their towns. 14 When he disembarked and saw the vast crowd, his heart was moved with pity for them, and he cured their sick. 15 When it was evening, the disciples approached him and said, "This is a deserted place and it is already late; dismiss the crowds so that they can go to the villages and buy food for themselves." 16 [Jesus] said to them, "There is no need for them to go away; give them some food yourselves." 17 But they said to him, "Five loaves and two fish are all we have here." 18 Then he said, "Bring them here to me," 19† and he ordered the crowds to sit down on the grass. Taking the five loaves and the two fish, and looking up to heaven, he said the blessing, broke the loaves, and gave them to the disciples, who in turn gave them to the crowds. 20† They all ate and were satisfied, and they picked up the fragments left over—twelve wicker baskets full. 21 Those who ate were about five thousand men, not counting women and children.

The Walking on the Water.† 22* Then he made the disciples get into the boat and precede him to the other side, while he dismissed the crowds. 23* After doing so, he went up on the mountain by himself to pray. When it was evening he was there alone. 24 Meanwhile the boat, already a few miles offshore, was being tossed about by the waves, for the wind was against it. 25† During the fourth watch of the night, he came toward them, walking on the sea. 26 When the disciples saw him walking on the sea they were terrified. "It is a ghost," they said, and they cried out in fear. 27 At once [Jesus] spoke to them, "Take courage, it is I; do not be afraid." 28 Peter said to him in reply, "Lord, if it is you, command me to come to you on the water." 29 He said, "Come." Peter got out of the boat and began to walk on the water toward Jesus. 30* But when he saw how [strong] the wind was he became frightened; and, beginning to sink, he cried out, "Lord, save me!" 31† Immediately Jesus stretched out his hand and caught him, and said to him, "O you of little faith, why did you doubt?" 32 After they got into the boat, the wind died down. 33*† Those who were in the boat did him homage, saying, "Truly, you are the Son of God."

The Healings at Gennesaret. 34* After making the crossing, they came to land at Gennesaret. 35 When the men of that place recognized him, they sent word to all the surrounding country. People brought to him all those who were sick 36* and begged him that they might touch only the tassel on his cloak, and as many as touched it were healed.

---

*

13-21: 15, 32-38; Mk 6, 32-44; Lk 9, 10-17; Jn 6, 1-13.
22-33: Mk 6, 45-52; Jn 6, 16-21.
23: Mk 1, 35; Lk 5, 16; 6, 12.
30-31: 8, 25-26.
33: 16, 16.
34-36: Mk 6, 53-56.
36: 9, 20-22.

---

†

14, 13-21: The feeding of the five thousand is the only miracle of Jesus that is recounted in all four gospels. The principal reason for that may be that it was seen as anticipating the Eucharist and the final banquet in the kingdom (8, 11; 26, 29), but it looks not only forward but backward, to the feeding of Israel with manna in the desert at the time of the Exodus (Ex 16), a miracle that in some contemporary Jewish expectation would be repeated in the messianic age (2 Baruch 29, 8). It may also be meant to recall Elisha's feeding a hundred men with small provisions (2 Kgs 4, 42-44).

14, 19: The *taking,* saying the blessing, breaking, and giving to the disciples correspond to the actions of Jesus over the bread at the Last Supper (26, 26). Since they were usual at any Jewish meal, that correspondence does not necessarily indicate a eucharistic reference here. Matthew's silence about Jesus' dividing the fish among the people (Mk 6, 41) is perhaps more significant in that regard.

14, 20: *The fragments left over:* as in Elisha's miracle, food was *left over* after all had been fed. The word *fragments* (Greek *klasmata*) is used, in the singular, of the broken bread of the Eucharist in *Didache* 9, 3-4.

14, 22-33: The disciples, laboring against the turbulent sea, are saved by Jesus. For his power over the waters, see the note on 8, 26. Here that power is expressed also by his *walking on the sea* (25; cf Ps 77, 20; Jb 9, 8). Matthew has inserted into the Marcan story (Mk 6, 45-52) material that belongs to his special traditions on Peter (28-31).

14, 25: *The fourth watch of the night:* between 3 a.m. and 6 a.m. The Romans divided the twelve hours between 6 p.m. and 6 a.m. into four equal parts called "watches."

14, 27: *It is I:* see the note on Mk 6, 50.

14, 31: *You of little faith:* see the note on 6, 30. *Why did you doubt?:* the verb is peculiar to Matthew and occurs elsewhere only in 28, 17.

14, 33: This confession is in striking contrast to the Marcan parallel (6, 51) where the disciples are "completely astounded."

CHAPTER 15

***The Tradition of the Elders.*†** 1* Then
Pharisees and scribes came to Jesus
from Jerusalem and said, 2*† "Why do
your disciples break the tradition of the
elders? They do not wash [their] hands
when they eat a meal." 3† He said to
them in reply, "And why do you break
the commandment of God for the sake
of your tradition? 4* For God said,
'Honor your father and your mother,'
and 'Whoever curses father or mother
shall die.' 5† But you say, 'Whoever says
to father or mother, "Any support you
might have had from me is dedicated
to God," 6 need not honor his father.'
You have nullified the word of God for
the sake of your tradition. 7 Hypocrites,
well did Isaiah prophesy about you
when he said:

8*† 'This people honors me with their
lips,
but their hearts are far from me;
9* in vain do they worship me,
teaching as doctrines human pre-
cepts.'"

10* He summoned the crowd and said
to them, "Hear and understand. 11 It is
not what enters one's mouth that defiles
that person; but what comes out of the
mouth is what defiles one." 12 Then his
disciples approached and said to him,
"Do you know that the Pharisees took
offense when they heard what you
said?" 13† He said in reply, "Every plant
that my heavenly Father has not
planted will be uprooted. 14* Let them
alone; they are blind guides [of the
blind]. If a blind person leads a blind
person, both will fall into a pit." 15† Then
Peter said to him in reply, "Explain
[this] parable to us." 16 He said to them,
"Are even you still without understand-
ing? 17 Do you not realize that every-
thing that enters the mouth passes into
the stomach and is expelled into the la-
trine? 18* But the things that come out
of the mouth come from the heart, and
they defile. 19† For from the heart come
evil thoughts, murder, adultery, un-
chastity, theft, false witness, blas-
phemy. 20 These are what defile a
person, but to eat with unwashed hands
does not defile."

***The Canaanite Woman's Faith.*†**
21* Then Jesus went from that place and
withdrew to the region of Tyre and Si-
don. 22 And behold, a Canaanite woman
of that district came and called out,
"Have pity on me, Lord, Son of David!
My daughter is tormented by a demon."
23 But he did not say a word in answer
to her. His disciples came and asked
him, "Send her away, for she keeps
calling out after us." 24† He said in re-
ply, "I was sent only to the lost sheep
of the house of Israel." 25* But the
woman came and did him homage, say-
ing, "Lord, help me." 26† He said in re-
ply, "It is not right to take the food of
the children and throw it to the dogs."
27 She said, "Please, Lord, for even the
dogs eat the scraps that fall from the
table of their masters." 28*† Then Jesus
said to her in reply, "O woman, great
is your faith! Let it be done for you as
you wish." And her daughter was
healed from that hour.

*

15, 1-20: Mk 7, 1-23.
2: Lk 11, 38.
4: Ex 20, 12; 21, 17; Lv 20, 9; Dt 5, 16; Prv 20, 20.
8: Is 29, 13 LXX.
9: Col 2, 23.
10: Mk 7, 14.
14: 23, 16.19.24; Lk 6, 39; Jn 9, 40.
18: 12, 34.
21-28: Mk 7, 24-30.
25: 10, 6.
28: 8, 10.

†

15, 1-20: This dispute begins with the question of the Pharisees and scribes why Jesus' disciples are breaking *the tradition of the elders* about washing one's hands before eating (2). Jesus' counterquestion accuses his opponents of breaking *the commandment of God for the sake of* their *tradition* (3) and illustrates this by their interpretation of the commandment of the Decalogue concerning parents (4-6). Denouncing them as hypocrites, he applies to them a derogatory prophecy of Isaiah (7-8). Then with a wider audience (*the crowd,* 10) he goes beyond the violation of tradition with which the dispute has started. The parable (11) is an attack on the Mosaic law concerning clean and unclean foods, similar to those antitheses that abrogate the law (5, 31-32.33-34.38-39). After a warning to his disciples not to follow the moral guidance of the Pharisees (13-14), he explains the *parable* (15) to them, saying that defilement comes not from what *enters the mouth* (17) but from the evil thoughts and deeds that rise from within, *from the heart* (18-20). The last verse returns to the starting point of the dispute (eating *with unwashed hands*). Because of Matthew's omission of Mk 7, 19b, some scholars think that Matthew has weakened the Marcan repudiation of the Mosaic food laws. But that half verse is ambiguous in the Greek, which may be the reason for its omission here.

15, 2: *The tradition of the elders:* see the note on Mk 7, 5. The purpose of the handwashing was to remove defilement caused by contact with what was ritually unclean.

15, 3-4: For the commandment see Ex 20, 12 (// Dt 5, 16); 21, 17. The honoring of one's parents had to do with supporting them in their needs.

15, 5: See the note on Mk 7, 11.

15, 8: The text of Is 29, 13 is quoted approximately according to the Septuagint.

15, 13-14: Jesus leads his disciples away from the teaching authority of the Pharisees.

15, 15: Matthew specifies *Peter* as the questioner, unlike Mk 7, 17. Given his tendency to present the disciples as more understanding than in his Marcan source, it is noteworthy that here he retains the Marcan rebuke, although in a slightly milder form. This may be due to his wish to correct the Jewish Christians within his church who still held to the food laws and thus separated themselves from Gentile Christians who did not observe them.

15, 19: The Marcan list of thirteen things that defile (7, 21-22) is here reduced to seven that partially cover the content of the Decalogue.

15, 21-28: See the note on 8, 5-13.

15, 24: See the note on 10, 5-6.

15, 26: *The children:* the people of Israel. *Dogs:* see the note on 7, 6.

15, 28: As in the case of the cure of the centurion's servant (8, 10), Matthew ascribes Jesus' granting the request to the woman's *great faith,* a point not made equally explicit in the Marcan parallel (7, 24-30).

The Healing of Many People. 29 Moving on from there Jesus walked by the Sea of Galilee, went up on the mountain, and sat down there. 30* Great crowds came to him, having with them the lame, the blind, the deformed, the mute, and many others. They placed them at his feet, and he cured them. 31 The crowds were amazed when they saw the mute speaking, the deformed made whole, the lame walking, and the blind able to see, and they glorified the God of Israel.

The Feeding of the Four Thousand.† 32* Jesus summoned his disciples and said, "My heart is moved with pity for the crowd, for they have been with me now for three days and have nothing to eat. I do not want to send them away hungry, for fear they may collapse on the way." 33 The disciples said to him, "Where could we ever get enough bread in this deserted place to satisfy such a crowd?" 34 Jesus said to them, "How many loaves do you have?" "Seven," they replied, "and a few fish." 35 He ordered the crowd to sit down on the ground. 36† Then he took the seven loaves and the fish, gave thanks, broke the loaves, and gave them to the disciples, who in turn gave them to the crowds. 37* They all ate and were satisfied. They picked up the fragments left over—seven baskets full. 38 Those who ate were four thousand men, not counting women and children. 39 And when he had dismissed the crowds, he got into the boat and came to the district of Magadan.

CHAPTER 16

The Demand for a Sign. 1*† The Pharisees and Sadducees came and, to test him, asked him to show them a sign from heaven. 2† He said to them in reply, "[In the evening you say, 'Tomorrow will be fair, for the sky is red'; 3* and, in the morning, 'Today will be stormy, for the sky is red and threatening.' You know how to judge the appearance of the sky, but you cannot judge the signs of the times.] 4*† An evil and unfaithful generation seeks a sign, but no sign will be given it except the sign of Jonah." Then he left them and went away.

The Leaven of the Pharisees and Sadducees.† 5* In coming to the other side of the sea, the disciples had forgotten to bring bread. 6*† Jesus said to them, "Look out, and beware of the leaven of the Pharisees and Sadducees." 7† They concluded among themselves, saying, "It is because we have brought no bread." 8 When Jesus became aware of this he said, "You of little faith, why do you conclude among yourselves that it is because you have no bread? 9* Do you not yet understand, and do you not remember the five loaves for the five thousand, and how many wicker baskets you took up? 10* Or the seven loaves for the four thousand, and how many baskets you took up? 11 How do you not comprehend that I was not speaking to you about bread? Beware of the leaven of the Pharisees and Sadducees." 12† Then they understood that he was not telling them to beware of the leaven of bread, but of the teaching of the Pharisees and Sadducees.

*

30: Is 35, 5-6.
32-39: Mk 8, 1-10.
37: 16, 10.
16, 1-10: Mk 8, 11-21.
3: Lk 12, 54-56.
4: 12, 39; Jon 2, 1.
5-12: Mk 8, 14-21.
6: Lk 12, 1.
9: 14, 17-21; Jn 6, 9.
10: 15, 34-38.

†

15, 32-39: Most probably this story is a doublet of that of the feeding of the five thousand (14, 13-21). It differs from it notably only in that Jesus takes the initiative, not the disciples (32), and in the numbers: the crowd has been with Jesus *three days* (32), *seven loaves* are multiplied (36), *seven baskets* of *fragments* remain after the feeding (37), and *four thousand* men are fed (38).

15, 36: *Gave thanks:* see 14, 19, "said the blessing." There is no difference in meaning. The thanksgiving was a blessing of God for his benefits.

16, 1: *A sign from heaven:* see the note on 12, 38-42.

16, 2-3: The answer of Jesus in these verses is omitted in many important textual witnesses, and it is very uncertain that it is an original part of this gospel. It resembles Lk 12, 54-56 and may have been inserted from there. It rebukes the Pharisees and Sadducees who are able to read indications of coming weather but not the indications of the coming kingdom in the signs that Jesus does offer, his mighty deeds and teaching.

16, 4: See the notes on 12, 39.40.

16, 5-12: Jesus' warning his disciples against *the teaching of the Pharisees and Sadducees* comes immediately before his promise to confer on Peter the authority to bind and to loose on earth (19), an authority that will be confirmed in heaven. Such authority most probably has to do, at least in part, with teaching. The rejection of the teaching authority of the Pharisees (see also 12, 12-14) prepares for a new one derived from Jesus.

16, 6: *Leaven:* see the note on 13, 33. *Sadducees:* Matthew's Marcan source speaks rather of "the leaven of Herod" (8, 15).

16, 7-11: The disciples, men *of little faith,* misunderstand Jesus' metaphorical use of *leaven,* forgetting that, as the feeding of the crowds shows, he is not at a loss to provide them with bread.

16, 12: After his rebuke, the disciples understand that by *leaven* he meant the corrupting influence of *the teaching of the Pharisees and Sadducees.* The evangelist probably understands this *teaching* as common to both groups. Since at the time of Jesus' ministry the two differed widely on points of teaching, e.g., the resurrection of the dead, and at the time of the evangelist the Sadducee party was no longer a force in Judaism, the supposed common *teaching* fits neither period. The disciples' eventual understanding of Jesus' warning contrasts with their continuing obtuseness in the Marcan parallel (8, 14-21).

Peter's Confession about Jesus.†

13*† When Jesus went into the region of
Caesarea Philippi he asked his disci-
ples, "Who do people say that the Son
of Man is?" 14*† They replied, "Some
say John the Baptist, others Elijah, still
others Jeremiah or one of the proph-
ets." 15 He said to them, "But who do
you say that I am?" 16*† Simon Peter
said in reply, "You are the Messiah, the
Son of the living God." 17† Jesus said
to him in reply, "Blessed are you, Simon
son of Jonah. For flesh and blood has
not revealed this to you, but my heav-
enly Father. 18*† And so I say to you,
you are Peter, and upon this rock I will
build my church, and the gates of the
netherworld shall not prevail against it.
19*† I will give you the keys to the king-
dom of heaven. Whatever you bind on
earth shall be bound in heaven; and
whatever you loose on earth shall be
loosed in heaven." 20*† Then he strictly
ordered his disciples to tell no one that
he was the Messiah.

The First Prediction of the Passion.†

21*† From that time on, Jesus began to
show his disciples that he must go to
Jerusalem and suffer greatly from the
elders, the chief priests, and the scribes,
and be killed and on the third day be

*

13-16: Mk 8, 27-29; Lk 9, 18-20.
14: 14, 2.
16: Jn 6, 69.
18: Jn 1, 42.
19: Is 22, 22; Rv 3, 7.
20: Mk 8, 30; Lk 9, 21.
21-28: Mk 8, 31—9, 1; Lk 9, 22-27.
21: 17, 22-23; 20, 17-19.

†

16, 13-20: The Marcan confession of Jesus as Messiah, made by Peter as spokesman for the other disciples (8, 27-29; cf also Lk 9, 18-20), is modified significantly here. The confession is of Jesus both as *Messiah* and as *Son of the living God* (16). Jesus' response, drawn principally from material peculiar to Matthew, attributes the confession to a divine revelation granted to Peter alone (17) and makes him the *rock* on which Jesus *will build* his *church* (18) and the disciple whose authority in the church *on earth* will be confirmed *in heaven*, i.e., by God (19).

16, 13: *Caesarea Philippi:* situated about twenty miles north of the Sea of Galilee in the territory ruled by Philip, a son of Herod the Great, tetrarch from 4 B.C. until his death in A.D. 34 (see the note on 14, 1). He rebuilt the town of Paneas, naming it *Caesarea* in honor of the emperor, and *Philippi* ("of Philip") to distinguish it from the seaport in Samaria that was also called Caesarea. *Who do people say that the Son of Man is?:* although the question differs from the Marcan parallel (8, 27: "Who . . . that I am?"), the meaning is the same, for Jesus here refers to himself as *the Son of Man* (cf 15).

16, 14: *John the Baptist:* see 14, 2. *Elijah:* cf Mal 3, 23-24; Sir 48, 10; and see the note on 3, 4. *Jeremiah:* an addition of Matthew to the Marcan source.

16, 16: *The Son of the living God:* see 2, 15; 3, 17. The addition of this exalted title to the Marcan confession eliminates whatever ambiguity was attached to the title Messiah. This, among other things, supports the view proposed by many scholars that Matthew has here combined his source's confession with a post-resurrectional confession of faith in Jesus as *Son of the living God* that belonged to the appearance of the risen Jesus to Peter; cf 1 Cor 15, 5; Lk 24, 34.

16, 17: *Flesh and blood:* a Semitic expression for human beings, especially in their weakness. *Has not revealed this . . . but my heavenly Father:* that Peter's faith is spoken of as coming not through human means but through a revelation from God is similar to Paul's description of his recognition of who Jesus was; see Gal 1, 15-16, ". . . when he [God] . . . was pleased to reveal his Son to me. . . ."

16, 18: *You are Peter, and upon this rock I will build my church:* the Aramaic word *kēpāʾ* meaning *rock* and transliterated into Greek as *Kēphas* is the name by which Peter is called in the Pauline letters (1 Cor 1, 12; 3, 22; 9, 5; 15, 4; Gal 1, 18; 2, 9.11.14) except in Gal 2, 7-8 ("Peter"). It is translated as *Petros* ("Peter") in Jn 1, 42. The presumed original Aramaic of Jesus' statement would have been, in English, "You are the Rock *(Kēpāʾ)* and upon this rock (*kēpāʾ*) I will build my church." The Greek text probably means the same, for the difference in gender between the masculine noun *petros,* the disciple's new name, and the feminine noun *petra* (rock) may be due simply to the unsuitability of using a feminine noun as the proper name of a male. Although the two words were generally used with slightly different nuances, they were also used interchangeably with the same meaning, "rock." *Church:* this word (Greek *ekklēsia*) occurs in the gospels only here and in 18, 17 (twice). There are several possibilities for an Aramaic original. Jesus' *church* means the community that he *will* gather and that, like a building, will have Peter as its solid foundation. That function of Peter consists in his being witness to Jesus as *the Messiah, the Son of the living God. The gates of the netherworld shall not prevail against it:* the netherworld (Greek *Hadēs,* the abode of the dead) is conceived of as a walled city whose *gates* will not close in upon the church of Jesus, i.e., it will not be overcome by the power of death.

16, 19: *The keys to the kingdom of heaven:* the image of *the keys* is probably drawn from Is 22, 15-25, where Eliakim, who succeeds Shebnah as master of the palace, is given "the key of the house of David," which he authoritatively "opens" and "shuts" (22, 22). *Whatever you bind . . . loosed in heaven:* there are many instances in rabbinic literature of the binding-loosing imagery. Of the several meanings given there to the metaphor, two are of special importance here: the giving of authoritative teaching, and the lifting or imposing of the ban of excommunication. It is disputed whether the image of *the keys* and that of binding and loosing are different metaphors meaning the same thing. In any case, the promise of the keys is given to Peter alone. In 18, 18 all the disciples are given the power of binding and loosing, but the context of that verse suggests that there the power of excommunication alone is intended. That *the keys* are those to *the kingdom of heaven* and that Peter's exercise of authority in the church *on earth* will be confirmed *in heaven* show an intimate connection between, but not an identification of, the church and *the kingdom of heaven.*

16, 20: Cf Mk 8, 30. Matthew makes explicit that the prohibition has to do with speaking of Jesus as *the Messiah;* see the note on Mk 8, 27-30.

16, 21-23: This first prediction of the passion follows Mk 8, 31-33 in the main and serves as a corrective to an understanding of Jesus' messiahship as solely one of glory and triumph. By his addition of *from that time on* (21) Matthew has emphasized that Jesus' revelation of his coming suffering and death marks a new phase of the gospel. Neither this nor the two later passion predictions (17, 22-23; 20, 17-19) can be taken as sayings that, as they stand, go back to Jesus himself. However, it is probable that he foresaw that his mission would entail suffering and perhaps death, but was confident that he would ultimately be vindicated by God (see 26, 29).

16, 21: *He:* the Marcan parallel (8, 31) has "the Son of Man." Since Matthew has already designated Jesus by that title (13), its omission here is not significant. The Matthean prediction is equally about the sufferings of the Son of Man. *Must:* this necessity is part of the tradition of all the synoptics; cf Mk 8, 31; Lk 9, 21. *The elders, the chief priests, and the scribes:* see the note on Mk 8, 31. *On the third day:* so also Lk 9, 22, against the Marcan "after three days" (8, 31). Matthew's formulation is, in the Greek, almost identical with the pre-Pauline fragment of the kerygma in 1 Cor 15, 4, and also with Hos 6, 2, which many take to be the Old Testament background to the confession that Jesus was raised *on the third day.* Josephus uses "after three days" and "on the third day" interchangeably (*Antiquities* 7, 11, 6 §§280-81; 8, 8, 1-2 §§214, 218) and there is probably no difference in meaning between the two phrases.

raised. [22]† Then Peter took him aside and began to rebuke him, "God forbid, Lord! No such thing shall ever happen to you." [23]* He turned and said to Peter, "Get behind me, Satan! You are an obstacle to me. You are thinking not as God does, but as human beings do."

The Conditions of Discipleship.†
[24]*† Then Jesus said to his disciples, "Whoever wishes to come after me must deny himself, take up his cross, and follow me. [25]*† For whoever wishes to save his life will lose it, but whoever loses his life for my sake will find it. [26] What profit would there be for one to gain the whole world and forfeit his life? Or what can one give in exchange for his life? [27]*† For the Son of Man will come with his angels in his Father's glory, and then he will repay everyone according to his conduct. [28]† Amen, I say to you, there are some standing here who will not taste death until they see the Son of Man coming in his kingdom."

CHAPTER 17

The Transfiguration of Jesus.†
[1]*† After six days Jesus took Peter, James, and John his brother, and led them up a high mountain by themselves. [2]*† And he was transfigured before them; his face shone like the sun and his clothes became white as light. [3]† And behold, Moses and Elijah appeared to them, conversing with him. [4]† Then Peter said to Jesus in reply, "Lord, it is good that we are here. If you wish, I will make three tents here, one for you, one for Moses, and one for Elijah." [5]*† While he was still speaking, behold, a bright cloud cast a shadow over them, then from the cloud came a voice that said, "This is my beloved Son, with whom I am well pleased; listen to him." [6]† When the disciples heard this, they fell prostrate and were very much afraid. [7] But Jesus came and touched them, saying, "Rise, and do not be afraid." [8] And when the disciples raised their eyes, they saw no one else but Jesus alone.

The Coming of Elijah.† [9]*† As they were coming down from the mountain, Jesus charged them, "Do not tell the vision to anyone until the Son of Man has been raised from the dead." [10]*† Then

*

23: 4, 10.
24: Lk 14, 27.
25: Lk 17, 33; Jn 12, 25.
27: 25, 31-33; Jb 34, 11; Ps 62, 13; Jer 17,

10; 2 Thes 1, 7-8.
17, 1-8: Mk 9, 2-8; Lk 9, 28-36.
2: 28, 3; Dn 7, 9; 10, 6; Rv 4, 4; 7, 9; 19, 14.
5: 3, 17; Dt 18, 15; 2 Pt 1, 17.
9-13: Mk 9, 9-13.
10: Mal 3, 23-24.

†

16, 22-23: Peter's refusal to accept Jesus' predicted suffering and death is seen as a satanic attempt to deflect Jesus from his God-appointed course, and the disciple is addressed in terms that recall Jesus' dismissal of the devil in the temptation account (4, 10: "Get away, Satan!"). Peter's satanic purpose is emphasized by Matthew's addition to the Marcan source of the words *You are an obstacle to me.*

16, 24-28: A readiness to follow Jesus even to giving up one's life for him is the condition for true discipleship; this will be repaid by him at the final judgment.

16, 24: *Deny himself:* to deny someone is to disown him (see 10, 33; 26, 34-35) and to deny oneself is to disown oneself as the center of one's existence.

16, 25: See the notes on 10, 38.39.

16, 27: The parousia and final judgment are described in 25, 31 in terms almost identical with these.

16, 28: *Coming in his kingdom:* since the *kingdom* of *the Son of Man* has been described as "the world" and Jesus' sovereignty precedes his final coming in glory (13, 38.41), the *coming* in this verse is not the parousia as in the preceding but the manifestation of Jesus' rule after his resurrection; see the notes on 13, 38.41.

17, 1-8: The account of the transfiguration confirms that Jesus is the *Son* of God (5) and points to fulfillment of the prediction that he will come *in his Father's glory* at the end of the age (16, 27). It has been explained by some as a resurrection appearance retrojected into the time of Jesus' ministry, but that is not probable since the account lacks many of the usual elements of the resurrection-appearance narratives. It draws upon motifs from the Old Testament and noncanonical Jewish apocalyptic literature that express the presence of the heavenly and the divine, e.g., brilliant light, white garments, and the overshadowing cloud.

17, 1: These three disciples are also taken apart from the others by Jesus in Gethsemane (26, 37). *A high mountain:* this has been identified with Tabor or Hermon, but probably no specific mountain was intended by the evangelist or by his Marcan source (9, 2). Its meaning is theological rather than geographical, possibly recalling the revelation to Moses on Mount Sinai (Ex 24, 12-18) and to Elijah at the same place (1 Kgs 19, 8-18; Horeb = Sinai).

17, 2: *His face shone like the sun:* this is a Matthean addition; cf Dn 10, 6. *His clothes became white as light:* cf Dn 7, 9, where the clothing of God appears "snow bright." For the *white* garments of other heavenly beings, see Rv 4, 4; 7, 9; 19, 14.

17, 3: See the note on Mk 9, 5.

17, 4: *Three tents:* the booths in which the Israelites lived during the feast of Tabernacles (cf Jn 7, 2) were meant to recall their ancestors' dwelling in booths during the journey from Egypt to the promised land (Lv 23, 39-42). The same Greek word, *skēnē,* here translated *tents,* is used in the LXX for the booths of that feast, and some scholars have suggested that there is an allusion here to that liturgical custom.

17, 5: *Cloud cast a shadow over them:* see the note on Mk 9, 7. *This is my beloved Son . . . listen to him:* cf 3, 17. The voice repeats the baptismal proclamation about Jesus, with the addition of the command *listen to him.* The latter is a reference to Dt 18, 15 in which the Israelites are commanded to *listen to* the prophet like Moses whom God will raise up for them. The command to *listen to* Jesus is general, but in this context it probably applies particularly to the preceding predictions of his passion and resurrection (16, 21) and of his coming (16, 27.28).

17, 6-7: A Matthean addition; cf Dn 10, 9-10.18-19.

17, 9-13: In response to the disciples' question about the expected return of Elijah, Jesus interprets the mission of the Baptist as the fulfillment of that expectation. But that was not suspected by those who opposed and finally killed him, and Jesus predicts a similar fate for himself.

17, 9: *The vision:* Matthew alone uses this word to describe the transfiguration. *Until the Son of Man has been raised from the dead:* only in the light of Jesus' resurrection can the meaning of his life and mission be truly understood; until then no testimony to *the vision* will lead people to faith.

17, 10: See the notes on 3, 4; 16, 14.

the disciples asked him, "Why do the
scribes say that Elijah must come
first?" 11*† He said in reply, "Elijah will
indeed come and restore all things;
12* but I tell you that Elijah has already
come, and they did not recognize him
but did to him whatever they pleased.
So also will the Son of Man suffer at
their hands." 13† Then the disciples un-
derstood that he was speaking to them
of John the Baptist.

The Healing of a Boy with a Demon.†
14* When they came to the crowd a man
approached, knelt down before him,
15† and said, "Lord, have pity on my
son, for he is a lunatic and suffers se-
verely; often he falls into fire, and often
into water. 16 I brought him to your dis-
ciples, but they could not cure him."
17*† Jesus said in reply, "O faithless and
perverse generation, how long will I be
with you? How long will I endure you?
Bring him here to me." 18† Jesus
rebuked him and the demon came
out of him, and from that hour the
boy was cured. 19 Then the disciples ap-
proached Jesus in private and said,
"Why could we not drive it out?"
20*† He said to them, "Because of
your little faith. Amen, I say to you,
if you have faith the size of a mustard
seed, you will say to this mountain,
'Move from here to there,' and it will
move. Nothing will be impossible for
you." [21]†

***The Second Prediction of the
Passion.***† 22* As they were gathering in
Galilee, Jesus said to them, "The Son
of Man is to be handed over to men,
23 and they will kill him, and he will be
raised on the third day." And they were
overwhelmed with grief.

Payment of the Temple Tax.†
24*† When they came to Capernaum, the
collectors of the temple tax approached
Peter and said, "Doesn't your teacher
pay the temple tax?" 25† "Yes," he said.
When he came into the house, before
he had time to speak, Jesus asked him,
"What is your opinion, Simon? From
whom do the kings of the earth take tolls
or census tax? From their subjects or
from foreigners?" 26† When he said,
"From foreigners," Jesus said to him,
"Then the subjects are exempt. 27† But

*

11: Lk 1, 17.
12-13: 11, 14.
14-21: Mk 9, 14-29; Lk 9, 37-43.
17: Dt 32, 5 LXX.
20: 21, 21; Lk 17, 6; 1 Cor 13, 2.
22-23: 16, 21; 20, 18-19.
24: Ex 30, 11-16; Neh 10, 33.

†

17, 11-12: The preceding question and this answer may reflect later controversy with Jews who objected to the Christian claims for Jesus that Elijah had not yet come.

17, 13: See 11, 14.

17, 14-20: Matthew has greatly shortened the Marcan story (9, 14-29). Leaving aside several details of the boy's illness, he concentrates on the need for faith, not so much on the part of the boy's father (as does Mark, for Matthew omits Mk 9, 22b-24) but on that of his own disciples whose inability to drive out the demon is ascribed to their *little faith* (20).

17, 15: *A lunatic:* this description of the boy is peculiar to Matthew. The word occurs in the New Testament only here and in 4, 24 and means one affected or struck by the moon. The symptoms of the boy's illness point to epilepsy, and attacks of this were thought to be caused by phases of the moon.

17, 17: *Faithless and perverse:* so Matthew and Luke (9, 41) against Mark's *faithless* (9, 19). The Greek word here translated *perverse* is the same as that in Dt 32, 5 LXX, where Moses speaks to his people. There is a problem in knowing to whom the reproach is addressed. Since the Matthean Jesus normally chides his disciples for their *little faith* (as in 20), it would appear that the charge of lack of faith could not be made against them and that the reproach is addressed to unbelievers among the Jews. However in v 20b (*if you have faith the size of a mustard seed*), which is certainly addressed to the disciples, they appear to have not even the smallest faith; if they had, they would have been able to cure the boy. In the light of v 20b the reproach of v 17 could have applied to the disciples. There seems to be an inconsistency between the charge of *little faith* in v 20a and that of not even a little in v 20b.

17, 18: *The demon came out of him:* not until this verse does Matthew indicate that the boy's illness is a case of demoniacal possession.

17, 20: The entire verse is an addition of Matthew who (according to the better attested text) omits the reason given for the disciples' inability in Mk 9, 29. *Little faith:* see the note on 6, 30. *Faith the size of a mustard seed . . . and it will move:* a combination of a Q saying (cf Lk 17, 6) with a Marcan saying (cf Mk 11, 23).

17, 21: Some manuscripts add, "But this kind does not come out except by prayer and fasting"; this is a variant of the better reading of Mk 9, 29.

17, 22-23: The second passion prediction (cf 16, 21-23) is the least detailed of the three and may be the earliest. In the Marcan parallel the disciples do not understand (9, 32); here they understand and are *overwhelmed with grief* at the prospect of Jesus' death (23).

17, 24-27: Like 14, 28-31 and 16, 16b-19, this episode comes from Matthew's special material on Peter. Although the question of *the collectors* concerns Jesus' payment of *the temple tax*, it is put to *Peter*. It is he who receives instruction from Jesus about freedom from the obligation of payment and yet why it should be made. The means of doing so is provided miraculously. The pericope deals with a problem of Matthew's church, whether its members should pay the temple tax, and the answer is given through a word of Jesus conveyed to Peter. Some scholars see here an example of the teaching authority of Peter exercised in the name of Jesus (see 16, 19). The specific problem was a Jewish Christian one and may have arisen when the Matthean church was composed largely of that group.

17, 24: *The temple tax:* before the destruction of the Jerusalem temple in A.D. 70 every male Jew above nineteen years of age was obliged to make an annual contribution to its upkeep (cf Ex 30, 11-16; Neh 10, 33). After the destruction the Romans imposed upon Jews the obligation of paying that tax for the temple of Jupiter Capitolinus. There is disagreement about which period the story deals with.

17, 25: *From their subjects or from foreigners?:* the Greek word here translated *subjects* literally means "sons."

17, 26: *Then the subjects are exempt:* just as *subjects* are not bound by laws applying to *foreigners,* neither are Jesus and his disciples, who belong to the kingdom of heaven, bound by the duty of paying the temple tax imposed on those who are not of the kingdom. If the Greek is translated "sons," the freedom of Jesus, the Son of God, and of his disciples, children ("sons") of the kingdom (cf 13, 38), is even more clear.

17, 27: *That we may not offend them:* though they are *exempt* (26), Jesus and his disciples are to avoid giving offense; therefore the tax is to be paid. *A coin worth twice the temple tax:* literally, "a stater," a Greek coin worth two double drachmas. Two double drachmas were equal to the Jewish shekel and the tax was a half-shekel. *For me and for you:* not only Jesus but Peter pays the tax, and this example serves as a standard for the conduct of all the disciples.

that we may not offend them, go to the
sea, drop in a hook, and take the first
fish that comes up. Open its mouth and
you will find a coin worth twice the tem-
ple tax. Give that to them for me and
for you."

CHAPTER 18†

The Greatest in the Kingdom.
1*† At that time the disciples ap-
proached Jesus and said, "Who is the
greatest in the kingdom of heaven?"
2 He called a child over, placed it in
their midst, 3*† and said, "Amen, I say
to you, unless you turn and become like
children, you will not enter the kingdom
of heaven. 4* Whoever humbles himself
like this child is the greatest in the king-
dom of heaven. 5† And whoever re-
ceives one child such as this in my name
receives me.

Temptations to Sin. 6*† "Whoever
causes one of these little ones who be-
lieve in me to sin, it would be better for
him to have a great millstone hung
around his neck and to be drowned in
the depths of the sea. 7† Woe to the
world because of things that cause sin!
Such things must come, but woe to the
one through whom they come! 8*† If
your hand or foot causes you to sin, cut
it off and throw it away. It is better for
you to enter into life maimed or crippled
than with two hands or two feet to be
thrown into eternal fire. 9 And if your
eye causes you to sin, tear it out and
throw it away. It is better for you to
enter into life with one eye than with
two eyes to be thrown into fiery Ge-
henna.

The Parable of the Lost Sheep.†
10*† "See that you do not despise one
of these little ones, for I say to you that
their angels in heaven always look upon
the face of my heavenly Father. [11]*†
12 What is your opinion? If a man has a
hundred sheep and one of them goes
astray, will he not leave the ninety-nine
in the hills and go in search of the stray?
13 And if he finds it, amen, I say to you,
he rejoices more over it than over the
ninety-nine that did not stray. 14 In just
the same way, it is not the will of your
heavenly Father that one of these little
ones be lost.

*

18, 1-5: Mk 9, 36-37; Lk 9, 46-48.
3: 19, 14; Mk 10, 15; Lk 18, 17.
4: 23, 12.
6-7: Mk 9, 42; Lk 17, 1-2.
8-9: 5, 29-30; Mk 9, 43-47.
10-14: Ez 34, 1-3.16; Lk 15, 3-7.
11: Lk 19, 10.

†

18, 1-35: This discourse of the fourth book of the gospel is often called the "church order" discourse, but it lacks most of the considerations usually connected with church order, such as various offices in the church and the duties of each, and deals principally with the relations that must obtain among the members of the church. Beginning with the warning that greatness in *the kingdom of heaven* is measured not by rank or power but by childlikeness (1-5), it deals with the care that the disciples must take not to cause the *little ones to sin* or to neglect them if they stray from the community (6-14), the correction of members who sin (15-18), the efficacy of the prayer of the disciples because of the presence of Jesus (19-20), and the forgiveness that must be repeatedly extended to sinful members who repent (21-35).

18, 1: The initiative is taken not by Jesus as in the Marcan parallel (9, 33-34) but by the disciples. *Kingdom of heaven:* this may mean *the kingdom* in its fullness, i.e., after the parousia and the final judgment. But what follows about causes of sin, church discipline, and forgiveness, all dealing with the present age, suggests that the question has to do with rank also in the church, where *the kingdom* is manifested here and now, although only partially and by anticipation; see the notes on 3, 2; 4, 17.

18, 3: *Become like children:* the child is held up as a model for the disciples not because of any supposed innocence of children but because of their complete dependence on, and trust in, their parents. So must the disciples be, in respect to God.

18, 5: Cf 10, 40.

18, 6: *One of these little ones:* the thought passes from the child of vv 2-4 to the disciples, *little ones* because of their becoming *like children.* It is difficult to know whether this is a designation of all who are disciples or of those who are insignificant in contrast to others, e.g., the leaders of the community. Since apart from this chapter the designation *little ones* occurs in Mt only in 10, 42 where it means disciples as such, that is its more likely meaning here. *Who believe in me:* since discipleship is impossible without at least some degree of faith, this further specification seems superfluous. However, it serves to indicate that the warning against causing a *little one* to sin is principally directed against whatever would lead such a one to a weakening or loss of faith. The Greek verb *skandalizein,* here translated *causes . . . to sin,* means literally "causes to stumble"; what the stumbling is depends on the context. It is used of falling away from faith in 13, 21. According to the better reading of Mk 9, 42, *in me* is a Matthean addition to the Marcan source. *It would be better . . . depths of the sea:* cf Mk 9, 42.

18, 7: This is a Q saying; cf Lk 17, 1. The inevitability of *things that cause sin* (literally, "scandals") does not take away the responsibility of *the one through whom they come.*

18, 8-9: These verses are a doublet of 5, 29-30. In that context they have to do with causes of sexual sin. As in the Marcan source from which they have been drawn (Mk 9, 42-48), they differ from the first warning about scandal, which deals with causing another person to sin, for they concern what *causes* oneself *to sin* and they do not seem to be related to another's loss of faith, as the first warning is. It is difficult to know how Matthew understood the logical connection between these verses and vv 6-7.

18, 10-14: The first and last verses are peculiar to Mt. The parable itself comes from Q; see Lk 15, 3-7. In Lk it serves as justification for Jesus' table-companionship with sinners; here, it is an exhortation for the disciples to seek out fellow disciples who have gone *astray.* Not only must no one cause a fellow disciple to sin, but those who have strayed must be sought out and, if possible, brought back to the community. The joy of the shepherd on finding the sheep, though not absent in Mt (13), is more emphasized in Lk. By his addition of vv 10 and 14, Matthew has drawn out explicitly the application of the parable to the care of the *little ones.*

18, 10: *Their angels in heaven . . . my heavenly Father:* for the Jewish belief in angels as guardians of nations and individuals, see Dn 10, 13.20-21; Tb 5, 4-7; 1QH 5, 20-22; as intercessors who present the prayers of human beings to God, see Tb 13, 12.15. The high worth of the *little ones* is indicated by their being represented before God by these heavenly beings.

18, 11: Some manuscripts add, "For the Son of Man has come to save what was lost"; cf 9, 13. This is practically identical with Lk 19, 10 and is probably a copyist's addition from that source.

A Brother Who Sins. † 15*† "If your
brother sins [against you], go and tell
him his fault between you and him
alone. If he listens to you, you have won
over your brother. 16*† If he does not
listen, take one or two others along with
you, so that 'every fact may be estab-
lished on the testimony of two or three
witnesses.' 17*† If he refuses to listen to
them, tell the church. If he refuses to
listen even to the church, then treat him
as you would a Gentile or a tax collec-
tor. 18*† Amen, I say to you, whatever
you bind on earth shall be bound in
heaven, and whatever you loose on
earth shall be loosed in heaven.
19*† Again, [amen,] I say to you, if two
of you agree on earth about anything
for which they are to pray, it shall be
granted to them by my heavenly Fa-
ther. 20*† For where two or three are
gathered together in my name, there
am I in the midst of them."

The Parable of the Unforgiving Servant. † 21* Then Peter approaching
asked him, "Lord, if my brother sins
against me, how often must I forgive
him? As many as seven times?"
22† Jesus answered, "I say to you, not
seven times but seventy-seven times.
23* That is why the kingdom of heaven
may be likened to a king who decided
to settle accounts with his servants.
24† When he began the accounting, a
debtor was brought before him who
owed him a huge amount. 25 Since he
had no way of paying it back, his master
ordered him to be sold, along with his
wife, his children, and all his property,
in payment of the debt. 26† At that, the
servant fell down, did him homage, and
said, 'Be patient with me, and I will pay
you back in full.' 27 Moved with compas-
sion the master of that servant let him
go and forgave him the loan. 28† When
that servant had left, he found one of
his fellow servants who owed him a
much smaller amount. He seized him
and started to choke him, demanding,
'Pay back what you owe.' 29 Falling to
his knees, his fellow servant begged

*

15: Lv 19, 17; Sir 19, 13; Gal 6, 1.
16: Dt 19, 15; Jn 8, 17; 1 Tm 5, 19.
17: 1 Cor 5, 1-13.
18: 16, 19; Jn 20, 23.
19: 7, 7-8; Jn 15, 7.
20: 1 Cor 5, 4.
21-22: 6, 12; Lk 17, 4.
23: 25, 19.

†

18, 15-20: Passing from the duty of Christian disciples toward those who have strayed from their number, the discourse now turns to how they are to deal with one who sins and yet remains within the community. First there is to be private correction (15); if this is unsuccessful, further correction before *two or three witnesses* (16); if this fails, the matter is to be brought before the assembled community (*the church*), and if the sinner refuses to attend to the correction of *the church,* he is to be expelled (17). The church's judgment will be ratified *in heaven,* i.e., by God (18). This three-step process of correction corresponds, though not exactly, to the procedure of the Qumran community; see 1QS 5, 25—6, 1; 6, 24—7, 25; CD 9, 2-8. The section ends with a saying about the favorable response of God to prayer, even to that of a very small number, for Jesus is in the midst of any gathering of his disciples, however small (19-20). Whether this prayer has anything to do with the preceding judgment is uncertain.

18, 15: *Your brother:* a fellow disciple; see 23, 8. The bracketed words, *against you,* are widely attested but they are not in the important codices Sinaiticus and Vaticanus or in some other textual witnesses. Their omission broadens the type of sin in question. *Won over:* literally, "gained."

18, 16: Cf Dt 19, 15.

18, 17: *The church:* the second of the only two instances of this word in the gospels; see the note on 16, 18. Here it refers not to the entire *church* of Jesus, as in 16, 18, but to the local congregation. *Treat him . . . a Gentile or a tax collector:* just as the observant Jew avoided the company of Gentiles and tax collectors, so must the congregation of Christian disciples separate itself from the arrogantly sinful member who refuses to repent even when convicted of his sin by the whole *church.* Such a one is to be set outside the fellowship of the community. The harsh language about *Gentile* and *tax collector* probably reflects a stage of the Matthean *church* when it was principally composed of Jewish Christians. That time had long since passed, but the principle of exclusion for such a sinner remained. Paul makes a similar demand for excommunication in 1 Cor 5, 1-13.

18, 18: Except for the plural of the verbs *bind* and *loose,* this verse is practically identical with 16, 19b, and many scholars understand it as granting to all the disciples what was previously given to Peter alone. For a different view, based on the different contexts of the two verses, see the note on 16, 19.

18, 19-20: Some take these verses as applying to prayer on the occasion of the church's gathering to deal with the sinner of v 17. Unless an *a fortiori* argument is supposed, this seems unlikely. God's answer to the prayer of *two or three* envisages a different situation from one that involves the entire congregation. In addition, the object of this prayer is expressed in most general terms as *anything for which they are to pray.*

18, 20: *For where two or three . . . midst of them:* the presence of Jesus guarantees the efficacy of the prayer. This saying is similar to one attributed to a rabbi executed in A.D. 135 at the time of the second Jewish revolt: ". . . When two sit and there are between them the words of the Torah, the divine presence (Shekinah) rests upon them" (*Pirqê ʾAbôt* 3, 3).

18, 21-35: The final section of the discourse deals with the forgiveness that the disciples are to give to their fellow disciples who sin against them. To the question of Peter how often forgiveness is to be granted (21), Jesus answers that it is to be given without limit (22) and illustrates this with the parable of the unmerciful servant (23-34), warning that his *heavenly Father* will give those who do not forgive the same treatment as that given to the unmerciful servant (35). Verses 21-22 correspond to Lk 17, 4; the parable and the final warning are peculiar to Mt. That the parable did not originally belong to this context is suggested by the fact that it really does not deal with repeated forgiveness, which is the point of Peter's question and Jesus' reply.

18, 22: *Seventy-seven times:* the Greek corresponds exactly to the LXX of Gn 4, 24. There is probably an allusion, by contrast, to the limitless vengeance of Lamech in the Gn text. In any case, what is demanded of the disciples is limitless forgiveness.

18, 24: *A huge amount:* literally, "ten thousand talents." The talent was a unit of coinage of high but varying value depending on its metal (gold, silver, copper) and its place of origin. It is mentioned in the New Testament only here and in 25, 14-30.

18, 26: *Pay you back in full:* an empty promise, given the size of the debt.

18, 28: *A much smaller amount:* literally, "a hundred denarii." A denarius was the normal daily wage of a laborer. The difference between the two debts is enormous and brings out the absurdity of the conduct of the Christian who has received the great forgiveness of God and yet refuses to forgive the relatively minor offenses done to him.

him, 'Be patient with me, and I will pay you back.' 30 But he refused. Instead, he had him put in prison until he paid back the debt. 31 Now when his fellow servants saw what had happened, they were deeply disturbed, and went to their master and reported the whole affair. 32 His master summoned him and said to him, 'You wicked servant! I forgave you your entire debt because you begged me to. 33* Should you not have had pity on your fellow servant, as I had pity on you?' 34† Then in anger his master handed him over to the torturers until he should pay back the whole debt. 35*† So will my heavenly Father do to you, unless each of you forgives his brother from his heart."

VI: MINISTRY IN JUDEA AND JERUSALEM†

CHAPTER 19

Marriage and Divorce.† 1† When Jesus finished these words, he left Galilee and went to the district of Judea across the Jordan. 2 Great crowds followed him, and he cured them there. 3*† Some Pharisees approached him, and tested him, saying, "Is it lawful for a man to divorce his wife for any cause whatever?" 4*† He said in reply, "Have you not read that from the beginning the Creator 'made them male and female' 5* and said, 'For this reason a man shall leave his father and mother and be joined to his wife, and the two shall become one flesh'? 6 So they are no longer two, but one flesh. Therefore, what God has joined together, no human being must separate." 7*† They said to him, "Then why did Moses command that the man give the woman a bill of divorce and dismiss [her]?" 8 He said to them, "Because of the hardness of your hearts Moses allowed you to divorce your wives, but from the beginning it was not so. 9*† I say to you, whoever divorces his wife (unless the marriage is unlawful) and marries another commits adultery." 10 [His] disciples said to him, "If that is the case of a man with his wife, it is better not to marry." 11† He answered, "Not all can accept [this] word,

*

33: Sir 28, 4.
35: 6, 15; Jas 2, 13.
19, 3-9: Mk 10, 2-12.
4: Gn 1, 27.
5: Gn 2, 24; 1 Cor 6, 16; Eph 5, 31.
7: Dt 24, 1-4.
9: 5, 32; Lk 16, 18; 1 Cor 7, 10-11.

†

18, 34: Since the debt is so great as to be unpayable, the punishment will be endless.

18, 35: The Father's forgiveness, already given, will be withdrawn at the final judgment for those who have not imitated his forgiveness by their own.

19, 1—23, 39: The narrative section of the fifth book of the gospel. The first part (19, 1—20, 34) has for its setting the journey of Jesus from Galilee to Jerusalem; the second (21, 1—23, 39) deals with Jesus' ministry in Jerusalem up to the final great discourse of the gospel (chs 24-25). Matthew follows the Marcan sequence of events, though adding material both special to this gospel and drawn from Q. The second part ends with the denunciation of the scribes and Pharisees (23, 1-36) followed by Jesus' lament over Jerusalem (37-39). This long and important speech raises a problem for the view that Mt is structured around five other discourses of Jesus (see Introduction) and that this one has no such function in the gospel. However, it is to be noted that this speech lacks the customary concluding formula that follows the five discourses (see the note on 7, 28), and that those discourses are all addressed either exclusively (chs 10, 18, 24-25) or primarily (chs 5-7, 13) to the disciples, whereas this is addressed primarily to the scribes and Pharisees (13-36). Consequently, it seems plausible to maintain that the evangelist did not intend to give it the structural importance of the five other discourses, and that, in spite of its being composed of sayings-material, it belongs to the narrative section of this book. In that regard, it is similar to the sayings-material of 11, 7-30. Some have proposed that Matthew wished to regard it as part of the final discourse of chs 24-25, but the intervening material (24, 1-4) and the change in matter and style of those chapters do not support that view.

19, 1-12: In giving Jesus' teaching on divorce (3-9), Matthew here follows his Marcan source (10, 2-12) as he does Q in 5, 31-32 (cf Lk 16, 18). Verses 10-12 are peculiar to Mt.

19, 1: *When Jesus finished these words:* see the note on 7, 28-29. *The district of Judea across the Jordan:* an inexact designation of the territory. Judea did not extend *across the Jordan;* the territory east of the river was Perea. The route to Jerusalem by way of Perea avoided passage through Samaria.

19, 3: *Tested him:* the verb is used of attempts of Jesus' opponents to embarrass him by challenging him to do something they think impossible (16, 1; Mk 8, 11; Lk 11, 16) or by having him say something that they can use against him (22, 18.35; Mk 10, 2; 12, 15). *For any cause whatever:* this is peculiar to Mt and has been interpreted by some as meaning that Jesus was being asked to take sides in the dispute between the schools of Hillel and Shammai on the reasons for divorce, the latter holding a stricter position than the former. It is unlikely, however, that to ask Jesus' opinion about the differing views of two Jewish schools, both highly respected, could be described as "testing" him, for the reason indicated above.

19, 4-6: Matthew recasts his Marcan source, omitting Jesus' question about Moses' command (Mk 10, 3) and having him recall at once two Genesis texts that show the will and purpose of *the Creator* in making human beings *male and female* (Gn 1, 27), namely, that *a man* may *be joined to his wife* in marriage in the intimacy of *one flesh* (Gn 2, 24). *What God has* thus *joined* must not be separated by any *human being.* (The NAB translation of the Hebrew *bāśār* of Gn 2, 24 as "body" rather than "flesh" obscures the reference of Mt to that text.)

19, 7: See Dt 24, 1-4.

19, 9: Moses' concession to human sinfulness (*the hardness of your hearts,* 8) is repudiated by Jesus, and the original will of the Creator is reaffirmed against that concession. *(Unless the marriage is unlawful):* see the note on 5, 31-32. There is some evidence suggesting that Jesus' absolute prohibition of divorce was paralleled in the Qumran community (see 11QTemple 57, 17-19; CD 4, 12b—5, 14). Matthew removes Mark's setting of this verse as spoken to the disciples alone "in the house" (Mk 10, 10) and also his extension of the divorce prohibition to the case of a woman's divorcing her husband (10, 12), probably because in Palestine, unlike the places where Roman and Greek law prevailed, the woman was not allowed to initiate the divorce.

19, 11: *[This] word:* probably the disciples' *it is better not to marry* (10). Jesus agrees but says that celibacy is not for all but only for those *to whom that is granted* by God.

but only those to whom that is granted.
12† Some are incapable of marriage be-
cause they were born so; some, because
they were made so by others; some, be-
cause they have renounced marriage
for the sake of the kingdom of heaven.
Whoever can accept this ought to accept
it."

***Blessing of the Children.*†** 13* Then
children were brought to him that he
might lay his hands on them and pray.
The disciples rebuked them, 14* but Je-
sus said, "Let the children come to me,
and do not prevent them; for the king-
dom of heaven belongs to such as
these." 15 After he placed his hands on
them, he went away.

***The Rich Young Man.*†** 16*† Now
someone approached him and said,
"Teacher, what good must I do to gain
eternal life?" 17† He answered him,
"Why do you ask me about the good?
There is only One who is good. If you
wish to enter into life, keep the com-
mandments." 18*† He asked him,
"Which ones?" And Jesus replied,
" 'You shall not kill; you shall not com-
mit adultery; you shall not steal; you
shall not bear false witness; 19 honor
your father and your mother'; and 'you
shall love your neighbor as yourself.' "
20† The young man said to him, "All of
these I have observed. What do I still
lack?" 21*† Jesus said to him, "If you
wish to be perfect, go, sell what you
have and give to [the] poor, and
you will have treasure in heaven. Then
come, follow me." 22 When the young
man heard this statement, he went
away sad, for he had many possessions.
23† Then Jesus said to his disciples,
"Amen, I say to you, it will be hard for
one who is rich to enter the kingdom
of heaven. 24* Again I say to you, it is
easier for a camel to pass through the
eye of a needle than for one who is rich
to enter the kingdom of God." 25† When
the disciples heard this, they were
greatly astonished and said, "Who then
can be saved?" 26* Jesus looked at them
and said, "For human beings this is
impossible, but for God all things are
possible." 27* Then Peter said to him in
reply, "We have given up everything
and followed you. What will there be for
us?" 28*† Jesus said to them, "Amen, I
say to you that you who have followed
me, in the new age, when the Son of
Man is seated on his throne of glory,

*

13-15: Mk 10, 13-16; Lk 18, 15-17.
14: 18, 3; Acts 8, 36.
16-30: Mk 10, 17-31; Lk 18, 18-30.
18-19: Ex 20, 12-16; Dt 5, 16-20 / Lv 19, 18; Rom 13, 9.
21: 5, 48; 6, 20.
24: 7, 14.
26: Gn 18, 14; Jb 42, 2; Lk 1, 37.
27: 4, 20.22.
28: 25, 31; Dn 7, 9.22; Lk 22, 30; Rv 3, 21; 20, 4.

†

19, 12: *Incapable of marriage:* literally, "eunuchs." Three classes are mentioned, eunuchs from birth, eunuchs by castration, and those who have voluntarily *renounced marriage* (literally, "have made themselves eunuchs") *for the sake of the kingdom,* i.e., to devote themselves entirely to its service. Some scholars take the last class to be those who have been divorced by their spouses and have refused to enter another marriage. But it is more likely that it is rather those who have chosen never to marry, since that suits better the optional nature of the decision: *whoever can . . . ought to accept it.*

19, 13-15: This account is understood by some as intended to justify the practice of infant baptism. That interpretation is based principally on the command not to *prevent* the children from coming, since that word sometimes has a baptismal connotation in the New Testament; see Acts 8, 36.

19, 16-30: Cf Mk 10, 17-31. This story does not set up a "two-tier" morality, that of those who seek (only) *eternal life* (16) and that of those who *wish to be perfect* (21). It speaks rather of the obstacle that riches constitute for the following of Jesus and of the impossibility, humanly speaking, for one who has *many possessions* (22) *to enter the kingdom* (24). Actual renunciation of riches is not demanded of all; Matthew counts the rich Joseph of Arimathea as a disciple of Jesus (27, 57). But only the poor in spirit (5, 3) can *enter the kingdom* and, as here, such poverty may entail the sacrifice of one's *possessions.* The Twelve, who *have given up everything* (27) to follow Jesus, will have as their reward a share in Jesus' (the Son of Man's) *judging the twelve tribes of Israel* (28), and all who have similarly sacrificed family or property for his sake *will inherit eternal life* (29).

19, 16: *Gain eternal life:* this is equivalent to "entering into life" (17) and "being saved" (25); the *life* is that of the new age after the final judgment (see 25, 46). It probably is also equivalent here to "entering the kingdom of heaven" (23) or "the kingdom of God" (24), but see the notes on 3, 2; 4, 17; 18, 1 for the wider reference of *the kingdom* in Mt.

19, 17: By Matthew's reformulation of the Marcan question and reply (Mk 10, 17-18) Jesus' repudiation of the term "good" for himself has been softened. Yet the Marcan assertion that "no one is good but God alone" stands, with only unimportant verbal modification.

19, 18-19: The first five commandments cited are from the Decalogue (see Ex 20, 12-16; Dt 5, 16-20). Matthew omits Mark's "you shall not defraud" (10, 19; see Dt 24, 14) and adds Lv 19, 18. This combination of commandments of the Decalogue with Lv 19, 18 is partially the same as Paul's enumeration of the demands of Christian morality in Rom 13, 9.

19, 20: *Young man:* in Mt alone of the synoptics the questioner is said to be a *young man;* thus the Marcan "from my youth" (10, 20) is omitted.

19, 21: *If you wish to be perfect: to be perfect* is demanded of all Christians; see 5, 48. In the case of this man, it involves selling his possessions and giving to the poor; only so can he *follow* Jesus.

19, 23-24: Riches are an obstacle to entering *the kingdom* that cannot be overcome by human power. The comparison with the impossibility of a camel's passing *through the eye of a needle* should not be mitigated by such suppositions as that *the eye of a needle* means a low or narrow gate. *The kingdom of God:* as in 12, 28; 21, 31.43, instead of Mt's usual *kingdom of heaven.*

19, 25-26: See the note on Mk 10, 23-27.

19, 28: This saying, directed to the Twelve, is from Q; see Lk 22, 29-30. *The new age:* the Greek word here translated "new age" occurs in the New Testament only here and in Ti 3, 5. Literally, it means "rebirth" or "regeneration," and is used in Ti of spiritual rebirth through baptism. Here it means the "rebirth" effected by the coming of the kingdom. Since that coming has various stages (see the notes on 3, 2; 4, 17), *the new age* could be taken as referring to the time after the resurrection when the Twelve will govern the true Israel, i.e., the church of Jesus. (For "judge" in the sense of "govern," cf Jgs 12, 8.9.11; 15, 20; 16, 31; Ps 2, 10). But since it is connected here with the time when *the Son of Man* will be *seated on his throne of glory,* language that Matthew uses in 25, 31 for the time of final judgment, it is more likely that what the Twelve are promised is that they will be joined with Jesus then in judging the people of Israel.

will yourselves sit on twelve thrones,
judging the twelve tribes of Israel.
[29] And everyone who has given up
houses or brothers or sisters or father
or mother or children or lands for the
sake of my name will receive a hundred
times more, and will inherit eternal
life. [30]*† But many who are first will be
last, and the last will be first.

CHAPTER 20

The Workers in the Vineyard.†
[1] "The kingdom of heaven is like a land-
owner who went out at dawn to hire
laborers for his vineyard. [2] After agree-
ing with them for the usual daily wage,
he sent them into his vineyard. [3] Going
out about nine o'clock, he saw others
standing idle in the marketplace,
[4]† and he said to them, 'You too go into
my vineyard, and I will give you what
is just.' [5] So they went off. [And] he went
out again around noon, and around
three o'clock, and did likewise. [6] Going
out about five o'clock, he found others
standing around, and said to them,
'Why do you stand here idle all day?'
[7] They answered, 'Because no one has
hired us.' He said to them, 'You too go
into my vineyard.' [8]*† When it was eve-
ning the owner of the vineyard said to
his foreman, 'Summon the laborers and
give them their pay, beginning with the
last and ending with the first.' [9] When
those who had started about five o'clock
came, each received the usual daily
wage. [10] So when the first came, they
thought that they would receive more,
but each of them also got the usual
wage. [11] And on receiving it they grum-
bled against the landowner, [12] saying,
'These last ones worked only one hour,
and you have made them equal to us,
who bore the day's burden and the
heat.' [13]† He said to one of them in reply,
'My friend, I am not cheating you. Did
you not agree with me for the usual
daily wage? [14]† Take what is yours and
go. What if I wish to give this last one
the same as you? [15] [Or] am I not free
to do as I wish with my own money?
Are you envious because I am gener-
ous?' [16]† Thus, the last will be first, and
the first will be last."

The Third Prediction of the Passion.†
[17]* As Jesus was going up to Jerusalem,
he took the twelve [disciples] aside by
themselves, and said to them on the
way, [18] "Behold, we are going up to Je-
rusalem, and the Son of Man will be
handed over to the chief priests and the
scribes, and they will condemn him to
death, [19] and hand him over to the Gen-
tiles to be mocked and scourged and
crucified, and he will be raised on the
third day."

The Request of James and John.†
[20]*† Then the mother of the sons of Zeb-
edee approached him with her sons and
did him homage, wishing to ask him for
something. [21] He said to her, "What do
you wish?" She answered him, "Com-
mand that these two sons of mine sit,
one at your right and the other at your
left, in your kingdom." [22]† Jesus said in
reply, "You do not know what you are
asking. Can you drink the cup that I am
going to drink?" They said to him, "We
can." [23] He replied, "My cup you will
indeed drink, but to sit at my right and
at my left [, this] is not mine to give
but is for those for whom it has been
prepared by my Father." [24]* When the
ten heard this, they became indignant
at the two brothers. [25] But Jesus sum-
moned them and said, "You know that

---

*

30: 20, 16.
20, 8: Lv 19, 13; Dt 24, 15.
17-19: 16, 21; 17, 22-23; Mk 10, 32-34; Lk 18, 31-33.
20-28: Mk 10, 35-45.
24-27: Lk 22, 25-27.

†

19, 30: Different interpretations have been given to this saying, which comes from Mk 10, 31. In view of Matthew's associating it with the following parable (20, 1-15) and substantially repeating it (in reverse order) at the end of that parable (20, 16), it may be that his meaning is that all who respond to the call of Jesus, at whatever time (*first* or *last*), will be the same in respect to inheriting the benefits of the kingdom, which is the gift of God.

20, 1-16: This parable is peculiar to Mt. It is difficult to know whether the evangelist composed it or received it as part of his traditional material and, if the latter is the case, what its original reference was. In its present context its close association with 19, 30 suggests that its teaching is the equality of all the disciples in the reward of inheriting eternal life.

20, 4: *What is just:* although the wage is not stipulated as in the case of those first hired, it will be fair.

20, 8: *Beginning with the last . . . the first:* this element of the parable has no other purpose than to show how *the first* knew what *the last* were given (12).

20, 13: *I am not cheating you:* literally, "I am not treating you unjustly."

20, 14-15: The owner's conduct involves no violation of justice (4.13), and that all the workers receive the same wage is due only to his generosity to the latest arrivals; the resentment of the first comes from envy.

20, 16: See the note on 19, 30.

20, 17-19: Cf Mk 10, 32-34. This is the third and the most detailed of the passion predictions (16, 21-23; 17, 22-23). It speaks of Jesus' being *handed over to the Gentiles* (27, 2), his being *mocked* (27, 27-30), *scourged* (27, 26), and *crucified* (27, 31.35). In all but the last of these points Matthew agrees with his Marcan source, but whereas Mk speaks of Jesus' being killed (10, 34), Mt has the specific *to be . . . crucified.*

20, 20-28: Cf Mk 10, 35-45. The request of the sons of Zebedee, made through their mother, for the highest places of honor in the *kingdom,* and the indignation of *the* other *ten* disciples at this request, show that neither *the two brothers* nor the others have understood that what makes for greatness in the kingdom is not lordly power but humble service. Jesus gives the example, and his ministry of service will reach its highest point when he gives his life for the deliverance of the human race from sin.

20, 20-21: The reason for Matthew's making *the mother* the petitioner (cf Mk 10, 35) is not clear. Possibly he intends an allusion to Bathsheba's seeking the kingdom for Solomon; see 1 Kgs 1, 11-21. *Your kingdom:* see the note on 16, 28.

20, 22: *You do not know what you are asking:* the Greek verbs are plural and, with the rest of the verse, indicate that the answer is addressed not to the woman but to her sons. *Drink the cup:* see the note on Mk 10, 38-40. Matthew omits the Marcan "or be baptized with the baptism with which I am baptized" (10, 38).

the rulers of the Gentiles lord it over
them, and the great ones make their au-
thority over them felt. 26 But it shall not
be so among you. Rather, whoever
wishes to be great among you shall be
your servant; 27* whoever wishes to be
first among you shall be your slave.
28*† Just so, the Son of Man did not
come to be served but to serve and to
give his life as a ransom for many."

The Healing of Two Blind Men.†
29* As they left Jericho, a great crowd
followed him. 30*† Two blind men were
sitting by the roadside, and when they
heard that Jesus was passing by, they
cried out, "[Lord,] Son of David, have
pity on us!" 31 The crowd warned them
to be silent, but they called out all the
more, "Lord, Son of David, have pity
on us!" 32 Jesus stopped and called them
and said, "What do you want me to do
for you?" 33 They answered him, "Lord,
let our eyes be opened." 34 Moved with
pity, Jesus touched their eyes. Immedi-
ately they received their sight, and fol-
lowed him.

CHAPTER 21

The Entry into Jerusalem.† 1*† When
they drew near Jerusalem and came to
Bethphage on the Mount of Olives, Je-
sus sent two disciples, 2† saying to them,
"Go into the village opposite you, and
immediately you will find an ass teth-
ered, and a colt with her. Untie them
and bring them here to me. 3 And if any-
one should say anything to you, reply,
'The master has need of them.' Then he
will send them at once." 4† This hap-
pened so that what had been spoken
through the prophet might be fulfilled:

5* "Say to daughter Zion,
'Behold, your king comes to you,
meek and riding on an ass,
and on a colt, the foal of a beast
of burden.' "

6 The disciples went and did as Jesus
had ordered them. 7† They brought the
ass and the colt and laid their cloaks
over them, and he sat upon them.
8*† The very large crowd spread their
cloaks on the road, while others cut
branches from the trees and strewed
them on the road. 9*† The crowds pre-
ceding him and those following kept
crying out and saying:

"Hosanna to the Son of David;
blessed is he who comes in the
name of the Lord;
hosanna in the highest."

10† And when he entered Jerusalem the
whole city was shaken and asked, "Who

*

27: Mk 9, 35.
28: 26, 28; Is 53, 12; Rom 5, 6; 1 Tm 2, 6.

29-34: Mk 10, 46-52; Lk 18, 35-43.
30: 9, 27.
21, 1-11: Mk 11, 1-11; Lk 19, 28-38; Jn 12, 12-15.
5: Is 62, 11; Zec 9, 9.
8: 2 Kgs 9, 13.
9: Ps 118, 25-26.

†

20, 28: *Ransom:* this noun, which occurs in the New Testament only here and in the Marcan parallel (10, 45), does not necessarily express the idea of liberation by payment of some price. The cognate verb is used frequently in the LXX of God's liberating Israel from Egypt or from Babylonia after the Exile; see Ex 6, 6; 15, 13; Ps 77 (76 LXX), 16; Is 43, 1; 44, 22. The liberation brought by Jesus' death will be *for many;* cf Is 53, 12. *Many* does not mean that some are excluded, but is a Semitism designating the collectivity who benefit from the service of the one, and is equivalent to "all." While there are few verbal contacts between this saying and the fourth Servant Song (Is 52, 13—53, 12), the ideas of that passage are reflected here.

20, 29-34: The cure of the blind men is probably symbolic of what will happen to the disciples, now blind to the meaning of Jesus' passion and to the necessity of their sharing his suffering. As the men are given sight, so, after the resurrection, will the disciples come to see that to which they are now blind. Matthew has abbreviated his Marcan source (10, 46-52) and has made Mk's one man two. Such doubling is characteristic of this gospel; see 8, 28-34 (// Mk 5, 1-20) and the note on 9, 27-31.

20, 30: *[Lord]:* some important textual witnesses omit this, but that may be because copyists assimilated this verse to 9, 27. *Son of David:* see the note on 9, 27.

21, 1-11: Jesus' coming to Jerusalem is in accordance with the divine will that he must go there (cf 16, 21) to suffer, die, and be raised. He prepares for his entry into the city in such a way as to make it a fulfillment of the prophecy of Zec 9, 9 (2) that emphasizes the humility of the *king* who *comes* (5). That prophecy, absent from the Marcan parallel account (11, 1-11) although found also in the Johannine account of the entry (12, 15), is the center of the Matthean story. During the procession from Bethphage to Jerusalem, Jesus is acclaimed as the Davidic messianic king by the crowds who accompany him (9). On his arrival *the whole city was shaken,* and to the inquiry of the amazed populace about Jesus' identity the crowds with him reply that he is *the prophet, from Nazareth in Galilee* (10.11).

21, 1: *Bethphage:* a village that can no longer be certainly identified. Mk mentions it before Bethany (11, 1), which suggests that it lay to the east of the latter. *The Mount of Olives:* the hill east of Jerusalem that is spoken of in Zec 14, 4 as the place where the Lord will come to rescue Jerusalem from the enemy nations.

21, 2: *An ass tethered, and a colt with her:* instead of the one animal of Mk 11, 2, Mt has two, as demanded by his understanding of Zec 9, 9.

21, 4-5: *The prophet:* this fulfillment citation is actually composed of two distinct Old Testament texts, Is 62, 11 (*Say to daughter Zion*) and Zec 9, 9. The *ass* and the *colt* are the same animal in the prophecy, mentioned twice in different ways, the common Hebrew literary device of poetic parallelism. That Matthew takes them as two is one of the reasons why some scholars think that he was a Gentile rather than a Jewish Christian who would presumably not make that mistake (see Introduction).

21, 7: *Upon them:* upon the two animals; an awkward picture resulting from Matthew's misunderstanding of the prophecy.

21, 8: *Spread . . . on the road:* cf 2 Kgs 9, 13. There is a similarity between the cutting and strewing of the *branches* and the festivities of Tabernacles (Lv 23, 39-40); see also 2 Mc 10, 5-8 where the celebration of the rededication of the temple is compared to that of Tabernacles.

21, 9: *Hosanna:* the Hebrew means "(O LORD) grant salvation"; see Ps 118, 25, but that invocation had become an acclamation of jubilation and welcome. *Blessed is he . . . in the name of the Lord:* see Ps 118, 26 and the note on Jn 12, 13. *In the highest:* probably only an intensification of the acclamation, although *Hosanna in the highest* could be taken as a prayer, "May God save (him)."

21, 10: *Was shaken:* in the gospels this verb is peculiar to Mt where it is used also of the earthquake at the time of the crucifixion (27, 51) and of the terror of the guards of Jesus' tomb at the appearance of the angel (28, 4). For Matthew's use of the cognate noun, see the note on 8, 24.

is this?" 11† And the crowds replied,
"This is Jesus the prophet, from Naza-
reth in Galilee."

***The Cleansing of the Temple.*†**
12*† Jesus entered the temple area and
drove out all those engaged in selling
and buying there. He overturned the ta-
bles of the money changers and the
seats of those who were selling doves.
13*† And he said to them, "It is written:

'My house shall be a house of
prayer,'
but you are making it a den of
thieves."

14*† The blind and the lame approached
him in the temple area, and he cured
them. 15† When the chief priests and the
scribes saw the wondrous things he was
doing, and the children crying out in
the temple area, "Hosanna to the Son
of David," they were indignant 16*† and
said to him, "Do you hear what they
are saying?" Jesus said to them, "Yes;
and have you never read the text, 'Out
of the mouths of infants and nurslings
you have brought forth praise'?"
17 And leaving them, he went out of the
city to Bethany, and there he spent the
night.

***The Cursing of the Fig Tree.*†**
18* When he was going back to the city
in the morning, he was hungry.
19* Seeing a fig tree by the road, he went
over to it, but found nothing on it except
leaves. And he said to it, "May no fruit
ever come from you again." And imme-
diately the fig tree withered. 20 When the
disciples saw this, they were amazed
and said, "How was it that the fig tree
withered immediately?" 21*† Jesus said
to them in reply, "Amen, I say to you,
if you have faith and do not waver, not
only will you do what has been done to
the fig tree, but even if you say to this
mountain, 'Be lifted up and thrown into
the sea,' it will be done. 22* Whatever
you ask for in prayer with faith, you will
receive."

***The Authority of Jesus Questioned.*†**
23*† When he had come into the temple
area, the chief priests and the elders of
the people approached him as he was
teaching and said, "By what authority
are you doing these things? And who
gave you this authority?" 24† Jesus said
to them in reply, "I shall ask you one
question, and if you answer it for me,
then I shall tell you by what authority
I do these things. 25 Where was John's
baptism from? Was it of heavenly or of
human origin?" They discussed this
among themselves and said, "If we say
'Of heavenly origin,' he will say to us,
'Then why did you not believe him?'
26*† But if we say, 'Of human origin,'
we fear the crowd, for they all regard
John as a prophet." 27† So they said to
Jesus in reply, "We do not know." He
himself said to them, "Neither shall I
tell you by what authority I do these
things.

*

12-17: Mk 11, 15-19; Lk 19, 45-48; Jn 2, 14-22.
12: Lv 5, 7.
13: Is 56, 7; Jer 7, 11.
14: 2 Sm 5, 8 LXX.
16: Ps 8, 2 LXX; Wis 10, 21.
18-22: Mk 11, 12-14.20-24.
19: Jer 8, 13; Lk 13, 6-9.
21: 17, 20; Lk 17, 6.
22: 7, 7; 1 Jn 3, 22.
23-27: Mk 11, 27-33; Lk 20, 1-8.
23: Jn 2, 18.
26: 14, 5.

†

21, 11: *The prophet:* see 16, 14 ("one of the prophets") and 21, 46.

21, 12-17: Matthew changes the order of Mk (11, 11.12.15) and places the cleansing of the temple on the same day as the entry into Jerusalem, immediately after it. The activities going on in *the temple area* were not secular but connected with the temple worship. Thus Jesus' attack on those so engaged and his charge that they were *making* God's *house of prayer a den of thieves* (12-13) constituted a claim to authority over the religious practices of Israel and were a challenge to the priestly authorities. Verses 14-17 are peculiar to Mt. Jesus' healings and his countenancing the children's cries of praise rouse the indignation of *the chief priests and the scribes* (15). These two groups appear in the infancy narrative (2, 4) and have been mentioned in the first and third passion predictions (16, 21; 20, 18). Now, as the passion approaches, they come on the scene again, exhibiting their hostility to Jesus.

21, 12: These activities were carried on in the court of the Gentiles, the outermost court of *the temple area.* Animals for sacrifice were sold; the *doves* were for those who could not afford a more expensive offering; see Lv 5, 7. *Tables of the money changers:* only the coinage of Tyre could be used for the purchases; other money had to be exchanged for that.

21, 13: *'My house . . . prayer':* cf Is 56, 7. Matthew omits the final words of the quotation, "for all peoples" ("all nations"), possibly because for him the worship of the God of Israel by all nations belongs to the time after the resurrection; see 28, 19. *A den of thieves:* the phrase is taken from Jer 7, 11.

21, 14: *The blind and the lame:* according to 2 Sm 5, 8 (LXX) *the blind and the lame* were forbidden to enter "the house of the Lord," the temple. These are the last of Jesus' healings in Mt.

21, 15: *The wondrous things:* the healings.

21, 16: *'Out of the mouths . . . praise':* cf Ps 8, 3 (LXX).

21, 18-22: In Mk the effect of Jesus' cursing the fig tree is not immediate; see 11, 14.20. By making it so, Matthew has heightened the miracle. Jesus' act seems arbitrary and ill-tempered, but it is a prophetic action similar to those of Old Testament prophets that vividly symbolize some part of their preaching; see, e.g., Ez 12, 1-20. It is a sign of the judgment that is to come upon the Israel that with all its apparent piety lacks the fruit of good deeds (3, 10) and will soon bear the punishment of its fruitlessness (43). Some scholars propose that this story is the development in tradition of a parable of Jesus about the destiny of a fruitless tree, such as Lk 13, 6-9. Jesus' answer to the question of the amazed disciples (20) makes the miracle an example of the power of prayer made with unwavering *faith* (21-22).

21, 21: See 17, 20.

21, 23-27: Cf Mk 11, 27-33. This is the first of five controversies between Jesus and the religious authorities of Judaism in 21, 23—22, 46, presented in the form of questions and answers.

21, 23: *These things:* probably his entry into the city, his cleansing of the temple, and his healings there.

21, 24: To reply by counterquestion was common in rabbinical debate.

21, 26: *We fear . . . as a prophet:* cf 14, 5.

21, 27: Since through embarrassment on the one hand and fear on the other the religious authorities claim ignorance of the origin of John's baptism, they show themselves incapable of speaking with authority; hence Jesus refuses to discuss with them the grounds of his authority.

The Parable of the Two Sons. †
28 "What is your opinion? A man had
two sons. He came to the first and said,
'Son, go out and work in the vineyard
today.' 29 He said in reply, 'I will not,'
but afterwards he changed his mind
and went. 30 The man came to the other
son and gave the same order. He said
in reply, 'Yes, sir,' but did not go.
31† Which of the two did his father's
will?" They answered, "The first." Je-
sus said to them, "Amen, I say to you,
tax collectors and prostitutes are enter-
ing the kingdom of God before you.
32*† When John came to you in the way
of righteousness, you did not believe
him; but tax collectors and prostitutes
did. Yet even when you saw that, you
did not later change your minds and be-
lieve him.

The Parable of the Tenants. †
33*† "Hear another parable. There was
a landowner who planted a vineyard,
put a hedge around it, dug a wine press
in it, and built a tower. Then he leased
it to tenants and went on a journey.
34† When vintage time drew near, he
sent his servants to the tenants to obtain
his produce. 35 But the tenants seized
the servants and one they beat, another
they killed, and a third they stoned.
36 Again he sent other servants, more
numerous than the first ones, but they
treated them in the same way.
37 Finally, he sent his son to them, think-
ing, 'They will respect my son.' 38† But
when the tenants saw the son, they said
to one another, 'This is the heir. Come,
let us kill him and acquire his inheri-
tance.' 39*† They seized him, threw him
out of the vineyard, and killed him.
40 What will the owner of the vineyard
do to those tenants when he comes?"
41† They answered him, "He will put
those wretched men to a wretched
death and lease his vineyard to other
tenants who will give him the produce
at the proper times." 42*† Jesus said to
them, "Did you never read in the scrip-
tures:

'The stone that the builders rejected
has become the cornerstone;
by the Lord has this been done,
and it is wonderful in our eyes'?

43† Therefore, I say to you, the kingdom
of God will be taken away from you and
given to a people that will produce its
fruit. [44† The one who falls on this stone
will be dashed to pieces; and it will

---

*

32: Lk 7, 29-30.
33-46: Mk 12, 1-12; Lk 20, 9-19.
33: Is 5, 1-2.7.
39: Heb 13, 12.
42: Ps 118, 22-23; Is 28, 16; Acts 4, 11; 1 Pt 2, 7.

†

21, 28-32: The series of controversies is interrupted by three parables on the judgment of Israel (21, 28—22, 14) of which this, peculiar to Mt, is the first. The second (21, 33-46) comes from Mk (12, 1-12), and the third (22, 1-14) from Q; see Lk 14, 15-24. This interruption of the controversies is similar to that in Mk, although Mk has only one parable between the first and second controversy. As regards Mt's first parable, vv 28-30 if taken by themselves could point simply to the difference between saying and doing, a theme of much importance in this gospel (cf 7, 21; 12, 50); that may have been the parable's original reference. However, it is given a more specific application by the addition of vv 31-32. The two sons represent, respectively, the religious leaders and the religious outcasts who followed John's call to repentance. By the answer they give to Jesus' question (31) the leaders condemn themselves. There is much confusion in the textual tradition of the parable. Of the three different forms of the text given by important textual witnesses, one has the leaders answer that the son who agreed to go but did not was the one who did the father's will. Although some scholars accept that as the original reading, their arguments in favor of it seem unconvincing. The choice probably lies only between a reading that puts the son who agrees and then disobeys before the son who at first refuses and then obeys, and the reading followed in the present translation. The witnesses to the latter reading are slightly better than those that support the other.

21, 31: *Entering . . . before you:* this probably means "they enter; you do not."

21, 32: Cf Lk 7, 29-30. Although the thought is similar to that of the Lucan text, the formulation is so different that it is improbable that the saying comes from Q. *Came to you . . . way of righteousness:* several meanings are possible: that John himself was righteous, that he taught righteousness to others, or that he had an important place in God's plan of salvation. For the last, see the note on 3, 14-15.

21, 33-46: Cf Mk 12, 1-12. In this parable there is a close correspondence between most of the details of the story and the situation that it illustrates, the dealings of God with his people. Because of that heavy allegorizing, some scholars think that it does not in any way go back to Jesus, but represents the theology of the later church. That judgment applies to the Marcan parallel as well, although the allegorizing has gone farther in Mt. There are others who believe that while many of the allegorical elements are due to church sources, they have been added to a basic parable spoken by Jesus. This view is now supported by the Gospel of Thomas, #65, where a less allegorized and probably more primitive form of the parable is found.

21, 33: *Planted a vineyard . . . a tower:* cf Is 5, 1-2. The *vineyard* is defined in Is 5, 7 as "the house of Israel."

21, 34-35: *His servants:* Mt has two sendings of *servants* as against Mk's three sendings of a single servant (11, 2-5a) followed by a statement about the sending of "many others" (11, 2.5b). That these *servants* stand for the prophets sent by God to Israel is clearly implied but not made explicit here, but see 23, 37. *His produce:* cf Mk 12, 2, "some of the produce." The *produce* is the good works demanded by God, and his claim to them is total.

21, 38: *Acquire his inheritance:* if a Jewish proselyte died without heir, the tenants of his land would have final claim on it.

21, 39: *Threw him out . . . and killed him:* the change in the Marcan order where the son is killed and his corpse then thrown out (12, 8) was probably made because of the tradition that Jesus died outside the city of Jerusalem; see Jn 19, 17; Heb 13, 12.

21, 41: *They answered:* in Mk 12, 9 the question is answered by Jesus himself; here the leaders answer and so condemn themselves; cf v 31. Matthew adds that the new *tenants* to whom the vineyard will be transferred *will give* the owner *the produce at the proper times.*

21, 42: Cf Ps 118, 22-23. The psalm was used in the early church as a prophecy of Jesus' resurrection; see Acts 4, 11; 1 Pt 2, 7. If, as some think, the original parable ended at v 39, it was thought necessary to complete it by a reference to Jesus' vindication by God.

21, 43: Peculiar to Mt. *Kingdom of God:* see the note on 19, 23-24. Its presence here instead of Mt's usual "kingdom of heaven" may indicate that the saying came from Matthew's own traditional material. *A people that will produce its fruit:* believing Israelites and Gentiles, the church of Jesus.

21, 44: The majority of textual witnesses omit this verse. It is probably an early addition to Mt from Lk 20, 18 with which it is practically identical.

crush anyone on whom it falls.]"
45† When the chief priests and the Phar-
isees heard his parables, they knew that
he was speaking about them. 46 And al-
though they were attempting to arrest
him, they feared the crowds, for they
regarded him as a prophet.

CHAPTER 22

The Parable of the Wedding Feast.†

1* Jesus again in reply spoke to them
in parables, saying, 2† "The kingdom of
heaven may be likened to a king who
gave a wedding feast for his son.
3† He dispatched his servants to sum-
mon the invited guests to the feast, but
they refused to come. 4 A second time
he sent other servants, saying, 'Tell
those invited: "Behold, I have prepared
my banquet, my calves and fattened
cattle are killed, and everything is
ready; come to the feast."' 5 Some ig-
nored the invitation and went away, one
to his farm, another to his business.
6* The rest laid hold of his servants,
mistreated them, and killed them.
7† The king was enraged and sent his
troops, destroyed those murderers, and
burned their city. 8 Then he said to his
servants, 'The feast is ready, but those
who were invited were not worthy to
come. 9 Go out, therefore, into the main
roads and invite to the feast whomever
you find.' 10† The servants went out into
the streets and gathered all they found,
bad and good alike, and the hall was
filled with guests. 11† But when the king
came in to meet the guests he saw a man
there not dressed in a wedding gar-
ment. 12 He said to him, 'My friend, how
is it that you came in here without a
wedding garment?' But he was reduced
to silence. 13*† Then the king said to his
attendants, 'Bind his hands and feet,
and cast him into the darkness outside,
where there will be wailing and grind-
ing of teeth.' 14 Many are invited, but
few are chosen."

Paying Taxes to the Emperor.†

15*† Then the Pharisees went off and
plotted how they might entrap him in
speech. 16† They sent their disciples to
him, with the Herodians, saying,
"Teacher, we know that you are a truth-
ful man and that you teach the way of
God in accordance with the truth. And
you are not concerned with anyone's
opinion, for you do not regard a per-
son's status. 17† Tell us, then, what is
your opinion: Is it lawful to pay the cen-
sus tax to Caesar or not?" 18 Knowing
their malice, Jesus said, "Why are you
testing me, you hypocrites? 19† Show me
the coin that pays the census tax." Then
they handed him the Roman coin.
20 He said to them, "Whose image is this
and whose inscription?" 21*† They re-
plied, "Caesar's." At that he said to
them, "Then repay to Caesar what be-
longs to Caesar and to God what belongs
to God." 22 When they heard this they
were amazed, and leaving him they
went away.

---

*

22, 1-14: Lk 14, 15-24.
6: 21, 35.
13: 8, 12; 25, 30.
15-22: Mk 12, 13-17; Lk 20, 20-26.
21: Rom 13, 7.

---

†

21, 45: *The Pharisees:* Matthew inserts into the group of Jewish leaders (23) those who represented the Judaism of his own time.

22, 1-14: This parable is from Q; see Lk 14, 15-24. It has been given many allegorical traits by Matthew, e.g., the burning of the *city* of the guests who refused the invitation (7), which corresponds to the destruction of Jerusalem by the Romans in A.D. 70. It has similarities with the preceding parable of the tenants: the sending of two groups of *servants* (3.4), the murder of the *servants* (6), the punishment of the *murderers* (7), and the entrance of a new group into a privileged situation of which the others had proved themselves unworthy (8-10). The parable ends with a section that is peculiar to Mt (11-14), which some take as a distinct parable. Mt presents the *kingdom* in its double aspect, already present and something that can be entered here and now (1-10), and something that will be possessed only by those present members who can stand the scrutiny of the final judgment (11-14). The parable is not only a statement of God's judgment on Israel but a warning to Matthew's church.

22, 2: *Wedding feast:* the Old Testament's portrayal of final salvation under the image of a banquet (Is 25, 6) is taken up also in 8, 11; cf Lk 13, 15.

22, 3-4: *Servants . . . other servants:* probably Christian missionaries in both instances; cf 23, 34.

22, 7: See the note on vv 1-14.

22, 10: *Bad and good alike:* cf 13, 47.

22, 11: *A wedding garment:* the repentance, change of heart and mind, that is the condition for entrance into the kingdom (3, 2; 4, 17) must be continued in a life of good deeds (7, 21-23).

22, 13: *Wailing and grinding of teeth:* the Christian who lacks the wedding garment of good deeds will suffer the same fate as those Jews who have rejected Jesus; see the note on 8, 11-12.

22, 15-22: The series of controversies between Jesus and the representatives of Judaism (see the note on 21, 23-27) is resumed. As in the first (21, 23-27), here and in the following disputes Matthew follows his Marcan source with few modifications.

22, 15: *The Pharisees:* while Matthew retains the Marcan union of Pharisees and Herodians in this account, he clearly emphasizes the Pharisees' part. They alone are mentioned here, and the Herodians are joined with them only in a prepositional phrase of v 16. *Entrap him in speech:* the question that they will pose is intended to force Jesus to take either a position contrary to that held by the majority of the people or one that will bring him into conflict with the Roman authorities.

22, 16: *Herodians:* see the note on Mk 3, 6. They would favor payment of the tax; the Pharisees did not.

22, 17: *Is it lawful:* the law to which they refer is the law of God.

22, 19: *They handed him the Roman coin:* their readiness in producing the money implies their use of it and their acceptance of the financial advantages of the Roman administration in Palestine.

22, 21: *Caesar's:* the emperor Tiberius (A.D. 14-37). *Repay to Caesar what belongs to Caesar:* those who willingly use the coin that is Caesar's should *repay* him in kind. The answer avoids taking sides in the question of the lawfulness of the tax. *To God what belongs to God:* Jesus raises the debate to a new level. Those who have hypocritically asked about tax in respect to its relation to the law of God should be concerned rather with repaying *God* with the good deeds that are his due; cf 21, 41.43.

The Question about the Resurrection.† [23]*† On that day Sadducees approached him, saying that there is no resurrection. They put this question to him, [24]*† saying, "Teacher, Moses said, 'If a man dies without children, his brother shall marry his wife and raise up descendants for his brother.' [25] Now there were seven brothers among us. The first married and died and, having no descendants, left his wife to his brother. [26] The same happened with the second and the third, through all seven. [27] Finally the woman died. [28] Now at the resurrection, of the seven, whose wife will she be? For they all had been married to her." [29]† Jesus said to them in reply, "You are misled because you do not know the scriptures or the power of God. [30] At the resurrection they neither marry nor are given in marriage but are like the angels in heaven. [31]† And concerning the resurrection of the dead, have you not read what was said to you by God, [32]* 'I am the God of Abraham, the God of Isaac, and the God of Jacob'? He is not the God of the dead but of the living." [33] When the crowds heard this, they were astonished at his teaching.

The Greatest Commandment.† [34]* When the Pharisees heard that he had silenced the Sadducees, they gathered together, [35]† and one of them [a scholar of the law] tested him by asking, [36]† "Teacher, which commandment in the law is the greatest?" [37]*† He said to him, "You shall love the Lord, your God, with all your heart, with all your soul, and with all your mind. [38] This is the greatest and the first commandment. [39]*† The second is like it: You shall love your neighbor as yourself. [40]*† The whole law and the prophets depend on these two commandments."

The Question about David's Son.† [41]*† While the Pharisees were gathered together, Jesus questioned them, [42]† saying, "What is your opinion about the Messiah? Whose son is he?" They replied, "David's." [43] He said to them, "How, then, does David, inspired by the Spirit, call him 'lord,' saying:

*

23-33:	Mk 12, 18-27; Lk 20, 27-40.	37:	Dt 6, 5.
24:	Gn 38, 8; Dt 25, 5-6.	39:	Lv 19, 18; Jas 2, 8.
32:	Ex 3, 6.	40:	Rom 13, 8-10; Gal 5, 14.
34-40:	Mk 12, 28-34; Lk 10, 25-28.	41-46:	Mk 12, 35-37; Lk 20, 41-44.

†

22, 23-33: Here Jesus' opponents are the *Sadducees,* members of the powerful priestly party of his time; see the note on 3, 7. Denying the resurrection of the dead, a teaching of relatively late origin in Judaism (cf Dn 12, 2), they appeal to a law of the Pentateuch (Dt 25, 5-10) and present a case based on it that would make resurrection from the dead ridiculous (24-28). Jesus chides them for knowing neither *the scriptures* nor *the power of God* (29). His argument in respect to God's *power* contradicts the notion, held even by many proponents as well as by opponents of the teaching, that the life of those raised from the dead would be essentially a continuation of the type of life they had had before death (30). His argument based on the scriptures (31-32) is of a sort that was accepted as valid among Jews of the time.

22, 23: *Saying that there is no resurrection:* in the Marcan parallel (12, 18) the Sadducees are correctly defined as those "who say there is no resurrection"; see also Lk 20, 27. Matthew's rewording of Mk can mean that these particular Sadducees deny the resurrection, which would imply that he was not aware that the denial was characteristic of the party. For some scholars this is an indication of his being a Gentile Christian; see the note on 21, 4-5.

22, 24: *'If a man dies . . . his brother':* this is known as the "law of the levirate," from the Latin *levir,* "brother-in-law." Its purpose was to continue the family line of the deceased *brother* (Dt 25, 6).

22, 29: The sexual relationships of this world will be transcended; the risen body will be the work of the creative *power of God.*

22, 31-32: Cf Ex 3, 6. In the Pentateuch, which the Sadducees accepted as normative for Jewish belief and practice, God speaks even now (*to you*) of himself as the God of the patriarchs who died centuries ago. He identifies himself in relation to them, and because of their relation to him, the living God, they too are alive. This might appear no argument for the resurrection, but simply for life after death as conceived in Wis 3, 1-3. But the general thought of early first-century Judaism was not influenced by that conception; for it human immortality was connected with the existence of the body.

22, 34-40: The Marcan parallel (12, 28-34) is an exchange between Jesus and a scribe who is impressed by the way in which Jesus has conducted himself in the previous controversy (12, 28), who compliments him for the answer he gives him (12, 32), and who is said by Jesus to be "not far from the kingdom of God" (12, 34). Matthew has sharpened that scene. The questioner, as the representative of other Pharisees, tests Jesus by his question (34-35), and both his reaction to Jesus' reply and Jesus' commendation of him are lacking.

22, 35: *[A scholar of the law]:* meaning "scribe." Although this reading is supported by the vast majority of textual witnesses, it is the only time that the Greek word so translated occurs in Mt. It is relatively frequent in Lk, and there is reason to think that it may have been added here by a copyist since it occurs in the Lucan parallel (10, 25-28). *Tested:* see the note on 19, 3.

22, 36: For the devout Jew all the commandments were to be kept with equal care, but there is evidence of preoccupation in Jewish sources with the question put to Jesus.

22, 37-38: Cf Dt 6, 5. Matthew omits the first part of Mk's fuller quotation (12, 29; Dt 6, 4-5), probably because he considered its monotheistic emphasis needless for his church. The love of God must engage the total person (*heart, soul, mind*).

22, 39: Jesus goes beyond the extent of the question put to him and joins to *the greatest and the first commandment* a *second,* that of *love* of *neighbor,* Lv 19, 18; see the note on 19, 18-19. This combination of the two commandments may already have been made in Judaism.

22, 40: The double commandment is the source from which *the whole law and the prophets* are derived.

22, 41-46: Having answered the questions of his opponents in the preceding three controversies, Jesus now puts a question to them about the sonship of the Messiah. Their easy response (43a) is countered by his quoting a verse of Ps 110 that raises a problem for their response (43b-45). They are unable to solve it and *from that day on* their questioning of him is ended.

22, 41: *The Pharisees . . . questioned them:* Mk is not specific about who are questioned (12, 35).

22, 42-44: *David's:* this view of the Pharisees was based on such Old Testament texts as Is 11, 1-9; Jer 23, 5; and Ez 34, 23; see also the extrabiblical Psalms of Solomon 17, 21. *How, then . . . saying:* Jesus cites Ps 110, 1, accepting the Davidic authorship of the psalm, a common view of his time. The psalm was probably composed for the enthronement of a Davidic king of Judah. Matthew assumes that the Pharisees interpret it as referring to the Messiah, although there is no clear evidence that it was so interpreted in the Judaism of Jesus' time. It was widely used in the early church as referring to the exaltation of the risen Jesus. *My lord:* understood as the Messiah.

44* 'The Lord said to my lord,
"Sit at my right hand
until I place your enemies under
your feet" '?
45† If David calls him 'lord,' how can he
be his son?" 46* No one was able to an-
swer him a word, nor from that day on
did anyone dare to ask him any more
questions.

CHAPTER 23†

Denunciation of the Scribes and
Pharisees. 1* Then Jesus spoke to the
crowds and to his disciples, 2† saying,
"The scribes and the Pharisees have
taken their seat on the chair of Moses.
3 Therefore, do and observe all things
whatsoever they tell you, but do not fol-
low their example. For they preach but
they do not practice. 4*† They tie up
heavy burdens [hard to carry] and lay
them on people's shoulders, but they
will not lift a finger to move them.
5*† All their works are performed to be
seen. They widen their phylacteries and
lengthen their tassels. 6*† They love
places of honor at banquets, seats of
honor in synagogues, 7 greetings in
marketplaces, and the salutation
'Rabbi.' 8† As for you, do not be called
'Rabbi.' You have but one teacher, and
you are all brothers. 9 Call no one on
earth your father; you have but one
Father in heaven. 10 Do not be called
'Master'; you have but one master, the
Messiah. 11* The greatest among you
must be your servant. 12* Whoever ex-
alts himself will be humbled; but who-
ever humbles himself will be exalted.
13*† "Woe to you, scribes and Phari-
sees, you hypocrites. You lock the king-
dom of heaven before human beings.
You do not enter yourselves, nor do you
allow entrance to those trying to enter.
[14]†

*
44: Ps 110, 1; Acts 2, 35; Heb 1, 13.
46: Lk 20, 40.
23, 1-39: Mk 12, 38-39; Lk 11, 37-52; 13, 34-35.
4: Lk 11, 46.
5: 6, 1-6; Ex 13, 9.16; Nm 15, 38-39; Dt 6, 8; 11, 18.
6-7: Mk 12, 38-39; Lk 11, 43; 20, 46.
11: 20, 26.
12: Lk 14, 11; 18, 14.
13: Lk 11, 52.

†
22, 45: Since Matthew presents Jesus both as Messiah (16, 16) and as Son of David (1, 1; see also the note on 9, 27), the question is not meant to imply Jesus' denial of Davidic sonship. It probably means that although he is the Son of David, he is someone greater, Son of Man and Son of God, and recognized as greater by David who calls him my *'lord.'*

23, 1-39: The final section of the narrative part of the fifth book of the gospel is a denunciation by Jesus of the scribes and the Pharisees (see the note on 3, 7). It depends in part on Mk and Q (cf Mk 12, 38-39; Lk 11, 37-52; 13, 34-35), but in the main it is peculiar to Mt. (For the reasons against considering this extensive body of sayings-material either as one of the structural discourses of this gospel or as part of the one that follows in chs 24-25, see the note on 19, 1—23, 39.) While the tradition of a deep opposition between Jesus and the Pharisees is well founded, this speech reflects an opposition that goes beyond that of Jesus' ministry and must be seen as expressing the bitter conflict between Pharisaic Judaism and the church of Matthew at the time when the gospel was composed. The complaint often made that the speech ignores the positive qualities of Pharisaism and of its better representatives is true, but the complaint overlooks the circumstances that gave rise to the invective. Nor is the speech purely anti-Pharisaic. The evangelist discerns in his church many of the same faults that he finds in its opponents and warns his fellow Christians to look to their own conduct and attitudes.

23, 2-3: *Have taken their seat . . . Moses:* it is uncertain whether this is simply a metaphor for Mosaic teaching authority or refers to an actual *chair* on which the teacher sat. It has been proved that there was a seat so designated in synagogues of a later period than that of this gospel. *Do and observe . . . they tell you:* since the Matthean Jesus abrogates Mosaic law (5, 31-42), warns his disciples against the teaching of the Pharisees (14, 1-12), and, in this speech, denounces the Pharisees as blind guides in respect to their teaching on oaths (16-22), this commandment to *observe all things whatsoever they* (the scribes and Pharisees) *tell you* cannot be taken as the evangelist's understanding of the proper standard of conduct for his church. The saying may reflect a period when the Matthean community was largely Jewish Christian and was still seeking to avoid a complete break with the synagogue. Matthew has incorporated this traditional material into the speech in accordance with his view of the course of salvation history, in which he portrays the time of Jesus' ministry as marked by the fidelity to the law, although with significant pointers to the new situation that would exist after his death and resurrection (see the note on 5, 17-20). The crowds and the disciples (1) are exhorted not to *follow* the *example* of the Jewish leaders, whose deeds do not conform to their teaching (3).

23, 4: *Tie up heavy burdens:* see the note on 11, 28.

23, 5: To the charge of preaching but not practicing (3), Jesus adds that of acting in order to earn praise. The disciples have already been warned against this same fault (see the note on 6, 1-18). *Phylacteries:* the Mosaic law required that during prayer small boxes containing parchments on which verses of scripture were written be worn on the left forearm and the forehead (see Ex 13, 9.16; Dt 6, 8; 11, 18). *Tassels:* see the note on 9, 20. The widening of *phylacteries* and the lengthening of *tassels* were for the purpose of making these evidences of piety more noticeable.

23, 6-7: Cf Mk 12, 38-39. *'Rabbi':* literally, "my great one," a title of respect for teachers and leaders.

23, 8-12: These verses, warning against the use of various titles, are addressed to the disciples alone. While only the title *'Rabbi'* has been said to be used in addressing the scribes and Pharisees (7), the implication is that *Father* and *'Master'* also were. The prohibition of these titles to the disciples suggests that their use was present in Matthew's church. The Matthean Jesus forbids not only the titles but the spirit of superiority and pride that is shown by their acceptance. *Whoever exalts . . . will be exalted:* cf Lk 14, 11.

23, 13-36: This series of seven "woes," directed against the *scribes and Pharisees* and addressed to them, is the heart of the speech. The phrase *woe to* occurs often in the prophetic and apocalyptic literature, expressing horror of a sin and punishment for those who commit it. *Hypocrites:* see the note on 6, 2. The hypocrisy of the *scribes and Pharisees* consists in the difference between their speech and action (3) and in demonstrations of piety that have no other purpose than to enhance their reputation as religious persons (5).

23, 13: *You lock the kingdom of heaven:* cf 16, 19 where Jesus tells Peter that he will give him the keys to *the kingdom of heaven.* The purpose of the authority expressed by that metaphor is to give entrance into the kingdom (the kingdom is closed only to those who reject the authority); here the charge is made that the authority of the *scribes and Pharisees* is exercised in such a way as to be an obstacle to entrance. Cf Lk 11, 52 where the accusation against the "scholars of the law" (Mt's *scribes*) is that they "have taken away the key of knowledge."

23, 14: Some manuscripts add a verse here or after v 12, "Woe to you, scribes and Pharisees, you hypocrites. You devour the houses of widows and, as a pretext, recite lengthy prayers. Because of this, you will receive a very severe condemnation." Cf Mk 12, 40; Lk 20, 47. This "woe" is almost identical with Mk 12, 40 and seems to be an interpolation derived from that text.

15† "Woe to you, scribes and Phari-
sees, you hypocrites. You traverse sea
and land to make one convert, and
when that happens you make him a
child of Gehenna twice as much as
yourselves.
16*† "Woe to you, blind guides, who
say, 'If one swears by the temple, it
means nothing, but if one swears by the
gold of the temple, one is obligated.'
17 Blind fools, which is greater, the gold,
or the temple that made the gold sa-
cred? 18 And you say, 'If one swears by
the altar, it means nothing, but if one
swears by the gift on the altar, one is
obligated.' 19 You blind ones, which is
greater, the gift, or the altar that makes
the gift sacred? 20* One who swears by
the altar swears by it and all that is upon
it; 21 one who swears by the temple
swears by it and by him who dwells in
it; 22 one who swears by heaven swears
by the throne of God and by him who
is seated on it.
23*† "Woe to you, scribes and Phari-
sees, you hypocrites. You pay tithes of
mint and dill and cummin, and have ne-
glected the weightier things of the law:
judgment and mercy and fidelity. [But]
these you should have done, without ne-
glecting the others. 24*† Blind guides,
who strain out the gnat and swallow the
camel!
25*† "Woe to you, scribes and Phari-
sees, you hypocrites. You cleanse the
outside of cup and dish, but inside they
are full of plunder and self-indulgence.
26 Blind Pharisee, cleanse first the inside
of the cup, so that the outside also may
be clean.
27† "Woe to you, scribes and Phari-
sees, you hypocrites. You are like
whitewashed tombs, which appear
beautiful on the outside, but inside are
full of dead men's bones and every kind
of filth. 28* Even so, on the outside you
appear righteous, but inside you are
filled with hypocrisy and evildoing.
29† "Woe to you, scribes and Phari-
sees, you hypocrites. You build the
tombs of the prophets and adorn the
memorials of the righteous, 30* and you
say, 'If we had lived in the days of our
ancestors, we would not have joined
them in shedding the prophets' blood.'
31* Thus you bear witness against your-
selves that you are the children of those
who murdered the prophets; 32 now fill
up what your ancestors measured out!
33* You serpents, you brood of vipers,
how can you flee from the judgment of
Gehenna? 34*† Therefore, behold, I

*

16: 15, 14.
20-22: 5, 34-35.
23: Lv 27, 30; Dt 14, 22; Lk 11, 42.
24: Lv 11, 41-45.
25-26: Mk 7, 4; Lk 11, 39.
28: Lk 16, 15; 18, 9.
30: Lk 11, 47.
31: Acts 7, 52.
33: 3, 7; 12, 34.
34-36: 5, 12; Gn 4, 8; 2 Chr 24, 20-22; Zec 1, 1; Lk 11, 49-51; Rv 18, 24.

†

23, 15: In the first century A.D. until the First Jewish Revolt against Rome (A.D. 66-70), many Pharisees conducted a vigorous missionary campaign among Gentiles. *Convert:* literally, "proselyte," a Gentile who accepted Judaism fully by submitting to circumcision and all other requirements of Mosaic law. *Child of Gehenna:* worthy of everlasting punishment; for *Gehenna,* see the note on 5, 22. *Twice as much as yourselves:* possibly this refers simply to the zeal of the *convert,* surpassing that of the one who converted him.

23, 16-22: An attack on the casuistry that declared some oaths binding (*one is obligated*) and others not (*it means nothing*) and held the binding oath to be the one made by something of lesser value (*the gold; the gift on the altar*). Such teaching, which inverts the order of values, reveals the teachers to be *blind guides;* cf 15, 14. Since the Matthean Jesus forbids all oaths to his disciples (5, 33-37), this *woe* does not set up a standard for Christian moral conduct, but ridicules the Pharisees on their own terms.

23, 23: The Mosaic law ordered tithing of the produce of the land (Lv 27, 30; Dt 14, 22-23), and the scribal tradition is said here to have extended this law to even the smallest herbs. The practice is criticized not in itself but because it shows the Pharisees' preoccupation with matters of less importance while they neglect *the weightier things of the law.*

23, 24: Cf Lv 11, 41-45 that forbids the eating of any "swarming creature." The Pharisees' scrupulosity about minor matters and neglect of greater ones (23) is further brought out by this contrast between straining liquids that might contain a tiny "swarming creature" and yet swallowing *the camel.* The latter was one of the unclean animals forbidden by the law (Lv 11, 4), but it is hardly possible that the scribes and Pharisees are being denounced as guilty of so gross a violation of the food laws. To *swallow the camel* is only a hyperbolic way of speaking of their neglect of what is important.

23, 25-26: The ritual washing of utensils for dining (cf Mk 7, 4) is turned into a metaphor illustrating a concern for appearances while inner purity is ignored. The *scribes and Pharisees* are compared to cups carefully washed on the outside but filthy within. *Self-indulgence:* the Greek word here translated means lack of self-control, whether in drinking or in sexual conduct.

23, 27-28: The sixth *woe,* like the preceding one, deals with concern for externals and neglect of what is *inside.* Since contact with dead bodies, even when one was unaware of it, caused ritual impurity (Nm 19, 11-22), tombs were whitewashed so that no one would contract such impurity inadvertently.

23, 29-36: The final *woe* is the most serious indictment of all. It portrays the *scribes and Pharisees* as standing in the same line as their *ancestors* who murdered *the prophets* and *the righteous.*

23, 29-32: In spite of honoring the slain dead by building their *tombs* and adorning their *memorials,* and claiming that they would not have joined in their ancestors' crimes if they *had lived in* their *days,* the *scribes and Pharisees* are true *children* of their ancestors and are defiantly ordered by Jesus to *fill up* what those *ancestors measured out.* This order reflects the Jewish notion that there was an allotted measure of suffering that had to be completed before God's final judgment would take place.

23, 34-36: There are important differences between the Matthean and the Lucan form of this Q material; cf Lk 11, 49-51. In Lk the one who sends the emissaries is the "wisdom of God." If, as many scholars think, that is the original wording of Q, Matthew, by making Jesus the sender, has presented him as the personified divine wisdom. In Lk, wisdom's emissaries are the Old Testament "prophets" and the Christian "apostles." Mt's *prophets and wise men and scribes* are probably Christian disciples alone; cf 10, 41 and see the note on 13, 52. *You will kill:* see 24, 9. *Scourge in your synagogues . . . town to town:* see 10, 17.23 and the note on 10, 17. *All the righteous blood shed upon the earth:* the slaying of the disciples is in continuity with all the shedding of *righteous blood* beginning with that of *Abel.* The persecution of Jesus' disciples by *this generation* involves the persecutors in the guilt of their murderous ancestors. *The blood of Zechariah:* see the note on Lk 11, 51. By identifying him as *the son of Barachiah* Matthew understands him to be Zechariah the Old Testament minor prophet; see Zec 1, 1.

send to you prophets and wise men and
scribes; some of them you will kill and
crucify, some of them you will scourge
in your synagogues and pursue from
town to town, [35] so that there may come
upon you all the righteous blood shed
upon earth, from the righteous blood
of Abel to the blood of Zechariah, the
son of Barachiah, whom you mur-
dered between the sanctuary and
the altar. [36] Amen, I say to you, all
these things will come upon this genera-
tion.

The Lament over Jerusalem.†
[37*] "Jerusalem, Jerusalem, you who kill
the prophets and stone those sent to
you, how many times I yearned to
gather your children together, as a hen
gathers her young under her wings, but
you were unwilling! [38*] Behold, your
house will be abandoned, desolate.
[39*] I tell you, you will not see me again
until you say, 'Blessed is he who comes
in the name of the Lord.' "

CHAPTER 24†

***The Destruction of the Temple
Foretold.*** [1*] Jesus left the temple area
and was going away, when his disciples
approached him to point out the temple
buildings. [2†] He said to them in re-
ply, "You see all these things, do
you not? Amen, I say to you, there
will not be left here a stone upon an-
other stone that will not be thrown
down."

The Beginning of Calamities. [3†] As he
was sitting on the Mount of Olives, the
disciples approached him privately and
said, "Tell us, when will this happen,
and what sign will there be of your com-
ing, and of the end of the age?" [4†] Jesus
said to them in reply, "See that no one
deceives you. [5] For many will come in
my name, saying, 'I am the Messiah,'
and they will deceive many. [6*†] You
will hear of wars and reports of wars;
see that you are not alarmed, for these
things must happen, but it will not yet
be the end. [7*] Nation will rise against
nation, and kingdom against kingdom;
there will be famines and earthquakes
from place to place. [8†] All these are the

*

37-39: Lk 13, 34-35; 19, 41-44.
37: 21, 35.
38: Jer 12, 7.
39: Ps 118, 26.
24, 1-44: Mk 13, 1-37; Lk 21, 5-36.
6: Dn 2, 28 LXX.
7: Is 19, 2.

†

23, 37-39: Cf Lk 13, 34-35. The denunciation of Pharisaic Judaism ends with this lament over *Jerusalem,* which has repeatedly rejected and murdered those whom God has *sent to* her. *How many times:* this may refer to various visits of Jesus to the city, an aspect of his ministry found in Jn but otherwise not in the synoptics. *As a hen . . . under her wings:* for imagery similar to this, see Pss 17, 8; 91, 4. *Your house . . . desolate:* probably an allusion to the destruction of the temple in A.D. 70. *You will not see me . . . in the name of the Lord:* Israel will not see Jesus again until he comes in glory for the final judgment. The acclamation has been interpreted in contrasting ways, as an indication that Israel will at last accept Jesus at that time, and as its troubled recognition of him as its dreaded judge who will pronounce its condemnation; in support of the latter view see 24, 30.

24, 1—25, 46: The discourse of the fifth book, the last of the five around which the gospel is structured. It is called the "eschatological" discourse since it deals with the coming of the new age (the *eschaton*) in its fullness, with events that will precede it, and with how the disciples are to conduct themselves while awaiting an event that is as certain as its exact time is unknown to all but the Father (24, 36). The discourse may be divided into two parts, 24, 1-44 and 24, 45—25, 46. In the first, Matthew follows his Marcan source (13, 1-37) closely. The second is drawn from Q and from the evangelist's own traditional material. Both parts show Matthew's editing of his sources by deletions, additions, and modifications. The vigilant waiting that is emphasized in the second part does not mean a cessation of ordinary activity and concentration only on what is to come, but a faithful accomplishment of duties at hand, with awareness that the end, for which the disciples must always be ready, will entail the great judgment by which the everlasting destiny of all will be determined.

24, 2: As in Mk, Jesus predicts the destruction of the temple. By omitting the Marcan story of the widow's contribution (12, 41-44) that immediately precedes the prediction in that gospel, Matthew has established a close connection between it and 23, 38, ". . . your house will be abandoned desolate."

24, 3: *The Mount of Olives:* see the note on 21, 1. *The disciples:* cf Mk 13, 3-4 where only Peter, James, John, and Andrew put the question that is answered by the discourse. In both gospels, however, the question is put *privately:* the ensuing discourse is only for those who are *disciples* of Jesus. *When will this happen . . . end of the age?:* Matthew distinguishes carefully between the destruction of the temple (*this*) and the *coming* of Jesus that will bring *the end of the age.* In Mk the two events are more closely connected, a fact that may be explained by Mark's believing that the one would immediately succeed the other. *Coming:* this translates the Greek word *parousia,* which is used in the gospels only here and in vv 27, 37, and 39. It designated the official visit of a ruler to a city or the manifestation of a saving deity, and it was used by Christians to refer to the final coming of Jesus in glory, a term first found in the New Testament with that meaning in 1 Thes 2, 19. *The end of the age:* see the note on 13, 39.

24, 4-14: This section of the discourse deals with calamities in the world (6-7) and in the church (9-12). The former *must happen* before *the end* comes (6), but they are only *the beginning of the labor pains* (8). (It may be noted that the Greek word translated *the end* in v 6 and in vv 13-14 is not the same as the phrase "the end of the age" in v 3, although the meaning is the same.) The latter are sufferings of the church, both from within and without, that will last until the *gospel* is *preached . . . to all nations. Then the end will come* and those who have endured the sufferings with fidelity *will be saved* (13-14).

24, 6-7: The disturbances mentioned here are a commonplace of apocalyptic language, as is the assurance that they *must happen* (see Dn 2, 28 LXX), for that is the plan of God. *Kingdom against kingdom:* see Is 19, 2.

24, 8: *The labor pains:* the tribulations leading up to the end of the age are compared to the pains of a woman about to give birth. There is much attestation for rabbinic use of the phrase "the woes (or birth pains) of the Messiah" after the New Testament period, but in at least one instance it is attributed to a rabbi who lived in the late first century A.D. In this Jewish usage it meant the distress of the time preceding the coming of the Messiah; here, the *labor pains* precede the coming of the Son of Man in glory.

beginning of the labor pains. 9*† Then
they will hand you over to persecution,
and they will kill you. You will be hated
by all nations because of my name.
10 And then many will be led into sin;
they will betray and hate one another.
11 Many false prophets will arise and de-
ceive many; 12 and because of the in-
crease of evildoing, the love of many
will grow cold. 13* But the one who per-
severes to the end will be saved.
14*† And this gospel of the kingdom will
be preached throughout the world as a
witness to all nations, and then the end
will come.

The Great Tribulation.† 15*† "When
you see the desolating abomination spo-
ken of through Daniel the prophet
standing in the holy place (let the
reader understand), 16† then those in
Judea must flee to the mountains,
17*† a person on the housetop must not
go down to get things out of his house,
18 a person in the field must not return
to get his cloak. 19 Woe to pregnant
women and nursing mothers in those
days. 20† Pray that your flight not be in
winter or on the sabbath, 21*† for at that
time there will be great tribulation, such
as has not been since the beginning of
the world until now, nor ever will be.
22 And if those days had not been short-
ened, no one would be saved; but for
the sake of the elect they will be short-
ened. 23* If anyone says to you then,
'Look, here is the Messiah!' or, 'There
he is!' do not believe it. 24 False messi-
ahs and false prophets will arise, and
they will perform signs and wonders so
great as to deceive, if that were possible,
even the elect. 25 Behold, I have told it
to you beforehand. 26† So if they say to
you, 'He is in the desert,' do not go out
there; if they say, 'He is in the inner
rooms,' do not believe it. 27* For just as
lightning comes from the east and is
seen as far as the west, so will the com-
ing of the Son of Man be. 28 Wherever
the corpse is, there the vultures will
gather.

The Coming of the Son of Man.
29*† "Immediately after the tribulation
of those days,

the sun will be darkened,
and the moon will not give its
light,
and the stars will fall from the sky,

---

*

9: 10, 17.
13: 10, 22.
14: 28, 19; Rom 10, 18.
15: Dn 9, 27; 11, 31; 12, 11; Mk 13, 14.
17: Lk 17, 31.
21: Dn 12, 1.
23: Lk 17, 23.
27-28: Lk 17, 24.37.
29: Is 13, 10.13; Ez 32, 7; Am 8, 9.

---

†

24, 9-12: Matthew has used Mk 13, 9-12 in his missionary discourse (10, 17-21) and omits it here. Besides the sufferings, including death, and the hatred of *all nations* that the disciples will have to endure, there will be worse affliction within the church itself. This is described in vv 10-12, which are peculiar to Mt. *Will be led into sin:* literally, "will be scandalized," probably meaning that they will become apostates; see 13, 21 where "fall away" translates the same Greek word as here. *Betray:* in the Greek this is the same word as the *hand over* of v 9. The handing over to persecution and hatred from outside will have their counterpart within the church. *False prophets:* these are Christians; see the note on 7, 15-20. *Evildoing:* see 7, 23. Because of the apocalyptic nature of much of this discourse, the literal meaning of this description of the church should not be pressed too hard. However, there is reason to think that Mt's addition of these verses reflects in some measure the condition of his community.

24, 14: Except for the last part (*and then the end will come*), this verse substantially repeats Mk 13, 10. The Matthean addition raises a problem since what follows in vv 15-23 refers to the horrors of the First Jewish Revolt including the destruction of the temple, and Matthew, writing after that time, knew that the parousia of Jesus was still in the future. A solution may be that the evangelist saw the events of those verses as foreshadowing the cosmic disturbances that he associates with the parousia (29) so that the period in which the former took place could be understood as belonging to *the end.*

24, 15-28: Cf Mk 13, 14-23; Lk 17, 23-24.37. A further stage in the tribulations that will precede the coming of the Son of Man, and an answer to the question of v 3a, "when will this (the destruction of the temple) happen?"

24, 15: *The desolating abomination:* in 167 B.C. the Syrian king Antiochus IV Epiphanes desecrated the temple by setting up in it a statue of Zeus Olympios (see 1 Mc 1, 54). That event is referred to in Dn 12, 11 LXX as the "desolating abomination" (NAB "horrible abomination") and the same Greek term is used here; cf also Dn 9, 27; 11, 31. Although the desecration had taken place before Dn was written, it is presented there as a future event, and Matthew sees that "prophecy" fulfilled in the desecration of the temple by the Romans. *In the holy place:* the temple; more precise than Mk's *where he should not* (13, 14). *Let the reader understand:* this parenthetical remark, taken from Mk 13, 14, invites *the reader* to realize the meaning of Dn's "prophecy."

24, 16: The tradition that the Christians of Jerusalem fled from that city to Pella, a city of Transjordan, at the time of the First Jewish Revolt is found in Eusebius (*Ecclesiastical History,* 3, 5, 3), who attributes the flight to "a certain oracle given by revelation before the war." The tradition is not improbable but the Matthean command, derived from its Marcan source, is vague in respect to the place of flight (*to the mountains*), although some scholars see it as applicable to the flight to Pella.

24, 17-19: Haste is essential, and the journey will be particularly difficult for women who are burdened with unborn or infant children.

24, 20: *On the sabbath:* this addition to *in winter* (cf Mk 13, 18) has been understood as an indication that Mt was addressed to a church still observing the Mosaic law of sabbath rest and the scribal limitations upon the length of journeys that might lawfully be made on that day. That interpretation conflicts with Mt's view on sabbath observance (cf 12, 1-14). The meaning of the addition may be that those undertaking on the sabbath a journey such as the one here ordered would be offending the sensibilities of law-observant Jews and would incur their hostility.

24, 21: For the unparalleled distress of that time, see Dn 12, 1.

24, 26-28: Claims that the Messiah is to be found in some distant or secret place must be ignored. *The coming of the Son of Man* will be as clear as *lightning* is to all and as *the corpse* of an animal is to *vultures;* cf Lk 17, 24.37. Here there is clear identification of *the Son of Man* and the Messiah; cf v 23.

24, 29: The answer to the question of v 3b, "What will be the sign of your coming?" *Immediately after . . . those days:* the shortening of time between the preceding *tribulation* and the parousia has been explained as Matthew's use of a supposed device of Old Testament prophecy whereby certainty that a predicted event will occur is expressed by depicting it as imminent. While it is questionable that that is an acceptable understanding of the Old Testament predictions, it may be applicable here, for Matthew knew that the parousia had not come *immediately after* the fall of Jerusalem, and it is unlikely that he is attributing a mistaken calculation of time to Jesus. *The sun . . . be shaken:* cf Is 13, 10.13.

and the powers of the heavens will
be shaken.
30*† And then the sign of the Son of Man
will appear in heaven, and all the tribes
of the earth will mourn, and they will
see the Son of Man coming upon the
clouds of heaven with power and great
glory. 31*† And he will send out his an-
gels with a trumpet blast, and they will
gather his elect from the four winds,
from one end of the heavens to the
other.

The Lesson of the Fig Tree.†
32 "Learn a lesson from the fig tree.
When its branch becomes tender and
sprouts leaves, you know that summer
is near. 33 In the same way, when you
see all these things, know that he is
near, at the gates. 34† Amen, I say to
you, this generation will not pass away
until all these things have taken place.
35* Heaven and earth will pass away,
but my words will not pass away.

The Unknown Day and Hour.†
36*† "But of that day and hour no one
knows, neither the angels of heaven,
nor the Son, but the Father alone.
37*† For as it was in the days of Noah,
so it will be at the coming of the Son of
Man. 38 In [those] days before the flood,
they were eating and drinking, marry-
ing and giving in marriage, up to the
day that Noah entered the ark. 39 They
did not know until the flood came and
carried them all away. So will it be
[also] at the coming of the Son of Man.
40*† Two men will be out in the field; one
will be taken, and one will be left.
41 Two women will be grinding at the
mill; one will be taken, and one will be
left. 42*† Therefore, stay awake! For
you do not know on which day your
Lord will come. 43* Be sure of this: if the
master of the house had known the hour
of night when the thief was coming, he
would have stayed awake and not let
his house be broken into. 44 So too, you
also must be prepared, for at an hour
you do not expect, the Son of Man will
come.

The Faithful or the Unfaithful Servant.† 45*† "Who, then, is the faith-
ful and prudent servant, whom the mas-
ter has put in charge of his household
to distribute to them their food at the
proper time? 46 Blessed is that servant
whom his master on his arrival finds do-
ing so. 47 Amen, I say to you, he will put
him in charge of all his property.
48† But if that wicked servant says to
himself, 'My master is long delayed,'
49 and begins to beat his fellow servants,
and eat and drink with drunkards,
50 the servant's master will come on an
unexpected day and at an unknown
hour 51*† and will punish him severely
and assign him a place with the hypo-
crites, where there will be wailing and
grinding of teeth.

CHAPTER 25

The Parable of the Ten Virgins.†
1† "Then the kingdom of heaven will be
like ten virgins who took their lamps
and went out to meet the bridegroom.
2† Five of them were foolish and five

*

30: Dn 7, 13; Zec 12, 12-14; Rv 1, 7.
31: Is 27, 13; 1 Cor 15, 52; 1 Thes 4, 16.
35: Is 40, 8.
36: Acts 1, 7.
37-39: Gn 6, 5—7, 23; Lk 17, 26-27; 2 Pt 3, 6.
40-41: Lk 17, 34-35.
42-44: 25, 13; Lk 12, 39-40.
43: 1 Thes 5, 2.
45-51: Lk 12, 41-46.
51: 13, 42; 25, 30.

†

24, 30: *The sign of the Son of Man:* perhaps this means *the sign* that is the glorious appearance *of the Son of Man;* cf 12, 39-40 where "the sign of Jonah" is Jonah's being in the "belly of the whale." *Tribes of the earth will mourn:* peculiar to Mt; cf Zec 12, 12-14. *Coming upon the clouds . . . glory:* cf Dn 7, 13, although there the "one like a son of man" comes to God to receive kingship; here *the Son of Man* comes from heaven for judgment.

24, 31: *Send out his angels:* cf 13, 41 where they are sent out to collect the wicked for punishment. *Trumpet blast:* cf Is 27, 13; 1 Thes 4, 16.

24, 32-35: Cf Mk 13, 28-31.

24, 34: The difficulty raised by this verse cannot be satisfactorily removed by the supposition that *this generation* means the Jewish people throughout the course of their history, much less the entire human race. Perhaps for Matthew it means the *generation* to which he and his community belonged.

24, 36-44: The statement of v 34 is now counterbalanced by one that declares that the exact time of the parousia is known only to *the Father* (36), and the disciples are warned to be always ready for it. This section is drawn from Mk and Q (cf Lk 17, 26-27.34-35; 12, 39-40).

24, 36: Many textual witnesses omit *nor the Son,* which follows Mk 13, 32. Since its omission can be explained by reluctance to attribute this ignorance to *the Son,* the reading that includes it is probably original.

24, 37-39: Cf Lk 17, 26-27. *In the days of Noah:* the Old Testament account of the flood lays no emphasis upon what is central for Matthew, i.e., the unexpected coming of the flood upon those who were unprepared for it.

24, 40-41: Cf Lk 17, 34-35. *Taken . . . left:* the former probably means *taken* into the kingdom; the latter, *left* for destruction. People in the same situation will be dealt with in opposite ways. In this context, the discrimination between them will be based on their readiness for the coming of the Son of Man.

24, 42-44: Cf Lk 12, 39-40. The theme of vigilance and readiness is continued with the bold comparison of the Son of Man to a thief who comes to break into a house.

24, 45-51: The second part of the discourse (see the note on 24, 1—25, 46) begins with this parable of *the faithful* or unfaithful *servant;* cf Lk 12, 41-46. It is addressed to the leaders of Matthew's church; *the servant has* been *put in charge* of his master's *household* (45) even though that *household* is composed of those who are his *fellow servants* (49).

24, 45: *To distribute . . . proper time:* readiness for the master's return means a vigilance that is accompanied by faithful performance of the duty assigned.

24, 48: *My master . . . delayed:* the note of delay is found also in the other parables of this section; cf 25, 5.19.

24, 51: *Punish him severely:* the Greek verb, found in the New Testament only here and in the Lucan parallel (12, 46), means, literally, "cut in two." *With the hypocrites:* see the note on 6, 2. Matthew classes the unfaithful Christian leader with the unbelieving leaders of Judaism. *Wailing and grinding of teeth:* see the note on 8, 11-12.

25, 1-13: Peculiar to Mt.

25, 1: *Then:* at the time of the parousia. *Kingdom . . . will be like:* see the note on 13, 24-30.

25, 2-4: *Foolish . . . wise:* cf the contrasted "wise man" and "fool" of 7, 24.26, where the two are distinguished by good deeds and lack of them, and such deeds may be signified by the *oil* of this parable.

were wise. 3 The foolish ones, when tak-
ing their lamps, brought no oil with
them, 4 but the wise brought flasks of
oil with their lamps. 5 Since the bride-
groom was long delayed, they all be-
came drowsy and fell asleep. 6 At
midnight, there was a cry, 'Behold, the
bridegroom! Come out to meet him!'
7 Then all those virgins got up and trim-
med their lamps. 8 The foolish ones said
to the wise, 'Give us some of your oil,
for our lamps are going out.' 9 But the
wise ones replied, 'No, for there may
not be enough for us and you. Go in-
stead to the merchants and buy some
for yourselves.' 10 While they went off
to buy it, the bridegroom came and
those who were ready went into the
wedding feast with him. Then the door
was locked. 11*† Afterwards the other
virgins came and said, 'Lord, Lord,
open the door for us!' 12 But he said in
reply, 'Amen, I say to you, I do not know
you.' 13*† Therefore, stay awake, for
you know neither the day nor the hour.

The Parable of the Talents.† 14*† "It
will be as when a man who was going
on a journey called in his servants and
entrusted his possessions to them.
15† To one he gave five talents; to an-
other, two; to a third, one—to each ac-
cording to his ability. Then he went
away. Immediately 16 the one who re-
ceived five talents went and traded with
them, and made another five.
17 Likewise, the one who received two
made another two. 18† But the man who
received one went off and dug a hole
in the ground and buried his master's
money. 19 After a long time the master
of those servants came back and settled
accounts with them. 20† The one who
had received five talents came forward
bringing the additional five. He said,
'Master, you gave me five talents. See,
I have made five more.' 21* His master
said to him, 'Well done, my good and
faithful servant. Since you were faithful
in small matters, I will give you great
responsibilities. Come, share your mas-
ter's joy.' 22 [Then] the one who had re-
ceived two talents also came forward
and said, 'Master, you gave me two tal-
ents. See, I have made two more.'
23 His master said to him, 'Well done,
my good and faithful servant. Since you
were faithful in small matters, I will
give you great responsibilities. Come,
share your master's joy.' 24 Then the one
who had received the one talent came
forward and said, 'Master, I knew you
were a demanding person, harvesting
where you did not plant and gathering
where you did not scatter; 25 so out of
fear I went off and buried your talent
in the ground. Here it is back.' 26† His
master said to him in reply, 'You
wicked, lazy servant! So you knew that
I harvest where I did not plant and
gather where I did not scatter? 27 Should
you not then have put my money in the
bank so that I could have got it back
with interest on my return? 28 Now then!
Take the talent from him and give it to
the one with ten. 29*† For to everyone
who has, more will be given and he will
grow rich; but from the one who has not,
even what he has will be taken away.
30† And throw this useless servant into
the darkness outside, where there will
be wailing and grinding of teeth.'

The Judgment of the Nations.†
31*† "When the Son of Man comes in his
glory, and all the angels with him, he
will sit upon his glorious throne,

*

25, 11-12: 7, 21.23; Lk 13, 25.27.
13: 24, 42; Mk 13, 33.
14-30: Lk 19, 12-27.
21: Lk 16, 10.
29: 13, 12; Mk 4, 25; Lk 8, 18; 19, 26.
31: 16, 27; Dt 33, 2 LXX.

†

25, 11-12: *Lord, Lord:* cf 7, 21. *I do not know you:* cf 7, 23, where the Greek verb is different but synonymous.

25, 13: *Stay awake:* some scholars see this command as an addition to the original parable of Matthew's traditional material, since in v 5 all the virgins, wise and foolish, fall asleep. But the wise virgins are adequately equipped for their task, and *stay awake* may mean no more than to be prepared; cf 24, 42.44.

25, 14-30: Cf Lk 19, 12-27.

25, 14: *It will be as when . . . journey:* literally, "For just as a man who was going on a journey." Although the comparison is not completed, the sense is clear; the kingdom of heaven is like the situation here described. Faithful use of one's gifts will lead to participation in the fullness of the kingdom, lazy inactivity to exclusion from it.

25, 15: *Talents:* see the note on 18, 24.

25, 18: *Buried his master's money:* see the note on 13, 44.

25, 20-23: Although the first two servants have received and doubled large sums, their faithful trading is regarded by the master as fidelity *in small matters* only, compared with the *great responsibilities* now to be given to them. The latter are unspecified. *Share your master's joy:* probably the joy of the banquet of the kingdom; cf 8, 11.

25, 26-28: *Wicked, lazy servant:* this man's inactivity is not negligible but seriously culpable. As punishment, he loses the gift he had received, that is now given to the first servant, whose possessions are already great.

25, 29: See the note on 13, 12 where there is a similar application of this maxim.

25, 30: See the note on 8, 11-12.

25, 31-46: The conclusion of the discourse, which is peculiar to Mt, portrays the final judgment that will accompany the parousia. Although often called a "parable," it is not really such, for the only parabolic elements are the depiction of *the Son of Man* as *a shepherd* and of *the righteous* and the wicked as *sheep* and *goats* respectively (32-33). The criterion of judgment will be the deeds of mercy that have been done for the *least* of Jesus' *brothers* (40). A difficult and important question is the identification of these *least brothers.* Are they all people who have suffered hunger, thirst, etc. (35.36) or a particular group of such sufferers? Scholars are divided in their response and arguments can be made for either side. But leaving aside the problem of what the traditional material that Matthew edited may have meant, it seems that a stronger case can be made for the view that in the evangelist's sense the sufferers are Christians, probably Christian missionaries whose sufferings were brought upon them by their preaching of the gospel. The criterion of judgment for *all the nations* is their treatment of those who have borne to the world the message of Jesus, and this means ultimately their acceptance or rejection of Jesus himself; cf 10, 40, "Whoever receives you, receives me."

25, 31: See the note on 16, 27.

32*† and all the nations will be assem-
bled before him. And he will separate
them one from another, as a shepherd
separates the sheep from the goats.
33 He will place the sheep on his right
and the goats on his left. 34 Then the
king will say to those on his right,
'Come, you who are blessed by my Fa-
ther. Inherit the kingdom prepared for
you from the foundation of the world.
35* For I was hungry and you gave me
food, I was thirsty and you gave me
drink, a stranger and you welcomed
me, 36 naked and you clothed me, ill and
you cared for me, in prison and you vis-
ited me.' 37† Then the righteous will an-
swer him and say, 'Lord, when did we
see you hungry and feed you, or thirsty
and give you drink? 38 When did we see
you a stranger and welcome you, or
naked and clothe you? 39 When did we
see you ill or in prison, and visit you?'
40* And the king will say to them in re-
ply, 'Amen, I say to you, whatever you
did for one of these least brothers of
mine, you did for me.' 41*† Then he will
say to those on his left, 'Depart from
me, you accursed, into the eternal fire
prepared for the devil and his angels.
42* For I was hungry and you gave
me no food, I was thirsty and you
gave me no drink, 43 a stranger and
you gave me no welcome, naked and
you gave me no clothing, ill and in
prison, and you did not care for me.'
44† Then they will answer and say,
'Lord, when did we see you hungry or
thirsty or a stranger or naked or ill or
in prison, and not minister to your
needs?' 45 He will answer them, 'Amen,
I say to you, what you did not do for
one of these least ones, you did not do
for me.' 46* And these will go off to eter-
nal punishment, but the righteous to
eternal life."

VII: THE PASSION AND RESURRECTION†

CHAPTER 26

The Conspiracy against Jesus.†
1 When Jesus finished all these words,
he said to his disciples, 2* "You know
that in two days' time it will be Pass-
over, and the Son of Man will be handed
over to be crucified." 3† Then the chief
priests and the elders of the people as-
sembled in the palace of the high priest,
who was called Caiaphas, 4* and they
consulted together to arrest Jesus by
treachery and put him to death. 5† But
they said, "Not during the festival, that
there may not be a riot among the peo-
ple."

The Anointing at Bethany.† 6* Now
when Jesus was in Bethany in the house
of Simon the leper, 7 a woman came up
to him with an alabaster jar of costly
perfumed oil, and poured it on his head
while he was reclining at table. 8 When
the disciples saw this, they were indig-
nant and said, "Why this waste? 9 It
could have been sold for much, and the
money given to the poor." 10 Since Jesus
knew this, he said to them, "Why do you
make trouble for the woman? She has
done a good thing for me. 11* The poor
you will always have with you; but you
will not always have me. 12† In pouring
this perfumed oil upon my body, she did
it to prepare me for burial. 13 Amen, I
say to you, wherever this gospel is pro-
claimed in the whole world, what she
has done will be spoken of, in memory
of her."

The Betrayal by Judas. 14*† Then one
of the Twelve, who was called Judas Is-

---

*

32: Ez 34, 17.
35-36: Is 58, 7; Ez 18, 7.
40: 10, 40.42.
41: 7, 23; Lk 13, 27.
42-43: Jb 22, 7; Jas 2, 15-16.
46: Dn 12, 2.
26, 2-5: Mk 14, 1-2; Lk 22, 1-2.
4: Jn 11, 47-53.
6-13: Mk 14, 3-9; Jn 12, 1-8.
11: Dt 15, 11.
14-16: Mk 14, 10-11; Lk 22, 3-6.

---

†

25, 32: *All the nations:* before the end the gospel will have been preached throughout the world (24, 14); thus the Gentiles will be judged on their response to it. But the phrase *all the nations* includes the Jews also, for at the judgment "the Son of Man . . . will repay everyone according to his conduct" (16, 27).

25, 37-40: *The righteous* will be astonished that in caring for the needs of the sufferers they were ministering to the *Lord* himself. *One of these least brothers of mine:* cf 10, 42.

25, 41: *Fire prepared . . . his angels:* cf 1 Enoch 10, 13 where it is said of the evil angels and Semyaza, their leader, "In those days they will lead them into the bottom of the fire—and in torment—in the prison (where) they will be locked up forever."

25, 44-45: The *accursed* (41) will be likewise astonished that their neglect of the sufferers was neglect of the *Lord* and will receive from him a similar answer.

26, 1—28, 20: The five books with alternating narrative and discourse (3, 1—25, 46) that give this gospel its distinctive structure lead up to the climactic events that are the center of Christian belief and the origin of the Christian church, the passion and resurrection of Jesus. In his passion narrative (chs 26-27) Matthew follows his Marcan source closely but with omissions (e.g., Mk 14, 51-52) and additions (e.g., 27, 3-10.19). Some of the additions indicate that he utilized traditions that he had received from elsewhere; others are due to his own theological insight (e.g., 26, 28, ". . . for the forgiveness of sins"; 27, 52). In his editing Matthew also altered Mk in some minor details. But there is no need to suppose that he knew any passion narrative other than Mark's.

26, 1-2: *When Jesus finished all these words:* see the note on 7, 28-29. *"You know . . . crucified":* Matthew turns Mk's statement of the time (14, 1) into Jesus' final prediction of his passion. *Passover:* see the note on Mk 14, 1.

26, 3: *Caiaphas* was high priest from A.D. 18 to 36.

26, 5: *Not during the festival:* the plan to delay Jesus' arrest and execution until after *the festival* was not carried out, for according to the synoptics he was arrested on the night of Nisan 14 and put to death the following day. No reason is given why the plan was changed.

26, 6-13: See the notes on Mk 14, 3-9 and Jn 12, 1-8.

26, 12: *To prepare me for burial:* cf Mk 14, 8. In accordance with the interpretation of this act as Jesus' *burial* anointing, Matthew, more consistent than Mark, changes the purpose of the visit of the women to Jesus' tomb; they do not go to anoint him (Mk 16, 1) but "to see the tomb" (28, 1).

26, 14: *Iscariot:* see the note on Lk 6, 16.

cariot, went to the chief priests 15*† and
said, "What are you willing to give me
if I hand him over to you?" They paid
him thirty pieces of silver, 16 and from
that time on he looked for an opportu-
nity to hand him over.

Preparations for the Passover.
17*† On the first day of the Feast of Un-
leavened Bread, the disciples ap-
proached Jesus and said, "Where do
you want us to prepare for you to eat
the Passover?" 18† He said, "Go into the
city to a certain man and tell him, 'The
teacher says, "My appointed time
draws near; in your house I shall cele-
brate the Passover with my disci-
ples."'" 19 The disciples then did as
Jesus had ordered, and prepared the
Passover.

The Betrayer. 20 When it was evening,
he reclined at table with the Twelve.
21† And while they were eating, he said,
"Amen, I say to you, one of you will be-
tray me." 22 Deeply distressed at this,
they began to say to him one after an-
other, "Surely it is not I, Lord?" 23 He
said in reply, "He who has dipped his
hand into the dish with me is the one
who will betray me. 24*† The Son of Man
indeed goes, as it is written of him, but
woe to that man by whom the Son of
Man is betrayed. It would be better for
that man if he had never been born."
25† Then Judas, his betrayer, said in re-
ply, "Surely it is not I, Rabbi?" He an-
swered, "You have said so."

The Lord's Supper.† 26*† While they
were eating, Jesus took bread, said the
blessing, broke it, and giving it to his
disciples said, "Take and eat; this is my
body." 27† Then he took a cup, gave
thanks, and gave it to them, saying,
"Drink from it, all of you, 28* for this is
my blood of the covenant, which will be
shed on behalf of many for the forgive-
ness of sins. 29† I tell you, from now on
I shall not drink this fruit of the vine
until the day when I drink it with you
new in the kingdom of my Father."
30† Then, after singing a hymn, they
went out to the Mount of Olives.

Peter's Denial Foretold. 31*† Then
Jesus said to them, "This night all of
you will have your faith in me shaken,
for it is written:

'I will strike the shepherd,
and the sheep of the flock will be
dispersed';

32 but after I have been raised up, I shall
go before you to Galilee." 33 Peter said
to him in reply, "Though all may have
their faith in you shaken, mine will
never be." 34*† Jesus said to him,

---

* 15: Zec 11, 12.
17-25: Mk 14, 12-21; Lk 22, 7-23.
17: Ex 12, 14-20.
24: Is 53, 8-10.
26-30: Mk 14, 22-26; Lk 22, 14-23; 1 Cor 11, 23-25.
26-27: 1 Cor 10, 16.
28: Ex 24, 8; Is 53, 12.
31-35: Mk 14, 7-31.
31: Zec 13, 7; Jn 16, 32.
34-35: Lk 22, 33-34; Jn 13, 37-38.
34: 26, 69-75.

---

† 26, 15: The motive of avarice is introduced by Judas's question about the price for betrayal, which is absent in the Marcan source (14, 10-11). *Hand him over:* the same Greek verb is used to express the saving purpose of God by which Jesus is handed over to death (cf 17, 22; 20, 18; 26, 2) and the human malice that hands him over. *Thirty pieces of silver:* the price of the betrayal is found only in Mt. It is derived from Zec 11, 12 where it is the wages paid to the rejected shepherd, a cheap price (Zec 11, 13). That amount is also the compensation paid to one whose slave has been gored by an ox (Ex 21, 32).

26, 17: *The first day of the Feast of Unleavened Bread:* see the note on Mk 14, 1. Matthew omits Mk's "when they sacrificed the Passover lamb."

26, 18: By omitting much of Mk 14, 13-15, adding *My appointed time draws near,* and turning the question into a statement, *in your house I shall celebrate the Passover,* Matthew has given this passage a solemnity and majesty greater than that of his source.

26, 21: Given Matthew's interest in the fulfillment of the Old Testament, it is curious that he omits the Marcan designation of Jesus' betrayer as "one who is eating with me" (14, 18), since that is probably an allusion to Ps 41, 10. However, the shocking fact that the betrayer is one who shares table fellowship with Jesus is emphasized in v 23.

26, 24: *It would be better . . . born:* the enormity of the deed is such that it would be better not to exist than to do it.

26, 25: Peculiar to Mt. *You have said so:* cf 26, 64; 27, 11. This is a half-affirmative. Emphasis is laid on the pronoun and the answer implies that the statement would not have been made if the question had not been asked.

26, 26-29: See the note on Mk 14, 22-24. The Marcan-Matthean is one of the two major New Testament traditions of the words of Jesus when instituting the Eucharist. The other (and earlier) is the Pauline-Lucan (1 Cor 11, 23-25; Lk 22, 19-20). Each shows the influence of Christian liturgical usage, but the Marcan-Matthean is more developed in that regard than the Pauline-Lucan. The words over the bread and cup succeed each other without the intervening meal mentioned in 1 Cor 11, 25; Lk 22, 20; and there is parallelism between the consecratory words (*this is my body . . . this is my blood*). Matthew follows Mk closely but with some changes.

26, 26: See the note on 14, 19. *Said the blessing:* a prayer blessing God. *Take and eat:* literally, *Take, eat. Eat* is an addition to Mk's "take it" (literally, "take"; 14, 22). *This is my body:* the bread is identified with Jesus himself.

26, 27-28: *Gave thanks:* see the note on 15, 36. *Gave it to them . . . all of you:* cf Mk 14, 23-24. In the Marcan sequence the disciples drink and then Jesus says the interpretative words. Matthew has changed this into a command to *drink* followed by those words. *My blood:* see Lv 17, 11 for the concept that the *blood* is "the seat of life" and that when placed on the altar it "makes atonement." *Which will be shed:* the present participle, "being shed" or "going to be shed," is future in relation to the Last Supper. *On behalf of:* Greek *peri;* see the note on Mk 14, 24. *Many:* see the note on 20, 28. *For the forgiveness of sins:* a Matthean addition. The same phrase occurs in Mk 1, 4 in connection with John's baptism but Matthew avoids it there (3, 11). He places it here probably because he wishes to emphasize that it is the sacrificial death of Jesus that brings *forgiveness of sins.*

26, 29: Although his death will interrupt the table fellowship he has had with the disciples, Jesus confidently predicts his vindication by God and a new table fellowship with them at the banquet of the kingdom.

26, 30: See the note on Mk 14, 26.

26, 31: *Will have . . . shaken:* literally, "will be scandalized in me"; see the note on 24, 9-12. *I will strike . . . dispersed:* cf Zec 13, 7.

26, 34: *Before the cock crows:* see the note on 14, 25. The third watch of the night was called "cockcrow." *Deny me:* see the note on 16, 24.

"Amen, I say to you, this very night be-
fore the cock crows, you will deny me
three times." 35 Peter said to him, "Even
though I should have to die with you, I
will not deny you." And all the disciples
spoke likewise.

***The Agony in the Garden.*†** 36*† Then
Jesus came with them to a place called
Gethsemane, and he said to his disci-
ples, "Sit here while I go over there and
pray." 37*† He took along Peter and the
two sons of Zebedee, and began to feel
sorrow and distress. 38*† Then he said
to them, "My soul is sorrowful even to
death. Remain here and keep watch
with me." 39*† He advanced a little and
fell prostrate in prayer, saying, "My
Father, if it is possible, let this cup pass
from me; yet, not as I will, but as you
will." 40 When he returned to his disci-
ples he found them asleep. He said to
Peter, "So you could not keep watch
with me for one hour? 41† Watch and
pray that you may not undergo the test.
The spirit is willing, but the flesh is
weak." 42*† Withdrawing a second time,
he prayed again, "My Father, if it is
not possible that this cup pass with-
out my drinking it, your will be done!"
43 Then he returned once more and
found them asleep, for they could not
keep their eyes open. 44 He left them
and withdrew again and prayed a
third time, saying the same thing again.
45* Then he returned to his disciples
and said to them, "Are you still sleep-
ing and taking your rest? Behold, the
hour is at hand when the Son of Man is
to be handed over to sinners. 46 Get
up, let us go. Look, my betrayer is at
hand."

The Betrayal and Arrest of Jesus.
47* While he was still speaking, Judas,
one of the Twelve, arrived, accompa-
nied by a large crowd, with swords and
clubs, who had come from the chief
priests and the elders of the people.
48 His betrayer had arranged a sign with
them, saying, "The man I shall kiss is
the one; arrest him." 49† Immediately
he went over to Jesus and said, "Hail,
Rabbi!" and he kissed him. 50 Jesus an-
swered him, "Friend, do what you have
come for." Then stepping forward they
laid hands on Jesus and arrested him.
51 And behold, one of those who accom-
panied Jesus put his hand to his sword,
drew it, and struck the high priest's ser-
vant, cutting off his ear. 52 Then Jesus
said to him, "Put your sword back into
its sheath, for all who take the sword
will perish by the sword. 53 Do you think
that I cannot call upon my Father and
he will not provide me at this moment
with more than twelve legions of an-
gels? 54 But then how would the scrip-
tures be fulfilled which say that it must
come to pass in this way?" 55† At that
hour Jesus said to the crowds, "Have
you come out as against a robber, with
swords and clubs to seize me? Day af-
ter day I sat teaching in the temple
area, yet you did not arrest me. 56* But
all this has come to pass that the
writings of the prophets may be ful-
filled." Then all the disciples left him
and fled.

---

*

36-46: Mk 14, 32-42; Lk 22, 39-46.
36: Jn 18, 1.
37-39: Heb 5, 7.
38: Ps 42, 6.12; Jon 4, 9.
39: Jn 4, 34; 6, 38; Phil 2, 8.
42: 6, 10; Heb 10, 9.
45: Jn 12, 23; 13, 1; 17, 1.
47-56: Mk 14, 43-50; Lk 22, 47-53; Jn 18, 3-11.
56: 26, 31.

---

†

26, 36-56: Cf Mk 14, 32-52. The account of Jesus in Gethsemane is divided between that of his agony (36-46) and that of his betrayal and arrest (47-56). Jesus' *sorrow and distress* (37) in face of death is unrelieved by the presence of his three disciples who, though urged to *watch with* him (38.41), fall asleep (40.43). He prays that *if . . . possible* his death may be avoided (39) but that his Father's will be done (39.42.44). Knowing then that his death must take place, he announces to his companions that *the hour* for his being *handed over* has come (45). Judas arrives with an armed band provided by the Sanhedrin and greets Jesus with a kiss, the prearranged sign for his identification (47-49). After his arrest, he rebukes a disciple who has attacked *the high priest's servant* with a *sword* (51-54), and chides those who have come out to seize him with *swords and clubs* as if he were *a robber* (55-56). In both rebukes Jesus declares that the treatment he is now receiving is the fulfillment of the scriptures (55.56). The subsequent flight of *all the disciples* is itself the fulfillment of his own prediction (cf 31). In this episode, Matthew follows Mk with a few alterations.

26, 36: *Gethsemane:* the Hebrew name means "oil press" and designates an olive orchard on the western slope of the Mount of Olives; see the note on 21, 1. The name appears only in Mt and Mk. The place is called a "garden" in Jn 18, 1.

26, 37: *Peter and the two sons of Zebedee:* cf 17, 1.

26, 38: Cf Ps 42, 6.12. In the Septuagint (Ps 41, 5.12) the same Greek word for *sorrowful* is used as here. *To death:* i.e., "enough to die"; cf Jon 4, 9.

26, 39: *My Father:* see the note on Mk 14, 36. Matthew omits the Aramaic *ʾabbāʾ* and adds the qualifier *my. This cup:* see the note on Mk 10, 38-40.

26, 41: *Undergo the test:* see the note on 6, 13. In that verse "the final test" translates the same Greek word as is here translated *the test,* and these are the only instances of the use of that word in Mt. It is possible that the passion of Jesus is seen here as an anticipation of the great tribulation that will precede the parousia (see the notes on 24, 8; 24, 21) to which 6, 13 refers, and that just as Jesus prays to be delivered from death (39), so he exhorts the disciples to pray that they will not have to *undergo the* great *test* that his passion would be for them. Some scholars, however, understand *not undergo* (literally, "not enter") *the test* as meaning not that the disciples may be spared *the test* but that they may not yield to the temptation of falling away from Jesus because of his passion even though they will have to endure it.

26, 42: *Your will be done:* cf 6, 10.

26, 49: *Rabbi:* see the note on 23, 6-7. Jesus is so addressed twice in Mt (cf 25), both times by Judas. For the significance of the closely related address "teacher" in Mt, see the note on 8, 19.

26, 55: *Day after day . . . arrest me:* cf Mk 14, 49. This suggests that Jesus had taught for a relatively long period in Jerusalem, whereas 21, 1-11 puts his coming to the city for the first time only a few days before.

Jesus before the Sanhedrin. †
57*† Those who had arrested Jesus led him away to Caiaphas the high priest, where the scribes and the elders were assembled. 58 Peter was following him at a distance as far as the high priest's courtyard, and going inside he sat down with the servants to see the outcome.
59† The chief priests and the entire Sanhedrin kept trying to obtain false testimony against Jesus in order to put him to death, 60*† but they found none, though many false witnesses came forward. Finally two came forward 61 who stated, "This man said, 'I can destroy the temple of God and within three days rebuild it.' " 62 The high priest rose and addressed him, "Have you no answer? What are these men testifying against you?" 63*† But Jesus was silent. Then the high priest said to him, "I order you to tell us under oath before the living God whether you are the Messiah, the Son of God." 64*† Jesus said to him in reply, "You have said so. But I tell you:

From now on you will see 'the Son of Man
seated at the right hand of the Power'
and 'coming on the clouds of heaven.' "

65† Then the high priest tore his robes and said, "He has blasphemed! What further need have we of witnesses? You have now heard the blasphemy; 66 what is your opinion?" They said in reply, "He deserves to die!" 67*† Then they spat in his face and struck him, while some slapped him, 68 saying, "Prophesy for us, Messiah: who is it that struck you?"

Peter's Denial of Jesus. 69* Now Peter was sitting outside in the courtyard. One of the maids came over to him and said, "You too were with Jesus the Galilean." 70† But he denied it in front of everyone, saying, "I do not know what you are talking about!" 71 As he went out to the gate, another girl saw him and said to those who were there, "This man was with Jesus the Nazorean." 72 Again he denied it with an oath, "I do not know the man!" 73† A little later the bystanders came over and said to Peter, "Surely you too are one of them; even your speech gives you away." 74 At that he began to curse and to swear, "I do not know the man." And immediately a cock crowed. 75* Then Peter remembered the word that Jesus had spoken: "Before the cock crows you will deny me three times." He went out and began to weep bitterly.

MATTHEW

*

57-68: Mk 14, 53-65; Lk 22, 54-55.63-71; Jn 18, 12-14.19-24.
60-61: Dt 19, 15; Jn 2, 19; Acts 6, 14.
63: Is 53, 7.
64: Ps 110, 1; Dn 7, 13.
67: Wis 2, 19; Is 50, 6.
69-75: Mk 14, 66-72; Lk 22, 56-62; Jn 18, 17-18.25-27.
75: 26, 34.

†

26, 57-68: Following Mk 14, 53-65, Matthew presents the nighttime appearance of Jesus before *the Sanhedrin* as a real trial. After *many false witnesses* bring charges against him that do not suffice for the death sentence (60), *two came forward* who charge him with claiming to be able to *destroy the temple . . . and within three days* to *rebuild it* (60-61). Jesus makes no answer even when challenged to do so by *the high priest,* who then orders him to declare *under oath . . . whether* he is *the Messiah, the Son of God* (62-63). Matthew changes Mk's clear affirmative response (14, 62) to the same one as that given to Judas (cf 25), but follows Mk almost verbatim in Jesus' predicting that his judges will see him (*the Son of Man*) *seated at the right hand of* God *and coming on the clouds of heaven* (64). *The high priest* then charges him with blasphemy (65), a charge with which the other members of *the Sanhedrin* agree by declaring that *he deserves to die* (66). They then attack him (67) and mockingly demand that he *prophesy* (68). This account contains elements that are contrary to the judicial procedures prescribed in the Mishnah, the Jewish code of law that dates in written form from ca. A.D. 200, e.g., trial on a feast day, a night session of the court, pronouncement of a verdict of condemnation at the same session at which testimony was received. Consequently, some scholars regard the account entirely as a creation of the early Christians without historical value. However, it is disputable whether the norms found in the Mishnah were in force at the time of Jesus. More to the point is the question whether the Matthean-Marcan night trial derives from a combination of two separate incidents, a nighttime preliminary investigation (cf Jn 18, 13.19-24) and a formal trial on the following morning (cf Lk 22, 66-71).

26, 57: *Caiaphas:* see the note on 26, 3.

26, 59: *Sanhedrin:* see the note on Lk 22, 66.

26, 60-61: *Two:* cf Dt 19, 15. *I can destroy . . . rebuild it:* there are significant differences from the Marcan parallel (14, 58). Matthew omits "made with hands" and "not made with hands" and changes Mk's "will destroy" and "will build another" to *can destroy* and (can) *rebuild.* The charge is probably based on Jesus' prediction of the temple's destruction; see the notes on 23, 37-39; 24, 2; and Jn 2, 19. A similar prediction by Jeremiah was considered as deserving death; cf Jer 7, 1-15; 26, 1-8.

26, 63: *Silent:* possibly an allusion to Is 53, 7. *I order you . . . living God:* peculiar to Mt; cf Mk 14, 61.

26, 64: *You have said so:* see the note on 26, 25. *From now on . . . heaven:* the Son of Man who is to be crucified (cf 20, 19) will be seen in glorious majesty (cf Ps 110, 1) and *coming on the clouds of heaven* (cf Dn 7, 13). *The Power:* see the note on Mk 14, 61-62.

26, 65: *Blasphemed:* the punishment for *blasphemy* was death by stoning (see Lv 24, 10-16). According to the Mishnah, to be guilty of *blasphemy* one had to pronounce "the Name itself," i.e. Yahweh; cf *Sanhedrin* 7, 4.5. Those who judge the gospel accounts of Jesus' trial by the later Mishnah standards point out that Jesus uses the surrogate "the Power," and hence no Jewish court would have regarded him as guilty of *blasphemy;* others hold that the Mishnah's narrow understanding of *blasphemy* was a later development.

26, 67-68: The physical abuse, apparently done to Jesus by the members of the Sanhedrin themselves, recalls the sufferings of the Isaian Servant of the Lord; cf Is 50, 6. The mocking challenge to *prophesy* is probably motivated by Jesus' prediction of his future glory (64).

26, 70: *Denied it in front of everyone:* see 10, 33. Peter's repentance (75) saves him from the fearful destiny of which Jesus speaks there.

26, 73: *Your speech . . . away:* Matthew explicates Mk's "you too are a Galilean" (14, 70).

CHAPTER 27

***Jesus before Pilate.*†** 1*† When it was morning, all the chief priests and the elders of the people took counsel against Jesus to put him to death. 2 They bound him, led him away, and handed him over to Pilate, the governor.

The Death of Judas. 3*† Then Judas, his betrayer, seeing that Jesus had been condemned, deeply regretted what he had done. He returned the thirty pieces of silver to the chief priests and elders, 4 saying, "I have sinned in betraying innocent blood." They said, "What is that to us? Look to it yourself." 5† Flinging the money into the temple, he departed and went off and hanged himself. 6 The chief priests gathered up the money, but said, "It is not lawful to deposit this in the temple treasury, for it is the price of blood." 7 After consultation, they used it to buy the potter's field as a burial place for foreigners. 8 That is why that field even today is called the Field of Blood. 9† Then was fulfilled what had been said through Jeremiah the prophet, "And they took the thirty pieces of silver, the value of a man with a price on his head, a price set by some of the Israelites, 10* and they paid it out for the potter's field just as the Lord had commanded me."

Jesus Questioned by Pilate. 11*† Now Jesus stood before the governor, and he questioned him, "Are you the king of the Jews?" Jesus said, "You say so." 12*† And when he was accused by the chief priests and elders, he made no answer. 13 Then Pilate said to him, "Do you not hear how many things they are testifying against you?" 14 But he did not answer him one word, so that the governor was greatly amazed.

***The Sentence of Death.*†** 15* Now on the occasion of the feast the governor was accustomed to release to the crowd one prisoner whom they wished. 16† And at that time they had a notorious prisoner called [Jesus] Barabbas. 17 So when they had assembled, Pilate said to them, "Which one do you want me to release to you, [Jesus] Barabbas, or Jesus called Messiah?" 18† For he knew that it was out of envy that they had handed him over. 19† While he was still seated on the bench, his wife sent him a message, "Have nothing to do with that righteous man. I suffered much in a dream today because of him." 20* The chief priests and the elders persuaded the crowds to ask for Barabbas but to destroy Jesus. 21 The

---

*

27, 1-2: Mk 15, 1; Lk 23, 1; Jn 18, 28.
3-10: Acts 1, 18-19.
3: 26, 15.
10: Zec 11, 12-13.
11-14: Mk 15, 2-5; Lk 23, 2-3; Jn 18, 29-38.
12: Is 53, 7.
15-26: Mk 15, 6-15; Lk 23, 17-25; Jn 18, 39—19, 16.
20: Acts 3, 14.

---

†

27, 1-31: Cf Mk 15, 1-20. Matthew's account of the Roman trial before *Pilate* is introduced by a consultation of the Sanhedrin after which Jesus is *handed over to . . . the governor* (1-2). Matthew follows his Marcan source closely but adds some material that is peculiar to him, the death of *Judas* (3-10), possibly the name *Jesus* as the name of *Barabbas* also (16-17), the intervention of Pilate's *wife* (19), Pilate's washing *his hands* in token of his disclaiming responsibility for Jesus' death (24), and the assuming of that responsibility by *the whole people* (25).

27, 1-2: There is scholarly disagreement about the meaning of the Sanhedrin's taking *counsel* (*symboulion elabon;* cf 12, 14; 22, 15; 27, 7; 28, 12); see the note on Mk 15, 1. Some understand it as a discussion about the strategy for putting their death sentence against *Jesus* into effect since they lacked the right to do so themselves. Others see it as the occasion for their passing that sentence, holding that Matthew, unlike Mark (14, 64), does not consider that it had been passed in the night session (26, 66). Even in the latter interpretation, their handing *him over to Pilate* is best explained on the hypothesis that they did not have competence to put their sentence into effect, as is stated in Jn 18, 31.

27, 3: *The thirty pieces of silver:* see 26, 15.

27, 5-8: For another tradition about the death of Judas, cf Acts 1, 18-19. The two traditions agree only in the purchase of a *field* with *the money* paid to Judas for his betrayal of Jesus and the name given to the *field, the Field of Blood.* In Acts Judas himself buys the field and its name comes from his own blood shed in his fatal accident on it. *The potter's field:* this designation of the field is based on the fulfillment citation in v 10.

27, 9-10: Cf 26, 15. Matthew's attributing this text to Jeremiah is puzzling, for there is no such text in that book, and *the thirty pieces of silver* thrown by Judas "into the temple" (5) recall rather Zec 11, 12-13. It is usually said that the attribution of the text to Jeremiah is due to Matthew's combining the Zechariah text with texts from Jeremiah that speak of a *potter* (18, 2-3), the buying of a *field* (32, 6-9), or the breaking of a potter's flask at Topheth in the valley of Ben-Hinnom with the prediction that it will become a burial place (19, 1-13).

27, 11: *King of the Jews:* this title is used of Jesus only by pagans. The Matthean instances are, besides this verse, 2, 2; 27, 29.37. Matthew equates it with "Messiah"; cf 2, 2.4 and 27, 17.22 where he has changed "the king of the Jews" of his Marcan source (15, 9.12) to "(Jesus) called Messiah." The normal political connotation of both titles would be of concern to the Roman *governor. You say so:* see the note on 26, 25. An unqualified affirmative response is not made because Jesus' kingship is not what Pilate would understand it to be.

27, 12-14: Cf 26, 62-63. As in the trial before the Sanhedrin, Jesus' silence may be meant to recall Is 53, 7. *Greatly amazed:* possibly an allusion to Is 52, 14-15.

27, 15-26: The choice that Pilate offers *the crowd* between *Barabbas* and *Jesus* is said to be in accordance with a custom of releasing at the Passover feast *one prisoner* chosen by *the crowd* (15). This custom is mentioned also in Mk 15, 6 and Jn 18, 39 but not in Lk; see the note on Lk 23, 17. Outside of the gospels there is no direct attestation of it, and scholars are divided in their judgment of the historical reliability of the claim that there was such a practice.

27, 16-17: *[Jesus] Barabbas:* it is possible that the double name is the original reading; *Jesus* was a common Jewish name; see the note on 1, 21. This reading is found in only a few textual witnesses, although its absence in the majority can be explained as an omission of *Jesus* made for reverential reasons. That name is bracketed because of its uncertain textual attestation. The Aramaic name *Barabbas* means "son of the father"; the irony of the choice offered between him and Jesus, the true son of the Father, would be evident to those addressees of Mt who knew that.

27, 18: Cf Mk 14, 10. This is an example of the tendency, found in varying degree in all the gospels, to present Pilate in a relatively favorable light and emphasize the hostility of the Jewish authorities and eventually of the people.

27, 19: Jesus' innocence is declared by a Gentile woman. *In a dream:* in Mt's infancy narrative, dreams are the means of divine communication; cf 1, 20; 2, 12.13.19.22.

governor said to them in reply, "Which
of the two do you want me to release
to you?" They answered, "Barabbas!"
22† Pilate said to them, "Then what shall
I do with Jesus called Messiah?" They
all said, "Let him be crucified!" 23 But
he said, "Why? What evil has he done?"
They only shouted the louder, "Let him
be crucified!" 24*† When Pilate saw that
he was not succeeding at all, but that
a riot was breaking out instead, he took
water and washed his hands in the sight
of the crowd, saying, "I am innocent of
this man's blood. Look to it yourselves."
25 And the whole people said in reply,
"His blood be upon us and upon our
children." 26† Then he released Barab-
bas to them, but after he had Jesus
scourged, he handed him over to be cru-
cified.

Mockery by the Soldiers. 27*† Then
the soldiers of the governor took Jesus
inside the praetorium and gathered the
whole cohort around him. 28† They
stripped off his clothes and threw a
scarlet military cloak about him.
29*† Weaving a crown out of thorns,
they placed it on his head, and a reed
in his right hand. And kneeling before
him, they mocked him, saying, "Hail,
King of the Jews!" 30*† They spat upon
him and took the reed and kept striking
him on the head. 31 And when they had
mocked him, they stripped him of the
cloak, dressed him in his own clothes,
and led him off to crucify him.

The Way of the Cross. 32*† As they
were going out, they met a Cyrenian
named Simon; this man they pressed
into service to carry his cross.

The Crucifixion. 33* And when they
came to a place called Golgotha (which
means Place of the Skull), 34*† they
gave Jesus wine to drink mixed with
gall. But when he had tasted it, he re-
fused to drink. 35*† After they had cru-
cified him, they divided his garments
by casting lots; 36 then they sat down
and kept watch over him there. 37† And
they placed over his head the written
charge against him: This is Jesus, the
King of the Jews. 38† Two revolutionar-
ies were crucified with him, one on his
right and the other on his left.
39*† Those passing by reviled him,
shaking their heads 40* and saying,
"You who would destroy the temple and
rebuild it in three days, save yourself,
if you are the Son of God, [and] come
down from the cross!" 41 Likewise the
chief priests with the scribes and elders
mocked him and said, 42† "He saved
others; he cannot save himself. So he
is the king of Israel! Let him come down
from the cross now, and we will believe
in him. 43*† He trusted in God; let him

*

24: Dt 21, 1-8.
27-31: Mk 15, 16-20; Jn 19, 2-3.
29: 27, 11.
30: Is 50, 6.
32: Mk 15, 21; Lk 23, 26.
33-44: Mk 15, 22-32; Lk 23, 32-38; Jn 19, 17-19.23-24.
34: Ps 69, 21.
35: Ps 22, 19.
39: Ps 22, 8.
40: 4, 3.6; 26, 61.
43: Ps 22, 9; Wis 2, 12-20.

†

27, 22: *Let him be crucified:* incited by the chief priests and elders (20), the crowds demand that Jesus be executed by crucifixion, a peculiarly horrible form of Roman capital punishment. The Marcan parallel, "Crucify him" (15, 3), addressed to Pilate, is changed by Matthew to the passive, probably to emphasize the responsibility of the crowds.

27, 24-25: Peculiar to Mt. *Took water . . . blood:* cf Dt 21, 1-8, the handwashing prescribed in the case of a murder when the killer is unknown. The elders of the city nearest to where the corpse is found must wash their hands, declaring, "Our hands did not shed this blood." *Look to it yourselves:* cf v 4. *The whole people:* Matthew sees in those who speak these words *the* entire *people* (Greek *laos*) of Israel. *His blood . . . and upon our children:* cf Jer 26, 15. The responsibility for Jesus' death is accepted by the nation that was God's special possession (Ex 19, 5), his own *people* (Hos 2, 25), and they thereby lose that high privilege; see 21, 43 and the note on that verse. The controversy between Matthew's church and Pharisaic Judaism about which was the true people of God is reflected here. As the Second Vatican Council has pointed out, guilt for Jesus' death is not attributable to all the Jews of his time or to any Jews of later times.

27, 26: *He had Jesus scourged:* the usual preliminary to crucifixion.

27, 27: *The praetorium:* the residence of the Roman *governor.* His usual place of residence was at Caesarea Maritima on the Mediterranean coast, but he went to Jerusalem during the great feasts, when the influx of pilgrims posed the danger of a nationalistic riot. It is disputed whether *the praetorium* in Jerusalem was the old palace of Herod in the west of the city or the fortress of Antonia northwest of the temple area. *The whole cohort:* normally six hundred soldiers.

27, 28: *Scarlet military cloak:* so Mt as against the royal purple of Mk 15, 17 and Jn 19, 2.

27, 29: *Crown out of thorns:* probably of long *thorns* that stood upright so that it resembled the "radiant" *crown,* a diadem with spikes worn by Hellenistic kings. The soldiers' purpose was mockery, not torture. *A reed:* peculiar to Mt; a mock scepter.

27, 30: *Spat upon him:* cf 26, 67 where there also is a possible allusion to Is 50, 6.

27, 32: See the note on Mk 15, 21. *Cyrenian named Simon:* Cyrenaica was a Roman province on the north coast of Africa and Cyrene was its capital city. The city had a large population of Greek-speaking Jews. *Simon* may have been living in Palestine or have come there for the Passover as a pilgrim. *Pressed into service:* see the note on 5, 41.

27, 34: *Wine . . . mixed with gall:* cf Mk 15, 23 where the drink is "wine drugged with myrrh," a narcotic. Mt's text is probably an inexact allusion to Ps 69, 22. That psalm belongs to the class called the individual lament, in which a persecuted just man prays for deliverance in the midst of great suffering and also expresses confidence that his prayer will be heard. That theme of the suffering Just One is frequently applied to the sufferings of Jesus in the passion narratives.

27, 35: The clothing of an executed criminal went to his executioner(s), but the description of that procedure in the case of Jesus, found in all the gospels, is plainly inspired by Ps 22, 19. However, that psalm verse is quoted only in Jn 19, 24.

27, 37: The offense of a person condemned to death by crucifixion was written on a tablet that was displayed on his cross. The *charge* against *Jesus* was that he had claimed to be *the King of the Jews* (cf 11), i.e., the Messiah (cf 17.22).

27, 38: *Revolutionaries:* see the note on Jn 18, 40 where the same Greek word as that found here is used for Barabbas.

27, 39-40: *Reviled him . . . heads:* cf Ps 22, 8. *You who would destroy . . . three days:* cf 26, 61. *If you are the Son of God:* the same words as those of the devil in the temptation of Jesus; cf 4, 3.6.

27, 42: *King of Israel:* in their mocking of Jesus the members of the Sanhedrin call themselves and their people not "the Jews" but *Israel.*

27, 43: Peculiar to Mt. *He trusted in God . . . wants him:* cf Ps 22, 9. *He said . . . of God:* probably an allusion to Wis 2, 12-20 where the theme of the suffering Just One appears.

deliver him now if he wants him. For
he said, 'I am the Son of God.' " 44 The
revolutionaries who were crucified with
him also kept abusing him in the same
way.

The Death of Jesus. 45*† From noon
onward, darkness came over the whole
land until three in the afternoon.
46*† And about three o'clock Jesus cried
out in a loud voice, "*Eli, Eli, lema sa-
bachthani?*" which means, "My God,
my God, why have you forsaken me?"
47† Some of the bystanders who heard
it said, "This one is calling for Elijah."
48* Immediately one of them ran to get
a sponge; he soaked it in wine, and put-
ting it on a reed, gave it to him to drink.
49 But the rest said, "Wait, let us see if
Elijah comes to save him." 50† But Jesus
cried out again in a loud voice, and gave
up his spirit. 51*† And behold, the veil
of the sanctuary was torn in two from
top to bottom. The earth quaked, rocks
were split, 52* tombs were opened, and
the bodies of many saints who had
fallen asleep were raised. 53 And coming
forth from their tombs after his resur-
rection, they entered the holy city and
appeared to many. 54† The centurion
and the men with him who were keeping
watch over Jesus feared greatly when
they saw the earthquake and all that
was happening, and they said, "Truly,
this was the Son of God!" 55† There were
many women there, looking on from a
distance, who had followed Jesus from
Galilee, ministering to him. 56* Among
them were Mary Magdalene and Mary
the mother of James and Joseph, and
the mother of the sons of Zebedee.

The Burial of Jesus. † 57* When it was
evening, there came a rich man from
Arimathea named Joseph, who was
himself a disciple of Jesus. 58 He went
to Pilate and asked for the body of Je-
sus; then Pilate ordered it to be handed
over. 59 Taking the body, Joseph
wrapped it [in] clean linen 60 and laid
it in his new tomb that he had hewn in
the rock. Then he rolled a huge stone
across the entrance to the tomb and de-
parted. 61 But Mary Magdalene and the
other Mary remained sitting there, fac-
ing the tomb.

The Guard at the Tomb. † 62† The next
day, the one following the day of prepa-
ration, the chief priests and the Phari-
sees gathered before Pilate 63* and said,
"Sir, we remember that this imposter
while still alive said, 'After three days
I will be raised up.' 64† Give orders,
then, that the grave be secured until the

*

45-46: Mk 15, 33-41; Lk 23, 44-49; Jn 19, 28-30.
45: Am 8, 9.
46: Ps 22, 2.
48: Ps 69, 21.
51: Ex 26, 31-36; Ps 68, 9; 77, 19.
52: Dn 12, 1-3.
56: 13, 55.
57-61: Mk 15, 42-47; Lk 23, 50-56; Jn 19, 38-42.
57: Is 53, 9.
63: 12, 40; 16, 21; 17, 23; 20, 19.

†

27, 45: Cf Amos 8, 9 where on the day of the Lord "the sun will set at midday."

27, 46: *Eli, Eli, lema sabachthani?:* Jesus cries out in the words of Ps 22, 2a, a psalm of lament that is the Old Testament passage most frequently drawn upon in this narrative. In Mk the verse is cited entirely in Aramaic, which Matthew partially retains but changes the invocation of God to the Hebrew *Eli*, possibly because that is more easily related to the statement of the following verse about Jesus' calling for Elijah.

27, 47: *Elijah:* see the note on 3, 4. This prophet, taken up into heaven (2 Kgs 2, 11), was believed to come to the help of those in distress, but the evidences of that belief are all later than the gospels.

27, 50: *Gave up his spirit:* of the Marcan parallel (15, 37), "breathed his last." Matthew's alteration expresses both Jesus' control over his destiny and his obedient giving up of his life to God.

27, 51-53: *Veil of the sanctuary . . . bottom:* cf Mk 15, 38; Lk 23, 45. Lk puts this event immediately before the death of Jesus. There were two veils in the Mosaic tabernacle on the model of which the temple was constructed, the outer one before the entrance of the Holy Place and the inner one before the Holy of Holies (see Ex 26, 31-36). Only the high priest could pass through the latter and that only on the Day of Atonement (see Lv 16, 1-18). Probably the *torn veil* of the gospels is the inner one. The meaning of the scene may be that now, because of Jesus' death, all people have access to the presence of God, or that the temple, its holiest part standing exposed, is now profaned and will soon be destroyed. *The earth quaked . . . appeared to many:* peculiar to Mt. The earthquake, the splitting of the *rocks,* and especially the resurrection of the dead *saints* indicate the coming of the final age. In the Old Testament the coming of God is frequently portrayed with the imagery of an earthquake (see Pss 68, 9; 77, 19), and Jesus speaks of the earthquakes that will accompany the "labor pains" that signify the beginning of the dissolution of the old world (24, 7-8). For the expectation of the resurrection of the dead at the coming of the new and final age, see Dn 12, 1-3. Matthew knows that the end of the old age has not yet come (28, 20), but the new age has broken in with the death (and resurrection; cf the earthquake in 28, 2) of Jesus; see the note on 16, 28. *After his resurrection:* this qualification seems to be due to Matthew's wish to assert the primacy of Jesus' *resurrection* even though he has placed the resurrection of the dead *saints* immediately after Jesus' death.

27, 54: Cf Mk 15, 39. The Christian confession of faith is made by Gentiles, not only *the centurion,* as in Mk, but the other soldiers *who were keeping watch over Jesus* (cf 36).

27, 55-56: *Looking on from a distance:* cf Ps 38, 12. *Mary Magdalene . . . Joseph:* these two women are mentioned again in v 61 and 28, 1 and are important as witnesses of the reality of the empty tomb. A *James* and *Joseph* are referred to in 13, 55 as brothers of Jesus.

27, 57-61: Cf Mk 15, 42-47. Matthew drops Mk's designation of *Joseph* of *Arimathea* as "a distinguished member of the council" (the Sanhedrin), and makes him *a rich man* and *a disciple of Jesus.* The former may be an allusion to Is 53, 9 (the Hebrew reading of that text is disputed and the one followed in the NAB OT has nothing about the rich, but they are mentioned in the LXX version). That the tomb was the *new tomb* of *a rich man* and that it was seen by the women are indications of an apologetic intent of Matthew; there could be no question about the identity of Jesus' burial place. *The other Mary:* the mother of James and Joseph (56).

27, 62-66: Peculiar to Mt. The story prepares for 28, 11-15 and the Jewish charge that the tomb was empty because the *disciples* had stolen the body of Jesus (28, 13.15).

27, 62: *The next day . . . preparation:* the sabbath. According to the synoptic chronology, in that year *the day of preparation* (for the sabbath) was the Passover; cf Mk 15, 42. *The Pharisees:* the principal opponents of Jesus during his ministry and, in Matthew's time, of the Christian church, join with *the chief priests* to guarantee against a possible attempt of Jesus' *disciples* to steal his body.

27, 64: *This last imposture . . . the first:* the claim that Jesus *has been raised from the dead* is clearly the *last imposture; the first* may be either his claim that he would *be raised up* (63) or his claim that he was the one with whose ministry the kingdom of God had come (see 12, 28).

third day, lest his disciples come and steal him and say to the people, 'He has been raised from the dead.' This last imposture would be worse than the first." 65† Pilate said to them, "The guard is yours; go secure it as best you can." 66 So they went and secured the tomb by fixing a seal to the stone and setting the guard.

CHAPTER 28†

The Resurrection of Jesus. 1*† After the sabbath, as the first day of the week was dawning, Mary Magdalene and the other Mary came to see the tomb. 2*† And behold, there was a great earthquake; for an angel of the Lord descended from heaven, approached, rolled back the stone, and sat upon it. 3* His appearance was like lightning and his clothing was white as snow. 4 The guards were shaken with fear of him and became like dead men. 5 Then the angel said to the women in reply, "Do not be afraid! I know that you are seeking Jesus the crucified. 6† He is not here, for he has been raised just as he said. Come and see the place where he lay. 7* Then go quickly and tell his disciples, 'He has been raised from the dead, and he is going before you to Galilee; there you will see him.' Behold, I have told you." 8† Then they went away quickly from the tomb, fearful yet overjoyed, and ran to announce this to his disciples. 9*† And behold, Jesus met them on their way and greeted them. They approached, embraced his feet, and did him homage. 10 Then Jesus said to them, "Do not be afraid. Go tell my brothers to go to Galilee, and there they will see me."

The Report of the Guard. † 11 While they were going, some of the guard went into the city and told the chief priests all that had happened. 12 They assembled with the elders and took counsel; then they gave a large sum of money to the soldiers, 13 telling them, "You are to say, 'His disciples came by night and stole him while we were asleep.' 14 And if this gets to the ears of the governor, we will satisfy [him] and keep you out of trouble." 15 The soldiers took the money and did as they were instructed. And this story has circulated among the Jews to the present [day].

The Commissioning of the Disciples. †
16*† The eleven disciples went to Gali-

*

28, 1-10: Mk 16, 1-8; Lk 24, 1-12; Jn 20, 1-10.
2: 25, 51.
3: 17, 2.
7: 26, 32.
9-10: Jn 20, 17.
16-20: Mk 16, 14-16; Lk 24, 36-49; Jn 20, 19-23.

†

27, 65: *The guard is yours:* literally, "have a guard" or "you have a guard." Either the imperative or the indicative could mean that Pilate granted the petitioners some Roman soldiers as guards, which is the sense of the present translation. However, if the verb is taken as an indicative it could also mean that Pilate told them to use their own Jewish guards.

28, 1-20: Except for vv 1-8, based on Mk 16, 1-8, the material of this final chapter is peculiar to Mt. Even where he follows Mk, Matthew has altered his source so greatly that a very different impression is given from that of the Marcan account. The two points that are common to the resurrection testimony of all the gospels are that the tomb of Jesus had been found empty and that the risen Jesus had appeared to certain persons, or, in the original form of Mk, that such an appearance was promised as soon to take place (see Mk 16, 7). On this central and all-important basis, Matthew has constructed an account that interprets the resurrection as the turning of the ages (2-4), shows the Jewish opposition to Jesus as continuing *to the present* in the claim that the resurrection is a deception perpetrated by the *disciples* who stole his body from the tomb (11-15), and marks a new stage in the mission of *the disciples* once limited to Israel (10, 5-6); now they are to *make disciples of all nations.* In this work they will be strengthened by the presence of the exalted Son of Man, who will be with them *until* the kingdom comes in fullness at *the end of the age* (16-20).

28, 1: *After the sabbath . . . dawning:* since the sabbath ended at sunset, this could mean in the early evening, for *dawning* can refer to the appearance of the evening star; cf Lk 23, 54. However, it is probable that Matthew means the morning dawn of the day after the sabbath, as in the similar though slightly different text of Mk, "when the sun had risen" (16, 2). *Mary Magdalene and the other Mary:* see the notes on 27, 55-56; 57-61. *To see the tomb:* cf Mk 16, 1-2 where the purpose of the women's visit is to anoint Jesus' body.

28, 2-4: Peculiar to Mt. *A great earthquake:* see the note on 27, 51-53. *Descended from heaven:* this trait is peculiar to Mt, although his interpretation of the "young man" of his Marcan source (16, 5) as an *angel* is probably true to Mk's intention; cf Lk 24, 23 where the "two men" of 24, 4 are said to be "angels." *Rolled back the stone . . . upon it:* not to allow the risen Jesus to leave the tomb but to make evident that the tomb is empty (see 6). Unlike the apocryphal Gospel of Peter (9, 35—11, 44), the New Testament does not describe the resurrection of Jesus, nor is there anyone who sees it. *His appearance was like lightning . . . snow:* see the note on 17, 2.

28, 6-7: Cf Mk 16, 6-7. *Just as he said:* a Matthean addition referring to Jesus' predictions of his resurrection, e.g., 16, 21; 17, 23; 20, 19. *Tell his disciples:* like the angel of the Lord of the infancy narrative, the angel interprets a fact and gives a commandment about what is to be done; cf 1, 20-21. Matthew omits Mk's "and Peter" (16, 7); considering his interest in Peter, this omission is curious. Perhaps the reason is that the Marcan text may allude to a first appearance of Jesus to Peter alone (cf 1 Cor 15, 5; Lk 24, 34) which Matthew has already incorporated into his account of Peter's confession at Caesarea Philippi; see the note on 16, 16. *He is going . . . Galilee:* like Mk 16, 7, a reference to Jesus' prediction at the Last Supper (26, 32; Mk 14, 28). Matthew changes Mk's "as he told you" to a declaration of the angel.

28, 8: Contrast Mk 16, 8 where the women in their fear "said nothing to anyone."

28, 9-10: Although these verses are peculiar to Mt, there are similarities between them and Jn's account of the appearance of Jesus to Mary Magdalene (20, 17). In both there is a touching of Jesus' body, and a command of Jesus to bear a message to his disciples, designated as his *brothers.* Matthew may have drawn upon a tradition that appears in a different form in Jn. Jesus' words to the women are mainly a repetition of those of the angel (5a; 7b).

28, 11-15: This account indicates that the dispute between Christians and Jews about the empty tomb was not whether the tomb was empty but why.

28, 16-20: This climactic scene has been called a "proleptic parousia," for it gives a foretaste of the final glorious coming of the Son of Man (26, 64). Then his triumph will be manifest to all; now it is revealed only to *the disciples,* who are commissioned to announce it to *all nations* and bring them to belief in Jesus and obedience to his commandments.

28, 16: *The eleven:* the number recalls the tragic defection of Judas Iscariot. *To the mountain . . . ordered them:* since the message to *the disciples* was simply that they were to go to Galilee (10), some think that *the mountain* comes from a tradition of the message known to Matthew and alluded to here. For the significance of *the mountain,* see the note on 17, 1.

lee, to the mountain to which Jesus had
ordered them. 17† When they saw him,
they worshiped, but they doubted.
18*† Then Jesus approached and said to
them, "All power in heaven and on
earth has been given to me. 19*† Go,
therefore, and make disciples of all na-
tions, baptizing them in the name of the
Father, and of the Son, and of the holy
Spirit, 20*† teaching them to observe all
that I have commanded you. And be-
hold, I am with you always, until the
end of the age."

---

* 18: Dn 7, 14 LXX.
19: Acts 1, 8.
20: 1, 23; 13, 39; 24, 3.

---

† 28, 17: *But they doubted:* the Greek can also be translated, "but some doubted." The verb occurs elsewhere in the New Testament only in 14, 31 where it is associated with Peter's being of "little faith." For the meaning of that designation, see the note on 6, 30.

28, 18: *All power . . . me:* the Greek word here translated *power* is the same as that found in the LXX translation of Dn 7, 13-14 where one "like a son of man" is given *power* and an everlasting kingdom by God. The risen Jesus here claims universal power, i.e., *in heaven and on earth.*

28, 19: *Therefore:* since universal power belongs to the risen Jesus (18), he gives the eleven a mission that is universal. They are to *make disciples of all nations.* While *all nations* is understood by some scholars as referring only to *all* Gentiles, it is probable that it included the Jews as well. *Baptizing them:* baptism is the means of entrance into the community of the risen one, the Church. *In the name of the Father . . . holy Spirit:* this is perhaps the clearest expression in the New Testament of trinitarian belief. It may have been the baptismal formula of Matthew's church, but primarily it designates the effect of baptism, the union of the one baptized with the Father, Son, and holy Spirit.

28, 20: *All that I have commanded you:* the moral teaching found in this gospel, preeminently that of the Sermon on the Mount (chs 5-7). The commandments of Jesus are the standard of Christian conduct, not the Mosaic law as such, even though some of the Mosaic commandments have now been invested with the authority of Jesus. *Behold, I am with you always:* the promise of Jesus' real though invisible presence echoes the name Emmanuel given to him in the infancy narrative; see the note on 1, 23. *End of the age:* see the notes on 13, 39 and 24, 3.

The Gospel According to

MARK

This shortest of all New Testament gospels is likely the first to have been written, yet it often tells of Jesus' ministry in more detail than either Matthew or Luke (for example, the miracle stories at 5, 1-20 or 9, 14-29). It recounts what Jesus did in a vivid style, where one incident follows directly upon another. In this almost breathless narrative, Mark stresses Jesus' message about the kingdom of God now breaking into human life as good news (1, 14-15) and Jesus himself as the gospel of God (1, 1; 8, 35; 10, 29). Jesus is the Son whom God has sent to rescue humanity by serving and by sacrificing his life (10, 45).

The opening verse about good news in Mark (1, 1) serves as a title for the entire book. The action begins with the appearance of John the Baptist, a messenger of God attested by scripture. But John points to a mightier one, Jesus, at whose baptism God speaks from heaven, declaring Jesus his Son. The Spirit descends upon Jesus, who eventually, it is promised, will baptize "with the holy Spirit." This presentation of who Jesus really is (1, 1-13) is rounded out with a brief reference to the temptation of Jesus and how Satan's attack fails. Jesus as Son of God will be victorious, a point to be remembered as one reads of Jesus' death and the enigmatic ending to Mark's Gospel.

The key verses at 1, 14-15, which are programmatic, summarize what Jesus proclaims as gospel: fulfillment, the nearness of the kingdom, and therefore the need for repentance and for faith. After the call of the first four disciples, all fishermen (1, 16-20), we see Jesus engaged in teaching (1, 21.22.27), preaching (1, 38.39), and healing (1, 29-31.34.40-45), and exorcising demons (1, 22-27.34.39). The content of Jesus' teaching is only rarely stated, and then chiefly in parables (ch 4) about the kingdom. His cures, especially on the sabbath (3, 1-5); his claim, like God, to forgive sins (2, 3-12); his table fellowship with tax collectors and sinners (2, 14-17); and the statement that his followers need not now fast but should rejoice while Jesus is present (2, 18-22), all stir up opposition that will lead to Jesus' death (3, 6).

In Mark, Jesus is portrayed as immensely popular with the people in Galilee during his ministry (2, 2; 3, 7; 4, 1). He appoints twelve disciples to help preach and drive out demons, just as he does (3, 13-19). He continues to work many miracles; the blocks 4, 35—6, 44 and 6, 45—7, 10 are cycles of stories about healings, miracles at the Sea of Galilee, and marvelous feedings of the crowds. Jesus' teaching in ch 7 exalts the word of God over "the tradition of the elders" and sees defilement as a matter of the heart, not of unclean foods. Yet opposition mounts. Scribes charge that Jesus is possessed by Beelzebul (3, 22). His relatives think him "out of his mind" (3, 21). Jesus' kinship is with those who do the will of God, in a new eschatological family, not even with mother, brothers, or sisters by blood ties (3, 31-35; cf 6, 1-6). But all too often his own disciples do not understand Jesus (4, 13.40; 6, 52; 8, 17-21). The fate of John the Baptist (6, 17-29) hints ominously at Jesus' own passion (9, 13; cf 8, 31).

A breakthrough seemingly comes with Peter's confession that Jesus is the Christ (Messiah; 8, 27-30). But Jesus himself emphasizes his passion (8, 31; 9, 31; 10, 33-34), not glory in the kingdom (10, 35-45). Momentarily he is glimpsed in his true identity when he is transfigured before three of the disciples (9, 2-8), but by and large Jesus is depicted in Mark as moving obediently along the way to his cross in Jerusalem. Occasionally there are miracles (9, 17-27; 10, 46-52; 11, 12-14.20-21, the only such account in Jerusalem), sometimes teachings (10, 2-11.23-31), but the greatest concern is with discipleship (8, 34—9, 1; 9, 33-50). For the disciples do not grasp the mystery being revealed (9, 32; 10, 32.38). One of them will betray him, Judas (14, 10-11.43-45); one will deny him, Peter (14, 27.31.54.66-72); all eleven men will desert Jesus (14, 27.50).

The passion account, with its condemnation of Jesus by the Sanhedrin (14, 53.55-65; 15, 1a) and sentencing by Pilate (15, 1b-15), is prefaced with the entry into Jerusalem (11, 1-11), ministry and controversies there (11, 15—12, 44), Jesus' Last Supper with the disciples (14, 1-26), and his arrest at Gethsemane (14, 32-52). A chapter of apocalyptic tone about the destruction of the temple (13, 1-2.14-23) and the coming of the Son of Man (13, 24-27), a discourse filled with promises (13, 11.31) and admonitions to be watchful (13, 2.23.37), is significant for Mark's Gospel, for it helps one see that God, in Jesus, will be victorious after the cross and at the end of history.

The Gospel of Mark ends in the most ancient manuscripts with an abrupt scene at Jesus' tomb, which the women find empty (16, 1-8). His own prophecy of 14, 28 is reiterated, that Jesus goes before the disciples into Galilee; "there you will see him." These words may imply resurrection appearances there, or Jesus' parousia there, or the start of Christian mission, or a return to the roots depicted in 1, 9.14-15 in Galilee. Other hands have attached additional endings after 16, 8; see the note on 16, 9-20.

The framework of Mark's Gospel is partly geographical: Galilee (1, 14—9, 49), through the area "across the Jordan" (10, 1) and through Jericho (10, 46-52), to Jerusalem (11, 1—16, 8). Only rarely does Jesus go into Gentile territory (5, 1-20; 7, 24-37), but those who acknowledge him there and the centurion who confesses Jesus at the cross (15, 39) presage the gospel's expansion into the world beyond Palestine.

Mark's Gospel is even more oriented to christology. Jesus is the Son of God (1, 11; 9, 7; 15, 39; cf 1, 1; 14, 61). He is the Messiah, the anointed king of Davidic descent (12, 35; 15, 32), the Greek for which, Christos, *has, by the time Mark wrote, become in effect a proper name (1, 1; 9, 41). Jesus is also seen as Son of Man, a term used in Mark not simply as a substitute for "I" or for humanity in general (cf 2, 10.27-28; 14, 21) or with reference to a mighty figure who is to come (13, 26; 14, 62), but also in connection with Jesus' predestined, necessary path of suffering and vindication (8, 31; 10, 45).*

The unfolding of Mark's story about Jesus is sometimes viewed by interpreters as centered around the term "mystery." The word is employed just once, at 4, 11, in the singular, and its content there is the kingdom, the open secret that God's reign is now breaking into human life with its reversal of human values. There is a related sense in which Jesus' real identity remained a secret during his lifetime, according to Mark, although demons and demoniacs knew it (1, 24; 3, 11; 5, 7); Jesus warned against telling of his mighty deeds and revealing his identity (1, 44; 3, 12; 5, 43; 7, 36; 8, 26.30), an injunction sometimes broken (1, 45; cf 5, 19-20). Further, Jesus teaches by parables, according to Mark, in such a way that those "outside" the kingdom do not understand, but only those to whom the mystery has been granted by God.

Mark thus shares with Paul, as well as with other parts of the New Testament, an emphasis on election (13, 20.22) and upon the gospel as Christ and his cross (cf 1 Cor 1, 23). Yet in Mark the person of Jesus is also depicted with an unaffected naturalness. He reacts to events with authentic human emotion: pity (1, 44), anger (3, 5), triumph (4, 40), sympathy (5, 36; 6, 34), surprise (6, 9), admiration (7, 29; 10, 21), sadness (14, 33-34), and indignation (14, 48-49).

Although the book is anonymous, apart from the ancient heading "According to Mark" in manuscripts, it has traditionally been assigned to John Mark, in whose mother's house (at Jerusalem) Christians assembled (Acts 12, 12). This Mark was a cousin of Barnabas (Col 4, 10) and accompanied Barnabas and Paul on a missionary journey (Acts 12, 25; 13, 3; 15, 36-39). He appears in Pauline letters (2 Tm 4, 11; Phlm 24) and with Peter (1 Pt 5, 13). Papias (ca. A.D. 135) described Mark as Peter's "interpreter," a view found in other patristic writers. Petrine influence should not, however, be exaggerated. The evangelist has put together various oral and possibly written sources—miracle stories, parables, sayings, stories of controversies, and the passion—so as to speak of the crucified Messiah for Mark's own day.

Traditionally, the gospel is said to have been written shortly before A.D. 70 in Rome, at a time of impending persecution and when destruction loomed over Jerusalem. Its audience seems to have been Gentile, unfamiliar with Jewish customs (hence 7, 3-4.11). The book aimed to equip such Christians to stand faithful in the face of persecution (13, 9-13), while going on with the proclamation of the gospel begun in Galilee (13, 10; 14, 9). Modern research often proposes as the author an unknown Hellenistic Jewish Christian, possibly in Syria, and perhaps shortly after the year 70.

The principal divisions of the Gospel according to Mark are the following:

- *I: The Preparation for the Public Ministry of Jesus (1, 1-13)*
- *II: The Mystery of Jesus (1, 14—8, 26)*
- *III: The Mystery Begins to Be Revealed (8, 27—9, 32)*
- *IV: The Full Revelation of the Mystery (9, 33—16, 8)*
- *The Longer Ending (16, 9-20)*
- *The Shorter Ending*
- *The Freer Logion (in the note on 16, 9-20)*

I: THE PREPARATION FOR THE PUBLIC MINISTRY OF JESUS†

CHAPTER 1

1† The beginning of the gospel of Jesus Christ [the Son of God].

The Preaching of John the Baptist.†
2* As it is written in Isaiah the prophet:

"Behold, I am sending my messenger ahead of you;
he will prepare your way.
3* A voice of one crying out in the desert:
'Prepare the way of the Lord,
make straight his paths.' "

4 John [the] Baptist appeared in the desert proclaiming a baptism of repentance for the forgiveness of sins.
5 People of the whole Judean countryside and all the inhabitants of Jerusalem were going out to him and were being baptized by him in the Jordan River as they acknowledged their sins.
6† John was clothed in camel's hair, with a leather belt around his waist. He fed on locusts and wild honey. 7 And this is what he proclaimed: "One mightier than I is coming after me. I am not worthy to stoop and loosen the thongs of his sandals. 8*† I have baptized you with water; he will baptize you with the holy Spirit."
The Baptism of Jesus. 9* It happened in those days that Jesus came from Nazareth of Galilee and was baptized in

---

*

1, 2-8: Mt 3, 1-11; Lk 3, 2-16.
2: Mal 3, 1.
3: Is 40, 3; Jn 1, 23.
8: Jn 1, 27; Acts 1, 5; 11, 16.
9-11: Mt 3, 13-17; Lk 3, 21-23; Jn 1, 32-33.

†

1, 1-13: The prologue of the Gospel according to Mark begins with the title (1) followed by three events preparatory to Jesus' preaching: (1) the appearance in the Judean wilderness of John, baptizer, preacher of repentance, and precursor of Jesus (2-8); (2) the baptism of Jesus, at which a voice from heaven acknowledges Jesus to be God's Son, and the holy Spirit descends on him (9-11); (3) the temptation of Jesus by Satan (12-13).

1, 1: *The gospel of Jesus Christ [the Son of God]:* the "good news" of salvation in and through Jesus, crucified and risen, acknowledged by the Christian community as Messiah (8, 29; 14, 61-62) and Son of God (1, 11; 9, 7; 15, 39), although some important manuscripts here omit *the Son of God.*

1, 2-3: Although Mark attributes the prophecy to Isaiah, the text is a combination of Mal 3, 1; Is 40, 3; and Ex 23, 20; cf Mt 11, 10; Lk 7, 27. John's ministry is seen as God's prelude to the saving mission of his Son. *The way of the Lord:* this prophecy of Deutero-Isaiah concerning the end of the Babylonian exile is here applied to the coming of Jesus; John the Baptist is to prepare the way for him.

1, 6: *Clothed in camel's hair . . . waist:* the Baptist's garb recalls that of Elijah in 2 Kgs 1, 8. Jesus speaks of the Baptist as Elijah who has already come (9, 11-13; Mt 17, 10-12; cf Mal 3, 23-24; Lk 1, 17).

1, 8-9: Through the life-giving baptism with the holy Spirit (8), Jesus will create a new people of God. But first he identifies himself with the people of Israel in submitting to John's baptism of repentance and in bearing on their behalf the burden of God's decisive judgment (9; cf 4). As in the desert of Sinai, so here in the wilderness of Judea, Israel's sonship with God is to be renewed.

the Jordan by John. 10† On coming up out of the water he saw the heavens being torn open and the Spirit, like a dove, descending upon him. 11* And a voice came from the heavens, "You are my beloved Son; with you I am well pleased."

***The Temptation of Jesus.*†** 12* At once the Spirit drove him out into the desert, 13 and he remained in the desert for forty days, tempted by Satan. He was among wild beasts, and the angels ministered to him.

II: THE MYSTERY OF JESUS

***The Beginning of the Galilean Ministry.*†** 14* After John had been arrested, Jesus came to Galilee proclaiming the gospel of God: 15* "This is the time of fulfillment. The kingdom of God is at hand. Repent, and believe in the gospel."

***The Call of the First Disciples.*†** 16* As he passed by the Sea of Galilee, he saw Simon and his brother Andrew casting their nets into the sea; they were fishermen. 17 Jesus said to them, "Come after me, and I will make you fishers of men." 18 Then they left their nets and followed him. 19 He walked along a little farther and saw James, the son of Zebedee, and his brother John. They too were in a boat mending their nets. 20 Then he called them. So they left their father Zebedee in the boat along with the hired men and followed him.

***The Cure of a Demoniac.*†** 21* Then they came to Capernaum, and on the sabbath he entered the synagogue and taught. 22* The people were astonished at his teaching, for he taught them as one having authority and not as the scribes. 23† In their synagogue was a man with an unclean spirit; 24† he cried out, "What have you to do with us, Jesus of Nazareth? Have you come to destroy us? I know who you are—the Holy One of God!" 25 Jesus rebuked him and said, "Quiet! Come out of him!" 26 The unclean spirit convulsed him and with a loud cry came out of him. 27 All were amazed and asked one another, "What is this? A new teaching with authority. He commands even the unclean spirits and they obey him." 28 His fame spread everywhere throughout the whole region of Galilee.

The Cure of Simon's Mother-in-Law. 29* On leaving the synagogue he entered the house of Simon and Andrew with James and John. 30 Simon's mother-in-law lay sick with a fever. They immediately told him about her. 31 He approached, grasped her hand, and helped her up. Then the fever left her and she waited on them.

Other Healings. 32 When it was evening, after sunset, they brought to him all who were ill or possessed by demons. 33 The whole town was gathered at the door. 34 He cured many who were sick with various diseases, and he drove out many demons, not permitting them to speak because they knew him.

Jesus Leaves Capernaum. 35* Rising very early before dawn, he left and went off to a deserted place, where he prayed. 36 Simon and those who were with him pursued him 37 and on finding him said, "Everyone is looking for you." 38 He told them, "Let us go on to

*

11: Ps 2, 7.
12-13: Mt 4, 1-11; Lk 4, 1-13.
14-15: Mt 4, 12-17; Lk 4, 14-15.
15: Mt 3, 2.
16-20: Mt 4, 18-22; Lk 5, 2-11.
21-28: Lk 4, 31-37.
22: Mt 7, 28-29.
29-34: Mt 8, 14-16; Lk 4, 38-41.
35-39: Lk 4, 42-44.

†

1, 10-11: *He saw the heavens . . . and the Spirit . . . upon him:* indicating divine intervention in fulfillment of promise. Here the descent of the Spirit on Jesus is meant, anointing him for his ministry; cf Is 11, 2; 42, 1; 61, 1; 63, 9. *A voice . . . with you I am well pleased:* God's acknowledgment of Jesus as his unique Son, the object of his love. His approval of Jesus is the assurance that Jesus will fulfill his messianic mission of salvation.

1, 12-13: The same Spirit who descended on Jesus in his baptism now drives him into the desert for forty days. The result is radical confrontation and temptation by Satan who attempts to frustrate the work of God. The presence of wild beasts may indicate the horror and danger of the desert regarded as the abode of demons or may reflect the paradise motif of harmony among all creatures; cf Is 11, 6-9. The presence of ministering angels to sustain Jesus recalls the angel who guided the Israelites in the desert in the first Exodus (14, 19; 23, 20) and the angel who supplied nourishment to Elijah in the wilderness (1 Kgs 19, 5-7). The combined forces of good and evil were present to Jesus in the desert. His sustained obedience brings forth the new Israel of God there where Israel's rebellion had brought death and alienation.

1, 14-15: *After John had been arrested:* in the plan of God, Jesus was not to proclaim the good news of salvation prior to the termination of the Baptist's active mission. *Galilee:* in the Marcan account, scene of the major part of Jesus' public ministry before his arrest and condemnation. *The gospel of God:* not only the good news from God but about God at work in Jesus Christ. *This is the time of fulfillment:* i.e., of God's promises. *The kingdom of God . . . repent:* see the note on Mt 3, 2.

1, 16-20: These verses narrate the call of the first disciples. See the notes on Mt 4, 18-22 and 4, 20.

1, 21-45: The account of a single day's ministry of Jesus on a sabbath in and outside the synagogue of Capernaum (21-31) combines teaching and miracles of exorcism and healing. Mention is not made of the content of the teaching but of the effect of astonishment and alarm on the people. Jesus' teaching with authority, making an absolute claim on the hearer, was in the best tradition of the ancient prophets, not of the scribes. The narrative continues with events that evening (32-34; see the notes on Mt 8, 14-17) and the next day (35-39). The cleansing in vv 40-45 stands as an isolated story.

1, 23: *An unclean spirit:* so called because of the spirit's resistance to the holiness of God. The spirit knows and fears the power of Jesus to destroy his influence; cf 32.34; 3, 11; 6, 13.

1, 24: *What have you to do with us?:* see the note on Jn 2, 4.

1, 24-25: *The Holy One of God:* not a confession but an attempt to ward off Jesus' power, reflecting the notion that use of the precise name of an opposing spirit would guarantee mastery over him. Jesus silenced the cry of the unclean spirit and drove him out of the man.

the nearby villages that I may preach there also. For this purpose have I come." 39 So he went into their synagogues, preaching and driving out demons throughout the whole of Galilee.

The Cleansing of a Leper. 40*† A leper came to him [and kneeling down] begged him and said, "If you wish, you can make me clean." 41* Moved with pity, he stretched out his hand, touched him, and said to him, "I do will it. Be made clean." 42* The leprosy left him immediately, and he was made clean. 43 Then, warning him sternly, he dismissed him at once. 44* Then he said to him, "See that you tell no one anything, but go, show yourself to the priest and offer for your cleansing what Moses prescribed; that will be proof for them." 45 The man went away and began to publicize the whole matter. He spread the report abroad so that it was impossible for Jesus to enter a town openly. He remained outside in deserted places, and people kept coming to him from everywhere.

CHAPTER 2

The Healing of a Paralytic.† 1*† When Jesus returned to Capernaum after some days, it became known that he was at home. 2 Many gathered together so that there was no longer room for them, not even around the door, and he preached the word to them. 3 They came bringing to him a paralytic carried by four men. 4 Unable to get near Jesus because of the crowd, they opened up the roof above him. After they had broken through, they let down the mat on which the paralytic was lying. 5† When Jesus saw their faith, he said to the paralytic, "Child, your sins are forgiven." 6† Now some of the scribes were sitting there asking themselves, 7*† "Why does this man speak that way? He is blaspheming. Who but God alone can forgive sins?" 8 Jesus immediately knew in his mind what they were thinking to themselves, so he said, "Why are you thinking such things in your hearts? 9 Which is easier, to say to the paralytic, 'Your sins are forgiven,' or to say, 'Rise, pick up your mat and walk'? 10† But that you may know that the Son of Man has authority to forgive sins on earth"—11 he said to the paralytic, "I say to you, rise, pick up your mat, and go home." 12 He rose, picked up his mat at once, and went away in the sight of everyone. They were all astounded and glorified God, saying, "We have never seen anything like this."

The Call of Levi. 13*† Once again he went out along the sea. All the crowd came to him and he taught them. 14*† As he passed by, he saw Levi, son of Alphaeus, sitting at the customs post. He said to him, "Follow me." And he got up and followed him. 15† While he was at table in his house, many tax collectors and sinners sat with Jesus and his disciples; for there were many who followed him. 16† Some scribes who were Pharisees saw that he was eating with sinners and tax collectors and said to his disciples, "Why does he eat with tax collectors and sinners?" 17† Jesus heard this and said to them [that], "Those who are well do not need a physician, but the sick do. I did not come to call the righteous but sinners."

MARK

*

40-44: Mt 8, 2-4; Lk 5, 12-14.
41: 5, 30.
42: Lk 17, 14.
44: Lv 14, 2-32.
2, 1-12: Mt 9, 2-8; Lk 5, 18-26.
7: Is 43, 25.
13: 4, 1.
14-17: Mt 9, 9-13; Lk 5, 27-32.

†

1, 40: *A leper:* for the various forms of skin disease, see Lv 13, 1-50 and the note on Lv 13, 2-4. There are only two instances in the Old Testament in which God is shown to have cured a leper (Nm 12, 10-15 and 2 Kgs 5, 1-14). The law of Moses provided for the ritual purification of a leper. In curing the leper, Jesus assumes that the priests will reinstate the cured man into the religious community. See also the note on Lk 5, 14.

2, 1—3, 6: This section relates a series of conflicts between Jesus and the scribes and Pharisees in which the growing opposition of the latter leads to their plot to put Jesus to death (3, 6).

2, 1-2: *He was at home:* to the crowds that gathered in and outside the house Jesus *preached the word,* i.e., the gospel concerning the nearness of the kingdom and the necessity of repentance and faith (1, 14).

2, 5: It was the faith of the paralytic and those who carried him that moved Jesus to heal the sick man. Accounts of other miracles of Jesus reveal more and more his emphasis on faith as the requisite for exercising his healing powers (5, 34; 9, 23-24; 10, 52).

2, 6: *Scribes:* trained in oral interpretation of the written law; in Mark's gospel, adversaries of Jesus, with one exception (12, 28.34).

2, 7: *He is blaspheming:* an accusation made here and repeated during the trial of Jesus (14, 60-64).

2, 10: *But that you may know that the Son of Man . . . on earth:* although vv 8-9 are addressed to the scribes, the sudden interruption of thought and structure in v 10 seems not addressed to them nor to the paralytic. Moreover, the early public use of the designation "Son of Man" to unbelieving scribes is most unlikely. The most probable explanation is that Mark's insertion of v 10 is a commentary addressed to Christians for whom he recalls this miracle and who already accept in faith that Jesus is Messiah and Son of God.

2, 13: *He taught them:* see the note on 1, 21-45.

2, 14: *As he passed by:* see the note on 1, 16-20. *Levi, son of Alphaeus:* see the note on Mt 9, 9. *Customs post:* such tax collectors paid a fixed sum for the right to collect customs duties within their districts. Since whatever they could collect above this amount constituted their profit, the abuse of extortion was widespread among them. Hence, Jewish customs officials were regarded as sinners (16), outcasts of society, and disgraced along with their families. *He got up and followed him:* i.e., became a disciple of Jesus.

2, 15: *In his house:* cf v 1; Mt 9, 10. Lk 5, 29 clearly calls it Levi's house.

2, 16-17: This and the following conflict stories reflect a similar pattern: a statement of fact, a question of protest, and a reply by Jesus.

2, 17: *Do not need a physician:* this maxim of Jesus with its implied irony was uttered to silence his adversaries who objected that he ate with *tax collectors and sinners* (16). Because the scribes and Pharisees were self-righteous, they were not capable of responding to Jesus' call to repentance and faith in the gospel.

***The Question about Fasting.*†** [18]* The disciples of John and of the Pharisees were accustomed to fast. People came to him and objected, "Why do the disciples of John and the disciples of the Pharisees fast, but your disciples do not fast?" [19]† Jesus answered them, "Can the wedding guests fast while the bridegroom is with them? As long as they have the bridegroom with them they cannot fast. [20] But the days will come when the bridegroom is taken away from them, and then they will fast on that day. [21] No one sews a piece of unshrunken cloth on an old cloak. If he does, its fullness pulls away, the new from the old, and the tear gets worse. [22] Likewise, no one pours new wine into old wineskins. Otherwise, the wine will burst the skins, and both the wine and the skins are ruined. Rather, new wine is poured into fresh wineskins."

***The Disciples and the Sabbath.*†** [23]* As he was passing through a field of grain on the sabbath, his disciples began to make a path while picking the heads of grain. [24]* At this the Pharisees said to him, "Look, why are they doing what is unlawful on the sabbath?" [25]† He said to them, "Have you never read what David did when he was in need and he and his companions were hungry? [26]* How he went into the house of God when Abiathar was high priest and ate the bread of offering that only the priests could lawfully eat, and shared it with his companions?" [27]*† Then he said to them, "The sabbath was made for man, not man for the sabbath. [28]† That is why the Son of Man is lord even of the sabbath."

CHAPTER 3

***A Man with a Withered Hand.*†** [1]* Again he entered the synagogue. There was a man there who had a withered hand. [2] They watched him closely to see if he would cure him on the sabbath so that they might accuse him. [3] He said to the man with the withered hand, "Come up here before us." [4] Then he said to them, "Is it lawful to do good on the sabbath rather than to do evil, to save life rather than to destroy it?" But they remained silent. [5]* Looking around at them with anger and grieved at their hardness of heart, he said to the man, "Stretch out your hand." He stretched it out and his hand was restored. [6]† The Pharisees went out and immediately took counsel with the Herodians against him to put him to death.

***The Mercy of Jesus.*†** [7]* Jesus withdrew toward the sea with his disciples. A large number of people [followed] from Galilee and from Judea. [8] Hearing what he was doing, a large number of people came to him also from Jerusalem, from Idumea, from beyond the Jordan, and from the neighborhood of Tyre and Sidon. [9] He told his disciples to have a boat ready for him because of the crowd, so that they would not crush him. [10]* He had cured many and, as a result, those who had diseases were pressing upon him to touch him. [11]*† And whenever unclean spirits saw him they would fall down before him and shout, "You are the Son of God." [12] He warned them sternly not to make him known.

*

18-22: Mt 9, 14-17; Lk 5, 33-39.
23-28: Mt 12, 1-8; Lk 6, 1-5.
24: Dt 23, 25.
26: 1 Sm 21, 2-7/ Lv 24, 5-9.
27: 2 Mc 5, 19.
3, 1-6: Mt 12, 9-14; Lk 6, 6-11.
5: Lk 14, 4.
7-12: Mt 4, 23-25; 12, 15; Lk 6, 17-19.
10: 5, 30.
11: 1, 34; Lk 4, 41.

†

2, 18-22: This conflict over the question of fasting has the same pattern as vv 16-17; see the notes on Mt 9, 15 and 9, 16-17.

2, 19: *Can the wedding guests fast?:* the bridal metaphor expresses a new relationship of love between God and his people in the person and mission of Jesus to his disciples. It is the inauguration of the new and joyful messianic time of fulfillment and the passing of the old. Any attempt at assimilating the Pharisaic practice of fasting, or of extending the preparatory discipline of John's disciples beyond the arrival of the bridegroom, would be as futile as sewing *a piece of unshrunken cloth on an old cloak* or pouring *new wine into old wineskins* with the resulting destruction of both cloth and wine (21-22). Fasting is rendered superfluous during the earthly ministry of Jesus; cf v 20.

2, 23-28: This conflict regarding the sabbath follows the same pattern as in vv 18-22.

2, 25-26: *Have you never read what David did?:* Jesus defends the action of his disciples on the basis of 1 Sm 21, 2-7 in which an exception is made to the regulation of Lv 24, 9 because of the extreme hunger of David and his men. According to 1 Sm, the priest who gave the bread to David was Ahimelech, father of Abiathar.

2, 27: *The sabbath was made for man:* a reaffirmation of the divine intent of the sabbath to benefit Israel as contrasted with the restrictive Pharisaic tradition added to the law.

2, 28: *The Son of Man is lord even of the sabbath:* Mark's comment on the theological meaning of the incident is to benefit his Christian readers; see the note on 2, 10.

3, 1-5: Here Jesus is again depicted in conflict with his adversaries over the question of sabbath-day observance. His opponents were already ill disposed toward him because they regarded Jesus as a violator of the sabbath. Jesus' question *Is it lawful to do good on the sabbath rather than to do evil?* places the matter in the broader theological context outside the casuistry of the scribes. The answer is obvious. Jesus heals the man with the withered hand in the sight of all and reduces his opponents to silence; cf Jn 5, 17-18.

3, 6: In reporting the plot of the Pharisees and Herodians to put Jesus to death after this series of conflicts in Galilee, Mark uses a pattern that recurs in his account of later controversies in Jerusalem (11, 17-18; 12, 13-17). The help of the Herodians, supporters of Herod Antipas, tetrarch of Galilee and Perea, is needed to take action against Jesus. Both series of conflicts point to their gravity and to the impending passion of Jesus.

3, 7-19: This overview of the Galilean ministry manifests the power of Jesus to draw people to himself through his teaching and deeds of power. The crowds of Jews from many regions surround Jesus (7-12). This phenomenon prepares the way for creating a new people of Israel. The choice and mission of the Twelve is the prelude (13-19).

3, 11-12: See the note on 1, 24-25.

The Mission of the Twelve. 13*† He went up the mountain and summoned those whom he wanted and they came to him. 14*† He appointed twelve [whom he also named apostles] that they might be with him and he might send them forth to preach 15 and to have authority to drive out demons: 16† [he appointed the twelve:] Simon, whom he named Peter; 17* James, son of Zebedee, and John the brother of James, whom he named Boanerges, that is, sons of thunder; 18 Andrew, Philip, Bartholomew, Matthew, Thomas, James the son of Alphaeus; Thaddeus, Simon the Cananean, 19 and Judas Iscariot who betrayed him.

Blasphemy of the Scribes.† 20*† He came home. Again [the] crowd gathered, making it impossible for them even to eat. 21* When his relatives heard of this they set out to seize him, for they said, "He is out of his mind." 22*† The scribes who had come from Jerusalem said, "He is possessed by Beelzebul," and "By the prince of demons he drives out demons."

Jesus and Beelzebul. 23 Summoning them, he began to speak to them in parables, "How can Satan drive out Satan? 24 If a kingdom is divided against itself, that kingdom cannot stand. 25 And if a house is divided against itself, that house will not be able to stand. 26 And if Satan has risen up against himself and is divided, he cannot stand; that is the end of him. 27 But no one can enter a strong man's house to plunder his property unless he first ties up the strong man. Then he can plunder his house. 28* Amen, I say to you, all sins and all blasphemies that people utter will be forgiven them. 29† But whoever blasphemes against the holy Spirit will never have forgiveness, but is guilty of an everlasting sin." 30 For they had said, "He has an unclean spirit."

Jesus and His Family. 31* His mother and his brothers arrived. Standing outside they sent word to him and called him. 32† A crowd seated around him told him, "Your mother and your brothers [and your sisters] are outside asking for you." 33 But he said to them in reply, "Who are my mother and [my] brothers?" 34 And looking around at those seated in the circle he said, "Here are my mother and my brothers. 35 [For] whoever does the will of God is my brother and sister and mother."

CHAPTER 4

The Parable of the Sower.† 1*† On another occasion he began to teach by the sea. A very large crowd gathered around him so that he got into a boat on the sea and sat down. And the whole crowd was beside the sea on land. 2 And he taught them at length in parables, and in the course of his instruction he said to them, 3† "Hear this! A sower went out to sow. 4 And as he sowed, some seed fell on the path, and the birds came and ate it up. 5 Other seed fell on rocky ground where it had little soil. It sprang up at once because the soil was not deep. 6 And when the sun rose, it was scorched and it withered for lack of roots. 7 Some seed fell among thorns, and the thorns grew up and choked it and it produced no grain. 8 And some seed fell on rich soil and produced fruit.

*

13-19: Mt 10, 1-4; Lk 6, 12-16.
14: 6, 7.
17: Mt 16, 18; Jn 1, 42.
20: 2, 2.
21: Jn 10, 20.
22-30: Mt 12, 24-32; Lk 11, 15-22; 12, 10.
28: Lk 12, 10.
31-35: Mt 12, 46-50; Lk 8, 19-21.
4, 1-12: Mt 13, 1-13; Lk 8, 4-10.
1: 2, 13; Lk 5, 1.

†

3, 13: *He went up the mountain:* here and elsewhere the mountain is associated with solemn moments and acts in the mission and self-revelation of Jesus (6, 46; 9, 2-8; 13, 3). Jesus acts with authority as he *summoned those whom he wanted and they came to him.*

3, 14-15: *He appointed twelve [whom he also named apostles] that they might be with him:* literally "he made," i.e., instituted them as apostles to extend his messianic mission through them (6, 7-13). See the notes on Mt 10, 1 and 10, 2-4.

3, 16: *Simon, whom he named Peter:* Mark indicates that Simon's name was changed on this occasion. Peter is first in all lists of the apostles (Mt 10, 2; Lk 6, 14; Acts 1, 13; cf 1 Cor 15, 5-8).

3, 20-35: Within the narrative of the coming of Jesus' relatives (20-21) is inserted the account of the unbelieving scribes from Jerusalem who attributed Jesus' power over demons to Beelzebul (22-30); see the note on 5, 21-43. There were those even among the relatives of Jesus who disbelieved and regarded Jesus as *out of his mind* (21). Against this background, Jesus is informed of the arrival of his mother and brothers [and sisters] (32). He responds by showing that not family ties but doing God's will (35) is decisive in the kingdom; cf the note on Mt 12, 46-50.

3, 20: *He came home:* cf 2, 1-2 and see the note on 2, 15.

3, 22: *By Beelzebul:* see the note on Mt 10, 25. Two accusations are leveled against Jesus: (1) that *he is possessed* by an unclean spirit, and (2) *by the prince of demons he drives out demons.* Jesus answers the second charge by a parable (24-27) and responds to the first charge in vv 28-29.

3, 29: *Whoever blasphemes against the holy Spirit:* this sin is called *an everlasting sin* because it attributes to Satan, who is the power of evil, what is actually the work of the holy Spirit, namely, victory over the demons.

3, 32: *Your brothers:* see the note on 6, 3.

4, 1-34: *In parables* (2): see the note on Mt 13, 3. The use of parables is typical of Jesus' enigmatic method of teaching the crowds (2-9.12) as compared with the interpretation of the parables he gives to his disciples (10-25.33-34), to each group according to its capacity to understand (9-11). The key feature of the parable at hand is the sowing of the seed (3), representing the breakthrough of the kingdom of God into the world. The various types of soil refer to the diversity of response accorded the word of God (4-7). The climax of the parable is the harvest of thirty, sixty, and a hundredfold, indicating the consummation of the kingdom (8). Thus both the present and the future action of God, from the initiation to the fulfillment of the kingdom, is presented through this and other parables (26-29.30-32).

4, 1: *By the sea:* the shore of the Sea of Galilee or a boat near the shore (2, 13; 3, 7-8) is the place where Mark depicts Jesus teaching the crowds. By contrast the mountain is the scene of Jesus at prayer (6, 46) or in the process of forming his disciples (3, 13; 9, 2).

4, 3-8: See the note on Mt 13, 3-8.

It came up and grew and yielded thirty,
sixty, and a hundredfold." 9 He added,
"Whoever has ears to hear ought to
hear."

The Purpose of the Parables. 10 And
when he was alone, those present along
with the Twelve questioned him about
the parables. 11† He answered them,
"The mystery of the kingdom of God
has been granted to you. But to those
outside everything comes in parables,
12* so that

'they may look and see but not perceive,
and hear and listen but not understand,
in order that they may not be converted and be forgiven.' "

13*† Jesus said to them, "Do you not un-
derstand this parable? Then how will
you understand any of the parables?
14 The sower sows the word. 15 These are
the ones on the path where the word is
sown. As soon as they hear, Satan
comes at once and takes away the word
sown in them. 16 And these are the ones
sown on rocky ground who, when they
hear the word, receive it at once with
joy. 17 But they have no root; they last
only for a time. Then when tribulation
or persecution comes because of the
word, they quickly fall away. 18 Those
sown among thorns are another sort.
They are the people who hear the word,
19 but worldly anxiety, the lure of riches,
and the craving for other things intrude
and choke the word, and it bears no
fruit. 20 But those sown on rich soil are
the ones who hear the word and accept
it and bear fruit thirty and sixty and a
hundredfold."

Parable of the Lamp. 21* He said to
them, "Is a lamp brought in to be placed
under a bushel basket or under a bed,
and not to be placed on a lampstand?
22* For there is nothing hidden except
to be made visible; nothing is secret ex-
cept to come to light. 23 Anyone who has
ears to hear ought to hear." 24* He also
told them, "Take care what you hear.
The measure with which you measure
will be measured out to you, and still
more will be given to you. 25* To the one
who has, more will be given; from the
one who has not, even what he has will
be taken away."

Seed Grows of Itself.† 26* He said,
"This is how it is with the kingdom of
God; it is as if a man were to scatter
seed on the land 27 and would sleep and
rise night and day and the seed would
sprout and grow, he knows not how.
28 Of its own accord the land yields fruit,
first the blade, then the ear, then the
full grain in the ear. 29 And when the
grain is ripe, he wields the sickle at
once, for the harvest has come."

The Mustard Seed. 30* He said, "To
what shall we compare the kingdom of
God, or what parable can we use for it?
31 It is like a mustard seed that, when
it is sown in the ground, is the smallest
of all the seeds on the earth. 32† But once
it is sown, it springs up and becomes
the largest of plants and puts forth large
branches, so that the birds of the sky
can dwell in its shade." 33* With many
such parables he spoke the word to
them as they were able to understand
it. 34 Without parables he did not speak
to them, but to his own disciples he ex-
plained everything in private.

The Calming of a Storm at Sea.†
35* On that day, as evening drew on, he
said to them, "Let us cross to the other
side." 36 Leaving the crowd, they took
him with them in the boat just as he was.
And other boats were with him. 37 A vio-
lent squall came up and waves were
breaking over the boat, so that it was
already filling up. 38 Jesus was in the
stern, asleep on a cushion. They woke
him and said to him, "Teacher, do you
not care that we are perishing?" 39† He
woke up, rebuked the wind, and said to
the sea, "Quiet! Be still!" The wind
ceased and there was great calm.
40 Then he asked them, "Why are you
terrified? Do you not yet have faith?"
41*† They were filled with great awe and

*

12: Is 6, 9; Jn 12, 40; Acts 28, 26; Rom 11, 8.
13-20: Mt 13, 18-23; Lk 8, 11-15.
21-25: Lk 8, 16-18.
21: Mt 5, 15; Lk 11, 33.
22: Mt 10, 26; Lk 12, 2.
24: Mt 7, 2; Lk 6, 38.
25: Mt 13, 12; Lk 19, 26.
26-29: Jas 5, 7.
30-32: Mt 13, 31-32; Lk 13, 18-19.
33-34: Mt 13, 34.
35-40: Mt 8, 18.23-37; Lk 8, 22-25.
41: 1, 27.

†

4, 11-12: These verses are to be viewed against their background in 3, 6.22 concerning the unbelief and opposition Jesus encountered in his ministry. It is against this background that the distinction in Jesus' method becomes clear of presenting the kingdom to the disbelieving crowd in one manner and to the disciples in another. To the former it is presented in parables and the truth remains hidden; for the latter the parable is interpreted and the mystery is partially revealed because of their faith; see the notes on Mt 13, 11 and 13, 13.

4, 13-20: See the note on Mt 13, 18-23.

4, 26-29: Only Mark records the parable of the seed's growth. Sower and harvester are the same. The emphasis is on the power of the seed to grow of itself without human intervention (27). Mysteriously it produces *blade* and *ear* and *full grain* (28). Thus the kingdom of God initiated by Jesus in proclaiming the word develops quietly yet powerfully until it is fully established by him at the final judgment (29); cf Rv 14, 15.

4, 32: The universality of the kingdom of God is indicated here; cf Ez 17, 23; 31, 6; Dn 4, 17-19.

4, 35—5, 43: After the chapter on parables, Mark narrates four miracle stories: 4, 35-41; 5, 1-20; and two joined together in 5, 21-43. See also the notes on Mt 8, 23-34 and 9, 8-26.

4, 39: *Quiet! Be still!*: as in the case of silencing a demon (1, 25), Jesus rebukes the wind and subdues the turbulence of the sea by a mere word; see the note on Mt 8, 26.

4, 41: Jesus is here depicted as exercising power over wind and sea. In the Christian community this event was seen as a sign of Jesus' saving presence amid persecutions that threatened its existence.

said to one another, "Who then is this
whom even wind and sea obey?"

CHAPTER 5

***The Healing of the Gerasene De-
moniac.*** 1*† They came to the other
side of the sea, to the territory of the
Gerasenes. 2† When he got out of the
boat, at once a man from the tombs who
had an unclean spirit met him. 3 The
man had been dwelling among the
tombs, and no one could restrain him
any longer, even with a chain. 4 In fact,
he had frequently been bound with
shackles and chains, but the chains had
been pulled apart by him and the shack-
les smashed, and no one was strong
enough to subdue him. 5 Night and day
among the tombs and on the hillsides
he was always crying out and bruising
himself with stones. 6 Catching sight of
Jesus from a distance, he ran up and
prostrated himself before him, 7† crying
out in a loud voice, "What have you to
do with me, Jesus, Son of the Most High
God? I adjure you by God, do not tor-
ment me!" 8 (He had been saying to
him, "Unclean spirit, come out of the
man!") 9*† He asked him, "What is your
name?" He replied, "Legion is my
name. There are many of us." 10 And
he pleaded earnestly with him not to
drive them away from that territory.

11† Now a large herd of swine was
feeding there on the hillside. 12 And they
pleaded with him, "Send us into the
swine. Let us enter them." 13 And he let
them, and the unclean spirits came out
and entered the swine. The herd of
about two thousand rushed down a
steep bank into the sea, where they
were drowned. 14 The swineherds ran
away and reported the incident in the
town and throughout the countryside.
And people came out to see what had
happened. 15 As they approached Jesus,
they caught sight of the man who had
been possessed by Legion, sitting there
clothed and in his right mind. And they
were seized with fear. 16 Those who wit-
nessed the incident explained to them
what had happened to the possessed
man and to the swine. 17 Then they be-
gan to beg him to leave their district.
18 As he was getting into the boat, the
man who had been possessed pleaded
to remain with him. 19† But he would not
permit him but told him instead, "Go
home to your family and announce to
them all that the Lord in his pity has
done for you." 20 Then the man went off
and began to proclaim in the Decapolis
what Jesus had done for him; and all
were amazed.

***Jairus's Daughter and the Woman
with a Hemorrhage.***† 21* When Jesus
had crossed again [in the boat] to the
other side, a large crowd gathered
around him, and he stayed close to the
sea. 22* One of the synagogue officials,
named Jairus, came forward. Seeing
him he fell at his feet 23† and pleaded
earnestly with him, saying, "My daugh-
ter is at the point of death. Please, come
lay your hands on her that she may get
well and live." 24 He went off with him,
and a large crowd followed him and
pressed upon him.

25 There was a woman afflicted with
hemorrhages for twelve years. 26 She
had suffered greatly at the hands of
many doctors and had spent all that she
had. Yet she was not helped but only
grew worse. 27 She had heard about Je-
sus and came up behind him in the
crowd and touched his cloak. 28† She
said, "If I but touch his clothes, I shall
be cured." 29 Immediately her flow of
blood dried up. She felt in her body that
she was healed of her affliction. 30 Jesus,
aware at once that power had gone out
from him, turned around in the crowd
and asked, "Who has touched my
clothes?" 31 But his disciples said to him,
"You see how the crowd is pressing
upon you, and yet you ask, 'Who
touched me?' " 32 And he looked around
to see who had done it. 33 The woman,
realizing what had happened to her, ap-
proached in fear and trembling. She fell
down before Jesus and told him the
whole truth. 34* He said to her, "Daugh-
ter, your faith has saved you. Go in
peace and be cured of your affliction."

MARK

*

5, 1-20: Mt 8, 28-34; Lk 8, 26-39.
9: Mt 12, 45; Lk 8, 2; 11, 26.
21: 2, 13.
22-43: Mt 9, 18-26; Lk 8, 41-56.
34: Lk 7, 30.

†

5, 1: *The territory of the Gerasenes:* the reference is to pagan territory; cf Is 65, 1. Another reading is "Gadarenes"; see the note on Mt 8, 28.

5, 2-6: The man was an outcast from society, dominated by unclean spirits (8.13), living among the tombs. The prostration before Jesus (6) indicates Jesus' power over evil spirits.

5, 7: *What have you to do with me?:* cf 1, 24 and see the note on Jn 2, 4.

5, 9: *Legion is my name:* the demons were numerous and the condition of the possessed man was extremely serious; cf Mt 12, 45.

5, 11: *Herd of swine:* see the note on Mt 8, 30.

5, 19: *Go home:* Jesus did not accept the man's request *to remain with him* as a disciple (18), yet invited him to announce to his own people what the Lord had done for him, i.e., proclaim the gospel message to his pagan family; cf 1, 14.39; 3, 14; 13, 10.

5, 21-43: The story of the raising to life of Jairus's daughter is divided into two parts: vv 21-24 and 35-43. Between these two separated parts the account of the cure of the hemorrhage victim (25-34) is interposed. This technique of intercalating or sandwiching one story within another occurs several times in Mk: 3, 19b-21 (22-30) 31-35; 6, 6b-13 (14-29) 30; 11, 12-14 (15-19) 20-25; 14, 53 (54) 55-65 (66-73).

5, 23: *Lay your hands on her:* this act for the purpose of healing is frequent in Mk (6, 5; 7, 32-35; 8, 23-25; 16, 18) and is also found in Mt 9, 18; Lk 4, 40; 13, 13; Acts 9, 17; 28, 8.

5, 28: Both in the case of Jairus and his daughter (23) and in the case of the hemorrhage victim, the inner conviction that physical contact (30) accompanied by faith in Jesus' saving power could effect a cure was rewarded.

35† While he was still speaking, people from the synagogue official's house arrived and said, "Your daughter has died; why trouble the teacher any longer?" 36 Disregarding the message that was reported, Jesus said to the synagogue official, "Do not be afraid; just have faith." 37 He did not allow anyone to accompany him inside except Peter, James, and John, the brother of James. 38 When they arrived at the house of the synagogue official, he caught sight of a commotion, people weeping and wailing loudly. 39*† So he went in and said to them, "Why this commotion and weeping? The child is not dead but asleep." 40 And they ridiculed him. Then he put them all out. He took along the child's father and mother and those who were with him and entered the room where the child was. 41† He took the child by the hand and said to her, "*Talitha koum,*" which means, "Little girl, I say to you, arise!" 42 The girl, a child of twelve, arose immediately and walked around. [At that] they were utterly astounded. 43 He gave strict orders that no one should know this and said that she should be given something to eat.

CHAPTER 6

The Rejection at Nazareth. 1*† He departed from there and came to his native place, accompanied by his disciples. 2† When the sabbath came he began to teach in the synagogue, and many who heard him were astonished. They said, "Where did this man get all this? What kind of wisdom has been given him? What mighty deeds are wrought by his hands! 3*† Is he not the carpenter, the son of Mary, and the brother of James and Joses and Judas and Simon? And are not his sisters here with us?" And they took offense at him. 4*† Jesus said to them, "A prophet is not without honor except in his native place and among his own kin and in his own house." 5† So he was not able to perform any mighty deed there, apart from curing a few sick people by laying his hands on them. 6 He was amazed at their lack of faith.

The Mission of the Twelve. He went around to the villages in the vicinity teaching. 7*† He summoned the Twelve and began to send them out two by two and gave them authority over unclean spirits. 8† He instructed them to take nothing for the journey but a walking stick—no food, no sack, no money in their belts. 9 They were, however, to wear sandals but not a second tunic. 10† He said to them, "Wherever you enter a house, stay there until you leave from there. 11 Whatever place does not welcome you or listen to you, leave there and shake the dust off your feet in testimony against them." 12 So they went off and preached repentance. 13*† They drove out many demons, and

---

*

39-40: Acts 9, 40.
6, 1-6: Mt 13, 54-58; Lk 4, 16-30.
3: 15, 40; Mt 12, 46; Jn 6, 42.
4: Jn 4, 44.
7-11: Mt 10, 1.9-14; Lk 9, 15; 10, 4-11.
13: Jas 5, 14.

---

†

5, 35: The faith of Jairus was put to a twofold test: (1) that his daughter might be cured and, now that she had died, (2) that she might be restored to life. His faith contrasts with the lack of faith of the crowd.

5, 39: *Not dead but asleep:* the New Testament often refers to death as sleep (Mt 27, 52; Jn 11, 11; 1 Cor 15, 6; 1 Thes 4, 13-15); see the note on Mt 9, 24.

5, 41: *Arise:* the Greek verb *egeirein* is the verb generally used to express resurrection from death (6, 14.16; Mt 11, 5; Lk 7, 14) and Jesus' own resurrection (16, 6; Mt 28, 6; Lk 24, 6).

6, 1: *His native place:* the Greek word *patris* here refers to Nazareth (cf 1, 9; Lk 4, 16.23-24), though it can also mean native land.

6, 2-6: See the note on Mt 13, 54-58.

6, 3: *Is he not the carpenter?:* no other gospel calls Jesus a carpenter. Some witnesses have "the carpenter's son," as in Mt 13, 55. *Son of Mary:* contrary to Jewish custom, which calls a man the son of his father, this expression may reflect Mark's own faith that God is the Father of Jesus (1, 1.11; 8, 38; 13, 32; 14, 36). *The brother of James . . . Simon:* in Semitic usage, the terms 'brother,' 'sister' are applied not only to children of the same parents, but to nephews, nieces, cousins, half-brothers, and half-sisters; cf Gn 14, 16; 29, 15; Lv 10, 4. While one cannot suppose that the meaning of a Greek word should be sought in the first place from Semitic usage, the Septuagint often translates the Hebrew *ʾāh* by the Greek word *adelphos,* "brother," as in the cited passages, a fact that may argue for a similar breadth of meaning in some New Testament passages. For instance, there is no doubt that in v 17, "brother" is used of Philip, who was actually the half-brother of Herod Antipas. On the other hand, Mark may have understood the terms literally; see also Mt 3, 31-32; 12, 46; 13, 55-56; Lk 8, 19; Jn 7, 3.5. The question of meaning here would not have arisen but for the faith of the church in Mary's perpetual virginity.

6, 4: *A prophet is not without honor except . . . in his own house:* a saying that finds parallels in other literatures, especially Jewish and Greek, but without reference to a prophet. Comparing himself to previous Hebrew prophets whom the people rejected, Jesus intimates his own eventual rejection by the nation especially in view of the dishonor his own relatives had shown him (3, 21) and now his townspeople as well.

6, 5: *He was not able to perform any mighty deed there:* according to Mark, Jesus' power could not take effect because of a person's lack of faith.

6, 7-13: The preparation for the mission of the Twelve is seen in the call (1) of the first disciples to be fishers of men (1, 16-20), (2) then of the Twelve set apart to be with Jesus and to receive authority to preach and expel demons (3, 13-19). Now they are given the specific mission to exercise that authority in word and power as representatives of Jesus during the time of their formation.

6, 8-9: In Mk the use of a *walking stick* (8) and *sandals* (9) is permitted, but not in Mt 10, 10 nor in Lk 10, 4. Mark does not mention any prohibition to visit pagan territory and to enter Samaritan towns. These differences indicate a certain adaptation to conditions in and outside of Palestine and suggest in Mark's account a later activity in the church. For the rest, Jesus required of his apostles a total dependence on God for food and shelter; cf vv 35-44; 8, 1-9.

6, 10-11: Remaining in the same house as a guest (10) rather than moving to another offering greater comfort avoided any impression of seeking advantage for oneself and prevented dishonor to one's host. Shaking the dust off one's feet served as testimony against those who rejected the call to repentance.

6, 13: *Anointed with oil . . . cured them:* a common medicinal remedy, but seen here as a vehicle of divine power for healing.

they anointed with oil many who were
sick and cured them.
Herod's Opinion of Jesus. † 14*† King
Herod heard about it, for his fame had
become widespread, and people were
saying, "John the Baptist has been
raised from the dead; that is why
mighty powers are at work in him."
15* Others were saying, "He is Elijah";
still others, "He is a prophet like any
of the prophets." 16 But when Herod
learned of it, he said, "It is John whom
I beheaded. He has been raised up."
The Death of John the Baptist. †
17* Herod was the one who had John ar-
rested and bound in prison on account
of Herodias, the wife of his brother
Philip, whom he had married. 18* John
had said to Herod, "It is not lawful for
you to have your brother's wife."
19† Herodias harbored a grudge against
him and wanted to kill him but was un-
able to do so. 20 Herod feared John,
knowing him to be a righteous and holy
man, and kept him in custody. When he
heard him speak he was very much per-
plexed, yet he liked to listen to him.
21 She had an opportunity one day when
Herod, on his birthday, gave a banquet
for his courtiers, his military officers,
and the leading men of Galilee.
22 Herodias's own daughter came in and
performed a dance that delighted
Herod and his guests. The king said to
the girl, "Ask of me whatever you wish
and I will grant it to you." 23* He even
swore [many things] to her, "I will
grant you whatever you ask of me, even
to half of my kingdom." 24 She went out
and said to her mother, "What shall I
ask for?" She replied, "The head of
John the Baptist." 25 The girl hurried
back to the king's presence and made
her request, "I want you to give me at
once on a platter the head of John the
Baptist." 26 The king was deeply dis-
tressed, but because of his oaths and the
guests he did not wish to break his word
to her. 27* So he promptly dispatched an
executioner with orders to bring back
his head. He went off and beheaded him
in the prison. 28 He brought in the head
on a platter and gave it to the girl. The
girl in turn gave it to her mother.
29 When his disciples heard about it,
they came and took his body and laid
it in a tomb.
The Return of the Twelve. 30*† The
apostles gathered together with Jesus
and reported all they had done and
taught. 31*† He said to them, "Come
away by yourselves to a deserted place
and rest a while." People were coming
and going in great numbers, and they
had no opportunity even to eat. 32* So
they went off in the boat by themselves
to a deserted place. 33 People saw them
leaving and many came to know about
it. They hastened there on foot from all
the towns and arrived at the place be-
fore them.
The Feeding of the Five Thousand.
34 When he disembarked and saw the
vast crowd, his heart was moved with
pity for them, for they were like sheep
without a shepherd; and he began to
teach them many things. 35† By now it
was already late and his disciples ap-
proached him and said, "This is a de-
serted place and it is already very late.
36 Dismiss them so that they can go to
the surrounding farms and villages and
buy themselves something to eat."
37 He said to them in reply, "Give them
some food yourselves." But they said
to him, "Are we to buy two hundred
days' wages worth of food and give it
to them to eat?" 38 He asked them, "How
many loaves do you have? Go and see."
And when they had found out they said,
"Five loaves and two fish." 39 So he gave
orders to have them sit down in groups
on the green grass. 40† The people took
their places in rows by hundreds and
by fifties. 41† Then, taking the five

MARK

*

14-16: Lk 9, 7-8.
14-29: Mt 14, 1-12.
15: Mt 16, 14.
17: Lk 3, 19-20.
18: Lv 18, 16.
23: Est 5, 3.
27-28: Lk 9, 9.
30: Lk 9, 10.
31: 3, 20; Mt 14, 13; Lk 9, 10.
32-44: Mt 14, 13-21; Lk 9, 10-17; Jn 6, 1-13.

†

6, 14-16: The various opinions about Jesus anticipate the theme of his identity that reaches its climax in 8, 27-30.

6, 14: *King Herod:* see the note on Mt 14, 1.

6, 17-29: Similarities are to be noted between Mark's account of the imprisonment and death of John the Baptist in this pericope, and that of the passion of Jesus (15, 1-47). Herod and Pilate, each in turn, acknowledges the holiness of life of one over whom he unjustly exercises the power of condemnation and death (26-27; 15, 9-10.14-15). The hatred of Herodias toward John parallels that of the Jewish leaders toward Jesus. After the deaths of John and of Jesus, well-disposed persons request the bodies of the victims of Herod and of Pilate in turn to give them respectful burial (29; 15, 45-46).

6, 19: *Herodias:* see the note on Mt 14, 3.

6, 30: *Apostles:* here, and in some manuscripts at 3, 14, Mark calls apostles (i.e., those sent forth) the Twelve whom Jesus sends as his emissaries, empowering them to preach, to expel demons, and to cure the sick (13). Only after Pentecost is the title used in the technical sense.

6, 31-34: The withdrawal of Jesus with his disciples to a desert place to rest attracts a great number of people to follow them. Toward this people of the new exodus Jesus is moved with pity; he satisfies their spiritual hunger by teaching them many things, thus gradually showing himself the faithful shepherd of a new Israel; cf Nm 27, 17; Ez 34, 15.

6, 35-44: See the note on Mt 14, 13-21. Compare this section with 8, 1-9. The various accounts of the multiplication of loaves and fishes, two each in Mark and in Matthew and one each in Luke and in John, indicate the wide interest of the early church in their eucharistic gatherings; see, e.g., v 41; 8, 6; 14, 22; and recall also the sign of bread in Ex 16; Dt 8, 3-16; Pss 78, 24-25; 105, 40; Wis 16, 20-21.

6, 40: *The people . . . in rows by hundreds and by fifties:* reminiscent of the groupings of Israelites encamped in the desert (Ex 18, 21-25) and of the wilderness tradition of the prophets depicting the transformation of the wasteland into pastures where the true shepherd feeds his flock (Ez 34, 25-26) and makes his people beneficiaries of messianic grace.

6, 41: On the language of this verse as eucharistic (cf 14, 22), see the notes on Mt 14, 19.20. Jesus observed the Jewish table ritual of blessing God before partaking of food.

loaves and the two fish and looking up
to heaven, he said the blessing, broke
the loaves, and gave them to [his] disci-
ples to set before the people; he also di-
vided the two fish among them all.
42 They all ate and were satisfied.
43 And they picked up twelve wicker
baskets full of fragments and what was
left of the fish. 44 Those who ate [of the
loaves] were five thousand men.

The Walking on the Water. †
45*† Then he made his disciples get into
the boat and precede him to the other
side toward Bethsaida, while he dis-
missed the crowd. 46† And when he had
taken leave of them, he went off to the
mountain to pray. 47 When it was eve-
ning, the boat was far out on the sea
and he was alone on shore. 48† Then he
saw that they were tossed about while
rowing, for the wind was against them.
About the fourth watch of the night, he
came towards them walking on the sea.
He meant to pass by them. 49 But when
they saw him walking on the sea, they
thought it was a ghost and cried out.
50† They had all seen him and were ter-
rified. But at once he spoke with them,
"Take courage, it is I, do not be afraid!"
51 He got into the boat with them and
the wind died down. They were [com-
pletely] astounded. 52*† They had not
understood the incident of the loaves.
On the contrary, their hearts were
hardened.

The Healings at Gennesaret.
53* After making the crossing, they
came to land at Gennesaret and tied up
there. 54 As they were leaving the boat,
people immediately recognized him.
55 They scurried about the surrounding
country and began to bring in the sick
on mats to wherever they heard he was.
56* Whatever villages or towns or coun-
tryside he entered, they laid the sick in
the marketplaces and begged him that
they might touch only the tassel on his
cloak; and as many as touched it were
healed.

CHAPTER 7

The Tradition of the Elders. † 1* Now
when the Pharisees with some scribes
who had come from Jerusalem gath-
ered around him, 2 they observed that
some of his disciples ate their meals
with unclean, that is, unwashed, hands.
3† (For the Pharisees and, in fact, all
Jews, do not eat without carefully wash-
ing their hands, keeping the tradition
of the elders. 4 And on coming from the
marketplace they do not eat without pu-
rifying themselves. And there are many
other things that they have traditionally
observed, the purification of cups and
jugs and kettles [and beds].) 5† So the
Pharisees and scribes questioned him,
"Why do your disciples not follow the
tradition of the elders but instead eat
a meal with unclean hands?" 6* He re-
sponded, "Well did Isaiah prophesy
about you hypocrites, as it is written:

'This people honors me with their lips,
but their hearts are far from me;
7 In vain do they worship me,
teaching as doctrines human precepts.'

8 You disregard God's commandment
but cling to human tradition." 9 He went
on to say, "How well you have set aside
the commandment of God in order to
uphold your tradition! 10* For Moses
said, 'Honor your father and your
mother,' and 'Whoever curses father or
mother shall die.' 11† Yet you say, 'If a
person says to father or mother, "Any
support you might have had from me
is *qorban*"' (meaning, dedicated to
God), 12 you allow him to do nothing
more for his father or mother. 13 You
nullify the word of God in favor of your
tradition that you have handed on. And
you do many such things." 14* He sum-
moned the crowd again and said to
them, "Hear me, all of you, and under-
stand. 15 Nothing that enters one from

*

45-51: Mt 14, 22-32; Jn 6, 15-21.
52: 4, 13.
53-56: Mt 14, 34-36.
56: 5, 27-28; Acts 5, 15.
7, 1-23: Mt 15, 1-20.
6: Is 29, 13.
10: Ex 21, 17; Lv 20, 9; Dt 5, 16; Eph 6, 2.
14-23: Mt 15, 10-20.

†

6, 45-52: See the note on Mt 14, 22-33.

6, 45: *To the other side toward Bethsaida:* a village at the northeastern shore of the Sea of Galilee.

6, 46: *He went off to the mountain to pray:* see 1, 35-38. In Jn 6, 15 Jesus withdrew to evade any involvement in the false messianic hopes of the multitude.

6, 48: *Walking on the sea:* see the notes on Mt 14, 22-33 and on Jn 6, 19.

6, 50: *It is I, do not be afraid!:* literally, "I am." This may reflect the divine revelatory formula of Ex 3, 14; Is 41, 4.10.14; 43, 1-3.10.13. Mark implies the hidden identity of Jesus as Son of God.

6, 52: *They had not understood . . . the loaves:* the revelatory character of this sign and that of the walking on the sea completely escaped the disciples. *Their hearts were hardened:* in 3, 5-6 hardness of heart was attributed to those who did not accept Jesus and plotted his death. Here the same disposition prevents the disciples from comprehending Jesus' self-revelation through signs; cf 8, 17.

7, 1-23: See the note on Mt 15, 1-20. Against the Pharisees' narrow, legalistic, and external practices of piety in matters of purification (2-5), external worship (6-7), and observance of commandments, Jesus sets in opposition the true moral intent of the divine law (8-13). But he goes beyond contrasting the law and Pharisaic interpretation of it. The parable of vv 14-15 in effect sets aside the law itself in respect to clean and unclean food. He thereby opens the way for unity between Jew and Gentile in the kingdom of God, intimated by Jesus' departure for pagan territory beyond Galilee. For similar contrast see 2, 1—3, 6; 3, 20-35; 6, 1-6.

7, 3: *Carefully washing their hands:* refers to ritual purification.

7, 5: *Tradition of the elders:* the body of detailed, unwritten, human laws regarded by the scribes and Pharisees to have the same binding force as that of the Mosaic law; cf Gal 1, 14.

7, 11: *Qorban:* a formula for a gift to God, dedicating the offering to the temple, so that the giver might continue to use it for himself but not give it to others, even needy parents.

outside can defile that person; but the things that come out from within are what defile." [16]†

17*† When he got home away from the crowd his disciples questioned him about the parable. 18 He said to them, "Are even you likewise without understanding? Do you not realize that everything that goes into a person from outside cannot defile, 19*† since it enters not the heart but the stomach and passes out into the latrine?" (Thus he declared all foods clean.) 20 "But what comes out of a person, that is what defiles. 21* From within people, from their hearts, come evil thoughts, unchastity, theft, murder, 22 adultery, greed, malice, deceit, licentiousness, envy, blasphemy, arrogance, folly. 23 All these evils come from within and they defile."

The Syrophoenician Woman's Faith.†

24* From that place he went off to the district of Tyre. He entered a house and wanted no one to know about it, but he could not escape notice. 25 Soon a woman whose daughter had an unclean spirit heard about him. She came and fell at his feet. 26* The woman was a Greek, a Syrophoenician by birth, and she begged him to drive the demon out of her daughter. 27† He said to her, "Let the children be fed first. For it is not right to take the food of the children and throw it to the dogs." 28 She replied and said to him, "Lord, even the dogs under the table eat the children's scraps." 29 Then he said to her, "For saying this, you may go. The demon has gone out of your daughter." 30 When the woman went home, she found the child lying in bed and the demon gone.

The Healing of a Deaf Man. 31* Again he left the district of Tyre and went by way of Sidon to the Sea of Galilee, into the district of the Decapolis. 32 And people brought to him a deaf man who had a speech impediment and begged him to lay his hand on him. 33 He took him off by himself away from the crowd. He put his finger into the man's ears and, spitting, touched his tongue; 34 then he looked up to heaven and groaned, and said to him, "*Ephphatha!*" (that is, "Be opened!") 35 And [immediately] the man's ears were opened, his speech impediment was removed, and he spoke plainly. 36† He ordered them not to tell anyone. But the more he ordered them not to, the more they proclaimed it. 37* They were exceedingly astonished and they said, "He has done all things well. He makes the deaf hear and [the] mute speak."

CHAPTER 8

The Feeding of the Four Thousand.†

1* In those days when there again was a great crowd without anything to eat, he summoned the disciples and said, 2 "My heart is moved with pity for the crowd, because they have been with me now for three days and have nothing to eat. 3 If I send them away hungry to their homes, they will collapse on the way, and some of them have come a great distance." 4 His disciples answered him, "Where can anyone get enough bread to satisfy them here in this deserted place?" 5 Still he asked them, "How many loaves do you have?" "Seven," they replied. 6† He ordered the crowd to sit down on the ground. Then, taking the seven loaves he gave thanks, broke them, and gave them to his disciples to distribute, and they distributed them to the crowd. 7 They also had a few fish. He said the blessing over them and ordered them distributed also. 8 They ate and were satisfied. They picked up the fragments left over—seven baskets. 9 There were about four thousand people.

He dismissed them 10 and got into the boat with his disciples and came to the region of Dalmanutha.

---

*

17: 4, 10.13.
19: Acts 10, 15.
21: Jer 17, 9.
24-30: Mt 15, 21-28.
26: Mt 8, 29.
31-37: Mt 15, 29-31.
37: Mt 15, 31.
8, 1-10: 6, 34-44; Mt 15, 32-39.

---

†

7, 16: Verse 16, "Anyone who has ears to hear ought to hear," is omitted because it is lacking in some of the best Greek manuscripts and was probably transferred here by scribes from 4, (9).23.

7, 17: *Away from the crowd . . . the parable:* in this context of privacy the term *parable* refers to something hidden, about to be revealed to the disciples; cf 4, 10-11.34. Jesus sets the Mosaic food laws in the context of the kingdom of God where they are abrogated, and he declares moral defilement the only cause of uncleanness.

7, 19: *(Thus he declared all foods clean):* if this bold declaration goes back to Jesus, its force was not realized among Jewish Christians in the early church; cf Acts 10, 1—11, 18.

7, 24-37: The withdrawal of Jesus to the district of Tyre may have been for a respite (24), but he soon moved onward to Sidon and, by way of the Sea of Galilee, to the Decapolis. These districts provided a Gentile setting for the extension of his ministry of healing because the people there acknowledged his power (29.37). The actions attributed to Jesus (33-35) were also used by healers of the time.

7, 27-28: The figure of a household in which children at table are fed first and then their leftover food is given to the dogs under the table is used effectively to acknowledge the prior claim of the Jews to the ministry of Jesus; however, Jesus accedes to the Gentile woman's plea for the cure of her afflicted daughter because of her faith.

7, 36: *The more they proclaimed it:* the same verb *proclaim* attributed here to the crowd in relation to the miracles of Jesus is elsewhere used in Mark for the preaching of the gospel on the part of Jesus, of his disciples, and of the Christian community (1, 14; 13, 10; 14, 9). Implied in the action of the crowd is a recognition of the salvific mission of Jesus; see the note on Mt 11, 5-6.

8, 1-10: The two accounts of the multiplication of loaves and fishes (8, 1-10 and 6, 31-44) have eucharistic significance. Their similarity of structure and themes but dissimilarity of detail are considered by many to refer to a single event that, however, developed in two distinct traditions, one Jewish Christian and the other Gentile Christian, since Jesus in Mark's presentation (7, 24-37) has extended his saving mission to the Gentiles.

8, 6: See the note on 6, 41.

***The Demand for a Sign.*†** 11* The Pharisees came forward and began to argue with him, seeking from him a sign from heaven to test him. 12 He sighed from the depth of his spirit and said, "Why does this generation seek a sign? Amen, I say to you, no sign will be given to this generation." 13 Then he left them, got into the boat again, and went off to the other shore.

The Leaven of the Pharisees. 14* They had forgotten to bring bread, and they had only one loaf with them in the boat. 15† He enjoined them, "Watch out, guard against the leaven of the Pharisees and the leaven of Herod." 16 They concluded among themselves that it was because they had no bread. 17* When he became aware of this he said to them, "Why do you conclude that it is because you have no bread? Do you not yet understand or comprehend? Are your hearts hardened? 18* Do you have eyes and not see, ears and not hear? And do you not remember, 19 when I broke the five loaves for the five thousand, how many wicker baskets full of fragments you picked up?" They answered him, "Twelve." 20 "When I broke the seven loaves for the four thousand, how many full baskets of fragments did you pick up?" They answered [him], "Seven." 21 He said to them, "Do you still not understand?"

***The Blind Man of Bethsaida.*†** 22 When they arrived at Bethsaida, they brought to him a blind man and begged him to touch him. 23* He took the blind man by the hand and led him outside the village. Putting spittle on his eyes he laid his hands on him and asked, "Do you see anything?" 24 Looking up he replied, "I see people looking like trees and walking." 25 Then he laid hands on his eyes a second time and he saw clearly; his sight was restored and he could see everything distinctly. 26 Then he sent him home and said, "Do not even go into the village."

III: THE MYSTERY BEGINS TO BE REVEALED

***Peter's Confession about Jesus.*†** 27* Now Jesus and his disciples set out for the villages of Caesarea Philippi. Along the way he asked his disciples, "Who do people say that I am?" 28 They said in reply, "John the Baptist, others Elijah, still others one of the prophets." 29 And he asked them, "But who do you say that I am?" Peter said to him in reply, "You are the Messiah." 30 Then he warned them not to tell anyone about him.

The First Prediction of the Passion. 31*† He began to teach them that the Son of Man must suffer greatly and be rejected by the elders, the chief priests, and the scribes, and be killed, and rise after three days. 32 He spoke this openly. Then Peter took him aside and began to rebuke him. 33 At this he turned around and, looking at his disciples, rebuked Peter and said, "Get behind me, Satan. You are thinking not as God does, but as human beings do."

***The Conditions of Discipleship.*†** 34* He summoned the crowd with his disciples and said to them, "Whoever

*

11-13: Mt 12, 38-39; 16, 1-4.
11: Lk 11, 16.
14-21: Mt 16, 5-12; Lk 12, 1.
17: 4, 13.
18: Jer 5, 21; Ez 12, 2.
23: 7, 33; Jn 9, 6.
27-30: Mt 16, 13-20; Lk 9, 18-21.
31-38: Mt 16, 21-27; Lk 9, 22-26.
34: Mt 10, 38-39; 16, 24-27; Lk 14, 26-27.

†

8, 11-12: The objection of the Pharisees that Jesus' miracles are unsatisfactory for proving the arrival of God's kingdom is comparable to the request of the crowd for a sign in Jn 6, 30-31. Jesus' response shows that a sign originating in human demand will not be provided; cf Nm 14, 11.22.

8, 15: *The leaven of the Pharisees . . . of Herod:* the corruptive action of leaven (1 Cor 5, 6-8; Gal 5, 9) was an apt symbol of the evil dispositions both of the Pharisees (11-13; 7, 5-13) and of Herod (6, 14-29) toward Jesus. The disciples of Jesus are warned against sharing such rebellious attitudes toward Jesus; cf vv 17, 21.

8, 22-26: Jesus' actions and the gradual cure of the blind man probably have the same purpose as in the case of the deaf man (7, 31-37). Some commentators regard the cure as an intended symbol of the gradual enlightenment of the disciples concerning Jesus' messiahship.

8, 27-30: This episode is the turning point in Mark's account of Jesus in his public ministry. Popular opinions concur in regarding him as a prophet. The disciples by contrast believe him to be the Messiah. Jesus acknowledges this identification but prohibits them from making his messianic office known to avoid confusing it with ambiguous contemporary ideas on the nature of that office. See further the notes on Mt 16, 13-20.

8, 31: *Son of Man:* an enigmatic title. It is used in Dn 7, 13-14 as a symbol of "the saints of the Most High," the faithful Israelites who receive the everlasting kingdom from the Ancient One (God). They are represented by a human figure that contrasts with the various beasts who represent the previous kingdoms of the earth. In the Jewish apocryphal books of 1 Enoch and 4 Ezra the "Son of Man" is not, as in Dn, a group, but a unique figure of extraordinary spiritual endowments, who will be revealed as the one through whom the everlasting kingdom decreed by God will be established. It is possible though doubtful that this individualization of the Son of Man figure had been made in Jesus' time, and therefore his use of the title in that sense is questionable. Of itself, this expression means simply a human being, or, indefinitely, someone, and there are evidences of this use in pre-Christian times. Its use in the New Testament is probably due to Jesus' speaking of himself in that way, "a human being," and the later church's taking this in the sense of the Jewish apocrypha and applying it to him with that meaning. *Rejected by the elders, the chief priests, and the scribes:* the supreme council called the Sanhedrin was made up of seventy-one members of these three groups and presided over by the high priest. It exercised authority over the Jews in religious matters. See the note on Mt 8, 20.

8, 34-35: This utterance of Jesus challenges all believers to authentic discipleship and total commitment to himself through self-renunciation and acceptance of the cross of suffering, even to the sacrifice of life itself. *Whoever wishes to save his life will lose it . . . will save it:* an expression of the ambivalence of life and its contrasting destiny. Life seen as mere self-centered earthly existence and lived in denial of Christ ends in destruction, but when lived in loyalty to Christ, despite earthly death, it arrives at fullness of life.

wishes to come after me must deny himself, take up his cross, and follow me. 35*† For whoever wishes to save his life will lose it, but whoever loses his life for my sake and that of the gospel will save it. 36 What profit is there for one to gain the whole world and forfeit his life? 37 What could one give in exchange for his life? 38* Whoever is ashamed of me and of my words in this faithless and sinful generation, the Son of Man will be ashamed of when he comes in his Father's glory with the holy angels."

CHAPTER 9

1*† He also said to them, "Amen, I say to you, there are some standing here who will not taste death until they see that the kingdom of God has come in power."

The Transfiguration of Jesus.† 2* After six days Jesus took Peter, James, and John and led them up a high mountain apart by themselves. And he was transfigured before them, 3 and his clothes became dazzling white, such as no fuller on earth could bleach them. 4 Then Elijah appeared to them along with Moses, and they were conversing with Jesus. 5† Then Peter said to Jesus in reply, "Rabbi, it is good that we are here! Let us make three tents: one for you, one for Moses, and one for Elijah." 6 He hardly knew what to say, they were so terrified. 7† Then a cloud came, casting a shadow over them; then from the cloud came a voice, "This is my beloved Son. Listen to him." 8 Suddenly, looking around, they no longer saw anyone but Jesus alone with them.

The Coming of Elijah.† 9* As they were coming down from the mountain, he charged them not to relate what they had seen to anyone, except when the Son of Man had risen from the dead. 10 So they kept the matter to themselves, questioning what rising from the dead meant. 11* Then they asked him, "Why do the scribes say that Elijah must come first?" 12 He told them, "Elijah will indeed come first and restore all things, yet how is it written regarding the Son of Man that he must suffer greatly and be treated with contempt? 13* But I tell you that Elijah has come and they did to him whatever they pleased, as it is written of him."

The Healing of a Boy with a Demon.† 14* When they came to the disciples, they saw a large crowd around them and scribes arguing with them. 15 Immediately on seeing him, the whole crowd was utterly amazed. They ran up to him and greeted him. 16 He asked them, "What are you arguing about with them?" 17 Someone from the crowd answered him, "Teacher, I have brought to you my son possessed by a mute spirit. 18 Wherever it seizes him, it throws him down; he foams at the mouth, grinds his teeth, and becomes rigid. I asked your disciples to drive it out, but they were unable to do so." 19 He said to them in reply, "O faithless generation, how long will I be with you? How long will I endure you? Bring him to me." 20 They brought the boy to him. And when he saw him, the spirit immediately threw the boy into convulsions. As he fell to the ground, he began to roll around and foam at the mouth. 21 Then he questioned his father, "How long has this been happening to him?" He replied, "Since childhood. 22 It has often thrown him into fire and into water to kill him. But if you can do anything, have compassion on us and help us." 23 Jesus said to him, " 'If you can!' Everything is possible to one who has faith." 24 Then the boy's father cried out, "I do believe, help my unbelief!"

MARK

*

35:	Jn 12, 25.	9:	8, 31.
38:	Mt 10, 33; Lk 12, 8.	11-12:	Is 53, 3; Mal 3, 23.
9, 1:	Mt 16, 28; Lk 9, 27.	13:	1 Kgs 19, 2-10.
2-13:	Mt 17, 1-13; Lk 9, 28-36.	14-29:	Mt 17, 14-21; Lk 9, 37-43.

†

8, 35: *For my sake and that of the gospel:* Mark here, as at 10, 29, equates Jesus with the gospel.

9, 1: *There are some standing . . . come in power:* understood by some to refer to the establishment by God's power of his kingdom on earth in and through the church; more likely, as understood by others, a reference to the imminent parousia.

9, 2-8: Mk and Mt 17, 1 place the transfiguration of Jesus six days after the first prediction of his passion and death and his instruction to the disciples on the doctrine of the cross; Lk 9, 28 has "about eight days." Thus the transfiguration counterbalances the prediction of the passion by affording certain of the disciples insight into the divine glory that Jesus possessed. His glory will overcome his death and that of his disciples; cf 2 Cor 3, 18; 2 Pt 1, 16-19. The heavenly voice (7) prepares the disciples to understand that in the divine plan Jesus must die ignominiously before his messianic glory is made manifest; cf Lk 24, 25-27. See further the note on Mt 17, 1-8.

9, 5: Moses and Elijah represent respectively law and prophecy in the Old Testament and are linked to Mt. Sinai; cf Ex 19, 16—20, 17; 1 Kgs 19, 2.8-14. They now appear with Jesus as witnesses to the fulfillment of the law and the prophets taking place in the person of Jesus as he appears in glory.

9, 7: *A cloud came, casting a shadow over them:* even the disciples enter into the mystery of his glorification. In the Old Testament the cloud covered the meeting tent, indicating the Lord's presence in the midst of his people (Ex 40, 34-35) and came to rest upon the temple in Jerusalem at the time of its dedication (1 Kgs 8, 10).

9, 9-13: At the transfiguration of Jesus his disciples had seen Elijah. They were perplexed because, according to the rabbinical interpretation of Mal 3, 23-24, Elijah was to come first. Jesus' response shows that Elijah has come, in the person of John the Baptist, to prepare for the day of the Lord. Jesus *must suffer greatly and be treated with contempt* (12) like the Baptist (13); cf 6, 17-29.

9, 14-29: The disciples' failure to effect a cure seems to reflect unfavorably on Jesus (14-18.22). In response Jesus exposes their lack of trust in God (19) and scores their lack of prayer (29), i.e., of conscious reliance on God's power when acting in Jesus' name. For Mt, see the note on 17, 14-20. Luke 9, 37-43 centers attention on Jesus' sovereign power.

25 Jesus, on seeing a crowd rapidly
gathering, rebuked the unclean spirit
and said to it, "Mute and deaf spirit, I
command you: come out of him and
never enter him again!" 26 Shouting and
throwing the boy into convulsions, it
came out. He became like a corpse,
which caused many to say, "He is
dead!" 27 But Jesus took him by the
hand, raised him, and he stood up.
28 When he entered the house, his disci-
ples asked him in private, "Why could
we not drive it out?" 29† He said to them,
"This kind can only come out through
prayer."

The Second Prediction of the Passion.
30* They left from there and began a
journey through Galilee, but he did not
wish anyone to know about it. 31 He was
teaching his disciples and telling them,
"The Son of Man is to be handed over
to men and they will kill him, and three
days after his death he will rise."
32 But they did not understand the say-
ing, and they were afraid to question
him.

IV: THE FULL REVELATION OF THE MYSTERY

The Greatest in the Kingdom.†
33* They came to Capernaum and, once
inside the house, he began to ask them,
"What were you arguing about on the
way?" 34 But they remained silent. They
had been discussing among themselves
on the way who was the greatest.
35* Then he sat down, called the Twelve,
and said to them, "If anyone wishes to
be first, he shall be the last of all and
the servant of all." 36 Taking a child he
placed it in their midst, and putting his
arms around it he said to them,
37* "Whoever receives one child such as
this in my name, receives me; and
whoever receives me, receives not me
but the one who sent me."

Another Exorcist.† 38* John said to
him, "Teacher, we saw someone driving
out demons in your name, and we tried
to prevent him because he does not fol-
low us." 39 Jesus replied, "Do not pre-
vent him. There is no one who performs
a mighty deed in my name who can at
the same time speak ill of me. 40* For
whoever is not against us is for us.
41* Anyone who gives you a cup of water
to drink because you belong to Christ,
amen, I say to you, will surely not lose
his reward.

Temptations to Sin. 42* "Whoever
causes one of these little ones who be-
lieve [in me] to sin, it would be better
for him if a great millstone were put
around his neck and he were thrown
into the sea. 43† If your hand causes you
to sin, cut it off. It is better for you to
enter into life maimed than with two
hands to go into Gehenna, into the un-
quenchable fire. [44]† 45 And if your foot
causes you to sin, cut it off. It is better
for you to enter into life crippled than
with two feet to be thrown into Gehenna.
[46] 47 And if your eye causes you to sin,
pluck it out. Better for you to enter into
the kingdom of God with one eye than
with two eyes to be thrown into Ge-
henna, 48* where 'their worm does not
die, and the fire is not quenched.'

The Simile of Salt. 49† "Everyone will
be salted with fire. 50* Salt is good, but
if salt becomes insipid, with what will
you restore its flavor? Keep salt in your-
selves and you will have peace with one
another."

CHAPTER 10

Marriage and Divorce. 1 He set out
from there and went into the district of
Judea [and] across the Jordan. Again
crowds gathered around him and, as
was his custom, he again taught them.
2*† The Pharisees approached and
asked, "Is it lawful for a husband to di-
vorce his wife?" They were testing him.
3 He said to them in reply, "What did
Moses command you?" 4* They replied,
"Moses permitted him to write a bill of
divorce and dismiss her." 5 But Jesus
told them, "Because of the hardness of

---

*

30: Jn 7, 1.
30-32: 8, 31; Mt 17, 22-23; Lk 9, 43-45.
33-37: Mt 18, 1-5; Lk 9, 46-48.
35: Mt 20, 27.
37: Mt 10, 40; 18, 5; Jn 13, 20.
38-41: Nm 11, 28; Lk 9, 49-50; 1 Cor 12, 3.
40: Mt 12, 30.
41: Mt 10, 42; 1 Cor 3, 23.
42-47: Mt 5, 29-30; 18, 6-9; Lk 17, 1-2.
48: Is 66, 24.
50: Lv 2, 13; Mt 5, 13; Lk 14, 34-35; Col 4, 6.
10, 2-12: Mt 19, 3-9.
4: Dt 24, 1-4.

---

†

9, 29: *This kind can only come out through prayer:* a variant reading adds "and through fasting."

9, 33-37: Mark probably intends this incident and the sayings that follow as commentary on the disciples' lack of understanding (32). Their role in Jesus' work is one of service, especially to the poor and lowly. Children were the symbol Jesus used for the *anawim,* the poor in spirit, the lowly in the Christian community.

9, 38-41: Jesus warns against jealousy and intolerance toward others, such as exorcists who do *not follow us.* The saying in v 40 is a broad principle of the divine tolerance. Even the smallest courtesies shown to those who teach in Jesus' name do not go unrewarded.

9, 43.45.47: *Gehenna:* see the note on Mt 5, 22.

9, 44.46: These verses, lacking in some important early manuscripts, are here omitted as scribal additions. They simply repeat v 48, itself a modified citation of Is 66, 24.

9, 49: *Everyone will be salted with fire:* so the better manuscripts. Some add "every sacrifice will be salted with salt." The purifying and preservative use of salt in food (Lv 2, 13) and the refinement effected through fire refer here to comparable effects in the spiritual life of the disciples of Jesus.

10, 2-9: In the dialogue between Jesus and the Pharisees on the subject of divorce, Jesus declares that the law of Moses permitted divorce (Dt 24, 1) only *because of the hardness of your hearts* (4-5). In citing Gn 1, 27 and 2, 24, Jesus proclaims permanence to be the divine intent from the beginning concerning human marriage (6-8). He reaffirms this with the declaration that *what God has joined together, no human being must separate* (9). See further the notes on Mt 5, 31-32 and 19, 3-9.

your hearts he wrote you this commandment. 6* But from the beginning of creation, 'God made them male and female. 7* For this reason a man shall leave his father and mother [and be joined to his wife], 8 and the two shall become one flesh.' So they are no longer two but one flesh. 9 Therefore what God has joined together, no human being must separate." 10 In the house the disciples again questioned him about this. 11* He said to them, "Whoever divorces his wife and marries another commits adultery against her; 12 and if she divorces her husband and marries another, she commits adultery."

Blessing of the Children. 13* And people were bringing children to him that he might touch them, but the disciples rebuked them. 14 When Jesus saw this he became indignant and said to them, "Let the children come to me; do not prevent them, for the kingdom of God belongs to such as these. 15*† Amen, I say to you, whoever does not accept the kingdom of God like a child will not enter it." 16 Then he embraced them and blessed them, placing his hands on them.

The Rich Man. 17* As he was setting out on a journey, a man ran up, knelt down before him, and asked him, "Good teacher, what must I do to inherit eternal life?" 18† Jesus answered him, "Why do you call me good? No one is good but God alone. 19* You know the commandments: 'You shall not kill; you shall not commit adultery; you shall not steal; you shall not bear false witness; you shall not defraud; honor your father and your mother.'" 20 He replied and said to him, "Teacher, all of these I have observed from my youth." 21 Jesus, looking at him, loved him and said to him, "You are lacking in one thing. Go, sell what you have, and give to [the] poor and you will have treasure in heaven; then come, follow me." 22 At that statement his face fell, and he went away sad, for he had many possessions.

23*† Jesus looked around and said to his disciples, "How hard it is for those who have wealth to enter the kingdom of God!" 24 The disciples were amazed at his words. So Jesus again said to them in reply, "Children, how hard it is to enter the kingdom of God! 25 It is easier for a camel to pass through [the] eye of [a] needle than for one who is rich to enter the kingdom of God." 26 They were exceedingly astonished and said among themselves, "Then who can be saved?" 27 Jesus looked at them and said, "For human beings it is impossible, but not for God. All things are possible for God." 28 Peter began to say to him, "We have given up everything and followed you." 29 Jesus said, "Amen, I say to you, there is no one who has given up house or brothers or sisters or mother or father or children or lands for my sake and for the sake of the gospel 30 who will not receive a hundred times more now in this present age: houses and brothers and sisters and mothers and children and lands, with persecutions, and eternal life in the age to come. 31* But many that are first will be last, and [the] last will be first."

MARK

The Third Prediction of the Passion. 32* They were on the way, going up to Jerusalem, and Jesus went ahead of them. They were amazed, and those who followed were afraid. Taking the Twelve aside again, he began to tell them what was going to happen to him. 33 "Behold, we are going up to Jerusalem, and the Son of Man will be handed over to the chief priests and the scribes, and they will condemn him to death and hand him over to the Gentiles 34 who will mock him, spit upon him, scourge him, and put him to death, but after three days he will rise."

Ambition of James and John. 35* Then James and John, the sons of Zebedee, came to him and said to him, "Teacher, we want you to do for us whatever we ask of you." 36 He replied, "What do you wish [me] to do for you?" 37 They answered him, "Grant that in your glory we may sit one at your right and the other at your left." 38*† Jesus

*

6: Gn 1, 27.
7-8: Gn 2, 24; 1 Cor 6, 16; Eph 5, 31.
11-12: Mt 5, 32; Lk 16, 18; 1 Cor 7, 10-11.
13-16: Mt 19, 13-15; Lk 18, 15-17.
13: Lk 9, 47.
15: Mt 18, 3.
17-31: Mt 19, 16-30; Lk 18, 18-30.
19: Ex 20, 12-16; Dt 5, 16-21.
23: Prv 11, 28.
31: Mt 19, 30; Lk 13, 30.
32-34: 8, 31; Mt 20, 17-19; Lk 18, 31-33.
35-45: Mt 20, 20-28.
38: Lk 12, 50.

†

10, 15: *Whoever does not accept the kingdom of God like a child:* i.e., in total dependence upon and obedience to the gospel; cf Mt 18, 3-4.

10, 18: *Why do you call me good?:* Jesus repudiates the term "good" for himself and directs it to God, the source of all goodness who alone can grant the gift of eternal life; cf Mt 19, 16-17.

10, 23-27: In the Old Testament wealth and material goods are considered a sign of God's favor (Jb 1, 10; Ps 128, 1-2; Is 3, 10). The words of Jesus in 23-25 provoke astonishment among the disciples because of their apparent contradiction of the Old Testament concept (24.26). Since wealth, power, and merit generate false security, Jesus rejects them utterly as a claim to enter the kingdom. Achievement of salvation is beyond human capability and depends solely on the goodness of God who offers it as a gift (27).

10, 38-40: *Can you drink the cup . . . I am baptized?:* the metaphor of drinking the cup is used in the Old Testament to refer to acceptance of the destiny assigned by God; see the note on Ps 11, 6. In Jesus' case, this involves divine judgment on sin that Jesus the innocent one is to expiate on behalf of the guilty (14, 24; Is 53, 5). His baptism is to be his crucifixion and death for the salvation of the human race; cf Lk 12, 50. The request of James and John for a share in the glory (35-37) must of necessity involve a share in Jesus' sufferings, the endurance of tribulation and suffering for the gospel (39). The authority of assigning places of honor in the kingdom is reserved to God (40).

said to them, "You do not know what
you are asking. Can you drink the cup
that I drink or be baptized with the bap-
tism with which I am baptized?" 39 They
said to him, "We can." Jesus said to
them, "The cup that I drink, you will
drink, and with the baptism with which
I am baptized, you will be baptized;
40 but to sit at my right or at my left is
not mine to give but is for those for
whom it has been prepared." 41 When
the ten heard this, they became indig-
nant at James and John. 42*† Jesus
summoned them and said to them, "You
know that those who are recognized as
rulers over the Gentiles lord it over
them, and their great ones make their
authority over them felt. 43 But it shall
not be so among you. Rather, whoever
wishes to be great among you will be
your servant; 44 whoever wishes to be
first among you will be the slave of all.
45 For the Son of Man did not come to
be served but to serve and to give his
life as a ransom for many."

***The Blind Bartimaeus.*†** 46* They
came to Jericho. And as he was leaving
Jericho with his disciples and a sizable
crowd, Bartimaeus, a blind man, the
son of Timaeus, sat by the roadside beg-
ging. 47 On hearing that it was Jesus of
Nazareth, he began to cry out and say,
"Jesus, son of David, have pity on me."
48 And many rebuked him, telling him
to be silent. But he kept calling out all
the more, "Son of David, have pity on
me." 49 Jesus stopped and said, "Call
him." So they called the blind man, say-
ing to him, "Take courage; get up, he
is calling you." 50 He threw aside his
cloak, sprang up, and came to Jesus.
51 Jesus said to him in reply, "What do
you want me to do for you?" The blind
man replied to him, "Master, I want to
see." 52 Jesus told him, "Go your way;
your faith has saved you." Immediately
he received his sight and followed him
on the way.

CHAPTER 11

***The Entry into Jerusalem.*†** 1* When
they drew near to Jerusalem, to Beth-
phage and Bethany at the Mount of Ol-
ives, he sent two of his disciples 2 and
said to them, "Go into the village oppo-
site you, and immediately on entering
it, you will find a colt tethered on which
no one has ever sat. Untie it and bring
it here. 3 If anyone should say to you,
'Why are you doing this?' reply, 'The
Master has need of it and will send it
back here at once.' " 4 So they went off
and found a colt tethered at a gate out-
side on the street, and they untied it.
5 Some of the bystanders said to them,
"What are you doing, untying the colt?"
6 They answered them just as Jesus had
told them to, and they permitted them
to do it. 7 So they brought the colt to Je-
sus and put their cloaks over it. And he
sat on it. 8 Many people spread their
cloaks on the road, and others spread
leafy branches that they had cut from
the fields. 9* Those preceding him as
well as those following kept crying out:

"Hosanna!
Blessed is he who comes in the
name of the Lord!
10 Blessed is the kingdom of our fa-
ther David that is to come!
Hosanna in the highest!"

11* He entered Jerusalem and went into
the temple area. He looked around at
everything and, since it was already
late, went out to Bethany with the
Twelve.

***Jesus Curses a Fig Tree.*†** 12* The
next day as they were leaving Bethany
he was hungry. 13 Seeing from a dis-
tance a fig tree in leaf, he went over to
see if he could find anything on it. When
he reached it he found nothing but
leaves; it was not the time for figs.
14 And he said to it in reply, "May no
one ever eat of your fruit again!" And
his disciples heard it.

***Cleansing of the Temple.*†** 15* They
came to Jerusalem, and on entering the
temple area he began to drive out those
selling and buying there. He overturned
the tables of the money changers and
the seats of those who were selling
doves. 16 He did not permit anyone to
carry anything through the temple
area. 17* Then he taught them saying,
"Is it not written:

'My house shall be called a house
of prayer for all peoples'?
But you have made it a den of
thieves."

*

42-45: Lk 22, 25-27.
46-52: Mt 20, 29-34; Lk 18, 35-43.
11, 1-10: Mt 21, 1-9; Lk 19, 29-38; Jn 12, 12-15.
9-10: 2 Sm 7, 16; Ps 118, 26.
11: Mt 21, 10.17.
12-14: Mt 21, 18-20; Lk 13, 6-9.
15-18: Mt 21, 12-13; Lk 19, 45-46; Jn 2, 14-16.
17: Is 56, 7; Jer 7, 11.

†

10, 42-45: Whatever authority is to be exercised by the disciples must, like that of Jesus, be rendered as service to others (45) rather than for personal aggrandizement (42-44). The service of Jesus is his passion and death for the sins of the human race (45); cf 14, 24; Is 53, 11-12; Mt 26, 28; Lk 22, 19-20.

10, 46-52: See the notes on Mt 9, 27-31 and 20, 29-34.

11, 1-11: In Mark's account Jesus takes the initiative in ordering the preparation for his entry into Jerusalem (1-6) even as he later orders the preparation of his last Passover Supper (14, 12-16). In vv 9-10 the greeting Jesus receives stops short of proclaiming him Messiah. He is greeted rather as the prophet of the coming messianic kingdom. Contrast Mt 21, 9.

11, 12-14: Jesus' search for fruit on the fig tree recalls the prophets' earlier use of this image to designate Israel; cf Jer 8, 13; 29, 17; Jl 1, 7; Hos 9, 10.16. Cursing the fig tree is a parable in action representing Jesus' judgment (20) on barren Israel and the fate of Jerusalem for failing to receive his teaching; cf Is 34, 4; Hos 2, 14; Lk 13, 6-9.

11, 15-19: See the note on Mt 21, 12-17.

18 The chief priests and the scribes came
to hear of it and were seeking a way to
put him to death, yet they feared him
because the whole crowd was aston-
ished at his teaching. 19* When evening
came, they went out of the city.
The Withered Fig Tree. 20* Early in
the morning, as they were walking
along, they saw the fig tree withered to
its roots. 21 Peter remembered and said
to him, "Rabbi, look! The fig tree that
you cursed has withered." 22 Jesus said
to them in reply, "Have faith in God.
23* Amen, I say to you, whoever says
to this mountain, 'Be lifted up and
thrown into the sea,' and does not doubt
in his heart but believes that what he
says will happen, it shall be done for
him. 24* Therefore I tell you, all that you
ask for in prayer, believe that you will
receive it and it shall be yours. 25* When
you stand to pray, forgive anyone
against whom you have a grievance, so
that your heavenly Father may in turn
forgive you your transgressions.[26]† "
The Authority of Jesus Questioned.†
27* They returned once more to Jerusa-
lem. As he was walking in the temple
area, the chief priests, the scribes, and
the elders approached him 28 and said
to him, "By what authority are you do-
ing these things? Or who gave you this
authority to do them?" 29 Jesus said to
them, "I shall ask you one question. An-
swer me, and I will tell you by what au-
thority I do these things. 30 Was John's
baptism of heavenly or of human ori-
gin? Answer me." 31 They discussed this
among themselves and said, "If we say,
'Of heavenly origin,' he will say,
'[Then] why did you not believe him?'
32 But shall we say, 'Of human
origin'?"—they feared the crowd, for
they all thought John really was a
prophet. 33 So they said to Jesus in reply,
"We do not know." Then Jesus said to
them, "Neither shall I tell you by what
authority I do these things."

CHAPTER 12

Parable of the Tenants.† 1* He began
to speak to them in parables. "A man
planted a vineyard, put a hedge around
it, dug a wine press, and built a tower.
Then he leased it to tenant farmers and
left on a journey. 2 At the proper time
he sent a servant to the tenants to obtain
from them some of the produce of the
vineyard. 3 But they seized him, beat
him, and sent him away empty-handed.
4 Again he sent them another servant.
And that one they beat over the head
and treated shamefully. 5 He sent yet
another whom they killed. So, too, many
others; some they beat, others they
killed. 6 He had one other to send, a be-
loved son. He sent him to them last of
all, thinking, 'They will respect my son.'
7 But those tenants said to one another,
'This is the heir. Come, let us kill him,
and the inheritance will be ours.'
8 So they seized him and killed him, and
threw him out of the vineyard. 9 What
[then] will the owner of the vineyard
do? He will come, put the tenants to
death, and give the vineyard to others.
10* Have you not read this scripture
passage:

'The stone that the builders rejected
has become the cornerstone;
11 by the Lord has this been done,
and it is wonderful in our eyes'?"

12 They were seeking to arrest him, but
they feared the crowd, for they realized
that he had addressed the parable
to them. So they left him and went
away.
Paying Taxes to the Emperor.†
13*† They sent some Pharisees and He-
rodians to him to ensnare him in his
speech. 14 They came and said to him,
"Teacher, we know that you are a truth-
ful man and that you are not concerned
with anyone's opinion. You do not re-
gard a person's status but teach the way
of God in accordance with the truth. Is
it lawful to pay the census tax to Caesar
or not? Should we pay or should we not
pay?" 15 Knowing their hypocrisy he
said to them, "Why are you testing me?
Bring me a denarius to look at." 16 They
brought one to him and he said to them,
"Whose image and inscription is this?"
They replied to him, "Caesar's." 17* So

MARK

*

19: Lk 21, 37.
20-24: Mt 21, 20-22.
23: Mt 17, 20-21; Lk 17, 6.
24: Mt 7, 7; Jn 11, 22; 14, 13.
25: Mt 6, 14; 18, 35.
27-33: Mt 21, 23-27; Lk 20, 1-8.
12, 1-12: Mt 21, 33-46; Lk 20, 9-19.
1: Is 5, 1-7; Jer 2, 21.
10-11: Ps 118, 22-23; Is 28, 16.
13-27: Mt 22, 15-33; Lk 20, 20-39.
13: 3, 6.
17: Rom 13, 7.

†

11, 26: This verse, which reads, "But if you do not forgive, neither will your heavenly Father forgive your transgressions," is omitted in the best manuscripts. It was probably added by copyists under the influence of Mt 6, 15.

11, 27-33: The mounting hostility toward Jesus came from the chief priests, the scribes, and the elders (27); the Herodians and the Pharisees (12, 13); and the Sadducees (12, 18). By their rejection of God's messengers, John the Baptist and Jesus, they incurred the divine judgment implied in vv 27-33 and confirmed in the parable of the vineyard tenants (12, 1-12).

12, 1-12: The vineyard denotes Israel (Is 5, 1-7). The tenant farmers are the religious leaders of Israel. God is the owner of the vineyard. His servants are his messengers, the prophets. The beloved son is Jesus (1, 11; 9, 7; Mt 3, 17; 17, 5; Lk 3, 22; 9, 35). The punishment of the tenants refers to the religious leaders, and the transfer of the vineyard to others refers to the people of the new Israel.

12, 13-34: In the ensuing conflicts (cf also 2, 1—3, 6) Jesus vanquishes his adversaries by his responses to their questions and reduces them to silence (34).

12, 13-17: See the note on Mt 22, 15-22.

Jesus said to them, "Repay to Caesar
what belongs to Caesar and to God what
belongs to God." They were utterly
amazed at him.

The Question about the Resurrection. † 18 Some Sadducees, who say
there is no resurrection, came to him
and put this question to him, 19* saying,
"Teacher, Moses wrote for us, 'If some-
one's brother dies, leaving a wife but
no child, his brother must take the wife
and raise up descendants for his
brother.' 20 Now there were seven broth-
ers. The first married a woman and
died, leaving no descendants. 21 So the
second married her and died, leaving
no descendants, and the third likewise.
22 And the seven left no descendants.
Last of all the woman also died. 23 At
the resurrection [when they arise]
whose wife will she be? For all seven
had been married to her." 24 Jesus said
to them, "Are you not misled because
you do not know the scriptures or the
power of God? 25 When they rise from
the dead, they neither marry nor are
given in marriage, but they are like the
angels in heaven. 26* As for the dead be-
ing raised, have you not read in the
Book of Moses, in the passage about the
bush, how God told him, 'I am the God
of Abraham, [the] God of Isaac, and
[the] God of Jacob'? 27 He is not God
of the dead but of the living. You are
greatly misled."

The Greatest Commandment. †
28* One of the scribes, when he came
forward and heard them disputing and
saw how well he had answered them,
asked him, "Which is the first of all the
commandments?" 29 Jesus replied,
"The first is this: 'Hear, O Israel! The
Lord our God is Lord alone! 30* You
shall love the Lord your God with all
your heart, with all your soul, with all
your mind, and with all your strength.'
31* The second is this: 'You shall love
your neighbor as yourself.' There is no
other commandment greater than
these." 32 The scribe said to him, "Well
said, teacher. You are right in say-
ing, 'He is One and there is no other
than he.' 33* And 'to love him with
all your heart, with all your understand-
ing, with all your strength, and to
love your neighbor as yourself' is
worth more than all burnt offerings
and sacrifices." 34* And when Jesus
saw that [he] answered with under-
standing, he said to him, "You are not
far from the kingdom of God." And no
one dared to ask him any more ques-
tions.

The Question about David's Son. †
35* As Jesus was teaching in the temple
area he said, "How do the scribes claim
that the Messiah is the son of David?
36* David himself, inspired by the holy
Spirit, said:

'The Lord said to my lord,
"Sit at my right hand
until I place your enemies under
your feet." '

37 David himself calls him 'lord'; so how
is he his son?" [The] great crowd heard
this with delight.

Denunciation of the Scribes. † 38* In
the course of his teaching he said, "Be-
ware of the scribes, who like to go
around in long robes and accept greet-
ings in the marketplaces, 39 seats of
honor in synagogues, and places of
honor at banquets. 40 They devour the
houses of widows and, as a pretext, re-
cite lengthy prayers. They will receive
a very severe condemnation."

The Poor Widow's Contribution. †
41* He sat down opposite the treasury
and observed how the crowd put money
into the treasury. Many rich people put
in large sums. 42 A poor widow also
came and put in two small coins worth
a few cents. 43 Calling his disciples to
himself, he said to them, "Amen, I say
to you, this poor widow put in more than
all the other contributors to the trea-
sury. 44 For they have all contributed
from their surplus wealth, but she, from
her poverty, has contributed all she
had, her whole livelihood."

CHAPTER 13

The Destruction of the Temple Foretold. † 1* As he was making his way
out of the temple area one of his disci-
ples said to him, "Look, teacher, what
stones and what buildings!" 2 Jesus said
to him, "Do you see these great build-
ings? There will not be one stone left
upon another that will not be thrown
down."

---

*

19: Dt 25, 5.
26: Ex 3, 6.
28-34: Mt 22, 34-40; Lk 10, 25-28.
30: Dt 6, 4-5.
31: Lv 19, 18; Rom 13, 9; Gal 5, 14; Jas 2, 8.
33: Dt 6, 4; Ps 40, 7-9.
34: Mt 22, 46; Lk 20, 40.
35-37: Mt 22, 41-45; Lk 20, 41-44.
36: Ps 110, 1.
38-40: Mt 23, 1-7; Lk 11, 43; 20, 45-47.
41-44: Lk 21, 1-4.
13, 1-2: Mt 24, 1-2; Lk 21, 5-6.

---

†

12, 18-27: See the note on Mt 22, 23-33.

12, 28-34: See the note on Mt 22, 34-40.

12, 35-37: Jesus questions the claim of the scribes about the Davidic descent of the Messiah, not to deny it (Mt 1, 1; Acts 2, 20.34; Rom 1, 3; 2 Tm 2, 8) but to imply that he is more than this. His superiority derives from his transcendent origin, to which David himself attested when he spoke of the Messiah with the name "Lord" (Ps 110, 1). See also the note on Mt 22, 41-46.

12, 38-40: See the notes on 7, 1-23 and Mt 23, 1-39.

12, 41-44: See the note on Lk 21, 1-4.

13, 1-2: The reconstructed temple with its precincts, begun under Herod the Great ca. 20 B.C., was completed only some seven years before it was destroyed by fire in A.D. 70 at the hands of the Romans; cf Jer 26, 18; Mt 24, 1-2. For the dating of the reconstruction of the temple, see further the note on Jn 2, 20.

The Signs of the End. † 3* As he was
sitting on the Mount of Olives opposite
the temple area, Peter, James, John,
and Andrew asked him privately,
4 "Tell us, when will this happen, and
what sign will there be when all these
things are about to come to an end?"
5* Jesus began to say to them, "See that
no one deceives you. 6 Many will come
in my name saying, 'I am he,' and they
will deceive many. 7 When you hear of
wars and reports of wars do not be
alarmed; such things must happen, but
it will not yet be the end. 8 Nation will
rise against nation and kingdom
against kingdom. There will be earth-
quakes from place to place and there
will be famines. These are the begin-
nings of the labor pains.

The Coming Persecution. 9* "Watch
out for yourselves. They will hand you
over to the courts. You will be beaten
in synagogues. You will be arraigned
before governors and kings because of
me, as a witness before them. 10† But
the gospel must first be preached to all
nations. 11* When they lead you away
and hand you over, do not worry be-
forehand about what you are to say. But
say whatever will be given to you at that
hour. For it will not be you who are
speaking but the holy Spirit. 12 Brother
will hand over brother to death, and
the father his child; children will rise
up against parents and have them
put to death. 13 You will be hated by
all because of my name. But the one
who perseveres to the end will be
saved.

The Great Tribulation. 14*† "When
you see the desolating abomination
standing where he should not (let the
reader understand), then those in Ju-
dea must flee to the mountains,
15* [and] a person on a housetop must
not go down or enter to get anything
out of his house, 16 and a person in a
field must not return to get his cloak.
17 Woe to pregnant women and nursing
mothers in those days. 18 Pray that this
does not happen in winter. 19* For those
times will have tribulation such as has
not been since the beginning of God's
creation until now, nor ever will be.
20 If the Lord had not shortened those
days, no one would be saved; but for
the sake of the elect whom he chose,
he did shorten the days. 21 If anyone
says to you then, 'Look, here is the
Messiah! Look, there he is!' do not be-
lieve it. 22 False messiahs and false
prophets will arise and will perform
signs and wonders in order to mislead,
if that were possible, the elect. 23 Be
watchful! I have told it all to you before-
hand.

The Coming of the Son of Man.
24* "But in those days after that tribula-
tion

the sun will be darkened,
and the moon will not give its
light,
25 and the stars will be falling from the
sky,
and the powers in the heavens will
be shaken.

26*† And then they will see 'the Son of
Man coming in the clouds' with great
power and glory, 27 and then he will
send out the angels and gather [his]
elect from the four winds, from the end
of the earth to the end of the sky.

The Lesson of the Fig Tree.
28* "Learn a lesson from the fig tree.
When its branch becomes tender and
sprouts leaves, you know that summer
is near. 29 In the same way, when you
see these things happening, know that
he is near, at the gates. 30 Amen, I say
to you, this generation will not pass
away until all these things have taken
place. 31 Heaven and earth will pass
away, but my words will not pass away.

Need for Watchfulness. 32 "But of that
day or hour, no one knows, neither the
angels in heaven, nor the Son, but only
the Father. 33* Be watchful! Be alert!
You do not know when the time will
come. 34* It is like a man traveling
abroad. He leaves home and places his
servants in charge, each with his work,
and orders the gatekeeper to be on the

*

3-8: Mt 24, 3-8; Lk 21, 7-11.
5: Eph 5, 6; 2 Thes 2, 3.
9-13: Mt 24, 9-14; Lk 21, 12-19.
11-12: Mt 10, 19-22; Lk 12, 11-12.
14-23: Mt 24, 15-22; Lk 21, 20-24.
14: Dn 9, 27; Mt 24, 15.
15: Lk 17, 31.
19: Dn 12, 1.
24-27: Mt 24, 29-31; Lk 21, 25-27.
24: Is 13, 10; Ez 32, 7; Jl 2, 10.
26: 14, 62; Dn 7, 13-14.
28-32: Mt 24, 32-36; Lk 21, 29-33.
33-37: Mt 24, 42; 25, 13-15.
34: Mt 25, 14-30; Lk 19, 12-27.

†

13, 3-37: Jesus' prediction of the destruction of the temple (2) provoked questions that the four named disciples put to him in private regarding the time and the sign *when all these things are about to come to an end* (3-4). The response to their questions was Jesus' eschatological discourse prior to his imminent death. It contained instruction and consolation exhorting the disciples and the church to faith and obedience through the trials that would confront them (5-13). The sign is the presence of *the desolating abomination* (14; see Dn 9, 27), i.e., of the Roman power profaning the temple. Flight from Jerusalem is urged rather than defense of the city through misguided messianic hope (14-23). Intervention will occur only after destruction (24-27), which will happen before the end of the first Christian generation (28-31). No one but the Father knows the precise time, or that of the parousia (32); hence the necessity of constant vigilance (33-37). Luke sets the parousia at a later date, after "the time of the Gentiles" (Lk 21, 24). See also the notes on Mt 24, 1—25, 46.

13, 10: *The gospel . . . to all nations:* the period of the Christian mission.

13, 14: The participle *standing* is masculine, in contrast to the neuter at Mt 24, 15.

13, 26: *Son of Man . . . with great power and glory:* Jesus cites this text from Dn 7, 13 in his response to the high priest, *Are you the Messiah?* (14, 61). In Ex 34, 5; Lv 16, 2; and Nm 11, 25 the clouds indicate the presence of the divinity. Thus in his role of Son of Man, Jesus is a heavenly being who will come in power and glory.

watch. 35 Watch, therefore; you do not
know when the lord of the house is com-
ing, whether in the evening, or at mid-
night, or at cockcrow, or in the morning.
36 May he not come suddenly and find
you sleeping. 37 What I say to you, I say
to all: 'Watch!' "

CHAPTER 14

The Conspiracy against Jesus. †
1*† The Passover and the Feast of Un-
leavened Bread were to take place in
two days' time. So the chief priests and
the scribes were seeking a way to arrest
him by treachery and put him to death.
2 They said, "Not during the festival, for
fear that there may be a riot among the
people."
The Anointing at Bethany. † 3* When
he was in Bethany reclining at table in
the house of Simon the leper, a woman
came with an alabaster jar of perfumed
oil, costly genuine spikenard. She broke
the alabaster jar and poured it on his
head. 4 There were some who were in-
dignant. "Why has there been this waste
of perfumed oil? 5 It could have been
sold for more than three hundred days'
wages and the money given to the
poor." They were infuriated with her.
6 Jesus said, "Let her alone. Why do you
make trouble for her? She has done a
good thing for me. 7 The poor you will
always have with you, and whenever
you wish you can do good to them, but
you will not always have me. 8 She has
done what she could. She has antici-
pated anointing my body for burial.
9 Amen, I say to you, wherever the gos-
pel is proclaimed to the whole world,
what she has done will be told in mem-
ory of her."
The Betrayal by Judas. 10* Then Ju-
das Iscariot, one of the Twelve, went off
to the chief priests to hand him over to
them. 11 When they heard him they were
pleased and promised to pay him
money. Then he looked for an opportu-
nity to hand him over.
Preparations for the Passover.
12*† On the first day of the Feast of Un-
leavened Bread, when they sacrificed
the Passover lamb, his disciples said to
him, "Where do you want us to go and
prepare for you to eat the Passover?"
13† He sent two of his disciples and said
to them, "Go into the city and a man
will meet you, carrying a jar of water.
Follow him. 14 Wherever he enters, say
to the master of the house, 'The Teacher
says, "Where is my guest room where
I may eat the Passover with my disci-
ples?" ' 15 Then he will show you a large
upper room furnished and ready. Make
the preparations for us there." 16 The
disciples then went off, entered the city,
and found it just as he had told them;
and they prepared the Passover.
The Betrayer. 17* When it was eve-
ning, he came with the Twelve. 18† And
as they reclined at table and were eat-
ing, Jesus said, "Amen, I say to you,
one of you will betray me, one who is
eating with me." 19 They began to be
distressed and to say to him, one by one,
"Surely it is not I?" 20 He said to them,
"One of the Twelve, the one who dips
with me into the dish. 21† For the Son
of Man indeed goes, as it is written of
him, but woe to that man by whom the
Son of Man is betrayed. It would be bet-
ter for that man if he had never been
born."
The Lord's Supper. † 22* While they
were eating, he took bread, said the
blessing, broke it, and gave it to them,

---

*
14, 1-2: Mt 26, 2-5; Lk 22, 1-2; Jn 11, 45-53.
3-9: Mt 26, 6-13; Jn 12, 1-8.
10-11: Mt 26, 14-16; Lk 22, 3-6.
12-16: Mt 26, 17-19; Lk 22, 7-13.
17-21: Mt 26, 20-24; Lk 22, 21-23; Jn 13, 21-26.
22-25: Mt 26, 26-30; Lk 22, 19-20; 1 Cor 11, 23-25.

---

†
14, 1—16, 8: In the movement of Mark's gospel the cross is depicted as Jesus' way to glory in accordance with the divine will. Thus the passion narrative is seen as the climax of Jesus' ministry.

14, 1: *The Passover and the Feast of Unleavened Bread:* the connection between the two festivals is reflected in Ex 12, 3-20; 34, 18; Lv 23, 4-8; Nm 9, 2-14; 28, 16-17; Dt 16, 1-8. The Passover commemorated the redemption from slavery and the departure of the Israelites from Egypt by night. It began at sundown after the Passover lamb was sacrificed in the temple in the afternoon of the fourteenth day of the month of Nisan. With the Passover supper on the same evening was associated the eating of unleavened bread. The latter was continued through Nisan 21, a reminder of the affliction of the Israelites and of the haste surrounding their departure. Praise and thanks to God for his goodness in the past were combined at this dual festival with the hope of future salvation. *The chief priests . . . to death:* the intent to put Jesus to death was plotted for a long time but delayed for fear of the crowd (3, 6; 11, 18; 12, 12).

14, 3-9: At Bethany on the Mount of Olives, a few miles from Jerusalem, *in the house of Simon the leper,* Jesus defends a woman's loving action of anointing his head with perfumed oil in view of his impending death and burial as a criminal, in which case his body would not be anointed. See further the note on Jn 12, 7. He assures the woman of the remembrance of her deed in the worldwide preaching of the good news.

14, 12: *The first day of the Feast of Unleavened Bread . . . the Passover lamb:* a less precise designation of the day for sacrificing the Passover lamb as evidenced by some rabbinical literature. For a more exact designation, see the note on 14, 1. It was actually Nisan 14.

14, 13: *A man . . . carrying a jar of water:* perhaps a prearranged signal, for only women ordinarily carried water in jars. The Greek word used here, however, implies simply a person and not necessarily a male.

14, 18: *One of you will betray me, one who is eating with me:* contrasts the intimacy of table fellowship at the Passover meal with the treachery of the traitor; cf Ps 41, 10.

14, 21: *The Son of Man indeed goes, as it is written of him:* a reference to Ps 41, 10 cited by Jesus concerning Judas at the Last Supper; cf Jn 13, 18-19.

14, 22-24: The actions and words of Jesus express within the framework of the Passover meal and the transition to a new covenant the sacrifice of himself through the offering of his body and blood in anticipation of his passion and death. His *blood of the covenant* both alludes to the ancient rite of Ex 24, 4-8 and indicates the new community that the sacrifice of Jesus will bring into being (Mt 26, 26-28; Lk 22, 19-20; 1 Cor 11, 23-25).

and said, "Take it; this is my body."
23 Then he took a cup, gave thanks, and
gave it to them, and they all drank from
it. 24† He said to them, "This is my blood
of the covenant, which will be shed for
many. 25 Amen, I say to you, I shall not
drink again the fruit of the vine until
the day when I drink it new in the king-
dom of God." 26*† Then, after singing
a hymn, they went out to the Mount of
Olives.

Peter's Denial Foretold.† 27* Then
Jesus said to them, "All of you will have
your faith shaken, for it is written:

> 'I will strike the shepherd,
> and the sheep will be dispersed.'

28 But after I have been raised up, I shall
go before you to Galilee." 29 Peter said
to him, "Even though all should have
their faith shaken, mine will not be."
30 Then Jesus said to him, "Amen, I say
to you, this very night before the cock
crows twice you will deny me three
times." 31 But he vehemently replied,
"Even though I should have to die with
you, I will not deny you." And they all
spoke similarly.

The Agony in the Garden.† 32* Then
they came to a place named Gethsem-
ane, and he said to his disciples, "Sit
here while I pray." 33 He took with him
Peter, James, and John, and began to
be troubled and distressed. 34 Then he
said to them, "My soul is sorrowful even
to death. Remain here and keep
watch." 35 He advanced a little and fell
to the ground and prayed that if it were
possible the hour might pass by him;
36† he said, "Abba, Father, all things are
possible to you. Take this cup away
from me, but not what I will but what
you will." 37 When he returned he found
them asleep. He said to Peter, "Simon,
are you asleep? Could you not keep
watch for one hour? 38*† Watch and
pray that you may not undergo the test.
The spirit is willing but the flesh is
weak." 39 Withdrawing again, he
prayed, saying the same thing. 40 Then
he returned once more and found them
asleep, for they could not keep their
eyes open and did not know what to an-
swer him. 41 He returned a third time
and said to them, "Are you still sleeping
and taking your rest? It is enough. The
hour has come. Behold, the Son of Man
is to be handed over to sinners. 42 Get
up, let us go. See, my betrayer is at
hand."

The Betrayal and Arrest of Jesus.
43* Then, while he was still speaking,
Judas, one of the Twelve, arrived, ac-
companied by a crowd with swords and
clubs who had come from the chief
priests, the scribes, and the elders.
44 His betrayer had arranged a signal
with them, saying, "The man I shall kiss
is the one; arrest him and lead him
away securely." 45 He came and imme-
diately went over to him and said,
"Rabbi." And he kissed him. 46 At this
they laid hands on him and arrested
him. 47 One of the bystanders drew his
sword, struck the high priest's servant,
and cut off his ear. 48 Jesus said to them
in reply, "Have you come out as against
a robber, with swords and clubs, to seize
me? 49 Day after day I was with you
teaching in the temple area, yet you did
not arrest me; but that the scriptures
may be fulfilled." 50 And they all left
him and fled. 51 Now a young man fol-
lowed him wearing nothing but a linen
cloth about his body. They seized him,
52 but he left the cloth behind and ran
off naked.

Jesus before the Sanhedrin.
53*† They led Jesus away to the high
priest, and all the chief priests and the
elders and the scribes came together.
54 Peter followed him at a distance into
the high priest's courtyard and was
seated with the guards, warming himself

MARK

---

*

26-31: Mt 26, 30-35; Lk 22, 34.39; Jn 13, 36-38.
27: Zec 13, 7; Jn 16, 32.
32-42: Mt 26, 36-46; Lk 22, 40-46.
32: Jn 18, 1.
38: Rom 7, 5.
43-50: Mt 26, 47-56; Lk 22, 47-53; Jn 18, 3-11.
53-65: Mt 26, 57-68; Lk 22, 54-55.63-65.67-71; Jn 18, 12-13.

---

†

14, 24: *Which will be shed:* see the note on Mt 26, 27-28. *For many:* the Greek preposition *hyper* is a different one from that at Mt 26, 28 but the same as that found at Lk 22, 19.20 and 1 Cor 11, 24. The sense of both words is vicarious, and it is difficult in Hellenistic Greek to distinguish between them. For *many* in the sense of "all," see the note on Mt 20, 28.

14, 26: *After singing a hymn:* Pss 114-118, thanksgiving songs concluding the Passover meal.

14, 27-31: Jesus predicted that the Twelve would waver in their faith, even abandon him, despite their protestations to the contrary. Yet he reassured them that after his resurrection he would regather them in Galilee (16, 7; cf Mt 26, 32; 28, 7.10.16; Jn 21), where he first summoned them to be his followers as he began to preach the good news (1, 14-20).

14, 32-34: The disciples who had witnessed the raising to life of the daughter of Jairus (5, 37) and the transfiguration of their Master (9, 2) were now invited to witness his degradation and agony and to watch and pray with him.

14, 36: *Abba, Father:* an Aramaic term, here also translated by Mark, Jesus' special way of addressing God with filial intimacy. The word *ʾabbāʾ* seems not to have been used in earlier or contemporaneous Jewish sources to address God without some qualifier. Cf Rom 8, 15; Gal 4, 6 for other occurrences of the Aramaic word in the Greek New Testament. *Not what I will but what you will:* note the complete obedient surrender of the human will of Jesus to the divine will of the Father; cf Jn 4, 34; 8, 29; Rom 5, 19; Phil 2, 8; Heb 5, 8.

14, 38: *The spirit is willing but the flesh is weak:* the spirit is drawn to what is good yet found in conflict with the flesh, inclined to sin; cf Ps 51, 7.12. Everyone is faced with this struggle, the full force of which Jesus accepted on our behalf and, through his bitter passion and death, achieved the victory.

14, 53: *They led Jesus away . . . came together:* Mark presents a formal assembly of the whole Sanhedrin (chief priests, elders, and scribes) at night, leading to the condemnation of Jesus (64), in contrast to Lk 22, 66.71, where Jesus is condemned in a daytime meeting of the council; see also Jn 18, 13.19-24.

MARK

at the fire. 55 The chief priests and the
entire Sanhedrin kept trying to obtain
testimony against Jesus in order to put
him to death, but they found none.
56 Many gave false witness against him,
but their testimony did not agree.
57† Some took the stand and testified
falsely against him, alleging, 58* "We
heard him say, 'I will destroy this tem-
ple made with hands and within three
days I will build another not made with
hands.' " 59 Even so their testimony did
not agree. 60 The high priest rose before
the assembly and questioned Jesus,
saying, "Have you no answer? What are
these men testifying against you?"
61† But he was silent and answered
nothing. Again the high priest asked
him and said to him, "Are you the Mes-
siah, the son of the Blessed One?"
62* Then Jesus answered, "I am;

and 'you will see the Son of Man
seated at the right hand of the Power
and coming with the clouds of heaven.' "

63 At that the high priest tore his gar-
ments and said, "What further need
have we of witnesses? 64 You have heard
the blasphemy. What do you think?"
They all condemned him as deserving
to die. 65* Some began to spit on him.
They blindfolded him and struck him
and said to him, "Prophesy!" And the
guards greeted him with blows.

Peter's Denial of Jesus. 66* While Pe-
ter was below in the courtyard, one of
the high priest's maids came along.
67 Seeing Peter warming himself, she
looked intently at him and said, "You
too were with the Nazarene, Jesus."
68† But he denied it saying, "I neither
know nor understand what you are
talking about." So he went out into the
outer court. [Then the cock crowed.]
69 The maid saw him and began again
to say to the bystanders, "This man is
one of them." 70 Once again he denied
it. A little later the bystanders said to
Peter once more, "Surely you are one
of them; for you too are a Galilean."
71 He began to curse and to swear, "I
do not know this man about whom you
are talking." 72* And immediately a
cock crowed a second time. Then Peter
remembered the word that Jesus had
said to him, "Before the cock crows
twice you will deny me three times." He
broke down and wept.

CHAPTER 15

Jesus before Pilate. 1*† As soon as
morning came, the chief priests with the
elders and the scribes, that is, the whole
Sanhedrin, held a council. They bound
Jesus, led him away, and handed him
over to Pilate. 2† Pilate questioned him,
"Are you the king of the Jews?" He said
to him in reply, "You say so." 3 The
chief priests accused him of many
things. 4 Again Pilate questioned him,
"Have you no answer? See how many
things they accuse you of." 5 Jesus gave
him no further answer, so that Pilate
was amazed.

***The Sentence of Death.*†** 6* Now on
the occasion of the feast he used to re-
lease to them one prisoner whom they
requested. 7† A man called Barabbas
was then in prison along with the rebels
who had committed murder in a rebel-
lion. 8 The crowd came forward and be-
gan to ask him to do for them as he was
accustomed. 9 Pilate answered, "Do you
want me to release to you the king of
the Jews?" 10 For he knew that it was
out of envy that the chief priests had
handed him over. 11 But the chief priests
stirred up the crowd to have him release
Barabbas for them instead. 12 Pilate
again said to them in reply, "Then what
[do you want] me to do with [the man
you call] the king of the Jews?" 13† They
shouted again, "Crucify him." 14 Pilate
said to them, "Why? What evil has he
done?" They only shouted the louder,
"Crucify him." 15† So Pilate, wishing to
satisfy the crowd, released Barabbas to
them and, after he had Jesus scourged,
handed him over to be crucified.

*

58: 15, 29; 2 Cor 5, 1.
62: 13, 26; Ps 110, 1; Dn 7, 13; Mt 24, 30.
65: Lk 22, 63-65.
66-72: Mt 26, 69-75; Lk 22, 56-62; Jn 18, 16-18.25-27.
72: Jn 13, 38.
15, 1-5: Mt 27, 1-2.11-14; Lk 23, 1-3.
1: Jn 18, 28.
6-15: Mt 27, 15-26; Lk 23, 17-25; Jn 18, 39-40.

†

14, 57-58: See the notes on Mt 26, 60-61 and Jn 2, 19.

14, 61-62: *The Blessed One:* a surrogate for the divine name, which Jews did not pronounce. *I am:* indicates Jesus' acknowledgment that he is the Messiah and Son of God; cf 1, 1. Contrast Mt 26, 64 and Lk 22, 67-70, in which Jesus leaves his interrogators to answer their own question. *You will see the Son of Man . . . with the clouds of heaven:* an allusion to Dn 7, 13 and Ps 110, 1, portending the enthronement of Jesus as judge in the transcendent glory of God's kingdom. *The Power:* another surrogate for the name of God.

14, 68: *[Then the cock crowed]:* found in most manuscripts, perhaps in view of vv 30 and 72, but omitted in others.

15, 1: *Held a council:* the verb here, *poieō*, can mean either "convene a council" or "take counsel." This reading is preferred to a variant "reached a decision" (cf 3, 6), which 14, 64 describes as having happened at the night trial; see the note on Mt 27, 1-2. *Handed him over to Pilate:* lacking authority to execute their sentence of condemnation (14, 64), the Sanhedrin had recourse to Pilate to have Jesus tried and put to death (15); cf Jn 18, 31.

15, 2: *The king of the Jews:* in the accounts of the evangelists a certain irony surrounds the use of this title as an accusation against Jesus (see the note on 15, 26). While Pilate uses this term (2.9.12), he is aware of the evil motivation of the chief priests who handed Jesus over for trial and condemnation (10; Lk 23, 14-16.20; Mt 27, 18.24; Jn 18, 38; 19, 4.6.12).

15, 6-15: See the note on Mt 27, 15-26.

15, 7: *Barabbas:* see the note on Mt 27, 16-17.

15, 13: *Crucify him:* see the note on Mt 27, 22.

15, 15: See the note on Mt 27, 26.

Mockery by the Soldiers. 16*† The soldiers led him away inside the palace, that is, the praetorium, and assembled the whole cohort. 17 They clothed him in purple and, weaving a crown of thorns, placed it on him. 18 They began to salute him with, "Hail, King of the Jews!" 19 and kept striking his head with a reed and spitting upon him. They knelt before him in homage. 20 And when they had mocked him, they stripped him of the purple cloak, dressed him in his own clothes, and led him out to crucify him.

The Way of the Cross. 21*† They pressed into service a passer-by, Simon, a Cyrenian, who was coming in from the country, the father of Alexander and Rufus, to carry his cross.

The Crucifixion. 22* They brought him to the place of Golgotha (which is translated Place of the Skull). 23 They gave him wine drugged with myrrh, but he did not take it. 24*† Then they crucified him and divided his garments by casting lots for them to see what each should take. 25† It was nine o'clock in the morning when they crucified him. 26† The inscription of the charge against him read, "The King of the Jews." 27* With him they crucified two revolutionaries, one on his right and one on his left. [28]† 29*† Those passing by reviled him, shaking their heads and saying, "Aha! You who would destroy the temple and rebuild it in three days, 30 save yourself by coming down from the cross." 31 Likewise the chief priests, with the scribes, mocked him among themselves and said, "He saved others; he cannot save himself. 32* Let the Messiah, the King of Israel, come down now from the cross that we may see and believe." Those who were crucified with him also kept abusing him.

The Death of Jesus. 33 At noon darkness came over the whole land until three in the afternoon. 34*† And at three o'clock Jesus cried out in a loud voice, "*Eloi, Eloi, lema sabachthani?*" which is translated, "My God, my God, why have you forsaken me?" 35† Some of the bystanders who heard it said, "Look, he is calling Elijah." 36 One of them ran, soaked a sponge with wine, put it on a reed, and gave it to him to drink, saying, "Wait, let us see if Elijah comes to take him down." 37 Jesus gave a loud cry and breathed his last. 38† The veil of the sanctuary was torn in two from top to bottom. 39*† When the centurion who stood facing him saw how he breathed his last he said, "Truly this man was the Son of God!" 40*† There were also women looking on from a distance. Among them were Mary Magdalene, Mary the mother of the younger James and of Joses, and Salome. 41 These women had followed him when he was in Galilee and ministered to him. There were also many other women who had come up with him to Jerusalem.

The Burial of Jesus. 42* When it was already evening, since it was the day of preparation, the day before the sabbath, 43† Joseph of Arimathea, a distinguished member of the council, who was himself awaiting the kingdom of God, came and courageously went to Pilate and asked for the body of Jesus. 44 Pilate was amazed that he was already dead. He summoned the centurion and asked him if Jesus had already died. 45 And when he learned of it from the centurion, he gave the body to Joseph. 46 Having bought a linen cloth, he took him down, wrapped him in the linen cloth and laid him in a tomb that had been hewn out of the rock. Then he rolled a stone against the entrance to the tomb. 47 Mary Magdalene and Mary the mother of Joses watched where he was laid.

*

16-20: Mt 27, 27-31; Jn 19, 2-3.
21: Mt 27, 32; Lk 23, 26.
22-38: Mt 27, 33-51; Lk 23, 32-46; Jn 19, 17-30.
24: Ps 22, 18.
27: Lk 23, 33.
29: Jn 2, 19.
32: Lk 23, 39.
34: Ps 22, 2.
39-41: Mt 27, 54-56; Lk 23, 47-49.
40: 6, 3; Lk 8, 2-3.
42-47: Mt 27, 57-61; Lk 23, 50-56; Jn 19, 38-42.

†

15, 16: *Praetorium:* see the note on Mt 27, 27.

15, 21: *They pressed into service . . . Simon, a Cyrenian:* a condemned person was constrained to bear his own instrument of torture, at least the crossbeam. The precise naming of Simon and his sons is probably due to their being known among early Christian believers to whom Mark addressed his gospel. See also the notes on Mt 27, 32 and Lk 23, 26-32.

15, 24: See the notes on Mt 27, 35 and Jn 19, 23-25a.

15, 25: *It was nine o'clock in the morning:* literally, "the third hour," thus between 9 a.m. and 12 noon. Cf vv 33.34.42 for Mark's chronological sequence, which may reflect liturgical or catechetical considerations rather than the precise historical sequence of events; contrast the different chronologies in the other gospels, especially Jn 19, 14.

15, 26: *The inscription . . . the King of the Jews:* the political reason for the death penalty falsely charged by the enemies of Jesus. See further the notes on Mt 27, 37 and Jn 19, 19.

15, 28: This verse, "And the scripture was fulfilled that says, 'And he was counted among the wicked,' " is omitted in the earliest and best manuscripts. It contains a citation from Is 53, 12, and was probably introduced from Lk 22, 37.

15, 29: See the note on Mt 27, 39-40.

15, 34: An Aramaic rendering of Ps 22, 2. See also the note on Mt 27, 46.

15, 35: *Elijah:* a verbal link with *Eloi* (34). See the note on 9, 9-13; cf Mal 3, 23-24. See also the note on Mt 27, 47.

15, 38: See the note on Mt 27, 51-53.

15, 39: The closing portion of Mark's gospel returns to the theme of its beginning in the Gentile centurion's climactic declaration of belief that Jesus *was the Son of God.* It indicates the fulfillment of the good news announced in the prologue (1, 1) and may be regarded as the firstfruit of the passion and death of Jesus.

15, 40-41: See the note on Mt 27, 55-56.

15, 43: *Joseph of Arimathea:* see the note on Mt 27, 57-61.

CHAPTER 16

The Resurrection of Jesus.† 1* When
the sabbath was over, Mary Magdalene,
Mary, the mother of James, and Salome
bought spices so that they might go and
anoint him. 2 Very early when the sun
had risen, on the first day of the week,
they came to the tomb. 3 They were say-
ing to one another, "Who will roll back
the stone for us from the entrance to
the tomb?" 4 When they looked up, they
saw that the stone had been rolled back;
it was very large. 5* On entering the
tomb they saw a young man sitting on
the right side, clothed in a white robe,
and they were utterly amazed. 6 He said
to them, "Do not be amazed! You seek
Jesus of Nazareth, the crucified. He has
been raised; he is not here. Behold the
place where they laid him. 7* But go and
tell his disciples and Peter, 'He is going
before you to Galilee; there you will see
him, as he told you.' " 8 Then they went
out and fled from the tomb, seized with
trembling and bewilderment. They said
nothing to anyone, for they were afraid.

THE LONGER ENDING†

The Appearance to Mary Magdalene. [9* When he had risen, early on
the first day of the week, he appeared
first to Mary Magdalene, out of whom
he had driven seven demons. 10* She
went and told his companions who were
mourning and weeping. 11 When they
heard that he was alive and had been
seen by her, they did not believe.
The Appearance to Two Disciples.
12* After this he appeared in another
form to two of them walking along on
their way to the country. 13 They re-
turned and told the others; but they did
not believe them either.
The Commissioning of the Eleven.
14* [But] later, as the eleven were at ta-
ble, he appeared to them and rebuked
them for their unbelief and hardness of
heart because they had not believed
those who saw him after he had been
raised. 15* He said to them, "Go into the
whole world and proclaim the gospel to
every creature. 16 Whoever believes and
is baptized will be saved; whoever does
not believe will be condemned. 17 These
signs will accompany those who be-
lieve: in my name they will drive out
demons, they will speak new languages.
18* They will pick up serpents [with
their hands], and if they drink any
deadly thing, it will not harm them.
They will lay hands on the sick, and
they will recover."
The Ascension of Jesus. 19* So then
the Lord Jesus, after he spoke to them,
was taken up into heaven and took his
seat at the right hand of God. 20* But
they went forth and preached every-
where, while the Lord worked with
them and confirmed the word through
accompanying signs.]

THE SHORTER ENDING

[And they reported all the instruc-
tions briefly to Peter's companions. Af-
terwards Jesus himself, through them,
sent forth from east to west the sacred
and imperishable proclamation of eter-
nal salvation. Amen.]

---

*

16, 1-8:	Mt 28, 1-8; Lk 24, 1-10; Jn 20, 1-10.
1-2:	Mt 28, 1; Lk 23, 56.
5:	Jn 20, 12.
7:	14, 28.
9-20:	Mt 28, 1-10; Jn 20, 11-18.
10-11:	Lk 24, 10-11; Jn 20, 18.
12-14:	Lk 24, 13-35.
14:	Lk 24, 36-49; 1 Cor 15, 5.
15-16:	13, 10; Mt 28, 18-20; Lk 24, 47; Jn 20, 21.
18:	Mt 10, 1; Lk 10, 19; Acts 28, 3-6.
19:	Lk 24, 50-53.
20:	1 Tm 3, 16.

---

†

16, 1-8: The purpose of this narrative is to show that the tomb is empty and that Jesus *has been raised* (6) and *is going before you to Galilee* (7) in fulfillment of 14, 28. The women find the tomb empty, and an angel stationed there announces to them what has happened. They are told to proclaim the news to Peter and the disciples in order to prepare them for a reunion with him. Mark's composition of the gospel ends at v 8 with the women telling no one, because they were afraid. This abrupt termination causes some to believe that the original ending of this gospel may have been lost. See the following note.

16, 9-20: This passage, termed the Longer Ending to the Marcan gospel by comparison with a much briefer conclusion found in some less important manuscripts, has traditionally been accepted as a canonical part of the gospel and was defined as such by the Council of Trent. Early citations of it by the Fathers indicate that it was composed by the second century, although vocabulary and style indicate that it was written by someone other than Mark. It is a general resume of the material concerning the appearances of the risen Jesus, reflecting, in particular, traditions found in Luke (24) and John (20).

The Shorter Ending: Found after v 8 before the Longer Ending in four seventh-to-ninth-century Greek manuscripts as well as in one Old Latin version, where it appears alone without the Longer Ending.

The Freer Logion: Found after v 14 in a fourth-fifth century manuscript preserved in the Freer Gallery of Art, Washington, DC, this ending was known to Jerome in the fourth century. It reads: "And they excused themselves, saying, 'This age of lawlessness and unbelief is under Satan, who does not allow the truth and power of God to prevail over the unclean things dominated by the spirits [*or,* does not allow the unclean things dominated by the spirits to grasp the truth and power of God]. Therefore reveal your righteousness now.' They spoke to Christ. And Christ responded to them, 'The limit of the years of Satan's power is completed, but other terrible things draw near. And for those who sinned I was handed over to death, that they might return to the truth and no longer sin, in order that they might inherit the spiritual and incorruptible heavenly glory of righteousness. But . . . .' "

The Gospel According to

LUKE

The Gospel according to Luke is the first part of a two-volume work that continues the biblical history of God's dealings with humanity found in the Old Testament, showing how God's promises to Israel have been fulfilled in Jesus and how the salvation promised to Israel and accomplished by Jesus has been extended to the Gentiles. The stated purpose of the two volumes is to provide Theophilus and others like him with certainty—assurance—about earlier instruction they have received (1, 4). To accomplish his purpose, Luke shows that the preaching and teaching of the representatives of the early church are grounded in the preaching and teaching of Jesus, who during his historical ministry (Acts 1, 21-22) prepared his specially chosen followers and commissioned them to be witnesses to his resurrection and to all else that he did (Acts 10, 37-42). This continuity between the historical ministry of Jesus and the ministry of the apostles is Luke's way of guaranteeing the fidelity of the church's teaching to the teaching of Jesus.

Luke's story of Jesus and the church is dominated by a historical perspective. This history is first of all salvation history. God's divine plan for human salvation was accomplished during the period of Jesus, who through the events of his life (22, 22) fulfilled the Old Testament prophecies (4, 21; 18, 31; 22, 37; 24, 26-27.44), and this salvation is now extended to all humanity in the period of the church (Acts 4, 12). This salvation history, moreover, is a part of human history. Luke relates the story of Jesus and the church to events in contemporary Palestinian (1, 5; 3, 1-2; Acts 4, 6) and Roman (2, 1-2; 3, 1; Acts 11, 28; 18, 2.12) history, for, as Paul says in Acts 26, 26, "this was not done in a corner." Finally, Luke relates the story of Jesus and the church to contemporaneous church history. Luke is concerned with presenting Christianity as a legitimate form of worship in the Roman world, a religion that is capable of meeting the spiritual needs of a world empire like that of Rome. To this end, Luke depicts the Roman governor Pilate declaring Jesus innocent of any wrongdoing three times (Acts 23, 29; 25, 25; 26, 31-32). At the same time Luke argues in Acts that Christianity is the logical development and proper fulfillment of Judaism and is therefore deserving of the same toleration and freedom traditionally accorded Judaism by Rome (Acts 13, 16-41; 23, 6-9; 24, 10-21; 26, 2-23).

The prominence given to the period of the church in the story has important consequences for Luke's interpretation of the teachings of Jesus. By presenting the time of the church as a distinct phase of salvation history, Luke accordingly shifts the early Christian emphasis away from the expectation of an imminent parousia to the day-to-day concerns of the Christian community in the world. He does this in the gospel by regularly emphasizing the words "each day" (9, 23; cf Mk 8, 34; 11, 3; 16, 19; 19, 47) in the sayings of Jesus. Although Luke still believes the parousia to be a reality that will come unexpectedly (12, 38.45-46), he is more concerned with presenting the words and deeds of Jesus as guides for the conduct of Christian disciples in the interim period between the ascension and the parousia and with presenting Jesus himself as the model of Christian life and piety.

Throughout the gospel, Luke calls upon the Christian disciple to identify with the master Jesus, who is caring and tender toward the poor and lowly, the outcast, the sinner, and the afflicted, toward all those who recognize their dependence on God (4, 18; 6, 20-23; 7, 36-50; 14, 12-14; 15, 1-32; 16, 19-31; 18, 9-14; 19, 1-10; 21, 1-4), but who is severe toward the proud and self-righteous, and particularly toward those who place their material wealth before the service of God and his people (6, 24-26; 12, 13-21; 16, 13-15.19-31; 18, 9-14.15-25; cf 1, 50-53). No gospel

L U K E

writer is more concerned than Luke with the mercy and compassion of Jesus (7, 41-43; 10, 29-37; 13, 6-9; 15, 11-32). No gospel writer is more concerned with the role of the Spirit in the life of Jesus and the Christian disciple (1, 35.41; 2, 25-27; 4, 1.14.18; 10, 21; 11, 13; 24, 49), with the importance of prayer (3, 21; 5, 16; 6, 12; 9, 28; 11, 1-13; 18, 1-8), or with Jesus' concern for women (7, 11-17.36-50; 8, 2-3; 10, 38-42). While Jesus calls all humanity to repent (5, 32; 10, 13; 11, 32; 13, 1-5; 15, 7-10; 16, 30; 17, 3-4; 24, 47), he is particularly demanding of those who would be his disciples. Of them he demands absolute and total detachment from family and material possessions (9, 57-62; 12, 32-34; 14, 25-35). To all who respond in faith and repentance to the word Jesus preaches, he brings salvation (2, 30-32; 3, 6; 7, 50; 8, 48.50; 17, 19; 19, 9) and peace (2, 14; 7, 50; 8, 48; 19, 38.42) and life (10, 25-28; 18, 26-30).

Early Christian tradition, from the late second century on, identifies the author of this gospel and of the Acts of the Apostles as Luke, a Syrian from Antioch, who is mentioned in the New Testament in Col 4, 14, Phlm 24, and 2 Tm 4, 11. The prologue of the gospel makes it clear that Luke is not part of the first generation of Christian disciples but is himself dependent upon the traditions he received from those who were eyewitnesses and ministers of the word (1, 2). His two-volume work marks him as someone who was highly literate both in the Old Testament traditions according to the Greek versions and in Hellenistic Greek writings.

Among the likely sources for the composition of this gospel (1, 3) were the Gospel of Mark, a written collection of sayings of Jesus known also to the author of the Gospel of Matthew (Q; see Introduction to Matthew), and other special traditions that were used by Luke alone among the gospel writers. Some hold that Luke used Mark only as a complementary source for rounding out the material he took from other traditions. Because of its dependence on the Gospel of Mark and because details in Luke's Gospel (13, 35a; 19, 43-44; 21, 20; 23, 28-31) imply that the author was acquainted with the destruction of the city of Jerusalem by the Romans in A.D. 70, the Gospel of Luke is dated by most scholars after that date; many propose A.D. 80-90 as the time of composition.

Luke's consistent substitution of Greek names for the Aramaic or Hebrew names occurring in his sources (e.g., 23, 33 // Mk 15, 22; 18, 41 // Mk 10, 51), his omission from the gospel of specifically Jewish Christian concerns found in his sources (e.g., Mk 7, 1-23), his interest in Gentile Christians (2, 30-32; 3, 6.38; 4, 16-30; 13, 28-30; 14, 15-24; 17, 11-19; 24, 47-48), and his incomplete knowledge of Palestinian geography, customs, and practices are among the characteristics of this gospel that suggest that Luke was a non-Palestinian writing to a non-Palestinian audience that was largely made up of Gentile Christians.

The principal divisions of the Gospel according to Luke are the following:

- *I: The Prologue (1, 1-4)*
- *II: The Infancy Narrative (1, 5—2, 52)*
- *III: The Preparation for the Public Ministry (3, 1—4, 13)*
- *IV: The Ministry in Galilee (4, 14—9, 50)*
- *V: The Journey to Jerusalem: Luke's Travel Narrative (9, 51—19, 27)*
- *VI: The Teaching Ministry in Jerusalem (19, 28—21, 38)*
- *VII: The Passion Narrative (22, 1—23, 56)*
- *VIII: The Resurrection Narrative (24, 1-53)*

I: THE PROLOGUE†

CHAPTER 1

1* Since many have undertaken to
compile a narrative of the events that
have been fulfilled among us, 2* just as
those who were eyewitnesses from the
beginning and ministers of the word
have handed them down to us, 3 I too
have decided, after investigating ev-
erything accurately anew, to write it
down in an orderly sequence for you,
most excellent Theophilus, 4 so that you
may realize the certainty of the teach-
ings you have received.

II: THE INFANCY NARRATIVE†

Announcement of the Birth of John.
5*† In the days of Herod, King of Judea,
there was a priest named Zechariah of
the priestly division of Abijah; his wife
was from the daughters of Aaron, and
her name was Elizabeth. 6 Both were
righteous in the eyes of God, observing
all the commandments and ordinances
of the Lord blamelessly. 7*† But they
had no child, because Elizabeth was
barren and both were advanced in
years. 8 Once when he was serving as
priest in his division's turn before God,
9* according to the practice of the
priestly service, he was chosen by lot
to enter the sanctuary of the Lord to
burn incense. 10 Then, when the whole
assembly of the people was praying out-
side at the hour of the incense offering,
11 the angel of the Lord appeared to him,
standing at the right of the altar of in-
cense. 12 Zechariah was troubled by
what he saw, and fear came upon him.
13*† But the angel said to him, "Do not
be afraid, Zechariah, because your
prayer has been heard. Your wife Eliza-
beth will bear you a son, and you shall
name him John. 14 And you will have
joy and gladness, and many will rejoice
at his birth, 15*† for he will be great in
the sight of [the] Lord. He will drink
neither wine nor strong drink. He will
be filled with the holy Spirit even from
his mother's womb, 16 and he will turn
many of the children of Israel to the
Lord their God. 17*† He will go before
him in the spirit and power of Elijah
to turn the hearts of fathers toward chil-
dren and the disobedient to the under-
standing of the righteous, to prepare a
people fit for the Lord." 18 Then Zecha-
riah said to the angel, "How shall I

---

*

1, 1-4: Acts 1, 1; 1 Cor 15, 3.
2: 24, 48; Jn 15, 27; Acts 1, 21-22.
5: 1 Chr 24, 10.
7: Gn 18, 11; Jgs 13, 2-5; 1 Sm 1, 5-6.
9: Ex 30, 7.
13: 1, 57.60.63; Mt 1, 20-21.
15: 7, 33; Nm 6, 1-21; Jgs 13, 4; 1 Sm 1, 11 LXX.
17: Sir 48, 10; Mal 3, 1; 3, 23-24; Mt 11, 14; 17, 11-13.

---

†

1, 1-4: The Gospel according to Luke is the only one of the synoptic gospels to begin with a literary prologue. Making use of a formal, literary construction and vocabulary, the author writes the prologue in imitation of Hellenistic Greek writers and, in so doing, relates his story about Jesus to contemporaneous Greek and Roman literature. Luke is not only interested in the words and deeds of Jesus, but also in the larger context of the birth, ministry, death, and resurrection of Jesus as the fulfillment of the promises of God in the Old Testament. As a second- or third-generation Christian, Luke acknowledges his debt to earlier *eyewitnesses* and *ministers of the word,* but claims that his contribution to this developing tradition is a complete and accurate account, told in an orderly manner, and intended to provide *Theophilus* ("friend of God," literally) and other readers with certainty about earlier teachings they have received.

1, 5—2, 52: Like the Gospel according to Matthew, this gospel opens with an infancy narrative, a collection of stories about the birth and childhood of Jesus. The narrative uses early Christian traditions about the birth of Jesus, traditions about the birth and circumcision of John the Baptist, and canticles such as the Magnificat (1, 46-55) and Benedictus (1, 67-79), composed of phrases drawn from the Greek Old Testament. It is largely, however, the composition of Luke who writes in imitation of Old Testament birth stories, combining historical and legendary details, literary ornamentation and interpretation of scripture, to answer in advance the question, "Who is Jesus Christ?" The focus of the narrative, therefore, is primarily christological. In this section Luke announces many of the themes that will become prominent in the rest of the gospel: the centrality of Jerusalem and the temple, the journey motif, the universality of salvation, joy and peace, concern for the lowly, the importance of women, the presentation of Jesus as savior, Spirit-guided revelation and prophecy, and the fulfillment of Old Testament promises. The account presents parallel scenes (diptychs) of angelic announcements of the birth of John the Baptist and of Jesus, and of the birth, circumcision, and presentation of John and Jesus. In this parallelism, the ascendency of Jesus over John is stressed: John is prophet of the Most High (1, 76); Jesus is Son of the Most High (1, 32). John is great in the sight of the Lord (1, 15); Jesus will be Great (a LXX attribute, used absolutely, of God) (1, 32). John will go before the Lord (1, 16-17); Jesus will be Lord (1, 43; 2, 11).

1, 5: *In the days of Herod, King of Judea:* Luke relates the story of salvation history to events in contemporary world history. Here and in 3, 1-2, he connects his narrative with events in Palestinian history; in 2, 1-2 and 3, 1, he casts the Jesus story in the light of events of Roman history. Herod the Great, the son of the Idumean Antipater, was declared "King of Judea" by the Roman Senate in 40 B.C., but became the undisputed ruler of Palestine only in 37 B.C. He continued as king until his death in 4 B.C. *Priestly division of Abijah:* a reference to the eighth of the twenty-four divisions of priests who, for a week at a time, twice a year, served in the Jerusalem temple.

1, 7: *They had no child:* though childlessness was looked upon in contemporaneous Judaism as a curse or punishment for sin, it is intended here to present Elizabeth in a situation similar to that of some of the great mothers of important Old Testament figures: Sarah (Gn 15, 3; 16, 1); Rebekah (Gn 25, 21); Rachel (Gn 29, 31; 30, 1); the mother of Samson and wife of Manoah (Jgs 13, 2-3); Hannah (1 Sm 1, 2).

1, 13: *Do not be afraid:* a stereotyped Old Testament phrase spoken to reassure the recipient of a heavenly vision (Gn 15, 1; Jos 1, 9; Dn 10, 12.19 and elsewhere in 1, 30; 2, 10). *You shall name him John:* the name means "Yahweh has shown favor," an indication of John's role in salvation history.

1, 15: *He will drink neither wine nor strong drink:* like Samson (Jgs 13, 4-5) and Samuel (1 Sm 1, 11 LXX and 4QSam[a]), John is to be consecrated by Nazirite vow and set apart for the Lord's service.

1, 17: *He will go before him in the spirit and power of Elijah:* John is to be the messenger sent before Yahweh, as described in Mal 3, 1-2. He is cast, moreover, in the role of the Old Testament fiery reformer, the prophet Elijah, who according to Mal 3, 23 (4, 5) is sent before "the great and terrible day of the Lord comes."

LUKE

know this? For I am an old man, and my wife is advanced in years." 19*† And the angel said to him in reply, "I am Gabriel, who stand before God. I was sent to speak to you and to announce to you this good news. 20*† But now you will be speechless and unable to talk until the day these things take place, because you did not believe my words, which will be fulfilled at their proper time."

21 Meanwhile the people were waiting for Zechariah and were amazed that he stayed so long in the sanctuary. 22 But when he came out, he was unable to speak to them, and they realized that he had seen a vision in the sanctuary. He was gesturing to them but remained mute. 23 Then, when his days of ministry were completed, he went home. 24 After this time his wife Elizabeth conceived, and she went into seclusion for five months, saying, 25* "So has the Lord done for me at a time when he has seen fit to take away my disgrace before others."

Announcement of the Birth of Jesus.† 26 In the sixth month, the angel Gabriel was sent from God to a town of Galilee called Nazareth, 27* to a virgin betrothed to a man named Joseph, of the house of David, and the virgin's name was Mary. 28* And coming to her, he said, "Hail, favored one! The Lord is with you." 29 But she was greatly troubled at what was said and pondered what sort of greeting this might be. 30 Then the angel said to her, "Do not be afraid, Mary, for you have found favor with God. 31* Behold, you will conceive in your womb and bear a son, and you shall name him Jesus. 32*† He will be great and will be called Son of the Most High, and the Lord God will give him the throne of David his father, 33* and he will rule over the house of Jacob forever, and of his kingdom there will be no end." 34† But Mary said to the angel, "How can this be, since I have no relations with a man?" 35* And the angel said to her in reply, "The holy Spirit will come upon you, and the power of the Most High will overshadow you. Therefore the child to be born will be called holy, the Son of God. 36† And behold, Elizabeth, your relative, has also conceived a son in her old age, and this is the sixth month for her who was called barren; 37* for nothing will be impossible for God." 38 Mary said, "Behold, I am the handmaid of the Lord. May it be done to me according to your word." Then the angel departed from her.

Mary Visits Elizabeth. 39 During those days Mary set out and traveled to the hill country in haste to a town of Judah, 40 where she entered the house of Zechariah and greeted Elizabeth. 41* When Elizabeth heard Mary's greeting, the infant leaped in her womb, and Elizabeth, filled with the holy Spirit, 42* cried out in a loud voice and said, "Most blessed are you among women, and blessed is the fruit of your womb. 43† And how does this happen to me, that the mother of my Lord should come to me? 44 For at the moment the sound of your greeting reached my ears, the infant in my womb leaped for joy. 45*† Blessed are you who believed that what was spoken to you by the Lord would be fulfilled."

*

19: Dn 8, 16; 9, 21.
20: 1, 45.
25: Gn 30, 23.
27: 2, 5; Mt 1, 16.18.
28: Jgs 6, 12; Ru 2, 4; Jdt 13, 18.
31: Gn 16, 11; Jgs 13, 3; Is 7, 14; Mt 1, 21-23.
32-33: 2 Sm 7, 12.13.16; Is 9, 7.
33: Dn 2, 44; 7, 14; Mi 4, 7; Mt 28, 18.
35: Mt 1, 20.
37: Gn 18, 14; Jer 32, 27; Mt 19, 26.
41: 1, 15; Gn 25, 22 LXX.
42: 11, 27-28; Jgs 5, 24; Jdt 13, 18 / Dt 28, 4.
45: 1; 20.

†

1, 19: *I am Gabriel:* "the angel of the Lord" is identified as Gabriel, the angel who in Dn 9, 20-25 announces the seventy weeks of years and the coming of an anointed one, a prince. By alluding to Old Testament themes in vv 17 and 19, such as the coming of the day of the Lord and the dawning of the messianic era, Luke is presenting his interpretation of the significance of the births of John and Jesus.

1, 20: *You will be speechless and unable to talk:* Zechariah's becoming mute is the sign given in response to his question in v 18. When Mary asks a similar question in 1, 34, unlike Zechariah who was punished for his doubt, she, in spite of her doubt, is praised and reassured (35-37).

1, 26-38: The announcement to Mary of the birth of Jesus is parallel to the announcement to Zechariah of the birth of John. In both the angel Gabriel appears to the parent who is troubled by the vision (11-12.26-29) and then told by the angel not to fear (13.30). After the announcement is made (14-17.31-33) the parent objects (18.34) and a sign is given to confirm the announcement (20.36). The particular focus of the announcement of the birth of Jesus is on his identity as Son of David (32-33) and Son of God (32.35).

1, 32: *Son of the Most High:* cf 1, 76 where John is described as "prophet of the Most High." "Most High" is a title for God commonly used by Luke (35.76; 6, 35; 8, 28; Acts 7, 48; 16, 17).

1, 34: Mary's questioning response is a denial of sexual relations and is used by Luke to lead to the angel's declaration about the Spirit's role in the conception of this child (35). According to Luke, the virginal conception of Jesus takes place through the holy Spirit, the power of God, and therefore Jesus has a unique relationship to Yahweh: he is Son of God.

1, 36-37: The sign given to Mary in confirmation of the angel's announcement to her is the pregnancy of her aged relative Elizabeth. If a woman past the childbearing age could become pregnant, why, the angel implies, should there be doubt about Mary's pregnancy, for *nothing will be impossible for God.*

1, 43: Even before his birth, Jesus is identified in Lk as the *Lord.*

1, 45: *Blessed are you who believed:* Luke portrays Mary as a believer whose faith stands in contrast to the disbelief of Zechariah (20). Mary's role as believer in the infancy narrative should be seen in connection with the explicit mention of her presence among "those who believed" after the resurrection at the beginning of the Acts of the Apostles (14).

The Canticle of Mary. † 46* And Mary
said:

"My soul proclaims the greatness of
the Lord;
47* my spirit rejoices in God my savior.
48* For he has looked upon his handmaid's lowliness;
behold, from now on will all ages
call me blessed.
49* The Mighty One has done great
things for me,
and holy is his name.
50* His mercy is from age to age
to those who fear him.
51* He has shown might with his arm,
dispersed the arrogant of mind
and heart.
52* He has thrown down the rulers from
their thrones
but lifted up the lowly.
53* The hungry he has filled with good
things;
the rich he has sent away
empty.
54* He has helped Israel his servant,
remembering his mercy,
55* according to his promise to our fathers,
to Abraham and to his descendants forever."

56 Mary remained with her about three
months and then returned to her
home.

The Birth of John. † 57 When the time
arrived for Elizabeth to have her child
she gave birth to a son. 58* Her neighbors and relatives heard that the Lord
had shown his great mercy toward her,
and they rejoiced with her. 59*† When
they came on the eighth day to circumcise the child, they were going to call
him Zechariah after his father, 60* but
his mother said in reply, "No. He will
be called John." 61 But they answered
her, "There is no one among your relatives who has this name." 62 So they
made signs, asking his father what he
wished him to be called. 63 He asked for
a tablet and wrote, "John is his name,"
and all were amazed. 64* Immediately
his mouth was opened, his tongue freed,
and he spoke blessing God. 65 Then fear
came upon all their neighbors, and all
these matters were discussed throughout the hill country of Judea. 66 All who
heard these things took them to heart,
saying, "What, then, will this child be?"
For surely the hand of the Lord was
with him.

The Canticle of Zechariah. 67 Then
Zechariah his father, filled with the holy
Spirit, prophesied, saying:

68*†"Blessed be the Lord, the God of Israel,
for he has visited and brought redemption to his people.
69*†He has raised up a horn for our salvation
within the house of David his servant,

---

*

46-55: 1 Sm 2, 1-10.
46: Ps 35, 9; Is 61, 10; Hb 3, 18.
47: Ti 3, 4; Jude 25.
48: 11, 27; 1 Sm 1, 11; 2 Sm 16, 12; 2 Kgs 14, 26; Ps 113, 7.
49: Dt 10, 21; Pss 71, 19; 111, 9; 126, 2-3.
50: Pss 89, 2; 103, 13.17.
51: Pss 89, 10; 118, 15; Jer 32, 17 (39, 17 LXX).
52: 1 Sm 2, 7; 2 Sm 22, 28; Jb 5, 11; 12, 19; Ps 147, 6; Sir 10, 14; Jas 4, 6; 1 Pt 5, 5.
53: 1 Sm 2, 5; Ps 107, 9.
54: Ps 98, 3; Is 41, 8-9.
55: Gn 13, 15; 17, 7; 18, 18; 22, 17-18; Mi 7, 20.
58: 1, 14.
59: 2, 21; Gn 17, 10.12; Lv 12, 3.
60: 1, 13.
64: 1, 20.
68: 7, 16; Pss 41, 13; 72, 18; 106, 48; 111, 9.
69: Ps 18, 3.

---

†

1, 46-55: Although Mary is praised for being the mother of the Lord and because of her belief, she reacts as the servant in a psalm of praise, the Magnificat. Because there is no specific connection of the canticle to the context of Mary's pregnancy and her visit to Elizabeth, the Magnificat (with the possible exception of v 48) may have been a Jewish Christian hymn that Luke found appropriate at this point in his story. Even if not composed by Luke, it fits in well with themes found elsewhere in Lk: joy and exultation in the Lord; the lowly being singled out for God's favor; the reversal of human fortunes; the fulfillment of Old Testament promises. The loose connection between the hymn and the context is further seen in the fact that a few Old Latin manuscripts identify the speaker of the hymn as Elizabeth, even though the overwhelming textual evidence makes Mary the speaker.

1, 57-66: The birth and circumcision of John above all emphasize John's incorporation into the people of Israel by the sign of the covenant (Gn 17, 1-12). The narrative of John's circumcision also prepares the way for the subsequent description of the circumcision of Jesus in 2, 21. At the beginning of his two-volume work Luke shows those who play crucial roles in the inauguration of Christianity to be wholly a part of the people of Israel. At the end of the Acts of the Apostles (21, 20; 22, 3; 23, 6-9; 24, 14-16; 26, 2-8.22-23) he will argue that Christianity is the direct descendant of Pharisaic Judaism.

1, 59: The practice of Palestinian Judaism at this time was to name the child at birth; moreover, though naming a male child after the father is not completely unknown, the usual practice was to name the child after the grandfather (see 61). The naming of the child John and Zechariah's recovery from his loss of speech should be understood as fulfilling the angel's announcement to Zechariah in 1, 13 and 20.

1, 68-79: Like the canticle of Mary (46-55) the canticle of Zechariah is only loosely connected with its context. Apart from vv 76-77, the hymn in speaking of *a horn for our salvation* (69) and *the daybreak from on high* (78) applies more closely to Jesus and his work than to John. Again like Mary's canticle, it is largely composed of phrases taken from the Greek Old Testament and may have been a Jewish Christian hymn of praise that Luke adapted to fit the present context by inserting vv 76-77 to give Zechariah's reply to the question asked in v 66.

1, 69: *A horn for our salvation:* the horn is a common Old Testament figure for strength (Pss 18, 3; 75, 5-6; 89, 18; 112, 9; 148, 14). This description is applied to God in Ps 18, 3 and is here transferred to Jesus. The connection of the phrase with *the house of David* gives the title messianic overtones and may indicate an allusion to a phrase in Hannah's song of praise (1 Sm 2, 10), "the horn of his anointed."

70 even as he promised through the mouth of his holy prophets from of old:
71* salvation from our enemies and from the hand of all who hate us,
72* to show mercy to our fathers
and to be mindful of his holy covenant
73* and of the oath he swore to Abraham our father,
and to grant us that, 74 rescued from the hand of enemies,
without fear we might worship him
75* in holiness and righteousness
before him all our days.
76*†And you, child, will be called prophet of the Most High,
for you will go before the Lord to prepare his ways,
77 to give his people knowledge of salvation
through the forgiveness of their sins,
78*†because of the tender mercy of our God
by which the daybreak from on high will visit us
79 to shine on those who sit in darkness and death's shadow,
to guide our feet into the path of peace."

80* The child grew and became strong in spirit, and he was in the desert until the day of his manifestation to Israel.

CHAPTER 2

***The Birth of Jesus.*†** 1† In those days
a decree went out from Caesar Augustus that the whole world should be enrolled.
2 This was the first enrollment,
when Quirinius was governor of Syria.
3 So all went to be enrolled, each to his
own town. 4* And Joseph too went up
from Galilee from the town of Nazareth to Judea, to the city of David that is called Bethlehem, because he was of the house and family of David,
5* to be enrolled with Mary, his betrothed, who
was with child. 6 While they were there,
the time came for her to have her child,
7*† and she gave birth to her firstborn son. She wrapped him in swaddling clothes and laid him in a manger, because there was no room for them in the inn.
8† Now there were shepherds in that
region living in the fields and keeping
the night watch over their flock. 9* The
angel of the Lord appeared to them and the glory of the Lord shone around them, and they were struck with great
fear. 10 The angel said to them, "Do not
be afraid; for behold, I proclaim to you good news of great joy that will be for

*

71: Ps 106, 10.
72: Ps 106, 45-46.
72-73: Gn 17, 7; Lv 26, 42; Ps 105, 8-9; Mi 7, 20.
73-74: Gn 22, 16-17.
75: Ti 2, 12.
76: Is 40, 3; Mal 3, 1; Mt 3, 3; 11, 10.
78: Mal 3, 20.
78-79: Is 60, 1-2.
80: 2, 40; Mt 3, 1.
2, 4: Mi 5, 2; Mt 2, 6.
5: 1, 27; Mt 1, 18.
7: Mt 1, 25.
9: 1, 11.26.

†

1, 76: *You will go before the Lord:* here *the Lord* is most likely a reference to Jesus (contrast 15-17 where Yahweh is meant) and John is presented as the precursor of Jesus.

1, 78: *The daybreak from on high:* three times in the LXX (Jer 23, 5; Zec 3, 8; 6, 12), the Greek word used here for *daybreak* translates the Hebrew word for "scion, branch," an Old Testament messianic title.

2, 1-2: Although universal registrations of Roman citizens are attested in 28 B.C., 8 B.C., and A.D. 14 and enrollments in individual provinces of those who are not Roman citizens are also attested, such a universal census of the Roman world under Caesar Augustus is unknown outside the New Testament. Moreover, there are notorious historical problems connected with Luke's dating the census *when Quirinius was governor of Syria,* and the various attempts to resolve the difficulties have proved unsuccessful. P. Sulpicius Quirinius became legate of the province of Syria in A.D. 6-7 when Judea was annexed to the province of Syria. At that time, a provincial census of Judea was taken up. If Quirinius had been legate of Syria previously, it would have to have been before 10 B.C. because the various legates of Syria from 10 B.C. to 4 B.C. (the death of Herod) are known, and such a dating for an earlier census under Quirinius would create additional problems for dating the beginning of Jesus' ministry (3, 1.23). A previous legateship after 4 B.C. (and before A.D. 6) would not fit with the dating of Jesus' birth in the days of Herod (1, 5; Mt 2, 1). Luke may simply be combining Jesus' birth in Bethlehem with his vague recollection of a census under Quirinius (see also Acts 5, 37) to underline the significance of this birth for the whole Roman world: through this child born in Bethlehem peace and salvation come to the empire.

2, 1: *Caesar Augustus:* the reign of the Roman emperor Caesar Augustus is usually dated from 27 B.C. to his death in A.D. 14. According to Greek inscriptions, Augustus was regarded in the Roman Empire as "savior" and "god," and he was credited with establishing a time of peace, the *pax Augusta,* throughout the Roman world during his long reign. It is not by chance that Luke relates the birth of Jesus to the time of Caesar Augustus: the real savior (11) and peacebearer (14; see also 19, 38) is the child born in Bethlehem. The great emperor is simply God's agent (like the Persian king Cyrus in Is 44, 28—45, 1) who provides the occasion for God's purposes to be accomplished. *The whole world:* that is, the whole Roman world: Rome, Italy, and the Roman provinces.

2, 7: *Firstborn son:* the description of Jesus as *firstborn son* does not necessarily mean that Mary had other sons. It is a legal description indicating that Jesus possessed the rights and privileges of the firstborn son (Gn 27; Ex 13, 2; Nm 3, 12-13; 18, 15-16; Dt 21, 15-17). See the notes on Mt 1, 25 and Mk 6, 3. *Wrapped him in swaddling clothes:* there may be an allusion here to the birth of another descendant of David, his son Solomon, who though a great king was wrapped in swaddling clothes like any other infant (Wis 7, 4-6). *Laid him in a manger:* a feeding trough for animals. A possible allusion to Is 1, 3 LXX.

2, 8-20: The annoucement of Jesus' birth to the shepherds is in keeping with Luke's theme that the lowly are singled out as the recipients of God's favors and blessings (see also 1, 48.52).

all the people. 11*† For today in the city
of David a savior has been born for you
who is Messiah and Lord. 12 And this
will be a sign for you: you will find an
infant wrapped in swaddling clothes
and lying in a manger." 13 And sud-
denly there was a multitude of the heav-
enly host with the angel, praising God
and saying:

14*† "Glory to God in the highest
and on earth peace to those on
whom his favor rests."

The Visit of the Shepherds. 15 When
the angels went away from them to
heaven, the shepherds said to one an-
other, "Let us go, then, to Bethlehem
to see this thing that has taken place,
which the Lord has made known to us."
16 So they went in haste and found Mary
and Joseph, and the infant lying in the
manger. 17 When they saw this, they
made known the message that had been
told them about this child. 18 All who
heard it were amazed by what had been
told them by the shepherds. 19 And
Mary kept all these things, reflecting on
them in her heart. 20 Then the shepherds
returned, glorifying and praising God
for all they had heard and seen, just as
it had been told to them.

***The Circumcision and Naming of
Jesus.*** 21*† When eight days were com-
pleted for his circumcision, he was
named Jesus, the name given him by
the angel before he was conceived in
the womb.

The Presentation in the Temple.†
22*† When the days were completed for
their purification according to the law
of Moses, they took him up to Jerusalem
to present him to the Lord, 23* just as
it is written in the law of the Lord, "Ev-
ery male that opens the womb shall be
consecrated to the Lord," 24 and to offer
the sacrifice of "a pair of turtledoves
or two young pigeons," in accordance
with the dictate in the law of the Lord.

25† Now there was a man in Jerusalem
whose name was Simeon. This man was
righteous and devout, awaiting the con-
solation of Israel, and the holy Spirit
was upon him. 26 It had been revealed
to him by the holy Spirit that he should
not see death before he had seen the
Messiah of the Lord. 27 He came in
the Spirit into the temple; and when the
parents brought in the child Jesus to
perform the custom of the law in regard
to him, 28 he took him into his arms and
blessed God, saying:

29 "Now, Master, you may let your
servant go
in peace, according to your word,
30* for my eyes have seen your salva-
tion,
31 which you prepared in sight of all
the peoples,
32* a light for revelation to the Gentiles,
and glory for your people Israel."

33 The child's father and mother were
amazed at what was said about him;

*

11: Mt 1, 21; 16, 16; Jn 4, 42; Acts 2, 36; 5, 31; Phil 2, 11.
14: 19, 38.
21: 1, 31; Gn 17, 12; Mt 1, 21.
22-24: Lv 12, 2-8.
23: Ex 13, 2.12.
30-31: 3, 6; Is 40, 5 LXX; 52, 10.
32: Is 42, 6; 46, 13; 49, 6; Acts 13, 47; 26, 23.

†

2, 11: The basic message of the infancy narrative is contained in the angel's announcement: this child is *savior, Messiah,* and *Lord.* Luke is the only synoptic gospel writer to use the title *savior* for Jesus (11; Acts 5, 31; 13, 23; see also 1, 69; 19, 9; Acts 4, 12). As savior, Jesus is looked upon by Luke as the one who rescues humanity from sin and delivers humanity from the condition of alienation from God. The title *christos,* "Christ," is the Greek equivalent of the Hebrew *māšîaḥ,* "Messiah," "anointed one." Among certain groups in first-century Palestinian Judaism, the title was applied to an expected royal leader from the line of David who would restore the kingdom to Israel (see Acts 1, 6). The political overtones of the title are played down in Lk and instead the Messiah of the Lord (26) or the Lord's anointed is the one who now brings salvation to all humanity, Jew and Gentile (29-32). *Lord* is the most frequently used title for Jesus in Lk and Acts. In the New Testament it is also applied to Yahweh, as it is in the Old Testament. When used of Jesus it points to his transcendence and dominion over humanity.

2, 14: *On earth peace to those on whom his favor rests:* the peace that results from the Christ event is for those whom God has favored with his grace. This reading is found in the oldest representatives of the Western and Alexandrian text traditions and is the preferred one; the Byzantine text tradition, on the other hand, reads: "on earth peace, good will toward men." The peace of which Luke's gospel speaks (14; 7, 50; 8, 48; 10, 5-6; 19, 38.42; 24, 36) is more than the absence of war of the *pax Augusta;* it also includes the security and well-being characteristic of peace in the Old Testament.

2, 21: Just as John before him had been incorporated into the people of Israel through his circumcision, so too this child (see the note on 1, 57-66).

2, 22-40: The presentation of Jesus in the temple depicts the parents of Jesus as devout Jews, faithful observers of the law of the Lord (23.24.39), i.e., the law of Moses. In this respect, they are described in a fashion similar to the parents of John (1, 6) and Simeon (25) and Anna (36-37).

2, 22: *Their purification:* syntactically, *their* must refer to Mary and Joseph, even though the Mosaic law never mentions the purification of the husband. Recognizing the problem, some Western scribes have altered the text to read "his purification," understanding the presentation of Jesus in the temple as a form of purification; the Vulgate version has a Latin form that could be either "his" or "her." According to the Mosaic law (Lv 12, 2-8), the woman who gives birth to a boy is unable for forty days to touch anything sacred or to enter the temple area by reason of her legal impurity. At the end of this period she is required to offer a year-old lamb as a burnt offering and a turtledove or young pigeon as an expiation of sin. The woman who could not afford a lamb offered instead two turtledoves or two young pigeons, as Mary does here. *They took him up to Jerusalem to present him to the Lord:* as the firstborn son (7) Jesus was consecrated to the Lord as the law required (Ex 13, 2.12), but there was no requirement that this be done at the temple. The concept of a presentation at the temple is probably derived from 1 Sm 1, 24-28, where Hannah offers the child Samuel for sanctuary services. The law further stipulated (Nm 3, 47-48) that the firstborn son should be redeemed by the parents through their payment of five shekels to a member of a priestly family. About this legal requirement Luke is silent.

2, 25: *Awaiting the consolation of Israel:* Simeon here and later Anna who speak about the child to all who were awaiting the redemption of Jerusalem represent the hopes and expectations of faithful and devout Jews who at this time were looking forward to the restoration of God's rule in Israel. The birth of Jesus brings these hopes to fulfillment.

34* and Simeon blessed them and said
to Mary his mother, "Behold, this child
is destined for the fall and rise of many
in Israel, and to be a sign that will be
contradicted 35† (and you yourself a
sword will pierce) so that the thoughts
of many hearts may be revealed."
36 There was also a prophetess, Anna,
the daughter of Phanuel, of the tribe of
Asher. She was advanced in years, hav-
ing lived seven years with her husband
after her marriage, 37 and then as a
widow until she was eighty-four. She
never left the temple, but worshiped
night and day with fasting and prayer.
38* And coming forward at that very
time, she gave thanks to God and spoke
about the child to all who were awaiting
the redemption of Jerusalem.

The Return to Nazareth. 39* When
they had fulfilled all the prescriptions
of the law of the Lord, they returned
to Galilee, to their own town of Naza-
reth. 40* The child grew and became
strong, filled with wisdom; and the favor
of God was upon him.

The Boy Jesus in the Temple.†
41* Each year his parents went to Jeru-
salem for the feast of Passover, 42 and
when he was twelve years old, they
went up according to festival custom.
43 After they had completed its days, as
they were returning, the boy Jesus re-
mained behind in Jerusalem, but his
parents did not know it. 44 Thinking that
he was in the caravan, they journeyed
for a day and looked for him among
their relatives and acquaintances,
45 but not finding him, they returned to
Jerusalem to look for him. 46 After three
days they found him in the temple, sit-
ting in the midst of the teachers, listen-
ing to them and asking them questions,
47 and all who heard him were as-
tounded at his understanding and his
answers. 48 When his parents saw him,
they were astonished, and his mother
said to him, "Son, why have you done
this to us? Your father and I have been
looking for you with great anxiety."
49† And he said to them, "Why were you
looking for me? Did you not know that
I must be in my Father's house?"
50 But they did not understand what he
said to them. 51* He went down with
them and came to Nazareth, and was
obedient to them; and his mother kept
all these things in her heart. 52* And Je-
sus advanced [in] wisdom and age and
favor before God and man.

III: THE PREPARATION FOR THE PUBLIC MINISTRY

CHAPTER 3

The Preaching of John the Baptist.†
1*† In the fifteenth year of the reign of
Tiberius Caesar, when Pontius Pilate
was governor of Judea, and Herod was
tetrarch of Galilee, and his brother
Philip tetrarch of the region of Ituraea
and Trachonitis, and Lysanias was te-
trarch of Abilene, 2*† during the high

*

34: 12, 51; Is 8, 14; Jn 9, 39; Rom 9, 33; 1 Cor 1, 23; 1 Pt 2, 7-8.
38: Is 52, 9.
39: Mt 2, 23.
40: 1, 80; 2, 52.
41: Ex 12, 24-27; 23, 15; Dt 16, 1-8.
51: 2, 19.
52: 1, 80; 2, 40; 1 Sm 2, 26.
3, 1-20: Mt 3, 1-12; Mk 1, 1-8; Jn 1, 19-28.
2: 1, 80.

†

2, 35: *(And you yourself a sword will pierce):* Mary herself will not be untouched by the various reactions to the role of Jesus (34). Her blessedness as mother of the Lord will be challenged by her son who describes true blessedness as "hearing the word of God and observing it" (11, 27-28 and 8, 20-21).

2, 41-52: This story's concern with an incident from Jesus' youth is unique in the canonical gospel tradition. It presents Jesus in the role of the faithful Jewish boy, raised in the traditions of Israel, and fulfilling all that the law requires. With this episode, the infancy narrative ends just as it began, in the setting of the Jerusalem temple.

2, 49: *I must be in my Father's house:* this phrase can also be translated, "I must be about my Father's work." In either translation, Jesus refers to God as his Father. His divine sonship, and his obedience to his heavenly Father's will, take precedence over his ties to his family.

3, 1-20: Although Luke is indebted in this section to his sources, the Gospel of Mark and a collection of sayings of John the Baptist, he has clearly marked this introduction to the ministry of Jesus with his own individual style. Just as the gospel began with a long periodic sentence (1, 1-4), so too this section (1-2). He casts the call of John the Baptist in the form of an Old Testament prophetic call (2) and extends the quotation from Isaiah found in Mk 1, 3 (Is 40, 3) by the addition of Is 40, 4-5 in vv 5-6. In doing so, he presents his theme of the universality of salvation, which he has announced earlier in the words of Simeon (2, 30-32). Moreover, in describing the expectation of the people (15), Luke is characterizing the time of John's preaching in the same way as he had earlier described the situation of other devout Israelites in the infancy narrative (2, 25-26.37-38). In vv 7-18 Luke presents the preaching of John the Baptist who urges the crowds to reform in view of *the coming wrath* (7.9: eschatological preaching), and who offers the crowds certain standards for reforming social conduct (10-14: ethical preaching), and who announces to the crowds the coming of *one mightier than* he (15-18: messianic preaching).

3, 1: *Tiberius Caesar:* Tiberius succeeded Augustus as emperor in A.D. 14 and reigned until A.D. 37. The fifteenth year of his reign, depending on the method of calculating his first regnal year, would have fallen between A.D. 27 and 29. *Pontius Pilate:* prefect of Judea from A.D. 26 to 36. The Jewish historian Josephus describes him as a greedy and ruthless prefect who had little regard for the local Jewish population and their religious practices (see 13, 1). *Herod:* i.e., Herod Antipas, the son of Herod the Great. He ruled over Galilee and Perea from 4 B.C. to A.D. 39. His official title *tetrarch* means literally, "ruler of a quarter," but came to designate any subordinate prince. *Philip:* also a son of Herod the Great, tetrarch of the territory to the north and east of the Sea of Galilee from 4 B.C. to A.D. 34. Only two small areas of this territory are mentioned by Luke. *Lysanias:* nothing is known about this Lysanias who is said here to have been tetrarch of Abilene, a territory northwest of Damascus.

3, 2: *During the high priesthood of Annas and Caiaphas:* after situating the call of John the Baptist in terms of the

priesthood of Annas and Caiaphas, the
word of God came to John the son of
Zechariah in the desert. 3*† He went
throughout [the] whole region of the
Jordan, proclaiming a baptism of re-
pentance for the forgiveness of sins,
4*† as it is written in the book of the
words of the prophet Isaiah:

> "A voice of one crying out in the
> desert:
> 'Prepare the way of the Lord,
> make straight his paths.
> 5 Every valley shall be filled
> and every mountain and hill shall
> be made low.
> The winding roads shall be made
> straight,
> and the rough ways made smooth,
> 6* and all flesh shall see the salvation
> of God.' "

7* He said to the crowds who came out
to be baptized by him, "You brood of
vipers! Who warned you to flee from the
coming wrath? 8* Produce good fruits
as evidence of your repentance; and do
not begin to say to yourselves, 'We have
Abraham as our father,' for I tell you,
God can raise up children to Abraham
from these stones. 9* Even now the ax
lies at the root of the trees. Therefore
every tree that does not produce good
fruit will be cut down and thrown into
the fire."

10 And the crowds asked him, "What
then should we do?" 11 He said to them
in reply, "Whoever has two cloaks
should share with the person who has
none. And whoever has food should do
likewise." 12* Even tax collectors came
to be baptized and they said to him,
"Teacher, what should we do?" 13 He
answered them, "Stop collecting more
than what is prescribed." 14 Soldiers
also asked him, "And what is it that we
should do?" He told them, "Do not prac-
tice extortion, do not falsely accuse
anyone, and be satisfied with your
wages."

15* Now the people were filled with ex-
pectation, and all were asking in their
hearts whether John might be the Mes-
siah. 16*† John answered them all, say-
ing, "I am baptizing you with water, but
one mightier than I is coming. I am not
worthy to loosen the thongs of his san-
dals. He will baptize you with the holy
Spirit and fire. 17*† His winnowing fan
is in his hand to clear his threshing floor
and to gather the wheat into his barn,
but the chaff he will burn with un-
quenchable fire." 18 Exhorting them in
many other ways, he preached good
news to the people. 19*† Now Herod the
tetrarch, who had been censured by
him because of Herodias, his brother's
wife, and because of all the evil deeds
Herod had committed, 20 added still an-
other to these by [also] putting John in
prison.

The Baptism of Jesus. † 21*† After all
the people had been baptized and Jesus
also had been baptized and was pray-
ing, heaven was opened 22*† and the

LUKE

*

3: Acts 13, 24; 19, 4.
4-6: Is 40, 3-5.
4: Jn 1, 23.
6: 2, 30-31.
7: Mt 12, 34.
8: Jn 8, 39.
9: Mt 7, 19; Jn 15, 6.
12: 7, 29.
15-16: Acts 13, 25.
16: 7, 19-20; Jn 1, 27; Acts 1, 5; 11, 16.
17: Mt 3, 12.
19-20: Mt 14, 3-4; Mk 6, 17-18.
21-22: Mt 3, 13-17; Mk 1, 9-11.
22: 9, 35; Ps 2, 7; Is 42, 1; Mt 12, 18; 17, 5; Mk 9, 7; Jn 1, 32; 2 Pt 1, 17.

†

civil rulers of the period, Luke now mentions the religious leadership of Palestine (see the note on 1, 5). Annas had been high priest A.D. 6-15. After being deposed by the Romans in A.D. 15 he was succeeded by various members of his family and eventually by his son-in-law, Caiaphas, who was high priest A.D. 18-36. Luke refers to Annas as high priest at this time (but see Jn 18, 13.19), possibly because of the continuing influence of Annas or because the title continued to be used for the ex-high priest. *The word of God came to John:* Luke is alone among the New Testament writers in associating the preaching of John with a call from God. Luke is thereby identifying John with the prophets whose ministries began with similar calls. In 7, 26 John will be described as "more than a prophet"; he is also the precursor of Jesus (7, 27), a transitional figure inaugurating the period of the fulfillment of prophecy and promise.

3, 3: See the note on Mt 3, 2.

3, 4: The Essenes from Qumran used the same passage to explain why their community was in the desert studying and observing the law and the prophets (1QS 8, 12-15).

3, 16: *He will baptize you with the holy Spirit and fire:* in contrast to John's baptism with water, Jesus is said to baptize with the holy Spirit and with fire. From the point of view of the early Christian community, the Spirit and fire must have been understood in the light of the fire symbolism of the pouring out of the Spirit at Pentecost (Acts 2, 1-4); but as part of John's preaching, the Spirit and fire should be related to their purifying and refining characteristics (Ez 36, 25-27; Mal 3, 2-3). See the note on Mt 3, 11.

3, 17: *Winnowing fan:* see the note on Mt 3, 12.

3, 19-20: Luke separates the ministry of John the Baptist from that of Jesus by reporting the imprisonment of John before the baptism of Jesus (21-22). Luke uses this literary device to serve his understanding of the periods of salvation history. With John the Baptist, the time of promise, the period of Israel, comes to an end; with the baptism of Jesus and the descent of the Spirit upon him, the time of fulfillment, the period of Jesus, begins. In his second volume, the Acts of the Apostles, Luke will introduce the third epoch in salvation history, the period of the church.

3, 21-22: This episode in Luke focuses on the heavenly message identifying Jesus as *Son* and, through the allusion to Is 42, 1, as Servant of Yahweh. The relationship of Jesus to the Father has already been announced in the infancy narrative (1, 32.35; 2, 49); it occurs here at the beginning of Jesus' Galilean ministry and will reappear in 9, 35 before another major section of Luke's gospel, the travel narrative (9, 51—19, 27). Elsewhere in Luke's writings (4, 18; Acts 10, 38), this incident will be interpreted as a type of anointing of Jesus.

3, 21: *Was praying:* Luke regularly presents Jesus at prayer at important points in his ministry: here at his baptism; at the choice of the Twelve (6, 12); before Peter's confession (9, 18); at the transfiguration (9, 28); when he teaches his disciples to pray (11, 1); at the Last Supper (22, 32); on the Mount of Olives (22, 41); on the cross (23, 46).

3, 22: *You are my beloved Son; with you I am well pleased:* this is the best attested reading in the Greek manuscripts. The Western reading, "You are my Son, this day I have begotten you," is derived from Ps 2, 7.

holy Spirit descended upon him in bod-
ily form like a dove. And a voice came
from heaven, "You are my beloved Son;
with you I am well pleased."

The Genealogy of Jesus.† 23* When
Jesus began his ministry he was about
thirty years of age. He was the son, as
was thought, of Joseph, the son of Heli,
24 the son of Matthat, the son of Levi,
the son of Melchi, the son of Jannai, the
son of Joseph, 25 the son of Mattathias,
the son of Amos, the son of Nahum, the
son of Esli, the son of Naggai, 26 the son
of Maath, the son of Mattathias, the
son of Semein, the son of Josech, the
son of Joda, 27* the son of Joanan,
the son of Rhesa, the son of Zerubbabel,
the son of Shealtiel, the son of Neri,
28 the son of Melchi, the son of Addi, the
son of Cosam, the son of Elmadam, the
son of Er, 29 the son of Joshua, the son
of Eliezer, the son of Jorim, the son of
Matthat, the son of Levi, 30 the son of
Simeon, the son of Judah, the son of Jo-
seph, the son of Jonam, the son of Eli-
akim, 31*† the son of Melea, the son of
Menna, the son of Mattatha, the son of
Nathan, the son of David, 32 the son of
Jesse, the son of Obed, the son of Boaz,
the son of Sala, the son of Nahshon,
33* the son of Amminadab, the son of
Admin, the son of Arni, the son of
Hezron, the son of Perez, the son of Ju-
dah, 34* the son of Jacob, the son of
Isaac, the son of Abraham, the son
of Terah, the son of Nahor, 35 the son of
Serug, the son of Reu, the son of Peleg,
the son of Eber, the son of Shelah,
36* the son of Cainan, the son of Ar-
phaxad, the son of Shem, the son of
Noah, the son of Lamech, 37 the son of
Methuselah, the son of Enoch, the son
of Jared, the son of Mahalaleel, the
son of Cainan, 38 the son of Enos, the son
of Seth, the son of Adam, the son of God.

CHAPTER 4

The Temptation of Jesus.† 1*† Filled
with the holy Spirit, Jesus returned
from the Jordan and was led by the
Spirit into the desert 2*† for forty days,
to be tempted by the devil. He ate noth-
ing during those days, and when they
were over he was hungry. 3 The devil
said to him, "If you are the Son of God,
command this stone to become bread."
4* Jesus answered him, "It is written,
'One does not live by bread alone.' "
5 Then he took him up and showed him
all the kingdoms of the world in a single
instant. 6* The devil said to him, "I shall
give to you all this power and their
glory; for it has been handed over to
me, and I may give it to whomever I
wish. 7 All this will be yours, if you wor-
ship me." 8* Jesus said to him in reply,
"It is written:

> 'You shall worship the Lord, your
> God,
> and him alone shall you serve.' "

9† Then he led him to Jerusalem, made
him stand on the parapet of the temple,
and said to him, "If you are the Son of
God, throw yourself down from here,
10* for it is written:

> 'He will command his angels con-
> cerning you,
> to guard you,'

11* and:

> 'With their hands they will support
> you,
> lest you dash your foot against a
> stone.' "

12* Jesus said to him in reply, "It also
says, 'You shall not put the Lord, your
God, to the test.' " 13*† When the devil
had finished every temptation, he de-
parted from him for a time.

IV: THE MINISTRY IN GALILEE

***The Beginning of the Galilean
Ministry.*** 14*† Jesus returned to Galilee

---

*

23-38: Mt 1, 1-17.
23: 4, 22; Jn 6, 42.
27: 1 Chr 3, 17; Ez 3, 2.
31: 2 Sm 5, 14.
31-32: 1 Sm 16, 1.18.
31-33: Ru 4, 17-22; 1 Chr 2, 1-15.
33: Gn 29, 35; 38, 29.
34: Gn 21, 3; 25, 26; 1 Chr 1, 34; 28, 34.
34-36: Gn 11, 10-26; 1 Chr 1, 24-27.
36-38: Gn 4, 25—5, 32; 1 Chr 1, 1-4.
4, 1-13: Mt 4, 1-11; Mk 1, 12-13.
2: Heb 4, 15.
4: Dt 8, 3.
6: Jer 27, 5; Mt 28, 18.
8: Dt 6, 13.
10: Ps 91, 11.
11: Ps 91, 12.
12: Dt 6, 16; 1 Cor 10, 9.
13: 22, 3; Jn 13, 2.27; Heb 4, 15.
14-15: Mt 4, 12-17; Mk 1, 14-15.
14: 5, 15; Mt 3, 16.

---

†

3, 23-38: Whereas Mt 1, 2 begins the genealogy of Jesus with Abraham to emphasize Jesus' bonds with the people of Israel, Luke's universalism leads him to trace the descent of Jesus beyond Israel to Adam and beyond that to God (38) to stress again Jesus' divine sonship.

3, 31: *The son of Nathan, the son of David:* in keeping with Jesus' prophetic role in Lk and Acts (e.g., 7, 16.39; 9, 8; 13, 33; 24, 19; Acts 3, 22-23; 7, 37) Luke traces Jesus' Davidic ancestry through the prophet Nathan (see 2 Sm 7, 2) rather than through King Solomon, as Mt 1, 6-7.

4, 1-13: See the note on Mt 4, 1-11.

4, 1: *Filled with the holy Spirit:* as a result of the descent of the Spirit upon him at his baptism (3, 21-22), Jesus is now equipped to overcome the devil. Just as the Spirit is prominent at this early stage of Jesus' ministry (1.14.18), so too it will be at the beginning of the period of the church in Acts (Acts 1, 4; 2, 4.17).

4, 2: *For forty days:* the mention of forty days recalls the forty years of the wilderness wanderings of the Israelites during the Exodus (Dt 8, 2).

4, 9: *To Jerusalem:* the Lucan order of the temptations concludes on the parapet of the temple in Jerusalem, the city of destiny in Luke-Acts. It is in Jerusalem that Jesus will ultimately face his destiny (9, 51; 13, 33).

4, 13: *For a time:* the devil's opportune time will occur before the passion and death of Jesus (Lk 22, 3.31-32.53).

4, 14: *News of him spread:* a Lucan theme; see v 37; 5, 15; 7, 17.

in the power of the Spirit, and news of
him spread throughout the whole re-
gion. 15 He taught in their synagogues
and was praised by all.

***The Rejection at Nazareth.*†** 16*† He
came to Nazareth, where he had grown
up, and went according to his custom
into the synagogue on the sabbath day.
He stood up to read 17 and was handed
a scroll of the prophet Isaiah. He un-
rolled the scroll and found the passage
where it was written:

18*†"The Spirit of the Lord is upon me,
because he has anointed me
to bring glad tidings to the poor.
He has sent me to proclaim liberty
to captives
and recovery of sight to the blind,
to let the oppressed go free,
19 and to proclaim a year acceptable
to the Lord."

20 Rolling up the scroll, he handed it
back to the attendant and sat down, and
the eyes of all in the synagogue looked
intently at him. 21† He said to them,
"Today this scripture passage is ful-
filled in your hearing." 22* And all spoke
highly of him and were amazed at the
gracious words that came from his
mouth. They also asked, "Isn't this the
son of Joseph?" 23† He said to them,
"Surely you will quote me this proverb,
'Physician, cure yourself,' and say, 'Do
here in your native place the things that
we heard were done in Capernaum.'"
24 And he said, "Amen, I say to you, no
prophet is accepted in his own native
place. 25*† Indeed, I tell you, there were
many widows in Israel in the days of
Elijah when the sky was closed for three
and a half years and a severe famine
spread over the entire land. 26*† It was
to none of these that Elijah was sent,
but only to a widow in Zarephath in the
land of Sidon. 27* Again, there were
many lepers in Israel during the time
of Elisha the prophet; yet not one of
them was cleansed, but only Naaman
the Syrian." 28 When the people in the
synagogue heard this, they were all
filled with fury. 29 They rose up, drove
him out of the town, and led him to the
brow of the hill on which their town had
been built, to hurl him down headlong.
30 But he passed through the midst of
them and went away.

***The Cure of a Demoniac.*†** 31* Jesus
then went down to Capernaum, a town
of Galilee. He taught them on the sab-
bath, 32* and they were astonished at his
teaching because he spoke with author-
ity. 33* In the synagogue there was a
man with the spirit of an unclean de-
mon, and he cried out in a loud voice,
34*† "Ha! What have you to do with us,
Jesus of Nazareth? Have you come to
destroy us? I know who you are—the
Holy One of God!" 35 Jesus rebuked him
and said, "Be quiet! Come out of him!"
Then the demon threw the man down
in front of them and came out of him
without doing him any harm. 36 They
were all amazed and said to one an-
other, "What is there about his word?
For with authority and power he com-
mands the unclean spirits, and they

LUKE

*

16-30: Mt 13, 53-58; Mk 6, 1-6.
18-19: Is 61, 1-2; 58, 6.
22: 3, 23; Jn 6, 42.
25: 1 Kgs 17, 1-7; 18, 1; Jas 5, 17.
26: 1 Kgs 17, 9.
27: 2 Kgs 5, 1-14.
31-37: Mk 1, 21-28.
31: Mt 4, 13; Jn 2, 12.
32: Mt 7, 28-29.
33-34: 8, 28; Mt 8, 29; Mk 1, 23-24; 5, 7.
34: 4, 41; Jn 6, 69.

†

4, 16-30: Luke has transposed to the beginning of Jesus' ministry an incident from his Marcan source, which situated it near the end of the Galilean ministry (Mk 6, 1-6a). In doing so, Luke turns the initial admiration (22) and subsequent rejection of Jesus (28-29) into a foreshadowing of the whole future ministry of Jesus. Moreover, the rejection of Jesus in his own hometown hints at the greater rejection of him by Israel (Acts 13, 46).

4, 16: *According to his custom:* Jesus' practice of regularly attending synagogue is carried on by the early Christians' practice of meeting in the temple (Acts 2, 46; 3, 1; 5, 12).

4, 18: *The Spirit of the Lord is upon me, because he has anointed me:* see the note on 3, 21-22. As this incident develops, Jesus is portrayed as a prophet whose ministry is compared to that of the prophets Elijah and Elisha. Prophetic anointings are known in first-century Palestinian Judaism from the Qumran literature that speaks of prophets as God's anointed ones. *To bring glad tidings to the poor:* more than any other gospel writer Luke is concerned with Jesus' attitude toward the economically and socially poor (see 6, 20.24; 12, 16-21; 14, 12-14; 16, 19-26; 19, 8). At times, the poor in Luke's gospel are associated with the downtrodden, the oppressed and afflicted, the forgotten and the neglected (18; 6, 20-22; 7, 22; 14, 12-14), and it is they who accept Jesus' message of salvation.

4, 21: *Today this scripture passage is fulfilled in your hearing:* this sermon inaugurates the time of fulfillment of Old Testament prophecy. Luke presents the ministry of Jesus as fulfilling Old Testament hopes and expectations (7, 22); for Luke, even Jesus' suffering, death, and resurrection are done in fulfillment of the scriptures (24, 25-27.44-46; Acts 3, 18).

4, 23: *The things that we heard were done in Capernaum:* Luke's source for this incident reveals an awareness of an earlier ministry of Jesus in Capernaum that Luke has not yet made use of because of his transposition of this Nazareth episode to the beginning of Jesus' Galilean ministry. It is possible that by use of the future tense *you will quote me . . .*, Jesus is being portrayed as a prophet.

4, 25-26: The references to Elijah and Elisha serve several purposes in this episode: they emphasize Luke's portrait of Jesus as a prophet like Elijah and Elisha; they help to explain why the initial admiration of the people turns to rejection; and they provide the scriptural justification for the future Christian mission to the Gentiles.

4, 26: *A widow in Zarephath in the land of Sidon:* like Naaman the Syrian in v 27, a non-Israelite becomes the object of the prophet's ministry.

4, 31-44: The next several incidents in Jesus' ministry take place in Capernaum and are based on Luke's source, Mk 1, 21-39. To the previous portrait of Jesus as prophet (16-30) they now add a presentation of him as teacher (31-32), exorcist (32-37.41), healer (38-40), and proclaimer of God's kingdom (43).

4, 34: *What have you to do with us?:* see the note on Jn 2, 4. *Have you come to destroy us?:* the question reflects the current belief that before the day of the Lord control over humanity would be wrested from the evil spirits, evil destroyed, and God's authority over humanity reestablished. The synoptic gospel tradition presents Jesus carrying out this task.

come out." 37 And news of him spread
everywhere in the surrounding region.

The Cure of Simon's Mother-in-Law.
38*† After he left the synagogue, he en-
tered the house of Simon. Simon's
mother-in-law was afflicted with a se-
vere fever, and they interceded with
him about her. 39 He stood over her, re-
buked the fever, and it left her. She got
up immediately and waited on them.

Other Healings. 40* At sunset, all who
had people sick with various diseases
brought them to him. He laid his hands
on each of them and cured them.
41*† And demons also came out from
many, shouting, "You are the Son of
God." But he rebuked them and did not
allow them to speak because they knew
that he was the Messiah.

Jesus Leaves Capernaum. 42*† At
daybreak, Jesus left and went to a de-
serted place. The crowds went looking
for him, and when they came to him,
they tried to prevent him from leaving
them. 43* But he said to them, "To the
other towns also I must proclaim the
good news of the kingdom of God, be-
cause for this purpose I have been
sent." 44† And he was preaching in the
synagogues of Judea.

CHAPTER 5

The Call of Simon the Fisherman.†
1* While the crowd was pressing in on
Jesus and listening to the word of God,
he was standing by the Lake of Gennes-
aret. 2 He saw two boats there alongside
the lake; the fishermen had disem-
barked and were washing their nets.
3 Getting into one of the boats, the one
belonging to Simon, he asked him to put
out a short distance from the shore.
Then he sat down and taught the crowds
from the boat. 4* After he had finished
speaking, he said to Simon, "Put out
into deep water and lower your nets for
a catch." 5 Simon said in reply, "Master,
we have worked hard all night and have
caught nothing, but at your command
I will lower the nets." 6 When they had
done this, they caught a great number
of fish and their nets were tearing.
7 They signaled to their partners in the
other boat to come to help them. They
came and filled both boats so that they
were in danger of sinking. 8 When Si-
mon Peter saw this, he fell at the knees
of Jesus and said, "Depart from me,
Lord, for I am a sinful man." 9 For as-
tonishment at the catch of fish they had
made seized him and all those with him,
10* and likewise James and John, the
sons of Zebedee, who were partners of
Simon. Jesus said to Simon, "Do not be
afraid; from now on you will be catching
men." 11*† When they brought their
boats to the shore, they left everything
and followed him.

The Cleansing of a Leper. 12*† Now
there was a man full of leprosy in one
of the towns where he was; and when
he saw Jesus, he fell prostrate, pleaded
with him, and said, "Lord, if you wish,
you can make me clean." 13 Jesus
stretched out his hand, touched him,
and said, "I do will it. Be made clean."
And the leprosy left him immediately.
14*† Then he ordered him not to tell
anyone, but "Go, show yourself to the
priest and offer for your cleansing what
Moses prescribed; that will be proof for
them." 15 The report about him spread
all the more, and great crowds assem-

---

*

38-39: Mt 8, 14-15; Mk 1, 29-31.
40-41: Mt 8, 16; Mk 1, 32-34.
41: 4, 34; Mt 8, 29; Mk 3, 11-12.
42-44: Mk 1, 35-39.
43: 8, 1; Mk 1, 14-15.
5, 1-11: Mt 4, 18-22; Mk 1, 16-20.
1-3: Mt 13, 1-2; Mk 2, 13; 3, 9-10; 4, 1-2.
4-9: Jn 21, 1-11.
10: Jer 16, 16.
11: Mt 19, 27.
12-16: Mt 8, 2-4; Mk 1, 40-45.
14: 8, 56; Lv 14, 2-32; Mk 7, 36.

---

†

4, 38: *The house of Simon:* because of Luke's arrangement of material, the reader has not yet been introduced to Simon (cf Mk 1, 16-18.29-31). Situated as it is before the call of Simon (5, 1-11), it helps the reader to understand Simon's eagerness to do what Jesus says (5, 5) and to follow him (5, 11).

4, 41: *They knew that he was the Messiah:* that is, the Christ (see the note on 2, 11).

4, 42: *They tried to prevent him from leaving them:* the reaction of these strangers in Capernaum is presented in contrast to the reactions of those in his hometown who rejected him (28-30).

4, 44: *In the synagogues of Judea:* instead of *Judea,* which is the best reading of the manuscript tradition, the Byzantine text tradition and other manuscripts read "Galilee," a reading that harmonizes Lk with Mt 4, 23 and Mk 1, 39. Up to this point Luke has spoken only of a ministry of Jesus in Galilee. Luke may be using *Judea* to refer to the land of Israel, the territory of the Jews, and not to a specific portion of it.

5, 1-11: This incident has been transposed from his source, Mk 1, 16-20, which places it immediately after Jesus makes his appearance in Galilee. By this transposition Luke uses this example of Simon's acceptance of Jesus to counter the earlier rejection of him by his hometown people, and since several incidents dealing with Jesus' power and authority have already been narrated, Luke creates a plausible context for the acceptance of Jesus by Simon and his partners. Many commentators have noted the similarity between the wondrous catch of fish reported here (4-9) and the post-resurrectional appearance of Jesus in Jn 21, 1-11. There are traces in Luke's story that the post-resurrectional context is the original one: in v 8 Simon addresses Jesus as *Lord* (a post-resurrectional title for Jesus—see 24, 34; Acts 2, 36—that has been read back into the historical ministry of Jesus) and recognizes himself as a sinner (an appropriate recognition for one who has denied knowing Jesus—22, 54-62). As used by Luke, the incident looks forward to Peter's leadership in Luke-Acts (6, 14; 9, 20; 22, 31-32; 24, 34; Acts 1, 15; 2, 14-40; 10, 11-18; 15, 7-12) and symbolizes the future success of Peter as fisherman (Acts 2, 41).

5, 11: *They left everything:* in Mk 1, 16-20 and Mt 4, 18-22 the fishermen who follow Jesus leave their nets and their father; in Luke, they leave *everything* (see also 28; 12, 33; 14, 33; 18, 22), an indication of Luke's theme of complete detachment from material possessions.

5, 12: *Full of leprosy:* see the note on Mk 1, 40.

5, 14: *Show yourself to the priest . . . what Moses prescribed:* this is a reference to Lv 14, 2-9 that gives detailed instructions for the purification of one who had been a victim of leprosy and thereby excluded from contact with others (see Lv 13, 45-46.49; Nm 5, 2-3). *That will be proof for them:* see the note on Mt 8, 4.

bled to listen to him and to be cured of
their ailments, 16* but he would with-
draw to deserted places to pray.
The Healing of a Paralytic.† 17*† One
day as Jesus was teaching, Pharisees
and teachers of the law were sitting
there who had come from every village
of Galilee and Judea and Jerusalem,
and the power of the Lord was with him
for healing. 18 And some men brought
on a stretcher a man who was para-
lyzed; they were trying to bring him in
and set [him] in his presence. 19† But
not finding a way to bring him in be-
cause of the crowd, they went up on the
roof and lowered him on the stretcher
through the tiles into the middle in front
of Jesus. 20† When he saw their faith,
he said, "As for you, your sins are for-
given." 21*† Then the scribes and Phari-
sees began to ask themselves, "Who is
this who speaks blasphemies? Who but
God alone can forgive sins?" 22* Jesus
knew their thoughts and said to them
in reply, "What are you thinking in your
hearts? 23 Which is easier, to say, 'Your
sins are forgiven,' or to say, 'Rise and
walk'? 24*† But that you may know that
the Son of Man has authority on earth
to forgive sins"—he said to the man who
was paralyzed, "I say to you, rise, pick
up your stretcher, and go home."
25 He stood up immediately before them,
picked up what he had been lying on,
and went home, glorifying God. 26 Then
astonishment seized them all and they
glorified God, and, struck with awe,
they said, "We have seen incredible
things today."
The Call of Levi. 27* After this he
went out and saw a tax collector named
Levi sitting at the customs post. He said
to him, "Follow me." 28† And leaving
everything behind, he got up and fol-
lowed him. 29* Then Levi gave a great
banquet for him in his house, and a
large crowd of tax collectors and others
were at table with them. 30 The Phari-
sees and their scribes complained to his
disciples, saying, "Why do you eat and
drink with tax collectors and sinners?"
31 Jesus said to them in reply, "Those
who are healthy do not need a physi-
cian, but the sick do. 32 I have not come
to call the righteous to repentance but
sinners."
The Question about Fasting. 33* And
they said to him, "The disciples of John
fast often and offer prayers, and the
disciples of the Pharisees do the same;
but yours eat and drink." 34† Jesus an-
swered them, "Can you make the wed-
ding guests fast while the bridegroom
is with them? 35 But the days will come,
and when the bridegroom is taken away
from them, then they will fast in those
days." 36† And he also told them a para-
ble. "No one tears a piece from a new
cloak to patch an old one. Otherwise,
he will tear the new and the piece from
it will not match the old cloak.
37 Likewise, no one pours new wine into
old wineskins. Otherwise, the new wine
will burst the skins, and it will be spilled,
and the skins will be ruined. 38 Rather,
new wine must be poured into fresh
wineskins. 39† [And] no one who has
been drinking old wine desires new, for
he says, 'The old is good.' "

LUKE

CHAPTER 6

Debates about the Sabbath.† 1* While
he was going through a field of grain
on a sabbath, his disciples were picking
the heads of grain, rubbing them in
their hands, and eating them. 2 Some
Pharisees said, "Why are you doing
what is unlawful on the sabbath?"
3* Jesus said to them in reply, "Have
you not read what David did when he
and those [who were] with him were
hungry? 4*† [How] he went into the
house of God, took the bread of offering,
which only the priests could lawfully
eat, ate of it, and shared it with his com-

*

16: Mk 1, 35.
17-26: Mt 9, 1-8; Mk 2, 1-12.
21: 7, 49; Is 43, 25.
22: 6, 8; 9, 47.
24-25: Jn 5, 8-9.27.
27-32: Mt 9, 9-13; Mk 2, 13-17.
29-30: 15, 1-2.
33-39: Mt 9, 14-17; Mk 2, 18-22.
6, 1-5: Mt 12, 1-8; Mk 2, 23-28.
1: Dt 23, 26.
3-4: 1 Sm 21, 1-6.
4: Lv 24, 5-9.

†

5, 17—6, 11: From his Marcan source, Luke now introduces a series of controversies with Pharisees: controversy over Jesus' power to forgive sins (17-26); controversy over his eating and drinking with tax collectors and sinners (27-32); controversy over not fasting (33-36); and finally two episodes narrating controversies over observance of the sabbath (1-11).

5, 17: *Pharisees:* see the note on Mt 3, 7.

5, 19: *Through the tiles:* Luke has adapted the story found in Mk to his non-Palestinian audience by changing "opened up the roof" (Mk 2, 4, a reference to Palestinian straw and clay roofs) to *through the tiles,* a detail that reflects the Hellenistic Greco-Roman house with tiled roof.

5, 20: *As for you, your sins are forgiven:* literally, "O man, your sins are forgiven you." The connection between the forgiveness of sins and the cure of the paralytic reflects the belief of first-century Palestine (based on the Old Testament: Ex 20, 5; Dt 5, 9) that sickness and infirmity are the result of sin, one's own or that of one's ancestors (see also 13, 2; Jn 5, 14; 9, 2).

5, 21: *The scribes:* see the note on Mk 2, 6.

5, 24: See the notes on Mt 9, 6 and Mk 2, 10.

5, 28: *Leaving everything behind:* see the note on 5, 11.

5, 34-35: See the notes on Mt 9, 15 and Mk 2, 19.

5, 34: *Wedding guests:* literally, "sons of the bridal chamber."

5, 36-39: See the notes on Mt 9, 16-17 and Mk 2, 19.

5, 39: *The old is good:* this saying is meant to be ironic and offers an explanation for the rejection by some of the new wine that Jesus offers: satisfaction with old forms will prevent one from sampling the new.

6, 1-11: The two episodes recounted here deal with gathering grain and healing, both of which were forbidden on the sabbath. In his defense of his disciples' conduct and his own charitable deed, Jesus argues that satisfying human needs such as hunger and performing works of mercy take precedence even over the sacred sabbath rest. See also the notes on Mt 12, 1-14 and Mk 2, 25-26.

6, 4: *The bread of offering:* see the note on Mt 12, 5-6.

panions." 5 Then he said to them, "The
Son of Man is lord of the sabbath."
6* On another sabbath he went into
the synagogue and taught, and there
was a man there whose right hand was
withered. 7* The scribes and the Phari-
sees watched him closely to see if he
would cure on the sabbath so that they
might discover a reason to accuse him.
8* But he realized their intentions and
said to the man with the withered hand,
"Come up and stand before us." And
he rose and stood there. 9 Then Jesus
said to them, "I ask you, is it lawful to
do good on the sabbath rather than to
do evil, to save life rather than to de-
stroy it?" 10 Looking around at them all,
he then said to him, "Stretch out your
hand." He did so and his hand was re-
stored. 11 But they became enraged and
discussed together what they might do
to Jesus.
The Mission of the Twelve. † 12*† In
those days he departed to the moun-
tain to pray, and he spent the night in
prayer to God. 13† When day came, he
called his disciples to himself, and from
them he chose Twelve, whom he also
named apostles: 14*† Simon, whom he
named Peter, and his brother Andrew,
James, John, Philip, Bartholomew,
15† Matthew, Thomas, James the son of
Alphaeus, Simon who was called a
Zealot, 16† and Judas the son of James,
and Judas Iscariot, who became a trai-
tor.
Ministering to a Great Multitude.
17*† And he came down with them and
stood on a stretch of level ground. A
great crowd of his disciples and a large
number of the people from all Judea
and Jerusalem and the coastal region
of Tyre and Sidon 18 came to hear him
and to be healed of their diseases; and
even those who were tormented by un-
clean spirits were cured. 19 Everyone in
the crowd sought to touch him because
power came forth from him and healed
them all.
Sermon on the Plain. † 20*† And rais-
ing his eyes toward his disciples he said:

"Blessed are you who are poor,
for the kingdom of God is yours.
21* Blessed are you who are now hun-
gry,
for you will be satisfied.
Blessed are you who are now weep-
ing,
for you will laugh.
22* Blessed are you when people hate
you,
and when they exclude and insult
you,
and denounce your name as evil
on account of the Son of Man.
23* Rejoice and leap for joy on that day!
Behold, your reward will be
great in heaven. For their an-

---

*

6-11: Mt 12, 9-14; Mk 3, 1-6.
7: 14, 1.
8: 5, 22; 9, 47.
12-16: Mt 10, 1-4; Mk 3, 13-19.
14-16: Acts 1, 13.
17-19: Mt 4, 23-25; Mk 3, 7-10.
20-26: Mt 5, 1-12.
21: Ps 126, 5-6; Is 61, 3; Jer 31, 25; Rv 7, 16-17.
22: Jn 15, 19; 16, 2; 1 Pt 4, 14.
23: 11, 47-48; 2 Chr 36, 16; Mt 23, 30-31.

†

6, 12-16: See the notes on Mt 10, 1—11, 1 and Mk 3, 14-15.

6, 12: *Spent the night in prayer:* see the note on 3, 21.

6, 13: *He chose Twelve:* the identification of this group as the *Twelve* is a part of early Christian tradition (see 1 Cor 15, 5), and in Mt and Lk, the Twelve are associated with the twelve tribes of Israel (22, 29-30; Mt 19, 28). After the fall of Judas from his position among the Twelve, the need is felt on the part of the early community to reconstitute this group before the Christian mission begins at Pentecost (Acts 1, 15-26). From Luke's perspective, they are an important group who because of their association with Jesus from the time of his baptism to his ascension (Acts 1, 21-22) provide the continuity between the historical Jesus and the church of Luke's day and who as the original eyewitnesses guarantee the fidelity of the church's beliefs and practices to the teachings of Jesus (1, 1-4). *Whom he also named apostles:* only Luke among the gospel writers attributes to Jesus the bestowal of the name *apostles* upon the Twelve. See the note on Mt 10, 2-4. "Apostle" becomes a technical term in early Christianity for a missionary sent out to preach the word of God. Although Luke seems to want to restrict the title to the Twelve (only in Acts 4, 4.14 are Paul and Barnabas termed apostles), other places in the New Testament show an awareness that the term was more widely applied (1 Cor 15, 5-7; Gal 1, 19; 1 Cor 1, 1; 9, 1; Rom 16, 7).

6, 14: *Simon, whom he named Peter:* see the note on Mk 3, 16.

6, 15: *Simon who was called a Zealot:* the Zealots were the instigators of the First Revolt of Palestinian Jews against Rome in A.D. 66-70. Because the existence of the Zealots as a distinct group during the lifetime of Jesus is the subject of debate, the meaning of the identification of Simon as a Zealot is unclear.

6, 16: *Judas Iscariot:* the name *Iscariot* may mean "man from Kerioth."

6, 17: *The coastal region of Tyre and Sidon:* not only Jews from Judea and Jerusalem, but even Gentiles from outside Palestine come to hear Jesus (see 2, 31-32; 3, 6; 4, 24-27).

6, 20-49: Luke's "Sermon on the Plain" is the counterpart to Mt's "Sermon on the Mount" (Mt 5, 1—7, 27). It is addressed to the disciples of Jesus, and, like the sermon in Mt, it begins with beatitudes (20-22) and ends with the parable of the two houses (46-49). Almost all the words of Jesus reported by Lk are found in Mt's version, but because Mt includes sayings that were related to specifically Jewish Christian problems (e.g., Mt 5, 17-20; 6, 1-8.16-18) that Luke did not find appropriate for his predominantly Gentile Christian audience, the "Sermon on the Mount" is considerably longer. Lk's sermon may be outlined as follows: an introduction consisting of blessings and woes (20-26); the love of one's enemies (27-36); the demands of loving one's neighbor (37-42); good deeds as proof of one's goodness (43-45); a parable illustrating the result of listening to and acting on the words of Jesus (46-49). At the core of the sermon is Jesus' teaching on the love of one's enemies (27-36) that has as its source of motivation God's graciousness and compassion for all humanity (35-36) and Jesus' teaching on the love of one's neighbor (37-42) that is characterized by forgiveness and generosity.

6, 20-26: The introductory portion of the sermon consists of blessings and woes that address the real economic and social conditions of humanity (the poor—the rich; the hungry—the satisfied; those grieving—those laughing; the outcast—the socially acceptable). By contrast, Matthew emphasizes the religious and spiritual values of disciples in the kingdom inaugurated by Jesus ("poor in spirit," 5, 5; "hunger and thirst for righteousness," 5, 6). In the sermon, *blessed* extols the fortunate condition of persons who are favored with the blessings of God; the woes, addressed as they are to the disciples of Jesus, threaten God's profound displeasure on those so blinded by their present fortunate situation that they do not recognize and appreciate the real values of God's kingdom. In all the blessings and woes, the present condition of the persons addressed will be reversed in the future.

cestors treated the prophets in
the same way.
24* But woe to you who are rich,
for you have received your conso-
lation.
25* But woe to you who are filled now,
for you will be hungry.
Woe to you who laugh now,
for you will grieve and weep.
26* Woe to you when all speak well of
you,
for their ancestors treated the
false prophets in this way.

Love of Enemies.† 27* "But to you
who hear I say, love your enemies, do
good to those who hate you, 28* bless
those who curse you, pray for those who
mistreat you. 29 To the person who
strikes you on one cheek, offer the other
one as well, and from the person who
takes your cloak, do not withhold even
your tunic. 30 Give to everyone who asks
of you, and from the one who takes what
is yours do not demand it back. 31* Do
to others as you would have them do
to you. 32 For if you love those who love
you, what credit is that to you? Even
sinners love those who love them.
33 And if you do good to those who do
good to you, what credit is that to you?
Even sinners do the same. 34* If you
lend money to those from whom you ex-
pect repayment, what credit [is] that to
you? Even sinners lend to sinners, and
get back the same amount. 35* But
rather, love your enemies and do good
to them, and lend expecting nothing
back; then your reward will be great
and you will be children of the Most
High, for he himself is kind to the un-
grateful and the wicked. 36 Be merciful,
just as [also] your Father is merciful.

Judging Others.† 37* "Stop judg-
ing and you will not be judged. Stop
condemning and you will not be con-
demned. Forgive and you will be for-
given. 38* Give and gifts will be given to
you; a good measure, packed together,
shaken down, and overflowing, will be
poured into your lap. For the measure
with which you measure will in return
be measured out to you." 39* And he told
them a parable, "Can a blind person
guide a blind person? Will not both fall
into a pit? 40* No disciple is superior to
the teacher; but when fully trained, ev-
ery disciple will be like his teacher.
41 Why do you notice the splinter in your
brother's eye, but do not perceive the
wooden beam in your own? 42 How can
you say to your brother, 'Brother, let
me remove that splinter in your eye,'
when you do not even notice the wooden
beam in your own eye? You hypocrite!
Remove the wooden beam from your
eye first; then you will see clearly to re-
move the splinter in your brother's eye.

A Tree Known by Its Fruit.† 43* "A
good tree does not bear rotten fruit, nor
does a rotten tree bear good fruit.
44 For every tree is known by its own
fruit. For people do not pick figs from
thornbushes, nor do they gather grapes
from brambles. 45 A good person out of
the store of goodness in his heart pro-
duces good, but an evil person out of a
store of evil produces evil; for from the
fullness of the heart the mouth speaks.

The Two Foundations. 46* "Why do
you call me, 'Lord, Lord,' but not do
what I command? 47*† I will show you
what someone is like who comes to me,
listens to my words, and acts on them.
48 That one is like a person building a
house, who dug deeply and laid the
foundation on rock; when the flood
came, the river burst against that house
but could not shake it because it had
been well built. 49 But the one who lis-
tens and does not act is like a person
who built a house on the ground without
a foundation. When the river burst
against it, it collapsed at once and was
completely destroyed."

CHAPTER 7

The Healing of a Centurion's Slave.†
1*† When he had finished all his words
to the people, he entered Capernaum.
2† A centurion there had a slave who
was ill and about to die, and he was
valuable to him. 3 When he heard about
Jesus, he sent elders of the Jews to him,

*

24: Jas 5, 1.
25: Is 65, 13-14.
26: Jas 4, 4.
27-36: Mt 5, 38-48.
27: Prv 25, 21; Rom 12, 20-21.
28: Rom 12, 14; 1 Pt 3, 9.
31: Mt 7, 12.
34: Dt 15, 7-8.
35: Lv 25, 35-36.
37-42: Mt 7, 1-5.
37: Mt 6, 14; Jas 2, 13.
38: Mk 4, 24.
39: Mt 15, 14; 23, 16-17.24.
40: Mt 10, 24-25; Jn 13, 16; 15, 20.
43-45: Mt 7, 16-20; 12, 33.35.
46: Mt 7, 21; Rom 2, 13; Jas 1, 22.
47-49: Mt 7, 24-27.
7, 1-10: Mt 8, 5-13; Jn 4, 43-54.

†

6, 27-36: See the notes on Mt 5, 43-48 and 5, 48.
6, 37-42: See the notes on Mt 7, 1-12; 7, 1; 7, 5.
6, 43-46: See the notes on Mt 7, 15-20 and 12, 33.
6, 47-49: See the note on Mt 7, 24-27.

7, 1—8, 3: The episodes in this section present a series of reactions to the Galilean ministry of Jesus and reflect some of Luke's particular interests: the faith of a Gentile (1-10); the prophet Jesus' concern for a widowed mother (11-17); the ministry of Jesus directed to the afflicted and unfortunate of Is 61, 1 (18-23); the relation between John and Jesus and their role in God's plan for salvation (24-35); a forgiven sinner's manifestation of love (36-50); the association of women with the ministry of Jesus (8, 1-3).

7, 1-10: This story about the faith of the centurion, a Gentile who cherishes the Jewish nation (5), prepares for the story in Acts of the conversion by Peter of the Roman centurion Cornelius who is similarly described as one who is generous to the Jewish nation (Acts 10, 2). See also Acts 10, 34-35 in the speech of Peter: "God shows no partiality . . . the person who fears him and acts righteously is acceptable to him." See also the notes on Mt 8, 5-13 and Jn 4, 43-54.

7, 2: *A centurion:* see the note on Mt 8, 5.

asking him to come and save the life
of his slave. 4 They approached Jesus
and strongly urged him to come, saying,
"He deserves to have you do this for
him, 5 for he loves our nation and he
built the synagogue for us." 6† And Je-
sus went with them, but when he was
only a short distance from the house,
the centurion sent friends to tell him,
"Lord, do not trouble yourself, for I am
not worthy to have you enter under my
roof. 7 Therefore, I did not consider my-
self worthy to come to you; but say the
word and let my servant be healed.
8 For I too am a person subject to au-
thority, with soldiers subject to me. And
I say to one, 'Go,' and he goes; and to
another, 'Come here,' and he comes;
and to my slave, 'Do this,' and he does
it." 9 When Jesus heard this he was
amazed at him and, turning, said to the
crowd following him, "I tell you, not
even in Israel have I found such faith."
10 When the messengers returned to the
house, they found the slave in good
health.

Raising of the Widow's Son.† 11* Soon
afterward he journeyed to a city called
Nain, and his disciples and a large
crowd accompanied him. 12* As he drew
near to the gate of the city, a man who
had died was being carried out, the only
son of his mother, and she was a widow.
A large crowd from the city was with
her. 13 When the Lord saw her, he was
moved with pity for her and said to her,
"Do not weep." 14 He stepped forward
and touched the coffin; at this the bear-
ers halted, and he said, "Young man, I
tell you, arise!" 15* The dead man sat
up and began to speak, and Jesus gave
him to his mother. 16* Fear seized them
all, and they glorified God, exclaiming,
"A great prophet has arisen in our
midst," and "God has visited his peo-
ple." 17 This report about him spread
through the whole of Judea and in all
the surrounding region.

The Messengers from John the Baptist.† 18* The disciples of John told
him about all these things. John sum-
moned two of his disciples 19* and sent
them to the Lord to ask, "Are you the
one who is to come, or should we look
for another?" 20 When the men came to
him, they said, "John the Baptist has
sent us to you to ask, 'Are you the one
who is to come, or should we look for
another?' " 21 At that time he cured
many of their diseases, sufferings, and
evil spirits; he also granted sight to
many who were blind. 22* And he said
to them in reply, "Go and tell John what
you have seen and heard: the blind re-
gain their sight, the lame walk, lepers
are cleansed, the deaf hear, the dead
are raised, the poor have the good news
proclaimed to them. 23† And blessed is
the one who takes no offense at me."

Jesus' Testimony to John.† 24* When
the messengers of John had left, Jesus
began to speak to the crowds about
John. "What did you go out to the desert
to see—a reed swayed by the wind?
25 Then what did you go out to see?
Someone dressed in fine garments?
Those who dress luxuriously and live
sumptuously are found in royal palaces.
26* Then what did you go out to see? A
prophet? Yes, I tell you, and more than
a prophet. 27* This is the one about
whom scripture says:

> 'Behold, I am sending my messenger ahead of you,
> he will prepare your way before you.'

28 I tell you, among those born of
women, no one is greater than John; yet
the least in the kingdom of God is
greater than he." 29* (All the people
who listened, including the tax collec-
tors, and who were baptized with the
baptism of John, acknowledged the
righteousness of God; 30 but the Phari-
sees and scholars of the law, who were
not baptized by him, rejected the plan
of God for themselves.)

31*† "Then to what shall I compare
the people of this generation? What are
they like? 32 They are like children who

*

11-17: 4, 25-26; 1 Kgs 17, 17-24.
12: 8, 42; 1 Kgs 17, 17.
15: 1 Kgs 17, 23; 2 Kgs 4, 36.
16: 1, 68; 19, 44.
18-23: Mt 11, 2-6.
19: Mal 3, 1; Rv 1, 4.8; 4, 8.
22: 4, 18; Is 35, 5-6; 61, 1.
24-30: Mt 11, 7-15.
26: 1, 76.
27: Is 40, 3 / Mal 3, 1.
29-30: 3, 7.12; Mt 21, 32.
31-35: Mt 11, 16-19.

†

7, 6: *I am not worthy to have you enter under my roof:* to enter the house of a Gentile was considered unclean for a Jew; cf Acts 10, 28.

7, 11-17: In the previous incident Jesus' power was displayed for a Gentile whose servant was dying; in this episode it is displayed toward a widowed mother whose only son has already died. Jesus' power over death prepares for his reply to John's disciples in v 22: "the dead are raised." This resuscitation in alluding to the prophet Elijah's resurrection of the only son of a widow of Zarephath (1 Kgs 7, 8-24) leads to the reaction of the crowd: "A great prophet has arisen in our midst" (16).

7, 18-23: In answer to John's question, *Are you the one who is to come?*—a probable reference to the return of the fiery prophet of reform, Elijah, "before the day of the Lord comes, the great and terrible day" (Mal 3, 23)—Jesus responds that his role is rather to bring the blessings spoken of in Is 61, 1 to the oppressed and neglected of society (22; cf 4, 18).

7, 23: *Blessed is the one who takes no offense at me:* this beatitude is pronounced on the person who recognizes Jesus' true identity in spite of previous expectations of what "the one who is to come" would be like.

7, 24-30: In his testimony to John, Jesus reveals his understanding of the relationship between them: John is the precursor of Jesus (27); John is the messenger spoken of in Mal 3, 1 who in Mal 3, 23 is identified as Elijah. Taken with the previous episode, it can be seen that Jesus identifies John as precisely the person John envisioned Jesus to be: the Elijah who prepares the way for the coming of the day of the Lord.

7, 31-35: See the note on Mt 11, 16-19.

sit in the marketplace and call to one
another,

> 'We played the flute for you, but you
> did not dance.
> We sang a dirge, but you did not
> weep.'

33 For John the Baptist came neither
eating food nor drinking wine, and you
said, 'He is possessed by a demon.'
34* The Son of Man came eating and
drinking and you said, 'Look, he is a
glutton and a drunkard, a friend of tax
collectors and sinners.' 35 But wisdom is
vindicated by all her children."

The Pardon of the Sinful Woman.†
36*† A Pharisee invited him to dine with
him, and he entered the Pharisee's
house and reclined at table. 37* Now
there was a sinful woman in the city
who learned that he was at table in the
house of the Pharisee. Bringing an ala-
baster flask of ointment, 38 she stood be-
hind him at his feet weeping and began
to bathe his feet with her tears. Then
she wiped them with her hair, kissed
them, and anointed them with the oint-
ment. 39 When the Pharisee who had in-
vited him saw this he said to himself,
"If this man were a prophet, he would
know who and what sort of woman this
is who is touching him, that she is a sin-
ner." 40 Jesus said to him in reply, "Si-
mon, I have something to say to you."
"Tell me, teacher," he said. 41† "Two
people were in debt to a certain cred-
itor; one owed five hundred days' wages
and the other owed fifty. 42 Since they
were unable to repay the debt, he for-
gave it for both. Which of them will love
him more?" 43 Simon said in reply, "The
one, I suppose, whose larger debt was
forgiven." He said to him, "You have
judged rightly." 44 Then he turned to the
woman and said to Simon, "Do you see
this woman? When I entered your
house, you did not give me water for
my feet, but she has bathed them with
her tears and wiped them with her hair.
45 You did not give me a kiss, but she
has not ceased kissing my feet since the
time I entered. 46 You did not anoint my
head with oil, but she anointed my feet
with ointment. 47† So I tell you, her
many sins have been forgiven; hence,
she has shown great love. But the one
to whom little is forgiven, loves little."
48* He said to her, "Your sins are for-
given." 49* The others at table said to
themselves, "Who is this who even for-
gives sins?" 50 But he said to the woman,
"Your faith has saved you; go in peace."

CHAPTER 8

Galilean Women Follow Jesus.†
1* Afterward he journeyed from one
town and village to another, preaching
and proclaiming the good news of the
kingdom of God. Accompanying him
were the Twelve 2* and some women
who had been cured of evil spirits and
infirmities, Mary, called Magdalene,
from whom seven demons had gone out,
3 Joanna, the wife of Herod's steward
Chuza, Susanna, and many others who
provided for them out of their re-
sources.

The Parable of the Sower.† 4*† When
a large crowd gathered, with people
from one town after another journeying
to him, he spoke in a parable. 5 "A sower
went out to sow his seed. And as he
sowed, some seed fell on the path and
was trampled, and the birds of the sky
ate it up. 6 Some seed fell on rocky
ground, and when it grew, it withered
for lack of moisture. 7 Some seed fell
among thorns, and the thorns grew with
it and choked it. 8* And some seed fell

*

34: 15, 2.
36: 11, 37; 14, 1. 10; Mt 27, 55-56; Mk 15, 40-41; Jn 19, 5.
37: Mt 26, 7; Mk 14, 3.
37-38: Jn 12, 3.
48: 5, 20; Mt 9, 20; Mk 2, 5.
49: 5, 21.
8, 1: 4, 43.
2-3: 23, 49; 24,
4-8: Mt 13, 1-9; Mk 4, 1-9.
8: 14, 35; Mt 11, 15; 13, 43; Mk 4, 23.

†

7, 36-50: In this story of the pardoning of the sinful woman Luke presents two different reactions to the ministry of Jesus. A Pharisee, suspecting Jesus to be a prophet, invites Jesus to a festive banquet in his house, but the Pharisee's self-righteousness leads to little forgiveness by God and consequently little love shown toward Jesus. The sinful woman, on the other hand, manifests a faith in God (50) that has led her to seek forgiveness for her sins, and because so much was forgiven, she now overwhelms Jesus with her display of love; cf the similar contrast in attitudes in 18, 9-14. The whole episode is a powerful lesson on the relation between forgiveness and love.

7, 36: *Reclined at table:* the normal posture of guests at a banquet. Other oriental banquet customs alluded to in this story include the reception by the host with a kiss (45), washing the feet of the guests (44), and the anointing of the guests' heads (46).

7, 41: *Days' wages:* one denarius is the normal daily wage of a laborer.

7, 47: *Her many sins have been forgiven; hence, she has shown great love:* literally, "her many sins have been forgiven, seeing that she has loved much." That the woman's sins have been forgiven is attested by the great love she shows toward Jesus. Her love is the consequence of her forgiveness. This is also the meaning demanded by the parable in vv 41-43.

8, 1-3: Luke presents Jesus as an itinerant preacher traveling in the company of the Twelve and of the Galilean women who are sustaining them out of their means. These Galilean women will later accompany Jesus on his journey to Jerusalem and become witnesses to his death (23, 49) and resurrection (24, 9-11, where Mary Magdalene and Joanna are specifically mentioned; cf also Acts 1, 14). The association of women with the ministry of Jesus is most unusual in the light of the attitude of first-century Palestinian Judaism toward women. The more common attitude is expressed in Jn 4, 27, and early rabbinic documents caution against speaking with women in public.

8, 4-21: The focus in this section is on how one should hear the word of God and act on it. It includes the parable of the sower and its explanation (4-15), a collection of sayings on how one should act on the word that is heard (16-18), and the identification of the mother and brothers of Jesus as the ones who hear the word and act on it (19-21). See also the notes on Mt 13, 1-53 and Mk 4, 1-34.

8, 4-8: See the note on Mt 13, 3-8.

on good soil, and when it grew, it produced fruit a hundredfold." After saying this, he called out, "Whoever has ears to hear ought to hear."

The Purpose of the Parables. 9* Then his disciples asked him what the meaning of this parable might be. 10* He answered, "Knowledge of the mysteries of the kingdom of God has been granted to you; but to the rest, they are made known through parables so that 'they may look but not see, and hear but not understand.'

The Parable of the Sower Explained.† 11* "This is the meaning of the parable. The seed is the word of God. 12 Those on the path are the ones who have heard, but the devil comes and takes away the word from their hearts that they may not believe and be saved. 13 Those on rocky ground are the ones who, when they hear, receive the word with joy, but they have no root; they believe only for a time and fall away in time of trial. 14 As for the seed that fell among thorns, they are the ones who have heard, but as they go along, they are choked by the anxieties and riches and pleasures of life, and they fail to produce mature fruit. 15 But as for the seed that fell on rich soil, they are the ones who, when they have heard the word, embrace it with a generous and good heart, and bear fruit through perseverance.

The Parable of the Lamp.† 16* "No one who lights a lamp conceals it with a vessel or sets it under a bed; rather, he places it on a lampstand so that those who enter may see the light. 17* For there is nothing hidden that will not become visible, and nothing secret that will not be known and come to light. 18* Take care, then, how you hear. To anyone who has, more will be given, and from the one who has not, even what he seems to have will be taken away."

Jesus and His Family. 19*† Then his mother and his brothers came to him but were unable to join him because of the crowd. 20* He was told, "Your mother and your brothers are standing outside and they wish to see you." 21† He said to them in reply, "My mother and my brothers are those who hear the word of God and act on it."

The Calming of a Storm at Sea.† 22* One day he got into a boat with his disciples and said to them, "Let us cross to the other side of the lake." So they set sail, 23 and while they were sailing he fell asleep. A squall blew over the lake, and they were taking in water and were in danger. 24 They came and woke him saying, "Master, master, we are perishing!" He awakened, rebuked the wind and the waves, and they subsided and there was a calm. 25 Then he asked them, "Where is your faith?" But they were filled with awe and amazed and said to one another, "Who then is this, who commands even the winds and the sea, and they obey him?"

The Healing of the Gerasene Demoniac. 26*† Then they sailed to the territory of the Gerasenes, which is opposite Galilee. 27 When he came ashore a man from the town who was possessed by demons met him. For a long time he had not worn clothes; he did not live in a house, but lived among the tombs. 28* When he saw Jesus, he cried out and fell down before him; in a loud voice he shouted, "What have you to do with me, Jesus, son of the Most High God? I beg you, do not torment me!" 29 For he had ordered the unclean spirit to come out of the man. (It had taken hold of him many times, and he used to be bound with chains and shackles as a restraint, but he would break his bonds and be driven by the demon into deserted places.) 30† Then Jesus asked

*

9-10: Mt 13, 10-13; Mk 4, 10-12.
10: Is 6, 9.
11-15: Mt 13, 18-23; Mk 4, 13-20.
11: 1 Pt 1, 23.
16-18: Mk 4, 21-25.
16: 11, 33; Mt 5, 15.
17: 12, 2; Mt 10, 26.
18: 19, 26; Mt 13, 12; 25, 29.
19-21: Mt 12, 46-50; Mk 3, 31-35.
20-21: 11, 27-28.
22-25: Mt 8, 18.23-27; Mk 4, 35-41.
26-39: Mt 8, 28-34; Mk 5, 1-20.
28-29: 4, 33-35; Mt 8, 29; Mk 1, 23-24.

†

8, 11-15: On the interpretation of the parable of the sower, see the note on Mt 13, 18-23.

8, 16-18: These sayings continue the theme of responding to the word of God. Those who hear the word must become a light to others (16); even the mysteries of the kingdom that have been made known to the disciples (9-10) must come to light (17); a generous and persevering response to the word of God leads to a still more perfect response to the word.

8, 19: *His brothers:* see the note on Mk 6, 3.

8, 21: The family of Jesus is not constituted by physical relationship with him but by obedience to the word of God. In this, Luke agrees with the Marcan parallel (3, 31-35), although by omitting Mk 3, 33 and especially Mk 3, 20-21 Luke has softened the Marcan picture of Jesus' natural family. Probably he did this because Mary has already been presented in 1, 38 as the obedient handmaid of the Lord who fulfills the requirement for belonging to the eschatological family of Jesus; cf also 11, 27-28.

8, 22-56: This section records four miracles of Jesus that manifest his power and authority: (1) the calming of a storm on the lake (22-25); (2) the exorcism of a demoniac (26-39); (3) the cure of a hemorrhaging woman (40-48); (4) the raising of Jairus's daughter to life (49-56). They parallel the same sequence of stories at Mk 4, 35—5, 43.

8, 26: *Gerasenes:* other manuscripts read Gadarenes or Gergesenes. See also the note on Mt 8, 28. *Opposite Galilee:* probably Gentile territory (note the presence in the area of pigs—unclean animals to Jews) and an indication that the person who receives salvation (36) is a Gentile.

8, 30: *What is your name?:* the question reflects the popular belief that knowledge of the spirit's name brought control over the spirit. *Legion:* to Jesus' question the demon replies with a Latin word transliterated into Greek. The Roman legion at this period consisted of 5,000 to 6,000 foot soldiers; hence the name implies a very large number of demons.

him, "What is your name?" He replied, "Legion," because many demons had entered him. 31† And they pleaded with him not to order them to depart to the abyss.

32 A herd of many swine was feeding there on the hillside, and they pleaded with him to allow them to enter those swine; and he let them. 33 The demons came out of the man and entered the swine, and the herd rushed down the steep bank into the lake and was drowned. 34 When the swineherds saw what had happened, they ran away and reported the incident in the town and throughout the countryside. 35† People came out to see what had happened and, when they approached Jesus, they discovered the man from whom the demons had come out sitting at his feet. He was clothed and in his right mind, and they were seized with fear. 36 Those who witnessed it told them how the possessed man had been saved. 37 The entire population of the region of the Gerasenes asked Jesus to leave them because they were seized with great fear. So he got into a boat and returned. 38 The man from whom the demons had come out begged to remain with him, but he sent him away, saying, 39 "Return home and recount what God has done for you." The man went off and proclaimed throughout the whole town what Jesus had done for him.

Jairus's Daughter and the Woman with a Hemorrhage.† 40* When Jesus returned, the crowd welcomed him, for they were all waiting for him. 41 And a man named Jairus, an official of the synagogue, came forward. He fell at the feet of Jesus and begged him to come to his house, 42† because he had an only daughter, about twelve years old, and she was dying. As he went, the crowds almost crushed him. 43† And a woman afflicted with hemorrhages for twelve years, who [had spent her whole livelihood on doctors and] was unable to be cured by anyone, 44 came up behind him and touched the tassel on his cloak. Immediately her bleeding stopped. 45 Jesus then asked, "Who touched me?" While all were denying it, Peter said, "Master, the crowds are pushing and pressing in upon you." 46* But Jesus said, "Someone has touched me; for I know that power has gone out from me." 47 When the woman realized that she had not escaped notice, she came forward trembling. Falling down before him, she explained in the presence of all the people why she had touched him and how she had been healed immediately. 48* He said to her, "Daughter, your faith has saved you; go in peace."

49 While he was still speaking, someone from the synagogue official's house arrived and said, "Your daughter is dead; do not trouble the teacher any longer." 50 On hearing this, Jesus answered him, "Do not be afraid; just have faith and she will be saved." 51 When he arrived at the house he allowed no one to enter with him except Peter and John and James, and the child's father and mother. 52*† All were weeping and mourning for her, when he said, "Do not weep any longer, for she is not dead, but sleeping." 53 And they ridiculed him, because they knew that she was dead. 54 But he took her by the hand and called to her, "Child, arise!" 55 Her breath returned and she immediately arose. He then directed that she should be given something to eat. 56 Her parents were astounded, and he instructed them to tell no one what had happened.

CHAPTER 9

The Mission of the Twelve.† 1* He summoned the Twelve and gave them power and authority over all demons and to cure diseases, 2 and he sent them to proclaim the kingdom of God and to heal [the sick]. 3† He said to them, "Take nothing for the journey, neither

*

40-56: Mt 9, 18-26; Mk 5, 21-43.
46: 6, 19.
48: 7, 50; 17, 19; 18, 42.
52: 7, 13.
9, 1-6: Mt 10, 1.5-15; Mk 6, 7-13.

†

8, 31: *Abyss:* the place of the dead (Rom 10, 7) or the prison of Satan (Rv 20, 3) or the subterranean "watery deep" that symbolizes the chaos before the order imposed by creation (Gn 1, 2).

8, 35: *Sitting at his feet:* the former demoniac takes the position of a disciple before the master (10, 39; Acts 22, 3).

8, 40-56: Two interwoven miracle stories, one a healing and the other a resuscitation, present Jesus as master over sickness and death. In the Lucan account, faith in Jesus is responsible for the cure (48) and for the raising to life (50).

8, 42: *An only daughter:* cf the son of the widow of Nain whom Luke describes as an "only" son (7, 12; see also 9, 38).

8, 43: *Afflicted with hemorrhages for twelve years:* according to the Mosaic law (Lv 15, 25-30) this condition would render the woman unclean and unfit for contact with other people.

8, 52: *Sleeping:* her death is a temporary condition; cf Jn 11, 11-14.

9, 1-6: Armed with the power and authority that Jesus himself has been displaying in the previous episodes, the Twelve are now sent out to continue the work that Jesus has been performing throughout his Galilean ministry: (1) proclaiming the kingdom (4, 43; 8, 1); (2) exorcising demons (4, 33-37.41; 8, 26-39) and (3) healing the sick (4, 38-40; 5, 12-16.17-26; 6, 6-10; 7, 1-10.17.22; 8, 40-56).

9, 3: *Take nothing for the journey:* the absolute detachment required of the disciple (14, 33) leads to complete reliance on God (12, 22-31).

walking stick, nor sack, nor food, nor
money, and let no one take a second
tunic. 4* Whatever house you enter, stay
there and leave from there. 5*† And as
for those who do not welcome you, when
you leave that town, shake the dust
from your feet in testimony against
them." 6 Then they set out and went
from village to village proclaiming the
good news and curing diseases every-
where.

Herod's Opinion of Jesus.† 7*† Herod
the tetrarch heard about all that was
happening, and he was greatly per-
plexed because some were saying,
"John has been raised from the dead";
8 others were saying, "Elijah has ap-
peared"; still others, "One of the an-
cient prophets has arisen." 9*† But
Herod said, "John I beheaded. Who
then is this about whom I hear such
things?" And he kept trying to see
him.

The Return of the Twelve and the Feeding of the Five Thousand.
10* When the apostles returned, they ex-
plained to him what they had done. He
took them and withdrew in private to
a town called Bethsaida. 11 The crowds,
meanwhile, learned of this and followed
him. He received them and spoke to
them about the kingdom of God, and
he healed those who needed to be cured.
12 As the day was drawing to a close,
the Twelve approached him and said,
"Dismiss the crowd so that they can go
to the surrounding villages and farms
and find lodging and provisions; for we
are in a deserted place here." 13* He
said to them, "Give them some food
yourselves." They replied, "Five loaves
and two fish are all we have, unless we
ourselves go and buy food for all these
people." 14 Now the men there num-
bered about five thousand. Then he said
to his disciples, "Have them sit down
in groups of [about] fifty." 15 They did
so and made them all sit down.
16*† Then taking the five loaves and the
two fish, and looking up to heaven, he
said the blessing over them, broke
them, and gave them to the disciples to
set before the crowd. 17 They all ate and
were satisfied. And when the leftover
fragments were picked up, they filled
twelve wicker baskets.

Peter's Confession about Jesus.†
18*† Once when Jesus was praying in
solitude, and the disciples were with
him, he asked them, "Who do the
crowds say that I am?" 19* They said
in reply, "John the Baptist; others, Eli-
jah; still others, 'One of the ancient
prophets has arisen.' " 20† Then he said
to them, "But who do you say that I
am?" Peter said in reply, "The Mes-
siah of God." 21 He rebuked them and
directed them not to tell this to any-
one.

The First Prediction of the Passion.
22* He said, "The Son of Man must suf-
fer greatly and be rejected by the el-
ders, the chief priests, and the scribes,
and be killed and on the third day be
raised."

The Conditions of Discipleship.
23*† Then he said to all, "If anyone
wishes to come after me, he must deny
himself and take up his cross daily and
follow me. 24* For whoever wishes to
save his life will lose it, but whoever
loses his life for my sake will save it.
25 What profit is there for one to gain the
whole world yet lose or forfeit himself?
26* Whoever is ashamed of me and of

*

4: 10, 5-7.
5: 10, 10-11; Acts 13, 51.
7-9: Mt 14, 1-12; Mk 6, 14-29.
7-8: 9, 19; Mt 16, 14; Mk 8, 28.
9: 23, 8.
10-17: Mt 14, 13-21; Mk 6, 30-44; Jn 6, 1-14.
13-17: 2 Kgs 4, 42-44.
16: 22, 19; 24, 30-31; Acts 2, 42; 20, 11; 27, 35.
18-21: Mt 16, 13-20; Mk 8, 27-30.
19: 9, 7-8.
22: 24, 7.26; Mt 16, 21; 20, 18-19; Mk 8, 31; 10, 33-34.
23-27: Mt 16, 24-28; Mk 8, 34—9, 1.
23: 14, 27; Mt 10, 38.
24: 17, 33; Mt 10, 39; Jn 12, 25.
26: 12, 9; Mt 10, 33; 2 Tm 2, 12.

†

9, 5: *Shake the dust from your feet:* see the note on Mt 10, 14.

9, 7-56: This section in which Luke gathers together incidents that focus on the identity of Jesus is introduced by a question that Herod is made to ask in this gospel: "Who then is this about whom I hear such things?" (9). In subsequent episodes, Luke reveals to the reader various answers to Herod's question: Jesus is one in whom God's power is present and who provides for the needs of God's people (10-17); Peter declares Jesus to be "the Messiah of God" (18-21); Jesus says he is the suffering Son of Man (22.43-45); Jesus is the Master to be followed, even to death (23-27); Jesus is God's Son, his Chosen One (28-36).

9, 7: *Herod the tetrarch:* see the note on 3, 1.

9, 9: *And he kept trying to see him:* this indication of Herod's interest in Jesus prepares for 13, 31-33 and for 23, 8-12 where Herod's curiosity about Jesus' power to perform miracles remains unsatisfied.

9, 16: *Then taking . . . :* the actions of Jesus recall the institution of the Eucharist in 22, 19; see also the note on Mt 14, 19.

9, 18-22: This incident is based on Mk 8, 27-33, but Luke has eliminated Peter's refusal to accept Jesus as suffering Son of Man (Mk 8, 32) and the rebuke of Peter by Jesus (Mk 8, 33). Elsewhere in the gospel, Luke softens the harsh portrait of Peter and the other apostles found in his Marcan source (cf 22, 39-46, which similarly lacks a rebuke of Peter that occurs in the source, Mk 14, 37-38).

9, 18: *When Jesus was praying in solitude:* see the note on 3, 21.

9, 20: *The Messiah of God:* on the meaning of this title in first-century Palestinian Judaism, see the notes on 2, 11 and on Mt 16, 13-20 and Mk 8, 27-30.

9, 23: *Daily:* this is a Lucan addition to a saying of Jesus, removing the saying from a context that envisioned the imminent suffering and death of the disciple of Jesus (as does the saying in Mk 8, 34-35) to one that focuses on the demands of daily Christian existence.

my words, the Son of Man will be ashamed of when he comes in his glory and in the glory of the Father and of the holy angels. 27 Truly I say to you, there are some standing here who will not taste death until they see the kingdom of God."

***The Transfiguration of Jesus.*†**
28*† About eight days after he said this, he took Peter, John, and James and went up the mountain to pray. 29 While he was praying his face changed in appearance and his clothing became dazzling white. 30† And behold, two men were conversing with him, Moses and Elijah, 31*† who appeared in glory and spoke of his exodus that he was going to accomplish in Jerusalem. 32*† Peter and his companions had been overcome by sleep, but becoming fully awake, they saw his glory and the two men standing with him. 33† As they were about to part from him, Peter said to Jesus, "Master, it is good that we are here; let us make three tents, one for you, one for Moses, and one for Elijah." But he did not know what he was saying. 34† While he was still speaking, a cloud came and cast a shadow over them, and they became frightened when they entered the cloud. 35*† Then from the cloud came a voice that said, "This is my chosen Son; listen to him." 36† After the voice had spoken, Jesus was found alone. They fell silent and did not at that time tell anyone what they had seen.

***The Healing of a Boy with a Demon.*†**
37* On the next day, when they came down from the mountain, a large crowd met him. 38 There was a man in the crowd who cried out, "Teacher, I beg you, look at my son; he is my only child. 39 For a spirit seizes him and he suddenly screams and it convulses him until he foams at the mouth; it releases him only with difficulty, wearing him out. 40 I begged your disciples to cast it out but they could not." 41 Jesus said in reply, "O faithless and perverse generation, how long will I be with you and endure you? Bring your son here." 42 As he was coming forward, the demon threw him to the ground in a convulsion; but Jesus rebuked the unclean spirit, healed the boy, and returned him to his father. 43* And all were astonished by the majesty of God.

The Second Prediction of the Passion.
While they were all amazed at his every deed, he said to his disciples, 44 "Pay attention to what I am telling you. The Son of Man is to be handed over to men." 45 But they did not understand this saying; its meaning was hidden from them so that they should not understand it, and they were afraid to ask him about this saying.

***The Greatest in the Kingdom.*†**
46* An argument arose among the disciples about which of them was the greatest. 47 Jesus realized the intention of their hearts and took a child and placed it by his side 48* and said to them, "Whoever receives this child in my name receives me, and whoever receives me receives the one who sent me. For the one who is least among all of you is the one who is the greatest."

Another Exorcist. 49* Then John said in reply, "Master, we saw someone casting out demons in your name and we tried to prevent him because he does not follow in our company." 50 Jesus said to him, "Do not prevent him, for whoever is not against you is for you."

*

28-36: Mt 17, 1-8; Mk 9, 2-8.
31: 9, 22; 13, 33.
32: Jn 1, 14; 2 Pt 1, 16.
35: 3, 22; Dt 18, 15; Ps 2, 7; Is 42, 1; Mt 3, 17; 12, 18; Mk 1, 11; 2 Pt 1, 17-18.
37-43: Mt 17, 14-18; Mk 9, 14-27.
43-45: 18, 32-34; Mt 17, 22-23; Mk 9, 30-32.
46-48: Mt 18, 1-5; Mk 9, 33-37.
46: 22, 24.
48: 10, 16; Mt 10, 40; Jn 13, 20.
49-50: Mk 9, 38-40.

†

9, 28-36: Situated shortly after the first announcement of the passion, death, and resurrection, this scene of Jesus' transfiguration provides the heavenly confirmation to Jesus' declaration that his suffering will end in glory (32); see also the notes on Mt 17, 1-8 and Mk 9, 2-8.

9, 28: *Up the mountain to pray:* the "mountain" is the regular place of prayer in Lk (see 6, 12; 22, 39-41).

9, 30: *Moses and Elijah:* the two figures represent the Old Testament law and the prophets. At the end of this episode, the heavenly voice will identify Jesus as the one to be listened to now (35). See also the note on Mk 9, 5.

9, 31: *His exodus that he was going to accomplish in Jerusalem:* Luke identifies the subject of the conversation as the *exodus* of Jesus, a reference to the death, resurrection, and ascension of Jesus that will take place in Jerusalem, the city of destiny (see 9, 51). The mention of *exodus,* however, also calls to mind the Israelite Exodus from Egypt to the promised land.

9, 32: *They saw his glory:* the *glory* that is proper to God is here attributed to Jesus (see 24, 26).

9, 33: *Let us make three tents:* in a possible allusion to the feast of Tabernacles, Peter may be likening his joy on the occasion of the transfiguration to the joyful celebration of this harvest festival.

9, 34: *Over them:* it is not clear whether *them* refers to Jesus, Moses, and Elijah, or to the disciples. For the cloud casting its shadow, see the note on Mk 9, 7.

9, 35: Like the heavenly voice that identified Jesus at his baptism prior to his undertaking the Galilean ministry (3, 22), so too here before the journey to the city of destiny is begun (51) the heavenly voice again identifies Jesus as Son. *Listen to him:* the two representatives of Israel of old depart (33) and Jesus is left alone (36) as the teacher whose words must be heeded (see also Acts 3, 22).

9, 36: *At that time:* i.e., before the resurrection.

9, 37-43a: See the note on Mk 9, 14-29.

9, 46-50: These two incidents focus on attitudes that are opposed to Christian discipleship: rivalry and intolerance of outsiders.

V: THE JOURNEY TO JERUSALEM: LUKE'S TRAVEL NARRATIVE†

Departure for Jerusalem; Samaritan Inhospitality. † [51]*† When the days for his being taken up were fulfilled, he resolutely determined to journey to Jerusalem, [52]*† and he sent messengers ahead of him. On the way they entered a Samaritan village to prepare for his reception there, [53] but they would not welcome him because the destination of his journey was Jerusalem. [54]* When the disciples James and John saw this they asked, "Lord, do you want us to call down fire from heaven to consume them?" [55] Jesus turned and rebuked them, [56] and they journeyed to another village.

The Would-be Followers of Jesus. † [57]* As they were proceeding on their journey someone said to him, "I will follow you wherever you go." [58] Jesus answered him, "Foxes have dens and birds of the sky have nests, but the Son of Man has nowhere to rest his head." [59] And to another he said, "Follow me." But he replied, "[Lord,] let me go first and bury my father." [60]† But he answered him, "Let the dead bury their dead. But you, go and proclaim the kingdom of God." [61]* And another said, "I will follow you, Lord, but first let me say farewell to my family at home." [62] [To him] Jesus said, "No one who sets a hand to the plow and looks to what was left behind is fit for the kingdom of God."

CHAPTER 10

The Mission of the Seventy-two. † [1]*† After this the Lord appointed seventy[-two] others whom he sent ahead of him in pairs to every town and place he intended to visit. [2]* He said to them, "The harvest is abundant but the laborers are few; so ask the master of the harvest to send out laborers for his harvest. [3]* Go on your way; behold, I am sending you like lambs among wolves. [4]*† Carry no money bag, no sack, no sandals; and greet no one along the way. [5]† Into whatever house you enter, first say, 'Peace to this household.' [6]† If a peaceful person lives there, your peace will rest on him; but if not, it will return to you. [7]* Stay in the same house and eat and drink what is offered to you, for the laborer deserves his payment. Do not move about from one house to another. [8]* Whatever town you enter and they welcome you, eat what is set before you, [9]* cure the sick in it and say to them, 'The kingdom of God is at hand for you.' [10]* Whatever town you enter and they do not receive you, go out into the streets and say, [11]* 'The dust of your town that clings to our feet, even that

*

51: 9, 53; 13, 22.33; 17, 11; 18, 31; 19, 28; 24, 51; Acts 1, 2.9-11.22.
52: Mal 3, 1.
54: 2 Kgs 1, 10.12.
57-60: Mt 8, 19-22.
61-62: 1 Kgs 19, 20.
10, 1: Mk 6, 7.
2: Mt 9, 37-38; Jn 4, 35.
3: Mt 10, 16.
4: 9, 3; 2 Kgs 4, 29.
4-11: Mt 10, 7-14.
7: 9, 4; Mt 10, 10; 1 Cor 9, 6-14; 1 Tm 5, 18.
8: 1 Cor 10, 27.
9: Mt 3, 2; 4, 17; Mk 1, 15.
10-11: 9, 5.
11: Acts 13, 51; 18, 6.

†

9, 51—18, 14: The Galilean ministry of Jesus finishes with the previous episode and a new section of Luke's gospel begins, the journey to Jerusalem. This journey is based on Mk 10, 1-52, but Luke uses his Marcan source only in 18, 15—19, 27. Before that point he has inserted into his gospel a distinctive collection of sayings of Jesus and stories about him that he has drawn from Q, a collection of sayings of Jesus used also by Matthew, and from his own special traditions. All of the material collected in this section is loosely organized within the framework of a journey of Jesus to Jerusalem, the city of destiny, where his exodus (suffering, death, resurrection, ascension) is to take place (9, 31), where salvation is accomplished, and from where the proclamation of God's saving word is to go forth (24, 47; Acts 1, 8). Much of the material in the Lucan travel narrative is teaching for the disciples. During the course of this journey Jesus is preparing his chosen Galilean witnesses for the role they will play after his exodus (9, 31): they are to be his witnesses to the people (Acts 10, 39; 13, 31) and thereby provide certainty to the readers of Luke's gospel that the teachings they have received are rooted in the teachings of Jesus (1, 1-4).

9, 51-55: Just as the Galilean ministry began with a rejection of Jesus in his hometown, so too the travel narrative begins with the rejection of him by Samaritans. In this episode Jesus disassociates himself from the attitude expressed by his disciples that those who reject him are to be punished severely. The story alludes to 2 Kgs 1, 10.12, where the prophet Elijah takes the course of action Jesus rejects, and Jesus thereby rejects the identification of himself with Elijah.

9, 51: *Days for his being taken up:* like the reference to his exodus in v 31, this is probably a reference to all the events (suffering, death, resurrection, ascension) of his last days in Jerusalem. *He resolutely determined:* literally, "he set his face."

9, 52: *Samaritan:* Samaria was the territory between Judea and Galilee west of the Jordan river. For ethnic and religious reasons, the Samaritans and the Jews were bitterly opposed to one another (see Jn 4, 9).

9, 57-62: In these sayings Jesus speaks of the severity and the unconditional nature of Christian discipleship. Even family ties and filial obligations, such as burying one's parents, cannot distract one no matter how briefly from proclaiming the kingdom of God. The first two sayings are paralleled in Mt 8, 19-22; see also the notes there.

9, 60: *Let the dead bury their dead:* i.e., let the spiritually dead (those who do not follow) bury their physically dead. See also the note on Mt 8, 22.

10, 1-12: Only the Gospel of Luke contains two episodes in which Jesus sends out his followers on a mission: the first (9, 1-6) is based on the mission in Mk 6, 6b-13 and recounts the sending out of the Twelve; here in vv 1-12 a similar report based on Q becomes the sending out of seventy-two in this gospel. The episode continues the theme of Jesus preparing witnesses to himself and his ministry. These witnesses include not only the Twelve but also the seventy-two who may represent the Christian mission in Luke's own day. Note that the instructions given to the Twelve and to the seventy-two are similar and that what is said to the seventy-two in v 4 is directed to the Twelve in 22, 35.

10, 1: *Seventy[-two]:* important representatives of the Alexandrian and Caesarean text types read "seventy," while other important Alexandrian texts and Western readings have "seventy-two."

10, 4: *Carry no money bag . . . greet no one along the way:* because of the urgency of the mission and the single-mindedness required of missionaries, attachment to material possessions should be avoided and even customary greetings should not distract from the fulfillment of the task.

10, 5: *First say, 'Peace to this household':* see the notes on 2, 14 and Mt 10, 13.

10, 6: *A peaceful person:* literally, "a son of peace."

we shake off against you.' Yet know this: the kingdom of God is at hand. [12]* I tell you, it will be more tolerable for Sodom on that day than for that town.

Reproaches to Unrepentant Towns.† [13]* "Woe to you, Chorazin! Woe to you, Bethsaida! For if the mighty deeds done in your midst had been done in Tyre and Sidon, they would long ago have repented, sitting in sackcloth and ashes. [14] But it will be more tolerable for Tyre and Sidon at the judgment than for you. [15]*† And as for you, Capernaum, 'Will you be exalted to heaven? You will go down to the netherworld.' [16]* Whoever listens to you listens to me. Whoever rejects you rejects me. And whoever rejects me rejects the one who sent me."

Return of the Seventy-two. [17] The seventy[-two] returned rejoicing, and said, "Lord, even the demons are subject to us because of your name." [18]*† Jesus said, "I have observed Satan fall like lightning from the sky. [19]* Behold, I have given you the power 'to tread upon serpents' and scorpions and upon the full force of the enemy and nothing will harm you. [20]* Nevertheless, do not rejoice because the spirits are subject to you, but rejoice because your names are written in heaven."

Praise of the Father. [21]*† At that very moment he rejoiced [in] the holy Spirit and said, "I give you praise, Father, Lord of heaven and earth, for although you have hidden these things from the wise and the learned you have revealed them to the childlike. Yes, Father, such has been your gracious will. [22]* All things have been handed over to me by my Father. No one knows who the Son is except the Father, and who the Father is except the Son and anyone to whom the Son wishes to reveal him."

The Privileges of Discipleship. [23]* Turning to the disciples in private he said, "Blessed are the eyes that see what you see. [24] For I say to you, many prophets and kings desired to see what you see, but did not see it, and to hear what you hear, but did not hear it."

The Greatest Commandment.† [25]*† There was a scholar of the law who stood up to test him and said, "Teacher, what must I do to inherit eternal life?" [26] Jesus said to him, "What is written in the law? How do you read it?" [27]* He said in reply, "You shall love the Lord, your God, with all your heart, with all your being, with all your strength, and with all your mind, and your neighbor as yourself." [28]* He replied to him, "You have answered correctly; do this and you will live."

The Parable of the Good Samaritan. [29] But because he wished to justify himself, he said to Jesus, "And who is my neighbor?" [30] Jesus replied, "A man fell victim to robbers as he went down from Jerusalem to Jericho. They stripped and beat him and went off leaving him half-dead. [31]† A priest happened to be going down that road, but when he saw him, he passed by on the opposite side. [32] Likewise a Levite came to the place, and when he saw him, he passed by on the opposite side. [33] But a Samaritan traveler who came upon him was moved with compassion at the sight. [34] He approached the victim, poured oil and wine over his wounds and bandaged them. Then he lifted him up on his own animal, took him to an inn and cared for him. [35] The next day he took out two silver coins and gave them to the innkeeper with the instruction, 'Take care of him. If you spend more than what I have given you, I shall repay you on my way back.' [36] Which of these three, in your opinion, was neighbor to the

*

- 12: Mt 10, 15; 11, 24.
- 13-15: Mt 11, 20-24.
- 13-14: Is 23; Ez 26-28; Jl 3, 4-8; Am 1, 1-10; Zec 9, 2-4.
- 15: Is 14, 13-15.
- 16: Mt 10, 40; Jn 5, 23; 13, 20; 15, 23.
- 18: Is 14, 12; Jn 12, 31; Rv 12, 7-12.
- 19: Ps 19, 13; Mk 16, 18.
- 20: Ex 32, 32; Dn 12, 1; Mt 7, 22; Phil 4, 3; Heb 12, 23; Rv 3, 5; 21, 27.
- 21-22: Mt 11, 25-27.
- 21: 1 Cor 1, 26-28.
- 22: Jn 3, 35; 10, 15.
- 23-24: Mt 13, 16-17.
- 25-28: Mt 22, 34-40; Mk 12, 28-34.
- 25: 18, 18; Mt 19, 16; Mk 10, 17.
- 27: Lv 19, 18; Dt 6, 5; 10, 12; Jos 22, 5; Mt 19, 19; 22, 37-39; Rom 13, 9; Gal 5, 14; Jas 2, 8.
- 28: Lv 18, 5; Prv 19, 16; Rom 10, 5; Gal 3, 12.

†

10, 13-16: The call to repentance that is a part of the proclamation of the kingdom brings with it a severe judgment for those who hear it and reject it.

10, 15: *The netherworld:* the underworld, the place of the dead (Acts 2, 27.31), here contrasted with heaven; see also the note on Mt 11, 23.

10, 18: *I have observed Satan fall like lightning:* the effect of the mission of the seventy-two is characterized by the Lucan Jesus as a symbolic fall of Satan. As the kingdom of God is gradually being established, evil in all its forms is being defeated; the dominion of Satan over humanity is at an end.

10, 21: *Revealed them to the childlike:* a restatement of the theme announced in 8, 10: the mysteries of the kingdom are revealed to the disciples. See also the note on Mt 11, 25-27.

10, 25-37: In response to a question from a Jewish legal expert about inheriting eternal life, Jesus illustrates the superiority of love over legalism through the story of the good Samaritan. The law of love proclaimed in the "Sermon on the Plain" (6, 27-36) is exemplified by one whom the legal expert would have considered ritually impure (see Jn 4, 9). Moreover, the identity of the "neighbor" requested by the legal expert (29) turns out to be a Samaritan, the enemy of the Jew (see the note on 9, 52).

10, 25: *Scholar of the law:* an expert in the Mosaic law, and probably a member of the group elsewhere identified as the scribes (5, 21).

10, 31-32: *Priest . . . Levite:* those religious representatives of Judaism who would have been expected to be models of "neighbor" to the victim pass him by.

robbers' victim?" 37 He answered, "The
one who treated him with mercy." Jesus
said to him, "Go and do likewise."
***Martha and Mary.*†** 38* As they con-
tinued their journey he entered a village
where a woman whose name was Mar-
tha welcomed him. 39† She had a sister
named Mary [who] sat beside the Lord
at his feet listening to him speak.
40 Martha, burdened with much serving,
came to him and said, "Lord, do you
not care that my sister has left me by
myself to do the serving? Tell her to help
me." 41 The Lord said to her in reply,
"Martha, Martha, you are anxious and
worried about many things. 42† There is
need of only one thing. Mary has chosen
the better part and it will not be taken
from her."

CHAPTER 11

***The Lord's Prayer.*†** 1*† He was
praying in a certain place, and when
he had finished, one of his disciples said
to him, "Lord, teach us to pray just as
John taught his disciples." 2† He said
to them, "When you pray, say:

Father, hallowed be your name,
your kingdom come.
3† Give us each day our daily bread
4 and forgive us our sins
for we ourselves forgive everyone
in debt to us,
and do not subject us to the final
test."

Further Teachings on Prayer. 5* And
he said to them, "Suppose one of you
has a friend to whom he goes at mid-
night and says, 'Friend, lend me three
loaves of bread, 6 for a friend of mine
has arrived at my house from a journey
and I have nothing to offer him,' 7 and
he says in reply from within, 'Do not
bother me; the door has already been
locked and my children and I are al-
ready in bed. I cannot get up to give
you anything.' 8 I tell you, if he does not
get up to give him the loaves because
of their friendship, he will get up to give
him whatever he needs because of his
persistence.
The Answer to Prayer. 9* "And I tell
you, ask and you will receive; seek and
you will find; knock and the door will
be opened to you. 10 For everyone who
asks, receives; and the one who seeks,
finds; and to the one who knocks, the
door will be opened. 11 What father
among you would hand his son a snake
when he asks for a fish? 12 Or hand him
a scorpion when he asks for an egg?
13† If you then, who are wicked, know
how to give good gifts to your children,
how much more will the Father in
heaven give the holy Spirit to those who
ask him?"

Jesus and Beelzebul. 14* He was driv-
ing out a demon [that was] mute, and
when the demon had gone out, the mute
person spoke and the crowds were
amazed. 15* Some of them said, "By the
power of Beelzebul, the prince of de-
mons, he drives out demons."
16* Others, to test him, asked him for a
sign from heaven. 17 But he knew their
thoughts and said to them, "Every
kingdom divided against itself will be
laid waste and house will fall against
house. 18 And if Satan is divided against
himself, how will his kingdom stand?
For you say that it is by Beelzebul that
I drive out demons. 19† If I, then, drive
out demons by Beelzebul, by whom do
your own people drive them out? There-
fore they will be your judges. 20* But if
it is by the finger of God that [I] drive
out demons, then the kingdom of God
has come upon you. 21 When a strong
man fully armed guards his palace, his
possessions are safe. 22† But when one

*

38-39: Jn 11, 1; 12, 2-3.
11, 1-4: Mt 6, 9-15.
5-8: 18, 1-5.
9-13: Mt 7, 7-11.
9: Mt 21, 22; Mk 11, 24; Jn 14, 13; 15, 7; 1 Jn 5, 14-15.
14-23: Mt 12, 22-30; Mk 3, 20-27.
15: Mt 9, 34.
16: Mt 12, 38; 16, 1; Mk 8, 11; 1 Cor 1, 22.
20: Ex 8, 19.

†

10, 38-42: The story of Martha and Mary further illustrates the importance of hearing the words of the teacher and the concern with women in Lk.

10, 39: *Sat beside the Lord at his feet:* it is remarkable for first-century Palestinian Judaism that a woman would assume the posture of a disciple at the master's feet (see also 8, 35; Acts 22, 3), and it reveals a characteristic attitude of Jesus toward women in this gospel (see 8, 2-3).

10, 42: *There is need of only one thing:* some ancient versions read, "there is need of few things"; another important, although probably inferior, reading found in some manuscripts is, "there is need of few things, or of one."

11, 1-13: Luke presents three episodes concerned with prayer. The first (1-4) recounts Jesus teaching his disciples the Christian communal prayer, the "Our Father"; the second (5-8), the importance of persistence in prayer; the third (9-13), the effectiveness of prayer.

11, 1-4: The Matthean form of the "Our Father" occurs in the "Sermon on the Mount" (Mt 6, 9-15); the shorter Lucan version is presented while Jesus is at prayer (see the note on 3, 21) and his disciples ask him to teach them to pray just as John taught his disciples to pray. In answer to their question, Jesus presents them with an example of a Christian communal prayer that stresses the fatherhood of God and acknowledges him as the one to whom the Christian disciple owes daily sustenance (3), forgiveness (4), and deliverance from the final trial (4). See also the notes on Mt 6, 9-13.

11, 2: *Your kingdom come:* in place of this petition, some early church Fathers record: "May your holy Spirit come upon us and cleanse us," a petition that may reflect the use of the "Our Father" in a baptismal liturgy.

11, 3-4: *Daily bread:* see the note on Mt 6, 11. *The final test:* see the note on Mt 6, 13.

11, 13: *The holy Spirit:* this is a Lucan editorial alteration of a traditional saying of Jesus (see Mt 7, 11). Luke presents the gift of the holy Spirit as the response of the Father to the prayer of the Christian disciple.

11, 19: *Your own people:* the Greek reads "your sons." Other Jewish exorcists (see Acts 19, 13-20), who recognize that the power of God is active in the exorcism, would themselves convict the accusers of Jesus. See also the note on Mt 12, 27.

11, 22: *One stronger:* i.e., Jesus. Cf 3, 16 where John the Baptist identifies Jesus as "more powerful than I."

stronger than he attacks and overcomes
him, he takes away the armor on which
he relied and distributes the spoils.
23* Whoever is not with me is against
me, and whoever does not gather with
me scatters.

The Return of the Unclean Spirit.
24* "When an unclean spirit goes out of
someone, it roams through arid regions
searching for rest but, finding none, it
says, 'I shall return to my home from
which I came.' 25 But upon returning, it
finds it swept clean and put in order.
26* Then it goes and brings back seven
other spirits more wicked than itself
who move in and dwell there, and the
last condition of that person is worse
than the first."

***True Blessedness.*†** 27* While he was
speaking, a woman from the crowd
called out and said to him, "Blessed is
the womb that carried you and the
breasts at which you nursed." 28 He re-
plied, "Rather, blessed are those who
hear the word of God and observe it."

***The Demand for a Sign.*†** 29* While
still more people gathered in the crowd,
he said to them, "This generation is an
evil generation; it seeks a sign, but no
sign will be given it, except the sign of
Jonah. 30 Just as Jonah became a sign
to the Ninevites, so will the Son of Man
be to this generation. 31* At the judg-
ment the queen of the south will rise
with the men of this generation and she
will condemn them, because she came
from the ends of the earth to hear the
wisdom of Solomon, and there is some-
thing greater than Solomon here.
32* At the judgment the men of Nineveh
will arise with this generation and con-
demn it, because at the preaching of
Jonah they repented, and there is some-
thing greater than Jonah here.

The Simile of Light. 33* "No one who
lights a lamp hides it away or places it
[under a bushel basket], but on a lamp-
stand so that those who enter might see
the light. 34* The lamp of the body is
your eye. When your eye is sound, then
your whole body is filled with light, but
when it is bad, then your body is in
darkness. 35 Take care, then, that the
light in you not become darkness.
36 If your whole body is full of light, and
no part of it is in darkness, then it will
be as full of light as a lamp illuminating
you with its brightness."

***Denunciation of the Pharisees and
Scholars of the Law.*†** 37* After he had
spoken, a Pharisee invited him to dine
at his home. He entered and reclined
at table to eat. 38* The Pharisee was
amazed to see that he did not observe
the prescribed washing before the meal.
39* The Lord said to him, "Oh you Phar-
isees! Although you cleanse the outside
of the cup and the dish, inside you are
filled with plunder and evil. 40 You fools!
Did not the maker of the outside also
make the inside? 41 But as to what is
within, give alms, and behold, every-
thing will be clean for you. 42* Woe to
you Pharisees! You pay tithes of mint
and of rue and of every garden herb,
but you pay no attention to judgment
and to love for God. These you should
have done, without overlooking the oth-
ers. 43* Woe to you Pharisees! You love
the seat of honor in synagogues and
greetings in marketplaces. 44*† Woe to
you! You are like unseen graves over
which people unknowingly walk."

45*† Then one of the scholars of the
law said to him in reply, "Teacher, by
saying this you are insulting us too."
46 And he said, "Woe also to you schol-
ars of the law! You impose on people
burdens hard to carry, but you your-
selves do not lift one finger to touch
them. 47* Woe to you! You build the
memorials of the prophets whom your
ancestors killed. 48 Consequently, you
bear witness and give consent to the
deeds of your ancestors, for they killed
them and you do the building.
49*† Therefore, the wisdom of God said,
'I will send to them prophets and apos-
tles; some of them they will kill and per-
secute' 50 in order that this generation

LUKE

*

23: 9, 50; Mk 9, 40.
24-26: Mt 12, 43-45.
26: Jn 5, 14.
27: 1, 28.42.48.
29-32: Mt 12, 38-42; Mk 8, 12.
29: Mt 16, 1.4; Jn 6, 30; 1 Cor 1, 22.
31: 1 Kgs 10, 1-10; 2 Chr 9, 1-12.
32: Jon 3, 8.10.
33: 8, 16; Mt 5, 15; Mk 4, 21.
34-36: Mt 6, 22-23.
37-54: 20, 45-47; Mt 23, 1-36; Mk 12, 38-40.
37: 7, 36; 14, 1.
38: Mt 15, 2; Mk 7, 2-5.
39-41: Mt 23, 25-26.
42: Lv 27, 30; Mt 23, 23.
43: 20, 46; Mt 23, 6; Mk 12, 38-39.
44: Mt 23, 27.
45: Mt 23, 4.
47-48: Mt 23, 29-32.
49-51: Mt 23, 34-36.

†

11, 27-28: The beatitude in v 28 should not be interpreted as a rebuke of the mother of Jesus; see the note on 8, 21. Rather, it emphasizes (like 2, 35) that attentiveness to God's word is more important than biological relationship to Jesus.

11, 29-32: The "sign of Jonah" in Lk is the preaching of the need for repentance by a prophet who comes from afar. Cf Mt 12, 38-42 (and see the notes there) where the "sign of Jonah" is interpreted by Jesus as his death and resurrection.

11, 37-54: This denunciation of the Pharisees (39-44) and the scholars of the law (45-52) is set by Luke in the context of Jesus' dining at the home of a Pharisee. Controversies with or reprimands of Pharisees are regularly set by Luke within the context of Jesus' eating with Pharisees (see 5, 29-39; 7, 36-50; 14, 1-24). A different compilation of similar sayings is found in Mt 23 (see also the notes there).

11, 44: *Unseen graves:* contact with the dead or with human bones or graves (see Nm 19, 16) brought ritual impurity. Jesus presents the Pharisees as those who insidiously lead others astray through their seeming attention to the law.

11, 45: *Scholars of the law:* see the note on 10, 25.

11, 49: *I will send to them prophets and apostles:* Jesus connects the mission of the church (apostles) with the mission of the Old Testament prophets who often suffered the rebuke of their contemporaries.

might be charged with the blood of all the prophets shed since the foundation of the world, 51*† from the blood of Abel to the blood of Zechariah who died between the altar and the temple building. Yes, I tell you, this generation will be charged with their blood! 52* Woe to you, scholars of the law! You have taken away the key of knowledge. You yourselves did not enter and you stopped those trying to enter." 53* When he left, the scribes and Pharisees began to act with hostility toward him and to interrogate him about many things, 54* for they were plotting to catch him at something he might say.

CHAPTER 12

The Leaven of the Pharisees. 1*† Meanwhile, so many people were crowding together that they were trampling one another underfoot. He began to speak, first to his disciples, "Beware of the leaven—that is, the hypocrisy—of the Pharisees.

Courage under Persecution.† 2* "There is nothing concealed that will not be revealed, nor secret that will not be known. 3 Therefore whatever you have said in the darkness will be heard in the light, and what you have whispered behind closed doors will be proclaimed on the housetops. 4 I tell you, my friends, do not be afraid of those who kill the body but after that can do no more. 5† I shall show you whom to fear. Be afraid of the one who after killing has the power to cast into Gehenna; yes, I tell you, be afraid of that one. 6† Are not five sparrows sold for two small coins? Yet not one of them has escaped the notice of God. 7* Even the hairs of your head have all been counted. Do not be afraid. You are worth more than many sparrows. 8 I tell you, everyone who acknowledges me before others the Son of Man will acknowledge before the angels of God. 9* But whoever denies me before others will be denied before the angels of God.

Sayings about the holy Spirit.† 10* "Everyone who speaks a word against the Son of Man will be forgiven, but the one who blasphemes against the holy Spirit will not be forgiven. 11* When they take you before synagogues and before rulers and authorities, do not worry about how or what your defense will be or about what you are to say. 12 For the holy Spirit will teach you at that moment what you should say."

Saying against Greed.† 13 Someone in the crowd said to him, "Teacher, tell my brother to share the inheritance with me." 14* He replied to him, "Friend, who appointed me as your judge and arbitrator?" 15* Then he said to the crowd, "Take care to guard against all greed, for though one may be rich, one's life does not consist of possessions."

Parable of the Rich Fool. 16 Then he told them a parable. "There was a rich man whose land produced a bountiful harvest. 17 He asked himself, 'What shall I do, for I do not have space to store my harvest?' 18 And he said, 'This is what I shall do: I shall tear down my barns and build larger ones. There I shall store all my grain and other goods 19* and I shall say to myself, "Now as for you, you have so many good things stored up for many years, rest, eat, drink, be merry!"' 20 But God said to him, 'You fool, this night your life will be demanded of you; and the things you have prepared, to whom will they belong?' 21† Thus will it be for the one who stores up treasure for himself but is not rich in what matters to God."

Dependence on God. 22* He said to [his] disciples, "Therefore I tell you, do not worry about your life and what you will eat, or about your body and what you will wear. 23 For life is more than food and the body more than clothing. 24* Notice the ravens: they do not sow or reap; they have neither storehouse nor barn, yet God feeds them. How much more important are you than

---

*

51: Gn 4, 8; 2 Chr 24, 20-22.
52: Mt 23, 13.
53: 6, 11; Mt 22, 15-22.
54: 20, 20.
12, 1: Mt 16, 6; Mk 8, 15.
2-9: Mt 10, 26-33.
2: 8, 17; Mk 4, 22.
7: 12, 24; 21, 18; Acts 27, 34.
9: 9, 26; Mk 8, 38; 2 Tm 2, 12.
10: Mt 12, 31-32; Mk 3, 28-29.
11-12: 21, 12-15; Mt 10, 17-20; Mk 13, 11.
14: Ex 2, 14; Acts 7, 27.
15: 1 Tm 6, 9-10.
19-21: Mt 6, 19-21; 1 Tm 6, 17.
19-20: Sir 11, 19.
22-32: Mt 6, 25-34.
24: 12, 7.

---

†

11, 51: *From the blood of Abel to the blood of Zechariah:* the murder of Abel is the first murder recounted in the Old Testament (Gn 4, 8). The Zechariah mentioned here may be the Zechariah whose murder is recounted in 2 Chr 24, 20-22, the last murder presented in the Hebrew canon of the Old Testament.

12, 1: See the notes on Mk 8, 15 and Mt 16, 5-12.

12, 2-9: Luke presents a collection of sayings of Jesus exhorting his followers to acknowledge him and his mission fearlessly and assuring them of God's protection even in times of persecution. They are paralleled in Mt 10, 26-33.

12, 5: *Gehenna:* see the note on Mt 5, 22.

12, 6: *Two small coins:* the Roman copper coin, the assarion (Latin *as*), was worth about one-sixteenth of a denarius (see the note on 7, 41).

12, 10-12: The sayings about the holy Spirit are set in the context of fearlessness in the face of persecution (2-9; cf Mt 12, 31-32). The holy Spirit will be presented in Luke's second volume, the Acts of the Apostles, as the power responsible for the guidance of the Christian mission and the source of courage in the face of persecution.

12, 13-34: Luke has joined together sayings contrasting those whose focus and trust in life is on material possessions, symbolized here by the rich fool of the parable (16-21), with those who recognize their complete dependence on God (21), those whose radical detachment from material possessions symbolizes their heavenly treasure (33-34).

12, 21: *Rich in what matters to God:* literally, "rich for God."

birds! 25 Can any of you by worrying add a moment to your lifespan? 26 If even the smallest things are beyond your control, why are you anxious about the rest? 27* Notice how the flowers grow. They do not toil or spin. But I tell you, not even Solomon in all his splendor was dressed like one of them. 28 If God so clothes the grass in the field that grows today and is thrown into the oven tomorrow, will he not much more provide for you, O you of little faith? 29 As for you, do not seek what you are to eat and what you are to drink, and do not worry anymore. 30 All the nations of the world seek for these things, and your Father knows that you need them. 31 Instead, seek his kingdom, and these other things will be given you besides. 32* Do not be afraid any longer, little flock, for your Father is pleased to give you the kingdom. 33* Sell your belongings and give alms. Provide money bags for yourselves that do not wear out, an inexhaustible treasure in heaven that no thief can reach nor moth destroy. 34 For where your treasure is, there also will your heart be.

***Vigilant and Faithful Servants.*†** 35* "Gird your loins and light your lamps 36* and be like servants who await their master's return from a wedding, ready to open immediately when he comes and knocks. 37 Blessed are those servants whom the master finds vigilant on his arrival. Amen, I say to you, he will gird himself, have them recline at table, and proceed to wait on them. 38 And should he come in the second or third watch and find them prepared in this way, blessed are those servants. 39* Be sure of this: if the master of the house had known the hour when the thief was coming, he would not have let his house be broken into. 40 You also must be prepared, for at an hour you do not expect, the Son of Man will come."

41 Then Peter said, "Lord, is this parable meant for us or for everyone?" 42 And the Lord replied, "Who, then, is the faithful and prudent steward whom the master will put in charge of his servants to distribute [the] food allowance at the proper time? 43 Blessed is that servant whom his master on arrival finds doing so. 44 Truly, I say to you, he will put him in charge of all his property. 45† But if that servant says to himself, 'My master is delayed in coming,' and begins to beat the menservants and the maidservants, to eat and drink and get drunk, 46 then that servant's master will come on an unexpected day and at an unknown hour and will punish him severely and assign him a place with the unfaithful. 47* That servant who knew his master's will but did not make preparations nor act in accord with his will shall be beaten severely; 48 and the servant who was ignorant of his master's will but acted in a way deserving of a severe beating shall be beaten only lightly. Much will be required of the person entrusted with much, and still more will be demanded of the person entrusted with more.

***Jesus: A Cause of Division.*†** 49 "I have come to set the earth on fire, and how I wish it were already blazing! 50*† There is a baptism with which I must be baptized, and how great is my anguish until it is accomplished! 51* Do you think that I have come to establish peace on the earth? No, I tell you, but rather division. 52 From now on a household of five will be divided, three against two and two against three; 53* a father will be divided against his son and a son against his father, a mother against her daughter and a daughter against her mother, a mother-in-law against her daughter-in-law and a daughter-in-law against her mother-in-law."

Signs of the Times. 54* He also said to the crowds, "When you see [a] cloud rising in the west you say immediately that it is going to rain—and so it does; 55 and when you notice that the wind is blowing from the south you say that it is going to be hot—and so it is. 56 You hypocrites! You know how to interpret the appearance of the earth and the sky; why do you not know how to interpret the present time?

Settlement with an Opponent. 57* "Why do you not judge for yourselves what is right? 58 If you are to go with your opponent before a magistrate, make an effort to settle the matter on the way; otherwise your opponent will turn you over to the judge, and the judge hand you over to the constable, and the constable throw you into prison.

LUKE

*

27: 1 Kgs 10, 4-7; 2 Chr 9, 3-6.
32: 22, 29; Rv 1, 6.
33: 18, 22; Mt 6, 20-21; Mk 10, 21.
35-46: Mt 24, 45-51.
36: Mt 25, 1-13; Mk 13, 35-37.
39-40: Mt 24, 43-44; 1 Thes 5, 2.
47: Jas 4, 17.
50: Mk 10, 38-39.
51-53: Mt 10, 34-35.
51: 2, 14.
53: Mi 7, 6.
54-56: Mt 16, 2-3.
57-59: Mt 5, 25-26.

†

12, 35-48: This collection of sayings relates to Luke's understanding of the end time and the return of Jesus. Luke emphasizes for his readers the importance of being faithful to the instructions of Jesus in the period before the parousia.

12, 45: *My master is delayed in coming:* this statement indicates that early Christian expectations for the imminent return of Jesus had undergone some modification. Luke cautions his readers against counting on such a delay and acting irresponsibly. Cf the similar warning in Mt 24, 48.

12, 49-53: Jesus' proclamation of the kingdom is a refining and purifying fire. His message that meets with acceptance or rejection will be a source of conflict and dissension even within families.

12, 50: *Baptism:* i.e., his death.

59† I say to you, you will not be released
until you have paid the last penny."

CHAPTER 13

A Call to Repentance. † 1† At that
time some people who were present
there told him about the Galileans
whose blood Pilate had mingled with
the blood of their sacrifices. 2* He said
to them in reply, "Do you think that be-
cause these Galileans suffered in this
way they were greater sinners than all
other Galileans? 3* By no means! But I
tell you, if you do not repent, you will
all perish as they did! 4† Or those eigh-
teen people who were killed when the
tower at Siloam fell on them—do you
think they were more guilty than every-
one else who lived in Jerusalem?
5 By no means! But I tell you, if you do
not repent, you will all perish as they
did!"

The Parable of the Barren Fig Tree. †
6* And he told them this parable:
"There once was a person who had a
fig tree planted in his orchard, and
when he came in search of fruit on it
but found none, 7 he said to the gar-
dener, 'For three years now I have
come in search of fruit on this fig tree
but have found none. [So] cut it down.
Why should it exhaust the soil?' 8 He
said to him in reply, 'Sir, leave it for
this year also, and I shall cultivate the
ground around it and fertilize it; 9 it may
bear fruit in the future. If not you can
cut it down.'"

***Cure of a Crippled Woman on the
Sabbath.*** † 10 He was teaching in a syna-
gogue on the sabbath. 11 And a woman
was there who for eighteen years had
been crippled by a spirit; she was bent
over, completely incapable of standing
erect. 12 When Jesus saw her, he called
to her and said, "Woman, you are set
free of your infirmity." 13 He laid his
hands on her, and she at once stood up
straight and glorified God. 14* But the
leader of the synagogue, indignant that
Jesus had cured on the sabbath, said
to the crowd in reply, "There are six
days when work should be done. Come
on those days to be cured, not on the
sabbath day." 15*† The Lord said to him
in reply, "Hypocrites! Does not each
one of you on the sabbath untie his ox
or his ass from the manger and lead it
out for watering? 16*† This daughter of
Abraham, whom Satan has bound for
eighteen years now, ought she not to
have been set free on the sabbath day
from this bondage?" 17 When he said
this, all his adversaries were hu-
miliated; and the whole crowd re-
joiced at all the splendid deeds done by
him.

The Parable of the Mustard Seed. †
18* Then he said, "What is the kingdom
of God like? To what can I compare it?
19* It is like a mustard seed that a per-
son took and planted in the garden.
When it was fully grown, it became a
large bush and 'the birds of the sky
dwelt in its branches.'"

The Parable of the Yeast. 20* Again
he said, "To what shall I compare the
kingdom of God? 21 It is like yeast that
a woman took and mixed [in] with three
measures of wheat flour until the whole
batch of dough was leavened."

*

13, 2: Jn 9, 2.
3-5: Jn 8, 24.
6-9: Jer 8, 13; Hb 3, 17; Mt 21, 19; Mk 11, 13.
14: 6, 7; 14, 3; Ex 20, 8-11; Dt 5, 12-15; Mt 12, 10; Mk 3, 2-4; Jn 5, 16; 7, 23; 9, 14.16.
15: 14, 5; Dt 22, 4; Mt 12, 11.
16: 19, 9.
18-19: Mt 13, 31-32; Mk 4, 30-32.
19: Ez 17, 23-24; 31, 6.
20-21: Mt 13, 33.

†

12, 59: *The last penny:* Greek, *lepton,* a very small amount. Mt 5, 26 has for "the last penny" the Greek word *kodrantēs* (Latin *quadrans,* "farthing").

13, 1-5: The death of the Galileans at the hands of Pilate (1) and the accidental death of those on whom the tower fell (4) are presented by the Lucan Jesus as timely reminders of the need for all to repent, for the victims of these tragedies should not be considered outstanding sinners who were singled out for punishment.

13, 1: The slaughter of the Galileans by Pilate is unknown outside Lk; but from what is known about Pilate from the Jewish historian Josephus, such a slaughter would be in keeping with the character of Pilate. Josephus reports that Pilate had disrupted a religious gathering of the Samaritans on Mt. Gerizim with a slaughter of the participants (*Antiquities* 18, 4, 1 §§86-87), and that on another occasion Pilate had killed many Jews who had opposed him when he appropriated money from the temple treasury to build an aqueduct in Jerusalem (*Jewish War* 2, 9, 4 §§175-77; *Antiquities* 18, 3, 2 §§60-62).

13, 4: Like the incident mentioned in v 1, nothing of this accident in Jerusalem is known outside Lk and the New Testament.

13, 6-9: Following on the call to repentance in vv 1-5, the parable of the barren fig tree presents a story about the continuing patience of God with those who have not yet given evidence of their repentance (see 3, 8). The parable may also be alluding to the delay of the end time, when punishment will be meted out, and the importance of preparing for the end of the age because the delay will not be permanent (8-9).

13, 10-17: The cure of the crippled woman on the sabbath and the controversy that results furnishes a parallel to an incident that will be reported by Lk in 14, 1-6, the cure of the man with dropsy on the sabbath. A characteristic of Luke's style is the juxtaposition of an incident that reveals Jesus' concern for a man with an incident that reveals his concern for a woman; cf, e.g., 7, 11-17 and 8, 49-56.

13, 15-16: If the law as interpreted by Jewish tradition allowed for the untying of bound animals on the sabbath, how much more should this woman who has been bound by Satan's power be freed on the sabbath from her affliction.

13, 16: *Whom Satan has bound:* affliction and infirmity are taken as evidence of Satan's hold on humanity. The healing ministry of Jesus reveals the gradual wresting from Satan of control over humanity and the establishment of God's kingdom.

13, 18-21: Two parables are used to illustrate the future proportions of the kingdom of God that will result from its deceptively small beginning in the preaching and healing ministry of Jesus. They are paralleled in Mt 13, 31-33 and Mk 4, 30-32.

***The Narrow Door; Salvation and Rejection.*†** 22 He passed through towns and villages, teaching as he went and making his way to Jerusalem. 23 Someone asked him, "Lord, will only a few people be saved?" He answered them, 24* "Strive to enter through the narrow gate, for many, I tell you, will attempt to enter but will not be strong enough. 25* After the master of the house has arisen and locked the door, then will you stand outside knocking and saying, 'Lord, open the door for us.' He will say to you in reply, 'I do not know where you are from.' 26 And you will say, 'We ate and drank in your company and you taught in our streets.' 27* Then he will say to you, 'I do not know where [you] are from. Depart from me, all you evildoers!' 28* And there will be wailing and grinding of teeth when you see Abraham, Isaac, and Jacob and all the prophets in the kingdom of God and you yourselves cast out. 29* And people will come from the east and the west and from the north and the south and will recline at table in the kingdom of God. 30* For behold, some are last who will be first, and some are first who will be last."

Herod's Desire to Kill Jesus. 31 At that time some Pharisees came to him and said, "Go away, leave this area because Herod wants to kill you." 32† He replied, "Go and tell that fox, 'Behold, I cast out demons and I perform healings today and tomorrow, and on the third day I accomplish my purpose. 33*† Yet I must continue on my way today, tomorrow, and the following day, for it is impossible that a prophet should die outside of Jerusalem.'

The Lament over Jerusalem. 34* "Jerusalem, Jerusalem, you who kill the prophets and stone those sent to you, how many times I yearned to gather your children together as a hen gathers her brood under her wings, but you were unwilling! 35* Behold, your house will be abandoned. [But] I tell you, you will not see me until [the time comes when] you say, 'Blessed is he who comes in the name of the Lord.' "

CHAPTER 14

***Healing of the Man with Dropsy on the Sabbath.*†** 1* On a sabbath he went to dine at the home of one of the leading Pharisees, and the people there were observing him carefully. 2† In front of him there was a man suffering from dropsy. 3* Jesus spoke to the scholars of the law and Pharisees in reply, asking, "Is it lawful to cure on the sabbath or not?" 4 But they kept silent; so he took the man and, after he had healed him, dismissed him. 5*† Then he said to them, "Who among you, if your son or ox falls into a cistern, would not immediately pull him out on the sabbath day?" 6* But they were unable to answer his question.

***Conduct of Invited Guests and Hosts.*†** 7* He told a parable to those who had been invited, noticing how they were choosing the places of honor at the table. 8* "When you are invited by someone to a wedding banquet, do not recline at table in the place of honor. A more distinguished guest than you may have been invited by him, 9 and the host who invited both of you may approach you and say, 'Give your place to this man,' and then you would proceed with embarrassment to take the lowest place. 10 Rather, when you are invited, go and take the lowest place so that when the host comes to you he may say, 'My friend, move up to a higher position.' Then you will enjoy the esteem of your companions at the table. 11* For everyone who exalts himself will be humbled, but the one who humbles himself will be exalted." 12* Then he said to the host who invited him, "When you hold a

LUKE

*

24-30: Mt 7, 13-14.21-23.
24: Mk 10, 25.
25: Mt 25, 10-12.
27: Ps 6, 9; Mt 7, 23; 25, 41.
28-29: Mt 8, 11-12.
29: Ps 107, 2-3.
30: Mt 19, 20; 20, 16; Mk 10, 31.
33: 2, 38; Jn 6, 30; 8, 20.
34-35: 19, 41-44; Mt 23, 37-39.
35: 19, 38; 1 Kgs 9, 7-8; Ps 118, 26; Jer 7, 4-7.13-15; 12, 7; 22, 5.
14, 1-6: 6, 6-11; 13, 10-17.
1: 11, 37.
3: 6, 9; Mk 3, 4.
5: 13, 15; Dt 22, 4; Mt 12, 11.
6: Mt 22, 46.
7: 11, 43; Mt 23, 6; Mk 12, 38-39.
8-10: Prv 25, 6-7.
11: 18, 14.
12: 6, 32-35.

†

13, 22-30: These sayings of Jesus follow in Lk upon the parables of the kingdom (18-21) and stress that great effort is required for entrance into the kingdom (24) and that there is an urgency to accept the present opportunity to enter because the narrow door will not remain open indefinitely (25). Lying behind the sayings is the rejection of Jesus and his message by his Jewish contemporaries (26) whose places at table in the kingdom will be taken by Gentiles from the four corners of the world (29). Those called last (the Gentiles) will precede those to whom the invitation to enter was first extended (the Jews). See also 14, 15-24.

13, 32: Nothing, not even Herod's desire to kill Jesus, stands in the way of Jesus' role in fulfilling God's will and in establishing the kingdom through his exorcisms and healings.

13, 33: *It is impossible that a prophet should die outside of Jerusalem:* Jerusalem is the city of destiny and the goal of the journey of the prophet Jesus. Only when he reaches the holy city will his work be accomplished.

14, 1-6: See the note on 13, 10-17.

14, 2: *Dropsy:* an abnormal swelling of the body because of the retention and accumulation of fluid.

14, 5: *Your son or ox:* this is the reading of many of the oldest and most important New Testament manuscripts. Because of the strange collocation of *son* and *ox*, some copyists have altered it to "your ass or ox," on the model of the saying in 13, 15.

14, 7-14: The banquet scene found only in Luke provides the opportunity for these teachings of Jesus on humility and presents a setting to display Luke's interest in Jesus' attitude toward the rich and the poor (see the notes on 4, 18; 6, 20-26; 12, 13-34).

lunch or a dinner, do not invite your
friends or your brothers or your rela-
tives or your wealthy neighbors, in case
they may invite you back and you have
repayment. 13 Rather, when you hold a
banquet, invite the poor, the crippled,
the lame, the blind; 14* blessed indeed
will you be because of their inability to
repay you. For you will be repaid at the
resurrection of the righteous."

The Parable of the Great Feast.†
15 One of his fellow guests on hearing
this said to him, "Blessed is the one who
will dine in the kingdom of God."
16* He replied to him, "A man gave a
great dinner to which he invited many.
17 When the time for the dinner came,
he dispatched his servant to say to those
invited, 'Come, everything is now
ready.' 18 But one by one, they all began
to excuse themselves. The first said to
him, 'I have purchased a field and must
go to examine it; I ask you, consider me
excused.' 19 And another said, 'I have
purchased five yoke of oxen and am on
my way to evaluate them; I ask you,
consider me excused.' 20 And another
said, 'I have just married a woman, and
therefore I cannot come.' 21 The servant
went and reported this to his master.
Then the master of the house in a rage
commanded his servant, 'Go out
quickly into the streets and alleys of the
town and bring in here the poor and the
crippled, the blind and the lame.'
22 The servant reported, 'Sir, your or-
ders have been carried out and still
there is room.' 23 The master then or-
dered the servant, 'Go out to the high-
ways and hedgerows and make people
come in that my home may be filled.
24 For, I tell you, none of those men who
were invited will taste my dinner.' "

Sayings on Discipleship.† 25 Great
crowds were traveling with him, and he
turned and addressed them, 26*† "If
anyone comes to me without hating his
father and mother, wife and children,
brothers and sisters, and even his own
life, he cannot be my disciple.
27* Whoever does not carry his own
cross and come after me cannot be my
disciple. 28 Which of you wishing to con-
struct a tower does not first sit down and
calculate the cost to see if there is
enough for its completion? 29 Otherwise,
after laying the foundation and finding
himself unable to finish the work the on-
lookers should laugh at him 30 and say,
'This one began to build but did not have
the resources to finish.' 31 Or what king
marching into battle would not first sit
down and decide whether with ten thou-
sand troops he can successfully oppose
another king advancing upon him with
twenty thousand troops? 32 But if not,
while he is still far away, he will send
a delegation to ask for peace terms.
33* In the same way, everyone of you
who does not renounce all his posses-
sions cannot be my disciple.

The Simile of Salt.† 34* "Salt is good,
but if salt itself loses its taste, with what
can its flavor be restored? 35* It is fit nei-
ther for the soil nor for the manure pile;
it is thrown out. Whoever has ears to
hear ought to hear."

CHAPTER 15

The Parable of the Lost Sheep.†
1* The tax collectors and sinners were
all drawing near to listen to him,
2* but the Pharisees and scribes began
to complain, saying, "This man wel-
comes sinners and eats with them."
3 So to them he addressed this parable.
4* "What man among you having a hun-
dred sheep and losing one of them
would not leave the ninety-nine in the
desert and go after the lost one until he
finds it? 5 And when he does find it, he
sets it on his shoulders with great joy
6 and, upon his arrival home, he calls
together his friends and neighbors and
says to them, 'Rejoice with me because
I have found my lost sheep.' 7* I tell you,
in just the same way there will be more
joy in heaven over one sinner who
repents than over ninety-nine righ-
teous people who have no need of re-
pentance.

*

14: Jn 5, 29.
16-24: Mt 22, 2-10.
26-27: Mt 10, 37-38.
26: 9, 57-62; 18, 29; Jn 12, 25.
27: 9, 23; Mt 16, 24; Mk 8, 34.
33: 5, 11.
34: Mt 5, 13; Mk 9, 50.
35: 8, 8; Mt 11, 15; 13, 9; Mk 4, 9.23.
15, 1-7: Mt 9, 10-13.
2: 5, 30; 19, 7.
4-7: Mt 18, 12-14.
4-6: 19, 10.
4: Ez 34, 11-12.16.
7: Ez 18, 23.

†

14, 15-24: The parable of the great dinner is a further illustration of the rejection by Israel, God's chosen people, of Jesus' invitation to share in the banquet in the kingdom and the extension of the invitation to other Jews whose identification as the poor, crippled, blind, and lame (21) classifies them among those who recognize their need for salvation, and to Gentiles (23). A similar parable is found in Mt 22, 1-10.

14, 25-33: This collection of sayings, most of which are peculiar to Lk, focuses on the total dedication necessary for the disciple of Jesus. No attachment to family (26) or possessions (33) can stand in the way of the total commitment demanded of the disciple. Also, acceptance of the call to be a disciple demands readiness to accept persecution and suffering (27) and a realistic assessment of the hardships and costs (28-32).

14, 26: *Hating his father . . . :* cf the similar saying in Mt 10, 37. The disciple's family must take second place to the absolute dedication involved in following Jesus (see also 9, 59-62).

14, 34-35: The simile of salt follows the sayings of Jesus that demanded of the disciple total dedication and detachment from family and possessions and illustrates the condition of one who does not display this total commitment. The half-hearted disciple is like salt that cannot serve its intended purpose. See the simile of salt in Mt 5, 13 and the note there.

15, 1-32: To the parable of the lost sheep (1-7) that Luke shares with Matthew (Mt 18, 12-14), Luke adds two parables (the lost coin, 8-10; the prodigal son, 11-32) from his own special tradition to illustrate Jesus' particular concern for the lost and God's love for the repentant sinner.

The Parable of the Lost Coin. 8† “Or
what woman having ten coins and los-
ing one would not light a lamp and
sweep the house, searching carefully
until she finds it? 9 And when she does
find it, she calls together her friends and
neighbors and says to them, ‘Rejoice
with me because I have found the coin
that I lost.’ 10 In just the same way, I
tell you, there will be rejoicing among
the angels of God over one sinner who
repents.”

The Parable of the Lost Son. 11 Then
he said, “A man had two sons, 12 and
the younger son said to his father, ‘Fa-
ther, give me the share of your estate
that should come to me.’ So the father
divided the property between them.
13* After a few days, the younger son
collected all his belongings and set off
to a distant country where he squan-
dered his inheritance on a life of dissi-
pation. 14 When he had freely spent
everything, a severe famine struck that
country, and he found himself in dire
need. 15 So he hired himself out to one
of the local citizens who sent him to his
farm to tend the swine. 16 And he longed
to eat his fill of the pods on which the
swine fed, but nobody gave him any.
17 Coming to his senses he thought, ‘How
many of my father’s hired workers have
more than enough food to eat, but here
am I, dying from hunger. 18 I shall get
up and go to my father and I shall say
to him, “Father, I have sinned against
heaven and against you. 19 I no longer
deserve to be called your son; treat me
as you would treat one of your hired
workers.” ’ 20 So he got up and went
back to his father. While he was still a
long way off, his father caught sight of
him, and was filled with compassion. He
ran to his son, embraced him and kissed
him. 21 His son said to him, ‘Father, I
have sinned against heaven and against
you; I no longer deserve to be called
your son.’ 22 But his father ordered his
servants, ‘Quickly bring the finest robe
and put it on him; put a ring on his finger
and sandals on his feet. 23 Take the fat-
tened calf and slaughter it. Then let us
celebrate with a feast, 24 because this
son of mine was dead, and has come
to life again; he was lost, and has been
found.’ Then the celebration began.
25 Now the older son had been out in the
field and, on his way back, as he neared
the house, he heard the sound of music
and dancing. 26 He called one of the ser-
vants and asked what this might mean.
27 The servant said to him, ‘Your brother
has returned and your father has
slaughtered the fattened calf because
he has him back safe and sound.’
28 He became angry, and when he re-
fused to enter the house, his father
came out and pleaded with him. 29 He
said to his father in reply, ‘Look, all
these years I served you and not once
did I disobey your orders; yet you never
gave me even a young goat to feast on
with my friends. 30 But when your son
returns who swallowed up your prop-
erty with prostitutes, for him you
slaughter the fattened calf.’ 31 He said
to him, ‘My son, you are here with me
always; everything I have is yours.
32 But now we must celebrate and re-
joice, because your brother was dead
and has come to life again; he was lost
and has been found.’ ”

LUKE

CHAPTER 16

***The Parable of the Dishonest Stew-
ard.*** † 1 Then he also said to his disci-
ples, “A rich man had a steward who
was reported to him for squandering his
property. 2 He summoned him and said,
‘What is this I hear about you? Prepare
a full account of your stewardship, be-
cause you can no longer be my stew-
ard.’ 3 The steward said to himself,
‘What shall I do, now that my master
is taking the position of steward away
from me? I am not strong enough to dig
and I am ashamed to beg. 4 I know what
I shall do so that, when I am removed
from the stewardship, they may wel-
come me into their homes.’ 5 He called
in his master’s debtors one by one. To
the first he said, ‘How much do you owe
my master?’ 6† He replied, ‘One hun-
dred measures of olive oil.’ He said to
him, ‘Here is your promissory note. Sit
down and quickly write one for fifty.’
7† Then to another he said, ‘And you,
how much do you owe?’ He replied, ‘One
hundred kors of wheat.’ He said to him,
‘Here is your promissory note; write one
for eighty.’ 8* And the master com-

*

15, 13: Prv 29, 3.
16, 8: Eph 5, 8; 1 Thes 5, 5.

†

15, 8: *Ten coins:* literally, “ten drachmas.” A drachma was a Greek silver coin.

16, 1-8a: The parable of the dishonest steward has to be understood in the light of the Palestinian custom of agents acting on behalf of their masters and the usurious practices common to such agents. The dishonesty of the steward consisted in the squandering of his master’s property (1) and not in any subsequent graft. The master commends the dishonest steward who has forgone his own usurious commission on the business transaction by having the debtors write new notes that reflected only the real amount owed the master (i.e., minus the steward’s profit). The dishonest steward acts in this way in order to ingratiate himself with the debtors because he knows he is being dismissed from his position (3). The parable, then, teaches the prudent use of one’s material goods in light of an imminent crisis.

16, 6: *One hundred measures:* literally, “one hundred *baths.*” A *bath* is a Hebrew unit of liquid measurement equivalent to eight or nine gallons.

16, 7: *One hundred kors:* a *kor* is a Hebrew unit of dry measure for grain or wheat equivalent to ten or twelve bushels.

mended that dishonest steward for act-
ing prudently.
Application of the Parable.† "For the
children of this world are more prudent
in dealing with their own generation
than are the children of light. 9*† I tell
you, make friends for yourselves with
dishonest wealth, so that when it fails,
you will be welcomed into eternal dwell-
ings. 10*† The person who is trustworthy
in very small matters is also trustwor-
thy in great ones; and the person who
is dishonest in very small matters is also
dishonest in great ones. 11 If, therefore,
you are not trustworthy with dishonest
wealth, who will trust you with true
wealth? 12 If you are not trustworthy
with what belongs to another, who will
give you what is yours? 13*† No servant
can serve two masters. He will either
hate one and love the other, or be de-
voted to one and despise the other. You
cannot serve God and mammon."
A Saying against the Pharisees.†
14† The Pharisees, who loved money,
heard all these things and sneered at
him. 15* And he said to them, "You jus-
tify yourselves in the sight of others, but
God knows your hearts; for what is of
human esteem is an abomination in the
sight of God.
Sayings about the Law. 16*† "The law
and the prophets lasted until John; but
from then on the kingdom of God is pro-
claimed, and everyone who enters does
so with violence. 17* It is easier for
heaven and earth to pass away than for
the smallest part of a letter of the law
to become invalid.
Sayings about Divorce. 18* "Ev-
eryone who divorces his wife and mar-
ries another commits adultery, and the
one who marries a woman divorced
from her husband commits adultery.
***The Parable of the Rich Man and
Lazarus.***† 19† "There was a rich man
who dressed in purple garments and
fine linen and dined sumptuously each
day. 20 And lying at his door was a poor
man named Lazarus, covered with
sores, 21* who would gladly have eaten
his fill of the scraps that fell from the
rich man's table. Dogs even used to
come and lick his sores. 22 When the
poor man died, he was carried away by
angels to the bosom of Abraham. The
rich man also died and was buried,
23† and from the netherworld, where he
was in torment, he raised his eyes and
saw Abraham far off and Lazarus at his
side. 24 And he cried out, 'Father Abra-
ham, have pity on me. Send Lazarus to
dip the tip of his finger in water and cool
my tongue, for I am suffering torment
in these flames.' 25* Abraham replied,
'My child, remember that you received
what was good during your lifetime
while Lazarus likewise received what
was bad; but now he is comforted here,
whereas you are tormented.
26 Moreover, between us and you a great
chasm is established to prevent anyone
from crossing who might wish to go
from our side to yours or from your side
to ours.' 27 He said, 'Then I beg you, fa-
ther, send him to my father's house,
28 for I have five brothers, so that he
may warn them, lest they too come to
this place of torment.' 29 But Abraham
replied, 'They have Moses and the
prophets. Let them listen to them.'
30† He said, 'Oh no, father Abraham, but
if someone from the dead goes to them,
they will repent.' 31* Then Abraham
said, 'If they will not listen to Moses and
the prophets, neither will they be per-
suaded if someone should rise from the
dead.'"

*

9: 12, 33.
10: 19, 17; Mt 25, 20-23.
13: Mt 6, 24.
15: 18, 9-14.
16: Mt 11, 12-13.
17: Mt 5, 18.
18: Mt 5, 32; 19, 9; Mk 10, 11-12; 1 Cor 7, 10-11.
21: Mt 15, 27; Mk 7, 28.
25: 6, 24-25.
31: Jn 5, 46-47; 11, 44-48.

†

16, 8b-13: Several originally independent sayings of Jesus are gathered here by Luke to form the concluding application of the parable of the dishonest steward.

16, 8b-9: The first conclusion recommends the prudent use of one's wealth (in the light of the coming of the end of the age) after the manner of the children of this world, represented in the parable by the dishonest steward.

16, 9: *Dishonest wealth:* literally, "mammon of iniquity." Mammon is the Greek transliteration of a Hebrew or Aramaic word that is usually explained as meaning "that in which one trusts." The characterization of this wealth as *dishonest* expresses a tendency of wealth to lead one to dishonesty. *Eternal dwellings:* or, "eternal tents," i.e., heaven.

16, 10-12: The second conclusion recommends constant fidelity to those in positions of responsibility.

16, 13: The third conclusion is a general statement about the incompatibility of serving God and being a slave to riches. To be dependent upon wealth is opposed to the teachings of Jesus who counseled complete dependence on the Father as one of the characteristics of the Christian disciple (12, 22-39). *God and mammon:* see the note on 16, 9. Mammon is used here as if it were itself a god.

16, 14-18: The two parables about the use of riches in ch 16 are separated by several isolated sayings of Jesus on the hypocrisy of the Pharisees (14-15), on the law (16-17), and on divorce (18).

16, 14-15: The Pharisees are here presented as examples of those who are slaves to wealth (see 16, 13) and, consequently, they are unable to serve God.

16, 16: John the Baptist is presented in Luke's gospel as a transitional figure between the period of Israel, the time of promise, and the period of Jesus, the time of fulfillment. With John, the fulfillment of the Old Testament promises has begun.

16, 19-31: The parable of the rich man and Lazarus again illustrates Luke's concern with Jesus' attitude toward the rich and the poor. The reversal of the fates of the rich man and Lazarus (22-23) illustrates the teachings of Jesus in Luke's "Sermon on the Plain" (6, 20-21.24-25).

16, 19: The oldest Greek manuscript of Lk dating from ca. A.D. 175-225 records the name of the rich man as an abbreviated form of "Nineveh," but there is very little textual support in other manuscripts for this reading. "Dives" of popular tradition is the Latin Vulgate's translation for "rich man."

16, 23: *The netherworld:* see the note on 10, 15.

16, 30-31: A foreshadowing in Luke's gospel of the rejection of the call to repentance even after Jesus' resurrection.

CHAPTER 17

Temptations to Sin. 1* He said to his
disciples, "Things that cause sin will in-
evitably occur, but woe to the person
through whom they occur. 2 It would be
better for him if a millstone were put
around his neck and he be thrown into
the sea than for him to cause one of
these little ones to sin. 3*† Be on your
guard! If your brother sins, rebuke him;
and if he repents, forgive him. 4* And
if he wrongs you seven times in one day
and returns to you seven times saying,
'I am sorry,' you should forgive him."

Saying of Faith. 5 And the apostles
said to the Lord, "Increase our faith."
6* The Lord replied, "If you have faith
the size of a mustard seed, you would
say to [this] mulberry tree, 'Be up-
rooted and planted in the sea,' and it
would obey you.

Attitude of a Servant.† 7 "Who among
you would say to your servant who has
just come in from plowing or tending
sheep in the field, 'Come here immedi-
ately and take your place at table'?
8 Would he not rather say to him, 'Pre-
pare something for me to eat. Put on
your apron and wait on me while I eat
and drink. You may eat and drink when
I am finished'? 9 Is he grateful to that
servant because he did what was com-
manded? 10 So should it be with you.
When you have done all you have been
commanded, say, 'We are unprofitable
servants; we have done what we were
obliged to do.' "

The Cleansing of Ten Lepers.†
11*† As he continued his journey to Je-
rusalem, he traveled through Samaria
and Galilee. 12 As he was entering a vil-
lage, ten lepers met [him]. They stood
at a distance from him 13* and raised
their voice, saying, "Jesus, Master!
Have pity on us!" 14*† And when he saw
them, he said, "Go show yourselves to
the priests." As they were going they
were cleansed. 15 And one of them, real-
izing he had been healed, returned, glo-
rifying God in a loud voice; 16 and he
fell at the feet of Jesus and thanked him.
He was a Samaritan. 17 Jesus said in re-
ply, "Ten were cleansed, were they not?
Where are the other nine? 18 Has none
but this foreigner returned to give
thanks to God?" 19* Then he said to him,
"Stand up and go; your faith has saved
you."

The Coming of the Kingdom of God.†
20* Asked by the Pharisees when the
kingdom of God would come, he said
in reply, "The coming of the kingdom
of God cannot be observed, 21*† and no
one will announce, 'Look, here it is,' or,
'There it is.' For behold, the kingdom
of God is among you."

The Day of the Son of Man. 22 Then
he said to his disciples, "The days will
come when you will long to see one of
the days of the Son of Man, but you will
not see it. 23* There will be those who
will say to you, 'Look, there he is,' [or]
'Look, here he is.' Do not go off, do not
run in pursuit. 24* For just as lightning
flashes and lights up the sky from one
side to the other, so will the Son of Man
be [in his day]. 25* But first he must suf-
fer greatly and be rejected by this gen-
eration. 26* As it was in the days of
Noah, so it will be in the days of the
Son of Man; 27 they were eating and
drinking, marrying and giving in mar-
riage up to the day that Noah entered
the ark, and the flood came and de-
stroyed them all. 28* Similarly, as it was
in the days of Lot: they were eating,
drinking, buying, selling, planting,
building; 29 on the day when Lot left
Sodom, fire and brimstone rained from
the sky to destroy them all. 30 So it will
be on the day the Son of Man is re-
vealed. 31* On that day, a person who

*

17, 1-2: Mt 18, 6-7.
3: Mt 18, 15.
4: Mt 6, 14; 18, 21-22.35; Mk 11, 25.
6: Mt 17, 20; 21, 21; Mk 11, 23.
11: 9, 51-53; 13, 22.33; 18, 31; 19, 28; Jn 4, 4.
13: 18, 38; Mt 9, 27; 15, 22.
14: 5, 14; Lv 14, 2-32; Mt 8, 4; Mk 1, 44.
19: 7, 50; 18, 42.
20: Jn 3, 3.
21: 17, 23; Mt 24, 23; Mk 13, 21.
23: 17, 21; Mt 24, 23.26; Mk 13, 21.
24: Mt 24, 27.
25: 9, 22; 18, 32-33; Mt 16, 21; 17, 22-23; 20, 18-19; Mk 8, 31; 9, 31; 10, 33-34.
26-27: Gn 6-8; Mt 24, 37-39.
28-29: Gn 18, 20-21; 19, 1-29.
31: Mt 24, 17-18; Mk 13, 15-16.
31-32: Gn 19, 17.26.

†

17, 3a: *Be on your guard:* the translation takes v 3a as the conclusion to the saying on scandal in vv 1-2. It is not impossible that it should be taken as the beginning of the saying on forgiveness in vv 3b-4.

17, 7-10: These sayings of Jesus, peculiar to Luke, which continue his response to the apostles' request to increase their faith (5-6), remind them that Christian disciples can make no claim on God's graciousness; in fulfilling the exacting demands of discipleship, they are only doing their duty.

17, 11-19: This incident recounting the thankfulness of the cleansed Samaritan leper is narrated only in Luke's gospel and provides an instance of Jesus holding up a non-Jew (18) as an example to his Jewish contemporaries (cf 10, 33 where a similar purpose is achieved in the story of the good Samaritan). Moreover, it is the faith in Jesus manifested by the foreigner that has brought him salvation (19; cf the similar relationship between faith and salvation in 7, 50; 8, 48.50).

17, 11: *Through Samaria and Galilee:* or, "between Samaria and Galilee."

17, 14: See the note on 5, 14.

17, 20-37: To the question of the Pharisees about the time of the coming of God's kingdom, Jesus replies that the kingdom is *among you* (20-21). The emphasis has thus been shifted from an imminent observable coming of the kingdom to something that is already present in Jesus' preaching and healing ministry. Luke has also appended further traditional sayings of Jesus about the unpredictable suddenness of the day of the Son of Man, and assures his readers that in spite of the delay of that day (12, 45), it will bring judgment unexpectedly on those who do not continue to be vigilant.

17, 21: *Among you:* the Greek preposition translated as *among* can also be translated as "within." In the light of other statements in Luke's gospel about the presence of the kingdom (see 10, 9.11; 11, 20) "among" is to be preferred.

is on the housetop and whose belongings are in the house must not go down to get them, and likewise a person in the field must not return to what was left behind. 32 Remember the wife of Lot. 33* Whoever seeks to preserve his life will lose it, but whoever loses it will save it. 34 I tell you, on that night there will be two people in one bed; one will be taken, the other left. 35* And there will be two women grinding meal together; one will be taken, the other left." [36]† 37* They said to him in reply, "Where, Lord?" He said to them, "Where the body is, there also the vultures will gather."

CHAPTER 18

The Parable of the Persistent Widow.† 1* Then he told them a parable about the necessity for them to pray always without becoming weary. He said, 2 "There was a judge in a certain town who neither feared God nor respected any human being. 3 And a widow in that town used to come to him and say, 'Render a just decision for me against my adversary.' 4 For a long time the judge was unwilling, but eventually he thought, 'While it is true that I neither fear God nor respect any human being, 5*† because this widow keeps bothering me I shall deliver a just decision for her lest she finally come and strike me.'" 6 The Lord said, "Pay attention to what the dishonest judge says. 7 Will not God then secure the rights of his chosen ones who call out to him day and night? Will he be slow to answer them? 8 I tell you, he will see to it that justice is done for them speedily. But when the Son of Man comes, will he find faith on earth?"

The Parable of the Pharisee and the Tax Collector. 9* He then addressed this parable to those who were convinced of their own righteousness and despised everyone else. 10 "Two people went up to the temple area to pray; one was a Pharisee and the other was a tax collector. 11 The Pharisee took up his position and spoke this prayer to himself, 'O God, I thank you that I am not like the rest of humanity—greedy, dishonest, adulterous—or even like this tax collector. 12* I fast twice a week, and I pay tithes on my whole income.' 13* But the tax collector stood off at a distance and would not even raise his eyes to heaven but beat his breast and prayed, 'O God, be merciful to me a sinner.' 14* I tell you, the latter went home justified, not the former; for everyone who exalts himself will be humbled, and the one who humbles himself will be exalted."

Saying on Children and the Kingdom.† 15*† People were bringing even infants to him that he might touch them, and when the disciples saw this, they rebuked them. 16 Jesus, however, called the children to himself and said, "Let the children come to me and do not prevent them; for the kingdom of God belongs to such as these. 17* Amen, I say to you, whoever does not accept the kingdom of God like a child will not enter it."

The Rich Official. 18* An official asked him this question, "Good teacher, what must I do to inherit eternal life?" 19 Jesus answered him, "Why do you call me good? No one is good but God alone. 20* You know the commandments, 'You shall not commit adultery; you shall not kill; you shall not steal; you shall not bear false witness; honor your father and your mother.'" 21 And he replied, "All of these I have observed from my youth." 22*† When Jesus heard

*

33: 9, 24; Mt 10, 39; 16, 25; Mk 8, 35; Jn 12, 25.
35: Mt 24, 40-41.
37: Jb 39, 30; Mt 24, 28.
18, 1: Rom 12, 12; Col 4, 2; 1 Thes 5, 17.
5: 11, 8.
9: 16, 5; Mt 23, 25-28.
12: Mt 23, 23.
13: Ps 51, 3.
14: 14, 11; Mt 23, 12.
15-17: Mt 19, 13-15; Mk 10, 13-16.
17: Mt 18, 3.
18-30: Mt 19, 16-30; Mk 10, 17-31.
18: 10, 25.
20: Ex 20, 12-16; Dt 5, 16-20.
22: 12, 33; Sir 29, 11; Mt 6, 20.

†

17, 36: The inclusion of v 36, "There will be two men in the field; one will be taken, the other left behind," in some Western manuscripts appears to be a scribal assimilation to Mt 24, 40.

18, 1-14: The particularly Lucan material in the travel narrative concludes with two parables on prayer. The first (1-8) teaches the disciples the need of persistent prayer so that they not fall victims to apostasy (8). The second (9-14) condemns the self-righteous, critical attitude of the Pharisee and teaches that the fundamental attitude of the Christian disciple must be the recognition of sinfulness and complete dependence on God's graciousness. The second parable recalls the story of the pardoning of the sinful woman (7, 36-50) where a similar contrast is presented between the critical attitude of the Pharisee Simon and the love shown by the pardoned sinner.

18, 5: *Strike me:* the Greek verb translated as *strike* means "to strike under the eye" and suggests the extreme situation to which the persistence of the widow might lead. It may, however, be used here in the much weaker sense of "to wear one out."

18, 15—19, 27: Luke here includes much of the material about the journey to Jerusalem found in his Marcan source (10, 1-52) and adds to it the story of Zacchaeus (19, 1-10) from his own particular tradition and the parable of the gold coins (minas) (19, 11-27) from Q, the source common to Lk and Mt.

18, 15-17: The sayings on children furnish a contrast to the attitude of the Pharisee in the preceding episode (9-14) and that of the wealthy official in the following one (18-23) who think that they can lay claim to God's favor by their own merit. The attitude of the disciple should be marked by the receptivity and trustful dependence characteristic of the child.

18, 22: Detachment from material possessions results in the total dependence on God demanded of one who would inherit eternal life. *Sell all that you have:* the original saying (cf Mk 10, 21) has characteristically been made more demanding by Luke's addition of "all."

this he said to him, "There is still one thing left for you: sell all that you have and distribute it to the poor, and you will have a treasure in heaven. Then come, follow me." 23 But when he heard this he became quite sad, for he was very rich.

On Riches and Renunciation. 24 Jesus looked at him [now sad] and said, "How hard it is for those who have wealth to enter the kingdom of God! 25 For it is easier for a camel to pass through the eye of a needle than for a rich person to enter the kingdom of God." 26 Those who heard this said, "Then who can be saved?" 27* And he said, "What is impossible for human beings is possible for God." 28 Then Peter said, "We have given up our possessions and followed you." 29* He said to them, "Amen, I say to you, there is no one who has given up house or wife or brothers or parents or children for the sake of the kingdom of God 30 who will not receive [back] an overabundant return in this present age and eternal life in the age to come."

The Third Prediction of the Passion.†
31*† Then he took the Twelve aside and said to them, "Behold, we are going up to Jerusalem and everything written by the prophets about the Son of Man will be fulfilled. 32* He will be handed over to the Gentiles and he will be mocked and insulted and spat upon; 33 and after they have scourged him they will kill him, but on the third day he will rise." 34* But they understood nothing of this; the word remained hidden from them and they failed to comprehend what he said.

The Healing of the Blind Beggar.
35* Now as he approached Jericho a blind man was sitting by the roadside begging, 36 and hearing a crowd going by, he inquired what was happening. 37 They told him, "Jesus of Nazareth is passing by." 38*† He shouted, "Jesus, Son of David, have pity on me!" 39 The people walking in front rebuked him, telling him to be silent, but he kept calling out all the more, "Son of David, have pity on me!" 40 Then Jesus stopped and ordered that he be brought to him; and when he came near, Jesus asked him, 41* "What do you want me to do for you?" He replied, "Lord, please let me see." 42* Jesus told him, "Have sight; your faith has saved you." 43 He immediately received his sight and followed him, giving glory to God. When they saw this, all the people gave praise to God.

CHAPTER 19

Zacchaeus the Tax Collector.† 1 He came to Jericho and intended to pass through the town. 2 Now a man there named Zacchaeus, who was a chief tax collector and also a wealthy man, 3 was seeking to see who Jesus was; but he could not see him because of the crowd, for he was short in stature. 4 So he ran ahead and climbed a sycamore tree in order to see Jesus, who was about to pass that way. 5 When he reached the place, Jesus looked up and said to him, "Zacchaeus, come down quickly, for today I must stay at your house." 6 And he came down quickly and received him with joy. 7* When they all saw this, they began to grumble, saying, "He has gone to stay at the house of a sinner." 8* But Zacchaeus stood there and said to the Lord, "Behold, half of my possessions, Lord, I shall give to the poor, and if I have extorted anything from anyone I shall repay it four times over." 9*† And Jesus said to him, "Today salvation has come to this house because this man too is a descendant of Abraham. 10*† For the Son of Man

LUKE

*

27: Mk 14, 36.
29-30: 14, 26.
31-34: 24, 25-27.44; Mt 20, 17-19; Mk 10, 32-34; Acts 3, 18.
32-33: 9, 22.44.
34: Mk 9, 32.
35-43: Mt 20, 29-34; Mk 10, 46-52.
38-39: 17, 13; Mt 9, 27; 15, 22.
41: Mk 10, 36.
42: 7, 50; 17, 19.
19, 7: 5, 30; 15, 2.
8: Ex 21, 37; Nm 5, 6-7; 2 Sm 12, 6.
9: 13, 16; Mt 21, 31.
10: 15, 4-10; Ez 34, 16.

†

18, 31-33: The details included in this third announcement of Jesus' suffering and death suggest that the literary formulation of the announcement has been directed by the knowledge of the historical passion and death of Jesus.

18, 31: *Everything written by the prophets . . . will be fulfilled:* this is a Lucan addition to the words of Jesus found in the Marcan source (Mk 10, 32-34). Luke understands the events of Jesus' last days in Jerusalem to be the fulfillment of Old Testament prophecy, but, as is usually the case in Luke-Acts, the author does not specify which Old Testament prophets he has in mind; cf 24, 25.27.44; Acts 3, 8; 13, 27; 26, 22-23.

18, 38: *Son of David:* the blind beggar identifies Jesus with a title that is related to Jesus' role as Messiah (see the note on 2, 11). Through this Son of David, salvation comes to the blind man. Note the connection between salvation and house of David mentioned earlier in Zechariah's canticle (1, 69). See also the note on Mt 9, 27.

19, 1-10: The story of the tax collector Zacchaeus is unique to this gospel. While a rich man (2), Zacchaeus provides a contrast to the rich man of 18, 18-23 who cannot detach himself from his material possessions to become a follower of Jesus. Zacchaeus, according to Luke, exemplifies the proper attitude toward wealth: he promises to give half of his possessions to the poor (8) and consequently is the recipient of salvation (9-10).

19, 9: *A descendant of Abraham:* literally, "a son of Abraham." The tax collector Zacchaeus, whose repentance is attested by his determination to amend his former ways, shows himself to be a true descendant of Abraham, the true heir to the promises of God in the Old Testament. Underlying Luke's depiction of Zacchaeus as a descendant of Abraham, the father of the Jews (1, 73; 16, 22-31), is his recognition of the central place occupied by Israel in the plan of salvation.

19, 10: This verse sums up for Luke his depiction of the role of Jesus as savior in this gospel.

has come to seek and to save what was
lost."

***The Parable of the Ten Gold Coins.*†**
11* While they were listening to him
speak, he proceeded to tell a parable
because he was near Jerusalem and
they thought that the kingdom of God
would appear there immediately.
12* So he said, "A nobleman went off to
a distant country to obtain the kingship
for himself and then to return. 13† He
called ten of his servants and gave them
ten gold coins and told them, 'Engage
in trade with these until I return.'
14 His fellow citizens, however, despised
him and sent a delegation after him to
announce, 'We do not want this man to
be our king.' 15 But when he returned
after obtaining the kingship, he had the
servants called, to whom he had given
the money, to learn what they had
gained by trading. 16 The first came for-
ward and said, 'Sir, your gold coin has
earned ten additional ones.' 17* He re-
plied, 'Well done, good servant! You
have been faithful in this very small
matter; take charge of ten cities.'
18 Then the second came and reported,
'Your gold coin, sir, has earned five
more.' 19 And to this servant too he said,
'You, take charge of five cities.' 20 Then
the other servant came and said, 'Sir,
here is your gold coin; I kept it stored
away in a handkerchief, 21 for I was
afraid of you, because you are a de-
manding person; you take up what you
did not lay down and you harvest what
you did not plant.' 22 He said to him,
'With your own words I shall condemn
you, you wicked servant. You knew I
was a demanding person, taking up
what I did not lay down and harvesting
what I did not plant; 23 why did you not
put my money in a bank? Then on my
return I would have collected it with in-
terest.' 24 And to those standing by he
said, 'Take the gold coin from him and
give it to the servant who has ten.'
25 But they said to him, 'Sir, he has ten
gold coins.' 26* 'I tell you, to everyone
who has, more will be given, but from
the one who has not, even what he has
will be taken away. 27 Now as for those
enemies of mine who did not want me
as their king, bring them here and slay
them before me.' "

VI: THE TEACHING MINISTRY IN JERUSALEM†

The Entry into Jerusalem. 28* After
he had said this, he proceeded on his
journey up to Jerusalem. 29* As he drew
near to Bethphage and Bethany at the
place called the Mount of Olives, he sent
two of his disciples. 30* He said, "Go into
the village opposite you, and as you en-
ter it you will find a colt tethered on
which no one has ever sat. Untie it and
bring it here. 31 And if anyone should
ask you, 'Why are you untying it?' you
will answer, 'The Master has need of
it.' " 32* So those who had been sent
went off and found everything just as
he had told them. 33 And as they were
untying the colt, its owners said to them,
"Why are you untying this colt?"
34 They answered, "The Master has
need of it." 35* So they brought it to Je-
sus, threw their cloaks over the colt, and
helped Jesus to mount. 36 As he rode
along, the people were spreading their
cloaks on the road; 37 and now as he was
approaching the slope of the Mount of
Olives, the whole multitude of his disci-
ples began to praise God aloud with joy
for all the mighty deeds they had seen.
38*† They proclaimed:

"Blessed is the king who comes
 in the name of the Lord.
Peace in heaven
 and glory in the highest."

*

11-27: Mt 25, 14-30.
12: Mk 13, 34.
17: 16, 10.
26: 8, 18; Mt 13, 12; Mk 4, 25.
28-40: Mt 21, 1-11; Mk 11, 1-11; Jn 12, 12-19.
29: Zec 14, 4.
30: Nm 19, 2; Dt 21, 3; 1 Sm 6, 7; Zec 9, 9.
32: 22, 13.
35-36: 2 Kgs 9, 13.
38: 2, 14; Ps 118, 26.

†

19, 11-27: In this parable Luke has combined two originally distinct parables: (1) a parable about the conduct of faithful and productive servants (13.15b-26) and (2) a parable about a rejected king (12.14-15a.27). The story about the conduct of servants occurs in another form in Mt 25, 14-20. The story about the rejected king may have originated with a contemporary historical event. After the death of Herod the Great, his son Archelaus traveled to Rome to receive the title of king. A delegation of Jews appeared in Rome before Caesar Augustus to oppose the request of Archelaus. Although not given the title of king, Archelaus was made ruler over Judea and Samaria. As the story is used by Luke, however, it furnishes a correction to the expectation of the imminent end of the age and of the establishment of the kingdom in Jerusalem (11). Jesus is not on his way to Jerusalem to receive the kingly power; for that, he must go away and only after returning from the distant country (a reference to the parousia) will reward and judgment take place.

19, 13: *Ten gold coins:* literally, "ten minas." A mina was a monetary unit that in ancient Greece was the equivalent of one hundred drachmas.

19, 28—21, 38: With the royal entry of Jesus into Jerusalem, a new section of Luke's gospel begins, the ministry of Jesus in Jerusalem before his death and resurrection. Luke suggests that this was a lengthy ministry in Jerusalem (19, 47; 20, 1; 21, 37-38; 22, 53) and it is characterized by Jesus' daily teaching in the temple (21, 37-38). For the story of the entry of Jesus into Jerusalem, see also Mt 21, 1-11; Mk 11, 1-10; Jn 12, 12-19 and the notes there.

19, 38: *Blessed is the king who comes in the name of the Lord:* only in Lk is Jesus explicitly given the title *king* when he enters Jerusalem in triumph. Luke has inserted this title into the words of Ps 118, 26 that heralded the arrival of the pilgrims coming to the holy city and to the temple. Jesus is thereby acclaimed as *king* (see 1, 32) and as the one *who comes* (see Mal 3, 1; Lk 7, 19). *Peace in heaven . . . :* the acclamation of the disciples of Jesus in Lk echoes the announcement of the angels at the birth of Jesus (2, 14). The peace Jesus brings is associated with the salvation to be accomplished here in Jerusalem.

39† Some of the Pharisees in the crowd said to him, "Teacher, rebuke your disciples." 40 He said in reply, "I tell you, if they keep silent, the stones will cry out!"

***The Lament for Jerusalem.*†** 41* As he drew near, he saw the city and wept over it, 42* saying, "If this day you only knew what makes for peace—but now it is hidden from your eyes. 43*† For the days are coming upon you when your enemies will raise a palisade against you; they will encircle you and hem you in on all sides. 44* They will smash you to the ground and your children within you, and they will not leave one stone upon another within you because you did not recognize the time of your visitation."

***The Cleansing of the Temple.*†** 45* Then Jesus entered the temple area and proceeded to drive out those who were selling things, 46* saying to them, "It is written, 'My house shall be a house of prayer, but you have made it a den of thieves.' " 47* And every day he was teaching in the temple area. The chief priests, the scribes, and the leaders of the people, meanwhile, were seeking to put him to death, 48 but they could find no way to accomplish their purpose because all the people were hanging on his words.

CHAPTER 20†

The Authority of Jesus Questioned. 1* One day as he was teaching the people in the temple area and proclaiming the good news, the chief priests and scribes, together with the elders, approached him 2* and said to him, "Tell us, by what authority are you doing these things? Or who is the one who gave you this authority?" 3 He said to them in reply, "I shall ask you a question. Tell me, 4* was John's baptism of heavenly or of human origin?" 5* They discussed this among themselves, and said, "If we say, 'Of heavenly origin,' he will say, 'Why did you not believe him?' 6 But if we say, 'Of human origin,' then all the people will stone us, for they are convinced that John was a prophet." 7 So they answered that they did not know from where it came. 8 Then Jesus said to them, "Neither shall I tell you by what authority I do these things."

***The Parable of the Tenant Farmers.*†** 9* Then he proceeded to tell the people this parable. "[A] man planted a vineyard, leased it to tenant farmers, and then went on a journey for a long time. 10* At harvest time he sent a servant to the tenant farmers to receive some of the produce of the vineyard. But they beat the servant and sent him away empty-handed. 11 So he proceeded to send another servant, but him also they beat and insulted and sent away empty-handed. 12 Then he proceeded to send a third, but this one too they wounded and threw out. 13* The owner of the vineyard said, 'What shall I do? I shall send my beloved son; maybe they will respect him.' 14 But when the tenant farmers saw him they said to one another, 'This is the heir. Let us kill him that the inheritance may become ours.' 15† So they threw him out of the vineyard and killed him. What will the owner of the vineyard do to them? 16 He will come and put those tenant farmers to death and turn over the vineyard to others." When the people heard this, they exclaimed, "Let it not be so!" 17* But he

LUKE

*

41-44: 13, 34-35.
41: 2 Kgs 8, 11-12; Jer 14, 17; 15, 5.
42: 8, 10; Is 6, 9-10; Mt 13, 14; Mk 4, 12; Acts 28, 26-27; Rom 11, 8.10.
43: Is 29, 3.
44: 1, 68; 21, 6; Ps 137, 9; Mt 24, 2; Mk 13, 2.
45-46: Mt 21, 12-13; Mk 11, 15-17; Jn 2, 13-17.
45: Mal 3, 1 / Hos 9, 15.
46: Is 56, 7; Jer 7, 11.
47-48: 20, 19; 22, 2; Mt 21, 46; Mk 11, 18; 12, 12; 14, 1-2; Jn 5, 18; 7, 30.
47: 21, 37; 22, 53; Jn 18, 20.
20, 1-8: Mt 21, 23-27; Mk 11, 27-33.
2: Acts 4, 7.
4: 3, 3.16.
5: Mt 21, 32.
9-19: Mt 21, 33-46; Mk 12, 1-12.
9: Is 5, 1-7.
10-12: 2 Chr 36, 15-16.
13: 3, 22.
17: Ps 118, 22; Is 28, 16.

†

19, 39: *Rebuke your disciples:* this command, found only in Lk, was given so that the Roman authorities would not interpret the acclamation of Jesus as king as an uprising against them; cf 23, 2-3.

19, 41-44: The lament for Jerusalem is found only in Lk. By not accepting Jesus (the one who mediates peace), Jerusalem will not find peace but will become the victim of devastation.

19, 43-44: Luke may be describing the actual disaster that befell Jerusalem in A.D. 70 when it was destroyed by the Romans during the First Revolt.

19, 45-46: Immediately upon entering the holy city, Jesus in a display of his authority enters the temple (see Mal 3, 1-3) and lays claim to it after cleansing it that it might become a proper place for his teaching ministry in Jerusalem (19, 47; 20, 1; 21, 37; 22, 53). See Mt 21, 12-17; Mk 11, 15-19; Jn 2, 13-17 and the notes there.

20, 1-47: The Jerusalem religious leaders or their representatives, in an attempt to incriminate Jesus with the Romans and to discredit him with the people, pose a number of questions to him (about his authority, 2; about payment of taxes, 22; about the resurrection, 28-33).

20, 9-19: This parable about an absentee landlord and a tenant farmers' revolt reflects the social and economic conditions of rural Palestine in the first century. The synoptic gospel writers use the parable to describe how the rejection of the landlord's son becomes the occasion for the vineyard to be taken away from those to whom it was entrusted (the religious leadership of Judaism that rejects the teaching and preaching of Jesus; 19).

20, 15: *They threw him out of the vineyard and killed him:* cf Mk 12, 8. Luke has altered his Marcan source and reports that the murder of the son takes place outside the vineyard to reflect the tradition of Jesus' death outside the walls of the city of Jerusalem (see Heb 13, 12).

looked at them and asked, "What then
does this scripture passage mean:

'The stone which the builders re-
jected
has become the cornerstone'?

18 Everyone who falls on that stone will
be dashed to pieces; and it will crush
anyone on whom it falls." 19* The
scribes and chief priests sought to lay
their hands on him at that very hour,
but they feared the people, for they
knew that he had addressed this para-
ble to them.

Paying Taxes to the Emperor.
20*† They watched him closely and sent
agents pretending to be righteous who
were to trap him in speech, in order to
hand him over to the authority and
power of the governor. 21* They posed
this question to him, "Teacher, we know
that what you say and teach is correct,
and you show no partiality, but teach
the way of God in accordance with the
truth. 22† Is it lawful for us to pay tribute
to Caesar or not?" 23 Recognizing their
craftiness he said to them, 24† "Show me
a denarius; whose image and name does
it bear?" They replied, "Caesar's."
25* So he said to them, "Then repay to
Caesar what belongs to Caesar and to
God what belongs to God." 26 They were
unable to trap him by something he
might say before the people, and so
amazed were they at his reply that they
fell silent.

The Question about the Resurrection.
27*† Some Sadducees, those who deny
that there is a resurrection, came for-
ward and put this question to him,
28*† saying, "Teacher, Moses wrote for
us, 'If someone's brother dies leaving
a wife but no child, his brother must
take the wife and raise up descendants
for his brother.' 29 Now there were seven
brothers; the first married a woman but
died childless. 30 Then the second
31 and the third married her, and like-
wise all the seven died childless.
32 Finally the woman also died. 33 Now
at the resurrection whose wife will that
woman be? For all seven had been mar-
ried to her." 34 Jesus said to them, "The
children of this age marry and remarry;
35 but those who are deemed worthy to
attain to the coming age and to the res-
urrection of the dead neither marry nor
are given in marriage. 36† They can no
longer die, for they are like angels; and
they are the children of God because
they are the ones who will rise. 37* That
the dead will rise even Moses made
known in the passage about the bush,
when he called 'Lord' the God of Abra-
ham, the God of Isaac, and the God of
Jacob; 38* and he is not God of the dead,
but of the living, for to him all are
alive." 39 Some of the scribes said in re-
ply, "Teacher, you have answered
well." 40* And they no longer dared to
ask him anything.

The Question about David's Son.†
41* Then he said to them, "How do they
claim that the Messiah is the Son of Da-
vid? 42* For David himself in the Book
of Psalms says:

'The Lord said to my lord,
"Sit at my right hand
43 till I make your enemies your
footstool."'

44 Now if David calls him 'lord,' how can
he be his son?"

Denunciation of the Scribes.
45* Then, within the hearing of all the
people, he said to [his] disciples, 46* "Be
on guard against the scribes, who like
to go around in long robes and love
greetings in marketplaces, seats
of honor in synagogues, and places
of honor at banquets. 47 They de-
vour the houses of widows and, as a
pretext, recite lengthy prayers. They
will receive a very severe condemna-
tion."

*

19: 19, 47-48; 22, 2; Mt 21, 46; Mk 11, 18; 12, 12; 14, 1-2; Jn 5, 18; 7, 30.
20-26: Mt 22, 15-22; Mk 12, 13-17.
20: 11, 54.
21: Jn 3, 2.
25: Rom 13, 6-7.
27-40: Mt 22, 23-33; Mk 12, 18-27.
27: Acts 23, 8.
28: Gn 38, 8; Dt 25, 5.
37: Ex 3, 2.6.15-16.
38: Rom 14, 8-9.
40: Mt 22, 46; Mk 12, 34.
41-44: Mt 22, 41-45; Mk 12, 35-37.
42-43: Ps 110, 1.
45-47: 11, 37-54; Mt 23, 1-36; Mk 12, 38-40.
46: 14, 7-11.

†

20, 20: *The governor:* i.e., Pontius Pilate, the Roman administrator responsible for the collection of taxes and maintenance of order in Palestine.

20, 22: Through their question the agents of the Jerusalem religious leadership hope to force Jesus to take sides on one of the sensitive political issues of first-century Palestine. The issue of nonpayment of taxes to Rome becomes one of the focal points of the First Jewish Revolt (A.D. 66-70) that resulted in the Roman destruction of Jerusalem and the temple. See also the note on Mt 22, 15-22.

20, 24: *Denarius:* a Roman silver coin (see the note on 7, 41).

20, 27: *Sadducees:* see the note on Mt 3, 7.

20, 28-33: The Sadducees' question, based on the law of levirate marriage recorded in Dt 25, 5-10, ridicules the idea of the resurrection. Jesus rejects their naive understanding of the resurrection (35-36) and then argues on behalf of the resurrection of the dead on the basis of the written law (37-38) that the Sadducees accept. See also the notes on Mt 22, 23-33.

20, 36: *Because they are the ones who will rise:* literally, "being sons of the resurrection."

20, 41-44: After successfully answering the three questions of his opponents, Jesus now asks them a question. Their inability to respond implies that they have forfeited their position and authority as the religious leaders of the people because they do not understand the scriptures. This series of controversies between the religious leadership of Jerusalem and Jesus reveals Jesus as the authoritative teacher whose words are to be listened to (see 9, 35). See also the notes on Mt 22, 41-46.

CHAPTER 21

The Poor Widow's Contribution.†
1* When he looked up he saw some
wealthy people putting their offerings
into the treasury 2 and he noticed a poor
widow putting in two small coins.
3 He said, "I tell you truly, this poor
widow put in more than all the rest;
4 for those others have all made offer-
ings from their surplus wealth, but she,
from her poverty, has offered her whole
livelihood."

The Destruction of the Temple Foretold.† 5* While some people were
speaking about how the temple was
adorned with costly stones and votive
offerings, he said, 6* "All that you see
here—the days will come when there
will not be left a stone upon another
stone that will not be thrown down."

The Signs of the End. 7* Then they
asked him, "Teacher, when will this
happen? And what sign will there be
when all these things are about to hap-
pen?" 8*† He answered, "See that you
not be deceived, for many will come in
my name, saying, 'I am he,' and 'The
time has come.' Do not follow them!
9 When you hear of wars and insurrec-
tions, do not be terrified; for such things
must happen first, but it will not imme-
diately be the end." 10* Then he said to
them, "Nation will rise against nation,
and kingdom against kingdom. 11 There
will be powerful earthquakes, famines,
and plagues from place to place; and
awesome sights and mighty signs will
come from the sky.

The Coming Persecution.
12*† "Before all this happens, however,
they will seize and persecute you, they
will hand you over to the synagogues
and to prisons, and they will have you
led before kings and governors because
of my name. 13 It will lead to your giving
testimony. 14 Remember, you are not to
prepare your defense beforehand,
15*† for I myself shall give you a wisdom
in speaking that all your adversaries
will be powerless to resist or refute.
16* You will even be handed over by
parents, brothers, relatives, and
friends, and they will put some of you
to death. 17 You will be hated by all be-
cause of my name, 18* but not a hair on
your head will be destroyed. 19* By your
perseverance you will secure your lives.

The Great Tribulation.† 20* "When
you see Jerusalem surrounded by ar-
mies, know that its desolation is at
hand. 21* Then those in Judea must flee
to the mountains. Let those within the
city escape from it, and let those in the
countryside not enter the city, 22 for
these days are the time of punishment
when all the scriptures are fulfilled.
23* Woe to pregnant women and nursing
mothers in those days, for a terrible ca-
lamity will come upon the earth and a
wrathful judgment upon this people.
24*† They will fall by the edge of the
sword and be taken as captives to all
the Gentiles; and Jerusalem will be
trampled underfoot by the Gentiles un-
til the times of the Gentiles are fulfilled.

The Coming of the Son of Man.
25* "There will be signs in the sun, the
moon, and the stars, and on earth na-
tions will be in dismay, perplexed by the
roaring of the sea and the waves.
26*† People will die of fright in anticipa-

LUKE

*

21, 1-4: Mk 12, 41-44.
5-6: Mt 24, 1-2; Mk 13, 1-2.
6: 19, 44.
7-19: Mt 24, 3-14; Mk 13, 3-13.
8: 17, 23; Mk 13, 5.6.21; 1 Jn 2, 18.
10: 2 Chr 15, 6; Is 19, 2.
12-15: 12, 11-12; Mt 10, 17-20; Mk 13, 9-11.
12: Jn 16, 2; Acts 25, 24.
15: Acts 6, 10.
16-18: Mt 10, 21-22.
16: 12, 52-53.
18: 12, 7; 1 Sm 14, 45; Mt 10, 30; Acts 27, 34.
19: 8, 15.
20-24: Mt 24, 15-21; Mk 13, 14-19.
20-22: 19, 41-44.
21: 17, 31.
23: 1 Cor 7, 26.
24: Tb 14, 5; Ps 79, 1; Is 63, 18; Jer 21, 7; Rom 11, 25; Rv 11, 2.
25-28: Mt 24, 29-31; Mk 13, 24-27.
25: Wis 5, 22; Is 13, 10; Ez 32, 7; Jl 2, 10; 3, 3-4; 4, 15; Rv 6, 12-14.
26: Hg 2, 6.21.

†

21, 1-4: The widow is another example of the poor ones in this gospel whose detachment from material possessions and dependence on God leads to their blessedness (6, 20). Her simple offering provides a striking contrast to the pride and pretentiousness of the scribes denounced in the preceding section (20, 45-47). The story is taken from Mk 12, 41-44.

21, 5-36: Jesus' eschatological discourse in Lk is inspired by Mk 13, but Luke has made some significant alterations to the words of Jesus found there. Luke maintains, though in a modified form, the belief in the early expectation of the end of the age (see 27.28. 31.32.36), but, by focusing attention throughout the gospel on the importance of the day-to-day following of Jesus and by reinterpreting the meaning of some of the signs of the end from Mk 13, he has come to terms with what seemed to the early Christian community to be a delay of the parousia. Mark, for example, described the desecration of the Jerusalem temple by the Romans (Mk 13, 14) as the apocalyptic symbol (see Dn 9, 27; 12, 11) accompanying the end of the age and the coming of the Son of Man. Luke (21, 20-24), however, removes the apocalyptic setting and separates the historical destruction of Jerusalem from the signs of the coming of the Son of Man by a period that he refers to as "the times of the Gentiles" (21, 24). See also the notes on Mt 24, 1-36 and Mk 13, 1-37.

21, 8: *The time has come:* in Lk, the proclamation of the imminent end of the age has itself become a false teaching.

21, 12: *Before all this happens . . . :* to Luke and his community, some of the signs of the end just described (10-11) still lie in the future. Now in dealing with the persecution of the disciples (12-19) and the destruction of Jerusalem (20-24) Luke is pointing to eschatological signs that have already been fulfilled.

21, 15: *A wisdom in speaking:* literally, "a mouth and wisdom."

21, 20-24: The actual destruction of Jerusalem by Rome in A.D. 70 upon which Luke and his community look back provides the assurance that, just as Jesus' prediction of Jerusalem's destruction was fulfilled, so too will be his announcement of their final redemption (27-28).

21, 24: *The times of the Gentiles:* a period of indeterminate length separating the destruction of Jerusalem from the cosmic signs accompanying the coming of the Son of Man.

21, 26: *The powers of the heavens:* the heavenly bodies mentioned in v 25 and thought of as cosmic armies.

tion of what is coming upon the world,
for the powers of the heavens will be
shaken. 27* And then they will see the
Son of Man coming in a cloud with
power and great glory. 28* But when
these signs begin to happen, stand erect
and raise your heads because your re-
demption is at hand."
The Lesson of the Fig Tree. 29* He
taught them a lesson. "Consider the fig
tree and all the other trees. 30 When
their buds burst open, you see for your-
selves and know that summer is now
near; 31 in the same way, when you see
these things happening, know that the
kingdom of God is near. 32* Amen, I say
to you, this generation will not pass
away until all these things have taken
place. 33* Heaven and earth will pass
away, but my words will not pass away.
Exhortation to be Vigilant.
34* "Beware that your hearts do not be-
come drowsy from carousing and
drunkenness and the anxieties of daily
life, and that day catch you by surprise
35 like a trap. For that day will assault
everyone who lives on the face of the
earth. 36* Be vigilant at all times and
pray that you have the strength to es-
cape the tribulations that are imminent
and to stand before the Son of Man."
Ministry in Jerusalem. 37* During the
day, Jesus was teaching in the temple
area, but at night he would leave and
stay at the place called the Mount of
Olives. 38 And all the people would get
up early each morning to listen to him
in the temple area.

VII: THE PASSION NARRATIVE†

CHAPTER 22

The Conspiracy against Jesus.
1*† Now the feast of Unleavened Bread,
called the Passover, was drawing near,
2* and the chief priests and the scribes
were seeking a way to put him to death,
for they were afraid of the people.
3*† Then Satan entered into Judas, the
one surnamed Iscariot, who was
counted among the Twelve, 4 and he
went to the chief priests and temple
guards to discuss a plan for handing
him over to them. 5 They were pleased
and agreed to pay him money. 6 He ac-
cepted their offer and sought a favor-
able opportunity to hand him over to
them in the absence of a crowd.
Preparations for the Passover.
7* When the day of the feast of Unleav-
ened Bread arrived, the day for sacri-
ficing the Passover lamb, 8 he sent out
Peter and John, instructing them, "Go
and make preparations for us to eat the
Passover." 9 They asked him, "Where
do you want us to make the prepara-
tions?" 10† And he answered them,
"When you go into the city, a man will
meet you carrying a jar of water. Follow
him into the house that he enters
11 and say to the master of the house,
'The teacher says to you, "Where is the
guest room where I may eat the Pass-
over with my disciples?"' 12 He will
show you a large upper room that is fur-
nished. Make the preparations there."
13* Then they went off and found every-
thing exactly as he had told them, and
there they prepared the Passover.
The Last Supper. 14* When the hour
came, he took his place at table with
the apostles. 15† He said to them, "I have
eagerly desired to eat this Passover
with you before I suffer, 16* for, I tell
you, I shall not eat it [again] until there
is fulfillment in the kingdom of God."
17† Then he took a cup, gave thanks, and
said, "Take this and share it among
yourselves; 18 for I tell you [that] from
this time on I shall not drink of the fruit
of the vine until the kingdom of God

---

*

27: Dn 7, 13-14; Mt 26, 64; Rv 1, 7.
28: 2, 38.
29-33: Mt 24, 32-35; Mk 13, 28-31.
32: 9, 27; Mt 16, 28.
33: 16, 17.
34: 12, 45-46; Mt 24, 48-50; 1 Thes 5, 3.6-7.
36: Mk 13, 33.
37: 19, 47; 22, 39.
22, 1-2: Mt 26, 1-5; Mk 14, 1-2; Jn 11, 47-53.
2: 19, 47-48; 20, 19; Mt 21, 46; Mk 12, 12; Jn 5, 18; 7, 30.
3-6: Mt 26, 14-16; Mk 14, 10-11; Jn 13, 2.27.
3: Acts 1, 17.
7-13: Mt 26, 17-19; Mk 14, 12-16.
7: Ex 12, 6.14-20.
13: 19, 32.
14-20: Mt 26, 20.26-30; Mk 14, 17.22-26; 1 Cor 11, 23-25.
16: 13, 29.

---

†

22, 1—23, 56a: The passion narrative. Luke is still dependent upon Mk for the composition of the passion narrative but has incorporated much of his own special tradition into the narrative. Among the distinctive sections in Lk are: (1) the tradition of the institution of the Eucharist (22, 15-20); (2) Jesus' farewell discourse (22, 21-38); (3) the mistreatment and interrogation of Jesus (22, 63-71); (4) Jesus before Herod and his second appearance before Pilate (23, 6-16); (5) words addressed to the women followers on the way to the crucifixion (23, 27-32); (6) words to the penitent thief (23, 39-41); (7) the death of Jesus (23, 46.47b-49). Luke stresses the innocence of Jesus (23, 4.14-15.22) who is the victim of the powers of evil (22, 3.31.53) and who goes to his death in fulfillment of his Father's will (22, 42.46). Throughout the narrative Luke emphasizes the mercy, compassion, and healing power of Jesus (22, 51; 23, 43) who does not go to death lonely and deserted, but is accompanied by others who follow him on the way of the cross (23, 26-31.49).

22, 1: *Feast of Unleavened Bread, called the Passover:* see the note on Mk 14, 1.

22, 3: *Satan entered into Judas:* see the note on 4, 13.

22, 10: *A man will meet you carrying a jar of water:* see the note on Mk 14, 13.

22, 15: *This Passover:* Luke clearly identifies this last supper of Jesus with the apostles as a Passover meal that commemorated the deliverance of the Israelites from slavery in Egypt. Jesus reinterprets the significance of the Passover by setting it in the context of the kingdom of God (16). The "deliverance" associated with the Passover finds its new meaning in the blood that will be shed (20).

22, 17: Because of a textual problem in vv 19 and 20, some commentators interpret this cup as the eucharistic cup.

comes." 19*† Then he took the bread, said the blessing, broke it, and gave it to them, saying, "This is my body, which will be given for you; do this in memory of me." 20* And likewise the cup after they had eaten, saying, "This cup is the new covenant in my blood, which will be shed for you.

The Betrayal Foretold. 21* "And yet behold, the hand of the one who is to betray me is with me on the table; 22 for the Son of Man indeed goes as it has been determined; but woe to that man by whom he is betrayed." 23 And they began to debate among themselves who among them would do such a deed.

The Role of the Disciples.† 24* Then an argument broke out among them about which of them should be regarded as the greatest. 25*† He said to them, "The kings of the Gentiles lord it over them and those in authority over them are addressed as 'Benefactors'; 26* but among you it shall not be so. Rather, let the greatest among you be as the youngest, and the leader as the servant. 27 For who is greater: the one seated at table or the one who serves? Is it not the one seated at table? I am among you as the one who serves. 28 It is you who have stood by me in my trials; 29* and I confer a kingdom on you, just as my Father has conferred one on me, 30* that you may eat and drink at my table in my kingdom; and you will sit on thrones judging the twelve tribes of Israel.

Peter's Denial Foretold.† 31*† "Simon, Simon, behold Satan has demanded to sift all of you like wheat, 32 but I have prayed that your own faith may not fail; and once you have turned back, you must strengthen your brothers." 33* He said to him, "Lord, I am prepared to go to prison and to die with you." 34* But he replied, "I tell you, Peter, before the cock crows this day, you will deny three times that you know me."

Instructions for the Time of Crisis. 35* He said to them, "When I sent you forth without a money bag or a sack or sandals, were you in need of anything?" "No, nothing," they replied. 36*† He said to them, "But now one who has a money bag should take it, and likewise a sack, and one who does not have a sword should sell his cloak and buy one. 37* For I tell you that this scripture must be fulfilled in me, namely, 'He was counted among the wicked'; and indeed what is written about me is coming to fulfillment." 38† Then they said, "Lord, look, there are two swords here." But he replied, "It is enough!"

The Agony in the Garden. 39* Then going out he went, as was his custom, to the Mount of Olives, and the disciples followed him. 40* When he arrived at the place he said to them, "Pray that you may not undergo the test." 41* After withdrawing about a stone's throw from them and kneeling, he prayed, 42* saying, "Father, if you are willing, take this cup away from me; still, not my will but yours be done." [43† And to strengthen him an angel from heaven appeared to him. 44 He was in such agony and he prayed so fervently that his sweat became like drops of blood falling on the ground.] 45 When he rose from prayer and returned to his disciples, he found them sleeping from grief. 46* He said to them, "Why are you sleeping? Get up and pray that you may not undergo the test."

The Betrayal and Arrest of Jesus. 47* While he was still speaking, a crowd

---

*

19: 24, 30; Acts 27, 35.
20: Ex 24, 8; Jer 31, 31; 32, 40; Zec 9, 11.
21-23: Ps 41, 10; Mt 26, 21-25; Mk 14, 18-21; Jn 13, 21-30.
24: 9, 46; Mt 18, 1; Mk 9, 34.
25-27: Mt 20, 25-27; Mk 10, 42-44; Jn 13, 3-16.
26: Mt 23, 11; Mk 9, 35.
29: 12, 32.
30: Mt 19, 28.
31-34: Mt 26, 33-35; Mk 14, 29-31; Jn 13, 37-38.
31: Jb 1, 6-12; Am 9, 9.
33: 22, 54.
34: 22, 54-62.
35: 9, 3; 10, 4; Mt 10, 9-10; Mk 6, 7-9.
36: 22, 49.
37: Is 53, 12.
39-46: Mt 26, 30.36-46; Mk 14, 26.32-42; Jn 18, 1-2.
40: 22, 46.
41: Heb 5, 7-8.
42: Mt 6, 10.
46: 22, 40.
47-53: Mt 26, 47-56; Mk 14, 43-50; Jn 18, 3-4.

---

†

22, 19c-20: *Which will be given . . . do this in memory of me:* these words are omitted in some important Western text manuscripts and a few Syriac manuscripts. Other ancient text types, including the oldest papyrus manuscript of Lk dating from the late second or early third century, contain the longer reading presented here. The Lucan account of the words of institution of the Eucharist bears a close resemblance to the words of institution in the Pauline tradition (see 1 Cor 11, 23-26). See also the notes on Mt 26, 26-29; 26, 27-28; and Mk 14, 22-24.

22, 24-38: The Gospel of Luke presents a brief farewell discourse of Jesus; compare the lengthy farewell discourses and prayer in Jn, chs 13-17.

22, 25: *'Benefactors':* this word occurs as a title of rulers in the Hellenistic world.

22, 31: *All of you:* literally, "you." The translation reflects the meaning of the Greek text that uses a second person plural pronoun here.

22, 31-32: Jesus' prayer for Simon's faith and the commission to strengthen his brothers anticipates the post-resurrectional prominence of Peter in the first half of Acts, where he appears as the spokesman for the Christian community and the one who begins the mission to the Gentiles (Acts 10-11).

22, 36: In contrast to the ministry of the Twelve and of the seventy-two during the period of Jesus (9, 3; 10, 4), in the future period of the church the missionaries must be prepared for the opposition they will face in a world hostile to their preaching.

22, 38: *It is enough!:* the farewell discourse ends abruptly with these words of Jesus spoken to the disciples when they take literally what was intended as figurative language about being prepared to face the world's hostility.

22, 43-44: These verses, though very ancient, were probably not part of the original text of Lk. They are absent from the oldest papyrus manuscripts of Lk and from manuscripts of wide geographical distribution.

approached and in front was one of the
Twelve, a man named Judas. He went
up to Jesus to kiss him. 48 Jesus said to
him, "Judas, are you betraying the Son
of Man with a kiss?" 49* His disciples
realized what was about to happen, and
they asked, "Lord, shall we strike with
a sword?" 50* And one of them struck
the high priest's servant and cut off his
right ear. 51† But Jesus said in reply,
"Stop, no more of this!" Then he
touched the servant's ear and healed
him. 52* And Jesus said to the chief
priests and temple guards and elders
who had come for him, "Have you come
out as against a robber, with swords and
clubs? 53* Day after day I was with you
in the temple area, and you did not seize
me; but this is your hour, the time for
the power of darkness."

Peter's Denial of Jesus. 54* After ar-
resting him they led him away and took
him into the house of the high priest;
Peter was following at a distance.
55 They lit a fire in the middle of the
courtyard and sat around it, and Peter
sat down with them. 56 When a maid saw
him seated in the light, she looked in-
tently at him and said, "This man too
was with him." 57 But he denied it say-
ing, "Woman, I do not know him."
58 A short while later someone else saw
him and said, "You too are one of
them"; but Peter answered, "My friend,
I am not." 59 About an hour later, still
another insisted, "Assuredly, this man
too was with him, for he also is a Gali-
lean." 60 But Peter said, "My friend, I
do not know what you are talking
about." Just as he was saying this, the
cock crowed, 61*† and the Lord turned
and looked at Peter; and Peter remem-
bered the word of the Lord, how he had
said to him, "Before the cock crows to-
day, you will deny me three times."
62 He went out and began to weep bit-
terly. 63* The men who held Jesus in
custody were ridiculing and beating
him. 64 They blindfolded him and ques-
tioned him, saying, "Prophesy! Who is
it that struck you?" 65 And they reviled
him in saying many other things
against him.

Jesus before the Sanhedrin.†
66*† When day came the council of el-
ders of the people met, both chief priests
and scribes, and they brought him be-
fore their Sanhedrin. 67* They said, "If
you are the Messiah, tell us," but he re-
plied to them, "If I tell you, you will not
believe, 68 and if I question, you will not
respond. 69* But from this time on the
Son of Man will be seated at the right
hand of the power of God." 70 They all
asked, "Are you then the Son of God?"
He replied to them, "You say that I am."
71 Then they said, "What further need
have we for testimony? We have heard
it from his own mouth."

CHAPTER 23

Jesus before Pilate.† 1* Then the
whole assembly of them arose and
brought him before Pilate. 2* They
brought charges against him, saying,
"We found this man misleading our
people; he opposes the payment of taxes
to Caesar and maintains that he is the
Messiah, a king." 3* Pilate asked him,
"Are you the king of the Jews?" He said
to him in reply, "You say so." 4* Pilate
then addressed the chief priests and the
crowds, "I find this man not guilty."
5 But they were adamant and said, "He
is inciting the people with his teaching
throughout all Judea, from Galilee
where he began even to here."

Jesus before Herod.† 6 On hearing
this Pilate asked if the man was a Gali-
lean; 7* and upon learning that he was
under Herod's jurisdiction, he sent him
to Herod who was in Jerusalem at that
time. 8* Herod was very glad to see Je-
sus; he had been wanting to see him for
a long time, for he had heard about him

*

49: 22, 36.
50: Jn 18, 26.
52: 22, 37.
53: 19, 47; 21, 37; Jn 7, 30; 8, 20; Col 1, 13.
54-62: Mt 26, 57-58.69-75; Mk 14, 53-54.66-72; Jn 18, 12-18.25-27.
54: 22, 33.
61: 22, 34.
63-65: Mt 26, 67-68; Mk 14, 65.
66-71: Mt 26, 59-66; Mk 14, 55-64.
66: Mt 27, 1; Mk 15, 1.
67: Jn 3, 12; 8, 45; 10, 24.
69: Ps 110, 1; Dn 7, 13-14; Acts 7, 56.
23, 1-5: Mt 27, 1-2.11-14; Mk 15, 1-5; Jn 18, 28-38.
2: 20, 22-25; Acts 17, 7; 24, 5.
3: 22, 70; 1 Tm 6, 13.
4: 23, 14.22.41; Mt 27, 24; Jn 19, 4.6; Acts 13, 28.
7: 3, 1; 9, 7.
8: 9, 9; Acts 4, 27-28.

†

22, 51: *And healed him:* only Luke recounts this healing of the injured servant.

22, 61: Only Luke recounts that *the Lord turned and looked at Peter.* This look of Jesus leads to Peter's weeping bitterly over his denial (62).

22, 66-71: Luke recounts one daytime trial of Jesus (66-71) and hints at some type of preliminary nighttime investigation (54-65). Mark (and Matthew who follows Mk) has transferred incidents of this day into the nighttime interrogation with the result that there appear to be two Sanhedrin trials of Jesus in Mk (and Mt); see the note on Mk 14, 53.

22, 66: *Sanhedrin:* the word is a Hebraized form of a Greek word meaning a "council," and refers to the elders, chief priests, and scribes who met under the high priest's leadership to decide religious and legal questions that did not pertain to Rome's interests. Jewish sources are not clear on the competence of the Sanhedrin to sentence and to execute during this period.

23, 1-5.13-25: Twice Jesus is brought before Pilate in Luke's account, and each time Pilate explicitly declares Jesus innocent of any wrongdoing (4.14.22). This stress on the innocence of Jesus before the Roman authorities is also characteristic of John's gospel (Jn 18, 38; 19, 4.6). Luke presents the Jerusalem Jewish leaders as the ones who force the hand of the Roman authorities (1-2.5.10.13. 18.21.23-25).

23, 6-12: The appearance of Jesus before Herod is found only in this gospel. Herod has been an important figure in Lk (9, 7-9; 13, 31-33) and has been presented as someone who has been curious about Jesus for a long time. His curiosity goes unrewarded. It is faith in Jesus, not curiosity, that is rewarded (7, 50; 8, 48.50; 17, 19).

and had been hoping to see him perform
some sign. 9* He questioned him at
length, but he gave him no answer.
10* The chief priests and scribes, mean-
while, stood by accusing him harshly.
11* [Even] Herod and his soldiers
treated him contemptuously and
mocked him, and after clothing him in
resplendent garb, he sent him back to
Pilate. 12 Herod and Pilate became
friends that very day, even though they
had been enemies formerly. 13 Pilate
then summoned the chief priests, the
rulers, and the people 14* and said to
them, "You brought this man to me and
accused him of inciting the people to re-
volt. I have conducted my investigation
in your presence and have not found
this man guilty of the charges you have
brought against him, 15 nor did Herod,
for he sent him back to us. So no capital
crime has been committed by him.
16* Therefore I shall have him flogged
and then release him." [17]†

The Sentence of Death. 18* But all to-
gether they shouted out, "Away with
this man! Release Barabbas to us."
19 (Now Barabbas had been imprisoned
for a rebellion that had taken place in
the city and for murder.) 20 Again Pilate
addressed them, still wishing to release
Jesus, 21 but they continued their shout-
ing, "Crucify him! Crucify him!"
22 Pilate addressed them a third time,
"What evil has this man done? I found
him guilty of no capital crime. There-
fore I shall have him flogged and then
release him." 23 With loud shouts, how-
ever, they persisted in calling for his
crucifixion, and their voices prevailed.
24 The verdict of Pilate was that their
demand should be granted. 25 So he re-
leased the man who had been impris-
oned for rebellion and murder, for
whom they asked, and he handed Jesus
over to them to deal with as they
wished.

The Way of the Cross.† 26* As they led
him away they took hold of a certain
Simon, a Cyrenian, who was coming in
from the country; and after laying the
cross on him, they made him carry it
behind Jesus. 27 A large crowd of people
followed Jesus, including many women
who mourned and lamented him.
28* Jesus turned to them and said,
"Daughters of Jerusalem, do not weep
for me; weep instead for yourselves and
for your children, 29 for indeed, the days
are coming when people will say,
'Blessed are the barren, the wombs that
never bore and the breasts that never
nursed.' 30* At that time people will say
to the mountains, 'Fall upon us!' and to
the hills, 'Cover us!' 31 for if these things
are done when the wood is green what
will happen when it is dry?" 32 Now two
others, both criminals, were led away
with him to be executed.

The Crucifixion. 33* When they came
to the place called the Skull, they cruci-
fied him and the criminals there, one
on his right, the other on his left.
34*† [Then Jesus said, "Father, forgive
them, they know not what they do."]
They divided his garments by casting
lots. 35* The people stood by and
watched; the rulers, meanwhile,
sneered at him and said, "He saved oth-
ers, let him save himself if he is the cho-
sen one, the Messiah of God." 36* Even
the soldiers jeered at him. As they ap-
proached to offer him wine 37 they
called out, "If you are King of the Jews,
save yourself." 38 Above him there was
an inscription that read, "This is the
King of the Jews."

39† Now one of the criminals hanging
there reviled Jesus, saying, "Are you
not the Messiah? Save yourself and us."
40 The other, however, rebuking him,
said in reply, "Have you no fear of God,
for you are subject to the same condem-
nation? 41* And indeed, we have been
condemned justly, for the sentence we
received corresponds to our crimes, but
this man has done nothing criminal."
42* Then he said, "Jesus, remember me
when you come into your kingdom."
43* He replied to him, "Amen, I say to

*

9: Mk 15, 5.
10: Mt 27, 12; Mk 15, 3.
11: Mt 27, 28-30; Mk 15, 17-19; Jn 19, 2-3.
14: 23, 4.22.41.
16: 23, 22; Jn 19, 12-14.
18-25: Mt 27, 20-26; Mk 15, 6-7.11-15; Jn 18, 38b-40; 19, 14-16; Acts 3, 13-14.
26-32: Mt 27, 32.38; Mk 15, 21.27; Jn 19, 17.
28-31: 19, 41-44; 21, 23-24.
30: Hos 10, 8; Rv 6, 16.
33-43: Mt 27, 33-44; Mk 15, 22-32; Jn 19, 17-24.
33: 22, 37; Is 53, 12.
34: Nm 15, 27-31; Ps 22, 19; Mt 5, 44; Acts 7, 60.
35-36: Ps 22, 8-9.
35: 4, 23.
36: Ps 69, 22; Mt 27, 48; Mk 15, 36.
41: 23, 4.14.22.
42: 9, 27; 23, 2.3.38.
43: 2 Cor 12, 3; Rv 2, 7.

†

23, 17: This verse, "He was obliged to release one prisoner for them at the festival," is not part of the original text of Lk. It is an explanatory gloss from Mk 15, 6 (also Mt 27, 15) and is not found in many early and important Greek manuscripts. On its historical background, see the notes on Mt 27, 15-26.

23, 26-32: An important Lucan theme throughout the gospel has been the need for the Christian disciple to follow in the footsteps of Jesus. Here this theme comes to the fore with the story of Simon of Cyrene who takes up the cross and follows Jesus (see 9, 23; 14, 27) and with the large crowd who likewise follow Jesus on the way of the cross. See also the note on Mk 15, 21.

23, 34a: *[Then Jesus said, "Father, forgive them, they know not what they do."]*: this portion of v 34 does not occur in the oldest papyrus manuscript of Lk and in other early Greek manuscripts and ancient versions of wide geographical distribution.

23, 39-43: This episode is recounted only in this gospel. The penitent sinner receives salvation through the crucified Jesus. Jesus' words to the penitent thief reveal Luke's understanding that the destiny of the Christian is "to be with Jesus."

you, today you will be with me in Paradise."

The Death of Jesus. 44*† It was now about noon and darkness came over the whole land until three in the afternoon 45* because of an eclipse of the sun. Then the veil of the temple was torn down the middle. 46* Jesus cried out in a loud voice, "Father, into your hands I commend my spirit"; and when he had said this he breathed his last. 47† The centurion who witnessed what had happened glorified God and said, "This man was innocent beyond doubt." 48* When all the people who had gathered for this spectacle saw what had happened, they returned home beating their breasts; 49* but all his acquaintances stood at a distance, including the women who had followed him from Galilee and saw these events.

The Burial of Jesus. 50* Now there was a virtuous and righteous man named Joseph who, though he was a member of the council, 51* had not consented to their plan of action. He came from the Jewish town of Arimathea and was awaiting the kingdom of God. 52 He went to Pilate and asked for the body of Jesus. 53* After he had taken the body down, he wrapped it in a linen cloth and laid him in a rock-hewn tomb in which no one had yet been buried. 54 It was the day of preparation, and the sabbath was about to begin. 55* The women who had come from Galilee with him followed behind, and when they had seen the tomb and the way in which his body was laid in it, 56* they returned and prepared spices and perfumed oils. Then they rested on the sabbath according to the commandment.

VIII: THE RESURRECTION NARRATIVE†

CHAPTER 24

The Resurrection of Jesus. 1* But at daybreak on the first day of the week they took the spices they had prepared and went to the tomb. 2 They found the stone rolled away from the tomb; 3 but when they entered, they did not find the body of the Lord Jesus. 4* While they were puzzling over this, behold, two men in dazzling garments appeared to them. 5* They were terrified and bowed their faces to the ground. They said to them, "Why do you seek the living one among the dead? 6† He is not here, but he has been raised. Remember what he said to you while he was still in Galilee, 7* that the Son of Man must be handed over to sinners and be crucified, and rise on the third day." 8* And they remembered his words. 9*† Then they returned from the tomb and announced all these things to the eleven and to all the others. 10* The women were Mary Magdalene, Joanna, and Mary the mother of James; the others who accompanied them also told this to the apostles, 11 but their story seemed like nonsense and they did not believe them. 12*† But Peter got up and ran to the tomb, bent down, and saw the burial cloths alone; then he went home amazed at what had happened.

***The Appearance on the Road to Emmaus.*†** 13*† Now that very day two

LUKE

*

44-49: Mt 27, 45-56; Mk 15, 33-41; Jn 19, 25-30.
44-45: Am 8, 9.
45: Ex 26, 31-33; 36, 35.
46: Ps 31, 6; Acts 7, 59.
48: 18, 13; Zec 12, 10.
49: 8, 1-3; 23, 55-56; 24, 10; Ps 38, 12.
50-56: Mt 27, 57-61; Mk 15, 42-47; Jn 19, 38-42; Acts 13, 29.
51: 2, 25.38.
53: 19, 30; Acts 13, 29.
55: 8, 2; 23, 49; 24, 10.
56: Ex 12, 16; 20, 10; Dt 5, 14.
24, 1-8: Mt 28, 1-8; Mk 16, 1-8; Jn 20, 1-17.
4: 2 Mc 3, 26; Acts 1, 10.
5: Acts 2, 9.
7: 9, 22.44; 17, 25; 18, 32-33; Mt 16, 21; 17, 22-23; Mk 9, 31; Acts 17, 3.
8: Jn 2, 22.
9-11: Mk 16, 10-11; Jn 20, 18.
10: 8, 2-3; Mk 16, 9.
12: Jn 20, 3-7.
13: Mk 16, 12-13.

†

23, 44: *Noon . . . three in the afternoon:* literally, the sixth and ninth hours. See the note on Mk 15, 25.

23, 47: *This man was innocent:* or, "This man was righteous."

24, 1-53: The resurrection narrative in Lk consists of five sections: (1) the women at the empty tomb (23, 56b—24, 12); (2) the appearance to the two disciples on the way to Emmaus (24, 13-35); (3) the appearance to the disciples in Jerusalem (24, 36-43); (4) Jesus' final instructions (24, 44-49); (5) the ascension (24, 50-53). In Lk, all the resurrection appearances take place in and around Jerusalem; moreover, they are all recounted as having taken place on Easter Sunday. A consistent theme throughout the narrative is that the suffering, death, and resurrection of Jesus were accomplished in fulfillment of Old Testament promises and of Jewish hopes (19a.21.26-27.44.46). In his second volume, Acts, Luke will argue that Christianity is the fulfillment of the hopes of Pharisaic Judaism and its logical development (see Acts 24, 10-21).

24, 6a: *He is not here, but he has been raised:* this part of the verse is omitted in important representatives of the Western text tradition, but its presence in other text types and the slight difference in wording from Mt 28, 6 and Mk 16, 6 argue for its retention.

24, 9: The women in this gospel do not flee from the tomb and tell no one, as in Mk 16, 8, but return and tell the disciples about their experience. The initial reaction to the testimony of the women is disbelief (11).

24, 12: This verse is missing from the Western textual tradition but is found in the best and oldest manuscripts of other text types.

24, 13-35: This episode focuses on the interpretation of scripture by the risen Jesus and the recognition of him in the breaking of the bread. The references to the quotations of scripture and explanation of it (25-27), the kerygmatic proclamation (34), and the liturgical gesture (30) suggest that the episode is primarily catechetical and liturgical rather than apologetic.

24, 13: *Seven miles:* literally, "sixty stades." A stade was 607 feet. Some manuscripts read "160 stades" or more than eighteen miles. The exact location of Emmaus is disputed.

of them were going to a village seven
miles from Jerusalem called Emmaus,
14 and they were conversing about all
the things that had occurred. 15 And it
happened that while they were convers-
ing and debating, Jesus himself drew
near and walked with them, 16*† but
their eyes were prevented from recog-
nizing him. 17 He asked them, "What are
you discussing as you walk along?"
They stopped, looking downcast. 18 One
of them, named Cleopas, said to him in
reply, "Are you the only visitor to Jeru-
salem who does not know of the things
that have taken place there in these
days?" 19* And he replied to them,
"What sort of things?" They said to him,
"The things that happened to Jesus the
Nazarene, who was a prophet mighty
in deed and word before God and all
the people, 20 how our chief priests and
rulers both handed him over to a sen-
tence of death and crucified him.
21* But we were hoping that he would
be the one to redeem Israel; and besides
all this, it is now the third day since this
took place. 22* Some women from our
group, however, have astounded us:
they were at the tomb early in the morn-
ing 23 and did not find his body; they
came back and reported that they had
indeed seen a vision of angels who an-
nounced that he was alive. 24* Then
some of those with us went to the tomb
and found things just as the women had
described, but him they did not see."
25* And he said to them, "Oh, how fool-
ish you are! How slow of heart to believe
all that the prophets spoke! 26† Was it
not necessary that the Messiah should
suffer these things and enter into his
glory?" 27* Then beginning with Moses
and all the prophets, he interpreted to
them what referred to him in all the
scriptures. 28 As they approached the
village to which they were going, he
gave the impression that he was going
on farther. 29 But they urged him, "Stay
with us, for it is nearly evening and the
day is almost over." So he went in to
stay with them. 30 And it happened that,
while he was with them at table, he took
bread, said the blessing, broke it, and
gave it to them. 31 With that their eyes
were opened and they recognized him,
but he vanished from their sight.
32 Then they said to each other, "Were
not our hearts burning [within us] while
he spoke to us on the way and opened
the scriptures to us?" 33 So they set out
at once and returned to Jerusalem
where they found gathered together the
eleven and those with them 34* who
were saying, "The Lord has truly been
raised and has appeared to Simon!"
35 Then the two recounted what had
taken place on the way and how he was
made known to them in the breaking
of the bread.

The Appearance to the Disciples in Jerusalem.† 36* While they were still
speaking about this, he stood in their
midst and said to them, "Peace be with
you." 37* But they were startled and ter-
rified and thought that they were seeing
a ghost. 38 Then he said to them, "Why
are you troubled? And why do questions
arise in your hearts? 39† Look at my
hands and my feet, that it is I myself.
Touch me and see, because a ghost does
not have flesh and bones as you can see
I have." 40* And as he said this, he
showed them his hands and his feet.
41 While they were still incredulous for
joy and were amazed, he asked them,
"Have you anything here to eat?"
42* They gave him a piece of baked fish;
43 he took it and ate it in front of them.
44* He said to them, "These are my
words that I spoke to you while I was
still with you, that everything written
about me in the law of Moses and in the
prophets and psalms must be fulfilled."
45* Then he opened their minds to un-
derstand the scriptures. 46*† And he
said to them, "Thus it is written that the
Messiah would suffer and rise from the
dead on the third day 47* and that re-
pentance, for the forgiveness of sins,
would be preached in his name to all
the nations, beginning from Jerusalem.

*

16: Jn 20, 14; 21, 4.
19: Mt 2, 23; 21, 11; Acts 2, 22.
21: 1, 54.68; 2, 38.
22-23: 24, 1-11; Mt 28, 1-8; Mk 16, 1-8.
24: Jn 20, 3-10.
25-26: 9, 22; 18, 31; 24, 44; Acts 3, 24; 17, 3.
27: 24, 44; Dt 18, 25; Ps 22, 1-18; Is 53; 1 Pt 1, 10-11.
34: 1 Cor 15, 4-5.
36-53: Mk 16, 14-19; Jn 20, 19-20.
36: 1 Cor 15, 5.
37: Mt 14, 26.
40-41: Jn 21, 5.9-10.13.
42: Acts 10, 41.
44: 18, 31; 24, 27; Mt 16, 21; Jn 5, 39.46.
45: Jn 20, 9.
46: 9, 22; Is 53; Hos 6, 2.
47: Mt 3, 2; 28, 19-20; Mk 16, 15-16; Acts 10, 41.

†

24, 16: A consistent feature of the resurrection stories is that the risen Jesus was different and initially unrecognizable (37; Mk 16, 12; Jn 20, 14; 21, 4).

24, 26: *That the Messiah should suffer . . . :* Luke is the only New Testament writer to speak explicitly of a suffering Messiah (26.46; Acts 3, 18; 17, 3; 26, 23). The idea of a suffering Messiah is not found in the Old Testament or in other Jewish literature prior to the New Testament period, although the idea is hinted at in Mk 8, 31-33. See the notes on Mt 26, 63 and 26, 67-68.

24, 36-43.44-49: The Gospel of Luke, like each of the other gospels (Mt 28, 16-20; Mk 16, 14-15; Jn 20, 19-23), focuses on an important appearance of Jesus to the Twelve in which they are commissioned for their future ministry. As in vv 6 and 12, so in vv 36 and 40 there are omissions in the Western text.

24, 39-42: The apologetic purpose of this story is evident in the concern with the physical details and the report that Jesus ate food.

24, 46: See the note on 24, 26.

48* You are witnesses of these things.
49*† And [behold] I am sending the
promise of my Father upon you; but
stay in the city until you are clothed
with power from on high."

The Ascension.† 50* Then he led them
[out] as far as Bethany, raised his
hands, and blessed them. 51 As he
blessed them he parted from them and
was taken up to heaven. 52* They did
him homage and then returned to Jeru-
salem with great joy, 53† and they were
continually in the temple praising God.

LUKE

*

48: Acts 1, 8.
49: Jn 14, 26; Acts 1, 4; 2, 3-4.
50-51: Mk 16, 19; Acts 1, 9-11.
52: Acts 1, 12.

†

24, 49: *The promise of my Father:* i.e., the gift of the holy Spirit.

24, 50-53: Luke brings his story about the time of Jesus to a close with the report of the ascension. He will also begin the story of the time of the church with a recounting of the ascension. In the gospel, Luke recounts the ascension of Jesus on Easter Sunday night, thereby closely associating it with the resurrection. In Acts (1, 3.9-11; 13, 31) he historicizes the ascension by speaking of a forty-day period between the resurrection and the ascension. The Western text omits some phrases in vv 51 and 52, perhaps to avoid any chronological conflict with Acts 1 about the time of the ascension.

24, 53: The Gospel of Luke ends as it began (1, 9), in the Jerusalem temple.

The Gospel According to

JOHN

The Gospel according to John is quite different in character from the three synoptic gospels. It is highly literary and symbolic. It does not follow the same order or reproduce the same stories as the synoptic gospels. To a much greater degree, it is the product of a developed theological reflection and grows out of a different circle and tradition. It was probably written in the 90s of the first century.

The Gospel of John begins with a magnificent prologue, which states many of the major themes and motifs of the gospel, much as an overture does for a musical work. The prologue proclaims Jesus as the preexistent and incarnate Word of God who has revealed the Father to us. The rest of the first chapter forms the introduction to the gospel proper and consists of the Baptist's testimony about Jesus (there is no baptism of Jesus in this gospel—John simply points him out as the Lamb of God), followed by stories of the call of the first disciples, in which various titles predicated of Jesus in the early church are presented.

The gospel narrative contains a series of "signs"—the gospel's word for the wondrous deeds of Jesus. The author is primarily interested in the significance of these deeds, and so interprets them for the reader by various reflections, narratives, and discourses. The first sign is the transformation of water into wine at Cana (2, 1-11); this represents the replacement of the Jewish ceremonial washings and symbolizes the entire creative and transforming work of Jesus. The second sign, the cure of the royal official's son (4, 46-54) simply by the word of Jesus at a distance, signifies the power of Jesus' life-giving word. The same theme is further developed by other signs, probably for a total of seven. The third sign, the cure of the paralytic at the pool with five porticoes in ch 5, continues the theme of water offering newness of life. In the preceding chapter, to the woman at the well in Samaria Jesus had offered living water springing up to eternal life, a symbol of the revelation that Jesus brings; here Jesus' life-giving word replaces the water of the pool that failed to bring life. Chapter 6 contains two signs, the multiplication of loaves and the walking on the waters of the Sea of Galilee. These signs are connected much as the manna and the crossing of the Red Sea are in the Passover narrative and symbolize a new exodus. The multiplication of the loaves is interpreted for the reader by the discourse that follows, where the bread of life is used first as a figure for the revelation of God in Jesus and then for the Eucharist. After a series of dialogues reflecting Jesus' debates with the Jewish authorities at the Feast of Tabernacles in chs 7 and 8, the sixth sign is presented in ch 9, the sign of the young man born blind. This is a narrative illustration of the theme of conflict in the preceding two chapters; it proclaims the triumph of light over darkness, as Jesus is presented as the Light of the world. This is interpreted by a narrative of controversy between the Pharisees and the young man who had been given his sight by Jesus, ending with a discussion of spiritual blindness and spelling out the symbolic meaning of the cure. And finally, the seventh sign, the raising of Lazarus in ch 11, is the climax of signs. Lazarus is presented as a token of the real life that Jesus, the Resurrection and the Life, who will now ironically be put to death because of his gift of life to Lazarus, will give to all who believe in him once he has been raised from the dead.

After the account of the seven signs, the "hour" of Jesus arrives, and the author passes from sign to reality, as he moves into the discourses in the upper room that interpret the meaning of the passion, death, and resurrection narratives that follow. The whole gospel of John is a progressive revelation of the glory of God's only Son, who comes to reveal the Father and then returns in glory to the Father.

J O H N

The author's purpose is clearly expressed in what must have been the original ending of the gospel at the end of ch 20: "Now Jesus did many other signs in the presence of [his] disciples that are not written in this book. But these are written that you may [come to] believe that Jesus is the Messiah, the Son of God, and that through this belief you may have life in his name."

Critical analysis makes it difficult to accept the idea that the gospel as it now stands was written by one person. Chapter 21 seems to have been added after the gospel was completed; it exhibits a Greek style somewhat different from that of the rest of the work. The prologue (1, 1-18) apparently contains an independent hymn, subsequently adapted to serve as a preface to the gospel. Within the gospel itself there are also some inconsistencies, e.g., there are two endings of Jesus' discourse in the upper room (14, 31; 18, 1). To solve these problems, scholars have proposed various rearrangements that would produce a smoother order. However, most have come to the conclusion that the inconsistencies were probably produced by subsequent editing in which homogeneous materials were added to a shorter original.

Other difficulties for any theory of eyewitness authorship of the gospel in its present form are presented by its highly developed theology and by certain elements of its literary style. For instance, some of the wondrous deeds of Jesus have been worked into highly effective dramatic scenes (ch 9); there has been a careful attempt to have these followed by discourses that explain them (chs 5 and 6); and the sayings of Jesus have been woven into long discourses of a quasi-poetic form resembling the speeches of personified Wisdom in the Old Testament.

The gospel contains many details about Jesus not found in the synoptic gospels, e.g., that Jesus engaged in a baptizing ministry (3, 22) before he changed to one of preaching and signs; that Jesus' public ministry lasted for several years (see the note on 2, 13); that he traveled to Jerusalem for various festivals and met serious opposition long before his death (2, 14-25; chs 5 and 7-8); and that he was put to death on the day before Passover (18, 28). These events are not always in chronological order because of the development and editing that took place. However, the accuracy of much of the detail of the fourth gospel constitutes a strong argument that the Johannine tradition rests upon the testimony of an eyewitness. Although tradition identified this person as John, the son of Zebedee, most modern scholars find that the evidence does not support this.

The fourth gospel is not simply history; the narrative has been organized and adapted to serve the evangelist's theological purposes as well. Among them are the opposition to the synagogue of the day and to John the Baptist's followers, who tried to exalt their master at Jesus' expense, the desire to show that Jesus was the Messiah, and the desire to convince Christians that their religious belief and practice must be rooted in Jesus. Such theological purposes have impelled the evangelist to emphasize motifs that were not so clear in the synoptic account of Jesus' ministry, e.g., the explicit emphasis on his divinity.

The polemic between synagogue and church produced bitter and harsh invective, especially regarding the hostility toward Jesus of the authorities—Pharisees and Sadducees—who are combined and referred to frequently as "the Jews" (see the note on 1, 19). These opponents are even described in 8, 44 as springing from their father the devil, whose conduct they imitate in opposing God by rejecting Jesus, whom God has sent. On the other hand, the author of this gospel seems to take pains to show that women are not inferior to men in the Christian community: the woman at the well in Samaria (ch 4) is presented as a prototype of a missionary (4, 4-42), and the first witness of the resurrection is a woman (20, 11-18).

The final editing of the gospel and arrangement in its present form probably dates from between A.D. 90 and 100. Traditionally, Ephesus has been favored as the place of composition, though many support a location in Syria, perhaps the city of Antioch, while some have suggested other places, including Alexandria.

The principal divisions of the Gospel according to John are the following:

I: Prologue (1, 1-18)
II: The Book of Signs (1, 19—12, 50)
III: The Book of Glory (13, 1—20, 31)
IV: Epilogue: The Resurrection Appearance in Galilee (21, 1-25)

I: PROLOGUE†

CHAPTER 1

1*† In the beginning was the Word,
and the Word was with God,
and the Word was God.
2 He was in the beginning with God.
3*† All things came to be through him,
and without him nothing came to be.
What came to be 4* through him was life,
and this life was the light of the human race;
5*† the light shines in the darkness,
and the darkness has not overcome it.

6*† A man named John was sent from
God. 7*† He came for testimony, to tes-
tify to the light, so that all might believe
through him. 8* He was not the light, but
came to testify to the light. 9* The true
light, which enlightens everyone, was
coming into the world.

10 He was in the world,
and the world came to be through him,
but the world did not know him.
11† He came to what was his own,
but his own people did not accept him.

12* But to those who did accept him
he gave power to become children of
God, to those who believe in his
name, 13*† who were born not by
natural generation nor by human
choice nor by a man's decision but of
God.

*

1, 1: 10, 30; Gn 1, 1-5; Jb 28, 12-27; Prv 8, 22-25; Wis 9, 1-2; 1 Jn 1, 1-2; Col 1, 1.15; Rv 3, 14; 19, 13.
3: Ps 33, 9; Wis 9, 1; Sir 42, 15; 1 Cor 8, 6; Col 1, 16; Heb 1, 2; Rv 3, 14.
4: 5, 26; 8, 12; 1 Jn 1, 2.
5: 3, 19; 8, 12; 9, 5; 12, 35.46; Wis 7, 29-30; 1 Thes 5, 4; 1 Jn 2, 8.
6: Mt 3, 1; Mk 1, 4; Lk 3, 2-3.
7: 1, 19-34; 5, 33.
8: 5, 35.
9: 3, 19; 8, 12; 9, 39; 12, 46.
12: 3, 11-12; 5, 43-44; 12, 46-50; Gal 3, 26; 4, 6-7; Eph 1, 5; 1 Jn 3, 2.
13: 3, 5-6.

†

1, 1-18: The prologue states the main themes of the gospel: life, light, truth, the world, testimony, and the preexistence of Jesus Christ, the incarnate *Logos,* who reveals God the Father. In origin, it was probably an early Christian hymn. Its closest parallel is in other christological hymns, Col 1, 15-20 and Phil 2, 6-11. Its core (1-5.10-11.14) is poetic in structure, with short phrases linked by "staircase parallelism," in which the last word of one phrase becomes the first word of the next. Prose inserts (at least 6-8 and 15) deal with John the Baptist.

1, 1: *In the beginning:* also the first words of the Old Testament (Gn 1, 1). *Was:* this verb is used three times with different meanings in this verse: existence, relationship, and predication. *The Word* (Greek *logos*): this term combines God's dynamic, creative word (Genesis), personified preexistent Wisdom as the instrument of God's creative activity (Proverbs), and the ultimate intelligibility of reality (Hellenistic philosophy). *With God:* the Greek preposition here connotes communication with another. *Was God:* lack of a definite article with "God" in Greek signifies predication rather than identification.

1, 3: *What came to be:* while the oldest manuscripts have no punctuation here, the corrector of Bodmer Papyrus P75, some manuscripts, and the Ante-Nicene Fathers take this phrase with what follows, as staircase parallelism. Connection with v 3 reflects fourth-century anti-Arianism.

1, 5: The ethical dualism of light and darkness is paralleled in intertestamental literature and in the Dead Sea Scrolls. *Overcome:* "comprehend" is another possible translation, but cf 12, 35; Wis 7, 29-30.

1, 6: John was *sent* just as Jesus was "sent" (4, 34) in divine mission. Other references to John the Baptist in this gospel emphasize the differences between them and John's subordinate role.

1, 7: *Testimony:* the testimony theme of Jn is introduced, which portrays Jesus as if on trial throughout his ministry. All testify to Jesus: John the Baptist, the Samaritan woman, scripture, his works, the crowds, the Spirit, and his disciples.

1, 11: *What was his own . . . his own people:* first a neuter, literally, "his own property/possession" (probably = Israel), then a masculine, "his own people" (the Israelites).

1, 13: Believers in Jesus become children of God not through any of the three natural causes mentioned but through God who is the immediate cause of the new spiritual life. *Were born:* the Greek verb can mean "begotten" (by a male) or "born" (from a female or of parents). The variant "he who was begotten," asserting Jesus' virginal conception, is weakly attested in Old Latin and Syriac versions.

14*†And the Word became flesh
and made his dwelling among us,
and we saw his glory,
the glory as of the Father's only
Son,
full of grace and truth.

15*† John testified to him and cried out,
saying, "This was he of whom I said,
'The one who is coming after me ranks
ahead of me because he existed before
me.' " 16† From his fullness we have all
received, grace in place of grace,
17* because while the law was given
through Moses, grace and truth came
through Jesus Christ. 18*† No one has
ever seen God. The only Son, God, who
is at the Father's side, has revealed
him.

JOHN

II: THE BOOK OF SIGNS

John the Baptist's Testimony to
Himself.† 19 †And this is the testimony
of John. When the Jews from Jerusalem
sent priests and Levites [to him] to ask
him, "Who are you?" 20*† he admitted
and did not deny it, but admitted, "I am
not the Messiah." 21*† So they asked
him, "What are you then? Are you Eli-
jah?" And he said, "I am not." "Are you
the Prophet?" He answered, "No."
22 So they said to him, "Who are you,
so we can give an answer to those who
sent us? What do you have to say for
yourself?" 23*† He said:

"I am 'the voice of one crying out
in the desert,
"Make straight the way of the
Lord," '

as Isaiah the prophet said." 24† Some
Pharisees were also sent. 25* They
asked him, "Why then do you baptize
if you are not the Messiah or Elijah or
the Prophet?" 26*† John answered
them, "I baptize with water; but there
is one among you whom you do not rec-
ognize, 27 the one who is coming after
me, whose sandal strap I am not worthy
to untie." 28† This happened in Bethany
across the Jordan, where John was bap-
tizing.

John the Baptist's Testimony to Jesus.
29*† The next day he saw Jesus coming
toward him and said, "Behold, the

---

*

14: Ex 16, 10; 24, 17; 25, 8-9; 33, 22; 34, 6; Sir 24, 4.8; Is 60, 1; Ez 43, 7; Jl 4, 17; Hb 2, 14; 1 Jn 1, 2; 4, 2; 2 Jn 7.
15: 1, 30; 3, 27-30.
17: 7, 19; Ex 31, 18; 34, 28.
18: 5, 37; 6, 46; Ex 33, 20; Jgs 13, 21-22; 1 Tm 6, 16; 1 Jn 4, 12.
20: 3, 28; Lk 3, 15; Acts 13, 25.
21: Dt 18, 15.18; 2 Kgs 2, 11; Sir 48, 10; Mal 3, 1.23; Mt 11, 14; 17, 11-13; Mk 9, 13; Acts 3, 22.
23: Is 40, 3; Mt 3, 3; Mk 1, 2; Lk 3, 4.
25: Ez 36, 25; Zec 13, 1; Mt 16, 14.
26: Mt 3, 11; Mk 1, 7-8; Lk 3, 16; Acts 13, 25.
29: 1, 36; Ex 12; Is 53, 7; Rv 5-7; 17, 14.

---

†

1, 14: *Flesh:* the whole person, used probably against docetistic tendencies (cf 1 Jn 4, 2; 2 Jn 7). *Made his dwelling:* literally, "pitched his tent/tabernacle." Cf the tabernacle or tent of meeting that was the place of God's presence among his people (Ex 25, 8-9). The incarnate Word is the new mode of God's presence among his people. The Greek verb has the same consonants as the Aramaic word for God's presence (Shekinah). *Glory:* God's visible manifestation of majesty in power, which once filled the tabernacle (Ex 40, 34) and the temple (1 Kgs 8, 10-11.27), is now centered in Jesus. *Only Son:* Greek, *monogenēs,* but see the note on 1, 18. *Grace and truth:* these words may represent two Old Testament terms describing Yahweh in covenant relationship with Israel (cf Ex 34, 6), thus God's "love" and "fidelity." The Word shares Yahweh's covenant qualities.

1, 15: This verse, interrupting vv 14 and 16, seems drawn from v 30.

1, 16: *Grace in place of grace:* replacement of the Old Covenant with the New (cf 17). Other possible translations are "grace upon grace" (accumulation) and "grace for grace" (correspondence).

1, 18: *The only Son, God:* while the vast majority of later textual witnesses have another reading, "the Son, the only one" or "the only Son," the translation above follows the best and earliest manuscripts, *monogenēs theos,* but takes the first term to mean not just "Only One" but to include a filial relationship with the Father, as at Lk 9, 38 ("only child") or Heb 11, 17 ("only son") and as translated at Jn 1, 14. The Logos is thus "only Son" and God but not Father/God.

1, 19-51: The testimony of John the Baptist about the Messiah and Jesus' self-revelation to the first disciples. This section constitutes the introduction to the gospel proper and is connected with the prose inserts in the prologue. It develops the major theme of testimony in four scenes: John's negative testimony about himself; his positive testimony about Jesus; the revelation of Jesus to Andrew and Peter; the revelation of Jesus to Philip and Nathanael.

1, 19: *The Jews:* throughout most of the gospel, the "Jews" does not refer to the Jewish people as such but to the hostile authorities, both Pharisees and Sadducees, particularly in Jerusalem, who refuse to believe in Jesus. The usage reflects the atmosphere, at the end of the first century, of polemics between church and synagogue, or possibly it refers to Jews as representative of a hostile world (10-11).

1, 20: *Messiah:* the anointed agent of Yahweh, usually considered to be of Davidic descent. See further the note on 1, 41.

1, 21: *Elijah:* the Baptist did not claim to be Elijah returned to earth (cf Mal 3, 23; Mt 11, 14). *The Prophet:* probably the prophet like Moses (Dt 18, 15; cf Acts 3, 22).

1, 23: This is a repunctuation and reinterpretation (as in the synoptic gospels and Septuagint) of the Hebrew text of Is 40, 3, which reads, "A voice cries out: In the desert prepare the way of the LORD."

1, 24: *Some Pharisees:* other translations, such as "Now they had been sent from the Pharisees," misunderstand the grammatical construction. This is a different group from that in v 19; the priests and Levites would have been Sadducees, not Pharisees.

1, 26: *I baptize with water:* the synoptics add "but he will baptize you with the holy Spirit" (Mk 1, 8) or ". . . holy Spirit and fire" (Mt 3, 11; Lk 3, 16). John's emphasis is on purification and preparation for a better baptism.

1, 28: *Bethany across the Jordan:* site unknown. Another reading is "Bethabara."

1, 29: *The Lamb of God:* the background for this title may be the victorious apocalyptic lamb who would destroy evil in the world (Rv 5-7; 17, 14); the paschal lamb, whose blood saved Israel (Ex 12); and/or the suffering servant led like a lamb to the slaughter as a sin-offering (Is 53, 7.10).

Lamb of God, who takes away the sin of the world. 30*† He is the one of whom I said, 'A man is coming after me who ranks ahead of me because he existed before me.' 31† I did not know him, but the reason why I came baptizing with water was that he might be made known to Israel." 32*† John testified further, saying, "I saw the Spirit come down like a dove from the sky and remain upon him. 33* I did not know him, but the one who sent me to baptize with water told me, 'On whomever you see the Spirit come down and remain, he is the one who will baptize with the holy Spirit.' 34*† Now I have seen and testified that he is the Son of God."

The First Disciples. 35* The next day John was there again with two of his disciples, 36† and as he watched Jesus walk by, he said, "Behold, the Lamb of God." 37† The two disciples heard what he said and followed Jesus. 38 Jesus turned and saw them following him and said to them, "What are you looking for?" They said to him, "Rabbi" (which translated means Teacher), "where are you staying?" 39† He said to them, "Come, and you will see." So they went and saw where he was staying, and they stayed with him that day. It was about four in the afternoon. 40 Andrew, the brother of Simon Peter, was one of the two who heard John and followed Jesus. 41*† He first found his own brother Simon and told him, "We have found the Messiah" (which is translated Anointed). 42*† Then he brought him to Jesus. Jesus looked at him and said, "You are Simon the son of John; you will be called Kephas" (which is translated Peter).

43† The next day he decided to go to Galilee, and he found Philip. And Jesus said to him, "Follow me." 44 Now Philip was from Bethsaida, the town of Andrew and Peter. 45* Philip found Nathanael and told him, "We have found the one about whom Moses wrote in the law, and also the prophets, Jesus, son of Joseph, from Nazareth." 46 But Nathanael said to him, "Can anything good come from Nazareth?" Philip said to him, "Come and see." 47† Jesus saw Nathanael coming toward him and said of him, "Here is a true Israelite. There is no duplicity in him." 48*† Nathanael said to him, "How do you know me?" Jesus answered and said to him, "Before Philip called you, I saw you under the fig tree." 49*† Nathanael answered him, "Rabbi, you are the Son of God; you are the King of Israel." 50† Jesus answered and said to him, "Do you believe because I told you that I saw you under the fig tree? You will see greater things than this." 51*† And he said to him, "Amen, amen, I say to you, you will see the sky opened and the angels of God ascending and descending on the Son of Man."

JOHN

*

30: 1, 15; Mt 3, 11; Mk 1, 7; Lk 3, 16.
32: Sg 5, 2; Is 11, 2; Hos 11, 11; Mt 3, 16; Mk 1, 10; Lk 3, 21-22.
33: Is 42, 1; Mt 3, 11; Mk 1, 8; Lk 3, 16.
34: Is 42, 1; Mt 3, 17; Mk 1, 11; Lk 9, 35.
35-51: Mt 4, 18-22; Mk 1, 16-20; Lk 5, 1-11.
41: 4, 25.
42: Mt 16, 18; Mk 3, 16.
45: 21, 2.
48: Mi 4, 4; Zec 3, 10.
49: 12, 13; Ex 4, 22; Dt 14, 1; 2 Sm 7, 14; Jb 1, 6; 2, 1; 38, 7; Pss 2, 7; 29, 1; 89, 27; Wis 2, 18; Sir 4, 10; Dn 3, 25; Hos 11, 1; Mt 14, 33; 16, 16; Mk 13, 32.
51: Gn 28, 10-17; Dn 7, 13.

†

1, 30: *He existed before me:* possibly as Elijah (to come, 27); for the evangelist and his audience, Jesus' preexistence would be implied (see the note on 1, 1).

1, 31: *I did not know him:* this gospel shows no knowledge of the tradition (Lk 1) about the kinship of Jesus and John the Baptist. *The reason why I came baptizing with water:* in this gospel, John's baptism is not connected with forgiveness of sins; its purpose is revelatory, that Jesus may be made known to Israel.

1, 32: *Like a dove:* a symbol of the new creation (Gn 8, 8) or the community of Israel (Hos 11, 11). *Remain:* the first use of a favorite verb in Jn, emphasizing the permanency of the relationship between Father and Son (as here) and between the Son and the Christian. Jesus is the permanent bearer of the Spirit.

1, 34: *The Son of God:* this reading is supported by good Greek manuscripts, including the Chester Beatty and Bodmer Papyri and the Vatican Codex, but is suspect because it harmonizes this passage with the synoptic version: "This is my beloved Son" (Mt 3, 17; Mk 1, 11; Lk 3, 22). The poorly attested alternate reading, "God's chosen One," is probably a reference to the Servant of Yahweh (Is 42, 1).

1, 36: John the Baptist's testimony makes his disciples' following of Jesus plausible.

1, 37: *The two disciples:* Andrew (40) and, traditionally, John, son of Zebedee (see the note on 13, 23).

1, 39: *Four in the afternoon:* literally, the tenth hour, from sunrise, in the Roman calculation of time. Some suggest that the next day, beginning at sunset, was the sabbath; they would have stayed with Jesus to avoid travel on it.

1, 41: *Messiah:* the Hebrew word *māšîaḥ,* "anointed one" (see the note on Lk 2, 11), appears in Greek as the transliterated *messias* only here and in 4, 25. Elsewhere the Greek translation *christos* is used.

1, 42: *Simon, the son of John:* in Mt 16, 17, Simon is called *Bariōna,* "son of Jonah," a different tradition for the name of Simon's father. *Kephas:* in Aramaic = the Rock; cf Mt 16, 18. Neither the Greek equivalent *Petros* nor, with one isolated exception, *Kephas* is attested as a personal name before Christian times.

1, 43: *He:* grammatically, could be Peter, but logically is probably Jesus.

1, 47: *A true Israelite. There is no duplicity in him:* Jacob was the first to bear the name "Israel" (Gn 32, 29), but Jacob was a man of duplicity (Gn 27, 35-36).

1, 48: *Under the fig tree:* a symbol of messianic peace (cf Mi 4, 4; Zec 3, 10).

1, 49: *Son of God:* this title is used in the Old Testament, among other ways, as a title of adoption for the Davidic king (2 Sm 7, 14; Pss 2, 7; 89, 27), and thus here, with *King of Israel,* in a messianic sense. For the evangelist, Son of God also points to Jesus' divinity (cf 20, 28).

1, 50: Possibly a statement: "You [singular] believe because I saw you under the fig tree."

1, 51: The double "Amen" is characteristic of John. *You* is plural in Greek. The allusion is to Jacob's ladder (Gn 28, 12).

CHAPTER 2

***The Wedding at Cana.*†** 1*† On the
third day there was a wedding in Cana
in Galilee, and the mother of Jesus was
there. 2 Jesus and his disciples were also
invited to the wedding. 3 When the wine
ran short, the mother of Jesus said to
him, "They have no wine." 4*† [And]
Jesus said to her, "Woman, how does
your concern affect me? My hour has
not yet come." 5* His mother said to the
servers, "Do whatever he tells you."
6*† Now there were six stone water jars
there for Jewish ceremonial washings,
each holding twenty to thirty gallons.
7 Jesus told them, "Fill the jars with wa-
ter." So they filled them to the brim.
8† Then he told them, "Draw some out
now and take it to the headwaiter." So
they took it. 9 And when the headwaiter
tasted the water that had become wine,
without knowing where it came from
(although the servers who had drawn
the water knew), the headwaiter called
the bridegroom 10 and said to him, "Ev-
eryone serves good wine first, and then
when people have drunk freely, an infe-
rior one; but you have kept the good
wine until now." 11*† Jesus did this as
the beginning of his signs in Cana in
Galilee and so revealed his glory, and
his disciples began to believe in him.

12† After this, he and his mother, [his]
brothers, and his disciples went down
to Capernaum and stayed there only a
few days.

***Cleansing of the Temple.*†** 13*† Since
the Passover of the Jews was near, Je-
sus went up to Jerusalem. 14*† He found
in the temple area those who sold oxen,
sheep, and doves, as well as the money-
changers seated there. 15 He made a
whip out of cords and drove them all
out of the temple area, with the sheep
and oxen, and spilled the coins of the
money-changers and overturned their
tables, 16* and to those who sold doves
he said, "Take these out of here, and
stop making my Father's house a mar-
ketplace." 17*† His disciples recalled
the words of scripture, "Zeal for your
house will consume me." 18* At this the
Jews answered and said to him, "What
sign can you show us for doing this?"
19*† Jesus answered and said to them,
"Destroy this temple and in three days
I will raise it up." 20† The Jews said,
"This temple has been under construc-
tion for forty-six years, and you will
raise it up in three days?" 21 But he was
speaking about the temple of his body.

---

*

2, 1: 4, 46; Jgs 14, 12; Tb 11, 8.
4: 7, 30; 8, 20; 12, 23; 13, 1; Jgs 11, 12; 1 Kgs 17, 18; 2 Kgs 3, 13; 2 Chr 35, 21; Hos 14, 9; Mk 1, 24; 5, 7; 7, 30; 8, 20; 12, 23; 13, 1.
5: Gn 41, 55.
6: 3, 25; Lv 11, 33; Am 9, 13-14; Mt 15, 2; 23, 25-26; Mk 7, 2-4; Lk 11, 38.
11: 4, 54.
13-22: Mt 21, 12-13; Mk 11, 15-17; Lk 19, 45-46.
14: Ex 30, 11-16; Lv 5, 7.
16: Zec 14, 21.
17: Ps 69, 9.
18: 6, 30.
19: Mt 24, 2; 26, 61; 27, 40; Mk 13, 2; 14, 58; 15, 29; Lk 21, 6; Acts 6, 14.

---

†

2, 1—6, 71: Signs revealing Jesus as the Messiah to all Israel. "Sign" (*sēmeion*) is John's symbolic term for Jesus' wondrous deeds (see Introduction). The Old Testament background lies in the Exodus story (cf Dt 11, 3; 29, 2). John is interested primarily in what the *sēmeia* signify: God's intervention in human history in a new way through Jesus.

2, 1-11: The first sign. This story of replacement of Jewish ceremonial washings (6) presents the initial revelation about Jesus at the outset of his ministry. He manifests his glory; the disciples believe. There is no synoptic parallel.

2, 1: *Cana:* unknown from the Old Testament. *The mother of Jesus:* she is never named in John.

2, 4: This verse may seek to show that Jesus did not work miracles to help his family and friends, as in the apocryphal gospels. *Woman:* a normal, polite form of address, but unattested in reference to one's mother. Cf also 19, 26. *How does your concern affect me?:* literally, "What is this to me and to you?"—a Hebrew expression of either hostility (Jgs 11, 12; 2 Chr 35, 21; 1 Kgs 17, 18) or denial of common interest (Hos 14, 9; 2 Kgs 3, 13). Cf Mk 1, 24; 5, 7, used by demons to Jesus. *My hour has not yet come:* the translation as a question ("Has not my hour now come?"), while preferable grammatically and supported by Greek Fathers, seems unlikely from a comparison with 7, 6.30. The "hour" is that of Jesus' passion, death, resurrection, and ascension (13, 1).

2, 6: *Twenty to thirty gallons:* literally, "two or three measures"; the Attic liquid measure contained 39.39 liters. The vast quantity recalls prophecies of abundance in the last days; cf Am 9, 13-14; Hos 14, 7; Jer 31, 12.

2, 8: *Headwaiter:* used of the official who managed a banquet, but there is no evidence of such a functionary in Palestine. Perhaps here a friend of the family acted as master of ceremonies; cf Sir 32, 1.

2, 11: *The beginning of his signs:* the first of seven (see Introduction).

2, 12—3, 21: The next three episodes take place in Jerusalem. Only the first is paralleled in the synoptic gospels.

2, 12: This transitional verse may be a harmonization with the synoptic tradition in Lk 4, 31 and Mt 4, 13. There are many textual variants. John depicts no extended ministry in Capernaum as do the synoptics.

2, 13-22: This episode indicates the post-resurrectional replacement of the temple by the person of Jesus.

2, 13: *Passover:* this is the first Passover mentioned in John; a second is mentioned in 6, 4, a third in 13, 1. Taken literally, they point to a ministry of at least two years.

2, 14-22: The other gospels place the cleansing of the temple in the last days of Jesus' life (Mt, on the day Jesus entered Jerusalem; Mk, on the next day). The order of events in the gospel narratives is often determined by theological motives rather than by chronological data.

2, 14: *Oxen, sheep, and doves:* intended for sacrifice. The doves were the offerings of the poor (Lv 5, 7). *Money-changers:* for a temple tax paid by every male Jew more than nineteen years of age, with a half-shekel coin (Ex 30, 11-16), in Tyrian currency. See the note on Mt 17, 24.

2, 17: Ps 69, 10, changed to future tense to apply to Jesus.

2, 19: This saying about the destruction of the temple occurs in various forms (Mt 24, 2; 27, 40; Mk 13, 2; 15, 29; Lk 21, 6; cf Acts 6, 14). Mt 26, 61 has: "I *can* destroy the temple of God. . ."; see the note there. In Mk 14, 58, there is a metaphorical contrast with a new temple: "I will destroy this temple *made with hands* and within three days I will build another *not made with hands.*" Here it is symbolic of Jesus' resurrection and the resulting community (see 21 and Rv 21, 2). *In three days:* an Old Testament expression for a short, indefinite period of time; cf Hos 6, 2.

2, 20: *Forty-six years:* based on references in Josephus (*Jewish Wars* 1, 21, 1 §401; *Antiquities* 15, 11, 1 §380), possibly the spring of A.D. 28. Cf the note on Lk 3, 1.

22* Therefore, when he was raised from
the dead, his disciples remembered that
he had said this, and they came to be-
lieve the scripture and the word Jesus
had spoken.
23* While he was in Jerusalem for the
feast of Passover, many began to be-
lieve in his name when they saw the
signs he was doing. 24 But Jesus would
not trust himself to them because he
knew them all, 25* and did not need any-
one to testify about human nature. He
himself understood it well.

CHAPTER 3

Nicodemus.† 1*† Now there was a
Pharisee named Nicodemus, a ruler of
the Jews. 2* He came to Jesus at night
and said to him, "Rabbi, we know that
you are a teacher who has come from
God, for no one can do these signs that
you are doing unless God is with him."
3† Jesus answered and said to him,
"Amen, amen, I say to you, no one can
see the kingdom of God without being
born from above." 4* Nicodemus said to
him, "How can a person once grown old
be born again? Surely he cannot reen-
ter his mother's womb and be born
again, can he?" 5* Jesus answered,
"Amen, amen, I say to you, no one can
enter the kingdom of God without being
born of water and Spirit. 6* What is born
of flesh is flesh and what is born of spirit
is spirit. 7 Do not be amazed that I told
you, 'You must be born from above.'
8*† The wind blows where it wills, and
you can hear the sound it makes, but
you do not know where it comes from
or where it goes; so it is with everyone
who is born of the Spirit." 9 Nicodemus
answered and said to him, "How can
this happen?" 10 Jesus answered and
said to him, "You are the teacher of Is-
rael and you do not understand this?
11* Amen, amen, I say to you, we speak
of what we know and we testify to what
we have seen, but you people do not ac-
cept our testimony. 12* If I tell you about
earthly things and you do not believe,
how will you believe if I tell you about
heavenly things? 13* No one has gone
up to heaven except the one who has
come down from heaven, the Son of
Man. 14*† And just as Moses lifted up
the serpent in the desert, so must the
Son of Man be lifted up, 15† so that ev-
eryone who believes in him may have
eternal life."
16*† For God so loved the world that
he gave his only Son, so that everyone
who believes in him might not perish
but might have eternal life. 17*† For
God did not send his Son into the world
to condemn the world, but that the
world might be saved through him.
18* Whoever believes in him will not be
condemned, but whoever does not be-
lieve has already been condemned, be-
cause he has not believed in the name
of the only Son of God. 19*† And this is
the verdict, that the light came into the
world, but people preferred darkness to
light, because their works were evil.
20* For everyone who does wicked
things hates the light and does not come
toward the light, so that his works might
not be exposed. 21* But whoever lives
the truth comes to the light, so that his
works may be clearly seen as done in
God.

JOHN

---

*

22: 5, 39; 12, 16; 14, 26; 20, 9; Mt 12, 6; Lk 24, 6-8; Rv 21, 22.
23: 4, 45.
25: 1 Kgs 8, 39; Pss 33, 15; 94, 11; Sir 42, 18; Jer 17, 10; 20, 12.
3, 1: 7, 50-51; 19, 39.
2: 9, 4.16.33; 10, 21; 11, 10; 13, 30; Mt 22, 16; Mk 12, 14; Lk 20, 21.
4: 1, 13.
5: 1, 32; 7, 39; 19, 30.34-35; Is 32, 15; 44, 3; Ez 36, 25-27; Jl 3, 1-2.
6: 6, 63; 1 Cor 15, 44-50.
8: Eccl 11, 4-5; Acts 2, 2-4.
11: 3, 32.34; 8, 14; Mt 11, 27.
12: 6, 62-65; Wis 9, 16-17; 1 Cor 15, 40; 2 Cor 5, 1; Phil 2, 10; 3, 19-20.
13: 1, 18; 6, 62; Dn 7, 13; Rom 10, 6; Eph 4, 9.
14: 8, 28; 12, 32.34; Nm 21, 4-9; Wis 16, 5-7.
16: 1 Jn 4, 9.
17: 5, 22.30; 8, 15-18; 12, 47.
18: 5, 24; Mk 16, 16.
19: 1, 5.9-11; 8, 12; 9, 5.
20: Jb 24, 13-17.
21: Gn 47, 29 LXX; Jos 2, 14 LXX; 2 Sm 2, 6 LXX; 15, 20 LXX; Tb 4, 6 LXX; 13, 6; Is 26, 10 LXX; Mt 5, 14-16.

---

†

3, 1-21: Jesus instructs Nicodemus on the necessity of a new birth from above. This scene in Jerusalem at Passover exemplifies the faith engendered by signs (2, 23). It continues the self-manifestation of Jesus in Jerusalem begun in ch 2. This is the first of the Johannine discourses, shifting from dialogue to monologue (11-15) to reflection of the evangelist (16-21). The shift from singular through v 10 to plural in v 11 may reflect the early church's controversy with the Jews.

3, 1: *A ruler of the Jews:* most likely a member of the Jewish council, the Sanhedrin; see the note on Mk 8, 31.

3, 3: *Born:* see the note on 1, 13. *From above:* the Greek adverb *anōthen* means both "from above" and "again." Jesus means "from above" (see 31), but Nicodemus misunderstands it as "again." This misunderstanding serves as a springboard for further instruction.

3, 8: *Wind:* the Greek word *pneuma* (as well as the Hebrew *rûaḥ*) means both "wind" and "spirit." In the play on the double meaning, "wind" is primary.

3, 14: *Lifted up:* in Nm 21, 9, Moses simply "mounted" a serpent upon a pole. John here substitutes a verb implying glorification. Jesus, exalted to glory at his cross and resurrection, represents healing for all.

3, 15: *Eternal life:* used here for the first time in John, this term stresses quality of life rather than duration.

3, 16: *Gave:* as a gift in the incarnation, and also "over to death" in the crucifixion; cf Rom 8, 32.

3, 17-19: *Condemn:* the Greek root means both judgment and condemnation. Jesus' purpose is to save, but his coming provokes judgment; some condemn themselves by turning from the light.

3, 19: Judgment is not only future but is partially realized here and now.

Final Witness of the Baptist.†
22* After this, Jesus and his disciples
went into the region of Judea, where he
spent some time with them baptizing.
23† John was also baptizing in Aenon
near Salim, because there was an abun-
dance of water there, and people came
to be baptized, 24*† for John had not yet
been imprisoned. 25† Now a dispute
arose between the disciples of John and
a Jew about ceremonial washings.
26* So they came to John and said to
him, "Rabbi, the one who was with you
across the Jordan, to whom you testi-
fied, here he is baptizing and everyone
is coming to him." 27* John answered
and said, "No one can receive anything
except what has been given him from
heaven. 28* You yourselves can testify
that I said [that] I am not the Messiah,
but that I was sent before him. 29*† The
one who has the bride is the bride-
groom; the best man, who stands and
listens for him, rejoices greatly at the
bridegroom's voice. So this joy of mine
has been made complete. 30* He must
increase; I must decrease."

The One from Heaven.† 31* The one
who comes from above is above all. The
one who is of the earth is earthly and
speaks of earthly things. But the one
who comes from heaven [is above all].
32* He testifies to what he has seen and
heard, but no one accepts his testimony.
33* Whoever does accept his testimony
certifies that God is trustworthy. 34† For
the one whom God sent speaks the
words of God. He does not ration his
gift of the Spirit. 35* The Father loves
the Son and has given everything over
to him. 36* Whoever believes in the Son
has eternal life, but whoever disobeys
the Son will not see life, but the wrath
of God remains upon him.

CHAPTER 4

1† Now when Jesus learned that the
Pharisees had heard that Jesus was
making and baptizing more disciples
than John 2† (although Jesus himself
was not baptizing, just his disciples),
3 he left Judea and returned to Galilee.

The Samaritan Woman. 4† He had to
pass through Samaria. 5*† So he came
to a town of Samaria called Sychar,
near the plot of land that Jacob had
given to his son Joseph. 6 Jacob's well
was there. Jesus, tired from his journey,
sat down there at the well. It was about
noon.

7 A woman of Samaria came to draw
water. Jesus said to her, "Give me a
drink." 8 His disciples had gone into the
town to buy food. 9*† The Samaritan
woman said to him, "How can you, a
Jew, ask me, a Samaritan woman, for
a drink?" (For Jews use nothing in com-
mon with Samaritans.) 10*† Jesus an-
swered and said to her, "If you knew
the gift of God and who is saying to you,
'Give me a drink,' you would have
asked him and he would have given you
living water." 11† [The woman] said to
him, "Sir, you do not even have a bucket
and the cistern is deep; where then can
you get this living water? 12* Are you
greater than our father Jacob, who gave
us this cistern and drank from it himself
with his children and his flocks?"
13 Jesus answered and said to her, "Ev-
eryone who drinks this water will be
thirsty again; 14* but whoever drinks
the water I shall give will never thirst;

*

22-23: 4, 1-2.
24: Mt 4, 12; 14, 3; Mk 1, 14; 6, 17; Lk 3, 20.
26: 1, 26.32-34.36.
27: 19, 11; 1 Cor 4, 7; 2 Cor 3, 5; Heb 5, 4.
28: 1, 20-23; Lk 3, 15.
29: 15, 11; 17, 13; Mt 9, 15.
30: 2 Sm 3, 1.
31: 8, 23.
32: 3, 11.
33-34: 8, 26; 12, 44-50; 1 Jn 5, 10.
35: 13, 3; Mt 11, 27; 28, 18; Lk 10, 22.
36: 3, 16; 1 Jn 5, 13.
4, 5: Gn 33, 18-19; 48, 22; Jos 24, 32.
9: Sir 50, 25-26; Mt 10, 5.
10: Sir 24, 20-21; Is 55, 1; Jer 2, 13.
12: 8, 53; Mt 12, 41.
14: 6, 35.58; 7, 37-39; Is 44, 3; 49, 10; Jl 4, 18; Rv 7, 16; 21, 6.

†

3, 22-26: Jesus' ministry in Judea is only loosely connected with 2, 13—3, 21; cf 1, 19-36. Perhaps John the Baptist's further testimony was transposed here to give meaning to "water" in v 5. Jesus is depicted as baptizing (22); contrast 4, 2.

3, 23: *Aenon near Salim:* site uncertain, either in the upper Jordan valley or in Samaria.

3, 24: A remark probably intended to avoid objections based on a chronology like that of the synoptics (Mt 4, 12; Mk 1, 14).

3, 25: *A Jew:* some think Jesus is meant. Many manuscripts read "Jews."

3, 29: *The best man:* literally, "the friend of the groom," the *shoshben* of Jewish tradition, who arranged the wedding. Competition between him and the groom would be unthinkable.

3, 31-36: It is uncertain whether these are words by the Baptist, Jesus, or the evangelist. They are reflections on the two preceding scenes.

3, 34: *His gift:* of God or to Jesus, perhaps both. This verse echoes vv 5 and 8.

4, 1-42: Jesus in Samaria. The self-revelation of Jesus continues with his second discourse, on his mission to "half-Jews." It continues the theme of replacement, here with regard to cult (21). Water (7-15) serves as a symbol (as at Cana and in the Nicodemus episode).

4, 2: An editorial refinement of 3, 22, perhaps directed against followers of John the Baptist who claimed that Jesus imitated him.

4, 4: *He had to:* a theological necessity; geographically, Jews often bypassed Samaria by taking a route across the Jordan.

4, 5: *Sychar:* Jerome identifies this with Shechem, a reading found in Syriac manuscripts.

4, 9: Samaritan women were regarded by Jews as ritually impure, and therefore Jews were forbidden to drink from any vessel they had handled.

4, 10: *Living water:* the water of life, i.e., the revelation that Jesus brings; the woman thinks of "flowing water," so much more desirable than stagnant cistern water. On John's device of such misunderstanding, cf the note on 3, 3.

4, 11: *Sir:* the Greek *kyrios* means "master" or "lord," as a respectful mode of address for a human being or a deity; cf 4, 19. It is also the word used in the Septuagint for the Hebrew *ʾădônai,* substituted for the tetragrammaton YHWH.

the water I shall give will become in him
a spring of water welling up to eternal
life." 15 The woman said to him, "Sir,
give me this water, so that I may not
be thirsty or have to keep coming here
to draw water."
16 Jesus said to her, "Go call your hus-
band and come back." 17 The woman
answered and said to him, "I do not
have a husband." Jesus answered her,
"You are right in saying, 'I do not have
a husband.' 18* For you have had five
husbands, and the one you have now
is not your husband. What you have said
is true." 19* The woman said to him,
"Sir, I can see that you are a prophet.
20*† Our ancestors worshiped on this
mountain; but you people say that the
place to worship is in Jerusalem."
21 Jesus said to her, "Believe me,
woman, the hour is coming when you
will worship the Father neither on this
mountain nor in Jerusalem. 22* You
people worship what you do not under-
stand; we worship what we understand,
because salvation is from the Jews.
23† But the hour is coming, and is now
here, when true worshipers will worship
the Father in Spirit and truth; and in-
deed the Father seeks such people to
worship him. 24* God is Spirit, and those
who worship him must worship in Spirit
and truth." 25*† The woman said to him,
"I know that the Messiah is coming, the
one called the Anointed; when he
comes, he will tell us everything."
26*† Jesus said to her, "I am he, the one
who is speaking with you."
27† At that moment his disciples re-
turned, and were amazed that he was
talking with a woman, but still no one
said, "What are you looking for?" or
"Why are you talking with her?" 28 The
woman left her water jar and went into
the town and said to the people,
29 "Come see a man who told me every-
thing I have done. Could he possibly be
the Messiah?" 30 They went out of the
town and came to him. 31 Meanwhile,
the disciples urged him, "Rabbi, eat."
32 But he said to them, "I have food to
eat of which you do not know." 33 So the
disciples said to one another, "Could
someone have brought him something
to eat?" 34* Jesus said to them, "My food
is to do the will of the one who sent me
and to finish his work. 35*† Do you not
say, 'In four months the harvest will be
here'? I tell you, look up and see the
fields ripe for the harvest. 36*† The
reaper is already receiving his payment
and gathering crops for eternal life, so
that the sower and reaper can rejoice
together. 37* For here the saying is veri-
fied that 'One sows and another reaps.'
38 I sent you to reap what you have not
worked for; others have done the work,
and you are sharing the fruits of their
work."
39† Many of the Samaritans of that
town began to believe in him because
of the word of the woman who testified,
"He told me everything I have done."
40 When the Samaritans came to him,
they invited him to stay with them; and
he stayed there two days. 41 Many more
began to believe in him because of his
word, 42* and they said to the woman,
"We no longer believe because of your
word; for we have heard for ourselves,
and we know that this is truly the savior
of the world."

Return to Galilee.† 43 After the two
days, he left there for Galilee. 44*† For
Jesus himself testified that a prophet
has no honor in his native place. 45 When
he came into Galilee, the Galileans wel-
comed him, since they had seen all he
had done in Jerusalem at the feast; for
they themselves had gone to the feast.

Second Sign at Cana.† 46* Then he re-

JOHN

*

18: 2 Kgs 17, 24-34.
19: 9, 17; Hos 1, 3.
20: Dt 11, 29; 27, 4; Jos 8, 33; Ps 122, 1-5.
22: 2 Kgs 17, 27; Ps 76, 2-3.
24: 2 Cor 3, 17.
25: 1, 41.
26: 9, 37.
34: 5, 30.36; 6, 38; 9, 4; 17, 4.
35: Mt 9, 37-38; Lk 10, 2; Rv 14, 15.
36: Ps 126, 5-6; Am 9, 13-14.
37: Dt 20, 6; 28, 30; Jb 31, 8; Mi 6, 15.
42: 1 Jn 4, 14.
44: Mt 13, 57; Mk 6, 4; Lk 4, 24.
46-54: 2, 1-11; Mt 8, 5-13; 15, 21-28; Mk 7, 24-30; Lk 7, 1-10.

†

4, 20: *This mountain:* Gerizim, on which a temple was erected in the fourth century B.C. by Samaritans to rival Mt. Zion in Jerusalem; cf Dt 27, 4 (Mt. Ebal = the Jews' term for Gerizim).

4, 23: *In Spirit and truth:* not a reference to an interior worship within one's own spirit. The Spirit is the spirit given by God that reveals truth and enables one to worship God appropriately (14, 16-17). Cf "born of water and Spirit" (3, 5).

4, 25: The expectations of the Samaritans are expressed here in Jewish terminology. They did not expect a messianic king of the house of David but a prophet like Moses (Dt 18, 15).

4, 26: *I am he:* it could also be translated "I am," an Old Testament self-designation of Yahweh (Is 43, 3, etc.); cf 6, 20; 8, 24.28.58; 13, 19; 18, 5.6.8. See the note on Mk 6, 50.

4, 27: *Talking with a woman:* a religious and social restriction that Jesus is pictured treating as unimportant.

4, 35: *'In four months . . .':* probably a proverb; cf Mt 9, 37-38.

4, 36: *Already:* this word may go with the preceding verse rather than with 36.

4, 39: The woman is presented as a missionary, described in virtually the same words as the disciples are in Jesus' prayer (17, 20).

4, 43-54: Jesus' arrival in Cana in Galilee; the second sign. This section introduces another theme, that of the life-giving word of Jesus. It is explicitly linked to the first sign (2, 11). The royal official believes (50). The natural life given his son is a sign of eternal life.

4, 44: Probably a reminiscence of a tradition as in Mk 6, 4. Cf Gospel of Thomas #31: "No prophet is acceptable in his village, no physician heals those who know him."

4, 46-54: The story of the cure of the royal official's son may be a third version of the cure of the centurion's son (Mt 8, 5-13) or servant (Lk 7, 1-10). Cf also Mt 15, 21-28 // Mk 7, 24-30.

turned to Cana in Galilee, where he had made the water wine. Now there was a royal official whose son was ill in Capernaum. 47 When he heard that Jesus had arrived in Galilee from Judea, he went to him and asked him to come down and heal his son, who was near death. 48* Jesus said to him, "Unless you people see signs and wonders, you will not believe." 49 The royal official said to him, "Sir, come down before my child dies." 50* Jesus said to him, "You may go; your son will live." The man believed what Jesus said to him and left. 51 While he was on his way back, his slaves met him and told him that his boy would live. 52 He asked them when he began to recover. They told him, "The fever left him yesterday, about one in the afternoon." 53 The father realized that just at that time Jesus had said to him, "Your son will live," and he and his whole household came to believe. 54* [Now] this was the second sign Jesus did when he came to Galilee from Judea.

CHAPTER 5†

Cure on a Sabbath. 1*† After this, there was a feast of the Jews, and Jesus went up to Jerusalem. 2*† Now there is in Jerusalem at the Sheep [Gate] a pool called in Hebrew Bethesda, with five porticoes. 3† In these lay a large number of ill, blind, lame, and crippled. [4]† 5 One man was there who had been ill for thirty-eight years. 6 When Jesus saw him lying there and knew that he had been ill for a long time, he said to him, "Do you want to be well?" 7 The sick man answered him, "Sir, I have no one to put me into the pool when the water is stirred up; while I am on my way, someone else gets down there before me." 8* Jesus said to him, "Rise, take up your mat, and walk." 9* Immediately the man became well, took up his mat, and walked.

Now that day was a sabbath. 10* So the Jews said to the man who was cured, "It is the sabbath, and it is not lawful for you to carry your mat." 11 He answered them, "The man who made me well told me, 'Take up your mat and walk.' " 12 They asked him, "Who is the man who told you, 'Take it up and walk'?" 13* The man who was healed did not know who it was, for Jesus had slipped away, since there was a crowd there. 14*† After this Jesus found him in the temple area and said to him, "Look, you are well; do not sin any more, so that nothing worse may happen to you." 15 The man went and told the Jews that Jesus was the one who had made him well. 16* Therefore, the Jews began to persecute Jesus because he did this on a sabbath. 17*† But Jesus answered them, "My Father is at work until now, so I am at work." 18* For this reason the Jews tried all the more to kill him, because he not only broke the sabbath but he also called God his own father, making himself equal to God.

The Work of the Son. 19*† Jesus answered and said to them, "Amen, amen, I say to you, a son cannot do anything on his own, but only what he sees his

*

48: 2, 18.23; Wis 8, 8; Mt 12, 38; 1 Cor 1, 22.
50: 1 Kgs 17, 23.
54: 2, 11.
5, 1: 6, 4.
2: Neh 3, 1.32; 12, 39.
8: Mt 9, 6; Mk 2, 11; Lk 5, 24; Acts 3, 6.
9: Mk 2, 12; Lk 5, 25 / 9, 14.
10: Ex 20, 8; Jer 17, 21-27; Mk 3, 2; Lk 13, 10; 14, 1.
13: Mt 8, 18; 13, 36; Mk 4, 36; 7, 17.
14: 8, 11; 9, 2; Ez 18, 20.
16: 7, 23; Mt 12, 8.
17: Ex 20, 11.
18: 7, 1.25; 8, 37.40; 10, 33.36; 14, 28; Gn 3, 5-6; Wis 2, 16; Mt 26, 4; 2 Thes 2, 4.
19: 3, 34; 8, 26; 12, 49; 9, 4; 10, 30.

†

5, 1-47: The self-revelation of Jesus continues in Jerusalem at a feast. The third sign (cf 2, 11; 4, 54) is performed, the cure of a paralytic by Jesus' life-giving word. The water of the pool fails to bring life; Jesus' word does.

5, 1: The reference in vv 45-46 to Moses suggests that the feast was Pentecost. The connection of that feast with the giving of the law to Moses on Sinai, attested in later Judaism, may already have been made in the first century. The feast could also be Passover (cf 6, 4). John stresses that the day was a sabbath (9).

5, 2: There is no noun with *Sheep.* "Gate" is supplied on the grounds that there must have been a gate in the NE wall of the temple area where animals for sacrifice were brought in; cf Neh 3, 1.32; 12, 39. *Hebrew:* more precisely, Aramaic. *Bethesda:* preferred to variants "Be(th)zatha" and "Bethsaida"; *bêt-ʾešdatayin* is given as the name of a double pool northeast of the temple area in the Qumran Copper Roll. *Five porticoes:* a pool excavated in Jerusalem actually has five porticoes.

5, 3: The Caesarean and Western recensions, followed by the Vulgate, add "waiting for the movement of the water." Apparently an intermittent spring in the pool bubbled up occasionally (see 7). This turbulence was believed to cure.

5, 4: Toward the end of the second century in the West and among the fourth-century Greek Fathers, an additional verse was known: "For [from time to time] an angel of the Lord used to come down into the pool; and the water was stirred up, so the first one to get in [after the stirring of the water] was healed of whatever disease afflicted him." The angel was a popular explanation of the turbulence and the healing powers attributed to it. This verse is missing from all early Greek manuscripts and the earliest versions, including the original Vulgate. Its vocabulary is markedly non-Johannine.

5, 14: While the cure of the paralytic in Mk 2, 1-12 is associated with the forgiveness of sins, Jesus never drew a one-to-one connection between sin and suffering (cf 9, 3; Lk 12, 1-5), as did Ez 18, 20.

5, 17: Sabbath observance (10) was based on God's resting on the seventh day (cf Gn 2, 2-3; Ex 20, 11). Philo and some rabbis insisted that God's providence remains active on the sabbath, keeping all things in existence, giving life in birth and taking it away in death. Other rabbis taught that God rested from creating, but not from judging (= ruling, governing). Jesus here claims the same authority to work as the Father, and, in the discourse that follows, the same divine prerogatives: power over life and death (21.24-26) and judgment (22.27).

5, 19: This proverb or parable is taken from apprenticeship in a trade: the activity of a son is modeled on that of his father. Jesus' dependence on the Father is justification for doing what the Father does.

father doing; for what he does, his son
will do also. 20* For the Father loves his
Son and shows him everything that he
himself does, and he will show him
greater works than these, so that you
may be amazed. 21*† For just as the Fa-
ther raises the dead and gives life, so
also does the Son give life to whomever
he wishes. 22*† Nor does the Father
judge anyone, but he has given all judg-
ment to his Son, 23 so that all may honor
the Son just as they honor the Father.
Whoever does not honor the Son does
not honor the Father who sent him.
24* Amen, amen, I say to you, whoever
hears my word and believes in the one
who sent me has eternal life and will
not come to condemnation, but has
passed from death to life. 25* Amen,
amen, I say to you, the hour is coming
and is now here when the dead will hear
the voice of the Son of God, and those
who hear will live. 26* For just as the
Father has life in himself, so also he
gave to his Son the possession of life in
himself. 27* And he gave him power to
exercise judgment, because he is the
Son of Man. 28*† Do not be amazed at
this, because the hour is coming in
which all who are in the tombs will hear
his voice 29* and will come out, those
who have done good deeds to the resur-
rection of life, but those who have done
wicked deeds to the resurrection of con-
demnation.

30* "I cannot do anything on my own;
I judge as I hear, and my judgment is
just, because I do not seek my own will
but the will of the one who sent me.

Witnesses to Jesus. 31* "If I testify on
my own behalf, my testimony cannot be
verified. 32† But there is another who
testifies on my behalf, and I know that
the testimony he gives on my behalf is
true. 33* You sent emissaries to John,
and he testified to the truth. 34* I do not
accept testimony from a human being,
but I say this so that you may be saved.
35*† He was a burning and shining
lamp, and for a while you were content
to rejoice in his light. 36* But I have tes-
timony greater than John's. The works
that the Father gave me to accomplish,
these works that I perform testify on my
behalf that the Father has sent me.
37* Moreover, the Father who sent me
has testified on my behalf. But you have
never heard his voice nor seen his form,
38* and you do not have his word re-
maining in you, because you do not be-
lieve in the one whom he has sent.
39*† You search the scriptures, because
you think you have eternal life through
them; even they testify on my behalf.
40 But you do not want to come to me
to have life.

Unbelief of Jesus' Hearers. 41† "I do
not accept human praise; 42* moreover,
I know that you do not have the love
of God in you. 43* I came in the name
of my Father, but you do not accept me;
yet if another comes in his own name,
you will accept him. 44* How can you
believe, when you accept praise from
one another and do not seek the praise
that comes from the only God? 45* Do
not think that I will accuse you before
the Father: the one who will accuse you
is Moses, in whom you have placed your
hope. 46* For if you had believed Moses,
you would have believed me, because
he wrote about me. 47 But if you do not
believe his writings, how will you be-
lieve my words?"

CHAPTER 6

Multiplication of the Loaves.†

1*† After this, Jesus went across the Sea

*

20: 3, 35.
21: 11, 25; Dt 32, 39; 1 Sm 2, 6; 2 Kgs 5, 7; Tb 13, 2; Wis 16, 13; Is 26, 19; Dn 7, 10.13; 12, 2; Rom 4, 17; 2 Cor 1, 9.
22: Acts 10, 42; 17, 31.
24: 3, 18; 8, 51; 1 Jn 3, 14.
25: 5, 28; 8, 51; 11, 25-26; Eph 2, 1; 5, 14; Rv 3, 1.
26: 1, 4; 1 Jn 5, 11.
27: 5, 22; Dn 7, 13.22; Mt 25, 31; Lk 21, 36.
28: 11, 43.
29: Dn 12, 2; Mt 16, 27; 25, 46; Acts 24, 15; 2 Cor 5, 10.
30: 6, 38.
31-32: 8, 13-14.18.
33: 1, 19-27; Mt 11, 10-11.
34: 1 Jn 5, 9.
35: 1, 8; Ps 132, 17; Sir 48, 1.
36: 10, 25.
37: 8, 18; Dt 4, 12.15; 1 Jn 5, 9.
38: 1 Jn 2, 14.
39: 12, 16; 19, 28; 20, 9; Lk 24, 27.44; 1 Pt 1, 10.
42: 1 Jn 2, 15.
43: Mt 24, 5.24.
44: 12, 43.
45: Dt 31, 26.
46: 5, 39; Dt 18, 15; Lk 16, 31; 24, 44.
6, 1-13: Mt 14, 13-21; Mk 6, 32-44; Lk 9, 10-17.

†

5, 21: *Gives life:* in the Old Testament, a divine prerogative (Dt 32, 39; 1 Sm 2, 6; 2 Kgs 5, 7; Tob 13, 2; Is 26, 19; Dan 12, 2).

5, 22: *Judgment:* another divine prerogative, often expressed as acquittal or condemnation (Dt 32, 36; Ps 43, 1).

5, 28-29: While vv 19-27 present realized eschatology, vv 28-29 are future eschatology; cf Dn 12, 2.

5, 32: *Another:* likely the Father, who in four different ways gives testimony to Jesus, as indicated in the verse groupings 33-34, 36, 37-38, 39-40.

5, 35: *Lamp:* cf Ps 132, 17: "I will place a lamp for my Anointed (= David)," and possibly the description of Elijah in Sir 48, 1. But only *for a while,* indicating the temporary and subordinate nature of John's mission.

5, 39: *You search:* this may be an imperative: "Search the scriptures, because you think that you have eternal life through them."

5, 41: *Praise:* the same Greek word means "praise" or "honor" (from others) and "glory" (from God). There is a play on this in v 44.

6, 1-15: This story of the multiplication of the loaves is the fourth sign (cf the note on 5, 1-47). It is the only miracle story found in all four gospels (occurring twice in Mk and Mt). See the notes on Mt 14, 13-21 and 15, 32-39. John differs on the roles of Philip and Andrew, the proximity of Passover (4), and the allusion to Elisha (see 9). The story here symbolizes the food that is really available through Jesus. It connotes a new exodus and has eucharistic overtones.

6, 1: *[Of Tiberias]:* the awkward apposition represents a later name of the Sea of Galilee. It was probably originally a marginal gloss.

of Galilee [of Tiberias]. 2 A large crowd
followed him, because they saw the
signs he was performing on the sick.
3 Jesus went up on the mountain, and
there he sat down with his disciples.
4* The Jewish feast of Passover was
near. 5*† When Jesus raised his eyes
and saw that a large crowd was coming
to him, he said to Philip, "Where can
we buy enough food for them to eat?"
6† He said this to test him, because he
himself knew what he was going to do.
7*† Philip answered him, "Two hundred
days' wages worth of food would not be
enough for each of them to have a little
[bit]." 8 One of his disciples, Andrew,
the brother of Simon Peter, said to him,
9*† "There is a boy here who has five
barley loaves and two fish; but what
good are these for so many?" 10*† Jesus
said, "Have the people recline." Now
there was a great deal of grass in that
place. So the men reclined, about five
thousand in number. 11* Then Jesus
took the loaves, gave thanks, and distrib-
uted them to those who were reclining,
and also as much of the fish as they
wanted. 12 When they had had their fill,
he said to his disciples, "Gather the
fragments left over, so that nothing will
be wasted." 13† So they collected them,
and filled twelve wicker baskets with
fragments from the five barley loaves
that had been more than they could eat.
14*† When the people saw the sign he
had done, they said, "This is truly the
Prophet, the one who is to come into the
world." 15* Since Jesus knew that they
were going to come and carry him off
to make him king, he withdrew again
to the mountain alone.

***Walking on the Water.*†** 16* When it
was evening, his disciples went down
to the sea, 17 embarked in a boat, and
went across the sea to Capernaum. It
had already grown dark, and Jesus had
not yet come to them. 18 The sea was
stirred up because a strong wind was
blowing. 19*† When they had rowed
about three or four miles, they saw Je-
sus walking on the sea and coming near
the boat, and they began to be afraid.
20† But he said to them, "It is I. Do not
be afraid." 21 They wanted to take him
into the boat, but the boat immediately
arrived at the shore to which they were
heading.

***The Bread of Life Discourse.*†** 22 The
next day, the crowd that remained
across the sea saw that there had been
only one boat there, and that Jesus had
not gone along with his disciples in the
boat, but only his disciples had left.
23† Other boats came from Tiberias near
the place where they had eaten the
bread when the Lord gave thanks.
24 When the crowd saw that neither Je-
sus nor his disciples were there, they
themselves got into boats and came to
Capernaum looking for Jesus. 25 And
when they found him across the sea
they said to him, "Rabbi, when did you
get here?" 26 Jesus answered them and
said, "Amen, amen, I say to you, you
are looking for me not because you saw
signs but because you ate the loaves and
were filled. 27*† Do not work for food
that perishes but for the food that en-
dures for eternal life, which the Son of
Man will give you. For on him the Fa-
ther, God, has set his seal." 28 So they
said to him, "What can we do to accom-
plish the works of God?" 29 Jesus an-
swered and said to them, "This is the
work of God, that you believe in the one
he sent." 30* So they said to him, "What
sign can you do, that we may see and
believe in you? What can you do?
31*† Our ancestors ate manna in the des-
ert, as it is written:

> 'He gave them bread from heaven
> to eat.' "

---

*

4: 2, 13; 11, 55.
5: Nm 11, 13.
7: Mt 20, 2.
9: 2 Kgs 4, 42-44.
10: Mt 14, 21; Mk 6, 44.
11: 21, 13.
14: Dt 18, 15.18; Mal 3, 1.23; Acts 3, 22.
15: 18, 36.
16-21: Mt 14, 22-27; Mk 6, 45-52.
19: Jb 9, 8; Pss 29, 3-4; 77, 20; Is 43, 16.
27: 6, 50.51.54.58.
30: Mt 16, 1-4; Lk 11, 29-30.
31: Ex 16, 4-5; Nm 11, 7-9; Ps 78, 24.

---

†

6, 5: Jesus takes the initiative (in the synoptics, the disciples do), possibly pictured as (cf 14) the new Moses (cf Nm 11, 13).

6, 6: Probably the evangelist's comment; in this gospel Jesus is never portrayed as ignorant of anything.

6, 7: *Days' wages:* literally, "denarii"; a Roman denarius is a day's wage in Mt 20, 2.

6, 9: *Barley loaves:* the food of the poor. There seems an allusion to the story of Elisha multiplying the barley bread in 2 Kgs 4, 42-44.

6, 10: *Grass:* implies springtime, and therefore Passover. *Five thousand:* so Mk 6, 39.44 and parallels.

6, 13: *Baskets:* the word describes the typically Palestinian wicker basket, as in Mk 6, 43 and parallels.

6, 14: *The Prophet:* probably the prophet like Moses (see the note on 1, 21). *The one who is to come into the world:* probably Elijah; cf Mal 3, 1.23.

6, 16-21: The fifth sign is a nature miracle, portraying Jesus sharing Yahweh's power. Cf the parallel stories following the multiplication of the loaves in Mk 6, 45-52 and Mt 14, 22-33.

6, 19: *Walking on the sea:* although the Greek (cf 16) could mean "on the seashore" or "by the sea" (cf 21, 1), the parallels, especially Mt 14, 25, make clear that Jesus walked upon the water. John may allude to Job 9, 8: God "treads upon the crests of the sea."

6, 20: *It is I:* literally, "I am." See also the notes on 4, 26 and Mk 6, 50.

6, 22-71: Discourse on the bread of life; replacement of the manna. Verses 22-34 serve as an introduction, vv 35-59 constitute the discourse proper, vv 60-71 portray the reaction of the disciples and Peter's confession.

6, 23: Possibly a later interpolation, to explain how the crowd got to Capernaum.

6, 27: *The food that endures for eternal life:* cf 4, 14, on water "springing up to eternal life."

6, 31: *Bread from heaven:* cf Ex 16, 4.15.32-34 and the notes there; Ps 78, 24. The manna, thought to have been hidden by Jeremiah (2 Mc 2, 5-8), was expected to reappear miraculously at Passover, in the last days.

32* So Jesus said to them, "Amen, amen,
I say to you, it was not Moses who gave
the bread from heaven; my Father
gives you the true bread from heaven.
33 For the bread of God is that which
comes down from heaven and gives life
to the world."

34* So they said to him, "Sir, give us
this bread always." 35*† Jesus said to
them, "I am the bread of life; whoever
comes to me will never hunger, and
whoever believes in me will never thirst.
36* But I told you that although you
have seen [me], you do not believe.
37 Everything that the Father gives me
will come to me, and I will not reject
anyone who comes to me, 38* because I
came down from heaven not to do my
own will but the will of the one who sent
me. 39* And this is the will of the one
who sent me, that I should not lose any-
thing of what he gave me, but that I
should raise it [on] the last day. 40* For
this is the will of my Father, that every-
one who sees the Son and believes in
him may have eternal life, and I shall
raise him [on] the last day."

41 The Jews murmured about him be-
cause he said, "I am the bread that
came down from heaven," 42* and they
said, "Is this not Jesus, the son of Jo-
seph? Do we not know his father and
mother? Then how can he say, 'I have
come down from heaven'?" 43*† Jesus
answered and said to them, "Stop mur-
muring among yourselves. 44 No one
can come to me unless the Father who
sent me draw him, and I will raise him
on the last day. 45* It is written in the
prophets:

'They shall all be taught by God.'

Everyone who listens to my Father and
learns from him comes to me. 46* Not
that anyone has seen the Father except
the one who is from God; he has seen
the Father. 47 Amen, amen, I say to you,
whoever believes has eternal life.
48 I am the bread of life. 49* Your ances-
tors ate the manna in the desert, but
they died; 50 this is the bread that comes
down from heaven so that one may eat
it and not die. 51* I am the living bread
that came down from heaven; whoever
eats this bread will live forever; and the
bread that I will give is my flesh for the
life of the world."

52 The Jews quarreled among them-
selves, saying, "How can this man give
us [his] flesh to eat?" 53 Jesus said to
them, "Amen, amen, I say to you, unless
you eat the flesh of the Son of Man and
drink his blood, you do not have life
within you. 54† Whoever eats my flesh
and drinks my blood has eternal life,
and I will raise him on the last day.
55 For my flesh is true food, and my
blood is true drink. 56 Whoever eats my
flesh and drinks my blood remains in
me and I in him. 57* Just as the living
Father sent me and I have life because
of the Father, so also the one who feeds
on me will have life because of me.
58 This is the bread that came down from
heaven. Unlike your ancestors who ate
and still died, whoever eats this bread
will live forever." 59 These things he
said while teaching in the synagogue in
Capernaum.

The Words of Eternal Life. † 60 Then
many of his disciples who were listening
said, "This saying is hard; who can ac-
cept it?" 61 Since Jesus knew that his
disciples were murmuring about this, he
said to them, "Does this shock you?
62† What if you were to see the Son of
Man ascending to where he was before?
63† It is the spirit that gives life, while
the flesh is of no avail. The words I have
spoken to you are spirit and life. 64* But
there are some of you who do not be-
lieve." Jesus knew from the beginning
the ones who would not believe and the
one who would betray him. 65 And he
said, "For this reason I have told you
that no one can come to me unless it is
granted him by my Father."

66 As a result of this, many [of] his dis-
ciples returned to their former way of
life and no longer accompanied him.
67 Jesus then said to the Twelve, "Do
you also want to leave?" 68 Simon Peter
answered him, "Master, to whom shall
we go? You have the words of eternal
life. 69* We have come to believe and are

*

32: Mt 6, 11.
34: 4, 15.
35: Is 55, 1-3; Am 8, 11-13.
36: 20, 29.
38: 4, 34; Mt 26, 39; Heb 10, 9.
39: 10, 28-29; 17, 12; 18, 9.
40: 1 Jn 2, 25.
42: Mt 13, 54-57; Mk 6, 1-4; Lk 4, 22.
43: Ex 16, 2.7.8; Lk 4, 22.
45: Is 54, 13; Jer 31, 33-34.
46: 1, 18; 7, 29; Ex 33, 20.
49: 1 Cor 10, 3.5.
51: Mt 26, 26-27; Lk 22, 19.
57: 5, 26.
64: 13, 11.
69: 11, 27; Mt 16, 16; Mk 1, 24; Lk 4, 34.

†

6, 35-59: Up to v 50, "bread of life" is a figure for God's revelation in Jesus; in vv 51-58, the eucharistic theme comes to the fore. There may thus be a break between vv 50 and 51.

6, 43: *Murmuring:* the word may reflect the Greek of Ex 16, 2.7.8.

6, 54-58: *Eats:* the verb used in these verses is not the classical Greek verb used of human eating, but that of animal eating: "munch," "gnaw." This may be part of John's emphasis on the reality of the flesh and blood of Jesus (cf 55), but the same verb eventually became the ordinary verb in Greek meaning "eat."

6, 60-71: These verses refer more to themes of vv 35-50 than to those of 51-58 and seem to be addressed to members of the Johannine community who found it difficult to accept the high christology reflected in the bread of life discourse.

6, 62: This unfinished conditional sentence is obscure. Probably there is a reference to vv 49-51. Jesus claims to be *the bread that comes down from heaven* (50); this claim provokes incredulity (60); and so Jesus is pictured as asking what his disciples will say when he goes up to heaven.

6, 63: *Spirit . . . flesh:* probably not a reference to the eucharistic body of Jesus but to the supernatural and the natural, as in 3, 6. *Spirit and life:* all Jesus said about the bread of life is the revelation of the Spirit.

convinced that you are the Holy One
of God." 70 Jesus answered them, "Did
I not choose you twelve? Yet is not one
of you a devil?" 71* He was referring to
Judas, son of Simon the Iscariot; it was
he who would betray him, one of the
Twelve.

CHAPTER 7

The Feast of Tabernacles. † 1* After
this, Jesus moved about within Galilee;
but he did not wish to travel in Judea,
because the Jews were trying to kill
him. 2* But the Jewish feast of Taberna-
cles was near. 3† So his brothers said
to him, "Leave here and go to Judea,
so that your disciples also may see the
works you are doing. 4* No one works
in secret if he wants to be known pub-
licly. If you do these things, manifest
yourself to the world." 5 For his broth-
ers did not believe in him. 6† So Jesus
said to them, "My time is not yet here,
but the time is always right for you.
7* The world cannot hate you, but it
hates me, because I testify to it that its
works are evil. 8† You go up to the feast.
I am not going up to this feast, because
my time has not yet been fulfilled."
9 After he had said this, he stayed on
in Galilee.
10 But when his brothers had gone up
to the feast, he himself also went up,
not openly but [as it were] in secret.
11 The Jews were looking for him at the
feast and saying, "Where is he?"
12 And there was considerable murmur-
ing about him in the crowds. Some said,
"He is a good man," [while] others said,
"No; on the contrary, he misleads the
crowd." 13* Still, no one spoke openly
about him because they were afraid of
the Jews.

The First Dialogue. † 14 When the
feast was already half over, Jesus went
up into the temple area and began to
teach. 15*† The Jews were amazed and
said, "How does he know scripture
without having studied?" 16 Jesus an-
swered them and said, "My teaching is
not my own but is from the one who sent
me. 17*† Whoever chooses to do his will
shall know whether my teaching is from
God or whether I speak on my own.
18 Whoever speaks on his own seeks his
own glory, but whoever seeks the glory
of the one who sent him is truthful, and
there is no wrong in him. 19* Did not Mo-
ses give you the law? Yet none of you
keeps the law. Why are you trying to
kill me?" 20*† The crowd answered,
"You are possessed! Who is trying to kill
you?" 21*† Jesus answered and said to
them, "I performed one work and all
of you are amazed 22* because of it. Mo-
ses gave you circumcision—not that it
came from Moses but rather from the
patriarchs—and you circumcise a man
on the sabbath. 23* If a man can receive
circumcision on a sabbath so that the
law of Moses may not be broken, are
you angry with me because I made a
whole person well on a sabbath? 24* Stop
judging by appearances, but judge
justly."
25 So some of the inhabitants of Jeru-
salem said, "Is he not the one they are
trying to kill? 26† And look, he is speak-
ing openly and they say nothing to him.
Could the authorities have realized that
he is the Messiah? 27* But we know
where he is from. When the Messiah
comes, no one will know where he is
from." 28* So Jesus cried out in the tem-
ple area as he was teaching and said,
"You know me and also know where I
am from. Yet I did not come on my own,

*

71: 12, 4; 13, 2.27.
7, 1: 5, 18; 8, 37.40.
2: Ex 23, 16; Lv 23, 34; Nm 29, 12; Dt 16, 13-16; Zec 14, 16-19.
4: 14, 22.
7: 15, 18.
13: 9, 22; 19, 38; 20, 19.
15: Lk 2, 47.
17: 6, 29.
19: Acts 7, 53.
20: 8, 48-49; 10, 20.
21: 5, 1-9.
22: Gn 17, 10; Lv 12, 3.
23: 5, 2-9.16; Mt 12, 11-12; Lk 14, 5.
24: 8, 15; Lv 19, 15; Is 11, 3-4.
27: Heb 7, 3.
28: 8, 19.

†

7—8: These chapters contain events about the feast of Tabernacles (Sukkoth, Ingathering: Ex 23, 16; Tents, Booths: Dt 16, 13-16), with its symbols of booths (originally built to shelter harvesters), rain (water from Siloam poured on the temple altar), and lights (illumination of the four torches in the Court of the Women). They continue the theme of the replacement of feasts (Passover, 2, 13; 6, 4; Hanukkah, 10, 22; Pentecost, 5, 1), here accomplished by Jesus as the Living Water. These chapters comprise seven miscellaneous controversies and dialogues. There is a literary inclusion with Jesus in hiding in 7, 4.10 and 8, 59. There are frequent references to attempts on his life: 7, 1.13.19.25.30.32.44; 8, 37.40.59.

7, 3: *Brothers:* these relatives (cf 2, 12 and see the note on Mk 6, 3) are never portrayed as disciples until after the resurrection (Acts 1, 14). Mt 13, 55 and Mk 6, 3 give the names of four of them. Jesus has already performed works/signs in Judea; cf 2, 23; 3, 2; 4, 45; 5, 8.

7, 6: *Time:* the Greek word means "opportune time," here a synonym for Jesus' "hour" (see the note on 2, 4), his death and resurrection. In the wordplay, any time is suitable for Jesus' brothers, because they are not dependent on God's will.

7, 8: *I am not going up:* an early attested reading "not yet" seems a correction, since Jesus in the story does go up to the feast. "Go up," in a play on words, refers not only to going up to Jerusalem but also to exaltation at the cross, resurrection, and ascension; cf 3, 14; 6, 62; 20, 17.

7, 14-31: Jesus teaches in the temple; debate with the Jews.

7, 15: *Without having studied:* literally, "How does he know letters without having learned?" Children were taught to read and write by means of the scriptures. But here more than Jesus' literacy is being discussed; the people are wondering how he can teach like a rabbi. Rabbis were trained by other rabbis and traditionally quoted their teachers.

7, 17: *To do his will:* presumably a reference back to the "work" of 6, 29: belief in the one whom God has sent.

7, 20: *You are possessed:* literally, "You have a demon." The insane were thought to be possessed by a demoniacal spirit.

7, 21: *One work:* the cure of the paralytic (5, 1-9) because of the reference to the sabbath (22; 5, 9-10).

7, 26: *The authorities:* the members of the Sanhedrin (same term as 3, 1).

but the one who sent me, whom you do
not know, is true. 29* I know him, be-
cause I am from him, and he sent me."
30* So they tried to arrest him, but no
one laid a hand upon him, because his
hour had not yet come. 31* But many of
the crowd began to believe in him, and
said, "When the Messiah comes, will he
perform more signs than this man has
done?"

Officers Sent to Arrest Jesus. † 32 The
Pharisees heard the crowd murmuring
about him to this effect, and the chief
priests and the Pharisees sent guards
to arrest him. 33* So Jesus said, "I will
be with you only a little while longer,
and then I will go to the one who sent
me. 34* You will look for me but not find
[me], and where I am you cannot
come." 35† So the Jews said to one an-
other, "Where is he going that we will
not find him? Surely he is not going to
the dispersion among the Greeks to
teach the Greeks, is he? 36 What is the
meaning of his saying, 'You will look
for me and not find [me], and where I
am you cannot come'?"

Rivers of Living Water. † 37* On the
last and greatest day of the feast, Jesus
stood up and exclaimed, "Let anyone
who thirsts come to me and drink.
38*† Whoever believes in me, as scrip-
ture says:

> 'Rivers of living water will flow from
> within him.' "

39*† He said this in reference to the
Spirit that those who came to believe
in him were to receive. There was, of
course, no Spirit yet, because Jesus had
not yet been glorified.

***Discussion about the Origins of the
Messiah.*** † 40* Some in the crowd who
heard these words said, "This is truly
the Prophet." 41 Others said, "This is the
Messiah." But others said, "The Mes-
siah will not come from Galilee, will he?
42* Does not scripture say that the Mes-
siah will be of David's family and come
from Bethlehem, the village where Da-
vid lived?" 43 So a division occurred in
the crowd because of him. 44 Some of
them even wanted to arrest him, but no
one laid hands on him.

45 So the guards went to the chief
priests and Pharisees, who asked them,
"Why did you not bring him?" 46 The
guards answered, "Never before has
anyone spoken like this one." 47 So the
Pharisees answered them, "Have you
also been deceived? 48* Have any of the
authorities or the Pharisees believed
in him? 49 But this crowd, which does
not know the law, is accursed."
50* Nicodemus, one of their members
who had come to him earlier, said to
them, 51* "Does our law condemn a per-
son before it first hears him and finds
out what he is doing?" 52 They answered
and said to him, "You are not from Gali-
lee also, are you? Look and see that no
prophet arises from Galilee."

A Woman Caught in Adultery. †
[53 Then each went to his own house,

CHAPTER 8

1*† while Jesus went to the Mount of
Olives. 2 But early in the morning he ar-
rived again in the temple area, and all
the people started coming to him, and
he sat down and taught them. 3 Then the
scribes and the Pharisees brought a
woman who had been caught in adul-
tery and made her stand in the middle.
4 They said to him, "Teacher, this
woman was caught in the very act of
committing adultery. 5*† Now in the
law, Moses commanded us to stone such
women. So what do you say?" 6† They
said this to test him, so that they could

JOHN

*

29: 6, 46; 8, 55.
30: 7, 44; 8, 20; Lk 4, 29-30.
31: 2, 11; 10, 42; 11, 45.
33: 13, 33; 16, 16.
34: 8, 21; 12, 36; 13, 33.36; 16, 5; Dt 4, 29; Prv 1, 28; Is 55, 6; Hos 5, 6.
37: Rv 21, 6.
38: 4, 10.14; 19, 34; Is 12, 3; Ez 47, 1.
39: 16, 7.
40: Dt 18, 15.18.
42: 2 Sm 7, 12-14; Pss 89, 3-4; 132, 11; Mi 5, 1; Mt 2, 5-6.
48: 12, 42.
50: 3, 1; 19, 39.
51: Dt 1, 16-17.
8, 1-2: Lk 21, 37-38.
5: Lv 20, 10; Dt 22, 22-29.

†

7, 32-36: Jesus announces his approaching departure (cf also 8, 21; 12, 36; 13, 33) and complete control over his destiny.

7, 35: *Dispersion:* or "diaspora": Jews living outside Palestine. *Greeks:* probably refers to the Gentiles in the Mediterranean area; cf 12, 20.

7, 37-39: Promise of living water through the Spirit.

7, 38: *Living water:* not an exact quotation from any Old Testament passage; in the gospel context the gift of the Spirit is meant; cf 3, 5. *From within him:* either Jesus or the believer; if Jesus, it continues the Jesus-Moses motif (water from the rock, Ex 17, 6; Nm 20, 11) as well as Jesus as the new temple (cf Ez 47, 1). Grammatically, it goes better with the believer.

7, 39: *No Spirit yet:* Codex Vaticanus and early Latin, Syriac, and Coptic versions add "given." In this gospel, the sending of the Spirit cannot take place until Jesus' glorification through his death, resurrection, and ascension; cf 20, 22.

7, 40-53: Discussion of the Davidic lineage of the Messiah.

7, 53—8, 11: The story of the woman caught in adultery is a later insertion here, missing from all early Greek manuscripts. A Western text-type insertion, attested mainly in Old Latin translations, it is found in different places in different manuscripts: here, or after 7, 36, or at the end of this gospel, or after Lk 21, 38, or at the end of that gospel. There are many non-Johannine features in the language, and there are also many doubtful readings within the passage. The style and motifs are similar to those of Luke, and it fits better with the general situation at the end of Lk 21, but it was probably inserted here because of the allusion to Jer 17, 13 (cf the note on 8, 6) and the statement, "I do not judge anyone," in 8, 15. The Catholic Church accepts this passage as canonical scripture.

8, 1: *Mount of Olives:* not mentioned elsewhere in the gospel tradition outside of passion week.

8, 5: Lv 20, 10 and Dt 22, 22 mention only death, but Dt 22, 23-24 prescribes stoning for a betrothed virgin.

8, 6: Cf Jer 17, 13 (RSV): "Those who turn away from thee shall be written in the earth, for they have forsaken the LORD, the fountain of living water"; cf 7, 38.

have some charge to bring against him.
Jesus bent down and began to write on
the ground with his finger. 7*† But when
they continued asking him, he straight-
ened up and said to them, "Let the one
among you who is without sin be the first
to throw a stone at her." 8 Again he bent
down and wrote on the ground. 9 And
in response, they went away one by one,
beginning with the elders. So he was left
alone with the woman before him.
10* Then Jesus straightened up and said
to her, "Woman, where are they? Has
no one condemned you?" 11* She re-
plied, "No one, sir." Then Jesus said,
"Neither do I condemn you. Go, [and]
from now on do not sin any more."]

The Light of the World. † 12* Jesus
spoke to them again, saying, "I am the
light of the world. Whoever follows me
will not walk in darkness, but will have
the light of life." 13 So the Pharisees said
to him, "You testify on your own behalf,
so your testimony cannot be verified."
14*† Jesus answered and said to them,
"Even if I do testify on my own be-
half, my testimony can be verified, be-
cause I know where I came from and
where I am going. But you do not know
where I come from or where I am going.
15*† You judge by appearances, but I do
not judge anyone. 16* And even if I
should judge, my judgment is valid, be-
cause I am not alone, but it is I and the
Father who sent me. 17*† Even in your
law it is written that the testimony of
two men can be verified. 18* I testify on
my behalf and so does the Father who
sent me." 19* So they said to him,
"Where is your father?" Jesus an-
swered, "You know neither me nor my
Father. If you knew me, you would
know my Father also." 20* He spoke
these words while teaching in the trea-
sury in the temple area. But no one ar-
rested him, because his hour had not
yet come.

Jesus, the Father's Ambassador. †
21*† He said to them again, "I am going
away and you will look for me, but you
will die in your sin. Where I am going
you cannot come." 22† So the Jews said,
"He is not going to kill himself, is he,
because he said, 'Where I am going you
cannot come'?" 23* He said to them,
"You belong to what is below, I belong
to what is above. You belong to this
world, but I do not belong to this world.
24*† That is why I told you that you will
die in your sins. For if you do not believe
that I AM, you will die in your sins."
25*† So they said to him, "Who are you?"
Jesus said to them, "What I told you
from the beginning. 26* I have much to
say about you in condemnation. But the
one who sent me is true, and what I
heard from him I tell the world."
27 They did not realize that he was
speaking to them of the Father. 28* So
Jesus said [to them], "When you lift up
the Son of Man, then you will realize
that I AM, and that I do nothing on my
own, but I say only what the Father
taught me. 29 The one who sent me is
with me. He has not left me alone, be-
cause I always do what is pleasing to
him." 30 Because he spoke this way,
many came to believe in him.

Jesus and Abraham. † 31† Jesus then
said to those Jews who believed in him,
"If you remain in my word, you will
truly be my disciples, 32* and you will
know the truth, and the truth will set
you free." 33*† They answered him, "We
are descendants of Abraham and have
never been enslaved to anyone. How
can you say, 'You will become free'?"

---

*

7: Dt 17, 7.
10: Ez 33, 11.
11: 5, 14.
12: 1, 4-5.9; 12, 46; Ex 13, 22; Is 42, 6; Zec 14, 8.
14: 5, 31.
15: 12, 47; 1 Sm 16, 7.
16: 5, 30.
17: Dt 17, 6; 19, 15; Nm 35, 30.
18: 5, 23.37.
19: 7, 28; 14, 7; 15, 21.
20: 7, 30.
21: 7, 34; 13, 33.
23: 3, 31; 17, 14; 18, 36.
24: Ex 3, 14; Dt 32, 39; Is 43, 10.
25: 10, 24.
26: 12, 44-50.
28: 3, 14; 12, 32.34.
32: Is 42, 7; Gal 4, 31.
33: Mt 3, 9.

---

†

8, 7: The first stones were to be thrown by the witnesses (Dt 17, 7).

8, 12-20: Jesus the light of the world. Jesus replaces the four torches of the illumination of the temple as the light of joy.

8, 14: *My testimony can be verified:* this seems to contradict 5, 31, but the emphasis here is on Jesus' origin from the Father and his divine destiny. *Where I am going:* indicates Jesus' passion and glorification.

8, 15: *By appearances:* literally, "according to the flesh." *I do not judge anyone:* superficial contradiction of 5, 22.27.30; here the emphasis is that the judgment is not by material standards.

8, 17: *Your law:* a reflection of later controversy between church and synagogue.

8, 21-30: He whose ambassador I am is with me. Jesus' origin is from God; he can reveal God.

8, 21: *You will die in your sin:* i.e., of disbelief; cf v 24. *Where I am going you cannot come:* except through faith in Jesus' passion-resurrection.

8, 22: The Jews suspect that he is referring to his death. Johannine irony is apparent here; Jesus' death will not be self-inflicted but destined by God.

8, 24.28: *I AM:* an expression that late Jewish tradition understood as Yahweh's own self-designation (Is 43, 10); see the note on 4, 26. Jesus is here placed on a par with Yahweh.

8, 25: *What I told you from the beginning:* this verse seems textually corrupt, with several other possible translations: "(I am) what I say to you"; "Why do I speak to you at all?" The earliest attested reading (Bodmer Papyrus P^{66}) has (in a second hand), "I told you at the beginning what I am also telling you (now)." The answer here (cf Prv 8, 22) seems to hinge on a misunderstanding of v 24 "*that* I AM" as "*what* I am."

8, 31-59: Jesus' origin ("before Abraham") and destiny are developed; the truth will free them from sin (34) and death (51).

8, 31: *Those Jews who believed in him:* a rough editorial suture, since in v 37 they are described as trying to kill Jesus.

8, 33: *Have never been enslaved to anyone:* since, historically, the Jews were enslaved almost continuously, this verse is probably Johannine irony, about slavery to sin.

34* Jesus answered them, "Amen,
amen, I say to you, everyone who com-
mits sin is a slave of sin. 35*† A slave
does not remain in a household forever,
but a son always remains. 36 So if a son
frees you, then you will truly be free.
37 I know that you are descendants of
Abraham. But you are trying to kill me,
because my word has no room among
you. 38† I tell you what I have seen in
the Father's presence; then do what you
have heard from the Father."
39*† They answered and said to him,
"Our father is Abraham." Jesus said to
them, "If you were Abraham's children,
you would be doing the works of Abra-
ham. 40 But now you are trying to kill
me, a man who has told you the truth
that I heard from God; Abraham did not
do this. 41* You are doing the works of
your father!" [So] they said to him, "We
are not illegitimate. We have one Fa-
ther, God." 42* Jesus said to them, "If
God were your Father, you would love
me, for I came from God and am here;
I did not come on my own, but he sent
me. 43 Why do you not understand what
I am saying? Because you cannot bear
to hear my word. 44* You belong to your
father the devil and you willingly carry
out your father's desires. He was a mur-
derer from the beginning and does not
stand in truth, because there is no truth
in him. When he tells a lie, he speaks
in character, because he is a liar and
the father of lies. 45 But because I speak
the truth, you do not believe me. 46* Can
any of you charge me with sin? If I am
telling the truth, why do you not believe
me? 47* Whoever belongs to God hears
the words of God; for this reason you
do not listen, because you do not belong
to God."
48† The Jews answered and said to
him, "Are we not right in saying that
you are a Samaritan and are pos-
sessed?" 49 Jesus answered, "I am not
possessed; I honor my Father, but you
dishonor me. 50* I do not seek my own
glory; there is one who seeks it and he
is the one who judges. 51* Amen, amen,
I say to you, whoever keeps my word
will never see death." 52 [So] the Jews
said to him, "Now we are sure that you
are possessed. Abraham died, as did the
prophets, yet you say, 'Whoever keeps
my word will never taste death.'
53*† Are you greater than our father
Abraham, who died? Or the prophets,
who died? Who do you make yourself
out to be?" 54 Jesus answered, "If I glo-
rify myself, my glory is worth nothing;
but it is my Father who glorifies me, of
whom you say, 'He is our God.' 55* You
do not know him, but I know him. And
if I should say that I do not know him,
I would be like you a liar. But I do know
him and I keep his word. 56*† Abraham
your father rejoiced to see my day; he
saw it and was glad." 57† So the Jews
said to him, "You are not yet fifty years
old and you have seen Abraham?"
58*† Jesus said to them, "Amen, amen,
I say to you, before Abraham came to
be, I AM." 59* So they picked up stones
to throw at him; but Jesus hid and went
out of the temple area.

CHAPTER 9

The Man Born Blind.† 1* As he
passed by he saw a man blind from
birth. 2*† His disciples asked him,
"Rabbi, who sinned, this man or his
parents, that he was born blind?"
3* Jesus answered, "Neither he nor his
parents sinned; it is so that the works
of God might be made visible through
him. 4* We have to do the works of the
one who sent me while it is day. Night
is coming when no one can work.
5* While I am in the world, I am the light

JOHN

*

34: Rom 6, 16-17.
35: Gn 21, 10; Gal 4, 30; Heb 3, 5-6.
39: Gn 26, 5; Rom 4, 11-17; Jas 2, 21-23.
41: Mal 2, 10.
42: 1 Jn 5, 1.
44: Gn 3, 4; Wis 1, 13; 2, 24; Acts 13, 10; 1 Jn 3, 8-15.
46: Heb 4, 15; 1 Pt 2, 22; 1 Jn 3, 5.
47: 10, 26; 1 Jn 4, 6.
50: 7, 18.
51: 5, 24-29; 6, 40.47; 11, 25-26.
53: 4, 12.
55: 7, 28-29.
56: Gn 17, 17; Mt 13, 17; Lk 17, 22.
58: 1, 30; 17, 5.
59: 10, 31.39; 11, 8; Lk 4, 29-30.
9, 1-2: Is 42, 7.
2: Ex 20, 5; Ez 18, 20; Lk 13, 2.
3: 5, 14; 11, 4.
4: 11, 9-10; 12, 35-36.
5: 8, 12.

†

8, 35: *A slave . . . a son:* an allusion to Ishmael and Isaac (Gn 16 and 21), or to the release of a slave after six years (Ex 21, 2; Dt 15, 12).

8, 38: *The Father:* i.e., God. It is also possible, however, to understand the second part of the verse as a sarcastic reference to descent of the Jews from the devil (44), "You do what you have heard from [your] father."

8, 39: *The works of Abraham:* Abraham believed; cf Rom 4, 11-17; Jas 2, 21-23.

8, 48: *Samaritan:* therefore interested in magical powers; cf Acts 7, 14-24.

8, 53: *Are you greater than our father Abraham?:* cf 4, 12.

8, 56: *He saw it:* this seems a reference to the birth of Isaac (Gn 17, 7; 21, 6), the beginning of the fulfillment of promises about Abraham's seed.

8, 57: The evidence of the third-century Bodmer Papyrus P^{75} and the first hand of Codex Sinaiticus indicates that the text originally read: "How can Abraham have seen you?"

8, 58: *Came to be, I AM:* the Greek word used for "came to be" is the one used of all creation in the prologue, while the word used for "am" is the one reserved for the Logos.

9, 1—10, 21: Sabbath healing of the man born blind. This fifth sign is introduced to illustrate the saying, "I am the light of the world" (8, 12; 9, 5). The narrative of conflict about Jesus contrasts Jesus (light) with the Jews (blindness, 39-41). The theme of water is reintroduced in the reference to the pool of Siloam. Ironically, Jesus is being judged by the Jews, yet the Jews are judged by the Light of the world; cf 3, 19-21.

9, 2: See the note on 5, 14, and Ex 20, 5, that parents' sins were visited upon their children. Jesus denies such a cause and emphasizes the purpose: the infirmity was providential.

of the world." 6* When he had said this, he spat on the ground and made clay with the saliva, and smeared the clay on his eyes, 7*† and said to him, "Go wash in the Pool of Siloam" (which means Sent). So he went and washed, and came back able to see.

8 His neighbors and those who had seen him earlier as a beggar said, "Isn't this the one who used to sit and beg?" 9 Some said, "It is," but others said, "No, he just looks like him." He said, "I am." 10 So they said to him, "[So] how were your eyes opened?" 11 He replied, "The man called Jesus made clay and anointed my eyes and told me, 'Go to Siloam and wash.' So I went there and washed and was able to see." 12 And they said to him, "Where is he?" He said, "I don't know."

13 They brought the one who was once blind to the Pharisees. 14*† Now Jesus had made clay and opened his eyes on a sabbath. 15 So then the Pharisees also asked him how he was able to see. He said to them, "He put clay on my eyes, and I washed, and now I can see." 16* So some of the Pharisees said, "This man is not from God, because he does not keep the sabbath." [But] others said, "How can a sinful man do such signs?" And there was a division among them. 17* So they said to the blind man again, "What do you have to say about him, since he opened your eyes?" He said, "He is a prophet."

18 Now the Jews did not believe that he had been blind and gained his sight until they summoned the parents of the one who had gained his sight. 19 They asked them, "Is this your son, who you say was born blind? How does he now see?" 20 His parents answered and said, "We know that this is our son and that he was born blind. 21 We do not know how he sees now, nor do we know who opened his eyes. Ask him, he is of age; he can speak for himself." 22*† His parents said this because they were afraid of the Jews, for the Jews had already agreed that if anyone acknowledged him as the Messiah, he would be expelled from the synagogue. 23* For this reason his parents said, "He is of age; question him."

24*† So a second time they called the man who had been blind and said to him, "Give God the praise! We know that this man is a sinner." 25 He replied, "If he is a sinner, I do not know. One thing I do know is that I was blind and now I see." 26 So they said to him, "What did he do to you? How did he open your eyes?" 27 He answered them, "I told you already and you did not listen. Why do you want to hear it again? Do you want to become his disciples, too?" 28 They ridiculed him and said, "You are that man's disciple; we are disciples of Moses! 29* We know that God spoke to Moses, but we do not know where this one is from." 30 The man answered and said to them, "This is what is so amazing, that you do not know where he is from, yet he opened my eyes. 31* We know that God does not listen to sinners, but if one is devout and does his will, he listens to him. 32† It is unheard of that anyone ever opened the eyes of a person born blind. 33* If this man were not from God, he would not be able to do anything." 34 They answered and said to him, "You were born totally in sin, and are you trying to teach us?" Then they threw him out.

35 When Jesus heard that they had thrown him out, he found him and said, "Do you believe in the Son of Man?" 36 He answered and said, "Who is he, sir, that I may believe in him?" 37* Jesus said to him, "You have seen him and the one speaking with you is he." 38 He said, "I do believe, Lord," and he worshiped him. 39*† Then Jesus said, "I came into this world for judgment, so that those who do not see might see, and those who do see might become blind."

40* Some of the Pharisees who were with him heard this and said to him, "Surely we are not also blind, are we?" 41* Jesus said to them, "If you were blind, you would have no sin; but now you are saying, 'We see,' so your sin remains.

---

*

6: 5, 11; Mk 7, 33; 8, 23.
7: 2 Kgs 5, 10-14.
14: 5, 9.
16: 3, 2; Mt 12, 10-11; Lk 13, 10-11; 14, 1-4.
17: 4, 19.
22: 7, 13; 12, 42; 16, 2; 19, 38.
23: 12, 42.
24: Jos 7, 19; 1 Sm 6, 5 LXX.
29: Ex 33, 11.
31: 10, 21; Pss 34, 16; 66, 18; Prv 15, 29; Is 1, 15.
33: 3, 2.
37: 4, 26; Dn 7, 13.
39: Mt 13, 33-35.
40: Mt 15, 14; 23, 26; Rom 2, 19.
41: 15, 22.

---

†

9, 7: *Go wash:* perhaps a test of faith; cf 2 Kgs 5, 10-14. The water tunnel Siloam (= Sent) is used as a symbol of Jesus, sent by his Father.

9, 14: In using spittle, kneading clay, and healing, Jesus had broken the sabbath rules laid down by Jewish tradition.

9, 22: This comment of the evangelist (in terms used again in 12, 42 and 16, 2) envisages a situation after Jesus' ministry. Rejection/excommunication from the synagogue of Jews who confessed Jesus as Messiah seems to have begun ca. A.D. 85, when the curse against the *mînîm* or heretics was introduced into the "Eighteen Benedictions."

9, 24: *Give God the praise!:* an Old Testament formula of adjuration to tell the truth; cf Jos 7, 19; 1 Sm 6, 5 LXX. Cf 5, 41.

9, 32: *A person born blind:* the only Old Testament cure from blindness is found in Tobit (cf Tb 7, 7; 11, 7-13; 14, 1-2), but Tobit was not born blind.

9, 39-41: These verses spell out the symbolic meaning of the cure; the Pharisees are not the innocent blind, willing to accept the testimony of others.

CHAPTER 10

The Good Shepherd. † 1*† "Amen,
amen, I say to you, whoever does not
enter a sheepfold through the gate but
climbs over elsewhere is a thief and a
robber. 2 But whoever enters through
the gate is the shepherd of the sheep.
3 The gatekeeper opens it for him, and
the sheep hear his voice, as he calls his
own sheep by name and leads them out.
4*† When he has driven out all his own,
he walks ahead of them, and the sheep
follow him, because they recognize his
voice. 5 But they will not follow a
stranger; they will run away from him,
because they do not recognize the voice
of strangers." 6† Although Jesus used
this figure of speech, they did not realize
what he was trying to tell them.

7† So Jesus said again, "Amen, amen,
I say to you, I am the gate for the sheep.
8† All who came [before me] are thieves
and robbers, but the sheep did not listen
to them. 9 I am the gate. Whoever enters
through me will be saved, and will come
in and go out and find pasture. 10 A thief
comes only to steal and slaughter and
destroy; I came so that they might have
life and have it more abundantly.
11* I am the good shepherd. A good
shepherd lays down his life for the
sheep. 12* A hired man, who is not a
shepherd and whose sheep are not his
own, sees a wolf coming and leaves the
sheep and runs away, and the wolf
catches and scatters them. 13 This is be-
cause he works for pay and has no con-
cern for the sheep. 14 I am the good
shepherd, and I know mine and mine
know me, 15* just as the Father knows
me and I know the Father; and I will
lay down my life for the sheep. 16*† I
have other sheep that do not belong to
this fold. These also I must lead, and
they will hear my voice, and there will
be one flock, one shepherd. 17* This is
why the Father loves me, because I lay
down my life in order to take it up again.
18*† No one takes it from me, but I lay
it down on my own. I have power to lay
it down, and power to take it up again.
This command I have received from my
Father."

19* Again there was a division among
the Jews because of these words.
20* Many of them said, "He is possessed
and out of his mind; why listen to him?"
21* Others said, "These are not the
words of one possessed; surely a demon
cannot open the eyes of the blind, can
he?"

Feast of the Dedication. 22*† The
feast of the Dedication was then taking
place in Jerusalem. It was winter.
23† And Jesus walked about in the tem-
ple area on the Portico of Solomon.
24*† So the Jews gathered around him
and said to him, "How long are you go-
ing to keep us in suspense? If you are
the Messiah, tell us plainly." 25*† Jesus
answered them, "I told you and you do
not believe. The works I do in my Fa-
ther's name testify to me. 26* But you
do not believe, because you are not
among my sheep. 27 My sheep hear my
voice; I know them, and they follow me.
28* I give them eternal life, and they
shall never perish. No one can take
them out of my hand. 29*† My Father,
who has given them to me, is greater
than all, and no one can take them out

JOHN

---

*

10, 1-5: Gn 48, 15; 49, 24; Pss 23, 1-4; 80, 2; Jer 23, 1-4; Ez 34, 1-31; Mi 7, 14.
4: Mi 2, 12-13.
11: Ps 23, 1-4; Is 40, 11; 49, 9-10; Heb 13, 20; Rv 7, 17.
12: Zec 11, 17.
15: 15, 13; 1 Jn 3, 16.
16: 11, 52; Is 56, 8; Jer 23, 3; Ez 34, 23; 37, 24; Mi 2, 12.
17: Heb 10, 10.
18: 19, 11.
19: 7, 43; 9, 16.
20: 7, 20; 8, 48.
21: 3, 2.
22: 1 Mc 4, 54.59.
24: Lk 22, 67.
25: 8, 25 / 5, 36; 10, 38.
26: 8, 45.47.
28: Dt 32, 39.
29: Wis 3, 1; Is 43, 13.

---

†

10, 1-21: The good shepherd discourse continues the theme of attack on the Pharisees that ends ch 9. The figure is allegorical: the hired hands are the Pharisees who excommunicated the cured blind man. It serves as a commentary on ch 9. For the shepherd motif, used of Yahweh in the Old Testament, cf Ex 34; Gn 48, 15; 49, 24; Mi 7, 14; Pss 23, 1-4; 80, 1.

10, 1: *Sheepfold:* a low stone wall open to the sky.

10, 4: *Recognize his voice:* the Pharisees do not recognize Jesus, but the people of God, symbolized by the blind man, do.

10, 6: *Figure of speech:* John uses a different word for illustrative speech than the "parable" of the synoptics, but the idea is similar.

10, 7-10: In vv 7-8, the figure is of a gate for the shepherd to come to the sheep; in vv 9-10, the figure is of a gate for the sheep to *come in and go out.*

10, 8: *[Before me]:* these words are omitted in many good early manuscripts and versions.

10, 16: *Other sheep:* the Gentiles, possibly a reference to "God's dispersed children" of 11, 52 destined to be gathered into one, or "apostolic Christians" at odds with the community of the beloved disciple.

10, 18: *Power to take it up again:* contrast the role of the Father as the efficient cause of the resurrection in Acts 2, 24; 4, 10; etc.; Rom 1, 4; 4, 24. Yet even here is added: *This command I have received from my Father.*

10, 22: *Feast of the Dedication:* an eight-day festival of lights (Hebrew, Hanukkah) held in December, three months after the feast of Tabernacles (7, 2), to celebrate the Maccabees' rededication of the altar and reconsecration of the temple in 164 B.C., after their desecration by Antiochus IV Epiphanes (Dn 8, 13; 9, 27; cf 1 Mc 4, 36-59; 2 Mc 1, 18—2, 19; 10, 1-8).

10, 23: *Portico of Solomon:* on the east side of the temple area, offering protection against the cold winds from the desert.

10, 24: *Keep us in suspense:* literally, "How long will you take away our life?" Cf 11, 48-50. *If you are the Messiah, tell us plainly:* cf Lk 22, 67. This is the climax of Jesus' encounters with the Jewish authorities. There has never yet been an open confession before them.

10, 25: *I told you:* probably at 8, 25, which was an evasive answer.

10, 29: The textual evidence for the first clause is very divided; it may also be translated: "As for the Father, what he has given me is greater than all," or "My Father is greater than all, in what he has given me."

of the Father's hand. 30*† The Father
and I are one."
31* The Jews again picked up rocks to
stone him. 32 Jesus answered them, "I
have shown you many good works from
my Father. For which of these are you
trying to stone me?" 33* The Jews an-
swered him, "We are not stoning you
for a good work but for blasphemy. You,
a man, are making yourself God."
34*† Jesus answered them, "Is it not
written in your law, 'I said, "You are
gods" '? 35 If it calls them gods to whom
the word of God came, and scripture
cannot be set aside, 36*† can you say
that the one whom the Father has con-
secrated and sent into the world blas-
phemes because I said, 'I am the Son
of God'? 37 If I do not perform my Fa-
ther's works, do not believe me; 38* but
if I perform them, even if you do not
believe me, believe the works, so that
you may realize [and understand] that
the Father is in me and I am in the Fa-
ther." 39 [Then] they tried again to ar-
rest him; but he escaped from their
power.
40* He went back across the Jordan
to the place where John first baptized,
and there he remained. 41† Many came
to him and said, "John performed no
sign, but everything John said about
this man was true." 42* And many there
began to believe in him.

JOHN

CHAPTER 11

The Raising of Lazarus.† 1* Now a
man was ill, Lazarus from Bethany, the
village of Mary and her sister Martha.
2 Mary was the one who had anointed
the Lord with perfumed oil and dried
his feet with her hair; it was her brother
Lazarus who was ill. 3 So the sisters sent
word to him, saying, "Master, the one
you love is ill." 4*† When Jesus heard
this he said, "This illness is not to end
in death, but is for the glory of God, that
the Son of God may be glorified through
it." 5 Now Jesus loved Martha and her
sister and Lazarus. 6 So when he heard
that he was ill, he remained for two days
in the place where he was. 7 Then after
this he said to his disciples, "Let us go
back to Judea." 8* The disciples said to
him, "Rabbi, the Jews were just trying
to stone you, and you want to go back
there?" 9* Jesus answered, "Are there
not twelve hours in a day? If one walks
during the day, he does not stumble, be-
cause he sees the light of this world.
10† But if one walks at night, he stum-
bles, because the light is not in him."
11 He said this, and then told them, "Our
friend Lazarus is asleep, but I am going
to awaken him." 12 So the disciples said
to him, "Master, if he is asleep, he will
be saved." 13* But Jesus was talking
about his death, while they thought that
he meant ordinary sleep. 14 So then
Jesus said to them clearly, "Laza-
rus has died. 15 And I am glad for you
that I was not there, that you may
believe. Let us go to him." 16*† So
Thomas, called Didymus, said to his fel-
low disciples, "Let us also go to die with
him."
17 When Jesus arrived, he found that
Lazarus had already been in the tomb
for four days. 18† Now Bethany was
near Jerusalem, only about two miles
away. 19* And many of the Jews had
come to Martha and Mary to comfort
them about their brother. 20 When Mar-
tha heard that Jesus was coming, she
went to meet him; but Mary sat at home.
21* Martha said to Jesus, "Lord, if you
had been here, my brother would not
have died. 22 [But] even now I know that

*

30: 1, 1; 12, 45; 14, 9; 17, 21.
31: 8, 59.
33: 5, 18; 19, 7; Lv 24, 16.
34: Ps 82, 6.
36: 5, 18.
38: 14, 10-11.20.
40: 1, 28.
42: 2, 23; 7, 31; 8, 30.
11, 1-2: 12, 1-8; Lk 10, 38-42; 16, 19-31.
4: 9, 3.24.
8: 8, 59; 10, 31.
9: 8, 12; 9, 4.
9-10: 12, 35; 1 Jn 2, 10.
13: Mt 9, 24.
16: 14, 5.22.
19: 12, 9.17-18.
21: 11, 32.

†

10, 30: This is justification for v 29; it asserts unity of power and reveals that the words and deeds of Jesus are the words and deeds of God.

10, 34: This is a reference to the judges of Israel who, since they exercised the divine prerogative to judge (Dt 1, 17), were called "gods"; cf Ex 21, 6, besides Ps 82, 6, from which the quotation comes.

10, 36: *Consecrated:* this may be a reference to the rededicated altar at the Hanukkah feast; see the note on 10, 22.

10, 41: *Performed no sign:* this is to stress the inferior role of John the Baptist. The Transjordan topography recalls the great witness of John the Baptist to Jesus, as opposed to the hostility of the authorities in Jerusalem.

11, 1-44: The raising of Lazarus, the longest continuous narrative in John outside of the passion account, is the climax of the signs. It leads directly to the decision of the Sanhedrin to kill Jesus. The theme of life predominates. Lazarus is a token of the real life that Jesus dead and raised will give to all who believe in him. Johannine irony is found in the fact that Jesus' gift of life leads to his own death. The story is not found in the synoptics, but cf Mk 5, 21 and parallels; Lk 7, 11-17. There are also parallels between this story and Luke's parable of the rich man and poor Lazarus (Lk 16, 19-31). In both a man named Lazarus dies; in Luke, there is a request that he return to convince his contemporaries of the need for faith and repentance, while in John, Lazarus does return and some believe but others do not.

11, 4: *Not to end in death:* this is misunderstood by the disciples as referring to physical death, but it is meant as spiritual death.

11, 10: *The light is not in him:* the ancients apparently did not grasp clearly the entry of light *through* the eye; they seem to have thought of it as being *in* the eye; cf Lk 11, 34; Mt 6, 23.

11, 16: *Called Didymus: Didymus* is the Greek word for twin. Thomas is derived from the Aramaic word for twin; in an ancient Syriac version and in the Gospel of Thomas (#80, 11-12) his given name, Judas, is supplied.

11, 18: *About two miles:* literally, "about fifteen stades"; a stade was 607 feet.

whatever you ask of God, God will give you." 23 Jesus said to her, "Your brother will rise." 24* Martha said to him, "I know he will rise, in the resurrection on the last day." 25* Jesus told her, "I am the resurrection and the life; whoever believes in me, even if he dies, will live, 26 and everyone who lives and believes in me will never die. Do you believe this?" 27*† She said to him, "Yes, Lord. I have come to believe that you are the Messiah, the Son of God, the one who is coming into the world."

28 When she had said this, she went and called her sister Mary secretly, saying, "The teacher is here and is asking for you." 29 As soon as she heard this, she rose quickly and went to him. 30 For Jesus had not yet come into the village, but was still where Martha had met him. 31 So when the Jews who were with her in the house comforting her saw Mary get up quickly and go out, they followed her, presuming that she was going to the tomb to weep there. 32 When Mary came to where Jesus was and saw him, she fell at his feet and said to him, "Lord, if you had been here, my brother would not have died." 33† When Jesus saw her weeping and the Jews who had come with her weeping, he became perturbed and deeply troubled, 34 and said, "Where have you laid him?" They said to him, "Sir, come and see." 35* And Jesus wept. 36 So the Jews said, "See how he loved him." 37 But some of them said, "Could not the one who opened the eyes of the blind man have done something so that this man would not have died?"

38 So Jesus, perturbed again, came to the tomb. It was a cave, and a stone lay across it. 39 Jesus said, "Take away the stone." Martha, the dead man's sister, said to him, "Lord, by now there will be a stench; he has been dead for four days." 40 Jesus said to her, "Did I not tell you that if you believe you will see the glory of God?" 41† So they took away the stone. And Jesus raised his eyes and said, "Father, I thank you for hearing me. 42* I know that you always hear me; but because of the crowd here I have said this, that they may believe that you sent me." 43† And when he had said this, he cried out in a loud voice, "Lazarus, come out!" 44 The dead man came out, tied hand and foot with burial bands, and his face was wrapped in a cloth. So Jesus said to them, "Untie him and let him go."

Session of the Sanhedrin. 45* Now many of the Jews who had come to Mary and seen what he had done began to believe in him. 46 But some of them went to the Pharisees and told them what Jesus had done. 47* So the chief priests and the Pharisees convened the Sanhedrin and said, "What are we going to do? This man is performing many signs. 48† If we leave him alone, all will believe in him, and the Romans will come and take away both our land and our nation." 49*† But one of them, Caiaphas, who was high priest that year, said to them, "You know nothing, 50 nor do you consider that it is better for you that one man should die instead of the people, so that the whole nation may not perish." 51 He did not say this on his own, but since he was high priest for that year, he prophesied that Jesus was going to die for the nation, 52† and not only for the nation, but also to gather into one the dispersed children of God. 53* So from that day on they planned to kill him.

54† So Jesus no longer walked about in public among the Jews, but he left for the region near the desert, to a town called Ephraim, and there he remained with his disciples.

The Last Passover. 55*† Now the Passover of the Jews was near, and many went up from the country to Jerusalem before Passover to purify themselves. 56 They looked for Jesus and said to one another as they were in the temple area, "What do you think? That he will not come to the feast?" 57 For the chief priests and the Pharisees had given orders that if anyone knew where he was, he should inform them, so that they might arrest him.

*

24: 5, 29; 6, 39-40.44.54; 12, 48; Is 2, 2; Mi 4, 1; Acts 23, 8; 24, 15.
25: 5, 24; 8, 51; 14, 6; Dn 12, 2.
27: 1, 9; 6, 69.
35: Lk 19, 41.
42: 12, 30.
45: Lk 16, 31.
47: 12, 19; Mt 26, 3-5; Lk 22, 2; Acts 4, 16.
49-50: 18, 13-14.
53: 5, 18; 7, 1; Mt 12, 14.
55: 2, 13; 5, 1; 6, 4; 18, 28; Ex 19, 10-11.15; Nm 9, 6-14; 19, 12; Dt 16, 6; 2 Chr 30, 1-3.15-18.

†

11, 27: The titles here are a summary of titles given to Jesus earlier in the gospel.

11, 33: *Became perturbed:* a startling phrase in Greek, literally, "He snorted in spirit," perhaps in anger at the presence of evil (death).

11, 41: *Father:* in Aramaic, *ʾabbāʾ*. See the note on Mk 14, 36.

11, 43: *Cried out in a loud voice:* a dramatization of 5, 28: "the hour is coming when all who are in the tombs will hear his voice."

11, 48: *The Romans will come:* Johannine irony; this is precisely what happened after Jesus' death.

11, 49: *That year:* emphasizes the conjunction of the office and the year. Actually, Caiaphas was high priest A.D. 18-36. The Jews attributed a gift of prophecy, sometimes unconscious, to the high priest.

11, 52: *Dispersed children of God:* perhaps the "other sheep" of 10, 16.

11, 54: Ephraim is usually located about twelve miles northeast of Jerusalem, where the mountains descend into the Jordan valley.

11, 55: *Purify:* prescriptions for purity were based on Ex 19, 10-11.15; Nm 9, 6-14; 2 Chr 30, 1-3.15-18.

CHAPTER 12

The Anointing at Bethany.† 1* Six
days before Passover Jesus came to
Bethany, where Lazarus was, whom Je-
sus had raised from the dead. 2* They
gave a dinner for him there, and Martha
served, while Lazarus was one of those
reclining at table with him. 3*† Mary
took a liter of costly perfumed oil made
from genuine aromatic nard and
anointed the feet of Jesus and dried
them with her hair; the house was filled
with the fragrance of the oil. 4 Then Ju-
das the Iscariot, one [of] his disciples,
and the one who would betray him, said,
5† "Why was this oil not sold for three
hundred days' wages and given to the
poor?" 6* He said this not because he
cared about the poor but because he was
a thief and held the money bag and used
to steal the contributions. 7† So Jesus
said, "Leave her alone. Let her keep
this for the day of my burial. 8* You al-
ways have the poor with you, but you
do not always have me."

9* [The] large crowd of the Jews
found out that he was there and came,
not only because of Jesus, but also to
see Lazarus, whom he had raised from
the dead. 10 And the chief priests plotted
to kill Lazarus too, 11* because many of
the Jews were turning away and believ-
ing in Jesus because of him.

The Entry into Jerusalem.† 12* On
the next day, when the great crowd that
had come to the feast heard that Jesus
was coming to Jerusalem, 13*† they took
palm branches and went out to meet
him, and cried out:

"Hosanna!
Blessed is he who comes in the
name of the Lord,
[even] the king of Israel."

14 Jesus found an ass and sat upon it,
as is written:

15*†"Fear no more, O daughter Zion;
see, your king comes, seated upon
an ass's colt."

16*† His disciples did not understand
this at first, but when Jesus had been
glorified they remembered that these
things were written about him and that
they had done this for him. 17† So the
crowd that was with him when he called
Lazarus from the tomb and raised him
from death continued to testify. 18 This
was [also] why the crowd went to meet
him, because they heard that he had
done this sign. 19*† So the Pharisees
said to one another, "You see that you
are gaining nothing. Look, the whole
world has gone after him."

The Coming of Jesus' Hour.†
20*† Now there were some Greeks
among those who had come up to wor-
ship at the feast. 21*† They came to
Philip, who was from Bethsaida in Gali-
lee, and asked him, "Sir, we would like
to see Jesus." 22* Philip went and told
Andrew; then Andrew and Philip went
and told Jesus. 23*† Jesus answered
them, "The hour has come for the Son of
Man to be glorified. 24*† Amen, amen, I
say to you, unless a grain of wheat falls

---

*

12, 1-11: Mt 26, 6-13; Mk 14, 3-9.
1-2: 11, 1.
2: Lk 10, 38-42.
3: 11, 2.
6: 13, 29.
8: Dt 15, 11.
9: 11, 19.
11: 11, 45.
12-19: Mt 21, 1-16; Mk 11, 1-10; Lk 19, 28-40.
13: 1, 49; Lv 23, 40; 1 Mc 13, 51; 2 Mc 10, 7; Rv 7, 9.
15: Is 40, 9; Zec 9, 9.
16: 2, 22.
19: 11, 47-48.
20: Acts 10, 2.
21: 1, 44.
22: 1, 40.
23: 2, 4.
24: Is 53, 10-12; 1 Cor 15, 36.

---

†

12, 1-8: This is probably the same scene of anointing found in Mk 14, 3-9 (see the note there) and Mt 26, 6-13. The anointing by a penitent woman in Lk 7, 36-38 is different. Details from these various episodes have become interchanged.

12, 3: *The feet of Jesus:* so Mk 14, 3; but in Mt 26, 6, Mary anoints Jesus' head as a sign of regal, messianic anointing.

12, 5: *Days' wages:* literally, "denarii." A denarius is a day's wage in Mt 20, 2; see the note on 6, 7.

12, 7: Jesus' response reflects the rabbinical discussion of what was the greatest act of mercy, almsgiving or burying the dead. Those who favored proper burial of the dead thought it an essential condition for sharing in the resurrection.

12, 12-19: In Jn, the entry into Jerusalem follows the anointing whereas in the synoptics it precedes. In John, the crowd, not the disciples, are responsible for the triumphal procession.

12, 13: *Palm branches:* used to welcome great conquerors; cf 1 Mc 13, 51; 2 Mc 10, 7. They may be related to the *lûlāb,* the twig bundles used at the feast of Tabernacles. *Hosanna:* see Ps 118, 25-26. The Hebrew word means: "(O Lord), grant salvation." *He who comes in the name of the Lord:* referred in Ps 118, 26 to a pilgrim entering the temple gates, but here a title for Jesus (see the notes on Mt 11, 3 and Jn 6, 14; 11, 27). *The king of Israel:* perhaps from Zep 3, 14-15, in connection with the next quotation from Zec 9, 9.

12, 15: *Daughter Zion:* Jerusalem. *Ass's colt:* symbol of peace, as opposed to the war-horse.

12, 16: *They had done this:* the antecedent of *they* is ambiguous.

12, 17-18: There seem to be two different crowds in these verses. There are some good witnesses to the text that have another reading for v 17: "Then the crowd that was with him began to testify that he had called Lazarus out of the tomb and raised him from the dead."

12, 19: *The whole world:* the sense is that everyone is following Jesus, but John has an ironic play on *world;* he alludes to the universality of salvation (3, 17; 4, 42).

12, 20-36: This announcement of glorification by death is an illustration of "the whole world" (19) going after him.

12, 20: *Greeks:* not used here in a nationalistic sense. These are probably Gentile proselytes to Judaism; cf 7, 35.

12, 21-22: *Philip . . . Andrew:* the approach is made through disciples who have distinctly Greek names, suggesting that access to Jesus was mediated to the Greek world through his disciples. Philip and Andrew were from Bethsaida (1, 44); Galileans were mostly bilingual. *See:* here seems to mean "have an interview with."

12, 23: Jesus' response suggests that only after the crucifixion could the gospel encompass both Jew and Gentile.

12, 24: This verse implies that through his death Jesus will be accessible to all. *It remains just a grain of wheat:* this saying is found in the synoptic triple and double traditions (Mk 8, 35 // Mt 16, 25 // Lk 9, 24; Mt 10, 39 // Lk 17, 33). John adds the phrases (25) *in this world* and *for eternal life.*

to the ground and dies, it remains just
a grain of wheat; but if it dies, it pro-
duces much fruit. 25*† Whoever loves
his life loses it, and whoever hates his
life in this world will preserve it for eter-
nal life. 26* Whoever serves me must fol-
low me, and where I am, there also will
my servant be. The Father will honor
whoever serves me.
27*† "I am troubled now. Yet what
should I say? 'Father, save me from this
hour'? But it was for this purpose that
I came to this hour. 28* Father, glorify
your name." Then a voice came from
heaven, "I have glorified it and will glo-
rify it again." 29* The crowd there heard
it and said it was thunder; but others
said, "An angel has spoken to him."
30* Jesus answered and said, "This
voice did not come for my sake but for
yours. 31*† Now is the time of judgment
on this world; now the ruler of this world
will be driven out. 32* And when I am
lifted up from the earth, I will draw ev-
eryone to myself." 33 He said this indi-
cating the kind of death he would die.
34*† So the crowd answered him, "We
have heard from the law that the
Messiah remains forever. Then how
can you say that the Son of Man must
be lifted up? Who is this Son of Man?"
35* Jesus said to them, "The light
will be among you only a little while.
Walk while you have the light, so that
darkness may not overcome you. Who-
ever walks in the dark does not
know where he is going. 36* While you
have the light, believe in the light, so
that you may become children of the
light."

Unbelief and Belief among the Jews.
After he had said this, Jesus left and
hid from them. 37*† Although he had
performed so many signs in their
presence they did not believe in him,
38*† in order that the word which
Isaiah the prophet spoke might be ful-
filled:

"Lord, who has believed our
preaching,
to whom has the might of the Lord
been revealed?"

39 For this reason they could not believe,
because again Isaiah said:

40* "He blinded their eyes
and hardened their heart,
so that they might not see with their
eyes
and understand with their heart
and be converted,
and I would heal them."

41*† Isaiah said this because he saw
his glory and spoke about him.
42* Nevertheless, many, even among
the authorities, believed in him, but be-
cause of the Pharisees they did not ac-
knowledge it openly in order not to be
expelled from the synagogue. 43* For
they preferred human praise to the
glory of God.

Recapitulation. 44* Jesus cried out
and said, "Whoever believes in me be-
lieves not only in me but also in the one
who sent me, 45* and whoever sees me
sees the one who sent me. 46* I came into
the world as light, so that everyone who
believes in me might not remain in
darkness. 47* And if anyone hears my
words and does not observe them, I do
not condemn him, for I did not come
to condemn the world but to save the
world. 48* Whoever rejects me and does
not accept my words has something to
judge him: the word that I spoke, it will
condemn him on the last day,
49* because I did not speak on my own,
but the Father who sent me commanded
me what to say and speak. 50 And I know
that his commandment is eternal life.
So what I say, I say as the Father told
me."

*

25: Mt 10, 39; 16, 25; Mk 8, 35; Lk 9, 24; 17, 33.
26: 14, 3; 17, 24; Mt 16, 24; Mk 8, 34; Lk 9, 23.
27: 6, 38; 18, 11; Mt 26, 38-39; Mk 14, 34-36; Lk 22, 42; Heb 5, 7-8.
28: 2, 11; 17, 5; Dn 4, 31.34.
29: Ex 9, 28; 2 Sm 22, 14; Jb 37, 4; Ps 29, 3; Lk 22, 43; Acts 23, 9.
30: 11, 42.
31: 16, 11; Lk 10, 18; Rv 12, 9.
32: 3, 14; 8, 28; Is 52, 13.
34: Pss 89, 5; 110, 4; Is 9, 7; Dn 7, 13-14; Rv 20, 1-6.
35: 9, 4; 11, 10; Jb 5, 14.
36: Eph 5, 8.
37-43: Dt 29, 2-4; Mk 4, 11-12; Rom 9-11.
38: Is 53, 1; Rom 10, 16.
40: Is 6, 9-10; Mt 13, 13-15; Mk 4, 12.
41: 5, 39; Is 6, 1.4.
42: 9, 22.
43: 5, 44.
44: 13, 20; 14, 1.
45: 14, 7-9.
46: 1, 9; 8, 12.
47: 3, 17.
48: Lk 10, 16; Heb 4, 12.
49: 14, 10.31; Dt 18, 18-19.

†

12, 25: *His life:* the Greek word *psychē* refers to a person's natural life. It does not mean "soul," for Hebrew anthropology did not postulate body/soul dualism in the way that is familiar to us.

12, 27: *I am troubled:* perhaps an allusion to the Gethsemane agony scene of the synoptics.

12, 31: *Ruler of this world:* Satan.

12, 34: There is no passage in the Old Testament that states precisely that *the Messiah remains forever.* Perhaps the closest is Ps 89, 37.

12, 37-50: These verses, on unbelief of the Jews, provide an epilogue to the Book of Signs.

12, 38-41: John gives a historical explanation of the disbelief of the Jewish people, not a psychological one. The Old Testament had to be fulfilled; the disbelief that met Isaiah's message was a foreshadowing of the disbelief that Jesus encountered. In v 42 and also in 3, 20, we see that there is no negation of freedom.

12, 41: *His glory:* Isaiah saw the glory of Yahweh enthroned in the heavenly temple, but in John the antecedent of *his* is Jesus.

III: THE BOOK OF GLORY†

CHAPTER 13

The Washing of the Disciples' Feet.†
1*† Before the feast of Passover, Jesus
knew that his hour had come to pass
from this world to the Father. He loved
his own in the world and he loved them
to the end. 2*† The devil had already
induced Judas, son of Simon the Iscar-
iot, to hand him over. So, during supper,
3* fully aware that the Father had put
everything into his power and that he
had come from God and was returning
to God, 4 he rose from supper and took
off his outer garments. He took a towel
and tied it around his waist. 5*† Then
he poured water into a basin and began
to wash the disciples' feet and dry them
with the towel around his waist. 6 He
came to Simon Peter, who said to him,
"Master, are you going to wash my
feet?" 7 Jesus answered and said to him,
"What I am doing, you do not under-
stand now, but you will understand
later." 8* Peter said to him, "You will
never wash my feet." Jesus answered
him, "Unless I wash you, you will have
no inheritance with me." 9 Simon Peter
said to him, "Master, then not only my
feet, but my hands and head as well."
10*† Jesus said to him, "Whoever has
bathed has no need except to have his
feet washed, for he is clean all over; so
you are clean, but not all." 11* For he
knew who would betray him; for this rea-
son, he said, "Not all of you are clean."
12 So when he had washed their feet
[and] put his garments back on and re-
clined at table again, he said to them,
"Do you realize what I have done for
you? 13* You call me 'teacher' and 'mas-
ter,' and rightly so, for indeed I am.
14 If I, therefore, the master and
teacher, have washed your feet, you
ought to wash one another's feet.
15* I have given you a model to follow,
so that as I have done for you, you
should also do. 16*† Amen, amen, I say
to you, no slave is greater than his mas-
ter nor any messenger greater than the
one who sent him. 17 If you understand
this, blessed are you if you do it. 18* I
am not speaking of all of you. I know
those whom I have chosen. But so that
the scripture might be fulfilled, 'The one
who ate my food has raised his heel
against me.' 19 From now on I am telling
you before it happens, so that when it
happens you may believe that I AM.
20* Amen, amen, I say to you, whoever
receives the one I send receives me, and
whoever receives me receives the one
who sent me."

Announcement of Judas's Betrayal.
21* When he had said this, Jesus was
deeply troubled and testified, "Amen,
amen, I say to you, one of you will be-
tray me." 22 The disciples looked at one
another, at a loss as to whom he meant.
23*† One of his disciples, the one whom
Jesus loved, was reclining at Jesus'
side. 24 So Simon Peter nodded to him
to find out whom he meant. 25* He
leaned back against Jesus' chest and
said to him, "Master, who is it?"
26† Jesus answered, "It is the one to
whom I hand the morsel after I have
dipped it." So he dipped the morsel and
[took it and] handed it to Judas, son of
Simon the Iscariot. 27* After he took the
morsel, Satan entered him. So Jesus
said to him, "What you are going to do,
do quickly." 28 [Now] none of those re-
clining at table realized why he said this
to him. 29* Some thought that since Ju-
das kept the money bag, Jesus had told
him, "Buy what we need for the feast,"
or to give something to the poor. 30 So
he took the morsel and left at once. And
it was night.

*

13, 1: 2, 4; 7, 30; 8, 20; Mt 26, 17.45; Mk 14, 12.41; Lk 22, 7.
2: 6, 71; 17, 12; Mt 26, 20-21; Mk 14, 17-18; Lk 22, 3.
3: 3, 35.
5: 1 Sm 25, 41.
8: 2 Sm 20, 1.
10: 15, 3.
11: 6, 70.
13: Mt 23, 8.10.
15: Lk 22, 27; 1 Pt 2, 21.
16: 15, 20; Mt 10, 24; Lk 6, 40.
18: Ps 41, 10.
20: Mt 10, 40; Mk 9, 37; Lk 9, 48.
21-30: Mt 26, 21-25; Mk 14, 18-21; Lk 22, 21-23.
23: 19, 26; 20, 2; 21, 7.20; Mt 10, 37.
25: 21, 20.
27: 13, 2; Lk 22, 3.
29: 12, 5-6.

†

13, 1—19, 42: The Book of Glory. There is a major break here; the word "sign" is used again only in 20, 30. In this phase of Jesus' return to the Father, the discourses (chs 13-17) precede the traditional narrative of the passion (chs 18-20) to interpret them for the Christian reader. This is the only extended example of esoteric teaching of disciples in John.

13, 1-20: Washing of the disciples' feet. This episode occurs in John at the place of the narration of the institution of the Eucharist in the synoptics. It may be a dramatization of Lk 22, 27: "I am your servant." It is presented as a "model" ("pattern") of the crucifixion. It symbolizes cleansing from sin by sacrificial death.

13, 1: *Before the feast of Passover:* this would be Thursday evening, before the day of preparation; in the synoptics, the Last Supper is a Passover meal taking place, in John's chronology, on Friday evening. *To the end:* or, "completely."

13, 2: *Induced:* literally, "The devil put into the heart that Judas should hand him over."

13, 5: The act of washing another's feet was one that could not be required of the lowliest Jewish slave. It is an allusion to the humiliating death of the crucifixion.

13, 10: *Bathed:* many have suggested that this passage is a symbolic reference to baptism. The Greek root involved is used in baptismal contexts in 1 Cor 6, 11; Eph 5, 26; Ti 3, 5; Heb 10, 22.

13, 16: *Messenger:* the Greek has *apostolos,* the only occurrence of the term in John. It is not used in the technical sense here.

13, 23: *The one whom Jesus loved:* also mentioned in 19, 26; 20, 2; 21, 7. A disciple, called "another disciple" or "the other disciple," is mentioned in 18, 15 and 20, 2; in the latter reference he is identified with the disciple whom Jesus loved. There is also an unnamed disciple in 1, 35-40; see the note on 1, 37.

13, 26: *Morsel:* probably the bitter herb dipped in salt water.

***The New Commandment.*†** 31† When he had left, Jesus said, "Now is the Son of Man glorified, and God is glorified in him. 32* [If God is glorified in him,] God will also glorify him in himself, and he will glorify him at once. 33* My children, I will be with you only a little while longer. You will look for me, and as I told the Jews, 'Where I go you cannot come,' so now I say it to you. 34*† I give you a new commandment: love one another. As I have loved you, so you also should love one another. 35 This is how all will know that you are my disciples, if you have love for one another."

Peter's Denial Predicted. 36* Simon Peter said to him, "Master, where are you going?" Jesus answered [him], "Where I am going, you cannot follow me now, though you will follow later." 37 Peter said to him, "Master, why can't I follow you now? I will lay down my life for you." 38* Jesus answered, "Will you lay down your life for me? Amen, amen, I say to you, the cock will not crow before you deny me three times."

CHAPTER 14

***Last Supper Discourses.*†** 1† "Do not let your hearts be troubled. You have faith in God; have faith also in me. 2 In my Father's house there are many dwelling places. If there were not, would I have told you that I am going to prepare a place for you? 3*† And if I go and prepare a place for you, I will come back again and take you to myself, so that where I am you also may be. 4† Where [I] am going you know the way." 5 Thomas said to him, "Master, we do not know where you are going; how can we know the way?" 6*† Jesus said to him, "I am the way and the truth and the life. No one comes to the Father except through me. 7*† If you know me, then you will also know my Father. From now on you do know him and have seen him." 8*† Philip said to him, "Master, show us the Father, and that will be enough for us." 9* Jesus said to him, "Have I been with you for so long a time and you still do not know me, Philip? Whoever has seen me has seen the Father. How can you say, 'Show us the Father'? 10* Do you not believe that I am in the Father and the Father is in me? The words that I speak to you I do not speak on my own. The Father who dwells in me is doing his works. 11* Believe me that I am in the Father and the Father is in me, or else, believe because of the works themselves. 12* Amen, amen, I say to you, whoever believes in me will do the works that I do, and will do greater ones than these, because I am going to the Father. 13* And whatever you ask in my name, I will do, so that the Father may be glorified in the Son. 14 If you ask anything of me in my name, I will do it.

The Advocate. 15* "If you love me, you will keep my commandments. 16*† And I will ask the Father, and he will give you another Advocate to be with you always, 17*† the Spirit of truth, which the world cannot accept, because it neither sees nor knows it. But you know it, because it remains with you,

*

32: 17, 1-5.
33: 7, 33; 8, 21.
34: 15, 12-13.17; Lv 19, 18; 1 Thes 4, 9; 1 Jn 2, 7-10; 3, 23; 2 Jn 5.
36: Mk 14, 27; Lk 22, 23.
38: 18, 27; Mt 26, 33-35; Mk 14, 29-31; Lk 22, 33-34.
14, 3: 12, 26; 17, 24; 1 Jn 2, 28.
6: 8, 31-47.
7: 8, 19; 12, 45.
8: Ex 24, 9-10; 33, 18.
9: 1, 18; 10, 30; 12, 45; 2 Cor 4, 4; Col 1, 15; Heb 1, 3.
10: 1, 1; 10, 37-38; 12, 49.
11: 10, 38.
12: 1, 50; 5, 20.
13: 15, 7.16; 16, 23-24; Mt 7, 7-11.
15: 15, 10; Dt 6, 4-9; Ps 119; Wis 6, 18; 1 Jn 5, 3; 2 Jn 6.
16: 15, 26; Lk 24, 49; 1 Jn 2, 1.
17: 16, 13; Mt 28, 20; 2 Jn 1-2.

†

13, 31—17, 26: Two farewell discourses and a prayer. These seem to be Johannine compositions, including sayings of Jesus at the Last Supper and on other occasions, modeled on similar farewell discourses in Greek literature and the Old Testament (of Moses, Joshua, David).

13, 31-38: Introduction: departure and return. Terms of coming and going predominate. These verses form an introduction to the last discourse of Jesus, which extends through chs 14 to 17. In it John has collected Jesus' words to *his own* (13, 1). There are indications that several speeches have been fused together, e.g., in 14, 31 and 17, 1.

13, 34: *I give you a new commandment:* this puts Jesus on a par with Yahweh. The commandment itself is not new; cf Lv 19, 18 and the note there.

14, 1-31: Jesus' departure and return. This section is a dialogue marked off by a literary inclusion in vv 1 and 27: "Do not let your hearts be troubled."

14, 1: *You have faith:* could also be imperative: "Have faith."

14, 3: *Come back again:* a rare Johannine reference to the parousia; cf 1 Jn 2, 28.

14, 4: *The way:* here, of Jesus himself; also a designation of Christianity in Acts 9, 2; 19, 9.23; 22, 4; 24, 14.22.

14, 6: *The truth:* in John, the divinely revealed reality of the Father manifested in the person and works of Jesus. The possession of truth confers knowledge and liberation from sin (8, 32).

14, 7: An alternative reading, "If you knew me, then you would have known my Father also," would be a rebuke, as in 8, 19.

14, 8: *Show us the Father:* Philip is pictured asking for a theophany like Ex 24, 9-10; 33, 18.

14, 16: *Another Advocate:* Jesus is the first advocate (paraclete); see 1 Jn 2, 1, where Jesus is an advocate in the sense of intercessor in heaven. The Greek term derives from legal terminology for an advocate or defense attorney, and can mean spokesman, mediator, intercessor, comforter, consoler, although no one of these terms encompasses the meaning in John. The Paraclete in John is a teacher, a witness to Jesus, and a prosecutor of the world, who represents the continued presence on earth of the Jesus who has returned to the Father.

14, 17: *The Spirit of truth:* this term is also used at Qumran, where it is a moral force put into a person by God, as opposed to the spirit of perversity. It is more personal in John; it will teach the realities of the new order (26), and testify to the truth (6). While it has been customary to use masculine personal pronouns in English for the Advocate, the Greek word for "spirit" is neuter, and the Greek text and manuscript variants fluctuate between masculine and neuter pronouns.

and will be in you. 18† I will not leave
you orphans; I will come to you. 19* In
a little while the world will no longer
see me, but you will see me, because I
live and you will live. 20* On that day
you will realize that I am in my Father
and you are in me and I in you.
21* Whoever has my commandments
and observes them is the one who loves
me. And whoever loves me will be loved
by my Father, and I will love him and
reveal myself to him." 22*† Judas, not
the Iscariot, said to him, "Master,
[then] what happened that you will re-
veal yourself to us and not to the
world?" 23* Jesus answered and said to
him, "Whoever loves me will keep my
word, and my Father will love him, and
we will come to him and make our
dwelling with him. 24 Whoever does not
love me does not keep my words; yet
the word you hear is not mine but that
of the Father who sent me.

25 "I have told you this while I am with
you. 26* The Advocate, the holy Spirit
that the Father will send in my name—
he will teach you everything and re-
mind you of all that [I] told you.
27*† Peace I leave with you; my peace
I give to you. Not as the world gives do
I give it to you. Do not let your hearts
be troubled or afraid. 28*† You heard me
tell you, 'I am going away and I will
come back to you.' If you loved me, you
would rejoice that I am going to the Fa-
ther; for the Father is greater than I.
29* And now I have told you this before
it happens, so that when it happens you
may believe. 30† I will no longer speak
much with you, for the ruler of the world
is coming. He has no power over me,
31* but the world must know that I love
the Father and that I do just as the Fa-
ther has commanded me. Get up, let
us go.

CHAPTER 15

***The Vine and the Branches.*†** 1*† "I
am the true vine, and my Father is the
vine grower. 2† He takes away every
branch in me that does not bear fruit,
and everyone that does he prunes so
that it bears more fruit. 3* You are al-
ready pruned because of the word that
I spoke to you. 4 Remain in me, as I re-
main in you. Just as a branch cannot
bear fruit on its own unless it remains
on the vine, so neither can you unless
you remain in me. 5 I am the vine, you
are the branches. Whoever remains in
me and I in him will bear much fruit,
because without me you can do nothing.
6*† Anyone who does not remain in me
will be thrown out like a branch and
wither; people will gather them and
throw them into a fire and they will be
burned. 7* If you remain in me and my
words remain in you, ask for whatever
you want and it will be done for you.
8* By this is my Father glorified, that
you bear much fruit and become my
disciples. 9* As the Father loves me, so
I also love you. Remain in my love.
10* If you keep my commandments, you
will remain in my love, just as I have
kept my Father's commandments and
remain in his love.

11* "I have told you this so that my
joy might be in you and your joy might
be complete. 12* This is my command-
ment: love one another as I love you.
13*† No one has greater love than this,
to lay down one's life for one's friends.
14 You are my friends if you do what I
command you. 15*† I no longer call you

---

*

19: 16, 16.
20: 10, 38; 17, 21; Is 2, 17; 4, 2-3.
21: 16, 27; 1 Jn 2, 5; 3, 24.
22: 7, 4; Acts 10, 40-41.
23: Rv 3, 20.
26: 15, 26; 16, 7.13-14; Ps 51, 13; Is 63, 10.
27: 16, 33; Eph 2, 14-18.
28: 8, 40.
29: 13, 19; 16, 4.
31: 6, 38.
15, 1: Ps 80, 9-17; Is 5, 1-7; Jer 2, 21; Ez 15, 2; 17, 5-10; 19, 10.
3: 13, 10.
6: Ez 15, 6-7; 19, 10-14.
7: 14, 13; Mt 7, 7; Mk 11, 24; 1 Jn 5, 14.
8: Mt 5, 16.
9: 17, 23.
10: 8, 29; 14, 15.
11: 16, 22; 17, 13.
12: 13, 34.
13: Rom 5, 6-8; 1 Jn 3, 16.
15: Dt 34, 5; Jos 24, 29; 2 Chr 20, 7; Ps 89, 21; Is 41, 8; Rom 8, 15; Gal 4, 7; Jas 2, 23.

---

†

14, 18: *I will come to you:* indwelling, not parousia.

14, 22: *Judas, not the Iscariot:* probably not the brother of Jesus in Mk 6, 3 // Mt 13, 55 or the apostle named Jude in Lk 6, 16, but Thomas (see the note on 11, 16), although other readings have "Judas the Cananean."

14, 27: *Peace:* the traditional Hebrew salutation *šālôm;* but Jesus' "Shalom" is a gift of salvation, connoting the bounty of messianic blessing.

14, 28: *The Father is greater than I:* because he *sent, gave,* etc., and Jesus is "a man who has told you the truth that I heard from God" (8. 40).

14, 30: *The ruler of the world:* Satan; cf 12, 31; 16, 11.

15, 1—16, 4: Discourse on the union of Jesus with his disciples. His words become a monologue and go beyond the immediate crisis of the departure of Jesus.

15, 1-17: Like 10, 1-5, this passage resembles a parable. Israel is spoken of as a vineyard at Is 5, 1-7; Mt 21, 33-46 and as a vine at Ps 80, 9-17; Jer 2, 21; Ez 15, 2; 17, 5-10; 19, 10; Hos 10, 1. The identification of the vine as the Son of Man in Ps 80, 16, and Wisdom's description of herself as a vine in Sir 24, 17, are further background for portrayal of Jesus by this figure. There may be secondary eucharistic symbolism here; cf Mk 14, 25, "the fruit of the vine."

15, 2: *Takes away . . . prunes:* in Greek there is a play on two related verbs.

15, 6: Branches were cut off and dried on the wall of the vineyard for later use as fuel.

15, 13: *For one's friends:* or: "those whom one loves." In 9-13a, the words for love are related to the Greek *agapaō.* In 13b-15, the words for love are related to the Greek *phileō.* For John, the two roots seem synonymous and mean "to love"; cf also 21, 15-17. The word *philos* is used here.

15, 15: *Slaves . . . friends:* in the Old Testament, Moses (Dt 34, 5), Joshua (Jos 24, 29), and David (Ps 89, 21) were called "servants" or "slaves of Yahweh"; only Abraham (Is 41, 8; 2 Chr 20, 7; cf Jas 2, 23) was called a "friend of God."

slaves, because a slave does not know
what his master is doing. I have called
you friends, because I have told you ev-
erything I have heard from my Father.
16* It was not you who chose me, but I
who chose you and appointed you to go
and bear fruit that will remain, so that
whatever you ask the Father in my
name he may give you. 17* This I com-
mand you: love one another.

The World's Hatred.† 18* "If the
world hates you, realize that it hated
me first. 19* If you belonged to the world,
the world would love its own; but be-
cause you do not belong to the world,
and I have chosen you out of the world,
the world hates you. 20*† Remember the
word I spoke to you, 'No slave is greater
than his master.' If they persecuted me,
they will also persecute you. If they kept
my word, they will also keep yours.
21*† And they will do all these things to
you on account of my name, because
they do not know the one who sent me.
22*† If I had not come and spoken to
them, they would have no sin; but as it
is they have no excuse for their sin.
23* Whoever hates me also hates my Fa-
ther. 24* If I had not done works among
them that no one else ever did, they
would not have sin; but as it is, they
have seen and hated both me and my
Father. 25*† But in order that the word
written in their law might be fulfilled,
'They hated me without cause.'

26*† "When the Advocate comes
whom I will send you from the Father,
the Spirit of truth that proceeds from
the Father, he will testify to me. 27* And
you also testify, because you have been
with me from the beginning.

CHAPTER 16

1 "I have told you this so that you may
not fall away. 2*† They will expel you
from the synagogues; in fact, the hour
is coming when everyone who kills you
will think he is offering worship to God.
3* They will do this because they have
not known either the Father or me.
4* I have told you this so that when their
hour comes you may remember that I
told you.

Jesus' Departure; Coming of the Advocate.† "I did not tell you this from
the beginning, because I was with you.
5*† But now I am going to the one who
sent me, and not one of you asks me,
'Where are you going?' 6 But because I
told you this, grief has filled your
hearts. 7* But I tell you the truth, it is
better for you that I go. For if I do not
go, the Advocate will not come to you.
But if I go, I will send him to you.
8† And when he comes he will convict
the world in regard to sin and righ-
teousness and condemnation: 9* sin, be-
cause they do not believe in me;
10 righteousness, because I am going to
the Father and you will no longer see
me; 11* condemnation, because the
ruler of this world has been condemned.

12 "I have much more to tell you, but
you cannot bear it now. 13*† But when
he comes, the Spirit of truth, he will
guide you to all truth. He will not speak
on his own, but he will speak what he
hears, and will declare to you the things
that are coming. 14 He will glorify me,
because he will take from what is mine

*

16: 14, 13; Dt 7, 6.
17: 13, 34; 1 Jn 3, 23; 4, 21.
18: 7, 7; 14, 17; Mt 10, 22; 24, 9; Mk 13, 13; Lk 6, 22; 1 Jn 3, 13.
19: 17, 14-16; 1 Jn 4, 5.
20: 13, 16; Mt 10, 24.
21: 8, 19; 16, 3.
22: 8, 21.24; 9, 41.
23: 5, 23; Lk 10, 16; 1 Jn 2, 23.
24: 3, 2; 9, 32; Dt 4, 32-33.
25: Ps 35, 19; 69, 4.
26: 14, 16.26; Mt 10, 19-20.
27: Lk 1, 2; Acts 1, 8.
16, 2: 9, 22; 12, 42; Mt 10, 17; Lk 21, 12; Acts 26, 11.
3: 15, 21.
4: 13, 19; 14, 29.
5: 7, 33; 13, 36; 14, 5.
7: 7, 39; 14, 16-17.26; 15, 26.
9: 8, 21-24; 15, 22.
11: 12, 31.
13: 14, 17.26; 15, 26; Pss 25, 5; 143, 10; 1 Jn 2, 27; Rv 7, 17.

†

15, 18—16, 4: The hostile reaction of the world. There are synoptic parallels, predicting persecution, especially at Mt 10, 17-25; 24, 9-10.

15, 20: *The word I spoke to you:* a reference to 13, 16.

15, 21: *On account of my name:* the idea of persecution for Jesus' name is frequent in the New Testament (Mt 10, 22; 24, 9; Acts 9, 14). For John, association with Jesus' name implies union with Jesus.

15, 22.24: Jesus' words (*spoken*) and deeds (*works*) are the great motives of credibility. *They have seen and hated:* probably means that they have seen his works and still have hated; but the Greek can be read: "have seen both me and my Father and still have hated both me and my Father." *Works . . . that no one else ever did:* so Yahweh in Dt 4, 32-33.

15, 25: *In their law:* law is here used as a larger concept than the Pentateuch, for the reference is to Ps 35, 19 or 69, 5. See the notes on 10, 34; 12, 34. *Their* law reflects the argument of the church with the synagogue.

15, 26: *Whom I will send:* in 14, 16.26, the Paraclete is to be sent by the Father, at the request of Jesus. Here the Spirit comes from both Jesus and the Father in mission; there is no reference here to the eternal procession of the Spirit.

16, 2: *Hour:* of persecution, not Jesus' "hour" (see the note on 2, 4).

16, 4b-33: A duplicate of 14, 1-31 on departure and return.

16, 5: *Not one of you asks me:* the difficulty of reconciling this with Simon Peter's question in 13, 36 and Thomas's words in 14, 5 strengthens the supposition that the last discourse has been made up of several collections of Johannine material.

16, 8-11: These verses illustrate the forensic character of the Paraclete's role: in the forum of the disciples' conscience he prosecutes the world. He leads believers to see (a) that the basic sin was and is refusal to believe in Jesus; (b) that, although Jesus was found guilty and apparently died in disgrace, in reality righteousness has triumphed, for Jesus has returned to his Father; (c) finally, that it is *the ruler of this world,* Satan, who has been condemned through Jesus' death (12, 32).

16, 13: *Declare to you the things that are coming:* not a reference to new predictions about the future, but interpretation of what has already occurred or been said.

and declare it to you. 15 Everything that the Father has is mine; for this reason I told you that he will take from what is mine and declare it to you.

16* "A little while and you will no longer see me, and again a little while later and you will see me." 17 So some of his disciples said to one another, "What does this mean that he is saying to us, 'A little while and you will not see me, and again a little while and you will see me,' and 'Because I am going to the Father'?" 18 So they said, "What is this 'little while' [of which he speaks]? We do not know what he means." 19 Jesus knew that they wanted to ask him, so he said to them, "Are you discussing with one another what I said, 'A little while and you will not see me, and again a little while and you will see me'? 20* Amen, amen, I say to you, you will weep and mourn, while the world rejoices; you will grieve, but your grief will become joy. 21* When a woman is in labor, she is in anguish because her hour has arrived; but when she has given birth to a child, she no longer remembers the pain because of her joy that a child has been born into the world. 22* So you also are now in anguish. But I will see you again, and your hearts will rejoice, and no one will take your joy away from you. 23* On that day you will not question me about anything. Amen, amen, I say to you, whatever you ask the Father in my name he will give you. 24 Until now you have not asked anything in my name; ask and you will receive, so that your joy may be complete.

25*† "I have told you this in figures of speech. The hour is coming when I will no longer speak to you in figures but I will tell you clearly about the Father. 26* On that day you will ask in my name, and I do not tell you that I will ask the Father for you. 27 For the Father himself loves you, because you have loved me and have come to believe that I came from God. 28* I came from the Father and have come into the world. Now I am leaving the world and going back to the Father." 29 His disciples said, "Now you are talking plainly, and not in any figure of speech. 30† Now we realize that you know everything and that you do not need to have anyone question you. Because of this we believe that you came from God." 31 Jesus answered them, "Do you believe now? 32*† Behold, the hour is coming and has arrived when each of you will be scattered to his own home and you will leave me alone. But I am not alone, because the Father is with me. 33* I have told you this so that you might have peace in me. In the world you will have trouble, but take courage, I have conquered the world."

CHAPTER 17

***The Prayer of Jesus.*†** 1*† When Jesus had said this, he raised his eyes to heaven and said, "Father, the hour has come. Give glory to your son, so that your son may glorify you, 2*† just as you gave him authority over all people, so that he may give eternal life to all you gave him. 3*† Now this is eternal life, that they should know you, the only true God, and the one whom you sent, Jesus Christ. 4 I glorified you on earth by accomplishing the work that you gave me to do. 5* Now glorify me, Father, with you, with the glory that I had with you before the world began.

6† "I revealed your name to those whom you gave me out of the world. They belonged to you, and you gave them to me, and they have kept your word. 7 Now they know that everything you gave me is from you, 8 because the words you gave to me I have given to them, and they accepted them and truly understood that I came from you, and they have believed that you sent me.

---

*

16: 7, 33; 14, 19.
20: Ps 126, 6.
21: Is 26, 17-18; Jer 31, 13; Mic 4, 9.
22: 14, 19; 15, 11; 20, 20.
23: 14, 13.
25: Mt 13, 34-35.
26: 14, 13.
28: 1, 1.
32: 8, 29; Zec 13, 7; Mt 26, 31; Mk 14, 27.
33: 14, 27.
17, 1: 13, 31.
2: 3, 35; Mt 28, 18.
3: 1, 17; Wis 14, 7; 15, 3; 1 Jn 5, 20.
5: 1, 1.2; 12, 28; Phil 2, 6.9-11.

---

†

16, 25: See the note on 10, 6. Here, possibly a reference to 15, 1-16 or 16, 21.

16, 30: The reference is seemingly to the fact that Jesus could anticipate their question in v 19. The disciples naively think they have the full understanding that is the climax of "the hour" of Jesus' death, resurrection, and ascension (25), but the only part of the hour that is at hand for them is their share in the passion (32).

16, 32: *You will be scattered:* cf Mk 14, 27 and Mt 26, 31, where both cite Zec 13, 7 about the sheep being dispersed.

17, 1-26: Climax of the last discourse(s). Since the sixteenth century, this chapter has been called the "high priestly prayer" of Jesus. He speaks as intercessor, with words addressed directly to the Father and not to the disciples, who supposedly only overhear. Yet the prayer is one of petition, for immediate (6-19) and future (20-21) disciples. Many phrases reminiscent of the Lord's Prayer occur. Although still in the world (13), Jesus looks on his earthly ministry as a thing of the past (4.12). Whereas Jesus has up to this time stated that the disciples could follow him (13, 33.36), now he wishes tnem to be with him in union with the Father (12-14).

17, 1: The action of looking up to heaven and the address *Father* are typical of Jesus at prayer; cf 11, 41 and Lk 11, 2.

17, 2: Another possible interpretation is to treat the first line of the verse as parenthetical and the second as an appositive to the clause that ends v 1: *so that your son may glorify you (just as . . . all people), so that he may give eternal life. . . .*

17, 3: This verse was clearly added in the editing of the gospel as a reflection on the preceding verse; Jesus nowhere else refers to himself as Jesus Christ.

17, 6: *I revealed your name:* perhaps the name *I AM;* cf 8, 24. 28.58; 13, 19.

9* I pray for them. I do not pray for the
world but for the ones you have given
me, because they are yours, 10* and ev-
erything of mine is yours and every-
thing of yours is mine, and I have been
glorified in them. 11 And now I will no
longer be in the world, but they are in
the world, while I am coming to you.
Holy Father, keep them in your name
that you have given me, so that they
may be one just as we are. 12* When I
was with them I protected them in your
name that you gave me, and I guarded
them, and none of them was lost except
the son of destruction, in order that the
scripture might be fulfilled. 13* But now
I am coming to you. I speak this in the
world so that they may share my joy
completely. 14* I gave them your word,
and the world hated them, because they
do not belong to the world any more
than I belong to the world. 15*† I do not
ask that you take them out of the world
but that you keep them from the evil
one. 16 They do not belong to the world
any more than I belong to the world.
17* Consecrate them in the truth. Your
word is truth. 18* As you sent me into
the world, so I sent them into the world.
19 And I consecrate myself for them, so
that they also may be consecrated in
truth.

20 "I pray not only for them, but also
for those who will believe in me through
their word, 21* so that they may all be
one, as you, Father, are in me and I in
you, that they also may be in us, that
the world may believe that you sent me.
22 And I have given them the glory you
gave me, so that they may be one, as
we are one, 23 I in them and you in me,
that they may be brought to perfection
as one, that the world may know that
you sent me, and that you loved them
even as you loved me. 24*† Father, they
are your gift to me. I wish that where I
am they also may be with me, that they
may see my glory that you gave me,
because you loved me before the foun-
dation of the world. 25* Righteous Fa-
ther, the world also does not know you,
but I know you, and they know that you
sent me. 26† I made known to them your
name and I will make it known, that the
love with which you loved me may be
in them and I in them."

CHAPTER 18

Jesus Arrested.† 1*† When he had
said this, Jesus went out with his disci-
ples across the Kidron valley to where
there was a garden, into which he and
his disciples entered. 2 Judas his be-
trayer also knew the place, because Je-
sus had often met there with his
disciples. 3*† So Judas got a band of sol-
diers and guards from the chief priests
and the Pharisees and went there with
lanterns, torches, and weapons. 4 Jesus,
knowing everything that was going to
happen to him, went out and said to
them, "Whom are you looking for?"
5† They answered him, "Jesus the
Nazorean." He said to them, "I AM."
Judas his betrayer was also with them.
6 When he said to them, "I AM," they
turned away and fell to the ground.
7 So he again asked them, "Whom are
you looking for?" They said, "Jesus the
Nazorean." 8 Jesus answered, "I told
you that I AM. So if you are looking for
me, let these men go." 9*† This was to
fulfill what he had said, "I have not lost
any of those you gave me." 10† Then Si-
mon Peter, who had a sword, drew it,
struck the high priest's slave, and cut
off his right ear. The slave's name was
Malchus. 11*† Jesus said to Peter, "Put
your sword into its scabbard. Shall I not
drink the cup that the Father gave me?"

12* So the band of soldiers, the tri-
bune, and the Jewish guards seized Je-

JOHN

*

9: 17, 20.
10: 16, 15; 2 Thes 1, 10.12.
12: 13, 18; 18, 9; Ps 41, 10; Mt 26, 24; Acts 1, 16.
13: 15, 11.
14: 15, 19.
15: Mt 6, 13; 2 Thes 3, 3; 1 Jn 5, 18.
17: 1 Pt 1, 22
18: 20, 21-22.
21: 10, 30; 14, 10-11.20.
24: 14, 3; 1 Thes 4, 17.
25: 1, 10.
18, 1: 2 Sm 15, 23; Mt 26, 30.36; Mk 14, 26.32; Lk 22, 39.
3: Mt 26, 47-51; Mk 14, 43-44; Lk 22, 47.
9: 6, 39; 10, 28; 17, 12.
11: Mt 20, 22; 26, 39; Mk 10, 38; Lk 22, 42.
12-14: Mt 26, 57-58; Mk 14, 53-54; Lk 22, 54-55.

†

17, 15: Note the resemblance to the petition of the Lord's Prayer, "deliver us from the evil one." Both probably refer to the devil rather than to abstract evil.

17, 24: *Where I am:* Jesus prays for the believers ultimately to join him in heaven. Then they will not see his glory as in a mirror but clearly (2 Cor 3, 18; 1 Jn 3, 2).

17, 26: *I will make it known:* through the Advocate.

18, 1-14: John does not mention the agony in the garden and the kiss of Judas, nor does he identify the place as Gethsemane or the Mount of Olives.

18, 1: *Jesus went out:* see 14, 31, where it seems he is leaving the supper room. *Kidron valley:* literally, "the winter-flowing Kidron"; this wadi has water only during the winter rains.

18, 3: *Band of soldiers:* seems to refer to Roman troops, either the full cohort of 600 men (1/10 of a legion), or more likely the maniple of 200 under their tribune (12). In this case, John is hinting at Roman collusion in the action against Jesus before he was brought to Pilate. The lanterns and torches may be symbolic of the hour of darkness.

18, 5: *Nazorean:* the form found in Mt 26, 71 (see the note on Mt 2, 23) is here used, not *Nazarene* of Mark. *I AM:* or "I am he," but probably intended by the evangelist as an expression of divinity (cf their appropriate response in 6); see the note on 8, 24. John sets the confusion of the arresting party against the background of Jesus' divine majesty.

18, 9: The citation may refer to 6, 39; 10, 28; or 17, 12.

18, 10: Only John gives the names of the two antagonists; both John and Luke mention the right ear.

18, 11: The theme of the cup is found in the synoptic account of the agony (Mk 14, 36 and parallels).

sus, bound him, 13*† and brought him
to Annas first. He was the father-in-law
of Caiaphas, who was high priest that
year. 14* It was Caiaphas who had coun-
seled the Jews that it was better that
one man should die rather than the peo-
ple.

Peter's First Denial. † 15* Simon Peter
and another disciple followed Jesus.
Now the other disciple was known to the
high priest, and he entered the court-
yard of the high priest with Jesus.
16 But Peter stood at the gate outside.
So the other disciple, the acquaintance
of the high priest, went out and spoke
to the gatekeeper and brought Peter in.
17 Then the maid who was the gate-
keeper said to Peter, "You are not one
of this man's disciples, are you?" He
said, "I am not." 18 Now the slaves and
the guards were standing around a
charcoal fire that they had made, be-
cause it was cold, and were warming
themselves. Peter was also standing
there keeping warm.

The Inquiry before Annas. 19* The
high priest questioned Jesus about his
disciples and about his doctrine.
20*† Jesus answered him, "I have spo-
ken publicly to the world. I have always
taught in a synagogue or in the temple
area where all the Jews gather, and in
secret I have said nothing. 21 Why ask
me? Ask those who heard me what I
said to them. They know what I said."
22* When he had said this, one of the
temple guards standing there struck
Jesus and said, "Is this the way you an-
swer the high priest?" 23 Jesus an-
swered him, "If I have spoken wrongly,
testify to the wrong; but if I have spoken
rightly, why do you strike me?"
24*† Then Annas sent him bound to
Caiaphas the high priest.

Peter Denies Jesus Again. 25* Now
Simon Peter was standing there keep-
ing warm. And they said to him, "You
are not one of his disciples, are you?"
He denied it and said, "I am not."
26 One of the slaves of the high priest,
a relative of the one whose ear Peter
had cut off, said, "Didn't I see you in
the garden with him?" 27† Again Peter
denied it. And immediately the cock
crowed.

The Trial before Pilate. 28*† Then
they brought Jesus from Caiaphas to
the praetorium. It was morning. And
they themselves did not enter the prae-
torium, in order not to be defiled so that
they could eat the Passover. 29 So Pilate
came out to them and said, "What
charge do you bring [against] this
man?" 30 They answered and said to
him, "If he were not a criminal, we
would not have handed him over to
you." 31† At this, Pilate said to them,
"Take him yourselves, and judge him
according to your law." The Jews an-
swered him, "We do not have the right
to execute anyone," 32*† in order that
the word of Jesus might be fulfilled that
he said indicating the kind of death he
would die. 33 So Pilate went back into
the praetorium and summoned Jesus
and said to him, "Are you the King of
the Jews?" 34 Jesus answered, "Do you
say this on your own or have others told
you about me?" 35* Pilate answered, "I
am not a Jew, am I? Your own nation
and the chief priests handed you over
to me. What have you done?" 36* Jesus
answered, "My kingdom does not be-
long to this world. If my kingdom did
belong to this world, my attendants
[would] be fighting to keep me from be-
ing handed over to the Jews. But as it
is, my kingdom is not here." 37*† So Pi-
late said to him, "Then you are a king?"
Jesus answered, "You say I am a king.
For this I was born and for this I came
into the world, to testify to the truth.
Everyone who belongs to the truth lis-
tens to my voice." 38* Pilate said to him,
"What is truth?"

---

*

13: Lk 3, 2.
14: 11, 49-50.
15-18: Mt 26, 58.69-70; Mk 14, 54.66-68; Lk 22, 54-57.
19-24: Mt 26, 59-66; Mk 14, 55-64; Lk 22, 66-71.
20: 6, 59; 7, 14.26; Is 48, 16; Mt 26, 55; Mk 4, 23; Lk 19, 47; 22, 53.
22: Acts 23, 2.
24: Mt 26, 57.
25-27: Mt 26, 71-75; Mk 14, 69-72; Lk 22, 58-62.
28-38a: Mt 27, 1-2.11-25; Mk 15, 1-5; Lk 23, 1-5.
32: 3, 14; 8, 28; 12, 32-33.
35: 1, 11.
36: 1, 10; 8, 23.
37: 8, 47; 1 Tm 6, 13.
38b-40: Mt 27, 15-26; Mk 15, 6-15; Lk 23, 18-25; Acts 3, 14.

---

†

18, 13: *Annas:* only John mentions an inquiry before Annas; cf 16.19-24; see the note on Lk 3, 2. It is unlikely that this nighttime interrogation before Annas is the same as the trial before Caiaphas placed by Matthew and Mark at night and by Luke in the morning.

18, 15-16: *Another disciple . . . the other disciple:* see the note on 13, 23.

18, 20: *I have always taught . . . in the temple area:* cf Mk 14, 49 for a similar statement.

18, 24: *Caiaphas:* see Mt 26, 3.57; Lk 3, 2; and the notes there. John may leave room here for the trial before Caiaphas described in the synoptic gospels.

18, 27: Cockcrow was the third Roman division of the night, lasting from midnight to 3 a.m.

18, 28: *Praetorium:* see the note on Mt 27, 27. *Morning:* literally, "the early hour," or fourth Roman division of the night, 3 to 6 a.m. *The Passover:* the synoptic gospels give the impression that the Thursday night supper was the Passover meal (Mk 14, 12); for John that meal is still to be eaten Friday night.

18, 31: *We do not have the right to execute anyone:* only John gives this reason for their bringing Jesus to Pilate. Jewish sources are not clear on the competence of the Sanhedrin at this period to sentence and to execute for political crimes.

18, 32: The Jewish punishment for blasphemy was stoning (Lv 24, 16). In coming to the Romans to ensure that Jesus would be crucified, the Jewish authorities fulfilled his prophecy that he would be *exalted* (3, 14; 12, 32-33). There is some historical evidence, however, for Jews crucifying Jews.

18, 37: *You say I am a king:* see Mt 26, 64 for a similar response to the high priest. It is at best a reluctant affirmative.

When he had said this, he again went
out to the Jews and said to them, "I find
no guilt in him. 39† But you have a cus-
tom that I release one prisoner to you
at Passover. Do you want me to release
to you the King of the Jews?" 40† They
cried out again, "Not this one but Bar-
abbas!" Now Barabbas was a revolu-
tionary.

CHAPTER 19

1*† Then Pilate took Jesus and had
him scourged. 2 And the soldiers wove
a crown out of thorns and placed it on
his head, and clothed him in a purple
cloak, 3 and they came to him and said,
"Hail, King of the Jews!" And they
struck him repeatedly. 4* Once more Pi-
late went out and said to them, "Look,
I am bringing him out to you, so that
you may know that I find no guilt in
him." 5* So Jesus came out, wearing the
crown of thorns and the purple cloak.
And he said to them, "Behold, the
man!" 6* When the chief priests and the
guards saw him they cried out, "Crucify
him, crucify him!" Pilate said to them,
"Take him yourselves and crucify him.
I find no guilt in him." 7*† The Jews an-
swered, "We have a law, and according
to that law he ought to die, because he
made himself the Son of God." 8 Now
when Pilate heard this statement, he
became even more afraid, 9* and went
back into the praetorium and said to Je-
sus, "Where are you from?" Jesus did
not answer him. 10 So Pilate said to him,
"Do you not speak to me? Do you not
know that I have power to release you
and I have power to crucify you?"
11* Jesus answered [him], "You would
have no power over me if it had not been
given to you from above. For this reason
the one who handed me over to you has
the greater sin." 12*† Consequently, Pi-
late tried to release him; but the Jews
cried out, "If you release him, you are
not a Friend of Caesar. Everyone who
makes himself a king opposes Caesar."
13† When Pilate heard these words he
brought Jesus out and seated him on the
judge's bench in the place called Stone
Pavement, in Hebrew, Gabbatha.
14† It was preparation day for Passover,
and it was about noon. And he said to
the Jews, "Behold, your king!" 15 They
cried out, "Take him away, take him
away! Crucify him!" Pilate said to them,
"Shall I crucify your king?" The chief
priests answered, "We have no king but
Caesar." 16† Then he handed him over
to them to be crucified.

The Crucifixion of Jesus. So they took
Jesus, 17*† and carrying the cross him-
self he went out to what is called the
Place of the Skull, in Hebrew, Golgotha.
18 There they crucified him, and with
him two others, one on either side,
with Jesus in the middle. 19† Pilate also
had an inscription written and put on
the cross. It read, "Jesus the Nazorean,
the King of the Jews." 20 Now many
of the Jews read this inscription, be-
cause the place where Jesus was cruci-
fied was near the city; and it was written
in Hebrew, Latin, and Greek. 21* So the
chief priests of the Jews said to Pilate,
"Do not write 'The King of the Jews,'
but that he said, 'I am the King of the
Jews.'" 22 Pilate answered, "What I
have written, I have written."
23*† When the soldiers had crucified

*

19, 1-16: Mt 27, 27-31; Mk 15, 16-20; Lk 23, 13-25.
4: 18, 38.
5: Is 52, 14.
6: 18, 31; 19, 15.
7: 10, 33-36; Lv 24, 16.
9: 7, 28.
11: 3, 27; 10, 18; Rom 13, 1.
12: Acts 17, 7.
17-22: Mt 27, 32-37; Mk 15, 21-26; Lk 23, 26-35.
21: 18, 33; Lk 19, 14.
23-27: Mt 27, 38-44; Mk 15, 27-32; Lk 23, 36-43.
23-24: Ps 22, 19; Mt 27, 35; Mk 15, 24; Lk 23, 34.

†

18, 39: See the note on Mt 27, 15.

18, 40: *Barabbas:* see the note on Mt 27, 16-17. *Revolutionary:* a guerrilla warrior fighting for nationalistic aims, though the term can also denote a robber. See the note on Mt 27, 38.

19, 1: Luke places the mockery of Jesus at the midpoint in the trial when Jesus was sent to Herod. Mark and Matthew place the scourging and mockery at the end of the trial after the sentence of death. Scourging was an integral part of the crucifixion penalty.

19, 7: *Made himself the Son of God:* this question was not raised in John's account of the Jewish interrogations of Jesus as it was in the synoptic account. Nevertheless, see 5, 18; 8, 53; 10, 36.

19, 12: *Friend of Caesar:* a Roman honorific title bestowed upon high-ranking officials for merit.

19, 13: *Seated him:* others translate "(Pilate) sat down." In John's thought, Jesus is the real judge of the world, and John may here be portraying him seated on the judgment bench. *Stone Pavement:* in Greek *lithostrotos;* under the fortress Antonia, one of the conjectured locations of the praetorium, a massive stone pavement has been excavated. *Gabbatha* (Aramaic rather than Hebrew) probably means "ridge, elevation."

19, 14: *Noon:* Mk 15, 25 has Jesus crucified "at the third hour," which means either 9 a.m. or the period from 9 to 12. Noon, the time when, according to John, Jesus was sentenced to death, was the hour at which the priests began to slaughter Passover lambs in the temple; see Jn 1, 29.

19, 16: *He handed him over to them to be crucified:* in context this would seem to mean "handed him over to the chief priests." Lk 23, 25 has a similar ambiguity. There is a polemic tendency in the gospels to place the guilt of the crucifixion on the Jewish authorities and to exonerate the Romans from blame. But John later mentions the Roman soldiers (23), and it was to these soldiers that Pilate handed Jesus over.

19, 17: *Carrying the cross himself:* a different picture from that of the synoptics, especially Lk 23, 26, where Simon of Cyrene is made to carry the cross, walking behind Jesus. In John's theology, Jesus remained in complete control and master of his destiny (cf 10, 18). *Place of the Skull:* the Latin word for skull is *Calvaria;* hence "Calvary." *Golgotha* is actually an Aramaic rather than a Hebrew word.

19, 19: The inscription differs with slightly different words in each of the four gospels. John's form is fullest and gives the equivalent of the Latin *INRI = Iesus Nazarenus Rex Iudaeorum.* Only John mentions its polyglot character (20) and Pilate's role in keeping the title unchanged (21-22).

19, 23-25a: While all four gospels describe the soldiers casting lots to divide Jesus' garments (see the note on Mt 27, 35), only John quotes the underlying passage from Ps 22, 19, and only John sees each line of the poetic parallelism literally carried out in two separate actions (23a; 23b-24).

Jesus, they took his clothes and divided them into four shares, a share for each soldier. They also took his tunic, but the tunic was seamless, woven in one piece from the top down. [24] So they said to one another, "Let's not tear it, but cast lots for it to see whose it will be," in order that the passage of scripture might be fulfilled [that says]:

> "They divided my garments among them,
> and for my vesture they cast lots."

This is what the soldiers did. [25]*† Standing by the cross of Jesus were his mother and his mother's sister, Mary the wife of Clopas, and Mary of Magdala. [26]*† When Jesus saw his mother and the disciple there whom he loved, he said to his mother, "Woman, behold, your son." [27] Then he said to the disciple, "Behold, your mother." And from that hour the disciple took her into his home.

[28]*† After this, aware that everything was now finished, in order that the scripture might be fulfilled, Jesus said, "I thirst." [29]† There was a vessel filled with common wine. So they put a sponge soaked in wine on a sprig of hyssop and put it up to his mouth. [30]*† When Jesus had taken the wine, he said, "It is finished." And bowing his head, he handed over the spirit.

The Blood and Water. [31]* Now since it was preparation day, in order that the bodies might not remain on the cross on the sabbath, for the sabbath day of that week was a solemn one, the Jews asked Pilate that their legs be broken and they be taken down. [32] So the soldiers came and broke the legs of the first and then of the other one who was crucified with Jesus. [33] But when they came to Jesus and saw that he was already dead, they did not break his legs, [34]*† but one soldier thrust his lance into his side, and immediately blood and water flowed out. [35]*† An eyewitness has testified, and his testimony is true; he knows that he is speaking the truth, so that you also may [come to] believe. [36]* For this happened so that the scripture passage might be fulfilled:

> "Not a bone of it will be broken."

[37]* And again another passage says:

> "They will look upon him whom they have pierced."

The Burial of Jesus.† [38]* After this, Joseph of Arimathea, secretly a disciple of Jesus for fear of the Jews, asked Pilate if he could remove the body of Jesus. And Pilate permitted it. So he came and took his body. [39]* Nicodemus, the one who had first come to him at night, also came bringing a mixture of myrrh and aloes weighing about one hundred pounds. [40] They took the body of Jesus and bound it with burial cloths along with the spices, according to the Jewish burial custom. [41] Now in the place where he had been crucified there was a garden, and in the garden a new tomb, in which no one had yet been buried. [42] So they laid Jesus there because of the Jewish preparation day; for the tomb was close by.

*

25: Mt 27, 55; Mk 15, 40-41; Lk 8, 2; 23, 49.
26: 13, 23.
28-30: Mt 27, 45-56; Mk 15, 33-41; Lk 23, 44-49.
28: Pss 22, 16; 69, 22.
30: 4, 34; 10, 18; 17, 4; Lk 23, 46.
31: Ex 12, 16; Dt 21, 23.
34: Nm 20, 11; 1 Jn 5, 6.
35: 7, 37-39; 21, 24.
36: Ex 12, 46; Nm 9, 12; Ps 34, 21.
37: Nm 21, 9; Zec 12, 10; Rv 1, 7.
38-42: Mt 27, 57-60; Mk 15, 42-46; Lk 34, 50-54.
39: 3, 1-2; 7, 50; Ps 45, 9.

†

19, 25: It is not clear whether four women are meant, or three (i.e., *Mary the wife of Cl[e]opas* [cf Lk 24, 18] is in apposition with *his mother's sister*) or two (his mother and his mother's sister, i.e., Mary of Cl[e]opas and Mary of Magdala). Only John mentions the mother of Jesus here. The synoptics have a group of women looking on from a distance at the cross (Mk 15, 40).

19, 26-27: This scene has been interpreted literally, of Jesus' concern for his mother; and symbolically, e.g., in the light of the Cana story in ch 2 (the presence of the mother of Jesus, the address *woman*, and the mention of the *hour*) and of the upper room in ch 13 (the presence of the beloved disciple; the *hour*). Now that the hour has come (28), Mary (a symbol of the church?) is given a role as the mother of Christians (personified by the beloved disciple); or, as a representative of those seeking salvation, she is supported by the disciple who interprets Jesus' revelation; or Jewish and Gentile Christianity (or Israel and the Christian community) are reconciled.

19, 28: *The scripture . . . fulfilled:* either in the scene of vv 25-27, or in the *I thirst* of v 28. If the latter, Pss 22, 16 and 69, 22 deserve consideration.

19, 29: *Wine:* John does not mention the drugged wine, a narcotic that Jesus refused as the crucifixion began (Mk 15, 23), but only this final gesture of kindness at the end (Mk 15, 36). *Hyssop,* a small plant, is scarcely suitable for carrying a sponge (Mark mentions a reed) and may be a symbolic reference to the hyssop used to daub the blood of the paschal lamb on the doorpost of the Hebrews (Ex 12, 22).

19, 30: *Handed over the spirit:* there is a double nuance of dying (giving up the last breath or spirit) and that of passing on the holy Spirit; see 7, 39, which connects the giving of the Spirit with Jesus' glorious return to the Father, and 20, 22, where the author portrays the conferral of the Spirit.

19, 34-35: John probably emphasizes these verses to show the reality of Jesus' death, against the Docetist heretics. In the blood and water there may also be a symbolic reference to the Eucharist and baptism.

19, 35: *He knows:* it is not certain from the Greek that this *he* is the *eyewitness* of the first part of the sentence. *May [come to] believe:* see the note on 20, 31.

19, 38-42: In the first three gospels there is no anointing on Friday. In Mt and Lk, the women come to the tomb on Sunday morning precisely to anoint Jesus.

CHAPTER 20†

The Empty Tomb. † 1*† On the first
day of the week, Mary of Magdala came
to the tomb early in the morning, while
it was still dark, and saw the stone re-
moved from the tomb. 2† So she ran and
went to Simon Peter and to the other
disciple whom Jesus loved, and told
them, "They have taken the Lord from
the tomb, and we don't know where they
put him." 3† So Peter and the other dis-
ciple went out and came to the tomb.
4 They both ran, but the other disciple
ran faster than Peter and arrived at the
tomb first; 5 he bent down and saw the
burial cloths there, but did not go in.
6*† When Simon Peter arrived after
him, he went into the tomb and saw the
burial cloths there, 7* and the cloth that
had covered his head, not with the
burial cloths but rolled up in a separate
place. 8 Then the other disciple also
went in, the one who had arrived at the
tomb first, and he saw and believed.
9*† For they did not yet understand the
scripture that he had to rise from the
dead. 10 Then the disciples returned
home.

***The Appearance to Mary of Mag-
dala.*** † 11* But Mary stayed outside the
tomb weeping. And as she wept, she
bent over into the tomb 12 and saw two
angels in white sitting there, one at the
head and one at the feet where the body
of Jesus had been. 13 And they said to
her, "Woman, why are you weeping?"
She said to them, "They have taken my
Lord, and I don't know where they laid
him." 14* When she had said this, she
turned around and saw Jesus there, but
did not know it was Jesus. 15* Jesus said
to her, "Woman, why are you weeping?
Whom are you looking for?" She
thought it was the gardener and said
to him, "Sir, if you carried him away,
tell me where you laid him, and I will
take him." 16† Jesus said to her,
"Mary!" She turned and said to him in
Hebrew, "Rabbouni," which means
Teacher. 17*† Jesus said to her, "Stop
holding on to me, for I have not yet as-
cended to the Father. But go to my
brothers and tell them, 'I am going to
my Father and your Father, to my God
and your God.'" 18 Mary of Magdala
went and announced to the disciples, "I
have seen the Lord," and what he told
her.

Appearance to the Disciples. †
19*† On the evening of that first day of
the week, when the doors were locked,
where the disciples were, for fear of the
Jews, Jesus came and stood in their
midst and said to them, "Peace be with
you." 20*† When he had said this, he
showed them his hands and his side.
The disciples rejoiced when they saw
the Lord. 21*† [Jesus] said to them

*

20, 1-10: Mt 28, 1-10; Mk 16, 1-11; Lk 24, 1-12.
1: 19, 25.
6: Lk 24, 12.
7: 11, 44; 19, 40.
9: Acts 2, 26-27; 1 Cor 15, 4.
11-18: Mk 16, 9-11.
14: 21, 4; Mk 16, 12; Lk 24, 16; 1 Cor 15, 43-44.
15-17: Mt 28, 9-10.
17: Acts 1, 9.
19-23: Mt 28, 16-20; Mk 16, 14-18; Lk 24, 36-44.
20: 14, 27.
21: 17, 18; Mt 28, 19; Mk 16, 15; Lk 24, 47-48.

JOHN

†

20, 1-31: The risen Jesus reveals his glory and confers the Spirit. This story fulfills the basic need for testimony to the resurrection. What we have here is not a record but a series of single stories.

20, 1-10: The story of the empty tomb is found in both the Matthean and the Lucan traditions; John's version seems to be a fusion of the two.

20, 1: *Still dark:* according to Mark the sun had risen, Matthew describes it as "dawning," and Luke refers to early dawn. Mary sees the stone removed, not the empty tomb.

20, 2: Mary runs away, not directed by an angel/young man as in the synoptic accounts. The plural "we" in the second part of her statement might reflect a tradition of more women going to the tomb.

20, 3-10: The basic narrative is told of Peter alone in Lk 24, 12, a verse missing in important manuscripts and which may be borrowed from tradition similar to John. Cf also Lk 24, 24.

20, 6-8: Some special feature about the state of the burial cloths caused the beloved disciple to believe. Perhaps the details emphasized that the grave had not been robbed.

20, 9: Probably a general reference to the scriptures is intended, as in Lk 24, 26 and 1 Cor 15, 4. Some individual Old Testament passages suggested are Ps 16, 10; Hos 6, 2; Jon 2, 1.2.11.

20, 11-18: This appearance to Mary is found only in Jn, but cf Mt 28, 8-10 and Mk 16, 9-11.

20, 16: *Rabbouni:* Hebrew or Aramaic for "my master."

20, 17: *Stop holding on to me:* see Mt 28, 9, where the women take hold of his feet. *I have not yet ascended:* for John and many of the New Testament writers, the ascension in the theological sense of going to the Father to be glorified took place with the resurrection as one action. This scene in John dramatizes such an understanding, for by Easter night Jesus is glorified and can give the Spirit. Therefore his ascension takes place immediately after he has talked to Mary. In such a view, the ascension after forty days described in Acts 1, 1-11 would be simply a termination of earthly appearances or, perhaps better, an introduction to the conferral of the Spirit upon the early church, modeled on Elisha's being able to have a (double) share in the spirit of Elijah if he saw him being taken up (same verb as ascending) into heaven (2 Kgs 2, 9-12). *To my Father and your Father, to my God and your God:* this echoes Ru 1, 16: "Your people shall be my people, and your God my God." The Father of Jesus will now become the Father of the disciples because, once ascended, Jesus can give them the Spirit that comes from the Father and they can be reborn as God's children (3, 5). That is why he calls them *my brothers.*

20, 19-29: The appearances to the disciples, without or with Thomas (cf 11, 16; 14, 5), have rough parallels in the other gospels only for vv 19-23; cf Lk 24, 36-39; Mk 16, 14-18.

20, 19: *The disciples:* by implication from v 24, this means ten of the Twelve, presumably in Jerusalem. *Peace be with you:* although this could be an ordinary greeting, John intends here to echo 14, 27. The theme of rejoicing in v 20 echoes 16, 22.

20, 20: *Hands and . . . side:* Lk 24, 39-40 mentions "hands and feet," based on Ps 22, 17.

20, 21: By means of this sending, the Eleven were made apostles, that is, "those sent" (cf 17, 18), though John does not use the noun in reference to them (see the note on 13, 16). A solemn mission or "sending" is also the subject of the post-resurrection appearances to the Eleven in Mt 28, 19; Lk 24, 47; Mk 16, 15.

again, "Peace be with you. As the Fa-
ther has sent me, so I send you."
22*† And when he had said this, he
breathed on them and said to them,
"Receive the holy Spirit. 23*† Whose
sins you forgive are forgiven them, and
whose sins you retain are retained."

Thomas. 24 Thomas, called Didymus,
one of the Twelve, was not with them
when Jesus came. 25* So the other disci-
ples said to him, "We have seen the
Lord." But he said to them, "Unless I
see the mark of the nails in his hands
and put my finger into the nailmarks
and put my hand into his side, I will
not believe." 26* Now a week later his
disciples were again inside and Thomas
was with them. Jesus came, although
the doors were locked, and stood in
their midst and said, "Peace be with
you." 27 Then he said to Thomas, "Put
your finger here and see my hands, and
bring your hand and put it into my side,
and do not be unbelieving, but believe."
28*† Thomas answered and said to him,
"My Lord and my God!" 29*† Jesus said
to him, "Have you come to believe be-
cause you have seen me? Blessed are
those who have not seen and have be-
lieved."

Conclusion.† 30* Now Jesus did many
other signs in the presence of [his] dis-
ciples that are not written in this book.
31* But these are written that you may
[come to] believe that Jesus is the Mes-
siah, the Son of God, and that through
this belief you may have life in his
name.

IV: EPILOGUE THE RESURRECTION APPEARANCE IN GALILEE

CHAPTER 21

***The Appearance to the Seven
Disciples.***† 1* After this, Jesus revealed
himself again to his disciples at the Sea
of Tiberias. He revealed himself in this
way. 2† Together were Simon Peter,
Thomas called Didymus, Nathanael
from Cana in Galilee, Zebedee's sons,
and two others of his disciples.
3*† Simon Peter said to them, "I am go-
ing fishing." They said to him, "We also
will come with you." So they went out
and got into the boat, but that night they
caught nothing. 4* When it was already
dawn, Jesus was standing on the shore;
but the disciples did not realize that it
was Jesus. 5* Jesus said to them, "Chil-
dren, have you caught anything to eat?"
They answered him, "No." 6 So he said
to them, "Cast the net over the right side
of the boat and you will find some-
thing." So they cast it, and were not able
to pull it in because of the number of
fish. 7 So the disciple whom Jesus loved
said to Peter, "It is the Lord." When Si-
mon Peter heard that it was the Lord,
he tucked in his garment, for he was
lightly clad, and jumped into the sea.
8 The other disciples came in the boat,
for they were not far from shore, only
about a hundred yards, dragging the
net with the fish. 9*† When they climbed
out on shore, they saw a charcoal fire
with fish on it and bread. 10 Jesus said
to them, "Bring some of the fish you just
caught." 11*† So Simon Peter went over
and dragged the net ashore full of one
hundred fifty-three large fish. Even
though there were so many, the net was
not torn. 12† Jesus said to them, "Come,

*

22: Gn 2, 7; Ez 37, 9; 1 Cor 15, 45.
23: Mt 16, 19; 18, 18.
25: 1 Jn 1, 1.
26: 21, 14.
28: 1, 1.
29: 4, 48; Lk 1, 45; 1 Pt 1, 8.
30: 21, 25.
31: 3, 14.15; 1 Jn 5, 13.
21, 1: Mt 26, 32; 28, 7.
3: Mt 4, 18; Lk 5, 4-10.
4: 20, 14; Mt 28, 17; Lk 24, 16.
5: Lk 24, 41.
9: Lk 24, 41-43.
11: 2 Chr 2, 16.

†

20, 22: This action recalls Gn 2, 7, where God breathed on the first man and gave him life; just as Adam's life came from God, so now the disciples' new spiritual life comes from Jesus. Cf also the revivification of the dry bones in Ez 37. This is the author's version of Pentecost. Cf also the note on 19, 30.

20, 23: The Council of Trent defined that this power to forgive sins is exercised in the sacrament of penance. See Mt 16, 19 and 18, 18.

20, 28: *My Lord and my God:* this forms a literary inclusion with the first verse of the gospel: "and the Word was God."

20, 29: This verse is a beatitude on future generations; faith, not sight, matters.

20, 30-31: These verses are clearly a conclusion to the gospel and express its purpose. While many manuscripts read *come to believe,* possibly implying a missionary purpose for John's gospel, a small number of quite early ones read "continue to believe," suggesting that the audience consists of Christians whose faith is to be deepened by the book; cf 19, 35.

21, 1-23: There are many non-Johannine peculiarities in this chapter, some suggesting Lucan Greek style; yet this passage is closer to John than 7, 53—8, 11. There are many Johannine features as well. Its closest parallels in the synoptic gospels are found in Lk 5, 1-11 and Mt 14, 28-31. Perhaps the tradition was ultimately derived from John but preserved by some disciple other than the writer of the rest of the gospel. The appearances narrated seem to be independent of those in ch 20. Even if a later addition, the chapter was added before publication of the gospel, for it appears in all manuscripts.

21, 2: *Zebedee's sons:* the only reference to James and John in this gospel (but see the note on 1, 37). Perhaps the phrase was originally a gloss to identify, among the five, the *two others of his disciples.* The anonymity of the latter phrase is more Johannine (1, 35). The total of seven may suggest the community of the disciples in its fullness.

21, 3-6: This may be a variant of Luke's account of the catch of fish; see the note on Lk 5, 1-11.

21, 9.12-13: It is strange that Jesus already has fish since none have yet been brought ashore. This meal may have had eucharistic significance for early Christians since v 13 recalls Jn 6, 11, which uses the vocabulary of Jesus' action at the Last Supper; but see also the note on Mt 14, 19.

21, 11: The exact number 153 is probably meant to have a symbolic meaning in relation to the apostles' universal mission; Jerome claims that Greek zoologists catalogued 153 species of fish. Or 153 is the sum of the numbers from 1 to 17. Others invoke Ez 47, 10.

21, 12: *None . . . dared to ask him:* is Jesus' appearance strange to them? Cf Lk 24, 16; Mk 16, 12; Jn 20, 14. The disciples do, however, recognize Jesus *before* the breaking of the bread (opposed to Lk 24, 35).

have breakfast." And none of the disci-
ples dared to ask him, "Who are you?"
because they realized it was the Lord.
13* Jesus came over and took the bread
and gave it to them, and in like manner
the fish. 14*† This was now the third time
Jesus was revealed to his disciples after
being raised from the dead.

Jesus and Peter.† 15† When they had
finished breakfast, Jesus said to Simon
Peter, "Simon, son of John, do you love
me more than these?" He said to him,
"Yes, Lord, you know that I love you."
He said to him, "Feed my lambs."
16 He then said to him a second time,
"Simon, son of John, do you love me?"
He said to him, "Yes, Lord, you know
that I love you." He said to him, "Tend
my sheep." 17* He said to him the third
time, "Simon, son of John, do you love
me?" Peter was distressed that he had
said to him a third time, "Do you love
me?" and he said to him, "Lord, you
know everything; you know that I love
you." [Jesus] said to him, "Feed my
sheep. 18*† Amen, amen, I say to you,
when you were younger, you used to
dress yourself and go where you
wanted; but when you grow old, you will
stretch out your hands, and someone
else will dress you and lead you where
you do not want to go." 19* He said this
signifying by what kind of death he
would glorify God. And when he had
said this, he said to him, "Follow me."

The Beloved Disciple. 20* Peter
turned and saw the disciple following
whom Jesus loved, the one who had also
reclined upon his chest during the sup-
per and had said, "Master, who is the
one who will betray you?" 21 When Peter
saw him, he said to Jesus, "Lord, what
about him?" 22*† Jesus said to him,
"What if I want him to remain until I
come? What concern is it of yours? You
follow me." 23† So the word spread
among the brothers that that disciple
would not die. But Jesus had not told
him that he would not die, just "What
if I want him to remain until I come?
[What concern is it of yours?]"

Conclusion. 24*† It is this disciple who
testifies to these things and has written
them, and we know that his testimony
is true. 25* There are also many other
things that Jesus did, but if these were
to be described individually, I do not
think the whole world would contain the
books that would be written.

*

13: Lk 24, 42.
14: 20, 19.26.
17: 13, 37-38; 18, 15-18.25-27; Mt 26, 69-75; Mk 14, 66-72; Lk 22, 55-62.
18: Acts 21, 11.14; 2 Pt 1, 14.
19: 13, 36.
20: 13, 25.
22: Mt 16, 28.
24: 19, 35.
25: 20, 30.

†

21, 14: This verse connects chs 20 and 21; cf 20, 19.26.

21, 15-23: This section constitutes Peter's rehabilitation and emphasizes his role in the church.

21, 15-17: In these three verses there is a remarkable variety of synonyms: two different Greek verbs for *love* (see the note on 15, 13); two verbs for *feed/tend;* two nouns for *sheep;* two verbs for *know.* But apparently there is no difference of meaning. The threefold confession of Peter is meant to counteract his earlier threefold denial (18, 17.25.27). The First Vatican Council cited these verses in defining that Jesus after his resurrection gave Peter the jurisdiction of supreme shepherd and ruler over the whole flock.

21, 15: *More than these:* probably "more than these disciples do" rather than "more than you love them" or "more than you love these things [fishing, etc.]."

21, 18: Originally probably a proverb about old age, now used as a figurative reference to the crucifixion of Peter.

21, 22: *Until I come:* a reference to the parousia.

21, 23: This whole scene takes on more significance if the disciple is already dead. The death of the apostolic generation caused problems in the church because of a belief that Jesus was to have returned first. Loss of faith sometimes resulted; cf 2 Pt 3, 4.

21, 24: *Who . . . has written them:* this does not necessarily mean he wrote them with his own hand. The same expression is used in 19, 22 of Pilate, who certainly would not have written the inscription himself. *We know:* i.e., the Christian community; cf 1, 14.16.

The Acts of the

APOSTLES

ACTS

The Acts of the Apostles, the second volume of Luke's two-volume work, continues Luke's presentation of biblical history, describing how the salvation promised to Israel in the Old Testament and accomplished by Jesus has now under the guidance of the holy Spirit been extended to the Gentiles. This was accomplished through the divinely chosen representatives (10, 41) whom Jesus prepared during his historical ministry (1, 21-22) and commissioned after his resurrection as witnesses to all that he taught (l, 8; 10, 37-43; Lk 24, 48). Luke's preoccupation with the Christian community as the Spirit-guided bearer of the word of salvation rules out of his book detailed histories of the activity of most of the preachers. Only the main lines of the roles of Peter and Paul serve Luke's interest.

Peter was the leading member of the Twelve (1, 13.15), a miracle worker like Jesus in the gospel (3, 1-10; 5, 1-11.15; 9, 32-35.36-42), the object of divine care (5, 17-21; 12, 6-11), and the spokesman for the Christian community (2, 14-36; 3, 12-26; 4, 8-12; 5, 29-32; 10, 34-43; 15, 7-11), who, according to Luke, was largely responsible for the growth of the community in the early days (2, 4; 4, 4). Paul eventually joined the community at Antioch (11, 25-26), which subsequently commissioned him and Barnabas to undertake the spread of the gospel to Asia Minor. This missionary venture generally failed to win the Jews of the diaspora to the gospel but enjoyed success among the Gentiles (13, 14—14, 27).

Paul's refusal to impose the Mosaic law upon his Gentile converts provoked very strong objection among the Jewish Christians of Jerusalem (15, 1), but both Peter and James supported his position (15, 6-21). Paul's second and third missionary journeys (16, 36—21, 16) resulted in the same pattern of failure among the Jews generally but of some success among the Gentiles. Paul, like Peter, is presented as a miracle worker (14, 8-18; 19, 12; 20, 7-12; 28, 7-10) and the object of divine care (16, 25-31).

In Acts, Luke has provided a broad survey of the church's development from the resurrection of Jesus to Paul's first Roman imprisonment, the point at which the book ends. In telling this story, Luke describes the emergence of Christianity from its origins in Judaism to its position as a religion of worldwide status and appeal. Originally a Jewish Christian community in Jerusalem, the church was placed in circumstances impelling it to include within its membership people of other cultures: the Samaritans (8, 4-25), at first an occasional Gentile (8, 26-30; 10, 1-48), and finally the Gentiles on principle (11, 20-21). Fear on the part of the Jewish people that Christianity, particularly as preached to the Gentiles, threatened their own cultural heritage caused them to be suspicious of Paul's gospel (13, 42-45; 15, 1-5; 28, 17-24). The inability of Christian missionaries to allay this apprehension inevitably created a situation in which the gospel was preached more and more to the Gentiles. Toward the end of Paul's career, the Christian communities, with the exception of those in Palestine itself (9, 31), were mainly of Gentile membership. In tracing the emergence of Christianity from Judaism, Luke is insistent upon the prominence of Israel in the divine plan of salvation (see the note on 1, 26; see also 2, 5-6; 3, 13-15; 10, 36; 13, 16-41; 24, 14-15) and that the extension of salvation to the Gentiles has been a part of the divine plan from the beginning (see 15, 13-18; 26, 22-23).

In the development of the church from a Jewish Christian origin in Jerusalem, with its roots in Jewish religious tradition, to a series of Christian communities among the Gentiles of the Roman empire, Luke perceives the action of God in history laying open the heart of all humanity to the divine message of salvation. His approach to the history of the church is motivated by his theological interests.

His history of the apostolic church is the story of a Spirit-guided community and a Spirit-guided spread of the Word of God (1, 8). The travels of Peter and Paul are in reality the travels of the Word of God as it spreads from Jerusalem, the city of destiny for Jesus, to Rome, the capital of the civilized world of Luke's day. Nonetheless, the historical data he utilizes are of value for the understanding of the church's early life and development and as general background to the Pauline epistles. In the interpretation of Acts, care must be exercised to determine Luke's theological aims and interests and to evaluate his historical data without either exaggerating their literal accuracy or underestimating their factual worth.

Finally, an apologetic concern is evident throughout Acts. By stressing the continuity between Judaism and Christianity (13, 16-41; 23, 6-9; 24, 10-21; 26, 2-23), Luke argues that Christianity is deserving of the same toleration accorded Judaism by Rome. Part of Paul's defense before Roman authorities is to show that Christianity is not a disturber of the peace of the Roman Empire (24, 5.12-13; 25, 7-8). Moreover, when he stands before Roman authorities, he is declared innocent of any crime against the empire (18, 13-15; 23, 29; 25, 25-27; 26, 31-32). Luke tells his story with the hope that Christianity will be treated as fairly.

Concerning the date of Acts, see the Introduction to the Gospel according to Luke.

The principal divisions of the Acts of the Apostles are the following:

I: THE PREPARATION FOR THE CHRISTIAN MISSION

CHAPTER 1†

The Promise of the Spirit. 1* In the first book, Theophilus, I dealt with all that Jesus did and taught 2* until the day he was taken up, after giving instructions through the holy Spirit to the apostles whom he had chosen. 3*† He presented himself alive to them by many proofs after he had suffered, appearing to them during forty days and speaking about the kingdom of God. 4*† While meeting with them, he enjoined them not to depart from Jerusalem, but to wait for "the promise of the Father about which you have heard me speak; 5* for John baptized with water, but in a few days you will be baptized with the holy Spirit."

The Ascension of Jesus. 6† When they had gathered together they asked him,

*

1, 1: Lk 1, 1-4. 2: Mt 28, 19-20; Lk 24, 44-49; Jn 20, 22; 1 Tm 3, 16. 3: 10, 41; 13, 31. 4: Jn 14, 16.17.26. 5: 11, 16; Mt 3, 11; Mk 1, 8; Lk 3, 16; Jn 1, 26; Eph 1, 13.

†

1, 1-26: This introductory material (1-2) connects Acts with the Gospel of Luke, shows that the apostles were instructed by the risen Jesus (3-5), points out that the parousia or second coming in glory of Jesus will occur as certainly as his ascension occurred (6-11), and lists the members of the Twelve, stressing their role as a body of divinely mandated witnesses to his life, teaching, and resurrection (12-26).

1, 3: *Appearing to them during forty days:* Luke considered especially sacred the interval in which the appearances and instructions of the risen Jesus occurred and expressed it therefore in terms of the sacred number forty (cf Dt 8, 2). In his gospel, however, Luke connects the ascension of Jesus with the resurrection by describing the ascension on Easter Sunday evening (Lk 24, 50-53). What should probably be understood as one event (resurrection, glorification, ascension, sending of the Spirit—the paschal mystery) has been historicized by Luke when he writes of a visible ascension of Jesus after forty days and the descent of the Spirit at Pentecost. For Luke, the ascension marks the end of the appearances of Jesus except for the extraordinary appearance to Paul. With regard to Luke's understanding of salvation history, the ascension also marks the end of the time of Jesus (Lk 24, 50-53) and signals the beginning of the time of the church.

1, 4: *The promise of the Father:* the holy Spirit, as is clear from the next verse. This gift of the Spirit was first promised in Jesus' final instructions to his chosen witnesses in Luke's gospel (Lk 24, 49) and formed part of the continuing instructions of the risen Jesus on the kingdom of God, of which Luke speaks in v. 3.

1, 6: The question of the disciples implies that in believing Jesus to be the Christ (see the note on Lk 2, 11) they had expected him to be a political leader who would restore self-rule to Israel during his historical ministry. When this had not taken place, they ask if it is to take place at this time, the period of the church.

"Lord, are you at this time going to restore the kingdom to Israel?" 7*† He answered them, "It is not for you to know the times or seasons that the Father has established by his own authority. 8*† But you will receive power when the holy Spirit comes upon you, and you will be my witnesses in Jerusalem, throughout Judea and Samaria, and to the ends of the earth." 9* When he had said this, as they were looking on, he was lifted up, and a cloud took him from their sight. 10* While they were looking intently at the sky as he was going, suddenly two men dressed in white garments stood beside them. 11* They said, "Men of Galilee, why are you standing there looking at the sky? This Jesus who has been taken up from you into heaven will return in the same way as you have seen him going into heaven." 12* Then they returned to Jerusalem from the mount called Olivet, which is near Jerusalem, a sabbath day's journey away.

The First Community in Jerusalem. 13 When they entered the city they went to the upper room where they were staying, Peter and John and James and Andrew, Philip and Thomas, Bartholomew and Matthew, James son of Alphaeus, Simon the Zealot, and Judas son of James. 14* All these devoted themselves with one accord to prayer, together with some women, and Mary the mother of Jesus, and his brothers.

The Choice of Judas' Successor. 15 During those days Peter stood up in the midst of the brothers (there was a group of about one hundred and twenty persons in the one place). He said, 16* "My brothers, the scripture had to be fulfilled which the holy Spirit spoke beforehand through the mouth of David, concerning Judas, who was the guide for those who arrested Jesus. 17 He was numbered among us and was allotted a share in this ministry. 18*† He bought a parcel of land with the wages of his iniquity, and falling headlong, he burst open in the middle, and all his insides spilled out. 19 This became known to everyone who lived in Jerusalem, so that the parcel of land was called in their language 'Akeldama,' that is, Field of Blood. 20* For it is written in the Book of Psalms:

'Let his encampment become desolate,
and may no one dwell in it.'

And:

'May another take his office.'

21 Therefore, it is necessary that one of the men who accompanied us the whole time the Lord Jesus came and went among us, 22* beginning from the baptism of John until the day on which he was taken up from us, become with us a witness to his resurrection." 23 So they proposed two, Joseph called Barsabbas, who was also known as Justus, and Matthias. 24 Then they prayed, "You, Lord, who know the hearts of all, show which one of these two you have chosen 25 to take the place in this apostolic ministry from which Judas turned away to go to his own place." 26*† Then they gave lots to them, and the lot fell upon Matthias, and he was counted with the eleven apostles.

CHAPTER 2

The Coming of the Spirit.† 1* When the time for Pentecost was fulfilled, they were all in one place together. 2*† And suddenly there came from the sky a noise like a strong driving wind, and it filled the entire house in which they were. 3*† Then there appeared to them

*

7: Mt 24, 36; 1 Thes 5, 1-2.
8: 2, 1-13; 10, 39; Is 43, 10; Mt 28, 19; Lk 24, 47-48.
9: 2 Kgs 2, 11; Mk 16, 19; Lk 24, 51.
10: Jn 20, 17.
11: Lk 24, 51; Eph 4, 8-10; 1 Pt 3, 22; Rv 1, 7.
12-14: Lk 6, 14-16.
14: Lk 23, 49.
16: Ps 41, 10; Lk 22, 47.
18: Mt 27, 3-10.
20: Pss 69, 26; 109, 8; Jn 17, 12.
22: 1, 8-9; 10, 39.
26: Prv 16, 33.
2, 1: Lv 23, 15-21; Dt 16, 9-11.
2-3: Jn 3, 8.
3: Lk 3, 16.

†

1, 7: This verse echoes the tradition that the precise time of the parousia is not revealed to human beings; cf Mk 13, 32; I Thes 5, 1-3.

1, 8: Just as Jerusalem was the city of destiny in the Gospel of Luke (the place where salvation was accomplished), so here at the beginning of Acts, Jerusalem occupies a central position. It is the starting point for the mission of the Christian disciples to "the ends of the earth," the place where the apostles were situated and the doctrinal focal point in the early days of the community (15, 2.6). *The ends of the earth:* for Luke, this means Rome.

1, 18: Luke records a popular tradition about the death of Judas that differs from the one in Mt 27, 5, according to which Judas hanged himself. Here, although the text is not certain, Judas is depicted as purchasing a piece of property with the betrayal money and being killed on it in a fall.

1, 26: The need to replace Judas was probably dictated by the symbolism of the number twelve, recalling the twelve tribes of Israel. This symbolism also indicates that for Luke (see Lk 22, 30) the Christian church is a reconstituted Israel.

2, 1-41: Luke's pentecostal narrative consists of an introduction (1-13), a speech ascribed to Peter declaring the resurrection of Jesus and its messianic significance (14-36), and a favorable response from the audience (37-41). It is likely that the narrative telescopes events that took place over a period of time and on a less dramatic scale. The Twelve were not originally in a position to proclaim publicly the messianic office of Jesus without incurring immediate reprisal from those religious authorities in Jerusalem who had brought about Jesus' death precisely to stem the rising tide in his favor.

2, 2: *There came from the sky a noise like a strong driving wind:* wind and spirit are associated in Jn 3, 8. The sound of a great rush of wind would herald a new action of God in the history of salvation.

2, 3: *Tongues as of fire:* see Ex 19, 18 where fire symbolizes the presence of God to initiate the covenant on Sinai. Here the holy Spirit acts upon the apostles, preparing them to proclaim the new covenant with its unique gift of the Spirit (38).

tongues as of fire, which parted and
came to rest on each one of them.
4*† And they were all filled with the holy
Spirit and began to speak in different
tongues, as the Spirit enabled them to
proclaim.
5 Now there were devout Jews from
every nation under heaven staying in
Jerusalem. 6 At this sound, they gath-
ered in a large crowd, but they were
confused because each one heard them
speaking in his own language. 7* They
were astounded, and in amazement
they asked, "Are not all these people
who are speaking Galileans? 8 Then how
does each of us hear them in his own
native language? 9 We are Parthians,
Medes, and Elamites, inhabitants of
Mesopotamia, Judea and Cappadocia,
Pontus and Asia, 10 Phrygia and Pam-
phylia, Egypt and the districts of Libya
near Cyrene, as well as travelers from
Rome, 11* both Jews and converts to Ju-
daism, Cretans and Arabs, yet we hear
them speaking in our own tongues of
the mighty acts of God." 12 They were
all astounded and bewildered, and said
to one another, "What does this mean?"
13* But others said, scoffing, "They have
had too much new wine."

II: THE MISSION IN JERUSALEM

Peter's Speech at Pentecost.† 14 Then
Peter stood up with the Eleven, raised
his voice, and proclaimed to them, "You
who are Jews, indeed all of you staying
in Jerusalem. Let this be known to you,
and listen to my words. 15 These people
are not drunk, as you suppose, for it is
only nine o'clock in the morning.
16 No, this is what was spoken through
the prophet Joel:

17* 'It will come to pass in the last days,'
God says,
'that I will pour out a portion of
my spirit
upon all flesh.
Your sons and your daughters shall
prophesy,
your young men shall see visions,
your old men shall dream
dreams.
18 Indeed, upon my servants and my
handmaids
I will pour out a portion of my
spirit in those days,
and they shall prophesy.
19 And I will work wonders in the
heavens above
and signs on the earth below:
blood, fire, and a cloud of
smoke.
20 The sun shall be turned to darkness,
and the moon to blood,
before the coming of the great
and splendid day of the Lord,
21* and it shall be that everyone shall
be saved who calls on the name
of the Lord.'

22* You who are Israelites, hear these
words. Jesus the Nazorean was a man
commended to you by God with mighty
deeds, wonders, and signs, which God
worked through him in your midst, as
you yourselves know. 23* This man, de-
livered up by the set plan and fore-
knowledge of God, you killed, using
lawless men to crucify him. 24* But God
raised him up, releasing him from the
throes of death, because it was impossi-
ble for him to be held by it. 25* For David
says of him:

'I saw the Lord ever before me,
with him at my right hand I shall
not be disturbed.
26 Therefore my heart has been glad
and my tongue has exulted;
my flesh, too, will dwell in hope,
27* because you will not abandon my
soul to the netherworld,
nor will you suffer your holy one
to see corruption.
28 You have made known to me the
paths of life;
you will fill me with joy in your
presence.'

29 My brothers, one can confidently say
to you about the patriarch David that
he died and was buried, and his tomb
is in our midst to this day. 30* But since
he was a prophet and knew that God
had sworn an oath to him that he would
set one of his descendants upon his
throne, 31* he foresaw and spoke of the
resurrection of the Messiah, that nei-
ther was he abandoned to the nether-
world nor did his flesh see corruption.
32 God raised this Jesus; of this we are
all witnesses. 33*† Exalted at the right
hand of God, he received the promise
of the holy Spirit from the Father and
poured it forth, as you [both] see and
hear. 34* For David did not go up into
heaven, but he himself said:

*

4: 1, 5; 4, 31; 8, 15.17; 10, 44; 11, 15-16; 15, 8; 19, 6; Ps 104, 30; Jn 20, 33.
7: 1, 11.
11: 10, 46.
13: 1 Cor 14, 23.
17: Is 2, 2; 44, 3; Jl 3, 1-5.
21: Rom 10, 13.
22: 10, 38; Lk 24, 19.
23: 1 Thes 2, 15.
24: 13, 34.
25-28: Ps 16, 8-11.
27: 13, 35.
30: 2 Sm 7, 12; Ps 132, 11.
31: 13, 35; Ps 16, 10.
33: 1, 4-5.
34-35: Ps 110, 1.

†

2, 4: *To speak in different tongues:* ecstatic prayer in praise of God, interpreted in vv 6 and 11 as speaking in foreign languages, symbolizing the worldwide mission of the church.

2, 14-36: The first of six discourses in Acts (along with 3, 12-26; 4, 8-12; 5, 29-32; 10, 34-43; 13, 16-41) dealing with the resurrection of Jesus and its messianic import. Five of these are attributed to Peter, the final one to Paul. Modern scholars term these discourses in Acts the "kerygma," the Greek word for proclamation (cf I Cor 15, 11).

2, 33: *At the right hand of God:* or "by the right hand of God."

'The Lord said to my Lord,
"Sit at my right hand
35 until I make your enemies your
footstool." '

36* Therefore let the whole house of Is-
rael know for certain that God has
made him both Lord and Messiah, this
Jesus whom you crucified."
37* Now when they heard this, they
were cut to the heart, and they asked
Peter and the other apostles, "What are
we to do, my brothers?" 38*† Peter
[said] to them, "Repent and be bap-
tized, every one of you, in the name of
Jesus Christ for the forgiveness of your
sins; and you will receive the gift of the
holy Spirit. 39* For the promise is made
to you and to your children and to all
those far off, whomever the Lord our
God will call." 40* He testified with
many other arguments, and was ex-
horting them, "Save yourselves from
this corrupt generation." 41* Those who
accepted his message were baptized,
and about three thousand persons were
added that day.
Communal Life.† 42* They devoted
themselves to the teaching of the apos-
tles and to the communal life, to the
breaking of the bread and to the pray-
ers. 43* Awe came upon everyone, and
many wonders and signs were done
through the apostles. 44* All who be-
lieved were together and had all things
in common; 45 they would sell their
property and possessions and divide
them among all according to each one's
need. 46 Every day they devoted them-
selves to meeting together in the temple
area and to breaking bread in their
homes. They ate their meals with exul-
tation and sincerity of heart, 47 praising
God and enjoying favor with all the peo-
ple. And every day the Lord added to
their number those who were being
saved.

CHAPTER 3

Cure of a Crippled Beggar.† 1† Now
Peter and John were going up to the
temple area for the three o'clock hour
of prayer. 2* And a man crippled from
birth was carried and placed at the gate
of the temple called "the Beautiful
Gate" every day to beg for alms from
the people who entered the temple.
3 When he saw Peter and John about to
go into the temple, he asked for alms.
4 But Peter looked intently at him, as
did John, and said, "Look at us."
5 He paid attention to them, expecting
to receive something from them.
6*† Peter said, "I have neither silver nor
gold, but what I do have I give you: in
the name of Jesus Christ the Nazorean,
[rise and] walk." 7 Then Peter took him
by the right hand and raised him up,
and immediately his feet and ankles
grew strong. 8* He leaped up, stood, and
walked around, and went into the tem-
ple with them, walking and jumping
and praising God. 9 When all the people
saw him walking and praising God,
10 they recognized him as the one who
used to sit begging at the Beautiful Gate
of the temple, and they were filled with
amazement and astonishment at what
had happened to him.
Peter's Speech. 11* As he clung to Pe-
ter and John, all the people hurried in
amazement toward them in the portico
called "Solomon's Portico." 12* When
Peter saw this, he addressed the people,
"You Israelites, why are you amazed at
this, and why do you look so intently
at us as if we had made him walk by

*

36: 9, 22; Rom 10, 9; Phil 2, 11.
37: Lk 3, 10.
38: 3, 19; 16, 31; Lk 3, 3.
39: Is 57, 19; Jl 3, 5; Eph 2, 17.
40: Dt 32, 5; Ps 78, 8; Lk 9, 41; Phil 2, 15.
41: 2, 47; 4, 4; 5, 14; 6, 7; 11, 21.24; 21, 20.
42-47: 4, 32-35.
42: 1, 14; 6, 4.
43: 5, 12-16.
44: 4, 32.34-35.
3, 2-8: 14, 8-10.
6: 4, 10.
8: Is 35, 6; Lk 7, 22.
11: 5, 12; Jn 10, 23.
12: 14, 15.

†

2, 38: *Repent and be baptized:* repentance is a positive concept, a change of mind and heart toward God reflected in the actual goodness of one's life. It is in accord with the apostolic teaching derived from Jesus (42) and ultimately recorded in the four gospels. Luke presents baptism in Acts as the expected response to the apostolic preaching about Jesus and associates it with the conferring of the Spirit (1, 5; 10, 44-48; 11, 16).

2, 42-47: The first of three summary passages (along with 4, 32-37 and 5, 12-16) that outline, somewhat idyllically, the chief characteristics of the Jerusalem community: adherence to the teachings of the Twelve and the centering of its religious life in the eucharistic liturgy (42); a system of distribution of goods that led wealthier Christians to sell their possessions when the needs of the community's poor required it (44 and the note on 4, 32-37); and continued attendance at the temple, since in this initial stage there was little or no thought of any dividing line between Christianity and Judaism (46).

3, 1—4, 31: This section presents a series of related events: the dramatic cure of a lame beggar (3, 1-10) produces a large audience for the kerygmatic discourse of Peter (3, 11-26). The Sadducees, taking exception to the doctrine of resurrection, have Peter, John, and apparently the beggar as well, arrested (4, 1-4) and brought to trial before the Sanhedrin. The issue concerns the authority by which Peter and John publicly teach religious doctrine in the temple (4, 5-7). Peter replies with a brief summary of the kerygma, implying that his authority is prophetic (4, 8-12). The court warns the apostles to abandon their practice of invoking prophetic authority in the name of Jesus (4, 13-18). When Peter and John reply that the prophetic role cannot be abandoned to satisfy human objections, the court nevertheless releases them, afraid to do otherwise since the beggar, lame from birth and over forty years old, is a well-known figure in Jerusalem and the facts of his cure are common property (4, 19-22). The narrative concludes with a prayer of the Christian community imploring divine aid against threats of persecution (4, 23-31).

3, 1: *For the three o'clock hour of prayer:* literally, "at the ninth hour of prayer." With the day beginning at 6 a.m., the ninth hour would be 3 p.m.

3, 6-10: The miracle has a dramatic cast; it symbolizes the saving power of Christ and leads the beggar to enter the temple, where he hears Peter's proclamation of salvation through Jesus.

our own power or piety? 13*† The God
of Abraham, [the God] of Isaac, and
[the God] of Jacob, the God of our an-
cestors, has glorified his servant Jesus
whom you handed over and denied in
Pilate's presence, when he had decided
to release him. 14*† You denied the Holy
and Righteous One and asked that a
murderer be released to you. 15*† The
author of life you put to death, but God
raised him from the dead; of this we are
witnesses. 16 And by faith in his name,
this man, whom you see and know, his
name has made strong, and the faith
that comes through it has given him this
perfect health, in the presence of all of
you. 17*† Now I know, brothers, that you
acted out of ignorance, just as your
leaders did; 18*† but God has thus
brought to fulfillment what he had an-
nounced beforehand through the mouth
of all the prophets, that his Messiah
would suffer. 19* Repent, therefore, and
be converted, that your sins may be
wiped away, 20† and that the Lord may
grant you times of refreshment and
send you the Messiah already ap-
pointed for you, Jesus, 21† whom heaven
must receive until the times of universal
restoration of which God spoke through
the mouth of his holy prophets from of
old. 22*† For Moses said:

'A prophet like me will the Lord,
your God, raise up for you
from among your own kinsmen;
to him you shall listen in all that he
may say to you.
23* Everyone who does not listen to that
prophet
will be cut off from the people.'

24 Moreover, all the prophets who spoke,
from Samuel and those afterwards, also
announced these days. 25* You are the
children of the prophets and of the cov-
enant that God made with your ances-
tors when he said to Abraham, 'In your
offspring all the families of the earth
shall be blessed.' 26* For you first, God
raised up his servant and sent him to
bless you by turning each of you from
your evil ways."

CHAPTER 4

1† While they were still speaking to
the people, the priests, the captain of
the temple guard, and the Sadducees
confronted them, 2* disturbed that they
were teaching the people and proclaim-
ing in Jesus the resurrection of the
dead. 3 They laid hands on them and put
them in custody until the next day,
since it was already evening. 4 But
many of those who heard the word
came to believe and [the] number of
men grew to [about] five thousand.

Before the Sanhedrin. 5 On the next
day, their leaders, elders, and scribes
were assembled in Jerusalem, 6 with
Annas the high priest, Caiaphas, John,
Alexander, and all who were of the
high-priestly class. 7 They brought
them into their presence and ques-

*

13: Ex 3, 6.15; Is 52, 13; Lk 23, 14-25.
14: Mt 27, 20-21; Mk 15, 11; Lk 23, 18; Jn 18, 40.
15: 4, 10; 5, 31 / 1, 8; 2, 32.
17: 13, 27; Lk 23, 34; 1 Cor 2, 8; 1 Tm 1, 13.
18: Lk 18, 31.
19: 2, 38.
22: 7, 37; Dt 18, 15.18.
23: Lv 23, 29; Dt 18, 19.
25: Gn 12, 3; 18, 18; 22, 18; Sir 44, 19-21; Gal 3, 8-9.
26: 13, 46; Rom 1, 16.
4, 2: 23, 6-8; 24, 21.

†

3, 13: *Has glorified:* through the resurrection and ascension of Jesus, God reversed the judgment against him on the occasion of his trial. *Servant:* the Greek word can also be rendered as "son" or even "child" here and also in 3, 26; 4, 25 (applied to David); 4, 27; and 4, 30. Scholars are of the opinion, however, that the original concept reflected in the words identified Jesus with the suffering Servant of the Lord of Is 52, 13—53, 12.

3, 14: *The Holy and Righteous One:* so designating Jesus emphasizes his special relationship to the Father (see Lk 1, 35; 4, 34) and emphasizes his sinlessness and religious dignity that are placed in sharp contrast with the guilt of those who rejected him in favor of Barabbas.

3, 15: *The author of life:* other possible translations of the Greek title are "leader of life" or "pioneer of life." The title clearly points to Jesus as the source and originator of salvation.

3, 17: *Ignorance:* a Lucan motif, explaining away the actions not only of the people but also of their leaders in crucifying Jesus. On this basis the presbyters in Acts could continue to appeal to the Jews in Jerusalem to believe in Jesus, even while affirming their involvement in his death because they were unaware of his messianic dignity. See also 13, 27 and Lk 23, 34.

3, 18: *Through the mouth of all the prophets:* Christian prophetic insight into the Old Testament saw the crucifixion and death of Jesus as the main import of messianic prophecy. The Jews themselves did not anticipate a suffering Messiah; they usually understood the Servant Song in Is 52, 13—53, 12 to signify their own suffering as a people. In his typical fashion (cf Lk 18, 31; 24, 25.27.44), Luke does not specify the particular Old Testament prophecies that were fulfilled by Jesus. See also the note on Lk 24, 26.

3, 20: *The Lord . . . and send you the Messiah already appointed for you, Jesus:* an allusion to the parousia or second coming of Christ, judged to be imminent in the apostolic age. This reference to its nearness is the only explicit one in Acts. Some scholars believe that this verse preserves a very early christology, in which the title "Messiah" (Greek "Christ") is applied to him as of his parousia, his second coming (contrast 2, 36). This view of a future messiahship of Jesus is not found elsewhere in the New Testament.

3, 21: *The times of universal restoration:* like "the times of refreshment" (20), an apocalyptic designation of the messianic age, fitting in with the christology of v 20 that associates the messiahship of Jesus with his future coming.

3, 22: A loose citation of Dt 18, 15, which teaches that the Israelites are to learn the will of Yahweh from no one but their prophets. At the time of Jesus, some Jews expected a unique prophet to come in fulfillment of this text. Early Christianity applied this tradition and text to Jesus and used them especially in defense of the divergence of Christian teaching from traditional Judaism.

4, 1: *The priests, the captain of the temple guard, and the Sadducees:* the priests performed the temple liturgy; the temple guard was composed of Levites, whose captain ranked next after the high priest. The Sadducees, a party within Judaism at this time, rejected those doctrines, including bodily resurrection, which they believed alien to the ancient Mosaic religion. The Sadducees were drawn from priestly families and from the lay aristocracy.

tioned them, "By what power or by
what name have you done this?"
8* Then Peter, filled with the holy Spirit,
answered them, "Leaders of the people
and elders: 9 If we are being examined
today about a good deed done to a crip-
ple, namely, by what means he was
saved, 10 then all of you and all the peo-
ple of Israel should know that it was in
the name of Jesus Christ the Nazorean
whom you crucified, whom God raised
from the dead; in his name this man
stands before you healed. 11*† He is 'the
stone rejected by you, the builders,
which has become the cornerstone.'
12*† There is no salvation through any-
one else, nor is there any other name
under heaven given to the human race
by which we are to be saved."

13 Observing the boldness of Peter and
John and perceiving them to be unedu-
cated, ordinary men, they were
amazed, and they recognized them as
the companions of Jesus. 14 Then when
they saw the man who had been cured
standing there with them, they could
say nothing in reply. 15 So they ordered
them to leave the Sanhedrin, and con-
ferred with one another, saying,
16 "What are we to do with these men?
Everyone living in Jerusalem knows
that a remarkable sign was done
through them, and we cannot deny it.
17* But so that it may not be spread any
further among the people, let us give
them a stern warning never again to
speak to anyone in this name."

18 So they called them back and or-
dered them not to speak or teach at all
in the name of Jesus. 19* Peter and
John, however, said to them in reply,
"Whether it is right in the sight of God
for us to obey you rather than God, you
be the judges. 20 It is impossible for us
not to speak about what we have seen
and heard." 21 After threatening them
further, they released them, finding no
way to punish them, on account of the
people who were all praising God for
what had happened. 22 For the man on
whom this sign of healing had been
done was over forty years old.

Prayer of the Community. 23 After
their release they went back to their
own people and reported what the chief
priests and elders had told them.
24 And when they heard it, they raised
their voices to God with one accord and
said, "Sovereign Lord, maker of heaven
and earth and the sea and all that is in
them, 25* you said by the holy Spirit
through the mouth of our father David,
your servant:

'Why did the Gentiles rage
and the peoples entertain folly?
26 The kings of the earth took their
stand
and the princes gathered together
against the Lord and against his
anointed.'

27*† Indeed they gathered in this city
against your holy servant Jesus whom
you anointed, Herod and Pontius Pilate,
together with the Gentiles and the peo-
ples of Israel, 28 to do what your hand
and [your] will had long ago planned
to take place. 29 And now, Lord, take
note of their threats, and enable your
servants to speak your word with all
boldness, 30 as you stretch forth [your]
hand to heal, and signs and wonders are
done through the name of your holy ser-
vant Jesus." 31*† As they prayed, the
place where they were gathered shook,
and they were all filled with the holy
Spirit and continued to speak the word
of God with boldness.

Life in the Christian Community.†
32 The community of believers was of
one heart and mind, and no one claimed
that any of his possessions was his own,
but they had everything in common.
33 With great power the apostles bore
witness to the resurrection of the Lord
Jesus, and great favor was accorded
them all. 34* There was no needy person
among them, for those who owned prop-
erty or houses would sell them, bring
the proceeds of the sale, 35 and put them
at the feet of the apostles, and they were
distributed to each according to need.

36* Thus Joseph, also named by the
apostles Barnabas (which is translated
"son of encouragement"), a Levite, a

*

8: Mt 10, 20.
11: Ps 118, 22; Is 28, 16; Mt 21, 42; Mk 12, 10; Lk 20, 17; Rom 9, 33; 1 Pt 2, 7.
12: Mt 1, 21; 1 Cor 3, 11.
17: 5, 28.
19: 5, 29-32.
25-26: Ps 2, 1-2.
27: Lk 23, 12-13.
31: 2, 4.
34-35: 2, 44-45.
36-37: 9, 27; 11, 22.30; 12, 25; 13, 15; 1 Cor 9, 6; Gal 2, 1.9.13; Col 4, 10.

†

4, 11: Early Christianity applied this citation from Ps 118, 22 to Jesus; cf Mk 12, 10; 1 Pt 2, 7.

4, 12: In the Roman world of Luke's day, salvation was often attributed to the emperor who was hailed as "savior" and "god." Luke, in the words of Peter, denies that deliverance comes through anyone other than Jesus.

4, 27: *Herod:* Herod Antipas, ruler of Galilee and Perea from 4 B.C. to A.D. 39, who executed John the Baptist and before whom Jesus was arraigned; cf Lk 23, 6-12.

4, 31: *The place . . . shook:* the earthquake is used as a sign of the divine presence in Ex 19, 18; Is 6, 4. Here the shaking of the building symbolizes God's favorable response to the prayer. Luke may have had as an additional reason for using the symbol in this sense the fact that it was familiar in the Hellenistic world. Ovid and Virgil also employ it.

4, 32-37: This is the second summary characterizing the Jerusalem community (see the note on 2, 42-47). It emphasizes the system of the distribution of goods and introduces Barnabas, who appears later in Acts as the friend and companion of Paul, and who, as noted here (37), endeared himself to the community by a donation of money through the sale of property. This sharing of material possessions continues a practice that Luke describes during the historical ministry of Jesus (Lk 8, 3) and is in accord with the sayings of Jesus in Luke's gospel (Lk 12, 33; 16, 9.11.13).

Cypriot by birth, 37 sold a piece of property that he owned, then brought the money and put it at the feet of the apostles.

CHAPTER 5

***Ananias and Sapphira.*†** 1 A man named Ananias, however, with his wife Sapphira, sold a piece of property. 2 He retained for himself, with his wife's knowledge, some of the purchase price, took the remainder, and put it at the feet of the apostles. 3* But Peter said, "Ananias, why has Satan filled your heart so that you lied to the holy Spirit and retained part of the price of the land? 4 While it remained unsold, did it not remain yours? And when it was sold, was it not still under your control? Why did you contrive this deed? You have lied not to human beings, but to God." 5 When Ananias heard these words, he fell down and breathed his last, and great fear came upon all who heard of it. 6 The young men came and wrapped him up, then carried him out and buried him.

7 After an interval of about three hours, his wife came in, unaware of what had happened. 8 Peter said to her, "Tell me, did you sell the land for this amount?" She answered, "Yes, for that amount." 9 Then Peter said to her, "Why did you agree to test the Spirit of the Lord? Listen, the footsteps of those who have buried your husband are at the door, and they will carry you out." 10 At once, she fell down at his feet and breathed her last. When the young men entered they found her dead, so they carried her out and buried her beside her husband. 11* And great fear came upon the whole church and upon all who heard of these things.

***Signs and Wonders of the Apostles.*†** 12* Many signs and wonders were done among the people at the hands of the apostles. They were all together in Solomon's portico. 13 None of the others dared to join them, but the people esteemed them. 14 Yet more than ever, believers in the Lord, great numbers of men and women, were added to them. 15* Thus they even carried the sick out into the streets and laid them on cots and mats so that when Peter came by, at least his shadow might fall on one or another of them. 16 A large number of people from the towns in the vicinity of Jerusalem also gathered, bringing the sick and those disturbed by unclean spirits, and they were all cured.

***Trial before the Sanhedrin.*†** 17* Then the high priest rose up and all his companions, that is, the party of the Sadducees, and, filled with jealousy, 18 laid hands upon the apostles and put them in the public jail. 19* But during the night, the angel of the Lord opened the doors of the prison, led them out, and said, 20 "Go and take your place in the temple area, and tell the people everything about this life." 21 When they heard this, they went to the temple early in the morning and taught. When the high priest and his companions arrived, they convened the Sanhedrin, the full senate of the Israelites, and sent to the jail to have them brought in. 22 But the court officers who went did not find them in the prison, so they came back and reported, 23 "We found the jail securely locked and the guards stationed outside the doors, but when we opened them, we found no one inside." 24 When they heard this report, the captain of the temple guard and the chief priests were at a loss about them, as to what this would come to. 25 Then someone came in and reported to them, "The men whom you put in prison are in the temple area and are teaching the people." 26* Then the captain and the court officers went and brought them in, but without force, because they were afraid of being stoned by the people.

27 When they had brought them in and made them stand before the Sanhedrin, the high priest questioned them, 28* "We gave you strict orders [did we not?] to stop teaching in that name. Yet you have filled Jerusalem with your teaching and want to bring this man's blood upon us." 29* But Peter and the apostles said in reply, "We must obey God rather

ACTS

*

5, 3: Lk 22, 3; Jn 13, 2.
11: 2, 43; 5, 5; 19, 17.
12: 2, 43; 6, 8; 14, 3; 15, 12.
15: 19, 11-12; Mk 6, 56.
17: 4, 1-3.6.
19: 12, 7-10; 16, 25-26.
26: Lk 20, 19.
28: Mt 27, 25.
29: 4, 19.

†

5, 1-11: The sin of Ananias and Sapphira did not consist in the withholding of part of the money but in their deception of the community. Their deaths are ascribed to a lie to the holy Spirit (3.9), i.e., they accepted the honor accorded them by the community for their generosity, but in reality they were not deserving of it.

5, 12-16: This, the third summary portraying the Jerusalem community, underscores the Twelve as its bulwark, especially because of their charismatic power to heal the sick; cf 2, 42-47; 4, 32-37.

5, 17-42: A second action against the community is taken by the Sanhedrin in the arrest and trial of the Twelve; cf 4, 1-3. The motive is the jealousy of the religious authorities over the popularity of the apostles (17) who are now charged with the defiance of the Sanhedrin's previous order to them to abandon their prophetic role (28; cf 4, 18). In this crisis the apostles are favored by a miraculous release from prison (18-24). (For similar incidents involving Peter and Paul, see 12, 6-11; 16, 25-29.) The real significance of such an event, however, would be manifest only to people of faith, not to unbelievers; since the Sanhedrin already judged the Twelve to be inauthentic prophets, it could disregard reports of their miracles. When the Twelve immediately resumed public teaching, the Sanhedrin determined to invoke upon them the penalty of death (33) prescribed in Dt 13, 6-10. Gamaliel's advice against this course finally prevailed, but it did not save the Twelve from the punishment of scourging (40) in a last endeavor to shake their conviction of their prophetic mission.

than men. 30*† The God of our ancestors raised Jesus, though you had him killed by hanging him on a tree. 31*† God exalted him at his right hand as leader and savior to grant Israel repentance and forgiveness of sins. 32* We are witnesses of these things, as is the holy Spirit that God has given to those who obey him."

33 When they heard this, they became infuriated and wanted to put them to death. 34*† But a Pharisee in the Sanhedrin named Gamaliel, a teacher of the law, respected by all the people, stood up, ordered the men to be put outside for a short time, 35 and said to them, "Fellow Israelites, be careful what you are about to do to these men. 36† Some time ago, Theudas appeared, claiming to be someone important, and about four hundred men joined him, but he was killed, and all those who were loyal to him were disbanded and came to nothing. 37 After him came Judas the Galilean at the time of the census. He also drew people after him, but he too perished and all who were loyal to him were scattered. 38 So now I tell you, have nothing to do with these men, and let them go. For if this endeavor or this activity is of human origin, it will destroy itself. 39 But if it comes from God, you will not be able to destroy them; you may even find yourselves fighting against God." They were persuaded by him. 40* After recalling the apostles, they had them flogged, ordered them to stop speaking in the name of Jesus, and dismissed them. 41* So they left the presence of the Sanhedrin, rejoicing that they had been found worthy to suffer dishonor for the sake of the name. 42* And all day long, both at the temple and in their homes, they did not stop teaching and proclaiming the Messiah, Jesus.

CHAPTER 6

The Need for Assistants. † 1* At that time, as the number of disciples continued to grow, the Hellenists complained against the Hebrews because their widows were being neglected in the daily distribution. 2† So the Twelve called together the community of the disciples and said, "It is not right for us to neglect the word of God to serve at table. 3 Brothers, select from among you seven reputable men, filled with the Spirit and wisdom, whom we shall appoint to this task, 4 whereas we shall devote ourselves to prayer and to the ministry of the word." 5 The proposal was acceptable to the whole community, so they chose Stephen, a man filled with faith and the holy Spirit, also Philip, Prochorus, Nicanor, Timon, Parmenas, and Nicholas of Antioch, a convert to Judaism. 6*† They presented these men to the apostles who prayed and laid hands on them. 7* The word of God continued to spread, and the number of the disciples in Jerusalem increased greatly; even a large group of priests were becoming obedient to the faith.

Accusation against Stephen. † 8 Now Stephen, filled with grace and power,

*

30: 2, 23-24.
31: 2, 38.
32: Lk 24, 48; Jn 15, 26.
34: 22, 3.
40: Mt 10, 17; Acts 4, 17-18.
41: Mt 5, 10-11; 1 Pt 4, 13.
42: 2, 46; 5, 20-21.25; 8, 35; 17, 3; 18, 5.28; 19, 4-5.
6, 1: 2, 45; 4, 34-35.
6: 1, 24; 13, 3; 14, 23.
7: 9, 31; 12, 24; 16, 5; 19, 20; 28, 30-31.

†

5, 30: *Hanging him on a tree:* that is, crucifying him (cf also Gal 3, 13).

5, 31: *At his right hand:* see the note on 2, 33.

5, 34: *Gamaliel:* in 22, 3, Paul identifies himself as a disciple of this Rabbi Gamaliel I who flourished in Jerusalem between A.D. 25 and 50.

5, 36-37: Gamaliel offers examples of unsuccessful contemporary movements to argue that if God is not the origin of this movement preached by the apostles it will perish by itself. The movement initiated by Theudas actually occurred when C. Cuspius Fadus was governor, A.D. 44-46. Luke's placing of Judas the Galilean after Theudas and at the time of the census (see the note on Lk 2, 1-2) is an indication of the vagueness of his knowledge of these events.

6, 1-7: *The Hellenists . . . the Hebrews:* the Hellenists were not necessarily Jews from the diaspora, but were more probably Palestinian Jews who spoke only Greek. The Hebrews were Palestinian Jews who spoke Hebrew or Aramaic and who may also have spoken Greek. Both groups belong to the Jerusalem Jewish Christian community. The conflict between them leads to a restructuring of the community that will better serve the community's needs. The real purpose of the whole episode, however, is to introduce Stephen as a prominent figure in the community whose long speech and martyrdom will be recounted in ch 7.

6, 2-4: The essential function of the Twelve is the "service of the word," including development of the kerygma by formulation of the teachings of Jesus.

6, 2: *To serve at table:* some commentators think that it is not the serving of food that is described here but rather the keeping of the accounts that recorded the distribution of food to the needy members of the community. In any case, after Stephen and the others are chosen, they are never presented carrying out the task for which they were appointed (2-3). Rather, two of their number, Stephen and Philip, are presented as preachers of the Christian message. They, the Hellenist counterpart of the Twelve, are active in the ministry of the word.

6, 6: *They . . . laid hands on them:* the customary Jewish way of designating persons for a task and invoking upon them the divine blessing and power to perform it.

6, 8—8, 1: The summary (6, 7) on the progress of the Jerusalem community, illustrated by the conversion of the priests, is followed by a lengthy narrative regarding Stephen. Stephen's defense is not a response to the charges made against him but takes the form of a discourse that reviews the fortunes of God's word to Israel and leads to a prophetic declaration: a plea for the hearing of that word as announced by Christ and now possessed by the Christian community.

The charges that Stephen depreciated the importance of the temple and the Mosaic law and elevated Jesus to a stature above Moses (6, 13-14) were in fact true. Before the Sanhedrin, no defense against them was possible. With Stephen, who thus perceived the fuller implications of the teachings of Jesus, the differences between Judaism and Christianity began to appear. Luke's account of Stephen's martyrdom and its aftermath shows how the major impetus behind the Christian movement passed from Jerusalem, where the temple and law prevailed, to Antioch in Syria, where these influences were less pressing.

was working great wonders and signs among the people. 9 Certain members of the so-called Synagogue of Freedmen, Cyrenians, and Alexandrians, and people from Cilicia and Asia, came forward and debated with Stephen, 10* but they could not withstand the wisdom and the spirit with which he spoke. 11* Then they instigated some men to say, "We have heard him speaking blasphemous words against Moses and God." 12 They stirred up the people, the elders, and the scribes, accosted him, seized him, and brought him before the Sanhedrin. 13† They presented false witnesses who testified, "This man never stops saying things against [this] holy place and the law. 14* For we have heard him claim that this Jesus the Nazorean will destroy this place and change the customs that Moses handed down to us." 15 All those who sat in the Sanhedrin looked intently at him and saw that his face was like the face of an angel.

CHAPTER 7

Stephen's Discourses. 1 Then the high priest asked, "Is this so?" 2*† And he replied, "My brothers and fathers, listen. The God of glory appeared to our father Abraham while he was in Mesopotamia, before he had settled in Haran, 3* and said to him, 'Go forth from your land and [from] your kinsfolk to the land that I will show you.' 4* So he went forth from the land of the Chaldeans and settled in Haran. And from there, after his father died, he made him migrate to this land where you now dwell. 5* Yet he gave him no inheritance in it, not even a foot's length, but he did promise to give it to him and his descendants as a possession, even though he was childless. 6* And God spoke thus, 'His descendants shall be aliens in a land not their own, where they shall be enslaved and oppressed for four hundred years; 7* but I will bring judgment on the nation they serve,' God said, 'and after that they will come out and worship me in this place.' 8* Then he gave him the covenant of circumcision, and so he became the father of Isaac, and circumcised him on the eighth day, as Isaac did Jacob, and Jacob the twelve patriarchs.

9* "And the patriarchs, jealous of Joseph, sold him into slavery in Egypt; but God was with him 10* and rescued him from all his afflictions. He granted him favor and wisdom before Pharaoh, the king of Egypt, who put him in charge of Egypt and [of] his entire household. 11* Then a famine and great affliction struck all Egypt and Canaan, and our ancestors could find no food; 12* but when Jacob heard that there was grain in Egypt, he sent our ancestors there a first time. 13* The second time, Joseph made himself known to his brothers, and Joseph's family became known to Pharaoh. 14* Then Joseph sent for his father Jacob, inviting him and his whole clan, seventy-five persons; 15* and Jacob went down to Egypt. And he and our ancestors died 16* and were brought back to Shechem and placed in the tomb that Abraham had purchased for a sum of money from the sons of Hamor at Shechem.

17* "When the time drew near for the fulfillment of the promise that God pledged to Abraham, the people had increased and become very numerous in Egypt, 18* until another king who knew nothing of Joseph came to power [in Egypt]. 19 He dealt shrewdly with our people and oppressed [our] ancestors by forcing them to expose their infants, that they might not survive. 20* At this time Moses was born, and he was extremely beautiful. For three months he was nursed in his father's house; 21* but when he was exposed, Pharaoh's daughter adopted him and brought him up as her own son. 22 Moses was educated [in] all the wisdom of the Egyptians and was powerful in his words and deeds.

*

10: Lk 21, 15.
11: Mt 26, 59-61; Mk 14, 55-58; Acts 21, 21.
14: Mt 26, 59-61; 27, 40; Jn 2, 19.
7, 2: Gn 11, 31; 12, 1; Ps 29, 3.
3: Gn 12, 1.
4: Gn 12, 5; 15, 7.
5: Gn 12, 7; 13, 15; 15, 2; 16, 1; Dt 2, 5.
6-7: Gn 15, 13-14.
7: Ex 3, 12.
8: Gn 17, 10-14; 21, 2-4.
9: Gn 37, 11.28; 39, 2.3.21.23.
10: Gn 41, 37-43; Ps 105, 21; Wis 10, 13-14.
11: Gn 41, 54-57; 42, 5.
12: Gn 42, 1-2.
13: Gn 45, 3-4.16.
14: Gn 45, 9-11.18-19; 46, 27; Ex 1, 5 LXX; Dt 10, 22.
15: Gn 46, 5-6; 49, 33.
16: Gn 23, 3-20; 33, 19; 49, 29-30; 50, 13; Jos 24, 32.
17: Ex 1, 7.
18: Ex 1, 8.
20: Ex 2, 2; Heb 11, 23.
21: Ex 2, 3-10.

†

6, 13: *False witnesses:* here, and in his account of Stephen's execution (7, 54-60), Luke parallels the martyrdom of Stephen with the death of Jesus.

7, 2-53: Stephen's speech represents Luke's description of Christianity's break from its Jewish matrix. Two motifs become prominent in the speech: (1) Israel's reaction to God's chosen leaders in the past reveals that the people have consistently rejected them; and (2) Israel has misunderstood God's choice of the Jerusalem temple as the place where he is to be worshiped.

7, 2: *God . . . appeared to our father Abraham . . . in Mesopotamia:* the first of a number of minor discrepancies between the data of the Old Testament and the data of Stephen's discourse. According to Gn 12, 1, God first spoke to Abraham in Haran. The main discrepancies are these: in v 16 it is said that Jacob was buried in Shechem, whereas Gn 50, 13 says he was buried at Hebron; in the same verse it is said that the tomb was purchased by Abraham, but in Gn 33, 19 and Jos 24, 32 the purchase is attributed to Jacob himself.

23* "When he was forty years old, he decided to visit his kinsfolk, the Israelites. 24 When he saw one of them treated unjustly, he defended and avenged the oppressed man by striking down the Egyptian. 25 He assumed [his] kinsfolk would understand that God was offering them deliverance through him, but they did not understand. 26* The next day he appeared to them as they were fighting and tried to reconcile them peacefully, saying, 'Men, you are brothers. Why are you harming one another?' 27 Then the one who was harming his neighbor pushed him aside, saying, 'Who appointed you ruler and judge over us? 28 Are you thinking of killing me as you killed the Egyptian yesterday?' 29* Moses fled when he heard this and settled as an alien in the land of Midian, where he became the father of two sons.

30* "Forty years later, an angel appeared to him in the desert near Mount Sinai in the flame of a burning bush. 31 When Moses saw it, he was amazed at the sight, and as he drew near to look at it, the voice of the Lord came, 32 'I am the God of your fathers, the God of Abraham, of Isaac, and of Jacob.' Then Moses, trembling, did not dare to look at it. 33 But the Lord said to him, 'Remove the sandals from your feet, for the place where you stand is holy ground. 34 I have witnessed the affliction of my people in Egypt and have heard their groaning, and I have come down to rescue them. Come now, I will send you to Egypt.' 35* This Moses, whom they had rejected with the words, 'Who appointed you ruler and judge?' God sent as [both] ruler and deliverer, through the angel who appeared to him in the bush. 36* This man led them out, performing wonders and signs in the land of Egypt, at the Red Sea, and in the desert for forty years. 37* It was this Moses who said to the Israelites, 'God will raise up for you, from among your own kinsfolk, a prophet like me.' 38* It was he who, in the assembly in the desert, was with the angel who spoke to him on Mount Sinai and with our ancestors, and he received living utterances to hand on to us.

39* "Our ancestors were unwilling to obey him; instead, they pushed him aside and in their hearts turned back to Egypt, 40* saying to Aaron, 'Make us gods who will be our leaders. As for that Moses who led us out of the land of Egypt, we do not know what has happened to him.' 41* So they made a calf in those days, offered sacrifice to the idol, and reveled in the works of their hands. 42* Then God turned and handed them over to worship the host of heaven, as it is written in the book of the prophets:

'Did you bring me sacrifices and offerings
for forty years in the desert, O house of Israel?
43 No, you took up the tent of Moloch
and the star of [your] god Rephan,
the images that you made to worship.
So I shall take you into exile beyond Babylon.'

44* "Our ancestors had the tent of testimony in the desert just as the One who spoke to Moses directed him to make it according to the pattern he had seen. 45* Our ancestors who inherited it brought it with Joshua when they dispossessed the nations that God drove out from before our ancestors, up to the time of David, 46* who found favor in the sight of God and asked that he might find a dwelling place for the house of Jacob. 47* But Solomon built a house for him. 48* Yet the Most High does not dwell in houses made by human hands. As the prophet says:

49* 'The heavens are my throne,
the earth is my footstool.
What kind of house can you build for me?
says the Lord,
or what is to be my resting place?
50 Did not my hand make all these things?'

Conclusion. 51 "You stiff-necked people, uncircumcised in heart and ears, you always oppose the holy Spirit; you are just like your ancestors. 52* Which of the prophets did your ancestors not persecute? They put to death those who foretold the coming of the righteous one, whose betrayers and murderers you have now become. 53* You received the law as transmitted by angels, but you did not observe it."

Stephen's Martyrdom. 54 When they heard this, they were infuriated, and they ground their teeth at him. 55*† But

---

*

23-24: Ex 2, 11-12.
26-28: Ex 2, 13-14.
29: Ex 2, 15.21-22; 18, 3-4.
30-34: Ex 3, 2-3.
35: Ex 2, 14.
36: Ex 7, 3.10; 14, 21; Nm 14, 33.
37: Dt 18, 15; Acts 3, 22.
38: Ex 19, 3; 20, 1-17; Dt 5, 4-22; 6, 4-25.
39: Nm 14, 3.
40: Ex 32, 1.23.
41: Ex 32, 4-6.
42-43: Am 5, 25-27.
42: Jer 7, 18; 8, 2; 19, 13.
44: Ex 25, 9.40.
45: Jos 3, 14-17; 18, 1; 2 Sm 7, 5-7.
46: 2 Sm 7, 1-2; 1 Kgs 8, 17; Ps 132, 1-5.
47: 1 Kgs 6, 1; 1 Chr 17, 12.
48: 17, 24.
49: Is 66, 1-2.
52: 2 Chr 36, 16; Mt 23, 31.34.
53: Gal 3, 19; Heb 2, 2.
55-56: Mt 26, 64; Mk 14, 62; Lk 22, 69; Acts 2, 34.

†

7, 55: *He . . . saw . . . Jesus standing at the right hand of God:* Stephen affirms to the Sanhedrin that the prophecy Jesus made before them has been fulfilled (Mk 14, 62).

he, filled with the holy Spirit, looked up
intently to heaven and saw the glory of
God and Jesus standing at the right
hand of God, 56 and he said, "Behold, I
see the heavens opened and the Son of
Man standing at the right hand of God."
57† But they cried out in a loud voice,
covered their ears, and rushed upon
him together. 58* They threw him out of
the city, and began to stone him. The
witnesses laid down their cloaks at the
feet of a young man named Saul.
59*† As they were stoning Stephen, he
called out, "Lord Jesus, receive my
spirit." 60* Then he fell to his knees and
cried out in a loud voice, "Lord, do not
hold this sin against them"; and when
he said this, he fell asleep.

CHAPTER 8†

1*† Now Saul was consenting to his ex-
ecution.
Persecution of the Church. On that
day, there broke out a severe persecu-
tion of the church in Jerusalem, and all
were scattered throughout the country-
side of Judea and Samaria, except the
apostles. 2 Devout men buried Stephen
and made a loud lament over him.
3*† Saul, meanwhile, was trying to de-
stroy the church; entering house after
house and dragging out men and
women, he handed them over for im-
prisonment.

III: THE MISSION IN JUDEA AND SAMARIA

Philip in Samaria. 4* Now those who
had been scattered went about preach-
ing the word. 5* Thus Philip went down
to [the] city of Samaria and proclaimed
the Messiah to them. 6 With one accord,
the crowds paid attention to what was
said by Philip when they heard it and
saw the signs he was doing. 7* For un-
clean spirits, crying out in a loud voice,
came out of many possessed people,
and many paralyzed and crippled peo-
ple were cured. 8 There was great joy
in that city.
Simon the Magician.† 9 A man named
Simon used to practice magic in the city
and astounded the people of Samaria,
claiming to be someone great. 10 All of
them, from the least to the greatest,
paid attention to him, saying, "This
man is the 'Power of God' that is called
'Great.'" 11 They paid attention to him
because he had astounded them by his
magic for a long time, 12* but once they
began to believe Philip as he preached
the good news about the kingdom of
God and the name of Jesus Christ, men
and women alike were baptized. 13 Even
Simon himself believed and, after being
baptized, became devoted to Philip; and
when he saw the signs and mighty
deeds that were occurring, he was as-
tounded.
14 Now when the apostles in Jerusa-
lem heard that Samaria had accepted
the word of God, they sent them Peter
and John, 15 who went down and prayed
for them, that they might receive the
holy Spirit, 16† for it had not yet fallen
upon any of them; they had only been
baptized in the name of the Lord Jesus.
17* Then they laid hands on them and
they received the holy Spirit.
18† When Simon saw that the Spirit
was conferred by the laying on of the
apostles' hands, he offered them money
19 and said, "Give me this power too, so
that anyone upon whom I lay my hands

*

58: 22, 20.
59: Ps 31, 6; Lk 23, 46.
60: Mt 27, 46.50; Mk 15, 34; Lk 23, 46.
8, 1: 22, 20.
3: 9, 1.13; 22, 4; 26, 9-11; 1 Cor 5, 9; Gal 1, 13.
4: 11, 19.
5: 6, 5; 21, 8-9.
7: Mk 16, 17.
12: 1, 3; 19, 8; 28, 23.31.
17: 2, 4; 4, 31; 10, 44-47; 15, 8-9; 19, 2.6.

†

7, 57: *Covered their ears:* Stephen's declaration, like that of Jesus, is a scandal to the court, which regards it as blasphemy.

7, 59: Compare Lk 23, [34].46.

8, 1-40: Some idea of the severity of the persecution that now breaks out against the Jerusalem community can be gathered from 22, 4 and 26, 9-11. Luke, however, concentrates on the fortunes of the word of God among people, indicating how the dispersal of the Jewish community resulted in the conversion of the Samaritans (4-17.25). His narrative is further expanded to include the account of Philip's acceptance of an Ethiopian (26-39).

8, 1: *All were scattered . . . except the apostles:* this observation leads some modern scholars to conclude that the persecution was limited to the Hellenist Christians and that the Hebrew Christians were not molested, perhaps because their attitude toward the law and temple was still more in line with that of their fellow Jews (see the charge leveled against the Hellenist Stephen in 6, 13-14). Whatever the facts, it appears that the Twelve took no public stand regarding Stephen's position, choosing, instead, to await the development of events.

8, 3: *Saul . . . was trying to destroy the church:* like Stephen, Saul was able to perceive that the Christian movement contained the seeds of doctrinal divergence from Judaism. A pupil of Gamaliel, according to 22, 3, and totally dedicated to the law as the way of salvation (Gal 1, 13-14), Saul accepted the task of crushing the Christian movement, at least insofar as it detracted from the importance of the temple and the law. His vehement opposition to Christianity reveals how difficult it was for a Jew of his time to accept a messianism that differed so greatly from the general expectation.

8, 9-13.18-24: Sorcerers were well known in the ancient world. Probably the incident involving Simon and his altercation with Peter is introduced to show that the miraculous charisms possessed by members of the Christian community (6-7) were not to be confused with the magic of sorcerers.

8, 16: Here and in 10, 44-48 and 19, 1-6, Luke distinguishes between baptism in the name of the Lord Jesus and the reception of the Spirit. In each case, the Spirit is conferred through members of the Twelve (Peter and John) or their representative (Paul). This may be Luke's way of describing the role of the church in the bestowal of the Spirit. Elsewhere in Acts, baptism and the Spirit are more closely related (1, 5; 11, 16).

8, 18-20: Simon attempts to buy the gift of God (20) with money. Peter's cursing of Simon's attempt so to use his money expresses a typically Lucan attitude toward material wealth (cf Lk 6, 24; 12, 16-21; 16, 13).

may receive the holy Spirit." 20 But Pe-
ter said to him, "May your money per-
ish with you, because you thought that
you could buy the gift of God with
money. 21 You have no share or lot in
this matter, for your heart is not upright
before God. 22 Repent of this wickedness
of yours and pray to the Lord that, if
possible, your intention may be for-
given. 23 For I see that you are filled with
bitter gall and are in the bonds of iniq-
uity." 24 Simon said in reply, "Pray for
me to the Lord, that nothing of what you
have said may come upon me." 25 So
when they had testified and proclaimed
the word of the Lord, they returned to
Jerusalem and preached the good news
to many Samaritan villages.

Philip and the Ethiopian.† 26 Then
the angel of the Lord spoke to Philip,
"Get up and head south on the road that
goes down from Jerusalem to Gaza, the
desert route." 27*† So he got up and set
out. Now there was an Ethiopian eu-
nuch, a court official of the Candace,
that is, the queen of the Ethiopians, in
charge of her entire treasury, who had
come to Jerusalem to worship, 28 and
was returning home. Seated in his char-
iot, he was reading the prophet Isaiah.
29 The Spirit said to Philip, "Go and join
up with that chariot." 30† Philip ran up
and heard him reading Isaiah the
prophet and said, "Do you understand
what you are reading?" 31* He replied,
"How can I, unless someone instructs
me?" So he invited Philip to get in and
sit with him. 32* This was the scripture
passage he was reading:

"Like a sheep he was led to the
slaughter,
and as a lamb before its shearer
is silent,
so he opened not his mouth.
33 In [his] humiliation justice was de-
nied him.
Who will tell of his posterity?
For his life is taken from the
earth."

34 Then the eunuch said to Philip in re-
ply, "I beg you, about whom is the
prophet saying this? About himself, or
about someone else?" 35 Then Philip
opened his mouth and, beginning with
this scripture passage, he proclaimed
Jesus to him. 36* As they traveled along
the road they came to some water, and
the eunuch said, "Look, there is water.
What is to prevent my being baptized?"
[37]† 38 Then he ordered the chariot to
stop, and Philip and the eunuch both
went down into the water, and he bap-
tized him. 39* When they came out of the
water, the Spirit of the Lord snatched
Philip away, and the eunuch saw him
no more, but continued on his way re-
joicing. 40* Philip came to Azotus, and
went about proclaiming the good news
to all the towns until he reached Caes-
area.

CHAPTER 9

Saul's Conversion.† 1* Now Saul, still
breathing murderous threats against
the disciples of the Lord, went to the
high priest 2† and asked him for letters
to the synagogues in Damascus, that,
if he should find any men or women who
belonged to the Way, he might bring
them back to Jerusalem in chains.
3* On his journey, as he was nearing
Damascus, a light from the sky sud-
denly flashed around him. 4* He fell to
the ground and heard a voice saying to
him, "Saul, Saul, why are you persecut-
ing me?" 5* He said, "Who are you, sir?"
The reply came, "I am Jesus, whom you
are persecuting. 6* Now get up and go
into the city and you will be told what

*

27: Is 56, 3-5.
31: Jn 16, 13.
32-33: Is 53, 7-8 LXX.
36: 10, 47.
39: 1 Kgs 18, 12.
40: 21, 8.
9, 1: 8, 3; 9, 13; 22, 4; 1 Cor 15, 9; Gal 1, 13-14.
1-2: 9, 14; 26, 10.
3: 1 Cor 9, 1; 15, 8; Gal 1, 16.
4: 22, 6; 26, 14.
5: 22, 8; 26, 15; Mt 25, 40.
6: 22, 10; 26, 16.

†

8, 26-40: In the account of the conversion of the Ethiopian eunuch, Luke adduces additional evidence to show that the spread of Christianity outside the confines of Judaism itself was in accord with the plan of God. He does not make clear whether the Ethiopian was originally a convert to Judaism or, as is more probable, a "God-fearer" (10, 1), i.e., one who accepted Jewish monotheism and ethic and attended the synagogue but did not consider himself bound by other regulations such as circumcision and observance of the dietary laws. The story of his conversion to Christianity is given a strong supernatural cast by the introduction of an angel (26), instruction from the holy Spirit (29), and the strange removal of Philip from the scene (39).

8, 27: *The Candace:* Candace is not a proper name here but the title of a Nubian queen.

8, 30-34: Philip is brought alongside the carriage at the very moment when the Ethiopian is pondering the meaning of Is 53, 7-8, a passage that Christianity, from its earliest origins, has applied to Jesus; cf the note on 3, 13.

8, 37: The oldest and best manuscripts of Acts omit this verse, which is a Western text reading: "And Philip said, 'If you believe with all your heart, you may.' And he said in reply, 'I believe that Jesus Christ is the Son of God.' "

9, 1-19: This is the first of three accounts of Paul's conversion (with 22, 3-16 and 26, 2-18) with some differences of detail owing to Luke's use of different sources. Paul's experience was not visionary but was precipitated by the appearance of Jesus, as he insists in 1 Cor 15, 8. The words of Jesus, "Saul, Saul, why are you persecuting me?" related by Luke with no variation in all three accounts, exerted a profound and lasting influence on the thought of Paul. Under the influence of this experience he gradually developed his understanding of justification by faith (see the letters to the Galatians and Romans) and of the identification of the Christian community with Jesus Christ (see 1 Cor 12, 27). That Luke would narrate this conversion three times is testimony to the importance he attaches to it. This first account occurs when the word is first spread to the Gentiles. At this point, the conversion of the hero of the Gentile mission is recounted. The emphasis in the account is on Paul as a divinely chosen instrument (15).

9, 2: *The Way:* a name used by the early Christian community for itself (18, 26; 19, 9.23; 22, 4; 24, 14.22). The Essene community at Qumran used the same designation to describe its mode of life.

you must do." 7* The men who were traveling with him stood speechless, for they heard the voice but could see no one. 8*† Saul got up from the ground, but when he opened his eyes he could see nothing; so they led him by the hand and brought him to Damascus. 9 For three days he was unable to see, and he neither ate nor drank.

Saul's Baptism. 10* There was a disciple in Damascus named Ananias, and the Lord said to him in a vision, "Ananias." He answered, "Here I am, Lord." 11* The Lord said to him, "Get up and go to the street called Straight and ask at the house of Judas for a man from Tarsus named Saul. He is there praying, 12 and [in a vision] he has seen a man named Ananias come in and lay [his] hands on him, that he may regain his sight." 13*† But Ananias replied, "Lord, I have heard from many sources about this man, what evil things he has done to your holy ones in Jerusalem. 14* And here he has authority from the chief priests to imprison all who call upon your name." 15* But the Lord said to him, "Go, for this man is a chosen instrument of mine to carry my name before Gentiles, kings, and Israelites, 16 and I will show him what he will have to suffer for my name." 17 So Ananias went and entered the house; laying his hands on him, he said, "Saul, my brother, the Lord has sent me, Jesus who appeared to you on the way by which you came, that you may regain your sight and be filled with the holy Spirit." 18 Immediately things like scales fell from his eyes and he regained his sight. He got up and was baptized, 19† and when he had eaten, he recovered his strength.

Saul Preaches in Damascus. He stayed some days with the disciples in Damascus, 20† and he began at once to proclaim Jesus in the synagogues, that he is the Son of God. 21 All who heard him were astounded and said, "Is not this the man who in Jerusalem ravaged those who call upon this name, and came here expressly to take them back in chains to the chief priests?" 22 But Saul grew all the stronger and confounded [the] Jews who lived in Damascus, proving that this is the Messiah.

Saul Visits Jerusalem. 23 After a long time had passed, the Jews conspired to kill him, 24* but their plot became known to Saul. Now they were keeping watch on the gates day and night so as to kill him, 25 but his disciples took him one night and let him down through an opening in the wall, lowering him in a basket.

26*† When he arrived in Jerusalem he tried to join the disciples, but they were all afraid of him, not believing that he was a disciple. 27 Then Barnabas took charge of him and brought him to the apostles, and he reported to them how on the way he had seen the Lord and that he had spoken to him, and how in Damascus he had spoken out boldly in the name of Jesus. 28 He moved about freely with them in Jerusalem, and spoke out boldly in the name of the Lord. 29† He also spoke and debated with the Hellenists, but they tried to kill him. 30* And when the brothers learned of this, they took him down to Caesarea and sent him on his way to Tarsus.

The Church at Peace.† 31 The church throughout all Judea, Galilee, and Samaria was at peace. It was being built up and walked in the fear of the Lord, and with the consolation of the holy Spirit it grew in numbers.

Peter Heals Aeneas at Lydda. 32 As Peter was passing through every region, he went down to the holy ones living in Lydda. 33 There he found a man named Aeneas, who had been confined to bed for eight years, for he was paralyzed. 34 Peter said to him, "Aeneas, Jesus Christ heals you. Get up and make your bed." He got up at once. 35 And all the inhabitants of Lydda and Sharon saw him, and they turned to the Lord.

Peter Restores Tabitha to Life. 36† Now in Joppa there was a disciple named Tabitha (which translated means Dorcas). She was completely occupied with good deeds and almsgiving. 37 Now during those days she fell sick

*

7: 22, 9; 26, 13-14.
8: 22, 11.
10-19: 22, 12-16.
11: 21, 39.
13: 8, 3; 9, 1.
14: 9, 1-2; 26, 10; 1 Cor 1, 2; 2 Tm 2, 22.
15: 22, 15; 26, 1; 27, 24.
24-25: 2 Cor 11, 32-33.
26-27: Gal 1, 18.
30: 11, 25.

†

9, 8: *He could see nothing:* a temporary blindness (18) symbolizing the religious blindness of Saul as persecutor (cf 26, 18).

9, 13: *Your holy ones:* literally, "your saints."

9, 19-30: This is a brief resume of Paul's initial experience as an apostolic preacher. At first he found himself in the position of being regarded as an apostate by the Jews and suspect by the Christian community of Jerusalem. His acceptance by the latter was finally brought about through his friendship with Barnabas (27).

9, 20: *Son of God:* the title "Son of God" occurs in Acts only here, but cf the citation of Ps 2, 7 in Paul's speech at Antioch in Pisidia (13, 33).

9, 26: This visit of Paul to Jerusalem is mentioned by Paul in Gal 1, 18.

9, 29: *Hellenists:* see the note on 6, 1-7.

9, 31-43: In the context of the period of peace enjoyed by the community through the cessation of Paul's activities against it, Luke introduces two traditions concerning the miraculous power exercised by Peter as he was making a tour of places where the Christian message had already been preached. The towns of Lydda, Sharon, and Joppa were populated by both Jews and Gentiles and their Christian communities may well have been mixed.

9, 36: *Tabitha* (*Dorcas*), respectively the Aramaic and Greek words for "gazelle," exemplifies the right attitude toward material possessions expressed by Jesus in the Lucan Gospel (Lk 6, 30; 11, 41; 12, 33; 18, 22; 19, 8).

and died, so after washing her, they laid
[her] out in a room upstairs. 38 Since
Lydda was near Joppa, the disciples,
hearing that Peter was there, sent two
men to him with the request, "Please
come to us without delay." 39 So Peter
got up and went with them. When he
arrived, they took him to the room up-
stairs where all the widows came to him
weeping and showing him the tunics
and cloaks that Dorcas had made while
she was with them. 40* Peter sent them
all out and knelt down and prayed.
Then he turned to her body and said,
"Tabitha, rise up." She opened her
eyes, saw Peter, and sat up. 41 He gave
her his hand and raised her up, and
when he had called the holy ones and
the widows, he presented her alive.
42 This became known all over Joppa,
and many came to believe in the Lord.
43*† And he stayed a long time in Joppa
with Simon, a tanner.

IV: THE INAUGURATION OF THE GENTILE MISSION

CHAPTER 10

The Vision of Cornelius. † 1*† Now in
Caesarea there was a man named Cor-
nelius, a centurion of the Cohort called
the Italica, 2† devout and God-fearing
along with his whole household, who
used to give alms generously to the Jew-
ish people and pray to God constantly.
3† One afternoon about three o'clock, he
saw plainly in a vision an angel of God
come in to him and say to him, "Cornel-
ius." 4 He looked intently at him and,
seized with fear, said, "What is it, sir?"
He said to him, "Your prayers and
almsgiving have ascended as a memo-
rial offering before God. 5 Now send
some men to Joppa and summon one
Simon who is called Peter. 6* He is stay-
ing with another Simon, a tanner, who
has a house by the sea." 7† When the
angel who spoke to him had left, he
called two of his servants and a de-
vout soldier from his staff, 8 explained
everything to them, and sent them to
Joppa.
The Vision of Peter. † 9† The next day,
while they were on their way and near-
ing the city, Peter went up to the roof
terrace to pray at about noontime.
10 He was hungry and wished to eat, and
while they were making preparations
he fell into a trance. 11* He saw heaven
opened and something resembling a
large sheet coming down, lowered to the
ground by its four corners. 12 In it were
all the earth's four-legged animals and
reptiles and the birds of the sky. 13 A
voice said to him, "Get up, Peter.
Slaughter and eat." 14* But Peter said,
"Certainly not, sir. For never have I
eaten anything profane and unclean."
15* The voice spoke to him again, a sec-
ond time, "What God has made clean,
you are not to call profane." 16 This hap-
pened three times, and then the object
was taken up into the sky.
17† While Peter was in doubt about the
meaning of the vision he had seen, the
men sent by Cornelius asked for Si-
mon's house and arrived at the en-
trance. 18 They called out inquiring
whether Simon, who is called Peter, was
staying there. 19* As Peter was ponder-
ing the vision, the Spirit said [to him],
"There are three men here looking for
you. 20 So get up, go downstairs, and ac-
company them without hesitation, be-
cause I have sent them." 21 Then Peter
went down to the men and said, "I am
the one you are looking for. What is the
reason for your being here?" 22* They
answered, "Cornelius, a centurion, an
upright and God-fearing man, re-
spected by the whole Jewish nation, was
directed by a holy angel to summon you
to his house and to hear what you have
to say." 23 So he invited them in and
showed them hospitality.

---

*

40: Mk 5, 40-41.
43: 10, 6.
10, 1-8: 10, 30-33.
6: 9, 43.
11-20: 11, 5-12.
14: Lv 11, 1-47; Ez 4, 14.
15: Mk 7, 15-19; Gal 2, 12.
19: 13, 2.
22: Lk 7, 4-5.

---

†

9, 43: The fact that Peter lodged with a tanner would have been significant to both the Gentile and Jewish Christians, for Judaism considered the tanning occupation unclean.

10, 1-48: The narrative centers on the conversion of Cornelius, a Gentile and a "God-fearer" (see the note on 8, 26-40). Luke considers the event of great importance, as is evident from his long treatment of it. The incident is again related in 11, 1-18 where Peter is forced to justify his actions before the Jerusalem community and alluded to in 15, 7-11 where at the Jerusalem "Council" Peter supports Paul's missionary activity among the Gentiles. The narrative divides itself into a series of distinct episodes, concluding with Peter's presentation of the Christian kerygma (34-43) and a pentecostal experience undergone by Cornelius' household preceding their reception of baptism (44-48).

10, 1: *The Cohort called the Italica:* this battalion was an auxiliary unit of archers formed originally in Italy but transferred to Syria shortly before A.D. 69.

10, 2: *Used to give alms generously:* like Tabitha (9, 36), Cornelius exemplifies the proper attitude toward wealth (see the note on 9, 36).

10, 3: *About three o'clock:* literally, "about the ninth hour." See the note on 3, 1.

10, 7: *A devout soldier:* by using this adjective, Luke probably intends to classify him as a "God-fearer" (see the note on 8, 26-40).

10, 9-16: The vision is intended to prepare Peter to share the food of Cornelius' household without qualms of conscience (48). The necessity of such instructions to Peter reveals that at first not even the apostles fully grasped the implications of Jesus' teaching on the law. In Acts, the initial insight belongs to Stephen.

10, 9: *At about noontime:* literally, "about the sixth hour."

10, 17-23: The arrival of the Gentile emissaries with their account of the angelic apparition illuminates Peter's vision: he is to be prepared to admit Gentiles, who were considered unclean like the animals of his vision, into the Christian community.

The next day he got up and went with them, and some of the brothers from Joppa went with him. [24]† On the following day he entered Caesarea. Cornelius was expecting them and had called together his relatives and close friends. [25]* When Peter entered, Cornelius met him and, falling at his feet, paid him homage. [26] Peter, however, raised him up, saying, "Get up. I myself am also a human being." [27] While he conversed with him, he went in and found many people gathered together [28]*† and said to them, "You know that it is unlawful for a Jewish man to associate with, or visit, a Gentile, but God has shown me that I should not call any person profane or unclean. [29] And that is why I came without objection when sent for. May I ask, then, why you summoned me?"

[30]† Cornelius replied, "Four days ago at this hour, three o'clock in the afternoon, I was at prayer in my house when suddenly a man in dazzling robes stood before me and said, [31] 'Cornelius, your prayer has been heard and your almsgiving remembered before God. [32] Send therefore to Joppa and summon Simon, who is called Peter. He is a guest in the house of Simon, a tanner, by the sea.' [33] So I sent for you immediately, and you were kind enough to come. Now therefore we are all here in the presence of God to listen to all that you have been commanded by the Lord."

Peter's Speech.† [34]*† Then Peter proceeded to speak and said, "In truth, I see that God shows no partiality. [35] Rather, in every nation whoever fears him and acts uprightly is acceptable to him. [36]*† You know the word [that] he sent to the Israelites as he proclaimed peace through Jesus Christ, who is Lord of all, [37]* what has happened all over Judea, beginning in Galilee after the baptism that John preached, [38]*† how God anointed Jesus of Nazareth with the holy Spirit and power. He went about doing good and healing all those oppressed by the devil, for God was with him. [39]† We are witnesses of all that he did both in the country of the Jews and [in] Jerusalem. They put him to death by hanging him on a tree. [40] This man God raised [on] the third day and granted that he be visible, [41]* not to all the people, but to us, the witnesses chosen by God in advance, who ate and drank with him after he rose from the dead. [42]*† He commissioned us to preach to the people and testify that he is the one appointed by God as judge of the living and the dead. [43] To him all the prophets bear witness, that everyone who believes in him will receive forgiveness of sins through his name."

The Baptism of Cornelius. [44]*† While Peter was still speaking these things, the holy Spirit fell upon all who were listening to the word. [45] The circumcised believers who had accompanied Peter were astounded that the gift of the holy Spirit should have been poured out on the Gentiles also, [46] for they could hear them speaking in tongues and glorifying God. Then Peter responded, [47]* "Can anyone withhold the water for baptizing these people, who have received the holy Spirit even as we have?" [48] He ordered them to be baptized in the name of Jesus Christ. [49] Then they invited him to stay for a few days.

*

25-26: 14, 13-15; Rv 19, 10.
28: Gal 2, 11-16.
34: Dt 17, 2; 2 Chr 19, 7; Jb 34, 19; Wis 6, 7; Rom 2, 11; Gal 2, 6; Eph 6, 9; 1 Pt 1, 17.
36: Is 52, 7; Na 2, 1.
37: Mt 4, 12; Mk 1, 14; Lk 4, 14.
38: Is 61, 1; Lk 4, 18.
41: Lk 24, 41-43.
42: 1, 8; 3, 15; 17, 31; Lk 24, 48; Rom 14, 9; 2 Tm 4, 1.
44: 11, 15; 15, 8.
47: 8, 36.

†

10, 24-27: So impressed is Cornelius with the apparition that he invites close personal friends to join him in his meeting with Peter. But his understanding of the person he is about to meet is not devoid of superstition, suggested by his falling down before him. For a similar experience of Paul and Barnabas, see 14, 11-18.

10, 28: Peter now fully understands the meaning of his vision; see the note on 10, 17-23.

10, 30: *Four days ago:* literally, "from the fourth day up to this hour."

10, 34-43: Peter's speech to the household of Cornelius typifies early Christian preaching to Gentiles.

10, 34-35: The revelation of God's choice of Israel to be the people of God did not mean he withheld the divine favor from other people.

10, 36-43: These words are more directed to Luke's Christian readers than to the household of Cornelius, as indicated by the opening words, "You know." They trace the continuity between the preaching and teaching of Jesus of Nazareth and the proclamation of Jesus by the early community. The emphasis on this divinely ordained continuity (41) is meant to assure Luke's readers of the fidelity of Christian tradition to the words and deeds of Jesus.

10, 36: *To the Israelites:* Luke, in the words of Peter, speaks of the prominent position occupied by Israel in the history of salvation.

10, 38: *Jesus of Nazareth:* God's revelation of his plan for the destiny of humanity through Israel culminated in Jesus of Nazareth. Consequently, the ministry of Jesus is an integral part of God's revelation. This viewpoint explains why the early Christian communities were interested in conserving the historical substance of the ministry of Jesus, a tradition leading to the production of the four gospels.

10, 39: *We are witnesses:* the apostolic testimony was not restricted to the resurrection of Jesus but also included his historical ministry. This witness, however, was theological in character; the Twelve, divinely mandated as prophets, were empowered to interpret his sayings and deeds in the light of his redemptive death and resurrection. The meaning of these words and deeds was to be made clear to the developing Christian community as the bearer of the word of salvation (cf 1, 21-26). *Hanging him on a tree:* see the note on 5, 30.

10, 42: *As judge of the living and the dead:* the apostolic preaching to the Jews appealed to their messianic hope, while the preaching to Gentiles stressed the coming divine judgment; cf 1 Thes 1, 10.

10, 44: Just as the Jewish Christians received the gift of the Spirit, so too do the Gentiles.

CHAPTER 11

***The Baptism of the Gentiles Ex-
plained.*** † 1 Now the apostles and the
brothers who were in Judea heard that
the Gentiles too had accepted the word
of God. 2 So when Peter went up to Jeru-
salem the circumcised believers con-
fronted him, 3† saying, "You entered
the house of uncircumcised people and
ate with them." 4 Peter began and ex-
plained it to them step by step, saying,
5* "I was at prayer in the city of Joppa
when in a trance I had a vision, some-
thing resembling a large sheet coming
down, lowered from the sky by its four
corners, and it came to me. 6 Looking
intently into it, I observed and saw the
four-legged animals of the earth, the
wild beasts, the reptiles, and the birds
of the sky. 7 I also heard a voice say to
me, 'Get up, Peter. Slaughter and eat.'
8 But I said, 'Certainly not, sir, because
nothing profane or unclean has ever en-
tered my mouth.' 9 But a second time a
voice from heaven answered, 'What
God has made clean, you are not to call
profane.' 10 This happened three times,
and then everything was drawn up
again into the sky. 11 Just then three
men appeared at the house where we
were, who had been sent to me from
Caesarea. 12† The Spirit told me to ac-
company them without discriminating.
These six brothers also went with me,
and we entered the man's house.
13* He related to us how he had seen
[the] angel standing in his house, say-
ing, 'Send someone to Joppa and sum-
mon Simon, who is called Peter, 14 who
will speak words to you by which you
and all your household will be saved.'
15* As I began to speak, the holy Spirit
fell upon them as it had upon us at the
beginning, 16* and I remembered the
word of the Lord, how he had said,
'John baptized with water but you will
be baptized with the holy Spirit.' 17* If
then God gave them the same gift he
gave to us when we came to believe in
the Lord Jesus Christ, who was I to be
able to hinder God?" 18 When they
heard this, they stopped objecting and
glorified God, saying, "God has then
granted life-giving repentance to the
Gentiles too."

The Church at Antioch. † 19* Now
those who had been scattered by the
persecution that arose because of Ste-
phen went as far as Phoenicia, Cyprus,
and Antioch, preaching the word to no
one but Jews. 20 There were some Cypri-
ots and Cyrenians among them, how-
ever, who came to Antioch and began
to speak to the Greeks as well, pro-
claiming the Lord Jesus. 21 The hand of
the Lord was with them and a great
number who believed turned to the
Lord. 22 The news about them reached
the ears of the church in Jerusalem, and
they sent Barnabas [to go] to Antioch.
23 When he arrived and saw the grace
of God, he rejoiced and encouraged
them all to remain faithful to the Lord
in firmness of heart, 24 for he was a good
man, filled with the holy Spirit and
faith. And a large number of people was
added to the Lord. 25 Then he went to
Tarsus to look for Saul, 26† and when he
had found him he brought him to Anti-
och. For a whole year they met with
the church and taught a large num-
ber of people, and it was in Antioch
that the disciples were first called Chris-
tians.

The Prediction of Agabus. † 27 At that
time some prophets came down from
Jerusalem to Antioch, 28* and one of
them named Agabus stood up and pre-
dicted by the Spirit that there would be
a severe famine all over the world, and
it happened under Claudius. 29* So the
disciples determined that, according to
ability, each should send relief to the
brothers who lived in Judea. 30† This
they did, sending it to the presbyters
in care of Barnabas and Saul.

*

11, 5-12: 10, 11-20.
13: 10, 3-5.22.30-32.
15: 10, 44.
16: 1, 5; 19, 4; Lk 3, 16.
17: 15, 8-9.
19: 8, 1-4.
28: 21, 10.
29-30: 12, 25.

†

11, 1-18: The Jewish Christians of Jerusalem were scandalized to learn of Peter's sojourn in the house of the Gentile Cornelius. Nonetheless, they had to accept the divine directions given to both Peter and Cornelius. They concluded that the setting aside of the legal barriers between Jew and Gentile was an exceptional ordinance of God to indicate that the apostolic kerygma was also to be directed to the Gentiles. Only in ch 15 at the "Council" in Jerusalem does the evangelization of the Gentiles become the official position of the church leadership in Jerusalem.

11, 3: *You entered . . . :* alternatively, this could be punctuated as a question.

11, 12: *These six brothers:* companions from the Christian community of Joppa (see 10, 23).

11, 19-26: The Jewish Christian antipathy to the mixed community was reflected by the early missionaries generally. The few among them who entertained a different view succeeded in introducing Gentiles into the community at Antioch (in Syria). When the disconcerted Jerusalem community sent Barnabas to investigate, he was so favorably impressed by what he observed that he persuaded his friend Saul to participate in the Antioch mission.

11, 26: *Christians:* "Christians" is first applied to the members of the community at Antioch because the Gentile members of the community enable it to stand out clearly from Judaism.

11, 27-30: It is not clear whether the prophets from Jerusalem came to Antioch to request help in view of the coming famine or whether they received this insight during their visit there. The former supposition seems more likely. Suetonius and Tacitus speak of famines during the reign of Claudius (A.D. 41-54), while the Jewish historian Josephus mentions a famine in Judea in A.D. 46-48. Luke is interested, rather, in showing the charity of the Antiochene community toward the Jewish Christians of Jerusalem despite their differences on mixed communities.

11, 30: *Presbyters:* this is the same Greek word that elsewhere is translated "elders," primarily in reference to the Jewish community.

ACTS

CHAPTER 12

Herod's Persecution of the
Christians.† 1 About that time King
Herod laid hands upon some members
of the church to harm them. 2† He had
James, the brother of John, killed by
the sword, 3† and when he saw that this
was pleasing to the Jews he proceeded
to arrest Peter also. (It was [the] feast
of Unleavened Bread.) 4 He had him
taken into custody and put in prison un-
der the guard of four squads of four sol-
diers each. He intended to bring him
before the people after Passover.
5* Peter thus was being kept in prison,
but prayer by the church was fervently
being made to God on his behalf.

6 On the very night before Herod was
to bring him to trial, Peter, secured by
double chains, was sleeping between
two soldiers, while outside the door
guards kept watch on the prison.
7 Suddenly the angel of the Lord stood
by him and a light shone in the cell. He
tapped Peter on the side and awakened
him, saying, "Get up quickly." The
chains fell from his wrists. 8 The angel
said to him, "Put on your belt and your
sandals." He did so. Then he said to
him, "Put on your cloak and follow me."
9 So he followed him out, not realizing
that what was happening through the
angel was real; he thought he was see-
ing a vision. 10 They passed the first
guard, then the second, and came to the
iron gate leading out to the city, which
opened for them by itself. They
emerged and made their way down an
alley, and suddenly the angel left him.
11 Then Peter recovered his senses and
said, "Now I know for certain that [the]
Lord sent his angel and rescued me
from the hand of Herod and from all
that the Jewish people had been expect-
ing." 12* When he realized this, he went
to the house of Mary, the mother of John
who is called Mark, where there were
many people gathered in prayer.
13 When he knocked on the gateway
door, a maid named Rhoda came to an-
swer it. 14 She was so overjoyed when
she recognized Peter's voice that, in-
stead of opening the gate, she ran in and
announced that Peter was standing at
the gate. 15 They told her, "You are out
of your mind," but she insisted that it
was so. But they kept saying, "It is his
angel." 16 But Peter continued to knock,
and when they opened it, they saw him
and were astounded. 17† He motioned to
them with his hand to be quiet and ex-
plained [to them] how the Lord had led
him out of the prison, and said, "Report
this to James and the brothers." Then
he left and went to another place.
18* At daybreak there was no small
commotion among the soldiers over
what had become of Peter. 19 Herod, af-
ter instituting a search but not finding
him, ordered the guards tried and exe-
cuted. Then he left Judea to spend some
time in Caesarea.

Herod's Death.† 20 He had long been
very angry with the people of Tyre and
Sidon, who now came to him in a body.
After winning over Blastus, the king's
chamberlain, they sued for peace be-
cause their country was supplied with
food from the king's territory. 21 On an
appointed day, Herod, attired in royal
robes, [and] seated on the rostrum, ad-
dressed them publicly. 22 The assem-
bled crowd cried out, "This is the voice
of a god, not of a man." 23 At once the
angel of the Lord struck him down be-
cause he did not ascribe the honor to
God, and he was eaten by worms and
breathed his last. 24* But the word of
God continued to spread and grow.

Mission of Barnabas and Saul.
25*† After Barnabas and Saul com-
pleted their relief mission, they re-
turned to Jerusalem, taking with them
John, who is called Mark.

CHAPTER 13

1† Now there were in the church at
Antioch prophets and teachers: Barna-
bas, Symeon who was called Niger, Lu-
cius of Cyrene, Manaen who was a close
friend of Herod the tetrarch, and Saul.
2 While they were worshiping the Lord

*

12, 5: Jas 5, 16.
12: 12, 25; 15, 37.
18: 5, 22-24.
24: 6, 7.
25: 11, 29-30.

†

12, 1-19: Herod Agrippa ruled Judea A.D. 41-44. While Luke does not assign a motive for his execution of James and his intended execution of Peter, the broad background lies in Herod's support of Pharisaic Judaism. The Jewish Christians had lost the popularity they had had in Jerusalem (2, 47), perhaps because of suspicions against them traceable to the teaching of Stephen.

12, 2: *James, the brother of John:* this James, the son of Zebedee, was beheaded by Herod Agrippa ca. A.D. 44.

12, 3.4: *Feast of Unleavened Bread . . . Passover:* see the note on Lk 22, l.

12, 17: *To James:* this James is not the son of Zebedee mentioned in v 2, but is James, the "brother of the Lord" (Gal 1, 19), who in chs 15 and 21 is presented as leader of the Jerusalem Christian community. *He left and went to another place:* the conjecture that Peter left for Rome at this time has nothing to recommend it. His chief responsibility was still the leadership of the Jewish Christian community in Palestine (see Gal 2, 7). The concept of the great missionary effort of the church was yet to come (see 13, 1-3).

12, 20-23: Josephus gives a similar account of Herod's death that occurred in A.D. 44. Early Christian tradition considered the manner of it to be a divine punishment upon his evil life. See 2 Kgs 19, 35 for the figure of the angel of the Lord in such a context.

12, 25: *They returned to Jerusalem:* many manuscripts read "from Jerusalem," since 11, 30 implies that Paul and Barnabas are already in Jerusalem. This present verse could refer to a return visit or subsequent relief mission.

13, 1-3: The impulse for the first missionary effort in Asia Minor is ascribed to the prophets of the Antiochene community, under the inspiration of the holy Spirit. Just as the Jerusalem community had earlier been the center of missionary activity, so too Antioch becomes the center from which the missionaries Barnabas and Saul are sent out.

and fasting, the holy Spirit said, "Set
apart for me Barnabas and Saul for the
work to which I have called them."
3 Then, completing their fasting and
prayer, they laid hands on them and
sent them off.

First Mission Begins in Cyprus. †
4 So they, sent forth by the holy Spirit,
went down to Seleucia and from there
sailed to Cyprus. 5† When they arrived
in Salamis, they proclaimed the word
of God in the Jewish synagogues. They
had John also as their assistant.
6† When they had traveled through the
whole island as far as Paphos, they met
a magician named Bar-Jesus who was
a Jewish false prophet. 7 He was with
the proconsul Sergius Paulus, a man of
intelligence, who had summoned Bar-
nabas and Saul and wanted to hear the
word of God. 8 But Elymas the magician
(for that is what his name means) op-
posed them in an attempt to turn the
proconsul away from the faith. 9† But
Saul, also known as Paul, filled with the
holy Spirit, looked intently at him
10 and said, "You son of the devil, you
enemy of all that is right, full of every
sort of deceit and fraud. Will you not
stop twisting the straight paths of [the]
Lord? 11 Even now the hand of the Lord
is upon you. You will be blind, and un-
able to see the sun for a time." Immedi-
ately a dark mist fell upon him, and he
went about seeking people to lead him
by the hand. 12 When the proconsul saw
what had happened, he came to believe,
for he was astonished by the teaching
about the Lord.

Paul's Arrival at Antioch in Pisidia.
13* From Paphos, Paul and his compan-
ions set sail and arrived at Perga in
Pamphylia. But John left them and re-
turned to Jerusalem. 14 They continued
on from Perga and reached Antioch in
Pisidia. On the sabbath they entered
[into] the synagogue and took their
seats. 15 After the reading of the law and
the prophets, the synagogue officials
sent word to them, "My brothers, if one
of you has a word of exhortation for the
people, please speak."

Paul's Address in the Synagogue. †
16† So Paul got up, motioned with his
hand, and said, "Fellow Israelites and
you others who are God-fearing, listen.
17* The God of this people Israel chose
our ancestors and exalted the people
during their sojourn in the land of
Egypt. With uplifted arms he led them
out of it 18*† and for about forty years
he put up with them in the desert.
19* When he had destroyed seven na-
tions in the land of Canaan, he gave
them their land as an inheritance
20*† at the end of about four hundred
and fifty years. After these things he
provided judges up to Samuel [the]
prophet. 21* Then they asked for a king.
God gave them Saul, son of Kish, a man
from the tribe of Benjamin, for forty
years. 22* Then he removed him and
raised up David as their king; of him
he testified, 'I have found David, son of
Jesse, a man after my own heart; he will
carry out my every wish.' 23* From this
man's descendants God, according to
his promise, has brought to Israel a sav-
ior, Jesus. 24* John heralded his coming
by proclaiming a baptism of repentance
to all the people of Israel; 25* and as
John was completing his course, he
would say, 'What do you suppose that
I am? I am not he. Behold, one is coming
after me; I am not worthy to unfasten
the sandals of his feet.'

26 "My brothers, children of the fam-
ily of Abraham, and those others among
you who are God-fearing, to us this
word of salvation has been sent. 27 The
inhabitants of Jerusalem and their
leaders failed to recognize him, and by
condemning him they fulfilled the ora-
cles of the prophets that are read sab-

*

13, 13: 15, 38.
17: Ex 6, 1.6; 12, 51.
18: Ex 16, 1.35; Nm 14, 34.
19: Dt 7, 1; Jos 14, 1-2.
20: Jgs 2, 16; 1 Sm 3, 20.
21: 1 Sm 8, 5.19; 9, 16; 10, 1.20-21.24; 11, 15.
22: 1 Sm 13, 14; 16, 12-13; Ps 89, 20-21.
23: Is 11, 1.
24: Mt 3, 1-2; Mk 1, 4-5; Lk 3, 2-3.
25: Mt 3, 11; Mk 1, 7; Lk 3, 16; Jn 1, 20.27.

†

13, 4—14, 27: The key event in Luke's account of the first missionary journey is the experience of Paul and Barnabas at Pisidian Antioch (13, 14-52). The Christian kerygma proclaimed by Paul in the synagogue was favorably received. Some Jews and "God-fearers" (see the note on 8, 26-40) became interested and invited the missionaries to speak again on the following sabbath (13, 42). By that time, however, the appearance of a large number of Gentiles from the city had so disconcerted the Jews that they became hostile toward the apostles (13, 44-50). This hostility of theirs appears in all three accounts of Paul's missionary journeys in Acts, the Jews of Iconium (14, 1-2) and Beroea (17, 11) being notable exceptions.

13, 5: *John:* that is, John Mark (see 12, 12.25).

13, 6: *A magician named Bar-Jesus who was a Jewish false prophet:* that is, he posed as a prophet. Again Luke takes the opportunity to dissociate Christianity from the magical acts of the time (7-11); see also 8, 18-24.

13, 9: *Saul, also known as Paul:* there is no reason to believe that his name was changed from Saul to Paul upon his conversion. The use of a double name, one Semitic (Saul), the other Greco-Roman (Paul), is well attested (cf 1, 23, Joseph Justus; 12, 12.25, John Mark).

13, 16-41: This is the first of several speeches of Paul to Jews proclaiming that the Christian church is the logical development of Pharisaic Judaism (see also 24, 10-21; 26, 2-23).

13, 16: *Who are God-fearing:* see the note on 8, 26-40.

13, 18: *Put up with:* some manuscripts read "sustained."

13, 20: *At the end of about four hundred and fifty years:* the manuscript tradition makes it uncertain whether the mention of four hundred and fifty years refers to the sojourn in Egypt before the Exodus, the wilderness period and the time of the conquest (see Ex 12, 40-41), as the translation here suggests, or to the time between the conquest and the time of Samuel, the period of the judges, if the text is read, "After these things, for about four hundred and fifty years, he provided judges."

bath after sabbath. 28* For even though they found no grounds for a death sentence, they asked Pilate to have him put to death, 29* and when they had accomplished all that was written about him, they took him down from the tree and placed him in a tomb. 30* But God raised him from the dead, 31*† and for many days he appeared to those who had come up with him from Galilee to Jerusalem. These are [now] his witnesses before the people. 32 We ourselves are proclaiming this good news to you that what God promised our ancestors 33* he has brought to fulfillment for us, [their] children, by raising up Jesus, as it is written in the second psalm, 'You are my son; this day I have begotten you.' 34* And that he raised him from the dead never to return to corruption he declared in this way, 'I shall give you the benefits assured to David.' 35* That is why he also says in another psalm, 'You will not suffer your holy one to see corruption.' 36* Now David, after he had served the will of God in his lifetime, fell asleep, was gathered to his ancestors, and did see corruption. 37 But the one whom God raised up did not see corruption. 38† You must know, my brothers, that through him forgiveness of sins is being proclaimed to you, [and] in regard to everything from which you could not be justified under the law of Moses, 39* in him every believer is justified. 40 Be careful, then, that what was said in the prophets not come about:

41* 'Look on, you scoffers,
 be amazed and disappear.
For I am doing a work in your days,
 a work that you will never believe
 even if someone tells you.' "

42 As they were leaving, they invited them to speak on these subjects the following sabbath. 43 After the congregation had dispersed, many Jews and worshipers who were converts to Judaism followed Paul and Barnabas, who spoke to them and urged them to remain faithful to the grace of God.

Address to the Gentiles. 44 On the following sabbath almost the whole city gathered to hear the word of the Lord. 45 When the Jews saw the crowds, they were filled with jealousy and with violent abuse contradicted what Paul said. 46*† Both Paul and Barnabas spoke out boldly and said, "It was necessary that the word of God be spoken to you first, but since you reject it and condemn yourselves as unworthy of eternal life, we now turn to the Gentiles. 47* For so the Lord has commanded us, 'I have made you a light to the Gentiles, that you may be an instrument of salvation to the ends of the earth.' "

48 The Gentiles were delighted when they heard this and glorified the word of the Lord. All who were destined for eternal life came to believe, 49 and the word of the Lord continued to spread through the whole region. 50 The Jews, however, incited the women of prominence who were worshipers and the leading men of the city, stirred up a persecution against Paul and Barnabas, and expelled them from their territory. 51*† So they shook the dust from their feet in protest against them and went to Iconium. 52 The disciples were filled with joy and the holy Spirit.

CHAPTER 14

Paul and Barnabas at Iconium. 1 In Iconium they entered the Jewish synagogue together and spoke in such a way that a great number of both Jews and Greeks came to believe, 2 although the disbelieving Jews stirred up and poisoned the minds of the Gentiles against the brothers. 3* So they stayed for a considerable period, speaking out boldly for the Lord, who confirmed the word about his grace by granting signs and wonders to occur through their hands. 4 The people of the city were divided: some were with the Jews; others, with the apostles. 5* When there was an attempt by both the Gentiles and the Jews, together with their leaders, to attack and stone them, 6 they realized it and fled to the Lycaonian cities of Lys-

*

28: Mt 27, 20.22-23; Mk 15, 13-14; Lk 23, 4.14-15.21-23; Jn 19, 4-6.15.
29: Mt 27, 59-60; Mk 15, 46; Lk 23, 53; Jn 19, 38.41-42.
30: 2, 24.32; 3, 15; 4, 10; 17, 31.
31: 1, 3.8; 10, 39.41; Mt 28, 8-10.16-20; Mk 16, 9.12-20; Lk 24, 13-53; Jn 20, 11-29; 21, 1-23.
33: Ps 2, 7.
34: Is 55, 3.
35: Ps 16, 10.
36: 2, 29; 1 Kgs 2, 10.
39: Rom 3, 20.
41: Hb 1, 5.
46: 3, 26; Rom 1, 16.
47: Is 49, 6.
51: Mt 10, 14; Mk 6, 11; Lk 9, 5; 10, 11.
14, 3: Mk 16, 17-20.
5: 2 Tm 3, 11.

†

13, 31: The theme of the Galilean witnesses is a major one in the Gospel of Luke and in Acts and is used to signify the continuity between the teachings of Jesus and the teachings of the church and to guarantee the fidelity of the church's teachings to the words of Jesus.

13, 38-39: *Justified:* the verb is the same as that used in Paul's letters to speak of the experience of justification and, as in Paul, is here connected with the term "to have faith" ("every believer"). But this seems the only passage about Paul in Acts where justification is mentioned. In Lucan fashion it is paralleled with "forgiveness of sins" (a theme at 2, 38; 3, 19; 5, 31; 10, 43) based on Jesus' resurrection (37) rather than his cross, and is put negatively (38). Therefore, some would translate, "in regard to everything from which you could not be acquitted . . . every believer is acquitted."

13, 46: The refusal to believe frustrates God's plan for his chosen people; however, no adverse judgment is made here concerning their ultimate destiny. Again, Luke, in the words of Paul, speaks of the priority of Israel in the plan for salvation (see 10, 36).

13, 51: See the note on Lk 9, 5.

tra and Derbe and to the surrounding
countryside, 7 where they continued to
proclaim the good news.
Paul and Barnabas at Lystra. † 8 At
Lystra there was a crippled man, lame
from birth, who had never walked.
9 He listened to Paul speaking, who
looked intently at him, saw that he had
the faith to be healed, 10 and called out
in a loud voice, "Stand up straight on
your feet." He jumped up and began to
walk about. 11* When the crowds saw
what Paul had done, they cried out in
Lycaonian, "The gods have come down
to us in human form." 12† They called
Barnabas "Zeus" and Paul "Hermes,"
because he was the chief speaker.
13 And the priest of Zeus, whose temple
was at the entrance to the city, brought
oxen and garlands to the gates, for he
together with the people intended to of-
fer sacrifice.
14† The apostles Barnabas and Paul
tore their garments when they heard
this and rushed out into the crowd,
shouting, 15*† "Men, why are you doing
this? We are of the same nature as you,
human beings. We proclaim to you good
news that you should turn from these
idols to the living God, 'who made
heaven and earth and sea and all that
is in them.' 16* In past generations he
allowed all Gentiles to go their own
ways; 17* yet, in bestowing his goodness,
he did not leave himself without wit-
ness, for he gave you rains from heaven
and fruitful seasons, and filled you with
nourishment and gladness for your
hearts." 18 Even with these words, they
scarcely restrained the crowds from of-
fering sacrifice to them.
19* However, some Jews from Antioch
and Iconium arrived and won over the
crowds. They stoned Paul and dragged
him out of the city, supposing that he
was dead. 20 But when the disciples
gathered around him, he got up and en-
tered the city. On the following day he
left with Barnabas for Derbe.
End of the First Mission. 21 After they
had proclaimed the good news to that
city and made a considerable number
of disciples, they returned to Lystra and
to Iconium and to Antioch. 22* They
strengthened the spirits of the disciples
and exhorted them to persevere in the
faith, saying, "It is necessary for us to
undergo many hardships to enter the
kingdom of God." 23† They appointed
presbyters for them in each church and,
with prayer and fasting, commended
them to the Lord in whom they had put
their faith. 24 Then they traveled
through Pisidia and reached Pam-
phylia. 25 After proclaiming the word at
Perga they went down to Attalia.
26* From there they sailed to Antioch,
where they had been commended to the
grace of God for the work they had now
accomplished. 27 And when they ar-
rived, they called the church together
and reported what God had done with
them and how he had opened the door
of faith to the Gentiles. 28 Then they
spent no little time with the disciples.

CHAPTER 15

Council of Jerusalem. † 1*† Some who
had come down from Judea were in-
structing the brothers, "Unless you are
circumcised according to the Mosaic
practice, you cannot be saved."
2 Because there arose no little dissen-
sion and debate by Paul and Barnabas
with them, it was decided that Paul,
Barnabas, and some of the others
should go up to Jerusalem to the apos-
tles and presbyters about this question.
3 They were sent on their journey by the
church, and passed through Phoenicia
and Samaria telling of the conversion
of the Gentiles, and brought great joy
to all the brothers. 4 When they arrived
in Jerusalem, they were welcomed by
the church, as well as by the apostles
and the presbyters, and they reported
what God had done with them. 5 But
some from the party of the Pharisees
who had become believers stood up and

*

11: 28, 6.
15: 3, 12; 10, 26; Ex 20, 11; Ps 146, 6.
16: 17, 30.
17: Wis 13, 1.
19-20: 2 Cor 11, 25; 2 Tm 3, 11.
22: 1 Thes 3, 3.
26: 13, 1-3.
15, 1-4: Gal 2, 1-9.
1: Lv 12, 3; Gal 5, 2.

†

14, 8-18: In an effort to convince his hearers that the divine power works through his word, Paul cures the cripple. However, the pagan tradition of the occasional appearance of gods among human beings leads the people astray in interpreting the miracle. The incident reveals the cultural difficulties with which the church had to cope. Note the similarity of the miracle worked here by Paul to the one performed by Peter in 3, 2-10.

14, 12: *Zeus . . . Hermes:* in Greek religion, Zeus was the chief of the Olympian gods, the "father of gods and men"; Hermes was a son of Zeus and was usually identified as the herald and messenger of the gods.

14, 14: *Tore their garments:* a gesture of protest.

14, 15-17: This is the first speech of Paul to Gentiles recorded by Luke in Acts (cf 17, 22-31). Rather than showing how Christianity is the logical outgrowth of Judaism, as he does in speeches before Jews, Luke says that God excuses past Gentile ignorance and then presents a natural theology arguing for the recognition of God's existence and presence through his activity in natural phenomena.

14, 23: *They appointed presbyters:* the communities are given their own religious leaders by the traveling missionaries. The structure in these churches is patterned on the model of the Jerusalem community (11, 30; 15, 2.5.22; 21, 18).

15, 1-35: The Jerusalem "Council" marks the official rejection of the rigid view that Gentile converts were obliged to observe the Mosaic law completely. From here to the end of Acts, Paul and the Gentile mission become the focus of Luke's writing.

15, 1-5: When some of the converted Pharisees of Jerusalem discover the results of the first missionary journey of Paul, they urge that the Gentiles be taught to follow the Mosaic law. Recognizing the authority of the Jerusalem church, Paul and Barnabas go there to settle the question of whether Gentiles can embrace a form of Christianity that does not include this obligation.

said, "It is necessary to circumcise
them and direct them to observe the
Mosaic law."
6† The apostles and the presbyters
met together to see about this matter.
7*† After much debate had taken place,
Peter got up and said to them, "My
brothers, you are well aware that from
early days God made his choice among
you that through my mouth the Gentiles
would hear the word of the gospel and
believe. 8* And God, who knows the
heart, bore witness by granting them
the holy Spirit just as he did us. 9* He
made no distinction between us and
them, for by faith he purified their
hearts. 10* Why, then, are you now put-
ting God to the test by placing on the
shoulders of the disciples a yoke that
neither our ancestors nor we have been
able to bear? 11*† On the contrary, we
believe that we are saved through the
grace of the Lord Jesus, in the same
way as they." 12 The whole assembly fell
silent, and they listened while Paul and
Barnabas described the signs and won-
ders God had worked among the Gen-
tiles through them.
James on Dietary Law.† 13 After they
had fallen silent, James responded,
"My brothers, listen to me. 14† Symeon
has described how God first concerned
himself with acquiring from among the
Gentiles a people for his name. 15 The
words of the prophets agree with this,
as is written:

16* 'After this I shall return
and rebuild the fallen hut of David;
from its ruins I shall rebuild it
and raise it up again,
17 so that the rest of humanity may
seek out the Lord,
even all the Gentiles on whom my
name is invoked.
Thus says the Lord who accomplishes these things,
18 known from of old.'

19* It is my judgment, therefore, that we
ought to stop troubling the Gentiles who
turn to God, 20* but tell them by letter
to avoid pollution from idols, unlawful
marriage, the meat of strangled ani-
mals, and blood. 21 For Moses, for gen-
erations now, has had those who
proclaim him in every town, as he has
been read in the synagogues every sab-
bath."
Letter of the Apostles. 22 Then the
apostles and presbyters, in agreement
with the whole church, decided to
choose representatives and to send
them to Antioch with Paul and Barna-
bas. The ones chosen were Judas, who
was called Barsabbas, and Silas, lead-
ers among the brothers. 23 This is the
letter delivered by them: "The apostles
and the presbyters, your brothers, to
the brothers in Antioch, Syria, and Cili-
cia of Gentile origin: greetings. 24 Since
we have heard that some of our number
[who went out] without any mandate
from us have upset you with their teach-
ings and disturbed your peace of mind,
25 we have with one accord decided to
choose representatives and to send
them to you along with our beloved Bar-
nabas and Paul, 26 who have dedicated
their lives to the name of our Lord Jesus
Christ. 27 So we are sending Judas and
Silas who will also convey this same
message by word of mouth: 28* 'It is the
decision of the holy Spirit and of us not
to place on you any burden beyond
these necessities, 29* namely, to abstain
from meat sacrificed to idols, from
blood, from meats of strangled animals,
and from unlawful marriage. If you
keep free of these, you will be doing
what is right. Farewell.'"
Delegates at Antioch. 30 And so they
were sent on their journey. Upon their
arrival in Antioch they called the as-
sembly together and delivered the let-
ter. 31 When the people read it, they
were delighted with the exhortation.
32 Judas and Silas, who were themselves

*

7: 10, 27-43.
8: 10, 44-48.
9: 10, 34-35.
10: Mt 23, 4; Gal 5, 1.
11: Gal 2, 16; 3, 11; Eph 2, 5-8.
16-18: Am 9, 11-12.
19-20: 15, 28-29; 21, 25.
20: Gn 9, 4; Lv 3, 17; 17, 10-14.
28-29: 15, 19-20.
29: Gn 9, 4; Lv 3, 17; 17, 10-14.

†

15, 6-12: The gathering is possibly the same as that recalled by Paul in Gal 2, 1-10. Note that in v 2 it is only the apostles and presbyters, a small group, with whom Paul and Barnabas are to meet. Here Luke gives the meeting a public character because he wishes to emphasize its doctrinal significance (see 22).

15, 7-11: Paul's refusal to impose the Mosaic law on the Gentile Christians is supported by Peter on the ground that within his own experience God bestowed the holy Spirit upon Cornelius and his household without preconditions concerning the adoption of the Mosaic law (see 10, 44-47).

15, 11: In support of Paul, Peter formulates the fundamental meaning of the gospel: that all are invited to be saved through faith in the power of Christ.

15, 13-35: Some scholars think that this apostolic decree suggested by James, the immediate leader of the Jerusalem community, derives from another historical occasion than the meeting in question. This seems to be the case if the meeting is the same as the one related in Gal 2, 1-10. According to that account, nothing was imposed upon Gentile Christians in respect to Mosaic law; whereas the decree instructs Gentile Christians of mixed communities to abstain from meats sacrificed to idols and from blood-meats, and to avoid marriage within forbidden degrees of consanguinity and affinity (Lv 18), all of which practices were especially abhorrent to Jews. Luke seems to have telescoped two originally independent incidents here: the first a Jerusalem "Council" that dealt with the question of circumcision, and the second a Jerusalem decree dealing mainly with Gentile observance of dietary laws (see 21, 25 where Paul seems to be learning of the decree for the first time).

15, 14: *Symeon:* elsewhere in Acts he is called either Peter or Simon. The presence of the name Symeon here suggests that, in the source Luke is using for this part of the Jerusalem "Council" incident, the name may have originally referred to someone other than Peter (see 13, 1 where the Antiochene Symeon Niger is mentioned). As the text now stands, however, it is undoubtedly a reference to Simon Peter (7).

prophets, exhorted and strengthened the brothers with many words. 33 After they had spent some time there, they were sent off with greetings of peace from the brothers to those who had commissioned them. [34]† 35 But Paul and Barnabas remained in Antioch, teaching and proclaiming with many others the word of the Lord.

V: THE MISSION OF PAUL TO THE ENDS OF THE EARTH

Paul and Barnabas Separate.† 36 After some time, Paul said to Barnabas, "Come, let us make a return visit to see how the brothers are getting on in all the cities where we proclaimed the word of the Lord." 37 Barnabas wanted to take with them also John, who was called Mark, 38* but Paul insisted that they should not take with them someone who had deserted them at Pamphylia and who had not continued with them in their work. 39 So sharp was their disagreement that they separated. Barnabas took Mark and sailed to Cyprus. 40 But Paul chose Silas and departed after being commended by the brothers to the grace of the Lord. 41 He traveled through Syria and Cilicia bringing strength to the churches.

CHAPTER 16

Paul in Lycaonia: Timothy. 1* He reached [also] Derbe and Lystra where there was a disciple named Timothy, the son of a Jewish woman who was a believer, but his father was a Greek. 2* The brothers in Lystra and Iconium spoke highly of him, 3† and Paul wanted him to come along with him. On account of the Jews of that region, Paul had him circumcised, for they all knew that his father was a Greek. 4 As they traveled from city to city, they handed on to the people for observance the decisions reached by the apostles and presbyters in Jerusalem. 5 Day after day the churches grew stronger in faith and increased in number.

Through Asia Minor. 6 They traveled through the Phrygian and Galatian territory because they had been prevented by the holy Spirit from preaching the message in the province of Asia. 7† When they came to Mysia, they tried to go on into Bithynia, but the Spirit of Jesus did not allow them, 8 so they crossed through Mysia and came down to Troas. 9 During [the] night Paul had a vision. A Macedonian stood before him and implored him with these words, "Come over to Macedonia and help us." 10† When he had seen the vision, we sought passage to Macedonia at once, concluding that God had called us to proclaim the good news to them.

Into Europe.† 11 We set sail from Troas, making a straight run for Samothrace, and on the next day to Neapolis, 12 and from there to Philippi, a leading city in that district of Macedonia and a Roman colony. We spent some time in that city. 13 On the sabbath we went outside the city gate along the river where we thought there would be a place of prayer. We sat and spoke with the women who had gathered there. 14† One of them, a woman named Lydia, a dealer in purple cloth, from the city of Thyatira, a worshiper of God, listened, and the Lord opened her heart to pay attention to what Paul was saying. 15 After she and her household had been baptized, she offered us an invitation, "If you consider me a believer in the Lord, come and stay at my home," and she prevailed on us.

Imprisonment at Philippi. 16† As we were going to the place of prayer, we met a slave girl with an oracular spirit,

*

38: 13, 13.
16, 1: 1 Tm 1, 2; 2 Tm 1, 5.
2: Phil 2, 20.

†

15, 34: Some manuscripts add, in various wordings, "But Silas decided to remain there."

15, 36—18, 22: This continuous narrative recounts Paul's second missionary journey. On the internal evidence of the Lucan account, it lasted about three years. Paul first visited the communities he had established on his first journey (16, 1-5), then pushed on into Macedonia, where he established communities at Philippi, Thessalonica, and Beroea (16, 7—17, 5). To escape the hostility of the Jews of Thessalonica, he left for Greece and while resident in Athens attempted, without success, to establish an effective Christian community there. From Athens he proceeded to Corinth and, after a stay of a year and a half, returned to Antioch by way of Ephesus and Jerusalem (17, 16—18, 22). Luke does not concern himself with the structure or statistics of the communities but aims to show the general progress of the gospel in the Gentile world as well as its continued failure to take root in the Jewish community.

16, 3: *Paul had him circumcised:* he did this in order that Timothy might be able to associate with the Jews and so perform a ministry among them. Paul did not object to the Jewish Christians' adherence to the law. But he insisted that the law could not be imposed on the Gentiles. Paul himself lived in accordance with the law, or as exempt from the law, according to particular circumstances (see 1 Cor 9, 19-23).

16, 7: *The Spirit of Jesus:* this is an unusual formulation in Luke's writings. The parallelism with v 6 indicates its meaning, the holy Spirit.

16, 10-17: This is the first of the so-called "we-sections" in Acts, where Luke writes as one of Paul's companions. The other passages are 20, 5-15; 21, 1-18; 27, 1—28, 16. Scholars debate whether Luke may not have used the first person plural simply as a literary device to lend color to the narrative. The realism of the narrative, however, lends weight to the argument that the "we" includes Luke or another companion of Paul whose data Luke used as a source.

16, 11-40: The church at Philippi became a flourishing community to which Paul addressed one of his letters (see Introduction to the Letter to the Philippians).

16, 14: *A worshiper of God:* a "God-fearer." See the note on 8, 26-40.

16, 16: *With an oracular spirit:* literally, "with a Python spirit." The Python was the serpent or dragon that guarded the Delphic oracle. It later came to designate a "spirit that pronounced oracles" and also a ventriloquist who, it was thought, had such a spirit in the belly.

who used to bring a large profit to her
owners through her fortune-telling.
17 She began to follow Paul and us,
shouting, "These people are slaves of
the Most High God, who proclaim to you
a way of salvation." 18 She did this for
many days. Paul became annoyed,
turned, and said to the spirit, "I com-
mand you in the name of Jesus Christ
to come out of her." Then it came out
at that moment.

19 When her owners saw that their
hope of profit was gone, they seized
Paul and Silas and dragged them to the
public square before the local authori-
ties. 20† They brought them before the
magistrates and said, "These people are
Jews and are disturbing our city 21 and
are advocating customs that are not
lawful for us Romans to adopt or prac-
tice." 22* The crowd joined in the attack
on them, and the magistrates had them
stripped and ordered them to be beaten
with rods. 23 After inflicting many blows
on them, they threw them into prison
and instructed the jailer to guard them
securely. 24 When he received these in-
structions, he put them in the innermost
cell and secured their feet to a stake.

Deliverance from Prison. 25 About
midnight, while Paul and Silas were
praying and singing hymns to God as
the prisoners listened, 26 there was sud-
denly such a severe earthquake that the
foundations of the jail shook; all the
doors flew open, and the chains of all
were pulled loose. 27 When the jailer
woke up and saw the prison doors wide
open, he drew [his] sword and was
about to kill himself, thinking that the
prisoners had escaped. 28 But Paul
shouted out in a loud voice, "Do no
harm to yourself; we are all here."
29 He asked for a light and rushed in
and, trembling with fear, he fell down
before Paul and Silas. 30 Then he
brought them out and said, "Sirs, what
must I do to be saved?" 31 And they said,
"Believe in the Lord Jesus and you and
your household will be saved." 32 So
they spoke the word of the Lord to him
and to everyone in his house. 33 He took
them in at that hour of the night and
bathed their wounds; then he and all his
family were baptized at once. 34 He
brought them up into his house and pro-
vided a meal and with his household re-
joiced at having come to faith in God.

35† But when it was day, the magis-
trates sent the lictors with the order,
"Release those men." 36 The jailer re-
ported the[se] words to Paul, "The
magistrates have sent orders that you
be released. Now, then, come out and
go in peace." 37*† But Paul said to them,
"They have beaten us publicly, even
though we are Roman citizens and have
not been tried, and have thrown us into
prison. And now, are they going to re-
lease us secretly? By no means. Let
them come themselves and lead us out."
38* The lictors reported these words to
the magistrates, and they became
alarmed when they heard that they
were Roman citizens. 39 So they came
and placated them, and led them out
and asked that they leave the city.
40 When they had come out of the prison,
they went to Lydia's house where they
saw and encouraged the brothers, and
then they left.

CHAPTER 17

Paul in Thessalonica. 1* When they
took the road through Amphipolis and
Apollonia, they reached Thessalonica,
where there was a synagogue of the
Jews. 2 Following his usual custom,
Paul joined them, and for three sab-
baths he entered into discussions with
them from the scriptures, 3* ex-
pounding and demonstrating that the
Messiah had to suffer and rise from
the dead, and that "This is the Messiah,
Jesus, whom I proclaim to you." 4 Some
of them were convinced and joined Paul
and Silas; so, too, a great number of
Greeks who were worshipers, and not
a few of the prominent women. 5* But
the Jews became jealous and recruited
some worthless men loitering in the
public square, formed a mob, and set
the city in turmoil. They marched on
the house of Jason, intending to bring
them before the people's assembly.
6† When they could not find them, they
dragged Jason and some of the brothers
before the city magistrates, shouting,
"These people who have been creating
a disturbance all over the world have
now come here, 7*† and Jason has wel-
comed them. They all act in opposition
to the decrees of Caesar and claim in-
stead that there is another king, Jesus."
8 They stirred up the crowd and the city
magistrates who, upon hearing these
charges, 9 took a surety payment from

---

*

22-23: 2 Cor 11, 25; Phil 1, 30; 1 Thes 2, 2.
37: 22, 25.
38: 22, 29.
17, 1: 1 Thes 2, 1-2.
3: 3, 18; Lk 24, 25-26.46.
5: Rom 16, 21.
7: Lk 23, 2; Jn 19, 12-15.

---

†

16, 20: *Magistrates:* in Greek, *stratēgoi,* the popular designation of the *duoviri,* the highest officials of the Roman colony of Philippi.

16, 35: *The lictors:* the equivalent of police officers, among whose duties were the apprehension and punishment of criminals.

16, 37: Paul's Roman citizenship granted him special privileges in regard to criminal process. Roman law forbade under severe penalty the beating of Roman citizens (see also 22, 25).

17, 6-7: The accusations against Paul and his companions echo the charges brought against Jesus in Lk 23, 2.

17, 7: *There is another king, Jesus:* a distortion into a political sense of the apostolic proclamation of Jesus and the kingdom of God (see 8, 12).

Jason and the others before releasing
them.
Paul in Beroea. 10 The brothers im-
mediately sent Paul and Silas to Beroea
during the night. Upon arrival they
went to the synagogue of the Jews.
11* These Jews were more fair-minded
than those in Thessalonica, for they re-
ceived the word with all willingness and
examined the scriptures daily to deter-
mine whether these things were so.
12 Many of them became believers, as
did not a few of the influential Greek
women and men. 13 But when the Jews
of Thessalonica learned that the word
of God had now been proclaimed by
Paul in Beroea also, they came there
too to cause a commotion and stir up
the crowds. 14* So the brothers at once
sent Paul on his way to the seacoast,
while Silas and Timothy remained be-
hind. 15 After Paul's escorts had taken
him to Athens, they came away with in-
structions for Silas and Timothy to join
him as soon as possible.
Paul in Athens.† 16 While Paul was
waiting for them in Athens, he grew ex-
asperated at the sight of the city full of
idols. 17 So he debated in the synagogue
with the Jews and with the worshipers,
and daily in the public square with
whoever happened to be there. 18† Even
some of the Epicurean and Stoic philos-
ophers engaged him in discussion.
Some asked, "What is this scavenger
trying to say?" Others said, "He sounds
like a promoter of foreign deities," be-
cause he was preaching about 'Jesus'
and 'Resurrection.' 19*† They took him
and led him to the Areopagus and said,
"May we learn what this new teaching
is that you speak of? 20 For you bring
some strange notions to our ears; we
should like to know what these things
mean." 21 Now all the Athenians as well
as the foreigners residing there used
their time for nothing else but telling
or hearing something new.
Paul's Speech at the Areopagus.†
22 Then Paul stood up at the Areopagus
and said:
"You Athenians, I see that in every
respect you are very religious. 23† For
as I walked around looking carefully at
your shrines, I even discovered an altar
inscribed, 'To an Unknown God.' What
therefore you unknowingly worship, I
proclaim to you. 24* The God who made
the world and all that is in it, the Lord
of heaven and earth, does not dwell in
sanctuaries made by human hands,
25 nor is he served by human hands be-
cause he needs anything. Rather it is
he who gives to everyone life and breath
and everything. 26† He made from one
the whole human race to dwell on the
entire surface of the earth, and he fixed
the ordered seasons and the boundaries
of their regions, 27* so that people might
seek God, even perhaps grope for him
and find him, though indeed he is not
far from any one of us. 28† For 'In him
we live and move and have our being,'
as even some of your poets have said,
'For we too are his offspring.' 29* Since
therefore we are the offspring of God,
we ought not to think that the divinity
is like an image fashioned from gold,
silver, or stone by human art and imagi-
nation. 30 God has overlooked the times
of ignorance, but now he demands that
all people everywhere repent 31* be-
cause he has established a day on
which he will 'judge the world with jus-
tice' through a man he has appointed,

*

11: Jn 5, 39.
14: 1 Thes 3, 1-2.
19: 1 Cor 1, 22.
24: 7, 48-50; Gn 1, 1; 1 Kgs 8, 27; Is 42, 5.
27: Jer 23, 23; Wis 13, 6; Rom 1, 19.
29: 19, 26; Is 40, 18-20; 44, 10-17; Rom 1, 22-23.
31: 10, 42.

†

17, 16-21: Paul's presence in Athens sets the stage for the great discourse before a Gentile audience in vv 22-31. Although Athens was a politically insignificant city at this period, it still lived on the glories of its past and represented the center of Greek culture. The setting describes the conflict between Christian preaching and Hellenistic philosophy.

17, 18: *Epicurean and Stoic philosophers:* for the followers of Epicurus (342-271 B.C.), the goal of life was happiness attained through sober reasoning and the searching out of motives for all choice and avoidance. The Stoics were followers of Zeno, a younger contemporary of Alexander the Great. Zeno and his followers believed in a type of pantheism that held that the spark of divinity was present in all reality and that, in order to be free, each person must live "according to nature." *This scavenger:* literally, "seed-picker," as of a bird that picks up grain. The word is later used of scrap collectors and of people who take other people's ideas and propagate them as if they were their own. *Promoter of foreign deities:* according to Xenophon, Socrates was accused of promoting new deities. The accusation against Paul echoes the charge against Socrates. *'Jesus' and 'Resurrection':* the Athenians are presented as misunderstanding Paul from the outset; they think he is preaching about Jesus and a goddess named *Anastasis,* i.e., Resurrection.

17, 19: *To the Areopagus:* the "Areopagus" refers either to the Hill of Ares west of the Acropolis or to the Council of Athens, which at one time met on the hill but which at this time assembled in the Royal Colonnade (*Stoa Basileios*).

17, 22-31: In Paul's appearance at the Areopagus he preaches his climactic speech to Gentiles in the cultural center of the ancient world. The speech is more theological than christological. Paul's discourse appeals to the Greek world's belief in divinity as responsible for the origin and existence of the universe. It contests the common belief in a multiplicity of gods supposedly exerting their powers through their images. It acknowledges that the attempt to find God is a constant human endeavor. It declares, further, that God is the judge of the human race, that the time of the judgment has been determined, and that it will be executed through a man whom God raised from the dead. The speech reflects sympathy with pagan religiosity, handles the subject of idol worship gently, and appeals for a new examination of divinity, not from the standpoint of creation but from the standpoint of judgment.

17, 23: *'To an Unknown God':* ancient authors such as Pausanias, Philostratus, and Tertullian speak of Athenian altars with no specific dedication as altars of "unknown gods" or "nameless altars."

17, 26: *From one:* many manuscripts read "from one blood." *Fixed . . . seasons:* or "fixed limits to the epochs."

17, 28: *'In him we live and move and have our being':* some scholars understand this saying to be based on an earlier saying of Epimenides of Knossos (6th century B.C.). *'For we too are his offspring':* here Paul is quoting Aratus of Soli, a third-century B.C. poet from Cilicia.

and he has provided confirmation for
all by raising him from the dead."
32 When they heard about resur-
rection of the dead, some began to scoff,
but others said, "We should like to hear
you on this some other time." 33 And so
Paul left them. 34 But some did join him,
and became believers. Among them
were Dionysius, a member of the Court
of the Areopagus, a woman named Da-
maris, and others with them.

CHAPTER 18

Paul in Corinth. 1 After this he left
Athens and went to Corinth. 2*† There
he met a Jew named Aquila, a native
of Pontus, who had recently come from
Italy with his wife Priscilla because
Claudius had ordered all the Jews to
leave Rome. He went to visit them
3 and, because he practiced the same
trade, stayed with them and worked, for
they were tentmakers by trade. 4 Every
sabbath, he entered into discussions in
the synagogue, attempting to convince
both Jews and Greeks.
5 When Silas and Timothy came down
from Macedonia, Paul began to occupy
himself totally with preaching the word,
testifying to the Jews that the Messiah
was Jesus. 6*† When they opposed him
and reviled him, he shook out his gar-
ments and said to them, "Your blood
be on your heads! I am clear of respon-
sibility. From now on I will go to the
Gentiles." 7*† So he left there and went
to a house belonging to a man named
Titus Justus, a worshiper of God; his
house was next to a synagogue.
8*† Crispus, the synagogue official,
came to believe in the Lord along with
his entire household, and many of the
Corinthians who heard believed and
were baptized. 9* One night in a vision
the Lord said to Paul, "Do not be afraid.
Go on speaking, and do not be silent,
10 for I am with you. No one will attack
and harm you, for I have many people
in this city." 11 He settled there for a
year and a half and taught the word of
God among them.
Accusations before Gallio. 12† But
when Gallio was proconsul of Achaia,
the Jews rose up together against Paul
and brought him to the tribunal,
13† saying, "This man is inducing people
to worship God contrary to the law."
14 When Paul was about to reply, Gallio
spoke to the Jews, "If it were a matter
of some crime or malicious fraud, I
should with reason hear the complaint
of you Jews; 15 but since it is a question
of arguments over doctrine and titles
and your own law, see to it yourselves.
I do not wish to be a judge of such mat-
ters." 16 And he drove them away from
the tribunal. 17 They all seized Sos-
thenes, the synagogue official, and beat
him in full view of the tribunal. But none
of this was of concern to Gallio.
Return to Syrian Antioch. 18*† Paul
remained for quite some time, and after
saying farewell to the brothers he sailed
for Syria, together with Priscilla and
Aquila. At Cenchreae he had his hair
cut because he had taken a vow. 19 When
they reached Ephesus, he left them
there, while he entered the synagogue
and held discussions with the Jews.
20 Although they asked him to stay for
a longer time, he did not consent,
21 but as he said farewell he promised,
"I shall come back to you again, God
willing." Then he set sail from Ephesus.
22† Upon landing at Caesarea, he went
up and greeted the church and then
went down to Antioch. 23† After staying
there some time, he left and traveled
in orderly sequence through the Gala-
tian country and Phrygia, bringing
strength to all the disciples.
Apollos.† 24* A Jew named Apollos, a
native of Alexandria, an eloquent
speaker, arrived in Ephesus. He was an
authority on the scriptures. 25 He had
been instructed in the Way of the Lord
and, with ardent spirit, spoke and
taught accurately about Jesus, al-
though he knew only the baptism of

*

18, 2: Rom 16, 3.
6: 13, 51; Mt 10, 14; 27, 24-25; Mk 6, 11; Lk 9, 5; 10, 10-11.
7: 13, 46-47; 28, 28.
8: 1 Cor 1, 14.
9-10: Jer 1, 8.
18: 21, 24; Nm 6, 18.
24: 1 Cor 1, 12.

†

18, 2: *Aquila . . . Priscilla:* both may already have been Christians at the time of their arrival in Corinth (see 26). According to 1 Cor 16, 19, their home became a meeting place for Christians. *Claudius:* the Emperor Claudius expelled the Jews from Rome ca. A.D. 40. The Roman historian Suetonius gives as reason for the expulsion disturbances among the Jews "at the instigation of Chrestos," probably meaning disputes about the messiahship of Jesus.

18, 6: *Shook out his garments:* a gesture indicating Paul's repudiation of his mission to the Jews there; cf 28, 17-31.

18, 7: *A worshiper of God:* see the note on 8, 26-40.

18, 8: *Crispus:* in 1 Cor 1, 14, Paul mentions that Crispus was one of the few he himself baptized at Corinth.

18, 12: *When Gallio was proconsul of Achaia:* Gallio's proconsulship in Achaia is dated to A.D. 51-52 from an inscription discovered at Delphi. This has become an important date in establishing a chronology of the life and missionary work of Paul.

18, 13: *Contrary to the law:* Gallio (15) understands this to be a problem of Jewish, not Roman, law.

18, 18: *He had his hair cut because he had taken a vow:* a reference to a Nazirite vow (see Nm 6, 1-21, especially, 6, 18) taken by Paul (see also 21, 23-27).

18, 22: *He went up and greeted the church:* "going up" suggests a visit to the church in Jerusalem.

18, 23—21, 16: Luke's account of Paul's third missionary journey devotes itself mainly to his work at Ephesus (19, 1—20, 1). There is a certain restiveness on Paul's part and a growing conviction that the Spirit bids him return to Jerusalem and prepare to go to Rome (19, 21).

18, 24-25: Apollos appears as a preacher who knows the teaching of Jesus in the context of John's baptism of repentance. Aquila and Priscilla instruct him more fully. He is referred to in 1 Cor 1, 12; 3, 5-6.22.

John. 26† He began to speak boldly in
the synagogue; but when Priscilla and
Aquila heard him, they took him aside
and explained to him the Way [of God]
more accurately. 27 And when he
wanted to cross to Achaia, the brothers
encouraged him and wrote to the disci-
ples there to welcome him. After his ar-
rival he gave great assistance to those
who had come to believe through grace.
28 He vigorously refuted the Jews in
public, establishing from the scriptures
that the Messiah is Jesus.

CHAPTER 19

Paul in Ephesus. † 1 While Apollos
was in Corinth, Paul traveled through
the interior of the country and came
[down] to Ephesus where he found
some disciples. 2 He said to them, "Did
you receive the holy Spirit when you be-
came believers?" They answered him,
"We have never even heard that there
is a holy Spirit." 3 He said, "How were
you baptized?" They replied, "With the
baptism of John." 4* Paul then said,
"John baptized with a baptism of repen-
tance, telling the people to believe in the
one who was to come after him, that is,
in Jesus." 5 When they heard this, they
were baptized in the name of the Lord
Jesus. 6* And when Paul laid [his]
hands on them, the holy Spirit came
upon them, and they spoke in tongues
and prophesied. 7 Altogether there were
about twelve men.

8 He entered the synagogue, and for
three months debated boldly with per-
suasive arguments about the kingdom
of God. 9 But when some in their obsti-
nacy and disbelief disparaged the Way
before the assembly, he withdrew and
took his disciples with him and began
to hold daily discussions in the lecture
hall of Tyrannus. 10 This continued for
two years with the result that all the in-
habitants of the province of Asia heard
the word of the Lord, Jews and Greeks
alike. 11 So extraordinary were the
mighty deeds God accomplished at the
hands of Paul 12* that when face cloths
or aprons that touched his skin were ap-
plied to the sick, their diseases left them
and the evil spirits came out of them.

The Jewish Exorcists. 13 Then some
itinerant Jewish exorcists tried to in-
voke the name of the Lord Jesus over
those with evil spirits, saying, "I adjure
you by the Jesus whom Paul preaches."
14 When the seven sons of Sceva, a Jew-
ish high priest, tried to do this, 15 the
evil spirit said to them in reply, "Jesus
I recognize, Paul I know, but who are
you?" 16 The person with the evil spirit
then sprang at them and subdued them
all. He so overpowered them that they
fled naked and wounded from that
house. 17 When this became known to all
the Jews and Greeks who lived in Ephe-
sus, fear fell upon them all, and the
name of the Lord Jesus was held in
great esteem. 18 Many of those who had
become believers came forward and
openly acknowledged their former
practices. 19 Moreover, a large number
of those who had practiced magic col-
lected their books and burned them in
public. They calculated their value and
found it to be fifty thousand silver
pieces. 20 Thus did the word of the Lord
continue to spread with influence and
power.

Paul's Plans. 21* When this was con-
cluded, Paul made up his mind to travel
through Macedonia and Achaia, and
then to go on to Jerusalem, saying, "Af-
ter I have been there, I must visit Rome
also." 22 Then he sent to Macedonia two
of his assistants, Timothy and Erastus,
while he himself stayed for a while in
the province of Asia.

The Riot of the Silversmiths. 23 About
that time a serious disturbance broke
out concerning the Way. 24† There was
a silversmith named Demetrius who
made miniature silver shrines of Ar-
temis and provided no little work for the
craftsmen. 25 He called a meeting of
these and other workers in related
crafts and said, "Men, you know well
that our prosperity derives from this
work. 26* As you can now see and hear,
not only in Ephesus but throughout
most of the province of Asia this Paul
has persuaded and misled a great num-
ber of people by saying that gods made
by hands are not gods at all. 27 The dan-
ger grows, not only that our business
will be discredited, but also that the
temple of the great goddess Artemis will
be of no account, and that she whom
the whole province of Asia and all the
world worship will be stripped of her
magnificence."

28 When they heard this, they were
filled with fury and began to shout,

---

*

19, 4: 1, 5; 11, 16; 13, 24-25; Mt 3, 11; Mk 1, 8; Lk 3, 16.
6: 8, 15-17; 10, 44.46.
12: 5, 15-16; Lk 8, 44-47.
21: 23, 11; Rom 1, 13; 15, 22-32.
26: 17, 29.

†

18, 26: *The Way [of God]:* for the Way, see the note on 9, 2. Other manuscripts here read "the Way of the Lord," "the word of the Lord," or simply "the Way."

19, 1-6: Upon his arrival in Ephesus, Paul discovers other people at the same religious stage as Apollos, though they seem to have considered themselves followers of Christ, not of the Baptist. On the relation between baptism and the reception of the Spirit, see the note on 8, 16.

19, 24: *Miniature silver shrines of Artemis:* the temple of Artemis at Ephesus was one of the seven wonders of the ancient world. Artemis, originally the Olympian virgin hunter, moon goddess, and goddess of wild nature, was worshiped at Ephesus as an Asian mother goddess and goddess of fertility. She was one of the most widely worshiped female deities in the Hellenistic world (see 18, 27).

"Great is Artemis of the Ephesians!"
29* The city was filled with confusion,
and the people rushed with one accord
into the theater, seizing Gaius and Aris-
tarchus, the Macedonians, Paul's trav-
eling companions. 30 Paul wanted to go
before the crowd, but the disciples
would not let him, 31† and even some of
the Asiarchs who were friends of his
sent word to him advising him not to
venture into the theater. 32 Meanwhile,
some were shouting one thing, others
something else; the assembly was in
chaos, and most of the people had no
idea why they had come together.
33 Some of the crowd prompted Alexan-
der, as the Jews pushed him forward,
and Alexander signaled with his hand
that he wished to explain something to
the gathering. 34 But when they recog-
nized that he was a Jew, they all
shouted in unison, for about two hours,
"Great is Artemis of the Ephesians!"
35† Finally the town clerk restrained the
crowd and said, "You Ephesians, what
person is there who does not know that
the city of the Ephesians is the guardian
of the temple of the great Artemis and
of her image that fell from the sky?
36 Since these things are undeniable,
you must calm yourselves and not do
anything rash. 37 The men you brought
here are not temple robbers, nor have
they insulted our goddess. 38 If Deme-
trius and his fellow craftsmen have a
complaint against anyone, courts are in
session, and there are proconsuls. Let
them bring charges against one an-
other. 39 If you have anything further
to investigate, let the matter be settled
in the lawful assembly, 40† for, as it is,
we are in danger of being charged with
rioting because of today's conduct.
There is no cause for it. We shall [not]
be able to give a reason for this demon-
stration." With these words he dis-
missed the assembly.

CHAPTER 20

Journey to Macedonia and Greece.
1* When the disturbance was over, Paul
had the disciples summoned and, after
encouraging them, he bade them fare-
well and set out on his journey to Mace-
donia. 2 As he traveled throughout those
regions, he provided many words of en-
couragement for them. Then he arrived
in Greece, 3 where he stayed for three
months. But when a plot was made
against him by the Jews as he was about
to set sail for Syria, he decided to return
by way of Macedonia.
Return to Troas. 4* Sopater, the son
of Pyrrhus, from Beroea, accompanied
him, as did Aristarchus and Secundus
from Thessalonica, Gaius from Derbe,
Timothy, and Tychicus and Trophimus
from Asia 5*† who went on ahead
and waited for us at Troas. 6† We sailed
from Philippi after the feast of Unleav-
ened Bread, and rejoined them five
days later in Troas, where we spent a
week.
Eutychus Restored to Life. 7† On the
first day of the week when we gathered
to break bread, Paul spoke to them be-
cause he was going to leave on the next
day, and he kept on speaking until mid-
night. 8 There were many lamps in the
upstairs room where we were gathered,
9 and a young man named Eutychus
who was sitting on the window sill was
sinking into a deep sleep as Paul talked
on and on. Once overcome by sleep, he
fell down from the third story and when
he was picked up, he was dead.
10*† Paul went down, threw himself
upon him, and said as he embraced him,
"Don't be alarmed; there is life in him."
11 Then he returned upstairs, broke the
bread, and ate; after a long conversa-
tion that lasted until daybreak, he de-
parted. 12 And they took the boy away
alive and were immeasurably com-
forted.
Journey to Miletus. 13 We went ahead
to the ship and set sail for Assos where
we were to take Paul on board, as he
had arranged, since he was going over-
land. 14 When he met us in Assos, we
took him aboard and went on to Mity-
lene. 15 We sailed away from there on the
next day and reached a point off Chios,
and a day later we reached Samos, and

*

29: Col 4, 10.
20, 1: 1 Cor 16, 1.
4: Rom 16, 21.
5: 21, 29; 2 Tm 4, 20.
10: 1 Kgs 17, 17-24; 2 Kgs 4, 30-37; Mt 9, 24; Mk 5, 39; Lk 8, 52.

†

19, 31: *Asiarchs:* the precise status and role of the Asiarchs is disputed. They appear to have been people of wealth and influence who promoted the Roman imperial cult and who may also have been political representatives in a league of cities in the Roman province of Asia.

19, 35: *Guardian of the temple:* this title was accorded by Rome to cities that provided a temple for the imperial cult. Inscriptional evidence indicates that Ephesus was acknowledged as the temple keeper of Artemis and of the imperial cult. *That fell from the sky:* many scholars think that this refers to a meteorite that was worshiped as an image of the goddess.

19, 40: Some manuscripts omit the negative in *[not] be able,* making the meaning, "There is no cause for which we shall be able to give a reason for this demonstration."

20, 5: The second "we-section" of Acts begins here. See the note on 16, 10-17.

20, 6: *Feast of Unleavened Bread:* see the note on Lk 22, 1.

20, 7: *The first day of the week:* the day after the sabbath and the first day of the Jewish week, apparently chosen originally by the Jerusalem community for the celebration of the liturgy of the Eucharist in order to relate it to the resurrection of Christ.

20, 10: The action of Paul in throwing himself upon the dead boy recalls that of Elijah in 1 Kgs 17, 21 where the son of the widow of Zarephath is revived and that of Elisha in 2 Kgs 4, 34 where the Shunamite woman's son is restored to life.

on the following day we arrived at Mile-
tus. 16† Paul had decided to sail past
Ephesus in order not to lose time in the
province of Asia, for he was hurrying
to be in Jerusalem, if at all possible, for
the day of Pentecost.

Paul's Farewell Speech at Miletus.
17 From Miletus he had the presbyters
of the church at Ephesus summoned.
18 When they came to him, he addressed
them, "You know how I lived among
you the whole time from the day I first
came to the province of Asia. 19 I served
the Lord with all humility and with the
tears and trials that came to me because
of the plots of the Jews, 20 and I did not
at all shrink from telling you what was
for your benefit, or from teaching you
in public or in your homes. 21 I earnestly
bore witness for both Jews and Greeks
to repentance before God and to faith
in our Lord Jesus. 22 But now, compelled
by the Spirit, I am going to Jerusalem.
What will happen to me there I do not
know, 23* except that in one city after
another the holy Spirit has been warn-
ing me that imprisonment and hard-
ships await me. 24* Yet I consider life
of no importance to me, if only I may
finish my course and the ministry that
I received from the Lord Jesus, to bear
witness to the gospel of God's grace.

25 "But now I know that none of you
to whom I preached the kingdom during
my travels will ever see my face again.
26 And so I solemnly declare to you this
day that I am not responsible for the
blood of any of you, 27 for I did not
shrink from proclaiming to you the en-
tire plan of God. 28*† Keep watch over
yourselves and over the whole flock of
which the holy Spirit has appointed you
overseers, in which you tend the church
of God that he acquired with his own
blood. 29* I know that after my depar-
ture savage wolves will come among
you, and they will not spare the flock.
30* And from your own group, men will
come forward perverting the truth to
draw the disciples away after them.
31* So be vigilant and remember that for
three years, night and day, I unceas-
ingly admonished each of you with
tears. 32 And now I commend you to God
and to that gracious word of his that
can build you up and give you the inher-
itance among all who are consecrated.
33 I have never wanted anyone's silver
or gold or clothing. 34* You know well
that these very hands have served my
needs and my companions. 35* In every
way I have shown you that by hard
work of that sort we must help the weak,
and keep in mind the words of the Lord
Jesus who himself said, 'It is more
blessed to give than to receive.' "

36 When he had finished speaking he
knelt down and prayed with them all.
37 They were all weeping loudly as they
threw their arms around Paul and
kissed him, 38 for they were deeply dis-
tressed that he had said that they would
never see his face again. Then they es-
corted him to the ship.

CHAPTER 21

Arrival at Tyre.† 1 When we had
taken leave of them we set sail, made
a straight run for Cos, and on the next
day for Rhodes, and from there to Pat-
ara. 2 Finding a ship crossing to Phoe-
nicia, we went on board and put out to
sea. 3 We caught sight of Cyprus but
passed by it on our left and sailed on
toward Syria and put in at Tyre where
the ship was to unload cargo. 4 There
we sought out the disciples and stayed
for a week. They kept telling Paul
through the Spirit not to embark for Je-
rusalem. 5 At the end of our stay we left
and resumed our journey. All of them,
women and children included, escorted
us out of the city, and after kneeling on
the beach to pray, 6 we bade farewell
to one another. Then we boarded the
ship, and they returned home.

Arrival at Ptolemais and Caesarea.
7 We continued the voyage and came
from Tyre to Ptolemais, where we
greeted the brothers and stayed a day
with them. 8*† On the next day we re-
sumed the trip and came to Caesarea,
where we went to the house of Philip
the evangelist, who was one of the
Seven, and stayed with him. 9 He had
four virgin daughters gifted with proph-
ecy. 10† We had been there several days
when a prophet named Agabus came

* 23: 9, 16.
24: 2 Tm 4, 7.
28: Jn 21, 15-17; 1 Pt 5, 2.
29: Jn 10, 12.
30: Mt 7, 15; 2 Pt 2, 1-3; 1 Jn 2, 18-19.
31: 1 Thes 2, 11.
34: 1 Cor 4, 12; 1 Thes 2, 9; 2 Thes 3, 8.
35: Sir 4, 31.
21, 8: 6, 5; 8, 5-6.

† 20, 16-35: Apparently aware of difficulties at Ephesus and neighboring areas, Paul calls the presbyters together at Miletus, about thirty miles from Ephesus. He reminds them of his dedication to the gospel (18-21), speaks of what he is about to suffer for the gospel (22-27), and admonishes them to guard the community against false prophets, sure to arise upon his departure (28-31). He concludes by citing a saying of Jesus (35) not recorded in the gospel tradition. Luke presents this farewell to the Ephesian presbyters as Paul's last will and testament.

20, 28: *Overseers:* see the note on Phil 1, 1. *The church of God:* because the clause "that he acquired with his own blood" following "the church of God" suggests that "his own blood" refers to God's blood, some early copyists changed "the church of God" to "the church of the Lord." Some prefer the translation "acquired with the blood of his own," i.e., Christ.

21, 1-18: The third "we-section" of Acts (see the note on 16, 10-17).

21, 8: *One of the Seven:* see the note on 6, 2-4.

21, 10: *Agabus:* mentioned in 11, 28 as the prophet who predicted the famine that occurred when Claudius was emperor.

down from Judea. 11*† He came up to
us, took Paul's belt, bound his own feet
and hands with it, and said, "Thus says
the holy Spirit: This is the way the Jews
will bind the owner of this belt in Jeru-
salem, and they will hand him over to
the Gentiles." 12 When we heard this, we
and the local residents begged him not
to go up to Jerusalem. 13* Then Paul
replied, "What are you doing, weeping
and breaking my heart? I am prepared
not only to be bound but even to die in
Jerusalem for the name of the Lord Je-
sus." 14*† Since he would not be dis-
suaded we let the matter rest, saying,
"The Lord's will be done."

Paul and James in Jerusalem.
15 After these days we made prepara-
tions for our journey, then went up to
Jerusalem. 16 Some of the disciples from
Caesarea came along to lead us to the
house of Mnason, a Cypriot, a disciple
of long standing, with whom we were
to stay. 17† When we reached Jerusalem
the brothers welcomed us warmly.
18 The next day, Paul accompanied us
on a visit to James, and all the presby-
ters were present. 19 He greeted them,
then proceeded to tell them in detail
what God had accomplished among the
Gentiles through his ministry. 20 They
praised God when they heard it but said
to him, "Brother, you see how many
thousands of believers there are from
among the Jews, and they are all zeal-
ous observers of the law. 21 They have
been informed that you are teaching all
the Jews who live among the Gentiles
to abandon Moses and that you are tell-
ing them not to circumcise their chil-
dren or to observe their customary
practices. 22 What is to be done? They
will surely hear that you have arrived.
23*† So do what we tell you. We have
four men who have taken a vow.
24† Take these men and purify yourself
with them, and pay their expenses that
they may have their heads shaved. In
this way everyone will know that there
is nothing to the reports they have been
given about you but that you yourself
live in observance of the law. 25*† As for
the Gentiles who have come to believe,
we sent them our decision that they ab-
stain from meat sacrificed to idols, from
blood, from the meat of strangled ani-
mals, and from unlawful marriage."
26* So Paul took the men, and on the
next day after purifying himself to-
gether with them entered the temple to
give notice of the day when the purifica-
tion would be completed and the offer-
ing made for each of them.

Paul's Arrest. 27 When the seven days
were nearly completed, the Jews from
the province of Asia noticed him in the
temple, stirred up the whole crowd, and
laid hands on him, 28*† shouting, "Fel-
low Israelites, help us. This is the man
who is teaching everyone everywhere
against the people and the law and this
place, and what is more, he has even
brought Greeks into the temple and de-
filed this sacred place." 29 For they had
previously seen Trophimus the Ephe-
sian in the city with him and supposed
that Paul had brought him into the tem-
ple. 30 The whole city was in turmoil with
people rushing together. They seized
Paul and dragged him out of the temple,
and immediately the gates were closed.
31† While they were trying to kill him,
a report reached the cohort commander
that all Jerusalem was rioting. 32 He im-
mediately took soldiers and centurions
and charged down on them. When they
saw the commander and the soldiers
they stopped beating Paul. 33 The cohort
commander came forward, arrested
him, and ordered him to be secured with
two chains; he tried to find out who he
might be and what he had done. 34 Some
in the mob shouted one thing, others
something else; so, since he was unable
to ascertain the truth because of the up-
roar, he ordered Paul to be brought into
the compound. 35 When he reached the
steps, he was carried by the soldiers be-

ACTS

*

11: 11, 28; 20, 23.
13: 19, 15-16.
14: Mt 6, 10; 26, 39; Mk 14, 36; Lk 22, 42.
23-27: 18, 18; Nm 6, 1-21.
25: 15, 19-20.28-29.
26: 1 Cor 9, 20.
28: Rom 15, 31.

†

21, 11: The symbolic act of Agabus recalls those of Old Testament prophets. Compare Is 20, 2; Ez 4, 1; Jer 13, 1.

21, 14: The Christian disciples' attitude reflects that of Jesus (see Lk 22, 42).

21, 17-26: The leaders of the Jewish Christians of Jerusalem inform Paul that the Jews there believe he has encouraged the Jews of the diaspora to abandon the Mosaic law. According to Acts, Paul had no objection to the retention of the law by the Jewish Christians of Jerusalem and left the Jews of the diaspora who accepted Christianity free to follow the same practice.

21, 23-26: The leaders of the community suggest that Paul, on behalf of four members of the Jerusalem community, make the customary payment for the sacrifices offered at the termination of the Nazirite vow (see Nm 6, 1-24) in order to impress favorably the Jewish Christians in Jerusalem with his high regard for the Mosaic law. Since Paul himself had once made this vow (18, 18), his respect for the law would be on public record.

21, 24: *Pay their expenses:* according to Nm 6, 14-15 the Nazirite had to present a yearling lamb for a holocaust, a yearling ewe lamb for a sin offering, and a ram for a peace offering, along with food and drink offerings, upon completion of the period of the vow.

21, 25: Paul is informed about the apostolic decree, seemingly for the first time (see the note on 15, 13-35). The allusion to the decree was probably introduced here by Luke to remind his readers that the Gentile Christians themselves were asked to respect certain Jewish practices deriving from the law.

21, 28: The charges against Paul by the diaspora Jews are identical to the charges brought against Stephen by diaspora Jews in 6, 13. *Brought Greeks into the temple:* non-Jews were forbidden, under penalty of death, to go beyond the Court of the Gentiles. Inscriptions in Greek and Latin on a stone balustrade marked off the prohibited area.

21, 31: *Cohort commander:* literally, "the leader of a thousand in a cohort." At this period the Roman cohort commander usually led six hundred soldiers, a tenth of a legion; but the number in a cohort varied.

cause of the violence of the mob, 36*† for a crowd of people followed and shouted, "Away with him!"

37 Just as Paul was about to be taken into the compound, he said to the cohort commander, "May I say something to you?" He replied, "Do you speak Greek? 38*† So then you are not the Egyptian who started a revolt some time ago and led the four thousand assassins into the desert?" 39 Paul answered, "I am a Jew, of Tarsus in Cilicia, a citizen of no mean city; I request you to permit me to speak to the people." 40† When he had given his permission, Paul stood on the steps and motioned with his hand to the people; and when all was quiet he addressed them in Hebrew.

CHAPTER 22

Paul's Defense before the Jerusalem Jews.† 1 "My brothers and fathers, listen to what I am about to say to you in my defense." 2 When they heard him addressing them in Hebrew they became all the more quiet. And he continued, 3* "I am a Jew, born in Tarsus in Cilicia, but brought up in this city. At the feet of Gamaliel I was educated strictly in our ancestral law and was zealous for God, just as all of you are today. 4* I persecuted this Way to death, binding both men and women and delivering them to prison. 5 Even the high priest and the whole council of elders can testify on my behalf. For from them I even received letters to the brothers and set out for Damascus to bring back to Jerusalem in chains for punishment those there as well.

6* "On that journey as I drew near to Damascus, about noon a great light from the sky suddenly shone around me. 7* I fell to the ground and heard a voice saying to me, 'Saul, Saul, why are you persecuting me?' 8* I replied, 'Who are you, sir?' And he said to me, 'I am Jesus the Nazorean whom you are persecuting.' 9* My companions saw the light but did not hear the voice of the one who spoke to me. 10* I asked, 'What shall I do, sir?' The Lord answered me, 'Get up and go into Damascus, and there you will be told about everything appointed for you to do.' 11* Since I could see nothing because of the brightness of that light, I was led by hand by my companions and entered Damascus.

12* "A certain Ananias, a devout observer of the law, and highly spoken of by all the Jews who lived there, 13 came to me and stood there and said, 'Saul, my brother, regain your sight.' And at that very moment I regained my sight and saw him. 14 Then he said, 'The God of our ancestors designated you to know his will, to see the Righteous One, and to hear the sound of his voice; 15† for you will be his witness before all to what you have seen and heard. 16 Now, why delay? Get up and have yourself baptized and your sins washed away, calling upon his name.'

17 "After I had returned to Jerusalem and while I was praying in the temple, I fell into a trance 18 and saw the Lord saying to me, 'Hurry, leave Jerusalem at once, because they will not accept your testimony about me.' 19* But I replied, 'Lord, they themselves know that from synagogue to synagogue I used to imprison and beat those who believed in you. 20* And when the blood of your witness Stephen was being shed, I myself stood by giving my approval and keeping guard over the cloaks of his murderers.' 21*† Then he said to me, 'Go, I shall send you far away to the Gentiles.' "

Paul Imprisoned. 22*† They listened to him until he said this, but then they raised their voices and shouted, "Take such a one as this away from the earth. It is not right that he should live." 23 And as they were yelling and throwing off their cloaks and flinging dust into the air, 24 the cohort commander or-

*

36: 22, 22; Lk 23, 18; Jn 19, 15.
38: 5, 36-37.
22, 3: 5, 34; 26, 4-5; 2 Cor 11, 22; Gal 1, 13-14; Phil 3, 5-6.
4: 8, 3; 9, 1-2; 22, 19; 26, 9-11; Phil 3, 6.
6: 9, 3; 26, 13; 1 Cor 15, 8.
7: 9, 4; 26, 14.
8: 9, 5; 26, 15; Mt 25, 40.
9: 9, 7; 26, 13-14.
10: 9, 6; 26, 16.
11: 9, 8.
12-16: 9, 10-19.
19: 8, 3; 9, 1-2; 22, 4-5; 26, 9-11.
20: 7, 58; 8, 1.
21: 9, 15; Gal 2, 7-9.
22: 21, 36; Lk 23, 18; Jn 19, 15.

†

21, 36: *Away with him:* at the trial of Jesus before Pilate in Lk 23, 18, the people similarly shout, "Away with this man."

21, 38: *The Egyptian:* according to the Jewish historian Josephus, an Egyptian gathered a large crowd on the Mount of Olives to witness the destruction of the walls of Jerusalem that would fall at the Egyptian "prophet's" word. The commotion was put down by the Roman authorities and the Egyptian escaped, but only after thousands had been killed. *Four thousand assassins:* literally, *sicarii.* According to Josephus, these were political nationalists who removed their opponents by assassination with a short dagger, called in Latin a *sica.*

21, 40: *In Hebrew:* meaning, perhaps, in Aramaic, which at this time was the Semitic tongue in common use.

22, 1-21: Paul's first defense speech is presented to the Jerusalem crowds. Luke here presents Paul as a devout Jew (3) and zealous persecutor of the Christian community (4-5), and then recounts the conversion of Paul for the second time in Acts (see the note on 9, 1-19).

22, 15: *His witness:* like the Galilean followers during the historical ministry of Jesus, Paul too, through his experience of the risen Christ, is to be a witness to the resurrection (compare 1, 8; 10, 39-41; Lk 24, 48).

22, 21: Paul endeavors to explain that his position on the law has not been identical with that of his audience because it has been his prophetic mission to preach to the Gentiles to whom the law was not addressed and who had no faith in it as a way of salvation.

22, 22: Paul's suggestion that his prophetic mission to the Gentiles did not involve his imposing the law on them provokes the same opposition as occurred in Pisidian Antioch (13, 45).

dered him to be brought into the com-
pound and gave instruction that he be
interrogated under the lash to deter-
mine the reason why they were making
such an outcry against him. 25*† But
when they had stretched him out for the
whips, Paul said to the centurion on
duty, "Is it lawful for you to scourge a
man who is a Roman citizen and has
not been tried?" 26 When the centurion
heard this, he went to the cohort com-
mander and reported it, saying, "What
are you going to do? This man is a Ro-
man citizen." 27 Then the commander
came and said to him, "Tell me, are you
a Roman citizen?" "Yes," he answered.
28 The commander replied, "I acquired
this citizenship for a large sum of
money." Paul said, "But I was born
one." 29 At once those who were going
to interrogate him backed away from
him, and the commander became
alarmed when he realized that he was
a Roman citizen and that he had had
him bound.

Paul before the Sanhedrin. 30 The
next day, wishing to determine the truth
about why he was being accused by the
Jews, he freed him and ordered the
chief priests and the whole Sanhedrin
to convene. Then he brought Paul down
and made him stand before them.

CHAPTER 23

1* Paul looked intently at the Sanhe-
drin and said, "My brothers, I have con-
ducted myself with a perfectly clear
conscience before God to this day."
2† The high priest Ananias ordered his
attendants to strike his mouth. 3*† Then
Paul said to him, "God will strike you,
you whitewashed wall. Do you indeed
sit in judgment upon me according to
the law and yet in violation of the law
order me to be struck?" 4 The atten-
dants said, "Would you revile God's
high priest?" 5*† Paul answered,
"Brothers, I did not realize he was the
high priest. For it is written, 'You shall
not curse a ruler of your people.' "

6* Paul was aware that some were
Sadducees and some Pharisees, so he
called out before the Sanhedrin, "My
brothers, I am a Pharisee, the son of
Pharisees; [I] am on trial for hope in
the resurrection of the dead." 7 When
he said this, a dispute broke out between
the Pharisees and Sadducees, and the
group became divided. 8* For the Sad-
ducees say that there is no resurrection
or angels or spirits, while the Pharisees
acknowledge all three. 9 A great uproar
occurred, and some scribes belonging
to the Pharisee party stood up and
sharply argued, "We find nothing
wrong with this man. Suppose a spirit
or an angel has spoken to him?" 10 The
dispute was so serious that the com-
mander, afraid that Paul would be torn
to pieces by them, ordered his troops
to go down and rescue him from their
midst and take him into the compound.
11*† The following night the Lord stood
by him and said, "Take courage. For
just as you have borne witness to my
cause in Jerusalem, so you must also
bear witness in Rome."

Transfer to Caesarea. 12 When day
came, the Jews made a plot and bound
themselves by oath not to eat or drink
until they had killed Paul. 13 There were
more than forty who formed this con-
spiracy. 14 They went to the chief priests
and elders and said, "We have bound
ourselves by a solemn oath to taste
nothing until we have killed Paul.
15 You, together with the Sanhedrin,
must now make an official request to
the commander to have him bring him
down to you, as though you meant to
investigate his case more thoroughly.
We on our part are prepared to kill him
before he arrives." 16 The son of Paul's
sister, however, heard about the am-
bush; so he went and entered the com-
pound and reported it to Paul. 17† Paul
then called one of the centurions and
requested, "Take this young man to the
commander; he has something to report
to him." 18 So he took him and brought
him to the commander and explained,
"The prisoner Paul called me and asked
that I bring this young man to you; he
has something to say to you." 19 The
commander took him by the hand, drew
him aside, and asked him privately,
"What is it you have to report to me?"
20 He replied, "The Jews have conspired
to ask you to bring Paul down to the
Sanhedrin tomorrow, as though they
meant to inquire about him more thor-
oughly, 21 but do not believe them. More
than forty of them are lying in wait for
him; they have bound themselves by

*

25: 16, 37.
23, 1: 24, 16.
3: Ez 13, 10-15; Mt 23, 27.
5: Ex 22, 27.
6: 24, 15.21; 26, 5; Phil 3, 5.
8: Mt 22, 23; Lk 20, 27.
11: 19, 21.

†

22, 25: *Is it lawful for you to scourge a man who is a Roman citizen and has not been tried?:* see the note on 16, 37.

23, 2: *The high priest Ananias:* Ananias, son of Nedebaeus, was high priest from A.D. 47 to 59.

23, 3: *God will strike you:* Josephus reports that Ananias was later assassinated in A.D. 66 at the beginning of the First Revolt.

23, 5: Luke portrays Paul as a model of one who is obedient to the Mosaic law. Paul, because of his reverence for the law (Ex 22, 27), withdraws his accusation of hypocrisy, "white-washed wall" (cf Mt 23, 27), when he is told Ananias is the high priest.

23, 11: The occurrence of the vision of Christ consoling Paul and assuring him that he will be his witness in Rome prepares the reader for the final section of Acts: the journey of Paul and the word he preaches to Rome under the protection of the Romans.

23, 17: *Centurions:* a centurion was a military officer in charge of one hundred soldiers.

oath not to eat or drink until they have killed him. They are now ready and only wait for your consent." 22 As the commander dismissed the young man he directed him, "Tell no one that you gave me this information."

23† Then he summoned two of the centurions and said, "Get two hundred soldiers ready to go to Caesarea by nine o'clock tonight, along with seventy horsemen and two hundred auxiliaries. 24 Provide mounts for Paul to ride and give him safe conduct to Felix the governor." 25 Then he wrote a letter with this content: 26† "Claudius Lysias to his excellency the governor Felix, greetings. 27* This man, seized by the Jews and about to be murdered by them, I rescued after intervening with my troops when I learned that he was a Roman citizen. 28 I wanted to learn the reason for their accusations against him so I brought him down to their Sanhedrin. 29* I discovered that he was accused in matters of controversial questions of their law and not of any charge deserving death or imprisonment. 30 Since it was brought to my attention that there will be a plot against the man, I am sending him to you at once, and have also notified his accusers to state [their case] against him before you."

31 So the soldiers, according to their orders, took Paul and escorted him by night to Antipatris. 32 The next day they returned to the compound, leaving the horsemen to complete the journey with him. 33 When they arrived in Caesarea they delivered the letter to the governor and presented Paul to him. 34 When he had read it and asked to what province he belonged, and learned that he was from Cilicia, 35 he said, "I shall hear your case when your accusers arrive." Then he ordered that he be held in custody in Herod's praetorium.

CHAPTER 24

Trial before Felix. 1 Five days later the high priest Ananias came down with some elders and an advocate, a certain Tertullus, and they presented formal charges against Paul to the governor. 2 When he was called, Tertullus began to accuse him, saying, "Since we have attained much peace through you, and reforms have been accomplished in this nation through your provident care, 3 we acknowledge this in every way and everywhere, most excellent Felix, with all gratitude. 4 But in order not to detain you further, I ask you to give us a brief hearing with your customary graciousness. 5*† We found this man to be a pest; he creates dissension among Jews all over the world and is a ringleader of the sect of the Nazoreans. 6* He even tried to desecrate our temple, but we arrested him. [7]† 8 If you examine him you will be able to learn from him for yourself about everything of which we are accusing him." 9 The Jews also joined in the attack and asserted that these things were so.

10† Then the governor motioned to him to speak and Paul replied, "I know that you have been a judge over this nation for many years and so I am pleased to make my defense before you. 11 As you can verify, not more than twelve days have passed since I went up to Jerusalem to worship. 12 Neither in the temple, nor in the synagogues, nor anywhere in the city did they find me arguing with anyone or instigating a riot among the people. 13 Nor can they prove to you the accusations they are now making against me. 14* But this I do admit to you, that according to the Way, which they call a sect, I worship the God of our ancestors and I believe everything that is in accordance with the law and written in the prophets. 15* I have the same hope in God as they themselves have that there will be a resurrection of the righteous and the unrighteous. 16* Because of this, I always strive to keep my conscience clear before God and man. 17* After many years, I came to bring alms for my nation and offerings. 18* While I was so engaged, they found me, after my purification, in the temple without a crowd or disturbance. 19 But some Jews

*

27: 21, 30-34; 22, 27.
29: 18, 14-15; 25, 18-19.
24, 5: 24, 14; Lk 23, 2.
6: 21, 28.
14: 24, 5.
15: Dn 12, 2; Jn 5, 28-29.
16: 23, 1.
17: Rom 15, 25-26; Gal 2, 10.
18-19: 21, 26-30.

†

23, 23: *By nine o'clock tonight:* literally, "by the third hour of the night." The night hours began at 6 p.m. *Two hundred auxiliaries:* the meaning of the Greek is not certain. It seems to refer to spearmen from the local police force and not from the cohort of soldiers, which would have numbered only 500-1000 men.

23, 26-30: The letter emphasizes the fact that Paul is a Roman citizen and asserts the lack of evidence that he is guilty of a crime against the empire. The tone of the letter implies that the commander became initially involved in Paul's case because of his Roman citizenship, but this is not an exact description of what really happened (see 21, 31-33; 22, 25-29).

23, 26: M. Antonius Felix was procurator of Judea from A.D. 52 to 60. His procuratorship was marked by cruelty toward and oppression of his Jewish subjects.

24, 5: *Nazoreans:* that is, followers of Jesus of Nazareth.

24, 7: The Western text has added here a verse (really 6b-8a) that is not found in the best Greek manuscripts. It reads, "and would have judged him according to our own law, but the cohort commander Lysias came and violently took him out of our hands and ordered his accusers to come before you."

24, 10-21: Whereas the advocate Tertullus referred to Paul's activities on his missionary journeys, the apostle narrowed the charges down to the riot connected with the incident in the temple (see 21, 27-30; 24, 17-20). In his defense, Paul stresses the continuity between Christianity and Judaism.

from the province of Asia, who should
be here before you to make whatever
accusation they might have against
me—20 or let these men themselves state
what crime they discovered when I
stood before the Sanhedrin, 21* unless
it was my one outcry as I stood among
them, that 'I am on trial before you to-
day for the resurrection of the dead.' "
22 Then Felix, who was accurately in-
formed about the Way, postponed the
trial, saying, "When Lysias the com-
mander comes down, I shall decide
your case." 23 He gave orders to the cen-
turion that he should be kept in custody
but have some liberty, and that he
should not prevent any of his friends
from caring for his needs.
Captivity in Caesarea.† 24 Several
days later Felix came with his wife Dru-
silla, who was Jewish. He had Paul sum-
moned and listened to him speak about
faith in Christ Jesus. 25 But as he spoke
about righteousness and self-restraint
and the coming judgment, Felix be-
came frightened and said, "You may go
for now; when I find an opportunity I
shall summon you again." 26 At the
same time he hoped that a bribe would
be offered him by Paul, and so he sent
for him very often and conversed with
him.
27† Two years passed and Felix was
succeeded by Porcius Festus. Wishing
to ingratiate himself with the Jews, Fe-
lix left Paul in prison.

CHAPTER 25

Appeal to Caesar. 1 Three days after
his arrival in the province, Festus went
up from Caesarea to Jerusalem
2† where the chief priests and Jewish
leaders presented him their formal
charges against Paul. They asked him
3 as a favor to have him sent to Jerusa-
lem, for they were plotting to kill him
along the way. 4 Festus replied that Paul
was being held in custody in Caesarea
and that he himself would be returning
there shortly. 5 He said, "Let your au-
thorities come down with me, and if this
man has done something improper, let
them accuse him."
6 After spending no more than eight
or ten days with them, he went down
to Caesarea, and on the following day
took his seat on the tribunal and or-
dered that Paul be brought in. 7 When
he appeared, the Jews who had come
down from Jerusalem surrounded him
and brought many serious charges
against him, which they were unable to
prove. 8 In defending himself Paul said,
"I have committed no crime either
against the Jewish law or against the
temple or against Caesar." 9† Then Fes-
tus, wishing to ingratiate himself with
the Jews, said to Paul in reply, "Are you
willing to go up to Jerusalem and there
stand trial before me on these
charges?" 10 Paul answered, "I am
standing before the tribunal of Caesar;
this is where I should be tried. I have
committed no crime against the Jews,
as you very well know. 11 If I have com-
mitted a crime or done anything de-
serving death, I do not seek to escape
the death penalty; but if there is no sub-
stance to the charges they are bringing
against me, then no one has the right
to hand me over to them. I appeal to
Caesar." 12 Then Festus, after confer-
ring with his council, replied, "You
have appealed to Caesar. To Caesar you
will go."
Paul before King Agrippa. 13† When
a few days had passed, King Agrippa
and Bernice arrived in Caesarea on a
visit to Festus. 14* Since they spent sev-
eral days there, Festus referred Paul's
case to the king, saying, "There is a
man here left in custody by Felix.
15 When I was in Jerusalem the chief
priests and the elders of the Jews
brought charges against him and de-
manded his condemnation. 16 I an-
swered them that it was not Roman
practice to hand over an accused per-
son before he has faced his accusers
and had the opportunity to defend him-
self against their charge. 17 So when
[they] came together here, I made no
delay; the next day I took my seat on
the tribunal and ordered the man to be
brought in. 18* His accusers stood
around him, but did not charge him with
any of the crimes I suspected. 19 Instead
they had some issues with him about
their own religion and about a certain
Jesus who had died but who Paul
claimed was alive. 20 Since I was at a
loss how to investigate this controversy,
I asked if he were willing to go to Jeru-
salem and there stand trial on these
charges. 21 And when Paul appealed

*

21: 23, 6; 24, 15.
25, 14: 24, 27.
18-19: 18, 14-15; 23, 29.

†

24, 24-25: The way of Christian discipleship greatly disquiets Felix, who has entered into an adulterous marriage with Drusilla, daughter of Herod Agrippa I. This marriage provides the background for the topics Paul speaks about and about which Felix does not want to hear.

24, 27: Very little is known of Porcius Festus who was a procurator of Judea from A.D. 60 to 62.

25, 2: Even after two years the animosity toward Paul in Jerusalem had not subsided (see 24, 27).

25, 9-12: Paul refuses to acknowledge that the Sanhedrin in Jerusalem has any jurisdiction over him now (11). Paul uses his right as a Roman citizen to appeal his case to the jurisdiction of the Emperor (Nero, ca. A.D. 60) (12). This move broke the deadlock between Roman protective custody of Paul and the plan of his enemies to kill him (3).

25, 13: *King Agrippa and Bernice:* brother and sister, children of Herod Agrippa I whose activities against the Jerusalem community are mentioned in 12, 1-19. Agrippa II was a petty ruler over small areas in northern Palestine and some villages in Perea. His influence on the Jewish population of Palestine was insignificant.

that he be held in custody for the Em-
peror's decision, I ordered him held un-
til I could send him to Caesar."
22 Agrippa said to Festus, "I too should
like to hear this man." He replied, "To-
morrow you will hear him."
23 The next day Agrippa and Bernice
came with great ceremony and entered
the audience hall in the company of co-
hort commanders and the prominent
men of the city and, by command of
Festus, Paul was brought in. 24 And Fes-
tus said, "King Agrippa and all you here
present with us, look at this man about
whom the whole Jewish populace peti-
tioned me here and in Jerusalem, clam-
oring that he should live no longer.
25 I found, however, that he had done
nothing deserving death, and so when
he appealed to the Emperor, I decided
to send him. 26 But I have nothing defi-
nite to write about him to our sovereign;
therefore I have brought him before all
of you, and particularly before you,
King Agrippa, so that I may have some-
thing to write as a result of this investi-
gation. 27 For it seems senseless to me
to send up a prisoner without indicating
the charges against him."

CHAPTER 26

King Agrippa Hears Paul. 1 Then
Agrippa said to Paul, "You may now
speak on your own behalf." So Paul
stretched out his hand and began his
defense. 2† "I count myself fortunate,
King Agrippa, that I am to defend my-
self before you today against all the
charges made against me by the Jews,
3 especially since you are an expert in
all the Jewish customs and controver-
sies. And therefore I beg you to listen
patiently. 4† My manner of living from
my youth, a life spent from the begin-
ning among my people and in Jerusa-
lem, all [the] Jews know. 5* They have
known about me from the start, if they
are willing to testify, that I have lived
my life as a Pharisee, the strictest party
of our religion. 6* But now I am standing
trial because of my hope in the promise
made by God to our ancestors. 7 Our
twelve tribes hope to attain to that
promise as they fervently worship God
day and night; and on account of this
hope I am accused by Jews, O king.
8 Why is it thought unbelievable among
you that God raises the dead? 9* I my-
self once thought that I had to do many
things against the name of Jesus the
Nazorean, 10* and I did so in Jerusalem.
I imprisoned many of the holy ones with
the authorization I received from the
chief priests, and when they were to be
put to death I cast my vote against
them. 11 Many times, in synagogue after
synagogue, I punished them in an at-
tempt to force them to blaspheme; I was
so enraged against them that I pursued
them even to foreign cities.
12 "On one such occasion I was travel-
ing to Damascus with the authorization
and commission of the chief priests.
13* At midday, along the way, O king, I
saw a light from the sky, brighter than
the sun, shining around me and my
traveling companions. 14*† We all fell to
the ground and I heard a voice saying
to me in Hebrew, 'Saul, Saul, why are
you persecuting me? It is hard for you
to kick against the goad.' 15* And I said,
'Who are you, sir?' And the Lord re-
plied, 'I am Jesus whom you are perse-
cuting. 16*† Get up now, and stand on
your feet. I have appeared to you for
this purpose, to appoint you as a servant
and witness of what you have seen [of
me] and what you will be shown.
17* I shall deliver you from this people
and from the Gentiles to whom I send
you, 18*† to open their eyes that they
may turn from darkness to light and
from the power of Satan to God, so that
they may obtain forgiveness of sins and
an inheritance among those who have
been consecrated by faith in me.'
19 "And so, King Agrippa, I was not
disobedient to the heavenly vision.
20 On the contrary, first to those in Da-
mascus and in Jerusalem and through-
out the whole country of Judea, and
then to the Gentiles, I preached the
need to repent and turn to God, and to
do works giving evidence of repen-
tance. 21* That is why the Jews seized
me [when I was] in the temple and tried
to kill me. 22*† But I have enjoyed God's

*

26, 5: Phil 3, 5-6; Gal 1, 13-14; 2 Cor 11, 22.
6-8: 23, 6; 24, 15.21; 28, 20.
9-11: 8, 3; 9, 1-2; 22, 19; Phil 3, 6.
10: 9, 14.
13-14: 9, 7.
13: 9, 3; 22, 6.
14: 9, 4; 22, 7.
15: 9, 5; 22, 8; Mt 25, 40.
16: 9, 6; 22, 10; Ez 2, 1.
17: Jer 1, 7.
18: Is 42, 7.16; 61, 1 LXX; Col 1, 13.
21: 21, 31.
22-23: 3, 18; Lk 24, 26-27.44-47.

†

26, 2-23: Paul's final defense speech in Acts is now made before a king (see 9, 15). In the speech Paul presents himself as a zealous Pharisee and Christianity as the logical development of Pharisaic Judaism. The story of his conversion is recounted for the third time in Acts in this speech (see the note on 9, 1-19).

26, 4: *Among my people:* that is, among the Jews.

26, 14: *In Hebrew:* see the note on 21, 40. *It is hard for you to kick against the goad:* this proverb is commonly found in Greek literature and in this context signifies the senselessness and ineffectiveness of any opposition to the divine influence in his life.

26, 16: The words of Jesus directed to Paul here reflect the dialogues between Christ and Ananias (9, 15) and between Ananias and Paul (22, 14-15) in the two previous accounts of Paul's conversion.

26, 18: *To open their eyes:* though no mention is made of Paul's blindness in this account (cf 9, 8-9.12.18; 22, 11-13), the task he is commissioned to perform is the removal of other people's spiritual blindness.

26, 22: *Saying nothing different from what the prophets and Moses foretold:* see the note on Lk 18, 31.

help to this very day, and so I stand here testifying to small and great alike, saying nothing different from what the prophets and Moses foretold, 23*† that the Messiah must suffer and that, as the first to rise from the dead, he would proclaim light both to our people and to the Gentiles."

Reactions to Paul's Speech. 24 While Paul was so speaking in his defense, Festus said in a loud voice, "You are mad, Paul; much learning is driving you mad." 25 But Paul replied, "I am not mad, most excellent Festus; I am speaking words of truth and reason. 26† The king knows about these matters and to him I speak boldly, for I cannot believe that [any] of this has escaped his notice; this was not done in a corner. 27† King Agrippa, do you believe the prophets? I know you believe." 28 Then Agrippa said to Paul, "You will soon persuade me to play the Christian." 29 Paul replied, "I would pray to God that sooner or later not only you but all who listen to me today might become as I am except for these chains."

30 Then the king rose, and with him the governor and Bernice and the others who sat with them. 31† And after they had withdrawn they said to one another, "This man is doing nothing [at all] that deserves death or imprisonment." 32* And Agrippa said to Festus, "This man could have been set free if he had not appealed to Caesar."

CHAPTER 27

Departure for Rome.† 1† When it was decided that we should sail to Italy, they handed Paul and some other prisoners over to a centurion named Julius of the Cohort Augusta. 2* We went on board a ship from Adramyttium bound for ports in the province of Asia and set sail. Aristarchus, a Macedonian from Thessalonica, was with us. 3 On the following day we put in at Sidon where Julius was kind enough to allow Paul to visit his friends who took care of him. 4 From there we put out to sea and sailed around the sheltered side of Cyprus because of the headwinds, 5 and crossing the open sea off the coast of Cilicia and Pamphylia we came to Myra in Lycia.

Storm and Shipwreck. 6 There the centurion found an Alexandrian ship that was sailing to Italy and put us on board. 7 For many days we made little headway, arriving at Cnidus only with difficulty, and because the wind would not permit us to continue our course we sailed for the sheltered side of Crete off Salmone. 8 We sailed past it with difficulty and reached a place called Fair Havens, near which was the city of Lasea.

9*† Much time had now passed and sailing had become hazardous because the time of the fast had already gone by, so Paul warned them, 10 "Men, I can see that this voyage will result in severe damage and heavy loss not only to the cargo and the ship, but also to our lives." 11 The centurion, however, paid more attention to the pilot and to the owner of the ship than to what Paul said. 12 Since the harbor was unfavorably situated for spending the winter, the majority planned to put out to sea from there in the hope of reaching Phoenix, a port in Crete facing west-northwest, there to spend the winter.

13 A south wind blew gently, and thinking they had attained their objective, they weighed anchor and sailed along close to the coast of Crete. 14 Before long an offshore wind of hurricane force called a "Northeaster" struck. 15 Since the ship was caught up in it and could not head into the wind we gave way and let ourselves be driven. 16 We passed along the sheltered side of an island named Cauda and managed only with difficulty to get the dinghy under control. 17 They hoisted it aboard, then used cables to undergird the ship. Because of their fear that they would run aground on the shoal of Syrtis, they lowered the drift anchor and were carried along in this way. 18 We were being pounded by the storm so violently that the next day they jettisoned

---

*

23: Is 42, 6; 49, 6; Lk 2, 32; 1 Cor 15, 20-23.
32: 25, 11-12.
27, 2: 19, 29; 20, 4.
9: Lv 16, 29-31.

---

†

26, 23: *That the Messiah must suffer:* see the note on Lk 24, 26.

26, 26: *Not done in a corner:* for Luke, this Greek proverb expresses his belief that he is presenting a story about Jesus and the church that is already well known. As such, the entire history of Christianity is public knowledge and incontestable. Luke presents his story in this way to provide "certainty" to his readers about the instructions they have received (Lk 1, 4).

26, 27-28: If the Christian missionaries proclaim nothing different from what the Old Testament prophets had proclaimed (22-23), then the logical outcome for the believing Jew, according to Luke, is to become a Christian.

26, 31-32: In recording the episode of Paul's appearance before Agrippa, Luke wishes to show that, when Paul's case was judged impartially, no grounds for legal action against him were found (see 23, 29; 25, 25).

27, 1—28, 16: Here Luke has written a stirring account of adventure on the high seas, incidental to his main purpose of showing how well Paul got along with his captors and how his prophetic influence saved the lives of all on board. The recital also establishes the existence of Christian communities in Puteoli and Rome. This account of the voyage and shipwreck also constitutes the final "we-section" in Acts (see the note on 16, 10-17).

27, 1: *Cohort Augusta:* the presence of a Cohort Augusta in Syria during the first century A.D. is attested in inscriptions. Whatever the historical background to this information given by Luke may be, the name Augusta serves to increase the prominence and prestige of the prisoner Paul whose custodians bear so important a Roman name.

27, 9: *The time of the fast:* the fast kept on the occasion of the Day of Atonement (Lv 16, 29-31), which occurred in late September or early October.

some cargo, 19 and on the third day with their own hands they threw even the ship's tackle overboard. 20 Neither the sun nor the stars were visible for many days, and no small storm raged. Finally, all hope of our surviving was taken away.

21 When many would no longer eat, Paul stood among them and said, "Men, you should have taken my advice and not have set sail from Crete and you would have avoided this disastrous loss. 22 I urge you now to keep up your courage; not one of you will be lost, only the ship. 23 For last night an angel of the God to whom [I] belong and whom I serve stood by me 24* and said, 'Do not be afraid, Paul. You are destined to stand before Caesar; and behold, for your sake, God has granted safety to all who are sailing with you.' 25 Therefore, keep up your courage, men; I trust in God that it will turn out as I have been told. 26 We are destined to run aground on some island."

27 On the fourteenth night, as we were still being driven about on the Adriatic Sea, toward midnight the sailors began to suspect that they were nearing land. 28 They took soundings and found twenty fathoms; a little farther on, they again took soundings and found fifteen fathoms. 29 Fearing that we would run aground on a rocky coast, they dropped four anchors from the stern and prayed for day to come. 30 The sailors then tried to abandon ship; they lowered the dinghy to the sea on the pretext of going to lay out anchors from the bow. 31 But Paul said to the centurion and the soldiers, "Unless these men stay with the ship, you cannot be saved." 32 So the soldiers cut the ropes of the dinghy and set it adrift.

33 Until the day began to dawn, Paul kept urging all to take some food. He said, "Today is the fourteenth day that you have been waiting, going hungry and eating nothing. 34 I urge you, therefore, to take some food; it will help you survive. Not a hair of the head of anyone of you will be lost." 35*† When he said this, he took bread, gave thanks to God in front of them all, broke it, and began to eat. 36 They were all encouraged, and took some food themselves. 37 In all, there were two hundred seventy-six of us on the ship. 38 After they had eaten enough, they lightened the ship by throwing the wheat into the sea.

39 When day came they did not recognize the land, but made out a bay with a beach. They planned to run the ship ashore on it, if they could. 40 So they cast off the anchors and abandoned them to the sea, and at the same time they unfastened the lines of the rudders, and hoisting the foresail into the wind, they made for the beach. 41 But they struck a sandbar and ran the ship aground. The bow was wedged in and could not be moved, but the stern began to break up under the pounding [of the waves]. 42 The soldiers planned to kill the prisoners so that none might swim away and escape, 43 but the centurion wanted to save Paul and so kept them from carrying out their plan. He ordered those who could swim to jump overboard first and get to the shore, 44 and then the rest, some on planks, others on debris from the ship. In this way, all reached shore safely.

CHAPTER 28

Winter in Malta. 1 Once we had reached safety we learned that the island was called Malta. 2 The natives showed us extraordinary hospitality; they lit a fire and welcomed all of us because it had begun to rain and was cold. 3 Paul had gathered a bundle of brushwood and was putting it on the fire when a viper, escaping from the heat, fastened on his hand. 4† When the natives saw the snake hanging from his hand, they said to one another, "This man must certainly be a murderer; though he escaped the sea, Justice has not let him remain alive." 5 But he shook the snake off into the fire and suffered no harm. 6* They were expecting him to swell up or suddenly to fall down dead but, after waiting a long time and seeing nothing unusual happen to him, they changed their minds and began to say that he was a god. 7 In the vicinity of that place were lands belonging to a man named Publius, the chief of the island. He welcomed us and received us cordially as his guests for three days. 8 It so happened that the father of Publius was sick with a fever and dysentery. Paul visited him and, after praying, laid his hands on him and healed him. 9 After this had taken place, the rest of the sick on the island came to Paul and were cured. 10 They paid us great honor and when we eventually set sail they brought us the provisions we needed.

Arrival in Rome. 11† Three months later we set sail on a ship that had wintered at the island. It was an Alexandrian ship with the Dioscuri as its figurehead. 12 We put in at Syracuse and

---

* 24: 23, 11.
35: Mt 15, 36; Mk 6, 41; 8, 6; Lk 22, 19; 1 Cor 11, 23-24.
28, 6: 14, 11.

---

† 27, 35: *He took bread . . . :* the words recall the traditional language of the celebration of the Eucharist (see Lk 22, 19).

28, 4: *Justice:* in Greek mythology, the pursuing goddess of vengeance and justice.

28, 11: *Dioscuri:* that is, the Twin Brothers, Castor and Pollux, the sons of Zeus and the patrons of the sailors.

stayed there three days, 13 and from
there we sailed round the coast and ar-
rived at Rhegium. After a day, a south
wind came up and in two days we
reached Puteoli. 14 There we found
some brothers and were urged to stay
with them for seven days. And thus we
came to Rome. 15 The brothers from
there heard about us and came as far
as the Forum of Appius and Three Tav-
erns to meet us. On seeing them, Paul
gave thanks to God and took courage.
16† When he entered Rome, Paul was al-
lowed to live by himself, with the soldier
who was guarding him.

Testimony to Jews in Rome.†
17* Three days later he called together
the leaders of the Jews. When they had
gathered he said to them, "My brothers,
although I had done nothing against our
people or our ancestral customs, I was
handed over to the Romans as a pris-
oner from Jerusalem. 18* After trying
my case the Romans wanted to release
me, because they found nothing against
me deserving the death penalty. 19* But
when the Jews objected, I was obliged
to appeal to Caesar, even though I had
no accusation to make against my own
nation. 20*† This is the reason, then, I
have requested to see you and to speak
with you, for it is on account of the hope
of Israel that I wear these chains."
21 They answered him, "We have re-
ceived no letters from Judea about you,
nor has any of the brothers arrived with
a damaging report or rumor about you.
22* But we should like to hear you pre-
sent your views, for we know that this
sect is denounced everywhere."

23 So they arranged a day with him
and came to his lodgings in great num-
bers. From early morning until evening,
he expounded his position to them,
bearing witness to the kingdom of God
and trying to convince them about Je-
sus from the law of Moses and the
prophets. 24 Some were convinced by
what he had said, while others did not
believe. 25† Without reaching any
agreement among themselves they be-
gan to leave; then Paul made one final
statement. "Well did the holy Spirit
speak to your ancestors through the
prophet Isaiah, saying:

26* 'Go to this people and say:
You shall indeed hear but not un-
derstand.
You shall indeed look but never
see.
27 Gross is the heart of this people;
they will not hear with their ears;
they have closed their eyes,
so they may not see with their
eyes
and hear with their ears
and understand with their heart
and be converted,
and I heal them.'

28* Let it be known to you that this sal-
vation of God has been sent to the Gen-
tiles; they will listen." [29]†

30† He remained for two full years in
his lodgings. He received all who came
to him, 31 and with complete assurance
and without hindrance he proclaimed
the kingdom of God and taught about
the Lord Jesus Christ.

ACTS

*

17: 24, 12-13; 25, 8.
18: 23, 29; 25, 25; 26, 31-32.
19: 25, 11.
20: 23, 6; 24, 15.21; 26, 6-8.
22: 24, 5.14.
26: Is 6, 9-10; Mt 13, 14-15; Mk 4, 12; Lk 8, 10; Jn 12, 40; Rom 11, 8.
28: 13, 46; 18, 6; Ps 67, 2; Is 40, 5 LXX; Lk 3, 6.

†

28, 16: With Paul's arrival in Rome, the programmatic spread of the word of the Lord to "the ends of the earth" (1, 8) is accomplished. In Rome, Paul is placed under house arrest, and under this mild form of custody he is allowed to proclaim the word in the capital of the civilized world of his day.

28, 17-22: Paul's first act in Rome is to learn from the leaders of the Jewish community whether the Jews of Jerusalem plan to pursue their case against him before the Roman jurisdiction. He is informed that no such plan is afoot, but that the Jews of Rome have heard the Christian teaching denounced. Paul's offer to explain it to them is readily accepted.

28, 20: *The hope of Israel:* in the words of Paul (23, 6), Luke has identified this hope as hope in the resurrection of the dead.

28, 25-28: Paul's final words in Acts reflect a major concern of Luke's writings: how the salvation promised in the Old Testament, accomplished by Jesus, and offered first to Israel (13, 26), has now been offered to and accepted by the Gentiles. Quoting Is 6, 9-10, Paul presents the scriptural support for his indictment of his fellow Jews who refuse to accept the message he proclaims. Their rejection leads to its proclamation among the Gentiles.

28, 29: The Western text has added here a verse that is not found in the best Greek manuscripts: "And when he had said this, the Jews left, seriously arguing among themselves."

28, 30-31: Although the ending of Acts may seem to be abrupt, Luke has now completed his story with the establishment of Paul and the proclamation of Christianity in Rome. Paul's confident and unhindered proclamation of the gospel in Rome forms the climax to the story whose outline was provided in 1, 8: "You will be my witnesses in Jerusalem . . . and to the ends of the earth."

NEW TESTAMENT LETTERS

In the New Testament canon, between the Acts of the Apostles and Revelation, there are twenty-one documents that take the form of letters or epistles. Most of these are actual letters, but some are more like treatises in the guise of letters. In a few cases even some of the more obvious elements of the letter form are absent; see the Introductions to Hebrews and to 1 John.

The virtually standard form found in these documents, though with some variation, is dependent upon the conventions of letter writing common in the ancient world, but these were modified to suit the purposes of Christian writers. The New Testament letters usually begin with a greeting including an identification of the sender or senders and of the recipients. Next comes a prayer, usually in the form of a thanksgiving. The body of the letter provides an exposition of Christian teaching, usually provoked by concrete circumstances, and generally also draws conclusions regarding ethical behavior. There often follows a discussion of practical matters, such as the writer's travel plans, and the letter concludes with further advice and a formula of farewell.

Fourteen of the twenty-one letters have been traditionally attributed to Paul. One of these, the Letter to the Hebrews, does not itself claim to be the work of Paul; when it was accepted into the canon after much discussion, it was attached at the very end of the Pauline corpus. The other thirteen identify Paul as their author, but most scholars believe that some of them were actually written by his disciples; see the Introductions to Ephesians, Colossians, 2 Thessalonians, and 1 Timothy.

Four of the letters in the Pauline corpus (Ephesians, Philippians, Colossians, and Philemon) are called the "Captivity Epistles" because in each of them the author speaks of being in prison at the time of writing. Three others (1-2 Timothy and Titus) are known as the "Pastoral Epistles" because, addressed to individuals rather than communities, they give advice to disciples about caring for the flock. The letters of the Pauline corpus are arranged in roughly descending order of length from Romans to Philemon, with Hebrews added at the end.

The other seven letters of the New Testament that follow the Pauline corpus are collectively referred to as the "Catholic Epistles." This term, which means "universal," refers to the fact that most of them are directed not to a single Christian community, as are most of the Pauline letters, but to a wider audience; see the Introduction to the catholic letters. Three of them (1-2-3 John) are closely related to the fourth gospel and thus belong to the Johannine corpus. The catholic letters, like those of the Pauline corpus, are also arranged in roughly descending order of length, but the three Johannine letters are kept together and Jude is placed at the end.

The genuine letters of Paul are earlier in date than any of our written gospels. The dates of the other New Testament letters are more difficult to determine, but for the most part they belong to the second and third Christian generations rather than to the first.

The Letter to the

ROMANS

Of all the letters of Paul, that to the Christians at Rome has long held pride of place. It is the longest and most systematic unfolding of the apostle's thought, expounding the gospel of God's righteousness that saves all who believe (1, 16-17); it reflects a universal outlook, with special implications for Israel's relation to the church (chs 9-11). Yet, like all Paul's letters, Romans too arose out of a specific situation, when the apostle wrote from Greece, likely Corinth, between A.D. 56 and 58 (cf Acts 20, 2-3).

Paul at that time was about to leave for Jerusalem with a collection of funds for the impoverished Jewish Christian believers there, taken up from his predominantly Gentile congregations (15, 25-27). He planned then to travel on to Rome and to enlist support there for a mission to Spain (15, 24.28). Such a journey had long been on his mind (1, 9-13; 15, 23). Now, with much missionary preaching successfully accomplished in the East (15, 19), he sought new opportunities in the West (15, 20-21), in order to complete the divine plan of evangelization in the Roman world. Yet he recognized that the visit to Jerusalem would be hazardous (15, 30-32), and we know from Acts that Paul was arrested there and came to Rome only in chains, as a prisoner (Acts 21-28, especially 21, 30-33 and 28, 14.30-31).

The existence of a Christian community in Rome antedates Paul's letter there. When it arose, likely within the sizable Jewish population at Rome, and how, we do not know. The Roman historian Suetonius mentions an edict of the Emperor Claudius about A.D. 49 ordering the expulsion of Jews from Rome in connection with a certain "Chrestus," probably involving a dispute in the Jewish community over Jesus as the Messiah ("Christus"). According to Acts 18, 2, Aquila and Priscilla (or Prisca, as in Rom 16, 3) were among those driven out; from them, in Corinth, Paul may have learned about conditions in the church at Rome.

Opinions vary as to whether Jewish or Gentile Christians predominated in the house churches (cf 16, 5) in the capital city of the empire at the time Paul wrote. Perhaps already by then Gentile Christians were in the majority. Paul speaks in Romans of both Jews and Gentiles (3, 9.29; see the note on 1, 14). The letter also refers to those "weak in faith" (14, 1) and those "who are strong" (15, 1); this terminology may reflect not so much differences between believers of Jewish and of Gentile background, respectively, as an ascetic tendency in some converts (14, 2) combined with Jewish laws about clean and unclean foods (14, 14.20). The issues were similar to problems that Paul had faced in Corinth (1 Cor 8). If Romans 16 is part of the Letter to Rome (see the note on 16, 1-23), then Paul had considerable information about conditions in Rome through all these people there whom he knew, and our letter does not just reflect a generalized picture of an earlier situation in Corinth.

In any case, Paul writes to introduce himself and his message to the Christians at Rome, seeking to enlist their support for the proposed mission to Spain. He therefore employs formulations likely familiar to the Christians at Rome; see the note on the confessional material at 1, 3-4 and compare 3, 25-26 and 4, 25. He cites the Old Testament frequently (1, 17; 3, 10-18; ch 4; 9, 7.12-13.15.17.25-29.33; 10, 5-13.15-21; 15, 9-12). The gospel Paul presents is meant to be a familiar one to those in Rome, even though they heard it first from other preachers.

As the outline below shows, this gospel of Paul (see 16, 25) finds its center in salvation and justification through faith in Christ (1, 16-17). While God's wrath is revealed against all sin and wickedness of Gentile and Jew alike (1, 18—3, 20), God's power to save by divine righteous or justifying action in Christ is also revealed (1, 16-17; 3, 21—5, 21). The consequences and implications for those who believe are set forth (6, 1—8, 39), as are results for those in Israel (chs 9-11) who, to Paul's great sorrow (9, 1-5), disbelieve. The apostle's hope is that, just as rejection of the gospel by some in Israel has led to a ministry of salvation for non-Jews, so one day, in God's mercy, "all Israel" will be saved (11, 11-15.25-29.30-32). The fuller ethical response of believers is also drawn out, both with reference to life in Christ's body (ch 12) and with regard to the world (13, 1-7), on the basis of the eschatological situation (13, 11-14) and conditions in the community (14, 1—15, 13).

Others have viewed Romans more in the light of Paul's earlier, quite polemical Letter to the Galatians and so see the theme as the relationship between Judaism and Christianity, a topic judged to be much in the minds of the Roman Christians. Each of these religious faiths claimed to be the way of salvation based upon a covenant between God and a people chosen and made the beneficiary of divine gifts. But Christianity regarded itself as the prophetic development and fulfillment of the faith of the Old Testament, declaring that the preparatory Mosaic covenant must now give way to the new and more perfect covenant in Jesus Christ. Paul himself had been the implacable advocate of freedom of Gentiles from the laws of the Mosaic covenant and, especially in Galatia, had refused to allow attempts to impose them on Gentile converts to the gospel. He had witnessed the personal hostilities that developed between the adherents of the two faiths and had written his strongly worded letter to the Galatians against those Jewish Christians who were seeking to persuade Gentile Christians to adopt the religious practices of Judaism. For him, the purity of the religious understanding of Jesus as the source of salvation would be seriously impaired if Gentile Christians were obligated to amalgamate the two religious faiths.

Still others find the theme of Israel and the church as expressed in Romans 9-11 to be the heart of Romans. Then the implication of Paul's exposition of justification by faith rather than by means of law is that the divine plan of salvation works itself out on a broad theological plane to include the whole of humanity, despite the differences in the content of the given religious system to which a human culture is heir. Romans presents a plan of salvation stretching from Adam through Abraham and Moses to Christ (chs 4 and 5) and on to the future revelation at Christ's parousia (8, 18-25). Its outlook is universal.

Paul's Letter to the Romans is a powerful exposition of the doctrine of the supremacy of Christ and of faith in Christ as the source of salvation. It is an implicit plea to the Christians at Rome, and to all Christians, to hold fast to that faith. They are to resist any pressure put on them to accept a doctrine of salvation through works of the law (see the note on 10, 4). At the same time they are not to exaggerate Christian freedom as an abdication of responsibility for others (12, 1-2) or as a repudiation of God's law and will (see the notes on 3, 9-26; 3, 31; 7, 7-12.13-25).

The principal divisions of the Letter to the Romans are the following:

I: Address (1, 1-15)
II: Humanity Lost without the Gospel (1, 16—3, 20)
III: Justification through Faith in Christ (3, 21—5, 21)
IV: Justification and the Christian Life (6, 1—8, 39)
V: Jews and Gentiles in God's Plan (9, 1—11, 36)
VI: The Duties of Christians (12, 1—15, 13)
VII: Conclusion (15, 14—16, 27)

I: ADDRESS

CHAPTER 1

***Greeting.*†** 1*† Paul, a slave of Christ
Jesus, called to be an apostle and set
apart for the gospel of God, 2* which he
promised previously through his proph-
ets in the holy scriptures, 3*† the gospel
about his Son, descended from David
according to the flesh, 4* but established
as Son of God in power according to the
spirit of holiness through resurrection
from the dead, Jesus Christ our Lord.
5*† Through him we have received the
grace of apostleship, to bring about the
obedience of faith, for the sake of his
name, among all the Gentiles, 6* among
whom are you also, who are called to
belong to Jesus Christ; 7*† to all the
beloved of God in Rome, called to be
holy. Grace to you and peace from
God our Father and the Lord Jesus
Christ.

Thanksgiving. 8*† First, I give
thanks to my God through Jesus Christ
for all of you, because your faith is her-
alded throughout the world. 9* God is
my witness, whom I serve with my spirit
in proclaiming the gospel of his Son,
that I remember you constantly,
10*† always asking in my prayers that
somehow by God's will I may at last find
my way clear to come to you. 11* For I
long to see you, that I may share with
you some spiritual gift so that you may
be strengthened, 12 that is, that you and
I may be mutually encouraged by one
another's faith, yours and mine. 13*† I
do not want you to be unaware, broth-
ers, that I often planned to come to you,
though I was prevented until now, that
I might harvest some fruit among you,
too, as among the rest of the Gentiles.
14† To Greeks and non-Greeks alike, to
the wise and the ignorant, I am under
obligation; 15* that is why I am eager
to preach the gospel also to you in
Rome.

*

1, 1: Gal 1, 10; Phil 1, 1; Jas 1, 1 / Acts 9, 15; 13, 2; 1 Cor 1, 1; Gal 1, 15; Ti 1, 1.
2: 16, 25-26; Ti 1, 2.
3: 9, 5; 2 Sm 7, 12; Mt 1, 1; Mk 12, 35; Jn 7, 42; Acts 13, 22-23; 2 Tm 2, 8; Rv 22, 16.
4: 10, 9; Acts 13, 33; Phil 3, 10.
5: 15, 15; Gal 2, 7.9 / 15, 18; Acts 9, 15; 26, 16-18; Gal 1, 16; 2, 7.9.
6: 1 Cor 1, 9.
7: Nm 6, 25-26; 1 Cor 1, 2-3; 2 Cor 1, 1-2.
8: 16, 19; 1 Thes 1, 8.
9: 2 Cor 1, 23; Eph 1, 16; Phil 1, 8; 1 Thes 1, 2; 2, 5.10; 2 Tm 1, 3.
10: 15, 23.32; Acts 18, 21; 1 Cor 4, 19; 1 Thes 2, 17.
11: 1 Thes 2, 17; 3, 10.
13: 15, 22; Jn 15, 16; Acts 19, 21.
15: Acts 28, 30-31.

†

1, 1-7: In Paul's letters the greeting or *praescriptio* follows a standard form, though with variations. It is based upon the common Greco-Roman epistolary practice, but with the addition of Semitic and specifically Christian elements. The three basic components are: name of sender; name of addressee; greeting. In identifying himself, Paul often adds phrases to describe his apostolic mission; this element is more developed in Rom than in any other letter. Elsewhere he associates co-workers with himself in the greeting: Sosthenes (1 Cor), Timothy (2 Cor; Phil; Phlm), Silvanus (1-2 Thes). The standard secular greeting was the infinitive *chairein,* "greetings." Paul uses instead the similar-sounding *charis,* "grace," together with the Semitic greeting *šālôm* (Greek *eirēnē*), "peace." These gifts, foreshadowed in God's dealings with Israel (see Nm 6, 24-26), have been poured out abundantly in Christ, and Paul wishes them to his readers. In Rom the Pauline *praescriptio* is expanded and expressed in a formal tone; it emphasizes Paul's office as apostle to the Gentiles. Verses 3-4 stress the gospel or kerygma, v 2 the fulfillment of God's promise, and vv 1 and 5 Paul's office. On his call, see Gal 1, 15-16; 1 Cor 9, 1; 15, 8-10; Acts 9, 1-22; 22, 3-16; 26, 4-18.

1, 1: *Slave of Christ Jesus:* Paul applies the term slave to himself in order to express his undivided allegiance to the Lord of the church, the Master of all, including slaves and masters. "No one can serve (i.e., be a slave to) two masters," said Jesus (Mt 6, 24). It is this aspect of the slave-master relationship rather than its degrading implications that Paul emphasizes when he discusses Christian commitment.

1, 3-4: Paul here cites an early confession that proclaims Jesus' sonship as messianic descendant of David (cf Mt 22, 42; 2 Tm 2, 8; Rv 22, 16) and as Son of God by the resurrection. As "life-giving spirit" (1 Cor 15, 45), Jesus Christ is able to communicate the Spirit to those who believe in him.

1, 5: Paul recalls his apostolic office, implying that the Romans know something of his history. *The obedience of faith:* as Paul will show at length in chs 6-8 and 12-15, faith in God's justifying action in Jesus Christ relates one to God's gift of the new life that is made possible through the death and resurrection of Jesus Christ and the activity of the holy Spirit (see especially 8, 1-11).

1, 7: *Called to be holy:* Paul often refers to Christians as "the holy ones" or "the saints." The Israelite community was called a "holy assembly" because they had been separated for the worship and service of the Lord (see Lv 11, 44; 23, 1-44). The Christian community regarded its members as sanctified by baptism (6, 22; 15, 16; 1 Cor 6, 11; Eph 5, 26-27). Christians are called to holiness (1 Cor 1, 2; 1 Thes 4, 7), that is, they are called to make their lives conform to the gift they have already received.

1, 8: In Greco-Roman letters, the greeting was customarily followed by a prayer. The Pauline letters usually include this element (except Gal and Ti), expressed in Christian thanksgiving formulas and usually stating the principal theme of the letter. In 2 Cor the thanksgiving becomes a blessing, and in Eph it is preceded by a lengthy blessing. Sometimes the thanksgiving is blended into the body of the letter, especially in 1 Thes. In Rom it is stated briefly.

1, 10-12: Paul lays the groundwork for his more detailed statement in 15, 22-24 about his projected visit to Rome.

1, 13: *Brothers* is idiomatic for all Paul's "kin in Christ," all those who believe in the gospel; it includes women as well as men (cf 4, 3).

1, 14: *Greeks and non-Greeks:* literally, "Greeks and barbarians." As a result of Alexander's conquests, Greek became the standard international language of the Mediterranean world. *Greeks* in Paul's statement therefore means people who know Greek or who have been influenced by Greek culture. *Non-Greeks* were people whose cultures remained substantially unaffected by Greek influences. Greeks called such people "barbarians" (cf Acts 28, 2), meaning people whose speech was foreign. Roman citizens would scarcely classify themselves as such, and Nero, who was reigning when Paul wrote this letter, prided himself on his admiration for Greek culture. *Under obligation:* Paul will expand on the theme of obligation in 13, 8; 15, 1.27.

II: HUMANITY LOST WITHOUT THE GOSPEL

God's Power for Salvation. † 16* For
I am not ashamed of the gospel. It
is the power of God for the salvation
of everyone who believes: for Jew
first, and then Greek. 17*† For in it
is revealed the righteousness of God
from faith to faith; as it is written,
"The one who is righteous by faith will
live."

Punishment of Idolators. † 18*† The
wrath of God is indeed being revealed
from heaven against every impiety and
wickedness of those who suppress the
truth by their wickedness. 19* For what
can be known about God is evident to
them, because God made it evident to
them. 20* Ever since the creation of the
world, his invisible attributes of eternal
power and divinity have been able to
be understood and perceived in what he
has made. As a result, they have no ex-
cuse; 21* for although they knew God
they did not accord him glory as God
or give him thanks. Instead, they be-
came vain in their reasoning, and their
senseless minds were darkened.
22* While claiming to be wise, they be-
came fools 23* and exchanged the glory
of the immortal God for the likeness
of an image of mortal man or of birds
or of four-legged animals or of
snakes.

24*† Therefore, God handed them
over to impurity through the lusts of
their hearts for the mutual degradation
of their bodies. 25* They exchanged the
truth of God for a lie and revered and
worshiped the creature rather than the
creator, who is blessed forever. Amen.
26 Therefore, God handed them over to
degrading passions. Their females ex-
changed natural relations for unnatu-
ral, 27* and the males likewise gave up
natural relations with females and
burned with lust for one another. Males
did shameful things with males and
thus received in their own persons the
due penalty for their perversity. 28 And
since they did not see fit to acknowledge
God, God handed them over to their un-
discerning mind to do what is improper.
29* They are filled with every form of
wickedness, evil, greed, and malice; full
of envy, murder, rivalry, treachery,
and spite. They are gossips 30 and scan-
dalmongers and they hate God. They
are insolent, haughty, boastful, inge-
nious in their wickedness, and rebellious
toward their parents. 31 They are sense-
less, faithless, heartless, ruthless.
32* Although they know the just decree
of God that all who practice such things
deserve death, they not only do them
but give approval to those who practice
them.

*

16: Ps 119, 46; 1 Cor 1, 18.24 / 2, 9; Acts 3, 26; 13, 46.
17: 3, 21-22; Hb 2, 4; Gal 3, 11; Heb 10, 38.
18: 2, 5.8-9; Is 66, 15; Eph 5, 6; Col 3, 6.
19-32: Wis 13-19; Acts 14, 15-17; 17, 23-29.
20: Jb 12, 7-9; Pss 8, 4; 19, 2; Sir 17, 7-9; Is 40, 26; Acts 14, 17; 17, 25-28.
21: Eph 4, 17-18.
22: Wis 13, 1-9; Is 5, 21; Jer 10, 14; Acts 17, 29-30; 1 Cor 1, 19-21.
23: Dt 4, 15-19; Ps 106, 20; Wis 11, 15; 12, 24; 13, 10-19; Jer 2, 11.
24: Wis 12, 25; 14, 22-31; Acts 7, 41-42; Eph 4, 19.
25: 9, 5; Jer 13, 25-27.
27: Lv 18, 22; 20, 13; Wis 14, 26; 1 Cor 6, 9; 1 Tm 1, 10.
29-31: 13, 13; Mt 15, 19; Mk 7, 21-22; Gal 5, 19-21; 2 Tm 3, 2-4.
32: Acts 8, 1; 2 Thes 2, 12.

†

1, 16-17: The principal theme of the letter is salvation through faith. *I am not ashamed of the gospel:* Paul is not ashamed to proclaim the gospel, despite the criticism that Jews and Gentiles leveled against the proclamation of the crucified savior; cf 1 Cor 1, 23-24. Paul affirms, however, that it is precisely through the crucifixion and resurrection of Jesus that God's saving will and power become manifest. *Jew first* (cf 2, 9-10) means that Jews especially, in view of the example of Abraham (ch 4), ought to be the leaders in the response of faith.

1, 17: *In it is revealed the righteousness of God from faith to faith:* the gospel centers in Jesus Christ, in whom God's saving presence and righteousness in history have been made known. Faith is affirmation of the basic purpose and meaning of the Old Testament as proclamation of divine promise (2; 4, 13) and exposure of the inability of humanity to effect its salvation even through covenant law. Faith is the gift of the holy Spirit and denotes acceptance of salvation as God's righteousness, that is, God's gift of a renewed relationship in forgiveness and power for a new life. Faith is response to God's total claim on people and their doctiny. *The one who is righteous by faith will live:* see the note on Hb 2, 4.

1, 18—3, 20: Paul aims to show that all humanity is in a desperate plight and requires God's special intervention if it is to be saved.

1, 18-32: In this passage Paul uses themes and rhetoric common in Jewish-Hellenistic mission proclamation (cf Wis 13, 1—14, 31) to indict especially the non-Jewish world. The close association of idolatry and immorality is basic, but the generalization needs in all fairness to be balanced against the fact that non-Jewish Christian society on many levels displayed moral attitudes and performance whose quality would challenge much of contemporary Christian culture. Romans themselves expressed abhorrence over devotion accorded to animals in Egypt. Paul's main point is that the wrath of God does not await the end of the world but goes into action at each present moment in humanity's history when misdirected piety serves as a facade for self-interest.

1, 18: *The wrath of God:* God's reaction to human sinfulness, an Old Testament phrase that expresses the irreconcilable opposition between God and evil (see Is 9, 11.16.18.20; 10, 4; 30, 27). It is not contrary to God's universal love for his creatures, but condemns Israel's turning aside from the covenant obligations. Hosea depicts Yahweh as suffering intensely at the thought of having to punish Israel (Hos 11, 8-9). God's wrath was to be poured forth especially on the "Day of Yahweh" and thus took on an eschatological connotation (see Zep 1, 15).

1, 24: In order to expose the depth of humanity's rebellion against the Creator, *God handed them over to impurity through the lusts of their hearts.* Instead of curbing people's evil interests, God abandoned them to self-indulgence, thereby removing the facade of apparent conformity to the divine will. Subsequently Paul will show that the Mosaic law produces the same effect; cf 5, 20; 7, 13-24. The divine judgment expressed here is related to the theme of hardness of heart described in 9, 17-18.

CHAPTER 2

***God's Just Judgment.*†** 1*† Therefore, you are without excuse, every one of you who passes judgment. For by the standard by which you judge another you condemn yourself, since you, the judge, do the very same things. 2 We know that the judgment of God on those who do such things is true. 3* Do you suppose, then, you who judge those who engage in such things and yet do them yourself, that you will escape the judgment of God? 4* Or do you hold his priceless kindness, forbearance, and patience in low esteem, unaware that the kindness of God would lead you to repentance? 5* By your stubbornness and impenitent heart, you are storing up wrath for yourself for the day of wrath and revelation of the just judgment of God, 6*† who will repay everyone according to his works: 7 eternal life to those who seek glory, honor, and immortality through perseverance in good works, 8* but wrath and fury to those who selfishly disobey the truth and obey wickedness. 9 Yes, affliction and distress will come upon every human being who does evil, Jew first and then Greek. 10* But there will be glory, honor, and peace for everyone who does good, Jew first and then Greek. 11*† There is no partiality with God.

***Judgment by the Interior Law.*†** 12* All who sin outside the law will also perish without reference to it, and all who sin under the law will be judged in accordance with it. 13* For it is not those who hear the law who are just in the sight of God; rather, those who observe the law will be justified. 14* For when the Gentiles who do not have the law by nature observe the prescriptions of the law, they are a law for themselves even though they do not have the law. 15† They show that the demands of the law are written in their hearts, while their conscience also bears witness and their conflicting thoughts accuse or even defend them 16* on the day when, according to my gospel, God will judge people's hidden works through Christ Jesus.

***Judgment by the Mosaic Law.*†** 17* Now if you call yourself a Jew and rely on the law and boast of God 18* and know his will and are able to discern what is important since you are instructed from the law, 19* and if you are confident that you are a guide for the blind and a light for those in darkness, 20* that you are a trainer of the foolish and teacher of the simple, because in the law you have the formulation of knowledge and truth—21* then you who teach another, are you failing to teach yourself? You who preach against stealing, do you steal? 22 You who forbid adultery, do you commit adultery? You who detest idols, do you rob temples? 23 You who boast of the law, do you dishonor God by breaking the law? 24*† For, as it is written, "Because of you the name of God is reviled among the Gentiles."

25* Circumcision, to be sure, has value if you observe the law; but if you break the law, your circumcision has become uncircumcision. 26* Again, if an uncircumcised man keeps the precepts of the law, will he not be considered circumcised? 27 Indeed, those who are physi-

*

2, 1: Mt 7, 1-2.
3: Wis 16, 15-16.
4: 3, 25-26; 9, 22; Wis 11, 23; 15, 1; 2 Pt 3, 9.15.
5: Ex 33, 3; Acts 7, 51; Rv 6, 17; 11, 18.
6: Ps 62, 12; Prv 24, 12; Sir 16, 14; Mt 16, 27; Jn 5, 29; 2 Cor 5, 10.
8: 2 Thes 1, 8.
10: 1, 16; 3, 9.
11: Dt 10, 17; 2 Chr 19, 7; Sir 35, 12-13; Acts 10, 34; Gal 2, 6; Eph 6, 9; Col 3, 25; 1 Pt 1, 17.
12: 3, 19.
13: Mt 7, 21; Lk 6, 46-49; 8, 21; Jas 1, 22-25; 1 Jn 3, 7.
14: Acts 10, 35.
16: Acts 10, 42; 17, 31.
17: Is 48, 1-2; Mi 3, 11; Phil 3, 4-6.
18: Phil 1, 10.
19: Mt 15, 14; Lk 6, 39.
20: 2 Tm 3, 15.
21: Ps 50, 16-21; Mt 23, 3-4.
24: Is 52, 5; Ez 36, 20; 2 Pt 2, 2.
25-29: Jer 4, 4; 9, 24-25.
25: 1 Cor 7, 19; Gal 5, 3.
26: Gal 5, 6.

†

2, 1—3, 20: After his general indictment of the Gentile, Paul shows that in spite of special revelation Jews enjoy no advantage in moral status before God (3, 1-8). With the entire human race now declared guilty before God (3, 9-20), Paul will then be able to display the solution for the total problem: salvation through God's redemptive work that is revealed in Christ Jesus for all who believe (3, 21-31).

2, 1-11: As a first step in his demonstration that Jews enjoy no real moral supremacy over Gentiles, Paul explains that the final judgment will be a review of performance, not of privilege. From this perspective Gentiles stand on an equal footing with Jews, and Jews cannot condemn the sins of Gentiles without condemning themselves.

2, 6: *Will repay everyone according to his works:* Paul reproduces the Septuagint text of Ps 62, 12 and Prv 24, 12.

2, 11: *No partiality with God:* this sentence is not at variance with the statements in vv 9-10. Since Jews are the first to go under indictment, it is only fair that they be given first consideration in the distribution of blessings. Basic, of course, is the understanding that God accepts no bribes (Dt 10, 17).

2, 12-16: Jews cannot reasonably demand from Gentiles the standard of conduct inculcated in the Old Testament since God did not address its revelation to them. Rather, God made it possible for Gentiles to know instinctively the difference between right and wrong. But, as Paul explained in 1, 18-32, humanity misread the evidence of God's existence, power, and divinity, and "while claiming to be wise, they became fools" (1, 22).

2, 15: Paul expands on the thought of Jer 31, 33; Wis 17, 11.

2, 17-29: Mere possession of laws is no evidence of virtue. By eliminating circumcision as an elitist moral sign, Paul clears away the last obstacle to his presentation of justification through faith without claims based on the receipt of circumcision and its attendant legal obligations.

2, 24: According to Is 52, 5 the suffering of Israel prompts her enemies to revile God. Paul uses the passage in support of his point that the present immorality of Israelites is the cause of such defamation.

ROMANS

cally uncircumcised but carry out the
law will pass judgment on you, with
your written law and circumcision, who
break the law. [28]* One is not a Jew out-
wardly. True circumcision is not out-
ward, in the flesh. [29]* Rather, one is a
Jew inwardly, and circumcision is of
the heart, in the spirit, not the letter;
his praise is not from human beings but
from God.

CHAPTER 3

Answers to Objections.† [1] What ad-
vantage is there then in being a Jew?
Or what is the value of circumcision?
[2]* Much, in every respect. [For] in the
first place, they were entrusted with the
utterances of God. [3]* What if some were
unfaithful? Will their infidelity nullify
the fidelity of God? [4]*† Of course not!
God must be true, though every human
being is a liar, as it is written:

> "That you may be justified in your
> words,
> and conquer when you are
> judged."

[5]* But if our wickedness provides proof
of God's righteousness, what can we
say? Is God unjust, humanly speaking,
to inflict his wrath? [6] Of course not! For
how else is God to judge the world?
[7] But if God's truth redounds to his glory
through my falsehood, why am I still
being condemned as a sinner? [8]* And
why not say—as we are accused and as
some claim we say—that we should do
evil that good may come of it? Their
penalty is what they deserve.
Universal Bondage to Sin.† [9]* Well,
then, are we better off? Not entirely, for
we have already brought the charge
against Jews and Greeks alike that they
are all under the domination of sin,
[10]* as it is written:

> "There is no one just, not one,
> 11 there is no one who understands,
> there is no one who seeks God.
> 12 All have gone astray; all alike are
> worthless;
> there is not one who does good,
> [there is not] even one.
> 13* Their throats are open graves;
> they deceive with their tongues;
> the venom of asps is on their lips;
> 14* their mouths are full of bitter
> cursing.
> 15* Their feet are quick to shed blood;
> 16 ruin and misery are in their ways,
> 17 and the way of peace they know not.
> 18* There is no fear of God before
> their eyes."

[19]*† Now we know that what the law
says is addressed to those under the
law, so that every mouth may be si-
lenced and the whole world stand ac-
countable to God, [20]*† since no human
being will be justified in his sight by ob-
serving the law; for through the law
comes consciousness of sin.

III: JUSTIFICATION THROUGH FAITH IN CHRIST

Justification apart from the Law.†
[21]*† But now the righteousness of God
has been manifested apart from the
law, though testified to by the law and
the prophets, [22]* the righteousness of
God through faith in Jesus Christ for
all who believe. For there is no distinc-
tion; [23]* all have sinned and are de-
prived of the glory of God. [24]* They are

---

*

28: Jn 7, 24; 8, 15.39.
29: Dt 30, 6; Jer 4, 4; 9, 25; Col 2, 11 / 1 Cor 4, 5; 2 Cor 10, 18.
3, 2: 9, 4; Dt 4, 7-8; Pss 103, 7; 147, 19-20.
3: 9, 6; 11, 1.29; Ps 89, 30-37; 2 Tm 2, 13.
4: Ps 116, 11 / Ps 51, 6.
5: 9, 14; Jb 34, 12-17.
8: 6, 1.
9: 1, 18—2, 25; 3, 23; Sir 8, 5.
10-11: Pss 14, 1-3; 53, 2-4; Eccl 7, 20.
13: Pss 5, 10; 140, 4.
14: Ps 10, 7.
15-17: Prv 1, 16; Is 59, 7-8.
18: Ps 36, 2.
19: 7, 7.
20: Ps 143, 2; Gal 2, 16 / 7, 7.
21: Is 51, 6-8; Acts 10, 43.
22: 1, 17; Gal 2, 16; Phil 3, 9.
23: 3, 9; 5, 12.
24: Eph 2, 8; Ti 3, 7 / 5, 1-2; Eph 1, 7.

---

†

3, 1-4: In keeping with the popular style of diatribe, Paul responds to the objection that his teaching on the sinfulness of all humanity detracts from the religious prerogatives of Israel. He stresses that Jews have remained the vehicle of God's revelation despite their sins, though this depends on the fidelity of God.

3, 4: *Though every human being is a liar:* these words reproduce the Greek text of Ps 116, 11. The rest of the verse is from Ps 51, 6.

3, 9-20: *Well, then, are we better off?:* this phrase can also be translated "Are we at a disadvantage?" but the latter version does not substantially change the overall meaning of the passage. Having explained that Israel's privileged status is guaranteed by God's fidelity, Paul now demonstrates the infidelity of the Jews by a catena of citations from scripture, possibly derived from an existing collection of *testimonia.* These texts show that all human beings share the common burden of sin. They are linked together by mention of organs of the body: throat, tongue, lips, mouth, feet, eyes.

3, 19: *The law:* Paul here uses the term in its broadest sense to mean all of the scriptures; none of the preceding texts is from the Torah or Pentateuch.

3, 20: *No human being will be justified in his sight:* these words are freely cited from Ps 143, 2. In place of the psalmist's "no living person," Paul substitutes "no human being" (literally "no flesh," a Hebraism), and he adds "by observing the law."

3, 21-31: These verses provide a clear statement of Paul's "gospel," i.e., the principle of justification by faith in Christ. God has found a means of rescuing humanity from its desperate plight: Paul's general term for this divine initiative is *the righteousness of God* (21). Divine mercy declares the guilty innocent and makes them so. God does this not as a result of the law but apart from it (21), and not because of any merit in human beings but through forgiveness of their sins (24), in virtue of the redemption wrought in Christ Jesus for all who believe (22.24-25). God has manifested his righteousness in the coming of Jesus Christ, whose saving activity inaugurates a new era in human history.

3, 21: *But now:* Paul adopts a common phrase used by Greek authors to describe movement from disaster to prosperity. The expressions indicate that vv 21-26 are the consolatory answer to vv 9-20.

justified freely by his grace through the redemption in Christ Jesus, 25*† whom God set forth as an expiation, through faith, by his blood, to prove his righteousness because of the forgiveness of sins previously committed, 26 through the forbearance of God—to prove his righteousness in the present time, that he might be righteous and justify the one who has faith in Jesus.

27*† What occasion is there then for boasting? It is ruled out. On what principle, that of works? No, rather on the principle of faith. 28* For we consider that a person is justified by faith apart from works of the law. 29* Does God belong to Jews alone? Does he not belong to Gentiles, too? Yes, also to Gentiles, 30* for God is one and will justify the circumcised on the basis of faith and the uncircumcised through faith. 31*† Are we then annulling the law by this faith? Of course not! On the contrary, we are supporting the law.

CHAPTER 4

Abraham Justified by Faith.† 1* What then can we say that Abraham found, our ancestor according to the flesh? 2† Indeed, if Abraham was justified on the basis of his works, he has reason to boast; but this was not so in the sight of God. 3*† For what does the scripture say? "Abraham believed God, and it was credited to him as righteousness." 4* A worker's wage is credited not as a gift, but as something due. 5 But when one does not work, yet believes in the one who justifies the ungodly, his faith is credited as righteousness. 6 So also David declares the blessedness of the person to whom God credits righteousness apart from works:

7* "Blessed are they whose iniquities
are forgiven
and whose sins are covered.
8 Blessed is the man whose sin the
Lord does not record."

9*† Does this blessedness apply only to the circumcised, or to the uncircumcised as well? Now we assert that "faith was credited to Abraham as righteousness." 10 Under what circumstances was it credited? Was he circumcised or not? He was not circumcised, but uncircumcised. 11* And he received the sign of circumcision as a seal on the righteousness received through faith while he was uncircumcised. Thus he was to be the father of all the uncircumcised who believe, so that to them [also] righteousness might be credited, 12 as well as the father of the circumcised who not only are circumcised, but also follow the path of faith that our father Abraham walked while still uncircumcised.

Inheritance through Faith. 13* It was not through the law that the promise was made to Abraham and his descendants that he would inherit the world, but through the righteousness that comes from faith. 14* For if those who adhere to the law are the heirs, faith is null and the promise is void. 15*† For the law produces wrath; but where there is no law, neither is there viola-

*

25: Lv 16, 12-15; Acts 17, 31; 1 Jn 4, 10.
27: 8, 2; 1 Cor 1, 29-31.
28: 5, 1; Gal 2, 16.
29: 10, 12.
30: Dt 6, 4; Gal 3, 20; Jas 2, 19 / 4, 11-12.
31: 8, 4; Mt 5, 17.
4, 1: Gal 3, 6-9.
3: Gn 15, 6; Gal 3, 6; Jas 2, 14.20-24.
4: 11, 6.
7-8: Ps 32, 1-2.
9: 4, 3.
11: Gn 17, 10-11; Gal 3, 6-8.
13: Gn 12, 7; 18, 18; 22, 17-18; Sir 44, 21; Gal 3, 16-18.29.
14: Gal 3, 18.
15: 3, 20; 5, 13; 7, 8; Gal 3, 19.

†

3, 25: *Expiation:* this rendering is preferable to "propitiation," which suggests hostility on the part of God toward sinners. As Paul will be at pains to point out (5, 8-10), it is humanity that is hostile to God.

3, 27-31: People cannot boast of their own holiness, since it is God's free gift (27), both to the Jew who practices circumcision out of faith and to the Gentile who accepts faith without the Old Testament religious culture symbolized by circumcision (29-30).

3, 27: *Principle of faith:* literally, "law of faith." Paul is fond of wordplay involving the term "law"; cf 7, 21.23; 8, 2. Since "law" in Greek may also connote "custom" or "principle," his readers and hearers would have sensed no contradiction in the use of the term after the negative statement concerning law in v 20.

3, 31: *We are supporting the law:* giving priority to God's intentions. God is the ultimate source of law, and the essence of law is fairness. On the basis of the Mosaic covenant, God's justice is in question if those who sinned against the law are permitted to go free (see 23-26). In order to rescue all humanity rather than condemn it, God thinks of an alternative: the law or "principle" of faith (27). What can be more fair than to admit everyone into the divine presence on the basis of forgiveness grasped by faith? Indeed, this principle of faith antedates the Mosaic law, as Paul will demonstrate in ch 4, and does not therefore mark a change in divine policy.

4, 1-25: This is an expanded treatment of the significance of Abraham's faith, which Paul discusses in Gal 3, 6-18; see the notes there.

4, 2-5: Verse 2 corresponds to v 4, and v 3 to v 5. The Greek term here rendered *credited* means "made an entry." The context determines whether it is credit or debit. Verse 8 speaks of "recording sin" as a debit. Paul's repeated use of accountants' terminology in this and other passages can be traced both to the Old Testament texts he quotes and to his business activity as a tentmaker. The commercial term in Gn 15, 6, "credited it to him," reminds Paul in vv 7-8 of Ps 32, 2, in which the same term is used and applied to forgiveness of sins. Thus Paul is able to argue that Abraham's faith involved receipt of forgiveness of sins and that all believers benefit as he did through faith.

4, 3: Jas 2, 24 appears to conflict with Paul's statement. However, James combats the error of extremists who used the doctrine of justification through faith as a screen for moral self- determination. Paul discusses the subject of holiness in greater detail than does James and beginning with ch 6 shows how justification through faith introduces one to the gift of a new life in Christ through the power of the holy Spirit.

4, 9: *Blessedness:* evidence of divine favor.

4, 15: Law has the negative function of bringing the deep-seated rebellion against God to the surface in specific sins; see the note on 1, 18-32.

tion. [16]* For this reason, it depends on
faith, so that it may be a gift, and the
promise may be guaranteed to all his
descendants, not to those who only ad-
here to the law but to those who follow
the faith of Abraham, who is the father
of all of us, [17]* as it is written, "I have
made you father of many nations." He
is our father in the sight of God, in
whom he believed, who gives life to the
dead and calls into being what does not
exist. [18]* He believed, hoping against
hope, that he would become "the father
of many nations," according to what
was said, "Thus shall your descendants
be." [19]* He did not weaken in faith when
he considered his own body as [al-
ready] dead (for he was almost a hun-
dred years old) and the dead womb of
Sarah. [20]† He did not doubt God's prom-
ise in unbelief; rather, he was empow-
ered by faith and gave glory to God
[21]* and was fully convinced that what
he had promised he was also able to do.
[22]* That is why "it was credited to him
as righteousness." [23] But it was not for
him alone that it was written that "it
was credited to him"; [24]* it was also for
us, to whom it will be credited, who be-
lieve in the one who raised Jesus our
Lord from the dead, [25]* who was
handed over for our transgressions and
was raised for our justification.

CHAPTER 5

Faith, Hope, and Love.†
[1]*† Therefore, since we have been justi-
fied by faith, we have peace with God
through our Lord Jesus Christ,
[2]* through whom we have gained access
[by faith] to this grace in which we
stand, and we boast in hope of the glory
of God. [3] Not only that, but we even
boast of our afflictions, knowing that af-
fliction produces endurance, [4]* and en-
durance, proven character, and proven
character, hope, [5]* and hope does not
disappoint, because the love of God has
been poured out into our hearts through
the holy Spirit that has been given to
us. [6] For Christ, while we were still help-
less, yet died at the appointed time for
the ungodly. [7]† Indeed, only with diffi-
culty does one die for a just person,
though perhaps for a good person one
might even find courage to die. [8]* But
God proves his love for us in that while
we were still sinners Christ died for us.
[9]* How much more then, since we are
now justified by his blood, will we be
saved through him from the wrath.
[10]* Indeed, if, while we were enemies,
we were reconciled to God through the
death of his Son, how much more, once
reconciled, will we be saved by his life.
[11] Not only that, but we also boast of God
through our Lord Jesus Christ, through
whom we have now received reconcilia-
tion.

Humanity's Sin through Adam.†
[12]*† Therefore, just as through one per-
son sin entered the world, and through
sin, death, and thus death came to all,
inasmuch as all sinned—[13]* for up to the
time of the law, sin was in the world,
though sin is not accounted when there
is no law. [14]* But death reigned from

*

16: Sir 44, 19; Gal 3, 7-9.
17: Gn 17, 5; Heb 11, 19 / Is 48, 13.
18: Gn 15, 5.
19-20: Gn 17, 17; Heb 11, 11.
21: Gn 18, 14; Lk 1, 37.
22: Gn 15, 6.
24: 10, 9; 1 Pt 1, 21.
25: Is 53, 4-5.12; 1 Cor 15, 17; 1 Pt 1, 3 / 8, 11.
5, 1: 3, 24-28; Gal 2, 16.
2: Eph 2, 18; 3, 12.
4: 2 Cor 12, 9-10; Jas 1, 2-4; 1 Pt 1, 5-7; 4, 12-14.
5: 8, 14-16; Pss 22, 5-6; 25, 20.
8: Jn 3, 16; 1 Jn 4, 10.19.
9: 1, 18; 1 Thes 1, 10.
10: 8, 7-8; 2 Cor 5, 18; Col 1, 21-22.
12: Gn 2, 17; 3, 1-19; Wis 2, 24 / 3, 19.23.
13: 4, 15.
14: 1 Cor 15, 21.

†

4, 20: *He did not doubt God's promise in unbelief:* any doubts Abraham might have had were resolved in commitment to God's promise. Heb 11, 8-12 emphasizes the faith of Abraham and Sarah.

5, 1-11: Popular piety frequently construed reverses and troubles as punishment for sin; cf Jn 9, 2. Paul therefore assures believers that God's justifying action in Jesus Christ is a declaration of peace. The crucifixion of Jesus Christ displays God's initiative in certifying humanity for unimpeded access into the divine presence. Reconciliation is God's gift of pardon to the entire human race. Through faith one benefits personally from this pardon or, in Paul's term, is justified. The ultimate aim of God is to liberate believers from the pre-Christian self as described in chs 1-3. Since this liberation will first find completion in the believer's resurrection, salvation is described as future in 5, 10. Because this fullness of salvation belongs to the future it is called the Christian *hope*. Paul's Greek term for *hope* does not, however, suggest a note of uncertainty, to the effect: "I wonder whether God really means it." Rather, God's promise in the gospel fills believers with expectation and anticipation for the climactic gift of unalloyed commitment in the holy Spirit to the performance of the will of God. The persecutions that attend Christian commitment are to teach believers patience and to strengthen this hope, which will not disappoint them because the holy Spirit dwells in their hearts and imbues them with God's love (5).

5, 1: *We have peace:* a number of manuscripts, versions, and church Fathers read "Let us have peace"; cf 14, 19.

5, 7: In the world of Paul's time the *good person* is especially one who is magnanimous to others.

5, 12-21: Paul reflects on the sin of Adam (Gn 3, 1-13) in the light of the redemptive mystery of Christ. Sin, as used in the singular by Paul, refers to the dreadful power that has gripped humanity, which is now in revolt against the Creator and engaged in the exaltation of its own desires and interests. But no one has a right to say, "Adam made me do it," for all are culpable (12): Gentiles under the demands of the law written in their hearts (2, 14-15), and Jews under the Mosaic covenant. Through the Old Testament law, the sinfulness of humanity that was operative from the beginning (13) found further stimulation, with the result that sins were generated in even greater abundance. According to vv 15-21, God's act in Christ is in total contrast to the disastrous effects of the virus of sin that invaded humanity through Adam's crime.

5, 12: *Inasmuch as all sinned:* others translate "because all sinned," and understand v 13 as a parenthetical remark. Unlike Wis 2, 24, Paul does not ascribe the entry of death to the devil.

Adam to Moses, even over those who did not sin after the pattern of the trespass of Adam, who is the type of the one who was to come.

Grace and Life through Christ. 15 But the gift is not like the transgression. For if by that one person's transgression the many died, how much more did the grace of God and the gracious gift of the one person Jesus Christ overflow for the many. 16 And the gift is not like the result of the one person's sinning. For after one sin there was the judgment that brought condemnation; but the gift, after many transgressions, brought acquittal. 17 For if, by the transgression of one person, death came to reign through that one, how much more will those who receive the abundance of grace and of the gift of justification come to reign in life through the one person Jesus Christ. 18* In conclusion, just as through one transgression condemnation came upon all, so through one righteous act acquittal and life came to all. 19* For just as through the disobedience of one person the many were made sinners, so through the obedience of one the many will be made righteous. 20*† The law entered in so that transgression might increase but, where sin increased, grace overflowed all the more, 21* so that, as sin reigned in death, grace also might reign through justification for eternal life through Jesus Christ our Lord.

IV: JUSTIFICATION AND THE CHRISTIAN LIFE

CHAPTER 6

Freedom from Sin; Life in God.† 1* What then shall we say? Shall we persist in sin that grace may abound? Of course not! 2* How can we who died to sin yet live in it? 3* Or are you unaware that we who were baptized into Christ Jesus were baptized into his death? 4* We were indeed buried with him through baptism into death, so that, just as Christ was raised from the dead by the glory of the Father, we too might live in newness of life.

5* For if we have grown into union with him through a death like his, we shall also be united with him in the resurrection. 6* We know that our old self was crucified with him, so that our sinful body might be done away with, that we might no longer be in slavery to sin. 7 For a dead person has been absolved from sin. 8* If, then, we have died with Christ, we believe that we shall also live with him. 9* We know that Christ, raised from the dead, dies no more; death no longer has power over him. 10* As to his death, he died to sin once and for all; as to his life, he lives for God. 11* Consequently, you too must think of yourselves as [being] dead to sin and living for God in Christ Jesus.

12*† Therefore, sin must not reign over your mortal bodies so that you obey their desires. 13* And do not present the parts of your bodies to sin as weapons for wickedness, but present yourselves to God as raised from the dead to life and the parts of your bodies to God as weapons for righteousness. 14* For sin is not to have any power over you, since you are not under the law but under grace.

15* What then? Shall we sin because we are not under the law but under grace? Of course not! 16* Do you not know that if you present yourselves to someone as obedient slaves, you are slaves of the one you obey, either of sin, which leads to death, or of obedience, which leads to righteousness? 17† But

ROMANS

*

18: 1 Cor 15, 21-22.
19: Is 53, 11; Phil 2, 8-9.
20: 4, 15; 7, 7-8; Gal 3, 19.
21: 6, 23.
6, 1: 3, 5-8.
2: 1 Pt 4, 1.
3: Gal 3, 27.
4: Col 2, 12; 1 Pt 3, 21-22.
5: Phil 3, 10-11; 2 Tm 2, 11.
6: Gal 5, 24; 6, 14; Eph 4, 22-23.
8: 1 Thes 4, 17.
9: Acts 13, 34; 1 Cor 15, 26; 2 Tm 1, 10; Rv 1, 18.
10: Heb 9, 26-28; 1 Pt 3, 18.
11: 2 Cor 5, 15; 1 Pt 2, 24.
12: Gn 4, 7.
13: 12, 1; Eph 2, 5; 5, 14 / Col 3, 5.
14: Gal 5, 18; 1 Jn 3, 6.
15: 5, 17.21.
16: Jn 8, 31-34; 2 Pt 2, 19.
16-18: Jn 8, 32-36.

†

5, 20: *The law entered in:* sin had made its entrance (12); now the law comes in alongside sin. See the notes on 1, 18-32; 5, 12-21. *Where sin increased, grace overflowed all the more:* Paul declares that grace outmatches the productivity of sin.

6, 1-11: To defend the gospel against the charge that it promotes moral laxity (cf 3, 5-8), Paul expresses himself in the typical style of spirited diatribe. God's display of generosity or grace is not evoked by sin but, as stated in 5, 8, is the expression of God's love, and this love pledges eternal life to all believers (5, 21). Paul views the present conduct of the believers from the perspective of God's completed salvation when the body is resurrected and directed totally by the holy Spirit. Through baptism believers share the death of Christ and thereby escape from the grip of sin. Through the resurrection of Christ the power to live anew becomes reality for them, but the fullness of participation in Christ's resurrection still lies in the future. But life that is lived in dedication to God now is part and parcel of that future. Hence anyone who sincerely claims to be interested in that future will scarcely be able to say, "Let us sin so that grace may prosper" (cf 1).

6, 12-19: Christians have been released from the grip of sin, but sin endeavors to reclaim its victims. The antidote is constant remembrance that divine grace has claimed them and identifies them as people who are alive only for God's interests.

6, 17: In contrast to humanity, which was handed over to self-indulgence (1, 24-32), believers are *entrusted* ("handed over") to God's *pattern of teaching,* that is, the new life God aims to develop in Christians through the productivity of the holy Spirit. Throughout this passage Paul uses the slave-master model in order to emphasize the fact that one cannot give allegiance to both God and sin.

thanks be to God that, although you
were once slaves of sin, you have be-
come obedient from the heart to the pat-
tern of teaching to which you were
entrusted. 18 Freed from sin, you have
become slaves of righteousness. 19 I am
speaking in human terms because of the
weakness of your nature. For just as
you presented the parts of your bodies
as slaves to impurity and to lawlessness
for lawlessness, so now present them as
slaves to righteousness for sanctifica-
tion. 20*† For when you were slaves of
sin, you were free from righteousness.
21* But what profit did you get then from
the things of which you are now
ashamed? For the end of those things
is death. 22*† But now that you have
been freed from sin and have become
slaves of God, the benefit that you have
leads to sanctification, and its end is
eternal life. 23* For the wages of sin is
death, but the gift of God is eternal life
in Christ Jesus our Lord.

CHAPTER 7

***Freedom from the Law.*†** 1 Are you
unaware, brothers (for I am speaking
to people who know the law), that the
law has jurisdiction over one as long as
one lives? 2* Thus a married woman is
bound by law to her living husband; but
if her husband dies, she is released from
the law in respect to her husband.
3 Consequently, while her husband is
alive she will be called an adulteress if
she consorts with another man. But if
her husband dies she is free from that
law, and she is not an adulteress if she
consorts with another man.
4 In the same way, my brothers, you
also were put to death to the law
through the body of Christ, so that you
might belong to another, to the one who
was raised from the dead in order that
we might bear fruit for God. 5* For
when we were in the flesh, our sinful
passions, awakened by the law, worked
in our members to bear fruit for death.
6* But now we are released from the
law, dead to what held us captive, so
that we may serve in the newness of the
spirit and not under the obsolete letter.
***Acquaintance with Sin through the
Law.*†** 7*† What then can we say? That
the law is sin? Of course not! Yet I did
not know sin except through the law,
and I did not know what it is to covet
except that the law said, "You shall not
covet." 8* But sin, finding an opportu-
nity in the commandment, produced in
me every kind of covetousness. Apart
from the law sin is dead. 9 I once lived
outside the law, but when the com-
mandment came, sin became alive;
10* then I died, and the commandment
that was for life turned out to be death
for me. 11* For sin, seizing an opportu-
nity in the commandment, deceived me
and through it put me to death. 12* So
then the law is holy, and the command-
ment is holy and righteous and good.
***Sin and Death.*†** 13* Did the good,
then, become death for me? Of course
not! Sin, in order that it might be shown
to be sin, worked death in me through
the good, so that sin might become sin-
ful beyond measure through the com-
mandment. 14* We know that the law is
spiritual; but I am carnal, sold into slav-
ery to sin. 15 What I do, I do not under-
stand. For I do not do what I want, but
I do what I hate. 16 Now if I do what I
do not want, I concur that the law is
good. 17 So now it is no longer I who do
it, but sin that dwells in me. 18* For I
know that good does not dwell in me,
that is, in my flesh. The willing is ready
at hand, but doing the good is not.
19 For I do not do the good I want, but
I do the evil I do not want. 20 Now if [I]
do what I do not want, it is no longer I
who do it, but sin that dwells in me.
21 So, then, I discover the principle that

*

20: Jn 8, 34.
21: 8, 6.13; Prv 12, 28; Ez 16, 61.63.
22: 1 Pt 1, 9.
23: Gn 2, 17; Gal 6, 7-9; Jas 1, 15.
7, 2: 1 Cor 7, 39.
5: 6, 21; 8, 6.13.
6: 8, 2; 2 Cor 3, 6.
7: 3, 20; Ex 20, 17; Dt 5, 21.
8: 5, 13.20; 1 Cor 15, 56 / 4, 15.
10: Lv 18, 5.
11: Gn 3, 13; Heb 3, 13.
12: 1 Tm 1, 8.
13: 4, 15; 5, 20.
14: 8, 7-8; Ps 51, 7.
18: Gn 6, 5; 8, 21; Phil 2, 13.

†

6, 20: *You were free from righteousness:* expressed ironically, for such freedom is really tyranny. The commercial metaphors in vv 21-23 add up only one way: sin is a bad bargain.

6, 22: *Sanctification:* or holiness.

7, 1-6: Paul reflects on the fact that Christians have a different understanding of the law because of their faith in Christ. Law binds the living, not the dead, as exemplified in marriage, which binds in life but is dissolved through death. Similarly, Christians who through baptism have died with Christ to sin (cf 6, 2-4) are freed from the law that occasioned transgressions, which in turn were productive of death. Now that Christians are joined to Christ, the power of Christ's resurrection makes it possible for them to bear the fruit of newness of life for God.

7, 7-25: In this passage Paul uses the first person singular in the style of diatribe for the sake of argument. He aims to depict the disastrous consequences when a Christian reintroduces the law as a means to attain the objective of holiness pronounced in 6, 22.

7, 7-12: The apostle defends himself against the charge of identifying the law with sin. Sin does not exist in law but in human beings, whose sinful inclinations are not overcome by the proclamation of law.

7, 13-25: Far from improving the sinner, law encourages sin to expose itself in transgressions or violations of specific commandments (see 1, 24; 5, 20). Thus persons who do not experience the justifying grace of God, and Christians who revert to dependence on law as the criterion for their relationship with God, will recognize a rift between their reasoned desire for the goodness of the law and their actual performance that is contrary to the law. Unable to free themselves from the slavery of sin and the power of death, they can only be rescued from defeat in the conflict by the power of God's grace working through Jesus Christ.

when I want to do right, evil is at hand. 22 For I take delight in the law of God, in my inner self, 23*† but I see in my members another principle at war with the law of my mind, taking me captive to the law of sin that dwells in my members. 24 Miserable one that I am! Who will deliver me from this mortal body? 25* Thanks be to God through Jesus Christ our Lord. Therefore, I myself, with my mind, serve the law of God but, with my flesh, the law of sin.

CHAPTER 8

***The Flesh and the Spirit.*†** 1 Hence, now there is no condemnation for those who are in Christ Jesus. 2* For the law of the spirit of life in Christ Jesus has freed you from the law of sin and death. 3* For what the law, weakened by the flesh, was powerless to do, this God has done: by sending his own Son in the likeness of sinful flesh and for the sake of sin, he condemned sin in the flesh, 4* so that the righteous decree of the law might be fulfilled in us, who live not according to the flesh but according to the spirit. 5 For those who live according to the flesh are concerned with the things of the flesh, but those who live according to the spirit with the things of the spirit. 6* The concern of the flesh is death, but the concern of the spirit is life and peace. 7* For the concern of the flesh is hostility toward God; it does not submit to the law of God, nor can it; 8* and those who are in the flesh cannot please God. 9* But you are not in the flesh; on the contrary, you are in the spirit, if only the Spirit of God dwells in you. Whoever does not have the Spirit of Christ does not belong to him. 10* But if Christ is in you, although the body is dead because of sin, the spirit is alive because of righteousness. 11 If the Spirit of the one who raised Jesus from the dead dwells in you, the one who raised Christ from the dead will give life to your mortal bodies also, through his Spirit that dwells in you. 12 Consequently, brothers, we are not debtors to the flesh, to live according to the flesh. 13* For if you live according to the flesh, you will die, but if by the spirit you put to death the deeds of the body, you will live.

***Children of God through Adoption.*†** 14* For those who are led by the Spirit of God are children of God. 15*† For you did not receive a spirit of slavery to fall back into fear, but you received a spirit of adoption, through which we cry, "*Abba*, Father!" 16* The Spirit itself bears witness with our spirit that we are children of God, 17* and if children, then heirs, heirs of God and joint heirs with Christ, if only we suffer with him so that we may also be glorified with him.

***Destiny of Glory.*†** 18* I consider that the sufferings of this present time are as nothing compared with the glory to be revealed for us. 19 For creation awaits with eager expectation the revelation of the children of God; 20* for creation was made subject to futility, not of its own accord but because of the one who subjected it, in hope 21* that creation itself would be set free from slavery to corruption and share in the glorious freedom of the children of God. 22* We know that all creation is groaning in labor pains even until now; 23* and not only that, but we ourselves, who have the firstfruits of the Spirit, we also groan within ourselves as we wait for adoption, the redemption of our bod-

*

23: Gal 5, 17; 1 Pt 2, 11.
25: 1 Cor 15, 57.
8, 2: 7, 23-24; 2 Cor 3, 17.
3: Acts 13, 38; 15, 10 / Jn 3, 16-17; 2 Cor 5, 21; Gal 3, 13; 4, 4; Phil 2, 7; Col 1, 22; Heb 2, 17; 4, 15; 1 Jn 4, 9.
4: Gal 5, 16-25.
6: 6, 21; 7, 5; 8, 13; Gal 6, 8.
7: 5, 10; Jas 4, 4.
8: 1 Jn 2, 16.
9: 1 Cor 3, 16.
10: Gal 2, 20; 1 Pt 4, 6.
13: Gal 5, 24; 6, 8; Eph 4, 22-24.
14: Gal 5, 18.
15: Mk 14, 36; Gal 4, 5-6; 2 Tm 1, 7.
16: Jn 1, 12; Gal 3, 26-29.
17: Gal 4, 7; 1 Pt 4, 13; 5, 1.
18: 2 Cor 4, 17.
20: Gn 3, 17-19.
21: 2 Pt 3, 12-13; Rv 21, 1.
22: 2 Cor 5, 2-5.
23: 2 Cor 1, 22; Gal 5, 5.

†

7, 23: As in 3, 27, Paul plays on the term *law,* which in Greek can connote custom, system, or *principle.*

8, 1-13: After his warning in ch 7 against the wrong route to fulfillment of the objective of holiness expressed in 6, 22, Paul points his addressees to the correct way. Through the redemptive work of Christ, Christians have been liberated from the terrible forces of sin and death. Holiness was impossible so long as the *flesh* (or our "old self"), that is, self-interested hostility toward God (7), frustrated the divine objectives expressed in the law. What is worse, sin used the law to break forth into all manner of lawlessness (8). All this is now changed. At the cross God broke the power of sin and pronounced sentence on it (3). Christians still retain the flesh, but it is alien to their new being, which is life in the spirit, namely the new self, governed by the holy Spirit. Under the direction of the holy Spirit Christians are able to fulfill the divine will that formerly found expression in the law (4). The same Spirit who enlivens Christians for holiness will also resurrect their bodies at the last day (11). Christian life is therefore the experience of a constant challenge to put to death the evil deeds of the body through life of the spirit (13).

8, 14-17: Christians, by reason of the Spirit's presence within them, enjoy not only new life but also a new relationship to God, that of adopted children and heirs through Christ, whose sufferings and glory they share.

8, 15: *Abba:* see the note on Mk 14, 36.

8, 18-27: The glory that believers are destined to share with Christ far exceeds the sufferings of the present life. Paul considers the destiny of the created world to be linked with the future that belongs to the believers. As it shares in the penalty of corruption brought about by sin, so also will it share in the benefits of redemption and future glory that comprise the ultimate liberation of God's people (19-22). After patient endurance in steadfast expectation, the full harvest of the Spirit's presence will be realized. On earth believers enjoy the firstfruits, i.e., the Spirit, as a guarantee of the total liberation of their bodies from the influence of the rebellious old self (23).

ies. 24* For in hope we were saved. Now
hope that sees for itself is not hope. For
who hopes for what one sees? 25 But if
we hope for what we do not see, we wait
with endurance.
26 In the same way, the Spirit too
comes to the aid of our weakness; for
we do not know how to pray as we ought,
but the Spirit itself intercedes with inex-
pressible groanings. 27* And the one
who searches hearts knows what is the
intention of the Spirit, because it inter-
cedes for the holy ones according to
God's will.

God's Indomitable Love in Christ.†
28*† We know that all things work for
good for those who love God, who are
called according to his purpose.
29*† For those he foreknew he also pre-
destined to be conformed to the image
of his Son, so that he might be the first-
born among many brothers. 30* And
those he predestined he also called;
and those he called he also justified; and
those he justified he also glorified.
31*† What then shall we say to this?
If God is for us, who can be against us?
32* He who did not spare his own Son but
handed him over for us all, how will he
not also give us everything else along
with him? 33* Who will bring a charge
against God's chosen ones? It is God
who acquits us. 34* Who will condemn?
It is Christ [Jesus] who died, rather, was
raised, who also is at the right hand of
God, who indeed intercedes for us.
35 What will separate us from the love
of Christ? Will anguish, or distress, or
persecution, or famine, or nakedness, or
peril, or the sword? 36* As it is written:

> "For your sake we are being slain
> all the day;
> we are looked upon as sheep to
> be slaughtered."

37* No, in all these things we conquer
overwhelmingly through him who loved
us. 38*† For I am convinced that neither
death, nor life, nor angels, nor princi-
palities, nor present things, nor future
things, nor powers, 39† nor height, nor
depth, nor any other creature will be
able to separate us from the love of God
in Christ Jesus our Lord.

V: JEWS AND GENTILES IN GOD'S PLAN†

CHAPTER 9

Paul's Love for Israel.† 1* I speak the
truth in Christ, I do not lie; my con-
science joins with the holy Spirit in
bearing me witness 2 that I have great
sorrow and constant anguish in my
heart. 3* For I could wish that I myself
were accursed and separated from
Christ for the sake of my brothers, my
kin according to the flesh. 4* They are
Israelites; theirs the adoption, the glory,
the covenants, the giving of the law, the
worship, and the promises; 5*† theirs

*

24: 2 Cor 5, 7; Heb 11, 1.
27: Ps 139, 1; 1 Cor 4, 5.
28-29: Eph 1, 4-14; 3, 11.
29: Eph 1, 5; 1 Pt 1, 2.
30: Is 45, 25; 2 Thes 2, 13-14.
31: Ps 118, 6; Heb 13, 6.
32: Jn 3, 16.
33-34: Is 50, 8.
34: Ps 110, 1; Heb 7, 25; 1 Jn 2, 1.
36: Ps 44, 23; 1 Cor 4, 9; 15, 30; 2 Cor 4, 11; 2 Tm 3, 12.
37: 1 Jn 5, 4.
38-39: 1 Cor 3, 22; Eph 1, 21; 1 Pt 3, 22.
9, 1: 2 Cor 11, 31; 1 Tm 2, 7.
3: Ex 32, 32.
4-5: 3, 2; Ex 4, 22; Dt 7, 6; 14, 1-2.
5: Mt 1, 1-16; Lk 3, 23-38 / 1, 25; Ps 41, 14.

†

8, 28-30: These verses outline the Christian vocation as it was designed by God: *to be conformed to the image of his Son,* who is to *be the firstborn among many brothers* (29). God's redemptive action on behalf of the believers has been in process before the beginning of the world. Those whom God chooses are *those he foreknew* (29) or elected. Those who are *called* (30) are *predestined* or predetermined. These expressions do not mean that God is arbitrary. Rather, Paul uses them to emphasize the thought and care that God has taken for the Christian's salvation.

8, 28: *We know that all things work for good for those who love God:* a few ancient authorities have God as the subject of the verb, and some translators render: "We know that God makes everything work for good for those who love God. . . ."

8, 29: *Image:* while man and woman were originally created in God's image (Gn 1, 26-27), it is through baptism into Christ, the image of God (2 Cor 4, 4; Col 1, 15), that we are renewed according to the image of the Creator (Col 3, 10).

8, 31-39: The all-conquering power of God's love has overcome every obstacle to Christians' salvation and every threat to separate them from God. That power manifested itself fully when God's own Son was delivered up to death for their salvation. Through him Christians can overcome all their afflictions and trials.

8, 38: *Present things* and *future things* may refer to astrological data. Paul appears to be saying that the gospel liberates believers from dependence on astrologers.

8, 39: *Height, depth* may refer to positions in the zodiac, positions of heavenly bodies relative to the horizon. In astrological documents the term for "height" means "exaltation" or the position of greatest influence exerted by a planet. Since hostile spirits were associated with the planets and stars, Paul includes *powers* (38) in his list of malevolent forces.

9, 1—11, 36: Israel's unbelief and its rejection of Jesus as savior astonished and puzzled Christians. It constituted a serious problem for them in view of God's specific preparation of Israel for the advent of the Messiah. Paul addresses himself here to the essential question of how the divine plan could be frustrated by Israel's unbelief. At the same time, he discourages both complacency and anxiety on the part of Gentiles. To those who might boast of their superior advantage over Jews, he warns that their enjoyment of the blessings assigned to Israel can be terminated. To those who might anxiously ask, "How can we be sure that Israel's fate will not be ours?" he replies that only unbelief can deprive one of salvation.

9, 1-5: The apostle speaks in strong terms of the depth of his grief over the unbelief of his own people. He would willingly undergo a curse himself for the sake of their coming to the knowledge of Christ (3; cf Lv 27, 28-29). His love for them derives from God's continuing choice of them and from the spiritual benefits that God bestows on them and through them on all of humanity (4-5).

9, 5: Some editors punctuate this verse differently and prefer the translation, "Of whom is Christ according to the flesh, who is God over all." However, Paul's point is that *God who is over all* aimed to use Israel, which had been entrusted with every privilege, in outreach to the entire world through the Messiah.

the patriarchs, and from them, according to the flesh, is the Messiah. God who is over all be blessed forever. Amen.

God's Free Choice. 6* But it is not that the word of God has failed. For not all who are of Israel are Israel, 7* nor are they all children of Abraham because they are his descendants; but "It is through Isaac that descendants shall bear your name." 8* This means that it is not the children of the flesh who are the children of God, but the children of the promise are counted as descendants. 9* For this is the wording of the promise, "About this time I shall return and Sarah will have a son." 10*† And not only that, but also when Rebecca had conceived children by one husband, our father Isaac— 11 before they had yet been born or had done anything, good or bad, in order that God's elective plan might continue, 12* not by works but by his call—she was told, "The older shall serve the younger." 13*† As it is written:

"I loved Jacob
but hated Esau."

14*† What then are we to say? Is there injustice on the part of God? Of course not! 15* For he says to Moses:

"I will show mercy to whom I will,
I will take pity on whom I will."

16* So it depends not upon a person's will or exertion, but upon God, who shows mercy. 17* For the scripture says to Pharaoh, "This is why I have raised you up, to show my power through you that my name may be proclaimed throughout the earth." 18*† Consequently, he has mercy upon whom he wills, and he hardens whom he wills.

19*† You will say to me then, "Why [then] does he still find fault? For who can oppose his will?" 20* But who indeed are you, a human being, to talk back to God? Will what is made say to its maker, "Why have you created me so?" 21 Or does not the potter have a right over the clay, to make out of the same lump one vessel for a noble purpose and another for an ignoble one? 22* What if God, wishing to show his wrath and make known his power, has endured with much patience the vessels of wrath made for destruction? 23 This was to make known the riches of his glory to the vessels of mercy, which he has prepared previously for glory, 24 namely, us whom he has called, not only from the Jews but also from the Gentiles.

Witness of the Prophets. 25*† As indeed he says in Hosea:

"Those who were not my people I will call 'my people,'
and her who was not beloved I will call 'beloved.'

26* And in the very place where it was said to them, 'You are not my people,'
there they shall be called children of the living God."

27* And Isaiah cries out concerning Israel, "Though the number of the Israelites were like the sand of the sea, only a remnant will be saved; 28 for decisively and quickly will the Lord execute sentence upon the earth." 29* And as Isaiah predicted:

"Unless the Lord of hosts had left us descendants,
we would have become like Sodom
and have been made like Gomorrah."

ROMANS

*

6: Nm 23, 19 / Mt 3, 9.
7: Gn 21, 12; Gal 3, 29.
8: Gal 4, 23.28.
9: Gn 18, 10.14.
10: Gn 25, 21.
12: 11, 5-6 / Gn 25, 23-24.
13: Mal 1, 3.
14: Dt 32, 4.
15: Ex 33, 19.
16: Eph 2, 8; Ti 3, 5.
17: Ex 9, 16.
18: 11, 30-32; Ex 4, 21; 7, 3.
19: 3, 7; Wis 12, 12.
20-21: Wis 15, 7; Is 29, 16; 45, 9; Jer 18, 6.
22: 2, 4; Wis 12, 20-21; Jer 50, 25.
25: Hos 2, 25.
26: Hos 2, 1.
27-28: Is 10, 22-23; Hos 2, 1 / 11, 5 / Is 28, 22.
29: Is 1, 9; Mt 10, 15.

†

9, 10: *Children by one husband, our father Isaac:* Abraham had two children, Ishmael and Isaac, by two wives, Hagar and Sarah, respectively. In that instance Isaac, although born later than Ishmael, became the bearer of the messianic promise. In the case of twins born to Rebecca, God's elective procedure is seen even more dramatically, and again the younger, contrary to Semitic custom, is given the preference.

9, 13: The literal rendering, *"Jacob I loved, but Esau I hated,"* suggests an attitude of divine hostility that is not implied in Paul's statement. In Semitic usage "hate" means to love less; cf Lk 14, 26 with Mt 10, 37. Israel's unbelief reflects the mystery of the divine election that is always operative within it. Mere natural descent from Abraham does not ensure the full possession of the divine gifts; it is God's sovereign prerogative to bestow this fullness upon, or to withhold it from, whomsoever he wishes; cf Mt 3, 9; Jn 8, 39. The choice of Jacob over Esau is a case in point.

9, 14-18: The principle of divine election does not invite Christians to theoretical inquiry concerning the nonelected, nor does this principle mean that God is unfair in his dealings with humanity. The instruction concerning divine election is a part of the gospel and reveals that the gift of faith is the enactment of God's mercy (16). God raised up Moses to display that mercy, and Pharaoh to display divine severity in punishing those who obstinately oppose their Creator.

9, 18: The basic biblical principle is: those who will not see or hear *shall* not see or hear. On the other hand, the same God who thus makes stubborn or hardens the heart can reconstruct it through the work of the holy Spirit.

9, 19-29: The apostle responds to the objection that if God rules over faith through the principle of divine election, God cannot then accuse unbelievers of sin (19). For Paul, this objection is in the last analysis a manifestation of human insolence, and his "answer" is less an explanation of God's ways than the rejection of an argument that places humanity on a level with God. At the same time, Paul shows that God is far less arbitrary than appearances suggest, for God endures *with much patience* (22) a person like the Pharaoh of the Exodus.

9, 25: *Beloved:* in Semitic discourse means "preferred" or "favorite" (cf 13). See Hos 2, 1, which is transposed after Hos 3, 5 in the NAB.

Righteousness Based on Faith.†

30* What then shall we say? That Gen-
tiles, who did not pursue righteousness,
have achieved it, that is, righteousness
that comes from faith; 31* but that Is-
rael, who pursued the law of righteous-
ness, did not attain to that law?
32*† Why not? Because they did it not
by faith, but as if it could be done by
works. They stumbled over the stone
that causes stumbling, 33* as it is writ-
ten:

> "Behold, I am laying a stone in Zion
> that will make people stumble
> and a rock that will make them fall,
> and whoever believes in him shall
> not be put to shame."

CHAPTER 10

1*† Brothers, my heart's desire and
prayer to God on their behalf is for sal-
vation. 2* I testify with regard to them
that they have zeal for God, but it is not
discerning. 3* For, in their unawareness
of the righteousness that comes from
God and their attempt to establish their
own [righteousness], they did not sub-
mit to the righteousness of God. 4*† For
Christ is the end of the law for the justi-
fication of everyone who has faith.

5*† Moses writes about the righteous-
ness that comes from [the] law, "The
one who does these things will live by
them." 6* But the righteousness that
comes from faith says, "Do not say in
your heart, 'Who will go up into
heaven?' (that is, to bring Christ down)
7*† or 'Who will go down into the abyss?'
(that is, to bring Christ up from the
dead)." 8* But what does it say?

> "The word is near you,
> in your mouth and in your heart"

(that is, the word of faith that we
preach), 9*† for, if you confess with
your mouth that Jesus is Lord and be-
lieve in your heart that God raised him
from the dead, you will be saved.
10 For one believes with the heart and
so is justified, and one confesses with
the mouth and so is saved. 11* For the
scripture says, "No one who believes in
him will be put to shame." 12* For there
is no distinction between Jew and
Greek; the same Lord is Lord of all, en-
riching all who call upon him. 13* For
"everyone who calls on the name of the
Lord will be saved."

14*† But how can they call on him in
whom they have not believed? And how
can they believe in him of whom they
have not heard? And how can they hear
without someone to preach? 15*† And
how can people preach unless they are
sent? As it is written, "How beautiful
are the feet of those who bring [the]
good news!" 16* But not everyone has
heeded the good news; for Isaiah says,
"Lord, who has believed what was
heard from us?" 17* Thus faith comes
from what is heard, and what is heard
comes through the word of Christ.
18* But I ask, did they not hear? Cer-
tainly they did; for

> "Their voice has gone forth to all
> the earth,

---

*

30: 10, 4.20.
31: 10, 3.
32: Is 8, 14.
33: Is 28, 16; 1 Pt 2, 6-8.
10, 1: 9, 1.3.
2: Acts 22, 3.
3: 9, 31-32; Phil 3, 9.
4: Acts 13, 38-39; 2 Cor 3, 14; Heb 8, 13.
5: Lv 18, 5; Gal 3, 12.
6: Dt 9, 4; 30, 12.
7: Dt 30, 13; 1 Pt 3, 19.
8: Dt 30, 14.
9: 1 Cor 12, 3.
11: 9, 33; Is 28, 16.
12: 1, 16; 3, 22.29; Acts 10, 34; 15, 9.11; Gal 3, 28; Eph 2, 14.
13: Jl 3, 5; Acts 2, 21.
14: Acts 8, 31.
15: Is 52, 7; Na 2, 1; Eph 6, 15.
16: Is 53, 1; Jn 12, 38.
17: Jn 17, 20.
18: Ps 19, 5; Mt 24, 14.

---

†

9, 30-33: In the conversion of the Gentiles and, by contrast, of relatively few Jews, the Old Testament prophecies are seen to be fulfilled; cf 25-29. Israel feared that the doctrine of justification through faith would jeopardize the validity of the Mosaic law, and so they never reached their goal of righteousness that they had sought to attain through meticulous observance of the law (31). Since Gentiles, including especially Greeks and Romans, had a great regard for righteousness, Paul's statement concerning Gentiles in v 30 is to be understood from a Jewish perspective: quite evidently they had not been interested in "God's" righteousness, for it had not been revealed to them; but now in response to the proclamation of the gospel they respond in faith.

9, 32: Paul discusses Israel as a whole from the perspective of contemporary Jewish rejection of Jesus as Messiah. The Old Testament and much of Jewish noncanonical literature in fact reflect a fervent faith in divine mercy.

10, 1-13: Despite Israel's lack of faith in God's act in Christ, Paul does not abandon hope for her salvation (1). However, Israel must recognize that the Messiah's arrival in the person of Jesus Christ means the termination of the Mosaic law as the criterion for understanding oneself in a valid relationship to God. Faith in God's saving action in Jesus Christ takes precedence over any such legal claim (6).

10, 4: The Mosaic legislation has been superseded by God's action in Jesus Christ. Others understand *end* here in the sense that Christ is the goal of the law, i.e., the true meaning of the Mosaic law, which cannot be correctly understood apart from him. Still others believe that both meanings are intended.

10, 5-6: The subject of the verb *says* (6) is *righteousness* personified. Both of the statements in vv 5 and 6 derive from Moses, but Paul wishes to contrast the language of law and the language of faith.

10, 7: Here Paul blends Dt 30, 13 and Ps 107, 26.

10, 9-11: To confess Jesus as Lord was frequently quite hazardous in the first century (cf Mt 10, 18; 1 Thes 2, 2; 1 Pt 2, 18-21; 3, 14). For a Jew it could mean disruption of normal familial and other social relationships, including great economic sacrifice. In the face of penalties imposed by the secular world, Christians are assured that *no one who believes in* Jesus *will be put to shame* (11).

10, 14-21: The gospel has been sufficiently proclaimed to Israel, and Israel has adequately understood God's plan for the messianic age, which would see the gospel brought to the uttermost parts of the earth. As often in the past, Israel has not accepted the prophetic message; cf Acts 7, 51-53.

10, 15: *How beautiful are the feet of those who bring [the] good news:* in Semitic fashion, the parts of the body that bring the messenger with welcome news are praised; cf Lk 11, 27.

and their words to the ends of the
world."
19* But I ask, did not Israel understand?
First Moses says:
"I will make you jealous of those
who are not a nation;
with a senseless nation I will make
you angry."
20* Then Isaiah speaks boldly and says:
"I was found [by] those who were
not seeking me;
I revealed myself to those who
were not asking for me."
21 But regarding Israel he says, "All day
long I stretched out my hands to a dis-
obedient and contentious people."

CHAPTER 11

The Remnant of Israel. † 1* I ask,
then, has God rejected his people? Of
course not! For I too am an Israelite, a
descendant of Abraham, of the tribe of
Benjamin. 2 God has not rejected his
people whom he foreknew. Do you not
know what the scripture says about Eli-
jah, how he pleads with God against Is-
rael? 3* "Lord, they have killed your
prophets, they have torn down your al-
tars, and I alone am left, and they are
seeking my life." 4* But what is God's
response to him? "I have left for myself
seven thousand men who have not knelt
to Baal." 5* So also at the present time
there is a remnant, chosen by grace.
6* But if by grace, it is no longer because
of works; otherwise grace would no
longer be grace. 7* What then? What Is-
rael was seeking it did not attain, but
the elect attained it; the rest were hard-
ened, 8* as it is written:
"God gave them a spirit of deep
sleep,
eyes that should not see
and ears that should not hear,
down to this very day."
9* And David says:
"Let their table become a snare and
a trap,
a stumbling block and a retribu-
tion for them;
10 let their eyes grow dim so that they
may not see,
and keep their backs bent for-
ever."

The Gentiles' Salvation. † 11* Hence I
ask, did they stumble so as to fall? Of
course not! But through their transgres-
sion salvation has come to the Gentiles,
so as to make them jealous. 12 Now if
their transgression is enrichment for
the world, and if their diminished num-
ber is enrichment for the Gentiles, how
much more their full number.
13* Now I am speaking to you Gen-
tiles. Inasmuch then as I am the apostle
to the Gentiles, I glory in my ministry
14 in order to make my race jealous and
thus save some of them. 15 For if their
rejection is the reconciliation of the
world, what will their acceptance be but
life from the dead? 16*† If the firstfruits
are holy, so is the whole batch of dough;
and if the root is holy, so are the
branches.
17* But if some of the branches were
broken off, and you, a wild olive shoot,
were grafted in their place and have
come to share in the rich root of the ol-
ive tree, 18* do not boast against the
branches. If you do boast, consider that
you do not support the root; the root
supports you. 19 Indeed you will say,
"Branches were broken off so that I
might be grafted in." 20* That is so.
They were broken off because of unbe-
lief, but you are there because of faith.
So do not become haughty, but stand
in awe. 21* For if God did not spare the
natural branches, [perhaps] he will not
spare you either. 22* See, then, the kind-
ness and severity of God: severity to-
ward those who fell, but God's kindness
to you, provided you remain in his kind-
ness; otherwise you too will be cut off.
23* And they also, if they do not remain

*

19: 11, 11.14; Dt 32, 21.
20-21: 9, 30; Is 65, 1-2.
11, 1: 2 Cor 11, 22; Phil 3, 5.
1-2: 1 Sm 12, 22; Ps 94, 14.
3: 1 Kgs 19, 10.14.
4: 1 Kgs 19, 18.
5: 9, 27.
6: 4, 4; Gal 3, 18.
7: 9, 31.
8: Dt 29, 3; Is 29, 10; Mt 13, 13-15; Acts 28, 26-27.
9-10: Pss 69, 23-24; 35, 8.
11: Acts 13, 46; 18, 6; 28, 28 / 10, 19; Dt 32, 21.
13: 1, 5.
16: Nm 15, 17-21; Ez 44, 30; Neh 10, 36-38.
17: Eph 2, 11-19.
18: 1 Cor 1, 31.
20: 12, 16.
21: 1 Cor 10, 12.
22: Jn 15, 2.4; Heb 3, 14.
23: 2 Cor 3, 16.

†

11, 1-10: Although Israel has been unfaithful to the prophetic message of the gospel (10, 14-21), God remains faithful to Israel. Proof of the divine fidelity lies in the existence of Jewish Christians like Paul himself. The unbelieving Jews, says Paul, have been blinded by the Christian teaching concerning the Messiah.

11, 11-15: The unbelief of the Jews has paved the way for the preaching of the gospel to the Gentiles and for their easier acceptance of it outside the context of Jewish culture. Through his mission to the Gentiles Paul also hopes to fill his fellow Jews with jealousy. Hence he hastens to fill the entire Mediterranean world with the gospel. Once all the Gentile nations have heard the gospel, Israel as a whole is expected to embrace it. This will be tantamount to resurrection of the dead, that is, the reappearance of Jesus Christ with all the believers at the end of time.

11, 16-24: Israel remains holy in the eyes of God and stands as a witness to the faith described in the Old Testament because of *the firstfruits* (or the first piece baked) (16), that is, the converted remnant, and *the root* that *is holy,* that is, the patriarchs (16). The Jews' failure to believe in Christ is a warning to Gentile Christians to be on guard against any semblance of anti-Jewish arrogance, that is, failure to recognize their total dependence on divine grace.

in unbelief, will be grafted in, for God is able to graft them in again. 24 For if you were cut from what is by nature a wild olive tree, and grafted, contrary to nature, into a cultivated one, how much more will they who belong to it by nature be grafted back into their own olive tree.

God's Irrevocable Call. † 25* I do not want you to be unaware of this mystery, brothers, so that you will not become wise [in] your own estimation: a hardening has come upon Israel in part, until the full number of the Gentiles comes in, 26* and thus all Israel will be saved, as it is written:

"The deliverer will come out of Zion,
he will turn away godlessness from Jacob;
27* and this is my covenant with them
when I take away their sins."

28* In respect to the gospel, they are enemies on your account; but in respect to election, they are beloved because of the patriarchs. 29* For the gifts and the call of God are irrevocable.

Triumph of God's Mercy. † 30 Just as you once disobeyed God but have now received mercy because of their disobedience, 31 so they have now disobeyed in order that, by virtue of the mercy shown to you, they too may [now] receive mercy. 32* For God delivered all to disobedience, that he might have mercy upon all.

33*† Oh, the depth of the riches and wisdom and knowledge of God! How inscrutable are his judgments and how unsearchable his ways!

34*† "For who has known the mind of the Lord
or who has been his counselor?"
35*† "Or who has given him anything
that he may be repaid?"

36* For from him and through him and for him are all things. To him be glory forever. Amen.

VI: THE DUTIES OF CHRISTIANS†

CHAPTER 12

Sacrifice of Body and Mind. † 1* I urge you therefore, brothers, by the mercies of God, to offer your bodies as a living sacrifice, holy and pleasing to God, your spiritual worship. 2* Do not conform yourself to this age but be transformed by the renewal of your mind, that you may discern what is the will of God, what is good and pleasing and perfect.

Many Parts in One Body. 3* For by the grace given to me I tell everyone among you not to think of himself more highly than one ought to think, but to think soberly, each according to the measure of faith that God has apportioned. 4* For as in one body we have many parts, and all the parts do not have the same function, 5† so we, though many, are one body in Christ and individually parts of one another.

---

*

25: Prv 3, 7 / 12, 16; Mk 13, 10; Lk 21, 24; Jn 10, 16.
26: Mt 23, 39.
26-27: Ps 14, 7; Is 59, 20-21.
27: Is 27, 9; Jer 31, 33-34.
28: 15, 8; 1 Thes 2, 15-16.
29: 9, 6; Nm 23, 19; Is 54, 10.
32: Gal 3, 22; 1 Tm 2, 4.
33: Jb 11, 7-8; Ps 139, 6.17-18; Wis 17, 1; Is 55, 8-9.
34: Jb 15, 8; Wis 9, 13; Is 40, 13; Jer 23, 18; 1 Cor 2, 11-16.
35: Jb 41, 3; Is 40, 14.
36: 1 Cor 8, 6; Col 1, 16-17.
12, 1: 2 Cor 1, 3 / 6, 13; 1 Pt 2, 5.
2: Eph 4, 17.22-23; 1 Pt 1, 14 / Eph 5, 10.17; Phil 1, 10.
3: 15, 15 / Phil 2, 3 / 1 Cor 12, 11; Eph 4, 7.
4-5: 1 Cor 12, 12.27; Eph 4, 25.

---

†

11, 25-29: In God's design, Israel's unbelief is being used to grant the light of faith to the Gentiles. Meanwhile, Israel remains dear to God (cf 9, 13), still the object of special providence, the mystery of which will one day be revealed.

11, 30-32: Israel, together with the Gentiles who have been handed over to all manner of vices (ch 1), has been *delivered . . . to disobedience.* The conclusion of v 32 repeats the thought of 5, 20, "Where sin increased, grace overflowed all the more."

11, 33-36: This final reflection celebrates the wisdom of God's plan of salvation. As Paul has indicated throughout these chapters, both Jew and Gentile, despite the religious recalcitrance of each, have received the gift of faith. The methods used by God in making this outreach to the world stagger human comprehension but are at the same time a dazzling invitation to abiding faith.

11, 34: The citation is from the Greek text of Is 40, 13. Paul does not explicitly mention Isaiah in this verse, nor Job in v 35.

11, 35: Paul quotes from an old Greek version of Jb 41, 3a, which differs from the Hebrew text (Jb 41, 11a).

12, 1—13, 14: Since Christ marks the termination of the Mosaic law as the primary source of guidance for God's people (10, 4), the apostle explains how Christians can function, in the light of the gift of justification through faith, in their relation to one another and the state.

12, 1-8: The Mosaic code included elaborate directions on sacrifices and other cultic observances. The gospel, however, invites believers to present their *bodies as a living sacrifice* (1). Instead of being limited by specific legal maxims, Christians are liberated for the exercise of good judgment as they are confronted with the many and varied decisions required in the course of daily life. To assist them, God distributes a variety of gifts to the fellowship of believers, including those of prophecy, teaching, and exhortation (6-8). Prophets assist the community to understand the will of God as it applies to the present situation (6). Teachers help people to understand themselves and their responsibilities in relation to others (7). One who *exhorts* offers encouragement to the community to exercise their faith in the performance of all that is pleasing to God (8). Indeed, this very section, beginning with v 1, is a specimen of Paul's own style of exhortation.

12, 5: *One body in Christ:* on the church as the body of Christ, see 1 Cor 12, 12-27.

6*† Since we have gifts that differ ac-
cording to the grace given to us, let us
exercise them: if prophecy, in propor-
tion to the faith; 7 if ministry, in minis-
tering; if one is a teacher, in teaching;
8† if one exhorts, in exhortation; if one
contributes, in generosity; if one is over
others, with diligence; if one does acts
of mercy, with cheerfulness.

Mutual Love. 9* Let love be sincere;
hate what is evil, hold on to what is
good; 10* love one another with mutual
affection; anticipate one another in
showing honor. 11* Do not grow slack in
zeal, be fervent in spirit, serve the Lord.
12* Rejoice in hope, endure in affliction,
persevere in prayer. 13* Contribute to
the needs of the holy ones, exercise hos-
pitality. 14*† Bless those who persecute
[you], bless and do not curse them.
15* Rejoice with those who rejoice, weep
with those who weep. 16* Have the same
regard for one another; do not be
haughty but associate with the lowly;
do not be wise in your own estimation.
17* Do not repay anyone evil for evil; be
concerned for what is noble in the sight
of all. 18* If possible, on your part, live
at peace with all. 19* Beloved, do not
look for revenge but leave room for the
wrath; for it is written, "Vengeance is
mine, I will repay, says the Lord."
20* Rather, "if your enemy is hungry,
feed him; if he is thirsty, give him some-
thing to drink; for by so doing you will
heap burning coals upon his head."
21 Do not be conquered by evil but con-
quer evil with good.

CHAPTER 13

Obedience to Authority.† 1* Let ev-
ery person be subordinate to the higher
authorities, for there is no authority ex-
cept from God, and those that exist
have been established by God.
2 Therefore, whoever resists authority
opposes what God has appointed, and
those who oppose it will bring judgment
upon themselves. 3* For rulers are not
a cause of fear to good conduct, but to
evil. Do you wish to have no fear of au-
thority? Then do what is good and you
will receive approval from it, 4* for it
is a servant of God for your good. But
if you do evil, be afraid, for it does not
bear the sword without purpose; it is the
servant of God to inflict wrath on the
evildoer. 5* Therefore, it is necessary to
be subject not only because of the wrath
but also because of conscience. 6 This
is why you also pay taxes, for the au-
thorities are ministers of God, devoting
themselves to this very thing. 7* Pay to
all their dues, taxes to whom taxes are
due, toll to whom toll is due, respect to
whom respect is due, honor to whom
honor is due.

Love Fulfills the Law.† 8* Owe noth-
ing to anyone, except to love one an-
other; for the one who loves another has
fulfilled the law. 9* The command-
ments, "You shall not commit adultery;

---

*

6-8: 1 Cor 12, 4-11.28-31; Eph 4, 7-12; 1 Pt 4, 10-11 / 2 Cor 9, 7.
9: 2 Cor 6, 6; 1 Tm 1, 5; 1 Pt 1, 22 / Am 5, 15.
10: Jn 13, 34; 1 Thes 4, 9; 1 Pt 2, 17; 2 Pt 1, 7 / Phil 2, 3.
11: Acts 18, 25.
12: 5, 2-3; Col 4, 2; 1 Thes 5, 17.
13: Heb 13, 2; 1 Pt 4, 9.
14-21: Mt 5, 38-48; 1 Cor 4, 12; 1 Pt 3, 9.
14: Lk 6, 27-28.
15: Ps 35, 13; Sir 7, 34; 1 Cor 12, 26.
16: 15, 5; Phil 2, 2-3 / 11, 20; Prv 3, 7; Is 5, 21.
17: Prv 3, 4; 1 Thes 5, 15; 1 Pt 3, 9.
18: Heb 12, 14.
19: Lv 19, 18; Dt 32, 35.41; Mt 5, 39; 1 Cor 6, 6-7; Heb 10, 30.
20: Prv 25, 21-22; Mt 5, 44.
13, 1: Prv 8, 15-16; Wis 6, 3; Jn 19, 11; 1 Pt 2, 13-17; Ti 3, 1.
3: 1 Pt 2, 13-14; 3, 13.
4: 12, 19.
5: 1 Pt 2, 19.
7: Mt 22, 21; Mk 12, 17; Lk 20, 25.
8: Jn 13, 34; Gal 5, 14.
9: Ex 20, 13-17 / Lv 19, 18; Dt 5, 17-21; Mt 5, 43-44; 19, 18-19; 22, 39; Mk 12, 31; Lk 10, 27; Gal 5, 14; Jas 2, 8.

---

†

12, 6: Everyone has some gift that can be used for the benefit of the community. When the instruction on justification through faith is correctly grasped, the possesser of a gift will understand that it is not an instrument of self-aggrandizement. Possession of a gift is not an index to quality of faith. Rather, the gift is a challenge to faithful use.

12, 8: *Over others:* usually taken to mean "rule over" but possibly "serve as a patron." Wealthier members in Greco-Roman communities were frequently asked to assist in public service projects. In view of the references to contributing *in generosity* and to *acts of mercy,* Paul may have in mind people like Phoebe (16, 1-2), who is called a *benefactor* (or "patron") because of the services she rendered to many Christians, including Paul.

12, 14-21: Since God has justified the believers, it is not necessary for them to take justice into their own hands by taking vengeance. God will ultimately deal justly with all, including those who inflict injury on the believers. This question of personal rights as a matter of justice prepares the way for more detailed consideration of the state as adjudicator.

13, 1-7: Paul must come to grips with the problem raised by a message that declares people free from the law. How are they to relate to Roman authority? The problem was exacerbated by the fact that imperial protocol was interwoven with devotion to various deities. Paul builds on the traditional instruction exhibited in Wis 6, 1-3, according to which kings and magistrates rule by consent of God. From this perspective, then, believers who render obedience to the governing authorities are obeying the one who is highest in command. At the same time, it is recognized that Caesar has the responsibility to make just ordinances and to commend uprightness; cf Wis 6, 4-21. That Caesar is not entitled to obedience when such obedience would nullify God's prior claim to the believers' moral decision becomes clear in the light of the following verses.

13, 8-10: When love directs the Christian's moral decisions, the interest of law in basic concerns, such as familial relationships, sanctity of life, and security of property, is safeguarded (9). Indeed, says Paul, the same applies to any *other commandment* (9), whether one in the Mosaic code or one drawn up by local magistrates under imperial authority. Love anticipates the purpose of public legislation, namely, to secure the best interests of the citizenry. Since Caesar's obligation is to punish the wrongdoer (4), the Christian who acts in love is free from all legitimate indictment.

you shall not kill; you shall not steal;
you shall not covet," and whatever
other commandment there may be, are
summed up in this saying, [namely]
"You shall love your neighbor as your-
self." [10]* Love does no evil to the neigh-
bor; hence, love is the fulfillment of the
law.

Awareness of the End of Time.†
[11]* And do this because you know the
time; it is the hour now for you to awake
from sleep. For our salvation is nearer
now than when we first believed;
[12]* the night is advanced, the day is at
hand. Let us then throw off the works
of darkness [and] put on the armor of
light; [13]*† let us conduct ourselves prop-
erly as in the day, not in orgies and
drunkenness, not in promiscuity and li-
centiousness, not in rivalry and jeal-
ousy. [14]* But put on the Lord Jesus
Christ, and make no provision for the
desires of the flesh.

CHAPTER 14

To Live and Die for Christ.† [1]* Wel-
come anyone who is weak in faith,
but not for disputes over opinions.
[2]* One person believes that one may eat
anything, while the weak person eats
only vegetables. [3]* The one who eats
must not despise the one who abstains,
and the one who abstains must not pass
judgment on the one who eats; for God
has welcomed him. [4]* Who are you to
pass judgment on someone else's ser-
vant? Before his own master he stands
or falls. And he will be upheld, for the
Lord is able to make him stand.
[5]*† [For] one person considers one day
more important than another, while an-
other person considers all days alike.
Let everyone be fully persuaded in his
own mind. [6] Whoever observes the day,
observes it for the Lord. Also whoever
eats, eats for the Lord, since he gives
thanks to God; while whoever abstains,
abstains for the Lord and gives thanks
to God. [7] None of us lives for oneself,
and no one dies for oneself. [8]*† For if
we live, we live for the Lord, and if we
die, we die for the Lord; so then,
whether we live or die, we are the
Lord's. [9]* For this is why Christ died
and came to life, that he might be Lord
of both the dead and the living. [10]* Why
then do you judge your brother? Or you,
why do you look down on your brother?
For we shall all stand before the
judgment seat of God; [11]* for it is writ-
ten:

> "As I live, says the Lord, every knee
> shall bend before me,
> and every tongue shall give praise
> to God."

[12]* So [then] each of us shall give an
account of himself [to God].

***Consideration for the Weak Con-
science.*** [13]* Then let us no longer
judge one another, but rather resolve
never to put a stumbling block or hin-
drance in the way of a brother. [14]* I
know and am convinced in the Lord Je-
sus that nothing is unclean in itself; still,
it is unclean for someone who thinks it
unclean. [15]* If your brother is being hurt
by what you eat, your conduct is no
longer in accord with love. Do not be-
cause of your food destroy him for
whom Christ died. [16]* So do not let your
good be reviled. [17]* For the kingdom of
God is not a matter of food and drink,
but of righteousness, peace, and joy in
the holy Spirit; [18] whoever serves Christ
in this way is pleasing to God and ap-
proved by others. [19]*† Let us then pur-
sue what leads to peace and to building
up one another. [20]* For the sake of food,

*

10: Mt 22, 40; 1 Cor 13, 4-7.
11: Eph 5, 8-16; 1 Thes 5, 5-7.
12: Jn 8, 12; 1 Thes 5, 4-8; 1 Jn 2, 8 / 2 Cor 6, 7; 10, 4; Eph 5, 11; 6, 13-17.
13: Lk 21, 34; Eph 5, 18.
14: Gal 3, 27; 5, 16; Eph 4, 24; 6, 11.
14, 1-23: 1 Cor 8, 1-13.
1: 15, 1.7; 1 Cor 9, 22.
2: Gn 1, 29; 9, 3; 1 Cor 8, 1-13; 10, 14-33.
3: Col 2, 16.
4: 2, 1; Mt 7, 11; Jas 4, 11-12.
5: Gal 4, 10.
8: Lk 20, 38; 2 Cor 5, 15; Gal 2, 20; 1 Thes 5, 10.
9: Acts 10, 42.
10: Acts 17, 31; 2 Cor 5, 10.
11: Is 49, 18 / Is 45, 23; Phil 2, 10-11.
12: Gal 6, 5.
13: 1 Cor 8, 9.13.
14: Mk 7, 5.20; Acts 10, 15; 1 Cor 10, 25-27; 1 Tm 4, 4.
15: 1 Cor 8, 11-13.
16: 2, 24; Ti 2, 5.
17: 1 Cor 8, 8.
19: 12, 18 / 15, 2.
20-21: 1 Cor 8, 11-13; 10, 28-29; Ti 1, 15.

†

13, 11-14: These verses provide the motivation for the love that is encouraged in vv 8-10.

13, 13: *Let us conduct ourselves properly as in the day:* the behavior described in 1, 29-30 is now to be reversed. Secular moralists were fond of making references to people who could not wait for nightfall to do their carousing. Paul says that Christians claim to be people of the new day that will dawn with the return of Christ. Instead of planning for nighttime behavior they should be concentrating on conduct that is consonant with avowed interest in the Lord's return.

14, 1—15, 6: Since Christ spells termination of the law, which included observance of specific days and festivals as well as dietary instruction, the jettisoning of long-practiced customs was traumatic for many Christians brought up under the Mosaic code. Although Paul acknowledges that in principle no food is a source of moral contamination (14), he recommends that the consciences of Christians who are scrupulous in this regard be respected by other Christians (21). On the other hand, those who have scruples are not to sit in judgment on those who know that the gospel has liberated them from such ordinances (10). See 1 Cor 8 and 10.

14, 5: Since the problem to be overcome was humanity's perverted mind or judgment (1, 28), Paul indicates that the *mind* of the Christian is now able to function with appropriate discrimination (cf 12, 2).

14, 8: *The Lord:* Jesus, our Master. The same Greek word, *kyrios,* was applied to both rulers and holders of slaves. Throughout the Letter to the Romans Paul emphasizes God's total claim on the believer; see the note on 1, 1.

14, 19: Some manuscripts, versions, and church Fathers read, "We then pursue . . ."; cf 5, 1.

do not destroy the work of God. Every-
thing is indeed clean, but it is wrong for
anyone to become a stumbling block by
eating; 21 it is good not to eat meat or
drink wine or do anything that causes
your brother to stumble. 22 Keep the
faith [that] you have to yourself in the
presence of God; blessed is the one who
does not condemn himself for what he
approves. 23*† But whoever has doubts
is condemned if he eats, because this
is not from faith; for whatever is not
from faith is sin.

CHAPTER 15

Patience and Self-Denial. 1* We who
are strong ought to put up with the fail-
ings of the weak and not to please our-
selves; 2* let each of us please our
neighbor for the good, for building up.
3*† For Christ did not please himself;
but, as it is written, "The insults of those
who insult you fall upon me." 4* For
whatever was written previously was
written for our instruction, that by en-
durance and by the encouragement of
the scriptures we might have hope.
5*† May the God of endurance and en-
couragement grant you to think in har-
mony with one another, in keeping with
Christ Jesus, 6 that with one accord you
may with one voice glorify the God and
Father of our Lord Jesus Christ.
God's Fidelity and Mercy. † 7* Wel-
come one another, then, as Christ wel-
comed you, for the glory of God. 8* For
I say that Christ became a minister of
the circumcised to show God's truthful-
ness, to confirm the promises to the pa-
triarchs, 9* but so that the Gentiles
might glorify God for his mercy. As it
is written:

"Therefore, I will praise you among
the Gentiles
and sing praises to your name."

10*† And again it says:

"Rejoice, O Gentiles, with his peo-
ple."

11* And again:

"Praise the Lord, all you Gentiles,
and let all the peoples praise
him."

12* And again Isaiah says:

"The root of Jesse shall come,
raised up to rule the Gentiles;
in him shall the Gentiles hope."

13* May the God of hope fill you with all
joy and peace in believing, so that you
may abound in hope by the power of
the holy Spirit.

VII: CONCLUSION

Apostle to the Gentiles. † 14† I myself
am convinced about you, my brothers,
that you yourselves are full of goodness,
filled with all knowledge, and able to
admonish one another. 15* But I have
written to you rather boldly in some re-
spects to remind you, because of the
grace given me by God 16* to be a minis-
ter of Christ Jesus to the Gentiles in per-
forming the priestly service of the
gospel of God, so that the offering up
of the Gentiles may be acceptable,
sanctified by the holy Spirit. 17 In Christ
Jesus, then, I have reason to boast in
what pertains to God. 18* For I will not
dare to speak of anything except what
Christ has accomplished through me to
lead the Gentiles to obedience by word
and deed, 19† by the power of signs and
wonders, by the power of the Spirit [of
God], so that from Jerusalem all the
way around to Illyricum I have finished
preaching the gospel of Christ.
20*† Thus I aspire to proclaim the gospel

ROMANS

*

14, 23: Ti 1, 15; Jas 4, 17.
15, 1: 14, 1-2.
2: 14, 1.19; 1 Cor 9, 19; 10, 24.33.
3: Ps 69, 10.
4: 4, 23-24; 1 Mc 12, 9; 1 Cor 10, 11; 2 Tm 3, 16.
5: 12, 16; Phil 2, 2; 4, 2.
7: 14, 1.
8: Mt 15, 24 / Mi 7, 20; Acts 3, 25.
9: 11, 30 / 2 Sm 22, 50; Ps 18, 50.
10: Dt 32, 43.
11: Ps 117, 1.
12: Is 11, 10; Rv 5, 5; 22, 16.
13: 5, 1-2.
15: 1, 5; 12, 3.
16: 11, 13; Phil 2, 17.
18: Acts 15, 12; 2 Cor 12, 12.
20: 2 Cor 10, 13-18.

†

14, 23: *Whatever is not from faith is sin:* Paul does not mean that all the actions of unbelievers are sinful. He addresses himself to the question of intracommunity living. *Sin* in the singular is the dreadful power described in 5, 12-14.

15, 3: Liberation from the law of Moses does not make the scriptures of the old covenant irrelevant. Much consolation and motivation for Christian living can be derived from the Old Testament, as in the citation from Ps 69, 10. Because this psalm is quoted several times in the New Testament, it has been called indirectly messianic.

15, 5: *Think in harmony:* a Greco-Roman ideal. Not rigid uniformity of thought and expression but thoughtful consideration of other people's views finds expression here.

15, 7-13: True oneness of mind is found in pondering the ultimate mission of the church: to bring it about that God's name be glorified throughout the world and that Jesus Christ be universally recognized as God's gift to all humanity. Paul here prepares his addressees for the climactic appeal he is about to make.

15, 10: Paul's citation of Dt 32, 43 follows the Greek version.

15, 14-33: Paul sees himself as apostle and benefactor in the priestly service of the gospel and so sketches plans for a mission in Spain, supported by those in Rome.

15, 14: *Full of goodness:* the opposite of what humanity was filled with according to 1, 29-30.

15, 19: *Illyricum:* Roman province northwest of Greece on the eastern shore of the Adriatic.

15, 20: *I aspire:* Paul uses terminology customarily applied to philanthropists. Unlike some philanthropists of his time, Paul does not engage in cheap competition for public acclaim. This explanation of his missionary policy is to assure the Christians in Rome that he is also not planning to remain in that city and build on other people's foundations (cf 2 Cor 10, 12-18). However, he does solicit their help in sending him on his way to Spain, which was considered the limit of the western world. Thus Paul's addressees realize that evangelization may be understood in the broader sense of mission or, as in Rom 1, 15, of instruction within the Christian community that derives from the gospel.

not where Christ has already been
named, so that I do not build on anoth-
er's foundation, 21*† but as it is written:

> "Those who have never been told
> of him shall see,
> and those who have never heard
> of him shall understand."

Paul's Plans; Need for Prayers.
22 That is why I have so often been pre-
vented from coming to you. 23* But now,
since I no longer have any opportunity
in these regions and since I have de-
sired to come to you for many years,
24* I hope to see you in passing as I go
to Spain and to be sent on my way there
by you, after I have enjoyed being with
you for a time. 25*† Now, however, I
am going to Jerusalem to minister to
the holy ones. 26† For Macedonia and
Achaia have decided to make some
contribution for the poor among the
holy ones in Jerusalem; 27* they decided
to do it, and in fact they are indebted
to them, for if the Gentiles have come
to share in their spiritual blessings, they
ought also to serve them in material
blessings. 28 So when I have completed
this and safely handed over this contri-
bution to them, I shall set out by way
of you to Spain; 29 and I know that in
coming to you I shall come in the full-
ness of Christ's blessing.
30* I urge you, [brothers,] by our Lord
Jesus Christ and by the love of the
Spirit, to join me in the struggle by your
prayers to God on my behalf, 31 that I
may be delivered from the disobedient
in Judea, and that my ministry for Jeru-
salem may be acceptable to the holy
ones, 32 so that I may come to you with
joy by the will of God and be refreshed
together with you. 33* The God of peace
be with all of you. Amen.

CHAPTER 16

Phoebe Commended. † 1*† I com-
mend to you Phoebe our sister, who is
[also] a minister of the church at Cen-
chreae, 2 that you may receive her in
the Lord in a manner worthy of the holy
ones, and help her in whatever she may
need from you, for she has been a bene-
factor to many and to me as well.
Paul's Greetings. 3*† Greet Prisca
and Aquila, my co-workers in Christ Je-
sus, 4 who risked their necks for my life,
to whom not only I am grateful but also
all the churches of the Gentiles;
5*† greet also the church at their house.
Greet my beloved Epaenetus, who was
the firstfruits in Asia for Christ. 6 Greet
Mary, who has worked hard for you.
7† Greet Andronicus and Junia, my rel-
atives and my fellow prisoners; they are
prominent among the apostles and they
were in Christ before me. 8 Greet Am-
pliatus, my beloved in the Lord. 9 Greet
Urbanus, our co-worker in Christ, and
my beloved Stachys. 10 Greet Apelles,
who is approved in Christ. Greet those
who belong to the family of Aristobulus.
11 Greet my relative Herodion. Greet
those in the Lord who belong to the fam-
ily of Narcissus. 12 Greet those workers
in the Lord, Tryphaena and Tryphosa.
Greet the beloved Persis, who has
worked hard in the Lord. 13*† Greet Ru-
fus, chosen in the Lord, and his mother
and mine. 14 Greet Asyncritus, Phlegon,
Hermes, Patrobas, Hermas, and the
brothers who are with them. 15 Greet
Philologus, Julia, Nereus and his sister,
and Olympas, and all the holy ones who
are with them. 16* Greet one another
with a holy kiss. All the churches of
Christ greet you.

---

*

21: Is 52, 15.
23: 1, 10-13; Acts 19, 21-22.
24: 1 Cor 16, 6.
25: Acts 19, 21; 20, 22.
26: 1 Cor 16, 1; 2 Cor 8, 1-4; 9, 2.12.
27: 9, 4 / 1 Cor 9, 11.
30: 2 Cor 1, 11; Phil 1, 27; Col 4, 3; 2 Thes 3, 1.
33: 16, 20; 2 Cor 13, 11; Phil 4, 9; 1 Thes 5, 23; 2 Thes 3, 16; Heb 13, 20.
16, 1: Acts 18, 18.
3: Acts 18, 2.18-26; 1 Cor 16, 19; 2 Tm 4, 19.
5: 1 Cor 16, 19; Col 4, 15; Phlm 2 / 1 Cor 16, 15.
13: Mk 15, 21.
16: 1 Cor 16, 20; 2 Cor 13, 12; 1 Thes 5, 26; 1 Pt 5, 14.

†

15, 21: The citation from Is 52, 15 concerns the Servant of the Lord. According to Isaiah, the Servant is first of all Israel, which was to bring the knowledge of Yahweh to the nations. In chs 9-11 Paul showed how Israel failed in this mission. Therefore, he himself undertakes almost singlehandedly Israel's responsibility as the Servant and moves as quickly as possible with the gospel through the Roman empire.

15, 25-27: Paul may have viewed the contribution he was gathering from Gentile Christians for the poor in Jerusalem (cf 2 Cor 8 and 9) as a fulfillment of the vision of Is 60, 5-6. In confidence that the messianic fulfillment was taking place, Paul stresses in chs 14-16 the importance of harmonious relationships between Jews and Gentiles.

15, 26: *Achaia:* the Roman province of southern Greece.

16, 1-23: Some authorities regard these verses as a later addition to the letter, but in general the evidence favors the view that they were included in the original. Paul endeavors through the long list of greetings (3-16; 21-23) to establish strong personal contact with congregations that he has not personally encountered before. The combination of Jewish and Gentile names dramatically attests the unity in the gospel that transcends previous barriers of nationality, religious ceremony, or racial status.

16, 1: *Minister:* in Greek, *diakonos;* see the note on Phil 1, 1.

16, 3: *Prisca and Aquila:* presumably the couple mentioned at Acts 18, 2; 1 Cor 16, 19; 2 Tm 4, 19.

16, 5: *The church at their house:* i.e., that meets there. Such local assemblies (cf 1 Cor 16, 19; Col 4, 15; Phlm 2) might consist of only one or two dozen Christians each. It is understandable, therefore, that such smaller groups might experience difficulty in relating to one another on certain issues. *Firstfruits:* cf 8, 23; 11, 16; 1 Cor 16, 15.

16, 7: The name Junia is a woman's name. One ancient Greek manuscript and a number of ancient versions read the name "Julia." Most editors have interpreted it as a man's name, Junias.

16, 13: This Rufus cannot be identified to any degree of certainty with the Rufus of Mk 15, 21.

***Against Factions.*†** [17]* I urge you,
brothers, to watch out for those who
create dissensions and obstacles, in op-
position to the teaching that you
learned; avoid them. [18]* For such peo-
ple do not serve our Lord Christ but
their own appetites, and by fair and
flattering speech they deceive the
hearts of the innocent. [19]* For while
your obedience is known to all, so that
I rejoice over you, I want you to be wise
as to what is good, and simple as to what
is evil; [20]*† then the God of peace
will quickly crush Satan under your
feet. The grace of our Lord Jesus be with
you.

Greetings from Corinth. [21]* Timothy,
my co-worker, greets you; so do Lucius
and Jason and Sosipater, my relatives.
[22] I, Tertius, the writer of this letter,
greet you in the Lord. [23]*† Gaius, who
is host to me and to the whole church,
greets you. Erastus, the city treasurer,
and our brother Quartus greet you.
[24]†

***Doxology.*†** [[25]*† Now to him who can
strengthen you, according to my gospel
and the proclamation of Jesus Christ,
according to the revelation of the my-
stery kept secret for long ages [26]* but
now manifested through the prophetic
writings and, according to the com-
mand of the eternal God, made known
to all nations to bring about the obedi-
ence of faith, [27]* to the only wise God,
through Jesus Christ be glory forever
and ever. Amen.]

*

17: Mt 7, 15; Ti 3, 10.
18: Phil 3, 18-19 / Col 2, 4; 2 Pt 2, 3.
19: 1, 8; Mt 10, 16; 1 Cor 14, 20.
20: 15, 33; Gn 3, 15; Lk 10, 19 / 1 Cor 16, 23; 1 Thes 5, 28; 2 Thes 3, 18.
21: Acts 16, 1-2; 19, 22; 20, 4; 1 Cor 4, 17; 16, 10; Phil 2, 19-22; Heb 13, 23.
23: Acts 19, 29; 1 Cor 1, 14 / 2 Tm 4, 20.
25: 1 Cor 2, 7; Eph 1, 9; 3, 3-9; Col 1, 26.
26: 2 Tm 1, 10 / 1, 5; Eph 3, 4-5.9; 1 Pt 1, 20.
27: 11, 36; Gal 1, 5; Eph 3, 20-21; Phil 4, 20; 1 Tm 1, 17; 2 Tm 4, 18; Heb 13, 21; 1 Pt 4, 11; 2 Pt 3, 18; Jude 25, Rv 1, 6.

†

16, 17-18: Paul displays genuine concern for the congregations in Rome by warning them against self-seeking teachers. It would be a great loss, he intimates, if their obedience, which is known to all (cf 1, 8), would be diluted.

16, 20: This verse contains the only mention of Satan in Romans.

16, 23: This Erastus is not necessarily to be identified with the Erastus of Acts 19, 22 or of 2 Tm 4, 20.

16, 24: Some manuscripts add, similarly to v 20, "The grace of our Lord Jesus Christ be with you all. Amen."

16, 25-27: This doxology is assigned variously to the end of chs 14, 15, and 16 in the manuscript tradition. Some manuscripts omit it entirely. Whether written by Paul or not, it forms an admirable conclusion to the letter at this point.

16, 25: Paul's gospel reveals *the mystery kept secret for long ages:* justification and salvation through faith, with all the implications for Jews and Gentiles that Paul has developed in the letter.

The First Letter to the

CORINTHIANS

Paul's first letter to the church of Corinth provides us with a fuller insight into the life of an early Christian community of the first generation than any other book of the New Testament. Through it we can glimpse both the strengths and the weaknesses of this small group in a great city of the ancient world, men and women who had accepted the good news of Christ and were now trying to realize in their lives the implications of their baptism. Paul, who had founded the community and continued to look after it as a father, responds both to questions addressed to him and to situations of which he had been informed. In doing so, he reveals much about himself, his teaching, and the way in which he conducted his work of apostleship. Some things are puzzling because we have the correspondence only in one direction. For the person studying this letter, it seems to raise as many questions as it answers, but without it our knowledge of church life in the middle of the first century would be much poorer.

Paul established a Christian community in Corinth about the year 51, on his second missionary journey. The city, a commercial crossroads, was a melting pot full of devotees of various pagan cults and marked by a measure of moral depravity not unusual in a great seaport. The Acts of the Apostles suggests that moderate success attended Paul's efforts among the Jews in Corinth at first, but that they soon turned against him (Acts 18, 1-8). More fruitful was his year and a half spent among the Gentiles (Acts 18, 11), which won to the faith many of the city's poor and underprivileged (1, 26). After his departure the eloquent Apollos, an Alexandrian Jewish Christian, rendered great service to the community, expounding "from the scriptures that the Messiah is Jesus" (Acts 18, 24-28).

While Paul was in Ephesus on his third journey (16, 8; Acts 19, 1-20), he received disquieting news about Corinth. The community there was displaying open factionalism, as certain members were identifying themselves exclusively with individual Christian leaders and interpreting Christian teaching as a superior wisdom for the initiated few (1, 10—4, 21). The community lacked the decisiveness to take appropriate action against one of its members who was living publicly in an incestuous union (5, 1-13). Other members engaged in legal conflicts in pagan courts of law (6, 1-11); still others may have participated in religious prostitution (6, 12-20) or temple sacrifices (10, 14-22).

The community's ills were reflected in its liturgy. In the celebration of the Eucharist certain members discriminated against others, drank too freely at the agape, or fellowship meal, and denied Christian social courtesies to the poor among the membership (11, 17-22). Charisms such as ecstatic prayer, attributed freely to the impulse of the holy Spirit, were more highly prized than works of charity (13, 1-2.8), and were used at times in a disorderly way (14, 1-40). Women appeared at the assembly without the customary head-covering (11, 3-16), and perhaps were quarreling over their right to address the assembly (14, 34-35).

Still other problems with which Paul had to deal concerned matters of conscience discussed among the faithful members of the community: the eating of meat that had been sacrificed to idols (8, 1-13), the use of sex in marriage (7, 1-7), and the attitude to be taken by the unmarried toward marriage in view of the possible proximity of Christ's second coming (7, 25-40). There was also a doctrinal matter that called for Paul's attention, for some members of the community, despite their belief in the resurrection of Christ, were denying the possibility of general bodily resurrection.

To treat this wide spectrum of questions, Paul wrote this letter from Ephesus about the year 56. The majority of the Corinthian Christians may well have been quite faithful. Paul writes on their behalf to guard against the threats posed to the community by the views and conduct of various minorities. He writes with confidence in the authority of his apostolic mission, and he presumes that the Corinthians, despite their deficiencies, will recognize and accept it. On the other hand, he does not hesitate to exercise his authority as his judgment dictates in each situation, even going so far as to promise a direct confrontation with recalcitrants, should the abuses he scores remain uncorrected (4, 18-21).

The letter illustrates well the mind and character of Paul. Although he is impelled to insist on his office as founder of the community, he recognizes that he is only one servant of God among many and generously acknowledges the labors of Apollos (3, 5-8). He provides us in this letter with many valuable examples of his method of theological reflection and exposition. He always treats the questions at issue on the level of the purity of Christian teaching and conduct. Certain passages of the letter are of the greatest importance for the understanding of early Christian teaching on the Eucharist (10, 14-22; 11, 17-34) and on the resurrection of the body (15, 1-58).

Paul's authorship of 1 Corinthians, apart from a few verses that some regard as later interpolations, has never been seriously questioned. Some scholars have proposed, however, that the letter as we have it contains portions of more than one original Pauline letter. We know that Paul wrote at least two other letters to Corinth (see 5, 9; 2 Cor 2, 3-4) in addition to the two that we now have; this theory holds that the additional letters are actually contained within the two canonical ones. Most commentators, however, find 1 Corinthians quite understandable as a single coherent work.

The principal divisions of the First Letter to the Corinthians are the following:

I: Address (1, 1-9)
II: Disorders in the Corinthian Community (1, 10—6, 20)
  A. Divisions in the Church (1, 10—4, 21)
  B. Moral Disorders (5, 1—6, 20)
III: Answers to the Corinthians' Questions (7, 1—11, 1)
  A. Marriage and Virginity (7, 1-40)
  B. Offerings to Idols (8, 1—11, 1)
IV: Problems in Liturgical Assemblies (11, 2—14, 40)
  A. Women's Headdresses (11, 3-16)
  B. The Lord's Supper (11, 17-34)
  C. Spiritual Gifts (12, 1—14, 40)
V: The Resurrection (15, 1-58)
  A. The Resurrection of Christ (15, 1-11)
  B. The Resurrection of the Dead (15, 12-34)
  C. The Manner of the Resurrection (15, 35-58)
VI: Conclusion (16, 1-24)

1 CORINTHIANS

I: ADDRESS†

CHAPTER 1

Greeting. [1]*† Paul, called to be an apostle of Christ Jesus by the will of God, and Sosthenes our brother, [2]* to the church of God that is in Corinth, to you who have been sanctified in Christ Jesus, called to be holy, with all those everywhere who call upon the name of our Lord Jesus Christ, their Lord and ours. [3] Grace to you and peace from God our Father and the Lord Jesus Christ.

Thanksgiving. [4] I give thanks to my

* 1, 1: Rom 1, 1. 2: Acts 18, 1-11.

† 1, 1-9: Paul follows the conventional form for the opening of a Hellenistic letter (cf Rom 1, 1-7), but expands the opening with details carefully chosen to remind the readers of their situation and to suggest some of the issues the letter will discuss.

1, 1: *Called . . . by the will of God:* Paul's mission and the church's existence are grounded in God's initiative. God's call, grace, and fidelity are central ideas in this introduction, emphasized by repetition and wordplays in the Greek.

God always on your account for the grace of God bestowed on you in Christ Jesus, 5 that in him you were enriched in every way, with all discourse and all knowledge, 6† as the testimony to Christ was confirmed among you, 7* so that you are not lacking in any spiritual gift as you wait for the revelation of our Lord Jesus Christ. 8* He will keep you firm to the end, irreproachable on the day of our Lord Jesus [Christ]. 9* God is faithful, and by him you were called to fellowship with his Son, Jesus Christ our Lord.

II: DISORDERS IN THE CORINTHIAN COMMUNITY

A. Divisions in the Church†

Groups and Slogans. 10* I urge you, brothers, in the name of our Lord Jesus Christ, that all of you agree in what you say, and that there be no divisions among you, but that you be united in the same mind and in the same purpose. 11 For it has been reported to me about you, my brothers, by Chloe's people, that there are rivalries among you. 12*† I mean that each of you is saying, "I belong to Paul," or "I belong to Apollos," or "I belong to Kephas," or "I belong to Christ." 13† Is Christ divided? Was Paul crucified for you? Or were you baptized in the name of Paul? 14* I give thanks [to God] that I baptized none of you except Crispus and Gaius, 15 so that no one can say you were baptized in my name. 16* (I baptized the household of Stephanas also; beyond that I do not know whether I baptized anyone else.) 17*† For Christ did not send me to baptize but to preach the gospel, and not with the wisdom of human eloquence, so that the cross of Christ might not be emptied of its meaning.

Paradox of the Cross. 18* The message of the cross is foolishness to those who are perishing, but to us who are being saved it is the power of God. 19* For it is written:

"I will destroy the wisdom of the wise,
and the learning of the learned I will set aside."

20* Where is the wise one? Where is the scribe? Where is the debater of this age? Has not God made the wisdom of the world foolish? 21† For since in the wisdom of God the world did not come to know God through wisdom, it was the will of God through the foolishness of the proclamation to save those who have faith. 22* For Jews demand signs and Greeks look for wisdom, 23* but we proclaim Christ crucified, a stumbling block to Jews and foolishness to Gentiles, 24 but to those who are called, Jews and Greeks alike, Christ the power of God and the wisdom of God. 25 For the foolishness of God is wiser than human wisdom, and the weakness of God is stronger than human strength.

The Corinthians and Paul. † 26 Consider your own calling, brothers. Not many of you were wise by human standards, not many were powerful, not

*

- 7: Ti 2, 13.
- 8: Phil 1, 6.
- 9: 1 Jn 1, 3.
- 10: Phil 2, 2.
- 12: 3, 4.22; 16, 12; Acts 18, 24-28.
- 14: Acts 18, 8 / Rom 16, 23.
- 16: 16, 15-17.
- 17: 2, 1.4.
- 18: 2, 14 / Rom 1, 16.
- 19: Is 29, 14.
- 20: Is 19, 12.
- 22: Mt 12, 38; 16, 1 / Acts 17, 18-21.
- 23: 2, 2; Gal 3, 1 / Gal 5, 11.

†

1, 6: *The testimony:* this defines the purpose of Paul's mission (see also 15, 15 and the note on 2, 1). The forms of his testimony include oral preaching and instruction, his letters, and the life he leads as an apostle.

1, 10—4, 21: The first problem Paul addresses is that of divisions within the community. Although we are unable to reconstruct the situation in Corinth completely, Paul clearly traces the divisions back to a false self-image on the part of the Corinthians, coupled with a false understanding of the apostles who preached to them (cf 4, 6.9; 9, 1-5) and of the Christian message itself. In these chapters he attempts to deal with those underlying factors and to bring the Corinthians back to a more correct perspective.

1, 12: *I belong to:* the activities of Paul and Apollos in Corinth are described in Acts 18. *Kephas* (i.e., "the Rock," a name by which Paul designates Peter also in 3, 22; 9, 5; 15, 5 and in Gal 1, 18; 2, 9.11.14) may well have passed through Corinth; he could have baptized some members of the community either there or elsewhere. The reference to *Christ* may be intended ironically here.

1, 13-17: The reference to baptism and the contrast with preaching the gospel in v 17a suggest that some Corinthians were paying special allegiance to the individuals who initiated them into the community.

1, 17b-18: The basic theme of chs 1-4 is announced. Adherence to individual leaders has something to do with differences in rhetorical ability and also with certain presuppositions regarding wisdom, eloquence, and effectiveness (power), which Paul judges to be in conflict with the gospel and the cross.

1, 17b: *Not with the wisdom of human eloquence:* both of the nouns employed here involve several levels of meaning, on which Paul deliberately plays as his thought unfolds. *Wisdom* (*sophia*) may be philosophical and speculative, but in biblical usage the term primarily denotes practical knowledge such as is demonstrated in the choice and effective application of means to achieve an end. The same term can designate the arts of building (cf 3, 10) or of persuasive speaking (cf 2, 4) or effectiveness in achieving salvation. *Eloquence* (*logos*): this translation emphasizes one possible meaning of the term *logos* (cf the references to rhetorical style and persuasiveness in 2, 1.4). But the term itself may denote an internal reasoning process, plan, or intention, as well as an external word, speech, or message. So by his expression *ouk en sophia logou* in the context of gospel preaching, Paul may intend to exclude both human ways of reasoning or thinking about things and human rhetorical technique. *Human:* this adjective does not stand in the Greek text but is supplied from the context. Paul will begin immediately to distinguish between *sophia* and *logos* from their divine counterparts and play them off against each other.

1, 21-25: True wisdom and power are to be found paradoxically where one would least expect them, in the place of their apparent negation. To human eyes the crucified Christ symbolizes impotence and absurdity.

1, 26—2, 5: The pattern of God's wisdom and power is exemplified in their own experience, if they interpret it rightly (1, 26-31), and can also be read in their experience of Paul as he first appeared among them preaching the gospel (2, 1-5).

many were of noble birth. 27* Rather, God chose the foolish of the world to shame the wise, and God chose the weak of the world to shame the strong, 28 and God chose the lowly and despised of the world, those who count for nothing, to reduce to nothing those who are something, 29*† so that no human being might boast before God. 30* It is due to him that you are in Christ Jesus, who became for us wisdom from God, as well as righteousness, sanctification, and redemption, 31* so that, as it is written, "Whoever boasts, should boast in the Lord."

CHAPTER 2

1*† When I came to you, brothers, proclaiming the mystery of God, I did not come with sublimity of words or of wisdom. 2* For I resolved to know nothing while I was with you except Jesus Christ, and him crucified. 3† I came to you in weakness and fear and much trembling, 4*† and my message and my proclamation were not with persuasive [words of] wisdom, but with a demonstration of spirit and power, 5* so that your faith might rest not on human wisdom but on the power of God.

The True Wisdom.† 6 Yet we do speak a wisdom to those who are mature, but not a wisdom of this age, nor of the rulers of this age who are passing away. 7† Rather we speak God's wisdom, mysterious, hidden, which God predetermined before the ages for our glory, 8† and which none of the rulers of this age knew, for if they had known it, they would not have crucified the Lord of glory. 9* But as it is written:

"What eye has not seen, and ear has not heard,
and what has not entered the human heart,
what God has prepared for those who love him,"

10* this God has revealed to us through the Spirit.

For the Spirit scrutinizes everything, even the depths of God. 11 Among human beings, who knows what pertains to a person except the spirit of the person that is within? Similarly, no one knows what pertains to God except the Spirit of God. 12 We have not received the spirit of the world but the Spirit that is from God, so that we may understand the things freely given us by God. 13† And we speak about them not with words taught by human wisdom, but with words taught by the Spirit, describing spiritual realities in spiritual terms.

14† Now the natural person does not accept what pertains to the Spirit of God, for to him it is foolishness, and he cannot understand it, because it is judged spiritually. 15† The spiritual person, however, can judge everything but is not subject to judgment by anyone.

16* For "who has known the mind of the Lord, so as to counsel him?" But we have the mind of Christ.

*

27: Jas 2, 5.
29: Eph 2, 9.
30: Rom 4, 17 / 6, 11; Rom 3, 24-26; 2 Cor 5, 21 / Eph 1, 7; Col 1, 14; 1 Thes 5, 23.
31: Jer 9, 23; 2 Cor 10, 17.
2, 1: 1, 17.
2: 1, 23; Gal 6, 14.
4: 4, 20; Rom 15, 19; 1 Thes 1, 5.
5: 2 Cor 4, 7.
9: Is 64, 3.
10: Mt 11, 25; 13, 11; 16, 17.
16: Wis 9, 13; Is 40, 13; Rom 11, 34.

†

1, 29-31: "Boasting (about oneself)" is a Pauline expression for the radical sin, the claim to autonomy on the part of a creature, the illusion that we live and are saved by our own resources. "Boasting in the Lord" (31), on the other hand, is the acknowledgment that we live only from God and for God.

2, 1: *The mystery of God:* God's secret, known only to himself, is his plan for the salvation of his people; it is clear from 1, 18-25; 2, 2.8-10 that this secret involves Jesus and the cross. In place of *mystery,* other good manuscripts read "testimony" (cf 1, 6).

2, 3: The *weakness* of the crucified Jesus is reflected in Paul's own bearing (cf 2 Cor 10-13). *Fear and much trembling:* reverential fear based on a sense of God's transcendence permeates Paul's existence and preaching. Compare his advice to the Philippians to work out their salvation with "fear and trembling" (Phil 2, 12), because God is at work in them just as his exalting power was paradoxically at work in the emptying, humiliation, and obedience of Jesus to death on the cross (Phil 2, 6-11).

2, 4: Among many manuscript readings here the best is either "not with the persuasion of wisdom" or "not with persuasive words of wisdom," which differ only by a nuance. Whichever reading is accepted, the inefficacy of human wisdom for salvation is contrasted with the power of the cross.

2, 6—3, 4: Paul now asserts paradoxically what he has previously been denying. To the Greeks who "are looking for wisdom" (1, 22), he does indeed bring a wisdom, but of a higher order and an entirely different quality, the only wisdom really worthy of the name. The Corinthians would be able to grasp Paul's preaching as wisdom and enter into a wisdom-conversation with him if they were more open to the Spirit and receptive to the new insight and language that the Spirit teaches.

2, 7-10a: *God's wisdom:* his plan for our salvation. This was his own eternal secret that no one else could fathom, but in this new age of salvation he has graciously revealed it to us. For the pattern of God's secret, hidden to others and now revealed to the Church, cf also Rom 11, 25-36; 16, 25-27; Eph 1, 3-10; 3, 3-11; Col 1, 25-28.

2, 8: *The rulers of this age:* this suggests not only the political leaders of the Jews and Romans under whom Jesus was crucified (cf Acts 4, 25-28) but also the cosmic powers behind them (cf Eph 1, 20-23; 3, 10). *They would not have crucified the Lord of glory:* they became the unwitting executors of God's plan, which will paradoxically bring about their own conquest and submission (15, 24-28).

2, 13: *In spiritual terms:* the Spirit teaches spiritual people a new mode of perception (12) and an appropriate language by which they can share their self-understanding, their knowledge about what God has done in them. The final phrase in v 13 can also be translated "describing spiritual realities to spiritual people," in which case it prepares for vv 14-16.

2, 14: *The natural person:* see the note on 3, 1.

2, 15: *The spiritual person . . . is not subject to judgment:* since spiritual persons have been given knowledge of what pertains to God (11-12), they share in God's own capacity to judge. One to whom the mind of the Lord (and of Christ) is revealed (16) can be said to share in some sense in God's exemption from counseling and criticism.

CHAPTER 3

1† Brothers, I could not talk to you as
spiritual people, but as fleshly people,
as infants in Christ. 2* I fed you milk,
not solid food, because you were unable
to take it. Indeed, you are still not able,
even now, 3*† for you are still of the
flesh. While there is jealousy and rivalry
among you, are you not of the flesh,
and behaving in an ordinary human
way? 4* Whenever someone says, "I be-
long to Paul," and another, "I belong
to Apollos," are you not merely hu-
man?

The Role of God's Ministers.† 5† What
is Apollos, after all, and what is Paul?
Ministers through whom you became
believers, just as the Lord assigned
each one. 6* I planted, Apollos watered,
but God caused the growth. 7 Therefore,
neither the one who plants nor the one
who waters is anything, but only God,
who causes the growth. 8 The one who
plants and the one who waters are
equal, and each will receive wages in
proportion to his labor. 9* For we are
God's co-workers; you are God's field,
God's building.

10† According to the grace of God
given to me, like a wise master builder
I laid a foundation, and another is
building upon it. But each one must be
careful how he builds upon it, 11 for no
one can lay a foundation other than the
one that is there, namely, Jesus Christ.
12 If anyone builds on this foundation
with gold, silver, precious stones, wood,
hay, or straw, 13*† the work of each will
come to light, for the Day will disclose
it. It will be revealed with fire, and the
fire [itself] will test the quality of each
one's work. 14 If the work stands that
someone built upon the foundation, that
person will receive a wage. 15† But if
someone's work is burned up, that one
will suffer loss; the person will be saved,
but only as through fire. 16* Do you not
know that you are the temple of God,
and that the Spirit of God dwells in you?
17† If anyone destroys God's temple,
God will destroy that person; for the
temple of God, which you are, is holy.

18* Let no one deceive himself. If any-
one among you considers himself wise
in this age, let him become a fool so as
to become wise. 19* For the wisdom of
this world is foolishness in the eyes of
God, for it is written:

> "He catches the wise in their own
> ruses,"

20* and again:

> "The Lord knows the thoughts of
> the wise, that they are vain."

21*† So let no one boast about human
beings, for everything belongs to you,
22 Paul or Apollos or Kephas, or the
world or life or death, or the present
or the future: all belong to you, 23 and
you to Christ, and Christ to God.

*

3, 2: Heb 5, 12-14.
3: Jas 3, 13-16.
4: 1, 12.
6: Acts 18, 1-11.24-28.
9: Eph 2, 20-22; 1 Pt 2, 5.
13: Mt 3, 11-12; 2 Thes 1, 7-10.
16: 6, 19; 2 Cor 6, 16; Eph 2, 20-22.
18: 8, 2; Is 5, 21; Gal 6, 3.
19: 1, 20 / Jb 5, 13.
20: Ps 94, 11.
21: 4, 6 / Rom 8, 32.

†

3, 1-4: The Corinthians desire a sort of wisdom dialogue or colloquy with Paul; they are looking for solid, adult food, and he appears to disappoint their expectations. Paul counters: if such a dialogue has not yet taken place, the reason is that they are still at an immature stage of development (cf 2, 6).

3, 1: *Spiritual people . . . fleshly people:* Paul employs two clusters of concepts and terms to distinguish what later theology will call the "natural" and the "supernatural." (1) The natural person (2, 14) is one whose existence, perceptions, and behavior are determined by purely natural principles, the *psychē* (2, 14) and the *sarx* (flesh, a biblical term that connotes creatureliness, 1.3). Such persons are only infants (1); they remain on a purely human level (*anthrōpoi,* 4). (2) On the other hand, they are called to be animated by a higher principle, the *pneuma,* God's spirit. They are to become spiritual (*pneumatikoi,* 1) and mature (2, 6) in their perceptions and behavior (cf Gal 5, 16-26). The culmination of existence in the Spirit is described in 15, 44-49.

3, 3-4: Jealousy, rivalry, and divisions in the community are symptoms of their arrested development; they reveal the immaturity both of their self-understanding (4) and of the judgments about their apostles (21).

3, 5—4, 5: The Corinthians tend to evaluate their leaders by the criteria of human wisdom and to exaggerate their importance. Paul views the role of the apostles in the light of his theology of spiritual gifts (cf chs 12-14, where the charism of the apostle heads the lists). The essential aspects of all spiritual gifts (12, 4-6 presents them as gifts of grace, as services, and as modes of activity) are exemplified by the apostolate, which is a gift of grace (3, 10) through which God works (3, 9) and a form of service (3, 5) for the common good (elsewhere expressed by the verb "build up," suggested here by the image of the building, 3, 9). The apostles serve the church, but their accountability is to God and to Christ (4, 1-5).

3, 5: *Ministers:* for other expressions of Paul's understanding of himself as minister or steward to the church, cf 4, 1; 9, 17.19-27; 2 Cor 3, 6-9; 4, 1; 5, 18; 6, 3-4; and 11, 23 (the climax of Paul's defense).

3, 10-11: There are diverse functions in the service of the community, but each individual's task is serious, and each will stand accountable for the quality of his contribution.

3, 13: *The Day:* the great day of Yahweh, the day of judgment, which can be a time of either gloom or joy. *Fire* both destroys and purifies.

3, 15: *Will be saved:* although Paul can envision very harsh divine punishment (cf 17), he appears optimistic about the success of divine corrective means both here and elsewhere (cf 5, 5; 11, 32 [discipline]). The text of v 15 has sometimes been used to support the notion of purgatory, though it does not envisage this.

3, 17: *Holy:* i.e., "belonging to God." The cultic sanctity of the community is a fundamental theological reality to which Paul frequently alludes (cf 1, 2.30; 6, 11; 7, 14).

3, 21-23: These verses pick up the line of thought of 1, 10-13. If the Corinthians were genuinely wise (18-20), their perceptions would be reversed, and they would see everything in the world and all those with whom they exist in the church in their true relations with one another. Paul assigns all the persons involved in the theological universe a position on a scale: God, Christ, church members, church leaders. Read from top to bottom, the scale expresses ownership; read from bottom to top, the obligation to serve. This picture should be complemented by similar statements such as those in 8, 6 and 15, 20-28.

CHAPTER 4

1* Thus should one regard us: as ser-
vants of Christ and stewards of the mys-
teries of God. 2 Now it is of course
required of stewards that they be found
trustworthy. 3 It does not concern me in
the least that I be judged by you or any
human tribunal; I do not even pass
judgment on myself; 4* I am not con-
scious of anything against me, but I do
not thereby stand acquitted; the one
who judges me is the Lord. 5 Therefore,
do not make any judgment before the
appointed time, until the Lord comes,
for he will bring to light what is hidden
in darkness and will manifest the mo-
tives of our hearts, and then everyone
will receive praise from God.

Paul's Life as Pattern. † 6† I have ap-
plied these things to myself and Apollos
for your benefit, brothers, so that you
may learn from us not to go beyond
what is written, so that none of you will
be inflated with pride in favor of one
person over against another. 7 Who con-
fers distinction upon you? What do you
possess that you have not received? But
if you have received it, why are you
boasting as if you did not receive it?
8† You are already satisfied; you have
already grown rich; you have become
kings without us! Indeed, I wish that you
had become kings, so that we also might
become kings with you.

9*† For as I see it, God has exhibited
us apostles as the last of all, like people
sentenced to death, since we have be-
come a spectacle to the world, to angels
and human beings alike. 10* We are
fools on Christ's account, but you
are wise in Christ; we are weak, but you
are strong; you are held in honor, but
we in disrepute. 11* To this very hour
we go hungry and thirsty, we are poorly
clad and roughly treated, we wander
about homeless 12* and we toil, working
with our own hands. When ridiculed, we
bless; when persecuted, we endure;
13 when slandered, we respond gently.
We have become like the world's rub-
bish, the scum of all, to this very mo-
ment.

14† I am writing you this not to shame
you, but to admonish you as my beloved
children. 15* Even if you should have
countless guides to Christ, yet you do
not have many fathers, for I became
your father in Christ Jesus through the
gospel. 16* Therefore, I urge you, be imi-
tators of me. 17* For this reason I am
sending you Timothy, who is my be-
loved and faithful son in the Lord; he
will remind you of my ways in Christ
[Jesus], just as I teach them every-
where in every church.

18† Some have become inflated with
pride, as if I were not coming to you.
19 But I will come to you soon, if the Lord
is willing, and I shall ascertain not the
talk of these inflated people but their
power. 20* For the kingdom of God is
not a matter of talk but of power.

*

4, 1: Ti 1, 7; 1 Pt 4, 10.
4: 2 Cor 1, 12 / Rom 2, 16; 2 Cor 5, 10.
9: 15, 31; Rom 8, 36; 2 Cor 4, 8-12; 11, 23 / Heb 10, 33.
10: 1, 18; 3, 18; 2 Cor 11, 19 / 2, 3; 2 Cor 13, 9.
11: Rom 8, 35; 2 Cor 11, 23-27.
12: Acts 9, 6-14; 18, 3; 20, 34; 1 Thes 2, 9 / 1 Pt 3, 9.
15: Gal 4, 19; Phlm 10.
16: 11, 1; Phil 3, 17; 4, 9; 1 Thes 1, 6; 2 Thes 3, 7.9.
17: 16, 10; Acts 19, 22.
20: 2, 4; 1 Thes 1, 5.

†

4, 6-21: This is an emotionally charged peroration to the discussion about divisions. It contains several exhortations and statements of Paul's purpose in writing (cf 6.14-17.21) that counterbalance the initial exhortation at 1, 10.

4, 6: *That you may learn from us not to go beyond what is written:* the words "to go" are not in the Greek, but have here been added as the minimum necessary to elicit sense from this difficult passage. It probably means that the Corinthians should avoid the false wisdom of vain speculation, contenting themselves with Paul's proclamation of the cross, which is the fulfillment of God's promises in the Old Testament (what is written). *Inflated with pride:* literally, "puffed up," i.e., arrogant, filled with a sense of self-importance. The term is particularly Pauline, found in the New Testament only in 1 Cor 4, 6.18-19; 5, 2; 8, 1; 13, 4; Col 2, 18 (cf the related noun at 2 Cor 12, 20). It sometimes occurs in conjunction with the theme of "boasting," as in vv 6-7 here.

4, 8: *Satisfied . . . rich . . . kings:* these three statements could also be punctuated as questions continuing the series begun in v 7. In any case these expressions reflect a tendency at Corinth toward an overrealized eschatology, a form of self-deception that draws Paul's irony. The underlying attitude has implications for the Corinthians' thinking about other issues, notably morality and the resurrection, that Paul will address later in the letter.

4, 9-13: A rhetorically effective catalogue of the circumstances of apostolic existence, in the course of which Paul ironically contrasts his own sufferings with the Corinthians' illusion that they have passed beyond the folly of the passion and have already reached the condition of glory. His language echoes that of the beatitudes and woes, which assert a future reversal of present conditions. Their present sufferings ("to this very hour," 11) place the apostles in the class of those to whom the beatitudes promise future relief (Mt 5, 3-11; Lk 6, 20-23); whereas the Corinthians' image of themselves as "already" filled, rich, ruling (8), as wise, strong, and honored (10) places them paradoxically in the position of those whom the woes threaten with future undoing (Lk 6, 24-26). They have lost sight of the fact that the reversal is predicted for the future.

4, 14-17: *My beloved children:* the close of the argument is dominated by the tender metaphor of the father who not only gives his children life but also educates them. Once he has begotten them through his preaching, Paul continues to present the gospel to them existentially, by his life as well as by his word, and they are to learn, as children do, by imitating their parents (16). The reference to the *rod* in v 21 belongs to the same image-complex. So does the image of the *ways* in v 17: the ways that Paul teaches everywhere, "his ways in Christ Jesus," mean a behavior pattern quite different from the human ways along which the Corinthians are walking (3, 3).

4, 18-21: Verse 20 picks up the contrast between a certain kind of talk (*logos*) and true power (*dynamis*) from 1, 17-18 and 2, 4-5. The kingdom, which many of them imagine to be fully present in their lives (8), will be rather unexpectedly disclosed in the strength of Paul's encounter with them, if they make a powerful intervention on his part necessary. Compare the similar ending to an argument in 2 Cor 13, 1-4.10.

21* Which do you prefer? Shall I come to you with a rod, or with love and a gentle spirit?

B. Moral Disorders†

CHAPTER 5

***A Case of Incest.*†** 1* It is widely reported that there is immorality among you, and immorality of a kind not found even among pagans—a man living with his father's wife. 2† And you are inflated with pride. Should you not rather have been sorrowful? The one who did this deed should be expelled from your midst. 3* I, for my part, although absent in body but present in spirit, have already, as if present, pronounced judgment on the one who has committed this deed, 4 in the name of [our] Lord Jesus: when you have gathered together and I am with you in spirit with the power of the Lord Jesus, 5*† you are to deliver this man to Satan for the destruction of his flesh, so that his spirit may be saved on the day of the Lord.

6*† Your boasting is not appropriate. Do you not know that a little yeast leavens all the dough? 7*† Clear out the old yeast, so that you may become a fresh batch of dough, inasmuch as you are unleavened. For our paschal lamb, Christ, has been sacrificed. 8* Therefore let us celebrate the feast, not with the old yeast, the yeast of malice and wickedness, but with the unleavened bread of sincerity and truth.

9† I wrote you in my letter not to associate with immoral people, 10* not at all referring to the immoral of this world or the greedy and robbers or idolaters; for you would then have to leave the world. 11* But I now write to you not to associate with anyone named a brother, if he is immoral, greedy, an idolater, a slanderer, a drunkard, or a robber, not even to eat with such a person. 12 For why should I be judging outsiders? Is it not your business to judge those within? 13* God will judge those outside. "Purge the evil person from your midst."

CHAPTER 6

***Lawsuits before Unbelievers.*†** 1 How can any one of you with a case against another dare to bring it to the unjust for judgment instead of to the holy ones? 2*† Do you not know that the holy ones will judge the world? If the world is to be judged by you, are you unqualified for the lowest law courts? 3 Do you not know that we will judge angels? Then why not everyday matters? 4 If, therefore, you have courts for everyday matters, do you seat as judges people of no standing in the church? 5 I say this to shame you. Can it be that there is not one among you wise enough to be able to settle a case between brothers? 6 But rather brother goes to court against brother, and that before unbelievers?

7* Now indeed [then] it is, in any case, a failure on your part that you have lawsuits against one another. Why not rather put up with injustice? Why not rather let yourselves be cheated?

*

21: 2 Cor 1, 23; 10, 2.
5, 1: Lv 18, 7-8; 20, 11; Dt 27, 20.
3: Col 2, 5.
5: 1 Tm 1, 20.
6: Gal 5, 9.
7: Ex 12, 1-13; Dt 16, 1-2; 1 Pt 1, 19.
8: Ex 12, 15-20; 13, 7; Dt 16, 3.
10: 10, 27; Jn 17, 15.
11: Mt 18, 17; 2 Thes 3, 6.14; 2 Jn 10.
13: Dt 13, 6; 17, 7; 22, 24.
6, 2: Wis 3, 8; Mt 19, 28; Rv 20, 4.
7: Mt 5, 38-42; Rom 12, 17-21; 1 Thes 5, 15.

†

5, 1—6, 20: Paul now takes up a number of other matters that require regulation. These have come to his attention by hearsay (5, 1), probably in reports brought by "Chloe's people" (1, 11).

5, 1-13: Paul first deals with the incestuous union of a man with his stepmother (1-8) and then attempts to clarify general admonitions he has given about associating with fellow Christians guilty of immorality (9-13). Each of these three brief paragraphs expresses the same idea: the need of separation between the holy and the unholy.

5, 2: *Inflated with pride:* this remark and the reference to *boasting* in v 6 suggest that they are proud of themselves despite the infection in their midst, tolerating and possibly even approving the situation. The attitude expressed in 6, 2.13 may be influencing their thinking in this case.

5, 5: *Deliver this man to Satan:* once the sinner is expelled from the church, the sphere of Jesus' lordship and victory over sin, he will be in the region outside over which Satan is still master. *For the destruction of his flesh:* the purpose of the penalty is medicinal: through affliction, sin's grip over him may be destroyed and the path to repentance and reunion laid open. With Paul's instructions for an excommunication ceremony here, contrast his recommendations for the reconciliation of a sinner in 2 Cor 2, 5-11.

5, 6: *A little yeast:* yeast, which induces fermentation, is a natural symbol for a source of corruption that becomes all-pervasive. The expression is proverbial.

5, 7-8: In the Jewish calendar, Passover was followed immediately by the festival of Unleavened Bread. In preparation for this feast all traces of old bread were removed from the house, and during the festival only unleavened bread was eaten. The sequence of these two feasts provides Paul with an image of Christian existence: Christ's death (the true Passover celebration) is followed by the life of the Christian community, marked by newness, purity, and integrity (a perpetual feast of unleavened bread). Paul may have been writing around Passover time (cf 16, 5); this is a little Easter homily, the earliest in Christian literature.

5, 9-13: Paul here corrects a misunderstanding of his earlier directives against associating with immoral fellow Christians. He concedes the impossibility of avoiding contact with sinners in society at large but urges the Corinthians to maintain the inner purity of their own community.

6, 1-11: Christians at Corinth are suing one another before pagan judges in Roman courts. A barrage of rhetorical questions (1-9) betrays Paul's indignation over this practice, which he sees as an infringement upon the holiness of the Christian community.

6, 2-3: The principle to which Paul appeals is an eschatological prerogative promised to Christians: they are to share with Christ the judgment of the world (cf Dn 7, 22.27). Hence they ought to be able to settle minor disputes within the community.

8 Instead, you inflict injustice and cheat,
and this to brothers. 9*† Do you not
know that the unjust will not inherit the
kingdom of God? Do not be deceived;
neither fornicators nor idolaters nor
adulterers nor boy prostitutes nor prac-
ticing homosexuals 10 nor thieves nor
the greedy nor drunkards nor slander-
ers nor robbers will inherit the kingdom
of God. 11* That is what some of you
used to be; but now you have had your-
selves washed, you were sanctified, you
were justified in the name of the Lord
Jesus Christ and in the Spirit of our God.
Sexual Immorality.† 12*† "Every-
thing is lawful for me," but not every-
thing is beneficial. "Everything is lawful
for me," but I will not let myself be
dominated by anything. 13 "Food for the
stomach and the stomach for food," but
God will do away with both the one and
the other. The body, however, is not for
immorality, but for the Lord, and the
Lord is for the body; 14* God raised the
Lord and will also raise us by his power.
15*† Do you not know that your bodies
are members of Christ? Shall I then take
Christ's members and make them the
members of a prostitute? Of course not!
16* [Or] do you not know that anyone
who joins himself to a prostitute be-
comes one body with her? For "the
two," it says, "will become one flesh."
17* But whoever is joined to the Lord be-
comes one spirit with him. 18† Avoid im-
morality. Every other sin a person
commits is outside the body, but the im-
moral person sins against his own body.
19*† Do you not know that your body is
a temple of the holy Spirit within you,
whom you have from God, and that you
are not your own? 20* For you have been
purchased at a price. Therefore, glorify
God in your body.

III: ANSWERS TO THE CORINTHIANS' QUESTIONS

A. Marriage and Virginity†

CHAPTER 7

Advice to the Married.† 1† Now in re-
gard to the matters about which you
wrote: "It is a good thing for a man not
to touch a woman," 2 but because of
cases of immorality every man should
have his own wife, and every woman

---

*

9: 15, 50; Gal 5, 19-21; Eph 5, 5.
11: Ti 3, 3-7.
12: 10, 23.
14: Rom 8, 11; 2 Cor 4, 14.
15: 12, 27; Rom 6, 12-13; 12, 5; Eph 5, 30.
16: Gn 2, 24; Mt 19, 5; Mk 10, 8; Eph 5, 31.
17: Rom 8, 9-10; 2 Cor 3, 17.
19: 3, 16-17; Rom 5, 5.
20: 3, 23; 7, 23; Acts 20, 28 / Rom 12, 1; Phil 1, 20.

---

†

6, 9-10: A catalogue of typical vices that exclude from the kingdom of God and that should be excluded from God's church. Such lists (cf 5, 10) reflect the common moral sensibility of the New Testament period.

6, 9: The Greek word translated as *boy prostitutes* designated catamites, i.e., boys or young men who were kept for purposes of prostitution, a practice not uncommon in the Greco-Roman world. In Greek mythology this was the function of Ganymede, the "cupbearer of the gods," whose Latin name was Catamitus. The term translated *practicing homosexuals* refers to adult males who indulged in homosexual practices with such boys. See similar condemnations of such practices in Rom 1, 26-27; 1 Tm 1, 10.

6, 12-20: Paul now turns to the opinion of some Corinthians that sexuality is a morally indifferent area (12-13). This leads him to explain the mutual relation between the Lord Jesus and our bodies (13b) in a densely packed paragraph that contains elements of a profound theology of sexuality (15-20).

6, 12-13: *Everything is lawful for me:* the Corinthians may have derived this slogan from Paul's preaching about Christian freedom, but they mean something different by it: they consider sexual satisfaction a matter as indifferent as food, and they attribute no lasting significance to bodily functions (13a). Paul begins to deal with the slogan by two qualifications, which suggest principles for judging sexual activity. *Not everything is beneficial:* cf 10, 23, and the whole argument of chs 8-10 on the finality of freedom and moral activity. *Not let myself be dominated:* certain apparently free actions may involve in fact a secret servitude in conflict with the lordship of Jesus.

6, 15b-16: *A prostitute:* the reference may be specifically to religious prostitution, an accepted part of pagan culture at Corinth and elsewhere; but the prostitute also serves as a symbol for any sexual relationship that conflicts with Christ's claim over us individually. *The two . . . will become one flesh:* the text of Gn 2, 24 is applied positively to human marriage in Mt and Mk, and in Eph 5, 29-32: love of husband and wife reflect the love of Christ for his church. The application of the text to union with a prostitute is jarring, for such a union is a parody, an antitype of marriage, which does conflict with Christ's claim over us. This explains the horror expressed in 15b.

6, 18: *Against his own body:* expresses the intimacy and depth of sexual disorder, which violates the very orientation of our bodies.

6, 19-20: Paul's vision becomes trinitarian. *A temple:* sacred by reason of God's gift, his indwelling Spirit. *Not your own:* but "for the Lord," who acquires ownership by the act of redemption. *Glorify God in your body:* the argument concludes with a positive imperative to supplement the negative "avoid immorality" of v 18. Far from being a terrain that is morally indifferent, the area of sexuality is one in which our relationship with God (and his Christ and his Spirit) is very intimately expressed: he is either highly glorified or deeply offended.

7, 1-40: Paul now begins to answer questions addressed to him by the Corinthians (7, 1—11, 1). The first of these concerns marriage. This chapter contains advice both to the married (1-16) and to the unmarried (25-38) or widowed (39-40); these two parts are separated by vv 17-24, which enunciate a principle applicable to both.

7, 1-16: It seems that some Christians in Corinth were advocating asceticism in sexual matters. The pattern *it is a good thing . . ., but* occurs twice (1-2.8-9; cf 26), suggesting that in this matter as in others the Corinthians have seized upon a genuine value but are exaggerating or distorting it in some way. Once again Paul calls them to a more correct perspective and a better sense of their own limitations. The phrase *it is a good thing* (1) may have been the slogan of the ascetic party at Corinth.

7, 1-7: References to Paul's own behavior (7-8) suggest that his celibate way of life and his preaching to the unmarried (cf 25-35) have given some the impression that asceticism within marriage, i.e., suspension of normal sexual relations, would be a laudable ideal. Paul points to their experience of widespread immorality to caution them against overestimating their own strength (2); as individuals they may not have the particular gift that makes such asceticism feasible (7) and hence are to abide by the principle to be explained in vv 17-24.

her own husband. 3 The husband should fulfill his duty toward his wife, and likewise the wife toward her husband. 4 A wife does not have authority over her own body, but rather her husband, and similarly a husband does not have authority over his own body, but rather his wife. 5 Do not deprive each other, except perhaps by mutual consent for a time, to be free for prayer, but then return to one another, so that Satan may not tempt you through your lack of self-control. 6† This I say by way of concession, however, not as a command. 7*† Indeed, I wish everyone to be as I am, but each has a particular gift from God, one of one kind and one of another.

8*† Now to the unmarried and to widows, I say: it is a good thing for them to remain as they are, as I do, 9 but if they cannot exercise self-control they should marry, for it is better to marry than to be on fire. 10*† To the married, however, I give this instruction (not I, but the Lord): a wife should not separate from her husband 11—and if she does separate she must either remain single or become reconciled to her husband—and a husband should not divorce his wife.

12† To the rest I say (not the Lord): if any brother has a wife who is an unbeliever, and she is willing to go on living with him, he should not divorce her; 13 and if any woman has a husband who is an unbeliever, and he is willing to go on living with her, she should not divorce her husband. 14* For the unbelieving husband is made holy through his wife, and the unbelieving wife is made holy through the brother. Otherwise your children would be unclean, whereas in fact they are holy.

15† If the unbeliever separates, however, let him separate. The brother or sister is not bound in such cases; God has called you to peace. 16 For how do you know, wife, whether you will save your husband; or how do you know, husband, whether you will save your wife?

The Life That the Lord Has Assigned.† 17 Only, everyone should live as the Lord has assigned, just as God called each one. I give this order in all the churches. 18* Was someone called after he had been circumcised? He should not try to undo his circumcision. Was an uncircumcised person called? He should not be circumcised. 19* Circumcision means nothing, and uncircumcision means nothing; what matters is keeping God's commandments. 20 Everyone should remain in the state in which he was called.

21 Were you a slave when you were called? Do not be concerned but, even if you can gain your freedom, make the most of it. 22* For the slave called in the Lord is a freed person in the Lord, just as the free person who has been called is a slave of Christ. 23* You have been purchased at a price. Do not become slaves to human beings. 24 Brothers, everyone should continue before God in the state in which he was called.

Advice to Virgins and Widows.† 25 Now in regard to virgins, I have no commandment from the Lord, but I give my opinion as one who by the Lord's mercy is trustworthy. 26* So this is what I think best because of the present distress: that it is a good thing for a person to remain as he is. 27 Are you bound to a wife? Do not seek a separation. Are you free of a wife? Then do not look for a wife. 28 If you marry, however, you do not sin, nor does an unmarried woman sin if she marries; but such people will experience affliction in their earthly life, and I would like to spare you that.

29*† I tell you, brothers, the time is running out. From now on, let those having wives act as not having them, 30 those weeping as not weeping, those rejoicing as not rejoicing, those buying as not owning, 31 those using the world

---

*

7, 7: Mt 19, 11-12.
8: 1 Tm 5, 11-16 / 9, 5;
10-11: Mt 5, 32; 19, 9.
14: Rom 11, 16.
18: 1 Mc 1, 15 / Acts 15, 1-2.
19: Rom 2, 25.29; Gal 5, 6; 6, 15.
22: Eph 6, 5-9; Col 3, 11; Phlm 16.
23: 6, 20.
26: 8.
29: Rom 13, 11.

†

7, 6: *By way of concession:* this refers most likely to the concession mentioned in v 5a: temporary interruption of relations for a legitimate purpose.

7, 7: *A particular gift from God:* use of the term *charisma* suggests that marriage and celibacy may be viewed in the light of Paul's theology of spiritual gifts (chs 12-14).

7, 8: Paul was obviously unmarried when he wrote this verse. Some interpreters believe that he had previously been married and widowed; there is no clear evidence either for or against this view, which was expressed already at the end of the second century by Clement of Alexandria.

7, 10-11: *(Not I, but the Lord):* Paul reminds the married of Jesus' principle of nonseparation (Mk 10, 9). This is one of his rare specific references to the teaching of Jesus.

7, 12-14: *To the rest:* marriages in which only one partner is a baptized Christian. Jesus' prohibition against divorce is not addressed to them, but Paul extends the principle of nonseparation to such unions, provided they are marked by peacefulness and shared sanctification.

7, 15-16: *If the unbeliever separates:* the basis of the "Pauline privilege" in Catholic marriage legislation.

7, 17-24: On the ground that distinct human conditions are less significant than the whole new existence opened up by God's call, Paul urges them to be less concerned with changing their states of life than with answering God's call where it finds them. The principle applies both to the married state (1-16) and to the unmarried (25-38).

7, 25-28: Paul is careful to explain that the principle of v 17 does not bind under sin but that present earthly conditions make it advantageous for the unmarried to remain as they are (28). These remarks must be complemented by the statement about "particular gifts" from v 7.

7, 29-31: *The world . . . is passing away:* Paul advises Christians to go about the ordinary activities of life in a manner different from those who are totally immersed in them and unaware of their transitoriness.

as not using it fully. For the world in
its present form is passing away.
32 I should like you to be free of anxi-
eties. An unmarried man is anxious
about the things of the Lord, how he
may please the Lord. 33* But a married
man is anxious about the things of the
world, how he may please his wife,
34* and he is divided. An unmarried
woman or a virgin is anxious about the
things of the Lord, so that she may be
holy in both body and spirit. A married
woman, on the other hand, is anxious
about the things of the world, how she
may please her husband. 35* I am telling
you this for your own benefit, not to im-
pose a restraint upon you, but for the
sake of propriety and adherence to the
Lord without distraction.
36† If anyone thinks he is behaving
improperly toward his virgin, and if a
critical moment has come and so it has
to be, let him do as he wishes. He is com-
mitting no sin; let them get married.
37 The one who stands firm in his re-
solve, however, who is not under com-
pulsion but has power over his own will,
and has made up his mind to keep his
virgin, will be doing well. 38 So then, the
one who marries his virgin does well;
the one who does not marry her will do
better.
39*† A wife is bound to her husband
as long as he lives. But if her husband
dies, she is free to be married to whom-
ever she wishes, provided that it be
in the Lord. 40* She is more blessed,
though, in my opinion, if she remains
as she is, and I think that I too have
the Spirit of God.

B. Offerings to Idols†

CHAPTER 8

Knowledge Insufficient. 1*† Now in
regard to meat sacrificed to idols: we
realize that "all of us have knowledge";
knowledge inflates with pride, but love
builds up. 2 If anyone supposes he
knows something, he does not yet know
as he ought to know. 3* But if one loves
God, one is known by him.
4* So about the eating of meat sacri-
ficed to idols: we know that "there is
no idol in the world," and that "there
is no God but one." 5 Indeed, even
though there are so-called gods in
heaven and on earth (there are, to be
sure, many "gods" and many "lords"),
6*† yet for us there is

one God, the Father,
from whom all things are and for
whom we exist,
and one Lord, Jesus Christ,
through whom all things are and
through whom we exist.

Practical Rules. 7* But not all have
this knowledge. There are some who
have been so used to idolatry up until
now that, when they eat meat sacrificed
to idols, their conscience, which is
weak, is defiled.
8*† Now food will not bring us closer
to God. We are no worse off if we do
not eat, nor are we better off if we do.
9* But make sure that this liberty of

*

33: Lk 14, 20.
34: 1 Tm 5, 5.
35: Lk 10, 39-42.
39: Rom 7, 2.
40: 25.
8, 1: Rom 15, 14 / 13, 1-13; Rom 14, 15.19.
3: Rom 8, 29; Gal 4, 9;
4: 10, 19; Dt 6, 4.
6: Mal 2, 10 / Rom 11, 36; Eph 4, 5-6 / 1, 2-3 / Jn 1, 3; Col 1, 16.
7: 10, 28; Rom 14, 23 / Rom 14, 1; 15, 1.
8: Rom 14, 17.
9: Rom 14, 13.20-21.

†

7, 36-38: The passage is difficult to interpret, because it is unclear whether Paul is thinking of a father and his unmarried daughter (or slave), or of a couple engaged in a betrothal or spiritual marriage. The general principles already enunciated apply: there is no question of sin, even if they should marry, but staying as they are is "better" (for the reasons mentioned in 28-35). Once again the *charisma* of v 7, which applies also to the unmarried (8-9), is to be presupposed.

7, 36: *A critical moment has come:* either because the woman will soon be beyond marriageable age, or because their passions are becoming uncontrollable (cf 9).

7, 39-40: Application of the principles to the case of widows. If they do choose to remarry, they ought to prefer Christian husbands.

8, 1—11, 1: The Corinthians' second question concerns meat that has been sacrificed to idols; in this area they were exhibiting a disordered sense of liberation that Paul here tries to rectify. These chapters contain a sustained and unified argument that illustrates Paul's method of theological reflection on a moral dilemma. Although the problem with which he is dealing is dated, the guidelines for moral decisions that he offers are of lasting validity.

Essentially Paul urges them to take a communitarian rather than an individualistic view of their Christian freedom. Many decisions that they consider pertinent only to their private relationship with God have, in fact, social consequences. Nor can moral decisions be determined by merely theoretical considerations; they must be based on concrete circumstances, specifically on the value and needs of other individuals and on mutual responsibility within the community. Paul here introduces the theme of "building up" (*oikodomē*), i.e., of contributing by individual action to the welfare and growth of the community. This theme will be further developed in ch 14; see the note on 14, 3b-5. Several years later Paul would again deal with the problem of meat sacrificed to idols in Rom 14, 1—15, 6.

8, 1a: *Meat sacrificed to idols:* much of the food consumed in the city could have passed through pagan religious ceremonies before finding its way into markets and homes. *"All of us have knowledge":* a slogan, similar to 6, 12, which reveals the self-image of the Corinthians. Verse 4 will specify the content of this knowledge.

8, 6: This verse rephrases the monotheistic confession of v 4 in such a way as to contrast it with polytheism (5) and to express our relationship with the one God in concrete, i.e., in personal and Christian terms. *And for whom we exist:* since the Greek contains no verb here and the action intended must be inferred from the preposition *eis,* another translation is equally possible: "toward whom we return." *Through whom all things:* the earliest reference in the New Testament to Jesus' role in creation.

8, 8-9: Although the food in itself is morally neutral, extrinsic circumstances may make the eating of it harmful. *A stumbling block:* the image is that of tripping or causing someone to fall (cf 13; 9, 12; 10, 12.32; 2 Cor 6, 3; Rom 14, 13.20-21). This is a basic moral imperative for Paul, a counterpart to the positive imperative to "build one another up"; compare the expression "giving offense" as opposed to "pleasing" in 10, 32-33.

yours in no way becomes a stumbling
block to the weak. 10 If someone sees
you, with your knowledge, reclining at
table in the temple of an idol, may not
his conscience too, weak as it is, be
"built up" to eat the meat sacrificed to
idols? 11* Thus through your knowledge,
the weak person is brought to destruc-
tion, the brother for whom Christ died.
12 When you sin in this way against your
brothers and wound their consciences,
weak as they are, you are sinning
against Christ. 13*† Therefore, if food
causes my brother to sin, I will never
eat meat again, so that I may not cause
my brother to sin.

CHAPTER 9†

Paul's Rights as an Apostle. 1* Am I
not free? Am I not an apostle? Have I
not seen Jesus our Lord? Are you not
my work in the Lord? 2 Although I may
not be an apostle for others, certainly
I am for you, for you are the seal of my
apostleship in the Lord.
3† My defense against those who
would pass judgment on me is this.
4† Do we not have the right to eat and
drink? 5 Do we not have the right to take
along a Christian wife, as do the rest
of the apostles, and the brothers of the
Lord, and Kephas? 6* Or is it only my-
self and Barnabas who do not have the
right not to work? 7* Who ever serves
as a soldier at his own expense? Who
plants a vineyard without eating its pro-
duce? Or who shepherds a flock without
using some of the milk from the flock?
8 Am I saying this on human authority,
or does not the law also speak of these
things? 9* It is written in the law of Mo-
ses, "You shall not muzzle an ox while
it is treading out the grain." Is God con-
cerned about oxen, 10* or is he not really
speaking for our sake? It was written
for our sake, because the plowman
should plow in hope, and the thresher
in hope of receiving a share. 11* If we
have sown spiritual seed for you, is it
a great thing that we reap a material
harvest from you? 12*† If others share
this rightful claim on you, do not we still
more?
Reason for Not Using His Rights.
Yet we have not used this right. On the
contrary, we endure everything so as
not to place an obstacle to the gospel
of Christ. 13*† Do you not know that
those who perform the temple services
eat [what] belongs to the temple, and
those who minister at the altar share
in the sacrificial offerings? 14* In the
same way, the Lord ordered that those
who preach the gospel should live by
the gospel.
15*† I have not used any of these
rights, however, nor do I write this that
it be done so in my case. I would rather
die. Certainly no one is going to nullify
my boast. 16* If I preach the gospel, this
is no reason for me to boast, for an obli-
gation has been imposed on me, and
woe to me if I do not preach it! 17* If I
do so willingly, I have a recompense,
but if unwillingly, then I have been en-
trusted with a stewardship. 18* What
then is my recompense? That, when I

*

11: Rom 14, 15.20.
13: Mt 18, 6; Rom 14, 20-21.
9, 1: 19 / 2 Cor 12, 12 / 15, 8-9; Acts 9, 17; 26, 16.
6: Acts 4, 36-37; 13, 1-2; Gal 2, 1.9.13; Col 4, 10.
7: 2 Tm 2, 3-4.
9: Dt 25, 4; 1 Tm 5, 18.
10: 2 Tm 2, 6.
11: Rom 15, 27.
12: 2 Cor 11, 7-12; 12, 13-18; 2 Thes 3, 6-12.
13: Nm 18, 8.31; Dt 18, 1-5.
14: Mt 10, 10; Lk 10, 7-8.
15: 2 Cor 11, 9-10.
16: Acts 26, 14-18.
17: 4, 1; Gal 2, 7.
18: 2 Cor 11, 7-12.

†

8, 13: His own course is clear: he will avoid any action that might harm another Christian. This statement prepares for the paradigmatic development in ch 9.

9, 1-27: This chapter is an emotionally charged expansion of Paul's appeal to his own example in 8, 13; its purpose is to reinforce the exhortation of 8, 9. The two opening questions introduce the themes of Paul's freedom and his apostleship (1), themes that the chapter will develop in reverse order, vv 1-18 treating the question of his apostleship and the rights that flow from it, and vv 19-27 exploring dialectically the nature of Paul's freedom. The language is highly rhetorical, abounding in questions, wordplays, paradoxes, images, and appeals to authority and experience. The argument is unified by repetitions; its articulations are highlighted by inclusions and transitional verses.

9, 3: *My defense against those who would pass judgment on me:* the reference to a defense (*apologia*) is surprising, and suggests that Paul is incorporating some material here that he has previously used in another context. The defense will touch on two points: the fact of Paul's rights as an apostle (4-12a and 13-14) and his nonuse of those rights (12b and 15-18).

9, 4-12a: Apparently some believe that Paul is not equal to the other apostles and therefore does not enjoy equal privileges. His defense on this point (here and in 13-14) reinforces the assertion of his apostolic character in v 2. It consists of a series of analogies from natural equity (7) and religious custom (13) designed to establish his equal right to support from the churches (4-6.11-12a); these analogies are confirmed by the authority of the law (8-10) and of Jesus himself (14).

9, 12b: It appears, too, that suspicion or misunderstanding has been created by Paul's practice of not living from his preaching. The first reason he asserts in defense of this practice is an entirely apostolic one; it anticipates the developments to follow in vv 19-22. He will give a second reason in vv 15-18.

9, 13-14: The position of these verses produces an interlocking of the two points of Paul's defense. These arguments by analogy (13) and from authority (14) belong with those of vv 7-10 and ground the first point. But Paul defers them until he has had a chance to mention "the gospel of Christ" (12b), after which it is more appropriate to mention Jesus' injunction to his preachers and to argue by analogy from the sacred temple service to his own liturgical service, the preaching of the gospel (cf Rom 1, 9; 15, 16).

9, 15-18: Paul now assigns a more personal motive to his nonuse of his right to support. His preaching is not a service spontaneously undertaken on his part but a stewardship imposed by a sort of divine compulsion. Yet to merit any reward he must bring some spontaneous quality to his service, and this he does by freely renouncing his right to support. The material here is quite similar to that contained in Paul's "defense" at 2 Cor 11, 5-12; 12, 11-18.

preach, I offer the gospel free of charge so as not to make full use of my right in the gospel.

***All Things to All.*†** 19* Although I am free in regard to all, I have made myself a slave to all so as to win over as many as possible. 20 To the Jews I became like a Jew to win over Jews; to those under the law I became like one under the law—though I myself am not under the law—to win over those under the law. 21 To those outside the law I became like one outside the law—though I am not outside God's law but within the law of Christ—to win over those outside the law. 22* To the weak I became weak, to win over the weak. I have become all things to all, to save at least some. 23 All this I do for the sake of the gospel, so that I too may have a share in it.

24*† Do you not know that the runners in the stadium all run in the race, but only one wins the prize? Run so as to win. 25* Every athlete exercises discipline in every way. They do it to win a perishable crown, but we an imperishable one. 26 Thus I do not run aimlessly; I do not fight as if I were shadowboxing. 27† No, I drive my body and train it, for fear that, after having preached to others, I myself should be disqualified.

CHAPTER 10

***Warning against Overconfidence.*†** 1* I do not want you to be unaware, brothers, that our ancestors were all under the cloud and all passed through the sea, 2* and all of them were baptized into Moses in the cloud and in the sea. 3 All ate the same spiritual food, 4*† and all drank the same spiritual drink, for they drank from a spiritual rock that followed them, and the rock was the Christ. 5* Yet God was not pleased with most of them, for they were struck down in the desert.

6*† These things happened as examples for us, so that we might not desire evil things, as they did. 7* And do not become idolaters, as some of them did, as it is written, "The people sat down to eat and drink, and rose up to revel." 8* Let us not indulge in immorality as some of them did, and twenty-three thousand fell within a single day. 9*† Let us not test Christ as some of them did, and suffered death by serpents. 10* Do not grumble as some of them did, and suffered death by the destroyer. 11† These things happened to them as an example, and they have been written down as a warning to us, upon whom the end of the ages has come. 12† Therefore, whoever thinks he is standing secure should take care not to fall. 13* No trial has come to you but what is human. God is faithful and will not let you be tried beyond your strength; but with the trial he will also provide a way out, so that you may be able to bear it.

***Warning against Idolatry.*†** 14* Therefore, my beloved, avoid idolatry. 15 I am speaking as to sensible people; judge for yourselves what I am saying. 16* The cup of blessing that we bless, is it not a participation in the blood of Christ? The bread that we

*

19: Mt 20, 26-27.
22: 10, 33; Rom 15, 1; 2 Cor 11, 29.
24: Heb 12, 1.
25: 2 Tm 2, 5 / 2 Tm 4, 7-8; Jas 1, 12; 1 Pt 5, 4.
10, 1: Ex 13, 21-22; 14, 19-20 / Ex 14, 21-22.26-30.
2: Rom 6, 3; Gal 3, 27 / Ex 16, 4-35.
4: Ex 17, 1-7; Nm 20, 7-11; Dt 8, 15.
5: Nm 14, 28-38; Jude 5.
6: Nm 11, 4.34.
7: Ex 32, 6.
8: Nm 25, 1-9.
9: Nm 21, 5-9.
10: Nm 14, 2-37; 16, 1-35.
13: Mt 6, 13; Jas 1, 13-14 / 1, 9.
14: 1 Jn 5, 21.
16: Mt 26, 26-29; Acts 2, 42.

†

9, 19-23: In a rhetorically balanced series of statements Paul expands and generalizes the picture of his behavior and explores the paradox of apostolic freedom. It is not essentially freedom *from* restraint but freedom *for* service—a possibility of constructive activity.

9, 24-27: A series of miniparables from sports, appealing to readers familiar with Greek gymnasia and the nearby Isthmian games.

9, 27: *For fear that . . . I myself should be disqualified:* a final paradoxical turn to the argument: what appears at first a free, spontaneous renunciation of rights (12-18) seems subsequently to be required for fulfillment of Paul's stewardship (to preach effectively he must reach his hearers wherever they are, 19-22), and finally is seen to be necessary for his own salvation (23-27). Mention of the possibility of disqualification provides a transition to ch 10.

10, 1-5: Paul embarks unexpectedly upon a panoramic survey of the events of the Exodus period. The privileges of Israel in the wilderness are described in terms that apply strictly only to the realities of the new covenant ("baptism," "spiritual food and drink"); interpreted in this way they point forward to the Christian experience (1-4). But those privileges did not guarantee God's permanent pleasure (5).

10, 4: *A spiritual rock that followed them:* the Torah speaks only about a rock from which water issued, but rabbinic legend amplified this into a spring that followed the Israelites throughout their migration. Paul uses this legend as a literary type: he makes the rock itself accompany the Israelites, and he gives it a spiritual sense. *The rock was the Christ:* in the Old Testament, Yahweh is the Rock of his people (cf Dt 32, Moses' song to Yahweh the Rock). Paul now applies this image to the Christ, the source of the living water, the true Rock that accompanied Israel, guiding their experiences in the desert.

10, 6-13: This section explicitates the typological value of these Old Testament events: the desert experiences of the Israelites are examples, meant as warnings, to deter us from similar sins (idolatry, immorality, etc.) and from a similar fate.

10, 9: *Christ:* to avoid Paul's concept of Christ present in the wilderness events, some manuscripts read "the Lord."

10, 11: *Upon whom the end of the ages has come:* it is our period in time toward which past ages have been moving and in which they arrive at their goal.

10, 12-13: *Take care not to fall:* the point of the whole comparison with Israel is to caution against overconfidence, a sense of complete security (12). This warning is immediately balanced by a reassurance, based, however, on God (13).

10, 14-22: The warning against idolatry from v 7 is now repeated (14) and explained in terms of the effect of sacrifices: all sacrifices, Christian (16-17), Jewish (18), or pagan (20), establish communion. But communion with Christ is exclusive, incompatible with any other such communion (21). Compare the line of reasoning at 6, 15.

break, is it not a participation in the body of Christ? [17]* Because the loaf of bread is one, we, though many, are one body, for we all partake of the one loaf.

[18]* Look at Israel according to the flesh; are not those who eat the sacrifices participants in the altar? [19] So what am I saying? That meat sacrificed to idols is anything? Or that an idol is anything? [20]*† No, I mean that what they sacrifice, [they sacrifice] to demons, not to God, and I do not want you to become participants with demons. [21]* You cannot drink the cup of the Lord and also the cup of demons. You cannot partake of the table of the Lord and of the table of demons. [22]* Or are we provoking the Lord to jealous anger? Are we stronger than he?

***Seek the Good of Others.*†** [23]*† "Everything is lawful," but not everything is beneficial. "Everything is lawful," but not everything builds up. [24]* No one should seek his own advantage, but that of his neighbor. [25]† Eat anything sold in the market, without raising questions on grounds of conscience, [26]* for "the earth and its fullness are the Lord's." [27] If an unbeliever invites you and you want to go, eat whatever is placed before you, without raising questions on grounds of conscience. [28] But if someone says to you, "This was offered in sacrifice," do not eat it on account of the one who called attention to it and on account of conscience; [29] I mean not your own conscience, but the other's. For why should my freedom be determined by someone else's conscience? [30]* If I partake thankfully, why am I reviled for that over which I give thanks?

[31] So whether you eat or drink, or whatever you do, do everything for the glory of God. [32]† Avoid giving offense, whether to Jews or Greeks or the church of God, [33]* just as I try to please everyone in every way, not seeking my own benefit but that of the many, that they may be saved.

CHAPTER 11

[1]* Be imitators of me, as I am of Christ.

IV: PROBLEMS IN LITURGICAL ASSEMBLIES†

[2]* I praise you because you remember me in everything and hold fast to the traditions, just as I handed them on to you.

A. Women's Headdresses†

Man and Woman. [3]*† But I want you to know that Christ is the head of every man, and a husband the head of his wife, and God the head of Christ. [4]† Any man who prays or prophesies

*

17: Rom 12, 5; Eph 4, 4.
18: Lv 7, 6.
20: Dt 32, 17.
21: 2 Cor 6, 14-18.
22: Dt 32, 21 / Eccl 6, 10.
23: 6, 12.
24: Rom 15, 2; Phil 2, 4.21.
26: Pss 24, 1; 50, 12.
30: Rom 14, 6; 1 Tm 4, 3-4.
33: 9, 22; Rom 15, 2.
11, 1: 4, 16; Phil 3, 17.
2: 15, 3; 2 Thes 2, 15.
3: Eph 5, 23.

†

10, 20: *To demons:* although Jews denied divinity to pagan gods, they often believed that there was some nondivine reality behind the idols, such as the dead, or angels, or demons. The explanation Paul offers in v 20 is drawn from Dt 32, 7: the power behind the idols, with which the pagans commune, consists of demonic powers hostile to God.

10, 23—11, 1: By way of peroration Paul returns to the opening situation (ch 8) and draws conclusions based on the intervening considerations (chs 9-10).

10, 23-24: He repeats in the context of this new problem the slogans of liberty from 6, 12, with similar qualifications. Liberty is not merely an individual perfection, nor an end in itself, but is to be used for the common good. The language of v 24 recalls the descriptions of Jesus' self-emptying in Phil 2.

10, 25-30: A summary of specific situations in which the eating of meat sacrificed to idols could present problems of conscience. Three cases are considered. In the first (the marketplace, 25-26) and the second (at table, 27), there is no need to be concerned with whether food has passed through a pagan sacrifice or not, for the principle of 8, 4-6 still stands, and the whole creation belongs to the one God. But in the third case (28), the situation changes if someone present explicitly raises the question of the sacrificial origin of the food; eating in such circumstances may be subject to various interpretations, some of which could be harmful to individuals. Paul is at pains to insist that the enlightened Christian conscience need not change its judgment about the neutrality, even the goodness, of the food in itself (29-30); yet the total situation is altered to the extent that others are potentially endangered, and this calls for a different response, for the sake of others.

10, 32—11, 1: In summary, the general rule of mutually responsible use of their Christian freedom is enjoined first negatively (32), then positively, as exemplified in Paul (33), and finally grounded in Christ, the pattern for Paul's behavior and theirs (11, 1; cf Rom 15, 1-3).

11, 2—14, 40: This section of the letter is devoted to regulation of conduct at the liturgy. The problems Paul handles have to do with the dress of women in the assembly (11, 3-16), improprieties in the celebration of community meals (11, 17-34), and the use of charisms or spiritual gifts (12, 1—14, 40). The statement in 11, 2 introduces all of these discussions, but applies more appropriately to the second (cf the mention of praise in 11, 17 and of tradition in 11, 23).

11, 3-16: Women have been participating in worship at Corinth without the head-covering normal in Greek society of the period. Paul's stated goal is to bring them back into conformity with contemporary practice and propriety. In his desire to convince, he reaches for arguments from a variety of sources, though he has space to develop them only sketchily and is perhaps aware that they differ greatly in persuasiveness.

11, 3: *A husband the head of his wife:* the specific problem suggests to Paul the model of the head as a device for clarifying relations within a hierarchical structure. The model is similar to that developed later in greater detail and nuance in Eph 5, 21-33. It is a hybrid model, for it grafts onto a strictly theological scale of existence (cf 3, 21-23) the hierarchy of sociosexual relations prevalent in the ancient world: men, dominant, reflect the active function of Christ in relation to his church; women, submissive, reflect the passive role of the church with respect to its savior. This gives us the functional scale: God, Christ, man, woman.

11, 4-6: From man's direct relation to Christ, Paul infers that his head should not be covered. But woman, related not directly to Christ on the scale but to her husband, requires a covering as a sign of that relationship. *Shameful . . . to have her hair cut off:* certain less honored classes in society, such as lesbians and prostitutes, are thought to have worn their hair close-cropped.

with his head covered brings shame upon his head. 5 But any woman who prays or prophesies with her head unveiled brings shame upon her head, for it is one and the same thing as if she had had her head shaved. 6 For if a woman does not have her head veiled, she may as well have her hair cut off. But if it is shameful for a woman to have her hair cut off or her head shaved, then she should wear a veil.

7*† A man, on the other hand, should not cover his head, because he is the image and glory of God, but woman is the glory of man. 8* For man did not come from woman, but woman from man; 9* nor was man created for woman, but woman for man; 10† for this reason a woman should have a sign of authority on her head, because of the angels. 11*† Woman is not independent of man or man of woman in the Lord. 12* For just as woman came from man, so man is born of woman; but all things are from God.

13† Judge for yourselves: is it proper for a woman to pray to God with her head unveiled? 14 Does not nature itself teach you that if a man wears his hair long it is a disgrace to him, 15 whereas if a woman has long hair it is her glory, because long hair has been given [her] for a covering? 16 But if anyone is inclined to be argumentative, we do not have such a custom, nor do the churches of God.

B. The Lord's Supper†

An Abuse at Corinth. 17 In giving this instruction, I do not praise the fact that your meetings are doing more harm than good. 18* First of all, I hear that when you meet as a church there are divisions among you, and to a degree I believe it; 19† there have to be factions among you in order that [also] those who are approved among you may become known. 20 When you meet in one place, then, it is not to eat the Lord's supper, 21 for in eating, each one goes ahead with his own supper, and one goes hungry while another gets drunk. 22* Do you not have houses in which you can eat and drink? Or do you show contempt for the church of God and make those who have nothing feel ashamed? What can I say to you? Shall I praise you? In this matter I do not praise you.

Tradition of the Institution.† 23* For I received from the Lord what I also handed on to you, that the Lord Jesus, on the night he was handed over, took bread, 24 and, after he had given thanks, broke it and said, "This is my body that is for you. Do this in remembrance of me." 25* In the same way also the cup, after supper, saying, "This cup is the new covenant in my blood. Do this, as often as you drink it, in remembrance of me." 26 For as often as you eat this bread and drink the cup, you proclaim the death of the Lord until he comes.

27† Therefore whoever eats the bread or drinks the cup of the Lord unworthily will have to answer for the body and blood of the Lord. 28† A person should

---

*

7: Gn 1, 26-27; 5, 1.
8: Gn 2, 21-23.
9: Gn 2, 18.
11: Gal 3, 27-28.
12: 8, 6; Rom 11, 36.
18: 1, 10-12; Gal 5, 20.
22: Jas 2, 1-7.
23: 2; 15, 3 / 10, 16-17; Mt 26, 26-29; Mk 14, 22-25; Lk 22, 14-20.
25: Ex 24, 8; 2 Cor 3, 6; Heb 8, 6-13.

---

†

11, 7-9: The hierarchy of v 3 is now expressed in other metaphors: the image (*eikōn*) and the reflected glory (*doxa*). Paul is alluding basically to the text of Gn 1, 27, in which mankind as a whole, the male-female couple, is created in God's image and given the command to multiply and together dominate the lower creation. But Gn 1, 24 is interpreted here in the light of the second creation narrative in Gn 2, in which each of the sexes is created separately (first the man and then the woman *from* man and *for* him, to be his helpmate, Gn 2, 20-23), and under the influence of the story of the fall, as a result of which the husband rules over the woman (Gn 3, 16). This interpretation splits the single image of God into two, at different degrees of closeness.

11, 10: *A sign of authority:* "authority" (*exousia*) may possibly be due to mistranslation of an Aramaic word for "veil"; in any case, the connection with v 9 indicates that the covering is a sign of woman's subordination. *Because of the angels:* a surprising additional reason, which the context does not clarify. Presumably the reference is to cosmic powers who might inflict harm on women or whose function is to watch over women or the cult.

11, 11-12: These parenthetical remarks relativize the argument from Gn 2-3. *In the Lord:* in the Christian economy the relation between the sexes is characterized by a mutual dependence, which is not further specified. And even in the natural order conditions have changed: the mode of origin described in Gn 2 has been reversed (12a). But the ultimately significant fact is the origin that all things have in common (12b).

11, 13-16: The argument for conformity to common church practice is summed up and pressed home. Verses 14-15 contain a final appeal to the sense of propriety that contemporary Greek society would consider "natural" (cf 5-6).

11, 17-34: Paul turns to another abuse connected with the liturgy, and a more serious one, for it involves neglect of basic Christian tradition concerning the meaning of the Lord's Supper. Paul recalls that tradition for them and reminds them of its implications.

11, 19: *That . . . those who are approved among you may become known:* Paul situates their divisions within the context of the eschatological separation of the authentic from the inauthentic and the final revelation of the difference. The notion of authenticity-testing recurs in the injunction to self-examination in view of present and future judgment (28-32).

11, 23-25: This is the earliest written account of the institution of the Lord's Supper in the New Testament. The narrative emphasizes Jesus' action of self-giving (expressed in the words over the bread and the cup) and his double command to repeat his own action.

11, 27: It follows that the only proper way to celebrate the Eucharist is one that corresponds to Jesus' intention, which fits with the meaning of his command to reproduce his action in the proper spirit. If the Corinthians eat and drink unworthily, i.e., without having grasped and internalized the meaning of his death for them, they *will have to answer for the body and blood,* i.e., will be guilty of a sin against the Lord himself (cf 8, 12).

11, 28: *Examine himself:* the Greek word is similar to that for "approved" in v 19, which means "having been tested and found true." The self-testing required for proper eating involves *discerning the body* (29), which, from the context, must mean understanding the sense of Jesus' death (26), perceiving the imperative to unity that follows from the fact that Jesus gives himself to all and requires us to repeat his sacrifice in the same spirit (18-25).

examine himself, and so eat the bread and drink the cup. 29† For anyone who eats and drinks without discerning the body, eats and drinks judgment on himself. 30 That is why many among you are ill and infirm, and a considerable number are dying. 31 If we discerned ourselves, we would not be under judgment; 32* but since we are judged by [the] Lord, we are being disciplined so that we may not be condemned along with the world.

33 Therefore, my brothers, when you come together to eat, wait for one another. 34 If anyone is hungry, he should eat at home, so that your meetings may not result in judgment. The other matters I shall set in order when I come.

C. Spiritual Gifts†

CHAPTER 12

Unity and Variety. 1 Now in regard to spiritual gifts, brothers, I do not want you to be unaware. 2*† You know how, when you were pagans, you were constantly attracted and led away to mute idols. 3* Therefore, I tell you that nobody speaking by the spirit of God says, "Jesus be accursed." And no one can say, "Jesus is Lord," except by the holy Spirit.

4*† There are different kinds of spiritual gifts but the same Spirit; 5 there are different forms of service but the same Lord; 6 there are different workings but the same God who produces all of them in everyone. 7 To each individual the manifestation of the Spirit is given for some benefit. 8* To one is given through the Spirit the expression of wisdom; to another the expression of knowledge according to the same Spirit; 9 to another faith by the same Spirit; to another gifts of healing by the one Spirit; 10* to another mighty deeds; to another prophecy; to another discernment of spirits; to another varieties of tongues; to another interpretation of tongues. 11* But one and the same Spirit produces all of these, distributing them individually to each person as he wishes.

One Body, Many Parts.† 12* As a body is one though it has many parts, and all the parts of the body, though many, are one body, so also Christ. 13* For in one Spirit we were all baptized into one body, whether Jews or Greeks, slaves or free persons, and we were all given to drink of one Spirit.

14 Now the body is not a single part, but many. 15 If a foot should say, "Because I am not a hand I do not belong to the body," it does not for this reason belong any less to the body. 16 Or if an ear should say, "Because I am not an eye I do not belong to the body," it does not for this reason belong any less to the body. 17 If the whole body were an eye, where would the hearing be? If the whole body were hearing, where would the sense of smell be? 18 But as it is, God placed the parts, each one of them, in the body as he intended. 19 If they were all one part, where would the body be? 20 But as it is, there are many parts, yet one body. 21 The eye cannot say to the hand, "I do not need you," nor again the head to the feet, "I do not need you." 22 Indeed, the parts of the body that seem to be weaker are all the more necessary, 23 and those parts of the body that we consider less honorable we surround with greater honor, and our less presentable parts are treated with greater propriety, 24 whereas our more presentable parts do not need this. But God has so constructed the body as to give greater honor to a part that is without it, 25 so that there may be no division in the body, but that the parts may have the same concern for one another. 26 If [one] part suffers, all the parts suffer with it; if one part is honored, all the parts share its joy.

*

32: Dt 8, 5; Heb 12, 5-11.
12, 2: Eph 2, 11-18.
3: Rom 10, 9; 1 Jn 4, 2-3.
4: Rom 12, 6; Eph 4, 7.11.
8: 2, 6-13.
10: 14, 5.26.39; Acts 2, 4.
11: 7, 7; Eph 4, 7.
12: 10, 17; Rom 12, 4-5; Eph 2, 16; Col 3, 15.
13: Gal 3, 28; Eph 2, 13-18; Col 3, 11 / Jn 7, 37-39.

†

11, 29-32: *Judgment:* there is a series of wordplays in these verses that would be awkward to translate literally into English; it includes all the references to judgment (*krima,* 29.34; *krinō,* 31.32), discernment (*diakrinō,* 29.31), and condemnation (*katakrinō,* 32). The judgment is concretely described as the illness, infirmity, and death that have visited the community. These are signs that the power of Jesus' death is not yet completely recognized and experienced. Yet even the judgment incurred is an expression of God's concern; it is a medicinal measure meant to rescue us from condemnation with God's enemies.

12, 1—14, 40: Ecstatic and charismatic activity were common in early Christian experience, as they were in other ancient religions. But the Corinthians seem to have developed a disproportionate esteem for certain phenomena, especially tongues, to the detriment of order in the liturgy. Paul's response to this development provides us with the fullest exposition we have of his theology of the charisms.

12, 2-3: There is an experience of the Spirit and an understanding of ecstatic phenomena that are specifically Christian and that differ, despite apparent similarities, from those of the pagans. It is necessary to discern which spirit is leading one; ecstatic phenomena must be judged by their effect (2). Verse 3 illustrates this by an example: power to confess Jesus as Lord can come only from the Spirit, and it is inconceivable that the Spirit would move anyone to curse the Lord.

12, 4-6: There are some features common to all charisms, despite their diversity: all are *gifts* (*charismata*), grace from outside ourselves; all are *forms of service* (*diakoniai*), an expression of their purpose and effect; and all are *workings* (*energēmata*), in which God is at work. Paul associates each of these aspects with what later theology will call one of the persons of the Trinity, an early example of "appropriation."

12, 12-26: The image of *a body* is introduced to explain Christ's relationship with believers (12). Verse 13 applies this model to the church: by baptism all, despite diversity of ethnic or social origins, are integrated into one organism. Verses 14-26 then develop the need for diversity of function among the parts of a body without threat to its unity.

Application to Christ. † 27* Now you
are Christ's body, and individually
parts of it. 28*† Some people God has
designated in the church to be, first,
apostles; second, prophets; third, teach-
ers; then, mighty deeds; then, gifts of
healing, assistance, administration,
and varieties of tongues. 29 Are all apos-
tles? Are all prophets? Are all teachers?
Do all work mighty deeds? 30 Do all
have gifts of healing? Do all speak
in tongues? Do all interpret? 31 Strive
eagerly for the greatest spiritual
gifts.
The Way of Love. But I shall show
you a still more excellent way.

CHAPTER 13†

1*† If I speak in human and angelic
tongues but do not have love, I am a
resounding gong or a clashing cymbal.
2* And if I have the gift of prophecy and
comprehend all mysteries and all
knowledge; if I have all faith so as to
move mountains but do not have love,
I am nothing. 3* If I give away every-
thing I own, and if I hand my body over
so that I may boast but do not have love,
I gain nothing.
4*† Love is patient, love is kind. It
is not jealous, [love] is not pompous,
it is not inflated, 5* it is not rude, it
does not seek its own interests, it is
not quick-tempered, it does not brood
over injury, 6 it does not rejoice over
wrongdoing but rejoices with the truth.
7* It bears all things, believes all
things, hopes all things, endures all
things.
8† Love never fails. If there are proph-
ecies, they will be brought to nothing;
if tongues, they will cease; if knowledge,
it will be brought to nothing. 9 For we
know partially and we prophesy par-
tially, 10 but when the perfect comes, the
partial will pass away. 11 When I was
a child, I used to talk as a child, think as
a child, reason as a child; when I be-
came a man, I put aside childish things.
12* At present we see indistinctly, as in
a mirror, but then face to face. At pres-
ent I know partially; then I shall know
fully, as I am fully known. 13*† So faith,
hope, love remain, these three; but the
greatest of these is love.

CHAPTER 14

Prophecy Greater than Tongues. †
1* Pursue love, but strive eagerly for the
spiritual gifts, above all that you may
prophesy. 2† For one who speaks in a
tongue does not speak to human beings
but to God, for no one listens; he utters
mysteries in spirit. 3*† On the other
hand, one who prophesies does speak
to human beings, for their building up,

*

27: Rom 12, 5-8; Eph 1, 23; 4, 12; 5, 30; Col 1, 18.24.
28: Eph 2, 20; 3, 5; 4, 11.
13, 1: 8, 1; 16, 14; Rom 12, 9-10; 13, 8-10.
2: 4, 1; 14, 2 / 1, 5; 8, 1-3; 12, 8 / Mt 17, 20; 21, 21; Col 2, 3.
3: Mt 6, 2.
4: Eph 4, 2 / 4, 6.18; 5, 2; 8, 1.
5: 10, 24.33; Phil 2, 4.21; 1 Thes 5, 15.
7: Prv 10, 12; 1 Pt 4, 8.
12: 2 Cor 5, 7; Heb 11, 1 / 2 Tm 2, 19; 1 Jn 3, 2.
13: Col 1, 4; 1 Thes 1, 3; 5, 8.
14, 1: 5.12.39.
3: 4-5.12.17.26; 3, 9; 8, 1.10; 10, 23.

†

12, 27-30: Paul now applies the image again to the church as a whole and its members (27). The lists in vv 28-30 spell out the parallelism by specifying the diversity of functions found in the church (cf Rom 12, 6-8; Eph 4, 11).

12, 28: *First, apostles:* apostleship was not mentioned in vv 8-10, nor is it at issue in these chapters, but Paul gives it pride of place in his listing. It is not just one gift among others but a prior and fuller gift that includes the others. They are all demonstrated in Paul's apostolate, but he may have developed his theology of charisms by reflecting first of all on his own grace of apostleship (cf 3, 5—4, 14; 9, 1-27; 2 Cor 2, 14—6, 13; 10, 1—13, 30, esp. 11, 23 and 12, 12).

13, 1-13: This chapter involves a shift of perspective and a new point. All or part of the material may once have been an independent piece in the style of Hellenistic eulogies of virtues, but it is now integrated, by editing, into the context of chs 12-14 (cf the reference to tongues and prophecy) and into the letter as a whole (cf the references to knowledge and to behavior). The function of ch 13 within the discussion of spiritual gifts is to relativize all the charisms by contrasting them with the more basic, pervasive, and enduring value that gives them their purpose and their effectiveness. The rhetoric of this chapter is striking.

13, 1-3: An inventory of gifts, arranged in careful gradation: neither tongues (on the lowest rung), nor prophecy, knowledge, or faith, nor even self-sacrifice has value unless informed by love.

13, 4-7: This paragraph is developed by personification and enumeration, defining love by what it does or does not do. The Greek contains fifteen verbs; it is natural to translate many of them by adjectives in English.

13, 8-13: The final paragraph announces its topic, *Love never fails* (8), then develops the permanence of love in contrast to the charisms (9-12), and finally asserts love's superiority even over the other "theological virtues" (13).

13, 13: In speaking of love, Paul is led by spontaneous association to mention faith and hope as well. They are already a well-known triad (cf 1 Thes 1, 3), three interrelated (cf 7) features of Christian life, more fundamental than any particular charism. *The greatest . . . is love:* love is operative even within the other members of the triad (7), so that it has a certain primacy among them. Or, if the perspective is temporal, love will remain (cf "never fails," 8) even when faith has yielded to sight and hope to possession.

14, 1-5: Verse 1b returns to the thought of 12, 31a and reveals Paul's primary concern. The series of contrasts in vv 2-5 discloses the problem at Corinth: a disproportionate interest in tongues, with a corresponding failure to appreciate the worth of prophecy. Paul attempts to clarify the relative values of those gifts by indicating the kind of communication achieved in each and the kind of effect each produces.

14, 2-3a: They involve two kinds of communication: tongues, private speech toward God in inarticulate terms that need interpretation to be intelligible to others (see 27-28); prophecy, communication with others in the community.

14, 3b-5: They produce two kinds of effect. One who speaks in tongues *builds himself up;* it is a matter of individual experience and personal perfection, which inevitably recalls Paul's previous remarks about being inflated, seeking one's own good, pleasing oneself. But a prophet *builds up the church:* the theme of "building up" or "edifying" others, the main theme of the letter, comes to clearest expression in this chapter (3.4.5.12.17). It has been anticipated at 8, 1 and 10, 23, and by the related concept of "the beneficial" in 6, 12; 10, 23; 12, 7; etc.

encouragement, and solace. 4 Whoever
speaks in a tongue builds himself up,
but whoever prophesies builds up the
church. 5 Now I should like all of you
to speak in tongues, but even more to
prophesy. One who prophesies is
greater than one who speaks in tongues,
unless he interprets, so that the church
may be built up.
6† Now, brothers, if I should come to
you speaking in tongues, what good will
I do you if I do not speak to you by way
of revelation, or knowledge, or proph-
ecy, or instruction? 7 Likewise, if inani-
mate things that produce sound, such
as flute or harp, do not give out the tones
distinctly, how will what is being played
on flute or harp be recognized? 8 And
if the bugle gives an indistinct sound,
who will get ready for battle? 9 Sim-
ilarly, if you, because of speaking in
tongues, do not utter intelligible speech,
how will anyone know what is being
said? For you will be talking to the air.
10 It happens that there are many differ-
ent languages in the world, and none
is meaningless; 11 but if I do not know
the meaning of a language, I shall be a
foreigner to one who speaks it, and one
who speaks it a foreigner to me. 12 So
with yourselves: since you strive ea-
gerly for spirits, seek to have an abun-
dance of them for building up the
church.

Need for Interpretation.†
13 Therefore, one who speaks in a tongue
should pray to be able to interpret.
14† [For] if I pray in a tongue, my spirit
is at prayer but my mind is unproduc-
tive. 15* So what is to be done? I will pray
with the spirit, but I will also pray with
the mind. I will sing praise with the
spirit, but I will also sing praise with
the mind. 16 Otherwise, if you pronounce
a blessing [with] the spirit, how shall
one who holds the place of the unin-
structed say the "Amen" to your
thanksgiving, since he does not know
what you are saying? 17 For you may
be giving thanks very well, but the other
is not built up. 18 I give thanks to
God that I speak in tongues more
than any of you, 19 but in the church
I would rather speak five words
with my mind, so as to instruct others
also, than ten thousand words in a
tongue.

Functions of These Gifts.†
20* Brothers, stop being childish in your
thinking. In respect to evil be like in-
fants, but in your thinking be mature.
21* It is written in the law:

"By people speaking strange
tongues
and by the lips of foreigners
I will speak to this people,
and even so they will not listen to
me,
says the Lord." 22 Thus, tongues are a
sign not for those who believe but for
unbelievers, whereas prophecy is not
for unbelievers but for those who be-
lieve.
23*† So if the whole church meets in
one place and everyone speaks in
tongues, and then uninstructed people
or unbelievers should come in, will they
not say that you are out of your minds?
24 But if everyone is prophesying, and
an unbeliever or uninstructed person
should come in, he will be convinced by
everyone and judged by everyone,
25* and the secrets of his heart will be
disclosed, and so he will fall down and
worship God, declaring, "God is really
in your midst."

Rules of Order.† 26* So what is to be

---

*
15: Eph 5, 19; Col 3, 16.
20: Mt 10, 16; Rom 16, 19; Eph 4, 14.
21: Is 28, 11-12; Dt 28, 49.
23: Acts 2, 6.13.
25: 4, 5 / Is 45, 14; Zec 8, 23.
26: Eph 4, 12.

---

†
14, 6-12: Sound, in order to be useful, must be intelligible. This principle is illustrated by a series of analogies from music (7-8) and from ordinary human speech (10-11); it is applied to the case at hand in v 9 and v 12.

14, 13-19: The charism of interpretation lifts tongues to the level of intelligibility, enabling them to produce the same effect as prophecy (cf 5.26-28).

14, 14-15: *My spirit:* Paul emphasizes the exclusively ecstatic, nonrational quality of tongues. The tongues at Pentecost are also described as an ecstatic experience (Acts 2, 4.12-13), though Luke superimposes further interpretations of his own. *My mind:* the ecstatic element, dominant in earliest Old Testament prophecy as depicted in 1 Sam 10, 5-13; 19, 20-24, seems entirely absent from Paul's notion of prophecy and completely relegated to tongues. He emphasizes the role of reason when he specifies instruction as a function of prophecy (6.19.31). But he does not exclude intuition and emotion; cf references to encouragement and consolation (3.31) and the scene describing the ideal exercise of prophecy (24-25).

14, 20-22: The Corinthians pride themselves on tongues as a sign of God's favor, a means of direct communication with him (2.28). To challenge them to a more mature appraisal, Paul draws from scripture a less flattering explanation of what speaking in tongues may signify. Isaiah threatened the people that if they failed to listen to their prophets, the Lord would speak to them (in punishment) through the lips of Assyrian conquerors (Is 28, 11-12). Paul compresses Isaiah's text and makes God address his people directly. Equating tongues with foreign languages (cf 10-11), Paul concludes from Isaiah that *tongues are a sign not for those who believe,* i.e., not a mark of God's pleasure for those who listen to him but a mark of his displeasure with those in the community who are faithless, who have not heeded the message that he has sent through the prophets.

14, 23-25: Paul projects the possible missionary effect of two hypothetical liturgical experiences, one consisting wholly of tongues, the other entirely of prophecy. *Uninstructed* (*idiōtai*): the term may simply mean people who do not speak or understand tongues, as in v 16, where it seems to designate Christians. But coupled with the term "unbelievers" it may be another way of designating those who have not been initiated into the community of faith; some believe it denotes a special class of non-Christians who are close to the community, such as catechumens. *Unbelievers* (*apistoi*): he has shifted from the inner-community perspective of v 22; the term here designates non-Christians (cf 6, 6; 7, 15; 10, 27).

14, 26-33a: Paul concludes with specific directives regarding exercise of the gifts in their assemblies. Verse 26 enunciates the basic criterion in the use of any gift: it must contribute to "building up."

done, brothers? When you assemble,
one has a psalm, another an instruction,
a revelation, a tongue, or an interpreta-
tion. Everything should be done for
building up. 27 If anyone speaks in a
tongue, let it be two or at most three,
and each in turn, and one should inter-
pret. 28 But if there is no interpreter, the
person should keep silent in the church
and speak to himself and to God.
29 Two or three prophets should speak,
and the others discern. 30 But if a reve-
lation is given to another person sitting
there, the first one should be silent.
31 For you can all prophesy one by one,
so that all may learn and all be encour-
aged. 32 Indeed, the spirits of prophets
are under the prophets' control, 33 since
he is not the God of disorder but of
peace.
†As in all the churches of the holy
ones, 34* women should keep silent in
the churches, for they are not allowed
to speak, but should be subordinate, as
even the law says. 35 But if they want
to learn anything, they should ask their
husbands at home. For it is improper
for a woman to speak in the church.
36 Did the word of God go forth from
you? Or has it come to you alone?
37 If anyone thinks that he is a prophet
or a spiritual person, he should recog-
nize that what I am writing to you is a
commandment of the Lord. 38 If anyone
does not acknowledge this, he is not ac-
knowledged. 39 So, [my] brothers, strive
eagerly to prophesy, and do not for-
bid speaking in tongues, 40 but every-
thing must be done properly and in
order.

V: THE RESURRECTION

A. The Resurrection of Christ

CHAPTER 15†

The Gospel Teaching.† 1 Now I am
reminding you, brothers, of the gospel
I preached to you, which you indeed re-
ceived and in which you also stand.
2 Through it you are also being saved,
if you hold fast to the word I preached
to you, unless you believed in vain.
3*† For I handed on to you as of first
importance what I also received: that
Christ died for our sins in accordance
with the scriptures; 4* that he was bur-
ied; that he was raised on the third day
in accordance with the scriptures;
5* that he appeared to Kephas, then to
the Twelve. 6 After that, he appeared to
more than five hundred brothers at
once, most of whom are still living,
though some have fallen asleep. 7 After
that he appeared to James, then to all
the apostles. 8* Last of all, as to one born
abnormally, he appeared to me. 9*† For
I am the least of the apostles, not fit to
be called an apostle, because I perse-
cuted the church of God. 10 But by the
grace of God I am what I am, and his
grace to me has not been ineffective.
Indeed, I have toiled harder than all of
them; not I, however, but the grace of
God [that is] with me. 11 Therefore,
whether it be I or they, so we preach
and so you believed.

*

34: 1 Tm 2, 11-15; 1 Pt 3, 1.
15, 3: 11, 23 / 1 Pt 2, 24; 3, 18 / Is 53, 4-12.
4: Acts 2, 23-24 / Ps 16, 8-11; Hos 6, 1-2; Jon 2, 1.
5: Mk 16, 14; Mt 28, 16-17; Lk 24, 36; Jn 20, 19.
8: 9, 1; Acts 9, 3-6; Gal 1, 16.
9: Acts 8, 3; 9, 1-2; Gal 1, 23; Eph 3, 8; 1 Tm 1, 15.

†

14, 33b-36: Verse 33b may belong with what precedes, so that the new paragraph would begin only with v 34. Verses 34-35 change the subject. These two verses have the theme of submission in common with ch 11, despite differences in vocabulary, and a concern with what is or is not becoming; but it is difficult to harmonize the injunction to silence here with ch 11, which appears to take it for granted that women do pray and prophesy aloud in the assembly (cf 11, 5.13). Hence the verses are often considered an interpolation, reflecting the discipline of later churches; such an interpolation would have to have antedated our manuscripts, all of which contain them, though some transpose them to the very end of the chapter.

15, 1-58: Some consider this chapter an earlier Pauline composition inserted into the present letter. The problem that Paul treats is clear to a degree: some of the Corinthians are denying the resurrection of the dead (12), apparently because of their inability to imagine how any kind of bodily existence could be possible after death (35). It is plausibly supposed that their attitude stems from Greek anthropology, which looks with contempt upon matter and would be content with the survival of the soul, and perhaps also from an overrealized eschatology of gnostic coloration, such as that reflected in 2 Tm 2, 18, which considers the resurrection a purely spiritual experience already achieved in baptism and in the forgiveness of sins. Paul, on the other hand, will affirm both the essential corporeity of the resurrection and its futurity.

His response moves through three steps: a recall of the basic kerygma about Jesus' resurrection (1-11), an assertion of the logical inconsistencies involved in denial of the resurrection (12-34), and an attempt to perceive theologically what the properties of the resurrected body must be (35-58).

15, 1-11: Paul recalls the tradition (3-7), which he can presuppose as common ground and which provides a starting point for his argument. This is the fundamental content of all Christian preaching and belief (1-2.11).

15, 3-7: The language by which Paul expresses the essence of the "gospel" (1) is not his own but is drawn from older credal formulas. This credo highlights Jesus' death for our sins (confirmed by his burial) and Jesus' resurrection (confirmed by his appearances) and presents both of them as fulfillment of prophecy. *In accordance with the scriptures:* conformity of Jesus' passion with the scriptures is asserted in Mt 16, 1; Lk 24, 25-27.32.44-46. Application of some Old Testament texts (Pss 2, 7; 16, 8-11) to his resurrection is illustrated by Acts 2, 27-31; 13, 29-39; and Is 52, 13—53, 12 and Hos 6, 2 may also have been envisaged.

15, 9-11: A persecutor may have appeared disqualified (*ouk . . . hikanos*) from apostleship, but in fact God's grace has qualified him. Cf the remarks in 2 Cor about his qualifications (2, 16; 3, 5) and his greater labors (11, 23). These verses are parenthetical, but a nerve has been touched (the references to his abnormal birth and his activity as a persecutor may echo taunts from Paul's opponents), and he is instinctively moved to self-defense.

B. The Resurrection of the Dead

Results of Denial. † 12 But if Christ is
preached as raised from the dead, how
can some among you say there is no res-
urrection of the dead? 13* If there is no
resurrection of the dead, then neither
has Christ been raised. 14 And if Christ
has not been raised, then empty [too]
is our preaching; empty, too, your faith.
15* Then we are also false witnesses to
God, because we testified against God
that he raised Christ, whom he did not
raise if in fact the dead are not raised.
16 For if the dead are not raised, neither
has Christ been raised, 17† and if Christ
has not been raised, your faith is vain;
you are still in your sins. 18 Then those
who have fallen asleep in Christ have
perished. 19 If for this life only we have
hoped in Christ, we are the most pitiable
people of all.

Christ the Firstfruits. † 20*† But now
Christ has been raised from the dead,
the firstfruits of those who have fallen
asleep. 21† For since death came
through a human being, the resur-
rection of the dead came also through
a human being. 22* For just as in Adam
all die, so too in Christ shall all be
brought to life, 23* but each one in
proper order: Christ the firstfruits; then,
at his coming, those who belong to
Christ; 24*† then comes the end, when
he hands over the kingdom to his God
and Father, when he has destroyed ev-
ery sovereignty and every authority
and power. 25* For he must reign until
he has put all his enemies under his feet.
26*† The last enemy to be destroyed is
death, 27*† for "he subjected everything
under his feet." But when it says that
everything has been subjected, it is
clear that it excludes the one who sub-
jected everything to him. 28* When
everything is subjected to him, then
the Son himself will [also] be sub-
jected to the one who subjected every-
thing to him, so that God may be all
in all.

Practical Arguments. † 29† Otherwise,
what will people accomplish by having
themselves baptized for the dead? If the
dead are not raised at all, then why are
they having themselves baptized for
them?

30*† Moreover, why are we endanger-
ing ourselves all the time? 31* Every day
I face death; I swear it by the pride in
you [brothers] that I have in Christ Je-
sus our Lord. 32* If at Ephesus I fought
with beasts, so to speak, what benefit
was it to me? If the dead are not raised:

> "Let us eat and drink,
> for tomorrow we die."

33 Do not be led astray:

> "Bad company corrupts good morals."

34* Become sober as you ought and stop
sinning. For some have no knowledge
of God; I say this to your shame.

---

*

13: 1 Thes 4, 14.
15: Acts 5, 32.
20: Rom 8, 11; Col 1, 18; 1 Thes 4, 14.
22: Gn 3, 17-19; Rom 5, 12-19.
23: 1 Thes 4, 15-17.
24: Eph 1, 22.
25: Ps 110, 1.
26: Rom 6, 9; 2 Tm 1, 10; Rv 20, 14; 21, 4.
27: Ps 8, 7; Eph 1, 22; Phil 3, 21.
28: Eph 4, 6; Col 3, 11.
30: 2 Cor 4, 8-12; 11, 23-27.
31: Ps 44, 23; Rom 8, 36.
32: 4, 9; 2 Cor 4, 10-11 / Wis 2, 5-7; Is 22, 13.
34: Mt 22, 29; Mk 12, 24.

†

15, 12-19: Denial of the resurrection (12) involves logical inconsistencies. The basic one, stated twice (13.16), is that if there is no such thing as (bodily) resurrection, then it has not taken place even in Christ's case.

15, 17-18: The consequences for the Corinthians are grave: both forgiveness of sins and salvation are an illusion, despite their strong convictions about both. Unless Christ is risen, their faith does not save.

15, 20-28: After a triumphant assertion of the reality of Christ's resurrection (20a), Paul explains its positive implications and consequences. As a soteriological event of both human (20-23) and cosmic (24-28) dimensions, Jesus' resurrection logically and necessarily involves ours as well.

15, 20: *The firstfruits:* the portion of the harvest offered in thanksgiving to God implies the consecration of the entire harvest to come. Christ's resurrection is not an end in itself; its finality lies in the whole harvest, ourselves.

15, 21-22: Our human existence, both natural and supernatural, is corporate, involves solidarity. *In Adam . . . in Christ:* the Hebrew word *ʾādām* in Genesis is both a common noun for mankind and a proper noun for the first man. Paul here presents Adam as at least a literary type of Christ; the parallelism and contrast between them will be developed further in vv 45-49 and in Rom 5, 12-21.

15, 24-28: Paul's perspective expands to cosmic dimensions, as he describes the climax of history, *the end.* His viewpoint is still christological, as in vv 20-23. Verses 24 and 28 describe Christ's final relations to his enemies and his Father in language that is both royal and military; vv 25-28 insert a proof from scripture (Pss 110, 1; 8, 7) into this description. But the viewpoint is also theological, for God is the ultimate agent and end, and likewise soteriological, for we are the beneficiaries of all the action.

15, 26: *The last enemy . . . is death:* a parenthesis that specifies the final fulfillment of the two Old Testament texts just referred to, Ps 110, 1 and Ps 8, 7. Death is not just one cosmic power among many, but the ultimate effect of sin in the universe (cf 56; Rom 5, 12). Christ defeats death where it prevails, in our bodies. The destruction of the last enemy is concretely the "coming to life" (22) of "those who belong to Christ" (23).

15, 27b-28: *The one who subjected everything to him:* the Father is the ultimate agent in the drama, and the final end of the process, to whom the Son and everything else is ordered (24.28). *That God may be all in all:* his reign is a dynamic exercise of creative power, an outpouring of life and energy through the universe, with no further resistance. This is the supremely positive meaning of "subjection": that God may fully be God.

15, 29-34: Paul concludes his treatment of logical inconsistencies with a listing of miscellaneous Christian practices that would be meaningless if the resurrection were not a fact.

15, 29: *Baptized for the dead:* this practice is not further explained here, nor is it necessarily mentioned with approval, but Paul cites it as something in their experience that attests in one more way to belief in the resurrection.

15, 30-34: A life of sacrifice, such as Paul describes in 4, 9-13 and 2 Cor, would be pointless without the prospect of resurrection; a life of pleasure, such as that expressed in the Epicurean slogan of v 32, would be far more consistent. *I fought with beasts:* since Paul does not elsewhere mention a combat with beasts at Ephesus, he may be speaking figuratively about struggles with adversaries.

C. The Manner of the Resurrection†

35† But someone may say, "How are
the dead raised? With what kind of body
will they come back?"
The Resurrection Body.† 36* You
fool! What you sow is not brought to life
unless it dies. 37 And what you sow is
not the body that is to be but a bare ker-
nel of wheat, perhaps, or of some other
kind; 38* but God gives it a body as
he chooses, and to each of the seeds its
own body. 39† Not all flesh is the same,
but there is one kind for human be-
ings, another kind of flesh for ani-
mals, another kind of flesh for birds,
and another for fish. 40 There are both
heavenly bodies and earthly bodies,
but the brightness of the heavenly is
one kind and that of the earthly an-
other. 41 The brightness of the sun is
one kind, the brightness of the moon an-
other, and the brightness of the stars
another. For star differs from star in
brightness.
42† So also is the resurrection of the
dead. It is sown corruptible; it is raised
incorruptible. 43* It is sown dishonor-
able; it is raised glorious. It is sown
weak; it is raised powerful. 44 It is sown
a natural body; it is raised a spiritual
body. If there is a natural body, there
is also a spiritual one.
45*† So, too, it is written, "The first
man, Adam, became a living being," the
last Adam a life-giving spirit. 46 But the
spiritual was not first; rather the natural
and then the spiritual. 47 The first man
was from the earth, earthly; the sec-
ond man, from heaven. 48 As was the
earthly one, so also are the earthly,
and as is the heavenly one, so also are
the heavenly. 49*† Just as we have
borne the image of the earthly one,
we shall also bear the image of the
heavenly one.
The Resurrection Event.† 50*† This I
declare, brothers: flesh and blood can-
not inherit the kingdom of God, nor does
corruption inherit incorruption.
51*† Behold, I tell you a mystery. We
shall not all fall asleep, but we will all
be changed, 52* in an instant, in the
blink of an eye, at the last trumpet. For
the trumpet will sound, the dead will be
raised incorruptible, and we shall be
changed. 53* For that which is corrupt-
ible must clothe itself with incorrupt-
ibility, and that which is mortal must
clothe itself with immortality. 54*† And
when this which is corruptible clothes
itself with incorruptibility and this
which is mortal clothes itself with im-
mortality, then the word that is written
shall come about:

"Death is swallowed up in victory.
55* Where, O death, is your victory?
Where, O death, is your sting?"

*

36: Jn 12, 24.
38: Gn 1, 11.
43: Phil 3, 20-21; Col 3, 4.
45: Gn 2, 7 / Jn 5, 21-29; 2 Cor 3, 6.17.
49: Gn 5, 3 / Rom 8, 29; Phil 3, 21.
50: Jn 3, 3-6.
51: 1 Thes 4, 14-17.
52: Jl 2, 1; Zec 9, 14; Mt 24, 31; Rv 11, 15-18.
53: 2 Cor 5, 2-4.
54: Is 25, 8; 2 Cor 5, 4; 2 Tm 1, 10; Heb 2, 14-15.
55: Hos 13, 14.

†

15, 35-58: Paul imagines two objections that the Corinthians could raise: one concerning the manner of the resurrection (*how?*), the other pertaining to the qualities of the risen body (*what kind?*). These questions probably lie behind their denial of the resurrection (12), and seem to reflect the presumption that no kind of body other than the one we now possess would be possible. Paul deals with these objections in inverse order, in vv 36-49 and vv 50-58. His argument is fundamentally theological and its appeal is to the understanding.

15, 35-49: Paul approaches the question of the nature of the risen body (*what kind of body?*) by means of two analogies: the seed (36-44) and the first man, Adam (45-49).

15, 36-38: The analogy of the seed: there is a change of attributes from seed to plant; the old life-form must be lost for the new to emerge. By speaking about the seed as a *body* that dies and comes to life, Paul keeps the point of the analogy before the reader's mind.

15, 39-41: The expression "its own body" (38) leads to a development on the marvelous diversity evident in bodily life.

15, 42-44: The principles of qualitative difference before and after death (36-38) and of diversity on different levels of creation (39-41) are now applied to the human body. Before: a body animated by a lower, natural life-principle (*psychē*) and endowed with the properties of natural existence (corruptibility, lack of glory, weakness). After: a body animated by a higher life-principle (*pneuma;* cf 45) and endowed with other qualities (incorruptibility, glory, power, spirituality), which are properties of God himself.

15, 45: The analogy of *the first man, Adam,* is introduced by a citation from Gn 2, 7. Paul alters the text slightly, adding the adjective *first,* and translating the Hebrew *ʾādām* twice, so as to give it its value both as a common noun (*man*) and as a proper name (*Adam*). Verse 45b then specifies similarities and differences between the two Adams. *The last Adam,* Christ (cf 21-22) has become *a . . . spirit* (*pneuma*), a life-principle transcendent with respect to the natural soul (*psychē*) of the first Adam (on the terminology here, cf the note on 3, 1). Further, he is not just alive, but *life-giving,* a source of life for others.

15, 49: *We shall also bear the image:* although it has less manuscript support, this reading better fits the context's emphasis on futurity and the transforming action of God; on future transformation as conformity to the image of the Son, cf Rom 8, 29; Phil 3, 21. The majority reading, "let us bear the image," suggests that the image of the heavenly man is already present and exhorts us to conform to it.

15, 50-57: These verses, an answer to the first question of v 35, explain theologically how the change of properties from one image to another will take place: God has the power to transform, and he will exercise it.

15, 50-53: *Flesh and blood . . . corruption:* living persons and the corpses of the dead, respectively. In both cases, the gulf between creatures and God is too wide to be bridged unless God himself transforms us.

15, 51-52: *A mystery:* the last moment in God's plan is disclosed; cf the notes on 2, 1.7-10a. The final trumpet and the awakening of the dead are stock details of the apocalyptic scenario. *We shall not all fall asleep:* Paul expected that some of his contemporaries might still be alive at Christ's return; after the death of Paul and his whole generation, copyists altered this statement in various ways. *We will all be changed:* the statement extends to all Christians, for Paul is not directly speaking about anyone else. Whether they have died before the end or happen still to be alive, all must be transformed.

15, 54-55: *Death is swallowed up in victory:* scripture itself predicts death's overthrow. *O death:* in his prophetic vision Paul may be making Hosea's words his own, or imagining this cry of triumph on the lips of the risen church.

56*† The sting of death is sin, and the power of sin is the law. 57* But thanks be to God who gives us the victory through our Lord Jesus Christ.

58 Therefore, my beloved brothers, be firm, steadfast, always fully devoted to the work of the Lord, knowing that in the Lord your labor is not in vain.

VI: CONCLUSION

CHAPTER 16

***The Collection.*†** 1*† Now in regard to the collection for the holy ones, you also should do as I ordered the churches of Galatia. 2 On the first day of the week each of you should set aside and save whatever one can afford, so that collections will not be going on when I come. 3 And when I arrive, I shall send those whom you have approved with letters of recommendation to take your gracious gift to Jerusalem. 4† If it seems fitting that I should go also, they will go with me.

***Paul's Travel Plans.*†** 5* I shall come to you after I pass through Macedonia (for I am going to pass through Macedonia), 6 and perhaps I shall stay or even spend the winter with you, so that you may send me on my way wherever I may go. 7* For I do not wish to see you now just in passing, but I hope to spend some time with you, if the Lord permits. 8*† I shall stay in Ephesus until Pentecost, 9* because a door has opened for me wide and productive for work, but there are many opponents.

10* If Timothy comes, see that he is without fear in your company, for he is doing the work of the Lord just as I am. 11 Therefore no one should disdain him. Rather, send him on his way in peace that he may come to me, for I am expecting him with the brothers. 12* Now in regard to our brother Apollos, I urged him strongly to go to you with the brothers, but it was not at all his will that he go now. He will go when he has an opportunity.

Exhortation and Greetings. 13 Be on your guard, stand firm in the faith, be courageous, be strong. 14 Your every act should be done with love.

15* I urge you, brothers—you know that the household of Stephanas is the firstfruits of Achaia and that they have devoted themselves to the service of the holy ones—16 be subordinate to such people and to everyone who works and toils with them. 17 I rejoice in the arrival of Stephanas, Fortunatus, and Achaicus, because they made up for your absence, 18* for they refreshed my spirit as well as yours. So give recognition to such people.

19*† The churches of Asia send you greetings. Aquila and Prisca together with the church at their house send you many greetings in the Lord. 20* All the brothers greet you. Greet one another with a holy kiss.

21* I, Paul, write you this greeting in my own hand. 22*† If anyone does not love the Lord, let him be accursed. *Marana tha.* 23* The grace of the Lord Jesus be with you. 24 My love to all of you in Christ Jesus.

*

56: Rom 4, 15; 7, 7.13.
57: Jn 16, 33; 1 Jn 5, 4.
16, 1: Acts 24, 17; Rom 15, 25-32; 2 Cor 8-9; Gal 2, 10.
5: Acts 19, 21; Rom 15, 26; 2 Cor 1, 15-16.
7: Acts 18, 21.
8: 15, 32; Acts 18, 19; 19, 1-10.
9: Acts 14, 27; 2 Cor 2, 12.
10: 4, 17; Acts 16, 1; 19, 22; Phil 2, 19-23.
12: 1, 12; 3, 4-6.22; Acts 18, 24-28.
15: 1, 16.
18: 1 Thes 5, 12-13.
19: Acts 18, 2.18.26; Rom 16, 3-5.
20: Rom 16, 16; 2 Cor 13, 12; 1 Thes 5, 26; 1 Pt 5, 14.
21: Gal 6, 11; Col 4, 18; 2 Thes 3, 17.
22: 12, 3; Rom 9, 3; Gal 1, 8-9; Rv 22, 20.
23: Rom 16, 20.

†

15, 56: *The sting of death is sin:* an explanation of Hosea's metaphor. Death, scorpion-like, is equipped with a sting, sin, by which it injects its poison. Christ defeats sin, the cause of death (Gn 3, 19; Rom 5, 12).

16, 1-4: This paragraph contains our earliest evidence for a project that became a major undertaking of Paul's ministry. The collection for the church at Jerusalem was a symbol in his mind for the unity of Jewish and Gentile Christianity. Cf Gal 2, 10; Rom 15, 25-29; 2 Cor 8-9 and the notes to this last passage.

16, 1: *In regard to the collection:* it has already begun in Galatia and Macedonia (cf 2 Cor 8), and presumably he has already instructed the Corinthians about its purpose.

16, 4: *That I should go also:* presumably Paul delivered the collection on his final visit to Jerusalem; cf Rom 15, 25-32; Acts 24, 14.

16, 5-12: The travel plans outlined here may not have materialized precisely as Paul intended; cf 2 Cor 1, 8—2, 13; 7, 4-16.

16, 8: *In Ephesus until Pentecost:* this tells us the place from which he wrote the letter and suggests he may have composed it about Easter time (cf 5, 7-8).

16, 19-24: These paragraphs conform to the normal epistolary conclusion, but their language is overlaid with liturgical coloration as well. The *greetings* of the Asian churches are probably to be read, along with the letter, in the liturgy at Corinth, and the union of the church is to be expressed by *a holy kiss* (19-20). Paul adds to this his own greeting (21) and blessings (23-24).

16, 22: *Accursed:* literally, "anathema." This expression (cf 12, 3) is a formula for exclusion from the community; it may imply here a call to self-examination before celebration of the Eucharist, in preparation for the Lord's coming and judgment (cf 11, 17-34). *Marana tha:* an Aramaic expression, probably used in the early Christian liturgy. As understood here ("O Lord, come!"), it is a prayer for the early return of Christ. If the Aramaic words are divided differently (*Maran atha,* "Our Lord has come"), it becomes a credal declaration. The former interpretation is supported by what appears to be a Greek equivalent of this acclamation in Rv 22, 20: "Amen. Come, Lord Jesus!"

The Second Letter to the

CORINTHIANS

The Second Letter to the Corinthians is the most personal of all of Paul's extant writings, and it reveals much about his character. In it he deals with one or more crises that have arisen in the Corinthian church. The confrontation with these problems caused him to reflect deeply on his relationship with the community and to speak about it frankly. One moment he is venting his feelings of frustration and uncertainty, the next he is pouring out his relief and affection. The importance of the issues at stake between them calls forth from him an enormous effort of personal persuasion, as well as doctrinal considerations that are of great value for us. Paul's ability to produce profound theological foundations for what may at first sight appear to be rather commonplace circumstances is perhaps nowhere better exemplified than in Second Corinthians. The emotional tone of the letter, its lack of order, and our ignorance of some of its background do not make it easy to follow, but it amply repays the effort required of the reader.

Second Corinthians is rich and varied in content. The interpretation of Exodus in chapter 3, for instance, offers a striking example of early apologetic use of the Old Testament. Paul's discussion of the collection in chs 8-9 contains a theology of sharing of possessions, of community of goods among Christian churches, which is both balanced and sensitive. Furthermore, the closing chapters provide an illustration of early Christian invective and polemic, because the conflict with intruders forces Paul to assert his authority. But in those same chapters Paul articulates the vision and sense of values that animate his own apostolate, revealing his faith that Jesus' passion and resurrection are the pattern for all Christian life and expressing a spirituality of ministry unsurpassed in the New Testament.

The letter is remarkable for its rhetoric. Paul falls naturally into the style and argumentation of contemporary philosophic preachers, employing with ease the stock devices of the "diatribe." By a barrage of questions, by challenges both serious and ironic, by paradox heaped upon paradox, even by insults hurled at his opponents, he strives to awaken in his hearers a true sense of values and an appropriate response. All his argument centers on the destiny of Jesus, in which a paradoxical reversal of values is revealed. But Paul appeals to his own personal experience as well. In passages of great rhetorical power (4, 7-15; 6, 3-10; 11, 21-29; 12, 5-10; 13, 3-4) he enumerates the circumstances of his ministry and the tribulations he has had to endure for Jesus and the gospel, in the hope of illustrating the pattern of Jesus' existence in his own and of drawing the Corinthians into a reappraisal of the values they cherish. Similar passages in the same style in his other letters (cf especially Rom 8, 31-39; 1 Cor 1, 26-31; 4, 6-21; 9, 1-27; 13, 1-13; Phil 4, 10-19) confirm Paul's familiarity with contemporary rhetoric and demonstrate how effectively it served to express his vision of Christian life and ministry.

Second Corinthians was occasioned by events and problems that developed after Paul's first letter reached Corinth. We have no information about these circumstances except what is contained in the letter itself, which of course supposes that they are known to the readers. Consequently the reconstruction of the letter's background is an uncertain enterprise about which there is not complete agreement.

The letter deals principally with these three topics: (1) a crisis between Paul and the Corinthians, occasioned at least partially by changes in his travel plans (1, 12—2, 13), and the successful resolution of that crisis (7, 5-16); (2) further directives and encouragement in regard to the collection for the church in Jerusalem (8, 1—9, 15); (3) the definition and defense of Paul's ministry as an apostle. Paul's reflections on this matter are occasioned by visitors from other churches who passed through Corinth, missionaries who differed from Paul in a variety of ways, both in theory and in practice. Those differences led to comparisons. Either the visitors themselves or some of the local church members appear to have sown confusion among the Corinthians with regard to Paul's authority or his style, or both. Paul deals at length with aspects of this situation in 2, 14—7, 4 and again in 10, 1—13, 10, though the manner of treatment and the thrust of the argument differ in each of these sections.

Scholars have noticed a lack of continuity in this document. For example, the long section of 2, 14—7, 4 seems abruptly spliced into the narrative of a crisis and its resolution. Identical or similar topics, moreover, seem to be treated several times during the letter (compare 2, 14—7, 4 with 10, 1—13, 10, and 8, 1-24 with 9, 1-15). Many judge, therefore, that this letter as it stands incorporates several briefer letters sent to Corinth over a certain span of time. If this is so, then Paul himself or, more likely, some other editor clearly took care to gather those letters together and impose some literary unity upon the collection, thus producing the document that has come down to us as the Second Letter to the Corinthians. Others continue to regard it as a single letter, attributing its inconsistencies to changes of perspective in Paul that may have been occasioned by the arrival of fresh news from Corinth during its composition. The letter, or at least some sections of it, appears to have been composed in Macedonia (2, 12-13; 7, 5-6; 8, 1-4; 9, 2-4). It is generally dated about the autumn of A.D. 57; if it is a compilation, of course, the various parts may have been separated by intervals of at least some months.

The principal divisions of the Second Letter to the Corinthians are the following:

I: Address (1, 1-11)
II: The Crisis between Paul and the Corinthians (1, 12—7, 16)
- *A. Past Relationships (1, 12—2, 13)*
- *B. Paul's Ministry (2, 14—7, 4)*
- *C. Resolution of the Crisis (7, 5-16)*

III: The Collection for Jerusalem (8, 1—9, 15)
IV: Paul's Defense of His Ministry (10, 1—13, 10)
V: Conclusion (13, 11-13)

I: ADDRESS

CHAPTER 1

Greeting. † 1* Paul, an apostle of
Christ Jesus by the will of God, and Tim-
othy our brother, to the church of God
that is in Corinth, with all the holy ones
throughout Achaia: 2 grace to you and
peace from God our Father and the
Lord Jesus Christ.

Thanksgiving. 3*† Blessed be the God
and Father of our Lord Jesus Christ, the
Father of compassion and God of all en-
couragement, 4* who encourages us in
our every affliction, so that we may be
able to encourage those who are in any
affliction with the encouragement with
which we ourselves are encouraged by
God. 5† For as Christ's sufferings over-

* 1, 1: Eph 1, 1; Col 1, 1 / 1, 19; Acts 16 / Rom 1, 7; 1 Cor 1, 2.
3: 1 Cor 15, 24; Eph 1, 3; 1 Pt 1, 3 / Rom 15, 5.
4: 7, 6-7.13; 1 Thes 3, 6-8; 2 Thes 2, 16.

† 1, 1-11: The opening follows the usual Pauline form, except that the thanksgiving takes the form of a doxology or glorification of God (3). This introduces a meditation on the experience of suffering and encouragement shared by Paul and the Corinthians (4-7), drawn, at least in part, from Paul's reflections on a recent affliction (8-10). The section ends with a modified and delayed allusion to thanksgiving (11).

1, 3: *God of all encouragement:* Paul expands a standard Jewish blessing so as to state the theme of the paragraph. The theme of "encouragement" or "consolation" (*paraklēsis*) occurs ten times in this opening, against a background formed by multiple references to "affliction" and "suffering."

1, 5: *Through Christ:* the Father of compassion is the Father of our Lord Jesus (3); Paul's sufferings and encouragement (or "consolation") are experienced in union with Christ. Cf Lk 2, 25: the "consolation of Israel" is Jesus himself.

flow to us, so through Christ does our
encouragement also overflow. 6 If we
are afflicted, it is for your encourage-
ment and salvation; if we are encour-
aged, it is for your encouragement,
which enables you to endure the same
sufferings that we suffer. 7† Our hope
for you is firm, for we know that as you
share in the sufferings, you also share
in the encouragement.
8*† We do not want you to be unaware,
brothers, of the affliction that came to
us in the province of Asia; we were ut-
terly weighed down beyond our
strength, so that we despaired even of
life. 9*† Indeed, we had accepted within
ourselves the sentence of death, that we
might trust not in ourselves but in God
who raises the dead. 10* He rescued
us from such great danger of death,
and he will continue to rescue us; in
him we have put our hope [that] he
will also rescue us again, 11* as you
help us with prayer, so that thanks may
be given by many on our behalf for the
gift granted us through the prayers of
many.

II: THE CRISIS BETWEEN PAUL AND THE CORINTHIANS

A. Past Relationships†

***Paul's Sincerity and Constancy.*†**
12 For our boast is this, the testimony
of our conscience that we have con-
ducted ourselves in the world, and espe-
cially toward you, with the simplicity
and sincerity of God, [and] not by hu-
man wisdom but by the grace of God.
13 For we write you nothing but what
you can read and understand, and I
hope that you will understand com-
pletely, 14* as you have come to under-
stand us partially, that we are your
boast as you also are ours, on the day
of [our] Lord Jesus.
15† With this confidence I formerly in-
tended to come to you so that you might
receive a double favor, 16* namely, to
go by way of you to Macedonia, and
then to come to you again on my return
from Macedonia, and have you send me
on my way to Judea. 17*† So when I in-
tended this, did I act lightly? Or do I
make my plans according to human
considerations, so that with me it is
"yes, yes" and "no, no"? 18† As God is
faithful, our word to you is not "yes"
and "no." 19* For the Son of God, Jesus
Christ, who was proclaimed to you by
us, Silvanus and Timothy and me, was
not "yes" and "no," but "yes" has been
in him. 20* For however many are the
promises of God, their Yes is in him;
therefore, the Amen from us also goes
through him to God for glory. 21*† But
the one who gives us security with you
in Christ and who anointed us is God;
22* he has also put his seal upon us and
given the Spirit in our hearts as a first
installment.

---

*

8: Acts 20, 18-19; 1 Cor 15, 32.
9: 4, 7-11; Rom 4, 17.
10: 2 Tm 4, 18.
11: 4, 15; 9, 12.
14: Phil 2, 16; 1 Thes 2, 19-20.
16: 1 Cor 16, 5-9; Acts 19, 21.
17: Mt 5, 37; Jas 5, 12.
19: Acts 16, 1-3; 1 Thes 1, 1; 2 Thes 1, 1.
20: 1 Cor 14, 16; Rv 3, 14.
21: 1 Jn 2, 20.27.
22: Eph 1, 13-14; 4, 30 / 5, 5; Rom 5, 5; 8, 16.23.

---

†

1, 7: *You also share in the encouragement:* the eschatological reversal of affliction and encouragement that Christians expect (cf Mt 5, 4; Lk 6, 24) permits some present experience of reversal in the Corinthians' case, as in Paul's.

1, 8: *Asia:* a Roman province in western Asia Minor, the capital of which was Ephesus.

1, 9-10: *The sentence of death:* it is unclear whether Paul is alluding to a physical illness or to an external threat to life. The result of the situation was to produce an attitude of faith in God alone. *God who raises the dead:* rescue is the constant pattern of God's activity; his final act of encouragement is the resurrection.

1, 12—2, 13: The autobiographical remarks about the crisis in Asia Minor lead into consideration of a crisis that has arisen between Paul and the Corinthians. Paul will return to this question, after a long digression, in 7, 5-16. Both of these sections deal with travel plans Paul had made, changes in the plans, alternative measures adopted, a breach that opened between him and the community, and finally a reconciliation between them.

1, 12-14: Since Paul's own conduct will be under discussion here, he prefaces the section with a statement about his habitual behavior and attitude toward the community. He protests his openness, single-mindedness, and conformity to God's grace; he hopes that his relationship with them will be marked by mutual understanding and pride, which will constantly increase until it reaches its climax at the judgment. Two references to boasting frame this paragraph (12.14), the first appearances of a theme that will be important in the letter, especially in chs 10-13; the term is used in a positive sense here (cf the note on 1 Cor 1, 29-31).

1, 15: *I formerly intended to come:* this plan reads like a revision of the one mentioned in 1 Cor 16, 5. Not until 1, 23—2, 1 will Paul tell us something his original readers already knew, that he has canceled one or the other of these projected visits.

1, 17: *Did I act lightly?:* the subsequent change of plans casts suspicion on the original intention, creating the impression that Paul is vacillating and inconsistent or that *human considerations* keep dictating shifts in his goals and projects (cf the counterclaim of 12). *"Yes, yes" and "no, no":* stating something and denying it in the same or the next breath; being of two minds at once, or from one moment to the next.

1, 18-22: *As God is faithful:* unable to deny the change in plans, Paul nonetheless asserts the firmness of the original plan and claims a profound constancy in his life and work. He grounds his defense in God himself, who is firm and reliable; this quality can also be predicated in various ways of those who are associated with him. Christ, Paul, and the Corinthians all participate in analogous ways in the constancy of God. A number of the terms here, which appear related only conceptually in Greek or English, would be variations of the same root, *ʾmn,* in a Semitic language, and thus naturally associated in a Semitic mind, such as Paul's. These include the words *yes* (17-20), *faithful* (18), *Amen* (20), *gives us security* (21), *faith, stand firm* (24).

1, 21-22: The commercial terms *gives us security, seal, first installment* are here used analogously to refer to the process of initiation into the Christian life, perhaps specifically to baptism. The passage is clearly trinitarian. The Spirit is the *first installment* or "down payment" of the full messianic benefits that God guarantees to Christians. Cf Eph 1, 13-14.

Paul's Change of Plan. † 23* But I call
upon God as witness, on my life, that
it is to spare you that I have not yet gone
to Corinth. 24 Not that we lord it over
your faith; rather, we work together
for your joy, for you stand firm in the
faith.

CHAPTER 2

1 For I decided not to come to you again
in painful circumstances. 2 For if I in-
flict pain upon you, then who is there
to cheer me except the one pained by
me? 3† And I wrote as I did so that when
I came I might not be pained by those
in whom I should have rejoiced, confi-
dent about all of you that my joy is that
of all of you. 4 For out of much affliction
and anguish of heart I wrote to you with
many tears, not that you might be
pained but that you might know the
abundant love I have for you.

The Offender. † 5 If anyone has
caused pain, he has caused it not to me,
but in some measure (not to exagger-
ate) to all of you. 6 This punishment by
the majority is enough for such a per-
son, 7* so that on the contrary you
should forgive and encourage him
instead, or else the person may be
overwhelmed by excessive pain.
8 Therefore, I urge you to reaffirm your
love for him. 9* For this is why I wrote,
to know your proven character,
whether you were obedient in every-
thing. 10 Whomever you forgive any-
thing, so do I. For indeed what I have
forgiven, if I have forgiven anything,
has been for you in the presence of
Christ, 11* so that we might not be taken
advantage of by Satan, for we are not
unaware of his purposes.

Paul's Anxiety. † 12* When I went to
Troas for the gospel of Christ, although
a door was opened for me in the Lord,
13*† I had no relief in my spirit because
I did not find my brother Titus. So I took
leave of them and went on to Macedo-
nia.

B. Paul's Ministry†

Ministers of a New Covenant. †
14† But thanks be to God, who always
leads us in triumph in Christ and mani-
fests through us the odor of the knowl-
edge of him in every place. 15* For we

*

23: 13, 2.
2, 7: Col 3, 13.
9: 7, 15.
11: Eph 4, 27.
12: Acts 16, 8.
13: 7, 6; 1 Tm 1, 3.
15: 4, 3; 1 Cor 1, 18.

†

1, 23-24: *I have not yet gone to Corinth:* some suppose that Paul received word of some affair in Corinth, which he decided to regulate by letter even before the first of his projected visits (cf 16). Others conjecture that he did pay the first visit, was offended there (cf 2, 5), returned to Ephesus, and sent a letter (2, 3-9) in place of the second visit. The expressions *to spare you* (23) and *work together for your joy* (24) introduce the major themes of the next two paragraphs, which are remarkable for insistent repetition of key words and ideas. These form two clusters of terms in the English translation: (1) cheer, rejoice, encourage, joy; (2) pain, affliction, anguish. These clusters reappear when Paul resumes treatment of this subject in 7, 5-16.

2, 3-4: *I wrote as I did:* we learn for the first time about the sending of a letter in place of the proposed visit. Paul mentions the letter in passing, but emphasizes his motivation in sending it: to avoid being saddened by them (cf 1), and to help them realize the depth of his love. Another motive will be added in 7, 12: to bring to light their own concern for him. *With many tears:* it has been suggested that we may have all or part of this "tearful letter" somewhere in the Corinthian correspondence, either in 1 Cor 5 (the case of the incestuous man), or in 1 Cor as a whole, or in 2 Cor 10-13. None of these hypotheses is entirely convincing. See the note on 13, 1.

2, 5-11: The nature of the *pain* (5) is unclear, though some believe an individual at Corinth rejected Paul's authority, thereby scandalizing many in the community. In any case, action has been taken, and Paul judges the measures adequate to right the situation (6). The follow-up directives he now gives are entirely positive: forgive, encourage, love. *Overwhelmed* (7): a vivid metaphor (literally "swallowed") that Paul employs positively at 5, 4 and in 1 Cor 15, 54 (7). It is often used to describe satanic activity (cf 1 Pt 5, 8); note the reference to Satan here in v 11.

2, 12-13: *I had no relief:* Paul does not explain the reason for his anxiety until he resumes the thread of his narrative at 7, 5: he was waiting to hear how the Corinthians would respond to his letter. Since 7, 5-16 describes their response in entirely positive terms, we never learn in detail why he found it necessary to defend and justify his change of plans, as in 1, 15-24. Was this portion of the letter written before the arrival of Titus with his good news (7, 6-7)?

2, 13: *Macedonia*: a Roman province in northern Greece.

2, 14—7, 4: This section constitutes a digression within the narrative of the crisis and its resolution (1, 12—2, 13 and 7, 5-16). The main component (2, 14—6, 10) treats the nature of Paul's ministry and his qualifications for it; this material bears some similarity to the defense of his ministry in chs 10-13, but it may well come from a period close to the crisis. This is followed by a supplementary block of material quite different in character and tone (6, 14—7, 1). These materials may have been brought together into their present position during final editing of the letter; appeals to the Corinthians link them to one another (6, 11-13) and lead back to the interrupted narrative (7, 2-4).

2, 14—6, 10: The question of Paul's adequacy (16; cf 3, 5) and his credentials (3, 1-2) has been raised. Paul responds by an extended treatment of the nature of his ministry. It is a ministry of glory (3, 7—4, 6), of life (4, 7—5, 10), of reconciliation (5, 11—6, 10).

2, 14-16a: The initial statement plunges us abruptly into another train of thought. Paul describes his personal existence and his function as a preacher in two powerful images (14) that constitute a prelude to the development to follow.

2, 14a: *Leads us in triumph in Christ:* this metaphor of a festive parade in honor of a conquering military hero can suggest either a positive sharing in Christ's triumph or an experience of defeat, being led in captivity and submission (cf 4, 8-11; 1 Cor 4, 9). Paul is probably aware of the ambiguity, as he is in the case of the next metaphor.

2, 14b-16a: *The odor of the knowledge of him:* incense was commonly used in triumphal processions. The metaphor suggests the gradual diffusion of the knowledge of God through the apostolic preaching. *The aroma of Christ:* the image shifts from the fragrance Paul diffuses to the aroma that he is. Paul is probably thinking of the "sweet odor" of the sacrifices in the Old Testament (e.g., Gn 8, 21; Ex 29, 18) and perhaps of the metaphor of wisdom as a sweet odor (Sir 24, 15). *Death . . . life:* the aroma of Christ that comes to them through Paul is perceived differently by various classes of people. To some his preaching and his life (cf 1 Cor 1, 17—2, 6) are perceived as *death,* and the effect is death for them; others perceive him, despite appearances, as *life,* and the effect is life for them. This fragrance thus produces a separation and a judgment (cf the function of the "light" in John's gospel).

are the aroma of Christ for God among those who are being saved and among those who are perishing, [16]† to the latter an odor of death that leads to death, to the former an odor of life that leads to life. Who is qualified for this? [17]* For we are not like the many who trade on the word of God; but as out of sincerity, indeed as from God and in the presence of God, we speak in Christ.

CHAPTER 3

[1]*† Are we beginning to commend ourselves again? Or do we need, as some do, letters of recommendation to you or from you? [2]† You are our letter, written on our hearts, known and read by all, [3]*† shown to be a letter of Christ administered by us, written not in ink but by the Spirit of the living God, not on tablets of stone but on tablets that are hearts of flesh.

[4]† Such confidence we have through Christ toward God. [5]* Not that of ourselves we are qualified to take credit for anything as coming from us; rather, our qualification comes from God, [6]*† who has indeed qualified us as ministers of a new covenant, not of letter but of spirit; for the letter brings death, but the Spirit gives life.

Contrast with the Old Covenant. †
[7]*† Now if the ministry of death, carved in letters on stone, was so glorious that the Israelites could not look intently at the face of Moses because of its glory that was going to fade, [8]† how much more will the ministry of the Spirit be glorious? [9] For if the ministry of condemnation was glorious, the ministry of righteousness will abound much more in glory. [10] Indeed, what was endowed with glory has come to have no glory in this respect because of the glory that surpasses it. [11] For if what was going to fade was glorious, how much more will what endures be glorious.

[12]† Therefore, since we have such hope, we act very boldly [13]† and not like Moses, who put a veil over his face so that the Israelites could not look intently at the cessation of what was fad-

*

17: 4, 2; 1 Cor 5, 8.
3, 1: Acts 18, 27; Rom 16, 1; 1 Cor 16, 3.
3: Ex 24, 12; 31, 18; 32, 15-19 / Jer 31, 33; Ez 11, 19; 36, 26-27.
5: Jn 3, 27.
6: Eph 3, 7 / Jer 31, 31-34.
7: Ex 34, 29-35.

†

2, 16b-17: *Qualified:* Paul may be echoing either the self-satisfied claims of other preachers or their charges about Paul's deficiencies. No one is really qualified, but the apostle contrasts himself with those who dilute or falsify the preaching for personal advantage and insists on his totally good conscience: his ministry is from God, and he has exercised it with fidelity and integrity (cf 3, 5-6).

3, 1: Paul seems to allude to certain preachers who pride themselves on their written credentials. Presumably they reproach him for not possessing similar credentials and compel him to spell out his own qualifications (4, 2; 5, 12; 6, 4). The Corinthians themselves should have performed this function for Paul (5, 12; cf 12, 11). Since he is forced to find something that can recommend him, he points to them: their very existence constitutes his *letter* of recommendation (1-2). Others who engage in self-commendation will also be mentioned in 10, 12-18.

3, 2-3: Mention of "letters of recommendation" generates a series of metaphors in which Paul plays on the word "letter": (1) the community is Paul's letter of recommendation (2a); (2) they are a letter engraved on his affections for all to see and read (2b); (3) they are a letter from Christ that Paul merely delivers (3a); (4) they are a letter written by the Spirit on the tablets of human hearts (3b). One image dissolves into another.

3, 3b: This verse contrasts Paul's letter with those *written . . . in ink* (like the credentials of other preachers) and those *written . . . on tablets of stone* (like the law of Moses). These contrasts suggest that the other preachers may have claimed special relationship with Moses. If they were Judaizers zealous for the Mosaic law, that would explain the detailed contrast between the old and the new covenants (6; 4, 7—6, 10). If they were charismatics who claimed Moses as their model, that would explain the extended treatment of Moses himself and his glory (3, 7—4, 6). *Hearts of flesh:* cf Ezekiel's contrast between the heart of flesh that the Spirit gives and the heart of stone that it replaces (Ez 36, 26); the context is covenant renewal and purification that makes observance of the law possible.

3, 4-6: These verses resume 2, 1—3, 3. Paul's confidence (4) is grounded in his sense of God-given mission (2, 17), the specifics of which are described in vv 1-3. Verses 5-6 return to the question of his qualifications (2, 16), attributing them entirely to God. Verse 6 further spells out the situation described in v 3b and "names" it: Paul is living within *a new covenant,* characterized by the Spirit, which *gives life.* The usage of a *new covenant* is derived from Jer 31, 31-33, a passage that also speaks of writing on the heart; cf 2.

3, 6b: This verse serves as a topic sentence for 3, 7—6, 10. For the contrast between *letter* and *spirit,* cf Rom 2, 29; 7, 5-6.

3, 7—4, 6: Paul now develops the contrast enunciated in 3, 6b in terms of the relative glory of the two covenants, insisting on the greater glory of the new. His polemic seems directed against individuals who appeal to the glorious Moses and fail to perceive any comparable glory either in Paul's life as an apostle or in the gospel he preaches. He asserts in response that Christians have a glory of their own that far surpasses that of Moses.

3, 7: *The ministry of death:* from his very first words, Paul describes the Mosaic covenant and ministry from the viewpoint of their limitations. They lead to *death* rather than life (6-7; cf 4, 7—5, 10), to *condemnation* rather than reconciliation (9; cf 5, 11—6, 10). *Was so glorious:* the basic text to which Paul alludes is Ex 34, 29-35, to which his opponents have undoubtedly laid claim. *Going to fade:* Paul concedes the glory of Moses' covenant and ministry, but grants them only temporary significance.

3, 8-11: *How much more:* the argument "from the less to the greater" is repeated three times (8.9.11). Verse 10 expresses another point of view: the difference in glory is so great that only the new covenant and ministry can properly be called "glorious" at all.

3, 12: *Such hope:* the glory is not yet an object of experience, but that does not lessen Paul's confidence. *Boldly:* the term *parrēsia* expresses outspoken declaration of Christian conviction (cf 4, 1-2). Paul has nothing to hide and no reason for timidity.

3, 13-14a: *Not like Moses:* in Exodus Moses veiled his face to protect the Israelites from God's reflected glory. Without impugning Moses' sincerity, Paul attributes another effect to the veil. Since it lies between God's glory and the Israelites, it explains how they could fail to notice the glory disappearing. *Their thoughts were rendered dull:* the problem lay with their understanding. This will be expressed in vv 14b-16 by a shift in the place of the veil: it is no longer over Moses' face but over their perception.

ing. 14† Rather, their thoughts were
rendered dull, for to this present day
the same veil remains unlifted when
they read the old covenant, because
through Christ it is taken away. 15* To
this day, in fact, whenever Moses is
read, a veil lies over their hearts,
16* but whenever a person turns to the
Lord the veil is removed. 17† Now the
Lord is the Spirit, and where the Spirit
of the Lord is, there is freedom. 18*† All
of us, gazing with unveiled face on the
glory of the Lord, are being trans-
formed into the same image from glory
to glory, as from the Lord who is the
Spirit.

CHAPTER 4

Integrity in the Ministry.†

1 Therefore, since we have this ministry
through the mercy shown us, we are not
discouraged. 2* Rather, we have re-
nounced shameful, hidden things; not
acting deceitfully or falsifying the word
of God, but by the open declaration
of the truth we commend ourselves to
everyone's conscience in the sight of
God. 3*† And even though our gospel is
veiled, it is veiled for those who are per-
ishing, 4* in whose case the god of this
age has blinded the minds of the unbe-
lievers, so that they may not see the light
of the gospel of the glory of Christ, who
is the image of God. 5† For we do not
preach ourselves but Jesus Christ as
Lord, and ourselves as your slaves for
the sake of Jesus. 6*† For God who said,
"Let light shine out of darkness," has
shone in our hearts to bring to light the
knowledge of the glory of God on the
face of [Jesus] Christ.

The Paradox of the Ministry.† 7† But
we hold this treasure in earthen vessels,
that the surpassing power may be of
God and not from us. 8*† We are af-
flicted in every way, but not con-
strained; perplexed, but not driven to
despair; 9 persecuted, but not aban-
doned; struck down, but not destroyed;
10*† always carrying about in the body
the dying of Jesus, so that the life of
Jesus may also be manifested in our

*

15: Rom 11, 7-10.
16: Ex 34, 34.
18: Rom 8, 29-30; 12, 2; Gal 4, 19; Phil 3, 10.20-21 / 4, 4-6; 1 Cor 15, 49; Col 1, 15; 3, 9-11; 1 Jn 3, 2.
4, 2: 2, 17; 1 Thes 2, 4-7.
3: 2, 15-16; 2 Thes 2, 10.
4: Jn 12, 31-36 / 1 Tm 1, 11.
6: Gn 1, 3; Is 9, 1; Acts 26, 13-23; Gal 1, 15-16 / Jn 8, 12; Heb 1, 3.
8: 6, 4-10; 1 Cor 4, 9-13.
10: Col 1, 24.

†

3, 14b-16: The parallelism in these verses makes it necessary to interpret corresponding parts in relation to one another. *To this present day:* this signals the shift of Paul's attention to his contemporaries; his argument is typological, as in 1 Cor 10. The Israelites of Moses' time typify the Jews of Paul's time, and perhaps also Christians of Jewish origin or mentality who may not recognize the temporary character of Moses' glory. *When they read the old covenant:* the lasting dullness prevents proper appraisal of Moses' person and covenant. When his writings are read in the synagogue, a veil still impedes their understanding. *Through Christ:* i.e., in the new covenant. *Whenever a person turns to the Lord:* Moses in Exodus appeared before God without the veil and gazed on his face unprotected. Paul applies that passage to converts to Christianity: when they turn to the Lord fully and authentically, the impediment to their understanding is removed.

3, 17: *The Lord is the Spirit:* the "Lord" to whom the Christian turns (16) is the Spirit of whom Paul has been speaking, the life-giving Spirit of the living God (6.8), the inaugurator of the new covenant and ministry, who is also the Spirit of Christ. *The Spirit of the Lord:* the Lord here is the living God (3), but there may also be an allusion to Christ as Lord (14.16). *Freedom:* i.e., from the ministry of death (7) and the covenant that condemned (9).

3, 18: Another application of the veil image. *All of us . . . with unveiled face:* Christians (Israelites from whom the veil has been removed) are like Moses, standing in God's presence, beholding and reflecting his glory. *Gazing:* the verb may also be translated "contemplating as in a mirror"; 4, 6 would suggest that the mirror is Christ himself. *Are being transformed:* elsewhere Paul speaks of transformation, conformity to Jesus, God's image, as a reality of the end time, and even v 12 speaks of the glory as an object of hope. But the life-giving Spirit, the distinctive gift of the new covenant, is already present in the community (cf 1, 22, the "first installment"), and the process of transformation has already begun. *Into the same image:* into the image of God, which is Christ (4, 4).

4, 1-2: A ministry of this sort generates confidence and forthrightness; cf 1, 12-14; 2, 17.

4, 3-4: *Though our gospel is veiled:* the final application of the image. Paul has been reproached either for obscurity in his preaching or for his manner of presenting the gospel. But he confidently asserts that there is no veil over his gospel. If some fail to perceive its light, that is because of unbelief. The veil lies over their eyes (3, 14), a blindness induced by Satan, and a sign that they are headed for destruction (cf 2, 15).

4, 5: *We do not preach ourselves:* the light seen in his gospel is the glory of Christ (4). Far from preaching himself, the preacher should be a transparent medium through whom Jesus is perceived (cf 10-11). *Your slaves:* Paul draws attention away from individuals as such and toward their role in relation to God, Christ, and the community; cf 1 Cor 3, 5; 4, 1.

4, 6: Autobiographical allusion to the episode at Damascus clarifies the origin and nature of Paul's service; cf Acts 9, 1-19; 22, 3-16; 26, 2-18. *"Let light shine out of darkness":* Paul seems to be thinking of Gn 1, 3 and presenting his apostolic ministry as a new creation. There may also be an allusion to Is 9, 1, suggesting his prophetic calling as servant of the Lord and light to the nations; cf Is 42, 6.16; 49, 6; 60, 1-2, and the use of light imagery in Acts 26, 13-23. *To bring to light the knowledge:* Paul's role in the process of revelation, expressed at the beginning under the image of the odor and aroma (2, 14-15), is restated now, at the end of this first moment of the development, in the imagery of light and glory (3-6).

4, 7—5, 10: Paul now confronts the difficulty that his present existence does not appear glorious at all; it is marked instead by suffering and death. He deals with this by developing the topic already announced in 3, 3.6, asserting his faith in the presence and ultimate triumph of life, in his own and every Christian existence, despite the experience of death.

4, 7: *This treasure:* the glory that he preaches and into which they are being transformed. *In earthen vessels:* the instruments God uses are human and fragile; some imagine small terracotta lamps in which light is carried.

4, 8-9: A catalogue of his apostolic trials and afflictions. Yet in these the negative never completely prevails; there is always some experience of rescue, of salvation.

4, 10-11: Both the negative and the positive sides of the experience are grounded christologically. The logic is similar to that of 1, 3-11. His sufferings are connected with Christ's, and his deliverance is a sign that he is to share in Jesus' resurrection.

body. 11* For we who live are constantly being given up to death for the sake of Jesus, so that the life of Jesus may be manifested in our mortal flesh.

12† So death is at work in us, but life in you. 13*† Since, then, we have the same spirit of faith, according to what is written, "I believed, therefore I spoke," we too believe and therefore speak, 14* knowing that the one who raised the Lord Jesus will raise us also with Jesus and place us with you in his presence. 15* Everything indeed is for you, so that the grace bestowed in abundance on more and more people may cause the thanksgiving to overflow for the glory of God.

16*† Therefore, we are not discouraged; rather, although our outer self is wasting away, our inner self is being renewed day by day. 17* For this momentary light affliction is producing for us an eternal weight of glory beyond all comparison, 18* as we look not to what is seen but to what is unseen; for what is seen is transitory, but what is unseen is eternal.

CHAPTER 5

Our Future Destiny. 1*† For we know that if our earthly dwelling, a tent, should be destroyed, we have a building from God, a dwelling not made with hands, eternal in heaven. 2*† For in this tent we groan, longing to be further clothed with our heavenly habitation 3† if indeed, when we have taken it off, we shall not be found naked. 4*† For while we are in this tent we groan and are weighed down, because we do not wish to be unclothed but to be further clothed, so that what is mortal may be swallowed up by life. 5*† Now the one who has prepared us for this very thing is God, who has given us the Spirit as a first installment.

6† So we are always courageous, although we know that while we are at home in the body we are away from the Lord, 7 for we walk by faith, not by sight. 8* Yet we are courageous, and we would rather leave the body and go home to the Lord. 9 Therefore, we aspire to please him, whether we are at home or away. 10*† For we must all appear be-

*

11: Rom 8, 36; 1 Cor 15, 31.
13: Ps 116, 10.
14: Rom 4, 24-25; 8, 11; 1 Cor 6, 14; 1 Thes 4, 14.
15: 1, 11.
16: 4, 1.1
17: Mt 5, 11-12; Rom 8, 18.
18: Rom 8, 24-25; Heb 11, 1.
5, 1: Is 38, 12 / Col 3, 1-4 / Mk 14, 58; Col 2, 11; Heb 9, 11.24.
2: Rom 8, 23 / 1 Cor 15, 51-54.
4: Is 25, 8; 1 Cor 15, 54.
5: 1, 22.
8: Phil 1, 21-23.
10: Mt 16, 27; 25, 31-46; Rom 2, 16; 14, 10-11.

†

4, 12-15: His experience does not terminate in himself, but in others (12.15; cf 1, 4-5). Ultimately, everything is ordered even beyond the community, toward God (15; cf 1, 11).

4, 13-14: Like the Psalmist, Paul clearly proclaims his faith, affirming life within himself despite death (10-11) and the life-giving effect of his experience upon the church (12.14-15). *And place us with you in his presence:* Paul imagines God presenting him and them to Jesus at the parousia and the judgment; cf 11, 2; Rom 14, 10.

4, 16-18: In a series of contrasts Paul explains the extent of his faith in life. Life is not only already present and revealing itself (8-11.16) but will outlast his experience of affliction and dying: it is eternal (17-18).

4, 16: *Not discouraged:* i.e., despite the experience of death. Paul is still speaking of himself personally, but he assumes his faith and attitude will be shared by all Christians. *Our outer self:* the individual subject of ordinary perception and observation, in contrast to the interior and hidden self, which undergoes renewal. *Is being renewed day by day:* this suggests a process that has already begun; cf 3, 18. The renewal already taking place even in Paul's dying is a share in the life of Jesus, but this is recognized only by faith (13.18; 5, 7).

5, 1: *Our earthly dwelling:* the same contrast is restated in the imagery of a dwelling. The language recalls Jesus' saying about the destruction of the temple and the construction of another building *not made with hands* (Mk 14, 58), a prediction later applied to Jesus' own body (Jn 2, 20).

5, 2-5: Verses 2-3 and 4 are largely parallel in structure. *We groan, longing:* see the note on 5, 5. *Clothed with our heavenly habitation:* Paul mixes his metaphors, adding the image of the garment to that of the building. *Further clothed:* the verb means strictly "to put one garment on over another." Paul may desire to put the resurrection body on over his mortal body, without dying; vv 2 and 4 permit this meaning but do not impose it. Or perhaps he imagines the resurrection body as a garment put on over the Christ-garment first received in baptism (Gal 3, 27) and preserved by moral behavior (Rom 13, 12-14; Col 3, 12; cf Mt 22, 11-13). Some support for this interpretation may be found in the context; cf the references to baptism (5), to judgment according to works (10), and to present renewal (4, 16), an idea elsewhere combined with the image of "putting on" a new nature (Eph 4, 22-24; Col 3, 1-5.9-10).

5, 3: *When we have taken it off:* the majority of witnesses read "when we have put it on," i.e., when we have been clothed (in the resurrection body), then we shall not be without a body (naked). This seems mere tautology, though some understand it to mean: whether we are "found" (by God at the judgment) clothed or naked depends upon whether we have preserved or lost our original investiture in Christ (cf the previous note). In this case to "put it on" does not refer to the resurrection body, but to keeping intact the Christ-garment of baptism. The translation follows the western reading (Codex Bezae, Tertullian), the sense of which is clear: to "take it off" is to shed our mortal body in death, after which we shall be clothed in the resurrection body and hence not "naked" (cf 1 Cor 15, 51-53).

5, 4: *We do not wish to be unclothed:* a clear allusion to physical death (4, 16; 5, 1). Unlike the Greeks, who found dissolution of the body desirable (cf Socrates), Paul has a Jewish horror of it. He seems to be thinking of the "intermediate period," an interval between death and resurrection. *Swallowed up by life:* cf 1 Cor 15, 54.

5, 5: God has created us for resurrected bodily life and already prepares us for it by the gift of the Spirit in baptism. *The Spirit as a first installment:* the striking parallel to 5, 1-5 in Rom 8, 17-30 describes Christians who have received the "firstfruits" (cf "first installment" here) of the Spirit as "groaning" (cf 2.4 here) for the resurrection, the complete redemption of their bodies. In place of clothing and building, Rom 8 uses other images for the resurrection: adoption and conformity to the image of the Son.

5, 6-9: Tension between present and future is expressed by another spatial image, the metaphor of the country and its citizens. At present we are like citizens in exile or far away from home. The Lord is the distant homeland, believed in but unseen (7).

5, 10: *We must all appear:* the verb is ambiguous: we are scheduled to "appear" for judgment, at which we will be "revealed" as we are (cf 11; 2, 14; 4, 10-11).

fore the judgment seat of Christ, so that
each one may receive recompense, ac-
cording to what he did in the body,
whether good or evil.

The Ministry of Reconciliation.†
11* Therefore, since we know the fear
of the Lord, we try to persuade others;
but we are clearly apparent to God, and
I hope we are also apparent to your con-
sciousness. 12* We are not commending
ourselves to you again but giving you
an opportunity to boast of us, so that
you may have something to say to those
who boast of external appearance
rather than of the heart. 13† For if we
are out of our minds, it is for God; if
we are rational, it is for you. 14*† For
the love of Christ impels us, once we
have come to the conviction that one
died for all; therefore, all have died.
15* He indeed died for all, so that those
who live might no longer live for them-
selves but for him who for their sake
died and was raised.

16† Consequently, from now on we re-
gard no one according to the flesh; even
if we once knew Christ according to the
flesh, yet now we know him so no longer.
17* So whoever is in Christ is a new cre-
ation: the old things have passed away;
behold, new things have come. 18† And
all this is from God, who has reconciled
us to himself through Christ and given
us the ministry of reconciliation,
19* namely, God was reconciling the
world to himself in Christ, not counting
their trespasses against them and en-
trusting to us the message of reconcilia-
tion. 20* So we are ambassadors for
Christ, as if God were appealing
through us. We implore you on behalf
of Christ, be reconciled to God. 21*† For
our sake he made him to be sin who did
not know sin, so that we might become
the righteousness of God in him.

CHAPTER 6

The Experience of the Ministry.†
1*† Working together, then, we appeal
to you not to receive the grace of God
in vain. 2*† For he says:

> "In an acceptable time I heard you,
> and on the day of salvation I
> helped you."

Behold, now is a very acceptable time;
behold, now is the day of salvation.
3*† We cause no one to stumble in any-
thing, in order that no fault may be
found with our ministry; 4*† on the con-

*

11: 1, 12-14.
12: 3, 1 / 1, 14; Phil 1, 26.
14: Rom 6, 1-6.
15: Rom 4, 25; 6, 4-11; 14, 9; Col 3, 3-4.
17: Gal 6, 15; Eph 2, 15 / Is 43, 18-21; Rv 21, 5.
19: Rom 5, 10-11; Col 1, 20.
20: Eph 6, 20; Phlm 9.
21: Is 53, 6-9; Gal 3, 13 / Rom 3, 24-26; 1 Cor 1, 30; 1 Pt 2, 24; 1 Jn 3, 5-8.
6, 1: 1 Cor 3, 9; 1 Thes 3, 2.
2: Is 49, 8.
3: 1 Cor 9, 12; 10, 32 / 8, 20-21.
4: 4, 8-11; 11, 23-27; 1 Cor 4, 9-13.

†

5, 11-15: This paragraph is transitional. Paul sums up much that has gone before. Still playing on the term "appearance," he reasserts his transparency before God and the Corinthians, in contrast to the self-commendation, boasting, and preoccupation with externals that characterize some others (cf 1, 12-14; 2, 14; 3, 1; 3, 7—4, 6). Verse 14 recalls 3, 7—4, 6, and sums up 4, 7—5, 10.

5, 13: *Out of our minds:* this verse confirms that a concern for ecstasy and charismatic experience may lie behind the discussion about "glory" in 3, 7—4, 6. Paul also enjoys such experiences but, unlike others, does not make a public display of them or consider them ends in themselves. *Rational:* the Greek virtue *sōphrosynē,* to which Paul alludes, implies reasonableness, moderation, good judgment, self-control.

5, 14-15: These verses echo 4, 14 and resume the treatment of "life despite death" from 4, 7—5, 10.

5, 16-17: *Consequently:* the death of Christ described in vv 14-15 produces a whole new order (17) and a new mode of perception (16). *According to the flesh:* the natural mode of perception, characterized as "fleshly," is replaced by a mode of perception proper to the Spirit. Elsewhere Paul contrasts what Christ looks like according to the old criteria (weakness, powerlessness, folly, death) and according to the new (wisdom, power, life); cf vv 15.21; 1 Cor 1, 17—3, 3. Similarly, he describes the paradoxical nature of Christian existence, e.g., in 4, 10-11.14. *A new creation:* rabbis used this expression to describe the effect of the entrance of a proselyte or convert into Judaism or of the remission of sins on the Day of Atonement. The new order created *in Christ* is the new covenant (3, 6).

5, 18-21: Paul attempts to explain the meaning of God's action by a variety of different categories; his attention keeps moving rapidly back and forth from God's act to his own ministry as well. *Who has reconciled us to himself:* i.e., he has brought all into oneness. *Not counting their trespasses:* the reconciliation is described as an act of justification (cf "righteousness," 21); this contrasts with the covenant that condemned (3, 8). *The ministry of reconciliation:* Paul's role in the wider picture is described: entrusted with the message of reconciliation (19), he is Christ's ambassador, through whom God appeals (20a). In v 20b Paul acts in the capacity just described.

5, 21: This is a statement of God's purpose, expressed paradoxically in terms of sharing and exchange of attributes. As Christ became our righteousness (1 Cor 1, 30), we become God's righteousness (cf vv 14-15).

6, 1-10: This paragraph is a single long sentence in the Greek, interrupted by the parenthesis of v 2. The one main verb is "we appeal." In this paragraph Paul both exercises his ministry of reconciliation (cf 5, 20) and describes how his ministry is exercised: the "message of reconciliation" (5, 19) is lived existentially in his apostolic experience.

6, 1: *Not to receive . . . in vain:* i.e., conform to the gift of justification and new creation. The context indicates how this can be done concretely: become God's righteousness (5, 21), not live for oneself (5, 15), be reconciled with Paul (6, 11-13; 7, 2-3).

6, 2: *In an acceptable time:* Paul cites the Septuagint text of Is 49, 8; the Hebrew reads "in a time of favor"; it is parallel to "on the day of salvation." *Now:* God is bestowing favor and salvation at this very moment, as Paul is addressing his letter to them.

6, 3: *Cause no one to stumble:* the language echoes that of 1 Cor 8-10, as does the expression "no longer live for themselves" in 5, 15. *That no fault may be found:* i.e., at the eschatological judgment (cf 1 Cor 4, 2-5).

6, 4a: This is the central assertion, the topic statement for the catalogue that follows. *We commend ourselves:* Paul's self-commendation is ironical (with an eye on the charges mentioned in 3, 1-3) and paradoxical (pointing mostly to experiences that would not normally be considered points of pride but are perceived as such by faith). Cf also the self-commendation in 11, 23-29. *As ministers of God:* the same Greek word, *diakonos,* means "minister" and "servant"; cf 11, 23, the central assertion in a similar context, and 1 Cor 3, 5.

6, 4b-5: *Through much endurance:* this phrase functions as a subtitle; it is followed by an enumeration of nine specific types of trials endured.

trary, in everything we commend our-
selves as ministers of God, through
much endurance, in afflictions, hard-
ships, constraints, [5]* beatings, impris-
onments, riots, labors, vigils, fasts;
[6]*† by purity, knowledge, patience,
kindness, in a holy spirit, in unfeigned
love, [7]* in truthful speech, in the power
of God; with weapons of righteousness
at the right and at the left; [8]† through
glory and dishonor, insult and praise.
We are treated as deceivers and yet are
truthful; [9]* as unrecognized and yet ac-
knowledged; as dying and behold we
live; as chastised and yet not put to
death; [10]* as sorrowful yet always re-
joicing; as poor yet enriching many; as
having nothing and yet possessing all
things.

[11]† We have spoken frankly to you,
Corinthians; our heart is open wide.
[12]* You are not constrained by us; you
are constrained by your own affec-
tions. [13]* As recompense in kind (I
speak as to my children), be open your-
selves.

Call to Holiness.† [14]† Do not be yoked
with those who are different, with un-
believers. For what partnership do
righteousness and lawlessness have? Or
what fellowship does light have with
darkness? [15] What accord has Christ
with Beliar? Or what has a believer in
common with an unbeliever? [16]*† What
agreement has the temple of God with
idols? For we are the temple of the liv-
ing God; as God said:

"I will live with them and move
among them,
and I will be their God
and they shall be my people.
17* Therefore, come forth from them
and be separate," says the Lord,
"and touch nothing unclean;
then I will receive you
18* and I will be a father to you,
and you shall be sons and daugh-
ters to me,
says the Lord Almighty."

CHAPTER 7

[1] Since we have these promises, be-
loved, let us cleanse ourselves from ev-
ery defilement of flesh and spirit, mak-
ing holiness perfect in the fear of God.

[2]† Make room for us; we have not
wronged anyone, or ruined anyone, or
taken advantage of anyone. [3]* I do not
say this in condemnation, for I have al-
ready said that you are in our hearts,
that we may die together and live to-
gether. [4] I have great confidence in you,
I have great pride in you; I am filled
with encouragement, I am overflowing
with joy all the more because of all our
affliction.

C. Resolution of the Crisis†

Paul's Joy in Macedonia.† [5]*† For
even when we came into Macedonia,

*

5: Acts 16, 23.
6: Gal 5, 22-23.
7: 10, 4; Rom 13, 12; Eph 6, 11-17.
9: 4, 10-11; Rom 8, 36.
10: Rom 8, 32; 1 Cor 3, 21.
12: 7, 3.
13: Gal 4, 19.
16: 1 Cor 10, 20-21 / 1 Cor 3, 16-17; 6, 19 / Ex 25, 8; 29, 45; Lv 26, 12; Jer 31, 1; 32, 38; Ez 37, 27.
17: Is 52, 11; Ez 20, 34.41; Rv 18, 4; 21, 27.
18: 2 Sm 7, 14; Ps 2, 7; Is 43, 6; Jer 31, 9; Rv 21, 7 / Rv 4, 8; 11, 17; 15, 3; 21, 22.
7, 3: 6, 11-13.
5: 2, 13.

†

6, 6-7a: A list of virtuous qualities in two groups of four, the second fuller than the first.

6, 8b-10: A series of seven rhetorically effective antitheses, contrasting negative external impressions with positive inner reality. Paul perceives his existence as a reflection of Jesus' own and affirms an inner reversal that escapes outward observation. The final two members illustrate two distinct kinds of paradox or apparent contradiction that are characteristic of apostolic experience.

6, 11-13: Paul's tone becomes quieter, but his appeal for acceptance and affection is emotionally charged. References to the heart and their mutual relations bring the development begun in 2, 14—3, 3 to an effective conclusion.

6, 14—7, 1: Language and thought shift noticeably here. Suddenly we are in a different atmosphere, dealing with a quite different problem. Both the vocabulary and the thought, with their contrast between good and evil, are more characteristic of Qumran documents or the Book of Revelation than they are of Paul. Hence, critics suspect that this section was inserted by another hand.

6, 14-16a: The opening injunction to separate from unbelievers is reinforced by five rhetorical questions to make the point that Christianity is not compatible with paganism. Their opposition is emphasized also by the accumulation of five distinct designations for each group. These verses are a powerful statement of God's holiness and the exclusiveness of his claims.

6, 16c-18: This is a chain of scriptural citations carefully woven together. God's covenant relation to his people and his presence among them (16) is seen as conditioned on cultic separation from the profane and cultically impure (17); that relation is translated into the personal language of the parent-child relationship, an extension to the community of the language of 2 Sm 7, 14 (18). Some remarkable parallels to this chain are found in the final chapters of Revelation. God's presence among his people (21, 22) is expressed there, too, by applying 2 Sm 7, 14 to the community (21, 7). There is a call to separation (18, 4) and exclusion of the unclean from the community and its liturgy (21, 27). The title "Lord Almighty" (*Pantokratōr*) occurs in the New Testament only here in 18 and nine times in Rv.

7, 2-4: These verses continue the thought of 6, 11-13, before the interruption of 6, 14—7, 1. Verse 4 serves as a transition to the next section: the four themes it introduces (confidence; pride or "boasting"; encouragement; joy in affliction) are developed in vv 5-16. All have appeared previously in the letter.

7, 5-16: This section functions as a peroration or formal summing up of the whole first part of the letter, chs 1-7. It deals with the restoration of right relations between Paul and the Corinthians, and it is marked by fullness and intensity of emotion.

7, 5-7: Paul picks up the thread of the narrative interrupted at 2, 13 (5) and describes the resolution of the tense situation there depicted (6-7). Finally Titus arrives and his coming puts an end to Paul's restlessness (2, 13; 7, 5); casts out his fears, and reverses his mood. The theme of encouragement and affliction is reintroduced (cf 1, 3-11); here, too, encouragement is traced back to God and is described as contagious (6). The language of joy and sorrow also reappears in v 7 (cf 1, 23—2, 1 and the note on 1, 23-24).

7, 5: *Macedonia:* see the note on 2, 13.

our flesh had no rest, but we were af-
flicted in every way—external conflicts,
internal fears. 6* But God, who encour-
ages the downcast, encouraged us by
the arrival of Titus, 7 and not only by
his arrival but also by the encourage-
ment with which he was encouraged in
regard to you, as he told us of your
yearning, your lament, your zeal for
me, so that I rejoiced even more.
8*† For even if I saddened you by my
letter, I do not regret it; and if I did re-
gret it ([for] I see that that letter sad-
dened you, if only for a while), 9 I rejoice
now, not because you were saddened,
but because you were saddened into re-
pentance; for you were saddened in a
godly way, so that you did not suffer
loss in anything because of us. 10 For
godly sorrow produces a salutary re-
pentance without regret, but worldly
sorrow produces death. 11 For behold
what earnestness this godly sorrow has
produced for you, as well as readiness
for a defense, and indignation, and fear,
and yearning, and zeal, and punish-
ment. In every way you have shown
yourselves to be innocent in the matter.
12* So then even though I wrote to you,
it was not on account of the one who
did the wrong, or on account of the one
who suffered the wrong, but in order
that your concern for us might be made
plain to you in the sight of God. 13† For
this reason we are encouraged.

And besides our encouragement, we
rejoice even more because of the joy of
Titus, since his spirit has been refreshed
by all of you. 14 For if I have boasted
to him about you, I was not put to
shame. No, just as everything we said
to you was true, so our boasting before
Titus proved to be the truth. 15* And his
heart goes out to you all the more, as
he remembers the obedience of all of
you, when you received him with fear
and trembling. 16 I rejoice, because
I have confidence in you in every re-
spect.

III: THE COLLECTION FOR JERUSALEM†

CHAPTER 8

Generosity in Giving.† 1*† We want
you to know, brothers, of the grace of
God that has been given to the churches
of Macedonia, 2† for in a severe test of
affliction, the abundance of their joy
and their profound poverty overflowed
in a wealth of generosity on their part.
3† For according to their means, I can
testify, and beyond their means, spon-
taneously, 4* they begged us insistently
for the favor of taking part in the ser-
vice to the holy ones, 5† and this, not
as we expected, but they gave them-
selves first to the Lord and to us through

*

6: 7, 13-14; 1 Thes 3, 6-8.
8: 2, 2-4; Heb 12, 11.
12: 2, 3.9; 7, 8.
15: 2, 9.
8, 1: 11, 9; Rom 15, 26.
4: Acts 24, 17; Rom 15, 31.

†

7, 8-12: Paul looks back on the episode from the viewpoint of its ending. The goal of their common activity, promotion of their joy (1, 24), has been achieved, despite and because of the sorrow they felt. That sorrow was God-given. Its salutary effects are enumerated fully and impressively in vv 10-11; not the least important of these is that it has revealed to them the attachment they have to Paul.

7, 13-16: Paul summarizes the effect of the experience on Titus: encouragement, joy, love, relief. Finally, he describes its effects on himself: encouragement, joy, confidence, pride or "boasting" (i.e., the satisfaction resulting from a boast that proves well-founded; cf 4; 1, 12.14).

8, 1—9, 15: Paul turns to a new topic, the collection for the church in Jerusalem. There is an early precedent for this project in the agreement mentioned in Gal 2, 6-10. According to Acts, the church at Antioch had sent Saul and Barnabas to Jerusalem with relief (Acts 11, 27-30). Subsequently Paul organized a project of relief for Jerusalem among his own churches. Our earliest evidence for it comes in 1 Cor 16, 1-4, after it had already begun (see the notes there); by the time Paul wrote Rom 15, 25-28 the collection was completed and ready for delivery. Chapters 8 and 9 contain what appear to be two letters on the subject. In them Paul gives us his fullest exposition of the meaning he sees in the enterprise, presenting it as an act of Christian charity and as an expression of the unity of the church, both present and eschatological. These chapters are especially rich in the recurrence of key words, on which Paul plays; it is usually impossible to do justice to these wordplays in the translation.

8, 1-24: This is a letter of recommendation for Titus and two unnamed companions, written from Macedonia probably at least a year later than 1 Cor 16. The recommendation proper is prefaced by remarks about the ideals of sharing and equality within the Christian community (1-15). Phil 4, 10-20 shows that Paul has reflected on his personal experience of need and relief in his relations with the community at Philippi; he now develops his reflections on the larger scale of relations between his Gentile churches and the mother church in Jerusalem.

8, 1-5: The example of the Macedonians, a model of what ought to be happening at Corinth, provides Paul with the occasion for expounding his theology of "giving."

8, 1: *The grace of God:* the fundamental theme is expressed by the Greek noun *charis,* which will be variously translated throughout these chapters as "grace" (8, 1; 9, 8.14), "favor" (8, 4), "gracious act" (8, 6.7.9) or "gracious work" (8, 19), to be compared to "gracious gift" (1 Cor 16, 3). The related term, *eucharistia,* "thanksgiving," also occurs at 9, 11.12. The wordplay is not superficial; various mutations of the same root signal inner connection between aspects of a single reality, and Paul consciously exploits the similarities in vocabulary to highlight that connection.

8, 2: Three more terms are now introduced. *Test* (*dokimē*): the same root is translated as "to test" (8) and "evidence" (9, 13); it means to be tried and found genuine. *Abundance:* variations on the same root lie behind "overflow" (8, 2; 9, 12), "excel" (8, 7), "surplus" (8, 14), "superfluous" (9, 1), "make abundant" and "have an abundance" (9, 8). These expressions of fullness contrast with references to need (8, 14; 9, 12). *Generosity:* the word *haplotēs* has nuances of both simplicity and sincerity; here and in 9, 11.13 it designates the singleness of purpose that manifests itself in generous giving.

8, 3-4: Paul emphasizes the spontaneity of the Macedonians and the nature of their action. *They begged us insistently:* the same root is translated as "urge," "appeal," "encourage" (8, 6.17; 9, 5). *Taking part:* the same word is translated "contribution" in 9, 13 and a related term as "partner" in 8, 23. *Service* (*diakonia*): this word occurs also in 9, 1.13 as "service"; in 9, 12 it is translated "administration," and in 8, 19.20 the corresponding verb is rendered "administer."

8, 5: *They gave themselves . . . to the Lord and to us:* on its deepest level their attitude is one of self-giving.

the will of God, 6*† so that we urged Titus that, as he had already begun, he should also complete for you this gracious act also. 7*† Now as you excel in every respect, in faith, discourse, knowledge, all earnestness, and in the love we have for you, may you excel in this gracious act also.

8 I say this not by way of command, but to test the genuineness of your love by your concern for others. 9*† For you know the gracious act of our Lord Jesus Christ, that for your sake he became poor although he was rich, so that by his poverty you might become rich. 10* And I am giving counsel in this matter, for it is appropriate for you who began not only to act but to act willingly last year: 11† complete it now, so that your eager willingness may be matched by your completion of it out of what you have. 12† For if the eagerness is there, it is acceptable according to what one has, not according to what one does not have; 13 not that others should have relief while you are burdened, but that as a matter of equality 14 your surplus at the present time should supply their needs, so that their surplus may also supply your needs, that there may be equality. 15* As it is written:

"Whoever had much did not have more,
and whoever had little did not have less."

Titus and His Collaborators. † 16 But thanks be to God who put the same concern for you into the heart of Titus, 17 for he not only welcomed our appeal but, since he is very concerned, he has gone to you of his own accord. 18*† With him we have sent the brother who is praised in all the churches for his preaching of the gospel. 19* And not only that, but he has also been appointed our traveling companion by the churches in this gracious work administered by us for the glory of the Lord [himself] and for the expression of our eagerness. 20† This we desire to avoid, that anyone blame us about this lavish gift administered by us, 21* for we are concerned for what is honorable not only in the sight of the Lord but also in the sight of others. 22 And with them we have sent our brother whom we often tested in many ways and found earnest, but who is now much more earnest because of his great confidence in you. 23 As for Titus, he is my partner and co-worker for you; as for our brothers, they are apostles of the churches, the glory of Christ. 24† So give proof before the churches of your love and of our boasting about you to them.

CHAPTER 9

God's Indescribable Gift. † 1 Now about the service to the holy ones, it is superfluous for me to write to you, 2*† for I know your eagerness, about which I boast of you to the Macedonians, that Achaia has been ready since last year; and your zeal has stirred up most of them. 3† Nonetheless, I sent the brothers so that our boast about you might not prove empty in this case, so

---

*

6: 2, 13; 7, 6-7.13-14; 8, 16.23; 12, 18.
7: 1 Cor 1, 5.
9: 6, 10; Phil 2, 6-8.
10: 9, 2; 1 Cor 16, 1-4.
15: Ex 16, 18.
18: 12, 18.
19: 1 Cor 16, 3-4.
21: Rom 12, 17.
9, 2: 8, 10; Rom 15, 26.

---

†

8, 6: *Titus:* 1 Cor 16 seemed to leave the organization up to the Corinthians, but apparently Paul has sent Titus to initiate the collection as well; 8, 16-17 will describe Titus' attitude as one of shared concern and cooperation.

8, 7: The charitable service Paul is promoting is seen briefly and in passing within the perspective of Paul's theology of the charisms. *Earnestness* (*spoudē*): this or related terms occur also in v 22 ("earnest") and 8, 8.16.17 ("concern").

8, 9: The dialectic of Jesus' experience, expressed earlier in terms of life and death (5, 15), sin and righteousness (5, 21), is now rephrased in terms of poverty and wealth. Many scholars think this is a reference to Jesus' preexistence with God (his "wealth") and to his incarnation and death (his "poverty"), and they point to the similarity between this verse and Phil 2, 6-8. Others interpret the wealth and poverty as succeeding phases of Jesus' earthly existence, e.g., his sense of intimacy with God and then the desolation and the feeling of abandonment by God in his death (cf Mk 15, 34).

8, 11: *Eager:* the word *prothymia* also occurs in 8, 12.19; 9, 2.

8, 12-15: Paul introduces the principle of *equality* into the discussion. The goal is not impoverishment but sharing of resources; balance is achieved at least over the course of time. In v 15 Paul grounds his argument unexpectedly in the experience of Israel gathering manna in the desert: equality was achieved, independently of personal exertion, by God, who gave with an even hand according to need. Paul touches briefly here on the theme of "living from God."

8, 16-24: In recommending Titus and his companions, Paul stresses their personal and apostolic qualities, their good dispositions toward the Corinthians, and their authority as messengers of the churches and representatives of Christ.

8, 18: *The brother:* we do not know the identity of this coworker of Paul, nor of the third companion mentioned below in v 22.

8, 20-22: *That anyone blame us:* 12, 16-18 suggests that misunderstandings may indeed have arisen concerning Paul's management of the collection through the messengers mentioned here, but those same verses seem to imply that the Corinthians by and large would recognize the honesty of Paul's conduct in this area as in others (cf 6, 3).

8, 24: As Paul began by holding up the Macedonians as examples to be imitated, he closes by exhorting the Corinthians to show their love (by accepting the envoys and by cooperating as the Macedonians do), thus justifying the pride Paul demonstrates because of them before other churches.

9, 1-15: Quite possibly this was originally an independent letter, though it deals with the same subject and continues many of the same themes. In that case, it may have been written a few weeks later than ch 8, while the delegation there mentioned was still on its way.

9, 2: *Achaia:* see the note on Rom 15, 26.

9, 3: *I sent the brothers:* the Greek aorist tense here could be epistolary, referring to the present; in that case Paul would be sending them now, and ch 9 would merely conclude the letter of recommendation begun in ch 8. But the aorist may also refer to a sending that is past as Paul writes; then ch 9, with its apparently fresh beginning, is a follow-up message entrusted to another carrier.

that you might be ready, as I said,
4 for fear that if any Macedonians come
with me and find you not ready we
might be put to shame (to say nothing
of you) in this conviction. 5 So I thought
it necessary to encourage the brothers
to go on ahead to you and arrange in
advance for your promised gift, so that
in this way it might be ready as a boun-
tiful gift and not as an exaction.
6* Consider this: whoever sows spar-
ingly will also reap sparingly, and
whoever sows bountifully will also reap
bountifully. 7* Each must do as already
determined, without sadness or com-
pulsion, for God loves a cheerful giver.
8† Moreover, God is able to make every
grace abundant for you, so that in all
things, always having all you need, you
may have an abundance for every good
work. 9* As it is written:

> "He scatters abroad, he gives to the poor;
> his righteousness endures forever."

10* The one who supplies seed to the
sower and bread for food will supply
and multiply your seed and increase the
harvest of your righteousness.
11† You are being enriched in every
way for all generosity, which through
us produces thanksgiving to God,
12 for the administration of this public
service is not only supplying the needs
of the holy ones but is also overflowing
in many acts of thanksgiving to God.
13* Through the evidence of this service,
you are glorifying God for your obedi-
ent confession of the gospel of Christ
and the generosity of your contribution
to them and to all others, 14 while in
prayer on your behalf they long for you,
because of the surpassing grace of God
upon you. 15* Thanks be to God for his
indescribable gift!

IV: PAUL'S DEFENSE OF HIS MINISTRY†

CHAPTER 10

***Accusation of Weakness.*†** 1† Now I
myself, Paul, urge you through the gen-
tleness and clemency of Christ, I who
am humble when face to face with you,
but brave toward you when absent,
2*† I beg you that, when present, I may
not have to be brave with that confi-
dence with which I intend to act boldly
against some who consider us as acting
according to the flesh. 3† For, although
we are in the flesh, we do not battle ac-
cording to the flesh, 4* for the weapons
of our battle are not of flesh but are
enormously powerful, capable of de-
stroying fortresses. We destroy argu-
ments 5 and every pretension raising
itself against the knowledge of God, and
take every thought captive in obedience
to Christ, 6* and we are ready to punish

*

6: Prv 11, 24-25.
7: Prv 22, 8 LXX.
9: Ps 112, 9.
10: Is 55, 10.
13: 8, 4; Rom 15, 31.
15: Rom 5, 15-16.
10, 2: 13, 2.10; 1 Cor 4, 21.
4: 6, 7; 13, 2-3; 1 Cor 1, 25; Eph 6, 10-14.
6: 2, 9.

†

9, 8-10: The behavior to which he exhorts them is grounded in God's own pattern of behavior. God is capable of overwhelming generosity, as scripture itself attests (9), so that they need not fear being short. He will provide in abundance, both supplying their natural needs and increasing their righteousness. Paul challenges them to godlike generosity and reminds them of the fundamental motive for encouragement: God himself cannot be outdone.

9, 11-15: Paul's vision broadens to take in all the interested parties in one dynamic picture. His language becomes liturgically colored and conveys a sense of fullness. With a final play on the words *charis* and *eucharistia* (see the note on 8, 1), he describes a circle that closes on itself: the movement of grace overflowing from God to them and handed on from them through Paul to others is completed by the prayer of praise and thanksgiving raised on their behalf to God.

10, 1—13, 10: These final chapters have their own unity of structure and theme and could well have formed the body of a separate letter. They constitute an *apologia* on Paul's part, i.e., a legal defense of his behavior and his ministry; the writing is emotionally charged and highly rhetorical. In the central section (11, 16—12, 10), the *apologia* takes the form of a boast. This section is prepared for by a prologue (11, 1-15) and followed by an epilogue (12, 11-18), which are similar in content and structure. These sections, in turn, are framed by an introduction (10, 1-18) and a conclusion (12, 19—13, 10), both of which assert Paul's apostolic authority and confidence and define the purpose of the letter. The structure that results from this disposition of the material is chiastic, i.e., the first element corresponds to the last, the second to the second last, etc., following the pattern *a b c b' a'*.

10, 1-18: Paul asserts his apostolic authority and expresses the confidence this generates in him. He writes in response to certain opinions that have arisen in the community and certain charges raised against him and in preparation for a forthcoming visit in which he intends to set things in order. This section gives us an initial glimpse of the situation in Corinth that Paul must address; much of its thematic material will be taken up again in the finale (12, 19—13, 10).

10, 1-2: A strong opening plunges us straight into the conflict. Contrasts dominate here: presence versus absence, gentleness-clemency-humility versus boldness-confidence-bravery. *Through the gentleness and clemency of Christ:* the figure of the gentle Christ, presented in a significant position before any specifics of the situation are suggested, forms a striking contrast to the picture of the bold and militant Paul (2-6); this tension is finally resolved in 13, 3-4. *Absent . . . present:* this same contrast, with a restatement of the purpose of the letter, recurs in 13, 10, which forms an inclusion with 10, 1-2.

10, 2b-4a: *Flesh:* the Greek word *sarx* can express both the physical life of the body without any pejorative overtones (as in "we are in the flesh," 3) and our natural life insofar as it is marked by limitation and weakness (as in the other expressions) in contrast to the higher life and power conferred by the Spirit; cf the note on 1 Cor 3, 1. The wordplay is intended to express the paradoxical situation of a life already taken over by the Spirit but not yet seen as such except by faith. Lack of empirical evidence of the Spirit permits misunderstanding and misjudgment, but Paul resolutely denies that his behavior and effectiveness are as limited as some suppose.

10, 3b-6: Paul is involved in combat. The strong military language and imagery are both an assertion of his confidence in the divine power at his disposal and a declaration of war against those who underestimate his resources. The threat is echoed in 13, 2-3.

every disobedience, once your obedi-
ence is complete.
7*† Look at what confronts you.
Whoever is confident of belonging to
Christ should consider that as he
belongs to Christ, so do we. 8* And
even if I should boast a little too much
of our authority, which the Lord
gave for building you up and not for
tearing you down, I shall not be
put to shame. 9† May I not seem as
one frightening you through letters.
10* For someone will say, "His let-
ters are severe and forceful, but his
bodily presence is weak, and his
speech contemptible." 11* Such a per-
son must understand that what we
are in word through letters when ab-
sent, that we also are in action when
present.
12*† Not that we dare to class or com-
pare ourselves with some of those who
recommend themselves. But when they
measure themselves by one another
and compare themselves with one
another, they are without understand-
ing. 13† But we will not boast beyond
measure but will keep to the limits
God has apportioned us, namely, to
reach even to you. 14 For we are not
overreaching ourselves, as though
we did not reach you; we indeed first
came to you with the gospel of Christ.
15 We are not boasting beyond mea-
sure, in other people's labors; yet our
hope is that, as your faith increases,
our influence among you may be
greatly enlarged, within our proper
limits, 16* so that we may preach the gos-
pel even beyond you, not boasting of
work already done in another's sphere.
17*† "Whoever boasts, should boast
in the Lord." 18*† For it is not the one
who recommends himself who is
approved, but the one whom the Lord
recommends.

CHAPTER 11

***Preaching without Charge.*†** 1*† If
only you would put up with a little fool-
ishness from me! Please put up with me.
2*† For I am jealous of you with the jeal-
ousy of God, since I betrothed you to
one husband to present you as a chaste
virgin to Christ. 3*† But I am afraid that,
as the serpent deceived Eve by his cun-
ning, your thoughts may be corrupted
from a sincere [and pure] commitment
to Christ. 4*† For if someone comes and
preaches another Jesus than the one we
preached, or if you receive a different
spirit from the one you received or a
different gospel from the one you ac-
cepted, you put up with it well enough.

*

7: 1 Cor 1, 12.
8: 13, 10.
10: 1 Cor 2, 3.
11: 13, 1-2.
12: 3, 1-2; 4, 2; 5, 12; 6, 4; 10, 18; 12, 11.
16: Rom 15, 20-21.
17: Jer 9, 22-23; 1 Cor 1, 31.
18: 13, 3-9.
11, 1: 11, 21; 12, 11.
2: Hos 2, 21-22; Eph 5, 26-27.
3: Gn 3, 1-6.
4: Gal 1, 6-9.

†

10, 7-8: *Belonging to Christ . . . so do we:* these phrases already announce the pattern of Paul's boast in 11, 21b-29, especially 11, 22-23. *For building you up and not for tearing you down:* Paul draws on the language by which Jeremiah described the purpose of the prophetic power the Lord gave to him (Jer 1, 9-10; 12, 16-17; 24, 6). Though Paul's power may have destructive effects on others (2-6), its intended effect on the community is entirely constructive (cf 13, 10). *I shall not be put to shame:* his assertions will not be refuted; they will be revealed as true at the judgment.

10, 9-10: Paul cites the complaints of some who find him lacking in personal forcefulness and holds out the threat of a personal *parousia* (both "return" and "presence") that will be forceful, indeed will be a demonstration of Christ's own power (cf 13, 2-4).

10, 12-18: Paul now qualifies his claim to boldness, indicating its limits. He distinguishes his own behavior from that of others, revealing those "others" as they appear to him: as self-recommending, immoderately boastful, encroaching on territory not assigned to them, and claiming credit not due to them.

10, 13: *Will keep to the limits:* the notion of proper limits is expressed here by two terms with overlapping meanings, *metron* and *kanōn,* which are played off against several expressions denoting overreaching or expansion beyond a legitimate sphere.

10, 17: *Boast in the Lord:* there is a legitimate boasting, in contrast to the immoderate boasting to which vv 13 and 15 allude. God's work through Paul in the community is the object of his boast (13-16; 1, 12-14) and constitutes his recommendation (3, 1-3). Cf the notes on 1, 12-14 and 1 Cor 1, 29-31.

10, 18: *Approved:* to be approved is to come successfully through the process of testing for authenticity (cf 13, 3-7 and the note on 8, 2). *Whom the Lord recommends:* self-commendation is a premature and unwarranted anticipation of the final judgment, which the Lord alone will pass (cf 1 Cor 4, 3-5). Paul alludes to this judgment throughout chs 10-13, frequently in final or transitional positions; cf 11, 15; 12, 19a; 13, 3-7.

11, 1-15: Although these verses continue to reveal information about Paul's opponents and the differences he perceives between them and himself, 11, 1 signals a turn in Paul's thought. This section constitutes a prologue to the boasting that he will undertake in 11, 16—12, 10, and it bears remarkable similarities to the section that follows the central boast, 12, 11-18.

11, 1: *Put up with a little foolishness from me:* this verse indicates more clearly than the general statement of intent in 10, 13 the nature of the project Paul is about to undertake. He alludes ironically to the Corinthians' toleration for others. *Foolishness:* Paul qualifies his project as folly from beginning to end; see the note on 11, 16—12, 10.

11, 2: Paul gives us a sudden glimpse of the theological values that are at stake. *The jealousy of God:* the perspective is that of the covenant, described in imagery of love and marriage, as in the prophets; cf 1 Cor 10, 22. *I betrothed you:* Paul, like a father (cf 12, 14), betroths the community to Christ as his bride (cf Eph 5, 21-33) and will present her to him at his second coming. Cf Mt 25, 1-13 and the nuptial imagery in Rv 21.

11, 3: *As the serpent deceived Eve:* before Christ can return for the community Paul fears a repetition of the primal drama of seduction. Corruption of minds is satanic activity (see 2, 11; 4, 4). Satanic imagery recurs in 11, 13-15.20; 12, 7b.16-17; see the notes on these passages.

11, 4: *Preaches another Jesus:* the danger is specified, and Paul's opponents are identified with the cunning serpent. The battle for minds has to do with the understanding of Jesus, the Spirit, the gospel; the Corinthians have flirted with another understanding than the one that Paul handed on to them as traditional and normative.

5*† For I think that I am not in any way
inferior to these "superapostles."
6*† Even if I am untrained in speaking,
I am not so in knowledge; in every way
we have made this plain to you in all
things.
7*† Did I make a mistake when I hum-
bled myself so that you might be ex-
alted, because I preached the gospel of
God to you without charge? 8 I plun-
dered other churches by accepting from
them in order to minister to you. 9* And
when I was with you and in need, I did
not burden anyone, for the brothers who
came from Macedonia supplied my
needs. So I refrained and will refrain
from burdening you in any way. 10* By
the truth of Christ in me, this boast of
mine shall not be silenced in the regions
of Achaia. 11*† And why? Because I do
not love you? God knows I do!
12 And what I do I will continue to do,
in order to end this pretext of those who
seek a pretext for being regarded as we
are in the mission of which they boast.
13† For such people are false apostles,
deceitful workers, who masquerade as
apostles of Christ. 14 And no wonder, for
even Satan masquerades as an angel of
light. 15 So it is not strange that his min-
isters also masquerade as ministers of
righteousness. Their end will corre-
spond to their deeds.

Paul's Boast: His Labors. † 16† I re-
peat, no one should consider me foolish;
but if you do, accept me as a fool, so
that I too may boast a little. 17 What I
am saying I am not saying according
to the Lord but as in foolishness, in this
boastful state. 18 Since many boast ac-
cording to the flesh, I too will boast.
19 For you gladly put up with fools, since
you are wise yourselves. 20† For you put
up with it if someone enslaves you, or
devours you, or gets the better of you,
or puts on airs, or slaps you in the face.
21† To my shame I say that we were too
weak!
But what anyone dares to boast of (I
am speaking in foolishness) I also dare.
22*† Are they Hebrews? So am I. Are
they Israelites? So am I. Are they de-
scendants of Abraham? So am I.
23*† Are they ministers of Christ? (I

*

5: 12, 11.
6: 1 Cor 1, 5.17; 2, 1-5.
7: 12, 13-18; Acts 18, 3; 1 Cor 9, 6-18.
9: Phil 4, 15.18.
10: 1 Cor 9, 15.
11: 12, 15.
22: Acts 22, 3 / Rom 11, 1; Phil 3, 5-6.
23: 6, 5; Acts 16, 22-24; 1 Cor 15, 31-32.

†

11, 5: *These "superapostles":* this term, employed again in 12, 11b, designates the opponents of whom Paul has spoken in ch 10 and again in 11, 4. They appear to be intruders at Corinth. Their preaching is marked at least by a different emphasis and style, and they do not hesitate to accept support from the community. Perhaps these itinerants appeal to the authority of church leaders in Jerusalem and even carry letters of recommendation from them. But it is not those distant leaders whom Paul is attacking here. The intruders are "superapostles" not in the sense of the "pillars" at Jerusalem (Gal 2), but in their own estimation. They consider themselves superior to Paul as apostles and ministers of Christ, and they are obviously enjoying some success among the Corinthians. Paul rejects their claim to be apostles in any superlative sense (*hyperlian*), judging them bluntly as "false apostles," ministers of Satan masquerading as apostles of Christ (13-15). On the contrary, he himself will claim to be a superminister of Christ (*hyper egō*, 23).

11, 6: Apparently found deficient in both rhetorical ability (cf 10, 10) and knowledge (cf 10, 5), Paul concedes the former charge but not the latter. *In every way:* in all their contacts with him revelation has been taking place. Paul, through whom God reveals the knowledge of himself (2, 14), and in whom the death and life of Jesus are revealed (4, 10-11; cf 6, 4), also demonstrates his own role as the bearer of true knowledge. Cf 1 Cor 1, 18—2, 16.

11, 7-10: Abruptly Paul passes to another reason for complaints: his practice of preaching without remuneration (cf 1 Cor 9, 3-18). He deftly defends his practice by situating it from the start within the pattern of Christ's own self-humiliation (cf 10, 1) and reduces objections to absurdity by rhetorical questions (cf 12, 13).

11, 11-12: Paul rejects lack of affection as his motive (possibly imputed to him by his opponents) and states his real motive, a desire to emphasize the disparity between himself and the others (cf 19-21). The topic of his gratuitous service will be taken up once more in 12, 13-18. 1 Cor 9, 15-18 gives a different but complementary explanation of his motivation.

11, 13-15: Paul picks up again the imagery of v 3 and applies it to the opponents: they are false apostles of Christ, really serving another master. *Deceitful . . . masquerade:* deception and simulation, like cunning (3), are marks of the satanic. *Angel of light:* recalls the contrast between light and darkness, Christ and Beliar at 6, 14-15. *Ministers of righteousness:* recalls the earlier contrast between the ministry of condemnation and that of righteousness (3, 9). *Their end:* the section closes with another allusion to the judgment, when all participants in the final conflict will be revealed or unmasked and dealt with as they deserve.

11, 16—12, 10: Paul now accepts the challenge of his opponents and indulges in boasting similar to theirs, but with differences that he has already signaled in 10, 12-18 and that become clearer as he proceeds. He defines the nature of his project and unmistakably labels it as folly at the beginning and the end (11, 16-23; 12, 11). Yet his boast does not spring from ignorance (11, 21; 12, 6) nor is it concerned merely with human distinctions (11, 18). Paul boasts "in moderation" (10, 13.15) and "in the Lord" (10, 17).

11, 16-29: The first part of Paul's boast focuses on labors and afflictions, in which authentic service of Christ consists.

11, 16-21: These verses recapitulate remarks already made about the foolishness of boasting and the excessive toleration of the Corinthians. They form a prelude to the boast proper.

11, 20: Paul describes the activities of the "others" in terms that fill out the picture drawn in vv 3-4.13-15. Much of the vocabulary suggests fleshly or even satanic activity. *Enslaves:* cf Gal 2, 4. *Devours:* cf 1 Pt 5, 8. *Gets the better:* the verb *lambanō* means "to take," but is used in a variety of senses; here it may imply financial advantage, as in the English colloquialism "to take someone." It is similarly used at 12, 16 and is there connected with cunning and deceit. *Puts on airs:* the same verb is rendered "raise oneself" (10, 5) and "be too elated" (12, 7).

11, 21: Paul ironically concedes the charge of personal weakness from 10, 1-18 but will refute the other charge there mentioned, that of lack of boldness, accepting the challenge to demonstrate it by his boast.

11, 22: The opponents apparently pride themselves on their "Jewishness." Paul, too, can claim to be a Jew by race, religion, and promise. *Descendants of Abraham:* elsewhere Paul distinguishes authentic from inauthentic heirs of Abraham and the promise (Rom 4, 13-18; 9, 7-13; 11, 1; Gal 3, 9.27-29; cf Jn 8, 33-47). Here he grants his opponents this title in order to concentrate on the principal claim that follows.

11, 23a: *Ministers of Christ . . . I am still more:* the central point of the boast (cf the note on 11, 5). *Like an insane person:* the climax of his folly.

11, 23b-29: Service of the humiliated and crucified Christ is demonstrated by trials endured for him. This rhetorically impressive catalogue enumerates many of the labors and perils Paul encountered on his missionary journeys.

am talking like an insane person.) I am
still more, with far greater labors, far
more imprisonments, far worse beat-
ings, and numerous brushes with death.
24* Five times at the hands of the Jews
I received forty lashes minus one.
25* Three times I was beaten with rods,
once I was stoned, three times I was
shipwrecked, I passed a night and a day
on the deep; 26 on frequent journeys, in
dangers from rivers, dangers from rob-
bers, dangers from my own race, dan-
gers from Gentiles, dangers in the city,
dangers in the wilderness, dangers at
sea, dangers among false brothers;
27* in toil and hardship, through many
sleepless nights, through hunger and
thirst, through frequent fastings,
through cold and exposure. 28 And apart
from these things, there is the daily
pressure upon me of my anxiety for all
the churches. 29* Who is weak, and I am
not weak? Who is led to sin, and I am
not indignant?
Paul's Boast: His Weakness.† 30 If I
must boast, I will boast of the things that
show my weakness. 31† The God and
Father of the Lord Jesus knows, he who
is blessed forever, that I do not lie.
32 At Damascus, the governor under
King Aretas guarded the city of Damas-
cus, in order to seize me, 33* but I was
lowered in a basket through a window
in the wall and escaped his hands.

CHAPTER 12

1† I must boast; not that it is profitable,
but I will go on to visions and revela-
tions of the Lord. 2 I know someone
in Christ who, fourteen years ago
(whether in the body or out of the body
I do not know, God knows), was caught
up to the third heaven. 3 And I know that
this person (whether in the body or out
of the body I do not know, God knows)
4* was caught up into Paradise and
heard ineffable things, which no one
may utter. 5† About this person I will
boast, but about myself I will not boast,
except about my weaknesses. 6 Al-
though if I should wish to boast, I
would not be foolish, for I would be tell-
ing the truth. But I refrain, so that no
one may think more of me than what
he sees in me or hears from me
7*† because of the abundance of the
revelations. Therefore, that I might not
become too elated, a thorn in the flesh
was given to me, an angel of Satan, to
beat me, to keep me from being too
elated. 8*† Three times I begged the
Lord about this, that it might leave me,
9*† but he said to me, "My grace is suffi-
cient for you, for power is made perfect
in weakness." I will rather boast most
gladly of my weaknesses, in order that
the power of Christ may dwell with me.
10*† Therefore, I am content with weak-

*

24: Dt 25, 2-3.
25: Acts 14, 19; 27, 43-44.
27: 1 Cor 4, 11.
29: 1 Cor 9, 22.
33: Acts 9, 23-25.
12, 4: Lk 23, 43; Rv 2, 7.
7: Nm 33, 55; Jos 23, 13; Ez 28, 24.
8: Mt 26, 39-44.
9: 4, 7.
10: 6, 4-5; Rom 5, 3 / Phil 4, 13.

†

11, 30—12, 10: The second part of Paul's boast, marked by a change of style and a shift in focus. After recalling the project in which he is engaged, he states a new topic: his weaknesses as matter for boasting. Everything in this section, even the discussion of privileges and distinctions, will be integrated into this perspective.

11, 31-32: The episode at Damascus is symbolic. It aptly illustrates Paul's weakness but ends in deliverance (cf 4, 7-11).

12, 1-4: *In the body or out of the body:* he seemed no longer confined to bodily conditions, but he does not claim to understand the mechanics of the experience. *Caught up:* i.e., in ecstasy. *The third heaven . . . Paradise:* ancient cosmologies depicted a multitiered universe. Jewish intertestamental literature contains much speculation about the number of heavens. Seven is the number usually mentioned, but the Testament of Levi (2, 7-10; 3, 1-4) speaks of three; God himself dwelt in the third of these. Without giving us any clear picture of the cosmos, Paul indicates a mental journey to a nonearthly space, set apart by God, in which secrets were revealed to him. *Ineffable things:* i.e., privileged knowledge, which it was not possible or permitted to divulge.

12, 5-7: *This person:* the indirect way of referring to himself has the effect of emphasizing the distance between that experience and his everyday life, just as the indirect *someone in Christ* (2) and all the passive verbs emphasize his passivity and receptivity in the experience. The revelations were not a personal achievement, nor were they meant to draw attention to any quality of his own.

12, 7b: *That I might not become too elated:* God assures that there is a negative component to his experience, so that he cannot lose proper perspective; cf 1, 9; 4, 7-11. *A thorn in the flesh:* variously interpreted as a sickness or physical disability, a temptation, or a handicap connected with his apostolic activity. But since Hebrew "thorn in the flesh," like English "thorn in my side," refers to persons (cf Nm 33, 55; Ez 28, 24), Paul may be referring to some especially persistent and obnoxious opponent. The language of vv 7-8 permits this interpretation. If this is correct, the frequent appearance of singular pronouns in depicting the opposition may not be merely a stylistic variation; the singular may be provoked and accompanied by the image of one individual in whom criticism of Paul's preaching, way of life, and apostolic consciousness is concentrated, and who embodies all the qualities Paul attributes to the group. *An angel of Satan:* a personal messenger from Satan; cf the satanic language already applied to the opponents in 11, 3.13-15.20.

12, 8: *Three times:* his prayer was insistent, like that of Jesus in Gethsemane, a sign of how intolerable he felt the thorn to be.

12, 9: *But he said to me:* Paul's petition is denied; release and healing are withheld for a higher purpose. The Greek perfect tense indicates that Jesus' earlier response still holds at the time of writing. *My grace is sufficient for you:* this is not a statement about the sufficiency of grace in general. Jesus speaks directly to Paul's situation. *Is made perfect:* i.e., is given most fully and manifests itself fully.

12, 9b-10a: Paul draws the conclusion from the autobiographical anecdote and integrates it into the subject of this part of the boast. *Weaknesses:* the apostolic hardships he must endure, including active personal hostility, as specified in a final catalogue (10a). *That the power of Christ may dwell with me:* Paul pinpoints the ground for the paradoxical strategy he has adopted in his self-defense.

12, 10b: *When I am weak, then I am strong:* Paul recognizes a twofold pattern in the resolution of the weakness-power (and death-life) dialectic, each of which looks to Jesus as the model and is experienced in him. The first is personal, involving a reversal in oneself (Jesus, 13, 4a; Paul, 1, 9-10; 4, 10-11; 6, 9). The second is apostolic, involving an effect on others (Jesus, 5, 14-15; Paul, 1, 6; 4, 12; 13, 9). The specific kind of "effectiveness in ministry" that Paul promises to demonstrate on his arrival (13, 4b; cf 10, 1-11) involves elements of both; this, too, will be modeled on Jesus' experience and a participation in that experience (9; 13, 3b).

nesses, insults, hard ships, persecutions, and constraints, for the sake of Christ; for when I am weak, then I am strong.

***Selfless Concern for the Church.*†**
11* I have been foolish. You compelled me, for I ought to have been commended by you. For I am in no way inferior to these "superapostles," even though I am nothing. 12*† The signs of an apostle were performed among you with all endurance, signs and wonders, and mighty deeds. 13*† In what way were you less privileged than the rest of the churches, except that on my part I did not burden you? Forgive me this wrong!

14 Now I am ready to come to you this third time. And I will not be a burden, for I want not what is yours, but you. Children ought not to save for their parents, but parents for their children. 15 I will most gladly spend and be utterly spent for your sakes. If I love you more, am I to be loved less? 16* But granted that I myself did not burden you, yet I was crafty and got the better of you by deceit. 17 Did I take advantage of you through any of those I sent to you? 18* I urged Titus to go and sent the brother with him. Did Titus take advantage of you? Did we not walk in the same spirit? And in the same steps?

***Final Warnings and Appeals.*†**
19† Have you been thinking all along that we are defending ourselves before you? In the sight of God we are speaking in Christ, and all for building you up, beloved. 20*† For I fear that when I come I may find you not such as I wish, and that you may find me not as you wish; that there may be rivalry, jealousy, fury, selfishness, slander, gossip, conceit, and disorder. 21† I fear that when I come again my God may humiliate me before you, and I may have to mourn over many of those who sinned earlier and have not repented of the impurity, immorality, and licentiousness they practiced.

CHAPTER 13

1*† This third time I am coming to you. "On the testimony of two or three witnesses a fact shall be established." 2† I warned those who sinned earlier and all the others, and I warn them now while absent, as I did when present on my second visit, that if I come again I will not be lenient, 3† since you are looking for proof of Christ speaking in me.

*

11: 11, 5.
12: Rom 15, 19; 1 Thes 1, 5.
13: 11, 9-12.
16: 11, 3.13.
18: 2, 13; 8, 16.23.
20: 1 Cor 1, 11; 3, 3.
13, 1: Dt 19, 15; Mt 18, 16; Jn 8, 17; Heb 10, 28.

†

12, 11-18: This brief section forms an epilogue or concluding observation to Paul's boast, corresponding to the prologue in 11, 1-15. A four-step sequence of ideas is common to these two sections: Paul qualifies his boast as folly (11, 1; 12, 11a), asserts his noninferiority to the "superapostles" (11, 5; 12, 11b), exemplifies this by allusion to charismatic endowments (11, 6; 12, 12), and finally denies that he has been a financial burden to the community (11, 7-12; 12, 13-18).

12, 12: Despite weakness and affliction (suggested by the mention of *endurance*), his ministry has been accompanied by demonstrations of power (cf 1 Cor 2, 3-4). *Signs of an apostle:* visible proof of belonging to Christ and of mediating Christ's power, which the opponents require as touchstones of apostleship (11; cf 13, 3).

12, 13-18: Paul insists on his intention to continue refusing support from the community (cf 11, 8-12). In defending his practice and his motivation, he once more protests his love (cf 11, 11) and rejects the suggestion of secret self-enrichment. He has recourse here again to language applied to his opponents earlier: "cunning" (11, 3), "deceit" (11, 13), "got the better of you" (see the note on 11, 20), "take advantage" (2, 11).

12, 19—13, 10: This concludes the development begun in ch 10. In the chiastic arrangement of the material (see the note on 10, 1—13, 10), this final part corresponds to the opening; there are important similarities of content between the two sections as well.

12, 19: This verse looks back at the previous chapters and calls them by their proper name, a defense, an *apologia* (cf 1 Cor 9, 3). Yet Paul insists on an important distinction: he has indeed been speaking for their benefit, but the ultimate judgment to which he submits is God's (cf 1 Cor 4, 3-5). This verse also leads into the final section, announcing two of its themes: judgment and building up.

12, 20: *I fear that . . . :* earlier Paul expressed fear that the Corinthians were being victimized, exploited, seduced from right thinking by his opponents (11, 3-4.19-21). Here he alludes unexpectedly to moral disorders among the Corinthians themselves. The catalogue suggests the effects of factions that have grown up around rival apostles.

12, 21: *Again:* one can also translate, "I fear that when I come my God may again humiliate me." Paul's allusion to the humiliation and mourning that may await him recall the mood he described in 2, 1-4, but there is no reference here to any individual such as there is in 2, 5-11. The crisis of ch 2 has happily been resolved by integration of the offender and repentance (7, 4-16), whereas 12, 21 is preoccupied with still unrepentant sinners. The sexual sins recall 1 Cor 5-7.

13, 1: *This third time I am coming:* designation of the forthcoming visit as the "third" (cf 12, 14) may indicate that, in addition to his founding sojourn in Corinth, Paul had already made the first of two visits mentioned as planned in 1, 15, and the next visit will be the long-postponed second of these. If so, the materials in 1, 12—2, 13 plus 7, 4-16 and chs 10-13 may date from the same period of time, presumably of some duration, between Paul's second and third visit, though it is not clear that they are addressing the same crisis. The chronology is too unsure and the relations between sections of 2 Cor too unclear to yield any certainty. The hypothesis that chs 10-13 are themselves the "tearful letter" mentioned at 2, 3-4 creates more problems than it solves.

13, 2: *I warned those who sinned earlier:* mention of unrepentant sinners (12, 21 and here) and of an oral admonition given them on an earlier visit complicates the picture at the very end of Paul's development. It provides, in fact, a second explanation for the show of power that has been threatened from the beginning (10, 1-6), but a different reason for it, quite unsuspected until now. It is not clear whether Paul is merely alluding to a dimension of the situation that he has not previously had occasion to mention, or whether some other community crisis, not directly connected with that behind chs 10-13, has influenced the final editing. *I will not be lenient:* contrast Paul's hesitation and reluctance to inflict pain in 1, 23 and 2, 1-4. The next visit will bring the showdown.

13, 3-4: Paul now gives another motive for severity when he comes, the charge of weakness leveled against him as an apostle. The motive echoes more closely the opening section (10, 1-18) and the intervening development (especially 11, 30—12, 10). *Proof of Christ speaking in me:* the threat of 10, 1-2 is reworded to recall Paul's conformity with the pattern of Christ, his insertion into the interplay of death and life, weakness and power (cf the note on 12, 10b).

He is not weak toward you but powerful
in you. 4 For indeed he was crucified out
of weakness, but he lives by the power
of God. So also we are weak in him, but
toward you we shall live with him by
the power of God.
5† Examine yourselves to see whether
you are living in faith. Test yourselves.
Do you not realize that Jesus Christ is
in you?—unless, of course, you fail the
test. 6 I hope you will discover that we
have not failed. 7 But we pray to God
that you may not do evil, not that we
may appear to have passed the test but
that you may do what is right, even
though we may seem to have failed.
8 For we cannot do anything against the
truth, but only for the truth. 9 For we
rejoice when we are weak but you are
strong. What we pray for is your im-
provement.
10*† I am writing this while I am away,
so that when I come I may not have to
be severe in virtue of the authority that
the Lord has given me to build up and
not to tear down.

V: CONCLUSION†

11 Finally, brothers, rejoice. Mend
your ways, encourage one another,
agree with one another, live in peace,
and the God of love and peace will be
with you. 12* Greet one another with a
holy kiss. All the holy ones greet you.
13* The grace of the Lord Jesus Christ
and the love of God and the fellowship
of the holy Spirit be with all of you.

*

10: 10, 8.
12: Rom 16, 16; 1 Cor 16, 20 / Phil 4, 22; 1 Thes 5, 26; 1 Pt 5, 14.
13: Rom 16, 20; 1 Cor 16, 23.

†

13, 5-9: Paul turns the challenge mentioned in v 3 on them: they are to put themselves to the test to demonstrate whether Christ is in them. These verses involve a complicated series of plays on the theme of *dokimē* (testing, proof, passing and failing a test). Behind this stands the familiar distinction between present human judgment and final divine judgment. This is the final appearance of the theme (cf 10, 18; 11, 15; 12, 19).

13, 10: *Authority . . . to build up and not to tear down:* Paul restates the purpose of his letter in language that echoes 10, 2.8, emphasizing the positive purpose of his authority in their regard. This verse forms an inclusion with the topic sentence of the section (12, 19), as well as with the opening of this entire portion of the letter (10, 1-2).

13, 11-13: These verses may have originally concluded chs 10-13, but they have nothing specifically to do with the material of that section. It is also possible to consider them a conclusion to the whole of 2 Cor in its present edited form. The exhortations are general, including a final appeal for peace in the community. The letter ends calmly, after its many storms, with the prospect of ecclesial unity and divine blessing. The final verse is one of the clearest trinitarian passages in the New Testament.

The Letter to the

GALATIANS

The Galatians to whom the letter is addressed were Paul's converts, most likely among the descendants of Celts who had invaded western and central Asia Minor in the third century B.C. and had settled in the territory around Ancyra (modern Ankara, Turkey). Paul had passed through this area on his second missionary journey (Acts 16, 6) and again on his third (Acts 18, 23). It is less likely that the recipients of this letter were Paul's churches in the southern regions of Pisidia, Lycaonia, and Pamphylia where he had preached earlier in the Hellenized cities of Perge, Iconium, Pisidian Antioch, Lystra, and Derbe (Acts 13, 13—14, 27); this area was part of the Roman province of Galatia, and some scholars think that South Galatia was the destination of this letter.

If it is addressed to the Galatians in the north, the letter was probably written around A.D. 54 or 55, most likely from Ephesus after Paul's arrival there for a stay of several years on his third missionary journey (Acts 19; 20, 31). On the South Galatian theory, the date would be earlier, perhaps A.D. 48-50. Involved is the question of how one relates the events of 2, 1-10 to the "Council of Jerusalem" described in Acts 15 (see the notes on each passage).

In any case, the new Christians whom Paul is addressing were converts from paganism (4, 8-9) who were now being enticed by other missionaries to add the observances of the Jewish law, including the rite of circumcision, to the cross of Christ as a means of salvation. For, since Paul's visit, some other interpretation of Christianity had been brought to these neophytes, probably by converts from Judaism (the name "Judaizers" is sometimes applied to them); it has specifically been suggested that they were Jewish Christians who had come from the austere Essene sect.

These interlopers insisted on the necessity of following certain precepts of the Mosaic law along with faith in Christ. They were undermining Paul's authority also, asserting that he had not been trained by Jesus himself, that his gospel did not agree with that of the original and true apostles in Jerusalem, that he had kept from his converts in Galatia the necessity of accepting circumcision and other key obligations of the Jewish law, in order more easily to win them to Christ, and that his gospel was thus not the full and authentic one held by "those of repute" in Jerusalem (2, 2). Some scholars also see in chapters 5 and 6 another set of opponents against whom Paul writes, people who in their emphasis on the Spirit set aside all norms for conduct and became libertines in practice.

When Paul learned of the situation, he wrote this defense of his apostolic authority and of the correct understanding of the faith. He set forth the unique importance of Christ and his redemptive sacrifice on the cross, the freedom that Christians enjoy from the old burdens of the law, the total sufficiency of Christ and of faith in Christ as the way to God and to eternal life, and the beauty of the new life of the Spirit. Galatians is thus a summary of basic Pauline theology. Its themes were more fully and less polemically developed in the Letter to the Romans.

Autobiographically, the letter gives us Paul's own accounts of how he came to faith (1, 15-24), the agreement in "the truth of the gospel" (2, 5.14) that he shared with the Jewish Christian leaders in Jerusalem, James, Kephas, and John (2, 1-10), and the rebuke he had to deliver to Kephas in Antioch for inconsistency, contrary to the gospel, on the issue of table fellowship in the racially mixed church of Jewish and Gentile Christians in Antioch (2, 11-14; cf 15-21). At the conclusion of the letter (6, 11-18), Paul wrote in his own hand (cf 2 Thes 3, 17-18) a vivid summary of the message to the Galatians.

In his vigorous emphasis on the absolute preeminence of Christ and his cross as God's way to salvation and holiness, Paul stresses Christian freedom and the ineffectiveness of the Mosaic law for gaining divine favor and blessings (3, 19-29). The pious Jew saw in the law a way established by God to win divine approval by a life of meticulous observance of ritual, social, and moral regulations. But Paul's profound insight into the higher designs of God in Christ led him to understand and welcome the priority of promise and faith (shown in the experience of Abraham, 3, 6-18) and the supernatural gifts of the Spirit (3, 2-5; 5, 16—6, 10). His enthusiasm for this new vision of the life of grace in Christ and of the uniquely salvific role of Christ's redemptive death on the cross shines through this whole letter.

The principal divisions of the Letter to the Galatians are the following:

- *I: Address (1, 1-5)*
- *II: Loyalty to the Gospel (1, 6-10)*
- *III: Paul's Defense of His Gospel and His Authority (1, 11—2, 21)*
- *IV: Faith and Liberty (3, 1—4, 31)*
- *V: Exhortation to Christian Living (5, 1—6, 10)*
- *VI: Conclusion (6, 11-18)*

I: ADDRESS

CHAPTER 1

Greeting.† 1*† Paul, an apostle not
from human beings nor through a hu-
man being but through Jesus Christ and
God the Father who raised him from
the dead, 2† and all the brothers who are
with me, to the churches of Galatia:
3 grace to you and peace from God our
Father and the Lord Jesus Christ,
4*† who gave himself for our sins that
he might rescue us from the present evil
age in accord with the will of our God
and Father, 5* to whom be glory forever
and ever. Amen.

II: LOYALTY TO THE GOSPEL†

6*† I am amazed that you are so
quickly forsaking the one who called
you by [the] grace [of Christ] for a dif-
ferent gospel 7 (not that there is an-
other). But there are some who are
disturbing you and wish to pervert the
gospel of Christ. 8*† But even if we or
an angel from heaven should preach [to
you] a gospel other than the one that
we preached to you, let that one be ac-
cursed! 9 As we have said before, and
now I say again, if anyone preaches
to you a gospel other than the one that
you received, let that one be ac-
cursed!
10*† Am I now currying favor with hu-
man beings or God? Or am I seeking
to please people? If I were still trying
to please people, I would not be a slave
of Christ.

GALATIANS

*

1, 1-3: Rom 1, 1-7; 1 Cor 1, 1-3.
1: 1, 11-12.
4: 2, 20; Eph 5, 2; 1 Tm 2, 6 / 1 Jn 5, 19 / Rom 12, 2; Eph 5, 16; Heb 10, 10.
5: Rom 16, 27; 2 Tm 4, 18.
6-7: 5, 8.10; Acts 15, 1.24; 2 Cor 11, 4.
8-9: 1 Cor 16, 22 / 5, 3.21; 2 Cor 13, 2.
10: 2 Cor 5, 11 / 1 Thes 2, 4.

†

1, 1-5: See the note on Rom 1, 1-7, concerning the greeting.

1, 1: *Apostle:* because of attacks on his authority in Galatia, Paul defends his apostleship. He is not an apostle commissioned by a congregation (Phil 2, 25; 2 Cor 8, 23) or even by prophets (1 Tm 1, 18 and 4, 14) but *through Jesus Christ and God the Father.*

1, 2: *All the brothers:* fellow believers in Christ, male and female; cf 3, 27-28. Paul usually mentions the co-sender(s) at the start of a letter, but the use of *all* is unique, adding weight to the letter. *Galatia:* central Turkey more likely than the Roman province of Galatia; see Introduction.

1, 4: The greeting in v 3 is expanded by a christological formula that stresses deliverance through the Lord Jesus from a world dominated by Satan; cf 2 Cor 4, 4; Eph 2, 2; 6, 12.

1, 6-10: In place of the usual thanksgiving (see the note on Rom 1, 8), Paul, with little to be thankful for in the Galatian situation, expresses amazement at the way his converts are deserting the gospel of Christ for a perverted message. He reasserts the one gospel he has preached (7-9) and begins to defend himself (10).

1, 6: *The one who called you:* God or Christ, though in actuality Paul was the divine instrument to call the Galatians.

1, 8: *Accursed:* in Greek, *anathema;* cf Rom 9, 3; 1 Cor 12, 3; 16, 22.

1, 10: This charge by Paul's opponents, that he sought to conciliate people with flattery and to curry favor with God, might refer to his mission practices (cf 1 Cor 9, 19-23) but the word *still* suggests it refers to his pre-Christian days (cf 14; Phil 3, 6). The self-description *slave of Christ* is one Paul often uses in a greeting (Rom 1, 1).

III: PAUL'S DEFENSE OF HIS GOSPEL AND HIS AUTHORITY†

His Call by Christ. 11* Now I want
you to know, brothers, that the gospel
preached by me is not of human origin.
12† For I did not receive it from a human
being, nor was I taught it, but it came
through a revelation of Jesus Christ.
13*† For you heard of my former way
of life in Judaism, how I persecuted the
church of God beyond measure and
tried to destroy it, 14* and progressed
in Judaism beyond many of my con-
temporaries among my race, since I
was even more a zealot for my ancestral
traditions. 15* But when [God], who
from my mother's womb had set me
apart and called me through his grace,
was pleased 16*† to reveal his Son to me,
so that I might proclaim him to the Gen-
tiles, I did not immediately consult flesh
and blood, 17† nor did I go up to Jerusa-
lem to those who were apostles before
me; rather, I went into Arabia and then
returned to Damascus.
18*† Then after three years I went up
to Jerusalem to confer with Kephas and
remained with him for fifteen days.
19*† But I did not see any other of the
apostles, only James the brother of the
Lord. 20* (As to what I am writing to
you, behold, before God, I am not ly-
ing.) 21* Then I went into the regions of
Syria and Cilicia. 22 And I was unknown
personally to the churches of Judea that
are in Christ; 23* they only kept hearing
that "the one who once was persecuting
us is now preaching the faith he once
tried to destroy." 24 So they glorified
God because of me.

CHAPTER 2

The Council of Jerusalem.† 1*† Then
after fourteen years I again went up to
Jerusalem with Barnabas, taking Titus
along also. 2*† I went up in accord with
a revelation, and I presented to them
the gospel that I preach to the Gen-
tiles—but privately to those of repute—
so that I might not be running, or have
run, in vain. 3*† Moreover, not even Ti-

*

11-12: 1 Cor 15, 1 / 1, 1; Eph 3, 3.
13: Acts 8, 1-3; 9, 1-2; 1 Cor 15, 9.
14: Acts 26, 4-5.
15: Is 49, 1; Jer 1, 4.
16: 1, 11-12; Rom 1, 5; 1 Cor 15, 10; Acts 9, 3-9 / 2, 2.7 / Mt 16, 17.
18: Acts 9, 26-30 / Jn 1, 42.
19: 2, 9; Mt 13, 55; Acts 12, 17.
20: Rom 9, 1; 2 Cor 11, 31.
21: Acts 9, 30.
23: 1, 13.
2, 1: Acts 15, 2.
2: 1, 11-12.16 / 1, 16 / Phil 2, 16.
3: 2 Cor 2, 13; 7, 6-7; 8, 16-17; 12, 18; Ti 1, 4 / 2, 14; 6, 12.

†

1, 11—2, 21: Paul's presentation on behalf of his message and of his apostleship reflects rhetorical forms of his day: he first narrates the facts about certain past events (1, 12—2, 14) and then states his contention regarding justification by faith as the gospel message (2, 15-21). Further arguments follow from both experience and scripture in chs 3 and 4, before he draws out the ethical consequences (5, 1—6, 10). The specific facts that he takes up here to show that his gospel is not a human invention (1, 11) but *came through a revelation of Jesus Christ* (1, 12) deal with his own calling as a Christian missionary (1, 13-17), his initial relations with the apostles in Jerusalem (1, 18-24), a later journey to Jerusalem (2, 1-10), and an incident in Antioch involving Kephas and persons from James (2, 11-14). The content of Paul's revealed gospel is then set forth in the heart of the letter (2, 15-21).

1, 12: Although Paul received his gospel *through a revelation* from Christ, this did not exclude his use of early Christian confessional formulations. See the note on 1, 4.

1, 13-17: Along with Phil 3, 4-11, which also moves from autobiography to its climax in a discussion on justification by faith (cf Gal 2, 15-21), this passage is Paul's chief account of the change from his *former way of life* (13) to service as a Christian missionary (16); cf Acts 9, 1-22; 22, 4-16; 26, 9-18. Paul himself does not use the term "conversion" but stresses revelation (12.16). In v 15 his language echoes the Old Testament prophetic call of Jeremiah. Unlike the account in Acts (cf 22, 4-16), the calling of Paul here includes the mission to proclaim Christ *to the Gentiles* (16).

1, 16: *Flesh and blood:* human authorities (cf Mt 16, 17; 1 Cor 15, 50). Paul's apostleship comes from God (1).

1, 17: *Arabia:* probably the region of the Nabataean Arabs, east and south of Damascus.

1, 18-24: Paul's first journey to Jerusalem as a Christian, according to Galatians (cf Acts 9, 23-31 and the note on Acts 12, 25). He is quite explicit about contacts there, testifying under oath (20). On returning to *Syria* (perhaps specifically Damascus, cf v 17) *and Cilicia* (including his home town Tarsus, cf Acts 9, 30; 22, 3), Paul most likely engaged in missionary work. He underscores the fact that Christians in Judea knew of him only by reputation.

1, 18: *After three years:* two years and more, since Paul's call. To *confer with* Kephas may mean simply "pay a visit" or more specifically "get information from" him about Jesus, over a two-week period. *Kephas:* Aramaic name of Simon (Peter); cf Mt 16, 16-18 and the notes there.

1, 19: *James the brother of the Lord:* not one of the Twelve, but a brother of Jesus (see the note on Mk 6, 3). He played an important role in the Jerusalem church (see the note on Gal 2, 9), the leadership of which he took over from Peter (Acts 12, 17). Paul may have regarded James as an apostle.

2, 1-10: Paul's second journey to Jerusalem, according to Galatians, involved a private meeting with *those of repute* (2). At issue was a Gentile, Titus, and the question of circumcision, which *false brothers* (4) evidently demanded for him. Paul insists that the gospel he preaches (2; cf 1, 9.11) remained intact with no addition by those of repute (6); that *Titus* was not *compelled* to accept circumcision (3); and that he and the reputed *pillars* in Jerusalem agreed on how each would advance the missionary task (7-10). Usually, 1-10 is equated with the "Council of Jerusalem," as it is called, described in Acts 15. See the notes on Acts 15, 6-12 and 15, 13-35, the latter concerning the "decree" that Paul does not mention.

2, 1: *After fourteen years:* thirteen or more years, probably reckoned from the return to Syria and Cilicia (1, 21), though possibly from Paul's calling as a Christian (1, 15). *Barnabas:* cf 9.13; 1 Cor 9, 6. A Jewish Christian missionary, with whom Paul worked (Acts 4, 36-37; 11, 22.25.30; 12, 25; 13, 1-3; 15, 2). *Titus:* a missionary companion of Paul (2 Cor 2, 13; 7, 6.13-15; 8, 6.16.23; 12, 18), non-Jewish (Gal 2, 3), never mentioned in Acts.

2, 2: *A revelation:* cf 1, 1.12. Paul emphasizes it was God's will, not Jerusalem authority, that led to the journey. Acts 15, 2 states that the church in Antioch appointed Paul and Barnabas for the task. *Those of repute:* leaders of the Jerusalem church; the term, while positive, may be slightly ironic (cf 6.9). *Run, in vain:* while Paul presents a positive picture in what follows, his missionary work in Galatia would have been to no purpose if his opponents were correct that circumcision is needed for complete faith in Christ.

2, 3: *Not even* a Gentile Christian like Titus was compelled to receive the rite of circumcision. The Greek text could be interpreted that he voluntarily accepted circumcision, but this is unlikely in the overall argument.

tus, who was with me, although he was
a Greek, was compelled to be circum-
cised, 4*† but because of the false broth-
ers secretly brought in, who slipped in
to spy on our freedom that we have in
Christ Jesus, that they might enslave
us—5*† to them we did not submit even
for a moment, so that the truth of the
gospel might remain intact for you.
6* But from those who were reputed to
be important (what they once were
makes no difference to me; God shows
no partiality)—those of repute made me
add nothing. 7*† On the contrary, when
they saw that I had been entrusted with
the gospel to the uncircumcised, just as
Peter to the circumcised, 8 for the one
who worked in Peter for an apostolate
to the circumcised worked also in me
for the Gentiles, 9*† and when they rec-
ognized the grace bestowed upon me,
James and Kephas and John, who were
reputed to be pillars, gave me and Bar-
nabas their right hands in partnership,
that we should go to the Gentiles and
they to the circumcised. 10*† Only,
we were to be mindful of the poor,
which is the very thing I was eager to
do.

***Peter's Inconsistency at Antioch.*†**

11*† And when Kephas came to Antioch,
I opposed him to his face because he
clearly was wrong. 12*† For, until some
people came from James, he used to eat
with the Gentiles; but when they came,
he began to draw back and separated
himself, because he was afraid of the
circumcised. 13*† And the rest of the
Jews [also] acted hypocritically along
with him, with the result that even Bar-
nabas was carried away by their hypoc-
risy. 14*† But when I saw that they were
not on the right road in line with the
truth of the gospel, I said to Kephas in
front of all, "If you, though a Jew, are
living like a Gentile and not like a Jew,
how can you compel the Gentiles to live
like Jews?"

***Faith and Works.*†** 15 We, who are
Jews by nature and not sinners from
among the Gentiles, 16*† [yet] who
know that a person is not justified by
works of the law but through faith in
Jesus Christ, even we have believed in
Christ Jesus that we may be justified by
faith in Christ and not by works of the
law, because by works of the law no one
will be justified. 17† But if, in seeking to
be justified in Christ, we ourselves are
found to be sinners, is Christ then a min-
ister of sin? Of course not! 18† But if I
am building up again those things that
I tore down, then I show myself to be a

*

4: 5, 1; Acts 15, 1.24.
5: 2, 14; 4, 16.
6: Dt 10, 17; Rom 2, 11.
7: 1, 15-16; Acts 9, 15; 15, 12; 22, 21; Rom 1, 5.
9: Rom 15, 15 / 1, 18-19; Jn 1, 42; Acts 12, 17 / 2, 1.
10: Acts 11, 29-30; Rom 15, 25-28; 1 Cor 16, 1-4; 2 Cor 8, 9.
11: 1, 18 / Acts 11, 19-30; 15, 1-2.
12: Acts 10, 15.28; 11, 3.
13: 2, 1.9.
14: 2, 5 / 1, 18; 2, 9 / 2, 3.
16: 3, 2.11; Ps 143, 1-2; Rom 3, 20.28; 4, 5; 11, 6; Eph 2, 8-9; Phil 3, 9.

†

2, 4: *False brothers:* Jewish Christians who took the position that Gentile Christians must first become Jews through circumcision and observance of the Mosaic law in order to become Christians; cf Acts 15, 1.

2, 5: *The truth of the gospel:* the true gospel, in contrast to the false one of the opponents (1, 6-9); the gospel of grace, used as a norm (14).

2, 7-9: Some think that actual "minutes" of the meeting are here quoted. Paul's apostleship to the Gentiles (1, 16) is recognized alongside that of Peter to the Jews. Moreover, the right to proclaim the gospel without requiring circumcision and the Jewish law is sealed by a handshake. That Paul and colleagues *should go to the Gentiles* did not exclude his preaching to the Jews as well (Rom 1, 13-16) or Kephas to Gentile areas.

2, 9: *James and Kephas and John:* see the notes on 1, 18 and 19; on Peter and John as leaders in the Jerusalem church, cf Acts 3, 1 and 8, 14. The order here, with James first, may reflect his prominence in Jerusalem after Peter (Kephas) departed (Acts 12, 17).

2, 10: *The poor:* Jerusalem Christians or a group within the church there (cf Rom 15, 26). The collection for them was extremely important in Paul's thought and labor (cf Rom 15, 25-28; 1 Cor 16, 1-4; 2 Cor 8 and 9).

2, 11-14: The decision reached in Jerusalem (3-7) recognized the freedom of Gentile Christians from the Jewish law. But the problem of table fellowship between Jewish Christians, who possibly still kept kosher food regulations, and Gentile believers was not yet settled. When Kephas first came to the racially mixed community of Jewish and Gentile Christians in Antioch (12), he ate with non-Jews. Pressure from persons arriving later from Jerusalem caused him and Barnabas to draw back. Paul therefore publicly rebuked Peter's inconsistency toward the gospel (14). Some think that what Paul said on that occasion extends through v 16 or v 21.

2, 11: *Clearly was wrong:* literally, "stood condemned," by himself and also by Paul. His action in breaking table fellowship was especially grievous if the eating involved the meal at the Lord's supper (cf 1 Cor 11, 17-25).

2, 12: *Some people came from James:* strict Jewish Christians (cf Acts 15, 1.5; 21, 20-21), either sent by James (1, 19; 2, 9) or claiming to be from the leader of the Jerusalem church. *The circumcised:* presumably Jewish Christians, not Jews.

2, 13: *The Jews:* Jewish Christians, like Barnabas. *Hypocrisy:* literally, "pretense," "play-acting"; moral insincerity.

2, 14: *Compel the Gentiles to live like Jews:* that is, conform to Jewish practices, such as circumcision (3-5) or regulations about food (12).

2, 15-21: Following on the series of incidents cited above, Paul's argument, whether spoken to Kephas at Antioch or only now articulated, is pertinent to the Galatian situation, where believers were having themselves circumcised (6, 12-13) and obeying other aspects of Jewish law (4, 9-10; 5, 1-4). He insists that salvation is by faith in Christ, not by works of the law. His teaching on the gospel concerns justification by faith (16) in relation to sin (17), law (19), life in Christ (19-20), and grace (21).

2, 16: *No one will be justified:* Ps 143, 2 is reflected.

2, 17: *A minister of sin:* literally, "a servant of sin" (cf Rom 15, 8), an agent of sin, one who promotes it. This is possibly a claim by opponents that justification on the basis of faith in Christ makes Christ an abettor of sin when Christians *are found to be sinners.* Paul denies the conclusion (cf Rom 6, 1-4).

2, 18: To return to observance of the law as the means to salvation would entangle one not only in inevitable transgressions of it but also in the admission that it was wrong to have abandoned the law in the first place.

transgressor. [19]*† For through the law I died to the law, that I might live for God. I have been crucified with Christ; [20]* yet I live, no longer I, but Christ lives in me; insofar as I now live in the flesh, I live by faith in the Son of God who has loved me and given himself up for me. [21]* I do not nullify the grace of God; for if justification comes through the law, then Christ died for nothing.

IV: FAITH AND LIBERTY

CHAPTER 3

Justification by Faith. † [1]*† O stupid Galatians! Who has bewitched you, before whose eyes Jesus Christ was publicly portrayed as crucified? [2]*† I want to learn only this from you: did you receive the Spirit from works of the law, or from faith in what you heard? [3]*† Are you so stupid? After beginning with the Spirit, are you now ending with the flesh? [4]† Did you experience so many things in vain?—if indeed it was in vain. [5]* Does, then, the one who supplies the Spirit to you and works mighty deeds among you do so from works of the law or from faith in what you heard? [6]*† Thus Abraham "believed God, and it was credited to him as righteousness."

[7]*† Realize then that it is those who have faith who are children of Abraham. [8]* Scripture, which saw in advance that God would justify the Gentiles by faith, foretold the good news to Abraham, saying, "Through you shall all the nations be blessed." [9]* Consequently, those who have faith are blessed along with Abraham who had faith. [10]*† For all who depend on works of the law are under a curse; for it is written, "Cursed be everyone who does not persevere in doing all the things written in the book of the law." [11]* And that no one is justified before God by the law is clear, for "the one who is righteous by faith will live." [12]* But the law does not depend on faith; rather, "the one who does these things will live by them." [13]* Christ ransomed us from the curse of the law by becoming a curse for us, for it is written, "Cursed be everyone who hangs on a tree," [14]* that the blessing of Abraham might be extended to the Gentiles through Christ Jesus, so that we might receive the promise of the Spirit through faith.

The Law Did Not Nullify the Promise. † [15]* Brothers, in human terms I say that no one can annul or amend even a human will once ratified.

*

19: 6, 14; Rom 6, 6.8.10; 7, 6.
20: 1, 4; Rom 8, 10-11; Col 3, 3-4.
21: 5, 2.
3, 1: 5, 7; 1 Cor 1, 23.
2: 2, 16 / 3, 14; Rom 10, 17.
3: 5, 16-18.
5: 2, 16.
6: Gn 15, 6; Rom 4, 3; Jas 2, 23.
7: 3, 29; Rom 4, 11-12 / Sir 44, 19-21.
8: Gn 12, 3; 18, 17-19; Acts 3, 25.
9: Rom 4, 16.
10: Dt 27, 26; Jas 2, 10.
11: 2, 16; Hb 2, 4; Rom 1, 17.
12: Lv 18, 5; Rom 10, 5.
13: Dt 21, 23; Rom 8, 3; 2 Cor 5, 21.
14: 3, 2-3.5; Is 44, 3; Jl 3, 1-2; Acts 2, 33.
15: Rom 3, 5 / Heb 9, 16-17.

†

2, 19: *Through the law I died to the law:* this is variously explained: the law revealed sin (Rom 7, 7-9) and led to death and then to belief in Christ; or, the law itself brought the insight that law cannot justify (16; Ps 143, 2); or, the "law of Christ" (6, 2) led to abandoning the Mosaic law; or, the law put Christ to death (cf 3, 13) and so provided a way to our salvation, through baptism into Christ, through which we die (*crucified with Christ;* see Rom 6, 6). Cf also 3, 19-25 on the role of the law in reference to salvation.

3, 1-14: Paul's contention that justification comes not through the law or the works of the law but by faith in Christ and in his death (2, 16.21) is supported by appeals to Christian experience (1-5) and to scripture (6-14). The gift of God's Spirit to the Galatians came from the gospel received in faith, not from doing what the law enjoins. The story of Abraham shows that faith in God brings *righteousness* (6; Gn 15, 6). The promise to Abraham (8; Gn 12, 3) extends to the Gentiles (14).

3, 1: *Stupid:* not just senseless, for they were in danger of deserting their salvation.

3, 2: *Faith in what you heard:* Paul's message received with faith. The Greek can also mean "the proclamation of the faith" or "a hearing that comes from faith."

3, 3: On the contrast of *Spirit* and *flesh,* cf Rom 8, 1-11. Having received the Spirit, they need not be circumcised now.

3, 4: *Experience so many things:* probably the *mighty deeds* of v 5 but possibly the experience of sufferings.

3, 6: *Abraham . . . righteousness:* see Gn 15, 6; Rom 4, 3. The Galatians like Abraham heard with faith and experienced justification. This first argument forms the basis for the further scriptural evidence that follows.

3, 7-9: *Faith* is what matters, for *Abraham* and the *children of Abraham,* in contrast to the claims of the opponents that circumcision and observance of the law are needed to bring the promised blessing of Gn 12, 3; cf Gn 18, 18; Sir 44, 21; Acts 3, 25.

3, 10-14: Those *who depend* not on promise and faith but *on works of the law are under a curse* because they do *not persevere in doing all the things written in the book of the law* (10; Dt 27, 26) in order to gain life (12; Lv 18, 5; cf Rom 10, 5). But scripture teaches that *no one is justified before God by the law* (11; Hb 2, 4, adapted from the Greek version of Habakkuk; cf Rom 1, 17; Heb 10, 38). Salvation, then, depends on faith in Christ who died on the cross (13), taking upon himself a curse found in Dt 21, 23 (about executed criminals hanged in public view), to free us from *the curse of the law* (13). That the Gentile Galatians have received the promised Spirit (14) by faith and in no other way returns the argument to the experience cited in vv 1-5.

3, 15-18: A third argument to support Paul's position that salvation is not through the law but by promise (1-14) comes from legal practice and scriptural history. A legal agreement or *human will,* duly *ratified,* is unalterable (15). God's *covenant* with *Abraham* and its repeated promises (Gn 12, 2-3.7; 13, 15; 17, 7-8; 22, 16-18; 24, 7) is not superseded by *the law,* which came much later, in the time of Moses. *The inheritance* (of the Spirit and the blessings) is by promise, not by law (18). Paul's argument hinges on the fact that the same Greek word, *diathēkē,* can be rendered as *will* or testament (15) and as *covenant* (17).

16*† Now the promises were made to
Abraham and to his descendant. It does
not say, "And to descendants," as re-
ferring to many, but as referring to one,
"And to your descendant," who is
Christ. 17*† This is what I mean: the law,
which came four hundred and thirty
years afterward, does not annul a cove-
nant previously ratified by God, so as
to cancel the promise. 18*† For if the in-
heritance comes from the law, it is no
longer from a promise; but God be-
stowed it on Abraham through a prom-
ise.
19*† Why, then, the law? It was added
for transgressions, until the descendant
came to whom the promise had been
made; it was promulgated by angels at
the hand of a mediator. 20* Now there
is no mediator when only one party is
involved, and God is one. 21* Is the law
then opposed to the promises [of God]?
Of course not! For if a law had been
given that could bring life, then righ-
teousness would in reality come from
the law. 22* But scripture confined all
things under the power of sin, that
through faith in Jesus Christ the prom-
ise might be given to those who believe.

What Faith Has Brought Us.†

23* Before faith came, we were held
in custody under law, confined for
the faith that was to be revealed.
24*† Consequently, the law was our dis-
ciplinarian for Christ, that we might be
justified by faith. 25* But now that faith
has come, we are no longer under a dis-
ciplinarian. 26*† For through faith you
are all children of God in Christ Jesus.
27*† For all of you who were baptized
into Christ have clothed yourselves with
Christ. 28* There is neither Jew nor
Greek, there is neither slave nor free
person, there is not male and female;
for you are all one in Christ Jesus.
29* And if you belong to Christ, then you
are Abraham's descendant, heirs ac-
cording to the promise.

CHAPTER 4

God's Free Children in Christ.†

1† I mean that as long as the heir is not
of age, he is no different from a slave,
although he is the owner of everything,
2 but he is under the supervision of
guardians and administrators until the
date set by his father. 3*† In the same
way we also, when we were not of age,
were enslaved to the elemental powers
of the world. 4* But when the fullness
of time had come, God sent his Son,
born of a woman, born under the law,
5* to ransom those under the law, so that
we might receive adoption. 6*† As proof

*

16: Gn 12, 7; 13, 15; 17, 8; 22, 17; 24, 7; Mt 1, 1.
17: Ex 12, 40.
18: Rom 4, 16; 11, 6.
19: Rom 4, 15; 5, 20; 7, 7.13 / Acts 7, 38.53.
20: Dt 6, 4.
21: Rom 7, 7.10; 8, 2-4.
22: Rom 3, 9-20.23; 11, 32.
23: 4, 3-5; 5, 18.
24: 2, 16.
25: Rom 10, 4.
26: 4, 5-7; Jn 1, 12; Rom 8, 14-17.
27: Rom 6, 3; 13, 14; Eph 4, 24.
28: Rom 10, 12; 1 Cor 12, 13; Col 3, 11.
29: 3, 7.14.16.18; Rom 4, 16-17; 9, 7 / 4, 1.7; Rom 4, 13-14; 8, 17; Heb 6, 12; Jas 2, 5.
4, 3: 3, 23 / 4, 9; Col 2, 20.
4: Mk 1, 15.
5: 3, 13.26.
6: 3, 26; Rom 8, 15.

†

3, 16: *Descendant:* literally, "and to his seed." The Hebrew, as in Gn 12, 7; 15, 18; 22, 17-18, is a collective singular, traditionally rendered as a plural, *descendants,* but taken by Paul in its literal number to refer to *Christ* as descendant of Abraham.

3, 17: *Four hundred and thirty years afterward:* follows Ex 12, 40 in the Greek (Septuagint) version, in contrast to Gn 15, 13 and Acts 7, 6, for chronology.

3, 18: This refutes the opponents' contention that the promises of God are fulfilled only as a reward for human observance of the law.

3, 19-22: A digression: if the Mosaic law, then, does not save or *bring life,* why was it given? Elsewhere, Paul says the law served to show what sin is (Rom 3, 20; 7, 7-8). Here the further implication is that the law in effect served to produce transgressions. Moreover, it was received at second hand *by angels,* through a *mediator,* not directly from God (19). The law does not, however, oppose God's purposes, for it carries out its function (22), so that *righteousness* comes by *faith* and *promise,* not by human works of the law.

3, 19: *The descendant:* Christ (16). *By angels:* Dt 33, 2-4 stressed their presence as enhancing the importance of the law; Paul uses their role to diminish its significance (cf Acts 7, 38.53). *A mediator:* Moses. But in a covenant of promise, where all depends on the one God, no mediator is needed (20).

3, 23-29: Paul adds a further argument in support of righteousness or justification by faith and through God's promise rather than by works of the law (2, 16; 3, 22): as *children of God, baptized into Christ,* the Galatians are all *Abraham's descendant* and *heirs* of *the promise* to Abraham (8.14.16-18.29). The teaching in 23-25, that since *faith* (Christianity) *has come, we are no longer under* the law, could be taken with the previous paragraph on the role of the Mosaic law, but it also fits here as a contrast between the situation *before faith* (23) and the results after faith has come (25-29).

3, 24-25: *Disciplinarian:* the Greek *paidagōgos* referred to a slave who escorted a child to school but did not teach or tutor; hence, a guardian or monitor. Applying this to the law fits the role of the law described in vv 19-25.

3, 26: *Children of God:* literally "sons," in contrast to the young child under the disciplinarian in vv 24-25. The term includes males and females (28).

3, 27-28: Likely a formula used at baptism that expresses racial, social-economic, and sexual equality in Christ (cf Col 3, 11).

3, 27: *Clothed yourselves with Christ:* literally, "have put on Christ"; cf Rom 13, 14; Eph 4, 24; Col 3, 10. Baptismal imagery, traceable to the Old Testament (Jb 29, 14; Is 59, 17) but also found in pagan mystery cults.

4, 1-7: What Paul has argued in 3, 26-29 is now elaborated in terms of the Christian as *the heir* (1.7; cf 3, 18.29) freed from control by others. Again, as in 3, 2-5, the proof that Christians are children of God is the gift of the Spirit of Christ relating them intimately to God.

4, 1.3: *Not of age:* an infant or minor.

4, 3: *The elemental powers of the world:* while the term can refer to the "elements" like earth, air, fire, and water or to elementary forms of religion, the sense here is more likely that of celestial beings that were thought in pagan circles to control the world; cf 8; Col 2, 8.20.

4, 6: *Children:* see the note on 3, 26; here in contrast to the infant or young person *not of age* (1.3). *Abba:* cf Mk 14, 36 and the note; Rom 8, 15.

that you are children, God sent the
spirit of his Son into our hearts, crying
out, "Abba, Father!" 7* So you are no
longer a slave but a child, and if a child
then also an heir, through God.

***Do Not Throw This Freedom Away.*†**

8*† At a time when you did not know
God, you became slaves to things that
by nature are not gods; 9* but now that
you have come to know God, or rather
to be known by God, how can you turn
back again to the weak and destitute
elemental powers? Do you want to be
slaves to them all over again? 10*† You
are observing days, months, seasons,
and years. 11† I am afraid on your ac-
count that perhaps I have labored for
you in vain.

***Appeal to Former Loyalty.*†** 12*† I
implore you, brothers, be as I am, be-
cause I have also become as you are.
You did me no wrong; 13† you know that
it was because of a physical illness that
I originally preached the gospel to you,
14 and you did not show disdain or con-
tempt because of the trial caused you
by my physical condition, but rather
you received me as an angel of God,
as Christ Jesus. 15† Where now is that
blessedness of yours? Indeed, I can tes-
tify to you that, if it had been possible,
you would have torn out your eyes and
given them to me. 16 So now have I be-
come your enemy by telling you the
truth? 17*† They show interest in you,
but not in a good way; they want to iso-
late you, so that you may show interest
in them. 18 Now it is good to be shown
interest for good reason at all times, and
not only when I am with you. 19* My
children, for whom I am again in labor
until Christ be formed in you! 20 I would
like to be with you now and to change
my tone, for I am perplexed because of
you.

***An Allegory on Christian Freedom.*†**

21 Tell me, you who want to be under
the law, do you not listen to the law?
22* For it is written that Abraham had
two sons, one by the slave woman and
the other by the freeborn woman.
23* The son of the slave woman was born
naturally, the son of the freeborn
through a promise. 24* Now this is an
allegory. These women represent two
covenants. One was from Mount Sinai,
bearing children for slavery; this is Ha-
gar. 25† Hagar represents Sinai, a
mountain in Arabia; it corresponds to
the present Jerusalem, for she is in
slavery along with her children.
26* But the Jerusalem above is free-
born, and she is our mother. 27*† For it
is written:

"Rejoice, you barren one who bore
no children;
break forth and shout, you who
were not in labor;
for more numerous are the children
of the deserted one
than of her who has a husband."

28* Now you, brothers, like Isaac, are
children of the promise. 29 But just as
then the child of the flesh persecuted

*

7: 3, 29; Rom 8, 16-17.
8: 1 Cor 12, 2.
9: 4, 3; Col 2, 20.
10: Col 2, 16-20.
12: 1 Cor 11, 1.
17: 1, 7; 6, 12; Acts 20, 30.
19: 1 Cor 4, 14-15; 2 Cor 6, 13; 1 Thes 2, 7-8.
22: Gn 16, 15; 21, 2-3.
23: Gn 17, 16; Rom 4, 19-20; 9, 7-9.
24: 3, 17 / Ex 19, 20 / Gn 16, 1.
26: Heb 12, 22; Rv 21, 2.
27: Is 54, 1.
28: Rom 9, 8.

†

4, 8-11: On the basis of the arguments advanced from 3, 1 through 4, 7, Paul now launches his appeal to the Galatians with the question, *how can you turn back* to the slavery of the law (9)? The question is posed with reference to bondage to the *elemental powers* (see the note on 4, 3) because the Galatians had originally been converted to Christianity from paganism, not Judaism (8). The use of the direct question is like 3, 3-5.

4, 8: *Things that by nature are not gods:* or "gods that by nature do not exist."

4, 10: This is likely a reference to ritual observances from the Old Testament, promoted by opponents: sabbaths or Yom Kippur, new moon, Passover or Pentecost, sabbatical years.

4, 11: Cf 2, 2. If the Galatians become *slaves . . . all over again* to the law (9), Paul will have worked in vain among them.

4, 12-20: A strongly personal section. Paul appeals to past ties between the Galatians and himself. He speaks sharply of the opponents (17-18) and pastorally to the Galatians (19-20).

4, 12: *Because I have also become as you are:* a terse phrase in Greek, meaning "Be as I, Paul, am," i.e., living by faith, independent of the law, for, in spite of my background in Judaism (1, 13), I have become as you Galatians are now, a brother in Christ.

4, 13: *Physical illness:* because its nature is not described, some assume an eye disease (15); others, epilepsy; some relate it to 2 Cor 12, 7-9. *Originally:* this may also be translated "formerly" or "on the first (of two) visit(s)"; cf Acts 16, 6; 18, 23.

4, 15: *That blessedness of yours:* possibly a reference to the Galatians' initial happy reception of Paul (14) and of his gospel (1, 6; 3, 1-4) and their felicitation at such blessedness, but the phrase could also refer ironically to earlier praise by Paul of the Galatians, no longer possible when they turn from the gospel to the claims of the opponents (17-18; 1, 7). If the word is a more literal reference to a beatitude, Gal 3, 26-28 may be in view.

4, 17: *Isolate you:* that is, from the blessings of the gospel and/or from Paul.

4, 21-31: Paul supports his appeal for the gospel (9; 1, 6-9; 2, 16; 3, 2) by a further argument from scripture (cf 3, 6-18). It involves the relationship of *Abraham* (3, 6-16) to his wife, Sarah, the *freeborn woman,* and to Hagar, *the slave woman,* and the contrast between the sons born to each, *Isaac,* child of promise, and Ishmael, son of Hagar (Gn 16 and 21). Only through Isaac is the promise of God preserved. This *allegory* (24), with its equation of the Sinai covenant and Mosaic law with slavery and of the promise of God with freedom, Paul uses only in light of previous arguments. His quotation of Gn 21, 10 at v 30 suggests on a scriptural basis that the Galatians should expel those who are troubling them (1, 7).

4, 25: *Hagar represents Sinai . . . :* some manuscripts have what seems a geographical note, "For Sinai is a mountain in Arabia."

4, 27: Is 54, 1 in the Septuagint translation is applied to Sarah as the *barren one* (in Gn 15) who ultimately becomes the mother not only of Isaac but now of numerous children, i.e., of all those who believe, the *children of the promise* (28).

the child of the spirit, it is the same now.
30* But what does the scripture say?

> "Drive out the slave woman and her
> son!
> For the son of the slave woman
> shall not share the inheritance
> with the son"

of the freeborn. 31* Therefore, brothers,
we are children not of the slave woman
but of the freeborn woman.

V: EXHORTATION TO CHRISTIAN LIVING

CHAPTER 5

The Importance of Faith. † 1*† For
freedom Christ set us free; so stand firm
and do not submit again to the yoke of
slavery.
2* It is I, Paul, who am telling you that
if you have yourselves circumcised,
Christ will be of no benefit to you.
3*† Once again I declare to every man
who has himself circumcised that he is
bound to observe the entire law. 4 You
are separated from Christ, you who are
trying to be justified by law; you have
fallen from grace. 5* For through the
Spirit, by faith, we await the hope of
righteousness. 6*† For in Christ Jesus,
neither circumcision nor uncircumci-
sion counts for anything, but only faith
working through love.
Be Not Misled. † 7† You were running
well; who hindered you from following
[the] truth? 8*† That enticement does
not come from the one who called you.
9* A little yeast leavens the whole batch
of dough. 10* I am confident of you in
the Lord that you will not take a differ-
ent view, and that the one who is trou-
bling you will bear the condemnation,
whoever he may be. 11*† As for me,
brothers, if I am still preaching circum-
cision, why am I still being persecuted?
In that case, the stumbling block of the
cross has been abolished. 12† Would that
those who are upsetting you might also
castrate themselves!
Freedom for Service. † 13*† For you
were called for freedom, brothers. But
do not use this freedom as an opportu-
nity for the flesh; rather, serve one an-
other through love. 14*† For the whole
law is fulfilled in one statement, namely,
"You shall love your neighbor as your-
self." 15 But if you go on biting and de-
vouring one another, beware that you
are not consumed by one another.
16*† I say, then: live by the Spirit and
you will certainly not gratify the desire
of the flesh. 17* For the flesh has desires
against the Spirit, and the Spirit against
the flesh; these are opposed to each
other, so that you may not do what you
want. 18* But if you are guided by the
Spirit, you are not under the law.
19*† Now the works of the flesh are obvi-
ous: immorality, impurity, licentious-
ness, 20* idolatry, sorcery, hatreds,
rivalry, jealousy, outbursts of fury, acts
of selfishness, dissensions, factions,
21† occasions of envy, drinking bouts,
orgies, and the like. I warn you, as I
warned you before, that those who do
such things will not inherit the kingdom
of God. 22* In contrast, the fruit of the

---

*

30: Gn 21, 10.
31: 3, 29; Jn 8, 35.
5, 1: 2, 4; 4, 5.9; Jn 8, 32.36.
2: 2, 21; Acts 15, 1-29.
3: 3, 10; Rom 2, 25; Jas 2, 10.
5: Rom 8, 23.25.
6: 3, 28; 6, 15; 1 Cor 7, 19.
8: 1, 6.
9: 1 Cor 5, 6.
10: 1, 7.
11: 6, 12.14; 1 Cor 1, 23.
13: 5, 1 / Rom 6, 18; 1 Cor 8, 9; 1 Pt 2, 16.
14: Lv 19, 18; Mt 22, 39; Rom 13, 8-10.
16: 5, 24-25; Rom 8, 5.
17: Rom 7, 15.23; 8, 6.
18: Rom 6, 14; 8, 14.
19-21: Rom 1, 29-31; 1 Cor 6, 9-10; Col 3, 5-6.8.
20: Rv 22, 15.
22: Eph 5, 9 / 1 Cor 13, 4-7; 2 Cor 6, 6; 1 Tm 4, 12; 2 Pt 1, 6.

---

†

5, 1-6: Paul begins the exhortations, continuing through 6, 10, with an appeal to the Galatians to side with freedom instead of slavery (1). He reiterates his message of justification or righteousness by faith instead of law and circumcision (2-5); cf 2, 16; 3, 3. Faith, not circumcision, is what counts (6).

5, 1: *Freedom:* Paul stresses as the conclusion from the allegory in 4, 21-31 this result of Christ's work for us. It is a principle previously mentioned (2, 4), the responsible use of which v 13 will emphasize.

5, 3: Cf 3, 10-12. Just as those who seek to live by the law must carry out all its contents, so those who have faith and live by promise must stand firm in their freedom (1.13).

5, 6: Cf Rom 2, 25-26; 1 Cor 7, 19; Gal 6, 15. The Greek for *faith working through love* or "faith expressing itself through love" can also be rendered as "faith energized by (God's) love."

5, 7-12: Paul addresses the Galatians directly: with questions (7.11), a proverb (9), a statement (8), and biting sarcasm (12), seeking to persuade the Galatians to break with those trying to add law and circumcision to Christ as a basis for salvation.

5, 7: *Running well:* as in an athletic contest; cf 2, 2; 1 Cor 9, 24-26; Phil 2, 16; 3, 14.

5, 8: *The one who called you:* see the note on 1, 6.

5, 11: *Preaching circumcision:* this could refer to Paul's pre-Christian period (possibly as a missionary for Judaism); more probably it arose as a charge from opponents, based perhaps on the story in Acts 16, 1-3 that Paul had circumcised Timothy "on account of the Jews." Unlike the Gentile Titus in Gal 2, 3, Timothy was the son of a Jewish mother. *The stumbling block of the cross:* cf 1 Cor 1, 23.

5, 12: A sarcastic half-wish that their knife would go beyond mere circumcision; cf Phil 3, 2 and the note there.

5, 13-26: In light of another reminder of the freedom of the gospel (13; cf 1), Paul elaborates on what believers are called to do and be: they fulfill the law by love of neighbor (14-15), walking in the Spirit (16-26), as is illustrated by concrete *fruit of the Spirit* in their lives.

5, 13: *Serve . . . through love:* cf v 6.

5, 14: Lv 19, 18, emphasized by Jesus (Mt 22, 39; Lk 10, 27); cf Rom 13, 8-10.

5, 16-25: *Spirit . . . flesh:* cf 3, 3 and the note on Rom 8, 1-13.

5, 19-23: Such lists of vices and virtues (cf Rom 1, 29-31; 1 Cor 6, 9-10) were common in the ancient world. Paul contrasts *works of the flesh* (19) with *fruit* (not "works") *of the Spirit* (22). Not law, but the Spirit, leads to such traits.

5, 21: *Occasions of envy:* after the Greek word *phthonoi,* "envies," some manuscripts add a similar sounding one, *phonoi,* "murders."

Spirit is love, joy, peace, patience, kind-
ness, generosity, faithfulness,
23* gentleness, self-control. Against
such there is no law. 24* Now those who
belong to Christ [Jesus] have crucified
their flesh with its passions and desires.
25* If we live in the Spirit, let us also fol-
low the Spirit. 26* Let us not be con-
ceited, provoking one another, envious
of one another.

CHAPTER 6

***Life in the Community of Christ.*†**
1* Brothers, even if a person is caught
in some transgression, you who are
spiritual should correct that one in a
gentle spirit, looking to yourself, so that
you also may not be tempted. 2*† Bear
one another's burdens, and so you will
fulfill the law of Christ. 3* For if anyone
thinks he is something when he is noth-
ing, he is deluding himself. 4† Each one
must examine his own work, and then
he will have reason to boast with regard
to himself alone, and not with regard
to someone else; 5* for each will bear
his own load.
6*† One who is being instructed in the
word should share all good things with
his instructor. 7 Make no mistake: God
is not mocked, for a person will reap
only what he sows, 8* because the one
who sows for his flesh will reap corrup-
tion from the flesh, but the one who sows
for the spirit will reap eternal life from
the spirit. 9* Let us not grow tired of do-
ing good, for in due time we shall reap
our harvest, if we do not give up.
10*† So then, while we have the opportu-
nity, let us do good to all, but especially
to those who belong to the family of the
faith.

VI: CONCLUSION

***Final Appeal.*†** 11*† See with what
large letters I am writing to you in my
own hand! 12*† It is those who want to
make a good appearance in the flesh
who are trying to compel you to have
yourselves circumcised, only that they
may not be persecuted for the cross of
Christ. 13† Not even those having them-
selves circumcised observe the law
themselves; they only want you to be
circumcised so that they may boast of
your flesh. 14*† But may I never boast
except in the cross of our Lord Jesus
Christ, through which the world has
been crucified to me, and I to the world.
15*† For neither does circumcision
mean anything, nor does uncircumci-
sion, but only a new creation. 16*† Peace
and mercy be to all who follow this rule
and to the Israel of God.
17*† From now on, let no one make
troubles for me; for I bear the marks
of Jesus on my body.
18* The grace of our Lord Jesus Christ
be with your spirit, brothers. Amen.

*

23: 1 Tm 1, 9.
24: 2, 19; Rom 6, 6; 8, 13.
25: 5, 16.
26: Phil 2, 3.
6, 1: Mt 18, 15; Jas 5, 19 / 1 Cor 10, 12-13.
2: Col 3, 13 / 1 Cor 9, 21.
3-4: 1 Cor 3, 18; 8, 2; 2 Cor 12, 11.
5: Rom 14, 12.
6: 1 Cor 9, 14.
8: Prv 11, 18; Rom 8, 6.13.
9: 2 Thes 3, 13; Heb 12, 1-3.
10: 1 Thes 5, 15.
11: 1 Cor 16, 21.
12: 5, 2.11.
14: 2, 20; 1 Cor 2, 2.
15: 5, 6; 1 Cor 7, 19 / 2 Cor 5, 17.
16: Pss 125, 5; 128, 6.
17: 2 Cor 4, 10.
18: Phil 4, 23; 2 Tm 4, 22; Phlm 25.

†

6, 1-10: The ethical exhortations begun at 5, 1 continue with a variety of admonitions to the community (*brothers:* see the note on 1, 2). Nearly every sentence contains a separate item of practical advice; the faith and freedom of the gospel underlie each maxim. Tensions and temptation within communal life have previously been addressed in 5, 15.26, and v 1 continues with a case in which *a person is caught in some transgression* such as those in 5, 19-21; cf 2, 17.

6, 2: *The law of Christ:* cf Rom 8, 2; 1 Cor 9, 21; Gal 5, 14. The principle of love for others is meant. To *bear one another's burdens* is to "serve one another through love" (5, 13).

6, 4-5: Self-examination is the cure for self-deception. Compare what you are with what you were before, and give the glory to God; cf Rom 6, 19-22. *Load:* used elsewhere of a soldier's pack. Correcting one's own conduct avoids burdening others with it.

6, 6: Implies oral instruction in the faith by catechists; these are to be remunerated for their service; cf Rom 15, 27.

6, 10: *The family of the faith:* the Christian household or church. Doing good has a universal object (*to all*), but the local community makes specific the reality of those to be served.

6, 11-18: A postscript in Paul's own hand, as was his practice (see 1 Cor 16, 21; 2 Thes 3, 17). Paul summarizes his appeal against his opponents (12-13), then returns to his message of glorying in the cross, not in circumcision, as the means of salvation (14-15; cf 5, 11). A benediction follows at v 16. In the polemical spirit that the attack on his apostleship called forth (1, 11—2, 21), Paul reasserts his missionary credentials (17) before giving a final benediction (18).

6, 11: *Large letters:* in contrast to the finer hand of the scribe who wrote the letter up to this point. The larger Greek letters make Paul's message even more emphatic. Some find a hint of poor eyesight on Paul's part. See the note on 4, 13.

6, 12-15: The Jewish Christian opponents wished *not to be persecuted,* possibly by Jews. But since Judaism seems to have had a privileged status as a religion in the Roman empire, circumcised Christians might, if taken as Jews, thereby avoid persecution from the Romans. In any case, Paul instead stresses conformity with *the cross of our Lord Jesus Christ;* cf 2, 19-21; 5, 11.

6, 13: *Those having themselves circumcised:* other manuscripts read, "those who have had themselves circumcised."

6, 14: *Through which:* or "through whom."

6, 15: *New creation:* or "new creature"; cf 2 Cor 5, 17.

6, 16: *This rule:* the principle in vv 14 and 15. *The Israel of God:* while the church may be meant (the phrase can be translated "to all who follow this rule, even the Israel of God"; cf 10; 1 Cor 10, 18), the reference may also be to God's ancient people, Israel; cf Pss 125, 5; 128, 6.

6, 17: *The marks of Jesus:* slaves were often branded by marks (*stigmata*) burned into their flesh to show to whom they belonged; so also were devotees of pagan gods. Paul implies that instead of outdated circumcision, his body bears the scars of his apostolic labors (2 Cor 11, 22-31), such as floggings (Acts 16, 22; 2 Cor 11, 25) and stonings (Acts 14, 19), that mark him as belonging to the Christ who suffered (cf Rom 6, 3; 2 Cor 4, 10; Col 1, 24) and will protect his own.

The Letter to the

EPHESIANS

Ephesians is the great Pauline letter about the church. It deals, however, not so much with a congregation in the city of Ephesus in Asia Minor as with the worldwide church, the head of which is Christ (4, 15), the purpose of which is to be the instrument for making God's plan of salvation known throughout the universe (3, 9-10). Yet this ecclesiology is anchored in God's saving love, shown in Jesus Christ (2, 4-10), and the whole of redemption is rooted in the plan and accomplishment of the triune God (1, 3-14). The language is often that of doxology (1, 3-14) and prayer (cf 1, 15-23; 3, 14-19), indeed of liturgy and hymns (3, 20-21; 5, 14).

The majestic chapters of Ephesians emphasize the unity in the church of Christ that has come about for both Jews and Gentiles within God's household (1, 15—2, 22, especially 2, 11-22) and indeed the "seven unities" of church, Spirit, hope; one Lord, faith, and baptism; and the one God (4, 4-6). Yet the concern is not with the church for its own sake but rather as the means for mission in the world (3, 1—4, 24). The gifts Christ gives its members are to lead to growth and renewal (4, 7-24). Ethical admonition is not lacking either; all aspects of human life and relationships are illumined by the light of Christ (4, 25—6, 20).

The letter is seemingly addressed by Paul to Christians in Ephesus (1, 1), a place where the apostle labored for well over two years (Acts 19, 10). Yet there is a curiously impersonal tone to the writing for a community with which Paul was so intimately acquainted (cf 3, 2 and 4, 21). There are no personal greetings (cf 6, 23). More significantly, important early manuscripts omit the words "in Ephesus" (see the note on 1, 1). Many therefore regard the letter as an encyclical or "circular letter" sent to a number of churches in Asia Minor, the addressees to be designated in each place by its bearer, Tychicus (6, 21-22). Others think that Ephesians is the letter referred to in Colossians 4, 16 as "to the Laodiceans."

Paul, who is designated as the sole author at 1, 1, is described in almost unparalleled terms with regard to the significant role he has in God's plan for bringing the Gentiles to faith in Christ (3, 1-12). Yet at the time of writing he is clearly in prison (3, 1; 4, 1; 6, 20), suffering afflictions (3, 13). Traditionally this "Captivity Epistle" has, along with Colossians, Philippians, and Philemon, been dated to an imprisonment in Rome, likely in A.D. 61-63. Others appeal to an earlier imprisonment, perhaps in Caesarea (Acts 23, 27—27, 2). Since the early nineteenth century, however, much of critical scholarship has considered the letter's style and use of words (especially when compared with Colossians), its concept of the church, and other points of doctrine put forward by the writer as grounds for serious doubt about authorship by Paul. The letter may then be the work of a secretary writing at the apostle's direction or of a later disciple who sought to develop Paul's ideas for a new situation around A.D. 80-100.

The principal divisions of the Letter to the Ephesians are the following:

I: Address (1, 1-14)
II: Unity of the Church in Christ (1, 15—2, 22)
III: World Mission of the Church (3, 1—4, 24)
IV: Daily Conduct, an Expression of Unity (4, 25—6, 20)
V: Conclusion (6, 21-24)

I: ADDRESS

CHAPTER 1

Greeting.† 1*† Paul, an apostle of
Christ Jesus by the will of God, to the
holy ones who are [in Ephesus] faithful
in Christ Jesus: 2* grace to you and
peace from God our Father and the
Lord Jesus Christ.

The Father's Plan of Salvation.†
3*† Blessed be the God and Father of our
Lord Jesus Christ, who has blessed us
in Christ with every spiritual blessing
in the heavens, 4* as he chose us in him,
before the foundation of the world, to
be holy and without blemish before him.
In love 5* he destined us for adoption
to himself through Jesus Christ, in ac-
cord with the favor of his will, 6* for the
praise of the glory of his grace that he
granted us in the beloved.

Fulfillment through Christ. 7* In him
we have redemption by his blood, the
forgiveness of transgressions, in accord
with the riches of his grace 8* that he
lavished upon us. In all wisdom and in-
sight, 9*† he has made known to us the
mystery of his will in accord with his
favor that he set forth in him 10* as a
plan for the fullness of times, to sum
up all things in Christ, in heaven and
on earth.

Inheritance through the Spirit.
11* In him we were also chosen, destined
in accord with the purpose of the one
who accomplishes all things according
to the intention of his will, 12† so that
we might exist for the praise of his
glory, we who first hoped in Christ.
13*† In him you also, who have heard
the word of truth, the gospel of your sal-
vation, and have believed in him, were
sealed with the promised holy Spirit,
14*† which is the first installment of our
inheritance toward redemption as
God's possession, to the praise of his
glory.

II: UNITY OF THE CHURCH IN CHRIST

The Church as Christ's Body.†
15*† Therefore, I, too, hearing of your
faith in the Lord Jesus and of your love
for all the holy ones, 16* do not cease
giving thanks for you, remembering
you in my prayers, 17* that the God of
our Lord Jesus Christ, the Father of
glory, may give you a spirit of wisdom
and revelation resulting in knowledge
of him. 18* May the eyes of [your] hearts
be enlightened, that you may know

*

1, 1: Rom 1, 7; 1 Cor 1, 1-2; Col 1, 1.
2: Col 1, 2.
3: 2, 6; 2 Cor 1, 3.
4: 5, 27; Jn 15, 16; 17, 24; Rom 8, 29; 2 Thes 2, 13.
5: Jn 1, 12; 1 Jn 3, 1.
6: Mt 3, 17; Col 1, 13.
7: 2, 7-13; Rom 3, 24; Col 1, 14.20.
8: Col 1, 9.
9: 3, 3.9; Rom 16, 25.
10: Gal 4, 4; Col 1, 16.20.
11: Is 46, 10; Rom 8, 28; Col 1, 12; Rv 4, 11.
13: 4, 30; Acts 2, 33; Col 1, 5-6.
14: 2 Cor 1, 22; 5, 5.
15: Col 1, 3-4; Phlm 4-5.
16: Col 1, 3.9.
17: 3, 14.16; Col 1, 9-10; 1 Jn 5, 20.
18: 4, 4; Col 1, 12.27.

†

1, 1-2: For the epistolary form used at the beginning of letters, see the note on Rom 1, 1-7. Twenty-two of the thirty Greek words in vv 1-2 also occur in Col 1, 1-2.

1, 1: *[In Ephesus]:* the phrase is lacking in important early witnesses such as P46 (3rd cent.), and Sinaiticus and Vaticanus (4th cent.), appearing in the latter two as a fifth-century addition. Basil and Origen mention its absence from manuscripts. See Introduction. Without the phrase, the Greek can be rendered, as in Col 1, 2, "to the holy ones and faithful brothers in Christ."

1, 3-14: While a Pauline letter usually continues after the greeting with a prayer of thanksgiving, as in 15-23 below, Ephesians first inserts a blessing of God for the blessings Christians have experienced, as in 2 Cor 1, 3-4 and 1 Pt 1, 3-12. The blessing here, akin to a Jewish *berakah,* is rich in images almost certainly drawn from hymns and liturgy. Many ideas here are also found in Col 1, 3-23. Certain phrases are frequently repeated, such as *in Christ* (3.10.12) or *in him* (4.7.9.11.13) or *in the Beloved* (6) and *(for) the praise of (his) glory* (6.12.14). Some terms like *chose* (4) and *destined* (5) reflect Old Testament theology (Dt 7, 7; 9, 4-6; 23, 5) or Pauline themes (*redemption,* 7.14; *grace,* 6.7) or specific emphases in Col (*forgiveness,* Col 1, 14).

A triadic structure is discernible in vv 3-14: *God* the *Father* (3-6.8.11), *Christ* (3.5.7-10.12), and the *Spirit* (13-14). The spiritual blessings Christians have received through Christ (3) are gratefully enumerated: the call to holiness (4; cf Col 1, 22); the gift of divine *adoption* establishing a unique spiritual relationship with God the Father through Christ (5; cf Gal 4, 5); liberation from sin through Christ's sacrificial death (7); revelation of God's plan of salvation in Christ (9; cf 3, 3-4; Rom 16, 25); the gift of election and faith in Christ bestowed upon Jewish Christians (see the note on 12, *we who first hoped in Christ*); and finally, the same gift granted to Gentiles (13, *you also*). In the Christ-centered faith and existence of the Christian communities the apostle sees the predetermined *plan* of God to bring all creation under the final rule of Christ (4-5.9-10) being *made known* (9) and carried through, to God's *glory* (6.12.14).

1, 3: *In the heavens:* literally, "in the heavenlies" or "in the heavenly places," a term in Eph for the divine realm.

1, 9: *Mystery:* as in Rom 16, 25; Col 1, 26.27 and elsewhere, a secret of God now revealed in the *plan* to save and *sum up all things in Christ* (10); cf 3, 3-6.

1, 12: *We who first hoped:* probably Jewish Christians (contrast 13, *you,* the Gentiles); possibly the people of Israel, "we who already enjoyed the hope of Christ," or perhaps present hope in contrast to future redemption (cf 14).

1, 13: *Sealed:* by God, in baptism; cf 4, 30; 2 Cor 1, 22.

1, 14: *First installment:* down payment by God on full salvation, as at 2 Cor 1, 22.

1, 15-23: See the note on Rom 1, 8 for the thanksgiving form in a letter. Much of the content parallels thoughts in Col 1, 3-20. The prayer moves from God and Christ (17.20-21) to the Ephesians (17-19) and the church (22-23). Paul asks that the blessing imparted by God the Father (3) to the Ephesians will be strengthened in them through the message of the gospel (13.17-19). Those blessings are seen in the context of God's *might* in establishing the sovereignty of Christ over all other creatures (19-21) and in appointing him *head* of the church (22-23). For the allusion to angelic spirits in v 21, see Rom 8, 38 and Col 1, 16. Here, as in 1 Cor 15, 24-25 and Col 2, 15, every such *principality* and *power* is made subject to Christ.

1, 15: *Your faith . . . your love:* some manuscripts omit the latter phrase, but cf Col 1, 4.

what is the hope that belongs to his call, what are the riches of glory in his inheritance among the holy ones, 19* and what is the surpassing greatness of his power for us who believe, in accord with the exercise of his great might, 20* which he worked in Christ, raising him from the dead and seating him at his right hand in the heavens, 21* far above every principality, authority, power, and dominion, and every name that is named not only in this age but also in the one to come. 22* And he put all things beneath his feet and gave him as head over all things to the church, 23*† which is his body, the fullness of the one who fills all things in every way.

CHAPTER 2†

Generosity of God's Plan.† 1*† You were dead in your transgressions and sins 2*† in which you once lived following the age of this world, following the ruler of the power of the air, the spirit that is now at work in the disobedient. 3* All of us once lived among them in the desires of our flesh, following the wishes of the flesh and the impulses, and we were by nature children of wrath, like the rest. 4 But God, who is rich in mercy, because of the great love he had for us, 5*† even when we were dead in our transgressions, brought us to life with Christ (by grace you have been saved), 6* raised us up with him, and seated us with him in the heavens in Christ Jesus, 7* that in the ages to come he might show the immeasurable riches of his grace in his kindness to us in Christ Jesus. 8* For by grace you have been saved through faith, and this is not from you; it is the gift of God; 9* it is not from works, so no one may boast. 10* For we are his handiwork, created in Christ Jesus for the good works that God has prepared in advance, that we should live in them.

One in Christ.† 11 Therefore, remember that at one time you, Gentiles in the flesh, called the uncircumcision by those called the circumcision, which is done in the flesh by human hands, 12*† were at that time without Christ, alienated from the community of Israel and strangers to the covenants of promise, without hope and without God in the world. 13* But now in Christ Jesus you who once were far off have become near by the blood of Christ.

*

19: 2 Cor 13, 4; Col 1, 11; 2, 12.
20: Ps 110, 1; Heb 1, 3.
21: Phil 2, 9; Col 1, 16; 1 Pt 3, 22.
22: 4, 15; Ps 8, 7; Mt 28, 18; Col 1, 18.
23: 4, 10.12; Rom 12, 5; 1 Cor 12, 27; Col 1, 19.
2, 1: Col 1, 21; 2, 13.
2: 6, 12; Jn 12, 31; Col 1, 13.
3: Col 3, 6-7.
5: Rom 5, 8; 6, 13; Col 2, 13.
6: Rom 8, 10-11; Phil 3, 20; Col 2, 12.
7: 1, 7.
8: Rom 3, 24; Gal 2, 16.
9: 1 Cor 1, 29.
10: 4, 24; Ti 2, 14.
12: Rom 9, 4; Col 1, 21.27.
13: 2, 17; Is 57, 19; Col 1, 20.

†

1, 23: *His body:* the church (22); cf the note on Col 1, 18. Only in Eph and Col is Christ the *head* of the *body,* in contrast to the view in 1 Cor 12 and Rom 12, 4-8 where Christ is equated with the entire body or community. *Fullness:* see the note on Col 1, 19. Some take *the one who fills* as God, others as Christ (cf 4, 10). If in Christ "dwells the fullness of the deity bodily" (Col 2, 9), then, as God "fills" Christ, Christ in turn fills the church and the believer (3, 19; 5, 18). But the difficult phrases here may also allow the church to be viewed as the "complement" of Christ who is "being filled" as God's plan for the universe is carried out through the church (cf 3, 9-10).

2, 1-22: The gospel of *salvation* (1, 13) that God *worked in Christ* (1, 20) is reiterated in terms of what God's *great love* (4), expressed in Christ, means for us. The passage sometimes addresses *you,* Gentiles (1-2.8.11-13.19.22), but other times speaks of *all of us* who believe (3-7.10.14.18). In urging people to *remember* their grim past when they were *dead* in sins (1-3.11-12) and what they are *now in Christ* (4-10.13), the author sees both Jew and Gentile reconciled with God, now *one new person,* a new humanity, *one body, the household of God, a temple* and *dwelling place* of God's Spirit (15-16.19-22). The presentation falls into two parts, the second stressing more the meaning for the church.

2, 1-10: The recipients of Paul's letter have experienced, in their redemption from *transgressions and sins,* the effect of Christ's supremacy over the power of the devil (1-2; cf 6, 11-12), who rules not from the netherworld but from the *air* between God in heaven and human beings on earth. Both Jew and Gentile have experienced, through Christ, God's free gift of salvation that already marks them for a future heavenly destiny (3-7). The language *dead, raised us up,* and *seated us . . . in the heavens* closely parallels Jesus' own passion and Easter experience. The terms in vv 8-9 describe salvation in the way Paul elsewhere speaks of justification: *by grace, through faith, the gift of God, not from works;* cf Gal 2, 16-21; Rom 3, 24-28. Christians are a newly created people in Christ, fashioned by God for a life of goodness (10).

2, 1-7: These verses comprise one long sentence in Greek, the main verb coming in v 5, God *brought us to life,* the object you/us *dead in . . . transgressions* being repeated in 1 and 5; cf Col 2, 13.

2, 2: *Age of this world:* or "aeon," a term found in gnostic thought, possibly synonymous with *the rulers of this world,* but also reflecting the Jewish idea of "two ages," this present evil age and "the age to come"; cf 1 Cor 3, 19; 5, 10; 7, 31; Gal 1, 4; Ti 2, 12. *The disobedient:* literally, "the sons of disobedience," a Semitism as at Is 30, 9.

2, 5: Our relation through baptism *with Christ,* the risen Lord, is depicted in terms of realized eschatology, as already exaltation, though v 7 brings in the future aspect too.

2, 11-22: The Gentiles lacked Israel's messianic expectation, lacked the various *covenants* God made with *Israel,* lacked *hope* of salvation and knowledge of the true *God* (11-12); but through Christ all these religious barriers between Jew and Gentile have been transcended (13-14) by the abolition of the Mosaic covenant-law (15) for the sake of uniting Jew and Gentile into a single religious community (15-16), imbued with the same holy *Spirit* and worshiping the same *Father* (18). The Gentiles are now included in God's *household* (19) as it arises upon the *foundation* of *apostles* assisted by those endowed with the prophetic gift (3, 5), the preachers of Christ (20; cf 1 Cor 12, 28). With Christ as the *capstone* (20; cf Is 28, 16; Mt 21, 42), they are being built into the holy *temple* of God's people where the divine presence dwells (21-22).

2, 12: *The community of Israel:* or "commonwealth"; cf 4, 18. *The covenants:* cf Rom 9, 4: with Abraham, with Moses, with David.

14*† For he is our peace, he who made
both one and broke down the dividing
wall of enmity, through his flesh,
15*† abolishing the law with its com-
mandments and legal claims, that he
might create in himself one new person
in place of the two, thus establishing
peace, 16* and might reconcile both with
God, in one body, through the cross,
putting that enmity to death by it.
17* He came and preached peace to you
who were far off and peace to those who
were near, 18* for through him we both
have access in one Spirit to the Father.
19* So then you are no longer strang-
ers and sojourners, but you are fellow
citizens with the holy ones and mem-
bers of the household of God, 20*† built
upon the foundation of the apostles and
prophets, with Christ Jesus himself as
the capstone. 21* Through him the whole
structure is held together and grows
into a temple sacred in the Lord;
22* in him you also are being built to-
gether into a dwelling place of God in
the Spirit.

III: WORLD MISSION OF THE CHURCH

CHAPTER 3

Commission to Preach God's Plan.†
1*† Because of this, I, Paul, a prisoner
of Christ [Jesus] for you Gentiles—
2*† if, as I suppose, you have heard of
the stewardship of God's grace that
was given to me for your benefit,
3*† [namely, that] the mystery was
made known to me by revelation, as I
have written briefly earlier. 4 When you
read this you can understand my in-
sight into the mystery of Christ,
5* which was not made known to human
beings in other generations as it has
now been revealed to his holy apostles
and prophets by the Spirit, 6* that the
Gentiles are coheirs, members of the
same body, and copartners in the prom-
ise in Christ Jesus through the gospel.
7* Of this I became a minister by the
gift of God's grace that was granted me
in accord with the exercise of his power.
8* To me, the very least of all the holy
ones, this grace was given, to preach
to the Gentiles the inscrutable riches of
Christ, 9*† and to bring to light [for all]
what is the plan of the mystery hidden
from ages past in God who created all
things, 10*† so that the manifold wisdom
of God might now be made known
through the church to the principalities
and authorities in the heavens. 11 This
was according to the eternal purpose
that he accomplished in Christ Jesus
our Lord, 12* in whom we have boldness
of speech and confidence of access
through faith in him. 13* So I ask you
not to lose heart over my afflictions for
you; this is your glory.
Prayer for the Readers.† 14† For this
reason I kneel before the Father,
15 from whom every family in heaven
and on earth is named, 16* that he may

*

14: Gal 3, 28.
15: 2 Cor 5, 17; Col 2, 14.
16: Col 1, 20.22.
17: Is 57, 19; Zec 9, 10.
18: 3, 12.
19: Heb 12, 22-23.
20: Is 28, 16; Rv 21, 14.
21: 1 Cor 3, 16; Col 2, 19.
22: 1 Pt 2, 5.
3, 1: Phil 1, 7.13; Col 1, 24-29; 4, 18; Phlm 1, 9; 2 Tm 2, 9.
2: Col 1, 25.
3: 1, 9-10; Col 1, 26.
5: Col 1, 26.
6: 2, 13.18-19.
7: Rom 15, 15; Col 1, 25.29.
8: 1 Cor 15, 8-10; Gal 1, 16; 2, 7-9.
9: Rom 16, 25; Col 1, 26-27.
10: 1 Pt 1, 12.
12: Rom 5, 1-2; Heb 4, 16.
13: Col 1, 22.24; 2 Tm 2, 10.
16: 6, 10; Rom 7, 22; 2 Cor 4, 16; Col 1, 11.

†

2, 14-16: The elaborate imagery here combines pictures of Christ as *our peace* (Is 9, 5), his crucifixion, the ending of the Mosaic law (cf Col 2, 14), reconciliation (2 Cor 5, 18-21), and the destruction of *the dividing wall* such as kept people from God in the temple or a barrier in the heavens.

2, 15: *One new person:* a corporate body, the Christian community, made up of Jews and Gentiles, replacing ancient divisions; cf Rom 1, 16.

2, 20: *Capstone:* the Greek can also mean cornerstone or keystone.

3, 1-13: Paul reflects on his mission to the Gentiles. He alludes to his call and appointment to the apostolic office (2-3) and how his *insight* through revelation, as well as that of the other apostles and charismatic prophets in the church (4-5), has deepened understanding of God's plan of salvation in Christ. Paul is the special herald (7) of a new *promise* to the *Gentiles* (6): that the divine plan includes them in the spiritual benefits promised to Israel. Not only is this unique apostolic role his; Paul also has been given the task of explaining to all the divine *plan* of salvation (8-9), once *hidden.* Through *the church,* God's plan to save through Christ is becoming manifest to angelic beings (10; cf 1, 21), in accord with God's *purpose* (11). The fulfillment of the plan in Christ gives the whole church more *confidence* through *faith* in God (12). The readers of this letter are also thereby encouraged to greater confidence despite Paul's imprisonment (13).

3, 1: *A prisoner of Christ:* see Introduction. Paul abruptly departs from his train of thought at the end of v 1, leaving an incomplete sentence.

3, 2: *Stewardship:* the Greek is the same term employed at 1, 10 for the *plan* that God administers (Col 1, 25) and in which Paul plays a key role.

3, 3-4: *The mystery:* God's resolve to deliver Gentiles along with Israel through Christ; cf the notes on 1, 10; 3, 9.

3, 9: *[For all]:* while some think this phrase was added so as to yield the sense "to enlighten all about the plan . . . ," it is more likely that some manuscripts and Fathers omitted it accidentally or to avoid the idea that *all* conflicted with Paul's assignment to preach to *the Gentiles* (8) specifically.

3, 10: *Principalities and authorities:* see the note on 1, 15-23 regarding v 21.

3, 14-21: The apostle prays that those he is addressing may, like the rest of the church, deepen their understanding of God's plan of salvation in Christ. It is a plan that affects the whole universe (15) with *the breadth and length and height and depth* of God's love in Christ (18) or possibly the universe in all its dimensions. The apostle prays that they may perceive the redemptive love of Christ for them and be completely immersed in the fullness of God (19). The prayer concludes with a doxology to God (20-21).

3, 14-15: *Every family:* in the Greek there is wordplay on the word for *the Father* (*patria, patēr*). The phrase could also mean "God's whole family" (cf 2, 21).

grant you in accord with the riches of his glory to be strengthened with power through his Spirit in the inner self, 17* and that Christ may dwell in your hearts through faith; that you, rooted and grounded in love, 18* may have strength to comprehend with all the holy ones what is the breadth and length and height and depth, 19* and to know the love of Christ that surpasses knowledge, so that you may be filled with all the fullness of God.

20* Now to him who is able to accomplish far more than all we ask or imagine, by the power at work within us, 21 to him be glory in the church and in Christ Jesus to all generations, forever and ever. Amen.

CHAPTER 4

***Unity in the Body.*†** 1* I, then, a prisoner for the Lord, urge you to live in a manner worthy of the call you have received, 2* with all humility and gentleness, with patience, bearing with one another through love, 3* striving to preserve the unity of the spirit through the bond of peace: 4*† one body and one Spirit, as you were also called to the one hope of your call; 5* one Lord, one faith, one baptism; 6* one God and Father of all, who is over all and through all and in all.

Diversity of Gifts. 7* But grace was given to each of us according to the measure of Christ's gift. 8*† Therefore, it says:

> "He ascended on high and took
> prisoners captive;
> he gave gifts to men."

9 What does "he ascended" mean except that he also descended into the lower [regions] of the earth? 10 The one who descended is also the one who ascended far above all the heavens, that he might fill all things.

11*† And he gave some as apostles, others as prophets, others as evangelists, others as pastors and teachers, 12† to equip the holy ones for the work of ministry, for building up the body of Christ, 13*† until we all attain to the unity of faith and knowledge of the Son of God, to mature manhood, to the extent of the full stature of Christ, 14* so that we may no longer be infants, tossed by waves and swept along by every wind of teaching arising from human trickery, from their cunning in the interests of deceitful scheming. 15*† Rather, living the truth in love, we should grow in every way into him who is the head, Christ, 16* from whom the whole body, joined and held together by every supporting ligament, with the proper functioning of each part, brings about the body's growth and builds itself up in love.

***Renewal in Christ.*†** 17* So I declare and testify in the Lord that you must no longer live as the Gentiles do, in the futility of their minds; 18* darkened in understanding, alienated from the life

*

3, 17: Jn 14, 23; Col 1, 23; 2, 7.
18: Col 2, 2.
19: Col 2, 3.9.
20: Rom 16, 25-27; Col 1, 29.
4, 1: 3, 1; Col 1, 10.
2: Col 3, 12-13.
3: Col 3, 14-15.
4: Rom 12, 5; 1 Cor 10, 17; 12, 12-13.
5: 1 Cor 8, 6.
6: 1 Cor 12, 6.
7: Rom 12, 3.6; 1 Cor 12, 28.
8: Ps 68, 19; Col 2, 15.
11: 1 Cor 12, 28.
13: Col 1, 28.
14: 1 Cor 14, 20; Col 2, 4.8; Heb 13, 9; Jas 1, 6.
15: 1 Cor 11, 3; Col 1, 18; 2, 19.
16: Col 2, 19.
17: Rom 1, 21.
18: Col 1, 21; 1 Pt 1, 14.

†

4, 1-16: A general plea for unity in the church. Christians have been fashioned through the *Spirit* into a single harmonious religious community (*one body,* 4.12; cf 16), belonging to a single *Lord* (in contrast to the many gods of the pagan world), and by one way of salvation through *faith,* brought out especially by the significance of *baptism* (1-6; cf Rom 6, 1-11). But Christian unity is more than adherence to a common belief. It is manifested in the exalted Christ's gifts to individuals to serve so as to make the community more Christlike (11-16). This teaching on Christ as the source of the gifts is introduced in v 8 by a citation of Ps 68, 18, which depicts Yahweh triumphantly leading Israel to salvation in Jerusalem. It is here understood of Christ, ascending *above all the heavens,* the *head* of the church; through his redemptive death, resurrection, and ascension he has become the source of the church's spiritual gifts. The "descent" of Christ (9-10) refers more probably to the incarnation (cf Phil 2, 6-8) than to Christ's presence after his death in the world of the dead (cf 1 Pt 3, 19).

4, 4-6: The "seven unities" (church, *Spirit, hope; Lord, faith* in Christ [1, 13], *baptism; one God*) reflect the triune structure of later creeds in reverse.

4, 8-10: While the emphasis is on an ascension and gift-giving by Christ, there is also a reference in taking *prisoners captive* to the aeons and powers mentioned at 1, 21; 2, 2; 3, 10; and 6, 12.

4, 11: Concerning this list of ministers, cf 1 Cor 12, 28 and Rom 12, 6-8. *Evangelists:* missionary preachers (cf Acts 21, 8 and 2 Tm 4, 5), not those who wrote gospels. *Pastors and teachers:* a single group in the Greek, shepherding congregations.

4, 12: The ministerial leaders in v 11 are to equip the whole people of God for their *work of ministry.*

4, 13: *Mature manhood:* literally, "a perfect man" (cf Col 1, 28), possibly the "one new person" of 2, 15, though there *anthrōpos* suggests humanity, while here *anēr* is the term for male. This personage becomes visible in the church's growing to its fullness in the unity of those who believe in Christ.

4, 15-16: *The head, Christ:* cf Col 1, 18 and contrast 1 Cor 12, 12-27 and Rom 12, 4-5 where Christ is identified with the whole body, including the head. The imagery may derive from ancient views in medicine, the *head* coordinating and caring for the body, each *ligament* (perhaps the ministers of v 11) supporting the whole. But as at 2, 19-22, where the temple is depicted as a growing organism, there may also be the idea here of growing toward the capstone, Christ.

4, 17-24: Paul begins to indicate how the new life in Christ contrasts with the Gentiles' old way of existence. Literally, *the old self* (22) and *the new self* (24) are "the old man" and "the new man" (*anthrōpos,* person), as at 2, 15; cf the note on 4, 13.

of God because of their ignorance, because of their hardness of heart, [19]* they have become callous and have handed themselves over to licentiousness for the practice of every kind of impurity to excess. [20] That is not how you learned Christ, [21] assuming that you have heard of him and were taught in him, as truth is in Jesus, [22]* that you should put away the old self of your former way of life, corrupted through deceitful desires, [23]* and be renewed in the spirit of your minds, [24]*† and put on the new self, created in God's way in righteousness and holiness of truth.

IV: DAILY CONDUCT, AN EXPRESSION OF UNITY†

Rules for the New Life. [25]* Therefore, putting away falsehood, speak the truth, each one to his neighbor, for we are members one of another. [26]*† Be angry but do not sin; do not let the sun set on your anger, [27]* and do not leave room for the devil. [28]*† The thief must no longer steal, but rather labor, doing honest work with his [own] hands, so that he may have something to share with one in need. [29]* No foul language should come out of your mouths, but only such as is good for needed edification, that it may impart grace to those who hear. [30]† And do not grieve the holy Spirit of God, with which you were sealed for the day of redemption. [31]* All bitterness, fury, anger, shouting, and reviling must be removed from you, along with all malice. [32]* [And] be kind to one another, compassionate, forgiving one another as God has forgiven you in Christ.

CHAPTER 5

[1]*† So be imitators of God, as beloved children, [2]* and live in love, as Christ loved us and handed himself over for us as a sacrificial offering to God for a fragrant aroma. [3]* Immorality or any impurity or greed must not even be mentioned among you, as is fitting among holy ones, [4]* no obscenity or silly or suggestive talk, which is out of place, but instead, thanksgiving. [5]* Be sure of this, that no immoral or impure or greedy person, that is, an idolater, has any inheritance in the kingdom of Christ and of God.

Duty to Live in the Light. [6]*† Let no one deceive you with empty arguments, for because of these things the wrath of God is coming upon the disobedient. [7] So do not be associated with them. [8]* For you were once darkness, but now you are light in the Lord. Live as children of light, [9]* for light produces every kind of goodness and righteousness and truth. [10]* Try to learn what is pleasing to the Lord. [11]* Take no part in the fruitless works of darkness; rather expose them, [12] for it is shameful even to mention the things done by them in secret; [13]* but everything exposed by the light becomes visible, [14]*† for everything that becomes visible is light. Therefore, it says:

"Awake, O sleeper,
and arise from the dead,
and Christ will give you light."

[15]*† Watch carefully then how you live, not as foolish persons but as wise, [16] making the most of the opportunity, because the days are evil. [17] Therefore, do not continue in ignorance, but try to understand what is the will of the Lord. [18]* And do not get drunk on wine, in which lies debauchery, but be filled with the Spirit, [19]* addressing one another [in] psalms and hymns and spiritual songs, singing and playing to the Lord in your hearts, [20]* giving thanks always and for everything in the name of our Lord Jesus Christ to God the Father.

*

19: Col 3, 5.
22: Rom 8, 13; Gal 6, 8; Col 3, 9.
23: Rom 12, 2.
24: Gn 1, 26-27; Col 3, 10.
25: Zec 8, 16.
26: Ps 4, 5 LXX; Mt 5, 22.
27: 2 Cor 2, 11.
28: 1 Thes 4, 11.
29: 5, 4; Col 3, 16; 4, 6.
31: Col 3, 8.
32: Mt 6, 14; Col 3, 12-13.
5, 1: Mt 5, 45.48.
2: Ex 29, 18; Ps 40, 7; Gal 2, 20; 1 Jn 3, 16.
3: Gal 5, 19; Col 3, 5.
4: 4, 29; Col 3, 8.
5: 1 Cor 6, 9-10; Gal 5, 21; Col 3, 5.
6: Rom 1, 18; Col 2, 4.8.
8: 2, 11-13; Jn 12, 36; Col 1, 12-13.
9: Gal 5, 22.
10: Rom 12, 2.
11: Rom 13, 12.
13: Jn 3, 20-21.
14: Is 26, 19; 60, 1.
15-16: Col 4, 5.
18: Prv 23, 31 LXX; Lk 21, 34.
19: Ps 33, 2-3; Col 3, 16.
20: Col 3, 17.

†

4, 24: *Put on:* in baptism. See the note on Gal 3, 27.

4, 25—6, 20: For similar exhortations to a morally good life in response to God's gift of faith, see the notes on Rom 12, 1—13, 14 and Gal 5, 13-26.

4, 26: If angry, seek reconciliation that day, not giving the devil (6, 11) opportunity to lead into sin.

4, 28: *Honest work:* literally, "the good." *His [own] hands:* some manuscripts have the full phrase as in 1 Cor 4, 12.

4, 30: See the note on 1, 13.

5, 1: *Imitators of God:* in forgiving (4, 32) and in loving (as exhibited in how *Christ loved us*).

5, 6: See the note on 2, 2.

5, 14: An early Christian hymn, possibly from a baptismal liturgy. For the content compare 2, 5-6; 3, 9 and Is 60, 1.

5, 15-16.19-20: The wording is similar to Col 4, 5 and 3, 16-17.

Wives and Husbands.† 21*† Be subor-
dinate to one another out of reverence
for Christ. 22* Wives should be subordi-
nate to their husbands as to the Lord.
23* For the husband is head of his wife
just as Christ is head of the church, he
himself the savior of the body. 24 As the
church is subordinate to Christ, so wives
should be subordinate to their husbands
in everything. 25* Husbands, love your
wives, even as Christ loved the church
and handed himself over for her 26* to
sanctify her, cleansing her by the bath
of water with the word, 27* that he might
present to himself the church in splen-
dor, without spot or wrinkle or any such
thing, that she might be holy and with-
out blemish. 28 So [also] husbands
should love their wives as their own
bodies. He who loves his wife loves him-
self. 29 For no one hates his own flesh
but rather nourishes and cherishes it,
even as Christ does the church,
30* because we are members of his body.

31* "For this reason a man shall leave
[his] father and [his] mother
and be joined to his wife,
and the two shall become one flesh."

32* This is a great mystery, but I speak
in reference to Christ and the church.
33 In any case, each one of you should
love his wife as himself, and the wife
should respect her husband.

CHAPTER 6

Children and Parents. 1* Children,
obey your parents [in the Lord], for this
is right. 2* "Honor your father and
mother." This is the first commandment
with a promise, 3 "that it may go well
with you and that you may have a long
life on earth." 4* Fathers, do not pro-
voke your children to anger, but bring
them up with the training and instruc-
tion of the Lord.

Slaves and Masters. 5* Slaves, be
obedient to your human masters with
fear and trembling, in sincerity of
heart, as to Christ, 6* not only when be-
ing watched, as currying favor, but as
slaves of Christ, doing the will of God
from the heart, 7 willingly serving the
Lord and not human beings, 8 knowing
that each will be requited from the Lord
for whatever good he does, whether he
is slave or free. 9* Masters, act in the
same way towards them, and stop bul-
lying, knowing that both they and you
have a Master in heaven and that with
him there is no partiality.

Battle against Evil.† 10 Finally, draw
your strength from the Lord and from
his mighty power. 11* Put on the armor
of God so that you may be able to stand
firm against the tactics of the devil.
12* For our struggle is not with flesh and
blood but with the principalities, with
the powers, with the world rulers of this
present darkness, with the evil spirits
in the heavens. 13* Therefore, put on the
armor of God, that you may be able to
resist on the evil day and, having done
everything, to hold your ground. 14* So
stand fast with your loins girded in
truth, clothed with righteousness as a
breastplate, 15* and your feet shod in
readiness for the gospel of peace.
16* In all circumstances, hold faith as
a shield, to quench all [the] flaming
arrows of the evil one. 17* And
take the helmet of salvation and the
sword of the Spirit, which is the word of
God.

Constant Prayer. 18* With all prayer
and supplication, pray at every oppor-
tunity in the Spirit. To that end, be
watchful with all perseverance and sup-

*

21: 1 Pt 5, 5.
22: Col 3, 18—4, 1; 1 Pt 3, 1-7.
23: 1 Cor 11, 3; Col 1, 18.
25: Col 3, 19; 1 Tm 2, 6.
26: Rom 6, 4; Ti 3, 5-7.
27: 2 Cor 11, 2; Col 1, 22.
30: Rom 12, 5; 1 Cor 6, 15.
31: Gn 2, 24; Mt 19, 5; Mk 10, 7-8.
32: Rv 19, 7.
6, 1: Prv 6, 20; Sir 3, 1-6; Col 3, 20.
2-3: Ex 20, 12; Dt 5, 16.
4: Col 3, 21-22.
5: Col 3, 22-25; 1 Tm 6, 1-2; Ti 2, 9-10.
6: 1 Pt 2, 18.
9: Col 4, 1.
11: Rom 13, 12; 2 Cor 6, 7; 10, 4; Jas 4, 7.
12: 1, 21; 2, 2; Col 1, 13.
13: Rom 13, 12.
14: Wis 5, 17-20; Is 11, 5; Lk 12, 35; 1 Thes 5, 8.
15: Is 52, 7.
16: 1 Pt 5, 9.
17: Is 59, 17; 1 Thes 5, 8.
18: Mt 26, 41; Col 4, 2-3.

†

5, 21—6, 9: Cf the notes on Col 3, 18—4, 1 and 1 Pt 2, 18—3, 7 for a similar listing of household duties where the inferior is admonished first (*wives,* 5, 22; *children,* 6, 1; *slaves,* 6, 5), then the superior (*husbands,* 5, 25; *fathers,* 6, 4; *masters,* 6, 9). Paul varies this pattern by an emphasis on mutuality (see 5, 20); use of Old Testament material about *father and mother* in 6, 2; the judgment to come for slave-owners (*you have a Master in heaven,* 6, 9); and above all the initial principle of subordination *to one another* under *Christ,* thus effectively undermining exclusive claims to domination by one party. Into the section on *wives* and *husbands* an elaborate teaching on *Christ* and *the church* has been woven (5, 22-33).

5, 21-33: The apostle exhorts married Christians to a strong mutual love. Holding with Gn 2, 24 that marriage is a divine institution (31), Paul sees Christian marriage as taking on a new meaning symbolic of the intimate relationship of love between Christ and the church. The wife should serve her husband in the same spirit as that of the church's service to Christ (22.24), and the husband should care for his wife with the devotion of Christ to the church (25-30). Paul gives to the Genesis passage its highest meaning in the light of the union of Christ and the church, of which Christlike loyalty and devotion in Christian marriage are a clear reflection (31-33).

6, 10-20: A general exhortation to courage and prayer. Drawing upon the imagery and ideas of Is 11, 5; 59, 16-17; and Wis 5, 17-23, Paul describes the Christian in terms of the dress and equipment of Roman soldiers. He observes, however, that the Christian's readiness for combat is not directed against human beings but against the spiritual powers of evil (10-17; cf 1, 21; 2, 2; 3, 10). Unique importance is placed upon prayer (18-20).

plication for all the holy ones [19*] and
also for me, that speech may be given
me to open my mouth, to make known
with boldness the mystery of the gospel
[20*] for which I am an ambassador in
chains, so that I may have the courage
to speak as I must.

V: CONCLUSION

***A Final Message.*†** [21*] So that you
also may have news of me and of what
I am doing, Tychicus, my beloved
brother and trustworthy minister in the
Lord, will tell you everything. [22*] I am
sending him to you for this very pur-
pose, so that you may know about us
and that he may encourage your hearts.
[23] Peace be to the brothers, and love
with faith, from God the Father and the
Lord Jesus Christ. [24*] Grace be with all
who love our Lord Jesus Christ in im-
mortality.

*

19: Acts 4, 29; Col 4, 3; 2 Thes 3, 1.
20: 2 Cor 5, 20; Col 4, 4.
21: Acts 20, 4; Col 4, 7; 2 Tm 4, 12.
22: Col 4, 8.
24: 1 Pt 1, 8.

†

6, 21-24: *Tychicus:* the bearer of the letter; see the note on Col 4, 7. Verses 21-22 parallel Col 4, 7-8, often word for word. If Ephesians is addressed to several Christian communities (see Introduction), it is understandable that no greetings to individual members of these communities should have been included in it.

EPHESIANS

The Letter to the

PHILIPPIANS

Philippi, in northeastern Greece, was a city of some importance in the Roman province of Macedonia. Lying on the great road from the Adriatic coast to Byzantium, the Via Egnatia, and in the midst of rich agricultural plains near the gold deposits of Mt. Pangaeus, it was in Paul's day a Roman town (Acts 16, 21), with a Greek-Macedonian population and a small group of Jews (see Acts 16, 13). Originally founded in the sixth century B.C. as Krenides by the Thracians, the town was taken over after 360 B.C. by Philip II of Macedon, the father of Alexander the Great, and was renamed for himself, "Philip's City." The area became Roman in the second century B.C. On the plains near Philippi in October 42 B.C., Antony and Octavian decisively defeated the forces of Brutus and Cassius, the slayers of Julius Caesar. Octavian (Augustus) later made Philippi a Roman colony and settled many veterans of the Roman armies there.

Paul, according to Acts (16, 9-40), established at Philippi the first Christian community in Europe. He came to Philippi, via its harbor town of Neapolis (modern Kavalla), on his second missionary journey, probably in A.D. 49 or 50, accompanied by Silas and Timothy (Acts 15, 40; 16, 3; cf Phil 1, 1) and Luke, if he is to be included in the "we" references of Acts 16, 10-17. The Acts account tells of the conversion of a business woman, Lydia; the exorcism of a slave girl; and, after an earthquake, while Paul and Silas were imprisoned in Philippi, the faith and baptism of a jailer and his family. None of these persons, however, is directly mentioned in Philippians (cf the notes on 4, 2 and 4, 3). Acts 16 concludes its account by describing how Paul (and Silas), asked by the magistrates to leave Philippi, went on to Thessalonica (Acts 17, 1-10), where several times his loyal Philippians continued to support him with financial aid (Phil 4, 16). Later, Paul may have passed through Philippi on his way from Ephesus to Greece (Acts 20, 1-2), and he definitely stopped there on his fateful trip to Jerusalem (Acts 20, 6).

Paul's letter to the Christians at Philippi was written while he was in a prison somewhere (1, 7.13.14.17), indeed in danger of death (1, 20-23). Although under guard for preaching Christ, Paul rejoices at the continuing progress of the gospel (1, 12-26) and expresses gratitude for the Philippians' renewed concern and help in an expression of thanks most clearly found at 4, 10-20. Much of the letter is devoted to instruction about unity and humility within the Christian community at Philippi (1, 27—2, 18) and exhortations to growth, joy, and peace in their life together (4, 1-9). The letter seems to be drawing to a close at the end of what we number as ch 2, as Paul reports the plans of his helper Timothy and of Epaphroditus (whom the Philippians had sent to aid Paul) to come to Philippi (2, 19—3, 1), and even Paul's own expectation that he will go free and come to Philippi (1, 25-26; 2, 24). Yet quite abruptly at 3, 2, Paul erupts into warnings against false teachers who threaten to impose on the Philippians the burdens of the Mosaic law, including circumcision. The section that follows, 3, 2-21, is a vigorous attack on these Judaizers (cf Gal 2, 11—3, 29) or Jewish Christian teachers (cf 2 Cor 11, 12-23), giving us insights into Paul's own life story (3, 4-6) and into the doctrine of justification, the Christian life, and ultimate hope (3, 7-21).

The location of Paul's imprisonment when he wrote to the Philippians, and thus the date of the letter, are uncertain. The traditional view has been that it stems from Paul's confinement in Rome, between A.D. 59 and 63 (cf Acts 28, 14-31). One modern view suggests the period when he was imprisoned at Caesarea, on the coast of Palestine, A.D. 57 or 58 (Acts 23, 23—26, 32); another suggests Corinth (cf 2 Cor 11, 9). Much recent scholarship favors Ephesus, around A.D. 55, a situation referred to in 2 Cor 1, 8 concerning "the affliction that came to us" in Asia Minor (cf also 1 Cor 15, 32). The reference at 1, 13 to the "praetorium" (cf also 4, 22) can be understood to mean the imperial guard or government house at Ephesus (or Caesarea), or the praetorian camp in Rome. Involved in a decision are the several journeys back and forth between Philippi and wherever Paul is imprisoned, mentioned in the letter (2, 25-28; 4, 14); this factor causes many to prefer Ephesus because of its proximity to Philippi. The Ephesian hypothesis dates the composition of Philippians to the mid-50s when most of Paul's major letters were written.

There is also a likelihood, according to some scholars, that the letter as we have it is a composite from parts of three letters by Paul to the Philippians. Seemingly 4, 10-20 is a brief note of appreciation for help sent through Epaphroditus. The long section from 1, 3 to 3, 1 is then another letter, with news of Paul's imprisonment and reports on Timothy and Epaphroditus (who has fallen ill while with Paul), along with exhortations to the Philippians about Christian conduct; and 3, 2-21 a third communication warning about threats to Philippian Christianity. The other verses in ch 4 and 1, 1-2, are variously assigned by critics to these three underlying letters, which an editor presumably put together to produce a picture of Paul writing earnestly from prison (chs 1-2), facing opponents of the faith (ch 3), and with serene joy advising and thanking his Philippians (ch 4). If all four chapters were originally a unity, then one must assume that a break occurred between the writing of 3, 1 and 3, 2, possibly involving the receipt of bad news from Philippi, and that Paul had some reasons for delaying his words of thanks for the aid brought by Epaphroditus till the end of his letter.

This beautiful letter is rich in insights into Paul's theology and his apostolic love and concern for the gospel and his converts. In Philippians, Paul reveals his human sensitivity and tenderness, his enthusiasm for Christ as the key to life and death (1, 21), and his deep feeling for those in Christ who dwell in Philippi. With them he shares his hopes and convictions, his anxieties and fears, revealing the total confidence in Christ that constitutes faith (3, 8-10). The letter incorporates a hymn about the salvation that God has brought about through Christ (2, 6-11), applied by Paul to the relations of Christians with one another (2, 1-5). Philippians has been termed "the letter of joy" (4, 4.10). It is the rejoicing of faith, based on true understanding of Christ's unique role in the salvation of all who profess his lordship (2, 11; 3, 8-12.14.20-21).

The principal divisions of the Letter to the Philippians are the following:

I: Address (1, 1-11)
II: Progress of the Gospel (1, 12-26)
III: Instructions for the Community (1, 27—2, 18)
IV: Travel Plans of Paul and His Assistants (2, 19—3, 1)
V: Polemic: Righteousness and the Goal in Christ (3, 2-21)
VI: Instructions for the Community (4, 1-9)
VII: Gratitude for the Philippians' Generosity (4, 10-20)
VIII: Farewell (4, 21-23)

I: ADDRESS

CHAPTER 1

***Greeting.*†** 1*† Paul and Timothy,
slaves of Christ Jesus, to all the holy
ones in Christ Jesus who are in Philippi,
with the overseers and ministers:
2*† grace to you and peace from God
our Father and the Lord Jesus Christ.
***Thanksgiving.*†** 3* I give thanks to
my God at every remembrance of you,
4 praying always with joy in my every
prayer for all of you, 5 because of your
partnership for the gospel from the first
day until now. 6*† I am confident of this,
that the one who began a good work in
you will continue to complete it until the
day of Christ Jesus. 7 It is right that I
should think this way about all of you,
because I hold you in my heart, you who
are all partners with me in grace, both
in my imprisonment and in the defense
and confirmation of the gospel. 8* For
God is my witness, how I long for all
of you with the affection of Christ Jesus.
9* And this is my prayer: that your love
may increase ever more and more in
knowledge and every kind of percep-
tion, 10* to discern what is of value, so
that you may be pure and blameless for
the day of Christ, 11* filled with the fruit
of righteousness that comes through Je-
sus Christ for the glory and praise of
God.

II: PROGRESS OF THE GOSPEL†

12* I want you to know, brothers, that
my situation has turned out rather to
advance the gospel, 13*† so that my im-
prisonment has become well known in
Christ throughout the whole praetorium
and to all the rest, 14† and so that the
majority of the brothers, having taken
encouragement in the Lord from my
imprisonment, dare more than ever to
proclaim the word fearlessly.
15 Of course, some preach Christ from
envy and rivalry, others from good will.
16 The latter act out of love, aware that
I am here for the defense of the gospel;
17 the former proclaim Christ out of self-
ish ambition, not from pure motives,
thinking that they will cause me trouble
in my imprisonment. 18*† What differ-
ence does it make, as long as in every
way, whether in pretense or in truth,
Christ is being proclaimed? And in that
I rejoice.
Indeed I shall continue to rejoice,
19*† for I know that this will result in

---

*

1, 1: Rom 1, 1; 2 Cor 1, 1; 1 Thes 1, 1; Phlm 1 / 1 Tm 3, 1-13.
2: Rom 1, 7; Gal 1, 3; Phlm 3.
3: Rom 1, 8; 1 Cor 1, 4; 1 Thes 1, 2.
6: 2, 13 / 1, 10; 2, 16; 1 Cor 1, 8.
8: Rom 1, 9; 2 Cor 1, 23; 1 Thes 2, 5.
9: Eph 3, 14-19; Col 1, 9-10; Phlm 6.
10: Rom 2, 18; 12, 2 / 1, 6.
11: Jn 15, 8.
12-13: Eph 3, 1; 6, 20; 2 Tm 2, 9; Phlm 9.
13: 4, 22.
18: 4, 10.
19: Jb 13, 16 / 2 Cor 1, 11.

---

†

1, 1-2: See the note on Rom 1, 1-7, concerning the greeting.

1, 1: *Slaves:* Paul usually refers to himself at the start of a letter as an apostle. Here he substitutes a term suggesting the unconditional obligation of himself and Timothy to the service of Christ, probably because, in view of the good relationship with the Philippians, he wishes to stress his status as a co-servant rather than emphasize his apostolic authority. Reference to Timothy is a courtesy: Paul alone writes the letter, as the singular verb throughout shows (3-26), and the reference (2, 19-24) to Timothy in the third person. *Overseers:* the Greek term *episkopos* literally means "one who oversees" or "one who supervises," but since the second century it has come to designate the "bishop," the official who heads a local church. In New Testament times this office had not yet developed into the form that it later assumed, though it seems to be well on the way to such development in the Pastorals; see 1 Tm 3, 2 and Ti 1, 7, where it is translated *bishop.* At Philippi, however (and at Ephesus, according to Acts 20, 28), there was more than one *episkopos,* and the precise function of these officials is uncertain. In order to distinguish this office from the later stages into which it developed, the term is here translated as *overseers. Ministers:* the Greek term *diakonoi* is used frequently in the New Testament to designate "servants," "attendants," or "ministers." Paul refers to himself and to other apostles as "ministers of God" (2 Cor 6, 4) or "ministers of Christ" (2 Cor 11, 23). In the Pastorals (1 Tm 3, 8.12) the *diakonos* has become an established official in the local church; hence the term is there translated as *deacon.* The *diakonoi* at Philippi seem to represent an earlier stage of development of the office; we are uncertain about their precise functions. Hence the term is here translated as *ministers.* See Rom 16, 1, where Phoebe is described as a *diakonos* (*minister*) of the church of Cenchreae.

1, 2: The gifts come *from* Christ the Lord, not simply through him from the Father; compare the christology in 2, 6-11.

1, 3-11: As in Rom 1, 8-15 and all the Pauline letters except Galatians, a thanksgiving follows, including a direct prayer for the Philippians (9-11); see the note on Rom 1, 8. On their *partnership for the gospel* (5), cf 29-30; 4, 10-20. Their devotion to the faith and to Paul made them his pride and joy (4, 1). The characteristics thus manifested are evidence of the community's continuing preparation for the Lord's parousia (6.10). Paul's especially warm relationship with the Philippians is suggested here (7.8) as elsewhere in the letter. The eschatology serves to underscore a concern for ethical growth (9-11), which appears throughout the letter.

1, 6: *The day of Christ Jesus:* the parousia or triumphant return of Christ, when those loyal to him will be with him and share in his eternal glory; cf 10; 2, 16; 3, 20-21; 1 Thes 4, 17; 5, 10; 2 Thes 1, 10; 1 Cor 1, 8.

1, 12-26: The body of the letter begins with an account of Paul's present *situation,* i.e., his *imprisonment* (12-13; see Introduction), and then goes on with advice for the Philippians (1, 27—2, 18). The *advance of the gospel* (12) and the *progress* of the Philippians *in the faith* (25) frame what is said.

1, 13: *Praetorium:* either the praetorian guard in the city where Paul was imprisoned or the governor's official residence in a Roman province (cf Mk 15, 16; Acts 23, 35). See Introduction on possible sites.

1, 14-18: Although Paul is imprisoned, Christians there nonetheless go on preaching Christ. But they do so with varied motives, *some* with personal hostility toward Paul, others out of personal ambition.

1, 18: *Rejoice:* a major theme in the letter; see Introduction.

1, 19-25: Paul earnestly debates his prospects of martyrdom or continued missionary labor. While he may *long to depart this life* and thus *be with Christ* (23), his overall and final expectation is that he will be delivered from this imprisonment and *continue in the service* of the Philippians and of others (19.25; 2, 24). In either case, Christ is central (20.21); if to live means Christ for Paul, death means to be united with Christ in a deeper sense.

1, 19: *Result in deliverance for me:* an echo of Jb 13, 16, hoping that God will turn suffering to ultimate good and deliverance from evil.

deliverance for me through your
prayers and support from the Spirit of
Jesus Christ. 20* My eager expectation
and hope is that I shall not be put to
shame in any way, but that with all
boldness, now as always, Christ will be
magnified in my body, whether by life
or by death. 21* For to me life is Christ,
and death is gain. 22* If I go on living
in the flesh, that means fruitful labor
for me. And I do not know which I shall
choose. 23* I am caught between the
two. I long to depart this life and be with
Christ, [for] that is far better. 24 Yet that
I remain [in] the flesh is more necessary
for your benefit. 25 And this I know with
confidence, that I shall remain and con-
tinue in the service of all of you for your
progress and joy in the faith, 26 so that
your boasting in Christ Jesus may
abound on account of me when I come
to you again.

III: INSTRUCTIONS FOR THE COMMUNITY

***Steadfastness in Faith.*†** 27* Only,
conduct yourselves in a way worthy of
the gospel of Christ, so that, whether I
come and see you or am absent, I may
hear news of you, that you are standing
firm in one spirit, with one mind strug-
gling together for the faith of the gospel,
28 not intimidated in any way by your
opponents. This is proof to them of de-
struction, but of your salvation. And
this is God's doing. 29* For to you has
been granted, for the sake of Christ, not
only to believe in him but also to suffer
for him. 30*† Yours is the same struggle
as you saw in me and now hear about
me.

CHAPTER 2

***Plea for Unity and Humility.*†** 1 If
there is any encouragement in Christ,
any solace in love, any participation in
the Spirit, any compassion and mercy,
2* complete my joy by being of the same
mind, with the same love, united in
heart, thinking one thing. 3* Do nothing
out of selfishness or out of vainglory;
rather, humbly regard others as more
important than yourselves, 4* each
looking out not for his own interests, but
[also] everyone for those of others.
5† Have among yourselves the same
attitude that is also yours in Christ Je-
sus,

6*† Who, though he was in the form of
God,
did not regard equality with God
something to be grasped.
7*† Rather, he emptied himself,
taking the form of a slave,
coming in human likeness;
and found human in appearance,
8*† he humbled himself,
becoming obedient to death,
even death on a cross.
9*† Because of this, God greatly exalted
him

*

20: 1 Cor 6, 20; 1 Pt 4, 16.
21: Gal 2, 20.
22: Rom 1, 13.
23: 2 Cor 5, 8.
27: Eph 4, 1; Col 1, 10; 1 Thes 2, 12 / 4, 3.
29: Mt 5, 10; 10, 38; Mk 8, 34; Acts 5, 41.
30: 1, 13; Acts 16, 22-24.
2, 2: Rom 15, 5; 1 Cor 1, 10.
3: Rom 12, 3.10; Gal 5, 26.
4: 1 Cor 10, 24.33; 13, 5.
6: Jn 1, 1-2; 17, 5; Col 2, 9; Heb 1, 3.
7: Is 53, 3.11; Jn 1, 14; Rom 8, 3; 2 Cor 8, 9; Gal 4, 4; Heb 2, 14.17.
8: Mt 26, 39; Jn 10, 17; Heb 5, 8; 12, 2.
9: Acts 2, 33; Mt 23, 12; Eph 1, 20-21; Heb 1, 3-4.

†

1, 27-30: Ethical admonition begins at this early point in the letter, emphasizing steadfastness and congregational unity in the face of possible suffering. The *opponents* (28) are those in Philippi, probably pagans, who oppose the gospel cause. *This is proof . . .* (28) may refer to the whole outlook and conduct of the Philippians, turning out for their salvation but to the judgment of the opponents (cf 2 Cor 2, 15-16), or possibly the sentence refers to the opinion of the opponents, who hold that the obstinacy of the Christians points to the destruction of such people as defy Roman authority (though in reality, Paul holds, such faithfulness leads to salvation).

1, 30: A reference to Paul's earlier imprisonment in Philippi (Acts 16, 19-24; 1 Thes 2, 2) and to his present confinement.

2, 1-11: The admonition to likemindedness and unity (2-5) is based on the believers' threefold experience with Christ, God's love, and the Spirit. The appeal to humility (3) and to obedience (12) is rooted in christology, specifically in a statement about Christ Jesus (6-11) and his humbling of self and obedience to the point of death (8).

2, 5: *Have . . . the same attitude that is also yours in Christ Jesus:* or, "that also Christ Jesus had." While it is often held that Christ here functions as a model for moral imitation, it is not the historical Jesus but the entire Christ event that vv 6-11 depict. Therefore, the appeal is to have in relations among yourselves that same relationship you have in Jesus Christ, i.e., serving one another as you serve Christ (4).

2, 6-11: Perhaps an early Christian hymn quoted here by Paul. The short rhythmic lines fall into two parts, vv 6-8 where the subject of every verb is Christ, and vv 9-11 where the subject is God. The general pattern is thus of Christ's humiliation and then exaltation. More precise analyses propose a division into six three-line stanzas (6; 7abc; 7d-8; 9; 10; 11) or into three stanzas (6-7ab; 7cd-8; 9-11). Phrases such as *even death on a cross* (8c) are considered by some to be additions (by Paul) to the hymn, as are vv 10c and 11c.

2, 6: Either a reference to Christ's preexistence and those aspects of divinity that he was willing to give up in order to serve in human form, or to what the man Jesus refused to grasp at to attain divinity. Many see an allusion to the Genesis story: unlike Adam, Jesus, *though . . . in the form of God* (Gn 1, 26-27), did not reach out for *equality with God,* in contrast with the first Adam in Gn 3, 5-6.

2, 7: *Taking the form of a slave, coming in human likeness:* or ". . . taking the form of a slave. // Coming in human likeness, and found human in appearance." While it is common to take vv 6 and 7 as dealing with Christ's preexistence and v 8 with his incarnate life, so that lines 7b and c are parallel, it is also possible to interpret so as to exclude any reference to preexistence (see the note on 2, 6) and to take vv 6-8 as presenting two parallel stanzas about Jesus' human state (6-7b; 7cd-8); in the latter alternative, *coming in human likeness* begins the second stanza and parallels 6a to some extent.

2, 8: There may be reflected here language about the servant of the Lord, Is 52, 13—53, 12, especially 53, 12.

2, 9: *The name:* "Lord" (11), revealing the true nature of the one who is named.

and bestowed on him the name
that is above every name,
10*† that at the name of Jesus
every knee should bend,
of those in heaven and on earth
and under the earth,
11*† and every tongue confess that
Jesus Christ is Lord,
to the glory of God the Father.

Obedience and Service in the World.†
12*† So then, my beloved, obedient as
you have always been, not only when I
am present but all the more now when
I am absent, work out your salvation
with fear and trembling. 13* For God is
the one who, for his good purpose,
works in you both to desire and to work.
14* Do everything without grumbling or
questioning, 15*† that you may be
blameless and innocent, children of
God without blemish in the midst of a
crooked and perverse generation,
among whom you shine like lights in the
world, 16* as you hold on to the word
of life, so that my boast for the day
of Christ may be that I did not run in
vain or labor in vain. 17*† But, even if
I am poured out as a libation upon
the sacrificial service of your faith, I
rejoice and share my joy with all of
you. 18* In the same way you also should
rejoice and share your joy with
me.

IV: TRAVEL PLANS OF PAUL AND HIS ASSISTANTS†

Timothy and Paul. 19*† I hope, in the
Lord Jesus, to send Timothy to you
soon, so that I too may be heartened by
hearing news of you. 20 For I have no
one comparable to him for genuine in-
terest in whatever concerns you. 21* For
they all seek their own interests, not
those of Jesus Christ. 22 But you know
his worth, how as a child with a father
he served along with me in the cause
of the gospel. 23 He it is, then, whom I
hope to send as soon as I see how things
go with me, 24† but I am confident in
the Lord that I myself will also come
soon.

Epaphroditus. 25*† With regard to
Epaphroditus, my brother and co-
worker and fellow soldier, your messen-
ger and minister in my need, I consider
it necessary to send him to you. 26 For
he has been longing for all of you and
was distressed because you heard that
he was ill. 27 He was indeed ill, close to
death; but God had mercy on him, not
just on him but also on me, so that I
might not have sorrow upon sorrow.
28 I send him therefore with the greater
eagerness, so that, on seeing him, you
may rejoice again, and I may have less
anxiety. 29* Welcome him then in the
Lord with all joy and hold such people
in esteem, 30 because for the sake of the
work of Christ he came close to death,
risking his life to make up for those
services to me that you could not per-
form.

CHAPTER 3

Concluding Admonitions. 1*† Fi-
nally, my brothers, rejoice in the
Lord. Writing the same things to you is
no burden for me but is a safeguard for
you.

*

10: Is 45, 23; Jn 5, 23; Rom 14, 11; Rv 5, 13.
11: Acts 2, 36; Rom 10, 9; 1 Cor 12, 3.
12: Ps 2, 11; 1 Cor 2, 3; 2 Cor 7, 15.
13: 1, 6; 1 Cor 12, 6; 15, 10; 2 Cor 3, 5.
14: 1 Cor 10, 10; 1 Pt 4, 9.
15: 1 Thes 3, 13 / Dt 32, 5; Mt 10, 16; Acts 2, 40 / Dn 12, 3; Mt 5, 14.16; Eph 5, 8.
16: 1 Thes 2, 19 / Is 49, 4; 65, 23; Gal 2, 2.
17: Rom 15, 16; 2 Tm 4, 6.
18: 3, 1; 4, 4.
19: Acts 16, 1-3; 17, 14-15; 1 Cor 4, 17; 16, 10.
21: 1 Cor 13, 5; 2 Tm 4, 10.
25: 4, 10-11.15-16.18.
29: 1 Cor 16, 18.
3, 1: 2, 18; 4, 4.

†

2, 10-11: *Every knee should bend . . . every tongue confess:* into this language of Is 45, 23 there has been inserted a reference to the three levels in the universe, according to ancient thought, *heaven, earth, under the earth.*

2, 11: *Jesus Christ is Lord:* a common early Christian acclamation; cf 1 Cor 12, 3; Rom 10, 9. But doxology to God the Father is not overlooked here (11c) in the final version of the hymn.

2, 12-18: Paul goes on to draw out further ethical implications for daily life (14-18) from the salvation God works in Christ.

2, 12: *Fear and trembling:* a common Old Testament expression indicating awe and seriousness in the service of God (cf Ex 15, 16; Jdt 2, 28; Ps 2, 11; Is 19, 16).

2, 15-16: *Generation . . . as you hold on to . . . :* or ". . . generation. Among them shine like lights in the world because you hold the word of life. . . ."

2, 17: *Libation:* in ancient religious ritual, the pouring out on the ground of a liquid offering as a sacrifice. Paul means that he may be facing death.

2, 19—3, 1: The plans of Paul and his assistants for future travel are regularly a part of a Pauline letter near its conclusion; cf Rom 15, 22-29; 1 Cor 16, 5-12.

2, 19: *Timothy:* already known to the Philippians (Acts 16, 1-15; cf 1 Cor 4, 17; 16, 10).

2, 24: *I myself will also come soon:* cf 1, 19-25 for the significance of this statement.

2, 25: *Epaphroditus:* sent by the Philippians as their *messenger* (literally, "apostle") to aid Paul in his imprisonment, he had fallen seriously ill; Paul commends him as he sends him back to Philippi.

3, 1: *Finally . . . rejoice:* the adverb often signals the close of a letter; cf 4, 8; 2 Cor 13, 11. While the verb could also be translated "good-bye" or "farewell," although it is never so used in Greek epistolography, the theme of joy has been frequent in the letter (1, 18; 2, 2.18); note also 4, 4 and the addition of "always" there as evidence for the meaning "rejoice." To write *the same things* may refer to what Paul has previously taught in Philippi or to what he has just written or to what follows.

V: POLEMIC: RIGHTEOUSNESS AND THE GOAL IN CHRIST†

Against Legalistic Teachers.†
2*† Beware of the dogs! Beware of the
evil-workers! Beware of the mutilation!
3*† For we are the circumcision, we who
worship through the Spirit of God, who
boast in Christ Jesus and do not put our
confidence in flesh, 4* although I myself
have grounds for confidence even in the
flesh.

Paul's Autobiography. If anyone else
thinks he can be confident in flesh, all
the more can I. 5*† Circumcised on the
eighth day, of the race of Israel, of the
tribe of Benjamin, a Hebrew of Hebrew
parentage, in observance of the law a
Pharisee, 6* in zeal I persecuted the
church, in righteousness based on the
law I was blameless.

Righteousness from God. 7*† [But]
whatever gains I had, these I have come
to consider a loss because of Christ.
8 More than that, I even consider every-
thing as a loss because of the supreme
good of knowing Christ Jesus my Lord.
For his sake I have accepted the loss
of all things and I consider them so
much rubbish, that I may gain Christ
9* and be found in him, not having any
righteousness of my own based on the
law but that which comes through faith
in Christ, the righteousness from God,
depending on faith 10* to know him and
the power of his resurrection and [the]
sharing of his sufferings by being con-
formed to his death, 11* if somehow I
may attain the resurrection from the
dead.

Forward in Christ.† 12*† It is not that
I have already taken hold of it or have
already attained perfect maturity, but
I continue my pursuit in hope that I may
possess it, since I have indeed been
taken possession of by Christ [Jesus].
13 Brothers, I for my part do not con-
sider myself to have taken possession.
Just one thing: forgetting what lies be-
hind but straining forward to what lies
ahead, 14* I continue my pursuit toward
the goal, the prize of God's upward call-
ing, in Christ Jesus. 15 Let us, then, who
are "perfectly mature" adopt this atti-
tude. And if you have a different atti-
tude, this too God will reveal to you.
16† Only, with regard to what we have
attained, continue on the same course.

Wrong Conduct and Our Goal.†
17*† Join with others in being imitators
of me, brothers, and observe those who
thus conduct themselves according to
the model you have in us. 18* For many,
as I have often told you and now tell
you even in tears, conduct themselves
as enemies of the cross of Christ.
19* Their end is destruction. Their God
is their stomach; their glory is in their
"shame." Their minds are occupied
with earthly things. 20*† But our citizen-
ship is in heaven, and from it we also
await a savior, the Lord Jesus Christ.

---

*

2: Ps 22, 17.21; Rv 22, 15 / 2 Cor 11, 13 / Gal 5, 6.12.
3: Rom 2, 28-29; Col 2, 11.
4: 2 Cor 11, 18.21-23.
5: Lk 1, 59; 2, 21 / Acts 22, 3; 23, 6; 26, 5.
6: Acts 8, 3; 22, 4; 26, 9-11.
7: Mt 13, 44.46; Lk 14, 33.
9: Rom 3, 21-22.
10: Rom 6, 3-5; 8, 17; Gal 6, 17.
11: Jn 11, 23-26; Acts 4, 2; Rv 20, 5-6.
12: 1 Tm 6, 12.19.
14: 1 Cor 9, 24-25; 2 Tm 4, 7.
17: 1 Cor 4, 16; 11, 1; 1 Thes 1, 7; 1 Pt 5, 3.
18: 1 Cor 1, 17.23; Gal 6, 12.
19: Rom 8, 5-6; 16, 18.
20: Eph 2, 6.19; Col 3, 1-3; Heb 12, 22.

---

†

3, 2-21: An abrupt change in content and tone, either because Paul at this point responds to disturbing news he has just heard about a threat to the faith of the Philippians in the form of false teachers, or because part of another Pauline letter was inserted here; see Introduction. The chapter describes these teachers in strong terms as *dogs.* The persons meant are evidently different from the rival preachers of 1, 14-18 and the opponents of 1, 28. Since vv 2-4 emphasize Jewish terms like *circumcision* (2-3.5), some relate them to the "Judaizers" of the Letter to the Galatians. Other phrases make them appear more like the false teachers of 2 Cor 11, 12-15, the *evil-workers.* The latter part of the chapter depicts the *many* who are *enemies* of Christ's cross in terms that may sound more Gentile or even "gnostic" than Jewish (18-19). Accordingly, some see two groups of false teachers in ch 3, others one group characterized by a claim of having attained "perfect maturity" (12-15).

3, 2-11: Paul sets forth the Christian claim, especially using personal, autobiographical terms that are appropriate to the situation. He presents his own experience in coming to know Christ Jesus in terms of *righteousness* or justification (cf Rom 1, 16-17; 3, 21—5, 11; Gal 2, 5-11), contrasting *the righteousness from God* through faith and that of one's own *based on the law* as two exclusive ways of pleasing God.

3, 2: *Beware of the mutilation:* literally, "incision," an ironic wordplay on "circumcision"; cf Gal 5, 12. There may be an association with the self-inflicted mutilations of the prophets of Baal (1 Kgs 18, 28) and of devotees of Cybele who slashed themselves in religious frenzy.

3, 3: *We are the circumcision:* the true people of God, seed and offspring of Abraham (Gal 3, 7.29; 6, 15). *Spirit of God:* some manuscripts read "worship God by the Spirit."

3, 5: *Circumcised on the eighth day:* as the law required (Gn 17, 12; Lv 12, 3).

3, 7: *Loss:* his knowledge of Christ led Paul to reassess the ways of truly pleasing and serving God. His reevaluation indicates the profound and lasting effect of his experience of the meaning of Christ on the way to Damascus some twenty years before (Gal 1, 15-16; Acts 9, 1-22).

3, 12-16: To be *taken possession of by Christ* does not mean that one has already arrived at perfect spiritual maturity. Paul and the Philippians instead press on, trusting in God.

3, 12: *Attained perfect maturity:* possibly an echo of the concept in the mystery religions of being an initiate, admitted to divine secrets.

3, 16: Some manuscripts add, probably to explain Paul's cryptic phrase, "thinking alike."

3, 17-21: Paul and those who live a life centered in Christ, envisaging both his suffering and resurrection, provide a model that is the opposite of opponents who reject Christ's cross (cf 1 Cor 1, 23).

3, 17: *Being imitators of me:* not arrogance, but humble simplicity, since all his converts know that Paul is wholly dedicated to imitating Christ (1 Cor 11, 1; cf also Phil 4, 9; 1 Thes 1, 6; 2 Thes 3, 7.9; 1 Cor 4, 6).

3, 20: *Citizenship:* Christians constitute a colony of heaven, as Philippi was a *colonia* of Rome (Acts 16, 12). The hope Paul expresses involves the final coming of Christ, not a status already attained, such as the opponents claim.

[21]* He will change our lowly body to
conform with his glorified body by the
power that enables him also to bring all
things into subjection to himself.

VI: INSTRUCTIONS FOR THE COMMUNITY†

CHAPTER 4

Live in Concord. [1]* Therefore, my
brothers, whom I love and long for, my
joy and crown, in this way stand firm
in the Lord, beloved.

[2]† I urge Euodia and I urge Syntyche
to come to a mutual understanding in
the Lord. [3]*† Yes, and I ask you also,
my true yokemate, to help them, for
they have struggled at my side in pro-
moting the gospel, along with Clement
and my other co-workers, whose names
are in the book of life.

Joy and Peace. [4]*† Rejoice in the
Lord always. I shall say it again: re-
joice! [5]*† Your kindness should be
known to all. The Lord is near. [6]* Have
no anxiety at all, but in everything, by
prayer and petition, with thanksgiving,
make your requests known to God.
[7]* Then the peace of God that surpasses
all understanding will guard your
hearts and minds in Christ Jesus.

[8]*† Finally, brothers, whatever is
true, whatever is honorable, whatever
is just, whatever is pure, whatever is
lovely, whatever is gracious, if there is
any excellence and if there is anything
worthy of praise, think about these
things. [9]*† Keep on doing what you
have learned and received and heard
and seen in me. Then the God of peace
will be with you.

VII: GRATITUDE FOR THE PHILIPPIANS' GENEROSITY†

[10]* I rejoice greatly in the Lord that
now at last you revived your concern
for me. You were, of course, concerned
about me but lacked an opportunity.
[11]* Not that I say this because of need,
for I have learned, in whatever situation
I find myself, to be self-sufficient.
[12] I know indeed how to live in humble
circumstances; I know also how to live
with abundance. In every circumstance
and in all things I have learned the se-
cret of being well fed and of going hun-
gry, of living in abundance and of being
in need. [13]* I have the strength for ev-
erything through him who empowers
me. [14] Still, it was kind of you to share
in my distress.

[15]† You Philippians indeed know that
at the beginning of the gospel, when I
left Macedonia, not a single church
shared with me in an account of giving
and receiving, except you alone. [16] For
even when I was at Thessalonica you
sent me something for my needs, not
only once but more than once. [17] It is
not that I am eager for the gift; rather,
I am eager for the profit that accrues
to your account. [18]*† I have received
full payment and I abound. I am very
well supplied because of what I received
from you through Epaphroditus, "a fra-
grant aroma," an acceptable sacrifice,
pleasing to God. [19]* My God will fully
supply whatever you need, in accord
with his glorious riches in Christ Jesus.
[20]* To our God and Father, glory for-
ever and ever. Amen.

*

21: Rom 8, 23.29; 1 Cor 15, 42-57; 2 Cor 3, 18; 5, 1-5 / 1 Cor 15, 27-28.
4, 1: 1 Thes 2, 19-20.
3: Ex 32, 32-33; Ps 69, 29; Dn 12, 1; Lk 10, 20; Rv 3, 5; 13, 8; 17, 8; 20, 12.15; 21, 27.
4: 2, 18; 3, 1.
5: Ti 3, 2 / Ps 145, 18; Heb 10, 37; Jas 5, 8-9.
6: Mt 6, 25-34; 1 Pt 5, 7 / Col 4, 2.
7: Jn 14, 27; Col 3, 15.
8: Rom 12, 17.
9: 1 Thes 4, 1 / Rom 15, 33; 16, 20; 1 Cor 14, 33; 1 Thes 5, 23.
10: 1, 18; 2, 25; 1 Cor 9, 11; 2 Cor 11, 9.
11-12: 1 Cor 4, 11; 2 Cor 6, 10; 11, 27 / 2 Cor 12, 9-10.
13: Col 1, 29; 2 Tm 4, 17.
18: Gn 8, 21; Ex 29, 18; Eph 5, 2; Heb 13, 16.
19: 1 Thes 3, 11.13.
20: Rom 16, 27; Eph 5, 20.

†

4, 1-9: This series of ethical admonitions rests especially on the view of Christ and his coming (cf 5) in 3, 20-21. Paul's instructions touch on unity within the congregation, joy, prayer, and the Christian outlook on life.

4, 2: *Euodia . . . Syntyche:* two otherwise unknown women in the Philippian congregation; on the advice to them, cf 2, 2-4.

4, 3: *Yokemate:* or "comrade," although the Greek *syzygos* could also be a proper name. *Clement:* otherwise unknown, although later writers sought to identify him with Clement, bishop of Rome (Eusebius, *Ecclesiastical History* 3.15.1).

4, 4: *Rejoice:* see the note on 3, 1.

4, 5: *Kindness:* considerateness, forbearance, fairness. *The Lord is near:* most likely a reference to Christ's parousia (1, 6.10; 3, 20-21; 1 Cor 16, 22), although some sense an echo of Ps 119, 151 and the perpetual presence of the Lord.

4, 8: The language employs terms from Roman Stoic thought.

4, 9: Cf the note on 3, 17.

4, 10-20: Paul, more directly than anywhere else in the letter (cf 1, 3-5), here thanks the Philippians for their gift of money sent through Epaphroditus (2, 25). Paul's own policy was *to be self-sufficient* as a missionary, supporting himself by his own labor (1 Thes 2, 5-9; 1 Cor 9, 15-18; cf Acts 18, 2-3). In spite of this reliance on self and on God to provide (11-13), Paul accepted gifts from the Philippians *not only once but more than once* (16) when he was in Thessalonica (Acts 17, 1-9), as he does now, in prison (*my distress,* 14). While commercial terms appear in the passage, like *an account of giving and receiving* (15) and *received full payment* (18), Paul is most concerned about the spiritual growth of the Philippians (10.17.19); he emphasizes that God will care for their needs, through Christ.

4, 15: *The beginning of the gospel:* it was at Philippi that Paul first preached Christ in Europe, going on from there to Thessalonica and Beroea (Acts 16, 9—17, 14).

4, 18: *Aroma . . . sacrifice:* Old Testament cultic language (cf Gn 8, 21; Ex 29, 18.25.41; Lv 1, 9.13; Ez 20, 41) applied to the Philippians' gift; cf Eph 5, 2; 2 Cor 2, 14-16.

VIII: FAREWELL†

21 Give my greetings to every holy
one in Christ Jesus. The brothers who
are with me send you their greetings;
22*† all the holy ones send you their
greetings, especially those of Caesar's
household. 23 The grace of the Lord Je-
sus Christ be with your spirit.

* 22: 1, 13.

† 4, 21-23: On the usual greetings at the conclusion of a letter, see the note on 1 Cor 16, 19-24. Inclusion of greetings from *all the holy ones* in the place from which Paul writes would involve even the Christians of 1, 14-18 who had their differences with Paul.

4, 22: *Those of Caesar's household:* minor officials or even slaves and freedmen, found in Ephesus or Rome, among other places.

The Letter to the

COLOSSIANS

This letter is addressed to a congregation at Colossae in the Lycus Valley in Asia Minor, east of Ephesus. At the time of writing, Paul had not visited there, the letter says (1, 4; 2, 1). The community had apparently been established by Epaphras of Colossae (1, 7; 4, 12; Phlm 23). Problems, however, had arisen, brought on by teachers who emphasized Christ's relation to the universe (cosmos). Their teachings stressed angels (2, 18; "principalities and powers," 2, 15), which were connected with astral powers and cultic practices (see the note on 2, 16) and rules about food and drink and ascetical disciplines (2, 16.18). These teachings, Paul insists, detract from the person and work of Christ for salvation as set forth magnificently in a hymnic passage at 1, 15-20 and reiterated throughout the letter. Such teachings are but "shadows"; Christ is "reality" (2, 17).

For help in dealing with these problems that the new teachers posed at Colossae, Epaphras sought out Paul, who was then imprisoned (4, 10.18) at a place that the letter does not mention. Paul, without entering into debate over the existence of angelic spirits or their function, simply affirms that Christ possesses the sum total of redemptive power (1, 19) and that the spiritual renewal of the human person occurs through contact in baptism with the person of Christ, who died and rose again (2, 9-14). It is unnecessary for the Christian to be concerned about placating spirits (2, 15) or avoiding imagined defilement through ascetical practices in regard to food and drink (2, 20-23). True Christian asceticism consists in the conquering of personal sins (3, 5-10) and the practice of love of neighbor in accordance with the standard set by Christ (3, 12-16).

Paul commends the community as a whole (1, 3-8); this seems to indicate that, though the Colossians have been under pressure to adopt the false doctrines, they have not yet succumbed. The apostle expresses his prayerful concern for them (1, 9-14). His preaching has cost him persecution, suffering, and imprisonment, but he regards these as reflective of the sufferings of Christ, a required discipline for the sake of the gospel (see the note on 1, 24; cf 1, 29; 2, 1). His instructions to the Christian family and to slaves and masters require a new spirit of reflection and action. Love, obedience, and service are to be rendered "in the Lord" (3, 18—4, 1).

Colossians follows the outline of a typical Pauline letter. It is distinguished by the poetic lines in 1, 15-20 concerning who Christ is and what Christ means in creation and redemption. This hymn may be compared with similar passages in Philippians 2, 6-11; 1 Timothy 3, 16; and John 1, 1-18. It was apparently familiar liturgical material to the author, the audience, and the false teachers. In 1, 21—2, 7, however, Paul interprets the relation between the body of Christ, which he insists is the church (1, 18), and the world or cosmos to be one not simply of Christ's preexistence and rule but one of missionary advance into the world by the spreading of the word (1, 25.28). In this labor of the missionary body of Christ, Paul as a minister plays a prime part in bringing Christ and the gospel as hope to the Gentiles (1, 23.25.27). To "every creature under heaven" the word is to be proclaimed, so that everyone receives Christ, is established in faith, and walks in Christ (1, 28; 2, 6.7).

Paul wrote the Letter to the Colossians while in prison, but his several imprisonments leave the specific place and date of composition uncertain. On this point the same problem exists as with Ephesians and Philippians (see the Introductions to these letters). Traditionally the house arrest at Rome, in which Paul enjoyed a certain restricted freedom in preaching (see Acts 28, 16-28), or a second Roman imprisonment has been claimed as the setting. Others suggest a still earlier imprisonment at Caesarea (see Acts 23, 12—27, 1) or in Ephesus (see Acts 19). Still others regard the letter as the work of some pupil or follower of Paul, writing in his name. In any case, the contents are often closely paralleled by thoughts in Ephesians.

The principal divisions of the Letter to the Colossians are the following:

- *I: Address (1, 1-14)*
- *II: The Preeminence of Christ (1, 15—2, 3)*
- *III: Warnings against False Teachers (2, 4-23)*
- *IV: The Ideal Christian Life in the World (3, 1—4, 6)*
- *V: Conclusion (4, 7-18)*

I: ADDRESS

CHAPTER 1

Greeting.† 1* Paul, an apostle of
Christ Jesus by the will of God, and Tim-
othy our brother, 2 to the holy ones
and faithful brothers in Christ in Colos-
sae: grace to you and peace from God
our Father.
Thanksgiving.† 3* We always give
thanks to God, the Father of our Lord
Jesus Christ, when we pray for you,
4 for we have heard of your faith in
Christ Jesus and the love that you have
for all the holy ones 5* because of the
hope reserved for you in heaven. Of this
you have already heard through the
word of truth, the gospel, 6 that has
come to you. Just as in the whole world
it is bearing fruit and growing, so also
among you, from the day you heard it
and came to know the grace of God in
truth, 7*† as you learned it from Epa-
phras our beloved fellow slave, who is
a trustworthy minister of Christ on your
behalf 8 and who also told us of your
love in the Spirit.
Prayer for Continued Progress.†
9* Therefore, from the day we heard
this, we do not cease praying for you
and asking that you may be filled with
the knowledge of his will through all
spiritual wisdom and understanding
10 to live in a manner worthy of the Lord,
so as to be fully pleasing, in every good
work bearing fruit and growing in the
knowledge of God, 11 strengthened with
every power, in accord with his glorious
might, for all endurance and patience,
with joy 12*† giving thanks to the Fa-
ther, who has made you fit to share in
the inheritance of the holy ones in light.
13 He delivered us from the power of
darkness and transferred us to the
kingdom of his beloved Son, 14* in whom
we have redemption, the forgiveness of
sins.

*

1, 1: Eph 1, 1.
3: Eph 1, 15-16; Phlm 4-5.
5: Eph 1, 13.18; 1 Pt 1, 4.
7: Phlm 23.
9: Eph 1, 15-17; 5, 17; Phil 1, 9.
12: 3, 17; Jn 8, 12; Acts 26, 18; 1 Tm 6, 16; 1 Pt 2, 9.
14: Eph 1, 7.

†

1, 1-2: For the epistolary form used by Paul at the beginning of his letters, see the note on Rom 1, 1-7. On *holy ones* or "God's people," see the note on Rom 1, 7. Awareness of their calling helps this group to be *faithful brothers* and sisters *in Christ*, i.e., dedicated to the tasks implied in their calling.

1, 3-8: On thanksgiving at the start of a letter, see the note on Rom 1, 8. The apostle, recalling his own prayers for them and the good report about them he has received (3-4), congratulates the Colossians upon their acceptance of Christ and their faithful efforts to live the gospel (3, 6-8). To encourage them he mentions the success of the gospel elsewhere (6) and assures them that his knowledge of their community is accurate, since he has been in personal contact with Epaphras (7-8), who likely had evangelized Colossae and other cities in the Lycus Valley of Asia Minor (cf 4, 12.13; Phlm 23). On *faith, love,* and *hope* (4.5.8), see the note on 1 Cor 13, 13; cf 1 Thes 1, 3; 5, 8.

1, 7: *Epaphras:* now with Paul but a Colossian, founder of the church there.

1, 9-14: Moved by Epaphras' account, the apostle has prayed and continues to pray fervently for the Colossians that, in their response to the gospel, they *may be filled with the knowledge of* God's *will* (9; cf 3, 10). Paul expects a mutual interaction between their life according to the gospel and this knowledge (10), yielding results (*fruit,* 10; cf 6) *in every good work:* growth, strength, *endurance, patience, with joy* (11), and the further giving of thanks (12).

1, 12-14: A summary about *redemption* by *the Father* precedes the statement in vv 15-20 about the *beloved Son* who is God's love in person (13). Christians share *the inheritance . . . in light* with *the holy ones,* here probably the angels (12). The imagery reflects the Exodus (*delivered . . . transferred*) and Jesus' theme of *the kingdom. Redemption* is explained as *forgiveness of sins* (cf Acts 2, 38; Rom 3, 24-25; Eph 1, 7).

II: THE PREEMINENCE OF CHRIST

His Person and Work†

15*†He is the image of the invisible God,
the firstborn of all creation.
16*†For in him were created all things
in heaven and on earth,
the visible and the invisible,
whether thrones or dominions or
principalities or powers;
all things were created through
him and for him.
17 He is before all things,
and in him all things hold together.
18*†He is the head of the body, the
church.
He is the beginning, the firstborn
from the dead,
that in all things he himself might
be preeminent.
19† For in him all the fullness was
pleased to dwell,
20*† and through him to reconcile all
things for him,
making peace by the blood of his
cross
[through him], whether those on
earth or those in heaven.

21*† And you who once were alienated
and hostile in mind because of evil
deeds 22 he has now reconciled in his
fleshly body through his death, to present you holy, without blemish, and irreproachable before him, 23 provided that
you persevere in the faith, firmly grounded, stable, and not shifting from the hope of the gospel that you heard, which has been preached to every creature under heaven, of which I, Paul, am a minister.

Christ in Us.† 24† Now I rejoice in my
sufferings for your sake, and in my flesh I am filling up what is lacking in the afflictions of Christ on behalf of his body, which is the church, 25 of which I
am a minister in accordance with God's stewardship given to me to bring to completion for you the word of God,
26* the mystery hidden from ages and from generations past. But now it has been manifested to his holy ones,
27* to whom God chose to make known the riches of the glory of this mystery among the Gentiles; it is Christ in you, the hope for glory. 28* It is he whom we
proclaim, admonishing everyone and teaching everyone with all wisdom, that we may present everyone perfect in Christ. 29* For this I labor and struggle,
in accord with the exercise of his power working within me.

*

15: Ps 89, 28; Jn 1, 3.18; 2 Cor 4, 4.
16: 1 Cor 8, 6; Eph 1, 10.21.
18: 1 Cor 11, 3; 12, 12.27; 15, 20; Eph 1, 22-23; Rv 1, 5.
20: 2 Cor 5, 18-19; Eph 1, 10.
21: Eph 2, 14-16.
26: Rom 16, 25-26; 1 Cor 2, 7; Eph 3, 3.9.
27: 3, 4; Rom 8, 10.
28: Eph 4, 13.
29: 2, 1; 4, 12; Phil 4, 13.

†

1, 15-20: As the poetic arrangement indicates, these lines are probably an early Christian hymn, known to the Colossians and taken up into the letter from liturgical use (cf Phil 2, 6-11; 1 Tm 3, 16). They present Christ as the mediator of creation (15-18a) and of redemption (18b-20). There is a parallelism between *firstborn of all creation* (15) and *firstborn from the dead* (18). While many of the phrases were at home in Greek philosophical use and even in gnosticism, the basic ideas also reflect Old Testament themes about Wisdom found in Prv 8, 22-31; Wis 7, 22—8, 1; and Sir 1, 4. See also the notes on what is possibly a hymn in Jn 1, 1-18.

1, 15: *Image:* cf Gn 1, 27. Whereas the man and the woman were originally created in the image and likeness of God (see also Gn 1, 26), Christ as image (2 Cor 4, 4) of *the invisible God* (Jn 1, 18) now shares this new nature in baptism with those redeemed (cf 3, 10-11).

1, 16-17: Christ (though not mentioned by name) is preeminent and supreme as God's agent in the creation of *all things* (cf Jn 1, 3), as prior to *all things* (17; cf Heb 1, 3).

1, 18: *Church:* such a reference seemingly belongs under "redemption" in the following lines, not under the "creation" section of the hymn. Stoic thought sometimes referred to the world as "the body of Zeus." Pauline usage is to speak of the church as the body of Christ (1 Cor 12, 12-27; Rom 12, 4-5). Some think that the author of Colossians has inserted the reference to the church here so as to define "head of the body" in Paul's customary way. See v 24. *Preeminent:* when Christ was raised by God as *firstborn from the dead* (cf Acts 26, 23; Rv 1, 5), he was placed over the community, the church, that he had brought into being, but he is also indicated as crown of the whole new creation, over *all things.* His further role is to *reconcile all things* (20) for God or possibly "to himself."

1, 19: *Fullness:* in gnostic usage this term referred to a spiritual world of beings above, between God and the world; many later interpreters take it to refer to *the fullness of the deity* (2, 9); the reference could also be to the fullness of grace (cf Jn 1, 16).

1, 20: *The blood of his cross:* the most specific reference in the hymn to redemption through Christ's death, a central theme in Paul; cf 2, 14-15; 1 Cor 1, 17.18.23. *[Through him]:* the phrase, lacking in some manuscripts, seems superfluous but parallels the reference to reconciliation through Christ earlier in the verse.

1, 21-23: Paul, in applying this hymn to the Colossians, reminds them that they have experienced the reconciling effect of Christ's death. He sees the effects of the cross in the redemption of human beings, not of cosmic powers such as those referred to in vv 16 and 20 (*all things*). Paul also urges adherence to Christ in faith and begins to point to his own role as minister (23), sufferer (24), and proclaimer (27-28) of this gospel.

1, 24—2, 3: As the community at Colossae was not personally known to Paul (see Introduction), he here invests his teaching with greater authority by presenting a brief sketch of his apostolic ministry and sufferings as they reflect those of Christ on behalf of the church (24). The preaching of God's word (25) carries out the divine plan (*the mystery,* 26) to make Christ known to the Gentiles (27). It teaches the God-given wisdom about Christ (28), whose power works mightily in the apostle (29). Even in those communities that do not know him personally (2, 1), he can increase the perception of God in Christ, unite the faithful more firmly in love, and so bring encouragement to them (2). He hopes that his apostolic authority will make the Colossians perceive more readily the defects in the teaching of others who have sought to delude them, the next concern in the letter.

1, 24: *What is lacking:* although variously interpreted, this phrase does not imply that Christ's atoning death on the cross was defective. It may refer to the apocalyptic concept of a quota of "messianic woes" to be endured before the end comes; cf Mk 13, 8.19-20.24 and the note on Mt 23, 29-32. Others suggest that Paul's mystical unity with Christ allowed him to call his own *sufferings the afflictions of Christ.*

CHAPTER 2

1† For I want you to know how great a
struggle I am having for you and for
those in Laodicea and all who have not
seen me face to face, 2* that their hearts
may be encouraged as they are brought
together in love, to have all the richness
of fully assured understanding, for the
knowledge of the mystery of God,
Christ, 3* in whom are hidden all the
treasures of wisdom and knowledge.

III: WARNINGS AGAINST FALSE TEACHERS†

A General Admonition. 4* I say this
so that no one may deceive you by spe-
cious arguments. 5* For even if I am ab-
sent in the flesh, yet I am with you in
spirit, rejoicing as I observe your good
order and the firmness of your faith in
Christ. 6 So, as you received Christ Jesus
the Lord, walk in him, 7* rooted in him
and built upon him and established in
the faith as you were taught, abounding
in thanksgiving. 8*† See to it that no one
captivate you with an empty, seductive
philosophy according to human tradi-
tion, according to the elemental powers
of the world and not according to Christ.
Sovereign Role of Christ. 9*† For in
him dwells the whole fullness of the de-
ity bodily, 10 and you share in this full-
ness in him, who is the head of every
principality and power. 11*† In him you
were also circumcised with a circumci-
sion not administered by hand, by strip-
ping off the carnal body, with the
circumcision of Christ. 12* You were
buried with him in baptism, in which
you were also raised with him through
faith in the power of God, who raised
him from the dead. 13* And even when
you were dead [in] transgressions and
the uncircumcision of your flesh, he
brought you to life along with him, hav-
ing forgiven us all our transgressions;
14*† obliterating the bond against us,
with its legal claims, which was opposed
to us, he also removed it from our midst,
nailing it to the cross; 15*† despoiling
the principalities and the powers, he
made a public spectacle of them, lead-
ing them away in triumph by it.
Practices Contrary to Faith. 16*† Let
no one, then, pass judgment on you in
matters of food and drink or with re-
gard to a festival or new moon or sab-
bath. 17* These are shadows of things to
come; the reality belongs to Christ.
18*† Let no one disqualify you, delight-
ing in self-abasement and worship of
angels, taking his stand on visions, in-
flated without reason by his fleshly
mind, 19* and not holding closely to the
head, from whom the whole body, sup-
ported and held together by its liga-
ments and bonds, achieves the growth
that comes from God.
20 If you died with Christ to the ele-
mental powers of the world, why do you
submit to regulations as if you were still
living in the world? 21 "Do not handle!
Do not taste! Do not touch!" 22* These
are all things destined to perish with

*

2, 2: 1, 26-27; Eph 3, 18-19.
3: Prv 2, 4-5; Is 45, 3; Rom 11, 33; 1 Cor 1, 30.
4: Eph 4, 14.
5: 1 Cor 5, 3; Phil 1, 27.
7: Eph 2, 20-22; 3, 17.
8: Gal 4, 3; Eph 5, 6.
9: 1, 19; Eph 3, 19.
11: 1, 22; Jer 4, 4; Rom 2, 25-29; Phil 3, 3.
12: Rom 6, 3-4.
13: Eph 2, 1.5.
14: Eph 2, 14-15.
15: 1, 16.20; 2 Cor 2, 14; Eph 1, 21.
16: Rom 14, 3-4; 1 Tm 4, 3.
17: Heb 8, 5; 10, 1.
18: 2, 23; Mt 24, 4.
19: Eph 2, 21-22; 4, 16.
22: Is 29, 13.

†

2, 1: *Laodicea:* chief city in Phrygia, northwest of Colossae; cf 4, 13.16; Rv 3, 14-22.

2, 4-23: In face of the threat posed by false teachers (4), the Colossians are admonished to adhere to the gospel as it was first preached to them (6), steeping themselves in it with grateful hearts (7). They must reject religious teachings originating in any source except the gospel (8) because in Christ alone will they have access to God, *the deity* (9). So fully has Christ enlightened them that they need no other source of religious knowledge or virtue (10). They do not require *circumcision* (11), for *in baptism* their whole being has been affected by Christ (12) through forgiveness of sin and resurrection to a new life (13; cf 3, 1 and Rom 6, 1-11).

On the cross Christ canceled the record of the debt that stood against us with all its claims (14), i.e., he eliminated the law (cf Eph 2, 15) that human beings could not observe—and that could not save them. He forgave sins against the law (14) and exposed as false and misleading (15) all other powers (cf 1, 16) that purport to offer salvation. Therefore, the Colossians are not to accept judgments from such teachers on *food and drink* or to keep certain religious festivals or engage in certain cultic practices (16), for the Colossians would thereby risk severing themselves from Christ (19). If, when they accepted the gospel, they believed in Christ as their savior, they must be convinced that their salvation cannot be achieved by appeasing ruling spirits through dietary practices or through a wisdom gained simply by means of harsh asceticism (20-23).

2, 8: *Elemental powers of the world:* see the note on Gal 4, 3.

2, 9: *Fullness of the deity:* the divine nature, not just attributes; see the note on 1, 19.

2, 11: A description of baptism (12) in symbolic terms of the Old Testament rite for entry into the community. The false teachers may have demanded physical circumcision of the Colossians.

2, 14: The elaborate metaphor here about how God canceled the legal claims against us through Christ's cross depicts not Christ being nailed to the cross by men but *the bond . . . with its legal claims* being nailed to the cross by God.

2, 15: The picture derives from the *public spectacle* and *triumph* of a Roman emperor's victory parade, where captives marched in subjection. *The principalities and the powers* are here conquered, not reconciled (cf 1, 16.20). An alternate rendering for *by it* (the cross) is "by him" (Christ).

2, 16: *Festival or new moon or sabbath:* yearly, monthly, and weekly observances determined by religious powers associated with a calendar set by the heavenly bodies, sun, moon, and stars (cf 8).

2, 18: Ascetic practices encouraged by the false teachers included subjection of self humbly to their rules, worship of angels, and cultivation of visions, though exact details are unclear.

use; they accord with human precepts and teachings. 23 While they have a semblance of wisdom in rigor of devotion and self-abasement [and] severity to the body, they are of no value against gratification of the flesh.

IV: THE IDEAL CHRISTIAN LIFE IN THE WORLD

CHAPTER 3

Mystical Death and Resurrection.† 1* If then you were raised with Christ, seek what is above, where Christ is seated at the right hand of God. 2 Think of what is above, not of what is on earth. 3* For you have died, and your life is hidden with Christ in God. 4 When Christ your life appears, then you too will appear with him in glory.

Renunciation of Vice.† 5*† Put to death, then, the parts of you that are earthly: immorality, impurity, passion, evil desire, and the greed that is idolatry. 6*† Because of these the wrath of God is coming [upon the disobedient]. 7 By these you too once conducted yourselves, when you lived in that way. 8*† But now you must put them all away: anger, fury, malice, slander, and obscene language out of your mouths. 9* Stop lying to one another, since you have taken off the old self with its practices 10*† and have put on the new self, which is being renewed, for knowledge, in the image of its creator. 11*† Here there is not Greek and Jew, circumcision and uncircumcision, barbarian, Scythian, slave, free; but Christ is all and in all.

12* Put on then, as God's chosen ones, holy and beloved, heartfelt compassion, kindness, humility, gentleness, and patience, 13* bearing with one another and forgiving one another, if one has a grievance against another; as the Lord has forgiven you, so must you also do. 14* And over all these put on love, that is, the bond of perfection. 15* And let the peace of Christ control your hearts, the peace into which you were also called in one body. And be thankful. 16* Let the word of Christ dwell in you richly, as in all wisdom you teach and admonish one another, singing psalms, hymns, and spiritual songs with gratitude in your hearts to God. 17* And whatever you do, in word or in deed, do everything in the name of the Lord Jesus, giving thanks to God the Father through him.

The Christian Family.† 18* Wives, be subordinate to your husbands, as is proper in the Lord. 19 Husbands, love your wives, and avoid any bitterness toward them. 20* Children, obey your parents in everything, for this is pleasing to the Lord. 21* Fathers, do not provoke your children, so they may not become discouraged.

Slaves and Masters.† 22* Slaves, obey your human masters in everything, not only when being watched, as currying favor, but in simplicity of heart, fearing the Lord. 23 Whatever you do, do from the heart, as for the Lord and not for others, 24 knowing that you will receive from the Lord the due payment of the inheritance; be slaves of the Lord Christ. 25* For the wrongdoer will receive recompense for the wrong he committed, and there is no partiality.

CHAPTER 4

1 Masters, treat your slaves justly and fairly, realizing that you too have a Master in heaven.

---

*

3, 1: 2, 12; Ps 110, 1; Phil 3, 20; Eph 2, 6.
3: Rom 6, 2-5.
5: Mt 15, 19; Rom 1, 29-30; Gal 5, 19-21; Eph 5, 3.5.
6: Rom 1, 18.
8: Eph 4, 22.25.31.
9: Rom 6, 4.6; Eph 4, 22-25; Heb 12, 1; 1 Pt 2, 1; 4, 2.
10: Gn 1, 26-27.
11: 1 Cor 12, 13; Gal 3, 27-28.
12: Eph 4, 1-2.32; 1 Thes 5, 15.
13: Mt 6, 14; 18, 21-35; Eph 4, 32.
14: Rom 13, 8-10.
15: Rom 12, 5; 1 Cor 12, 12; Eph 2, 16; 4, 3-4; Phil 4, 7.
16: Eph 5, 19-20.
17: 1 Cor 10, 31.
18: Eph 5, 22; Ti 2, 5; 1 Pt 3, 1.
20: Eph 6, 1.
21: Eph 6, 4.
22: Eph 6, 5; 1 Tm 6, 1; Ti 2, 9-10; 1 Pt 2, 18.
25: Rom 2, 11.

†

3, 1-4: By retaining the message of the gospel that the risen, living Christ is the source of their salvation, the Colossians will be free from false religious evaluations of the things of the world (1-2). They have died to these; but one day *when Christ . . . appears,* they will live with Christ in the presence of God (3-4).

3, 5-17: In lieu of false asceticism and superstitious festivals, the apostle reminds the Colossians of the moral life that is to characterize their response to God through Christ. He urges their participation in the liturgical hymns and prayers that center upon God's plan of salvation in Christ (16).

3, 5.8: The two lists of five vices each are similar to enumerations at Rom 1, 29-31 and Gal 5, 19-21.

3, 6: *The wrath of God:* see the note on Rom 1, 18. Many manuscripts add, as at Eph 5, 6, "upon the disobedient."

3, 8-10: *Put . . . away; have taken off; have put on:* the terms may reflect baptismal practice, taking off garments and putting on new ones after being united with Christ, here translated into ethical terms.

3, 10: *Image:* see the note on 1, 15.

3, 11: *Scythian:* a barbarous people from north of the Black Sea.

3, 18—4, 6: After general recommendations that connect family life and the social condition of slavery with the service of Christ (3, 18—4, 1), Paul requests prayers for himself, especially in view of his imprisonment (2-3), and recommends friendly relations and meaningful discussions of Christian teaching with *outsiders,* i.e., non-Christians (5-6). See the note on Eph 5, 21—6, 9.

3, 22-25: *Slaves:* within this table of duties in family and societal relations, involving wives and husbands, children and parents (18-21), such as also appears in Eph 5, 22—6, 9, slaves here receive special attention because of the case of Onesimus the slave returning to his master (4, 9; Phlm 10-12).

Prayer and Apostolic Spirit. [2]* Persevere in prayer, being watchful in it with thanksgiving; [3]* at the same time, pray for us, too, that God may open a door to us for the word, to speak of the mystery of Christ, for which I am in prison, [4] that I may make it clear, as I must speak. [5]* Conduct yourselves wisely toward outsiders, making the most of the opportunity. [6] Let your speech always be gracious, seasoned with salt, so that you know how you should respond to each one.

V: CONCLUSION

Tychicus and Onesimus.† [7]*† Tychicus, my beloved brother, trustworthy minister, and fellow slave in the Lord, will tell you all the news of me. [8] I am sending him to you for this very purpose, so that you may know about us and that he may encourage your hearts, [9]* together with Onesimus, a trustworthy and beloved brother, who is one of you. They will tell you about everything here.

From Paul's Co-Workers. [10]*† Aristarchus, my fellow prisoner, sends you greetings, as does Mark the cousin of Barnabas (concerning whom you have received instructions; if he comes to you, receive him), [11]† and Jesus, who is called Justus, who are of the circumcision; these alone are my co-workers for the kingdom of God, and they have been a comfort to me. [12]*† Epaphras sends you greetings; he is one of you, a slave of Christ [Jesus], always striving for you in his prayers so that you may be perfect and fully assured in all the will of God. [13]† For I can testify that he works very hard for you and for those in Laodicea and those in Hierapolis. [14]*† Luke the beloved physician sends greetings, as does Demas.

A Message for the Laodiceans. [15]† Give greetings to the brothers in Laodicea and to Nympha and to the church in her house. [16]† And when this letter is read before you, have it read also in the church of the Laodiceans, and you yourselves read the one from Laodicea. [17]*† And tell Archippus, "See that you fulfill the ministry that you received in the Lord."

[18]*† The greeting is in my own hand, Paul's. Remember my chains. Grace be with you.

*

4, 2: Lk 18, 1; Rom 12, 12; Eph 6, 18-20; 1 Thes 5, 17.
3: Rom 15, 30; 1 Cor 16, 9; Eph 6, 19; 2 Thes 3, 1.
5: Eph 5, 15-16.
7: Acts 20, 4; Eph 6, 21-22; Phil 1, 12.
9: Phlm 10-11.
10: Acts 19, 29; 20, 4; 27, 2 / Acts 12, 12.25; 13, 13; 15, 37.40; 2 Tm 4, 11; Phlm 24; 1 Pt 5, 13.
12: 1, 7; Rom 15, 30.
14: Phlm 24; 2 Tm 4, 10-11.
17: Phlm 2.
18: 1 Cor 16, 21; Gal 6, 11; Eph 3, 1; 2 Thes 3, 17

†

4, 7-18: Paul concludes with greetings and information concerning various Christians known to the Colossians.

4, 7: *Tychicus:* Acts 20, 4 mentions his role in the collection for Jerusalem; Eph 6, 21 repeats what is said here; see also 2 Tm 4, 12; Ti 3, 12.

4, 10: *Aristarchus:* a Thessalonian who was with Paul at Ephesus and Caesarea and on the voyage to Rome (Acts 19, 29; 20, 4; 27, 2). *Mark:* also referred to at Phlm 24 and 2 Tm 4, 11 and, as "John Mark," in Acts (12, 12.25; 13, 13; 15, 37-40). See also 1 Pt 5, 13 and the note there. Traditionally the author of the second gospel.

4, 11: *Jesus:* a then common Jewish name, the Greek form of Joshua.

4, 12: *Epaphras:* see the notes on 1, 3-8 and 1, 7.

4, 13: *Laodicea:* see the note on 2, 1. *Hierapolis:* a city northeast of Laodicea and northwest of Colossae.

4, 14: *Luke:* only here described as a medical doctor; cf Phlm 24 and 2 Tm 4, 11. Traditionally the author of the third gospel. *Demas:* cf Phlm 24; he later deserted Paul (2 Tm 4, 10).

4, 15: *Nympha and . . . her house:* some manuscripts read a masculine for the house-church leader, "Nymphas and . . . his house."

4, 16: *The one from Laodicea:* either a letter by Paul that has been lost or the Letter to the Ephesians (cf the note on Eph 1, 1, *in Ephesus*).

4, 17: *Fulfill the ministry:* usually taken to mean that *Archippus,* the son of Philemon and Apphia (Phlm 1-2), is "pastor" at Colossae. An alternate interpretation is that Archippus, not Philemon, is the owner of the slave Onesimus and that Paul is asking Archippus to complete the service he has received in the Lord by sending Onesimus back to minister to Paul in his captivity (cf Phlm 20).

4, 18: *My own hand:* a postscript in Paul's own hand was his custom; cf Gal 6, 11-18 and 2 Thes 3, 17-18.

The First Letter to the

THESSALONIANS

When Paul parted from Barnabas (Acts 15, 36-41) at the beginning of what is called his second missionary journey, he chose Silvanus (Silas) as his traveling companion. Soon afterwards he took Timothy along with him (Acts 16, 1-3). Paul was now clearly at the head of his own missionary band. About A.D. 50, he arrived in Greece for the first time. In making converts in Philippi and, soon afterwards, in Thessalonica, he was beset by persecution from Jews and Gentiles alike. Moving on to Beroea, he was again harassed by enemies from Thessalonica and hurriedly left for Athens (Acts 16, 11—17, 15). Silvanus and Timothy remained behind for a while. Paul soon sent Timothy back to Thessalonica to strengthen that community in its trials (3, 1-5). Timothy and Silvanus finally returned to Paul when he reached Corinth (Acts 18, 1-18), probably in the early summer of A.D. 51. Timothy's return with a report on conditions at Thessalonica served as the occasion for Paul's first letter (3, 6-8).

The letter begins with a brief address (1, 1) and concludes with a greeting (5, 26-28). The body of the letter consists of two major parts. The first (1, 2—3, 13) is a set of three sections of thanksgiving connected by two apologiae *(defenses) dealing, respectively, with the missionaries' previous conduct and their current concerns. Paul's thankful optimism regarding the Thessalonians' spiritual welfare is tempered by his insistence on their recognition of the selfless love shown by the missionaries. In an age of itinerant peddlers of new religions, Paul found it necessary to emphasize not only the content of his gospel but also his manner of presenting it, for both attested to God's grace as freely bestowed and powerfully effected.*

The second part of the letter (4, 1—5, 25) is specifically hortatory or parenetic. The superabundant love for which Paul has just prayed (3, 12-13) is to be shown practically by living out the norms of conduct that he has communicated to them. Specific "imperatives" of Christian life, principles for acting morally, stem from the "indicative" of one's relationship to God through Christ by the sending of the holy Spirit. Thus, moral conduct is the practical, personal expression of one's Christian faith, love, and hope.

The principal divisions of the First Letter to the Thessalonians are the following:

I: Address (1, 1-10)
II: Previous Relations with the Thessalonians (2, 1—3, 13)
III: Specific Exhortations (4, 1—5, 25)
IV: Final Greeting (5, 26-28)

1 THESSALONIANS

I: ADDRESS

CHAPTER 1

Greeting. 1*† Paul, Silvanus, and Timothy to the church of the Thessalonians in God the Father and the Lord Jesus Christ: grace to you and peace.
Thanksgiving for Their Faith. 2* We give thanks to God always for all of you, remembering you in our prayers, unceasingly 3† calling to mind your work of faith and labor of love and endurance in hope of our Lord Jesus Christ, before our God and Father, 4* knowing, brothers loved by God, how you were chosen.

*

1, 1: Acts 15, 40; 16, 1-3.19; 17, 14-15; 2 Thes 1, 1-2.
2: 2 Thes 1, 3.
4: 2 Thes 2, 13.

†

1, 1: On the address, see the note on Rom 1, 1-7.

1, 3: *Faith . . . love . . . hope:* this, along with 5, 8, is the earliest mention in Christian literature of the three "theological virtues" (see 1 Cor 13, 13). The order here stresses eschatological hope, in line with the letter's emphasis on the Lord's second, triumphal coming, or parousia (10; 2, 12.19; 3, 13; 4, 13—5, 11; 5, 23).

[5]* For our gospel did not come to you
in word alone, but also in power and in
the holy Spirit and [with] much convic-
tion. You know what sort of people we
were [among] you for your sake.
[6]† And you became imitators of us and
of the Lord, receiving the word in great
affliction, with joy from the holy Spirit,
[7]* so that you became a model for all
the believers in Macedonia and in
Achaia. [8]* For from you the word of the
Lord has sounded forth not only in
Macedonia and [in] Achaia, but in ev-
ery place your faith in God has gone
forth, so that we have no need to say
anything. [9]* For they themselves
openly declare about us what sort of re-
ception we had among you, and how
you turned to God from idols to serve
the living and true God [10]* and to await
his Son from heaven, whom he raised
from [the] dead, Jesus, who delivers us
from the coming wrath.

II: PREVIOUS RELATIONS WITH THE THESSALONIANS

CHAPTER 2

Paul's Ministry Among Them. [1] For
you yourselves know, brothers, that our
reception among you was not without
effect. [2]* Rather, after we had suffered
and been insolently treated, as you
know, in Philippi, we drew courage
through our God to speak to you the
gospel of God with much struggle.
[3] Our exhortation was not from delusion
or impure motives, nor did it work
through deception. [4]*† But as we were
judged worthy by God to be entrusted
with the gospel, that is how we speak,
not as trying to please human beings,
but rather God, who judges our hearts.
[5] Nor, indeed, did we ever appear with
flattering speech, as you know, or with
a pretext for greed—God is witness—
[6]* nor did we seek praise from human
beings, either from you or from others,
[7]† although we were able to impose our
weight as apostles of Christ. Rather, we
were gentle among you, as a nursing
mother cares for her children. [8] With
such affection for you, we were deter-
mined to share with you not only the
gospel of God, but our very selves as
well, so dearly beloved had you become
to us. [9]* You recall, brothers, our toil
and drudgery. Working night and day
in order not to burden any of you, we
proclaimed to you the gospel of God.
[10] You are witnesses, and so is God, how
devoutly and justly and blamelessly we
behaved toward you believers. [11]* As
you know, we treated each one of
you as a father treats his children,
[12]* exhorting and encouraging you and
insisting that you conduct yourselves as
worthy of the God who calls you into
his kingdom and glory.

Further Thanksgiving. [13] And for this
reason we too give thanks to God un-
ceasingly, that, in receiving the word
of God from hearing us, you received
not a human word but, as it truly is, the
word of God, which is now at work in
you who believe. [14]† For you, brothers,
have become imitators of the churches
of God that are in Judea in Christ Jesus.
For you suffer the same things from
your compatriots as they did from the
Jews, [15]*† who killed both the Lord Je-
sus and the prophets and persecuted us;
they do not please God, and are opposed
to everyone, [16]* trying to prevent us
from speaking to the Gentiles that they
may be saved, thus constantly filling up
the measure of their sins. But the wrath
of God has finally begun to come upon
them.

Paul's Recent Travel Plans.
[17]* Brothers, when we were bereft of
you for a short time, in person, not in
heart, we were all the more eager in our
great desire to see you in person.
[18]* We decided to go to you—I, Paul, not
only once but more than once—yet Sa-
tan thwarted us. [19]* For what is our

*

5: Acts 13, 52; 17, 1-9.
7: 2 Thes 1, 4; 1 Cor 4, 16; 11, 1 / 2, 14; Phil 3, 17.
8: Rom 1, 8.
9: Acts 14, 15; Gal 4, 8 / 4, 5.
10: Rom 2, 1-16; 5, 9; 13, 4 / 5, 9.
2, 2: Acts 16, 19—17, 10.
4: Gal 1, 10.
6: Jn 5, 41.44; 1 Cor 10, 31; 2 Cor 4, 17.
9: Acts 20, 34; 1 Cor 4, 12; 9, 3-18; 2 Thes 3, 7-9.
11: Acts 20, 31.
12: 1 Pt 5, 10 / 4, 7; 2 Thes 2, 14.
15: Acts 2, 23; 7, 52.
16: Gn 15, 16; 2 Mc 6, 14 / Rom 1, 18; 2, 5-6.
17: 3, 10; Rom 1, 10-11.
18: Rom 15, 22.
19: 2 Cor 1, 14; Phil 2, 16; 4, 1.

†

1, 6: *Imitators:* the Pauline theme of "imitation" (see 2, 14; 1 Cor 4, 16; 11, 1; 2 Thes 3, 9) is rooted in Paul's view of solidarity in Christ through sharing in Jesus' cross and in the Spirit of the risen Lord.

2, 4: *Judged worthy:* Paul regards "worthiness" not as grounded in one's own talent or moral self-righteousness but in God's discernment of genuinely selfless attitudes and actions (see 2 Cor 10, 17-18).

2, 7: *Gentle:* many excellent manuscripts read "infants" (*nēpioi*), but "gentle" (*ēpioi*) better suits the context here.

2, 14: Luke's picture of the persecutions at Philippi (by Gentiles) and in Thessalonica and Beroea (by Jews) seems to be considerably schematized (Acts 16, 11-40; 17, 1-15). Paul pictures the Thessalonian community as composed of converts from paganism (1, 9) and speaks here of persecution by their (pagan) compatriots rather than by Jews.

2, 15-16: Paul is speaking of historical opposition on the part of Palestinian Jews in particular and does so only some twenty years after Jesus' crucifixion. Even so, he quickly proceeds to depict the persecutors typologically, in apocalyptic terms. His remarks give no grounds for anti-Semitism to those willing to understand him, especially in view of Paul's pride in his own ethnic and religious background (Rom 9, 1-5; 10, 1; 11, 1-3; Phil 3, 4-6). Sinful conduct (16) is itself an anticipation of the ultimate wrath or judgment of God (Rom 1, 18—2, 5), whether or not it is perceived as such.

hope or joy or crown to boast of in the
presence of our Lord Jesus at his com-
ing if not you yourselves? 20 For you are
our glory and joy.

CHAPTER 3

1* That is why, when we could bear
it no longer, we decided to remain alone
in Athens 2* and sent Timothy, our
brother and co-worker for God in the
gospel of Christ, to strengthen and en-
courage you in your faith, 3† so that no
one be disturbed in these afflictions. For
you yourselves know that we are des-
tined for this. 4* For even when we were
among you, we used to warn you in ad-
vance that we would undergo affliction,
just as has happened, as you know.
5 For this reason, when I too could bear
it no longer, I sent to learn about your
faith, for fear that somehow the tempter
had put you to the test and our toil might
come to nothing.
6 But just now Timothy has returned
to us from you, bringing us the good
news of your faith and love, and that
you always think kindly of us and long
to see us as we long to see you. 7 Because
of this, we have been reassured about
you, brothers, in our every distress
and affliction, through your faith. 8 For
we now live, if you stand firm in the
Lord.
***Concluding Thanksgiving and
Prayer.*** † 9 What thanksgiving, then,
can we render to God for you, for all
the joy we feel on your account before
our God? 10 Night and day we pray be-
yond measure to see you in person and
to remedy the deficiencies of your faith.
11 Now may God himself, our Father,
and our Lord Jesus direct our way to
you, 12* and may the Lord make you in-
crease and abound in love for one an-
other and for all, just as we have for
you, 13* so as to strengthen your hearts,
to be blameless in holiness before our
God and Father at the coming of our
Lord Jesus with all his holy ones.
[Amen.]

III: SPECIFIC EXHORTATIONS

CHAPTER 4

General Exhortations. 1 Finally,
brothers, we earnestly ask and exhort
you in the Lord Jesus that, as you re-
ceived from us how you should conduct
yourselves to please God—and as you
are conducting yourselves—you do so
even more. 2† For you know what in-
structions we gave you through the
Lord Jesus.
Holiness in Sexual Conduct. † 3 This is
the will of God, your holiness: that you
refrain from immorality, 4 that each of
you know how to acquire a wife for him-
self in holiness and honor, 5* not in lust-
ful passion as do the Gentiles who do
not know God; 6 not to take advantage
of or exploit a brother in this matter,
for the Lord is an avenger in all these
things, as we told you before and sol-
emnly affirmed. 7 For God did not call
us to impurity but to holiness.
8* Therefore, whoever disregards this,
disregards not a human being but God,
who [also] gives his holy Spirit to you.
Mutual Charity. 9* On the subject of
mutual charity you have no need for
anyone to write you, for you yourselves
have been taught by God to love one
another. 10* Indeed, you do this for all
the brothers throughout Macedonia.
Nevertheless we urge you, brothers, to
progress even more, 11 and to aspire to
live a tranquil life, to mind your own
affairs, and to work with your [own]
hands, as we instructed you, 12 that you
may conduct yourselves properly to-
ward outsiders and not depend on any-
one.
Hope for the Christian Dead. 13 We do
not want you to be unaware, brothers,
about those who have fallen asleep, so
that you may not grieve like the rest,
who have no hope. 14* For if we believe
that Jesus died and rose, so too will God,

*

3, 1: Acts 17, 14.
2: Acts 16, 1-2; 1 Cor 3, 5-9.
4: Acts 14, 22; 2 Thes 2, 5-7; 2 Tm 3, 12.
12: 4, 9-10; 2 Thes 1, 3.
13: 5, 23; 1 Cor 1, 8.
4, 5: Ps 79, 6; Jer 10, 25; 2 Thes 1, 8; 1 Pt 3, 7.
8: Lk 10, 16.
9: Jn 6, 45; 13, 34; 1 Jn 2, 20-21.27; 4, 7.
10: 2 Thes 3, 6-12.
14: 1 Cor 15, 3-4.12.20.

†

3, 3: *We are destined:* the Greek phraseology and the context suggest Paul's concern to alert his readers to difficulties he knew they would necessarily face and to enable them to see their present experience in the light of what he warned them would happen in the future. This line of thought is followed in 2 Thes 2, 1-15.

3, 9-10: The tension between Paul's optimism concerning the Thessalonians' faith and his worries about their perseverance remains unresolved. Perhaps this is accounted for not only by the continuing harassment but also by the shortness of his own stay in Thessalonica (even if that were over twice as long as the conventional three weeks that Luke assigns to it, Acts 17, 2).

4, 2: *Instructions:* these include specific guidelines on the basis of the Lord's authority, not necessarily sayings Jesus actually uttered. More profoundly, as v 8 implies, the instructions are practical principles that Paul worked out in accordance with his understanding of the role of the Spirit.

4, 3-8: Many think that this passage deals with a variety of moral regulations (fornication, adultery, sharp business practices). It can be more specifically interpreted as bringing general norms to bear on a specific problem, namely, marriage within degrees of consanguinity (as between uncle and niece) forbidden in Jewish law but allowed according to a Greek heiress law, which would insure retention of an inheritance within the family and perhaps thereby occasion divorce. In that case, "immorality" (3) should be rendered as "unlawful marriage" and "this matter" (6) as "a lawsuit." The phrase in v 4, "acquire a wife for himself," has often been interpreted to mean "control one's body."

through Jesus, bring with him those who have fallen asleep. 15*† Indeed, we tell you this, on the word of the Lord, that we who are alive, who are left until the coming of the Lord, will surely not precede those who have fallen asleep. 16* For the Lord himself, with a word of command, with the voice of an archangel and with the trumpet of God, will come down from heaven, and the dead in Christ will rise first. 17† Then we who are alive, who are left, will be caught up together with them in the clouds to meet the Lord in the air. Thus we shall always be with the Lord. 18 Therefore, console one another with these words.

CHAPTER 5

Vigilance. 1* Concerning times and seasons, brothers, you have no need for anything to be written to you. 2* For you yourselves know very well that the day of the Lord will come like a thief at night. 3 When people are saying, "Peace and security," then sudden disaster comes upon them, like labor pains upon a pregnant woman, and they will not escape.

4* But you, brothers, are not in darkness, for that day to overtake you like a thief. 5† For all of you are children of the light and children of the day. We are not of the night or of darkness. 6* Therefore, let us not sleep as the rest do, but let us stay alert and sober. 7 Those who sleep go to sleep at night, and those who are drunk get drunk at night. 8* But since we are of the day, let us be sober, putting on the breastplate of faith and love and the helmet that is hope for salvation. 9 For God did not destine us for wrath, but to gain salvation through our Lord Jesus Christ, 10† who died for us, so that whether we are awake or asleep we may live together with him. 11* Therefore, encourage one another and build one another up, as indeed you do.

Church Order. 12 We ask you, brothers, to respect those who are laboring among you and who are over you in the Lord and who admonish you, 13 and to show esteem for them with special love on account of their work. Be at peace among yourselves.

14 We urge you, brothers, admonish the idle, cheer the fainthearted, support the weak, be patient with all. 15* See that no one returns evil for evil; rather, always seek what is good [both] for each other and for all. 16 Rejoice always. 17 Pray without ceasing. 18* In all circumstances give thanks, for this is the will of God for you in Christ Jesus. 19† Do not quench the Spirit. 20 Do not despise prophetic utterances. 21 Test everything; retain what is good. 22 Refrain from every kind of evil.

Concluding Prayer. 23*† May the God of peace himself make you perfectly holy and may you entirely, spirit, soul, and body, be preserved blameless for the coming of our Lord Jesus Christ. 24 The one who calls you is faithful, and he will also accomplish it. 25 Brothers, pray for us [too].

IV: FINAL GREETING

26† Greet all the brothers with a holy kiss. 27 I adjure you by the Lord that this letter be read to all the brothers. 28 The grace of our Lord Jesus Christ be with you.

*

15: 1 Cor 15, 51; Rv 14, 13; 20, 4-6.
16: Mt 24, 31; 1 Cor 15, 23.52.
5, 1: Mt 24, 36-45.
2: 2 Pt 3, 10.
4: Eph 5, 8-9.
6: Mt 24, 42; Rom 13, 12-13; 1 Pt 5, 8.
8: Is 59, 17; Rom 13, 11-14; Eph 6, 11.14-17.
11: Rom 15, 2; 1 Cor 8, 1; 14, 12.26; Eph 4, 29.
15: Prv 20, 22; Mt 5, 38-42; Rom 12, 17.
18: Eph 5, 20.
23: 2 Thes 3, 16.

†

4, 15: *Coming of the Lord:* Paul here assumes that the second coming, or parousia, will occur within his own lifetime but insists that the time or season is unknown (5, 1-2). Nevertheless, the most important aspect of the parousia for him was the fulfillment of union with Christ. His pastoral exhortation focuses first on hope for the departed faithful, then (5, 1-3) on the need of preparedness for those who have to achieve their goal.

4, 17: *Will be caught up together:* literally, snatched up, carried off; cf 2 Cor 12, 2; Rv 12, 5. From the Latin verb here used, *rapiemur,* has come the idea of "the rapture," when believers will be transported away from the woes of the world; this construction combines this verse with Mt 24, 40-41 (see the note there) // Lk 17, 34-35 and passages from Rv in a scheme of millennial dispensationalism.

5, 5: *Children of the light:* that is, belonging to the daylight of God's personal revelation and expected to achieve it (an analogous development of imagery that appears in Jn 12, 36).

5, 10: Characteristically, Paul plays on words suggesting ultimate and anticipated death and life. Union with the crucified and risen Lord at his parousia is anticipated in some measure in contrasted states of our temporal life. The essential element he urges is our indestructible personal union in Christ's own life (see Rom 5, 1-10).

5, 19-21: Paul's buoyant encouragement of charismatic freedom sometimes occasioned excesses that he or others had to remedy (see 1 Cor 14; 2 Thes 2, 1-15; 2 Pt 3, 1-16).

5, 23: Another possible translation is, "May the God of peace himself make you perfectly holy and sanctify your spirit fully, and may both soul and body be preserved blameless for the coming of our Lord Jesus Christ." In either case, Paul is not offering an anthropological or philosophical analysis of human nature. Rather, he looks to the wholeness of what may be called the supernatural and natural aspects of a person's service of God.

5, 26: *Kiss:* the holy embrace (see Rom 16, 16; 1 Cor 16, 20; 2 Cor 13, 12; 1 Pt 5, 14) was a greeting of respect and affection, perhaps given during a liturgy at which Paul's letter would have been read.

The Second Letter to the

THESSALONIANS

This letter is addressed to the same church as the letter that precedes it in the canon and contains many expressions parallel to those in the First Letter to the Thessalonians, indeed verbatim with them. Yet other aspects of the contents of the Second Letter to the Thessalonians suggest a more impersonal tone and changed circumstances in the situation at Thessalonica.

The letter begins with an address (1, 1-2) that expands only slightly on that of 1 Thes 1, 1. It ends with a greeting insisting on its Pauline authority in the face of false claims made in Paul's name (see the note on 2, 2). The body of the letter falls into three short parts, of which the second is notoriously difficult (ch 2).

The opening thanksgiving and prayer (1, 3-12) speak of the Thessalonians' increasing faith and love in the face of outside persecution. God's eventual judgment against persecutors and his salvation for the faithful are already evidenced by the very fact of persecution. The second part (2, 1-17), the heart of the letter, deals with a problem threatening the faith of the community. A message involving a prophetic oracle and apparently a forged letter, possibly presented at a liturgical gathering (cf 2, 2 and 1 Cor 14, 26-33), to the effect that the day of the Lord and all that it means have already come, has upset the life of the Thessalonian church.

The writer counters their preoccupation with the date of the parousia (or coming again of the Lord Jesus from heaven, 2, 1) by recalling Paul's teaching concerning what must happen first and by going on to describe what will happen at the Lord's coming (2, 8); he indicates the twofold process by which the "activity of Satan" and God's actions (2, 9-11) are working out, namely, a growing division between believers and those who succumb to false prophecy and "the lie." He concludes by insisting on Pauline traditions and by praying for divine strength (2, 13-17). The closing part of the letter (3, 1-16) deals in particular with the apostle's directives and model style of life and with correction of disorderly elements within the community.

Traditional opinion holds that this letter was written shortly after 1 Thessalonians. Occasionally it has been argued that 2 Thessalonians was written first or that the two letters are addressed to different segments within the church at Thessalonica (2 Thessalonians being directed to the Jewish Christians there) or even that 2 Thessalonians was originally written to some other nearby place where Paul carried out mission work, such as Philippi or Beroea. Increasingly in recent times, however, the opinion has been advanced that 2 Thessalonians is a pseudepigraph, that is, a letter written authoritatively in Paul's name, to maintain apostolic traditions in a later period, perhaps during the last two decades of the first century.

In any case, the presumed audience of Second Thessalonians and certain features of its style and content require that it be read and studied in a Pauline context, particularly that provided by 1 Thessalonians. At the same time, and especially if the letter is regarded as not by Paul himself, its apocalyptic presentation of preconditions for the parousia (2, 1-12) may profit from and require recourse to a wider biblical basis for interpretation, namely Old Testament books such as Daniel and Isaiah and especially, in the New Testament, the synoptic apocalyptic discourse (Mk 13; Mt 24-25; Lk 21, 5-36) and the Book of Revelation.

The principal divisions of the Second Letter to the Thessalonians are the following:

I: Address (1, 1-12)
II: Warning against Deception Concerning the Parousia (2, 1-17)

III: Concluding Exhortations (3, 1-16)
IV: Final Greetings (3, 17-18)

I: ADDRESS

CHAPTER 1

Greeting. † 1* Paul, Silvanus, and Tim-
othy to the church of the Thessaloni-
ans in God our Father and the Lord
Jesus Christ: 2 grace to you and peace
from God [our] Father and the Lord Je-
sus Christ.
Thanksgiving. † 3* We ought to thank
God always for you, brothers, as is fit-
ting, because your faith flourishes ever
more, and the love of every one of you
for one another grows ever greater.
4 Accordingly, we ourselves boast of you
in the churches of God regarding your
endurance and faith in all your perse-
cutions and the afflictions you endure.
5* This is evidence of the just judg-
ment of God, so that you may be consid-
ered worthy of the kingdom of God for
which you are suffering. 6 For it is
surely just on God's part to repay with
afflictions those who are afflicting you,
7 and to grant rest along with us to you
who are undergoing afflictions, at the
revelation of the Lord Jesus from
heaven with his mighty angels, 8* in
blazing fire, inflicting punishment on
those who do not acknowledge God and
on those who do not obey the gospel of
our Lord Jesus. 9* These will pay the
penalty of eternal ruin, separated from
the presence of the Lord and from the
glory of his power, 10*† when he comes
to be glorified among his holy ones and
to be marveled at on that day among
all who have believed, for our testimony
to you was believed.
Prayer. 11* To this end, we always
pray for you, that our God may make
you worthy of his calling and power-
fully bring to fulfillment every good
purpose and every effort of faith,
12*† that the name of our Lord Jesus
may be glorified in you, and you in him,
in accord with the grace of our God and
Lord Jesus Christ.

II: WARNING AGAINST DECEPTION CONCERNING THE PAROUSIA

CHAPTER 2

Christ and the Lawless One. † 1* We
ask you, brothers, with regard to the
coming of our Lord Jesus Christ and our
assembling with him, 2*† not to be
shaken out of your minds suddenly, or
to be alarmed either by a "spirit," or

*

1, 1: 1 Thes 1, 1.
3: 1 Cor 1, 4; 1 Thes 1, 2; 3, 12.
5: Phil 1, 28; 1 Thes 2, 12.
8: Ps 79, 5-6; Is 66, 15; Jer 10, 25.
9: Is 2, 10.19.21.
10: Ps 89, 8; Dn 7, 18-22.27; 1 Thes 3, 13.
11: 1 Thes 1, 2-3.
12: Is 66, 5.
2, 1: 1 Thes 4, 13-17.
2: Mt 24, 6; 1 Cor 14, 26.32-33; 1 Thes 5, 1-2.

†

1, 1-2: On the address, see the note on Rom 1, 1-7 and cf 1 Thes 1, 1.

1, 3-12: On the thanksgiving, see the note on Rom 1, 8 and cf 1 Thes 1, 2-10. Paul's gratitude to God for the faith and love of the Thessalonians (3) and his Christian pride in their faithful endurance (4-5) contrast with the condemnation announced for those who afflict them, a judgment to be carried out at the parousia (6-10), which is described in vivid language drawn from Old Testament apocalyptic. A prayer for the fulfillment of God's purpose in the Thessalonians (11-12) completes the section, as is customary in a Pauline letter (cf 1 Thes 1, 2-3).

1, 10: *Among his holy ones:* in the Old Testament, this term can refer to an angelic throng (cf also Jude 14), but here, in parallel with *among all who have believed,* it can refer to the triumphant people of God.

1, 12: *The grace of our God and Lord Jesus Christ:* the Greek can also be translated, "the grace of our God and of the Lord Jesus Christ."

2, 1-17: The Thessalonians have been *shaken* by a message purporting to come from Paul himself that *the day of the Lord* is already present. He warns against this deception in eschatology by citing a scenario of events that must first occur (3-12) before the end will come. The overall point Paul makes is the need to reject such lies as Satan sends; he also reaffirms the Thessalonians in their calling (13-14). They are to uphold what Paul himself has taught (15). There is a concluding prayer for their strengthening (16-17). As in 1, 8-10, the Old Testament provides a good deal of coloring; cf especially Is 14, 13-14; 66, 15.18-21; Ez 28, 2-9; Dn 11, 36-37. The contents of 2, 3b-8 may come from a previously existing apocalypse. The details have been variously interpreted.

An alternative to the possibilities noted below understands that an oracular utterance, supposedly coming from a prophetic spirit (2-3a), has so disrupted the community's thinking that its effects may be compared to those of the mania connected with the worship of the Greek god Dionysus. On this view, the writer seems to allude in vv 6-8 to Dionysiac "seizure," although, of course, ironically, somewhat as Paul alludes to witchcraft ("an evil eye") in Gal 3, 1 in speaking of the threat to faith posed by those disturbing the Galatians (Gal 1, 6-7; 5, 10b). On this view of 2 Thes 2, the Greek participles *katechon* (rendered above as *what is restraining*) and *katechōn* (*the one who restrains*) are to be translated "the seizing power" in v 6 and "the seizer" in v 7. They then allude to a pseudocharismatic force or spirit of Dionysiac character that has suddenly taken hold of the Thessalonian community (see 2). The addressees *know* (6) this force or spirit because of the problem it is causing. This pseudocharismatic force or spirit is a kind of anticipation and advance proof of the ultimate, climactic figure (*the lawless one* or the rebel, 3), of which the community has been warned (see the note on 1 Thes 3, 3). It is, however, only the beginning of the end that the latter's manifestation entails; the end is not yet. For in the course of *the mystery of lawlessness* (7), false prophetism, after it ceases in the Thessalonian community, will be manifested in the world at large (8-12), where it will also be eliminated in turn by the Lord Jesus.

2, 2: *"Spirit":* a Spirit-inspired utterance or ecstatic revelation. *An oral statement:* literally, a "word" or pronouncement, not necessarily of ecstatic origin. *A letter allegedly sent by us:* possibly a forged letter, so that Paul calls attention in 3, 17 to his practice of concluding a genuine letter with a summary note or greeting in his own hand, as at Gal 6, 11-18 and elsewhere.

by an oral statement, or by a letter al-
legedly from us to the effect that the
day of the Lord is at hand. 3† Let no one
deceive you in any way. For unless the
apostasy comes first and the lawless one
is revealed, the one doomed to perdi-
tion, 4*† who opposes and exalts himself
above every so-called god and object
of worship, so as to seat himself in the
temple of God, claiming that he is a
god—5 do you not recall that while I was
still with you I told you these things?
6† And now you know what is restrain-
ing, that he may be revealed in his time.
7*† For the mystery of lawlessness is al-
ready at work. But the one who re-
strains is to do so only for the present,
until he is removed from the scene.
8* And then the lawless one will be re-
vealed, whom the Lord [Jesus] will kill
with the breath of his mouth and render
powerless by the manifestation of his
coming, 9* the one whose coming
springs from the power of Satan in
every mighty deed and in signs and
wonders that lie, 10 and in every wicked
deceit for those who are perishing be-
cause they have not accepted the love
of truth so that they may be saved.
11 Therefore, God is sending them a de-
ceiving power so that they may believe
the lie, 12 that all who have not believed
the truth but have approved wrong-
doing may be condemned.

13*† But we ought to give thanks to
God for you always, brothers loved by
the Lord, because God chose you as the
firstfruits for salvation through sanctifi-
cation by the Spirit and belief in truth.
14* To this end he has [also] called you
through our gospel to possess the glory
of our Lord Jesus Christ. 15† Therefore,
brothers, stand firm and hold fast to the
traditions that you were taught, either
by an oral statement or by a letter of
ours.

16 May our Lord Jesus Christ himself
and God our Father, who has loved us
and given us everlasting encourage-
ment and good hope through his grace,
17 encourage your hearts and
strengthen them in every good deed
and word.

III: CONCLUDING EXHORTATIONS

CHAPTER 3†

Request for Prayers. 1* Finally,
brothers, pray for us, so that the word
of the Lord may speed forward and be
glorified, as it did among you, 2 and that
we may be delivered from perverse and
wicked people, for not all have faith.
3* But the Lord is faithful; he will
strengthen you and guard you from the
evil one. 4* We are confident of you in
the Lord that what we instruct you, you
[both] are doing and will continue to do.
5 May the Lord direct your hearts to the
love of God and to the endurance of
Christ.

*

4: Dn 11, 36-37; Ez 28, 2.
7: Mt 13, 36-43; Acts 20, 29; Gal 5, 10; 2 Pt 2, 1; Rv 22, 11.
8: Is 11, 4; Rv 19, 15.
9: Mt 24, 24; Rv 13, 13.
13: 1 Thes 2, 13; 5, 9.
14: Rom 5, 1-10; 8, 29-30; 1 Thes 4, 7; 5, 9.
3, 1: Eph 6, 19; Col 4, 3.
3: 1 Thes 5, 24 / 1 Cor 16, 13 / Mt 6, 13.
4: 2 Cor 7, 16; 1 Thes 4, 1-2.

†

2, 3b-5: This incomplete sentence (anacoluthon, 4) recalls what the Thessalonians had already been taught, an apocalyptic scenario depicting, in terms borrowed especially from Dn 11, 36-37 and related verses, human self-assertiveness against God in *the temple of God* itself. *The lawless one* represents the climax of such activity in this account.

2, 4: *Seat himself in the temple of God:* a reflection of the language in Dn 7, 23-25; 8, 9-12; 9, 27; 11, 36-37; and 12, 11 about the attempt of Antiochus IV Epiphanes to set up a statue of Zeus in the Jerusalem temple and possibly of the Roman emperor Caligula to do a similar thing (Mk 13, 14). Here the imagery suggests an attempt to install someone in the place of God, *claiming that he is a god* (cf Ez 28, 2). Usually, it is the Jerusalem temple that is assumed to be meant; on the alternative view sketched above (see the note on 2, 1-17), *the temple* refers to the Christian community.

2, 6-7: *What is restraining . . . the one who restrains:* neuter and masculine, respectively, of a force and person holding back the lawless one. The Thessalonians know what is meant (6), but the terms, seemingly found only in this passage and in writings dependent on it, have been variously interpreted. Traditionally, v 6 has been applied to the Roman empire and v 7 to the Roman emperor (in Paul's day, Nero) as bulwarks holding back chaos (cf Rom 13, 1-7). A second interpretation suggests that cosmic or angelic powers are binding Satan (9) and so restraining him; some relate this to an anti-Christ figure (1 Jn 2, 18) or to Michael the archangel (Rv 12, 7-9; 20, 1-3). A more recent view suggests that it is the preaching of the Christian gospel that restrains the end, for in God's plan the end cannot come until the gospel is preached to all nations (Mk 13, 10); in that case, Paul as missionary preacher par excellence is "the one who restrains," whose removal (death) will bring the end (7). On the alternative view (see the note on 2, 1-17), the phrases should be referred to that which and to him who seizes (a prophet) in ecstasy so as to have him speak pseudo-oracles.

2, 7-12: *The lawless one* and *the one who restrains* are involved in an activity or process, *the mystery of lawlessness,* behind which *Satan* stands (9). The action of *the Lord [Jesus]* in overcoming the lawless one is described in Old Testament language (*with the breath of his mouth;* cf Is 11, 4; Jb 4, 9; Rv 19, 15). His *coming* is literally the Lord's "parousia." The biblical concept of the "holy war," eschatologically conceived, may underlie the imagery.

2, 13: *As the firstfruits:* there is also strong manuscript evidence for the reading, "God chose you from the beginning," thus providing a focus on God's activity from beginning to end; *firstfruits* is a Pauline term, however; cf Rom 8, 23; 11, 16; 16, 5, among other references.

2, 15: Reference to *an oral statement* and *a letter* (2) and the content here, including a formula of conclusion (cf 1 Cor 16, 13; Gal 5, 1), suggest that vv 1-15 or even 1-17 are to be taken as a literary unit, notwithstanding the incidental thanksgiving formula in v 13.

3, 1-18: The final chapter urges the Thessalonians to pray for Paul and his colleagues (1-2) and reiterates confidence in the Thessalonians (3-5), while admonishing them about a specific problem in their community that has grown out of the intense eschatological speculation, namely, not to work but to become instead disorderly busybodies (6-15). A benediction (16) and postscript in Paul's own hand round out the letter. On vv 17-18, cf the note on 2, 2.

Neglect of Work. 6† We instruct you,
brothers, in the name of [our] Lord Je-
sus Christ, to shun any brother who con-
ducts himself in a disorderly way and
not according to the tradition they re-
ceived from us. 7 For you know how one
must imitate us. For we did not act in
a disorderly way among you, 8* nor did
we eat food received free from anyone.
On the contrary, in toil and drudgery,
night and day we worked, so as not to
burden any of you. 9* Not that we do
not have the right. Rather, we wanted
to present ourselves as a model for you,
so that you might imitate us. 10* In fact,
when we were with you, we instructed
you that if anyone was unwilling to
work, neither should that one eat.
11* We hear that some are conducting
themselves among you in a disorderly
way, by not keeping busy but minding
the business of others. 12 Such people we
instruct and urge in the Lord Jesus
Christ to work quietly and to eat their
own food. 13 But you, brothers, do not
be remiss in doing good. 14 If anyone
does not obey our word as expressed
in this letter, take note of this person
not to associate with him, that he may
be put to shame. 15* Do not regard him
as an enemy but admonish him as a
brother. 16* May the Lord of peace him-
self give you peace at all times and in
every way. The Lord be with all of you.

IV: FINAL GREETINGS

17* This greeting is in my own hand,
Paul's. This is the sign in every letter;
this is how I write. 18 The grace of our
Lord Jesus Christ be with all of you.

*

8: 1 Thes 2, 9.
9: Mt 10, 10; Phil 3, 17.
10: 1 Thes 4, 11.
11: 1 Thes 5, 14.
15: 2 Cor 2, 7; Gal 6, 1.
16: Jn 14, 27; Rom 15, 33.
17: 1 Cor 16, 21; Gal 6, 11.

†

3, 6: Some members of the community, probably because they regarded the parousia as imminent or the new age of the Lord to be already here (2, 2), had apparently ceased to work for a living. The disciplinary problem they posed could be rooted in distorted thinking about Paul's own teaching (cf 1 Thes 2, 16; 3, 3-4; 5, 4-5) or, more likely, in a forged letter (2, 2) and the type of teaching dealt with in 2, 1-15. The apostle's own moral teaching, reflected in his selfless labors for others, was rooted in a deep doctrinal concern for the gospel message (cf 1 Thes 2, 3-10).

The First Letter to

TIMOTHY

The three letters, First and Second Timothy and Titus, form a distinct group within the Pauline corpus. In the collection of letters by the Apostle to the Gentiles, they differ from the others in form and contents. All three suggest they were written late in Paul's career. The opponents are not "Judaizers" as in Galatians but false teachers stressing "knowledge" (gnōsis; *see the note on 1 Tm 6, 20-21). Attention is given especially to correct doctrine and church organization. Jesus' second coming recedes into the background compared to references in Paul's earlier letters (though not Colossians and Ephesians). The three letters are addressed not to congregations but to those who shepherd congregations (Latin,* pastores*). These letters were first named "Pastoral Epistles" in the eighteenth century because they all are concerned with the work of a pastor in caring for the community or communities under his charge.*

The first of the Pastorals, 1 Timothy, is presented as having been written from Macedonia. Timothy, whom Paul converted, was of mixed Jewish and Gentile parentage (Acts 16, 1-3). He was the apostle's companion on both the second and the third missionary journeys (Acts 16, 3; 19, 22) and was often sent by him on special missions (Acts 19, 22; 1 Cor 4, 17; 1 Thes 3, 2). In 1 Timothy (1, 3), he is described as the administrator of the entire Ephesian community.

The letter instructs Timothy on his duty to restrain false and useless teaching (1, 3-11; 4, 1-5; 6, 3-16) and proposes principles pertaining to his relationship with the older members of the community (5, 1-2) and with the presbyters (5, 17-22). It gives rules for aid to widows (5, 3-8) and their selection for charitable ministrations (5, 9-16) and also deals with liturgical celebrations (2, 1-15), selections for the offices of bishop and deacon (3, 1-13), relation of slaves with their masters (6, 1-2), and obligations of the wealthier members of the community (6, 17-19). This letter also reminds Timothy of the prophetic character of his office (1, 12-20) and encourages him in his exercise of it (4, 6-16). The central passage of the letter (3, 14-16) expresses the principal motive that should guide the conduct of Timothy—preservation of the purity of the church's doctrine against false teaching. On this same note the letter concludes (6, 20-21).

From the late second century to the nineteenth, Pauline authorship of the three Pastoral Epistles went unchallenged. Since then, the attribution of these letters to Paul has been questioned. Most scholars are convinced that Paul could not have been responsible for the vocabulary and style, the concept of church organization, or the theological expressions found in these letters. A second group believes, on the basis of statistical evidence, that the vocabulary and style are Pauline, even if at first sight the contrary seems to be the case. They state that the concept of church organization in the letters is not as advanced as the questioners of Pauline authorship hold since the notion of hierarchical order in a religious community existed in Israel before the time of Christ, as evidenced in the Dead Sea Scrolls. Finally, this group sees affinities between the theological thought of the Pastorals and that of the unquestionably genuine letters of Paul. Other scholars, while conceding a degree of validity to the positions mentioned above, suggest that the apostle made use of a secretary who was responsible for the composition of the letters. A fourth group of scholars believes that these letters are the work of a compiler, that they are based on traditions about Paul in his later years, and that they include, in varying amounts, actual fragments of genuine Pauline correspondence.

If Paul is considered the more immediate author, the Pastorals are to be dated between the end of his first Roman imprisonment (Acts 28, 16) and his execution under Nero (A.D. 63-67); if they are regarded as only more remotely Pauline, their date may be as late as the early second century. In spite of these problems of authorship and dating, the Pastorals are illustrative of early Christian life and remain an important element of canonical scripture.

The principal divisions of the First Letter to Timothy are the following:

- *I: Address (1, 1-2)*
- *II: Sound Teaching (1, 3-20)*
- *III: Problems of Discipline (2, 1—4, 16)*
- *IV: Duties toward Others (5, 1—6, 2a)*
- *V: False Teaching and True Wealth (6, 2b-19)*
- *VI: Final Recommendation and Warning (6, 20-21)*

I: ADDRESS

CHAPTER 1

Greeting.† [1]* Paul, an apostle of
Christ Jesus by command of God our
savior and of Christ Jesus our hope,
[2]* to Timothy, my true child in faith:
grace, mercy, and peace from God the
Father and Christ Jesus our Lord.

II: SOUND TEACHING

Warning against False Doctrine.†
[3]* I repeat the request I made of you
when I was on my way to Macedonia,
that you stay in Ephesus to instruct cer-
tain people not to teach false doctrines
[4]*† or to concern themselves with
myths and endless genealogies, which
promote speculations rather than the
plan of God that is to be received by
faith. [5]* The aim of this instruction is
love from a pure heart, a good con-
science, and a sincere faith. [6]* Some
people have deviated from these and
turned to meaningless talk, [7] wanting to
be teachers of the law, but without un-
derstanding either what they are saying
or what they assert with such assur-
ance.
[8]*† We know that the law is good, pro-
vided that one uses it as law, [9] with the
understanding that law is meant not for
a righteous person but for the lawless
and unruly, the godless and sinful, the
unholy and profane, those who kill their
fathers or mothers, murderers, [10]*† the
unchaste, practicing homosexuals, kid-
napers, liars, perjurers, and whatever
else is opposed to sound teaching,
[11]* according to the glorious gospel of
the blessed God, with which I have been
entrusted.

Gratitude for God's Mercy.† [12]* I am
grateful to him who has strengthened
me, Christ Jesus our Lord, because he
considered me trustworthy in appoint-
ing me to the ministry. [13]* I was once a
blasphemer and a persecutor and an ar-
rogant man, but I have been mercifully
treated because I acted out of ignorance
in my unbelief. [14]* Indeed, the grace of
our Lord has been abundant, along with
the faith and love that are in Christ Je-
sus. [15]*† This saying is trustworthy and

1 TIMOTHY

---

*

1, 1: 2, 3; Lk 1, 47; Ti 1, 3; 2, 10 / Col 1, 27.
2: 2 Tm 1, 2; Ti 1, 4.
3: Acts 20, 1.
4: 4, 7; Ti 1, 14; 3, 9; 2 Pt 1, 16.
5: Rom 13, 10.
6: 6, 4.20; Ti 1, 10.
8: Rom 7, 12.16.
10: 4, 6; 6, 3; 2 Tm 4, 3; Ti 1, 9; 2, 1.
11: Ti 1, 3.
12: Phil 4, 13 / Acts 9, 15; Gal 1, 15-16.
13: Acts 8, 3; 9, 1-2; 1 Cor 15, 9; Gal 1, 13.
14: Rom 5, 20; 2 Tm 1, 13.
15: Lk 15, 2; 19, 10.

---

†

1, 1-2: For the Pauline use of the conventional epistolary form, see the note on Rom 1, 1-7.

1, 3-7: Here Timothy's initial task *in Ephesus* (cf Acts 20, 17-35) is outlined: to suppress the idle religious speculations, probably about Old Testament figures (3-4, but see the note on 6, 20-21), which do not contribute to the development of love within the community (5) but rather encourage similar useless conjectures (6-7).

1, 4: *The plan of God that is to be received by faith:* the Greek may also possibly mean "God's trustworthy plan" or "the training in faith that God requires."

1, 8-11: Those responsible for the speculations that are to be suppressed by Timothy do not present the Old Testament from the Christian viewpoint. The Christian values the Old Testament not as a system of law but as the first stage in God's revelation of his saving plan, which is brought to fulfillment in the good news of salvation through faith in Jesus Christ.

1, 10: *Practicing homosexuals:* see 1 Cor 6, 9 and the note there.

1, 12-17: Present gratitude for the Christian apostleship leads Paul to recall an earlier time when he had been a fierce persecutor of the Christian communities (cf Acts 26, 9-11) until his conversion by intervention of divine mercy through the appearance of Jesus. This and his subsequent apostolic experience testify to the saving purpose of Jesus' incarnation. The fact of his former ignorance of the truth has not kept the apostle from regarding himself as having been the worst of sinners (15). Yet he was chosen to be an apostle, that God might manifest his firm will to save sinful humanity through Jesus Christ (16). The recounting of so great a mystery leads to a spontaneous outpouring of adoration (17).

1, 15: *This saying is trustworthy:* this phrase regularly introduces in the Pastorals a basic truth of early Christian faith; cf 3, 1; 4, 9; 2 Tm 2, 11; Ti 3, 8.

deserves full acceptance: Christ Jesus
came into the world to save sinners. Of
these I am the foremost. 16 But for that
reason I was mercifully treated, so that
in me, as the foremost, Christ Jesus
might display all his patience as an ex-
ample for those who would come to be-
lieve in him for everlasting life. 17*† To
the king of ages, incorruptible, invisi-
ble, the only God, honor and glory for-
ever and ever. Amen.
Responsibility of Timothy. † 18*† I en-
trust this charge to you, Timothy,
my child, in accordance with the pro-
phetic words once spoken about you.
Through them may you fight a good
fight 19* by having faith and a good
conscience. Some, by rejecting con-
science, have made a shipwreck of
their faith, 20*† among them Hyme-
naeus and Alexander, whom I have
handed over to Satan to be taught not
to blaspheme.

III: PROBLEMS OF DISCIPLINE

CHAPTER 2

Prayer and Conduct. † 1* First of all,
then, I ask that supplications, prayers,
petitions, and thanksgivings be offered
for everyone, 2 for kings and for all in
authority, that we may lead a quiet and
tranquil life in all devotion and dignity.
3* This is good and pleasing to God our
savior, 4* who wills everyone to be
saved and to come to knowledge of the
truth.

5* For there is one God.
There is also one mediator between
God and the human race,
Christ Jesus, himself human,
6*† who gave himself as ransom for all.

This was the testimony at the proper
time. 7* For this I was appointed
preacher and apostle (I am speaking
the truth, I am not lying), teacher of the
Gentiles in faith and truth.
8† It is my wish, then, that in every
place the men should pray, lifting up
holy hands, without anger or argument.
9* Similarly, [too,] women should adorn
themselves with proper conduct, with
modesty and self-control, not with
braided hairstyles and gold ornaments,
or pearls, or expensive clothes, 10* but
rather, as befits women who profess
reverence for God, with good deeds.
11* A woman must receive instruction
silently and under complete control.
12† I do not permit a woman to teach
or to have authority over a man. She
must be quiet. 13* For Adam was formed
first, then Eve. 14* Further, Adam was
not deceived, but the woman was de-
ceived and transgressed. 15* But she
will be saved through motherhood, pro-
vided women persevere in faith and
love and holiness, with self-control.

---

*

17: Rom 16, 27.
18: 4, 14 / 6, 12; 2 Tm 4, 7; Jude 3.
19: 3, 9.
20: 2 Tm 2, 17; 4, 14 / 1 Cor 5, 5.
2, 1: Eph 6, 18; Phil 4, 6.
3: 1, 1; 4, 10.
4: 2 Tm 3, 7; 2 Pt 3, 9.
5: 1 Cor 8, 6; Heb 8, 6; 9, 15; 12, 24 / Rom 5, 15.
6: Mk 10, 45; Gal 1, 4; 2, 20; Eph 5, 25; Ti 2, 14.
7: Acts 9, 15; 1 Cor 9, 1; Gal 2, 7-8.
9: 1 Pt 3, 3-5.
10: 5, 10; 1 Pt 3, 1.
11-12: 1 Cor 14, 34-35.
13: Gn 1, 27; 2, 7.22; 1 Cor 11, 8-9.
14: Gn 3, 6.13; 2 Cor 11, 3.
15: 5, 14.

---

†

1, 17: *King of ages:* through Semitic influence, the Greek expression could mean "everlasting king"; it could also mean "king of the universe."

1, 18-20: Timothy is to be mindful of his calling, which is here compared to the way Barnabas and Saul were designated by Christ as prophets for missionary service; cf Acts 13, 1-3. Such is probably the sense of the allusion to the prophetic words (18). His task is not to yield, whether in doctrine or in conduct, to erroneous opinions, taking warning from what has already happened at Ephesus in the case of Hymenaeus and Alexander (19-20).

1, 18: *The prophetic words once spoken about you:* the Greek may also be translated, "the prophecies that led (me) to you." It probably refers to testimonies given by charismatic figures in the Christian communities. *Fight a good fight:* this translation preserves the play on words in Greek. The Greek terms imply a lengthy engagement in battle and might well be translated "wage a good campaign."

1, 20: *Hymenaeus:* mentioned in 2 Tm 2, 17 as saying that the resurrection has already taken place (in baptism). *Alexander:* probably the Alexander mentioned in 2 Tm 4, 14 as the coppersmith who "did me a great deal of harm." *Whom I have handed over to Satan:* the same terms are used in the condemnation of the incestuous man in 1 Cor 5, 5.

2, 1-7: This marked insistence that the liturgical prayer of the community concern itself with the needs of all, whether Christian or not, and especially of those in authority, may imply that a disposition existed at Ephesus to refuse prayer for pagans. In actuality, such prayer aids the community to achieve peaceful relationships with non-Christians (2) and contributes to salvation, since it derives its value from the presence within the community of Christ, who is the one and only savior of all (3-6). The vital apostolic mission to the Gentiles (7) reflects Christ's purpose of universal salvation.

Verse 5 contains what may well have been a very primitive creed. Some interpreters have called it a Christian version of the Jewish *shema:* "Hear, O Israel, the LORD is our God, the LORD alone . . ." (Dt 6, 4-5). The assertion in v 7, "I am speaking the truth, I am not lying," reminds one of similar affirmations in Rom 9, 1; 2 Cor 11, 31; and Gal 1, 20.

2, 6: *The testimony:* to make sense of this overly concise phrase, many manuscripts supply "to which" (or "to whom"); two others add "was given." The translation has supplied "this was."

2, 8-15: The prayer of the community should be unmarred by internal dissension (8); cf Mt 5, 21-26; 6, 14; Mk 11, 25. At the liturgical assembly the dress of women should be appropriate to the occasion (9); their chief adornment is to be reputation for good works (10). Women are not to take part in the charismatic activity of the assembly (11-12; cf 1 Cor 14, 34) or exercise authority; their conduct there should reflect the role of man's helpmate (13; cf Gn 2, 18) and not the later relationship of Eve to Adam (14; cf Gn 3, 6-7). As long as women perform their role as wives and mothers in faith and love, their salvation is assured (15).

2, 12: *A man:* this could also mean "her husband."

CHAPTER 3

Qualifications of Various Ministers.†
1*† This saying is trustworthy: whoever aspires to the office of bishop desires a noble task. 2 Therefore, a bishop must be irreproachable, married only once, temperate, self-controlled, decent, hospitable, able to teach, 3* not a drunkard, not aggressive, but gentle, not contentious, not a lover of money. 4 He must manage his own household well, keeping his children under control with perfect dignity; 5 for if a man does not know how to manage his own household, how can he take care of the church of God? 6† He should not be a recent convert, so that he may not become conceited and thus incur the devil's punishment. 7* He must also have a good reputation among outsiders, so that he may not fall into disgrace, the devil's trap.

8† Similarly, deacons must be dignified, not deceitful, not addicted to drink, not greedy for sordid gain, 9 holding fast to the mystery of the faith with a clear conscience. 10 Moreover, they should be tested first; then, if there is nothing against them, let them serve as deacons. 11*† Women, similarly, should be dignified, not slanderers, but temperate and faithful in everything. 12 Deacons may be married only once and must manage their children and their households well. 13 Thus those who serve well as deacons gain good standing and much confidence in their faith in Christ Jesus.

The Mystery of Our Religion.† 14 I am writing you about these matters, although I hope to visit you soon. 15* But if I should be delayed, you should know how to behave in the household of God, which is the church of the living God, the pillar and foundation of truth. 16*† Undeniably great is the mystery of devotion,

> Who was manifested in the flesh,
> vindicated in the spirit,
> seen by angels,
> proclaimed to the Gentiles,
> believed in throughout the world,
> taken up in glory.

CHAPTER 4

False Asceticism.† 1* Now the Spirit explicitly says that in the last times some will turn away from the faith by paying attention to deceitful spirits and demonic instructions 2 through the hypocrisy of liars with branded consciences. 3* They forbid marriage and require abstinence from foods that God created to be received with thanksgiving by those who believe and know the truth. 4* For everything created by God is good, and nothing is to be rejected when received with thanksgiving,

---

*

3, 1-7: Ti 1, 6-9.
3: Heb 13, 5.
7: 2 Cor 8, 21; 2 Tm 2, 26.
11: Ti 2, 3.
15: Eph 2, 19-22.
16: Jn 1, 14; Rom 1, 3-4.
4, 1: 2 Tm 3, 1; 4, 3; 2 Pt 3, 3; Jude 18.
3: Gn 9, 3; Rom 14, 6; 1 Cor 10, 30-31.
4: Gn 1, 31; Acts 10, 15.

†

3, 1-7: The passage begins by commending those who aspire to the office of bishop (*episkopos;* see the note on Phil 1, 1) within the community, but this first sentence (1) may also imply a warning about the great responsibilities involved. The writer proceeds to list the qualifications required: personal stability and graciousness; talent for teaching (2); moderation in habits and temperament (3); managerial ability (4); and experience in Christian living (5-6). Moreover, the candidate's previous life should provide no grounds for the charge that he did not previously practice what he now preaches. No list of qualifications for presbyters appears in 1 Tm. The presbyter-bishops here and in Ti (see the note on Ti 1, 5-9) lack certain functions reserved here for Paul and Timothy.

3, 1: *This saying is trustworthy:* the saying introduced is so unlike others after this phrase that some later Western manuscripts read, "This saying is popular." It is understood by some interpreters as concluding the preceding section (2, 8-15). *Bishop:* literally, "overseer"; see the note on Phil 1, 1.

3, 6: *The devil's punishment:* this phrase could mean the punishment once incurred by the devil (objective genitive) or a punishment brought about by the devil (subjective genitive).

3, 8-13: Deacons, besides possessing the virtue of moderation (8), are to be outstanding for their faith (9) and well respected within the community (10). Women in the same role, although some interpreters take them to mean wives of deacons, must be dignified, temperate, dedicated, and not given to malicious talebearing (11). Deacons must have shown stability in marriage and have a good record with their families (12), for such experience prepares them well for the exercise of their ministry on behalf of the community (13). See further the note on Phil 1, 1.

3, 11: *Women:* this seems to refer to women deacons but may possibly mean wives of deacons. The former is preferred because the word is used absolutely; if deacons' wives were meant, a possessive "their" would be expected. Moreover, they are also introduced by the word "similarly," as in v 8; this parallel suggests that they too exercised ecclesiastical functions.

3, 14-16: In case there is some delay in the visit to Timothy at Ephesus planned for the near future, the present letter is being sent on ahead to arm and enlighten him in his task of preserving sound Christian conduct in the Ephesian church. The care he must exercise over this community is required by the profound nature of Christianity. It centers in Christ, appearing in human flesh, vindicated by the holy Spirit; the mystery of his person was revealed to the angels, announced to the Gentiles, and accepted by them in faith. He himself was taken up (through his resurrection and ascension) to the divine glory (16). This passage apparently includes part of a liturgical hymn used among the Christian communities in and around Ephesus. It consists of three couplets in typical Hebrew balance: flesh-spirit (contrast), seen-proclaimed (complementary), world-glory (contrast).

3, 16: *Who:* the reference is to Christ, who is himself "the mystery of our devotion." Some predominantly Western manuscripts read "which," harmonizing the gender of the pronoun with that of the Greek word for mystery; many later (eighth/ninth century on), predominantly Byzantine manuscripts read "God," possibly for theological reasons.

4, 1-5: Doctrinal deviations from the true Christian message within the church have been prophesied, though the origin of the prophecy is not specified (1-2); cf Acts 20, 29-30. The letter warns against a false asceticism that prohibits marriage and regards certain foods as forbidden, though they are part of God's good creation (3).

5† for it is made holy by the invocation
of God in prayer.
Counsel to Timothy.† 6 If you will give
these instructions to the brothers, you
will be a good minister of Christ Jesus,
nourished on the words of the faith and
of the sound teaching you have fol-
lowed. 7* Avoid profane and silly
myths. Train yourself for devotion,
8* for, while physical training is of lim-
ited value, devotion is valuable in every
respect, since it holds a promise of life
both for the present and for the future.
9* This saying is trustworthy and de-
serves full acceptance. 10*† For this we
toil and struggle, because we have set
our hope on the living God, who is the
savior of all, especially of those who be-
lieve.
11† Command and teach these things.
12*† Let no one have contempt for your
youth, but set an example for those who
believe, in speech, conduct, love, faith,
and purity. 13† Until I arrive, attend to
the reading, exhortation, and teaching.
14*† Do not neglect the gift you have,
which was conferred on you through the
prophetic word with the imposition of
hands of the presbyterate. 15 Be diligent
in these matters, be absorbed in them,
so that your progress may be evident
to everyone. 16 Attend to yourself and
to your teaching; persevere in both
tasks, for by doing so you will save both
yourself and those who listen to you.

IV: DUTIES TOWARD OTHERS

CHAPTER 5

1*† Do not rebuke an older man, but
appeal to him as a father. Treat younger
men as brothers, 2 older women as
mothers, and younger women as sisters
with complete purity.
Rules for Widows. 3 Honor widows
who are truly widows. 4 But if a widow
has children or grandchildren, let these
first learn to perform their religious
duty to their own family and to make
recompense to their parents, for this is
pleasing to God. 5* The real widow, who
is all alone, has set her hope on God
and continues in supplications and
prayers night and day. 6 But the one
who is self-indulgent is dead while she
lives. 7 Command this, so that they may
be irreproachable. 8 And whoever does
not provide for relatives and especially
family members has denied the faith
and is worse than an unbeliever.
9 Let a widow be enrolled if she is not
less than sixty years old, married only
once, 10* with a reputation for good
works, namely, that she has raised chil-
dren, practiced hospitality, washed the
feet of the holy ones, helped those in
distress, involved herself in every good
work. 11 But exclude younger widows,
for when their sensuality estranges
them from Christ, they want to marry
12 and will incur condemnation for
breaking their first pledge. 13* And fur-
thermore, they learn to be idlers, going
about from house to house, and not only
idlers but gossips and busybodies as
well, talking about things that ought not
to be mentioned. 14* So I would like
younger widows to marry, have chil-
dren, and manage a home, so as to give
the adversary no pretext for maligning
us. 15 For some have already turned
away to follow Satan. 16† If any woman
believer has widowed relatives, she

*

7: 1, 4; 2 Tm 2, 16; Ti 1, 14.
8: 6, 6.
9: 1, 15; 2 Tm 2, 11; Ti 3, 8.
10: 2, 4; Ti 2, 11.
12: 1 Cor 16, 11; Ti 2, 15 / Phil 3, 17.
14: 5, 22; Acts 6, 6; 8, 17; 2 Tm 1, 6.
5, 1: Lv 19, 32; Ti 2, 2.
5: Jer 49, 11; Lk 2, 37; 18, 7.
10: Jn 13, 14; Heb 13, 2.
13: 2 Thes 3, 11.
14: 1 Cor 7, 9.

†

4, 5: *The invocation of God in prayer:* literally, "the word of God and petition." The use of "word of God" without an article in Greek suggests that it refers to the name of God being invoked in blessing rather than to the "word of God" proclaimed to the community.

4, 6-10: Timothy is urged to be faithful, both in his teaching and in his own life, as he looks only to God for salvation.

4, 10: *Struggle:* other manuscripts and patristic witnesses read "suffer reproach."

4, 11-16: Timothy is urged to preach and teach with confidence, relying on the gifts and the mission that God has bestowed on him.

4, 12: *Youth:* some commentators find this reference a sign of pseudepigraphy. Timothy had joined Paul as a missionary already in A.D. 49, some fifteen years before the earliest supposed date of composition.

4, 13: *Reading:* the Greek word refers to private or public reading. Here, it probably designates the public reading of scripture in the Christian assembly.

4, 14: *Prophetic word:* this may mean the utterance of a Christian prophet designating the candidate or a prayer of blessing accompanying the rite. *Imposition of hands:* this gesture was used in the Old Testament to signify the transmission of authority from Moses to Joshua (Nm 27, 18-23; Dt 34, 9). The early Christian community used it as a symbol of installation into an office: the Seven (Acts 6, 6) and Paul and Barnabas (Acts 13, 3). *Of the presbyterate:* this would mean that each member of the college of presbyters imposed hands and appears to contradict 2 Tm 1, 6, in which Paul says that he imposed hands on Timothy. This latter text, however, does not exclude participation by others in the rite. Some prefer to translate "for the presbyterate," and thus understand it to designate the office into which Timothy was installed rather than the agents who installed him.

5, 1-16: After a few words of general advice based on common sense (1-2), the letter takes up, in its several aspects, the subject of widows. The first responsibility for their care belongs to the family circle, not to the Christian community as such (3-4.16). The widow left without the aid of relatives may benefit the community by her prayer, and the community should consider her material sustenance its responsibility (5-8). Widows who wish to work directly for the Christian community should not be accepted unless they are well beyond the probability of marriage, i.e., sixty years of age, married only once, and with a reputation for good works (9-10). Younger widows are apt to be troublesome and should be encouraged to remarry (11-15).

5, 16: *Woman believer:* some early Latin manuscripts and Fathers have a masculine here, while most later manuscripts and patristic quotations conflate the two readings, perhaps to avoid unfair restriction to women.

must assist them; the church is not to be burdened, so that it will be able to help those who are truly widows.

Rules for Presbyters.† [17]* Presbyters who preside well deserve double honor, especially those who toil in preaching and teaching. [18]* For the scripture says, "You shall not muzzle an ox when it is threshing," and, "A worker deserves his pay." [19]* Do not accept an accusation against a presbyter unless it is supported by two or three witnesses. [20]* Reprimand publicly those who do sin, so that the rest also will be afraid. [21] I charge you before God and Christ Jesus and the elect angels to keep these rules without prejudice, doing nothing out of favoritism. [22]* Do not lay hands too readily on anyone, and do not share in another's sins. Keep yourself pure. [23] Stop drinking only water, but have a little wine for the sake of your stomach and your frequent illnesses.

[24] Some people's sins are public, preceding them to judgment; but other people are followed by their sins. [25] Similarly, good works are also public; and even those that are not cannot remain hidden.

CHAPTER 6

Rules for Slaves.† [1]*† Those who are under the yoke of slavery must regard their masters as worthy of full respect, so that the name of God and our teaching may not suffer abuse. [2]* Those whose masters are believers must not take advantage of them because they are brothers but must give better service because those who will profit from their work are believers and are beloved.

V: FALSE TEACHING AND TRUE WEALTH

† Teach and urge these things. [3]* Whoever teaches something different and does not agree with the sound words of our Lord Jesus Christ and the religious teaching [4] is conceited, understanding nothing, and has a morbid disposition for arguments and verbal disputes. From these come envy, rivalry, insults, evil suspicions, [5]* and mutual friction among people with corrupted minds, who are deprived of the truth, supposing religion to be a means of gain. [6]*† Indeed, religion with contentment is a great gain. [7]* For we brought nothing into the world, just as we shall not be able to take anything out of it. [8]* If we have food and clothing, we shall be content with that. [9]* Those who want to be rich are falling into temptation and into a trap and into many foolish and harmful desires, which plunge them into ruin and destruction. [10] For the love of money is the root of all evils, and some people in their desire for it have strayed from the faith and have pierced themselves with many pains.

Exhortations to Timothy.† [11]*† But you, man of God, avoid all this. Instead, pursue righteousness, devotion, faith, love, patience, and gentleness. [12]* Compete well for the faith. Lay hold of eternal life, to which you were called when you made the noble confession in the presence of many witnesses. [13]* I charge [you] before God, who gives life to all things, and before Christ Jesus, who gave testimony under Pontius

*

17: 1 Cor 16, 18; Phil 2, 29.
18: Dt 25, 4; 1 Cor 9, 8 / Mt 10, 10; Lk 10, 7.
19: Dt 17, 6; 19, 15; Mt 18, 16; 2 Cor 13, 1.
20: Gal 2, 14; Eph 5, 11; 2 Tm 4, 2; Ti 1, 9.13.
22: 4, 14; 2 Tm 1, 6.
6, 1: Eph 6, 5; Ti 2, 9-10.
2: Phlm 16.
3: Gal 1, 6-9; 2 Tm 1, 13; Ti 1, 1.
5: 2 Tm 3, 8; 4, 4; Ti 1, 14.
6: 4, 8; Phil 4, 11-12; Heb 13, 5.
7: Jb 1, 21; Eccl 5, 14.
8: Prv 30, 8.
9: Prv 23, 4; 28, 22.
11: 2 Tm 2, 22.
12: 1 Cor 9, 26; 2 Tm 4, 7.
13: Jn 18, 36-37; 19, 11.

†

5, 17-25: The function of presbyters is not exactly the same as that of the *episkopos*, "bishop" (3, 1); in fact, the relation of the two at the time of this letter is obscure (but cf the note on Ti 1, 5-9). The Pastorals seem to reflect a transitional stage that developed in many regions of the church into the monarchical episcopate of the second and third centuries. The presbyters possess the responsibility of preaching and teaching, for which functions they are supported by the community (17-18). The realization that their position subjects them to adverse criticism is implied in the direction to Timothy (19-20) to make sure of the truth of any accusation against them before public reproof is given. He must be as objective as possible in weighing charges against presbyters (21), learning from his experience to take care in selecting them (22). Some scholars take v 22 as a reference not to ordination of presbyters but to reconciliation of public sinners. The letter now sounds an informal note of personal concern in its advice to Timothy not to be so ascetic that he even avoids wine (23). Judgment concerning the fitness of candidates to serve as presbyters is easy with persons of open conduct, more difficult and prolonged with those of greater reserve (24-25).

6, 1-2: Compare the tables for household duties, such as that of Col 3, 18—4, 1. Domestic relationships derive new meaning from the Christian faith.

6, 1: *Our teaching:* this refers to the teaching of the Christian community.

6, 2b-10: Timothy is exhorted to maintain steadfastly the position outlined in this letter, not allowing himself to be pressured into any other course. He must realize that false teachers can be discerned by their pride, envy, quarrelsomeness, and greed for material gain. Verse 6 is rather obscure and is interpreted, and therefore translated, variously. The suggestion seems to be that the important gain that religion brings is spiritual, but that there is material gain, too, up to the point of what is needed for physical sustenance (cf 17-19).

6, 6: *Contentment:* the word *autarkeia* is a technical Greek philosophical term for the virtue of independence from material goods (Aristotle, Cynics, Stoics).

6, 11-16: Timothy's position demands total dedication to God and faultless witness to Christ (11-14) operating from an awareness, through faith, of the coming revelation in Jesus of the invisible God (15-16).

6, 11: *Man of God:* a title applied to Moses and the prophets (Dt 33, 1; 1 Sm 2, 27; 1 Kgs 12, 22; 13, 1; etc.).

Pilate for the noble confession, 14 to keep the commandment without stain or reproach until the appearance of our Lord Jesus Christ 15* that the blessed and only ruler will make manifest at the proper time, the King of kings and Lord of lords, 16* who alone has immortality, who dwells in unapproachable light, and whom no human being has seen or can see. To him be honor and eternal power. Amen.

Right Use of Wealth.† 17* Tell the rich in the present age not to be proud and not to rely on so uncertain a thing as wealth but rather on God, who richly provides us with all things for our enjoyment. 18 Tell them to do good, to be rich in good works, to be generous, ready to share, 19* thus accumulating as treasure a good foundation for the future, so as to win the life that is true life.

VI: FINAL RECOMMENDATION AND WARNING†

20* O Timothy, guard what has been entrusted to you. Avoid profane babbling and the absurdities of so-called knowledge. 21* By professing it, some people have deviated from the faith.

Grace be with all of you.

*

15: 2 Mc 13, 4; Rv 17, 14.
16: Ex 33, 20; Ps 104, 2.
17: Ps 62, 11; Lk 12, 20.
19: Mt 6, 20.
20: 2 Tm 1, 14 / 4, 7.
21: 1, 6; 2 Tm 2, 18.

†

6, 17-19: Timothy is directed to instruct the rich, advising them to make good use of their wealth by aiding the poor.

6, 20-21: A final solemn warning against the heretical teachers, with what seems to be a specific reference to gnosticism, the great rival and enemy of the church for two centuries and more (the Greek word for "knowledge" is *gnōsis*). If gnosticism is being referred to here, it is probable that the warnings against "speculations" and "myths and genealogies" (cf especially 1, 4; Ti 3, 9) involve allusions to that same kind of heresy. Characteristic of the various gnostic systems of speculation was an elaborate mythology of innumerable superhuman intermediaries, on a descending scale ("genealogies"), between God and the world. Thus would be explained the emphasis upon Christ's being the *one* mediator (as in 2, 5). Although fully developed gnosticism belonged to the second and later centuries, there are signs that incipient forms of it belonged to Paul's own period.

The Second Letter to

TIMOTHY

The authorship and date of this letter, as one of the Pastoral Epistles, are discussed in the Introduction to the First Letter to Timothy.

The tone here is more personal than in First Timothy, for this letter addresses Timothy in vivid terms (1, 6-14; 2, 1-13) and depicts Paul's courage and hope in the face of discouragements late in the course of his apostolic ministry (1, 15-18; 3, 10-17; 4, 9-18). Indeed, the letter takes on the character of a final exhortation and testament from Paul to the younger Timothy (4, 1-8). Paul is portrayed as a prisoner (1, 8.16; 2, 9) in Rome (1, 17), and there is a hint that Timothy may be in Ephesus (2, 17). The letter reveals that, with rare exceptions, Christians have not rallied to Paul's support (1, 15-18) and takes a pessimistic view of the outcome of his case (4, 6). It describes Paul as fully aware of what impends, looking to God, not to human beings, for his deliverance (4, 3-8.18). It recalls his mission days with Timothy (1, 3-5; cf Acts 16, 1-4). It points to his preaching of the gospel as the reason for his imprisonment and offers Timothy, as a motive for steadfastness, his own example of firmness in faith despite adverse circumstances (1, 6-14). The letter suggests that Timothy should prepare others to replace himself as Paul has prepared Timothy to replace him (2, 1-2). Paul urges him not to desist out of fear from preserving and spreading the Christian message (2, 3-7). It presents the resurrection of Jesus and his messianic role as the heart of the gospel for which Paul has been ready to lay down his life (2, 8-9) and thus not only to express his own conviction fully but to support the conviction of others (2, 10-13).

This letter, like the preceding one, urges Timothy to protect the community from the inevitable impact of false teaching (2, 14—3, 9), without fear of the personal attacks that may result (3, 10-13). It recommends that he rely on the power of the scriptures, on proclamation of the word, and on sound doctrine (3, 14—4, 2), without being troubled by those who do not accept him (4, 3-5). The letter poignantly observes in passing that Paul has need of his reading materials and his cloak (4, 13) and, what will be best of all, a visit from Timothy.

On the theory of authorship by Paul himself, Second Timothy appears to be the last of the three Pastoral Epistles. The many scholars who argue that the Pastorals are products of the Pauline school often incline toward Second Timothy as the earliest of the three and the one most likely to have actual fragments of material from Paul himself.

The principal divisions of the Second Letter to Timothy are the following:

I: Address (1, 1-5)
II: Exhortations to Timothy (1, 6—2, 13)
III: Instructions Concerning False Teaching (2, 14—4, 8)
IV: Personal Requests and Final Greetings (4, 9-22)

I: ADDRESS

CHAPTER 1

Greeting.† 1*† Paul, an apostle of Christ Jesus by the will of God for the promise of life in Christ Jesus, 2 to Timothy, my dear child: grace, mercy, and peace from God the Father and Christ Jesus our Lord.

* 1, 1: 1 Tm 4, 8.

† 1, 1-2: For the formula of address and greeting, see the note on Rom 1, 1-7.

1, 1: *The promise of life in Christ Jesus:* that God grants through union with Christ in faith and love; cf Col 3, 4; 1 Tm 4, 8.

Thanksgiving. 3*† I am grateful to God, whom I worship with a clear conscience as my ancestors did, as I remember you constantly in my prayers, night and day. 4† I yearn to see you again, recalling your tears, so that I may be filled with joy, 5* as I recall your sincere faith that first lived in your grandmother Lois and in your mother Eunice and that I am confident lives also in you.

II: EXHORTATIONS TO TIMOTHY

The Gifts Timothy Has Received. 6*† For this reason, I remind you to stir into flame the gift of God that you have through the imposition of my hands. 7* For God did not give us a spirit of cowardice but rather of power and love and self-control. 8*† So do not be ashamed of your testimony to our Lord, nor of me, a prisoner for his sake; but bear your share of hardship for the gospel with the strength that comes from God.

9*† He saved us and called us to a holy life, not according to our works but according to his own design and the grace bestowed on us in Christ Jesus before time began, 10* but now made manifest through the appearance of our savior Christ Jesus, who destroyed death and brought life and immortality to light through the gospel, 11*† for which I was appointed preacher and apostle and teacher. 12*† On this account I am suffering these things; but I am not ashamed, for I know him in whom I have believed and am confident that he is able to guard what has been entrusted to me until that day. 13* Take as your norm the sound words that you heard from me, in the faith and love that are in Christ Jesus. 14* Guard this rich trust with the help of the holy Spirit that dwells within us.

Paul's Suffering. 15*† You know that everyone in Asia deserted me, including Phygelus and Hermogenes. 16*† May the Lord grant mercy to the family of Onesiphorus because he often gave me new heart and was not ashamed of my chains. 17 But when he came to Rome, he promptly searched for me and found me. 18*† May the Lord grant him to find mercy from the Lord on that day. And you know very well the services he rendered in Ephesus.

CHAPTER 2

Timothy's Conduct. † 1 So you, my child, be strong in the grace that is in Christ Jesus. 2 And what you heard from me through many witnesses entrust to faithful people who will have the ability to teach others as well. 3* Bear your share of hardship along with me like a good soldier of Christ Jesus. 4* To satisfy the one who recruited him, a soldier does not become entangled in the business affairs of life. 5* Similarly, an athlete cannot receive the winner's crown except by competing according to the rules. 6* The hardworking farmer ought to have the first share of the crop. 7* Reflect on what I am saying, for the Lord will give you understanding in everything.

*

3: 1 Tm 3, 9 / Phil 3, 5.
5: 1 Tm 1, 5 / Acts 16, 1.
6: 1 Tm 4, 14; 5, 22 / Acts 6, 6; 8, 17.
7: Rom 5, 5; 8, 15; 1 Cor 2, 4.
8: 2, 3.15; Rom 1, 16.
9: Eph 2, 8-9; Ti 3, 5 / Eph 1, 4; Ti 1, 2.
10: Rom 16, 26; 1 Pt 1, 20 / 1 Tm 6, 14 / Phil 3, 20; Ti 1, 4; 2, 13; 2 Pt 1, 11 / 1 Cor 15, 54-55; Heb 2, 14 / 1 Cor 15, 53-54.
11: 1 Tm 2, 7.
12: 1 Pt 4, 16 / 1 Tm 1, 10-11.
13: 1 Tm 1, 14.
14: 1 Tm 6, 20 / Rom 8, 11.
15: 4, 16.
16: 4, 19.
18: Jude 21.
2, 3: 1, 8; 4, 5; Phlm 2.
4: 1 Cor 9, 6.
5: 1 Cor 9, 25.
6: 1 Cor 9, 7-10.
7: Prv 2, 6.

†

1, 3: *As my ancestors did:* this emphasizes the continuity of Judaism and Christianity; for a similar view, see Rom 9, 3-5; Phil 3, 4-6.

1, 4-5: Purportedly written from prison in Rome (8.17; 4, 6-8) shortly before the writer's death, the letter recalls the earlier sorrowful parting from Timothy, commending him for his faith and expressing the longing to see him again.

1, 6: *The gift of God:* the grace resulting from the conferral of an ecclesiastical office. *The imposition of my hands:* see the note on 1 Tm 4, 14.

1, 8: *Do not be ashamed of your testimony to our Lord:* i.e., of preaching and suffering for the sake of the gospel.

1, 9-10: Redemption from sin and the call to holiness of life are not won by personal deeds but are freely and graciously bestowed according to God's eternal plan; cf Eph 1, 4.

1, 11: *Teacher:* the overwhelming majority of manuscripts and Fathers read "teacher of the nations," undoubtedly a harmonization with 1 Tm 2, 7.

1, 12: *He is able to guard . . . until that day:* the intervening words can also be translated "what I have entrusted to him" (i.e., the fruit of his ministry) as well as "what has been entrusted to me" (i.e., the faith). The same difficult term occurs in v 14, where it is modified by the adjective "rich" and used without a possessive.

1, 15: Keen disappointment is expressed, here and later (4, 16), that the Christians of the province of Asia, especially Phygelus and Hermogenes, should have abandoned the writer and done nothing to defend his case in court.

1, 16-18: *The family of Onesiphorus because he . . . of my chains:* Onesiphorus seems to have died before this letter was written. His family is mentioned twice (here and in 4, 19), though it was Onesiphorus himself who was helpful to Paul in prison and rendered much service to the community of Ephesus. Because the apostle complains of abandonment by all in Asia during his second imprisonment and trial, the assistance of Onesiphorus seems to have been given to Paul during his first Roman imprisonment (A.D. 61-63).

1, 18: *Lord . . . Lord:* the first "Lord" here seems to refer to Christ, the second "Lord" to the Father.

2, 1-7: This passage manifests a characteristic deep concern for safeguarding the faith and faithfully transmitting it through trustworthy people (1-2; cf 1, 14; 1 Tm 6, 20; Ti 1, 9). Comparisons to the soldier's detachment, the athlete's sportsmanship, and the farmer's arduous work as the price of recompense (4-6) emphasize the need of singleness of purpose in preaching the word, even at the cost of hardship, for the sake of Christ (3).

8*† Remember Jesus Christ, raised from the dead, a descendant of David: such is my gospel, 9* for which I am suffering, even to the point of chains, like a criminal. But the word of God is not chained. 10* Therefore, I bear with everything for the sake of those who are chosen, so that they too may obtain the salvation that is in Christ Jesus, together with eternal glory. 11* This saying is trustworthy:

If we have died with him
  we shall also live with him;
12* if we persevere
  we shall also reign with him.
But if we deny him
  he will deny us.
13* If we are unfaithful
  he remains faithful,
  for he cannot deny himself.

III: INSTRUCTIONS CONCERNING FALSE TEACHING

***Warning against Useless Disputes.*†**
14*† Remind people of these things and charge them before God to stop disputing about words. This serves no useful purpose since it harms those who listen. 15* Be eager to present yourself as acceptable to God, a workman who causes no disgrace, imparting the word of truth without deviation. 16* Avoid profane, idle talk, for such people will become more and more godless, 17* and their teaching will spread like gangrene. Among them are Hymenaeus and Philetus, 18* who have deviated from the truth by saying that [the] resurrection has already taken place and are upsetting the faith of some. 19* Nevertheless, God's solid foundation stands, bearing this inscription, "The Lord knows those who are his"; and, "Let everyone who calls upon the name of the Lord avoid evil."

20 In a large household there are vessels not only of gold and silver but also of wood and clay, some for lofty and others for humble use. 21* If anyone cleanses himself of these things, he will be a vessel for lofty use, dedicated, beneficial to the master of the house, ready for every good work. 22*† So turn from youthful desires and pursue righteousness, faith, love, and peace, along with those who call on the Lord with purity of heart. 23* Avoid foolish and ignorant debates, for you know that they breed quarrels. 24* A slave of the Lord should not quarrel, but should be gentle with everyone, able to teach, tolerant, 25* correcting opponents with kindness. It may be that God will grant them repentance that leads to knowledge of the truth, 26*† and that they may return to their senses out of the devil's snare, where they are entrapped by him, for his will.

CHAPTER 3

***The Dangers of the Last Days.*†**
1* But understand this: there will be terrifying times in the last days. 2* People will be self-centered and lovers of money, proud, haughty, abusive, disobedient to their parents, ungrateful, irreligious, 3 callous, implacable, slanderous, licentious, brutal, hating what is good, 4 traitors, reckless, conceited,

*

8: Rom 1, 3; 1 Cor 15, 4.20 / Rom 2, 16; Gal 1, 11; 2, 2.
9: Phil 1, 12-14.
10: Col 1, 24; 1 Tm 1, 15.
11: Rom 6, 8.
12: Mt 10, 22.33; Lk 12, 9.
13: Nm 23, 19; Rom 3, 3-4; 1 Cor 10, 13; Ti 1, 2.
14: 1 Tm 6, 4.
15: 1, 8; 2 Cor 6, 7; Eph 1, 13; Col 1, 5.
16: 1 Tm 4, 7.
17: 1 Tm 1, 20.
18: 2 Thes 2, 2.
19: Is 28, 16; 1 Cor 3, 10-15 / Nm 16, 5; Jn 10, 14.
21: 3, 17.
22: Gal 5, 22; 1 Tm 6, 11 / Rom 10, 13; 1 Cor 1, 2.
23: 1 Tm 1, 4; 4, 7; 6, 4; Ti 3, 9.
24: 1 Tm 3, 2-3.
25: 3, 7; 1 Tm 2, 4.
26: 1 Tm 3, 7.
3, 1: 1 Tm 4, 1; 2 Pt 3, 3; Jude 18.
2-4: Rom 1, 29-31.

†

2, 8-13: The section begins with a sloganlike summary of Paul's gospel about Christ (8) and concludes with what may be part of an early Christian hymn (11b-12a; most exegetes include the rest of v 12 and all of v 13 as part of the quotation). The poetic lines suggest that through baptism Christians die spiritually with Christ and hope to live with him and reign with him forever, but the Christian life includes endurance, witness, and even suffering, as the final judgment will show and as Paul's own case makes clear; while he is imprisoned for preaching the gospel (9), his sufferings are helpful to the elect for obtaining the salvation and glory available in Christ (10), who will be true to those who are faithful and will disown those who deny him (12-13).

2, 14-19: For those who dispute about mere words (cf 23-24) and indulge in irreligious talk to the detriment of their listeners (16-19), see the notes on 1 Tm 1, 3-7; 6, 20-21. Hymenaeus and Philetus (17), while accepting the Christian's mystical death and resurrection in Christ through baptism, claimed that baptized Christians are already risen with Christ in this life and thus that there is no future bodily resurrection or eternal glory to come. The first quotation in v 19 is from Nm 16, 5; the other quotation is from some unidentified Jewish or Christian writing.

2, 14: *Before God:* many ancient manuscripts read "before the Lord."

2, 22: *Those who call on the Lord:* those who believe in Christ and worship him as Lord, i.e., Christians (Acts 9, 14-16.20-21; Rom 10, 12-13; cf 19, literally, "Everyone who names the name of the Lord").

2, 26: Some interpreters would render this passage, "Thus they may come to their senses and, forced to do his (i.e., God's) will, may escape the devil's trap." This interpretation of the Greek is possible, but the one accepted in the text seems more likely.

3, 1-9: The moral depravity and false teaching that will be rampant in the last days are already at work (1-5). The frivolous and superficial, too, devoid of the true spirit of religion, will be easy victims of those who pervert them by falsifying the truth (6-8), just as Jannes and Jambres, Pharaoh's magicians of Egypt (Ex 7, 11-12.22), discredited the truth in Moses' time. Exodus does not name the magicians, but the two names are widely found in much later Jewish, Christian, and even pagan writings. Their origins are legendary.

lovers of pleasure rather than lovers of
God, 5* as they make a pretense of reli-
gion but deny its power. Reject them.
6* For some of these slip into homes and
make captives of women weighed down
by sins, led by various desires,
7* always trying to learn but never able
to reach a knowledge of the truth.
8* Just as Jannes and Jambres opposed
Moses, so they also oppose the truth—
people of depraved mind, unqualified
in the faith. 9 But they will not make
further progress, for their foolishness
will be plain to all, as it was with those
two.

***Paul's Example and Teaching.*†**
10 You have followed my teaching, way
of life, purpose, faith, patience, love,
endurance, 11* persecutions, and suffer-
ings, such as happened to me in Anti-
och, Iconium, and Lystra, persecutions
that I endured. Yet from all these things
the Lord delivered me. 12* In fact, all
who want to live religiously in Christ Je-
sus will be persecuted. 13 But wicked
people and charlatans will go from bad
to worse, deceivers and deceived.
14* But you, remain faithful to what you
have learned and believed, because you
know from whom you learned it, 15* and
that from infancy you have known [the]
sacred scriptures, which are capable of
giving you wisdom for salvation
through faith in Christ Jesus. 16*† All
scripture is inspired by God and is
useful for teaching, for refutation, for
correction, and for training in righ-
teousness, 17* so that one who belongs
to God may be competent, equipped for
every good work.

CHAPTER 4

***Solemn Charge.*†** 1* I charge you in
the presence of God and of Christ Jesus,
who will judge the living and the dead,
and by his appearing and his kingly
power: 2* proclaim the word; be per-
sistent whether it is convenient or
inconvenient; convince, reprimand, en-
courage through all patience and teach-
ing. 3*† For the time will come when
people will not tolerate sound doctrine
but, following their own desires and in-
satiable curiosity, will accumulate
teachers 4* and will stop listening to the
truth and will be diverted to myths.
5 But you, be self-possessed in all cir-
cumstances; put up with hardship; per-
form the work of an evangelist; fulfill
your ministry.

Reward for Fidelity. 6*† For I am al-
ready being poured out like a libation,
and the time of my departure is at hand.
7*† I have competed well; I have fin-
ished the race; I have kept the faith.
8*† From now on the crown of righ-
teousness awaits me, which the Lord,
the just judge, will award to me on that
day, and not only to me, but to all who
have longed for his appearance.

IV: PERSONAL REQUESTS AND FINAL GREETINGS

***Paul's Loneliness.*†** 9 Try to join me
soon, 10*† for Demas, enamored of the
present world, deserted me and went to

---

*

5: Rom 2, 20-22; Ti 1, 16.
6: Ti 1, 11.
7: 2, 25.
8: Ex 7, 11.22; 1 Tm 6, 5.
11: Acts 13, 50; 14, 5.19 / Ps 34, 20.
12: Jn 15, 20; Acts 14, 22.
14: 2, 2.
15: Jn 5, 39.
16: Rom 15, 4; 2 Pt 1, 19-21.
17: 2, 21.
4, 1: 1 Tm 5, 21; 6, 14 / Acts 10, 42; Rom 14, 9-10; 1 Pt 4, 5.
2: Acts 20, 20.31; 1 Tm 5, 20.
3: 1 Tm 4, 1.
4: 1 Tm 1, 4; 4, 7; Ti 1, 14.
6: Phil 2, 17.
7: 1 Tm 1, 18; 6, 12; Jude 3 / Acts 20, 24; 1 Cor 9, 24; Heb 12, 1.
8: 2, 5; Wis 5, 16; 1 Cor 9, 25; Phil 3, 14; Jas 1, 12; 1 Pt 5, 4; Rv 2, 10.
10: Col 4, 14; Phlm 24 / 2 Cor 2, 13; 7, 6-7; 8, 23; Gal 2, 3; Ti 1, 4.

---

†

3, 10-17: Paul's example for Timothy includes persecution, a frequent emphasis in the Pastorals. Timothy is to be steadfast to what he has been taught and to scripture. The scriptures are the source of wisdom, i.e., of belief in and loving fulfillment of God's word revealed in Christ, through whom salvation is given.

3, 16: *All scripture is inspired by God:* this could possibly also be translated, "All scripture inspired by God is useful for. . . ." In this classic reference to inspiration, God is its principal author, with the writer as the human collaborator. Thus the scriptures are the word of God in human language. See also 2 Pt 1, 20-21.

3, 16-17: *Useful for teaching . . . every good work:* because as God's word the scriptures share his divine authority. It is exercised through those who are ministers of the word.

4, 1-5: The gravity of the obligation incumbent on Timothy to preach the word can be gauged from the solemn adjuration: in the presence of God, and of Christ coming as universal judge, and by his appearance and his kingly power (1). Patience, courage, constancy, and endurance are required despite the opposition, hostility, indifference, and defection of many to whom the truth has been preached (2-5).

4, 3: *Insatiable curiosity:* literally, "with itching ears."

4, 6: The apostle recognizes his death through martyrdom to be imminent. He regards it as an act of worship in which his blood will be poured out in sacrifice; cf Ex 29, 38-40; Phil 2, 17.

4, 7: At the close of his life Paul could testify to the accomplishment of what Christ himself foretold concerning him at the time of his conversion, "I will show him what he will have to suffer for my name" (Acts 9, 16).

4, 8: When the world is judged at the parousia, all who have eagerly looked for the Lord's appearing and have sought to live according to his teachings will be rewarded. The crown is a reference to the laurel wreath placed on the heads of victorious athletes and conquerors in war; cf 2, 5; 1 Cor 9, 25.

4, 9-13: Demas either abandoned the work of the ministry for worldly affairs or, perhaps, gave up the faith itself (10). Luke (11) may have accompanied Paul on parts of his second and third missionary journeys (Acts 16, 10-12; 20, 5-7). Notice the presence of the first personal pronoun "we" in these Acts passages, suggesting to some that Luke (or at least some traveling companion of Paul's) was the author of Acts. Mark, once rejected by Paul (Acts 13, 13; 15, 39), is now to render him a great service (11); cf Col 4, 10; Phlm 24. For Tychicus, see Eph 6, 21; cf also Acts 20, 4; Col 4, 7.

4, 10: *Galatia:* some manuscripts read "Gaul" or "Gallia."

Thessalonica, Crescens to Galatia, and
Titus to Dalmatia. 11* Luke is the only
one with me. Get Mark and bring him
with you, for he is helpful to me in the
ministry. 12* I have sent Tychicus to
Ephesus. 13* When you come, bring the
cloak I left with Carpus in Troas, the
papyrus rolls, and especially the parch-
ments.
14*† Alexander the coppersmith did
me a great deal of harm; the Lord will
repay him according to his deeds.
15 You too be on guard against him,
for he has strongly resisted our preach-
ing.
16* At my first defense no one ap-
peared on my behalf, but everyone de-
serted me. May it not be held against
them! 17* But the Lord stood by me and
gave me strength, so that through me
the proclamation might be completed
and all the Gentiles might hear it. And
I was rescued from the lion's mouth.
18* The Lord will rescue me from every
evil threat and will bring me safe to his
heavenly kingdom. To him be glory for-
ever and ever. Amen.
Final Greeting. 19*† Greet Prisca and
Aquila and the family of Onesiphorus.
20*† Erastus remained in Corinth, while
I left Trophimus sick at Miletus. 21† Try
to get here before winter. Eubulus, Pu-
dens, Linus, Claudia, and all the broth-
ers send greetings.
22* The Lord be with your spirit.
Grace be with all of you.

*

11: Col 4, 14; Phlm 24 / Col 4, 10; Phlm 24.
12: Acts 20, 4; Eph 6, 21; Col 4, 7.
13: Acts 16, 8; 20, 6.
14: 1 Tm 1, 20 / 2 Sm 3, 39; Pss 28, 4; 62, 12; Prv 24, 12; Rom 2, 6.
16: 1, 15.
17: Acts 23, 11; 27, 23; Phil 4, 13 / 1 Mc 2, 60; Ps 22, 22; Dn 6, 23.
18: 2 Cor 1, 10 / Rom 16, 27.
19: Acts 18, 2; Rom 16, 3; 1 Cor 16, 19 / 1, 16.
20: Acts 19, 22; Rom 16, 24 / Acts 20, 4; 21, 29.
22: Gal 6, 18; Phil 4, 23; Col 4, 18; 1 Tm 6, 21; Ti 3, 15.

†

4, 14-18: *Alexander:* an opponent of Paul's preaching (14-15), perhaps the one who is mentioned in 1 Tm 1, 20. Despite Paul's abandonment by his friends in the province of Asia (cf 1, 15-16), the divine assistance brought this first trial to a successful issue, even to the point of making the gospel message known to those who participated in or witnessed the trial (16-17).

4, 19: *Prisca and Aquila:* they assisted Paul in his ministry in Corinth (Acts 18, 2-3) and Ephesus (Acts 18, 19.26; 1 Cor 16, 19). They risked death to save his life, and all the Gentile communities are indebted to them (Rom 16, 3-5).

4, 20: *Erastus:* he was the treasurer of the city of Corinth (Rom 16, 24); cf also Acts 19, 22. *Trophimus:* from the province of Asia, he accompanied Paul from Greece to Troas (Acts 20, 4-5).

4, 21: *Linus:* Western tradition sometimes identified this Linus with the supposed successor of Peter as bishop of Rome, and Claudia as the mother of Linus (*Apostolic Constitutions,* fourth century).

The Letter to

TITUS

The third of the Pastoral Epistles in the New Testament is addressed to a different co-worker of Paul than are First and Second Timothy. The situation is different, too, for Titus is addressed as the person in charge of developing the church on the large Mediterranean island of Crete (1, 5), a place Paul had never, according to the New Testament, visited. The tone is closer to that of First Timothy as three topics of church life and structure are discussed: presbyter-bishops (see the note on 1, 5-9), groups with which one must work in the church (2, 1-10), and admonitions for conduct based on the grace and love of God that appeared in Jesus Christ (2, 11—3, 10). The warmer personal tone of Second Timothy is replaced by emphasis on church office and on living in the society of the day, in which deceivers and heretics abound (1, 10-16; 3, 9-10).

The Pauline assistant who is addressed, Titus, was a Gentile Christian, but we are nowhere informed of his place of birth or residence. He went from Antioch with Paul and Barnabas to Jerusalem (Gal 2, 1; cf Acts 15, 2). According to 2 Corinthians (2, 13; 7, 6.13-14), he was with Paul on his third missionary journey; his name, however, does not appear in Acts. Besides being the bearer of Paul's severe letter to the Corinthians (2 Cor 7, 6-8), he had the responsibility of taking up the collection in Corinth for the Christian community of Jerusalem (2 Cor 8, 6.16-19.23). In the present letter (1, 5), he is mentioned as the administrator of the Christian community in Crete, charged with the task of organizing it through the appointment of presbyters and bishops (1, 5-9; here the two terms refer to the same personages).

The letter instructs Titus about the character of the assistants he is to choose in view of the pastoral difficulties peculiar to Crete (1, 5-16). It suggests the special individual and social virtues that the various age groups and classes in the Christian community should be encouraged to acquire (2, 1-10). The motivation for transformation of their lives comes from christology, especially the redemptive sacrifice of Christ and his future coming, as applied through baptism and justification (2, 11-14; 3, 4-8). The community is to serve as a leaven for Christianizing the social world about it (3, 1-3). Good works are to be the evidence of their faith in God (3, 8); those who engage in religious controversy are, after suitable warning, to be ignored (3, 9-11).

The authorship and date of the Letter to Titus are discussed in the Introduction to 1 Timothy. Those who assume authorship by Paul himself usually place Titus after 1 Timothy and before 2 Timothy. Others see it as closely related to 1 Timothy, in a growing emphasis on church structure and opposition to heresy, later than the letters of Paul himself and 2 Timothy. It has also been suggested that, if the three Pastorals once circulated as a literary unit, Titus was meant to be read ahead of 1 and 2 Timothy.

The principal divisions of the Letter to Titus are the following:

I: Address (1, 1-4)
II: Pastoral Charge (1, 5-16)
III: Teaching the Christian Life (2, 1—3, 15)

I: ADDRESS

CHAPTER 1

***Greeting.*†** 1* Paul, a slave of God and apostle of Jesus Christ for the sake of the faith of God's chosen ones and the recognition of religious truth, 2* in the hope of eternal life that God, who does not lie, promised before time began, 3* who indeed at the proper time revealed his word in the proclamation with which I was entrusted by the command of God our savior, 4* to Titus, my true child in our common faith: grace and peace from God the Father and Christ Jesus our savior.

II: PASTORAL CHARGE

***Titus in Crete.*†** 5 For this reason I left you in Crete so that you might set right what remains to be done and appoint presbyters in every town, as I directed you, 6* on condition that a man be blameless, married only once, with believing children who are not accused of licentiousness or rebellious. 7 For a bishop as God's steward must be blameless, not arrogant, not irritable, not a drunkard, not aggressive, not greedy for sordid gain, 8 but hospitable, a lover of goodness, temperate, just, holy, and self-controlled, 9* holding fast to the true message as taught so that he will be able both to exhort with sound doctrine and to refute opponents. 10† For there are also many rebels, idle talkers and deceivers, especially the Jewish Christians. 11 It is imperative to silence them, as they are upsetting whole families by teaching for sordid gain what they should not. 12† One of them, a prophet of their own, once said, "Cretans have always been liars, vicious beasts, and lazy gluttons." 13* That testimony is true. Therefore, admonish them sharply, so that they may be sound in the faith, 14* instead of paying attention to Jewish myths and regulations of people who have repudiated the truth. 15* To the clean all things are clean, but to those who are defiled and unbelieving nothing is clean; in fact, both their minds and their consciences are tainted. 16 They claim to know God, but by their deeds they deny him. They are vile and disobedient and unqualified for any good deed.

TITUS

III: TEACHING THE CHRISTIAN LIFE

CHAPTER 2

***Christian Behavior.*†** 1* As for yourself, you must say what is consistent with sound doctrine, namely, 2 that older men should be temperate, dignified, self-controlled, sound in faith, love, and endurance. 3 Similarly, older women should be reverent in their behavior, not slanderers, not addicted to drink, teaching what is good, 4 so that they may train younger women to love their husbands and children, 5* to be self-controlled, chaste, good homemakers, under the control of their husbands, so that the word of God may not be discredited.

6 Urge the younger men, similarly, to control themselves, 7 showing yourself as a model of good deeds in every respect, with integrity in your teaching, dignity, 8 and sound speech that cannot be criticized, so that the opponent will be put to shame without anything bad to say about us.

9* Slaves are to be under the control of their masters in all respects, giving them satisfaction, not talking back to

*

1, 1: 1 Tm 2, 4; 4, 3; 2 Tm 2, 25; 3, 7; Heb 10, 26.
2: 3, 7; 2 Tm 1, 1; 1 Jn 2, 25.
3: 2, 10; 3, 4; Ps 24, 5; 1 Tm 1, 1; 2, 3; 4, 10; Jude 25.
4: 2, 13; 3, 6; Phil 3, 20; 2 Tm 1, 10; 2 Pt 1, 1.11; 2, 20; 3, 2.18.
6-7: 1 Tm 3, 2-7; 2 Tm 2, 24-26.
9: 1, 13; 2, 1-2.8; 1 Tm 1, 10; 6, 3; 2 Tm 1, 13; 4, 3.
13: 1, 9.
14: 3, 9; 1 Tm 1, 4; 4, 7; 2 Tm 4, 4; 2 Pt 1, 16.
15: Mk 7, 18-23; Acts 10, 15; Rom 14, 14-23.
2, 1: 1, 9.13; 2, 8; 1 Tm 1, 10; 6, 3; 2 Tm 1, 13; 4, 3.
5: 1 Cor 11, 3; 14, 34; Eph 5, 22-24; Col 3, 18; 1 Tm 2, 11-15; 1 Pt 3, 1-6.
9: 1 Cor 7, 21-22; Eph 6, 5-8; Col 3, 22-25; 1 Tm 6, 1-2; 1 Pt 2, 18.

†

1, 1-4: On the epistolary form, see the note on Rom 1, 1-7. The apostolate is the divinely appointed mission to lead others to the true faith and through it to eternal salvation (1-3).

1, 5-9: This instruction on the selection and appointment of presbyters, substantially identical with that in 1 Tm 3, 1-7 on a bishop (see the note there), was aimed at strengthening the authority of Titus by apostolic mandate; cf 2, 15. In vv 5.7 and Acts 20, 17.28, the terms *episkopos* and *presbyteros* ("bishop" and "presbyter") refer to the same persons. Deacons are not mentioned in Titus. See also the note on Phil 1, 1.

1, 10-16: This adverse criticism of the defects within the community is directed especially against certain Jewish Christians, who busy themselves with useless speculations over persons mentioned in the Old Testament, insist on the observance of Jewish ritual purity regulations, and thus upset whole families by teaching things they have no right to teach; cf 3, 9; 1 Tm 1, 3-10.

1, 10: *Jewish Christians:* literally, "those of the circumcision."

1, 12: *Cretans . . . gluttons:* quoted from Epimenides, a Cretan poet of the sixth century B.C.

2, 1-10: One of Titus' main tasks in Crete is to become acquainted with the character of the Cretans and thereby learn to cope with its deficiencies (see 1, 12). The counsel is not only for Titus himself but for various classes of people with whom he must deal: older men and women (2-4), younger women and men (4-7), and slaves (9-10); cf Eph 6, 1-9; Col 3, 18—4, 1.

them 10* or stealing from them, but ex-
hibiting complete good faith, so as to
adorn the doctrine of God our savior in
every way.

Transformation of Life.† 11* For the
grace of God has appeared, saving all
12 and training us to reject godless ways
and worldly desires and to live temper-
ately, justly, and devoutly in this age,
13*† as we await the blessed hope, the
appearance of the glory of the great
God and of our savior Jesus Christ,
14* who gave himself for us to deliver
us from all lawlessness and to cleanse
for himself a people as his own, eager
to do what is good.

15* Say these things. Exhort and cor-
rect with all authority. Let no one look
down on you.

CHAPTER 3

1*† Remind them to be under the con-
trol of magistrates and authorities, to
be obedient, to be open to every good
enterprise. 2 They are to slander no one,
to be peaceable, considerate, exercising
all graciousness toward everyone.
3* For we ourselves were once foolish,
disobedient, deluded, slaves to various
desires and pleasures, living in malice
and envy, hateful ourselves and hating
one another.

4* But when the kindness and gener-
ous love
of God our savior appeared,
5* not because of any righteous deeds
we had done
but because of his mercy,
he saved us through the bath of re-
birth
and renewal by the holy Spirit,
6* whom he richly poured out on us
through Jesus Christ our savior,
7* so that we might be justified by his
grace
and become heirs in hope of eter-
nal life.

8*† This saying is trustworthy.

Advice to Titus. I want you to insist
on these points, that those who have
believed in God be careful to devote
themselves to good works; these are ex-
cellent and beneficial to others.
9*† Avoid foolish arguments, genealo-
gies, rivalries, and quarrels about the
law, for they are useless and futile.
10* After a first and second warning,
break off contact with a heretic,
11 realizing that such a person is per-
verted and sinful and stands self-
condemned.

Directives, Greetings, and Blessing.†
12* When I send Artemas to you, or
Tychicus, try to join me at Nicopolis,
where I have decided to spend the win-
ter. 13* Send Zenas the lawyer and
Apollos on their journey soon, and see
to it that they have everything they
need. 14* But let our people, too, learn
to devote themselves to good works to
supply urgent needs, so that they may
not be unproductive.

15* All who are with me send you
greetings. Greet those who love us in
the faith.

Grace be with all of you.

---

*

10: 1, 3; 3, 4; Ps 24, 5; 1 Tm 1, 1; 2, 3; 4, 10; Jude 25.
11: 1 Tm 2, 4; 4, 10.
13: 1 Cor 1, 7; Phil 3, 20; 1 Thes 1, 10 / 2 Tm 1, 10 / 1, 4; 3, 6; 2 Pt 1, 1.11; 2, 20; 3, 2.18.
14: Gal 1, 4; 2, 20; Eph 5, 2.25; 1 Tm 2, 6; 1 Pt 1, 18-19 / Ps 130, 8.
15: 1 Tm 4, 12.
3, 1: Rom 13, 1-7; 1 Tm 2, 1-2; 1 Pt 2, 13-14.
3: 1 Cor 6, 9-11; Eph 2, 1-3; 5, 8; Col 3, 5-7; 1 Pt 4, 3.
4: 1, 3; 2, 10; Ps 24, 5; 1 Tm 1, 1; 2, 3; 4, 10; Jude 25.
5: Dt 9, 5; Eph 2, 4-5.8-9; 2 Tm 1, 9.
6: 1, 4; 2, 13; Phil 3, 20; 2 Tm 1, 10; 2 Pt 1, 1.11; 2, 20; 3, 2.18.
7: 1, 2; 2 Tm 1, 1; 1 Jn 2, 25.
8: 1 Tm 1, 15; 3, 1; 4, 9; 2 Tm 2, 11.
9: 1 Tm 1, 4; 4, 7; 2 Tm 2, 23.
10: Mt 18, 15-18; Rom 16, 17; 1 Cor 5, 11; 2 Thes 3, 6.14-15.
12: Acts 20, 4; Eph 6, 21; Col 4, 7; 2 Tm 4, 12.
13: Acts 18, 24-26; 1 Cor 1, 12; 3, 4-6.22; 4, 6; 16, 12.
14: 2, 14; 3, 8; Heb 10, 24; 1 Pt 3, 13.
15: Heb 13, 25.

---

†

2, 11-15: Underlying the admonitions for moral improvement in 1-10 as the moving force is the constant appeal to God's revelation of salvation in Christ, with its demand for transformation of life.

2, 13: *The blessed hope, the appearance:* literally, "the blessed hope and appearance," but the use of a single article in Greek strongly suggests an epexegetical, i.e., explanatory sense. *Of the great God and of our savior Jesus Christ:* another possible translation is "of our great God and savior Jesus Christ."

3, 1-8: The list of Christian duties continues from 2, 9-10, undergirded again as in 2, 11-13 by appeal to what God in Christ has done (4-7; cf 2, 11-14). The spiritual renewal of the Cretans, signified in God's merciful gift of baptism (4-7), should be reflected in their improved attitude toward civil authority and in their Christian relationship with all (1-3).

3, 1: *Magistrates and authorities:* some interpreters understand these terms as referring to the principalities and powers of the heavenly hierarchy. *To be open to every good enterprise:* this implies being good citizens. It could also be translated "ready to do every sort of good work" (as Christians); cf 14.

3, 8-11: In matters of good conduct and religious doctrine, Titus is to stand firm.

3, 9: See the note on 1 Tm 6, 20-21.

3, 12-15: *Artemas* or *Tychicus* (2 Tm 4, 12) is to replace Titus, who will join Paul in his winter sojourn at Nicopolis in Epirus, on the western coast of Greece.

The Letter to

PHILEMON

This short letter addressed to three specific individuals was written by Paul during an imprisonment, perhaps in Rome between A.D. 61 and 63 (see the Introduction to Colossians for other possible sites). It concerns Onesimus, a slave from Colossae (Col 4, 9), who had run away from his master, perhaps guilty of theft in the process (18). Onesimus was converted to Christ by Paul (10). Paul sends him back to his master (12) with this letter asking that he be welcomed willingly by his old master (8-10.14.17) not just as a slave but as a brother in Christ (16). Paul uses very strong arguments (especially 19) in his touching appeal on behalf of Onesimus. It is unlikely that Paul is subtly hinting that he would like to retain Onesimus as his own slave, lent to Paul by his master. Rather, he suggests he would like to have Onesimus work with him for the gospel (13.20-21). There is, however, little evidence connecting this Onesimus with a bishop of Ephesus of the same name mentioned by Ignatius of Antioch (ca. A.D. 110).

Paul's letter deals with an accepted institution of antiquity, human slavery. But Paul breathes into this letter the spirit of Christ and of equality within the Christian community. He does not attack slavery directly, for this is something the Christian communities of the first century were in no position to do, and the expectation that Christ would soon come again militated against social reforms. Yet Paul, by presenting Onesimus as "brother, beloved . . . to me, but even more so to you" (16), voiced an idea revolutionary in that day and destined to break down worldly barriers of division "in the Lord."

Address and Greeting. 1*† Paul, a
prisoner for Christ Jesus, and Timothy
our brother, to Philemon, our beloved
and our co-worker, 2*† to Apphia our
sister, to Archippus our fellow soldier,
and to the church at your house.
3*† Grace to you and peace from God
our Father and the Lord Jesus Christ.
Thanksgiving. 4*† I give thanks to
my God always, remembering you in
my prayers, 5† as I hear of the love and
the faith you have in the Lord Jesus and
for all the holy ones, 6*† so that your
partnership in the faith may become ef-
fective in recognizing every good there
is in us that leads to Christ.
Plea for Onesimus. 7*† For I have ex-
perienced much joy and encourage-
ment from your love, because the hearts
of the holy ones have been refreshed
by you, brother. 8† Therefore, al-
though I have the full right in Christ to
order you to do what is proper, 9*† I
rather urge you out of love, being as I
am, Paul, an old man, and now also a
prisoner for Christ Jesus. 10* I urge you
on behalf of my child Onesimus, whose

---

*

1: 9; Eph 3, 1; 4, 1; Phil 1, 7.13.
2: Col 4, 17.
3: Rom 1, 7; Gal 1, 3; Phil 1, 2.
4-5: Rom 1, 8-9; Eph 1, 15-16.
6: Phil 1, 9; Col 1, 9.
7: 2 Cor 7, 4.
9: 1; Eph 3, 1; 4, 1; Phil 1, 7.13.
10: 1 Cor 4, 14-15; Gal 4, 19; Col 4, 9.

---

†

1: *Prisoner:* as often elsewhere (cf Rom, 1 Cor, Gal especially), the second word in Greek enunciates the theme and sets the tone of the letter. Here it is the prisoner appealing rather than the apostle commanding.

2: *Apphia our sister:* sister is here used (like brother) to indicate a fellow Christian. *The church at your house: your* here is singular. It more likely refers to Philemon than to the last one named, Archippus; Philemon is then the owner of the slave Onesimus (10). An alternate view is that the actual master of the slave is Archippus and that the one to whom the letter is addressed, Philemon, is the most prominent Christian there; see the note on Col 4, 17.

3: *Grace . . . and peace:* for this greeting, which may be a combination of Greek and Aramaic epistolary formulae, see the note on Rom 1, 1-7.

4: *In my prayers:* literally, "at the time of my prayers."

5: *Holy ones:* a common term for members of the Christian community (so also 7).

6: *In us:* some good ancient manuscripts have *in you* (plural). *That leads to Christ: leads to* translates the Greek preposition *eis,* indicating direction or purpose.

7: *Encouragement:* the Greek word *paraklēsis* is cognate with the verb translated "urge" in vv 9.10, and serves as an introduction to Paul's plea. *Hearts:* literally, "bowels," expressing in Semitic fashion the seat of the emotions, one's "inmost self." The same Greek word is used in v 12 and again in v 20, where it forms a literary inclusion marking off the body of the letter.

8: *Full right:* often translated "boldness," the Greek word *parrēsia* connotes the full franchise of speech, as the right of a citizen to speak before the body politic, claimed by the Athenians as their privilege (Euripides).

9: *Old man:* some editors conjecture that Paul here used a similar Greek word meaning "ambassador" (cf Eph 6, 20). This conjecture heightens the contrast with "prisoner" but is totally without manuscript support.

father I have become in my imprison-
ment, 11† who was once useless to you
but is now useful to [both] you and me.
12 I am sending him, that is, my own
heart, back to you. 13*† I should have
liked to retain him for myself, so that
he might serve me on your behalf in my
imprisonment for the gospel, 14* but I
did not want to do anything without
your consent, so that the good you do
might not be forced but voluntary.
15† Perhaps this is why he was away
from you for a while, that you might
have him back forever, 16*† no longer
as a slave but more than a slave, a
brother, beloved especially to me, but
even more so to you, as a man and in
the Lord. 17 So if you regard me as a
partner, welcome him as you would me.
18† And if he has done you any injustice
or owes you anything, charge it to me.
19* I, Paul, write this in my own hand:
I will pay. May I not tell you that you
owe me your very self. 20 Yes, brother,
may I profit from you in the Lord. Re-
fresh my heart in Christ.
21 With trust in your compliance I
write to you, knowing that you will do
even more than I say. 22* At the same
time prepare a guest room for me, for
I hope to be granted to you through your
prayers.

Final Greetings.† 23* Epaphras, my
fellow prisoner in Christ Jesus, greets
you, 24* as well as Mark, Aristarchus,
Demas, and Luke, my co-workers.
25 The grace of the Lord Jesus Christ be
with your spirit.

*

13: Phil 2, 30.
14: 2 Cor 9, 7; 1 Pt 5, 2.
16: 1 Tm 6, 2.
19: Gal 6, 11; 2 Thes 3, 17.
22: Heb 13, 19.
23: Col 1, 7; 4, 12-13.
24: Acts 12, 12.15; 13, 13; 15, 37-39; 19, 29; 20, 4; 27, 2; Col 4, 10.14; 2 Tm 4, 10-13.

†

11: *Useless . . . useful:* here Paul plays on the name Onesimus, which means "useful" or "beneficial." The verb translated "profit" in v 20 is cognate.

13: *Serve:* the Greek *diakoneō* could connote a ministry.

15: *Was away from:* literally, "was separated from," but the same verb means simply "left" in Acts 18, 1. It is a euphemism for his running away.

16: *As a man:* literally, "in the flesh." With this and the following phrase, Paul describes the natural and spiritual orders.

18-19: *Charge it to me . . . I will pay:* technical legal and commercial terms in account keeping and acknowledgment of indebtedness.

23-24: *Epaphras:* a Colossian who founded the church there (Col 1, 7) and perhaps also in Laodicea and Hierapolis (Col 2, 1; 4, 12-13). *Aristarchus:* a native of Thessalonica and fellow worker of Paul (Acts 19, 29; 20, 4; 27, 2). For Mark, Demas, and Luke, see 2 Tm 4, 9-13 and the note there.

The Letter to the

HEBREWS

As early as the second century, this treatise, which is of great rhetorical power and force in its admonition to faithful pilgrimage under Christ's leadership, bore the title "To the Hebrews." It was assumed to be directed to Jewish Christians. Usually Hebrews was attached in Greek manuscripts to the collection of letters by Paul. Although no author is mentioned (for there is no address), a reference to Timothy (13, 23) suggested connections to the circle of Paul and his assistants. Yet the exact audience, the author, and even whether Hebrews is a letter have long been disputed.

The author saw the addressees in danger of apostasy from their Christian faith. This danger was due not to any persecution from outsiders but to a weariness with the demands of Christian life and a growing indifference to their calling (2, 1; 4, 14; 6, 1-12; 10, 23-32). The author's main theme, the priesthood and sacrifice of Jesus (chs 3-10), is not developed for its own sake but as a means of restoring their lost fervor and strengthening them in their faith. Another important theme of the letter is that of the pilgrimage of the people of God to the heavenly Jerusalem (11, 10; 12, 1-3.18-29; 13, 14). This theme is intimately connected with that of Jesus' ministry in the heavenly sanctuary (9, 11—10, 22).

The author calls this work a "message of encouragement" (13, 22), a designation that is given to a synagogue sermon in Acts 13, 15. Hebrews is probably therefore a written homily, to which the author gave an epistolary ending (13, 22-25).

The author begins with a reminder of the preexistence, incarnation, and exaltation of Jesus (1, 3) that proclaimed him the climax of God's word to humanity (1, 1-3). He dwells upon the dignity of the person of Christ, superior to the angels (1, 4—2, 2). Christ is God's final word of salvation communicated (in association with accredited witnesses to his teaching: cf 2, 3-4) not merely by word but through his suffering in the humanity common to him and to all others (2, 5-16). This enactment of salvation went beyond the pattern known to Moses, faithful prophet of God's word though he was, for Jesus as high priest expiated sin and was faithful to God with the faithfulness of God's own Son (2, 17—3, 6).

Just as the infidelity of the people thwarted Moses' efforts to save them, so the infidelity of any Christian may thwart God's plan in Christ (3, 6—4, 13). Christians are to reflect that it is their humanity that Jesus took upon himself, with all its defects save sinfulness, and that he bore the burden of it until death out of obedience to God. God declared this work of his Son to be the cause of salvation for all (4, 14—5, 10). Although Christians recognize this fundamental teaching, they may grow weary of it and of its implications, and therefore require other reflections to stimulate their faith (5, 11—6, 20).

Therefore, the author presents to the readers for their reflection the everlasting priesthood of Christ (7, 1-28), a priesthood that fulfills the promise of the Old Testament (8, 1-13). It also provides the meaning God ultimately intended in the sacrifices of the Old Testament (9, 1-28): these pointed to the unique sacrifice of Christ, which alone obtains forgiveness of sins (10, 1-18). The trial of faith experienced by the readers should resolve itself through their consideration of Christ's ministry in the heavenly sanctuary and his perpetual intercession there on their behalf (7, 25; 8, 1-13). They should also be strengthened by the assurance of his foreordained parousia, and by the fruits of faith that they have already enjoyed (10, 19-39).

It is in the nature of faith to recognize the reality of what is not yet seen and is the object of hope, and the saints of the Old Testament give striking example of that faith (11, 1-40). The perseverance to which the author exhorts the readers is shown forth in the early life of Jesus. Despite the afflictions of his ministry and the supreme trial of his suffering and death, he remained confident of the triumph that God would bring him (12, 1-3). The difficulties of human life have meaning when they are accepted as God's discipline (12, 4-13), and if Christians persevere in fidelity to the word in which they have believed, they are assured of possessing forever the unshakable kingdom of God (12, 14-29).

The letter concludes with specific moral commandments (13, 1-17), in the course of which the author recalls again his central theme of the sacrifice of Jesus and the courage needed to associate oneself with it in faith (13, 9-16).

As early as the end of the second century, the church of Alexandria in Egypt accepted Hebrews as a letter of Paul, and that became the view commonly held in the East. Pauline authorship was contested in the West into the fourth century, but then accepted. In the sixteenth century, doubts about that position were again raised, and the modern consensus is that the letter was not written by Paul. There is, however, no widespread agreement on any of the other suggested authors, e.g., Barnabas, Apollos, or Prisc(ill)a and Aquila. The document itself has no statement about its author.

Among the reasons why Pauline authorship has been abandoned are the great difference of vocabulary and style between Hebrews and Paul's letters, the alternation of doctrinal teaching with moral exhortation, the different manner of citing the Old Testament, and the resemblance between the thought of Hebrews and that of Alexandrian Judaism. The Greek of the letter is in many ways the best in the New Testament.

Since the letter of Clement of Rome to the Corinthians, written about A.D. 96, most probably cites Hebrews, the upper limit for the date of composition is reasonably certain. While the letter's references in the present tense to the Old Testament sacrificial worship do not necessarily show that temple worship was still going on, many older commentators and a growing number of recent ones favor the view that it was and that the author wrote before the destruction of the temple of Jerusalem in A.D. 70. In that case, the argument of the letter is more easily explained as directed toward Jewish Christians rather than those of Gentile origin, and the persecutions they have suffered in the past (cf 10, 32-34) may have been connected with the disturbances that preceded the expulsion of the Jews from Rome in A.D. 49 under the emperor Claudius. These were probably caused by disputes between Jews who accepted Jesus as the Messiah and those who did not.

The principal divisions of the Letter to the Hebrews are the following:

I: Introduction (1, 1-4)
II: The Son Higher than the Angels (1, 5—2, 18)
III: Jesus, Faithful and Compassionate High Priest (3, 1—5, 10)
IV: Jesus' Eternal Priesthood and Eternal Sacrifice (5, 11—10, 39)
V: Examples, Discipline, Disobedience (11, 1—12, 29)
VI: Final Exhortation, Blessing, Greetings (13, 1-25)

I: INTRODUCTION†

CHAPTER 1

1 In times past, God spoke in partial
and various ways to our ancestors
through the prophets;
2* in these last
days, he spoke to us through a son, whom he made heir of all things and through whom he created the universe,

3* who is the refulgence of his glory,
the very imprint of his being,
and who sustains all things by his
mighty word.
When he had accomplished purification from sins,
he took his seat at the right hand
of the Majesty on high,

4* as far superior to the angels
as the name he has inherited is
more excellent than theirs.

II: THE SON HIGHER THAN THE ANGELS

Messianic Enthronement.†
5* For to which of the angels did God ever say:

"You are my son; this day I have
begotten you"?

Or again:

"I will be a father to him, and he
shall be a son to me"?

6*† And again, when he leads the firstborn into the world, he says:

"Let all the angels of God worship
him."

7* Of the angels he says:

"He makes his angels winds
and his ministers a fiery flame";

8*† but of the Son:

"Your throne, O God, stands forever and ever;
and a righteous scepter is the
scepter of your kingdom.

9 You loved justice and hated wickedness;
therefore God, your God,
anointed you
with the oil of gladness above
your companions";

10* and:

"At the beginning, O Lord, you established the earth,
and the heavens are the works of
your hands.

11 They will perish, but you remain;
and they will all grow old like a
garment.

12 You will roll them up like a cloak,
and like a garment they will be
changed.
But you are the same, and your
years will have no end."

13* But to which of the angels has he ever said:

"Sit at my right hand
until I make your enemies your
footstool"?

14* Are they not all ministering spirits

---

*

1, 2: Is 2, 2; Jer 23, 20; Ez 38, 16; Dn 10, 14 / Jn 3, 17; Rom 8, 3; Gal 4, 4 / Prv 8, 30; Wis 7, 22; Jn 1, 3; 1 Cor 8, 6; Col 1, 16.
3: Wis 7, 26; 2 Cor 4, 4; Col 1, 15 / 8, 1; 10, 12; 12, 2; Mk 16, 19; Acts 2, 33; 7, 55-56; Rom 8, 34; Eph 1, 20; Col 3, 1; 1 Pt 3, 22.
4: Eph 1, 21; Phil 2, 9-11.
5: Ps 2, 7 / 2 Sm 7, 14.
6: Dt 32, 43 LXX; Ps 97, 7.
7: Ps 104, 4 LXX.
8: Ps 45, 7-8.
10-12: Ps 102, 26-28.
13: Ps 110, 1.
14: Ps 91, 11; Dn 7, 10.

---

†

1, 1-4: The letter opens with an introduction consisting of a reflection on the climax of God's revelation to the human race in his Son. The divine communication was initiated and maintained during Old Testament times in fragmentary and varied ways through *the prophets* (1), including Abraham, Moses, and all through whom God spoke. But now *in these last days* (2), the final age, God's revelation of his saving purpose is achieved *through a son,* i.e., one who is Son, whose role is redeemer and mediator of creation. He was made *heir of all things* through his death and exaltation to glory, yet he existed before he appeared as man; through him God *created the universe.* Verses 3-4, which may be based upon a liturgical hymn, assimilate the Son to the personified Wisdom of the Old Testament as *refulgence of* God's *glory* and *imprint of his being* (3; cf Wis 7, 26). These same terms are used of the Logos in Philo. The author now turns from the cosmological role of the preexistent Son to the redemptive work of Jesus: he brought about purification from sins and has been exalted to the right hand of God (see Ps 110, 1). The once-humiliated and crucified Jesus has been declared God's Son, and this name shows his superiority to the angels. The reason for the author's insistence on that superiority is, among other things, that in some Jewish traditions angels were mediators of the old covenant (see Acts 7, 53; Gal 3, 19). Finally, Jesus' superiority to the angels emphasizes the superiority of the new covenant to the old because of the heavenly priesthood of Jesus.

1, 5-14: Jesus' superiority to the angels is now demonstrated by a series of seven Old Testament texts. Some scholars see in the stages of Jesus' exaltation an order corresponding to that of enthronement ceremonies in the ancient Near East, especially in Egypt, namely, elevation to divine status (5-6); presentation to the angels and proclamation of everlasting lordship (7-12); enthronement and conferral of royal power (13). The citations from the Psalms in vv 5 and 13 were traditionally used of Jesus' messianic sonship (cf Acts 13, 33) through his resurrection and exaltation (cf Acts 2, 33-35); those in vv 8 and 10-12 are concerned with his divine kingship and his creative function. The central quotation in v 7 serves to contrast the angels with the Son. The author quotes it according to the Septuagint translation, which is quite different in meaning from that of the Hebrew ("You make the winds your messengers, and flaming fire your ministers"). The angels are only *sent to serve . . . those who are to inherit salvation* (14).

1, 6: *And again, when he leads:* the Greek could also be translated "And when he again leads" in reference to the parousia.

1, 8-12: *O God:* the application of the name "God" to the Son derives from the preexistence mentioned in vv 2-3; the psalmist had already used it of the Hebrew king in the court style of the original. See the note on Ps 45, 7. It is also important for the author's christology that in vv 10-12 an Old Testament passage addressed to God is redirected to Jesus.

sent to serve, for the sake of those who
are to inherit salvation?

CHAPTER 2

Exhortation to Faithfulness.†

1 Therefore, we must attend all the more
to what we have heard, so that we may
not be carried away. 2* For if the word
announced through angels proved firm,
and every transgression and disobedi-
ence received its just recompense,
3* how shall we escape if we ignore so
great a salvation? Announced origi-
nally through the Lord, it was con-
firmed for us by those who had heard.
4* God added his testimony by signs,
wonders, various acts of power, and dis-
tribution of the gifts of the holy Spirit
according to his will.

Exaltation through Abasement.†

5 For it was not to angels that he sub-
jected the world to come, of which we
are speaking. 6* Instead, someone has
testified somewhere:

"What is man that you are mindful
of him,
or the son of man that you care
for him?
7 You made him for a little while
lower than the angels;
you crowned him with glory and
honor,
8* subjecting all things under his
feet."

In "subjecting" all things [to him], he
left nothing not "subject to him." Yet
at present we do not see "all things sub-
ject to him," 9* but we do see Jesus
"crowned with glory and honor" be-
cause he suffered death, he who "for a
little while" was made "lower than the
angels," that by the grace of God he
might taste death for everyone.
10* For it was fitting that he, for whom
and through whom all things exist, in
bringing many children to glory, should
make the leader to their salvation per-
fect through suffering. 11 He who con-
secrates and those who are being
consecrated all have one origin. There-
fore, he is not ashamed to call them
"brothers," 12* saying:

"I will proclaim your name to my
brothers,
in the midst of the assembly I will
praise you";

13* and again:

"I will put my trust in him";

and again:

"Behold, I and the children God has
given me."

14* Now since the children share in
blood and flesh, he likewise shared in
them, that through death he might de-
stroy the one who has the power of
death, that is, the devil, 15 and free those
who through fear of death had been
subject to slavery all their life. 16 Surely
he did not help angels but rather the
descendants of Abraham; 17* therefore,
he had to become like his brothers in
every way, that he might be a merciful
and faithful high priest before God to
expiate the sins of the people. 18 Because
he himself was tested through what he
suffered, he is able to help those who
are being tested.

*

2, 2: Acts 7, 38.53; Gal 3, 19.
3: 10, 29; 12, 25.
4: Mk 16, 20; Acts 14, 3; 19, 11.
6: Ps 8, 5-7.
8: Mt 28, 18; 1 Cor 15, 25-28; Eph 1, 20-23; Phil 3, 21; 1 Pt 3, 22.
9: Phil 2, 6-11.
10: 12, 2; Is 53, 4 / Rom 11, 36; 1 Cor 8, 6.
12: Ps 22, 23.
13: Is 8, 17.18.
14: Is 25, 8; Hos 13, 14; Jn 12, 31; Rom 6, 9; 1 Cor 15, 54-55; 2 Tm 1, 10; Rv 12, 10.
17: 4, 15; 5, 1-3.

†

2, 1-4: The author now makes a transition into exhortation, using an a fortiori argument (as at 7, 21-22; 9, 13-14; 10, 28-29; 12, 25). The *word announced through angels* (2), the Mosaic law, is contrasted with the more powerful word that Christians have received (3-4). Christ's supremacy strengthens Christians against being *carried away* from their faith.

2, 5-18: The humanity and the suffering of Jesus do not constitute a valid reason for relinquishing the Christian faith. Ps 8 (6-7) is also applied to Jesus in 1 Cor 15, 27; Eph 1, 22; and probably 1 Pt 3, 22. This christological interpretation, therefore, probably reflects a common early Christian tradition, which may have originated in the expression *the son of man* (6). The psalm contrasts God's greatness with man's relative insignificance but also stresses the superiority of man to the rest of creation, of which he is lord. Heb applies this christologically: Jesus lived a truly human existence, *lower than the angels,* in the days of his earthly life, particularly in his suffering and death; now, *crowned with glory and honor,* he is raised above all creation. The author considers all things as already *subject to him* because of his exaltation (8-9), though *we do not see* this yet. The reference to Jesus as *leader* (10) sounds the first note of an important leitmotif in Heb: the journey of the people of God to the sabbath rest (4, 9), the heavenly sanctuary, following Jesus, their "forerunner" (6, 20). It was fitting that God should make him *perfect through suffering,* consecrated by obedient suffering. Because he is perfected as high priest, Jesus is then able to consecrate his people (11); access to God is made possible by each of these two consecrations. If Jesus is able to help human beings, it is because he has become one of us; we are his "brothers." The author then cites three Old Testament texts as proofs of this unity between ourselves and the Son. Psalm 22, 23 is interpreted so as to make Jesus the singer of this lament, which ends with joyful praise of the Lord in the assembly of "brothers." The other two texts are from Is 8, 17.18. The first of these seems intended to display in Jesus an example of the trust in God that his followers should emulate. The second curiously calls these followers "children"; probably this is to be understood to mean children of Adam, but the point is our solidarity with Jesus. By sharing human nature, including the ban of death, Jesus broke the power of the devil over death (14); the author shares the view of Hellenistic Judaism that death was not intended by God and that it had been introduced into the world by the devil. The *fear of death* (15) is a religious fear based on the false conception that death marks the end of a person's relations with God (cf Ps 115, 17-18; Is 38, 18). Jesus deliberately allied himself with *the descendants of Abraham* (16) in order to be *a merciful and faithful high priest.* This is the first appearance of the central theme of Heb, Jesus the great high priest expiating *the sins of the people* (17), as one who experienced the same tests as they (18).

III: JESUS, FAITHFUL AND COMPASSIONATE HIGH PRIEST

CHAPTER 3

Jesus, Superior to Moses.†
1 Therefore, holy "brothers," sharing in
a heavenly calling, reflect on Jesus, the
apostle and high priest of our confes-
sion, 2* who was faithful to the one who
appointed him, just as Moses was
"faithful in [all] his house." 3* But he
is worthy of more "glory" than Moses,
as the founder of a house has more
"honor" than the house itself. 4 Every
house is founded by someone, but the
founder of all is God. 5 Moses was
"faithful in all his house" as a "servant"
to testify to what would be spoken,
6*† but Christ was faithful as a son
placed over his house. We are his house,
if [only] we hold fast to our confidence
and pride in our hope.

Israel's Infidelity a Warning.†
7* Therefore, as the holy Spirit says:

"Oh, that today you would hear his voice,
8 'Harden not your hearts as at the rebellion
in the day of testing in the desert,
9* where your ancestors tested and tried me
and saw my works 10 for forty years.
Because of this I was provoked with that generation
and I said, "They have always been of erring heart,
and they do not know my ways."
11 As I swore in my wrath,
"They shall not enter into my rest." ' "

12 Take care, brothers, that none of you
may have an evil and unfaithful heart,
so as to forsake the living God.
13 Encourage yourselves daily while it
is still "today," so that none of you may
grow hardened by the deceit of sin.
14* We have become partners of Christ
if only we hold the beginning of the real-
ity firm until the end, 15* for it is said:

"Oh, that today you would hear his voice:
'Harden not your hearts as at the rebellion.' "

16* Who were those who rebelled when
they heard? Was it not all those who
came out of Egypt under Moses?
17* With whom was he "provoked for
forty years"? Was it not those who had
sinned, whose corpses fell in the desert?
18* And to whom did he "swear that
they should not enter into his rest," if
not to those who were disobedient?
19 And we see that they could not enter
for lack of faith.

CHAPTER 4

The Sabbath Rest. 1 Therefore, let us
be on our guard while the promise of
entering into his rest remains, that none
of you seem to have failed. 2 For in fact
we have received the good news just as
they did. But the word that they heard

*

3, 2: Nm 12, 7.
3: 2 Cor 3, 7-8.
6: 10, 21; Eph 2, 19; 1 Tm 3, 15; 1 Pt 4, 17.
7-11: Ps 95, 7-11.
9: Ex 17, 7; Nm 20, 2-5.
14: Rom 8, 17.
15: Ps 95, 7-8.
16-19: Nm 14, 1-38; Dt 1, 19-40.
17: Nm 14, 29.
18: Nm 14, 22-23; Dt 1, 35.

†

3, 1-6: The author now takes up the two qualities of Jesus mentioned in 2, 17, but in inverse order: faithfulness (3, 1—4, 13) and mercy (4, 14—5, 10). Christians are called *holy "brothers"* because of their common relation to him (2, 11), the *apostle*, a designation for Jesus used only here in the New Testament (cf Jn 13, 16; 17, 3), meaning one sent as God's final word to us (1, 2). He is compared with Moses probably because he is seen as mediator of the new covenant (9, 15) just as Moses was of the old (9, 19-22, including his sacrifice). But when the author of Heb speaks of Jesus' sacrifice, he does not consider Moses as the Old Testament antitype, but rather the high priest on the Day of Atonement (9, 6-15). Moses' faithfulness *"in [all] his house"* refers back to Nm 12, 7, on which this section is a midrashic commentary. In vv 3-6, the author does not indicate that he thinks of either Moses or Christ as the founder of the household. *His house* (2.5.6) means God's house, not that of Moses or Christ; in the case of Christ, compare v 6 with 10, 21. The *house* of v 6 is the Christian community; the author suggests its continuity with Israel by speaking not of two houses but of only one. Verse 6 brings out the reason why Jesus is superior to Moses: the latter was the faithful *servant* laboring *in* the house founded by God, but Jesus is God's *son,* placed *over* the house.

3, 6: The majority of manuscripts add "firm to the end," but these words are not found in the three earliest and best witnesses and are probably an interpolation derived from v 14.

3, 7—4, 13: The author appeals for steadfastness of faith in Jesus, basing his warning on the experience of Israel during the Exodus. In the Old Testament the Exodus had been invoked as a symbol of the return of Israel from the Babylonian exile (Is 42, 9; 43, 16-21; 51, 9-11). In the New Testament the redemption was similarly understood as a new exodus, both in the experience of Jesus himself (Lk 9, 31) and in that of his followers (1 Cor 10, 1-4). The author cites Ps 95, 7-11, a salutary example of hardness of heart, as a warning against the danger of growing weary and giving up the journey. To call God *living* (12) means that he reveals himself in his works (cf Jos 3, 10; Jer 10, 10). The *rest* (11) into which Israel was to enter was only a foreshadowing of that rest to which Christians are called. They are to remember the example of Israel's revolt in the desert that cost a whole generation the loss of the promised land (15-19; cf Nm 14, 20-29). In 4, 1-11, the symbol of *rest* is seen in deeper dimension: because the promise to the ancient Hebrews foreshadowed that given to Christians, it is *good news;* and because the promised land was the place of rest that God provided for his people, it was a share in his own rest, which he enjoyed after he had finished his creative work (3-4; cf Gn 2, 2). The author attempts to read this meaning of God's rest into Ps 95, 7-11 (6-9). The Greek form of the name of Joshua, who led Israel into the promised land, is Jesus (8). The author plays upon the name but stresses the superiority of Jesus, who leads his followers into heavenly rest. Verses 12 and 13 are meant as a continuation of the warning, for the word of God brings judgment as well as salvation. Some would capitalize *the word of God* and see it as a personal title of Jesus, comparable to that of Jn 1, 1-18.

did not profit them, for they were not
united in faith with those who listened.
3* For we who believed enter into [that]
rest, just as he has said:

"As I swore in my wrath,
'They shall not enter into my rest,'"

and yet his works were accomplished
at the foundation of the world. 4* For
he has spoken somewhere about the
seventh day in this manner, "And God
rested on the seventh day from all his
works"; 5* and again, in the previously
mentioned place, "They shall not enter
into my rest." 6 Therefore, since it re-
mains that some will enter into it, and
those who formerly received the good
news did not enter because of disobedi-
ence, 7* he once more set a day, "to-
day," when long afterwards he spoke
through David, as already quoted:

"Oh, that today you would hear his
voice:
'Harden not your hearts.'"

8* Now if Joshua had given them rest,
he would not have spoken afterwards
of another day. 9 Therefore, a sabbath
rest still remains for the people of God.
10 And whoever enters into God's rest,
rests from his own works as God did
from his. 11 Therefore, let us strive to
enter into that rest, so that no one may
fall after the same example of disobedi-
ence.

12* Indeed, the word of God is living
and effective, sharper than any two-
edged sword, penetrating even between
soul and spirit, joints and marrow, and
able to discern reflections and thoughts
of the heart. 13* No creature is con-
cealed from him, but everything
is naked and exposed to the eyes of
him to whom we must render an ac-
count.

Jesus, Compassionate High Priest.†
14* Therefore, since we have a great
high priest who has passed through the
heavens, Jesus, the Son of God, let us
hold fast to our confession. 15* For we
do not have a high priest who is unable
to sympathize with our weaknesses, but
one who has similarly been tested in ev-
ery way, yet without sin. 16* So let us
confidently approach the throne of
grace to receive mercy and to find grace
for timely help.

CHAPTER 5

1† Every high priest is taken from
among men and made their representa-
tive before God, to offer gifts and sacri-
fices for sins. 2† He is able to deal
patiently with the ignorant and erring,
for he himself is beset by weakness
3* and so, for this reason, must make
sin offerings for himself as well as for
the people. 4* No one takes this honor
upon himself but only when called by
God, just as Aaron was. 5* In the same
way, it was not Christ who glorified him-
self in becoming high priest, but rather
the one who said to him:

"You are my son;
this day I have begotten you";

6*† just as he says in another place:

"You are a priest forever
according to the order of Melchiz-
edek."

7*† In the days when he was in the flesh,
he offered prayers and supplications

HEBREWS

*

4, 3: 3, 11; Ps 95, 11.
4: Gn 2, 2.
5: Ps 95, 11.
7: 3, 7-8.15; Ps 95, 7-8.
8: Dt 31, 7; Jos 22, 4.
12: Wis 18, 15-16; Is 49, 2; Eph 6, 17; Rv 1, 16; 2, 12.
13: Jb 34, 21-22; Pss 90, 8; 139, 2-4.
14: 9, 11.24.
15: 2, 17-18; 5, 2.
16: 8, 1; 10, 19.22.35; 12, 2; Eph 3, 12.
5, 3: Lv 9, 7; 16, 15-17.30.34.
4: Ex 28, 1.
5: Ps 2, 7.
6: Ps 110, 4.
7: Mt 26, 38-44; Mk 14, 34-40; Lk 22, 41-46; Jn 12, 27.

†

4, 14-16: These verses, which return to the theme first sounded in 2, 16—3, 1, serve as an introduction to the section that follows. The author here alone calls Jesus *a great high priest* (14), a designation used by Philo for the Logos; perhaps he does so in order to emphasize Jesus' superiority over the Jewish high priest. He has *been tested in every way, yet without sin* (15); this indicates an acquaintance with the tradition of Jesus' temptations, not only at the beginning (as in Mk 1, 13) but throughout his public life (cf Lk 22, 28). Although the reign of the exalted Jesus is a theme that occurs elsewhere in Heb, and Jesus' throne is mentioned in 1, 8, *the throne of grace* (16) refers to the throne of God. The similarity of v 16 to 10, 19-22 indicates that the author is thinking of our confident access to God, made possible by the priestly work of Jesus.

5, 1-10: The true humanity of Jesus (see the note on 2, 5-18) makes him a more rather than a less effective high priest to the Christian community. In Old Testament tradition, the high priest was identified with the people, guilty of personal sin just as they were (1-3). Even so, the office was of divine appointment (4), as was also the case with the sinless Christ (5). For v 6, see the note on Ps 110, 4. Although Jesus was Son of God, he was destined as a human being to learn obedience by accepting the suffering he had to endure (8). Because of his perfection through this experience of human suffering, he is the cause of salvation for all (9), a *high priest according to the order of Melchizedek* (10; cf 6 and 7, 3).

5, 1: *To offer gifts and sacrifices for sins:* the author is thinking principally of the Day of Atonement rite, as is clear from 9, 7. This ritual was celebrated to atone for "all the sins of the Israelites" (Lv 16, 34).

5, 2: *Deal patiently:* the Greek word *metriopathein* occurs only here in the Bible; this term was used by the Stoics to designate the golden mean between excess and defect of passion. Here it means rather the ability to sympathize.

5, 6-8: The author of Heb is the only New Testament writer to cite v 4 of Ps 110, here and in 7, 17.21, to show that Jesus has been called by God to his role as priest. Verses 7-8 deal with his ability to sympathize with sinners, because of his own experience of the trials and weakness of human nature, especially fear of death. In his present exalted state, weakness is foreign to him, but he understands what we suffer because of his previous earthly experience.

5, 7: *He offered prayers . . . to the one who was able to save him from death:* at Gethsemane (cf Mk 14, 35), though some see a broader reference (see the note on Jn 12, 27).

with loud cries and tears to the one who
was able to save him from death, and
he was heard because of his reverence.
8*† Son though he was, he learned obe-
dience from what he suffered; 9* and
when he was made perfect, he became
the source of eternal salvation for all
who obey him, 10* declared by God high
priest according to the order of Mel-
chizedek.

IV: JESUS' ETERNAL PRIESTHOOD AND ETERNAL SACRIFICE

Exhortation to Spiritual Renewal.†
11 About this we have much to say, and
it is difficult to explain, for you have be-
come sluggish in hearing. 12* Although
you should be teachers by this time, you
need to have someone teach you again
the basic elements of the utterances of
God. You need milk, [and] not solid
food. 13 Everyone who lives on milk
lacks experience of the word of righ-
teousness, for he is a child. 14 But solid
food is for the mature, for those whose
faculties are trained by practice to dis-
cern good and evil.

CHAPTER 6

1* Therefore, let us leave behind the
basic teaching about Christ and ad-
vance to maturity, without laying the
foundation all over again: repentance
from dead works and faith in God,
2*† instruction about baptisms and lay-
ing on of hands, resurrection of the
dead and eternal judgment. 3 And we
shall do this, if only God permits.
4*† For it is impossible in the case of
those who have once been enlightened
and tasted the heavenly gift and shared
in the holy Spirit 5† and tasted the good
word of God and the powers of the age
to come, 6*† and then have fallen away,
to bring them to repentance again, since
they are recrucifying the Son of God for
themselves and holding him up to con-
tempt. 7* Ground that has absorbed the
rain falling upon it repeatedly and
brings forth crops useful to those for
whom it is cultivated receives a blessing
from God. 8* But if it produces thorns
and thistles, it is rejected; it will soon
be cursed and finally burned.

9 But we are sure in your regard, be-
loved, of better things related to salva-
tion, even though we speak in this way.
10 For God is not unjust so as to overlook
your work and the love you have dem-
onstrated for his name by having
served and continuing to serve the holy
ones. 11* We earnestly desire each of
you to demonstrate the same eagerness
for the fulfillment of hope until the end,
12*† so that you may not become slug-
gish, but imitators of those who, through
faith and patience, are inheriting the
promises.

God's Promise Immutable. 13*† When
God made the promise to Abraham,
since he had no one greater by whom
to swear, "he swore by himself," 14* and

---

*

8: Rom 5, 19; Phil 2, 8.
9: 7, 24-25.28.
10: 6, 20; Ps 110, 4.
12: 1 Cor 3, 1-3.
6, 1: 9, 14.
2: 9, 10; Mk 7, 4 / Acts 6, 6; 8, 17; 13, 3; 19, 6; 1 Tm 4, 14; 5, 22; 2 Tm 1, 6.
4: 10, 26.32; Ps 34, 6; 2 Cor 4, 6.
6: 2 Pt 2, 21.
7: Gn 1, 11-12; Dt 11, 11.
8: Gn 3, 17-18; Mt 7, 16; 13, 7; Mk 4, 7; Lk 8, 7.
11: 3, 14.
12: 5, 11; Gal 3, 14; Eph 1, 13-14.
13: Gn 22, 16.
14: Gn 22, 17.

---

†

5, 8: *Son though he was:* two different though not incompatible views of Jesus' sonship coexist in Heb, one associating it with his exaltation, the other with his preexistence. The former view is the older one (cf Rom 1, 4).

5, 11—6, 20: The central section of Heb (5, 11—10, 39) opens with a reprimand and an appeal. Those to whom the author directs his teaching about Jesus' priesthood, which is *difficult to explain,* have become *sluggish in hearing* and forgetful of even *the basic elements* (5, 12). But rather than treating of basic teachings, the author apparently believes that the challenge of more advanced ones may shake them out of their inertia (*therefore,* 6, 1). The six examples of *basic teaching* in 6, 1-3 are probably derived from a traditional catechetical list. No effort is made to address apostates, for their very hostility to the Christian message cuts them off completely from Christ (6, 4-8). This harsh statement seems to rule out repentance after apostasy, but perhaps the author deliberately uses hyperbole in order to stress the seriousness of abandoning Christ. With 6, 9 a milder tone is introduced, and the criticism of the community (6, 1-3.9) is now balanced by an expression of confidence that its members are living truly Christian lives, and that God will justly reward their efforts (10). The author is concerned especially about their persevering (11-12), citing in this regard the achievement of Abraham, who relied on God's promise and on God's oath (13-18; cf Gn 22, 16), and proposes to them as a firm anchor of Christian hope the high priesthood of Christ, who is now living with God (19-20).

6, 2: *Instruction about baptisms:* not simply about Christian baptism but about the difference between it and similar Jewish rites, such as proselyte baptism, John's baptism, and the washings of the Qumran sectaries. *Laying on of hands:* in Acts 8, 17; 19, 6 this rite effects the infusion of the holy Spirit; in Acts 6, 6; 13, 3; 1 Tm 4, 14; 5, 22; 2 Tm 1, 6 it is a means of conferring some ministry or mission in the early Christian community.

6, 4: *Enlightened and tasted the heavenly gift:* this may refer to baptism and the Eucharist, respectively, but more probably means the neophytes' enlightenment by faith and their experience of salvation.

6, 5: *Tasted the good word of God and the powers of the age to come:* the proclamation of the *word of God* was accompanied by signs of the Spirit's power (1 Thes 1, 5; 1 Cor 2, 4).

6, 6: *They are recrucifying the Son of God for themselves:* a colorful description of the malice of apostasy, which is portrayed as again crucifying and deriding the Son of God.

6, 12: *Imitators of those . . . inheriting the promises:* the author urges the addressees to imitate the faith of the holy people of the Old Testament, who now possess the promised goods of which they lived in hope. This theme will be treated fully in ch 11.

6, 13: *He swore by himself:* God's promise to Abraham, which he confirmed by an oath ("I swear by myself," Gen 22, 16) was the basis for the hope of all Abraham's descendants.

said, "I will indeed bless you and multi-
ply" you. 15*† And so, after patient
waiting, he obtained the promise.
16 Human beings swear by someone
greater than themselves; for them an
oath serves as a guarantee and puts an
end to all argument. 17* So when God
wanted to give the heirs of his promise
an even clearer demonstration of the
immutability of his purpose, he inter-
vened with an oath, 18*† so that by two
immutable things, in which it was im-
possible for God to lie, we who have
taken refuge might be strongly encour-
aged to hold fast to the hope that lies
before us. 19*† This we have as an an-
chor of the soul, sure and firm, which
reaches into the interior behind the veil,
20* where Jesus has entered on our be-
half as forerunner, becoming high
priest forever according to the order of
Melchizedek.

CHAPTER 7

Melchizedek, a Type of Christ.†

1*† This "Melchizedek, king of Salem
and priest of God Most High," "met
Abraham as he returned from his de-
feat of the kings" and "blessed him."
2† And Abraham apportioned to him
"a tenth of everything." His name
first means righteous king, and he
was also "king of Salem," that is, king
of peace. 3*† Without father, mother,
or ancestry, without beginning of days
or end of life, thus made to resemble
the Son of God, he remains a priest for-
ever.

4*† See how great he is to whom the
patriarch "Abraham [indeed] gave a
tenth" of his spoils. 5* The descendants
of Levi who receive the office of priest-
hood have a commandment according
to the law to exact tithes from the peo-
ple, that is, from their brothers, al-
though they also have come from the
loins of Abraham. 6 But he who was not
of their ancestry received tithes from
Abraham and blessed him who had
received the promises. 7† Unques-
tionably, a lesser person is blessed by
a greater. 8 In the one case, mortal men
receive tithes; in the other, a man of
whom it is testified that he lives on.
9† One might even say that Levi himself,
who receives tithes, was tithed through
Abraham, 10 for he was still in his fa-
ther's loins when Melchizedek met him.

11*† If, then, perfection came through
the levitical priesthood, on the basis of
which the people received the law, what
need would there still have been for an-
other priest to arise according to the or-
der of Melchizedek, and not reckoned
according to the order of Aaron?
12 When there is a change of priesthood,
there is necessarily a change of law as
well. 13† Now he of whom these things
are said belonged to a different tribe,
of which no member ever officiated at

*

15: 12; Rom 4, 20.
17: 12.
18: Nm 23, 19; 1 Sm 15, 29; Jn 8, 17; 2 Tm 2, 13.
19: 10, 20; Ex 26, 31-33; Lv 16, 2.
20: 5, 10; Ps 110, 4.
7, 1: Gn 14, 17-20.
3: 4, 14; 6, 6; 10, 29.
4: Gn 14, 20.
5: Nm 18, 21 / Gn 35, 11.
11: 5, 6; Ps 110, 4.

†

6, 15: *He obtained the promise:* this probably refers not to Abraham's temporary possession of the land but to the eschatological blessings that Abraham and the other patriarchs have now come to possess.

6, 18: *Two immutable things:* the promise and the oath, both made by God.

6, 19: *Anchor . . . into the interior behind the veil:* a mixed metaphor. The Holy of Holies, beyond the veil that separates it from the Holy Place (Ex 26, 31-33), is seen as the earthly counterpart of the heavenly abode of God. This theme will be developed in ch 9.

7, 1-3: Recalling the meeting between Melchizedek and Abraham described in Gn 14, 17-20, the author enhances the significance of this priest by providing the popular etymological meaning of his name and that of the city over which he ruled (2). Since Genesis gives no information on the parentage or the death of Melchizedek, he is seen here as a type of Christ, representing a priesthood that is unique and eternal (3).

7, 1: The author here assumes that Melchizedek was a priest of the God of Israel (cf Gn 14, 22 and the note there).

7, 2: In Gn 14, the Hebrew text does not state explicitly who gave tithes to whom. The author of Heb supplies Abraham as the subject, according to a contemporary interpretation of the passage. This supports the argument of the midrash and makes it possible to see in Melchizedek a type of Jesus. The messianic blessings of righteousness and peace are foreshadowed in the names "Melchizedek" and "Salem."

7, 3: *Without father, mother, or ancestry, without beginning of days or end of life:* this is perhaps a quotation from a hymn about Melchizedek. The rabbis maintained that anything not mentioned in the Torah does not exist. Consequently, since the Old Testament nowhere mentions Melchizedek's ancestry, birth, or death, the conclusion can be drawn that he *remains . . . forever.*

7, 4-10: The tithe that Abraham gave to Melchizedek (4), a practice later followed by the levitical priesthood (5), was a gift (6) acknowledging a certain superiority in Melchizedek, the foreign priest (7). This is further indicated by the fact that the institution of the levitical priesthood was sustained by hereditary succession in the tribe of Levi, whereas the absence of any mention of Melchizedek's death in Gn implies that his personal priesthood is permanent (8). The levitical priesthood itself, through Abraham, its ancestor, paid tithes to Melchizedek, thus acknowledging the superiority of his priesthood over its own (9-10).

7, 7: *A lesser person is blessed by a greater:* though this sounds like a principle, there are some examples in the Old Testament that do not support it (cf 2 Sm 14, 22; Jb 31, 20). The author may intend it as a statement of a liturgical rule.

7, 9: *Levi:* for the author this name designates not only the son of Jacob mentioned in Genesis but the priestly tribe that was thought to be descended from him.

7, 11-14: The levitical priesthood was not typified by the priesthood of Melchizedek, for Ps 110, 4 speaks of a priesthood of a new order, the order of Melchizedek, to arise in messianic times (11). Since the levitical priesthood served the Mosaic law, a new priesthood (12) would not come into being without a change in the law itself. Thus Jesus was not associated with the Old Testament priesthood, for he was a descendant of the tribe of Judah, which had never exercised the priesthood (13-14).

7, 13: *He of whom these things are said:* Jesus, the priest "according to the order of Melchizedek." According to the author's interpretation, Ps 110 spoke prophetically of Jesus.

the altar. 14*† It is clear that our Lord
arose from Judah, and in regard to that
tribe Moses said nothing about priests.
15† It is even more obvious if another
priest is raised up after the likeness of
Melchizedek, 16† who has become so,
not by a law expressed in a command-
ment concerning physical descent but
by the power of a life that cannot be
destroyed. 17* For it is testified:

> "You are a priest forever
> according to the order of Melchiz-
> edek."

18* On the one hand, a former com-
mandment is annulled because of its
weakness and uselessness, 19† for the
law brought nothing to perfection; on
the other hand, a better hope is intro-
duced, through which we draw near to
God. 20† And to the degree that this hap-
pened not without the taking of an
oath—for others became priests without
an oath, 21* but he with an oath, through
the one who said to him:

> "The Lord has sworn, and he will
> not repent:
> 'You are a priest forever' "—

22*† to that same degree has Jesus
[also] become the guarantee of an
[even] better covenant. 23 Those priests
were many because they were pre-
vented by death from remaining in of-
fice, 24* but he, because he remains
forever, has a priesthood that does not
pass away. 25*† Therefore, he is always
able to save those who approach God
through him, since he lives forever to
make intercession for them.
26*† It was fitting that we should have
such a high priest: holy, innocent, unde-
filed, separated from sinners, higher
than the heavens. 27*† He has no need,
as did the high priests, to offer sacrifice
day after day, first for his own sins and
then for those of the people; he did that
once for all when he offered himself.
28* For the law appoints men subject to
weakness to be high priests, but the
word of the oath, which was taken after
the law, appoints a son, who has been
made perfect forever.

CHAPTER 8

Heavenly Priesthood of Jesus.†

1* The main point of what has been said
is this: we have such a high priest, who
has taken his seat at the right hand of
the throne of the Majesty in heaven,

---

*

14: Gn 49, 10; Is 11, 1; Mt 1, 1-2.16.20; 2, 6; Lk 1, 27; 2, 4; Rom 1, 3; Rv 5, 5.
17: 5, 6; Ps 110, 4.
18: 10, 1.
21: Ps 110, 4.
22: 8, 6-10; 9, 15-20; 10, 29; 12, 24; 13, 20.
24: 5, 6; 13, 8.
25: Rom 8, 34; 1 Jn 2, 1; Rv 1, 18.
26: 4, 14.15.
27: 5, 3; 9, 12.25-28; 10, 11-14; Ex 29, 38-39; Lv 16, 6.11.15-17; Nm 28, 3-4; Is 53, 10; Rom 6, 10.
28: 5, 1.2.9.
8, 1: 1, 3; 4, 14; 7, 26-28.

---

†

7, 14: *Judah:* the author accepts the early Christian tradition that Jesus was descended from the family of David (cf Mt 1, 1-2.16.20; Lk 1, 27; 2, 4; Rom 1, 3). The Qumran community expected two Messiahs, one descended from Aaron and one from David; Heb shows no awareness of this view or at least does not accept it. Our author's view is not attested in contemporaneous Judaism.

7, 15-19: Jesus does not exercise a priesthood through family lineage but through his immortal existence (15-16), fulfilling Ps 110, 4 (17; cf 3). Thus he abolishes forever both the levitical priesthood and the law it serves, because neither could effectively sanctify people (18) by leading them into direct communication with God (19).

7, 16: *A life that cannot be destroyed:* the life to which Jesus has attained by virtue of his resurrection; it is his exaltation rather than his divine nature that makes him priest. The Old Testament speaks of the Aaronic priesthood as eternal (see Ex 40, 15); our author does not explicitly consider this possible objection to his argument but implicitly refutes it in vv 23-24.

7, 19: *A better hope:* this hope depends upon the sacrifice of the Son of God; through it we "approach the throne of grace" (4, 16); cf 6, 19.20.

7, 20-25: As was the case with the promise to Abraham (6, 13), though not with the levitical priesthood, the eternal priesthood of the order of Melchizedek was confirmed by God's oath (20-21); cf Ps 110, 4. Thus Jesus becomes the guarantee of a permanent covenant (22) that does not require a succession of priests as did the levitical priesthood (23) because his high priesthood is eternal and unchangeable (24). Consequently, Jesus is able to save all who draw near to God through him since he is their ever-living intercessor (25).

7, 20: *An oath:* God's oath in Ps 110, 4.

7, 22: *An [even] better covenant:* better than the Mosaic covenant because it will be eternal, like the priesthood of Jesus upon which it is based. Verse 12 argued that a change of priesthood involves a change of law; since "law" and "covenant" are used correlatively, a new covenant is likewise instituted.

7, 25: *To make intercession:* the intercession of the exalted Jesus, not the sequel to his completed sacrifice but its eternal presence in heaven; cf Rom 8, 34.

7, 26-28: Jesus is precisely the high priest whom the human race requires, holy and sinless, installed far above humanity (26); one having no need to offer sacrifice daily for sins but making a single offering of himself (27) once for all. The law could only appoint high priests with human limitations, but the fulfillment of God's oath regarding the priesthood of Melchizedek (Ps 110, 4) makes the Son of God the perfect priest forever (28).

7, 26: This verse with its list of attributes is reminiscent of v 3 and is perhaps a hymnic counterpart to it, contrasting the exalted Jesus with Melchizedek.

7, 27: Such daily sacrifice is nowhere mentioned in the Mosaic law; only on the Day of Atonement is it prescribed that the high priest must *offer sacrifice . . . for his own sins and then for those of the people* (Lv 16, 11-19). *Once for all:* this translates the Greek words *ephapax/hapax* that occur eleven times in Heb.

8, 1-6: The Christian community has in Jesus the kind of high priest described in 7, 26-28. In virtue of his ascension Jesus has taken his place at God's right hand in accordance with Ps 110, 1 (1), where he presides over the heavenly sanctuary established by God himself (2). Like every high priest, he has his offering to make (3; cf 9, 12.14), but it differs from that of the levitical priesthood in which he had no share (4) and which was in any case but a shadowy reflection of the true offering in the heavenly sanctuary (5). But Jesus' ministry in the heavenly sanctuary is that of mediator of a superior covenant that accomplishes what it signifies (6).

2*† a minister of the sanctuary and of
the true tabernacle that the Lord, not
man, set up. 3* Now every high priest
is appointed to offer gifts and sacrifices;
thus the necessity for this one also to
have something to offer. 4* If then he
were on earth, he would not be a priest,
since there are those who offer gifts ac-
cording to the law. 5* They worship in
a copy and shadow of the heavenly
sanctuary, as Moses was warned when
he was about to erect the tabernacle.
For he says, "See that you make every-
thing according to the pattern shown
you on the mountain." 6* Now he has
obtained so much more excellent a min-
istry as he is mediator of a better cove-
nant, enacted on better promises.

Old and New Covenants.† 7 For if that
first covenant had been faultless, no
place would have been sought for a sec-
ond one. 8*† But he finds fault with them
and says:

"Behold, the days are coming, says the Lord,
when I will conclude a new covenant with the house of Israel
and the house of Judah.
9 It will not be like the covenant I made with their fathers
the day I took them by the hand to lead them forth from the land of Egypt;
for they did not stand by my covenant
and I ignored them, says the Lord.
10* But this is the covenant I will establish with the house of Israel
after those days, says the Lord:
I will put my laws in their minds
and I will write them upon their hearts.
I will be their God,
and they shall be my people.
11 And they shall not teach, each one his fellow citizen
and kinsman, saying, 'Know the Lord,'
for all shall know me,
from least to greatest.
12 For I will forgive their evildoing
and remember their sins no more."

13*† When he speaks of a "new" cove-
nant, he declares the first one obsolete.
And what has become obsolete and has
grown old is close to disappearing.

CHAPTER 9

The Worship of the First Covenant.†
1 Now [even] the first covenant had reg-
ulations for worship and an earthly
sanctuary. 2*† For a tabernacle was
constructed, the outer one, in which
were the lampstand, the table, and the
bread of offering; this is called the Holy
Place. 3*† Behind the second veil was
the tabernacle called the Holy of Holies,
4*† in which were the gold altar of in-
cense and the ark of the covenant en-
tirely covered with gold. In it were the
gold jar containing the manna, the staff
of Aaron that had sprouted, and the
tablets of the covenant. 5*† Above it
were the cherubim of glory overshad-
owing the place of expiation. Now is
not the time to speak of these in detail.

*

2: 9, 11; Ex 33, 7; Nm 24, 6 LXX.
3: 5, 1.
4: 7, 13.
5: 9, 23; Ex 25, 40; Acts 7, 44; Col 2, 17.
6: 7, 22; 9, 15.
8: Jer 31, 31-34.
10: 10, 16-17.
13: Rom 10, 4.
9, 2: Ex 25, 23-30.
3: Ex 26, 31-34.
4: Ex 16, 32-34; 25, 10.16.21; 30, 1-10; Lv 16, 12-13; Nm 17, 2-7.16-26.
5: Ex 25, 16-22; 26, 34; Lv 16, 14-15.

†

8, 2: *The sanctuary:* the Greek term could also mean "holy things" but bears the meaning "sanctuary" elsewhere in Heb (9, 8.12.24.25; 10, 19; 13, 11). *The true tabernacle:* the heavenly tabernacle *that the Lord . . . set up* is contrasted with the earthly tabernacle that Moses set up in the desert. *True* means "real" in contradistinction to a mere "copy and shadow" (5); compare the Johannine usage (e.g., Jn 1, 9; 6, 32; 15, 1). The idea that the earthly sanctuary is a reflection of a heavenly model may be based upon Ex 25, 9, but probably also derives from the Platonic concept of a real world of which our observable world is merely a shadow.

8, 7-13: Since the first covenant was deficient in accomplishing what it signified, it had to be replaced (7), as Jeremiah (31, 31-34) had prophesied (8-12). Even in the time of Jeremiah, the first covenant was antiquated (13). In 7, 22-24, the superiority of the new covenant was seen in the permanence of its priesthood; here the superiority is based on better promises, made explicit in the citation of Jer 31 (LXX: 38), 31-34, namely, in the immediacy of the people's knowledge of God (11) and in the forgiveness of sin (12).

8, 8-12: In citing Jer the author follows the Septuagint; some apparent departures from it may be the result of a different Septuagintal text rather than changes deliberately introduced.

8, 13: *Close to disappearing:* from the prophet's perspective, not that of the author of Heb.

9, 1-10: The regulations for worship under the old covenant permitted all the priests to enter the Holy Place (2, 6), but only the high priest to enter the Holy of Holies and then only once a year (3-5.7). The description of the sanctuary and its furnishings is taken essentially from Ex 25-26. This exclusion of the people from the Holy of Holies signified that they were not allowed to stand in God's presence (8) because their offerings and sacrifices, which were merely symbols of their need of spiritual renewal (10), could not obtain forgiveness of sins (9).

9, 2: *The outer one:* the author speaks of *the outer tabernacle* (6) and *the inner one* (7) rather than of one Mosaic tabernacle divided into two parts or sections.

9, 3: *The second veil:* what is meant is the veil that divided the Holy Place from the Holy of Holies. It is here called *the second,* because there was another veil at the entrance to the Holy Place, or "outer tabernacle" (Ex 26, 36).

9, 4: *The gold altar of incense:* Ex 30, 6 locates this altar in the Holy Place, i.e., the first tabernacle, rather than in the Holy of Holies. Neither is there any Old Testament support for the assertion that the jar of manna and the staff of Aaron were in the ark of the covenant. For the tablets of the covenant, see Ex 25, 16.

9, 5: *The place of expiation:* the gold "mercy seat" (Greek *hilastērion,* as in Rom 3, 25), where the blood of the sacrificial animals was sprinkled on the Day of Atonement (Lv 16, 14-15). This rite achieved "expiation" or atonement for the sins of the preceding year.

6*† With these arrangements for wor-
ship, the priests, in performing their
service, go into the outer tabernacle re-
peatedly, 7*† but the high priest alone
goes into the inner one once a year, not
without blood that he offers for himself
and for the sins of the people. 8 In this
way the holy Spirit shows that the way
into the sanctuary had not yet been re-
vealed while the outer tabernacle still
had its place. 9† This is a symbol of the
present time, in which gifts and sacri-
fices are offered that cannot perfect the
worshiper in conscience 10* but only in
matters of food and drink and various
ritual washings: regulations concerning
the flesh, imposed until the time of the
new order.

Sacrifice of Jesus.† 11*† But when
Christ came as high priest of the good
things that have come to be, passing
through the greater and more perfect
tabernacle not made by hands, that is,
not belonging to this creation, 12* he en-
tered once for all into the sanctuary, not
with the blood of goats and calves but
with his own blood, thus obtaining eter-
nal redemption. 13*† For if the blood of
goats and bulls and the sprinkling of a
heifer's ashes can sanctify those who
are defiled so that their flesh is
cleansed, 14*† how much more will the
blood of Christ, who through the eter-
nal spirit offered himself unblem-
ished to God, cleanse our consciences
from dead works to worship the living
God.

15*† For this reason he is mediator of
a new covenant: since a death has taken
place for deliverance from transgres-
sions under the first covenant, those
who are called may receive the prom-
ised eternal inheritance. 16† Now where
there is a will, the death of the testator
must be established. 17 For a will takes
effect only at death; it has no force while
the testator is alive. 18 Thus not even the
first covenant was inaugurated without
blood. 19*† When every commandment
had been proclaimed by Moses to all the
people according to the law, he took the
blood of calves [and goats], together
with water and crimson wool and hys-
sop, and sprinkled both the book itself
and all the people, 20* saying, "This is
'the blood of the covenant which God
has enjoined upon you.' " 21*† In the
same way, he sprinkled also the taber-
nacle and all the vessels of worship with

*

6: Ex 27, 21; 30, 7; Lv 24, 8.
7: Ex 30, 10; Lv 16, 1-14.
10: 13, 9; Lv 11; 14, 8; Nm 19, 11-21; Col 2, 16.
11: 4, 14; 10, 1.20.
12: 7, 27; Mt 26, 28.
13: 10, 4; Lv 16, 6-16; Nm, 19, 9.14-21.
14: 10, 10; Rom 5, 9; 1 Tm 3, 9; Ti 2, 14; 1 Pt 1, 18-19; 1 Jn 1, 7; Rv 1, 5.
15: 1 Tm 2, 5.
19: 12-13.
20: Ex 24, 3-8; Mt 26, 28; Mk 14, 24.
21: Ex 40, 9; Lv 8, 15.19.

†

9, 6: *In performing their service:* the priestly services that had to be performed regularly in the Holy Place or *outer tabernacle* included burning incense on the incense altar twice each day (Ex 30, 7), replacing the loaves on the table of the bread of offering once each week (Lv 24, 8), and constantly caring for the lamps on the lampstand (Ex 27, 21).

9, 7: *Not without blood:* blood was essential to Old Testament sacrifice because it was believed that life was located in the blood. Hence blood was especially sacred, and its outpouring functioned as a meaningful symbol of cleansing from sin and reconciliation with God. Unlike Heb, the Old Testament never says that the blood is "offered." The author is perhaps retrojecting into his description of Mosaic ritual a concept that belongs to the New Testament antitype, as Paul does when he speaks of the Israelites' passage through the sea as a "baptism" (1 Cor 10, 2).

9, 9: *The present time:* this expression is equivalent to the "present age," used in contradistinction to the "age to come."

9, 11-14: Christ, the high priest of the spiritual blessings foreshadowed in the Old Testament sanctuary, has actually entered the true sanctuary of heaven that is not of human making (11). His place there is permanent, and his offering is his own blood that won eternal redemption (12). If the sacrifice of animals could bestow legal purification (13), how much more effective is the blood of the sinless, divine Christ who spontaneously offered himself to purge the human race of sin and render it fit for the service of God (14).

9, 11: *The good things that have come to be:* the majority of later manuscripts here read "the good things to come"; cf 10, 1.

9, 13: *A heifer's ashes:* ashes from a red heifer that had been burned were mixed with water and used for the cleansing of those who had become ritually defiled by touching a corpse; see Nm 19, 9.14-21.

9, 14: *Through the eternal spirit:* this expression does not refer either to the holy Spirit or to the divine nature of Jesus but to the life of the risen Christ, "a life that cannot be destroyed" (7, 16).

9, 15-22: Jesus' role as *mediator of the new covenant* is based upon his sacrificial *death* (cf 8, 6). His death has effected *deliverance from transgressions,* i.e., deliverance from sins committed under the old covenant, which the Mosaic sacrifices were incapable of effacing. Until this happened, the *eternal inheritance* promised by God could not be obtained (15). This effect of his work follows the human pattern by which a last will and testament becomes effective only with the death of the testator (16-17). The Mosaic covenant was also associated with death, for Moses made use of blood to seal the pact between God and the people (18-21). In Old Testament tradition, guilt could normally not be remitted without the use of blood (22; cf Lv 17, 11).

9, 16-17: *A will . . . death of the testator:* the same Greek word *diathēkē,* meaning "covenant" in vv 15 and 18, is used here with the meaning *will.* The new covenant, unlike the old, is at the same time a will that requires *the death of the testator.* Jesus as eternal Son is the one who established the new covenant together with his Father, author of both covenants; at the same time he is the testator whose death puts his *will* into effect.

9, 19-20: A number of details here are different from the description of this covenant rite in Ex 24, 5-8. Exodus mentions only calves ("young bulls," NAB), not goats (but this addition in Heb is of doubtful authenticity), says nothing of the use of *water and crimson wool and hyssop* (these features probably came from a different rite; cf Lv 14, 3-7; Nm 19, 6-18), and describes Moses as splashing blood on the altar, whereas Heb says he sprinkled it on the book (but both book and altar are meant to symbolize the agreement of God). The words of Moses are also slightly different from those in Exodus and are closer to the words of Jesus at the Last Supper in Mk 14, 24 // Mt 26, 28.

9, 21: According to Ex, the tabernacle did not yet exist at the time of the covenant rite. Moreover, nothing is said of sprinkling it with blood at its subsequent dedication (Ex 40, 9-11).

blood. 22*† According to the law almost
everything is purified by blood, and
without the shedding of blood there is
no forgiveness.
23*† Therefore, it was necessary for
the copies of the heavenly things to be
purified by these rites, but the heavenly
things themselves by better sacrifices
than these. 24* For Christ did not enter
into a sanctuary made by hands, a copy
of the true one, but heaven itself, that
he might now appear before God on our
behalf. 25 Not that he might offer himself
repeatedly, as the high priest enters
each year into the sanctuary with blood
that is not his own; 26*† if that were so,
he would have had to suffer repeatedly
from the foundation of the world. But
now once for all he has appeared at the
end of the ages to take away sin by
his sacrifice. 27* Just as it is appointed
that human beings die once, and af-
ter this the judgment, 28*† so also
Christ, offered once to take away
the sins of many, will appear a sec-
ond time, not to take away sin but to
bring salvation to those who eagerly
await him.

CHAPTER 10

One Sacrifice instead of Many.†

1*† Since the law has only a shadow of
the good things to come, and not the
very image of them, it can never make
perfect those who come to worship by
the same sacrifices that they offer con-
tinually each year. 2 Otherwise, would
not the sacrifices have ceased to be of-
fered, since the worshipers, once
cleansed, would no longer have had
any consciousness of sins? 3* But in
those sacrifices there is only a yearly
remembrance of sins, 4* for it is im-
possible that the blood of bulls and
goats take away sins. 5*† For this rea-
son, when he came into the world, he
said:

> "Sacrifice and offering you did not
> desire,
> but a body you prepared for me;
> 6 holocausts and sin offerings you
> took no delight in.
> 7 Then I said, 'As is written of me in
> the scroll,
> Behold, I come to do your will, O
> God.' "

8*† First he says, "Sacrifices and offer-
ings, holocausts and sin offerings, you
neither desired nor delighted in." These
are offered according to the law.
9* Then he says, "Behold, I come to do
your will." He takes away the first to
establish the second. 10* By this "will,"
we have been consecrated through the
offering of the body of Jesus Christ once
for all.

*

22: Lv 17, 11.
23: Jb 15, 15.
24: 7, 25; Rom 8, 34; 1 Jn 2, 1-2.
26: 7, 27; Jn 1, 29; Gal 4, 4.
27: Gn 3, 19.
28: 10, 10; Is 53, 12.
10, 1: 8, 5; Col 2, 17.
3: Lv 16, 21; Nm 5, 15 LXX.
4: Is 1, 11; Mi 6, 6-8.
5-7: Ps 40, 7-9.
8: 5-6; Ps 40, 7.
9: 7; Ps 40, 8; Mt 26, 39; Mk 14, 36; Lk 22, 42; Jn 6, 38.
10: 9, 12.14.

†

9, 22: *Without the shedding of blood there is no forgiveness:* in fact, ancient Israel did envisage other means of obtaining forgiveness; the Old Testament mentions contrition of heart (Ps 51, 19), fasting (Jl 2, 12), and almsgiving (Sir 3, 29). The author is limiting his horizon to the sacrificial cult, which did always involve the shedding of blood for its expiatory and unitive value.

9, 23-28: Since the blood of animals became a cleansing symbol among Old Testament prefigurements, it was necessary that the realities foreshadowed be brought into being by a shedding of blood that was infinitely more effective by reason of its worth (23). Christ did not simply prefigure the heavenly realities (24) by performing an annual sacrifice with a blood not his own (25); he offered the single sacrifice of himself as the final annulment of sin (26). Just as death is the unrepeatable act that ends a person's life, so Christ's offering of himself for all is the unrepeatable sacrifice that has once for all achieved redemption (27-28).

9, 26: *At the end of the ages:* the use of expressions such as this shows that the author of Heb, despite his interest in the Platonic concept of an eternal world above superior to temporal reality here below, nevertheless still clings to the Jewish Christian eschatology with its sequence of "the present age" and "the age to come."

9, 28: *To take away the sins of many:* the reference is to Is 53, 12. Since the Greek verb *anapherō* can mean both "to take away" and "to bear," the author no doubt intended to play upon both senses: Jesus took away sin by bearing it himself. See the similar wordplay in Jn 1, 29. *Many* is used in the Semitic meaning of "all" in the inclusive sense, as in Mk 14, 24. *To those who eagerly await him:* Jesus will appear *a second time* at the parousia, as the high priest reappeared on the Day of Atonement, emerging from the Holy of Holies, which he had entered *to take away sin.* This dramatic scene is described in Sir 50, 5-11.

10, 1-10: Christian faith now realizes that the Old Testament sacrifices did not effect the spiritual benefits to come but only prefigured them (1). For if the sacrifices had actually effected the forgiveness of sin, there would have been no reason for their constant repetition (2). They were rather a continual reminder of the people's sins (3). It is not reasonable to suppose that human sins could be removed by the blood of animal sacrifices (4). Christ, therefore, is here shown to understand his mission in terms of Ps 40, 6-8, cited according to the Septuagint (5-7). Jesus acknowledged that the Old Testament sacrifices did not remit the sins of the people and so, perceiving the will of God, offered his own body for this purpose (8-10).

10, 1: *A shadow of the good things to come:* the term *shadow* was used in 8, 5 to signify the earthly counterpart of the Platonic heavenly reality. But here it means a prefiguration of what is to come in Christ, as it is used in the Pauline literature; cf Col 2, 17.

10, 5-7: A passage from Ps 40, 7-9a is placed in the mouth of the Son at his incarnation. As usual, the author follows the Septuagint text. There is a notable difference in v 5 (= Ps 40, 7b), where the Masoretic text reads "ears you have dug for me" ("ears open to obedience you gave me," NAB), but most Septuagint manuscripts have "a body you prepared for me," a reading obviously more suited to the interpretation of Heb.

10, 8: *Sacrifices and offerings, holocausts and sin offerings:* these four terms taken from the preceding passage of Ps 40 (with the first two changed to plural forms) are probably intended as equivalents to the four principal types of Old Testament sacrifices: peace offerings (Lv 3, here called *sacrifices*); cereal offerings (Lv 2, here called *offerings*); *holocausts* (Lv 1); and *sin offerings* (Lv 4-5). This last category includes the guilt offerings of Lv 5, 14-26.

11*† Every priest stands daily at his
ministry, offering frequently those
same sacrifices that can never take
away sins. 12* But this one offered one
sacrifice for sins, and took his seat for-
ever at the right hand of God; 13† now
he waits until his enemies are made his
footstool. 14* For by one offering he has
made perfect forever those who are be-
ing consecrated. 15† The holy Spirit also
testifies to us, for after saying:

16* "This is the covenant I will establish
with them after those days, says
the Lord:
'I will put my laws in their hearts,
and I will write them upon their
minds,' "

17*† he also says:

"Their sins and their evildoing
I will remember no more."

18 Where there is forgiveness of these,
there is no longer offering for sin.

Recalling the Past.† 19* Therefore,
brothers, since through the blood of Je-
sus we have confidence of entrance into
the sanctuary 20*† by the new and living
way he opened for us through the veil,
that is, his flesh, 21*† and since we have
"a great priest over the house of God,"
22*† let us approach with a sincere heart
and in absolute trust, with our hearts
sprinkled clean from an evil conscience
and our bodies washed in pure water.
23* Let us hold unwaveringly to our con-
fession that gives us hope, for he who
made the promise is trustworthy.
24 We must consider how to rouse one
another to love and good works. 25*† We
should not stay away from our assem-
bly, as is the custom of some, but en-
courage one another, and this all the
more as you see the day drawing near.

26*† If we sin deliberately after re-
ceiving knowledge of the truth, there no
longer remains sacrifice for sins 27* but
a fearful prospect of judgment and a
flaming fire that is going to consume the
adversaries. 28*† Anyone who rejects
the law of Moses is put to death without
pity on the testimony of two or three
witnesses. 29* Do you not think that a
much worse punishment is due the one
who has contempt for the Son of God,
considers unclean the covenant-blood
by which he was consecrated, and in-
sults the spirit of grace? 30* We know the
one who said:

*

11: 7, 27; Dt 10, 8; 18, 7.
12-13: Ps 110, 1.
14: 9, 28.
16: 8, 10; Jer 31, 33.
17: 8, 12; Jer 31, 34.
19: 3, 6; 4, 16; 6, 19-20; Eph 1, 7; 3, 12.
20: Jn 14, 6 / 6, 19-20; 9, 8.11-12; Mt 27, 51; Mk 15, 38; Lk 23, 45.
21: 3, 6.
22: 9, 13-14; Ez 36, 25; 1 Cor 6, 11; Ti 3, 5; 1 Pt 3, 21.
23: 3, 1.6; 4, 14; 1 Cor 10, 13.
25: Rom 13, 12; 1 Cor 3, 13.
26: 3, 12; 6, 4-8.
27: 31; 9, 27; Is 26, 11 LXX; Zep 1, 18.
28: Dt 17, 6.
29: 6, 6.
30: Dt 32, 35.36; Rom 12, 19.

†

10, 11-18: Whereas the levitical priesthood offered daily sacrifices that were ineffectual in remitting sin (11), Jesus offered a single sacrifice that won him a permanent place at God's right hand. There he has only to await the final outcome of his work (12-13; cf Ps 110, 1). Thus he has brought into being in his own person the new covenant prophesied by Jeremiah (31, 33-34) that has rendered meaningless all other offerings for sin (14-18).

10, 13: *Until his enemies are made his footstool:* Ps 110, 1 is again used; the reference here is to the period of time between the enthronement of Jesus and his second coming. The identity of the *enemies* is not specified; cf 1 Cor 15, 25-27.

10, 15-17: The testimony of the scriptures is now invoked to support what has just preceded. The passage cited is a portion of the new covenant prophecy of Jer 31, 31-34, which the author previously used in 8, 8-12.

10, 17: *He also says:* these words are not in the Greek text, which has only *kai,* "also," but the expression *after saying* in v 15 seems to require such a phrase to divide the Jeremiah text into two sayings. Others understand "the Lord says" of v 16 (here rendered *says the Lord*) as outside the quotation and consider v 16b as part of the second saying. Two ancient versions and a number of minuscules introduce the words "then he said" or a similar expression at the beginning of v 17.

10, 19-39: Practical consequences from these reflections on the priesthood and the sacrifice of Christ should make it clear that Christians may now have direct and confident access to God through the person of Jesus (19-20), who rules God's house as high priest (21). They should approach God with sincerity and faith, in the knowledge that through baptism their sins have been remitted (22), reminding themselves of the hope they expressed in Christ at that event (23). They are to encourage one another to Christian love and activity (24), not refusing, no matter what the reason, to participate in the community's assembly, especially in view of the parousia (25; cf 1 Thes 4, 13-18). If refusal to participate in the assembly indicates rejection of Christ, no sacrifice exists to obtain forgiveness for so great a sin (26); only the dreadful judgment of God remains (27). For if violation of the Mosaic law could be punished by death, how much worse will be the punishment of those who have turned their backs on Christ by despising his sacrifice and disregarding the gifts of the holy Spirit (28-29). Judgment belongs to the Lord, and he enacts it by his living presence (30-31). There was a time when the spirit of their community caused them to welcome and share their sufferings (32-34). To revitalize that spirit is to share in the courage of the Old Testament prophets (cf Is 26, 20; Hb 2, 3-4), the kind of courage that must distinguish the faith of the Christian (35-39).

10, 20: *Through the veil, that is, his flesh:* the term *flesh* is used pejoratively. As the temple veil kept people from entering the Holy of Holies (it was rent at Christ's death, Mk 15, 38), so the flesh of Jesus constituted an obstacle to approaching God.

10, 21: *The house of God:* this refers back to 3, 6, "we are his house."

10, 22: *With our hearts sprinkled clean from an evil conscience:* as in 9, 13 (see the note there), the sprinkling motif refers to the Mosaic rite of cleansing from ritual impurity. This could produce only an external purification, whereas sprinkling with the blood of Christ (9, 14) cleanses the *conscience. Washed in pure water:* baptism is elsewhere referred to as a washing; cf 1 Cor 6, 11; Eph 5, 26.

10, 25: *Our assembly:* the liturgical *assembly* of the Christian community, probably for the celebration of the Eucharist. *The day:* this designation for the parousia also occurs in the Pauline letters, e.g., Rom 2, 16; 1 Cor 3, 13; 1 Thes 5, 2.

10, 26: *If we sin deliberately:* verse 29 indicates that the author is here thinking of apostasy; cf 3, 12; 6, 4-8.

10, 28: *Rejects the law of Moses:* evidently not any sin against the law, but idolatry. Dt 17, 2-7 prescribed capital punishment for idolaters who were convicted on the testimony of two or three witnesses.

"Vengeance is mine; I will repay,"
and again:
"The Lord will judge his people."

31* It is a fearful thing to fall into the
hands of the living God.
32*† Remember the days past when,
after you had been enlightened, you en-
dured a great contest of suffering.
33* At times you were publicly exposed
to abuse and affliction; at other times
you associated yourselves with those so
treated. 34* You even joined in the suf-
ferings of those in prison and joyfully
accepted the confiscation of your prop-
erty, knowing that you had a better and
lasting possession. 35* Therefore, do not
throw away your confidence; it will
have great recompense. 36* You need
endurance to do the will of God and re-
ceive what he has promised.

37*† "For, after just a brief moment,
he who is to come shall come;
he shall not delay.
38* But my just one shall live by faith,
and if he draws back I take no
pleasure in him."

39 We are not among those who draw
back and perish, but among those who
have faith and will possess life.

V: EXAMPLES, DISCIPLINE, DISOBEDIENCE

CHAPTER 11†

Faith of the Ancients. 1*† Faith is the
realization of what is hoped for and evi-
dence of things not seen. 2 Because of
it the ancients were well attested.
3*† By faith we understand that the uni-
verse was ordered by the word of God,
so that what is visible came into being
through the invisible. 4*† By faith Abel
offered to God a sacrifice greater than
Cain's. Through this he was attested to
be righteous, God bearing witness to his
gifts, and through this, though dead, he
still speaks. 5* By faith Enoch was
taken up so that he should not see death,
and "he was found no more because
God had taken him." Before he was
taken up, he was attested to have
pleased God. 6*† But without faith it is
impossible to please him, for anyone
who approaches God must believe that
he exists and that he rewards those who
seek him. 7* By faith Noah, warned
about what was not yet seen, with rever-
ence built an ark for the salvation of
his household. Through this he con-
demned the world and inherited the
righteousness that comes through faith.
8* By faith Abraham obeyed when
he was called to go out to a place that he
was to receive as an inheritance; he
went out, not knowing where he was to

HEBREWS

*

31: 27; Mt 10, 28; Lk 12, 4-5.
32: 6, 4.
33: 1 Cor 4, 9.
34: 13, 3; Mt 6, 19-20; Lk 12, 33-34.
35: 4, 16.
36: Lk 21, 19.
37: Is 26, 20; Hb 2, 3.
38: Hb 2, 4; Rom 1, 17; Gal 3, 11.
11, 1: 1, 3; 3, 14; Rom 8, 24; 2 Cor 4, 18.
3: Gn 1, 3; Ps 33, 6; Wis 9, 1; Jn 1, 3.
4: 12, 24; Gn 4, 4.10.
5: Gn 5, 24; Sir 44, 16.
6: Wis 4, 10.
7: Gn 6, 8-22; Sir 44, 17-18; Mt 24, 37-39; Lk 17, 26-27; 1 Pt 3, 20; 2 Pt 2, 5.
8: Gn 12, 1-4; 15, 7-21; Sir 44, 19-22; Acts 7, 2-8; Rom 4, 16-22.

†

10, 32: *After you had been enlightened:* "enlightenment" is an ancient metaphor for baptism (cf Eph 5, 14; Jn 9, 11), but see 6, 4 and the note there.

10, 37-38: In support of his argument, the author uses Hb 2, 3-4 in a wording almost identical with the text of the Codex Alexandrinus of the Septuagint but with the first and second lines of v 4 inverted. He introduces it with a few words from Is 26, 20: *after just a brief moment.* Note the Pauline usage of Hb 2, 4 in Rom 1, 17; Gal 3, 11.

11, 1-40: This chapter draws upon the people and events of the Old Testament to paint an inspiring portrait of religious faith, firm and unyielding in the face of any obstacles that confront it. These pages rank among the most eloquent and lofty to be found in the Bible. They expand the theme announced in 6, 12, to which the author now returns (10, 39). The material of this chapter is developed chronologically. Verses 3-7 draw upon the first nine chapters of Gn; vv 8-22, upon the period of the patriarchs; vv 23-31, upon the time of Moses; vv 32-38, upon the history of the judges, the prophets, and the Maccabean martyrs. The author gives the most extensive description of faith provided in the New Testament, though his interest does not lie in a technical, theological definition. In view of the needs of his audience he describes what authentic faith does, not what it is in itself. Through faith God guarantees the blessings to be hoped for from him, providing evidence in the gift of faith that what he promises will eventually come to pass (1). Because they accepted in faith God's guarantee of the future, the biblical personages discussed in vv 3-38 were themselves commended by God (2). Christians have even greater reason to remain firm in faith since they, unlike the Old Testament men and women of faith, have perceived the beginning of God's fulfillment of his messianic promises (39-40).

11, 1: *Faith is the realization . . . evidence:* the author is not attempting a precise definition. There is dispute about the meaning of the Greek words *hypostasis* and *elenchos,* here translated *realization* and *evidence,* respectively. *Hypostasis* usually means "substance," "being" (as translated in 1, 3), or "reality" (as translated in 3, 14); here it connotes something more subjective, and so *realization* has been chosen rather than "assurance" (RSV). *Elenchos,* usually "proof," is used here in an objective sense and so translated *evidence* rather than the transferred sense of "(inner) conviction" (RSV).

11, 3: *By faith . . . God:* this verse does not speak of the faith of the Old Testament men and women but is in the first person plural. Hence it seems out of place in the sequence of thought.

11, 4: The "Praise of the Ancestors" in Sir 44, 1—50, 21 gives a similar list of heroes. The Cain and Abel narrative in Gn 4, 1-16 does not mention Abel's faith. It says, however, that God "looked with favor on Abel and his offering" (Gn 4, 4); in view of v 6 the author probably understood God's favor to have been activated by Abel's faith. *Though dead, he still speaks:* possibly because his blood "cries out to me from the soil" (Gn 4, 10), but more probably a way of saying that the repeated story of Abel provides ongoing witness to faith.

11, 6: One must believe not only that God *exists* but that he is concerned about human conduct; the Old Testament defines folly as the denial of this truth; cf Ps 52, 2.

go. 9* By faith he sojourned in the prom-
ised land as in a foreign country, dwell-
ing in tents with Isaac and Jacob, heirs
of the same promise; 10* for he was look-
ing forward to the city with foundations,
whose architect and maker is God.
11* By faith he received power to gener-
ate, even though he was past the normal
age—and Sarah herself was sterile—for
he thought that the one who had made
the promise was trustworthy. 12* So it
was that there came forth from one
man, himself as good as dead, descen-
dants as numerous as the stars in the
sky and as countless as the sands on
the seashore.

13* All these died in faith. They did
not receive what had been promised but
saw it and greeted it from afar and ac-
knowledged themselves to be strangers
and aliens on earth, 14 for those who
speak thus show that they are seeking
a homeland. 15 If they had been thinking
of the land from which they had come,
they would have had opportunity to re-
turn. 16* But now they desire a better
homeland, a heavenly one. Therefore,
God is not ashamed to be called their
God, for he has prepared a city for
them.

17* By faith Abraham, when put to the
test, offered up Isaac, and he who had
received the promises was ready to of-
fer his only son, 18* of whom it was said,
"Through Isaac descendants shall bear
your name." 19*† He reasoned that God
was able to raise even from the dead,
and he received Isaac back as a symbol.
20*† By faith regarding things still to
come Isaac blessed Jacob and Esau.
21* By faith Jacob, when dying, blessed
each of the sons of Joseph and "bowed
in worship, leaning on the top of his
staff." 22* By faith Joseph, near the end
of his life, spoke of the Exodus of the
Israelites and gave instructions about
his bones.

23* By faith Moses was hidden by his
parents for three months after his birth,
because they saw that he was a beauti-
ful child, and they were not afraid of
the king's edict. 24*† By faith Moses,
when he had grown up, refused to be
known as the son of Pharaoh's daugh-
ter; 25 he chose to be ill-treated along
with the people of God rather than enjoy
the fleeting pleasure of sin. 26 He consid-
ered the reproach of the Anointed
greater wealth than the treasures of
Egypt, for he was looking to the recom-
pense. 27* By faith he left Egypt, not
fearing the king's fury, for he perse-
vered as if seeing the one who is invisible.
28* By faith he kept the Passover and
sprinkled the blood, that the Destroyer
of the firstborn might not touch them.
29* By faith they crossed the Red Sea
as if it were dry land, but when the
Egyptians attempted it they were
drowned. 30* By faith the walls of Jeri-
cho fell after being encircled for seven
days. 31* By faith Rahab the harlot did
not perish with the disobedient, for she
had received the spies in peace.

32* What more shall I say? I have not
time to tell of Gideon, Barak, Samson,
Jephthah, of David and Samuel and the
prophets, 33* who by faith conquered
kingdoms, did what was righteous, ob-
tained the promises; they closed the
mouths of lions, 34* put out raging fires,
escaped the devouring sword; out of
weakness they were made powerful, be-
came strong in battle, and turned back
foreign invaders. 35* Women received
back their dead through resurrection.
Some were tortured and would not ac-
cept deliverance, in order to obtain a
better resurrection. 36* Others endured
mockery, scourging, even chains and
imprisonment. 37* They were stoned,
sawed in two, put to death at sword's
point; they went about in skins of sheep
or goats, needy, afflicted, tormented.
38* The world was not worthy of them.
They wandered about in deserts and on
mountains, in caves and in crevices in
the earth.

39 Yet all these, though approved be-
cause of their faith, did not receive what

---

*

9: Gn 12, 8; 13, 12; 23, 4; 26, 3; 35, 27.
10: 12, 22; 13, 14; Rv 21, 10-22.
11: Gn 17, 19; 21, 2; Rom 4, 19-21 / 1 Cor 10, 13.
12: Gn 15, 5; 22, 17; 32, 13; Ex 32, 13; Dt 10, 22; Dn 3, 36 LXX.
13: Gn 23, 4; Ps 39, 13.
16: 13, 14; Ex 3, 6.
17: Gn 22, 1-10; Sir 44, 20; 1 Mc 2, 52; Jas 2, 21.
18: Gn 21, 12 LXX; Rom 9, 7.
19: Rom 4, 16-22.
20: Gn 27, 27-40.
21: Gn 27, 38-40; 47, 31 LXX; 48, 15-16.
22: Gn 50, 24-25.
23: Ex 2, 2; Acts 7, 20.
24-25: Ex 2, 10-15; Acts 7, 23-29.
27: Ex 2, 15; Acts 7, 29.
28: Ex 12, 21-23; Wis 18, 25; 1 Cor 10, 10.
29: Ex 14, 22-28.
30: Jos 6, 12-21.
31: Jos 2, 1-21; 6, 22-25; Jas 2, 25.
32: Jgs 4, 6-22; 6, 11—8, 32; 11, 1—12, 7.
33: Dn 6, 23.
34: Dn 3, 22-25.49-50.
35: 1 Kgs 17, 17-24; 2 Kgs 4, 18-37; 2 Mc 6, 18—7, 42.
36: 2 Chr 36, 16; Jer 20, 2; 37, 15.
37: 2 Chr 24, 21.
38: 1 Mc 2, 28-30.

†

11, 19: *As a symbol:* Isaac's "return from death" is seen as a *symbol* of Christ's resurrection. Others understand the words *en parabolē* to mean "in figure," i.e., the word *dead* is used figuratively of Isaac, since he did not really die. But in the one other place that *parabolē* occurs in Heb, it means symbol (9, 9).

11, 20-22: Each of these three patriarchs, Isaac, Jacob, and Joseph, had faith in the future fulfillment of God's promise and renewed this faith when near death.

11, 24-27: The reason given for Moses' departure from Egypt differs from the account in Ex 2, 11-15. The author also gives a christological interpretation of his decision to share the trials of his people.

had been promised. [40]† God had fore-
seen something better for us, so that
without us they should not be made per-
fect.

CHAPTER 12

God our Father.† [1]† Therefore, since
we are surrounded by so great a cloud
of witnesses, let us rid ourselves of ev-
ery burden and sin that clings to us and
persevere in running the race that lies
before us [2]* while keeping our eyes
fixed on Jesus, the leader and perfecter
of faith. For the sake of the joy that lay
before him he endured the cross, de-
spising its shame, and has taken his seat
at the right of the throne of God.
[3] Consider how he endured such opposi-
tion from sinners, in order that you may
not grow weary and lose heart. [4] In your
struggle against sin you have not yet
resisted to the point of shedding blood.
[5]* You have also forgotten the exhorta-
tion addressed to you as sons:

"My son, do not disdain the disci-
pline of the Lord
or lose heart when reproved by
him;
[6] for whom the Lord loves, he disci-
plines;
he scourges every son he ac-
knowledges."

[7]* Endure your trials as "discipline";
God treats you as sons. For what "son"
is there whom his father does not disci-
pline? [8] If you are without discipline, in
which all have shared, you are not sons
but bastards. [9]* Besides this, we have
had our earthly fathers to discipline us,
and we respected them. Should we not
[then] submit all the more to the Father
of spirits and live? [10] They disciplined
us for a short time as seemed right to
them, but he does so for our benefit, in
order that we may share his holiness.
[11]* At the time, all discipline seems a
cause not for joy but for pain, yet later
it brings the peaceful fruit of righteous-
ness to those who are trained by it.
[12]* So strengthen your drooping
hands and your weak knees. [13]* Make
straight paths for your feet, that what
is lame may not be dislocated but
healed.

Penalties of Disobedience. [14]* Strive
for peace with everyone, and for that
holiness without which no one will see
the Lord. [15]*† See to it that no one be
deprived of the grace of God, that no
bitter root spring up and cause trouble,
through which many may become de-
filed, [16]* that no one be an immoral or
profane person like Esau, who sold his
birthright for a single meal. [17]* For you
know that later, when he wanted to in-
herit his father's blessing, he was re-
jected because he found no opportunity
to change his mind, even though he
sought the blessing with tears.
[18]*† You have not approached that
which could be touched and a blazing
fire and gloomy darkness and storm
[19]* and a trumpet blast and a voice
speaking words such that those who
heard begged that no message be fur-
ther addressed to them, [20]* for they
could not bear to hear the command:
"If even an animal touches the moun-
tain, it shall be stoned." [21]* Indeed, so
fearful was the spectacle that Moses
said, "I am terrified and trembling."
[22]* No, you have approached Mount
Zion and the city of the living God, the
heavenly Jerusalem, and countless an-

*

12, 2: 2, 10; Ps 110, 1; Phil 2, 6-8.
5-6: Prv 3, 11-12 / Dt 8, 5; 1 Cor 11, 32.
7: Prv 13, 24; Sir 30, 1.
9: Nm 16, 22; 27, 16 LXX.
11: 2 Cor 4, 17; Phil 1, 11; Jas 3, 18.
12: Is 35, 3; Sir 25, 23; Jb 4, 3-4.
13: Prv 4, 26 LXX.
14: Rom 12, 18; 14, 19.
15: Dt 29, 18 (17 LXX).
16: Gn 25, 33.
17: Gn 27, 34-38.
18: Ex 19, 12-14; Dt 4, 11; 5, 22-23.
19: Ex 19, 16.19; 20, 18-19.
20: Ex 19, 12-13.
21: Dt 9, 19.
22: Gal 4, 26; Rv 21, 2.

†

11, 40: *So that without us they should not be made perfect:* the heroes of the Old Testament obtained their recompense only after the saving work of Christ had been accomplished. Thus they already enjoy what Christians who are still struggling do not yet possess in its fullness.

12, 1-13: Christian life is to be inspired not only by the Old Testament men and women of faith (1) but above all by Jesus. As the architect of Christian faith, he had himself to endure the cross before receiving the glory of his triumph (2). Reflection on his sufferings should give his followers courage to continue the struggle, if necessary even to the shedding of blood (3-4). Christians should regard their own sufferings as the affectionate correction of the Lord, who loves them as a father loves his children.

12, 1: *That clings to us:* the meaning is uncertain, since the Greek word *euperistatos,* translated *cling,* occurs only here. The papyrus P46 and one minuscule read *euperispastos,* "easily distracting," which also makes good sense.

12, 15-17: Esau serves as an example in two ways: his *profane* attitude illustrates the danger of apostasy, and his inability to secure a blessing afterward illustrates the impossibility of repenting after falling away (see 6, 4-6).

12, 18-29: As a final appeal for adherence to Christian teaching, the two covenants, of Moses and of Christ, are compared. The Mosaic covenant, the author argues, is shown to have originated in fear of God and threats of divine punishment (18-21). The covenant in Christ gives us direct access to God (22), makes us members of the Christian community, God's children, a sanctified people (23), who have Jesus as mediator to speak for us (24). Not to heed the voice of the risen Christ is a graver sin than the rejection of the word of Moses (25-26). Though Christians fall away, God's kingdom in Christ will remain and his justice will punish those guilty of deserting it (28-29).

12, 18-24: This remarkably beautiful passage contrasts two great assemblies of people: that of the Israelites gathered at Mount Sinai for the sealing of the old covenant and the promulgation of the Mosaic law, and that of the followers of Jesus gathered at *Mount Zion, the heavenly Jerusalem,* the assembly of the *new covenant.* This latter scene, marked by the presence of *countless angels* and of *Jesus* with his redeeming *blood,* is reminiscent of the celestial liturgies of the Book of Revelation.

gels in festal gathering, 23*† and the as-
sembly of the firstborn enrolled in
heaven, and God the judge of all, and
the spirits of the just made perfect,
24*† and Jesus, the mediator of a new
covenant, and the sprinkled blood that
speaks more eloquently than that of
Abel.
25* See that you do not reject the one
who speaks. For if they did not escape
when they refused the one who warned
them on earth, how much more in our
case if we turn away from the one who
warns from heaven. 26* His voice shook
the earth at that time, but now he has
promised, "I will once more shake not
only earth but heaven." 27* That phrase,
"once more," points to [the] removal
of shaken, created things, so that what
is unshaken may remain. 28* Therefore,
we who are receiving the unshakable
kingdom should have gratitude, with
which we should offer worship pleasing
to God in reverence and awe. 29* For
our God is a consuming fire.

VI: FINAL EXHORTATION, BLESSING, GREETINGS

CHAPTER 13

1† Let mutual love continue. 2* Do not
neglect hospitality, for through it some
have unknowingly entertained angels.
3* Be mindful of prisoners as if sharing
their imprisonment, and of the ill-
treated as of yourselves, for you also
are in the body. 4* Let marriage be hon-
ored among all and the marriage bed
be kept undefiled, for God will judge the
immoral and adulterers. 5* Let your life
be free from love of money but be con-
tent with what you have, for he has said,
"I will never forsake you or abandon
you." 6* Thus we may say with confi-
dence:

"The Lord is my helper,
[and] I will not be afraid.
What can anyone do to me?"

7 Remember your leaders who spoke the
word of God to you. Consider the out-
come of their way of life and imitate
their faith. 8* Jesus Christ is the same
yesterday, today, and forever.
9*† Do not be carried away by all
kinds of strange teaching. It is good to
have our hearts strengthened by grace
and not by foods, which do not benefit
those who live by them. 10† We have an
altar from which those who serve the
tabernacle have no right to eat. 11* The
bodies of the animals whose blood the
high priest brings into the sanctuary as
a sin offering are burned outside the
camp. 12* Therefore, Jesus also suffered
outside the gate, to consecrate the peo-
ple by his own blood. 13 Let us then go
to him outside the camp, bearing the re-
proach that he bore. 14* For here we
have no lasting city, but we seek the one
that is to come. 15* Through him [then]
let us continually offer God a sacrifice
of praise, that is, the fruit of lips that
confess his name. 16* Do not neglect
to do good and to share what you
have; God is pleased by sacrifices of that
kind.
17† Obey your leaders and defer to
them, for they keep watch over you and
will have to give an account, that they
may fulfill their task with joy and not
with sorrow, for that would be of no ad-
vantage to you.
18 Pray for us, for we are confident
that we have a clear conscience, wish-
ing to act rightly in every respect.
19 I especially ask for your prayers that
I may be restored to you very soon.

*

23: Lk 10, 20; Rv 5, 11.
24: 7, 22; 8, 6; 9, 15 / 11, 4; Gn 4, 10.
25: Ex 20, 19.
26: Ex 19, 18; Jgs 5, 4-5; Ps 68, 9; Hg 2, 6.
27: Is 66, 22; Mt 24, 35; Mk 13, 31; Lk 21, 33.
28: Dn 7, 14.18 / Rom 1, 9.
29: Dt 4, 24; Is 33, 14.
13, 2: Gn 18, 3; 19, 2-3; Jgs 6, 11-22; Tb 5, 4.
3: Mt 25, 36.
4: 1 Cor 5, 13; Eph 5, 5.
5: Dt 31, 6.8; Jos 1, 5.
6: Pss 27, 1-3; 118, 6.
8: 1, 12; 7, 24; Rv 1, 17.
9: Rom 14, 17; 1 Cor 8, 8; Eph 4, 14; Col 2, 16.
11: Ex 29, 14; Lv 16, 27.
12: Mt 21, 39; Mk 12, 8; Lk 20, 15; Jn 19, 17.
14: 11, 10.14.
15: Hos 14, 3.
16: Phil 4, 18.

†

12, 23: *The assembly of the firstborn enrolled in heaven:* this expression may refer to the angels of v 22, or to the heroes of the Old Testament (see ch 11), or to the entire assembly of the new covenant.

12, 24: *Speaks more eloquently:* the blood of Abel, the first human blood to be shed, is contrasted with that of Jesus. Abel's blood cried out from the earth for vengeance, but the blood of Jesus has opened the way for everyone, providing cleansing and access to God (10, 19).

13, 1-16: After recommendations on social and moral matters (1-6), the letter turns to doctrinal issues. The fact that the original leaders are dead should not cause the recipients of this letter to lose their faith (7), for Christ still lives and he remains always the same (8). They must not rely for their personal sanctification on regulations concerning foods (9), nor should they entertain the notion that Judaism and Christianity can be intermingled (10; cf the notes on Gal 2, 11-14 and 2, 15-21). As Jesus died separated from his own people, so must the Christian community remain apart from the religious doctrines of Judaism (11-14). Christ must be the heart and center of the community (15-16).

13, 9: *Strange teaching:* this doctrine about *foods* probably refers to the Jewish food laws; in view of v 10, however, the author may be thinking of the Mosaic sacrificial banquets.

13, 10: *We have an altar:* this does not refer to the Eucharist, which is never clearly mentioned in Heb, but to the sacrifice of Christ.

13, 17-25: Recommending obedience to the leaders of the community, the author asks for prayers (17-19). The letter concludes with a blessing (20-21), a final request for the acceptance of its message (22), information regarding Timothy (23), and general greetings (24-25).

20*† May the God of peace, who
brought up from the dead the great
shepherd of the sheep by the blood of
the eternal covenant, Jesus our Lord,
21 furnish you with all that is good, that
you may do his will. May he carry out
in you what is pleasing to him through
Jesus Christ, to whom be glory forever
[and ever]. Amen.
22 Brothers, I ask you to bear with this
message of encouragement, for I have
written to you rather briefly. 23* I must
let you know that our brother Timothy
has been set free. If he comes soon, I
shall see you together with him.
24 Greetings to all your leaders and to
all the holy ones. Those from Italy send
you greetings. 25* Grace be with all of
you.

HEBREWS

*

20: Is 63, 11; Zec 9, 11; Jn 10, 11; Acts 2, 24; Rom 15, 33.
23: Acts 16, 1.
25: Ti 3, 15

†

13, 20-21: These verses constitute one of the most beautiful blessings in the New Testament. The resurrection of Jesus is presupposed throughout Heb, since it is included in the author's frequently expressed idea of his exaltation, but this is the only place where it is explicitly mentioned.

THE CATHOLIC LETTERS

In addition to the thirteen letters attributed to Paul and the Letter to the Hebrews, the New Testament contains seven other letters. Three of these are attributed to John, two to Peter, and one each to James and Jude, all personages of the apostolic age. The term "catholic letter" first appears, with reference only to 1 John, in the writings of Apollonius of Ephesus, a second-century apologist, known only from a citation in Eusebius' Ecclesiastical History. *Eusebius himself (A.D. 260-340) used the term to refer to all seven letters.*

The reason for the term "catholic," which means "universal," was the perception that these letters, unlike those of Paul, which were directed to a particular local church, were apparently addressed more generally to the universal church. This designation is not entirely accurate, however. On the one hand, Hebrews has no specifically identified addressees, and originally this was probably true of Ephesians as well. On the other hand, 3 John is addressed to a named individual, 2 John to a specific, though unnamed, community, and 1 Peter to a number of churches that are specified as being located in Asia Minor.

While all seven of these writings begin with an epistolary formula, several of them do not appear to be real letters in the modern sense of the term. In the ancient world it was not unusual to cast an exhortation in the form of a letter for literary effect, a phenomenon comparable to the "open letter" that is sometimes used today.

With the exception of 1 Peter and 1 John, the ancient church showed reluctance to include the catholic letters in the New Testament canon. The reason for this was widespread doubt whether they had actually been written by the apostolic figures to whom they are attributed. The early Christians saw the New Testament as the depository of apostolic faith; therefore, they wished to include only the testimony of apostles. Today we distinguish more clearly between the authorship of a work and its canonicity: even though written by other, later witnesses than those whose names they bear, these writings nevertheless testify to the apostolic faith and constitute canonical scripture. By the late fourth or early fifth centuries, most objections had been overcome in both the Greek and Latin churches (though not in the Syriac), and all seven of the catholic letters have since been acknowledged as canonical.

The Letter of

JAMES

*The person to whom this letter is ascribed can scarcely be one of the two members of the Twelve who bore the name James (see Mt 10, 2-3; Mk 3, 17-18; Lk 6, 14-15), for he is not identified as an apostle but only as "slave of God and of the Lord Jesus Christ" (1, 1). This designation most probably refers to the third New Testament personage named James, a relative of Jesus who is usually called "brother of the Lord" (see Mt 13, 55; Mk 6, 3). He was the leader of the Jewish Christian community in Jerusalem whom Paul acknowledged as one of the "pillars" (Gal 2, 9). In Acts he appears as the authorized spokesman for the Jewish Christian position in the early Church (Acts 12, 17; 15, 13-21). According to the Jewish historian Josephus (*Antiquities *20, 9, 1 §§200-203), he was stoned to death by the Jews under the high priest Ananus II in A.D. 62.*

The letter is addressed to "the twelve tribes in the dispersion." In Old Testament terminology the term "twelve tribes" designates the people of Israel; the "dispersion" or "diaspora" refers to the non-Palestinian Jews who had settled throughout the Greco-Roman world (see Jn 7, 35). Since in Christian thought the church is the new Israel, the address probably designates the Jewish Christian churches located in Palestine, Syria, and elsewhere. Or perhaps the letter is meant more generally for all Christian communities, and the "dispersion" has the symbolic meaning of exile from our true home, as it has in the address of 1 Peter (1, 1). The letter is so markedly Jewish in character that some scholars have regarded it as a Jewish document subsequently "baptized" by a few Christian insertions, but such an origin is scarcely tenable in view of the numerous contacts discernible between the Letter of James and other New Testament literature.

*From the viewpoint of its literary form, James is a letter only in the most conventional sense; it has none of the characteristic features of a real letter except the address. It belongs rather to the genre of *parenesis* or exhortation and is concerned almost exclusively with ethical conduct. It therefore falls within the tradition of Jewish wisdom literature, such as can be found in the Old Testament (Proverbs, Sirach) and in the extracanonical Jewish literature (*Testaments of the Twelve Patriarchs*, the *Books of Enoch*, the *Manual of Discipline* found at Qumran). More specifically, it consists of sequences of didactic proverbs, comparable to Tob 4, 5-19, to many passages in Sirach, and to sequences of sayings in the synoptic gospels. Numerous passages in James treat of subjects that also appear in the synoptic sayings of Jesus, especially in Matthew's Sermon on the Mount, but the correspondences are too general to establish any literary dependence. James represents a type of early Christianity that emphasized sound teaching and responsible moral behavior. Ethical norms are derived not primarily from christology, as in Paul, but from a concept of salvation that involves conversion, baptism, forgiveness of sin, and expectation of judgment (1, 17; 4, 12).*

Paradoxically, this very Jewish work is written in an excellent Greek style, which ranks among the best in the New Testament and appears to be the work of a trained Hellenistic writer. Those who continue to regard James of Jerusalem as its author are therefore obliged to suppose that a secretary must have put the letter into its present literary form. This assumption is not implausible in the light of ancient practice. Some regard the letter as one of the earliest writings in the New Testament and feel that its content accurately reflects what we would expect of the leader of Jewish Christianity. Moreover, they argue that the type of Jewish Christianity reflected in the letter cannot be situated historically after the fall of Jerusalem in A.D. 70.

Others, however, believe it more likely that James is a pseudonymous work of a later period. In addition to its Greek style, they observe further that (a) the prestige that the writer is assumed to enjoy points to the later legendary reputation of James; (b) the discussion of the importance of good works seems to presuppose a debate subsequent to that in Paul's own day; (c) the author does not rely upon prescriptions of the Mosaic law, as we would expect from the historical James; (d) the letter contains no allusions to James's own history and to his relationship with Jesus or to the early Christian community of Jerusalem. For these reasons, many recent interpreters assign James to the period A.D. 90-100.

The principal divisions of the Letter of James are the following:

I: Address (1, 1)
II: The Value of Trials and Temptation (1, 2-18)
III: Exhortations and Warnings (1, 19—5, 12)
IV: The Power of Prayer (5, 13-20)

I: ADDRESS

CHAPTER 1

1*† James, a slave of God and of the Lord Jesus Christ, to the twelve tribes in the dispersion, greetings.

II: THE VALUE OF TRIALS AND TEMPTATION

Perseverance in Trial. 2*† Consider it all joy, my brothers, when you encounter various trials, 3† for you know that the testing of your faith produces perseverance. 4 And let perseverance be perfect, so that you may be perfect and complete, lacking in nothing. 5*† But if any of you lacks wisdom, he should ask God who gives to all generously and ungrudgingly, and he will be given it. 6* But he should ask in faith, not doubting, for the one who doubts is like a wave of the sea that is driven and tossed about by the wind. 7 For that person must not suppose that he will receive anything from the Lord, 8 since he is a man of two minds, unstable in all his ways.

9*† The brother in lowly circumstances should take pride in his high standing, 10* and the rich one in his lowliness, for he will pass away "like the flower of the field." 11 For the sun comes up with its scorching heat and dries up the grass, its flower droops, and the beauty of its appearance vanishes. So will the rich person fade away in the midst of his pursuits.

Temptation. 12*† Blessed is the man who perseveres in temptation, for when he has been proved he will receive the crown of life that he promised to those who love him. 13*† No one experiencing temptation should say, "I am being tempted by God"; for God is not subject to temptation to evil, and he himself tempts no one. 14 Rather, each person is tempted when he is lured and enticed by his own desire. 15 Then desire conceives and brings forth sin, and when sin reaches maturity it gives birth to death.

*

1, 1: Jn 7, 35; 1 Pt 1, 1.
2: Rom 5, 3-5; 1 Pt 1, 6; 4, 13-16.
5: Prv 2, 2-6; Wis 9, 4.9-12.
6: Mt 7, 7; Mk 11, 24.
9: 2, 5.
10: Is 40, 6-7.
12: 1 Cor 9, 25; 2 Tm 4, 8; 1 Pt 5, 4; Rv 2, 10.
13: Sir 15, 11-20; 1 Cor 10, 13.

†

1, 1: *James, a slave of God and of the Lord Jesus Christ:* a declaration of the writer's authority for instructing the Christian communities; cf Rom 1, 1. Regarding the identity of the author, see Introduction. *Dispersion:* see Introduction.

1, 2: *Consider it all joy . . . various trials:* a frequent teaching of the New Testament derived from the words and sufferings of Jesus (Mt 5, 10-12; Jn 10, 11; Acts 5, 41).

1, 3-8: The sequence of testing, perseverance, and being perfect and complete indicates the manner of attaining spiritual maturity and full preparedness for the coming of Christ (5, 7-12; cf 1 Pt 1, 6-7; Rom 5, 3-5). These steps require wisdom (5).

1, 5: *Wisdom:* a gift that God readily grants to all who ask in faith and that sustains the Christian in times of trial. It is a kind of knowledge or understanding not accessible to the unbeliever or those who doubt, which gives the recipient an understanding of the real importance of events. In this way a Christian can deal with adversity with great calm and hope (cf 1 Cor 2, 6-12).

1, 9-11: Throughout his letter (see 2, 5; 4, 10.13-16; 5, 1-6), the author reaffirms the teaching of Jesus that worldly prosperity is not necessarily a sign of God's favor but can even be a hindrance to proper humility before God (cf Lk 6, 20-25; 12, 16-21; 16, 19-31).

1, 12: *Temptation:* the Greek word used here is the same one used for "trials" in v 2. *The crown of life:* in ancient Palestine, crowns or wreaths of flowers were worn at festive occasions as signs of joy and honor. In the Hellenistic world, wreaths were given as a reward to great statesmen, soldiers, athletes. *Life:* here means eternal life. *He promised:* some manuscripts read "God" or "the Lord," while the best witnesses do not specify the subject of "promised."

1, 13-15: It is contrary to what we know of God for God to be the author of human temptation (13). In the commission of a sinful act, one is first beguiled by passion (14), then consent is given, which in turn causes the sinful act. When sin permeates the entire person, it incurs the ultimate penalty of death (15).

16† Do not be deceived, my beloved
brothers: 17† all good giving and every
perfect gift is from above, coming down
from the Father of lights, with whom
there is no alteration or shadow caused
by change. 18*† He willed to give us
birth by the word of truth that we may
be a kind of firstfruits of his creatures.

III: EXHORTATIONS AND WARNINGS

Doers of the Word.† 19* Know this,
my dear brothers: everyone should be
quick to hear, slow to speak, slow to
wrath, 20* for the wrath of a man does
not accomplish the righteousness of
God. 21* Therefore, put away all filth
and evil excess and humbly welcome
the word that has been planted in you
and is able to save your souls.
22* Be doers of the word and not hear-
ers only, deluding yourselves. 23 For if
anyone is a hearer of the word and not
a doer, he is like a man who looks at
his own face in a mirror. 24 He sees him-
self, then goes off and promptly forgets
what he looked like. 25*† But the one
who peers into the perfect law of free-
dom and perseveres, and is not a hearer
who forgets but a doer who acts, such
a one shall be blessed in what he does.
26*† If anyone thinks he is religious
and does not bridle his tongue but de-
ceives his heart, his religion is vain.
27*† Religion that is pure and undefiled
before God and the Father is this: to
care for orphans and widows in their
affliction and to keep oneself unstained
by the world.

CHAPTER 2

Sin of Partiality.† 1 My brothers,
show no partiality as you adhere to the
faith in our glorious Lord Jesus Christ.
2 For if a man with gold rings on his fin-
gers and in fine clothes comes into your
assembly, and a poor person in shabby
clothes also comes in, 3 and you pay at-
tention to the one wearing the fine
clothes and say, "Sit here, please,"
while you say to the poor one, "Stand
there," or "Sit at my feet," 4† have you
not made distinctions among your-
selves and become judges with evil de-
signs?
5*† Listen, my beloved brothers. Did
not God choose those who are poor in
the world to be rich in faith and heirs
of the kingdom that he promised to
those who love him? 6 But you dishon-
ored the poor person. Are not the rich
oppressing you? And do they them-
selves not haul you off to court? 7* Is
it not they who blaspheme the noble
name that was invoked over you?
8*† However, if you fulfill the royal law
according to the scripture, "You shall
love your neighbor as yourself," you are
doing well. 9* But if you show partiality,
you commit sin, and are convicted by
the law as transgressors. 10* For who-
ever keeps the whole law, but falls short
in one particular, has become guilty in
respect to all of it. 11* For he who said,
"You shall not commit adultery," also
said, "You shall not kill." Even if you
do not commit adultery but kill, you
have become a transgressor of the law.
12*† So speak and so act as people who

JAMES

*

18: Jn 1, 12-13; 1 Pt 1, 23.
19: Prv 14, 17; Sir 5, 11.
20: Eph 4, 26.
21: Col 3, 8.
22: Mt 7, 26; Rom 2, 13.
25: 2, 12; Ps 19, 8; Rom 8, 2.
26: 3, 2; Ps 34, 14.
27: Ex 22, 21.
2, 5: 1 Cor 1, 26-28; Rv 2, 9.
7: 1 Pt 4, 4.
8: Lv 19, 18; Mt 22, 39; Rom 13, 9.
9: Dt 1, 17.
10: Gal 3, 10.
11: Ex 20, 13-14; Dt 5, 17-18.
12: 1, 25; Rom 8, 2.

†

1, 16-18: The author here stresses that God is the source of all good and of good alone, and the evil of temptation does not come from him.

1, 17: *All good giving and every perfect gift* may be a proverb written in hexameter. *Father of lights:* God is here called the Father of the heavenly luminaries, i.e., the stars, sun, and moon that he created (Gn 1, 14-18). Unlike orbs moving from nadir to zenith, he never changes or diminishes in brightness.

1, 18: Acceptance of the gospel message, *the word of truth,* constitutes new birth (Jn 3, 5-6) and makes the recipient the *firstfruits* (i.e., the cultic offering of the earliest grains, symbolizing the beginning of an abundant harvest) of a new creation; cf 1 Cor 15, 20; Rom 8, 23.

1, 19-25: To *be quick to hear* the gospel is to accept it readily and to act in conformity with it, removing from one's soul whatever is opposed to it, so that it may take root and effect salvation (19-21). To listen to the gospel message but not practice it is failure to improve oneself (22-24). Only conformity of life to the perfect law of true freedom brings happiness (25).

1, 25: *Peers into the perfect law:* the image of a person doing this is paralleled to that of hearing God's word. The *perfect law* applies the Old Testament description of the Mosaic law to the gospel of Jesus Christ that brings freedom.

1, 26-27: A practical application of v 22 is now made.

1, 26: For control of the tongue, see the note on 3, 1-12.

1, 27: In the Old Testament, orphans and widows are classical examples of the defenseless and oppressed.

2, 1-13: In the Christian community there must be no discrimination or favoritism based on status or wealth (2-4; cf Mt 5, 3; 11, 5; 23, 6; 1 Cor 1, 27-29). Divine favor rather consists in God's election and promises (5). The rich who oppress the poor blaspheme the name of Christ (6-7). By violating one law of love of neighbor, they offend against the whole law (8-11). On the other hand, conscious awareness of the final judgment helps the faithful to fulfill the whole law (12).

2, 4: When Christians show favoritism to the rich they are guilty of the worst kind of prejudice and discrimination. The author says that such Christians set themselves up as judges who judge not by divine law but by the basest, self-serving motives.

2, 5: The poor, "God's poor" of the Old Testament, were seen by Jesus as particularly open to God for belief in and reliance on him alone (Lk 6, 20). God's law cannot tolerate their oppression in any way (9).

2, 8: *Royal:* literally, "kingly"; because the Mosaic law came from God, the universal king. There may be an allusion to Jesus' uses of this commandment in his preaching of the kingdom of God (Mt 22, 39; Mk 12, 31; Lk 10, 27).

2, 12-13: The law upon which the last judgment will be based is the law of freedom. As Jesus taught, mercy (which participates in God's own loving mercy) includes forgiveness of those who wrong us (see Mt 6, 12.14-15).

JAMES

will be judged by the law of freedom.
13* For the judgment is merciless to one
who has not shown mercy; mercy tri-
umphs over judgment.
Faith and Works.† 14* What good is it,
my brothers, if someone says he has
faith but does not have works? Can that
faith save him? 15 If a brother or sister
has nothing to wear and has no food for
the day, 16* and one of you says to them,
"Go in peace, keep warm, and eat well,"
but you do not give them the necessities
of the body, what good is it? 17 So also
faith of itself, if it does not have works,
is dead.
18 Indeed someone might say, "You
have faith and I have works." Demon-
strate your faith to me without works,
and I will demonstrate my faith to you
from my works. 19 You believe that God
is one. You do well. Even the demons
believe that and tremble. 20 Do you want
proof, you ignoramus, that faith without
works is useless? 21* Was not Abraham
our father justified by works when he
offered his son Isaac upon the altar?
22 You see that faith was active along
with his works, and faith was completed
by the works. 23* Thus the scripture was
fulfilled that says, "Abraham believed
God, and it was credited to him as righ-
teousness," and he was called "the
friend of God." 24 See how a person is
justified by works and not by faith
alone. 25* And in the same way, was not
Rahab the harlot also justified by works
when she welcomed the messengers
and sent them out by a different route?
26 For just as a body without a spirit is
dead, so also faith without works is
dead.

CHAPTER 3

Power of the Tongue.† 1 Not many of
you should become teachers, my broth-
ers, for you realize that we will be
judged more strictly, 2* for we all fall
short in many respects. If anyone does
not fall short in speech, he is a per-
fect man, able to bridle his whole body
also. 3 If we put bits into the mouths of
horses to make them obey us, we also
guide their whole bodies. 4 It is the
same with ships: even though they are
so large and driven by fierce winds,
they are steered by a very small rud-
der wherever the pilot's inclination
wishes. 5 In the same way the tongue is
a small member and yet has great pre-
tensions.
Consider how small a fire can set a
huge forest ablaze. 6 The tongue is also
a fire. It exists among our members as
a world of malice, defiling the whole
body and setting the entire course of our
lives on fire, itself set on fire by Ge-
henna. 7 For every kind of beast and
bird, of reptile and sea creature, can be
tamed and has been tamed by the hu-
man species, 8* but no human being can
tame the tongue. It is a restless evil, full
of deadly poison. 9 With it we bless the
Lord and Father, and with it we curse
human beings who are made in the like-
ness of God. 10 From the same mouth
come blessing and cursing. This need
not be so, my brothers. 11 Does a spring
gush forth from the same opening both
pure and brackish water? 12* Can a fig
tree, my brothers, produce olives, or a
grapevine figs? Neither can salt water
yield fresh.
True Wisdom.† 13* Who among you is
wise and understanding? Let him show
his works by a good life in the humility
that comes from wisdom. 14 But if you
have bitter jealousy and selfish ambi-
tion in your hearts, do not boast and be
false to the truth. 15 Wisdom of this kind
does not come down from above but is
earthly, unspiritual, demonic. 16 For
where jealousy and selfish ambition ex-
ist, there is disorder and every foul
practice. 17* But the wisdom from above
is first of all pure, then peaceable, gen-
tle, compliant, full of mercy and good
fruits, without inconstancy or insincer-
ity. 18* And the fruit of righteousness is
sown in peace for those who cultivate
peace.

*

13: Mt 5, 7; 6, 14-15; 18, 32-33.
14: Mt 25, 31-46; Gal 5, 6.
16: 1 Jn 3, 17.
21: Gn 22, 9-12; Heb 11, 17.
23: Gn 15, 6; Rom 4, 3; Gal 3, 6 / 2 Chr 20, 7; Is 41, 8.
25: Jos 2, 1-21.
3, 2: 1, 26; Prv 13, 3; Sir 28, 12-26.
8: Ps 140, 4.
12: Mt 7, 16-17.
13: Eph 4, 1-2.
17: 1, 17; Wis 7, 22-23.
18: Mt 5, 9.

†

2, 14-26: The theme of these verses is the relationship of faith and works (deeds). It has been argued that the teaching here contradicts that of Paul (see especially Rom 4, 5-6). The problem can only be understood if the different viewpoints of the two authors are seen. Paul argues against those who claim to participate in God's salvation because of their good deeds as well as because they have committed themselves to trust in God through Jesus Christ (Paul's concept of faith). Paul certainly understands, however, the implications of true faith for a life of love and generosity (see Gal 5, 6.13-15). The author of James is well aware that proper conduct can only come about with an authentic commitment to God in faith (18.26). Many think he was seeking to correct a misunderstanding of Paul's view.

3, 1-12: The use and abuse of the important role of teaching in the church (1) are here related to the good and bad use of the tongue (9-12), the instrument through which teaching was chiefly conveyed (see Sir 5, 11—6, 1; 28, 12-26).

3, 13-18: This discussion of true wisdom is related to the previous reflection on the role of the teacher as one who is in control of his speech. The qualities of the wise man endowed from above are detailed (17-18; cf Gal 5, 22-23), in contrast to the qualities of earthbound wisdom (14-16; cf 2 Cor 12, 20).

CHAPTER 4

Causes of Division. † 1*† Where do the
wars and where do the conflicts among
you come from? Is it not from your pas-
sions that make war within your mem-
bers? 2 You covet but do not possess.
You kill and envy but you cannot obtain;
you fight and wage war. You do not pos-
sess because you do not ask. 3 You ask
but do not receive, because you ask
wrongly, to spend it on your passions.
4*† Adulterers! Do you not know that to
be a lover of the world means enmity
with God? Therefore, whoever wants to
be a lover of the world makes himself
an enemy of God. 5† Or do you suppose
that the scripture speaks without mean-
ing when it says, "The spirit that he has
made to dwell in us tends toward jeal-
ousy"? 6*† But he bestows a greater
grace; therefore, it says:

"God resists the proud,
but gives grace to the humble."

7* So submit yourselves to God. Resist
the devil, and he will flee from you.
8* Draw near to God, and he will draw
near to you. Cleanse your hands, you
sinners, and purify your hearts, you of
two minds. 9 Begin to lament, to mourn,
to weep. Let your laughter be turned
into mourning and your joy into dejec-
tion. 10* Humble yourselves before the
Lord and he will exalt you.

11† Do not speak evil of one another,
brothers. Whoever speaks evil of a
brother or judges his brother speaks
evil of the law and judges the law. If
you judge the law, you are not a doer
of the law but a judge. 12* There is one
lawgiver and judge who is able to save
or to destroy. Who then are you to judge
your neighbor?

Warning against Presumption. †
13 Come now, you who say, "Today or
tomorrow we shall go into such and
such a town, spend a year there doing
business, and make a profit"—14*† you
have no idea what your life will be like
tomorrow. You are a puff of smoke that
appears briefly and then disappears.
15† Instead you should say, "If the Lord
wills it, we shall live to do this or that."
16 But now you are boasting in your ar-
rogance. All such boasting is evil.
17*† So for one who knows the right
thing to do and does not do it, it is a
sin.

CHAPTER 5

Warning to the Rich. † 1* Come now,
you rich, weep and wail over your im-
pending miseries. 2* Your wealth has
rotted away, your clothes have become
moth-eaten, 3* your gold and silver
have corroded, and that corrosion will
be a testimony against you; it will de-
vour your flesh like a fire. You have
stored up treasure for the last days.
4* Behold, the wages you withheld from
the workers who harvested your fields
are crying aloud, and the cries of the
harvesters have reached the ears of the
Lord of hosts. 5* You have lived on earth
in luxury and pleasure; you have fat-
tened your hearts for the day of slaugh-

*

4, 1: Rom 7, 23; 1 Pt 2, 11.
4: Mt 6, 24; Lk 16, 13; Rom 8, 7; 1 Jn 2, 15-16.
6: Jb 22, 29; Prv 3, 34; Mt 23, 12; 1 Pt 5, 5.
7: 1 Pt 5, 8-9.
8: Zec 1, 3; Mal 3, 7.
10: Jb 5, 11; Mt 23, 12; Lk 14, 11; 18, 14; 1 Pt 5, 6.
12: Mt 7, 1; Rom 2, 1; 14, 4.
14: Prv 27, 1 / Ps 39, 6-7.
17: Lk 12, 47.
5, 1: Lk 6, 24.
2: Mt 6, 19.
3: Ps 21, 10; Prv 11, 4; Jdt 16, 17.
4: Lv 19, 13; Dt 24, 14-15; Mal 3, 5.
5: Jer 12, 3; Lk 16, 19-25.

†

4, 1-12: The concern here is with the origin of conflicts in the Christian community. These are occasioned by love *of the world,* which *means enmity with God* (4). Further, the conflicts are bound up with failure to pray properly (cf Mt 7, 7-11; Jn 14, 13; 15, 7; 16, 23), that is, not asking God at all or using God's kindness only for one's pleasure (2-3). In contrast, the proper dispositions are submission to God, repentance, humility, and resistance to evil (7-10).

4, 1: *Passions:* the Greek word here (literally, "pleasures") does not indicate that pleasure is evil. Rather, as the text points out (2-3), it is the manner in which one deals with needs and desires that determines good or bad. The motivation for any action can be wrong, especially if one does not pray properly but seeks only selfish enjoyment (3).

4, 4: *Adulterers:* a common biblical image for the covenant between God and his people is the marriage bond. In this image, breaking the covenant with God is likened to the unfaithfulness of adultery.

4, 5: The meaning of this saying is difficult because the author of Jas cites, probably from memory, a passage that is not in any extant manuscript of the Bible. Other translations of the text with a completely different meaning are possible: "The Spirit that he (God) made to dwell in us yearns (for us) jealously," or, "He (God) yearns jealously for the spirit that he has made to dwell in us." If this last translation is correct, the author perhaps had in mind an apocryphal religious text that echoes the idea that God is zealous for his creatures; cf Ex 20, 5; Dt 4, 24; Zec 8, 2.

4, 6: The point of this whole argument is that God wants the happiness of all, but that selfishness and pride can make that impossible. We must work with him in humility (10).

4, 11: Slander of a fellow Christian does not break just one commandment but makes mockery of the authority of law in general and therefore of God.

4, 13-17: The uncertainty of life (14), its complete dependence on God, and the necessity of submitting to God's will (15) all help one know and do what is right (17). To disregard this is to live in pride and arrogance (16); failure to do what is right is a sin (17).

4, 14: Some important Greek manuscripts here have, "You who have no idea what tomorrow will bring. Why, what is your life?"

4, 15: *If the Lord wills it:* often in piety referred to as the *"conditio Jacobaea,"* the condition James says we should employ to qualify all our plans.

4, 17: *It is a sin:* those who live arrogantly, forgetting the contingency of life and our dependence on God (13-16), are guilty of sin.

5, 1-6: Continuing with the theme of the transitory character of life on earth, the author points out the impending ruin of the godless. He denounces the unjust rich, whose victims cry to heaven for judgment on their exploiters (4-6). The decay and corrosion of the costly garments and metals, which symbolize wealth, prove them worthless and portend the destruction of their possessors (2-3).

ter. 6*† You have condemned; you have murdered the righteous one; he offers you no resistance.

Patience and Oaths.† 7† Be patient, therefore, brothers, until the coming of the Lord. See how the farmer waits for the precious fruit of the earth, being patient with it until it receives the early and the late rains. 8* You too must be patient. Make your hearts firm, because the coming of the Lord is at hand. 9 Do not complain, brothers, about one another, that you may not be judged. Behold, the Judge is standing before the gates. 10 Take as an example of hardship and patience, brothers, the prophets who spoke in the name of the Lord. 11* Indeed we call blessed those who have persevered. You have heard of the perseverance of Job, and you have seen the purpose of the Lord, because "the Lord is compassionate and merciful."

12*† But above all, my brothers, do not swear, either by heaven or by earth or with any other oath, but let your "Yes" mean "Yes" and your "No" mean "No," that you may not incur condemnation.

IV: THE POWER OF PRAYER

Anointing of the Sick. 13 Is anyone among you suffering? He should pray. Is anyone in good spirits? He should sing praise. 14*† Is anyone among you sick? He should summon the presbyters of the church, and they should pray over him and anoint [him] with oil in the name of the Lord, 15† and the prayer of faith will save the sick person, and the Lord will raise him up. If he has committed any sins, he will be forgiven.

Confession and Intercession. 16 Therefore, confess your sins to one another and pray for one another, that you may be healed. The fervent prayer of a righteous person is very powerful. 17* Elijah was a human being like us; yet he prayed earnestly that it might not rain, and for three years and six months it did not rain upon the land. 18* Then he prayed again, and the sky gave rain and the earth produced its fruit.

Conversion of Sinners. 19* My brothers, if anyone among you should stray from the truth and someone bring him back, 20*† he should know that whoever brings back a sinner from the error of his way will save his soul from death and will cover a multitude of sins.

---

*

6: Wis 2, 10-20.
8: Lk 21, 19; Heb 10, 36 / Heb 10, 25; 1 Pt 4, 7.
11: Ex 34, 6; Ps 103, 8.
12. Mt 5, 34-37.
14: Mk 6, 13.
17: 1 Kgs 17, 1; Lk 4, 25.
18: 1 Kgs 18, 45.
19: Mt 18, 15; Gal 6, 1.
20: Prv 10, 12; 1 Pt 4, 8

---

†

5, 6: The author does not have in mind any specific crime in his readers' communities but rather echoes the Old Testament theme of the harsh oppression of the righteous poor (see Prv 1, 11; Wis 2, 10.12.20).

5, 7-11: Those oppressed by the unjust rich are reminded of the need for patience, both in bearing the sufferings of human life (9) and in their expectation of the coming of the Lord. It is then that they will receive their reward (7-8.10-11; cf Heb 10, 25; 1 Jn 2, 18).

5, 7: *The early and the late rains:* an expression related to the agricultural season in ancient Palestine (see Dt 11, 14; Jer 5, 24; Jl 2, 23).

5, 12: This is the threat of condemnation for the abuse of swearing oaths (cf Mt 5, 33-37). *By heaven or by earth:* these words were substitutes for the original form of an oath, to circumvent its binding force and to avoid pronouncing the holy name of God (see Ex 22, 10).

5, 14: In case of sickness a Christian should ask for the presbyters of the church, i.e., those who have authority in the church (cf Acts 15, 2.22-23; 1 Tm 5, 17; Ti 1, 5). They are to pray over the person and anoint with oil; oil was used for medicinal purposes in the ancient world (see Is 1, 6; Lk 10, 34). In Mk 6, 13, the Twelve anoint the sick with oil on their missionary journey. *In the name of the Lord:* by the power of Jesus Christ.

5, 15: The results of the prayer and anointing are physical health and forgiveness of sins. The Roman Catholic Church (Council of Trent, Session 14) declared that this anointing of the sick is a sacrament "instituted by Christ and promulgated by blessed James the apostle."

5, 20: When a Christian is instrumental in the conversion of a sinner, the result is forgiveness of sins and a reinstatement of the sinner to the life of grace.

The First Letter of

PETER

This letter begins with an address by Peter to Christian communities located in five provinces of Asia Minor (1, 1), including areas evangelized by Paul (Acts 16, 6-7; 18, 23). Christians there are encouraged to remain faithful to their standards of belief and conduct in spite of threats of persecution. Numerous allusions in the letter suggest that the churches addressed were largely of Gentile composition (1, 14.18; 2, 9-10; 4, 3-4), though considerable use is made of the Old Testament (1, 24; 2, 6-7.9-10.22; 3, 10-12).

The contents following the address both inspire and admonish these "chosen sojourners" (1, 1) who, in seeking to live as God's people, feel an alienation from their previous religious roots and the society around them. Appeal is made to Christ's resurrection and the future hope it provides (1, 3-5) and to the experience of baptism as new birth (1, 3.23-25; 3, 21). The suffering and death of Christ serve as both source of salvation and example (1, 19; 2, 21-25; 3, 18). What Christians are in Christ, as a people who have received mercy and are to proclaim and live according to God's call (2, 9-10), is repeatedly spelled out for all sorts of situations in society (2, 11-17), work (even as slaves, 2, 18-20), the home (3, 1-7), and general conduct (3, 8-12; 4, 1-11). But over all hangs the possibility of suffering as a Christian (3, 13-17). In 4, 12-19 persecution is described as already occurring, so that some have supposed the letter was addressed both to places where such a "trial by fire" was already present and to places where it might break out.

*The letter constantly mingles moral exhortation (*paraklēsis*) with its catechetical summaries of mercies in Christ. Encouragement to fidelity in spite of suffering is based upon a vision of the meaning of Christian existence. The emphasis on baptism and allusions to various features of the baptismal liturgy suggest that the author has incorporated into his exposition numerous homiletic, credal, hymnic, and sacramental elements of the baptismal rite that had become traditional at an early date.*

From Irenaeus in the late second century until modern times, Christian tradition regarded Peter the apostle as author of this document. Since he was martyred at Rome during the persecution of Nero between A.D. 64 and 67, it was supposed that the letter was written from Rome shortly before his death. This is supported by its reference to "Babylon" (5, 13), a code name for Rome in the early church.

Some modern scholars, however, on the basis of a number of features that they consider incompatible with Petrine authenticity, regard the letter as the work of a later Christian writer. Such features include the cultivated Greek in which it is written, difficult to attribute to a Galilean fisherman, together with its use of the Greek Septuagint translation when citing the Old Testament; the similarity in both thought and expression to the Pauline literature; and the allusions to widespread persecution of Christians, which did not occur until at least the reign of Domitian (A.D. 81-96). In this view the letter would date from the end of the first century or even the beginning of the second, when there is evidence for persecution of Christians in Asia Minor (the letter of Pliny the Younger to Trajan, A.D. 111-12).

Other scholars believe, however, that these objections can be met by appeal to use of a secretary, Silvanus, mentioned in 5, 12. Such secretaries often gave literary expression to the author's thoughts in their own style and language. The persecutions may refer to local harassment rather than to systematic repression by the state. Hence there is nothing in the document incompatible with Petrine authorship in the 60s.

Still other scholars take a middle position. The many literary contacts with the

Pauline literature, James, and 1 John suggest a common fund of traditional formulations rather than direct dependence upon Paul. Such liturgical and catechetical traditions must have been very ancient and in some cases of Palestinian origin.

Yet it is unlikely that Peter addressed a letter to the Gentile churches of Asia Minor while Paul was still alive. This suggests a period after the death of the two apostles, perhaps A.D. 70-90. The author would be a disciple of Peter in Rome, representing a Petrine group that served as a bridge between the Palestinian origins of Christianity and its flowering in the Gentile world. The problem addressed would not be official persecution but the difficulty of living the Christian life in a hostile, secular environment that espoused different values and subjected the Christian minority to ridicule and oppression.

The principal divisions of the First Letter of Peter are the following:

- *I: Address (1, 1-2)*
- *II: The Gift and Call of God in Baptism (1, 3—2, 10)*
- *III: The Christian in a Hostile World (2, 11—4, 11)*
- *IV: Advice to the Persecuted (4, 12—5, 11)*
- *V: Conclusion (5, 12-14)*

I: ADDRESS

CHAPTER 1

Greeting.*† 1*† Peter, an apostle of
Jesus Christ, to the chosen sojourners
of the dispersion in Pontus, Galatia,
Cappadocia, Asia, and Bithynia, 2* in
the foreknowledge of God the Father,
through sanctification by the Spirit, for
obedience and sprinkling with the blood
of Jesus Christ: may grace and peace
be yours in abundance.

II: THE GIFT AND CALL OF GOD IN BAPTISM

Blessing.*† 3* Blessed be the God and
Father of our Lord Jesus Christ, who
in his great mercy gave us a new birth
to a living hope through the resur-
rection of Jesus Christ from the dead,
4* to an inheritance that is imperish-
able, undefiled, and unfading, kept in
heaven for you 5 who by the power of
God are safeguarded through faith, to
a salvation that is ready to be revealed
in the final time. 6*† In this you rejoice,
although now for a little while you may
have to suffer through various trials,
7* so that the genuineness of your faith,
more precious than gold that is perish-
able even though tested by fire, may
prove to be for praise, glory, and honor
at the revelation of Jesus Christ.
8* Although you have not seen him you
love him; even though you do not see
him now yet believe in him, you rejoice
with an indescribable and glorious joy,
9 as you attain the goal of [your] faith,
the salvation of your souls.
10† Concerning this salvation, proph-
ets who prophesied about the grace that
was to be yours searched and investi-
gated it, 11* investigating the time and
circumstances that the Spirit of Christ
within them indicated when it testified

*

1, 1: Jas 1, 1.
2: Rom 8, 29.
3: Ti 3, 5.
4: Mt 6, 19-20.
6: Jas 1, 2-3.
7: 1 Cor 3, 13.
8: 2 Cor 5, 6-7.
11: Is 52, 13—53, 12; Dn 9, 24.

†

1, 1-2: The introductory formula names *Peter* as the writer (but see Introduction). In his comments to the presbyters (5, 1), the author calls himself a "fellow presbyter." He addresses himself to the Gentile converts of Asia Minor. Their privileged status as a *chosen* and sanctified people makes them worthy of God's *grace* and *peace*. In contrast is their actual existence as aliens and *sojourners*, scattered among pagans, far from their true country.

1, 1: *Dispersion:* literally, diaspora; see Jas 1, 1 and Introduction to that letter. *Pontus . . . Bithynia:* five provinces in Asia Minor, listed in clockwise order from the north, perhaps in the sequence in which a messenger might deliver the letter.

1, 3-5: A prayer of praise and thanksgiving to God who bestows the gift of new life and hope in baptism (*new birth,* 3) *through the resurrection of Jesus Christ from the dead.* The new birth is a sign of an *imperishable inheritance* (4), of *salvation* that is still in the future (*to be revealed in the final time,* 5).

1, 6-9: As the glory of Christ's resurrection was preceded by his sufferings and death, the new life of faith that it bestows is to be subjected to many *trials* (6) while achieving its goal: the glory of the fullness of *salvation* (9) at the coming of Christ (7).

1, 10-12: The *Spirit of Christ* (11) is here shown to have been present in the prophets, moving them to search, investigate, and prophesy about the *grace* of *salvation* that was to come (10), and in the apostles impelling them to preach the fulfillment of salvation in the message of Christ's sufferings and glory (12).

in advance to the sufferings destined for
Christ and the glories to follow them.
12 It was revealed to them that they were
serving not themselves but you with re-
gard to the things that have now been
announced to you by those who
preached the good news to you
[through] the holy Spirit sent from
heaven, things into which angels longed
to look.

Obedience. † 13† Therefore, gird up
the loins of your mind, live soberly, and
set your hopes completely on the grace
to be brought to you at the revelation
of Jesus Christ. 14† Like obedient chil-
dren, do not act in compliance with the
desires of your former ignorance
15* but, as he who called you is holy, be
holy yourselves in every aspect of your
conduct, 16* for it is written, "Be holy
because I [am] holy."

Reverence. 17* Now if you invoke as
Father him who judges impartially ac-
cording to each one's works, conduct
yourselves with reverence during the
time of your sojourning, 18* realizing
that you were ransomed from your
futile conduct, handed on by your an-
cestors, not with perishable things like
silver or gold 19*† but with the precious
blood of Christ as of a spotless unblem-
ished lamb. 20 He was known before
the foundation of the world but re-
vealed in the final time for you, 21 who
through him believe in God who raised
him from the dead and gave him
glory, so that your faith and hope are
in God.

Mutual Love. † 22* Since you have pu-
rified yourselves by obedience to the
truth for sincere mutual love, love one
another intensely from a [pure] heart.
23*† You have been born anew, not from
perishable but from imperishable seed,
through the living and abiding word of
God, 24* for:

"All flesh is like grass,
and all its glory like the flower of
the field;
the grass withers,
and the flower wilts;
25 but the word of the Lord remains
forever."

This is the word that has been pro-
claimed to you.

CHAPTER 2

God's House and People. † 1* Rid
yourselves of all malice and all deceit,
insincerity, envy, and all slander;
2 like newborn infants, long for pure
spiritual milk so that through it you may
grow into salvation, 3*† for you have
tasted that the Lord is good. 4*† Come
to him, a living stone, rejected by hu-
man beings but chosen and precious in
the sight of God, 5*† and, like living
stones, let yourselves be built into a
spiritual house to be a holy priesthood
to offer spiritual sacrifices acceptable
to God through Jesus Christ. 6* For it
says in scripture:

"Behold, I am laying a stone in
Zion,
a cornerstone, chosen and pre-
cious,
and whoever believes in it shall not
be put to shame."

7* Therefore, its value is for you who
have faith, but for those without faith:

"The stone which the builders re-
jected
has become the cornerstone,"

8* and

"A stone that will make people
stumble,
and a rock that will make them
fall."

They stumble by disobeying the word,
as is their destiny.

*

15: Mt 5, 48; 1 Jn 3, 3.
16: Lv 11, 44; 19, 2.
17: 2, 11.
18: Is 52, 3; 1 Cor 6, 20.
19: Ex 12, 5; Jn 1, 29; Heb 9, 14.
22: Rom 12, 10.
23: 1 Jn 3, 9.
24: Is 40, 6-8.
2, 1-2: Jas 1, 21.
3: Ps 34, 9.
4: Ps 118, 22; Mt 21, 42; Acts 4, 11.
5: Eph 2, 21-22.
6: Is 28, 16.
7: Ps 118, 22; Mt 21, 42; Lk 20, 17; Acts 4, 11.
8: Is 8, 14; Rom 9, 33.

†

1, 13-25: These verses are concerned with the call of God's people to holiness and to mutual love by reason of their redemption through the blood of Christ (18-21).

1, 13: *Gird up the loins of your mind:* a figure reminiscent of the rite of Passover when the Israelites were in flight from their oppressors (Ex 12, 11), and also suggesting the vigilance of the Christian people in expectation of the parousia of Christ (Lk 12, 35).

1, 14-16: The *ignorance* here referred to (14) was their former lack of knowledge of God, leading inevitably to godless conduct. Holiness (15-16), on the contrary, is the result of their call to the knowledge and love of God.

1, 19: Christians have received the redemption prophesied by Isaiah (52, 3), through the blood (Jewish symbol of life) of the spotless lamb (Is 53, 7.10; Jn 1, 29; Rom 3, 24-25; cf 1 Cor 6, 20).

1, 22-25: The new birth of Christians (23) derives from Christ, the *imperishable seed* or sowing that produces a new and lasting existence in those who accept the gospel (24-25), with the consequent duty of loving *one another* (22).

1, 23: *The living and abiding word of God:* or, "the word of the living and abiding God."

2, 1-3: Growth toward salvation is seen here as two steps: first, stripping away all that is contrary to the new life in Christ; second, the nourishment (*pure spiritual milk*) that the newly baptized have received.

2, 3: *Tasted that the Lord is good:* cf Ps 34, 9.

2, 4-8: Christ is the cornerstone (cf Is 28, 16) that is the foundation of the spiritual edifice of the Christian community (5). To unbelievers, Christ is an obstacle and a stumbling block on which they are destined to fall (8); cf Rom 11, 11.

2, 5: *Let yourselves be built:* the form of the Greek word could also be indicative passive, "you are being built" (cf 9).

9*† But you are "a chosen race, a royal priesthood, a holy nation, a people of his own, so that you may announce the praises" of him who called you out of darkness into his wonderful light.

10* Once you were "no people"
but now you are God's people;
you "had not received mercy"
but now you have received mercy.

III: THE CHRISTIAN IN A HOSTILE WORLD

Christian Examples. † 11*† Beloved, I urge you as aliens and sojourners to keep away from worldly desires that wage war against the soul. 12 Maintain good conduct among the Gentiles, so that if they speak of you as evildoers, they may observe your good works and glorify God on the day of visitation.

Christian Citizens. † 13* Be subject to every human institution for the Lord's sake, whether it be to the king as supreme 14 or to governors as sent by him for the punishment of evildoers and the approval of those who do good. 15 For it is the will of God that by doing good you may silence the ignorance of foolish people. 16* Be free, yet without using freedom as a pretext for evil, but as slaves of God. 17* Give honor to all, love the community, fear God, honor the king.

Christian Slaves. † 18* Slaves, be subject to your masters with all reverence, not only to those who are good and equitable but also to those who are perverse. 19 For whenever anyone bears the pain of unjust suffering because of consciousness of God, that is a grace. 20 But what credit is there if you are patient when beaten for doing wrong? But if you are patient when you suffer for doing what is good, this is a grace before God. 21*† For to this you have been called, because Christ also suffered for you, leaving you an example that you should follow in his footsteps.

22*† "He committed no sin,
and no deceit was found in his mouth."

23* When he was insulted, he returned no insult; when he suffered, he did not threaten; instead, he handed himself over to the one who judges justly. 24* He himself bore our sins in his body upon the cross, so that, free from sin, we might live for righteousness. By his wounds you have been healed. 25*† For you had gone astray like sheep, but you have now returned to the shepherd and guardian of your souls.

CHAPTER 3

Christian Spouses. † 1 Likewise, you wives should be subordinate to your husbands so that, even if some disobey the word, they may be won over without a word by their wives' conduct 2* when they observe your reverent and chaste behavior. 3* Your adornment should not

---

*

9: Ex 19, 6; Is 61, 6; Rv 1, 6; 20, 6.
10: Hos 1, 9; 2, 25 / Hos 1, 6.
11: Gal 5, 24.
13: Rom 13, 1-7.
16: Gal 5, 13.
17: Prv 24, 21; Mt 22, 21.
18: Eph 6, 5.
21: Mt 16, 24.
22: Is 53, 9.
23: Mt 5, 39.
24: Is 53, 4.12 / Is 53, 5.
25: Is 53, 6.
3, 2: 1 Cor 7, 12-16; Eph 5, 22-24; Col 3, 18; 1 Tm 2, 9-15.
3: 1 Tm 2, 9-10.

---

†

2, 9-10: The prerogatives of ancient Israel mentioned here are now more fully and fittingly applied to the Christian people: "a chosen race" (cf Is 43, 20-21) indicates their divine election (Eph 1, 4-6); "a royal priesthood" (cf Ex 19, 6) to serve and worship God in Christ, thus continuing the priestly functions of his life, passion, and resurrection; "a holy nation" (Ex 19, 6) reserved for God, a people he claims for his own (cf Mal 3, 17) in virtue of their baptism into his death and resurrection. This transcends all natural and national divisions and unites the people into one community to glorify the one who led them from the darkness of paganism to the light of faith in Christ. From being "no people" deprived of all mercy, they have become the very people of God, the chosen recipients of his mercy (cf Hos 1, 9; 2, 25).

2, 11—3, 12: After explaining the doctrinal basis for the Christian community, the author makes practical applications in terms of the virtues that should prevail in all the social relationships of the members of the community: good example to Gentile neighbors (2, 11-12); respect for human authority (2, 13-17); obedience, patience, and endurance of hardship in domestic relations (2, 18-25); Christian behavior of husbands and wives (3, 1-7); mutual charity (3, 8-12).

2, 11: *Aliens and sojourners:* no longer signifying absence from one's native land (Gn 23, 4), this image denotes rather their estrangement from the world during their earthly pilgrimage (see also 1, 1.17).

2, 13-17: True Christian freedom is the result of being servants of God (16; see the note on 2, 18-23). It includes reverence for God, esteem for every individual, and committed love for fellow Christians (17). Although persecution may threaten, subjection to human government is urged (13.17) and concern for the impact of Christians' conduct on those who are not Christians (12.15).

2, 18-21: Most of the labor in the commercial cities of first-century Asia Minor was performed by a working class of slaves. The sense of freedom contained in the gospel undoubtedly caused great tension among Christian slaves: witness the special advice given concerning them here and in 1 Cor 7, 21-24; Eph 6, 5-8; Col 3, 22-25; Phlm. The point made here does not have so much to do with the institution of slavery, which the author does not challenge, but with the nonviolent reaction (20) of slaves to unjust treatment. Their patient suffering is compared to that of Jesus (21), which won righteousness for all humanity.

2, 21: *Suffered:* some ancient manuscripts and versions read "died" (cf 3, 18).

2, 22-25: After the quotation of Is 53, 9b, the passage describes Jesus' passion with phrases concerning the Suffering Servant from Is 53, 4-12, perhaps as employed in an early Christian confession of faith; cf 1, 18-21 and 3, 18-22.

2, 25: *The shepherd and guardian of your souls:* the familiar shepherd and flock figures express the care, vigilance, and love of God for his people in the Old Testament (Ps 23; Is 40, 11; Jer 23, 4-5; Ez 34, 11-16) and of Jesus for all humanity in the New Testament (Mt 18, 10-14; Lk 15, 4-7; Jn 10, 1-16; Heb 13, 20).

3, 1-6: The typical marital virtues of women of the ancient world, obedience, reverence, and chastity (1-2), are outlined here by the author, who gives them an entirely new motivation: Christian wives are to be virtuous so that they may be instrumental in the conversion of their husbands. In imitation of *holy women* in the past (5) they are to cultivate the interior life (4) instead of excessive concern with their appearance (3).

be an external one: braiding the hair,
wearing gold jewelry, or dressing in fine
clothes, 4 but rather the hidden charac-
ter of the heart, expressed in the im-
perishable beauty of a gentle and calm
disposition, which is precious in the
sight of God. 5 For this is also how the
holy women who hoped in God once
used to adorn themselves and were sub-
ordinate to their husbands; 6 thus Sarah
obeyed Abraham, calling him "lord."
You are her children when you do what
is good and fear no intimidation.
7*† Likewise, you husbands should
live with your wives in understanding,
showing honor to the weaker female
sex, since we are joint heirs of the gift
of life, so that your prayers may not be
hindered.
Christian Conduct.† 8 Finally, all of
you, be of one mind, sympathetic, lov-
ing toward one another, compassionate,
humble. 9* Do not return evil for evil,
or insult for insult; but, on the contrary,
a blessing, because to this you were
called, that you might inherit a blessing.
10* For:

"Whoever would love life
and see good days
must keep the tongue from evil
and the lips from speaking deceit,
11 must turn from evil and do good,
seek peace and follow after it.
12 For the eyes of the Lord are on the
righteous
and his ears turned to their
prayer,
but the face of the Lord is against
evildoers."

Christian Suffering.† 13 Now who is
going to harm you if you are enthusias-
tic for what is good? 14 But even if you
should suffer because of righteousness,
blessed are you. Do not be afraid or ter-
rified with fear of them, 15* but sanctify
Christ as Lord in your hearts. Always
be ready to give an explanation to any-
one who asks you for a reason for your
hope, 16 but do it with gentleness and
reverence, keeping your conscience
clear, so that, when you are maligned,
those who defame your good conduct
in Christ may themselves be put to
shame. 17 For it is better to suffer for
doing good, if that be the will of God,
than for doing evil.
18*† For Christ also suffered for sins
once, the righteous for the sake of the
unrighteous, that he might lead you to
God. Put to death in the flesh, he was
brought to life in the spirit. 19† In it he
also went to preach to the spirits in
prison, 20* who had once been disobe-
dient while God patiently waited in the
days of Noah during the building of the
ark, in which a few persons, eight in all,
were saved through water. 21*† This
prefigured baptism, which saves you
now. It is not a removal of dirt from the
body but an appeal to God for a clear
conscience, through the resurrection of
Jesus Christ, 22* who has gone into
heaven and is at the right hand of God,
with angels, authorities, and powers
subject to him.

CHAPTER 4

Christian Restraint.† 1 Therefore,
since Christ suffered in the flesh, arm
yourselves also with the same attitude
(for whoever suffers in the flesh has
broken with sin), 2 so as not to spend
what remains of one's life in the flesh
on human desires, but on the will of
God. 3* For the time that has passed is
sufficient for doing what the Gentiles
like to do: living in debauchery, evil de-
sires, drunkenness, orgies, carousing,
and wanton idolatry. 4 They are sur-
prised that you do not plunge into the
same swamp of profligacy, and they vil-

*

7: Eph 5, 25-33; Col 3, 19.
9: Mt 5, 44; Lk 6, 28; Rom 12, 14.
10-12: Ps 34, 13-17.
15: Is 8, 12.
18: 1 Cor 15, 45.
20: Gn 7, 7.17; 2 Pt 2, 5.
21: Eph 5, 26; Heb 10, 22.
22: Eph 1, 20-21.
4, 3: Eph 2, 2-3; 4, 17-19; Col 3, 7; Ti 3, 3.

†

3, 7: Husbands who do not respect their wives will have as little success in prayer as those who, according to Paul, have no love: their prayers will be "a resounding gong or a clashing cymbal" (1 Cor 13, 1). Consideration for others is shown as a prerequisite for effective prayer also in Mt 5, 23-24; 1 Cor 11, 20-22; Jas 4, 3. After all, whatever the social position of women in the world and in the family, they are equal recipients of the gift of God's salvation. Paul is very clear on this point, too (see 1 Cor 11, 11-12; Gal 3, 28).

3, 8-12: For the proper ordering of Christian life in its various aspects as described in 2, 11—3, 9, there is promised the blessing expressed in Ps 34, 13-17. In the Old Testament this refers to longevity and prosperity; here, it also refers to eternal life.

3, 13-22: This exposition, centering on v 17, runs as follows: by his suffering and death Christ the righteous one saved the unrighteous (18); by his resurrection he received new life in the spirit, which he communicates to believers through the baptismal bath that cleanses their consciences from sin. As Noah's family was saved *through water,* so Christians are saved through the waters of baptism (19-22). Hence they need not share the fear of sinners; they should rather rejoice in suffering because of their hope in Christ. Thus their innocence disappoints their accusers (13-16; cf Mt 10, 28; Rom 8, 35-39).

3, 18: *Suffered:* very many ancient manuscripts and versions read "died." *Put to death in the flesh:* affirms that Jesus truly died as a human being. *Brought to life in the spirit:* that is, in the new and transformed existence freed from the limitations and weaknesses of natural human life (cf 1 Cor 15, 45).

3, 19: *The spirits in prison:* it is not clear just who these spirits are. They may be the spirits of the sinners who died in the flood, or angelic powers, hostile to God, who have been overcome by Christ (cf 22; Gn 6, 4; Enoch 6-36, especially 21, 6; 2 Enoch 7, 1-5).

3, 21: *Appeal to God:* this could also be translated "pledge," that is, a promise on the part of Christians to live with a good conscience before God, or a pledge from God of forgiveness and therefore a good conscience for us.

4, 1-6: Willingness to suffer with Christ equips the Christian with the power to conquer sin (1). Christ is here portrayed as the judge to whom those guilty of pagan vices must render an account (5; cf Jn 5, 22-27; Acts 10, 42; 2 Tm 4, 1).

ify you; 5* but they will give an account
to him who stands ready to judge the
living and the dead. 6† For this is why
the gospel was preached even to the
dead that, though condemned in the
flesh in human estimation, they might
live in the spirit in the estimation of
God.

Christian Charity.† 7 The end of all
things is at hand. Therefore, be serious
and sober for prayers. 8*† Above all, let
your love for one another be intense,
because love covers a multitude of sins.
9* Be hospitable to one another without
complaining. 10* As each one has re-
ceived a gift, use it to serve one another
as good stewards of God's varied grace.
11*† Whoever preaches, let it be with the
words of God; whoever serves, let it be
with the strength that God supplies, so
that in all things God may be glorified
through Jesus Christ, to whom belong
glory and dominion forever and ever.
Amen.

IV: ADVICE TO THE PERSECUTED

Trial of Persecution.† 12* Beloved, do
not be surprised that a trial by fire is
occurring among you, as if something
strange were happening to you. 13* But
rejoice to the extent that you share in
the sufferings of Christ, so that when
his glory is revealed you may also re-
joice exultantly. 14* If you are insulted
for the name of Christ, blessed are you,
for the Spirit of glory and of God rests
upon you. 15 But let no one among you
be made to suffer as a murderer, a thief,
an evildoer, or as an intriguer. 16 But
whoever is made to suffer as a Christian
should not be ashamed but glorify God
because of the name. 17* For it is time
for the judgment to begin with the
household of God; if it begins with us,
how will it end for those who fail to obey
the gospel of God?

18* "And if the righteous one is barely
saved,
where will the godless and the sin-
ner appear?"

19 As a result, those who suffer in accord
with God's will hand their souls over to
a faithful creator as they do good.

CHAPTER 5

Advice to Presbyters.† 1† So I exhort
the presbyters among you, as a fellow
presbyter and witness to the sufferings
of Christ and one who has a share in
the glory to be revealed. 2* Tend the
flock of God in your midst, [overseeing]
not by constraint but willingly, as God
would have it, not for shameful profit
but eagerly. 3 Do not lord it over those
assigned to you, but be examples to the
flock. 4*† And when the chief Shepherd
is revealed, you will receive the unfad-
ing crown of glory.

Advice to the Community.†
5*† Likewise, you younger members, be
subject to the presbyters. And all of you,
clothe yourselves with humility in your
dealings with one another, for:

"God opposes the proud
but bestows favor on the humble."

6* So humble yourselves under the
mighty hand of God, that he may exalt
you in due time. 7* Cast all your worries
upon him because he cares for you.
8* Be sober and vigilant. Your oppo-
nent the devil is prowling around like
a roaring lion looking for [someone] to

---

*

5: Acts 10, 42; 2 Tm 4, 1.
8: Prv 10, 12; Jas 5, 20.
9: Heb 13, 2.
10: Rom 12, 6-8; 1 Cor 12, 4-11.
11: 1 Cor 10, 31.
12: 1, 6-7; 3, 14.17.
13: Rom 5, 3-5; 8, 17; 2 Tm 2, 12.
14: Acts 5, 41 / Is 11, 2.
17: Lk 23, 31; 2 Thes 1, 8.
18: Prv 11, 31 LXX.
5, 2: Acts 20, 28; Ti 1, 7.
4: Wis 5, 15-16; 1 Cor 9, 25; 2 Tm 4, 8; Jas 1, 12.
5: Prv 3, 34.
6: Jb 22, 29; Jas 4, 10.
7: Ps 55, 23; Mt 6, 25-33; Lk 12, 22-31; Phil 4, 6.
8: 1 Thes 5, 6.

---

†

4, 6: *The dead:* these may be the sinners of the flood generation who are possibly referred to in 3, 19. But many scholars think that there is no connection between these two verses, and that *the dead* here are Christians who have died since hearing the preaching of the gospel.

4, 7-11: The inner life of the eschatological community is outlined as *the end* (the parousia of Christ) and the judgment draws near in terms of seriousness, sobriety, prayer, and love expressed through hospitality and the use of one's gifts for the glory of God and of Christ.

4, 8: *Love covers a multitude of sins:* a maxim based on Prv 10, 12; see also Ps 32, 1; Jas 5, 20.

4, 11: Some scholars feel that this doxology concludes the part of the homily addressed specifically to the newly baptized, begun in 1, 3; others that it concludes a baptismal liturgy. Such doxologies do occur within a New Testament letter, e.g., Rom 9, 5. Some propose that v 11 was an alternate ending, with 4, 12—5, 14 being read in places where persecution was more pressing. But such doxologies usually do not occur at the end of letters (the only examples are 2 Pt 3, 18, Jude 25, and Rom 16, 27, the last probably a liturgical insertion).

4, 12-19: The suffering to which the author has already frequently referred is presented in more severe terms. This has led some scholars to see these verses as referring to an actual persecution. Others see the heightening of the language as only a rhetorical device used at the end of the letter to emphasize the suffering motif.

5, 1-4: In imitation of Christ, the chief shepherd, those entrusted with a pastoral office are to tend the flock by their care and example.

5, 1: *Presbyters:* the officially appointed leaders and teachers of the Christian community (cf 1 Tm 5, 17-18; Ti 1, 5-8; Jas 5, 14).

5, 4: See the note on 2, 25.

5, 5-11: The community is to be subject to the presbyters and to show humility toward one another and trust in God's love and care (5-7). With sobriety, alertness, and steadfast faith they must resist the evil one; their sufferings are shared with Christians everywhere (8-9). They will be strengthened and called to eternal glory (10-11).

5, 5: *Younger members:* this may be a designation for office-holders of lesser rank.

devour. [9] Resist him, steadfast in faith,
knowing that your fellow believers
throughout the world undergo the same
sufferings. [10]* The God of all grace who
called you to his eternal glory through
Christ [Jesus] will himself restore, con-
firm, strengthen, and establish you af-
ter you have suffered a little. [11] To him
be dominion forever. Amen.

V: CONCLUSION

[12]† I write you this briefly through Sil-
vanus, whom I consider a faithful
brother, exhorting you and testifying
that this is the true grace of God. Re-
main firm in it. [13]† The chosen one at
Babylon sends you greeting, as does
Mark, my son. [14]* Greet one another
with a loving kiss. Peace to all of you
who are in Christ.

*

10: Rom 8, 18; 2 Cor 4, 17.
14: Rom 16, 16; 1 Cor 16, 20; 2 Cor 13, 12.

†

5, 12: *Silvanus:* the companion of Paul (see 2 Cor 1, 19; 1 Thes 1, 1; 2 Thes 1, 1). Jews and Jewish Christians, like Paul, often had a Hebrew name (Saoul, Silas) and a Greek or Latin name (Paul, Silvanus). On Silvanus's possible role as amanuensis, see Introduction.

5, 13: *The chosen one:* feminine, referring to the Christian community (*ekklēsia*) at *Babylon,* the code name for Rome in Rv 14, 8; 17, 5; 18, 2. *Mark, my son:* traditionally a prominent disciple of Peter and co-worker at the church in Rome, perhaps the John Mark referred to in Acts 12, 12.25; 13, 5.13; and in 15, 37-39, a companion of Barnabas. Perhaps this is the same Mark mentioned as Barnabas's cousin in Col 4, 10, a co-worker with Paul in Phlm 24 (see also 2 Tm 4, 11).

The Second Letter of

PETER

This letter can be appreciated both for its positive teachings and for its earnest warnings. It seeks to strengthen readers in faith (1, 1), hope for the future (3, 1-10), knowledge (1, 2.6.8), love (1, 7), and other virtues (1, 5-6). This aim is carried out especially by warning against false teachers, the condemnation of whom occupies the long central section of the letter (2, 1-22). A particular crisis is the claim by "scoffers" that there will be no second coming of Jesus, a doctrine that the author vigorously affirms (3, 1-10). The concept of God's "promises" is particularly precious in the theology of 2 Peter (1, 4; 3, 4.9.13). Closing comments at 3, 17-18 well sum up the twin concerns: that you not "be led into" error and "fall" but instead "grow in grace" and "knowledge" of Jesus Christ.

Second Peter is clearly structured in its presentation of these points. It reminds its readers of the divine authenticity of Christ's teaching (1, 3-4), continues with reflections on Christian conduct (1, 5-15), then returns to the exalted dignity of Jesus by incorporating into the text the apostolic witness to his transfiguration (1, 16-18). It takes up the question of the interpretation of scripture by pointing out that it is possible to misunderstand the sacred writings (1, 19-21) and that divine punishment will overtake false teachers (2, 1-22). It proclaims that the parousia is the teaching of the Lord and of the apostles and is therefore an eventual certainty (3, 1-13). At the same time, it warns that the meaning of Paul's writings on this question should not be distorted (3, 14-18).

In both content and style this letter is very different from 1 Peter, which immediately precedes it in the canon. The opening verse attributes it to "Symeon Peter, a slave and apostle of Jesus Christ." Moreover, the author in 3, 1 calls his work a "second letter," referring probably to 1 Peter as his first, and in 1, 18 counts himself among those present at the transfiguration of Jesus.

Nevertheless, acceptance of 2 Peter into the New Testament canon met with great resistance in the early church. The oldest certain reference to it comes from Origen in the early third century. While he himself accepted both Petrine letters as canonical, he testifies that others rejected 2 Peter. As late as the fifth century some local churches still excluded it from the canon, but eventually it was universally adopted. The principal reason for the long delay was the persistent doubt that the letter stemmed from the apostle Peter.

Among modern scholars there is wide agreement that 2 Peter is a pseudonymous work, i.e., one written by a later author who attributed it to Peter according to a literary convention popular at the time. It gives the impression of being more remote in time from the apostolic period than 1 Peter; indeed, many think it is the latest work in the New Testament and assign it to the first or even the second quarter of the second century.

The principal reasons for this view are the following. The author refers to the apostles and "our ancestors" as belonging to a previous generation, now dead (3, 2-4). A collection of Paul's letters exists and appears to be well known, but disputes have arisen about the interpretation of them (3, 14-16). The passage about false teachers (2, 1-18) contains a number of literary contacts with Jude 4-16, and it is generally agreed that 2 Peter depends upon Jude, not vice versa. Finally, the principal problem exercising the author is the false teaching of "scoffers" who have concluded from the delay of the parousia that the Lord is not going to return. This could scarcely have been an issue during the lifetime of Simon Peter.

The Christians to whom the letter is addressed are not identified, though it may be the intent of 3, 1 to identify them with the churches of Asia Minor to which 1 Peter was sent. Except for the epistolary greeting in 1, 1-2, 2 Peter does not have the features of a genuine letter at all, but is rather a general exhortation cast in the form of a letter. The author must have been a Jewish Christian of the dispersion for, while his Jewish heritage is evident in various features of his thought and style, he writes in the rather stilted literary Greek of the Hellenistic period. He appeals to tradition against the twin threat of doctrinal error and moral laxity, which appear to reflect an early stage of what later developed into full-blown gnosticism. Thus he forms a link between the apostolic period and the church of subsequent ages.

The principal divisions of the Second Letter of Peter are the following:

I: Address (1, 1-2)
II: Exhortation to Christian Virtue (1, 3-21)
III: Condemnation of the False Teachers (2, 1-22)
IV: The Delay of the Second Coming (3, 1-16)
V: Final Exhortation and Doxology (3, 17-18)

I: ADDRESS

CHAPTER 1

Greeting. 1† Symeon Peter, a slave and apostle of Jesus Christ, to those who have received a faith of equal value to ours through the righteousness of our God and savior Jesus Christ: 2† may grace and peace be yours in abundance through knowledge of God and of Jesus our Lord.

II: EXHORTATION TO CHRISTIAN VIRTUE

The Power of God's Promise.† 3*† His divine power has bestowed on us everything that makes for life and devotion, through the knowledge of him who called us by his own glory and power. 4* Through these, he has bestowed on us the precious and very great promises, so that through them you may come to share in the divine nature, after escaping from the corruption that is in the world because of evil desire. 5*† For this very reason, make every effort to supplement your faith with virtue, virtue with knowledge, 6 knowledge with self-control, self-control with endurance, endurance with devotion, 7 devotion with mutual affection, mutual affection with love. 8 If these are yours and increase in abundance, they will keep you from being idle or unfruitful in the knowledge of our Lord Jesus Christ. 9* Anyone who lacks them is blind and shortsighted, forgetful of the cleansing of his past sins. 10† Therefore, brothers, be all the more eager to make your call and election firm, for, in doing so, you will never stumble. 11 For, in this way, entry into the eternal kingdom of our Lord and savior Jesus Christ will be richly provided for you.

Apostolic Witness.† 12 Therefore, I will always remind you of these things, even though you already know them and are established in the truth you have. 13† I think it right, as long as I am in this "tent," to stir you up by a re-

---

*

1, 3: 2 Cor 4, 6; 1 Pt 2, 9.
4: 2 Cor 7, 1; 1 Jn 2, 15.
5-7: Gal 5, 22-23.
9: 1 Jn 2, 9.11.

---

†

1, 1: *Symeon Peter:* on the authorship of 2 Peter, see Introduction; on the spelling here of the Hebrew name *Šimʿôn,* cf Acts 15, 14. The greeting is especially similar to those in 1 Peter and Jude. The words translated *our God and savior Jesus Christ* could also be rendered "our God and the savior Jesus Christ"; cf 11; 2, 20; 3, 2.18.

1, 2: *Knowledge:* a key term in the letter (3.8; 2, 20; 3, 18), perhaps used as a Christian emphasis against gnostic claims.

1, 3-4: Christian life in its fullness is a gift of divine power effecting a knowledge of Christ and the bestowal of divine promises (3, 4.9). *To share in the divine nature,* escaping from a corrupt world, is a thought found elsewhere in the Bible but expressed only here in such Hellenistic terms, since it is said to be accomplished through *knowledge* (3); cf 2, 2, 20; but see also Jn 15, 4; 17, 22-23; Rom 8, 14-17; Heb 3, 14; 1 Jn 1, 3; 3, 2.

1, 3: *By his own glory and power:* the most ancient papyrus and the best codex read "through glory and power."

1, 5-9: Note the climactic gradation of qualities (5-7), beginning with faith and leading to the fullness of Christian life, which is love; cf Rom 5, 3-4; Gal 5, 6.22 for a similar series of "virtues," though the program and sense here are different than in Paul. The fruit of these is knowledge of Christ (8) referred to in v 3; their absence is spiritual blindness (9).

1, 10-11: Perseverance in the Christian vocation is the best preventative against losing it and the safest provision for attaining its goal, the kingdom. *Kingdom of . . . Christ,* instead of "God," is unusual; cf Col 1, 13 and Mt 13, 41, as well as the *righteousness of . . . Christ* (1).

1, 12-19: The purpose in writing is to call to mind the apostle's witness to the truth, even as he faces the end of his life (12-15), his eyewitness testimony to Christ (16-18), and the true prophetic message (19) through the Spirit in scripture (20-21), in contrast to what false teachers are setting forth (ch 2).

1, 13: *Tent:* a biblical image for transitory human life (Is 38, 12), here combined with a verb that suggests not folding or packing up a tent but its being discarded in death (cf 2 Cor 5, 1-4).

minder, 14* since I know that I will soon have to put it aside, as indeed our Lord Jesus Christ has shown me. 15 I shall also make every effort to enable you always to remember these things after my departure.

16*† We did not follow cleverly devised myths when we made known to you the power and coming of our Lord Jesus Christ, but we had been eyewitnesses of his majesty. 17*† For he received honor and glory from God the Father when that unique declaration came to him from the majestic glory, "This is my Son, my beloved, with whom I am well pleased." 18† We ourselves heard this voice come from heaven while we were with him on the holy mountain. 19* Moreover, we possess the prophetic message that is altogether reliable. You will do well to be attentive to it, as to a lamp shining in a dark place, until day dawns and the morning star rises in your hearts. 20† Know this first of all, that there is no prophecy of scripture that is a matter of personal interpretation, 21 for no prophecy ever came through human will; but rather human beings moved by the holy Spirit spoke under the influence of God.

III: CONDEMNATION OF THE FALSE TEACHERS

CHAPTER 2

False Teachers.† 1* There were also false prophets among the people, just as there will be false teachers among you, who will introduce destructive heresies and even deny the Master who ransomed them, bringing swift destruction on themselves. 2* Many will follow their licentious ways, and because of them the way of truth will be reviled. 3* In their greed they will exploit you with fabrications, but from of old their condemnation has not been idle and their destruction does not sleep.

Lessons from the Past.† 4*† For if God did not spare the angels when they sinned, but condemned them to the chains of Tartarus and handed them over to be kept for judgment; 5*† and if he did not spare the ancient world, even though he preserved Noah, a herald of righteousness, together with seven others, when he brought a flood upon the godless world; 6* and if he condemned the cities of Sodom and Gomorrah [to destruction], reducing them to ashes, making them an example for the godless [people] of what is coming; 7 and if he rescued Lot, a righteous man oppressed by the licentious conduct of unprincipled people 8 (for day after day that righteous man living among them was tormented in his righteous soul at the lawless deeds that he saw and heard), 9* then the Lord knows how to rescue the devout from trial and to keep the unrighteous under punishment for the day of judgment, 10*† and especially those who follow the flesh with its depraved desire and show contempt for lordship.

*

14: Is 38, 12; Jn 21, 18-19.
16: Lk 9, 28-36; Jn 1, 14.
17: Ps 2, 7; Mt 17, 4-6.
19: Lk 1, 78-79; Rv 2, 28.
2, 1: Mt 24, 11.24; 1 Tm 4, 1; Jude 4.
2: Is 52, 5.
3: Rom 16, 18.
4: Jude 6.
5: Gn 8, 15-19; Heb 11, 7.
6: Gn 19, 24-25; Jude 7.
9: 1 Cor 10, 13; Rv 3, 10.
10: Jude 8.

†

1, 16: *Coming:* in Greek *parousia,* used at 3, 4.12 of the second coming of Christ. The word was used in the extrabiblical writings for the visitation of someone in authority; in Greek cult and Hellenistic Judaism it was used for the manifestation of the divine presence. What the apostles *made known* has been interpreted to refer to Jesus' transfiguration (17) or to his entire first coming or to his future coming in power (ch 3).

1, 17: The author assures the readers of the reliability of the apostolic message (including Jesus' power, glory, and coming; cf the note on 1, 16) by appeal to the transfiguration of Jesus in glory (cf Mt 17, 1-8 and parallels) and by appeal to the prophetic message (19; perhaps Nm 24, 17). Here, as elsewhere, the New Testament insists on continued reminders as necessary to preserve the historical facts about Jesus and the truths of the faith; cf 3, 1-2; 1 Cor 11, 2; 15, 1-3. *My Son, my beloved:* or, "my beloved Son."

1, 18: *We:* at Jesus' transfiguration, referring to Peter, James, and John (Mt 17, 1).

1, 20-21: Often cited, along with 2 Tm 3, 16, on the "inspiration" of scripture or against private interpretation, these verses in context are directed against the false teachers of ch 2 and clever tales (16). The prophetic word in scripture comes admittedly through *human beings* (21), but *moved by the holy Spirit,* not from their own interpretation, and is a matter of what the author and Spirit intended, not the *personal interpretation* of false teachers. Instead of *under the influence of God,* some manuscripts read "holy ones of God."

2, 1-3: The pattern of *false prophets* among the Old Testament people of God will recur through *false teachers* in the church. Such destructive opinions of heretical sects bring loss of faith in Christ, contempt for the way of salvation (cf 21), and immorality.

2, 4-6: The false teachers will be punished just as surely and as severely as were the fallen *angels* (4; cf Jude 6; Gn 6, 1-4), the sinners of Noah's day (5; Gn 7, 21-23), and the inhabitants of the cities of the Plain (6; Jude 7; Gn 19, 25). Whereas there are three examples in Jude 5-7 (Exodus and wilderness; rebellious angels; Sodom and Gomorrah), 2 Peter omitted the first of these, has inserted a new illustration about Noah (5) between Jude's second and third examples, and listed the resulting three examples in their Old Testament order (Gn 6; 7; 19).

2, 4: *Chains of Tartarus:* cf Jude 6; other manuscripts in 2 Peter read "pits of Tartarus." *Tartarus:* a term borrowed from Greek mythology to indicate the infernal regions.

2, 5-10a: Although God did not spare the sinful, he kept and saved the righteous, such as *Noah* (5) and *Lot* (7), and he *knows how to rescue the devout* (9), who are contrasted with the false teachers of the author's day. On Noah, cf Gn 5, 32—9, 29, especially 7, 1. On Lot, cf Gn 13 and 19.

2, 10b-22: Some take 10b and 11 with the preceding paragraph. Others begin the new paragraph with 10a, supplying from v 9 *The Lord knows how . . . to keep . . . under punishment,* with reference to God and probably specifically Christ (1). The conduct of the false teachers is described and condemned in language similar to that of Jude 8-16. This arrogance knows no bounds; animal-like, they are due to be caught and destroyed. They seduce even those who have knowledge of Christ (20).

False Teachers Denounced. † Bold and arrogant, they are not afraid to revile glorious beings, 11*† whereas angels, despite their superior strength and power, do not bring a reviling judgment against them from the Lord. 12* But these people, like irrational animals born by nature for capture and destruction, revile things that they do not understand, and in their destruction they will also be destroyed, 13*† suffering wrong as payment for wrongdoing. Thinking daytime revelry a delight, they are stains and defilements as they revel in their deceits while carousing with you. 14 Their eyes are full of adultery and insatiable for sin. They seduce unstable people, and their hearts are trained in greed. Accursed children! 15*† Abandoning the straight road, they have gone astray, following the road of Balaam, the son of Bosor, who loved payment for wrongdoing, 16* but he received a rebuke for his own crime: a mute beast spoke with a human voice and restrained the prophet's madness.

17* These people are waterless springs and mists driven by a gale; for them the gloom of darkness has been reserved. 18*† For, talking empty bombast, they seduce with licentious desires of the flesh those who have barely escaped from people who live in error. 19* They promise them freedom, though they themselves are slaves of corruption, for a person is a slave of whatever overcomes him. 20* For if they, having escaped the defilements of the world through the knowledge of [our] Lord and savior Jesus Christ, again become entangled and overcome by them, their last condition is worse than their first. 21*† For it would have been better for them not to have known the way of righteousness than after knowing it to turn back from the holy commandment handed down to them. 22*† What is expressed in the true proverb has happened to them, "The dog returns to its own vomit," and "A bathed sow returns to wallowing in the mire."

IV: THE DELAY OF THE SECOND COMING

CHAPTER 3

Denial of the Parousia. † 1 This is now, beloved, the second letter I am writing to you; through them by way of reminder I am trying to stir up your sincere disposition, 2* to recall the words previously spoken by the holy prophets and the commandment of the Lord and savior through your apostles. 3*† Know this first of all, that in the last days scoffers will come [to] scoff, living according to their own desires 4*† and saying, "Where is the promise of his coming? From the time when our ancestors fell asleep, everything has remained as it was from the beginning of creation." 5*† They deliberately ignore the fact that the heavens existed of old and earth was formed out of water and through water by the word of God; 6*† through these the world that then existed was destroyed, deluged with water. 7* The present heavens and earth have been reserved by the same word for fire, kept for the day of judgment and of destruction of the godless.

*

11: Jude 9.
12: Ps 49, 13-15; Jude 10.
13: Jude 12.
15: Nm 31, 16; Jude 11.
16: Nm 22, 28-33.
17: Jude 12-13.
18: Jude 16.
19: Jn 8, 34; Rom 6, 16-17.
20: Mt 12, 45.
21: Ez 3, 20.
22: Prv 26, 11.
3, 2: Jude 17.
3: 1 Tm 4, 1; 2 Tm 3, 1; Jude 18.
4: Is 5, 19.
5: Gn 1, 2.6.8; Ps 24, 2.
6: Gn 7, 21.
7: Is 51, 6; Mt 3, 12.

†

2, 10b: *Glorious beings:* literally, "glories"; cf Jude 8. While some think that illustrious personages are meant or even political officials behind whom (fallen) angels stand, it is more likely that the reference is to glorious angelic beings (cf Jude 9).

2, 11: *From the Lord:* some manuscripts read "before the Lord"; cf Jude 9.

2, 13: *Suffering wrong:* some manuscripts read "receiving a reward." *In their deceits:* some manuscripts read "in their love feasts" (Jude 12).

2, 15: *Balaam, the son of Bosor:* in Nm 22, 5, Balaam is said to be the son of Beor, and it is this name that turns up in a few ancient Greek manuscripts by way of "correction" of the text. Balaam is not portrayed in such a bad light in Nm 22. His evil reputation and his *madness* (16), and possibly his surname Bosor, may have come from a Jewish tradition about him in the first/second century, of which we no longer have any knowledge.

2, 18: *Barely escaped:* some manuscripts read "really escaped."

2, 21: *Commandment handed down:* cf 3, 2 and Jude 3.

2, 22: The second proverb is of unknown origin, while the first appears in Prv 26, 11.

3, 1-4: The false teachers not only flout Christian morality (cf Jude 8-19); they also deny the second coming of Christ and the judgment (4; cf 7). They seek to justify their licentiousness by arguing that the promised return of Christ has not been realized and the world is the same, no better than it was before (3-4). The author wishes to strengthen the faithful against such errors by reminding them in this *second letter* of the instruction in 1 Pt and of the teaching of the *prophets* and of Christ, conveyed through the *apostles* (1-2; cf Jude 17); cf 1 Pt 1, 10-12.16-21, especially 16-21; Eph 2, 20.

3, 3: *Scoffers:* cf Jude 18, where, however, only the passions of the scoffers are mentioned, not a denial on their part of Jesus' parousia.

3, 4-7: The false teachers tried to justify their immorality by pointing out that the promised *coming* (*parousia*) of the Lord has not yet occurred, even though early Christians expected it in their day. They thus insinuate that God is not guiding the world's history anymore, since nothing has changed and the first generation of Christians, *our ancestors* (4), has all died by this time. The author replies that, just as God destroyed the earth by water in the flood (5-6, cf 2, 5), so he will destroy it along with the false teachers on judgment day (7). *The word of God,* which called the world into being (Gn 1; Ps 33, 6) and *destroyed* it by the waters of a flood, will destroy it again by fire on *the day of judgment* (5-7).

3, 5: *Formed out of water and through water:* Gn 1, 2.6-8 is reflected as well as Greek views that water was the basic element from which all is derived.

3, 6: *Destroyed, deluged with water:* cf 2, 5; Gn 7, 11—8, 2.

8*† But do not ignore this one fact, beloved, that with the Lord one day is like a thousand years and a thousand years like one day. 9* The Lord does not delay his promise, as some regard "delay," but he is patient with you, not wishing that any should perish but that all should come to repentance. 10*† But the day of the Lord will come like a thief, and then the heavens will pass away with a mighty roar and the elements will be dissolved by fire, and the earth and everything done on it will be found out.

Exhortation to Preparedness.† 11* Since everything is to be dissolved in this way, what sort of persons ought [you] to be, conducting yourselves in holiness and devotion, 12*† waiting for and hastening the coming of the day of God, because of which the heavens will be dissolved in flames and the elements melted by fire. 13*† But according to his promise we await new heavens and a new earth in which righteousness dwells.

14 Therefore, beloved, since you await these things, be eager to be found without spot or blemish before him, at peace. 15* And consider the patience of our Lord as salvation, as our beloved brother Paul, according to the wisdom given to him, also wrote to you, 16† speaking of these things as he does in all his letters. In them there are some things hard to understand that the ignorant and unstable distort to their own destruction, just as they do the other scriptures.

V: FINAL EXHORTATION AND DOXOLOGY†

17* Therefore, beloved, since you are forewarned, be on your guard not to be led into the error of the unprincipled and to fall from your own stability. 18* But grow in grace and in the knowledge of our Lord and savior Jesus Christ. To him be glory now and to the day of eternity. [Amen.]

---

*

8: Ps 90, 4.
9: Ez 18, 23; 1 Tm 2, 4.
10: Is 66, 15-16; Mt 24, 29.
11: Acts 3, 19-21.
12: Is 34, 4; Heb 10, 27.
13: Is 65, 17; 66, 22; Rom 8, 21; Rv 21, 1.27.
15: Rom 8, 19; Jude 24.
17: Mk 13, 5; Heb 2, 1.
18: Rom 16, 27.

---

†

3, 8-10: The scoffers' objection (4) is refuted also by showing that *delay* of the Lord's second coming is not a failure to fulfill his word but rather a sign of his patience: God is giving time for repentance before the final judgment (cf Wis 11, 23-26; Ez 18, 23; 33, 11).

3, 8: Cf Ps 90, 4.

3, 10: *Like a thief:* Mt 24, 43; 1 Thes 5, 2; Rv 3, 3. *Will be found out:* cf 1 Cor 3, 13-15. Some few versions read, as the sense may demand, "will not be found out"; many manuscripts read "will be burned up"; there are further variants in other manuscripts, versions, and Fathers. Total destruction is assumed (11).

3, 11-16: The second coming of Christ and the judgment of the world are the doctrinal bases for the moral exhortation to readiness through vigilance and a virtuous life; cf Mt 24, 42.50-51; Lk 12, 40; 1 Thes 5, 1-11; Jude 20-21.

3, 12: *Flames . . . fire:* although this is the only New Testament passage about a final conflagration, the idea was common in apocalyptic and Greco-Roman thought. *Hastening:* eschatology is here used to motivate ethics (11), as elsewhere in the New Testament. Jewish sources and Acts 3, 19-20 assume that proper ethical conduct can help bring the promised day of the Lord; cf 9. Some render the phrase, however, "desiring it earnestly."

3, 13: *New heavens and a new earth:* cf Is 65, 17; 66, 22. The divine promises will be fulfilled after the day of judgment will have passed. The universe will be transformed by the reign of God's *righteousness* or justice; cf Is 65, 17-18; Acts 3, 21; Rom 8, 18-25; Rv 21, 1.

3, 16: *These things:* the teachings of this letter find parallels in Paul, e.g., God's will to save (Rom 2, 4; 9, 22-23; 1 Cor 1, 7-8), the coming of Christ (1 Thes 4, 16-17; 1 Cor 15, 23-52), and preparedness for the judgment (Col 1, 22-23; Eph 1, 4-14; 4, 30; 5, 5-14). *Other scriptures:* used to guide the faith and life of the Christian community. The letters of Paul are thus here placed on the same level as books of the Old Testament. Possibly other New Testament writings could also be included.

3, 17-18: To avoid the dangers of *error* and loss of *stability,* Christians are *forewarned* to be *on guard* and to *grow in grace and knowledge* (1, 2) of Christ. The doxology (18) recalls 1 Pt 4, 11. Some manuscripts add *Amen.*

The First Letter of

JOHN

Early Christian tradition identified this work as a letter of John the apostle. Because of its resemblance to the fourth gospel in style, vocabulary, and ideas, it is generally agreed that both works are the product of the same school of Johannine Christianity. The terminology and the presence or absence of certain theological ideas in 1 John suggest that it was written after the gospel; it may have been composed as a short treatise on ideas that were developed more fully in the fourth gospel. To others, the evidence suggests that 1 John was written after the fourth gospel as part of a debate on the proper interpretation of that gospel. Whatever its relation to the gospel, 1 John may be dated toward the end of the first century. Unlike 2 and 3 John, it lacks in form the salutation and epistolary conclusion of a letter. These features, its prologue, and its emphasis on doctrinal teaching make it more akin to a theological treatise than to most other New Testament letters.

The purpose of the letter is to combat certain false ideas, especially about Jesus, and to deepen the spiritual and social awareness of the Christian community (3, 17). Some former members (2, 19) of the community refused to acknowledge Jesus as the Christ (2, 22) and denied that he was a true man (4, 2). The specific heresy described in this letter cannot be identified exactly, but it is a form of docetism or gnosticism; the former doctrine denied the humanity of Christ to insure that his divinity was untainted, and the latter viewed the appearance of Christ as a mere stepping-stone to higher knowledge of God. These theological errors are rejected by an appeal to the reality and continuity of the apostolic witness to Jesus. The author affirms that authentic Christian love, ethics, and faith take place only within the historical revelation and sacrifice of Jesus Christ. The fullness of Christian life as fellowship with the Father must be based on true belief and result in charitable living; knowledge of God and love for one another are inseparable, and error in one area inevitably affects the other. Although the author recognizes that Christian doctrine presents intangible mysteries of faith about Christ, he insists that the concrete Christian life brings to light the deeper realities of the gospel.

The structure and language of the letter are straightforward yet repetitious. The author sets forth the striking contrasts between light and darkness, Christians and the world, and truth and error to illustrate the threats and responsibilities of Christian life. The result is not one of theological argument but one of intense religious conviction expressed in simple truths. The letter is of particular value for its declaration of the humanity and divinity of Christ as an apostolic teaching and for its development of the intrinsic connection between Christian moral conduct and Christian doctrine.

The principal divisions of the First Letter of John are the following:

- *I: Prologue (1, 1-4)*
- *II: God as Light (1, 5—3, 10)*
- *III: Love for One Another (3, 11—5, 12)*
- *IV: Epilogue (5, 13-21)*

I: PROLOGUE

CHAPTER 1

The Word of Life†

1* What was from the beginning,
what we have heard,
what we have seen with our eyes,
what we looked upon
and touched with our hands
concerns the Word of life—
2* for the life was made visible;
we have seen it and testify to it
and proclaim to you the eternal life
that was with the Father and was
made visible to us—
3* what we have seen and heard
we proclaim now to you,
so that you too may have fellowship
with us;
for our fellowship is with the Father
and with his Son, Jesus Christ.
4* We are writing this so that our joy
may be complete.

II: GOD AS LIGHT

God is Light.† 5 Now this is the mes-
sage that we have heard from him and
proclaim to you: God is light, and in him
there is no darkness at all. 6* If we say,
"We have fellowship with him," while
we continue to walk in darkness, we lie
and do not act in truth. 7* But if we walk
in the light as he is in the light, then
we have fellowship with one another,
and the blood of his Son Jesus cleanses
us from all sin. 8*† If we say, "We are
without sin," we deceive ourselves, and
the truth is not in us. 9* If we acknowl-
edge our sins, he is faithful and just and
will forgive our sins and cleanse us from
every wrongdoing. 10* If we say, "We
have not sinned," we make him a liar,
and his word is not in us.

CHAPTER 2

Christ and His Commandments.
1*† My children, I am writing this to you
so that you may not commit sin. But if
anyone does sin, we have an Advocate
with the Father, Jesus Christ the righ-
teous one. 2* He is expiation for our sins,
and not for our sins only but for those
of the whole world. 3*† The way we may
be sure that we know him is to keep his
commandments. 4* Whoever says, "I
know him," but does not keep his com-
mandments is a liar, and the truth is
not in him. 5* But whoever keeps his
word, the love of God is truly perfected
in him. This is the way we may know
that we are in union with him: 6 whoever
claims to abide in him ought to live
[just] as he lived.

The New Commandment.†
7* Beloved, I am writing no new com-
mandment to you but an old command-
ment that you had from the beginning.
The old commandment is the word that
you have heard. 8*† And yet I do write
a new commandment to you, which
holds true in him and among you, for
the darkness is passing away, and the
true light is already shining. 9* Whoever
says he is in the light, yet hates his
brother, is still in the darkness.
10* Whoever loves his brother remains
in the light, and there is nothing in him
to cause a fall. 11 Whoever hates his
brother is in darkness; he walks in dark-

---

*

1, 1: 2, 13; Jn 1, 1.14; 20, 20.25.27.
2: Jn 15, 27; 17, 5.
3: Jn 17, 21; Acts 4, 20.
4: Jn 15, 11; 2 Jn 12.
6: Jn 12, 35.
7: Mt 26, 28; Rom 3, 24-25; Heb 9, 14; 1 Pt 1, 19; Rv 1, 5.
8: 2 Chr 6, 36; Prv 20, 9.
9: Prv 28, 13; Jas 5, 16.
10: 5, 10.
2, 1: Jn 14, 16; Heb 7, 25.
2: 4, 10.
3: Jn 14, 15; 15, 10.
4: 4, 20.
5: Jn 14, 23.
7: 3, 11; Dt 6, 5; Mt 22, 37-40.
8: Jn 13, 34 / Jn 1, 5; Rom 13, 12.
9: Jn 8, 12.
10: Eccl 2, 14; Jn 11, 10.

---

†

1, 1-4: There is a striking parallel to the prologue of the gospel of John (Jn 1, 1-18), but the emphasis here is not on the preexistent Word but rather on the apostles' witness to the incarnation of *life* by their experience of the historical Jesus. He is *the Word of life* (1; cf Jn 1, 4), *the eternal life that was with the Father and was made visible* (2; cf Jn 1, 14), and was *heard, seen, looked upon,* and *touched* by the apostles. The purpose of their teaching is to share that *life*, called *fellowship . . . with the Father and with his Son, Jesus Christ,* with those who receive their witness (3; Jn 1, 14.16).

1, 5-7: *Light* is to be understood here as truth and goodness; *darkness* here is error and depravity (cf Jn 3, 19-21; 17, 17; Eph 5, 8). To *walk* in light or darkness is to live according to truth or error, not merely intellectual but moral as well. Fellowship with God and with one another consists in a life according to the truth as found in God and in Christ.

1, 8-10: Denial of the condition of sin is self-deception and even contradictory of divine revelation; there is also the continual possibility of sin's recurrence. Forgiveness and deliverance from sin through Christ are assured through acknowledgment of them and repentance.

2, 1: *Children:* like the term "beloved," this is an expression of pastoral love (cf Jn 13, 33; 21, 5; 1 Cor 4, 14). *Advocate:* for the use of the term, see Jn 14, 16. Forgiveness of sin is assured through Christ's intercession and expiation or "offering"; the death of Christ effected the removal of sin.

2, 3-6: *The way we may be sure:* to those who claim, "I have known Christ and therefore I know him," our author insists on not mere intellectual knowledge but obedience to God's commandments in a life conformed to the example of Christ; this confirms our knowledge of him and is *the love of God . . . perfected.* Disparity between moral life and the commandments proves improper belief.

2, 7-11: The author expresses the continuity and freshness of mutual charity in Christian experience. Through Christ the commandment of love has become the *light* defeating the *darkness* of evil in a new age. All hatred as darkness is incompatible with the light and Christian life. Note also the characteristic Johannine polemic in which a positive assertion is emphasized by the negative statement of its opposite.

2, 8: *Which holds true in him and among you:* literally, "a thing that holds true in him and in you."

ness and does not know where he is going because the darkness has blinded his eyes.

Members of the Community. † 12*† I am writing to you, children, because your sins have been forgiven for his name's sake.

13* I am writing to you, fathers, because you know him who is from the beginning.

I am writing to you, young men, because you have conquered the evil one.

14 I write to you, children, because you know the Father.

I write to you, fathers, because you know him who is from the beginning.

I write to you, young men, because you are strong and the word of God remains in you, and you have conquered the evil one.

15*† Do not love the world or the things of the world. If anyone loves the world, the love of the Father is not in him. 16† For all that is in the world, sensual lust, enticement for the eyes, and a pretentious life, is not from the Father but is from the world. 17* Yet the world and its enticement are passing away. But whoever does the will of God remains forever.

Antichrists. 18*† Children, it is the last hour; and just as you heard that the antichrist was coming, so now many antichrists have appeared. Thus we know this is the last hour. 19† They went out from us, but they were not really of our number; if they had been, they would have remained with us. Their desertion shows that none of them was of our number. 20*† But you have the anointing that comes from the holy one, and you all have knowledge. 21* I write to you not because you do not know the truth but because you do, and because every lie is alien to the truth. 22*† Who is the liar? Whoever denies that Jesus is the Christ. Whoever denies the Father and the Son, this is the antichrist. 23* No one who denies the Son has the Father, but whoever confesses the Son has the Father as well.

Life from God's Anointing. 24*† Let what you heard from the beginning remain in you. If what you heard from the beginning remains in you, then you will remain in the Son and in the Father. 25* And this is the promise that he made us: eternal life. 26 I write you these things about those who would deceive you. 27 As for you, the anointing that you received from him remains in you, so that you do not need anyone to teach you. But his anointing teaches you about everything and is true and not false; just as it taught you, remain in him.

Children of God. † 28 And now, children, remain in him, so that when he appears we may have confidence and not be put to shame by him at his coming. 29 If you consider that he is righteous, you also know that everyone who acts in righteousness is begotten by him.

CHAPTER 3

1*† See what love the Father has bestowed on us that we may be called the children of God. Yet so we are. The reason the world does not know us is that it did not know him. 2*† Beloved, we are God's children now; what we shall be has not yet been revealed. We do know that when it is revealed we shall be like him, for we shall see him as he is. 3* Everyone who has this hope based on

*

12: 1 Cor 6, 11.
13: 1, 1; Jn 1, 1.
15: Rom 8, 7-8; Jas 4, 4; 2 Pt 1, 4.
17: Is 40, 8; Mt 7, 21; 1 Cor 7, 31; 1 Pt 4, 2.
18: 1 Tim 4, 1.
20: Jn 14, 26.
21: 3, 19; 2 Pt 1, 12.
22: 2 Thes 2, 4.
23: Jn 14, 7-9.
24: Jn 14, 23.
25: Jn 5, 24; 10, 28; 17, 2.
3, 1: Jn 1, 12; Eph 1, 5 / Jn 15, 21; 17, 25.
2: Phil 3, 21.
3: 2, 6.

†

2, 12-17: The Christian community that has experienced the grace of God through forgiveness of sin and knowledge of Christ is armed against the evil one.

2, 12: *For his name's sake:* because of Christ our sins are forgiven.

2, 15: *The world:* all that is hostile toward God and alienated from him. Love of the *world* and love of God are thus mutually exclusive; cf Jas 4, 4.

2, 16: *Sensual lust:* literally, "the lust of the flesh," inordinate desire for physical gratification. *Enticement for the eyes:* literally, "the lust of the eyes," avarice or covetousness; the eyes are regarded as the windows of the soul. *Pretentious life:* literally, "pride of life," arrogance or ostentation in one's earthly style of life that reflects a willful independence from God and others.

2, 18: *It is the last hour:* literally, "a last hour," the period between the death and resurrection of Christ and his second coming. *The antichrist:* opponent or adversary of Christ; the term appears only in 1-2 John, but "pseudochrists" (translated "false messiahs") in Mt 24, 24 and Mk 13, 22, and Paul's "lawless one" in 2 Thes 2, 3, are similar figures. *Many antichrists:* Mt, Mk, and Rv seem to indicate a collectivity of persons, here related to the false teachers.

2, 19: *Not really of our number:* the apostate teachers only proved their lack of faith by leaving the community.

2, 20: *The anointing that comes from the holy one:* this anointing is in the Old Testament sense of receiving the Spirit of God. The *Holy One* probably refers to Christ. True knowledge is the gift of the Spirit (cf Is 11, 2), and the function of the Spirit is to lead Christians to the truth (Jn 14, 17.26; 16, 13).

2, 22-23: Certain gnostics denied that the earthly Jesus was the Christ; to deny knowledge of the Son is to deny the Father, since only through the Son has God been fully revealed (Jn 1, 18; 14, 8-9).

2, 24: Continuity with the apostolic witness as proclaimed in the prologue is the safeguard of right belief.

2, 28-29: Our confidence at his judgment is based on the daily assurance of salvation. Our actions reflect our true relation to him.

3, 1-3: The greatest sign of God's love is the gift of his Son (Jn 3, 16) that has made Christians true children of God. This relationship is a present reality and also part of the life to come; true knowledge of God will ultimately be gained, and Christians prepare themselves now by virtuous lives in imitation of the Son.

3, 2: *When it is revealed:* or "when he is revealed" (the subject of the verb could be Christ).

him makes himself pure, as he is pure. ***Avoiding Sin.*** 4† Everyone who commits sin commits lawlessness, for sin is lawlessness. 5* You know that he was revealed to take away sins, and in him there is no sin. 6 No one who remains in him sins; no one who sins has seen him or known him. 7 Children, let no one deceive you. The person who acts in righteousness is righteous, just as he is righteous. 8* Whoever sins belongs to the devil, because the devil has sinned from the beginning. Indeed, the Son of God was revealed to destroy the works of the devil. 9† No one who is begotten by God commits sin, because God's seed remains in him; he cannot sin because he is begotten by God. 10 In this way, the children of God and the children of the devil are made plain; no one who fails to act in righteousness belongs to God, nor anyone who does not love his brother.

III: LOVE FOR ONE ANOTHER

11*† For this is the message you have heard from the beginning: we should love one another, 12* unlike Cain who belonged to the evil one and slaughtered his brother. Why did he slaughter him? Because his own works were evil, and those of his brother righteous. 13* Do not be amazed, [then,] brothers, if the world hates you. 14* We know that we have passed from death to life because we love our brothers. Whoever does not love remains in death. 15* Everyone who hates his brother is a murderer, and you know that no murderer has eternal life remaining in him. 16* The way we came to know love was that he laid down his life for us; so we ought to lay down our lives for our brothers. 17* If someone who has worldly means sees a brother in need and refuses him compassion, how can the love of God remain in him? 18* Children, let us love not in word or speech but in deed and truth.

Confidence before God.† 19† [Now] this is how we shall know that we belong to the truth and reassure our hearts before him 20 in whatever our hearts condemn, for God is greater than our hearts and knows everything. 21 Beloved, if [our] hearts do not condemn us, we have confidence in God 22* and receive from him whatever we ask, because we keep his commandments and do what pleases him. 23* And his commandment is this: we should believe in the name of his Son, Jesus Christ, and love one another just as he commanded us. 24* Those who keep his commandments remain in him, and he in them, and the way we know that he remains in us is from the Spirit that he gave us.

CHAPTER 4

Testing the Spirits.† 1* Beloved, do not trust every spirit but test the spirits to see whether they belong to God, because many false prophets have gone out into the world. 2* This is how you can know the Spirit of God: every spirit that acknowledges Jesus Christ come in the flesh belongs to God, 3*† and every spirit that does not acknowledge Jesus does not belong to God. This is the spirit of the antichrist that, as you heard, is to come, but in fact is already in the world. 4 You belong to God, children, and you have conquered them, for the one who is in you is greater than the

*

5: Is 53, 9; Jn 1, 29; 8, 46; 1 Pt 2, 22.
8: Jn 8, 44; 12, 31-32.
11: 2, 7; Jn 13, 34; 15, 12.17.
12: Gn 4, 8; Jude 11.
13: Mt 24, 9; Jn 15, 18; 17, 14.
14: Lv 19, 17; Jn 5, 24.
15: Jn 8, 44.
16: Mt 20, 28; Jn 10, 11; 15, 13.
17: Dt 15, 7.11; Jas 2, 15-16.
18: Jas 1, 22.
22: 5, 15; Mt 7, 7-11; 21, 22; Jn 14, 13-14.
23: Jn 13, 34; 15, 17.
24: 4, 13; Jn 14, 21-23.
4, 1: 2, 18; Mt 24, 24.
2: 1 Cor 12, 3; 1 Thes 5, 21.
3: 1, 22.

†

3, 4: *Lawlessness:* a reference to the activity of the antichrist, so it is expressed as hostility toward God and a rejection of Christ. The author goes on to contrast the states of sin and righteousness. Christians do not escape sin but realize that when they sin they cease to have fellowship with God. Virtue and sin distinguish the children of God from the children of the devil.

3, 9: A habitual sinner is a child of the devil, while a child of God, who by definition is in fellowship with God, cannot sin. *Seed:* Christ or the Spirit who shares the nature of God with the Christian.

3, 11-18: Love, even to the point of self-sacrifice, is the point of the commandment. The story of Cain and Abel (12-15; Gn 4, 1-16) presents the rivalry of two brothers, in a contrast of evil and righteousness, where envy led to murder. For Christians, proof of deliverance is love toward others, after the example of Christ. This includes concrete acts of charity, out of our material abundance.

3, 19-24: Living a life of faith in Jesus and of Christian love assures us of abiding in God no matter what our feelings may at times tell us. Our obedience gives us confidence in prayer and trust in God's judgment. This obedience includes our belief in Christ and love for one another.

3, 19b-20: This difficult passage may also be translated "we shall be at peace before him in whatever our hearts condemn, for . . ." or "and before God we shall convince our hearts, if our hearts condemn us, that God is greater than our hearts."

4, 1-6: Deception is possible in spiritual phenomena and may be tested by its relation to Christian doctrine (cf 1 Cor 12, 3): those who fail to acknowledge Jesus Christ in the flesh are false prophets and belong to the antichrist. Even though these false prophets are well received in the world, the Christian who belongs to God has a greater power in the truth.

4, 3: *Does not acknowledge Jesus:* some ancient manuscripts add "Christ" and/or "to have come in the flesh" (cf 2), and others read "every spirit that annuls (or severs) Jesus."

one who is in the world. [5]* They belong to the world; accordingly, their teaching belongs to the world, and the world listens to them. [6]* We belong to God, and anyone who knows God listens to us, while anyone who does not belong to God refuses to hear us. This is how we know the spirit of truth and the spirit of deceit.

***God's Love and Christian Life.*†** [7] Beloved, let us love one another, because love is of God; everyone who loves is begotten by God and knows God. [8] Whoever is without love does not know God, for God is love. [9]* In this way the love of God was revealed to us: God sent his only Son into the world so that we might have life through him. [10]* In this is love: not that we have loved God, but that he loved us and sent his Son as expiation for our sins. [11] Beloved, if God so loved us, we also must love one another. [12]* No one has ever seen God. Yet, if we love one another, God remains in us, and his love is brought to perfection in us.

[13]† This is how we know that we remain in him and he in us, that he has given us of his Spirit. [14] Moreover, we have seen and testify that the Father sent his Son as savior of the world. [15] Whoever acknowledges that Jesus is the Son of God, God remains in him and he in God. [16] We have come to know and to believe in the love God has for us.

God is love, and whoever remains in love remains in God and God in him. [17]* In this is love brought to perfection among us, that we have confidence on the day of judgment because as he is, so are we in this world. [18] There is no fear in love, but perfect love drives out fear because fear has to do with punishment, and so one who fears is not yet perfect in love. [19] We love because he first loved us. [20]*† If anyone says, "I love God," but hates his brother, he is a liar; for whoever does not love a brother whom he has seen cannot love God whom he has not seen. [21]* This is the commandment we have from him: whoever loves God must also love his brother.

CHAPTER 5

***Faith is Victory over the World.*†** [1]* Everyone who believes that Jesus is the Christ is begotten by God, and everyone who loves the father loves [also] the one begotten by him. [2] In this way we know that we love the children of God when we love God and obey his commandments. [3]* For the love of God is this, that we keep his commandments. And his commandments are not burdensome, [4]* for whoever is begotten by God conquers the world. And the victory that conquers the world is our faith. [5]* Who [indeed] is the victor over the world but the one who believes that Jesus is the Son of God?

[6]*† This is the one who came through water and blood, Jesus Christ, not by water alone, but by water and blood. The Spirit is the one that testifies, and the Spirit is truth. [7] So there are three that testify, [8]* the Spirit, the water, and the blood, and the three are of one accord. [9]* If we accept human testimony, the testimony of God is surely greater. Now the testimony of God is this, that he has testified on behalf of his Son. [10]* Whoever believes in the Son of God has this testimony within himself. Whoever does not believe God has made him a liar by not believing the testimony God has given about his Son. [11]* And this is the testimony: God gave us eternal life, and this life is in his Son. [12] Whoever possesses the Son has life; whoever does not possess the Son of God does not have life.

*

5: Jn 15, 19.
6: Jn 8, 47; 10, 16.
9: Jn 3, 16.
10: Rom 5, 8.
12: Jn 1, 18; 1 Tm 6, 16.
17: 2, 28.
20: 2, 4.
21: Jn 13, 34; 14, 15.21; 15, 17.
5, 1: Jn 8, 42; 1 Pt 1, 23.
3: Jn 14, 15.
4: Jn 16, 33.
5: 1 Cor 15, 57.
6: Jn 15, 26; 19, 34.
8: Jn 5, 32.36; 15, 26.
9: Jn 5, 32.37.
10: 3, 33.
11: 1, 2; Jn 1, 4; 5, 21.26; 17, 3.

†

4, 7-12: Love as we share in it testifies to the nature of God and to his presence in our lives. One who loves shows that one is a child of God and knows God, for God's very being is love; one without love is without God. The revelation of the nature of God's love is found in the free gift of his Son to us, so that we may share life with God and be delivered from our sins. The love we have for one another must be of the same sort: authentic, merciful; this unique Christian love is our proof that we know God and can "see" the invisible God.

4, 13-21: The testimony of the Spirit and that of faith join the testimony of love to confirm our knowledge of God. Our love is grounded in the confession of Jesus as the Son of God and the example of God's love for us. Christian life is founded on the knowledge of God as love and on his continuing presence that relieves us from fear of judgment (16-18). What Christ is gives us confidence, even as we live and love in this world. Yet Christian love is not abstract but lived in the concrete manner of love for one another.

4, 20: *Cannot love God:* some ancient manuscripts read "how can he love . . . ?"

5, 1-5: Children of God are identified not only by their love for others (4, 7-9) and for God (5, 1-2) but by their belief in the divine sonship of Jesus Christ. Faith, the acceptance of Jesus in his true character and the obedience in love to God's commands (3), is the source of the Christian's power in the world and conquers the world of evil (4-5), even as Christ overcame the world (Jn 16, 33).

5, 6-12: *Water and blood* (6) refers to Christ's baptism (Mt 3, 16-17) and to the shedding of his blood on the cross (Jn 19, 34). *The Spirit* was present at the baptism (Mt 3, 16; Mk 1, 10; Lk 3, 22; Jn 1, 32.34). *The testimony* to Christ as the Son of God is confirmed by divine witness (7-9), greater by far than the two legally required human witnesses (Dt 17, 6). To deny this is to deny God's truth; cf Jn 8, 17-18. The gist of the divine witness or *testimony* is that *eternal life* (11-12) is given in Christ and nowhere else. To *possess the Son* is not acceptance of a doctrine but of a person who lives now and provides life.

IV: EPILOGUE†

Prayer for Sinners. [13]* I write these
things to you so that you may know that
you have eternal life, you who believe
in the name of the Son of God. [14]* And
we have this confidence in him, that if
we ask anything according to his will,
he hears us. [15] And if we know that he
hears us in regard to whatever we ask,
we know that what we have asked him
for is ours. [16]* If anyone sees his brother
sinning, if the sin is not deadly, he
should pray to God and he will give him
life. This is only for those whose sin is
not deadly. There is such a thing as
deadly sin, about which I do not say that
you should pray. [17] All wrongdoing is
sin, but there is sin that is not deadly.
[18] We know that no one begotten by
God sins; but the one begotten by God
he protects, and the evil one cannot
touch him. [19] We know that we belong
to God, and the whole world is under
the power of the evil one. [20]* We also
know that the Son of God has come and
has given us discernment to know the
one who is true. And we are in the one
who is true, in his Son Jesus Christ. He
is the true God and eternal life.
[21] Children, be on your guard against
idols.

*

13: Jn 1, 12; 20, 31.
14: 3, 21-22; Mt 7, 7; Jn 14, 13-14.
16: Mt 12, 31.
20: Jer 24, 7; Jn 17, 3; Eph 1, 17

†

5, 13-21: As children of God we have confidence in prayer because of our intimate relationship with him (14-15). In love, we pray (16-17) for those who are in *sin,* but not in *deadly sin* (literally, "sin unto death"), probably referring to apostasy or activities brought on under the antichrist; cf Mk 3, 29; Heb 6, 4-6; 10, 26-31. Even in the latter case, however, prayer, while not enjoined, is not forbidden. The letter concludes with a summary of the themes of the letter (18-20). There is a sharp antithesis between the children of God and those belonging to the world and to the evil one. The Son reveals the God of truth; Christians dwell in the true God, *in his Son,* and have eternal life. The final verse (21) voices a perennial warning about *idols,* any type of rival to God.

The Second Letter of

JOHN

Written in response to similar problems, the Second and Third Letters of John are of the same length, perhaps determined by the practical consideration of the writing space on one piece of papyrus. In each letter the writer calls himself "the Presbyter," and their common authorship is further evidenced by internal similarities in style and wording, especially in the introductions and conclusions. The literary considerations that link 2 and 3 John also link them with the First Letter and the Gospel of John. The concern with "truth," christology, mutual love, the new commandment, antichrist, and the integrity of witness to the earthly Jesus mark these works as products of the Johannine school. The identity of the Presbyter is problematic. The use of the title implies more than age, and refers to his position of leadership in the early church. The absence of a proper name indicates that he was well known and acknowledged in authority by the communities to which he writes. Although traditionally attributed to John the apostle, these letters were probably written by a disciple or scribe of an apostle. The traditional place and date of composition, Ephesus at the end of the first century, are plausible for both letters.

The Second Letter is addressed to "the chosen Lady" and "to her children." This literary image of a particular Christian community reflects the specific destination and purpose of the letter. Unlike 1 John, this brief letter is not a theological treatise but a reply to problems within the church. The Johannine themes of love and truth are used to support practical advice on Christian living. The Presbyter encourages community members to show their Christianity by adhering to the great commandment of mutual love and to the historical truth about Jesus. The false teaching present among them is a spiritualizing christology that may tempt some members to discount teachings about the incarnation and death of Jesus the Christ; cf 1 Jn 4, 2. For their protection the Presbyter forbids hospitality toward unknown or "progressive" Christians to prevent their infiltration of the community. The Second Letter preserves the Johannine concerns of doctrinal purity and active love in the form of pastoral advice to a threatened community.

1*† The Presbyter to the chosen Lady
and to her children whom I love in
truth—and not only I but also all who
know the truth—2 because of the truth
that dwells in us and will be with us for-
ever. 3† Grace, mercy, and peace will
be with us from God the Father and
from Jesus Christ the Father's Son in
truth and love.
4*† I rejoiced greatly to find some of
your children walking in the truth just
as we were commanded by the Father.
5* But now, Lady, I ask you, not as
though I were writing a new command-
ment but the one we have had from the
beginning: let us love one another.
6*† For this is love, that we walk ac-

*

1: Jn 8, 32; 3 Jn 1.
4: 3 Jn 3.
5: Jn 13, 34; 15, 12; 1 Jn 4, 7.
6: Jn 13, 34; 14, 15; 1 Jn 5, 3.

†

1: *The chosen Lady:* literally, "elected"; this could also be translated "Kyria (a woman's name) chosen (by God)" or "the lady Electa" or "Electa Kyria." The adjective "chosen" is applied to all Christians at the beginning of other New Testament letters (1 Pt 1, 1; Ti 1, 1). The description is of a specific community with "children" who are its members. *The truth:* the affirmation of Jesus in the flesh and in contrast to false teaching (7).

3: *Grace, mercy, and peace:* like 1 and 2 Tm this letter adds *mercy* to the terms used frequently in a salutation to describe Christian blessing; it appears only here in the Johannine writings. The author also puts the blessing in relation to *truth* and *love,* the watchwords of the Johannine teaching. *The Father's Son:* the title that affirms the close relationship of Christ to God; similar variations of this title occur elsewhere (Jn 1, 14; 3, 35), but the precise wording is not found elsewhere in the New Testament.

4: *Some of your children:* this refers to those whom the Presbyter has recently encountered, but it may also indicate the presence of false doctrine in the community: the Presbyter encourages those who have remained faithful. *Walking in the truth:* an expression used in the Johannine writings to describe a way of living in which the Christian faith is visibly expressed; cf 1 Jn 1, 6-7; 2, 6.11; 3 Jn 3.

6: *His commandments:* cf 1 Jn 3, 23; 2, 7-8; 4, 21; obedience to the commandment of faith and love includes all others.

cording to his commandments; this is
the commandment, as you heard from
the beginning, in which you should
walk.
7*† Many deceivers have gone out
into the world, those who do not acknowledge Jesus Christ as coming in
the flesh; such is the deceitful one and
the antichrist. 8† Look to yourselves
that you do not lose what we worked
for but may receive a full recompense.
9*† Anyone who is so "progressive" as
not to remain in the teaching of the
Christ does not have God; whoever remains in the teaching has the Father
and the Son. 10*† If anyone comes to you
and does not bring this doctrine, do not
receive him in your house or even greet
him; 11 for whoever greets him shares
in his evil works.
12*† Although I have much to write to
you, I do not intend to use paper and
ink. Instead, I hope to visit you and to
speak face to face so that our joy may
be complete. 13† The children of your
chosen sister send you greetings.

*

7: 1 Jn 2, 22; 4, 2.
9: Jn 8, 31; 1 Jn 2, 23; 4, 15.
10: Rom 16, 17; 2 Thes 3, 6.
12: Jn 15, 11; 1 Jn 1, 4; 3 Jn 13

†

7: *The antichrist:* see 1 Jn 2, 18-19.22; 4, 3.

8: *You* (plural): it is not certain whether this means the Christians addressed or includes the Presbyter, since some of the ancient Greek manuscripts and Greek Fathers have "we."

9: *Anyone who is so "progressive":* literally, "Anyone who goes ahead." Some gnostic groups held the doctrine of the Christ come in the flesh to be a first step in belief, which the more advanced and spiritual believer surpassed and abandoned in his knowledge of the spiritual Christ. The author affirms that fellowship with God may be gained only by holding to the complete doctrine of Jesus Christ (1 Jn 2, 22-23; 4, 2; 5, 5-6).

10-11: At this time false teachers were considered so dangerous and divisive as to be shunned completely. From this description they seem to be wandering preachers. We see here a natural suspicion of early Christians concerning such itinerants and can envisage the problems faced by missionaries such as those mentioned in 3 Jn 10.

12: *Our joy:* a number of other Greek manuscripts read "your joy."

13: *Chosen sister:* the community of which the Presbyter is now a part greets you (singular), the community of the Lady addressed.

The Third Letter of

JOHN

The Third Letter of John preserves a brief glimpse into the problems of missionary activity and local autonomy in the early church. In contrast to the other two letters of John, this work was addressed to a specific individual, Gaius. This letter is less theological in content and purpose. The author's goal was to secure hospitality and material support for his missionaries, and the Presbyter is writing to another member of the church who has welcomed missionaries in the past. The Presbyter commends Gaius for his hospitality and encourages his future help. He indicates he may come to challenge the policy of Diotrephes that is based on evil gossip.

The problems of the Presbyter in this short letter provide us with valuable evidence of the flexible and personal nature of authority in the early church. The Presbyter writes to Gaius, whom perhaps he had converted or instructed, on the basis of their personal links. The brothers have also confirmed him as a loyal Christian in action and belief. Gaius accepted the missionaries from the Presbyter and presumably will accept Demetrius on the Presbyter's recommendation. In contrast, Diotrephes refuses to receive either letters or friends of the Presbyter. Although he is portrayed as ambitious and hostile, he perhaps exemplifies the cautious and sectarian nature of early Christianity; for its own protection the local community mistrusted missionaries as false teachers. Most interestingly, Diotrephes seems comfortable in ignoring the requests of the Presbyter. The Presbyter seems to acknowledge that only a personal confrontation with Diotrephes will remedy the situation (10). The division, however, may also rest on doctrinal disagreement in which Gaius and the other "friends" accept the teaching of the Presbyter, and Diotrephes does not; the missionaries are not received for suspicion of theological error. Diotrephes has thus been viewed by some as an overly ambitious local upstart trying to thwart the advance of orthodox Christianity, by others as an orthodox church official suspicious of the teachings of the Presbyter and those in the Johannine school who think as he does, or by still others as a local leader anxious to keep the debates in the Johannine community out of his own congregation.

This brief letter and the situation that it mirrors show us how little we know about some details of early development in the church: schools of opinion existed around which questions of faith and life were discussed, and personal ties as well as doctrine and authority played a role in what happened amid divisions and unity.

1*† The Presbyter to the beloved
Gaius whom I love in truth.
2 Beloved, I hope you are prospering
in every respect and are in good health,
just as your soul is prospering. 3*† I re-
joiced greatly when some of the broth-
ers came and testified to how truly you
walk in the truth. 4* Nothing gives me
greater joy than to hear that my chil-
dren are walking in the truth.
5*† Beloved, you are faithful in all you
do for the brothers, especially for
strangers; 6*† they have testified to

*

1: 2 Jn 1.
3: 5; Gal 6, 10; 2 Jn 4.
4: 1 Thes 2, 11-12; 1 Tm 1, 2; 2 Tm 1, 2; 1 Jn 2, 1; 2 Jn 4.
5: Rom 12, 13; Gal 6, 10; Heb 13, 2.
6: Acts 15, 3; Col 1, 10; 1 Thes 2, 12.

†

1: *Beloved Gaius:* a frequent form of address for fellow Christians in New Testament epistolary literature.

3: *The brothers:* in this letter, the term may refer to Christians who have been missionaries and received hospitality from Gaius (5-6). *Walk in the truth:* the common Johannine term to describe Christian living; this description presents Gaius as following the teachings of the Presbyter in contrast to Diotrephes.

5: *You are faithful in all you do:* Gaius's aid to the missionaries is a manifestation of his true Christian faith.

6: *Help them . . . to continue their journey:* the Presbyter asks Gaius not only to continue to welcome the missionaries to his community but also to equip them for further travels.

your love before the church. Please help
them in a way worthy of God to continue
their journey. 7† For they have set out
for the sake of the Name and are ac-
cepting nothing from the pagans.
8 Therefore, we ought to support such
persons, so that we may be co-workers
in the truth.
9† I wrote to the church, but Diot-
rephes, who loves to dominate, does not
acknowledge us. 10† Therefore, if I
come, I will draw attention to what he
is doing, spreading evil nonsense about
us. And not content with that, he will
not receive the brothers, hindering
those who wish to do so and expelling
them from the church.
11*† Beloved, do not imitate evil but
imitate good. Whoever does what is
good is of God; whoever does what is
evil has never seen God. 12*† Demetrius
receives a good report from all, even
from the truth itself. We give our testi-
monial as well, and you know our testi-
mony is true.
13* I have much to write to you, but I
do not wish to write with pen and ink.
14 Instead, I hope to see you soon, when
we can talk face to face. 15*† Peace be
with you. The friends greet you; greet
the friends there each by name.

*

11: 1 Jn 2, 29; 3, 6.10.
12: Jn 19, 35; 21, 24; 1 Tm 3, 7.
13: 2 Jn 12.
15: Jn 20, 19.21.26; Eph 6, 23; 1 Pt 5, 14.

†

7: *The Name:* of Jesus Christ (cf Acts 5, 41; 1 Jn 2, 12; 3, 23; 5, 13). *Accepting nothing:* not expecting support from the pagans to whom they preach the gospel, so that they will not be considered as beggars; they required support from other Christians; cf Paul's complaints to the Corinthians (1 Cor 9, 3-12).

9: *Who loves to dominate:* the Presbyter does not deny Diotrephes' place as leader but indicates that his ambition may have caused him to disregard his letter and his influence.

10: *If I come:* the Presbyter may visit the community to challenge the actions of Diotrephes toward himself and the missionaries. *Will not receive the brothers:* Diotrephes may have been critical of the teachings of the Presbyter and sought to maintain doctrinal purity; cf 1 Jn 2, 19 and 2 Jn 10-11.

11: *Do not imitate evil:* Gaius should not be influenced by the behavior of Diotrephes.

12: *Demetrius:* because of the fear of false teachers, Demetrius, perhaps the bearer of the letter, is provided with a recommendation from the Presbyter; cf 2 Cor 3, 1; Rom 16, 1. *Even from the truth itself:* this refers probably to the manner of Demetrius's life that testifies to his true belief; cf Gaius above (v 3).

15: *Friends:* although a Johannine term for Christians (Jn 15, 15), the word here may refer to those in the community loyal to the Presbyter and to Gaius.

The Letter of

JUDE

This letter is by its address attributed to "Jude, a slave of Jesus Christ and brother of James" (1). Since he is not identified as an apostle, this designation can hardly be meant to refer to the Jude or Judas who is listed as one of the Twelve (Lk 6, 16; Acts 1, 13; cf Jn 14, 22). The person intended is almost certainly the other Jude, named in the gospels among the relatives of Jesus (Mt 13, 55; Mk 6, 3), and the James who is listed there as his brother is the one to whom the Letter of James is attributed (see the Introduction to James). Nothing else is known of this Jude, and the apparent need to identify him by reference to his better-known brother indicates that he was a rather obscure personage in the early church.

The letter is addressed in the most general terms to "those who are called, beloved in God the Father and kept safe for Jesus Christ" (1), hence apparently to all Christians. But since its purpose is to warn the addressees against false teachers, the author must have had in mind one or more specific Christian communities located in the unidentified region where the errors in question constituted a danger. While the letter contains some Semitic features, there is nothing to identify the addressees specifically as Jewish Christians; indeed, the errors envisaged seem to reflect an early form of gnosticism, opposed to law, that points rather to the cultural context of the Gentile world. Like James and 2 Peter, the Letter of Jude manifests none of the typical features of the letter form except the address.

There is so much similarity between Jude and 2 Peter, especially Jude 4-16 and 2 Peter 2, 1-18, that there must be a literary relationship between them. Since there is no evidence for the view that both authors borrowed from the same source, it is usually supposed that one of them borrowed from the other. Most scholars believe that Jude is the earlier of the two, principally because he quotes two apocryphal Jewish works, the Assumption of Moses (9) and the Book of Enoch (14-15) as part of his structured argument, whereas 2 Peter omits both references. Since there was controversy in the early church about the propriety of citing noncanonical literature that included legendary material, it is more probable that a later writer would omit such references than that he would add them.

Many interpreters today consider Jude a pseudonymous work dating from the end of the first century or even later. In support of this view they adduce the following arguments: (a) the apostles are referred to as belonging to an age that has receded into the past (17-18); (b) faith is understood as a body of doctrine handed down by a process of tradition (3); (c) the author's competent Greek style shows that he must have had a Hellenistic cultural formation; (d) the gnostic character of the errors envisaged fits better into the early second century than into a period several decades earlier. While impressive, these arguments are not entirely compelling and do not completely rule out the possibility of composition around the year A.D. 80, when the historical Jude may still have been alive.

This little letter is an urgent note by an author who intended to write more fully about salvation to an unknown group of readers, but who was forced by dangers from false teachers worming their way into the community (3-4) to dash off a warning against them (5-16) and to deliver some pressing Christian admonitions (17-23). The letter is justly famous for its majestic closing doxology (24-25).

Address and Greeting. 1*† Jude, a slave of Jesus Christ and brother of James, to those who are called, beloved in God the Father and kept safe for Jesus Christ: 2* may mercy, peace, and love be yours in abundance.

Occasion for Writing.† 3* Beloved, although I was making every effort to write to you about our common salvation, I now feel a need to write to encourage you to contend for the faith that was once for all handed down to the holy ones. 4* For there have been some intruders, who long ago were designated for this condemnation, godless persons, who pervert the grace of our God into licentiousness and who deny our only Master and Lord, Jesus Christ.

The False Teachers. 5*† I wish to remind you, although you know all things, that [the] Lord who once saved a people from the land of Egypt later destroyed those who did not believe. 6*† The angels too, who did not keep to their own domain but deserted their proper dwelling, he has kept in eternal chains, in gloom, for the judgment of the great day. 7*† Likewise, Sodom, Gomorrah, and the surrounding towns, which, in the same manner as they, indulged in sexual promiscuity and practiced unnatural vice, serve as an example by undergoing a punishment of eternal fire.

8† Similarly, these dreamers nevertheless also defile the flesh, scorn lordship, and revile glorious beings. 9*† Yet the archangel Michael, when he argued with the devil in a dispute over the body of Moses, did not venture to pronounce a reviling judgment upon him but said, "May the Lord rebuke you!" 10* But these people revile what they do not understand and are destroyed by what they know by nature like irrational animals. 11*† Woe to them! They followed the way of Cain, abandoned themselves to Balaam's error for the sake of gain, and perished in the rebellion of Korah. 12*† These are blemishes on your love feasts, as they carouse fearlessly and look after themselves. They are waterless clouds blown about by winds, fruitless trees in late autumn, twice dead and uprooted. 13 They are like wild waves of the sea, foaming up their shameless deeds, wandering stars for whom the gloom of darkness has been reserved forever.

14*† Enoch, of the seventh generation from Adam, prophesied also about them when he said, "Behold, the Lord has come with his countless holy ones 15 to execute judgment on all and to convict everyone for all the godless deeds that they committed and for all the harsh words godless sinners have uttered against him." 16* These people are complainers, disgruntled ones who live by their desires; their mouths utter bombast as they fawn over people to gain advantage.

---

*

1: Mt 13, 55; Mk 6, 3; Acts 12, 17; Rom 1, 7.
2: Gal 6, 16; 1 Tm 1, 2; 2 Pt 1, 2.
3: 17.20; 1 Tm 6, 12.
4: Gal 2, 4; 2 Tm 3, 6; 2 Pt 2, 1.
5: Nm 14, 35; 1 Cor 10, 5; Heb 3, 16.17.
6: 2 Pt 2, 4.9.
7: Dt 29, 22-24; Mt 25, 41; 2 Thes 1, 8-9; 2 Pt 2, 6; 3, 7.
9: Dn 10, 21; 12, 1.
10: 2 Pt 2, 12.
11: Gn 4, 8-16; 1 Jn 3, 12 / Nm 31, 15-16; 2 Pt 2, 15; Rv 2, 14 / Nm 16, 19-35.
12: 2 Pt 2, 13.17.
14-15: Mt 16, 27; Heb 12, 22-23.
16: 18; 1 Cor 10, 10; 2 Pt 2, 10.18.

---

†

1: *Jude . . . brother of James:* for the identity of the author of this letter, see Introduction. *To those who are called:* the vocation to the Christian faith is God's free gift to those whom he loves and whom he safely protects in Christ until the Lord's second coming.

3-4: *Our common salvation:* the teachings of the Christian faith derived from the apostolic preaching and to be kept by the Christian community.

5: For this first example of divine punishment on those who had been saved but did not then keep faith, see Nm 14, 28-29 and the note there. Some manuscripts have the word "once" (*hapax* as at 3) after "you know"; some commentators have suggested that it means "knowing one thing" or "you know all things once for all." Instead of "[the] Lord" manuscripts vary, having "Jesus," "God," or no subject stated.

6: This second example draws on Gn 6, 1-4 as elaborated in the apocryphal Book of Enoch (cf 14): heavenly beings came to earth and had sexual intercourse with women. God punished them by casting them out of heaven into darkness and bondage.

7: *Practiced unnatural vice:* literally, "went after alien flesh." This example derives from Gn 19, 1-25, especially 4-11, when the townsmen of Sodom violated both hospitality and morality by demanding that Lot's two visitors (really messengers of Yahweh) be handed over to them so that they could abuse them sexually. *Unnatural vice:* this refers to the desire for intimacies by human beings with angels (the reverse of the example in 6). Sodom (whence "sodomy") and Gomorrah became proverbial as object lessons for God's punishment on sin (Is 1, 9; Jer 50, 40; Am 4, 11; Mt 10, 15; 2 Pt 2, 6).

8: *Dreamers:* the writer returns to the false teachers of v 4, applying charges from the three examples in vv 5, 6, 7. This may apply to claims they make for revelations they have received by night (to the author, hallucinations). *Defile the flesh:* this may mean bodily pollutions from the erotic dreams of sexual license (7). *Lordship . . . glorious beings:* these may reflect the Lord (5; Jesus, 4) whom they spurn and the angels (6; cf the note on 2 Pt 2, 10, here, as there, literally, "glories").

9: *The archangel Michael . . . judgment:* a reference to an incident in the apocryphal *Assumption of Moses.* Dt 34, 6 had said of Moses, literally in Greek, "they buried him" or "he (God?) buried him" (taken to mean "he was buried"). The later account tells how Michael, who was sent to bury him, was challenged by the devil's interest in the body. Our author draws out the point that if an archangel refrained from reviling even the devil, how wrong it is for mere human beings to revile glorious beings (angels).

11: *Cain . . . Balaam . . . Korah:* examples of rebellious men and of the punishment their conduct incurred; cf Gn 4, 8-16; Nm 16, 1-35; 31, 16. See the note on 2 Pt 2, 15.

12: *Blemishes on your love feasts:* or "hidden rocks" or "submerged reefs" (cf 13). The opponents engaged in scandalous conduct in connection with community gatherings called *love feasts* (agape meals), which were associated with eucharistic celebrations at certain stages of early Christian practice; cf 1 Cor 11, 18-34 and the note on 2 Pt 2, 13.

14-15: Cited from the apocryphal *Book of Enoch* 1, 9.

Exhortations. 17* But you, beloved,
remember the words spoken before-
hand by the apostles of our Lord Jesus
Christ, 18*† for they told you, "In [the]
last time there will be scoffers who will
live according to their own godless de-
sires." 19* These are the ones who cause
divisions; they live on the natural plane,
devoid of the Spirit. 20* But you, be-
loved, build yourselves up in your most
holy faith; pray in the holy Spirit.
21* Keep yourselves in the love of God
and wait for the mercy of our Lord Je-
sus Christ that leads to eternal life.
22† On those who waver, have mercy;
23† save others by snatching them out
of the fire; on others have mercy with
fear, abhorring even the outer garment
stained by the flesh.

***Doxology.*†** 24* To the one who is able
to keep you from stumbling and to pre-
sent you unblemished and exultant, in
the presence of his glory, 25* to the only
God, our savior, through Jesus Christ
our Lord be glory, majesty, power, and
authority from ages past, now, and for
ages to come. Amen.

*

17: Heb 2, 3; 2 Pt 3, 2.
18: 1 Tm 4, 1; 2 Tm 3, 1-5; 2 Pt 3, 3.
19: 1 Cor 2, 14; Jas 3, 15.
20: 2; Eph 6, 18; Col 2, 7.
21: Ti 2, 13.
24: 2 Cor 4, 14; 1 Pt 4, 13.
25: Rom 11, 36; 1 Tm 1, 17.

†

18: This is the substance of much early Christian preaching rather than a direct quotation of any of the various New Testament passages on this theme (see Mk 13, 22; Acts 20, 30; 1 Tm 4, 1-3; 2 Pt 3, 3).

22: *Have mercy:* some manuscripts read "convince," "confute," or "reprove." Others have "even though you waver" or "doubt" instead of *who waver.*

23: *With fear:* some manuscripts connect the phrase "with fear" with the imperative "save" or with the participle "snatching." Other manuscripts omit the phrase "on others have mercy," so that only two groups are envisioned. Rescue of those led astray and caution in the endeavor are both enjoined. *Outer garment stained by the flesh:* the imagery may come from Zec 3, 3-5, just as that of *snatching . . . out of the fire* comes from Zec 3, 2; the very garments of the godless are to be abhorred because of their contagion.

24-25: With this liturgical statement about the power of God to keep the faithful from stumbling, and praise to him through Jesus Christ, the letter reaches its conclusion by returning to the themes with which it began (1-2).

The Revelation to

JOHN

The Apocalypse, or Revelation to John, the last book of the Bible, is one of the most difficult to understand because it abounds in unfamiliar and extravagant symbolism, which at best appears unusual to the modern reader. Symbolic language, however, is one of the chief characteristics of apocalyptic literature, of which this book is an outstanding example. Such literature enjoyed wide popularity in both Jewish and Christian circles from ca. 200 B.C. to A.D. 200.

This book contains an account of visions in symbolic and allegorical language borrowed extensively from the Old Testament, especially Ezekiel, Zechariah, and Daniel. Whether or not these visions were real experiences of the author or simply literary conventions employed by him is an open question.

This much, however, is certain: symbolic descriptions are not to be taken as literal descriptions, nor is the symbolism meant to be pictured realistically. One would find it difficult and repulsive to visualize a lamb with seven horns and seven eyes; yet Jesus Christ is described in precisely such words (5, 6). The author used these images to suggest Christ's universal (seven) power (horns) and knowledge (eyes). A significant feature of apocalyptic writing is the use of symbolic colors, metals, garments (1, 13-16; 3, 18; 4, 4; 6, 1-8; 17, 4; 19, 8), and numbers (four *signifies the world,* six *imperfection,* seven *totality or perfection,* twelve *Israel's tribes or the apostles,* one thousand *immensity). Finally the vindictive language in the book (6, 9-10; 18, 1—19, 4) is also to be understood symbolically and not literally. The cries for vengeance on the lips of Christian martyrs that sound so harsh are in fact literary devices the author employed to evoke in the reader and hearer a feeling of horror for apostasy and rebellion that will be severely punished by God.*

REVELATION

The lurid descriptions of the punishment of Jezebel (2, 22) and of the destruction of the great harlot, Babylon (16, 9—19, 2), are likewise literary devices. The metaphor of Babylon as harlot would be wrongly construed if interpreted literally. On the other hand, the stylized figure of the woman clothed with the sun (12, 1-6), depicting the New Israel, may seem to be a negative stereotype. It is necessary to look beyond the literal meaning to see that these images mean to convey a sense of God's wrath at sin in the former case and trust in God's providential care over the church in the latter.

The Book of Revelation cannot be adequately understood except against the historical background that occasioned its writing. Like Daniel and other apocalypses, it was composed as resistance literature to meet a crisis. The book itself suggests that the crisis was ruthless persecution of the early church by the Roman authorities; the harlot Babylon symbolizes pagan Rome, the city on seven hills (17, 9). The book is, then, an exhortation and admonition to Christians of the first century to stand firm in the faith and to avoid compromise with paganism, despite the threat of adversity and martyrdom; they are to await patiently the fulfillment of God's mighty promises. The triumph of God in the world of men and women remains a mystery, to be accepted in faith and longed for in hope. It is a triumph that unfolded in the history of Jesus of Nazareth and continues to unfold in the history of the individual Christian who follows the way of the cross, even, if necessary, to a martyr's death.

Though the perspective is eschatological—ultimate salvation and victory are said to take place at the end of the present age when Christ will come in glory at the parousia—the book presents the decisive struggle of Christ and his followers against Satan and his cohorts as already over. Christ's overwhelming defeat of the kingdom of Satan ushered in the everlasting reign of God (11, 15; 12, 10).

Even the forces of evil unwittingly carry out the divine plan (17, 17), for God is the sovereign Lord of history.

The Book of Revelation had its origin in a time of crisis, but it remains valid and meaningful for Christians of all time. In the face of apparently insuperable evil, either from within or from without, all Christians are called to trust in Jesus' promise, "Behold, I am with you always, until the end of the age" (Mt 28, 20). Those who remain steadfast in their faith and confidence in the risen Lord need have no fear. Suffering, persecution, even death by martyrdom, though remaining impenetrable mysteries of evil, do not comprise an absurd dead end. No matter what adversity or sacrifice Christians may endure, they will in the end triumph over Satan and his forces because of their fidelity to Christ the victor. This is the enduring message of the book; it is a message of hope and consolation and challenge for all who dare to believe.

The author of the book calls himself John (1, 1.4.9; 22, 8), who because of his Christian faith has been exiled to the rocky island of Patmos, a Roman penal colony. Although he never claims to be John the apostle, whose name is attached to the fourth gospel, he was so identified by several of the early church Fathers, including Justin, Irenaeus, Clement of Alexandria, Tertullian, Cyprian, and Hippolytus. This identification, however, was denied by other Fathers, including Denis of Alexandria, Eusebius of Caesarea, Cyril of Jerusalem, Gregory Nazianzen, and John Chrysostom. Indeed, vocabulary, grammar, and style make it doubtful that the book could have been put into its present form by the same person(s) responsible for the fourth gospel. Nevertheless, there are definite linguistic and theological affinities between the two books. The tone of the letters to the seven churches (1, 4—3, 22) is indicative of the great authority the author enjoyed over the Christian communities in Asia. It is possible, therefore, that he was a disciple of John the apostle, who is traditionally associated with that part of the world. The date of the book in its present form is probably near the end of the reign of Domitian (A.D. 81-96), a fierce persecutor of the Christians.

The principal divisions of the Book of Revelation are the following:

- *I: Prologue (1, 1-3)*
- *II: Letters to the Churches of Asia (1, 4—3, 22)*
- *III: God and the Lamb in Heaven (4, 1—5, 14)*
- *IV: The Seven Seals, Trumpets, and Plagues, with Interludes (6, 1—16, 21)*
- *V: The Punishment of Babylon and the Destruction of Pagan Nations (17, 1—20, 15)*
- *VI: The New Creation (21, 1—22, 5)*
- *VII: Epilogue (22, 6-21)*

I: PROLOGUE†

CHAPTER 1

1* **The revelation of Jesus Christ,
which God gave to him, to show his ser-
vants what must happen soon. He made
it known by sending his angel to his ser-
vant John, 2 who gives witness to the
word of God and to the testimony of Je-
sus Christ by reporting what he saw.
3*† Blessed is the one who reads aloud
and blessed are those who listen to this
prophetic message and heed what is
written in it, for the appointed time is
near.**

*

1, 1: 22, 6-8.20; Dn 2, 28 / 19, 10.

3: 22, 7 / Lk 11, 28.

†

1, 1-3: This prologue describes the source, contents, and audience of the book and forms an inclusion with the epilogue (22, 6-21), with its similar themes and expressions.

1, 3: *Blessed is the one:* this is the first of seven beatitudes in this book; the others are in 14, 13; 16, 15; 19, 9; 20, 6; 22, 7.14. *This prophetic message:* literally, "the words of the prophecy"; so 22, 7.10.18.19 by inclusion. *The appointed time:* when Jesus will return in glory; cf 1, 7; 3, 11; 22, 7.10.12.20.

II: LETTERS TO THE CHURCHES OF ASIA

***Greeting.*†** 4*† John, to the seven
churches in Asia: grace to you and
peace from him who is and who was and
who is to come, and from the seven spir-
its before his throne, 5*† and from Jesus
Christ, the faithful witness, the firstborn
of the dead and ruler of the kings of
the earth. To him who loves us and has
freed us from our sins by his blood,
6* who has made us into a kingdom,
priests for his God and Father, to him
be glory and power forever [and ever].
Amen.

7* Behold, he is coming amid the
clouds,
and every eye will see him,
even those who pierced him.
All the peoples of the earth will la-
ment him.
Yes. Amen.

8*† "I am the Alpha and the Omega,"
says the Lord God, "the one who is and
who was and who is to come, the al-
mighty."

***The First Vision.*†** 9† I, John, your
brother, who share with you the dis-
tress, the kingdom, and the endurance
we have in Jesus, found myself on the
island called Patmos because I pro-
claimed God's word and gave testimony
to Jesus. 10† I was caught up in spirit
on the Lord's day and heard behind me
a voice as loud as a trumpet, 11† which
said, "Write on a scroll what you see
and send it to the seven churches: to
Ephesus, Smyrna, Pergamum, Thya-
tira, Sardis, Philadelphia, and Laodi-
cea." 12† Then I turned to see whose
voice it was that spoke to me, and when
I turned, I saw seven gold lampstands
13*† and in the midst of the lampstands
one like a son of man, wearing an ankle-
length robe, with a gold sash around his
chest. 14† The hair of his head was as
white as white wool or as snow, and his
eyes were like a fiery flame. 15† His feet
were like polished brass refined in a fur-
nace, and his voice was like the sound
of rushing water. 16*† In his right hand
he held seven stars. A sharp two-edged
sword came out of his mouth, and
his face shone like the sun at its bright-
est.

17*† When I caught sight of him, I fell
down at his feet as though dead. He
touched me with his right hand and
said, "Do not be afraid. I am the first
and the last, 18† the one who lives. Once
I was dead, but now I am alive forever
and ever. I hold the keys to death and
the netherworld. 19† Write down, there-
fore, what you have seen, and what is
happening, and what will happen after-

*

4: 8; 4, 8; 11, 17; 16, 5; Ex 3, 14.
5: 3, 14; 1 Cor 15, 20; Col 1, 18 / Heb 9, 14; 1 Pt 1, 19; 1 Jn 1, 7.
6: Ex 19, 6; 1 Pt 2, 9.
7: Dn 7, 13 / Zec 12, 10; Mt 24, 30; Jn 19, 37.
8: 17; 21, 6; 22, 13; Is 41, 4; 44, 6; 48, 12.
13: Dn 7, 13; 10, 5.
16: Heb 4, 12.
17: Dn 8, 18 / 1, 8.

†

1, 4-8: Although Revelation begins and ends (22, 21) with Christian epistolary formulae, there is nothing between chs 4 and 22 resembling a letter. The author here employs the standard word order for greetings in Greek letter writing: "N. to N., greetings . . ."; see the note on Rom 1, 1.

1, 4: *Seven churches in Asia:* Asia refers to the Roman province of that name in western Asia Minor (modern Turkey); these representative churches are mentioned by name in v 11, and each is the recipient of a message (2, 1—3, 22). *Seven* is the biblical number suggesting fullness and completeness; thus the seer is writing for the whole church.

1, 5: *Freed us:* the majority of Greek manuscripts and several early versions read "washed us"; but "freed us" is supported by the best manuscripts and fits well with Old Testament imagery, e.g., Is 40, 2.

1, 8: *The Alpha and the Omega:* the first and last letters of the Greek alphabet. In 22, 13 the same words occur together with the expressions "the First and the Last, the Beginning and the End"; cf 17; 2, 8; 21, 6; Is 41, 4; 44, 6.

1, 9-20: In this first vision, the seer is commanded to write what he sees to the seven churches (9-11). He sees Christ in glory, whom he depicts in stock apocalyptic imagery (12-16), and hears him describe himself in terms meant to encourage Christians by emphasizing his victory over death (17-20).

1, 9: *Island called Patmos:* one of the Sporades islands in the Aegean Sea, some fifty miles south of Ephesus, used by the Romans as a penal colony. *Because I proclaimed God's word:* literally, "on account of God's word."

1, 10: *The Lord's day:* Sunday. *As loud as a trumpet:* the imagery is derived from the theophany at Sinai (Ex 19, 16.19; cf Heb 12, 19 and the trumpet in other eschatological settings in Is 27, 13; Jl 2, 1; Mt 24, 31; 1 Cor 15, 52; 1 Thes 4, 16).

1, 11: *Scroll:* a papyrus roll.

1, 12-16: A symbolic description of Christ in glory. The metaphorical language is not to be understood literally; cf Introduction.

1, 13: *Son of man:* see the note on Mk 8, 31. *Ankle-length robe:* Christ is priest; cf Ex 28, 4; 29, 5; Wis 18, 24; Zec 3, 4. *Gold sash:* Christ is king; cf Ex 28, 4; 1 Mc 10, 89; 11, 58; Dn 10, 5.

1, 14: *Hair . . . as white as white wool or as snow:* Christ is eternal, clothed with the dignity that belonged to the "Ancient of Days"; cf 18; Dn 7, 9. *His eyes were like a fiery flame:* Christ is portrayed as all-knowing; cf 2, 23; Ps 7, 10; Jer 17, 10; and similar expressions in 2, 18; 19, 12; cf Dn 10, 6.

1, 15: *His feet . . . furnace:* Christ is depicted as unchangeable; cf Ez 1, 27; Dn 10, 6. The Greek word translated "refined" is unconnected grammatically with any other word in the sentence. *His voice . . . water:* Christ speaks with divine authority; cf Ez 1, 24.

1, 16: *Seven stars:* in the pagan world, Mithras and the Caesars were represented with seven stars in their right hand, symbolizing their universal dominion. *A sharp two-edged sword:* this refers to the word of God (cf Eph 6, 17; Heb 4, 12) that will destroy unrepentant sinners; cf 2, 16; 19, 15; Wis 18, 15; Is 11, 4; 49, 2. *His face . . . brightest:* this symbolizes the divine majesty of Christ; cf 10, 1; 21, 23; Jgs 5, 31; Is 60, 19; Mt 17, 2.

1, 17: It was an Old Testament belief that for sinful human beings to see God was to die; cf Ex 19, 21; 33, 20; Jgs 6, 22-23; Is 6, 5.

1, 18: *Netherworld:* Greek Hades, Hebrew Sheol, the abode of the dead; cf 20, 13-14; Nm 16, 33.

1, 19: *What you have seen, and what is happening, and what will happen afterwards:* the three parts of the Book of Revelation, the vision (10-20), the situation in the seven churches (chs 2-3), and the events of chs 6-22.

wards. [20]† This is the secret meaning of the seven stars you saw in my right hand, and of the seven gold lampstands: the seven stars are the angels of the seven churches, and the seven lampstands are the seven churches.

CHAPTER 2

***To Ephesus.*†** [1]† "To the angel of the church in Ephesus, write this:

" 'The one who holds the seven stars in his right hand and walks in the midst of the seven gold lampstands says this: [2]† "I know your works, your labor, and your endurance, and that you cannot tolerate the wicked; you have tested those who call themselves apostles but are not, and discovered that they are impostors. [3] Moreover, you have endurance and have suffered for my name, and you have not grown weary. [4] Yet I hold this against you: you have lost the love you had at first. [5] Realize how far you have fallen. Repent, and do the works you did at first. Otherwise, I will come to you and remove your lampstand from its place, unless you repent. [6]† But you have this in your favor: you hate the works of the Nicolaitans, which I also hate.

[7]*† " ' "Whoever has ears ought to hear what the Spirit says to the churches. To the victor I will give the right to eat from the tree of life that is in the garden of God." '

***To Smyrna.*†** [8]† "To the angel of the church in Smyrna, write this:

" 'The first and the last, who once died but came to life, says this: [9]*† "I know your tribulation and poverty, but you are rich. I know the slander of those who claim to be Jews and are not, but rather are members of the assembly of Satan. [10] Do not be afraid of anything that you are going to suffer. Indeed, the devil will throw some of you into prison, that you may be tested, and you will face an ordeal for ten days. Remain faithful until death, and I will give you the crown of life.

[11]*† " ' "Whoever has ears ought to hear what the Spirit says to the churches. The victor shall not be harmed by the second death." '

***To Pergamum.*†** [12]† "To the angel of the church in Pergamum, write this:

" 'The one with the sharp two-edged sword says this: [13]† "I know that you live where Satan's throne is, and yet you hold fast to my name and have not denied your faith in me, not even in the days of Antipas, my faithful witness, who was martyred among you, where Satan lives. [14]*† Yet I have a few things

---

* 2, 7: 11.17.29; 3, 6.13.22; 13, 9; Mt 11, 15.
9: Jas 2, 5.
11: 20, 6.14; 21, 8.
14: Nm 22-24; 25, 1-3; 31, 16; 2 Pt 2, 15; Jude 11.

---

† 1, 20: *Secret meaning:* literally, "mystery." *Angels:* these are the presiding spirits of the seven churches. Angels were thought to be in charge of the physical world (cf 7, 1; 14, 18; 16, 5) and of nations (Dn 10, 13; 12, 1), communities (the seven churches), and individuals (Mt 18, 10; Acts 12, 15). Some have seen in the "angel" of each of the seven churches its pastor or a personification of the spirit of the congregation.

2, 1—3, 22: Each of the seven letters follows the same pattern: address; description of the exalted Christ; blame and/or praise for the church addressed; threat and/or admonition; final exhortation and promise to all Christians.

2, 1-7: The letter to Ephesus praises the members of the church there for their works and virtues, including discerning false teachers (2-3), but admonishes them to repent and return to their former devotion (4-5). It concludes with a reference to the Nicolaitans (see the note on 6) and a promise that the victor will have access to eternal life (7).

2, 1: *Ephesus:* this great ancient city had a population of ca. 250,000; it was the capital of the Roman province of Asia and the commercial, cultural, and religious center of Asia. The other six churches were located in the same province, situated roughly in a circle; they were selected for geographical reasons rather than for the size of their Christian communities. *Walks in the midst of the seven gold lampstands:* this signifies that Christ is always present in the church; see the note on 1, 4.

2, 2: *Who call themselves . . . impostors:* this refers to unauthorized and perverse missionaries; cf Acts 20, 29-30.

2, 6: *Nicolaitans:* these are perhaps the impostors of v 2; see the note on vv 14-15. There is little evidence for connecting this group with Nicolaus, the proselyte from Antioch, mentioned in Acts 6, 5.

2, 7: *Victor:* referring to any Christian individual who holds fast to the faith and does God's will in the face of persecution. *The tree of life that is in the garden of God:* this is a reference to the tree in the primeval paradise (Gn 2, 9); cf 22, 2.14.19. The decree excluding humanity from the tree of life has been revoked by Christ.

2, 8-11: The letter to Smyrna encourages the Christians in this important commercial center by telling them that although they are impoverished, they are nevertheless rich, and calls those Jews who are slandering them members of the assembly of Satan (9). There is no admonition; rather, the Christians are told that they will suffer much, even death, but the time of tribulation will be short compared to their eternal reward (10), and they will thus escape final damnation (11).

2, 8: *Smyrna:* modern Izmir, ca. thirty miles north of Ephesus, and the chief city of Lydia, with a temple to the goddess Roma. It was renowned for its loyalty to Rome, and it also had a large Jewish community very hostile toward Christians.

2, 9-10: The church in Smyrna was materially poor but spiritually rich. Accusations made by Jewish brethren there occasioned the persecution of Christians; cf Acts 14, 2.19; 17, 5.13.

2, 11: *The second death:* this refers to the eternal death, when sinners will receive their final punishment; cf 20, 6.14-15; 21, 8.

2, 12-17: The letter to Pergamum praises the members of the church for persevering in their faith in Christ even in the midst of a pagan setting and in face of persecution and martyrdom (13). But it admonishes them about members who advocate an unprincipled morality (14; cf 2 Pt 2, 15; Jude 11) and others who follow the teaching of the Nicolaitans (15; see the note there). It urges them to repent (16) and promises them the hidden manna and Christ's amulet (17).

2, 12: *Pergamum:* modern Bergama, ca. forty-five miles northeast of Smyrna, a center for various kinds of pagan worship. It also had an outstanding library (the word *parchment* is derived from its name).

2, 13: *Satan's throne:* the reference is to emperor worship and other pagan practices that flourished in Pergamum, perhaps specifically to the white marble altar erected and dedicated to Zeus by Eumenes II (197-160 B.C.).

2, 14-15: Like Balaam, the biblical prototype of the religious compromiser (cf Nm 25, 1-3; 31, 16; 2 Pt 2, 15; Jude 11), the Nicolaitans in Pergamum and Ephesus (6) accommodated their Christian faith to paganism. They abused the principle of liberty enunciated by Paul (1 Cor 9, 19-23).

against you. You have some people there who hold to the teaching of Balaam, who instructed Balak to put a stumbling block before the Israelites: to eat food sacrificed to idols and to play the harlot. 15 Likewise, you also have some people who hold to the teaching of [the] Nicolaitans. 16 Therefore, repent. Otherwise, I will come to you quickly and wage war against them with the sword of my mouth.

17*† " ' "Whoever has ears ought to hear what the Spirit says to the churches. To the victor I shall give some of the hidden manna; I shall also give a white amulet upon which is inscribed a new name, which no one knows except the one who receives it." '

To Thyatira.† 18† "To the angel of the church in Thyatira, write this:

" 'The Son of God, whose eyes are like a fiery flame and whose feet are like polished brass, says this: 19 "I know your works, your love, faith, service, and endurance, and that your last works are greater than the first. 20† Yet I hold this against you, that you tolerate the woman Jezebel, who calls herself a prophetess, who teaches and misleads my servants to play the harlot and to eat food sacrificed to idols. 21 I have given her time to repent, but she refuses to repent of her harlotry. 22 So I will cast her on a sickbed and plunge those who commit adultery with her into intense suffering unless they repent of her works. 23*† I will also put her children to death. Thus shall all the churches come to know that I am the searcher of hearts and minds and that I will give each of you what your works deserve. 24† But I say to the rest of you in Thyatira, who do not uphold this teaching and know nothing of the so-called deep secrets of Satan: on you I will place no further burden, 25 except that you must hold fast to what you have until I come.

REVELATION

26*† " ' "To the victor, who keeps to my
ways until the end,
I will give authority over the nations.
27 He will rule them with an iron rod.
Like clay vessels will they be
smashed,

28 just as I received authority from my Father. And to him I will give the morning star.

29 " ' "Whoever has ears ought to hear what the Spirit says to the churches." '

CHAPTER 3

To Sardis.† 1† "To the angel of the church in Sardis, write this:

" 'The one who has the seven spirits of God and the seven stars says this: "I know your works, that you have the reputation of being alive, but you are dead. 2 Be watchful and strengthen what is left, which is going to die, for I have not found your works complete in the sight of my God. 3* Remember then how you accepted and heard; keep it, and repent. If you are not watchful, I will come like a thief, and you will never know at what hour I will come upon you. 4* However, you have a few people in Sardis who have not soiled their garments; they will walk with me dressed in white, because they are worthy.

5*† " ' "The victor will thus be dressed

*

17: Is 62, 2; 65, 15.
23: 1 Sm 16, 7; Jer 11, 20; 17, 10.
26: 12, 5; Ps 2, 8-9.
3, 3: Mt 24, 42-44; Mk 13, 33; 1 Thes 5, 2; 2 Pt 3, 10.
4: 7, 13-14.
5: Ps 69, 29; Dn 12, 1 / Mt 10, 32.

†

2, 17: *The hidden manna:* this is the food of life; cf Ps 78, 24-25. *White amulet:* literally, "white stone," on which was written a magical name, whose power could be tapped by one who knew the secret name. It is used here as a symbol of victory and joy; cf 3, 4-5. *New name:* this is a reference to the Christian's rebirth in Christ; cf 3, 12; 19, 12; Is 62, 2; 65, 15.

2, 18-29: The letter to Thyatira praises the progress in virtue of this small Christian community (19) but admonishes them for tolerating a false prophet who leads them astray (20). Her fate is sealed, but there is hope of repentance for her followers (21-22). Otherwise, they too shall die (23). They are warned against Satanic power or knowledge (24-25). Those who remain faithful will share in the messianic reign, having authority over nations (26-27), and will in fact possess Christ himself (28).

2, 18: *Thyatira:* modern Akhisar, ca. forty miles southeast of Pergamum, a frontier town famous for its workers' guilds (cf Acts 16, 14), membership in which may have involved festal meals in pagan temples.

2, 20: The scheming and treacherous Jezebel of old (cf 1 Kgs 19, 1-2; 21, 1-14; 2 Kgs 9, 22.30-34) introduced pagan customs into the religion of Israel; this new Jezebel was doing the same to Christianity.

2, 23: *Children:* spiritual descendants.

2, 24: *The so-called deep secrets of Satan:* literally, "the deep things of Satan," a scathing reference to the perverse teaching of the Nicolaitans (15).

2, 26-28: The Christian who perseveres in faith will share in Christ's messianic authority (cf Ps 2, 8-9) and resurrection victory over death, symbolized by the morning star; cf 22, 16.

2, 26: *Who keeps to my ways:* literally, "who keeps my works."

3, 1-6: The letter to Sardis does not praise the community but admonishes its members to watchfulness, mutual support, and repentance (2-3). The few who have remained pure and faithful will share Christ's victory and will be inscribed in the book of life (4-5).

3, 1: *Sardis:* this city, located ca. thirty miles southeast of Thyatira, was once the capital of Lydia, known for its wealth at the time of Croesus (6th century B.C.). Its citadel, reputed to be unassailable, was captured by surprise, first by Cyrus and later by Antiochus. The church is therefore warned to be on guard.

3, 5: *In white:* white is a sign of victory and joy as well as resurrection; see the note on 2, 17. *The book of life:* the roll in which the names of the redeemed are kept; cf 13, 8; 17, 8; 20, 12.15; 21, 27; Phil 4, 3; Dn 12, 1. They will be acknowledged by Christ in heaven; cf Mt 10, 32.

in white, and I will never erase his name
from the book of life but will acknowl-
edge his name in the presence of my
Father and of his angels.
6“ ‘ “Whoever has ears ought to hear
what the Spirit says to the churches.” ’
To Philadelphia.† 7*† “To the an-
gel of the church in Philadelphia, write
this:

“ ‘The holy one, the true,
who holds the key of David,
who opens and no one shall close,
who closes and no one shall open,

says this:
8† “ ‘ “I know your works (behold, I
have left an open door before you,
which no one can close). You have lim-
ited strength, and yet you have kept my
word and have not denied my name.
9* Behold, I will make those of the as-
sembly of Satan who claim to be Jews
and are not, but are lying, behold I will
make them come and fall prostrate at
your feet, and they will realize that I
love you. 10† Because you have kept my
message of endurance, I will keep
you safe in the time of trial that is go-
ing to come to the whole world to test
the inhabitants of the earth. 11* I am
coming quickly. Hold fast to what you
have, so that no one may take your
crown.
12*† “ ‘ “The victor I will make into a
pillar in the temple of my God, and he
will never leave it again. On him I will
inscribe the name of my God and the
name of the city of my God, the new
Jerusalem, which comes down out of
heaven from my God, as well as my new
name.
13“ ‘ “Whoever has ears ought to
hear what the Spirit says to the
churches.” ’
To Laodicea.† 14*† “To the angel of
the church in Laodicea, write this:
“ ‘The Amen, the faithful and true
witness, the source of God’s creation,
says this: 15† “I know your works; I
know that you are neither cold nor hot.
I wish you were either cold or hot.
16† So, because you are lukewarm, nei-
ther hot nor cold, I will spit you out of
my mouth. 17*† For you say, ‘I am rich
and affluent and have no need of any-
thing,’ and yet do not realize that you
are wretched, pitiable, poor, blind, and
naked. 18† I advise you to buy from me
gold refined by fire so that you may be
rich, and white garments to put on so
that your shameful nakedness may not
be exposed, and buy ointment to smear
on your eyes so that you may see.
19* Those whom I love, I reprove and
chastise. Be earnest, therefore, and re-
pent.
20† “ ‘ “Behold, I stand at the door and
knock. If anyone hears my voice and
opens the door, [then] I will enter his
house and dine with him, and he with
me. 21* I will give the victor the right
to sit with me on my throne, as I myself
first won the victory and sit with my Fa-
ther on his throne.
22“ ‘ “Whoever has ears ought to hear
what the Spirit says to the churches.” ’ ”

*

7: Is 22, 22; Mt 16, 19.
9: 2, 9 / Is 45, 14; 60, 14.
11: 2, 25; 22, 7.20.
12: 21, 2-3; Ez 48, 35 / 19, 13.
14: 1, 5.
17: Prv 13, 7; Lk 12, 21.
19: Prv 3, 11-12; 1 Cor 11, 32; Heb 12, 5-11.
21: Lk 22, 28-30; Mt 19, 28.

†

3, 7-13: The letter to Philadelphia praises the Christians there for remaining faithful even with their limited strength (8). Members of the assembly of Satan are again singled out (9; see 2, 9 above). There is no admonition; rather, the letter promises that they will be kept safe at the great trial (10-11) and that the victors will become pillars of the heavenly temple, upon which three names will be inscribed: God, Jerusalem, and Christ (12).

3, 7: *Philadelphia:* modern Alasehir, ca. thirty miles southeast of Sardis, founded by Attalus II Philadelphus of Pergamum to be an "open door" (8) for Greek culture; it was destroyed by an earthquake in A.D. 17. Rebuilt by money from the Emperor Tiberius, the city was renamed Neo-Caesarea; this may explain the allusions to "name" in v 12. *Key of David:* to the heavenly city of David (cf Is 22, 22), "the new Jerusalem" (12), over which Christ has supreme authority.

3, 8: *An open door:* opportunities for sharing and proclaiming the faith; cf Acts 14, 27; 1 Cor 16, 9; 2 Cor 2, 12.

3, 10: *My message of endurance:* this does not refer to a saying of Jesus about patience but to the example of Christ's patient endurance. *The inhabitants of the earth:* literally, "those who live on the earth." This expression, which also occurs in 6, 10; 8, 13; 11, 10; 13, 8.12.14; 17, 2.8, always refers to the pagan world.

3, 12: *Pillar:* this may be an allusion to the rebuilding of the city; see the note on v 7. *New Jerusalem:* it is described in 21, 10—22, 5.

3, 14-22: The letter to Laodicea reprimands the community for being lukewarm (15-16), but no particular faults are singled out. Their material prosperity is contrasted with their spiritual poverty, the violet tunics that were the source of their wealth with the white robe of baptism, and their famous eye ointment with true spiritual perception (17-18). But Christ's chastisement is inspired by love and a desire to be allowed to share the messianic banquet with his followers in the heavenly kingdom (19-21).

3, 14: *Laodicea:* ca. forty miles southeast of Philadelphia and ca. eighty miles east of Ephesus, a wealthy industrial and commercial center, with a renowned medical school. It exported fine woolen garments and was famous for its eye salves. It was so wealthy that it was proudly rebuilt without outside aid after the devastating earthquake of A.D. 60/61. *The Amen:* this is a divine title (cf Hebrew text of Is 65, 16) applied to Christ; cf 2 Cor 1, 20. *Source of God's creation:* literally, "the beginning of God's creation," a concept found also in Jn 1, 3; Col 1, 16-17, Heb 1, 2; cf Prv 8, 22-31; Wis 9, 1-2.

3, 15-16: Halfhearted commitment to the faith is nauseating to Christ; cf Rom 12, 11.

3, 16: *Spit:* literally, "vomit." The image is that of a beverage that should be either hot or cold. Perhaps there is an allusion to the hot springs of Hierapolis across the Lycus river from Laodicea, which would have been lukewarm by the time they reached Laodicea.

3, 17: Economic prosperity occasioned spiritual bankruptcy.

3, 18: *Gold . . . fire:* God's grace. *White garments:* symbol of an upright life; the city was noted for its violet/purple cloth. *Ointment . . . eyes:* to remove spiritual blindness; one of the city's exports was eye ointment (see the note on 3, 14).

3, 20: Christ invites all to the messianic banquet in heaven; cf Is 25, 6; Lk 14, 15; 22, 30.

III: GOD AND THE LAMB IN HEAVEN

CHAPTER 4

Vision of Heavenly Worship.†
1† After this I had a vision of an open
door to heaven, and I heard the trum-
petlike voice that had spoken to me be-
fore, saying, "Come up here and I will
show you what must happen after-
wards." 2*† At once I was caught up in
spirit. A throne was there in heaven,
and on the throne sat 3 one whose
appearance sparkled like jasper and
carnelian. Around the throne was a
halo as brilliant as an emerald.
4*† Surrounding the throne I saw
twenty-four other thrones on which
twenty-four elders sat, dressed in white
garments and with gold crowns on their
heads. 5† From the throne came flashes
of lightning, rumblings, and peals of
thunder. Seven flaming torches burned
in front of the throne, which are the
seven spirits of God. 6*† In front of the
throne was something that resembled
a sea of glass like crystal.

In the center and around the throne,
there were four living creatures cov-
ered with eyes in front and in back.
7† The first creature resembled a lion,
the second was like a calf, the third had
a face like that of a human being, and
the fourth looked like an eagle in flight.
8*† The four living creatures, each of
them with six wings, were covered with
eyes inside and out. Day and night they
do not stop exclaiming:

"Holy, holy, holy is the Lord God
almighty,
who was, and who is, and who is
to come."

9 Whenever the living creatures give
glory and honor and thanks to the one
who sits on the throne, who lives forever
and ever, 10 the twenty-four elders fall
down before the one who sits on the
throne and worship him, who lives for-
ever and ever. They throw down their
crowns before the throne, exclaiming:

11* "Worthy are you, Lord our God,
to receive glory and honor and
power,
for you created all things;
because of your will they came to
be and were created."

CHAPTER 5

The Scroll and the Lamb.† 1*† I saw
a scroll in the right hand of the one who
sat on the throne. It had writing on both
sides and was sealed with seven seals.
2 Then I saw a mighty angel who pro-
claimed in a loud voice, "Who is worthy
to open the scroll and break its seals?"
3 But no one in heaven or on earth or
under the earth was able to open the
scroll or to examine it. 4 I shed many
tears because no one was found worthy
to open the scroll or to examine it.
5*† One of the elders said to me, "Do
not weep. The lion of the tribe of Judah,
the root of David, has triumphed, en-
abling him to open the scroll with its
seven seals."

6*† Then I saw standing in the midst
of the throne and the four living crea-
tures and the elders, a Lamb that
seemed to have been slain. He had
seven horns and seven eyes; these are

*

4, 2-3: Is 6, 1 / Ez 1, 26-28.
4: Is 24, 23.
6: Ex 24, 10.
8: Is 6, 2-3 / 1, 4.8; 11, 17; 16, 5.
11: Rom 4, 17; 16, 27.
5, 1: Is 29, 11.
5: Is 11, 1.10; Rom 15, 12.
6: Jn 1, 29.

†

4, 1-11: The seer now describes a vision of the heavenly court in worship of God enthroned. He reverently avoids naming or describing God but pictures twenty-four elders in priestly and regal attire (4) and God's throne and its surroundings made of precious gems and other symbols that traditionally express the majesty of God (5-6). Universal creation is represented by the four living creatures (6-7). Along with the twenty-four elders, they praise God unceasingly in humble adoration (8-11).

4, 1: The ancients viewed heaven as a solid vault, entered by way of actual doors.

4, 2-8: Much of the imagery here is taken from Ez 1 and 10.

4, 4: *Twenty-four elders:* these represent the twelve tribes of Israel and the twelve apostles; cf 21, 12-14.

4, 5: *Flashes of lightning, rumblings, and peals of thunder:* as in other descriptions of God's appearance or activity; cf 8, 5; 11, 19; 16, 18; Ex 19, 16; Ez 1, 4.13. *The seven spirits of God:* the seven "angels of the presence" as in 8, 2 and Tb 12, 15.

4, 6: *A sea of glass like crystal:* an image adapted from Ez 1, 22-26. *Four living creatures:* these are symbols taken from Ez 1, 5-21; they are identified as cherubim in Ez 10, 20. *Covered with eyes:* these suggest God's knowledge and concern.

4, 7: *Lion . . . calf . . . human being . . . eagle:* these symbolize, respectively, what is noblest, strongest, wisest, and swiftest in creation. *Calf:* traditionally translated "ox," the Greek word refers to a heifer or young bull. Since the second century, these four creatures have been used as symbols of the evangelists Mark, Luke, Matthew, and John, respectively.

4, 8: *Six wings:* like the seraphim of Is 6, 2.

5, 1-14: The seer now describes a papyrus roll in God's right hand (1) with seven seals indicating the importance of the message. A mighty angel asks who is worthy to open the scroll, i.e., who can accomplish God's salvific plan (2). There is despair at first when no one in creation can do it (3-4). But the seer is comforted by an elder who tells him that Christ, called the lion of the tribe of Judah, has won the right to open it (5). Christ then appears as a Lamb, coming to receive the scroll from God (6-7), for which he is acclaimed as at a coronation (8-10). This is followed by a doxology of the angels (11-12) and then finally by the heavenly church united with all of creation (13-14).

5, 1: *A scroll:* a papyrus roll possibly containing a list of afflictions for sinners (cf Ez 2, 9-10) or God's plan for the world. *Sealed with seven seals:* it is totally hidden from all but God. Only the Lamb (7-9) has the right to carry out the divine plan.

5, 5: *The lion of the tribe of Judah, the root of David:* these are the messianic titles applied to Christ to symbolize his victory; cf 22, 16; Gn 49, 9; Is 11, 1.10; Mt 1, 1.

5, 6: Christ is the Paschal Lamb without blemish, whose blood saved the new Israel from sin and death; cf Ex 12; Is 53, 7; Jn 1, 29.36; Acts 8, 32; 1 Pt 1, 18-19. This is the main title for Christ in Rv, used twenty-eight times. *Seven horns and seven eyes:* Christ has the fullness (see the note on 1, 4) of power (horns) and knowledge (eyes); cf Zec 4, 10. *[Seven] spirits:* as in 1, 4; 3, 1; and 4, 5.

the [seven] spirits of God sent out into
the whole world. 7 He came and re-
ceived the scroll from the right hand
of the one who sat on the throne.
8 When he took it, the four living crea-
tures and the twenty-four elders fell
down before the Lamb. Each of the el-
ders held a harp and gold bowls filled
with incense, which are the prayers of
the holy ones. 9 They sang a new hymn:

"Worthy are you to receive the scroll
and to break open its seals,
for you were slain and with your blood you purchased for God
those from every tribe and tongue, people and nation.
10* You made them a kingdom and priests for our God,
and they will reign on earth."

11*† I looked again and heard the voices
of many angels who surrounded the
throne and the living creatures and the
elders. They were countless in number,
12 and they cried out in a loud voice:

"Worthy is the Lamb that was slain
to receive power and riches, wisdom and strength,
honor and glory and blessing."

13 Then I heard every creature in
heaven and on earth and under the
earth and in the sea, everything in the
universe, cry out:

"To the one who sits on the throne and to the Lamb
be blessing and honor, glory and might,
forever and ever."

14 The four living creatures answered,
"Amen," and the elders fell down and
worshiped.

IV: THE SEVEN SEALS, TRUMPETS, AND PLAGUES, WITH INTERLUDES†

CHAPTER 6

The First Six Seals. † 1† Then I
watched while the Lamb broke open the
first of the seven seals, and I heard one
of the four living creatures cry out in a
voice like thunder, "Come forward."
2*† I looked, and there was a white
horse, and its rider had a bow. He was
given a crown, and he rode forth victo-
rious to further his victories.
3 When he broke open the second seal,
I heard the second living creature cry
out, "Come forward." 4*† Another
horse came out, a red one. Its rider was
given power to take peace away from
the earth, so that people would slaugh-
ter one another. And he was given a
huge sword.
5† When he broke open the third seal,
I heard the third living creature cry out,
"Come forward." I looked, and there
was a black horse, and its rider held a
scale in his hand. 6*† I heard what
seemed to be a voice in the midst of the
four living creatures. It said, "A ration
of wheat costs a day's pay, and three
rations of barley cost a day's pay. But
do not damage the olive oil or the wine."
7 When he broke open the fourth seal,
I heard the voice of the fourth living
creature cry out, "Come forward."
8*† I looked, and there was a pale green
horse. Its rider was named Death, and
Hades accompanied him. They were
given authority over a quarter of the
earth, to kill with sword, famine, and
plague, and by means of the beasts of
the earth.
9† When he broke open the fifth seal,
I saw underneath the altar the souls of
those who had been slaughtered be-

---

*

10: 1, 6; Ex 19, 6; Is 61, 6.
11: Dn 7, 10; Jude 14-15.
6, 2: Zec 1, 8-10; 6, 1-3.
4: Ez 21, 14-16.
6: Lv 26, 26; Ez 4, 16-17.
8: Ez 14, 21.

---

†

5, 11: *Countless:* literally, "100,000,000 plus 1,000,000," used by the author to express infinity.

6, 1—16, 21: A series of seven disasters now begins as each seal is broken (6, 1—8, 1), followed by a similar series as seven trumpets sound (8, 2—11, 19) and as seven angels pour bowls on the earth causing plagues (15, 1—16, 21). These gloomy sequences are interrupted by longer or shorter scenes suggesting the triumph of God and his witnesses (e.g., chs 7, 10, 11, 12, 13, 14).

6, 1-17: This chapter provides a symbolic description of the contents of the sealed scroll. The breaking of the first four seals reveals four riders. The first rider (of a white horse) is a conquering power (1-2), the second (red horse) a symbol of bloody war (3-4), the third (black horse) a symbol of famine (5-6), the fourth (pale green horse) a symbol of Death himself, accompanied by Hades (the netherworld) as his page (7-8). Verse 8b summarizes the role of all four riders. The breaking of the fifth seal reveals Christian martyrs in an attitude of sacrifice as blood poured out at the foot of an altar begging God for vindication, which will come only when their quota is filled; but they are given a white robe symbolic of victory (9-11). The breaking of the sixth seal reveals typical apocalyptic signs in the sky and the sheer terror of all people at the imminent divine judgment (12-17).

6, 1-8: The imagery is adapted from Zec 1, 8-10; 6, 1-8.

6, 2: *White horse . . . bow:* this may perhaps allude specifically to the Parthians on the eastern border of the Roman empire. Expert in the use of the bow, they constantly harassed the Romans and won a major victory in A.D. 62; see the note on 9, 13-21. But the Old Testament imagery typifies the history of oppression of God's people at all times.

6, 4: *Huge sword:* this is a symbol of war and violence; cf Ez 21, 14-17.

6, 5: *Black horse:* this is a symbol of famine, the usual accompaniment of war in antiquity; cf Lv 26, 26; Ez 4, 16-17. The *scale* is a symbol of shortage of food with a corresponding rise in price.

6, 6: *A day's pay:* literally, "a denarius," a Roman silver coin that constitutes a day's wage in Mt 20, 2. Because of the famine, food was rationed and sold at an exorbitant price. A liter of flour was considered a day's ration in the Greek historians Herodotus and Diogenes Laertius. *Barley:* food of the poor (Jn 6, 9.13; cf 2 Kgs 7, 1.16.18); it was also used to feed animals; cf 1 Kgs 5, 8. *Do not damage:* the olive and the vine are to be used more sparingly in time of famine.

6, 8: *Pale green:* symbol of death and decay; cf Ez 14, 21.

6, 9: *The altar:* this altar corresponds to the altar of holocausts in the temple in Jerusalem; see also 11, 1. *Because of the witness . . . word of God:* literally, "because of the word of God and the witness they had borne."

cause of the witness they bore to the
word of God. 10† They cried out in a loud
voice, "How long will it be, holy and true
master, before you sit in judgment and
avenge our blood on the inhabitants of
the earth?" 11 Each of them was given
a white robe, and they were told to be
patient a little while longer until the
number was filled of their fellow ser-
vants and brothers who were going to
be killed as they had been.

12*† Then I watched while he broke
open the sixth seal, and there was a
great earthquake; the sun turned as
black as dark sackcloth and the whole
moon became like blood. 13† The stars
in the sky fell to the earth like unripe
figs shaken loose from the tree in a
strong wind. 14*† Then the sky was di-
vided like a torn scroll curling up, and
every mountain and island was moved
from its place. 15† The kings of the
earth, the nobles, the military officers,
the rich, the powerful, and every slave
and free person hid themselves in caves
and among mountain crags. 16* They
cried out to the mountains and the
rocks, "Fall on us and hide us from the
face of the one who sits on the throne
and from the wrath of the Lamb,
17† because the great day of their wrath
has come and who can withstand it?"

CHAPTER 7†

The 144,000 Sealed. 1*† After this I
saw four angels standing at the four
corners of the earth, holding back the
four winds of the earth so that no wind
could blow on land or sea or against any
tree. 2† Then I saw another angel come
up from the East, holding the seal of
the living God. He cried out in a loud
voice to the four angels who were given
power to damage the land and the sea,
3* "Do not damage the land or the sea
or the trees until we put the seal on the
foreheads of the servants of our God."
4*† I heard the number of those who had
been marked with the seal, one hundred
and forty-four thousand marked from
every tribe of the Israelites: 5† twelve
thousand were marked from the tribe
of Judah, twelve thousand from the
tribe of Reuben, twelve thousand from
the tribe of Gad, 6 twelve thousand from
the tribe of Asher, twelve thousand
from the tribe of Naphtali, twelve thou-
sand from the tribe of Manasseh,
7 twelve thousand from the tribe of Sim-
eon, twelve thousand from the tribe of
Levi, twelve thousand from the tribe of
Issachar, 8 twelve thousand from the
tribe of Zebulun, twelve thousand from
the tribe of Joseph, and twelve thou-
sand were marked from the tribe of
Benjamin.

Triumph of the Elect. 9† After this I
had a vision of a great multitude, which
no one could count, from every nation,
race, people, and tongue. They stood
before the throne and before the Lamb,
wearing white robes and holding palm
branches in their hands. 10† They cried
out in a loud voice:

"Salvation comes from our God,
who is seated on the throne,
and from the Lamb."

11 All the angels stood around the throne
and around the elders and the four liv-
ing creatures. They prostrated them-
selves before the throne, worshiped
God, 12 and exclaimed:

"Amen. Blessing and glory, wisdom
and thanksgiving,
honor, power, and might
be to our God forever and ever.
Amen."

*

12: Jl 3, 4; Mt 24, 29.
14: Is 34, 4 / 16, 20.
16: Is 2, 19; Hos 10, 8; Lk 23, 30.
7, 1: Jer 49, 36; Zec 6, 5.
3: Ex 12, 7-14; Ez 9, 4; 2 Cor 1, 22; Eph 1, 13; 4, 30.
4: 14, 1.

†

6, 10: *Holy and true master:* Old Testament usage as well as the context indicates that this is addressed to God rather than to Christ.

6, 12-14: Symbolic rather than literal description of the cosmic upheavals attending the day of the Lord when the martyrs' prayer for vindication (10) would be answered; cf Am 8, 8-9; Is 34, 4; 50, 3; Jl 2, 10; 3, 3-4; Mt 24, 4-36; Mk 13, 5-37; Lk 21, 8-36.

6, 12: *Dark sackcloth:* for mourning, sackcloth was made from the skin of a black goat.

6, 13: *Unripe figs:* literally, "summer (or winter) fruit."

6, 14: *Was divided:* literally, "was split," like a broken papyrus roll torn in two, each half then curling up to form a roll on either side.

6, 15: *Nobles:* literally, "courtiers," "grandees." *Military officers:* literally, "commanders of 1,000 men," used in Josephus and other Greek authors as the equivalent of the Roman *tribunus militum*. The listing of various ranks of society represents the universality of terror at the impending doom.

6, 17: *Their:* this reading is attested in the best manuscripts, but the vast majority read "his" in reference to the wrath of the Lamb in the preceding verse.

7, 1-17: An interlude of two visions precedes the breaking of the seventh seal, just as two more will separate the sixth and seventh trumpets (ch 10). In the first vision (1-8), the elect receive the seal of the living God as protection against the coming cataclysm; cf 14, 1; Ez 9, 4-6; 2 Cor 1, 22; Eph 1, 13; 4, 30. The second vision (9-17) portrays the faithful Christians before God's throne to encourage those on earth to persevere to the end, even to death.

7, 1: *The four corners of the earth:* the earth is seen as a table or rectangular surface.

7, 2: *East:* literally, "rising of the sun." The east was considered the source of light and the place of paradise (Gn 2, 8). *Seal:* whatever was marked by the impression of one's signet ring belonged to that person and was under his protection.

7, 4-9: *One hundred and forty-four thousand:* the square of twelve (the number of Israel's tribes) multiplied by a thousand, symbolic of the new Israel (cf 14, 1-5; Gal 6, 16; Jas 1, 1) that embraces people *from every nation, race, people, and tongue* (9).

7, 5-8: Judah is placed first because of Christ; cf "the Lion of the tribe of Judah" (5, 5). Dan is omitted because of a later tradition that the antichrist would arise from it.

7, 9: *White robes . . . palm branches:* symbols of joy and victory; see the note on 3, 5.

7, 10: *Salvation comes from:* literally, "(let) salvation (be ascribed) to." A similar hymn of praise is found at the fall of the dragon (12, 10) and of Babylon (19, 1).

13 Then one of the elders spoke up and
said to me, "Who are these wearing
white robes, and where did they come
from?" 14*† I said to him, "My lord, you
are the one who knows." He said to me,
"These are the ones who have survived
the time of great distress; they have
washed their robes and made them
white in the blood of the Lamb.

15 "For this reason they stand before
God's throne
and worship him day and night
in his temple.
The one who sits on the throne will
shelter them.
16* They will not hunger or thirst anymore,
nor will the sun or any heat strike
them.
17*†For the Lamb who is in the center
of the throne will shepherd
them
and lead them to springs of life-giving water,
and God will wipe away every
tear from their eyes."

CHAPTER 8†

The Seven Trumpets. 1*† When he
broke open the seventh seal, there was
silence in heaven for about half an hour.
2* And I saw that the seven angels who
stood before God were given seven
trumpets.

The Gold Censer. 3*† Another angel
came and stood at the altar, holding a
gold censer. He was given a great quantity
of incense to offer, along with the
prayers of all the holy ones, on the gold
altar that was before the throne. 4 The
smoke of the incense along with the
prayers of the holy ones went up before
God from the hand of the angel. 5* Then
the angel took the censer, filled it with
burning coals from the altar, and hurled
it down to the earth. There were peals
of thunder, rumblings, flashes of lightning,
and an earthquake.

The First Four Trumpets. 6* The
seven angels who were holding the
seven trumpets prepared to blow them.
7† When the first one blew his trumpet,
there came hail and fire mixed with
blood, which was hurled down to the
earth. A third of the land was burned
up, along with a third of the trees and
all green grass.
8*† When the second angel blew his
trumpet, something like a large burning
mountain was hurled into the sea. A
third of the sea turned to blood, 9† a
third of the creatures living in the sea
died, and a third of the ships were
wrecked.
10* When the third angel blew his
trumpet, a large star burning like a
torch fell from the sky. It fell on a third
of the rivers and on the springs of water.
11*† The star was called "Wormwood,"
and a third of all the water turned to
wormwood. Many people died from this
water, because it was made bitter.
12* When the fourth angel blew his
trumpet, a third of the sun, a third of
the moon, and a third of the stars were
struck, so that a third of them became
dark. The day lost its light for a third
of the time, as did the night.
13† Then I looked again and heard an
eagle flying high overhead cry out in a
loud voice, "Woe! Woe! Woe to the inhabitants
of the earth from the rest of
the trumpet blasts that the three angels
are about to blow!"

CHAPTER 9

***The Fifth Trumpet.*†** 1*† Then the
fifth angel blew his trumpet, and I saw

---

*

14: Mt 24, 21.
16: Is 49, 10.
17: 21, 4; Is 25, 8.
8, 1: Hb 2, 20; Zep 1, 7; Zec 2, 17.
2: 4, 5; Tb 12, 15.
3: Ps 141, 2; Tb 12, 12.
5: Ez 10, 2; Ps 11, 6 / 4, 5; 11, 19; 16, 18.
6: 16, 1-21.
8: Ex 7, 20.
10: Is 14, 12.
11: Jer 9, 14.
12: Ex 10, 21-23.
9, 1: 20, 1.

---

†

7, 14: *Time of great distress:* fierce persecution by the Romans; cf Introduction.

7, 17: *Life-giving water:* literally, "the water of life," God's grace, which flows from Christ; cf 21, 6; 22, 1.17; Jn 4, 10.14.

8, 1-13: The breaking of the seventh seal produces at first silence and then seven symbolic disasters, each announced by a trumpet blast, of which the first four form a unit as did the first four seals. A minor liturgy (3-5) is enclosed by a vision of seven angels (2.6). Then follow the first four trumpet blasts, each heralding catastrophes modeled on the plagues of Egypt affecting the traditional prophetic third (cf Ez 5, 12) of the earth, sea, fresh water, and stars (7-12). Finally, there is a vision of an eagle warning of the last three trumpet blasts (13).

8, 1: *Silence in heaven:* as in Zep 1, 7, a prelude to the eschatological woes that are to follow; cf Introduction.

8, 3: *Altar:* there seems to be only one altar in the heavenly temple, corresponding to the altar of holocausts in 6, 9, and here to the altar of incense in Jerusalem; cf also 9, 13; 11, 1; 14, 18; 16, 7.

8, 7: This woe resembles the seventh plague of Egypt (Ex 9, 23-24); cf Jl 3, 3.

8, 8-11: The background of these two woes is the first plague of Egypt (Ex 7, 20-21).

8, 9: *Creatures living in the sea:* literally, "creatures in the sea that had souls."

8, 11: *Wormwood:* an extremely bitter and malignant plant symbolizing the punishment God inflicts on the ungodly; cf Jer 9, 12-14; 23, 15.

8, 13: *Woe! Woe! Woe:* each of the three woes pronounced by the angel represents a separate disaster; cf 9, 12; 11, 14. The final woe, released by the seventh trumpet blast, includes the plagues of ch 16.

9, 1-12: The fifth trumpet heralds a woe containing elements from the eighth and ninth plagues of Egypt (Ex 10, 12-15.21-23) but specifically reminiscent of the invasion of locusts in Jl 1, 4—2, 10.

9, 1: *A star:* late Judaism represented fallen powers as stars (Is 14, 12-15; Lk 10, 18; Jude 13), but a comparison with 1, 20 and 20, 1 suggests that here it means an angel. *The passage to the abyss:* referring to Sheol, the netherworld, where Satan and the fallen angels are kept for a thousand years, to be cast afterwards into the pool of fire; cf 20, 7-10. The abyss was conceived of as a vast subterranean cavern full of fire. Its only link with the earth was a kind of passage or mine shaft, which was kept locked.

a star that had fallen from the sky to
the earth. It was given the key for the
passage to the abyss. 2* It opened the
passage to the abyss, and smoke came
up out of the passage like smoke from
a huge furnace. The sun and the air
were darkened by the smoke from the
passage. 3*† Locusts came out of the
smoke onto the land, and they were
given the same power as scorpions of
the earth. 4 They were told not to harm
the grass of the earth or any plant or
any tree, but only those people who did
not have the seal of God on their fore-
heads. 5† They were not allowed to kill
them but only to torment them for five
months; the torment they inflicted was
like that of a scorpion when it stings a
person. 6* During that time these people
will seek death but will not find it, and
they will long to die but death will es-
cape them.

7*† The appearance of the locusts was
like that of horses ready for battle.
On their heads they wore what looked
like crowns of gold; their faces were
like human faces, 8* and they had
hair like women's hair. Their teeth
were like lions' teeth, 9 and they had
chests like iron breastplates. The sound
of their wings was like the sound of
many horse-drawn chariots racing into
battle. 10 They had tails like scorpions,
with stingers; with their tails they had
power to harm people for five months.
11† They had as their king the angel of
the abyss, whose name in Hebrew is
Abaddon and in Greek Apollyon.

12 The first woe has passed, but there
are two more to come.

The Sixth Trumpet.† 13*† Then the
sixth angel blew his trumpet, and I
heard a voice coming from the [four]
horns of the gold altar before God,
14† telling the sixth angel who held the
trumpet, "Release the four angels who
are bound at the banks of the great river
Euphrates." 15 So the four angels were
released, who were prepared for this
hour, day, month, and year to kill a
third of the human race. 16 The number
of cavalry troops was two hundred mil-
lion; I heard their number. 17*† Now in
my vision this is how I saw the horses
and their riders. They wore red, blue,
and yellow breastplates, and the horses'
heads were like heads of lions, and out
of their mouths came fire, smoke, and
sulfur. 18 By these three plagues of fire,
smoke, and sulfur that came out of their
mouths a third of the human race was
killed. 19 For the power of the horses is
in their mouths and in their tails; for
their tails are like snakes, with heads
that inflict harm.

20*† The rest of the human race, who
were not killed by these plagues, did not
repent of the works of their hands, to
give up the worship of demons and idols
made from gold, silver, bronze, stone,
and wood, which cannot see or hear or
walk. 21 Nor did they repent of their
murders, their magic potions, their un-
chastity, or their robberies.

CHAPTER 10

The Angel with the Small Scroll.†
1† Then I saw another mighty angel
come down from heaven wrapped in a
cloud, with a halo around his head; his
face was like the sun and his feet were
like pillars of fire. 2† In his hand he held
a small scroll that had been opened. He
placed his right foot on the sea and his
left foot on the land, 3* and then he cried
out in a loud voice as a lion roars. When
he cried out, the seven thunders raised
their voices, too. 4 When the seven thun-
ders had spoken, I was about to write
it down; but I heard a voice from heaven
say, "Seal up what the seven thunders
have spoken, but do not write it down."
5 Then the angel I saw standing on the
sea and on the land raised his right
hand to heaven 6*† and swore by the

*

2: Gn 19, 28.
3: Ex 10, 12-15; Wis 16, 9.
6: Jb 3, 21.
7: Jl 2, 4.
8: Jl 1, 6.
13: Ex 30, 1-3.
17: Jb 41, 10-13.
20: Ps 135, 15-17; Is 17, 8; Dn 5, 4.
10, 3: Ps 29, 3-9; Jer 25, 30; Am 3, 8.
6: Dt 32, 40; Dn 12, 7 / Ez 12, 28.

†

9, 3: *Scorpions:* their poisonous sting was proverbial; Ez 2, 6; Lk 11, 12.

9, 5: *For five months:* more or less corresponding to the life-span of locusts.

9, 7-10: Eight characteristics are listed to show the eschatological and diabolical nature of these locusts.

9, 11: *Abaddon:* Hebrew (more precisely, Aramaic) for destruction or ruin. *Apollyon:* Greek for the "Destroyer."

9, 13-21: The sixth trumpet heralds a woe representing another diabolical attack symbolized by an invasion by the Parthians living east of the Euphrates; see the note on 6, 2. At the appointed time (15), the frightful horses act as God's agents of judgment. The imaginative details are not to be taken literally; see Introduction and the note on 6, 12-14.

9, 13: *[Four]:* many Greek manuscripts and versions omit the word. The horns were situated at the four corners of the altar (Ex 27, 2; 30, 2-3); see the note on 8, 3.

9, 14-15: *The four angels:* they are symbolic of the destructive activity that will be extended throughout the universe.

9, 17: *Blue:* literally, "hyacinth-colored." *Yellow:* literally, "sulfurous."

9, 20: *The works of their hands:* i.e., the gods their hands had made.

10, 1—11, 14: An interlude in two scenes (10, 1-11 and 11, 1-14) precedes the sounding of the seventh trumpet; cf 7, 1-17. The first vision describes an angel astride sea and land like a colossus, with a small scroll open, the contents of which indicate that the end is imminent (ch 10). The second vision is of the measuring of the temple and of two witnesses, whose martyrdom means that the kingdom of God is about to be inaugurated.

10, 1-4: *The seven thunders:* God's voice announcing judgment and doom; cf Ps 29, 3-9, where thunder, as the voice of Yahweh, is praised seven times.

10, 2: *He placed . . . on the land:* this symbolizes the universality of the angel's message, as does the figure of the small scroll open to be read.

10, 6: *Heaven and earth and sea:* the three parts of the universe. *No more delay:* cf Dn 12, 7; Hb 2, 3.

one who lives forever and ever, who
created heaven and earth and sea and
all that is in them, "There shall be no
more delay. 7*† At the time when you
hear the seventh angel blow his trum-
pet, the mysterious plan of God shall
be fulfilled, as he promised to his ser-
vants the prophets."
8 Then the voice that I had heard from
heaven spoke to me again and said,
"Go, take the scroll that lies open in the
hand of the angel who is standing on
the sea and on the land." 9† So I went
up to the angel and told him to give me
the small scroll. He said to me, "Take
and swallow it. It will turn your stomach
sour, but in your mouth it will taste as
sweet as honey." 10* I took the small
scroll from the angel's hand and swal-
lowed it. In my mouth it was like sweet
honey, but when I had eaten it, my
stomach turned sour. 11† Then someone
said to me, "You must prophesy again
about many peoples, nations, tongues,
and kings."

CHAPTER 11

The Two Witnesses. 1*† Then I was
given a measuring rod like a staff and
I was told, "Come and measure the tem-
ple of God and the altar, and count
those who are worshiping in it. 2† But
exclude the outer court of the temple;
do not measure it, for it has been
handed over to the Gentiles, who will
trample the holy city for forty-two
months. 3† I will commission my two
witnesses to prophesy for those twelve
hundred and sixty days, wearing sack-
cloth." 4*† These are the two olive trees
and the two lampstands that stand be-
fore the Lord of the earth. 5† If anyone
wants to harm them, fire comes out of
their mouths and devours their ene-
mies. In this way, anyone wanting to
harm them is sure to be slain. 6* They
have the power to close up the sky so
that no rain can fall during the time of
their prophesying. They also have
power to turn water into blood and to
afflict the earth with any plague as often
as they wish.
7*† When they have finished their tes-
timony, the beast that comes up from
the abyss will wage war against them
and conquer them and kill them.
8† Their corpses will lie in the main
street of the great city, which has the
symbolic names "Sodom" and
"Egypt," where indeed their Lord was
crucified. 9† Those from every people,
tribe, tongue, and nation will gaze on
their corpses for three and a half days,
and they will not allow their corpses to
be buried. 10 The inhabitants of the
earth will gloat over them and be glad
and exchange gifts because these two
prophets tormented the inhabitants of
the earth. 11* But after the three and a
half days, a breath of life from God en-
tered them. When they stood on their
feet, great fear fell on those who saw
them. 12* Then they heard a loud voice
from heaven say to them, "Come up
here." So they went up to heaven in a
cloud as their enemies looked on.
13† At that moment there was a great
earthquake, and a tenth of the city fell
in ruins. Seven thousand people were
killed during the earthquake; the rest
were terrified and gave glory to the God
of heaven.
14 The second woe has passed, but the
third is coming soon.

*

7: Am 3, 7.
10: Ez 3, 1-3.
11, 1: Ez 40, 3-5 / Zec 2, 5-9.
4: Zec 4, 3.14.
6: Ex 7, 17.
7: Dn 7, 21.
11: Ez 37, 5.10.
12: 2 Kgs 2, 11.

†

10, 7: *The mysterious plan of God:* literally, "the mystery of God," the end of the present age when the forces of evil will be put down (17, 1—19, 4.11-21; 20, 7-10; cf 2 Thes 2, 6-12; Rom 16, 25-26), and the establishment of the reign of God when all creation will be made new (21, 1—22, 5).

10, 9-10: The small scroll was sweet because it predicted the final victory of God's people; it was sour because it also announced their sufferings. Cf Ez 3, 1-3.

10, 11: This further prophecy is contained in chs 12-22.

11, 1: The temple and altar symbolize the new Israel; see the note on 7, 4-9. The worshipers represent Christians. The measuring of the temple (cf Ez 40, 3—42, 20; 47, 1-12; Zec 2, 5-6) suggests that God will preserve the faithful remnant (cf Is 4, 2-3) who remain true to Christ (14, 1-5).

11, 2: *The outer court:* the Court of the Gentiles. *Trample . . . forty-two months:* the duration of the vicious persecution of the Jews by Antiochus IV Epiphanes (Dn 7, 25; 12, 7); this persecution of three and a half years (half of seven, counted as 1260 days in 3; 12, 6) became the prototype of periods of trial for God's people; cf Lk 4, 25; Jas 5, 17. The reference here is to the persecution by the Romans; cf Introduction.

11, 3: The two witnesses, wearing sackcloth symbolizing lamentation and repentance, cannot readily be identified. Do they represent Moses and Elijah, or the Law and the Prophets, or Peter and Paul? Most probably they refer to the universal church, especially the Christian martyrs, fulfilling the office of witness (two because of Dt 19, 15; cf Mk 6, 7; Jn 8, 17).

11, 4: *The two olive trees and the two lampstands:* the martyrs who stand in the presence of the Lord; the imagery is taken from Zec 4, 1-3.11-14, where the olive trees refer to Zerubbabel and Joshua.

11, 5-6: These details are derived from stories of Moses, who turned *water into blood* (Ex 7, 17-20), and of Elijah, who called down fire from heaven (1 Kgs 18, 36-40; 2 Kgs 1, 10) and closed up the sky for three years (1 Kgs 17, 1; cf 18, 1).

11, 7: *The beast . . . from the abyss:* the Roman emperor Nero, who symbolizes the forces of evil, or the antichrist (13, 1.8; 17, 8); cf Dn 7, 2-8.11-12.19-22 and Introduction.

11, 8: *The great city:* this expression is used constantly in Rv for Babylon, i.e., Rome; cf 14, 8; 16, 19; 17, 18; 18, 2.10.21. *"Sodom" and "Egypt":* symbols of immorality (cf Is 1, 10) and oppression of God's people (cf Ex 1, 11-14). *Where indeed their Lord was crucified:* not the geographical but the symbolic Jerusalem that rejects God and his witnesses, i.e., Rome, called Babylon in chs 16-18; see the note on 17, 9 and Introduction.

11, 9-12: Over the martyrdom (7) of the two witnesses, now called prophets, the ungodly rejoice *for three and a half days,* a symbolic period of time; see the note on v 2. Afterwards they go in triumph to heaven, as did Elijah (2 Kgs 2, 11).

11, 13: *Seven thousand people:* a symbolic sum to represent all social classes (seven) and large numbers (thousands); cf Introduction.

The Seventh Trumpet. † 15 Then the
seventh angel blew his trumpet. There
were loud voices in heaven, saying,
"The kingdom of the world now belongs
to our Lord and to his Anointed, and
he will reign forever and ever." 16 The
twenty-four elders who sat on their
thrones before God prostrated them-
selves and worshiped God 17 and said:

"We give thanks to you, Lord God
almighty,
who are and who were.
For you have assumed your great
power
and have established your reign.
18* The nations raged,
but your wrath has come,
and the time for the dead to be
judged,
and to recompense your servants,
the prophets,
and the holy ones and those who
fear your name,
the small and the great alike,
and to destroy those who destroy
the earth."

19 Then God's temple in heaven was
opened, and the ark of his covenant
could be seen in the temple. There were
flashes of lightning, rumblings, and
peals of thunder, an earthquake, and a
violent hailstorm.

CHAPTER 12

The Woman and the Dragon. † 1*† A
great sign appeared in the sky, a
woman clothed with the sun, with the
moon under her feet, and on her head
a crown of twelve stars. 2† She was with
child and wailed aloud in pain as she
labored to give birth. 3*† Then another
sign appeared in the sky; it was a huge
red dragon, with seven heads and ten
horns, and on its heads were seven dia-
dems. 4* Its tail swept away a third of
the stars in the sky and hurled them
down to the earth. Then the dragon
stood before the woman about to give
birth, to devour her child when she
gave birth. 5*† She gave birth to a son,
a male child, destined to rule all the
nations with an iron rod. Her child
was caught up to God and his throne.
6† The woman herself fled into the
desert where she had a place prepared
by God, that there she might be taken
care of for twelve hundred and sixty
days.
7† Then war broke out in heaven; Mi-
chael and his angels battled against the
dragon. The dragon and its angels
fought back, 8 but they did not prevail
and there was no longer any place for
them in heaven. 9*† The huge dragon,
the ancient serpent, who is called the
Devil and Satan, who deceived the
whole world, was thrown down to earth,
and its angels were thrown down with
it.
10† Then I heard a loud voice in
heaven say:

"Now have salvation and power
come,
and the kingdom of our God
and the authority of his
Anointed.
For the accuser of our brothers
is cast out,
who accuses them before our
God day and night.
11 They conquered him by the blood
of the Lamb

---

* 12, 18: Ps 2, 1.5 / Am 3, 7.
12, 1: Gn 37, 9.
3: Dn 7, 7.
4: Dn 8, 10.
5: Is 66, 7 / Ps 2, 9.
9: Gn 3, 1-4 / Lk 10, 18.

---

† 11, 15-19: The seventh trumpet proclaims the coming of God's reign after the victory over diabolical powers; see the note on 10, 7.

12, 1—14, 20: This central section of Rv portrays the power of evil, represented by a dragon, in opposition to God and his people. First, the dragon pursues the woman about to give birth, but her son is saved and "caught up to God and his throne" (12, 5). Then Michael and his angels cast the dragon and his angels out of heaven (12, 7-9). After this, the dragon tries to attack the boy indirectly by attacking members of his church (12, 13-18). A beast, symbolizing the Roman empire, then becomes the dragon's agent, mortally wounded but restored to life and worshiped by all the world (13, 1-10). A second beast arises from the land, symbolizing the antichrist, which leads people astray by its prodigies to idolize the first beast (13, 11-18). This is followed by a vision of the Lamb and his faithful ones, and the proclamation of imminent judgment upon the world in terms of the wine of God's wrath (14, 1-20).

12, 1-6: The woman adorned with the sun, the moon, and the stars (images taken from Gn 37, 9-10) symbolizes God's people in the Old and the New Testament. The Israel of old gave birth to the Messiah (5) and then became the new Israel, the church, which suffers persecution by the dragon (6.13-17); cf Is 50, 1; 66, 7; Jer 50, 12. This corresponds to a widespread myth throughout the ancient world that a goddess pregnant with a savior was pursued by a horrible monster; by miraculous intervention, she bore a son who then killed the monster.

12, 2: Because of Eve's sin, the woman gives birth in distress and pain (Gn 3, 16; cf Is 66, 7-14).

12, 3: *Huge red dragon:* the Devil or Satan (cf 9; 20, 2), symbol of the forces of evil, a mythical monster known also as Leviathan (Ps 74, 13-14) or Rahab (Jb 26, 12-13; Ps 89, 11). *Seven diadems:* these are symbolic of the fullness of the dragon's sovereignty over the kingdoms of this world; cf Christ with many diadems (19, 12).

12, 5: *Rule . . . iron rod:* fulfilled in 19, 15; cf Ps 2, 9. *Was caught up to God:* reference to Christ's ascension.

12, 6: God protects the persecuted church in the desert, the traditional Old Testament place of refuge for the afflicted, according to the typology of the Exodus; see the note on 11, 2.

12, 7-12: Michael, mentioned only here in Rv, wins a victory over the dragon. A hymn of praise follows.

12, 7: *Michael:* the archangel, guardian and champion of Israel; cf Dn 10, 13.21; 12, 1; Jude 9. In Hebrew, the name Michael means "Who can compare with God?"; cf 13, 4.

12, 9: *The ancient serpent:* who seduced Eve (Gn 3, 1-6), mother of the human race; cf 20, 2; Eph 6, 11-12. *Was thrown down:* allusion to the expulsion of Satan from heaven; cf Lk 10, 18.

12, 10: *The accuser:* the meaning of the Hebrew word "Satan," found in v 9; Jb 1—2; Zec 3, 1; 1 Chr 21, 1; he continues to accuse Christ's disciples.

and by the word of their testi-
mony;
love for life did not deter them
from death.
12 Therefore, rejoice, you heavens,
and you who dwell in them.
But woe to you, earth and sea,
for the Devil has come down to
you in great fury,
for he knows he has but a short
time."

13* When the dragon saw that it had
been thrown down to the earth, it pur-
sued the woman who had given birth
to the male child. 14*† But the woman
was given the two wings of the great
eagle, so that she could fly to her place
in the desert, where, far from the ser-
pent, she was taken care of for a year,
two years, and a half-year. 15† The ser-
pent, however, spewed a torrent of wa-
ter out of his mouth after the woman
to sweep her away with the current.
16 But the earth helped the woman and
opened its mouth and swallowed the
flood that the dragon spewed out of its
mouth. 17*† Then the dragon became
angry with the woman and went off to
wage war against the rest of her off-
spring, those who keep God's com-
mandments and bear witness to Jesus.
18† It took its position on the sand of the
sea.

CHAPTER 13

The First Beast. † 1* Then I saw a
beast come out of the sea with ten horns
and seven heads; on its horns were ten
diadems, and on its heads blasphemous
name[s]. 2*† The beast I saw was like
a leopard, but it had feet like a bear's,
and its mouth was like the mouth of a
lion. To it the dragon gave its own power
and throne, along with great authority.
3† I saw that one of its heads seemed
to have been mortally wounded, but this
mortal wound was healed. Fascinated,
the whole world followed after the
beast. 4† They worshiped the dragon be-
cause it gave its authority to the beast;
they also worshiped the beast and said,
"Who can compare with the beast or
who can fight against it?"

5*† The beast was given a mouth ut-
tering proud boasts and blasphemies,
and it was given authority to act for
forty-two months. 6 It opened its mouth
to utter blasphemies against God, blas-
pheming his name and his dwelling and
those who dwell in heaven. 7* It was also
allowed to wage war against the holy
ones and conquer them, and it was
granted authority over every tribe, peo-
ple, tongue, and nation. 8* All the in-
habitants of the earth will worship it,
all whose names were not written from
the foundation of the world in the book
of life, which belongs to the Lamb who
was slain.

9* Whoever has ears ought to hear
these words.
10* Anyone destined for captivity goes
into captivity.
Anyone destined to be slain by the
sword shall be slain by the
sword.

Such is the faithful endurance of the
holy ones.

The Second Beast. † 11 Then I saw an-
other beast come up out of the earth; it
had two horns like a lamb's but spoke
like a dragon. 12 It wielded all the au-
thority of the first beast in its sight and
made the earth and its inhabitants wor-
ship the first beast, whose mortal wound
had been healed. 13* It performed great
signs, even making fire come down
from heaven to earth in the sight of ev-
eryone. 14 It deceived the inhabitants of
the earth with the signs it was allowed
to perform in the sight of the first beast,
telling them to make an image for the
beast who had been wounded by the
sword and revived. 15* It was then per-

---

*

13: Gn 3, 15.
14: Ex 19, 4; Dn 7, 25; 12, 7.
17: Gn 3, 15.
13, 1: 2 Thes 2, 3-12.
2: Dn 7, 3-6.
5: Dn 7, 8.11.25; 8, 14; 9, 27; 11, 36; 12, 7.
7: Dn 7, 21.
8: 3, 5; 17, 8; 20, 12.
9: Mt 13, 9.
10: Jer 15, 2.
13: Dt 13, 2-4; Mt 24, 24; 2 Thes 2, 9-10.
15: Dn 3, 5-7.15.

†

12, 14: *Great eagle:* symbol of the power and swiftness of divine help; cf Ex 19, 4; Dt 32, 11; Is 40, 31.

12, 15: The serpent is depicted as the sea monster; cf 13, 1; Is 27, 1; Ez 32, 2; Ps 74, 13-14.

12, 17: Although the church is protected by God's special providence (16), the individual Christian is to expect persecution and suffering.

12, 18: *It took its position:* many later manuscripts and versions read "I took my position," thus connecting the sentence to the following paragraph.

13, 1-10: This wild beast, combining features of the four beasts in Dn 7, 2-28, symbolizes the Roman empire; the seven heads represent the emperors; see the notes on 17, 10 and 17, 12-14. The blasphemous names are the divine titles assumed by the emperors.

13, 2: Satan (12, 9), the prince of this world (Jn 12, 31), commissioned the beast to persecute the church (5-7).

13, 3: This may be a reference to the popular legend that Nero would come back to life and rule again after his death (which occurred in A.D. 68 from a self-inflicted stab wound in the throat); cf v 14; 17, 8. Domitian (A.D. 81-96) embodied all the cruelty and impiety of Nero. Cf Introduction.

13, 4: *Worshiped the beast:* allusion to emperor worship, which Domitian insisted upon and ruthlessly enforced. *Who can compare with the beast:* perhaps a deliberate parody of the name Michael; see the note on 12, 7.

13, 5-6: Domitian, like Antiochus IV Epiphanes (Dn 7, 8.11.25), demanded that he be called by divine titles such as "our lord and god" and "Jupiter." See the note on 11, 2.

13, 5: *Forty-two months:* this is the same duration as the profanation of the holy city (11, 2), the prophetic mission of the two witnesses (11, 3), and the retreat of the woman into the desert (12, 6.14).

13, 11-18: The second beast is described in terms of the false prophets (cf 16, 13; 19, 20; 20, 10) who accompany the false messiahs (the first beast); cf Mt 24, 24; Mk 13, 22; 2 Thes 2, 9; cf also Dt 13, 2-4. Christians had either to worship the emperor and his image or to suffer martyrdom.

mitted to breathe life into the beast's image, so that the beast's image could speak and [could] have anyone who did not worship it put to death. 16* It forced all the people, small and great, rich and poor, free and slave, to be given a stamped image on their right hands or their foreheads, 17 so that no one could buy or sell except one who had the stamped image of the beast's name or the number that stood for its name.

18*† Wisdom is needed here; one who understands can calculate the number of the beast, for it is a number that stands for a person. His number is six hundred and sixty-six.

CHAPTER 14

***The Lamb's Companions.*†** 1*† Then I looked and there was the Lamb standing on Mount Zion, and with him a hundred and forty-four thousand who had his name and his Father's name written on their foreheads. 2 I heard a sound from heaven like the sound of rushing water or a loud peal of thunder. The sound I heard was like that of harpists playing their harps. 3* They were singing [what seemed to be] a new hymn before the throne, before the four living creatures and the elders. No one could learn this hymn except the hundred and forty-four thousand who had been ransomed from the earth. 4*† These are they who were not defiled with women; they are virgins and these are the ones who follow the Lamb wherever he goes. They have been ransomed as the firstfruits of the human race for God and the Lamb. 5*† On their lips no deceit has been found; they are unblemished.

***The Three Angels.*†** 6† Then I saw another angel flying high overhead, with everlasting good news to announce to those who dwell on earth, to every nation, tribe, tongue, and people. 7* He said in a loud voice, "Fear God and give him glory, for his time has come to sit in judgment. Worship him who made heaven and earth and sea and springs of water."

8*† A second angel followed, saying:

"Fallen, fallen is Babylon the great,
that made all the nations drink the wine of her licentious passion."

9 A third angel followed them and said in a loud voice, "Anyone who worships the beast or its image, or accepts its mark on forehead or hand, 10† will also drink the wine of God's fury, poured full strength into the cup of his wrath, and will be tormented in burning sulfur before the holy angels and before the Lamb. 11* The smoke of the fire that torments them will rise forever and ever, and there will be no relief day or night for those who worship the beast or its image or accept the mark of its name." 12*† Here is what sustains the holy ones who keep God's commandments and their faith in Jesus.

13*† I heard a voice from heaven say, "Write this: Blessed are the dead who die in the Lord from now on." "Yes," said the Spirit, "let them find rest from their labors, for their works accompany them."

---

*

16: 14, 9; 16, 2; 19, 20; 20, 4.
18: 17, 9.
14, 1: Jl 3, 5; Ob 17; Acts 2, 21.
3: Pss 33, 3; 96, 1; 98, 1; Is 42, 10.
4: Jer 2, 2; Jas 1, 18.
5: Zep 3, 13.
7: 2, 10; Mt 10, 28.
8: 18, 2-3; Is 21, 9; Jer 51, 8 / Is 51, 17; Jer 25, 15-17.
11: 19, 3.
12: 12, 17.
13: Mt 11, 28-29; 2 Thes 1, 7; Heb 4, 10.

---

†

13, 18: Each of the letters of the alphabet in Hebrew as well as in Greek has a numerical value. Many possible combinations of letters will add up to 666, and many candidates have been nominated for this infamous number. The most likely is the emperor Caesar Nero (see the note on 13, 3), the Greek form of whose name in Hebrew letters gives the required sum. (The Latin form of this name equals 616, which is the reading of a few manuscripts.) Nero personifies the emperors who viciously persecuted the church. It has also been observed that "6" represents imperfection, falling short of the perfect number "7," and is represented here in a triple or superlative form.

14, 1-5: Now follows a tender and consoling vision of the Lamb and his companions.

14, 1: *Mount Zion:* in Jerusalem, the traditional place where the true remnant, the Israel of faith, is to be gathered in the messianic reign; cf 2 Kgs 19, 30-31; Jl 3, 5; Ob 17; Mi 4, 6-8; Zep 3, 12-20. *A hundred and forty-four thousand:* see the note on 7, 4-9. *His Father's name . . . foreheads:* in contrast to the pagans who were marked with the name or number of the beast (13, 16-17).

14, 4: *Virgins:* metaphorically, because they never indulged in any idolatrous practices, which are considered in the Old Testament to be adultery and fornication (2, 14-15.20-22; 17, 1-6; cf Ez 16, 1-58; 23, 1-49). The parallel passages (7, 3; 22, 4) indicate that the 144,000 whose foreheads are sealed represent all Christian people.

14, 5: *No deceit:* because they did not deny Christ or do homage to the beast. Lying is characteristic of the opponents of Christ (Jn 8, 44), but the Suffering Servant spoke no falsehood (Is 53, 9; 1 Pt 2, 22). *Unblemished:* a cultic term taken from the vocabulary of sacrificial ritual.

14, 6-13: Three angels proclaim imminent judgment on the pagan world, calling all peoples to worship God the creator. Babylon (Rome) will fall, and its supporters will be tormented forever.

14, 6: *Everlasting good news:* that God's eternal reign is about to begin; see the note on 10, 7.

14, 8: This verse anticipates the lengthy dirge over Babylon (Rome) in 18, 1—19, 4. The oracle of Is 21, 9 to Babylon is applied here.

14, 10-11: *The wine of God's fury:* image taken from Is 51, 17; Jer 25, 15-16; 49, 12; 51, 7; Ez 23, 31-34. Eternal punishment in the fiery pool of burning sulfur (or "fire and brimstone"; cf Gn 19, 24) is also reserved for the Devil, the beast, and the false prophet (19, 20; 20, 10; 21, 8).

14, 12: In addition to *faith in Jesus,* the seer insists upon the necessity and value of works, as in 2, 23; 20, 12-13; 22, 12; cf Mt 16, 27; Rom 2, 6.

14, 13: See the note on 1, 3. According to Jewish thought, people's actions followed them as witnesses before the court of God.

The Harvest of the Earth. † 14* Then
I looked and there was a white cloud,
and sitting on the cloud one who looked
like a son of man, with a gold crown
on his head and a sharp sickle in his
hand. 15* Another angel came out of the
temple, crying out in a loud voice to the
one sitting on the cloud, "Use your
sickle and reap the harvest, for the time
to reap has come, because the earth's
harvest is fully ripe." 16 So the one who
was sitting on the cloud swung his sickle
over the earth, and the earth was har-
vested.

17 Then another angel came out of the
temple in heaven who also had a sharp
sickle. 18† Then another angel [came]
from the altar, [who] was in charge of
the fire, and cried out in a loud voice
to the one who had the sharp sickle,
"Use your sharp sickle and cut the clus-
ters from the earth's vines, for its
grapes are ripe." 19* So the angel swung
his sickle over the earth and cut the
earth's vintage. He threw it into the
great wine press of God's fury. 20† The
wine press was trodden outside the city
and blood poured out of the wine press
to the height of a horse's bridle for two
hundred miles.

CHAPTER 15

The Seven Last Plagues. † 1† Then
I saw in heaven another sign, great
and awe-inspiring: seven angels
with the seven last plagues, for
through them God's fury is accom-
plished.

2*† Then I saw something like a sea
of glass mingled with fire. On the sea
of glass were standing those who had
won the victory over the beast and its
image and the number that signified its
name. They were holding God's harps,
3*† and they sang the song of Moses, the
servant of God, and the song of the
Lamb:

"Great and wonderful are your
works,
Lord God almighty.
Just and true are your ways,
O king of the nations.
4* Who will not fear you, Lord,
or glorify your name?
For you alone are holy.
All the nations will come
and worship before you,
for your righteous acts have been
revealed."

5† After this I had another vision. The
temple that is the heavenly tent of testi-
mony opened, 6* and the seven angels
with the seven plagues came out of the
temple. They were dressed in clean
white linen, with a gold sash around
their chests. 7 One of the four living
creatures gave the seven angels seven
gold bowls filled with the fury of God,
who lives forever and ever. 8* Then the
temple became so filled with the smoke
from God's glory and might that no one
could enter it until the seven plagues
of the seven angels had been accom-
plished.

CHAPTER 16

The Seven Bowls. † 1 I heard a loud
voice speaking from the temple to
the seven angels, "Go and pour out the
seven bowls of God's fury upon the
earth."

2† The first angel went and poured out
his bowl on the earth. Festering and
ugly sores broke out on those who had
the mark of the beast or worshiped its
image.

3† The second angel poured out his
bowl on the sea. The sea turned to blood
like that from a corpse; every creature
living in the sea died.

4* The third angel poured out his bowl
on the rivers and springs of water.
These also turned to blood. 5* Then I

---

*

14: 1, 7; Dn 7, 13.
15: Jl 4, 13; Mt 13, 36-43.
19: 19, 15; Is 63, 1-6.
15, 2: 7, 9.14; 13, 15-18.
3: Pss 92, 6; 98, 1 / Dt 32, 4; Ps 145, 17.
4: Ps 86, 9-10; Jer 10, 7.
6: 19, 8.
8: 1 Kgs 8, 10; Is 6, 4.
16, 4: Ex 7, 14-24.
5: 1, 4.

---

†

14, 14-20: The reaping of the harvest symbolizes the gathering of the elect in the final judgment, while the reaping and treading of the grapes symbolizes the doom of the ungodly (cf Jl 4, 12-13; Is 63, 1-6) that will come in 19, 11-21.

14, 18: *Altar:* there was only one altar in the heavenly temple; see the notes above on 6, 9; 8, 3; 11, 1.

14, 20: *Two hundred miles:* literally sixteen hundred stades. The *stadion,* a Greek unit of measurement, was about 607 feet in length, approximately the length of a furlong.

15, 1—16, 21: The seven bowls, the third and last group of seven after the seven seals and the seven trumpets, foreshadow the final cataclysm. Again, the series is introduced by a heavenly prelude, in which the victors over the beast sing the canticle of Moses (15, 2-4).

15, 1-4: A vision of the victorious martyrs precedes the vision of woe in 15, 5—16, 21; cf 7, 9-12.

15, 2: *Mingled with fire:* fire symbolizes the sanctity involved in facing God, reflected in the trials that have prepared the victorious Christians or in God's wrath.

15, 3: *The song of Moses:* the song that Moses and the Israelites sang after their escape from the oppression of Egypt (Ex 15, 1-18). The martyrs have escaped from the oppression of the Devil. *Nations:* many other Greek manuscripts and versions read "ages."

15, 5-8: Seven angels receive the bowls of God's wrath.

15, 5: *Tent of testimony:* the name of the meeting tent in the Greek text of Ex 40. Cf 2 Mc 2, 4-7.

16, 1-21: These seven bowls, like the seven seals (6, 1-17; 8, 1) and the seven trumpets (8, 2—9, 21; 11, 15-19), bring on a succession of disasters modeled in part on the plagues of Egypt (Ex 7—12). See the note on 6, 12-14.

16, 2: Like the sixth Egyptian plague (Ex 9, 8-11).

16, 3-4: Like the first Egyptian plague (Ex 7, 20-21). The same woe followed the blowing of the second trumpet (8, 8-9).

heard the angel in charge of the waters say:

"You are just, O Holy One,
who are and who were,
in passing this sentence.
6* For they have shed the blood of the holy ones and the prophets,
and you [have] given them blood to drink;
it is what they deserve."

7* Then I heard the altar cry out,

"Yes, Lord God almighty,
your judgments are true and just."

8 The fourth angel poured out his bowl on the sun. It was given the power to burn people with fire. 9* People were burned by the scorching heat and blasphemed the name of God who had power over these plagues, but they did not repent or give him glory.

10*† The fifth angel poured out his bowl on the throne of the beast. Its kingdom was plunged into darkness, and people bit their tongues in pain 11* and blasphemed the God of heaven because of their pains and sores. But they did not repent of their works.

12† The sixth angel emptied his bowl on the great river Euphrates. Its water was dried up to prepare the way for the kings of the East. 13*† I saw three unclean spirits like frogs come from the mouth of the dragon, from the mouth of the beast, and from the mouth of the false prophet. 14* These were demonic spirits who performed signs. They went out to the kings of the whole world to assemble them for the battle on the great day of God the almighty. 15*† ("Behold, I am coming like a thief." Blessed is the one who watches and keeps his clothes ready, so that he may not go naked and people see him exposed.) 16† They then assembled the kings in the place that is named Armageddon in Hebrew.

17* The seventh angel poured out his bowl into the air. A loud voice came out of the temple from the throne, saying, "It is done." 18* Then there were lightning flashes, rumblings, and peals of thunder, and a great earthquake. It was such a violent earthquake that there has never been one like it since the human race began on earth. 19† The great city was split into three parts, and the gentile cities fell. But God remembered great Babylon, giving it the cup filled with the wine of his fury and wrath. 20† Every island fled, and mountains disappeared. 21* Large hailstones like huge weights came down from the sky on people, and they blasphemed God for the plague of hail because this plague was so severe.

V: THE PUNISHMENT OF BABYLON AND THE DESTRUCTION OF PAGAN NATIONS

CHAPTER 17

Babylon the Great.† 1*† Then one of the seven angels who were holding the seven bowls came and said to me, "Come here. I will show you the judgment on the great harlot who lives near the many waters. 2*† The kings of the earth have had intercourse with her, and the inhabitants of the earth became drunk on the wine of her harlotry." 3*† Then he carried me away in spirit to a deserted place where I saw a woman seated on a scarlet beast that was covered with blasphemous names, with seven heads and ten horns. 4*† The woman was wearing purple and scarlet and adorned with gold, precious stones, and pearls. She held in her hand a gold cup that was filled with the abominable and sordid deeds of her harlotry. 5 On her forehead was written a name, which is a mystery, "Babylon the great, the mother of harlots and of the abominations of the earth." 6 I saw that the woman was drunk on the blood of the

---

*

6: Ez 35, 6; Mt 23, 34-35.
7: Dn 3, 27; Tb 3, 2.
9: Am 4, 6.
10: Ex 10, 21-23.
11: Ex 9, 8-11 / Jer 5, 3.
13: Ex 8, 2-3.
14: 1 Cor 1, 8.
15: Mt 24, 42-44 / 3, 17.
17: Is 66, 6.
18: Mk 13, 19.
21: Ex 9, 22-26.
17, 1: Jer 50, 38; 51, 13.
2: Jer 51, 7.
3: 13, 1.
4: 18, 16.

---

†

16, 10: *The throne of the beast:* symbol of the forces of evil. *Darkness:* like the ninth Egyptian plague (Ex 10, 21-23); cf 9, 2.

16, 12: *The kings of the East:* Parthians; see the notes on 6, 2 and 17, 12-13. *East:* literally, "rising of the sun," as in 7, 2.

16, 13: *Frogs:* possibly an allusion to the second Egyptian plague (Ex 7, 26—8, 11). *The false prophet:* identified with the two-horned second beast (13, 11-18 and the note there).

16, 15: *Like a thief:* as in 3, 3 (cf Mt 24, 42-44; 1 Thes 5, 2). *Blessed:* see the note on 1, 3.

16, 16: *Armageddon:* in Hebrew, this means "Mountain of Megiddo." Since Megiddo was the scene of many decisive battles in antiquity (Jgs 5, 19-20; 2 Kgs 9, 27; 2 Chr 35, 20-24), the town became the symbol of the final disastrous rout of the forces of evil.

16, 19: *The great city:* Rome and the empire.

16, 20-21: See the note on 6, 12-14. *Hailstones:* as in the seventh Egyptian plague (Ex 9, 23-24); cf 8, 7. *Like huge weights:* literally, "weighing a talent," about one hundred pounds.

17, 1—19, 10: The punishment of Babylon is now described as a past event and, metaphorically, under the image of the great harlot who leads people astray into idolatry.

17, 1-6: Babylon, the symbolic name (5) of Rome, is graphically described as "the great harlot."

17, 2: *Intercourse . . . harlotry:* see the note on 14, 4. The pagan kings subject to Rome adopted the cult of the emperor.

17, 3: *Scarlet beast:* see the note on 13, 1-10. *Blasphemous names:* divine titles assumed by the Roman emperors; see the note on 13, 5-6.

17, 4: Reference to the great wealth and idolatrous cults of Rome.

holy ones and on the blood of the wit-
nesses to Jesus.
Meaning of the Beast and Harlot.†
When I saw her I was greatly amazed.
7 The angel said to me, "Why are you
amazed? I will explain to you the mys-
tery of the woman and of the beast that
carries her, the beast with the seven
heads and the ten horns. 8*† The beast
that you saw existed once but now exists
no longer. It will come up from the
abyss and is headed for destruction.
The inhabitants of the earth whose
names have not been written in the book
of life from the foundation of the world
shall be amazed when they see the
beast, because it existed once but exists
no longer, and yet it will come again.
9*† Here is a clue for one who has wis-
dom. The seven heads represent seven
hills upon which the woman sits. They
also represent seven kings: 10† five have
already fallen, one still lives, and the
last has not yet come, and when he
comes he must remain only a short
while. 11† The beast that existed once
but exists no longer is an eighth king,
but really belongs to the seven and is
headed for destruction. 12*† The ten
horns that you saw represent ten kings
who have not yet been crowned; they
will receive royal authority along with
the beast for one hour. 13 They are of
one mind and will give their power and
authority to the beast. 14* They will fight
with the Lamb, but the Lamb will con-
quer them, for he is Lord of lords and
king of kings, and those with him are
called, chosen, and faithful."
15 Then he said to me, "The waters
that you saw where the harlot lives rep-
resent large numbers of peoples, na-
tions, and tongues. 16*† The ten horns
that you saw and the beast will hate the
harlot; they will leave her desolate and
naked; they will eat her flesh and con-
sume her with fire. 17 For God has put
it into their minds to carry out his pur-
pose and to make them come to an
agreement to give their kingdom to the
beast until the words of God are accom-
plished. 18 The woman whom you saw
represents the great city that has sover-
eignty over the kings of the earth."

CHAPTER 18

The Fall of Babylon.† 1* After this I
saw another angel coming down from
heaven, having great authority, and the
earth became illumined by his splendor.
2*† He cried out in a mighty voice:

"Fallen, fallen is Babylon the great.
She has become a haunt for demons.
She is a cage for every unclean spirit,
a cage for every unclean bird,
[a cage for every unclean] and disgusting [beast].
3*† For all the nations have drunk
the wine of her licentious passion.
The kings of the earth had intercourse with her,
and the merchants of the earth grew rich from her drive for luxury."

4*† Then I heard another voice from
heaven say:

"Depart from her, my people,
so as not to take part in her sins
and receive a share in her plagues,
5* for her sins are piled up to the sky,
and God remembers her crimes.
6* Pay her back as she has paid others.
Pay her back double for her deeds.
Into her cup pour double what she poured.
7* To the measure of her boasting and wantonness
repay her in torment and grief;
for she said to herself,
'I sit enthroned as queen;
I am no widow,
and I will never know grief.'

*

8: 13, 3-4 / 3, 5; 13, 8; 20, 12.
9: 13, 18.
12: Dn 7, 24.
14: 19, 11-21; 2 Mc 13, 4; 1 Tm 6, 15 / Rom 1, 6; 1 Pt 2, 9; Jude 1.
16: Ez 16, 37-41; 23, 25-29.
18, 1: Ez 43, 2.
2: 14, 8; Is 21, 9; Jer 50, 2-3; 51, 8.
3: 17, 2; Jer 51, 7.
4: Is 48, 20; Jer 50, 8.
5: Jer 51, 9.
6: Jer 50, 15 / Jer 16, 18.
7: Is 47, 8-9.

†

17, 6b-18: An interpretation of the vision is here given.

17, 8: Allusion to the belief that the dead Nero would return to power (11); see the note on 13, 3.

17, 9: *Here is a clue:* literally, "Here a mind that has wisdom." *Seven hills:* of Rome.

17, 10: There is little agreement as to the identity of the Roman emperors alluded to here. The number seven (9) suggests that all the emperors are meant; see the note on 1, 4.

17, 11: *The beast:* Nero; see the note on v 8.

17, 12-13: *Ten kings who have not yet been crowned:* perhaps Parthian satraps who are to accompany the revived Nero (the beast) in his march on Rome to regain power; see the note on 13, 3. In 19, 11-21, the Lamb and his companions will conquer them.

17, 16-18: *The ten horns:* the ten pagan kings (12) who unwittingly fulfill God's will against harlot Rome, the great city; cf Ez 16, 37.

18, 1—19, 4: A stirring dirge over the fall of Babylon-Rome. The perspective is prophetic, as if the fall of Rome had already taken place. The imagery here, as elsewhere in this book, is not to be taken literally. The vindictiveness of some of the language, borrowed from the scathing Old Testament prophecies against Babylon, Tyre, and Nineveh (Is 23; 24; 27; Jer 50-51; Ez 26-27), is meant to portray symbolically the inexorable demands of God's holiness and justice; cf Introduction. The section concludes with a joyous canticle on the future glory of heaven.

18, 2: Many Greek manuscripts and versions omit *a cage for every unclean . . . beast.*

18, 3-24: Rome is condemned for her immorality, symbol of idolatry (see the note on 14, 4), and for persecuting the church; cf 19, 2.

18, 4: *Depart from her:* not evacuation of the city but separation from sinners, as always in apocalyptic literature.

8 Therefore, her plagues will come in
one day,
pestilence, grief, and famine;
she will be consumed by fire.
For mighty is the Lord God who
judges her."

9 The kings of the earth who had inter-
course with her in their wantonness will
weep and mourn over her when they
see the smoke of her pyre. 10 They will
keep their distance for fear of the
torment inflicted on her, and they will
say:

"Alas, alas, great city,
Babylon, mighty city.
In one hour your judgment has
come."

11† The merchants of the earth will weep
and mourn for her, because there will
be no more markets for their cargo:
12 their cargo of gold, silver, precious
stones, and pearls; fine linen, purple
silk, and scarlet cloth; fragrant wood of
every kind, all articles of ivory and all
articles of the most expensive wood,
bronze, iron, and marble; 13† cinnamon,
spice, incense, myrrh, and frankin-
cense; wine, olive oil, fine flour, and
wheat; cattle and sheep, horses and
chariots, and slaves, that is, human be-
ings.

REVELATION

14* "The fruit you craved
has left you.
All your luxury and splendor are
gone,
never again will one find them."

15 The merchants who deal in these
goods, who grew rich from her, will
keep their distance for fear of the tor-
ment inflicted on her. Weeping and
mourning, 16* they cry out:

"Alas, alas, great city,
wearing fine linen, purple and
scarlet,
adorned [in] gold, precious
stones, and pearls.
17 In one hour this great wealth has
been ruined."

Every captain of a ship, every traveler
at sea, sailors, and seafaring merchants
stood at a distance 18 and cried out
when they saw the smoke of her pyre,
"What city could compare with the great
city?" 19* They threw dust on their
heads and cried out, weeping and mourn-
ing:

"Alas, alas, great city,
in which all who had ships at sea
grew rich from her wealth.
In one hour she has been ruined.
20* Rejoice over her, heaven,
you holy ones, apostles, and
prophets.
For God has judged your case
against her."

21* A mighty angel picked up a stone
like a huge millstone and threw it into
the sea and said:

"With such force will Babylon the
great city be thrown down,
and will never be found again.
22* No melodies of harpists and musi-
cians,
flutists and trumpeters,
will ever be heard in you again.
No craftsmen in any trade
will ever be found in you again.
No sound of the millstone
will ever be heard in you again.
23* No light from a lamp
will ever be seen in you again.
No voices of bride and groom
will ever be heard in you again.
Because your merchants were the
great ones of the world,
all nations were led astray by
your magic potion.
24* In her was found the blood of proph-
ets and holy ones
and all who have been slain on the
earth."

CHAPTER 19

1† After this I heard what sounded like
the loud voice of a great multitude in
heaven, saying:

"Alleluia!
Salvation, glory, and might belong
to our God,
2* for true and just are his judg-
ments.
He has condemned the great harlot
who corrupted the earth with her
harlotry.
He has avenged on her the blood of
his servants."

3* They said a second time:

"Alleluia! Smoke will rise from her
forever and ever."

4 The twenty-four elders and the four
living creatures fell down and wor-
shiped God who sat on the throne, say-
ing, "Amen. Alleluia."

---

*

14: Hos 10, 5 / Am 6, 7.
16: 17, 4.
19: Ez 27, 27-32.
20: 19, 1-2; Dt 32, 43.
21: Jer 51, 63-64; Ez 26, 21.
22: Is 24, 8; Ez 26, 13.
23: Jer 7, 34; 16, 9; 25, 10.
24: 16, 6.
19, 2: Dn 3, 27 / Jer 51, 48-49.
3: 14, 11; Is 34, 10.

---

†

18, 11: Ironically, the merchants weep not so much for Babylon-Rome, but for their lost markets; cf Ez 27, 36.

18, 13: *Spice:* an unidentified spice plant called in Greek *amōmon.*

19, 1.3.4.6: *Alleluia:* found only here in the New Testament, this frequent exclamation of praise in the Hebrew psalms was important in Jewish liturgy.

The Victory Song.† 5* A voice coming
from the throne said:

"Praise our God, all you his servants,
[and] you who revere him, small and great."

6 Then I heard something like the sound
of a great multitude or the sound of
rushing water or mighty peals of thunder, as they said:

"Alleluia!
The Lord has established his reign,
[our] God, the almighty.
7*† Let us rejoice and be glad
and give him glory.
For the wedding day of the Lamb has come,
his bride has made herself ready.
8*† She was allowed to wear
a bright, clean linen garment."

(The linen represents the righteous
deeds of the holy ones.)
9*† Then the angel said to me, "Write
this: Blessed are those who have been
called to the wedding feast of the
Lamb." And he said to me, "These
words are true; they come from God."
10*† I fell at his feet to worship him. But
he said to me, "Don't! I am a fellow servant of yours and of your brothers who
bear witness to Jesus. Worship God.
Witness to Jesus is the spirit of prophecy."

The King of Kings.† 11* Then I saw
the heavens opened, and there was a
white horse; its rider was [called]
"Faithful and True." He judges and
wages war in righteousness. 12*† His
eyes were [like] a fiery flame, and on
his head were many diadems. He had
a name inscribed that no one knows except himself. 13*† He wore a cloak that
had been dipped in blood, and his name
was called the Word of God. 14* The armies of heaven followed him, mounted
on white horses and wearing clean
white linen. 15*† Out of his mouth came
a sharp sword to strike the nations. He
will rule them with an iron rod, and he
himself will tread out in the wine press
the wine of the fury and wrath of God
the almighty. 16* He has a name written
on his cloak and on his thigh, "King of
kings and Lord of lords."
17† Then I saw an angel standing on
the sun. He cried out [in] a loud voice
to all the birds flying high overhead,
"Come here. Gather for God's great
feast, 18* to eat the flesh of kings, the
flesh of military officers, and the flesh
of warriors, the flesh of horses and of
their riders, and the flesh of all, free and
slave, small and great." 19 Then I saw
the beast and the kings of the earth and
their armies gathered to fight against
the one riding the horse and against his
army. 20*† The beast was caught and
with it the false prophet who had performed in its sight the signs by which
he led astray those who had accepted
the mark of the beast and those who had
worshiped its image. The two were
thrown alive into the fiery pool burning
with sulfur. 21 The rest were killed by
the sword that came out of the mouth
of the one riding the horse, and all the
birds gorged themselves on their flesh.

CHAPTER 20

The Thousand-year Reign.†
1*† Then I saw an angel come down
from heaven, holding in his hand the
key to the abyss and a heavy chain.

*

5: 11, 18; Ps 115, 13.
7: Mt 22, 9; Eph 5, 27.
8: 15, 6; Is 61, 10; Mt 22, 11-12.
9: Mt 8, 11; Lk 14, 15.
10: 22, 8-9.
11: Is 11, 4.
12: 1, 14-16; 2, 18 / Lk 10, 22.
13: Is 63, 1 / Jn 1, 1.
14: 15, 6; 19, 8.
15: 14, 20; Is 63, 3.
16: 17, 14; 2 Mc 13, 4.
18: Ez 39, 17-20.
20: 14, 10.
20, 1: 9, 1.

†

19, 5-10: A victory song follows, sung by the entire church, celebrating the marriage of the Lamb, the union of the Messiah with the community of the elect.

19, 7: *The wedding day of the Lamb:* symbol of God's reign about to begin (21, 1—22, 5); see the note on 10, 7. *His bride:* the church; cf 2 Cor 11, 2; Eph 5, 22-27. Marriage is one of the biblical metaphors used to describe the covenant relationship between God and his people; cf Hos 2, 16-22; Is 54, 5-6; 62, 5; Ez 16, 6-14. Hence, idolatry and apostasy are viewed as adultery and harlotry (Hos 2, 4-15; Ez 16, 15-63); see the note on 14, 4.

19, 8: See the note on 14, 12.

19, 9: *Blessed:* see the note on 1, 3.

19, 10: *The spirit of prophecy:* as the prophets were inspired to proclaim God's word, so the Christian is called to give witness to the Word of God (13) made flesh; cf 1, 2; 6, 9; 12, 17.

19, 11-16: Symbolic description of the exalted Christ (cf 1, 13-16) who together with the armies of heaven overcomes the beast and its followers; cf 17, 14.

19, 12: *A name:* in Semitic thought, the name conveyed the reality of the person; cf Mt 11, 27; Lk 10, 22.

19, 13: *Had been dipped in:* other Greek manuscripts and versions read "had been sprinkled with"; cf v 15. *The Word of God:* Christ is the revelation of the Father; cf Jn 1, 1.14; 1 Jn 2, 14.

19, 15: The treading of the wine press is a prophetic symbol used to describe the destruction of God's enemies; cf Is 63, 1-6; Jl 4, 13.

19, 17-21: The certainty of Christ's victory is proclaimed by an angel, followed by a reference to the mustering of enemy forces and a fearsome description of their annihilation. The gruesome imagery is borrowed from Ez 39, 4.17-20.

19, 20: *Beast . . . false prophet:* see the notes on ch 13. *The fiery pool . . . sulfur:* symbol of God's punishment (14, 10; 20, 10.14-15), different from the abyss; see the note on 9, 1.

20, 1-6: Like the other numerical values in this book, the thousand years are not to be taken literally; they symbolize the long period of time between the chaining up of Satan (a symbol for Christ's resurrection-victory over death and the forces of evil) and the end of the world. During this time God's people share in the glorious reign of God that is present to them by virtue of their baptismal victory over death and sin; cf Rom 6, 1-8; Jn 5, 24-25; 16, 33; 1 Jn 3, 14; Eph 2, 1.

20, 1: *Abyss:* see the note on 9, 1.

2*† He seized the dragon, the ancient
serpent, which is the Devil or Satan, and
tied it up for a thousand years 3 and
threw it into the abyss, which he locked
over it and sealed, so that it could no
longer lead the nations astray until the
thousand years are completed. After
this, it is to be released for a short time.
4*† Then I saw thrones; those who sat
on them were entrusted with judgment.
I also saw the souls of those who had
been beheaded for their witness to Jesus
and for the word of God, and who had
not worshiped the beast or its image nor
had accepted its mark on their fore-
heads or hands. They came to life and
they reigned with Christ for a thousand
years. 5 The rest of the dead did not
come to life until the thousand years
were over. This is the first resurrection.
6† Blessed and holy is the one who
shares in the first resurrection. The sec-
ond death has no power over these; they
will be priests of God and of Christ, and
they will reign with him for [the] thou-
sand years.
7† When the thousand years are com-
pleted, Satan will be released from his
prison. 8*† He will go out to deceive the
nations at the four corners of the earth,
Gog and Magog, to gather them for bat-
tle; their number is like the sand of the
sea. 9*† They invaded the breadth of
the earth and surrounded the camp of
the holy ones and the beloved city. But
fire came down from heaven and con-
sumed them. 10 The Devil who had led
them astray was thrown into the pool
of fire and sulfur, where the beast and
the false prophet were. There they will
be tormented day and night forever and
ever.

The Large White Throne. † 11* Next I
saw a large white throne and the one
who was sitting on it. The earth and the
sky fled from his presence and there
was no place for them. 12*† I saw the
dead, the great and the lowly, standing
before the throne, and scrolls were
opened. Then another scroll was
opened, the book of life. The dead were
judged according to their deeds, by
what was written in the scrolls. 13† The
sea gave up its dead; then Death and
Hades gave up their dead. All the dead
were judged according to their deeds.
14*† Then Death and Hades were
thrown into the pool of fire. (This pool
of fire is the second death.) 15 Anyone
whose name was not found written in
the book of life was thrown into the pool
of fire.

VI: THE NEW CREATION†

CHAPTER 21

The New Heaven and the New Earth.
1*† Then I saw a new heaven and a new
earth. The former heaven and the for-
mer earth had passed away, and the sea
was no more. 2*† I also saw the holy
city, a new Jerusalem, coming down out
of heaven from God, prepared as a
bride adorned for her husband. 3*† I
heard a loud voice from the throne say-
ing, "Behold, God's dwelling is with the
human race. He will dwell with them
and they will be his people and God
himself will always be with them [as
their God]. 4* He will wipe every tear
from their eyes, and there shall be no
more death or mourning, wailing or
pain, [for] the old order has passed
away."
5*† The one who sat on the throne
said, "Behold, I make all things new."
Then he said, "Write these words down,
for they are trustworthy and true."
6*† He said to me, "They are accom-
plished. I [am] the Alpha and the
Omega, the beginning and the end. To
the thirsty I will give a gift from the
spring of life-giving water. 7*† The vic-

---

*

2: Gn 3, 1.
4: Mt 19, 28.
8: Ez 38, 2.9.16.
9: Ez 38, 22.
11: 2 Pt 3, 7.10.12.
12: Rom 2, 6.
14: 1 Cor 15, 26.54-55.
21, 1: Is 65, 17; 66, 22; Rom 8, 19-23; 2 Pt 3, 13.
2: 19, 7-9.
3: Ez 37, 27.
4: 7, 17; Is 25, 8; 35, 10.
5: Is 43, 19; 2 Cor 5, 17.
6: 22, 17; Ps 36, 8-9; Is 55, 1.
7: 2 Sm 7, 14.

---

†

20, 2: *Dragon . . . serpent . . . Satan:* see the notes on 12, 3.9.10.15.

20, 4: *Beast . . . mark:* see ch 13 and its notes.

20, 6: *Blessed:* see the note on 1, 3. *Second death:* see the note on 2, 11. *Priests:* as in 1, 6; 5, 10; cf 1 Pt 2, 9.

20, 7-10: A description of the symbolic battle to take place when Satan is released at the end of time, when the thousand years are over; see the note on vv 1-6.

20, 8: *Gog and Magog:* symbols of all pagan nations; the names are taken from Ez 38, 1—39, 20.

20, 9: *The breadth of the earth:* Palestine. *The beloved city:* Jerusalem; see the note on 14, 1.

20, 11-15: A description of the final judgment. After the intermediate reign of Christ, all the dead are raised and judged, thus inaugurating the new age.

20, 12: *The book of life:* see the note on 3, 5. *Judged . . . scrolls:* see the note on 14, 12.

20, 13: *Hades:* the netherworld; see the note on 1, 18.

20, 14: *Second death:* see the note on 2, 11.

21, 1—22, 5: A description of God's eternal kingdom in heaven under the symbols of a new heaven and a new earth; cf Is 65, 17-25; 66, 22; Mt 19, 28.

21, 1: *Sea . . . no more:* because as home of the dragon it was doomed to disappear; cf Jb 7, 12.

21, 2: *New Jerusalem . . . bride:* symbol of the church (Gal 4, 26); see the note on 19, 7.

21, 3: *People:* other ancient manuscripts read a plural, "peoples."

21, 3-4: Language taken from Ez 37, 27; Is 25, 8; 35, 10; cf 7, 17.

21, 5: *The one . . . on the throne:* God himself; cf 4, 1-11.

21, 6: *They are accomplished:* God's reign has already begun; see the note on 20, 1-6. *Alpha . . . Omega:* see the note on 1, 8. *Life-giving water:* see the note on 7, 17.

21, 7: *The victor:* over the forces of evil; see the conclusions of the seven letters (2, 7.11.17.26; 3, 5.12.21). *He will be my son:* the victorious Christian enjoys divine affiliation by adoption (Gal 4, 4-7; Rom 8, 14-17); see the note on 2, 26-28.

tor will inherit these gifts, and I shall
be his God, and he will be my son.
8*† But as for cowards, the unfaithful,
the depraved, murderers, the unchaste,
sorcerers, idol-worshipers, and deceiv-
ers of every sort, their lot is in the burn-
ing pool of fire and sulfur, which is the
second death."

***The New Jerusalem.*† 9†** One of the
seven angels who held the seven bowls
filled with the seven last plagues came
and said to me, "Come here. I will show
you the bride, the wife of the Lamb."
10* He took me in spirit to a great, high
mountain and showed me the holy city
Jerusalem coming down out of heaven
from God. 11* It gleamed with the splen-
dor of God. Its radiance was like that
of a precious stone, like jasper, clear as
crystal. 12 It had a massive, high wall,
with twelve gates where twelve angels
were stationed and on which names
were inscribed, [the names] of the
twelve tribes of the Israelites. 13* There
were three gates facing east, three
north, three south, and three west.
14*† The wall of the city had twelve
courses of stones as its foundation,
on which were inscribed the twelve
names of the twelve apostles of the
Lamb.

15† The one who spoke to me held a
gold measuring rod to measure the city,
its gates, and its wall. 16† The city was
square, its length the same as [also] its
width. He measured the city with the
rod and found it fifteen hundred miles
in length and width and height. 17† He
also measured its wall: one hundred and
forty-four cubits according to the stan-
dard unit of measurement the angel
used. 18† The wall was constructed of
jasper, while the city was pure gold,
clear as glass. 19* The foundations of the
city wall were decorated with every
precious stone; the first course of stones
was jasper, the second sapphire, the
third chalcedony, the fourth emerald,
20 the fifth sardonyx, the sixth carne-
lian, the seventh chrysolite, the eighth
beryl, the ninth topaz, the tenth chryso-
prase, the eleventh hyacinth, and the
twelfth amethyst. 21 The twelve gates
were twelve pearls, each of the gates
made from a single pearl; and the street
of the city was of pure gold, transparent
as glass.

22*† I saw no temple in the city, for
its temple is the Lord God almighty and
the Lamb. 23*† The city had no need of
sun or moon to shine on it, for the glory
of God gave it light, and its lamp was
the Lamb. 24*† The nations will walk by
its light, and to it the kings of the earth
will bring their treasure. 25 During the
day its gates will never be shut, and
there will be no night there. 26 The trea-
sure and wealth of the nations will be
brought there, 27* but nothing unclean
will enter it, nor any[one] who does
abominable things or tells lies. Only
those will enter whose names are writ-
ten in the Lamb's book of life.

CHAPTER 22

1*† Then the angel showed me the river
of life-giving water, sparkling like crys-
tal, flowing from the throne of God and
of the Lamb 2† down the middle of its
street. On either side of the river grew
the tree of life that produces fruit twelve
times a year, once each month; the
leaves of the trees serve as medicine for
the nations. 3 Nothing accursed will be
found there anymore. The throne of
God and of the Lamb will be in it, and
his servants will worship him. 4† They
will look upon his face, and his name
will be on their foreheads. 5* Night will
be no more, nor will they need light
from lamp or sun, for the Lord God shall
give them light, and they shall reign
forever and ever.

*

8: 22, 15; Rom 1, 29-32.
10: Ez 40, 2.
11: Heb 11, 10.
13: Ez 48, 31-35.
14: Eph 2, 20.
19: Is 54, 11-12.
22: Jn 2, 19-20.
23: Is 60, 1-2.19-20.
24: Is 60, 11.
27: Is 35, 8; 52, 1; Zec 13, 2 / Rv 3, 5; 20, 12.
22, 1: Ez 47, 1-12.
5: Is 60, 20.

†

21, 8: *Cowards:* their conviction is so weak that they deny Christ in time of trial and become traitors. *Second death:* see the note on 2, 11.

21, 9—22, 5: Symbolic descriptions of the new Jerusalem, the church. Most of the images are borrowed from Ez 40—48.

21, 9: *The bride, the wife of the Lamb:* the church (2), the new Jerusalem (10); cf 2 Cor 11, 2.

21, 14: *Courses of stones . . . apostles:* literally, "twelve foundations"; cf Eph 2, 19-20.

21, 15-17: The city is shaped like a gigantic cube, a symbol of perfection (cf 1 Kgs 6, 19-20). The measurements of the city and its wall are multiples of the symbolic number twelve; see the note on 7, 4-9.

21, 16: *Fifteen hundred miles:* literally, twelve thousand stades, about 12,000 furlongs (see the note on 14, 20); the number is symbolic: twelve (the apostles as leaders of the new Israel) multiplied by 1,000 (the immensity of Christians); cf Introduction. *In length and width and height:* literally, "its length and width and height are the same."

21, 17: *One hundred and forty-four cubits:* the cubit was about eighteen inches in length. *Standard unit of measurement the angel used:* literally, "by a human measure, i.e., an angel's."

21, 18-21: The gold and precious gems symbolize the beauty and excellence of the church; cf Ex 28, 15-21; Tb 13, 16-17; Is 54, 11-12.

21, 22: Christ is present throughout the church; hence, no temple is needed as an earthly dwelling for God; cf Mt 18, 20; 28, 20; Jn 4, 21.

21, 23: *Lamp . . . Lamb:* cf Jn 8, 12.

21, 24-27: All men and women of good will are welcome in the church; cf Is 60, 1.3.5.11. *The . . . book of life:* see the note on 3, 5.

22, 1.17: *Life-giving water:* see the note on 7, 17.

22, 2: *The tree of life:* cf v 14; see the note on 2, 7. *Fruit . . . medicine:* cf Ez 47, 12.

22, 4: *Look upon his face:* cf Mt 5, 8; 1 Cor 13, 12; 1 Jn 3, 2.

VII: EPILOGUE†

6* And he said to me, "These words
are trustworthy and true, and the Lord,
the God of prophetic spirits, sent his an-
gel to show his servants what must hap-
pen soon." 7*† "Behold, I am coming
soon." Blessed is the one who keeps the
prophetic message of this book.
8 It is I, John, who heard and saw
these things, and when I heard and saw
them I fell down to worship at the feet
of the angel who showed them to me.
9* But he said to me, "Don't! I am a fel-
low servant of yours and of your broth-
ers the prophets and of those who keep
the message of this book. Worship God."
10† Then he said to me, "Do not seal
up the prophetic words of this book, for
the appointed time is near. 11 Let the
wicked still act wickedly, and the filthy
still be filthy. The righteous must still
do right, and the holy still be holy."
12* "Behold, I am coming soon. I bring
with me the recompense I will give to
each according to his deeds. 13*† I am
the Alpha and the Omega, the first and
the last, the beginning and the end."
14*† Blessed are they who wash their
robes so as to have the right to the tree
of life and enter the city through its
gates. 15* Outside are the dogs, the sor-
cerers, the unchaste, the murderers, the
idol-worshipers, and all who love and
practice deceit.
16*† "I, Jesus, sent my angel to give
you this testimony for the churches. I
am the root and offspring of David, the
bright morning star."
17*† The Spirit and the bride say,
"Come." Let the hearer say, "Come."
Let the one who thirsts come forward,
and the one who wants it receive the
gift of life-giving water.
18 I warn everyone who hears the
prophetic words in this book: if anyone
adds to them, God will add to him the
plagues described in this book, 19* and
if anyone takes away from the words
in this prophetic book, God will take
away his share in the tree of life and
in the holy city described in this book.
20*† The one who gives this testimony
says, "Yes, I am coming soon." Amen!
Come, Lord Jesus!
21 The grace of the Lord Jesus be with
all.

*

6: 1, 1.
7: 12.20 / 1, 3.
9: 19, 10.
12: 7.20 / Ps 62, 12; 2 Tm 4, 14.
13: 1, 8; 21, 6; Is 41, 4; 44, 6.
14: 7, 14-15; 22, 2.
15: 21, 8; Rom 1, 29-32.
16: 1, 1.11-12; 22, 6 / 2, 28.
17: 21, 6; Is 55, 1.
19: Dt 4, 2.
20: 7.12 / Acts 3, 20-21; 1 Cor 15, 23; 16, 22

†

22, 6-21: The book ends with an epilogue consisting of a series of warnings and exhortations and forming an inclusion with the prologue by resuming its themes and expressions; see the note on 1, 1-3.

22, 7.12.20: *I am coming soon:* Christ is the speaker; see the note on 1, 3.

22, 7.14: *Blessed:* see the note on 1, 3.

22, 10: *The appointed time:* see the note on 1, 3.

22, 13: Christ applies to himself words used by God in 1, 8.

22, 14: *The city:* heavenly Jerusalem; see the note on 21, 2.

22, 16: *The root . . . of David:* see the note on 5, 5. *Morning star:* see the note on 2, 26-28.

22, 17: *Bride:* the church; see the note on 21, 2.

22, 20: *Come, Lord Jesus:* a liturgical refrain, similar to the Aramaic expression *Marana tha*—"Our Lord, come!"—in 1 Cor 16, 22; cf the note there. It was a prayer for the coming of Christ in glory at the parousia; see the note on 1, 3.

LIST OF THE POPES

1. St. Peter d. 67
2. St. Linus, 67-76
3. St. Anacletus I, 76-88
4. St. Clement I, 88-97
5. St. Evaristus, 97-105
6. St. Alexander I, 105-115
7. St. Sixtus I, 115-125
8. St. Telesphorus, 125-36
9. St. Hyginus, 136-40
10. St. Pius I, 140-55
11. St. Anicetus, 155-66
12. St. Soter, 166-75
13. St. Eleuterius, 175-89
14. St. Victor I, 189-99
15. St. Zephyrinus, 199-217
16. St. Callistus I, 217-22
17. St. Urban I, 222-30
18. St. Pontian, 230-35
19. St. Anterus, 235-36
20. St. Fabian, 236-50
21. St. Cornelius, 251-53
22. St. Lucius I, 253-54
23. St. Stephen I, 254-57
24. St. Sixtus II, 257-58
25. St. Dionysius, 259-68
26. St. Felix I, 269-74
27. St. Eutychian, 275-83
28. St. Caius, 283-96
29. St. Marcellinus, 296-304
30. St. Marcellus I, 304-09
31. St. Eusebius, 309-11
32. St. Melchiades, 311-14
33. St. Sylvester I, 314-35
34. St. Marcus, 336
35. St. Julius I, 337-52
36. Liberius, 352-66
37. St. Damasus I, 366-84
38. St. Siricius, 384-99
39. St. Anastasius I, 399-401
40. St. Innocent I, 401-17
41. St. Zosimus, 417-18
42. St. Boniface I, 418-22
43. St. Celestine I, 422-32
44. St. Sixtus III, 432-40
45. St. Leo I, 440-61
46. St. Hilarius, 461-68
47. St. Simplicius, 468-83
48. St. Felix II, 483-92
49. St. Gelasius I, 492-96
50. Anastasius II, 496-98
51. St. Symmachus, 498-514
52. St. Hormisdas, 514-23
53. St. John I, 523-26
54. St. Felix III, 526-30
55. Boniface II, 530-32
56. John II, 533-35
57. St. Agapitus I, 535-36
58. St. Silverius, 536-37
59. Vigilius, 537-55
60. Pelagius I, 556-61
61. John III, 561-74
62. Benedict I, 575-79
63. Pelagius II, 579-90
64. St. Gregory I, 590-604
65. Sabinianus, 604-06
66. Boniface III, 607
67. St. Boniface IV, 608-15
68. St. Deusdedit, 615-18
69. Boniface V, 619-25
70. Honorius I, 625-38
71. Severinus, 638-40
72. John IV, 640-42
73. Theodore I, 642-49
74. St. Martin I, 649-55
75. St. Eugene I, 655-57
76. St. Vitalian, 657-72
77. Adeodatus, 672-76
78. Donus, 676-78
79. St. Agatho, 678-81
80. St. Leo II, 682-83
81. St. Benedict II, 684-85
82. John V, 685-86
83. Conon, 686-87
84. St. Sergius I, 687-701
85. John VI, 701-05
86. John VII, 705-07
87. Sisinnius, 708
88. Constantine, 708-15
89. St. Gregory II, 715-31
90. St. Gregory III, 731-41
91. St. Zacharias, 741-52
92. Stephen II, 752-57
93. St. Paul I, 757-67
94. Stephen III, 768-72
95. Adrian I, 772-95
96. St. Leo III, 795-816
97. Stephen IV, 816-17
98. St. Paschal I, 817-24
99. Eugene II, 824-27
100. Valentine, 827
101. Gregory IV, 827-44
102. Sergius II, 844-47
103. St. Leo IV, 847-55
104. Benedict III, 855-58
105. St. Nicholas I, 858-67
106. Adrian II, 867-72
107. John VIII, 872-82
108. Marinus I, 882-84
109. St. Adrian III, 884-85
110. Stephen V, 885-91
111. Formosus, 891-96
112. Boniface VI, 896
113. Stephen VI, 896-97
114. Romanus, 897
115. Theodore II, 897
116. John IX, 898-900
117. Benedict IV, 900-03
118. Leo V, 903
119. Sergius III, 904-11
120. Anastasius III, 911-13
121. Lando, 913-14
122. John X, 914-28
123. Leo VI, 928
124. Stephen VII, 928-31

125. John XI, 931-36
126. Leo VII, 936-39
127. Stephen VIII, 939-42
128. Marinus II, 942-46
129. Agaptus II, 946-55
130. John XII, 955-64
131. Leo VIII, 964-65
132. Benedict V, 965
133. John XIII, 965-72
134. Benedict VI, 973-74
135. Benedict VII, 974-83
136. John XIV, 983-84
137. John XV, 985-96
138. Gregory V, 996-99
139. Sylvester II, 999-1003
140. John XVII, 1003
141. John XVIII, 1003-09
142. Sergius IV, 1009-12
143. Benedict VIII, 1012-24
144. John XIX, 1024-32
145. Benedict IX, 1032-45
146. Sylvester III, 1045
147. Benedict IX, 1045, (2nd)
148. Gregory VI, 1045-46
149. Clement II, 1046-47
150. Benedict IX, 1047-48, (3rd)
151. Damasus II, 1048
152. St. Leo IX, 1049-54
153. Victor II, 1055-57
154. Stephen IX, 1057-58
155. Nicholas II, 1059-61
156. Alexander II, 1061-73
157. St. Gregory VII, 1073-85
158. Bl. Victor III, 1087
159. Bl. Urban II, 1088-99
160. Paschal II, 1099-1118
161. Gelasius II, 1118-19
162. Callistus II, 1119-24
163. Honorius II, 1124-30
164. Innocent II, 1130-43
165. Celestine II, 1143-44
166. Lucius, 1144-45
167. Bl. Eugene III, 1145-53
168. Anastasius IV, 1153-54
169. Adrian IV, 1154-59
170. Alexander III, 1159-81
171. Lucius III, 1181-85
172. Urban III, 1185-87
173. Gregory VIII, 1187
174. Clement III, 1187-91
175. Celestine III, 1191-98
176. Innocent III, 1198-1216
177. Honorius III, 1216-27
178. Gregory IX, 1227-41
179. Celestine IV, 1241
180. Innocent IV, 1243-54
181. Alexander IV, 1254-61
182. Urbaqn IV, 1261-64
183. Clement IV, 1265-68
184. Bl. Gregory X, 1271-76
185. Bl. Innocent V, 1276
186. Adrian V, 1276
187. John XXI, 1276-77
188. Nicholas III, 1277-80
189. Martin IV, 1281-85
190. Honorius IV, 1285-87
191. Nicholas IV, 1288-91
192. St. Celestine V, 1294
193. Boniface VIII, 1294-1303
194. Benedict XI, 1303-04
195. Clement V, 1305-14
196. John XXII, 1316-34
197. Benedict XII, 1334-42
198. Clement VI, 1342-52
199. Innocent VI, 1352-62
200. Bl. Urban V, 1362-70
201. Gregory XI, 1370-78
202. Urban VI, 1378-89
203. Boniface IX, 1389-1404
204. Innocent VII, 1404-06
205. Gregory XII, 1406-15 (resigned during Western Schism to permit a proper election of a successor)
206. Martin V, 1417-31
207. Eugene IV, 1431-47
208. Nicholas V, 1447-55
209. Callistus III, 1455-58
210. Pius II, 1458-64
211. Paul II, 1464-71
212. Sixtus IV, 1471-84
213. Innocent VIII, 1484-92
214. Alexander VI, 1492-1503
215. Pius III, 1503
216. Julius II, 1503-13
217. Leo X, 1513-21
218. Adrian VI, 1522-23
219. Clement VII, 1523-34
220. Paul III, 1534-49
221. Julius III, 1550-55
222. Marcellus II, 1555
223. Paul IV, 1555-59
224. Pius IV, 1559-65
225. St. Pius V, 1566-72
226. Gregory XIII, 1572-85
227. Sixtus V, 1585-90
228. Urban VII, 1590
229. Gregory XIV, 1590-91
230. Innocent IX, 1591
231. Clement VIII, 1592-1605
232. Leo XI, 1605
233. Paul V, 1605-21
234. Gregory XV, 1621-23
235. Urban VIII, 1623-44
236. Innocent X, 1644-55
237. Alexander VII, 1655-67
238. Clement IX, 1667-69
239. Clement X, 1670-76
240. Bl. Innocent XI, 1676-89
241. Alexander VIII, 1689-91
242. Innocent XII, 1691-1700
243. Clement XI, 1700-21
244. Innocent XIII, 1721-24
245. Benedict XIII, 1724-30
246. Clement XII, 1730-40
247. Benedict XIV, 1740-58
248. Clement XIII, 1758-69

249. Clement XIV, 1769-74
250. Pius VI, 1775-99
251. Pius VII, 1800-23
252. Leo XII, 1823-29
253. Pius VIII, 1829-30
254. Gregory XVI, 1831-46
255. Pius IX, 1846-78
256. Leo XIII, 1878-1903
257. St. Pius X, 1903-14
258. Benedict XV, 1914-22
259. Pius XI, 1922-1939
260. Pius XII, 1939-1958
261. John XXIII, 1958-1963
262. Paul VI, 1963-1978
263. John Paul I, 1978
264. John Paul II, 1978 (now reigning)

THE ENGLISH VERSIONS OF THE BIBLE

BY JOHN BERCHMANS DOCKERY, O.F.M.

Bibliography—The choice is very large. Only a selection of works which give a comprehensive treatment of the subject is offered here. The two classic works on the subject of English versions are: *The Cambridge History of the Bible: the West from the Reformation to the present day*, ed. S. L. Greenslade, Cambridge, 1963; H. Pope: *English Versions of the Bible*, revised and amplified by S. Bullough. St. Louis, Mo., 1952.

Other General Works: F. F. Bruce, *The English Bible: a history of translations*, London, 1961. A short, clear, up-to-date account of the history and development of the Bible in England; T. H. Darlow and H. F. Moule, *Historical Catalogue of Printed Editions of Holy Scripture*, London, 1903–11; vol. I English Editions; J. R. Dore, *Old Bibles: an Account of the Early versions of the English Bible*, 1882;[2] F. Kenyon, *Our Bible and the Ancient Manuscripts*, 1958[3], chs. X—XII; J. G. MacGregor, *The Bible in the Making*, 1961; W. F. Moulton, *The History of the English Bible*, last complete ed., 1911—abridged ed., 1937; E. H. Robertson, *The New Translations of the Bible*, 1959; H. W. Robinson (ed.), *The Bible in its Ancient and English Versions*, Oxford, 1940; Reprinted with appendix Oxford, 1954; L. A. Weigle, *The English New Testament from Tyndale to the RSV*, Nashville, 1949; London, 1950; B. F. Westcott: *A General View of the History of the English Bible*, 1905, 3rd revision by W. A. Wright.

Earliest English Bible—Some paraphrases and translations into the vernacular were made in England of at least some parts of the Bible about the end of the seventh century and continued by Bede and others. In those days the standard of literacy was low, books, before printing was invented, very scarce, and educated people were able to read Latin. In the ninth century King Alfred translated or caused to be translated several books of the Bible, as did Aldhelm and Aelfric. But the Bible in general use was the Latin Vulgate. "In no part of the western world was this version studied more diligently and copied more lovingly and faithfully than in Great Britain and Ireland," F. F. Bruce, *The English Bible*, 1. Possibly the finest MS of this Bible, the Codex Amiatinus was made in England at Jarrow or Wearmouth. One early form of translation was the interlinear gloss—i.e., a translation between the lines of a Latin MS. Thus the **Lindisfarne Gospels,** a magnificent MS in Latin, has an interlinear translation in the Northumbrian dialect of the tenth century. The Norman Conquest radically modified and slowed down the development of English as a national language and in consequence translations into the vernacular continued to be sporadic and partial until the fourteenth century, when English began to emerge as a national language, a blend of Norman French and the various Anglo-Saxon dialects. Some objected to the vernacular Scriptures and complained that "the jewel of the clergy has become the toy of the laity." Nevertheless the demand, inevitably, grew as English came to be more widely spoken by the educated classes. Hitherto they had been satisfied with either Latin or Norman-French Bibles. St. Thomas More, Cranmer and even Foxe the martyrologist affirm the existence of English versions, at least of large portions of the Bible before Wycliffe's time and MSS have survived of English translations of the Gospels (11th century) Mark, Luke, St. Paul's Epistles (14th century), Apocalypse (11th century).

John Wycliffe—However, it is now generally accepted that the first complete English version of the Bible was made toward the end of the fourteenth century by Wycliffe and his followers. Wycliffe was perhaps the most eminent theologian of his time at Oxford and a great popular preacher who fiercely attacked the abuses of the age. Unfortunately in doing so he expressed unorthodox views concerning the sacraments of Penance and the Eucharist, the use of relics and against the celibacy of the clergy. He strongly advocated a translation of the Scriptures into English so that the poor people could read God's Word for themselves. Such a version would also make it easier for him to propagate his teachings. Wycliffe and his companions made a translation of the NT in 1380, followed by one of the OT two years later, both of course from the Latin Vulgate and the latter including the deuterocanonical books. It is uncertain what part Wycliffe took in the translation. He may have translated the NT but most of the OT was the work of Nicholas of Hereford, one of his ardent supporters. Nicholas was vice-Chancellor of the University of Oxford but later retired to the Carthusian monastery at Coventry where he died. Hereford's work on the OT is scholarly and literal; that of his collaborators more free and colloquial. Many familiar phrases from the Wycliffite Bible are found in most later English versions, e.g., "strait is the gate and narewe the way"; "the beame and the mote." In 1384, after Wycliffe's death, John Purvey, one of his followers revised the translation. In the general prologue Purvey expressed his indebtedness to Nicholas of Lyra, the Franciscan scholar and expert in Hebrew and rabbinical studies who represented the culmination of a long tradition in these fields of knowledge.

Wycliffe's teachings were condemned repeatedly in England during the latter part of the fourteenth century and at the **Council of Oxford, 1408** translations of the Scriptures into the vernacular were forbidden unless and until they were fully approved by Church authority. The reason for this was the use made of the Wycliffite Bible in spreading the doctrines of Lollardy. In fact there was nothing unorthodox in the translation itself though, in the prologue, novel views on the Eucharist were expressed, incompatible with the faith. Finally in 1415 at the **Council of Florence** all Wycliffe's works were condemned. The actual Bibles, however, continued in use, shorn of their heretical prologue, and were in the possession of both religious houses and those of the nobility. Many of these Bibles may now be seen in the British Museum—mostly copies of the second Wycliffite version. The suggestion that these Bibles are really Catholic translations from the time before Wycliffe has now been abandoned. Once separated from the prologue there was no reason why they should not be used by Catholics and they came to be tacitly accepted. It should be noted that the Council of Oxford did not condemn vernacular translations. As Sir Thomas More said: "It neither forbiddeth the translations to be read that were already well done of old before Wycliffe's days, nor damneth his because it was new but because it was naught; nor prohibiteth new to be made but provideth that they shall not be read if they be made amiss till they be by good examination amended.' *A Dialogue against Heresies*.

First Printed Editions—The year 1525 saw the publication of the NT in Tyndale's translation and in 1530 there appeared his translation of the Pentateuch from the Hebrew. This was soon followed by Jonah. Unfortunately, like Wycliffe, Tyndale made his translation a vehicle for bitter attacks on the Church.

Tyndale was put to death in 1536 but left his translation of the OT in manuscript. The English ecclesiastical authorities condemned his Bible because it was considered to be part of the Lutheran reform. In their view much of the wording of the text and the prefaces emphasized basic principles of the reformers, e.g., justification by faith alone. The real reason for the condemnation seems rather to have been himself than his Bible, for his leanings toward Lutheranism were well known. It was on account of these opinions that he was compelled to carry out his work on the continent. His translation was a great improvement on that of Wycliffe, especially in literary merit, e.g., his translation of 1 Corinthians 13 has persevered through many versions. As regards orthodox Catholic teaching his translation gave some grounds for condemnation—his NT clearly reflects the influence of Luther's 1522 NT. The authorities objected to his rejection of "priest" for "elder," "church" for "congregation" and his notes were offensive to the Church. In 1543 Parliament banned it as a "crafty, false and untrue translation"; yet it is estimated that 80% of the words in the RV stand as in Tyndale's NT, and his Pentateuch formed the basis of most subsequent English versions. Cuthbert Tunstall, Bishop of London, had never encouraged Tyndale's efforts and, being especially perturbed by the circulation of this Bible, had it condemned and burned.

In the NT Tyndale used the Greek text of Erasmus and compared it with the Vulgate. In the OT he translated from the Hebrew, also comparing it with the Vulgate and Luther's German version. Tyndale's later corrections departed more from the Vulgate and from Wycliffe and his 1534 edition of the NT formed the basis for the AV, RV, and RSV. When Cranmer became Archbishop of Canterbury in 1533 the making of a new translation was committed to **Miles Coverdale** (1488-1569). He had been an Augustinian friar who left his Order under the influence of the Reformation, repudiated Catholicism and became the first Protestant Bishop of Exeter. In 1535 his English Bible was published. He did not claim Tyndale's knowledge of ancient languages but he made use of Tyndale's translation, together with Latin and German versions, as the title-page says, "translated from Douche and Latin." He followed Luther's example of putting the deuterocanonical books (he called them *Hagiographa* but later they were named *Apocrypha* by non-Catholics), at the end of the OT. Later English versions followed this example or omitted them. Coverdale's Bible was issued without royal authority but apparently there were no obstacles to its circulation. The second edition in 1537 received royal license, "set forth with the Kynges most gracious licence"; yet in 1546 King Henry forbade anyone to have a copy of either Tyndale's or Coverdale's NT. Because Coverdale's translation was not made from the original languages, it did not satisfy scholars. It may have been tactful of Coverdale not to mention Tyndale's Bible, but his NT is mainly Tyndale. It was essentially a "Protestant" version, e.g., "congregation" for "church," etc., but Coverdale was not a controversialist as Tyndale was. He was the first to introduce chapter summaries. One part of his Bible, the Psalter, has remained in the Prayer Book, as his English style has lent itself to singing.

In 1537 another English version appeared, known as the **Matthew Bible.** It was thought to be the work of a Thomas Matthew but now it is generally considered to be a composite translation edited by **John Rogers** (1500-55), a friend of Tyndale who became a Protestant under his influence. Some think that "Matthew" stands for Tyndale's own name, but in any case the pseudonym was probably used to protect the translator from the fate that overtook Tyndale. In fact Rogers became one of the first of the Marian martyrs. His work was a revision mainly of Tyndale with emendations from Coverdale. The king gave it royal license but did not authorize it for use in public worship. Numerous editions appeared; the last in 1551. This version welded together the best in Tyndale and Coverdale; his dependence on Tyndale is clear from his copious and offensive notes—it was the controversial nature of these that spoiled his work, though the Matthew Bible was an important influence on later versions.

The Great Bible, so called on account of its size (11″ x 16½″), was an attempt to supersede the two existing Bibles, Coverdale and Matthew, both considered unsatisfactory for one reason or another. Thomas Cromwell, deciding that these two Bibles stood in need of revision, assigned the work to Coverdale. It was now generally accepted by the reformers that the English Bible should be translated from the original languages. For this reason Coverdale worked on the Matthew Bible rather than on his own; but he was influenced by Tyndale's translation, especially in his retention of his ecclesiastical vocabulary. He used the last edition of Tyndale's NT of 1534–35, corrected by Sebastian Munster's Latin version of the Hebrew OT, the Latin Bible of Erasmus and the Complutensian Polyglot.

The Great Bible, often known as Cromwell's Bible first appeared in 1539 and though not considered heretical by Catholics, was defective in many places. It was the first English Bible to be authorized for public use in churches. In 1542 Convocation made an unsuccessful attempt to have it corrected by the Vulgate but a second edition had appeared in 1540, for which Cranmer himself had written the preface (hence often known as Cranmer's Bible), which became the standard text. There were seven editions of it in the next two years and many more before the last edition of 1569. As the publicly used Bible it remained unchallenged until the appearance of the Bishop's Bible in 1568. During Mary's reign no definite steps were taken to suppress it, though many English Bibles were burned. Neither Parliament nor royal proclamation denounced the Great Bible and when Elizabeth came to the throne, it was still in general use throughout the country.

Richard Taverner (1505-77) was a lawyer and a Greek scholar though he knew no Hebrew; he was a layman, the only one to produce an entire Bible, but licensed to preach by Edward VI. He revised the Matthew Bible and from the standpoint of scholarship, the result was a great improvement, particularly in his accurate rendering of the Greek article. He aimed at compression and vividness often substituting a Saxon word for a Latin word (e.g., "spokesman" for "advocate") and did not hesitate to coin words. He also introduced many strange spellings, e.g., "peax" for "peace," "hable" for "able." Owing to his lack of Hebrew, his standard of accuracy in the OT was not as high as in the NT; he merely polished up the text of Matthew's OT. His influence on later versions was slight but some of his words and expressions have survived, e.g., his use of "parable" for "similitude." The first edition of 1539 is the most reliable as later editions contain many alterations by Bishop Becke. Taverner's own marginal notes were not controversial and the Bible might have had a better reception had it not appeared so short a time before the Great Bible which entirely eclipsed it. The last edition was in 1552. It is of interest to note that a certain A. Marler was granted permission to sell copies of the Great Bible in 1541, unbound for 10/—and bound for 12/—a copy (in today's money about £30 and £36).

During the reign of Edward VI when all restrictions on reading the Bible were removed, thirty-five editions of the NT appeared and thirteen of the whole Bible. When the young king died and Mary Tudor succeeded, publications of the English Scriptures ceased and her reign witnessed only one edition, the NT from Geneva in 1557. It was at this time that a number of clerics left the country to join Knox and Calvin. Among these were Coverdale, Beza, and William Whittingham, sometime Fellow of All Souls, Oxford, and related by marriage to Calvin. These exiles decided to produce another English version, which became known as the **Geneva Bible.** Several hands took part in its completion. The NT was a revision of Tyndale's by Whittingham, more specifically Matthew's version of Tyndale, with some changes based on Beza's Latin NT of 1556. It was apparently only an interim edition for in 1560 there appeared the full Bible with a dedicatory epistle to Queen Elizabeth. The OT was a thorough revision of the Great Bible. Instead of the usual black letter type, Roman and italic types were used which rendered it much easier to read and this won it a place never achieved by previous Bibles. Its phrases find an echo in Scripture-quotations from Shakespeare to Bunyan. It remained the family Bible until the outbreak of the Civil War in 1642. For the first time in an English Bible the text was divided into verses. Its widespread popularity was due also to its quarto size. It was appointed to be read in the Churches in Scotland, though never in England. At least 140 editions of the whole Bible or NT were printed. It superseded the Great Bible and also held its own against the Bishops' Bible and even against the AV for a generation. The notes for the original 1560 edition emphasize "justification by faith alone" and make frequent attacks on Rome, thus making this first edition Protestant rather than Calvinistic. Later editions supply notes of a more Calvinistic nature; indeed this Bible played no small part in promoting English Puritanism. In spite of this, the AV was to benefit considerably from the scholarship of the Geneva translators. It formed a turning point in the history of the English Bible for it was more independent than the Great Bible which relied on Matthew, as Matthew relied on Tyndale. The Geneva Bible started afresh and a new way was opened for the later AV of 1611.

The growing popularity of the Geneva Bible made it impossible to continue reading the Great Bible in church. Apprehensive of the Calvinistic tendencies of the Geneva Bible Archbishop Matthew Parker in 1561 submitted a plan for the revision of the Great Bible. The **Bishops' Bible,** as it came to be called, took seven years to complete. The Great Bible was checked by the Hebrew text and the controversial notes were omitted; though it contained notes strongly Protestant in tone, these were neither anti-Catholic nor anti-Calvinist. On the whole the revision was inadequate and unsatisfactory, being little more than a safe and dignified compromise. It went through many editions until the last in 1606, but copies of the NT continued to be printed until 1619. In 1571 Convocation ordered this Bible to be used throughout the country and in 1572 there was a considerable revision of it, especially of the NT. Though not a work of high merit, it formed the official basis for the revision of 1611. It was the first text to be published in England by episcopal authority.

Catholic Bible—Meanwhile Catholics were considering a vernacular Bible and it was the professors of the English College at Douay who took up the work. Mainly from Oxford and exiled on account of their faith, even in Douay they were not left at rest; a storm on the political horizon threatened the existence of the college and caused its transfer to Rheims for fifteen years (1578-93). The chief names concerned with this translation of the Bible were: (1) **William Allen** (1532-94) Fellow of Oriel College, Oxford, Principal of St. Mary's Hall and Canon of York, who, refusing to conform in 1561, withdrew to Louvain. He opened the English College at Douay in 1568 and later founded a similar college in Rome. He was created Cardinal and appointed to the Sistine commission for the revision of the Septuagint and the Vulgate. (2) **Gregory Martin** (d. 1582), scholar of St. John's College, Oxford, poet, Hebraist, and Greek scholar. He too refused to conform to the religious changes in England and went to Douay in 1570. (3) **Richard Bristow** (1538-81), Fellow of Exeter College, Oxford, was a convert to Catholicism. He taught at Douay and went as its rector to Rheims. (4) **William Reynolds** (1544-94), another convert to the Catholic Church, from New College, Oxford, also went to Douay.

On 16 October 1578 Gregory Martin began an E. translation of the Bible in order to meet "the heretical corruptions imposed upon the English nation." He determined "to translate two chapters a day with Dr. Alanus and Mr. Bristous as revisors." In 1582 there was printed at Rheims the NT translated "faithfully into English out of the authentical Latin . . . diligently conferred with the Greek . . . especially for the discovery of the corruptions of divers late translations and for clearing the controversies in religion of these days . . . ." The reason for the translation was "not of necessity . . . but upon consideration of the present time and condition of our country"; i.e., a vernacular version would not have been necessary in more peaceful times. The preface goes on to say that the Church "never wholly condemned all vulgar versions" but gave warning against indiscriminate interpretation. The Council of Oxford, called by Thomas Arundel, Archbishop of Canterbury, in 1408, had demanded diocesan approval for the publication of Bibles. The translators of the Rheims NT went on to explain that, lest any doctrinal error should creep in or the true sense of the Holy Ghost be missed, they had followed the Fathers and Jerome himself "in keeping religiously the very barbarisms of the vulgar Latin text," e.g., "supersubstantial bread" (Mt 6, 11); "similitude of the prevarication of Adam" (Rom. 5, 14). The annotations, considerable in extent, were added "to show the studious reader both the heretical corruptions and false deductions." Then follow the reasons why the Vulgate was used for the translation: its ancient character, its tradition, its accuracy and its sincerity as well as the decree of the Council of Trent. The Rheims translators set out to produce a literal translation as they clearly point out in their preface of 1582. Further light is thrown on the intentions of the translators by a book published in the same year, 1582, by Martin entitled, *A Discoverie of the manifold corruptions of the Holy Scriptures by the Hereticks of our dais, especially the English*

Sectaries and of their foule dealing herein by partial and false translations to the advantage of their heresies in the English Bibles used and authorised since the time of Schisme. In this work Martin makes a careful study of a number of phrases in the English Bibles and comparing them with the Hebrew or Greek expressions establishes the accuracy of the recently published Catholic Bible; he also asserts that many of the inaccuracies have been due to the influence of the new religious teachings. The following year this expression of strong Catholic views was answered in equally strong language by William Fulke, Master of Pembroke Hall, Cambridge, in his *Defense of the Sincere and true translation of the holie Scriptures into the English tong against the manifold cavils, frivolous quarrels and imprudent slanders of Gregory Martin, one of the readers of Popish divinitie in the trayterous Seminarie of Rhemes*.

The groundwork of the Rheims NT was supplied by the existing English versions from which Martin did not hesitate to borrow freely; his renderings often bear a striking resemblance to Coverdale's diglot of 1538. The translation also shows traces of a careful study of the Bishops' Bible and the Geneva Bible and through them of the earlier translators from Tyndale onward. But generally speaking, the Rheims NT follows Wycliffe, whereas Protestant translations follow Tyndale. The notes in the first edition of this Catholic NT were most probably contributed by Bristow. The preface, termed "ingenious" by its critics, gives reasons for publishing a new English translation. Many critics gratuitously suggested that the obscure style was deliberately adopted in order to prevent readers from understanding the Bible; the Catholic Church, they said, had been compelled by circumstances to produce vernacular Bibles but made it as difficult as possible to understand them! Later scholars, among them Carleton and Westcott, have praised the accuracy of the Rheims-Douay version. Among points to be specially noted is the careful treatment of the definite article arising from a study of the Greek text, as Taverner had shown. In 1589 William Fulke, continuing his controversy, published the Bishops' version and the Rheims NT in parallel columns. This secured for the Catholic NT a publicity which it would not have otherwise obtained and this publicity was indirectly responsible for the marked influence of the Rheims NT on the AV.

It was not until 1609-10 that the Catholic OT was published in two volumes. In the preface the editors declare that the work had been "completed long since but lack of funds prevented its publication before." Another reason for the delay may have been that this OT, based on an unofficial Louvain text, might be corrected by the Sistine edition of the Vulgate published in 1590. It is again stated in the preface that the real purpose of the translation was polemical: "Now since Luther and his followers have pretended that the Catholic Roman faith and doctrine should be contrary to God's written word and that the Scriptures were not suffered in vulgar languages lest the people should see the truth and withal these new masters corruptly turning the Scriptures into diverse tongues, as might best serve their own opinions, against this false suggestion and practice, Catholic pastors have, for one especial remedy, set forth true and sincere translations in most languages of the Latin Church." Criticisms were made against the OT such as had been launched against the NT, especially its too close adherence to the Latin text. There was a partial reversal of this attitude when many of the improved translations of the Rheims NT were introduced into the AV (the Douay OT appeared too late to influence the AV), e.g., "converted" *(convertantur)* for "turn" (Mk 4, 12); "founded" *(fundata)* for "grounded" (Eph 3, 17); "centurion" *(centurio)* for "captain" (Acts 10, 22); "sign" *(signum)* for "badge, token" (Mt 26, 48); "clemency" *(clementia)* for "courtesy" (Acts 24, 4). Not only did the Rheims NT introduce such Latin words into the English language but it also influenced the AV in the direction of modernization, e.g., "moisture" for "moistness" (Lk 8, 6); "what man is there" for "what man is it" (Acts 19, 35); "distresses" for "anguishes" (2 Cor 12, 10). The Rheims-Douay gave a glossary ("explication") of new words and it is surprising how many have become well established, e.g., acquisition, advent, allegory, assumption, calumniate, character, evangelize, neophyte, resuscitate, victim, etc. The Psalter was thought to be the weakest part of the translation; but this was because Jerome's Gallican Psalter, made from the Septuagint, had been included in the Vulgate and not his translation from the Hebrew. In the Douay OT there were annotations of a doctrinal nature, most valuable at a time when the Catholic body in England was so short of pastors. The purpose of these notes was to interpret the text in conformity with the faith of the editors and the decrees of the Council of Trent, as well as to rebut the arguments of the reformers. The deuterocanonical books are found distributed among the other canonical books in the Catholic OT. At a time when there was almost no knowledge of the relative value of MSS of original texts, the Rheims-Douay Bible, based on the Latin, drew attention to an important fact. Since the Vulgate was made in the fourth century many readings contained in it might be more exact than those in very late and corrupt Greek MSS that were used to make translations in the sixteenth century. But obviously one must bear in mind the fact that the Vulgate MSS too were subject to error. No further edition of the Rheims-Douay version appeared for another hundred years.

Authorized Version (called in USA **King James Version**)—The official authority given to the Bishops' Bible caused the Puritans to agitate for a new translation, to which James I agreed. Almost all existing English Bibles, including the Rheims NT were used as sources with the Bishops' Bible of 1572 as the main text. The translators were to keep the "old ecclesiastical words" because it was feared that the Puritans would discard all ecclesiastical tradition. The completed work appeared in 1611 and became known later as the Authorized Version. It was, in fact, never officially authorized either by Church or State, though the king's "speciall command" conferred considerable authority and it became the official Bible of the Church of England until modern times. It was favorably accepted by the non-conformist Churches. Being translated from the original texts, it claimed to be more accurate than a translation from the Latin, but (as has already been seen) this did not necessarily follow. Its notes do not stress differences in theological views, and scholarly marginal notes add much to textual criticism. The Apocrypha were included as it was not until the Long Parliament of 1644 that the books of the Hebrew canon only were directed to be read in the Church of England. After the Restoration this policy was reversed but the non-conformists continued for the most part to disregard the deuterocanonical books. The AV weathered all attacks and nearly a thousand editions of all or part were published between 1611 and 1800. Alterations were found in many editions: "Thou art Christ" (Mt 16, 16) became "Thou art the Christ"; "The words of Jesus" (Mt 26, 75) became "the word of Jesus"; "For press" (Mk 2, 4) became "for the press"; "He came and worshipped" (Mk 5, 6) became "He ran and worshipped." The revisers were accused of being "damnable corrupters of God's word" for making such changes. Though the AV received no approbation from Convocation or Parliament, it obtained a pre-eminent place on its own merits, "the noblest monument of English prose." It was published in Scotland in 1633, in Ireland in 1714, and in the American colonies in 1752.

Later Catholic Editions—During the course of the hundred years following the publication of the only existing Catholic English Bible, its language became increasingly strange. "In a number of places it is unintelligible and all over so grating to the ears of such as are accustomed to speak, in a manner, another language, that most people will not be at the pains to reading them." As an example of the truth of this criticism by Dr. Nary Numbers 6, 17 reads in the Rheims-Douay edition, "The ram he shal immolate for a pacifique host to the Lord, offering withal the baskette of azymes and the libamentes that by custom are dew." With the authority of the Archbishop of Dublin, **Dr. Nary** published a modernized version of the NT in 1718. His sense of English rhythm was excellent and he had a high ideal of the translator's task, being probably ahead of his time in his understanding of it. He had another object in view, namely, to replace "Bibles that are so bulky that they cannot conveniently be carried about for public devotion; and so scarce and dear that the generality of people neither have nor can procure them for private use." In 1730 another President of the English College, Douay, **Dr. Robert Witham,** published a revision of the Rheims NT. In his preface, having praised the work of the original translators for producing such a true and literal translation and not a paraphrase, Witham thought that "the Rheims translators followed too scrupulously the Latin, even to the placing of words." He changed almost every verse in his revision of the NT. The censor of this edition was **Dr. Richard Challoner,** vice-president of the College at Douay. The same year Challoner returned to England to work on the mission and in 1738 a new revision of the NT appeared which was probably the work of Challoner, assisted by Francis Blyth, O.D.C. Both these men were converts from Protestantism and being familiar with the language of the AV did not hesitate to adopt many of its renderings. Thus, the young man who followed our Lord (Mk 14, 51), and, according to the Rheims translation was "clothed with sindon upon the bare," became "cloathed with linnen cloath over his naked body." Challoner's wide pastoral experience made him familiar with the needs of the people for whom the English Bible was required. This qualification more than made up for any lack of the profound scholarship that adorned the previous translators. Challoner's aim was to give his people a Bible they would read and understand and carry about with them; and this he did in the further revision of the NT of 1749. In this edition further alterations were made toward the AV and the expressions so familiar to modern readers of the Catholic Bible were introduced, e.g., instead of "But when I was made a man, I did away the things that belonged to a little one" Challoner wrote, "But when I became a man, I put away the things of a child" (1 Cor 13, 11). The next year, 1750, the whole Bible was published, "newly revised and corrected according to the Clementine edition of the Scriptures." It went through six editions in the lifetime of Challoner who died in his ninetieth year in 1781. His corrections in the OT almost amounted to a new translation. There must of necessity be a certain resemblance between any two Catholic versions, both translated from the Vulgate; but, this connection between the Douay and Challoner's being allowed for, Challoner's version is nearer to the AV than it is to the Douay in phraseology and diction. In the NT the Gospels are the best, the Epistles the least satisfactory part of his work. In the necessary simplifying of the English text, there was some loss of the dignity and rhythm of the original version of 1582; but Challoner produced what has been the Bible of English Catholics for nearly two hundred years. Nevertheless differing texts are found, due to the changes by different editors. For example, Bernard MacMahon produced a new edition in 1783 which professed to be a revision of Challoner and basically it is, but there are over five hundred variations and still more in an 1816 edition, known as Dr. Troy's Bible. Dr. Cotton maintained that the changes made in subsequent editions of the Rheims-Douay Bible produced a Bible further from the AV than Challoner's Bible ever was (H. Cotton, *Rhemes and Doway. An attempt to shew what has been done by the Roman Catholics for the diffusion of the Holy Scriptures in English*, Oxford, 1855. On this work cf H. Pope, op. cit., 92–97).

Revised Version—In the course of time, the need was felt for a revision of the AV as new sources of knowledge became available. In 1856 a petition for a royal commission was put before the House of Commons, but not until 1870 did the Convocation of Canterbury decide to undertake the work. A committee was formed of members of the Church of England as well as of other non-Catholic communions (Cardinal Newman was invited but felt unable to accept). They published the NT in 1881, the whole Bible in 1885, and the Apocrypha in 1894. In the preface to the NT the debt of the AV to the Rheims NT was at last publicly recognized. Though possessing greater accuracy than the AV, the RV lacked its style and dignity. But all agree that its appearance was a milestone in the history of the English Bible and a greater landmark than early critics ever suspected. Its scholarship has never been disputed.

The revisers were "to introduce as few alterations as possible into the text of the AV consistently with faithfulness," as the preface states. The Greek text they used, based on Septuagint (B) and (S), was the work of B. F. Westcott and F. J. A. Hort, both occupying professional chairs at Cambridge. For the OT the Massoretic text was employed. Toward the end of the nineteenth century, revisers in America were at work and produced in 1901 the **American Standard Version,** a recension of the RV in which were included words and phrases that were a matter of preference for Americans, e.g., "Holy Spirit" for "Holy Ghost." In general the American revisers desired a more extensive elimination of archaic words than the English revisers wished, e.g., the American version of the Lord's Prayer reverted to the "who art in heaven" of the Rheims NT. Perhaps the major defect of both the RV and the ASV of the NT is that they are too literal and follow the Greek order of words rather than the natural English word order.

The International Council of Education appointed in 1937 a committee of scholars to revise the American Standard Version and their work was published as the **Revised Standard Version** of the NT in 1946 and of the OT in 1952. The revision is "based on the consonantal Hebrew text" for the OT, and for the NT the best available texts. "The major reason for the revision of the King James' version . . . is the change since 1611 in English usage." Over twelve million copies of the RSV were sold within ten years.

Other Modern Non-Catholic Versions—Only briefly can mention be made of a number of modern English Protestant texts: (1) Richard Weymouth: NT in 1902, a careful, conservative, and literary translation; (2) Twentieth Century NT (1898, revised 1904), changed the traditional order of books to the chronological order; (3) James Moffat: the whole Bible (1913-24), a one-man translation, the first for nearly four hundred years and a complete breakaway from the style of the AV. It became most popular; (4) Basic English Bible, 1949 (it uses only a thousand words), has a simple direct style; (5) New English Bible, 1961, under the direction of Dr. C. H. Dodd, aims at rendering the original into idiomatic English designed primarily for private use; (6) J. B. Phillips's version has achieved a very wide circulation, especially of its separate parts in paperbacks: Epistles (London, 1947), Gospels (1952), Acts (1955), Revelation (1958); NT in one volume (1958). His principles of translation are: use only language that is commonly spoken; expand if necessary to make the meaning clear; keep the style flowing and easy to read; (7) New American Standard Bible, 1971, updated the ASV into more acceptable English style, and recent Hebrew and Greek textual discoveries were incorporated into the text; (8) New International Version, 1978, enlisted an international team of scholars and attempted a translation acceptable to all English-speaking peoples through the use of an eclectic Greek text, the Massoretic Hebrew text, and current English style; (9) New King James Bible (NT, 1979; NT with Psalms, 1980; complete Bible, 1982) is a complete revision of the 1611 AV or King James Version and endeavors to update the archaisms of the AV while retaining its style and beauty of language.

Modern Catholic Versions—In 1811 a revision of Challoner's version, which became known as Dr. Hay's version, went through a number of editions in Ireland. In the same year Thomas Haydock, printer and schoolmaster in Manchester, suggested that his brother, the Rev. George Haydock of Ushaw College, should prepare a new translation. It was mainly Challoner and published in fortnightly parts. Other editions of Challoner appeared but when Bible Societies began to produce their cheap copies, Catholics felt they should do something similar, so the "Catholic Board" inaugurated the "Roman Catholic Bible Society." After initial difficulties about the text and notes, the NT was published in 1815 "stereotyped from the edition published by authority in 1749," i.e., Challoner's revision, though the notes were abridged and the text modernized ("said" for "saith"; "my" for "mine"). Between 1816 and 1829 the text of Challoner's third revision was published in several editions. Dr. John Lingard made a translation of the Gospels from the Greek, using the Vulgate wherever possible. In 1857 Cardinal Wiseman approached Newman about the possibility of a new translation but nothing came of it. It must suffice to say that during the next hundred years ninety different editions of the NT were published and fifty-six of the complete Bible; a figure that does not include the vast number of editions appearing in America (See H. Pope: *English Versions*, 719–46).

Twentieth-Century Catholic Versions

The **Westminster Version** is an unofficial (i.e., not commissioned by the Hierarchy) English translation from the original languages. The NT under the direction of Cuthbert Lattey, S. J., was completed in 1936; but the OT remains unfinished. The translation of both Testaments, though uneven, is good, and the version is accompanied by copious notes and commentaries. It is interesting to notice that in the OT proper names appear as in the AV and not as in the Vulgate.

Confraternity Version of the New Testament (NT) was begun in the U.S.A. before the 1939–45 war as a translation from the Vulgate under the auspices of the Episcopal Committee of the Confraternity of Christian Doctrine. This translation of the NT was published in 1941.

New American Bible—Early in 1944 in conformity with the encyclical of Pope Pius XII, *Divino Afflante Spiritu*, the Episcopal Committee of the Confraternity of Christian Doctrine requested the Catholic Biblical Association of America to produce a completely new translation of the Bible from the original languages of Hebrew, Aramaic, and Greek, and to present the sense of biblical text as accurately as possible. The better understanding of these languages and the steady progress of the science of textual criticism allowed the translators and editors to approach more closely than ever before the sense of what the sacred authors actually wrote.

The OT, first published as a series of four volumes, was, upon completion of the NT in 1970, named the New American Bible. The translation has had great influence upon the American Catholic people, especially in widespread use in public worship.

Further advances in biblical scholarship and identification of pastoral needs brought about a revision of the NT text, completed and published in 1986. The revision fulfilled a fourfold purpose: (1) greater consistency of vocabulary, (2) sensitivity to the need of inclusive language in favor of women, (3) greater attention to public proclamation in sacred liturgy, and (4) provision of more abundant and upgraded explanatory material. The **Revised NT**, like the first edition, was accomplished with the collaboration of scholars from other Christian churches in response to the encouragement of Vatican Council II (*Dei Verbum* 22).

Knox Version—In 1939 Monsignor Ronald Knox was asked by the English Hierarchy to make a translation of the NT from the Vulgate. Knox's aim was to express the Bible "in timeless English" in a style that was "accurate, intelligible, idiomatic, readable." He pointed out that a literal translation was not always accurate. The NT, authorized by the Archbishops and Bishops of England and Wales, appeared in 1945. The preface stated that it was not intended to displace the Rheims version of the NT, "on the contrary we now have two official versions in the Church in this country." The translation was completely new, breaking away from all previous translations and became popular both in England and America. It had the overwhelming advantage of being the work of a single author who was a master of English. In 1949 his OT was published for private use only, though it bore the *imprimatur* of Cardinal Griffin. It represented what Knox himself claimed to be "my idea of how the OT ought to be translated." This meant that his translation was written in a freer, more personal style than was found in the NT. In this edition of the OT the book of Psalms was a translation from the Vulgate Gallican Psalter, but Knox gave in an appendix a translation into English of the new Latin psalter made in 1943 from the Hebrew by members of the Pontifical Biblical Institute. In the 1955 edition of Knox's Bible the Gallican Psalter is replaced by this new psalter.

RSV Catholic Edition—The whole story of the Bible from Wycliffe to modern times has been one of divergence and differences in English versions. In our own days a change in this long tradition is being effected and there is a movement in the direction of a common Bible. Thus the Second Vatican Council commended the making of present-day versions from the original text of the Bible for the use of the faithful, and added: "As opportunity offers, and with the approval of Church authority, such versions can be made in collaboration with our separated brothers and be available for use by all Christians" (*De divina Rev.*, 22). In England it was thought that one practical approach to this ideal would be to edit an existing version. The recently published RSV seemed to be the best starting point. The preliminary difficulties were surmounted and the NT was ready by 1956, but then Cardinal Griffin, who had approved the plan, died and things remained in abeyance until Archbishop Gray of St. Andrews and Edinburgh gave his *imprimatur* to the NT of the RSV Catholic edition in 1964.

In 1966 the whole Bible in **the RSV Catholic edition** was published. In it: (1) the deuterocanonical books (known to Protestants as the Apocrypha, are included, and moreover in their traditional Catholic order as in the Septuagint and the Vulgate; (2) in accordance with Canon Law, explanatory notes are supplied; (3) a small number of changes of wording has been made, where the textual evidence is evenly balanced; (4) some passages omitted in RSV have been restored. The publication of this Bible is a great step forward toward the ideal of a common Bible.

The **Jerusalem Bible** is a translation from the original languages following closely the critical text on which the well-known Bible de Jerusalem is based and providing an English version of the notes appended to the French translation. It thus provides for Catholics in English-speaking countries not only a version from the original languages but an annotated Bible for the first time in many years. The translation, the work of many hands, is adequate, and effectively brings out the meaning. It attempts to render the originals into good standard English, which at times can be beautiful but at others pedestrian. The whole Bible was published in 1966.

Meanwhile in the U.S.A. a promising and significant step of another kind was taken when the production of *the Anchor Bible* was begun. This is described by its editors as a project of international and interfaith scope: Protestant, Catholic, and Jewish scholars from many countries contribute individual volumes under the general editorship of William Foxwell Albright and David Noel Freedman. Each volume contains a new translation of the particular book concerned, together with introduction and notes; and while the work "is aimed at the general reader with no special formal training in biblical studies, yet it is written with the most exacting standards of scholarship."

TOPICAL INDEX

with

Real-Life

Application Notes

SUPERMAN YOU'RE NOT

Proverbs 20:1

Wine is arrogant, strong drink is riotous; none who goes astray for it is wise.

Prv 20:1

There's a good reason why fights often break out when people have had a few too many beers. It's because some people have a false sense of power when they're under the influence of alcohol or drugs. They think they're invincible—that is, until they wake up the next morning with a busted jaw, a splitting headache, or a DUI. Drugs and booze don't really give you more power; they actually take power away from you. Power actually comes from freedom—the freedom to think and act. However, when you're under the influence, you're no longer free. You're a slave to the chemicals whirling around in your body, directing you, controlling you, deceiving you. Why would anyone want to submit to being a slave to something from which they can control?

Higher Stakes

Zephaniah 3:6–7

I said, "Surely now you will fear me,
you will accept correction";
She should not fail to see
all I have visited upon her.
Yet all the more eagerly have they done
all their corrupt deeds.

Zep 3:6–7

When a seven-year-old and a three-year-old get into mischief, which one is held more responsible for the damage they do? The seven-year-old, of course, because that child "should've known better." Those who know more are judged tougher because their knowledge makes them guiltier.

The people of Israel had hoped that, despite their sins, God would judge them with a soft hand and save the tough judgment for other nations. But Zephaniah makes it clear that Israel will actually be judged harder because Israel *knew* better. They were God's chosen people. They had received a covenant (agreement) with God, clear guidelines for living, and mega-miracles to help them believe in God's promises. Yet they still turned away.

How about us? We've been given the gift of faith. We have the Word of God right in front of us to teach and guide us. We cannot justify our sin because "everyone else is doing it." Now we *know* better. Now we must strive to *live* better because of it.

TOPICAL INDEX

The Rainbow

Genesis 8:1—9:17

"This is the sign that I am giving for all ages to come, of the covenant between me and you and every living creature with you: I set my bow in the clouds to serve as a sign of the covenant between me and the earth. When I bring clouds over the earth, and the bow appears in the clouds, I will recall the covenant I have made between me and you and all living beings, so that the waters shall never again become a flood to destroy all mortal beings. As the bow appears in the clouds, I will see it and recall the everlasting covenant that I have established between God and all living beings—all mortal creatures that are on earth." **Gn 9:12–16**

Ever take off in an airplane during a storm? Rain, thunder, lightning, wind—you're wondering if you should start writing a will on a napkin. Then, all of a sudden, the plane lifts through the dark cloud cover and wham!—you're soaring through a clear, blue, sunny sky. When you're that high up, you're always above the storms. That's the same perspective we get through faith. God's viewpoint is always above the clouds. So regardless of the storm we may be stuck in, the Lord sees the bigger picture; God knows the sun is still shining in our lives, even if we can't see it.

Without storms, nature can't fully function. It needs that life-giving rain. So do we. Although sometimes intense pain comes with the storms of our lives, they can cleanse us, strengthen us, and bring us growth and maturity. Just remember that God's sun is still shining behind every dark cloud, ready to deliver a rainbow of hope and "congratulations" when the storms have finally passed.

C. Reactions to:
Rebellious .... Ex 14:4–8
.... Jb 2:9
Distrustful .... Ex 6:8, 9
Complaining .... Ru 1:20, 21
Questioning .... Jer 20:7–10
Lack of strength .... Prv 24:10
Arrogant .... Ps 10:6
Hopeful .... Lam 3:31–40
Submissive .... Jb 5:17–22
Joyful .... Jas 1:2–4

D. God's relation to, he:
Destroys nations with .... 2 Chr 15:5, 6
Sees and observes .... Ps 31:8
Delivers out of .... 1 Sm 10:19
Recues out of .... 2 Sm 4:9

E. Helps under:
By prayer .... Jon 2:1–7
By understanding God's purpose
.... Lam 3:31–40
.... Rom 5:3–5

Advocate, Christ our

His defense of believers by:
Pleading .... 1 Jn 2:1
Prayer .... Lk 22:31–34
Protection .... Heb 13:6
Perseverance .... 2 Tm 4:17, 18

Affection—*an inner feeling or emotion*

A. Kinds of:
Natural .... Rom 1:26, 27
Paternal .... Lk 15:20
Maternal .... 1 Kgs 3:16–27
Fraternal .... Gn 43:30–34
Filial .... Gn 49:29, 30
National .... Ps 137:1–6
Racial .... Rom 9:1–3
For wife .... Eph 5:25–33
For husband .... Ti 2:4
Christian .... Rom 12:10
Heavenly .... Col 3:1, 2

B. Good, characteristics of:
Loyal, intense .... Ru 1:14–18
Memorable .... 2 Sm 1:17–27
Natural, normal .... 2 Sm 13:37–39
Tested, tried .... Gn 22:1–19
Emotional .... Jn 11:33–36
Grateful .... Lk 7:36–50
Joyous .... Ps 126:1–6
Christ-centered .... Mt 10:37–42

C. Evil, characteristics of:
Unnatural .... Rom 1:18–32
Pretended .... Mt 26:47–49
Abnormal .... 2 Tm 3:2–4
Fleshly .... Rom 13:13, 14
Worldly .... 2 Tm 4:10
Defiling, degrading .... 2 Pt 2:10–12
Agonizing, in Hades .... Lk 16:23–28

Afraid—*overcome with fear*

A. Caused by:
Nakedness .... Gn 3:10
Unusual dream .... Gn 28:16, 17
God's presence .... Ex 3:6
Moses' approach .... Ex 34:30
A burning mountain .... Dt 5:5
Giant's raging .... 1 Sm 17:11, 23, 24
A prophet's words .... 1 Sm 28:20
Angel's sword .... 1 Chr 21:30
Gabriel's presence .... Dn 8:17
A terrifying storm .... Jon 1:5, 10
The angel Raphael's disclosure
.... Tb 12:15–19
Strong wind .... Mt 14:30
Changed person .... Mk 5:15
Heavenly hosts .... Lk 2:9

B. Overcome by:
The Lord's presence .... Ps 3:6, 7
Trusting God .... Ps 27:1–3
God's protection .... Ps 91:3–5
Stability of heart .... Ps 112:7, 8
God's coming judgment .... Is 10:24–26
The Messiah's advent .... Is 40:9–11
God's sovereign power .... Is 51:12, 13
Christ's comforting words .... Mt 14:27

Ambition, Christian

A. Good, if for:
The greatest gifts .... 1 Cor 12:31
Spiritual goals .... Phil 3:12–14
The gospel's extension
.... Rom 15:17–20
Acceptance before God .... 2 Cor 5:9, 10
Tranquil life .... 1 Thes 4:11

B. Evil, if it leads to:
Strife .... Mt 20:20–28
Sinful superiority .... Mt 18:1–6
A pharisaical spirit .... Mk 12:38–40
Selfish ambition .... Phil 1:14–17

Ambition, worldly

A. Inspired by:
The devil .... Gn 3:1–6
.... Lk 4:5–8

Angels All Around

Tobit 12:11–15

"I can now tell you that when you, Tobit, and Sarah prayed, it was I who presented and read the record of your prayer before the Glory of the Lord; and I did the same thing when you used to bury the dead. When you did not hesitate to get up and leave your dinner in order to go and bury the dead, I was sent to put you to the test. At the same time, however, God commissioned me to heal you and your daughter-in-law Sarah. I am Raphael, one of the seven angels who enter and serve before the Glory of the Lord." **Tb 12:12–15**

Angels are in. Rather, everyone's into angels. We've got big bad angels, little lovey dovey angels, angels with wings, angels on TV, angels with baseballs. It's a good thing, too; angels are for real. St. Paul says many of us have encountered angels without even knowing it. Angels are God's messengers and special assistants. They're our constant friends, protecting, guiding, and helping us—visibly or invisibly. They are especially important during our times of crisis, and sometimes appear in human form as Raphael does in the Book of Tobit. We should call on the angels often. Each one of us has a special guardian angel of our own, and that angel's purpose is to help in all our needs, especially in our spiritual walk.

Anxiety—*a disturbed state of mind produced by real or imaginary fears*

A. Caused by:
- Brother's hatred .... Gn 32:6–12
- Son's rebellion .... 2 Sm 18:24—19:1
- King's decree .... Est 4:1–16
- Child's absence .... Lk 2:48
- Son's sickness .... Jn 4:46–49
- Friend's delay .... 2 Cor 2:12, 13

B. Overcome by:
- Trust .... Ps 37:1–5
- Reliance upon the Holy Spirit .... Mk 13:11
- God's provision .... Lk 12:22–30
- Upward look .... Lk 21:25–28
- Assurance of God's sovereignty .... Rom 8:28
- Angel's word .... Ac 27:21–25
- Prayer and thanksgiving .... Phil 4:6
- God's care .... 1 Pt 5:6, 7

Apostasy—*a falling away from God's truth*

A. Kinds of:
- National .... 1 Kgs 12:26–33
- Individual .... 2 Kgs 21:1–9
- .... Heb 3:12
- Satanic .... Rv 12:7–9
- Angelic .... 2 Pt 2:4
- General .... 2 Tm 3:1–5
- Imputed .... Acts 21:21
- Final .... 2 Thes 2:3

B. Caused by:
- Satan .... Lk 22:31
- False teachers .... Acts 20:29, 30
- Perversion of Scripture .... 2 Tm 4:3, 4
- Persecution .... Mt 13:21
- Disobedience .... Heb 4:9–11
- Love of world .... 2 Tm 4:10
- Hardened heart .... Acts 7:54–57
- Spiritual blindness .... Acts 28:25–27

C. Manifested in:
- Resisting truth .... 2 Tm 3:7, 8
- Resorting to deception .... 2 Cor 11:13–15
- Reverting to immorality .... 2 Pt 2:14, 19–22

D. Safeguards against, found in:
- God's Word .... Ps 119:11
- .... 2 Tm 3:13–17
- Spiritual growth .... 2 Pt 1:5–11
- Indoctrination .... Acts 20:29–31
- Faithfulness .... Mt 24:42–51
- Spiritual perception .... 1 Jn 4:1–6
- Being grounded in the truth .... Eph 4:13–16
- Using God's armor .... Eph 6:10–20
- Preaching the Word .... 2 Tm 4:2

E. Examples of, seen in:
- Israelites .... Ex 32:1–35
- Saul .... 1 Sm 15:11
- Solomon .... 1 Kgs 11:1–10
- Amaziah .... 2 Chr 25:14–16
- Judas .... Mt 26:14–16
- Hymenaeus and Philetus .... 2 Tm 2:17, 18
- Demas .... 2 Tm 4:10
- Godless persons .... Jude 4

Appetite—*desire to fulfill some basic need*

A. Kinds of:
- Physical .... 1 Sm 14:31–33
- Sexual .... 1 Cor 7:1–9
- Lustful .... Mt 5:28
- Insatiable .... Prv 27:20
- Spiritual .... Ps 119:20, 131

B. Perversion of, by:
- Gluttony .... Prv 23:1, 2
- Adultery .... Prv 6:24–29
- .... Ez 23:1–49
- Impurity .... Rom 1:24–32

C. Loss of, by:
- Age .... 2 Sm 19:36
- Trouble .... 1 Sm 28:21–23
- Visions .... Dn 10:2–14
- Deep concern .... Jn 4:31–34

D. Spiritual, characteristics of:
- Satisfying .... Is 55:1, 2
- Sufficient .... Mt 5:6
- Spontaneous .... Jn 7:37–39
- Sanctifying .... 1 Pt 2:2
- Sublime .... Col 3:1–3

Arts and crafts in the Bible

- Baker .... Gn 40:1
- Barber .... Ez 5:1
- Brickmaker .... Ex 5:7
- Carpenter .... Mk 6:3
- Carver .... Ex 31:5
- Cook .... 1 Sm 8:13
- Coppersmith .... 2 Tm 4:14
- Draftsman .... Ez 4:1
- Dyer .... Ex 25:1–5
- Embalmer .... Gn 50:2, 3
- Engraver .... Ex 28:11
- .... Sir 38:27
- Fisherman .... Mt 4:18
- Gardener .... Jn 20:15
- Gatekeeper .... 2 Sm 18:24–26
- Goldsmith .... Is 40:19
- Jeweler .... Ex 28:17–21

GREAT BIBLE WOMEN

Judith 9—13

"O God, my God, hear me also, a widow. It is you who were the author of those events and of what preceded and followed them. The present, also, and the future you have planned. Whatever you devise comes into being; the things you decide on come forward and say, 'Here we are!' All your ways are in readiness, and your judgment is made with foreknowledge." **Jdt 9:5–6**

James Bond, move over. Here comes Judith, the ultimate undercover agent, on a mission from God. And she's a *she.* In fact, contrary to what you might think, the Bible is full of female superheroes. Judith is one of them. Her mission? To save the Israelites from the invading Assyrians.

Judith's technique may have been a little rough around the edges (she used the old "tempt the king with your beauty and then cut off his head" approach), but you've got to admire her incredible guts. Who said women can't get the job done? Don't think about saying that to Judith if you meet her someday in heaven.

Of course, the real secret to her success was her incredible faith. Check out the prayer she says before she goes undercover and risks her life (9:2–14). Not your average bedtime prayer. Judith shows us that true strength comes not from being physically strong, but rather from completely trusting in God's deliverance.

SELF-GIVING

Acts 20:17–35

And now I commend you to God and to that gracious word of his that can build you up and give you the inheritance among all who are consecrated. I have never wanted anyone's silver or gold or clothing. You know well that these very hands have served my needs and my companions. In every way I have shown you that by hard work of that sort we must help the weak, and keep in mind the words of the Lord Jesus who himself said, "It is more blessed to give than to receive." **Acts 20:32–35**

Have you ever taken something you really cared about and given it to someone else? Maybe it was a cross or a photo or a tape of your favorite band. Remember how great it made you feel? Sure, it was great to own that item, but it was even greater to give it away.

That's a "secret" of success and happiness. The greatest and happiest people who have walked the face of the earth have been the ones who have learned this secret. It's not that we give in order to gain this happiness. We give to follow Christ's example, and in doing so we are rewarded in unexpected ways. When you give of yourself and your belongings to others, God multiplies your gift by giving you back grace and fulfillment in return. In other words, giving is the best way to multiply your investments!

Jesus said, "More blessings come from giving than from receiving." And that happiness is in both this life and the one to come.

Bereavement—*the emotional state after a loved one's death*

A. General attitudes in:
- Anguish .... Ex 12:29, 30
- Great emotion .... 2 Sm 19:1
- Complaint .... Ru 1:20, 21
- Genuine sorrow .... Gn 37:33–35
- Submission .... Jb 1:18–21

B. Christian attitudes in:
- Unlike world's .... 1 Thes 4:13–18
- Yet sorrow allowed .... Jn 11:32–35
- .... Acts 9:39
- With hope of reunion .... Jn 11:20–27

C. Unusual circumstances of, mourning:
- Forbidden .... Lv 10:6
- Of great length .... Gn 50:1–11
- Turned to joy .... Jn 11:41–44

Bigotry—*excessive prejudice; blind fanaticism*

A. Characteristics of:
- Name-calling .... Jn 8:48, 49
- Spiritual blindness .... Jn 9:39–41
- Hatred .... Acts 7:54–58
- Self-righteousness .... Phil 3:4–6
- Ignorance .... 1 Tm 1:13

B. Examples of:
- Haman .... Est 3:8–10
- The Pharisees .... Jn 8:33–48
- The Jews .... 1 Thes 2:14–16
- Saul (Paul) .... Acts 9:1, 2
- Peter .... Acts 10:14, 28

Blasphemy—*cursing God*

A. Arises out of:
- Pride .... Ps 73:9, 11
- .... Ez 35:12, 13
- Hatred .... Ps 74:18
- Injustice .... Is 52:5
- Defiance .... Is 36:15–20
- Skepticism .... Ez 9:8
- .... Mal 3:13–15
- Self-deification .... Dn 11:36, 37
- .... 2 Thes 2:4
- Unworthy conduct .... 2 Sm 12:13, 14
- .... Rom 2:24

B. Instances of:
- Job's wife .... Jb 2:9
- Shelomith's son .... Lv 24:11–16, 23
- Sennacherib .... 2 Kgs 19:4, 10, 22
- The beast .... Dn 7:25
- .... Rv 13:1, 5, 6
- Saul of Tarsus .... 1 Tm 1:13
- Gentiles .... Rom 1:28–32
- Hymenaeus .... 1 Tm 1:20

C. Those falsely accused of:
- Naboth .... 1 Kgs 21:12, 13
- Jesus .... Mt 9:2, 3
- .... Mt 26:64, 65
- Stephen .... Acts 6:11–13

D. Guilt of:
- Punishable by death .... Lv 24:11, 16
- Christ accused of .... Jn 10:33, 36

Blessings—*the gift of God's grace*

A. Physical and temporal:
- Prosperity .... Mal 3:10–12
- Peace .... Tb 7:12
- Food, clothing .... Mt 6:26, 30–33
- Sowing, harvest .... Acts 14:17
- Longevity .... Ex 20:12
- Children .... Ps 127:3–5

B. National and Israelitish:
- General .... Gn 12:1–3
- Specific .... Rom 9:4, 5
- Fulfilled .... Rom 11:1–36
- Perverted .... Rom 2:17–29
- Rejected .... Acts 13:46–52

C. Spiritual and eternal:
- Salvation .... Jn 3:16
- Election .... Eph 1:3–5
- Regeneration .... 2 Cor 5:17
- Forgiveness .... Col 1:14
- Adoption .... Rom 8:15–17
- No condemnation .... Rom 8:1
- Holy Spirit .... Acts 1:8
- Justification .... Acts 13:38, 39
- New covenant .... Heb 8:6–13
- Fatherly correction .... Heb 12:5–11
- Christ's intercession .... Rom 8:34
- Results in life and peace .... Rom 8:3–14
- Perseverance .... Jn 10:27–29
- Of God's shared glory .... Rom 8:30

ANSWER THE PHONE

Isaiah 6:8

Then I heard the voice of the Lord saying, "Whom shall I send? Who will go for us?" "Here I am," I said; "send me!" **Is 6:8**

What would you do if you got a phone call and the voice on the other end said, "Hello, it's the Lord calling. Do you have a minute to talk?" You'd probably think the guy was a phone sicky and hang up. The fact is, God does call us, and we often hang up without realizing it! Maybe we're in the middle of another phone call, and we hear the second call come in. "Hello? Oh, listen God, I'm on the other line. Can I get back to you?" We're too busy right now to work on our relationship with God, but later, OK?

That day may never come. When God calls, we must be ready—even if it's today. When Christ walked the earth, he passed by many people who were busy with life. Some were fishing, some were collecting taxes or doing thousands of other things. All were called to listen and respond to his message, but only a few actually did. How about you? As Christ passes by you this very minute, will you choose to answer his call?

COMING HOME

Matthew 18:1–14

At that time the disciples approached Jesus and said, "Who is the greatest in the kingdom of heaven?" He called a child over, placed it in their midst, and said, "Amen, I say to you, unless you turn and become like children, you will not enter the kingdom of heaven. Whoever humbles himself like this child is the greatest in the kingdom of heaven. And whoever receives one child such as this in my name receives me." **Mt 18:1–5**

Remember those carefree days of childhood when we could merrily skip down the street, pick dandelions, and dream away the day? Then one day we woke up and went off on an incredible journey filled with school, homework, parties, sports, and hundreds of other things that now compete for our time. Before we knew it, we were lost in the fast lane. Now life has become one big machine, and we're getting worn out and confused.

That's when we long for those dandelion afternoons again—those days of innocence, purity, spontaneity, and trust. And that's why Jesus told us to become like little children! He wants us to surrender ourselves to the Father in heaven so that we can once again feel that security and freedom. God is waiting for us "children" with open arms. "Show me the way, Lord. I want to become a child again and place my trust in you."

DESERT WOES

Numbers 33:1–56

The LORD spoke to Moses on the plains of Moab beside the Jericho stretch of the Jordan and said to him: "Tell the Israelites: When you go across the Jordan into the land of Canaan, drive out all the inhabitants of the land before you; destroy all their stone figures and molten images, and demolish all their high places. You shall take possession of the land and settle in it, for I have given you the land as your property. You shall apportion the land among yourselves by lot, clan by clan, assigning a large heritage to a large group and a small heritage to a small group. Wherever anyone's lot falls, there shall his property be within the heritage of his ancestral tribe. But if you do not drive out the inhabitants of the land before you, those whom you allow to remain will become as barbs in your eyes and thorns in your sides, and they will harass you in the country where you live, and I will treat you as I had intended to treat them." **Nm 33:50–56**

"Okay, we can do this the easy way, or we can do it the hard way." Why is it that we so often pick "the hard way"? Most of the time we do so because of our lack of faith.

The Israelites had escaped from Egypt into the desert, and Moses was leading them to the Promised Land, but getting there was a lot harder than they had expected. They were hungry, tired, scared, and frustrated. Soon they were like impatient children crying, "I want it NOW, Daddy!" If only they could have trusted God and held on a little longer, they would've taken the "easy way" and arrived in the Promised Land in a short time. But their complaints and sins threw them off course, and God allowed them to wander in the desert forty more years before they finally reached the land of milk and honey.

We, too, have these choices in our lives. If we reject God when he allows us to enter a desert in our life, we may end up staying in that desert for a long time. If we trust God and wait on him, we may reach the Promised Land sooner than we think.

JESUS, HE KNOWS ME

Hebrews 4:12–16

No creature is concealed from him, but everything is naked and exposed to the eyes of him to whom we must render an account. Therefore, since we have a great high priest who has passed through the heavens, Jesus, the Son of God, let us hold fast to our confession. For we do not have a high priest who is unable to sympathize with our weaknesses, but one who has similarly been tested in every way, yet without sin. So let us confidently approach the throne of grace to receive mercy and to find grace for timely help. **Heb 4:13–16**

You run, but you can't hide. You could change your name. You could move to another country. You could even have plastic surgery done so that no one would ever recognize you. But guess what? Nothing is concealed from him.

God sees better than we see ourselves. Jesus sees us when we hate, lie, love, and cry. He's here when we hide behind our masks, wanting to be someone else, ashamed of who we are. He sees beyond our walls of fear, and pride, and yeah, our walls of attitude.

He sees our nakedness behind our hair, clothes, and makeup. He sees us when we're crushed, feeling hopeless. He knows everything we've ever done, and everything we do. And the incredible thing is he still loves us. Because Jesus loves to forgive.

LOVING ENEMIES

Luke 6:27–38

"But to you who hear I say, love your enemies, do good to those who hate you, bless those who curse you, pray for those who mistreat you. To the person who strikes you on one cheek, offer the other one as well, and from the person who takes your cloak, do not withhold even your tunic." **Lk 6:27–29**

"Man, I hate that guy. Every time I say 'hi' to him, he just keeps walking and doesn't say a word. Guy's got a serious attitude problem."

Do you have an "enemy" like this, or even worse? Well, Jesus had some things to say about the people who hate us. He said to love them! Notice, he didn't just say "like" your enemies. He said "love" them. Is he out of his mind? No, he's God. And if anybody should have a complaint about someone (especially about us), it should be him. After all, our sins—yours and mine—crucified him! But Jesus loves us nonetheless. And he wants us to do the same to others. That means being respectful, understanding, helpful, and giving without expecting anything in return—not even a "hello."

Remember not to judge. You never know why a person acts the way he or she does. Only God knows. And Jesus tells us to love—no matter what. The rest is up to him.

No Hiding Place

Matthew 5:14–16

You are the light of the world. A city set on a mountain cannot be hidden. Nor do they light a lamp and then put it under a bushel basket; it is set on a lampstand, where it gives light to all in the house. Just so, your light must shine before others, that they may see your good deeds and glorify your heavenly Father. **Mt 5:14–16**

Susan and Cindy were talking . . .

"Yeah, Susan, I was just reading this article about women's rights and the whole abortion issue. I'm totally pro-choice, you know. I think the whole thing is obviously an attempt by men to control women's bodies. What do you think?"

"Well, uh, I don't know, uh, well, er. . . ."

Sound familiar? Do you clam up when you're in a position where you need to defend what you believe? Are you afraid to tell people what you really think? Are you scared to say that you're a Catholic, that you go to church, and that you actually believe in God?

That's because you've got to place more trust in God. Go for it! Remember, you're light. You've got to shine or the world will never get out of its darkness. Maybe some of your friends will reject you, but do you know what? Chances are they'll come to you later looking for answers. Time will tell which one of you is right!

RULES . . . OR JEWELS?

Leviticus 11:1–47

"For I, the LORD, am your God; and you shall make and keep yourselves holy, because I am holy. You shall not make yourselves unclean, then, by any swarming creature that crawls on the ground. Since I, the LORD, brought you up from the land of Egypt that I might be your God, you shall be holy, because I am holy. This is the law for animals and birds and for all the creatures that move about in the water or swarm on the ground, that you may distinguish between the clean and the unclean, between creatures that may be eaten and those that may not be eaten."
Lv 11:44–47

When Stephanie first started taking piano lessons, she hated them—all those monotonous scales played over and over; all those boring exercises and lectures from her instructor. If she could have quit, she would have in a second. But her parents insisted she continue. "Someday you'll thank us," they claimed. *Yeah, right.*

It took some time, but after Stephanie had mastered the basics, she began to learn some of her favorite songs. She played her piano more and more each day—even started writing her own songs. One day her mom remarked, "Well, Steph, in the beginning we could hardly get you to play the piano. Now we can't get you to stop! It looks like all the lessons finally paid off."

God's relationship with humanity in the Old Testament reads a lot like Steph's story. The moral guidelines and rules the Jews established were like the scales and exercises that enabled them to experience the "music" God could bring into their lives. Some people saw these laws as oppressive, but to believers, they were a door to freedom—the freedom that comes from following God's plans for their lives.

In the New Testament, Jesus shows us that God wants to be loved from the heart. Jesus wants us to follow the Commandments, not from a sense of duty or fear, but because we're in a loving relationship with God. That's when we discover that—just as Steph's scales gave her the freedom to write songs—following God's rules and structures can actually give us the basics for building the rest of our lives.

A LOVE STORY

Psalm 63:2–12

O God, you are my God—
for you I long!
For you my body yearns;
for you my soul thirsts,
Like a land parched, lifeless,
and without water.
So I look to you in the sanctuary
to see your power and glory.
For your love is better than life;
my lips offer you worship!
Ps 63:2–4

Johnny met Jenny, and after they dated a few months, Johnny told her he loved her. After a while, though, Johnny hardly ever called or saw Jenny anymore. He ignored her—except for about one hour a week, when he'd show up at her house, mumble a few words, then go on his way. Is it any wonder Johnny and Jenny's relationship didn't last?

Well, you just read a perfect example of the relationship a lot of us have with God. God calls us, writes us (this book is the ultimate love letter), and even visits us. Too often our response is showing up at God's house once a week, mumbling a few responses, then checking out as soon as the final song starts.

Real love can only happen when people spend time together. People who are in love share their hopes and dreams, their pains and sorrows. And they *desire* to be in each other's presence.

Next time you pray (how about right now?) open the door to your heart and ask God to be your lifetime friend—now and forever.

THE PROSTITUTE

Hosea 2:4

Protest against your mother, protest!
for she is not my wife,
and I am not her husband.
Let her remove her harlotry from before her,
her adultery from between her breasts.

Hos 2:4

Consider this scenario: You meet someone, fall madly in love, and eventually get married. You pledge your lifelong fidelity to each other. Then your spouse tires of you and has an affair. Then another affair and another. In fact, your spouse becomes a prostitute, sleeping with anyone who will pay. How long could you stay with that person? How could you continue to love such an unfaithful spouse? What if that spouse were to reform and come home asking forgiveness—how difficult would it be to forgive and forget? Almost impossible!

Yet this is exactly what God asked Hosea to do—because God wanted people to understand what he has done for us, over and over again. Even after we've "cheated" on God through our sins, we are always welcomed home and promised that our Lord will "forgive and forget"—we must simply ask for it.

TOPICAL INDEX

LIVING IN DENIAL

Mark 14:66–72

While Peter was below in the courtyard, one of the high priest's maids came along. Seeing Peter warming himself, she looked intently at him and said, "You too were with the Nazarene, Jesus." But he denied it saying, "I neither know nor understand what you are talking about." So he went out into the outer court. (Then the cock crowed.) **Mk 14:66–68**

It's so easy to live in denial. We're embarrassed or afraid about something, so we deny it. Lying and covering up seem like the easiest solutions. But as long as we deny the truth, we won't be at peace. Living in truth *can* set us free, if we honestly look inside our hearts. That means taking a spotlight and shining it into our souls, looking at the wrongs we've done and the wrongs that have been done to us, and then making amends. Sometimes that means saying "I'm sorry," and other times it means doing something even more difficult—accepting someone else's "I'm sorry."

PUTTING OTHERS FIRST

Luke 14:7–11

For everyone who exalts himself will be humbled, but the one who humbles himself will be exalted. **Lk 14:11**

We live in a "me first" society. Being pushy, nosy, forceful, rude, self-seeking, and even bullheaded are applauded as being "assertive." Getting as close as possible to "famous people" somehow makes us important. But today's "stars" are tomorrow's "has-beens," and we can become "nobodies" instantly. That's humiliating.

Jesus offers us an alternative. Be grateful for everything we get, even if it's a ticket to the ball game in the "nosebleed" section. If we put others first, we'll show that God is Number One in our lives. And remember, God is now looking for people to star in a major new production called "Heaven." It's the longest-running production in history. It's gotten rave reviews. And every seat in the theater is in the front row! God needs new "stars" there. But they have to have a special talent on their resumé. It's called humility.

D. Fruits of:
- Faithfulness .... Mt 24:45–47
- Gentleness .... 1 Thes 2:7
- Patience .... Col 1:10–12
- Love .... 1 Jn 3:14
- Obedience .... Rom 15:18
- Peacefulness .... Jas 3:17, 18
- Self-control .... 2 Pt 1:6
- Self-denial .... Jn 12:25

Courage—*fearlessness in the face of danger*

A. Manifested:
- Among enemies .... Ezr 5:1–17
- In battle .... 1 Sm 17:46
- Against great foes .... Jgs 7:7–23
- Against great odds .... 1 Sm 17:32, 50
- When threatened .... Dn 3:16–18
- When intimidated .... Dn 6:7–13
- When facing death .... Jgs 16:28–30
- In youth .... 1 Sm 14:6–45
- In old age .... Jos 14:10–12
- Before a king .... Est 4:8, 16
- In moral crises .... Neh 13:1–31
- In preaching Christ .... Acts 3:12–26
- In rebuking .... Gal 2:11–15

B. Men, encouraged to:
- Leaders .... Dt 31:7
- Joshua .... Jos 1:5–7
- Gideon .... Jgs 7:7–11
- Philistines .... 1 Sm 4:9
- Zerubbabel .... Hg 2:4
- Solomon .... 1 Chr 28:20

C. Examples of:
- Caleb .... Jos 14:12
- Jonathan .... 1 Sm 14:6
- David .... 1 Sm 17:32
- Nehemiah .... Neh 6:11
- Daniel .... Dn 6:11
- Christ .... Jn 19:10, 11

Cross—*a method of execution*

A. Used literally of:
- Christ's death .... Mt 27:32

B. Used figuratively of:
- Duty .... Mt 10:38
- Christ's sufferings .... 1 Cor 1:17
- The Christian faith .... 1 Cor 1:18
- Reconciliation .... Eph 2:16

CARRYING THE CROSS

Mark 8:34–38

He summoned the crowd with his disciples and said to them, "Whoever wishes to come after me must deny himself, take up his cross, and follow me. For whoever wishes to save his life will lose it, but whoever loses his life for my sake and that of the gospel will save it. What profit is there for one to gain the whole world and forfeit his life?" **Mk 8:34–36**

You may be rich. You may be famous. You may be on the top of the world. But if you're a human being, you still have *a cross to bear*. It may be a birth defect, or a physical or mental challenge, or a disease or psychosis. For some, it may be brokenness from physical, emotional, or sexual abuse. Maybe it's a dysfunctional family, poverty, or unemployment. Whatever it is, each person knows his or her cross, because it's usually the thing we try to run away from. We want to avoid the pain, but Jesus showed us how to transform our pain into LIFE: by offering it to God. Jesus asked us to pick up that cross of pain and follow him. This enables us to grow spiritually so that we can better serve the needs of others.

Yes, we all have crosses. The difference is, a Christian carries the cross with the help of Christ. And that's how our cross leads us to . . . eternal life!

Dance—*an emotional movement of the body*

A. Kinds of:
- Joyful .... Ps 30:12
- Evil .... Ex 32:19

B. Designed to:
- Express joy in victory .... 1 Sm 18:6, 7
- Greet a returning son .... Lk 15:21–25
- Rejoice in the Lord .... 2 Sm 6:14–16
- Inflame lust .... Mt 14:6

C. Performed by:
- Children .... Mt 11:16, 17
- Women .... Jgs 11:34
- David .... 2 Sm 6:14–16
- Worshipers .... Ps 149:3

Death, eternal

A. Described as:
- Eternal punishment .... Mt 25:46
- Resurrection of condemnation .... Jn 5:29
- God's wrath .... 1 Thes 1:10
- Destruction .... 2 Thes 1:9 .... 2 Pt 2:12
- Second death .... Rv 20:14

B. Truths regarding:
- A consequence of man's sin .... Gn 3:17–19

For or Against?

Acts 9:1–6

On his journey, as he was nearing Damascus, a light from the sky suddenly flashed around him. He fell to the ground and heard a voice saying to him, "Saul, Saul, why are you persecuting me?" He said, "Who are you, sir?" The reply came, "I am Jesus, whom you are persecuting. Now get up and go into the city and you will be told what you must do."
Acts 9:3–6

Jim got in his car and jammed it into reverse. SLAM! He forgot to look in his rearview mirror before he backed out. His mom's car was right behind his. . . .

We have to think before we act. Sometimes one little failure to think can have disastrous effects. That's why Jesus wants us to always bring him into the important decisions we make in life. When we're faced with a choice between two things, we can ask ourselves, "Which way will lead me closer to God?"

We can ask other people we trust to help us choose as well. Sometimes those other people—particularly parents, teachers, and leaders at church—know the way better than we do because they've been down it before. They *know* that car is waiting behind us and we're about to slam into it!

Let's make it a habit to think before we act. Jesus is ready to help. He's always right behind us to be our support—we just have to look in the rearview mirror before we pull out.

RADICAL DEVOTION

Ruth 1:16–17

But Ruth said, "Do not ask me to abandon or forsake you! for wherever you go I will go, wherever you lodge I will lodge, your people shall be my people, and your God my God. Wherever you die I will die, and there be buried. May the LORD do so and so to me, and more besides, if aught but death separates me from you!" **Ru 1:16–17**

Ruth might have a tough time today. Why? Because devotion and commitment—the two words that describe her perfectly—seem in danger of being removed from our "disposable society," in which it's easier to replace devotion with "division" and commitment with "comfort."

When something in life becomes difficult, we tend to remove ourselves from it and seek something more comfortable. Getting rid of the uncomfortable things in life is as common as channel surfing the TV until you find a show you like. If Ruth had taken that approach, no one would have remembered her, she would not be one of Jesus' ancestors, and millions of people would never have been blessed by the story of her life.

Selfishness dies with the self, but self*less*ness lives on through others. Ruth is remembered because her love wasn't self-oriented; it was other-oriented. By committing herself to serving others, Ruth's love didn't die when she died. It lived on for thousands of years—all the way up to your reading of this passage today.

God shows us this same unending devotion. Through good and bad, God continues to love us. Where we go, God will go. When we call, God will be there. When we are in need, God will never fail us.

Difficulties—*problems hard to solve*

A. Kinds of:
Mental ... Ps 139:6
Moral ... Ps 38:2–23
Theological ... Jn 6:48–60

B. Examples of:
Birth of a child in old age ... Gn 18:9–15
Testing of Abraham ... Gn 22:1–14
Slaughter of Canaanites ... Ex 23:27–33
God's providence ... Ps 44:2–27
Prosperity of wicked ... Ps 73:1–28
Israel's unbelief ... Jn 12:39–41

C. Negative attitudes toward:
Rebellion against ... Nm 21:4, 5
Unbelief under ... Heb 3:12–19

D. Positive attitudes toward:
Submission under ... Nm 14:7–9
Prayer concerning ... Mk 11:23, 24
Admission of ... 2 Pt 3:15, 16

Disappointment—*the non-fulfillment of one's hopes*

A. Concerning one's:
Sons ... 1 Sm 2:12–17
Mate ... 1 Sm 25:23–31
Failure ... 2 Sm 17:23
Wisdom ... Eccl 1:12–18
Acceptance ... Jer 20:7–9
Mission ... Jon 4:1–9
Hopes ... Lk 24:17–24

B. Antidotes against:
Let trust prevail ... Hb 3:17–19
Put God first ... Hg 1:2–15
Accept God's plan ... Rom 8:28
Remember God's promises ... Heb 6:10–12

Discipleship—*adherence to a teacher's faith*

A. Tests of:
Obedience ... Jn 14:15
Faithfulness ... Jn 15:8
Perseverance ... Jn 8:31
Love ... Jn 13:35
Humility ... Mt 10:24, 25
Surrender of all ... Lk 14:26, 33
Bearing the cross ... Mt 16:24

B. Rewards of:
Acknowledged by Christ ... Mt 12:49, 50
Enlightened by Christ ... Jn 8:12
Guided by the Spirit ... Jn 16:13
Honored by the Father ... Jn 12:26

Discouragement—*depression of one's spirits*

A. Causes of:
Heavy burden ... Nm 11:10–15
Defeat ... Jos 7:7–9
Apparent failure ... 1 Kgs 19:2–4
Sickness ... Is 38:9–20

B. Responses to:
"Why are you here?" ... 1 Kgs 19:9–18
"Cast your care upon the LORD" ... Ps 55:22
"Come away by yourselves" ... Mk 6:31
"Raise your heads" ... Lk 21:28

Dishonesty—*untruthfulness*

A. Manifested in:
Half-truths ... Gn 12:11–20
Trickery ... Gn 27:6–29
Falsifying one's word ... Gn 34:1–31
Wicked devices ... Prv 1:10–19
Theft ... Jn 12:4–6
Unpaid wages ... Jas 5:4

B. Consequences of:
Uncovered by God ... 1 Kgs 21:17–26
Uncovered by men ... Jos 9:3–23
Condemned by conscience ... Mt 27:3–5

Generation ....Mt 12:39
Age...Gal 1:4
Our days...................................Eph 5:16
Conscience..............................Heb 10:22
Spirits.......................................Mt 12:45

C. Satan as "the Evil One":
Lord safeguards against ....Jn 17:15

D. The Christian should guard against:
Heart of unfaithfulness ....Heb 3:12
Judgments ....Jas 2:4
Boastings...................................Jas 4:16
Works ....2 Jn 9–11
Every kind...........................1 Thes 5:22

Example—*a pattern to follow*

A. Purposes of:
Set forth sin's punishment ....2 Pt 2:6
Show unbelief's consequences
....Heb 4:11
Restrain from evil............1 Cor 10:6–11
Illustrate humility..............Jn 13:14, 15
....1 Pt 3:5
Exemplify patience ....Jas 5:10, 11
....1 Pt 2:20–22
Portray Christian conduct........Phil 3:17

BE AN EXAMPLE

John 13:12–17

So when he had washed their feet (and) put his garments back on and reclined at table again, he said to them, "Do you realize what I have done for you? You call me 'teacher' and 'master,' and rightly so, for indeed I am. If I, therefore, the master and teacher, have washed your feet, you ought to wash one another's feet. I have given you a model to follow, so that as I have done for you, you should also do." **Jn 13:12–15**

If you want to learn how to play basketball well, you watch the top NBA players. If you want to learn how to ski well, you watch the Olympic champions. But if you want to learn how to live a good, holy life, Jesus is *the* example. Jesus showed us everything we need to know about living. He showed us that we must live to serve others. He cared for the sick and the poor, obeyed his Father's will, comforted those who were sorrowing, and gave his life on the cross after never having committed a single crime.

Jesus was the example. But guess what? We have to be an example, too. Because the only way people can see Jesus today is *through* us! How well do others see Christ in us? If people never had a chance to speak to us, would they still know we are Christians by the way we act? Remember, *we* may be the only Bible they read.

B. Of evil men:
Greed—Achan ....Jos 7:20, 21
Immorality—Eli's sons
....1 Sm 2:22–25
Rebellion—Saul..............1 Sm 15:17–23
Folly—Nabal...................1 Sm 25:25–37
Idolatry—Jeroboam ....1 Kgs 12:26–33

C. Of good men:
Faith—Caleb ....Jos 14:6–15
Fidelity—Joshua ....Jos 24:15–25
Courage—David.............1 Sm 17:32–37
Holy life—Daniel.................Ez 14:14, 20
Perseverance—Job ....Jas 5:10, 11
Christian living—Paul ....Phil 3:17

Faith—*confidence in the testimony of another*

A. Nature of:
Produced by the Spirit.........Gal 5:22, 23
Work of God ....Jn 6:29
God's gift ....Eph 2:8
Comes from the heart ....Rom 10:9, 10
Substance of unseen things.......Heb 11:1

BELIEVING WITHOUT SEEING

John 20:24–29

Thomas, called Didymus, one of the Twelve, was not with them when Jesus came. So the other disciples said to him, "We have seen the Lord." But he said to them, "Unless I see the mark of the nails in his hands and put my finger into the nailmarks and put my hand into his side, I will not believe." **Jn 20:24–25**

You don't always need to see to believe. When was the last time you saw an atom? A duck-billed platypus? How about George Washington? Most of us have never seen these, but *we believe* that they exist . . . or existed. It's the same with our belief in God. We've never seen Jesus "in person." We've never touched his hands and side. But Jesus *has* seen us. And if we know him, he *has* touched our hands and our side. We rely on what others tell us about history, and we believe. Now let's rely on what Jesus is telling us inside. Then we'll truly believe.

B. Results from:
Scriptures ....Jn 20:30, 31

SEA CRUISE

Exodus 14:21–31

Then Moses stretched out his hand over the sea, and the LORD swept the sea with a strong east wind throughout the night and so turned it into dry land. When the water was thus divided, the Israelites marched into the midst of the sea on dry land, with the water like a wall to their right and to their left. **Ex 14:21–22**

Imagine standing on a beach with your friends, looking out over the ocean, raising your arm out over the water, and telling it to open before you into dry land. Your friends would think you were a wee bit tweaked in the head. And they'd be right.

The difference between you standing on a beach and Moses standing in front of the Red Sea is that one of you has a powerful purpose, a driving faith, and God's unfailing promise. Can you guess which one that would be? Moses was on a mission from God, and nothing was going to stop him. He faced the impossible with faith, and it became possible. What you need to remember is that Moses isn't the only one called to such a task. All of us have a powerful purpose in this life, and all of us can see our faith make impossible things possible. It may not be through parting great bodies of water, but it will still be spectacular in its own way—if we *believe.*

SEEING IS BELIEVING

John 4:39–42

Many more began to believe in him because of his word, and they said to the woman, "We no longer believe because of your word; for we have heard for ourselves, and we know that this is truly the savior of the world." **Jn 4:41–42**

Why do I believe? Because my parents told me to? Because my teachers taught me to? Do I *really* believe or just know what everyone else has told me?

There comes a time when each one of us has to find out the truth about life, faith, and God by ourselves. We have to "own" our faith. We can only do that by seeking Jesus ourselves, in ways that are comfortable for us, with the help of the Church and other believers. When we see God with our own eyes of faith, then our faith will be our own.

I. Examples of, in Old Testament:
- Abel........Heb 11:4
- Enoch........Heb 11:5
- Noah........Heb 11:7
- Abraham........Rom 4:16–20
- Sarah........Heb 11:11
- Jacob........Heb 11:21
- Joseph........Heb 11:22
- Moses........Heb 11:23–29
- Caleb........Jos 14:6, 12
- Rahab........Heb 11:31
- Jonathan........1 Sm 14:6
- David........1 Sm 17:37
- Jehoshaphat........2 Chr 20:5, 12
- Three Hebrew captives........Dn 3:16, 17
- Job........Jb 19:25
- Others........Heb 11:32–39

J. Examples of, in New Testament:
- Roman centurion........Mt 8:5–10
- Jairus........Mk 5:22, 23
- Sick woman........Mk 5:25–34
- Syrophoenician woman........Mk 7:24–30
- Bartimaeus........Mk 10:46–52
- Sinful woman........Lk 7:36–50
- Ten lepers........Lk 17:11–19
- Royal official........Jn 4:46–54
- Mary and Martha........Jn 11:1–32
- Thomas........Jn 20:24–29
- Multitudes........Acts 5:14
- Stephen........Acts 6:8
- Samaritans........Acts 8:5–12
- Ethiopian official........Acts 8:26–39
- Barnabas........Acts 11:22–24
- Lydia........Acts 16:14, 15
- Philippian jailer........Acts 16:25–34
- Paul........Acts 27:23–25

Family

A. Founded on:
- Divine creation........Gn 1:27, 28
- Marriage........Mt 19:6
- Monogamy........Mt 19:5
- ....1 Tm 3:2, 12
- Honoring parents........Ex 20:12
- Subordination of children........Eph 6:1–3
- Training from fathers........Eph 6:4
- Common concern........Lk 16:27, 28

B. Disturbed by:
- Polygamy........Gn 16:1–6
- Jealousy........Gn 37:3, 4, 18–27
- Hatred........Gn 4:5, 8
- Deceit........Gn 37:31–35
- Ambition........2 Sm 15:1–16
- Waywardness........Lk 15:11–18
- Insubordination........Gn 34:6–31
- Unbelief........Jn 7:3–10
- Lust........Gn 34:1–31

C. Unity of:
- Husband and wife........1 Cor 7:3
- Parents and children........Jer 35:1–19
- Faith........2 Tm 1:5
- Baptism........Acts 16:14, 15

D. Worship in:
- Led by the father........Gn 18:19
- Instructed in the Scriptures........Eph 6:4
- Observing religious rites ....Acts 10:2, 47, 48
- Common consecration........Jos 24:15

Fasting—*abstaining from physical nourishment*

A. Occasions of:
- Public disasters........1 Sm 31:11–13
- Private emotions........1 Sm 1:7
- Grief........2 Sm 12:16
- Anxiety........Dn 6:18–20
- Approaching danger........Est 4:16
- National repentance........1 Sm 7:5, 6
- Sad news........Neh 1:4
- Sacred ordination........Acts 13:3

B. Accompaniments of:
- Prayer........Lk 2:37
- Confession........Neh 9:1, 2
- Mourning........Jl 2:12
- Humiliation........Neh 9:1

FAST . . . IT'S A BLAST

Mark 2:18–20

The disciples of John and of the Pharisees were accustomed to fast. People came to him and objected, "Why do the disciples of John and the disciples of the Pharisees fast, but your disciples do not fast?" Jesus answered them, "Can the wedding guests fast while the bridegroom is with them? As long as they have the bridegroom with them they cannot fast. But the days will come when the bridegroom is taken away from them, and then they will fast on that day." **Mk 2:18–20**

"Oh no. It's Good Friday again! Didn't we just have Good Friday? This means I have to fast again. . . ."

When we think of fasting, starvation usually comes to mind. Or fish. Or bread and water. But fasting wasn't meant to be a torture, but a blast of spiritual fortification! It's something we do to tune our spiritual radios to God's frequency. The space we create by "doing without" is the space that God fills.

Fasting is part of the practice of our Catholic faith during the season of Lent (the forty days before Easter), but it's also good to fast at other times as well. Try this: Do a music or TV fast—no TV or music for a week or a month! ("Aaaahhhhh, are you kidding?") Try a gossip fast—hold the latest dirt inside for a whole week! Or a video game fast. Whatever. Make up your own fast. Radical life alterations are guaranteed.

TOPICAL INDEX

Fear—*anxiety caused by approaching danger*

Fear, godly (reverence for God)

Fellowship—*sharing together*

NOBODY'S FOOL

Joshua 6:6–20

So he had the ark of the LORD circle the city, going once around it, after which they returned to camp for the night. Early the next morning, Joshua had the priests take up the ark of the LORD. The seven priests bearing the ram's horns marched in front of the ark of the LORD, blowing their horns. Ahead of these marched the picked troops, while the rear guard followed the ark of the LORD, and the blowing of horns was kept up continually. On this second day they again marched around the city once before returning to camp; and for six days in all they did the same. On the seventh day, beginning at daybreak, they marched around the city seven times in the same manner; on that day only did they march around the city seven times. The seventh time around, the priests blew the horns and Joshua said to the people, "Now shout, for the LORD has given you the city!" **Jos 6:11–16**

Call someone a fool, and you can expect one of the following in return: a frown, a frustration, or a fist. Being a fool is not on society's top ten list of promising careers. Yet every hero in the Bible was a fool in the world's eyes at one time or another.

Can you imagine being Joshua as he tells the Israelites, especially the soldiers, that the way they're going to conquer Jericho's walls is not by brute force but rather by strolling around the outside of the city blowing horns and shouting? No doubt some of the soldiers were having a hearty laugh and the rest of the people their doubts about this outlandish military approach! And no one would have been laughing more than the people of Jericho, who probably thought the Israelites were drunk. But just when God's strategy seemed the most ridiculous—BOOM—the walls of Jericho came tumbling down, and the city was conquered.

God loves to work this way. When we become fools for God, willing to do anything that is asked of us no matter how crazy it may seem, then God will work incredible miracles through us. Don't be anybody's fool—except God's.

PRAYER RULES GOD

2 Chronicles 33:10–13

In this distress, he began to appease the LORD, his God. He humbled himself abjectly before the God of his fathers and prayed to him. The LORD let himself be won over: he heard his prayer and restored him to his kingdom in Jerusalem. Then Manasseh understood that the LORD is indeed God. **2 Chr 33:12–13**

Have you ever been so hurt by someone that you think you could never forgive them? Now imagine if that person came to you and apologized. You might be able to forgive, but you'd still have a tough time giving the person a big hug and saying, "Hey, it's cool. I love you as much as I always have."

Yet that is exactly what God does for us, over and over again, every time we admit we've sinned. In this passage, God's justice has come down strong on Manasseh because of his sins and those of the people of Judah. In his distress, Manasseh called out to God, and asked for forgiveness. Immediately, God put the past sins aside, accepted Manasseh's repentance, and restored him to the kingdom.

There's an expression that says, "God rules humans, but prayer rules God." When we humble ourselves in prayer and repentance before God, we will find that God always responds with love and forgiveness.

GOD'S LOYALTY CODE

Obadiah 10

Because of violence to your brother Jacob,
disgrace shall cover you
and you shall be destroyed forever.
Ob 10

In the armed forces, there's a code of loyalty between soldiers, which says that you would willingly give your life to save the life of a fellow soldier. You'd stand in the line of fire to protect him; you'd rush onto the battlefield to rescue him if he was wounded; you'd be tortured and killed before you'd tell the enemy how to get to him.

God respects this kind of loyalty—especially when it's shown between family members. Here we see a sad division between the Edomites and the Israelites, who are cousins. Not only did the Edomites refuse to help the Israelites when they were attacked by Babylon. They even added to the attack by looting the conquered cities.

This is a wakeup call for all who have long-standing hatred or bitterness within their family. Now is the time to ask for God's strength to forgive and to ask forgiveness from God. Only then can we fully receive the Lord's forgiveness in our own lives.

Faithful Friends

Daniel 3:13–18

Shadrach, Meshach, and Abednego answered King Nebuchadnezzar, "There is no need for us to defend ourselves before you in this matter. If our God, whom we serve, can save us from the white-hot furnace and from your hands, O king, may he save us! But even if he will not, know, O king, that we will not serve your god or worship the golden statue which you set up." **Dn 3:16–18**

Have you ever noticed how much easier it is to handle something difficult if you're not the only one facing the challenge? Like studying for a final, doing chores, or stepping into a fiery furnace to be roasted alive. The incredible story of Shadrach, Meshach, and Abednego is an example of God's amazing miracles, as well as an example of "strength in numbers." These guys stuck together, and they were stronger because of it. They were like the Three Musketeers. They ate together, learned together, got promoted together, and were willing to die together. They supported each other in their commitment to God, even if it meant roasting in Nebuchadnezzar's furnace.

It's very important to have friends who support us in our faith. We need to surround ourselves with people who will spur us on to holiness, not drag us away from it. The old saying, "You are what company you keep" is absolutely true. God must be our best friend. As we "hang" with God more, that sometimes means we'll hang with certain friends less, because they're not interested in God. But the closer we get to God, the more we'll meet new, *true* friends, and these will be the friends who will stay united with us to the end—and beyond.

Going for the Gold

Philippians 3:1–21

It is not that I have already taken hold of it or have already attained perfect maturity, but I continue my pursuit in hope that I may possess it, since I have indeed been taken possession of by Christ (Jesus). Brothers, I for my part do not consider myself to have taken possession. Just one thing: forgetting what lies behind but straining forward to what lies ahead, I continue my pursuit toward the goal, the prize of God's upward calling, in Christ Jesus. **Phil 3:12–14**

The thrill of victory. The agony of defeat. The game: life. And we're all playing. Some of us are on the front line. Some of us are on the assist. And some of us are referees or coaches. But each one of us has a specific race to run, a specific gift to use, a specific *reason* for being here. We can run like turtles. Or we can run like there's no tomorrow. We can fall down and give up. Or we can pick ourselves up and try again. But one thing's for sure: Unless we run as a team, *none* of us is going to win. Teamwork will help us reach the goal: life with God in heaven, where we'll be a team forever.

COASTING OR ROASTING?

Deuteronomy 13:1–19

The LORD, your God, shall you follow, and him shall you fear; his commandment shall you observe, and his voice shall you heed, serving him and holding fast to him alone. **Dt 13:5**

All right, we need to talk about another side of God here. It's the *tough* side of God—the *just* side. The side no one likes to talk about, but look at it this way: The sun is warm and beautiful. It brings life, lights up the day, and can even give you a great tan to wow your friends. The sun can also fry you like an egg, roast you like a shish kebab, or flat out kill you. It's all in the way you approach the sun. If you respect its power, it will bring you life; if you ignore its power, it can bring you death.

Get it? God's love is powerful and bright. When you're living in that love, you will grow and flourish like a flower in the sun. When you're going against that love, it becomes "tough love" that can burn you. This punishment is actually God's *loving* way of burning away the junk in your life so that you can become spiritually fit. It's up to us whether we want to coast in God's love or roast in God's justice.

Crooked Threads

Genesis 37:1–36; 39:1—40:23

Israel loved Joseph best of all his sons, for he was the child of his old age; and he had made him a long tunic. When his brothers saw that their father loved him best of all his sons, they hated him so much that they would not even greet him. **Gn 37:3–4**

A lady opened a large box with a special present inside. She pulled out the gift and unraveled what appeared to be a large rug with tangled threads of various colors and no apparent pattern. Not knowing what to make of the mess, she turned to her family and offered a puzzled "Thank you." As the family laughed, her son replied, "Mom, turn it over. It's a tapestry!" Doing so, she discovered a beautiful image.

Sometimes our lives may seem like that jumble, but we aren't the first to have messed up lives. Think about poor Joseph. He was sold by his brothers, put in prison, forgotten. Like Joseph, many of us have lives that resemble the twisted, tangled back-side of a tapestry. We may experience tragedies and setbacks and find ourselves in a mess. That's when God can get hold of us, and with a simple flick of the wrist, he can turn us over so that we discover the masterpiece that our life really is. Each twisted thread in our past suddenly serves a purpose, and we realize everything that has happened in our lives can be worked for good.

The World's Opinion

Job 11:1–20

If you set your heart aright
and stretch out your hands toward him,
If you remove all iniquity from your conduct,
and let not injustice dwell in your tent,
Surely then you may lift up your face in innocence;
you may stand firm and unafraid.
For then you shall forget your misery,
or recall it like waters that have ebbed away.
Then your life shall be brighter than the noonday;
its gloom shall become as the morning,
And you shall be secure, because there is hope;
you shall look round you and lie down in safety,
and you shall take your rest with none to disturb.

Jb 11:13–19

"You can please some of the people some of the time, but you can't please all of the people all of the time." What does this really mean? It means that every one of us is going to have someone who hates, misjudges, or condemns us in this life. It doesn't matter who you are—even Mother Theresa was a villian in some people's eyes!

So what's most important is not what the world says about you, but rather what God says. Your friends may fail you, your family may fail you, even your dog may fail you, but God will never fail you.

That's what the Book of Job is really all about.

Job's "friends" told him he must have done something terribly wrong to have brought those curses upon his life (losing his family, his possessions, his health). They said, "Buddy, you're messed up! Obviously, you must have done something wrong." Thanks, guys. Appreciate the support.

Job's only true support came from his steadfast faith in God's goodness. Somehow, through all the suffering, he had to believe that God had a plan and that it was a good one. He held on firmly to that belief, and it paid off. In the end—well, you have to read the story to find out the ending. Let's just say, God rewards those who persevere in faith.

SEEING REALITY

Mark 10:46–52

Jesus said to him in reply, "What do you want me to do for you?" The blind man replied to him, "Master, I want to see." Jesus told him, "Go your way; your faith has saved you." Immediately he received his sight and followed him on the way. **Mk 10:51–52**

Sometimes we walk through life in a fog. Everything is hazy. We can't really see where we're headed. Then God comes to us with big, colorful glasses and says, "Here, try these on. I think you'll like what you see." We begin to see through the eyes of faith. For the first time we really see the truth.

But you know, those glasses might look funny to other people. Are we willing to take the ridicule, misunderstanding, and sacrifice that come with wearing them? And are we willing to turn away from falsehood and sin when we see them through those special glasses? If we are, then let us say, "Jesus, I believe. I want to see." He has plenty of glasses in stock.

REJECTION

John 15:18–27

"If the world hates you, realize that it hated me first. If you belonged to the world, the world would love its own; but because you do not belong to the world, and I have chosen you out of the world, the world hates you." **Jn 15:18–19**

You may be smart. You may be good-looking. You may be popular. But sooner or later, you'll find that it's impossible to go through life being liked by everyone. "You can please some of the people some of the time, but you can't please all of the people all the time." There will be people who disagree with us on hundreds of different issues. They'll reject us as being weird, old-fashioned, party-poopers, nerds, wimps, geeks, anti-or-pro-whatever wannabees. We'll be labeled and trashed like factory rejects.

Well, rejection is a part of life. If we expect to win everyone over to our side, we're just fooling ourselves. If Jesus couldn't do it, we won't be able to either. We can do our best and let God do the rest.

HOLY LIVING?

Ephesians 4:25–32

Therefore, putting away falsehood, speak the truth, each one to his neighbor, for we are members one of another. Be angry but do not sin; do not let the sun set on your anger, and do not leave room for the devil. The thief must no longer steal, but rather labor, doing honest work with his (own) hands, so that he may have something to share with one in need. No foul language should come out of your mouths, but only such as is good for needed edification, that it may impart grace to those who hear. And do not grieve the holy Spirit of God, with which you were sealed for the day of redemption. All bitterness, fury, anger, shouting, and reviling must be removed from you, along with all malice. (And) be kind to one another, compassionate, forgiving one another as God has forgiven you in Christ. **Eph 4:25–32**

Tommy had a reputation for being "BAD." His buddies thought that was pretty cool. In other words, they thought "bad" was *good*. Then one day Tommy got caught committing a crime, and he was thrown in jail. Apparently, the rest of society thought being bad was actually bad. Now Tommy was paying for it.

Being BAD (Basic Attitude Destroyers) has messed up the world. So St. Paul gives us a solution. It's being "RAD" (Radical Alternative Disciples). It's being right with God, and making a move in the right direction—toward holiness. It's waking up in the morning and saying, "Today, Lord, I'm going to be radical, in a good way, for you." Pretty soon even your friends might see that HOLY RADICAL is the only radical to be. (Check out Colossians 3:5–17 also.)

Holy Spirit

SPIRIT POWER

Joel 3:1–2

Then afterward I will pour out
  my spirit upon all mankind.
Your sons and daughters shall prophesy,
  your old men shall dream dreams,
  your young men shall see visions;
Even upon the servants and the handmaids,
  in those days, I will pour out my spirit.

Jl 3:1–2

When you come home one evening, try fixing your dinner, doing your homework, playing your new CD, watching your favorite TV show, and surfing the Internet—all without any electricity. You won't get very far. Every appliance, every light bulb, every electronic gadget relies on that electrical current to make it come alive. Without it, they're worthless.

That's how it is with us and the Holy Spirit. Without the power of God's Spirit flowing through us, we would be lifeless blobs. We depend on God for everything: our mind, our body, our soul, our very breath. Joel's prophecy of the coming of the Holy Spirit in a new and exciting way came to pass in the New Testament (see Acts 2). Now the Holy Spirit is available to all people through a relationship with Jesus Christ. Jesus is the socket we can "plug into" to access the power of the Holy Spirit.

Wealthy and Wise

Mark 12:38–44

He sat down opposite the treasury and observed how the crowd put money into the treasury. Many rich people put in large sums. A poor widow also came and put in two small coins worth a few cents. Calling his disciples to himself, he said to them, "Amen, I say to you, this poor widow put in more than all the other contributors to the treasury. For they have all contributed from their surplus wealth, but she, from her poverty, has contributed all she had, her whole livelihood." **Mk 12:41–44**

Being blessed with wealth can trap us into being greedy, stingy, and snobbish. It can also tempt us to "false charity," where our charitable works are a performance to satisfy our guilt. But God knows when we're giving from our hearts and when our donations are a real sacrifice. God knows when we cheat someone out of fair pay, when we get too much change at the checkout and keep it, or when we find a wallet and keep the money inside. God knows that we're really cheating ourselves.

WHY ME?

Exodus 3:11–15

God spoke further to Moses, "Thus shall you say to the Israelites: The LORD, the God of your fathers, the God of Abraham, the God of Isaac, the God of Jacob, has sent me to you.
'This is my name forever;
this is my title for all generations.' "
Ex 3:15

Scott, a high-school sophomore on the junior varsity football team, was amazed that his football coach asked him to try out for the varsity team. "But, Coach, I don't have all that it takes to handle that yet, do I?" Scott asked.

"You have the most important skill of all," his coach replied. "You're humble enough to let me show you how to succeed."

Moses wondered why in the world God would choose him for such a monumental task as leading almost a million folks out of Egypt to the Promised Land. God's reasoning was simple: Moses was willing to listen and obey. Unlike some leaders whose ego-inflated heads lead them to believe they can do anything by their own power, Moses knew he couldn't do anything without God's power. What God wants most is our total commitment to him. God is our coach, and God knows best how we can win big in the game of life. What could *you* do if you really turned your life over to God?

Clothe yourselves......1 Pt 5:5
Be humble......Eph 4:1, 2
Avoid false......Col 2:18–23

E. Examples of:
Abraham......Gn 18:27, 32
Jacob......Gn 32:10, 11
Moses......Ex 3:11
Joshua......Jos 7:6
David......1 Sm 18:18–23
Job......Jb 42:2–6
Jeremiah......Jer 1:6
Daniel......Dn 2:30
Elizabeth......Lk 1:43
John the Baptist......Jn 3:29, 30
Mary......Luke 1:46–48
Jesus......Mt 11:29
Paul......Acts 20:19

Hypocrisy, hypocrite—*showy, empty display of religion*

A. Kinds of:
Worldly......Mt 23:5–7
Legalistic......Rom 10:3
Evangelical......2 Pt 2:10–22
Satanic......2 Cor 11:13–15

B. Described as:
Self-righteous......Lk 18:11, 12
"Too sacred for you"......Is 65:5
Blind......Mt 23:17–26
Greedy......2 Pt 2:3
Showy......Mt 6:2, 5, 16
Highly critical......Mt 7:3–5
Indignant......Lk 13:14–16
Bound by traditions......Mt 15:1–9
Neglectful of major duties
......Mt 23:23, 24
Hearing but not obeying
......Ez 33:31, 32
Interested in the externals
......Lk 20:46, 47
Inwardly unregenerate......Lk 11:39

C. Examples of:
Jacob......Gn 27:6–35
Jacob's sons......Gn 37:29–35
Delilah......Jgs 16:4–20
Ishmael......Jer 41:6, 7
Herod......Mt 2:7, 8
Pharisees......Jn 8:4–9
Judas......Mt 26:25–49
Ananias and Sapphira......Acts 5:1–10
Kephas (Peter)......Gal 2:11–14

I AM—*a statement indicating divine existence or a divine name*

A. Revealed to:
Isaac......Gn 26:24
Jacob......Gn 28:13
Moses......Ex 6:6

B. Expressing uniqueness and existence of God:
His name......Ex 3:14
No other God......Is 45:18
......Hos 13:4
......Jl 2:27

C. Used by Christ as Yahweh:
Translated "It is I"......Mt 14:27
At his trial......Mk 14:62
"I AM"......Jn 8:24, 28, 58; 13:19

D. Used by Christ to call himself the:
Bread of life......Jn 6:35
Light of the world......Jn 8:12
Gate for the sheep......Jn 10:7
Good shepherd......Jn 10:11, 14
Resurrection and life......Jn 11:25
Way, truth, and life......Jn 14:6
True vine......Jn 15:1

Identifying with Christ

A. Proper time, when tempted:
Not to conform to world......Rom 12:2
With improper associations
......2 Cor 6:14–17

B. Results:
Hatred......Jn 17:14
Rejection......Lk 6:22, 23
Suffering......1 Pt 2:20, 21
Witness......1 Pt 3:15
Good conscience......1 Pt 3:16

C. Basis:
Future glory......Rom 8:18
Life of Christ......Gal 2:20
Reward......2 Tm 2:12

Immortality—*eternal existence*

A. Proof of, based upon:
Human beings' likeness to God
......Gn 1:26, 27
Translation of Enoch and Elijah
......Gn 5:24
......2 Kgs 2:11, 12
Promises of Christ......Jn 11:25, 26
......Jn 14:2, 3
Eternal rewards and punishments
......Mt 25:31–46
......Lk 16:19–31
Presence of God's Spirit in us
......Rom 8:11
Resurrection of Christ
......1 Cor 15:12–58
Resurrection of men......Dn 12:2, 3
......Jn 5:28, 29

TOPICAL INDEX

Sanctifying........................2 Tm 3:16, 17
Effective..................................Jer 23:29
....2 Tm 3:15

See Word of God

Integrity—*moral uprightness*

A. Manifested in:
Moral uprightness ....Gn 20:3–10
Unselfish service ....Nm 16:15
Performing vows................Jer 35:12–19
Rejecting bribes................Acts 8:18–23
Honest behavior.......................2 Cor 7:2

B. Illustrated in:
Job's life..............................Jb 2:3, 9, 10
The psalmist's plea.......................Ps 7:9
Nehemiah's service............Neh 5:14–19
Daniel's rule............................Dn 6:1–4
Paul's ministry........................2 Cor 4:2

Intercession—*prayer offered in behalf of others*

A. Purposes of:
Secure healing.....................Jas 5:14–16
Avert judgment.................Nm 14:11–21
Insure deliverance ....1 Sm 7:5–9
Give blessings.....................Nm 6:23–27
Obtain restoration................Jb 42:8–10
Encourage repentance ....Rom 10:1–4

It's Who You Know

Numbers 14:13–24

"Now then, let the power of my Lord be displayed in its greatness, even as you have said, 'The Lord is slow to anger and rich in kindness, forgiving wickedness and crime; yet not declaring the guilty guiltless, but punishing children to the third and fourth generation for their fathers' wickedness.' Pardon, then, the wickedness of this people in keeping with your great kindness, even as you have forgiven them from Egypt until now." **Nm 14:17–19**

In Hollywood there's an expression, "It's not what you know, it's *who* you know." Having "connections" is a sure path to success; sometimes it's the *only* path. It works in Hollywood today—just like it worked in Israel 3,000 years ago. You see, Moses had the *best* connections. He knew the Director of all directors, the Producer of all producers—God, Creator of the universe. True, Moses wasn't perfect, but God trusted him and worked through him. When the Israelites were sinking deep in sin, with God's wrath about to drown them, Moses pleaded with God to throw out a life preserver instead. This is why it's so important to pray for each other. God hears all our prayers and responds to our petitions for one another. After all, we've got friends in "high places," too.

B. Characteristics of:
Pleading ....Gn 18:23–33
Specific ....Gn 24:12–15
Victorious ....Ex 17:9–12
Very intense.......................Ex 32:31, 32
Quickly answered.............Nm 27:15–23
Confessing ....2 Sm 24:17
Personal ....1 Chr 29:19
Covenant pleading...............Neh 1:4–11
Unselfish.................................Acts 7:60

C. Examples of:
Moses ....Ex 32:11–13
Joshua......................................Jos 7:6–9
Jehoshaphat ....2 Chr 20:5–13
Isaiah ....2 Chr 32:20
Daniel.....................................Dn 9:3–19
Christ ....Jn 17:1–26
Paul...Col 1:9–12

Jealous, jealousy

A. Kinds of:
Divine ....Ex 20:5
Marital ....Nm 5:12–31
....Sir 9:1
Motherly.....................................Gn 30:1
Brotherly.............................Gn 37:4–28
Sectional ....2 Sm 19:41–43
National...................................Jgs 8:1–3

B. Good causes of:
Zeal for the Lord.....................Nm 25:11
Concern over Christians ....2 Cor 11:2

C. Evil causes of:
Favoritism ....Gn 37:3–11
Regard for names ....1 Cor 3:3–5
Carnality.............................2 Cor 12:20

Jealousy Kills

1 Samuel 23:14

David now lived in the refuges in the desert, or in the barren hill country near Ziph. Though Saul sought him continually, the Lord did not deliver David into his grasp. **1 Sm 23:14**

Any daytime soap opera will confirm one unfortunate fact: Jealousy kills. When we envy what someone else has—their talents, money, power—instead of being thankful for what we have, we're killing ourselves in a small way.

That's because God's perfect plan for us can only be fulfilled through the talents and treasures we have in *our* life, not those given to someone else. It's like trying to take a daisy and make it a rose. It just won't work, and you'll kill the daisy in the process.

Saul was king for the wrong reasons. He wanted power and fame. When David got more than he did, Saul's jealousy ate him alive. We must be careful not to fall into the same trap. By focusing on the unique gifts that God has given to us, we can become the person we are meant to be—whether we're called to be a "rose" or a "daisy" or even a blade of grass.

God's garden, as St. Therese of Lisieux said, would be boring with only one kind of flower. God knows it takes a variety of flowers, even little flowers, to make a perfect bouquet.

TOPICAL INDEX

THERE'S A SEASON

Ecclesiastes 3:1–22

There is an appointed time for everything,
and a time for every affair under the heavens.
A time to be born, and a time to die;
a time to plant, and a time to uproot the plant.
A time to kill, and a time to heal;
a time to tear down, and a time to build.
A time to weep, and a time to laugh;
a time to mourn, and a time to dance.
A time to scatter stones, and a time to gather them;
a time to embrace, and a time to be far from embraces.
A time to seek, and a time to lose;
a time to keep, and a time to cast away.
A time to rend, and a time to sew;
a time to be silent, and a time to speak.
A time to love, and a time to hate;
a time of war, and a time of peace.

Eccl 3:1–8

We can learn a lot about our lives by observing nature. In the dead of winter, when we see a thick sheet of ice and snow covering the ground, it's hard to imagine that green grass and flowers could ever occupy the same spot. Likewise, when we're in the depths of pain or difficulty in life, it's almost impossible to believe we'll ever know joy again. Yet spring does come—every time—and our joy does return. Having passed through a winter, we appreciate the spring all the more. We need the rain to appreciate the sun. We need darkness to understand the power of light. This is all part of the "seasons" that God has designed for nature and for our lives.

All things will change, and change often brings pain. Yet all pain will eventually give way to joy, if we trust in God's action in our lives. Easter's resurrection will always follow Good Friday's crucifixion.

DON'T JUDGE A BOOK

Ezra 1:2–4

"Thus says Cyrus, king of Persia: 'All the kingdoms of the earth the LORD, the God of heaven, has given to me, and he has also charged me to build him a house in Jerusalem, which is in Judah. Whoever, therefore, among you belongs to any part of his people, let him go up, and may his God be with him! Let everyone who has survived, in whatever place he may have dwelt, be assisted by the people of that place with silver, gold, goods, and cattle, together with free-will offerings for the house of God in Jerusalem.'" **Ezr 1:2–4**

Here's a question for you: How many times have you looked at people of another religion—or no religion at all—and considered them below you in their relationship with God? If you have, that's not all that unusual. In this passage, King Cyrus shows us that God looks into the heart of each person and sees the good (or bad) in us, regardless of our religion. Cyrus was a Persian king, not a Jew. Yet this outsider wound up being more faithful to God than many of the "chosen" people of God, the Jews.

We should be proud of our faith and encourage others to believe in Christ and the Church, but we must also remember that only God knows what's in a person's heart. That is why we should always leave judgment of another's relationship with God up to God alone.

A wise person once said, "When we get to heaven, we will be surprised by three things. First, that some people we thought would be there are not. Second, that others we never expected to be there are. And third, we'll be most surprised that WE are there."

Nature ....1 Cor 11:13, 14
Apostolic authority ....1 Cor 5:3, 4
Law of Christ ....Gal 6:2–4
Divine illumination.............Jos 7:10–15

Justification—*accounting the guilty just before God*

A. Negatively considered, not by:
The Law ....Rom 3:20, 28
Men's righteousness ....Rom 10:1–5
Human works alone..............Rom 4:1–5
The Mosaic Law ....Acts 15:1–29
....Gal 2:16
A dead faith ....Jas 2:14–26

B. Positively considered, by:
Grace ....Rom 5:17–21
Christ's:
Blood ....Rom 5:9
Resurrection ....Rom 4:25
Faith ....Rom 10:4
....Rom 3:26, 27

C. Fruits of:
Forgiveness of sins ....Acts 13:38, 39
Peace ....Rom 5:1
Sanctification ....Rom 6:22
Shared righteousness ....2 Cor 5:21
Outward righteousness ....Rom 8:4
Eternal life ....Ti 3:7

D. Evidence of:
Faith and good works...............Jas 2:18
Wisdom and good works
....Jas 3:13–18

Killing—*causing life to cease*

A. Reasons for:
Take another's wife ....Gn 12:12
Take another's property
....1 Kgs 21:19
Take revenge..........................Gn 27:42
Satisfy anger.........................Nm 22:29
Hate ....Jn 5:18
Destroy people..........................Ex 1:16
Seize a throne......................2 Kgs 15:25
Put down rebellion ....1 Kgs 12:27
Fulfill prophecy ....1 Kgs 16:1–11
Fear of punishment ....Acts 16:27
Get rid of an unwanted person
....Mt 21:38

B. Reasons against:
God's Law ....Ex 20:13
Regard for:
Life ....Gn 37:21
One's position ....1 Sm 11:1–13
....1 Sm 24:11

C. Of Christians:
Result of persecution ....Mt 24:9
Time will come............................Jn 16:2
Under antichrist ....Rv 11:7
....Rv 13:15

Kindness—*a friendly attitude toward others*

A. Kinds of:
Extraordinary..........................Acts 28:2
Acquired ....Col 3:12
Developed...............................Prv 31:26
Commended ....2 Cor 6:6
Divine ....Neh 9:17
Long-lasting ....Sir 40:17

B. Of God, described as:
Rich ....Neh 9:17
Enduring.......................................Is 54:8
Will never end ....Is 54:10
Manifested ....Ps 31:22
Through Christ ....Eph 2:7
Cause of man's salvation ....Ti 3:4–7

C. Manifestation of:
Rewarded...............................1 Sm 15:6
Recalled ....2 Sm 2:5, 6
Rebuffed....................................2 Sm 3:8
Remembered...........................2 Sm 9:1–7
Refused ....2 Sm 10:1–6

King, Christ as

A. In Old Testament prophecy:
Judah's tribe ....Gn 49:10
David's lineage ....2 Sm 7:1–29
Divine origin ....Is 9:6, 7
In righteousness ....Is 11:1–5
Will endure forever.....................Dn 2:44
Born in Bethlehem ....Mi 5:1, 2
He is coming ....Mal 3:1–5

B. Christ's right to rule, determined by:
Divine decree ....Ps 2:6, 7
Prophecy..................................Ps 45:7, 8
Birth ....Is 9:6, 7
Being seated at God's right hand
....Ps 16:8–11
....Ps 110:1, 2
....Acts 2:34–36
Crowning ....Zec 6:11–15

C. Described as:
Eternal...Rv 11:15
Spiritual ....Jn 18:36, 37
Not for immoral or impure person
....Eph 5:5
Of his beloved Son......................Col 1:13

TOPICAL INDEX

WANT A KING?

1 Samuel 8:19–22

The people, however, refused to listen to Samuel's warning and said, "Not so! There must be a king over us. We too must be like other nations, with a king to rule us and to lead us in warfare and fight our battles." When Samuel had listened to all the people had to say, he repeated it to the LORD, who then said to him, "Grant their request and appoint a king to rule them." Samuel thereupon said to the men of Israel, "Each of you go to his own city." **1 Sm 8:19–22**

Oh boy, these guys were asking for it now. Here's Israel with the ultimate King—God Almighty—ruling over them, yet they wanted a *human* king like all the other nations. It's a classic case of keeping up with the Joneses. "Everyone else has a king, so we want a king, too."

And so it goes. God is the Lord of our life, but we desire other "kings" (or queens) instead. We set up people, things, ambitions—even food—as the kings of our lives. One by one they let us down, and our kingdom crumbles.

Only God's reign in our life will truly satisfy us, but how do we bring this heavenly kingdom into our lives? Jesus tells us, "The kingdom of heaven is *within* you." That's the key. God's kingdom is not a vast palace or place; it is a bond of love that is born in your soul. From that bond, God builds a kingdom that no person could ever build, and no person can destroy. It's a kingdom that will last forever.

TRUST YOURSELF?

Proverbs 8:1–36

"So now, O children, listen to me;
instruction and wisdom do not reject!
Happy the man who obeys me,
and happy those who keep my ways,
Happy the man watching daily at my gates,
waiting at my doorposts;
For he who finds me finds life,
and wins favor from the LORD;
But he who misses me harms himself;
all who hate me love death."

Prv 8:32–36

St. John of the Cross said, "He who trusts himself, trusts an ass." Although we are perfectly capable of great wisdom, deep understanding, and Einstein-level genius, we are incapable of seeing ourselves or our situation "objectively" or "from the outside" the way others do. So having the guidance and wisdom of those around us is crucial. These days the prevailing attitude seems to be "No one's going to tell *me* what to do" and "I gotta be me." But you might call that the Christmas tree approach. All branches, no roots. Dying on arrival. All dressed up with nowhere to grow.

When we don't listen to the wisdom of others, especially our elders and religious leaders, we're cutting ourselves off from the life-giving roots of human tradition, history, and experience. We're saying, "Hey, your experience doesn't matter." And we're wrong. Because history *does* repeat itself. If we don't learn from other people's failures, we'll needlessly make the same mistakes. If we don't learn from their successes, we'll probably never be as successful as we could have been.

A healthy tree is one with branches *and* roots. This is the person who's smart enough to listen to the past—and bold enough to grow into the future.

TOPICAL INDEX

A Word About Life

John 1:1–5

In the beginning was the Word, and the Word was with God, and the Word was God. He was in the beginning with God. All things came to be through him, and without him nothing came to be. What came to be through him was life, and this life was the light of the human race; the light shines in the darkness, and the darkness has not overcome it. **Jn 1:1–5**

Listen . . .
One Word . . .
LIFE . . .
You want it?
You got it.
No . . . Not existence . . . Not
surviving . . .
Real LIFE:
No dark . . . LIGHT . . .
No death . . . LIFE . . .
No way . . . You say?
HE says: "THE WAY, THE TRUTH, THE LIFE."
Don't doubt it.

Lord's Supper

Real Food, Real Drink, Real Life

John 6:53–58

"Just as the living Father sent me and I have life because of the Father, so also the one who feeds on me will have life because of me. This is the bread that came down from heaven. Unlike your ancestors who ate and still died, whoever eats this bread will live forever." **Jn 6:57–58**

As Catholics, we have something special to celebrate . . . Jesus left us himself. He didn't lie at the Last Supper when he said about the bread and wine, "This is my body. This is my blood." He meant what he said. A miracle occurred, and it's been happening at Mass ever since. The Eucharist is really Jesus! He offered us himself in exchange for our sins. What a trade!

It would be stupid for us not to accept it. When we eat the Bread of Life, we nourish our souls so that they'll be up for the challenging mission of being his disciples in this world and for *everlasting life.* It's incredible! And it's real!

Love, Christian

King of Hearts

2 Samuel 11:2—12:25

Then David said to Nathan, "I have sinned against the LORD." Nathan answered David, "The LORD on his part has forgiven your sin; you shall not die." **2 Sm 12:13**

King David was a superhero with very human limitations. He would soar high in virtue and accomplishment, then he'd fall headfirst into failure and sin. He snuffed out a lion, slew Goliath, and dunked more enemies in battle than Michael Jordan has dunked basketballs. That's not what put him on God's "cool list." He committed adultery with Bathsheba and had her husband killed in battle, yet that's not what got him thrown off the cool list. What put him on the list and kept him there, enabling him to go down in history as Israel's greatest king, was the power of his heart.

David loved with the force of a hurricane. He loved his family, especially his children. He loved his best friend, Jonathan. He loved King Saul, even when Saul tried to kill him. Most of all, he loved God—so much that he wrote poetry, prayers, and songs for the Lord (see the Psalms).

It was this last love that made David "a man after his [God's] own heart." In loving the King of Love, David *became* a king of love.

Real Love

1 Corinthians 13:4–7

Love is patient, love is kind. It is not jealous, [love] is not pompous, it is not inflated. It is not rude, it does not seek its own interests, it is not quick-tempered, it does not brood over injury, it does not rejoice over wrongdoing but rejoices with the truth. It bears all things, believes all things, hopes all things, endures all things. **1 Cor 13:4–7**

How do we know when love is real? Try this one out. Replace the word *love* with the word *I,* then read this passage. Am I patient, kind, not jealous, and not snobbish? Then use your boyfriend's or girlfriend's name and read the passage to see if he/she doesn't brood over injuries or rejoice in what is wrong. Lastly, put in Jesus' name and read the whole passage again. That's what real love is all about.

Love of Christ, the

A. Objects of:
- Father ....Jn 14:31
- Believers ....Gal 2:20
- Church....................Eph 5:2, 25

B. Described as:
- Knowing....................Eph 3:19
- Personal ....Gal 2:20
- Victorious ....Rom 8:37
- Unbreakable....................Rom 8:35
- Intimate ....Jn 14:21
- Imitative ....1 Jn 3:16
- Like the Father's ....Jn 15:9
- Sacrificial ....Gal 2:20

C. Expressions of:
- In taking our nature..........Heb 2:16–18
- In dying for us ....Jn 15:13

God's Passion

Song of Songs 8:6–7

Set me as a seal on your heart,
as a seal on your arm;
For stern as death is love,
relentless as the nether world is devotion;
its flames are a blazing fire.
Deep waters cannot quench love,
nor floods sweep it away.
Were one to offer all he owns to purchase love,
he would be roundly mocked.
Sg 8:6–7

If anyone ever tells you God is against passionate love, tell that person to read The Song of Songs. We're talking romance novel dimensions here—true human love in its highest physical expression; the dance of lovers blessed in the context of marriage.

But this song of Solomon for his bride is not just about human love. It also represents divine love—God's passionate love for us. More specifically, it portrays Christ's radical love for the Church, the "bride of Christ." In the New Testament, marriage between a man and a woman is in fact seen as a symbol of Christ's marriage to the Church. In that marriage, Jesus lays down his life out of love for us, the Church, and we become inseparably one with him as husband and wife become one. That's something to sing a love song about.

Love of God, the

A. Objects of:
- Christ ....Jn 3:35
- Christians ....2 Thes 2:16
- Humanity ....Ti 3:4, 5
- Cheerful giver ....2 Cor 9:7

B. Described as:
- Great ....Eph 2:4
- Constant ....Jer 31:3
- Sacrificial....................Rom 5:9

Nobody Loves Me

1 John 4:7–21

We have come to know and to believe in the love God has for us. God is love, and whoever remains in love remains in God and God in him. In this is love brought to perfection among us, that we have confidence on the day of judgment because as he is, so are we in this world. There is no fear in love, but perfect love drives out fear because fear has to do with punishment, and so one who fears is not yet perfect in love. We love because he first loved us. **1 Jn 4:16–19**

"I've been hurt so many times I feel like nobody loves me. I don't even love myself. I don't even know what love is. Won't somebody love me?"

"I do. From the moment of your conception, I've held you in the palm of my hand. I lived for you, suffered for you, and died because I love you so much and I want you to be with me forever. Close your eyes. I am here. Rest your head on my shoulder as I hold you tight and whisper, 'I love you . . . I love you . . . I love you.' " God is love.

C. As seen in believers':
- Hearts ....Rom 5:5

Love, physical

THE POWER OF LOVE

Judges 16:4–20

Delilah said to Samson, "Tell me the secret of your great strength and how you may be bound so as to be kept helpless.". . . She importuned him continually and vexed him with her complaints till he was deathly weary of them. So he took her completely into his confidence and told her, "No razor has touched my head, for I have been consecrated to God from my mother's womb. If I am shaved, my strength will leave me, and I shall be as weak as any other man." When Delilah saw that he had taken her completely into his confidence, she summoned the lords of the Philistines, saying, "Come up this time, for he has opened his heart to me." So the lords of the Philistines came and brought up the money with them. She had him sleep on her lap, and called for a man who shaved off his seven locks of hair. Then she began to mistreat him, for his strength had left him. When she said, "The Philistines are upon you, Samson!", and he woke from his sleep, he thought he could make good his escape as he had done time and again, for he did not realize that the LORD had left him. **Jgs 16:6, 15–20**

Oh, ain't it the truth? Most of us would give up anything to be able to marry the girl or guy of our dreams. Of all the attractions on earth, the greatest is the person we're in love with, that we can't get enough of. Love is a powerful force, the most powerful force in the universe. Just remember that love is a power that can be used for good or bad. It can create life or destroy it. Samson learned this truth the hard way. His love for Delilah started out okay. In the long run, however, it led him to turn his back on God, and it stripped him of his incredible strength.

Today, there are a lot of Samsons and Delilahs. Many of us are involved in "love" that seems great at first, but it ends up stripping us of our power and purity. When we finally wake up from our slumber, we realize, like Samson, we've been betrayed. The very thing we thought would bring us joy led us instead to sorrow.

When our love isn't based in God's truth, it's not rooted in the source of life. If we really want to keep love connected to life, we have to *love God first*. From this greatest love, all other true love will flow.

Lust—*evil desire*

Malice—*active intent to harm others*

Mediator, Christ our

Meditation—*quiet contemplation of spiritual truths*

Mercy

Gimmee a Break

Psalm 130:1–8

Out of the depths I call to you, LORD;
Lord, hear my cry!
May your ears be attentive
to my cry for mercy.
If you, LORD, mark our sins,
Lord, who can stand?
But with you is forgiveness
and so you are revered.

Ps 130:1–4

If you added up every sin you've ever committed or ever will commit in your life—from the little bad words to the big bad deeds—you probably couldn't fit them in the pages of a really bad novel. Well, the Good Lord knows every one of our failings, and they'll all be recorded in the Book of Life. Scary as it may seem, everything that is hidden now will be known to all humanity on judgment day. And boy, what a trashy novel that will be!

When it comes right down to it, if God were to hold us accountable for every offense we've committed, we'd all be nice little ice cubes heading for the devil's microwave oven. You might say we "wouldn't have a prayer." But God is merciful. Because we *do* have a prayer. It's the prayer that asks for the Lord's forgiveness and gets it every single time.

Messiah, the

Of Judah's tribe ....Gn 49:10
....Heb 7:14
Root from Jesse ....Is 11:1–10
Son of David..................................Mt 1:1
Prophet ....Dt 18:15–19
....Acts 3:22, 23
Priest after Melchizedek's order
....Ps 110:4
....Heb 6:20
King of David's line ....Jer 23:5
......................................Lk 1:32, 33
Son of God ....Ps 2:7, 8
......................................Acts 13:33
Son of Man ....Mk 8:38
Immanuel.......................................Is 7:14
......................................Mt 1:22, 23
Shoot..Zec 3:8
Cornerstone ....Ps 118:22
....1 Pt 2:4, 7
Servant.....................................Is 42:1–4
.....................................Mt 12:18, 21

B. Mission of, to:
Introduce the new covenant
....................................Jer 31:31–34
....................................Mt 26:26–30
Preach the gospel ....Is 61:1–3
....Lk 4:17–19
Bring peace ....Is 9:6
Die for man's sin......................Is 53:4–6
......................................1 Pt 1:18, 19
Unite God's people...............Is 19:23–25
....Eph 2:11–22
Call the Gentiles........................Is 11:10
.....................................Rom 15:9–12
Be a priest ....Zec 6:12, 13
....Heb 1:3
....Heb 8:1
Rule from David's throne
......................................Acts 2:30–36
Destroy Satan ....Rom 16:20
....1 Jn 3:8
Bring in everlasting righteousness
....Dn 9:24
....Mt 3:15
....2 Cor 5:21

C. Old Testament passages used by early church concerning:
Worship ....Ps 72:11–16
....Mt 2:1–11
Flight to Egypt ....Hos 11:1
....Mt 2:13–15
Forerunner ....Mal 3:1
....Mk 1:1–8
Devotion for the Temple...........Ps 69:10
....Jn 2:17
Triumphal entry.....................Zec 9:9, 10
....Mt 21:1–11
Betrayal ....Ps 41:10
....Mk 14:10
Being sold ....Zec 11:12
....Mt 26:15
Silent defense ....Is 53:7
....Mt 26:62, 63
Being spit on...............................Is 50:6
....Mk 14:65
Being crucified with sinners
....Is 53:12
....Mt 27:38
Piercing of hands and feet ....Ps 22:17
....Jn 19:36, 37
Being mocked..........................Ps 22:7–9
....Mt 27:39–44
Dying drink...............................Ps 69:22
....Jn 19:29
Side pierced ....Zec 12:10
....Jn 19:34
Prayer for the enemies..........Ps 109:2–5
....Lk 23:34
Garments gambled for ....Ps 22:19
....Mk 15:24
Death without broken bones
....Ps 34:21
....Jn 19:33
Separation from God ....Ps 22:2
....Mt 27:46
Burial with the rich......................Is 53:9
....Mt 27:57–60
Preservation from decay ....Ps 16:8–10
....Acts 2:31
Ascension ....Ps 68:18, 19
....Eph 4:8–10
Exaltation ....Ps 2:6–11
....Phil 2:9, 10

See Christ

Minister—*one who serves*

A. Descriptive of:
Palace staff ....1 Kgs 10:5
Angels ....Ps 103:21
Priests and Levites.................Jl 1:9, 13
Servant..............................Mt 20:22–27
Ruler ....Rom 13:3–5
Christ..Rom 15:8
God's servants..........................1 Cor 3:5

B. Christian qualifications of:
Able to teach..............................1 Tm 3:2
Hard work ....1 Cor 15:10
Faithful ....Rom 15:17–19
Impartial ....1 Tm 5:21
Kind ....2 Tm 2:25
Obedient..............................Acts 16:9, 10
Persevering ....2 Cor 11:23–33
Prayerful......................................Acts 6:4

TOPICAL INDEX

Miracle

MIRACLES STILL HAPPEN

John 2:1–11

Now there were six stone water jars there for Jewish ceremonial washings, each holding twenty to thirty gallons. Jesus told them, "Fill the jars with water." So they filled them to the brim. Then he told them, "Draw some out now and take it to the headwaiter." So they took it. And when the headwaiter tasted the water that had become wine, without knowing where it came from . . . the headwaiter called the bridegroom and said to him, "Everyone serves good wine first, and then when people have drunk freely, an inferior one; but you have kept the good wine until now." Jesus did this as the beginning of his signs in Cana in Galilee and so revealed his glory, and his disciples began to believe in him. **Jn 2:6–11**

If Moses parted the Red Sea today, would you believe it? Is it possible that a real miracle could occur in this day and age? Yes! Miracles still happen. Sure, there are frauds and hoaxes, but real, honest miracles do occur. Thousands have been documented and some of the greatest have occurred with the help of Mary, the Mother of God. Ask your pastor or youth minister about the Miracle of the Sun at Fatima, Portugal, in 1917. Or go to Mexico City and see the miracle of the tilma (cactus coat) that Mary gave an Indian over 500 years ago. These and other miracles show us that God is still willing to do almost anything to get our attention. Check them out!

BURN THE BULL

1 Kings 18:20

So Ahab sent to all the Israelites and had the prophets assemble on Mount Carmel.
1 Kgs 18:20

Don't you just love it when God decides to pull out all the stops and perform a big-time miracle? It wasn't enough to just torch the bull au natural; Elijah had to drench it in so much water that even the greatest Boy Scout could never have lit up that hide. Then WHISH!—a fire bolt drops out of heaven and toasts that big beefy boy like a giant fireworks display. So cool!

Unfortunately, it doesn't usually happen that way. Even when it does, we still don't believe. That's why the greatest miracles in life are not the giant fireworks ones but rather the quiet ones that take place in our hearts. That's where the fire of the Holy Spirit swoops down and consumes the personal sacrifices we offer to God. We can place our worries, our sins, our struggles, all drenched in the tears of our pain on the altar of our hearts, and God will consume them in a blaze of glory.

MONEY LOVE

Luke 16:9–15

"The person who is trustworthy in very small matters is also trustworthy in great ones; and the person who is dishonest in very small matters is also dishonest in great ones. . . . No servant can serve two masters. He will either hate one and love the other, or be devoted to one and despise the other. You cannot serve God and mammon." **Lk 16:10, 13**

Money is everything. It makes us great. It makes us powerful. It makes us secure. We *are* "somebody" if we're rich. We've "made it" if we're rich. We can relax and "really live" if we're rich. We can do whatever we want if we're rich. And guess what, we can also *die* if we're rich. Then what? Our money gets us a bigger tombstone? Big wow!

Money doesn't guarantee *anything*. God does. We'll leave this life with exactly what we had when we came in: nothing but our soul. If we've made money Number One instead of God, then we'll even lose that. Remember that the only money that will matter to God when we die is the money we spent helping *other* people. Because mansions in heaven aren't built with money. They're built with love and virtue.

CARE FOR THE POOR

Luke 14:12–24

"When you hold a lunch or dinner, do not invite your friends or your brothers or your relatives or your wealthy neighbors, in case they may invite you back and you have repayment. Rather, when you hold a banquet, invite the poor, the crippled, the lame, the blind; blessed indeed will you be because of their inability to repay you. For you will be repaid at the resurrection of the righteous." **Lk 14:12–14**

Remember the other day when you passed a poor person on your way into Mel's Diner to eat? You figured, "Ah, forget this guy. He could get a job if he wanted to." Then you sat down to eat and ordered way more than you could finish. The waiter took a half-full plate back to the garbage disposal. Then you left, and that street person was still sitting there—hungry.

What's up? Don't you remember what Jesus said? That poor person is Jesus in disguise.

When was the last time we offered food or clothing to a homeless person on the street? When was the last time we asked our parents if we could invite a homeless or needy person to our home for a shower and something to eat—especially on a holiday like Thanksgiving when so many of them are alone? When was the last time we visited an elderly person and helped him or her around the house?

We can care for Jesus in the distressing disguise of those who need our help—the poor, the elderly, the imprisoned, the sick, the hungry. They're all around us. And that's Jesus himself waiting for a hand.

Father Knows Best

Job 38:1–15

Where were you when I founded the earth?
Tell me, if you have understanding.
Who determined its size; do you know?
Who stretched out the measuring line for it?
Into what were its pedestals sunk,
and who laid the cornerstone,
While the morning stars sang in chorus
and all the sons of God shouted for joy?

Jb 38:4–7

A teenage girl wanted to go to a party with her friends, but her parents said no, because they didn't trust the company she'd be with. Their daughter threw a fit, but having no choice, she stayed home. That night her friends had too much to drink and were killed in a car accident.

Simple story, simple message: Sometimes our parents know what's better for us than we do. God's conversation with Job drives this point home. God our Father in heaven knows a zillion times better than we do what is best for us. But how often we end up complaining like that teen daughter! "Oh, come on God, you're being too strict. This is no problem, no big deal. Trust me, I know what I'm doing."

Right. The only One we can really trust is God.

IS GOD TOO SLOW?

Exodus 32:1–14

When the people became aware of Moses' delay in coming down from the mountain, they gathered around Aaron and said to him, "Come, make us a god who will be our leader; as for the man Moses who brought us out of the land of Egypt, we do not know what has happened to him. Aaron replied, "Have your wives and sons and daughters take off the golden earrings they are wearing, and bring them to me." So all the people took off their earrings and brought them to Aaron, who accepted their offering, and fashioning this gold with a graving tool, made a molten calf. Then they cried out, "This is your God, O Israel, who brought you out of the land of Egypt." **Ex 32:1–4**

Some people—especially the Israelites in this passage—would say that if you ever need your car fixed, don't take it to God's repair shop, because the service is way too slow. In this passage, they got tired of waiting for God to solve their problems, so they just made up new gods for a quick fix.

Bad move. It's like the impatient car owner who insists on a fast, inexpensive fix for a car. Sure, it might look okay, and drive okay . . . for a while. But you know that jalopy will be back in the shop in no time. Those imitation parts and cheap labor will end up costing more in the long run. There is no cheap, quick, reliable imitation for God. Only God can truly fix us. It does take time, however, and we usually have to pay for the repairs in a currency we don't like to spend (you know, the stuff we don't want to let go of in this life). Unlike a fast fix, God's repairs come with a lifetime—and after-lifetime—guarantee.

C. Is a product of:
Good heart.....Lk 8:15
Affliction.....Rom 5:3, 4
Testing of faith.....Jas 1:3
Hope.....Rom 8:25

D. Necessary grace, in:
Times of crises.....Lk 21:15–19
Dealing with a church.....2 Cor 12:12
Opposing evil.....Rv 2:2
Soundness of doctrine.....Ti 2:2
Waiting for Christ's return.....Jas 5:7, 8

Peace

A. Kinds of:
International.....1 Sm 7:14
National.....1 Kgs 5:4
.....1 Mc 9:72, 73
Civil.....Rom 14:19
Domestic.....1 Cor 7:15
Individual.....Lk 8:48
False.....1 Thes 5:3
Hypocritical.....Jas 2:16
Spiritual.....Rom 5:1

B. Source of:
God.....Phil 4:7
Christ.....Jn 14:27
Holy Spirit.....Gal 5:22

C. Of Christ:
Predicted.....Is 9:6, 7
Promised.....Hg 2:9
Announced.....Is 52:7

D. Lord's relation to, he:
Reveals.....Jer 33:6
Gives.....Ps 29:11

E. Among believers, truths concerning:
Comes through Christ's atonement
.....Is 53:5
Results from reconciliation.....Col 1:20
Product of justification.....Rom 5:1
Obtained by faith.....Is 26:2, 3

F. Among believers, exhortations regarding:
Should live in.....2 Cor 13:11
Should pursue.....2 Tm 2:22

G. Leaders of:
King Alexander.....1 Mc 10:47

Penitence—*state of being sorry for one's sins*

A. Results of:
Forgiveness.....Ps 32:5, 6
Restoration.....Jb 22:23–29
Renewed fellowship.....Ps 51:12, 13

B. Examples of:
Job.....Jb 42:1–6
David.....Ps 51:2–19
Josiah.....2 Kgs 22:1, 19
Tax collector.....Lk 18:13
Criminal on the cross.....Lk 23:39–42

C. Elements:
Acknowledgment of sin
.....Jb 33:27, 28
.....Lk 15:18, 21
.....1 Jn 1:9
Broken heart.....Ps 34:19
.....Ps 51:19
Plea for mercy.....Lk 18:13

See Repentance

Perfection—*the extreme degree of excellence; pure; complete; mature*

A. Applied to natural things:
Day.....Prv 4:18
Gold.....2 Chr 4:20
Weights.....Dt 25:15
Example of.....Ez 28:12
Offering.....Lv 22:21

B. Applied to spiritual graces:
Perseverance.....Jas 1:4
Love.....Col 3:14
Holiness.....2 Cor 7:1
Faith.....1 Thes 3:10
Unity.....Jn 17:23
Strength.....2 Cor 12:9

C. Means of:
God.....1 Pt 5:10
Christ.....Heb 10:14
Sufferings.....Heb 2:10

D. Stages of:
Eternally accomplished.....Heb 10:14
Objective goal.....Mt 5:48
Subjective process.....2 Cor 7:1
Experience not yet reached.....Phil 3:12
Descriptive of the completed church
.....Heb 11:40
Heaven's eternal standard
.....1 Cor 13:10–12

Don't Mess with the Kid

1 Samuel 17:46–47

"Today the LORD shall deliver you into my hand; I will strike you down and cut off your head. This very day I will leave your corpse and the corpses of the Philistine army for the birds of the air and the beasts of the field; thus the whole land shall learn that Israel has a God. All this multitude, too, shall learn that it is not by sword or spear that the LORD saves. For the battle is the LORD's, and he shall deliver you into our hands." **1 Sm 17:46–47**

Can you see this Goliath brute galumphing onto the battlefield like a T-rex, and David skipping up like Bambi? The Philistines must have been laughing like hyenas at the spectacle. Obviously, Goliath would eat David for lunch—or at least as an appetizer.

But now the stage was set for a play featuring God's favorite theme: The weak would vanquish the strong because of God's power. The humble would triumph over the proud. David, a teenage shepherd boy, would conquer Goliath, the ultimate fighting machine. Very little actual effort was involved because David's strength didn't come from weapons and skill. It came from faith in God. The rock that flew from David's sling was mostly a "rock of faith" by which God won the battle through David. By trusting totally in God's power, David possessed the Rock that would give him victory over his enemies and a solid foundation for his life.

How Do I Pray?

Luke 11:1–13

He was praying in a certain place, and when he had finished, one of his disciples said to him, "Lord, teach us to pray just as John taught his disciples." He said to them, "When you pray, say: Father, hallowed be your name, your kingdom come. Give us each day our daily bread and forgive us our sins for we ourselves forgive everyone in debt to us, and do not subject us to the final test." **Lk 11:1–4**

"How am I supposed to pray? What do I say? God already knows it all. What's the point?"

The point is communication. Imagine if every time you went on a date with a person, that person didn't say a word. You wouldn't be dating that person too long! That's because a relationship goes nowhere if there's no communication. Same with God. You've got to spend time together, and you've got to talk.

How? There are many ways to pray, and none is "the best" way. But all forms of prayer are communication—talking and listening, a two-way street. You could start by just praising God and telling Jesus he's awesome. You could even sing it if you're gutsy enough. (What date doesn't enjoy having a song sung to him or her, no matter how bad it sounds?) Then you can thank God. Just start thinking of things you're thankful for. You won't believe how long the list will be once you get into it!

Praying is also telling God we're sorry for the sinful things we've done. Sometimes it's begging and pleading for something we really need. Then again, it could just be simply asking God to do what's best for us. Whatever it is, just remember . . . God has big ears!

Answered Prayers

John 11:17–44; Matthew 7:7–11

When Jesus arrived, he found that Lazarus had already been in the tomb for four days. Now Bethany was near Jerusalem, only about two miles away. And many of the Jews had come to Martha and Mary to comfort them about their brother. When Martha heard that Jesus was coming, she went to meet him; but Mary sat at home. Martha said to Jesus, "Lord, if you had been here, my brother would not have died. [But] even now I know that whatever you ask of God, God will give you." Jesus said to her, "Your brother will rise." **Jn 11:17–22**

"God, where were you? Why didn't you answer my prayers? Don't keep me hanging like this!"

We often feel like Mary and Martha when we don't get the results we want. But God *always* answers our prayers—sometimes with "Yes," sometimes with "No way," and sometimes with "Maybe later. It's not the right time yet." None of us likes to hear "no." And most of us hate waiting around for an answer (it's like waiting for the car in front of you to go when the light turned green five seconds ago).

But God knows what's best for us, and when. That means that sometimes, like Lazarus, we'll spend *four days* in the "tomb," wondering if God has heard our prayers. Just when we're about to give up, Jesus will stand before us and say, "Friend, come out! Your prayers have been heard!"

Everything = Nothing

Judges 3:1–14

Because the Israelites had offended the LORD by forgetting the LORD, their God, and

TOPICAL INDEX

serving the Baals and the Asherahs, the anger of the LORD flared up against them, and he allowed them to fall into the power of Cushan-rishathaim, king of Aram Naharaim, whom they served for eight years. But when the Israelites cried out to the LORD, he raised up for them a savior, Othniel, son of Caleb's younger brother Kenaz, who rescued them. The spirit of the LORD came upon him, and he judged Israel. When he went out to war, the LORD delivered Cushan-rishathaim, king of Aram, into his power, so that he made him subject. The land then was at rest for forty years, until Othniel, son of Kenaz, died. Again the Israelites offended the LORD, who because of this offense strengthened Eglon, king of Moab, against Israel. **Jgs 3:7–12**

Have you ever seen *Willie Wonka and the Chocolate Factory*? Great movie. The rich, spoiled kids lost everything, while the poor, sincere Charlie scored the inheritance of the Chocolate Factory. It's too bad the Israelites couldn't have seen the movie; it might have saved them a lot of grief.

It's simple. When we get everything we want, we become spoiled, like rotten fruit. Bit into a bruised, mushy apple lately? Not too tasty, eh? We *expect* things to go our way. We yell, "Unfair!" if life doesn't go the way we want. Our core—our heart and soul—becomes infected by our ego. Rotten.

This is what happened with the Israelites. As soon as God blessed them with comfort and success, they became spoiled. They thought it was because they deserved it. They didn't need God anymore. When that happens, it's only a matter of time until everything we've gotten collapses around us.

That's how it works. God has to reduce us when we get too big, or empty us when we get too full of ourselves. Because God can't fill what isn't empty. For God to work in our lives, there has to be room for him to work.

KILL 'EM, LORD

Jonah 4:1–11

But this was greatly displeasing to Jonah, and he became angry. "I beseech you, LORD," he prayed, "is not this what I said while I was still in my own country? This is why I fled at first to Tarshish. I knew that you are a gracious and merciful God, slow to anger, rich in clemency, loathe to punish. And now, LORD, please take my life from me; for it is better for me to die than to live." But the LORD asked, "Have you reason to be angry?" **Jon 4:1–4**

It's easy to get the Jonah syndrome. You start getting serious about your faith, reading the Bible, going to church, living a life closer to God, praying more—and soon you're soaring in the spiritual heights. But from "up there" the rest of the world looks like it's "down there." You start to feel like you're way above all the other "sinners" or nonbelievers who still wallow in their wickedness. You wish that God would just purge the earth of these horrible people whose sins deserve God's just punishments.

Hold on. You've just entered the land of spiritual pride. In some ways, this sin of "self-righteousness" is actually *worse* than the sins of those you're condemning. The truth is that all of us are sinners, even those of us who are following the Lord. If we have been fortunate enough, by God's grace, to enter God's kingdom before the doors are shut, then we must pray that God's mercy leaves those doors open for all to enter.

SEXUAL INTEGRITY

1 Corinthians 6:15–20

Avoid immorality. Every other sin a person commits is outside the body, but the immoral person sins against his own body. Do you not know that your body is a temple of the Holy Spirit within you, whom you have from God, and that you are not your own? For you have been purchased at a price. Therefore, glorify God in your body. **1 Cor 6:18–20**

"My body, a temple of the Holy Spirit?"

You'd have never guessed it, right? It sure doesn't look like a "temple." Especially not when sleazy clothes are in fashion. Or walking and dancing like we "want it" are in fashion. Not when celebrities are exploited as "sex objects."

But it's a fact. In baptism, God comes to dwell within us, and our bodies become temples of God's Holy Spirit. That's why God made our bodies and our sexuality pure and beautiful. Following God's plan for our sexual expression, in marriage, is true sexual freedom—free from fear, guilt, and abuse. That keeps us pure, happy, and whole. That keeps our temple in order.

SEXUAL PURITY

Tobit 8:4

When the girl's parents left the bedroom and closed the door behind them, Tobiah arose from bed and said to his wife, "My love, get up. Let us pray and beg our Lord to have mercy on us and to grant us deliverance." **Tb 8:4**

Few events are more exciting to watch than the Olympics. The top athletes from every country share a common bond and a common goal: using their personal best to win. It's not just the competition, the winning. It's calling on what they do best. They've trained for years. They've made huge sacrifices. They're ready to push themselves beyond the absolute limit. But in each event, only the most focused, gifted, and trained athlete will take home the gold. In this story of Sarah and Tobias, no less than seven other guys had tried to "take home the gold" by marrying Sarah. But they were marrying her for the wrong reasons, and each one of them was struck dead by a demon on their wedding night. (Man, what a way to go.)

Just when it seemed Sarah would never find a man who was worthy to win her love, in walks Tobias with a major advantage over all the previous suitors: His love was pure and true. Like a top athlete in an Olympic event, he was focused on achieving the prize—Sarah—with a pure, focused intention. That purity kept him from being snuffed by the demon like Sarah's previous husbands. That purity led to life.

The false love of Sarah's previous husbands was the same type of lust that we see a lot of today. This shallow emotion is based on sex, but it has no respect for the beauty of sexuality as God intended—that incredible sharing between a man and wife in a God-directed marriage. Pure lust only leads to death. Usually it's the emotional death that comes from a broken relationship or betrayal or the spiritual death that comes from living apart from God's will. Sometimes it's even a physical death from sexually transmitted diseases. Only the true love that Tobias showed Sarah can lead to life.

TOPICAL INDEX

TOPICAL INDEX

YOU LIE IN IT

Esther 5—8

Queen Esther replied: "If I have found favor with you, O king, and if it pleases your majesty, I ask that my life be spared, and I beg that you spare the lives of my people. For my people and I have been delivered to destruction, slaughter, and extinction. If we were to be sold into slavery I would remain silent, but as it is, the enemy will be unable to compensate for the harm done to the king." "Who and where," said King Ahasuerus to Queen Esther, "is the man who has dared to do this?" Esther replied, "The enemy oppressing us is this wicked Haman." At this, Haman was seized with dread of the king and queen. . . . That day King Ahasuerus gave the house of Haman, enemy of the Jews, to Queen Esther; and Mordecai was admitted to the king's presence, for Esther had revealed his relationship to her. The king removed his signet ring from Haman, and transferred it into the keeping of Mordecai; and Esther put Mordecai in charge of the house of Haman. **Est 7:3–6; 8:1–3**

Take a good read of these four chapters in Esther, because there's a heavy, big-time message in here. This chap Haman set out to destroy an innocent man—Mordecai. Haman's jealousy and anger led him to despise Mordecai and to build a gallows, upon which he attempted to have Mordecai hanged. But who ended up hanging on that gallows? Haman!

This is how it always goes, folks! Every attack you wage against other people—through your words, actions, or even thoughts—is actually an attack against yourself. Eventually, the hatred you put out will come back to haunt the one who created it (you), just like Frankenstein came back to destroy the doctor who gave him life. You know the saying: "Whenever you point an accusing finger at someone, there are three other fingers pointing back at you."

Take the safe route. Do unto others as you would have them do unto you. That way you'll never have problems lying comfortably in the bed you have made.

Owning Up to Responsibility

Matthew 27:20–26

The chief priests and the elders persuaded the crowds to ask for Barabbas but to destroy Jesus. The governor said to them in reply, "Which of the two do you want me to release to you?" They answered, "Barabbas!" Pilate said to them, "Then what shall I do with Jesus called Messiah?" They all said, "Let him be crucified!" But he said, "Why? What evil has he done?" They only shouted the louder, "Let him be crucified!" When Pilate saw that he was not succeeding at all, but that a riot was breaking out instead, he took water and washed his hands in the sight of the crowd, saying, "I am innocent of this man's blood. Look to it yourselves." **Mt 27:20–25**

How often do we do something wrong, push it to the back of our minds, then "wash our hands" free of guilt? It's easy to do. We'll do just about anything to avoid the truth of a dirty deed. We'll even smear the truth to make what we've done look right. But being a Christian means being bold enough to admit when we're wrong and accept the punishment that may follow our mistakes. Being responsible not only means doing our best to do what's right, but being honest and straight-forward when we've blown it. Is there something you haven't taken care of in this area? Do it today.

Hereditary Sins?

Ezekiel 18:5–20

You ask: "Why is not the son charged with the guilt of his father?" Because the son has done what is right and just, and has been careful to observe all my statutes, he shall surely live. Only the one who sins shall die. The son shall not be charged with the guilt of his father, nor shall the father be charged with the guilt of his son. The virtuous man's virtue shall be his own, as the wicked man's wickedness shall be his. **Ez 18:19–20**

These days we hear more and more people blaming their parents for the problems in their life. However, this passage shows us that we are responsible for our own sins. A sinful parent could have a virtuous child, and a sinful child could have a virtuous parent. Whatever our family experience has been, we must take responsibility for our own lives. If we've come from a negative experience at home, we must turn to God for the strength to break that mold and try to live a good life. In the end, we stand alone before God.

Building Blocks

Nehemiah 2:17

Afterward I said to them: "You see the evil plight in which we stand: how Jerusalem lies in ruins and its gates have been gutted by fire. Come, let us rebuild the wall of Jerusalem, so that we may no longer be an object of derision!" **Neh 2:17**

Remember when you played with building blocks as a kid? You'd get them all stacked up, then your brother or sister or some other Godzilla-type monster-kid would come along and reduce your nifty skyscraper to a heap of rubble. While you were thinking, "I could never get this thing rebuilt," Dad or Mom would step in to help, sitting down next to you. You'd end up building a grand cathedral to replace the measly skyscraper.

The Godzilla-happenings in our lives can often be blessings in disguise. After the monster subsides, we usually find that we've grown and learned from the pain. And—surprise! When we're sitting in the rubble of our mistakes, suddenly we see God, right there ready to get working with us to rebuild. But since we're weak and broken, God can do more of the building this time around.

TOPICAL INDEX

SOME KINDA LAMB

Psalm 23:1–6

The LORD is my shepherd;
  there is nothing I lack.
In green pastures you let me graze;
  to safe waters you lead me;
  you restore my strength.
You guide me along the right path
  for the sake of your name.
Even when I walk through a dark valley,
  I fear no harm for you are at my side;
  your rod and staff give me courage.
You set a table before me
  as my enemies watch;
You anoint my head with oil;
  my cup overflows.
Only goodness and love will pursue me
  all the days of my life;
I will dwell in the house of the LORD
  for years to come.

Ps 23:1–6

When you ask little kids what kind of animal they'd like to be, they usually

TOPICAL INDEX

pick a lion, a cheetah, a dog, cat, or bird. But what we should really want to be is a lamb. Maybe they're not the smartest creatures, nor the toughest, nor the most exciting. In fact, they look downright goofy after getting one of those wool-clipping crew cuts.

Yet that's the animal Jesus wants us to be like in our relationship with him. Why? Because he wants to be our shepherd, like the psalm says. He wants us to experience his guidance when we are lost. He wants us to feel his healing touch when we are sick. He wants us to know his protection when we're in danger. He wants to show us that when we offer him the wool of our lives (our time, talents, and treasures), he can spin wonderful garments of faith, hope, and love, which we will someday wear at the banquet in heaven.

Remember: When the wolves of this world came to destroy us, our Shepherd, Jesus, became a lamb to be sacrificed in our place.

Family Feuds

2 Samuel 15:13

An informant came to David with the report, "The Israelites have transferred their loyalty to Absalom." **2 Sm 15:13**

Is there anyone on earth who doesn't have a family tree affected by weak branches or infected roots? We've all come from imperfect families with strange legacies of saints and sinners, of family ties and family feuds, like the one we see here between King David and his son Absalom. But Jesus chose to be born into the lineage of David, which was tainted with adultery, murder, and almost every other kind of sin you can think of. In fact, Jesus entered directly into the human family *because* of its imperfections.

He wanted to show us that every part of the human experience—good and bad—can be transformed into building material for the kingdom of God. With God's grace, every blemish of hatred, abuse, infidelity, and division can be used to bring about a greater good.

IT HURTS TOO MUCH!

Colossians 1:24

Now I rejoice in my sufferings for your sake, and in my flesh I am filling up what is lacking in the afflictions of Christ on behalf of his body, which is the church. **Col 1:24**

Suffering seems senseless. It hurts. But it's a fact of life. We can hate it, rebel against it, reject it, or try to kill it. Or we can accept it, try to understand it, seek peace in it, and even learn to be happy with it. For a nonbeliever there's no hope or real explanation for suffering. For Christians, we can rejoice with Jesus because, in suffering, we are sharing intimately in his life. Each pain, each accident, each dilemma is a chance to turn away from or toward Christ. Do we choose to bring Christ into our suffering?

TOPICAL INDEX

TOPICAL INDEX

JUNK FOOD?

Genesis 3:1–8

Now the serpent was the most cunning of all the animals that the LORD God had made. The serpent asked the woman, "Did God really tell you not to eat from any of the trees in the garden?" The woman answered the serpent: "We may eat of the fruit of the trees in the garden; it is only about the fruit of the tree in the middle of the garden that God said, 'You shall not eat it or even touch it, lest you die.' " But the serpent said to the woman: "You certainly will not die! No, God knows well that the moment you eat of it your eyes will be opened and you will be like gods who know what is good and what is bad." The woman saw that the tree was desirable for gaining wisdom. So she also gave some to her husband, who was with her, and he ate it. **Gn 3:1–6**

Tricky, tricky, tricky. That rat, the devil—here taking the form of a serpent—knows that the best way to get us to do something bad is to make us believe it's actually good. Why is he able to do this when, like Eve, we all have a conscience chanting, "Do yourself a favor: Choose good and avoid evil." The Bible even says God's commandments are written on our hearts. *Hello?* Yet, here was Eve, checking out the forbidden fruit thinking, "It sure *looks* good. If the serpent was right about it letting me know the difference between right and wrong, then what's bad about that? This is the ultimate power snack! How could something that seems so good be bad?"

Ahh, yeah. It can happen to all of us. Little by little, we can be convinced that since something bad *appears* to be so good, it must *be* good. Temptations blur our ability to see right from wrong, and soon we can even swap the two. Drunk with desire, anger, or power, we think we're cruising into pleasure and success. In reality, we forget what's junk food and what's the power snack: We're about to have a head-on collision with pain and failure. There's only one way to know for sure: Always keep God in the driver's seat.

Anything, Except That

Genesis 22:1–19

God put Abraham to the test. He called to him, "Abraham!" "Ready!" he replied. Then God said: "Take your son Isaac, your only one, whom you love, and go to the land of Moriah. There you shall offer him up as a holocaust on a height that I will point out to you." Early the next morning Abraham saddled his donkey, took with him his son Isaac, and two of his servants as well, and with the wood that he had cut for the holocaust, set out for the place of which God had told him. . . . When they came to the place of which God had told him, Abraham built an altar there and arranged the wood on it. Next he tied up his son Isaac, and put him on top of the wood on the altar. Then he reached out and took the knife to slaughter his son. But the LORD's messenger called to him from heaven, "Abraham, Abraham!" "Yes, Lord," he answered. "Do not lay your hand on the boy," said the messenger. "Do not do the least thing to him. I know now how devoted you are to God, since you did not withhold from me your own beloved son." **Gn 22:1–3, 9–12**

One day a guy wanted to show a girl how much he really loved her, so he said, "Just to show you how much you mean to me, I'll let you have any one of my CDs." As she looked over his collection, he spotted his favorite CD and thought, "Oh, man, I hope she doesn't choose that one." Sure enough, that's the one she wanted.

God knows what our favorite CD is—and our favorite food, our favorite hobbies, our favorite *everything.* Yet God also wants to make sure that none of those things stand between us and our faith. So sometimes we're tested to see if we would be willing to give them up. "Anything you want, Lord," is easy to say if we can add "except *that.*" But *that* is exactly what God may ask us to give. For Abraham, sacrificing his son Isaac meant losing the most important person in his life. Abraham may not have been able to grasp why God would make such a request, but he had faith. God had promised him Isaac would grow up to be a father, so if Abraham really believed *everything* God said, then Abraham had to believe that both—the sacrifice and Isaac as a father—had to be true. Abraham was willing to let go of his greatest treasure, trusting that God would keep all his promises. Abraham was not disappointed. He got to keep his son, and, through Isaac, God blessed Abraham's lineage for generations. Abraham's human offering to God became a God-powered offering back to him.

That is the key: Everything we offer to God, no matter how great or small, is valuable to God, and nothing we can give to God will ever compare to what we'll receive in return.

Thankfulness—*gratitude for blessings*

Thanks

Luke 17:11–19

As he was entering a village, ten lepers met [him]. They stood at a distance from him and raised their voice, saying, "Jesus, Master!

Have pity on us!" And when he saw them, he said, "Go show yourselves to the priests." As they were going they were cleansed. And one of them, realizing he had been healed, returned, glorifying God in a loud voice; and he fell at the feet of Jesus and thanked him. **Lk 17:12–16**

Don't you hate it when you go out of your way to do something for someone, then they hardly even thank you? You feel like, "Man, I'm not going to go out of my way for that person again." Now, think about all that God has done for you. How many times have you really said "thank you"? It's so easy to forget to thank God. We start to take our blessings for granted, just like our friends or family sometimes take us for granted.

Take a moment now. What can I thank God for today? Am I thankful for my life? How about my family? How about my friends, pets, even snacks and movies? There are hundreds of things we can thank God for every day. It just takes one word . . . *thanks!*

THE TIME IS NOW

Matthew 25:1–13

At midnight, there was a cry, "Behold, the bridegroom! Come out to meet him!" Then all those virgins got up and trimmed their lamps. The foolish ones said to the wise, "Give us some of your oil, for our lamps are going out." But the wise ones replied, "No, for there may not be enough for us and you. Go instead to the merchants and buy some for yourselves." While they went off to buy it, the bridegroom came and those who were ready went into the wedding feast with him. Then the door was locked. **Mt 25:6–10**

It's easy to put things off until tomorrow. But tomorrow may never come. No one knows when Jesus will come back to earth or when we'll *leave* earth. Do you? Can you honestly say that you know you'll be here tomorrow?

We need to be prepared today!

The time to start living a new life with Jesus is *now.* Do we have sins to confess? Now's the time to do it. Do we have enemies we need to reconcile with? Now's the time to do it. Do we have things we know God is calling us to do, but we've just been too lazy or afraid to get going on them? Now's the time to do it.

Make a list now of the things you need to do. Get your house in order.

If not now, when?

Put a Leash on It

James 3:2–10

The tongue is a small member and yet has great pretensions. Consider how small a fire can set a huge forest ablaze. The tongue is also a fire. It exists among our members as a world of malice, defiling the whole body and setting the entire course of our lives on fire, itself set on fire by Gehenna. For every kind of beast and bird, of reptile and sea creature, can be tamed and has been tamed by the human species, but no human being can tame the tongue. It is a restless evil, full of deadly poison. **Jas 3:5–8**

Take this test, answering yes or no:

Do you feel compelled to know everybody's business?

Do you pump your friends for information?

Do you tell your friends everything you know about people?

Do you have difficulty keeping secrets?

Do you sometimes bend or exaggerate the truth to make yourself look better?

If you answered yes to any of these questions, your tongue may have a problem with gossip. The solution is simple. Put a leash on it. Try listening for a change.

Storms of Life

Mark 4:35–41

A violent squall came up and waves were breaking over the boat, so that it was already filling up. Jesus was in the stern, asleep on a cushion. They woke him and said to him, "Teacher, do you not care that we are perishing?" He woke up, rebuked the wind, and said to the sea, "Quiet! Be still!" The wind ceased and there was a great calm. **Mk 4:37–39**

Avoiding the storms of life is impossible. A death in the family. A friend's suicide. A miscarriage or stillbirth. Terminal diseases. A paralyzing accident. Unemployment. Broken relationships. An abusive home life. Trouble in school. We get hurt. We're shocked! We panic. We stress out.

The apostles did the same thing and Jesus was right there, *sleeping through it all*. Yeah, sometimes it seems like God is sleeping right through our difficult times—like we've been abandoned. But then Jesus arises and stretches out his powerful hands, and the storm passes. Jesus sent the Holy Spirit to help us keep our boat on course. And when we think we're drowning, we have to remember that he's there to calm the storm.

Trusting God

Luke 5:4–11

After he had finished speaking, he said to Simon, "Put out into deep water and lower your nets for a catch." Simon said in reply, "Master, we have worked hard all night and have caught nothing, but at your command I will lower the nets." When they had done this, they caught a great number of fish and their nets were tearing. **Lk 5:4–6**

Simon Peter probably looked at Jesus and thought, "Are you an idiot or what? I'm a fisherman, and I know what I'm doing. I'm telling you there isn't a fish in this stinkin' sea!"

But Peter obeyed Jesus anyway and caught hundreds of fish!

Sometimes God asks us to do things that seem totally stupid in the world's eyes and maybe even in ours. What God is really asking for is trust. Trust is the key to a relationship. And God wants our trust!

We can give it. The next time you hear God tell you to do something good that seems a little bit weird, go for it. You'll be amazed at what you and God can do together.

Trust the Unseen

2 Kings 5:9

Naaman came with his horses and chariots and stopped at the door of Elisha's house. **2 Kgs 5:9**

One day, as a boy was flying a kite, the kite went higher and higher until it disappeared into the clouds. A man came along and saw the boy holding the string, but couldn't see anything attached to it. "What are you doing there?" he asked.

"I'm flying a kite," the boy replied.

"But if you can't see it," the man protested, "how do you know it's still there?"

"Oh, I know it's there," the boy smiled. "I can still feel the tug."

Naaman was faced with a similar predicament when he was told by Elisha to go wash in the river to heal himself of leprosy. "You want me to do *what?*" He couldn't see how a simple bath would do anything more than humiliate him, and he didn't want to do it. But he felt the tug of his conscience telling him about a "higher plan" behind this silliness. He gave it a try—and it paid off; he was healed.

When the direction God is leading us just doesn't seem to make sense, all we can do is hold on by a thin string to that heavenly tug, trusting that God's plan will someday emerge from the clouds and be clear as day.

Truth—*that which agrees with final reality*

THE ANSWER

John 5:37–47

Moreover, the Father who sent me has testified on my behalf. But you have never heard his voice nor seen his form, and you do not have his word remaining in you, because you do not believe in the one whom he has sent. You search the scriptures, because you think you have eternal life through them; even they testify on my behalf. But you do not want to come to me to have life. **Jn 5:37–40**

Who do you believe? Cults supply us with pamphlets that contain life solutions . . . and we read them with lively interest. Politicians come around and say they have the answer . . . we accept it. Big-name celebrities get tons of time on the tube to tell us their solutions to the problems of the world . . . we believe them.

Then God, our Creator, sends Jesus to the world with all the ANSWERS, and funny thing, we have a hard time believing him. Could it be that we don't want to hear the real ANSWERS?

Sometimes the truth hurts. But lies hurt a lot more in the long run.

TRUTH OR DARE

Romans 1:18–32

The wrath of God is indeed being revealed from heaven against every impiety and wickedness of those who suppress the truth by their wickedness. For what can be known about God is evident to them, because God made it evident to them. Ever since the creation of the world, his invisible attributes of eternal power and divinity have been able to be understood and perceived in what he has made. As a result, they have no excuse; for although they knew God they did not accord him glory as God or give him thanks. Instead, they became vain in their reasoning, and their senseless minds were darkened. While claiming to be wise, they became fools and exchanged the glory of the immortal God for the likeness of an image of mortal man or of birds or of four-legged animals or of snakes. **Rom 1:18–23**

What happens when we stop seeking the truth? Lies become reality. Are we accepting the immorality and lawlessness that our godless society has presented to us on a screen?

Read about the Romans. How is our society different from theirs? How have we as a society continued to live the same lie as the Romans? In what ways have we dared to stand up for the truth and for God?

Jesus called us to stand out from the crowd and stand tall with him. So when we seem to be "fitting in" the shirt that the world around us has given us to wear, maybe we have to ask ourselves, "Is this the shirt God really wants on me?"

WE CAN OVERCOME

Joshua 23:1–16

Strive hard to observe and carry out all that is written in the book of the law of Moses, not straying from it in any way, or mingling with these nations while they survive among you. You must not invoke their gods, or swear by them, or serve them, or worship them, but you must remain loyal to the LORD, your God, as you have been to this day. . . . For if you ever abandon him and ally yourselves with the remnant of these nations while they survive among you, by intermarrying and intermingling with them, know for certain that the LORD, your God, will no longer drive these nations out of your way. Instead they will be a snare and a trap for you, a scourge for your sides and thorns for your eyes, until you perish from this good land which the LORD, your God, has given you. **Jos 23:6–8, 12–13**

Joshua knew his life was coming to an end. Recognizing that there was still much work to be done in claiming the land God promised them, he reminded the people that the Lord would help them drive out their enemies. Then, in his farewell message, he reminded them of several important rules: Obey the Word of God; stay away from the sinful enemies and their gods; and do not become friends with, nor marry, anyone from the sinful lands around Israel. Joshua warned that obedience to these rules was necessary for continued victory. God knows our weaknesses. His rules serve to protect us, not to cramp our style. We need to learn to recognize the temptations that have a strong pull in our lives and take steps to avoid them.

GOD NEVER ANSWERS?

1 Samuel 3:10

When Samuel went to sleep in his place, the LORD came and revealed his presence, calling out as before, "Samuel, Samuel!" Samuel answered, "Speak, for your servant is listening." **1 Sm 3:10**

You pray and you pray. You ask, and you plead, and you beg—but still, no answer from God! What's up? Is the Lord vacationing in another universe or something? Gone fishing?

No. Most likely the problem is not in the heavenly courts; it's looking you in the mirror (you know, that good-looking, really cool kid known as "you"). You see, the problem may be a spiritual hearing impediment on your part. God may have been answering your prayer, but you might not have been quiet long enough to listen!

Sometimes the only way we can fully hear God's message is in silence and "listening" prayer. In other words, we have to strap a muzzle over our mouth and pray Samuel's words: "Speak, for your servant is listening."

Like Samuel, we also have to seek the guidance of others, especially spiritual leaders such as our priests, sisters, teachers, campus ministers, and youth ministers. They may see God's direction in our life a lot easier than we can. Or they may help us clarify our vision.

A Genie or a God?

1 Kings 3:5

In Gibeon the LORD appeared to Solomon in a dream at night. God said, "Ask something of me and I will give it to you." **1 Kgs 3:5**

If you found a genie who could grant you three wishes, what would you ask for? Well, Solomon got better than a genie ready to grant his wish; he got God. Now there's a big difference between the two. A genie will give you anything you ask for, but God will only grant you a wish that is good for you. In this case, Solomon asked for the right thing: wisdom to lead his people well. Because this request pleased God, Solomon was also granted other gifts—in this case, all the power and money he could imagine. In fact, Solomon became the richest man in the world.

One thousand years later, Jesus said, "Seek first the kingdom [of God] and his righteousness, and all these things will be given you besides" (Mt 6:33). When God is number one in our lives, the true desires of our hearts will be granted, and our needs will be met—because our needs and our desires will finally be in line with God's will.

ACCEPTING GOD

Luke 1:34–37

But Mary said to the angel, "How can this be, since I have no relations with a man?" And the angel said to her in reply, "The Holy Spirit will come upon you, and the power of the Most High will overshadow you. Therefore the child to be born will be called holy, the Son of God. And behold, Elizabeth, your relative, has also conceived a son in her old age, and this is the sixth month for her who was called barren; for nothing will be impossible for God." Mary said, "Behold, I am the handmaid of the Lord. May it be done to me according to your word." Then the angel departed from her. **Lk 1:34–37**

Bob had it all under control. He said to himself, "This is how it's going to be. I'm going to graduate, go to college, get married, have three kids, and retire in Florida." Then Bob got cancer, and his whole life was turned upside down.

The point is, we have no idea what God has planned for us. Mary had planned on being a simple, quiet woman of Nazareth. She wasn't planning on taking on the most important mission in the history of the world. She wasn't planning on being the mother of the Savior. But one day, when Mary was the ripe old age of fifteen, God's angel said to her, "Here's the plan, Mary. Are you up for it?" And Mary said yes.

Her cousin Elizabeth "knew" she'd never be a mom. But God said, "Wrong. You *will* be a mom!" And she was.

To truly "follow" God, we must be open to whatever *God* wants. We have to "let go and let God." We may be surprised. We may be humbled. But for sure, we'll be on the most incredible adventure of our lives!

Wisdom—*knowledge gained by experience; the art of good living*

SAY WHAT?

Luke 12:8–12

"I tell you, everyone who acknowledges me before others the Son of Man will acknowledge before the angels of God. But whoever denies me before others will be denied before the angels of God." **Lk 12:8–9**

Sometimes we're put on the spot. We're speechless. What's the "right" thing to say when a) someone dies; b) we're teased about going to church; or c) a friend attacks us about our moral beliefs? If Jesus is the Lord of our lives, and if we quietly ask him in the middle of our panic what's the *best* thing to say, he'll give us the words we need to speak at that moment. We'll be amazed at what we come up with! We may speak boldly, fearlessly, and with authority. We may hear things coming out of our mouths that we never thought we knew. That's because God is speaking through us. And God knows a whole lot more than we'll ever know!

TOPICAL INDEX

WORK IT

Proverbs 12:24

The diligent hand will govern,
but the slothful will be enslaved.
Prv 12:24

Anyone who is at the top of a sport, art, or profession will tell you there's only one way to get there and stay there: hard work. Even the most gifted person will never reach the top without daily practice, training, and learning.

We might look at people who are leaders and think, "Oh, I could never be like that." But the truth is, each of us has gifts and talents that God has called us to use. For some that may mean high-profile leadership in politics or sports or entertainment. For others it may mean setting an example for just one person we meet. Whatever it may be, the only way we can discover and cultivate what God has given us is by hard work and perseverance. Hard work is the only prerequisite for leadership (see also Proverbs 10:5).

TOPICAL INDEX

We Live in a Material World

1 John 2:15–17

Do not love the world or the things of the world. If anyone loves the world, the love of the Father is not in him. For all that is in the world, sensual lust, enticement for the eyes, and a pretentious life, is not from the Father but is from the world. Yet the world and its enticement are passing away. But whoever does the will of God remains forever. **1 Jn 2:15–17**

Even though we'd hesitate to admit it, we're all a bit materialistic. We love our "things." Our cars, our clothes, our four-wheelers, our VCRs, TVs, and CDs—you name it, we *want* it.

But what things do we *really need* in order to live as productive members of society? Can we live without TV or music for a month? If not, why not? Can we do without a third pair of jeans? Will we be okay with $30 sneakers instead of $150 ones? What dust collectors could we give away to someone in need?

Someday all of us will get tired of our things, no matter what they are. And that's because there's only one "thing" that can really satisfy us—God. The sooner we realize that, the sooner we'll be happy.

NEVER TOO YOUNG

Jeremiah 1:6

'Ah, Lord GOD!" I said,
"I know not how to speak; I am too young."
Jer 1:6

What is it about young people—like Jeremiah—that makes God choose them to accomplish great tasks? Maybe it's because they're always up for a challenge. Maybe it's because they have the guts to try something new, radical, bold. Maybe it's because they're in the "addition" stage of life—they're growing, changing, expanding. Perhaps for all of these reasons and more, God has frequently called young people to have a tremendous impact on the world. In fact, the greatest spiritual role ever played by a human being was played by a teenager. Can you guess who that teen was? Mary, whose teenage "yes" to God brought Jesus Christ into this world.

What about you? Are you waiting until you're "old and wise" to say yes to God and change the world for the better? Are you afraid that you're too young to really make a difference? Well, think again. God wants to use you right now, right where you are—in your family, in your school, in your workplace, in your community. The world is awaiting the power of your youth.

Joshua....Jos 24:14–16
Gideon....Jgs 6:11–32
David....1 Sm 17:26–51
Elijah....1 Kgs 19:10
Jehu....2 Kgs 9:1–37
Josiah....2 Kgs 22:1–20
Ezra....Ezr 7:10
Nehemiah....Neh 4:1–17
Peter and John....Acts 4:8–20
Timothy....Phil 2:19–22
Epaphroditus....Phil 2:25–30
Epaphras....Col 4:12, 13

TOPICAL INDEX